AMERICAN

SALARIES

AND

WAGES

SURVEY

AMERICAN SALARIES AND WAGES SURVEY

Fourteenth Edition

Statistical Data Derived
from 340 Government,
Business & News
Sources

Joyce P. Simkin

GALE
A Cengage Company

Farmington Hills, Mich • San Francisco • New York • Waterville, Maine
Meriden, Conn • Mason, Ohio • Chicago

American Salaries and Wages Survey, 14th Edition

Joyce P. Simkin, Editor

Project Editor: Jim Craddock, Margaret Mazurkiewicz

Editorial: Monique D. Magee, Robert Lazich, Editorial Code and Data, Inc.

Manufacturing: Rita Wimberley

For product information and technology assistance, contact us at
Gale Customer Support, 1-800-877-4253.
For permission to use material from this text or product,
submit all requests online at **www.cengage.com/permissions.**
Further permissions questions can be emailed to
permissionrequest@cengage.com

Gale, A Cengage Company
27500 Drake Rd.
Farmington Hills, MI, 48331-3535

ISBN-13: 978-1-4103-2236-4

ISSN 1055-7628

Printed in the United States of America
1 2 3 4 5 6 7 21 20 19 18 17

CONTENTS

CONTENTS

INTRODUCTION

American Salaries & Wages Survey (*ASWS*), now in its fourteenth edition, is a compilation of 2,226 occupational combinations (2,754 occupations) and their corresponding salaries obtained from 340 sources—federal, state, and city government, as well as various trade associations and journals.

Incorporating wage data for the period 2011 through 2018 *ASWS* provides extensive compensation information for industry, economic planners and developers, human resources professionals, employment counselors, job seekers, and job changers. Most of the data shown were collected in May 2015 and released, for the first time, in March 2016.

Features of this edition include:

- Data from 340 sources.

- More than 84,230 individual entries.

- 2,226 occupational combinations representing 2,754 occupations.

- 881 geographical areas, including national data and 23 regions, 3 territories, 51 states, and 803 cities, of which 788 are reported as 327 metropolitan statistical areas and 461 as independent cities or urbanized counties.

- Occupational outline of contents with numerous cross references.

- Geographical outline of contents.

- Updated employment statistics for 2014 and 2024.

- Complete source listings for further research.

Sources

During the first decade of the twenty-first century publishers of trade journals, magazines, and newspapers have struggled. Since 2007 many have lost their battles and either cut back significantly on their publishing activities or stopped publishing all together. The economic recession that began in December 2007 complicated this situation from the perspective of a researcher into salary and wage data. By putting pressure on all sectors of the economy, the recession also impacted industry, trade, and professional associations. These associations conduct annual wage surveys of their members. Typically, these groups survey members of their professional societies to obtain data and report wages across the nation or within U.S. regions. Fewer large salary surveys are being conducted and fewer yet are being published by the shrinking number of trade journals on the market today.

This decline in unique source materials has meant that the research portion of producing *ASWS* has become a greater challenge with each edition since the turn of the century. All efforts are made to scour the data landscape gathering salary and wage data: (1) from all reliable sources; (2) covering as broad a spectrum of occupations as possible; and (3) from as large and varied a number of sources as possible.

In order to provide a comprehensive data base, wage information was sought at the city level, the county or state region level, the state level, the U.S. region level, and the national level. Most Federal data are from the Occupational Employment Statistics (OES) semi-annual survey, published annually. It samples and contacts approximately 200,000 establishments semi-annually and about 1.2 million establishments over a three year period. May 2015 data from this program are available for 820 detailed occupations, which represents an increase of more than 100 occupations from a decade ago. The fourteenth edition of *ASWS* contains 749 of these detailed occupations. Occupations categorized as "all other" (e.g., Education Administrators, All Other) are not included. Other occupations were identified using a variety of sources.

Occupational Titles

Federal data—and state data reported through the Federal government—follow the Standard Occupational Classification System (SOC). This system has now been adopted by the Occupational Employment Statistics program of the Bureau of Labor Statistics.

Occupational titles from other sources follow no particular standard. They are reproduced essentially as reported. Therefore it is possible to find both *Registered Nurse* under R and *Nurse Practitioner* under N. The Outline of Contents provides a cross-referenced alphabetical listing of all titles to help the user identify all variants of an occupation. Thus *Nurse* provides references to *Registered Nurse* and vice versa.

Wage Denominations

Wage figures presented in *ASWS* are given in the form provided by the original source—hourly, daily, weekly, monthly, or annual. A wage conversion chart is provided for your convenience in Appendix II. The denomination type is referred to by its first letter in the wage denomination column (H for hourly, W for weekly, etc.). The number of wage calculations varies from source to source; one source may provide only an average wage figure, another may report only a median. Many reports, however, give three or more calculated wage amounts—a mid-level value such as average or median, as well as a low and a high value. In some cases, ranges are provided. Occasionally the low and high figures will be replaced by or supplemented with percentile or quartile figures. *ASWS* presents, wherever possible, three points on the wage spectrum: Low, Mid, and High. The ideal entry will show Lowest Wage Paid, Average Wage Paid, and Highest

Wage Paid. But these figures are not always available; therefore, a coding system is used to specify what type of wage amount is being presented. For example,

FQ stands for First Quartile and means that 25% of the workers surveyed earned less than the dollar amount shown.

TQ stands for Third Quartile and means that 75% of the workers surveyed earned less than the dollar amount shown and 25% earned more than the dollar amount shown. All abbreviations of wage types are listed in alphabetical order at the bottom of every page in the data section.

Organization

Outlines of Contents

ASWS includes two outlines of contents providing access to the salaries listed. The Outline of Contents provides the reader with the means to find all listings of an occupation, despite variations in naming conventions. It lists the primary occupational classifications found in the main body of *ASWS,* in alphabetical order. In addition, the outline supplies derivations of those titles and cross-references them to their base forms. For example, the primary occupational title, Engineer, can be found in the data section. The Outline of Contents provides several additional titles including, but not limited to:

> *Aerospace Engineer*
> *Agricultural Engineer*
> *Biomedical Engineer*
> *Environmental Engineer*
> *Health and Safety Engineer*
> *Locomotive Engineer*
> *Nuclear Engineer*

The reader is advised to check the Outline of Contents when seeking wage information about a particular occupation in order to locate all available entries. The Geographic Outline is a listing of geographic locations down to the state level and the primary occupations provided for those locations. Metro areas and cities are not listed individually because the same occupations tend to be present at the state and local levels.

Main Body

The main body of *ASWS* is organized alphabetically by primary occupation first, then by secondary occupation and/or industry designation, then by geographic area. Data are presented in an eight-column table. The following is an explanation of these data columns from left to right.

Occupation/Type/Industry Column–

Lists the primary occupational title (e.g., Actuary), the secondary occupational title/type (e.g., Systems Software) and/or the industry designation (e.g., Banking or Manufacturing). In cases where both a secondary title and an industry designation are provided, the secondary title precedes the industry.

Location Column–

Specifies the geographical area to which the data refer. The column is organized by size of region in descending order: national data, U.S. regional (e.g., Southwest) data, statewide data, metropolitan statistical area (MSA) and New England city and town area (NECTA) data, county data, and city data. If the area is smaller than a U.S. state, the location is followed by its two-letter postal code (e.g., MI for Michigan). *Please note:* Cities appear alphabetically by state, so that California cities will appear ahead of those located in New Jersey, for instance.

Wage Denomination (Per) Column–

Specifies intervals at which the wage amount is paid to the employee. The single-letter codes are translated at the bottom of each page. Wages may be given in hourly, daily, weekly, monthly, or annual denominations. A wage conversion table is provided in Appendix II.

Low, Mid, and High Columns–

List the wage figures for each entry in U.S. dollars. Each amount is followed by an explanatory code. A typical code is AW, standing for Average Wage, or MW, standing for Median Wage. Sometimes references to "quartiles" may be found. The third quartile (TQ) wage, for instance, means that 75% of individuals earned less than the amount shown and 25% earned more.

Source Column–

Provides alphanumeric codes that refer to titles of sources from which data were obtained. A code like CABLS means that the source for this entry is the Bureau of Labor Statistics, based on data supplied by the State of California. These codes are explained in Appendix I.

Date Column–

Specifies the dates to which respective entries refer. If a particular source did not report a precise date, an approximate date ("2017") is provided.

Code Listings Block–

Offers an explanation for all wage codes and is presented at the bottom of each page. These abbreviations may also be found in the Abbreviations Table, Appendix III.

ASWS has four appendices, some of which have been mentioned above.

Appendix I - Sources

Appendix I lists 340 organizations which contributed data from one or multiple wage surveys or job banks. In some cases, additional explanations about the wage data are included. The appendix is organized alphabetically by source codes.

Appendix II - Salary Conversion Table

Appendix II is a table that translates an hourly wage into its weekly, monthly, and annual equivalents. The reader, however, should note that these equivalencies are only approximate since wages reported in hourly formats may pertain to work weeks of different lengths.

Appendix III - Abbreviations

Appendix III lists and explains the abbreviations used throughout *ASWS*. Source abbreviations, of course, are explained in Appendix I.

Appendix IV - Employment by Occupation - 2014 and 2024

Appendix IV reproduces a portion of the BLS Occupational Matrix, a data base that lists 819 detailed occupations and shows total employment in 2014 together with projections to the year 2024. The appendix provides three presentations—alphabetical, by largest employment, and by growth—to help the user gain further insight into wage trends in the United States.

Data Limitations

A number of points should be kept in mind when using *ASWS* for wage information. *ASWS* is a compilation of a large number of sources. Some are scientific surveys, some are job offers, and some are themselves compilations of other sources. No attempt was made to standardize the data from these sources. Therefore, the user should take great care drawing general conclusions. Variations and/or skewed data occur in title derivations, wage calculations, job descriptions, and methodology. Note, however, that data from the government surveys (sources that end in BLS) are largely comparable place to place. But, government survey data for some smaller metropolitan statistical areas may be skewed due to a low survey response rate.

In this edition, occupational titles are generally more uniform and follow Federal naming conventions much more consistently than in the first four editions. Ambiguous titles, however, continue to exist.

The editors have made a limited effort to edit the occupational titles presented. Grammatical forms and punctuation have been made consistent whenever possible. Titles are presented in singular forms (Nurse *vs* Nurses).

It is important to bear in mind that wage variations between different entries with the same occupational title may be due to differences in job responsibilities.

ASWS provides base salary figures only. Unless otherwise specified, supplemental compensation —i.e., fringe benefits, overtime, bonuses, etc.—have not been included. Wage figures shown do not include any cost of living adjustment.

Acknowledgments

ASWS was initially suggested to Gale by Ms. Flower L. Hund, Central Missouri State University, Warrensburg, MO. From the start, the editors have attempted to realize, in practice, Ms. Hund's original concepts; to the extent that they have succeeded, the credit is Ms. Hund's; she is, however, in no way responsible for shortcomings in *ASWS*. The editors would like to thank the many individuals in federal and state government agencies and in associations who helped in the creation of *ASWS* by providing reports, surveys, and income data so essential to this compilation.

Comments and Suggestions

Comments on *ASWS* or suggestions for improvement of its usefulness, format, and coverage are always welcome. Although we have made every effort to be as accurate and consistent as possible, errors may be noted by others; we will appreciate having these called to our attention. Please contact:

> *American Salaries & Wages Survey*
> Gale, A Cengage Company
> 27500 Drake Road
> Farmington Hills, MI 48331-3535
> Phone: (248) 699-GALE
> Toll-free: (800) 347-GALE
> Fax: (248) 699-8068
> E-mail: BusinessProducts@cengage.com
> URL: gale.cengage.com

OUTLINE OF CONTENTS

GEOGRAPHICAL OUTLINE OF CONTENTS

United States

1st Class Petty Officer
1st Sergeant
2nd Class Petty Officer
3D Animator
3D Modeler
3rd Class Petty Officer
Academic Advisor/Counselor
Academic Evaluator
Account Executive
Activities Coordinator
Actor
Addiction and Rehabilitation Counselor
Admissions Representative
Advancement Specialist
Advertising Sales Manager
Aerodrome Safety Inspector
Air Hostess
Airman
Airman 1st Class
Airplane Pilot
Airport Chauffeur
Airport Police Officer
Alligator Farmer
Ambulatory Healthcare Services Worker
Analytics Manager
Anesthesiologist
Animal Lawyer
Animation Checker
Application Development Manager
Applicator
Art Director
Art Museum Director
Assembly Line Worker
Assembly Professional
Assistant Coach
Assistant Professor
Assisted Living/Personal Care Director
Associate Justice
Associate Professor
Association Planner
Au Pair
Au Pair Extraordinaire
Audio Engineer
Avalanche Forcaster
Avionics Inspector
AWS Solutions Architect
Back-End Web Developer
Background Vocalist
Bandmember

Bereavement Coordinator
Big Data Engineer
Biogerontologist
Biomedical Laboratory Technician
Biostatistician
Birth Doula
Blood Bank Technology Specialist
Boom Operator
Boutique Agency Owner
Budget Director
Business Development Executive
Business Intelligence Developer
Business Lending Executive
Busker
Cake Designer
Call Center Representative
Campus Chaplain
Campus Minister
Cardiologist
Cartoonist
Category Manager
Certified Ethical Hacker
Certified Information Security Manager
Certified Professional Organizer
Chauffeur
Chef De Partie
Chemical Engineer
Chemist
Chief Academic Affairs Officer/ Provost
Chief Athletics Administrator
Chief Campus Marketing Administrator
Chief Executive Officer
Chief Financial Officer
Chief Health Affairs Officer
Chief Human Resources Officer
Chief Institutional Research Officer
Chief Justice
Chief Marketing Technologist
Chief Master Sergeant
Chief Medical Officer
Chief Nursing Officer
Chief Petty Officer
Chief Procurement Officer
Chief Security Officer
Chief Technology Officer
Children's Minister
Cinematographer/Videographer
Circuit Judge
City Letter Carrier
Civil Service Mariner

Clerk Stenographer
Climate Change Analyst
Clinical Neuropsychologist
Clinical Pharmacist
Clinical Podiatrist
Clinical Trial Nurse
Cloud Specialist
Command Sergeant Major
Commercial Jet Mechanic
Commissioned Officer
Communications Specialist
Communications/Switchboard Operator
Community Health Executive
Community Manager for Brands or Businesses
Compensation Analyst
Conservationist
Construction Manager
Content Curator
Continuing Education Specialist
Copywriter
Corporate In-House Counsel
Corporate Jet Mechanic
Corporate Meeting Professional
Corporate Planner
Corporate Recruiter
Costumer
Credential Specialist
Curriculum Writer
Customer Success Manager
Customer Support Professional
Customs Broker
Cybersecurity Specialist
Dairy Herdsperson
Data-Reporting Specialist
Data Scientist
Data Security Analyst
Delegate
Delivery Technician
Demand Planner
Dental Informaticist
Dental Sleep Doctor
Department Manager
Developmental Psychologist
DevOps Engineer
DevOps Specialist
Digital Media Influencer
Digital Remastering Engineer
Director
Director of Advertising
Director of E-Commerce
Director of Nursing

Disaster Housing Inspector
Disaster Medical Specialist
Disc Jockey
Dispatcher/Reservationist
District Judge
Docket/Calendar Clerk
Dog Walker
Dolly Grip
Education Services Worker
Electrical Engineer
Embedded Application Developer
Emergency Medical Technician
Endocrinologist
Endoscopy Technician
Engagement Manager
Enlisted Member
Enologist
Enterostomal Therapist
Enterprise Architect
Equine Dental Technician
Equity Research Associate
Event Coordinator
Event-Planning Assistant
Executive Director
Executive Sous Chef
F&I Manager
Field Engineer
Fighter
Film Loader
Financial Advisor
Financial Quantitative Analyst
Fire Protection Engineer
First-Year Associate Lawyer
Flash Animator
Fleet Manager
Food and Beverage Professional
Food Safety Specialist
Forensic Psychologist
Front-End Web Developer
Fueler Ramp Agent
Gem Worker
Genetic Counselor
Geneticist
Geophysicist
Gerontological Nurse Practitioner
Gerontology Nurse
Glass Blower.
Global Marketing Director
Golf Pro
Government Account Manager
Government Contracts Attorney
Government Fleet Manager
Government Meeting Professional

Tour Accountant
Traffic Manager
Trail Builder
Travel Analyst
Travel Director
Truck Driver
UH 72 Aircraft Mechanic
UI Designer
User Experience Designer
User Experience Researcher
Value Analysis Coordinator
Vermiculturist
Veterinarian
Veterinary Acupuncturist
Vice President of Loss Prevention
Vice President of the United States
Videogame Actor
Vineyard Manager
Warrant Officer
Wedding Planner
Wellness Coach
Wilderness Guide
Wind Turbine Service Technician
Wine Club Manager
Winemaker
Worship Minister
Zamboni Driver
Zoo Endocrinologist

Central

Information Technology Training
 Manager
Instructional Designer
Iron Worker
Public Relations Professional

Central Mountain

Iron Worker

East North Central

Automation Professional
Registered Polysomnographic
 Technologist

East South Central

Automation Professional
Registered Polysomnographic
 Technologist

Great Lakes

Gastroenterologist
Information Technology Training
 Manager
Instructional Designer
Iron Worker

Mid-Atlantic

Automation Professional
Information Architect
Iron Worker
Materials Handling Professional

Public Relations Professional
Registered Polysomnographic
 Technologist

Midwest

Information Architect
Librarian
Materials Handling Professional
Public Relations Professional
Truck Driver

Mountain

Automation Professional
Information Technology Training
 Manager
Instructional Designer
Librarian
Materials Handling Professional
Registered Polysomnographic
 Technologist

New England

Automation Professional
Iron Worker
Materials Handling Professional
Registered Polysomnographic
 Technologist

New York and New Jersey Region

Iron Worker

North Central

Gastroenterologist

Northeast

Information Architect
Information Technology Training
 Manager
Instructional Designer
Librarian
Public Relations Professional
Truck Driver

Northwest

Gastroenterologist
Iron Worker
Public Relations Professional

Pacific

Automation Professional
Information Technology Training
 Manager
Instructional Designer
Librarian
Registered Polysomnographic
 Technologist

Plains

Public Relations Professional

South

Materials Handling Professional

South Atlantic

Automation Professional
Registered Polysomnographic
 Technologist

South Central

Gastroenterologist
Iron Worker
Librarian

Southeast

Gastroenterologist
Information Architect
Information Technology Training
 Manager
Instructional Designer
Iron Worker
Librarian
Materials Handling Professional
Public Relations Professional
Truck Driver

Southwest

Gastroenterologist
Information Architect

West

Gastroenterologist
Iron Worker
Materials Handling Professional
Public Relations Professional
Truck Driver

West North Central

Automation Professional
Registered Polysomnographic
 Technologist

West South Central

Automation Professional
Registered Polysomnographic
 Technologist

Alabama

Accountant and Auditor
Actuary
Adhesive Bonding Machine
 Operator and Tender
Administrative Law Judge,
 Adjudicator, and Hearing Officer
Administrative Services Manager
Adult Basic, Secondary Education,
 and Literacy Teacher and
 Instructor
Advertising and Promotions
 Manager
Advertising Sales Agent
Aerospace Engineer
Aerospace Engineering and
 Operations Technician
Agent and Business Manager

Agricultural and Food Science
 Technician
Agricultural Engineer
Agricultural Equipment Operator
Agricultural Inspector
Agricultural Sciences Teacher
Air Traffic Controller
Aircraft Cargo Handling
 Supervisor
Aircraft Mechanic and Service
 Technician
Aircraft Structure, Surfaces,
 Rigging, and Systems Assembler
Airfield Operations Specialist
Airline Pilot, Copilot, and Flight
 Engineer
Ambulance Driver and Attendant
Amusement and Recreation
 Attendant
Animal Breeder
Animal Control Worker
Animal Trainer
Anthropologist and Archeologist
Anthropology and Archeology
 Teacher
Appraiser and Assessor of Real
 Estate
Arbitrator, Mediator, and
 Conciliator
Architect
Architectural and Civil Drafter
Architectural and Engineering
 Manager
Architecture Teacher
Archivist
Area, Ethnic, and Cultural Studies
 Teacher
Art, Drama, and Music Teacher
Art Director
Astronomer
Athletic Trainer
Atmospheric, Earth, Marine, and
 Space Sciences Teacher
Atmospheric and Space Scientist
Audio and Video Equipment
 Technician
Audio-Visual and Multimedia
 Collections Specialist
Audiologist
Automotive and Watercraft Service
 Attendant
Automotive Body and Related
 Repairer
Automotive Glass Installer and
 Repairer
Automotive Service Technician and
 Mechanic
Avionics Technician
Baggage Porter and Bellhop
Bailiff
Baker
Bartender
Bicycle Repairer
Bill and Account Collector
Billing and Posting Clerk
Biochemist and Biophysicist
Biological Science Teacher

Tool and Die Maker
Tool Grinder, Filer, and Sharpener
Tour Guide and Escort
Traffic Technician
Training and Development Manager
Training and Development Specialist
Transit and Railroad Police
Transportation, Storage, and
  Distribution Manager
Transportation Attendant
Transportation Inspector
Transportation Security Screener
Travel Agent
Travel Guide
Tree Trimmer and Pruner
Umpire, Referee, and Other Sports
  Official
Upholsterer
Urban and Regional Planner
Usher, Lobby Attendant, and Ticket
  Taker
Veterinarian
Veterinary Assistant and Laboratory
  Animal Caretaker
Veterinary Technologist and
  Technician
Vocational Education Teacher
Waiter and Waitress
Watch Repairer
Water and Wastewater Treatment
  Plant and System Operator
Web Developer
Weigher, Measurer, Checker, and
  Sampler, Recordkeeping
Welder, Cutter, Solderer, and Brazer
Welding, Soldering, and Brazing
  Machine Setter, Operator, and
  Tender
Wholesale and Retail Buyer
Woodworking Machine Setter,
  Operator, and Tender
Word Processor and Typist
Writer and Author
Zoologist and Wildlife Biologist

Georgia

Accountant and Auditor
Accounting Clerk
Actor
Actuary
Adhesive Bonding Machine
  Operator and Tender
Administrative Law Judge,
  Adjudicator, and Hearing Officer
Administrative Services Manager
Adult Basic, Secondary Education,
  and Literacy Teacher and
  Instructor
Advertising and Promotions
  Manager
Advertising Sales Agent
Aerospace Engineer
Aerospace Engineering and
  Operations Technician
Agent and Business Manager
Agricultural and Food Science
  Technician

Agricultural Engineer
Agricultural Equipment Operator
Agricultural Inspector
Agricultural Sciences Teacher
Air Traffic Controller
Aircraft Cargo Handling Supervisor
Aircraft Mechanic and Service
  Technician
Aircraft Structure, Surfaces,
  Rigging, and Systems Assembler
Airline Pilot, Copilot, and Flight
  Engineer
Airport Manager
Ambulance Driver and Attendant
Amusement and Recreation
  Attendant
Anesthesiologist
Animal Control Director
Animal Control Worker
Animal Trainer
Anthropologist and Archeologist
Anthropology and Archeology
  Teacher
Appraisal Technician
Appraiser
Appraiser and Assessor of Real
  Estate
Arbitrator, Mediator, and Conciliator
Architect
Architectural and Civil Drafter
Architectural and Engineering
  Manager
Architecture Teacher
Archivist
Area, Ethnic, and Cultural Studies
  Teacher
Art, Drama, and Music Teacher
Art Director
Athlete and Sports Competitor
Athletic Trainer
Atmospheric, Earth, Marine, and
  Space Sciences Teacher
Atmospheric and Space Scientist
Audio and Video Equipment
  Technician
Audio-Visual and Multimedia
  Collections Specialist
Audiologist
Automotive and Watercraft Service
  Attendant
Automotive Body and Related
  Repairer
Automotive Glass Installer and
  Repairer
Automotive Service Technician and
  Mechanic
Avionics Technician
Baggage Porter and Bellhop
Bailiff
Baker
Barber
Bartender
Baseball Player
Bicycle Repairer
Bill and Account Collector
Billing and Posting Clerk
Biochemist and Biophysicist

Biological Science Teacher
Biological Technician
Biomedical Engineer
Boilermaker
Bookkeeping, Accounting, and
  Auditing Clerk
Brickmason and Blockmason
Bridge and Lock Tender
Broadcast News Analyst
Broadcast Technician
Brokerage Clerk
Budget Analyst
Building Inspector
Bus and Truck Mechanic and Diesel
  Engine Specialist
Bus Driver
Business Teacher
Butcher and Meat Cutter
Buyer and Purchasing Agent
Cabinetmaker and Bench Carpenter
Camera and Photographic
  Equipment Repairer
Camera Operator
Captain, Mate, and Pilot of Water
  Vessels
Cardiovascular Technologist and
  Technician
Career/Technical Education Teacher
Cargo and Freight Agent
Carpenter
Carpet Installer
Cartographer and Photogrammetrist
Cashier
Cement Mason and Concrete
  Finisher
Chef and Head Cook
Chemical Engineer
Chemical Equipment Operator and
  Tender
Chemical Plant and System Operator
Chemical Technician
Chemist
Chemistry Teacher
Chief Appraiser
Chief Executive
Chief Jailer/Jail Administrator
Chief Registrar
Child, Family, and School Social
  Worker
Childcare Worker
Chiropractor
Choreographer
Civil Engineer
Civil Engineering Technician
Claims Adjuster, Examiner, and
  Investigator
Cleaner of Vehicles and Equipment
Cleaning, Washing, and Metal
  Pickling Equipment Operator and
  Tender
Clergy
Clerk
Clinical, Counseling, and School
  Psychologist
Coach and Scout

Coating, Painting, and Spraying
  Machine Setter, Operator, and
  Tender
Code Enforcement Officer
Coil Winder, Taper, and Finisher
Coin, Vending, and Amusement
  Machine Servicer and Repairer
Combined Food Preparation and
  Serving Worker
Commercial and Industrial
  Designer
Commercial Pilot
Communication Teacher
Communications Director
Community Health Worker
Compensation, Benefits, and Job
  Analysis Specialist
Compensation and Benefits
  Manager
Compliance Officer
Computer, Automated Teller, and
  Office Machine Repairer
Computer and Information
  Research Scientist
Computer and Information
  Systems Manager
Computer-Controlled Machine
  Tool Operator
Computer Hardware Engineer
Computer Network Architect
Computer Network Support
  Specialist
Computer Numerically Controlled
  Machine Tool Programmer
Computer Operator
Computer Programmer
Computer Science Teacher
Computer Systems Analyst
Computer User Support Specialist
Concierge
Conservation Scientist
Construction and Building Inspector
Construction Laborer
Construction Manager
Continuous Mining Machine
  Operator
Control and Valve Installer and
  Repairer
Conveyor Operator and Tender
Cook
Cooling and Freezing Equipment
  Operator and Tender
Coroner
Correctional Officer and Jailer
Correspondence Clerk
Cost Estimator
Costume Attendant
Counter and Rental Clerk
Counter Attendant
County Attorney
County Clerk
County Commission Chairperson
County Commissioner
County Manager/Administrator
Courier and Messenger
Court, Municipal, and License Clerk
Court Reporter

Geographical Outline of Contents

Geographical Outline of Contents

Crane and Tower Operator
Credit Analyst
Credit Authorizer, Checker, and Clerk
Credit Counselor
Criminal Justice and Law Enforcement Teacher
Crossing Guard
Crushing, Grinding, and Polishing Machine Setter, Operator, and Tender
Curator
Customer Service Representative
Cutter and Trimmer
Cutting, Punching, and Press Machine Setter, Operator, and Tender
Cutting and Slicing Machine Setter, Operator, and Tender
Dancer
Data Entry Keyer
Database Administrator
Demonstrator and Product Promoter
Dental Assistant
Dental Hygienist
Dental Laboratory Technician
Dentist
Desktop Publisher
Detective and Criminal Investigator
Diagnostic Medical Sonographer
Dietetic Technician
Dietitian and Nutritionist
Dining Room and Cafeteria Attendant and Bartender Helper
Director
Dishwasher
Dispatcher
Dredge Operator
Drilling and Boring Machine Tool Setter, Operator, and Tender
Driver/Sales Worker
Drywall and Ceiling Tile Installer
E-Government Business Analyst
Earth Driller
Economics Teacher
Economist
Editor
Education Administrator
Education Teacher
Educational, Guidance, School, and Vocational Counselor
Electric Motor, Power Tool, and Related Repairer
Electrical and Electronic Engineering Technician
Electrical and Electronic Equipment Assembler
Electrical and Electronics Drafter
Electrical and Electronics Installer and Repairer
Electrical and Electronics Repairer
Electrical Engineer
Electrical Power-Line Installer and Repairer
Electrician
Electro-Mechanical Technician

Electromechanical Equipment Assembler
Electronic Equipment Installer and Repairer
Electronic Home Entertainment Equipment Installer and Repairer
Electronics Engineer
Elementary School Teacher
Elevator Installer and Repairer
Eligibility Interviewer
Embalmer
Emergency Management Director
Emergency Medical Technician and Paramedic
Engine and Other Machine Assembler
Engineering Teacher
English Language and Literature Teacher
Environmental Engineer
Environmental Engineering Technician
Environmental Science and Protection Technician
Environmental Science Teacher
Environmental Scientist and Specialist
Excavating and Loading Machine and Dragline Operator
Executive Secretary and Executive Administrative Assistant
Exercise Physiologist
Extruding, Forming, Pressing, and Compacting Machine Setter, Operator, and Tender
Extruding and Drawing Machine Setter, Operator, and Tender
Extruding and Forming Machine Setter, Operator, and Tender
Fabric and Apparel Patternmaker
Fabric Mender
Faller
Family and General Practitioner
Farm, Ranch, and Other Agricultural Manager
Farm Equipment Mechanic and Service Technician
Farmworker
Farmworker and Laborer
Fashion Designer
Fence Erector
Fiberglass Laminator and Fabricator
File Clerk
Film and Video Editor
Financial Analyst
Financial Examiner
Financial Manager
Fine Artist, Including Painter, Sculptor, and Illustrator
Fire Inspector and Investigator
Firefighter
First-Line Supervisor
Fitness Trainer and Aerobics Instructor
Floor Layer
Floor Sander and Finisher
Floral Designer

Food and Tobacco Roasting, Baking, and Drying Machine Operator and Tender
Food Batchmaker
Food Cooking Machine Operator and Tender
Food Preparation Worker
Food Scientist and Technologist
Food Server
Food Service Manager
Foreign Language and Literature Teacher
Forensic Science Technician
Forest and Conservation Technician
Forest and Conservation Worker
Forester
Forging Machine Setter, Operator, and Tender
Foundry Mold and Coremaker
Fundraiser
Funeral Attendant
Funeral Service Manager
Furnace, Kiln, Oven, Drier, and Kettle Operator and Tender
Furniture Finisher
Gaming and Sports Book Writer and Runner
Gaming Dealer
Gaming Supervisor
Gas Plant Operator
General and Operations Manager
Genetic Counselor
Geological and Petroleum Technician
Geoscientist
Glazier
Grader and Sorter
Graduate Teaching Assistant
Graphic Designer
Grinding, Lapping, Polishing, and Buffing Machine Tool Setter, Operator, and Tender
Grinding and Polishing Worker
Hairdresser, Hairstylist, and Cosmetologist
Hazardous Materials Removal Worker
Health and Safety Engineer
Health Educator
Health Specialties Teacher
Healthcare Social Worker
Heat Treating Equipment Setter, Operator, and Tender
Heating, Air Conditioning, and Refrigeration Mechanic and Installer
Heavy and Tractor-Trailer Truck Driver
Helper
Highway Maintenance Worker
History Teacher
Home Appliance Repairer
Home Health Aide
Host and Hostess
Hotel, Motel, and Resort Desk Clerk
Human Resources Assistant
Human Resources Manager

Human Resources Specialist
Hydrologist
Industrial Engineer
Industrial Engineering Technician
Industrial Machinery Mechanic
Industrial Production Manager
Industrial Truck and Tractor Operator
Information Security Analyst
Inspector, Tester, Sorter, Sampler, and Weigher
Installer and Repairer
Instructional Coordinator
Insulation Worker
Insurance Appraiser
Insurance Claims and Policy Processing Clerk
Insurance Sales Agent
Insurance Underwriter
Interior Designer
Internist
Interpreter and Translator
Interviewer
Janitor and Cleaner
Jeweler and Precious Stone and Metal Worker
Judge, Magistrate Judge, and Magistrate
Judicial Law Clerk
Kindergarten Teacher
Labor Relations Specialist
Laborer and Freight, Stock, and Material Mover
Landscape Architect
Landscaping and Groundskeeping Worker
Lathe and Turning Machine Tool Setter, Operator, and Tender
Laundry and Dry-Cleaning Worker
Lawyer
Layout Worker
Legal Secretary
Legislator
Librarian
Library Assistant
Library Science Teacher
Library Technician
Licensed Practical and Licensed Vocational Nurse
Lifeguard, Ski Patrol, and Other Recreational Protective Service Worker
Light Truck or Delivery Services Driver
Loan Interviewer and Clerk
Loan Officer
Locker Room, Coatroom, and Dressing Room Attendant
Locksmith and Safe Repairer
Locomotive Engineer
Lodging Manager
Log Grader and Scaler
Logging Equipment Operator
Logistician
Machine Feeder and Offbearer
Machinist

OCCUPATIONS

Occupation/Type/Industry	Location	Per	Low	Mid	High	Source	Date
1st Class Petty Officer							
U.S. Navy, Active Duty, Pay Grade E-6	United States	M	2487 LO		3852 HI	DOD1	2017
1st Sergeant							
U.S. Army, Active Duty, Pay Grade E-8	United States	M	4136 LO		5899 HI	DOD1	2017
U.S. Marines, Active Duty, Pay Grade E-8	United States	M	4136 LO		5899 HI	DOD1	2017
2nd Class Petty Officer							
U.S. Navy, Active Duty, Pay Grade E-5	United States	M	2278 LO		3233 HI	DOD1	2017
3D Animator	United States	Y	65500 LO		94250 HI	RH02	2017
3D Modeler	United States	W		1826.92 MW		TAG01	2016
3rd Class Petty Officer							
U.S. Navy, Active Duty, Pay Grade E-4	United States	M	2089 LO		2354 HI	DOD1	2017
4-H Program Coordinator							
County Government	Oakland County, MI	B	1439 LO		1874 HI	MIOAK2	10/1/16
Absent Parent Locator							
State Government	Maryland	Y	27048 LO		47710 HI	MDGOV	2016
ACA Coordinator							
County Government	Douglas County, CO	Y			41005 HI	DCOGOV	2016
Academic Advisor/Counselor							
Baccalaureate Institution	United States	Y		42693 MW		CHE02	2015-2016
Master's Institution	United States	Y		42363 MW		CHE02	2015-2016
Research University	United States	Y		45074 MW		CHE02	2015-2016
Academic Evaluator							
College and University	United States	Y		41376 AW		HED01	2015-2016
Account Clerk Supervisor							
Jobs and Family Services, State Government	Ohio	H			24.72 HI	OHGOV	2015
Account Executive							
Copier Industry	United States	Y		89880 ATC		COPIER1	2016
Accountant and Auditor	Alabama	Y	44350 AE	68713 AW	80900 AEX	ALBLS	6/16
	Birmingham-Hoover MSA, AL	Y	48081 AE	70404 AW	81566 AEX	ALBLS	6/16
	Alaska	Y	59950 FQ	74400 MW	95550 TQ	USBLS	5/15
	Anchorage MSA, AK	Y	59970 FQ	75240 MW	98010 TQ	USBLS	5/15
	Arizona	Y	46290 FQ	58620 MW	76650 TQ	USBLS	5/15
	Phoenix-Mesa-Scottsdale MSA, AZ	Y	47580 FQ	60260 MW	78890 TQ	USBLS	5/15
	Tucson MSA, AZ	Y	43210 FQ	53370 MW	65490 TQ	USBLS	5/15
	Arkansas	Y	44010 FQ	57300 MW	76340 TQ	USBLS	5/15
	Little Rock-North Little Rock-Conway MSA, AR	Y	47140 FQ	60210 MW	79930 TQ	USBLS	5/15
	California	H	27.82 FQ	35.94 MW	46.99 TQ	CABLS	1/16-3/16
	Anaheim-Santa Ana-Irvine PMSA, CA	H	27.20 FQ	33.98 MW	44.02 TQ	CABLS	1/16-3/16
	Los Angeles-Long Beach-Glendale PMSA, CA	H	27.21 FQ	35.47 MW	46.80 TQ	CABLS	1/16-3/16
	Oakland-Hayward-Berkeley PMSA, CA	H	29.56 FQ	37.80 MW	49.84 TQ	CABLS	1/16-3/16
	Riverside-San Bernardino-Ontario MSA, CA	H	25.69 FQ	32.89 MW	40.96 TQ	CABLS	1/16-3/16

AE Average entry wage	**AWR** Average wage range	**H** Hourly	**LR** Low end range	**MTC** Median total compensation	**TCC** Total cash compensation
AEX Average experienced wage	**B** Biweekly	**HI** Highest wage paid	**M** Monthly	**MW** Median wage paid	**TQ** Third quartile wage
ATC Average total compensation	**D** Daily	**HR** High end range	**MCC** Median cash compensation	**MWR** Median wage range	**W** Weekly
AW Average wage paid	**FQ** First quartile wage	**LO** Lowest wage paid	**ME** Median entry wage	**S** See annotated source	**Y** Yearly

Occupation/Type/Industry	Location	Per	Low	Mid	High	Source	Date
Accountant and Auditor	Sacramento–Roseville–Arden-Arcade MSA, CA	H	25.89 FQ	33.59 MW	40.65 TQ	CABLS	1/16-3/16
	San Diego-Carlsbad MSA, CA	H	27.09 FQ	35.18 MW	45.71 TQ	CABLS	1/16-3/16
	San Francisco-Redwood City-South San Francisco PMSA, CA	H	32.03 FQ	40.71 MW	52.55 TQ	CABLS	1/16-3/16
	Colorado	Y	51790 FQ	67630 MW	89380 TQ	USBLS	5/15
	Denver-Aurora-Lakewood MSA, CO	Y	53710 FQ	69740 MW	91740 TQ	USBLS	5/15
	Connecticut	Y		74551 MW		CTBLS	1/16-3/16
	Bridgeport-Stamford-Norwalk MSA, CT	Y	62550 FQ	77530 MW	101680 TQ	USBLS	5/15
	Hartford-West Hartford-East Hartford MSA, CT	Y	58590 FQ	72310 MW	90270 TQ	USBLS	5/15
	Delaware	Y	56510 FQ	72320 MW	94420 TQ	USBLS	5/15
	Wilmington PMSA, DE-MD-NJ	Y	58510 FQ	74450 MW	96250 TQ	USBLS	5/15
	District of Columbia	Y	66890 FQ	87230 MW	114470 TQ	USBLS	5/15
	Washington-Arlington-Alexandria PMSA, DC-VA-MD-WV	Y	64160 FQ	82670 MW	105960 TQ	USBLS	5/15
	Florida	H	21.14 AE	30.24 MW	40.68 AEX	FLBLS	7/16-9/16
	Fort Lauderdale-Pompano Beach-Deerfield Beach PMSA, FL	H	22.21 AE	30.97 MW	42.91 AEX	FLBLS	7/16-9/16
	Miami-Miami Beach-Kendall PMSA, FL	H	22.19 AE	30.89 MW	42.05 AEX	FLBLS	7/16-9/16
	Orlando-Kissimmee-Sanford MSA, FL	H	21.53 AE	29.91 MW	38.41 AEX	FLBLS	7/16-9/16
	Tampa-St. Petersburg-Clearwater MSA, FL	H	22.09 AE	30.82 MW	41.11 AEX	FLBLS	7/16-9/16
	Georgia	Y	53190 FQ	69060 MW	91020 TQ	USBLS	5/15
	Atlanta-Sandy Springs-Roswell MSA, GA	Y	54620 FQ	70820 MW	93510 TQ	USBLS	5/15
	Augusta-Richmond County MSA, GA-SC	Y	46100 FQ	60340 MW	80410 TQ	USBLS	5/15
	Hawaii	Y	44590 FQ	55990 MW	70810 TQ	USBLS	5/15
	Urban Honolulu MSA, HI	Y	44860 FQ	56920 MW	72710 TQ	USBLS	5/15
	Idaho	Y	49990 FQ	61130 MW	78730 TQ	USBLS	5/15
	Boise City MSA, ID	Y	50110 FQ	63100 MW	77480 TQ	USBLS	5/15
	Illinois	Y	50030 FQ	65190 MW	86740 TQ	USBLS	5/15
	Chicago-Naperville-Arlington Heights PMSA, IL	Y	50850 FQ	66170 MW	87770 TQ	USBLS	5/15
	Lake County-Kenosha County PMSA, IL-WI	Y	53890 FQ	71030 MW	94260 TQ	USBLS	5/15
	Indiana	Y	46730 FQ	60060 MW	77190 TQ	USBLS	5/15
	Gary PMSA, IN	Y	47760 FQ	59080 MW	74780 TQ	USBLS	5/15
	Indianapolis-Carmel-Anderson MSA, IN	Y	50790 FQ	64010 MW	80070 TQ	USBLS	5/15
	Iowa	Y	45550 FQ	56690 MW	72270 TQ	USBLS	5/15
	Des Moines-West Des Moines MSA, IA	Y	49490 FQ	60550 MW	78400 TQ	USBLS	5/15
	Kansas	Y	45000 FQ	57360 MW	74770 TQ	USBLS	5/15
	Wichita MSA, KS	Y	46920 FQ	59320 MW	77450 TQ	USBLS	5/15
	Kentucky	Y	43350 FQ	56220 MW	74850 TQ	USBLS	5/15
	Louisville-Jefferson County MSA, KY-IN	Y	45090 FQ	57740 MW	75280 TQ	USBLS	5/15
	Louisiana	Y	47100 FQ	58370 MW	74140 TQ	USBLS	5/15
	Baton Rouge MSA, LA	Y	47990 FQ	57710 MW	71840 TQ	USBLS	5/15
	New Orleans-Metairie MSA, LA	Y	46900 FQ	59170 MW	76500 TQ	USBLS	5/15
	Maine	Y	46410 FQ	56770 MW	68880 TQ	USBLS	5/15
	Portland-South Portland MSA, ME	Y	51270 FQ	59620 MW	73720 TQ	USBLS	5/15
	Maryland	Y	48571 AE	80575 MW	96576 AEX	MDBLS	4/16
	Baltimore-Columbia-Towson MSA, MD	Y	54030 FQ	68820 MW	90820 TQ	USBLS	5/15
	Salisbury MSA, MD-DE	Y	45690 FQ	58780 MW	74250 TQ	USBLS	5/15
	Massachusetts	Y	59510 FQ	75420 MW	96280 TQ	USBLS	5/15
	Boston-Cambridge-Newton NECTA, MA	Y	61490 FQ	77920 MW	99770 TQ	USBLS	5/15
	Worcester MSA, MA-CT	Y	52770 FQ	64110 MW	81510 TQ	USBLS	5/15

Occupation/Type/Industry	Location	Per	Low	Mid	High	Source	Date
Accountant and Auditor	Michigan	Y	49070 FQ	63580 MW	83260 TQ	USBLS	5/15
	Detroit-Dearborn-Livonia PMSA, MI	Y	51730 FQ	67320 MW	88840 TQ	USBLS	5/15
	Grand Rapids-Wyoming MSA, MI	Y	47820 FQ	61050 MW	77110 TQ	USBLS	5/15
	Minnesota	Y	53051 FQ	64675 MW	80801 TQ	MNBLS	1/16-3/16
	Minneapolis-St. Paul-Bloomington MSA, MN-WI	Y	54433 FQ	66697 MW	83117 TQ	MNBLS	1/16-3/16
	Mississippi	Y	39470 FQ	51530 MW	66970 TQ	USBLS	5/15
	Jackson MSA, MS	Y	38310 FQ	50730 MW	63160 TQ	USBLS	5/15
	Missouri	Y	48410 FQ	62740 MW	82850 TQ	USBLS	5/15
	Kansas City MSA, MO-KS	Y	48600 FQ	61900 MW	80530 TQ	USBLS	5/15
	St. Louis MSA, MO-IL	Y	54050 FQ	68630 MW	89130 TQ	USBLS	5/15
	Montana	Y	43780 FQ	56960 MW	75280 TQ	USBLS	5/15
	Billings MSA, MT	Y	45950 FQ	61900 MW	76240 TQ	USBLS	5/15
	Nebraska	Y	46530 FQ	58795 MW	77230 TQ	NEBLS	7/16-9/16
	Omaha-Council Bluffs MSA, NE-IA	Y	49755 FQ	61715 MW	81610 TQ	NEBLS	7/16-9/16
	Nevada	Y	44520 FQ	56690 MW	74560 TQ	USBLS	5/15
	Las Vegas-Henderson-Paradise MSA, NV	Y	44360 FQ	56350 MW	73520 TQ	USBLS	5/15
	New Hampshire	H	23.41 AE	31.65 MW	40.27 AEX	NHBLS	6/16
	Manchester NECTA, NH	H	23.83 AE	30.85 MW	44.26 AEX	NHBLS	6/16
	Nashua NECTA, NH-MA	Y	59600 FQ	73550 MW	88270 TQ	USBLS	5/15
	New Jersey	Y	62640 FQ	78900 MW	100280 TQ	USBLS	5/15
	Camden PMSA, NJ	Y	63260 FQ	79290 MW	99090 TQ	USBLS	5/15
	Newark PMSA, NJ-PA	Y	62060 FQ	77820 MW	99840 TQ	USBLS	5/15
	Trenton MSA, NJ	Y	62390 FQ	79200 MW	97650 TQ	USBLS	5/15
	New Mexico	Y	45700 FQ	57130 MW	74160 TQ	USBLS	5/15
	Albuquerque MSA, NM	Y	47800 FQ	58570 MW	76450 TQ	USBLS	5/15
	New York	Y	53360 AE	81470 MW	113980 AEX	NYBLS	1/16-3/16
	Buffalo-Cheektowaga-Niagara Falls MSA, NY	Y	49850 FQ	63670 MW	85250 TQ	USBLS	5/15
	Nassau County-Suffolk County PMSA, NY	Y	63950 FQ	81230 MW	104780 TQ	USBLS	5/15
	New York-Jersey City-White Plains PMSA, NY-NJ	Y	64200 FQ	84530 MW	116160 TQ	USBLS	5/15
	Rochester MSA, NY	Y	52490 FQ	66540 MW	79840 TQ	USBLS	5/15
	North Carolina	Y	52830 FQ	64720 MW	84890 TQ	USBLS	5/15
	Charlotte-Concord-Gastonia MSA, NC-SC	Y	54770 FQ	68880 MW	93020 TQ	USBLS	5/15
	Raleigh MSA, NC	Y	52590 FQ	63000 MW	78590 TQ	USBLS	5/15
	North Dakota	Y	42750 FQ	52180 MW	65980 TQ	USBLS	5/15
	Fargo MSA, ND-MN	Y	44020 FQ	53960 MW	65740 TQ	USBLS	5/15
	Ohio	Y	50490 FQ	63350 MW	80460 TQ	USBLS	5/15
	Cincinnati MSA, OH-KY-IN	Y	49680 FQ	61630 MW	80950 TQ	USBLS	5/15
	Cleveland-Elyria MSA, OH	Y	53110 FQ	66520 MW	85230 TQ	USBLS	5/15
	Columbus MSA, OH	Y	51950 FQ	66390 MW	83750 TQ	USBLS	5/15
	Oklahoma	Y	43970 FQ	57050 MW	75410 TQ	USBLS	5/15
	Oklahoma City MSA, OK	Y	45100 FQ	58130 MW	75250 TQ	USBLS	5/15
	Tulsa MSA, OK	Y	48400 FQ	64080 MW	81510 TQ	USBLS	5/15
	Oregon	H	24.33 FQ	29.96 MW	38.14 TQ	ORBLS	2016
	Albany MSA, OR	Y	50440 FQ	62020 MW	86000 TQ	USBLS	5/15
	Portland-Vancouver-Hillsboro MSA, OR-WA	Y	51070 FQ	61880 MW	79390 TQ	USBLS	5/15
	Pennsylvania	Y	50940 FQ	65100 MW	85310 TQ	USBLS	5/15
	Allentown-Bethlehem-Easton MSA, PA-NJ	Y	52120 FQ	66590 MW	87440 TQ	USBLS	5/15
	Harrisburg-Carlisle MSA, PA	Y	50000 FQ	61380 MW	77740 TQ	USBLS	5/15
	Montgomery County-Bucks County-Chester County PMSA, PA	Y	54060 FQ	69970 MW	92150 TQ	USBLS	5/15
	Philadelphia PMSA, PA	Y	57190 FQ	74450 MW	97320 TQ	USBLS	5/15
	Pittsburgh MSA, PA	Y	50440 FQ	63280 MW	81010 TQ	USBLS	5/15
	Rhode Island	Y	57970 FQ	74190 MW	94860 TQ	USBLS	5/15
	Providence-Warwick MSA, RI-MA	Y	57970 FQ	74120 MW	94400 TQ	USBLS	5/15
	South Carolina	Y	43120 FQ	56030 MW	73250 TQ	USBLS	5/15
	Charleston-North Charleston MSA, SC	Y	41440 FQ	57210 MW	73810 TQ	USBLS	5/15
	Columbia MSA, SC	Y	41470 FQ	51820 MW	63600 TQ	USBLS	5/15

AE	Average entry wage	AWR	Average wage range	H	Hourly	LR	Low end range	MTC	Median total compensation	TCC	Total cash compensation
AEX	Average experienced wage	B	Biweekly	HI	Highest wage paid	M	Monthly	MCC	Median cash compensation	TQ	Third quartile wage
ATC	Average total compensation	D	Daily	HR	High end range	MCC	Median cash compensation	MWR	Median wage range	W	Weekly
AW	Average wage paid	FQ	First quartile wage	LO	Lowest wage paid	ME	Median entry wage	S	See annotated source	Y	Yearly

Occupation/Type/Industry	Location	Per	Low	Mid	High	Source	Date
Accountant and Auditor	Greenville-Anderson-Mauldin						
	MSA, SC	Y	51020 FQ	63350 MW	81710 TQ	USBLS	5/15
	South Dakota	Y	49520 FQ	58440 MW	71400 TQ	USBLS	5/15
	Sioux Falls MSA, SD	Y	51770 FQ	60800 MW	75550 TQ	USBLS	5/15
	Tennessee	Y	47040 FQ	58760 MW	75310 TQ	USBLS	5/15
	Knoxville MSA, TN	Y	48030 FQ	59830 MW	76980 TQ	USBLS	5/15
	Memphis MSA, TN-MS-AR	Y	46420 FQ	59310 MW	75500 TQ	USBLS	5/15
	Nashville-Davidson–						
	Murfreesboro–Franklin						
	MSA, TN	Y	47940 FQ	59210 MW	75760 TQ	USBLS	5/15
	Texas	Y	52790 FQ	69430 MW	94350 TQ	USBLS	5/15
	Austin-Round Rock MSA, TX	Y	49300 FQ	62560 MW	84120 TQ	USBLS	5/15
	Dallas-Plano-Irving PMSA, TX	Y	55690 FQ	72740 MW	95040 TQ	USBLS	5/15
	Fort Worth-Arlington PMSA,						
	TX	Y	53390 FQ	68430 MW	92410 TQ	USBLS	5/15
	Houston-The Woodlands-						
	Sugar Land MSA, TX	Y	57890 FQ	77030 MW	104980 TQ	USBLS	5/15
	San Antonio-New Braunfels						
	MSA, TX	Y	49590 FQ	64970 MW	90170 TQ	USBLS	5/15
	Utah	Y	48340 FQ	62860 MW	84350 TQ	USBLS	5/15
	Ogden-Clearfield MSA, UT	Y	51150 FQ	63980 MW	88820 TQ	USBLS	5/15
	Provo-Orem MSA, UT	Y	47680 FQ	63630 MW	77890 TQ	USBLS	5/15
	Salt Lake City MSA, UT	Y	49050 FQ	63730 MW	86620 TQ	USBLS	5/15
	Vermont	Y	51590 FQ	64950 MW	83090 TQ	USBLS	5/15
	Burlington-South Burlington						
	MSA, VT	Y	53120 FQ	66920 MW	87520 TQ	USBLS	5/15
	Virginia	Y	57490 FQ	74200 MW	95300 TQ	USBLS	5/15
	Richmond MSA, VA	Y	55090 FQ	67050 MW	88630 TQ	USBLS	5/15
	Virginia Beach-Norfolk-						
	Newport News MSA, VA-NC	Y	52560 FQ	68230 MW	88380 TQ	USBLS	5/15
	Washington	H	26.12 FQ	32.76 MW	43.00 TQ	WABLS	3/16
	Seattle-Bellevue-Everett						
	PMSA, WA	H	27.35 FQ	35.14 MW	46.36 TQ	WABLS	3/16
	Tacoma-Lakewood PMSA, WA	H	24.53 FQ	30.50 MW	37.79 TQ	WABLS	3/16
	West Virginia	Y	44480 FQ	58410 MW	75260 TQ	USBLS	5/15
	Huntington-Ashland MSA,						
	WV-KY-OH	Y	41750 FQ	57120 MW	74500 TQ	USBLS	5/15
	Wisconsin	Y	49970 FQ	61710 MW	78180 TQ	USBLS	5/15
	Madison MSA, WI	Y	51860 FQ	62610 MW	78120 TQ	USBLS	5/15
	Milwaukee-Waukesha-West						
	Allis MSA, WI	Y	52800 FQ	64710 MW	82720 TQ	USBLS	5/15
	Wyoming	Y	47490 FQ	57410 MW	74520 TQ	USBLS	5/15
	Cheyenne MSA, WY	Y	47490 FQ	53970 MW	63030 TQ	USBLS	5/15
	Puerto Rico	Y	25300 FQ	32200 MW	43670 TQ	USBLS	5/15
	San Juan-Carolina-Caguas						
	MSA, PR	Y	26090 FQ	33460 MW	45070 TQ	USBLS	5/15
	Virgin Islands	Y	33630 FQ	46710 MW	58350 TQ	USBLS	5/15
	Guam	Y	31090 FQ	37780 MW	47850 TQ	USBLS	5/15
Accounting Clerk							
County Government	Crisp County, GA	Y	33560 LO		41863 HI	GACTY04	2016
County Government	Dougherty County, GA	Y	23957 LO		35559 HI	GACTY04	2016
County Government	Gwinnett County, GA	Y	26911 LO		41712 HI	GACTY04	2016
Accounting Manager							
Municipal Government	Detroit, MI	M			5417 HI	DETGOV	2016
Activities Aide							
Veteran Services, State Government	Ohio	H	14.72 LO		16.54 HI	OHGOV	2015
Activities Coordinator							
Life Plan Community	United States	Y		36282 AW		LAGE2	2015
Actor	Arizona	H	10.86 FQ	14.73 MW	29.54 TQ	USBLS	5/15
	Colorado	H	9.03 FQ	11.15 MW	20.24 TQ	USBLS	5/15
	District of Columbia	H	10.69 FQ	17.53 MW	31.16 TQ	USBLS	5/15
	Florida	H	12.36 AE	16.87 MW	20.32 AEX	FLBLS	7/16-9/16
	Georgia	H	9.06 FQ	11.77 MW	17.21 TQ	USBLS	5/15
	Idaho	H	11.17 FQ	17.95 MW	27.22 TQ	USBLS	5/15
	Indiana	H	8.23 FQ	9.00 MW	10.84 TQ	USBLS	5/15
	Iowa	H	8.64 FQ	13.17 MW	33.79 TQ	USBLS	5/15
	Louisiana	H	8.89 FQ	15.85 MW	48.03 TQ	USBLS	5/15

AE Average entry wage	**AWR** Average wage range	**H** Hourly	**LR** Low end range	**MTC** Median total compensation	**TCC** Total cash compensation
AEX Average experienced wage	**B** Biweekly	**HI** Highest wage paid	**M** Monthly	**MW** Median wage paid	**TQ** Third quartile wage
ATC Average total compensation	**D** Daily	**HR** High end range	**MCC** Median cash compensation	**MWR** Median wage range	**W** Weekly
AW Average wage paid	**FQ** First quartile wage	**LO** Lowest wage paid	**ME** Median entry wage	**S** See annotated source	**Y** Yearly

Occupation/Type/Industry	Location	Per	Low	Mid	High	Source	Date
Actor	Maryland	H	9.00 AE	27.50 MW	36.50 AEX	MDBLS	4/16
	Massachusetts	H	9.50 FQ	11.35 MW	18.30 TQ	USBLS	5/15
	Michigan	H	10.28 FQ	13.27 MW	26.02 TQ	USBLS	5/15
	Minnesota	H	8.81 FQ	9.47 MW	15.89 TQ	MNBLS	1/16-3/16
	Missouri	H	12.04 FQ	15.02 MW	27.31 TQ	USBLS	5/15
	Nevada	H	20.77 FQ	27.03 MW	36.62 TQ	USBLS	5/15
	New Jersey	H	11.73 FQ	17.31 MW	30.50 TQ	USBLS	5/15
	North Carolina	H	9.61 FQ	11.68 MW	19.70 TQ	USBLS	5/15
	Ohio	H	9.07 FQ	10.58 MW	20.41 TQ	USBLS	5/15
	Oregon	H	10.39 FQ	11.24 MW	12.09 TQ	ORBLS	2016
	Pennsylvania	H	10.89 FQ	16.16 MW	20.65 TQ	USBLS	5/15
	South Carolina	H	11.11 FQ	16.24 MW	20.87 TQ	USBLS	5/15
	Tennessee	H	9.50 FQ	17.34 MW	54.67 TQ	USBLS	5/15
	Texas	H	11.99 FQ	18.85 MW	23.80 TQ	USBLS	5/15
	Utah	H	9.03 FQ	18.35 MW	21.91 TQ	USBLS	5/15
	Virginia	H	10.59 FQ	13.67 MW	18.22 TQ	USBLS	5/15
	Wisconsin	H	9.18 FQ	13.71 MW	27.73 TQ	USBLS	5/15
Television Comedy	United States	S		355200 AW		VAR01	2016
Television Drama	United States	S		402000 AW		VAR01	2016
Actuary	Alabama	Y	65787 AE	100475 AW	117824 AEX	ALBLS	6/16
	Birmingham-Hoover MSA, AL	Y	64217 AE	95256 AW	110780 AEX	ALBLS	6/16
	Arizona	Y	75710 FQ	86690 MW	96710 TQ	USBLS	5/15
	Phoenix-Mesa-Scottsdale MSA, AZ	Y	75280 FQ	86570 MW	96730 TQ	USBLS	5/15
	California	H	38.10 FQ	49.00 MW	66.49 TQ	CABLS	1/16-3/16
	Anaheim-Santa Ana-Irvine PMSA, CA	H	41.54 FQ	53.27 MW	69.66 TQ	CABLS	1/16-3/16
	Los Angeles-Long Beach-Glendale PMSA, CA	H	36.90 FQ	48.78 MW	64.34 TQ	CABLS	1/16-3/16
	Oakland-Hayward-Berkeley PMSA, CA	H	38.46 FQ	53.16 MW	73.76 TQ	CABLS	1/16-3/16
	Sacramento–Roseville–Arden-Arcade MSA, CA	H	33.69 FQ	44.46 MW	59.56 TQ	CABLS	1/16-3/16
	San Diego-Carlsbad MSA, CA	H	37.07 FQ	44.96 MW	61.52 TQ	CABLS	1/16-3/16
	San Francisco-Redwood City-South San Francisco PMSA, CA	H	38.73 FQ	47.32 MW	69.02 TQ	CABLS	1/16-3/16
	Colorado	Y	79660 FQ	132340 MW		USBLS	5/15
	Connecticut	Y		99471 MW		CTBLS	1/16-3/16
	Bridgeport-Stamford-Norwalk MSA, CT	Y	77420 FQ	95620 MW	128920 TQ	USBLS	5/15
	Hartford-West Hartford-East Hartford MSA, CT	Y	75430 FQ	98220 MW	127010 TQ	USBLS	5/15
	Delaware	Y	72440 FQ	99830 MW	121710 TQ	USBLS	5/15
	Wilmington PMSA, DE-MD-NJ	Y	72520 FQ	99830 MW	121330 TQ	USBLS	5/15
	District of Columbia	Y	94300 FQ	118080 MW	139520 TQ	USBLS	5/15
	Washington-Arlington-Alexandria PMSA, DC-VA-MD-WV	Y	93860 FQ	125220 MW	152780 TQ	USBLS	5/15
	Florida	H	30.88 AE	43.61 MW	58.49 AEX	FLBLS	7/16-9/16
	Fort Lauderdale-Pompano Beach-Deerfield Beach PMSA, FL	H	34.63 AE	44.81 MW	54.76 AEX	FLBLS	7/16-9/16
	Miami-Miami Beach-Kendall PMSA, FL	H	35.72 AE	44.89 MW	55.02 AEX	FLBLS	7/16-9/16
	Orlando-Kissimmee-Sanford MSA, FL	H	36.11 AE	46.97 MW	68.54 AEX	FLBLS	7/16-9/16
	Tampa-St. Petersburg-Clearwater MSA, FL	H	30.99 AE	44.75 MW	62.69 AEX	FLBLS	7/16-9/16
	Georgia	Y	61220 FQ	82410 MW	114100 TQ	USBLS	5/15
	Atlanta-Sandy Springs-Roswell MSA, GA	Y	60920 FQ	82180 MW	116790 TQ	USBLS	5/15
	Illinois	Y	67190 FQ	84840 MW	116240 TQ	USBLS	5/15
	Chicago-Naperville-Arlington Heights PMSA, IL	Y	66470 FQ	81880 MW	114590 TQ	USBLS	5/15
	Lake County-Kenosha County PMSA, IL-WI	Y	69480 FQ	102550 MW	179290 TQ	USBLS	5/15
	Indiana	Y	70360 FQ	91440 MW	120180 TQ	USBLS	5/15
	Indianapolis-Carmel-Anderson MSA, IN	Y	69150 FQ	90850 MW	119280 TQ	USBLS	5/15

AE	Average entry wage	AWR	Average wage range	H	Hourly	LR	Low end range	MTC	Median total compensation	TCC	Total cash compensation
AEX	Average experienced wage	B	Biweekly	HI	Highest wage paid	M	Monthly	MW	Median wage paid	TQ	Third quartile wage
ATC	Average total compensation	D	Daily	HR	High end range	MCC	Median cash compensation	MWR	Median wage range	W	Weekly
AW	Average wage paid	FQ	First quartile wage	LO	Lowest wage paid	ME	Median entry wage	S	See annotated source	Y	Yearly

5

Occupation/Type/Industry	Location	Per	Low	Mid	High	Source	Date
Actuary	Iowa	Y	68260 FQ	91000 MW	124090 TQ	USBLS	5/15
	Des Moines-West Des Moines MSA, IA	Y	67730 FQ	90330 MW	121220 TQ	USBLS	5/15
	Kansas	Y	85560 FQ	149760 MW	181660 TQ	USBLS	5/15
	Maine	Y	65700 FQ	101820 MW	142480 TQ	USBLS	5/15
	Portland-South Portland MSA, ME	Y	65830 FQ	103030 MW	143410 TQ	USBLS	5/15
	Baltimore-Columbia-Towson MSA, MD	Y	88740 FQ	121640 MW	149900 TQ	USBLS	5/15
	Massachusetts	Y	77830 FQ	101860 MW	138660 TQ	USBLS	5/15
	Boston-Cambridge-Newton NECTA, MA	Y	80150 FQ	104930 MW	146660 TQ	USBLS	5/15
	Worcester MSA, MA-CT	Y	79640 FQ	107270 MW	125450 TQ	USBLS	5/15
	Michigan	Y	64680 FQ	85910 MW	119260 TQ	USBLS	5/15
	Detroit-Dearborn-Livonia PMSA, MI	Y	66940 FQ	78570 MW	98590 TQ	USBLS	5/15
	Grand Rapids-Wyoming MSA, MI	Y	66890 FQ	87190 MW	116960 TQ	USBLS	5/15
	Minnesota	Y	76521 FQ	96259 MW	124676 TQ	MNBLS	1/16-3/16
	Minneapolis-St. Paul-Bloomington MSA, MN-WI	Y	76400 FQ	95916 MW	123416 TQ	MNBLS	1/16-3/16
	Mississippi	Y	47740 FQ	78320 MW	114410 TQ	USBLS	5/15
	Jackson MSA, MS	Y	47740 FQ	78320 MW	114410 TQ	USBLS	5/15
	Missouri	Y	62210 FQ	84950 MW	122020 TQ	USBLS	5/15
	St. Louis MSA, MO-IL	Y	62460 FQ	81960 MW	114360 TQ	USBLS	5/15
	Nebraska	Y	65110 FQ	78105 MW	115895 TQ	NEBLS	7/16-9/16
	Omaha-Council Bluffs MSA, NE-IA	Y	65565 FQ	77790 MW	112860 TQ	NEBLS	7/16-9/16
	New Hampshire	H	31.57 AE	46.45 MW	60.88 AEX	NHBLS	6/16
	New Jersey	Y	78830 FQ	101660 MW	144280 TQ	USBLS	5/15
	Camden PMSA, NJ	Y	78190 FQ	107060 MW	147480 TQ	USBLS	5/15
	Newark PMSA, NJ-PA	Y	77060 FQ	97760 MW	129320 TQ	USBLS	5/15
	Trenton MSA, NJ	Y	79420 FQ	96590 MW	124270 TQ	USBLS	5/15
	New York	Y	70680 AE	112160 MW	162310 AEX	NYBLS	1/16-3/16
	Buffalo-Cheektowaga-Niagara Falls MSA, NY	Y	57430 FQ	66410 MW	76330 TQ	USBLS	5/15
	Nassau County-Suffolk County PMSA, NY	Y	86530 FQ	95510 MW	109240 TQ	USBLS	5/15
	New York-Jersey City-White Plains PMSA, NY-NJ	Y	81800 FQ	117910 MW	170560 TQ	USBLS	5/15
	Rochester MSA, NY	Y	80160 FQ	98350 MW	136560 TQ	USBLS	5/15
	North Carolina	Y	67780 FQ	94380 MW	136460 TQ	USBLS	5/15
	Charlotte-Concord-Gastonia MSA, NC-SC	Y	70020 FQ	108720 MW	147340 TQ	USBLS	5/15
	Ohio	Y	67280 FQ	89430 MW	120550 TQ	USBLS	5/15
	Cincinnati MSA, OH-KY-IN	Y	65590 FQ	94360 MW	123390 TQ	USBLS	5/15
	Cleveland-Elyria MSA, OH	Y	58690 FQ	79410 MW	104260 TQ	USBLS	5/15
	Columbus MSA, OH	Y	71620 FQ	92670 MW	131450 TQ	USBLS	5/15
	Oklahoma	Y	62740 FQ	79500 MW	119950 TQ	USBLS	5/15
	Oklahoma City MSA, OK	Y	66260 FQ	83360 MW	119650 TQ	USBLS	5/15
	Oregon	H	29.03 FQ	38.25 MW	46.10 TQ	ORBLS	2016
	Portland-Vancouver-Hillsboro MSA, OR-WA	Y	64630 FQ	84930 MW	109980 TQ	USBLS	5/15
	Pennsylvania	Y	76630 FQ	101710 MW	140360 TQ	USBLS	5/15
	Allentown-Bethlehem-Easton MSA, PA-NJ	Y	84310 FQ	107590 MW	123050 TQ	USBLS	5/15
	Harrisburg-Carlisle MSA, PA	Y	72370 FQ	91750 MW	123320 TQ	USBLS	5/15
	Philadelphia PMSA, PA	Y	76380 FQ	101880 MW	128540 TQ	USBLS	5/15
	Pittsburgh MSA, PA	Y	71460 FQ	91660 MW	136540 TQ	USBLS	5/15
	Rhode Island	Y	65330 FQ	77800 MW	100680 TQ	USBLS	5/15
	Providence-Warwick MSA, RI-MA	Y	66270 FQ	79740 MW	105490 TQ	USBLS	5/15
	Columbia MSA, SC	Y	55870 FQ	75180 MW	105170 TQ	USBLS	5/15
	Tennessee	Y	67800 FQ	85350 MW	109280 TQ	USBLS	5/15
	Nashville-Davidson–Murfreesboro–Franklin MSA, TN	Y	63430 FQ	79400 MW	95380 TQ	USBLS	5/15
	Texas	Y	74730 FQ	101740 MW	143550 TQ	USBLS	5/15
	Austin-Round Rock MSA, TX	Y	66350 FQ	80530 MW	121680 TQ	USBLS	5/15
	Dallas-Plano-Irving PMSA, TX	Y	74280 FQ	100970 MW	143020 TQ	USBLS	5/15
	Fort Worth-Arlington PMSA, TX	Y	70890 FQ	92550 MW	181720 TQ	USBLS	5/15

AE Average entry wage	**AWR** Average wage range	**H** Hourly	**LR** Low end range	**MTC** Median total compensation	**TCC** Total cash compensation
AEX Average experienced wage	**B** Biweekly	**HI** Highest wage paid	**M** Monthly	**MCC** Median cash compensation	**TQ** Third quartile wage
ATC Average total compensation	**D** Daily	**HR** High end range	**MCC** Median cash compensation	**MWR** Median wage range	**W** Weekly
AW Average wage paid	**FQ** First quartile wage	**LO** Lowest wage paid	**ME** Median entry wage	**S** See annotated source	**Y** Yearly

Occupation/Type/Industry	Location	Per	Low	Mid	High	Source	Date
Actuary	Houston-The Woodlands-Sugar Land MSA, TX	Y	86710 FQ	119710 MW	148190 TQ	USBLS	5/15
	San Antonio-New Braunfels MSA, TX	Y	75990 FQ	102830 MW	138150 TQ	USBLS	5/15
	Utah	Y	42130 FQ	50910 MW	84600 TQ	USBLS	5/15
	Salt Lake City MSA, UT	Y	45630 FQ	71520 MW	94760 TQ	USBLS	5/15
	Richmond MSA, VA	Y	65820 FQ	89190 MW	137530 TQ	USBLS	5/15
	Washington	H	39.46 FQ	47.54 MW	64.30 TQ	WABLS	3/16
	Seattle-Bellevue-Everett PMSA, WA	H	40.83 FQ	49.10 MW	64.77 TQ	WABLS	3/16
	Wisconsin	Y	70490 FQ	95020 MW	130440 TQ	USBLS	5/15
	Madison MSA, WI	Y	69010 FQ	91480 MW	119720 TQ	USBLS	5/15
	Milwaukee-Waukesha-West Allis MSA, WI	Y	72190 FQ	107780 MW	161340 TQ	USBLS	5/15
Acupuncturist							
Department of Public Health, Mental Health, Community Care	San Francisco, CA	B	2514 LO		3056 HI	SFGOV	2016-2018
ADA Coordinator							
Municipal Government	Colorado Springs, CO	Y	62111 LO		85402 HI	COSPRS	2017
Adaptive Equipment Technician							
Veteran Services, State Government	Ohio	H			20.45 HI	OHGOV	2015
Addiction and Rehabilitation Counselor	United States	Y		39270 MW		FTIME	2016
Adhesive Bonding Machine Operator and Tender	Alabama	Y	25232 AE	38394 AW	44974 AEX	ALBLS	6/16
	Birmingham-Hoover MSA, AL	Y	22888 AE	31731 AW	36162 AEX	ALBLS	6/16
	Arizona	Y	21430 FQ	24390 MW	32620 TQ	USBLS	5/15
	Arkansas	Y	25580 FQ	33130 MW	37660 TQ	USBLS	5/15
	California	H	12.59 FQ	15.49 MW	19.65 TQ	CABLS	1/16-3/16
	Anaheim-Santa Ana-Irvine PMSA, CA	H	12.23 FQ	13.57 MW	14.90 TQ	CABLS	1/16-3/16
	Los Angeles-Long Beach-Glendale PMSA, CA	H	10.64 FQ	14.99 MW	19.08 TQ	CABLS	1/16-3/16
	Oakland-Hayward-Berkeley PMSA, CA	H	13.37 FQ	16.42 MW	18.88 TQ	CABLS	1/16-3/16
	Riverside-San Bernardino-Ontario MSA, CA	H	13.48 FQ	15.92 MW	21.36 TQ	CABLS	1/16-3/16
	Sacramento–Roseville–Arden-Arcade MSA, CA	H	11.04 FQ	15.33 MW	18.84 TQ	CABLS	1/16-3/16
	Colorado	Y	30240 FQ	34500 MW	38490 TQ	USBLS	5/15
	Denver-Aurora-Lakewood MSA, CO	Y	30250 FQ	34090 MW	37530 TQ	USBLS	5/15
	Connecticut	Y		38298 MW		CTBLS	1/16-3/16
	Hartford-West Hartford-East Hartford MSA, CT	Y	34640 FQ	38520 MW	45870 TQ	USBLS	5/15
	Florida	H	10.54 AE	13.94 MW	16.60 AEX	FLBLS	7/16-9/16
	Tampa-St. Petersburg-Clearwater MSA, FL	H	10.68 AE	18.16 MW	20.02 AEX	FLBLS	7/16-9/16
	Georgia	Y	22810 FQ	27190 MW	35750 TQ	USBLS	5/15
	Atlanta-Sandy Springs-Roswell MSA, GA	Y	22920 FQ	27280 MW	35910 TQ	USBLS	5/15
	Illinois	Y	30690 FQ	37520 MW	45960 TQ	USBLS	5/15
	Chicago-Naperville-Arlington Heights PMSA, IL	Y	31140 FQ	37960 MW	46690 TQ	USBLS	5/15
	Indiana	Y	23950 FQ	29780 MW	37900 TQ	USBLS	5/15
	Indianapolis-Carmel-Anderson MSA, IN	Y	33560 FQ	39330 MW	45310 TQ	USBLS	5/15
	Iowa	Y	25630 FQ	31640 MW	37500 TQ	USBLS	5/15
	Kansas	Y	23490 FQ	28100 MW	33970 TQ	USBLS	5/15
	Wichita MSA, KS	Y	21010 FQ	24920 MW	33880 TQ	USBLS	5/15
	Kentucky	Y	26920 FQ	32280 MW	37410 TQ	USBLS	5/15
	Louisville-Jefferson County MSA, KY-IN	Y	25740 FQ	30520 MW	38590 TQ	USBLS	5/15
	Louisiana	Y	29770 FQ	35760 MW	40960 TQ	USBLS	5/15
	Maine	Y	25680 FQ	27480 MW	29290 TQ	USBLS	5/15
	Maryland	Y	21152 AE	34193 MW	40714 AEX	MDBLS	4/16

Occupation/Type/Industry	Location	Per	Low	Mid	High	Source	Date
Adhesive Bonding Machine Operator and Tender	Baltimore-Columbia-Towson MSA, MD	Y	22390 FQ	33500 MW	44730 TQ	USBLS	5/15
	Massachusetts	Y	23510 FQ	30230 MW	40510 TQ	USBLS	5/15
	Michigan	Y	20780 FQ	24030 MW	31580 TQ	USBLS	5/15
	Grand Rapids-Wyoming MSA, MI	Y	25260 FQ	29470 MW	37610 TQ	USBLS	5/15
	Minnesota	Y	27690 FQ	33360 MW	37481 TQ	MNBLS	1/16-3/16
	Minneapolis-St. Paul-Bloomington MSA, MN-WI	Y	29482 FQ	34717 MW	38078 TQ	MNBLS	1/16-3/16
	Mississippi	Y	20900 FQ	24100 MW	28680 TQ	USBLS	5/15
	Jackson MSA, MS	Y	23840 FQ	29020 MW	34550 TQ	USBLS	5/15
	Missouri	Y	22550 FQ	27350 MW	34010 TQ	USBLS	5/15
	Kansas City MSA, MO-KS	Y	24830 FQ	29150 MW	34920 TQ	USBLS	5/15
	Nebraska	Y	32635 FQ	36930 MW	42525 TQ	NEBLS	7/16-9/16
	New Hampshire	H	14.79 AE	16.73 MW	17.27 AEX	NHBLS	6/16
	New Jersey	Y	25500 FQ	32300 MW	39510 TQ	USBLS	5/15
	Camden PMSA, NJ	Y	29920 FQ	52230 MW	57930 TQ	USBLS	5/15
	New York	Y	22740 AE	29580 MW	37510 AEX	NYBLS	1/16-3/16
	Buffalo-Cheektowaga-Niagara Falls MSA, NY	Y	27870 FQ	31700 MW	55830 TQ	USBLS	5/15
	Nassau County-Suffolk County PMSA, NY	Y	29000 FQ	35070 MW	42080 TQ	USBLS	5/15
	New York-Jersey City-White Plains PMSA, NY-NJ	Y	24540 FQ	31100 MW	36710 TQ	USBLS	5/15
	North Carolina	Y	21920 FQ	26190 MW	32720 TQ	USBLS	5/15
	Ohio	Y	29020 FQ	35940 MW	43240 TQ	USBLS	5/15
	Cincinnati MSA, OH-KY-IN	Y	26430 FQ	29840 MW	39610 TQ	USBLS	5/15
	Cleveland-Elyria MSA, OH	Y	27120 FQ	34080 MW	38080 TQ	USBLS	5/15
	Columbus MSA, OH	Y	28860 FQ	34800 MW	42150 TQ	USBLS	5/15
	Oklahoma	Y	21890 FQ	24850 MW	32260 TQ	USBLS	5/15
	Oregon	H	15.96 FQ	17.92 MW	20.37 TQ	ORBLS	2016
	Portland-Vancouver-Hillsboro MSA, OR-WA	Y	29770 FQ	35170 MW	42360 TQ	USBLS	5/15
	Pennsylvania	Y	28310 FQ	34070 MW	41690 TQ	USBLS	5/15
	Harrisburg-Carlisle MSA, PA	Y	30690 FQ	42770 MW	46920 TQ	USBLS	5/15
	Montgomery County-Bucks County-Chester County PMSA, PA	Y	28110 FQ	33520 MW	41100 TQ	USBLS	5/15
	Pittsburgh MSA, PA	Y	27430 FQ	31760 MW	40200 TQ	USBLS	5/15
	Rhode Island	Y	24250 FQ	31050 MW	37760 TQ	USBLS	5/15
	Providence-Warwick MSA, RI-MA	Y	24250 FQ	31050 MW	37760 TQ	USBLS	5/15
	South Carolina	Y	25330 FQ	29240 MW	34560 TQ	USBLS	5/15
	South Dakota	Y	25490 FQ	28240 MW	30980 TQ	USBLS	5/15
	Tennessee	Y	22610 FQ	27180 MW	35330 TQ	USBLS	5/15
	Memphis MSA, TN-MS-AR	Y	22260 FQ	26860 MW	35850 TQ	USBLS	5/15
	Nashville-Davidson–Murfreesboro–Franklin MSA, TN	Y	24520 FQ	29830 MW	37910 TQ	USBLS	5/15
	Texas	Y	25790 FQ	33580 MW	53100 TQ	USBLS	5/15
	Austin-Round Rock MSA, TX	Y	22210 FQ	27730 MW	33310 TQ	USBLS	5/15
	Fort Worth-Arlington PMSA, TX	Y	32650 FQ	38930 MW	69440 TQ	USBLS	5/15
	Houston-The Woodlands-Sugar Land MSA, TX	Y	18660 FQ	26760 MW	31280 TQ	USBLS	5/15
	San Antonio-New Braunfels MSA, TX	Y	30080 FQ	33880 MW	37500 TQ	USBLS	5/15
	Vermont	Y	20800 FQ	27810 MW	36920 TQ	USBLS	5/15
	Virginia	Y	24830 FQ	32920 MW	40050 TQ	USBLS	5/15
	Richmond MSA, VA	Y	26090 FQ	35270 MW	44770 TQ	USBLS	5/15
	Washington	H	15.13 FQ	19.96 MW	33.73 TQ	WABLS	3/16
	Tacoma-Lakewood PMSA, WA	H	16.04 FQ	17.58 MW	19.11 TQ	WABLS	3/16
	West Virginia	Y	24910 FQ	33680 MW	39540 TQ	USBLS	5/15
	Huntington-Ashland MSA, WV-KY-OH	Y	28920 FQ	51490 MW	57300 TQ	USBLS	5/15
	Wisconsin	Y	27740 FQ	33340 MW	37880 TQ	USBLS	5/15
	Milwaukee-Waukesha-West Allis MSA, WI	Y	23840 FQ	30120 MW	37100 TQ	USBLS	5/15
	Puerto Rico	Y	16860 FQ	18380 MW	21500 TQ	USBLS	5/15

AE	Average entry wage	AWR	Average wage range	H	Hourly
AEX	Average experienced wage	B	Biweekly	HI	Highest wage paid
ATC	Average total compensation	D	Daily	HR	High end range
AW	Average wage paid	FQ	First quartile wage	LO	Lowest wage paid

LR	Low end range	MTC	Median total compensation
M	Monthly	MW	Median wage paid
MCC	Median cash compensation	MWR	Median wage range
ME	Median entry wage	S	See annotated source

TCC	Total cash compensation		
TQ	Third quartile wage		
W	Weekly		
Y	Yearly		

Occupation/Type/Industry	Location	Per	Low	Mid	High	Source	Date
Administrative Analyst							
Police Department, Municipal Government	Anaheim, CA	Y			85847 HI	CACIT	6/28/16
Administrative Appeals Judge	Denver-Aurora LPA, CO	Y	134747 LO		172100 HI	OPM02	2017
	Albany-Schenectady LPA, NY	Y	125234 LO		172100 HI	OPM02	2017
	Cleveland-Akron-Canton LPA, OH	Y	129407 LO		172100 HI	OPM02	2017
	Portland-Vancouver-Salem LPA, OR-WA	Y	131828 LO		172100 HI	OPM02	2017
	Dallas-Fort Worth LPA, TX-OK	Y	132541 LO		172100 HI	OPM02	2017
Administrative Law Judge, Adjudicator, and Hearing Officer							
	Alabama	Y	74665 AE	129964 AW	157618 AEX	ALBLS	6/16
	Birmingham-Hoover MSA, AL	Y	83218 AE	137914 AW	165253 AEX	ALBLS	6/16
	Alaska	Y	89040 FQ	104360 MW	122990 TQ	USBLS	5/15
	Arizona	Y	63740 FQ	88890 MW	99570 TQ	USBLS	5/15
	Phoenix-Mesa-Scottsdale MSA, AZ	Y	71800 FQ	89880 MW	99610 TQ	USBLS	5/15
	Tucson MSA, AZ	Y	55970 FQ	87080 MW	101940 TQ	USBLS	5/15
	Arkansas	Y	17470 FQ	19390 MW	61520 TQ	USBLS	5/15
	Little Rock-North Little Rock-Conway MSA, AR	Y	18490 FQ	54270 MW	99680 TQ	USBLS	5/15
	California	H	48.90 FQ	58.59 MW	62.13 TQ	CABLS	1/16-3/16
	Anaheim-Santa Ana-Irvine PMSA, CA	H	40.67 FQ	51.38 MW	61.47 TQ	CABLS	1/16-3/16
	Oakland-Hayward-Berkeley PMSA, CA	H	54.22 FQ	58.59 MW	61.47 TQ	CABLS	1/16-3/16
	Riverside-San Bernardino-Ontario MSA, CA	H	54.84 FQ	61.46 MW	68.96 TQ	CABLS	1/16-3/16
	Sacramento–Roseville–Arden-Arcade MSA, CA	H	53.87 FQ	60.94 MW	61.47 TQ	CABLS	1/16-3/16
	San Francisco-Redwood City-South San Francisco PMSA, CA	H	51.41 FQ	61.46 MW	62.66 TQ	CABLS	1/16-3/16
	Colorado	Y	73670 FQ	103240 MW	127360 TQ	USBLS	5/15
	Denver-Aurora-Lakewood MSA, CO	Y	79330 FQ	104500 MW	127040 TQ	USBLS	5/15
	Connecticut	Y		100952 MW		CTBLS	1/16-3/16
	Delaware	Y	41570 FQ	47580 MW	81330 TQ	USBLS	5/15
	Wilmington PMSA, DE-MD-NJ	Y	41570 FQ	47570 MW	64160 TQ	USBLS	5/15
	Washington-Arlington-Alexandria PMSA, DC-VA-MD-WV	Y	105970 FQ	128790 MW	151920 TQ	USBLS	5/15
	Florida	H	18.90 AE	46.58 MW	58.48 AEX	FLBLS	7/16-9/16
	Fort Lauderdale-Pompano Beach-Deerfield Beach PMSA, FL	H	25.72 AE	56.53 MW	70.02 AEX	FLBLS	7/16-9/16
	Orlando-Kissimmee-Sanford MSA, FL	H	18.70 AE	49.31 MW	63.32 AEX	FLBLS	7/16-9/16
	Tampa-St. Petersburg-Clearwater MSA, FL	H	23.25 AE	47.94 MW	59.58 AEX	FLBLS	7/16-9/16
	Georgia	Y	37620 FQ	47690 MW	95940 TQ	USBLS	5/15
	Atlanta-Sandy Springs-Roswell MSA, GA	Y	39660 FQ	49320 MW	98630 TQ	USBLS	5/15
	Hawaii	Y	67620 FQ	85290 MW	98480 TQ	USBLS	5/15
	Idaho	Y	52380 FQ	69060 MW	94590 TQ	USBLS	5/15
	Boise City MSA, ID	Y	50230 FQ	66540 MW	87050 TQ	USBLS	5/15
	Illinois	Y	59130 FQ	79870 MW	107690 TQ	USBLS	5/15
	Chicago-Naperville-Arlington Heights PMSA, IL	Y	81790 FQ	103670 MW	140520 TQ	USBLS	5/15
	Indiana	Y	92520 FQ	115600 MW	138760 TQ	USBLS	5/15
	Indianapolis-Carmel-Anderson MSA, IN	Y	92240 FQ	109410 MW	124190 TQ	USBLS	5/15
	Iowa	Y	102590 FQ	113100 MW	113110 TQ	USBLS	5/15
	Des Moines-West Des Moines MSA, IA	Y	102590 FQ	113100 MW	113110 TQ	USBLS	5/15
	Kansas	Y	83450 FQ	103200 MW	148860 TQ	USBLS	5/15
	Kentucky	Y	34760 FQ	38490 MW	49150 TQ	USBLS	5/15

AE	Average entry wage	AWR	Average wage range	H	Hourly	LR	Low end range	MTC	Median total compensation	TCC	Total cash compensation
AEX	Average experienced wage	B	Biweekly	HI	Highest wage paid	M	Monthly	MW	Median wage paid	TQ	Third quartile wage
ATC	Average total compensation	D	Daily	HR	High end range	MCC	Median cash compensation	MWR	Median wage range	W	Weekly
AW	Average wage paid	FQ	First quartile wage	LO	Lowest wage paid	ME	Median entry wage	S	See annotated source	Y	Yearly

Occupation/Type/Industry	Location	Per	Low	Mid	High	Source	Date
Administrative Law Judge, Adjudicator, and Hearing Officer	Louisville-Jefferson County MSA, KY-IN	Y	34870 FQ	38700 MW	86240 TQ	USBLS	5/15
	Louisiana	Y	19430 FQ	56740 MW	97370 TQ	USBLS	5/15
	Baton Rouge MSA, LA	Y	17780 FQ	39530 MW	48700 TQ	USBLS	5/15
	New Orleans-Metairie MSA, LA	Y	83450 FQ	108500 MW	158350 TQ	USBLS	5/15
	Maine	Y	42310 FQ	50070 MW	63020 TQ	USBLS	5/15
	Maryland	Y	57087 AE	96772 MW	116614 AEX	MDBLS	4/16
	Baltimore-Columbia-Towson MSA, MD	Y	76800 FQ	96830 MW	115040 TQ	USBLS	5/15
	Massachusetts	Y	100360 FQ	126100 MW	168690 TQ	USBLS	5/15
	Boston-Cambridge-Newton NECTA, MA	Y	94290 FQ	118620 MW	168690 TQ	USBLS	5/15
	Michigan	Y	82420 FQ	99800 MW	118720 TQ	USBLS	5/15
	Detroit-Dearborn-Livonia PMSA, MI	Y	97810 FQ	111060 MW	144930 TQ	USBLS	5/15
	Minnesota	Y	87065 FQ	104011 MW	124585 TQ	MNBLS	1/16-3/16
	Minneapolis-St. Paul-Bloomington MSA, MN-WI	Y	87065 FQ	104011 MW	124585 TQ	MNBLS	1/16-3/16
	Mississippi	Y	37290 FQ	91820 MW	128670 TQ	USBLS	5/15
	Jackson MSA, MS	Y	40860 FQ	91830 MW	116270 TQ	USBLS	5/15
	Missouri	Y	60260 FQ	108500 MW	148860 TQ	USBLS	5/15
	Kansas City MSA, MO-KS	Y	103200 FQ	120900 MW	158330 TQ	USBLS	5/15
	St. Louis MSA, MO-IL	Y	67610 FQ	100160 MW	148860 TQ	USBLS	5/15
	Montana	Y	48730 FQ	59440 MW	75650 TQ	USBLS	5/15
	Nebraska	Y	94585 FQ	97375 MW	121655 TQ	NEBLS	7/16-9/16
	Omaha-Council Bluffs MSA, NE-IA	Y	97365 FQ	121640 MW	167360 TQ	NEBLS	7/16-9/16
	Nevada	Y	43560 FQ	59530 MW	91820 TQ	USBLS	5/15
	Las Vegas-Henderson-Paradise MSA, NV	Y	50580 FQ	72350 MW	102950 TQ	USBLS	5/15
	New Hampshire	H	22.61 AE	29.82 MW	39.99 AEX	NHBLS	6/16
	New Jersey	Y	84430 FQ	103220 MW	127450 TQ	USBLS	5/15
	Newark PMSA, NJ-PA	Y	81770 FQ	97250 MW	129670 TQ	USBLS	5/15
	New Mexico	Y	39820 FQ	47280 MW	62980 TQ	USBLS	5/15
	Albuquerque MSA, NM	Y	39810 FQ	47290 MW	66140 TQ	USBLS	5/15
	New York	Y	77260 AE	93270 MW	107610 AEX	NYBLS	1/16-3/16
	Buffalo-Cheektowaga-Niagara Falls MSA, NY	Y	74330 FQ	91600 MW	105480 TQ	USBLS	5/15
	Nassau County-Suffolk County PMSA, NY	Y	79240 FQ	90200 MW	99540 TQ	USBLS	5/15
	New York-Jersey City-White Plains PMSA, NY-NJ	Y	82670 FQ	91510 MW	99970 TQ	USBLS	5/15
	North Carolina	Y	49810 FQ	91820 MW	124580 TQ	USBLS	5/15
	Ohio	Y	64740 FQ	91080 MW	112800 TQ	USBLS	5/15
	Cincinnati MSA, OH-KY-IN	Y	72970 FQ	87320 MW	112690 TQ	USBLS	5/15
	Cleveland-Elyria MSA, OH	Y	67280 FQ	95440 MW	125690 TQ	USBLS	5/15
	Columbus MSA, OH	Y	64550 FQ	88800 MW	105210 TQ	USBLS	5/15
	Oklahoma	Y	72630 FQ	96050 MW	124300 TQ	USBLS	5/15
	Oklahoma City MSA, OK	Y	68180 FQ	99290 MW	134140 TQ	USBLS	5/15
	Oregon	H	24.63 FQ	31.24 MW	43.92 TQ	ORBLS	2016
	Portland-Vancouver-Hillsboro MSA, OR-WA	Y	56810 FQ	81220 MW	108530 TQ	USBLS	5/15
	Pennsylvania	Y	57310 FQ	81560 MW	105890 TQ	USBLS	5/15
	Harrisburg-Carlisle MSA, PA	Y	64100 FQ	79740 MW	102580 TQ	USBLS	5/15
	Montgomery County-Bucks County-Chester County PMSA, PA	Y	91800 FQ	111920 MW	168690 TQ	USBLS	5/15
	Philadelphia PMSA, PA	Y	45380 FQ	71510 MW	100910 TQ	USBLS	5/15
	Pittsburgh MSA, PA	Y	73090 FQ	93590 MW	116990 TQ	USBLS	5/15
	Rhode Island	Y	82210 FQ	97330 MW	116020 TQ	USBLS	5/15
	Providence-Warwick MSA, RI-MA	Y	82940 FQ	102860 MW	117040 TQ	USBLS	5/15
	South Carolina	Y	48870 FQ	91820 MW	136300 TQ	USBLS	5/15
	Columbia MSA, SC	Y	45820 FQ	53200 MW	94580 TQ	USBLS	5/15
	Tennessee	Y	49810 FQ	83450 MW	125020 TQ	USBLS	5/15
	Memphis MSA, TN-MS-AR	Y	68310 FQ	81900 MW	96510 TQ	USBLS	5/15

AE	Average entry wage	AWR	Average wage range	H	Hourly	LR	Low end range	MTC	Median total compensation	TCC	Total cash compensation
AEX	Average experienced wage	B	Biweekly	HI	Highest wage paid	M	Monthly	MW	Median wage paid	TQ	Third quartile wage
ATC	Average total compensation	D	Daily	HR	High end range	MCC	Median cash compensation	MWR	Median wage range	W	Weekly
AW	Average wage paid	FQ	First quartile wage	LO	Lowest wage paid	ME	Median entry wage	S	See annotated source	Y	Yearly

Occupation/Type/Industry	Location	Per	Low	Mid	High	Source	Date
Administrative Law Judge, Adjudicator, and Hearing Officer	Nashville-Davidson–Murfreesboro–Franklin MSA, TN	Y	52400 FQ	89040 MW	118520 TQ	USBLS	5/15
	Texas	Y	73190 FQ	86190 MW	114930 TQ	USBLS	5/15
	Austin-Round Rock MSA, TX	Y	86180 FQ	98250 MW	108500 TQ	USBLS	5/15
	Dallas-Plano-Irving PMSA, TX	Y	86190 FQ	114700 MW	155740 TQ	USBLS	5/15
	Fort Worth-Arlington PMSA, TX	Y	81170 FQ	86190 MW	155740 TQ	USBLS	5/15
	Houston-The Woodlands-Sugar Land MSA, TX	Y	66030 FQ	86190 MW	116060 TQ	USBLS	5/15
	San Antonio-New Braunfels MSA, TX	Y	86180 FQ	104760 MW	158330 TQ	USBLS	5/15
	Utah	Y	51850 FQ	68260 MW	91820 TQ	USBLS	5/15
	Salt Lake City MSA, UT	Y	53740 FQ	76440 MW	94590 TQ	USBLS	5/15
	Vermont	Y	49620 FQ	57620 MW	81460 TQ	USBLS	5/15
	Virginia	Y	53580 FQ	78930 MW	126250 TQ	USBLS	5/15
	Richmond MSA, VA	Y	53970 FQ	64910 MW	83810 TQ	USBLS	5/15
	Virginia Beach-Norfolk-Newport News MSA, VA-NC	Y	42010 FQ	54630 MW	148850 TQ	USBLS	5/15
	Washington	H	39.15 FQ	42.97 MW	52.12 TQ	WABLS	3/16
	Seattle-Bellevue-Everett PMSA, WA	H	41.92 FQ	47.78 MW	55.02 TQ	WABLS	3/16
	Tacoma-Lakewood PMSA, WA	H	41.07 FQ	46.60 MW	77.48 TQ	WABLS	3/16
	West Virginia	Y	77960 FQ	91050 MW	99240 TQ	USBLS	5/15
	Wisconsin	Y	88100 FQ	103620 MW	138290 TQ	USBLS	5/15
	Milwaukee-Waukesha-West Allis MSA, WI	Y	97860 FQ	112240 MW	153990 TQ	USBLS	5/15
	Puerto Rico	Y	57900 FQ	72870 MW	95680 TQ	USBLS	5/15
	San Juan-Carolina-Caguas MSA, PR	Y	58210 FQ	72330 MW	92790 TQ	USBLS	5/15
Administrative Nutritionist							
Municipal Government	Detroit, MI	M	5575 LO		5750 HI	DETGOV	2016
Administrative Services Manager	Alabama	Y	60842 AE	103285 AW	124502 AEX	ALBLS	6/16
	Birmingham-Hoover MSA, AL	Y	57910 AE	108215 AW	133358 AEX	ALBLS	6/16
	Alaska	Y	68090 FQ	84370 MW	106280 TQ	USBLS	5/15
	Anchorage MSA, AK	Y	68380 FQ	85860 MW	110510 TQ	USBLS	5/15
	Arizona	Y	60680 FQ	78040 MW	110070 TQ	USBLS	5/15
	Phoenix-Mesa-Scottsdale MSA, AZ	Y	62210 FQ	79810 MW	115730 TQ	USBLS	5/15
	Tucson MSA, AZ	Y	55360 FQ	75190 MW	98020 TQ	USBLS	5/15
	Arkansas	Y	52710 FQ	70460 MW	95090 TQ	USBLS	5/15
	Little Rock-North Little Rock-Conway MSA, AR	Y	53910 FQ	68960 MW	85750 TQ	USBLS	5/15
	California	H	33.10 FQ	45.35 MW	60.72 TQ	CABLS	1/16-3/16
	Anaheim-Santa Ana-Irvine PMSA, CA	H	34.68 FQ	50.29 MW	65.37 TQ	CABLS	1/16-3/16
	Los Angeles-Long Beach-Glendale PMSA, CA	H	33.72 FQ	44.84 MW	59.45 TQ	CABLS	1/16-3/16
	Oakland-Hayward-Berkeley PMSA, CA	H	33.99 FQ	45.52 MW	60.59 TQ	CABLS	1/16-3/16
	Riverside-San Bernardino-Ontario MSA, CA	H	29.92 FQ	42.72 MW	56.69 TQ	CABLS	1/16-3/16
	Sacramento–Roseville–Arden-Arcade MSA, CA	H	31.31 FQ	40.62 MW	52.19 TQ	CABLS	1/16-3/16
	San Diego-Carlsbad MSA, CA	H	31.57 FQ	42.54 MW	58.63 TQ	CABLS	1/16-3/16
	San Francisco-Redwood City-South San Francisco PMSA, CA	H	36.20 FQ	51.67 MW	69.10 TQ	CABLS	1/16-3/16
	Colorado	Y	67940 FQ	93590 MW	122480 TQ	USBLS	5/15
	Denver-Aurora-Lakewood MSA, CO	Y	73430 FQ	100700 MW	128970 TQ	USBLS	5/15
	Connecticut	Y		101117 MW		CTBLS	1/16-3/16
	Bridgeport-Stamford-Norwalk MSA, CT	Y	85350 FQ	103360 MW	130450 TQ	USBLS	5/15
	Hartford-West Hartford-East Hartford MSA, CT	Y	76330 FQ	97030 MW	124220 TQ	USBLS	5/15
	Delaware	Y	83690 FQ	102960 MW	123490 TQ	USBLS	5/15

AE Average entry wage	**AWR** Average wage range	**H** Hourly	**LR** Low end range	**MTC** Median total compensation	**TCC** Total cash compensation
AEX Average experienced wage	**B** Biweekly	**HI** Highest wage paid	**M** Monthly	**MW** Median wage paid	**TQ** Third quartile wage
ATC Average total compensation	**D** Daily	**HR** High end range	**MCC** Median cash compensation	**MWR** Median wage range	**W** Weekly
AW Average wage paid	**FQ** First quartile wage	**LO** Lowest wage paid	**ME** Median entry wage	**S** See annotated source	**Y** Yearly

11

Occupation/Type/Industry	Location	Per	Low	Mid	High	Source	Date
Administrative Services Manager	Wilmington PMSA, DE-MD-NJ	Y	84030 FQ	105440 MW	127000 TQ	USBLS	5/15
	District of Columbia	Y	73210 FQ	98200 MW	125440 TQ	USBLS	5/15
	Washington-Arlington-Alexandria PMSA, DC-VA-MD-WV	Y	77050 FQ	99920 MW	127690 TQ	USBLS	5/15
	Florida	H	32.21 AE	50.08 MW	63.53 AEX	FLBLS	7/16-9/16
	Fort Lauderdale-Pompano Beach-Deerfield Beach PMSA, FL	H	33.90 AE	53.57 MW	65.41 AEX	FLBLS	7/16-9/16
	Miami-Miami Beach-Kendall PMSA, FL	H	34.31 AE	55.75 MW	74.04 AEX	FLBLS	7/16-9/16
	Orlando-Kissimmee-Sanford MSA, FL	H	32.81 AE	52.19 MW	63.20 AEX	FLBLS	7/16-9/16
	Tampa-St. Petersburg-Clearwater MSA, FL	H	29.32 AE	47.57 MW	62.00 AEX	FLBLS	7/16-9/16
	Georgia	Y	56200 FQ	78960 MW	113390 TQ	USBLS	5/15
	Atlanta-Sandy Springs-Roswell MSA, GA	Y	60940 FQ	85570 MW	121340 TQ	USBLS	5/15
	Augusta-Richmond County MSA, GA-SC	Y	43400 FQ	70200 MW	101040 TQ	USBLS	5/15
	Hawaii	Y	49870 FQ	64620 MW	89320 TQ	USBLS	5/15
	Urban Honolulu MSA, HI	Y	52940 FQ	67550 MW	92410 TQ	USBLS	5/15
	Idaho	Y	44550 FQ	65800 MW	94550 TQ	USBLS	5/15
	Boise City MSA, ID	Y	44390 FQ	60110 MW	80080 TQ	USBLS	5/15
	Illinois	Y	50400 FQ	68610 MW	95600 TQ	USBLS	5/15
	Chicago-Naperville-Arlington Heights PMSA, IL	Y	53330 FQ	71130 MW	97900 TQ	USBLS	5/15
	Lake County-Kenosha County PMSA, IL-WI	Y	48180 FQ	63410 MW	90350 TQ	USBLS	5/15
	Indiana	Y	53420 FQ	69360 MW	93070 TQ	USBLS	5/15
	Gary PMSA, IN	Y	49890 FQ	63060 MW	81200 TQ	USBLS	5/15
	Indianapolis-Carmel-Anderson MSA, IN	Y	54960 FQ	71370 MW	94420 TQ	USBLS	5/15
	Iowa	Y	57410 FQ	73140 MW	92560 TQ	USBLS	5/15
	Des Moines-West Des Moines MSA, IA	Y	58440 FQ	78840 MW	100670 TQ	USBLS	5/15
	Kansas	Y	58910 FQ	76040 MW	98960 TQ	USBLS	5/15
	Wichita MSA, KS	Y	58690 FQ	73660 MW	95000 TQ	USBLS	5/15
	Kentucky	Y	51420 FQ	70720 MW	92730 TQ	USBLS	5/15
	Louisville-Jefferson County MSA, KY-IN	Y	55760 FQ	74600 MW	97670 TQ	USBLS	5/15
	Louisiana	Y	49360 FQ	66610 MW	92620 TQ	USBLS	5/15
	Baton Rouge MSA, LA	Y	49580 FQ	69050 MW	97280 TQ	USBLS	5/15
	New Orleans-Metairie MSA, LA	Y	53000 FQ	76420 MW	96810 TQ	USBLS	5/15
	Maine	Y	54050 FQ	70000 MW	89430 TQ	USBLS	5/15
	Portland-South Portland MSA, ME	Y	59630 FQ	78400 MW	97900 TQ	USBLS	5/15
	Maryland	Y	64074 AE	103839 MW	123722 AEX	MDBLS	4/16
	Baltimore-Columbia-Towson MSA, MD	Y	75410 FQ	95020 MW	123390 TQ	USBLS	5/15
	Salisbury MSA, MD-DE	Y	70550 FQ	87060 MW	106880 TQ	USBLS	5/15
	Massachusetts	Y	68880 FQ	93100 MW	125250 TQ	USBLS	5/15
	Boston-Cambridge-Newton NECTA, MA	Y	74540 FQ	100690 MW	132130 TQ	USBLS	5/15
	Worcester MSA, MA-CT	Y	64160 FQ	87890 MW	120850 TQ	USBLS	5/15
	Michigan	Y	57660 FQ	76670 MW	100120 TQ	USBLS	5/15
	Detroit-Dearborn-Livonia PMSA, MI	Y	57300 FQ	76360 MW	98720 TQ	USBLS	5/15
	Grand Rapids-Wyoming MSA, MI	Y	64700 FQ	85190 MW	113110 TQ	USBLS	5/15
	Minnesota	Y	69491 FQ	86470 MW	104201 TQ	MNBLS	1/16-3/16
	Minneapolis-St. Paul-Bloomington MSA, MN-WI	Y	71259 FQ	88238 MW	105715 TQ	MNBLS	1/16-3/16
	Mississippi	Y	39000 FQ	57670 MW	77910 TQ	USBLS	5/15
	Jackson MSA, MS	Y	46460 FQ	66670 MW	83220 TQ	USBLS	5/15
	Missouri	Y	57880 FQ	76000 MW	99840 TQ	USBLS	5/15
	Kansas City MSA, MO-KS	Y	60610 FQ	79240 MW	99470 TQ	USBLS	5/15
	St. Louis MSA, MO-IL	Y	60980 FQ	81620 MW	108590 TQ	USBLS	5/15
	Montana	Y	54000 FQ	70180 MW	92200 TQ	USBLS	5/15
	Billings MSA, MT	Y	51500 FQ	63860 MW	93960 TQ	USBLS	5/15

AE	Average entry wage	AWR	Average wage range	H	Hourly	LR	Low end range	MTC Median total compensation TCC Total cash compensation
AEX	Average experienced wage	B	Biweekly	HI	Highest wage paid	M	Monthly	MW Median wage paid TQ Third quartile wage
ATC	Average total compensation	D	Daily	HR	High end range	MCC	Median cash compensation	MWR Median wage range W Weekly
AW	Average wage paid	FQ	First quartile wage	LO	Lowest wage paid	ME	Median entry wage	S See annotated source Y Yearly

Occupation/Type/Industry	Location	Per	Low	Mid	High	Source	Date
Administrative Services Manager	Nebraska	Y	58960 FQ	77855 MW	106775 TQ	NEBLS	7/16-9/16
	Omaha-Council Bluffs MSA, NE-IA	Y	65680 FQ	84790 MW	114675 TQ	NEBLS	7/16-9/16
	Nevada	Y	58450 FQ	76410 MW	98140 TQ	USBLS	5/15
	Las Vegas-Henderson-Paradise MSA, NV	Y	56010 FQ	76450 MW	100070 TQ	USBLS	5/15
	New Hampshire	H	26.57 AE	38.99 MW	51.09 AEX	NHBLS	6/16
	Manchester NECTA, NH	H	25.10 AE	36.32 MW	51.74 AEX	NHBLS	6/16
	Nashua NECTA, NH-MA	Y	57620 FQ	79600 MW	99010 TQ	USBLS	5/15
	New Jersey	Y	92290 FQ	112320 MW	139370 TQ	USBLS	5/15
	Camden PMSA, NJ	Y	89260 FQ	108510 MW	132310 TQ	USBLS	5/15
	Newark PMSA, NJ-PA	Y	96830 FQ	115680 MW	145050 TQ	USBLS	5/15
	Trenton MSA, NJ	Y	90310 FQ	109380 MW	125100 TQ	USBLS	5/15
	New Mexico	Y	50870 FQ	71900 MW	94220 TQ	USBLS	5/15
	Albuquerque MSA, NM	Y	55300 FQ	74510 MW	99800 TQ	USBLS	5/15
	New York	Y	71280 AE	113570 MW	151600 AEX	NYBLS	1/16-3/16
	Buffalo-Cheektowaga-Niagara Falls MSA, NY	Y	68800 FQ	86450 MW	113140 TQ	USBLS	5/15
	Nassau County-Suffolk County PMSA, NY	Y	85920 FQ	109640 MW	140180 TQ	USBLS	5/15
	New York-Jersey City-White Plains PMSA, NY-NJ	Y	91360 FQ	119250 MW	156270 TQ	USBLS	5/15
	Rochester MSA, NY	Y	71480 FQ	86910 MW	104940 TQ	USBLS	5/15
	North Carolina	Y	72630 FQ	91320 MW	119300 TQ	USBLS	5/15
	Charlotte-Concord-Gastonia MSA, NC-SC	Y	77670 FQ	96180 MW	130250 TQ	USBLS	5/15
	Raleigh MSA, NC	Y	73250 FQ	95340 MW	129760 TQ	USBLS	5/15
	North Dakota	Y	56550 FQ	73650 MW	98640 TQ	USBLS	5/15
	Fargo MSA, ND-MN	Y	56370 FQ	73920 MW	97390 TQ	USBLS	5/15
	Ohio	Y	62080 FQ	77810 MW	98990 TQ	USBLS	5/15
	Cincinnati MSA, OH-KY-IN	Y	60650 FQ	76050 MW	97400 TQ	USBLS	5/15
	Cleveland-Elyria MSA, OH	Y	65600 FQ	79630 MW	98830 TQ	USBLS	5/15
	Columbus MSA, OH	Y	66900 FQ	84130 MW	109310 TQ	USBLS	5/15
	Oklahoma	Y	46430 FQ	60380 MW	80250 TQ	USBLS	5/15
	Oklahoma City MSA, OK	Y	49000 FQ	61950 MW	80100 TQ	USBLS	5/15
	Tulsa MSA, OK	Y	46610 FQ	62480 MW	86230 TQ	USBLS	5/15
	Oregon	H	27.05 FQ	36.13 MW	47.53 TQ	ORBLS	2016
	Portland-Vancouver-Hillsboro MSA, OR-WA	Y	58590 FQ	76180 MW	101780 TQ	USBLS	5/15
	Pennsylvania	Y	70080 FQ	91220 MW	118020 TQ	USBLS	5/15
	Allentown-Bethlehem-Easton MSA, PA-NJ	Y	68520 FQ	96340 MW	123050 TQ	USBLS	5/15
	Harrisburg-Carlisle MSA, PA	Y	73470 FQ	89880 MW	107210 TQ	USBLS	5/15
	Montgomery County-Bucks County-Chester County PMSA, PA	Y	75400 FQ	97280 MW	122420 TQ	USBLS	5/15
	Philadelphia PMSA, PA	Y	76410 FQ	98220 MW	129120 TQ	USBLS	5/15
	Pittsburgh MSA, PA	Y	61800 FQ	83700 MW	109290 TQ	USBLS	5/15
	Rhode Island	Y	81790 FQ	96940 MW	122350 TQ	USBLS	5/15
	Providence-Warwick MSA, RI-MA	Y	67090 FQ	90370 MW	115930 TQ	USBLS	5/15
	South Carolina	Y	53940 FQ	74810 MW	99180 TQ	USBLS	5/15
	Charleston-North Charleston MSA, SC	Y	55890 FQ	75120 MW	101970 TQ	USBLS	5/15
	Columbia MSA, SC	Y	57670 FQ	75830 MW	95800 TQ	USBLS	5/15
	Greenville-Anderson-Mauldin MSA, SC	Y	51170 FQ	71930 MW	98540 TQ	USBLS	5/15
	South Dakota	Y	67220 FQ	77990 MW	92760 TQ	USBLS	5/15
	Sioux Falls MSA, SD	Y	70520 FQ	82320 MW	96330 TQ	USBLS	5/15
	Tennessee	Y	48680 FQ	67370 MW	91470 TQ	USBLS	5/15
	Knoxville MSA, TN	Y	44270 FQ	63700 MW	85480 TQ	USBLS	5/15
	Memphis MSA, TN-MS-AR	Y	52260 FQ	69630 MW	90270 TQ	USBLS	5/15
	Nashville-Davidson–Murfreesboro–Franklin MSA, TN	Y	52220 FQ	70710 MW	96920 TQ	USBLS	5/15
	Texas	Y	66360 FQ	94270 MW	126000 TQ	USBLS	5/15
	Austin-Round Rock MSA, TX	Y	81350 FQ	102510 MW	125910 TQ	USBLS	5/15
	Dallas-Plano-Irving PMSA, TX	Y	76310 FQ	106030 MW	144600 TQ	USBLS	5/15
	Fort Worth-Arlington PMSA, TX	Y	57840 FQ	83290 MW	104710 TQ	USBLS	5/15
	Houston-The Woodlands-Sugar Land MSA, TX	Y	71770 FQ	100210 MW	142680 TQ	USBLS	5/15

AE	Average entry wage	AWR	Average wage range	H	Hourly
AEX	Average experienced wage	B	Biweekly	HI	Highest wage paid
ATC	Average total compensation	D	Daily	HR	High end range
AW	Average wage paid	FQ	First quartile wage	LO	Lowest wage paid

LR	Low end range	MTC	Median total compensation	TCC	Total cash compensation
M	Monthly	MW	Median wage paid	TQ	Third quartile wage
MCC	Median cash compensation	MWR	Median wage range	W	Weekly
ME	Median entry wage	S	See annotated source	Y	Yearly

Occupation/Type/Industry	Location	Per	Low	Mid	High	Source	Date
Administrative Services Manager	San Antonio-New Braunfels MSA, TX	Y	66620 FQ	91140 MW	123850 TQ	USBLS	5/15
	Utah	Y	55820 FQ	75530 MW	101690 TQ	USBLS	5/15
	Ogden-Clearfield MSA, UT	Y	55000 FQ	70190 MW	85300 TQ	USBLS	5/15
	Provo-Orem MSA, UT	Y	57020 FQ	81700 MW	103130 TQ	USBLS	5/15
	Salt Lake City MSA, UT	Y	58120 FQ	79150 MW	110430 TQ	USBLS	5/15
	Vermont	Y	64800 FQ	86160 MW	108310 TQ	USBLS	5/15
	Burlington-South Burlington MSA, VT	Y	58970 FQ	79880 MW	103900 TQ	USBLS	5/15
	Virginia	Y	70830 FQ	91220 MW	120190 TQ	USBLS	5/15
	Richmond MSA, VA	Y	68950 FQ	82300 MW	106740 TQ	USBLS	5/15
	Virginia Beach-Norfolk-Newport News MSA, VA-NC	Y	66900 FQ	85050 MW	113010 TQ	USBLS	5/15
	Washington	H	33.41 FQ	44.30 MW	56.48 TQ	WABLS	3/16
	Seattle-Bellevue-Everett PMSA, WA	H	38.22 FQ	47.76 MW	60.09 TQ	WABLS	3/16
	Tacoma-Lakewood PMSA, WA	H	26.89 FQ	36.84 MW	46.29 TQ	WABLS	3/16
	West Virginia	Y	51980 FQ	66210 MW	85920 TQ	USBLS	5/15
	Huntington-Ashland MSA, WV-KY-OH	Y	51040 FQ	64830 MW	85880 TQ	USBLS	5/15
	Wisconsin	Y	68560 FQ	88620 MW	114090 TQ	USBLS	5/15
	Madison MSA, WI	Y	74750 FQ	94330 MW	119820 TQ	USBLS	5/15
	Milwaukee-Waukesha-West Allis MSA, WI	Y	72380 FQ	93180 MW	118840 TQ	USBLS	5/15
	Wyoming	Y	57610 FQ	78790 MW	100150 TQ	USBLS	5/15
	Cheyenne MSA, WY	Y	52330 FQ	60870 MW	77040 TQ	USBLS	5/15
	Puerto Rico	Y	37070 FQ	48610 MW	67220 TQ	USBLS	5/15
	San Juan-Carolina-Caguas MSA, PR	Y	37700 FQ	48880 MW	68460 TQ	USBLS	5/15
	Virgin Islands	Y	52920 FQ	66990 MW	78570 TQ	USBLS	5/15
	Guam	Y	39340 FQ	49450 MW	62930 TQ	USBLS	5/15
Admissions Representative College and University	United States	Y		44745 MW		MCCS	2016
Adoption Consultant Child Protective Services, State Government	New Mexico	H	15.28 LO		26.59 HI	NMGOV	7/30/16
Adult Basic, Secondary Education, and Literacy Teacher and Instructor	Alabama	Y	22588 AE	38765 AW	46858 AEX	ALBLS	6/16
	Birmingham-Hoover MSA, AL	Y	17920 AE	35992 AW	45024 AEX	ALBLS	6/16
	Alaska	Y	36210 FQ	44560 MW	67270 TQ	USBLS	5/15
	Anchorage MSA, AK	Y	35770 FQ	41640 MW	72850 TQ	USBLS	5/15
	Arizona	Y	43750 FQ	49420 MW	59110 TQ	USBLS	5/15
	Phoenix-Mesa-Scottsdale MSA, AZ	Y	44560 FQ	49960 MW	59650 TQ	USBLS	5/15
	Tucson MSA, AZ	Y	19160 FQ	40830 MW	56340 TQ	USBLS	5/15
	Arkansas	Y	23620 FQ	38050 MW	50660 TQ	USBLS	5/15
	Little Rock-North Little Rock-Conway MSA, AR	Y	32750 FQ	36290 MW	39850 TQ	USBLS	5/15
	California	H	24.27 FQ	33.46 MW	42.99 TQ	CABLS	1/16-3/16
	Anaheim-Santa Ana-Irvine PMSA, CA	H	18.22 FQ	24.17 MW	31.71 TQ	CABLS	1/16-3/16
	Los Angeles-Long Beach-Glendale PMSA, CA	H	28.08 FQ	37.86 MW	44.44 TQ	CABLS	1/16-3/16
	Oakland-Hayward-Berkeley PMSA, CA	H	24.69 FQ	28.53 MW	34.25 TQ	CABLS	1/16-3/16
	Riverside-San Bernardino-Ontario MSA, CA	H	34.19 FQ	40.35 MW	47.97 TQ	CABLS	1/16-3/16
	Sacramento–Roseville–Arden-Arcade MSA, CA	H	21.47 FQ	33.53 MW	42.69 TQ	CABLS	1/16-3/16
	San Diego-Carlsbad MSA, CA	H	30.79 FQ	35.37 MW	40.18 TQ	CABLS	1/16-3/16
	San Francisco-Redwood City-South San Francisco PMSA, CA	H	22.87 FQ	28.01 MW	43.66 TQ	CABLS	1/16-3/16
	Colorado	Y	31600 FQ	40630 MW	48850 TQ	USBLS	5/15
	Denver-Aurora-Lakewood MSA, CO	Y	38560 FQ	44690 MW	50560 TQ	USBLS	5/15
	Connecticut	Y		66612 MW		CTBLS	1/16-3/16

AE	Average entry wage	AWR	Average wage range	H	Hourly	LR	Low end range	MTC	Median total compensation	TCC	Total cash compensation
AEX	Average experienced wage	B	Biweekly	HI	Highest wage paid	M	Monthly	MW	Median wage paid	TQ	Third quartile wage
ATC	Average total compensation	D	Daily	HR	High end range	MCC	Median cash compensation	MWR	Median wage range	W	Weekly
AW	Average wage paid	FQ	First quartile wage	LO	Lowest wage paid	ME	Median entry wage	S	See annotated source	Y	Yearly

Occupation/Type/Industry	Location	Per	Low	Mid	High	Source	Date
Adult Basic, Secondary Education, and Literacy Teacher and Instructor	Bridgeport-Stamford-Norwalk MSA, CT	Y	44210 FQ	75570 MW	90350 TQ	USBLS	5/15
	Hartford-West Hartford-East Hartford MSA, CT	Y	39380 FQ	48660 MW	71600 TQ	USBLS	5/15
	Norwich-New London-Westerly MSA, CT-RI	Y	68840 FQ	73910 MW	78980 TQ	USBLS	5/15
	Delaware	Y	52900 FQ	60170 MW	70460 TQ	USBLS	5/15
	Wilmington PMSA, DE-MD-NJ	Y	39400 FQ	53210 MW	69150 TQ	USBLS	5/15
	District of Columbia	Y	37600 FQ	48240 MW	64780 TQ	USBLS	5/15
	Washington-Arlington-Alexandria PMSA, DC-VA-MD-WV	Y	42430 FQ	50980 MW	67770 TQ	USBLS	5/15
	Florida	H	18.54 AE	23.05 MW	27.92 AEX	FLBLS	7/16-9/16
	Miami-Miami Beach-Kendall PMSA, FL	H	17.40 AE	18.91 MW	22.21 AEX	FLBLS	7/16-9/16
	Tampa-St. Petersburg-Clearwater MSA, FL	H	21.57 AE	22.99 MW	26.47 AEX	FLBLS	7/16-9/16
	Georgia	Y	31850 FQ	36650 MW	45060 TQ	USBLS	5/15
	Atlanta-Sandy Springs-Roswell MSA, GA	Y	29230 FQ	35730 MW	45700 TQ	USBLS	5/15
	Augusta-Richmond County MSA, GA-SC	Y	34100 FQ	46620 MW	59640 TQ	USBLS	5/15
	Hawaii	Y	42470 FQ	45690 MW	48920 TQ	USBLS	5/15
	Urban Honolulu MSA, HI	Y	42520 FQ	45700 MW	48870 TQ	USBLS	5/15
	Idaho	Y	33750 FQ	38020 MW	43570 TQ	USBLS	5/15
	Boise City MSA, ID	Y	32170 FQ	36180 MW	38800 TQ	USBLS	5/15
	Illinois	Y	38840 FQ	57960 MW	72960 TQ	USBLS	5/15
	Chicago-Naperville-Arlington Heights PMSA, IL	Y	48880 FQ	66690 MW	75300 TQ	USBLS	5/15
	Indiana	Y	29490 FQ	44320 MW	57050 TQ	USBLS	5/15
	Indianapolis-Carmel-Anderson MSA, IN	Y	24980 FQ	43850 MW	55750 TQ	USBLS	5/15
	Iowa	Y	38230 FQ	45470 MW	54540 TQ	USBLS	5/15
	Kansas	Y	30230 FQ	36770 MW	49140 TQ	USBLS	5/15
	Wichita MSA, KS	Y	34430 FQ	37840 MW	49110 TQ	USBLS	5/15
	Kentucky	Y	33670 FQ	37800 MW	45500 TQ	USBLS	5/15
	Louisville-Jefferson County MSA, KY-IN	Y	35380 FQ	41860 MW	50060 TQ	USBLS	5/15
	Louisiana	Y	25050 FQ	39370 MW	56050 TQ	USBLS	5/15
	Baton Rouge MSA, LA	Y	19830 FQ	29290 MW	53750 TQ	USBLS	5/15
	New Orleans-Metairie MSA, LA	Y	31450 FQ	46500 MW	61610 TQ	USBLS	5/15
	Maine	Y	31130 FQ	36240 MW	52770 TQ	USBLS	5/15
	Maryland	Y	34865 AE	55908 MW	66429 AEX	MDBLS	4/16
	Baltimore-Columbia-Towson MSA, MD	Y	37230 FQ	54490 MW	63930 TQ	USBLS	5/15
	Salisbury MSA, MD-DE	Y	51560 FQ	59790 MW	80110 TQ	USBLS	5/15
	Massachusetts	Y	36310 FQ	47470 MW	60300 TQ	USBLS	5/15
	Boston-Cambridge-Newton NECTA, MA	Y	19320 FQ	42190 MW	49560 TQ	USBLS	5/15
	Worcester MSA, MA-CT	Y	43840 FQ	50540 MW	63850 TQ	USBLS	5/15
	Michigan	Y	37800 FQ	53000 MW	68880 TQ	USBLS	5/15
	Detroit-Dearborn-Livonia PMSA, MI	Y	44940 FQ	66890 MW	80720 TQ	USBLS	5/15
	Grand Rapids-Wyoming MSA, MI	Y	50780 FQ	64030 MW	73950 TQ	USBLS	5/15
	Minnesota	Y	27984 FQ	44344 MW	60786 TQ	MNBLS	1/16-3/16
	Minneapolis-St. Paul-Bloomington MSA, MN-WI	Y	24848 FQ	32742 MW	53427 TQ	MNBLS	1/16-3/16
	Mississippi	Y	24480 FQ	33500 MW	43660 TQ	USBLS	5/15
	Jackson MSA, MS	Y	33540 FQ	44760 MW	52200 TQ	USBLS	5/15
	Missouri	Y	41190 FQ	50200 MW	59930 TQ	USBLS	5/15
	Kansas City MSA, MO-KS	Y	30180 FQ	47580 MW	61890 TQ	USBLS	5/15
	St. Louis MSA, MO-IL	Y	36310 FQ	43910 MW	50270 TQ	USBLS	5/15
	Montana	Y	41650 FQ	47380 MW	56680 TQ	USBLS	5/15
	Nebraska	Y	34880 FQ	45305 MW	54425 TQ	NEBLS	7/16-9/16
	Omaha-Council Bluffs MSA, NE-IA	Y	39045 FQ	47050 MW	55075 TQ	NEBLS	7/16-9/16

AE	Average entry wage	AWR	Average wage range	H	Hourly
AEX	Average experienced wage	B	Biweekly	HI	Highest wage paid
ATC	Average total compensation	D	Daily	HR	High end range
AW	Average wage paid	FQ	First quartile wage	LO	Lowest wage paid

LR	Low end range	MTC	Median total compensation	TCC	Total cash compensation
M	Monthly	MW	Median wage paid	TQ	Third quartile wage
MCC	Median cash compensation	MWR	Median wage range	W	Weekly
ME	Median entry wage	S	See annotated source	Y	Yearly

15

Occupation/Type/Industry	Location	Per	Low	Mid	High	Source	Date
Adult Basic, Secondary Education, and Literacy Teacher and Instructor	Nevada	Y	38490 FQ	46770 MW	65130 TQ	USBLS	5/15
	Las Vegas-Henderson-Paradise MSA, NV	Y	40790 FQ	47320 MW	65450 TQ	USBLS	5/15
	New Hampshire	H	17.92 AE	26.45 MW	30.39 AEX	NHBLS	6/16
	Nashua NECTA, NH-MA	Y	42370 FQ	54730 MW	71140 TQ	USBLS	5/15
	New Jersey	Y	40230 FQ	58380 MW	81960 TQ	USBLS	5/15
	Camden PMSA, NJ	Y	56760 FQ	79200 MW	84780 TQ	USBLS	5/15
	Trenton MSA, NJ	Y	53850 FQ	59080 MW	66360 TQ	USBLS	5/15
	New Mexico	Y	24950 FQ	34300 MW	44180 TQ	USBLS	5/15
	Albuquerque MSA, NM	Y	22980 FQ	27780 MW	41700 TQ	USBLS	5/15
	New York	Y	37580 AE	61780 MW	80050 AEX	NYBLS	1/16-3/16
	Buffalo-Cheektowaga-Niagara Falls MSA, NY	Y	60820 FQ	68220 MW	74390 TQ	USBLS	5/15
	Nassau County-Suffolk County PMSA, NY	Y	46690 FQ	69340 MW	79330 TQ	USBLS	5/15
	New York-Jersey City-White Plains PMSA, NY-NJ	Y	42490 FQ	61630 MW	84770 TQ	USBLS	5/15
	Rochester MSA, NY	Y	37930 FQ	44950 MW	55370 TQ	USBLS	5/15
	North Carolina	Y	35130 FQ	42510 MW	50640 TQ	USBLS	5/15
	Charlotte-Concord-Gastonia MSA, NC-SC	Y	36320 FQ	51420 MW	61600 TQ	USBLS	5/15
	Raleigh MSA, NC	Y	41120 FQ	49590 MW	73030 TQ	USBLS	5/15
	North Dakota	Y	28790 FQ	47190 MW	59110 TQ	USBLS	5/15
	Fargo MSA, ND-MN	Y	26630 FQ	42940 MW	57180 TQ	USBLS	5/15
	Ohio	Y	43500 FQ	52860 MW	65190 TQ	USBLS	5/15
	Cincinnati MSA, OH-KY-IN	Y	42130 FQ	48350 MW	59420 TQ	USBLS	5/15
	Cleveland-Elyria MSA, OH	Y	53270 FQ	62710 MW	72200 TQ	USBLS	5/15
	Columbus MSA, OH	Y	46270 FQ	57510 MW	72200 TQ	USBLS	5/15
	Oklahoma	Y	36810 FQ	45980 MW	57020 TQ	USBLS	5/15
	Oklahoma City MSA, OK	Y	50690 FQ	63620 MW	74740 TQ	USBLS	5/15
	Tulsa MSA, OK	Y	35500 FQ	43270 MW	50950 TQ	USBLS	5/15
	Oregon	H	20.39 FQ	24.56 MW	32.20 TQ	ORBLS	2016
	Portland-Vancouver-Hillsboro MSA, OR-WA	Y	44080 FQ	50900 MW	66070 TQ	USBLS	5/15
	Pennsylvania	Y	36290 FQ	50250 MW	59850 TQ	USBLS	5/15
	Allentown-Bethlehem-Easton MSA, PA-NJ	Y	39480 FQ	48870 MW	56370 TQ	USBLS	5/15
	Montgomery County-Bucks County-Chester County PMSA, PA	Y	48790 FQ	55950 MW	61150 TQ	USBLS	5/15
	Philadelphia PMSA, PA	Y	41120 FQ	51420 MW	59860 TQ	USBLS	5/15
	Pittsburgh MSA, PA	Y	26740 FQ	32790 MW	38650 TQ	USBLS	5/15
	Rhode Island	Y	42560 FQ	52410 MW	63190 TQ	USBLS	5/15
	Providence-Warwick MSA, RI-MA	Y	43050 FQ	51650 MW	62280 TQ	USBLS	5/15
	South Carolina	Y	34410 FQ	48940 MW	61440 TQ	USBLS	5/15
	Charleston-North Charleston MSA, SC	Y	28670 FQ	36300 MW	51790 TQ	USBLS	5/15
	Columbia MSA, SC	Y	32540 FQ	51020 MW	66270 TQ	USBLS	5/15
	Greenville-Anderson-Mauldin MSA, SC	Y	40180 FQ	46810 MW	57900 TQ	USBLS	5/15
	South Dakota	Y	29140 FQ	34300 MW	39450 TQ	USBLS	5/15
	Sioux Falls MSA, SD	Y	28790 FQ	33350 MW	37230 TQ	USBLS	5/15
	Tennessee	Y	37680 FQ	46890 MW	58870 TQ	USBLS	5/15
	Knoxville MSA, TN	Y	39270 FQ	46560 MW	55040 TQ	USBLS	5/15
	Memphis MSA, TN-MS-AR	Y	34250 FQ	42350 MW	56550 TQ	USBLS	5/15
	Nashville-Davidson–Murfreesboro–Franklin MSA, TN	Y	37760 FQ	45550 MW	63590 TQ	USBLS	5/15
	Texas	Y	33890 FQ	45700 MW	58450 TQ	USBLS	5/15
	Austin-Round Rock MSA, TX	Y	34100 FQ	41180 MW	46400 TQ	USBLS	5/15
	Dallas-Plano-Irving PMSA, TX	Y	43750 FQ	50740 MW	59730 TQ	USBLS	5/15
	Fort Worth-Arlington PMSA, TX	Y	26600 FQ	51500 MW	91390 TQ	USBLS	5/15
	Houston-The Woodlands-Sugar Land MSA, TX	Y	35090 FQ	46810 MW	62870 TQ	USBLS	5/15
	San Antonio-New Braunfels MSA, TX	Y	31170 FQ	37060 MW	48280 TQ	USBLS	5/15
	Utah	Y	31860 FQ	38020 MW	49410 TQ	USBLS	5/15

AE	Average entry wage	AWR	Average wage range	H	Hourly
AEX	Average experienced wage	B	Biweekly	HI	Highest wage paid
ATC	Average total compensation	D	Daily	HR	High end range
AW	Average wage paid	FQ	First quartile wage	LO	Lowest wage paid

LR	Low end range	MTC	Median total compensation	TCC	Total cash compensation
M	Monthly	MW	Median wage paid	TQ	Third quartile wage
MCC	Median cash compensation	MWR	Median wage range	W	Weekly
ME	Median entry wage	S	See annotated source	Y	Yearly

Occupation/Type/Industry	Location	Per	Low	Mid	High	Source	Date
Adult Basic, Secondary Education, and Literacy Teacher and Instructor	Provo-Orem MSA, UT	Y	31560 FQ	37620 MW	55380 TQ	USBLS	5/15
	Salt Lake City MSA, UT	Y	35200 FQ	40480 MW	49630 TQ	USBLS	5/15
	Vermont	Y	43570 FQ	54220 MW	70670 TQ	USBLS	5/15
	Burlington-South Burlington MSA, VT	Y	40610 FQ	54210 MW	74830 TQ	USBLS	5/15
	Virginia	Y	45740 FQ	53940 MW	61550 TQ	USBLS	5/15
	Richmond MSA, VA	Y	49300 FQ	55710 MW	61650 TQ	USBLS	5/15
	Virginia Beach-Norfolk-Newport News MSA, VA-NC	Y	46580 FQ	53560 MW	60210 TQ	USBLS	5/15
	Washington	H	22.85 FQ	28.01 MW	33.18 TQ	WABLS	3/16
	Seattle-Bellevue-Everett PMSA, WA	H	24.20 FQ	28.50 MW	33.21 TQ	WABLS	3/16
	Tacoma-Lakewood PMSA, WA	H	22.99 FQ	27.15 MW	32.65 TQ	WABLS	3/16
	West Virginia	Y	42530 FQ	54100 MW	90160 TQ	USBLS	5/15
	Huntington-Ashland MSA, WV-KY-OH	Y	40000 FQ	46970 MW	57830 TQ	USBLS	5/15
	Wisconsin	Y	38690 FQ	47830 MW	57670 TQ	USBLS	5/15
	Madison MSA, WI	Y	21090 FQ	22940 MW	46880 TQ	USBLS	5/15
	Milwaukee-Waukesha-West Allis MSA, WI	Y	36320 FQ	42840 MW	48750 TQ	USBLS	5/15
	Wyoming	Y	36280 FQ	47510 MW	59410 TQ	USBLS	5/15
	Puerto Rico	Y	27140 FQ	29980 MW	39910 TQ	USBLS	5/15
	San Juan-Carolina-Caguas MSA, PR	Y	26300 FQ	29210 MW	38360 TQ	USBLS	5/15
Adult Protective Social Worker							
Department of Public Health and Human Services, State Government	Missoula, MT	H			19.60 HI	MTGOV	2016
Advancement Specialist							
Baccalaureate Institution	United States	Y		36212 MW		CHE01	2015-2016
Master's Institution	United States	Y		40000 MW		CHE01	2015-2016
Research University	United States	Y		39598 MW		CHE01	2015-2016
Advertising and Promotions Manager	Alabama	Y	60247 AE	114375 AW	141434 AEX	ALBLS	6/16
	Birmingham-Hoover MSA, AL	Y	69257 AE	128848 AW	158643 AEX	ALBLS	6/16
	Alaska	Y	47710 FQ	67190 MW	97780 TQ	USBLS	5/15
	Anchorage MSA, AK	Y	46690 FQ	58830 MW	102790 TQ	USBLS	5/15
	Arizona	Y	68440 FQ	94180 MW	124580 TQ	USBLS	5/15
	Phoenix-Mesa-Scottsdale MSA, AZ	Y	65830 FQ	94010 MW	126040 TQ	USBLS	5/15
	Tucson MSA, AZ	Y	82490 FQ	92880 MW	111630 TQ	USBLS	5/15
	Arkansas	Y	59140 FQ	90400 MW	135840 TQ	USBLS	5/15
	California	H	31.51 FQ	47.97 MW	70.08 TQ	CABLS	1/16-3/16
	Anaheim-Santa Ana-Irvine PMSA, CA	H	32.10 FQ	43.96 MW	60.19 TQ	CABLS	1/16-3/16
	Los Angeles-Long Beach-Glendale PMSA, CA	H	32.67 FQ	51.87 MW	77.73 TQ	CABLS	1/16-3/16
	Oakland-Hayward-Berkeley PMSA, CA	H	34.68 FQ	47.93 MW	69.99 TQ	CABLS	1/16-3/16
	Riverside-San Bernardino-Ontario MSA, CA	H	18.43 FQ	29.66 MW	53.26 TQ	CABLS	1/16-3/16
	Sacramento–Roseville–Arden-Arcade MSA, CA	H	31.97 FQ	41.37 MW	63.46 TQ	CABLS	1/16-3/16
	San Diego-Carlsbad MSA, CA	H	28.83 FQ	36.26 MW	55.69 TQ	CABLS	1/16-3/16
	San Francisco-Redwood City-South San Francisco PMSA, CA	H	45.56 FQ	59.06 MW	74.75 TQ	CABLS	1/16-3/16
	Colorado	Y	74140 FQ	129790 MW	150640 TQ	USBLS	5/15
	Denver-Aurora-Lakewood MSA, CO	Y	68900 FQ	127560 MW	145200 TQ	USBLS	5/15
	Connecticut	Y		118934 MW		CTBLS	1/16-3/16
	Bridgeport-Stamford-Norwalk MSA, CT	Y	97000 FQ	133950 MW	160060 TQ	USBLS	5/15
	Hartford-West Hartford-East Hartford MSA, CT	Y	69410 FQ	87790 MW	155020 TQ	USBLS	5/15
	Delaware	Y	118860 FQ	141860 MW	165510 TQ	USBLS	5/15

AE	Average entry wage	**AWR**	Average wage range	**H**	Hourly	**LR** Low end range	**MTC** Median total compensation	**TCC** Total cash compensation
AEX	Average experienced wage	**B**	Biweekly	**HI**	Highest wage paid	**M** Monthly	**MW** Median wage paid	**TQ** Third quartile wage
ATC	Average total compensation	**D**	Daily	**HR**	High end range	**MCC** Median cash compensation	**MWR** Median wage range	**W** Weekly
AW	Average wage paid	**FQ**	First quartile wage	**LO**	Lowest wage paid	**ME** Median entry wage	**S** See annotated source	**Y** Yearly

Occupation/Type/Industry	Location	Per	Low	Mid	High	Source	Date
Advertising and Promotions Manager	Wilmington PMSA, DE-MD-NJ	Y	120490 FQ	143180 MW	166310 TQ	USBLS	5/15
	District of Columbia	Y	59920 FQ	90370 MW	117660 TQ	USBLS	5/15
	Washington-Arlington-Alexandria PMSA, DC-VA-MD-WV	Y	74280 FQ	99090 MW	140920 TQ	USBLS	5/15
	Florida	H	29.02 AE	49.84 MW	73.23 AEX	FLBLS	7/16-9/16
	Fort Lauderdale-Pompano Beach-Deerfield Beach PMSA, FL	H	35.02 AE	48.82 MW	64.11 AEX	FLBLS	7/16-9/16
	Miami-Miami Beach-Kendall PMSA, FL	H	36.99 AE	57.00 MW	77.00 AEX	FLBLS	7/16-9/16
	Orlando-Kissimmee-Sanford MSA, FL	H	35.58 AE	57.00 MW	79.22 AEX	FLBLS	7/16-9/16
	Tampa-St. Petersburg-Clearwater MSA, FL	H	21.59 AE	41.93 MW	59.99 AEX	FLBLS	7/16-9/16
	Georgia	Y	55810 FQ	89680 MW	131390 TQ	USBLS	5/15
	Atlanta-Sandy Springs-Roswell MSA, GA	Y	57050 FQ	92490 MW	136870 TQ	USBLS	5/15
	Hawaii	Y	58230 FQ	79560 MW	90960 TQ	USBLS	5/15
	Urban Honolulu MSA, HI	Y	71440 FQ	84950 MW	93620 TQ	USBLS	5/15
	Idaho	Y	42580 FQ	55330 MW	73960 TQ	USBLS	5/15
	Boise City MSA, ID	Y	44420 FQ	59410 MW	74160 TQ	USBLS	5/15
	Illinois	Y	45760 FQ	76860 MW	117460 TQ	USBLS	5/15
	Chicago-Naperville-Arlington Heights PMSA, IL	Y	44890 FQ	76780 MW	116080 TQ	USBLS	5/15
	Lake County-Kenosha County PMSA, IL-WI	Y	66570 FQ	95810 MW	130270 TQ	USBLS	5/15
	Indiana	Y	47060 FQ	69510 MW	96440 TQ	USBLS	5/15
	Gary PMSA, IN	Y	37400 FQ	52110 MW	67020 TQ	USBLS	5/15
	Indianapolis-Carmel-Anderson MSA, IN	Y	57860 FQ	81050 MW	115580 TQ	USBLS	5/15
	Iowa	Y	45480 FQ	71200 MW	100730 TQ	USBLS	5/15
	Des Moines-West Des Moines MSA, IA	Y	67290 FQ	91320 MW	121500 TQ	USBLS	5/15
	Kansas	Y	56690 FQ	68620 MW	80660 TQ	USBLS	5/15
	Wichita MSA, KS	Y	58930 FQ	71980 MW	92120 TQ	USBLS	5/15
	Kentucky	Y	49310 FQ	66100 MW	82570 TQ	USBLS	5/15
	Louisville-Jefferson County MSA, KY-IN	Y	48160 FQ	66800 MW	81110 TQ	USBLS	5/15
	Louisiana	Y	46310 FQ	58880 MW	75300 TQ	USBLS	5/15
	Baton Rouge MSA, LA	Y	53990 FQ	65260 MW	88330 TQ	USBLS	5/15
	New Orleans-Metairie MSA, LA	Y	45140 FQ	56020 MW	72650 TQ	USBLS	5/15
	Maine	Y	59130 FQ	74360 MW	99050 TQ	USBLS	5/15
	Portland-South Portland MSA, ME	Y	68580 FQ	79510 MW	122430 TQ	USBLS	5/15
	Maryland	Y	70011 AE	117299 MW	140944 AEX	MDBLS	4/16
	Baltimore-Columbia-Towson MSA, MD	Y	75950 FQ	102700 MW	135230 TQ	USBLS	5/15
	Massachusetts	Y	78140 FQ	110920 MW	153040 TQ	USBLS	5/15
	Boston-Cambridge-Newton NECTA, MA	Y	86350 FQ	116680 MW	167970 TQ	USBLS	5/15
	Worcester MSA, MA-CT	Y	55670 FQ	106390 MW	149600 TQ	USBLS	5/15
	Michigan	Y	60080 FQ	96020 MW	141050 TQ	USBLS	5/15
	Grand Rapids-Wyoming MSA, MI	Y	47470 FQ	59500 MW	76620 TQ	USBLS	5/15
	Minnesota	Y	87232 FQ	111954 MW	141716 TQ	MNBLS	1/16-3/16
	Minneapolis-St. Paul-Bloomington MSA, MN-WI	Y	90108 FQ	114494 MW	145089 TQ	MNBLS	1/16-3/16
	Mississippi	Y	43370 FQ	55660 MW	78710 TQ	USBLS	5/15
	Jackson MSA, MS	Y	42130 FQ	50030 MW	84260 TQ	USBLS	5/15
	Missouri	Y	71240 FQ	95930 MW	127800 TQ	USBLS	5/15
	Kansas City MSA, MO-KS	Y	68210 FQ	82930 MW	118230 TQ	USBLS	5/15
	St. Louis MSA, MO-IL	Y	73490 FQ	108240 MW	149510 TQ	USBLS	5/15
	Montana	Y	56220 FQ	73180 MW	99880 TQ	USBLS	5/15
	Nebraska	Y	49685 FQ	77715 MW	95840 TQ	NEBLS	7/16-9/16
	Omaha-Council Bluffs MSA, NE-IA	Y	47325 FQ	67135 MW	91215 TQ	NEBLS	7/16-9/16
	Nevada	Y	61610 FQ	78830 MW	100180 TQ	USBLS	5/15

AE	Average entry wage	AWR Average wage range	H Hourly	LR Low end range	MTC Median total compensation	TCC Total cash compensation
AEX	Average experienced wage	B Biweekly	HI Highest wage paid	M Monthly	MW Median wage paid	TQ Third quartile wage
ATC	Average total compensation	D Daily	HR High end range	MCC Median cash compensation	MWR Median wage range	W Weekly
AW	Average wage paid	FQ First quartile wage	LO Lowest wage paid	ME Median entry wage	S See annotated source	Y Yearly

Occupation/Type/Industry	Location	Per	Low	Mid	High	Source	Date
Advertising and Promotions Manager							
	Las Vegas-Henderson-Paradise MSA, NV	Y	62400 FQ	78380 MW	99620 TQ	USBLS	5/15
	New Hampshire	H	28.08 AE	42.03 MW	56.57 AEX	NHBLS	6/16
	Manchester NECTA, NH	H	36.29 AE	45.40 MW	52.04 AEX	NHBLS	6/16
	New Jersey	Y	86920 FQ	126720 MW	159780 TQ	USBLS	5/15
	Camden PMSA, NJ	Y	66950 FQ	94160 MW	140380 TQ	USBLS	5/15
	Newark PMSA, NJ-PA	Y	86080 FQ	124330 MW	161360 TQ	USBLS	5/15
	Trenton MSA, NJ	Y	92290 FQ	141290 MW		USBLS	5/15
	New Mexico	Y	52400 FQ	59240 MW	72930 TQ	USBLS	5/15
	Albuquerque MSA, NM	Y	51860 FQ	57280 MW	62710 TQ	USBLS	5/15
	New York	Y	95920 AE	177010 MW		NYBLS	1/16-3/16
	Buffalo-Cheektowaga-Niagara Falls MSA, NY	Y	55090 FQ	85560 MW	114100 TQ	USBLS	5/15
	Nassau County-Suffolk County PMSA, NY	Y	68220 FQ	80800 MW	129090 TQ	USBLS	5/15
	New York-Jersey City-White Plains PMSA, NY-NJ	Y	124350 FQ	176460 MW		USBLS	5/15
	Rochester MSA, NY	Y	53210 FQ	61930 MW	118330 TQ	USBLS	5/15
	North Carolina	Y	73230 FQ	108440 MW	131690 TQ	USBLS	5/15
	Charlotte-Concord-Gastonia MSA, NC-SC	Y	77180 FQ	115380 MW	132630 TQ	USBLS	5/15
	Raleigh MSA, NC	Y	69680 FQ	82890 MW	115620 TQ	USBLS	5/15
	North Dakota	Y	53050 FQ	67880 MW	89770 TQ	USBLS	5/15
	Fargo MSA, ND-MN	Y	57700 FQ	73760 MW	97870 TQ	USBLS	5/15
	Ohio	Y	65140 FQ	87750 MW	118940 TQ	USBLS	5/15
	Cincinnati MSA, OH-KY-IN	Y	72840 FQ	98440 MW	144960 TQ	USBLS	5/15
	Cleveland-Elyria MSA, OH	Y	49780 FQ	82500 MW	111520 TQ	USBLS	5/15
	Columbus MSA, OH	Y	75680 FQ	94230 MW	126450 TQ	USBLS	5/15
	Oklahoma	Y	38560 FQ	55560 MW	92420 TQ	USBLS	5/15
	Oklahoma City MSA, OK	Y	38720 FQ	56200 MW	83100 TQ	USBLS	5/15
	Tulsa MSA, OK	Y	38430 FQ	47120 MW	88980 TQ	USBLS	5/15
	Oregon	H	27.12 FQ	33.55 MW	46.83 TQ	ORBLS	2016
	Portland-Vancouver-Hillsboro MSA, OR-WA	Y	56260 FQ	70890 MW	98360 TQ	USBLS	5/15
	Pennsylvania	Y	72890 FQ	105730 MW	149810 TQ	USBLS	5/15
	Harrisburg-Carlisle MSA, PA	Y	62740 FQ	95770 MW	140740 TQ	USBLS	5/15
	Pittsburgh MSA, PA	Y	82850 FQ	96970 MW	138670 TQ	USBLS	5/15
	Rhode Island	Y	43720 FQ	57010 MW	118330 TQ	USBLS	5/15
	Providence-Warwick MSA, RI-MA	Y	43900 FQ	65400 MW	119450 TQ	USBLS	5/15
	South Carolina	Y	43240 FQ	68780 MW	95570 TQ	USBLS	5/15
	Columbia MSA, SC	Y	44210 FQ	72370 MW	96790 TQ	USBLS	5/15
	Greenville-Anderson-Mauldin MSA, SC	Y	47920 FQ	66530 MW	102540 TQ	USBLS	5/15
	Tennessee	Y	35130 FQ	60090 MW	107100 TQ	USBLS	5/15
	Memphis MSA, TN-MS-AR	Y	50730 FQ	67440 MW	95300 TQ	USBLS	5/15
	Nashville-Davidson–Murfreesboro–Franklin MSA, TN	Y	32130 FQ	64580 MW	116570 TQ	USBLS	5/15
	Texas	Y	59840 FQ	96920 MW	148230 TQ	USBLS	5/15
	Austin-Round Rock MSA, TX	Y	64560 FQ	91670 MW	122190 TQ	USBLS	5/15
	Dallas-Plano-Irving PMSA, TX	Y	76280 FQ	123390 MW	167120 TQ	USBLS	5/15
	Fort Worth-Arlington PMSA, TX	Y	61360 FQ	82250 MW	118760 TQ	USBLS	5/15
	Houston-The Woodlands-Sugar Land MSA, TX	Y	48040 FQ	85240 MW	115530 TQ	USBLS	5/15
	San Antonio-New Braunfels MSA, TX	Y	54050 FQ	110810 MW	131020 TQ	USBLS	5/15
	Utah	Y	46910 FQ	74010 MW	101540 TQ	USBLS	5/15
	Provo-Orem MSA, UT	Y	62060 FQ	89500 MW	111860 TQ	USBLS	5/15
	Salt Lake City MSA, UT	Y	44310 FQ	71990 MW	101090 TQ	USBLS	5/15
	Vermont	Y	65990 FQ	94940 MW	130280 TQ	USBLS	5/15
	Virginia	Y	80860 FQ	108120 MW	157450 TQ	USBLS	5/15
	Richmond MSA, VA	Y	64180 FQ	107500 MW	147680 TQ	USBLS	5/15
	Virginia Beach-Norfolk-Newport News MSA, VA-NC	Y	65460 FQ	95470 MW	152330 TQ	USBLS	5/15
	Washington	H	36.73 FQ	52.71 MW	62.82 TQ	WABLS	3/16
	Seattle-Bellevue-Everett PMSA, WA	H	39.58 FQ	53.94 MW	62.91 TQ	WABLS	3/16
	Tacoma-Lakewood PMSA, WA	H	28.12 FQ	48.69 MW	57.90 TQ	WABLS	3/16
	West Virginia	Y	41840 FQ	47290 MW	64760 TQ	USBLS	5/15

AE	Average entry wage	**AWR**	Average wage range	**H**	Hourly	**LR**	Low end range	**MTC**	Median total compensation	**TCC**	Total cash compensation
AEX	American experienced wage	**B**	Biweekly	**HI**	Highest wage paid	**M**	Monthly	**MW**	Median wage paid	**TQ**	Third quartile wage
ATC	Average total compensation	**D**	Daily	**HR**	High end range	**MCC**	Median cash compensation	**MWR**	Median wage range	**W**	Weekly
AW	Average wage paid	**FQ**	First quartile wage	**LO**	Lowest wage paid	**ME**	Median entry wage	**S**	See annotated source	**Y**	Yearly

Occupation/Type/Industry	Location	Per	Low	Mid	High	Source	Date
Advertising and Promotions Manager	Wisconsin	Y	64150 FQ	87690 MW	119370 TQ	USBLS	5/15
	Madison MSA, WI	Y	71580 FQ	95990 MW	138760 TQ	USBLS	5/15
	Milwaukee-Waukesha-West Allis MSA, WI	Y	68650 FQ	89640 MW	114220 TQ	USBLS	5/15
	Puerto Rico	Y	58690 FQ	72900 MW	88480 TQ	USBLS	5/15
	San Juan-Carolina-Caguas MSA, PR	Y	59930 FQ	73410 MW	89210 TQ	USBLS	5/15
	Guam	Y	42560 FQ	60630 MW	74430 TQ	USBLS	5/15
Advertising Sales Agent	Alabama	Y	20571 AE	45352 AW	57742 AEX	ALBLS	6/16
	Birmingham-Hoover MSA, AL	Y	24667 AE	55405 AW	70774 AEX	ALBLS	6/16
	Alaska	Y	33710 FQ	48040 MW	67810 TQ	USBLS	5/15
	Anchorage MSA, AK	Y	41210 FQ	56880 MW	72850 TQ	USBLS	5/15
	Arizona	Y	31850 FQ	44070 MW	70190 TQ	USBLS	5/15
	Phoenix-Mesa-Scottsdale MSA, AZ	Y	32970 FQ	45230 MW	72820 TQ	USBLS	5/15
	Tucson MSA, AZ	Y	29950 FQ	39140 MW	65580 TQ	USBLS	5/15
	Arkansas	Y	29470 FQ	38210 MW	55540 TQ	USBLS	5/15
	Little Rock-North Little Rock-Conway MSA, AR	Y	34500 FQ	45870 MW	61770 TQ	USBLS	5/15
	California	H	20.35 FQ	28.68 MW	42.43 TQ	CABLS	1/16-3/16
	Anaheim-Santa Ana-Irvine PMSA, CA	H	20.84 FQ	29.29 MW	41.71 TQ	CABLS	1/16-3/16
	Los Angeles-Long Beach-Glendale PMSA, CA	H	22.59 FQ	30.81 MW	44.47 TQ	CABLS	1/16-3/16
	Oakland-Hayward-Berkeley PMSA, CA	H	14.70 FQ	25.88 MW	38.17 TQ	CABLS	1/16-3/16
	Riverside-San Bernardino-Ontario MSA, CA	H	14.01 FQ	18.52 MW	25.42 TQ	CABLS	1/16-3/16
	Sacramento–Roseville–Arden-Arcade MSA, CA	H	15.24 FQ	22.00 MW	29.83 TQ	CABLS	1/16-3/16
	San Diego-Carlsbad MSA, CA	H	14.53 FQ	23.91 MW	36.73 TQ	CABLS	1/16-3/16
	San Francisco-Redwood City-South San Francisco PMSA, CA	H	21.40 FQ	32.23 MW	49.91 TQ	CABLS	1/16-3/16
	Colorado	Y	34190 FQ	46670 MW	72770 TQ	USBLS	5/15
	Denver-Aurora-Lakewood MSA, CO	Y	35630 FQ	49020 MW	75850 TQ	USBLS	5/15
	Connecticut	Y		48440 MW		CTBLS	1/16-3/16
	Bridgeport-Stamford-Norwalk MSA, CT	Y	43180 FQ	56000 MW	78360 TQ	USBLS	5/15
	Hartford-West Hartford-East Hartford MSA, CT	Y	33100 FQ	47000 MW	74740 TQ	USBLS	5/15
	Delaware	Y	34770 FQ	43040 MW	57600 TQ	USBLS	5/15
	Wilmington PMSA, DE-MD-NJ	Y	34160 FQ	41140 MW	56280 TQ	USBLS	5/15
	District of Columbia	Y	43190 FQ	56480 MW	80620 TQ	USBLS	5/15
	Washington-Arlington-Alexandria PMSA, DC-VA-MD-WV	Y	43540 FQ	56960 MW	80740 TQ	USBLS	5/15
	Florida	H	13.23 AE	21.02 MW	33.66 AEX	FLBLS	7/16-9/16
	Fort Lauderdale-Pompano Beach-Deerfield Beach PMSA, FL	H	15.03 AE	26.21 MW	41.94 AEX	FLBLS	7/16-9/16
	Miami-Miami Beach-Kendall PMSA, FL	H	14.29 AE	22.94 MW	41.46 AEX	FLBLS	7/16-9/16
	Orlando-Kissimmee-Sanford MSA, FL	H	12.33 AE	20.12 MW	28.03 AEX	FLBLS	7/16-9/16
	Tampa-St. Petersburg-Clearwater MSA, FL	H	13.78 AE	19.00 MW	30.80 AEX	FLBLS	7/16-9/16
	Georgia	Y	32290 FQ	45600 MW	82210 TQ	USBLS	5/15
	Atlanta-Sandy Springs-Roswell MSA, GA	Y	34180 FQ	49890 MW	96950 TQ	USBLS	5/15
	Augusta-Richmond County MSA, GA-SC	Y	24140 FQ	36110 MW	53940 TQ	USBLS	5/15
	Hawaii	Y	35160 FQ	46410 MW	61300 TQ	USBLS	5/15
	Urban Honolulu MSA, HI	Y	35290 FQ	43930 MW	59470 TQ	USBLS	5/15
	Idaho	Y	26810 FQ	37070 MW	48520 TQ	USBLS	5/15
	Boise City MSA, ID	Y	26370 FQ	36750 MW	48380 TQ	USBLS	5/15
	Illinois	Y	31890 FQ	47840 MW	72620 TQ	USBLS	5/15

Advertising Sales Agent

Occupation/Type/Industry	Location	Per	Low	Mid	High	Source	Date
Advertising Sales Agent	Chicago-Naperville-Arlington Heights PMSA, IL	Y	36950 FQ	49460 MW	74910 TQ	USBLS	5/15
	Lake County-Kenosha County PMSA, IL-WI	Y	27870 FQ	42800 MW	57850 TQ	USBLS	5/15
	Indiana	Y	28960 FQ	40060 MW	61250 TQ	USBLS	5/15
	Evansville MSA, IN-KY	Y	28680 FQ	44510 MW	60510 TQ	USBLS	5/15
	Gary PMSA, IN	Y	27180 FQ	36290 MW	61580 TQ	USBLS	5/15
	Indianapolis-Carmel-Anderson MSA, IN	Y	29890 FQ	45210 MW	66970 TQ	USBLS	5/15
	Iowa	Y	28390 FQ	37820 MW	56250 TQ	USBLS	5/15
	Des Moines-West Des Moines MSA, IA	Y	32890 FQ	49330 MW	70160 TQ	USBLS	5/15
	Kansas	Y	28630 FQ	44400 MW	62940 TQ	USBLS	5/15
	Wichita MSA, KS	Y	28540 FQ	46450 MW	65410 TQ	USBLS	5/15
	Kentucky	Y	28050 FQ	39750 MW	59300 TQ	USBLS	5/15
	Louisville-Jefferson County MSA, KY-IN	Y	33700 FQ	45220 MW	66700 TQ	USBLS	5/15
	Louisiana	Y	28390 FQ	36280 MW	47890 TQ	USBLS	5/15
	Baton Rouge MSA, LA	Y	35600 FQ	48680 MW	65460 TQ	USBLS	5/15
	New Orleans-Metairie MSA, LA	Y	29700 FQ	36890 MW	47520 TQ	USBLS	5/15
	Maine	Y	25870 FQ	35710 MW	48860 TQ	USBLS	5/15
	Portland-South Portland MSA, ME	Y	28860 FQ	37060 MW	54530 TQ	USBLS	5/15
	Maryland	Y	30989 AE	61762 MW	77149 AEX	MDBLS	4/16
	Baltimore-Columbia-Towson MSA, MD	Y	40920 FQ	58760 MW	91870 TQ	USBLS	5/15
	Salisbury MSA, MD-DE	Y	29770 FQ	39360 MW	54920 TQ	USBLS	5/15
	Massachusetts	Y	46260 FQ	66030 MW	88180 TQ	USBLS	5/15
	Boston-Cambridge-Newton NECTA, MA	Y	53350 FQ	73610 MW	91690 TQ	USBLS	5/15
	Worcester MSA, MA-CT	Y	34030 FQ	42900 MW	52660 TQ	USBLS	5/15
	Michigan	Y	26270 FQ	39040 MW	60290 TQ	USBLS	5/15
	Detroit-Dearborn-Livonia PMSA, MI	Y	31920 FQ	47300 MW	73060 TQ	USBLS	5/15
	Grand Rapids-Wyoming MSA, MI	Y	33140 FQ	45730 MW	60390 TQ	USBLS	5/15
	Minnesota	Y	36976 FQ	49309 MW	74548 TQ	MNBLS	1/16-3/16
	Minneapolis-St. Paul-Bloomington MSA, MN-WI	Y	41363 FQ	52404 MW	81919 TQ	MNBLS	1/16-3/16
	Mississippi	Y	20700 FQ	28410 MW	44730 TQ	USBLS	5/15
	Jackson MSA, MS	Y	22820 FQ	33820 MW	52620 TQ	USBLS	5/15
	Missouri	Y	24760 FQ	35700 MW	52610 TQ	USBLS	5/15
	Kansas City MSA, MO-KS	Y	34730 FQ	47220 MW	68620 TQ	USBLS	5/15
	St. Louis MSA, MO-IL	Y	22700 FQ	37540 MW	57320 TQ	USBLS	5/15
	Montana	Y	21640 FQ	30710 MW	45910 TQ	USBLS	5/15
	Billings MSA, MT	Y	25390 FQ	33810 MW	46930 TQ	USBLS	5/15
	Nebraska	Y	30310 FQ	40905 MW	59465 TQ	NEBLS	7/16-9/16
	Omaha-Council Bluffs MSA, NE-IA	Y	35625 FQ	51750 MW	68085 TQ	NEBLS	7/16-9/16
	Nevada	Y	42420 FQ	59480 MW	82280 TQ	USBLS	5/15
	Las Vegas-Henderson-Paradise MSA, NV	Y	42810 FQ	60820 MW	85990 TQ	USBLS	5/15
	New Hampshire	H	15.54 AE	26.23 MW	47.17 AEX	NHBLS	6/16
	Manchester NECTA, NH	H	18.36 AE	25.87 MW	34.67 AEX	NHBLS	6/16
	Nashua NECTA, NH-MA	Y	39370 FQ	55970 MW	168690 TQ	USBLS	5/15
	Portsmouth MSA, NH-ME	Y	29720 FQ	49550 MW	64830 TQ	USBLS	5/15
	New Jersey	Y	38120 FQ	57070 MW	85430 TQ	USBLS	5/15
	Camden PMSA, NJ	Y	34490 FQ	39850 MW	60650 TQ	USBLS	5/15
	Newark PMSA, NJ-PA	Y	42090 FQ	59480 MW	91610 TQ	USBLS	5/15
	Trenton MSA, NJ	Y	41100 FQ	69540 MW	84670 TQ	USBLS	5/15
	New Mexico	Y	25200 FQ	31110 MW	48750 TQ	USBLS	5/15
	Albuquerque MSA, NM	Y	26620 FQ	33470 MW	54460 TQ	USBLS	5/15
	New York	Y	38040 AE	69870 MW	109260 AEX	NYBLS	1/16-3/16
	Buffalo-Cheektowaga-Niagara Falls MSA, NY	Y	30550 FQ	37200 MW	52180 TQ	USBLS	5/15
	Nassau County-Suffolk County PMSA, NY	Y	45700 FQ	58080 MW	81170 TQ	USBLS	5/15
	New York-Jersey City-White Plains PMSA, NY-NJ	Y	49860 FQ	72840 MW	109160 TQ	USBLS	5/15
	Rochester MSA, NY	Y	31080 FQ	44080 MW	69380 TQ	USBLS	5/15
	North Carolina	Y	32360 FQ	46580 MW	63870 TQ	USBLS	5/15

AE	Average entry wage	AWR	Average wage range	H	Hourly
AEX	Average experienced wage	B	Biweekly	HI	Highest wage paid
ATC	Average total compensation	D	Daily	HR	High end range
AW	Average wage paid	FQ	First quartile wage	LO	Lowest wage paid

LR	Low end range	MTC	Median total compensation	TCC	Total cash compensation
M	Monthly	MW	Median wage paid	TQ	Third quartile wage
MCC	Median cash compensation	MWR	Median wage range	W	Weekly
ME	Median entry wage	S	See annotated source	Y	Yearly

Occupation/Type/Industry	Location	Per	Low	Mid	High	Source	Date
Advertising Sales Agent	Charlotte-Concord-Gastonia MSA, NC-SC	Y	40120 FQ	54050 MW	65020 TQ	USBLS	5/15
	Raleigh MSA, NC	Y	39660 FQ	48500 MW	77830 TQ	USBLS	5/15
	North Dakota	Y	25660 FQ	36610 MW	54740 TQ	USBLS	5/15
	Fargo MSA, ND-MN	Y	20720 FQ	32840 MW	38130 TQ	USBLS	5/15
	Ohio	Y	26660 FQ	39070 MW	59940 TQ	USBLS	5/15
	Cincinnati MSA, OH-KY-IN	Y	29920 FQ	42870 MW	72350 TQ	USBLS	5/15
	Cleveland-Elyria MSA, OH	Y	27870 FQ	45320 MW	70560 TQ	USBLS	5/15
	Columbus MSA, OH	Y	24640 FQ	38940 MW	58560 TQ	USBLS	5/15
	Oklahoma	Y	23220 FQ	38770 MW	71930 TQ	USBLS	5/15
	Oklahoma City MSA, OK	Y	21990 FQ	40710 MW	84070 TQ	USBLS	5/15
	Tulsa MSA, OK	Y	23350 FQ	42070 MW	54300 TQ	USBLS	5/15
	Oregon	H	14.15 FQ	19.72 MW	32.10 TQ	ORBLS	2016
	Portland-Vancouver-Hillsboro MSA, OR-WA	Y	30940 FQ	42620 MW	73890 TQ	USBLS	5/15
	Pennsylvania	Y	28320 FQ	42330 MW	63440 TQ	USBLS	5/15
	Allentown-Bethlehem-Easton MSA, PA-NJ	Y	32410 FQ	51810 MW	77240 TQ	USBLS	5/15
	Harrisburg-Carlisle MSA, PA	Y	29670 FQ	44430 MW	64540 TQ	USBLS	5/15
	Montgomery County-Bucks County-Chester County PMSA, PA	Y	26260 FQ	41400 MW	64590 TQ	USBLS	5/15
	Philadelphia PMSA, PA	Y	33850 FQ	50990 MW	71630 TQ	USBLS	5/15
	Pittsburgh MSA, PA	Y	32110 FQ	45240 MW	64740 TQ	USBLS	5/15
	Rhode Island	Y	30170 FQ	37650 MW	58800 TQ	USBLS	5/15
	Providence-Warwick MSA, RI-MA	Y	29460 FQ	37110 MW	56580 TQ	USBLS	5/15
	South Carolina	Y	28260 FQ	39220 MW	57910 TQ	USBLS	5/15
	Charleston-North Charleston MSA, SC	Y	26440 FQ	35820 MW	53580 TQ	USBLS	5/15
	Columbia MSA, SC	Y	26830 FQ	37350 MW	59780 TQ	USBLS	5/15
	Greenville-Anderson-Mauldin MSA, SC	Y	37190 FQ	47030 MW	66950 TQ	USBLS	5/15
	South Dakota	Y	33890 FQ	42060 MW	50360 TQ	USBLS	5/15
	Sioux Falls MSA, SD	Y	36100 FQ	43740 MW	54360 TQ	USBLS	5/15
	Tennessee	Y	26210 FQ	37300 MW	50250 TQ	USBLS	5/15
	Knoxville MSA, TN	Y	29260 FQ	45430 MW	64090 TQ	USBLS	5/15
	Memphis MSA, TN-MS-AR	Y	31320 FQ	37830 MW	61850 TQ	USBLS	5/15
	Nashville-Davidson–Murfreesboro–Franklin MSA, TN	Y	27930 FQ	38630 MW	49790 TQ	USBLS	5/15
	Texas	Y	26720 FQ	43100 MW	65240 TQ	USBLS	5/15
	Austin-Round Rock MSA, TX	Y	35840 FQ	50100 MW	69690 TQ	USBLS	5/15
	Dallas-Plano-Irving PMSA, TX	Y	29790 FQ	46950 MW	76530 TQ	USBLS	5/15
	Fort Worth-Arlington PMSA, TX	Y	25220 FQ	34890 MW	52760 TQ	USBLS	5/15
	Houston-The Woodlands-Sugar Land MSA, TX	Y	27650 FQ	47730 MW	68390 TQ	USBLS	5/15
	San Antonio-New Braunfels MSA, TX	Y	30560 FQ	43840 MW	60300 TQ	USBLS	5/15
	Utah	Y	34690 FQ	46510 MW	64830 TQ	USBLS	5/15
	Ogden-Clearfield MSA, UT	Y	32920 FQ	42220 MW	61110 TQ	USBLS	5/15
	Provo-Orem MSA, UT	Y	32950 FQ	43700 MW	54820 TQ	USBLS	5/15
	Salt Lake City MSA, UT	Y	36510 FQ	47420 MW	73680 TQ	USBLS	5/15
	Vermont	Y	32240 FQ	43230 MW	62800 TQ	USBLS	5/15
	Burlington-South Burlington MSA, VT	Y	37270 FQ	51570 MW	68530 TQ	USBLS	5/15
	Virginia	Y	36030 FQ	50780 MW	74940 TQ	USBLS	5/15
	Richmond MSA, VA	Y	39040 FQ	60930 MW	85520 TQ	USBLS	5/15
	Virginia Beach-Norfolk-Newport News MSA, VA-NC	Y	36050 FQ	52110 MW	64850 TQ	USBLS	5/15
	Washington	H	15.14 FQ	19.19 MW	29.14 TQ	WABLS	3/16
	Seattle-Bellevue-Everett PMSA, WA	H	15.75 FQ	19.36 MW	28.97 TQ	WABLS	3/16
	Tacoma-Lakewood PMSA, WA	H	14.46 FQ	17.84 MW	24.35 TQ	WABLS	3/16
	West Virginia	Y	20290 FQ	24900 MW	44410 TQ	USBLS	5/15
	Huntington-Ashland MSA, WV-KY-OH	Y	19440 FQ	24550 MW	40180 TQ	USBLS	5/15
	Wisconsin	Y	28960 FQ	39120 MW	52720 TQ	USBLS	5/15
	Madison MSA, WI	Y	32800 FQ	44920 MW	63690 TQ	USBLS	5/15
	Milwaukee-Waukesha-West Allis MSA, WI	Y	29520 FQ	39830 MW	50410 TQ	USBLS	5/15

AE	Average entry wage	AWR	Average wage range	H	Hourly	LR	Low end range	MTC	Median total compensation
AEX	Average experienced wage	B	Biweekly	HI	Highest wage paid	M	Monthly	MW	Median wage paid
ATC	Average total compensation	D	Daily	HR	High end range	MCC	Median cash compensation	MWR	Median wage range
AW	Average wage paid	FQ	First quartile wage	LO	Lowest wage paid	ME	Median entry wage	S	See annotated source

TCC Total cash compensation
TQ Third quartile wage
W Weekly
Y Yearly

Occupation/Type/Industry	Location	Per	Low	Mid	High	Source	Date
Advertising Sales Agent	Wyoming	Y	20630 FQ	29300 MW	45230 TQ	USBLS	5/15
	Cheyenne MSA, WY	Y	23750 FQ	39430 MW	58930 TQ	USBLS	5/15
	Puerto Rico	Y	17360 FQ	21510 MW	33070 TQ	USBLS	5/15
	San Juan-Carolina-Caguas MSA, PR	Y	17310 FQ	21370 MW	33200 TQ	USBLS	5/15
	Virgin Islands	Y	28510 FQ	40530 MW	47650 TQ	USBLS	5/15
	Guam	Y	25510 FQ	29660 MW	41580 TQ	USBLS	5/15
Advertising Sales Manager							
B2B Magazine	United States	Y		56100 AW		FOLIO02	4/22/15-5/22/15
Consumer Magazine	United States	Y		79300 AW		FOLIO02	4/22/15-5/22/15
Female	United States	Y		61400 AW		FOLIO02	4/22/15-5/22/15
Male	United States	Y		67800 AW		FOLIO02	4/22/15-5/22/15
Aerodrome Safety Inspector	United States	Y		123487 AW		AVJOB01	2016
Aerospace Engineer	Alabama	Y	76510 AE	112105 AW	129892 AEX	ALBLS	6/16
	Birmingham-Hoover MSA, AL	Y	64962 AE	79487 AW	86755 AEX	ALBLS	6/16
	Alaska	Y	75410 FQ	92810 MW	126650 TQ	USBLS	5/15
	Arizona	Y	72530 FQ	86830 MW	111120 TQ	USBLS	5/15
	Phoenix-Mesa-Scottsdale MSA, AZ	Y	71160 FQ	84060 MW	114440 TQ	USBLS	5/15
	Tucson MSA, AZ	Y	81300 FQ	92000 MW	108150 TQ	USBLS	5/15
	California	H	42.34 FQ	55.96 MW	71.44 TQ	CABLS	1/16-3/16
	Anaheim-Santa Ana-Irvine PMSA, CA	H	45.11 FQ	58.46 MW	71.70 TQ	CABLS	1/16-3/16
	Los Angeles-Long Beach-Glendale PMSA, CA	H	48.24 FQ	62.18 MW	76.05 TQ	CABLS	1/16-3/16
	Riverside-San Bernardino-Ontario MSA, CA	H	42.01 FQ	53.50 MW	59.18 TQ	CABLS	1/16-3/16
	Sacramento–Roseville–Arden-Arcade MSA, CA	H	49.72 FQ	60.39 MW	71.67 TQ	CABLS	1/16-3/16
	San Diego-Carlsbad MSA, CA	H	40.97 FQ	50.74 MW	62.98 TQ	CABLS	1/16-3/16
	San Francisco-Redwood City-South San Francisco PMSA, CA	H	43.73 FQ	53.72 MW	65.86 TQ	CABLS	1/16-3/16
	Colorado	Y	91830 FQ	123880 MW	159540 TQ	USBLS	5/15
	Denver-Aurora-Lakewood MSA, CO	Y	83690 FQ	111100 MW	150290 TQ	USBLS	5/15
	Connecticut	Y		107739 MW		CTBLS	1/16-3/16
	Bridgeport-Stamford-Norwalk MSA, CT	Y	91960 FQ	106670 MW	117840 TQ	USBLS	5/15
	Hartford-West Hartford-East Hartford MSA, CT	Y	91990 FQ	106870 MW	123630 TQ	USBLS	5/15
	Delaware	Y	81140 FQ	97000 MW	116860 TQ	USBLS	5/15
	Wilmington PMSA, DE-MD-NJ	Y	84940 FQ	101420 MW	125760 TQ	USBLS	5/15
	District of Columbia	Y	104170 FQ	132350 MW	151490 TQ	USBLS	5/15
	Washington-Arlington-Alexandria PMSA, DC-VA-MD-WV	Y	113160 FQ	143020 MW	164970 TQ	USBLS	5/15
	Florida	H	35.48 AE	50.69 MW	59.87 AEX	FLBLS	7/16-9/16
	Fort Lauderdale-Pompano Beach-Deerfield Beach PMSA, FL	H	37.08 AE	50.21 MW	59.12 AEX	FLBLS	7/16-9/16
	Miami-Miami Beach-Kendall PMSA, FL	H	30.48 AE	45.38 MW	55.35 AEX	FLBLS	7/16-9/16
	Orlando-Kissimmee-Sanford MSA, FL	H	37.89 AE	46.30 MW	50.71 AEX	FLBLS	7/16-9/16
	Tampa-St. Petersburg-Clearwater MSA, FL	H	31.38 AE	42.07 MW	47.44 AEX	FLBLS	7/16-9/16
	Georgia	Y	85070 FQ	106140 MW	125380 TQ	USBLS	5/15
	Atlanta-Sandy Springs-Roswell MSA, GA	Y	89960 FQ	109080 MW	123910 TQ	USBLS	5/15
	Illinois	Y	83440 FQ	101480 MW	122910 TQ	USBLS	5/15
	Chicago-Naperville-Arlington Heights PMSA, IL	Y	86710 FQ	105010 MW	124970 TQ	USBLS	5/15
	Indiana	Y	64330 FQ	75600 MW	92330 TQ	USBLS	5/15
	Indianapolis-Carmel-Anderson MSA, IN	Y	59250 FQ	75320 MW	93060 TQ	USBLS	5/15
	Iowa	Y	77680 FQ	106510 MW	135730 TQ	USBLS	5/15
	Kansas	Y	77650 FQ	97730 MW	122810 TQ	USBLS	5/15

AE	Average entry wage	AWR	Average wage range	
AEX	Average experienced wage	B	Biweekly	
ATC	Average total compensation	D	Daily	
AW	Average wage paid	FQ	First quartile wage	
H	Hourly	LR	Low end range	MTC Median total compensation
HI	Highest wage paid	M	Monthly	MW Median wage paid
HR	High end range	MCC	Median cash compensation	MWR Median wage range
LO	Lowest wage paid	ME	Median entry wage	S See annotated source
TCC	Total cash compensation			
TQ	Third quartile wage			
W	Weekly			
Y	Yearly			

Occupation/Type/Industry	Location	Per	Low	Mid	High	Source	Date
Aerospace Engineer	Wichita MSA, KS	Y	77560 FQ	96050 MW	117570 TQ	USBLS	5/15
	Louisiana	Y	74570 FQ	105220 MW	129130 TQ	USBLS	5/15
	Maine	Y	88940 FQ	109970 MW	121250 TQ	USBLS	5/15
	Maryland	Y	80204 AE	122448 MW	143570 AEX	MDBLS	4/16
	Baltimore-Columbia-Towson MSA, MD	Y	93700 FQ	118790 MW	151380 TQ	USBLS	5/15
	Massachusetts	Y	89200 FQ	108750 MW	130760 TQ	USBLS	5/15
	Boston-Cambridge-Newton NECTA, MA	Y	94140 FQ	114460 MW	137900 TQ	USBLS	5/15
	Michigan	Y	75620 FQ	89810 MW	108720 TQ	USBLS	5/15
	Minnesota	Y	74102 FQ	98003 MW	121652 TQ	MNBLS	1/16-3/16
	Minneapolis-St. Paul-Bloomington MSA, MN-WI	Y	81965 FQ	104414 MW	126450 TQ	MNBLS	1/16-3/16
	Mississippi	Y	88930 FQ	98100 MW	112950 TQ	USBLS	5/15
	Missouri	Y	83780 FQ	111950 MW	134340 TQ	USBLS	5/15
	Kansas City MSA, MO-KS	Y	91540 FQ	126950 MW	151950 TQ	USBLS	5/15
	St. Louis MSA, MO-IL	Y	81200 FQ	109320 MW	131110 TQ	USBLS	5/15
	Nebraska	Y	80965 FQ	95360 MW	123810 TQ	NEBLS	7/16-9/16
	Omaha-Council Bluffs MSA, NE-IA	Y	86575 FQ	116575 MW	146230 TQ	NEBLS	7/16-9/16
	New Hampshire	H	34.66 AE	46.63 MW	53.65 AEX	NHBLS	6/16
	New Jersey	Y	91150 FQ	116190 MW	142520 TQ	USBLS	5/15
	Newark PMSA, NJ-PA	Y	94740 FQ	122360 MW	147620 TQ	USBLS	5/15
	New Mexico	Y	79780 FQ	100850 MW	126750 TQ	USBLS	5/15
	Albuquerque MSA, NM	Y	80320 FQ	102720 MW	127980 TQ	USBLS	5/15
	New York	Y	79310 AE	113970 MW	132420 AEX	NYBLS	1/16-3/16
	New York-Jersey City-White Plains PMSA, NY-NJ	Y	95900 FQ	119490 MW	147070 TQ	USBLS	5/15
	North Carolina	Y	71220 FQ	91810 MW	113520 TQ	USBLS	5/15
	Charlotte-Concord-Gastonia MSA, NC-SC	Y	65100 FQ	74800 MW	92000 TQ	USBLS	5/15
	Ohio	Y	82800 FQ	107560 MW	128970 TQ	USBLS	5/15
	Cleveland-Elyria MSA, OH	Y	89670 FQ	112810 MW	133290 TQ	USBLS	5/15
	Columbus MSA, OH	Y	75920 FQ	101890 MW	128380 TQ	USBLS	5/15
	Oklahoma	Y	71360 FQ	86700 MW	105740 TQ	USBLS	5/15
	Oklahoma City MSA, OK	Y	72090 FQ	88910 MW	108500 TQ	USBLS	5/15
	Tulsa MSA, OK	Y	68900 FQ	79760 MW	95720 TQ	USBLS	5/15
	Oregon	H	32.47 FQ	39.81 MW	51.08 TQ	ORBLS	2016
	Portland-Vancouver-Hillsboro MSA, OR-WA	Y	70610 FQ	88240 MW	104260 TQ	USBLS	5/15
	Pennsylvania	Y	75670 FQ	98810 MW	120420 TQ	USBLS	5/15
	Montgomery County-Bucks County-Chester County PMSA, PA	Y	75680 FQ	98630 MW	121880 TQ	USBLS	5/15
	Pittsburgh MSA, PA	Y	63950 FQ	92620 MW	110030 TQ	USBLS	5/15
	Greenville-Anderson-Mauldin MSA, SC	Y	61850 FQ	83840 MW	110680 TQ	USBLS	5/15
	Tennessee	Y	72540 FQ	88650 MW	102840 TQ	USBLS	5/15
	Texas	Y	84520 FQ	108000 MW	133880 TQ	USBLS	5/15
	Austin-Round Rock MSA, TX	Y	86620 FQ	93690 MW	100710 TQ	USBLS	5/15
	Dallas-Plano-Irving PMSA, TX	Y	72440 FQ	90420 MW	114950 TQ	USBLS	5/15
	Fort Worth-Arlington PMSA, TX	Y	99320 FQ	120410 MW	145640 TQ	USBLS	5/15
	Houston-The Woodlands-Sugar Land MSA, TX	Y	90830 FQ	116050 MW	137150 TQ	USBLS	5/15
	San Antonio-New Braunfels MSA, TX	Y	70670 FQ	95360 MW	134460 TQ	USBLS	5/15
	Utah	Y	59540 FQ	80060 MW	95820 TQ	USBLS	5/15
	Ogden-Clearfield MSA, UT	Y	57540 FQ	77210 MW	93810 TQ	USBLS	5/15
	Salt Lake City MSA, UT	Y	70190 FQ	85390 MW	98140 TQ	USBLS	5/15
	Virginia	Y	99600 FQ	124930 MW	151700 TQ	USBLS	5/15
	Richmond MSA, VA	Y	94370 FQ	114240 MW	136460 TQ	USBLS	5/15
	Virginia Beach-Norfolk-Newport News MSA, VA-NC	Y	94590 FQ	116010 MW	135370 TQ	USBLS	5/15
	Tacoma-Lakewood PMSA, WA	H	50.82 FQ	60.39 MW	71.08 TQ	WABLS	3/16
	West Virginia	Y	70790 FQ	80640 MW	101500 TQ	USBLS	5/15
	Wisconsin	Y	78630 FQ	101860 MW	130840 TQ	USBLS	5/15
	Puerto Rico	Y	52270 FQ	56700 MW	61130 TQ	USBLS	5/15
	San Juan-Carolina-Caguas MSA, PR	Y	55300 FQ	69560 MW	87900 TQ	USBLS	5/15

AE	Average entry wage	AWR	Average wage range	H	Hourly
AEX	Average experienced wage	B	Biweekly	HI	Highest wage paid
ATC	Average total compensation	D	Daily	HR	High end range
AW	Average wage paid	FQ	First quartile wage	LO	Lowest wage paid

LR	Low end range	MTC	Median total compensation
M	Monthly	MW	Median wage paid
MCC	Median cash compensation	MWR	Median wage range
ME	Median entry wage	S	See annotated source

TCC	Total cash compensation	
TQ	Third quartile wage	
W	Weekly	
Y	Yearly	

Occupation/Type/Industry	Location	Per	Low	Mid	High	Source	Date
Aerospace Engineering and Operations Technician	Alabama	Y	38143 AE	63494 AW	76164 AEX	ALBLS	6/16
	Arizona	Y	41270 FQ	50390 MW	58830 TQ	USBLS	5/15
	Phoenix-Mesa-Scottsdale MSA, AZ	Y	42430 FQ	53540 MW	59480 TQ	USBLS	5/15
	Tucson MSA, AZ	Y	35050 FQ	50740 MW	59060 TQ	USBLS	5/15
	California	H	30.18 FQ	35.51 MW	41.48 TQ	CABLS	1/16-3/16
	Anaheim-Santa Ana-Irvine PMSA, CA	H	27.44 FQ	35.07 MW	43.79 TQ	CABLS	1/16-3/16
	Los Angeles-Long Beach-Glendale PMSA, CA	H	31.34 FQ	35.64 MW	40.49 TQ	CABLS	1/16-3/16
	Riverside-San Bernardino-Ontario MSA, CA	H	18.93 FQ	27.67 MW	33.67 TQ	CABLS	1/16-3/16
	San Diego-Carlsbad MSA, CA	H	32.78 FQ	35.94 MW	39.10 TQ	CABLS	1/16-3/16
	Colorado	Y	64400 FQ	75040 MW	88790 TQ	USBLS	5/15
	Denver-Aurora-Lakewood MSA, CO	Y	63940 FQ	75500 MW	86360 TQ	USBLS	5/15
	Connecticut	Y		77345 MW		CTBLS	1/16-3/16
	Washington-Arlington-Alexandria PMSA, DC-VA-MD-WV	Y	56460 FQ	67800 MW	78580 TQ	USBLS	5/15
	Florida	H	17.48 AE	28.35 MW	35.97 AEX	FLBLS	7/16-9/16
	Miami-Miami Beach-Kendall PMSA, FL	H	23.86 AE	33.25 MW	36.52 AEX	FLBLS	7/16-9/16
	Tampa-St. Petersburg-Clearwater MSA, FL	H	17.51 AE	26.68 MW	32.78 AEX	FLBLS	7/16-9/16
	Georgia	Y	55020 FQ	69300 MW	84240 TQ	USBLS	5/15
	Illinois	Y	43640 FQ	53790 MW	61300 TQ	USBLS	5/15
	Chicago-Naperville-Arlington Heights PMSA, IL	Y	43540 FQ	53680 MW	61210 TQ	USBLS	5/15
	Kansas	Y	45170 FQ	58310 MW	74540 TQ	USBLS	5/15
	Wichita MSA, KS	Y	45110 FQ	58560 MW	74950 TQ	USBLS	5/15
	Louisiana	Y	53370 FQ	66760 MW	79890 TQ	USBLS	5/15
	Maryland	Y	51162 AE	69537 MW	78725 AEX	MDBLS	4/16
	Baltimore-Columbia-Towson MSA, MD	Y	58820 FQ	75640 MW	90520 TQ	USBLS	5/15
	Michigan	Y	50510 FQ	57160 MW	64050 TQ	USBLS	5/15
	Grand Rapids-Wyoming MSA, MI	Y	48620 FQ	56770 MW	64160 TQ	USBLS	5/15
	Minnesota	Y	51199 FQ	61652 MW	85543 TQ	MNBLS	1/16-3/16
	Minneapolis-St. Paul-Bloomington MSA, MN-WI	Y	51088 FQ	61431 MW	85221 TQ	MNBLS	1/16-3/16
	Mississippi	Y	68080 FQ	84220 MW	93320 TQ	USBLS	5/15
	New Jersey	Y	50360 FQ	62650 MW	72740 TQ	USBLS	5/15
	New Mexico	Y	52540 FQ	61950 MW	74280 TQ	USBLS	5/15
	Albuquerque MSA, NM	Y	51790 FQ	62070 MW	74270 TQ	USBLS	5/15
	New York	Y	45030 AE	74880 MW	84220 AEX	NYBLS	1/16-3/16
	New York-Jersey City-White Plains PMSA, NY-NJ	Y	55950 FQ	76120 MW	90860 TQ	USBLS	5/15
	North Carolina	Y	39300 FQ	56680 MW	70230 TQ	USBLS	5/15
	Ohio	Y	59940 FQ	71230 MW	81670 TQ	USBLS	5/15
	Cleveland-Elyria MSA, OH	Y	61020 FQ	74900 MW	88020 TQ	USBLS	5/15
	Oklahoma	Y	44220 FQ	73920 MW	91370 TQ	USBLS	5/15
	Oregon	H	25.91 FQ	31.24 MW	37.52 TQ	ORBLS	2016
	Portland-Vancouver-Hillsboro MSA, OR-WA	Y	53390 FQ	64810 MW	77660 TQ	USBLS	5/15
	Pennsylvania	Y	42170 FQ	47690 MW	57910 TQ	USBLS	5/15
	Montgomery County-Bucks County-Chester County PMSA, PA	Y	41340 FQ	45670 MW	51130 TQ	USBLS	5/15
	Tennessee	Y	49660 FQ	54540 MW	59200 TQ	USBLS	5/15
	Texas	Y	45220 FQ	59610 MW	76250 TQ	USBLS	5/15
	Dallas-Plano-Irving PMSA, TX	Y	57080 FQ	73060 MW	89780 TQ	USBLS	5/15
	Fort Worth-Arlington PMSA, TX	Y	19160 FQ	51110 MW	79710 TQ	USBLS	5/15
	Houston-The Woodlands-Sugar Land MSA, TX	Y	56240 FQ	64440 MW	74860 TQ	USBLS	5/15
	Utah	Y	54720 FQ	61000 MW	75710 TQ	USBLS	5/15
	Ogden-Clearfield MSA, UT	Y	58000 FQ	70950 MW	85770 TQ	USBLS	5/15
	Salt Lake City MSA, UT	Y	53450 FQ	57440 MW	61440 TQ	USBLS	5/15
	Virginia	Y	44640 FQ	61980 MW	76830 TQ	USBLS	5/15

AE Average entry wage	**AWR** Average wage range	**H** Hourly	**LR** Low end range	**MTC** Median total compensation	**TCC** Total cash compensation
AEX Average experienced wage	**B** Biweekly	**HI** Highest wage paid	**M** Monthly	**MW** Median wage paid	**TQ** Third quartile wage
ATC Average total compensation	**D** Daily	**HR** High end range	**MCC** Median cash compensation	**MWR** Median wage range	**W** Weekly
AW Average wage paid	**FQ** First quartile wage	**LO** Lowest wage paid	**ME** Median entry wage	**S** See annotated source	**Y** Yearly

Occupation/Type/Industry	Location	Per	Low	Mid	High	Source	Date
Aerospace Engineering and Operations Technician	Virginia Beach-Norfolk-Newport News MSA, VA-NC	Y	49780 FQ	70030 MW	80150 TQ	USBLS	5/15
Affordable Housing Manager							
Community Development, Municipal Government	Sunnyvale, CA	Y			122193 HI	CACIT	6/28/16
Agent and Business Manager							
Artists, Performers, and Athletes	Alabama	Y	34521 AE	81074 AW	104351 AEX	ALBLS	6/16
Artists, Performers, and Athletes	Birmingham-Hoover MSA, AL	Y	33178 AE	71265 AW	90309 AEX	ALBLS	6/16
Artists, Performers, and Athletes	Arizona	Y	38050 FQ	71090 MW	83690 TQ	USBLS	5/15
Artists, Performers, and Athletes	Phoenix-Mesa-Scottsdale MSA, AZ	Y	40780 FQ	70680 MW	81310 TQ	USBLS	5/15
Artists, Performers, and Athletes	California	H	18.24 FQ	36.45 MW		CABLS	1/16-3/16
Artists, Performers, and Athletes	Los Angeles-Long Beach-Glendale PMSA, CA	H	18.17 FQ	37.27 MW		CABLS	1/16-3/16
Artists, Performers, and Athletes	Oakland-Hayward-Berkeley PMSA, CA	H	27.02 FQ	70.27 MW	80.05 TQ	CABLS	1/16-3/16
Artists, Performers, and Athletes	San Francisco-Redwood City-South San Francisco PMSA, CA	H	26.16 FQ	33.69 MW	56.40 TQ	CABLS	1/16-3/16
Artists, Performers, and Athletes	District of Columbia	Y	54130 FQ	74230 MW	151150 TQ	USBLS	5/15
Artists, Performers, and Athletes	Washington-Arlington-Alexandria PMSA, DC-VA-MD-WV	Y	38750 FQ	61910 MW	105110 TQ	USBLS	5/15
Artists, Performers, and Athletes	Florida	H	15.15 AE	26.68 MW	43.46 AEX	FLBLS	7/16-9/16
Artists, Performers, and Athletes	Fort Lauderdale-Pompano Beach-Deerfield Beach PMSA, FL	H	12.30 AE	25.14 MW	34.18 AEX	FLBLS	7/16-9/16
Artists, Performers, and Athletes	Miami-Miami Beach-Kendall PMSA, FL	H	16.22 AE	23.59 MW	36.82 AEX	FLBLS	7/16-9/16
Artists, Performers, and Athletes	Orlando-Kissimmee-Sanford MSA, FL	H	23.04 AE	38.15 MW	46.50 AEX	FLBLS	7/16-9/16
Artists, Performers, and Athletes	Tampa-St. Petersburg-Clearwater MSA, FL	H	13.00 AE	28.29 MW	45.21 AEX	FLBLS	7/16-9/16
Artists, Performers, and Athletes	Georgia	Y	43210 FQ	57820 MW	73050 TQ	USBLS	5/15
Artists, Performers, and Athletes	Atlanta-Sandy Springs-Roswell MSA, GA	Y	45340 FQ	59570 MW	73760 TQ	USBLS	5/15
Artists, Performers, and Athletes	Illinois	Y	34200 FQ	68280 MW	96260 TQ	USBLS	5/15
Artists, Performers, and Athletes	Chicago-Naperville-Arlington Heights PMSA, IL	Y	30750 FQ	51380 MW	174050 TQ	USBLS	5/15
Artists, Performers, and Athletes	Indiana	Y	42270 FQ	47010 MW	56850 TQ	USBLS	5/15
Artists, Performers, and Athletes	Indianapolis-Carmel-Anderson MSA, IN	Y	42540 FQ	46780 MW	54530 TQ	USBLS	5/15
Artists, Performers, and Athletes	Kansas	Y	35830 FQ	42680 MW	72450 TQ	USBLS	5/15
Artists, Performers, and Athletes	Louisiana	Y	64230 FQ	71230 MW	78220 TQ	USBLS	5/15
Artists, Performers, and Athletes	New Orleans-Metairie MSA, LA	Y	53820 FQ	67630 MW	78430 TQ	USBLS	5/15
Artists, Performers, and Athletes	Maryland	Y	24235 AE	63367 MW	82933 AEX	MDBLS	4/16
Artists, Performers, and Athletes	Massachusetts	Y	62760 FQ	85330 MW	97190 TQ	USBLS	5/15
Artists, Performers, and Athletes	Boston-Cambridge-Newton NECTA, MA	Y	66450 FQ	89480 MW	133740 TQ	USBLS	5/15
Artists, Performers, and Athletes	Michigan	Y	37140 FQ	57250 MW	76580 TQ	USBLS	5/15
Artists, Performers, and Athletes	Minnesota	Y	41538 FQ	58629 MW	92262 TQ	MNBLS	1/16-3/16
Artists, Performers, and Athletes	Minneapolis-St. Paul-Bloomington MSA, MN-WI	Y	41904 FQ	58629 MW	91134 TQ	MNBLS	1/16-3/16
Artists, Performers, and Athletes	Missouri	Y	32390 FQ	35330 MW	38270 TQ	USBLS	5/15
Artists, Performers, and Athletes	Kansas City MSA, MO-KS	Y	36300 FQ	44890 MW	84400 TQ	USBLS	5/15
Artists, Performers, and Athletes	St. Louis MSA, MO-IL	Y	32430 FQ	35280 MW	38130 TQ	USBLS	5/15
Artists, Performers, and Athletes	New Jersey	Y	41850 FQ	56750 MW	73530 TQ	USBLS	5/15
Artists, Performers, and Athletes	Newark PMSA, NJ-PA	Y	52600 FQ	58990 MW	73740 TQ	USBLS	5/15
Artists, Performers, and Athletes	New Mexico	Y	44510 FQ	67640 MW	75770 TQ	USBLS	5/15
Artists, Performers, and Athletes	Albuquerque MSA, NM	Y	46020 FQ	69100 MW	76030 TQ	USBLS	5/15
Artists, Performers, and Athletes	New York	Y	45080 AE	68870 MW	135450 AEX	NYBLS	1/16-3/16
Artists, Performers, and Athletes	Nassau County-Suffolk County PMSA, NY	Y	75570 FQ	87800 MW	96160 TQ	USBLS	5/15
Artists, Performers, and Athletes	New York-Jersey City-White Plains PMSA, NY-NJ	Y	50390 FQ	64930 MW	115010 TQ	USBLS	5/15
Artists, Performers, and Athletes	North Carolina	Y	41850 FQ	54640 MW	70300 TQ	USBLS	5/15
Artists, Performers, and Athletes	Charlotte-Concord-Gastonia MSA, NC-SC	Y	42500 FQ	53370 MW	64020 TQ	USBLS	5/15

Occupation/Type/Industry	Location	Per	Low	Mid	High	Source	Date
Agent and Business Manager							
Artists, Performers, and Athletes	Ohio	Y	51300 FQ	66470 MW	77720 TQ	USBLS	5/15
Artists, Performers, and Athletes	Oklahoma	Y	45130 FQ	54140 MW	60880 TQ	USBLS	5/15
Artists, Performers, and Athletes	Oklahoma City MSA, OK	Y	40060 FQ	51280 MW	61330 TQ	USBLS	5/15
Artists, Performers, and Athletes	Oregon	H	10.80 FQ	14.98 MW	24.25 TQ	ORBLS	2016
Artists, Performers, and Athletes	Portland-Vancouver-Hillsboro MSA, OR-WA	Y	19830 FQ	29240 MW	43030 TQ	USBLS	5/15
Artists, Performers, and Athletes	Pennsylvania	Y	36960 FQ	51030 MW	75120 TQ	USBLS	5/15
Artists, Performers, and Athletes	Philadelphia PMSA, PA	Y	18820 FQ	44210 MW	80010 TQ	USBLS	5/15
Artists, Performers, and Athletes	South Carolina	Y	34210 FQ	38430 MW	45670 TQ	USBLS	5/15
Artists, Performers, and Athletes	Tennessee	Y	36500 FQ	55340 MW	79980 TQ	USBLS	5/15
Artists, Performers, and Athletes	Nashville-Davidson–Murfreesboro–Franklin MSA, TN	Y	37150 FQ	56810 MW	81510 TQ	USBLS	5/15
Artists, Performers, and Athletes	Texas	Y	34270 FQ	59480 MW	103520 TQ	USBLS	5/15
Artists, Performers, and Athletes	Dallas-Plano-Irving PMSA, TX	Y	34470 FQ	61740 MW	99660 TQ	USBLS	5/15
Artists, Performers, and Athletes	Utah	Y	40710 FQ	51820 MW	57070 TQ	USBLS	5/15
Artists, Performers, and Athletes	Salt Lake City MSA, UT	Y	40110 FQ	51520 MW	56890 TQ	USBLS	5/15
Artists, Performers, and Athletes	Virginia	Y	34390 FQ	47490 MW	76400 TQ	USBLS	5/15
Artists, Performers, and Athletes	Washington	H	16.47 FQ	17.87 MW	19.28 TQ	WABLS	3/16
Artists, Performers, and Athletes	Seattle-Bellevue-Everett PMSA, WA	H	17.30 FQ	22.34 MW	64.64 TQ	WABLS	3/16
Agricultural and Food Science Technician							
	Alabama	Y	30998 AE	48071 AW	56603 AEX	ALBLS	6/16
	Arizona	Y	27960 FQ	33500 MW	37410 TQ	USBLS	5/15
	Phoenix-Mesa-Scottsdale MSA, AZ	Y	29240 FQ	33490 MW	37010 TQ	USBLS	5/15
	Arkansas	Y	28020 FQ	34730 MW	44500 TQ	USBLS	5/15
	California	H	15.50 FQ	18.53 MW	24.43 TQ	CABLS	1/16-3/16
	Los Angeles-Long Beach-Glendale PMSA, CA	H	16.06 FQ	18.87 MW	23.12 TQ	CABLS	1/16-3/16
	Oakland-Hayward-Berkeley PMSA, CA	H	17.37 FQ	21.65 MW	28.93 TQ	CABLS	1/16-3/16
	Riverside-San Bernardino-Ontario MSA, CA	H	10.07 FQ	12.13 MW	18.67 TQ	CABLS	1/16-3/16
	Sacramento–Roseville–Arden-Arcade MSA, CA	H	16.77 FQ	18.78 MW	24.18 TQ	CABLS	1/16-3/16
	San Diego-Carlsbad MSA, CA	H	13.83 FQ	16.77 MW	21.43 TQ	CABLS	1/16-3/16
	Colorado	Y	26060 FQ	37700 MW	45910 TQ	USBLS	5/15
	Connecticut	Y		23567 MW		CTBLS	1/16-3/16
	Washington-Arlington-Alexandria PMSA, DC-VA-MD-WV	Y	39070 FQ	49480 MW	62730 TQ	USBLS	5/15
	Florida	H	14.76 AE	17.65 MW	20.17 AEX	FLBLS	7/16-9/16
	Orlando-Kissimmee-Sanford MSA, FL	H	14.50 AE	16.67 MW	17.72 AEX	FLBLS	7/16-9/16
	Georgia	Y	28220 FQ	34470 MW	44110 TQ	USBLS	5/15
	Atlanta-Sandy Springs-Roswell MSA, GA	Y	27970 FQ	33440 MW	44060 TQ	USBLS	5/15
	Hawaii	Y	33900 FQ	42630 MW	50630 TQ	USBLS	5/15
	Urban Honolulu MSA, HI	Y	36800 FQ	44450 MW	52150 TQ	USBLS	5/15
	Idaho	Y	25380 FQ	32700 MW	38150 TQ	USBLS	5/15
	Boise City MSA, ID	Y	33260 FQ	37070 MW	43220 TQ	USBLS	5/15
	Illinois	Y	31170 FQ	39110 MW	51390 TQ	USBLS	5/15
	Chicago-Naperville-Arlington Heights PMSA, IL	Y	30160 FQ	36990 MW	47590 TQ	USBLS	5/15
	Indiana	Y	30090 FQ	36850 MW	45430 TQ	USBLS	5/15
	Indianapolis-Carmel-Anderson MSA, IN	Y	29280 FQ	37040 MW	45060 TQ	USBLS	5/15
	Iowa	Y	25550 FQ	33440 MW	43210 TQ	USBLS	5/15
	Des Moines-West Des Moines MSA, IA	Y	27680 FQ	35200 MW	49970 TQ	USBLS	5/15
	Kansas	Y	31060 FQ	37060 MW	45630 TQ	USBLS	5/15
	Kentucky	Y	18890 FQ	28290 MW	37500 TQ	USBLS	5/15
	Louisville-Jefferson County MSA, KY-IN	Y	33840 FQ	36780 MW	39720 TQ	USBLS	5/15
	Louisiana	Y	24000 FQ	30040 MW	38400 TQ	USBLS	5/15
	Maine	Y	26080 FQ	32970 MW	38270 TQ	USBLS	5/15
	Maryland	Y	29852 AE	47090 MW	55709 AEX	MDBLS	4/16
	Baltimore-Columbia-Towson MSA, MD	Y	29200 FQ	37590 MW	53760 TQ	USBLS	5/15

AE	Average entry wage	AWR	Average wage range	H	Hourly	LR	Low end range	MTC	Median total compensation	TCC	Total cash compensation
AEX	Average experienced wage	B	Biweekly	HI	Highest wage paid	M	Monthly	MW	Median wage paid	TQ	Third quartile wage
ATC	Average total compensation	D	Daily	HR	High end range	MCC	Median cash compensation	MWR	Median wage range	W	Weekly
AW	Average wage paid	FQ	First quartile wage	LO	Lowest wage paid	ME	Median entry wage	S	See annotated source	Y	Yearly

Occupation/Type/Industry	Location	Per	Low	Mid	High	Source	Date
Agricultural and Food Science Technician							
	Salisbury MSA, MD-DE	Y	35280 FQ	39200 MW	47490 TQ	USBLS	5/15
	Massachusetts	Y	35190 FQ	43250 MW	50660 TQ	USBLS	5/15
	Boston-Cambridge-Newton NECTA, MA	Y	33180 FQ	40940 MW	47340 TQ	USBLS	5/15
	Michigan	Y	30930 FQ	39470 MW	46720 TQ	USBLS	5/15
	Minnesota	Y	33356 FQ	38870 MW	47167 TQ	MNBLS	1/16-3/16
	Minneapolis-St. Paul-Bloomington MSA, MN-WI	Y	34667 FQ	40796 MW	50796 TQ	MNBLS	1/16-3/16
	Mississippi	Y	26100 FQ	31330 MW	39980 TQ	USBLS	5/15
	Missouri	Y	27520 FQ	34220 MW	44400 TQ	USBLS	5/15
	Kansas City MSA, MO-KS	Y	34890 FQ	41730 MW	48200 TQ	USBLS	5/15
	St. Louis MSA, MO-IL	Y	27750 FQ	34380 MW	45450 TQ	USBLS	5/15
	Montana	Y	34990 FQ	41750 MW	49820 TQ	USBLS	5/15
	Nebraska	Y	28360 FQ	33530 MW	40760 TQ	NEBLS	7/16-9/16
	Omaha-Council Bluffs MSA, NE-IA	Y	27875 FQ	35505 MW	47010 TQ	NEBLS	7/16-9/16
	New Hampshire	H	13.94 AE	20.95 MW	24.83 AEX	NHBLS	6/16
	New Jersey	Y	37840 FQ	48030 MW	59190 TQ	USBLS	5/15
	Newark PMSA, NJ-PA	Y	37480 FQ	66630 MW	86910 TQ	USBLS	5/15
	New Mexico	Y	33110 FQ	39140 MW	62320 TQ	USBLS	5/15
	New York	Y	34790 AE	48780 MW	60360 AEX	NYBLS	1/16-3/16
	New York-Jersey City-White Plains PMSA, NY-NJ	Y	37880 FQ	50150 MW	58590 TQ	USBLS	5/15
	Rochester MSA, NY	Y	39090 FQ	43730 MW	48080 TQ	USBLS	5/15
	North Carolina	Y	26190 FQ	33670 MW	39430 TQ	USBLS	5/15
	Charlotte-Concord-Gastonia MSA, NC-SC	Y	34300 FQ	37980 MW	46320 TQ	USBLS	5/15
	Raleigh MSA, NC	Y	32730 FQ	36840 MW	42540 TQ	USBLS	5/15
	North Dakota	Y	31470 FQ	38510 MW	49180 TQ	USBLS	5/15
	Fargo MSA, ND-MN	Y	33470 FQ	36340 MW	39130 TQ	USBLS	5/15
	Ohio	Y	29670 FQ	37200 MW	44830 TQ	USBLS	5/15
	Cincinnati MSA, OH-KY-IN	Y	28830 FQ	40730 MW	48390 TQ	USBLS	5/15
	Cleveland-Elyria MSA, OH	Y	37420 FQ	42550 MW	47020 TQ	USBLS	5/15
	Columbus MSA, OH	Y	27290 FQ	30620 MW	39070 TQ	USBLS	5/15
	Oklahoma	Y	30400 FQ	35480 MW	39860 TQ	USBLS	5/15
	Oklahoma City MSA, OK	Y	27490 FQ	34070 MW	42570 TQ	USBLS	5/15
	Tulsa MSA, OK	Y	29720 FQ	35220 MW	40730 TQ	USBLS	5/15
	Oregon	H	15.36 FQ	18.73 MW	24.40 TQ	ORBLS	2016
	Portland-Vancouver-Hillsboro MSA, OR-WA	Y	29890 FQ	38280 MW	56460 TQ	USBLS	5/15
	Pennsylvania	Y	30940 FQ	37390 MW	46260 TQ	USBLS	5/15
	Montgomery County-Bucks County-Chester County PMSA, PA	Y	24900 FQ	30080 MW	37770 TQ	USBLS	5/15
	Philadelphia PMSA, PA	Y	34420 FQ	41680 MW	48860 TQ	USBLS	5/15
	Pittsburgh MSA, PA	Y	32410 FQ	41780 MW	50290 TQ	USBLS	5/15
	South Carolina	Y	32540 FQ	37120 MW	43240 TQ	USBLS	5/15
	South Dakota	Y	23130 FQ	27780 MW	32890 TQ	USBLS	5/15
	Sioux Falls MSA, SD	Y	22130 FQ	24820 MW	32810 TQ	USBLS	5/15
	Tennessee	Y	26660 FQ	29120 MW	31590 TQ	USBLS	5/15
	Knoxville MSA, TN	Y	27840 FQ	38220 MW	46890 TQ	USBLS	5/15
	Memphis MSA, TN-MS-AR	Y	26590 FQ	28460 MW	30340 TQ	USBLS	5/15
	Nashville-Davidson–Murfreesboro–Franklin MSA, TN	Y	27320 FQ	29690 MW	34640 TQ	USBLS	5/15
	Texas	Y	22560 FQ	32340 MW	41190 TQ	USBLS	5/15
	Dallas-Plano-Irving PMSA, TX	Y	22770 FQ	33260 MW	40800 TQ	USBLS	5/15
	Houston-The Woodlands-Sugar Land MSA, TX	Y	34100 FQ	42210 MW	46440 TQ	USBLS	5/15
	Utah	Y	30290 FQ	37460 MW	45980 TQ	USBLS	5/15
	Vermont	Y	33200 FQ	36660 MW	40610 TQ	USBLS	5/15
	Virginia	Y	28840 FQ	35840 MW	43960 TQ	USBLS	5/15
	Washington	H	14.65 FQ	17.66 MW	22.60 TQ	WABLS	3/16
	Seattle-Bellevue-Everett PMSA, WA	H	16.06 FQ	19.75 MW	25.50 TQ	WABLS	3/16
	Tacoma-Lakewood PMSA, WA	H	14.00 FQ	16.59 MW	19.15 TQ	WABLS	3/16
	Wisconsin	Y	30810 FQ	38010 MW	46340 TQ	USBLS	5/15
	Madison MSA, WI	Y	31720 FQ	36420 MW	44650 TQ	USBLS	5/15
	Milwaukee-Waukesha-West Allis MSA, WI	Y	28310 FQ	36380 MW	47800 TQ	USBLS	5/15

Occupation/Type/Industry	Location	Per	Low	Mid	High	Source	Date
Agricultural and Food Science Technician	San Juan-Carolina-Caguas MSA, PR	Y	21570 FQ	25260 MW	30580 TQ	USBLS	5/15
Agricultural Engineer	Alabama	Y	65543 AE	87387 AW	98314 AEX	ALBLS	6/16
	California	H	34.38 FQ	41.08 MW	50.01 TQ	CABLS	1/16-3/16
	Florida	H	17.19 AE	21.80 MW	28.95 AEX	FLBLS	7/16-9/16
	Georgia	Y	53560 FQ	60850 MW	99520 TQ	USBLS	5/15
	Illinois	Y	59360 FQ	70190 MW	91260 TQ	USBLS	5/15
	Indiana	Y	64490 FQ	75220 MW	86580 TQ	USBLS	5/15
	Iowa	Y	71930 FQ	87250 MW	104200 TQ	USBLS	5/15
	Kansas	Y	63770 FQ	77920 MW	90600 TQ	USBLS	5/15
	Kentucky	Y	54630 FQ	64220 MW	77200 TQ	USBLS	5/15
	Maryland	Y	61098 AE	80359 MW	89990 AEX	MDBLS	4/16
	North Carolina	Y	61560 FQ	108500 MW	132380 TQ	USBLS	5/15
	Ohio	Y	58770 FQ	77500 MW	85060 TQ	USBLS	5/15
	Oregon	H	27.84 FQ	34.93 MW	37.21 TQ	ORBLS	2016
	Pennsylvania	Y	55260 FQ	66370 MW	88490 TQ	USBLS	5/15
	Texas	Y	53040 FQ	62160 MW	111800 TQ	USBLS	5/15
	Utah	Y	43240 FQ	52190 MW	64280 TQ	USBLS	5/15
	Virginia	Y	60590 FQ	74100 MW	96390 TQ	USBLS	5/15
	Washington	H	33.27 FQ	36.36 MW	42.34 TQ	WABLS	3/16
	Wisconsin	Y	68280 FQ	77070 MW	89790 TQ	USBLS	5/15
Agricultural Equipment Operator	Alabama	Y	17539 AE	27384 AW	32311 AEX	ALBLS	6/16
	Arizona	Y	19340 FQ	24310 MW	27720 TQ	USBLS	5/15
	Arkansas	Y	18210 FQ	21990 MW	29830 TQ	USBLS	5/15
	California	H	9.80 FQ	12.43 MW	14.83 TQ	CABLS	1/16-3/16
	Colorado	Y	26290 FQ	32180 MW	37470 TQ	USBLS	5/15
	Connecticut	Y		45189 MW		CTBLS	1/16-3/16
	Delaware	Y	21360 FQ	26850 MW	34580 TQ	USBLS	5/15
	Florida	H	8.85 AE	11.35 MW	15.79 AEX	FLBLS	7/16-9/16
	Georgia	Y	17490 FQ	19570 MW	27010 TQ	USBLS	5/15
	Idaho	Y	21170 FQ	28630 MW	34530 TQ	USBLS	5/15
	Illinois	Y	26560 FQ	31460 MW	38210 TQ	USBLS	5/15
	Indiana	Y	28340 FQ	33520 MW	42300 TQ	USBLS	5/15
	Iowa	Y	28600 FQ	33610 MW	38980 TQ	USBLS	5/15
	Kansas	Y	31000 FQ	34710 MW	38350 TQ	USBLS	5/15
	Kentucky	Y	17290 FQ	19160 MW	27930 TQ	USBLS	5/15
	Louisiana	Y	19930 FQ	24540 MW	38710 TQ	USBLS	5/15
	Maryland	Y	24542 AE	38265 MW	45127 AEX	MDBLS	4/16
	Massachusetts	Y	31330 FQ	35070 MW	38800 TQ	USBLS	5/15
	Michigan	Y	27950 FQ	34780 MW	42500 TQ	USBLS	5/15
	Minnesota	Y	28868 FQ	33439 MW	38918 TQ	MNBLS	1/16-3/16
	Mississippi	Y	20720 FQ	25780 MW	38870 TQ	USBLS	5/15
	Missouri	Y	19080 FQ	25260 MW	35060 TQ	USBLS	5/15
	Montana	Y	22670 FQ	27840 MW	39440 TQ	USBLS	5/15
	Nebraska	Y	27830 FQ	31200 MW	36970 TQ	NEBLS	7/16-9/16
	New Jersey	Y	32430 FQ	35090 MW	37740 TQ	USBLS	5/15
	New Mexico	Y	19390 FQ	22200 MW	25810 TQ	USBLS	5/15
	New York	Y	27950 AE	36750 MW	41380 AEX	NYBLS	1/16-3/16
	North Carolina	Y	17590 FQ	19670 MW	28940 TQ	USBLS	5/15
	North Dakota	Y	31900 FQ	35790 MW	40140 TQ	USBLS	5/15
	Ohio	Y	23140 FQ	33190 MW	39150 TQ	USBLS	5/15
	Oklahoma	Y	22580 FQ	28440 MW	35250 TQ	USBLS	5/15
	Oregon	H	10.82 FQ	12.11 MW	14.78 TQ	ORBLS	2016
	Pennsylvania	Y	21360 FQ	25860 MW	35200 TQ	USBLS	5/15
	South Carolina	Y	18130 FQ	21740 MW	30500 TQ	USBLS	5/15
	South Dakota	Y	26990 FQ	29210 MW	31450 TQ	USBLS	5/15
	Tennessee	Y	19110 FQ	23940 MW	28990 TQ	USBLS	5/15
	Texas	Y	18930 FQ	24230 MW	29860 TQ	USBLS	5/15
	Utah	Y	26400 FQ	28950 MW	31840 TQ	USBLS	5/15
	Virginia	Y	20790 FQ	25040 MW	29090 TQ	USBLS	5/15
	Washington	H	12.79 FQ	15.92 MW	19.14 TQ	WABLS	3/16
	Wisconsin	Y	27830 FQ	32250 MW	37290 TQ	USBLS	5/15
	Puerto Rico	Y	17130 FQ	18610 MW	20390 TQ	USBLS	5/15
Agricultural Inspector	Alabama	Y	25141 AE	40345 AW	47947 AEX	ALBLS	6/16
	Birmingham-Hoover MSA, AL	Y	34657 AE	44439 AW	49326 AEX	ALBLS	6/16
	Arizona	Y	28690 FQ	34120 MW	44280 TQ	USBLS	5/15
	Phoenix-Mesa-Scottsdale MSA, AZ	Y	29240 FQ	41270 MW	45430 TQ	USBLS	5/15

AE	Average entry wage	AWR	Average wage range	H	Hourly	LR	Low end range	MTC	Median total compensation	TCC	Total cash compensation
AEX	Average experienced wage	B	Biweekly	HI	Highest wage paid	M	Monthly	MW	Median wage paid	TQ	Third quartile wage
ATC	Average total compensation	D	Daily	HR	High end range	MCC	Median cash compensation	MWR	Median wage range	W	Weekly
AW	Average wage paid	FQ	First quartile wage	LO	Lowest wage paid	ME	Median entry wage	S	See annotated source	Y	Yearly

Occupation/Type/Industry	Location	Per	Low	Mid	High	Source	Date
Agricultural Inspector	Arkansas	Y	36610 FQ	44830 MW	50020 TQ	USBLS	5/15
	California	H	14.52 FQ	19.34 MW	26.34 TQ	CABLS	1/16-3/16
	Anaheim-Santa Ana-Irvine PMSA, CA	H	14.52 FQ	16.03 MW	17.62 TQ	CABLS	1/16-3/16
	Los Angeles-Long Beach-Glendale PMSA, CA	H	14.62 FQ	18.11 MW	30.74 TQ	CABLS	1/16-3/16
	Oakland-Hayward-Berkeley PMSA, CA	H	24.64 FQ	33.75 MW	43.11 TQ	CABLS	1/16-3/16
	Riverside-San Bernardino-Ontario MSA, CA	H	13.42 FQ	16.02 MW	23.18 TQ	CABLS	1/16-3/16
	Sacramento–Roseville–Arden-Arcade MSA, CA	H	12.21 FQ	14.24 MW	18.06 TQ	CABLS	1/16-3/16
	San Diego-Carlsbad MSA, CA	H	13.43 FQ	16.63 MW	22.33 TQ	CABLS	1/16-3/16
	Colorado	Y	37730 FQ	45300 MW	54020 TQ	USBLS	5/15
	Connecticut	Y		74085 MW		CTBLS	1/16-3/16
	Delaware	Y	39570 FQ	46160 MW	50130 TQ	USBLS	5/15
	Washington-Arlington-Alexandria PMSA, DC-VA-MD-WV	Y	41070 FQ	45150 MW	49130 TQ	USBLS	5/15
	Florida	H	10.37 AE	14.06 MW	18.39 AEX	FLBLS	7/16-9/16
	Orlando-Kissimmee-Sanford MSA, FL	H	13.07 AE	14.89 MW	18.77 AEX	FLBLS	7/16-9/16
	Tampa-St. Petersburg-Clearwater MSA, FL	H	13.39 AE	14.95 MW	18.66 AEX	FLBLS	7/16-9/16
	Georgia	Y	31940 FQ	41340 MW	48240 TQ	USBLS	5/15
	Atlanta-Sandy Springs-Roswell MSA, GA	Y	33380 FQ	45490 MW	51000 TQ	USBLS	5/15
	Idaho	Y	27830 FQ	34980 MW	38900 TQ	USBLS	5/15
	Illinois	Y	41180 FQ	56510 MW	67360 TQ	USBLS	5/15
	Chicago-Naperville-Arlington Heights PMSA, IL	Y	50280 FQ	63440 MW	70130 TQ	USBLS	5/15
	Indiana	Y	27940 FQ	40890 MW	48830 TQ	USBLS	5/15
	Iowa	Y	39510 FQ	47480 MW	56450 TQ	CABLS	5/15
	Kansas	Y	34710 FQ	39580 MW	46170 TQ	USBLS	5/15
	Kentucky	Y	34290 FQ	40890 MW	46170 TQ	USBLS	5/15
	Louisiana	Y	39380 FQ	47480 MW	57930 TQ	USBLS	5/15
	New Orleans-Metairie MSA, LA	Y	42220 FQ	54860 MW	62940 TQ	USBLS	5/15
	Maine	Y	33750 FQ	36460 MW	43330 TQ	USBLS	5/15
	Maryland	Y	31225 AE	44507 MW	51148 AEX	MDBLS	4/16
	Baltimore-Columbia-Towson MSA, MD	Y	37780 FQ	47010 MW	54130 TQ	USBLS	5/15
	Salisbury MSA, MD-DE	Y	39580 FQ	44840 MW	50110 TQ	USBLS	5/15
	Massachusetts	Y	63240 FQ	69030 MW	74750 TQ	USBLS	5/15
	Michigan	Y	52590 FQ	65140 MW	70820 TQ	USBLS	5/15
	Minnesota	Y	26658 FQ	42913 MW	51894 TQ	MNBLS	1/16-3/16
	Minneapolis-St. Paul-Bloomington MSA, MN-WI	Y	46475 FQ	55183 MW	62609 TQ	MNBLS	1/16-3/16
	Mississippi	Y	33810 FQ	43810 MW	48810 TQ	USBLS	5/15
	Jackson MSA, MS	Y	31480 FQ	43520 MW	49450 TQ	USBLS	5/15
	Missouri	Y	36120 FQ	42400 MW	48810 TQ	USBLS	5/15
	Kansas City MSA, MO-KS	Y	36220 FQ	42390 MW	50370 TQ	USBLS	5/15
	St. Louis MSA, MO-IL	Y	40290 FQ	51150 MW	64000 TQ	USBLS	5/15
	Montana	Y	22710 FQ	26470 MW	30370 TQ	USBLS	5/15
	Nebraska	Y	31945 FQ	43530 MW	50105 TQ	NEBLS	7/16-9/16
	New Jersey	Y	42940 FQ	57760 MW	66260 TQ	USBLS	5/15
	Camden PMSA, NJ	Y	29780 FQ	39490 MW	54550 TQ	USBLS	5/15
	New Mexico	Y	32350 FQ	36130 MW	46960 TQ	USBLS	5/15
	New York	Y	42290 AE	62580 MW	70230 AEX	NYBLS	1/16-3/16
	Nassau County-Suffolk County PMSA, NY	Y	39100 FQ	55950 MW	67230 TQ	USBLS	5/15
	New York-Jersey City-White Plains PMSA, NY-NJ	Y	52480 FQ	66110 MW	76860 TQ	USBLS	5/15
	North Carolina	Y	34050 FQ	42220 MW	48800 TQ	USBLS	5/15
	North Dakota	Y	27380 FQ	31160 MW	42480 TQ	USBLS	5/15
	Fargo MSA, ND-MN	Y	26770 FQ	29230 MW	40590 TQ	USBLS	5/15
	Ohio	Y	34270 FQ	45630 MW	53120 TQ	USBLS	5/15
	Oklahoma	Y	29380 FQ	36610 MW	45790 TQ	USBLS	5/15
	Oregon	H	14.99 FQ	20.83 MW	28.69 TQ	ORBLS	2016
	Portland-Vancouver-Hillsboro MSA, OR-WA	Y	46510 FQ	54420 MW	60960 TQ	USBLS	5/15
	Pennsylvania	Y	44340 FQ	51160 MW	59780 TQ	USBLS	5/15

AE	Average entry wage	AWR	Average wage range	H	Hourly	LR	Low end range	MTC	Median total compensation	TCC	Total cash compensation
AEX	Average experienced wage	B	Biweekly	HI	Highest wage paid	M	Monthly	MW	Median wage paid	TQ	Third quartile wage
ATC	Average total compensation	D	Daily	HR	High end range	MCC	Median cash compensation	MWR	Median wage range	W	Weekly
AW	Average wage paid	FQ	First quartile wage	LO	Lowest wage paid	ME	Median entry wage	S	See annotated source	Y	Yearly

Occupation/Type/Industry	Location	Per	Low	Mid	High	Source	Date
Agricultural Inspector	South Carolina	Y	30680 FQ	39580 MW	47470 TQ	USBLS	5/15
	Tennessee	Y	38820 FQ	43520 MW	48410 TQ	USBLS	5/15
	Nashville-Davidson– Murfreesboro–Franklin MSA, TN	Y	40950 FQ	47340 MW	56320 TQ	USBLS	5/15
	Texas	Y	40880 FQ	46780 MW	51650 TQ	USBLS	5/15
	Houston-The Woodlands- Sugar Land MSA, TX	Y	61850 FQ	67300 MW	70940 TQ	USBLS	5/15
	San Antonio-New Braunfels MSA, TX	Y	44840 FQ	50120 MW	53240 TQ	USBLS	5/15
	Virginia	Y	35730 FQ	43070 MW	48140 TQ	USBLS	5/15
	Richmond MSA, VA	Y	34470 FQ	43070 MW	48730 TQ	USBLS	5/15
	Virginia Beach-Norfolk- Newport News MSA, VA-NC	Y	26200 FQ	33410 MW	39070 TQ	USBLS	5/15
	Washington	H	21.84 FQ	23.71 MW	27.60 TQ	WABLS	3/16
	Seattle-Bellevue-Everett PMSA, WA	H	26.07 FQ	29.78 MW	34.87 TQ	WABLS	3/16
	Wisconsin	Y	39210 FQ	43530 MW	51540 TQ	USBLS	5/15
Agricultural Microbiologist State Government	North Carolina	Y	35474 LO		60604 HI	NCGOV	7/1/16
Agricultural Research Aide Michigan State University	East Lansing, MI	Y			43930 HI	MSUSAL	10/1/14-9/30/15
Agricultural Sciences Teacher							
Postsecondary	Alabama	Y	69538 AE	105113 AW	122900 AEX	ALBLS	6/16
Postsecondary	Arizona	Y	46010 FQ	66580 MW	90060 TQ	USBLS	5/15
Postsecondary	Arkansas	Y	64130 FQ	87470 MW	112510 TQ	USBLS	5/15
Postsecondary	California	Y		88677 AW		CABLS	1/16-3/16
Postsecondary	Colorado	Y	68340 FQ	88390 MW	110600 TQ	USBLS	5/15
Postsecondary	Florida	Y	78622 AE	102120 MW	131481 AEX	FLBLS	7/16-9/16
Postsecondary	Georgia	Y	85880 FQ	100370 MW	120910 TQ	USBLS	5/15
Postsecondary	Illinois	Y	53990 FQ	76230 MW	110030 TQ	USBLS	5/15
Postsecondary	Iowa	Y	68300 FQ	94540 MW	120560 TQ	USBLS	5/15
Postsecondary	Kansas	Y	64560 FQ	73720 MW	84850 TQ	USBLS	5/15
Postsecondary	Kentucky	Y	70720 FQ	91520 MW	109440 TQ	USBLS	5/15
Postsecondary	Louisiana	Y	61730 FQ	74930 MW	111260 TQ	USBLS	5/15
Postsecondary	Maryland	Y	45891 AE	91686 MW	114583 AEX	MDBLS	4/16
Postsecondary	Massachusetts	Y	64510 FQ	87770 MW	99000 TQ	USBLS	5/15
Postsecondary	Minnesota	Y	70745 FQ	93648 MW	120039 TQ	MNBLS	1/16-3/16
Postsecondary	Mississippi	Y	69100 FQ	82510 MW	96280 TQ	USBLS	5/15
Postsecondary	Missouri	Y	65230 FQ	83050 MW	113200 TQ	USBLS	5/15
Postsecondary	Montana	Y	66450 FQ	83850 MW	100320 TQ	USBLS	5/15
Postsecondary	Nebraska	Y	72700 FQ	93150 MW	116720 TQ	NEBLS	7/16-9/16
Postsecondary	New York	Y	55390 AE	101110 MW	131320 AEX	NYBLS	1/16-3/16
Postsecondary	North Carolina	Y	54150 FQ	77340 MW	108980 TQ	USBLS	5/15
Postsecondary	Ohio	Y	56060 FQ	84290 MW	113000 TQ	USBLS	5/15
Postsecondary	Oklahoma	Y	67280 FQ	87310 MW	114300 TQ	USBLS	5/15
Postsecondary	Oregon	Y	65527 FQ	88242 MW	114954 TQ	ORBLS	2016
Postsecondary	Pennsylvania	Y	80070 FQ	100680 MW	128820 TQ	USBLS	5/15
Postsecondary	South Dakota	Y	57240 FQ	74440 MW	93400 TQ	USBLS	5/15
Postsecondary	Tennessee	Y	59030 FQ	75040 MW	98870 TQ	USBLS	5/15
Postsecondary	Texas	Y	71340 FQ	95990 MW	126380 TQ	USBLS	5/15
Postsecondary	Utah	Y	55940 FQ	74140 MW	102880 TQ	USBLS	5/15
Postsecondary	Virginia	Y	35770 FQ	43770 MW	63290 TQ	USBLS	5/15
Postsecondary	Wisconsin	Y	64960 FQ	89570 MW	118360 TQ	USBLS	5/15
Postsecondary	Wyoming	Y	63980 FQ	77220 MW	93430 TQ	USBLS	5/15
Agriculture Enforcement Agent State Government	Ohio	H	23.28 LO		28.98 HI	OHGOV	2015
Agronomist State Government	North Carolina	Y	42667 LO		82872 HI	NCGOV	7/1/16
Air Hostess	United States	Y		12000-20000 AW		BUZZ01	2015
Air Quality Scientist State Government	Billings, MT	H	22.13 LO		30.37 HI	MTGOV	2016
Air Safety Investigator National Transportation Safety Board	Anchorage, AK	Y	91167 LO		143620 HI	APP01	2015

AE	Average entry wage	AWR	Average wage range	H	Hourly	LR	Low end range	MTC	Median total compensation	TCC	Total cash compensation
AEX	Average experienced wage	B	Biweekly	HI	Highest wage paid	M	Monthly	MW	Median wage paid	TQ	Third quartile wage
ATC	Average total compensation	D	Daily	HR	High end range	MCC	Median cash compensation	MWR	Median wage range	W	Weekly
AW	Average wage paid	FQ	First quartile wage	LO	Lowest wage paid	ME	Median entry wage	S	See annotated source	Y	Yearly

Occupation/Type/Industry	Location	Per	Low	Mid	High	Source	Date
Air Safety Investigator							
National Transportation Safety Board	Denver, CO	Y	42468 LO		153574 HI	APP01	2015
National Transportation Safety Board	Miami Springs, FL	Y			158700 HI	APP01	2015
National Transportation Safety Board	Randolph, NJ	Y			137163 HI	APP01	2015
Air Traffic Controller	Alabama	Y	66030 AE	91917 AW	104866 AEX	ALBLS	6/16
	Alaska	Y	87580 FQ	103760 MW	125140 TQ	USBLS	5/15
	Arizona	Y	76060 FQ	95920 MW	123440 TQ	USBLS	5/15
	Arkansas	Y	72880 FQ	87340 MW	102090 TQ	USBLS	5/15
	California	H	43.48 FQ	66.38 MW	77.93 TQ	CABLS	1/16-3/16
	Colorado	Y	114200 FQ	132810 MW	154520 TQ	USBLS	5/15
	Connecticut	Y		100864 MW		CTBLS	1/16-3/16
	Florida	H	38.94 AE	60.06 MW	69.30 AEX	FLBLS	7/16-9/16
	Georgia	Y	128170 FQ	138610 MW	162360 TQ	USBLS	5/15
	Hawaii	Y	80220 FQ	107200 MW	135330 TQ	USBLS	5/15
	Illinois	Y	90590 FQ	138740 MW	162050 TQ	USBLS	5/15
	Indiana	Y	86670 FQ	127200 MW	155680 TQ	USBLS	5/15
	Iowa	Y	64730 FQ	73660 MW	93140 TQ	USBLS	5/15
	Kansas	Y	82070 FQ	120590 MW	144560 TQ	USBLS	5/15
	Kentucky	Y	83010 FQ	102530 MW	125230 TQ	USBLS	5/15
	Louisiana	Y	71390 FQ	81600 MW	103580 TQ	USBLS	5/15
	Maryland	Y	78507 AE	109633 MW	125197 AEX	MDBLS	4/16
	Michigan	Y	82250 FQ	107840 MW	135170 TQ	USBLS	5/15
	Minnesota	Y	126209 FQ	142693 MW	161525 TQ	MNBLS	1/16-3/16
	Mississippi	Y	70040 FQ	81580 MW	99710 TQ	USBLS	5/15
	Missouri	Y	76470 FQ	99620 MW	128250 TQ	USBLS	5/15
	Montana	Y	57700 FQ	71550 MW	81600 TQ	USBLS	5/15
	Nebraska	Y	73855 FQ	90150 MW	104575 TQ	NEBLS	7/16-9/16
	Nevada	Y	101240 FQ	120580 MW	137160 TQ	USBLS	5/15
	New Hampshire	H	49.85 AE	72.18 MW	78.61 AEX	NHBLS	6/16
	New Jersey	Y	87960 FQ	109030 MW	140300 TQ	USBLS	5/15
	New Mexico	Y	99620 FQ	114590 MW	143980 TQ	USBLS	5/15
	New York	Y	79480 AE	145430 MW	163570 AEX	NYBLS	1/16-3/16
	North Carolina	Y	75570 FQ	89490 MW	120600 TQ	USBLS	5/15
	North Dakota	Y	74950 FQ	94700 MW	99610 TQ	USBLS	5/15
	Ohio	Y	111480 FQ	131640 MW	164050 TQ	USBLS	5/15
	Oklahoma	Y	73790 FQ	98580 MW	124930 TQ	USBLS	5/15
	Pennsylvania	Y	81590 FQ	111580 MW	149170 TQ	USBLS	5/15
	South Carolina	Y	71540 FQ	89590 MW	99440 TQ	USBLS	5/15
	South Dakota	Y	69160 FQ	73850 MW	83310 TQ	USBLS	5/15
	Tennessee	Y	103910 FQ	126620 MW	150840 TQ	USBLS	5/15
	Texas	Y	90600 FQ	133830 MW	158520 TQ	USBLS	5/15
	Virginia	Y	123570 FQ	137780 MW	170070 TQ	USBLS	5/15
	Washington	H	39.95 FQ	57.49 MW	66.67 TQ	WABLS	3/16
	West Virginia	Y	65760 FQ	80310 MW	90350 TQ	USBLS	5/15
	Wisconsin	Y	86430 FQ	103070 MW	116950 TQ	USBLS	5/15
	Puerto Rico	Y	86440 FQ	104480 MW	116780 TQ	USBLS	5/15
	Guam	Y	68720 FQ	75880 MW	90160 TQ	USBLS	5/15
Aircraft Attendant							
State Government	Ohio	H	15.41 LO		15.80 HI	OHGOV	2015
Aircraft Cargo Handling Supervisor	Alabama	Y	34969 AE	45830 AW	51271 AEX	ALBLS	6/16
	Alaska	Y	40850 FQ	47010 MW	79710 TQ	USBLS	5/15
	Anchorage MSA, AK	Y	40740 FQ	46910 MW	80670 TQ	USBLS	5/15
	Arizona	Y	29910 FQ	38630 MW	55570 TQ	USBLS	5/15
	Phoenix-Mesa-Scottsdale MSA, AZ	Y	31620 FQ	39970 MW	56430 TQ	USBLS	5/15
	Arkansas	Y	36360 FQ	46040 MW	57530 TQ	USBLS	5/15
	California	H	17.33 FQ	22.37 MW	30.82 TQ	CABLS	1/16-3/16
	Anaheim-Santa Ana-Irvine PMSA, CA	H	19.78 FQ	23.28 MW	27.29 TQ	CABLS	1/16-3/16
	Los Angeles-Long Beach-Glendale PMSA, CA	H	18.53 FQ	27.01 MW	34.85 TQ	CABLS	1/16-3/16
	Sacramento–Roseville–Arden-Arcade MSA, CA	H	17.50 FQ	23.57 MW	29.21 TQ	CABLS	1/16-3/16
	San Diego-Carlsbad MSA, CA	H	15.21 FQ	19.30 MW	27.13 TQ	CABLS	1/16-3/16
	San Francisco-Redwood City-South San Francisco PMSA, CA	H	17.09 FQ	21.86 MW	27.15 TQ	CABLS	1/16-3/16
	Colorado	Y	28860 FQ	36170 MW	50530 TQ	USBLS	5/15

AE	Average entry wage	AWR	Average wage range	H	Hourly	LR	Low end range	MTC	Median total compensation	TCC	Total cash compensation
AEX	Average experienced wage	B	Biweekly	HI	Highest wage paid	M	Monthly	MW	Median wage paid	TQ	Third quartile wage
ATC	Average total compensation	D	Daily	HR	High end range	MCC	Median cash compensation	MWR	Median wage range	W	Weekly
AW	Average wage paid	FQ	First quartile wage	LO	Lowest wage paid	ME	Median entry wage	S	See annotated source	Y	Yearly

Aircraft Cargo Handling Supervisor

Occupation/Type/Industry	Location	Per	Low	Mid	High	Source	Date
Aircraft Cargo Handling Supervisor							
	Denver-Aurora-Lakewood MSA, CO	Y	28850 FQ	35400 MW	47710 TQ	USBLS	5/15
	Connecticut	Y		48695 MW		CTBLS	1/16-3/16
	Washington-Arlington-Alexandria PMSA, DC-VA-MD-WV	Y	37330 FQ	46020 MW	57440 TQ	USBLS	5/15
	Florida	H	16.43 AE	23.33 MW	29.19 AEX	FLBLS	7/16-9/16
	Fort Lauderdale-Pompano Beach-Deerfield Beach PMSA, FL	H	16.37 AE	23.82 MW	29.57 AEX	FLBLS	7/16-9/16
	Miami-Miami Beach-Kendall PMSA, FL	H	16.72 AE	21.62 MW	27.63 AEX	FLBLS	7/16-9/16
	Orlando-Kissimmee-Sanford MSA, FL	H	16.53 AE	24.34 MW	30.01 AEX	FLBLS	7/16-9/16
	Tampa-St. Petersburg-Clearwater MSA, FL	H	18.24 AE	31.54 MW	33.27 AEX	FLBLS	7/16-9/16
	Georgia	Y	40670 FQ	47640 MW	60080 TQ	USBLS	5/15
	Atlanta-Sandy Springs-Roswell MSA, GA	Y	41630 FQ	48320 MW	62000 TQ	USBLS	5/15
	Hawaii	Y	43400 FQ	52640 MW	62540 TQ	USBLS	5/15
	Urban Honolulu MSA, HI	Y	43650 FQ	53320 MW	62640 TQ	USBLS	5/15
	Illinois	Y	38480 FQ	51370 MW	67060 TQ	USBLS	5/15
	Chicago-Naperville-Arlington Heights PMSA, IL	Y	37170 FQ	48620 MW	62910 TQ	USBLS	5/15
	Indiana	Y	41260 FQ	45880 MW	50450 TQ	USBLS	5/15
	Iowa	Y	35970 FQ	42290 MW	49910 TQ	USBLS	5/15
	Des Moines-West Des Moines MSA, IA	Y	37960 FQ	45840 MW	57150 TQ	USBLS	5/15
	Louisiana	Y	32860 FQ	43060 MW	52470 TQ	USBLS	5/15
	New Orleans-Metairie MSA, LA	Y	43130 FQ	52750 MW	62050 TQ	USBLS	5/15
	Maryland	Y	31789 AE	44414 MW	50726 AEX	MDBLS	4/16
	Baltimore-Columbia-Towson MSA, MD	Y	35440 FQ	43520 MW	53980 TQ	USBLS	5/15
	Massachusetts	Y	33460 FQ	42320 MW	56860 TQ	USBLS	5/15
	Michigan	Y	36810 FQ	47820 MW	63870 TQ	USBLS	5/15
	Detroit-Dearborn-Livonia PMSA, MI	Y	30690 FQ	40540 MW	50580 TQ	USBLS	5/15
	Minnesota	Y	35668 FQ	41394 MW	67546 TQ	MNBLS	1/16-3/16
	Minneapolis-St. Paul-Bloomington MSA, MN-WI	Y	36172 FQ	48189 MW	68120 TQ	MNBLS	1/16-3/16
	Missouri	Y	39030 FQ	52940 MW	62660 TQ	USBLS	5/15
	Kansas City MSA, MO-KS	Y	39120 FQ	53490 MW	70140 TQ	USBLS	5/15
	St. Louis MSA, MO-IL	Y	39530 FQ	54760 MW	62980 TQ	USBLS	5/15
	Nevada	Y	42640 FQ	50470 MW	58710 TQ	USBLS	5/15
	New Hampshire	H	15.74 AE	20.14 MW	30.03 AEX	NHBLS	6/16
	New Jersey	Y	36380 FQ	44100 MW	56370 TQ	USBLS	5/15
	Newark PMSA, NJ-PA	Y	35720 FQ	40960 MW	51630 TQ	USBLS	5/15
	New York	Y	34560 AE	51920 MW	65940 AEX	NYBLS	1/16-3/16
	New York-Jersey City-White Plains PMSA, NY-NJ	Y	39120 FQ	55500 MW	71680 TQ	USBLS	5/15
	North Carolina	Y	36710 FQ	48120 MW	62880 TQ	USBLS	5/15
	North Dakota	Y	46760 FQ	58430 MW	72080 TQ	USBLS	5/15
	Ohio	Y	34770 FQ	48130 MW	60280 TQ	USBLS	5/15
	Cincinnati MSA, OH-KY-IN	Y	35560 FQ	44360 MW	58560 TQ	USBLS	5/15
	Oklahoma	Y	41050 FQ	53640 MW	62600 TQ	USBLS	5/15
	Oklahoma City MSA, OK	Y	46710 FQ	60290 MW	105800 TQ	USBLS	5/15
	Tulsa MSA, OK	Y	34150 FQ	44450 MW	56830 TQ	USBLS	5/15
	Oregon	H	20.76 FQ	24.33 MW	30.32 TQ	ORBLS	2016
	Portland-Vancouver-Hillsboro MSA, OR-WA	Y	42340 FQ	49120 MW	61930 TQ	USBLS	5/15
	Pennsylvania	Y	39320 FQ	50320 MW	60690 TQ	USBLS	5/15
	South Carolina	Y	31790 FQ	38710 MW	53420 TQ	USBLS	5/15
	Tennessee	Y	26810 FQ	29960 MW	50740 TQ	USBLS	5/15
	Memphis MSA, TN-MS-AR	Y	26560 FQ	29500 MW	38460 TQ	USBLS	5/15
	Texas	Y	37910 FQ	53240 MW	60520 TQ	USBLS	5/15
	Austin-Round Rock MSA, TX	Y	41150 FQ	54180 MW	59040 TQ	USBLS	5/15
	Fort Worth-Arlington PMSA, TX	Y	47200 FQ	56310 MW	62480 TQ	USBLS	5/15
	Utah	Y	34020 FQ	41900 MW	63590 TQ	USBLS	5/15
	Salt Lake City MSA, UT	Y	33750 FQ	40280 MW	62800 TQ	USBLS	5/15

AE	Average entry wage	AWR	Average wage range	H	Hourly
AEX	Average experienced wage	B	Biweekly	HI	Highest wage paid
ATC	Average total compensation	D	Daily	HR	High end range
AW	Average wage paid	FQ	First quartile wage	LO	Lowest wage paid

LR	Low end range	MTC	Median total compensation	TCC	Total cash compensation
M	Monthly	MW	Median wage paid	TQ	Third quartile wage
MCC	Median cash compensation	MWR	Median wage range	W	Weekly
ME	Median entry wage	S	See annotated source	Y	Yearly

Occupation/Type/Industry	Location	Per	Low	Mid	High	Source	Date
Aircraft Cargo Handling Supervisor	Virginia	Y	38380 FQ	48630 MW	60700 TQ	USBLS	5/15
	Virginia Beach-Norfolk-Newport News MSA, VA-NC	Y	34760 FQ	46980 MW	60140 TQ	USBLS	5/15
	Washington	H	17.33 FQ	19.09 MW	22.86 TQ	WABLS	3/16
	Seattle-Bellevue-Everett PMSA, WA	H	17.41 FQ	19.21 MW	23.11 TQ	WABLS	3/16
	Wisconsin	Y	31320 FQ	43670 MW	60440 TQ	USBLS	5/15
	Milwaukee-Waukesha-West Allis MSA, WI	Y	36000 FQ	52410 MW	61390 TQ	USBLS	5/15
	Puerto Rico	Y	22210 FQ	26890 MW	36180 TQ	USBLS	5/15
	San Juan-Carolina-Caguas MSA, PR	Y	22630 FQ	27360 MW	37620 TQ	USBLS	5/15
Aircraft Mechanic and Service Technician	Alabama	Y	47291 AE	65069 AW	73958 AEX	ALBLS	6/16
	Birmingham-Hoover MSA, AL	Y	32229 AE	50892 AW	60218 AEX	ALBLS	6/16
	Alaska	Y	52420 FQ	61560 MW	72940 TQ	USBLS	5/15
	Anchorage MSA, AK	Y	52800 FQ	62850 MW	74480 TQ	USBLS	5/15
	Arizona	Y	47260 FQ	58680 MW	70240 TQ	USBLS	5/15
	Phoenix-Mesa-Scottsdale MSA, AZ	Y	46600 FQ	61070 MW	73020 TQ	USBLS	5/15
	Tucson MSA, AZ	Y	51300 FQ	57430 MW	62090 TQ	USBLS	5/15
	Arkansas	Y	41780 FQ	47980 MW	55480 TQ	USBLS	5/15
	Little Rock-North Little Rock-Conway MSA, AR	Y	44450 FQ	49770 MW	56540 TQ	USBLS	5/15
	California	H	24.39 FQ	31.14 MW	38.86 TQ	CABLS	1/16-3/16
	Anaheim-Santa Ana-Irvine PMSA, CA	H	19.24 FQ	25.46 MW	32.47 TQ	CABLS	1/16-3/16
	Los Angeles-Long Beach-Glendale PMSA, CA	H	24.09 FQ	32.45 MW	40.28 TQ	CABLS	1/16-3/16
	Oakland-Hayward-Berkeley PMSA, CA	H	25.91 FQ	30.43 MW	42.97 TQ	CABLS	1/16-3/16
	Riverside-San Bernardino-Ontario MSA, CA	H	21.45 FQ	30.93 MW	38.64 TQ	CABLS	1/16-3/16
	Sacramento–Roseville–Arden-Arcade MSA, CA	H	23.94 FQ	31.76 MW	37.21 TQ	CABLS	1/16-3/16
	San Diego-Carlsbad MSA, CA	H	25.14 FQ	28.94 MW	33.81 TQ	CABLS	1/16-3/16
	San Francisco-Redwood City-South San Francisco PMSA, CA	H	29.81 FQ	39.50 MW	43.81 TQ	CABLS	1/16-3/16
	Colorado	Y	49180 FQ	63800 MW	79000 TQ	USBLS	5/15
	Denver-Aurora-Lakewood MSA, CO	Y	57850 FQ	71470 MW	85100 TQ	USBLS	5/15
	Connecticut	Y		63219 MW		CTBLS	1/16-3/16
	Bridgeport-Stamford-Norwalk MSA, CT	Y	53610 FQ	62290 MW	75360 TQ	USBLS	5/15
	Hartford-West Hartford-East Hartford MSA, CT	Y	51140 FQ	63610 MW	72830 TQ	USBLS	5/15
	Delaware	Y	53360 FQ	59280 MW	64010 TQ	USBLS	5/15
	Wilmington PMSA, DE-MD-NJ	Y	51370 FQ	58640 MW	66500 TQ	USBLS	5/15
	Washington-Arlington-Alexandria PMSA, DC-VA-MD-WV	Y	52880 FQ	68410 MW	77060 TQ	USBLS	5/15
	Florida	H	17.46 AE	26.36 MW	32.46 AEX	FLBLS	7/16-9/16
	Fort Lauderdale-Pompano Beach-Deerfield Beach PMSA, FL	H	17.76 AE	27.53 MW	32.63 AEX	FLBLS	7/16-9/16
	Miami-Miami Beach-Kendall PMSA, FL	H	17.09 AE	25.09 MW	33.17 AEX	FLBLS	7/16-9/16
	Orlando-Kissimmee-Sanford MSA, FL	H	16.50 AE	32.63 MW	36.27 AEX	FLBLS	7/16-9/16
	Tampa-St. Petersburg-Clearwater MSA, FL	H	20.14 AE	28.00 MW	33.86 AEX	FLBLS	7/16-9/16
	Georgia	Y	51350 FQ	60580 MW	84550 TQ	USBLS	5/15
	Atlanta-Sandy Springs-Roswell MSA, GA	Y	56870 FQ	80020 MW	89990 TQ	USBLS	5/15
	Augusta-Richmond County MSA, GA-SC	Y	41370 FQ	55000 MW	67210 TQ	USBLS	5/15
	Hawaii	Y	54150 FQ	66110 MW	76360 TQ	USBLS	5/15

Occupation/Type/Industry	Location	Per	Low	Mid	High	Source	Date
Aircraft Mechanic and Service Technician	Urban Honolulu MSA, HI	Y	55610 FQ	67700 MW	75910 TQ	USBLS	5/15
	Idaho	Y	41790 FQ	49530 MW	57610 TQ	USBLS	5/15
	Boise City MSA, ID	Y	48500 FQ	55270 MW	59590 TQ	USBLS	5/15
	Illinois	Y	43170 FQ	59200 MW	73370 TQ	USBLS	5/15
	Chicago-Naperville-Arlington Heights PMSA, IL	Y	45130 FQ	61140 MW	75700 TQ	USBLS	5/15
	Lake County-Kenosha County PMSA, IL-WI	Y	51610 FQ	61620 MW	96340 TQ	USBLS	5/15
	Indiana	Y	40390 FQ	51740 MW	60930 TQ	USBLS	5/15
	Gary PMSA, IN	Y	53540 FQ	61170 MW	84520 TQ	USBLS	5/15
	Indianapolis-Carmel-Anderson MSA, IN	Y	39290 FQ	49660 MW	60820 TQ	USBLS	5/15
	Iowa	Y	41250 FQ	50540 MW	59090 TQ	USBLS	5/15
	Des Moines-West Des Moines MSA, IA	Y	38080 FQ	47970 MW	60800 TQ	USBLS	5/15
	Kansas	Y	54910 FQ	63900 MW	74080 TQ	USBLS	5/15
	Wichita MSA, KS	Y	52250 FQ	59780 MW	73750 TQ	USBLS	5/15
	Kentucky	Y	54350 FQ	92500 MW	111630 TQ	USBLS	5/15
	Louisville-Jefferson County MSA, KY-IN	Y	60660 FQ	105910 MW	115640 TQ	USBLS	5/15
	Louisiana	Y	47660 FQ	59300 MW	71700 TQ	USBLS	5/15
	New Orleans-Metairie MSA, LA	Y	45860 FQ	62450 MW	71900 TQ	USBLS	5/15
	Maine	Y	39730 FQ	47260 MW	52910 TQ	USBLS	5/15
	Maryland	Y	54882 AE	68311 MW	75025 AEX	MDBLS	4/16
	Baltimore-Columbia-Towson MSA, MD	Y	51650 FQ	60700 MW	82930 TQ	USBLS	5/15
	Massachusetts	Y	52520 FQ	63140 MW	73240 TQ	USBLS	5/15
	Boston-Cambridge-Newton NECTA, MA	Y	46170 FQ	56610 MW	67800 TQ	USBLS	5/15
	Worcester MSA, MA-CT	Y	65910 FQ	71250 MW	76580 TQ	USBLS	5/15
	Michigan	Y	36530 FQ	49060 MW	66710 TQ	USBLS	5/15
	Detroit-Dearborn-Livonia PMSA, MI	Y	42930 FQ	58090 MW	76330 TQ	USBLS	5/15
	Grand Rapids-Wyoming MSA, MI	Y	32380 FQ	41480 MW	55010 TQ	USBLS	5/15
	Minnesota	Y	36838 FQ	55573 MW	66203 TQ	MNBLS	1/16-3/16
	Minneapolis-St. Paul-Bloomington MSA, MN-WI	Y	32765 FQ	54628 MW	67973 TQ	MNBLS	1/16-3/16
	Mississippi	Y	41160 FQ	52930 MW	60940 TQ	USBLS	5/15
	Jackson MSA, MS	Y	29360 FQ	50680 MW	55960 TQ	USBLS	5/15
	Missouri	Y	42760 FQ	58480 MW	72460 TQ	USBLS	5/15
	Kansas City MSA, MO-KS	Y	26600 FQ	35980 MW	61660 TQ	USBLS	5/15
	St. Louis MSA, MO-IL	Y	48950 FQ	62810 MW	77560 TQ	USBLS	5/15
	Montana	Y	39860 FQ	50330 MW	60590 TQ	USBLS	5/15
	Billings MSA, MT	Y	39820 FQ	44230 MW	48630 TQ	USBLS	5/15
	Nebraska	Y	39555 FQ	48765 MW	55765 TQ	NEBLS	7/16-9/16
	Omaha-Council Bluffs MSA, NE-IA	Y	41145 FQ	50525 MW	64835 TQ	NEBLS	7/16-9/16
	Nevada	Y	47600 FQ	62020 MW	77020 TQ	USBLS	5/15
	Las Vegas-Henderson-Paradise MSA, NV	Y	45050 FQ	60130 MW	78340 TQ	USBLS	5/15
	New Hampshire	H	19.20 AE	30.47 MW	35.02 AEX	NHBLS	6/16
	Manchester NECTA, NH	H	18.65 AE	34.19 MW	42.18 AEX	NHBLS	6/16
	Nashua NECTA, NH-MA	Y	48300 FQ	64030 MW	78690 TQ	USBLS	5/15
	New Jersey	Y	58640 FQ	75960 MW	89550 TQ	USBLS	5/15
	Camden PMSA, NJ	Y	56730 FQ	60100 MW	62140 TQ	USBLS	5/15
	New Mexico	Y	39130 FQ	50340 MW	62490 TQ	USBLS	5/15
	Albuquerque MSA, NM	Y	44540 FQ	54750 MW	63030 TQ	USBLS	5/15
	New York	Y	43790 AE	60580 MW	71920 AEX	NYBLS	1/16-3/16
	Buffalo-Cheektowaga-Niagara Falls MSA, NY	Y	52900 FQ	61450 MW	71460 TQ	USBLS	5/15
	Nassau County-Suffolk County PMSA, NY	Y	44010 FQ	62360 MW	75730 TQ	USBLS	5/15
	New York-Jersey City-White Plains PMSA, NY-NJ	Y	53320 FQ	62260 MW	78370 TQ	USBLS	5/15
	Rochester MSA, NY	Y	48580 FQ	58200 MW	73680 TQ	USBLS	5/15
	North Carolina	Y	45670 FQ	54320 MW	66410 TQ	USBLS	5/15
	Charlotte-Concord-Gastonia MSA, NC-SC	Y	59890 FQ	69430 MW	75820 TQ	USBLS	5/15
	Raleigh MSA, NC	Y	46920 FQ	55580 MW	66950 TQ	USBLS	5/15

AE	Average entry wage	AWR	Average wage range	H	Hourly	LR	Low end range	MTC	Median total compensation	TCC	Total cash compensation
AEX	Average experienced wage	B	Biweekly	HI	Highest wage paid	M	Monthly	MW	Median wage paid	TQ	Third quartile wage
ATC	Average total compensation	D	Daily	HR	High end range	MCC	Median cash compensation	MWR	Median wage range	W	Weekly
AW	Average wage paid	FQ	First quartile wage	LO	Lowest wage paid	ME	Median entry wage	S	See annotated source	Y	Yearly

Occupation/Type/Industry	Location	Per	Low	Mid	High	Source	Date
Aircraft Mechanic and Service Technician	North Dakota	Y	41950 FQ	60830 MW	73350 TQ	USBLS	5/15
	Ohio	Y	44500 FQ	58370 MW	71860 TQ	USBLS	5/15
	Cincinnati MSA, OH-KY-IN	Y	39130 FQ	58060 MW	80860 TQ	USBLS	5/15
	Cleveland-Elyria MSA, OH	Y	42110 FQ	55510 MW	69650 TQ	USBLS	5/15
	Oklahoma	Y	44640 FQ	51890 MW	56260 TQ	USBLS	5/15
	Oklahoma City MSA, OK	Y	47900 FQ	53850 MW	55870 TQ	USBLS	5/15
	Tulsa MSA, OK	Y	33800 FQ	43850 MW	55160 TQ	USBLS	5/15
	Oregon	H	23.04 FQ	27.38 MW	32.09 TQ	ORBLS	2016
	Portland-Vancouver-Hillsboro MSA, OR-WA	Y	49710 FQ	58810 MW	70870 TQ	USBLS	5/15
	Pennsylvania	Y	45740 FQ	55550 MW	64370 TQ	USBLS	5/15
	Allentown-Bethlehem-Easton MSA, PA-NJ	Y	43600 FQ	55200 MW	69290 TQ	USBLS	5/15
	Harrisburg-Carlisle MSA, PA	Y	45730 FQ	53290 MW	58610 TQ	USBLS	5/15
	Montgomery County-Bucks County-Chester County PMSA, PA	Y	47660 FQ	55920 MW	63170 TQ	USBLS	5/15
	Philadelphia PMSA, PA	Y	46840 FQ	58760 MW	71380 TQ	USBLS	5/15
	Pittsburgh MSA, PA	Y	50860 FQ	57100 MW	62770 TQ	USBLS	5/15
	Rhode Island	Y	43860 FQ	54760 MW	71340 TQ	USBLS	5/15
	Providence-Warwick MSA, RI-MA	Y	44110 FQ	55770 MW	71800 TQ	USBLS	5/15
	South Carolina	Y	46260 FQ	52270 MW	59500 TQ	USBLS	5/15
	Charleston-North Charleston MSA, SC	Y	52020 FQ	57280 MW	71940 TQ	USBLS	5/15
	Columbia MSA, SC	Y	44720 FQ	51290 MW	55830 TQ	USBLS	5/15
	Greenville-Anderson-Mauldin MSA, SC	Y	50720 FQ	55310 MW	59900 TQ	USBLS	5/15
	South Dakota	Y	48810 FQ	55180 MW	61920 TQ	USBLS	5/15
	Sioux Falls MSA, SD	Y	46410 FQ	52600 MW	59610 TQ	USBLS	5/15
	Tennessee	Y	44170 FQ	52490 MW	61080 TQ	USBLS	5/15
	Knoxville MSA, TN	Y	44180 FQ	50140 MW	56580 TQ	USBLS	5/15
	Memphis MSA, TN-MS-AR	Y	50380 FQ	60550 MW	70400 TQ	USBLS	5/15
	Nashville-Davidson–Murfreesboro–Franklin MSA, TN	Y	43370 FQ	49990 MW	57790 TQ	USBLS	5/15
	Texas	Y	45730 FQ	57160 MW	69960 TQ	USBLS	5/15
	Austin-Round Rock MSA, TX	Y	48610 FQ	58130 MW	69890 TQ	USBLS	5/15
	Dallas-Plano-Irving PMSA, TX	Y	48500 FQ	66860 MW	87730 TQ	USBLS	5/15
	Fort Worth-Arlington PMSA, TX	Y	36830 FQ	56510 MW	69860 TQ	USBLS	5/15
	Houston-The Woodlands-Sugar Land MSA, TX	Y	56420 FQ	65910 MW	75400 TQ	USBLS	5/15
	San Antonio-New Braunfels MSA, TX	Y	42210 FQ	49060 MW	55500 TQ	USBLS	5/15
	Utah	Y	48460 FQ	56530 MW	59920 TQ	USBLS	5/15
	Ogden-Clearfield MSA, UT	Y	51730 FQ	56540 MW	56560 TQ	USBLS	5/15
	Provo-Orem MSA, UT	Y	24560 FQ	38810 MW	54920 TQ	USBLS	5/15
	Salt Lake City MSA, UT	Y	46230 FQ	55300 MW	62930 TQ	USBLS	5/15
	Vermont	Y	43650 FQ	58620 MW	66510 TQ	USBLS	5/15
	Burlington-South Burlington MSA, VT	Y	46260 FQ	60960 MW	68000 TQ	USBLS	5/15
	Virginia	Y	48330 FQ	65270 MW	76540 TQ	USBLS	5/15
	Richmond MSA, VA	Y	54480 FQ	61800 MW	78850 TQ	USBLS	5/15
	Virginia Beach-Norfolk-Newport News MSA, VA-NC	Y	55090 FQ	66600 MW	73980 TQ	USBLS	5/15
	Washington	H	26.80 FQ	33.67 MW	43.39 TQ	WABLS	3/16
	Tacoma-Lakewood PMSA, WA	H	28.30 FQ	31.52 MW	32.69 TQ	WABLS	3/16
	West Virginia	Y	35780 FQ	53230 MW	61710 TQ	USBLS	5/15
	Wisconsin	Y	41630 FQ	51210 MW	60160 TQ	USBLS	5/15
	Madison MSA, WI	Y	42210 FQ	50400 MW	55900 TQ	USBLS	5/15
	Milwaukee-Waukesha-West Allis MSA, WI	Y	43880 FQ	55400 MW	67200 TQ	USBLS	5/15
	Wyoming	Y	47670 FQ	53410 MW	60060 TQ	USBLS	5/15
	Cheyenne MSA, WY	Y	49640 FQ	53740 MW	59220 TQ	USBLS	5/15
	Puerto Rico	Y	19950 FQ	39250 MW	53260 TQ	USBLS	5/15
	San Juan-Carolina-Caguas MSA, PR	Y	19190 FQ	25080 MW	53820 TQ	USBLS	5/15

AE	Average entry wage	AWR	Average wage range	H	Hourly	LR	Low end range	MTC	Median total compensation	TCC	Total cash compensation
AEX	Average experienced wage	B	Biweekly	HI	Highest wage paid	M	Monthly	MW	Median wage paid	TQ	Third quartile wage
ATC	Average total compensation	D	Daily	HR	High end range	MCC	Median cash compensation	MWR	Median wage range	W	Weekly
AW	Average wage paid	FQ	First quartile wage	LO	Lowest wage paid	ME	Median entry wage	S	See annotated source	Y	Yearly

Occupation/Type/Industry	Location	Per	Low	Mid	High	Source	Date
Aircraft Pneudraulic Systems Mechanic							
United States Coast Guard	Elizabeth City, NC	Y	48523 LO		52238 HI	APP01	2015
Aircraft Structure, Surfaces, Rigging, and Systems Assembler	Alabama	Y	34373 AE	50753 AW	58937 AEX	ALBLS	6/16
	Arizona	Y	35740 FQ	49830 MW	60820 TQ	USBLS	5/15
	California	H	16.70 FQ	22.59 MW	30.80 TQ	CABLS	1/16-3/16
	Connecticut	Y		49516 MW		CTBLS	1/16-3/16
	Florida	H	14.84 AE	23.20 MW	27.66 AEX	FLBLS	7/16-9/16
	Georgia	Y	39980 FQ	50760 MW	59790 TQ	USBLS	5/15
	Idaho	Y	27080 FQ	29710 MW	37740 TQ	USBLS	5/15
	Illinois	Y	28560 FQ	43920 MW	57440 TQ	USBLS	5/15
	Louisiana	Y	31640 FQ	43300 MW	54190 TQ	USBLS	5/15
	Maryland	Y	29862 AE	38917 MW	43444 AEX	MDBLS	4/16
	Massachusetts	Y	37430 FQ	44140 MW	50030 TQ	USBLS	5/15
	Michigan	Y	37400 FQ	44020 MW	51510 TQ	USBLS	5/15
	Minnesota	Y	36732 FQ	47362 MW	59259 TQ	MNBLS	1/16-3/16
	New Jersey	Y	31730 FQ	37010 MW	48230 TQ	USBLS	5/15
	New York	Y	35350 AE	46470 MW	52560 AEX	NYBLS	1/16-3/16
	Ohio	Y	33990 FQ	42590 MW	54520 TQ	USBLS	5/15
	Oregon	H	13.01 FQ	16.05 MW	19.10 TQ	ORBLS	2016
	Texas	Y	29690 FQ	45210 MW	65890 TQ	USBLS	5/15
	Utah	Y	28250 FQ	32490 MW	38390 TQ	USBLS	5/15
	Wisconsin	Y	43510 FQ	51650 MW	72040 TQ	USBLS	5/15
Airfield Operations Specialist	Alabama	Y	37232 AE	55806 AW	65104 AEX	ALBLS	6/16
	Alaska	Y	53630 FQ	63590 MW	82670 TQ	USBLS	5/15
	Anchorage MSA, AK	Y	51700 FQ	63600 MW	79950 TQ	USBLS	5/15
	Arizona	Y	42210 FQ	49410 MW	57150 TQ	USBLS	5/15
	Phoenix-Mesa-Scottsdale MSA, AZ	Y	37510 FQ	46280 MW	58320 TQ	USBLS	5/15
	Tucson MSA, AZ	Y	46460 FQ	52790 MW	58290 TQ	USBLS	5/15
	California	H	22.40 FQ	32.08 MW	42.17 TQ	CABLS	1/16-3/16
	Oakland-Hayward-Berkeley PMSA, CA	H	26.37 FQ	34.79 MW	50.37 TQ	CABLS	1/16-3/16
	Riverside-San Bernardino-Ontario MSA, CA	H	22.55 FQ	27.84 MW	36.49 TQ	CABLS	1/16-3/16
	Sacramento–Roseville–Arden-Arcade MSA, CA	H	36.31 FQ	42.26 MW	46.28 TQ	CABLS	1/16-3/16
	San Diego-Carlsbad MSA, CA	H	14.19 FQ	18.27 MW	29.59 TQ	CABLS	1/16-3/16
	Colorado	Y	46560 FQ	54480 MW	61410 TQ	USBLS	5/15
	Denver-Aurora-Lakewood MSA, CO	Y	50000 FQ	55400 MW	61120 TQ	USBLS	5/15
	Connecticut	Y		57467 MW		CTBLS	1/16-3/16
	Florida	H	16.90 AE	25.51 MW	30.31 AEX	FLBLS	7/16-9/16
	Miami-Miami Beach-Kendall PMSA, FL	H	22.19 AE	29.61 MW	35.66 AEX	FLBLS	7/16-9/16
	Orlando-Kissimmee-Sanford MSA, FL	H	21.19 AE	27.96 MW	32.43 AEX	FLBLS	7/16-9/16
	Hawaii	Y	47930 FQ	55170 MW	58150 TQ	USBLS	5/15
	Illinois	Y	35910 FQ	52920 MW	64040 TQ	USBLS	5/15
	Chicago-Naperville-Arlington Heights PMSA, IL	Y	36520 FQ	50040 MW	62040 TQ	USBLS	5/15
	Indiana	Y	30240 FQ	37570 MW	50690 TQ	USBLS	5/15
	Gary PMSA, IN	Y	33410 FQ	37980 MW	47310 TQ	USBLS	5/15
	Iowa	Y	52010 FQ	58090 MW	64270 TQ	USBLS	5/15
	Kansas	Y	47570 FQ	53740 MW	58340 TQ	CABLS	5/15
	Kentucky	Y	51510 FQ	58440 MW	93500 TQ	USBLS	5/15
	Louisiana	Y	44380 FQ	55950 MW	68590 TQ	USBLS	5/15
	Boston-Cambridge-Newton NECTA, MA	Y	39040 FQ	52220 MW	60210 TQ	USBLS	5/15
	Michigan	Y	32000 FQ	43490 MW	58040 TQ	USBLS	5/15
	Detroit-Dearborn-Livonia PMSA, MI	Y	33640 FQ	52070 MW	59820 TQ	USBLS	5/15
	Minnesota	Y	43794 FQ	54369 MW	59238 TQ	MNBLS	1/16-3/16
	Minneapolis-St. Paul-Bloomington MSA, MN-WI	Y	45094 FQ	54299 MW	59037 TQ	MNBLS	1/16-3/16
	Missouri	Y	33320 FQ	38410 MW	50230 TQ	USBLS	5/15
	Kansas City MSA, MO-KS	Y	35810 FQ	50190 MW	57840 TQ	USBLS	5/15
	St. Louis MSA, MO-IL	Y	32020 FQ	36330 MW	43840 TQ	USBLS	5/15
	Nebraska	Y	22525 FQ	24850 MW	45480 TQ	NEBLS	7/16-9/16

AE	Average entry wage	AWR	Average wage range	H	Hourly	LR	Low end range	MTC	Median total compensation	TCC	Total cash compensation
AEX	Average experienced wage	B	Biweekly	HI	Highest wage paid	M	Monthly	MW	Median wage paid	TQ	Third quartile wage
ATC	Average total compensation	D	Daily	HR	High end range	MCC	Median cash compensation	MWR	Median wage range	W	Weekly
AW	Average wage paid	FQ	First quartile wage	LO	Lowest wage paid	ME	Median entry wage	S	See annotated source	Y	Yearly

Occupation/Type/Industry	Location	Per	Low	Mid	High	Source	Date
Airfield Operations Specialist	Nevada	Y	57680 FQ	64180 MW	87970 TQ	USBLS	5/15
	Las Vegas-Henderson-Paradise MSA, NV	Y	57610 FQ	63720 MW	87960 TQ	USBLS	5/15
	New Jersey	Y	35070 FQ	44900 MW	65720 TQ	USBLS	5/15
	Newark PMSA, NJ-PA	Y	37670 FQ	50170 MW	72300 TQ	USBLS	5/15
	New York	Y	28350 AE	43340 MW	53540 AEX	NYBLS	1/16-3/16
	Nassau County-Suffolk County PMSA, NY	Y	38610 FQ	44410 MW	49560 TQ	USBLS	5/15
	New York-Jersey City-White Plains PMSA, NY-NJ	Y	31220 FQ	40930 MW	50750 TQ	USBLS	5/15
	North Carolina	Y	28800 FQ	36000 MW	49690 TQ	USBLS	5/15
	Charlotte-Concord-Gastonia MSA, NC-SC	Y	28200 FQ	33010 MW	46330 TQ	USBLS	5/15
	Ohio	Y	25170 FQ	35700 MW	50070 TQ	USBLS	5/15
	Cincinnati MSA, OH-KY-IN	Y	52420 FQ	57000 MW	61590 TQ	USBLS	5/15
	Cleveland-Elyria MSA, OH	Y	21740 FQ	32790 MW	47890 TQ	USBLS	5/15
	Columbus MSA, OH	Y	25090 FQ	29770 MW	47640 TQ	USBLS	5/15
	Oklahoma	Y	28170 FQ	31150 MW	55610 TQ	USBLS	5/15
	Tulsa MSA, OK	Y	28760 FQ	43540 MW	57410 TQ	USBLS	5/15
	Oregon	H	18.76 FQ	30.02 MW	35.69 TQ	ORBLS	2016
	Portland-Vancouver-Hillsboro MSA, OR-WA	Y	55190 FQ	68820 MW	75660 TQ	USBLS	5/15
	Pennsylvania	Y	24470 FQ	53220 MW	87640 TQ	USBLS	5/15
	South Carolina	Y	35150 FQ	54860 MW	75450 TQ	USBLS	5/15
	Greenville-Anderson-Mauldin MSA, SC	Y	37650 FQ	51500 MW	112800 TQ	USBLS	5/15
	Texas	Y	38220 FQ	52160 MW	83050 TQ	USBLS	5/15
	Dallas-Plano-Irving PMSA, TX	Y	45920 FQ	66430 MW	105700 TQ	USBLS	5/15
	Houston-The Woodlands-Sugar Land MSA, TX	Y	35830 FQ	42960 MW	53780 TQ	USBLS	5/15
	Utah	Y	21690 FQ	42590 MW	56420 TQ	USBLS	5/15
	Salt Lake City MSA, UT	Y	50810 FQ	55670 MW	59890 TQ	USBLS	5/15
	Vermont	Y	35280 FQ	42240 MW	48530 TQ	USBLS	5/15
	Burlington-South Burlington MSA, VT	Y	40590 FQ	45330 MW	50070 TQ	USBLS	5/15
	Washington	H	17.20 FQ	23.78 MW	33.22 TQ	WABLS	3/16
	Seattle-Bellevue-Everett PMSA, WA	H	16.53 FQ	19.55 MW	33.36 TQ	WABLS	3/16
	Guam	Y	49650 FQ	59370 MW	69310 TQ	USBLS	5/15
State Government	West Yellowstone, MT	H			23.42 HI	MTGOV	2016
Airline Pilot, Copilot, and Flight Engineer							
	Alabama	Y	93594 AE	107386 AW	114277 AEX	ALBLS	6/16
	Alaska	Y	81280 FQ	115160 MW	172160 TQ	USBLS	5/15
	Anchorage MSA, AK	Y	86420 FQ	124750 MW	177810 TQ	USBLS	5/15
	Arizona	Y	86790 FQ	129390 MW	152050 TQ	USBLS	5/15
	Phoenix-Mesa-Scottsdale MSA, AZ	Y	86770 FQ	130940 MW	152760 TQ	USBLS	5/15
	Arkansas	Y	79920 FQ	98580 MW	113340 TQ	USBLS	5/15
	California	Y		148235 AW		CABLS	1/16-3/16
	Los Angeles-Long Beach-Glendale PMSA, CA	Y		122105 AW		CABLS	1/16-3/16
	San Francisco-Redwood City-South San Francisco PMSA, CA	Y		165645 AW		CABLS	1/16-3/16
	Colorado	Y	120410 FQ	163220 MW		USBLS	5/15
	Denver-Aurora-Lakewood MSA, CO	Y	133460 FQ	166480 MW		USBLS	5/15
	Washington-Arlington-Alexandria PMSA, DC-VA-MD-WV	Y	118730 FQ	159130 MW		USBLS	5/15
	Florida	Y	86315 AE	139253 MW	196185 AEX	FLBLS	7/16-9/16
	Fort Lauderdale-Pompano Beach-Deerfield Beach PMSA, FL	Y	67870 AE	95009 MW	106964 AEX	FLBLS	7/16-9/16
	Miami-Miami Beach-Kendall PMSA, FL	Y	104187 AE	158723 MW	222914 AEX	FLBLS	7/16-9/16
	Georgia	Y	71090 FQ	90030 MW	115640 TQ	USBLS	5/15
	Boise City MSA, ID	Y	83460 FQ	101370 MW	140720 TQ	USBLS	5/15
	Illinois	Y	88860 FQ	118130 MW	157550 TQ	USBLS	5/15
	Chicago-Naperville-Arlington Heights PMSA, IL	Y	89110 FQ	118410 MW	157920 TQ	USBLS	5/15

AE	Average entry wage	AWR	Average wage range	H	Hourly	LR	Low end range	MTC	Median total compensation	TCC	Total cash compensation
AEX	Average experienced wage	B	Biweekly	HI	Highest wage paid	M	Monthly	MW	Median wage paid	TQ	Third quartile wage
ATC	Average total compensation	D	Daily	HR	High end range	MCC	Median cash compensation	MWR	Median wage range	W	Weekly
AW	Average wage paid	FQ	First quartile wage	LO	Lowest wage paid	ME	Median entry wage	S	See annotated source	Y	Yearly

Occupation/Type/Industry	Location	Per	Low	Mid	High	Source	Date
Airline Pilot, Copilot, and Flight Engineer	Iowa	Y	91250 ꜰQ	100170 ᴍw	118360 ᴛQ	USBLS	5/15
	Kansas	Y	79930 ꜰQ	101380 ᴍw	117220 ᴛQ	USBLS	5/15
	Louisiana	Y	73730 ꜰQ	97160 ᴍw	112320 ᴛQ	USBLS	5/15
	Michigan	Y	92160 ꜰQ	111540 ᴍw	126550 ᴛQ	USBLS	5/15
	Detroit-Dearborn-Livonia PMSA, MI	Y	94410 ꜰQ	112390 ᴍw	127020 ᴛQ	USBLS	5/15
	Minnesota	Y	87144 ꜰQ	103718 ᴍw	120513 ᴛQ	MNBLS	1/16-3/16
	Minneapolis-St. Paul-Bloomington MSA, MN-WI	Y	87467 ꜰQ	103990 ᴍw	120695 ᴛQ	MNBLS	1/16-3/16
	Mississippi	Y	77220 ꜰQ	83460 ᴍw	101400 ᴛQ	USBLS	5/15
	Nebraska	Y	70195 ꜰQ	91210 ᴍw	107715 ᴛQ	NEBLS	7/16-9/16
	New Hampshire	Y	80741 ᴀᴇ	101027 ᴍw	111632 ᴀᴇx	NHBLS	6/16
	New Jersey	Y	98250 ꜰQ	118690 ᴍw	144350 ᴛQ	USBLS	5/15
	Newark PMSA, NJ-PA	Y	98150 ꜰQ	118860 ᴍw	145520 ᴛQ	USBLS	5/15
	New Mexico	Y	58560 ꜰQ	87160 ᴍw	102950 ᴛQ	USBLS	5/15
	Albuquerque MSA, NM	Y	55880 ꜰQ	69260 ᴍw	105250 ᴛQ	USBLS	5/15
	New York	Y	71490 ᴀᴇ	110940 ᴍw	134710 ᴀᴇx	NYBLS	1/16-3/16
	New York-Jersey City-White Plains PMSA, NY-NJ	Y	86120 ꜰQ	109580 ᴍw	135720 ᴛQ	USBLS	5/15
	North Carolina	Y	75920 ꜰQ	90860 ᴍw	104640 ᴛQ	USBLS	5/15
	Charlotte-Concord-Gastonia MSA, NC-SC	Y	78860 ꜰQ	92720 ᴍw	108540 ᴛQ	USBLS	5/15
	Ohio	Y	30880 ꜰQ	76810 ᴍw	122070 ᴛQ	USBLS	5/15
	Cincinnati MSA, OH-KY-IN	Y	84390 ꜰQ	98000 ᴍw	111740 ᴛQ	USBLS	5/15
	Columbus MSA, OH	Y	67230 ꜰQ	94240 ᴍw	111360 ᴛQ	USBLS	5/15
	Oklahoma	Y	76750 ꜰQ	101200 ᴍw	118050 ᴛQ	USBLS	5/15
	Tulsa MSA, OK	Y	75400 ꜰQ	101980 ᴍw	119070 ᴛQ	USBLS	5/15
	Portland-Vancouver-Hillsboro MSA, OR-WA	Y	47340 ꜰQ	107020 ᴍw		USBLS	5/15
	South Carolina	Y	84230 ꜰQ	98220 ᴍw	117210 ᴛQ	USBLS	5/15
	Tennessee	Y	71580 ꜰQ	96940 ᴍw	117190 ᴛQ	USBLS	5/15
	Memphis MSA, TN-MS-AR	Y	64870 ꜰQ	99740 ᴍw	121500 ᴛQ	USBLS	5/15
	Nashville-Davidson–Murfreesboro–Franklin MSA, TN	Y	84230 ꜰQ	95550 ᴍw	107350 ᴛQ	USBLS	5/15
	Texas	Y	134210 ꜰQ	158470 ᴍw		USBLS	5/15
	Dallas-Plano-Irving PMSA, TX	Y	141840 ꜰQ	161260 ᴍw		USBLS	5/15
	Fort Worth-Arlington PMSA, TX	Y	131580 ꜰQ	152740 ᴍw		USBLS	5/15
	San Antonio-New Braunfels MSA, TX	Y	77220 ꜰQ	77230 ᴍw	101400 ᴛQ	USBLS	5/15
	Utah	Y	57790 ꜰQ	88920 ᴍw	105520 ᴛQ	USBLS	5/15
	Richmond MSA, VA	Y	74250 ꜰQ	99360 ᴍw	151880 ᴛQ	USBLS	5/15
	Virginia Beach-Norfolk-Newport News MSA, VA-NC	Y	82050 ꜰQ	94230 ᴍw	105710 ᴛQ	USBLS	5/15
	Washington	Y		99112 ᴀw		WABLS	3/16
	Seattle-Bellevue-Everett PMSA, WA	Y		99143 ᴀw		WABLS	3/16
	West Virginia	Y	64690 ꜰQ	86250 ᴍw	98320 ᴛQ	USBLS	5/15
	Wisconsin	Y	86580 ꜰQ	100880 ᴍw	112240 ᴛQ	USBLS	5/15
	Wyoming	Y	39660 ꜰQ	69240 ᴍw	79930 ᴛQ	USBLS	5/15
Airman							
U.S. Air Force, Active Duty, Pay Grade E-2	United States	M		1793 ᴀw		DOD1	2017
Airman 1st Class							
U.S. Air Force, Active Duty, Pay Grade E-3	United States	M	1886 ʟᴏ		2126 ʜɪ	DOD1	2017
Airplane Pilot							
Film, Location	United States	D	1622 ʟᴏ			AFTRA2	7/1/16-6/30/17
Film, Studio	United States	D	1248 ʟᴏ			AFTRA2	7/1/16-6/30/17
Television, Location	United States	D	1622 ʟᴏ			AFTRA1	7/1/16-6/30/17
Television, Studio	United States	D	1248 ʟᴏ			AFTRA1	7/1/16-6/30/17
Airport Chauffeur	United States	H		14.38 ᴀw		AVJOB01	2016
Airport Escort Supervisor							
County Government	Clark County, NV	Y			50988 ʜɪ	TNV	2015
Airport Manager							
County Government	Fulton County, GA	Y	70291 ʟᴏ		105436 ʜɪ	GACTY04	2016

AE	Average entry wage	AWR	Average wage range	H	Hourly	LR	Low end range	MTC Median total compensation	TCC Total cash compensation
AEX	Average experienced wage	B	Biweekly	HI	Highest wage paid	M	Monthly	MW Median wage paid	TQ Third quartile wage
ATC	Average total compensation	D	Daily	HR	High end range	MCC	Median cash compensation	MWR Median wage range	W Weekly
AW	Average wage paid	FQ	First quartile wage	LO	Lowest wage paid	ME	Median entry wage	S See annotated source	Y Yearly

Occupation/Type/Industry	Location	Per	Low	Mid	High	Source	Date
Airport Manager							
County Government	Ware County, GA	Y	30912 LO		47036 HI	GACTY04	2016
Municipal Government	Fullerton, CA	Y			109304 HI	CACIT	6/28/16
Municipal Government	Mammoth Lakes, CA	Y			106295 HI	CACIT	6/28/16
Airport Police Officer	United States	H		21.34 AW		AVJOB01	2016
Municipal Government	Detroit, MI	M	2342 LO		3367 HI	DETGOV	2016
Airport Projects Supervisor							
Municipal Government	Fresno, CA	Y			86095 HI	CACIT	6/28/16
Airport Rental Agent							
County Government	Oakland County, MI	B	1583 LO		2060 HI	MIOAK2	10/1/16
Alligator Farmer	United States	Y		73000 AW		SKU01	2016
Ambulance Driver and Attendant							
Except Emergency Medical Technicians	Alabama	Y	17999 AE	24396 AW	27595 AEX	ALBLS	6/16
Except Emergency Medical Technicians	Birmingham-Hoover MSA, AL	Y	22401 AE	26710 AW	28860 AEX	ALBLS	6/16
Except Emergency Medical Technicians	Arkansas	Y	20830 FQ	25400 MW	34000 TQ	USBLS	5/15
Except Emergency Medical Technicians	Little Rock-North Little Rock-Conway MSA, AR	Y	23820 FQ	30070 MW	41740 TQ	USBLS	5/15
Except Emergency Medical Technicians	California	H	10.28 FQ	11.65 MW	14.23 TQ	CABLS	1/16-3/16
Except Emergency Medical Technicians	Anaheim-Santa Ana-Irvine PMSA, CA	H	10.05 FQ	11.53 MW	14.67 TQ	CABLS	1/16-3/16
Except Emergency Medical Technicians	Los Angeles-Long Beach-Glendale PMSA, CA	H	10.60 FQ	11.88 MW	14.51 TQ	CABLS	1/16-3/16
Except Emergency Medical Technicians	Oakland-Hayward-Berkeley PMSA, CA	H	11.07 FQ	12.98 MW	15.89 TQ	CABLS	1/16-3/16
Except Emergency Medical Technicians	Riverside-San Bernardino-Ontario MSA, CA	H	9.55 FQ	10.31 MW	11.51 TQ	CABLS	1/16-3/16
Except Emergency Medical Technicians	Colorado	Y	18700 FQ	21180 MW	27230 TQ	USBLS	5/15
Except Emergency Medical Technicians	Denver-Aurora-Lakewood MSA, CO	Y	18880 FQ	23140 MW	29390 TQ	USBLS	5/15
Except Emergency Medical Technicians	Connecticut	Y		29339 MW		CTBLS	1/16-3/16
Except Emergency Medical Technicians	Delaware	Y	24190 FQ	27830 MW	31060 TQ	USBLS	5/15
Except Emergency Medical Technicians	Wilmington PMSA, DE-MD-NJ	Y	23510 FQ	27810 MW	32370 TQ	USBLS	5/15
Except Emergency Medical Technicians	Washington-Arlington-Alexandria PMSA, DC-VA-MD-WV	Y	21140 FQ	23680 MW	33260 TQ	USBLS	5/15
Except Emergency Medical Technicians	Florida	H	10.20 AE	11.57 MW	13.52 AEX	FLBLS	7/16-9/16
Except Emergency Medical Technicians	Miami-Miami Beach-Kendall PMSA, FL	H	9.94 AE	13.83 MW	15.71 AEX	FLBLS	7/16-9/16
Except Emergency Medical Technicians	Georgia	Y	18950 FQ	24720 MW	29200 TQ	USBLS	5/15
Except Emergency Medical Technicians	Atlanta-Sandy Springs-Roswell MSA, GA	Y	23270 FQ	27350 MW	30180 TQ	USBLS	5/15
Except Emergency Medical Technicians	Augusta-Richmond County MSA, GA-SC	Y	18060 FQ	20130 MW	22770 TQ	USBLS	5/15
Except Emergency Medical Technicians	Idaho	Y	18760 FQ	22500 MW	28330 TQ	USBLS	5/15
Except Emergency Medical Technicians	Illinois	Y	18720 FQ	19870 MW	26290 TQ	USBLS	5/15
Except Emergency Medical Technicians	Chicago-Naperville-Arlington Heights PMSA, IL	Y	19130 FQ	20900 MW	26620 TQ	USBLS	5/15
Except Emergency Medical Technicians	Lake County-Kenosha County PMSA, IL-WI	Y	21290 FQ	22630 MW	23980 TQ	USBLS	5/15
Except Emergency Medical Technicians	Indiana	Y	19620 FQ	25290 MW	28950 TQ	USBLS	5/15
Except Emergency Medical Technicians	Indianapolis-Carmel-Anderson MSA, IN	Y	22320 FQ	26490 MW	30050 TQ	USBLS	5/15
Except Emergency Medical Technicians	Iowa	Y	18830 FQ	22900 MW	28490 TQ	USBLS	5/15
Except Emergency Medical Technicians	Kansas	Y	19100 FQ	24940 MW	30640 TQ	USBLS	5/15
Except Emergency Medical Technicians	Louisiana	Y	18620 FQ	22720 MW	32760 TQ	USBLS	5/15
Except Emergency Medical Technicians	Maine	Y	21700 FQ	26380 MW	29720 TQ	USBLS	5/15
Except Emergency Medical Technicians	Maryland	Y	21717 AE	27292 MW	30079 AEX	MDBLS	4/16
Except Emergency Medical Technicians	Baltimore-Columbia-Towson MSA, MD	Y	22280 FQ	25980 MW	31750 TQ	USBLS	5/15
Except Emergency Medical Technicians	Massachusetts	Y	23790 FQ	28350 MW	36160 TQ	USBLS	5/15
Except Emergency Medical Technicians	Boston-Cambridge-Newton NECTA, MA	Y	21780 FQ	24800 MW	30070 TQ	USBLS	5/15
Except Emergency Medical Technicians	Worcester MSA, MA-CT	Y	23760 FQ	27210 MW	30190 TQ	USBLS	5/15
Except Emergency Medical Technicians	Michigan	Y	19620 FQ	22490 MW	26190 TQ	USBLS	5/15
Except Emergency Medical Technicians	Detroit-Dearborn-Livonia PMSA, MI	Y	18280 FQ	19330 MW	20720 TQ	USBLS	5/15

AE	Average entry wage	AWR	Average wage range	H	Hourly
AEX	Average experienced wage	B	Biweekly	HI	Highest wage paid
ATC	Average total compensation	D	Daily	HR	High end range
AW	Average wage paid	FQ	First quartile wage	LO	Lowest wage paid

LR	Low end range	MTC	Median total compensation	TCC	Total cash compensation
M	Monthly	MW	Median wage paid	TQ	Third quartile wage
MCC	Median cash compensation	MWR	Median wage range	W	Weekly
ME	Median entry wage	S	See annotated source	Y	Yearly

Occupation/Type/Industry	Location	Per	Low	Mid	High	Source	Date
Ambulance Driver and Attendant							
Except Emergency Medical Technicians	Minnesota	Y	22361 FQ	24609 MW	31555 TQ	MNBLS	1/16-3/16
Except Emergency Medical Technicians	Minneapolis-St. Paul-Bloomington MSA, MN-WI	Y	19820 FQ	23913 MW	29710 TQ	MNBLS	1/16-3/16
Except Emergency Medical Technicians	Mississippi	Y	18020 FQ	20390 MW	24190 TQ	USBLS	5/15
Except Emergency Medical Technicians	Missouri	Y	21950 FQ	25210 MW	30390 TQ	USBLS	5/15
Except Emergency Medical Technicians	Kansas City MSA, MO-KS	Y	26040 FQ	29950 MW	40680 TQ	USBLS	5/15
Except Emergency Medical Technicians	St. Louis MSA, MO-IL	Y	17780 FQ	18380 MW	18970 TQ	USBLS	5/15
Except Emergency Medical Technicians	Montana	Y	18640 FQ	20430 MW	24250 TQ	USBLS	5/15
Except Emergency Medical Technicians	Nebraska	Y	24140 FQ	34830 MW	38655 TQ	NEBLS	7/16-9/16
Except Emergency Medical Technicians	New Hampshire	H	9.39 AE	11.32 MW	13.07 AEX	NHBLS	6/16
Except Emergency Medical Technicians	New Jersey	Y	22100 FQ	24550 MW	29030 TQ	USBLS	5/15
Except Emergency Medical Technicians	Camden PMSA, NJ	Y	22380 FQ	25200 MW	28710 TQ	USBLS	5/15
Except Emergency Medical Technicians	Newark PMSA, NJ-PA	Y	22310 FQ	24710 MW	29820 TQ	USBLS	5/15
Except Emergency Medical Technicians	New Mexico	Y	18390 FQ	21960 MW	28470 TQ	USBLS	5/15
Except Emergency Medical Technicians	Albuquerque MSA, NM	Y	18730 FQ	23060 MW	30660 TQ	USBLS	5/15
Except Emergency Medical Technicians	New York	Y	21960 AE	26020 MW	29520 AEX	NYBLS	1/16-3/16
Except Emergency Medical Technicians	Buffalo-Cheektowaga-Niagara Falls MSA, NY	Y	18780 FQ	19360 MW	22540 TQ	USBLS	5/15
Except Emergency Medical Technicians	Nassau County-Suffolk County PMSA, NY	Y	22970 FQ	26720 MW	31100 TQ	USBLS	5/15
Except Emergency Medical Technicians	New York-Jersey City-White Plains PMSA, NY-NJ	Y	22470 FQ	25350 MW	29270 TQ	USBLS	5/15
Except Emergency Medical Technicians	North Carolina	Y	27010 FQ	31810 MW	36710 TQ	USBLS	5/15
Except Emergency Medical Technicians	Charlotte-Concord-Gastonia MSA, NC-SC	Y	29860 FQ	33990 MW	37430 TQ	USBLS	5/15
Except Emergency Medical Technicians	North Dakota	Y	17400 FQ	19700 MW	33010 TQ	USBLS	5/15
Except Emergency Medical Technicians	Ohio	Y	18210 FQ	19450 MW	22530 TQ	USBLS	5/15
Except Emergency Medical Technicians	Cleveland-Elyria MSA, OH	Y	17970 FQ	18970 MW	20370 TQ	USBLS	5/15
Except Emergency Medical Technicians	Columbus MSA, OH	Y	19050 FQ	21510 MW	25080 TQ	USBLS	5/15
Except Emergency Medical Technicians	Oklahoma	Y	21960 FQ	25310 MW	28720 TQ	USBLS	5/15
Except Emergency Medical Technicians	Tulsa MSA, OK	Y	21340 FQ	25020 MW	29030 TQ	USBLS	5/15
Except Emergency Medical Technicians	Oregon	H	9.78 FQ	12.50 MW	14.31 TQ	ORBLS	2016
Except Emergency Medical Technicians	Pennsylvania	Y	20960 FQ	23110 MW	26920 TQ	USBLS	5/15
Except Emergency Medical Technicians	Allentown-Bethlehem-Easton MSA, PA-NJ	Y	21230 FQ	23400 MW	28200 TQ	USBLS	5/15
Except Emergency Medical Technicians	Montgomery County-Bucks County-Chester County PMSA, PA	Y	20910 FQ	22270 MW	23620 TQ	USBLS	5/15
Except Emergency Medical Technicians	Philadelphia PMSA, PA	Y	20770 FQ	23860 MW	28520 TQ	USBLS	5/15
Except Emergency Medical Technicians	Pittsburgh MSA, PA	Y	21910 FQ	28980 MW	35640 TQ	USBLS	5/15
Except Emergency Medical Technicians	Rhode Island	Y	24960 FQ	27890 MW	51310 TQ	USBLS	5/15
Except Emergency Medical Technicians	Providence-Warwick MSA, RI-MA	Y	23430 FQ	26610 MW	30660 TQ	USBLS	5/15
Except Emergency Medical Technicians	South Carolina	Y	20110 FQ	22100 MW	24080 TQ	USBLS	5/15
Except Emergency Medical Technicians	Columbia MSA, SC	Y	20710 FQ	22300 MW	23900 TQ	USBLS	5/15
Except Emergency Medical Technicians	Greenville-Anderson-Mauldin MSA, SC	Y	19660 FQ	22040 MW	24390 TQ	USBLS	5/15
Except Emergency Medical Technicians	South Dakota	Y	19750 FQ	21220 MW	23000 TQ	USBLS	5/15
Except Emergency Medical Technicians	Tennessee	Y	19510 FQ	22560 MW	26230 TQ	USBLS	5/15
Except Emergency Medical Technicians	Memphis MSA, TN-MS-AR	Y	18260 FQ	21310 MW	27790 TQ	USBLS	5/15
Except Emergency Medical Technicians	Texas	Y	19220 FQ	22720 MW	27300 TQ	USBLS	5/15
Except Emergency Medical Technicians	Austin-Round Rock MSA, TX	Y	21290 FQ	23770 MW	28350 TQ	USBLS	5/15
Except Emergency Medical Technicians	Dallas-Plano-Irving PMSA, TX	Y	19200 FQ	21170 MW	23430 TQ	USBLS	5/15
Except Emergency Medical Technicians	Houston-The Woodlands-Sugar Land MSA, TX	Y	16780 FQ	17960 MW	19150 TQ	USBLS	5/15
Except Emergency Medical Technicians	San Antonio-New Braunfels MSA, TX	Y	22290 FQ	27200 MW	30680 TQ	USBLS	5/15
Except Emergency Medical Technicians	Utah	Y	16670 FQ	17950 MW	19240 TQ	USBLS	5/15
Except Emergency Medical Technicians	Virginia	Y	18480 FQ	21370 MW	24790 TQ	USBLS	5/15
Except Emergency Medical Technicians	Virginia Beach-Norfolk-Newport News MSA, VA-NC	Y	21350 FQ	22940 MW	24520 TQ	USBLS	5/15
Except Emergency Medical Technicians	Washington	H	13.65 FQ	16.56 MW	19.14 TQ	WABLS	3/16
Except Emergency Medical Technicians	Seattle-Bellevue-Everett PMSA, WA	H	14.19 FQ	16.80 MW	19.12 TQ	WABLS	3/16
Except Emergency Medical Technicians	West Virginia	Y	17680 FQ	18710 MW	20140 TQ	USBLS	5/15
Except Emergency Medical Technicians	Huntington-Ashland MSA, WV-KY-OH	Y	19510 FQ	23180 MW	31140 TQ	USBLS	5/15
Except Emergency Medical Technicians	Wisconsin	Y	17630 FQ	19910 MW	25180 TQ	USBLS	5/15
Except Emergency Medical Technicians	Puerto Rico	Y	16490 FQ	17580 MW	18670 TQ	USBLS	5/15
Except Emergency Medical Technicians	San Juan-Carolina-Caguas MSA, PR	Y	16390 FQ	17470 MW	18560 TQ	USBLS	5/15

AE	Average entry wage	AWR	Average wage range	H	Hourly	LR	Low end range	MTC Median total compensation	TCC Total cash compensation
AEX	Average experienced wage	B	Biweekly	HI	Highest wage paid	M	Monthly	MW Median wage paid	TQ Third quartile wage
ATC	Average total compensation	D	Daily	HR	High end range	MCC	Median cash compensation	MWR Median wage range	W Weekly
AW	Average wage paid	FQ	First quartile wage	LO	Lowest wage paid	ME	Median entry wage	S See annotated source	Y Yearly

Occupation/Type/Industry	Location	Per	Low	Mid	High	Source	Date
Ambulance Secretary							
Municipal Government	Etna, CA	Y			7416 HI	CACIT	6/28/16
Ambulatory Healthcare Services							
Worker	United States	Y		52696 AW		IWRLD	2016
Amusement and Recreation							
Attendant	Alabama	Y	17493 AE	18708 AW	19315 AEX	ALBLS	6/16
	Birmingham-Hoover MSA, AL	Y	17452 AE	19007 AW	19779 AEX	ALBLS	6/16
	Alaska	Y	22080 FQ	26890 MW	34180 TQ	USBLS	5/15
	Anchorage MSA, AK	Y	21460 FQ	24490 MW	30030 TQ	USBLS	5/15
	Arizona	Y	18180 FQ	19640 MW	27670 TQ	USBLS	5/15
	Phoenix-Mesa-Scottsdale MSA, AZ	Y	18230 FQ	19770 MW	29230 TQ	USBLS	5/15
	Tucson MSA, AZ	Y	18110 FQ	19490 MW	25340 TQ	USBLS	5/15
	Arkansas	Y	16780 FQ	17950 MW	19110 TQ	USBLS	5/15
	Little Rock-North Little Rock-Conway MSA, AR	Y	16770 FQ	17930 MW	19100 TQ	USBLS	5/15
	California	H	9.43 FQ	9.82 MW	11.80 TQ	CABLS	1/16-3/16
	Anaheim-Santa Ana-Irvine PMSA, CA	H	9.41 FQ	9.60 MW	10.84 TQ	CABLS	1/16-3/16
	Los Angeles-Long Beach-Glendale PMSA, CA	H	9.48 FQ	10.47 MW	14.07 TQ	CABLS	1/16-3/16
	Oakland-Hayward-Berkeley PMSA, CA	H	9.50 FQ	10.83 MW	14.15 TQ	CABLS	1/16-3/16
	Riverside-San Bernardino-Ontario MSA, CA	H	9.42 FQ	9.67 MW	10.93 TQ	CABLS	1/16-3/16
	Sacramento–Roseville–Arden-Arcade MSA, CA	H	9.39 FQ	9.60 MW	10.81 TQ	CABLS	1/16-3/16
	San Diego-Carlsbad MSA, CA	H	9.39 FQ	9.81 MW	11.40 TQ	CABLS	1/16-3/16
	San Francisco-Redwood City-South San Francisco PMSA, CA	H	10.41 FQ	12.71 MW	14.85 TQ	CABLS	1/16-3/16
	Colorado	Y	18140 FQ	19160 MW	22580 TQ	USBLS	5/15
	Denver-Aurora-Lakewood MSA, CO	Y	17950 FQ	18780 MW	20050 TQ	USBLS	5/15
	Connecticut	Y		20232 MW		CTBLS	1/16-3/16
	Bridgeport-Stamford-Norwalk MSA, CT	Y	19610 FQ	31250 MW	46850 TQ	USBLS	5/15
	Hartford-West Hartford-East Hartford MSA, CT	Y	19200 FQ	19460 MW	21050 TQ	USBLS	5/15
	Delaware	Y	17830 FQ	19370 MW	23170 TQ	USBLS	5/15
	Wilmington PMSA, DE-MD-NJ	Y	18010 FQ	19750 MW	24310 TQ	USBLS	5/15
	District of Columbia	Y	20020 FQ	23670 MW	36070 TQ	USBLS	5/15
	Washington-Arlington-Alexandria PMSA, DC-VA-MD-WV	Y	17440 FQ	18880 MW	22270 TQ	USBLS	5/15
	Florida	H	9.01 AE	9.89 MW	11.57 AEX	FLBLS	7/16-9/16
	Fort Lauderdale-Pompano Beach-Deerfield Beach PMSA, FL	H	9.02 AE	9.56 MW	11.85 AEX	FLBLS	7/16-9/16
	Miami-Miami Beach-Kendall PMSA, FL	H	8.99 AE	10.01 MW	12.14 AEX	FLBLS	7/16-9/16
	Orlando-Kissimmee-Sanford MSA, FL	H	9.11 AE	10.28 MW	11.22 AEX	FLBLS	7/16-9/16
	Tampa-St. Petersburg-Clearwater MSA, FL	H	9.03 AE	9.68 MW	11.43 AEX	FLBLS	7/16-9/16
	Georgia	Y	16880 FQ	18330 MW	20050 TQ	USBLS	5/15
	Atlanta-Sandy Springs-Roswell MSA, GA	Y	16890 FQ	18370 MW	20630 TQ	USBLS	5/15
	Augusta-Richmond County MSA, GA-SC	Y	16720 FQ	17960 MW	19200 TQ	USBLS	5/15
	Hawaii	Y	19130 FQ	26770 MW	33410 TQ	USBLS	5/15
	Urban Honolulu MSA, HI	Y	17750 FQ	19530 MW	28300 TQ	USBLS	5/15
	Idaho	Y	16990 FQ	18470 MW	20420 TQ	USBLS	5/15
	Boise City MSA, ID	Y	16830 FQ	18180 MW	19550 TQ	USBLS	5/15
	Illinois	Y	18720 FQ	20260 MW	28090 TQ	USBLS	5/15
	Chicago-Naperville-Arlington Heights PMSA, IL	Y	18700 FQ	20150 MW	25760 TQ	USBLS	5/15

Occupation/Type/Industry	Location	Per	Low	Mid	High	Source	Date
Amusement and Recreation Attendant							
	Lake County-Kenosha County PMSA, IL-WI	Y	18260 FQ	19360 MW	23440 TQ	USBLS	5/15
	Indiana	Y	16810 FQ	18170 MW	19620 TQ	USBLS	5/15
	Gary PMSA, IN	Y	16790 FQ	18190 MW	19840 TQ	USBLS	5/15
	Indianapolis-Carmel-Anderson MSA, IN	Y	16930 FQ	18420 MW	20710 TQ	USBLS	5/15
	Iowa	Y	16660 FQ	17930 MW	19200 TQ	USBLS	5/15
	Des Moines-West Des Moines MSA, IA	Y	16520 FQ	17700 MW	18880 TQ	USBLS	5/15
	Kansas	Y	16760 FQ	18110 MW	19540 TQ	USBLS	5/15
	Wichita MSA, KS	Y	16680 FQ	17990 MW	19310 TQ	USBLS	5/15
	Kentucky	Y	16640 FQ	17920 MW	19190 TQ	USBLS	5/15
	Louisville-Jefferson County MSA, KY-IN	Y	16570 FQ	17850 MW	19130 TQ	USBLS	5/15
	Louisiana	Y	17220 FQ	19070 MW	24900 TQ	USBLS	5/15
	Baton Rouge MSA, LA	Y	17310 FQ	19200 MW	26200 TQ	USBLS	5/15
	New Orleans-Metairie MSA, LA	Y	19330 FQ	23070 MW	27300 TQ	USBLS	5/15
	Maine	Y	17290 FQ	18580 MW	20550 TQ	USBLS	5/15
	Portland-South Portland MSA, ME	Y	17180 FQ	18350 MW	19520 TQ	USBLS	5/15
	Maryland	Y	17871 AE	20140 MW	21275 AEX	MDBLS	4/16
	Baltimore-Columbia-Towson MSA, MD	Y	17720 FQ	18830 MW	21000 TQ	USBLS	5/15
	Salisbury MSA, MD-DE	Y	17910 FQ	19390 MW	22650 TQ	USBLS	5/15
	Massachusetts	Y	19310 FQ	21380 MW	24580 TQ	USBLS	5/15
	Boston-Cambridge-Newton NECTA, MA	Y	20140 FQ	22560 MW	25510 TQ	USBLS	5/15
	Worcester MSA, MA-CT	Y	19100 FQ	19580 MW	24210 TQ	USBLS	5/15
	Michigan	Y	17970 FQ	18890 MW	20840 TQ	USBLS	5/15
	Detroit-Dearborn-Livonia PMSA, MI	Y	18120 FQ	19190 MW	22830 TQ	USBLS	5/15
	Grand Rapids-Wyoming MSA, MI	Y	17890 FQ	18730 MW	19610 TQ	USBLS	5/15
	Minnesota	Y	18198 FQ	19501 MW	22975 TQ	MNBLS	1/16-3/16
	Minneapolis-St. Paul-Bloomington MSA, MN-WI	Y	18309 FQ	19783 MW	23601 TQ	MNBLS	1/16-3/16
	Mississippi	Y	17390 FQ	19490 MW	26140 TQ	USBLS	5/15
	Jackson MSA, MS	Y	17120 FQ	18910 MW	26590 TQ	USBLS	5/15
	Missouri	Y	17130 FQ	18340 MW	19770 TQ	USBLS	5/15
	Kansas City MSA, MO-KS	Y	17210 FQ	18640 MW	22700 TQ	USBLS	5/15
	St. Louis MSA, MO-IL	Y	17120 FQ	18260 MW	19390 TQ	USBLS	5/15
	Montana	Y	17940 FQ	19110 MW	22590 TQ	USBLS	5/15
	Billings MSA, MT	Y	17790 FQ	18800 MW	19960 TQ	USBLS	5/15
	Omaha-Council Bluffs MSA, NE-IA	Y	17610 FQ	18635 MW	20275 TQ	NEBLS	7/16-9/16
	Nevada	Y	17320 FQ	19240 MW	24100 TQ	USBLS	5/15
	Las Vegas-Henderson-Paradise MSA, NV	Y	17320 FQ	19230 MW	24280 TQ	USBLS	5/15
	New Hampshire	H	8.42 AE	9.57 MW	11.28 AEX	NHBLS	6/16
	Manchester NECTA, NH	H	8.40 AE	9.35 MW	10.35 AEX	NHBLS	6/16
	Nashua NECTA, NH-MA	Y	16940 FQ	18510 MW	21490 TQ	USBLS	5/15
	New Jersey	Y	18260 FQ	19020 MW	21050 TQ	USBLS	5/15
	Camden PMSA, NJ	Y	18100 FQ	18730 MW	19380 TQ	USBLS	5/15
	Newark PMSA, NJ-PA	Y	18410 FQ	19360 MW	23180 TQ	USBLS	5/15
	Trenton MSA, NJ	Y	18140 FQ	18790 MW	19570 TQ	USBLS	5/15
	New Mexico	Y	17610 FQ	19100 MW	24030 TQ	USBLS	5/15
	Albuquerque MSA, NM	Y	17540 FQ	18950 MW	23830 TQ	USBLS	5/15
	New York	Y	19250 AE	20280 MW	25300 AEX	NYBLS	1/16-3/16
	Buffalo-Cheektowaga-Niagara Falls MSA, NY	Y	18830 FQ	19520 MW	22600 TQ	USBLS	5/15
	Nassau County-Suffolk County PMSA, NY	Y	18880 FQ	19630 MW	24710 TQ	USBLS	5/15
	New York-Jersey City-White Plains PMSA, NY-NJ	Y	18800 FQ	19920 MW	24260 TQ	USBLS	5/15
	Rochester MSA, NY	Y	18630 FQ	19070 MW	19610 TQ	USBLS	5/15
	North Carolina	Y	16790 FQ	18210 MW	19910 TQ	USBLS	5/15
	Charlotte-Concord-Gastonia MSA, NC-SC	Y	16810 FQ	18250 MW	20030 TQ	USBLS	5/15
	Raleigh MSA, NC	Y	16650 FQ	17960 MW	19270 TQ	USBLS	5/15
	North Dakota	Y	17390 FQ	19320 MW	23610 TQ	USBLS	5/15

AE	Average entry wage	AWR	Average wage range	H	Hourly
AEX	Average experienced wage	B	Biweekly	HI	Highest wage paid
ATC	Average total compensation	D	Daily	HR	High end range
AW	Average wage paid	FQ	First quartile wage	LO	Lowest wage paid

LR	Low end range	MTC	Median total compensation	TCC	Total cash compensation
M	Monthly	MW	Median wage paid	TQ	Third quartile wage
MCC	Median cash compensation	MWR	Median wage range	W	Weekly
ME	Median entry wage	S	See annotated source	Y	Yearly

Occupation/Type/Industry	Location	Per	Low	Mid	High	Source	Date
Amusement and Recreation Attendant	Fargo MSA, ND-MN	Y	18100 FQ	20870 MW	24220 TQ	USBLS	5/15
	Ohio	Y	17780 FQ	18690 MW	19990 TQ	USBLS	5/15
	Cincinnati MSA, OH-KY-IN	Y	17790 FQ	18900 MW	21630 TQ	USBLS	5/15
	Cleveland-Elyria MSA, OH	Y	17920 FQ	18960 MW	22060 TQ	USBLS	5/15
	Columbus MSA, OH	Y	17840 FQ	18810 MW	20770 TQ	USBLS	5/15
	Oklahoma	Y	16850 FQ	18310 MW	20430 TQ	USBLS	5/15
	Oklahoma City MSA, OK	Y	16990 FQ	18580 MW	21530 TQ	USBLS	5/15
	Tulsa MSA, OK	Y	16640 FQ	17950 MW	19250 TQ	USBLS	5/15
	Oregon	H	9.64 FQ	10.65 MW	12.03 TQ	ORBLS	2016
	Portland-Vancouver-Hillsboro MSA, OR-WA	Y	19840 FQ	22420 MW	26710 TQ	USBLS	5/15
	Pennsylvania	Y	17120 FQ	18820 MW	22610 TQ	USBLS	5/15
	Allentown-Bethlehem-Easton MSA, PA-NJ	Y	17580 FQ	19690 MW	25480 TQ	USBLS	5/15
	Harrisburg-Carlisle MSA, PA	Y	17360 FQ	19210 MW	22830 TQ	USBLS	5/15
	Montgomery County-Bucks County-Chester County PMSA, PA	Y	17000 FQ	18580 MW	21280 TQ	USBLS	5/15
	Philadelphia PMSA, PA	Y	17460 FQ	19440 MW	25970 TQ	USBLS	5/15
	Pittsburgh MSA, PA	Y	17100 FQ	18780 MW	22770 TQ	USBLS	5/15
	Rhode Island	Y	19330 FQ	21700 MW	28380 TQ	USBLS	5/15
	Providence-Warwick MSA, RI-MA	Y	19210 FQ	20700 MW	26690 TQ	USBLS	5/15
	South Carolina	Y	16870 FQ	18380 MW	21310 TQ	USBLS	5/15
	Charleston-North Charleston MSA, SC	Y	17260 FQ	19150 MW	24960 TQ	USBLS	5/15
	Columbia MSA, SC	Y	16600 FQ	17940 MW	19300 TQ	USBLS	5/15
	Greenville-Anderson-Mauldin MSA, SC	Y	16750 FQ	18110 MW	19570 TQ	USBLS	5/15
	South Dakota	Y	18450 FQ	19220 MW	21620 TQ	USBLS	5/15
	Sioux Falls MSA, SD	Y	18650 FQ	19690 MW	22560 TQ	USBLS	5/15
	Tennessee	Y	16820 FQ	18290 MW	20290 TQ	USBLS	5/15
	Knoxville MSA, TN	Y	17610 FQ	20150 MW	23540 TQ	USBLS	5/15
	Memphis MSA, TN-MS-AR	Y	17150 FQ	18920 MW	21940 TQ	USBLS	5/15
	Nashville-Davidson–Murfreesboro–Franklin MSA, TN	Y	16800 FQ	18190 MW	19690 TQ	USBLS	5/15
	Texas	Y	16870 FQ	18300 MW	20010 TQ	USBLS	5/15
	Austin-Round Rock MSA, TX	Y	17000 FQ	18610 MW	25590 TQ	USBLS	5/15
	Dallas-Plano-Irving PMSA, TX	Y	16920 FQ	18470 MW	21730 TQ	USBLS	5/15
	Fort Worth-Arlington PMSA, TX	Y	17010 FQ	18600 MW	22090 TQ	USBLS	5/15
	Houston-The Woodlands-Sugar Land MSA, TX	Y	16700 FQ	17980 MW	19260 TQ	USBLS	5/15
	San Antonio-New Braunfels MSA, TX	Y	16920 FQ	18410 MW	20510 TQ	USBLS	5/15
	Utah	Y	17100 FQ	18770 MW	23250 TQ	USBLS	5/15
	Ogden-Clearfield MSA, UT	Y	17240 FQ	19020 MW	42940 TQ	USBLS	5/15
	Provo-Orem MSA, UT	Y	16850 FQ	18380 MW	21100 TQ	USBLS	5/15
	Salt Lake City MSA, UT	Y	16940 FQ	18480 MW	21040 TQ	USBLS	5/15
	Vermont	Y	19480 FQ	20780 MW	24540 TQ	USBLS	5/15
	Burlington-South Burlington MSA, VT	Y	19470 FQ	20960 MW	24320 TQ	USBLS	5/15
	Virginia	Y	16870 FQ	18340 MW	20450 TQ	USBLS	5/15
	Richmond MSA, VA	Y	16760 FQ	18070 MW	19390 TQ	USBLS	5/15
	Virginia Beach-Norfolk-Newport News MSA, VA-NC	Y	16710 FQ	18010 MW	19310 TQ	USBLS	5/15
	Washington	H	10.40 FQ	11.34 MW	12.70 TQ	WABLS	3/16
	Seattle-Bellevue-Everett PMSA, WA	H	10.46 FQ	11.32 MW	12.24 TQ	WABLS	3/16
	Tacoma-Lakewood PMSA, WA	H	10.66 FQ	11.76 MW	14.35 TQ	WABLS	3/16
	West Virginia	Y	17740 FQ	18830 MW	20990 TQ	USBLS	5/15
	Huntington-Ashland MSA, WV-KY-OH	Y	17550 FQ	18540 MW	19560 TQ	USBLS	5/15
	Wisconsin	Y	16960 FQ	18470 MW	20990 TQ	USBLS	5/15
	Madison MSA, WI	Y	16830 FQ	18260 MW	19870 TQ	USBLS	5/15
	Milwaukee-Waukesha-West Allis MSA, WI	Y	16910 FQ	18340 MW	19990 TQ	USBLS	5/15
	Wyoming	Y	17690 FQ	20390 MW	26810 TQ	USBLS	5/15
	Cheyenne MSA, WY	Y	17100 FQ	18950 MW	22870 TQ	USBLS	5/15
	Puerto Rico	Y	16560 FQ	17750 MW	18940 TQ	USBLS	5/15

AE	Average entry wage	AWR	Average wage range	H	Hourly	LR	Low end range	MTC	Median total compensation	TCC	Total cash compensation
AEX	Average experienced wage	B	Biweekly	HI	Highest wage paid	M	Monthly	MW	Median wage paid	TQ	Third quartile wage
ATC	Average total compensation	D	Daily	HR	High end range	MCC	Median cash compensation	MWR	Median wage range	W	Weekly
AW	Average wage paid	FQ	First quartile wage	LO	Lowest wage paid	ME	Median entry wage	S	See annotated source	Y	Yearly

Occupation/Type/Industry	Location	Per	Low	Mid	High	Source	Date
Amusement and Recreation Attendant	Ponce MSA, PR	Y	16360 FQ	17440 MW	18520 TQ	USBLS	5/15
	San Juan-Carolina-Caguas MSA, PR	Y	16590 FQ	17800 MW	19000 TQ	USBLS	5/15
	Virgin Islands	Y	19290 FQ	24570 MW	28520 TQ	USBLS	5/15
	Guam	Y	17870 FQ	18580 MW	19290 TQ	USBLS	5/15
Amusement Ride Inspector							
State Government	Maryland	Y	41358 LO		70265 HI	MDGOV	2016
Analytic Methodologist							
Central Intelligence Agency	District of Columbia	Y	51603 LO		76498 HI	CIA01	2016
Analytical Chemist							
Municipal Government	Detroit, MI	M	3700 LO		4217 HI	DETGOV	2016
Analytics Manager	United States	Y		109000 MW		HCHRON1	2017
Anatomy Resources Manager							
Michigan State University	East Lansing, MI	Y			59532 HI	MSUSAL	10/1/14-9/30/15
Anesthesiologist	Arizona	Y		242290 AW		USBLS	5/15
	Phoenix-Mesa-Scottsdale MSA, AZ	Y		236170 AW		USBLS	5/15
	Arkansas	Y		236230 AW		USBLS	5/15
	California	H		128.78 AW		CABLS	1/16-3/16
	Colorado	Y		266710 AW		USBLS	5/15
	Connecticut	Y		261445 AW		CTBLS	1/16-3/16
	District of Columbia	Y	133640 FQ	206050 AW		USBLS	5/15
	Washington-Arlington-Alexandria PMSA, DC-VA-MD-WV	Y	60460 FQ	183030 AW		USBLS	5/15
	Florida	H		123.33 AW		FLBLS	7/16-9/16
	Orlando-Kissimmee-Sanford MSA, FL	H	45.17 AE	55.69 MW	73.91 AEX	FLBLS	7/16-9/16
	Tampa-St. Petersburg-Clearwater MSA, FL	H		133.51 AW		FLBLS	7/16-9/16
	Georgia	Y		269720 AW		USBLS	5/15
	Atlanta-Sandy Springs-Roswell MSA, GA	Y		268270 AW		USBLS	5/15
	Idaho	Y	168640 FQ	212770 AW		USBLS	5/15
	Illinois	Y	102620 FQ	185920 AW		USBLS	5/15
	Chicago-Naperville-Arlington Heights PMSA, IL	Y	75010 FQ	112260 MW		USBLS	5/15
	Indiana	Y		261750 AW		USBLS	5/15
	Gary PMSA, IN	Y		242140 AW		USBLS	5/15
	Indianapolis-Carmel-Anderson MSA, IN	Y		257830 AW		USBLS	5/15
	Iowa	Y		280020 AW		USBLS	5/15
	Louisiana	Y		263740 AW		USBLS	5/15
	New Orleans-Metairie MSA, LA	Y		252460 AW		USBLS	5/15
	Maryland	Y		272422 MW		MDBLS	4/16
	Baltimore-Columbia-Towson MSA, MD	Y		253780 AW		USBLS	5/15
	Massachusetts	Y		258230 AW		USBLS	5/15
	Boston-Cambridge-Newton NECTA, MA	Y		243100 AW		USBLS	5/15
	Worcester MSA, MA-CT	Y		274580 AW		USBLS	5/15
	Minnesota	Y		267013 AW		MNBLS	1/16-3/16
	Mississippi	Y	43930 FQ	185490 MW		USBLS	5/15
	Missouri	Y	185410 FQ	238110 AW		USBLS	5/15
	Kansas City MSA, MO-KS	Y	178480 FQ	226120 AW		USBLS	5/15
	St. Louis MSA, MO-IL	Y		256100 AW		USBLS	5/15
	New Hampshire	H		134.54 AW		NHBLS	6/16
	New York	Y		260760 AW		NYBLS	1/16-3/16
	Buffalo-Cheektowaga-Niagara Falls MSA, NY	Y		236590 AW		USBLS	5/15
	Nassau County-Suffolk County PMSA, NY	Y		271060 AW		USBLS	5/15
	New York-Jersey City-White Plains PMSA, NY-NJ	Y		256070 AW		USBLS	5/15

AE Average entry wage	**AWR** Average wage range	**H** Hourly	**LR** Low end range	**MTC** Median total compensation	**TCC** Total cash compensation
AEX Average experienced wage	**B** Biweekly	**HI** Highest wage paid	**M** Monthly	**MW** Median wage paid	**TQ** Third quartile wage
ATC Average total compensation	**D** Daily	**HR** High end range	**MCC** Median cash compensation	**MWR** Median wage range	**W** Weekly
AW Average wage paid	**FQ** First quartile wage	**LO** Lowest wage paid	**ME** Median entry wage	**S** See annotated source	**Y** Yearly

Occupation/Type/Industry	Location	Per	Low	Mid	High	Source	Date
Anesthesiologist	Charlotte-Concord-Gastonia MSA, NC-SC	Y		245400 AW		USBLS	5/15
	North Dakota	Y		283200 AW		USBLS	5/15
	Ohio	Y		258960 AW		USBLS	5/15
	Cincinnati MSA, OH-KY-IN	Y	150210 FQ	216540 AW		USBLS	5/15
	Cleveland-Elyria MSA, OH	Y		245320 AW		USBLS	5/15
	Pennsylvania	Y		258610 AW		USBLS	5/15
	Harrisburg-Carlisle MSA, PA	Y	61590 FQ	210870 AW		USBLS	5/15
	Philadelphia PMSA, PA	Y		250270 AW		USBLS	5/15
	Providence-Warwick MSA, RI-MA	Y		266930 AW		USBLS	5/15
	South Carolina	Y		237790 AW		USBLS	5/15
	South Dakota	Y		279300 AW		USBLS	5/15
	Texas	Y		257570 AW		USBLS	5/15
	Dallas-Plano-Irving PMSA, TX	Y		243210 AW		USBLS	5/15
	Houston-The Woodlands-Sugar Land MSA, TX	Y		271280 AW		USBLS	5/15
	San Antonio-New Braunfels MSA, TX	Y		278040 AW		USBLS	5/15
	Utah	Y	131950 FQ	197720 AW		USBLS	5/15
	Salt Lake City MSA, UT	Y	145060 FQ	216790 AW		USBLS	5/15
	Vermont	Y	61660 FQ	217220 AW		USBLS	5/15
	Burlington-South Burlington MSA, VT	Y	61320 FQ	217580 AW		USBLS	5/15
	Virginia	Y	99690 FQ	201150 AW		USBLS	5/15
	Richmond MSA, VA	Y		257830 AW		USBLS	5/15
	Virginia Beach-Norfolk-Newport News MSA, VA-NC	Y	180510 FQ	216840 AW		USBLS	5/15
	Washington	H		124.90 AW		WABLS	3/16
	West Virginia	Y		262830 AW		USBLS	5/15
	Milwaukee-Waukesha-West Allis MSA, WI	Y		271960 AW		USBLS	5/15
	Puerto Rico	Y	57710 FQ	67180 MW	74400 TQ	USBLS	5/15
	San Juan-Carolina-Caguas MSA, PR	Y	62490 FQ	67780 MW	73080 TQ	USBLS	5/15
Academic Healthcare Institution	United States	Y		240489 AW		MLEVU1	2015
Private Practice	United States	Y		317481 AW		MLEVU1	2015
Animal Adoption Counselor							
Animal Care Facility, Municipal Government	Chula Vista, CA	Y			57088 HI	CACIT	6/28/16
Animal Autopsy Technician							
State Government	Maryland	Y	24056 LO		37204 HI	MDGOV	2016
Animal Breeder	Alabama	Y	24709 AE	37167 AW	43400 AEX	ALBLS	6/16
	California	H	12.85 FQ	15.36 MW	21.69 TQ	CABLS	1/16-3/16
	Iowa	Y	25180 FQ	34040 MW	38420 TQ	USBLS	5/15
	Kentucky	Y	27840 FQ	30780 MW	36930 TQ	USBLS	5/15
	Michigan	Y	27450 FQ	32360 MW	41550 TQ	USBLS	5/15
	Missouri	Y	20880 FQ	24910 MW	35000 TQ	USBLS	5/15
	Ohio	Y	40220 FQ	49990 MW	83380 TQ	USBLS	5/15
	South Dakota	Y	42220 FQ	45220 MW	48220 TQ	USBLS	5/15
	Texas	Y	29240 FQ	33860 MW	37550 TQ	USBLS	5/15
Animal Census Leader							
County Government	Oakland County, MI	H			13.36 HI	MIOAK2	10/1/16
Animal Collection Curator							
Municipal Zoo	Los Angeles, CA	Y			110290 HI	CACIT	6/23/16
Animal Control Director							
Municipal Government	Quitman City, GA	H			8.13 HI	GACTY01	2016
Animal Control Worker	Alabama	Y	22641 AE	31001 AW	35182 AEX	ALBLS	6/16
	Birmingham-Hoover MSA, AL	Y	22734 AE	32814 AW	37859 AEX	ALBLS	6/16
	Alaska	Y	41230 FQ	45820 MW	51430 TQ	USBLS	5/15
	Arizona	Y	31140 FQ	34990 MW	39130 TQ	USBLS	5/15
	Phoenix-Mesa-Scottsdale MSA, AZ	Y	33320 FQ	37350 MW	44030 TQ	USBLS	5/15
	Arkansas	Y	21700 FQ	26950 MW	30960 TQ	USBLS	5/15
	Little Rock-North Little Rock-Conway MSA, AR	Y	26920 FQ	29910 MW	35960 TQ	USBLS	5/15

AE Average entry wage	**AWR** Average wage range	**H** Hourly	**LR** Low end range	**MTC** Median total compensation	**TCC** Total cash compensation
AEX Average experienced wage	**B** Biweekly	**HI** Highest wage paid	**M** Monthly	**MW** Median wage paid	**TQ** Third quartile wage
ATC Average total compensation	**D** Daily	**HR** High end range	**MCC** Median cash compensation	**MWR** Median wage range	**W** Weekly
AW Average wage paid	**FQ** First quartile wage	**LO** Lowest wage paid	**ME** Median entry wage	**S** See annotated source	**Y** Yearly

Occupation/Type/Industry	Location	Per	Low	Mid	High	Source	Date
Animal Control Worker	California	H	18.52 FQ	23.24 MW	28.47 TQ	CABLS	1/16-3/16
	Anaheim-Santa Ana-Irvine PMSA, CA	H	25.50 FQ	27.96 MW	30.41 TQ	CABLS	1/16-3/16
	Los Angeles-Long Beach-Glendale PMSA, CA	H	22.49 FQ	26.84 MW	32.13 TQ	CABLS	1/16-3/16
	Oakland-Hayward-Berkeley PMSA, CA	H	19.53 FQ	24.44 MW	30.60 TQ	CABLS	1/16-3/16
	Riverside-San Bernardino-Ontario MSA, CA	H	16.55 FQ	21.69 MW	26.19 TQ	CABLS	1/16-3/16
	Sacramento–Roseville–Arden-Arcade MSA, CA	H	22.79 FQ	26.60 MW	29.96 TQ	CABLS	1/16-3/16
	San Diego-Carlsbad MSA, CA	H	18.67 FQ	21.80 MW	24.88 TQ	CABLS	1/16-3/16
	San Francisco-Redwood City-South San Francisco PMSA, CA	H	16.94 FQ	20.76 MW	26.73 TQ	CABLS	1/16-3/16
	Colorado	Y	33460 FQ	42040 MW	48420 TQ	USBLS	5/15
	Denver-Aurora-Lakewood MSA, CO	Y	42180 FQ	46750 MW	52040 TQ	USBLS	5/15
	Connecticut	Y		41014 MW		CTBLS	1/16-3/16
	Bridgeport-Stamford-Norwalk MSA, CT	Y	30440 FQ	43490 MW	58370 TQ	USBLS	5/15
	Hartford-West Hartford-East Hartford MSA, CT	Y	22290 FQ	42170 MW	56520 TQ	USBLS	5/15
	Washington-Arlington-Alexandria PMSA, DC-VA-MD-WV	Y	36050 FQ	45250 MW	63140 TQ	USBLS	5/15
	Florida	H	13.16 AE	16.73 MW	19.59 AEX	FLBLS	7/16-9/16
	Fort Lauderdale-Pompano Beach-Deerfield Beach PMSA, FL	H	14.68 AE	18.00 MW	20.39 AEX	FLBLS	7/16-9/16
	Orlando-Kissimmee-Sanford MSA, FL	H	14.30 AE	17.02 MW	18.20 AEX	FLBLS	7/16-9/16
	Tampa-St. Petersburg-Clearwater MSA, FL	H	15.86 AE	19.90 MW	22.11 AEX	FLBLS	7/16-9/16
	Georgia	Y	25430 FQ	29230 MW	34910 TQ	USBLS	5/15
	Atlanta-Sandy Springs-Roswell MSA, GA	Y	26560 FQ	29940 MW	35750 TQ	USBLS	5/15
	Idaho	Y	27370 FQ	32450 MW	36770 TQ	USBLS	5/15
	Illinois	Y	19640 FQ	29140 MW	43940 TQ	USBLS	5/15
	Chicago-Naperville-Arlington Heights PMSA, IL	Y	36450 FQ	50860 MW	61910 TQ	USBLS	5/15
	Indiana	Y	24690 FQ	32900 MW	38100 TQ	USBLS	5/15
	Indianapolis-Carmel-Anderson MSA, IN	Y	27150 FQ	33900 MW	37560 TQ	USBLS	5/15
	Iowa	Y	18920 FQ	30930 MW	44040 TQ	USBLS	5/15
	Kansas	Y	24570 FQ	30670 MW	37940 TQ	USBLS	5/15
	Wichita MSA, KS	Y	28390 FQ	34150 MW	41120 TQ	USBLS	5/15
	Kentucky	Y	22120 FQ	27310 MW	33010 TQ	USBLS	5/15
	Louisville-Jefferson County MSA, KY-IN	Y	25450 FQ	28960 MW	33890 TQ	USBLS	5/15
	Louisiana	Y	22170 FQ	28280 MW	36220 TQ	USBLS	5/15
	Baton Rouge MSA, LA	Y	21980 FQ	25760 MW	34500 TQ	USBLS	5/15
	New Orleans-Metairie MSA, LA	Y	26210 FQ	32490 MW	38770 TQ	USBLS	5/15
	Maine	Y	18440 FQ	22360 MW	30750 TQ	USBLS	5/15
	Maryland	Y	30692 AE	42009 MW	47668 AEX	MDBLS	4/16
	Baltimore-Columbia-Towson MSA, MD	Y	37430 FQ	43130 MW	48830 TQ	USBLS	5/15
	Massachusetts	Y	30840 FQ	38640 MW	48040 TQ	USBLS	5/15
	Boston-Cambridge-Newton NECTA, MA	Y	33970 FQ	39300 MW	48510 TQ	USBLS	5/15
	Worcester MSA, MA-CT	Y	27910 FQ	38440 MW	50840 TQ	USBLS	5/15
	Michigan	Y	31190 FQ	36390 MW	43100 TQ	USBLS	5/15
	Detroit-Dearborn-Livonia PMSA, MI	Y	31780 FQ	36510 MW	42880 TQ	USBLS	5/15
	Minnesota	Y	25126 FQ	37406 MW	50140 TQ	MNBLS	1/16-3/16
	Minneapolis-St. Paul-Bloomington MSA, MN-WI	Y	31286 FQ	47878 MW	56229 TQ	MNBLS	1/16-3/16
	Mississippi	Y	20130 FQ	23790 MW	28670 TQ	USBLS	5/15
	Missouri	Y	26640 FQ	31800 MW	37890 TQ	USBLS	5/15
	Kansas City MSA, MO-KS	Y	29580 FQ	36850 MW	43500 TQ	USBLS	5/15
	St. Louis MSA, MO-IL	Y	22930 FQ	32500 MW	40240 TQ	USBLS	5/15

AE Average entry wage	**AWR** Average wage range	**H** Hourly	**LR** Low end range	**MTC** Median total compensation	**TCC** Total cash compensation
AEX Average experienced wage	**B** Biweekly	**HI** Highest wage paid	**M** Monthly	**MW** Median wage paid	**TQ** Third quartile wage
ATC Average total compensation	**D** Daily	**HR** High end range	**MCC** Median cash compensation	**MWR** Median wage range	**W** Weekly
AW Average wage paid	**FQ** First quartile wage	**LO** Lowest wage paid	**ME** Median entry wage	**S** See annotated source	**Y** Yearly

47

Occupation/Type/Industry	Location	Per	Low	Mid	High	Source	Date
Animal Control Worker	Montana	Y	31840 FQ	36070 MW	41280 TQ	USBLS	5/15
	Nevada	Y	37680 FQ	49690 MW	60750 TQ	USBLS	5/15
	Las Vegas-Henderson-Paradise MSA, NV	Y	44950 FQ	56640 MW	68910 TQ	USBLS	5/15
	New Hampshire	H	9.87 AE	16.68 MW	19.44 AEX	NHBLS	6/16
	New Jersey	Y	32080 FQ	39500 MW	49880 TQ	USBLS	5/15
	Newark PMSA, NJ-PA	Y	34270 FQ	41120 MW	48210 TQ	USBLS	5/15
	New Mexico	Y	22450 FQ	27160 MW	33780 TQ	USBLS	5/15
	Albuquerque MSA, NM	Y	25840 FQ	29870 MW	34770 TQ	USBLS	5/15
	New York	Y	26340 AE	32730 MW	41320 AEX	NYBLS	1/16-3/16
	Buffalo-Cheektowaga-Niagara Falls MSA, NY	Y	24640 FQ	29060 MW	34970 TQ	USBLS	5/15
	Nassau County-Suffolk County PMSA, NY	Y	31850 FQ	47810 MW	64410 TQ	USBLS	5/15
	New York-Jersey City-White Plains PMSA, NY-NJ	Y	32970 FQ	40790 MW	55770 TQ	USBLS	5/15
	Rochester MSA, NY	Y	28870 FQ	34880 MW	40930 TQ	USBLS	5/15
	North Carolina	Y	27030 FQ	31130 MW	36440 TQ	USBLS	5/15
	Charlotte-Concord-Gastonia MSA, NC-SC	Y	26960 FQ	31080 MW	36630 TQ	USBLS	5/15
	Greensboro-High Point MSA, NC	Y	31660 FQ	35330 MW	39000 TQ	USBLS	5/15
	Ohio	Y	23920 FQ	30590 MW	37080 TQ	USBLS	5/15
	Cleveland-Elyria MSA, OH	Y	31520 FQ	35370 MW	39340 TQ	USBLS	5/15
	Columbus MSA, OH	Y	26450 FQ	30930 MW	36370 TQ	USBLS	5/15
	Oklahoma	Y	23040 FQ	28940 MW	36160 TQ	USBLS	5/15
	Oklahoma City MSA, OK	Y	32180 FQ	36520 MW	43560 TQ	USBLS	5/15
	Tulsa MSA, OK	Y	23820 FQ	28360 MW	34850 TQ	USBLS	5/15
	Oregon	H	19.39 FQ	22.60 MW	26.40 TQ	ORBLS	2016
	Portland-Vancouver-Hillsboro MSA, OR-WA	Y	45980 FQ	52150 MW	57760 TQ	USBLS	5/15
	Pennsylvania	Y	19840 FQ	37920 MW	45570 TQ	USBLS	5/15
	Rhode Island	Y	28300 FQ	37350 MW	46470 TQ	USBLS	5/15
	Providence-Warwick MSA, RI-MA	Y	29360 FQ	37410 MW	46630 TQ	USBLS	5/15
	South Carolina	Y	24300 FQ	28060 MW	32200 TQ	USBLS	5/15
	Columbia MSA, SC	Y	26240 FQ	29440 MW	35180 TQ	USBLS	5/15
	Greenville-Anderson-Mauldin MSA, SC	Y	22830 FQ	26500 MW	31310 TQ	USBLS	5/15
	South Dakota	Y	23200 FQ	28010 MW	32520 TQ	USBLS	5/15
	Tennessee	Y	24950 FQ	29710 MW	36200 TQ	USBLS	5/15
	Knoxville MSA, TN	Y	25280 FQ	29690 MW	36240 TQ	USBLS	5/15
	Memphis MSA, TN-MS-AR	Y	26850 FQ	34510 MW	42370 TQ	USBLS	5/15
	Nashville-Davidson–Murfreesboro–Franklin MSA, TN	Y	27400 FQ	30950 MW	36160 TQ	USBLS	5/15
	Texas	Y	27440 FQ	32760 MW	38000 TQ	USBLS	5/15
	Austin-Round Rock MSA, TX	Y	28320 FQ	33010 MW	37530 TQ	USBLS	5/15
	Dallas-Plano-Irving PMSA, TX	Y	32670 FQ	37010 MW	43010 TQ	USBLS	5/15
	Fort Worth-Arlington PMSA, TX	Y	31220 FQ	35330 MW	39660 TQ	USBLS	5/15
	Houston-The Woodlands-Sugar Land MSA, TX	Y	29450 FQ	34500 MW	40620 TQ	USBLS	5/15
	San Antonio-New Braunfels MSA, TX	Y	28940 FQ	33720 MW	38710 TQ	USBLS	5/15
	Utah	Y	27550 FQ	34250 MW	39050 TQ	USBLS	5/15
	Ogden-Clearfield MSA, UT	Y	25610 FQ	30410 MW	36540 TQ	USBLS	5/15
	Salt Lake City MSA, UT	Y	32900 FQ	36780 MW	40750 TQ	USBLS	5/15
	Vermont	Y	19190 FQ	23700 MW	31880 TQ	USBLS	5/15
	Burlington-South Burlington MSA, VT	Y	25010 FQ	30350 MW	36530 TQ	USBLS	5/15
	Virginia	Y	29930 FQ	35450 MW	43850 TQ	USBLS	5/15
	Richmond MSA, VA	Y	31200 FQ	35020 MW	38840 TQ	USBLS	5/15
	Virginia Beach-Norfolk-Newport News MSA, VA-NC	Y	30580 FQ	35170 MW	41100 TQ	USBLS	5/15
	Washington	H	17.92 FQ	23.17 MW	27.78 TQ	WABLS	3/16
	Seattle-Bellevue-Everett PMSA, WA	H	25.69 FQ	28.12 MW	30.71 TQ	WABLS	3/16
	Tacoma-Lakewood PMSA, WA	H	23.32 FQ	26.20 MW	28.74 TQ	WABLS	3/16
	West Virginia	Y	20780 FQ	22580 MW	24380 TQ	USBLS	5/15
	Wisconsin	Y	27390 FQ	33280 MW	39710 TQ	USBLS	5/15

AE	Average entry wage	AWR	Average wage range	H	Hourly
AEX	Average experienced wage	B	Biweekly	HI	Highest wage paid
ATC	Average total compensation	D	Daily	HR	High end range
AW	Average wage paid	FQ	First quartile wage	LO	Lowest wage paid

LR	Low end range	MTC	Median total compensation	TCC	Total cash compensation
M	Monthly	MW	Median wage paid	TQ	Third quartile wage
MCC	Median cash compensation	MWR	Median wage range	W	Weekly
ME	Median entry wage	S	See annotated source	Y	Yearly

Occupation/Type/Industry	Location	Per	Low	Mid	High	Source	Date
Animal Control Worker	Milwaukee-Waukesha-West Allis MSA, WI	Y	29460 FQ	34180 MW	39140 TQ	USBLS	5/15
	Wyoming	Y	32080 FQ	40510 MW	45840 TQ	USBLS	5/15
Animal Health Inspector							
Agriculture Department, State Government	Ohio	H	19.88 LO		26.51 HI	OHGOV	2015
Municipal Government	Northfield, MA	Y			2027 HI	FRCOG	2016
Municipal Government	Wendell, MA	Y			300 HI	FRCOG	2016
Animal Lawyer	United States	Y		132000 AW		SKU01	2016
Animal Regulations Officer							
Police Department, Municipal Government	National City, CA	Y			42049 HI	CACIT	6/28/16
Animal Scientist	Arkansas	Y	40190 FQ	45730 MW	55890 TQ	USBLS	5/15
	Florida	H	16.64 AE	20.96 MW	24.71 AEX	FLBLS	7/16-9/16
	Iowa	Y	46980 FQ	58410 MW	81250 TQ	USBLS	5/15
	Maryland	Y	55832 AE	82599 MW	95983 AEX	MDBLS	4/16
	Massachusetts	Y	35210 FQ	53200 MW	81610 TQ	USBLS	5/15
	Michigan	Y	44750 FQ	52230 MW	64040 TQ	USBLS	5/15
	Minnesota	Y	44012 FQ	54848 MW	77398 TQ	MNBLS	1/16-3/16
	Missouri	Y	39780 FQ	54780 MW	76860 TQ	USBLS	5/15
	Nebraska	Y	43315 FQ	68710 MW	147200 TQ	NEBLS	7/16-9/16
	New Jersey	Y	60270 FQ	74380 MW	88150 TQ	USBLS	5/15
	New York	Y	49180 AE	62200 MW	72190 AEX	NYBLS	1/16-3/16
	North Carolina	Y	43880 FQ	49990 MW	70300 TQ	USBLS	5/15
	Ohio	Y	54470 FQ	62530 MW	73970 TQ	USBLS	5/15
	Oklahoma	Y	51630 FQ	60730 MW	80960 TQ	USBLS	5/15
	Pennsylvania	Y	37820 FQ	55230 MW	70380 TQ	USBLS	5/15
	South Dakota	Y	45530 FQ	51420 MW	60160 TQ	USBLS	5/15
	Texas	Y	37290 FQ	55580 MW	82250 TQ	USBLS	5/15
	Wisconsin	Y	52280 FQ	65250 MW	78370 TQ	USBLS	5/15
Animal Trainer	Alabama	Y	18512 AE	31115 AW	37406 AEX	ALBLS	6/16
	Arizona	Y	18720 FQ	21640 MW	30360 TQ	USBLS	5/15
	Phoenix-Mesa-Scottsdale MSA, AZ	Y	18500 FQ	20760 MW	23660 TQ	USBLS	5/15
	Tucson MSA, AZ	Y	19800 FQ	31880 MW	36340 TQ	USBLS	5/15
	Arkansas	Y	19220 FQ	26160 MW	33710 TQ	USBLS	5/15
	California	H	10.96 FQ	15.03 MW	23.37 TQ	CABLS	1/16-3/16
	Anaheim-Santa Ana-Irvine PMSA, CA	H	10.79 FQ	13.55 MW	20.88 TQ	CABLS	1/16-3/16
	Los Angeles-Long Beach-Glendale PMSA, CA	H	11.04 FQ	19.98 MW	26.33 TQ	CABLS	1/16-3/16
	Oakland-Hayward-Berkeley PMSA, CA	H	11.24 FQ	14.89 MW	25.09 TQ	CABLS	1/16-3/16
	Riverside-San Bernardino-Ontario MSA, CA	H	9.62 FQ	11.85 MW	13.74 TQ	CABLS	1/16-3/16
	Sacramento–Roseville–Arden-Arcade MSA, CA	H	10.13 FQ	11.36 MW	16.04 TQ	CABLS	1/16-3/16
	San Diego-Carlsbad MSA, CA	H	17.21 FQ	22.08 MW	26.74 TQ	CABLS	1/16-3/16
	Colorado	Y	21300 FQ	24300 MW	30090 TQ	USBLS	5/15
	Denver-Aurora-Lakewood MSA, CO	Y	20880 FQ	23310 MW	27030 TQ	USBLS	5/15
	Connecticut	Y		26503 MW		CTBLS	1/16-3/16
	Hartford-West Hartford-East Hartford MSA, CT	Y	29890 FQ	33510 MW	36490 TQ	USBLS	5/15
	Delaware	Y	22730 FQ	35110 MW	43310 TQ	USBLS	5/15
	Wilmington PMSA, DE-MD-NJ	Y	33740 FQ	39450 MW	56230 TQ	USBLS	5/15
	Washington-Arlington-Alexandria PMSA, DC-VA-MD-WV	Y	20120 FQ	28490 MW	50330 TQ	USBLS	5/15
	Florida	H	9.12 AE	12.79 MW	23.44 AEX	FLBLS	7/16-9/16
	Fort Lauderdale-Pompano Beach-Deerfield Beach PMSA, FL	H	9.05 AE	9.52 MW	10.31 AEX	FLBLS	7/16-9/16
	Miami-Miami Beach-Kendall PMSA, FL	H	9.06 AE	12.90 MW	15.36 AEX	FLBLS	7/16-9/16
	Orlando-Kissimmee-Sanford MSA, FL	H	10.55 AE	14.34 MW	24.27 AEX	FLBLS	7/16-9/16
	Tampa-St. Petersburg-Clearwater MSA, FL	H	8.96 AE	9.46 MW	12.36 AEX	FLBLS	7/16-9/16

AE Average entry wage	**AWR** Average wage range	**H** Hourly	**LR** Low end range	**MTC** Median total compensation	**TCC** Total cash compensation
AEX Average experienced wage	**B** Biweekly	**HI** Highest wage paid	**M** Monthly	**MW** Median wage paid	**TQ** Third quartile wage
ATC Average total compensation	**D** Daily	**HR** High end range	**MCC** Median cash compensation	**MWR** Median wage range	**W** Weekly
AW Average wage paid	**FQ** First quartile wage	**LO** Lowest wage paid	**ME** Median entry wage	**S** See annotated source	**Y** Yearly

Occupation/Type/Industry	Location	Per	Low	Mid	High	Source	Date
Animal Trainer	Georgia	Y	21760 FQ	24960 MW	38350 TQ	USBLS	5/15
	Atlanta-Sandy Springs-Roswell MSA, GA	Y	22010 FQ	24480 MW	40920 TQ	USBLS	5/15
	Hawaii	Y	19750 FQ	25830 MW	30020 TQ	USBLS	5/15
	Idaho	Y	17620 FQ	19860 MW	22610 TQ	USBLS	5/15
	Boise City MSA, ID	Y	17290 FQ	19150 MW	21880 TQ	USBLS	5/15
	Illinois	Y	22090 FQ	30990 MW	54550 TQ	USBLS	5/15
	Chicago-Naperville-Arlington Heights PMSA, IL	Y	23500 FQ	37070 MW	54760 TQ	USBLS	5/15
	Lake County-Kenosha County PMSA, IL-WI	Y	19760 FQ	28050 MW	35810 TQ	USBLS	5/15
	Indiana	Y	17560 FQ	19770 MW	27850 TQ	USBLS	5/15
	Indianapolis-Carmel-Anderson MSA, IN	Y	18180 FQ	21340 MW	31150 TQ	USBLS	5/15
	Iowa	Y	20090 FQ	24540 MW	33570 TQ	USBLS	5/15
	Kansas	Y	17300 FQ	19120 MW	23250 TQ	USBLS	5/15
	Kentucky	Y	19850 FQ	28350 MW	36510 TQ	USBLS	5/15
	Louisville-Jefferson County MSA, KY-IN	Y	29930 FQ	37800 MW	45660 TQ	USBLS	5/15
	Louisiana	Y	18890 FQ	22600 MW	31520 TQ	USBLS	5/15
	New Orleans-Metairie MSA, LA	Y	21730 FQ	24120 MW	33680 TQ	USBLS	5/15
	Maine	Y	18510 FQ	22720 MW	29670 TQ	USBLS	5/15
	Maryland	Y	18000 AE	31187 MW	37780 AEX	MDBLS	4/16
	Baltimore-Columbia-Towson MSA, MD	Y	18530 FQ	29260 MW	38170 TQ	USBLS	5/15
	Massachusetts	Y	24290 FQ	30370 MW	39420 TQ	USBLS	5/15
	Boston-Cambridge-Newton NECTA, MA	Y	23210 FQ	28340 MW	34970 TQ	USBLS	5/15
	Michigan	Y	20050 FQ	24840 MW	41940 TQ	USBLS	5/15
	Detroit-Dearborn-Livonia PMSA, MI	Y	21400 FQ	24590 MW	34280 TQ	USBLS	5/15
	Grand Rapids-Wyoming MSA, MI	Y	20800 FQ	32020 MW	36940 TQ	USBLS	5/15
	Minnesota	Y	29165 FQ	46292 MW	58128 TQ	MNBLS	1/16-3/16
	Minneapolis-St. Paul-Bloomington MSA, MN-WI	Y	26751 FQ	46343 MW	58158 TQ	MNBLS	1/16-3/16
	Missouri	Y	20080 FQ	25250 MW	37190 TQ	USBLS	5/15
	Kansas City MSA, MO-KS	Y	17550 FQ	19500 MW	24380 TQ	USBLS	5/15
	St. Louis MSA, MO-IL	Y	21980 FQ	28400 MW	37830 TQ	USBLS	5/15
	Montana	Y	19910 FQ	22040 MW	24170 TQ	USBLS	5/15
	Omaha-Council Bluffs MSA, NE-IA	Y	21750 FQ	23805 MW	34680 TQ	NEBLS	7/16-9/16
	Nevada	Y	18480 FQ	21340 MW	24030 TQ	USBLS	5/15
	Las Vegas-Henderson-Paradise MSA, NV	Y	18320 FQ	21280 MW	24140 TQ	USBLS	5/15
	New Hampshire	H	10.68 AE	16.32 MW	21.03 AEX	NHBLS	6/16
	New Jersey	Y	22070 FQ	31460 MW	38640 TQ	USBLS	5/15
	Camden PMSA, NJ	Y	19630 FQ	23730 MW	36740 TQ	USBLS	5/15
	Newark PMSA, NJ-PA	Y	23430 FQ	36970 MW	55390 TQ	USBLS	5/15
	New Mexico	Y	22830 FQ	28770 MW	46280 TQ	USBLS	5/15
	New York	Y	23020 AE	35570 MW	52490 AEX	NYBLS	1/16-3/16
	Buffalo-Cheektowaga-Niagara Falls MSA, NY	Y	25140 FQ	29950 MW	37860 TQ	USBLS	5/15
	Nassau County-Suffolk County PMSA, NY	Y	26550 FQ	36180 MW	56270 TQ	USBLS	5/15
	New York-Jersey City-White Plains PMSA, NY-NJ	Y	26740 FQ	37180 MW	46480 TQ	USBLS	5/15
	Rochester MSA, NY	Y	31930 FQ	39470 MW	44870 TQ	USBLS	5/15
	North Carolina	Y	19040 FQ	24650 MW	46780 TQ	USBLS	5/15
	Charlotte-Concord-Gastonia MSA, NC-SC	Y	19990 FQ	22930 MW	34700 TQ	USBLS	5/15
	Raleigh MSA, NC	Y	16960 FQ	18520 MW	28430 TQ	USBLS	5/15
	North Dakota	Y	25700 FQ	27740 MW	29780 TQ	USBLS	5/15
	Ohio	Y	18510 FQ	21210 MW	30080 TQ	USBLS	5/15
	Cincinnati MSA, OH-KY-IN	Y	17930 FQ	19040 MW	23010 TQ	USBLS	5/15
	Cleveland-Elyria MSA, OH	Y	18560 FQ	20670 MW	23260 TQ	USBLS	5/15
	Columbus MSA, OH	Y	20400 FQ	30830 MW	40780 TQ	USBLS	5/15
	Oklahoma	Y	17750 FQ	20950 MW	26570 TQ	USBLS	5/15
	Oklahoma City MSA, OK	Y	17620 FQ	21470 MW	42230 TQ	USBLS	5/15
	Tulsa MSA, OK	Y	17150 FQ	19120 MW	21710 TQ	USBLS	5/15
	Oregon	H	10.87 FQ	12.15 MW	15.61 TQ	ORBLS	2016

AE	Average entry wage	AWR	Average wage range	H	Hourly
AEX	Average experienced wage	B	Biweekly	HI	Highest wage paid
ATC	Average total compensation	D	Daily	HR	High end range
AW	Average wage paid	FQ	First quartile wage	LO	Lowest wage paid

LR	Low end range	MTC	Median total compensation	TCC	Total cash compensation
M	Monthly	MW	Median wage paid	TQ	Third quartile wage
MCC	Median cash compensation	MWR	Median wage range	W	Weekly
ME	Median entry wage	S	See annotated source	Y	Yearly

Occupation/Type/Industry	Location	Per	Low	Mid	High	Source	Date
Animal Trainer	Portland-Vancouver-Hillsboro						
	MSA, OR-WA	Y	21860 FQ	24210 MW	37690 TQ	USBLS	5/15
	Pennsylvania	Y	19670 FQ	23980 MW	35080 TQ	USBLS	5/15
	Allentown-Bethlehem-Easton						
	MSA, PA-NJ	Y	20490 FQ	22270 MW	24050 TQ	USBLS	5/15
	Harrisburg-Carlisle MSA, PA	Y	20610 FQ	24980 MW	42380 TQ	USBLS	5/15
	Montgomery County-Bucks						
	County-Chester County						
	PMSA, PA	Y	19230 FQ	24090 MW	43090 TQ	USBLS	5/15
	Pittsburgh MSA, PA	Y	22170 FQ	25440 MW	28120 TQ	USBLS	5/15
	South Carolina	Y	22030 FQ	28930 MW	37240 TQ	USBLS	5/15
	Columbia MSA, SC	Y	26300 FQ	37100 MW	45010 TQ	USBLS	5/15
	Greenville-Anderson-Mauldin						
	MSA, SC	Y	22150 FQ	26680 MW	37960 TQ	USBLS	5/15
	Tennessee	Y	19060 FQ	24000 MW	31560 TQ	USBLS	5/15
	Knoxville MSA, TN	Y	23620 FQ	28510 MW	34460 TQ	USBLS	5/15
	Memphis MSA, TN-MS-AR	Y	21360 FQ	25050 MW	29290 TQ	USBLS	5/15
	Nashville-Davidson–						
	Murfreesboro–Franklin						
	MSA, TN	Y	18870 FQ	22460 MW	33400 TQ	USBLS	5/15
	Texas	Y	20080 FQ	24470 MW	34940 TQ	USBLS	5/15
	Austin-Round Rock MSA, TX	Y	23310 FQ	30580 MW	55450 TQ	USBLS	5/15
	Dallas-Plano-Irving PMSA, TX	Y	19620 FQ	22180 MW	24720 TQ	USBLS	5/15
	Fort Worth-Arlington PMSA,						
	TX	Y	21430 FQ	30340 MW	37070 TQ	USBLS	5/15
	Houston-The Woodlands-						
	Sugar Land MSA, TX	Y	19090 FQ	25830 MW	35770 TQ	USBLS	5/15
	San Antonio-New Braunfels						
	MSA, TX	Y	18320 FQ	21710 MW	33790 TQ	USBLS	5/15
	Utah	Y	18520 FQ	22780 MW	30070 TQ	USBLS	5/15
	Salt Lake City MSA, UT	Y	23040 FQ	26700 MW	29500 TQ	USBLS	5/15
	Virginia	Y	20390 FQ	25190 MW	44030 TQ	USBLS	5/15
	Virginia Beach-Norfolk-						
	Newport News MSA, VA-NC	Y	20440 FQ	23010 MW	27860 TQ	USBLS	5/15
	Washington	H	11.53 FQ	14.15 MW	20.33 TQ	WABLS	3/16
	Seattle-Bellevue-Everett						
	PMSA, WA	H	11.77 FQ	14.26 MW	21.26 TQ	WABLS	3/16
	West Virginia	Y	22350 FQ	28440 MW	36540 TQ	USBLS	5/15
	Wisconsin	Y	25240 FQ	31220 MW	37660 TQ	USBLS	5/15
	Milwaukee-Waukesha-West						
	Allis MSA, WI	Y	32600 FQ	36680 MW	42050 TQ	USBLS	5/15
Animation Checker	United States	W		1547.10 MW		TAG01	2016
Anthropologist and Archeologist	Alabama	Y	31467 AE	46267 AW	53667 AEX	ALBLS	6/16
	Alaska	Y	62440 FQ	74830 MW	94430 TQ	USBLS	5/15
	Arizona	Y	50910 FQ	66000 MW	79560 TQ	USBLS	5/15
	California	H	22.81 FQ	30.32 MW	38.96 TQ	CABLS	1/16-3/16
	Colorado	Y	47910 FQ	60000 MW	75320 TQ	USBLS	5/15
	Connecticut	Y		54671 MW		CTBLS	1/16-3/16
	District of Columbia	Y	72240 FQ	90830 MW	115040 TQ	USBLS	5/15
	Florida	H	20.20 AE	26.13 MW	33.74 AEX	FLBLS	7/16-9/16
	Georgia	Y	45730 FQ	58700 MW	81720 TQ	USBLS	5/15
	Hawaii	Y	44870 FQ	61710 MW	85180 TQ	USBLS	5/15
	Idaho	Y	51380 FQ	68330 MW	80540 TQ	USBLS	5/15
	Illinois	Y	43150 FQ	58320 MW	83520 TQ	USBLS	5/15
	Indiana	Y	36500 FQ	44400 MW	55530 TQ	USBLS	5/15
	Iowa	Y	50020 FQ	59710 MW	70430 TQ	USBLS	5/15
	Kentucky	Y	46450 FQ	58690 MW	83460 TQ	USBLS	5/15
	Louisiana	Y	33440 FQ	56510 MW	72540 TQ	USBLS	5/15
	Massachusetts	Y	67260 FQ	86980 MW	95070 TQ	USBLS	5/15
	Minnesota	Y	30080 FQ	64939 MW	89969 TQ	MNBLS	1/16-3/16
	Mississippi	Y	47990 FQ	58550 MW	64420 TQ	USBLS	5/15
	Missouri	Y	28550 FQ	43140 MW	64420 TQ	USBLS	5/15
	Montana	Y	37880 FQ	58550 MW	66370 TQ	USBLS	5/15
	Nebraska	Y	62475 FQ	72595 MW	83465 TQ	NEBLS	7/16-9/16
	Nevada	Y	46300 FQ	54870 MW	74980 TQ	USBLS	5/15
	New Jersey	Y	41960 FQ	56400 MW	77710 TQ	USBLS	5/15
	New Mexico	Y	42990 FQ	54730 MW	69590 TQ	USBLS	5/15
	New York	Y	52430 AE	80190 MW	99450 AEX	NYBLS	1/16-3/16
	North Carolina	Y	43500 FQ	50390 MW	63450 TQ	USBLS	5/15
	North Dakota	Y	29300 FQ	35250 MW	48400 TQ	USBLS	5/15

AE	Average entry wage	AWR	Average wage range	H	Hourly	LR	Low end range	MTC	Median total compensation	TCC	Total cash compensation
AEX	Average experienced wage	B	Biweekly	HI	Highest wage paid	M	Monthly	MW	Median wage paid	TQ	Third quartile wage
ATC	Average total compensation	D	Daily	HR	High end range	MCC	Median cash compensation	MWR	Median wage range	W	Weekly
AW	Average wage paid	FQ	First quartile wage	LO	Lowest wage paid	ME	Median entry wage	S	See annotated source	Y	Yearly

Occupation/Type/Industry	Location	Per	Low	Mid	High	Source	Date
Anthropologist and Archeologist	Ohio	Y	40800 FQ	54730 MW	76770 TQ	USBLS	5/15
	Oregon	H	24.91 FQ	33.65 MW	42.28 TQ	ORBLS	2016
	Pennsylvania	Y	55100 FQ	82320 MW	91870 TQ	USBLS	5/15
	Tennessee	Y	43860 FQ	53250 MW	75140 TQ	USBLS	5/15
	Texas	Y	39400 FQ	59220 MW	85850 TQ	USBLS	5/15
	Utah	Y	57580 FQ	66320 MW	74850 TQ	USBLS	5/15
	Virginia	Y	41600 FQ	66550 MW	79560 TQ	USBLS	5/15
	Washington	H	26.46 FQ	32.54 MW	39.98 TQ	WABLS	3/16
	West Virginia	Y	33140 FQ	36050 MW	38970 TQ	USBLS	5/15
	Wisconsin	Y	54360 FQ	68240 MW	79400 TQ	USBLS	5/15
	Wyoming	Y	52780 FQ	64440 MW	76130 TQ	USBLS	5/15

Anthropology and Archeology Teacher

Occupation/Type/Industry	Location	Per	Low	Mid	High	Source	Date
Postsecondary	Alabama	Y	48948 AE	90363 AW	111066 AEX	ALBLS	6/16
Postsecondary	Arizona	Y	55700 FQ	73040 MW	112570 TQ	USBLS	5/15
Postsecondary	Phoenix-Mesa-Scottsdale MSA, AZ	Y	56410 FQ	64360 MW	137360 TQ	USBLS	5/15
Postsecondary	Arkansas	Y	56190 FQ	73380 MW	96360 TQ	USBLS	5/15
Postsecondary	California	Y		99512 AW		CABLS	1/16-3/16
Postsecondary	Anaheim-Santa Ana-Irvine PMSA, CA	Y		98974 AW		CABLS	1/16-3/16
Postsecondary	Los Angeles-Long Beach-Glendale PMSA, CA	Y		111736 AW		CABLS	1/16-3/16
Postsecondary	Riverside-San Bernardino-Ontario MSA, CA	Y		115033 AW		CABLS	1/16-3/16
Postsecondary	Sacramento–Roseville–Arden-Arcade MSA, CA	Y		87287 AW		CABLS	1/16-3/16
Postsecondary	San Diego-Carlsbad MSA, CA	Y		99532 AW		CABLS	1/16-3/16
Postsecondary	Colorado	Y	37320 FQ	59950 MW	81000 TQ	USBLS	5/15
Postsecondary	Denver-Aurora-Lakewood MSA, CO	Y	36080 FQ	52680 MW	75480 TQ	USBLS	5/15
Postsecondary	Connecticut	Y		78014 MW		CTBLS	1/16-3/16
Postsecondary	Hartford-West Hartford-East Hartford MSA, CT	Y	63050 FQ	78530 MW	98550 TQ	USBLS	5/15
Postsecondary	District of Columbia	Y	58500 FQ	82660 MW	105750 TQ	USBLS	5/15
Postsecondary	Washington-Arlington-Alexandria PMSA, DC-VA-MD-WV	Y	54730 FQ	75920 MW	100440 TQ	USBLS	5/15
Postsecondary	Florida	Y	66599 AE	94645 MW	112393 AEX	FLBLS	7/16-9/16
Postsecondary	Tampa-St. Petersburg-Clearwater MSA, FL	Y	77548 AE	103850 MW	118542 AEX	FLBLS	7/16-9/16
Postsecondary	Georgia	Y	55660 FQ	63440 MW	78560 TQ	USBLS	5/15
Postsecondary	Hawaii	Y	48250 FQ	76080 MW	96960 TQ	USBLS	5/15
Postsecondary	Urban Honolulu MSA, HI	Y	46460 FQ	78000 MW	101540 TQ	USBLS	5/15
Postsecondary	Idaho	Y	43110 FQ	59060 MW	78360 TQ	USBLS	5/15
Postsecondary	Illinois	Y	52690 FQ	67700 MW	92980 TQ	USBLS	5/15
Postsecondary	Chicago-Naperville-Arlington Heights PMSA, IL	Y	53410 FQ	64960 MW	89620 TQ	USBLS	5/15
Postsecondary	Indiana	Y	56010 FQ	67940 MW	83000 TQ	USBLS	5/15
Postsecondary	Iowa	Y	63570 FQ	73320 MW	89850 TQ	USBLS	5/15
Postsecondary	Kentucky	Y	55660 FQ	69720 MW	91350 TQ	USBLS	5/15
Postsecondary	Louisiana	Y	54060 FQ	63030 MW	90260 TQ	USBLS	5/15
Postsecondary	Massachusetts	Y	81900 FQ	102980 MW	141260 TQ	USBLS	5/15
Postsecondary	Boston-Cambridge-Newton NECTA, MA	Y	90050 FQ	116300 MW	151530 TQ	USBLS	5/15
Postsecondary	Michigan	Y	65950 FQ	92140 MW	127290 TQ	USBLS	5/15
Postsecondary	Minnesota	Y	52550 FQ	72146 MW	96440 TQ	MNBLS	1/16-3/16
Postsecondary	Minneapolis-St. Paul-Bloomington MSA, MN-WI	Y	51774 FQ	69747 MW	97186 TQ	MNBLS	1/16-3/16
Postsecondary	Missouri	Y	50290 FQ	62060 MW	83960 TQ	USBLS	5/15
Postsecondary	St. Louis MSA, MO-IL	Y	41600 FQ	60230 MW	87450 TQ	USBLS	5/15
Postsecondary	New Jersey	Y	69920 FQ	92170 MW	122030 TQ	USBLS	5/15
Postsecondary	Newark PMSA, NJ-PA	Y	79660 FQ	100390 MW	139800 TQ	USBLS	5/15
Postsecondary	New Mexico	Y	62690 FQ	80210 MW	95920 TQ	USBLS	5/15
Postsecondary	New York	Y	50580 AE	86900 MW	119020 AEX	NYBLS	1/16-3/16
Postsecondary	Buffalo-Cheektowaga-Niagara Falls MSA, NY	Y	56400 FQ	79690 MW	105290 TQ	USBLS	5/15
Postsecondary	Nassau County-Suffolk County PMSA, NY	Y	53220 FQ	62560 MW	101600 TQ	USBLS	5/15
Postsecondary	New York-Jersey City-White Plains PMSA, NY-NJ	Y	62700 FQ	96730 MW	136760 TQ	USBLS	5/15

AE	Average entry wage	**AWR**	Average wage range	**H**	Hourly
AEX	Average experienced wage	**B**	Biweekly	**HI**	Highest wage paid
ATC	Average total compensation	**D**	Daily	**HR**	High end range
AW	Average wage paid	**FQ**	First quartile wage	**LO**	Lowest wage paid

LR	Low end range	**MTC**	Median total compensation	**TCC**	Total cash compensation
M	Monthly	**MW**	Median wage paid	**TQ**	Third quartile wage
MCC	Median cash compensation	**MWR**	Median wage range	**W**	Weekly
ME	Median entry wage	**S**	See annotated source	**Y**	Yearly

Occupation/Type/Industry	Location	Per	Low	Mid	High	Source	Date
Anthropology and Archeology Teacher							
Postsecondary	North Carolina	Y	54050 FQ	75240 MW	102550 TQ	USBLS	5/15
Postsecondary	Ohio	Y	59120 FQ	83600 MW	107950 TQ	USBLS	5/15
Postsecondary	Columbus MSA, OH	Y	53760 FQ	86470 MW	110980 TQ	USBLS	5/15
Postsecondary	Oregon	Y	70791 FQ	87012 MW	104020 TQ	ORBLS	2016
Postsecondary	Portland-Vancouver-Hillsboro MSA, OR-WA	Y	69210 FQ	78630 MW	93000 TQ	USBLS	5/15
Postsecondary	Pennsylvania	Y	62750 FQ	82600 MW	112450 TQ	USBLS	5/15
Postsecondary	Philadelphia PMSA, PA	Y	70560 FQ	92050 MW	132500 TQ	USBLS	5/15
Postsecondary	Pittsburgh MSA, PA	Y	60850 FQ	78490 MW	132150 TQ	USBLS	5/15
Postsecondary	Tennessee	Y	56180 FQ	70360 MW	89230 TQ	USBLS	5/15
Postsecondary	Memphis MSA, TN-MS-AR	Y	55900 FQ	67900 MW	78640 TQ	USBLS	5/15
Postsecondary	Texas	Y	55310 FQ	77460 MW	99430 TQ	USBLS	5/15
Postsecondary	Austin-Round Rock MSA, TX	Y	63820 FQ	77590 MW	95580 TQ	USBLS	5/15
Postsecondary	Houston-The Woodlands-Sugar Land MSA, TX	Y	51390 FQ	79050 MW	116660 TQ	USBLS	5/15
Postsecondary	San Antonio-New Braunfels MSA, TX	Y	24820 FQ	57350 MW	75960 TQ	USBLS	5/15
Postsecondary	Utah	Y	56760 FQ	73330 MW	90650 TQ	USBLS	5/15
Postsecondary	Virginia	Y	51860 FQ	64940 MW	89490 TQ	USBLS	5/15
Postsecondary	Washington	Y		70933 AW		WABLS	3/16
Postsecondary	Seattle-Bellevue-Everett PMSA, WA	Y		79912 AW		WABLS	3/16
Postsecondary	Tacoma-Lakewood PMSA, WA	Y		80967 AW		WABLS	3/16
Postsecondary	Wisconsin	Y	52440 FQ	62710 MW	79880 TQ	USBLS	5/15
Postsecondary	Milwaukee-Waukesha-West Allis MSA, WI	Y	56230 FQ	72250 MW	92230 TQ	USBLS	5/15
Antiterrorism Program Coordinator							
Department of Military Affairs, State Government	Fort Harrison, MT	H			27.30 HI	MTGOV	2016
Application Development Manager	United States	Y		120303 AW		CWRLD2	2016
Applicator							
Entry-Level, Full-Time	United States	Y		35945 AW		AGPRO	2016
Appraisal Technician							
County Government	Houston County, GA	H	14.71 LO		23.54 HI	GACTY04	2016
County Government	Lanier County, GA	H	8.00 LO		13.00 HI	GACTY04	2016
County Government	Murray County, GA	H	11.22 LO		17.94 HI	GACTY04	2016
Appraiser							
Personal Property, County Government	Barrow County, GA	Y	36568 LO		56680 HI	GACTY04	2016
Personal Property, County Government	Fayette County, GA	Y	36749 LO		71580 HI	GACTY04	2016
Personal Property, County Government	Peach County, GA	Y	28013 LO		42041 HI	GACTY04	2016
Appraiser and Assessor of Real Estate	Alabama	Y	31118 AE	54630 AW	66387 AEX	ALBLS	6/16
	Birmingham-Hoover MSA, AL	Y	33393 AE	54118 AW	64480 AEX	ALBLS	6/16
	Alaska	Y	55770 FQ	75120 MW	92250 TQ	USBLS	5/15
	Anchorage MSA, AK	Y	66750 FQ	83670 MW	97400 TQ	USBLS	5/15
	Arizona	Y	34390 FQ	47660 MW	72000 TQ	USBLS	5/15
	Phoenix-Mesa-Scottsdale MSA, AZ	Y	36190 FQ	50690 MW	73220 TQ	USBLS	5/15
	Tucson MSA, AZ	Y	38890 FQ	47630 MW	103800 TQ	USBLS	5/15
	Arkansas	Y	27550 FQ	35800 MW	51740 TQ	USBLS	5/15
	Little Rock-North Little Rock-Conway MSA, AR	Y	34700 FQ	52090 MW	60340 TQ	USBLS	5/15
	California	H	28.61 FQ	37.59 MW	45.60 TQ	CABLS	1/16-3/16
	Anaheim-Santa Ana-Irvine PMSA, CA	H	28.09 FQ	35.23 MW	44.31 TQ	CABLS	1/16-3/16
	Los Angeles-Long Beach-Glendale PMSA, CA	H	32.62 FQ	41.48 MW	47.02 TQ	CABLS	1/16-3/16
	Oakland-Hayward-Berkeley PMSA, CA	H	34.02 FQ	40.31 MW	47.49 TQ	CABLS	1/16-3/16
	Riverside-San Bernardino-Ontario MSA, CA	H	22.88 FQ	29.71 MW	38.49 TQ	CABLS	1/16-3/16

Occupation/Type/Industry	Location	Per	Low	Mid	High	Source	Date
Appraiser and Assessor of Real Estate							
	Sacramento–Roseville–Arden-Arcade MSA, CA	H	32.47 FQ	37.04 MW	42.36 TQ	CABLS	1/16-3/16
	San Diego-Carlsbad MSA, CA	H	29.48 FQ	35.70 MW	42.79 TQ	CABLS	1/16-3/16
	San Francisco-Redwood City-South San Francisco PMSA, CA	H	30.70 FQ	44.81 MW	56.67 TQ	CABLS	1/16-3/16
	Colorado	Y	38540 FQ	55530 MW	85630 TQ	USBLS	5/15
	Denver-Aurora-Lakewood MSA, CO	Y	35760 FQ	60300 MW	87910 TQ	USBLS	5/15
	Connecticut	Y		71225 MW		CTBLS	1/16-3/16
	Hartford-West Hartford-East Hartford MSA, CT	Y	61150 FQ	79360 MW	94790 TQ	USBLS	5/15
	Delaware	Y	46120 FQ	55030 MW	73760 TQ	USBLS	5/15
	Wilmington PMSA, DE-MD-NJ	Y	52490 FQ	61140 MW	86010 TQ	USBLS	5/15
	District of Columbia	Y	78240 FQ	92880 MW	107780 TQ	USBLS	5/15
	Washington-Arlington-Alexandria PMSA, DC-VA-MD-WV	Y	61070 FQ	83310 MW	96480 TQ	USBLS	5/15
	Florida	H	13.01 AE	21.87 MW	30.78 AEX	FLBLS	7/16-9/16
	Fort Lauderdale-Pompano Beach-Deerfield Beach PMSA, FL	H	21.00 AE	29.57 MW	47.87 AEX	FLBLS	7/16-9/16
	Miami-Miami Beach-Kendall PMSA, FL	H	10.86 AE	21.06 MW	28.11 AEX	FLBLS	7/16-9/16
	Orlando-Kissimmee-Sanford MSA, FL	H	11.14 AE	15.63 MW	27.39 AEX	FLBLS	7/16-9/16
	Tampa-St. Petersburg-Clearwater MSA, FL	H	15.80 AE	26.19 MW	34.37 AEX	FLBLS	7/16-9/16
	Georgia	Y	29390 FQ	41000 MW	59790 TQ	USBLS	5/15
	Atlanta-Sandy Springs-Roswell MSA, GA	Y	31510 FQ	48510 MW	63380 TQ	USBLS	5/15
	Augusta-Richmond County MSA, GA-SC	Y	32260 FQ	40690 MW	63850 TQ	USBLS	5/15
	Hawaii	Y	44800 FQ	53400 MW	66240 TQ	USBLS	5/15
	Urban Honolulu MSA, HI	Y	45540 FQ	56220 MW	71750 TQ	USBLS	5/15
	Idaho	Y	34040 FQ	42230 MW	56610 TQ	USBLS	5/15
	Boise City MSA, ID	Y	35800 FQ	49370 MW	92540 TQ	USBLS	5/15
	Illinois	Y	35290 FQ	55740 MW	76300 TQ	USBLS	5/15
	Chicago-Naperville-Arlington Heights PMSA, IL	Y	34800 FQ	60030 MW	76460 TQ	USBLS	5/15
	Lake County-Kenosha County PMSA, IL-WI	Y	41150 FQ	50390 MW	68270 TQ	USBLS	5/15
	Indiana	Y	29130 FQ	36480 MW	50250 TQ	USBLS	5/15
	Indianapolis-Carmel-Anderson MSA, IN	Y	33410 FQ	38730 MW	55520 TQ	USBLS	5/15
	Iowa	Y	41280 FQ	49560 MW	66940 TQ	USBLS	5/15
	Des Moines-West Des Moines MSA, IA	Y	41390 FQ	48480 MW	71440 TQ	USBLS	5/15
	Kansas	Y	31730 FQ	38910 MW	53490 TQ	USBLS	5/15
	Wichita MSA, KS	Y	24760 FQ	35140 MW	39370 TQ	USBLS	5/15
	Kentucky	Y	31860 FQ	53240 MW	73360 TQ	USBLS	5/15
	Louisville-Jefferson County MSA, KY-IN	Y	31720 FQ	66580 MW	86240 TQ	USBLS	5/15
	Louisiana	Y	33830 FQ	41800 MW	54610 TQ	USBLS	5/15
	Baton Rouge MSA, LA	Y	29630 FQ	38210 MW	50510 TQ	USBLS	5/15
	New Orleans-Metairie MSA, LA	Y	32200 FQ	40420 MW	56940 TQ	USBLS	5/15
	Maine	Y	36660 FQ	52860 MW	69390 TQ	USBLS	5/15
	Portland-South Portland MSA, ME	Y	41340 FQ	64110 MW	78640 TQ	USBLS	5/15
	Maryland	Y	29638 AE	60207 MW	75491 AEX	MDBLS	4/16
	Baltimore-Columbia-Towson MSA, MD	Y	33270 FQ	55300 MW	72790 TQ	USBLS	5/15
	Salisbury MSA, MD-DE	Y	40570 FQ	48200 MW	68220 TQ	USBLS	5/15
	Massachusetts	Y	43850 FQ	61350 MW	85320 TQ	USBLS	5/15
	Boston-Cambridge-Newton NECTA, MA	Y	56470 FQ	79580 MW	94260 TQ	USBLS	5/15
	Worcester MSA, MA-CT	Y	33530 FQ	42330 MW	57880 TQ	USBLS	5/15
	Michigan	Y	29560 FQ	47020 MW	61910 TQ	USBLS	5/15

AE	Average entry wage	AWR	Average wage range	H	Hourly
AEX	Average experienced wage	B	Biweekly	HI	Highest wage paid
ATC	Average total compensation	D	Daily	HR	High end range
AW	Average wage paid	FQ	First quartile wage	LO	Lowest wage paid

LR	Low end range	MTC	Median total compensation	TCC	Total cash compensation
M	Monthly	MW	Median wage paid	TQ	Third quartile wage
MCC	Median cash compensation	MWR	Median wage range	W	Weekly
ME	Median entry wage	S	See annotated source	Y	Yearly

Occupation/Type/Industry	Location	Per	Low	Mid	High	Source	Date
Appraiser and Assessor of Real Estate	Detroit-Dearborn-Livonia PMSA, MI	Y	43620 FQ	55490 MW	62680 TQ	USBLS	5/15
	Grand Rapids-Wyoming MSA, MI	Y	33830 FQ	47120 MW	62140 TQ	USBLS	5/15
	Minnesota	Y	46477 FQ	60783 MW	79652 TQ	MNBLS	1/16-3/16
	Minneapolis-St. Paul-Bloomington MSA, MN-WI	Y	48326 FQ	65092 MW	82762 TQ	MNBLS	1/16-3/16
	Mississippi	Y	28790 FQ	38140 MW	55380 TQ	USBLS	5/15
	Jackson MSA, MS	Y	27270 FQ	30630 MW	41530 TQ	USBLS	5/15
	Missouri	Y	34130 FQ	52220 MW	73740 TQ	USBLS	5/15
	Kansas City MSA, MO-KS	Y	30650 FQ	39880 MW	62480 TQ	USBLS	5/15
	St. Louis MSA, MO-IL	Y	52600 FQ	65040 MW	87820 TQ	USBLS	5/15
	Montana	Y	36120 FQ	43340 MW	54490 TQ	USBLS	5/15
	Nebraska	Y	30835 FQ	47410 MW	60550 TQ	NEBLS	7/16-9/16
	Omaha-Council Bluffs MSA, NE-IA	Y	29170 FQ	51215 MW	72615 TQ	NEBLS	7/16-9/16
	Nevada	Y	43080 FQ	49450 MW	63880 TQ	USBLS	5/15
	Las Vegas-Henderson-Paradise MSA, NV	Y	42050 FQ	47490 MW	58440 TQ	USBLS	5/15
	New Hampshire	H	20.54 AE	30.62 MW	38.71 AEX	NHBLS	6/16
	Manchester NECTA, NH	H	28.53 AE	41.43 MW	46.36 AEX	NHBLS	6/16
	New Jersey	Y	51830 FQ	63180 MW	84770 TQ	USBLS	5/15
	Camden PMSA, NJ	Y	43120 FQ	49500 MW	78550 TQ	USBLS	5/15
	Newark PMSA, NJ-PA	Y	57320 FQ	71830 MW	91620 TQ	USBLS	5/15
	Trenton MSA, NJ	Y	67130 FQ	75920 MW	90700 TQ	USBLS	5/15
	New Mexico	Y	29800 FQ	42070 MW	58830 TQ	USBLS	5/15
	Albuquerque MSA, NM	Y	31760 FQ	51240 MW	61410 TQ	USBLS	5/15
	New York	Y	35770 AE	51580 MW	75060 AEX	NYBLS	1/16-3/16
	Buffalo-Cheektowaga-Niagara Falls MSA, NY	Y	43420 FQ	58540 MW	75860 TQ	USBLS	5/15
	Nassau County-Suffolk County PMSA, NY	Y	46360 FQ	58580 MW	76900 TQ	USBLS	5/15
	New York-Jersey City-White Plains PMSA, NY-NJ	Y	38000 FQ	56640 MW	78410 TQ	USBLS	5/15
	Rochester MSA, NY	Y	40050 FQ	48210 MW	62680 TQ	USBLS	5/15
	North Carolina	Y	40830 FQ	50220 MW	76490 TQ	USBLS	5/15
	Charlotte-Concord-Gastonia MSA, NC-SC	Y	44450 FQ	65160 MW	103160 TQ	USBLS	5/15
	Raleigh MSA, NC	Y	55620 FQ	66330 MW	88970 TQ	USBLS	5/15
	North Dakota	Y	32740 FQ	46210 MW	59620 TQ	USBLS	5/15
	Fargo MSA, ND-MN	Y	38340 FQ	53350 MW	67230 TQ	USBLS	5/15
	Ohio	Y	34480 FQ	47750 MW	65760 TQ	USBLS	5/15
	Cleveland-Elyria MSA, OH	Y	49680 FQ	62400 MW	77370 TQ	USBLS	5/15
	Columbus MSA, OH	Y	34690 FQ	45090 MW	62760 TQ	USBLS	5/15
	Oklahoma	Y	30190 FQ	38670 MW	62600 TQ	USBLS	5/15
	Oklahoma City MSA, OK	Y	65520 FQ	74590 MW	89470 TQ	USBLS	5/15
	Tulsa MSA, OK	Y	29440 FQ	37170 MW	49080 TQ	USBLS	5/15
	Oregon	H	23.80 FQ	29.76 MW	35.43 TQ	ORBLS	2016
	Portland-Vancouver-Hillsboro MSA, OR-WA	Y	56870 FQ	66040 MW	77380 TQ	USBLS	5/15
	Pennsylvania	Y	37720 FQ	49950 MW	68260 TQ	USBLS	5/15
	Allentown-Bethlehem-Easton MSA, PA-NJ	Y	42730 FQ	47740 MW	61150 TQ	USBLS	5/15
	Harrisburg-Carlisle MSA, PA	Y	48480 FQ	51400 MW	61060 TQ	USBLS	5/15
	Montgomery County-Bucks County-Chester County PMSA, PA	Y	58890 FQ	69950 MW	79570 TQ	USBLS	5/15
	Philadelphia PMSA, PA	Y	43650 FQ	52920 MW	71300 TQ	USBLS	5/15
	Pittsburgh MSA, PA	Y	31500 FQ	38950 MW	59330 TQ	USBLS	5/15
	Rhode Island	Y	39930 FQ	52530 MW	71110 TQ	USBLS	5/15
	Providence-Warwick MSA, RI-MA	Y	39230 FQ	52260 MW	71050 TQ	USBLS	5/15
	South Carolina	Y	28530 FQ	38520 MW	49720 TQ	USBLS	5/15
	Charleston-North Charleston MSA, SC	Y	32240 FQ	45220 MW	63530 TQ	USBLS	5/15
	Columbia MSA, SC	Y	30580 FQ	50900 MW	60300 TQ	USBLS	5/15
	Greenville-Anderson-Mauldin MSA, SC	Y	28620 FQ	35280 MW	45370 TQ	USBLS	5/15
	South Dakota	Y	36730 FQ	46470 MW	61150 TQ	USBLS	5/15
	Tennessee	Y	37360 FQ	47340 MW	57930 TQ	USBLS	5/15
	Knoxville MSA, TN	Y	37980 FQ	46480 MW	60410 TQ	USBLS	5/15

AE Average entry wage	AWR Average wage range	H Hourly	LR Low end range	MTC Median total compensation	TCC Total cash compensation
AEX Average experienced wage	B Biweekly	HI Highest wage paid	M Monthly	MW Median wage paid	TQ Third quartile wage
ATC Average total compensation	D Daily	HR High end range	MCC Median cash compensation	MWR Median wage range	W Weekly
AW Average wage paid	FQ First quartile wage	LO Lowest wage paid	ME Median entry wage	S See annotated source	Y Yearly

Occupation/Type/Industry	Location	Per	Low	Mid	High	Source	Date
Appraiser and Assessor of Real Estate	Memphis MSA, TN-MS-AR	Y	44130 FQ	51750 MW	62120 TQ	USBLS	5/15
	Nashville-Davidson–Murfreesboro–Franklin MSA, TN	Y	39320 FQ	46980 MW	55330 TQ	USBLS	5/15
	Texas	Y	41920 FQ	56200 MW	80210 TQ	USBLS	5/15
	Austin-Round Rock MSA, TX	Y	54710 FQ	71680 MW	105630 TQ	USBLS	5/15
	Dallas-Plano-Irving PMSA, TX	Y	46350 FQ	66930 MW	100810 TQ	USBLS	5/15
	Fort Worth-Arlington PMSA, TX	Y	36170 FQ	46100 MW	63870 TQ	USBLS	5/15
	Houston-The Woodlands-Sugar Land MSA, TX	Y	47470 FQ	63390 MW	79820 TQ	USBLS	5/15
	San Antonio-New Braunfels MSA, TX	Y	43550 FQ	55740 MW	79540 TQ	USBLS	5/15
	Utah	Y	34840 FQ	43600 MW	51850 TQ	USBLS	5/15
	Ogden-Clearfield MSA, UT	Y	36750 FQ	53050 MW	90760 TQ	USBLS	5/15
	Provo-Orem MSA, UT	Y	40510 FQ	45420 MW	50300 TQ	USBLS	5/15
	Salt Lake City MSA, UT	Y	24900 FQ	40550 MW	49890 TQ	USBLS	5/15
	Vermont	Y	35090 FQ	44830 MW	56030 TQ	USBLS	5/15
	Burlington-South Burlington MSA, VT	Y	38480 FQ	45120 MW	56610 TQ	USBLS	5/15
	Virginia	Y	38090 FQ	54880 MW	74420 TQ	USBLS	5/15
	Richmond MSA, VA	Y	33580 FQ	50370 MW	66680 TQ	USBLS	5/15
	Virginia Beach-Norfolk-Newport News MSA, VA-NC	Y	38230 FQ	51490 MW	62510 TQ	USBLS	5/15
	Washington	H	25.23 FQ	32.30 MW	37.68 TQ	WABLS	3/16
	Seattle-Bellevue-Everett PMSA, WA	H	30.47 FQ	35.07 MW	40.59 TQ	WABLS	3/16
	Tacoma-Lakewood PMSA, WA	H	32.66 FQ	34.77 MW	36.89 TQ	WABLS	3/16
	West Virginia	Y	31920 FQ	39130 MW	47060 TQ	USBLS	5/15
	Wisconsin	Y	47540 FQ	62000 MW	80590 TQ	USBLS	5/15
	Madison MSA, WI	Y	63080 FQ	71480 MW	78190 TQ	USBLS	5/15
	Milwaukee-Waukesha-West Allis MSA, WI	Y	55760 FQ	65410 MW	83430 TQ	USBLS	5/15
	Wyoming	Y	38530 FQ	51930 MW	61520 TQ	USBLS	5/15
	Cheyenne MSA, WY	Y	44490 FQ	50200 MW	61510 TQ	USBLS	5/15
	Puerto Rico	Y	20880 FQ	25480 MW	31200 TQ	USBLS	5/15
	San Juan-Carolina-Caguas MSA, PR	Y	21950 FQ	26170 MW	31410 TQ	USBLS	5/15
Apprentice Lineworker							
Municipal Government	Alameda, CA	Y			70969 HI	CACIT	6/28/16
Aquarist							
Municipal Government	Detroit, MI	M	2692 LO		3767 HI	DETGOV	2016
Aquatic Coordinator							
Municipal Government	Bellflower, CA	Y			14393 HI	CACIT	6/28/16
Aquatic Systems Technician							
State Government	North Carolina	Y	35474 LO		55460 HI	NCGOV	7/1/16
Aquatics Instructor							
Municipal Government	Alameda, CA	Y		5478 AW		CACIT	6/28/16
Municipal Government	Carlsbad, CA	H	12.25 LO		15.25 HI	CCCA02	1/1/16
Aquatics Specialist							
Municipal Government	Carlsbad, CA	H	23.92 LO	27.61 MW	31.30 HI	CCCA01	6/28/16
Arbitrator, Mediator, and Conciliator	Alabama	Y	40610 AE	64279 AW	76123 AEX	ALBLS	6/16
	Arizona	Y	30060 FQ	36350 MW	50470 TQ	USBLS	5/15
	Phoenix-Mesa-Scottsdale MSA, AZ	Y	30140 FQ	36370 MW	51540 TQ	USBLS	5/15
	Tucson MSA, AZ	Y	30040 FQ	36580 MW	50010 TQ	USBLS	5/15
	Arkansas	Y	36450 FQ	43780 MW	50330 TQ	USBLS	5/15
	California	H	24.72 FQ	33.73 MW	46.96 TQ	CABLS	1/16-3/16
	Anaheim-Santa Ana-Irvine PMSA, CA	H	22.33 FQ	27.31 MW	34.22 TQ	CABLS	1/16-3/16
	Los Angeles-Long Beach-Glendale PMSA, CA	H	22.88 FQ	27.89 MW	42.39 TQ	CABLS	1/16-3/16

Occupation/Type/Industry	Location	Per	Low	Mid	High	Source	Date
Arbitrator, Mediator, and Conciliator	Oakland-Hayward-Berkeley PMSA, CA	H	24.86 FQ	30.51 MW	64.00 TQ	CABLS	1/16-3/16
	Riverside-San Bernardino-Ontario MSA, CA	H	25.39 FQ	31.70 MW	38.64 TQ	CABLS	1/16-3/16
	Sacramento–Roseville–Arden-Arcade MSA, CA	H	33.96 FQ	42.29 MW	47.27 TQ	CABLS	1/16-3/16
	San Diego-Carlsbad MSA, CA	H	33.79 FQ	38.50 MW	52.27 TQ	CABLS	1/16-3/16
	San Francisco-Redwood City-South San Francisco PMSA, CA	H	36.06 FQ	51.17 MW	59.45 TQ	CABLS	1/16-3/16
	Colorado	Y	42140 FQ	46680 MW	58800 TQ	USBLS	5/15
	District of Columbia	Y	70080 FQ	89670 MW	118070 TQ	USBLS	5/15
	Florida	H	17.86 AE	25.64 MW	41.83 AEX	FLBLS	7/16-9/16
	Fort Lauderdale-Pompano Beach-Deerfield Beach PMSA, FL	H	13.76 AE	14.75 MW	19.92 AEX	FLBLS	7/16-9/16
	Miami-Miami Beach-Kendall PMSA, FL	H	21.88 AE	29.26 MW	36.39 AEX	FLBLS	7/16-9/16
	Orlando-Kissimmee-Sanford MSA, FL	H	26.34 AE	27.65 MW	29.03 AEX	FLBLS	7/16-9/16
	Tampa-St. Petersburg-Clearwater MSA, FL	H	19.17 AE	34.58 MW	40.40 AEX	FLBLS	7/16-9/16
	Georgia	Y	42850 FQ	54700 MW	71690 TQ	USBLS	5/15
	Atlanta-Sandy Springs-Roswell MSA, GA	Y	43460 FQ	55040 MW	72500 TQ	USBLS	5/15
	Hawaii	Y	68970 FQ	79310 MW	101250 TQ	USBLS	5/15
	Illinois	Y	49140 FQ	74170 MW	110320 TQ	USBLS	5/15
	Chicago-Naperville-Arlington Heights PMSA, IL	Y	54940 FQ	80770 MW	115500 TQ	USBLS	5/15
	Indiana	Y	42070 FQ	50440 MW	56120 TQ	USBLS	5/15
	Indianapolis-Carmel-Anderson MSA, IN	Y	42080 FQ	50430 MW	55060 TQ	USBLS	5/15
	Iowa	Y	38390 FQ	55660 MW	72630 TQ	USBLS	5/15
	Des Moines-West Des Moines MSA, IA	Y	36200 FQ	54080 MW	68040 TQ	USBLS	5/15
	Kansas	Y	43290 FQ	49730 MW	65790 TQ	USBLS	5/15
	Louisiana	Y	46620 FQ	53570 MW	59070 TQ	USBLS	5/15
	Maine	Y	44120 FQ	64380 MW	106440 TQ	USBLS	5/15
	Maryland	Y	41393 AE	55667 MW	62803 AEX	MDBLS	4/16
	Baltimore-Columbia-Towson MSA, MD	Y	42250 FQ	48690 MW	59580 TQ	USBLS	5/15
	Massachusetts	Y	40170 FQ	51380 MW	76350 TQ	USBLS	5/15
	Boston-Cambridge-Newton NECTA, MA	Y	41710 FQ	52910 MW	88000 TQ	USBLS	5/15
	Michigan	Y	47820 FQ	65170 MW	75010 TQ	USBLS	5/15
	Grand Rapids-Wyoming MSA, MI	Y	38540 FQ	52160 MW	61460 TQ	USBLS	5/15
	Minnesota	Y	58689 FQ	75160 MW	119051 TQ	MNBLS	1/16-3/16
	Minneapolis-St. Paul-Bloomington MSA, MN-WI	Y	58396 FQ	75039 MW	105351 TQ	MNBLS	1/16-3/16
	Missouri	Y	27650 FQ	35690 MW	62440 TQ	USBLS	5/15
	St. Louis MSA, MO-IL	Y	26660 FQ	31370 MW	57490 TQ	USBLS	5/15
	Montana	Y	23550 FQ	40300 MW	56500 TQ	USBLS	5/15
	Nebraska	Y	43750 FQ	55215 MW	91245 TQ	NEBLS	7/16-9/16
	New Jersey	Y	90170 FQ	103370 MW	125570 TQ	USBLS	5/15
	New York	Y	50160 AE	85810 MW	101150 AEX	NYBLS	1/16-3/16
	Nassau County-Suffolk County PMSA, NY	Y	53480 FQ	78240 MW	95320 TQ	USBLS	5/15
	New York-Jersey City-White Plains PMSA, NY-NJ	Y	73270 FQ	93520 MW	116590 TQ	USBLS	5/15
	North Carolina	Y	46330 FQ	58340 MW	73270 TQ	USBLS	5/15
	Charlotte-Concord-Gastonia MSA, NC-SC	Y	48960 FQ	59130 MW	86030 TQ	USBLS	5/15
	Ohio	Y	52010 FQ	68390 MW	88180 TQ	USBLS	5/15
	Cleveland-Elyria MSA, OH	Y	67030 FQ	77860 MW	91270 TQ	USBLS	5/15
	Oklahoma	Y	16720 FQ	17910 MW	19100 TQ	USBLS	5/15
	Oregon	H	23.72 FQ	32.90 MW	39.15 TQ	ORBLS	2016
	Portland-Vancouver-Hillsboro MSA, OR-WA	Y	57890 FQ	69280 MW	77140 TQ	USBLS	5/15
	Pennsylvania	Y	49560 FQ	61280 MW	80040 TQ	USBLS	5/15
	Harrisburg-Carlisle MSA, PA	Y	59160 FQ	71900 MW	81850 TQ	USBLS	5/15

AE	Average entry wage	AWR	Average wage range	H	Hourly	LR	Low end range	MTC	Median total compensation	TCC	Total cash compensation
AEX	Average experienced wage	B	Biweekly	HI	Highest wage paid	M	Monthly	MW	Median wage paid	TQ	Third quartile wage
ATC	Average total compensation	D	Daily	HR	High end range	MCC	Median cash compensation	MWR	Median wage range	W	Weekly
AW	Average wage paid	FQ	First quartile wage	LO	Lowest wage paid	ME	Median entry wage	S	See annotated source	Y	Yearly

Occupation/Type/Industry	Location	Per	Low	Mid	High	Source	Date
Arbitrator, Mediator, and Conciliator	Philadelphia PMSA, PA	Y	46060 FQ	61680 MW	88630 TQ	USBLS	5/15
	Pittsburgh MSA, PA	Y	52970 FQ	60090 MW	83840 TQ	USBLS	5/15
	South Carolina	Y	37840 FQ	46650 MW	57850 TQ	USBLS	5/15
	Tennessee	Y	33100 FQ	41450 MW	61500 TQ	USBLS	5/15
	Nashville-Davidson–Murfreesboro–Franklin MSA, TN	Y	35110 FQ	42800 MW	68730 TQ	USBLS	5/15
	Texas	Y	40850 FQ	50920 MW	72960 TQ	USBLS	5/15
	Austin-Round Rock MSA, TX	Y	42720 FQ	48830 MW	62260 TQ	USBLS	5/15
	Dallas-Plano-Irving PMSA, TX	Y	24990 FQ	45270 MW	85890 TQ	USBLS	5/15
	Houston-The Woodlands-Sugar Land MSA, TX	Y	59680 FQ	72560 MW	92630 TQ	USBLS	5/15
	Washington	H	17.95 FQ	35.27 MW	42.97 TQ	WABLS	3/16
	Seattle-Bellevue-Everett PMSA, WA	H	14.88 FQ	35.27 MW	45.62 TQ	WABLS	3/16
	West Virginia	Y	33770 FQ	36830 MW	41270 TQ	USBLS	5/15
	Wisconsin	Y	42250 FQ	54800 MW	78970 TQ	USBLS	5/15
	Madison MSA, WI	Y	42250 FQ	46640 MW	65210 TQ	USBLS	5/15
	Puerto Rico	Y	31770 FQ	36530 MW	43200 TQ	USBLS	5/15
	San Juan-Carolina-Caguas MSA, PR	Y	31770 FQ	36530 MW	43200 TQ	USBLS	5/15
Arborist							
Municipal Government	Atherton, CA	Y			89535 HI	CACIT	7/5/16
Municipal Government	Campbell, CA	Y			75994 HI	CACIT	6/28/16
Municipal Government	Los Gatos, CA	Y			78407 HI	CACIT	6/28/16
Municipal Government	Menlo Park, CA	Y			91221 HI	CACIT	6/28/16
Arborist Technician							
Municipal Government	Glendale, CA	Y			56400 HI	CACIT	6/28/16
Municipal Government	San Francisco, CA	Y		70955 AW		CACIT	6/28/16
Architect							
Except Landscape and Naval	Alabama	Y	52679 AE	82412 AW	97274 AEX	ALBLS	6/16
Except Landscape and Naval	Birmingham-Hoover MSA, AL	Y	52485 AE	88212 AW	106081 AEX	ALBLS	6/16
Except Landscape and Naval	Alaska	Y	59730 FQ	88090 MW	104210 TQ	USBLS	5/15
Except Landscape and Naval	Anchorage MSA, AK	Y	78710 FQ	93690 MW	110580 TQ	USBLS	5/15
Except Landscape and Naval	Arizona	Y	50340 FQ	78440 MW	97140 TQ	USBLS	5/15
Except Landscape and Naval	Phoenix-Mesa-Scottsdale MSA, AZ	Y	48290 FQ	80230 MW	98360 TQ	USBLS	5/15
Except Landscape and Naval	Tucson MSA, AZ	Y	58670 FQ	74210 MW	90670 TQ	USBLS	5/15
Except Landscape and Naval	Arkansas	Y	52350 FQ	64350 MW	81880 TQ	USBLS	5/15
Except Landscape and Naval	Little Rock-North Little Rock-Conway MSA, AR	Y	59640 FQ	72980 MW	85530 TQ	USBLS	5/15
Except Landscape and Naval	California	H	34.68 FQ	42.93 MW	53.91 TQ	CABLS	1/16-3/16
Except Landscape and Naval	Anaheim-Santa Ana-Irvine PMSA, CA	H	37.51 FQ	44.80 MW	54.07 TQ	CABLS	1/16-3/16
Except Landscape and Naval	Los Angeles-Long Beach-Glendale PMSA, CA	H	34.79 FQ	42.82 MW	55.79 TQ	CABLS	1/16-3/16
Except Landscape and Naval	Oakland-Hayward-Berkeley PMSA, CA	H	41.03 FQ	45.70 MW	50.59 TQ	CABLS	1/16-3/16
Except Landscape and Naval	Riverside-San Bernardino-Ontario MSA, CA	H	34.72 FQ	39.52 MW	45.90 TQ	CABLS	1/16-3/16
Except Landscape and Naval	Sacramento–Roseville–Arden-Arcade MSA, CA	H	34.96 FQ	42.87 MW	53.72 TQ	CABLS	1/16-3/16
Except Landscape and Naval	San Diego-Carlsbad MSA, CA	H	32.86 FQ	40.62 MW	53.31 TQ	CABLS	1/16-3/16
Except Landscape and Naval	San Francisco-Redwood City-South San Francisco PMSA, CA	H	34.38 FQ	42.42 MW	55.31 TQ	CABLS	1/16-3/16
Except Landscape and Naval	Colorado	Y	51200 FQ	66330 MW	90000 TQ	USBLS	5/15
Except Landscape and Naval	Denver-Aurora-Lakewood MSA, CO	Y	55510 FQ	75570 MW	93550 TQ	USBLS	5/15
Except Landscape and Naval	Connecticut	Y		82590 MW		CTBLS	1/16-3/16
Except Landscape and Naval	Bridgeport-Stamford-Norwalk MSA, CT	Y	60250 FQ	87250 MW	105690 TQ	USBLS	5/15
Except Landscape and Naval	Hartford-West Hartford-East Hartford MSA, CT	Y	76080 FQ	87150 MW	95930 TQ	USBLS	5/15
Except Landscape and Naval	Delaware	Y	68550 FQ	84660 MW	98800 TQ	USBLS	5/15
Except Landscape and Naval	Wilmington PMSA, DE-MD-NJ	Y	67220 FQ	82080 MW	94440 TQ	USBLS	5/15
Except Landscape and Naval	District of Columbia	Y	57850 FQ	73940 MW	96940 TQ	USBLS	5/15

AE	Average entry wage	AWR	Average wage range	H	Hourly	LR	Low end range	MTC	Median total compensation	TCC	Total cash compensation
AEX	Average experienced wage	B	Biweekly	HI	Highest wage paid	M	Monthly	MW	Median wage paid	TQ	Third quartile wage
ATC	Average total compensation	D	Daily	HR	High end range	MCC	Median cash compensation	MWR	Median wage range	W	Weekly
AW	Average wage paid	FQ	First quartile wage	LO	Lowest wage paid	ME	Median entry wage	S	See annotated source	Y	Yearly

Occupation/Type/Industry	Location	Per	Low	Mid	High	Source	Date
Architect							
Except Landscape and Naval	Washington-Arlington-Alexandria PMSA, DC-VA-MD-WV	Y	58600 FQ	76810 MW	103060 TQ	USBLS	5/15
Except Landscape and Naval	Florida	H	24.09 AE	35.12 MW	47.10 AEX	FLBLS	7/16-9/16
Except Landscape and Naval	Fort Lauderdale-Pompano Beach-Deerfield Beach PMSA, FL	H	21.26 AE	30.38 MW	39.08 AEX	FLBLS	7/16-9/16
Except Landscape and Naval	Miami-Miami Beach-Kendall PMSA, FL	H	29.02 AE	36.64 MW	46.03 AEX	FLBLS	7/16-9/16
Except Landscape and Naval	Orlando-Kissimmee-Sanford MSA, FL	H	23.64 AE	32.24 MW	41.32 AEX	FLBLS	7/16-9/16
Except Landscape and Naval	Tampa-St. Petersburg-Clearwater MSA, FL	H	26.53 AE	39.21 MW	48.65 AEX	FLBLS	7/16-9/16
Except Landscape and Naval	Georgia	Y	62810 FQ	82540 MW	115440 TQ	USBLS	5/15
Except Landscape and Naval	Atlanta-Sandy Springs-Roswell MSA, GA	Y	64830 FQ	84750 MW	125300 TQ	USBLS	5/15
Except Landscape and Naval	Augusta-Richmond County MSA, GA-SC	Y	55260 FQ	75880 MW	105820 TQ	USBLS	5/15
Except Landscape and Naval	Hawaii	Y	67160 FQ	82050 MW	95290 TQ	USBLS	5/15
Except Landscape and Naval	Urban Honolulu MSA, HI	Y	67240 FQ	82060 MW	95290 TQ	USBLS	5/15
Except Landscape and Naval	Idaho	Y	44710 FQ	58220 MW	75030 TQ	USBLS	5/15
Except Landscape and Naval	Boise City MSA, ID	Y	48300 FQ	58030 MW	71120 TQ	USBLS	5/15
Except Landscape and Naval	Illinois	Y	61060 FQ	74160 MW	92640 TQ	USBLS	5/15
Except Landscape and Naval	Chicago-Naperville-Arlington Heights PMSA, IL	Y	63270 FQ	75110 MW	93710 TQ	USBLS	5/15
Except Landscape and Naval	Lake County-Kenosha County PMSA, IL-WI	Y	54290 FQ	61500 MW	75150 TQ	USBLS	5/15
Except Landscape and Naval	Indiana	Y	49540 FQ	68690 MW	89620 TQ	USBLS	5/15
Except Landscape and Naval	Gary PMSA, IN	Y	53680 FQ	74400 MW	110250 TQ	USBLS	5/15
Except Landscape and Naval	Indianapolis-Carmel-Anderson MSA, IN	Y	50110 FQ	68980 MW	90360 TQ	USBLS	5/15
Except Landscape and Naval	Iowa	Y	52810 FQ	67110 MW	82000 TQ	USBLS	5/15
Except Landscape and Naval	Des Moines-West Des Moines MSA, IA	Y	56040 FQ	69160 MW	81630 TQ	USBLS	5/15
Except Landscape and Naval	Kansas	Y	48500 FQ	64300 MW	78270 TQ	USBLS	5/15
Except Landscape and Naval	Wichita MSA, KS	Y	52700 FQ	61660 MW	74520 TQ	USBLS	5/15
Except Landscape and Naval	Kentucky	Y	46400 FQ	57720 MW	79350 TQ	USBLS	5/15
Except Landscape and Naval	Louisville-Jefferson County MSA, KY-IN	Y	53830 FQ	61960 MW	81550 TQ	USBLS	5/15
Except Landscape and Naval	Louisiana	Y	48890 FQ	64560 MW	88280 TQ	USBLS	5/15
Except Landscape and Naval	Baton Rouge MSA, LA	Y	41110 FQ	56730 MW	95310 TQ	USBLS	5/15
Except Landscape and Naval	New Orleans-Metairie MSA, LA	Y	56340 FQ	71720 MW	91680 TQ	USBLS	5/15
Except Landscape and Naval	Maine	Y	58980 FQ	70690 MW	81470 TQ	USBLS	5/15
Except Landscape and Naval	Portland-South Portland MSA, ME	Y	62610 FQ	71800 MW	80790 TQ	USBLS	5/15
Except Landscape and Naval	Maryland	Y	54187 AE	83364 MW	97952 AEX	MDBLS	4/16
Except Landscape and Naval	Baltimore-Columbia-Towson MSA, MD	Y	63630 FQ	78550 MW	98710 TQ	USBLS	5/15
Except Landscape and Naval	Salisbury MSA, MD-DE	Y	62770 FQ	75910 MW	104040 TQ	USBLS	5/15
Except Landscape and Naval	Massachusetts	Y	67630 FQ	81860 MW	104660 TQ	USBLS	5/15
Except Landscape and Naval	Boston-Cambridge-Newton NECTA, MA	Y	69280 FQ	84200 MW	106980 TQ	USBLS	5/15
Except Landscape and Naval	Michigan	Y	58670 FQ	74000 MW	92350 TQ	USBLS	5/15
Except Landscape and Naval	Detroit-Dearborn-Livonia PMSA, MI	Y	55150 FQ	73540 MW	93140 TQ	USBLS	5/15
Except Landscape and Naval	Grand Rapids-Wyoming MSA, MI	Y	59540 FQ	79740 MW	97490 TQ	USBLS	5/15
Except Landscape and Naval	Minnesota	Y	65816 FQ	86057 MW	105755 TQ	MNBLS	1/16-3/16
Except Landscape and Naval	Minneapolis-St. Paul-Bloomington MSA, MN-WI	Y	66683 FQ	87479 MW	107408 TQ	MNBLS	1/16-3/16
Except Landscape and Naval	Mississippi	Y	47960 FQ	61900 MW	81230 TQ	USBLS	5/15
Except Landscape and Naval	Jackson MSA, MS	Y	47660 FQ	61260 MW	80640 TQ	USBLS	5/15
Except Landscape and Naval	Missouri	Y	54930 FQ	75040 MW	96530 TQ	USBLS	5/15
Except Landscape and Naval	Kansas City MSA, MO-KS	Y	50050 FQ	69640 MW	88030 TQ	USBLS	5/15
Except Landscape and Naval	St. Louis MSA, MO-IL	Y	56400 FQ	79640 MW	100320 TQ	USBLS	5/15
Except Landscape and Naval	Montana	Y	52160 FQ	66020 MW	79800 TQ	USBLS	5/15
Except Landscape and Naval	Billings MSA, MT	Y	47520 FQ	63530 MW	84130 TQ	USBLS	5/15
Except Landscape and Naval	Nebraska	Y	56070 FQ	70605 MW	92230 TQ	NEBLS	7/16-9/16
Except Landscape and Naval	Omaha-Council Bluffs MSA, NE-IA	Y	58070 FQ	72555 MW	94760 TQ	NEBLS	7/16-9/16

AE	Average entry wage	AWR	Average wage range	H	Hourly	LR	Low end range	MTC	Median total compensation	TCC	Total cash compensation
AEX	Average experienced wage	B	Biweekly	HI	Highest wage paid	M	Monthly	MW	Median wage paid	TQ	Third quartile wage
ATC	Average total compensation	D	Daily	HR	High end range	MCC	Median cash compensation	MWR	Median wage range	W	Weekly
AW	Average wage paid	FQ	First quartile wage	LO	Lowest wage paid	ME	Median entry wage	S	See annotated source	Y	Yearly

Architect

Occupation/Type/Industry	Location	Per	Low	Mid	High	Source	Date
Architect							
Except Landscape and Naval	Nevada	Y	62970 FQ	80400 MW	98480 TQ	USBLS	5/15
Except Landscape and Naval	Las Vegas-Henderson-Paradise MSA, NV	Y	65200 FQ	83930 MW	99580 TQ	USBLS	5/15
Except Landscape and Naval	Manchester NECTA, NH	H	27.35 AE	41.88 MW	51.30 AEX	NHBLS	6/16
Except Landscape and Naval	New Jersey	Y	64610 FQ	84860 MW	105340 TQ	USBLS	5/15
Except Landscape and Naval	Camden PMSA, NJ	Y	60190 FQ	78440 MW	130540 TQ	USBLS	5/15
Except Landscape and Naval	Newark PMSA, NJ-PA	Y	64680 FQ	81640 MW	96880 TQ	USBLS	5/15
Except Landscape and Naval	Trenton MSA, NJ	Y	54410 FQ	66970 MW	91200 TQ	USBLS	5/15
Except Landscape and Naval	New Mexico	Y	44780 FQ	60910 MW	90950 TQ	USBLS	5/15
Except Landscape and Naval	Albuquerque MSA, NM	Y	45210 FQ	59660 MW	88830 TQ	USBLS	5/15
Except Landscape and Naval	New York	Y	56420 AE	77800 MW	101210 AEX	NYBLS	1/16-3/16
Except Landscape and Naval	Buffalo-Cheektowaga-Niagara Falls MSA, NY	Y	58020 FQ	72260 MW	91820 TQ	USBLS	5/15
Except Landscape and Naval	Nassau County-Suffolk County PMSA, NY	Y	54370 FQ	71400 MW	97590 TQ	USBLS	5/15
Except Landscape and Naval	New York-Jersey City-White Plains PMSA, NY-NJ	Y	63310 FQ	77810 MW	101910 TQ	USBLS	5/15
Except Landscape and Naval	Rochester MSA, NY	Y	60290 FQ	74430 MW	91080 TQ	USBLS	5/15
Except Landscape and Naval	North Carolina	Y	64170 FQ	76730 MW	94970 TQ	USBLS	5/15
Except Landscape and Naval	Charlotte-Concord-Gastonia MSA, NC-SC	Y	67320 FQ	79980 MW	98670 TQ	USBLS	5/15
Except Landscape and Naval	Raleigh MSA, NC	Y	57590 FQ	70770 MW	88160 TQ	USBLS	5/15
Except Landscape and Naval	North Dakota	Y	52890 FQ	66230 MW	76230 TQ	USBLS	5/15
Except Landscape and Naval	Fargo MSA, ND-MN	Y	55000 FQ	68100 MW	78030 TQ	USBLS	5/15
Except Landscape and Naval	Ohio	Y	55820 FQ	74140 MW	96110 TQ	USBLS	5/15
Except Landscape and Naval	Cincinnati MSA, OH-KY-IN	Y	53980 FQ	78590 MW	106710 TQ	USBLS	5/15
Except Landscape and Naval	Cleveland-Elyria MSA, OH	Y	55020 FQ	69830 MW	90020 TQ	USBLS	5/15
Except Landscape and Naval	Oklahoma	Y	53130 FQ	67650 MW	86800 TQ	USBLS	5/15
Except Landscape and Naval	Oklahoma City MSA, OK	Y	53200 FQ	62770 MW	84890 TQ	USBLS	5/15
Except Landscape and Naval	Tulsa MSA, OK	Y	51750 FQ	71680 MW	87910 TQ	USBLS	5/15
Except Landscape and Naval	Oregon	H	25.42 FQ	32.19 MW	40.70 TQ	ORBLS	2016
Except Landscape and Naval	Portland-Vancouver-Hillsboro MSA, OR-WA	Y	52820 FQ	67410 MW	85180 TQ	USBLS	5/15
Except Landscape and Naval	Pennsylvania	Y	55800 FQ	75250 MW	100010 TQ	USBLS	5/15
Except Landscape and Naval	Allentown-Bethlehem-Easton MSA, PA-NJ	Y	72530 FQ	87320 MW	103070 TQ	USBLS	5/15
Except Landscape and Naval	Harrisburg-Carlisle MSA, PA	Y	39750 FQ	65780 MW	85680 TQ	USBLS	5/15
Except Landscape and Naval	Montgomery County-Bucks County-Chester County PMSA, PA	Y	71710 FQ	86330 MW	97650 TQ	USBLS	5/15
Except Landscape and Naval	Philadelphia PMSA, PA	Y	55700 FQ	74610 MW	106660 TQ	USBLS	5/15
Except Landscape and Naval	Pittsburgh MSA, PA	Y	52150 FQ	70220 MW	95480 TQ	USBLS	5/15
Except Landscape and Naval	Rhode Island	Y	61650 FQ	84780 MW	99410 TQ	USBLS	5/15
Except Landscape and Naval	Providence-Warwick MSA, RI-MA	Y	59060 FQ	81990 MW	98430 TQ	USBLS	5/15
Except Landscape and Naval	South Carolina	Y	47860 FQ	65570 MW	86710 TQ	USBLS	5/15
Except Landscape and Naval	Charleston-North Charleston MSA, SC	Y	49030 FQ	64430 MW	73980 TQ	USBLS	5/15
Except Landscape and Naval	Columbia MSA, SC	Y	44130 FQ	63740 MW	103110 TQ	USBLS	5/15
Except Landscape and Naval	Greenville-Anderson-Mauldin MSA, SC	Y	63350 FQ	75220 MW	99170 TQ	USBLS	5/15
Except Landscape and Naval	South Dakota	Y	65010 FQ	73050 MW	84810 TQ	USBLS	5/15
Except Landscape and Naval	Sioux Falls MSA, SD	Y	64210 FQ	72280 MW	84840 TQ	USBLS	5/15
Except Landscape and Naval	Tennessee	Y	48100 FQ	63410 MW	81370 TQ	USBLS	5/15
Except Landscape and Naval	Knoxville MSA, TN	Y	43910 FQ	61050 MW	78610 TQ	USBLS	5/15
Except Landscape and Naval	Memphis MSA, TN-MS-AR	Y	50670 FQ	60390 MW	76290 TQ	USBLS	5/15
Except Landscape and Naval	Nashville-Davidson–Murfreesboro–Franklin MSA, TN	Y	46320 FQ	66640 MW	87520 TQ	USBLS	5/15
Except Landscape and Naval	Texas	Y	54670 FQ	73780 MW	96960 TQ	USBLS	5/15
Except Landscape and Naval	Austin-Round Rock MSA, TX	Y	53790 FQ	71180 MW	90310 TQ	USBLS	5/15
Except Landscape and Naval	Dallas-Plano-Irving PMSA, TX	Y	59980 FQ	83070 MW	101000 TQ	USBLS	5/15
Except Landscape and Naval	Fort Worth-Arlington PMSA, TX	Y	51560 FQ	72830 MW	104360 TQ	USBLS	5/15
Except Landscape and Naval	Houston-The Woodlands-Sugar Land MSA, TX	Y	56370 FQ	75020 MW	102910 TQ	USBLS	5/15
Except Landscape and Naval	San Antonio-New Braunfels MSA, TX	Y	45260 FQ	63260 MW	89580 TQ	USBLS	5/15
Except Landscape and Naval	Utah	Y	56950 FQ	71150 MW	88890 TQ	USBLS	5/15
Except Landscape and Naval	Ogden-Clearfield MSA, UT	Y	29690 FQ	55440 MW	77480 TQ	USBLS	5/15
Except Landscape and Naval	Salt Lake City MSA, UT	Y	58560 FQ	72310 MW	88900 TQ	USBLS	5/15

AE	Average entry wage	AWR	Average wage range	H	Hourly
AEX	Average experienced wage	B	Biweekly	HI	Highest wage paid
ATC	Average total compensation	D	Daily	HR	High end range
AW	Average wage paid	FQ	First quartile wage	LO	Lowest wage paid
LR	Low end range	MTC	Median total compensation	TCC	Total cash compensation
M	Monthly	MW	Median wage paid	TQ	Third quartile wage
MCC	Median cash compensation	MWR	Median wage range	W	Weekly
ME	Median entry wage	S	See annotated source	Y	Yearly

Occupation/Type/Industry	Location	Per	Low	Mid	High	Source	Date
Architect							
Except Landscape and Naval	Vermont	Y	53270 FQ	64770 MW	75700 TQ	USBLS	5/15
Except Landscape and Naval	Burlington-South Burlington MSA, VT	Y	60650 FQ	69760 MW	77600 TQ	USBLS	5/15
Except Landscape and Naval	Virginia	Y	56750 FQ	77230 MW	103930 TQ	USBLS	5/15
Except Landscape and Naval	Richmond MSA, VA	Y	43120 FQ	71640 MW	98940 TQ	USBLS	5/15
Except Landscape and Naval	Virginia Beach-Norfolk-Newport News MSA, VA-NC	Y	57230 FQ	78160 MW	94310 TQ	USBLS	5/15
Except Landscape and Naval	Washington	H	26.91 FQ	34.88 MW	44.88 TQ	WABLS	3/16
Except Landscape and Naval	Seattle-Bellevue-Everett PMSA, WA	H	26.67 FQ	34.44 MW	45.06 TQ	WABLS	3/16
Except Landscape and Naval	Tacoma-Lakewood PMSA, WA	H	30.08 FQ	38.70 MW	47.60 TQ	WABLS	3/16
Except Landscape and Naval	West Virginia	Y	54590 FQ	68920 MW	80740 TQ	USBLS	5/15
Except Landscape and Naval	Wisconsin	Y	53150 FQ	67730 MW	87830 TQ	USBLS	5/15
Except Landscape and Naval	Madison MSA, WI	Y	53000 FQ	77970 MW	98370 TQ	USBLS	5/15
Except Landscape and Naval	Milwaukee-Waukesha-West Allis MSA, WI	Y	55190 FQ	67910 MW	82780 TQ	USBLS	5/15
Except Landscape and Naval	Wyoming	Y	57100 FQ	69160 MW	89000 TQ	USBLS	5/15
Except Landscape and Naval	Puerto Rico	Y	41240 FQ	51410 MW	75810 TQ	USBLS	5/15
Except Landscape and Naval	San Juan-Carolina-Caguas MSA, PR	Y	42930 FQ	53500 MW	78030 TQ	USBLS	5/15
Except Landscape and Naval	Guam	Y	51690 FQ	61290 MW	88610 TQ	USBLS	5/15
Architectural and Civil Drafter	Alabama	Y	35452 AE	50467 AW	57979 AEX	ALBLS	6/16
	Birmingham-Hoover MSA, AL	Y	36420 AE	50813 AW	58010 AEX	ALBLS	6/16
	Alaska	Y	50870 FQ	61650 MW	72900 TQ	USBLS	5/15
	Anchorage MSA, AK	Y	49900 FQ	62700 MW	73730 TQ	USBLS	5/15
	Arizona	Y	42900 FQ	53580 MW	61490 TQ	USBLS	5/15
	Phoenix-Mesa-Scottsdale MSA, AZ	Y	44920 FQ	55020 MW	62490 TQ	USBLS	5/15
	Tucson MSA, AZ	Y	37710 FQ	45170 MW	53480 TQ	USBLS	5/15
	Arkansas	Y	36070 FQ	44990 MW	55550 TQ	USBLS	5/15
	Little Rock-North Little Rock-Conway MSA, AR	Y	36790 FQ	45310 MW	56180 TQ	USBLS	5/15
	California	H	21.84 FQ	27.61 MW	34.06 TQ	CABLS	1/16-3/16
	Anaheim-Santa Ana-Irvine PMSA, CA	H	20.87 FQ	27.09 MW	33.82 TQ	CABLS	1/16-3/16
	Los Angeles-Long Beach-Glendale PMSA, CA	H	21.09 FQ	28.07 MW	35.49 TQ	CABLS	1/16-3/16
	Oakland-Hayward-Berkeley PMSA, CA	H	24.71 FQ	28.13 MW	32.72 TQ	CABLS	1/16-3/16
	Riverside-San Bernardino-Ontario MSA, CA	H	19.34 FQ	23.82 MW	31.74 TQ	CABLS	1/16-3/16
	Sacramento–Roseville–Arden-Arcade MSA, CA	H	25.01 FQ	28.51 MW	32.17 TQ	CABLS	1/16-3/16
	San Diego-Carlsbad MSA, CA	H	22.95 FQ	28.31 MW	35.03 TQ	CABLS	1/16-3/16
	San Francisco-Redwood City-South San Francisco PMSA, CA	H	26.31 FQ	30.96 MW	37.52 TQ	CABLS	1/16-3/16
	Colorado	Y	42720 FQ	53050 MW	66380 TQ	USBLS	5/15
	Denver-Aurora-Lakewood MSA, CO	Y	42420 FQ	54350 MW	69650 TQ	USBLS	5/15
	Connecticut	Y		57349 MW		CTBLS	1/16-3/16
	Bridgeport-Stamford-Norwalk MSA, CT	Y	52100 FQ	57390 MW	62730 TQ	USBLS	5/15
	Hartford-West Hartford-East Hartford MSA, CT	Y	46380 FQ	55170 MW	65140 TQ	USBLS	5/15
	Delaware	Y	42200 FQ	49530 MW	62630 TQ	USBLS	5/15
	Wilmington PMSA, DE-MD-NJ	Y	42880 FQ	51920 MW	66130 TQ	USBLS	5/15
	District of Columbia	Y	43860 FQ	48660 MW	60400 TQ	USBLS	5/15
	Washington-Arlington-Alexandria PMSA, DC-VA-MD-WV	Y	42670 FQ	48770 MW	65120 TQ	USBLS	5/15
	Florida	H	16.85 AE	23.33 MW	27.69 AEX	FLBLS	7/16-9/16
	Fort Lauderdale-Pompano Beach-Deerfield Beach PMSA, FL	H	16.04 AE	23.79 MW	26.49 AEX	FLBLS	7/16-9/16
	Miami-Miami Beach-Kendall PMSA, FL	H	18.00 AE	24.92 MW	29.76 AEX	FLBLS	7/16-9/16
	Orlando-Kissimmee-Sanford MSA, FL	H	16.79 AE	23.78 MW	28.46 AEX	FLBLS	7/16-9/16

AE Average entry wage	**AWR** Average wage range	**H** Hourly	**LR** Low end range	**MTC** Median total compensation	**TCC** Total cash compensation
AEX Average experienced wage	**B** Biweekly	**HI** Highest wage paid	**M** Monthly	**MCC** Median cash compensation	**TQ** Third quartile wage
ATC Average total compensation	**D** Daily	**HR** High end range	**MCC** Median cash compensation	**MWR** Median wage range	**W** Weekly
AW Average wage paid	**FQ** First quartile wage	**LO** Lowest wage paid	**ME** Median entry wage	**S** See annotated source	**Y** Yearly

Architectural and Civil Drafter

Occupation/Type/Industry	Location	Per	Low	Mid	High	Source	Date
Architectural and Civil Drafter	Tampa-St. Petersburg-Clearwater MSA, FL	H	15.74 AE	21.72 MW	25.44 AEX	FLBLS	7/16-9/16
	Georgia	Y	39350 FQ	47930 MW	62020 TQ	USBLS	5/15
	Atlanta-Sandy Springs-Roswell MSA, GA	Y	41390 FQ	49060 MW	64560 TQ	USBLS	5/15
	Augusta-Richmond County MSA, GA-SC	Y	37300 FQ	45160 MW	54810 TQ	USBLS	5/15
	Hawaii	Y	40780 FQ	49720 MW	58840 TQ	USBLS	5/15
	Urban Honolulu MSA, HI	Y	40760 FQ	49050 MW	57990 TQ	USBLS	5/15
	Idaho	Y	36510 FQ	44650 MW	55130 TQ	USBLS	5/15
	Boise City MSA, ID	Y	36430 FQ	45100 MW	57430 TQ	USBLS	5/15
	Illinois	Y	38410 FQ	47320 MW	61060 TQ	USBLS	5/15
	Chicago-Naperville-Arlington Heights PMSA, IL	Y	38670 FQ	46990 MW	60750 TQ	USBLS	5/15
	Lake County-Kenosha County PMSA, IL-WI	Y	39640 FQ	46390 MW	56320 TQ	USBLS	5/15
	Indiana	Y	36420 FQ	46430 MW	61390 TQ	USBLS	5/15
	Gary PMSA, IN	Y	34380 FQ	41220 MW	59940 TQ	USBLS	5/15
	Indianapolis-Carmel-Anderson MSA, IN	Y	41000 FQ	53540 MW	68470 TQ	USBLS	5/15
	Iowa	Y	40890 FQ	50640 MW	60830 TQ	USBLS	5/15
	Des Moines-West Des Moines MSA, IA	Y	38650 FQ	50460 MW	60130 TQ	USBLS	5/15
	Kansas	Y	35370 FQ	43470 MW	53240 TQ	USBLS	5/15
	Wichita MSA, KS	Y	35640 FQ	42930 MW	53880 TQ	USBLS	5/15
	Kentucky	Y	35790 FQ	45840 MW	58750 TQ	USBLS	5/15
	Louisville-Jefferson County MSA, KY-IN	Y	36240 FQ	44880 MW	59150 TQ	USBLS	5/15
	Louisiana	Y	40300 FQ	50680 MW	66050 TQ	USBLS	5/15
	Baton Rouge MSA, LA	Y	44190 FQ	55180 MW	74280 TQ	USBLS	5/15
	New Orleans-Metairie MSA, LA	Y	39820 FQ	52500 MW	63800 TQ	USBLS	5/15
	Maine	Y	30190 FQ	42630 MW	55770 TQ	USBLS	5/15
	Portland-South Portland MSA, ME	Y	41320 FQ	50700 MW	62830 TQ	USBLS	5/15
	Maryland	Y	39759 AE	56192 MW	64408 AEX	MDBLS	4/16
	Baltimore-Columbia-Towson MSA, MD	Y	41900 FQ	53890 MW	61270 TQ	USBLS	5/15
	Salisbury MSA, MD-DE	Y	36940 FQ	43590 MW	50080 TQ	USBLS	5/15
	Massachusetts	Y	44490 FQ	56580 MW	68890 TQ	USBLS	5/15
	Boston-Cambridge-Newton NECTA, MA	Y	45790 FQ	57500 MW	69430 TQ	USBLS	5/15
	Worcester MSA, MA-CT	Y	40060 FQ	47270 MW	59510 TQ	USBLS	5/15
	Michigan	Y	39010 FQ	46120 MW	55530 TQ	USBLS	5/15
	Detroit-Dearborn-Livonia PMSA, MI	Y	40180 FQ	46580 MW	54870 TQ	USBLS	5/15
	Grand Rapids-Wyoming MSA, MI	Y	37760 FQ	47630 MW	57740 TQ	USBLS	5/15
	Minnesota	Y	43538 FQ	52459 MW	62116 TQ	MNBLS	1/16-3/16
	Minneapolis-St. Paul-Bloomington MSA, MN-WI	Y	45211 FQ	54223 MW	63124 TQ	MNBLS	1/16-3/16
	Mississippi	Y	37150 FQ	46730 MW	58140 TQ	USBLS	5/15
	Jackson MSA, MS	Y	41810 FQ	51770 MW	62430 TQ	USBLS	5/15
	Missouri	Y	38600 FQ	46580 MW	58220 TQ	USBLS	5/15
	Kansas City MSA, MO-KS	Y	37960 FQ	47000 MW	58760 TQ	USBLS	5/15
	St. Louis MSA, MO-IL	Y	39920 FQ	46990 MW	58450 TQ	USBLS	5/15
	Montana	Y	37140 FQ	46150 MW	56440 TQ	USBLS	5/15
	Billings MSA, MT	Y	38560 FQ	50200 MW	59840 TQ	USBLS	5/15
	Nebraska	Y	37970 FQ	45465 MW	54120 TQ	NEBLS	7/16-9/16
	Lincoln MSA, NE	Y	42010 FQ	46830 MW	53060 TQ	USBLS	5/15
	Omaha-Council Bluffs MSA, NE-IA	Y	35870 FQ	44750 MW	54460 TQ	NEBLS	7/16-9/16
	Nevada	Y	37350 FQ	49280 MW	61590 TQ	USBLS	5/15
	Las Vegas-Henderson-Paradise MSA, NV	Y	37640 FQ	50070 MW	62860 TQ	USBLS	5/15
	New Hampshire	H	18.69 AE	25.61 MW	29.39 AEX	NHBLS	6/16
	Manchester NECTA, NH	H	18.17 AE	25.22 MW	27.74 AEX	NHBLS	6/16
	Nashua NECTA, NH-MA	Y	50860 FQ	56090 MW	61290 TQ	USBLS	5/15
	New Jersey	Y	42400 FQ	52920 MW	66840 TQ	USBLS	5/15
	Camden PMSA, NJ	Y	48470 FQ	64370 MW	71970 TQ	USBLS	5/15
	Newark PMSA, NJ-PA	Y	38910 FQ	48490 MW	61790 TQ	USBLS	5/15
	Trenton MSA, NJ	Y	45270 FQ	56790 MW	106130 TQ	USBLS	5/15

Occupation/Type/Industry	Location	Per	Low	Mid	High	Source	Date
Architectural and Civil Drafter	New Mexico	Y	39100 FQ	46730 MW	62660 TQ	USBLS	5/15
	Albuquerque MSA, NM	Y	39530 FQ	45590 MW	57940 TQ	USBLS	5/15
	New York	Y	38770 AE	55000 MW	64360 AEX	NYBLS	1/16-3/16
	Buffalo-Cheektowaga-Niagara Falls MSA, NY	Y	40090 FQ	46120 MW	58150 TQ	USBLS	5/15
	Nassau County-Suffolk County PMSA, NY	Y	41380 FQ	53870 MW	61930 TQ	USBLS	5/15
	New York-Jersey City-White Plains PMSA, NY-NJ	Y	44880 FQ	55440 MW	66840 TQ	USBLS	5/15
	Rochester MSA, NY	Y	44360 FQ	53390 MW	62300 TQ	USBLS	5/15
	North Carolina	Y	42010 FQ	51210 MW	60290 TQ	USBLS	5/15
	Charlotte-Concord-Gastonia MSA, NC-SC	Y	47040 FQ	55610 MW	66050 TQ	USBLS	5/15
	Raleigh MSA, NC	Y	41930 FQ	48800 MW	57550 TQ	USBLS	5/15
	North Dakota	Y	39900 FQ	46990 MW	56650 TQ	USBLS	5/15
	Fargo MSA, ND-MN	Y	38390 FQ	45610 MW	54390 TQ	USBLS	5/15
	Ohio	Y	39110 FQ	48320 MW	58260 TQ	USBLS	5/15
	Cincinnati MSA, OH-KY-IN	Y	41260 FQ	51670 MW	61840 TQ	USBLS	5/15
	Cleveland-Elyria MSA, OH	Y	36760 FQ	45540 MW	57930 TQ	USBLS	5/15
	Columbus MSA, OH	Y	39100 FQ	50430 MW	57930 TQ	USBLS	5/15
	Oklahoma	Y	40430 FQ	48830 MW	59050 TQ	USBLS	5/15
	Oklahoma City MSA, OK	Y	36620 FQ	44870 MW	54030 TQ	USBLS	5/15
	Tulsa MSA, OK	Y	44900 FQ	52540 MW	63510 TQ	USBLS	5/15
	Oregon	H	20.29 FQ	25.25 MW	30.17 TQ	ORBLS	2016
	Portland-Vancouver-Hillsboro MSA, OR-WA	Y	43040 FQ	53610 MW	63430 TQ	USBLS	5/15
	Pennsylvania	Y	40680 FQ	51280 MW	62040 TQ	USBLS	5/15
	Allentown-Bethlehem-Easton MSA, PA-NJ	Y	45080 FQ	54460 MW	62820 TQ	USBLS	5/15
	Harrisburg-Carlisle MSA, PA	Y	41490 FQ	56360 MW	73190 TQ	USBLS	5/15
	Montgomery County-Bucks County-Chester County PMSA, PA	Y	36600 FQ	50050 MW	63340 TQ	USBLS	5/15
	Philadelphia PMSA, PA	Y	44320 FQ	56930 MW	71740 TQ	USBLS	5/15
	Pittsburgh MSA, PA	Y	43680 FQ	52640 MW	60990 TQ	USBLS	5/15
	Rhode Island	Y	45290 FQ	55370 MW	63920 TQ	USBLS	5/15
	Providence-Warwick MSA, RI-MA	Y	44110 FQ	53940 MW	63660 TQ	USBLS	5/15
	South Carolina	Y	39270 FQ	45360 MW	55140 TQ	USBLS	5/15
	Charleston-North Charleston MSA, SC	Y	41900 FQ	45660 MW	49490 TQ	USBLS	5/15
	Columbia MSA, SC	Y	34770 FQ	43970 MW	57330 TQ	USBLS	5/15
	Greenville-Anderson-Mauldin MSA, SC	Y	38960 FQ	45310 MW	57100 TQ	USBLS	5/15
	South Dakota	Y	32950 FQ	37970 MW	44990 TQ	USBLS	5/15
	Sioux Falls MSA, SD	Y	35640 FQ	43030 MW	48520 TQ	USBLS	5/15
	Tennessee	Y	40850 FQ	48710 MW	62840 TQ	USBLS	5/15
	Knoxville MSA, TN	Y	41110 FQ	51700 MW	60790 TQ	USBLS	5/15
	Memphis MSA, TN-MS-AR	Y	36510 FQ	44500 MW	57080 TQ	USBLS	5/15
	Nashville-Davidson–Murfreesboro–Franklin MSA, TN	Y	42850 FQ	52900 MW	66570 TQ	USBLS	5/15
	Texas	Y	41350 FQ	51150 MW	64720 TQ	USBLS	5/15
	Austin-Round Rock MSA, TX	Y	38250 FQ	48190 MW	59590 TQ	USBLS	5/15
	Dallas-Plano-Irving PMSA, TX	Y	43170 FQ	52990 MW	64750 TQ	USBLS	5/15
	Fort Worth-Arlington PMSA, TX	Y	40390 FQ	46720 MW	57340 TQ	USBLS	5/15
	Houston-The Woodlands-Sugar Land MSA, TX	Y	44770 FQ	56050 MW	76280 TQ	USBLS	5/15
	San Antonio-New Braunfels MSA, TX	Y	39040 FQ	45280 MW	53340 TQ	USBLS	5/15
	Utah	Y	39750 FQ	47120 MW	57810 TQ	USBLS	5/15
	Ogden-Clearfield MSA, UT	Y	36050 FQ	43160 MW	48800 TQ	USBLS	5/15
	Provo-Orem MSA, UT	Y	40620 FQ	47740 MW	59250 TQ	USBLS	5/15
	Salt Lake City MSA, UT	Y	40780 FQ	48950 MW	59540 TQ	USBLS	5/15
	Vermont	Y	37130 FQ	46040 MW	54820 TQ	USBLS	5/15
	Burlington-South Burlington MSA, VT	Y	39370 FQ	49190 MW	57070 TQ	USBLS	5/15
	Virginia	Y	40190 FQ	47520 MW	63280 TQ	USBLS	5/15
	Richmond MSA, VA	Y	42930 FQ	55000 MW	69030 TQ	USBLS	5/15
	Virginia Beach-Norfolk-Newport News MSA, VA-NC	Y	41450 FQ	48170 MW	59620 TQ	USBLS	5/15

AE	Average entry wage	AWR	Average wage range	H	Hourly	LR	Low end range	MTC Median total compensation TCC Total cash compensation
AEX	Average experienced wage	B	Biweekly	HI	Highest wage paid	M	Monthly	MW Median wage paid TQ Third quartile wage
ATC	Average total compensation	D	Daily	HR	High end range	MCC	Median cash compensation	MWR Median wage range W Weekly
AW	Average wage paid	FQ	First quartile wage	LO	Lowest wage paid	ME	Median entry wage	S See annotated source Y Yearly

Occupation/Type/Industry	Location	Per	Low	Mid	High	Source	Date
Architectural and Civil Drafter	Washington	H	21.05 FQ	26.54 MW	31.45 TQ	WABLS	3/16
	Seattle-Bellevue-Everett PMSA, WA	H	22.77 FQ	27.82 MW	33.09 TQ	WABLS	3/16
	Tacoma-Lakewood PMSA, WA	H	21.85 FQ	26.92 MW	30.72 TQ	WABLS	3/16
	Wenatchee MSA, WA	Y	42330 FQ	47580 MW	55640 TQ	USBLS	5/15
	West Virginia	Y	30450 FQ	38460 MW	49680 TQ	USBLS	5/15
	Huntington-Ashland MSA, WV-KY-OH	Y	32760 FQ	38720 MW	48780 TQ	USBLS	5/15
	Wisconsin	Y	37510 FQ	45340 MW	54930 TQ	USBLS	5/15
	Madison MSA, WI	Y	36830 FQ	45250 MW	55720 TQ	USBLS	5/15
	Milwaukee-Waukesha-West Allis MSA, WI	Y	37660 FQ	47290 MW	58350 TQ	USBLS	5/15
	Wyoming	Y	34170 FQ	41920 MW	50820 TQ	USBLS	5/15
	Cheyenne MSA, WY	Y	43720 FQ	47270 MW	56000 TQ	USBLS	5/15
	Puerto Rico	Y	20360 FQ	27110 MW	33710 TQ	USBLS	5/15
	San Juan-Carolina-Caguas MSA, PR	Y	21540 FQ	27550 MW	34730 TQ	USBLS	5/15
	Guam	Y	29310 FQ	35010 MW	42470 TQ	USBLS	5/15
Architectural and Engineering Manager	Alabama	Y	99124 AE	140491 AW	161175 AEX	ALBLS	6/16
	Birmingham-Hoover MSA, AL	Y	99503 AE	143248 AW	165121 AEX	ALBLS	6/16
	Alaska	Y	116450 FQ	146910 MW		USBLS	5/15
	Anchorage MSA, AK	Y	120260 FQ	154070 MW		USBLS	5/15
	Arizona	Y	102730 FQ	131500 MW	158810 TQ	USBLS	5/15
	Phoenix-Mesa-Scottsdale MSA, AZ	Y	103330 FQ	131800 MW	159880 TQ	USBLS	5/15
	Tucson MSA, AZ	Y	106940 FQ	137580 MW	162630 TQ	USBLS	5/15
	Arkansas	Y	86180 FQ	113860 MW	137270 TQ	USBLS	5/15
	Little Rock-North Little Rock-Conway MSA, AR	Y	88840 FQ	116140 MW	143500 TQ	USBLS	5/15
	California	H	60.66 FQ	76.58 MW		CABLS	1/16-3/16
	Anaheim-Santa Ana-Irvine PMSA, CA	H	54.10 FQ	71.52 MW		CABLS	1/16-3/16
	Los Angeles-Long Beach-Glendale PMSA, CA	H	58.38 FQ	73.66 MW		CABLS	1/16-3/16
	Oakland-Hayward-Berkeley PMSA, CA	H	66.98 FQ	81.97 MW		CABLS	1/16-3/16
	Riverside-San Bernardino-Ontario MSA, CA	H	49.67 FQ	62.88 MW	75.05 TQ	CABLS	1/16-3/16
	Sacramento–Roseville–Arden-Arcade MSA, CA	H	59.79 FQ	66.99 MW	75.39 TQ	CABLS	1/16-3/16
	San Diego-Carlsbad MSA, CA	H	57.54 FQ	75.20 MW		CABLS	1/16-3/16
	San Francisco-Redwood City-South San Francisco PMSA, CA	H	58.20 FQ	78.55 MW		CABLS	1/16-3/16
	Colorado	Y	125530 FQ	149530 MW	184870 TQ	USBLS	5/15
	Denver-Aurora-Lakewood MSA, CO	Y	129110 FQ	151020 MW	186420 TQ	USBLS	5/15
	Connecticut	Y		140496 MW		CTBLS	1/16-3/16
	Bridgeport-Stamford-Norwalk MSA, CT	Y	108940 FQ	132780 MW	164760 TQ	USBLS	5/15
	Hartford-West Hartford-East Hartford MSA, CT	Y	113520 FQ	136080 MW	157230 TQ	USBLS	5/15
	Delaware	Y	116660 FQ	139090 MW	162510 TQ	USBLS	5/15
	Wilmington PMSA, DE-MD-NJ	Y	119520 FQ	140920 MW	164280 TQ	USBLS	5/15
	District of Columbia	Y	127480 FQ	139520 MW	158370 TQ	USBLS	5/15
	Washington-Arlington-Alexandria PMSA, DC-VA-MD-WV	Y	127850 FQ	144770 MW	166220 TQ	USBLS	5/15
	Florida	H	40.47 AE	59.51 MW	73.57 AEX	FLBLS	7/16-9/16
	Fort Lauderdale-Pompano Beach-Deerfield Beach PMSA, FL	H	35.33 AE	55.14 MW	64.79 AEX	FLBLS	7/16-9/16
	Miami-Miami Beach-Kendall PMSA, FL	H	38.48 AE	57.75 MW	78.02 AEX	FLBLS	7/16-9/16
	Orlando-Kissimmee-Sanford MSA, FL	H	39.61 AE	58.44 MW	72.21 AEX	FLBLS	7/16-9/16
	Tampa-St. Petersburg-Clearwater MSA, FL	H	41.53 AE	60.41 MW	77.31 AEX	FLBLS	7/16-9/16
	Georgia	Y	103440 FQ	128410 MW	154870 TQ	USBLS	5/15

Occupation/Type/Industry	Location	Per	Low	Mid	High	Source	Date
Architectural and Engineering Manager	Atlanta-Sandy Springs-Roswell MSA, GA	Y	105780 FQ	130540 MW	156630 TQ	USBLS	5/15
	Augusta-Richmond County MSA, GA-SC	Y	113140 FQ	132730 MW	164820 TQ	USBLS	5/15
	Hawaii	Y	80690 FQ	109240 MW	129280 TQ	USBLS	5/15
	Urban Honolulu MSA, HI	Y	80620 FQ	110720 MW	130860 TQ	USBLS	5/15
	Idaho	Y	101340 FQ	130780 MW	157830 TQ	USBLS	5/15
	Boise City MSA, ID	Y	107830 FQ	136990 MW	162120 TQ	USBLS	5/15
	Illinois	Y	101150 FQ	122940 MW	152610 TQ	USBLS	5/15
	Chicago-Naperville-Arlington Heights PMSA, IL	Y	102540 FQ	122570 MW	150940 TQ	USBLS	5/15
	Lake County-Kenosha County PMSA, IL-WI	Y	101900 FQ	134690 MW	162270 TQ	USBLS	5/15
	Indiana	Y	89640 FQ	112370 MW	140140 TQ	USBLS	5/15
	Gary PMSA, IN	Y	87740 FQ	104900 MW	124760 TQ	USBLS	5/15
	Indianapolis-Carmel-Anderson MSA, IN	Y	91490 FQ	117530 MW	149880 TQ	USBLS	5/15
	Iowa	Y	99580 FQ	115360 MW	133680 TQ	USBLS	5/15
	Des Moines-West Des Moines MSA, IA	Y	99310 FQ	113440 MW	128270 TQ	USBLS	5/15
	Kansas	Y	90420 FQ	110400 MW	137850 TQ	USBLS	5/15
	Wichita MSA, KS	Y	98750 FQ	125910 MW	148610 TQ	USBLS	5/15
	Kentucky	Y	84190 FQ	106310 MW	125440 TQ	USBLS	5/15
	Louisville-Jefferson County MSA, KY-IN	Y	95490 FQ	114700 MW	132300 TQ	USBLS	5/15
	Louisiana	Y	105470 FQ	131550 MW	158690 TQ	USBLS	5/15
	Baton Rouge MSA, LA	Y	121530 FQ	144920 MW	179720 TQ	USBLS	5/15
	New Orleans-Metairie MSA, LA	Y	111720 FQ	133410 MW	156470 TQ	USBLS	5/15
	Maine	Y	95520 FQ	119010 MW	144810 TQ	USBLS	5/15
	Portland-South Portland MSA, ME	Y	104450 FQ	127980 MW	150070 TQ	USBLS	5/15
	Maryland	Y	104897 AE	144073 MW	163662 AEX	MDBLS	4/16
	Baltimore-Columbia-Towson MSA, MD	Y	115250 FQ	138430 MW	162080 TQ	USBLS	5/15
	Salisbury MSA, MD-DE	Y	105680 FQ	128130 MW	155290 TQ	USBLS	5/15
	Massachusetts	Y	107260 FQ	134180 MW	165000 TQ	USBLS	5/15
	Boston-Cambridge-Newton NECTA, MA	Y	105710 FQ	131440 MW	162480 TQ	USBLS	5/15
	Worcester MSA, MA-CT	Y	97140 FQ	119020 MW	149060 TQ	USBLS	5/15
	Michigan	Y	98400 FQ	119250 MW	145740 TQ	USBLS	5/15
	Detroit-Dearborn-Livonia PMSA, MI	Y	105860 FQ	137920 MW	169270 TQ	USBLS	5/15
	Grand Rapids-Wyoming MSA, MI	Y	89550 FQ	109590 MW	128940 TQ	USBLS	5/15
	Minnesota	Y	112574 FQ	135904 MW	170563 TQ	MNBLS	1/16-3/16
	Minneapolis-St. Paul-Bloomington MSA, MN-WI	Y	116364 FQ	141248 MW	177655 TQ	MNBLS	1/16-3/16
	Mississippi	Y	86790 FQ	108710 MW	129330 TQ	USBLS	5/15
	Jackson MSA, MS	Y	85090 FQ	100310 MW	124100 TQ	USBLS	5/15
	Missouri	Y	98610 FQ	124590 MW	154400 TQ	USBLS	5/15
	Kansas City MSA, MO-KS	Y	90600 FQ	111490 MW	137720 TQ	USBLS	5/15
	St. Louis MSA, MO-IL	Y	107280 FQ	133570 MW	159420 TQ	USBLS	5/15
	Montana	Y	93850 FQ	110410 MW	136430 TQ	USBLS	5/15
	Billings MSA, MT	Y	97280 FQ	119280 MW	147100 TQ	USBLS	5/15
	Nebraska	Y	100255 FQ	121375 MW	149425 TQ	NEBLS	7/16-9/16
	Omaha-Council Bluffs MSA, NE-IA	Y	107155 FQ	125935 MW	156160 TQ	NEBLS	7/16-9/16
	Nevada	Y	95110 FQ	125730 MW	160830 TQ	USBLS	5/15
	Las Vegas-Henderson-Paradise MSA, NV	Y	98920 FQ	129750 MW	166610 TQ	USBLS	5/15
	New Hampshire	H	47.22 AE	62.95 MW	77.51 AEX	NHBLS	6/16
	Manchester NECTA, NH	H	45.25 AE	59.35 MW	77.86 AEX	NHBLS	6/16
	Nashua NECTA, NH-MA	Y	121580 FQ	149200 MW	181820 TQ	USBLS	5/15
	New Jersey	Y	120580 FQ	145530 MW	178060 TQ	USBLS	5/15
	Camden PMSA, NJ	Y	114230 FQ	141360 MW	179900 TQ	USBLS	5/15
	Newark PMSA, NJ-PA	Y	121220 FQ	145880 MW	177780 TQ	USBLS	5/15
	Trenton MSA, NJ	Y	130610 FQ	165960 MW		USBLS	5/15
	New Mexico	Y	111210 FQ	144710 MW	172180 TQ	USBLS	5/15
	Albuquerque MSA, NM	Y	112330 FQ	146490 MW	171850 TQ	USBLS	5/15
	New York	Y	101850 AE	144670 MW	182000 AEX	NYBLS	1/16-3/16

AE	Average entry wage	AWR	Average wage range	H	Hourly	LR	Low end range	MTC	Median total compensation	TCC	Total cash compensation
AEX	Average experienced wage	B	Biweekly	HI	Highest wage paid	M	Monthly	MW	Median wage paid	TQ	Third quartile wage
ATC	Average total compensation	D	Daily	HR	High end range	MCC	Median cash compensation	MWR	Median wage range	W	Weekly
AW	Average wage paid	FQ	First quartile wage	LO	Lowest wage paid	ME	Median entry wage	S	See annotated source	Y	Yearly

Occupation/Type/Industry	Location	Per	Low	Mid	High	Source	Date
Architectural and Engineering Manager							
	Buffalo-Cheektowaga-Niagara Falls MSA, NY	Y	96430 FQ	114490 MW	133000 TQ	USBLS	5/15
	Nassau County-Suffolk County PMSA, NY	Y	118580 FQ	143740 MW	168870 TQ	USBLS	5/15
	New York-Jersey City-White Plains PMSA, NY-NJ	Y	123470 FQ	154470 MW		USBLS	5/15
	Rochester MSA, NY	Y	109320 FQ	125940 MW	154710 TQ	USBLS	5/15
	North Carolina	Y	101590 FQ	123670 MW	153420 TQ	USBLS	5/15
	Charlotte-Concord-Gastonia MSA, NC-SC	Y	105900 FQ	126450 MW	155020 TQ	USBLS	5/15
	Raleigh MSA, NC	Y	99710 FQ	125950 MW	156770 TQ	USBLS	5/15
	North Dakota	Y	93950 FQ	110610 MW	129550 TQ	USBLS	5/15
	Fargo MSA, ND-MN	Y	89150 FQ	106200 MW	122440 TQ	USBLS	5/15
	Ohio	Y	98560 FQ	120520 MW	146070 TQ	USBLS	5/15
	Cincinnati MSA, OH-KY-IN	Y	100870 FQ	122920 MW	150100 TQ	USBLS	5/15
	Cleveland-Elyria MSA, OH	Y	104050 FQ	124810 MW	149110 TQ	USBLS	5/15
	Columbus MSA, OH	Y	100740 FQ	119590 MW	147420 TQ	USBLS	5/15
	Oklahoma	Y	94190 FQ	118050 MW	141510 TQ	USBLS	5/15
	Oklahoma City MSA, OK	Y	90830 FQ	119080 MW	139280 TQ	USBLS	5/15
	Tulsa MSA, OK	Y	97710 FQ	118100 MW	144970 TQ	USBLS	5/15
	Oregon	H	54.96 FQ	68.42 MW	89.37 TQ	ORBLS	2016
	Portland-Vancouver-Hillsboro MSA, OR-WA	Y	115780 FQ	141040 MW	184930 TQ	USBLS	5/15
	Pennsylvania	Y	105770 FQ	133030 MW	161790 TQ	USBLS	5/15
	Allentown-Bethlehem-Easton MSA, PA-NJ	Y	100610 FQ	125170 MW	159470 TQ	USBLS	5/15
	Harrisburg-Carlisle MSA, PA	Y	92760 FQ	117310 MW	146640 TQ	USBLS	5/15
	Montgomery County-Bucks County-Chester County PMSA, PA	Y	113730 FQ	144410 MW	178100 TQ	USBLS	5/15
	Philadelphia PMSA, PA	Y	126270 FQ	147650 MW	180070 TQ	USBLS	5/15
	Pittsburgh MSA, PA	Y	107970 FQ	133700 MW	160760 TQ	USBLS	5/15
	Rhode Island	Y	113290 FQ	135610 MW	163360 TQ	USBLS	5/15
	Providence-Warwick MSA, RI-MA	Y	111730 FQ	132710 MW	158610 TQ	USBLS	5/15
	South Carolina	Y	95450 FQ	120800 MW	150700 TQ	USBLS	5/15
	Charleston-North Charleston MSA, SC	Y	92960 FQ	114420 MW	141320 TQ	USBLS	5/15
	Columbia MSA, SC	Y	81290 FQ	112210 MW	135770 TQ	USBLS	5/15
	Greenville-Anderson-Mauldin MSA, SC	Y	97790 FQ	128230 MW	165270 TQ	USBLS	5/15
	South Dakota	Y	93830 FQ	112510 MW	141350 TQ	USBLS	5/15
	Tennessee	Y	82960 FQ	109780 MW	139110 TQ	USBLS	5/15
	Knoxville MSA, TN	Y	89790 FQ	125080 MW	160680 TQ	USBLS	5/15
	Memphis MSA, TN-MS-AR	Y	84560 FQ	102290 MW	128210 TQ	USBLS	5/15
	Nashville-Davidson–Murfreesboro–Franklin MSA, TN	Y	81340 FQ	108750 MW	135020 TQ	USBLS	5/15
	Texas	Y	119050 FQ	151440 MW		USBLS	5/15
	Austin-Round Rock MSA, TX	Y	124160 FQ	153520 MW	186640 TQ	USBLS	5/15
	Dallas-Plano-Irving PMSA, TX	Y	116230 FQ	143170 MW	180720 TQ	USBLS	5/15
	Fort Worth-Arlington PMSA, TX	Y	97910 FQ	123070 MW	157570 TQ	USBLS	5/15
	Houston-The Woodlands-Sugar Land MSA, TX	Y	132740 FQ	169020 MW		USBLS	5/15
	San Antonio-New Braunfels MSA, TX	Y	104700 FQ	127490 MW	158180 TQ	USBLS	5/15
	Utah	Y	85100 FQ	113190 MW	141950 TQ	USBLS	5/15
	Ogden-Clearfield MSA, UT	Y	107390 FQ	128530 MW	151420 TQ	USBLS	5/15
	Provo-Orem MSA, UT	Y	86560 FQ	113580 MW	141620 TQ	USBLS	5/15
	Salt Lake City MSA, UT	Y	82270 FQ	108460 MW	138630 TQ	USBLS	5/15
	Vermont	Y	99330 FQ	110900 MW	124270 TQ	USBLS	5/15
	Burlington-South Burlington MSA, VT	Y	100430 FQ	110890 MW	121780 TQ	USBLS	5/15
	Virginia	Y	115450 FQ	140600 MW	171390 TQ	USBLS	5/15
	Richmond MSA, VA	Y	109080 FQ	132080 MW	165390 TQ	USBLS	5/15
	Virginia Beach-Norfolk-Newport News MSA, VA-NC	Y	115070 FQ	128230 MW	152000 TQ	USBLS	5/15
	Washington	H	58.17 FQ	69.99 MW	84.85 TQ	WABLS	3/16
	Seattle-Bellevue-Everett PMSA, WA	H	60.45 FQ	73.35 MW	88.43 TQ	WABLS	3/16

AE	Average entry wage	AWR	Average wage range	
AEX	Average experienced wage	B	Biweekly	
ATC	Average total compensation	D	Daily	
AW	Average wage paid	FQ	First quartile wage	

H	Hourly	LR	Low end range	
HI	Highest wage paid	M	Monthly	
HR	High end range	MCC	Median cash compensation	
LO	Lowest wage paid	ME	Median entry wage	

MTC	Median total compensation	TCC	Total cash compensation
MW	Median wage paid	TQ	Third quartile wage
MWR	Median wage range	W	Weekly
S	See annotated source	Y	Yearly

Occupation/Type/Industry	Location	Per	Low	Mid	High	Source	Date
Architectural and Engineering Manager	Tacoma-Lakewood PMSA, WA	H	48.27 FQ	60.88 MW	70.79 TQ	WABLS	3/16
	West Virginia	Y	105890 FQ	122390 MW	150610 TQ	USBLS	5/15
	Huntington-Ashland MSA, WV-KY-OH	Y	105770 FQ	118350 MW	135360 TQ	USBLS	5/15
	Wisconsin	Y	90850 FQ	110030 MW	131240 TQ	USBLS	5/15
	Madison MSA, WI	Y	98630 FQ	115490 MW	134400 TQ	USBLS	5/15
	Milwaukee-Waukesha-West Allis MSA, WI	Y	92490 FQ	113450 MW	139440 TQ	USBLS	5/15
	Wyoming	Y	92560 FQ	108250 MW	134860 TQ	USBLS	5/15
	Cheyenne MSA, WY	Y	90910 FQ	93700 MW	110960 TQ	USBLS	5/15
	Puerto Rico	Y	68260 FQ	97050 MW	125250 TQ	USBLS	5/15
	San Juan-Carolina-Caguas MSA, PR	Y	67250 FQ	97870 MW	126890 TQ	USBLS	5/15
	Guam	Y	63100 FQ	80050 MW	98620 TQ	USBLS	5/15
Architecture Teacher							
Postsecondary	Alabama	Y	71689 AE	101097 AW	115795 AEX	ALBLS	6/16
Postsecondary	Arizona	Y	50670 FQ	68750 MW	89720 TQ	USBLS	5/15
Postsecondary	Arkansas	Y	44120 FQ	57190 MW	82260 TQ	USBLS	5/15
Postsecondary	California	Y		89509 AW		CABLS	1/16-3/16
Postsecondary	Florida	Y	66089 AE	91489 MW	108967 AEX	FLBLS	7/16-9/16
Postsecondary	Georgia	Y	55940 FQ	72360 MW	93750 TQ	USBLS	5/15
Postsecondary	Illinois	Y	43390 FQ	63820 MW	77000 TQ	USBLS	5/15
Postsecondary	Kentucky	Y	57470 FQ	76380 MW	97620 TQ	USBLS	5/15
Postsecondary	Louisiana	Y	48650 FQ	67980 MW	90390 TQ	USBLS	5/15
Postsecondary	Maryland	Y	53739 AE	83529 MW	98424 AEX	MDBLS	4/16
Postsecondary	Massachusetts	Y	51990 FQ	75560 MW	105270 TQ	USBLS	5/15
Postsecondary	Michigan	Y	59240 FQ	78430 MW	103320 TQ	USBLS	5/15
Postsecondary	Mississippi	Y	56930 FQ	68310 MW	78800 TQ	USBLS	5/15
Postsecondary	Missouri	Y	53240 FQ	71220 MW	95680 TQ	USBLS	5/15
Postsecondary	Montana	Y	31680 FQ	52440 MW	73890 TQ	USBLS	5/15
Postsecondary	New Jersey	Y	62510 FQ	77000 MW	97110 TQ	USBLS	5/15
Postsecondary	New York	Y	41780 AE	80340 MW	137170 AEX	NYBLS	1/16-3/16
Postsecondary	North Carolina	Y	52640 FQ	66080 MW	83100 TQ	USBLS	5/15
Postsecondary	Ohio	Y	50320 FQ	70620 MW	94890 TQ	USBLS	5/15
Postsecondary	South Carolina	Y	57150 FQ	77230 MW	94550 TQ	USBLS	5/15
Postsecondary	Tennessee	Y	44170 FQ	53150 MW	78040 TQ	USBLS	5/15
Postsecondary	Texas	Y	48950 FQ	68540 MW	92350 TQ	USBLS	5/15
Postsecondary	Utah	Y	65030 FQ	78110 MW	106050 TQ	USBLS	5/15
Postsecondary	Virginia	Y	48720 FQ	67910 MW	93510 TQ	USBLS	5/15
Postsecondary	Wisconsin	Y	55620 FQ	69360 MW	83390 TQ	USBLS	5/15
Postsecondary	Puerto Rico	Y	37530 FQ	51510 MW	65330 TQ	USBLS	5/15
Archivist	Alabama	Y	36675 AE	59753 AW	71292 AEX	ALBLS	6/16
	Arizona	Y	40430 FQ	44530 MW	48410 TQ	USBLS	5/15
	Arkansas	Y	29200 FQ	40750 MW	70190 TQ	USBLS	5/15
	Little Rock-North Little Rock-Conway MSA, AR	Y	29370 FQ	39870 MW	72540 TQ	USBLS	5/15
	California	H	17.82 FQ	23.44 MW	33.50 TQ	CABLS	1/16-3/16
	Anaheim-Santa Ana-Irvine PMSA, CA	H	29.68 FQ	42.25 MW	45.34 TQ	CABLS	1/16-3/16
	Los Angeles-Long Beach-Glendale PMSA, CA	H	17.19 FQ	20.42 MW	27.44 TQ	CABLS	1/16-3/16
	Oakland-Hayward-Berkeley PMSA, CA	H	22.58 FQ	31.97 MW	38.87 TQ	CABLS	1/16-3/16
	Riverside-San Bernardino-Ontario MSA, CA	H	16.62 FQ	17.97 MW	39.40 TQ	CABLS	1/16-3/16
	San Diego-Carlsbad MSA, CA	H	17.99 FQ	21.90 MW	27.26 TQ	CABLS	1/16-3/16
	San Francisco-Redwood City-South San Francisco PMSA, CA	H	27.31 FQ	35.98 MW	44.59 TQ	CABLS	1/16-3/16
	Colorado	Y	39970 FQ	51790 MW	68160 TQ	USBLS	5/15
	Denver-Aurora-Lakewood MSA, CO	Y	44500 FQ	51880 MW	73680 TQ	USBLS	5/15
	Connecticut	Y		58019 MW		CTBLS	1/16-3/16
	District of Columbia	Y	54990 FQ	76390 MW	96240 TQ	USBLS	5/15
	Washington-Arlington-Alexandria PMSA, DC-VA-MD-WV	Y	57940 FQ	78930 MW	96750 TQ	USBLS	5/15
	Florida	H	16.89 AE	25.48 MW	29.28 AEX	FLBLS	7/16-9/16

AE Average entry wage	AWR Average wage range	H Hourly	LR Low end range	MTC Median total compensation	TCC Total cash compensation
AEX Average experienced wage	B Biweekly	HI Highest wage paid	M Monthly	MW Median wage paid	TQ Third quartile wage
ATC Average total compensation	D Daily	HR High end range	MCC Median cash compensation	MWR Median wage range	W Weekly
AW Average wage paid	FQ First quartile wage	LO Lowest wage paid	ME Median entry wage	S See annotated source	Y Yearly

Occupation/Type/Industry	Location	Per	Low	Mid	High	Source	Date
Archivist	Miami-Miami Beach-Kendall PMSA, FL	H	24.56 AE	27.68 MW	28.72 AEX	FLBLS	7/16-9/16
	Orlando-Kissimmee-Sanford MSA, FL	H	15.77 AE	25.32 MW	31.89 AEX	FLBLS	7/16-9/16
	Tampa-St. Petersburg-Clearwater MSA, FL	H	19.84 AE	26.98 MW	32.87 AEX	FLBLS	7/16-9/16
	Georgia	Y	35120 FQ	44860 MW	73090 TQ	USBLS	5/15
	Atlanta-Sandy Springs-Roswell MSA, GA	Y	38240 FQ	50720 MW	75790 TQ	USBLS	5/15
	Illinois	Y	52010 FQ	57940 MW	64020 TQ	USBLS	5/15
	Chicago-Naperville-Arlington Heights PMSA, IL	Y	53020 FQ	58000 MW	63010 TQ	USBLS	5/15
	Indiana	Y	31740 FQ	41490 MW	52970 TQ	USBLS	5/15
	Indianapolis-Carmel-Anderson MSA, IN	Y	31150 FQ	35950 MW	44870 TQ	USBLS	5/15
	Kansas	Y	24520 FQ	30510 MW	56040 TQ	USBLS	5/15
	Louisiana	Y	43740 FQ	52490 MW	58900 TQ	USBLS	5/15
	New Orleans-Metairie MSA, LA	Y	41650 FQ	47820 MW	56290 TQ	USBLS	5/15
	Maryland	Y	39377 AE	67714 MW	81883 AEX	MDBLS	4/16
	Baltimore-Columbia-Towson MSA, MD	Y	39330 FQ	48030 MW	57480 TQ	USBLS	5/15
	Massachusetts	Y	47300 FQ	57420 MW	84410 TQ	USBLS	5/15
	Boston-Cambridge-Newton NECTA, MA	Y	46110 FQ	59720 MW	92490 TQ	USBLS	5/15
	Michigan	Y	33620 FQ	47800 MW	66560 TQ	USBLS	5/15
	Minnesota	Y	28750 FQ	35292 MW	52802 TQ	MNBLS	1/16-3/16
	Minneapolis-St. Paul-Bloomington MSA, MN-WI	Y	29445 FQ	34566 MW	47005 TQ	MNBLS	1/16-3/16
	Missouri	Y	37600 FQ	44690 MW	72550 TQ	USBLS	5/15
	St. Louis MSA, MO-IL	Y	44280 FQ	54370 MW	74870 TQ	USBLS	5/15
	Nebraska	Y	29170 FQ	41035 MW	51270 TQ	NEBLS	7/16-9/16
	New Jersey	Y	46900 FQ	60780 MW	76340 TQ	USBLS	5/15
	New Mexico	Y	42560 FQ	48350 MW	56980 TQ	USBLS	5/15
	Albuquerque MSA, NM	Y	42430 FQ	49050 MW	56930 TQ	USBLS	5/15
	New York	Y	36560 AE	54310 MW	65690 AEX	NYBLS	1/16-3/16
	Nassau County-Suffolk County PMSA, NY	Y	37840 FQ	54400 MW	73720 TQ	USBLS	5/15
	New York-Jersey City-White Plains PMSA, NY-NJ	Y	43310 FQ	55070 MW	66780 TQ	USBLS	5/15
	North Carolina	Y	40620 FQ	45630 MW	53690 TQ	USBLS	5/15
	Ohio	Y	29420 FQ	37600 MW	52420 TQ	USBLS	5/15
	Cleveland-Elyria MSA, OH	Y	35110 FQ	46610 MW	62830 TQ	USBLS	5/15
	Oklahoma	Y	34560 FQ	46330 MW	58060 TQ	USBLS	5/15
	Oregon	H	19.99 FQ	24.53 MW	29.30 TQ	ORBLS	2016
	Pennsylvania	Y	28490 FQ	38430 MW	51640 TQ	USBLS	5/15
	Allentown-Bethlehem-Easton MSA, PA-NJ	Y	17060 FQ	18730 MW	30720 TQ	USBLS	5/15
	Philadelphia PMSA, PA	Y	34140 FQ	44790 MW	55290 TQ	USBLS	5/15
	Pittsburgh MSA, PA	Y	30880 FQ	35740 MW	42050 TQ	USBLS	5/15
	Rhode Island	Y	49970 FQ	59000 MW	73180 TQ	USBLS	5/15
	Providence-Warwick MSA, RI-MA	Y	50940 FQ	59780 MW	76770 TQ	USBLS	5/15
	South Carolina	Y	31380 FQ	40450 MW	50580 TQ	USBLS	5/15
	Charleston-North Charleston MSA, SC	Y	29130 FQ	42830 MW	53610 TQ	USBLS	5/15
	Tennessee	Y	34280 FQ	42580 MW	51400 TQ	USBLS	5/15
	Nashville-Davidson–Murfreesboro–Franklin MSA, TN	Y	38500 FQ	45430 MW	53820 TQ	USBLS	5/15
	Texas	Y	39740 FQ	55350 MW	77230 TQ	USBLS	5/15
	Austin-Round Rock MSA, TX	Y	40960 FQ	53480 MW	77210 TQ	USBLS	5/15
	Dallas-Plano-Irving PMSA, TX	Y	19350 FQ	77420 MW	84080 TQ	USBLS	5/15
	Houston-The Woodlands-Sugar Land MSA, TX	Y	49820 FQ	60210 MW	84310 TQ	USBLS	5/15
	Utah	Y	34490 FQ	40810 MW	44470 TQ	USBLS	5/15
	Salt Lake City MSA, UT	Y	34820 FQ	40640 MW	44460 TQ	USBLS	5/15
	Vermont	Y	36260 FQ	46510 MW	55940 TQ	USBLS	5/15
	Virginia	Y	39530 FQ	48280 MW	70080 TQ	USBLS	5/15
	Richmond MSA, VA	Y	40250 FQ	44500 MW	53080 TQ	USBLS	5/15
	Washington	H	21.40 FQ	27.85 MW	40.17 TQ	WABLS	3/16

AE	Average entry wage	AWR	Average wage range	H	Hourly	LR	Low end range
AEX	Average experienced wage	B	Biweekly	HI	Highest wage paid	M	Monthly
ATC	Average total compensation	D	Daily	HR	High end range	MCC	Median cash compensation
AW	Average wage paid	FQ	First quartile wage	LO	Lowest wage paid	ME	Median entry wage

MTC	Median total compensation	TCC	Total cash compensation
MW	Median wage paid	TQ	Third quartile wage
MWR	Median wage range	W	Weekly
S	See annotated source	Y	Yearly

Occupation/Type/Industry	Location	Per	Low	Mid	High	Source	Date
Archivist	Seattle-Bellevue-Everett						
	PMSA, WA	H	21.79 FQ	28.34 MW	39.99 TQ	WABLS	3/16
	Wisconsin	Y	34600 FQ	44460 MW	52540 TQ	USBLS	5/15
	Madison MSA, WI	Y	45730 FQ	50630 MW	54710 TQ	USBLS	5/15
	Milwaukee-Waukesha-West						
	Allis MSA, WI	Y	24280 FQ	38520 MW	51180 TQ	USBLS	5/15
	Puerto Rico	Y	18490 FQ	22940 MW	28730 TQ	USBLS	5/15
	San Juan-Carolina-Caguas						
	MSA, PR	Y	18410 FQ	22330 MW	27850 TQ	USBLS	5/15
Area, Ethnic, and Cultural Studies							
Teacher							
Postsecondary	Alabama	Y	47399 AE	75552 AW	89629 AEX	ALBLS	6/16
Postsecondary	Arizona	Y	47040 FQ	67400 MW	89870 TQ	USBLS	5/15
Postsecondary	California	Y		89407 AW		CABLS	1/16-3/16
Postsecondary	Colorado	Y	34090 FQ	47680 MW	74130 TQ	USBLS	5/15
Postsecondary	Connecticut	Y		69939 MW		CTBLS	1/16-3/16
Postsecondary	District of Columbia	Y	62670 FQ	82760 MW	122590 TQ	USBLS	5/15
Postsecondary	Florida	Y	59629 AE	96474 MW	146596 AEX	FLBLS	7/16-9/16
Postsecondary	Georgia	Y	49510 FQ	59920 MW	73060 TQ	USBLS	5/15
Postsecondary	Hawaii	Y	50710 FQ	68380 MW	91150 TQ	USBLS	5/15
Postsecondary	Idaho	Y	18540 FQ	46120 MW	77260 TQ	USBLS	5/15
Postsecondary	Illinois	Y	50650 FQ	64160 MW	77590 TQ	USBLS	5/15
Postsecondary	Indiana	Y	45110 FQ	62120 MW	92360 TQ	USBLS	5/15
Postsecondary	Kentucky	Y	59440 FQ	75340 MW	107550 TQ	USBLS	5/15
Postsecondary	Louisiana	Y	48220 FQ	68690 MW	95620 TQ	USBLS	5/15
Postsecondary	Maryland	Y	46505 AE	85111 MW	104414 AEX	MDBLS	4/16
Postsecondary	Massachusetts	Y	65820 FQ	86200 MW	120640 TQ	USBLS	5/15
Postsecondary	Michigan	Y	73780 FQ	101150 MW	143640 TQ	USBLS	5/15
Postsecondary	Minnesota	Y	59404 FQ	79162 MW	111410 TQ	MNBLS	1/16-3/16
Postsecondary	Missouri	Y	52740 FQ	71980 MW	100920 TQ	USBLS	5/15
Postsecondary	Montana	Y	41340 FQ	50000 MW	61690 TQ	USBLS	5/15
Postsecondary	New Jersey	Y	65100 FQ	90350 MW	123890 TQ	USBLS	5/15
Postsecondary	New Mexico	Y	57600 FQ	72560 MW	86160 TQ	USBLS	5/15
Postsecondary	New York	Y	50340 AE	80960 MW	118870 AEX	NYBLS	1/16-3/16
Postsecondary	North Carolina	Y	51780 FQ	71210 MW	92450 TQ	USBLS	5/15
Postsecondary	Ohio	Y	50460 FQ	73680 MW	102470 TQ	USBLS	5/15
Postsecondary	Oklahoma	Y	62450 FQ	85250 MW	95150 TQ	USBLS	5/15
Postsecondary	Oregon	Y	59306 FQ	75354 MW	96918 TQ	ORBLS	2016
Postsecondary	Pennsylvania	Y	55250 FQ	71160 MW	100820 TQ	USBLS	5/15
Postsecondary	Rhode Island	Y	63960 FQ	79870 MW	107050 TQ	USBLS	5/15
Postsecondary	South Carolina	Y	33870 FQ	49700 MW	71920 TQ	USBLS	5/15
Postsecondary	Tennessee	Y	43300 FQ	62760 MW	76420 TQ	USBLS	5/15
Postsecondary	Texas	Y	36420 FQ	58930 MW	86440 TQ	USBLS	5/15
Postsecondary	Utah	Y	51910 FQ	60800 MW	84440 TQ	USBLS	5/15
Postsecondary	Virginia	Y	49160 FQ	59690 MW	88590 TQ	USBLS	5/15
Postsecondary	Washington	Y		71765 AW		WABLS	3/16
Postsecondary	West Virginia	Y	42710 FQ	56590 MW	83400 TQ	USBLS	5/15
Postsecondary	Wisconsin	Y	43370 FQ	57320 MW	78330 TQ	USBLS	5/15
Postsecondary	Wyoming	Y	46500 FQ	61960 MW	78410 TQ	USBLS	5/15
Arson Investigations Chemist							
Municipal Government	Detroit, MI	M	3300 LO		3658 HI	DETGOV	2016
Art, Drama, and Music Teacher							
Postsecondary	Alabama	Y	39754 AE	64075 AW	76245 AEX	ALBLS	6/16
Postsecondary	Birmingham-Hoover MSA, AL	Y	42465 AE	63218 AW	73595 AEX	ALBLS	6/16
Postsecondary	Alaska	Y	64580 FQ	77880 MW	92820 TQ	USBLS	5/15
Postsecondary	Arizona	Y	41020 FQ	61180 MW	82750 TQ	USBLS	5/15
Postsecondary	Phoenix-Mesa-Scottsdale						
	MSA, AZ	Y	45520 FQ	63060 MW	86050 TQ	USBLS	5/15
Postsecondary	Arkansas	Y	44350 FQ	55380 MW	73460 TQ	USBLS	5/15
Postsecondary	Little Rock-North Little Rock-						
	Conway MSA, AR	Y	44980 FQ	57160 MW	77800 TQ	USBLS	5/15
Postsecondary	California	Y		89367 AW		CABLS	1/16-3/16
Postsecondary	Anaheim-Santa Ana-Irvine						
	PMSA, CA	Y		104665 AW		CABLS	1/16-3/16
Postsecondary	Los Angeles-Long Beach-						
	Glendale PMSA, CA	Y		87967 AW		CABLS	1/16-3/16
Postsecondary	Oakland-Hayward-Berkeley						
	PMSA, CA	Y		85065 AW		CABLS	1/16-3/16

AE	Average entry wage	**AWR** Average wage range	**H** Hourly	**LR** Low end range	**MTC** Median total compensation	**TCC** Total cash compensation
AEX	Average experienced wage	**B** Biweekly	**HI** Highest wage paid	**M** Monthly	**MW** Median wage paid	**TQ** Third quartile wage
ATC	Average total compensation	**D** Daily	**HR** High end range	**MCC** Median cash compensation	**MWR** Median wage range	**W** Weekly
AW	Average wage paid	**FQ** First quartile wage	**LO** Lowest wage paid	**ME** Median entry wage	**S** See annotated source	**Y** Yearly

Occupation/Type/Industry	Location	Per	Low	Mid	High	Source	Date
Art, Drama, and Music Teacher							
Postsecondary	Riverside-San Bernardino-Ontario MSA, CA	Y		92623 AW		CABLS	1/16-3/16
Postsecondary	Sacramento–Roseville–Arden-Arcade MSA, CA	Y		83158 AW		CABLS	1/16-3/16
Postsecondary	San Diego-Carlsbad MSA, CA	Y		95667 AW		CABLS	1/16-3/16
Postsecondary	San Francisco-Redwood City-South San Francisco PMSA, CA	Y		90249 AW		CABLS	1/16-3/16
Postsecondary	Colorado	Y	33950 FQ	53360 MW	67880 TQ	USBLS	5/15
Postsecondary	Denver-Aurora-Lakewood MSA, CO	Y	34810 FQ	54040 MW	67340 TQ	USBLS	5/15
Postsecondary	Connecticut	Y		61732 MW		CTBLS	1/16-3/16
Postsecondary	Bridgeport-Stamford-Norwalk MSA, CT	Y	34560 FQ	38100 MW	72840 TQ	USBLS	5/15
Postsecondary	Hartford-West Hartford-East Hartford MSA, CT	Y	56360 FQ	72190 MW	96750 TQ	USBLS	5/15
Postsecondary	Delaware	Y	49580 FQ	59950 MW	74270 TQ	USBLS	5/15
Postsecondary	Wilmington PMSA, DE-MD-NJ	Y	49580 FQ	60400 MW	75810 TQ	USBLS	5/15
Postsecondary	District of Columbia	Y	55950 FQ	75770 MW	98660 TQ	USBLS	5/15
Postsecondary	Washington-Arlington-Alexandria PMSA, DC-VA-MD-WV	Y	51720 FQ	68040 MW	92970 TQ	USBLS	5/15
Postsecondary	Florida	Y	42649 AE	69632 MW	99205 AEX	FLBLS	7/16-9/16
Postsecondary	Fort Lauderdale-Pompano Beach-Deerfield Beach PMSA, FL	Y	40469 AE	67048 MW	81805 AEX	FLBLS	7/16-9/16
Postsecondary	Miami-Miami Beach-Kendall PMSA, FL	Y	57689 AE	85012 MW	91540 AEX	FLBLS	7/16-9/16
Postsecondary	Orlando-Kissimmee-Sanford MSA, FL	Y	39447 AE	61318 MW	77304 AEX	FLBLS	7/16-9/16
Postsecondary	Georgia	Y	40380 FQ	56730 MW	78210 TQ	USBLS	5/15
Postsecondary	Atlanta-Sandy Springs-Roswell MSA, GA	Y	35170 FQ	53700 MW	73150 TQ	USBLS	5/15
Postsecondary	Augusta-Richmond County MSA, GA-SC	Y	30060 FQ	38700 MW	51870 TQ	USBLS	5/15
Postsecondary	Hawaii	Y	31330 FQ	54740 MW	81950 TQ	USBLS	5/15
Postsecondary	Urban Honolulu MSA, HI	Y	32770 FQ	59280 MW	85800 TQ	USBLS	5/15
Postsecondary	Idaho	Y	41330 FQ	53210 MW	67490 TQ	USBLS	5/15
Postsecondary	Boise City MSA, ID	Y	30570 FQ	49540 MW	62030 TQ	USBLS	5/15
Postsecondary	Illinois	Y	50170 FQ	73280 MW	97740 TQ	USBLS	5/15
Postsecondary	Chicago-Naperville-Arlington Heights PMSA, IL	Y	53250 FQ	75370 MW	97680 TQ	USBLS	5/15
Postsecondary	Lake County-Kenosha County PMSA, IL-WI	Y	29170 FQ	42380 MW	61700 TQ	USBLS	5/15
Postsecondary	Indiana	Y	46980 FQ	61780 MW	82280 TQ	USBLS	5/15
Postsecondary	Indianapolis-Carmel-Anderson MSA, IN	Y	47550 FQ	62200 MW	79630 TQ	USBLS	5/15
Postsecondary	Iowa	Y	49970 FQ	61510 MW	77100 TQ	USBLS	5/15
Postsecondary	Des Moines-West Des Moines MSA, IA	Y	52300 FQ	58640 MW	67280 TQ	USBLS	5/15
Postsecondary	Kansas	Y	42630 FQ	54370 MW	71650 TQ	USBLS	5/15
Postsecondary	Kentucky	Y	52490 FQ	70780 MW	90290 TQ	USBLS	5/15
Postsecondary	Louisville-Jefferson County MSA, KY-IN	Y	44100 FQ	61940 MW	82870 TQ	USBLS	5/15
Postsecondary	Louisiana	Y	34100 FQ	53570 MW	69860 TQ	USBLS	5/15
Postsecondary	New Orleans-Metairie MSA, LA	Y	19020 FQ	46230 MW	63980 TQ	USBLS	5/15
Postsecondary	Maine	Y	45890 FQ	70130 MW	94100 TQ	USBLS	5/15
Postsecondary	Portland-South Portland MSA, ME	Y	31040 FQ	50610 MW	85550 TQ	USBLS	5/15
Postsecondary	Maryland	Y	42704 AE	84793 MW	105837 AEX	MDBLS	4/16
Postsecondary	Massachusetts	Y	61790 FQ	85550 MW	114950 TQ	USBLS	5/15
Postsecondary	Boston-Cambridge-Newton NECTA, MA	Y	62910 FQ	87700 MW	116750 TQ	USBLS	5/15
Postsecondary	Worcester MSA, MA-CT	Y	60740 FQ	77300 MW	100020 TQ	USBLS	5/15
Postsecondary	Michigan	Y	40950 FQ	64600 MW	86960 TQ	USBLS	5/15
Postsecondary	Detroit-Dearborn-Livonia PMSA, MI	Y	44970 FQ	69200 MW	86260 TQ	USBLS	5/15
Postsecondary	Grand Rapids-Wyoming MSA, MI	Y	19030 FQ	43040 MW	67580 TQ	USBLS	5/15

AE	Average entry wage	AWR	Average wage range	H	Hourly	LR	Low end range	MTC	Median total compensation	TCC	Total cash compensation
AEX	Average experienced wage	B	Biweekly	HI	Highest wage paid	M	Monthly	MW	Median wage paid	TQ	Third quartile wage
ATC	Average total compensation	D	Daily	HR	High end range	MCC	Median cash compensation	MWR	Median wage range	W	Weekly
AW	Average wage paid	FQ	First quartile wage	LO	Lowest wage paid	ME	Median entry wage	S	See annotated source	Y	Yearly

70

Occupation/Type/Industry	Location	Per	Low	Mid	High	Source	Date
Art, Drama, and Music Teacher							
Postsecondary	Minnesota	Y	46824 FQ	64173 MW	83164 TQ	MNBLS	1/16-3/16
Postsecondary	Minneapolis-St. Paul-Bloomington MSA, MN-WI	Y	44405 FQ	62711 MW	80362 TQ	MNBLS	1/16-3/16
Postsecondary	Mississippi	Y	43050 FQ	54950 MW	67360 TQ	USBLS	5/15
Postsecondary	Jackson MSA, MS	Y	33760 FQ	39290 MW	55450 TQ	USBLS	5/15
Postsecondary	Missouri	Y	45660 FQ	62100 MW	85200 TQ	USBLS	5/15
Postsecondary	Kansas City MSA, MO-KS	Y	46210 FQ	60130 MW	79440 TQ	USBLS	5/15
Postsecondary	St. Louis MSA, MO-IL	Y	40760 FQ	62400 MW	92170 TQ	USBLS	5/15
Postsecondary	Montana	Y	36520 FQ	47750 MW	57960 TQ	USBLS	5/15
Postsecondary	Omaha-Council Bluffs MSA, NE-IA	Y	30055 FQ	39370 MW	63045 TQ	NEBLS	7/16-9/16
Postsecondary	Nevada	Y	35640 FQ	42180 MW	64170 TQ	USBLS	5/15
Postsecondary	Las Vegas-Henderson-Paradise MSA, NV	Y	35900 FQ	50140 MW	66460 TQ	USBLS	5/15
Postsecondary	New Hampshire	Y	50524 AE	77392 MW	108062 AEX	NHBLS	6/16
Postsecondary	New Jersey	Y	48440 FQ	66530 MW	89640 TQ	USBLS	5/15
Postsecondary	Camden PMSA, NJ	Y	46460 FQ	62530 MW	83500 TQ	USBLS	5/15
Postsecondary	Newark PMSA, NJ-PA	Y	44880 FQ	61910 MW	83200 TQ	USBLS	5/15
Postsecondary	New Mexico	Y	53720 FQ	61090 MW	78460 TQ	USBLS	5/15
Postsecondary	New York	Y	45680 AE	82490 MW	144100 AEX	NYBLS	1/16-3/16
Postsecondary	Buffalo-Cheektowaga-Niagara Falls MSA, NY	Y	37460 FQ	54250 MW	81320 TQ	USBLS	5/15
Postsecondary	Nassau County-Suffolk County PMSA, NY	Y	46000 FQ	64450 MW	91420 TQ	USBLS	5/15
Postsecondary	New York-Jersey City-White Plains PMSA, NY-NJ	Y	57710 FQ	86810 MW	145400 TQ	USBLS	5/15
Postsecondary	Rochester MSA, NY	Y	65080 FQ	89930 MW	138950 TQ	USBLS	5/15
Postsecondary	North Carolina	Y	45190 FQ	57640 MW	71870 TQ	USBLS	5/15
Postsecondary	Charlotte-Concord-Gastonia MSA, NC-SC	Y	45820 FQ	56760 MW	70590 TQ	USBLS	5/15
Postsecondary	Raleigh MSA, NC	Y	36760 FQ	48450 MW	59100 TQ	USBLS	5/15
Postsecondary	North Dakota	Y	48210 FQ	61590 MW	81200 TQ	USBLS	5/15.
Postsecondary	Fargo MSA, ND-MN	Y	54760 FQ	71180 MW	88250 TQ	USBLS	5/15
Postsecondary	Ohio	Y	45500 FQ	65190 MW	93370 TQ	USBLS	5/15
Postsecondary	Cincinnati MSA, OH-KY-IN	Y	44600 FQ	61710 MW	81240 TQ	USBLS	5/15
Postsecondary	Cleveland-Elyria MSA, OH	Y	46460 FQ	71040 MW	105040 TQ	USBLS	5/15
Postsecondary	Columbus MSA, OH	Y	43230 FQ	59380 MW	78810 TQ	USBLS	5/15
Postsecondary	Oklahoma	Y	38830 FQ	48030 MW	61150 TQ	USBLS	5/15
Postsecondary	Oklahoma City MSA, OK	Y	34690 FQ	43850 MW	52720 TQ	USBLS	5/15
Postsecondary	Oregon	Y	52428 FQ	67378 MW	88400 TQ	ORBLS	2016
Postsecondary	Portland-Vancouver-Hillsboro MSA, OR-WA	Y	49870 FQ	64420 MW	87780 TQ	USBLS	5/15
Postsecondary	Pennsylvania	Y	49740 FQ	66730 MW	88500 TQ	USBLS	5/15
Postsecondary	Allentown-Bethlehem-Easton MSA, PA-NJ	Y	40660 FQ	67360 MW	96180 TQ	USBLS	5/15
Postsecondary	Harrisburg-Carlisle MSA, PA	Y	52630 FQ	65330 MW	85000 TQ	USBLS	5/15
Postsecondary	Montgomery County-Bucks County-Chester County PMSA, PA	Y	48830 FQ	65840 MW	78380 TQ	USBLS	5/15
Postsecondary	Philadelphia PMSA, PA	Y	49190 FQ	65940 MW	88230 TQ	USBLS	5/15
Postsecondary	Pittsburgh MSA, PA	Y	49350 FQ	66750 MW	87540 TQ	USBLS	5/15
Postsecondary	Rhode Island	Y	63670 FQ	75300 MW	90250 TQ	USBLS	5/15
Postsecondary	Providence-Warwick MSA, RI-MA	Y	63580 FQ	75260 MW	90180 TQ	USBLS	5/15
Postsecondary	South Carolina	Y	39350 FQ	55360 MW	70800 TQ	USBLS	5/15
Postsecondary	Charleston-North Charleston MSA, SC	Y	17970 FQ	27550 MW	55320 TQ	USBLS	5/15
Postsecondary	Columbia MSA, SC	Y	40280 FQ	54700 MW	68780 TQ	USBLS	5/15
Postsecondary	Greenville-Anderson-Mauldin MSA, SC	Y	50300 FQ	64590 MW	80910 TQ	USBLS	5/15
Postsecondary	South Dakota	Y	48850 FQ	57850 MW	69740 TQ	USBLS	5/15
Postsecondary	Tennessee	Y	35420 FQ	49220 MW	65860 TQ	USBLS	5/15
Postsecondary	Knoxville MSA, TN	Y	34720 FQ	39870 MW	65640 TQ	USBLS	5/15
Postsecondary	Memphis MSA, TN-MS-AR	Y	39860 FQ	55370 MW	75270 TQ	USBLS	5/15
Postsecondary	Nashville-Davidson–Murfreesboro–Franklin MSA, TN	Y	33570 FQ	48450 MW	61440 TQ	USBLS	5/15
Postsecondary	Texas	Y	33930 FQ	56940 MW	74800 TQ	USBLS	5/15
Postsecondary	Austin-Round Rock MSA, TX	Y	44920 FQ	59360 MW	80920 TQ	USBLS	5/15
Postsecondary	Dallas-Plano-Irving PMSA, TX	Y	19340 FQ	54040 MW	70730 TQ	USBLS	5/15

AE	Average entry wage	AWR	Average wage range	H	Hourly	LR	Low end range	MTC	Median total compensation	TCC	Total cash compensation
AEX	Average experienced wage	B	Biweekly	HI	Highest wage paid	M	Monthly	MW	Median wage paid	TQ	Third quartile wage
ATC	Average total compensation	D	Daily	HR	High end range	MCC	Median cash compensation	MWR	Median wage range	W	Weekly
AW	Average wage paid	FQ	First quartile wage	LO	Lowest wage paid	ME	Median entry wage	S	See annotated source	Y	Yearly

Occupation/Type/Industry	Location	Per	Low	Mid	High	Source	Date
Art, Drama, and Music Teacher							
Postsecondary	Fort Worth-Arlington PMSA, TX	Y	28810 FQ	47810 MW	64410 TQ	USBLS	5/15
Postsecondary	Houston-The Woodlands-Sugar Land MSA, TX	Y	42820 FQ	63600 MW	80290 TQ	USBLS	5/15
Postsecondary	San Antonio-New Braunfels MSA, TX	Y	22100 FQ	38150 MW	66930 TQ	USBLS	5/15
Postsecondary	Utah	Y	44210 FQ	60580 MW	84740 TQ	USBLS	5/15
Postsecondary	Ogden-Clearfield MSA, UT	Y	23260 FQ	29990 MW	55090 TQ	USBLS	5/15
Postsecondary	Provo-Orem MSA, UT	Y	55990 FQ	80060 MW	97100 TQ	USBLS	5/15
Postsecondary	Salt Lake City MSA, UT	Y	43630 FQ	54160 MW	66340 TQ	USBLS	5/15
Postsecondary	Vermont	Y	37900 FQ	49750 MW	79190 TQ	USBLS	5/15
Postsecondary	Burlington-South Burlington MSA, VT	Y	35040 FQ	45770 MW	80640 TQ	USBLS	5/15
Postsecondary	Virginia	Y	38640 FQ	54280 MW	75140 TQ	USBLS	5/15
Postsecondary	Virginia Beach-Norfolk-Newport News MSA, VA-NC	Y	42360 FQ	59920 MW	79400 TQ	USBLS	5/15
Postsecondary	Washington	Y		61123 AW		WABLS	3/16
Postsecondary	Seattle-Bellevue-Everett PMSA, WA	Y		70781 AW		WABLS	3/16
Postsecondary	Tacoma-Lakewood PMSA, WA	Y		61752 AW		WABLS	3/16
Postsecondary	West Virginia	Y	44450 FQ	54140 MW	62070 TQ	USBLS	5/15
Postsecondary	Wisconsin	Y	42690 FQ	56920 MW	71800 TQ	USBLS	5/15
Postsecondary	Madison MSA, WI	Y	54860 FQ	80040 MW	93240 TQ	USBLS	5/15
Postsecondary	Milwaukee-Waukesha-West Allis MSA, WI	Y	41290 FQ	59130 MW	71850 TQ	USBLS	5/15
Postsecondary	Wyoming	Y	47450 FQ	58930 MW	70700 TQ	USBLS	5/15
Postsecondary	Puerto Rico	Y	27940 FQ	35090 MW	46170 TQ	USBLS	5/15
Postsecondary	San Juan-Carolina-Caguas MSA, PR	Y	27920 FQ	34910 MW	45420 TQ	USBLS	5/15
Art Director	Alabama	Y	50314 AE	73850 AW	85623 AEX	ALBLS	6/16
	Birmingham-Hoover MSA, AL	Y	50691 AE	76694 AW	89690 AEX	ALBLS	6/16
	Arizona	Y	49080 FQ	72640 MW	97530 TQ	USBLS	5/15
	Phoenix-Mesa-Scottsdale MSA, AZ	Y	55460 FQ	76240 MW	99690 TQ	USBLS	5/15
	Tucson MSA, AZ	Y	44980 FQ	55240 MW	76660 TQ	USBLS	5/15
	Arkansas	Y	35750 FQ	53250 MW	74310 TQ	USBLS	5/15
	Little Rock-North Little Rock-Conway MSA, AR	Y	56640 FQ	68180 MW	75690 TQ	USBLS	5/15
	California	H	36.34 FQ	53.85 MW	73.69 TQ	CABLS	1/16-3/16
	Anaheim-Santa Ana-Irvine PMSA, CA	H	32.09 FQ	41.43 MW	60.19 TQ	CABLS	1/16-3/16
	Los Angeles-Long Beach-Glendale PMSA, CA	H	38.03 FQ	55.70 MW	74.60 TQ	CABLS	1/16-3/16
	Oakland-Hayward-Berkeley PMSA, CA	H	32.39 FQ	52.47 MW	72.94 TQ	CABLS	1/16-3/16
	Riverside-San Bernardino-Ontario MSA, CA	H	28.24 FQ	35.57 MW	58.74 TQ	CABLS	1/16-3/16
	Sacramento–Roseville–Arden-Arcade MSA, CA	H	26.13 FQ	38.97 MW	54.71 TQ	CABLS	1/16-3/16
	San Diego-Carlsbad MSA, CA	H	33.86 FQ	44.93 MW	60.95 TQ	CABLS	1/16-3/16
	San Francisco-Redwood City-South San Francisco PMSA, CA	H	47.38 FQ	62.49 MW	79.59 TQ	CABLS	1/16-3/16
	Colorado	Y	58280 FQ	79280 MW	104510 TQ	USBLS	5/15
	Denver-Aurora-Lakewood MSA, CO	Y	60690 FQ	83170 MW	114180 TQ	USBLS	5/15
	Connecticut	Y		76797 MW		CTBLS	1/16-3/16
	Bridgeport-Stamford-Norwalk MSA, CT	Y	67660 FQ	79650 MW	96940 TQ	USBLS	5/15
	Hartford-West Hartford-East Hartford MSA, CT	Y	65630 FQ	94960 MW	120340 TQ	USBLS	5/15
	Delaware	Y	65540 FQ	78300 MW	91290 TQ	USBLS	5/15
	Wilmington PMSA, DE-MD-NJ	Y	65640 FQ	78230 MW	91320 TQ	USBLS	5/15
	District of Columbia	Y	83640 FQ	95100 MW	114450 TQ	USBLS	5/15
	Washington-Arlington-Alexandria PMSA, DC-VA-MD-WV	Y	79240 FQ	93560 MW	113340 TQ	USBLS	5/15
	Florida	H	26.73 AE	38.30 MW	48.42 AEX	FLBLS	7/16-9/16

AE	Average entry wage	AWR	Average wage range	H	Hourly	LR	Low end range	MTC	Median total compensation	TCC	Total cash compensation
AEX	Average experienced wage	B	Biweekly	HI	Highest wage paid	M	Monthly	MW	Median wage paid	TQ	Third quartile wage
ATC	Average total compensation	D	Daily	HR	High end range	MCC	Median cash compensation	MWR	Median wage range	W	Weekly
AW	Average wage paid	FQ	First quartile wage	LO	Lowest wage paid	ME	Median entry wage	S	See annotated source	Y	Yearly

Art Director

Occupation/Type/Industry	Location	Per	Low	Mid	High	Source	Date
Art Director	Fort Lauderdale-Pompano Beach-Deerfield Beach PMSA, FL	H	28.49 AE	36.59 MW	42.86 AEX	FLBLS	7/16-9/16
	Miami-Miami Beach-Kendall PMSA, FL	H	29.34 AE	41.56 MW	57.51 AEX	FLBLS	7/16-9/16
	Orlando-Kissimmee-Sanford MSA, FL	H	31.61 AE	43.61 MW	52.62 AEX	FLBLS	7/16-9/16
	Tampa-St. Petersburg-Clearwater MSA, FL	H	23.91 AE	37.22 MW	46.63 AEX	FLBLS	7/16-9/16
	Georgia	Y	65110 FQ	83030 MW	110960 TQ	USBLS	5/15
	Atlanta-Sandy Springs-Roswell MSA, GA	Y	65990 FQ	82690 MW	107130 TQ	USBLS	5/15
	Hawaii	Y	45170 FQ	55300 MW	69390 TQ	USBLS	5/15
	Urban Honolulu MSA, HI	Y	44540 FQ	55210 MW	71640 TQ	USBLS	5/15
	Idaho	Y	39140 FQ	57070 MW	77650 TQ	USBLS	5/15
	Illinois	Y	56000 FQ	73450 MW	117640 TQ	USBLS	5/15
	Chicago-Naperville-Arlington Heights PMSA, IL	Y	56620 FQ	74610 MW	122710 TQ	USBLS	5/15
	Lake County-Kenosha County PMSA, IL-WI	Y	66540 FQ	76780 MW	95290 TQ	USBLS	5/15
	Indiana	Y	52130 FQ	65940 MW	83130 TQ	USBLS	5/15
	Gary PMSA, IN	Y	46010 FQ	54390 MW	67600 TQ	USBLS	5/15
	Indianapolis-Carmel-Anderson MSA, IN	Y	55730 FQ	68060 MW	82390 TQ	USBLS	5/15
	Iowa	Y	48470 FQ	75980 MW	101090 TQ	USBLS	5/15
	Des Moines-West Des Moines MSA, IA	Y	64830 FQ	85890 MW	103600 TQ	USBLS	5/15
	Kansas	Y	44690 FQ	59630 MW	77640 TQ	USBLS	5/15
	Wichita MSA, KS	Y	48380 FQ	58850 MW	71730 TQ	USBLS	5/15
	Kentucky	Y	51850 FQ	68210 MW	81520 TQ	USBLS	5/15
	Louisville-Jefferson County MSA, KY-IN	Y	57390 FQ	73770 MW	91190 TQ	USBLS	5/15
	Louisiana	Y	62660 FQ	87520 MW	136300 TQ	USBLS	5/15
	Baton Rouge MSA, LA	Y	42160 FQ	49280 MW	60930 TQ	USBLS	5/15
	New Orleans-Metairie MSA, LA	Y	68930 FQ	101470 MW	145050 TQ	USBLS	5/15
	Maine	Y	49160 FQ	60420 MW	77930 TQ	USBLS	5/15
	Portland-South Portland MSA, ME	Y	50340 FQ	61100 MW	77990 TQ	USBLS	5/15
	Maryland	Y	52284 AE	90471 MW	109565 AEX	MDBLS	4/16
	Baltimore-Columbia-Towson MSA, MD	Y	64430 FQ	78170 MW	95290 TQ	USBLS	5/15
	Massachusetts	Y	71290 FQ	94260 MW	124360 TQ	USBLS	5/15
	Boston-Cambridge-Newton NECTA, MA	Y	78970 FQ	98110 MW	129100 TQ	USBLS	5/15
	Michigan	Y	54170 FQ	74950 MW	97880 TQ	USBLS	5/15
	Grand Rapids-Wyoming MSA, MI	Y	69110 FQ	78410 MW	93520 TQ	USBLS	5/15
	Minnesota	Y	57469 FQ	71864 MW	95533 TQ	MNBLS	1/16-3/16
	Minneapolis-St. Paul-Bloomington MSA, MN-WI	Y	58931 FQ	73729 MW	98184 TQ	MNBLS	1/16-3/16
	Mississippi	Y	29950 FQ	46390 MW	79920 TQ	USBLS	5/15
	Missouri	Y	77720 FQ	105780 MW	124950 TQ	USBLS	5/15
	Kansas City MSA, MO-KS	Y	66780 FQ	97260 MW	119700 TQ	USBLS	5/15
	St. Louis MSA, MO-IL	Y	72680 FQ	100410 MW	132830 TQ	USBLS	5/15
	Nebraska	Y	47120 FQ	61660 MW	81160 TQ	NEBLS	7/16-9/16
	Omaha-Council Bluffs MSA, NE-IA	Y	47440 FQ	61645 MW	80015 TQ	NEBLS	7/16-9/16
	Nevada	Y	59620 FQ	74070 MW	101330 TQ	USBLS	5/15
	Las Vegas-Henderson-Paradise MSA, NV	Y	59770 FQ	73470 MW	106550 TQ	USBLS	5/15
	New Hampshire	H	25.05 AE	36.29 MW	45.58 AEX	NHBLS	6/16
	New Jersey	Y	68430 FQ	90440 MW	117630 TQ	USBLS	5/15
	Camden PMSA, NJ	Y	68030 FQ	82100 MW	98610 TQ	USBLS	5/15
	Newark PMSA, NJ-PA	Y	79530 FQ	101260 MW	128000 TQ	USBLS	5/15
	Trenton MSA, NJ	Y	71200 FQ	90840 MW	121100 TQ	USBLS	5/15
	New Mexico	Y	50330 FQ	58500 MW	81900 TQ	USBLS	5/15
	Albuquerque MSA, NM	Y	51720 FQ	57740 MW	65480 TQ	USBLS	5/15
	New York	Y	72460 AE	117560 MW	159700 AEX	NYBLS	1/16-3/16
	Buffalo-Cheektowaga-Niagara Falls MSA, NY	Y	35790 FQ	54900 MW	114730 TQ	USBLS	5/15

AE	Average entry wage	AWR	Average wage range	H	Hourly	LR	Low end range	MTC	Median total compensation	TCC	Total cash compensation
AEX	Average experienced wage	B	Biweekly	HI	Highest wage paid	M	Monthly	MW	Median wage paid	TQ	Third quartile wage
ATC	Average total compensation	D	Daily	HR	High end range	MCC	Median cash compensation	MWR	Median wage range	W	Weekly
AW	Average wage paid	FQ	First quartile wage	LO	Lowest wage paid	ME	Median entry wage	S	See annotated source	Y	Yearly

Art Director

Occupation/Type/Industry	Location	Per	Low	Mid	High	Source	Date
Art Director	Nassau County-Suffolk County PMSA, NY	Y	70400 FQ	93990 MW	160680 TQ	USBLS	5/15
	New York-Jersey City-White Plains PMSA, NY-NJ	Y	90180 FQ	118250 MW	162110 TQ	USBLS	5/15
	Rochester MSA, NY	Y	54500 FQ	75020 MW	112290 TQ	USBLS	5/15
	North Carolina	Y	65250 FQ	81480 MW	113860 TQ	USBLS	5/15
	Charlotte-Concord-Gastonia MSA, NC-SC	Y	49730 FQ	72740 MW	93770 TQ	USBLS	5/15
	Raleigh MSA, NC	Y	67860 FQ	78850 MW	98820 TQ	USBLS	5/15
	North Dakota	Y	35960 FQ	67620 MW	87850 TQ	USBLS	5/15
	Ohio	Y	60670 FQ	78070 MW	95940 TQ	USBLS	5/15
	Cincinnati MSA, OH-KY-IN	Y	62040 FQ	76660 MW	92740 TQ	USBLS	5/15
	Cleveland-Elyria MSA, OH	Y	56000 FQ	69400 MW	87900 TQ	USBLS	5/15
	Columbus MSA, OH	Y	70310 FQ	87800 MW	108150 TQ	USBLS	5/15
	Oklahoma	Y	38940 FQ	54110 MW	73920 TQ	USBLS	5/15
	Oklahoma City MSA, OK	Y	36950 FQ	53270 MW	73390 TQ	USBLS	5/15
	Tulsa MSA, OK	Y	46460 FQ	57600 MW	80350 TQ	USBLS	5/15
	Oregon	H	29.94 FQ	38.00 MW	49.04 TQ	ORBLS	2016
	Portland-Vancouver-Hillsboro MSA, OR-WA	Y	64090 FQ	79910 MW	102460 TQ	USBLS	5/15
	Pennsylvania	Y	52270 FQ	69740 MW	96080 TQ	USBLS	5/15
	Allentown-Bethlehem-Easton MSA, PA-NJ	Y	53580 FQ	74390 MW	110100 TQ	USBLS	5/15
	Harrisburg-Carlisle MSA, PA	Y	42720 FQ	60380 MW	79880 TQ	USBLS	5/15
	Montgomery County-Bucks County-Chester County PMSA, PA	Y	58900 FQ	77440 MW	98780 TQ	USBLS	5/15
	Philadelphia PMSA, PA	Y	56130 FQ	77670 MW	100770 TQ	USBLS	5/15
	Pittsburgh MSA, PA	Y	45750 FQ	60940 MW	91230 TQ	USBLS	5/15
	Rhode Island	Y	44160 FQ	59220 MW	73230 TQ	USBLS	5/15
	Providence-Warwick MSA, RI-MA	Y	44620 FQ	60760 MW	73670 TQ	USBLS	5/15
	South Carolina	Y	38460 FQ	47180 MW	66850 TQ	USBLS	5/15
	Charleston-North Charleston MSA, SC	Y	41810 FQ	47620 MW	56760 TQ	USBLS	5/15
	Columbia MSA, SC	Y	57360 FQ	70120 MW	99930 TQ	USBLS	5/15
	Greenville-Anderson-Mauldin MSA, SC	Y	43520 FQ	47800 MW	69120 TQ	USBLS	5/15
	Tennessee	Y	51010 FQ	63240 MW	87480 TQ	USBLS	5/15
	Memphis MSA, TN-MS-AR	Y	33060 FQ	54650 MW	74770 TQ	USBLS	5/15
	Nashville-Davidson–Murfreesboro–Franklin MSA, TN	Y	55470 FQ	66190 MW	94070 TQ	USBLS	5/15
	Texas	Y	60800 FQ	79770 MW	107770 TQ	USBLS	5/15
	Austin-Round Rock MSA, TX	Y	60100 FQ	80690 MW	113300 TQ	USBLS	5/15
	Dallas-Plano-Irving PMSA, TX	Y	66700 FQ	87020 MW	117050 TQ	USBLS	5/15
	Fort Worth-Arlington PMSA, TX	Y	58580 FQ	73390 MW	92270 TQ	USBLS	5/15
	Houston-The Woodlands-Sugar Land MSA, TX	Y	64870 FQ	78860 MW	102310 TQ	USBLS	5/15
	San Antonio-New Braunfels MSA, TX	Y	54370 FQ	64550 MW	84960 TQ	USBLS	5/15
	Utah	Y	53430 FQ	71360 MW	98420 TQ	USBLS	5/15
	Provo-Orem MSA, UT	Y	50220 FQ	75900 MW	108630 TQ	USBLS	5/15
	Salt Lake City MSA, UT	Y	57210 FQ	73720 MW	98890 TQ	USBLS	5/15
	Vermont	Y	51360 FQ	64340 MW	88970 TQ	USBLS	5/15
	Virginia	Y	58440 FQ	89110 MW	125450 TQ	USBLS	5/15
	Richmond MSA, VA	Y	67240 FQ	97590 MW	179680 TQ	USBLS	5/15
	Virginia Beach-Norfolk-Newport News MSA, VA-NC	Y	55260 FQ	69020 MW	96490 TQ	USBLS	5/15
	Washington	H	36.66 FQ	45.96 MW	57.56 TQ	WABLS	3/16
	Seattle-Bellevue-Everett PMSA, WA	H	38.94 FQ	46.72 MW	57.77 TQ	WABLS	3/16
	Tacoma-Lakewood PMSA, WA	H	25.83 FQ	44.85 MW	55.19 TQ	WABLS	3/16
	West Virginia	Y	41070 FQ	56160 MW	79690 TQ	USBLS	5/15
	Wisconsin	Y	60330 FQ	80010 MW	104310 TQ	USBLS	5/15
	Madison MSA, WI	Y	64230 FQ	80790 MW	94670 TQ	USBLS	5/15
	Milwaukee-Waukesha-West Allis MSA, WI	Y	62750 FQ	87850 MW	118950 TQ	USBLS	5/15
	Puerto Rico	Y	35180 FQ	48540 MW	65700 TQ	USBLS	5/15
	San Juan-Carolina-Caguas MSA, PR	Y	35180 FQ	48540 MW	65700 TQ	USBLS	5/15

AE Average entry wage	**AWR** Average wage range	**H** Hourly	**LR** Low end range	**MTC** Median total compensation	**TCC** Total cash compensation
AEX Average experienced wage	**B** Biweekly	**HI** Highest wage paid	**M** Monthly	**MW** Median wage paid	**TQ** Third quartile wage
ATC Average total compensation	**D** Daily	**HR** High end range	**MCC** Median cash compensation	**MWR** Median wage range	**W** Weekly
AW Average wage paid	**FQ** First quartile wage	**LO** Lowest wage paid	**ME** Median entry wage	**S** See annotated source	**Y** Yearly

Occupation/Type/Industry	Location	Per	Low	Mid	High	Source	Date
Art Director							
Pharmaceutical, Medical Device, and Healthcare Industries	United States	Y		60300 AW		MMM01	7/16
Art Handler							
State Government	North Carolina	Y	27013 LO		40224 HI	NCGOV	7/1/16
Art Museum Director							
Museum With Annual Budget > $20 Million	United States	Y		487212 AW		FREEP01	2015
Artist Level Piano Technician							
Michigan State University	East Lansing, MI	Y			88619 HI	MSUSAL	10/1/14-9/30/15
Arts Instructor							
Public Library	Carlsbad, CA	H	21.50 LO		30.00 HI	CCCA02	1/1/16
Arts Program Assistant							
Street Artists Program	San Francisco, CA	B	2303 LO		2800 HI	SFGOV	2016-2018
Asbestos Abatement Worker							
Detroit Environmental Employment Program Graduate	Detroit, MI	H			22.00-25.00 HR	LSJ18	2017
Asbestos Inspector							
State Government	North Carolina	Y	44347 LO		72346 HI	NCGOV	7/1/16
Asian Services Coordinator							
Public Library	Alhambra, CA	Y			63814 HI	CACIT	6/28/16
Asphalt Plant Supervisor							
Public Works - Street Services, Municipal Government	Los Angeles, CA	Y		100491 AW		CACIT	6/23/16
Assembly Line Worker							
Entry-Level, Ford, General Motors, and Fiat Chrysler	United States	H			19.28 HI	LSJ01	2016
Assembly Professional							
Aerospace	United States	Y		91500 AW		ASSEM01	3/16
Fabricated Metal Products	United States	Y		99105 AW		ASSEM01	3/16
Medical Equipment and Supplies	United States	Y		69300 AW		ASSEM01	3/16
Assessor Chairperson							
Municipal Government	Ashfield, MA	Y			1500 HI	FRCOG	2016
Municipal Government	Erving, MA	Y			3516 HI	FRCOG	2016
Municipal Government	Shelburne, MA	Y			2590 HI	FRCOG	2016
Assistance Payments Worker							
State Government	Battle Creek, MI	B	1432.00 LO		2010.40 HI	MIGOV	2016
Assistant Coach							
Football, Conference USA	United States	Y		628000 AW		USAT01	2015
Football, FBS Conference	United States	Y		245000 AW		USAT01	2015
Football, Southeastern Conference	United States	Y		447000 AW		USAT01	2015
Football, Sun Belt Conference	United States	Y		542000 AW		USAT01	2015
Men's Soccer, Baccalaureate Institution	United States	Y		28982 MW		CHE02	2015-2016
Men's Soccer, Master's Institution	United States	Y		31308 MW		CHE02	2015-2016
Men's Soccer, Research University	United States	Y		41412 MW		CHE02	2015-2016
Strength and Conditioning, Baccalaureate Institution	United States	Y		41068 MW		CHE02	2015-2016
Strength and Conditioning, Master's Institution	United States	Y		35353 MW		CHE02	2015-2016
Strength and Conditioning, Research University	United States	Y		45996 MW		CHE02	2015-2016
Women's Soccer, Baccalaureate Institution	United States	Y		29886 MW		CHE02	2015-2016
Women's Soccer, Master's Institution	United States	Y		31858 MW		CHE02	2015-2016
Women's Soccer, Research University	United States	Y		44008 MW		CHE02	2015-2016
Assistant Lottery Ticket Sales Regional Manager							
Lottery Commission, State Government	Ohio	H	34.19 LO		39.64 HI	OHGOV	2015

AE	Average entry wage	AWR	Average wage range	H	Hourly	LR	Low end range	MTC	Median total compensation	TCC	Total cash compensation
AEX	Average experienced wage	B	Biweekly	HI	Highest wage paid	M	Monthly	MW	Median wage paid	TQ	Third quartile wage
ATC	Average total compensation	D	Daily	HR	High end range	MCC	Median cash compensation	MWR	Median wage range	W	Weekly
AW	Average wage paid	FQ	First quartile wage	LO	Lowest wage paid	ME	Median entry wage	S	See annotated source	Y	Yearly

75

Occupation/Type/Industry	Location	Per	Low	Mid	High	Source	Date
Assistant Market Manager							
Community Services Department, Municipal Government	Beverly Hills, CA	Y			21436 HI	CACIT	6/28/16
Assistant Professor							
Accounting	United States	Y		140300 AW		AACSB	2014-2015
Entrepreneurship	United States	Y		110900 AW		AACSB	2014-2015
Non-Tenure-Track	United States	Y		55479 AW		APAC02	2014-2015
Tenured/Tenure-Track	United States	Y		60195 AW		APAC02	2014-2015
Tenured/Tenure-Track, Research University	United States	Y		68968 AW		APAC02	2014-2015
Assistant Quartermaster General							
Adjutant General, State Government	Ohio	H	30.85 LO		44.80 HI	OHGOV	2015
Assistant Regional Scenic River Manager							
Natural Resources Department, State Government	Ohio	H	25.33 LO		28.15 HI	OHGOV	2015
Assisted Living/Personal Care Director							
Life Plan Community	United States	Y		71357 AW		LAGE1	2016
Assistive Technology Specialist							
State Government	New Mexico	H	15.28 LO		26.59 HI	NMGOV	7/30/16
Associate Justice							
United States Supreme Court	United States	Y			251800 HI	OPM01	2017
Associate Professor							
Accounting	United States	Y		134400 AW		AACSB	2014-2015
Entrepreneurship	United States	Y		128500 AW		AACSB	2014-2015
Non-Tenure-Track	United States	Y		65959 AW		APAC02	2014-2015
Tenured/Tenure-Track	United States	Y		70336 AW		APAC02	2014-2015
Tenured/Tenure-Track, Research University	United States	Y		79636 AW		APAC02	2014-2015
Associate Zoo Veterinarian							
Municipal Government	Detroit, MI	M	4133 LO		5775 HI	DETGOV	2016
Association Planner							
Meetings and Conventions	United States	Y		73187 AW		MANDC	2016
Astronomer	Alabama	Y	92860 AE	124378 AW	140137 AEX	ALBLS	6/16
	Tucson MSA, AZ	Y	62070 FQ	78360 MW	102600 TQ	USBLS	5/15
	California	H	41.84 FQ	65.26 MW	77.41 TQ	CABLS	1/16-3/16
	Los Angeles-Long Beach-Glendale PMSA, CA	H	38.27 FQ	50.99 MW	82.50 TQ	CABLS	1/16-3/16
	San Diego-Carlsbad MSA, CA	H	28.98 FQ	35.43 MW	51.56 TQ	CABLS	1/16-3/16
	Colorado	Y	74500 FQ	104630 MW	142460 TQ	USBLS	5/15
	Washington-Arlington-Alexandria PMSA, DC-VA-MD-WV	Y	107680 FQ	138870 MW	158690 TQ	USBLS	5/15
	Hawaii	Y	68830 FQ	106440 MW	165580 TQ	USBLS	5/15
	New Mexico	Y	105720 FQ	117610 MW	129800 TQ	USBLS	5/15
	Texas	Y	48000 FQ	61250 MW	98600 TQ	USBLS	5/15
	Houston-The Woodlands-Sugar Land MSA, TX	Y	100380 FQ	133440 MW	148260 TQ	USBLS	5/15
Astronomical Lecturer							
Recreation and Parks Department, Municipal Government	Los Angeles, CA	Y			76390 HI	CACIT	6/23/16
Astronomical Observer							
Recreation and Parks Department, Municipal Government	Los Angeles, CA	Y			82754 HI	CACIT	6/23/16
Athlete and Sports Competitor	Arkansas	Y	17050 FQ	18510 MW	33210 TQ	USBLS	5/15
	Connecticut	Y		61113 MW		CTBLS	1/16-3/16
	Florida	Y	26282 AE	34557 MW	62313 AEX	FLBLS	7/16-9/16
	Georgia	Y	19720 FQ	37100 MW	67590 TQ	USBLS	5/15
	Illinois	Y	23570 FQ	56120 MW	76170 TQ	USBLS	5/15
	Kentucky	Y	28630 FQ	45640 MW	62290 TQ	USBLS	5/15

AE	Average entry wage	**AWR**	Average wage range	**H**	Hourly	**LR** Low end range **MTC** Median total compensation **TCC** Total cash compensation
AEX	Average experienced wage	**B**	Biweekly	**HI**	Highest wage paid	**M** Monthly **MW** Median wage paid **TQ** Third quartile wage
ATC	Average total compensation	**D**	Daily	**HR**	High end range	**MCC** Median cash compensation **MWR** Median wage range **W** Weekly
AW	Average wage paid	**FQ**	First quartile wage	**LO**	Lowest wage paid	**ME** Median entry wage **S** See annotated source **Y** Yearly

Occupation/Type/Industry	Location	Per	Low	Mid	High	Source	Date
Athlete and Sports Competitor	Michigan	Y	31780 FQ	44580 MW	53110 TQ	USBLS	5/15
	Minnesota	Y	28719 FQ	38125 MW	50655 TQ	MNBLS	1/16-3/16
	Mississippi	Y	24960 FQ	31780 MW	46610 TQ	USBLS	5/15
	Missouri	Y	27830 FQ	35720 MW	49220 TQ	USBLS	5/15
	New Jersey	Y	42610 FQ	59630 MW	104200 TQ	USBLS	5/15
	New York	Y	35680 AE	59900 MW	88750 AEX	NYBLS	1/16-3/16
	Oregon	Y	31501 FQ	50131 MW	103219 TQ	ORBLS	2016
	South Carolina	Y	22310 FQ	34490 MW	56930 TQ	USBLS	5/15
	Texas	Y	41380 FQ	53080 MW		USBLS	5/15
	Utah	Y	36410 FQ	58380 MW	98190 TQ	USBLS	5/15
	Virginia	Y	19030 FQ	37680 MW	63840 TQ	USBLS	5/15
	Wisconsin	Y	30850 FQ	41170 MW	62460 TQ	USBLS	5/15
Athletic Equipment Attendant							
California State University	California	Y	23952 LO		52104 HI	CALST	2016-2017
Athletic Ticket Office Manager							
Michigan State University	East Lansing, MI	Y			102001 HI	MSUSAL	10/1/14-9/30/15
Athletic Trainer	Alabama	Y	32996 AE	44076 AW	49610 AEX	ALBLS	6/16
	Birmingham-Hoover MSA, AL	Y	31986 AE	40324 AW	44504 AEX	ALBLS	6/16
	Arizona	Y	32630 FQ	39850 MW	48510 TQ	USBLS	5/15
	Phoenix-Mesa-Scottsdale MSA, AZ	Y	31910 FQ	38060 MW	47330 TQ	USBLS	5/15
	Tucson MSA, AZ	Y	42250 FQ	47620 MW	63120 TQ	USBLS	5/15
	Arkansas	Y	27290 FQ	38820 MW	49320 TQ	USBLS	5/15
	Little Rock-North Little Rock-Conway MSA, AR	Y	18100 FQ	29910 MW	44890 TQ	USBLS	5/15
	California	Y		49771 AW		CABLS	1/16-3/16
	Anaheim-Santa Ana-Irvine PMSA, CA	Y		56933 AW		CABLS	1/16-3/16
	Los Angeles-Long Beach-Glendale PMSA, CA	Y		49375 AW		CABLS	1/16-3/16
	Oakland-Hayward-Berkeley PMSA, CA	Y		49680 AW		CABLS	1/16-3/16
	Riverside-San Bernardino-Ontario MSA, CA	Y		44881 AW		CABLS	1/16-3/16
	Sacramento–Roseville–Arden-Arcade MSA, CA	Y		52764 AW		CABLS	1/16-3/16
	San Diego-Carlsbad MSA, CA	Y		58465 AW		CABLS	1/16-3/16
	San Francisco-Redwood City-South San Francisco PMSA, CA	Y		57065 AW		CABLS	1/16-3/16
	Colorado	Y	35320 FQ	41420 MW	58560 TQ	USBLS	5/15
	Denver-Aurora-Lakewood MSA, CO	Y	34850 FQ	39040 MW	54270 TQ	USBLS	5/15
	Connecticut	Y		44110 MW		CTBLS	1/16-3/16
	Bridgeport-Stamford-Norwalk MSA, CT	Y	23390 FQ	41790 MW	50720 TQ	USBLS	5/15
	Hartford-West Hartford-East Hartford MSA, CT	Y	42010 FQ	46460 MW	53750 TQ	USBLS	5/15
	Delaware	Y	33050 FQ	37200 MW	47050 TQ	USBLS	5/15
	Wilmington PMSA, DE-MD-NJ	Y	33010 FQ	36970 MW	45980 TQ	USBLS	5/15
	District of Columbia	Y	42680 FQ	53220 MW	88580 TQ	USBLS	5/15
	Washington-Arlington-Alexandria PMSA, DC-VA-MD-WV	Y	36940 FQ	44860 MW	63160 TQ	USBLS	5/15
	Florida	Y	26813 AE	44954 MW	54377 AEX	FLBLS	7/16-9/16
	Fort Lauderdale-Pompano Beach-Deerfield Beach PMSA, FL	Y	24946 AE	42079 MW	49782 AEX	FLBLS	7/16-9/16
	Miami-Miami Beach-Kendall PMSA, FL	Y	24076 AE	46335 MW	53866 AEX	FLBLS	7/16-9/16
	Orlando-Kissimmee-Sanford MSA, FL	Y	43175 AE	55182 MW	60130 AEX	FLBLS	7/16-9/16
	Tampa-St. Petersburg-Clearwater MSA, FL	Y	31753 AE	42422 MW	49491 AEX	FLBLS	7/16-9/16
	Georgia	Y	40460 FQ	46030 MW	54110 TQ	USBLS	5/15
	Atlanta-Sandy Springs-Roswell MSA, GA	Y	40610 FQ	46010 MW	54250 TQ	USBLS	5/15
	Hawaii	Y	43610 FQ	50120 MW	57720 TQ	USBLS	5/15

AE	Average entry wage	**AWR**	Average wage range	**H**	Hourly
AEX	Average experienced wage	**B**	Biweekly	**HI**	Highest wage paid
ATC	Average total compensation	**D**	Daily	**HR**	High end range
AW	Average wage paid	**FQ**	First quartile wage	**LO**	Lowest wage paid

LR	Low end range	**MTC**	Median total compensation	**TCC**	Total cash compensation
M	Monthly	**MW**	Median wage paid	**TQ**	Third quartile wage
MCC	Median cash compensation	**MWR**	Median wage range	**W**	Weekly
ME	Median entry wage	**S**	See annotated source	**Y**	Yearly

Occupation/Type/Industry	Location	Per	Low	Mid	High	Source	Date
Athletic Trainer	Urban Honolulu MSA, HI	Y	44140 FQ	50700 MW	58220 TQ	USBLS	5/15
	Idaho	Y	32500 FQ	41150 MW	48440 TQ	USBLS	5/15
	Boise City MSA, ID	Y	33360 FQ	41520 MW	48640 TQ	USBLS	5/15
	Illinois	Y	37470 FQ	45960 MW	55680 TQ	USBLS	5/15
	Chicago-Naperville-Arlington Heights PMSA, IL	Y	37190 FQ	45600 MW	55280 TQ	USBLS	5/15
	Lake County-Kenosha County PMSA, IL-WI	Y	46970 FQ	54020 MW	59620 TQ	USBLS	5/15
	Indiana	Y	36570 FQ	42840 MW	48930 TQ	USBLS	5/15
	Gary PMSA, IN	Y	33970 FQ	38660 MW	45970 TQ	USBLS	5/15
	Indianapolis-Carmel-Anderson MSA, IN	Y	38250 FQ	43920 MW	49210 TQ	USBLS	5/15
	Iowa	Y	34200 FQ	39350 MW	46300 TQ	USBLS	5/15
	Des Moines-West Des Moines MSA, IA	Y	34470 FQ	40080 MW	47410 TQ	USBLS	5/15
	Kansas	Y	31540 FQ	38290 MW	47890 TQ	USBLS	5/15
	Kentucky	Y	33510 FQ	41460 MW	53230 TQ	USBLS	5/15
	Louisville-Jefferson County MSA, KY-IN	Y	35020 FQ	40350 MW	49270 TQ	USBLS	5/15
	Louisiana	Y	26600 FQ	38600 MW	51250 TQ	USBLS	5/15
	New Orleans-Metairie MSA, LA	Y	37090 FQ	48600 MW	58150 TQ	USBLS	5/15
	Maine	Y	33960 FQ	40020 MW	47730 TQ	USBLS	5/15
	Portland-South Portland MSA, ME	Y	33980 FQ	42770 MW	48080 TQ	USBLS	5/15
	Maryland	Y	30281 AE	44150 MW	51085 AEX	MDBLS	4/16
	Baltimore-Columbia-Towson MSA, MD	Y	34660 FQ	43240 MW	56140 TQ	USBLS	5/15
	Massachusetts	Y	39090 FQ	51080 MW	60710 TQ	USBLS	5/15
	Boston-Cambridge-Newton NECTA, MA	Y	44840 FQ	54630 MW	62380 TQ	USBLS	5/15
	Worcester MSA, MA-CT	Y	35020 FQ	39400 MW	50280 TQ	USBLS	5/15
	Michigan	Y	38420 FQ	44820 MW	51610 TQ	USBLS	5/15
	Detroit-Dearborn-Livonia PMSA, MI	Y	40360 FQ	45300 MW	50980 TQ	USBLS	5/15
	Grand Rapids-Wyoming MSA, MI	Y	36630 FQ	42970 MW	47750 TQ	USBLS	5/15
	Minnesota	Y	38689 FQ	44778 MW	50332 TQ	MNBLS	1/16-3/16
	Minneapolis-St. Paul-Bloomington MSA, MN-WI	Y	38074 FQ	44395 MW	49526 TQ	MNBLS	1/16-3/16
	Mississippi	Y	36870 FQ	44030 MW	50540 TQ	USBLS	5/15
	Jackson MSA, MS	Y	38940 FQ	46400 MW	54910 TQ	USBLS	5/15
	Missouri	Y	36600 FQ	43860 MW	51620 TQ	USBLS	5/15
	Kansas City MSA, MO-KS	Y	33750 FQ	40750 MW	47890 TQ	USBLS	5/15
	St. Louis MSA, MO-IL	Y	38090 FQ	47020 MW	55140 TQ	USBLS	5/15
	Montana	Y	32670 FQ	38390 MW	46560 TQ	USBLS	5/15
	Nebraska	Y	40110 FQ	45590 MW	52690 TQ	NEBLS	7/16-9/16
	Omaha-Council Bluffs MSA, NE-IA	Y	39760 FQ	43520 MW	47225 TQ	NEBLS	7/16-9/16
	Nevada	Y	39870 FQ	65580 MW	75410 TQ	USBLS	5/15
	New Hampshire	Y	36662 AE	46559 MW	53346 AEX	NHBLS	6/16
	Manchester NECTA, NH	Y	40681 AE	45920 MW	51276 AEX	NHBLS	6/16
	New Jersey	Y	43020 FQ	59070 MW	76990 TQ	USBLS	5/15
	Camden PMSA, NJ	Y	33370 FQ	51770 MW	74640 TQ	USBLS	5/15
	Newark PMSA, NJ-PA	Y	43720 FQ	61160 MW	76870 TQ	USBLS	5/15
	New York	Y	32100 AE	46970 MW	59730 AEX	NYBLS	1/16-3/16
	Buffalo-Cheektowaga-Niagara Falls MSA, NY	Y	32680 FQ	37750 MW	45780 TQ	USBLS	5/15
	Nassau County-Suffolk County PMSA, NY	Y	37220 FQ	51520 MW	60900 TQ	USBLS	5/15
	New York-Jersey City-White Plains PMSA, NY-NJ	Y	42400 FQ	56420 MW	73980 TQ	USBLS	5/15
	Rochester MSA, NY	Y	40220 FQ	45350 MW	52300 TQ	USBLS	5/15
	North Carolina	Y	33390 FQ	38960 MW	48790 TQ	USBLS	5/15
	Charlotte-Concord-Gastonia MSA, NC-SC	Y	34750 FQ	40330 MW	48350 TQ	USBLS	5/15
	Raleigh MSA, NC	Y	35220 FQ	47370 MW	58160 TQ	USBLS	5/15
	North Dakota	Y	32830 FQ	37760 MW	44790 TQ	USBLS	5/15
	Ohio	Y	39010 FQ	44680 MW	50530 TQ	USBLS	5/15
	Cincinnati MSA, OH-KY-IN	Y	36480 FQ	44230 MW	55490 TQ	USBLS	5/15
	Cleveland-Elyria MSA, OH	Y	37710 FQ	43600 MW	49220 TQ	USBLS	5/15
	Columbus MSA, OH	Y	42510 FQ	47880 MW	57820 TQ	USBLS	5/15

AE	Average entry wage	AWR	Average wage range	H	Hourly
AEX	Average experienced wage	B	Biweekly	HI	Highest wage paid
ATC	Average total compensation	D	Daily	HR	High end range
AW	Average wage paid	FQ	First quartile wage	LO	Lowest wage paid

LR	Low end range	MTC	Median total compensation
M	Monthly	MW	Median wage paid
MCC	Median cash compensation	MWR	Median wage range
ME	Median entry wage	S	See annotated source

TCC	Total cash compensation
TQ	Third quartile wage
W	Weekly
Y	Yearly

Occupation/Type/Industry	Location	Per	Low	Mid	High	Source	Date
Athletic Trainer	Oklahoma	Y	29500 FQ	38770 MW	47490 TQ	USBLS	5/15
	Oklahoma City MSA, OK	Y	29770 FQ	38360 MW	46120 TQ	USBLS	5/15
	Tulsa MSA, OK	Y	31990 FQ	37410 MW	47310 TQ	USBLS	5/15
	Oregon	Y	38886 FQ	46523 MW	56229 TQ	ORBLS	2016
	Portland-Vancouver-Hillsboro MSA, OR-WA	Y	36430 FQ	45190 MW	55630 TQ	USBLS	5/15
	Pennsylvania	Y	34560 FQ	41340 MW	50130 TQ	USBLS	5/15
	Allentown-Bethlehem-Easton MSA, PA-NJ	Y	36760 FQ	44240 MW	55140 TQ	USBLS	5/15
	Harrisburg-Carlisle MSA, PA	Y	23470 FQ	37400 MW	53030 TQ	USBLS	5/15
	Montgomery County-Bucks County-Chester County PMSA, PA	Y	36260 FQ	43540 MW	52290 TQ	USBLS	5/15
	Philadelphia PMSA, PA	Y	39230 FQ	47420 MW	57450 TQ	USBLS	5/15
	Pittsburgh MSA, PA	Y	34400 FQ	38330 MW	45560 TQ	USBLS	5/15
	Rhode Island	Y	37610 FQ	47360 MW	60640 TQ	USBLS	5/15
	Providence-Warwick MSA, RI-MA	Y	37680 FQ	47000 MW	59920 TQ	USBLS	5/15
	South Carolina	Y	33980 FQ	42120 MW	48670 TQ	USBLS	5/15
	Charleston-North Charleston MSA, SC	Y	37330 FQ	42610 MW	46780 TQ	USBLS	5/15
	Greenville-Anderson-Mauldin MSA, SC	Y	34790 FQ	40350 MW	47080 TQ	USBLS	5/15
	South Dakota	Y	36390 FQ	41960 MW	48090 TQ	USBLS	5/15
	Tennessee	Y	35410 FQ	41240 MW	48840 TQ	USBLS	5/15
	Knoxville MSA, TN	Y	35210 FQ	42230 MW	57100 TQ	USBLS	5/15
	Memphis MSA, TN-MS-AR	Y	35870 FQ	42440 MW	48610 TQ	USBLS	5/15
	Nashville-Davidson–Murfreesboro–Franklin MSA, TN	Y	36580 FQ	42280 MW	48360 TQ	USBLS	5/15
	Texas	Y	39590 FQ	50530 MW	63490 TQ	USBLS	5/15
	Austin-Round Rock MSA, TX	Y	29850 FQ	44860 MW	54600 TQ	USBLS	5/15
	Dallas-Plano-Irving PMSA, TX	Y	51270 FQ	58690 MW	69470 TQ	USBLS	5/15
	Fort Worth-Arlington PMSA, TX	Y	41590 FQ	47200 MW	59630 TQ	USBLS	5/15
	Houston-The Woodlands-Sugar Land MSA, TX	Y	50340 FQ	65680 MW	84200 TQ	USBLS	5/15
	San Antonio-New Braunfels MSA, TX	Y	26400 FQ	29300 MW	45130 TQ	USBLS	5/15
	Utah	Y	38500 FQ	45650 MW	56400 TQ	USBLS	5/15
	Salt Lake City MSA, UT	Y	39890 FQ	47180 MW	70830 TQ	USBLS	5/15
	Vermont	Y	37510 FQ	45280 MW	53570 TQ	USBLS	5/15
	Burlington-South Burlington MSA, VT	Y	39100 FQ	48510 MW	55320 TQ	USBLS	5/15
	Virginia	Y	36440 FQ	43300 MW	51610 TQ	USBLS	5/15
	Richmond MSA, VA	Y	34500 FQ	40130 MW	47790 TQ	USBLS	5/15
	Virginia Beach-Norfolk-Newport News MSA, VA-NC	Y	39940 FQ	45060 MW	51010 TQ	USBLS	5/15
	Washington	Y		48016 AW		WABLS	3/16
	Seattle-Bellevue-Everett PMSA, WA	Y		52764 AW		WABLS	3/16
	Tacoma-Lakewood PMSA, WA	Y		36512 AW		WABLS	3/16
	West Virginia	Y	34810 FQ	38890 MW	55320 TQ	USBLS	5/15
	Wisconsin	Y	40970 FQ	47630 MW	58450 TQ	USBLS	5/15
	Madison MSA, WI	Y	49840 FQ	56850 MW	65560 TQ	USBLS	5/15
	Milwaukee-Waukesha-West Allis MSA, WI	Y	40590 FQ	48880 MW	67200 TQ	USBLS	5/15
	Wyoming	Y	37560 FQ	44290 MW	50400 TQ	USBLS	5/15
Athletic Turf Manager							
Michigan State University	East Lansing, MI	Y			73960 HI	MSUSAL	10/1/14-9/30/15
Atmospheric, Earth, Marine, and Space Sciences Teacher							
Postsecondary	Alabama	Y	57123 AE	97753 AW	118058 AEX	ALBLS	6/16
Postsecondary	Arizona	Y	68150 FQ	93680 MW	127730 TQ	USBLS	5/15
Postsecondary	Arkansas	Y	54190 FQ	64360 MW	78380 TQ	USBLS	5/15
Postsecondary	California	Y		105649 AW		CABLS	1/16-3/16
Postsecondary	Colorado	Y	43020 FQ	73940 MW	108790 TQ	USBLS	5/15
Postsecondary	Georgia	Y	45900 FQ	62680 MW	91130 TQ	USBLS	5/15
Postsecondary	Idaho	Y	41270 FQ	66630 MW	94420 TQ	USBLS	5/15
Postsecondary	Illinois	Y	51800 FQ	62390 MW	107980 TQ	USBLS	5/15

AE	Average entry wage	AWR	Average wage range	H	Hourly	LR	Low end range	MTC	Median total compensation	TCC	Total cash compensation
AEX	Average experienced wage	B	Biweekly	HI	Highest wage paid	M	Monthly	MW	Median wage paid	TQ	Third quartile wage
ATC	Average total compensation	D	Daily	HR	High end range	MCC	Median cash compensation	MWR	Median wage range	W	Weekly
AW	Average wage paid	FQ	First quartile wage	LO	Lowest wage paid	ME	Median entry wage	S	See annotated source	Y	Yearly

Occupation/Type/Industry	Location	Per	Low	Mid	High	Source	Date
Atmospheric, Earth, Marine, and Space Sciences Teacher							
Postsecondary	Indiana	Y	87240 FQ	110630 MW	138790 TQ	USBLS	5/15
Postsecondary	Iowa	Y	63710 FQ	77170 MW	94900 TQ	USBLS	5/15
Postsecondary	Kentucky	Y	56650 FQ	77840 MW	100410 TQ	USBLS	5/15
Postsecondary	Louisiana	Y	64570 FQ	85960 MW	109390 TQ	USBLS	5/15
Postsecondary	Maine	Y	54030 FQ	75240 MW	99140 TQ	USBLS	5/15
Postsecondary	Maryland	Y	52592 AE	105443 MW	131869 AEX	MDBLS	4/16
Postsecondary	Massachusetts	Y	77400 FQ	101660 MW	140490 TQ	USBLS	5/15
Postsecondary	Michigan	Y	70510 FQ	87850 MW	107620 TQ	USBLS	5/15
Postsecondary	Minnesota	Y	51038 FQ	74687 MW	100765 TQ	MNBLS	1/16-3/16
Postsecondary	Mississippi	Y	49370 FQ	66980 MW	77780 TQ	USBLS	5/15
Postsecondary	Missouri	Y	70320 FQ	88170 MW	110950 TQ	USBLS	5/15
Postsecondary	Nebraska	Y	70360 FQ	83880 MW	114385 TQ	NEBLS	7/16-9/16
Postsecondary	New Hampshire	Y	56475 AE	76116 MW	92366 AEX	NHBLS	6/16
Postsecondary	New Mexico	Y	64760 FQ	86940 MW	104180 TQ	USBLS	5/15
Postsecondary	New York	Y	50060 AE	86550 MW	127250 AEX	NYBLS	1/16-3/16
Postsecondary	North Carolina	Y	64140 FQ	85490 MW	112200 TQ	USBLS	5/15
Postsecondary	North Dakota	Y	55380 FQ	85770 MW	110660 TQ	USBLS	5/15
Postsecondary	Ohio	Y	59280 FQ	79990 MW	111670 TQ	USBLS	5/15
Postsecondary	Oregon	Y	79399 FQ	104640 MW	124940 TQ	ORBLS	2016
Postsecondary	Pennsylvania	Y	55840 FQ	77240 MW	103610 TQ	USBLS	5/15
Postsecondary	Tennessee	Y	57420 FQ	79320 MW	96220 TQ	USBLS	5/15
Postsecondary	Texas	Y	54040 FQ	82160 MW	120350 TQ	USBLS	5/15
Postsecondary	Utah	Y	71520 FQ	91800 MW	117140 TQ	USBLS	5/15
Postsecondary	Vermont	Y	47360 FQ	59420 MW	77330 TQ	USBLS	5/15
Postsecondary	Virginia	Y	59510 FQ	85060 MW	113560 TQ	USBLS	5/15
Postsecondary	Washington	Y		84599 AW		WABLS	3/16
Postsecondary	Wisconsin	Y	56410 FQ	76710 MW	105010 TQ	USBLS	5/15
Postsecondary	Wyoming	Y	67880 FQ	83070 MW	109780 TQ	USBLS	5/15
Atmospheric and Space Scientist	Alabama	Y	57796 AE	84950 AW	98538 AEX	ALBLS	6/16
	Alaska	Y	70040 FQ	82080 MW	100290 TQ	USBLS	5/15
	Arizona	Y	70180 FQ	88920 MW	105710 TQ	USBLS	5/15
	Arkansas	Y	70010 FQ	84240 MW	105720 TQ	USBLS	5/15
	California	H	28.78 FQ	40.54 MW	54.74 TQ	CABLS	1/16-3/16
	Colorado	Y	74390 FQ	93660 MW	116330 TQ	USBLS	5/15
	Connecticut	Y		73165 MW		CTBLS	1/16-3/16
	District of Columbia	Y	67040 FQ	90810 MW	126950 TQ	USBLS	5/15
	Florida	H	23.12 AE	44.94 MW	54.74 AEX	FLBLS	7/16-9/16
	Georgia	Y	80440 FQ	94520 MW	112870 TQ	USBLS	5/15
	Hawaii	Y	84850 FQ	100660 MW	110750 TQ	USBLS	5/15
	Idaho	Y	83810 FQ	95930 MW	112160 TQ	USBLS	5/15
	Illinois	Y	82150 FQ	97040 MW	114270 TQ	USBLS	5/15
	Indiana	Y	64430 FQ	86970 MW	108500 TQ	USBLS	5/15
	Iowa	Y	70190 FQ	77880 MW	94590 TQ	USBLS	5/15
	Kansas	Y	38500 FQ	74870 MW	102610 TQ	USBLS	5/15
	Kentucky	Y	43680 FQ	84240 MW	102950 TQ	USBLS	5/15
	Louisiana	Y	77230 FQ	91820 MW	105720 TQ	USBLS	5/15
	Maryland	Y	71932 AE	107085 MW	124662 AEX	MDBLS	4/16
	Massachusetts	Y	62770 FQ	78410 MW	98730 TQ	USBLS	5/15
	Michigan	Y	74180 FQ	91250 MW	108500 TQ	USBLS	5/15
	Minnesota	Y	38014 FQ	48810 MW	81320 TQ	MNBLS	1/16-3/16
	Mississippi	Y	68330 FQ	79550 MW	97750 TQ	USBLS	5/15
	Missouri	Y	86240 FQ	101920 MW	108510 TQ	USBLS	5/15
	Montana	Y	64420 FQ	86250 MW	105720 TQ	USBLS	5/15
	Nebraska	Y	79550 FQ	91255 MW	105710 TQ	NEBLS	7/16-9/16
	Nevada	Y	63780 FQ	88900 MW	108510 TQ	USBLS	5/15
	New Hampshire	H	18.82 AE	40.85 MW	43.76 AEX	NHBLS	6/16
	New Jersey	Y	78540 FQ	101240 MW	134150 TQ	USBLS	5/15
	New Mexico	Y	83740 FQ	94810 MW	118360 TQ	USBLS	5/15
	New York	Y	51840 AE	88310 MW	104400 AEX	NYBLS	1/16-3/16
	North Carolina	Y	64170 FQ	91250 MW	108510 TQ	USBLS	5/15
	North Dakota	Y	71150 FQ	91230 MW	105350 TQ	USBLS	5/15
	Ohio	Y	75400 FQ	92930 MW	112670 TQ	USBLS	5/15
	Oklahoma	Y	61950 FQ	94000 MW	109690 TQ	USBLS	5/15
	Oregon	H	38.23 FQ	46.92 MW	54.36 TQ	ORBLS	2016
	Pennsylvania	Y	83650 FQ	93020 MW	105720 TQ	USBLS	5/15
	South Carolina	Y	66370 FQ	91260 MW	108500 TQ	USBLS	5/15
	South Dakota	Y	71760 FQ	84240 MW	102940 TQ	USBLS	5/15
	Tennessee	Y	55620 FQ	83450 MW	98390 TQ	USBLS	5/15
	Texas	Y	49990 FQ	67540 MW	96220 TQ	USBLS	5/15

AE	Average entry wage	**AWR**	Average wage range	**H**	Hourly	**LR**	Low end range	**MTC**	Median total compensation	**TCC**	Total cash compensation
AEX	Average experienced wage	**B**	Biweekly	**HI**	Highest wage paid	**M**	Monthly	**MW**	Median wage paid	**TQ**	Third quartile wage
ATC	Average total compensation	**D**	Daily	**HR**	High end range	**MCC**	Median cash compensation	**MWR**	Median wage range	**W**	Weekly
AW	Average wage paid	**FQ**	First quartile wage	**LO**	Lowest wage paid	**ME**	Median entry wage	**S**	See annotated source	**Y**	Yearly

Occupation/Type/Industry	Location	Per	Low	Mid	High	Source	Date
Atmospheric and Space Scientist	Utah	Y	74280 FQ	91250 MW	109280 TQ	USBLS	5/15
	Virginia	Y	77210 FQ	94330 MW	124950 TQ	USBLS	5/15
	Washington	H	33.79 FQ	43.71 MW	53.52 TQ	WABLS	3/16
	Wisconsin	Y	44280 FQ	86250 MW	108500 TQ	USBLS	5/15
	Wyoming	Y	61280 FQ	86240 MW	97380 TQ	USBLS	5/15
Attorney							
Court-Appointed, Michigan Appellate Assigned Counsel System	Michigan	H	50.00 LO		75.00 HI	LSJ11	2016
Experienced, Court-Appointed	Ingham County, MI	H			56.00 HI	LSJ08	2015
Experienced, Private Practice	Ingham County, MI	H		285.00 AW		LSJ08	2015
Au Pair	United States	W	195.75 LO			AIFS	2016
Au Pair Extraordinaire	United States	W	250.00 LO			AIFS	2016
Audio and Video Equipment Technician	Alabama	Y	22242 AE	37664 AW	45380 AEX	ALBLS	6/16
	Birmingham-Hoover MSA, AL	Y	27715 AE	43036 AW	50701 AEX	ALBLS	6/16
	Alaska	Y	33290 FQ	45360 MW	61670 TQ	USBLS	5/15
	Anchorage MSA, AK	Y	32570 FQ	47130 MW	68070 TQ	USBLS	5/15
	Arizona	Y	25270 FQ	36050 MW	48340 TQ	USBLS	5/15
	Phoenix-Mesa-Scottsdale MSA, AZ	Y	25670 FQ	37540 MW	49350 TQ	USBLS	5/15
	Tucson MSA, AZ	Y	22270 FQ	31940 MW	38560 TQ	USBLS	5/15
	Arkansas	Y	21680 FQ	29610 MW	39030 TQ	USBLS	5/15
	Little Rock-North Little Rock-Conway MSA, AR	Y	20000 FQ	27850 MW	36100 TQ	USBLS	5/15
	California	H	16.63 FQ	23.25 MW	32.31 TQ	CABLS	1/16-3/16
	Anaheim-Santa Ana-Irvine PMSA, CA	H	14.22 FQ	22.56 MW	30.25 TQ	CABLS	1/16-3/16
	Los Angeles-Long Beach-Glendale PMSA, CA	H	18.38 FQ	24.90 MW	35.83 TQ	CABLS	1/16-3/16
	Oakland-Hayward-Berkeley PMSA, CA	H	18.97 FQ	24.54 MW	31.99 TQ	CABLS	1/16-3/16
	Riverside-San Bernardino-Ontario MSA, CA	H	12.93 FQ	14.60 MW	18.35 TQ	CABLS	1/16-3/16
	Sacramento–Roseville–Arden-Arcade MSA, CA	H	11.57 FQ	16.64 MW	23.36 TQ	CABLS	1/16-3/16
	San Diego-Carlsbad MSA, CA	H	14.08 FQ	17.58 MW	23.93 TQ	CABLS	1/16-3/16
	San Francisco-Redwood City-South San Francisco PMSA, CA	H	18.34 FQ	22.96 MW	30.18 TQ	CABLS	1/16-3/16
	Colorado	Y	26580 FQ	36490 MW	49270 TQ	USBLS	5/15
	Denver-Aurora-Lakewood MSA, CO	Y	21840 FQ	36320 MW	49940 TQ	USBLS	5/15
	Connecticut	Y		49162 MW		CTBLS	1/16-3/16
	Bridgeport-Stamford-Norwalk MSA, CT	Y	31550 FQ	48630 MW	58930 TQ	USBLS	5/15
	Hartford-West Hartford-East Hartford MSA, CT	Y	34390 FQ	47870 MW	62320 TQ	USBLS	5/15
	District of Columbia	Y	41240 FQ	52700 MW	68300 TQ	USBLS	5/15
	Washington-Arlington-Alexandria PMSA, DC-VA-MD-WV	Y	35740 FQ	46390 MW	60780 TQ	USBLS	5/15
	Florida	H	12.25 AE	16.67 MW	21.61 AEX	FLBLS	7/16-9/16
	Fort Lauderdale-Pompano Beach-Deerfield Beach PMSA, FL	H	13.17 AE	15.73 MW	19.34 AEX	FLBLS	7/16-9/16
	Miami-Miami Beach-Kendall PMSA, FL	H	13.19 AE	17.19 MW	21.96 AEX	FLBLS	7/16-9/16
	Orlando-Kissimmee-Sanford MSA, FL	H	12.56 AE	16.78 MW	21.98 AEX	FLBLS	7/16-9/16
	Tampa-St. Petersburg-Clearwater MSA, FL	H	9.66 AE	14.93 MW	21.59 AEX	FLBLS	7/16-9/16
	Georgia	Y	29380 FQ	40370 MW	55480 TQ	USBLS	5/15
	Atlanta-Sandy Springs-Roswell MSA, GA	Y	31230 FQ	42400 MW	55760 TQ	USBLS	5/15
	Augusta-Richmond County MSA, GA-SC	Y	20160 FQ	27160 MW	38910 TQ	USBLS	5/15
	Hawaii	Y	27940 FQ	41560 MW	55340 TQ	USBLS	5/15
	Urban Honolulu MSA, HI	Y	27760 FQ	40840 MW	56210 TQ	USBLS	5/15

AE	Average entry wage	AWR	Average wage range	H	Hourly
AEX	Average experienced wage	B	Biweekly	HI	Highest wage paid
ATC	Average total compensation	D	Daily	HR	High end range
AW	Average wage paid	FQ	First quartile wage	LO	Lowest wage paid

LR	Low end range	MTC	Median total compensation
M	Monthly	MW	Median wage paid
MCC	Median cash compensation	MWR	Median wage range
ME	Median entry wage	S	See annotated source

TCC	Total cash compensation
TQ	Third quartile wage
W	Weekly
Y	Yearly

Occupation/Type/Industry	Location	Per	Low	Mid	High	Source	Date
Audio and Video Equipment Technician	Idaho	Y	21850 FQ	37740 MW	53290 TQ	USBLS	5/15
	Boise City MSA, ID	Y	23380 FQ	44380 MW	58860 TQ	USBLS	5/15
	Illinois	Y	28920 FQ	37660 MW	52770 TQ	USBLS	5/15
	Chicago-Naperville-Arlington Heights PMSA, IL	Y	30120 FQ	37940 MW	54650 TQ	USBLS	5/15
	Lake County-Kenosha County PMSA, IL-WI	Y	34100 FQ	46520 MW	66820 TQ	USBLS	5/15
	Indiana	Y	26150 FQ	31970 MW	39490 TQ	USBLS	5/15
	Gary PMSA, IN	Y	25210 FQ	31330 MW	35940 TQ	USBLS	5/15
	Indianapolis-Carmel-Anderson MSA, IN	Y	29010 FQ	35440 MW	44640 TQ	USBLS	5/15
	Iowa	Y	24440 FQ	30150 MW	44320 TQ	USBLS	5/15
	Des Moines-West Des Moines MSA, IA	Y	24320 FQ	33470 MW	50570 TQ	USBLS	5/15
	Kansas	Y	18550 FQ	28460 MW	41620 TQ	USBLS	5/15
	Wichita MSA, KS	Y	27190 FQ	33730 MW	43280 TQ	USBLS	5/15
	Kentucky	Y	29390 FQ	40890 MW	47940 TQ	USBLS	5/15
	Louisville-Jefferson County MSA, KY-IN	Y	35840 FQ	43820 MW	49270 TQ	USBLS	5/15
	Louisiana	Y	31010 FQ	41930 MW	60880 TQ	USBLS	5/15
	Baton Rouge MSA, LA	Y	19420 FQ	28980 MW	38300 TQ	USBLS	5/15
	New Orleans-Metairie MSA, LA	Y	34230 FQ	44640 MW	68070 TQ	USBLS	5/15
	Maine	Y	31110 FQ	35410 MW	40550 TQ	USBLS	5/15
	Portland-South Portland MSA, ME	Y	31880 FQ	35530 MW	39290 TQ	USBLS	5/15
	Maryland	Y	29605 AE	44475 MW	51910 AEX	MDBLS	4/16
	Baltimore-Columbia-Towson MSA, MD	Y	34470 FQ	40140 MW	53310 TQ	USBLS	5/15
	Massachusetts	Y	34240 FQ	43140 MW	57120 TQ	USBLS	5/15
	Boston-Cambridge-Newton NECTA, MA	Y	35200 FQ	44110 MW	58360 TQ	USBLS	5/15
	Worcester MSA, MA-CT	Y	34780 FQ	43670 MW	54290 TQ	USBLS	5/15
	Michigan	Y	32590 FQ	45430 MW	57940 TQ	USBLS	5/15
	Detroit-Dearborn-Livonia PMSA, MI	Y	30680 FQ	47090 MW	56960 TQ	USBLS	5/15
	Grand Rapids-Wyoming MSA, MI	Y	22720 FQ	29750 MW	39300 TQ	USBLS	5/15
	Minnesota	Y	29858 FQ	40473 MW	56995 TQ	MNBLS	1/16-3/16
	Minneapolis-St. Paul-Bloomington MSA, MN-WI	Y	31703 FQ	42963 MW	60251 TQ	MNBLS	1/16-3/16
	Mississippi	Y	17750 FQ	20120 MW	35880 TQ	USBLS	5/15
	Missouri	Y	26520 FQ	35710 MW	50350 TQ	USBLS	5/15
	Kansas City MSA, MO-KS	Y	19170 FQ	29970 MW	43260 TQ	USBLS	5/15
	St. Louis MSA, MO-IL	Y	28950 FQ	38180 MW	54870 TQ	USBLS	5/15
	Montana	Y	27370 FQ	37490 MW	45640 TQ	USBLS	5/15
	Billings MSA, MT	Y	28960 FQ	38320 MW	45600 TQ	USBLS	5/15
	Nebraska	Y	33125 FQ	39750 MW	49800 TQ	NEBLS	7/16-9/16
	Omaha-Council Bluffs MSA, NE-IA	Y	32950 FQ	40730 MW	51180 TQ	NEBLS	7/16-9/16
	Nevada	Y	40240 FQ	56340 MW	67930 TQ	USBLS	5/15
	Las Vegas-Henderson-Paradise MSA, NV	Y	43310 FQ	57480 MW	69100 TQ	USBLS	5/15
	New Hampshire	H	14.94 AE	18.88 MW	23.09 AEX	NHBLS	6/16
	Manchester NECTA, NH	H	16.91 AE	18.58 MW	21.24 AEX	NHBLS	6/16
	New Jersey	Y	40520 FQ	51720 MW	60840 TQ	USBLS	5/15
	Camden PMSA, NJ	Y	30620 FQ	36760 MW	45740 TQ	USBLS	5/15
	Newark PMSA, NJ-PA	Y	37140 FQ	45370 MW	55290 TQ	USBLS	5/15
	Trenton MSA, NJ	Y	44850 FQ	56160 MW	64050 TQ	USBLS	5/15
	New Mexico	Y	28480 FQ	34780 MW	52220 TQ	USBLS	5/15
	Albuquerque MSA, NM	Y	31780 FQ	37740 MW	68310 TQ	USBLS	5/15
	New York	Y	32060 AE	52370 MW	70810 AEX	NYBLS	1/16-3/16
	Buffalo-Cheektowaga-Niagara Falls MSA, NY	Y	31750 FQ	44120 MW	56440 TQ	USBLS	5/15
	Nassau County-Suffolk County PMSA, NY	Y	26730 FQ	42080 MW	59140 TQ	USBLS	5/15
	New York-Jersey City-White Plains PMSA, NY-NJ	Y	41420 FQ	55750 MW	76810 TQ	USBLS	5/15
	Rochester MSA, NY	Y	33820 FQ	42840 MW	56670 TQ	USBLS	5/15
	North Carolina	Y	26980 FQ	35430 MW	47290 TQ	USBLS	5/15

AE	Average entry wage	AWR	Average wage range	H	Hourly
AEX	Average experienced wage	B	Biweekly	HI	Highest wage paid
ATC	Average total compensation	D	Daily	HR	High end range
AW	Average wage paid	FQ	First quartile wage	LO	Lowest wage paid

LR	Low end range	MTC	Median total compensation	TCC	Total cash compensation
M	Monthly	MW	Median wage paid	TQ	Third quartile wage
MCC	Median cash compensation	MWR	Median wage range	W	Weekly
ME	Median entry wage	S	See annotated source	Y	Yearly

Occupation/Type/Industry	Location	Per	Low	Mid	High	Source	Date
Audio and Video Equipment Technician	Charlotte-Concord-Gastonia MSA, NC-SC	Y	25870 FQ	35050 MW	46680 TQ	USBLS	5/15
	Raleigh MSA, NC	Y	25910 FQ	30630 MW	43720 TQ	USBLS	5/15
	North Dakota	Y	19380 FQ	30070 MW	56850 TQ	USBLS	5/15
	Fargo MSA, ND-MN	Y	22390 FQ	38210 MW	57160 TQ	USBLS	5/15
	Ohio	Y	26700 FQ	35340 MW	49500 TQ	USBLS	5/15
	Cincinnati MSA, OH-KY-IN	Y	28490 FQ	35650 MW	46820 TQ	USBLS	5/15
	Cleveland-Elyria MSA, OH	Y	27230 FQ	34450 MW	47070 TQ	USBLS	5/15
	Columbus MSA, OH	Y	29100 FQ	36600 MW	53410 TQ	USBLS	5/15
	Oklahoma	Y	18830 FQ	29840 MW	45470 TQ	USBLS	5/15
	Oklahoma City MSA, OK	Y	18050 FQ	26900 MW	39000 TQ	USBLS	5/15
	Tulsa MSA, OK	Y	26700 FQ	41310 MW	56990 TQ	USBLS	5/15
	Oregon	H	15.67 FQ	18.60 MW	24.70 TQ	ORBLS	2016
	Portland-Vancouver-Hillsboro MSA, OR-WA	Y	33750 FQ	40570 MW	53370 TQ	USBLS	5/15
	Pennsylvania	Y	29270 FQ	37570 MW	51780 TQ	USBLS	5/15
	Allentown-Bethlehem-Easton MSA, PA-NJ	Y	28420 FQ	41990 MW	50790 TQ	USBLS	5/15
	Harrisburg-Carlisle MSA, PA	Y	28260 FQ	34890 MW	47580 TQ	USBLS	5/15
	Montgomery County-Bucks County-Chester County PMSA, PA	Y	35120 FQ	48560 MW	62830 TQ	USBLS	5/15
	Philadelphia PMSA, PA	Y	29900 FQ	36160 MW	47410 TQ	USBLS	5/15
	Pittsburgh MSA, PA	Y	30500 FQ	39040 MW	63830 TQ	USBLS	5/15
	Rhode Island	Y	35670 FQ	48050 MW	58080 TQ	USBLS	5/15
	Providence-Warwick MSA, RI-MA	Y	36050 FQ	48690 MW	58340 TQ	USBLS	5/15
	South Carolina	Y	23300 FQ	29600 MW	47990 TQ	USBLS	5/15
	Charleston-North Charleston MSA, SC	Y	24180 FQ	29850 MW	53020 TQ	USBLS	5/15
	Columbia MSA, SC	Y	22450 FQ	26960 MW	36280 TQ	USBLS	5/15
	Greenville-Anderson-Mauldin MSA, SC	Y	28190 FQ	38230 MW	48050 TQ	USBLS	5/15
	South Dakota	Y	21070 FQ	28800 MW	43260 TQ	USBLS	5/15
	Tennessee	Y	26970 FQ	34990 MW	53630 TQ	USBLS	5/15
	Knoxville MSA, TN	Y	24910 FQ	32730 MW	42440 TQ	USBLS	5/15
	Memphis MSA, TN-MS-AR	Y	31260 FQ	37830 MW	53340 TQ	USBLS	5/15
	Nashville-Davidson–Murfreesboro–Franklin MSA, TN	Y	27650 FQ	35890 MW	59370 TQ	USBLS	5/15
	Texas	Y	28750 FQ	37950 MW	56040 TQ	USBLS	5/15
	Austin-Round Rock MSA, TX	Y	32640 FQ	44180 MW	57580 TQ	USBLS	5/15
	Dallas-Plano-Irving PMSA, TX	Y	30990 FQ	39880 MW	58120 TQ	USBLS	5/15
	Fort Worth-Arlington PMSA, TX	Y	29200 FQ	37590 MW	62800 TQ	USBLS	5/15
	Houston-The Woodlands-Sugar Land MSA, TX	Y	27820 FQ	34110 MW	50170 TQ	USBLS	5/15
	San Antonio-New Braunfels MSA, TX	Y	27980 FQ	37870 MW	60190 TQ	USBLS	5/15
	Utah	Y	25530 FQ	35030 MW	50830 TQ	USBLS	5/15
	Provo-Orem MSA, UT	Y	33530 FQ	53120 MW	60400 TQ	USBLS	5/15
	Salt Lake City MSA, UT	Y	24850 FQ	34100 MW	44990 TQ	USBLS	5/15
	Vermont	Y	26890 FQ	30490 MW	37900 TQ	USBLS	5/15
	Burlington-South Burlington MSA, VT	Y	26560 FQ	29480 MW	34390 TQ	USBLS	5/15
	Virginia	Y	30400 FQ	38150 MW	53380 TQ	USBLS	5/15
	Richmond MSA, VA	Y	31930 FQ	41170 MW	67730 TQ	USBLS	5/15
	Roanoke MSA, VA	Y	24480 FQ	27470 MW	30550 TQ	USBLS	5/15
	Virginia Beach-Norfolk-Newport News MSA, VA-NC	Y	26910 FQ	33620 MW	44530 TQ	USBLS	5/15
	Washington	H	14.76 FQ	20.92 MW	30.21 TQ	WABLS	3/16
	Seattle-Bellevue-Everett PMSA, WA	H	16.47 FQ	23.25 MW	32.37 TQ	WABLS	3/16
	Tacoma-Lakewood PMSA, WA	H	14.46 FQ	20.13 MW	30.13 TQ	WABLS	3/16
	West Virginia	Y	23940 FQ	28620 MW	36430 TQ	USBLS	5/15
	Wisconsin	Y	26700 FQ	36080 MW	47410 TQ	USBLS	5/15
	Madison MSA, WI	Y	38260 FQ	45060 MW	52640 TQ	USBLS	5/15
	Milwaukee-Waukesha-West Allis MSA, WI	Y	28450 FQ	38660 MW	51800 TQ	USBLS	5/15
	Wyoming	Y	39020 FQ	44530 MW	49440 TQ	USBLS	5/15
	Puerto Rico	Y	18220 FQ	24800 MW	29390 TQ	USBLS	5/15

AE Average entry wage	**AWR** Average wage range	**H** Hourly	**LR** Low end range	**MTC** Median total compensation	**TCC** Total cash compensation
AEX Average experienced wage	**B** Biweekly	**HI** Highest wage paid	**M** Monthly	**MW** Median wage paid	**TQ** Third quartile wage
ATC Average total compensation	**D** Daily	**HR** High end range	**MCC** Median cash compensation	**MWR** Median wage range	**W** Weekly
AW Average wage paid	**FQ** First quartile wage	**LO** Lowest wage paid	**ME** Median entry wage	**S** See annotated source	**Y** Yearly

Occupation/Type/Industry	Location	Per	Low	Mid	High	Source	Date
Audio and Video Equipment Technician	San Juan-Carolina-Caguas MSA, PR	Y	18300 FQ	25250 MW	29430 TQ	USBLS	5/15
Audio Engineer	United States	Y		63000 AW		SKU01	2016
Audio-Visual and Multimedia Collections Specialist	Alabama	Y	20702 AE	26217 AW	28979 AEX	ALBLS	6/16
	Arizona	Y	31100 FQ	40910 MW	55800 TQ	USBLS	5/15
	Phoenix-Mesa-Scottsdale MSA, AZ	Y	30090 FQ	44290 MW	62300 TQ	USBLS	5/15
	Tucson MSA, AZ	Y	33780 FQ	37350 MW	42170 TQ	USBLS	5/15
	Arkansas	Y	39860 FQ	46660 MW	55630 TQ	USBLS	5/15
	California	H	17.40 FQ	20.52 MW	24.04 TQ	CABLS	1/16-3/16
	Anaheim-Santa Ana-Irvine PMSA, CA	H	18.82 FQ	21.45 MW	23.91 TQ	CABLS	1/16-3/16
	Los Angeles-Long Beach-Glendale PMSA, CA	H	17.45 FQ	20.56 MW	23.40 TQ	CABLS	1/16-3/16
	Oakland-Hayward-Berkeley PMSA, CA	H	18.45 FQ	21.91 MW	26.80 TQ	CABLS	1/16-3/16
	Riverside-San Bernardino-Ontario MSA, CA	H	16.26 FQ	17.83 MW	19.55 TQ	CABLS	1/16-3/16
	Sacramento–Roseville–Arden-Arcade MSA, CA	H	18.04 FQ	21.21 MW	24.82 TQ	CABLS	1/16-3/16
	San Diego-Carlsbad MSA, CA	H	17.60 FQ	21.15 MW	25.81 TQ	CABLS	1/16-3/16
	San Francisco-Redwood City-South San Francisco PMSA, CA	H	26.58 FQ	35.43 MW	41.29 TQ	CABLS	1/16-3/16
	Connecticut	Y		59622 MW		CTBLS	1/16-3/16
	Bridgeport-Stamford-Norwalk MSA, CT	Y	41800 FQ	50550 MW	61280 TQ	USBLS	5/15
	Hartford-West Hartford-East Hartford MSA, CT	Y	53850 FQ	69300 MW	82130 TQ	USBLS	5/15
	Delaware	Y	30420 FQ	39480 MW	51970 TQ	USBLS	5/15
	Wilmington PMSA, DE-MD-NJ	Y	29960 FQ	43000 MW	52460 TQ	USBLS	5/15
	District of Columbia	Y	49220 FQ	59750 MW	71280 TQ	USBLS	5/15
	Washington-Arlington-Alexandria PMSA, DC-VA-MD-WV	Y	31710 FQ	38690 MW	61660 TQ	USBLS	5/15
	Florida	H	11.14 AE	17.61 MW	21.67 AEX	FLBLS	7/16-9/16
	Georgia	Y	40340 FQ	61530 MW	72700 TQ	USBLS	5/15
	Atlanta-Sandy Springs-Roswell MSA, GA	Y	43290 FQ	68130 MW	75290 TQ	USBLS	5/15
	Illinois	Y	37740 FQ	48430 MW	59460 TQ	USBLS	5/15
	Chicago-Naperville-Arlington Heights PMSA, IL	Y	43020 FQ	50390 MW	59250 TQ	USBLS	5/15
	Lake County-Kenosha County PMSA, IL-WI	Y	24780 FQ	29390 MW	55370 TQ	USBLS	5/15
	Indiana	Y	29590 FQ	38570 MW	55680 TQ	USBLS	5/15
	Indianapolis-Carmel-Anderson MSA, IN	Y	31710 FQ	35780 MW	39830 TQ	USBLS	5/15
	Iowa	Y	24030 FQ	44760 MW	62540 TQ	USBLS	5/15
	Kansas	Y	47300 FQ	56430 MW	63350 TQ	USBLS	5/15
	Maryland	Y	28793 AE	49711 MW	60169 AEX	MDBLS	4/16
	Baltimore-Columbia-Towson MSA, MD	Y	44790 FQ	53660 MW	67450 TQ	USBLS	5/15
	Massachusetts	Y	48530 FQ	61720 MW	75440 TQ	USBLS	5/15
	Boston-Cambridge-Newton NECTA, MA	Y	50280 FQ	62960 MW	74880 TQ	USBLS	5/15
	Michigan	Y	25790 FQ	34730 MW	59310 TQ	USBLS	5/15
	Minnesota	Y	46310 FQ	64092 MW	73920 TQ	MNBLS	1/16-3/16
	Minneapolis-St. Paul-Bloomington MSA, MN-WI	Y	51753 FQ	67015 MW	75826 TQ	MNBLS	1/16-3/16
	Missouri	Y	36250 FQ	43500 MW	50570 TQ	USBLS	5/15
	St. Louis MSA, MO-IL	Y	41690 FQ	47090 MW	54720 TQ	USBLS	5/15
	Nebraska	Y	21025 FQ	22810 MW	28915 TQ	NEBLS	7/16-9/16
	New Hampshire	H	20.47 AE	29.67 MW	33.90 AEX	NHBLS	6/16
	New Jersey	Y	33460 FQ	51980 MW	64160 TQ	USBLS	5/15
	Newark PMSA, NJ-PA	Y	51870 FQ	59310 MW	69020 TQ	USBLS	5/15
	New York	Y	30160 AE	50750 MW	60740 AEX	NYBLS	1/16-3/16

AE	Average entry wage	AWR	Average wage range	H	Hourly
AEX	Average experienced wage	B	Biweekly	HI	Highest wage paid
ATC	Average total compensation	D	Daily	HR	High end range
AW	Average wage paid	FQ	First quartile wage	LO	Lowest wage paid

LR	Low end range	MTC	Median total compensation	TCC Total cash compensation
M	Monthly	MW	Median wage paid	TQ Third quartile wage
MCC	Median cash compensation	MWR	Median wage range	W Weekly
ME	Median entry wage	S	See annotated source	Y Yearly

Occupation/Type/Industry	Location	Per	Low	Mid	High	Source	Date
Audio-Visual and Multimedia Collections Specialist	Buffalo-Cheektowaga-Niagara Falls MSA, NY	Y	36640 FQ	45160 MW	62970 TQ	USBLS	5/15
	Nassau County-Suffolk County PMSA, NY	Y	48160 FQ	60500 MW	72370 TQ	USBLS	5/15
	New York-Jersey City-White Plains PMSA, NY-NJ	Y	47510 FQ	58080 MW	69620 TQ	USBLS	5/15
	Rochester MSA, NY	Y	27490 FQ	30760 MW	37740 TQ	USBLS	5/15
	North Carolina	Y	34590 FQ	43780 MW	54590 TQ	USBLS	5/15
	Ohio	Y	31680 FQ	45290 MW	63610 TQ	USBLS	5/15
	Cincinnati MSA, OH-KY-IN	Y	29620 FQ	57630 MW	80150 TQ	USBLS	5/15
	Cleveland-Elyria MSA, OH	Y	28490 FQ	51470 MW	64060 TQ	USBLS	5/15
	Columbus MSA, OH	Y	29540 FQ	43190 MW	69180 TQ	USBLS	5/15
	Oklahoma	Y	33540 FQ	40750 MW	46690 TQ	USBLS	5/15
	Oklahoma City MSA, OK	Y	33650 FQ	42840 MW	48240 TQ	USBLS	5/15
	Oregon	H	19.64 FQ	22.36 MW	26.12 TQ	ORBLS	2016
	Portland-Vancouver-Hillsboro MSA, OR-WA	Y	41460 FQ	46780 MW	55030 TQ	USBLS	5/15
	Pennsylvania	Y	39470 FQ	47920 MW	57430 TQ	USBLS	5/15
	Allentown-Bethlehem-Easton MSA, PA-NJ	Y	41800 FQ	46450 MW	54190 TQ	USBLS	5/15
	Montgomery County-Bucks County-Chester County PMSA, PA	Y	46880 FQ	55130 MW	61510 TQ	USBLS	5/15
	Philadelphia PMSA, PA	Y	37170 FQ	46680 MW	55700 TQ	USBLS	5/15
	Pittsburgh MSA, PA	Y	38490 FQ	51540 MW	58140 TQ	USBLS	5/15
	South Carolina	Y	28440 FQ	38200 MW	52830 TQ	USBLS	5/15
	Columbia MSA, SC	Y	27250 FQ	31150 MW	37890 TQ	USBLS	5/15
	Tennessee	Y	30850 FQ	42770 MW	65690 TQ	USBLS	5/15
	Nashville-Davidson– Murfreesboro–Franklin MSA, TN	Y	33440 FQ	62450 MW	74540 TQ	USBLS	5/15
	Texas	Y	41710 FQ	54380 MW	66180 TQ	USBLS	5/15
	Austin-Round Rock MSA, TX	Y	40280 FQ	48970 MW	62520 TQ	USBLS	5/15
	Dallas-Plano-Irving PMSA, TX	Y	32980 FQ	54000 MW	69150 TQ	USBLS	5/15
	Fort Worth-Arlington PMSA, TX	Y	52300 FQ	58410 MW	67180 TQ	USBLS	5/15
	Houston-The Woodlands-Sugar Land MSA, TX	Y	49990 FQ	58210 MW	68980 TQ	USBLS	5/15
	San Antonio-New Braunfels MSA, TX	Y	43120 FQ	54250 MW	66640 TQ	USBLS	5/15
	Utah	Y	23390 FQ	27620 MW	33870 TQ	USBLS	5/15
	Ogden-Clearfield MSA, UT	Y	27900 FQ	31350 MW	50360 TQ	USBLS	5/15
	Provo-Orem MSA, UT	Y	19820 FQ	22590 MW	26980 TQ	USBLS	5/15
	Salt Lake City MSA, UT	Y	24600 FQ	28120 MW	34380 TQ	USBLS	5/15
	Vermont	Y	30770 FQ	46550 MW	57580 TQ	USBLS	5/15
	Burlington-South Burlington MSA, VT	Y	29610 FQ	37370 MW	55320 TQ	USBLS	5/15
	Virginia	Y	29270 FQ	35190 MW	45310 TQ	USBLS	5/15
	Washington	H	17.93 FQ	21.44 MW	25.88 TQ	WABLS	3/16
	Seattle-Bellevue-Everett PMSA, WA	H	19.35 FQ	22.44 MW	27.15 TQ	WABLS	3/16
	West Virginia	Y	36430 FQ	44150 MW	51460 TQ	USBLS	5/15
	Wisconsin	Y	35160 FQ	43740 MW	54720 TQ	USBLS	5/15
	Milwaukee-Waukesha-West Allis MSA, WI	Y	33150 FQ	39260 MW	53560 TQ	USBLS	5/15
	Puerto Rico	Y	25780 FQ	42260 MW	46740 TQ	USBLS	5/15
	San Juan-Carolina-Caguas MSA, PR	Y	19720 FQ	40760 MW	46310 TQ	USBLS	5/15
Audiologist	Alabama	Y	36736 AE	61995 AW	74625 AEX	ALBLS	6/16
	Birmingham-Hoover MSA, AL	Y	42832 AE	65665 AW	77081 AEX	ALBLS	6/16
	Arizona	Y	62680 FQ	71190 MW	79870 TQ	USBLS	5/15
	Phoenix-Mesa-Scottsdale MSA, AZ	Y	62780 FQ	70860 MW	78850 TQ	USBLS	5/15
	Tucson MSA, AZ	Y	66890 FQ	72730 MW	79010 TQ	USBLS	5/15
	Arkansas	Y	52550 FQ	61530 MW	71730 TQ	USBLS	5/15
	California	H	39.26 FQ	44.29 MW	50.09 TQ	CABLS	1/16-3/16
	Anaheim-Santa Ana-Irvine PMSA, CA	H	36.04 FQ	41.50 MW	48.00 TQ	CABLS	1/16-3/16
	Los Angeles-Long Beach-Glendale PMSA, CA	H	41.44 FQ	44.70 MW	47.97 TQ	CABLS	1/16-3/16

AE	Average entry wage	AWR	Average wage range	H	Hourly	LR	Low end range	MTC	Median total compensation	TCC	Total cash compensation
AEX	Average experienced wage	B	Biweekly	HI	Highest wage paid	M	Monthly	MW	Median wage paid	TQ	Third quartile wage
ATC	Average total compensation	D	Daily	HR	High end range	MCC	Median cash compensation	MWR	Median wage range	W	Weekly
AW	Average wage paid	FQ	First quartile wage	LO	Lowest wage paid	ME	Median entry wage	S	See annotated source	Y	Yearly

Occupation/Type/Industry	Location	Per	Low	Mid	High	Source	Date
Audiologist	Oakland-Hayward-Berkeley PMSA, CA	H	41.81 FQ	49.42 MW	56.26 TQ	CABLS	1/16-3/16
	Riverside-San Bernardino-Ontario MSA, CA	H	33.55 FQ	43.36 MW	52.60 TQ	CABLS	1/16-3/16
	Sacramento–Roseville–Arden-Arcade MSA, CA	H	40.79 FQ	44.96 MW	49.13 TQ	CABLS	1/16-3/16
	San Diego-Carlsbad MSA, CA	H	41.00 FQ	48.47 MW	56.23 TQ	CABLS	1/16-3/16
	San Francisco-Redwood City-South San Francisco PMSA, CA	H	43.58 FQ	52.45 MW	58.65 TQ	CABLS	1/16-3/16
	Colorado	Y	72180 FQ	88190 MW	101820 TQ	USBLS	5/15
	Denver-Aurora-Lakewood MSA, CO	Y	72630 FQ	86610 MW	100800 TQ	USBLS	5/15
	Connecticut	Y		82651 MW		CTBLS	1/16-3/16
	Hartford-West Hartford-East Hartford MSA, CT	Y	65250 FQ	77530 MW	91100 TQ	USBLS	5/15
	Delaware	Y	69750 FQ	76110 MW	84220 TQ	USBLS	5/15
	Wilmington PMSA, DE-MD-NJ	Y	72240 FQ	81230 MW	91040 TQ	USBLS	5/15
	District of Columbia	Y	71250 FQ	93470 MW	132410 TQ	USBLS	5/15
	Washington-Arlington-Alexandria PMSA, DC-VA-MD-WV	Y	77520 FQ	93660 MW	118700 TQ	USBLS	5/15
	Florida	H	26.53 AE	36.65 MW	41.66 AEX	FLBLS	7/16-9/16
	Fort Lauderdale-Pompano Beach-Deerfield Beach PMSA, FL	H	33.12 AE	37.17 MW	41.88 AEX	FLBLS	7/16-9/16
	Miami-Miami Beach-Kendall PMSA, FL	H	29.09 AE	37.86 MW	41.28 AEX	FLBLS	7/16-9/16
	Orlando-Kissimmee-Sanford MSA, FL	H	22.91 AE	32.98 MW	38.47 AEX	FLBLS	7/16-9/16
	Tampa-St. Petersburg-Clearwater MSA, FL	H	36.56 AE	43.14 MW	44.07 AEX	FLBLS	7/16-9/16
	Georgia	Y	59380 FQ	76340 MW	96560 TQ	USBLS	5/15
	Atlanta-Sandy Springs-Roswell MSA, GA	Y	63380 FQ	78020 MW	96890 TQ	USBLS	5/15
	Hawaii	Y	60680 FQ	92710 MW	103810 TQ	USBLS	5/15
	Urban Honolulu MSA, HI	Y	60680 FQ	92710 MW	103810 TQ	USBLS	5/15
	Idaho	Y	46080 FQ	54200 MW	66650 TQ	USBLS	5/15
	Boise City MSA, ID	Y	46780 FQ	55020 MW	66720 TQ	USBLS	5/15
	Illinois	Y	63450 FQ	74570 MW	88810 TQ	USBLS	5/15
	Chicago-Naperville-Arlington Heights PMSA, IL	Y	65490 FQ	75650 MW	89390 TQ	USBLS	5/15
	Indiana	Y	58830 FQ	70280 MW	83700 TQ	USBLS	5/15
	Indianapolis-Carmel-Anderson MSA, IN	Y	56710 FQ	70020 MW	87010 TQ	USBLS	5/15
	Iowa	Y	56490 FQ	65510 MW	79720 TQ	USBLS	5/15
	Kansas	Y	45330 FQ	52900 MW	67800 TQ	USBLS	5/15
	Kentucky	Y	55860 FQ	61260 MW	72980 TQ	USBLS	5/15
	Louisville-Jefferson County MSA, KY-IN	Y	55370 FQ	59430 MW	63440 TQ	USBLS	5/15
	Louisiana	Y	53610 FQ	61320 MW	73550 TQ	USBLS	5/15
	Baton Rouge MSA, LA	Y	51850 FQ	59210 MW	69270 TQ	USBLS	5/15
	Maine	Y	63000 FQ	72330 MW	100900 TQ	USBLS	5/15
	Maryland	Y	54348 AE	79632 MW	92274 AEX	MDBLS	4/16
	Massachusetts	Y	64330 FQ	75600 MW	91710 TQ	USBLS	5/15
	Boston-Cambridge-Newton NECTA, MA	Y	72360 FQ	83080 MW	97000 TQ	USBLS	5/15
	Worcester MSA, MA-CT	Y	60680 FQ	67600 MW	75150 TQ	USBLS	5/15
	Michigan	Y	60150 FQ	70660 MW	79570 TQ	USBLS	5/15
	Detroit-Dearborn-Livonia PMSA, MI	Y	59760 FQ	68530 MW	76390 TQ	USBLS	5/15
	Grand Rapids-Wyoming MSA, MI	Y	54050 FQ	68720 MW	76960 TQ	USBLS	5/15
	Minnesota	Y	67056 FQ	75060 MW	84948 TQ	MNBLS	1/16-3/16
	Minneapolis-St. Paul-Bloomington MSA, MN-WI	Y	66713 FQ	73618 MW	80886 TQ	MNBLS	1/16-3/16
	Mississippi	Y	53400 FQ	61180 MW	76590 TQ	USBLS	5/15
	Missouri	Y	61740 FQ	72710 MW	88400 TQ	USBLS	5/15
	Kansas City MSA, MO-KS	Y	56370 FQ	64870 MW	77300 TQ	USBLS	5/15
	St. Louis MSA, MO-IL	Y	59430 FQ	73220 MW	92230 TQ	USBLS	5/15
	Montana	Y	59220 FQ	69850 MW	78200 TQ	USBLS	5/15

AE	Average entry wage	**AWR**	Average wage range	**H**	Hourly
AEX	Average experienced wage	**B**	Biweekly	**HI**	Highest wage paid
ATC	Average total compensation	**D**	Daily	**HR**	High end range
AW	Average wage paid	**FQ**	First quartile wage	**LO**	Lowest wage paid

LR	Low end range	**MTC**	Median total compensation	**TCC**	Total cash compensation
M	Monthly	**MW**	Median wage paid	**TQ**	Third quartile wage
MCC	Median cash compensation	**MWR**	Median wage range	**W**	Weekly
ME	Median entry wage	**S**	See annotated source	**Y**	Yearly

Occupation/Type/Industry	Location	Per	Low	Mid	High	Source	Date
Audiologist	Nebraska	Y	56465 FQ	63905 MW	78910 TQ	NEBLS	7/16-9/16
	Omaha-Council Bluffs MSA, NE-IA	Y	57730 FQ	67455 MW	78295 TQ	NEBLS	7/16-9/16
	Nevada	Y	19590 FQ	55650 MW	84850 TQ	USBLS	5/15
	Las Vegas-Henderson-Paradise MSA, NV	Y	18910 FQ	52280 MW	73710 TQ	USBLS	5/15
	New Jersey	Y	73130 FQ	84840 MW	97150 TQ	USBLS	5/15
	Camden PMSA, NJ	Y	71590 FQ	78890 MW	89770 TQ	USBLS	5/15
	Newark PMSA, NJ-PA	Y	73720 FQ	85160 MW	93790 TQ	USBLS	5/15
	New Mexico	Y	73140 FQ	93290 MW	145570 TQ	USBLS	5/15
	Albuquerque MSA, NM	Y	92810 FQ	140020 MW	153590 TQ	USBLS	5/15
	New York	Y	63770 AE	83020 MW	92590 AEX	NYBLS	1/16-3/16
	Buffalo-Cheektowaga-Niagara Falls MSA, NY	Y	50950 FQ	61020 MW	71490 TQ	USBLS	5/15
	Nassau County-Suffolk County PMSA, NY	Y	73110 FQ	83720 MW	93740 TQ	USBLS	5/15
	New York-Jersey City-White Plains PMSA, NY-NJ	Y	75600 FQ	89760 MW	109660 TQ	USBLS	5/15
	Rochester MSA, NY	Y	65030 FQ	76440 MW	95980 TQ	USBLS	5/15
	North Carolina	Y	60560 FQ	73200 MW	98470 TQ	USBLS	5/15
	Charlotte-Concord-Gastonia MSA, NC-SC	Y	63890 FQ	79130 MW	110430 TQ	USBLS	5/15
	Raleigh MSA, NC	Y	64310 FQ	69380 MW	75060 TQ	USBLS	5/15
	North Dakota	Y	67620 FQ	78080 MW	139540 TQ	USBLS	5/15
	Ohio	Y	54390 FQ	62560 MW	81810 TQ	USBLS	5/15
	Cincinnati MSA, OH-KY-IN	Y	60390 FQ	82920 MW	100840 TQ	USBLS	5/15
	Cleveland-Elyria MSA, OH	Y	53590 FQ	59360 MW	72220 TQ	USBLS	5/15
	Columbus MSA, OH	Y	56730 FQ	64180 MW	76910 TQ	USBLS	5/15
	Oklahoma	Y	80280 FQ	88840 MW	96490 TQ	USBLS	5/15
	Oklahoma City MSA, OK	Y	84630 FQ	91090 MW	97560 TQ	USBLS	5/15
	Oregon	H	31.51 FQ	39.62 MW	45.55 TQ	ORBLS	2016
	Portland-Vancouver-Hillsboro MSA, OR-WA	Y	79960 FQ	88730 MW	97120 TQ	USBLS	5/15
	Pennsylvania	Y	60190 FQ	71980 MW	85910 TQ	USBLS	5/15
	Allentown-Bethlehem-Easton MSA, PA-NJ	Y	82710 FQ	100270 MW	110740 TQ	USBLS	5/15
	Montgomery County-Bucks County-Chester County PMSA, PA	Y	61540 FQ	86060 MW	94600 TQ	USBLS	5/15
	Philadelphia PMSA, PA	Y	67830 FQ	73330 MW	78820 TQ	USBLS	5/15
	Pittsburgh MSA, PA	Y	68050 FQ	76890 MW	88800 TQ	USBLS	5/15
	South Carolina	Y	53660 FQ	80190 MW	97120 TQ	USBLS	5/15
	Tennessee	Y	57790 FQ	66290 MW	75010 TQ	USBLS	5/15
	Knoxville MSA, TN	Y	57060 FQ	65690 MW	72490 TQ	USBLS	5/15
	Nashville-Davidson–Murfreesboro–Franklin MSA, TN	Y	57360 FQ	65450 MW	76110 TQ	USBLS	5/15
	Texas	Y	54430 FQ	69770 MW	107300 TQ	USBLS	5/15
	Austin-Round Rock MSA, TX	Y	48380 FQ	54760 MW	60180 TQ	USBLS	5/15
	Dallas-Plano-Irving PMSA, TX	Y	64740 FQ	77140 MW	114250 TQ	USBLS	5/15
	Houston-The Woodlands-Sugar Land MSA, TX	Y	57840 FQ	69700 MW	82910 TQ	USBLS	5/15
	Utah	Y	56680 FQ	67910 MW	84010 TQ	USBLS	5/15
	Provo-Orem MSA, UT	Y	57540 FQ	63860 MW	83690 TQ	USBLS	5/15
	Salt Lake City MSA, UT	Y	56630 FQ	69150 MW	85460 TQ	USBLS	5/15
	Virginia	Y	60970 FQ	72940 MW	89150 TQ	USBLS	5/15
	Richmond MSA, VA	Y	55880 FQ	61670 MW	85240 TQ	USBLS	5/15
	Virginia Beach-Norfolk-Newport News MSA, VA-NC	Y	63780 FQ	70990 MW	77910 TQ	USBLS	5/15
	Washington	H	34.50 FQ	39.97 MW	48.77 TQ	WABLS	3/16
	Seattle-Bellevue-Everett PMSA, WA	H	35.25 FQ	40.47 MW	47.19 TQ	WABLS	3/16
	Tacoma-Lakewood PMSA, WA	H	33.90 FQ	37.02 MW	49.96 TQ	WABLS	3/16
	West Virginia	Y	39280 FQ	60130 MW	75430 TQ	USBLS	5/15
	Wisconsin	Y	63900 FQ	73870 MW	89060 TQ	USBLS	5/15
	Milwaukee-Waukesha-West Allis MSA, WI	Y	60810 FQ	73550 MW	87820 TQ	USBLS	5/15
Audiometrist Department of Public Health	San Francisco, CA	B	3217 LO		4106 HI	SFGOV	2016-2018

AE	Average entry wage	AWR	Average wage range	H	Hourly	LR
AEX	Average experienced wage	B	Biweekly	HI	Highest wage paid	M
ATC	Average total compensation	D	Daily	HR	High end range	MCC
AW	Average wage paid	FQ	First quartile wage	LO	Lowest wage paid	ME

AE   Average entry wage   AWR Average wage range   H   Hourly   LR   Low end range   MTC Median total compensation TCC Total cash compensation
AEX Average experienced wage   B   Biweekly   HI   Highest wage paid M   Monthly   MW   Median wage paid   TQ   Third quartile wage
ATC Average total compensation D   Daily   HR   High end range   MCC Median cash compensation MWR Median wage range   W   Weekly
AW   Average wage paid   FQ   First quartile wage   LO   Lowest wage paid   ME   Median entry wage   S   See annotated source   Y   Yearly

Occupation/Type/Industry	Location	Per	Low	Mid	High	Source	Date
Audit Technician							
City Administration	Anaheim, CA	Y			63555 HI	CACIT	6/28/16
Auditor							
Unclaimed Property, State Government	Dimondale, MI	H	24.24 LO		34.75 HI	MIGOV	2016
Auditorium Manager							
Municipal Government	Nashville, TN	Y			102924 HI	NTNGOV	2017
AutoCAD Technician							
Engineering Department, Municipal Government	El Centro, CA	Y			63425 HI	CACIT	10/20/16
Automated Fingerprint Technician							
Police Department, Municipal Government	Chula Vista, CA	Y		39422 AW		CACIT	6/28/16
Automation Professional	East North Central	Y		99623 AW		AUTOM	7/7/16-8/24/16
	East South Central	Y		102246 AW		AUTOM	7/7/16-8/24/16
	Mid-Atlantic	Y		107250 AW		AUTOM	7/7/16-8/24/16
	Mountain	Y		104892 AW		AUTOM	7/7/16-8/24/16
	New England	Y		112777 AW		AUTOM	7/7/16-8/24/16
	Pacific	Y		114505 AW		AUTOM	7/7/16-8/24/16
	South Atlantic	Y		105963 AW		AUTOM	7/7/16-8/24/16
	West North Central	Y		100308 AW		AUTOM	7/7/16-8/24/16
	West South Central	Y		127544 AW		AUTOM	7/7/16-8/24/16
Automotive and Watercraft Service Attendant	Alabama	Y	17618 AE	23388 AW	26278 AEX	ALBLS	6/16
	Birmingham-Hoover MSA, AL	Y	17464 AE	21578 AW	23635 AEX	ALBLS	6/16
	Alaska	Y	22130 FQ	25260 MW	30800 TQ	USBLS	5/15
	Anchorage MSA, AK	Y	25160 FQ	27840 MW	30550 TQ	USBLS	5/15
	Arizona	Y	18870 FQ	22090 MW	27430 TQ	USBLS	5/15
	Phoenix-Mesa-Scottsdale MSA, AZ	Y	18590 FQ	21440 MW	26650 TQ	USBLS	5/15
	Tucson MSA, AZ	Y	20910 FQ	24590 MW	30970 TQ	USBLS	5/15
	Arkansas	Y	18030 FQ	20570 MW	24920 TQ	USBLS	5/15
	Little Rock-North Little Rock-Conway MSA, AR	Y	18740 FQ	22440 MW	27750 TQ	USBLS	5/15
	California	H	10.19 FQ	11.99 MW	14.76 TQ	CABLS	1/16-3/16
	Anaheim-Santa Ana-Irvine PMSA, CA	H	9.61 FQ	12.08 MW	14.51 TQ	CABLS	1/16-3/16
	Los Angeles-Long Beach-Glendale PMSA, CA	H	11.36 FQ	13.51 MW	15.29 TQ	CABLS	1/16-3/16
	Oakland-Hayward-Berkeley PMSA, CA	H	10.58 FQ	14.74 MW	20.74 TQ	CABLS	1/16-3/16
	Riverside-San Bernardino-Ontario MSA, CA	H	10.55 FQ	11.92 MW	15.41 TQ	CABLS	1/16-3/16
	Sacramento–Roseville–Arden-Arcade MSA, CA	H	10.39 FQ	11.81 MW	13.71 TQ	CABLS	1/16-3/16
	San Diego-Carlsbad MSA, CA	H	10.56 FQ	12.09 MW	14.52 TQ	CABLS	1/16-3/16
	San Francisco-Redwood City-South San Francisco PMSA, CA	H	9.87 FQ	11.07 MW	12.25 TQ	CABLS	1/16-3/16
	Colorado	Y	20240 FQ	23420 MW	28900 TQ	USBLS	5/15
	Denver-Aurora-Lakewood MSA, CO	Y	21020 FQ	24610 MW	32900 TQ	USBLS	5/15
	Connecticut	Y		20395 MW		CTBLS	1/16-3/16
	Bridgeport-Stamford-Norwalk MSA, CT	Y	19270 FQ	19510 MW	23170 TQ	USBLS	5/15
	Delaware	Y	20560 FQ	24040 MW	29820 TQ	USBLS	5/15
	Wilmington PMSA, DE-MD-NJ	Y	18720 FQ	20550 MW	24440 TQ	USBLS	5/15
	Washington-Arlington-Alexandria PMSA, DC-VA-MD-WV	Y	18320 FQ	22370 MW	30180 TQ	USBLS	5/15
	Florida	H	9.23 AE	11.00 MW	12.87 AEX	FLBLS	7/16-9/16
	Fort Lauderdale-Pompano Beach-Deerfield Beach PMSA, FL	H	10.48 AE	11.55 MW	14.19 AEX	FLBLS	7/16-9/16
	Miami-Miami Beach-Kendall PMSA, FL	H	11.02 AE	11.44 MW	12.37 AEX	FLBLS	7/16-9/16

Occupation/Type/Industry	Location	Per	Low	Mid	High	Source	Date
Automotive and Watercraft Service Attendant	Orlando-Kissimmee-Sanford MSA, FL	H	10.01 AE	11.17 MW	12.77 AEX	FLBLS	7/16-9/16
	Tampa-St. Petersburg-Clearwater MSA, FL	H	8.99 AE	9.86 MW	12.21 AEX	FLBLS	7/16-9/16
	Georgia	Y	18030 FQ	20890 MW	25020 TQ	USBLS	5/15
	Atlanta-Sandy Springs-Roswell MSA, GA	Y	17970 FQ	20750 MW	24640 TQ	USBLS	5/15
	Augusta-Richmond County MSA, GA-SC	Y	17540 FQ	19530 MW	29710 TQ	USBLS	5/15
	Hawaii	Y	18430 FQ	21980 MW	33410 TQ	USBLS	5/15
	Urban Honolulu MSA, HI	Y	18110 FQ	21490 MW	32640 TQ	USBLS	5/15
	Idaho	Y	18160 FQ	21350 MW	26190 TQ	USBLS	5/15
	Boise City MSA, ID	Y	18500 FQ	23200 MW	29660 TQ	USBLS	5/15
	Illinois	Y	19650 FQ	22320 MW	26710 TQ	USBLS	5/15
	Chicago-Naperville-Arlington Heights PMSA, IL	Y	20120 FQ	22840 MW	29090 TQ	USBLS	5/15
	Lake County-Kenosha County PMSA, IL-WI	Y	20180 FQ	25580 MW	40200 TQ	USBLS	5/15
	Indiana	Y	18060 FQ	20890 MW	26110 TQ	USBLS	5/15
	Gary PMSA, IN	Y	17230 FQ	18820 MW	22590 TQ	USBLS	5/15
	Indianapolis-Carmel-Anderson MSA, IN	Y	18190 FQ	21730 MW	27060 TQ	USBLS	5/15
	Iowa	Y	20740 FQ	24610 MW	28740 TQ	USBLS	5/15
	Des Moines-West Des Moines MSA, IA	Y	23890 FQ	29630 MW	37640 TQ	USBLS	5/15
	Kansas	Y	17910 FQ	20260 MW	24520 TQ	USBLS	5/15
	Wichita MSA, KS	Y	18230 FQ	21080 MW	24560 TQ	USBLS	5/15
	Kentucky	Y	17810 FQ	20450 MW	24640 TQ	USBLS	5/15
	Louisville-Jefferson County MSA, KY-IN	Y	20250 FQ	24390 MW	29760 TQ	USBLS	5/15
	Louisiana	Y	20180 FQ	24080 MW	29400 TQ	USBLS	5/15
	Baton Rouge MSA, LA	Y	22330 FQ	26930 MW	31110 TQ	USBLS	5/15
	New Orleans-Metairie MSA, LA	Y	22450 FQ	27800 MW	32950 TQ	USBLS	5/15
	Maine	Y	17560 FQ	19010 MW	22220 TQ	USBLS	5/15
	Portland-South Portland MSA, ME	Y	17710 FQ	19500 MW	23990 TQ	USBLS	5/15
	Maryland	Y	18061 AE	23234 MW	25821 AEX	MDBLS	4/16
	Baltimore-Columbia-Towson MSA, MD	Y	18180 FQ	19870 MW	24690 TQ	USBLS	5/15
	Salisbury MSA, MD-DE	Y	21370 FQ	27280 MW	32710 TQ	USBLS	5/15
	Massachusetts	Y	20740 FQ	22720 MW	24810 TQ	USBLS	5/15
	Boston-Cambridge-Newton NECTA, MA	Y	20610 FQ	22290 MW	23960 TQ	USBLS	5/15
	Worcester MSA, MA-CT	Y	21820 FQ	24160 MW	27900 TQ	USBLS	5/15
	Michigan	Y	18550 FQ	20140 MW	23930 TQ	USBLS	5/15
	Detroit-Dearborn-Livonia PMSA, MI	Y	18900 FQ	21980 MW	27980 TQ	USBLS	5/15
	Grand Rapids-Wyoming MSA, MI	Y	18220 FQ	19230 MW	23260 TQ	USBLS	5/15
	Minnesota	Y	19739 FQ	23762 MW	29055 TQ	MNBLS	1/16-3/16
	Minneapolis-St. Paul-Bloomington MSA, MN-WI	Y	19518 FQ	23207 MW	28349 TQ	MNBLS	1/16-3/16
	Mississippi	Y	18030 FQ	20940 MW	25280 TQ	USBLS	5/15
	Jackson MSA, MS	Y	17560 FQ	19310 MW	23270 TQ	USBLS	5/15
	Missouri	Y	17960 FQ	20200 MW	27650 TQ	USBLS	5/15
	Kansas City MSA, MO-KS	Y	18590 FQ	21650 MW	25630 TQ	USBLS	5/15
	St. Louis MSA, MO-IL	Y	18020 FQ	19440 MW	23850 TQ	USBLS	5/15
	Montana	Y	25840 FQ	31080 MW	40720 TQ	USBLS	5/15
	Billings MSA, MT	Y	25340 FQ	29110 MW	35390 TQ	USBLS	5/15
	Nebraska	Y	19785 FQ	24905 MW	29685 TQ	NEBLS	7/16-9/16
	Omaha-Council Bluffs MSA, NE-IA	Y	19185 FQ	23745 MW	28450 TQ	NEBLS	7/16-9/16
	Nevada	Y	18510 FQ	22030 MW	28290 TQ	USBLS	5/15
	Las Vegas-Henderson-Paradise MSA, NV	Y	18230 FQ	21670 MW	28620 TQ	USBLS	5/15
	New Hampshire	H	8.42 AE	10.36 MW	12.58 AEX	NHBLS	6/16
	Manchester NECTA, NH	H	10.27 AE	12.62 MW	14.15 AEX	NHBLS	6/16
	Nashua NECTA, NH-MA	Y	17690 FQ	20390 MW	24330 TQ	USBLS	5/15
	New Jersey	Y	18460 FQ	19410 MW	21720 TQ	USBLS	5/15
	Camden PMSA, NJ	Y	18420 FQ	19340 MW	21520 TQ	USBLS	5/15

AE Average entry wage	**AWR** Average wage range	**H** Hourly	**LR** Low end range	**MTC** Median total compensation	**TCC** Total cash compensation
AEX Average experienced wage	**B** Biweekly	**HI** Highest wage paid	**M** Monthly	**MW** Median wage paid	**TQ** Third quartile wage
ATC Average total compensation	**D** Daily	**HR** High end range	**MCC** Median cash compensation	**MWR** Median wage range	**W** Weekly
AW Average wage paid	**FQ** First quartile wage	**LO** Lowest wage paid	**ME** Median entry wage	**S** See annotated source	**Y** Yearly

Occupation/Type/Industry	Location	Per	Low	Mid	High	Source	Date
Automotive and Watercraft Service Attendant	Newark PMSA, NJ-PA	Y	18210 FQ	18890 MW	19680 TQ	USBLS	5/15
	Trenton MSA, NJ	Y	18390 FQ	19230 MW	21250 TQ	USBLS	5/15
	New Mexico	Y	18300 FQ	21070 MW	27150 TQ	USBLS	5/15
	Albuquerque MSA, NM	Y	18140 FQ	20030 MW	26180 TQ	USBLS	5/15
	New York	Y	19290 AE	20770 MW	24550 AEX	NYBLS	1/16-3/16
	Buffalo-Cheektowaga-Niagara Falls MSA, NY	Y	19120 FQ	20430 MW	23460 TQ	USBLS	5/15
	Nassau County-Suffolk County PMSA, NY	Y	20190 FQ	22860 MW	28170 TQ	USBLS	5/15
	New York-Jersey City-White Plains PMSA, NY-NJ	Y	18740 FQ	19800 MW	22870 TQ	USBLS	5/15
	Rochester MSA, NY	Y	18750 FQ	19520 MW	22740 TQ	USBLS	5/15
	North Carolina	Y	17390 FQ	19260 MW	23280 TQ	USBLS	5/15
	Charlotte-Concord-Gastonia MSA, NC-SC	Y	17210 FQ	19140 MW	24110 TQ	USBLS	5/15
	Raleigh MSA, NC	Y	17130 FQ	18700 MW	21540 TQ	USBLS	5/15
	North Dakota	Y	22390 FQ	29480 MW	35800 TQ	USBLS	5/15
	Fargo MSA, ND-MN	Y	19530 FQ	22720 MW	26930 TQ	USBLS	5/15
	Ohio	Y	18830 FQ	21290 MW	25140 TQ	USBLS	5/15
	Cincinnati MSA, OH-KY-IN	Y	18820 FQ	21980 MW	26250 TQ	USBLS	5/15
	Cleveland-Elyria MSA, OH	Y	20960 FQ	23840 MW	34420 TQ	USBLS	5/15
	Columbus MSA, OH	Y	18450 FQ	20100 MW	24080 TQ	USBLS	5/15
	Oklahoma	Y	20750 FQ	23710 MW	28130 TQ	USBLS	5/15
	Oklahoma City MSA, OK	Y	20480 FQ	23950 MW	29450 TQ	USBLS	5/15
	Tulsa MSA, OK	Y	18800 FQ	21490 MW	24880 TQ	USBLS	5/15
	Oregon	H	9.84 FQ	11.08 MW	12.94 TQ	ORBLS	2016
	Portland-Vancouver-Hillsboro MSA, OR-WA	Y	22030 FQ	25300 MW	29350 TQ	USBLS	5/15
	Pennsylvania	Y	17660 FQ	19650 MW	23590 TQ	USBLS	5/15
	Allentown-Bethlehem-Easton MSA, PA-NJ	Y	17940 FQ	18970 MW	20090 TQ	USBLS	5/15
	Harrisburg-Carlisle MSA, PA	Y	17640 FQ	19540 MW	23680 TQ	USBLS	5/15
	Montgomery County-Bucks County-Chester County PMSA, PA	Y	17160 FQ	18390 MW	19620 TQ	USBLS	5/15
	Philadelphia PMSA, PA	Y	18120 FQ	20450 MW	23730 TQ	USBLS	5/15
	Pittsburgh MSA, PA	Y	17200 FQ	18860 MW	23260 TQ	USBLS	5/15
	Rhode Island	Y	19330 FQ	20020 MW	23770 TQ	USBLS	5/15
	Providence-Warwick MSA, RI-MA	Y	19450 FQ	20480 MW	24580 TQ	USBLS	5/15
	South Carolina	Y	18680 FQ	23020 MW	30280 TQ	USBLS	5/15
	Charleston-North Charleston MSA, SC	Y	19280 FQ	23080 MW	28280 TQ	USBLS	5/15
	Columbia MSA, SC	Y	20660 FQ	24960 MW	34910 TQ	USBLS	5/15
	Greenville-Anderson-Mauldin MSA, SC	Y	18460 FQ	22940 MW	29450 TQ	USBLS	5/15
	South Dakota	Y	19300 FQ	21720 MW	24120 TQ	USBLS	5/15
	Sioux Falls MSA, SD	Y	19630 FQ	22300 MW	24720 TQ	USBLS	5/15
	Tennessee	Y	17560 FQ	19630 MW	24190 TQ	USBLS	5/15
	Knoxville MSA, TN	Y	16830 FQ	18170 MW	19550 TQ	USBLS	5/15
	Memphis MSA, TN-MS-AR	Y	18260 FQ	22230 MW	29490 TQ	USBLS	5/15
	Nashville-Davidson–Murfreesboro–Franklin MSA, TN	Y	18020 FQ	21180 MW	25990 TQ	USBLS	5/15
	Texas	Y	18950 FQ	22640 MW	27960 TQ	USBLS	5/15
	Austin-Round Rock MSA, TX	Y	20110 FQ	22800 MW	26390 TQ	USBLS	5/15
	Dallas-Plano-Irving PMSA, TX	Y	20610 FQ	24810 MW	30320 TQ	USBLS	5/15
	Fort Worth-Arlington PMSA, TX	Y	19750 FQ	22210 MW	24720 TQ	USBLS	5/15
	Houston-The Woodlands-Sugar Land MSA, TX	Y	19430 FQ	24530 MW	29970 TQ	USBLS	5/15
	San Antonio-New Braunfels MSA, TX	Y	18110 FQ	21020 MW	26160 TQ	USBLS	5/15
	Utah	Y	18470 FQ	21740 MW	26160 TQ	USBLS	5/15
	Ogden-Clearfield MSA, UT	Y	17230 FQ	19070 MW	22850 TQ	USBLS	5/15
	Provo-Orem MSA, UT	Y	18170 FQ	21030 MW	24080 TQ	USBLS	5/15
	Salt Lake City MSA, UT	Y	19920 FQ	23820 MW	35110 TQ	USBLS	5/15
	Burlington-South Burlington MSA, VT	Y	19700 FQ	24280 MW	32440 TQ	USBLS	5/15
	Virginia	Y	17740 FQ	20220 MW	28590 TQ	USBLS	5/15
	Richmond MSA, VA	Y	17620 FQ	20680 MW	29830 TQ	USBLS	5/15

Occupation/Type/Industry	Location	Per	Low	Mid	High	Source	Date
Automotive and Watercraft Service Attendant	Virginia Beach-Norfolk-Newport News MSA, VA-NC	Y	17660 FQ	19540 MW	24080 TQ	USBLS	5/15
	Washington	H	10.94 FQ	12.23 MW	14.55 TQ	WABLS	3/16
	Seattle-Bellevue-Everett PMSA, WA	H	11.09 FQ	12.41 MW	14.54 TQ	WABLS	3/16
	Tacoma-Lakewood PMSA, WA	H	11.46 FQ	13.38 MW	15.73 TQ	WABLS	3/16
	West Virginia	Y	17950 FQ	19270 MW	22400 TQ	USBLS	5/15
	Huntington-Ashland MSA, WV-KY-OH	Y	18240 FQ	20410 MW	26630 TQ	USBLS	5/15
	Wisconsin	Y	17530 FQ	19530 MW	23440 TQ	USBLS	5/15
	Madison MSA, WI	Y	18230 FQ	20780 MW	24610 TQ	USBLS	5/15
	Milwaukee-Waukesha-West Allis MSA, WI	Y	17050 FQ	18750 MW	23540 TQ	USBLS	5/15
	Wyoming	Y	19980 FQ	24470 MW	30040 TQ	USBLS	5/15
	Cheyenne MSA, WY	Y	17440 FQ	19060 MW	21490 TQ	USBLS	5/15
	Puerto Rico	Y	16730 FQ	17910 MW	19100 TQ	USBLS	5/15
	San Juan-Carolina-Caguas MSA, PR	Y	16550 FQ	17700 MW	18840 TQ	USBLS	5/15
	Virgin Islands	Y	18350 FQ	21550 MW	25490 TQ	USBLS	5/15
	Guam	Y	17820 FQ	18470 MW	19120 TQ	USBLS	5/15
Automotive Body and Related Repairer	Alabama	Y	28192 AE	41474 AW	48115 AEX	ALBLS	6/16
	Birmingham-Hoover MSA, AL	Y	30358 AE	43600 AW	50220 AEX	ALBLS	6/16
	Alaska	Y	42200 FQ	55570 MW	62070 TQ	USBLS	5/15
	Anchorage MSA, AK	Y	49980 FQ	56630 MW	62650 TQ	USBLS	5/15
	Arizona	Y	34620 FQ	43020 MW	54510 TQ	USBLS	5/15
	Phoenix-Mesa-Scottsdale MSA, AZ	Y	34500 FQ	41950 MW	52530 TQ	USBLS	5/15
	Tucson MSA, AZ	Y	33030 FQ	43240 MW	56270 TQ	USBLS	5/15
	Arkansas	Y	26250 FQ	33200 MW	42400 TQ	USBLS	5/15
	Little Rock-North Little Rock-Conway MSA, AR	Y	25810 FQ	30300 MW	38840 TQ	USBLS	5/15
	California	H	15.84 FQ	19.58 MW	27.02 TQ	CABLS	1/16-3/16
	Anaheim-Santa Ana-Irvine PMSA, CA	H	15.23 FQ	19.69 MW	30.47 TQ	CABLS	1/16-3/16
	Los Angeles-Long Beach-Glendale PMSA, CA	H	14.46 FQ	18.44 MW	23.33 TQ	CABLS	1/16-3/16
	Oakland-Hayward-Berkeley PMSA, CA	H	18.51 FQ	23.54 MW	28.68 TQ	CABLS	1/16-3/16
	Riverside-San Bernardino-Ontario MSA, CA	H	14.58 FQ	18.09 MW	26.78 TQ	CABLS	1/16-3/16
	Sacramento–Roseville–Arden-Arcade MSA, CA	H	16.90 FQ	18.76 MW	24.04 TQ	CABLS	1/16-3/16
	San Diego-Carlsbad MSA, CA	H	15.68 FQ	18.31 MW	26.43 TQ	CABLS	1/16-3/16
	San Francisco-Redwood City-South San Francisco PMSA, CA	H	18.52 FQ	25.75 MW	36.21 TQ	CABLS	1/16-3/16
	Colorado	Y	36860 FQ	47550 MW	60290 TQ	USBLS	5/15
	Denver-Aurora-Lakewood MSA, CO	Y	39870 FQ	48030 MW	60520 TQ	USBLS	5/15
	Connecticut	Y		44125 MW		CTBLS	1/16-3/16
	Bridgeport-Stamford-Norwalk MSA, CT	Y	41210 FQ	47050 MW	54720 TQ	USBLS	5/15
	Hartford-West Hartford-East Hartford MSA, CT	Y	31630 FQ	39090 MW	55500 TQ	USBLS	5/15
	Delaware	Y	32640 FQ	39650 MW	55880 TQ	USBLS	5/15
	Wilmington PMSA, DE-MD-NJ	Y	33430 FQ	41460 MW	55790 TQ	USBLS	5/15
	District of Columbia	Y	46350 FQ	63170 MW	74260 TQ	USBLS	5/15
	Washington-Arlington-Alexandria PMSA, DC-VA-MD-WV	Y	43410 FQ	57890 MW	74320 TQ	USBLS	5/15
	Florida	H	13.16 AE	18.57 MW	23.58 AEX	FLBLS	7/16-9/16
	Fort Lauderdale-Pompano Beach-Deerfield Beach PMSA, FL	H	13.44 AE	19.46 MW	25.20 AEX	FLBLS	7/16-9/16
	Miami-Miami Beach-Kendall PMSA, FL	H	12.19 AE	17.01 MW	21.21 AEX	FLBLS	7/16-9/16

AE	Average entry wage	AWR	Average wage range	H	Hourly	LR	Low end range	MTC	Median total compensation	TCC	Total cash compensation
AEX	Average experienced wage	B	Biweekly	HI	Highest wage paid	M	Monthly	MW	Median wage paid	TQ	Third quartile wage
ATC	Average total compensation	D	Daily	HR	High end range	MCC	Median cash compensation	MWR	Median wage range	W	Weekly
AW	Average wage paid	FQ	First quartile wage	LO	Lowest wage paid	ME	Median entry wage	S	See annotated source	Y	Yearly

Occupation/Type/Industry	Location	Per	Low	Mid	High	Source	Date
Automotive Body and Related Repairer							
	Orlando-Kissimmee-Sanford MSA, FL	H	14.67 AE	20.19 MW	24.69 AEX	FLBLS	7/16-9/16
	Port St. Lucie MSA, FL	Y	32810 FQ	37630 MW	48640 TQ	USBLS	5/15
	Tampa-St. Petersburg-Clearwater MSA, FL	H	11.95 AE	17.60 MW	22.23 AEX	FLBLS	7/16-9/16
	Georgia	Y	29380 FQ	43790 MW	66330 TQ	USBLS	5/15
	Atlanta-Sandy Springs-Roswell MSA, GA	Y	29080 FQ	44550 MW	73640 TQ	USBLS	5/15
	Augusta-Richmond County MSA, GA-SC	Y	27760 FQ	38900 MW	60020 TQ	USBLS	5/15
	Hawaii	Y	37180 FQ	44960 MW	51870 TQ	USBLS	5/15
	Urban Honolulu MSA, HI	Y	38380 FQ	44500 MW	49700 TQ	USBLS	5/15
	Idaho	Y	33780 FQ	39710 MW	49040 TQ	USBLS	5/15
	Boise City MSA, ID	Y	34620 FQ	39340 MW	50150 TQ	USBLS	5/15
	Illinois	Y	30090 FQ	47700 MW	59160 TQ	USBLS	5/15
	Chicago-Naperville-Arlington Heights PMSA, IL	Y	33230 FQ	52790 MW	61090 TQ	USBLS	5/15
	Lake County-Kenosha County PMSA, IL-WI	Y	29020 FQ	41790 MW	55460 TQ	USBLS	5/15
	Indiana	Y	32490 FQ	42090 MW	55330 TQ	USBLS	5/15
	Gary PMSA, IN	Y	25850 FQ	30090 MW	45170 TQ	USBLS	5/15
	Indianapolis-Carmel-Anderson MSA, IN	Y	35930 FQ	50240 MW	66020 TQ	USBLS	5/15
	Iowa	Y	28670 FQ	35720 MW	44400 TQ	USBLS	5/15
	Des Moines-West Des Moines MSA, IA	Y	32140 FQ	39250 MW	53510 TQ	USBLS	5/15
	Kansas	Y	31070 FQ	38370 MW	54960 TQ	USBLS	5/15
	Wichita MSA, KS	Y	33290 FQ	48880 MW	69790 TQ	USBLS	5/15
	Kentucky	Y	29930 FQ	40180 MW	50900 TQ	USBLS	5/15
	Louisville-Jefferson County MSA, KY-IN	Y	36930 FQ	46430 MW	55940 TQ	USBLS	5/15
	Louisiana	Y	27190 FQ	35040 MW	48120 TQ	USBLS	5/15
	Baton Rouge MSA, LA	Y	20310 FQ	36640 MW	48460 TQ	USBLS	5/15
	New Orleans-Metairie MSA, LA	Y	27980 FQ	33560 MW	50630 TQ	USBLS	5/15
	Maine	Y	28970 FQ	35000 MW	41880 TQ	USBLS	5/15
	Portland-South Portland MSA, ME	Y	31960 FQ	38700 MW	49950 TQ	USBLS	5/15
	Maryland	Y	37716 AE	61760 MW	73782 AEX	MDBLS	4/16
	Baltimore-Columbia-Towson MSA, MD	Y	42590 FQ	60190 MW	82190 TQ	USBLS	5/15
	Salisbury MSA, MD-DE	Y	31220 FQ	38000 MW	49550 TQ	USBLS	5/15
	Massachusetts	Y	36540 FQ	45280 MW	55160 TQ	USBLS	5/15
	Boston-Cambridge-Newton NECTA, MA	Y	38260 FQ	46570 MW	55820 TQ	USBLS	5/15
	Worcester MSA, MA-CT	Y	34130 FQ	43130 MW	53610 TQ	USBLS	5/15
	Michigan	Y	32260 FQ	44820 MW	60780 TQ	USBLS	5/15
	Detroit-Dearborn-Livonia PMSA, MI	Y	43760 FQ	57730 MW	74170 TQ	USBLS	5/15
	Grand Rapids-Wyoming MSA, MI	Y	31040 FQ	41070 MW	50620 TQ	USBLS	5/15
	Minnesota	Y	35239 FQ	43797 MW	55744 TQ	MNBLS	1/16-3/16
	Minneapolis-St. Paul-Bloomington MSA, MN-WI	Y	37260 FQ	47649 MW	59305 TQ	MNBLS	1/16-3/16
	Mississippi	Y	25970 FQ	34580 MW	45410 TQ	USBLS	5/15
	Jackson MSA, MS	Y	32810 FQ	43010 MW	53070 TQ	USBLS	5/15
	Missouri	Y	33100 FQ	41860 MW	53190 TQ	USBLS	5/15
	Kansas City MSA, MO-KS	Y	34280 FQ	46650 MW	57830 TQ	USBLS	5/15
	St. Louis MSA, MO-IL	Y	34430 FQ	43330 MW	53610 TQ	USBLS	5/15
	Montana	Y	31190 FQ	38340 MW	47120 TQ	USBLS	5/15
	Billings MSA, MT	Y	32270 FQ	41660 MW	48390 TQ	USBLS	5/15
	Nebraska	Y	34260 FQ	41665 MW	51180 TQ	NEBLS	7/16-9/16
	Omaha-Council Bluffs MSA, NE-IA	Y	32675 FQ	40130 MW	48735 TQ	NEBLS	7/16-9/16
	Nevada	Y	34980 FQ	47870 MW	68980 TQ	USBLS	5/15
	Las Vegas-Henderson-Paradise MSA, NV	Y	35360 FQ	54520 MW	71280 TQ	USBLS	5/15
	New Hampshire	H	14.46 AE	18.62 MW	21.94 AEX	NHBLS	6/16
	Manchester NECTA, NH	H	16.36 AE	22.73 MW	26.79 AEX	NHBLS	6/16
	Nashua NECTA, NH-MA	Y	34950 FQ	40140 MW	50750 TQ	USBLS	5/15
	New Jersey	Y	35670 FQ	45820 MW	57140 TQ	USBLS	5/15

AE	Average entry wage	AWR	Average wage range	H	Hourly
AEX	Average experienced wage	B	Biweekly	HI	Highest wage paid
ATC	Average total compensation	D	Daily	HR	High end range
AW	Average wage paid	FQ	First quartile wage	LO	Lowest wage paid

LR	Low end range	MTC	Median total compensation	TCC	Total cash compensation
M	Monthly	MW	Median wage paid	TQ	Third quartile wage
MCC	Median cash compensation	MWR	Median wage range	W	Weekly
ME	Median entry wage	S	See annotated source	Y	Yearly

Occupation/Type/Industry	Location	Per	Low	Mid	High	Source	Date
Automotive Body and Related Repairer							
	Camden PMSA, NJ	Y	38480 FQ	51250 MW	60670 TQ	USBLS	5/15
	Newark PMSA, NJ-PA	Y	35870 FQ	46830 MW	58790 TQ	USBLS	5/15
	Trenton MSA, NJ	Y	34140 FQ	43050 MW	51130 TQ	USBLS	5/15
	New Mexico	Y	27570 FQ	40460 MW	50910 TQ	USBLS	5/15
	Albuquerque MSA, NM	Y	25160 FQ	40400 MW	51920 TQ	USBLS	5/15
	New York	Y	25370 AE	38710 MW	49680 AEX	NYBLS	1/16-3/16
	Buffalo-Cheektowaga-Niagara Falls MSA, NY	Y	19890 FQ	35300 MW	49480 TQ	USBLS	5/15
	Nassau County-Suffolk County PMSA, NY	Y	25480 FQ	31510 MW	55730 TQ	USBLS	5/15
	New York-Jersey City-White Plains PMSA, NY-NJ	Y	32760 FQ	41960 MW	54540 TQ	USBLS	5/15
	Rochester MSA, NY	Y	24920 FQ	34650 MW	44520 TQ	USBLS	5/15
	North Carolina	Y	35940 FQ	47010 MW	61610 TQ	USBLS	5/15
	Charlotte-Concord-Gastonia MSA, NC-SC	Y	41000 FQ	54140 MW	68170 TQ	USBLS	5/15
	North Dakota	Y	34610 FQ	42790 MW	55590 TQ	USBLS	5/15
	Fargo MSA, ND-MN	Y	34690 FQ	41890 MW	54360 TQ	USBLS	5/15
	Ohio	Y	31550 FQ	37960 MW	48910 TQ	USBLS	5/15
	Cincinnati MSA, OH-KY-IN	Y	32440 FQ	38890 MW	50890 TQ	USBLS	5/15
	Cleveland-Elyria MSA, OH	Y	32890 FQ	41680 MW	50870 TQ	USBLS	5/15
	Columbus MSA, OH	Y	32460 FQ	38780 MW	55080 TQ	USBLS	5/15
	Oklahoma	Y	30080 FQ	39370 MW	49890 TQ	USBLS	5/15
	Oklahoma City MSA, OK	Y	31230 FQ	37530 MW	50740 TQ	USBLS	5/15
	Tulsa MSA, OK	Y	28920 FQ	44140 MW	54150 TQ	USBLS	5/15
	Oregon	H	16.07 FQ	18.75 MW	26.72 TQ	ORBLS	2016
	Portland-Vancouver-Hillsboro MSA, OR-WA	Y	33170 FQ	38190 MW	54960 TQ	USBLS	5/15
	Pennsylvania	Y	31730 FQ	39010 MW	50100 TQ	USBLS	5/15
	Allentown-Bethlehem-Easton MSA, PA-NJ	Y	31650 FQ	41540 MW	50630 TQ	USBLS	5/15
	Harrisburg-Carlisle MSA, PA	Y	38690 FQ	53080 MW	69570 TQ	USBLS	5/15
	Montgomery County-Bucks County-Chester County PMSA, PA	Y	40660 FQ	51610 MW	62520 TQ	USBLS	5/15
	Philadelphia PMSA, PA	Y	30440 FQ	36940 MW	46400 TQ	USBLS	5/15
	Pittsburgh MSA, PA	Y	33050 FQ	38780 MW	48960 TQ	USBLS	5/15
	Rhode Island	Y	32130 FQ	44540 MW	52580 TQ	USBLS	5/15
	Providence-Warwick MSA, RI-MA	Y	33860 FQ	45140 MW	53740 TQ	USBLS	5/15
	South Carolina	Y	31350 FQ	38300 MW	49530 TQ	USBLS	5/15
	Charleston-North Charleston MSA, SC	Y	32600 FQ	43580 MW	58810 TQ	USBLS	5/15
	Columbia MSA, SC	Y	33960 FQ	42640 MW	53520 TQ	USBLS	5/15
	Greenville-Anderson-Mauldin MSA, SC	Y	32740 FQ	36610 MW	46510 TQ	USBLS	5/15
	South Dakota	Y	31570 FQ	36470 MW	43720 TQ	USBLS	5/15
	Sioux Falls MSA, SD	Y	34660 FQ	38590 MW	46770 TQ	USBLS	5/15
	Tennessee	Y	27090 FQ	37200 MW	48740 TQ	USBLS	5/15
	Knoxville MSA, TN	Y	24470 FQ	32530 MW	45280 TQ	USBLS	5/15
	Memphis MSA, TN-MS-AR	Y	32780 FQ	38390 MW	53220 TQ	USBLS	5/15
	Nashville-Davidson–Murfreesboro–Franklin MSA, TN	Y	25250 FQ	38270 MW	47840 TQ	USBLS	5/15
	Texas	Y	32080 FQ	40510 MW	55370 TQ	USBLS	5/15
	Austin-Round Rock MSA, TX	Y	34430 FQ	42230 MW	50180 TQ	USBLS	5/15
	Dallas-Plano-Irving PMSA, TX	Y	34540 FQ	44760 MW	58220 TQ	USBLS	5/15
	Fort Worth-Arlington PMSA, TX	Y	32470 FQ	37620 MW	46730 TQ	USBLS	5/15
	Houston-The Woodlands-Sugar Land MSA, TX	Y	30960 FQ	39810 MW	58260 TQ	USBLS	5/15
	San Antonio-New Braunfels MSA, TX	Y	34860 FQ	47010 MW	58840 TQ	USBLS	5/15
	Utah	Y	33520 FQ	44170 MW	57770 TQ	USBLS	5/15
	Ogden-Clearfield MSA, UT	Y	34780 FQ	39260 MW	51370 TQ	USBLS	5/15
	Provo-Orem MSA, UT	Y	34880 FQ	38920 MW	58910 TQ	USBLS	5/15
	Salt Lake City MSA, UT	Y	32590 FQ	48610 MW	59250 TQ	USBLS	5/15
	Vermont	Y	34310 FQ	41470 MW	51230 TQ	USBLS	5/15
	Burlington-South Burlington MSA, VT	Y	35680 FQ	44720 MW	54760 TQ	USBLS	5/15
	Virginia	Y	34940 FQ	45070 MW	61100 TQ	USBLS	5/15

AE	Average entry wage	AWR	Average wage range	H	Hourly	LR	Low end range	MTC	Median total compensation	TCC	Total cash compensation
AEX	Average experienced wage	B	Biweekly	HI	Highest wage paid	M	Monthly	MW	Median wage paid	TQ	Third quartile wage
ATC	Average total compensation	D	Daily	HR	High end range	MCC	Median cash compensation	MWR	Median wage range	W	Weekly
AW	Average wage paid	FQ	First quartile wage	LO	Lowest wage paid	ME	Median entry wage	S	See annotated source	Y	Yearly

Occupation/Type/Industry	Location	Per	Low	Mid	High	Source	Date
Automotive Body and Related Repairer	Richmond MSA, VA	Y	36200 FQ	44370 MW	53780 TQ	USBLS	5/15
	Virginia Beach-Norfolk-Newport News MSA, VA-NC	Y	32820 FQ	41900 MW	62570 TQ	USBLS	5/15
	Washington	H	16.65 FQ	21.73 MW	29.17 TQ	WABLS	3/16
	Seattle-Bellevue-Everett PMSA, WA	H	19.76 FQ	26.79 MW	37.14 TQ	WABLS	3/16
	Tacoma-Lakewood PMSA, WA	H	19.30 FQ	21.57 MW	23.84 TQ	WABLS	3/16
	West Virginia	Y	26400 FQ	34270 MW	45800 TQ	USBLS	5/15
	Huntington-Ashland MSA, WV-KY-OH	Y	18280 FQ	23050 MW	37230 TQ	USBLS	5/15
	Wisconsin	Y	30820 FQ	37040 MW	45550 TQ	USBLS	5/15
	Madison MSA, WI	Y	30660 FQ	36150 MW	45010 TQ	USBLS	5/15
	Milwaukee-Waukesha-West Allis MSA, WI	Y	29770 FQ	37100 MW	47180 TQ	USBLS	5/15
	Wyoming	Y	32030 FQ	47310 MW	58390 TQ	USBLS	5/15
	Puerto Rico	Y	17460 FQ	19250 MW	23850 TQ	USBLS	5/15
	San Juan-Carolina-Caguas MSA, PR	Y	17850 FQ	20190 MW	25230 TQ	USBLS	5/15
	Guam	Y	19890 FQ	26100 MW	29110 TQ	USBLS	5/15
Automotive Glass Installer and Repairer	Alabama	Y	23351 AE	32067 AW	36419 AEX	ALBLS	6/16
	Alaska	Y	27820 FQ	32940 MW	38070 TQ	USBLS	5/15
	Arizona	Y	27240 FQ	33620 MW	40090 TQ	USBLS	5/15
	Phoenix-Mesa-Scottsdale MSA, AZ	Y	22760 FQ	29670 MW	36110 TQ	USBLS	5/15
	Tucson MSA, AZ	Y	31930 FQ	38830 MW	54540 TQ	USBLS	5/15
	Arkansas	Y	22380 FQ	28240 MW	34190 TQ	USBLS	5/15
	California	H	14.49 FQ	17.85 MW	23.19 TQ	CABLS	1/16-3/16
	Riverside-San Bernardino-Ontario MSA, CA	H	19.21 FQ	21.79 MW	24.32 TQ	CABLS	1/16-3/16
	Sacramento–Roseville–Arden-Arcade MSA, CA	H	17.00 FQ	20.89 MW	25.44 TQ	CABLS	1/16-3/16
	Colorado	Y	29060 FQ	33790 MW	40400 TQ	USBLS	5/15
	Denver-Aurora-Lakewood MSA, CO	Y	31110 FQ	34880 MW	40510 TQ	USBLS	5/15
	Connecticut	Y		38391 MW		CTBLS	1/16-3/16
	Washington-Arlington-Alexandria PMSA, DC-VA-MD-WV	Y	29680 FQ	35510 MW	45260 TQ	USBLS	5/15
	Florida	H	10.02 AE	15.54 MW	20.39 AEX	FLBLS	7/16-9/16
	Fort Lauderdale-Pompano Beach-Deerfield Beach PMSA, FL	H	17.39 AE	19.48 MW	25.24 AEX	FLBLS	7/16-9/16
	Georgia	Y	21540 FQ	26870 MW	31880 TQ	USBLS	5/15
	Augusta-Richmond County MSA, GA-SC	Y	21020 FQ	26590 MW	30580 TQ	USBLS	5/15
	Idaho	Y	20160 FQ	29260 MW	41120 TQ	USBLS	5/15
	Illinois	Y	26090 FQ	29430 MW	37780 TQ	USBLS	5/15
	Indiana	Y	23270 FQ	32060 MW	37660 TQ	USBLS	5/15
	Indianapolis-Carmel-Anderson MSA, IN	Y	17500 FQ	25100 MW	37540 TQ	USBLS	5/15
	Iowa	Y	26190 FQ	31830 MW	37070 TQ	USBLS	5/15
	Kentucky	Y	26800 FQ	34380 MW	39500 TQ	USBLS	5/15
	Louisville-Jefferson County MSA, KY-IN	Y	28010 FQ	34550 MW	38530 TQ	USBLS	5/15
	Louisiana	Y	23080 FQ	32690 MW	41390 TQ	USBLS	5/15
	Maine	Y	29200 FQ	36040 MW	44430 TQ	USBLS	5/15
	Maryland	Y	27058 AE	39585 MW	45848 AEX	MDBLS	4/16
	Massachusetts	Y	24400 FQ	32620 MW	37730 TQ	USBLS	5/15
	Boston-Cambridge-Newton NECTA, MA	Y	23610 FQ	27680 MW	34130 TQ	USBLS	5/15
	Worcester MSA, MA-CT	Y	28610 FQ	42350 MW	46840 TQ	USBLS	5/15
	Michigan	Y	23450 FQ	30530 MW	43420 TQ	USBLS	5/15
	Detroit-Dearborn-Livonia PMSA, MI	Y	27530 FQ	40520 MW	46510 TQ	USBLS	5/15
	Minnesota	Y	35561 FQ	42238 MW	47025 TQ	MNBLS	1/16-3/16
	Minneapolis-St. Paul-Bloomington MSA, MN-WI	Y	38568 FQ	43686 MW	47548 TQ	MNBLS	1/16-3/16
	Mississippi	Y	26800 FQ	33340 MW	42210 TQ	USBLS	5/15

AE	Average entry wage	AWR	Average wage range	H	Hourly	LR	Low end range	MTC	Median total compensation	TCC	Total cash compensation
AEX	Average experienced wage	B	Biweekly	HI	Highest wage paid	M	Monthly	MW	Median wage paid	TQ	Third quartile wage
ATC	Average total compensation	D	Daily	HR	High end range	MCC	Median cash compensation	MWR	Median wage range	W	Weekly
AW	Average wage paid	FQ	First quartile wage	LO	Lowest wage paid	ME	Median entry wage	S	See annotated source	Y	Yearly

Occupation/Type/Industry	Location	Per	Low	Mid	High	Source	Date
Automotive Glass Installer and Repairer							
	Missouri	Y	23400 FQ	31330 MW	39170 TQ	USBLS	5/15
	St. Louis MSA, MO-IL	Y	25460 FQ	31530 MW	38350 TQ	USBLS	5/15
	Montana	Y	24110 FQ	30410 MW	36030 TQ	USBLS	5/15
	Nebraska	Y	31205 FQ	37815 MW	43980 TQ	NEBLS	7/16-9/16
	Omaha-Council Bluffs MSA, NE-IA	Y	25385 FQ	29390 MW	36055 TQ	NEBLS	7/16-9/16
	Nevada	Y	27590 FQ	34180 MW	42720 TQ	USBLS	5/15
	New Hampshire	H	14.67 AE	21.25 MW	24.62 AEX	NHBLS	6/16
	New Jersey	Y	25320 FQ	33980 MW	42900 TQ	USBLS	5/15
	Newark PMSA, NJ-PA	Y	29160 FQ	35430 MW	43510 TQ	USBLS	5/15
	New Mexico	Y	24960 FQ	29360 MW	34590 TQ	USBLS	5/15
	Buffalo-Cheektowaga-Niagara Falls MSA, NY	Y	32060 FQ	35240 MW	38420 TQ	USBLS	5/15
	New York-Jersey City-White Plains PMSA, NY-NJ	Y	18790 FQ	19380 MW	20040 TQ	USBLS	5/15
	North Carolina	Y	24480 FQ	31520 MW	37790 TQ	USBLS	5/15
	Charlotte-Concord-Gastonia MSA, NC-SC	Y	30590 FQ	35570 MW	41890 TQ	USBLS	5/15
	Raleigh MSA, NC	Y	23080 FQ	31250 MW	37200 TQ	USBLS	5/15
	North Dakota	Y	31380 FQ	34880 MW	38200 TQ	USBLS	5/15
	Ohio	Y	29090 FQ	38240 MW	48770 TQ	USBLS	5/15
	Cincinnati MSA, OH-KY-IN	Y	22450 FQ	43410 MW	56080 TQ	USBLS	5/15
	Columbus MSA, OH	Y	30090 FQ	39080 MW	52880 TQ	USBLS	5/15
	Oklahoma	Y	27770 FQ	32650 MW	38580 TQ	USBLS	5/15
	Oregon	H	10.45 FQ	18.11 MW	22.65 TQ	ORBLS	2016
	Portland-Vancouver-Hillsboro MSA, OR-WA	Y	40930 FQ	44720 MW	48510 TQ	USBLS	5/15
	Pennsylvania	Y	29090 FQ	36700 MW	44200 TQ	USBLS	5/15
	Pittsburgh MSA, PA	Y	34160 FQ	40730 MW	46160 TQ	USBLS	5/15
	Providence-Warwick MSA, RI-MA	Y	24640 FQ	33440 MW	36540 TQ	USBLS	5/15
	South Carolina	Y	31460 FQ	35470 MW	40400 TQ	USBLS	5/15
	South Dakota	Y	33140 FQ	38750 MW	46840 TQ	USBLS	5/15
	Tennessee	Y	23710 FQ	36250 MW	45280 TQ	USBLS	5/15
	Memphis MSA, TN-MS-AR	Y	37570 FQ	45770 MW	53000 TQ	USBLS	5/15
	Nashville-Davidson–Murfreesboro–Franklin MSA, TN	Y	33900 FQ	40480 MW	47390 TQ	USBLS	5/15
	Texas	Y	27300 FQ	34110 MW	44720 TQ	USBLS	5/15
	Austin-Round Rock MSA, TX	Y	34070 FQ	42640 MW	47450 TQ	USBLS	5/15
	Fort Worth-Arlington PMSA, TX	Y	29370 FQ	40100 MW	48560 TQ	USBLS	5/15
	Houston-The Woodlands-Sugar Land MSA, TX	Y	27970 FQ	32480 MW	43230 TQ	USBLS	5/15
	Utah	Y	26090 FQ	39160 MW	45170 TQ	USBLS	5/15
	Vermont	Y	23910 FQ	34060 MW	42500 TQ	USBLS	5/15
	Washington	H	13.93 FQ	17.81 MW	21.49 TQ	WABLS	3/16
	Seattle-Bellevue-Everett PMSA, WA	H	15.03 FQ	17.81 MW	21.15 TQ	WABLS	3/16
	Tacoma-Lakewood PMSA, WA	H	14.32 FQ	20.37 MW	22.76 TQ	WABLS	3/16
	West Virginia	Y	29640 FQ	34110 MW	37490 TQ	USBLS	5/15
	Wisconsin	Y	28280 FQ	36820 MW	44680 TQ	USBLS	5/15
	Wyoming	Y	21910 FQ	29550 MW	36560 TQ	USBLS	5/15
	Puerto Rico	Y	16260 FQ	17340 MW	18430 TQ	USBLS	5/15
Automotive Parts Technician							
Equipment Maintenance, Municipal Government	La Verne, CA	Y			38924 HI	CACIT	6/28/16
Automotive Research Assistant							
Municipal Government	Detroit, MI	M			3958 HI	DETGOV	2016
Automotive Service Technician and Mechanic							
	Alabama	Y	25151 AE	39654 AW	46905 AEX	ALBLS	6/16
	Birmingham-Hoover MSA, AL	Y	27134 AE	44525 AW	53221 AEX	ALBLS	6/16
	Alaska	Y	40720 FQ	51730 MW	64950 TQ	USBLS	5/15
	Anchorage MSA, AK	Y	40320 FQ	48390 MW	60990 TQ	USBLS	5/15
	Arizona	Y	28040 FQ	37900 MW	48970 TQ	USBLS	5/15
	Phoenix-Mesa-Scottsdale MSA, AZ	Y	30380 FQ	39110 MW	49270 TQ	USBLS	5/15
	Tucson MSA, AZ	Y	24260 FQ	33220 MW	46860 TQ	USBLS	5/15

AE	Average entry wage	AWR	Average wage range	H	Hourly
AEX	Average experienced wage	B	Biweekly	HI	Highest wage paid
ATC	Average total compensation	D	Daily	HR	High end range
AW	Average wage paid	FQ	First quartile wage	LO	Lowest wage paid

LR	Low end range	MTC	Median total compensation	TCC Total cash compensation
M	Monthly	MW	Median wage paid	TQ Third quartile wage
MCC	Median cash compensation	MWR	Median wage range	W Weekly
ME	Median entry wage	S	See annotated source	Y Yearly

Occupation/Type/Industry	Location	Per	Low	Mid	High	Source	Date
Automotive Service Technician and Mechanic	Arkansas	Y	24060 FQ	31870 MW	39750 TQ	USBLS	5/15
	Little Rock-North Little Rock-Conway MSA, AR	Y	27450 FQ	34030 MW	39910 TQ	USBLS	5/15
	California	H	15.01 FQ	19.77 MW	27.63 TQ	CABLS	1/16-3/16
	Anaheim-Santa Ana-Irvine PMSA, CA	H	17.66 FQ	23.22 MW	32.62 TQ	CABLS	1/16-3/16
	Los Angeles-Long Beach-Glendale PMSA, CA	H	13.47 FQ	17.26 MW	24.68 TQ	CABLS	1/16-3/16
	Oakland-Hayward-Berkeley PMSA, CA	H	16.89 FQ	24.00 MW	31.87 TQ	CABLS	1/16-3/16
	Riverside-San Bernardino-Ontario MSA, CA	H	14.24 FQ	19.12 MW	26.73 TQ	CABLS	1/16-3/16
	Sacramento–Roseville–Arden-Arcade MSA, CA	H	15.96 FQ	20.88 MW	26.94 TQ	CABLS	1/16-3/16
	San Diego-Carlsbad MSA, CA	H	13.86 FQ	19.13 MW	26.96 TQ	CABLS	1/16-3/16
	San Francisco-Redwood City-South San Francisco PMSA, CA	H	19.18 FQ	24.62 MW	35.07 TQ	CABLS	1/16-3/16
	Colorado	Y	28820 FQ	40780 MW	56900 TQ	USBLS	5/15
	Denver-Aurora-Lakewood MSA, CO	Y	26720 FQ	39060 MW	56750 TQ	USBLS	5/15
	Connecticut	Y		42244 MW		CTBLS	1/16-3/16
	Bridgeport-Stamford-Norwalk MSA, CT	Y	28280 FQ	45880 MW	59730 TQ	USBLS	5/15
	Hartford-West Hartford-East Hartford MSA, CT	Y	31160 FQ	40160 MW	47910 TQ	USBLS	5/15
	Delaware	Y	32410 FQ	38710 MW	53280 TQ	USBLS	5/15
	Wilmington PMSA, DE-MD-NJ	Y	32710 FQ	41760 MW	55690 TQ	USBLS	5/15
	District of Columbia	Y	44550 FQ	57360 MW	66170 TQ	USBLS	5/15
	Washington-Arlington-Alexandria PMSA, DC-VA-MD-WV	Y	34340 FQ	48560 MW	61670 TQ	USBLS	5/15
	Florida	H	11.92 AE	17.83 MW	22.62 AEX	FLBLS	7/16-9/16
	Fort Lauderdale-Pompano Beach-Deerfield Beach PMSA, FL	H	13.99 AE	19.20 MW	24.73 AEX	FLBLS	7/16-9/16
	Miami-Miami Beach-Kendall PMSA, FL	H	10.97 AE	18.02 MW	22.49 AEX	FLBLS	7/16-9/16
	Orlando-Kissimmee-Sanford MSA, FL	H	12.48 AE	17.79 MW	22.24 AEX	FLBLS	7/16-9/16
	Tampa-St. Petersburg-Clearwater MSA, FL	H	11.25 AE	17.95 MW	23.60 AEX	FLBLS	7/16-9/16
	Georgia	Y	24970 FQ	34620 MW	48040 TQ	USBLS	5/15
	Atlanta-Sandy Springs-Roswell MSA, GA	Y	26420 FQ	36580 MW	51070 TQ	USBLS	5/15
	Augusta-Richmond County MSA, GA-SC	Y	24570 FQ	38400 MW	54880 TQ	USBLS	5/15
	Hawaii	Y	32370 FQ	41030 MW	53160 TQ	USBLS	5/15
	Urban Honolulu MSA, HI	Y	32930 FQ	43700 MW	56850 TQ	USBLS	5/15
	Idaho	Y	28250 FQ	37900 MW	48540 TQ	USBLS	5/15
	Boise City MSA, ID	Y	30990 FQ	38510 MW	47660 TQ	USBLS	5/15
	Illinois	Y	26940 FQ	39210 MW	58720 TQ	USBLS	5/15
	Chicago-Naperville-Arlington Heights PMSA, IL	Y	27890 FQ	42640 MW	67760 TQ	USBLS	5/15
	Lake County-Kenosha County PMSA, IL-WI	Y	34910 FQ	45480 MW	59230 TQ	USBLS	5/15
	Indiana	Y	28490 FQ	37630 MW	49880 TQ	USBLS	5/15
	Gary PMSA, IN	Y	28400 FQ	41550 MW	58770 TQ	USBLS	5/15
	Indianapolis-Carmel-Anderson MSA, IN	Y	32840 FQ	43860 MW	57410 TQ	USBLS	5/15
	Iowa	Y	28220 FQ	37340 MW	48280 TQ	USBLS	5/15
	Des Moines-West Des Moines MSA, IA	Y	31550 FQ	42730 MW	54870 TQ	USBLS	5/15
	Kansas	Y	26420 FQ	35470 MW	46850 TQ	USBLS	5/15
	Wichita MSA, KS	Y	30270 FQ	39210 MW	52110 TQ	USBLS	5/15
	Kentucky	Y	23740 FQ	32170 MW	42630 TQ	USBLS	5/15
	Louisville-Jefferson County MSA, KY-IN	Y	26220 FQ	34200 MW	45080 TQ	USBLS	5/15
	Louisiana	Y	27040 FQ	35530 MW	46310 TQ	USBLS	5/15
	Baton Rouge MSA, LA	Y	31820 FQ	40300 MW	54370 TQ	USBLS	5/15

AE	Average entry wage	AWR	Average wage range	H	Hourly
AEX	Average experienced wage	B	Biweekly	HI	Highest wage paid
ATC	Average total compensation	D	Daily	HR	High end range
AW	Average wage paid	FQ	First quartile wage	LO	Lowest wage paid

LR	Low end range	MTC	Median total compensation
M	Monthly	MW	Median wage paid
MCC	Median cash compensation	MWR	Median wage range
ME	Median entry wage	S	See annotated source

TCC	Total cash compensation	
TQ	Third quartile wage	
W	Weekly	
Y	Yearly	

Occupation/Type/Industry	Location	Per	Low	Mid	High	Source	Date
Automotive Service Technician and Mechanic	New Orleans-Metairie MSA, LA	Y	28140 FQ	37640 MW	48680 TQ	USBLS	5/15
	Maine	Y	28600 FQ	36250 MW	45770 TQ	USBLS	5/15
	Portland-South Portland MSA, ME	Y	32050 FQ	42610 MW	53380 TQ	USBLS	5/15
	Maryland	Y	25993 AE	45238 MW	54860 AEX	MDBLS	4/16
	Baltimore-Columbia-Towson MSA, MD	Y	27540 FQ	42560 MW	56830 TQ	USBLS	5/15
	Salisbury MSA, MD-DE	Y	29770 FQ	36010 MW	45910 TQ	USBLS	5/15
	Massachusetts	Y	32790 FQ	43980 MW	57500 TQ	USBLS	5/15
	Boston-Cambridge-Newton NECTA, MA	Y	34830 FQ	49070 MW	61140 TQ	USBLS	5/15
	Worcester MSA, MA-CT	Y	30570 FQ	41570 MW	51170 TQ	USBLS	5/15
	Michigan	Y	25750 FQ	36950 MW	51910 TQ	USBLS	5/15
	Detroit-Dearborn-Livonia PMSA, MI	Y	26770 FQ	35800 MW	50910 TQ	USBLS	5/15
	Grand Rapids-Wyoming MSA, MI	Y	30150 FQ	38680 MW	49410 TQ	USBLS	5/15
	Minnesota	Y	31307 FQ	39644 MW	49258 TQ	MNBLS	1/16-3/16
	Minneapolis-St. Paul-Bloomington MSA, MN-WI	Y	32715 FQ	42862 MW	52536 TQ	MNBLS	1/16-3/16
	Mississippi	Y	22410 FQ	30970 MW	42780 TQ	USBLS	5/15
	Jackson MSA, MS	Y	22620 FQ	30430 MW	43470 TQ	USBLS	5/15
	Missouri	Y	27250 FQ	37320 MW	48950 TQ	USBLS	5/15
	Kansas City MSA, MO-KS	Y	26340 FQ	36100 MW	49420 TQ	USBLS	5/15
	St. Louis MSA, MO-IL	Y	33910 FQ	43400 MW	54030 TQ	USBLS	5/15
	Montana	Y	24230 FQ	34660 MW	47020 TQ	USBLS	5/15
	Billings MSA, MT	Y	28720 FQ	39350 MW	52120 TQ	USBLS	5/15
	Nebraska	Y	25550 FQ	35470 MW	46570 TQ	NEBLS	7/16-9/16
	Omaha-Council Bluffs MSA, NE-IA	Y	23615 FQ	35650 MW	49105 TQ	NEBLS	7/16-9/16
	Nevada	Y	28880 FQ	37610 MW	49710 TQ	USBLS	5/15
	Las Vegas-Henderson-Paradise MSA, NV	Y	28150 FQ	36460 MW	48820 TQ	USBLS	5/15
	New Hampshire	H	14.48 AE	20.83 MW	25.57 AEX	NHBLS	6/16
	Manchester NECTA, NH	H	14.29 AE	21.47 MW	25.15 AEX	NHBLS	6/16
	Nashua NECTA, NH-MA	Y	35340 FQ	44060 MW	53710 TQ	USBLS	5/15
	New Jersey	Y	33660 FQ	46490 MW	59560 TQ	USBLS	5/15
	Camden PMSA, NJ	Y	35670 FQ	46340 MW	58720 TQ	USBLS	5/15
	Newark PMSA, NJ-PA	Y	34670 FQ	51220 MW	61880 TQ	USBLS	5/15
	Trenton MSA, NJ	Y	33340 FQ	48550 MW	59020 TQ	USBLS	5/15
	New Mexico	Y	27570 FQ	36640 MW	49140 TQ	USBLS	5/15
	Albuquerque MSA, NM	Y	28500 FQ	38220 MW	50870 TQ	USBLS	5/15
	New York	Y	23070 AE	36750 MW	49110 AEX	NYBLS	1/16-3/16
	Buffalo-Cheektowaga-Niagara Falls MSA, NY	Y	21840 FQ	30180 MW	44750 TQ	USBLS	5/15
	Nassau County-Suffolk County PMSA, NY	Y	23830 FQ	41390 MW	59630 TQ	USBLS	5/15
	New York-Jersey City-White Plains PMSA, NY-NJ	Y	27080 FQ	37890 MW	55740 TQ	USBLS	5/15
	Rochester MSA, NY	Y	28000 FQ	36770 MW	47380 TQ	USBLS	5/15
	North Carolina	Y	26950 FQ	37460 MW	50440 TQ	USBLS	5/15
	Charlotte-Concord-Gastonia MSA, NC-SC	Y	29470 FQ	41370 MW	56550 TQ	USBLS	5/15
	Raleigh MSA, NC	Y	28380 FQ	40100 MW	51260 TQ	USBLS	5/15
	North Dakota	Y	31850 FQ	40920 MW	52230 TQ	USBLS	5/15
	Fargo MSA, ND-MN	Y	29600 FQ	42160 MW	49870 TQ	USBLS	5/15
	Ohio	Y	25100 FQ	35260 MW	47200 TQ	USBLS	5/15
	Cincinnati MSA, OH-KY-IN	Y	23120 FQ	33230 MW	47500 TQ	USBLS	5/15
	Cleveland-Elyria MSA, OH	Y	26700 FQ	37300 MW	49590 TQ	USBLS	5/15
	Columbus MSA, OH	Y	30020 FQ	38830 MW	51070 TQ	USBLS	5/15
	Oklahoma	Y	25320 FQ	35380 MW	48850 TQ	USBLS	5/15
	Oklahoma City MSA, OK	Y	27650 FQ	39630 MW	53510 TQ	USBLS	5/15
	Tulsa MSA, OK	Y	26330 FQ	35860 MW	47810 TQ	USBLS	5/15
	Oregon	H	14.16 FQ	19.66 MW	24.94 TQ	ORBLS	2016
	Portland-Vancouver-Hillsboro MSA, OR-WA	Y	31980 FQ	43740 MW	54380 TQ	USBLS	5/15
	Pennsylvania	Y	26730 FQ	35680 MW	46190 TQ	USBLS	5/15
	Allentown-Bethlehem-Easton MSA, PA-NJ	Y	31900 FQ	40460 MW	49390 TQ	USBLS	5/15
	Harrisburg-Carlisle MSA, PA	Y	25090 FQ	34570 MW	44590 TQ	USBLS	5/15

AE	Average entry wage	AWR	Average wage range	H	Hourly	LR	Low end range	MTC	Median total compensation	TCC	Total cash compensation
AEX	Average experienced wage	B	Biweekly	HI	Highest wage paid	M	Monthly	MW	Median wage paid	TQ	Third quartile wage
ATC	Average total compensation	D	Daily	HR	High end range	MCC	Median cash compensation	MWR	Median wage range	W	Weekly
AW	Average wage paid	FQ	First quartile wage	LO	Lowest wage paid	ME	Median entry wage	S	See annotated source	Y	Yearly

Occupation/Type/Industry	Location	Per	Low	Mid	High	Source	Date
Automotive Service Technician and Mechanic	Montgomery County-Bucks County-Chester County PMSA, PA	Y	32530 FQ	39410 MW	50220 TQ	USBLS	5/15
	Philadelphia PMSA, PA	Y	24240 FQ	36890 MW	48800 TQ	USBLS	5/15
	Pittsburgh MSA, PA	Y	25100 FQ	33690 MW	46080 TQ	USBLS	5/15
	Rhode Island	Y	32100 FQ	39770 MW	48370 TQ	USBLS	5/15
	Providence-Warwick MSA, RI-MA	Y	31960 FQ	39710 MW	48830 TQ	USBLS	5/15
	South Carolina	Y	24910 FQ	33950 MW	45340 TQ	USBLS	5/15
	Charleston-North Charleston MSA, SC	Y	31950 FQ	40160 MW	51830 TQ	USBLS	5/15
	Columbia MSA, SC	Y	28700 FQ	37420 MW	47890 TQ	USBLS	5/15
	Greenville-Anderson-Mauldin MSA, SC	Y	21930 FQ	31230 MW	43880 TQ	USBLS	5/15
	South Dakota	Y	28970 FQ	35540 MW	44550 TQ	USBLS	5/15
	Sioux Falls MSA, SD	Y	31810 FQ	38830 MW	46330 TQ	USBLS	5/15
	Tennessee	Y	26880 FQ	37130 MW	51650 TQ	USBLS	5/15
	Knoxville MSA, TN	Y	23720 FQ	33430 MW	45220 TQ	USBLS	5/15
	Memphis MSA, TN-MS-AR	Y	25300 FQ	37060 MW	51490 TQ	USBLS	5/15
	Nashville-Davidson–Murfreesboro–Franklin MSA, TN	Y	33880 FQ	46480 MW	57190 TQ	USBLS	5/15
	Texas	Y	27280 FQ	38600 MW	52210 TQ	USBLS	5/15
	Austin-Round Rock MSA, TX	Y	30720 FQ	39190 MW	49030 TQ	USBLS	5/15
	Dallas-Plano-Irving PMSA, TX	Y	30150 FQ	40750 MW	56200 TQ	USBLS	5/15
	Fort Worth-Arlington PMSA, TX	Y	29040 FQ	40280 MW	54760 TQ	USBLS	5/15
	Houston-The Woodlands-Sugar Land MSA, TX	Y	28370 FQ	40820 MW	54820 TQ	USBLS	5/15
	San Antonio-New Braunfels MSA, TX	Y	29030 FQ	38800 MW	52800 TQ	USBLS	5/15
	Utah	Y	26920 FQ	37750 MW	51580 TQ	USBLS	5/15
	Ogden-Clearfield MSA, UT	Y	32510 FQ	47230 MW	60810 TQ	USBLS	5/15
	Provo-Orem MSA, UT	Y	23370 FQ	35330 MW	49000 TQ	USBLS	5/15
	Salt Lake City MSA, UT	Y	27020 FQ	37920 MW	51310 TQ	USBLS	5/15
	Vermont	Y	28410 FQ	36140 MW	45340 TQ	USBLS	5/15
	Burlington-South Burlington MSA, VT	Y	26350 FQ	35270 MW	44050 TQ	USBLS	5/15
	Virginia	Y	30170 FQ	40560 MW	55400 TQ	USBLS	5/15
	Richmond MSA, VA	Y	32710 FQ	42520 MW	56480 TQ	USBLS	5/15
	Virginia Beach-Norfolk-Newport News MSA, VA-NC	Y	29790 FQ	39430 MW	52010 TQ	USBLS	5/15
	Washington	H	15.70 FQ	21.04 MW	26.97 TQ	WABLS	3/16
	Kennewick-Richland MSA, WA	Y	31420 FQ	43420 MW	56860 TQ	USBLS	5/15
	Seattle-Bellevue-Everett PMSA, WA	H	15.14 FQ	21.93 MW	27.87 TQ	WABLS	3/16
	Tacoma-Lakewood PMSA, WA	H	16.87 FQ	21.34 MW	26.38 TQ	WABLS	3/16
	West Virginia	Y	22410 FQ	29510 MW	40830 TQ	USBLS	5/15
	Huntington-Ashland MSA, WV-KY-OH	Y	21980 FQ	28810 MW	38530 TQ	USBLS	5/15
	Wisconsin	Y	28730 FQ	36670 MW	47310 TQ	USBLS	5/15
	Madison MSA, WI	Y	27060 FQ	36940 MW	49680 TQ	USBLS	5/15
	Milwaukee-Waukesha-West Allis MSA, WI	Y	31330 FQ	39570 MW	50790 TQ	USBLS	5/15
	Wyoming	Y	31300 FQ	39570 MW	53590 TQ	USBLS	5/15
	Cheyenne MSA, WY	Y	27750 FQ	36850 MW	53060 TQ	USBLS	5/15
	Puerto Rico	Y	17130 FQ	18710 MW	21870 TQ	USBLS	5/15
	San Juan-Carolina-Caguas MSA, PR	Y	17170 FQ	18800 MW	22270 TQ	USBLS	5/15
	Virgin Islands	Y	29200 FQ	35950 MW	43940 TQ	USBLS	5/15
	Guam	Y	21640 FQ	28520 MW	36680 TQ	USBLS	5/15
Autopsy Assistant							
Department of Veterans Affairs, Veterans Health Administration	Columbia, MO	Y	31944 LO		35140 HI	APP01	2015
Department of Veterans Affairs, Veterans Health Administration	San Antonio, TX	Y			40465 HI	APP01	2015
Department of Veterans Affairs, Veterans Health Administration	San Juan, PR	Y	33009 LO		39400 HI	APP01	2015

AE	Average entry wage	AWR Average wage range	H Hourly	LR Low end range	MTC Median total compensation	TCC Total cash compensation
AEX Average experienced wage	B Biweekly	HI Highest wage paid	M Monthly	MW Median wage paid	TQ Third quartile wage
ATC Average total compensation	D Daily	HR High end range	MCC Median cash compensation	MWR Median wage range	W Weekly
AW Average wage paid	FQ First quartile wage	LO Lowest wage paid	ME Median entry wage	S See annotated source	Y Yearly

Occupation/Type/Industry	Location	Per	Low	Mid	High	Source	Date
Autopsy Attendant							
County Government	Oakland County, MI	B	1583 LO		2060 HI	MIOAK2	10/1/16
Avalanche Forcaster	United States	H		25.00 AW		JM01	2017
Aviation Deputy							
County Government	Oakland County, MI	H	16.88 LO		21.73 HI	MIOAK2	10/1/16
Aviation Director							
Municipal Government	Colorado Springs, CO	Y	142288 LO		195647 HI	COSPRS	2017
Avionics Inspector	United States	H		25.50 AW		AVJOB05	2016
Avionics Technician	Alabama	Y	46966 AE	62750 AW	70652 AEX	ALBLS	6/16
	Birmingham-Hoover MSA, AL	Y	44617 AE	64215 AW	74019 AEX	ALBLS	6/16
	Alaska	Y	59010 FQ	70440 MW	83930 TQ	USBLS	5/15
	Arizona	Y	44060 FQ	54220 MW	62010 TQ	USBLS	5/15
	Phoenix-Mesa-Scottsdale MSA, AZ	Y	41460 FQ	52260 MW	61320 TQ	USBLS	5/15
	Tucson MSA, AZ	Y	51660 FQ	57440 MW	64410 TQ	USBLS	5/15
	Arkansas	Y	40750 FQ	49110 MW	60210 TQ	USBLS	5/15
	Little Rock-North Little Rock-Conway MSA, AR	Y	46210 FQ	52550 MW	61980 TQ	USBLS	5/15
	California	H	26.14 FQ	34.14 MW	41.59 TQ	CABLS	1/16-3/16
	Anaheim-Santa Ana-Irvine PMSA, CA	H	17.65 FQ	21.24 MW	32.95 TQ	CABLS	1/16-3/16
	Los Angeles-Long Beach-Glendale PMSA, CA	H	25.47 FQ	32.53 MW	39.92 TQ	CABLS	1/16-3/16
	Oakland-Hayward-Berkeley PMSA, CA	H	20.16 FQ	22.12 MW	24.07 TQ	CABLS	1/16-3/16
	Riverside-San Bernardino-Ontario MSA, CA	H	27.65 FQ	33.21 MW	35.75 TQ	CABLS	1/16-3/16
	Sacramento–Roseville–Arden-Arcade MSA, CA	H	30.79 FQ	33.64 MW	36.39 TQ	CABLS	1/16-3/16
	San Diego-Carlsbad MSA, CA	H	25.60 FQ	30.95 MW	40.45 TQ	CABLS	1/16-3/16
	San Francisco-Redwood City-South San Francisco PMSA, CA	H	38.51 FQ	41.69 MW	44.92 TQ	CABLS	1/16-3/16
	Colorado	Y	47670 FQ	69770 MW	84870 TQ	USBLS	5/15
	Denver-Aurora-Lakewood MSA, CO	Y	61230 FQ	71840 MW	83240 TQ	USBLS	5/15
	Connecticut	Y		56969 MW		CTBLS	1/16-3/16
	Hartford-West Hartford-East Hartford MSA, CT	Y	54760 FQ	65400 MW	73020 TQ	USBLS	5/15
	Delaware	Y	33380 FQ	56280 MW	62180 TQ	USBLS	5/15
	Wilmington PMSA, DE-MD-NJ	Y	29340 FQ	39030 MW	62090 TQ	USBLS	5/15
	Washington-Arlington-Alexandria PMSA, DC-VA-MD-WV	Y	48300 FQ	61940 MW	72520 TQ	USBLS	5/15
	Florida	H	18.41 AE	27.65 MW	33.12 AEX	FLBLS	7/16-9/16
	Fort Lauderdale-Pompano Beach-Deerfield Beach PMSA, FL	H	14.73 AE	27.62 MW	31.69 AEX	FLBLS	7/16-9/16
	Miami-Miami Beach-Kendall PMSA, FL	H	18.76 AE	25.74 MW	31.48 AEX	FLBLS	7/16-9/16
	Orlando-Kissimmee-Sanford MSA, FL	H	20.76 AE	34.24 MW	37.23 AEX	FLBLS	7/16-9/16
	Tampa-St. Petersburg-Clearwater MSA, FL	H	19.31 AE	24.83 MW	31.11 AEX	FLBLS	7/16-9/16
	Georgia	Y	52510 FQ	58130 MW	69250 TQ	USBLS	5/15
	Atlanta-Sandy Springs-Roswell MSA, GA	Y	53900 FQ	61810 MW	75090 TQ	USBLS	5/15
	Hawaii	Y	65450 FQ	74780 MW	81470 TQ	USBLS	5/15
	Urban Honolulu MSA, HI	Y	66060 FQ	74780 MW	81690 TQ	USBLS	5/15
	Idaho	Y	45800 FQ	52210 MW	58330 TQ	USBLS	5/15
	Illinois	Y	44450 FQ	53780 MW	66180 TQ	USBLS	5/15
	Chicago-Naperville-Arlington Heights PMSA, IL	Y	47220 FQ	60170 MW	71280 TQ	USBLS	5/15
	Indiana	Y	40980 FQ	48340 MW	57170 TQ	USBLS	5/15
	Indianapolis-Carmel-Anderson MSA, IN	Y	41230 FQ	47250 MW	55740 TQ	USBLS	5/15

AE	Average entry wage	AWR	Average wage range	
AEX	Average experienced wage	B	Biweekly	
ATC	Average total compensation	D	Daily	
AW	Average wage paid	FQ	First quartile wage	
H	Hourly	LR	Low end range	MTC Median total compensation
HI	Highest wage paid	M	Monthly	MW Median wage paid
HR	High end range	MCC	Median cash compensation	MWR Median wage range
LO	Lowest wage paid	ME	Median entry wage	S See annotated source
				TCC Total cash compensation
				TQ Third quartile wage
				W Weekly
				Y Yearly

Occupation/Type/Industry	Location	Per	Low	Mid	High	Source	Date
Avionics Technician	Des Moines-West Des Moines MSA, IA	Y	32130 FQ	41820 MW	59300 TQ	USBLS	5/15
	Kansas	Y	51840 FQ	58330 MW	65170 TQ	USBLS	5/15
	Wichita MSA, KS	Y	52460 FQ	58860 MW	66050 TQ	USBLS	5/15
	Kentucky	Y	50400 FQ	55600 MW	61760 TQ	USBLS	5/15
	Louisiana	Y	49060 FQ	63680 MW	78190 TQ	USBLS	5/15
	New Orleans-Metairie MSA, LA	Y	54650 FQ	71650 MW	89110 TQ	USBLS	5/15
	Baltimore-Columbia-Towson MSA, MD	Y	50950 FQ	56590 MW	61800 TQ	USBLS	5/15
	Massachusetts	Y	66620 FQ	70480 MW	76470 TQ	USBLS	5/15
	Michigan	Y	49120 FQ	61070 MW	72900 TQ	USBLS	5/15
	Minnesota	Y	51601 FQ	56810 MW	61507 TQ	MNBLS	1/16-3/16
	Minneapolis-St. Paul-Bloomington MSA, MN-WI	Y	50585 FQ	56820 MW	61406 TQ	MNBLS	1/16-3/16
	Mississippi	Y	39740 FQ	51210 MW	58610 TQ	USBLS	5/15
	Jackson MSA, MS	Y	38450 FQ	48710 MW	57190 TQ	USBLS	5/15
	Missouri	Y	52400 FQ	64560 MW	72060 TQ	USBLS	5/15
	Kansas City MSA, MO-KS	Y	45190 FQ	55210 MW	67930 TQ	USBLS	5/15
	St. Louis MSA, MO-IL	Y	50890 FQ	64040 MW	72250 TQ	USBLS	5/15
	Nevada	Y	46410 FQ	55290 MW	60350 TQ	USBLS	5/15
	Las Vegas-Henderson-Paradise MSA, NV	Y	52130 FQ	56710 MW	60970 TQ	USBLS	5/15
	New Hampshire	H	23.26 AE	28.83 MW	32.86 AEX	NHBLS	6/16
	Nashua NECTA, NH-MA	Y	49030 FQ	57190 MW	66310 TQ	USBLS	5/15
	New Jersey	Y	46370 FQ	55530 MW	60820 TQ	USBLS	5/15
	Newark PMSA, NJ-PA	Y	43800 FQ	51900 MW	60010 TQ	USBLS	5/15
	New York	Y	40720 AE	63420 MW	76030 AEX	NYBLS	1/16-3/16
	New York-Jersey City-White Plains PMSA, NY-NJ	Y	45710 FQ	58000 MW	70930 TQ	USBLS	5/15
	North Carolina	Y	48030 FQ	54230 MW	60720 TQ	USBLS	5/15
	Charlotte-Concord-Gastonia MSA, NC-SC	Y	51140 FQ	57290 MW	64230 TQ	USBLS	5/15
	Ohio	Y	49590 FQ	58520 MW	67340 TQ	USBLS	5/15
	Cleveland-Elyria MSA, OH	Y	51160 FQ	58340 MW	66840 TQ	USBLS	5/15
	Columbus MSA, OH	Y	52700 FQ	61050 MW	70790 TQ	USBLS	5/15
	Oklahoma	Y	49390 FQ	53860 MW	55870 TQ	USBLS	5/15
	Oklahoma City MSA, OK	Y	49900 FQ	53860 MW	55860 TQ	USBLS	5/15
	Tulsa MSA, OK	Y	43400 FQ	50350 MW	57180 TQ	USBLS	5/15
	Oregon	H	20.94 FQ	23.83 MW	29.17 TQ	ORBLS	2016
	Portland-Vancouver-Hillsboro MSA, OR-WA	Y	55910 FQ	63450 MW	76060 TQ	USBLS	5/15
	Pennsylvania	Y	49910 FQ	58450 MW	84590 TQ	USBLS	5/15
	Philadelphia PMSA, PA	Y	51370 FQ	60930 MW	89730 TQ	USBLS	5/15
	South Carolina	Y	48300 FQ	53130 MW	59680 TQ	USBLS	5/15
	Charleston-North Charleston MSA, SC	Y	52020 FQ	52040 MW	67550 TQ	USBLS	5/15
	Greenville-Anderson-Mauldin MSA, SC	Y	49250 FQ	54070 MW	58550 TQ	USBLS	5/15
	Tennessee	Y	39590 FQ	50710 MW	58850 TQ	USBLS	5/15
	Knoxville MSA, TN	Y	39090 FQ	53390 MW	59270 TQ	USBLS	5/15
	Memphis MSA, TN-MS-AR	Y	38000 FQ	49720 MW	61570 TQ	USBLS	5/15
	Nashville-Davidson–Murfreesboro–Franklin MSA, TN	Y	23030 FQ	41410 MW	52480 TQ	USBLS	5/15
	Texas	Y	37330 FQ	57230 MW	69500 TQ	USBLS	5/15
	Dallas-Plano-Irving PMSA, TX	Y	38760 FQ	54940 MW	64080 TQ	USBLS	5/15
	Fort Worth-Arlington PMSA, TX	Y	27210 FQ	56510 MW	77840 TQ	USBLS	5/15
	Houston-The Woodlands-Sugar Land MSA, TX	Y	59210 FQ	69570 MW	78110 TQ	USBLS	5/15
	San Antonio-New Braunfels MSA, TX	Y	18420 FQ	43150 MW	56580 TQ	USBLS	5/15
	Utah	Y	52540 FQ	56540 MW	56560 TQ	USBLS	5/15
	Ogden-Clearfield MSA, UT	Y	56540 FQ	56540 MW	56550 TQ	USBLS	5/15
	Salt Lake City MSA, UT	Y	43160 FQ	54280 MW	60130 TQ	USBLS	5/15
	Virginia	Y	50280 FQ	59830 MW	69810 TQ	USBLS	5/15
	Virginia Beach-Norfolk-Newport News MSA, VA-NC	Y	59820 FQ	65040 MW	69820 TQ	USBLS	5/15
	Washington	H	29.17 FQ	39.45 MW	44.82 TQ	WABLS	3/16
	West Virginia	Y	51240 FQ	59810 MW	68490 TQ	USBLS	5/15
	Wisconsin	Y	45650 FQ	52920 MW	61020 TQ	USBLS	5/15

AE Average entry wage	**AWR** Average wage range	**H** Hourly	**LR** Low end range	**MTC** Median total compensation	**TCC** Total cash compensation
AEX Average experienced wage	**B** Biweekly	**HI** Highest wage paid	**M** Monthly	**MW** Median wage paid	**TQ** Third quartile wage
ATC Average total compensation	**D** Daily	**HR** High end range	**MCC** Median cash compensation	**MWR** Median wage range	**W** Weekly
AW Average wage paid	**FQ** First quartile wage	**LO** Lowest wage paid	**ME** Median entry wage	**S** See annotated source	**Y** Yearly

Occupation/Type/Industry	Location	Per	Low	Mid	High	Source	Date
Avionics Technician	Puerto Rico	Y	40960 FQ	81740 MW	91510 TQ	USBLS	5/15
	San Juan-Carolina-Caguas MSA, PR	Y	53250 FQ	84600 MW	91510 TQ	USBLS	5/15
AWS Solutions Architect	United States	Y		125871 MW		LH01	2016
Babysitter	San Jose, CA	H		15.63 AW		CARE	2014
	Colorado Springs, CO	H		11.85 AW		CARE	2014
	Grand Rapids, MI	H		11.31 AW		CARE	2014
Back-End Web Developer	United States	Y		108580 AW		STOF2	2016
Background Investigator							
Police Department, Municipal Government	Covina, CA	Y			12805 HI	CACIT	6/28/16
Background Vocalist							
Theater/Arena-Level Touring Band	United States	W		100-8000 AWR		BBRD01	2014
Baggage Porter and Bellhop	Alabama	Y	17452 AE	19943 AW	21179 AEX	ALBLS	6/16
	Birmingham-Hoover MSA, AL	Y	17483 AE	20952 AW	22692 AEX	ALBLS	6/16
	Alaska	Y	18660 FQ	19120 MW	19900 TQ	USBLS	5/15
	Anchorage MSA, AK	Y	18640 FQ	19090 MW	19680 TQ	USBLS	5/15
	Arizona	Y	18000 FQ	19230 MW	22660 TQ	USBLS	5/15
	Phoenix-Mesa-Scottsdale MSA, AZ	Y	18040 FQ	19320 MW	22810 TQ	USBLS	5/15
	Tucson MSA, AZ	Y	17800 FQ	18840 MW	21660 TQ	USBLS	5/15
	Arkansas	Y	16910 FQ	18190 MW	19540 TQ	USBLS	5/15
	Little Rock-North Little Rock-Conway MSA, AR	Y	16970 FQ	18330 MW	19920 TQ	USBLS	5/15
	California	H	9.63 FQ	11.60 MW	14.88 TQ	CABLS	1/16-3/16
	Anaheim-Santa Ana-Irvine PMSA, CA	H	9.50 FQ	10.82 MW	13.65 TQ	CABLS	1/16-3/16
	Los Angeles-Long Beach-Glendale PMSA, CA	H	10.09 FQ	11.91 MW	16.00 TQ	CABLS	1/16-3/16
	Oakland-Hayward-Berkeley PMSA, CA	H	10.68 FQ	13.63 MW	20.24 TQ	CABLS	1/16-3/16
	Riverside-San Bernardino-Ontario MSA, CA	H	9.41 FQ	9.63 MW	11.70 TQ	CABLS	1/16-3/16
	Sacramento–Roseville–Arden-Arcade MSA, CA	H	9.39 FQ	9.54 MW	11.36 TQ	CABLS	1/16-3/16
	San Diego-Carlsbad MSA, CA	H	9.51 FQ	10.43 MW	12.41 TQ	CABLS	1/16-3/16
	San Francisco-Redwood City-South San Francisco PMSA, CA	H	13.27 FQ	15.03 MW	18.50 TQ	CABLS	1/16-3/16
	Colorado	Y	18290 FQ	19480 MW	24390 TQ	USBLS	5/15
	Denver-Aurora-Lakewood MSA, CO	Y	18120 FQ	19130 MW	21530 TQ	USBLS	5/15
	Connecticut	Y		20201 MW		CTBLS	1/16-3/16
	Hartford-West Hartford-East Hartford MSA, CT	Y	20460 FQ	23410 MW	33250 TQ	USBLS	5/15
	Delaware	Y	18040 FQ	19800 MW	24300 TQ	USBLS	5/15
	Wilmington PMSA, DE-MD-NJ	Y	17850 FQ	19300 MW	22650 TQ	USBLS	5/15
	District of Columbia	Y	22030 FQ	27310 MW	37200 TQ	USBLS	5/15
	Washington-Arlington-Alexandria PMSA, DC-VA-MD-WV	Y	19410 FQ	23010 MW	30880 TQ	USBLS	5/15
	Florida	H	8.99 AE	9.66 MW	12.38 AEX	FLBLS	7/16-9/16
	Fort Lauderdale-Pompano Beach-Deerfield Beach PMSA, FL	H	8.92 AE	9.19 MW	10.04 AEX	FLBLS	7/16-9/16
	Miami-Miami Beach-Kendall PMSA, FL	H	9.02 AE	12.30 MW	13.85 AEX	FLBLS	7/16-9/16
	Orlando-Kissimmee-Sanford MSA, FL	H	9.01 AE	9.51 MW	11.17 AEX	FLBLS	7/16-9/16
	Tampa-St. Petersburg-Clearwater MSA, FL	H	9.00 AE	9.32 MW	11.05 AEX	FLBLS	7/16-9/16
	Georgia	Y	17540 FQ	19630 MW	23980 TQ	USBLS	5/15
	Atlanta-Sandy Springs-Roswell MSA, GA	Y	17780 FQ	20060 MW	24560 TQ	USBLS	5/15
	Hawaii	Y	19360 FQ	23160 MW	30470 TQ	USBLS	5/15
	Urban Honolulu MSA, HI	Y	20180 FQ	23210 MW	29810 TQ	USBLS	5/15
	Idaho	Y	17260 FQ	19030 MW	23720 TQ	USBLS	5/15

AE Average entry wage	**AWR** Average wage range	**H** Hourly	**LR** Low end range	**MTC** Median total compensation	**TCC** Total cash compensation
AEX Average experienced wage	**B** Biweekly	**HI** Highest wage paid	**M** Monthly	**MW** Median wage paid	**TQ** Third quartile wage
ATC Average total compensation	**D** Daily	**HR** High end range	**MCC** Median cash compensation	**MWR** Median wage range	**W** Weekly
AW Average wage paid	**FQ** First quartile wage	**LO** Lowest wage paid	**ME** Median entry wage	**S** See annotated source	**Y** Yearly

Occupation/Type/Industry	Location	Per	Low	Mid	High	Source	Date
Baggage Porter and Bellhop	Illinois	Y	19820 FQ	25520 MW	34110 TQ	USBLS	5/15
	Chicago-Naperville-Arlington Heights PMSA, IL	Y	20100 FQ	26210 MW	34440 TQ	USBLS	5/15
	Indiana	Y	16510 FQ	17770 MW	19020 TQ	USBLS	5/15
	Indianapolis-Carmel-Anderson MSA, IN	Y	16410 FQ	17620 MW	18830 TQ	USBLS	5/15
	Iowa	Y	20200 FQ	22980 MW	37240 TQ	USBLS	5/15
	Kansas	Y	17190 FQ	18930 MW	22850 TQ	USBLS	5/15
	Wichita MSA, KS	Y	16950 FQ	18420 MW	21120 TQ	USBLS	5/15
	Kentucky	Y	17080 FQ	18700 MW	22040 TQ	USBLS	5/15
	Louisville-Jefferson County MSA, KY-IN	Y	16610 FQ	17960 MW	19380 TQ	USBLS	5/15
	Louisiana	Y	17180 FQ	18860 MW	22530 TQ	USBLS	5/15
	Baton Rouge MSA, LA	Y	17590 FQ	19690 MW	23640 TQ	USBLS	5/15
	New Orleans-Metairie MSA, LA	Y	17480 FQ	19380 MW	23890 TQ	USBLS	5/15
	Maine	Y	17180 FQ	18330 MW	19510 TQ	USBLS	5/15
	Portland-South Portland MSA, ME	Y	16970 FQ	17910 MW	18850 TQ	USBLS	5/15
	Maryland	Y	18250 AE	30950 MW	37301 AEX	MDBLS	4/16
	Baltimore-Columbia-Towson MSA, MD	Y	17990 FQ	19350 MW	24330 TQ	USBLS	5/15
	Massachusetts	Y	19310 FQ	20660 MW	24010 TQ	USBLS	5/15
	Boston-Cambridge-Newton NECTA, MA	Y	19310 FQ	20600 MW	23850 TQ	USBLS	5/15
	Michigan	Y	18590 FQ	20920 MW	26720 TQ	USBLS	5/15
	Detroit-Dearborn-Livonia PMSA, MI	Y	18950 FQ	21750 MW	28650 TQ	USBLS	5/15
	Minnesota	Y	18036 FQ	19198 MW	23156 TQ	MNBLS	1/16-3/16
	Minneapolis-St. Paul-Bloomington MSA, MN-WI	Y	17895 FQ	18935 MW	21904 TQ	MNBLS	1/16-3/16
	Mississippi	Y	16750 FQ	18050 MW	19360 TQ	USBLS	5/15
	Missouri	Y	17380 FQ	18840 MW	22230 TQ	USBLS	5/15
	Kansas City MSA, MO-KS	Y	18060 FQ	20590 MW	24540 TQ	USBLS	5/15
	St. Louis MSA, MO-IL	Y	17180 FQ	18430 MW	19990 TQ	USBLS	5/15
	Montana	Y	18520 FQ	20730 MW	24760 TQ	USBLS	5/15
	Omaha-Council Bluffs MSA, NE-IA	Y	17710 FQ	18780 MW	21265 TQ	NEBLS	7/16-9/16
	Nevada	Y	23670 FQ	27680 MW	30800 TQ	USBLS	5/15
	Las Vegas-Henderson-Paradise MSA, NV	Y	25260 FQ	28150 MW	31050 TQ	USBLS	5/15
	New Hampshire	H	8.43 AE	10.58 MW	12.92 AEX	NHBLS	6/16
	New Jersey	Y	19180 FQ	22700 MW	29250 TQ	USBLS	5/15
	Camden PMSA, NJ	Y	19420 FQ	22680 MW	27720 TQ	USBLS	5/15
	Newark PMSA, NJ-PA	Y	18830 FQ	21450 MW	27040 TQ	USBLS	5/15
	New Mexico	Y	17840 FQ	19950 MW	23250 TQ	USBLS	5/15
	Albuquerque MSA, NM	Y	17770 FQ	19650 MW	22720 TQ	USBLS	5/15
	New York	Y	20770 AE	32040 MW	38780 AEX	NYBLS	1/16-3/16
	Buffalo-Cheektowaga-Niagara Falls MSA, NY	Y	21190 FQ	24350 MW	37700 TQ	USBLS	5/15
	Nassau County-Suffolk County PMSA, NY	Y	19090 FQ	21440 MW	26750 TQ	USBLS	5/15
	New York-Jersey City-White Plains PMSA, NY-NJ	Y	23000 FQ	33030 MW	41640 TQ	USBLS	5/15
	Rochester MSA, NY	Y	18700 FQ	19200 MW	20630 TQ	USBLS	5/15
	North Carolina	Y	16920 FQ	18470 MW	20990 TQ	USBLS	5/15
	Charlotte-Concord-Gastonia MSA, NC-SC	Y	17580 FQ	19860 MW	22700 TQ	USBLS	5/15
	North Dakota	Y	20240 FQ	22400 MW	24550 TQ	USBLS	5/15
	Fargo MSA, ND-MN	Y	18600 FQ	21320 MW	23450 TQ	USBLS	5/15
	Ohio	Y	17990 FQ	19100 MW	22390 TQ	USBLS	5/15
	Cincinnati MSA, OH-KY-IN	Y	17710 FQ	18740 MW	23220 TQ	USBLS	5/15
	Cleveland-Elyria MSA, OH	Y	18270 FQ	19990 MW	23440 TQ	USBLS	5/15
	Columbus MSA, OH	Y	17690 FQ	18500 MW	19360 TQ	USBLS	5/15
	Oklahoma	Y	16960 FQ	18570 MW	21160 TQ	USBLS	5/15
	Oklahoma City MSA, OK	Y	16620 FQ	17860 MW	19100 TQ	USBLS	5/15
	Tulsa MSA, OK	Y	17430 FQ	19370 MW	21840 TQ	USBLS	5/15
	Oregon	H	9.69 FQ	10.37 MW	11.39 TQ	ORBLS	2016
	Portland-Vancouver-Hillsboro MSA, OR-WA	Y	19700 FQ	20900 MW	23120 TQ	USBLS	5/15
	Pennsylvania	Y	17600 FQ	19970 MW	24190 TQ	USBLS	5/15
	Harrisburg-Carlisle MSA, PA	Y	17380 FQ	19530 MW	23210 TQ	USBLS	5/15

AE	Average entry wage	AWR	Average wage range	H	Hourly	LR	Low end range	MTC	Median total compensation	TCC	Total cash compensation
AEX	Average experienced wage	B	Biweekly	HI	Highest wage paid	M	Monthly	MW	Median wage paid	TQ	Third quartile wage
ATC	Average total compensation	D	Daily	HR	High end range	MCC	Median cash compensation	MWR	Median wage range	W	Weekly
AW	Average wage paid	FQ	First quartile wage	LO	Lowest wage paid	ME	Median entry wage	S	See annotated source	Y	Yearly

Occupation/Type/Industry	Location	Per	Low	Mid	High	Source	Date
Baggage Porter and Bellhop	Montgomery County-Bucks County-Chester County						
	PMSA, PA	Y	19840 FQ	22320 MW	24830 TQ	USBLS	5/15
	Philadelphia PMSA, PA	Y	17420 FQ	19420 MW	24540 TQ	USBLS	5/15
	Pittsburgh MSA, PA	Y	17900 FQ	20540 MW	23700 TQ	USBLS	5/15
	Rhode Island	Y	19240 FQ	20740 MW	27270 TQ	USBLS	5/15
	Providence-Warwick MSA, RI-MA	Y	19140 FQ	19640 MW	25730 TQ	USBLS	5/15
	South Carolina	Y	16780 FQ	18190 MW	19880 TQ	USBLS	5/15
	Charleston-North Charleston MSA, SC	Y	16810 FQ	18190 MW	19720 TQ	USBLS	5/15
	South Dakota	Y	18700 FQ	19740 MW	23360 TQ	USBLS	5/15
	Tennessee	Y	17390 FQ	19380 MW	23060 TQ	USBLS	5/15
	Memphis MSA, TN-MS-AR	Y	16610 FQ	17860 MW	19100 TQ	USBLS	5/15
	Nashville-Davidson–Murfreesboro–Franklin MSA, TN	Y	17860 FQ	20730 MW	24320 TQ	USBLS	5/15
	Texas	Y	17000 FQ	18620 MW	21890 TQ	USBLS	5/15
	Austin-Round Rock MSA, TX	Y	16920 FQ	18430 MW	21830 TQ	USBLS	5/15
	Dallas-Plano-Irving PMSA, TX	Y	17050 FQ	18750 MW	22730 TQ	USBLS	5/15
	Fort Worth-Arlington PMSA, TX	Y	17390 FQ	19440 MW	22220 TQ	USBLS	5/15
	Houston-The Woodlands-Sugar Land MSA, TX	Y	16860 FQ	18370 MW	21620 TQ	USBLS	5/15
	San Antonio-New Braunfels MSA, TX	Y	17550 FQ	19600 MW	22910 TQ	USBLS	5/15
	Utah	Y	16820 FQ	18220 MW	19770 TQ	USBLS	5/15
	Salt Lake City MSA, UT	Y	16690 FQ	17950 MW	19210 TQ	USBLS	5/15
	Vermont	Y	19220 FQ	20920 MW	26170 TQ	USBLS	5/15
	Burlington-South Burlington MSA, VT	Y	19590 FQ	21990 MW	27590 TQ	USBLS	5/15
	Virginia	Y	17480 FQ	19500 MW	24410 TQ	USBLS	5/15
	Richmond MSA, VA	Y	17540 FQ	19770 MW	26040 TQ	USBLS	5/15
	Virginia Beach-Norfolk-Newport News MSA, VA-NC	Y	16930 FQ	18310 MW	19670 TQ	USBLS	5/15
	Washington	H	10.07 FQ	11.12 MW	12.37 TQ	WABLS	3/16
	Seattle-Bellevue-Everett PMSA, WA	H	10.12 FQ	11.24 MW	13.19 TQ	WABLS	3/16
	West Virginia	Y	17730 FQ	18810 MW	21340 TQ	USBLS	5/15
	Huntington-Ashland MSA, WV-KY-OH	Y	17600 FQ	18550 MW	19830 TQ	USBLS	5/15
	Wisconsin	Y	16830 FQ	18160 MW	19500 TQ	USBLS	5/15
	Madison MSA, WI	Y	16920 FQ	18290 MW	19760 TQ	USBLS	5/15
	Milwaukee-Waukesha-West Allis MSA, WI	Y	16670 FQ	17760 MW	18850 TQ	USBLS	5/15
	Wyoming	Y	19880 FQ	22040 MW	24210 TQ	USBLS	5/15
	Puerto Rico	Y	16530 FQ	17680 MW	18830 TQ	USBLS	5/15
	San Juan-Carolina-Caguas MSA, PR	Y	16530 FQ	17680 MW	18830 TQ	USBLS	5/15
	Virgin Islands	Y	18730 FQ	22150 MW	26790 TQ	USBLS	5/15
Bailiff	Alabama	Y	26759 AE	34461 AW	38312 AEX	ALBLS	6/16
	Arizona	Y	27510 FQ	30500 MW	38290 TQ	USBLS	5/15
	Arkansas	Y	25910 FQ	30650 MW	40060 TQ	USBLS	5/15
	California	H	16.45 FQ	22.54 MW	31.47 TQ	CABLS	1/16-3/16
	Colorado	Y	54050 FQ	66430 MW	73260 TQ	USBLS	5/15
	Florida	H	17.69 AE	22.35 MW	26.25 AEX	FLBLS	7/16-9/16
	Georgia	Y	17410 FQ	19310 MW	30100 TQ	USBLS	5/15
	Idaho	Y	31060 FQ	36430 MW	43420 TQ	USBLS	5/15
	Illinois	Y	25620 FQ	34180 MW	45190 TQ	USBLS	5/15
	Indiana	Y	29000 FQ	33630 MW	38240 TQ	USBLS	5/15
	Iowa	Y	26560 FQ	48800 MW	55580 TQ	USBLS	5/15
	Kansas	Y	28860 FQ	36170 MW	46700 TQ	USBLS	5/15
	Kentucky	Y	21090 FQ	24040 MW	29920 TQ	USBLS	5/15
	Louisiana	Y	26800 FQ	33570 MW	39220 TQ	USBLS	5/15
	Maine	Y	29180 FQ	31630 MW	37670 TQ	USBLS	5/15
	Maryland	Y	26493 AE	45260 MW	54644 AEX	MDBLS	4/16
	Michigan	Y	33200 FQ	36560 MW	41210 TQ	USBLS	5/15
	Minnesota	Y	30367 FQ	35800 MW	43172 TQ	MNBLS	1/16-3/16
	Mississippi	Y	18140 FQ	22160 MW	32150 TQ	USBLS	5/15
	Missouri	Y	29020 FQ	33880 MW	37760 TQ	USBLS	5/15
	Montana	Y	26700 FQ	29980 MW	34630 TQ	USBLS	5/15

AE	Average entry wage	AWR	Average wage range	H	Hourly
AEX	Average experienced wage	B	Biweekly	HI	Highest wage paid
ATC	Average total compensation	D	Daily	HR	High end range
AW	Average wage paid	FQ	First quartile wage	LO	Lowest wage paid

LR	Low end range	MTC	Median total compensation
M	Monthly	MW	Median wage paid
MCC	Median cash compensation	MWR	Median wage range
ME	Median entry wage	S	See annotated source

TCC	Total cash compensation		
TQ	Third quartile wage		
W	Weekly		
Y	Yearly		

Occupation/Type/Industry	Location	Per	Low	Mid	High	Source	Date
Bailiff	Nebraska	Y	39840 FQ	53745 MW	59715 TQ	NEBLS	7/16-9/16
	Nevada	Y	43120 FQ	49810 MW	56690 TQ	USBLS	5/15
	New Hampshire	H	11.01 AE	11.12 MW	11.40 AEX	NHBLS	6/16
	New Jersey	Y	28100 FQ	35640 MW	43200 TQ	USBLS	5/15
	New York	Y	41100 AE	66880 MW	70780 AEX	NYBLS	1/16-3/16
	North Carolina	Y	29840 FQ	34200 MW	37790 TQ	USBLS	5/15
	North Dakota	Y	23570 FQ	23580 MW	23590 TQ	USBLS	5/15
	Ohio	Y	34540 FQ	42360 MW	53000 TQ	USBLS	5/15
	Oklahoma	Y	29300 FQ	36920 MW	47630 TQ	USBLS	5/15
	Oregon	H	17.36 FQ	20.63 MW	22.92 TQ	ORBLS	2016
	Pennsylvania	Y	31270 FQ	40720 MW	45850 TQ	USBLS	5/15
	South Carolina	Y	17650 FQ	19920 MW	24050 TQ	USBLS	5/15
	South Dakota	Y	20790 FQ	22200 MW	23610 TQ	USBLS	5/15
	Tennessee	Y	25410 FQ	30670 MW	35920 TQ	USBLS	5/15
	Texas	Y	33270 FQ	42420 MW	52430 TQ	USBLS	5/15
	Utah	Y	36120 FQ	42290 MW	48290 TQ	USBLS	5/15
	Virginia	Y	31470 FQ	36350 MW	43170 TQ	USBLS	5/15
	Washington	H	16.80 FQ	24.18 MW	30.18 TQ	WABLS	3/16
	West Virginia	Y	22050 FQ	25610 MW	31920 TQ	USBLS	5/15
	Wisconsin	Y	21570 FQ	24050 MW	35390 TQ	USBLS	5/15
	Puerto Rico	Y	22840 FQ	29770 MW	35660 TQ	USBLS	5/15
Baker	Alabama	Y	17582 AE	22477 AW	24924 AEX	ALBLS	6/16
	Birmingham-Hoover MSA, AL	Y	17572 AE	23454 AW	26384 AEX	ALBLS	6/16
	Alaska	Y	28100 FQ	33320 MW	39180 TQ	USBLS	5/15
	Anchorage MSA, AK	Y	28770 FQ	34730 MW	41500 TQ	USBLS	5/15
	Arizona	Y	19290 FQ	23410 MW	28280 TQ	USBLS	5/15
	Phoenix-Mesa-Scottsdale MSA, AZ	Y	19140 FQ	22930 MW	27990 TQ	USBLS	5/15
	Tucson MSA, AZ	Y	20320 FQ	24040 MW	28710 TQ	USBLS	5/15
	Arkansas	Y	17480 FQ	19260 MW	23480 TQ	USBLS	5/15
	Little Rock-North Little Rock-Conway MSA, AR	Y	17470 FQ	19200 MW	22210 TQ	USBLS	5/15
	California	H	10.20 FQ	12.51 MW	15.23 TQ	CABLS	1/16-3/16
	Anaheim-Santa Ana-Irvine PMSA, CA	H	9.75 FQ	11.28 MW	14.48 TQ	CABLS	1/16-3/16
	Los Angeles-Long Beach-Glendale PMSA, CA	H	9.85 FQ	11.98 MW	14.45 TQ	CABLS	1/16-3/16
	Napa MSA, CA	Y	26410 FQ	29370 MW	34000 TQ	USBLS	5/15
	Oakland-Hayward-Berkeley PMSA, CA	H	12.17 FQ	13.90 MW	16.60 TQ	CABLS	1/16-3/16
	Riverside-San Bernardino-Ontario MSA, CA	H	10.22 FQ	12.22 MW	14.59 TQ	CABLS	1/16-3/16
	Sacramento–Roseville–Arden-Arcade MSA, CA	H	11.46 FQ	15.10 MW	18.03 TQ	CABLS	1/16-3/16
	San Diego-Carlsbad MSA, CA	H	9.81 FQ	11.41 MW	15.14 TQ	CABLS	1/16-3/16
	San Francisco-Redwood City-South San Francisco PMSA, CA	H	11.87 FQ	14.69 MW	18.71 TQ	CABLS	1/16-3/16
	Colorado	Y	20220 FQ	23880 MW	31070 TQ	USBLS	5/15
	Denver-Aurora-Lakewood MSA, CO	Y	20200 FQ	23730 MW	30540 TQ	USBLS	5/15
	Connecticut	Y		27029 MW		CTBLS	1/16-3/16
	Bridgeport-Stamford-Norwalk MSA, CT	Y	22150 FQ	26040 MW	31530 TQ	USBLS	5/15
	Hartford-West Hartford-East Hartford MSA, CT	Y	21460 FQ	25010 MW	31980 TQ	USBLS	5/15
	Delaware	Y	20310 FQ	26110 MW	31140 TQ	USBLS	5/15
	Dover MSA, DE	Y	18910 FQ	21970 MW	27210 TQ	USBLS	5/15
	Wilmington PMSA, DE-MD-NJ	Y	22400 FQ	28120 MW	33560 TQ	USBLS	5/15
	District of Columbia	Y	26440 FQ	35860 MW	43740 TQ	USBLS	5/15
	Washington-Arlington-Alexandria PMSA, DC-VA-MD-WV	Y	22120 FQ	28310 MW	37230 TQ	USBLS	5/15
	Florida	H	9.90 AE	12.22 MW	14.26 AEX	FLBLS	7/16-9/16
	Fort Lauderdale-Pompano Beach-Deerfield Beach PMSA, FL	H	10.67 AE	13.19 MW	15.08 AEX	FLBLS	7/16-9/16
	Miami-Miami Beach-Kendall PMSA, FL	H	9.13 AE	11.63 MW	13.61 AEX	FLBLS	7/16-9/16

AE	Average entry wage	**AWR**	Average wage range	**H**	Hourly	**LR**	Low end range	**MTC** Median total compensation	**TCC** Total cash compensation
AEX	Average experienced wage	**B**	Biweekly	**HI**	Highest wage paid	**M**	Monthly	**MW** Median wage paid	**TQ** Third quartile wage
ATC	Average total compensation	**D**	Daily	**HR**	High end range	**MCC**	Median cash compensation	**MWR** Median wage range	**W** Weekly
AW	Average wage paid	**FQ**	First quartile wage	**LO**	Lowest wage paid	**ME**	Median entry wage	**S** See annotated source	**Y** Yearly

Occupation/Type/Industry	Location	Per	Low	Mid	High	Source	Date
Baker	Orlando-Kissimmee-Sanford MSA, FL	H	9.86 AE	12.22 MW	14.82 AEX	FLBLS	7/16-9/16
	Tampa-St. Petersburg-Clearwater MSA, FL	H	9.99 AE	12.45 MW	14.14 AEX	FLBLS	7/16-9/16
	Georgia	Y	18530 FQ	21760 MW	25900 TQ	USBLS	5/15
	Atlanta-Sandy Springs-Roswell MSA, GA	Y	19150 FQ	22410 MW	26650 TQ	USBLS	5/15
	Augusta-Richmond County MSA, GA-SC	Y	18400 FQ	21590 MW	24600 TQ	USBLS	5/15
	Hawaii	Y	26400 FQ	33290 MW	42710 TQ	USBLS	5/15
	Urban Honolulu MSA, HI	Y	25660 FQ	31840 MW	41750 TQ	USBLS	5/15
	Idaho	Y	20310 FQ	23930 MW	29420 TQ	USBLS	5/15
	Boise City MSA, ID	Y	21630 FQ	24690 MW	31030 TQ	USBLS	5/15
	Illinois	Y	19760 FQ	24380 MW	29870 TQ	USBLS	5/15
	Chicago-Naperville-Arlington Heights PMSA, IL	Y	19730 FQ	25410 MW	30420 TQ	USBLS	5/15
	Lake County-Kenosha County PMSA, IL-WI	Y	19850 FQ	24120 MW	29270 TQ	USBLS	5/15
	Indiana	Y	19780 FQ	23040 MW	28840 TQ	USBLS	5/15
	Gary PMSA, IN	Y	18990 FQ	24090 MW	30350 TQ	USBLS	5/15
	Indianapolis-Carmel-Anderson MSA, IN	Y	20680 FQ	23050 MW	26520 TQ	USBLS	5/15
	Iowa	Y	20600 FQ	24980 MW	30310 TQ	USBLS	5/15
	Des Moines-West Des Moines MSA, IA	Y	21200 FQ	24730 MW	30380 TQ	USBLS	5/15
	Kansas	Y	18630 FQ	21890 MW	27320 TQ	USBLS	5/15
	Wichita MSA, KS	Y	20010 FQ	22460 MW	28280 TQ	USBLS	5/15
	Kentucky	Y	19100 FQ	22920 MW	29960 TQ	USBLS	5/15
	Louisville-Jefferson County MSA, KY-IN	Y	20670 FQ	25030 MW	33100 TQ	USBLS	5/15
	Louisiana	Y	17970 FQ	21270 MW	26240 TQ	USBLS	5/15
	Baton Rouge MSA, LA	Y	18340 FQ	22000 MW	26750 TQ	USBLS	5/15
	New Orleans-Metairie MSA, LA	Y	17860 FQ	20970 MW	26540 TQ	USBLS	5/15
	Maine	Y	20470 FQ	23880 MW	29050 TQ	USBLS	5/15
	Portland-South Portland MSA, ME	Y	20580 FQ	23820 MW	28760 TQ	USBLS	5/15
	Maryland	Y	19559 AE	28107 MW	32381 AEX	MDBLS	4/16
	Baltimore-Columbia-Towson MSA, MD	Y	20700 FQ	27890 MW	35220 TQ	USBLS	5/15
	Salisbury MSA, MD-DE	Y	19160 FQ	22640 MW	27330 TQ	USBLS	5/15
	Massachusetts	Y	22650 FQ	27990 MW	36190 TQ	USBLS	5/15
	Boston-Cambridge-Newton NECTA, MA	Y	22920 FQ	28500 MW	37510 TQ	USBLS	5/15
	Worcester MSA, MA-CT	Y	22380 FQ	25590 MW	33020 TQ	USBLS	5/15
	Michigan	Y	19180 FQ	23120 MW	29680 TQ	USBLS	5/15
	Detroit-Dearborn-Livonia PMSA, MI	Y	20140 FQ	23730 MW	30650 TQ	USBLS	5/15
	Grand Rapids-Wyoming MSA, MI	Y	20530 FQ	24110 MW	28580 TQ	USBLS	5/15
	Minnesota	Y	23944 FQ	29634 MW	35446 TQ	MNBLS	1/16-3/16
	Minneapolis-St. Paul-Bloomington MSA, MN-WI	Y	26314 FQ	30849 MW	36134 TQ	MNBLS	1/16-3/16
	Mississippi	Y	18420 FQ	21460 MW	25760 TQ	USBLS	5/15
	Jackson MSA, MS	Y	20520 FQ	22940 MW	26250 TQ	USBLS	5/15
	Missouri	Y	18090 FQ	21140 MW	27720 TQ	USBLS	5/15
	Kansas City MSA, MO-KS	Y	18830 FQ	23090 MW	28790 TQ	USBLS	5/15
	St. Louis MSA, MO-IL	Y	18540 FQ	22170 MW	30060 TQ	USBLS	5/15
	Montana	Y	20370 FQ	23720 MW	28550 TQ	USBLS	5/15
	Billings MSA, MT	Y	21700 FQ	24440 MW	29910 TQ	USBLS	5/15
	Nebraska	Y	18480 FQ	21620 MW	26910 TQ	NEBLS	7/16-9/16
	Omaha-Council Bluffs MSA, NE-IA	Y	21275 FQ	26205 MW	33760 TQ	NEBLS	7/16-9/16
	Nevada	Y	22890 FQ	32000 MW	43200 TQ	USBLS	5/15
	Las Vegas-Henderson-Paradise MSA, NV	Y	22980 FQ	35250 MW	44290 TQ	USBLS	5/15
	New Hampshire	H	9.74 AE	13.14 MW	14.65 AEX	NHBLS	6/16
	Manchester NECTA, NH	H	11.90 AE	13.55 MW	14.22 AEX	NHBLS	6/16
	Nashua NECTA, NH-MA	Y	18690 FQ	26540 MW	31680 TQ	USBLS	5/15
	New Jersey	Y	19780 FQ	24310 MW	33740 TQ	USBLS	5/15
	Camden PMSA, NJ	Y	18590 FQ	20220 MW	24620 TQ	USBLS	5/15
	Newark PMSA, NJ-PA	Y	19600 FQ	24490 MW	33550 TQ	USBLS	5/15

AE Average entry wage	**AWR** Average wage range	**H** Hourly	**LR** Low end range	**MTC** Median total compensation	**TCC** Total cash compensation
AEX Average experienced wage	**B** Biweekly	**HI** Highest wage paid	**M** Monthly	**MW** Median wage paid	**TQ** Third quartile wage
ATC Average total compensation	**D** Daily	**HR** High end range	**MCC** Median cash compensation	**MWR** Median wage range	**W** Weekly
AW Average wage paid	**FQ** First quartile wage	**LO** Lowest wage paid	**ME** Median entry wage	**S** See annotated source	**Y** Yearly

Occupation/Type/Industry	Location	Per	Low	Mid	High	Source	Date
Baker	Trenton MSA, NJ	Y	30950 FQ	33900 MW	36840 TQ	USBLS	5/15
	New Mexico	Y	19320 FQ	22880 MW	27870 TQ	USBLS	5/15
	Albuquerque MSA, NM	Y	18970 FQ	23910 MW	29850 TQ	USBLS	5/15
	New York	Y	19940 AE	24390 MW	31090 AEX	NYBLS	1/16-3/16
	Buffalo-Cheektowaga-Niagara Falls MSA, NY	Y	19280 FQ	24480 MW	30260 TQ	USBLS	5/15
	Nassau County-Suffolk County PMSA, NY	Y	19910 FQ	26280 MW	34330 TQ	USBLS	5/15
	New York-Jersey City-White Plains PMSA, NY-NJ	Y	19910 FQ	23680 MW	30390 TQ	USBLS	5/15
	Rochester MSA, NY	Y	19660 FQ	22550 MW	27520 TQ	USBLS	5/15
	North Carolina	Y	18560 FQ	22240 MW	28450 TQ	USBLS	5/15
	Charlotte-Concord-Gastonia MSA, NC-SC	Y	18660 FQ	21730 MW	25680 TQ	USBLS	5/15
	Raleigh MSA, NC	Y	18140 FQ	21650 MW	27060 TQ	USBLS	5/15
	North Dakota	Y	24400 FQ	28950 MW	34330 TQ	USBLS	5/15
	Fargo MSA, ND-MN	Y	25960 FQ	30200 MW	35810 TQ	USBLS	5/15
	Ohio	Y	19740 FQ	23050 MW	28390 TQ	USBLS	5/15
	Cincinnati MSA, OH-KY-IN	Y	19930 FQ	23890 MW	32030 TQ	USBLS	5/15
	Cleveland-Elyria MSA, OH	Y	20580 FQ	23450 MW	28570 TQ	USBLS	5/15
	Columbus MSA, OH	Y	20320 FQ	23070 MW	26750 TQ	USBLS	5/15
	Oklahoma	Y	18580 FQ	22020 MW	26380 TQ	USBLS	5/15
	Oklahoma City MSA, OK	Y	20060 FQ	23020 MW	26880 TQ	USBLS	5/15
	Tulsa MSA, OK	Y	17950 FQ	20890 MW	24460 TQ	USBLS	5/15
	Oregon	H	11.15 FQ	13.34 MW	17.01 TQ	ORBLS	2016
	Portland-Vancouver-Hillsboro MSA, OR-WA	Y	24030 FQ	29420 MW	36830 TQ	USBLS	5/15
	Pennsylvania	Y	19660 FQ	24340 MW	30970 TQ	USBLS	5/15
	Allentown-Bethlehem-Easton MSA, PA-NJ	Y	19350 FQ	23010 MW	28210 TQ	USBLS	5/15
	Harrisburg-Carlisle MSA, PA	Y	20060 FQ	25310 MW	29710 TQ	USBLS	5/15
	Montgomery County-Bucks County-Chester County PMSA, PA	Y	21910 FQ	28500 MW	35290 TQ	USBLS	5/15
	Philadelphia PMSA, PA	Y	22810 FQ	29620 MW	39060 TQ	USBLS	5/15
	Pittsburgh MSA, PA	Y	18750 FQ	23120 MW	29370 TQ	USBLS	5/15
	Rhode Island	Y	22520 FQ	27740 MW	34980 TQ	USBLS	5/15
	Providence-Warwick MSA, RI-MA	Y	22370 FQ	27600 MW	34660 TQ	USBLS	5/15
	South Carolina	Y	18150 FQ	21500 MW	25840 TQ	USBLS	5/15
	Charleston-North Charleston MSA, SC	Y	18870 FQ	22950 MW	28010 TQ	USBLS	5/15
	Columbia MSA, SC	Y	18660 FQ	21650 MW	24430 TQ	USBLS	5/15
	Greenville-Anderson-Mauldin MSA, SC	Y	17710 FQ	20260 MW	24480 TQ	USBLS	5/15
	South Dakota	Y	19890 FQ	22990 MW	27790 TQ	USBLS	5/15
	Sioux Falls MSA, SD	Y	21210 FQ	24510 MW	30150 TQ	USBLS	5/15
	Tennessee	Y	18320 FQ	21910 MW	29070 TQ	USBLS	5/15
	Knoxville MSA, TN	Y	18720 FQ	22140 MW	27310 TQ	USBLS	5/15
	Memphis MSA, TN-MS-AR	Y	23620 FQ	49950 MW	56440 TQ	USBLS	5/15
	Nashville-Davidson– Murfreesboro–Franklin MSA, TN	Y	20480 FQ	24100 MW	29310 TQ	USBLS	5/15
	Texas	Y	18450 FQ	22350 MW	28110 TQ	USBLS	5/15
	Austin-Round Rock MSA, TX	Y	21120 FQ	25030 MW	31390 TQ	USBLS	5/15
	Dallas-Plano-Irving PMSA, TX	Y	20460 FQ	25070 MW	30360 TQ	USBLS	5/15
	Fort Worth-Arlington PMSA, TX	Y	20100 FQ	25540 MW	28920 TQ	USBLS	5/15
	Houston-The Woodlands-Sugar Land MSA, TX	Y	17890 FQ	20450 MW	27260 TQ	USBLS	5/15
	San Antonio-New Braunfels MSA, TX	Y	21430 FQ	25520 MW	29370 TQ	USBLS	5/15
	Utah	Y	19660 FQ	25270 MW	32950 TQ	USBLS	5/15
	Ogden-Clearfield MSA, UT	Y	18870 FQ	23410 MW	30150 TQ	USBLS	5/15
	Provo-Orem MSA, UT	Y	20250 FQ	25170 MW	33820 TQ	USBLS	5/15
	Salt Lake City MSA, UT	Y	21140 FQ	27660 MW	37800 TQ	USBLS	5/15
	Vermont	Y	21750 FQ	25760 MW	30640 TQ	USBLS	5/15
	Burlington-South Burlington MSA, VT	Y	22100 FQ	26090 MW	31540 TQ	USBLS	5/15
	Virginia	Y	20600 FQ	25470 MW	31540 TQ	USBLS	5/15
	Richmond MSA, VA	Y	21210 FQ	25750 MW	30310 TQ	USBLS	5/15

AE	Average entry wage	AWR	Average wage range	H	Hourly	LR	Low end range	MTC	Median total compensation	TCC	Total cash compensation
AEX	Average experienced wage	B	Biweekly	HI	Highest wage paid	M	Monthly	MW	Median wage paid	TQ	Third quartile wage
ATC	Average total compensation	D	Daily	HR	High end range	MCC	Median cash compensation	MWR	Median wage range	W	Weekly
AW	Average wage paid	FQ	First quartile wage	LO	Lowest wage paid	ME	Median entry wage	S	See annotated source	Y	Yearly

Occupation/Type/Industry	Location	Per	Low	Mid	High	Source	Date
Baker	Virginia Beach-Norfolk-						
	Newport News MSA, VA-NC	Y	19320 FQ	24320 MW	28650 TQ	USBLS	5/15
	Washington	H	10.27 FQ	12.27 MW	15.61 TQ	WABLS	3/16
	Seattle-Bellevue-Everett						
	PMSA, WA	H	10.19 FQ	12.72 MW	15.60 TQ	WABLS	3/16
	Tacoma-Lakewood PMSA, WA	H	12.95 FQ	15.97 MW	18.53 TQ	WABLS	3/16
	West Virginia	Y	18290 FQ	20530 MW	24500 TQ	USBLS	5/15
	Huntington-Ashland MSA,						
	WV-KY-OH	Y	18270 FQ	19910 MW	23230 TQ	USBLS	5/15
	Wisconsin	Y	20760 FQ	24910 MW	30830 TQ	USBLS	5/15
	Madison MSA, WI	Y	22530 FQ	27870 MW	35690 TQ	USBLS	5/15
	Milwaukee-Waukesha-West						
	Allis MSA, WI	Y	21400 FQ	25990 MW	31880 TQ	USBLS	5/15
	Wyoming	Y	20340 FQ	23610 MW	29320 TQ	USBLS	5/15
	Cheyenne MSA, WY	Y	17670 FQ	19950 MW	23820 TQ	USBLS	5/15
	Puerto Rico	Y	16700 FQ	17900 MW	19110 TQ	USBLS	5/15
	San Juan-Carolina-Caguas						
	MSA, PR	Y	16800 FQ	18050 MW	19320 TQ	USBLS	5/15
	Virgin Islands	Y	22810 FQ	26120 MW	29190 TQ	USBLS	5/15
	Guam	Y	17870 FQ	18580 MW	19300 TQ	USBLS	5/15
Bandmember							
Late-Night Television Show	United States	W		10000-			
				50000 AWR		BBRD01	2014
Barber	California	H	10.20 FQ	11.91 MW	15.42 TQ	CABLS	1/16-3/16
	Colorado	Y	24430 FQ	29980 MW	38130 TQ	USBLS	5/15
	Connecticut	Y		24249 MW		CTBLS	1/16-3/16
	District of Columbia	Y	30520 FQ	48220 MW	59510 TQ	USBLS	5/15
	Florida	H	9.69 AE	12.48 MW	15.25 AEX	FLBLS	7/16-9/16
	Georgia	Y	19730 FQ	24340 MW	36900 TQ	USBLS	5/15
	Illinois	Y	22680 FQ	72990 MW	77850 TQ	USBLS	5/15
	Indiana	Y	20080 FQ	24190 MW	31140 TQ	USBLS	5/15
	Iowa	Y	20190 FQ	25940 MW	28770 TQ	USBLS	5/15
	Kentucky	Y	23180 FQ	33130 MW	36590 TQ	USBLS	5/15
	Louisiana	Y	18850 FQ	24960 MW	30310 TQ	USBLS	5/15
	Massachusetts	Y	31060 FQ	43250 MW	49830 TQ	USBLS	5/15
	Michigan	Y	18390 FQ	19770 MW	30310 TQ	USBLS	5/15
	Minnesota	Y	40970 FQ	43838 MW	46706 TQ	MNBLS	1/16-3/16
	Missouri	Y	19630 FQ	24660 MW	39100 TQ	USBLS	5/15
	New Jersey	Y	18620 FQ	20550 MW	23610 TQ	USBLS	5/15
	New York	Y	20380 AE	22720 MW	31360 AEX	NYBLS	1/16-3/16
	North Carolina	Y	17990 FQ	26200 MW	34810 TQ	USBLS	5/15
	Ohio	Y	19060 FQ	22050 MW	33900 TQ	USBLS	5/15
	Oklahoma	Y	34320 FQ	47740 MW	62570 TQ	USBLS	5/15
	Oregon	H	12.31 FQ	13.55 MW	14.81 TQ	ORBLS	2016
	Pennsylvania	Y	18200 FQ	23790 MW	35100 TQ	USBLS	5/15
	South Carolina	Y	21330 FQ	24180 MW	29140 TQ	USBLS	5/15
	Tennessee	Y	18810 FQ	24130 MW	30960 TQ	USBLS	5/15
	Texas	Y	18540 FQ	27680 MW	37320 TQ	USBLS	5/15
	Virginia	Y	25480 FQ	27890 MW	30310 TQ	USBLS	5/15
	Washington	H	12.37 FQ	15.70 MW	18.59 TQ	WABLS	3/16
	West Virginia	Y	20350 FQ	24350 MW	28740 TQ	USBLS	5/15
	Wisconsin	Y	17010 FQ	18650 MW	21690 TQ	USBLS	5/15
Barber Inspector							
State Government	Ohio	H	20.38 LO		31.89 HI	OHGOV	2015
Bartender	Alabama	Y	17483 AE	21148 AW	22981 AEX	ALBLS	6/16
	Birmingham-Hoover MSA, AL	Y	17442 AE	22456 AW	24968 AEX	ALBLS	6/16
	Alaska	Y	22970 FQ	27660 MW	34600 TQ	USBLS	5/15
	Anchorage MSA, AK	Y	23370 FQ	29480 MW	40830 TQ	USBLS	5/15
	Arizona	Y	18010 FQ	19250 MW	28110 TQ	USBLS	5/15
	Phoenix-Mesa-Scottsdale						
	MSA, AZ	Y	18090 FQ	19420 MW	28610 TQ	USBLS	5/15
	Tucson MSA, AZ	Y	18030 FQ	19290 MW	32500 TQ	USBLS	5/15
	Arkansas	Y	16930 FQ	18240 MW	19700 TQ	USBLS	5/15
	Little Rock-North Little Rock-						
	Conway MSA, AR	Y	16960 FQ	18300 MW	19930 TQ	USBLS	5/15
	California	H	9.68 FQ	11.85 MW	16.89 TQ	CABLS	1/16-3/16
	Anaheim-Santa Ana-Irvine						
	PMSA, CA	H	9.75 FQ	11.49 MW	15.32 TQ	CABLS	1/16-3/16

AE	Average entry wage	AWR	Average wage range	H	Hourly
AEX	Average experienced wage	B	Biweekly	HI	Highest wage paid
ATC	Average total compensation	D	Daily	HR	High end range
AW	Average wage paid	FQ	First quartile wage	LO	Lowest wage paid

LR	Low end range	MTC	Median total compensation
M	Monthly	MW	Median wage paid
MCC	Median cash compensation	MWR	Median wage range
ME	Median entry wage	S	See annotated source

TCC	Total cash compensation
TQ	Third quartile wage
W	Weekly
Y	Yearly

Bartender

Occupation/Type/Industry	Location	Per	Low	Mid	High	Source	Date
Bartender	Los Angeles-Long Beach-Glendale PMSA, CA	H	9.57 FQ	11.48 MW	17.68 TQ	CABLS	1/16-3/16
	Oakland-Hayward-Berkeley PMSA, CA	H	10.30 FQ	12.50 MW	15.30 TQ	CABLS	1/16-3/16
	Riverside-San Bernardino-Ontario MSA, CA	H	9.47 FQ	9.89 MW	11.95 TQ	CABLS	1/16-3/16
	Sacramento–Roseville–Arden-Arcade MSA, CA	H	9.57 FQ	11.86 MW	16.69 TQ	CABLS	1/16-3/16
	San Diego-Carlsbad MSA, CA	H	9.69 FQ	12.52 MW	17.53 TQ	CABLS	1/16-3/16
	San Francisco-Redwood City-South San Francisco PMSA, CA	H	11.19 FQ	14.14 MW	18.82 TQ	CABLS	1/16-3/16
	Colorado	Y	18080 FQ	19040 MW	22910 TQ	USBLS	5/15
	Denver-Aurora-Lakewood MSA, CO	Y	18060 FQ	19000 MW	22020 TQ	USBLS	5/15
	Connecticut	Y		19987 MW		CTBLS	1/16-3/16
	Bridgeport-Stamford-Norwalk MSA, CT	Y	19240 FQ	19680 MW	25550 TQ	USBLS	5/15
	Hartford-West Hartford-East Hartford MSA, CT	Y	19220 FQ	19520 MW	20780 TQ	USBLS	5/15
	Delaware	Y	18020 FQ	19820 MW	24560 TQ	USBLS	5/15
	Wilmington PMSA, DE-MD-NJ	Y	18480 FQ	21220 MW	25860 TQ	USBLS	5/15
	District of Columbia	Y	19920 FQ	23040 MW	31390 TQ	USBLS	5/15
	Washington-Arlington-Alexandria PMSA, DC-VA-MD-WV	Y	19910 FQ	24260 MW	36270 TQ	USBLS	5/15
	Florida	H	9.01 AE	10.42 MW	16.63 AEX	FLBLS	7/16-9/16
	Fort Lauderdale-Pompano Beach-Deerfield Beach PMSA, FL	H	9.01 AE	10.59 MW	17.23 AEX	FLBLS	7/16-9/16
	Miami-Miami Beach-Kendall PMSA, FL	H	9.02 AE	10.55 MW	19.69 AEX	FLBLS	7/16-9/16
	Orlando-Kissimmee-Sanford MSA, FL	H	9.02 AE	10.06 MW	22.23 AEX	FLBLS	7/16-9/16
	Tampa-St. Petersburg-Clearwater MSA, FL	H	9.06 AE	12.35 MW	16.30 AEX	FLBLS	7/16-9/16
	Georgia	Y	17020 FQ	18590 MW	22010 TQ	USBLS	5/15
	Atlanta-Sandy Springs-Roswell MSA, GA	Y	17050 FQ	18660 MW	22190 TQ	USBLS	5/15
	Augusta-Richmond County MSA, GA-SC	Y	16970 FQ	18540 MW	26840 TQ	USBLS	5/15
	Hawaii	Y	19870 FQ	30670 MW	48050 TQ	USBLS	5/15
	Urban Honolulu MSA, HI	Y	18530 FQ	25920 MW	39710 TQ	USBLS	5/15
	Idaho	Y	16920 FQ	18420 MW	21000 TQ	USBLS	5/15
	Boise City MSA, ID	Y	17020 FQ	18600 MW	21560 TQ	USBLS	5/15
	Illinois	Y	18500 FQ	19400 MW	23220 TQ	USBLS	5/15
	Chicago-Naperville-Arlington Heights PMSA, IL	Y	18570 FQ	19570 MW	23940 TQ	USBLS	5/15
	Lake County-Kenosha County PMSA, IL-WI	Y	18220 FQ	19340 MW	23320 TQ	USBLS	5/15
	Indiana	Y	17070 FQ	18720 MW	22620 TQ	USBLS	5/15
	Gary PMSA, IN	Y	16730 FQ	18060 MW	19440 TQ	USBLS	5/15
	Indianapolis-Carmel-Anderson MSA, IN	Y	17310 FQ	19170 MW	24470 TQ	USBLS	5/15
	Iowa	Y	16710 FQ	18020 MW	19340 TQ	USBLS	5/15
	Des Moines-West Des Moines MSA, IA	Y	16780 FQ	18090 MW	19430 TQ	USBLS	5/15
	Kansas	Y	16770 FQ	18100 MW	19460 TQ	USBLS	5/15
	Wichita MSA, KS	Y	16680 FQ	18010 MW	19360 TQ	USBLS	5/15
	Kentucky	Y	16730 FQ	18050 MW	19410 TQ	USBLS	5/15
	Louisville-Jefferson County MSA, KY-IN	Y	16750 FQ	18140 MW	19720 TQ	USBLS	5/15
	Louisiana	Y	16940 FQ	18480 MW	20830 TQ	USBLS	5/15
	Baton Rouge MSA, LA	Y	17430 FQ	19370 MW	22680 TQ	USBLS	5/15
	New Orleans-Metairie MSA, LA	Y	16960 FQ	18540 MW	21010 TQ	USBLS	5/15
	Maine	Y	17290 FQ	18600 MW	21930 TQ	USBLS	5/15
	Portland-South Portland MSA, ME	Y	17180 FQ	18390 MW	19680 TQ	USBLS	5/15
	Maryland	Y	18063 AE	24525 MW	27756 AEX	MDBLS	4/16

AE	Average entry wage	AWR	Average wage range	H	Hourly
AEX	Average experienced wage	B	Biweekly	HI	Highest wage paid
ATC	Average total compensation	D	Daily	HR	High end range
AW	Average wage paid	FQ	First quartile wage	LO	Lowest wage paid

LR	Low end range	MTC	Median total compensation	TCC	Total cash compensation
M	Monthly	MW	Median wage paid	TQ	Third quartile wage
MCC	Median cash compensation	MWR	Median wage range	W	Weekly
ME	Median entry wage	S	See annotated source	Y	Yearly

Occupation/Type/Industry	Location	Per	Low	Mid	High	Source	Date
Bartender	Baltimore-Columbia-Towson MSA, MD	Y	17810 FQ	18980 MW	24550 TQ	USBLS	5/15
	Salisbury MSA, MD-DE	Y	17680 FQ	18890 MW	24100 TQ	USBLS	5/15
	Massachusetts	Y	19130 FQ	19780 MW	31890 TQ	USBLS	5/15
	Boston-Cambridge-Newton NECTA, MA	Y	19200 FQ	25150 MW	40010 TQ	USBLS	5/15
	Worcester MSA, MA-CT	Y	19130 FQ	19520 MW	24760 TQ	USBLS	5/15
	Michigan	Y	17990 FQ	18920 MW	21590 TQ	USBLS	5/15
	Detroit-Dearborn-Livonia PMSA, MI	Y	18060 FQ	19040 MW	23560 TQ	USBLS	5/15
	Grand Rapids-Wyoming MSA, MI	Y	17960 FQ	18880 MW	21790 TQ	USBLS	5/15
	Minnesota	Y	18006 FQ	19107 MW	22066 TQ	MNBLS	1/16-3/16
	Mankato-North Mankato MSA, MN	Y	17570 FQ	18400 MW	19230 TQ	USBLS	5/15
	Minneapolis-St. Paul-Bloomington MSA, MN-WI	Y	18157 FQ	19470 MW	24065 TQ	MNBLS	1/16-3/16
	Mississippi	Y	16870 FQ	18280 MW	19880 TQ	USBLS	5/15
	Jackson MSA, MS	Y	17020 FQ	18570 MW	24900 TQ	USBLS	5/15
	Missouri	Y	17200 FQ	18470 MW	20250 TQ	USBLS	5/15
	Kansas City MSA, MO-KS	Y	17100 FQ	18460 MW	20000 TQ	USBLS	5/15
	St. Louis MSA, MO-IL	Y	17710 FQ	18760 MW	20840 TQ	USBLS	5/15
	Montana	Y	17800 FQ	18840 MW	20850 TQ	USBLS	5/15
	Billings MSA, MT	Y	18220 FQ	19890 MW	22980 TQ	USBLS	5/15
	Nebraska	Y	17580 FQ	18525 MW	19565 TQ	NEBLS	7/16-9/16
	Omaha-Council Bluffs MSA, NE-IA	Y	17640 FQ	18740 MW	21225 TQ	NEBLS	7/16-9/16
	Nevada	Y	18040 FQ	23440 MW	34080 TQ	USBLS	5/15
	Las Vegas-Henderson-Paradise MSA, NV	Y	18590 FQ	27610 MW	35270 TQ	USBLS	5/15
	New Hampshire	H	8.43 AE	9.11 MW	11.38 AEX	NHBLS	6/16
	Manchester NECTA, NH	H	8.42 AE	9.34 MW	12.83 AEX	NHBLS	6/16
	Nashua NECTA, NH-MA	Y	16840 FQ	18240 MW	19710 TQ	USBLS	5/15
	New Jersey	Y	19430 FQ	23070 MW	29370 TQ	USBLS	5/15
	Camden PMSA, NJ	Y	18480 FQ	19440 MW	23080 TQ	USBLS	5/15
	Newark PMSA, NJ-PA	Y	20360 FQ	24880 MW	30970 TQ	USBLS	5/15
	Trenton MSA, NJ	Y	20510 FQ	22400 MW	24300 TQ	USBLS	5/15
	New Mexico	Y	17370 FQ	18810 MW	23550 TQ	USBLS	5/15
	Albuquerque MSA, NM	Y	17360 FQ	18770 MW	22550 TQ	USBLS	5/15
	New York	Y	19280 AE	20190 MW	30700 AEX	NYBLS	1/16-3/16
	Buffalo-Cheektowaga-Niagara Falls MSA, NY	Y	18740 FQ	19290 MW	23100 TQ	USBLS	5/15
	Nassau County-Suffolk County PMSA, NY	Y	19050 FQ	22920 MW	33660 TQ	USBLS	5/15
	New York-Jersey City-White Plains PMSA, NY-NJ	Y	19140 FQ	23530 MW	31550 TQ	USBLS	5/15
	Rochester MSA, NY	Y	18880 FQ	19630 MW	24830 TQ	USBLS	5/15
	North Carolina	Y	17110 FQ	18780 MW	24610 TQ	USBLS	5/15
	Charlotte-Concord-Gastonia MSA, NC-SC	Y	17210 FQ	18940 MW	27930 TQ	USBLS	5/15
	Raleigh MSA, NC	Y	17550 FQ	20050 MW	35770 TQ	USBLS	5/15
	North Dakota	Y	17290 FQ	19150 MW	23200 TQ	USBLS	5/15
	Fargo MSA, ND-MN	Y	17070 FQ	18500 MW	20980 TQ	USBLS	5/15
	Ohio	Y	17810 FQ	18740 MW	19810 TQ	USBLS	5/15
	Cincinnati MSA, OH-KY-IN	Y	17550 FQ	18440 MW	19350 TQ	USBLS	5/15
	Cleveland-Elyria MSA, OH	Y	18000 FQ	19120 MW	22560 TQ	USBLS	5/15
	Columbus MSA, OH	Y	17850 FQ	18820 MW	20640 TQ	USBLS	5/15
	Oklahoma	Y	17000 FQ	18600 MW	22580 TQ	USBLS	5/15
	Oklahoma City MSA, OK	Y	17340 FQ	19230 MW	24000 TQ	USBLS	5/15
	Tulsa MSA, OK	Y	16690 FQ	18030 MW	19450 TQ	USBLS	5/15
	Oregon	H	9.58 FQ	9.84 MW	11.83 TQ	ORBLS	2016
	Portland-Vancouver-Hillsboro MSA, OR-WA	Y	19540 FQ	20330 MW	24740 TQ	USBLS	5/15
	Pennsylvania	Y	17230 FQ	19020 MW	22870 TQ	USBLS	5/15
	Allentown-Bethlehem-Easton MSA, PA-NJ	Y	17680 FQ	19820 MW	24830 TQ	USBLS	5/15
	Harrisburg-Carlisle MSA, PA	Y	17320 FQ	19210 MW	25800 TQ	USBLS	5/15
	Montgomery County-Bucks County-Chester County PMSA, PA	Y	18190 FQ	21520 MW	26930 TQ	USBLS	5/15
	Philadelphia PMSA, PA	Y	17230 FQ	19030 MW	23230 TQ	USBLS	5/15
	Pittsburgh MSA, PA	Y	17270 FQ	19120 MW	22750 TQ	USBLS	5/15

AE	Average entry wage	AWR	Average wage range	H	Hourly
AEX	Average experienced wage	B	Biweekly	HI	Highest wage paid
ATC	Average total compensation	D	Daily	HR	High end range
AW	Average wage paid	FQ	First quartile wage	LO	Lowest wage paid

LR	Low end range	MTC	Median total compensation
M	Monthly	MW	Median wage paid
MCC	Median cash compensation	MWR	Median wage range
ME	Median entry wage	S	See annotated source

TCC	Total cash compensation		
TQ	Third quartile wage		
W	Weekly		
Y	Yearly		

Occupation/Type/Industry	Location	Per	Low	Mid	High	Source	Date
Bartender	Rhode Island	Y	19090 FQ	19480 MW	22210 TQ	USBLS	5/15
	Providence-Warwick MSA, RI-MA	Y	19080 FQ	19460 MW	22440 TQ	USBLS	5/15
	South Carolina	Y	16880 FQ	18320 MW	20160 TQ	USBLS	5/15
	Charleston-North Charleston MSA, SC	Y	17150 FQ	18870 MW	31690 TQ	USBLS	5/15
	Columbia MSA, SC	Y	16720 FQ	17960 MW	19200 TQ	USBLS	5/15
	Greenville-Anderson-Mauldin MSA, SC	Y	16760 FQ	18070 MW	19390 TQ	USBLS	5/15
	South Dakota	Y	18580 FQ	19500 MW	22420 TQ	USBLS	5/15
	Sioux Falls MSA, SD	Y	18680 FQ	19720 MW	22500 TQ	USBLS	5/15
	Tennessee	Y	17030 FQ	18610 MW	22890 TQ	USBLS	5/15
	Knoxville MSA, TN	Y	16880 FQ	18320 MW	20820 TQ	USBLS	5/15
	Memphis MSA, TN-MS-AR	Y	16750 FQ	18060 MW	19410 TQ	USBLS	5/15
	Nashville-Davidson–Murfreesboro–Franklin MSA, TN	Y	17250 FQ	19090 MW	24710 TQ	USBLS	5/15
	Texas	Y	17130 FQ	18800 MW	28740 TQ	USBLS	5/15
	Austin-Round Rock MSA, TX	Y	17690 FQ	20290 MW	35100 TQ	USBLS	5/15
	Dallas-Plano-Irving PMSA, TX	Y	17310 FQ	19140 MW	36090 TQ	USBLS	5/15
	Fort Worth-Arlington PMSA, TX	Y	16860 FQ	18250 MW	19750 TQ	USBLS	5/15
	Houston-The Woodlands-Sugar Land MSA, TX	Y	17070 FQ	18670 MW	24500 TQ	USBLS	5/15
	San Antonio-New Braunfels MSA, TX	Y	17380 FQ	19330 MW	29250 TQ	USBLS	5/15
	Utah	Y	18440 FQ	22330 MW	29600 TQ	USBLS	5/15
	Ogden-Clearfield MSA, UT	Y	17350 FQ	19190 MW	22600 TQ	USBLS	5/15
	Provo-Orem MSA, UT	Y	17610 FQ	19680 MW	23300 TQ	USBLS	5/15
	Salt Lake City MSA, UT	Y	19390 FQ	24680 MW	32940 TQ	USBLS	5/15
	Vermont	Y	19710 FQ	24690 MW	36000 TQ	USBLS	5/15
	Burlington-South Burlington MSA, VT	Y	19540 FQ	23810 MW	34640 TQ	USBLS	5/15
	Virginia	Y	18860 FQ	26670 MW	37800 TQ	USBLS	5/15
	Richmond MSA, VA	Y	18200 FQ	24000 MW	33550 TQ	USBLS	5/15
	Virginia Beach-Norfolk-Newport News MSA, VA-NC	Y	18640 FQ	24520 MW	38040 TQ	USBLS	5/15
	Washington	H	10.45 FQ	12.22 MW	17.63 TQ	WABLS	3/16
	Seattle-Bellevue-Everett PMSA, WA	H	10.85 FQ	13.72 MW	20.59 TQ	WABLS	3/16
	Tacoma-Lakewood PMSA, WA	H	10.14 FQ	12.29 MW	15.10 TQ	WABLS	3/16
	West Virginia	Y	17500 FQ	18350 MW	19210 TQ	USBLS	5/15
	Huntington-Ashland MSA, WV-KY-OH	Y	17420 FQ	18300 MW	19180 TQ	USBLS	5/15
	Wisconsin	Y	16930 FQ	18460 MW	21120 TQ	USBLS	5/15
	Madison MSA, WI	Y	17490 FQ	19640 MW	27380 TQ	USBLS	5/15
	Milwaukee-Waukesha-West Allis MSA, WI	Y	17020 FQ	18650 MW	22400 TQ	USBLS	5/15
	Wyoming	Y	17000 FQ	18570 MW	22650 TQ	USBLS	5/15
	Cheyenne MSA, WY	Y	16650 FQ	17870 MW	19080 TQ	USBLS	5/15
	Puerto Rico	Y	16560 FQ	17700 MW	18840 TQ	USBLS	5/15
	San Juan-Carolina-Caguas MSA, PR	Y	16580 FQ	17730 MW	18870 TQ	USBLS	5/15
	Virgin Islands	Y	17090 FQ	18790 MW	23440 TQ	USBLS	5/15
	Guam	Y	17890 FQ	18610 MW	19340 TQ	USBLS	5/15
Baseball Player							
Arizona Diamondbacks	Phoenix, AZ	Y		1500000 MW		USAT03	2016
Atlanta Braves	Atlanta, GA	Y		948750 MW		USAT03	2016
Baltimore Orioles	Baltimore, MD	Y		2700000 MW		USAT03	2016
Boston Red Sox	Boston, MA	Y		2600000 MW		USAT03	2016
Chicago Cubs	Chicago, IL	Y		2250000 MW		USAT03	2016
Chicago White Sox	Chicago, IL	Y		2750000 MW		USAT03	2016
Cincinnati Reds	Cincinnati, OH	Y		525000 MW		USAT03	2016
Cleveland Indians	Cleveland, OH	Y		2000000 MW		USAT03	2016
Colorado Rockies	Denver, CO	Y		1300000 MW		USAT03	2016
Detroit Tigers	Detroit, MI	Y		900000 MW		USAT03	2016
Houston Astros	Houston, TX	Y		875000 MW		USAT03	2016
Kansas City Royals	Kansas City, MO	Y		4250000 MW		USAT03	2016
Los Angeles Angels	Los Angeles, CA	Y		1950000 MW		USAT03	2016
Los Angeles Dodgers	Los Angeles, CA	Y		3125000 MW		USAT03	2016
Miami Marlins	Miami, FL	Y		1425000 MW		USAT03	2016

AE	Average entry wage	**AWR**	Average wage range	**H**	Hourly	**LR**	Low end range	**MTC**	Median total compensation
AEX	Average experienced wage	**B**	Biweekly	**HI**	Highest wage paid	**M**	Monthly	**MW**	Median wage paid
ATC	Average total compensation	**D**	Daily	**HR**	High end range	**MCC**	Median cash compensation	**MWR**	Median wage range
AW	Average wage paid	**FQ**	First quartile wage	**LO**	Lowest wage paid	**ME**	Median entry wage	**S**	See annotated source

TCC Total cash compensation
TQ Third quartile wage
W Weekly
Y Yearly

Occupation/Type/Industry	Location	Per	Low	Mid	High	Source	Date
Baseball Player							
Milwaukee Brewers	Milwaukee, WI	Y		518100 MW		USAT03	2016
Minnesota Twins	Minneapolis, MN	Y		2150000 MW		USAT03	2016
Oakland Athletics	Oakland, CA	Y		1540000 MW		USAT03	2016
Philadelphia Phillies	Philadelphia, PA	Y		526000 MW		USAT03	2016
Pittsburgh Pirates	Pittsburgh, PA	Y		2750000 MW		USAT03	2016
St. Louis Cardinals	St. Louis, MO	Y		1650000 MW		USAT03	2016
San Diego Padres	San Diego, CA	Y		800000 MW		USAT03	2016
Seattle Mariners	Seattle, WA	Y		1500000 MW		USAT03	2016
Tampa Bay Rays	Tampa Bay, FL	Y		711300 MW		USAT03	2016
Texas Rangers	Arlington, TX	Y		1600000 MW		USAT03	2016
Washington Nationals	District of Columbia	Y		2937500 MW		USAT03	2016
Battalion Chief							
Fire Department, Municipal Government	Alhambra, CA	Y			99124 HI	CACIT	6/28/16
Fire Department, Municipal Government	Encinitas, CA	Y		128253 AW		CACIT	6/28/16
Fire Department, Municipal Government	Loma Linda, CA	Y		106178 AW		CACIT	6/28/16
Fire Department, Municipal Government	Los Angeles, CA	Y		141270 AW		CACIT	6/23/16
Fire Department, Municipal Government	Colorado Springs, CO	M			9436 HI	COSPRS	2017
Fire Department, Municipal Government	Detroit, MI	M	4442 LO		6650 HI	DETGOV	2016
Fire Department, Municipal Government	Seattle, WA	H	58.43 LO		69.05 HI	CSSS	1/1/14
Beach Maintenance Supervisor							
Municipal Government	Santa Monica, CA	Y			89220 HI	CACIT	6/28/16
Beach Maintenance Worker							
Municipal Government	Carpinteria, CA	Y			15492 HI	CACIT	6/28/16
Beach Services Manager							
Municipal Government	North Myrtle Beach, SC	Y			70577 HI	WMBFN	2017
Beautification Project Leader							
Municipal Government	El Monte, CA	Y			30515 HI	CACIT	6/24/16
Benefits Management Analyst							
Administrative Services, State Government	Ohio	H	26.13 LO		34.37 HI	OHGOV	2015
Bereavement Coordinator	United States	Y		52328 MW		FPAT	2015
Bibliographic Technician							
Library Services, Municipal Government	Santa Ana, CA	Y			57504 HI	CACIT	6/28/16
Bicycle Repairer	Alabama	Y	25954 AE	28049 AW	29087 AEX	ALBLS	6/16
	Arizona	Y	23720 FQ	28050 MW	35580 TQ	USBLS	5/15
	Arkansas	Y	18230 FQ	21290 MW	27710 TQ	USBLS	5/15
	California	H	11.98 FQ	15.44 MW	17.68 TQ	CABLS	1/16-3/16
	Colorado	Y	21790 FQ	27950 MW	34800 TQ	USBLS	5/15
	Connecticut	Y		26184 MW		CTBLS	1/16-3/16
	District of Columbia	Y	26410 FQ	31060 MW	35540 TQ	USBLS	5/15
	Florida	H	11.11 AE	16.31 MW	17.67 AEX	FLBLS	7/16-9/16
	Georgia	Y	21930 FQ	31440 MW	36350 TQ	USBLS	5/15
	Hawaii	Y	19920 FQ	27120 MW	30350 TQ	USBLS	5/15
	Idaho	Y	19960 FQ	26370 MW	34820 TQ	USBLS	5/15
	Illinois	Y	25900 FQ	28600 MW	31300 TQ	USBLS	5/15
	Indiana	Y	21100 FQ	24570 MW	30580 TQ	USBLS	5/15
	Iowa	Y	18460 FQ	23590 MW	28150 TQ	USBLS	5/15
	Kansas	Y	18000 FQ	20280 MW	27080 TQ	USBLS	5/15
	Kentucky	Y	24510 FQ	28520 MW	33040 TQ	USBLS	5/15
	Maine	Y	22680 FQ	26330 MW	30140 TQ	USBLS	5/15
	Massachusetts	Y	27390 FQ	32060 MW	37290 TQ	USBLS	5/15
	Michigan	Y	18810 FQ	21300 MW	27390 TQ	USBLS	5/15
	Minnesota	Y	20335 FQ	23694 MW	34595 TQ	MNBLS	1/16-3/16
	Missouri	Y	19230 FQ	27140 MW	29800 TQ	USBLS	5/15
	Montana	Y	19730 FQ	26030 MW	29710 TQ	USBLS	5/15
	Nevada	Y	27660 FQ	30910 MW	38390 TQ	USBLS	5/15
	New Hampshire	H	10.43 AE	11.62 MW	13.00 AEX	NHBLS	6/16
	New Mexico	Y	21970 FQ	25360 MW	28560 TQ	USBLS	5/15
	New York	Y	24540 AE	30850 MW	35830 AEX	NYBLS	1/16-3/16
	North Carolina	Y	21970 FQ	24700 MW	33080 TQ	USBLS	5/15
	Ohio	Y	21090 FQ	25340 MW	28820 TQ	USBLS	5/15
	Oklahoma	Y	21600 FQ	24760 MW	28260 TQ	USBLS	5/15
	Oregon	H	11.37 FQ	12.96 MW	14.35 TQ	ORBLS	2016
	Pennsylvania	Y	18540 FQ	22370 MW	30250 TQ	USBLS	5/15

AE	Average entry wage	AWR	Average wage range	H	Hourly
AEX	Average experienced wage	B	Biweekly	HI	Highest wage paid
ATC	Average total compensation	D	Daily	HR	High end range
AW	Average wage paid	FQ	First quartile wage	LO	Lowest wage paid

LR	Low end range
M	Monthly
MCC	Median cash compensation
ME	Median entry wage

MTC	Median total compensation
MW	Median wage paid
MWR	Median wage range
S	See annotated source

TCC	Total cash compensation
TQ	Third quartile wage
W	Weekly
Y	Yearly

Occupation/Type/Industry	Location	Per	Low	Mid	High	Source	Date
Bicycle Repairer	South Carolina	Y	20690 FQ	23050 MW	26310 TQ	USBLS	5/15
	Tennessee	Y	16900 FQ	18710 MW	23260 TQ	USBLS	5/15
	Texas	Y	24820 FQ	27940 MW	30900 TQ	USBLS	5/15
	Utah	Y	24490 FQ	27650 MW	30340 TQ	USBLS	5/15
	Vermont	Y	25230 FQ	31580 MW	35810 TQ	USBLS	5/15
	Virginia	Y	25330 FQ	27590 MW	29850 TQ	USBLS	5/15
	Washington	H	11.33 FQ	13.26 MW	15.93 TQ	WABLS	3/16
	Wisconsin	Y	18400 FQ	21730 MW	26640 TQ	USBLS	5/15
	Wyoming	Y	31410 FQ	34150 MW	36840 TQ	USBLS	5/15
Big Data Engineer	United States	Y	135000-196000 LR			INFOW01	2017
Bike Share Coordinator							
Strategic and Transportation Planning, Municipal Government	Santa Monica, CA	Y			13697 HI	CACIT	6/28/16
Bill and Account Collector	Alabama	Y	24188 AE	32917 AW	37287 AEX	ALBLS	6/16
	Birmingham-Hoover MSA, AL	Y	23704 AE	33000 AW	37648 AEX	ALBLS	6/16
	Alaska	Y	34900 FQ	41730 MW	48090 TQ	USBLS	5/15
	Anchorage MSA, AK	Y	34650 FQ	41510 MW	47650 TQ	USBLS	5/15
	Arizona	Y	26340 FQ	34020 MW	40580 TQ	USBLS	5/15
	Phoenix-Mesa-Scottsdale MSA, AZ	Y	28580 FQ	35270 MW	42100 TQ	USBLS	5/15
	Tucson MSA, AZ	Y	22200 FQ	24510 MW	32120 TQ	USBLS	5/15
	Arkansas	Y	25900 FQ	30010 MW	36630 TQ	USBLS	5/15
	Little Rock-North Little Rock-Conway MSA, AR	Y	27990 FQ	33740 MW	39270 TQ	USBLS	5/15
	California	H	15.64 FQ	18.93 MW	24.27 TQ	CABLS	1/16-3/16
	Anaheim-Santa Ana-Irvine PMSA, CA	H	16.57 FQ	19.54 MW	24.30 TQ	CABLS	1/16-3/16
	Los Angeles-Long Beach-Glendale PMSA, CA	H	15.53 FQ	18.78 MW	24.05 TQ	CABLS	1/16-3/16
	Oakland-Hayward-Berkeley PMSA, CA	H	16.63 FQ	20.55 MW	25.68 TQ	CABLS	1/16-3/16
	Riverside-San Bernardino-Ontario MSA, CA	H	13.18 FQ	16.14 MW	19.43 TQ	CABLS	1/16-3/16
	Sacramento–Roseville–Arden-Arcade MSA, CA	H	15.78 FQ	18.13 MW	21.64 TQ	CABLS	1/16-3/16
	San Diego-Carlsbad MSA, CA	H	15.65 FQ	18.23 MW	23.14 TQ	CABLS	1/16-3/16
	San Francisco-Redwood City-South San Francisco PMSA, CA	H	19.81 FQ	25.11 MW	31.22 TQ	CABLS	1/16-3/16
	Colorado	Y	29230 FQ	35580 MW	43570 TQ	USBLS	5/15
	Denver-Aurora-Lakewood MSA, CO	Y	31330 FQ	36730 MW	43940 TQ	USBLS	5/15
	Connecticut	Y		44311 MW		CTBLS	1/16-3/16
	Bridgeport-Stamford-Norwalk MSA, CT	Y	39550 FQ	46540 MW	55640 TQ	USBLS	5/15
	Hartford-West Hartford-East Hartford MSA, CT	Y	33900 FQ	42500 MW	49320 TQ	USBLS	5/15
	District of Columbia	Y	45780 FQ	57130 MW	71390 TQ	USBLS	5/15
	Washington-Arlington-Alexandria PMSA, DC-VA-MD-WV	Y	33560 FQ	42220 MW	54430 TQ	USBLS	5/15
	Florida	H	12.23 AE	16.48 MW	19.16 AEX	FLBLS	7/16-9/16
	Fort Lauderdale-Pompano Beach-Deerfield Beach PMSA, FL	H	13.06 AE	17.38 MW	19.92 AEX	FLBLS	7/16-9/16
	Miami-Miami Beach-Kendall PMSA, FL	H	13.71 AE	17.22 MW	20.42 AEX	FLBLS	7/16-9/16
	Orlando-Kissimmee-Sanford MSA, FL	H	12.70 AE	15.92 MW	18.21 AEX	FLBLS	7/16-9/16
	Tampa-St. Petersburg-Clearwater MSA, FL	H	13.15 AE	17.07 MW	19.68 AEX	FLBLS	7/16-9/16
	Georgia	Y	27740 FQ	34660 MW	42450 TQ	USBLS	5/15
	Atlanta-Sandy Springs-Roswell MSA, GA	Y	29980 FQ	36520 MW	44370 TQ	USBLS	5/15
	Augusta-Richmond County MSA, GA-SC	Y	18480 FQ	27380 MW	35440 TQ	USBLS	5/15
	Hawaii	Y	31780 FQ	36300 MW	42490 TQ	USBLS	5/15
	Urban Honolulu MSA, HI	Y	31880 FQ	36520 MW	43220 TQ	USBLS	5/15

AE	Average entry wage	AWR	Average wage range	H	Hourly
AEX	Average experienced wage	B	Biweekly	HI	Highest wage paid
ATC	Average total compensation	D	Daily	HR	High end range
AW	Average wage paid	FQ	First quartile wage	LO	Lowest wage paid

LR	Low end range	MTC	Median total compensation
M	Monthly	MW	Median wage paid
MCC	Median cash compensation	MWR	Median wage range
ME	Median entry wage	S	See annotated source

TCC	Total cash compensation		
TQ	Third quartile wage		
W	Weekly		
Y	Yearly		

Bill and Account Collector

Occupation/Type/Industry	Location	Per	Low	Mid	High	Source	Date
Bill and Account Collector	Idaho	Y	29160 FQ	34010 MW	38030 TQ	USBLS	5/15
	Boise City MSA, ID	Y	30480 FQ	34360 MW	37810 TQ	USBLS	5/15
	Illinois	Y	29500 FQ	36690 MW	47110 TQ	USBLS	5/15
	Chicago-Naperville-Arlington Heights PMSA, IL	Y	29840 FQ	36770 MW	47270 TQ	USBLS	5/15
	Lake County-Kenosha County PMSA, IL-WI	Y	35500 FQ	43770 MW	54240 TQ	USBLS	5/15
	Indiana	Y	27010 FQ	31110 MW	38230 TQ	USBLS	5/15
	Gary PMSA, IN	Y	26310 FQ	30080 MW	36540 TQ	USBLS	5/15
	Indianapolis-Carmel-Anderson MSA, IN	Y	27090 FQ	30870 MW	39520 TQ	USBLS	5/15
	Iowa	Y	27050 FQ	30400 MW	36610 TQ	USBLS	5/15
	Waterloo-Cedar Falls MSA, IA	Y	26150 FQ	28610 MW	32940 TQ	USBLS	5/15
	Kansas	Y	25930 FQ	31420 MW	37670 TQ	USBLS	5/15
	Wichita MSA, KS	Y	25150 FQ	30860 MW	36920 TQ	USBLS	5/15
	Kentucky	Y	26510 FQ	32810 MW	41990 TQ	USBLS	5/15
	Louisville-Jefferson County MSA, KY-IN	Y	28490 FQ	36980 MW	45400 TQ	USBLS	5/15
	Louisiana	Y	25840 FQ	30520 MW	36760 TQ	USBLS	5/15
	Baton Rouge MSA, LA	Y	28500 FQ	33650 MW	37950 TQ	USBLS	5/15
	New Orleans-Metairie MSA, LA	Y	27730 FQ	32300 MW	38620 TQ	USBLS	5/15
	Maine	Y	28330 FQ	32930 MW	39260 TQ	USBLS	5/15
	Portland-South Portland MSA, ME	Y	30900 FQ	36110 MW	42850 TQ	USBLS	5/15
	Maryland	Y	30725 AE	39735 MW	44240 AEX	MDBLS	4/16
	Baltimore-Columbia-Towson MSA, MD	Y	33580 FQ	38400 MW	45310 TQ	USBLS	5/15
	Salisbury MSA, MD-DE	Y	24720 FQ	28870 MW	34530 TQ	USBLS	5/15
	Massachusetts	Y	34580 FQ	41330 MW	49660 TQ	USBLS	5/15
	Boston-Cambridge-Newton NECTA, MA	Y	34860 FQ	41890 MW	50120 TQ	USBLS	5/15
	Worcester MSA, MA-CT	Y	34960 FQ	41480 MW	50450 TQ	USBLS	5/15
	Michigan	Y	28890 FQ	35470 MW	43870 TQ	USBLS	5/15
	Detroit-Dearborn-Livonia PMSA, MI	Y	32000 FQ	37600 MW	47290 TQ	USBLS	5/15
	Grand Rapids-Wyoming MSA, MI	Y	28470 FQ	34220 MW	39380 TQ	USBLS	5/15
	Minnesota	Y	28710 FQ	36011 MW	45821 TQ	MNBLS	1/16-3/16
	Minneapolis-St. Paul-Bloomington MSA, MN-WI	Y	30460 FQ	37387 MW	47216 TQ	MNBLS	1/16-3/16
	Mississippi	Y	24410 FQ	28870 MW	35770 TQ	USBLS	5/15
	Jackson MSA, MS	Y	25260 FQ	29450 MW	35910 TQ	USBLS	5/15
	Missouri	Y	24940 FQ	29640 MW	36960 TQ	USBLS	5/15
	Kansas City MSA, MO-KS	Y	26840 FQ	32550 MW	38520 TQ	USBLS	5/15
	St. Louis MSA, MO-IL	Y	24760 FQ	29530 MW	36840 TQ	USBLS	5/15
	Montana	Y	24520 FQ	29060 MW	36070 TQ	USBLS	5/15
	Billings MSA, MT	Y	23990 FQ	30310 MW	41870 TQ	USBLS	5/15
	Nebraska	Y	27985 FQ	33405 MW	40610 TQ	NEBLS	7/16-9/16
	Omaha-Council Bluffs MSA, NE-IA	Y	27470 FQ	31460 MW	37845 TQ	NEBLS	7/16-9/16
	Nevada	Y	27460 FQ	34010 MW	40190 TQ	USBLS	5/15
	Las Vegas-Henderson-Paradise MSA, NV	Y	28120 FQ	34430 MW	40780 TQ	USBLS	5/15
	New Hampshire	H	11.53 AE	15.58 MW	19.41 AEX	NHBLS	6/16
	Manchester NECTA, NH	H	12.19 AE	16.37 MW	19.53 AEX	NHBLS	6/16
	Nashua NECTA, NH-MA	Y	24690 FQ	30820 MW	37970 TQ	USBLS	5/15
	New Jersey	Y	28970 FQ	36240 MW	45950 TQ	USBLS	5/15
	Camden PMSA, NJ	Y	25720 FQ	30960 MW	37750 TQ	USBLS	5/15
	Newark PMSA, NJ-PA	Y	31320 FQ	38920 MW	48110 TQ	USBLS	5/15
	Trenton MSA, NJ	Y	33800 FQ	40840 MW	48850 TQ	USBLS	5/15
	New Mexico	Y	29530 FQ	34680 MW	39070 TQ	USBLS	5/15
	Albuquerque MSA, NM	Y	32140 FQ	35790 MW	39470 TQ	USBLS	5/15
	New York	Y	25600 AE	36540 MW	46750 AEX	NYBLS	1/16-3/16
	Buffalo-Cheektowaga-Niagara Falls MSA, NY	Y	24760 FQ	31230 MW	38240 TQ	USBLS	5/15
	Nassau County-Suffolk County PMSA, NY	Y	33390 FQ	39240 MW	48890 TQ	USBLS	5/15
	New York-Jersey City-White Plains PMSA, NY-NJ	Y	30370 FQ	40200 MW	52160 TQ	USBLS	5/15
	Rochester MSA, NY	Y	29300 FQ	35230 MW	43290 TQ	USBLS	5/15
	North Carolina	Y	28510 FQ	34010 MW	40010 TQ	USBLS	5/15

AE	Average entry wage	AWR	Average wage range	H	Hourly
AEX	Average experienced wage	B	Biweekly	HI	Highest wage paid
ATC	Average total compensation	D	Daily	HR	High end range
AW	Average wage paid	FQ	First quartile wage	LO	Lowest wage paid

LR	Low end range	MTC	Median total compensation
M	Monthly	MW	Median wage paid
MCC	Median cash compensation	MWR	Median wage range
ME	Median entry wage	S	See annotated source

TCC	Total cash compensation
TQ	Third quartile wage
W	Weekly
Y	Yearly

Bill and Account Collector

Occupation/Type/Industry	Location	Per	Low	Mid	High	Source	Date
Bill and Account Collector	Charlotte-Concord-Gastonia						
	MSA, NC-SC	Y	28490 FQ	34140 MW	39780 TQ	USBLS	5/15
	Raleigh MSA, NC	Y	31380 FQ	36400 MW	43460 TQ	USBLS	5/15
	North Dakota	Y	26530 FQ	32560 MW	40460 TQ	USBLS	5/15
	Fargo MSA, ND-MN	Y	25030 FQ	29990 MW	37510 TQ	USBLS	5/15
	Ohio	Y	26890 FQ	32110 MW	39480 TQ	USBLS	5/15
	Cincinnati MSA, OH-KY-IN	Y	27130 FQ	32130 MW	38740 TQ	USBLS	5/15
	Cleveland-Elyria MSA, OH	Y	25790 FQ	30530 MW	39370 TQ	USBLS	5/15
	Columbus MSA, OH	Y	26550 FQ	30880 MW	37360 TQ	USBLS	5/15
	Oklahoma	Y	25070 FQ	30220 MW	37220 TQ	USBLS	5/15
	Oklahoma City MSA, OK	Y	25280 FQ	30940 MW	38730 TQ	USBLS	5/15
	Tulsa MSA, OK	Y	26860 FQ	31700 MW	37300 TQ	USBLS	5/15
	Oregon	H	13.96 FQ	17.32 MW	21.12 TQ	ORBLS	2016
	Portland-Vancouver-Hillsboro						
	MSA, OR-WA	Y	31490 FQ	36890 MW	44730 TQ	USBLS	5/15
	Pennsylvania	Y	28270 FQ	34650 MW	41910 TQ	USBLS	5/15
	Allentown-Bethlehem-Easton						
	MSA, PA-NJ	Y	23360 FQ	28020 MW	35790 TQ	USBLS	5/15
	Harrisburg-Carlisle MSA, PA	Y	28100 FQ	34120 MW	39090 TQ	USBLS	5/15
	Montgomery County-Bucks						
	County-Chester County						
	PMSA, PA	Y	30530 FQ	37230 MW	45970 TQ	USBLS	5/15
	Philadelphia PMSA, PA	Y	31110 FQ	36700 MW	44990 TQ	USBLS	5/15
	Pittsburgh MSA, PA	Y	28080 FQ	33890 MW	39850 TQ	USBLS	5/15
	Rhode Island	Y	29440 FQ	38860 MW	47600 TQ	USBLS	5/15
	Providence-Warwick MSA, RI-						
	MA	Y	30230 FQ	39950 MW	48160 TQ	USBLS	5/15
	South Carolina	Y	26150 FQ	31340 MW	38340 TQ	USBLS	5/15
	Charleston-North Charleston						
	MSA, SC	Y	26280 FQ	35910 MW	46740 TQ	USBLS	5/15
	Columbia MSA, SC	Y	27970 FQ	32840 MW	37590 TQ	USBLS	5/15
	Greenville-Anderson-Mauldin						
	MSA, SC	Y	25980 FQ	29640 MW	36700 TQ	USBLS	5/15
	South Dakota	Y	25840 FQ	30130 MW	36550 TQ	USBLS	5/15
	Sioux Falls MSA, SD	Y	25660 FQ	30010 MW	36240 TQ	USBLS	5/15
	Tennessee	Y	25580 FQ	31530 MW	39270 TQ	USBLS	5/15
	Knoxville MSA, TN	Y	23920 FQ	28680 MW	36050 TQ	USBLS	5/15
	Memphis MSA, TN-MS-AR	Y	25260 FQ	31870 MW	38610 TQ	USBLS	5/15
	Nashville-Davidson–						
	Murfreesboro–Franklin						
	MSA, TN	Y	27650 FQ	34430 MW	42970 TQ	USBLS	5/15
	Texas	Y	26780 FQ	33900 MW	41470 TQ	USBLS	5/15
	Austin-Round Rock MSA, TX	Y	28860 FQ	35310 MW	44810 TQ	USBLS	5/15
	Dallas-Plano-Irving PMSA, TX	Y	32150 FQ	37790 MW	48450 TQ	USBLS	5/15
	Fort Worth-Arlington PMSA,						
	TX	Y	28780 FQ	34030 MW	38870 TQ	USBLS	5/15
	Houston-The Woodlands-						
	Sugar Land MSA, TX	Y	26120 FQ	33320 MW	42100 TQ	USBLS	5/15
	San Antonio-New Braunfels						
	MSA, TX	Y	27270 FQ	33110 MW	38020 TQ	USBLS	5/15
	Utah	Y	25060 FQ	28810 MW	34870 TQ	USBLS	5/15
	Ogden-Clearfield MSA, UT	Y	27310 FQ	31070 MW	37290 TQ	USBLS	5/15
	Provo-Orem MSA, UT	Y	27640 FQ	31660 MW	38210 TQ	USBLS	5/15
	Salt Lake City MSA, UT	Y	25790 FQ	29310 MW	35750 TQ	USBLS	5/15
	Vermont	Y	30780 FQ	36840 MW	46660 TQ	USBLS	5/15
	Burlington-South Burlington						
	MSA, VT	Y	31750 FQ	38410 MW	48680 TQ	USBLS	5/15
	Virginia	Y	27430 FQ	34180 MW	43630 TQ	USBLS	5/15
	Richmond MSA, VA	Y	29900 FQ	35380 MW	41960 TQ	USBLS	5/15
	Virginia Beach-Norfolk-						
	Newport News MSA, VA-NC	Y	25510 FQ	31130 MW	39300 TQ	USBLS	5/15
	Washington	H	14.46 FQ	17.67 MW	21.35 TQ	WABLS	3/16
	Seattle-Bellevue-Everett						
	PMSA, WA	H	13.39 FQ	17.65 MW	22.14 TQ	WABLS	3/16
	Tacoma-Lakewood PMSA, WA	H	16.57 FQ	18.43 MW	21.37 TQ	WABLS	3/16
	West Virginia	Y	27760 FQ	33720 MW	39210 TQ	USBLS	5/15
	Huntington-Ashland MSA,						
	WV-KY-OH	Y	32420 FQ	35830 MW	39240 TQ	USBLS	5/15
	Wisconsin	Y	29180 FQ	35210 MW	42980 TQ	USBLS	5/15
	Madison MSA, WI	Y	31700 FQ	39100 MW	50970 TQ	USBLS	5/15
	Milwaukee-Waukesha-West						
	Allis MSA, WI	Y	29400 FQ	35170 MW	42650 TQ	USBLS	5/15

AE	Average entry wage	**AWR**	Average wage range	**H**	Hourly
AEX	Average experienced wage	**B**	Biweekly	**HI**	Highest wage paid
ATC	Average total compensation	**D**	Daily	**HR**	High end range
AW	Average wage paid	**FQ**	First quartile wage	**LO**	Lowest wage paid

LR	Low end range	**MTC**	Median total compensation	**TCC** Total cash compensation
M	Monthly	**MW**	Median wage paid	**TQ** Third quartile wage
MCC	Median cash compensation	**MWR**	Median wage range	**W** Weekly
ME	Median entry wage	**S**	See annotated source	**Y** Yearly

Occupation/Type/Industry	Location	Per	Low	Mid	High	Source	Date
Bill and Account Collector	Wyoming	Y	27310 FQ	31960 MW	40910 TQ	USBLS	5/15
	Puerto Rico	Y	17650 FQ	19970 MW	26940 TQ	USBLS	5/15
	San Juan-Carolina-Caguas MSA, PR	Y	17950 FQ	21160 MW	28720 TQ	USBLS	5/15
	Virgin Islands	Y	25110 FQ	32580 MW	38380 TQ	USBLS	5/15
	Guam	Y	19500 FQ	23580 MW	29450 TQ	USBLS	5/15
Billing and Posting Clerk	Alabama	Y	24858 AE	32629 AW	36514 AEX	ALBLS	6/16
	Birmingham-Hoover MSA, AL	Y	27321 AE	34978 AW	38812 AEX	ALBLS	6/16
	Alaska	Y	34820 FQ	41350 MW	50220 TQ	USBLS	5/15
	Anchorage MSA, AK	Y	34640 FQ	40210 MW	48180 TQ	USBLS	5/15
	Arizona	Y	28510 FQ	33950 MW	38790 TQ	USBLS	5/15
	Phoenix-Mesa-Scottsdale MSA, AZ	Y	28710 FQ	34430 MW	39350 TQ	USBLS	5/15
	Tucson MSA, AZ	Y	28590 FQ	32900 MW	36860 TQ	USBLS	5/15
	Arkansas	Y	25420 FQ	29480 MW	35400 TQ	USBLS	5/15
	Little Rock-North Little Rock-Conway MSA, AR	Y	28090 FQ	33060 MW	38360 TQ	USBLS	5/15
	California	H	14.99 FQ	18.38 MW	23.03 TQ	CABLS	1/16-3/16
	Anaheim-Santa Ana-Irvine PMSA, CA	H	15.98 FQ	19.15 MW	23.67 TQ	CABLS	1/16-3/16
	Los Angeles-Long Beach-Glendale PMSA, CA	H	14.29 FQ	17.64 MW	21.87 TQ	CABLS	1/16-3/16
	Oakland-Hayward-Berkeley PMSA, CA	H	16.22 FQ	20.12 MW	25.11 TQ	CABLS	1/16-3/16
	Riverside-San Bernardino-Ontario MSA, CA	H	14.07 FQ	17.30 MW	21.41 TQ	CABLS	1/16-3/16
	Sacramento–Roseville–Arden-Arcade MSA, CA	H	16.37 FQ	19.95 MW	23.35 TQ	CABLS	1/16-3/16
	San Diego-Carlsbad MSA, CA	H	14.79 FQ	17.77 MW	21.33 TQ	CABLS	1/16-3/16
	San Francisco-Redwood City-South San Francisco PMSA, CA	H	20.39 FQ	24.75 MW	29.12 TQ	CABLS	1/16-3/16
	Colorado	Y	32880 FQ	38270 MW	46080 TQ	USBLS	5/15
	Denver-Aurora-Lakewood MSA, CO	Y	35010 FQ	40860 MW	47510 TQ	USBLS	5/15
	Connecticut	Y		43779 MW		CTBLS	1/16-3/16
	Bridgeport-Stamford-Norwalk MSA, CT	Y	36660 FQ	44430 MW	51380 TQ	USBLS	5/15
	Hartford-West Hartford-East Hartford MSA, CT	Y	35370 FQ	41620 MW	49120 TQ	USBLS	5/15
	Delaware	Y	29760 FQ	36010 MW	43410 TQ	USBLS	5/15
	Wilmington PMSA, DE-MD-NJ	Y	30820 FQ	37290 MW	45140 TQ	USBLS	5/15
	District of Columbia	Y	40380 FQ	51250 MW	66850 TQ	USBLS	5/15
	Washington-Arlington-Alexandria PMSA, DC-VA-MD-WV	Y	36200 FQ	43540 MW	50620 TQ	USBLS	5/15
	Florida	H	12.90 AE	16.47 MW	18.80 AEX	FLBLS	7/16-9/16
	Fort Lauderdale-Pompano Beach-Deerfield Beach PMSA, FL	H	13.96 AE	17.81 MW	20.21 AEX	FLBLS	7/16-9/16
	Miami-Miami Beach-Kendall PMSA, FL	H	12.11 AE	16.54 MW	18.95 AEX	FLBLS	7/16-9/16
	Orlando-Kissimmee-Sanford MSA, FL	H	13.11 AE	15.67 MW	18.52 AEX	FLBLS	7/16-9/16
	Tampa-St. Petersburg-Clearwater MSA, FL	H	13.47 AE	16.45 MW	18.52 AEX	FLBLS	7/16-9/16
	Georgia	Y	27430 FQ	33150 MW	39430 TQ	USBLS	5/15
	Atlanta-Sandy Springs-Roswell MSA, GA	Y	29370 FQ	35400 MW	43120 TQ	USBLS	5/15
	Augusta-Richmond County MSA, GA-SC	Y	25880 FQ	29360 MW	34740 TQ	USBLS	5/15
	Hawaii	Y	31240 FQ	38090 MW	45380 TQ	USBLS	5/15
	Urban Honolulu MSA, HI	Y	31650 FQ	38480 MW	45790 TQ	USBLS	5/15
	Idaho	Y	27500 FQ	32860 MW	37640 TQ	USBLS	5/15
	Boise City MSA, ID	Y	29090 FQ	34070 MW	38300 TQ	USBLS	5/15
	Illinois	Y	29800 FQ	35850 MW	43670 TQ	USBLS	5/15
	Chicago-Naperville-Arlington Heights PMSA, IL	Y	31080 FQ	36920 MW	45300 TQ	USBLS	5/15
	Lake County-Kenosha County PMSA, IL-WI	Y	32770 FQ	39530 MW	47770 TQ	USBLS	5/15

AE	Average entry wage	**AWR**	Average wage range	**H**	Hourly	**LR**	Low end range	**MTC**	Median total compensation	**TCC**	Total cash compensation
AEX	Average experienced wage	**B**	Biweekly	**HI**	Highest wage paid	**M**	Monthly	**MW**	Median wage paid	**TQ**	Third quartile wage
ATC	Average total compensation	**D**	Daily	**HR**	High end range	**MCC**	Median cash compensation	**MWR**	Median wage range	**W**	Weekly
AW	Average wage paid	**FQ**	First quartile wage	**LO**	Lowest wage paid	**ME**	Median entry wage	**S**	See annotated source	**Y**	Yearly

Occupation/Type/Industry	Location	Per	Low	Mid	High	Source	Date
Billing and Posting Clerk	Indiana	Y	27650 FQ	32930 MW	38800 TQ	USBLS	5/15
	Gary PMSA, IN	Y	28160 FQ	33020 MW	38950 TQ	USBLS	5/15
	Indianapolis-Carmel-Anderson MSA, IN	Y	28930 FQ	34530 MW	40810 TQ	USBLS	5/15
	Iowa	Y	29130 FQ	34400 MW	39520 TQ	USBLS	5/15
	Des Moines-West Des Moines MSA, IA	Y	33650 FQ	38720 MW	45070 TQ	USBLS	5/15
	Kansas	Y	27730 FQ	33390 MW	38530 TQ	USBLS	5/15
	Wichita MSA, KS	Y	25940 FQ	30350 MW	36370 TQ	USBLS	5/15
	Kentucky	Y	26720 FQ	32160 MW	38120 TQ	USBLS	5/15
	Louisville-Jefferson County MSA, KY-IN	Y	28510 FQ	34140 MW	38910 TQ	USBLS	5/15
	Louisiana	Y	25890 FQ	30660 MW	37140 TQ	USBLS	5/15
	Baton Rouge MSA, LA	Y	28460 FQ	34240 MW	39910 TQ	USBLS	5/15
	New Orleans-Metairie MSA, LA	Y	27570 FQ	32370 MW	38090 TQ	USBLS	5/15
	Maine	Y	28520 FQ	33420 MW	38470 TQ	USBLS	5/15
	Portland-South Portland MSA, ME	Y	32140 FQ	36520 MW	41990 TQ	USBLS	5/15
	Maryland	Y	28399 AE	38757 MW	43936 AEX	MDBLS	4/16
	Baltimore-Columbia-Towson MSA, MD	Y	32690 FQ	37800 MW	45600 TQ	USBLS	5/15
	Salisbury MSA, MD-DE	Y	28330 FQ	33420 MW	38230 TQ	USBLS	5/15
	Massachusetts	Y	33510 FQ	39650 MW	47570 TQ	USBLS	5/15
	Boston-Cambridge-Newton NECTA, MA	Y	35170 FQ	42080 MW	48990 TQ	USBLS	5/15
	Worcester MSA, MA-CT	Y	31250 FQ	36950 MW	44190 TQ	USBLS	5/15
	Michigan	Y	28890 FQ	34410 MW	39670 TQ	USBLS	5/15
	Detroit-Dearborn-Livonia PMSA, MI	Y	30040 FQ	35650 MW	42010 TQ	USBLS	5/15
	Grand Rapids-Wyoming MSA, MI	Y	29750 FQ	35250 MW	41480 TQ	USBLS	5/15
	Minnesota	Y	32432 FQ	37134 MW	43839 TQ	MNBLS	1/16-3/16
	Minneapolis-St. Paul-Bloomington MSA, MN-WI	Y	33574 FQ	38287 MW	45568 TQ	MNBLS	1/16-3/16
	Mississippi	Y	24120 FQ	29250 MW	35940 TQ	USBLS	5/15
	Jackson MSA, MS	Y	26730 FQ	30350 MW	36540 TQ	USBLS	5/15
	Missouri	Y	27280 FQ	33080 MW	39250 TQ	USBLS	5/15
	Kansas City MSA, MO-KS	Y	31230 FQ	36020 MW	42000 TQ	USBLS	5/15
	St. Louis MSA, MO-IL	Y	30020 FQ	35550 MW	42500 TQ	USBLS	5/15
	Montana	Y	27560 FQ	32310 MW	37610 TQ	USBLS	5/15
	Billings MSA, MT	Y	31100 FQ	34960 MW	38600 TQ	USBLS	5/15
	Nebraska	Y	28275 FQ	33435 MW	38590 TQ	NEBLS	7/16-9/16
	Omaha-Council Bluffs MSA, NE-IA	Y	29495 FQ	34675 MW	39505 TQ	NEBLS	7/16-9/16
	Nevada	Y	30690 FQ	36210 MW	43380 TQ	USBLS	5/15
	Las Vegas-Henderson-Paradise MSA, NV	Y	31270 FQ	36570 MW	43680 TQ	USBLS	5/15
	New Hampshire	H	15.00 AE	18.18 MW	20.21 AEX	NHBLS	6/16
	Manchester NECTA, NH	H	14.78 AE	17.90 MW	19.90 AEX	NHBLS	6/16
	Nashua NECTA, NH-MA	Y	33090 FQ	36350 MW	39800 TQ	USBLS	5/15
	New Jersey	Y	33360 FQ	38400 MW	46240 TQ	USBLS	5/15
	Camden PMSA, NJ	Y	30920 FQ	35850 MW	41910 TQ	USBLS	5/15
	Newark PMSA, NJ-PA	Y	34450 FQ	39670 MW	48990 TQ	USBLS	5/15
	Trenton MSA, NJ	Y	33230 FQ	38740 MW	45490 TQ	USBLS	5/15
	New Mexico	Y	26100 FQ	31980 MW	38200 TQ	USBLS	5/15
	Albuquerque MSA, NM	Y	26880 FQ	33720 MW	39500 TQ	USBLS	5/15
	New York	Y	28440 AE	38750 MW	46820 AEX	NYBLS	1/16-3/16
	Buffalo-Cheektowaga-Niagara Falls MSA, NY	Y	29810 FQ	34790 MW	39680 TQ	USBLS	5/15
	Nassau County-Suffolk County PMSA, NY	Y	33740 FQ	40830 MW	48350 TQ	USBLS	5/15
	New York-Jersey City-White Plains PMSA, NY-NJ	Y	32660 FQ	39340 MW	48370 TQ	USBLS	5/15
	Rochester MSA, NY	Y	27390 FQ	32990 MW	39700 TQ	USBLS	5/15
	North Carolina	Y	28160 FQ	33820 MW	39430 TQ	USBLS	5/15
	Charlotte-Concord-Gastonia MSA, NC-SC	Y	31050 FQ	37040 MW	44920 TQ	USBLS	5/15
	Raleigh MSA, NC	Y	33140 FQ	37270 MW	43460 TQ	USBLS	5/15
	North Dakota	Y	28610 FQ	34300 MW	39360 TQ	USBLS	5/15
	Fargo MSA, ND-MN	Y	28020 FQ	34100 MW	40350 TQ	USBLS	5/15
	Ohio	Y	28790 FQ	34290 MW	39360 TQ	USBLS	5/15

AE	Average entry wage	AWR	Average wage range	H	Hourly	LR	Low end range	MTC	Median total compensation	TCC	Total cash compensation
AEX	Average experienced wage	B	Biweekly	HI	Highest wage paid	M	Monthly	MW	Median wage paid	TQ	Third quartile wage
ATC	Average total compensation	D	Daily	HR	High end range	MCC	Median cash compensation	MWR	Median wage range	W	Weekly
AW	Average wage paid	FQ	First quartile wage	LO	Lowest wage paid	ME	Median entry wage	S	See annotated source	Y	Yearly

Occupation/Type/Industry	Location	Per	Low	Mid	High	Source	Date
Billing and Posting Clerk	Cincinnati MSA, OH-KY-IN	Y	31360 FQ	36110 MW	42060 TQ	USBLS	5/15
	Cleveland-Elyria MSA, OH	Y	29880 FQ	35290 MW	40930 TQ	USBLS	5/15
	Columbus MSA, OH	Y	30840 FQ	35710 MW	41020 TQ	USBLS	5/15
	Oklahoma	Y	26280 FQ	31480 MW	38830 TQ	USBLS	5/15
	Oklahoma City MSA, OK	Y	27610 FQ	32510 MW	38560 TQ	USBLS	5/15
	Tulsa MSA, OK	Y	27670 FQ	33960 MW	42480 TQ	USBLS	5/15
	Oregon	H	15.59 FQ	17.87 MW	21.08 TQ	ORBLS	2016
	Portland-Vancouver-Hillsboro MSA, OR-WA	Y	32750 FQ	37670 MW	45270 TQ	USBLS	5/15
	Pennsylvania	Y	28740 FQ	34740 MW	41700 TQ	USBLS	5/15
	Allentown-Bethlehem-Easton MSA, PA-NJ	Y	30060 FQ	35250 MW	41240 TQ	USBLS	5/15
	Harrisburg-Carlisle MSA, PA	Y	30920 FQ	35250 MW	39400 TQ	USBLS	5/15
	Montgomery County-Bucks County-Chester County PMSA, PA	Y	30420 FQ	37120 MW	45880 TQ	USBLS	5/15
	Philadelphia PMSA, PA	Y	32440 FQ	38180 MW	46860 TQ	USBLS	5/15
	Pittsburgh MSA, PA	Y	28300 FQ	33840 MW	38900 TQ	USBLS	5/15
	Rhode Island	Y	32550 FQ	37870 MW	45350 TQ	USBLS	5/15
	Providence-Warwick MSA, RI-MA	Y	32100 FQ	37250 MW	44720 TQ	USBLS	5/15
	South Carolina	Y	26390 FQ	31000 MW	37240 TQ	USBLS	5/15
	Charleston-North Charleston MSA, SC	Y	28810 FQ	34170 MW	38840 TQ	USBLS	5/15
	Columbia MSA, SC	Y	26550 FQ	31520 MW	38740 TQ	USBLS	5/15
	Greenville-Anderson-Mauldin MSA, SC	Y	27000 FQ	31500 MW	37000 TQ	USBLS	5/15
	South Dakota	Y	24080 FQ	27880 MW	31760 TQ	USBLS	5/15
	Sioux Falls MSA, SD	Y	24990 FQ	28670 MW	33560 TQ	USBLS	5/15
	Tennessee	Y	26810 FQ	31490 MW	37470 TQ	USBLS	5/15
	Knoxville MSA, TN	Y	25150 FQ	28800 MW	33940 TQ	USBLS	5/15
	Memphis MSA, TN-MS-AR	Y	27250 FQ	32800 MW	38360 TQ	USBLS	5/15
	Nashville-Davidson–Murfreesboro–Franklin MSA, TN	Y	29780 FQ	34830 MW	39550 TQ	USBLS	5/15
	Texas	Y	28110 FQ	34190 MW	40210 TQ	USBLS	5/15
	Austin-Round Rock MSA, TX	Y	29950 FQ	36410 MW	44510 TQ	USBLS	5/15
	Dallas-Plano-Irving PMSA, TX	Y	31810 FQ	36280 MW	42640 TQ	USBLS	5/15
	Fort Worth-Arlington PMSA, TX	Y	28180 FQ	34000 MW	40460 TQ	USBLS	5/15
	Houston-The Woodlands-Sugar Land MSA, TX	Y	31610 FQ	37160 MW	45060 TQ	USBLS	5/15
	San Antonio-New Braunfels MSA, TX	Y	27470 FQ	32120 MW	37350 TQ	USBLS	5/15
	Utah	Y	27590 FQ	32450 MW	37700 TQ	USBLS	5/15
	Ogden-Clearfield MSA, UT	Y	28530 FQ	33050 MW	37910 TQ	USBLS	5/15
	Provo-Orem MSA, UT	Y	27460 FQ	31120 MW	37170 TQ	USBLS	5/15
	Salt Lake City MSA, UT	Y	28870 FQ	33700 MW	38180 TQ	USBLS	5/15
	Vermont	Y	29960 FQ	35080 MW	40050 TQ	USBLS	5/15
	Burlington-South Burlington MSA, VT	Y	31060 FQ	36060 MW	42280 TQ	USBLS	5/15
	Virginia	Y	29820 FQ	36030 MW	43950 TQ	USBLS	5/15
	Richmond MSA, VA	Y	31010 FQ	35950 MW	42300 TQ	USBLS	5/15
	Virginia Beach-Norfolk-Newport News MSA, VA-NC	Y	28010 FQ	32420 MW	38020 TQ	USBLS	5/15
	Washington	H	15.91 FQ	18.94 MW	22.93 TQ	WABLS	3/16
	Seattle-Bellevue-Everett PMSA, WA	H	17.08 FQ	20.72 MW	24.43 TQ	WABLS	3/16
	Tacoma-Lakewood PMSA, WA	H	15.36 FQ	18.10 MW	21.60 TQ	WABLS	3/16
	West Virginia	Y	23450 FQ	28450 MW	34810 TQ	USBLS	5/15
	Huntington-Ashland MSA, WV-KY-OH	Y	24560 FQ	28370 MW	33030 TQ	USBLS	5/15
	Wisconsin	Y	30080 FQ	35390 MW	40820 TQ	USBLS	5/15
	Madison MSA, WI	Y	34660 FQ	39920 MW	48140 TQ	USBLS	5/15
	Milwaukee-Waukesha-West Allis MSA, WI	Y	31830 FQ	36100 MW	41560 TQ	USBLS	5/15
	Wyoming	Y	29940 FQ	34920 MW	39570 TQ	USBLS	5/15
	Cheyenne MSA, WY	Y	28990 FQ	34230 MW	39160 TQ	USBLS	5/15
	Puerto Rico	Y	17310 FQ	19110 MW	23080 TQ	USBLS	5/15
	San Juan-Carolina-Caguas MSA, PR	Y	17420 FQ	19370 MW	23440 TQ	USBLS	5/15
	Virgin Islands	Y	20310 FQ	26720 MW	33840 TQ	USBLS	5/15

AE	Average entry wage	AWR	Average wage range	H	Hourly	LR	Low end range	MTC	Median total compensation	TCC	Total cash compensation
AEX	Average experienced wage	B	Biweekly	HI	Highest wage paid	M	Monthly	MW	Median wage paid	TQ	Third quartile wage
ATC	Average total compensation	D	Daily	HR	High end range	MCC	Median cash compensation	MWR	Median wage range	W	Weekly
AW	Average wage paid	FQ	First quartile wage	LO	Lowest wage paid	ME	Median entry wage	S	See annotated source	Y	Yearly

Occupation/Type/Industry	Location	Per	Low	Mid	High	Source	Date
Billing and Posting Clerk	Guam	Y	19550 FQ	24180 MW	31790 TQ	USBLS	5/15
Bio-Defense Manager							
County Government	Cochise County, AZ	Y			57849 HI	AZGOV	2017
County Government	Pima County, AZ	Y			79809 HI	AZGOV	2017
Biochemist and Biophysicist	Alabama	Y	55981 AE	92677 AW	111015 AEX	ALBLS	6/16
	Arizona	Y	44550 FQ	55770 MW	84440 TQ	USBLS	5/15
	Arkansas	Y	49040 FQ	63580 MW	78820 TQ	USBLS	5/15
	Little Rock-North Little Rock-Conway MSA, AR	Y	48790 FQ	67830 MW	84910 TQ	USBLS	5/15
	California	H	36.35 FQ	48.60 MW	63.92 TQ	CABLS	1/16-3/16
	Los Angeles-Long Beach-Glendale PMSA, CA	H	32.31 FQ	45.17 MW	67.01 TQ	CABLS	1/16-3/16
	Oakland-Hayward-Berkeley PMSA, CA	H	41.88 FQ	55.46 MW	72.68 TQ	CABLS	1/16-3/16
	Sacramento–Roseville–Arden-Arcade MSA, CA	H	22.60 FQ	27.77 MW	43.54 TQ	CABLS	1/16-3/16
	San Diego-Carlsbad MSA, CA	H	31.44 FQ	41.97 MW	54.47 TQ	CABLS	1/16-3/16
	San Francisco-Redwood City-South San Francisco PMSA, CA	H	40.63 FQ	52.96 MW	66.08 TQ	CABLS	1/16-3/16
	Colorado	Y	46910 FQ	62910 MW	94090 TQ	USBLS	5/15
	Denver-Aurora-Lakewood MSA, CO	Y	59020 FQ	81270 MW	119280 TQ	USBLS	5/15
	Connecticut	Y		113481 MW		CTBLS	1/16-3/16
	Delaware	Y	63340 FQ	82460 MW	109680 TQ	USBLS	5/15
	Wilmington PMSA, DE-MD-NJ	Y	63220 FQ	84140 MW	112110 TQ	USBLS	5/15
	District of Columbia	Y	46200 FQ	55910 MW	72960 TQ	USBLS	5/15
	Washington-Arlington-Alexandria PMSA, DC-VA-MD-WV	Y	63480 FQ	93290 MW	126020 TQ	USBLS	5/15
	Florida	H	23.05 AE	35.93 MW	54.66 AEX	FLBLS	7/16-9/16
	Tampa-St. Petersburg-Clearwater MSA, FL	H	23.73 AE	31.01 MW	37.71 AEX	FLBLS	7/16-9/16
	Georgia	Y	40330 FQ	48890 MW	63120 TQ	USBLS	5/15
	Atlanta-Sandy Springs-Roswell MSA, GA	Y	40520 FQ	48650 MW	62050 TQ	USBLS	5/15
	Idaho	Y	34360 FQ	38340 MW	59970 TQ	USBLS	5/15
	Illinois	Y	70810 FQ	84960 MW	120500 TQ	USBLS	5/15
	Chicago-Naperville-Arlington Heights PMSA, IL	Y	67350 FQ	73610 MW	79860 TQ	USBLS	5/15
	Indiana	Y	78140 FQ	94200 MW	127190 TQ	USBLS	5/15
	Indianapolis-Carmel-Anderson MSA, IN	Y	79570 FQ	94770 MW	130670 TQ	USBLS	5/15
	Iowa	Y	52760 FQ	68730 MW	81940 TQ	USBLS	5/15
	Kansas	Y	47490 FQ	59780 MW	94170 TQ	USBLS	5/15
	Kentucky	Y	52320 FQ	64930 MW	80070 TQ	USBLS	5/15
	Louisiana	Y	36700 FQ	44830 MW	54790 TQ	USBLS	5/15
	Maine	Y	53660 FQ	64660 MW	84290 TQ	USBLS	5/15
	Maryland	Y	49510 AE	83960 MW	101186 AEX	MDBLS	4/16
	Baltimore-Columbia-Towson MSA, MD	Y	62480 FQ	74840 MW	98770 TQ	USBLS	5/15
	Massachusetts	Y	60500 FQ	88540 MW	116450 TQ	USBLS	5/15
	Boston-Cambridge-Newton NECTA, MA	Y	71910 FQ	97660 MW	121760 TQ	USBLS	5/15
	Worcester MSA, MA-CT	Y	46110 FQ	60080 MW	97470 TQ	USBLS	5/15
	Michigan	Y	50770 FQ	72840 MW	109080 TQ	USBLS	5/15
	Minnesota	Y	54707 FQ	71320 MW	90452 TQ	MNBLS	1/16-3/16
	Minneapolis-St. Paul-Bloomington MSA, MN-WI	Y	52993 FQ	67056 MW	87146 TQ	MNBLS	1/16-3/16
	Missouri	Y	54950 FQ	74400 MW	98850 TQ	USBLS	5/15
	Kansas City MSA, MO-KS	Y	52750 FQ	74650 MW	101810 TQ	USBLS	5/15
	St. Louis MSA, MO-IL	Y	55470 FQ	73920 MW	97470 TQ	USBLS	5/15
	Nebraska	Y	43375 FQ	50610 MW	88750 TQ	NEBLS	7/16-9/16
	Omaha-Council Bluffs MSA, NE-IA	Y	49010 FQ	89910 MW	104905 TQ	NEBLS	7/16-9/16
	New Hampshire	H	23.94 AE	34.48 MW	49.06 AEX	NHBLS	6/16
	New Jersey	Y	77760 FQ	110790 MW	140920 TQ	USBLS	5/15
	Camden PMSA, NJ	Y	57970 FQ	91030 MW	111120 TQ	USBLS	5/15
	Newark PMSA, NJ-PA	Y	87310 FQ	114330 MW	141890 TQ	USBLS	5/15

AE Average entry wage	**AWR** Average wage range	**H** Hourly	**LR** Low end range	**MTC** Median total compensation	**TCC** Total cash compensation
AEX Average experienced wage	**B** Biweekly	**HI** Highest wage paid	**M** Monthly	**MW** Median wage paid	**TQ** Third quartile wage
ATC Average total compensation	**D** Daily	**HR** High end range	**MCC** Median cash compensation	**MWR** Median wage range	**W** Weekly
AW Average wage paid	**FQ** First quartile wage	**LO** Lowest wage paid	**ME** Median entry wage	**S** See annotated source	**Y** Yearly

Occupation/Type/Industry	Location	Per	Low	Mid	High	Source	Date
Biochemist and Biophysicist	Trenton MSA, NJ	Y	73730 FQ	119320 MW	155450 TQ	USBLS	5/15
	New York	Y	45590 AE	67720 MW	101080 AEX	NYBLS	1/16-3/16
	Buffalo-Cheektowaga-Niagara Falls MSA, NY	Y	46350 FQ	59160 MW	85650 TQ	USBLS	5/15
	Nassau County-Suffolk County PMSA, NY	Y	44710 FQ	52800 MW	77040 TQ	USBLS	5/15
	New York-Jersey City-White Plains PMSA, NY-NJ	Y	60650 FQ	76730 MW	115970 TQ	USBLS	5/15
	Rochester MSA, NY	Y	67930 FQ	87470 MW	143570 TQ	USBLS	5/15
	North Carolina	Y	64180 FQ	83520 MW	108820 TQ	USBLS	5/15
	Raleigh MSA, NC	Y	64660 FQ	80990 MW	102620 TQ	USBLS	5/15
	Ohio	Y	61160 FQ	93160 MW	129860 TQ	USBLS	5/15
	Cincinnati MSA, OH-KY-IN	Y	65090 FQ	80570 MW	100050 TQ	USBLS	5/15
	Oklahoma	Y	29950 FQ	43720 MW	62790 TQ	USBLS	5/15
	Oregon	H	26.16 FQ	32.21 MW	48.10 TQ	ORBLS	2016
	Portland-Vancouver-Hillsboro MSA, OR-WA	Y	52170 FQ	63890 MW	100510 TQ	USBLS	5/15
	Pennsylvania	Y	67180 FQ	86560 MW	110380 TQ	USBLS	5/15
	Allentown-Bethlehem-Easton MSA, PA-NJ	Y	50850 FQ	72210 MW	95740 TQ	USBLS	5/15
	Montgomery County-Bucks County-Chester County PMSA, PA	Y	67150 FQ	89680 MW	114710 TQ	USBLS	5/15
	Philadelphia PMSA, PA	Y	66540 FQ	80210 MW	93700 TQ	USBLS	5/15
	Pittsburgh MSA, PA	Y	68250 FQ	82280 MW	96730 TQ	USBLS	5/15
	Rhode Island	Y	38910 FQ	52810 MW	72670 TQ	USBLS	5/15
	Providence-Warwick MSA, RI-MA	Y	38910 FQ	52810 MW	72670 TQ	USBLS	5/15
	South Carolina	Y	38070 FQ	47260 MW	74140 TQ	USBLS	5/15
	Tennessee	Y	37470 FQ	55790 MW	78030 TQ	USBLS	5/15
	Nashville-Davidson–Murfreesboro–Franklin MSA, TN	Y	35950 FQ	47140 MW	61230 TQ	USBLS	5/15
	Texas	Y	53540 FQ	70660 MW	102940 TQ	USBLS	5/15
	Austin-Round Rock MSA, TX	Y	66190 FQ	76710 MW	114940 TQ	USBLS	5/15
	Dallas-Plano-Irving PMSA, TX	Y	43950 FQ	90400 MW	142930 TQ	USBLS	5/15
	Houston-The Woodlands-Sugar Land MSA, TX	Y	51720 FQ	59750 MW	75530 TQ	USBLS	5/15
	Virginia	Y	62370 FQ	80020 MW	111310 TQ	USBLS	5/15
	Richmond MSA, VA	Y	61300 FQ	71820 MW	82660 TQ	USBLS	5/15
	Washington	H	26.28 FQ	40.17 MW	54.56 TQ	WABLS	3/16
	Seattle-Bellevue-Everett PMSA, WA	H	25.81 FQ	40.39 MW	54.94 TQ	WABLS	3/16
	Wisconsin	Y	48170 FQ	61380 MW	80130 TQ	USBLS	5/15
	Madison MSA, WI	Y	46410 FQ	59370 MW	76940 TQ	USBLS	5/15
	Milwaukee-Waukesha-West Allis MSA, WI	Y	64890 FQ	79790 MW	102020 TQ	USBLS	5/15
	Puerto Rico	Y	44320 FQ	49170 MW	60310 TQ	USBLS	5/15
Biogerontologist	United States	Y		60000-100000 AWR		EXHC06	2016
Biological Science Teacher							
Postsecondary	Alabama	Y	48387 AE	87427 AW	106947 AEX	ALBLS	6/16
Postsecondary	Arizona	Y	56940 FQ	78480 MW	107210 TQ	USBLS	5/15
Postsecondary	Phoenix-Mesa-Scottsdale MSA, AZ	Y	59020 FQ	81470 MW	105420 TQ	USBLS	5/15
Postsecondary	Arkansas	Y	47790 FQ	58570 MW	73960 TQ	USBLS	5/15
Postsecondary	Little Rock-North Little Rock-Conway MSA, AR	Y	49250 FQ	60020 MW	75170 TQ	USBLS	5/15
Postsecondary	California	Y		108449 AW		CABLS	1/16-3/16
Postsecondary	Anaheim-Santa Ana-Irvine PMSA, CA	Y		108896 AW		CABLS	1/16-3/16
Postsecondary	Los Angeles-Long Beach-Glendale PMSA, CA	Y		112761 AW		CABLS	1/16-3/16
Postsecondary	Riverside-San Bernardino-Ontario MSA, CA	Y		102291 AW		CABLS	1/16-3/16
Postsecondary	Sacramento–Roseville–Arden-Arcade MSA, CA	Y		126761 AW		CABLS	1/16-3/16
Postsecondary	San Diego-Carlsbad MSA, CA	Y		120572 AW		CABLS	1/16-3/16
Postsecondary	Colorado	Y	38930 FQ	58350 MW	85760 TQ	USBLS	5/15

AE	Average entry wage	**AWR**	Average wage range	**H**	Hourly
AEX	Average experienced wage	**B**	Biweekly	**HI**	Highest wage paid
ATC	Average total compensation	**D**	Daily	**HR**	High end range
AW	Average wage paid	**FQ**	First quartile wage	**LO**	Lowest wage paid

LR	Low end range	**MTC**	Median total compensation	**TCC**	Total cash compensation
M	Monthly	**MW**	Median wage paid	**TQ**	Third quartile wage
MCC	Median cash compensation	**MWR**	Median wage range	**W**	Weekly
ME	Median entry wage	**S**	See annotated source	**Y**	Yearly

Biological Science Teacher

Occupation/Type/Industry	Location	Per	Low	Mid	High	Source	Date
Biological Science Teacher							
Postsecondary	Denver-Aurora-Lakewood MSA, CO	Y	33890 FQ	45550 MW	71940 TQ	USBLS	5/15
Postsecondary	Connecticut	Y		80571 MW		CTBLS	1/16-3/16
Postsecondary	Bridgeport-Stamford-Norwalk MSA, CT	Y	62350 FQ	76730 MW	101820 TQ	USBLS	5/15
Postsecondary	Hartford-West Hartford-East Hartford MSA, CT	Y	65750 FQ	88400 MW	124730 TQ	USBLS	5/15
Postsecondary	District of Columbia	Y	56600 FQ	76840 MW	107750 TQ	USBLS	5/15
Postsecondary	Washington-Arlington-Alexandria PMSA, DC-VA-MD-WV	Y	51580 FQ	70190 MW	105660 TQ	USBLS	5/15
Postsecondary	Florida	Y	48695 AE	79769 MW	106086 AEX	FLBLS	7/16-9/16
Postsecondary	Miami-Miami Beach-Kendall PMSA, FL	Y	52983 AE	81191 MW	93145 AEX	FLBLS	7/16-9/16
Postsecondary	Orlando-Kissimmee-Sanford MSA, FL	Y	52223 AE	84218 MW	99515 AEX	FLBLS	7/16-9/16
Postsecondary	Tampa-St. Petersburg-Clearwater MSA, FL	Y	50740 AE	79948 MW	100826 AEX	FLBLS	7/16-9/16
Postsecondary	Georgia	Y	48840 FQ	62770 MW	86880 TQ	USBLS	5/15
Postsecondary	Atlanta-Sandy Springs-Roswell MSA, GA	Y	51050 FQ	62020 MW	84990 TQ	USBLS	5/15
Postsecondary	Hawaii	Y	74620 FQ	115670 MW	149130 TQ	USBLS	5/15
Postsecondary	Urban Honolulu MSA, HI	Y	84220 FQ	122890 MW	152580 TQ	USBLS	5/15
Postsecondary	Idaho	Y	44740 FQ	58440 MW	77860 TQ	USBLS	5/15
Postsecondary	Boise City MSA, ID	Y	42070 FQ	47800 MW	65070 TQ	USBLS	5/15
Postsecondary	Illinois	Y	58350 FQ	78510 MW	109290 TQ	USBLS	5/15
Postsecondary	Chicago-Naperville-Arlington Heights PMSA, IL	Y	58340 FQ	77200 MW	107880 TQ	USBLS	5/15
Postsecondary	Lake County-Kenosha County PMSA, IL-WI	Y	53170 FQ	61800 MW	86150 TQ	USBLS	5/15
Postsecondary	Indiana	Y	56800 FQ	78750 MW	113350 TQ	USBLS	5/15
Postsecondary	Indianapolis-Carmel-Anderson MSA, IN	Y	57020 FQ	77660 MW	109050 TQ	USBLS	5/15
Postsecondary	Iowa	Y	55680 FQ	73940 MW	105200 TQ	USBLS	5/15
Postsecondary	Des Moines-West Des Moines MSA, IA	Y	43200 FQ	56990 MW	70420 TQ	USBLS	5/15
Postsecondary	Kansas	Y	43510 FQ	55020 MW	69490 TQ	USBLS	5/15
Postsecondary	Kentucky	Y	50690 FQ	62430 MW	82040 TQ	USBLS	5/15
Postsecondary	Louisville-Jefferson County MSA, KY-IN	Y	47740 FQ	61580 MW	87810 TQ	USBLS	5/15
Postsecondary	Louisiana	Y	37200 FQ	51610 MW	73570 TQ	USBLS	5/15
Postsecondary	New Orleans-Metairie MSA, LA	Y	35190 FQ	46840 MW	76500 TQ	USBLS	5/15
Postsecondary	Maine	Y	55960 FQ	74320 MW	97670 TQ	USBLS	5/15
Postsecondary	Portland-South Portland MSA, ME	Y	54290 FQ	74900 MW	97370 TQ	USBLS	5/15
Postsecondary	Maryland	Y	48262 AE	89788 MW	110551 AEX	MDBLS	4/16
Postsecondary	Baltimore-Columbia-Towson MSA, MD	Y	58730 FQ	75440 MW	101330 TQ	USBLS	5/15
Postsecondary	Massachusetts	Y	61010 FQ	85980 MW	128520 TQ	USBLS	5/15
Postsecondary	Boston-Cambridge-Newton NECTA, MA	Y	59990 FQ	86140 MW	135100 TQ	USBLS	5/15
Postsecondary	Worcester MSA, MA-CT	Y	59890 FQ	81500 MW	123910 TQ	USBLS	5/15
Postsecondary	Michigan	Y	51470 FQ	77720 MW	108590 TQ	USBLS	5/15
Postsecondary	Detroit-Dearborn-Livonia PMSA, MI	Y	49760 FQ	66220 MW	91930 TQ	USBLS	5/15
Postsecondary	Grand Rapids-Wyoming MSA, MI	Y	43130 FQ	66480 MW	78560 TQ	USBLS	5/15
Postsecondary	Minnesota	Y	51804 FQ	66441 MW	80896 TQ	MNBLS	1/16-3/16
Postsecondary	Minneapolis-St. Paul-Bloomington MSA, MN-WI	Y	48487 FQ	63427 MW	77983 TQ	MNBLS	1/16-3/16
Postsecondary	Mississippi	Y	48870 FQ	61860 MW	77630 TQ	USBLS	5/15
Postsecondary	Jackson MSA, MS	Y	35540 FQ	45620 MW	62260 TQ	USBLS	5/15
Postsecondary	Missouri	Y	57650 FQ	80800 MW	114330 TQ	USBLS	5/15
Postsecondary	Kansas City MSA, MO-KS	Y	61420 FQ	81890 MW	113510 TQ	USBLS	5/15
Postsecondary	St. Louis MSA, MO-IL	Y	51480 FQ	74000 MW	106720 TQ	USBLS	5/15
Postsecondary	Montana	Y	40620 FQ	54120 MW	68360 TQ	USBLS	5/15
Postsecondary	Nebraska	Y	58040 FQ	78750 MW	103590 TQ	NEBLS	7/16-9/16
Postsecondary	Omaha-Council Bluffs MSA, NE-IA	Y	61100 FQ	85770 MW	107115 TQ	NEBLS	7/16-9/16
Postsecondary	Nevada	Y	38480 FQ	66620 MW	93840 TQ	USBLS	5/15

AE	Average entry wage	AWR	Average wage range	H	Hourly	LR	Low end range	MTC	Median total compensation	TCC	Total cash compensation
AEX	Average experienced wage	B	Biweekly	HI	Highest wage paid	M	Monthly	MW	Median wage paid	TQ	Third quartile wage
ATC	Average total compensation	D	Daily	HR	High end range	MCC	Median cash compensation	MWR	Median wage range	W	Weekly
AW	Average wage paid	FQ	First quartile wage	LO	Lowest wage paid	ME	Median entry wage	S	See annotated source	Y	Yearly

Occupation/Type/Industry	Location	Per	Low	Mid	High	Source	Date
Biological Science Teacher							
Postsecondary	New Hampshire	Y	59716 AE	99831 MW	134326 AEX	NHBLS	6/16
Postsecondary	New Jersey	Y	62140 FQ	84850 MW	117940 TQ	USBLS	5/15
Postsecondary	Camden PMSA, NJ	Y	57410 FQ	79310 MW	111890 TQ	USBLS	5/15
Postsecondary	Newark PMSA, NJ-PA	Y	69630 FQ	94210 MW	120590 TQ	USBLS	5/15
Postsecondary	New Mexico	Y	59210 FQ	74950 MW	94820 TQ	USBLS	5/15
Postsecondary	New York	Y	52550 AE	88300 MW	125930 AEX	NYBLS	1/16-3/16
Postsecondary	Buffalo-Cheektowaga-Niagara Falls MSA, NY	Y	51150 FQ	76360 MW	94110 TQ	USBLS	5/15
Postsecondary	Nassau County-Suffolk County PMSA, NY	Y	55410 FQ	75560 MW	112750 TQ	USBLS	5/15
Postsecondary	New York-Jersey City-White Plains PMSA, NY-NJ	Y	66850 FQ	100560 MW	144850 TQ	USBLS	5/15
Postsecondary	Rochester MSA, NY	Y	64590 FQ	81790 MW	102180 TQ	USBLS	5/15
Postsecondary	North Carolina	Y	53170 FQ	67890 MW	96860 TQ	USBLS	5/15
Postsecondary	Charlotte-Concord-Gastonia MSA, NC-SC	Y	51320 FQ	59230 MW	73150 TQ	USBLS	5/15
Postsecondary	Raleigh MSA, NC	Y	68370 FQ	93240 MW	119940 TQ	USBLS	5/15
Postsecondary	North Dakota	Y	76920 FQ	99960 MW	128390 TQ	USBLS	5/15
Postsecondary	Fargo MSA, ND-MN	Y	72390 FQ	90150 MW	110470 TQ	USBLS	5/15
Postsecondary	Ohio	Y	52940 FQ	77300 MW	105530 TQ	USBLS	5/15
Postsecondary	Cincinnati MSA, OH-KY-IN	Y	50240 FQ	70890 MW	96660 TQ	USBLS	5/15
Postsecondary	Cleveland-Elyria MSA, OH	Y	52170 FQ	73150 MW	101150 TQ	USBLS	5/15
Postsecondary	Columbus MSA, OH	Y	71670 FQ	102240 MW	115590 TQ	USBLS	5/15
Postsecondary	Oklahoma	Y	44860 FQ	60970 MW	88750 TQ	USBLS	5/15
Postsecondary	Oklahoma City MSA, OK	Y	41350 FQ	58460 MW	90350 TQ	USBLS	5/15
Postsecondary	Oregon	Y	66622 FQ	83500 MW	111802 TQ	ORBLS	2016
Postsecondary	Portland-Vancouver-Hillsboro MSA, OR-WA	Y	58370 FQ	76530 MW	98840 TQ	USBLS	5/15
Postsecondary	Pennsylvania	Y	57700 FQ	75940 MW	99450 TQ	USBLS	5/15
Postsecondary	Allentown-Bethlehem-Easton MSA, PA-NJ	Y	63260 FQ	92190 MW	122490 TQ	USBLS	5/15
Postsecondary	Harrisburg-Carlisle MSA, PA	Y	57580 FQ	75780 MW	98160 TQ	USBLS	5/15
Postsecondary	Montgomery County-Bucks County-Chester County PMSA, PA	Y	50270 FQ	67580 MW	92370 TQ	USBLS	5/15
Postsecondary	Philadelphia PMSA, PA	Y	62420 FQ	82880 MW	109810 TQ	USBLS	5/15
Postsecondary	Pittsburgh MSA, PA	Y	54430 FQ	67840 MW	84800 TQ	USBLS	5/15
Postsecondary	Rhode Island	Y	56500 FQ	71290 MW	96050 TQ	USBLS	5/15
Postsecondary	Providence-Warwick MSA, RI-MA	Y	55690 FQ	68900 MW	91260 TQ	USBLS	5/15
Postsecondary	South Carolina	Y	52620 FQ	65940 MW	82030 TQ	USBLS	5/15
Postsecondary	Columbia MSA, SC	Y	52460 FQ	71660 MW	94950 TQ	USBLS	5/15
Postsecondary	Greenville-Anderson-Mauldin MSA, SC	Y	52560 FQ	66490 MW	83780 TQ	USBLS	5/15
Postsecondary	South Dakota	Y	62590 FQ	79290 MW	97660 TQ	USBLS	5/15
Postsecondary	Tennessee	Y	40300 FQ	56140 MW	74990 TQ	USBLS	5/15
Postsecondary	Knoxville MSA, TN	Y	44140 FQ	64460 MW	95010 TQ	USBLS	5/15
Postsecondary	Memphis MSA, TN-MS-AR	Y	48140 FQ	61670 MW	83680 TQ	USBLS	5/15
Postsecondary	Nashville-Davidson–Murfreesboro–Franklin MSA, TN	Y	41350 FQ	51350 MW	67340 TQ	USBLS	5/15
Postsecondary	Texas	Y	51460 FQ	72770 MW	102530 TQ	USBLS	5/15
Postsecondary	Austin-Round Rock MSA, TX	Y	54940 FQ	75420 MW	99310 TQ	USBLS	5/15
Postsecondary	Dallas-Plano-Irving PMSA, TX	Y	56660 FQ	77490 MW	105880 TQ	USBLS	5/15
Postsecondary	Fort Worth-Arlington PMSA, TX	Y	42580 FQ	56450 MW	72200 TQ	USBLS	5/15
Postsecondary	Houston-The Woodlands-Sugar Land MSA, TX	Y	59050 FQ	79550 MW	128830 TQ	USBLS	5/15
Postsecondary	San Antonio-New Braunfels MSA, TX	Y	23630 FQ	72910 MW	101820 TQ	USBLS	5/15
Postsecondary	Utah	Y	62590 FQ	86950 MW	123820 TQ	USBLS	5/15
Postsecondary	Provo-Orem MSA, UT	Y	65360 FQ	85710 MW	100560 TQ	USBLS	5/15
Postsecondary	Salt Lake City MSA, UT	Y	62500 FQ	91830 MW	164910 TQ	USBLS	5/15
Postsecondary	Vermont	Y	36750 FQ	43830 MW	60480 TQ	USBLS	5/15
Postsecondary	Burlington-South Burlington MSA, VT.	Y	36850 FQ	43170 MW	50850 TQ	USBLS	5/15
Postsecondary	Virginia	Y	43450 FQ	59880 MW	87190 TQ	USBLS	5/15
Postsecondary	Richmond MSA, VA	Y	34190 FQ	42870 MW	59930 TQ	USBLS	5/15
Postsecondary	Virginia Beach-Norfolk-Newport News MSA, VA-NC	Y	44090 FQ	60810 MW	87190 TQ	USBLS	5/15
Postsecondary	Washington	Y		79648 AW		WABLS	3/16

AE	Average entry wage	AWR	Average wage range	H	Hourly	LR	Low end range	MTC	Median total compensation	TCC	Total cash compensation
AEX	Average experienced wage	B	Biweekly	HI	Highest wage paid	M	Monthly	MW	Median wage paid	TQ	Third quartile Teage
ATC	Average total compensation	D	Daily	HR	High end range	MCC	Median cash compensation	MWR	Median wage range	W	Weekly
AW	Average wage paid	FQ	First quartile wage	LO	Lowest wage paid	ME	Median entry wage	S	See annotated source	Y	Yearly

Biological Science Teacher

Occupation/Type/Industry	Location	Per	Low	Mid	High	Source	Date
Biological Science Teacher							
Postsecondary	Seattle-Bellevue-Everett PMSA, WA	Y		93830 AW		WABLS	3/16
Postsecondary	Tacoma-Lakewood PMSA, WA	Y		62706 AW		WABLS	3/16
Postsecondary	West Virginia	Y	49430 FQ	60310 MW	75130 TQ	USBLS	5/15
Postsecondary	Wisconsin	Y	53310 FQ	66470 MW	92670 TQ	USBLS	5/15
Postsecondary	Milwaukee-Waukesha-West Allis MSA, WI	Y	55730 FQ	70930 MW	90540 TQ	USBLS	5/15
Postsecondary	Wyoming	Y	62060 FQ	73350 MW	88680 TQ	USBLS	5/15
Postsecondary	Puerto Rico	Y	49880 FQ	64720 MW	81120 TQ	USBLS	5/15
Postsecondary	San Juan-Carolina-Caguas MSA, PR	Y	57030 FQ	72410 MW	87580 TQ	USBLS	5/15
Biological Technician	Alabama	Y	25636 AE	37919 AW	44065 AEX	ALBLS	6/16
	Birmingham-Hoover MSA, AL	Y	24647 AE	38479 AW	45401 AEX	ALBLS	6/16
	Alaska	Y	34890 FQ	38890 MW	46750 TQ	USBLS	5/15
	Anchorage MSA, AK	Y	31440 FQ	36390 MW	43210 TQ	USBLS	5/15
	Arizona	Y	28760 FQ	33660 MW	43820 TQ	USBLS	5/15
	Phoenix-Mesa-Scottsdale MSA, AZ	Y	30490 FQ	37240 MW	54300 TQ	USBLS	5/15
	Tucson MSA, AZ	Y	24890 FQ	28440 MW	31950 TQ	USBLS	5/15
	Arkansas	Y	31730 FQ	40790 MW	50720 TQ	USBLS	5/15
	Little Rock-North Little Rock-Conway MSA, AR	Y	30580 FQ	40860 MW	50250 TQ	USBLS	5/15
	California	H	18.41 FQ	24.18 MW	33.79 TQ	CABLS	1/16-3/16
	Anaheim-Santa Ana-Irvine PMSA, CA	H	17.18 FQ	22.12 MW	30.59 TQ	CABLS	1/16-3/16
	Los Angeles-Long Beach-Glendale PMSA, CA	H	17.33 FQ	23.37 MW	30.77 TQ	CABLS	1/16-3/16
	Oakland-Hayward-Berkeley PMSA, CA	H	20.48 FQ	26.86 MW	36.22 TQ	CABLS	1/16-3/16
	Riverside-San Bernardino-Ontario MSA, CA	H	17.36 FQ	22.93 MW	31.56 TQ	CABLS	1/16-3/16
	Sacramento–Roseville–Arden-Arcade MSA, CA	H	15.70 FQ	18.54 MW	23.22 TQ	CABLS	1/16-3/16
	San Diego-Carlsbad MSA, CA	H	18.16 FQ	22.84 MW	30.59 TQ	CABLS	1/16-3/16
	San Francisco-Redwood City-South San Francisco PMSA, CA	H	27.14 FQ	35.74 MW	42.92 TQ	CABLS	1/16-3/16
	San Rafael PMSA, CA	Y	42940 FQ	56540 MW	71790 TQ	USBLS	5/15
	Colorado	Y	34260 FQ	42700 MW	56020 TQ	USBLS	5/15
	Denver-Aurora-Lakewood MSA, CO	Y	34750 FQ	44340 MW	57750 TQ	USBLS	5/15
	Connecticut	Y		51080 MW		CTBLS	1/16-3/16
	Bridgeport-Stamford-Norwalk MSA, CT	Y	41520 FQ	49150 MW	66560 TQ	USBLS	5/15
	Hartford-West Hartford-East Hartford MSA, CT	Y	37530 FQ	43590 MW	48980 TQ	USBLS	5/15
	Delaware	Y	30740 FQ	43300 MW	58100 TQ	USBLS	5/15
	Wilmington PMSA, DE-MD-NJ	Y	30330 FQ	43040 MW	57600 TQ	USBLS	5/15
	District of Columbia	Y	35870 FQ	45930 MW	56610 TQ	USBLS	5/15
	Washington-Arlington-Alexandria PMSA, DC-VA-MD-WV	Y	39370 FQ	49260 MW	62000 TQ	USBLS	5/15
	Florida	H	12.76 AE	18.28 MW	22.19 AEX	FLBLS	7/16-9/16
	Fort Lauderdale-Pompano Beach-Deerfield Beach PMSA, FL	H	17.09 AE	25.00 MW	26.42 AEX	FLBLS	7/16-9/16
	Miami-Miami Beach-Kendall PMSA, FL	H	15.70 AE	20.68 MW	24.57 AEX	FLBLS	7/16-9/16
	Orlando-Kissimmee-Sanford MSA, FL	H	13.35 AE	19.58 MW	22.12 AEX	FLBLS	7/16-9/16
	Tampa-St. Petersburg-Clearwater MSA, FL	H	12.48 AE	16.98 MW	20.01 AEX	FLBLS	7/16-9/16
	Georgia	Y	35760 FQ	47820 MW	59370 TQ	USBLS	5/15
	Atlanta-Sandy Springs-Roswell MSA, GA	Y	42730 FQ	53650 MW	65730 TQ	USBLS	5/15
	Hawaii	Y	25950 FQ	32020 MW	38770 TQ	USBLS	5/15
	Urban Honolulu MSA, HI	Y	25950 FQ	32870 MW	40210 TQ	USBLS	5/15
	Idaho	Y	25900 FQ	31930 MW	36810 TQ	USBLS	5/15
	Boise City MSA, ID	Y	25910 FQ.	31940 MW	36510 TQ	USBLS	5/15

AE	Average entry wage	AWR	Average wage range	H	Hourly
AEX	Average experienced wage	B	Biweekly	HI	Highest wage paid
ATC	Average total compensation	D	Daily	HR	High end range
AW	Average wage paid	FQ	First quartile wage	LO	Lowest wage paid

LR	Low end range	MTC	Median total compensation
M	Monthly	MW	Median wage paid
MCC	Median cash compensation	MWR	Median wage range
ME	Median entry wage	S	See annotated source

TCC	Total cash compensation
TQ	Third quartile wage
W	Weekly
Y	Yearly

Occupation/Type/Industry	Location	Per	Low	Mid	High	Source	Date
Biological Technician	Illinois	Y	34850 FQ	41900 MW	52270 TQ	USBLS	5/15
	Chicago-Naperville-Arlington Heights PMSA, IL	Y	34960 FQ	40210 MW	48060 TQ	USBLS	5/15
	Indiana	Y	34830 FQ	43560 MW	52520 TQ	USBLS	5/15
	Indianapolis-Carmel-Anderson MSA, IN	Y	35430 FQ	43960 MW	52580 TQ	USBLS	5/15
	Iowa	Y	32450 FQ	38320 MW	48010 TQ	USBLS	5/15
	Des Moines-West Des Moines MSA, IA	Y	28560 FQ	32870 MW	37390 TQ	USBLS	5/15
	Kansas	Y	34240 FQ	40190 MW	49900 TQ	USBLS	5/15
	Kentucky	Y	20170 FQ	24780 MW	36200 TQ	USBLS	5/15
	Louisville-Jefferson County MSA, KY-IN	Y	28900 FQ	38230 MW	45160 TQ	USBLS	5/15
	Louisiana	Y	28910 FQ	37820 MW	51460 TQ	USBLS	5/15
	Baton Rouge MSA, LA	Y	24390 FQ	42740 MW	58150 TQ	USBLS	5/15
	New Orleans-Metairie MSA, LA	Y	25460 FQ	33250 MW	43520 TQ	USBLS	5/15
	Maine	Y	32850 FQ	40960 MW	50090 TQ	USBLS	5/15
	Portland-South Portland MSA, ME	Y	35740 FQ	45380 MW	55660 TQ	USBLS	5/15
	Maryland	Y	32781 AE	48856 MW	56893 AEX	MDBLS	4/16
	Massachusetts	Y	38070 FQ	47010 MW	58900 TQ	USBLS	5/15
	Boston-Cambridge-Newton NECTA, MA	Y	37940 FQ	47520 MW	59640 TQ	USBLS	5/15
	Worcester MSA, MA-CT	Y	37080 FQ	43880 MW	51720 TQ	USBLS	5/15
	Michigan	Y	28540 FQ	32970 MW	39580 TQ	USBLS	5/15
	Grand Rapids-Wyoming MSA, MI	Y	27390 FQ	30170 MW	35280 TQ	USBLS	5/15
	Minnesota	Y	35141 FQ	49122 MW	62519 TQ	MNBLS	1/16-3/16
	Minneapolis-St. Paul-Bloomington MSA, MN-WI	Y	32973 FQ	41562 MW	53759 TQ	MNBLS	1/16-3/16
	Mississippi	Y	23310 FQ	33030 MW	46280 TQ	USBLS	5/15
	Missouri	Y	30370 FQ	40360 MW	49210 TQ	USBLS	5/15
	Kansas City MSA, MO-KS	Y	34740 FQ	41610 MW	49330 TQ	USBLS	5/15
	St. Louis MSA, MO-IL	Y	31470 FQ	40790 MW	51650 TQ	USBLS	5/15
	Montana	Y	30460 FQ	34580 MW	43510 TQ	USBLS	5/15
	Billings MSA, MT	Y	30290 FQ	35260 MW	43530 TQ	USBLS	5/15
	Nebraska	Y	31930 FQ	38215 MW	47480 TQ	NEBLS	7/16-9/16
	Omaha-Council Bluffs MSA, NE-IA	Y	36850 FQ	45480 MW	56850 TQ	NEBLS	7/16-9/16
	Nevada	Y	33000 FQ	41870 MW	48340 TQ	USBLS	5/15
	Las Vegas-Henderson-Paradise MSA, NV	Y	35600 FQ	41190 MW	52310 TQ	USBLS	5/15
	New Hampshire	H	15.54 AE	21.35 MW	25.68 AEX	NHBLS	6/16
	Manchester NECTA, NH	H	15.14 AE	19.48 MW	24.78 AEX	NHBLS	6/16
	New Jersey	Y	34680 FQ	43180 MW	55210 TQ	USBLS	5/15
	Camden PMSA, NJ	Y	31050 FQ	38280 MW	52260 TQ	USBLS	5/15
	Newark PMSA, NJ-PA	Y	38270 FQ	48140 MW	59590 TQ	USBLS	5/15
	Trenton MSA, NJ	Y	34600 FQ	42530 MW	50180 TQ	USBLS	5/15
	New Mexico	Y	30170 FQ	39180 MW	46440 TQ	USBLS	5/15
	Albuquerque MSA, NM	Y	33790 FQ	42190 MW	48140 TQ	USBLS	5/15
	New York	Y	30140 AE	39900 MW	48890 AEX	NYBLS	1/16-3/16
	Buffalo-Cheektowaga-Niagara Falls MSA, NY	Y	32650 FQ	37160 MW	47380 TQ	USBLS	5/15
	Nassau County-Suffolk County PMSA, NY	Y	31920 FQ	39180 MW	54890 TQ	USBLS	5/15
	New York-Jersey City-White Plains PMSA, NY-NJ	Y	33620 FQ	42110 MW	54510 TQ	USBLS	5/15
	Rochester MSA, NY	Y	28950 FQ	36150 MW	44840 TQ	USBLS	5/15
	North Carolina	Y	32880 FQ	40040 MW	49160 TQ	USBLS	5/15
	Charlotte-Concord-Gastonia MSA, NC-SC	Y	17570 FQ	28550 MW	39750 TQ	USBLS	5/15
	Fargo MSA, ND-MN	Y	31930 FQ	44840 MW	54060 TQ	USBLS	5/15
	Ohio	Y	32320 FQ	38920 MW	49020 TQ	USBLS	5/15
	Cincinnati MSA, OH-KY-IN	Y	35390 FQ	43280 MW	55240 TQ	USBLS	5/15
	Cleveland-Elyria MSA, OH	Y	36530 FQ	43020 MW	48640 TQ	USBLS	5/15
	Columbus MSA, OH	Y	28990 FQ	35660 MW	44980 TQ	USBLS	5/15
	Oklahoma	Y	27280 FQ	38410 MW	46200 TQ	USBLS	5/15
	Oklahoma City MSA, OK	Y	26690 FQ	40390 MW	46990 TQ	USBLS	5/15
	Oregon	H	15.57 FQ	18.10 MW	21.99 TQ	ORBLS	2016
	Portland-Vancouver-Hillsboro MSA, OR-WA	Y	33260 FQ	39220 MW	48030 TQ	USBLS	5/15

AE	Average entry wage	AWR	Average wage range	
AEX	Average experianced wage	B	Biweekly	
ATC	Average total compensation	D	Daily	
AW	Average wage paid	FQ	First quartile wage	

H	Hourly	LR	Low end range
HI	Highest wage paid	M	Monthly
HR	High end range	MCC	Median cash compensation
LO	Lowest wage paid	ME	Median entry wage

MTC	Median total compensation	TCC	Total cash compensation
MW	Median wage paid	TQ	Third quartile wage
MWR	Median wage range	W	Weekly
S	See annotated source	Y	Yearly

Occupation/Type/Industry	Location	Per	Low	Mid	High	Source	Date
Biological Technician	Pennsylvania	Y	34100 FQ	43030 MW	55660 TQ	USBLS	5/15
	Allentown-Bethlehem-Easton MSA, PA-NJ	Y	31280 FQ	36810 MW	46770 TQ	USBLS	5/15
	Harrisburg-Carlisle MSA, PA	Y	29080 FQ	34770 MW	43900 TQ	USBLS	5/15
	Montgomery County-Bucks County-Chester County PMSA, PA	Y	34790 FQ	43630 MW	57990 TQ	USBLS	5/15
	Philadelphia PMSA, PA	Y	35670 FQ	47230 MW	57730 TQ	USBLS	5/15
	Pittsburgh MSA, PA	Y	32550 FQ	39640 MW	49730 TQ	USBLS	5/15
	Rhode Island	Y	34920 FQ	40880 MW	47570 TQ	USBLS	5/15
	Providence-Warwick MSA, RI-MA	Y	35920 FQ	42380 MW	48650 TQ	USBLS	5/15
	South Carolina	Y	28540 FQ	39020 MW	48800 TQ	USBLS	5/15
	Charleston-North Charleston MSA, SC	Y	25430 FQ	33530 MW	48390 TQ	USBLS	5/15
	Columbia MSA, SC	Y	18920 FQ	28200 MW	40060 TQ	USBLS	5/15
	Greenville-Anderson-Mauldin MSA, SC	Y	35400 FQ	41640 MW	46840 TQ	USBLS	5/15
	South Dakota	Y	27990 FQ	31950 MW	38870 TQ	USBLS	5/15
	Tennessee	Y	28250 FQ	36480 MW	48310 TQ	USBLS	5/15
	Knoxville MSA, TN	Y	26670 FQ	35980 MW	45380 TQ	USBLS	5/15
	Memphis MSA, TN-MS-AR	Y	31720 FQ	36600 MW	46530 TQ	USBLS	5/15
	Nashville-Davidson–Murfreesboro–Franklin MSA, TN	Y	28730 FQ	33010 MW	37990 TQ	USBLS	5/15
	Texas	Y	28990 FQ	39070 MW	50060 TQ	USBLS	5/15
	Austin-Round Rock MSA, TX	Y	35540 FQ	43620 MW	58800 TQ	USBLS	5/15
	Dallas-Plano-Irving PMSA, TX	Y	28020 FQ	39660 MW	55300 TQ	USBLS	5/15
	Fort Worth-Arlington PMSA, TX	Y	28480 FQ	37230 MW	51000 TQ	USBLS	5/15
	Houston-The Woodlands-Sugar Land MSA, TX	Y	30390 FQ	40430 MW	49420 TQ	USBLS	5/15
	San Antonio-New Braunfels MSA, TX	Y	33350 FQ	44200 MW	56550 TQ	USBLS	5/15
	Utah	Y	32100 FQ	41220 MW	57230 TQ	USBLS	5/15
	Provo-Orem MSA, UT	Y	31940 FQ	35600 MW	42580 TQ	USBLS	5/15
	Salt Lake City MSA, UT	Y	37990 FQ	51200 MW	69390 TQ	USBLS	5/15
	Vermont	Y	33040 FQ	40710 MW	48370 TQ	USBLS	5/15
	Burlington-South Burlington MSA, VT	Y	35410 FQ	43320 MW	50580 TQ	USBLS	5/15
	Virginia	Y	33660 FQ	40090 MW	50260 TQ	USBLS	5/15
	Richmond MSA, VA	Y	32790 FQ	36610 MW	42700 TQ	USBLS	5/15
	Virginia Beach-Norfolk-Newport News MSA, VA-NC	Y	35570 FQ	44530 MW	54300 TQ	USBLS	5/15
	Washington	H	16.19 FQ	19.14 MW	23.75 TQ	WABLS	3/16
	Seattle-Bellevue-Everett PMSA, WA	H	16.96 FQ	20.25 MW	24.43 TQ	WABLS	3/16
	Tacoma-Lakewood PMSA, WA	H	18.53 FQ	22.16 MW	33.11 TQ	WABLS	3/16
	West Virginia	Y	27940 FQ	34090 MW	47350 TQ	USBLS	5/15
	Wisconsin	Y	28560 FQ	35260 MW	44960 TQ	USBLS	5/15
	Madison MSA, WI	Y	29590 FQ	39180 MW	49660 TQ	USBLS	5/15
	Milwaukee-Waukesha-West Allis MSA, WI	Y	27790 FQ	32770 MW	39010 TQ	USBLS	5/15
	Wyoming	Y	31940 FQ	35600 MW	41580 TQ	USBLS	5/15
	Puerto Rico	Y	25430 FQ	35590 MW	43240 TQ	USBLS	5/15
	San Juan-Carolina-Caguas MSA, PR	Y	26420 FQ	36910 MW	44170 TQ	USBLS	5/15
Biologist							
Environmental Services, Municipal Government	San Jose, CA	Y		72983 AW		CACIT	6/28/16
Biomedical Coding Clerk							
Municipal Government	Detroit, MI	M	2292 LO		2800 HI	DETGOV	2016
Biomedical Engineer	Alabama	Y	70201 AE	89262 AW	98793 AEX	ALBLS	6/16
	Birmingham-Hoover MSA, AL	Y	65308 AE	86663 AW	97335 AEX	ALBLS	6/16
	Arizona	Y	70830 FQ	88980 MW	113730 TQ	USBLS	5/15
	Phoenix-Mesa-Scottsdale MSA, AZ	Y	73620 FQ	92660 MW	115280 TQ	USBLS	5/15
	Tucson MSA, AZ	Y	83710 FQ	105360 MW	135340 TQ	USBLS	5/15
	California	H	36.48 FQ	47.67 MW	60.88 TQ	CABLS	1/16-3/16

AE	Average entry wage	AWR	Average wage range	H	Hourly
AEX	Average experienced wage	B	Biweekly	HI	Highest paid
ATC	Average total compensation	D	Daily	HR	High end range
AW	Average wage paid	FQ	First quartile wage	LO	Lowest paid

LR	Low end range	MTC	Median total compensation	TCC	Total cash compensation
M	Monthly	MW	Median wage paid	TQ	Third quartile wage
MCC	Median cash compensation	MWR	Median wage range	W	Weekly
ME	Median entry wage	S	See annotated source	Y	Yearly

Occupation/Type/Industry	Location	Per	Low	Mid	High	Source	Date
Biomedical Engineer	Anaheim-Santa Ana-Irvine PMSA, CA	H	40.41 FQ	50.81 MW	72.38 TQ	CABLS	1/16-3/16
	Los Angeles-Long Beach-Glendale PMSA, CA	H	32.60 FQ	40.94 MW	50.83 TQ	CABLS	1/16-3/16
	Oakland-Hayward-Berkeley PMSA, CA	H	40.78 FQ	50.51 MW	63.79 TQ	CABLS	1/16-3/16
	Riverside-San Bernardino-Ontario MSA, CA	H	36.37 FQ	46.78 MW	57.31 TQ	CABLS	1/16-3/16
	Sacramento–Roseville–Arden-Arcade MSA, CA	H	21.74 FQ	28.10 MW	43.67 TQ	CABLS	1/16-3/16
	San Diego-Carlsbad MSA, CA	H	29.85 FQ	40.45 MW	52.43 TQ	CABLS	1/16-3/16
	San Francisco-Redwood City-South San Francisco PMSA, CA	H	41.75 FQ	49.04 MW	58.98 TQ	CABLS	1/16-3/16
	Colorado	Y	77900 FQ	95720 MW	120390 TQ	USBLS	5/15
	Denver-Aurora-Lakewood MSA, CO	Y	75600 FQ	89690 MW	107310 TQ	USBLS	5/15
	Connecticut	Y		91609 MW		CTBLS	1/16-3/16
	District of Columbia	Y	55030 FQ	69840 MW	86690 TQ	USBLS	5/15
	Washington-Arlington-Alexandria PMSA, DC-VA-MD-WV	Y	69350 FQ	83130 MW	115360 TQ	USBLS	5/15
	Florida	H	22.63 AE	35.17 MW	45.48 AEX	FLBLS	7/16-9/16
	Fort Lauderdale-Pompano Beach-Deerfield Beach PMSA, FL	H	25.21 AE	31.14 MW	56.05 AEX	FLBLS	7/16-9/16
	Miami-Miami Beach-Kendall PMSA, FL	H	21.48 AE	27.31 MW	35.64 AEX	FLBLS	7/16-9/16
	Orlando-Kissimmee-Sanford MSA, FL	H	20.82 AE	27.66 MW	32.30 AEX	FLBLS	7/16-9/16
	Tampa-St. Petersburg-Clearwater MSA, FL	H	23.74 AE	36.46 MW	42.45 AEX	FLBLS	7/16-9/16
	Georgia	Y	48980 FQ	63090 MW	91060 TQ	USBLS	5/15
	Atlanta-Sandy Springs-Roswell MSA, GA	Y	48530 FQ	63880 MW	90360 TQ	USBLS	5/15
	Idaho	Y	49670 FQ	56510 MW	62700 TQ	USBLS	5/15
	Illinois	Y	65390 FQ	83720 MW	97050 TQ	USBLS	5/15
	Chicago-Naperville-Arlington Heights PMSA, IL	Y	71660 FQ	85520 MW	97070 TQ	USBLS	5/15
	Lake County-Kenosha County PMSA, IL-WI	Y	59900 FQ	79630 MW	98330 TQ	USBLS	5/15
	Indiana	Y	55680 FQ	62620 MW	80030 TQ	USBLS	5/15
	Indianapolis-Carmel-Anderson MSA, IN	Y	54570 FQ	60170 MW	72560 TQ	USBLS	5/15
	Iowa	Y	66330 FQ	89160 MW	106540 TQ	USBLS	5/15
	Kansas	Y	77890 FQ	93640 MW	149360 TQ	USBLS	5/15
	Kentucky	Y	67200 FQ	74010 MW	86010 TQ	USBLS	5/15
	Louisville-Jefferson County MSA, KY-IN	Y	65810 FQ	74220 MW	82850 TQ	USBLS	5/15
	Louisiana	Y	59920 FQ	75030 MW	89040 TQ	USBLS	5/15
	Maine	Y	65160 FQ	86130 MW	107170 TQ	USBLS	5/15
	Portland-South Portland MSA, ME	Y	62560 FQ	78880 MW	102590 TQ	USBLS	5/15
	Maryland	Y	63779 AE	91898 MW	105957 AEX	MDBLS	4/16
	Baltimore-Columbia-Towson MSA, MD	Y	70830 FQ	85090 MW	100480 TQ	USBLS	5/15
	Massachusetts	Y	70360 FQ	90050 MW	113920 TQ	USBLS	5/15
	Boston-Cambridge-Newton NECTA, MA	Y	68680 FQ	88450 MW	111600 TQ	USBLS	5/15
	Worcester MSA, MA-CT	Y	63240 FQ	73450 MW	95080 TQ	USBLS	5/15
	Michigan	Y	60290 FQ	74830 MW	91550 TQ	USBLS	5/15
	Minnesota	Y	74495 FQ	97075 MW	123638 TQ	MNBLS	1/16-3/16
	Minneapolis-St. Paul-Bloomington MSA, MN-WI	Y	72983 FQ	96057 MW	122004 TQ	MNBLS	1/16-3/16
	Missouri	Y	57570 FQ	70270 MW	95370 TQ	USBLS	5/15
	Kansas City MSA, MO-KS	Y	70960 FQ	85470 MW	104500 TQ	USBLS	5/15
	St. Louis MSA, MO-IL	Y	62470 FQ	76650 MW	100810 TQ	USBLS	5/15
	New Hampshire	H	32.17 AE	48.20 MW	53.47 AEX	NHBLS	6/16
	Newark PMSA, NJ-PA	Y	100190 FQ	108940 MW	117830 TQ	USBLS	5/15
	New Mexico	Y	88580 FQ	99960 MW	117250 TQ	USBLS	5/15
	Albuquerque MSA, NM	Y	89090 FQ	100160 MW	116930 TQ	USBLS	5/15
	New York	Y	59220 AE	84080 MW	106990 AEX	NYBLS	1/16-3/16

Occupation/Type/Industry	Location	Per	Low	Mid	High	Source	Date
Biomedical Engineer	Buffalo-Cheektowaga-Niagara Falls MSA, NY	Y	71920 FQ	86570 MW	129400 TQ	USBLS	5/15
	New York-Jersey City-White Plains PMSA, NY-NJ	Y	74020 FQ	98730 MW	128530 TQ	USBLS	5/15
	Rochester MSA, NY	Y	72650 FQ	98590 MW	119610 TQ	USBLS	5/15
	North Carolina	Y	58060 FQ	73290 MW	95080 TQ	USBLS	5/15
	Raleigh MSA, NC	Y	71700 FQ	89840 MW	112470 TQ	USBLS	5/15
	Ohio	Y	54620 FQ	68220 MW	85670 TQ	USBLS	5/15
	Cincinnati MSA, OH-KY-IN	Y	55210 FQ	71290 MW	89560 TQ	USBLS	5/15
	Cleveland-Elyria MSA, OH	Y	54690 FQ	65780 MW	83250 TQ	USBLS	5/15
	Columbus MSA, OH	Y	60600 FQ	71240 MW	83000 TQ	USBLS	5/15
	Oklahoma	Y	51680 FQ	67930 MW	86640 TQ	USBLS	5/15
	Oklahoma City MSA, OK	Y	56960 FQ	79850 MW	93430 TQ	USBLS	5/15
	Oregon	H	34.49 FQ	38.74 MW	51.32 TQ	ORBLS	2016
	Portland-Vancouver-Hillsboro MSA, OR-WA	Y	70840 FQ	80000 MW	107370 TQ	USBLS	5/15
	Pennsylvania	Y	51770 FQ	73890 MW	95870 TQ	USBLS	5/15
	Allentown-Bethlehem-Easton MSA, PA-NJ	Y	75780 FQ	94710 MW	116510 TQ	USBLS	5/15
	Montgomery County-Bucks County-Chester County PMSA, PA	Y	64130 FQ	79630 MW	99560 TQ	USBLS	5/15
	Philadelphia PMSA, PA	Y	62470 FQ	77100 MW	95890 TQ	USBLS	5/15
	Pittsburgh MSA, PA	Y	37830 FQ	46040 MW	70390 TQ	USBLS	5/15
	Rhode Island	Y	61130 FQ	70580 MW	84050 TQ	USBLS	5/15
	Providence-Warwick MSA, RI-MA	Y	61810 FQ	71360 MW	87030 TQ	USBLS	5/15
	South Carolina	Y	51500 FQ	60390 MW	76790 TQ	USBLS	5/15
	Tennessee	Y	65340 FQ	79260 MW	93630 TQ	USBLS	5/15
	Knoxville MSA, TN	Y	57770 FQ	74380 MW	89950 TQ	USBLS	5/15
	Memphis MSA, TN-MS-AR	Y	67650 FQ	79490 MW	93000 TQ	USBLS	5/15
	Texas	Y	67110 FQ	85870 MW	103160 TQ	USBLS	5/15
	Austin-Round Rock MSA, TX	Y	66320 FQ	84670 MW	96600 TQ	USBLS	5/15
	Dallas-Plano-Irving PMSA, TX	Y	71370 FQ	87870 MW	104900 TQ	USBLS	5/15
	Houston-The Woodlands-Sugar Land MSA, TX	Y	53020 FQ	78630 MW	108400 TQ	USBLS	5/15
	San Antonio-New Braunfels MSA, TX	Y	62470 FQ	84230 MW	99500 TQ	USBLS	5/15
	Utah	Y	63510 FQ	78770 MW	96420 TQ	USBLS	5/15
	Ogden-Clearfield MSA, UT	Y	62960 FQ	77420 MW	94250 TQ	USBLS	5/15
	Salt Lake City MSA, UT	Y	64580 FQ	81000 MW	97540 TQ	USBLS	5/15
	Vermont	Y	83560 FQ	94330 MW	107220 TQ	USBLS	5/15
	Burlington-South Burlington MSA, VT	Y	83470 FQ	94160 MW	107350 TQ	USBLS	5/15
	Virginia	Y	67400 FQ	82810 MW	102620 TQ	USBLS	5/15
	Virginia Beach-Norfolk-Newport News MSA, VA-NC	Y	64070 FQ	79730 MW	94200 TQ	USBLS	5/15
	Washington	H	26.65 FQ	36.37 MW	55.45 TQ	WABLS	3/16
	Seattle-Bellevue-Everett PMSA, WA	H	26.21 FQ	35.31 MW	52.25 TQ	WABLS	3/16
	West Virginia	Y	51970 FQ	70630 MW	84950 TQ	USBLS	5/15
	Wisconsin	Y	61110 FQ	78600 MW	95420 TQ	USBLS	5/15
	Madison MSA, WI	Y	60800 FQ	77220 MW	96900 TQ	USBLS	5/15
	Milwaukee-Waukesha-West Allis MSA, WI	Y	61820 FQ	79880 MW	95130 TQ	USBLS	5/15
Biomedical Laboratory Technician	United States	Y		49310 MW		AAHS	2016
Biosolids Coordinator Water Department, Municipal Government	Santa Rosa, CA	Y			102984 HI	CACIT	6/28/16
Biostatistician	United States	Y		84000 AW		SKU01	2016
Birth Doula	United States	S		250-1000 AW		NATH	2017
Blacksmith California State University	California	Y	48072 LO		73704 HI	CALST	2016-2017
Blood Bank Technology Specialist	United States	Y		58000-78000 AWR		EXHC01	2016
Boilermaker	Alabama	Y	41940 AE	55138 AW	61742 AEX	ALBLS	6/16

AE	Average entry wage	AWR	Average wage range	H	Hourly	LR	Low end range	MTC	Median total compensation	TCC	Total cash compensation
AEX	Average experienced wage	B	Biweekly	HI	Highest wage paid	M	Monthly	MW	Median wage paid	TQ	Third quartile wage
ATC	Average total compensation	D	Daily	HR	High end range	MCC	Median cash compensation	MWR	Median wage range	W	Weekly
AW	Average wage paid	FQ	First quartile wage	LO	Lowest wage paid	ME	Median entry wage	S	See annotated source	Y	Yearly

Occupation/Type/Industry	Location	Per	Low	Mid	High	Source	Date
Boilermaker	Birmingham-Hoover MSA, AL	Y	41559 AE	50691 AW	55673 AEX	ALBLS	6/16
	Alaska	Y	63500 FQ	81090 MW	96200 TQ	USBLS	5/15
	Arizona	Y	44190 FQ	48610 MW	62110 TQ	USBLS	5/15
	California	H	28.98 FQ	39.92 MW	45.29 TQ	CABLS	1/16-3/16
	Anaheim-Santa Ana-Irvine PMSA, CA	H	27.57 FQ	40.60 MW	45.74 TQ	CABLS	1/16-3/16
	Los Angeles-Long Beach-Glendale PMSA, CA	H	31.92 FQ	42.18 MW	46.50 TQ	CABLS	1/16-3/16
	Oakland-Hayward-Berkeley PMSA, CA	H	32.11 FQ	36.74 MW	42.07 TQ	CABLS	1/16-3/16
	Colorado	Y	54530 FQ	68630 MW	80280 TQ	USBLS	5/15
	Denver-Aurora-Lakewood MSA, CO	Y	48130 FQ	58690 MW	84540 TQ	USBLS	5/15
	Connecticut	Y		64348 MW		CTBLS	1/16-3/16
	Washington-Arlington-Alexandria PMSA, DC-VA-MD-WV	Y	53470 FQ	62160 MW	77770 TQ	USBLS	5/15
	Florida	H	19.61 AE	25.13 MW	30.39 AEX	FLBLS	7/16-9/16
	Tampa-St. Petersburg-Clearwater MSA, FL	H	21.29 AE	29.49 MW	34.73 AEX	FLBLS	7/16-9/16
	Georgia	Y	51520 FQ	60750 MW	76940 TQ	USBLS	5/15
	Atlanta-Sandy Springs-Roswell MSA, GA	Y	44140 FQ	61980 MW	72560 TQ	USBLS	5/15
	Idaho	Y	45430 FQ	66190 MW	73940 TQ	USBLS	5/15
	Illinois	Y	40000 FQ	61740 MW	77820 TQ	USBLS	5/15
	Chicago-Naperville-Arlington Heights PMSA, IL	Y	37200 FQ	55000 MW	78330 TQ	USBLS	5/15
	Indiana	Y	59530 FQ	69460 MW	77180 TQ	USBLS	5/15
	Gary PMSA, IN	Y	67540 FQ	72000 MW	76460 TQ	USBLS	5/15
	Iowa	Y	65010 FQ	73040 MW	80920 TQ	USBLS	5/15
	Kansas	Y	41230 FQ	52610 MW	75490 TQ	USBLS	5/15
	Kentucky	Y	38660 FQ	55100 MW	68530 TQ	USBLS	5/15
	Louisville-Jefferson County MSA, KY-IN	Y	35730 FQ	39990 MW	58700 TQ	USBLS	5/15
	Louisiana	Y	43120 FQ	54660 MW	64720 TQ	USBLS	5/15
	Baton Rouge MSA, LA	Y	42170 FQ	53660 MW	65600 TQ	USBLS	5/15
	New Orleans-Metairie MSA, LA	Y	50900 FQ	57820 MW	65390 TQ	USBLS	5/15
	Maryland	Y	51793 AE	68285 MW	76531 AEX	MDBLS	4/16
	Massachusetts	Y	43320 FQ	60520 MW	76230 TQ	USBLS	5/15
	Worcester MSA, MA-CT	Y	49010 FQ	63590 MW	73980 TQ	USBLS	5/15
	Michigan	Y	62740 FQ	69560 MW	76280 TQ	USBLS	5/15
	Detroit-Dearborn-Livonia PMSA, MI	Y	59860 FQ	70350 MW	87780 TQ	USBLS	5/15
	Minnesota	Y	66635 FQ	72488 MW	78340 TQ	MNBLS	1/16-3/16
	Mississippi	Y	46350 FQ	58810 MW	81020 TQ	USBLS	5/15
	Jackson MSA, MS	Y	36630 FQ	41070 MW	47050 TQ	USBLS	5/15
	Missouri	Y	66740 FQ	77170 MW	90200 TQ	USBLS	5/15
	Kansas City MSA, MO-KS	Y	51630 FQ	84960 MW	95020 TQ	USBLS	5/15
	St. Louis MSA, MO-IL	Y	57840 FQ	69330 MW	79160 AEX	USBLS	5/15
	Montana	Y	55180 FQ	68660 MW	77730 TQ	USBLS	5/15
	Nebraska	Y	42685 FQ	51275 MW	59695 TQ	NEBLS	7/16-9/16
	Omaha-Council Bluffs MSA, NE-IA	Y	49050 FQ	55635 MW	62005 TQ	NEBLS	7/16-9/16
	Nevada	Y	39610 FQ	69010 MW	78700 TQ	USBLS	5/15
	New Hampshire	H	27.92 AE	35.55 MW	37.93 AEX	NHBLS	6/16
	New Jersey	Y	57330 FQ	72600 MW	83660 TQ	USBLS	5/15
	New Mexico	Y	46180 FQ	57560 MW	69390 TQ	USBLS	5/15
	New York	Y	48340 AE	74850 MW	84840 AEX	NYBLS	1/16-3/16
	New York-Jersey City-White Plains PMSA, NY-NJ	Y	78680 FQ	86510 MW	94370 TQ	USBLS	5/15
	North Carolina	Y	40470 FQ	48120 MW	56780 TQ	USBLS	5/15
	Charlotte-Concord-Gastonia MSA, NC-SC	Y	37920 FQ	44270 MW	50280 TQ	USBLS	5/15
	Ohio	Y	51230 FQ	57990 MW	68360 TQ	USBLS	5/15
	Cleveland-Elyria MSA, OH	Y	52040 FQ	57290 MW	62690 TQ	USBLS	5/15
	Oklahoma	Y	41590 FQ	55830 MW	68090 TQ	USBLS	5/15
	Tulsa MSA, OK	Y	55070 FQ	61890 MW	74330 TQ	USBLS	5/15
	Oregon	H	25.55 FQ	28.44 MW	31.49 TQ	ORBLS	2016
	Portland-Vancouver-Hillsboro MSA, OR-WA	Y	53750 FQ	59380 MW	66170 TQ	USBLS	5/15
	Pennsylvania	Y	54630 FQ	62760 MW	74100 TQ	USBLS	5/15

AE	Average entry wage	AWR	Average wage range	H	Hourly	LR	Low end range	MTC	Median total compensation	TCC	Total cash compensation
AEX	Average experienced wage	B	Biweekly	HI	Highest wage paid	M	Monthly	MW	Median wage paid	TQ	Third quartile wage
ATC	Average total compensation	D	Daily	HR	High end range	MCC	Median cash compensation	MWR	Median wage range	W	Weekly
AW	Average wage paid	FQ	First quartile wage	LO	Lowest wage paid	ME	Median entry wage	S	See annotated source	Y	Yearly

Occupation/Type/Industry	Location	Per	Low	Mid	High	Source	Date
Boilermaker	Pittsburgh MSA, PA	Y	65290 FQ	72070 MW	78850 TQ	USBLS	5/15
	South Carolina	Y	34330 FQ	51400 MW	58170 TQ	USBLS	5/15
	Columbia MSA, SC	Y	24050 FQ	52710 MW	58850 TQ	USBLS	5/15
	Tennessee	Y	46770 FQ	60610 MW	78130 TQ	USBLS	5/15
	Knoxville MSA, TN	Y	36070 FQ	71040 MW	78130 TQ	USBLS	5/15
	Memphis MSA, TN-MS-AR	Y	53900 FQ	58950 MW	64000 TQ	USBLS	5/15
	Texas	Y	47160 FQ	58730 MW	71980 TQ	USBLS	5/15
	Houston-The Woodlands-Sugar Land MSA, TX	Y	49020 FQ	57910 MW	72130 TQ	USBLS	5/15
	San Antonio-New Braunfels MSA, TX	Y	40370 FQ	48550 MW	71080 TQ	USBLS	5/15
	Utah	Y	45880 FQ	55470 MW	75810 TQ	USBLS	5/15
	Ogden-Clearfield MSA, UT	Y	42940 FQ	45890 MW	48840 TQ	USBLS	5/15
	Salt Lake City MSA, UT	Y	46900 FQ	53050 MW	82450 TQ	USBLS	5/15
	Virginia	Y	46730 FQ	52140 MW	59670 TQ	USBLS	5/15
	Richmond MSA, VA	Y	44070 FQ	49210 MW	56710 TQ	USBLS	5/15
	Virginia Beach-Norfolk-Newport News MSA, VA-NC	Y	46160 FQ	50820 MW	54850 TQ	USBLS	5/15
	Washington	H	23.36 FQ	27.69 MW	30.82 TQ	WABLS	3/16
	Seattle-Bellevue-Everett PMSA, WA	H	23.95 FQ	27.68 MW	30.42 TQ	WABLS	3/16
	West Virginia	Y	65230 FQ	71510 MW	77790 TQ	USBLS	5/15
	Huntington-Ashland MSA, WV-KY-OH	Y	68700 FQ	73400 MW	78100 TQ	USBLS	5/15
	Wisconsin	Y	45670 FQ	68050 MW	83480 TQ	USBLS	5/15
	Milwaukee-Waukesha-West Allis MSA, WI	Y	33960 FQ	39350 MW	47480 TQ	USBLS	5/15
	Wyoming	Y	58400 FQ	70070 MW	79610 TQ	USBLS	5/15
	Puerto Rico	Y	18460 FQ	21710 MW	26050 TQ	USBLS	5/15
Book Repairer							
Public Library	San Francisco, CA	Y		58767 AW		CACIT	6/28/16
Bookkeeping, Accounting, and Auditing Clerk	Alabama	Y	25837 AE	37514 AW	43357 AEX	ALBLS	6/16
	Birmingham-Hoover MSA, AL	Y	29403 AE	40502 AW	46047 AEX	ALBLS	6/16
	Alaska	Y	35590 FQ	43760 MW	53440 TQ	USBLS	5/15
	Anchorage MSA, AK	Y	36840 FQ	45160 MW	55480 TQ	USBLS	5/15
	Arizona	Y	29890 FQ	36040 MW	43870 TQ	USBLS	5/15
	Phoenix-Mesa-Scottsdale MSA, AZ	Y	30830 FQ	36600 MW	44720 TQ	USBLS	5/15
	Tucson MSA, AZ	Y	28920 FQ	34970 MW	41570 TQ	USBLS	5/15
	Arkansas	Y	26130 FQ	32300 MW	39650 TQ	USBLS	5/15
	Little Rock-North Little Rock-Conway MSA, AR	Y	27870 FQ	35100 MW	43460 TQ	USBLS	5/15
	California	H	16.45 FQ	20.97 MW	26.33 TQ	CABLS	1/16-3/16
	Anaheim-Santa Ana-Irvine PMSA, CA	H	17.07 FQ	21.74 MW	27.12 TQ	CABLS	1/16-3/16
	Los Angeles-Long Beach-Glendale PMSA, CA	H	16.05 FQ	20.57 MW	26.34 TQ	CABLS	1/16-3/16
	Oakland-Hayward-Berkeley PMSA, CA	H	18.60 FQ	22.84 MW	28.04 TQ	CABLS	1/16-3/16
	Riverside-San Bernardino-Ontario MSA, CA	H	15.32 FQ	19.58 MW	23.85 TQ	CABLS	1/16-3/16
	Sacramento–Roseville–Arden-Arcade MSA, CA	H	16.35 FQ	20.17 MW	24.39 TQ	CABLS	1/16-3/16
	San Diego-Carlsbad MSA, CA	H	16.47 FQ	20.72 MW	24.94 TQ	CABLS	1/16-3/16
	San Francisco-Redwood City-South San Francisco PMSA, CA	H	19.78 FQ	25.01 MW	30.00 TQ	CABLS	1/16-3/16
	Colorado	Y	28940 FQ	37020 MW	46710 TQ	USBLS	5/15
	Denver-Aurora-Lakewood MSA, CO	Y	30390 FQ	38500 MW	48240 TQ	USBLS	5/15
	Connecticut	Y		44403 MW		CTBLS	1/16-3/16
	Bridgeport-Stamford-Norwalk MSA, CT	Y	35890 FQ	46750 MW	57100 TQ	USBLS	5/15
	Hartford-West Hartford-East Hartford MSA, CT	Y	34020 FQ	42210 MW	51570 TQ	USBLS	5/15
	Delaware	Y	33060 FQ	39930 MW	48490 TQ	USBLS	5/15
	Wilmington PMSA, DE-MD-NJ	Y	33950 FQ	41450 MW	49690 TQ	USBLS	5/15
	District of Columbia	Y	43030 FQ	52380 MW	62800 TQ	USBLS	5/15

AE	Average entry wage	AWR	Average wage range	H	Hourly	LR	Low end range	MTC	Median total compensation	TCC	Total cash compensation
AEX	Average experienced wage	B	Biweekly	HI	Highest wage paid	M	Monthly	MW	Median wage paid	TQ	Third quartile wage
ATC	Average total compensation	D	Daily	HR	High end range	MCC	Median cash compensation	MWR	Median wage range	W	Weekly
AW	Average wage paid	FQ	First quartile wage	LO	Lowest wage paid	ME	Median entry wage	S	See annotated source	Y	Yearly

Occupation/Type/Industry	Location	Per	Low	Mid	High	Source	Date
Bookkeeping, Accounting, and Auditing Clerk							
	Washington-Arlington-Alexandria PMSA, DC-VA-MD-WV	Y	34850 FQ	44690 MW	55970 TQ	USBLS	5/15
	Florida	H	12.23 AE	17.29 MW	20.56 AEX	FLBLS	7/16-9/16
	Fort Lauderdale-Pompano Beach-Deerfield Beach PMSA, FL	H	12.27 AE	18.01 MW	21.24 AEX	FLBLS	7/16-9/16
	Miami-Miami Beach-Kendall PMSA, FL	H	12.80 AE	17.97 MW	21.27 AEX	FLBLS	7/16-9/16
	Orlando-Kissimmee-Sanford MSA, FL	H	12.53 AE	17.34 MW	20.48 AEX	FLBLS	7/16-9/16
	Tampa-St. Petersburg-Clearwater MSA, FL	H	12.14 AE	16.90 MW	19.91 AEX	FLBLS	7/16-9/16
	Georgia	Y	28210 FQ	36310 MW	46510 TQ	USBLS	5/15
	Atlanta-Sandy Springs-Roswell MSA, GA	Y	30850 FQ	38940 MW	49110 TQ	USBLS	5/15
	Augusta-Richmond County MSA, GA-SC	Y	26000 FQ	32570 MW	40270 TQ	USBLS	5/15
	Hawaii	Y	31780 FQ	37870 MW	45810 TQ	USBLS	5/15
	Urban Honolulu MSA, HI	Y	31910 FQ	38380 MW	46280 TQ	USBLS	5/15
	Idaho	Y	26490 FQ	33240 MW	40510 TQ	USBLS	5/15
	Boise City MSA, ID	Y	28050 FQ	34310 MW	41560 TQ	USBLS	5/15
	Illinois	Y	29630 FQ	38210 MW	47360 TQ	USBLS	5/15
	Chicago-Naperville-Arlington Heights PMSA, IL	Y	31420 FQ	40270 MW	48460 TQ	USBLS	5/15
	Lake County-Kenosha County PMSA, IL-WI	Y	34190 FQ	42140 MW	49200 TQ	USBLS	5/15
	Indiana	Y	27310 FQ	34540 MW	42700 TQ	USBLS	5/15
	Gary PMSA, IN	Y	27450 FQ	35170 MW	44610 TQ	USBLS	5/15
	Indianapolis-Carmel-Anderson MSA, IN	Y	30830 FQ	37950 MW	46750 TQ	USBLS	5/15
	Iowa	Y	26270 FQ	33170 MW	39820 TQ	USBLS	5/15
	Des Moines-West Des Moines MSA, IA	Y	30680 FQ	36660 MW	44540 TQ	USBLS	5/15
	Kansas	Y	26680 FQ	34220 MW	42210 TQ	USBLS	5/15
	Wichita MSA, KS	Y	28320 FQ	34360 MW	41930 TQ	USBLS	5/15
	Kentucky	Y	27010 FQ	34330 MW	42060 TQ	USBLS	5/15
	Louisville-Jefferson County MSA, KY-IN	Y	28770 FQ	35280 MW	42370 TQ	USBLS	5/15
	Louisiana	Y	28320 FQ	34520 MW	41080 TQ	USBLS	5/15
	Baton Rouge MSA, LA	Y	28330 FQ	35050 MW	42820 TQ	USBLS	5/15
	New Orleans-Metairie MSA, LA	Y	29950 FQ	36010 MW	43460 TQ	USBLS	5/15
	Maine	Y	29810 FQ	35840 MW	42380 TQ	USBLS	5/15
	Portland-South Portland MSA, ME	Y	31580 FQ	36510 MW	43750 TQ	USBLS	5/15
	Maryland	Y	29642 AE	43934 MW	51079 AEX	MDBLS	4/16
	Baltimore-Columbia-Towson MSA, MD	Y	34800 FQ	42790 MW	51570 TQ	USBLS	5/15
	Salisbury MSA, MD-DE	Y	29250 FQ	35300 MW	41680 TQ	USBLS	5/15
	Massachusetts	Y	34330 FQ	43150 MW	53400 TQ	USBLS	5/15
	Boston-Cambridge-Newton NECTA, MA	Y	36580 FQ	45760 MW	56380 TQ	USBLS	5/15
	Worcester MSA, MA-CT	Y	31590 FQ	38480 MW	48310 TQ	USBLS	5/15
	Michigan	Y	29440 FQ	36480 MW	45140 TQ	USBLS	5/15
	Detroit-Dearborn-Livonia PMSA, MI	Y	32350 FQ	38350 MW	47130 TQ	USBLS	5/15
	Grand Rapids-Wyoming MSA, MI	Y	28610 FQ	35250 MW	43220 TQ	USBLS	5/15
	Minnesota	Y	31896 FQ	38681 MW	47085 TQ	MNBLS	1/16-3/16
	Minneapolis-St. Paul-Bloomington MSA, MN-WI	Y	34019 FQ	41179 MW	48794 TQ	MNBLS	1/16-3/16
	Mississippi	Y	25310 FQ	32700 MW	42500 TQ	USBLS	5/15
	Jackson MSA, MS	Y	27710 FQ	35580 MW	46730 TQ	USBLS	5/15
	Missouri	Y	28050 FQ	35620 MW	44780 TQ	USBLS	5/15
	Kansas City MSA, MO-KS	Y	31320 FQ	37870 MW	45920 TQ	USBLS	5/15
	St. Louis MSA, MO-IL	Y	31200 FQ	38260 MW	47330 TQ	USBLS	5/15
	Montana	Y	25850 FQ	32810 MW	39930 TQ	USBLS	5/15
	Billings MSA, MT	Y	25630 FQ	33050 MW	42530 TQ	USBLS	5/15
	Nebraska	Y	26785 FQ	33020 MW	39065 TQ	NEBLS	7/16-9/16

AE	Average entry wage	AWR	Average wage range	H	Hourly
AEX	Average experienced wage	B	Biweekly	HI	Highest wage paid
ATC	Average total compensation	D	Daily	HR	High end range
AW	Average wage paid	FQ	First quartile wage	LO	Lowest wage paid

LR	Low end range	MTC	Median total compensation	TCC	Total cash compensation
M	Monthly	MW	Median wage paid	TQ	Third quartile wage
MCC	Median cash compensation	MWR	Median wage range	W	Weekly
ME	Median entry wage	S	See annotated source	Y	Yearly

Occupation/Type/Industry	Location	Per	Low	Mid	High	Source	Date
Bookkeeping, Accounting, and Auditing Clerk	Omaha-Council Bluffs MSA, NE-IA	Y	29375 FQ	35200 MW	41705 TQ	NEBLS	7/16-9/16
	Nevada	Y	29700 FQ	36770 MW	45990 TQ	USBLS	5/15
	Las Vegas-Henderson-Paradise MSA, NV	Y	29580 FQ	36220 MW	44690 TQ	USBLS	5/15
	New Hampshire	H	13.60 AE	19.02 MW	22.60 AEX	NHBLS	6/16
	Manchester NECTA, NH	H	14.09 AE	19.61 MW	24.20 AEX	NHBLS	6/16
	Nashua NECTA, NH-MA	Y	30940 FQ	38040 MW	46690 TQ	USBLS	5/15
	New Jersey	Y	34110 FQ	42680 MW	52630 TQ	USBLS	5/15
	Camden PMSA, NJ	Y	32600 FQ	39250 MW	48990 TQ	USBLS	5/15
	Newark PMSA, NJ-PA	Y	34200 FQ	43230 MW	53240 TQ	USBLS	5/15
	Trenton MSA, NJ	Y	37050 FQ	46000 MW	55690 TQ	USBLS	5/15
	New Mexico	Y	26810 FQ	33710 MW	41050 TQ	USBLS	5/15
	Albuquerque MSA, NM	Y	28300 FQ	35030 MW	42230 TQ	USBLS	5/15
	New York	Y	27930 AE	41530 MW	51230 AEX	NYBLS	1/16-3/16
	Buffalo-Cheektowaga-Niagara Falls MSA, NY	Y	30830 FQ	37040 MW	44900 TQ	USBLS	5/15
	Nassau County-Suffolk County PMSA, NY	Y	32630 FQ	43310 MW	53630 TQ	USBLS	5/15
	New York-Jersey City-White Plains PMSA, NY-NJ	Y	32840 FQ	43330 MW	55130 TQ	USBLS	5/15
	Rochester MSA, NY	Y	31100 FQ	36970 MW	45050 TQ	USBLS	5/15
	North Carolina	Y	28660 FQ	35670 MW	43670 TQ	USBLS	5/15
	Charlotte-Concord-Gastonia MSA, NC-SC	Y	30430 FQ	37350 MW	45700 TQ	USBLS	5/15
	Raleigh MSA, NC	Y	31870 FQ	37690 MW	45760 TQ	USBLS	5/15
	North Dakota	Y	30610 FQ	36490 MW	44600 TQ	USBLS	5/15
	Fargo MSA, ND-MN	Y	30460 FQ	36310 MW	44250 TQ	USBLS	5/15
	Ohio	Y	28750 FQ	35800 MW	43940 TQ	USBLS	5/15
	Cincinnati MSA, OH-KY-IN	Y	28600 FQ	35890 MW	44080 TQ	USBLS	5/15
	Cleveland-Elyria MSA, OH	Y	30430 FQ	36980 MW	45230 TQ	USBLS	5/15
	Columbus MSA, OH	Y	31690 FQ	37910 MW	46210 TQ	USBLS	5/15
	Oklahoma	Y	26410 FQ	33000 MW	40890 TQ	USBLS	5/15
	Oklahoma City MSA, OK	Y	27590 FQ	34270 MW	42720 TQ	USBLS	5/15
	Tulsa MSA, OK	Y	28690 FQ	35660 MW	44570 TQ	USBLS	5/15
	Oregon	H	15.30 FQ	18.39 MW	22.66 TQ	ORBLS	2016
	Portland-Vancouver-Hillsboro MSA, OR-WA	Y	32900 FQ	39080 MW	47320 TQ	USBLS	5/15
	Pennsylvania	Y	28890 FQ	36130 MW	44970 TQ	USBLS	5/15
	Allentown-Bethlehem-Easton MSA, PA-NJ	Y	29400 FQ	36310 MW	45080 TQ	USBLS	5/15
	Harrisburg-Carlisle MSA, PA	Y	29600 FQ	36170 MW	43960 TQ	USBLS	5/15
	Montgomery County-Bucks County-Chester County PMSA, PA	Y	32500 FQ	39850 MW	48440 TQ	USBLS	5/15
	Philadelphia PMSA, PA	Y	33570 FQ	41770 MW	51250 TQ	USBLS	5/15
	Pittsburgh MSA, PA	Y	28470 FQ	35200 MW	42940 TQ	USBLS	5/15
	Rhode Island	Y	32890 FQ	39080 MW	46810 TQ	USBLS	5/15
	Providence-Warwick MSA, RI-MA	Y	32640 FQ	38960 MW	46740 TQ	USBLS	5/15
	South Carolina	Y	26660 FQ	33580 MW	40720 TQ	USBLS	5/15
	Charleston-North Charleston MSA, SC	Y	27750 FQ	34720 MW	41710 TQ	USBLS	5/15
	Columbia MSA, SC	Y	28330 FQ	34550 MW	41740 TQ	USBLS	5/15
	Greenville-Anderson-Mauldin MSA, SC	Y	27870 FQ	34710 MW	41900 TQ	USBLS	5/15
	South Dakota	Y	26270 FQ	30340 MW	36220 TQ	USBLS	5/15
	Sioux Falls MSA, SD	Y	26590 FQ	30750 MW	37050 TQ	USBLS	5/15
	Tennessee	Y	27770 FQ	34470 MW	42700 TQ	USBLS	5/15
	Knoxville MSA, TN	Y	26950 FQ	32270 MW	40080 TQ	USBLS	5/15
	Memphis MSA, TN-MS-AR	Y	29100 FQ	36600 MW	45360 TQ	USBLS	5/15
	Nashville-Davidson–Murfreesboro–Franklin MSA, TN	Y	30920 FQ	37450 MW	45230 TQ	USBLS	5/15
	Texas	Y	29240 FQ	36950 MW	46910 TQ	USBLS	5/15
	Austin-Round Rock MSA, TX	Y	33050 FQ	40140 MW	49360 TQ	USBLS	5/15
	Dallas-Plano-Irving PMSA, TX	Y	33270 FQ	39970 MW	48510 TQ	USBLS	5/15
	Fort Worth-Arlington PMSA, TX	Y	30250 FQ	36930 MW	46750 TQ	USBLS	5/15
	Houston-The Woodlands-Sugar Land MSA, TX	Y	31710 FQ	39050 MW	49740 TQ	USBLS	5/15

AE	Average entry wage	AWR	Average wage range	H	Hourly	LR	Low end range	MTC	Median total compensation	TCC	Total cash compensation
AEX	Average experienced wage	B	Biweekly	HI	Highest wage paid	M	Monthly	MW	Median wage paid	TQ	Third quartile wage
ATC	Average total compensation	D	Daily	HR	High end range	MCC	Median cash compensation	MWR	Median wage range	W	Weekly
AW	Average wage paid	FQ	First quartile wage	LO	Lowest wage paid	ME	Median entry wage	S	See annotated source	Y	Yearly

Occupation/Type/Industry	Location	Per	Low	Mid	High	Source	Date
Bookkeeping, Accounting, and Auditing Clerk	San Antonio-New Braunfels						
	MSA, TX	Y	28460 FQ	35500 MW	44650 TQ	USBLS	5/15
	Utah	Y	28050 FQ	34900 MW	43090 TQ	USBLS	5/15
	Ogden-Clearfield MSA, UT	Y	28500 FQ	35630 MW	43520 TQ	USBLS	5/15
	Provo-Orem MSA, UT	Y	27090 FQ	33710 MW	41590 TQ	USBLS	5/15
	Salt Lake City MSA, UT	Y	29270 FQ	35820 MW	44220 TQ	USBLS	5/15
	Vermont	Y	31860 FQ	37900 MW	46180 TQ	USBLS	5/15
	Burlington-South Burlington MSA, VT	Y	32190 FQ	38880 MW	47650 TQ	USBLS	5/15
	Virginia	Y	30080 FQ	37470 MW	47470 TQ	USBLS	5/15
	Richmond MSA, VA	Y	32000 FQ	37580 MW	46350 TQ	USBLS	5/15
	Virginia Beach-Norfolk-Newport News MSA, VA-NC	Y	29320 FQ	35820 MW	44450 TQ	USBLS	5/15
	Washington	H	16.09 FQ	19.66 MW	23.73 TQ	WABLS	3/16
	Seattle-Bellevue-Everett PMSA, WA	H	16.93 FQ	20.77 MW	24.51 TQ	WABLS	3/16
	Tacoma-Lakewood PMSA, WA	H	15.90 FQ	19.37 MW	23.41 TQ	WABLS	3/16
	West Virginia	Y	24890 FQ	31000 MW	39270 TQ	USBLS	5/15
	Huntington-Ashland MSA, WV-KY-OH	Y	24960 FQ	31620 MW	40130 TQ	USBLS	5/15
	Wisconsin	Y	28520 FQ	35320 MW	42710 TQ	USBLS	5/15
	Madison MSA, WI	Y	32120 FQ	37900 MW	45230 TQ	USBLS	5/15
	Milwaukee-Waukesha-West Allis MSA, WI	Y	30630 FQ	36630 MW	44620 TQ	USBLS	5/15
	Wyoming	Y	28010 FQ	35450 MW	43890 TQ	USBLS	5/15
	Cheyenne MSA, WY	Y	28600 FQ	35940 MW	43810 TQ	USBLS	5/15
	Puerto Rico	Y	17550 FQ	19680 MW	25800 TQ	USBLS	5/15
	San Juan-Carolina-Caguas MSA, PR	Y	17810 FQ	20770 MW	27500 TQ	USBLS	5/15
	Virgin Islands	Y	20770 FQ	28830 MW	41000 TQ	USBLS	5/15
	Guam	Y	20570 FQ	26030 MW	33050 TQ	USBLS	5/15
Bookmobile Operator							
Public Library	Detroit, MI	M	1946 LO		2436 HI	DETGOV	2016
Boom Operator							
Made for Television Motion Picture	United States	W	1628 LO			MPEG01	7/31/16-7/29/17
Boutique Agency Owner							
Booking Agency	United States	Y		200000-2000000 AWR		BBRD01	2014
Bowling Alley Equipment Maintainer							
Michigan State University	East Lansing, MI	Y			42910 HI	MSUSAL	10/1/14-9/30/15
Box Office Treasurer							
Convention/Sports/Entertainment Department, Municipal Government	Anaheim, CA	Y			7086 HI	CACIT	6/28/16
Boxing Trainer							
Parks and Recreation Department, Municipal Government	Duarte, CA	Y			19550 HI	CACIT	6/28/16
Braillist							
Public Library	San Francisco, CA	B	1918 LO		2332 HI	SFGOV	2016-2018
Breath Alcohol Testing Inspector							
Health Department, State Government	Ohio	H	21.30 LO		21.47 HI	OHGOV	2015
Brickmason and Blockmason	Alabama	Y	32105 AE	41148 AW	45674 AEX	ALBLS	6/16
	Birmingham-Hoover MSA, AL	Y	30686 AE	46126 AW	53852 AEX	ALBLS	6/16
	Arizona	Y	29840 FQ	39000 MW	46210 TQ	USBLS	5/15
	Phoenix-Mesa-Scottsdale MSA, AZ	Y	27690 FQ	35650 MW	43440 TQ	USBLS	5/15
	Tucson MSA, AZ	Y	42740 FQ	47730 MW	55910 TQ	USBLS	5/15
	Arkansas	Y	29880 FQ	37440 MW	45140 TQ	USBLS	5/15
	Little Rock-North Little Rock-Conway MSA, AR	Y	33660 FQ	43080 MW	48900 TQ	USBLS	5/15
	California	H	21.77 FQ	28.23 MW	35.64 TQ	CABLS	1/16-3/16

AE Average entry wage | AWR Average wage range | H Hourly | LR Low end range | MTC Median total compensation | TCC Total cash compensation
AEX Average experienced wage | B Biweekly | HI Highest wage paid | M Monthly | MW Median wage range | TQ Third quartile wage
ATC Average total compensation | D Daily | HR High end range | MCC Median cash compensation | MWR Median wage range | W Weekly
AW Average wage paid | FQ First quartile wage | LO Lowest wage paid | ME Median entry wage | S See annotated source | Y Yearly

131

Occupation/Type/Industry	Location	Per	Low	Mid	High	Source	Date
Brickmason and Blockmason	Anaheim-Santa Ana-Irvine PMSA, CA	H	17.74 FQ	24.73 MW	29.63 TQ	CABLS	1/16-3/16
	Los Angeles-Long Beach-Glendale PMSA, CA	H	23.18 FQ	29.08 MW	35.60 TQ	CABLS	1/16-3/16
	Oakland-Hayward-Berkeley PMSA, CA	H	27.61 FQ	34.54 MW	43.46 TQ	CABLS	1/16-3/16
	Riverside-San Bernardino-Ontario MSA, CA	H	18.34 FQ	25.37 MW	30.97 TQ	CABLS	1/16-3/16
	Sacramento–Roseville–Arden-Arcade MSA, CA	H	28.03 FQ	32.49 MW	37.09 TQ	CABLS	1/16-3/16
	San Diego-Carlsbad MSA, CA	H	21.70 FQ	27.31 MW	34.56 TQ	CABLS	1/16-3/16
	San Francisco-Redwood City-South San Francisco PMSA, CA	H	26.47 FQ	40.47 MW	45.40 TQ	CABLS	1/16-3/16
	Colorado	Y	31030 FQ	48780 MW	57930 TQ	USBLS	5/15
	Denver-Aurora-Lakewood MSA, CO	Y	30250 FQ	51070 MW	57620 TQ	USBLS	5/15
	Connecticut	Y		67082 MW		CTBLS	1/16-3/16
	Bridgeport-Stamford-Norwalk MSA, CT	Y	45720 FQ	66120 MW	74090 TQ	USBLS	5/15
	Hartford-West Hartford-East Hartford MSA, CT	Y	54530 FQ	66240 MW	80460 TQ	USBLS	5/15
	Delaware	Y	44590 FQ	51450 MW	58280 TQ	USBLS	5/15
	Wilmington PMSA, DE-MD-NJ	Y	45880 FQ	52930 MW	59180 TQ	USBLS	5/15
	District of Columbia	Y	48750 FQ	57840 MW	62970 TQ	USBLS	5/15
	Washington-Arlington-Alexandria PMSA, DC-VA-MD-WV	Y	40570 FQ	48990 MW	60050 TQ	USBLS	5/15
	Florida	H	13.48 AE	17.17 MW	19.31 AEX	FLBLS	7/16-9/16
	Miami-Miami Beach-Kendall PMSA, FL	H	19.64 AE	25.92 MW	28.18 AEX	FLBLS	7/16-9/16
	Orlando-Kissimmee-Sanford MSA, FL	H	15.42 AE	17.80 MW	20.22 AEX	FLBLS	7/16-9/16
	Tampa-St. Petersburg-Clearwater MSA, FL	H	11.73 AE	15.31 MW	17.17 AEX	FLBLS	7/16-9/16
	Georgia	Y	28130 FQ	34500 MW	39610 TQ	USBLS	5/15
	Atlanta-Sandy Springs-Roswell MSA, GA	Y	31610 FQ	36390 MW	42570 TQ	USBLS	5/15
	Augusta-Richmond County MSA, GA-SC	Y	32970 FQ	35330 MW	37690 TQ	USBLS	5/15
	Hawaii	Y	50910 FQ	60760 MW	73500 TQ	USBLS	5/15
	Urban Honolulu MSA, HI	Y	51360 FQ	60310 MW	70340 TQ	USBLS	5/15
	Idaho	Y	34610 FQ	53100 MW	63570 TQ	USBLS	5/15
	Boise City MSA, ID	Y	29440 FQ	51390 MW	59080 TQ	USBLS	5/15
	Illinois	Y	56270 FQ	76920 MW	90430 TQ	USBLS	5/15
	Chicago-Naperville-Arlington Heights PMSA, IL	Y	62670 FQ	83870 MW	92840 TQ	USBLS	5/15
	Lake County-Kenosha County PMSA, IL-WI	Y	61230 FQ	84690 MW	93340 TQ	USBLS	5/15
	Indiana	Y	38470 FQ	48560 MW	61420 TQ	USBLS	5/15
	Gary PMSA, IN	Y	38530 FQ	50420 MW	71460 TQ	USBLS	5/15
	Indianapolis-Carmel-Anderson MSA, IN	Y	40510 FQ	48880 MW	63790 TQ	USBLS	5/15
	Iowa	Y	35430 FQ	42580 MW	54380 TQ	USBLS	5/15
	Des Moines-West Des Moines MSA, IA	Y	36460 FQ	42110 MW	53570 TQ	USBLS	5/15
	Kansas	Y	45190 FQ	53520 MW	62370 TQ	USBLS	5/15
	Wichita MSA, KS	Y	38970 FQ	45030 MW	51210 TQ	USBLS	5/15
	Kentucky	Y	35460 FQ	43520 MW	51800 TQ	USBLS	5/15
	Louisville-Jefferson County MSA, KY-IN	Y	34190 FQ	39760 MW	49570 TQ	USBLS	5/15
	Louisiana	Y	33060 FQ	40170 MW	45950 TQ	USBLS	5/15
	Baton Rouge MSA, LA	Y	40760 FQ	43870 MW	46990 TQ	USBLS	5/15
	New Orleans-Metairie MSA, LA	Y	33430 FQ	38280 MW	45500 TQ	USBLS	5/15
	Maine	Y	33620 FQ	37550 MW	50570 TQ	USBLS	5/15
	Portland-South Portland MSA, ME	Y	34390 FQ	43750 MW	57830 TQ	USBLS	5/15
	Maryland	Y	29809 AE	42999 MW	49594 AEX	MDBLS	4/16
	Baltimore-Columbia-Towson MSA, MD	Y	34410 FQ	43210 MW	49810 TQ	USBLS	5/15

AE	Average entry wage	**AWR**	Average wage range	**H**	Hourly	**LR**	Low end range	**MTC**	Median total compensation	**TCC** Total cash compensation
AEX	Average experienced wage	**B**	Biweekly	**HI**	Highest wage paid	**M**	Monthly	**MW**	Median wage paid	**TQ** Third quartile wage
ATC	Average total compensation	**D**	Daily	**HR**	High end range	**MCC**	Median cash compensation	**MWR**	Median wage range	**W** Weekly
AW	Average wage paid	**FQ**	First quartile wage	**LO**	Lowest wage paid	**ME**	Median entry wage	**S**	See annotated source	**Y** Yearly

Occupation/Type/Industry	Location	Per	Low	Mid	High	Source	Date
Brickmason and Blockmason	Salisbury MSA, MD-DE	Y	34540 FQ	39560 MW	45840 TQ	USBLS	5/15
	Massachusetts	Y	48140 FQ	72870 MW	101330 TQ	USBLS	5/15
	Boston-Cambridge-Newton NECTA, MA	Y	35630 FQ	84250 MW	109120 TQ	USBLS	5/15
	Worcester MSA, MA-CT	Y	43680 FQ	52040 MW	63370 TQ	USBLS	5/15
	Michigan	Y	39390 FQ	51170 MW	60280 TQ	USBLS	5/15
	Detroit-Dearborn-Livonia PMSA, MI	Y	42330 FQ	64640 MW	77950 TQ	USBLS	5/15
	Grand Rapids-Wyoming MSA, MI	Y	39210 FQ	45020 MW	52790 TQ	USBLS	5/15
	Minnesota	Y	53528 FQ	66605 MW	76746 TQ	MNBLS	1/16-3/16
	Minneapolis-St. Paul-Bloomington MSA, MN-WI	Y	55869 FQ	69118 MW	78683 TQ	MNBLS	1/16-3/16
	Mississippi	Y	30160 FQ	38130 MW	44820 TQ	USBLS	5/15
	Jackson MSA, MS	Y	32190 FQ	38990 MW	44510 TQ	USBLS	5/15
	Missouri	Y	54740 FQ	66090 MW	73630 TQ	USBLS	5/15
	Kansas City MSA, MO-KS	Y	53640 FQ	61600 MW	72020 TQ	USBLS	5/15
	St. Louis MSA, MO-IL	Y	60550 FQ	68130 MW	74230 TQ	USBLS	5/15
	Montana	Y	42800 FQ	49180 MW	58140 TQ	USBLS	5/15
	Billings MSA, MT	Y	36920 FQ	43290 MW	47970 TQ	USBLS	5/15
	Nebraska	Y	43960 FQ	51800 MW	58365 TQ	NEBLS	7/16-9/16
	Omaha-Council Bluffs MSA, NE-IA	Y	47590 FQ	53915 MW	59895 TQ	NEBLS	7/16-9/16
	Nevada	Y	34710 FQ	40050 MW	65010 TQ	USBLS	5/15
	Las Vegas-Henderson-Paradise MSA, NV	Y	34270 FQ	38700 MW	63750 TQ	USBLS	5/15
	New Hampshire	H	18.00 AE	24.09 MW	26.72 AEX	NHBLS	6/16
	Nashua NECTA, NH-MA	Y	37570 FQ	44950 MW	55430 TQ	USBLS	5/15
	New Jersey	Y	45730 FQ	62540 MW	75470 TQ	USBLS	5/15
	Camden PMSA, NJ	Y	61050 FQ	70970 MW	79310 TQ	USBLS	5/15
	Newark PMSA, NJ-PA	Y	47880 FQ	63160 MW	72230 TQ	USBLS	5/15
	Trenton MSA, NJ	Y	37580 FQ	52940 MW	72480 TQ	USBLS	5/15
	New Mexico	Y	30940 FQ	35970 MW	45170 TQ	USBLS	5/15
	Albuquerque MSA, NM	Y	29470 FQ	34400 MW	38210 TQ	USBLS	5/15
	New York	Y	38080 AE	63250 MW	80890 AEX	NYBLS	1/16-3/16
	Buffalo-Cheektowaga-Niagara Falls MSA, NY	Y	54750 FQ	64900 MW	72350 TQ	USBLS	5/15
	Nassau County-Suffolk County PMSA, NY	Y	52410 FQ	84800 MW	110510 TQ	USBLS	5/15
	New York-Jersey City-White Plains PMSA, NY-NJ	Y	43370 FQ	60380 MW	82170 TQ	USBLS	5/15
	Rochester MSA, NY	Y	33280 FQ	37930 MW	51250 TQ	USBLS	5/15
	North Carolina	Y	30730 FQ	35910 MW	42690 TQ	USBLS	5/15
	Charlotte-Concord-Gastonia MSA, NC-SC	Y	33310 FQ	36680 MW	40960 TQ	USBLS	5/15
	Raleigh MSA, NC	Y	24090 FQ	28520 MW	36850 TQ	USBLS	5/15
	North Dakota	Y	50870 FQ	59970 MW	72450 TQ	USBLS	5/15
	Fargo MSA, ND-MN	Y	51590 FQ	56140 MW	60700 TQ	USBLS	5/15
	Ohio	Y	40140 FQ	51650 MW	59660 TQ	USBLS	5/15
	Cincinnati MSA, OH-KY-IN	Y	43350 FQ	52870 MW	59460 TQ	USBLS	5/15
	Cleveland-Elyria MSA, OH	Y	48710 FQ	56090 MW	61990 TQ	USBLS	5/15
	Columbus MSA, OH	Y	38040 FQ	42870 MW	47710 TQ	USBLS	5/15
	Oklahoma	Y	36080 FQ	41940 MW	47180 TQ	USBLS	5/15
	Oklahoma City MSA, OK	Y	39300 FQ	43750 MW	48020 TQ	USBLS	5/15
	Tulsa MSA, OK	Y	34270 FQ	37820 MW	43500 TQ	USBLS	5/15
	Oregon	H	17.77 FQ	25.57 MW	32.26 TQ	ORBLS	2016
	Portland-Vancouver-Hillsboro MSA, OR-WA	Y	43450 FQ	59950 MW	78940 TQ	USBLS	5/15
	Pennsylvania	Y	39950 FQ	51680 MW	62900 TQ	USBLS	5/15
	Allentown-Bethlehem-Easton MSA, PA-NJ	Y	39630 FQ	64520 MW	73500 TQ	USBLS	5/15
	Harrisburg-Carlisle MSA, PA	Y	34520 FQ	37680 MW	54010 TQ	USBLS	5/15
	Montgomery County-Bucks County-Chester County PMSA, PA	Y	38390 FQ	56910 MW	75140 TQ	USBLS	5/15
	Philadelphia PMSA, PA	Y	61440 FQ	70980 MW	79690 TQ	USBLS	5/15
	Pittsburgh MSA, PA	Y	42540 FQ	51380 MW	58600 TQ	USBLS	5/15
	Rhode Island	Y	54200 FQ	61250 MW	72620 TQ	USBLS	5/15
	Providence-Warwick MSA, RI-MA	Y	55030 FQ	61600 MW	73020 TQ	USBLS	5/15
	South Carolina	Y	29950 FQ	34480 MW	39180 TQ	USBLS	5/15

AE	Average entry wage	AWR	Average wage range	H	Hourly	LR	Low end range	MTC	Median total compensation	TCC	Total cash compensation
AEX	Average experienced wage	B	Biweekly	HI	Highest wage paid	M	Monthly	MW	Median wage paid	TQ	Third quartile wage
ATC	Average total compensation	D	Daily	HR	High end range	MCC	Median cash compensation	MWR	Median wage range	W	Weekly
AW	Average wage paid	FQ	First quartile wage	LO	Lowest wage paid	ME	Median entry wage	S	See annotated source	Y	Yearly

Occupation/Type/Industry	Location	Per	Low	Mid	High	Source	Date
Brickmason and Blockmason	Charleston-North Charleston						
	MSA, SC	Y	28890 FQ	33370 MW	41680 TQ	USBLS	5/15
	Columbia MSA, SC	Y	31820 FQ	34600 MW	37390 TQ	USBLS	5/15
	Greenville-Anderson-Mauldin						
	MSA, SC	Y	28030 FQ	31390 MW	37590 TQ	USBLS	5/15
	South Dakota	Y	34310 FQ	45450 MW	65950 TQ	USBLS	,5/15
	Sioux Falls MSA, SD	Y	38750 FQ	64140 MW	72490 TQ	USBLS	5/15
	Tennessee	Y	38160 FQ	43750 MW	48810 TQ	USBLS	5/15
	Knoxville MSA, TN	Y	39930 FQ	44440 MW	48950 TQ	USBLS	5/15
	Memphis MSA, TN-MS-AR	Y	34550 FQ	43610 MW	50310 TQ	USBLS	5/15
	Nashville-Davidson–						
	Murfreesboro–Franklin						
	MSA, TN	Y	40040 FQ	44260 MW	48500 TQ	USBLS	5/15
	Texas	Y	34480 FQ	40520 MW	46320 TQ	USBLS	5/15
	Austin-Round Rock MSA, TX	Y	41590 FQ	44780 MW	47970 TQ	USBLS	5/15
	Dallas-Plano-Irving PMSA, TX	Y	34290 FQ	38940 MW	46940 TQ	USBLS	5/15
	Fort Worth-Arlington PMSA,						
	TX	Y	38140 FQ	43440 MW	47880 TQ	USBLS	5/15
	Houston-The Woodlands-						
	Sugar Land MSA, TX	Y	33230 FQ	38890 MW	45200 TQ	USBLS	5/15
	San Antonio-New Braunfels						
	MSA, TX	Y	40890 FQ	43940 MW	46990 TQ	USBLS	5/15
	Utah	Y	35820 FQ	42690 MW	48150 TQ	USBLS	5/15
	Ogden-Clearfield MSA, UT	Y	33930 FQ	40940 MW	45840 TQ	USBLS	5/15
	Provo-Orem MSA, UT	Y	34990 FQ	39540 MW	46320 TQ	USBLS	5/15
	Salt Lake City MSA, UT	Y	39600 FQ	44630 MW	49890 TQ	USBLS	5/15
	Vermont	Y	47620 FQ	53690 MW	58320 TQ	USBLS	5/15
	Burlington-South Burlington						
	MSA, VT	Y	51250 FQ	55640 MW	59960 TQ	USBLS	5/15
	Virginia	Y	38220 FQ	45240 MW	53730 TQ	USBLS	5/15
	Richmond MSA, VA	Y	37320 FQ	44630 MW	52080 TQ	USBLS	5/15
	Virginia Beach-Norfolk-						
	Newport News MSA, VA-NC	Y	41130 FQ	45690 MW	50270 TQ	USBLS	5/15
	Washington	H	28.81 FQ	34.95 MW	44.62 TQ	WABLS	3/16
	Tacoma-Lakewood PMSA, WA	H	30.11 FQ	33.14 MW	36.37 TQ	WABLS	3/16
	West Virginia	Y	31520 FQ	40760 MW	47020 TQ	USBLS	5/15
	Huntington-Ashland MSA,						
	WV-KY-OH	Y	28280 FQ	32230 MW	38730 TQ	USBLS	5/15
	Wisconsin	Y	43020 FQ	53110 MW	62800 TQ	USBLS	5/15
	Madison MSA, WI	Y	43020 FQ	56950 MW	68730 TQ	USBLS	5/15
	Milwaukee-Waukesha-West						
	Allis MSA, WI	Y	51840 FQ	59020 MW	70710 TQ	USBLS	5/15
	Wyoming	Y	45900 FQ	53090 MW	58740 TQ	USBLS	5/15
	Puerto Rico	Y	20910 FQ	25530 MW	38080 TQ	USBLS	5/15
	San Juan-Carolina-Caguas						
	MSA, PR	Y	22260 FQ	28570 MW	39390 TQ	USBLS	5/15
	Virgin Islands	Y	34530 FQ	39550 MW	51550 TQ	USBLS	5/15
	Guam	Y	26670 FQ	28280 MW	29890 TQ	USBLS	5/15
Bridge and Lock Tender	California	H	18.95 FQ	20.93 MW	26.97 TQ	CABLS	1/16-3/16
	Connecticut	Y		45782 MW		CTBLS	1/16-3/16
	Florida	H	11.14 AE	15.44 MW	19.75 AEX	FLBLS	7/16-9/16
	Georgia	Y	29760 FQ	37340 MW	45350 TQ	USBLS	5/15
	Illinois	Y	50790 FQ	54640 MW	57250 TQ	USBLS	5/15
	Indiana	Y	43720 FQ	53780 MW	56560 TQ	USBLS	5/15
	Iowa	Y	50790 FQ	54630 MW	57130 TQ	USBLS	5/15
	Kentucky	Y	49900 FQ	52200 MW	54650 TQ	USBLS	5/15
	Louisiana	Y	26460 FQ	31820 MW	45240 TQ	USBLS	5/15
	Michigan	Y	40040 FQ	46830 MW	59530 TQ	USBLS	5/15
	Minnesota	Y	52534 FQ	56980 MW	61446 TQ	MNBLS	1/16-3/16
	Mississippi	Y	27240 FQ	53180 MW	57270 TQ	USBLS	5/15
	Missouri	Y	48860 FQ	54630 MW	57130 TQ	USBLS	5/15
	New Jersey	Y	41800 FQ	53210 MW	57280 TQ	USBLS	5/15
	New York	Y	29430 AE	43560 MW	49860 AEX	NYBLS	1/16-3/16
	Ohio	Y	39990 FQ	50640 MW	54660 TQ	USBLS	5/15
	Oregon	H	10.68 FQ	11.91 MW	20.09 TQ	ORBLS	2016
	Pennsylvania	Y	47460 FQ	52080 MW	56020 TQ	USBLS	5/15
	Texas	Y	46630 FQ	55500 MW	58010 TQ	USBLS	5/15
	Washington	H	19.18 FQ	26.72 MW	29.77 TQ	WABLS	3/16
	West Virginia	Y	49560 FQ	51410 MW	54650 TQ	USBLS	5/15
	Wisconsin	Y	38510 FQ	47620 MW	58340 TQ	USBLS	5/15

AE	Average entry wage	AWR	Average wage range	H	Hourly	LR	Low end range	MTC	Median total compensation	TCC	Total cash compensation
AEX	Average experienced wage	B	Biweekly	HI	Highest wage paid	M	Monthly	MW	Median wage paid	TQ	Third quartile wage
ATC	Average total compensation	D	Daily	HR	High end range	MCC	Median cash compensation	MWR	Median wage range	W	Weekly
AW	Average wage paid	FQ	First quartile wage	LO	Lowest wage paid	ME	Median entry wage	S	See annotated source	Y	Yearly

Occupation/Type/Industry	Location	Per	Low	Mid	High	Source	Date
Broadcast News Analyst	Alabama	Y	45380 AE	100454 AW	127986 AEX	ALBLS	6/16
	Arizona	Y	43190 FQ	84460 MW	137310 TQ	USBLS	5/15
	Arkansas	Y	42470 FQ	60680 MW	90270 TQ	USBLS	5/15
	California	H	13.69 FQ	27.22 MW	48.06 TQ	CABLS	1/16-3/16
	Colorado	Y	32960 FQ	62410 MW	112890 TQ	USBLS	5/15
	Connecticut	Y		71887 MW		CTBLS	1/16-3/16
	Florida	H	28.07 AE	47.88 MW	83.42 AEX	FLBLS	7/16-9/16
	Georgia	Y	36140 FQ	50640 MW	93630 TQ	USBLS	5/15
	Idaho	Y	37290 FQ	61330 MW	92660 TQ	USBLS	5/15
	Illinois	Y	38730 FQ	69150 MW	119380 TQ	USBLS	5/15
	Indiana	Y	54960 FQ	75950 MW	104470 TQ	USBLS	5/15
	Kentucky	Y	43900 FQ	67820 MW	103060 TQ	USBLS	5/15
	Minnesota	Y	27439 FQ	43578 MW	65382 TQ	MNBLS	1/16-3/16
	Missouri	Y	30380 FQ	43190 MW	72310 TQ	USBLS	5/15
	Nevada	Y	40530 FQ	67240 MW	93130 TQ	USBLS	5/15
	New Jersey	Y	51300 FQ	74560 MW	139280 TQ	USBLS	5/15
	New York	Y	34310 AE	65970 MW	123710 AEX	NYBLS	1/16-3/16
	North Carolina	Y	47120 FQ	62320 MW	101190 TQ	USBLS	5/15
	Ohio	Y	36600 FQ	58900 MW	111430 TQ	USBLS	5/15
	Oklahoma	Y	66410 FQ	99790 MW	148900 TQ	USBLS	5/15
	South Carolina	Y	38070 FQ	57650 MW	101100 TQ	USBLS	5/15
	Tennessee	Y	28830 FQ	53200 MW	98580 TQ	USBLS	5/15
	Texas	Y	39290 FQ	70370 MW	120990 TQ	USBLS	5/15
	Utah	Y	42100 FQ	61220 MW	95980 TQ	USBLS	5/15
	Virginia	Y	52080 FQ	76210 MW	103260 TQ	USBLS	5/15
	Wisconsin	Y	31560 FQ	60610 MW	94420 TQ	USBLS	5/15
	Puerto Rico	Y	20670 FQ	44700 MW	80460 TQ	USBLS	5/15
Broadcast Technician	Alabama	Y	20580 AE	37083 AW	45329 AEX	ALBLS	6/16
	Birmingham-Hoover MSA, AL	Y	23516 AE	43525 AW	53525 AEX	ALBLS	6/16
	Alaska	Y	27470 FQ	37220 MW	46570 TQ	USBLS	5/15
	Anchorage MSA, AK	Y	24680 FQ	35410 MW	48630 TQ	USBLS	5/15
	Arizona	Y	24870 FQ	39430 MW	54070 TQ	USBLS	5/15
	Phoenix-Mesa-Scottsdale MSA, AZ	Y	31440 FQ	43520 MW	57360 TQ	USBLS	5/15
	Tucson MSA, AZ	Y	30870 FQ	38830 MW	53230 TQ	USBLS	5/15
	Arkansas	Y	19230 FQ	34410 MW	46740 TQ	USBLS	5/15
	Little Rock-North Little Rock-Conway MSA, AR	Y	32740 FQ	40070 MW	48390 TQ	USBLS	5/15
	California	H	14.43 FQ	25.10 MW	32.78 TQ	CABLS	1/16-3/16
	Anaheim-Santa Ana-Irvine PMSA, CA	H	9.64 FQ	11.33 MW	13.95 TQ	CABLS	1/16-3/16
	Los Angeles-Long Beach-Glendale PMSA, CA	H	17.55 FQ	27.69 MW	35.60 TQ	CABLS	1/16-3/16
	Oakland-Hayward-Berkeley PMSA, CA	H	15.14 FQ	19.02 MW	30.35 TQ	CABLS	1/16-3/16
	Riverside-San Bernardino-Ontario MSA, CA	H	17.33 FQ	26.14 MW	30.00 TQ	CABLS	1/16-3/16
	Sacramento–Roseville–Arden-Arcade MSA, CA	H	14.14 FQ	21.40 MW	28.10 TQ	CABLS	1/16-3/16
	San Diego-Carlsbad MSA, CA	H	11.29 FQ	15.25 MW	26.89 TQ	CABLS	1/16-3/16
	San Francisco-Redwood City-South San Francisco PMSA, CA	H	12.20 FQ	25.52 MW	36.50 TQ	CABLS	1/16-3/16
	Colorado	Y	28280 FQ	43620 MW	62870 TQ	USBLS	5/15
	Denver-Aurora-Lakewood MSA, CO	Y	33020 FQ	46020 MW	64520 TQ	USBLS	5/15
	Connecticut	Y		40671 MW		CTBLS	1/16-3/16
	Hartford-West Hartford-East Hartford MSA, CT	Y	25600 FQ	41980 MW	67300 TQ	USBLS	5/15
	District of Columbia	Y	45500 FQ	82740 MW	92890 TQ	USBLS	5/15
	Washington-Arlington-Alexandria PMSA, DC-VA-MD-WV	Y	44260 FQ	65920 MW	92190 TQ	USBLS	5/15
	Florida	H	11.42 AE	18.58 MW	24.13 AEX	FLBLS	7/16-9/16
	Fort Lauderdale-Pompano Beach-Deerfield Beach PMSA, FL	H	13.07 AE	18.79 MW	23.38 AEX	FLBLS	7/16-9/16
	Miami-Miami Beach-Kendall PMSA, FL	H	12.87 AE	19.81 MW	23.51 AEX	FLBLS	7/16-9/16
	Orlando-Kissimmee-Sanford MSA, FL	H	11.83 AE	22.43 MW	27.76 AEX	FLBLS	7/16-9/16

AE	Average entry wage	AWR	Average wage range	H	Hourly
AEX	Average experienced wage	B	Biweekly	HI	Highest wage paid
ATC	Average total compensation	D	Daily	HR	High end range
AW	Average wage paid	FQ	First quartile wage	LO	Lowest wage paid

LR Low end range   MTC Median total compensation   TCC Total cash compensation
M Monthly   MW Median wage paid   TQ Third quartile wage
MCC Median cash compensation   MWR Median wage range   W Weekly
ME Median entry wage   S See annotated source   Y Yearly

Broadcast Technician

Occupation/Type/Industry	Location	Per	Low	Mid	High	Source	Date
Broadcast Technician	Tampa-St. Petersburg-Clearwater MSA, FL	H	10.41 AE	18.93 MW	27.20 AEX	FLBLS	7/16-9/16
	Georgia	Y	23010 FQ	37500 MW	54150 TQ	USBLS	5/15
	Atlanta-Sandy Springs-Roswell MSA, GA	Y	30070 FQ	42680 MW	60360 TQ	USBLS	5/15
	Augusta-Richmond County MSA, GA-SC	Y	25440 FQ	31610 MW	56940 TQ	USBLS	5/15
	Hawaii	Y	26390 FQ	36470 MW	50370 TQ	USBLS	5/15
	Urban Honolulu MSA, HI	Y	25930 FQ	34520 MW	49840 TQ	USBLS	5/15
	Idaho	Y	19180 FQ	27850 MW	37030 TQ	USBLS	5/15
	Boise City MSA, ID	Y	18230 FQ	25040 MW	42170 TQ	USBLS	5/15
	Illinois	Y	19100 FQ	35050 MW	57480 TQ	USBLS	5/15
	Chicago-Naperville-Arlington Heights PMSA, IL	Y	18970 FQ	34840 MW	58910 TQ	USBLS	5/15
	Indiana	Y	18200 FQ	23000 MW	37200 TQ	USBLS	5/15
	Indianapolis-Carmel-Anderson MSA, IN	Y	25090 FQ	35910 MW	65060 TQ	USBLS	5/15
	Iowa	Y	19610 FQ	33420 MW	56420 TQ	USBLS	5/15
	Des Moines-West Des Moines MSA, IA	Y	27900 FQ	40810 MW	58110 TQ	USBLS	5/15
	Kansas	Y	18990 FQ	31940 MW	39040 TQ	USBLS	5/15
	Wichita MSA, KS	Y	22380 FQ	32780 MW	49960 TQ	USBLS	5/15
	Kentucky	Y	18910 FQ	29740 MW	44840 TQ	USBLS	5/15
	Louisville-Jefferson County MSA, KY-IN	Y	18140 FQ	23370 MW	42440 TQ	USBLS	5/15
	Louisiana	Y	20670 FQ	28860 MW	41240 TQ	USBLS	5/15
	Baton Rouge MSA, LA	Y	22480 FQ	41460 MW	57100 TQ	USBLS	5/15
	New Orleans-Metairie MSA, LA	Y	19790 FQ	26820 MW	39370 TQ	USBLS	5/15
	Maine	Y	23060 FQ	35540 MW	47790 TQ	USBLS	5/15
	Portland-South Portland MSA, ME	Y	23380 FQ	37120 MW	49020 TQ	USBLS	5/15
	Maryland	Y	20308 AE	45284 MW	57772 AEX	MDBLS	4/16
	Baltimore-Columbia-Towson MSA, MD	Y	22090 FQ	37900 MW	70250 TQ	USBLS	5/15
	Salisbury MSA, MD-DE	Y	18550 FQ	24040 MW	31130 TQ	USBLS	5/15
	Massachusetts	Y	31490 FQ	41960 MW	66970 TQ	USBLS	5/15
	Boston-Cambridge-Newton NECTA, MA	Y	32400 FQ	43490 MW	68770 TQ	USBLS	5/15
	Michigan	Y	23370 FQ	35230 MW	57950 TQ	USBLS	5/15
	Detroit-Dearborn-Livonia PMSA, MI	Y	39070 FQ	60040 MW	72900 TQ	USBLS	5/15
	Minnesota	Y	24344 FQ	32721 MW	52257 TQ	MNBLS	1/16-3/16
	Minneapolis-St. Paul-Bloomington MSA, MN-WI	Y	24899 FQ	32963 MW	54233 TQ	MNBLS	1/16-3/16
	Mississippi	Y	23450 FQ	32300 MW	51040 TQ	USBLS	5/15
	Jackson MSA, MS	Y	26800 FQ	31930 MW	45270 TQ	USBLS	5/15
	Missouri	Y	23410 FQ	35090 MW	47260 TQ	USBLS	5/15
	Kansas City MSA, MO-KS	Y	31940 FQ	35090 MW	38250 TQ	USBLS	5/15
	St. Louis MSA, MO-IL	Y	21700 FQ	33460 MW	51070 TQ	USBLS	5/15
	Montana	Y	22600 FQ	28320 MW	37360 TQ	USBLS	5/15
	Nebraska	Y	21305 FQ	36570 MW	50920 TQ	NEBLS	7/16-9/16
	Omaha-Council Bluffs MSA, NE-IA	Y	18970 FQ	30150 MW	54525 TQ	NEBLS	7/16-9/16
	Nevada	Y	24630 FQ	36940 MW	54100 TQ	USBLS	5/15
	Las Vegas-Henderson-Paradise MSA, NV	Y	25840 FQ	36960 MW	50720 TQ	USBLS	5/15
	Manchester NECTA, NH	H	8.29 AE	8.73 MW	11.22 AEX	NHBLS	6/16
	New Jersey	Y	32860 FQ	37520 MW	55490 TQ	USBLS	5/15
	Newark PMSA, NJ-PA	Y	23050 FQ	34910 MW	52830 TQ	USBLS	5/15
	New Mexico	Y	20000 FQ	27910 MW	37090 TQ	USBLS	5/15
	Albuquerque MSA, NM	Y	23640 FQ	30390 MW	41780 TQ	USBLS	5/15
	New York	Y	28920 AE	52080 MW	65880 AEX	NYBLS	1/16-3/16
	Buffalo-Cheektowaga-Niagara Falls MSA, NY	Y	23480 FQ	31780 MW	37470 TQ	USBLS	5/15
	Nassau County-Suffolk County PMSA, NY	Y	33870 FQ	50620 MW	71550 TQ	USBLS	5/15
	New York-Jersey City-White Plains PMSA, NY-NJ	Y	37630 FQ	54660 MW	74490 TQ	USBLS	5/15
	Rochester MSA, NY	Y	20000 FQ	25310 MW	36390 TQ	USBLS	5/15
	North Carolina	Y	22440 FQ	35150 MW	58620 TQ	USBLS	5/15
	North Dakota	Y	24520 FQ	33370 MW	55090 TQ	USBLS	5/15

AE	Average entry wage	AWR	Average wage range	H	Hourly	LR	Low end range	MTC	Median total compensation	TCC	Total cash compensation
AEX	Average experienced wage	B	Biweekly	HI	Highest wage paid	M	Monthly	MW	Median wage paid	TQ	Third quartile wage
ATC	Average total compensation	D	Daily	HR	High end range	MCC	Median cash compensation	MWR	Median wage range	W	Weekly
AW	Average wage paid	FQ	First quartile wage	LO	Lowest wage paid	ME	Median entry wage	S	See annotated source	Y	Yearly

Occupation/Type/Industry	Location	Per	Low	Mid	High	Source	Date
Broadcast Technician	Fargo MSA, ND-MN	Y	26770 FQ	43410 MW	58400 TQ	USBLS	5/15
	Ohio	Y	19440 FQ	29190 MW	51300 TQ	USBLS	5/15
	Cincinnati MSA, OH-KY-IN	Y	23640 FQ	35660 MW	56910 TQ	USBLS	5/15
	Cleveland-Elyria MSA, OH	Y	22950 FQ	34210 MW	58250 TQ	USBLS	5/15
	Columbus MSA, OH	Y	19050 FQ	31200 MW	51410 TQ	USBLS	5/15
	Oklahoma	Y	18810 FQ	29310 MW	50960 TQ	USBLS	5/15
	Tulsa MSA, OK	Y	17530 FQ	20920 MW	40230 TQ	USBLS	5/15
	Oregon	H	11.04 FQ	14.11 MW	23.65 TQ	ORBLS	2016
	Portland-Vancouver-Hillsboro MSA, OR-WA	Y	25460 FQ	31670 MW	53920 TQ	USBLS	5/15
	Pennsylvania	Y	21800 FQ	33600 MW	47990 TQ	USBLS	5/15
	Harrisburg-Carlisle MSA, PA	Y	26270 FQ	34920 MW	46080 TQ	USBLS	5/15
	Montgomery County-Bucks County-Chester County PMSA, PA	Y	28230 FQ	34790 MW	45270 TQ	USBLS	5/15
	Philadelphia PMSA, PA	Y	26960 FQ	36980 MW	56340 TQ	USBLS	5/15
	Pittsburgh MSA, PA	Y	18120 FQ	29710 MW	46750 TQ	USBLS	5/15
	Rhode Island	Y	33800 FQ	48570 MW	72990 TQ	USBLS	5/15
	Providence-Warwick MSA, RI-MA	Y	34110 FQ	48710 MW	72870 TQ	USBLS	5/15
	South Carolina	Y	29430 FQ	31310 MW	35360 TQ	USBLS	5/15
	Charleston-North Charleston MSA, SC	Y	29090 FQ	30970 MW	37440 TQ	USBLS	5/15
	Columbia MSA, SC	Y	29740 FQ	31770 MW	35390 TQ	USBLS	5/15
	Greenville-Anderson-Mauldin MSA, SC	Y	28190 FQ	30430 MW	33410 TQ	USBLS	5/15
	South Dakota	Y	27290 FQ	33650 MW	43360 TQ	USBLS	5/15
	Sioux Falls MSA, SD	Y	26650 FQ	31170 MW	39100 TQ	USBLS	5/15
	Tennessee	Y	27180 FQ	41330 MW	56750 TQ	USBLS	5/15
	Knoxville MSA, TN	Y	20140 FQ	33200 MW	53440 TQ	USBLS	5/15
	Memphis MSA, TN-MS-AR	Y	29830 FQ	42800 MW	63110 TQ	USBLS	5/15
	Nashville-Davidson–Murfreesboro–Franklin MSA, TN	Y	34290 FQ	44100 MW	58390 TQ	USBLS	5/15
	Texas	Y	20460 FQ	28070 MW	44180 TQ	USBLS	5/15
	Austin-Round Rock MSA, TX	Y	21840 FQ	29350 MW	47250 TQ	USBLS	5/15
	Dallas-Plano-Irving PMSA, TX	Y	24120 FQ	33970 MW	57630 TQ	USBLS	5/15
	Fort Worth-Arlington PMSA, TX	Y	23010 FQ	31200 MW	45330 TQ	USBLS	5/15
	Houston-The Woodlands-Sugar Land MSA, TX	Y	18790 FQ	27770 MW	44870 TQ	USBLS	5/15
	San Antonio-New Braunfels MSA, TX	Y	23500 FQ	31110 MW	45760 TQ	USBLS	5/15
	Utah	Y	23690 FQ	35700 MW	52020 TQ	USBLS	5/15
	Salt Lake City MSA, UT	Y	28390 FQ	37940 MW	54860 TQ	USBLS	5/15
	Vermont	Y	31690 FQ	35960 MW	41610 TQ	USBLS	5/15
	Burlington-South Burlington MSA, VT	Y	32850 FQ	36470 MW	42270 TQ	USBLS	5/15
	Virginia	Y	28100 FQ	42430 MW	57880 TQ	USBLS	5/15
	Richmond MSA, VA	Y	27150 FQ	40460 MW	52140 TQ	USBLS	5/15
	Virginia Beach-Norfolk-Newport News MSA, VA-NC	Y	30410 FQ	39080 MW	49420 TQ	USBLS	5/15
	Washington	H	11.05 FQ	14.56 MW	18.88 TQ	WABLS	3/16
	Seattle-Bellevue-Everett PMSA, WA	H	10.72 FQ	11.86 MW	17.63 TQ	WABLS	3/16
	West Virginia	Y	18340 FQ	22420 MW	46640 TQ	USBLS	5/15
	Wisconsin	Y	29710 FQ	47530 MW	64210 TQ	USBLS	5/15
	Madison MSA, WI	Y	32890 FQ	44830 MW	53210 TQ	USBLS	5/15
	Milwaukee-Waukesha-West Allis MSA, WI	Y	33120 FQ	58160 MW	76240 TQ	USBLS	5/15
	Wyoming	Y	27430 FQ	35430 MW	45930 TQ	USBLS	5/15
	Cheyenne MSA, WY	Y	29760 FQ	36290 MW	45280 TQ	USBLS	5/15
	Puerto Rico	Y	18670 FQ	26470 MW	34240 TQ	USBLS	5/15
	San Juan-Carolina-Caguas MSA, PR	Y	19860 FQ	28490 MW	35920 TQ	USBLS	5/15
	Guam	Y	22140 FQ	27540 MW	30410 TQ	USBLS	5/15
Broadcasting Services Program Manager							
Michigan State University	East Lansing, MI	Y			67344 HI	MSUSAL	10/1/14-9/30/15
Brokerage Clerk	Alabama	Y	35339 AE	48593 AW	55230 AEX	ALBLS	6/16

AE	Average entry wage	AWR	Average wage range	H	Hourly	LR Low end range	MTC Median total compensation	TCC Total cash compensation
AEX	Average experienced wage	B	Biweekly	HI	Highest wage paid	M Monthly	MW Median wage paid	TQ Third quartile wage
ATC	Average total compensation	D	Daily	HR	High end range	MCC Median cash compensation	MWR Median wage range	W Weekly
AW	Average wage paid	FQ	First quartile wage	LO	Lowest wage paid	ME Median entry wage	S See annotated source	Y Yearly

Brokerage Clerk

Occupation/Type/Industry	Location	Per	Low	Mid	High	Source	Date
Brokerage Clerk	Birmingham-Hoover MSA, AL	Y	36009 AE	46799 AW	52200 AEX	ALBLS	6/16
	Alaska	Y	40970 FQ	45840 MW	51820 TQ	USBLS	5/15
	Anchorage MSA, AK	Y	41520 FQ	46110 MW	52030 TQ	USBLS	5/15
	Arizona	Y	42020 FQ	48080 MW	58590 TQ	USBLS	5/15
	Phoenix-Mesa-Scottsdale MSA, AZ	Y	42130 FQ	48100 MW	58500 TQ	USBLS	5/15
	Tucson MSA, AZ	Y	40730 FQ	47720 MW	58360 TQ	USBLS	5/15
	Arkansas	Y	32500 FQ	40460 MW	54260 TQ	USBLS	5/15
	Little Rock-North Little Rock-Conway MSA, AR	Y	31290 FQ	39540 MW	57490 TQ	USBLS	5/15
	California	H	20.91 FQ	26.32 MW	34.34 TQ	CABLS	1/16-3/16
	Anaheim-Santa Ana-Irvine PMSA, CA	H	21.02 FQ	23.55 MW	27.77 TQ	CABLS	1/16-3/16
	Los Angeles-Long Beach-Glendale PMSA, CA	H	20.27 FQ	25.81 MW	32.59 TQ	CABLS	1/16-3/16
	Oakland-Hayward-Berkeley PMSA, CA	H	21.83 FQ	26.69 MW	31.26 TQ	CABLS	1/16-3/16
	Riverside-San Bernardino-Ontario MSA, CA	H	19.18 FQ	25.56 MW	31.81 TQ	CABLS	1/16-3/16
	Sacramento–Roseville–Arden-Arcade MSA, CA	H	14.73 FQ	23.58 MW	34.82 TQ	CABLS	1/16-3/16
	San Diego-Carlsbad MSA, CA	H	20.04 FQ	24.04 MW	32.37 TQ	CABLS	1/16-3/16
	San Francisco-Redwood City-South San Francisco PMSA, CA	H	22.46 FQ	30.26 MW	37.67 TQ	CABLS	1/16-3/16
	Colorado	Y	38300 FQ	48300 MW	59280 TQ	USBLS	5/15
	Denver-Aurora-Lakewood MSA, CO	Y	32080 FQ	46370 MW	58990 TQ	USBLS	5/15
	Connecticut	Y		53173 MW		CTBLS	1/16-3/16
	Bridgeport-Stamford-Norwalk MSA, CT	Y	38720 FQ	49880 MW	64240 TQ	USBLS	5/15
	Hartford-West Hartford-East Hartford MSA, CT	Y	46300 FQ	58080 MW	71950 TQ	USBLS	5/15
	Delaware	Y	43630 FQ	51750 MW	58650 TQ	USBLS	5/15
	Wilmington PMSA, DE-MD-NJ	Y	43940 FQ	51970 MW	58760 TQ	USBLS	5/15
	District of Columbia	Y	47100 FQ	54780 MW	62160 TQ	USBLS	5/15
	Washington-Arlington-Alexandria PMSA, DC-VA-MD-WV	Y	42620 FQ	52940 MW	61320 TQ	USBLS	5/15
	Florida	H	15.73 AE	23.19 MW	29.05 AEX	FLBLS	7/16-9/16
	Fort Lauderdale-Pompano Beach-Deerfield Beach PMSA, FL	H	15.53 AE	22.35 MW	28.38 AEX	FLBLS	7/16-9/16
	Miami-Miami Beach-Kendall PMSA, FL	H	18.89 AE	25.15 MW	31.70 AEX	FLBLS	7/16-9/16
	Orlando-Kissimmee-Sanford MSA, FL	H	14.45 AE	26.21 MW	33.61 AEX	FLBLS	7/16-9/16
	Tampa-St. Petersburg-Clearwater MSA, FL	H	16.47 AE	22.07 MW	25.89 AEX	FLBLS	7/16-9/16
	Georgia	Y	36470 FQ	46970 MW	60730 TQ	USBLS	5/15
	Atlanta-Sandy Springs-Roswell MSA, GA	Y	36940 FQ	47580 MW	62030 TQ	USBLS	5/15
	Hawaii	Y	36190 FQ	51410 MW	57540 TQ	USBLS	5/15
	Urban Honolulu MSA, HI	Y	36350 FQ	51490 MW	57620 TQ	USBLS	5/15
	Idaho	Y	35760 FQ	45960 MW	57240 TQ	USBLS	5/15
	Boise City MSA, ID	Y	36740 FQ	48020 MW	58020 TQ	USBLS	5/15
	Illinois	Y	37600 FQ	47100 MW	62180 TQ	USBLS	5/15
	Chicago-Naperville-Arlington Heights PMSA, IL	Y	37660 FQ	47480 MW	62870 TQ	USBLS	5/15
	Lake County-Kenosha County PMSA, IL-WI	Y	36890 FQ	45170 MW	57340 TQ	USBLS	5/15
	Indiana	Y	35920 FQ	43570 MW	53430 TQ	USBLS	5/15
	Indianapolis-Carmel-Anderson MSA, IN	Y	35990 FQ	44210 MW	54390 TQ	USBLS	5/15
	Iowa	Y	30640 FQ	37340 MW	48220 TQ	USBLS	5/15
	Des Moines-West Des Moines MSA, IA	Y	34470 FQ	46270 MW	56500 TQ	USBLS	5/15
	Kansas	Y	40710 FQ	47780 MW	59210 TQ	USBLS	5/15
	Kentucky	Y	32960 FQ	37540 MW	44850 TQ	USBLS	5/15
	Louisville-Jefferson County MSA, KY-IN	Y	34550 FQ	39430 MW	46560 TQ	USBLS	5/15

AE	Average entry wage	AWR	Average wage range	H	Hourly	LR	Low end range	MTC	Median total compensation	TCC	Total cash compensation
AEX	Average experienced wage	B	Biweekly	HI	Highest wage paid	M	Monthly	MW	Median wage paid	TQ	Third quartile wage
ATC	Average total compensation	D	Daily	HR	High end range	MCC	Median cash compensation	MWR	Median wage range	W	Weekly
AW	Average wage paid	FQ	First quartile wage	LO	Lowest wage paid	ME	Median entry wage	S	See annotated source	Y	Yearly

Occupation/Type/Industry	Location	Per	Low	Mid	High	Source	Date
Brokerage Clerk	Louisiana	Y	38590 FQ	51270 MW	63960 TQ	USBLS	5/15
	Baton Rouge MSA, LA	Y	40330 FQ	46780 MW	58000 TQ	USBLS	5/15
	New Orleans-Metairie MSA, LA	Y	42120 FQ	56740 MW	71890 TQ	USBLS	5/15
	Maine	Y	41660 FQ	46730 MW	56990 TQ	USBLS	5/15
	Portland-South Portland MSA, ME	Y	41520 FQ	46700 MW	57030 TQ	USBLS	5/15
	Maryland	Y	37073 AE	55489 MW	64697 AEX	MDBLS	4/16
	Baltimore-Columbia-Towson MSA, MD	Y	41470 FQ	51010 MW	64990 TQ	USBLS	5/15
	Massachusetts	Y	41660 FQ	48850 MW	60730 TQ	USBLS	5/15
	Boston-Cambridge-Newton NECTA, MA	Y	42070 FQ	49780 MW	61710 TQ	USBLS	5/15
	Michigan	Y	37000 FQ	45070 MW	55200 TQ	USBLS	5/15
	Detroit-Dearborn-Livonia PMSA, MI	Y	40280 FQ	52240 MW	60350 TQ	USBLS	5/15
	Grand Rapids-Wyoming MSA, MI	Y	27220 FQ	34280 MW	43270 TQ	USBLS	5/15
	Minnesota	Y	38823 FQ	45396 MW	53699 TQ	MNBLS	1/16-3/16
	Minneapolis-St. Paul-Bloomington MSA, MN-WI	Y	38985 FQ	45335 MW	53061 TQ	MNBLS	1/16-3/16
	Mississippi	Y	36530 FQ	42340 MW	48510 TQ	USBLS	5/15
	Jackson MSA, MS	Y	36580 FQ	42420 MW	48590 TQ	USBLS	5/15
	Missouri	Y	34860 FQ	39880 MW	47830 TQ	USBLS	5/15
	Kansas City MSA, MO-KS	Y	39510 FQ	50270 MW	59150 TQ	USBLS	5/15
	St. Louis MSA, MO-IL	Y	34740 FQ	39500 MW	46680 TQ	USBLS	5/15
	Montana	Y	33270 FQ	39950 MW	49320 TQ	USBLS	5/15
	Billings MSA, MT	Y	37840 FQ	47380 MW	63570 TQ	USBLS	5/15
	Nebraska	Y	35785 FQ	43325 MW	48855 TQ	NEBLS	7/16-9/16
	Omaha-Council Bluffs MSA, NE-IA	Y	35615 FQ	43170 MW	48805 TQ	NEBLS	7/16-9/16
	Nevada	Y	34070 FQ	46140 MW	57290 TQ	USBLS	5/15
	Las Vegas-Henderson-Paradise MSA, NV	Y	32210 FQ	39760 MW	52690 TQ	USBLS	5/15
	New Hampshire	H	17.88 AE	23.85 MW	30.10 AEX	NHBLS	6/16
	Manchester NECTA, NH	H	18.19 AE	24.11 MW	28.53 AEX	NHBLS	6/16
	Nashua NECTA, NH-MA	Y	40160 FQ	48420 MW	64690 TQ	USBLS	5/15
	New Jersey	Y	42680 FQ	50750 MW	61950 TQ	USBLS	5/15
	Camden PMSA, NJ	Y	40390 FQ	49590 MW	63870 TQ	USBLS	5/15
	Newark PMSA, NJ-PA	Y	44840 FQ	54410 MW	64000 TQ	USBLS	5/15
	Trenton MSA, NJ	Y	43440 FQ	49610 MW	58820 TQ	USBLS	5/15
	New Mexico	Y	33540 FQ	37140 MW	43940 TQ	USBLS	5/15
	Albuquerque MSA, NM	Y	33840 FQ	36770 MW	39690 TQ	USBLS	5/15
	New York	Y	38920 AE	59950 MW	73360 AEX	NYBLS	1/16-3/16
	Buffalo-Cheektowaga-Niagara Falls MSA, NY	Y	37520 FQ	52210 MW	66280 TQ	USBLS	5/15
	Nassau County-Suffolk County PMSA, NY	Per	39850 FQ	51750 MW	64920 TQ	USBLS	5/15
	New York-Jersey City-White Plains PMSA, NY-NJ	Y	44410 FQ	57300 MW	72230 TQ	USBLS	5/15
	Rochester MSA, NY	Y	41110 FQ	50620 MW	64910 TQ	USBLS	5/15
	North Carolina	Y	35500 FQ	43980 MW	52250 TQ	USBLS	5/15
	Charlotte-Concord-Gastonia MSA, NC-SC	Y	39970 FQ	46050 MW	53880 TQ	USBLS	5/15
	Raleigh MSA, NC	Y	34170 FQ	37880 MW	49200 TQ	USBLS	5/15
	North Dakota	Y	41070 FQ	49350 MW	59540 TQ	USBLS	5/15
	Ohio	Y	37060 FQ	44970 MW	55380 TQ	USBLS	5/15
	Cleveland-Elyria MSA, OH	Y	36120 FQ	42690 MW	49520 TQ	USBLS	5/15
	Columbus MSA, OH	Y	36010 FQ	45680 MW	57370 TQ	USBLS	5/15
	Oklahoma	Y	38330 FQ	46810 MW	60940 TQ	USBLS	5/15
	Oklahoma City MSA, OK	Y	40290 FQ	48200 MW	67120 TQ	USBLS	5/15
	Tulsa MSA, OK	Y	36570 FQ	45100 MW	59130 TQ	USBLS	5/15
	Oregon	H	20.65 FQ	24.10 MW	28.81 TQ	ORBLS	2016
	Portland-Vancouver-Hillsboro MSA, OR-WA	Y	44920 FQ	52730 MW	63750 TQ	USBLS	5/15
	Pennsylvania	Y	37260 FQ	45570 MW	56080 TQ	USBLS	5/15
	Allentown-Bethlehem-Easton MSA, PA-NJ	Y	41830 FQ	45830 MW	49840 TQ	USBLS	5/15
	Harrisburg-Carlisle MSA, PA	Y	37360 FQ	44730 MW	55280 TQ	USBLS	5/15
	Philadelphia PMSA, PA	Y	43110 FQ	49940 MW	59300 TQ	USBLS	5/15
	Pittsburgh MSA, PA	Y	36770 FQ	44450 MW	54290 TQ	USBLS	5/15
	Rhode Island	Y	42080 FQ	49620 MW	60670 TQ	USBLS	5/15

AE	Average entry wage	AWR	Average wage range	H	Hourly
AEX	Average experienced wage	B	Biweekly	HI	Highest wage paid
ATC	Average total compensation	D	Daily	HR	High end range
AW	Average wage paid	FQ	First quartile wage	LO	Lowest wage paid

LR	Low end range	MTC	Median total compensation	TCC	Total cash compensation
M	Monthly	MW	Median wage paid	TQ	Third quartile wage
MCC	Median cash compensation	MWR	Median wage range	W	Weekly
ME	Median entry wage	S	See annotated source	Y	Yearly

Occupation/Type/Industry	Location	Per	Low	Mid	High	Source	Date
Brokerage Clerk	Providence-Warwick MSA, RI-MA	Y	42070 FQ	49580 MW	60600 TQ	USBLS	5/15
	South Carolina	Y	37340 FQ	46130 MW	55450 TQ	USBLS	5/15
	Charleston-North Charleston MSA, SC	Y	43140 FQ	53720 MW	63610 TQ	USBLS	5/15
	Columbia MSA, SC	Y	32270 FQ	45050 MW	52950 TQ	USBLS	5/15
	Greenville-Anderson-Mauldin MSA, SC	Y	41800 FQ	46400 MW	51240 TQ	USBLS	5/15
	South Dakota	Y.	33270 FQ	36820 MW	40690 TQ	USBLS	5/15
	Sioux Falls MSA, SD	Y	33190 FQ	36670 MW	40140 TQ	USBLS	5/15
	Tennessee	Y	39630 FQ	46690 MW	61910 TQ	USBLS	5/15
	Knoxville MSA, TN	Y	38280 FQ	44870 MW	50820 TQ	USBLS	5/15
	Memphis MSA, TN-MS-AR	Y	40180 FQ	51060 MW	76960 TQ	USBLS	5/15
	Nashville-Davidson–Murfreesboro–Franklin MSA, TN	Y	42110 FQ	47350 MW	58220 TQ	USBLS	5/15
	Texas	Y	42930 FQ	53010 MW	66080 TQ	USBLS	5/15
	Austin-Round Rock MSA, TX	Y	38420 FQ	52210 MW	67050 TQ	USBLS	5/15
	Dallas-Plano-Irving PMSA, TX	Y	45480 FQ	55280 MW	68130 TQ	USBLS	5/15
	Fort Worth-Arlington PMSA, TX	Y	41460 FQ	51520 MW	64250 TQ	USBLS	5/15
	Houston-The Woodlands-Sugar Land MSA, TX	Y	47650 FQ	57560 MW	70660 TQ	USBLS	5/15
	San Antonio-New Braunfels MSA, TX	Y	42590 FQ	49520 MW	62040 TQ	USBLS	5/15
	Utah	Y	34220 FQ	43510 MW	53740 TQ	USBLS	5/15
	Salt Lake City MSA, UT	Y	33920 FQ	43650 MW	54230 TQ	USBLS	5/15
	Vermont	Y	36210 FQ	43830 MW	55280 TQ	USBLS	5/15
	Virginia	Y	36840 FQ	44490 MW	53580 TQ	USBLS	5/15
	Richmond MSA, VA	Y	35750 FQ	41820 MW	48610 TQ	USBLS	5/15
	Virginia Beach-Norfolk-Newport News MSA, VA-NC	Y	39960 FQ	45840 MW	52220 TQ	USBLS	5/15
	Washington	H	21.87 FQ	26.62 MW	30.30 TQ	WABLS	3/16
	Seattle-Bellevue-Everett PMSA, WA	H	21.59 FQ	26.53 MW	30.03 TQ	WABLS	3/16
	Tacoma-Lakewood PMSA, WA	H	19.75 FQ	24.54 MW	29.20 TQ	WABLS	3/16
	West Virginia	Y	36520 FQ	49940 MW	57620 TQ	USBLS	5/15
	Wisconsin	Y	33880 FQ	42000 MW	49400 TQ	USBLS	5/15
	Madison MSA, WI	Y	34330 FQ	44360 MW	59310 TQ	USBLS	5/15
	Milwaukee-Waukesha-West Allis MSA, WI	Y	33700 FQ	41610 MW	48830 TQ	USBLS	5/15
	Wyoming	Y	41760 FQ	48150 MW	55070 TQ	USBLS	5/15
Budget Analyst	Alabama	Y	52160 FQ	78625 AW	91857 AEX	ALBLS	6/16
	Birmingham-Hoover MSA, AL	Y	55614 AE	79322 AW	91170 AEX	ALBLS	6/16
	Alaska	Y	66090 FQ	77770 MW	94570 TQ	USBLS	5/15
	Anchorage MSA, AK	Y	66080 FQ	75430 MW	93480 TQ	USBLS	5/15
	Arizona	Y	54470 FQ	66010 MW	82460 TQ	USBLS	5/15
	Phoenix-Mesa-Scottsdale MSA, AZ	Y	54080 FQ	66000 MW	84920 TQ	USBLS	5/15
	Tucson MSA, AZ	Y	50020 FQ	59680 MW	70300 TQ	USBLS	5/15
	Arkansas	Y	47300 FQ	55630 MW	66460 TQ	USBLS	5/15
	Little Rock-North Little Rock-Conway MSA, AR	Y	50020 FQ	58200 MW	68390 TQ	USBLS	5/15
	California	H	31.71 FQ	39.47 MW	48.89 TQ	CABLS	1/16-3/16
	Anaheim-Santa Ana-Irvine PMSA, CA	H	35.92 FQ	44.14 MW	53.60 TQ	CABLS	1/16-3/16
	Los Angeles-Long Beach-Glendale PMSA, CA	H	33.47 FQ	42.52 MW	51.77 TQ	CABLS	1/16-3/16
	Oakland-Hayward-Berkeley PMSA, CA	H	33.70 FQ	39.72 MW	49.06 TQ	CABLS	1/16-3/16
	Riverside-San Bernardino-Ontario MSA, CA	H	22.11 FQ	30.18 MW	39.77 TQ	CABLS	1/16-3/16
	Sacramento–Roseville–Arden-Arcade MSA, CA	H	30.37 FQ	33.74 MW	43.13 TQ	CABLS	1/16-3/16
	San Diego-Carlsbad MSA, CA	H	33.20 FQ	38.33 MW	47.91 TQ	CABLS	1/16-3/16
	San Francisco-Redwood City-South San Francisco PMSA, CA	H	34.48 FQ	42.60 MW	53.46 TQ	CABLS	1/16-3/16
	Colorado	Y	62480 FQ	75160 MW	90880 TQ	USBLS	5/15
	Denver-Aurora-Lakewood MSA, CO	Y	64760 FQ	77880 MW	93450 TQ	USBLS	5/15

AE	Average entry wage	AWR Average wage range	H Hourly	LR Low end range	MTC Median total compensation	TCC Total cash compensation
AEX	Average experienced wage	B Biweekly	HI Highest wage paid	M Monthly	MW Median wage paid	TQ Third quartile wage
ATC	Average total compensation	D Daily	HR High end range	MCC Median cash compensation	MWR Median wage range	W Weekly
AW	Average wage paid	FQ First quartile wage	LO Lowest wage paid	ME Median entry wage	S See annotated source	Y Yearly

Budget Analyst

Occupation/Type/Industry	Location	Per	Low	Mid	High	Source	Date
Budget Analyst	Connecticut	Y		84529 MW		CTBLS	1/16-3/16
	Bridgeport-Stamford-Norwalk MSA, CT	Y	73750 FQ	87230 MW	101090 TQ	USBLS	5/15
	Hartford-West Hartford-East Hartford MSA, CT	Y	72460 FQ	83470 MW	96520 TQ	USBLS	5/15
	Delaware	Y	56230 FQ	70450 MW	86400 TQ	USBLS	5/15
	Wilmington PMSA, DE-MD-NJ	Y	65470 FQ	81190 MW	94170 TQ	USBLS	5/15
	District of Columbia	Y	76470 FQ	93860 MW	105970 TQ	USBLS	5/15
	Washington-Arlington-Alexandria PMSA, DC-VA-MD-WV	Y	76380 FQ	92890 MW	107770 TQ	USBLS	5/15
	Florida	H	22.43 AE	30.70 MW	36.93 AEX	FLBLS	7/16-9/16
	Fort Lauderdale-Pompano Beach-Deerfield Beach PMSA, FL	H	21.23 AE	27.68 MW	33.44 AEX	FLBLS	7/16-9/16
	Miami-Miami Beach-Kendall PMSA, FL	H	26.03 AE	32.83 MW	38.99 AEX	FLBLS	7/16-9/16
	Orlando-Kissimmee-Sanford MSA, FL	H	21.00 AE	31.01 MW	36.00 AEX	FLBLS	7/16-9/16
	Tampa-St. Petersburg-Clearwater MSA, FL	H	24.91 AE	36.07 MW	43.30 AEX	FLBLS	7/16-9/16
	Georgia	Y	53940 FQ	69050 MW	86590 TQ	USBLS	5/15
	Atlanta-Sandy Springs-Roswell MSA, GA	Y	54430 FQ	72190 MW	90470 TQ	USBLS	5/15
	Augusta-Richmond County MSA, GA-SC	Y	60510 FQ	72230 MW	94590 TQ	USBLS	5/15
	Savannah MSA, GA	Y	57540 FQ	66360 MW	77230 TQ	USBLS	5/15
	Hawaii	Y	60440 FQ	73700 MW	85980 TQ	USBLS	5/15
	Urban Honolulu MSA, HI	Y	63260 FQ	75210 MW	88200 TQ	USBLS	5/15
	Idaho	Y	56250 FQ	62930 MW	74180 TQ	USBLS	5/15
	Boise City MSA, ID	Y	55390 FQ	62850 MW	72550 TQ	USBLS	5/15
	Illinois	Y	58410 FQ	71980 MW	89410 TQ	USBLS	5/15
	Chicago-Naperville-Arlington Heights PMSA, IL	Y	59050 FQ	73050 MW	92880 TQ	USBLS	5/15
	Lake County-Kenosha County PMSA, IL-WI	Y	57350 FQ	67170 MW	81290 TQ	USBLS	5/15
	Indiana	Y	47450 FQ	59760 MW	76150 TQ	USBLS	5/15
	Indianapolis-Carmel-Anderson MSA, IN	Y	47750 FQ	60090 MW	75230 TQ	USBLS	5/15
	Iowa	Y	57300 FQ	67950 MW	78410 TQ	USBLS	5/15
	Des Moines-West Des Moines MSA, IA	Y	61840 FQ	75220 MW	83660 TQ	USBLS	5/15
	Wichita MSA, KS	Y	50040 FQ	58090 MW	67550 TQ	USBLS	5/15
	Kentucky	Y	44180 FQ	52080 MW	63590 TQ	USBLS	5/15
	Louisville-Jefferson County MSA, KY-IN	Y	53520 FQ	65190 MW	84050 TQ	USBLS	5/15
	Louisiana	Y	51600 FQ	62940 MW	77230 TQ	USBLS	5/15
	Baton Rouge MSA, LA	Y	46200 FQ	61280 MW	75120 TQ	USBLS	5/15
	New Orleans-Metairie MSA, LA	Y	54850 FQ	64430 MW	81900 TQ	USBLS	5/15
	Maine	Y	51490 FQ	59800 MW	69880 TQ	USBLS	5/15
	Portland-South Portland MSA, ME	Y	52700 FQ	62250 MW	80910 TQ	USBLS	5/15
	Maryland	Y	57674 AE	83634 MW	96614 AEX	MDBLS	4/16
	Baltimore-Columbia-Towson MSA, MD	Y	59690 FQ	75720 MW	96530 TQ	USBLS	5/15
	Massachusetts	Y	59410 FQ	72480 MW	89020 TQ	USBLS	5/15
	Boston-Cambridge-Newton NECTA, MA	Y	58280 FQ	71830 MW	88930 TQ	USBLS	5/15
	Worcester MSA, MA-CT	Y	60250 FQ	72890 MW	85790 TQ	USBLS	5/15
	Michigan	Y	67870 FQ	67880 MW	76820 TQ	USBLS	5/15
	Detroit-Dearborn-Livonia PMSA, MI	Y	67880 FQ	87370 MW	109100 TQ	USBLS	5/15
	Grand Rapids-Wyoming MSA, MI	Y	64860 FQ	67890 MW	75170 TQ	USBLS	5/15
	Minnesota	Y	50754 FQ	62480 MW	78728 TQ	MNBLS	1/16-3/16
	Minneapolis-St. Paul-Bloomington MSA, MN-WI	Y	53894 FQ	65163 MW	83493 TQ	MNBLS	1/16-3/16
	Mississippi	Y	48450 FQ	58770 MW	70100 TQ	USBLS	5/15
	Jackson MSA, MS	Y	35640 FQ	44320 MW	64900 TQ	USBLS	5/15
	Missouri	Y	54870 FQ	67660 MW	80040 TQ	USBLS	5/15

Occupation/Type/Industry	Location	Per	Low	Mid	High	Source	Date
Budget Analyst	Kansas City MSA, MO-KS	Y	58570 FQ	72550 MW	86660 TQ	USBLS	5/15
	St. Louis MSA, MO-IL	Y	59430 FQ	71030 MW	84230 TQ	USBLS	5/15
	Montana	Y	48500 FQ	57400 MW	64430 TQ	USBLS	5/15
	Nebraska	Y	49295 FQ	60525 MW	75215 TQ	NEBLS	7/16-9/16
	Omaha-Council Bluffs MSA, NE-IA	Y	51740 FQ	66280 MW	78215 TQ	NEBLS	7/16-9/16
	Nevada	Y	58180 FQ	67860 MW	79540 TQ	USBLS	5/15
	Las Vegas-Henderson-Paradise MSA, NV	Y	58080 FQ	64430 MW	77570 TQ	USBLS	5/15
	New Hampshire	H	25.30 AE	33.72 MW	39.56 AEX	NHBLS	6/16
	New Jersey	Y	60320 FQ	75270 MW	95090 TQ	USBLS	5/15
	Camden PMSA, NJ	Y	54260 FQ	66980 MW	83160 TQ	USBLS	5/15
	Newark PMSA, NJ-PA	Y	69510 FQ	87880 MW	107870 TQ	USBLS	5/15
	Trenton MSA, NJ	Y	64800 FQ	72950 MW	82220 TQ	USBLS	5/15
	New Mexico	Y	54860 FQ	67240 MW	84220 TQ	USBLS	5/15
	Albuquerque MSA, NM	Y	56550 FQ	70270 MW	84240 TQ	USBLS	5/15
	New York	Y	53400 AE	73280 MW	87390 AEX	NYBLS	1/16-3/16
	Buffalo-Cheektowaga-Niagara Falls MSA, NY	Y	56020 FQ	70030 MW	88000 TQ	USBLS	5/15
	Nassau County-Suffolk County PMSA, NY	Y	68090 FQ	84890 MW	98060 TQ	USBLS	5/15
	New York-Jersey City-White Plains PMSA, NY-NJ	Y	58610 FQ	72900 MW	91960 TQ	USBLS	5/15
	Rochester MSA, NY	Y	54660 FQ	69110 MW	85770 TQ	USBLS	5/15
	North Carolina	Y	56390 FQ	67740 MW	81900 TQ	USBLS	5/15
	Charlotte-Concord-Gastonia MSA, NC-SC	Y	58570 FQ	69520 MW	84130 TQ	USBLS	5/15
	Raleigh MSA, NC	Y	56430 FQ	67600 MW	82930 TQ	USBLS	5/15
	North Dakota	Y	54850 FQ	60530 MW	70280 TQ	USBLS	5/15
	Ohio	Y	59880 FQ	73380 MW	85140 TQ	USBLS	5/15
	Cincinnati MSA, OH-KY-IN	Y	55930 FQ	69760 MW	88580 TQ	USBLS	5/15
	Cleveland-Elyria MSA, OH	Y	56180 FQ	69950 MW	81840 TQ	USBLS	5/15
	Columbus MSA, OH	Y	65490 FQ	77510 MW	86970 TQ	USBLS	5/15
	Oklahoma	Y	48310 FQ	62600 MW	77680 TQ	USBLS	5/15
	Oklahoma City MSA, OK	Y	53490 FQ	68730 MW	79560 TQ	USBLS	5/15
	Tulsa MSA, OK	Y	46440 FQ	59560 MW	78790 TQ	USBLS	5/15
	Oregon	H	28.29 FQ	33.04 MW	38.24 TQ	ORBLS	2016
	Portland-Vancouver-Hillsboro MSA, OR-WA	Y	58210 FQ	68890 MW	78870 TQ	USBLS	5/15
	Pennsylvania	Y	55790 FQ	66500 MW	82830 TQ	USBLS	5/15
	Harrisburg-Carlisle MSA, PA	Y	55380 FQ	63230 MW	74020 TQ	USBLS	5/15
	Montgomery County-Bucks County-Chester County PMSA, PA	Y	55100 FQ	62610 MW	80480 TQ	USBLS	5/15
	Philadelphia PMSA, PA	Y	60610 FQ	74190 MW	89880 TQ	USBLS	5/15
	Pittsburgh MSA, PA	Y	54410 FQ	62860 MW	85880 TQ	USBLS	5/15
	Rhode Island	Y	60510 FQ	79140 MW	92250 TQ	USBLS	5/15
	Providence-Warwick MSA, RI-MA	Y	61690 FQ	79300 MW	92450 TQ	USBLS	5/15
	South Carolina	Y	44420 FQ	55660 MW	68720 TQ	USBLS	5/15
	Charleston-North Charleston MSA, SC	Y	47810 FQ	58080 MW	72230 TQ	USBLS	5/15
	Columbia MSA, SC	Y	56460 FQ	68310 MW	77220 TQ	USBLS	5/15
	Greenville-Anderson-Mauldin MSA, SC	Y	42010 FQ	48710 MW	59910 TQ	USBLS	5/15
	South Dakota	Y	50010 FQ	58280 MW	68320 TQ	USBLS	5/15
	Sioux Falls MSA, SD	Y	55470 FQ	65320 MW	75370 TQ	USBLS	5/15
	Tennessee	Y	51630 FQ	61730 MW	77530 TQ	USBLS	5/15
	Knoxville MSA, TN	Y	45620 FQ	60160 MW	78180 TQ	USBLS	5/15
	Memphis MSA, TN-MS-AR	Y	52680 FQ	61740 MW	77230 TQ	USBLS	5/15
	Nashville-Davidson–Murfreesboro–Franklin MSA, TN	Y	51950 FQ	61600 MW	75300 TQ	USBLS	5/15
	Texas	Y	56470 FQ	71580 MW	91550 TQ	USBLS	5/15
	Austin-Round Rock MSA, TX	Y	52660 FQ	63420 MW	77210 TQ	USBLS	5/15
	Dallas-Plano-Irving PMSA, TX	Y	61370 FQ	82140 MW	101250 TQ	USBLS	5/15
	Fort Worth-Arlington PMSA, TX	Y	59240 FQ	74300 MW	94450 TQ	USBLS	5/15
	Houston-The Woodlands-Sugar Land MSA, TX	Y	60290 FQ	79020 MW	112840 TQ	USBLS	5/15
	San Antonio-New Braunfels MSA, TX	Y	58570 FQ	71210 MW	85630 TQ	USBLS	5/15

AE	Average entry wage	AWR	Average wage range	H	Hourly
AEX	Average experienced wage	B	Biweekly	HI	Highest wage paid
ATC	Average total compensation	D	Daily	HR	High end range
AW	Average wage paid	FQ	First quartile wage	LO	Lowest wage paid

LR	Low end range	MTC	Median total compensation
M	Monthly	MW	Median wage paid
MCC	Median cash compensation	MWR	Median wage range
ME	Median entry wage	S	See annotated source

TCC	Total cash compensation
TQ	Third quartile wage
W	Weekly
Y	Yearly

Occupation/Type/Industry	Location	Per	Low	Mid	High	Source	Date
Budget Analyst	Utah	Y	60530 FQ	71830 MW	81900 TQ	USBLS	5/15
	Ogden-Clearfield MSA, UT	Y	68330 FQ	77220 MW	84240 TQ	USBLS	5/15
	Provo-Orem MSA, UT	Y	65830 FQ	72680 MW	79960 TQ	USBLS	5/15
	Salt Lake City MSA, UT	Y	58560 FQ	68560 MW	78280 TQ	USBLS	5/15
	Vermont	Y	48420 FQ	58560 MW	71100 TQ	USBLS	5/15
	Burlington-South Burlington MSA, VT	Y	48420 FQ	58090 MW	66350 TQ	USBLS	5/15
	Virginia	Y	65950 FQ	82520 MW	102120 TQ	USBLS	5/15
	Richmond MSA, VA	Y	58450 FQ	69130 MW	83050 TQ	USBLS	5/15
	Virginia Beach-Norfolk-Newport News MSA, VA-NC	Y	60390 FQ	72540 MW	85430 TQ	USBLS	5/15
	Washington	H	29.27 FQ	35.76 MW	45.27 TQ	WABLS	3/16
	Seattle-Bellevue-Everett PMSA, WA	H	29.88 FQ	37.54 MW	47.82 TQ	WABLS	3/16
	Tacoma-Lakewood PMSA, WA	H	30.49 FQ	34.85 MW	41.04 TQ	WABLS	3/16
	West Virginia	Y	48410 FQ	58570 MW	72540 TQ	USBLS	5/15
	Wisconsin	Y	57180 FQ	67420 MW	81040 TQ	USBLS	5/15
	Wyoming	Y	53250 FQ	65550 MW	76970 TQ	USBLS	5/15
	Cheyenne MSA, WY	Y	51720 FQ	62470 MW	75010 TQ	USBLS	5/15
	Puerto Rico	Y	32020 FQ	42260 MW	56320 TQ	USBLS	5/15
	San Juan-Carolina-Caguas MSA, PR	Y	28720 FQ	39000 MW	50380 TQ	USBLS	5/15
	Virgin Islands	Y	41940 FQ	48350 MW	58460 TQ	USBLS	5/15
	Guam	Y	43210 FQ	51630 MW	60290 TQ	USBLS	5/15
Budget Director							
10 or More Years of Experience	United States	Y		113000 MW		CNBC07	2016-2017
Building Inspector							
County Government	Lee County, GA	H	14.27 LO		22.12 HI	GACTY04	2016
Municipal Government	Montague, MA	Y			66933 HI	FRCOG	2016
Building Plans Engineer	San Francisco, CA	B	4848 LO		5893 HI	SFGOV	2016-2018
Building Plans Examiner							
Community Development, Municipal Government	Albany, CA	Y			73831 HI	CACIT	6/28/16
Building Trades Supervisor							
State Government	Lansing, MI	H	22.45 LO		30.89 HI	MIGOV	2016
Bus Aide							
Public Schools	Baldwin County, AL	Y	6696 LO		14200 HI	BCPSSS	2016-2017
Bus and Truck Mechanic and Diesel Engine Specialist	Alabama	Y	29036 AE	40548 AW	46305 AEX	ALBLS	6/16
	Birmingham-Hoover MSA, AL	Y	30734 AE	45420 AW	52763 AEX	ALBLS	6/16
	Alaska	Y	48260 FQ	62190 MW	74910 TQ	USBLS	5/15
	Anchorage MSA, AK	Y	46920 FQ	59990 MW	73520 TQ	USBLS	5/15
	Arizona	Y	35110 FQ	43980 MW	54960 TQ	USBLS	5/15
	Phoenix-Mesa-Scottsdale MSA, AZ	Y	35800 FQ	43950 MW	54640 TQ	USBLS	5/15
	Tucson MSA, AZ	Y	39010 FQ	50090 MW	60000 TQ	USBLS	5/15
	Arkansas	Y	29370 FQ	35920 MW	45600 TQ	USBLS	5/15
	Little Rock-North Little Rock-Conway MSA, AR	Y	33310 FQ	41690 MW	53480 TQ	USBLS	5/15
	California	H	19.62 FQ	25.10 MW	30.39 TQ	CABLS	1/16-3/16
	Anaheim-Santa Ana-Irvine PMSA, CA	H	18.68 FQ	23.52 MW	30.40 TQ	CABLS	1/16-3/16
	Los Angeles-Long Beach-Glendale PMSA, CA	H	20.44 FQ	26.75 MW	31.00 TQ	CABLS	1/16-3/16
	Oakland-Hayward-Berkeley PMSA, CA	H	23.12 FQ	28.63 MW	34.63 TQ	CABLS	1/16-3/16
	Riverside-San Bernardino-Ontario MSA, CA	H	17.56 FQ	21.94 MW	27.44 TQ	CABLS	1/16-3/16
	Sacramento–Roseville–Arden-Arcade MSA, CA	H	21.19 FQ	25.25 MW	30.31 TQ	CABLS	1/16-3/16
	San Diego-Carlsbad MSA, CA	H	20.24 FQ	25.52 MW	29.85 TQ	CABLS	1/16-3/16
	San Francisco-Redwood City-South San Francisco PMSA, CA	H	21.52 FQ	27.93 MW	35.28 TQ	CABLS	1/16-3/16
	Colorado	Y	38420 FQ	48210 MW	59500 TQ	USBLS	5/15

AE	Average entry wage	AWR	Average wage range	
AEX	Average experienced wage	B	Biweekly	
ATC	Average total compensation	D	Daily	
AW	Average wage paid	FQ	First quartile wage	
H	Hourly	LR	Low end range	MTC Median total compensation
HI	Highest wage paid	M	Monthly	MW Median wage paid
HR	High end range	MCC	Median cash compensation	MWR Median wage range
LO	Lowest wage paid	ME	Median entry wage	S See annotated source
				TCC Total cash compensation
				TQ Third quartile wage
				W Weekly
				Y Yearly

Occupation/Type/Industry	Location	Per	Low	Mid	High	Source	Date
Bus and Truck Mechanic and Diesel Engine Specialist	Denver-Aurora-Lakewood MSA, CO	Y	40670 FQ	51410 MW	61980 TQ	USBLS	5/15
	Connecticut	Y		53348 MW		CTBLS	1/16-3/16
	Bridgeport-Stamford-Norwalk MSA, CT	Y	51620 FQ	58610 MW	68050 TQ	USBLS	5/15
	Hartford-West Hartford-East Hartford MSA, CT	Y	39640 FQ	53680 MW	67470 TQ	USBLS	5/15
	Delaware	Y	41510 FQ	48490 MW	56690 TQ	USBLS	5/15
	Wilmington PMSA, DE-MD-NJ	Y	42190 FQ	50910 MW	57390 TQ	USBLS	5/15
	District of Columbia	Y	42100 FQ	53000 MW	68300 TQ	USBLS	5/15
	Washington-Arlington-Alexandria PMSA, DC-VA-MD-WV	Y	41780 FQ	50340 MW	64100 TQ	USBLS	5/15
	Florida	H	15.31 AE	21.10 MW	24.95 AEX	FLBLS	7/16-9/16
	Fort Lauderdale-Pompano Beach-Deerfield Beach PMSA, FL	H	17.41 AE	25.92 MW	29.69 AEX	FLBLS	7/16-9/16
	Miami-Miami Beach-Kendall PMSA, FL	H	14.52 AE	24.41 MW	27.89 AEX	FLBLS	7/16-9/16
	Orlando-Kissimmee-Sanford MSA, FL	H	16.15 AE	21.34 MW	25.21 AEX	FLBLS	7/16-9/16
	Tampa-St. Petersburg-Clearwater MSA, FL	H	15.41 AE	20.53 MW	23.39 AEX	FLBLS	7/16-9/16
	Georgia	Y	34270 FQ	42720 MW	52280 TQ	USBLS	5/15
	Atlanta-Sandy Springs-Roswell MSA, GA	Y	36810 FQ	45160 MW	54960 TQ	USBLS	5/15
	Augusta-Richmond County MSA, GA-SC	Y	33060 FQ	38940 MW	49800 TQ	USBLS	5/15
	Hawaii	Y	46790 FQ	56650 MW	65900 TQ	USBLS	5/15
	Urban Honolulu MSA, HI	Y	50580 FQ	57990 MW	66510 TQ	USBLS	5/15
	Idaho	Y	33510 FQ	39290 MW	46640 TQ	USBLS	5/15
	Boise City MSA, ID	Y	34200 FQ	39800 MW	47180 TQ	USBLS	5/15
	Illinois	Y	34480 FQ	46120 MW	59170 TQ	USBLS	5/15
	Chicago-Naperville-Arlington Heights PMSA, IL	Y	38490 FQ	51380 MW	62480 TQ	USBLS	5/15
	Lake County-Kenosha County PMSA, IL-WI	Y	35310 FQ	43740 MW	52010 TQ	USBLS	5/15
	Indiana	Y	33600 FQ	40850 MW	48430 TQ	USBLS	5/15
	Gary PMSA, IN	Y	37270 FQ	46070 MW	55400 TQ	USBLS	5/15
	Indianapolis-Carmel-Anderson MSA, IN	Y	35080 FQ	42620 MW	48980 TQ	USBLS	5/15
	Iowa	Y	31390 FQ	38830 MW	47940 TQ	USBLS	5/15
	Des Moines-West Des Moines MSA, IA	Y	37280 FQ	46840 MW	57080 TQ	USBLS	5/15
	Kansas	Y	33460 FQ	40900 MW	50760 TQ	USBLS	5/15
	Wichita MSA, KS	Y	34110 FQ	37880 MW	45910 TQ	USBLS	5/15
	Kentucky	Y	32100 FQ	38800 MW	48900 TQ	USBLS	5/15
	Louisville-Jefferson County MSA, KY-IN	Y	35160 FQ	43600 MW	56660 TQ	USBLS	5/15
	Louisiana	Y	33390 FQ	42770 MW	54460 TQ	USBLS	5/15
	Baton Rouge MSA, LA	Y	38550 FQ	47030 MW	56070 TQ	CTBLS	5/15
	New Orleans-Metairie MSA, LA	Y	35780 FQ	46920 MW	61260 TQ	USBLS	5/15
	Maine	Y	33230 FQ	39290 MW	46890 TQ	USBLS	5/15
	Portland-South Portland MSA, ME	Y	40370 FQ	44790 MW	49210 TQ	USBLS	5/15
	Maryland	Y	35471 AE	49928 MW	57156 AEX	MDBLS	4/16
	Baltimore-Columbia-Towson MSA, MD	Y	39870 FQ	48010 MW	59870 TQ	USBLS	5/15
	Salisbury MSA, MD-DE	Y	36760 FQ	43940 MW	52090 TQ	USBLS	5/15
	Massachusetts	Y	43450 FQ	53450 MW	64830 TQ	USBLS	5/15
	Boston-Cambridge-Newton NECTA, MA	Y	49830 FQ	60170 MW	70710 TQ	USBLS	5/15
	Worcester MSA, MA-CT	Y	44260 FQ	54380 MW	65220 TQ	USBLS	5/15
	Michigan	Y	34400 FQ	42380 MW	50660 TQ	USBLS	5/15
	Detroit-Dearborn-Livonia PMSA, MI	Y	35210 FQ	43290 MW	51370 TQ	USBLS	5/15
	Grand Rapids-Wyoming MSA, MI	Y	33730 FQ	41570 MW	49550 TQ	USBLS	5/15
	Minnesota	Y	37854 FQ	46241 MW	56338 TQ	MNBLS	1/16-3/16

AE	Average entry wage	**AWR**	Average wage range	**H**	Hourly	**LR**	Low end range	**MTC** Median total compensation	**TCC** Total cash compensation
AEX	Average experienced wage	**B**	Biweekly	**HI**	Highest wage paid	**M**	Monthly	**MW** Median wage paid	**TQ** Third quartile wage
ATC	Average total compensation	**D**	Daily	**HR**	High end range	**MCC**	Median cash compensation	**MWR** Median wage range	**W** Weekly
AW	Average wage paid	**FQ**	First quartile wage	**LO**	Lowest wage paid	**ME**	Median entry wage	**S** See annotated source	**Y** Yearly

Occupation/Type/Industry	Location	Per	Low	Mid	High	Source	Date
Bus and Truck Mechanic and Diesel Engine Specialist	Minneapolis-St. Paul-Bloomington MSA, MN-WI	Y	41605 FQ	48735 MW	58168 TQ	MNBLS	1/16-3/16
	Mississippi	Y	28910 FQ	35140 MW	43940 TQ	USBLS	5/15
	Jackson MSA, MS	Y	34770 FQ	44010 MW	54990 TQ	USBLS	5/15
	Missouri	Y	32650 FQ	41580 MW	50640 TQ	USBLS	5/15
	Kansas City MSA, MO-KS	Y	35470 FQ	43960 MW	52640 TQ	USBLS	5/15
	St. Louis MSA, MO-IL	Y	36270 FQ	45620 MW	55500 TQ	USBLS	5/15
	Montana	Y	30420 FQ	38260 MW	47960 TQ	USBLS	5/15
	Billings MSA, MT	Y	35190 FQ	44020 MW	55780 TQ	USBLS	5/15
	Nebraska	Y	33435 FQ	41280 MW	49730 TQ	NEBLS	7/16-9/16
	Omaha-Council Bluffs MSA, NE-IA	Y	34875 FQ	42490 MW	49385 TQ	NEBLS	7/16-9/16
	Nevada	Y	44050 FQ	55290 MW	66150 TQ	USBLS	5/15
	Las Vegas-Henderson-Paradise MSA, NV	Y	40310 FQ	52160 MW	61870 TQ	USBLS	5/15
	New Hampshire	H	16.68 AE	21.83 MW	25.46 AEX	NHBLS	6/16
	Manchester NECTA, NH	H	17.25 AE	23.05 MW	27.74 AEX	NHBLS	6/16
	Nashua NECTA, NH-MA	Y	40010 FQ	45460 MW	52190 TQ	USBLS	5/15
	New Jersey	Y	44700 FQ	55090 MW	62660 TQ	USBLS	5/15
	Camden PMSA, NJ	Y	43560 FQ	53840 MW	61620 TQ	USBLS	5/15
	Newark PMSA, NJ-PA	Y	52430 FQ	59010 MW	68720 TQ	USBLS	5/15
	Trenton MSA, NJ	Y	42160 FQ	53810 MW	61660 TQ	USBLS	5/15
	New Mexico	Y	32690 FQ	40580 MW	52290 TQ	USBLS	5/15
	Albuquerque MSA, NM	Y	38490 FQ	45870 MW	56200 TQ	USBLS	5/15
	New York	Y	35140 AE	51510 MW	62150 AEX	NYBLS	1/16-3/16
	Buffalo-Cheektowaga-Niagara Falls MSA, NY	Y	37880 FQ	45830 MW	55880 TQ	USBLS	5/15
	Nassau County-Suffolk County PMSA, NY	Y	42720 FQ	52310 MW	64900 TQ	USBLS	5/15
	New York-Jersey City-White Plains PMSA, NY-NJ	Y	45000 FQ	58100 MW	70240 TQ	USBLS	5/15
	Rochester MSA, NY	Y	34570 FQ	43110 MW	52890 TQ	USBLS	5/15
	North Carolina	Y	34000 FQ	41230 MW	50300 TQ	USBLS	5/15
	Charlotte-Concord-Gastonia MSA, NC-SC	Y	36430 FQ	44300 MW	53420 TQ	USBLS	5/15
	Raleigh MSA, NC	Y	33800 FQ	44340 MW	58800 TQ	USBLS	5/15
	North Dakota	Y	42130 FQ	51410 MW	59990 TQ	USBLS	5/15
	Fargo MSA, ND-MN	Y	41660 FQ	48980 MW	60830 TQ	USBLS	5/15
	Ohio	Y	34860 FQ	43920 MW	54470 TQ	USBLS	5/15
	Cincinnati MSA, OH-KY-IN	Y	37300 FQ	45920 MW	55160 TQ	USBLS	5/15
	Cleveland-Elyria MSA, OH	Y	41440 FQ	52290 MW	60160 TQ	USBLS	5/15
	Columbus MSA, OH	Y	35910 FQ	44730 MW	55220 TQ	USBLS	5/15
	Oklahoma	Y	32590 FQ	39010 MW	48160 TQ	USBLS	5/15
	Oklahoma City MSA, OK	Y	34220 FQ	39550 MW	47170 TQ	USBLS	5/15
	Tulsa MSA, OK	Y	34260 FQ	42470 MW	54490 TQ	USBLS	5/15
	Oregon	H	18.24 FQ	22.15 MW	26.58 TQ	ORBLS	2016
	Portland-Vancouver-Hillsboro MSA, OR-WA	Y	42780 FQ	51050 MW	59040 TQ	USBLS	5/15
	Pennsylvania	Y	35070 FQ	42890 MW	51420 TQ	USBLS	5/15
	Allentown-Bethlehem-Easton MSA, PA-NJ	Y	37700 FQ	44940 MW	52930 TQ	USBLS	5/15
	Harrisburg-Carlisle MSA, PA	Y	39190 FQ	47140 MW	56230 TQ	USBLS	5/15
	Montgomery County-Bucks County-Chester County PMSA, PA	Y	37900 FQ	46150 MW	57010 TQ	USBLS	5/15
	Philadelphia PMSA, PA	Y	39810 FQ	46960 MW	58140 TQ	USBLS	5/15
	Pittsburgh MSA, PA	Y	35750 FQ	43450 MW	52310 TQ	USBLS	5/15
	Rhode Island	Y	36930 FQ	45680 MW	54670 TQ	USBLS	5/15
	Providence-Warwick MSA, RI-MA	Y	38510 FQ	45240 MW	52460 TQ	USBLS	5/15
	South Carolina	Y	31800 FQ	38170 MW	48350 TQ	USBLS	5/15
	Charleston-North Charleston MSA, SC	Y	33050 FQ	41700 MW	48750 TQ	USBLS	5/15
	Columbia MSA, SC	Y	33110 FQ	40090 MW	51580 TQ	USBLS	5/15
	Greenville-Anderson-Mauldin MSA, SC	Y	31930 FQ	37760 MW	46290 TQ	USBLS	5/15
	South Dakota	Y	35200 FQ	41410 MW	48550 TQ	USBLS	5/15
	Sioux Falls MSA, SD	Y	37160 FQ	44100 MW	50990 TQ	USBLS	5/15
	Tennessee	Y	34170 FQ	43630 MW	52580 TQ	USBLS	5/15
	Knoxville MSA, TN	Y	31970 FQ	42250 MW	48700 TQ	USBLS	5/15
	Memphis MSA, TN-MS-AR	Y	37470 FQ	45890 MW	55190 TQ	USBLS	5/15

AE	Average entry wage	AWR	Average wage range	H	Hourly	LR	Low end range	MTC	Median total compensation	TCC	Total cash compensation
AEX	Average experienced wage	B	Biweekly	HI	Highest wage paid	M	Monthly	MW	Median wage paid	TQ	Third quartile wage
ATC	Average total compensation	D	Daily	HR	High end range	MCC	Median cash compensation	MWR	Median wage range	W	Weekly
AW	Average wage paid	FQ	First quartile wage	LO	Lowest wage paid	ME	Median entry wage	S	See annotated source	Y	Yearly

Occupation/Type/Industry	Location	Per	Low	Mid	High	Source	Date
Bus and Truck Mechanic and Diesel Engine Specialist	Nashville-Davidson–Murfreesboro–Franklin						
	MSA, TN	Y	36490 FQ	44650 MW	51540 TQ	USBLS	5/15
	Texas	Y	34260 FQ	42920 MW	53110 TQ	USBLS	5/15
	Austin-Round Rock MSA, TX	Y	34790 FQ	43520 MW	53830 TQ	USBLS	5/15
	Dallas-Plano-Irving PMSA, TX	Y	36990 FQ	46420 MW	55830 TQ	USBLS	5/15
	Fort Worth-Arlington PMSA, TX	Y	36970 FQ	43910 MW	50980 TQ	USBLS	5/15
	Houston-The Woodlands-Sugar Land MSA, TX	Y	36870 FQ	45790 MW	58280 TQ	USBLS	5/15
	San Antonio-New Braunfels MSA, TX	Y	35610 FQ	44210 MW	55250 TQ	USBLS	5/15
	Utah	Y	35040 FQ	42970 MW	52990 TQ	USBLS	5/15
	Ogden-Clearfield MSA, UT	Y	34340 FQ	41060 MW	48390 TQ	USBLS	5/15
	Provo-Orem MSA, UT	Y	33100 FQ	39100 MW	47790 TQ	USBLS	5/15
	Salt Lake City MSA, UT	Y	35710 FQ	45110 MW	56850 TQ	USBLS	5/15
	Vermont	Y	36230 FQ	42670 MW	49570 TQ	USBLS	5/15
	Burlington-South Burlington MSA, VT	Y	37060 FQ	45070 MW	57500 TQ	USBLS	5/15
	Virginia	Y	35530 FQ	43800 MW	52930 TQ	USBLS	5/15
	Richmond MSA, VA	Y	40380 FQ	47440 MW	56840 TQ	USBLS	5/15
	Virginia Beach-Norfolk-Newport News MSA, VA-NC	Y	37040 FQ	44720 MW	53460 TQ	USBLS	5/15
	Washington	H	20.43 FQ	25.16 MW	30.25 TQ	WABLS	3/16
	Seattle-Bellevue-Everett PMSA, WA	H	23.83 FQ	28.78 MW	34.70 TQ	WABLS	3/16
	Tacoma-Lakewood PMSA, WA	H	19.79 FQ	23.89 MW	28.32 TQ	WABLS	3/16
	West Virginia	Y	30020 FQ	35650 MW	42650 TQ	USBLS	5/15
	Huntington-Ashland MSA, WV-KY-OH	Y	29600 FQ	35030 MW	40110 TQ	USBLS	5/15
	Wisconsin	Y	35430 FQ	43480 MW	51620 TQ	USBLS	5/15
	Madison MSA, WI	Y	39550 FQ	47290 MW	58470 TQ	USBLS	5/15
	Milwaukee-Waukesha-West Allis MSA, WI	Y	39880 FQ	48420 MW	57460 TQ	USBLS	5/15
	Wyoming	Y	39730 FQ	51860 MW	68190 TQ	USBLS	5/15
	Cheyenne MSA, WY	Y	36750 FQ	47980 MW	57940 TQ	USBLS	5/15
	Puerto Rico	Y	17970 FQ	21450 MW	27870 TQ	USBLS	5/15
	San Juan-Carolina-Caguas MSA, PR	Y	18280 FQ	22660 MW	28820 TQ	USBLS	5/15
	Virgin Islands	Y	27450 FQ	41010 MW	54280 TQ	USBLS	5/15
	Guam	Y	26780 FQ	32240 MW	36230 TQ	USBLS	5/15
Bus Driver							
School or Special Client	Alabama	Y	17587 AE	19398 AW	20292 AEX	ALBLS	6/16
School or Special Client	Birmingham-Hoover MSA, AL	Y	17495 AE	19336 AW	20261 AEX	ALBLS	6/16
School or Special Client	Alaska	Y	32790 FQ	36460 MW	41830 TQ	USBLS	5/15
School or Special Client	Anchorage MSA, AK	Y	32970 FQ	35880 MW	38790 TQ	USBLS	5/15
School or Special Client	Arizona	Y	24680 FQ	27910 MW	31000 TQ	USBLS	5/15
School or Special Client	Phoenix-Mesa-Scottsdale MSA, AZ	Y	25340 FQ	28290 MW	31350 TQ	USBLS	5/15
School or Special Client	Tucson MSA, AZ	Y	24000 FQ	27020 MW	29730 TQ	USBLS	5/15
School or Special Client	Arkansas	Y	16880 FQ	18070 MW	19260 TQ	USBLS	5/15
School or Special Client	Little Rock-North Little Rock-Conway MSA, AR	Y	16840 FQ	18020 MW	19190 TQ	USBLS	5/15
School or Special Client	California	H	13.12 FQ	16.75 MW	20.54 TQ	CABLS	1/16-3/16
School or Special Client	Anaheim-Santa Ana-Irvine PMSA, CA	H	14.68 FQ	17.35 MW	21.74 TQ	CABLS	1/16-3/16
School or Special Client	Los Angeles-Long Beach-Glendale PMSA, CA	H	11.33 FQ	13.90 MW	17.62 TQ	CABLS	1/16-3/16
School or Special Client	Oakland-Hayward-Berkeley PMSA, CA	H	15.29 FQ	19.80 MW	22.23 TQ	CABLS	1/16-3/16
School or Special Client	Riverside-San Bernardino-Ontario MSA, CA	H	14.24 FQ	17.19 MW	19.66 TQ	CABLS	1/16-3/16
School or Special Client	Sacramento–Roseville–Arden-Arcade MSA, CA	H	11.82 FQ	16.79 MW	19.80 TQ	CABLS	1/16-3/16
School or Special Client	San Diego-Carlsbad MSA, CA	H	14.23 FQ	18.83 MW	23.87 TQ	CABLS	1/16-3/16
School or Special Client	San Francisco-Redwood City-South San Francisco PMSA, CA	H	15.96 FQ	22.67 MW	30.83 TQ	CABLS	1/16-3/16
School or Special Client	Colorado	Y	27180 FQ	32140 MW	37670 TQ	USBLS	5/15

AE	Average entry wage	AWR	Average wage range	H	Hourly
AEX	Average experienced wage	B	Biweekly	HI	Highest wage paid
ATC	Average total compensation	D	Daily	HR	High end range
AW	Average wage paid	FQ	First quartile wage	LO	Lowest wage paid

LR	Low end range	MTC	Median total compensation	TCC	Total cash compensation
M	Monthly	MW	Median wage paid	TQ	Third quartile wage
MCC	Median cash compensation	MWR	Median wage range	W	Weekly
ME	Median entry wage	S	See annotated source	Y	Yearly

Occupation/Type/Industry	Location	Per	Low	Mid	High	Source	Date
Bus Driver							
School or Special Client	Denver-Aurora-Lakewood MSA, CO	Y	28390 FQ	33720 MW	38430 TQ	USBLS	5/15
School or Special Client	Connecticut	Y		34637 MW		CTBLS	1/16-3/16
School or Special Client	Bridgeport-Stamford-Norwalk MSA, CT	Y	26310 FQ	32360 MW	37420 TQ	USBLS	5/15
School or Special Client	Hartford-West Hartford-East Hartford MSA, CT	Y	28710 FQ	34050 MW	38660 TQ	USBLS	5/15
School or Special Client	Delaware	Y	26020 FQ	30700 MW	36320 TQ	USBLS	5/15
School or Special Client	Wilmington PMSA, DE-MD-NJ	Y	28250 FQ	32690 MW	37470 TQ	USBLS	5/15
School or Special Client	District of Columbia	Y	27250 FQ	44020 MW	49230 TQ	USBLS	5/15
School or Special Client	Washington-Arlington-Alexandria PMSA, DC-VA-MD-WV	Y	27810 FQ	36810 MW	46690 TQ	USBLS	5/15
School or Special Client	Florida	H	10.49 AE	13.82 MW	15.68 AEX	FLBLS	7/16-9/16
School or Special Client	Fort Lauderdale-Pompano Beach-Deerfield Beach PMSA, FL	H	11.81 AE	14.05 MW	15.53 AEX	FLBLS	7/16-9/16
School or Special Client	Miami-Miami Beach-Kendall PMSA, FL	H	10.74 AE	13.58 MW	15.19 AEX	FLBLS	7/16-9/16
School or Special Client	Orlando-Kissimmee-Sanford MSA, FL	H	9.93 AE	13.41 MW	14.86 AEX	FLBLS	7/16-9/16
School or Special Client	Tampa-St. Petersburg-Clearwater MSA, FL	H	10.73 AE	13.57 MW	15.06 AEX	FLBLS	7/16-9/16
School or Special Client	Georgia	Y	18070 FQ	24200 MW	31460 TQ	USBLS	5/15
School or Special Client	Atlanta-Sandy Springs-Roswell MSA, GA	Y	18520 FQ	26560 MW	33080 TQ	USBLS	5/15
School or Special Client	Hawaii	Y	29580 FQ	41260 MW	47710 TQ	USBLS	5/15
School or Special Client	Urban Honolulu MSA, HI	Y	33330 FQ	43220 MW	51210 TQ	USBLS	5/15
School or Special Client	Idaho	Y	21040 FQ	24990 MW	29040 TQ	USBLS	5/15
School or Special Client	Boise City MSA, ID	Y	21360 FQ	24950 MW	28200 TQ	USBLS	5/15
School or Special Client	Illinois	Y	23140 FQ	29940 MW	38130 TQ	USBLS	5/15
School or Special Client	Chicago-Naperville-Arlington Heights PMSA, IL	Y	25310 FQ	30430 MW	37740 TQ	USBLS	5/15
School or Special Client	Lake County-Kenosha County PMSA, IL-WI	Y	25830 FQ	32480 MW	42740 TQ	USBLS	5/15
School or Special Client	Indiana	Y	18600 FQ	24350 MW	35350 TQ	USBLS	5/15
School or Special Client	Gary PMSA, IN	Y	22650 FQ	32580 MW	37630 TQ	USBLS	5/15
School or Special Client	Indianapolis-Carmel-Anderson MSA, IN	Y	18190 FQ	22010 MW	29890 TQ	USBLS	5/15
School or Special Client	Iowa	Y	20840 FQ	31840 MW	38220 TQ	USBLS	5/15
School or Special Client	Des Moines-West Des Moines MSA, IA	Y	22370 FQ	31820 MW	40110 TQ	USBLS	5/15
School or Special Client	Kansas	Y	20020 FQ	25320 MW	33580 TQ	USBLS	5/15
School or Special Client	Wichita MSA, KS	Y	20420 FQ	25190 MW	29700 TQ	USBLS	5/15
School or Special Client	Kentucky	Y	27410 FQ	32100 MW	37570 TQ	USBLS	5/15
School or Special Client	Louisville-Jefferson County MSA, KY-IN	Y	31060 FQ	38310 MW	47060 TQ	USBLS	5/15
School or Special Client	Louisiana	Y	17260 FQ	18960 MW	22410 TQ	USBLS	5/15
School or Special Client	Baton Rouge MSA, LA	Y	16740 FQ	18000 MW	19260 TQ	USBLS	5/15
School or Special Client	New Orleans-Metairie MSA, LA	Y	21510 FQ	24240 MW	29260 TQ	USBLS	5/15
School or Special Client	Maine	Y	28690 FQ	34000 MW	38590 TQ	USBLS	5/15
School or Special Client	Portland-South Portland MSA, ME	Y	32780 FQ	38910 MW	45390 TQ	USBLS	5/15
School or Special Client	Maryland	Y	24723 AE	35744 MW	41255 AEX	MDBLS	4/16
School or Special Client	Baltimore-Columbia-Towson MSA, MD	Y	24990 FQ	32940 MW	36990 TQ	USBLS	5/15
School or Special Client	Salisbury MSA, MD-DE	Y	24210 FQ	31030 MW	36200 TQ	USBLS	5/15
School or Special Client	Massachusetts	Y	25210 FQ	31270 MW	40010 TQ	USBLS	5/15
School or Special Client	Boston-Cambridge-Newton NECTA, MA	Y	24240 FQ	28160 MW	37830 TQ	USBLS	5/15
School or Special Client	Worcester MSA, MA-CT	Y	27440 FQ	32290 MW	36910 TQ	USBLS	5/15
School or Special Client	Michigan	Y	26050 FQ	31970 MW	37360 TQ	USBLS	5/15
School or Special Client	Detroit-Dearborn-Livonia PMSA, MI	Y	23650 FQ	28760 MW	34530 TQ	USBLS	5/15
School or Special Client	Grand Rapids-Wyoming MSA, MI	Y	25490 FQ	32400 MW	37070 TQ	USBLS	5/15
School or Special Client	Minnesota	Y	27381 FQ	33894 MW	38824 TQ	MNBLS	1/16-3/16
School or Special Client	Minneapolis-St. Paul-Bloomington MSA, MN-WI	Y	29982 FQ	34630 MW	38461 TQ	MNBLS	1/16-3/16

AE	Average entry wage	AWR	Average wage range	H	Hourly
AEX	Average experienced wage	B	Biweekly	HI	Highest wage paid
ATC	Average total compensation	D	Daily	HR	High end range
AW	Average wage paid	FQ	First quartile wage	LO	Lowest wage paid

LR	Low end range	MTC	Median total compensation	TCC	Total cash compensation
M	Monthly	MW	Median wage paid	TQ	Third quartile wage
MCC	Median cash compensation	MWR	Median wage range	W	Weekly
ME	Median entry wage	S	See annotated source	Y	Yearly

Occupation/Type/Industry	Location	Per	Low	Mid	High	Source	Date
Bus Driver							
School or Special Client	Mississippi	Y	17100 FQ	18660 MW	22270 TQ	USBLS	5/15
School or Special Client	Jackson MSA, MS	Y	16750 FQ	18050 MW	19460 TQ	USBLS	5/15
School or Special Client	Missouri	Y	19130 FQ	26660 MW	34850 TQ	USBLS	5/15
School or Special Client	Kansas City MSA, MO-KS	Y	22000 FQ	29140 MW	37350 TQ	USBLS	5/15
School or Special Client	St. Louis MSA, MO-IL	Y	20400 FQ	29140 MW	37970 TQ	USBLS	5/15
School or Special Client	Montana	Y	25530 FQ	31040 MW	37180 TQ	USBLS	5/15
School or Special Client	Billings MSA, MT	Y	23550 FQ	32010 MW	36760 TQ	USBLS	5/15
School or Special Client	Nebraska	Y	22050 FQ	31390 MW	37630 TQ	NEBLS	7/16-9/16
School or Special Client	Omaha-Council Bluffs MSA, NE-IA	Y	23430 FQ	32935 MW	36540 TQ	NEBLS	7/16-9/16
School or Special Client	Nevada	Y	32820 FQ	37520 MW	43800 TQ	USBLS	5/15
School or Special Client	Las Vegas-Henderson-Paradise MSA, NV	Y	35270 FQ	40280 MW	46040 TQ	USBLS	5/15
School or Special Client	New Hampshire	H	10.38 AE	15.02 MW	16.76 AEX	NHBLS	6/16
School or Special Client	Manchester NECTA, NH	H	13.44 AE	15.48 MW	17.70 AEX	NHBLS	6/16
School or Special Client	Nashua NECTA, NH-MA	Y	28390 FQ	32920 MW	37080 TQ	USBLS	5/15
School or Special Client	New Jersey	Y	26770 FQ	33040 MW	39270 TQ	USBLS	5/15
School or Special Client	Camden PMSA, NJ	Y	23080 FQ	28690 MW	35280 TQ	USBLS	5/15
School or Special Client	Newark PMSA, NJ-PA	Y	27840 FQ	33320 MW	38790 TQ	USBLS	5/15
School or Special Client	Trenton MSA, NJ	Y	29130 FQ	35720 MW	43350 TQ	USBLS	5/15
School or Special Client	New Mexico	Y	18580 FQ	23450 MW	29270 TQ	USBLS	5/15
School or Special Client	Albuquerque MSA, NM	Y	18120 FQ	20380 MW	24240 TQ	USBLS	5/15
School or Special Client	New York	Y	26690 AE	38230 MW	45610 AEX	NYBLS	1/16-3/16
School or Special Client	Buffalo-Cheektowaga-Niagara Falls MSA, NY	Y	27200 FQ	32250 MW	38830 TQ	USBLS	5/15
School or Special Client	Nassau County-Suffolk County PMSA, NY	Y	33510 FQ	41790 MW	51600 TQ	USBLS	5/15
School or Special Client	New York-Jersey City-White Plains PMSA, NY-NJ	Y	29890 FQ	38080 MW	46830 TQ	USBLS	5/15
School or Special Client	Rochester MSA, NY	Y	27210 FQ	34210 MW	42020 TQ	USBLS	5/15
School or Special Client	North Carolina	Y	22170 FQ	25940 MW	29250 TQ	USBLS	5/15
School or Special Client	Charlotte-Concord-Gastonia MSA, NC-SC	Y	22370 FQ	25990 MW	29220 TQ	USBLS	5/15
School or Special Client	Raleigh MSA, NC	Y	19110 FQ	22540 MW	26590 TQ	USBLS	5/15
School or Special Client	North Dakota	Y	30190 FQ	38590 MW	49040 TQ	USBLS	5/15
School or Special Client	Fargo MSA, ND-MN	Y	27200 FQ	31950 MW	52650 TQ	USBLS	5/15
School or Special Client	Ohio	Y	23310 FQ	32370 MW	39810 TQ	USBLS	5/15
School or Special Client	Cincinnati MSA, OH-KY-IN	Y	28730 FQ	35790 MW	42790 TQ	USBLS	5/15
School or Special Client	Cleveland-Elyria MSA, OH	Y	24120 FQ	33030 MW	41670 TQ	USBLS	5/15
School or Special Client	Columbus MSA, OH	Y	27070 FQ	33100 MW	38900 TQ	USBLS	5/15
School or Special Client	Oklahoma	Y	17660 FQ	19950 MW	26470 TQ	USBLS	5/15
School or Special Client	Oklahoma City MSA, OK	Y	17320 FQ	19110 MW	24400 TQ	USBLS	5/15
School or Special Client	Tulsa MSA, OK	Y	21910 FQ	26490 MW	29660 TQ	USBLS	5/15
School or Special Client	Oregon	H	12.38 FQ	14.98 MW	17.60 TQ	ORBLS	2016
School or Special Client	Portland-Vancouver-Hillsboro MSA, OR-WA	Y	30230 FQ	34910 MW	39210 TQ	USBLS	5/15
School or Special Client	Pennsylvania	Y	21730 FQ	28410 MW	36250 TQ	USBLS	5/15
School or Special Client	Allentown-Bethlehem-Easton MSA, PA-NJ	Y	25220 FQ	34060 MW	43440 TQ	USBLS	5/15
School or Special Client	Harrisburg-Carlisle MSA, PA	Y	22640 FQ	25510 MW	33690 TQ	USBLS	5/15
School or Special Client	Montgomery County-Bucks County-Chester County PMSA, PA	Y	31250 FQ	36700 MW	43510 TQ	USBLS	5/15
School or Special Client	Philadelphia PMSA, PA	Y	21480 FQ	27370 MW	32640 TQ	USBLS	5/15
School or Special Client	Pittsburgh MSA, PA	Y	20840 FQ	25930 MW	36470 TQ	USBLS	5/15
School or Special Client	Rhode Island	Y	32560 FQ	36860 MW	42060 TQ	USBLS	5/15
School or Special Client	Providence-Warwick MSA, RI-MA	Y	32600 FQ	37490 MW	43330 TQ	USBLS	5/15
School or Special Client	South Carolina	Y	18120 FQ	22440 MW	28730 TQ	USBLS	5/15
School or Special Client	Columbia MSA, SC	Y	17130 FQ	18830 MW	24190 TQ	USBLS	5/15
School or Special Client	Greenville-Anderson-Mauldin MSA, SC	Y	17900 FQ	21020 MW	26940 TQ	USBLS	5/15
School or Special Client	South Dakota	Y	25040 FQ	27670 MW	30260 TQ	USBLS	5/15
School or Special Client	Sioux Falls MSA, SD	Y	25230 FQ	28170 MW	31100 TQ	USBLS	5/15
School or Special Client	Tennessee	Y	18340 FQ	23710 MW	29880 TQ	USBLS	5/15
School or Special Client	Knoxville MSA, TN	Y	17720 FQ	20290 MW	24780 TQ	USBLS	5/15
School or Special Client	Memphis MSA, TN-MS-AR	Y	18910 FQ	23250 MW	29370 TQ	USBLS	5/15
School or Special Client	Nashville-Davidson–Murfreesboro–Franklin MSA, TN	Y	25030 FQ	29280 MW	35540 TQ	USBLS	5/15
School or Special Client	Texas	Y	18980 FQ	25860 MW	32290 TQ	USBLS	5/15

Occupation/Type/Industry	Location	Per	Low	Mid	High	Source	Date
Bus Driver							
School or Special Client	Austin-Round Rock MSA, TX	Y	19550 FQ	27950 MW	33600 TQ	USBLS	5/15
School or Special Client	Dallas-Plano-Irving PMSA, TX	Y	17960 FQ	20850 MW	29150 TQ	USBLS	5/15
School or Special Client	Fort Worth-Arlington PMSA, TX	Y	18880 FQ	23410 MW	30160 TQ	USBLS	5/15
School or Special Client	Houston-The Woodlands-Sugar Land MSA, TX	Y	22720 FQ	31670 MW	36780 TQ	USBLS	5/15
School or Special Client	San Antonio-New Braunfels MSA, TX	Y	18380 FQ	25460 MW	30160 TQ	USBLS	5/15
School or Special Client	Utah	Y	27450 FQ	34380 MW	39450 TQ	USBLS	5/15
School or Special Client	Ogden-Clearfield MSA, UT	Y	25680 FQ	29740 MW	35480 TQ	USBLS	5/15
School or Special Client	Provo-Orem MSA, UT	Y	29730 FQ	34380 MW	37440 TQ	USBLS	5/15
School or Special Client	Vermont	Y	28890 FQ	34170 MW	39800 TQ	USBLS	5/15
School or Special Client	Burlington-South Burlington MSA, VT	Y	27990 FQ	31560 MW	36920 TQ	USBLS	5/15
School or Special Client	Virginia	Y	22120 FQ	28730 MW	36470 TQ	USBLS	5/15
School or Special Client	Richmond MSA, VA	Y	25540 FQ	28550 MW	31590 TQ	USBLS	5/15
School or Special Client	Virginia Beach-Norfolk-Newport News MSA, VA-NC	Y	25080 FQ	27900 MW	30680 TQ	USBLS	5/15
School or Special Client	Washington	H	15.14 FQ	17.86 MW	20.87 TQ	WABLS	3/16
School or Special Client	Seattle-Bellevue-Everett PMSA, WA	H	16.09 FQ	20.17 MW	22.50 TQ	WABLS	3/16
School or Special Client	Tacoma-Lakewood PMSA, WA	H	14.39 FQ	18.50 MW	21.70 TQ	WABLS	3/16
School or Special Client	West Virginia	Y	21520 FQ	24060 MW	27950 TQ	USBLS	5/15
School or Special Client	Huntington-Ashland MSA, WV-KY-OH	Y	21510 FQ	26630 MW	34290 TQ	USBLS	5/15
School or Special Client	Wisconsin	Y	24660 FQ	29630 MW	35470 TQ	USBLS	5/15
School or Special Client	Madison MSA, WI	Y	26090 FQ	32700 MW	36620 TQ	USBLS	5/15
School or Special Client	Milwaukee-Waukesha-West Allis MSA, WI	Y	25330 FQ	30120 MW	35040 TQ	USBLS	5/15
School or Special Client	Wyoming	Y	26010 FQ	33230 MW	38570 TQ	USBLS	5/15
School or Special Client	Cheyenne MSA, WY	Y	24740 FQ	27740 MW	30430 TQ	USBLS	5/15
School or Special Client	Puerto Rico	Y	16620 FQ	17740 MW	18870 TQ	USBLS	5/15
School or Special Client	San Juan-Carolina-Caguas MSA, PR	Y	16630 FQ	17750 MW	18870 TQ	USBLS	5/15
School or Special Client	Virgin Islands	Y	21830 FQ	26570 MW	33970 TQ	USBLS	5/15
Transit and Intercity	Alabama	Y	18503 AE	26772 AW	30906 AEX	ALBLS	6/16
Transit and Intercity	Birmingham-Hoover MSA, AL	Y	20467 AE	30207 AW	35072 AEX	ALBLS	6/16
Transit and Intercity	Alaska	Y	40610 FQ	46430 MW	55670 TQ	USBLS	5/15
Transit and Intercity	Anchorage MSA, AK	Y	35220 FQ	52920 MW	60510 TQ	USBLS	5/15
Transit and Intercity	Arizona	Y	27650 FQ	35720 MW	44230 TQ	USBLS	5/15
Transit and Intercity	Phoenix-Mesa-Scottsdale MSA, AZ	Y	27830 FQ	37290 MW	44810 TQ	USBLS	5/15
Transit and Intercity	Tucson MSA, AZ	Y	28880 FQ	37390 MW	44080 TQ	USBLS	5/15
Transit and Intercity	Little Rock-North Little Rock-Conway MSA, AR	Y	28760 FQ	40790 MW	46320 TQ	USBLS	5/15
Transit and Intercity	California	H	14.56 FQ	19.81 MW	25.62 TQ	CABLS	1/16-3/16
Transit and Intercity	Anaheim-Santa Ana-Irvine PMSA, CA	H	13.62 FQ	16.09 MW	20.16 TQ	CABLS	1/16-3/16
Transit and Intercity	Los Angeles-Long Beach-Glendale PMSA, CA	H	14.06 FQ	19.04 MW	24.03 TQ	CABLS	1/16-3/16
Transit and Intercity	Riverside-San Bernardino-Ontario MSA, CA	H	14.71 FQ	20.21 MW	22.58 TQ	CABLS	1/16-3/16
Transit and Intercity	Sacramento–Roseville–Arden-Arcade MSA, CA	H	19.48 FQ	25.17 MW	29.11 TQ	CABLS	1/16-3/16
Transit and Intercity	San Diego-Carlsbad MSA, CA	H	12.72 FQ	14.48 MW	16.85 TQ	CABLS	1/16-3/16
Transit and Intercity	Colorado	Y	27290 FQ	35300 MW	42220 TQ	USBLS	5/15
Transit and Intercity	Denver-Aurora-Lakewood MSA, CO	Y	25290 FQ	33900 MW	41130 TQ	USBLS	5/15
Transit and Intercity	Connecticut	Y		39680 MW		CTBLS	1/16-3/16
Transit and Intercity	Hartford-West Hartford-East Hartford MSA, CT	Y	30040 FQ	38920 MW	51910 TQ	USBLS	5/15
Transit and Intercity	Delaware	Y	30090 FQ	36340 MW	51610 TQ	USBLS	5/15
Transit and Intercity	Wilmington PMSA, DE-MD-NJ	Y	30310 FQ	37880 MW	51610 TQ	USBLS	5/15
Transit and Intercity	District of Columbia	Y	27950 FQ	34790 MW	40120 TQ	USBLS	5/15
Transit and Intercity	Washington-Arlington-Alexandria PMSA, DC-VA-MD-WV	Y	31960 FQ	36790 MW	45630 TQ	USBLS	5/15
Transit and Intercity	Florida	H	12.19 AE	15.08 MW	18.80 AEX	FLBLS	7/16-9/16

AE Average entry wage	**AWR** Average wage range	**H** Hourly	**LR** Low end range	**MTC** Median total compensation	**TCC** Total cash compensation
AEX Average experienced wage	**B** Biweekly	**HI** Highest wage paid	**M** Monthly	**MW** Median wage paid	**TQ** Third quartile wage
ATC Average total compensation	**D** Daily	**HR** High end range	**MCC** Median cash compensation	**MWR** Median wage range	**W** Weekly
AW Average wage paid	**FQ** First quartile wage	**LO** Lowest wage paid	**ME** Median entry wage	**S** See annotated source	**Y** Yearly

Occupation/Type/Industry	Location	Per	Low	Mid	High	Source	Date
Bus Driver							
Transit and Intercity	Fort Lauderdale-Pompano Beach-Deerfield Beach PMSA, FL	H	12.21 AE	15.43 MW	21.91 AEX	FLBLS	7/16-9/16
Transit and Intercity	Miami-Miami Beach-Kendall PMSA, FL	H	14.17 AE	21.43 MW	23.95 AEX	FLBLS	7/16-9/16
Transit and Intercity	Tampa-St. Petersburg-Clearwater MSA, FL	H	12.94 AE	16.45 MW	18.72 AEX	FLBLS	7/16-9/16
Transit and Intercity	Georgia	Y	26400 FQ	30890 MW	40220 TQ	USBLS	5/15
Transit and Intercity	Atlanta-Sandy Springs-Roswell MSA, GA	Y	27190 FQ	31310 MW	41220 TQ	USBLS	5/15
Transit and Intercity	Augusta-Richmond County MSA, GA-SC	Y	17210 FQ	18530 MW	19840 TQ	USBLS	5/15
Transit and Intercity	Hawaii	Y	27730 FQ	44490 MW	54630 TQ	USBLS	5/15
Transit and Intercity	Urban Honolulu MSA, HI	Y	29660 FQ	46630 MW	55880 TQ	USBLS	5/15
Transit and Intercity	Idaho	Y	23880 FQ	28770 MW	38150 TQ	USBLS	5/15
Transit and Intercity	Boise City MSA, ID	Y	18860 FQ	26120 MW	31200 TQ	USBLS	5/15
Transit and Intercity	Illinois	Y	29690 FQ	44550 MW	67970 TQ	USBLS	5/15
Transit and Intercity	Chicago-Naperville-Arlington Heights PMSA, IL	Y	33080 FQ	57300 MW	71150 TQ	USBLS	5/15
Transit and Intercity	Lake County-Kenosha County PMSA, IL-WI	Y	30460 FQ	39400 MW	47740 TQ	USBLS	5/15
Transit and Intercity	Indiana	Y	31600 FQ	36570 MW	42910 TQ	USBLS	5/15
Transit and Intercity	Gary PMSA, IN	Y	33850 FQ	36640 MW	39430 TQ	USBLS	5/15
Transit and Intercity	Indianapolis-Carmel-Anderson MSA, IN	Y	33810 FQ	37430 MW	43140 TQ	USBLS	5/15
Transit and Intercity	Iowa	Y	22820 FQ	29320 MW	39350 TQ	USBLS	5/15
Transit and Intercity	Des Moines-West Des Moines MSA, IA	Y	23920 FQ	30210 MW	37730 TQ	USBLS	5/15
Transit and Intercity	Kansas	Y	22430 FQ	29010 MW	36320 TQ	USBLS	5/15
Transit and Intercity	Wichita MSA, KS	Y	23750 FQ	30230 MW	36410 TQ	USBLS	5/15
Transit and Intercity	Kentucky	Y	19210 FQ	28490 MW	39350 TQ	USBLS	5/15
Transit and Intercity	Louisville-Jefferson County MSA, KY-IN	Y	25080 FQ	34220 MW	43120 TQ	USBLS	5/15
Transit and Intercity	Louisiana	Y	22220 FQ	35010 MW	45300 TQ	USBLS	5/15
Transit and Intercity	New Orleans-Metairie MSA, LA	Y	24150 FQ	40700 MW	46270 TQ	USBLS	5/15
Transit and Intercity	Maine	Y	27060 FQ	31260 MW	39030 TQ	USBLS	5/15
Transit and Intercity	Portland-South Portland MSA, ME	Y	28640 FQ	33130 MW	47020 TQ	USBLS	5/15
Transit and Intercity	Maryland	Y	27251 AE	39407 MW	45485 AEX	MDBLS	4/16
Transit and Intercity	Baltimore-Columbia-Towson MSA, MD	Y	27580 FQ	30850 MW	35640 TQ	USBLS	5/15
Transit and Intercity	Salisbury MSA, MD-DE	Y	26130 FQ	28050 MW	29960 TQ	USBLS	5/15
Transit and Intercity	Massachusetts	Y	34570 FQ	44590 MW	65000 TQ	USBLS	5/15
Transit and Intercity	Boston-Cambridge-Newton NECTA, MA	Y	35040 FQ	50680 MW	69570 TQ	USBLS	5/15
Transit and Intercity	Worcester MSA, MA-CT	Y	27480 FQ	34890 MW	40330 TQ	USBLS	5/15
Transit and Intercity	Michigan	Y	26610 FQ	32340 MW	41430 TQ	USBLS	5/15
Transit and Intercity	Detroit-Dearborn-Livonia PMSA, MI	Y	28220 FQ	36660 MW	44850 TQ	USBLS	5/15
Transit and Intercity	Minneapolis-St. Paul-Bloomington MSA, MN-WI	Y	28359 FQ	33118 MW	47655 TQ	MNBLS	1/16-3/16
Transit and Intercity	Mississippi	Y	22070 FQ	28050 MW	34240 TQ	USBLS	5/15
Transit and Intercity	Missouri	Y	24110 FQ	36290 MW	43820 TQ	USBLS	5/15
Transit and Intercity	Kansas City MSA, MO-KS	Y	21020 FQ	30340 MW	39950 TQ	USBLS	5/15
Transit and Intercity	St. Louis MSA, MO-IL	Y	30820 FQ	40560 MW	45400 TQ	USBLS	5/15
Transit and Intercity	Montana	Y	27100 FQ	32870 MW	40730 TQ	USBLS	5/15
Transit and Intercity	Billings MSA, MT	Y	23140 FQ	36170 MW	44390 TQ	USBLS	5/15
Transit and Intercity	Nebraska	Y	25105 FQ	37675 MW	45910 TQ	NEBLS	7/16-9/16
Transit and Intercity	Omaha-Council Bluffs MSA, NE-IA	Y	23840 FQ	40810 MW	46005 TQ	NEBLS	7/16-9/16
Transit and Intercity	Nevada	Y	21860 FQ	25530 MW	31470 TQ	USBLS	5/15
Transit and Intercity	Las Vegas-Henderson-Paradise MSA, NV	Y	21860 FQ	25520 MW	31480 TQ	USBLS	5/15
Transit and Intercity	New Hampshire	H	11.66 AE	17.87 MW	22.14 AEX	NHBLS	6/16
Transit and Intercity	Nashua NECTA, NH-MA	Y	24300 FQ	30880 MW	51980 TQ	USBLS	5/15
Transit and Intercity	New Jersey	Y	37130 FQ	49430 MW	57180 TQ	USBLS	5/15
Transit and Intercity	Newark PMSA, NJ-PA	Y	42580 FQ	52160 MW	57990 TQ	USBLS	5/15
Transit and Intercity	Trenton MSA, NJ	Y	28680 FQ	34320 MW	54030 TQ	USBLS	5/15
Transit and Intercity	New Mexico	Y	25420 FQ	27940 MW	30450 TQ	USBLS	5/15
Transit and Intercity	Albuquerque MSA, NM	Y	25990 FQ	27920 MW	29850 TQ	USBLS	5/15

AE Average entry wage	**AWR** Average wage range	**H** Hourly	**LR** Low end range	**MTC** Median total compensation	**TCC** Total cash compensation
AEX Average experienced wage	**B** Biweekly	**HI** Highest wage paid	**M** Monthly	**MW** Median wage paid	**TQ** Third quartile wage
ATC Average total compensation	**D** Daily	**HR** High end range	**MCC** Median cash compensation	**MWR** Median wage range	**W** Weekly
AW Average wage paid	**FQ** First quartile wage	**LO** Lowest wage paid	**ME** Median entry wage	**S** See annotated source	**Y** Yearly

Bus Driver

Occupation/Type/Industry	Location	Per	Low	Mid	High	Source	Date
Bus Driver							
Transit and Intercity	New York	Y	33960 AE	55780 MW	62380 AEX	NYBLS	1/16-3/16
Transit and Intercity	Buffalo-Cheektowaga-Niagara Falls MSA, NY	Y	27240 FQ	32470 MW	38120 TQ	USBLS	5/15
Transit and Intercity	Nassau County-Suffolk County PMSA, NY	Y	38090 FQ	48260 MW	56780 TQ	USBLS	5/15
Transit and Intercity	New York-Jersey City-White Plains PMSA, NY-NJ	Y	39980 FQ	55390 MW	63750 TQ	USBLS	5/15
Transit and Intercity	Rochester MSA, NY	Y	36700 FQ	51600 MW	57300 TQ	USBLS	5/15
Transit and Intercity	North Carolina	Y	22980 FQ	29500 MW	38600 TQ	USBLS	5/15
Transit and Intercity	Raleigh MSA, NC	Y	21780 FQ	29730 MW	45940 TQ	USBLS	5/15
Transit and Intercity	North Dakota	Y	27870 FQ	33630 MW	37520 TQ	USBLS	5/15
Transit and Intercity	Ohio	Y	35300 FQ	46970 MW	56280 TQ	USBLS	5/15
Transit and Intercity	Cincinnati MSA, OH-KY-IN	Y	26990 FQ	38450 MW	52720 TQ	USBLS	5/15
Transit and Intercity	Cleveland-Elyria MSA, OH	Y	39270 FQ	47410 MW	55810 TQ	USBLS	5/15
Transit and Intercity	Columbus MSA, OH	Y	33460 FQ	38860 MW	52390 TQ	USBLS	5/15
Transit and Intercity	Oklahoma	Y	20350 FQ	25200 MW	32680 TQ	USBLS	5/15
Transit and Intercity	Oklahoma City MSA, OK	Y	30680 FQ	34000 MW	36890 TQ	USBLS	5/15
Transit and Intercity	Tulsa MSA, OK	Y	22970 FQ	26800 MW	31720 TQ	USBLS	5/15
Transit and Intercity	Oregon	H	13.75 FQ	20.23 MW	27.12 TQ	ORBLS	2016
Transit and Intercity	Portland-Vancouver-Hillsboro MSA, OR-WA	Y	28800 FQ	46390 MW	57480 TQ	USBLS	5/15
Transit and Intercity	Pennsylvania	Y	26800 FQ	35630 MW	50360 TQ	USBLS	5/15
Transit and Intercity	Allentown-Bethlehem-Easton MSA, PA-NJ	Y	27360 FQ	35090 MW	45120 TQ	USBLS	5/15
Transit and Intercity	Harrisburg-Carlisle MSA, PA	Y	34660 FQ	51430 MW	57100 TQ	USBLS	5/15
Transit and Intercity	Montgomery County-Bucks County-Chester County PMSA, PA	Y	24380 FQ	28160 MW	31700 TQ	USBLS	5/15
Transit and Intercity	Philadelphia PMSA, PA	Y	26660 FQ	28500 MW	30330 TQ	USBLS	5/15
Transit and Intercity	Pittsburgh MSA, PA	Y	33650 FQ	50740 MW	56820 TQ	USBLS	5/15
Transit and Intercity	Rhode Island	Y	32330 FQ	36590 MW	42010 TQ	USBLS	5/15
Transit and Intercity	Providence-Warwick MSA, RI-MA	Y	32540 FQ	36510 MW	41170 TQ	USBLS	5/15
Transit and Intercity	South Carolina	Y	23010 FQ	27400 MW	34430 TQ	USBLS	5/15
Transit and Intercity	Columbia MSA, SC	Y	21140 FQ	23340 MW	26860 TQ	USBLS	5/15
Transit and Intercity	Greenville-Anderson-Mauldin MSA, SC	Y	23930 FQ	27080 MW	29790 TQ	USBLS	5/15
Transit and Intercity	South Dakota	Y	22820 FQ	26020 MW	28930 TQ	USBLS	5/15
Transit and Intercity	Tennessee	Y	19440 FQ	28000 MW	40240 TQ	USBLS	5/15
Transit and Intercity	Knoxville MSA, TN	Y	17540 FQ	19240 MW	26250 TQ	USBLS	5/15
Transit and Intercity	Memphis MSA, TN-MS-AR	Y	25260 FQ	37130 MW	43800 TQ	USBLS	5/15
Transit and Intercity	Nashville-Davidson–Murfreesboro–Franklin MSA, TN	Y	19270 FQ	24390 MW	40350 TQ	USBLS	5/15
Transit and Intercity	Texas	Y	27090 FQ	36470 MW	44400 TQ	USBLS	5/15
Transit and Intercity	Austin-Round Rock MSA, TX	Y	29570 FQ	42920 MW	47390 TQ	USBLS	5/15
Transit and Intercity	Dallas-Plano-Irving PMSA, TX	Y	29580 FQ	41170 MW	45670 TQ	USBLS	5/15
Transit and Intercity	Fort Worth-Arlington PMSA, TX	Y	26560 FQ	29700 MW	37920 TQ	USBLS	5/15
Transit and Intercity	Houston-The Woodlands-Sugar Land MSA, TX	Y	32680 FQ	41060 MW	46010 TQ	USBLS	5/15
Transit and Intercity	San Antonio-New Braunfels MSA, TX	Y	25750 FQ	36750 MW	45420 TQ	USBLS	5/15
Transit and Intercity	Utah	Y	24560 FQ	30660 MW	38030 TQ	USBLS	5/15
Transit and Intercity	Ogden-Clearfield MSA, UT	Y	33260 FQ	35790 MW	38320 TQ	USBLS	5/15
Transit and Intercity	Provo-Orem MSA, UT	Y	19680 FQ	23030 MW	28160 TQ	USBLS	5/15
Transit and Intercity	Salt Lake City MSA, UT	Y	28250 FQ	32910 MW	41230 TQ	USBLS	5/15
Transit and Intercity	Vermont	Y	30610 FQ	35050 MW	39120 TQ	USBLS	5/15
Transit and Intercity	Virginia	Y	29490 FQ	36760 MW	44900 TQ	USBLS	5/15
Transit and Intercity	Richmond MSA, VA	Y	34300 FQ	41050 MW	45980 TQ	USBLS	5/15
Transit and Intercity	Virginia Beach-Norfolk-Newport News MSA, VA-NC	Y	29220 FQ	39900 MW	45530 TQ	USBLS	5/15
Transit and Intercity	Washington	H	16.08 FQ	24.12 MW	31.72 TQ	WABLS	3/16
Transit and Intercity	Seattle-Bellevue-Everett PMSA, WA	H	12.05 FQ	27.81 MW	33.90 TQ	WABLS	3/16
Transit and Intercity	West Virginia	Y	25720 FQ	30380 MW	35070 TQ	USBLS	5/15
Transit and Intercity	Wisconsin	Y	37680 FQ	45820 MW	52720 TQ	USBLS	5/15
Transit and Intercity	Madison MSA, WI	Y	44300 FQ	52370 MW	57650 TQ	USBLS	5/15
Transit and Intercity	Milwaukee-Waukesha-West Allis MSA, WI	Y	40860 FQ	47620 MW	54160 TQ	USBLS	5/15
Transit and Intercity	Wyoming	Y	23680 FQ	31710 MW	47650 TQ	USBLS	5/15

AE	Average entry wage	AWR	Average wage range	H	Hourly	LR	Low end range	MTC	Median total compensation	TCC	Total cash compensation
AEX	Average experienced wage	B	Biweekly	HI	Highest wage paid	M	Monthly	MW	Median wage paid	TQ	Third quartile wage
ATC	Average total compensation	D	Daily	HR	High end range	MCC	Median cash compensation	MWR	Median wage range	W	Weekly
AW	Average wage paid	FQ	First quartile wage	LO	Lowest wage paid	ME	Median entry wage	S	See annotated source	Y	Yearly

Occupation/Type/Industry	Location	Per	Low	Mid	High	Source	Date
Bus Driver							
Transit and Intercity	Puerto Rico	Y	21030 FQ	27400 MW	33280 TQ	USBLS	5/15
Transit and Intercity	San Juan-Carolina-Caguas MSA, PR	Y	21950 FQ	27970 MW	33620 TQ	USBLS	5/15
Transit and Intercity	Virgin Islands	Y	21790 FQ	25670 MW	28650 TQ	USBLS	5/15
Transit and Intercity	Guam	Y	18240 FQ	19340 MW	22470 TQ	USBLS	5/15
Business Development Executive							
Hospital	United States	Y		210300 MCC		MHLTH01	2015
Business Intelligence Developer	United States	Y		83000 MW		TSTR	2017
Business Lending Executive							
Credit Union	United States	Y		135287 MW		CUMGT	2016
Business Manager							
Police Department, Municipal Government	Bakersfield, CA	Y			86642 HI	CACIT	6/28/16
Business Teacher							
Postsecondary	Alabama	Y	41497 AE	92901 AW	118608 AEX	ALBLS	6/16
Postsecondary	Birmingham-Hoover MSA, AL	Y	31314 AE	96102 AW	128496 AEX	ALBLS	6/16
Postsecondary	Alaska	Y	82650 FQ	90890 MW	99770 TQ	USBLS	5/15
Postsecondary	Arizona	Y	52370 FQ	79770 MW	106110 TQ	USBLS	5/15
Postsecondary	Phoenix-Mesa-Scottsdale MSA, AZ	Y	53550 FQ	81410 MW	102910 TQ	USBLS	5/15
Postsecondary	Arkansas	Y	47860 FQ	61630 MW	93620 TQ	USBLS	5/15
Postsecondary	Little Rock-North Little Rock-Conway MSA, AR	Y	53340 FQ	72540 MW	112120 TQ	USBLS	5/15
Postsecondary	California	Y		100283 AW		CABLS	1/16-3/16
Postsecondary	Anaheim-Santa Ana-Irvine PMSA, CA	Y		98791 AW		CABLS	1/16-3/16
Postsecondary	Los Angeles-Long Beach-Glendale PMSA, CA	Y		114952 AW		CABLS	1/16-3/16
Postsecondary	Riverside-San Bernardino-Ontario MSA, CA	Y		95078 AW		CABLS	1/16-3/16
Postsecondary	Sacramento–Roseville–Arden-Arcade MSA, CA	Y		102068 AW		CABLS	1/16-3/16
Postsecondary	San Diego-Carlsbad MSA, CA	Y		95799 AW		CABLS	1/16-3/16
Postsecondary	San Francisco-Redwood City-South San Francisco PMSA, CA	Y		86942 AW		CABLS	1/16-3/16
Postsecondary	Colorado	Y	43780 FQ	75440 MW	121390 TQ	USBLS	5/15
Postsecondary	Denver-Aurora-Lakewood MSA, CO	Y	43630 FQ	77190 MW	129650 TQ	USBLS	5/15
Postsecondary	Connecticut	Y		68996 MW		CTBLS	1/16-3/16
Postsecondary	Hartford-West Hartford-East Hartford MSA, CT	Y	62080 FQ	80700 MW	122870 TQ	USBLS	5/15
Postsecondary	Delaware	Y	52100 FQ	74760 MW	98430 TQ	USBLS	5/15
Postsecondary	Wilmington PMSA, DE-MD-NJ	Y	46710 FQ	73700 MW	100290 TQ	USBLS	5/15
Postsecondary	District of Columbia	Y	54860 FQ	86780 MW	140020 TQ	USBLS	5/15
Postsecondary	Washington-Arlington-Alexandria PMSA, DC-VA-MD-WV	Y	48270 FQ	79970 MW	132810 TQ	USBLS	5/15
Postsecondary	Florida	Y	42673 AE	78819 MW	121142 AEX	FLBLS	7/16-9/16
Postsecondary	Fort Lauderdale-Pompano Beach-Deerfield Beach PMSA, FL	Y	43308 AE	69901 MW	91723 AEX	FLBLS	7/16-9/16
Postsecondary	Miami-Miami Beach-Kendall PMSA, FL	Y	45933 AE	89347 MW	127361 AEX	FLBLS	7/16-9/16
Postsecondary	Orlando-Kissimmee-Sanford MSA, FL	Y	39525 AE	75971 MW	118695 AEX	FLBLS	7/16-9/16
Postsecondary	Tampa-St. Petersburg-Clearwater MSA, FL	Y	39441 AE	73994 MW	118459 AEX	FLBLS	7/16-9/16
Postsecondary	Georgia	Y	45410 FQ	69750 MW	104790 TQ	USBLS	5/15
Postsecondary	Atlanta-Sandy Springs-Roswell MSA, GA	Y	44750 FQ	64290 MW	97740 TQ	USBLS	5/15
Postsecondary	Augusta-Richmond County MSA, GA-SC	Y	41530 FQ	47850 MW	79040 TQ	USBLS	5/15
Postsecondary	Hawaii	Y	39220 FQ	70960 MW	138980 TQ	USBLS	5/15
Postsecondary	Urban Honolulu MSA, HI	Y	39270 FQ	69840 MW	143980 TQ	USBLS	5/15
Postsecondary	Idaho	Y	37320 FQ	51690 MW	91830 TQ	USBLS	5/15

AE	Average entry wage	AWR	Average wage range	H	Hourly	LR	Low end range	MTC	Median total compensation	TCC	Total cash compensation
AEX	Average experienced wage	B	Biweekly	HI	Highest wage paid	M	Monthly	MW	Median wage paid	TQ	Third quartile wage
ATC	Average total compensation	D	Daily	HR	High end range	MCC	Median cash compensation	MWR	Median wage range	W	Weekly
AW	Average wage paid	FQ	First quartile wage	LO	Lowest wage paid	ME	Median entry wage	S	See annotated source	Y	Yearly

Business Teacher

Occupation/Type/Industry	Location	Per	Low	Mid	High	Source	Date
Business Teacher							
Postsecondary	Boise City MSA, ID	Y	25670 FQ	44430 MW	67610 TQ	USBLS	5/15
Postsecondary	Illinois	Y	54940 FQ	88500 MW	140380 TQ	USBLS	5/15
Postsecondary	Indiana	Y	53280 FQ	79180 MW	121160 TQ	USBLS	5/15
Postsecondary	Iowa	Y	52730 FQ	79680 MW	127650 TQ	USBLS	5/15
Postsecondary	Des Moines-West Des Moines MSA, IA	Y	50920 FQ	80140 MW	114020 TQ	USBLS	5/15
Postsecondary	Kansas	Y	40280 FQ	53540 MW	69470 TQ	USBLS	5/15
Postsecondary	Kentucky	Y	53460 FQ	81770 MW	128010 TQ	USBLS	5/15
Postsecondary	Louisville-Jefferson County MSA, KY-IN	Y	44580 FQ	67380 MW	112540 TQ	USBLS	5/15
Postsecondary	Louisiana	Y	42250 FQ	63930 MW	95980 TQ	USBLS	5/15
Postsecondary	Baton Rouge MSA, LA	Y	87760 FQ	132260 MW	166530 TQ	USBLS	5/15
Postsecondary	Maine	Y	51600 FQ	71260 MW	106530 TQ	USBLS	5/15
Postsecondary	Portland-South Portland MSA, ME	Y	51180 FQ	87970 MW	117090 TQ	USBLS	5/15
Postsecondary	Maryland	Y	48312 AE	99323 MW	124829 AEX	MDBLS	4/16
Postsecondary	Baltimore-Columbia-Towson MSA, MD	Y	61370 FQ.	86430 MW	110490 TQ	USBLS	5/15
Postsecondary	Salisbury MSA, MD-DE	Y	62790 FQ	73210 MW	93780 TQ	USBLS	5/15
Postsecondary	Massachusetts	Y	67310 FQ	114220 MW		USBLS	5/15
Postsecondary	Michigan	Y	59760 FQ	91880 MW	132750 TQ	USBLS	5/15
Postsecondary	Detroit-Dearborn-Livonia PMSA, MI	Y	61590 FQ	90710 MW	123310 TQ	USBLS	5/15
Postsecondary	Grand Rapids-Wyoming MSA, MI	Y	39280 FQ	77160 MW	116690 TQ	USBLS	5/15
Postsecondary	Minnesota	Y	52610 FQ	69112 MW	92186 TQ	MNBLS	1/16-3/16
Postsecondary	Minneapolis-St. Paul-Bloomington MSA, MN-WI	Y	52953 FQ	68840 MW	90382 TQ	MNBLS	1/16-3/16
Postsecondary	Mississippi	Y	54250 FQ	76520 MW	111750 TQ	USBLS	5/15
Postsecondary	Jackson MSA, MS	Y	44370 FQ	55100 MW	66710 TQ	USBLS	5/15
Postsecondary	Missouri	Y	44430 FQ	70290 MW	113020 TQ	USBLS	5/15
Postsecondary	Kansas City MSA, MO-KS	Y	44660 FQ	64920 MW	97130 TQ	USBLS	5/15
Postsecondary	St. Louis MSA, MO-IL	Y	38840 FQ	59270 MW	97560 TQ	USBLS	5/15
Postsecondary	Montana	Y	46620 FQ	66450 MW	94340 TQ	USBLS	5/15
Postsecondary	Nebraska	Y	48865 FQ	68345 MW	100045 TQ	NEBLS	7/16-9/16
Postsecondary	Omaha-Council Bluffs MSA, NE-IA	Y	43685 FQ	64950 MW	95450 TQ	NEBLS	7/16-9/16
Postsecondary	Nevada	Y	37640 FQ	65080 MW	115660 TQ	USBLS	5/15
Postsecondary	Las Vegas-Henderson-Paradise MSA, NV	Y	37610 FQ	68380 MW	112680 TQ	USBLS	5/15
Postsecondary	New Hampshire	Y	61628 AE	91920 MW	145046 AEX	NHBLS	6/16
Postsecondary	New Jersey	Y	58920 FQ	88350 MW	131620 TQ	USBLS	5/15
Postsecondary	Camden PMSA, NJ	Y	61270 FQ	96480 MW	134000 TQ	USBLS	5/15
Postsecondary	Newark PMSA, NJ-PA	Y	68650 FQ	100060 MW	145580 TQ	USBLS	5/15
Postsecondary	New Mexico	Y	56740 FQ	75770 MW	103000 TQ	USBLS	5/15
Postsecondary	Albuquerque MSA, NM	Y	56130 FQ	74440 MW	100880 TQ	USBLS	5/15
Postsecondary	New York	Y	41970 AE	76190 MW	128270 AEX	NYBLS	1/16-3/16
Postsecondary	Buffalo-Cheektowaga-Niagara Falls MSA, NY	Y	39460 FQ	74780 MW	111810 TQ	USBLS	5/15
Postsecondary	Nassau County-Suffolk County PMSA, NY	Y	45430 FQ	59630 MW	95440 TQ	USBLS	5/15
Postsecondary	New York-Jersey City-White Plains PMSA, NY-NJ	Y	52420 FQ	88730 MW	150090 TQ	USBLS	5/15
Postsecondary	Rochester MSA, NY	Y	37320 FQ	70560 MW	115710 TQ	USBLS	5/15
Postsecondary	North Carolina	Y	53140 FQ	68830 MW	103720 TQ	USBLS	5/15
Postsecondary	Charlotte-Concord-Gastonia MSA, NC-SC	Y	48940 FQ	65980 MW	87910 TQ	USBLS	5/15
Postsecondary	Raleigh MSA, NC	Y	48320 FQ	67620 MW	112430 TQ	USBLS	5/15
Postsecondary	North Dakota	Y	60700 FQ	95640 MW	159550 TQ	USBLS	5/15
Postsecondary	Fargo MSA, ND-MN	Y	90670 FQ	130440 MW	168220 TQ	USBLS	5/15
Postsecondary	Ohio	Y	44370 FQ	70500 MW	114540 TQ	USBLS	5/15
Postsecondary	Cleveland-Elyria MSA, OH	Y	47810 FQ	72900 MW	105600 TQ	USBLS	5/15
Postsecondary	Columbus MSA, OH	Y	48920 FQ	100080 MW	121800 TQ	USBLS	5/15
Postsecondary	Oklahoma	Y	40380 FQ	54250 MW	90520 TQ	USBLS	5/15
Postsecondary	Oklahoma City MSA, OK	Y	36820 FQ	47800 MW	83770 TQ	USBLS	5/15
Postsecondary	Tulsa MSA, OK	Y	47900 FQ	61650 MW	106040 TQ	USBLS	5/15
Postsecondary	Oregon	Y	53618 FQ	73484 MW	112655 TQ	ORBLS	2016
Postsecondary	Portland-Vancouver-Hillsboro MSA, OR-WA	Y	46780 FQ	59500 MW	88110 TQ	USBLS	5/15
Postsecondary	Pennsylvania	Y	48450 FQ	69990 MW	97570 TQ	USBLS	5/15

AE	Average entry wage	AWR	Average wage range	H	Hourly	LR	Low end range	MTC Median total compensation TCC Total cash compensation
AEX	Average experienced wage	B	Biweekly	HI	Highest wage paid	M	Monthly	MW Median wage paid TQ Third quartile wage
ATC	Average total compensation	D	Daily	HR	High end range	MCC	Median cash compensation	MWR Median wage range W Weekly
AW	Average wage paid	FQ	First quartile wage	LO	Lowest wage paid	ME	Median entry wage	S See annotated source Y Yearly

Occupation/Type/Industry	Location	Per	Low	Mid	High	Source	Date
Business Teacher							
Postsecondary	Allentown-Bethlehem-Easton MSA, PA-NJ	Y	55740 FQ	85650 MW	168710 TQ	USBLS	5/15
Postsecondary	Harrisburg-Carlisle MSA, PA	Y	57600 FQ	79540 MW	98280 TQ	USBLS	5/15
Postsecondary	Montgomery County-Bucks County-Chester County PMSA, PA	Y	23770 FQ	46770 MW	61020 TQ	USBLS	5/15
Postsecondary	Philadelphia PMSA, PA	Y	51250 FQ	73900 MW	106280 TQ	USBLS	5/15
Postsecondary	Pittsburgh MSA, PA	Y	39920 FQ	66640 MW	91580 TQ	USBLS	5/15
Postsecondary	Rhode Island	Y	65990 FQ	92570 MW	121260 TQ	USBLS	5/15
Postsecondary	Providence-Warwick MSA, RI-MA	Y	65150 FQ	91060 MW	120160 TQ	USBLS	5/15
Postsecondary	South Carolina	Y	51020 FQ	68020 MW	97810 TQ	USBLS	5/15
Postsecondary	Columbia MSA, SC	Y	46070 FQ	68580 MW	118750 TQ	USBLS	5/15
Postsecondary	Greenville-Anderson-Mauldin MSA, SC	Y	42540 FQ	66140 MW	110680 TQ	USBLS	5/15
Postsecondary	South Dakota	Y	45720 FQ	52750 MW	67080 TQ	USBLS	5/15
Postsecondary	Sioux Falls MSA, SD	Y	50910 FQ	56730 MW	63830 TQ	USBLS	5/15
Postsecondary	Tennessee	Y	43760 FQ	64590 MW	101800 TQ	USBLS	5/15
Postsecondary	Knoxville MSA, TN	Y	39020 FQ	63800 MW	118300 TQ	USBLS	5/15
Postsecondary	Memphis MSA, TN-MS-AR	Y	42170 FQ	59070 MW	105310 TQ	USBLS	5/15
Postsecondary	Nashville-Davidson–Murfreesboro–Franklin MSA, TN	Y	47430 FQ	66040 MW	95550 TQ	USBLS	5/15
Postsecondary	Texas	Y	51280 FQ	81730 MW	128160 TQ	USBLS	5/15
Postsecondary	Austin-Round Rock MSA, TX	Y	51560 FQ	80730 MW	133540 TQ	USBLS	5/15
Postsecondary	Fort Worth-Arlington PMSA, TX	Y	37770 FQ	57730 MW	85380 TQ	USBLS	5/15
Postsecondary	Houston-The Woodlands-Sugar Land MSA, TX	Y	53330 FQ	83960 MW	138190 TQ	USBLS	5/15
Postsecondary	San Antonio-New Braunfels MSA, TX	Y	32360 FQ	74150 MW	115690 TQ	USBLS	5/15
Postsecondary	Utah	Y	49840 FQ	76350 MW	114710 TQ	USBLS	5/15
Postsecondary	Ogden-Clearfield MSA, UT	Y	50910 FQ	63610 MW	104230 TQ	USBLS	5/15
Postsecondary	Provo-Orem MSA, UT	Y	59410 FQ	92950 MW	123900 TQ	USBLS	5/15
Postsecondary	Salt Lake City MSA, UT	Y	45990 FQ	58720 MW	95490 TQ	USBLS	5/15
Postsecondary	Vermont	Y	44170 FQ	64530 MW	75830 TQ	USBLS	5/15
Postsecondary	Burlington-South Burlington MSA, VT	Y	39760 FQ	58170 MW	87110 TQ	USBLS	5/15
Postsecondary	Virginia	Y	37220 FQ	56800 MW	97360 TQ	USBLS	5/15
Postsecondary	Virginia Beach-Norfolk-Newport News MSA, VA-NC	Y	40700 FQ	62980 MW	111700 TQ	USBLS	5/15
Postsecondary	Washington	Y		76736 AW		WABLS	3/16
Postsecondary	Seattle-Bellevue-Everett PMSA, WA	Y		85309 AW		WABLS	3/16
Postsecondary	West Virginia	Y	43260 FQ	57260 MW	74530 TQ	USBLS	5/15
Postsecondary	Huntington-Ashland MSA, WV-KY-OH	Y	47800 FQ	58750 MW	71070 TQ	USBLS	5/15
Postsecondary	Wisconsin	Y	52410 FQ	71980 MW	102570 TQ	USBLS	5/15
Postsecondary	Madison MSA, WI	Y	52810 FQ	66230 MW	106140 TQ	USBLS	5/15
Postsecondary	Milwaukee-Waukesha-West Allis MSA, WI	Y	47810 FQ	78210 MW	119590 TQ	USBLS	5/15
Postsecondary	Wyoming	Y	54370 FQ	70100 MW	97170 TQ	USBLS	5/15
Postsecondary	Puerto Rico	Y	40540 FQ	49260 MW	58740 TQ	USBLS	5/15
Postsecondary	San Juan-Carolina-Caguas MSA, PR	Y	30730 FQ	48070 MW	58870 TQ	USBLS	5/15
Busker	United States	D		50-100 AWR		BBRD01	2014
Butcher and Meat Cutter	Alabama	Y	22189 AE	30394 AW	34497 AEX	ALBLS	6/16
	Birmingham-Hoover MSA, AL	Y	21243 AE	28934 AW	32769 AEX	ALBLS	6/16
	Alaska	Y	31840 FQ	43350 MW	51870 TQ	USBLS	5/15
	Anchorage MSA, AK	Y	31460 FQ	42630 MW	51220 TQ	USBLS	5/15
	Arizona	Y	24040 FQ	29910 MW	36280 TQ	USBLS	5/15
	Phoenix-Mesa-Scottsdale MSA, AZ	Y	24040 FQ	29740 MW	36090 TQ	USBLS	5/15
	Tucson MSA, AZ	Y	26020 FQ	32250 MW	37370 TQ	USBLS	5/15
	Arkansas	Y	20530 FQ	23310 MW	28510 TQ	USBLS	5/15
	Little Rock-North Little Rock-Conway MSA, AR	Y	20860 FQ	27280 MW	36120 TQ	USBLS	5/15
	California	H	10.63 FQ	13.16 MW	18.59 TQ	CABLS	1/16-3/16

AE	Average entry wage	**AWR**	Average wage range	**H**	Hourly
AEX	Average experienced wage	**B**	Biweekly	**HI**	Highest wage paid
ATC	Average total compensation	**D**	Daily	**HR**	High end range
AW	Average wage paid	**FQ**	First quartile wage	**LO**	Lowest wage paid

LR	Low end range	**MTC**	Median total compensation	**TCC**	Total cash compensation
M	Monthly	**MW**	Median wage paid	**TQ**	Third quartile wage
MCC	Median cash compensation	**MWR**	Median wage range	**W**	Weekly
ME	Median entry wage	**S**	See annotated source	**Y**	Yearly

Butcher and Meat Cutter

Occupation/Type/Industry	Location	Per	Low	Mid	High	Source	Date
Butcher and Meat Cutter	Anaheim-Santa Ana-Irvine PMSA, CA	H	9.71 FQ	11.71 MW	15.72 TQ	CABLS	1/16-3/16
	Los Angeles-Long Beach-Glendale PMSA, CA	H	10.30 FQ	12.38 MW	16.31 TQ	CABLS	1/16-3/16
	Oakland-Hayward-Berkeley PMSA, CA	H	10.94 FQ	12.85 MW	18.56 TQ	CABLS	1/16-3/16
	Riverside-San Bernardino-Ontario MSA, CA	H	10.92 FQ	12.91 MW	18.92 TQ	CABLS	1/16-3/16
	Sacramento–Roseville–Arden-Arcade MSA, CA	H	11.35 FQ	17.24 MW	22.01 TQ	CABLS	1/16-3/16
	San Diego-Carlsbad MSA, CA	H	10.32 FQ	11.88 MW	15.11 TQ	CABLS	1/16-3/16
	San Francisco-Redwood City-South San Francisco PMSA, CA	H	12.07 FQ	19.30 MW	22.41 TQ	CABLS	1/16-3/16
	Colorado	Y	23700 FQ	30280 MW	38850 TQ	USBLS	5/15
	Denver-Aurora-Lakewood MSA, CO	Y	24610 FQ	32770 MW	40830 TQ	USBLS	5/15
	Connecticut	Y		41442 MW		CTBLS	1/16-3/16
	Bridgeport-Stamford-Norwalk MSA, CT	Y	38160 FQ	46170 MW	56340 TQ	USBLS	5/15
	Hartford-West Hartford-East Hartford MSA, CT	Y	31140 FQ	37840 MW	46050 TQ	USBLS	5/15
	Delaware	Y	24820 FQ	32730 MW	40900 TQ	USBLS	5/15
	Wilmington PMSA, DE-MD-NJ	Y	25870 FQ	32520 MW	38760 TQ	USBLS	5/15
	District of Columbia	Y	24610 FQ	42420 MW	47500 TQ	USBLS	5/15
	Washington-Arlington-Alexandria PMSA, DC-VA-MD-WV	Y	27270 FQ	41220 MW	46960 TQ	USBLS	5/15
	Florida	H	10.85 AE	14.98 MW	16.87 AEX	FLBLS	7/16-9/16
	Fort Lauderdale-Pompano Beach-Deerfield Beach PMSA, FL	H	12.01 AE	16.05 MW	18.08 AEX	FLBLS	7/16-9/16
	Miami-Miami Beach-Kendall PMSA, FL	H	9.10 AE	12.59 MW	14.87 AEX	FLBLS	7/16-9/16
	Orlando-Kissimmee-Sanford MSA, FL	H	11.42 AE	16.01 MW	17.18 AEX	FLBLS	7/16-9/16
	Tampa-St. Petersburg-Clearwater MSA, FL	H	11.85 AE	15.44 MW	16.92 AEX	FLBLS	7/16-9/16
	Georgia	Y	22560 FQ	27220 MW	31730 TQ	USBLS	5/15
	Atlanta-Sandy Springs-Roswell MSA, GA	Y	23860 FQ	27900 MW	32090 TQ	USBLS	5/15
	Augusta-Richmond County MSA, GA-SC	Y	22720 FQ	27730 MW	33420 TQ	USBLS	5/15
	Hawaii	Y	30220 FQ	41930 MW	48460 TQ	USBLS	5/15
	Urban Honolulu MSA, HI	Y	25450 FQ	43410 MW	49160 TQ	USBLS	5/15
	Idaho	Y	25220 FQ	32580 MW	38240 TQ	USBLS	5/15
	Boise City MSA, ID	Y	28700 FQ	33410 MW	37360 TQ	USBLS	5/15
	Illinois	Y	20570 FQ	25400 MW	34100 TQ	USBLS	5/15
	Chicago-Naperville-Arlington Heights PMSA, IL	Y	20820 FQ	25830 MW	34460 TQ	USBLS	5/15
	Lake County-Kenosha County PMSA, IL-WI	Y	20060 FQ	27770 MW	39080 TQ	USBLS	5/15
	Indiana	Y	24760 FQ	29700 MW	35410 TQ	USBLS	5/15
	Gary PMSA, IN	Y	26480 FQ	32830 MW	36930 TQ	USBLS	5/15
	Indianapolis-Carmel-Anderson MSA, IN	Y	26850 FQ	29820 MW	34540 TQ	USBLS	5/15
	Iowa	Y	20020 FQ	23960 MW	29700 TQ	USBLS	5/15
	Des Moines-West Des Moines MSA, IA	Y	19710 FQ	23300 MW	29060 TQ	USBLS	5/15
	Kansas	Y	24280 FQ	31710 MW	40460 TQ	USBLS	5/15
	Wichita MSA, KS	Y	25830 FQ	34290 MW	43820 TQ	USBLS	5/15
	Kentucky	Y	21660 FQ	26990 MW	34140 TQ	USBLS	5/15
	Louisville-Jefferson County MSA, KY-IN	Y	26280 FQ	31200 MW	37600 TQ	USBLS	5/15
	Louisiana	Y	20820 FQ	25600 MW	31160 TQ	USBLS	5/15
	Baton Rouge MSA, LA	Y	26010 FQ	29520 MW	34730 TQ	USBLS	5/15
	New Orleans-Metairie MSA, LA	Y	21850 FQ	26790 MW	33060 TQ	USBLS	5/15
	Maine	Y	23440 FQ	29780 MW	37290 TQ	USBLS	5/15
	Portland-South Portland MSA, ME	Y	24990 FQ	31250 MW	39630 TQ	USBLS	5/15

AE	Average entry wage	AWR	Average wage range	H	Hourly	LR	Low end range	MTC	Median total compensation	TCC	Total cash compensation
AEX	Average experienced wage	B	Biweekly	HI	Highest wage paid	M	Monthly	MW	Median wage paid	TQ	Third quartile wage
ATC	Average total compensation	D	Daily	HR	High end range	MCC	Median cash compensation	MWR	Median wage range	W	Weekly
AW	Average wage paid	FQ	First quartile wage	LO	Lowest wage paid	ME	Median entry wage	S	See annotated source	Y	Yearly

Butcher and Meat Cutter

Occupation/Type/Industry	Location	Per	Low	Mid	High	Source	Date
Butcher and Meat Cutter	Maryland	Y	26293 AE	38111 MW	44020 AEX	MDBLS	4/16
	Baltimore-Columbia-Towson MSA, MD	Y	30380 FQ	41130 MW	46590 TQ	USBLS	5/15
	Salisbury MSA, MD-DE	Y	21980 FQ	31540 MW	42340 TQ	USBLS	5/15
	Massachusetts	Y	29340 FQ	41340 MW	53600 TQ	USBLS	5/15
	Boston-Cambridge-Newton NECTA, MA	Y	29710 FQ	45280 MW	55430 TQ	USBLS	5/15
	Worcester MSA, MA-CT	Y	23670 FQ	34770 MW	49140 TQ	USBLS	5/15
	Michigan	Y	21690 FQ	28270 MW	35800 TQ	USBLS	5/15
	Detroit-Dearborn-Livonia PMSA, MI	Y	21450 FQ	28340 MW	36080 TQ	USBLS	5/15
	Grand Rapids-Wyoming MSA, MI	Y	22760 FQ	28270 MW	34230 TQ	USBLS	5/15
	Minnesota	Y	27134 FQ	34464 MW	48871 TQ	MNBLS	1/16-3/16
	Minneapolis-St. Paul-Bloomington MSA, MN-WI	Y	27933 FQ	39161 MW	53913 TQ	MNBLS	1/16-3/16
	Mississippi	Y	19370 FQ	25190 MW	30350 TQ	USBLS	5/15
	Jackson MSA, MS	Y	20870 FQ	26100 MW	29850 TQ	USBLS	5/15
	Missouri	Y	22760 FQ	28650 MW	36930 TQ	USBLS	5/15
	Kansas City MSA, MO-KS	Y	26980 FQ	34900 MW	43480 TQ	USBLS	5/15
	St. Louis MSA, MO-IL	Y	23230 FQ	30970 MW	39060 TQ	USBLS	5/15
	Montana	Y	23400 FQ	29420 MW	37070 TQ	USBLS	5/15
	Billings MSA, MT	Y	22940 FQ	28230 MW	36720 TQ	USBLS	5/15
	Nebraska	Y	21725 FQ	27450 MW	33925 TQ	NEBLS	7/16-9/16
	Omaha-Council Bluffs MSA, NE-IA	Y	23790 FQ	28500 MW	35220 TQ	NEBLS	7/16-9/16
	Nevada	Y	21970 FQ	31820 MW	43370 TQ	USBLS	5/15
	Las Vegas-Henderson-Paradise MSA, NV	Y	20840 FQ	32170 MW	43530 TQ	USBLS	5/15
	New Hampshire	H	11.70 AE	17.07 MW	20.11 AEX	NHBLS	6/16
	Manchester NECTA, NH	H	12.42 AE	17.23 MW	19.63 AEX	NHBLS	6/16
	Nashua NECTA, NH-MA	Y	24880 FQ	34550 MW	44350 TQ	USBLS	5/15
	New Jersey	Y	25270 FQ	42850 MW	54040 TQ	USBLS	5/15
	Camden PMSA, NJ	Y	30300 FQ	40670 MW	47970 TQ	USBLS	5/15
	Newark PMSA, NJ-PA	Y	22810 FQ	39410 MW	53700 TQ	USBLS	5/15
	Trenton MSA, NJ	Y	27360 FQ	41520 MW	49200 TQ	USBLS	5/15
	New Mexico	Y	19740 FQ	30140 MW	38080 TQ	USBLS	5/15
	Albuquerque MSA, NM	Y	22470 FQ	32120 MW	39780 TQ	USBLS	5/15
	New York	Y	23640 AE	35220 MW	46010 AEX	NYBLS	1/16-3/16
	Buffalo-Cheektowaga-Niagara Falls MSA, NY	Y	26530 FQ	33570 MW	45000 TQ	USBLS	5/15
	Nassau County-Suffolk County PMSA, NY	Y	23030 FQ	36120 MW	58020 TQ	USBLS	5/15
	New York-Jersey City-White Plains PMSA, NY-NJ	Y	27260 FQ	38350 MW	53710 TQ	USBLS	5/15
	Rochester MSA, NY	Y	18960 FQ	27530 MW	41990 TQ	USBLS	5/15
	North Carolina	Y	19250 FQ	26300 MW	32920 TQ	USBLS	5/15
	Charlotte-Concord-Gastonia MSA, NC-SC	Y	24040 FQ	30360 MW	35740 TQ	USBLS	5/15
	Raleigh MSA, NC	Y	25630 FQ	30160 MW	35240 TQ	USBLS	5/15
	North Dakota	Y	26160 FQ	32410 MW	37770 TQ	USBLS	5/15
	Fargo MSA, ND-MN	Y	27110 FQ	30170 MW	35060 TQ	USBLS	5/15
	Ohio	Y	26040 FQ	32220 MW	38430 TQ	USBLS	5/15
	Cincinnati MSA, OH-KY-IN	Y	27790 FQ	33510 MW	37680 TQ	USBLS	5/15
	Cleveland-Elyria MSA, OH	Y	26220 FQ	35060 MW	42430 TQ	USBLS	5/15
	Columbus MSA, OH	Y	25670 FQ	30590 MW	37000 TQ	USBLS	5/15
	Oklahoma	Y	20990 FQ	25960 MW	30270 TQ	USBLS	5/15
	Oklahoma City MSA, OK	Y	23360 FQ	28750 MW	35750 TQ	USBLS	5/15
	Tulsa MSA, OK	Y	19220 FQ	24460 MW	29480 TQ	USBLS	5/15
	Oregon	H	13.26 FQ	16.87 MW	19.69 TQ	ORBLS	2016
	Portland-Vancouver-Hillsboro MSA, OR-WA	Y	31680 FQ	38620 MW	44830 TQ	USBLS	5/15
	Pennsylvania	Y	26660 FQ	32710 MW	39320 TQ	USBLS	5/15
	Allentown-Bethlehem-Easton MSA, PA-NJ	Y	20610 FQ	31700 MW	41890 TQ	USBLS	5/15
	Harrisburg-Carlisle MSA, PA	Y	32190 FQ	34940 MW	37690 TQ	USBLS	5/15
	Montgomery County-Bucks County-Chester County PMSA, PA	Y	27290 FQ	31650 MW	41880 TQ	USBLS	5/15
	Philadelphia PMSA, PA	Y	28570 FQ	36940 MW	45180 TQ	USBLS	5/15
	Pittsburgh MSA, PA	Y	27260 FQ	32550 MW	40010 TQ	USBLS	5/15
	Rhode Island	Y	26380 FQ	30220 MW	38630 TQ	USBLS	5/15

AE	Average entry wage	AWR	Average wage range	H	Hourly
AEX	Average experienced wage	B	Biweekly	HI	Highest wage paid
ATC	Average total compensation	D	Daily	HR	High end range
AW	Average wage paid	FQ	First quartile wage	LO	Lowest wage paid

LR	Low end range	MTC	Median total compensation	TCC	Total cash compensation
M	Monthly	MW	Median wage paid	TQ	Third quartile wage
MCC	Median cash compensation	MWR	Median wage range	W	Weekly
ME	Median entry wage	S	See annotated source	Y	Yearly

Occupation/Type/Industry	Location	Per	Low	Mid	High	Source	Date
Butcher and Meat Cutter	Providence-Warwick MSA, RI-MA	Y	26280 FQ	30500 MW	40300 TQ	USBLS	5/15
	South Carolina	Y	22110 FQ	27980 MW	34390 TQ	USBLS	5/15
	Charleston-North Charleston MSA, SC	Y	19990 FQ	28310 MW	35320 TQ	USBLS	5/15
	Columbia MSA, SC	Y	25030 FQ	30610 MW	35980 TQ	USBLS	5/15
	Greenville-Anderson-Mauldin MSA, SC	Y	20650 FQ	25330 MW	30500 TQ	USBLS	5/15
	South Dakota	Y	24760 FQ	28510 MW	33440 TQ	USBLS	5/15
	Sioux Falls MSA, SD	Y	22030 FQ	26680 MW	33880 TQ	USBLS	5/15
	Tennessee	Y	22840 FQ	28460 MW	35030 TQ	USBLS	5/15
	Knoxville MSA, TN	Y	25030 FQ	29230 MW	34940 TQ	USBLS	5/15
	Memphis MSA, TN-MS-AR	Y	19910 FQ	26810 MW	35940 TQ	USBLS	5/15
	Nashville-Davidson–Murfreesboro–Franklin MSA, TN	Y	24860 FQ	30650 MW	36960 TQ	USBLS	5/15
	Texas	Y	19720 FQ	24510 MW	31850 TQ	USBLS	5/15
	Austin-Round Rock MSA, TX	Y	26410 FQ	32480 MW	36700 TQ	USBLS	5/15
	Dallas-Plano-Irving PMSA, TX	Y	18940 FQ	26500 MW	33000 TQ	USBLS	5/15
	Fort Worth-Arlington PMSA, TX	Y	19700 FQ	24080 MW	30660 TQ	USBLS	5/15
	Houston-The Woodlands-Sugar Land MSA, TX	Y	18200 FQ	22650 MW	32060 TQ	USBLS	5/15
	San Antonio-New Braunfels MSA, TX	Y	29470 FQ	33990 MW	37910 TQ	USBLS	5/15
	Utah	Y	24450 FQ	30430 MW	36170 TQ	USBLS	5/15
	Ogden-Clearfield MSA, UT	Y	24200 FQ	31420 MW	36600 TQ	USBLS	5/15
	Provo-Orem MSA, UT	Y	23140 FQ	29150 MW	34930 TQ	USBLS	5/15
	Salt Lake City MSA, UT	Y	25780 FQ	32410 MW	37300 TQ	USBLS	5/15
	Vermont	Y	26310 FQ	32930 MW	40120 TQ	USBLS	5/15
	Burlington-South Burlington MSA, VT	Y	25210 FQ	31790 MW	39030 TQ	USBLS	5/15
	Virginia	Y	24190 FQ	30530 MW	38530 TQ	USBLS	5/15
	Richmond MSA, VA	Y	28340 FQ	33660 MW	38570 TQ	USBLS	5/15
	Virginia Beach-Norfolk-Newport News MSA, VA-NC	Y	24620 FQ	32230 MW	37040 TQ	USBLS	5/15
	Washington	H	11.98 FQ	17.49 MW	22.17 TQ	WABLS	3/16
	Seattle-Bellevue-Everett PMSA, WA	H	11.59 FQ	17.81 MW	22.68 TQ	WABLS	3/16
	Tacoma-Lakewood PMSA, WA	H	14.41 FQ	19.28 MW	23.05 TQ	WABLS	3/16
	West Virginia	Y	21080 FQ	25510 MW	32960 TQ	USBLS	5/15
	Huntington-Ashland MSA, WV-KY-OH	Y	19150 FQ	23010 MW	31590 TQ	USBLS	5/15
	Wisconsin	Y	28560 FQ	36240 MW	44340 TQ	USBLS	5/15
	Madison MSA, WI	Y	29740 FQ	35870 MW	43140 TQ	USBLS	5/15
	Milwaukee-Waukesha-West Allis MSA, WI	Y	23910 FQ	32300 MW	44580 TQ	USBLS	5/15
	Wyoming	Y	25750 FQ	31650 MW	36450 TQ	USBLS	5/15
	Puerto Rico	Y	16790 FQ	18090 MW	19420 TQ	USBLS	5/15
	San Juan-Carolina-Caguas MSA, PR	Y	16840 FQ	18210 MW	19660 TQ	USBLS	5/15
	Virgin Islands	Y	21780 FQ	27360 MW	31570 TQ	USBLS	5/15
	Guam	Y	19000 FQ	21350 MW	25040 TQ	USBLS	5/15
Buyer and Purchasing Agent							
Farm Products	Alabama	Y	47333 AE	68129 AW	78532 AEX	ALBLS	6/16
Farm Products	Birmingham-Hoover MSA, AL	Y	50244 AE	74002 AW	85881 AEX	ALBLS	6/16
Farm Products	Arkansas	Y	36270 FQ	42680 MW	54640 TQ	USBLS	5/15
Farm Products	California	H	21.29 FQ	31.02 MW	43.15 TQ	CABLS	1/16-3/16
Farm Products	Anaheim-Santa Ana-Irvine PMSA, CA	H	22.75 FQ	32.22 MW	37.66 TQ	CABLS	1/16-3/16
Farm Products	Los Angeles-Long Beach-Glendale PMSA, CA	H	22.40 FQ	28.88 MW	39.05 TQ	CABLS	1/16-3/16
Farm Products	Oakland-Hayward-Berkeley PMSA, CA	H	18.20 FQ	25.55 MW	36.70 TQ	CABLS	1/16-3/16
Farm Products	Riverside-San Bernardino-Ontario MSA, CA	H	27.23 FQ	33.87 MW	40.74 TQ	CABLS	1/16-3/16
Farm Products	Sacramento–Roseville–Arden-Arcade MSA, CA	H	26.01 FQ	34.95 MW	51.59 TQ	CABLS	1/16-3/16
Farm Products	San Diego-Carlsbad MSA, CA	H	18.68 FQ	25.58 MW	37.35 TQ	CABLS	1/16-3/16

AE Average entry wage	**AWR** Average wage range	**H** Hourly	**LR** Low end range	**MTC** Median total compensation	**TCC** Total cash compensation
AEX Average experienced wage	**B** Biweekly	**HI** Highest wage paid	**M** Monthly	**MW** Median wage paid	**TQ** Third quartile wage
ATC Average total compensation	**D** Daily	**HR** High end range	**MCC** Median cash compensation	**MWR** Median wage range	**W** Weekly
AW Average wage paid	**FQ** First quartile wage	**LO** Lowest wage paid	**ME** Median entry wage	**S** See annotated source	**Y** Yearly

Occupation/Type/Industry	Location	Per	Low	Mid	High	Source	Date
Buyer and Purchasing Agent							
Farm Products	San Francisco-Redwood City-South San Francisco PMSA, CA	H	13.52 FQ	24.52 MW	45.12 TQ	CABLS	1/16-3/16
Farm Products	Colorado	Y	48690 FQ	59660 MW	73190 TQ	USBLS	5/15
Farm Products	Denver-Aurora-Lakewood MSA, CO	Y	50360 FQ	60060 MW	72320 TQ	USBLS	5/15
Farm Products	Connecticut	Y		36585 MW		CTBLS	1/16-3/16
Farm Products	District of Columbia	Y	59510 FQ	71100 MW	80000 TQ	USBLS	5/15
Farm Products	Washington-Arlington-Alexandria PMSA, DC-VA-MD-WV	Y	32950 FQ	64840 MW	77790 TQ	USBLS	5/15
Farm Products	Florida	H	20.86 AE	28.60 MW	34.96 AEX	FLBLS	7/16-9/16
Farm Products	Miami-Miami Beach-Kendall PMSA, FL	H	24.45 AE	29.38 MW	33.63 AEX	FLBLS	7/16-9/16
Farm Products	Orlando-Kissimmee-Sanford MSA, FL	H	23.19 AE	33.14 MW	41.14 AEX	FLBLS	7/16-9/16
Farm Products	Tampa-St. Petersburg-Clearwater MSA, FL	H	17.33 AE	23.45 MW	31.24 AEX	FLBLS	7/16-9/16
Farm Products	Georgia	Y	41460 FQ	49670 MW	74620 TQ	USBLS	5/15
Farm Products	Atlanta-Sandy Springs-Roswell MSA, GA	Y	43610 FQ	50670 MW	77620 TQ	USBLS	5/15
Farm Products	Augusta-Richmond County MSA, GA-SC	Y	46470 FQ	54640 MW	59930 TQ	USBLS	5/15
Farm Products	Hawaii	Y	19330 FQ	35850 MW	44500 TQ	USBLS	5/15
Farm Products	Urban Honolulu MSA, HI	Y	18100 FQ	32020 MW	45250 TQ	USBLS	5/15
Farm Products	Idaho	Y	52700 FQ	63850 MW	73980 TQ	USBLS	5/15
Farm Products	Illinois	Y	42880 FQ	54090 MW	67320 TQ	USBLS	5/15
Farm Products	Chicago-Naperville-Arlington Heights PMSA, IL	Y	44190 FQ	53210 MW	63810 TQ	USBLS	5/15
Farm Products	Indiana	Y	40500 FQ	54230 MW	61020 TQ	USBLS	5/15
Farm Products	Indianapolis-Carmel-Anderson MSA, IN	Y	41830 FQ	53590 MW	60790 TQ	USBLS	5/15
Farm Products	Iowa	Y	38200 FQ	56750 MW	70460 TQ	USBLS	5/15
Farm Products	Des Moines-West Des Moines MSA, IA	Y	55160 FQ	67070 MW	83060 TQ	USBLS	5/15
Farm Products	Kansas	Y	55280 FQ	64940 MW	79400 TQ	USBLS	5/15
Farm Products	Wichita MSA, KS	Y	55800 FQ	68850 MW	81030 TQ	USBLS	5/15
Farm Products	Kentucky	Y	28770 FQ	37280 MW	57550 TQ	USBLS	5/15
Farm Products	Louisville-Jefferson County MSA, KY-IN	Y	53240 FQ	67740 MW	80660 TQ	USBLS	5/15
Farm Products	Louisiana	Y	34460 FQ	46150 MW	59680 TQ	USBLS	5/15
Farm Products	Baton Rouge MSA, LA	Y	42290 FQ	49910 MW	60430 TQ	USBLS	5/15
Farm Products	Maine	Y	36950 FQ	42770 MW	48740 TQ	USBLS	5/15
Farm Products	Portland-South Portland MSA, ME	Y	35870 FQ	40580 MW	46600 TQ	USBLS	5/15
Farm Products	Maryland	Y	31005 AE	49626 MW	58936 AEX	MDBLS	4/16
Farm Products	Baltimore-Columbia-Towson MSA, MD	Y	31220 FQ	40110 MW	49500 TQ	USBLS	5/15
Farm Products	Massachusetts	Y	53660 FQ	72820 MW	104260 TQ	USBLS	5/15
Farm Products	Boston-Cambridge-Newton NECTA, MA	Y	53330 FQ	71800 MW	108040 TQ	USBLS	5/15
Farm Products	Michigan	Y	36800 FQ	54840 MW	79010 TQ	USBLS	5/15
Farm Products	Minnesota	Y	47411 FQ	60184 MW	74511 TQ	MNBLS	1/16-3/16
Farm Products	Minneapolis-St. Paul-Bloomington MSA, MN-WI	Y	48600 FQ	65325 MW	77397 TQ	MNBLS	1/16-3/16
Farm Products	Mississippi	Y	37660 FQ	62500 MW	70650 TQ	USBLS	5/15
Farm Products	Jackson MSA, MS	Y	35000 FQ	54050 MW	67160 TQ	USBLS	5/15
Farm Products	Missouri	Y	40200 FQ	50220 MW	60070 TQ	USBLS	5/15
Farm Products	Kansas City MSA, MO-KS	Y	54210 FQ	63590 MW	77800 TQ	USBLS	5/15
Farm Products	Montana	Y	22640 FQ	37690 MW	49130 TQ	USBLS	5/15
Farm Products	Nebraska	Y	46720 FQ	64880 MW	76205 TQ	NEBLS	7/16-9/16
Farm Products	Omaha-Council Bluffs MSA, NE-IA	Y	55850 FQ	68895 MW	77240 TQ	NEBLS	7/16-9/16
Farm Products	Nevada	Y	45230 FQ	58730 MW	70710 TQ	USBLS	5/15
Farm Products	Las Vegas-Henderson-Paradise MSA, NV	Y	46270 FQ	61010 MW	72000 TQ	USBLS	5/15
Farm Products	New Hampshire	H	20.61 AE	29.44 MW	35.62 AEX	NHBLS	6/16
Farm Products	Manchester NECTA, NH	H	22.36 AE	32.71 MW	37.91 AEX	NHBLS	6/16
Farm Products	New Jersey	Y	43890 FQ	51260 MW	72180 TQ	USBLS	5/15
Farm Products	New Mexico	Y	32060 FQ	40820 MW	49340 TQ	USBLS	5/15
Farm Products	Albuquerque MSA, NM	Y	32240 FQ	39900 MW	49550 TQ	USBLS	5/15

AE	Average entry wage	AWR	Average wage range	H	Hourly	LR	Low end range	MTC	Median total compensation	TCC	Total cash compensation
AEX	Average experienced wage	B	Biweekly	HI	Highest wage paid	M	Monthly	MCC	Median cash compensation	TQ	Third quartile wage
ATC	Average total compensation	D	Daily	HR	High end range	MCC	Median cash compensation	MWR	Median wage range	W	Weekly
AW	Average wage paid	FQ	First quartile wage	LO	Lowest wage paid	ME	Median entry wage	S	See annotated source	Y	Yearly

Occupation/Type/Industry	Location	Per	Low	Mid	High	Source	Date
Buyer and Purchasing Agent							
Farm Products	New York	Y	39580 AE	51280 MW	80770 AEX	NYBLS	1/16-3/16
Farm Products	Buffalo-Cheektowaga-Niagara Falls MSA, NY	Y	34520 FQ	38360 MW	46950 TQ	USBLS	5/15
Farm Products	Nassau County-Suffolk County PMSA, NY	Y	47320 FQ	59170 MW	86620 TQ	USBLS	5/15
Farm Products	New York-Jersey City-White Plains PMSA, NY-NJ	Y	44060 FQ	51290 MW	75930 TQ	USBLS	5/15
Farm Products	North Carolina	Y	43610 FQ	53620 MW	70620 TQ	USBLS	5/15
Farm Products	Charlotte-Concord-Gastonia MSA, NC-SC	Y	41190 FQ	47220 MW	69610 TQ	USBLS	5/15
Farm Products	North Dakota	Y	41520 FQ	55340 MW	70140 TQ	USBLS	5/15
Farm Products	Ohio	Y	44890 FQ	56820 MW	77060 TQ	USBLS	5/15
Farm Products	Cincinnati MSA, OH-KY-IN	Y	43450 FQ	58690 MW	75590 TQ	USBLS	5/15
Farm Products	Cleveland-Elyria MSA, OH	Y	37440 FQ	48910 MW	61730 TQ	USBLS	5/15
Farm Products	Columbus MSA, OH	Y	44040 FQ	52660 MW	63300 TQ	USBLS	5/15
Farm Products	Oklahoma	Y	29230 FQ	45920 MW	61430 TQ	USBLS	5/15
Farm Products	Oklahoma City MSA, OK	Y	40050 FQ	48030 MW	68850 TQ	USBLS	5/15
Farm Products	Tulsa MSA, OK	Y	31780 FQ	57020 MW	64250 TQ	USBLS	5/15
Farm Products	Oregon	H	19.54 FQ	23.69 MW	31.57 TQ	ORBLS	2016
Farm Products	Portland-Vancouver-Hillsboro MSA, OR-WA	Y	44340 FQ	53410 MW	64570 TQ	USBLS	5/15
Farm Products	Pennsylvania	Y	48940 FQ	60230 MW	76940 TQ	USBLS	5/15
Farm Products	Allentown-Bethlehem-Easton MSA, PA-NJ	Y	51720 FQ	65860 MW	89500 TQ	USBLS	5/15
Farm Products	Philadelphia PMSA, PA	Y	53190 FQ	57190 MW	61180 TQ	USBLS	5/15
Farm Products	Pittsburgh MSA, PA	Y	56000 FQ	69230 MW	80920 TQ	USBLS	5/15
Farm Products	Rhode Island	Y	28720 FQ	32900 MW	52790 TQ	USBLS	5/15
Farm Products	Providence-Warwick MSA, RI-MA	Y	29020 FQ	34720 MW	57260 TQ	USBLS	5/15
Farm Products	South Carolina	Y	40870 FQ	47660 MW	75320 TQ	USBLS	5/15
Farm Products	South Dakota	Y	54510 FQ	65960 MW	76830 TQ	USBLS	5/15
Farm Products	Sioux Falls MSA, SD	Y	52860 FQ	61650 MW	74570 TQ	USBLS	5/15
Farm Products	Texas	Y	32340 FQ	46990 MW	65310 TQ	USBLS	5/15
Farm Products	Dallas-Plano-Irving PMSA, TX	Y	41940 FQ	58430 MW	104790 TQ	USBLS	5/15
Farm Products	Fort Worth-Arlington PMSA, TX	Y	28420 FQ	46130 MW	58670 TQ	USBLS	5/15
Farm Products	Houston-The Woodlands-Sugar Land MSA, TX	Y	34480 FQ	50990 MW	69710 TQ	USBLS	5/15
Farm Products	San Antonio-New Braunfels MSA, TX	Y	37050 FQ	53530 MW	71780 TQ	USBLS	5/15
Farm Products	Utah	Y	42820 FQ	53020 MW	59540 TQ	USBLS	5/15
Farm Products	Ogden-Clearfield MSA, UT	Y	51470 FQ	55140 MW	58820 TQ	USBLS	5/15
Farm Products	Salt Lake City MSA, UT	Y	38520 FQ	48870 MW	59550 TQ	USBLS	5/15
Farm Products	Vermont	Y	33480 FQ	45920 MW	58480 TQ	USBLS	5/15
Farm Products	Burlington-South Burlington MSA, VT	Y	42940 FQ	48980 MW	69690 TQ	USBLS	5/15
Farm Products	Washington	H	22.37 FQ	28.12 MW	36.33 TQ	WABLS	3/16
Farm Products	Seattle-Bellevue-Everett PMSA, WA	H	27.56 FQ	35.65 MW	45.79 TQ	WABLS	3/16
Farm Products	Tacoma-Lakewood PMSA, WA	H	20.19 FQ	22.51 MW	26.18 TQ	WABLS	3/16
Farm Products	Wisconsin	Y	46260 FQ	60840 MW	74620 TQ	USBLS	5/15
Farm Products	Madison MSA, WI	Y	52980 FQ	65450 MW	76090 TQ	USBLS	5/15
Farm Products	Milwaukee-Waukesha-West Allis MSA, WI	Y	47920 FQ	64530 MW	74870 TQ	USBLS	5/15
Farm Products	Puerto Rico	Y	30520 FQ	42950 MW	55350 TQ	USBLS	5/15
Farm Products	San Juan-Carolina-Caguas MSA, PR	Y	30650 FQ	43390 MW	57870 TQ	USBLS	5/15
Cabinetmaker and Bench Carpenter	Alabama	Y	21222 AE	28554 AW	32214 AEX	ALBLS	6/16
	Birmingham-Hoover MSA, AL	Y	21983 AE	33222 AW	38836 AEX	ALBLS	6/16
	Alaska	Y	31050 FQ	37570 MW	46170 TQ	USBLS	5/15
	Anchorage MSA, AK	Y	31050 FQ	37570 MW	46170 TQ	USBLS	5/15
	Arizona	Y	20810 FQ	25560 MW	35410 TQ	USBLS	5/15
	Phoenix-Mesa-Scottsdale MSA, AZ	Y	19680 FQ	23910 MW	34120 TQ	USBLS	5/15
	Tucson MSA, AZ	Y	26300 FQ	32220 MW	40920 TQ	USBLS	5/15
	Arkansas	Y	26130 FQ	32940 MW	38610 TQ	USBLS	5/15
	Little Rock-North Little Rock-Conway MSA, AR	Y	28160 FQ	37590 MW	46950 TQ	USBLS	5/15
	California	H	11.90 FQ	15.68 MW	21.34 TQ	CABLS	1/16-3/16

AE	Average entry wage	AWR	Average wage range	H	Hourly	LR	Low end range	MTC	Median total compensation	TCC	Total cash compensation
AEX	Average experienced wage	B	Biweekly	HI	Highest wage paid	M	Monthly	MW	Median wage paid	TQ	Third quartile wage
ATC	Average total compensation	D	Daily	HR	High end range	MCC	Median cash compensation	MWR	Median wage range	W	Weekly
AW	Average wage paid	FQ	First quartile wage	LO	Lowest wage paid	ME	Median entry wage	S	See annotated source	Y	Yearly

Occupation/Type/Industry	Location	Per	Low	Mid	High	Source	Date
Cabinetmaker and Bench Carpenter							
	Anaheim-Santa Ana-Irvine PMSA, CA	H	12.24 FQ	16.38 MW	21.73 TQ	CABLS	1/16-3/16
	Los Angeles-Long Beach-Glendale PMSA, CA	H	11.93 FQ	16.57 MW	21.96 TQ	CABLS	1/16-3/16
	Oakland-Hayward-Berkeley PMSA, CA	H	15.78 FQ	20.77 MW	27.41 TQ	CABLS	1/16-3/16
	Riverside-San Bernardino-Ontario MSA, CA	H	10.39 FQ	12.45 MW	15.17 TQ	CABLS	1/16-3/16
	Sacramento–Roseville–Arden-Arcade MSA, CA	H	13.27 FQ	18.10 MW	25.67 TQ	CABLS	1/16-3/16
	San Diego-Carlsbad MSA, CA	H	14.26 FQ	17.36 MW	20.94 TQ	CABLS	1/16-3/16
	San Francisco-Redwood City-South San Francisco PMSA, CA	H	13.50 FQ	22.19 MW	28.21 TQ	CABLS	1/16-3/16
	Colorado	Y	28600 FQ	34910 MW	41740 TQ	USBLS	5/15
	Denver-Aurora-Lakewood MSA, CO	Y	28350 FQ	34750 MW	41730 TQ	USBLS	5/15
	Connecticut	Y		44627 MW		CTBLS	1/16-3/16
	Bridgeport-Stamford-Norwalk MSA, CT	Y	35370 FQ	41370 MW	48900 TQ	USBLS	5/15
	Hartford-West Hartford-East Hartford MSA, CT	Y	36060 FQ	44060 MW	51020 TQ	USBLS	5/15
	Delaware	Y	28560 FQ	36420 MW	44050 TQ	USBLS	5/15
	Wilmington PMSA, DE-MD-NJ	Y	25730 FQ	37220 MW	45160 TQ	USBLS	5/15
	District of Columbia	Y	37060 FQ	44760 MW	60220 TQ	USBLS	5/15
	Washington-Arlington-Alexandria PMSA, DC-VA-MD-WV	Y	31680 FQ	39710 MW	56700 TQ	USBLS	5/15
	Florida	H	10.93 AE	15.55 MW	19.43 AEX	FLBLS	7/16-9/16
	Fort Lauderdale-Pompano Beach-Deerfield Beach PMSA, FL	H	10.39 AE	15.38 MW	18.18 AEX	FLBLS	7/16-9/16
	Miami-Miami Beach-Kendall PMSA, FL	H	10.37 AE	14.38 MW	22.98 AEX	FLBLS	7/16-9/16
	Orlando-Kissimmee-Sanford MSA, FL	H	13.08 AE	17.32 MW	20.55 AEX	FLBLS	7/16-9/16
	Tampa-St. Petersburg-Clearwater MSA, FL	H	12.46 AE	15.54 MW	17.69 AEX	FLBLS	7/16-9/16
	Georgia	Y	24620 FQ	31140 MW	37050 TQ	USBLS	5/15
	Atlanta-Sandy Springs-Roswell MSA, GA	Y	24890 FQ	32810 MW	38060 TQ	USBLS	5/15
	Augusta-Richmond County MSA, GA-SC	Y	27030 FQ	33240 MW	37910 TQ	USBLS	5/15
	Hawaii	Y	33390 FQ	42890 MW	48010 TQ	USBLS	5/15
	Urban Honolulu MSA, HI	Y	31190 FQ	41430 MW	47510 TQ	USBLS	5/15
	Idaho	Y	20430 FQ	28300 MW	36440 TQ	USBLS	5/15
	Boise City MSA, ID	Y	19850 FQ	25560 MW	36810 TQ	USBLS	5/15
	Illinois	Y	30450 FQ	39140 MW	53290 TQ	USBLS	5/15
	Chicago-Naperville-Arlington Heights PMSA, IL	Y	32840 FQ	44510 MW	56960 TQ	USBLS	5/15
	Lake County-Kenosha County PMSA, IL-WI	Y	34540 FQ	41720 MW	48140 TQ	USBLS	5/15
	Indiana	Y	26370 FQ	31280 MW	41880 TQ	USBLS	5/15
	Gary PMSA, IN	Y	17750 FQ	19600 MW	24280 TQ	USBLS	5/15
	Indianapolis-Carmel-Anderson MSA, IN	Y	26930 FQ	30820 MW	39590 TQ	USBLS	5/15
	Iowa	Y	27280 FQ	31090 MW	38720 TQ	USBLS	5/15
	Des Moines-West Des Moines MSA, IA	Y	32580 FQ	38400 MW	45710 TQ	USBLS	5/15
	Kansas	Y	25850 FQ	32050 MW	38110 TQ	USBLS	5/15
	Wichita MSA, KS	Y	23780 FQ	30740 MW	36210 TQ	USBLS	5/15
	Kentucky	Y	22040 FQ	27400 MW	33940 TQ	USBLS	5/15
	Louisville-Jefferson County MSA, KY-IN	Y	25970 FQ	32170 MW	43220 TQ	USBLS	5/15
	Louisiana	Y	27500 FQ	32280 MW	37100 TQ	USBLS	5/15
	Baton Rouge MSA, LA	Y	27320 FQ	31840 MW	36140 TQ	USBLS	5/15
	New Orleans-Metairie MSA, LA	Y	33230 FQ	36500 MW	39770 TQ	USBLS	5/15
	Maine	Y	30590 FQ	35990 MW	43220 TQ	USBLS	5/15

AE	Average entry wage	**AWR**	Average wage range	**H**	Hourly	
AEX	Average experienced wage	**B**	Biweekly	**HI**	Highest wage paid	
ATC	Average total compensation	**D**	Daily	**HR**	High end range	
AW	Average wage paid	**FQ**	First quartile wage	**LO**	Lowest wage paid	

LR	Low end range	**MTC**	Median total compensation	**TCC**	Total cash compensation
M	Monthly	**MW**	Median wage paid	**TQ**	Third quartile wage
MCC	Median cash compensation	**MWR**	Median wage range	**W**	Weekly
ME	Median entry wage	**S**	See annotated source	**Y**	Yearly

Occupation/Type/Industry	Location	Per	Low	Mid	High	Source	Date
Cabinetmaker and Bench Carpenter	Portland-South Portland MSA, ME	Y	32740 FQ	37440 MW	47390 TQ	USBLS	5/15
	Maryland	Y	25849 AE	38501 MW	44827 AEX	MDBLS	4/16
	Baltimore-Columbia-Towson MSA, MD	Y	32840 FQ	37570 MW	45800 TQ	USBLS	5/15
	Salisbury MSA, MD-DE	Y	28880 FQ	33720 MW	38100 TQ	USBLS	5/15
	Massachusetts	Y	31490 FQ	38190 MW	48000 TQ	USBLS	5/15
	Boston-Cambridge-Newton NECTA, MA	Y	33270 FQ	38430 MW	48650 TQ	USBLS	5/15
	Worcester MSA, MA-CT	Y	34420 FQ	42080 MW	50700 TQ	USBLS	5/15
	Michigan	Y	28670 FQ	34880 MW	40770 TQ	USBLS	5/15
	Detroit-Dearborn-Livonia PMSA, MI	Y	22930 FQ	27240 MW	34300 TQ	USBLS	5/15
	Grand Rapids-Wyoming MSA, MI	Y	32200 FQ	35800 MW	39880 TQ	USBLS	5/15
	Minnesota	Y	32196 FQ	38362 MW	46643 TQ	MNBLS	1/16-3/16
	Minneapolis-St. Paul-Bloomington MSA, MN-WI	Y	34322 FQ	41905 MW	49215 TQ	MNBLS	1/16-3/16
	Mississippi	Y	21300 FQ	25380 MW	30800 TQ	USBLS	5/15
	Missouri	Y	24520 FQ	30240 MW	37380 TQ	USBLS	5/15
	Kansas City MSA, MO-KS	Y	26610 FQ	30990 MW	36590 TQ	USBLS	5/15
	St. Louis MSA, MO-IL	Y	28400 FQ	36820 MW	45070 TQ	USBLS	5/15
	Montana	Y	23230 FQ	29490 MW	39270 TQ	USBLS	5/15
	Billings MSA, MT	Y	23380 FQ	30880 MW	41980 TQ	USBLS	5/15
	Nebraska	Y	25340 FQ	29690 MW	36190 TQ	NEBLS	7/16-9/16
	Omaha-Council Bluffs MSA, NE-IA	Y	25830 FQ	29470 MW	34785 TQ	NEBLS	7/16-9/16
	Nevada	Y	28160 FQ	37450 MW	44930 TQ	USBLS	5/15
	Las Vegas-Henderson-Paradise MSA, NV	Y	26090 FQ	35530 MW	44040 TQ	USBLS	5/15
	New Hampshire	H	10.23 AE	17.01 MW	19.54 AEX	NHBLS	6/16
	Manchester NECTA, NH	H	18.32 AE	21.38 MW	22.34 AEX	NHBLS	6/16
	New Jersey	Y	34610 FQ	44000 MW	54220 TQ	USBLS	5/15
	Camden PMSA, NJ	Y	36910 FQ	45600 MW	53920 TQ	USBLS	5/15
	Newark PMSA, NJ-PA	Y	35300 FQ	42560 MW	52610 TQ	USBLS	5/15
	Trenton MSA, NJ	Y	44040 FQ	49770 MW	66980 TQ	USBLS	5/15
	New Mexico	Y	23580 FQ	29030 MW	35610 TQ	USBLS	5/15
	Albuquerque MSA, NM	Y	23790 FQ	29370 MW	35410 TQ	USBLS	5/15
	New York	Y	25650 AE	36030 MW	44920 AEX	NYBLS	1/16-3/16
	Buffalo-Cheektowaga-Niagara Falls MSA, NY	Y	29060 FQ	35830 MW	44740 TQ	USBLS	5/15
	Nassau County-Suffolk County PMSA, NY	Y	28220 FQ	35890 MW	52460 TQ	USBLS	5/15
	New York-Jersey City-White Plains PMSA, NY-NJ	Y	29620 FQ	39730 MW	50010 TQ	USBLS	5/15
	Rochester MSA, NY	Y	31770 FQ	36180 MW	42250 TQ	USBLS	5/15
	North Carolina	Y	24060 FQ	30090 MW	36950 TQ	USBLS	5/15
	Charlotte-Concord-Gastonia MSA, NC-SC	Y	25540 FQ	33440 MW	40710 TQ	USBLS	5/15
	Raleigh MSA, NC	Y	25180 FQ	31320 MW	37700 TQ	USBLS	5/15
	North Dakota	Y	34260 FQ	39140 MW	45480 TQ	USBLS	5/15
	Fargo MSA, ND-MN	Y	34130 FQ	37710 MW	45440 TQ	USBLS	5/15
	Ohio	Y	26510 FQ	31960 MW	38390 TQ	USBLS	5/15
	Cincinnati MSA, OH-KY-IN	Y	28650 FQ	34840 MW	41170 TQ	USBLS	5/15
	Cleveland-Elyria MSA, OH	Y	28060 FQ	35340 MW	42690 TQ	USBLS	5/15
	Columbus MSA, OH	Y	30130 FQ	36000 MW	43730 TQ	USBLS	5/15
	Oklahoma	Y	24440 FQ	32490 MW	37950 TQ	USBLS	5/15
	Oklahoma City MSA, OK	Y	24790 FQ	32550 MW	37600 TQ	USBLS	5/15
	Tulsa MSA, OK	Y	25890 FQ	32670 MW	38700 TQ	USBLS	5/15
	Oregon	H	13.05 FQ	15.63 MW	18.91 TQ	ORBLS	2016
	Portland-Vancouver-Hillsboro MSA, OR-WA	Y	27810 FQ	34600 MW	42780 TQ	USBLS	5/15
	Pennsylvania	Y	28900 FQ	35910 MW	44320 TQ	USBLS	5/15
	Allentown-Bethlehem-Easton MSA, PA-NJ	Y	29250 FQ	39410 MW	47040 TQ	USBLS	5/15
	Harrisburg-Carlisle MSA, PA	Y	32370 FQ	35570 MW	38760 TQ	USBLS	5/15
	Montgomery County-Bucks County-Chester County PMSA, PA	Y	27970 FQ	33540 MW	43940 TQ	USBLS	5/15
	Philadelphia PMSA, PA	Y	30410 FQ	50530 MW	59580 TQ	USBLS	5/15
	Pittsburgh MSA, PA	Y	31120 FQ	42350 MW	50350 TQ	USBLS	5/15

AE	Average entry wage	AWR	Average wage range	H	Hourly	LR	Low end range	MTC	Median total compensation	TCC	Total cash compensation
AEX	Average experienced wage	B	Biweekly	HI	Highest wage paid	M	Monthly	MW	Median wage paid	TQ	Third quartile wage
ATC	Average total compensation	D	Daily	HR	High end range	MCC	Median cash compensation	MWR	Median wage range	W	Weekly
AW	Average wage paid	FQ	First quartile wage	LO	Lowest wage paid	ME	Median entry wage	S	See annotated source	Y	Yearly

Occupation/Type/Industry	Location	Per	Low	Mid	High	Source	Date
Cabinetmaker and Bench Carpenter	Rhode Island	Y	30300 FQ	37270 MW	45860 TQ	USBLS	5/15
	Providence-Warwick MSA, RI-MA	Y	30740 FQ	37810 MW	46760 TQ	USBLS	5/15
	South Carolina	Y	28580 FQ	35560 MW	44650 TQ	USBLS	5/15
	Charleston-North Charleston MSA, SC	Y	27240 FQ	35430 MW	43390 TQ	USBLS	5/15
	Columbia MSA, SC	Y	19860 FQ	51480 MW	57140 TQ	USBLS	5/15
	Greenville-Anderson-Mauldin MSA, SC	Y	27830 FQ	32510 MW	38390 TQ	USBLS	5/15
	South Dakota	Y	24110 FQ	28680 MW	35220 TQ	USBLS	5/15
	Sioux Falls MSA, SD	Y	25360 FQ	30390 MW	37410 TQ	USBLS	5/15
	Tennessee	Y	23150 FQ	28660 MW	35180 TQ	USBLS	5/15
	Knoxville MSA, TN	Y	24610 FQ	30190 MW	35500 TQ	USBLS	5/15
	Memphis MSA, TN-MS-AR	Y	22490 FQ	26890 MW	33370 TQ	USBLS	5/15
	Nashville-Davidson–Murfreesboro–Franklin MSA, TN	Y	22400 FQ	30300 MW	38630 TQ	USBLS	5/15
	Texas	Y	20790 FQ	26400 MW	34360 TQ	USBLS	5/15
	Austin-Round Rock MSA, TX	Y	22230 FQ	27660 MW	34180 TQ	USBLS	5/15
	Dallas-Plano-Irving PMSA, TX	Y	20860 FQ	26280 MW	34010 TQ	USBLS	5/15
	Fort Worth-Arlington PMSA, TX	Y	20840 FQ	25870 MW	33630 TQ	USBLS	5/15
	Houston-The Woodlands-Sugar Land MSA, TX	Y	21830 FQ	27670 MW	36580 TQ	USBLS	5/15
	San Antonio-New Braunfels MSA, TX	Y	21010 FQ	26530 MW	33260 TQ	USBLS	5/15
	Utah	Y	26110 FQ	32100 MW	39570 TQ	USBLS	5/15
	Ogden-Clearfield MSA, UT	Y	25880 FQ	29560 MW	37370 TQ	USBLS	5/15
	Provo-Orem MSA, UT	Y	23350 FQ	29980 MW	36990 TQ	USBLS	5/15
	Salt Lake City MSA, UT	Y	27280 FQ	33660 MW	41770 TQ	USBLS	5/15
	Vermont	Y	28850 FQ	34520 MW	42860 TQ	USBLS	5/15
	Burlington-South Burlington MSA, VT	Y	30970 FQ	37500 MW	51680 TQ	USBLS	5/15
	Virginia	Y	25380 FQ	31940 MW	39080 TQ	USBLS	5/15
	Richmond MSA, VA	Y	26910 FQ	31160 MW	37330 TQ	USBLS	5/15
	Virginia Beach-Norfolk-Newport News MSA, VA-NC	Y	28200 FQ	35490 MW	43890 TQ	USBLS	5/15
	Washington	H	13.88 FQ	17.52 MW	21.75 TQ	WABLS	3/16
	Seattle-Bellevue-Everett PMSA, WA	H	13.75 FQ	17.10 MW	22.00 TQ	WABLS	3/16
	Tacoma-Lakewood PMSA, WA	H	14.15 FQ	17.88 MW	21.80 TQ	WABLS	3/16
	West Virginia	Y	27800 FQ	33310 MW	37310 TQ	USBLS	5/15
	Wisconsin	Y	26450 FQ	32530 MW	39080 TQ	USBLS	5/15
	Madison MSA, WI	Y	31880 FQ	36650 MW	42690 TQ	USBLS	5/15
	Milwaukee-Waukesha-West Allis MSA, WI	Y	30330 FQ	39130 MW	45960 TQ	USBLS	5/15
	Wyoming	Y	28780 FQ	34860 MW	41430 TQ	USBLS	5/15
	Puerto Rico	Y	16690 FQ	17920 MW	19150 TQ	USBLS	5/15
	San Juan-Carolina-Caguas MSA, PR	Y	16740 FQ	18090 MW	19470 TQ	USBLS	5/15
Cable TV Producer City Manager's Office	Moreno Valley, CA	Y		47019 AW		CACIT	6/28/16
CAD Specialist Public Safety Department, State Government	Ohio	H	18.97 LO		21.11 HI	OHGOV	2015
Cafeteria Worker Harvard University	Cambridge, MA	H		21.89 AW		NYT03	2016
Cake Designer	United States	Y		25000 AW		SKU01	2016
Call Center Analyst Municipal Government	Detroit, MI	M	3050 LO		3458 HI	DETGOV	2016
Call Center Representative	United States	Y		28000 AW		TJN02	2016
Camera and Photographic Equipment Repairer	Arizona	Y	29920 FQ	37830 MW	49680 TQ	USBLS	5/15
	California	H	15.54 FQ	19.59 MW	25.71 TQ	CABLS	1/16-3/16

Occupation/Type/Industry	Location	Per	Low	Mid	High	Source	Date
Camera and Photographic Equipment Repairer	Colorado	Y	34210 FQ	36880 MW	39540 TQ	USBLS	5/15
	Connecticut	Y		43549 MW		CTBLS	1/16-3/16
	Florida	H	21.37 AE	22.39 MW	24.88 AEX	FLBLS	7/16-9/16
	Georgia	Y	27620 FQ	32910 MW	38640 TQ	USBLS	5/15
	Illinois	Y	22080 FQ	28490 MW	37170 TQ	USBLS	5/15
	Indiana	Y	23390 FQ	28520 MW	46500 TQ	USBLS	5/15
	Iowa	Y	44060 FQ	53770 MW	60190 TQ	USBLS	5/15
	Louisiana	Y	32720 FQ	38140 MW	44120 TQ	USBLS	5/15
	Maryland	Y	27210 AE	37762 MW	43038 AEX	MDBLS	4/16
	Massachusetts	Y	37770 FQ	45290 MW	54000 TQ	USBLS	5/15
	Michigan	Y	28020 FQ	40280 MW	56790 TQ	USBLS	5/15
	Minnesota	Y	28752 FQ	44833 MW	53854 TQ	MNBLS	1/16-3/16
	Missouri	Y	27920 FQ	33430 MW	41610 TQ	USBLS	5/15
	New Jersey	Y	32020 FQ	45090 MW	58640 TQ	USBLS	5/15
	New York	Y	21300 AE	26050 MW	41250 AEX	NYBLS	1/16-3/16
	North Carolina	Y	22620 FQ	50980 MW	56980 TQ	USBLS	5/15
	Ohio	Y	35960 FQ	49710 MW	70500 TQ	USBLS	5/15
	Pennsylvania	Y	19730 FQ	27950 MW	39200 TQ	USBLS	5/15
	Texas	Y	50410 FQ	54950 MW	59480 TQ	USBLS	5/15
	Utah	Y	36220 FQ	45980 MW	61760 TQ	USBLS	5/15
	Washington	H	11.64 FQ	19.10 MW	22.87 TQ	WABLS	3/16
	Wisconsin	Y	52640 FQ	68350 MW	76480 TQ	USBLS	5/15
Camera Operator							
Television, Video, and Motion Picture	Alabama	Y	24229 AE	41069 AW	49488 AEX	ALBLS	6/16
Television, Video, and Motion Picture	Birmingham-Hoover MSA, AL	Y	29622 AE	41904 AW	48051 AEX	ALBLS	6/16
Television, Video, and Motion Picture	Arizona	Y	30450 FQ	41650 MW	54340 TQ	USBLS	5/15
Television, Video, and Motion Picture	Phoenix-Mesa-Scottsdale MSA, AZ	Y	30580 FQ	41130 MW	55130 TQ	USBLS	5/15
Television, Video, and Motion Picture	Tucson MSA, AZ	Y	30020 FQ	43430 MW	50290 TQ	USBLS	5/15
Television, Video, and Motion Picture	Arkansas	Y	28610 FQ	49310 MW	68150 TQ	USBLS	5/15
Television, Video, and Motion Picture	Little Rock-North Little Rock-Conway MSA, AR	Y	29610 FQ	48260 MW	68290 TQ	USBLS	5/15
Television, Video, and Motion Picture	California	H	19.85 FQ	29.02 MW	42.06 TQ	CABLS	1/16-3/16
Television, Video, and Motion Picture	Anaheim-Santa Ana-Irvine PMSA, CA	H	15.48 FQ	18.70 MW	25.78 TQ	CABLS	1/16-3/16
Television, Video, and Motion Picture	Los Angeles-Long Beach-Glendale PMSA, CA	H	19.86 FQ	29.28 MW	43.24 TQ	CABLS	1/16-3/16
Television, Video, and Motion Picture	Oakland-Hayward-Berkeley PMSA, CA	H	20.93 FQ	22.84 MW	24.80 TQ	CABLS	1/16-3/16
Television, Video, and Motion Picture	Riverside-San Bernardino-Ontario MSA, CA	H	26.74 FQ	33.41 MW	37.35 TQ	CABLS	1/16-3/16
Television, Video, and Motion Picture	Sacramento–Roseville–Arden-Arcade MSA, CA	H	25.71 FQ	29.09 MW	33.66 TQ	CABLS	1/16-3/16
Television, Video, and Motion Picture	San Francisco-Redwood City-South San Francisco PMSA, CA	H	24.80 FQ	28.69 MW	36.99 TQ	CABLS	1/16-3/16
Television, Video, and Motion Picture	Connecticut	Y		61783 MW		CTBLS	1/16-3/16
Television, Video, and Motion Picture	Hartford-West Hartford-East Hartford MSA, CT	Y	41010 FQ	62060 MW	111200 TQ	USBLS	5/15
Television, Video, and Motion Picture	District of Columbia	Y	70240 FQ	88710 MW	102830 TQ	USBLS	5/15
Television, Video, and Motion Picture	Washington-Arlington-Alexandria PMSA, DC-VA-MD-WV	Y	68680 FQ	87860 MW	101480 TQ	USBLS	5/15
Television, Video, and Motion Picture	Florida	H	15.39 AE	22.91 MW	29.66 AEX	FLBLS	7/16-9/16
Television, Video, and Motion Picture	Fort Lauderdale-Pompano Beach-Deerfield Beach PMSA, FL	H	14.55 AE	17.70 MW	21.19 AEX	FLBLS	7/16-9/16
Television, Video, and Motion Picture	Miami-Miami Beach-Kendall PMSA, FL	H	17.07 AE	28.26 MW	33.64 AEX	FLBLS	7/16-9/16
Television, Video, and Motion Picture	Orlando-Kissimmee-Sanford MSA, FL	H	16.37 AE	21.86 MW	25.13 AEX	FLBLS	7/16-9/16
Television, Video, and Motion Picture	Tampa-St. Petersburg-Clearwater MSA, FL	H	15.37 AE	26.87 MW	34.86 AEX	FLBLS	7/16-9/16
Television, Video, and Motion Picture	Georgia	Y	29470 FQ	55640 MW	69990 TQ	USBLS	5/15
Television, Video, and Motion Picture	Atlanta-Sandy Springs-Roswell MSA, GA	Y	28540 FQ	55620 MW	71560 TQ	USBLS	5/15
Television, Video, and Motion Picture	Hawaii	Y	41750 FQ	63230 MW	71940 TQ	USBLS	5/15
Television, Video, and Motion Picture	Urban Honolulu MSA, HI	Y	45920 FQ	64510 MW	72830 TQ	USBLS	5/15
Television, Video, and Motion Picture	Idaho	Y	27930 FQ	48370 MW	89550 TQ	USBLS	5/15
Television, Video, and Motion Picture	Boise City MSA, ID	Y	38490 FQ	52860 MW	87510 TQ	USBLS	5/15

AE Average entry wage	**AWR** Average wage range	**H** Hourly	**LR** Low end range	**MTC** Median total compensation	**TCC** Total cash compensation
AEX Average experienced wage	**B** Biweekly	**HI** Highest wage paid	**M** Monthly	**MW** Median wage paid	**TQ** Third quartile wage
ATC Average total compensation	**D** Daily	**HR** High end range	**MCC** Median cash compensation	**MWR** Median wage range	**W** Weekly
AW Average wage paid	**FQ** First quartile wage	**LO** Lowest wage paid	**ME** Median entry wage	**S** See annotated source	**Y** Yearly

Camera Operator

Occupation/Type/Industry	Location	Per	Low	Mid	High	Source	Date
Television, Video, and Motion Picture	Illinois	Y	27190 FQ	42210 MW	60800 TQ	USBLS	5/15
Television, Video, and Motion Picture	Chicago-Naperville-Arlington Heights PMSA, IL	Y	28420 FQ	49190 MW	62850 TQ	USBLS	5/15
Television, Video, and Motion Picture	Indiana	Y	29700 FQ	36360 MW	47500 TQ	USBLS	5/15
Television, Video, and Motion Picture	Indianapolis-Carmel-Anderson MSA, IN	Y	32030 FQ	37080 MW	46710 TQ	USBLS	5/15
Television, Video, and Motion Picture	Iowa	Y	26690 FQ	30350 MW	47980 TQ	USBLS	5/15
Television, Video, and Motion Picture	Des Moines-West Des Moines MSA, IA	Y	26220 FQ	29120 MW	53230 TQ	USBLS	5/15
Television, Video, and Motion Picture	Kansas	Y	23750 FQ	32240 MW	45280 TQ	USBLS	5/15
Television, Video, and Motion Picture	Kentucky	Y	27190 FQ	34340 MW	39450 TQ	USBLS	5/15
Television, Video, and Motion Picture	Louisville-Jefferson County MSA, KY-IN	Y	27450 FQ	33130 MW	37170 TQ	USBLS	5/15
Television, Video, and Motion Picture	Louisiana	Y	30400 FQ	42520 MW	48850 TQ	USBLS	5/15
Television, Video, and Motion Picture	Baton Rouge MSA, LA	Y	37580 FQ	45030 MW	54850 TQ	USBLS	5/15
Television, Video, and Motion Picture	New Orleans-Metairie MSA, LA	Y	29470 FQ	42120 MW	48650 TQ	USBLS	5/15
Television, Video, and Motion Picture	Maine	Y	19850 FQ	27190 MW	38220 TQ	USBLS	5/15
Television, Video, and Motion Picture	Portland-South Portland MSA, ME	Y	20900 FQ	27340 MW	38640 TQ	USBLS	5/15
Television, Video, and Motion Picture	Maryland	Y	37550 AE	53226 MW	61064 AEX	MDBLS	4/16
Television, Video, and Motion Picture	Baltimore-Columbia-Towson MSA, MD	Y	41360 FQ	47040 MW	58280 TQ	USBLS	5/15
Television, Video, and Motion Picture	Massachusetts	Y	33100 FQ	43650 MW	62590 TQ	USBLS	5/15
Television, Video, and Motion Picture	Boston-Cambridge-Newton NECTA, MA	Y	34720 FQ	45810 MW	63410 TQ	USBLS	5/15
Television, Video, and Motion Picture	Michigan	Y	34550 FQ	52090 MW	70340 TQ	USBLS	5/15
Television, Video, and Motion Picture	Detroit-Dearborn-Livonia PMSA, MI	Y	22140 FQ	33200 MW	37790 TQ	USBLS	5/15
Television, Video, and Motion Picture	Minnesota	Y	27187 FQ	36592 MW	47197 TQ	MNBLS	1/16-3/16
Television, Video, and Motion Picture	Minneapolis-St. Paul-Bloomington MSA, MN-WI	Y	30756 FQ	42197 MW	48598 TQ	MNBLS	1/16-3/16
Television, Video, and Motion Picture	Mississippi	Y	42710 FQ	51820 MW	71680 TQ	USBLS	5/15
Television, Video, and Motion Picture	Missouri	Y	33590 FQ	45950 MW	62540 TQ	USBLS	5/15
Television, Video, and Motion Picture	Kansas City MSA, MO-KS	Y	32460 FQ	37150 MW	52870 TQ	USBLS	5/15
Television, Video, and Motion Picture	St. Louis MSA, MO-IL	Y	30380 FQ	40670 MW	55710 TQ	USBLS	5/15
Television, Video, and Motion Picture	Montana	Y	32760 FQ	37640 MW	48460 TQ	USBLS	5/15
Television, Video, and Motion Picture	Nebraska	Y	22825 FQ	38510 MW	46970 TQ	NEBLS	7/16-9/16
Television, Video, and Motion Picture	Omaha-Council Bluffs MSA, NE-IA	Y	28655 FQ	43580 MW	48005 TQ	NEBLS	7/16-9/16
Television, Video, and Motion Picture	New Hampshire	H	14.26 AE	18.53 MW	20.17 AEX	NHBLS	6/16
Television, Video, and Motion Picture	New Jersey	Y	32440 FQ	44580 MW	72960 TQ	USBLS	5/15
Television, Video, and Motion Picture	Camden PMSA, NJ	Y	45070 FQ	61460 MW	102010 TQ	USBLS	5/15
Television, Video, and Motion Picture	Newark PMSA, NJ-PA	Y	34470 FQ	43850 MW	61540 TQ	USBLS	5/15
Television, Video, and Motion Picture	Trenton MSA, NJ	Y	43170 FQ	63790 MW	71820 TQ	USBLS	5/15
Television, Video, and Motion Picture	New Mexico	Y	48950 FQ	64430 MW	72980 TQ	USBLS	5/15
Television, Video, and Motion Picture	New York	Y	41000 AE	64960 MW	112320 AEX	NYBLS	1/16-3/16
Television, Video, and Motion Picture	Nassau County-Suffolk County PMSA, NY	Y	35080 FQ	43730 MW	57790 TQ	USBLS	5/15
Television, Video, and Motion Picture	Rochester MSA, NY	Y	25670 FQ	33140 MW	52070 TQ	USBLS	5/15
Television, Video, and Motion Picture	North Carolina	Y	28150 FQ	37160 MW	47180 TQ	USBLS	5/15
Television, Video, and Motion Picture	Charlotte-Concord-Gastonia MSA, NC-SC	Y	27200 FQ	36280 MW	45520 TQ	USBLS	5/15
Television, Video, and Motion Picture	Raleigh MSA, NC	Y	32400 FQ	38960 MW	45610 TQ	USBLS	5/15
Television, Video, and Motion Picture	North Dakota	Y	27310 FQ	31840 MW	47010 TQ	USBLS	5/15
Television, Video, and Motion Picture	Fargo MSA, ND-MN	Y	28530 FQ	35480 MW	45550 TQ	USBLS	5/15
Television, Video, and Motion Picture	Ohio	Y	27920 FQ	45440 MW	57160 TQ	USBLS	5/15
Television, Video, and Motion Picture	Cincinnati MSA, OH-KY-IN	Y	40910 FQ	53980 MW	60470 TQ	USBLS	5/15
Television, Video, and Motion Picture	Cleveland-Elyria MSA, OH	Y	36260 FQ	46680 MW	81890 TQ	USBLS	5/15
Television, Video, and Motion Picture	Columbus MSA, OH	Y	31340 FQ	49650 MW	55980 TQ	USBLS	5/15
Television, Video, and Motion Picture	Oklahoma	Y	24680 FQ	33440 MW	42060 TQ	USBLS	5/15
Television, Video, and Motion Picture	Oklahoma City MSA, OK	Y	23570 FQ	32660 MW	39310 TQ	USBLS	5/15
Television, Video, and Motion Picture	Tulsa MSA, OK	Y	31360 FQ	37210 MW	45830 TQ	USBLS	5/15
Television, Video, and Motion Picture	Oregon	H	21.93 FQ	28.77 MW	35.66 TQ	ORBLS	2016
Television, Video, and Motion Picture	Portland-Vancouver-Hillsboro MSA, OR-WA	Y	45600 FQ	59710 MW	74320 TQ	USBLS	5/15
Television, Video, and Motion Picture	Pennsylvania	Y	30170 FQ	39000 MW	46760 TQ	USBLS	5/15
Television, Video, and Motion Picture	Montgomery County-Bucks County-Chester County PMSA, PA	Y	34900 FQ	39730 MW	45410 TQ	USBLS	5/15
Television, Video, and Motion Picture	Philadelphia PMSA, PA	Y	35580 FQ	42500 MW	48520 TQ	USBLS	5/15

AE	Average entry wage	AWR	Average wage range	H	Hourly	LR	Low end range	MTC	Median total compensation	TCC	Total cash compensation
AEX	Average experienced wage	B	Biweekly	HI	Highest wage paid	M	Monthly	MW	Median wage paid	TQ	Third quartile wage
ATC	Average total compensation	D	Daily	HR	High end range	MCC	Median cash compensation	MWR	Median wage range	W	Weekly
AW	Average wage paid	FQ	First quartile wage	LO	Lowest wage paid	ME	Median entry wage	S	See annotated source	Y	Yearly

Occupation/Type/Industry	Location	Per	Low	Mid	High	Source	Date
Camera Operator							
Television, Video, and Motion Picture	Pittsburgh MSA, PA	Y	26800 FQ	40740 MW	46670 TQ	USBLS	5/15
Television, Video, and Motion Picture	South Carolina	Y	29220 FQ	38960 MW	55080 TQ	USBLS	5/15
Television, Video, and Motion Picture	Sioux Falls MSA, SD	Y	19230 FQ	23470 MW	34500 TQ	USBLS	5/15
Television, Video, and Motion Picture	Tennessee	Y	32600 FQ	43990 MW	61740 TQ	USBLS	5/15
Television, Video, and Motion Picture	Knoxville MSA, TN	Y	28060 FQ	50760 MW	86030 TQ	USBLS	5/15
Television, Video, and Motion Picture	Nashville-Davidson–Murfreesboro–Franklin MSA, TN	Y	34280 FQ	44370 MW	60830 TQ	USBLS	5/15
Television, Video, and Motion Picture	Texas	Y	31150 FQ	47540 MW	60720 TQ	USBLS	5/15
Television, Video, and Motion Picture	Austin-Round Rock MSA, TX	Y	36800 FQ	50680 MW	58340 TQ	USBLS	5/15
Television, Video, and Motion Picture	Dallas-Plano-Irving PMSA, TX	Y	40770 FQ	53220 MW	65340 TQ	USBLS	5/15
Television, Video, and Motion Picture	Houston-The Woodlands-Sugar Land MSA, TX	Y	27280 FQ	43260 MW	61360 TQ	USBLS	5/15
Television, Video, and Motion Picture	San Antonio-New Braunfels MSA, TX	Y	21940 FQ	33200 MW	50740 TQ	USBLS	5/15
Television, Video, and Motion Picture	Utah	Y	24400 FQ	34990 MW	55000 TQ	USBLS	5/15
Television, Video, and Motion Picture	Salt Lake City MSA, UT	Y	24010 FQ	34650 MW	51860 TQ	USBLS	5/15
Television, Video, and Motion Picture	Vermont	Y	27130 FQ	32910 MW	38150 TQ	USBLS	5/15
Television, Video, and Motion Picture	Burlington-South Burlington MSA, VT	Y	29070 FQ	33350 MW	37530 TQ	USBLS	5/15
Television, Video, and Motion Picture	Virginia	Y	41900 FQ	50450 MW	76130 TQ	USBLS	5/15
Television, Video, and Motion Picture	Richmond MSA, VA	Y	41430 FQ	45590 MW	49770 TQ	USBLS	5/15
Television, Video, and Motion Picture	Virginia Beach-Norfolk-Newport News MSA, VA-NC	Y	39240 FQ	58940 MW	75740 TQ	USBLS	5/15
Television, Video, and Motion Picture	Washington	H	17.47 FQ	23.52 MW	32.12 TQ	WABLS	3/16
Television, Video, and Motion Picture	Seattle-Bellevue-Everett PMSA, WA	H	17.99 FQ	23.84 MW	32.56 TQ	WABLS	3/16
Television, Video, and Motion Picture	West Virginia	Y	27830 FQ	32320 MW	41590 TQ	USBLS	5/15
Television, Video, and Motion Picture	Wisconsin	Y	18920 FQ	32630 MW	49770 TQ	USBLS	5/15
Television, Video, and Motion Picture	Madison MSA, WI	Y	19790 FQ	36840 MW	56980 TQ	USBLS	5/15
Television, Video, and Motion Picture	Milwaukee-Waukesha-West Allis MSA, WI	Y	19880 FQ	36660 MW	75950 TQ	USBLS	5/15
Television, Video, and Motion Picture	Wyoming	Y	39210 FQ	45400 MW	56340 TQ	USBLS	5/15
Television, Video, and Motion Picture	Puerto Rico	Y	18520 FQ	25000 MW	33850 TQ	USBLS	5/15
Television, Video, and Motion Picture	San Juan-Carolina-Caguas MSA, PR	Y	19280 FQ	26540 MW	35430 TQ	USBLS	5/15
Television, Video, and Motion Picture	Guam	Y	18730 FQ	21540 MW	27110 TQ	USBLS	5/15
Camp Manager							
Municipal Government	Arcadia, CA	Y			7881 HI	CACIT	6/28/16
Municipal Government	Los Angeles, CA	Y			63973 HI	CACIT	6/23/16
Campus Chaplain							
Baccalaureate Institution	United States	Y		56476 MW		CHE02	2015-2016
Master's Institution	United States	Y		49376 MW		CHE02	2015-2016
Research University	United States	Y		64900 MW		CHE02	2015-2016
Campus Minister							
Church of Christ	United States	Y		38700 AW		ACU	2/16-3/16
Campus Planner							
Michigan State University	East Lansing, MI	Y			112881 HI	MSUSAL	10/1/14-9/30/15
Cancer Registrar							
Health Department, State Government	Ohio	H	17.65 LO		24.69 HI	OHGOV	2015
Canine Handler							
Police Department, Municipal Government	Fountain Valley, CA	Y			87869 HI	CACIT	6/28/16
Police Department, Municipal Government	Menlo Park, CA	Y			114454 HI	CACIT	6/28/16
Cannabis Coach	District of Columbia	S	35000 LO		42000 HI	MDAY01	2017
Cannabis Testing Facility Scientist							
ACT Laboratories	Lansing, MI	Y			70000 HI	LSJ13	2018
Captain, Mate, and Pilot of Water Vessels	Alabama	Y	55714 AE	89418 AW	106275 AEX	ALBLS	6/16
	Alaska	Y	54200 FQ	70620 MW	85880 TQ	USBLS	5/15
	Arizona	Y	67810 FQ	87270 MW	103430 TQ	USBLS	5/15
	California	H	20.62 FQ	31.48 MW	39.79 TQ	CABLS	1/16-3/16
	Connecticut	Y		85451 MW		CTBLS	1/16-3/16

AE Average entry wage	**AWR** Average wage range	**H** Hourly	**LR** Low end range	**MTC** Median total compensation	**TCC** Total cash compensation
AEX Average experienced wage	**B** Biweekly	**HI** Highest wage paid	**M** Monthly	**MW** Median wage paid	**TQ** Third quartile wage
ATC Average total compensation	**D** Daily	**HR** High end range	**MCC** Median cash compensation	**MWR** Median wage range	**W** Weekly
AW Average wage paid	**FQ** First quartile wage	**LO** Lowest wage paid	**ME** Median entry wage	**S** See annotated source	**Y** Yearly

Occupation/Type/Industry	Location	Per	Low	Mid	High	Source	Date
Captain, Mate, and Pilot of Water Vessels	Delaware	Y	47630 FQ	62740 MW	76660 TQ	USBLS	5/15
	Florida	H	18.22 AE	29.89 MW	42.30 AEX	FLBLS	7/16-9/16
	Georgia	Y	26800 FQ	56580 MW	72180 TQ	USBLS	5/15
	Hawaii	Y	38360 FQ	46220 MW	56630 TQ	USBLS	5/15
	Illinois	Y	59190 FQ	71860 MW	86780 TQ	USBLS	5/15
	Indiana	Y	67460 FQ	73090 MW	78720 TQ	USBLS	5/15
	Iowa	Y	41840 FQ	52440 MW	72440 TQ	USBLS	5/15
	Kentucky	Y	60740 FQ	82830 MW	111200 TQ	USBLS	5/15
	Louisiana	Y	68430 FQ	91490 MW	121050 TQ	USBLS	5/15
	Maine	Y	43200 FQ	54880 MW	61530 TQ	USBLS	5/15
	Maryland	Y	48873 AE	83869 MW	101367 AEX	MDBLS	4/16
	Massachusetts	Y	43890 FQ	56190 MW	80840 TQ	USBLS	5/15
	Michigan	Y	27590 FQ	46510 MW	63340 TQ	USBLS	5/15
	Minnesota	Y	53502 FQ	59148 MW	86095 TQ	MNBLS	1/16-3/16
	Missouri	Y	41030 FQ	55060 MW	79120 TQ	USBLS	5/15
	New Jersey	Y	40270 FQ	59660 MW	80740 TQ	USBLS	5/15
	New York	Y	37860 AE	68980 MW	92820 AEX	NYBLS	1/16-3/16
	North Carolina	Y	33750 FQ	41790 MW	77820 TQ	USBLS	5/15
	Ohio	Y	43400 FQ	64520 MW	77150 TQ	USBLS	5/15
	Oklahoma	Y	43660 FQ	60970 MW	91590 TQ	USBLS	5/15
	Oregon	H	31.72 FQ	36.32 MW	42.75 TQ	ORBLS	2016
	Pennsylvania	Y	40370 FQ	72820 MW	94970 TQ	USBLS	5/15
	Rhode Island	Y	33140 FQ	47520 MW	62020 TQ	USBLS	5/15
	South Carolina	Y	36440 FQ	56580 MW	74660 TQ	USBLS	5/15
	Tennessee	Y	61310 FQ	93180 MW	111230 TQ	USBLS	5/15
	Texas	Y	62970 FQ	104120 MW	136310 TQ	USBLS	5/15
	Virginia	Y	56390 FQ	68510 MW	101330 TQ	USBLS	5/15
	Washington	H	35.86 FQ	39.86 MW	48.59 TQ	WABLS	3/16
	West Virginia	Y	53610 FQ	58320 MW	63030 TQ	USBLS	5/15
	Wisconsin	Y	42790 FQ	53410 MW	64990 TQ	USBLS	5/15
	Puerto Rico	Y	28350 FQ	55410 MW	84640 TQ	USBLS	5/15
	Virgin Islands	Y	32930 FQ	36980 MW	43210 TQ	USBLS	5/15
Cardiologist	United States	Y		410000 AW		TIME01	2016
Cardiovascular Technologist and Technician	Alabama	Y	27929 AE	46226 AW	55370 AEX	ALBLS	6/16
	Birmingham-Hoover MSA, AL	Y	36074 AE	52291 AW	36074 AEX	ALBLS	6/16
	Alaska	Y	66980 FQ	85170 MW	93840 TQ	USBLS	5/15
	Anchorage MSA, AK	Y	59360 FQ	83330 MW	94170 TQ	USBLS	5/15
	Arizona	Y	38480 FQ	59370 MW	78540 TQ	USBLS	5/15
	Phoenix-Mesa-Scottsdale MSA, AZ	Y	40210 FQ	60470 MW	79990 TQ	USBLS	5/15
	Arkansas	Y	28060 FQ	41670 MW	58370 TQ	USBLS	5/15
	Little Rock-North Little Rock-Conway MSA, AR	Y	32610 FQ	57040 MW	87020 TQ	USBLS	5/15
	California	H	24.11 FQ	32.90 MW	44.50 TQ	CABLS	1/16-3/16
	Anaheim-Santa Ana-Irvine PMSA, CA	H	25.30 FQ	34.46 MW	42.91 TQ	CABLS	1/16-3/16
	Los Angeles-Long Beach-Glendale PMSA, CA	H	22.92 FQ	30.86 MW	41.77 TQ	CABLS	1/16-3/16
	Oakland-Hayward-Berkeley PMSA, CA	H	29.68 FQ	38.09 MW	52.25 TQ	CABLS	1/16-3/16
	Riverside-San Bernardino-Ontario MSA, CA	H	18.73 FQ	29.10 MW	41.68 TQ	CABLS	1/16-3/16
	Sacramento–Roseville–Arden-Arcade MSA, CA	H	28.59 FQ	36.79 MW	50.99 TQ	CABLS	1/16-3/16
	San Diego-Carlsbad MSA, CA	H	23.04 FQ	32.41 MW	43.78 TQ	CABLS	1/16-3/16
	San Francisco-Redwood City-South San Francisco PMSA, CA	H	33.61 FQ	53.90 MW	65.58 TQ	CABLS	1/16-3/16
	Colorado	Y	49240 FQ	66770 MW	81040 TQ	USBLS	5/15
	Denver-Aurora-Lakewood MSA, CO	Y	51520 FQ	66360 MW	81280 TQ	USBLS	5/15
	Connecticut	Y		69401 MW		CTBLS	1/16-3/16
	Bridgeport-Stamford-Norwalk MSA, CT	Y	46580 FQ	64750 MW	74680 TQ	USBLS	5/15
	Hartford-West Hartford-East Hartford MSA, CT	Y	50110 FQ	70900 MW	86010 TQ	USBLS	5/15
	Delaware	Y	38780 FQ	55800 MW	70690 TQ	USBLS	5/15

AE	Average entry wage	AWR	Average wage range	H	Hourly	LR	Low end range	MTC	Median total compensation	TCC	Total cash compensation
AEX	Average experienced wage	B	Biweekly	HI	Highest wage paid	M	Monthly	MW	Median wage paid	TQ	Third quartile wage
ATC	Average total compensation	D	Daily	HR	High end range	MCC	Median cash compensation	MWR	Median wage range	W	Weekly
AW	Average wage paid	FQ	First quartile wage	LO	Lowest wage paid	ME	Median entry wage	S	See annotated source	Y	Yearly

Cardiovascular Technologist and Technician

Occupation/Type/Industry	Location	Per	Low	Mid	High	Source	Date
Cardiovascular Technologist and Technician	Wilmington PMSA, DE-MD-NJ	Y	37510 FQ	52130 MW	67500 TQ	USBLS	5/15
	District of Columbia	Y	57640 FQ	74090 MW	88870 TQ	USBLS	5/15
	Washington-Arlington-Alexandria PMSA, DC-VA-MD-WV	Y	42180 FQ	68850 MW	84930 TQ	USBLS	5/15
	Florida	H	13.52 AE	22.50 MW	28.26 AEX	FLBLS	7/16-9/16
	Fort Lauderdale-Pompano Beach-Deerfield Beach PMSA, FL	H	14.13 AE	21.50 MW	29.25 AEX	FLBLS	7/16-9/16
	Miami-Miami Beach-Kendall PMSA, FL	H	14.27 AE	21.42 MW	26.95 AEX	FLBLS	7/16-9/16
	Orlando-Kissimmee-Sanford MSA, FL	H	15.38 AE	26.99 MW	31.35 AEX	FLBLS	7/16-9/16
	Tampa-St. Petersburg-Clearwater MSA, FL	H	13.06 AE	19.62 MW	27.37 AEX	FLBLS	7/16-9/16
	Georgia	Y	36260 FQ	53770 MW	66560 TQ	USBLS	5/15
	Atlanta-Sandy Springs-Roswell MSA, GA	Y	35900 FQ	54290 MW	67330 TQ	USBLS	5/15
	Augusta-Richmond County MSA, GA-SC	Y	36680 FQ	50670 MW	63940 TQ	USBLS	5/15
	Hawaii	Y	44240 FQ	55330 MW	84460 TQ	USBLS	5/15
	Urban Honolulu MSA, HI	Y	45700 FQ	68860 MW	88490 TQ	USBLS	5/15
	Idaho	Y	51240 FQ	59820 MW	70470 TQ	USBLS	5/15
	Boise City MSA, ID	Y	51510 FQ	59070 MW	68510 TQ	USBLS	5/15
	Illinois	Y	38660 FQ	54660 MW	72120 TQ	USBLS	5/15
	Chicago-Naperville-Arlington Heights PMSA, IL	Y	39670 FQ	55930 MW	74030 TQ	USBLS	5/15
	Lake County-Kenosha County PMSA, IL-WI	Y	29120 FQ	34570 MW	43130 TQ	USBLS	5/15
	Indiana	Y	35180 FQ	51280 MW	67090 TQ	USBLS	5/15
	Gary PMSA, IN	Y	35970 FQ	48920 MW	64600 TQ	USBLS	5/15
	Indianapolis-Carmel-Anderson MSA, IN	Y	37420 FQ	53880 MW	68920 TQ	USBLS	5/15
	Iowa	Y	35010 FQ	46010 MW	60420 TQ	USBLS	5/15
	Des Moines-West Des Moines MSA, IA	Y	31930 FQ	41120 MW	58920 TQ	USBLS	5/15
	Kansas	Y	31120 FQ	53220 MW	65600 TQ	USBLS	5/15
	Kentucky	Y	28900 FQ	42470 MW	61630 TQ	USBLS	5/15
	Louisville-Jefferson County MSA, KY-IN	Y	34420 FQ	54000 MW	66350 TQ	USBLS	5/15
	Louisiana	Y	27380 FQ	39750 MW	55910 TQ	USBLS	5/15
	Baton Rouge MSA, LA	Y	18500 FQ	35450 MW	57880 TQ	USBLS	5/15
	New Orleans-Metairie MSA, LA	Y	32190 FQ	51260 MW	60380 TQ	USBLS	5/15
	Maine	Y	41640 FQ	56910 MW	72400 TQ	USBLS	5/15
	Maryland	Y	39619 AE	64772 MW	77348 AEX	MDBLS	4/16
	Baltimore-Columbia-Towson MSA, MD	Y	49000 FQ	67550 MW	83530 TQ	USBLS	5/15
	Salisbury MSA, MD-DE	Y	47360 FQ	60340 MW	72710 TQ	USBLS	5/15
	Massachusetts	Y	50630 FQ	71590 MW	91280 TQ	USBLS	5/15
	Boston-Cambridge-Newton NECTA, MA	Y	57610 FQ	77370 MW	96440 TQ	USBLS	5/15
	Worcester MSA, MA-CT	Y	44030 FQ	63140 MW	78920 TQ	USBLS	5/15
	Michigan	Y	41190 FQ	53170 MW	63910 TQ	USBLS	5/15
	Detroit-Dearborn-Livonia PMSA, MI	Y	42400 FQ	56100 MW	67720 TQ	USBLS	5/15
	Minnesota	Y	51511 FQ	66481 MW	76602 TQ	MNBLS	1/16-3/16
	Minneapolis-St. Paul-Bloomington MSA, MN-WI	Y	53739 FQ	69031 MW	78487 TQ	MNBLS	1/16-3/16
	Mississippi	Y	26490 FQ	35560 MW	55570 TQ	USBLS	5/15
	Jackson MSA, MS	Y	25730 FQ	29900 MW	51330 TQ	USBLS	5/15
	Missouri	Y	31530 FQ	42060 MW	60150 TQ	USBLS	5/15
	Kansas City MSA, MO-KS	Y	34210 FQ	53810 MW	67510 TQ	USBLS	5/15
	St. Louis MSA, MO-IL	Y	31010 FQ	39600 MW	59210 TQ	USBLS	5/15
	Montana	Y	53650 FQ	66010 MW	75280 TQ	USBLS	5/15
	Nebraska	Y	36195 FQ	50665 MW	63070 TQ	NEBLS	7/16-9/16
	Omaha-Council Bluffs MSA, NE-IA	Y	36000 FQ	49765 MW	64580 TQ	NEBLS	7/16-9/16
	Nevada	Y	46530 FQ	76990 MW	89700 TQ	USBLS	5/15

AE	Average entry wage	AWR	Average wage range	H	Hourly
AEX	Average experienced wage	B	Biweekly	HI	Highest wage paid
ATC	Average total compensation	D	Daily	HR	High end range
AW	Average wage paid	FQ	First quartile wage	LO	Lowest wage paid

LR	Low end range	MTC	Median total compensation	TCC	Total cash compensation
M	Monthly	MW	Median wage paid	TQ	Third quartile wage
MCC	Median cash compensation	MWR	Median wage range	W	Weekly
ME	Median entry wage	S	See annotated source	Y	Yearly

Occupation/Type/Industry	Location	Per	Low	Mid	High	Source	Date
Cardiovascular Technologist and Technician	Las Vegas-Henderson-Paradise MSA, NV	Y	45790 FQ	78200 MW	89750 TQ	USBLS	5/16
	New Hampshire	H	19.92 AE	30.91 MW	35.72 AEX	NHBLS	6/16
	Manchester NECTA, NH	H	24.17 AE	34.09 MW	38.44 AEX	NHBLS	6/16
	New Jersey	Y	63210 FQ	72100 MW	80660 TQ	USBLS	5/15
	Camden PMSA, NJ	Y	66940 FQ	74580 MW	84950 TQ	USBLS	5/15
	Newark PMSA, NJ-PA	Y	54110 FQ	66610 MW	76200 TQ	USBLS	5/15
	Trenton MSA, NJ	Y	46930 FQ	61980 MW	76420 TQ	USBLS	5/15
	New Mexico	Y	35810 FQ	54270 MW	70330 TQ	USBLS	5/15
	Albuquerque MSA, NM	Y	34880 FQ	48260 MW	68060 TQ	USBLS	5/15
	New York	Y	39360 AE	57740 MW	69480 AEX	NYBLS	1/16-3/16
	Buffalo-Cheektowaga-Niagara Falls MSA, NY	Y	41220 FQ	54260 MW	66990 TQ	USBLS	5/15
	Nassau County-Suffolk County PMSA, NY	Y	44740 FQ	59830 MW	77060 TQ	USBLS	5/15
	New York-Jersey City-White Plains PMSA, NY-NJ	Y	45790 FQ	63400 MW	76130 TQ	USBLS	5/15
	Rochester MSA, NY	Y	40520 FQ	58350 MW	69870 TQ	USBLS	5/15
	North Carolina	Y	53420 FQ	62260 MW	73740 TQ	USBLS	5/15
	Charlotte-Concord-Gastonia MSA, NC-SC	Y	53280 FQ	61220 MW	71370 TQ	USBLS	5/15
	North Dakota	Y	27540 FQ	33720 MW	55550 TQ	USBLS	5/15
	Ohio	Y	38280 FQ	54170 MW	67750 TQ	USBLS	5/15
	Cincinnati MSA, OH-KY-IN	Y	35830 FQ	48340 MW	68130 TQ	USBLS	5/15
	Cleveland-Elyria MSA, OH	Y	43140 FQ	56780 MW	68850 TQ	USBLS	5/15
	Columbus MSA, OH	Y	36630 FQ	54470 MW	71210 TQ	USBLS	5/15
	Oklahoma	Y	26850 FQ	37810 MW	57250 TQ	USBLS	5/15
	Oklahoma City MSA, OK	Y	27190 FQ	38780 MW	57990 TQ	USBLS	5/15
	Tulsa MSA, OK	Y	29230 FQ	41020 MW	59520 TQ	USBLS	5/15
	Oregon	H	22.42 FQ	33.26 MW	41.87 TQ	ORBLS	2016
	Portland-Vancouver-Hillsboro MSA, OR-WA	Y	45660 FQ	71290 MW	89720 TQ	USBLS	5/15
	Pennsylvania	Y	37180 FQ	49630 MW	64380 TQ	USBLS	5/15
	Allentown-Bethlehem-Easton MSA, PA-NJ	Y	40820 FQ	52090 MW	67030 TQ	USBLS	5/15
	Harrisburg-Carlisle MSA, PA	Y	47790 FQ	58420 MW	69140 TQ	USBLS	5/15
	Montgomery County-Bucks County-Chester County PMSA, PA	Y	39990 FQ	54380 MW	64930 TQ	USBLS	5/15
	Philadelphia PMSA, PA	Y	37600 FQ	53880 MW	73650 TQ	USBLS	5/15
	Pittsburgh MSA, PA	Y	33600 FQ	45530 MW	61070 TQ	USBLS	5/15
	Rhode Island	Y	50860 FQ	69500 MW	85610 TQ	USBLS	5/15
	Providence-Warwick MSA, RI-MA	Y	48480 FQ	69410 MW	85960 TQ	USBLS	5/15
	South Carolina	Y	29090 FQ	49380 MW	64180 TQ	USBLS	5/15
	Charleston-North Charleston MSA, SC	Y	47420 FQ	57710 MW	67540 TQ	USBLS	5/15
	Greenville-Anderson-Mauldin MSA, SC	Y	30410 FQ	41870 MW	57140 TQ	USBLS	5/15
	South Dakota	Y	36470 FQ	46640 MW	58230 TQ	USBLS	5/15
	Tennessee	Y	34670 FQ	50330 MW	62070 TQ	USBLS	5/15
	Knoxville MSA, TN	Y	29980 FQ	45900 MW	58220 TQ	USBLS	5/15
	Memphis MSA, TN-MS-AR	Y	32760 FQ	51330 MW	62190 TQ	USBLS	5/15
	Nashville-Davidson–Murfreesboro–Franklin MSA, TN	Y	35900 FQ	50010 MW	66430 TQ	USBLS	5/15
	Texas	Y	34840 FQ	51550 MW	70100 TQ	USBLS	5/15
	Austin-Round Rock MSA, TX	Y	33860 FQ	46450 MW	60120 TQ	USBLS	5/15
	Dallas-Plano-Irving PMSA, TX	Y	38420 FQ	54850 MW	72600 TQ	USBLS	5/15
	Fort Worth-Arlington PMSA, TX	Y	33200 FQ	51860 MW	78750 TQ	USBLS	5/15
	Houston-The Woodlands-Sugar Land MSA, TX	Y	35790 FQ	49860 MW	67260 TQ	USBLS	5/15
	San Antonio-New Braunfels MSA, TX	Y	41750 FQ	57540 MW	71240 TQ	USBLS	5/15
	Utah	Y	31220 FQ	47620 MW	70910 TQ	USBLS	5/15
	Ogden-Clearfield MSA, UT	Y	29280 FQ	37360 MW	71510 TQ	USBLS	5/15
	Provo-Orem MSA, UT	Y	27530 FQ	31620 MW	63310 TQ	USBLS	5/15
	Salt Lake City MSA, UT	Y	31140 FQ	40060 MW	68820 TQ	USBLS	5/15
	Vermont	Y	34560 FQ	51610 MW	69030 TQ	USBLS	5/15
	Virginia	Y	42540 FQ	59180 MW	73560 TQ	USBLS	5/15

AE	Average entry wage	AWR	Average wage range	H	Hourly
AEX	Average experienced wage	B	Biweekly	HI	Highest wage paid
ATC	Average total compensation	D	Daily	HR	High end range
AW	Average wage paid	FQ	First quartile wage	LO	Lowest wage paid

LR	Low end range	MTC	Median total compensation	TCC	Total cash compensation
M	Monthly	MW	Median wage paid	TQ	Third quartile wage
MCC	Median cash compensation	MWR	Median wage range	W	Weekly
ME	Median entry wage	S	See annotated source	Y	Yearly

Occupation/Type/Industry	Location	Per	Low	Mid	High	Source	Date
Cardiovascular Technologist and Technician	Richmond MSA, VA	Y	48500 FQ	61020 MW	72120 TQ	USBLS	5/15
	Virginia Beach-Norfolk-Newport News MSA, VA-NC	Y	45630 FQ	56300 MW	67380 TQ	USBLS	5/15
	Washington	H	22.66 FQ	33.11 MW	42.05 TQ	WABLS	3/16
	Seattle-Bellevue-Everett PMSA, WA	H	22.69 FQ	32.05 MW	42.17 TQ	WABLS	3/16
	West Virginia	Y	23230 FQ	30260 MW	47300 TQ	USBLS	5/15
	Huntington-Ashland MSA, WV-KY-OH	Y	28750 FQ	37340 MW	52900 TQ	USBLS	5/15
	Wisconsin	Y	32550 FQ	45720 MW	68550 TQ	USBLS	5/15
	Madison MSA, WI	Y	32600 FQ	63580 MW	82230 TQ	USBLS	5/15
	Milwaukee-Waukesha-West Allis MSA, WI	Y	33110 FQ	46050 MW	67050 TQ	USBLS	5/15
	Puerto Rico	Y	17510 FQ	19970 MW	27980 TQ	USBLS	5/15
	San Juan-Carolina-Caguas MSA, PR	Y	17280 FQ	19260 MW	26350 TQ	USBLS	5/15
	Guam	Y	28950 FQ	33820 MW	39180 TQ	USBLS	5/15
Career/Technical Education Teacher							
Middle School	Alabama	Y	42190 AE	51710 AW	56460 AEX	ALBLS	6/16
Middle School	Alaska	Y	71570 FQ	85550 MW	94550 TQ	USBLS	5/15
Middle School	Arizona	Y	33110 FQ	42890 MW	54520 TQ	USBLS	5/15
Middle School	Phoenix-Mesa-Scottsdale MSA, AZ	Y	32100 FQ	43820 MW	56590 TQ	USBLS	5/15
Middle School	Arkansas	Y	43440 FQ	50900 MW	57890 TQ	USBLS	5/15
Middle School	Little Rock-North Little Rock-Conway MSA, AR	Y	43480 FQ	51200 MW	58190 TQ	USBLS	5/15
Middle School	California	Y		54823 AW		CABLS	1/16-3/16
Middle School	Los Angeles-Long Beach-Glendale PMSA, CA	Y		66135 AW		CABLS	1/16-3/16
Middle School	Colorado	Y	43260 FQ	52840 MW	64110 TQ	USBLS	5/15
Middle School	Denver-Aurora-Lakewood MSA, CO	Y	44330 FQ	55920 MW	69140 TQ	USBLS	5/15
Middle School	Connecticut	Y		73997 MW		CTBLS	1/16-3/16
Middle School	Hartford-West Hartford-East Hartford MSA, CT	Y	59160 FQ	72560 MW	86890 TQ	USBLS	5/15
Middle School	District of Columbia	Y	40330 FQ	55080 MW	67120 TQ	USBLS	5/15
Middle School	Washington-Arlington-Alexandria PMSA, DC-VA-MD-WV	Y	53590 FQ	64540 MW	84540 TQ	USBLS	5/15
Middle School	Florida	Y	42445 AE	53941 MW	63757 AEX	FLBLS	7/16-9/16
Middle School	Orlando-Kissimmee-Sanford MSA, FL	Y	44615 AE	49195 MW	55600 AEX	FLBLS	7/16-9/16
Middle School	Tampa-St. Petersburg-Clearwater MSA, FL	Y	36522 AE	45290 MW	52873 AEX	FLBLS	7/16-9/16
Middle School	Georgia	Y	51070 FQ	58260 MW	68720 TQ	USBLS	5/15
Middle School	Atlanta-Sandy Springs-Roswell MSA, GA	Y	52500 FQ	61470 MW	74650 TQ	USBLS	5/15
Middle School	Idaho	Y	35780 FQ	43510 MW	58050 TQ	USBLS	5/15
Middle School	Illinois	Y	43930 FQ	57870 MW	75200 TQ	USBLS	5/15
Middle School	Chicago-Naperville-Arlington Heights PMSA, IL	Y	52090 FQ	65240 MW	82060 TQ	USBLS	5/15
Middle School	Indiana	Y	40110 FQ	49760 MW	60410 TQ	USBLS	5/15
Middle School	Iowa	Y	43820 FQ	50370 MW	58930 TQ	USBLS	5/15
Middle School	Kansas	Y	42600 FQ	49520 MW	59780 TQ	USBLS	5/15
Middle School	Louisiana	Y	42610 FQ	47860 MW	55060 TQ	USBLS	5/15
Middle School	New Orleans-Metairie MSA, LA	Y	44720 FQ	49730 MW	56220 TQ	USBLS	5/15
Middle School	Maryland	Y	45776 AE	61047 MW	68682 AEX	MDBLS	4/16
Middle School	Baltimore-Columbia-Towson MSA, MD	Y	49800 FQ	58730 MW	70310 TQ	USBLS	5/15
Middle School	Massachusetts	Y	59450 FQ	73520 MW	92280 TQ	USBLS	5/15
Middle School	Boston-Cambridge-Newton NECTA, MA	Y	60410 FQ	76430 MW	96320 TQ	USBLS	5/15
Middle School	Michigan	Y	49670 FQ	61940 MW	75830 TQ	USBLS	5/15
Middle School	Minnesota	Y	37419 FQ	47096 MW	59667 TQ	MNBLS	1/16-3/16
Middle School	Minneapolis-St. Paul-Bloomington MSA, MN-WI	Y	39657 FQ	48165 MW	59243 TQ	MNBLS	1/16-3/16
Middle School	Mississippi	Y	39500 FQ	46140 MW	54970 TQ	USBLS	5/15

AE	Average entry wage	AWR	Average wage range	H	Hourly	LR	Low end range	MTC	Median total compensation	TCC	Total cash compensation
AEX	Average experienced wage	B	Biweekly	HI	Highest wage paid	M	Monthly	MW	Median wage	TQ	Third quartile wage
ATC	Average total compensation	D	Daily	HR	High end range	MCC	Median cash compensation	MWR	Median wage range	W	Weekly
AW	Average wage paid	FQ	First quartile wage	LO	Lowest wage paid	ME	Median entry wage	S	See annotated source	Y	Yearly

Occupation/Type/Industry	Location	Per	Low	Mid	High	Source	Date
Career/Technical Education							
Teacher							
Middle School	Jackson MSA, MS	Y	36110 FQ	41760 MW	47040 TQ	USBLS	5/15
Middle School	Missouri	Y	40020 FQ	47140 MW	61060 TQ	USBLS	5/15
Middle School	Kansas City MSA, MO-KS	Y	50010 FQ	59360 MW	69040 TQ	USBLS	5/15
Middle School	Nebraska	Y	45420 FQ	53345 MW	61330 TQ	NEBLS	7/16-9/16
Middle School	Omaha-Council Bluffs MSA, NE-IA	Y	44160 FQ	51195 MW	59415 TQ	NEBLS	7/16-9/16
Middle School	New Hampshire	Y	49114 AE	65368 MW	69631 AEX	NHBLS	6/16
Middle School	Nashua NECTA, NH-MA	Y	61410 FQ	68080 MW	74070 TQ	USBLS	5/15
Middle School	New Jersey	Y	56810 FQ	64070 MW	89790 TQ	USBLS	5/15
Middle School	Camden PMSA, NJ	Y	57540 FQ	64080 MW	88210 TQ	USBLS	5/15
Middle School	New York	Y	45270 AE	63650 MW	84820 AEX	NYBLS	1/16-3/16
Middle School	Buffalo-Cheektowaga-Niagara Falls MSA, NY	Y	51330 FQ	62360 MW	73280 TQ	USBLS	5/15
Middle School	Nassau County-Suffolk County PMSA, NY	Y	79810 FQ	102880 MW	119270 TQ	USBLS	5/15
Middle School	New York-Jersey City-White Plains PMSA, NY-NJ	Y	50410 FQ	59680 MW	85990 TQ	USBLS	5/15
Middle School	Rochester MSA, NY	Y	45520 FQ	56790 MW	70070 TQ	USBLS	5/15
Middle School	North Carolina	Y	38130 FQ	44980 MW	53230 TQ	USBLS	5/15
Middle School	Charlotte-Concord-Gastonia MSA, NC-SC	Y	37890 FQ	45390 MW	54550 TQ	USBLS	5/15
Middle School	Raleigh MSA, NC	Y	40400 FQ	47380 MW	60920 TQ	USBLS	5/15
Middle School	Ohio	Y	43000 FQ	50810 MW	69390 TQ	USBLS	5/15
Middle School	Cincinnati MSA, OH-KY-IN	Y	52410 FQ	65450 MW	72800 TQ	USBLS	5/15
Middle School	Oklahoma	Y	39670 FQ	47780 MW	58650 TQ	USBLS	5/15
Middle School	Oklahoma City MSA, OK	Y	37890 FQ	46060 MW	55550 TQ	USBLS	5/15
Middle School	Tulsa MSA, OK	Y	45800 FQ	57940 MW	71840 TQ	USBLS	5/15
Middle School	Pennsylvania	Y	46190 FQ	57170 MW	73460 TQ	USBLS	5/15
Middle School	Allentown-Bethlehem-Easton MSA, PA-NJ	Y	48440 FQ	79380 MW	88690 TQ	USBLS	5/15
Middle School	Harrisburg-Carlisle MSA, PA	Y	46510 FQ	54790 MW	66220 TQ	USBLS	5/15
Middle School	Montgomery County-Bucks County-Chester County PMSA, PA	Y	46730 FQ	65880 MW	83270 TQ	USBLS	5/15
Middle School	Pittsburgh MSA, PA	Y	46130 FQ	53200 MW	61270 TQ	USBLS	5/15
Middle School	South Carolina	Y	41560 FQ	46770 MW	55780 TQ	USBLS	5/15
Middle School	Greenville-Anderson-Mauldin MSA, SC	Y	43510 FQ	50440 MW	59400 TQ	USBLS	5/15
Middle School	South Dakota	Y	40470 FQ	45580 MW	51300 TQ	USBLS	5/15
Middle School	Tennessee	Y	46990 FQ	53090 MW	58920 TQ	USBLS	5/15
Middle School	Texas	Y	47290 FQ	54260 MW	60580 TQ	USBLS	5/15
Middle School	Austin-Round Rock MSA, TX	Y	50890 FQ	58590 MW	68450 TQ	USBLS	5/15
Middle School	Dallas-Plano-Irving PMSA, TX	Y	48870 FQ	55250 MW	61330 TQ	USBLS	5/15
Middle School	Fort Worth-Arlington PMSA, TX	Y	47410 FQ	53460 MW	58850 TQ	USBLS	5/15
Middle School	Houston-The Woodlands-Sugar Land MSA, TX	Y	49020 FQ	55210 MW	60960 TQ	USBLS	5/15
Middle School	San Antonio-New Braunfels MSA, TX	Y	51660 FQ	55610 MW	59560 TQ	USBLS	5/15
Middle School	Utah	Y	40200 FQ	46410 MW	56250 TQ	USBLS	5/15
Middle School	Provo-Orem MSA, UT	Y	41160 FQ	47320 MW	59750 TQ	USBLS	5/15
Middle School	Vermont	Y	49910 FQ	57740 MW	66940 TQ	USBLS	5/15
Middle School	Burlington-South Burlington MSA, VT	Y	49920 FQ	58160 MW	67720 TQ	USBLS	5/15
Middle School	Virginia	Y	45930 FQ	54640 MW	65910 TQ	USBLS	5/15
Middle School	Richmond MSA, VA	Y	43170 FQ	47200 MW	52690 TQ	USBLS	5/15
Middle School	Virginia Beach-Norfolk-Newport News MSA, VA-NC	Y	46310 FQ	53530 MW	62340 TQ	USBLS	5/15
Middle School	Washington	Y		63680 AW		WABLS	3/16
Middle School	Seattle-Bellevue-Everett PMSA, WA	Y		64988 AW		WABLS	3/16
Middle School	Tacoma-Lakewood PMSA, WA	Y		64116 AW		WABLS	3/16
Middle School	Wisconsin	Y	48890 FQ	69570 MW	96550 TQ	USBLS	5/15
Middle School	Wyoming	Y	51640 FQ	59320 MW	68530 TQ	USBLS	5/15
Secondary School	Alabama	Y	43189 AE	53474 AW	58611 AEX	ALBLS	6/16
Secondary School	Birmingham-Hoover MSA, AL	Y	42108 AE	54462 AW	60640 AEX	ALBLS	6/16
Secondary School	Alaska	Y	61110 FQ	77700 MW	90070 TQ	USBLS	5/15
Secondary School	Arizona	Y	36900 FQ	45010 MW	55930 TQ	USBLS	5/15

AE	Average entry wage	AWR	Average wage range	H	Hourly	LR	Low end range	MTC	Median total compensation	TCC	Total cash compensation
AEX	Average experienced wage	B	Biweekly	HI	Highest wage paid	M	Monthly	MW	Median wage paid	TQ	Third quartile wage
ATC	Average total compensation	D	Daily	HR	High end range	MCC	Median cash compensation	MWR	Median wage range	W	Weekly
AW	Average wage paid	FQ	First quartile wage	LO	Lowest wage paid	ME	Median entry wage	S	See annotated source	Y	Yearly

Career/Technical Education Teacher

Occupation/Type/Industry	Location	Per	Low	Mid	High	Source	Date
Secondary School	Phoenix-Mesa-Scottsdale MSA, AZ	Y	36900 FQ	45750 MW	58600 TQ	USBLS	5/15
Secondary School	Tucson MSA, AZ	Y	37220 FQ	43950 MW	50580 TQ	USBLS	5/15
Secondary School	Arkansas	Y	42910 FQ	49750 MW	58740 TQ	USBLS	5/15
Secondary School	Little Rock-North Little Rock-Conway MSA, AR	Y	45170 FQ	53020 MW	61370 TQ	USBLS	5/15
Secondary School	California	Y		70943 AW		CABLS	1/16-3/16
Secondary School	Anaheim-Santa Ana-Irvine PMSA, CA	Y		82407 AW		CABLS	1/16-3/16
Secondary School	Los Angeles-Long Beach-Glendale PMSA, CA	Y		74809 AW		CABLS	1/16-3/16
Secondary School	Riverside-San Bernardino-Ontario MSA, CA	Y		78278 AW		CABLS	1/16-3/16
Secondary School	Sacramento–Roseville–Arden-Arcade MSA, CA	Y		70446 AW		CABLS	1/16-3/16
Secondary School	San Diego-Carlsbad MSA, CA	Y		68955 AW		CABLS	1/16-3/16
Secondary School	San Francisco-Redwood City-South San Francisco PMSA, CA	Y		67484 AW		CABLS	1/16-3/16
Secondary School	Colorado	Y	43390 FQ	53690 MW	65590 TQ	USBLS	5/15
Secondary School	Denver-Aurora-Lakewood MSA, CO	Y	51240 FQ	61390 MW	72590 TQ	USBLS	5/15
Secondary School	Connecticut	Y		78836 MW		CTBLS	1/16-3/16
Secondary School	Bridgeport-Stamford-Norwalk MSA, CT	Y	59960 FQ	73600 MW	88670 TQ	USBLS	5/15
Secondary School	Hartford-West Hartford-East Hartford MSA, CT	Y	60900 FQ	76200 MW	89720 TQ	USBLS	5/15
Secondary School	Wilmington PMSA, DE-MD-NJ	Y	64600 FQ	76690 MW	91170 TQ	USBLS	5/15
Secondary School	Washington-Arlington-Alexandria PMSA, DC-VA-MD-WV	Y	55850 FQ	69760 MW	87170 TQ	USBLS	5/15
Secondary School	Florida	Y	35494 AE	49747 MW	59719 AEX	FLBLS	7/16-9/16
Secondary School	Miami-Miami Beach-Kendall PMSA, FL	Y	44667 AE	51446 MW	61401 AEX	FLBLS	7/16-9/16
Secondary School	Orlando-Kissimmee-Sanford MSA, FL	Y	35888 AE	47636 MW	57862 AEX	FLBLS	7/16-9/16
Secondary School	Tampa-St. Petersburg-Clearwater MSA, FL	Y	39576 AE	50030 MW	57106 AEX	FLBLS	7/16-9/16
Secondary School	Georgia	Y	46500 FQ	56660 MW	67720 TQ	USBLS	5/15
Secondary School	Atlanta-Sandy Springs-Roswell MSA, GA	Y	45060 FQ	54870 MW	66430 TQ	USBLS	5/15
Secondary School	Augusta-Richmond County MSA, GA-SC	Y	40900 FQ	50140 MW	57950 TQ	USBLS	5/15
Secondary School	Idaho	Y	35530 FQ	41270 MW	49790 TQ	USBLS	5/15
Secondary School	Boise City MSA, ID	Y	35180 FQ	38950 MW	52690 TQ	USBLS	5/15
Secondary School	Illinois	Y	47290 FQ	62010 MW	80780 TQ	USBLS	5/15
Secondary School	Chicago-Naperville-Arlington Heights PMSA, IL	Y	55580 FQ	74540 MW	92550 TQ	USBLS	5/15
Secondary School	Lake County-Kenosha County PMSA, IL-WI	Y	47700 FQ	60380 MW	72240 TQ	USBLS	5/15
Secondary School	Indiana	Y	42410 FQ	53060 MW	63510 TQ	USBLS	5/15
Secondary School	Gary PMSA, IN	Y	46970 FQ	57700 MW	68800 TQ	USBLS	5/15
Secondary School	Indianapolis-Carmel-Anderson MSA, IN	Y	45200 FQ	55250 MW	64680 TQ	USBLS	5/15
Secondary School	Iowa	Y	43150 FQ	52120 MW	62370 TQ	USBLS	5/15
Secondary School	Des Moines-West Des Moines MSA, IA	Y	44970 FQ	53600 MW	68880 TQ	USBLS	5/15
Secondary School	Kansas	Y	41640 FQ	47890 MW	56620 TQ	USBLS	5/15
Secondary School	Wichita MSA, KS	Y	40210 FQ	48340 MW	59210 TQ	USBLS	5/15
Secondary School	Kentucky	Y	46960 FQ	55880 MW	65370 TQ	USBLS	5/15
Secondary School	Louisville-Jefferson County MSA, KY-IN	Y	44610 FQ	55070 MW	64780 TQ	USBLS	5/15
Secondary School	Louisiana	Y	46420 FQ	53560 MW	60750 TQ	USBLS	5/15
Secondary School	Baton Rouge MSA, LA	Y	50400 FQ	56600 MW	62870 TQ	USBLS	5/15
Secondary School	New Orleans-Metairie MSA, LA	Y	49920 FQ	56750 MW	64960 TQ	USBLS	5/15
Secondary School	Maine	Y	34320 FQ	38300 MW	51560 TQ	USBLS	5/15
Secondary School	Maryland	Y	47376 AE	67333 MW	77311 AEX	MDBLS	4/16

AE	Average entry wage	AWR	Average wage range	H	Hourly	LR	Low end range
AEX	Average experienced wage	B	Biweekly	HI	Highest wage paid	M	Monthly
ATC	Average total compensation	D	Daily	HR	High end range	MCC	Median cash compensation
AW	Average wage paid	FQ	First quartile wage	LO	Lowest wage paid	ME	Median entry wage

MTC	Median total compensation	TCC	Total cash compensation
MW	Median wage paid	TQ	Third quartile wage
MWR	Median wage range	W	Weekly
S	See annotated source	Y	Yearly

Career/Technical Education Teacher

Occupation/Type/Industry	Location	Per	Low	Mid	High	Source	Date
Secondary School	Baltimore-Columbia-Towson MSA, MD	Y	53680 FQ	68430 MW	87240 TQ	USBLS	5/15
Secondary School	Massachusetts	Y	63600 FQ	73660 MW	85570 TQ	USBLS	5/15
Secondary School	Boston-Cambridge-Newton NECTA, MA	Y	59280 FQ	71550 MW	84020 TQ	USBLS	5/15
Secondary School	Worcester MSA, MA-CT	Y	66260 FQ	75680 MW	87750 TQ	USBLS	5/15
Secondary School	Michigan	Y	47710 FQ	62310 MW	73270 TQ	USBLS	5/15
Secondary School	Detroit-Dearborn-Livonia PMSA, MI	Y	45840 FQ	56590 MW	70510 TQ	USBLS	5/15
Secondary School	Grand Rapids-Wyoming MSA, MI	Y	59580 FQ	70080 MW	78640 TQ	USBLS	5/15
Secondary School	Minnesota	Y	45040 FQ	56602 MW	72469 TQ	MNBLS	1/16-3/16
Secondary School	Minneapolis-St. Paul-Bloomington MSA, MN-WI	Y	56340 FQ	71068 MW	83729 TQ	MNBLS	1/16-3/16
Secondary School	Mississippi	Y	37830 FQ	43980 MW	49890 TQ	USBLS	5/15
Secondary School	Jackson MSA, MS	Y	37480 FQ	43670 MW	49840 TQ	USBLS	5/15
Secondary School	Missouri	Y	34590 FQ	45850 MW	58040 TQ	USBLS	5/15
Secondary School	Kansas City MSA, MO-KS	Y	44630 FQ	53730 MW	62440 TQ	USBLS	5/15
Secondary School	St. Louis MSA, MO-IL	Y	48550 FQ	58960 MW	73470 TQ	USBLS	5/15
Secondary School	Montana	Y	37600 FQ	48930 MW	61110 TQ	USBLS	5/15
Secondary School	Nebraska	Y	43510 FQ	52755 MW	61170 TQ	NEBLS	7/16-9/16
Secondary School	Omaha-Council Bluffs MSA, NE-IA	Y	43050 FQ	51460 MW	59760 TQ	NEBLS	7/16-9/16
Secondary School	Nevada	Y	48340 FQ	57500 MW	67800 TQ	USBLS	5/15
Secondary School	New Hampshire	Y	45926 AE	58689 MW	65476 AEX	NHBLS	6/16
Secondary School	Nashua NECTA, NH-MA	Y	54140 FQ	65640 MW	73420 TQ	USBLS	5/15
Secondary School	New Jersey	Y	58050 FQ	67900 MW	82910 TQ	USBLS	5/15
Secondary School	Camden PMSA, NJ	Y	55320 FQ	66990 MW	86120 TQ	USBLS	5/15
Secondary School	Newark PMSA, NJ-PA	Y	57080 FQ	63940 MW	76760 TQ	USBLS	5/15
Secondary School	New Mexico	Y	45860 FQ	54790 MW	65180 TQ	USBLS	5/15
Secondary School	Albuquerque MSA, NM	Y	51000 FQ	59180 MW	74390 TQ	USBLS	5/15
Secondary School	New York	Y	48750 AE	67870 MW	83600 AEX	NYBLS	1/16-3/16
Secondary School	Buffalo-Cheektowaga-Niagara Falls MSA, NY	Y	50260 FQ	59480 MW	71840 TQ	USBLS	5/15
Secondary School	Nassau County-Suffolk County PMSA, NY	Y	71290 FQ	96800 MW	115230 TQ	USBLS	5/15
Secondary School	New York-Jersey City-White Plains PMSA, NY-NJ	Y	63390 FQ	80240 MW	96560 TQ	USBLS	5/15
Secondary School	Rochester MSA, NY	Y	50860 FQ	60810 MW	76550 TQ	USBLS	5/15
Secondary School	North Carolina	Y	40110 FQ	46950 MW	55730 TQ	USBLS	5/15
Secondary School	Charlotte-Concord-Gastonia MSA, NC-SC	Y	41650 FQ	50050 MW	58900 TQ	USBLS	5/15
Secondary School	Raleigh MSA, NC	Y	41300 FQ	49020 MW	59370 TQ	USBLS	5/15
Secondary School	North Dakota	Y	43750 FQ	52500 MW	62430 TQ	USBLS	5/15
Secondary School	Fargo MSA, ND-MN	Y	44060 FQ	53460 MW	64060 TQ	USBLS	5/15
Secondary School	Ohio	Y	52450 FQ	63010 MW	75790 TQ	USBLS	5/15
Secondary School	Cincinnati MSA, OH-KY-IN	Y	55300 FQ	66100 MW	75180 TQ	USBLS	5/15
Secondary School	Cleveland-Elyria MSA, OH	Y	55140 FQ	72500 MW	87970 TQ	USBLS	5/15
Secondary School	Columbus MSA, OH	Y	57500 FQ	70610 MW	81230 TQ	USBLS	5/15
Secondary School	Oklahoma	Y	41030 FQ	46350 MW	54380 TQ	USBLS	5/15
Secondary School	Oklahoma City MSA, OK	Y	44750 FQ	53360 MW	60630 TQ	USBLS	5/15
Secondary School	Tulsa MSA, OK	Y	40300 FQ	46900 MW	59830 TQ	USBLS	5/15
Secondary School	Oregon	Y	43213 FQ	55043 MW	67019 TQ	ORBLS	2016
Secondary School	Portland-Vancouver-Hillsboro MSA, OR-WA	Y	52460 FQ	62310 MW	71400 TQ	USBLS	5/15
Secondary School	Pennsylvania	Y	50060 FQ	60440 MW	74740 TQ	USBLS	5/15
Secondary School	Allentown-Bethlehem-Easton MSA, PA-NJ	Y	54430 FQ	66010 MW	76290 TQ	USBLS	5/15
Secondary School	Harrisburg-Carlisle MSA, PA	Y	51660 FQ	59400 MW	71350 TQ	USBLS	5/15
Secondary School	Montgomery County-Bucks County-Chester County PMSA, PA	Y	55700 FQ	71580 MW	85320 TQ	USBLS	5/15
Secondary School	Philadelphia PMSA, PA	Y	55920 FQ	69020 MW	83980 TQ	USBLS	5/15
Secondary School	Pittsburgh MSA, PA	Y	47460 FQ	56370 MW	67200 TQ	USBLS	5/15
Secondary School	Rhode Island	Y	66490 FQ	79120 MW	88840 TQ	USBLS	5/15
Secondary School	Providence-Warwick MSA, RI-MA	Y	67120 FQ	76910 MW	87020 TQ	USBLS	5/15
Secondary School	South Carolina	Y	43620 FQ	51910 MW	61200 TQ	USBLS	5/15

AE	Average entry wage	AWR	Average wage range	H	Hourly	LR	Low end range	MTC	Median total compensation
AEX	Average experienced wage	B	Biweekly	HI	Highest wage paid	M	Monthly	MW	Median wage paid
ATC	Average total compensation	D	Daily	HR	High end range	MCC	Median cash compensation	MWR	Median wage range
AW	Average wage paid	FQ	First quartile wage	LO	Lowest wage paid	ME	Median entry wage	S	See annotated source

TCC	Total cash compensation
TQ	Third quartile wage
W	Weekly
Y	Yearly

Occupation/Type/Industry	Location	Per	Low	Mid	High	Source	Date
Career/Technical Education Teacher							
Secondary School	Charleston-North Charleston MSA, SC	Y	46530 FQ	54230 MW	68010 TQ	USBLS	5/15
Secondary School	Columbia MSA, SC	Y	41960 FQ	49530 MW	59070 TQ	USBLS	5/15
Secondary School	Greenville-Anderson-Mauldin MSA, SC	Y	41400 FQ	47230 MW	58380 TQ	USBLS	5/15
Secondary School	South Dakota	Y	37760 FQ	43960 MW	49590 TQ	USBLS	5/15
Secondary School	Sioux Falls MSA, SD	Y	39160 FQ	45720 MW	53460 TQ	USBLS	5/15
Secondary School	Tennessee	Y	41030 FQ	47270 MW	56540 TQ	USBLS	5/15
Secondary School	Knoxville MSA, TN	Y	41660 FQ	47200 MW	55710 TQ	USBLS	5/15
Secondary School	Memphis MSA, TN-MS-AR	Y	43480 FQ	51320 MW	59790 TQ	USBLS	5/15
Secondary School	Nashville-Davidson–Murfreesboro–Franklin MSA, TN	Y	41220 FQ	47190 MW	55840 TQ	USBLS	5/15
Secondary School	Texas	Y	47020 FQ	54430 MW	61210 TQ	USBLS	5/15
Secondary School	Austin-Round Rock MSA, TX	Y	45530 FQ	51850 MW	60290 TQ	USBLS	5/15
Secondary School	Dallas-Plano-Irving PMSA, TX	Y	48940 FQ	55400 MW	61510 TQ	USBLS	5/15
Secondary School	Fort Worth-Arlington PMSA, TX	Y	51840 FQ	57250 MW	62710 TQ	USBLS	5/15
Secondary School	Houston-The Woodlands-Sugar Land MSA, TX	Y	52360 FQ	59120 MW	69490 TQ	USBLS	5/15
Secondary School	San Antonio-New Braunfels MSA, TX	Y	50650 FQ	55210 MW	59780 TQ	USBLS	5/15
Secondary School	Utah	Y	34190 FQ	43450 MW	55730 TQ	USBLS	5/15
Secondary School	Salt Lake City MSA, UT	Y	36840 FQ	47570 MW	63530 TQ	USBLS	5/15
Secondary School	Vermont	Y	49440 FQ	58140 MW	67870 TQ	USBLS	5/15
Secondary School	Burlington-South Burlington MSA, VT	Y	56360 FQ	67170 MW	75670 TQ	USBLS	5/15
Secondary School	Virginia	Y	48910 FQ	59200 MW	74800 TQ	USBLS	5/15
Secondary School	Richmond MSA, VA	Y	50980 FQ	58690 MW	69670 TQ	USBLS	5/15
Secondary School	Virginia Beach-Norfolk-Newport News MSA, VA-NC	Y	53570 FQ	67020 MW	82050 TQ	USBLS	5/15
Secondary School	Washington	Y		63213 AW		WABLS	3/16
Secondary School	Seattle-Bellevue-Everett PMSA, WA	Y		64045 AW		WABLS	3/16
Secondary School	Spokane-Spokane Valley MSA, WA	Y	55770 FQ	65050 MW	73080 TQ	USBLS	5/15
Secondary School	Tacoma-Lakewood PMSA, WA	Y		62523 AW		WABLS	3/16
Secondary School	West Virginia	Y	40390 FQ	46470 MW	54590 TQ	USBLS	5/15
Secondary School	Huntington-Ashland MSA, WV-KY-OH	Y	40360 FQ	46790 MW	55050 TQ	USBLS	5/15
Secondary School	Wisconsin	Y	44460 FQ	53260 MW	62340 TQ	USBLS	5/15
Secondary School	Madison MSA, WI	Y	49900 FQ	56470 MW	63100 TQ	USBLS	5/15
Secondary School	Milwaukee-Waukesha-West Allis MSA, WI	Y	48270 FQ	58070 MW	70140 TQ	USBLS	5/15
Secondary School	Wyoming	Y	51020 FQ	59100 MW	68940 TQ	USBLS	5/15
Secondary School	Puerto Rico	Y	29850 FQ	35800 MW	42710 TQ	USBLS	5/15
Secondary School	San Juan-Carolina-Caguas MSA, PR	Y	29540 FQ	35630 MW	42910 TQ	USBLS	5/15
Cargo and Freight Agent	Alabama	Y	33103 AE	49860 AW	58239 AEX	ALBLS	6/16
	Birmingham-Hoover MSA, AL	Y	42234 AE	55034 AW	61444 AEX	ALBLS	6/16
	Alaska	Y	28170 FQ	33570 MW	41860 TQ	USBLS	5/15
	Anchorage MSA, AK	Y	27300 FQ	32440 MW	39170 TQ	USBLS	5/15
	Arizona	Y	32840 FQ	40160 MW	49900 TQ	USBLS	5/15
	Phoenix-Mesa-Scottsdale MSA, AZ	Y	33990 FQ	41620 MW	50590 TQ	USBLS	5/15
	Arkansas	Y	29970 FQ	36280 MW	46390 TQ	USBLS	5/15
	Little Rock-North Little Rock-Conway MSA, AR	Y	28780 FQ	35580 MW	48910 TQ	USBLS	5/15
	California	H	16.63 FQ	20.99 MW	27.24 TQ	CABLS	1/16-3/16
	Anaheim-Santa Ana-Irvine PMSA, CA	H	16.51 FQ	20.59 MW	26.51 TQ	CABLS	1/16-3/16
	Los Angeles-Long Beach-Glendale PMSA, CA	H	16.73 FQ	21.00 MW	26.85 TQ	CABLS	1/16-3/16
	Oakland-Hayward-Berkeley PMSA, CA	H	18.45 FQ	25.83 MW	42.01 TQ	CABLS	1/16-3/16
	Riverside-San Bernardino-Ontario MSA, CA	H	16.82 FQ	19.35 MW	23.56 TQ	CABLS	1/16-3/16
	Sacramento-Roseville–Arden-Arcade MSA, CA	H	20.94 FQ	26.60 MW	31.40 TQ	CABLS	1/16-3/16

AE	Average entry wage	AWR	Average wage range	H	Hourly
AEX	Average experienced wage	B	Biweekly	HI	Highest wage paid
ATC	Average total compensation	D	Daily	HR	High end range
AW	Average wage paid	FQ	First quartile wage	LO	Lowest wage paid

LR	Low end range	MTC	Median total compensation	TCC	Total cash compensation
M	Monthly	MW	Median wage paid	TQ	Third quartile wage
MCC	Median cash compensation	MWR	Median wage range	W	Weekly
ME	Median entry wage	S	See annotated source	Y	Yearly

Occupation/Type/Industry	Location	Per	Low	Mid	High	Source	Date
Cargo and Freight Agent	San Diego-Carlsbad MSA, CA	H	15.14 FQ	20.03 MW	26.09 TQ	CABLS	1/16-3/16
	San Francisco-Redwood City-South San Francisco PMSA, CA	H	14.77 FQ	20.69 MW	27.47 TQ	CABLS	1/16-3/16
	Colorado	Y	32380 FQ	43040 MW	56530 TQ	USBLS	5/15
	Denver-Aurora-Lakewood MSA, CO	Y	31430 FQ	43370 MW	56880 TQ	USBLS	5/15
	Connecticut	Y		50666 MW		CTBLS	1/16-3/16
	Bridgeport-Stamford-Norwalk MSA, CT	Y	40490 FQ	67530 MW	96620 TQ	USBLS	5/15
	Hartford-West Hartford-East Hartford MSA, CT	Y	35150 FQ	43950 MW	73410 TQ	USBLS	5/15
	District of Columbia	Y	28180 FQ	32050 MW	47740 TQ	USBLS	5/15
	Washington-Arlington-Alexandria PMSA, DC-VA-MD-WV	Y	24090 FQ	30380 MW	50440 TQ	USBLS	5/15
	Florida	H	13.19 AE	19.50 MW	25.03 AEX	FLBLS	7/16-9/16
	Fort Lauderdale-Pompano Beach-Deerfield Beach PMSA, FL	H	15.88 AE	20.01 MW	25.11 AEX	FLBLS	7/16-9/16
	Miami-Miami Beach-Kendall PMSA, FL	H	13.03 AE	18.59 MW	24.66 AEX	FLBLS	7/16-9/16
	Orlando-Kissimmee-Sanford MSA, FL	H	14.96 AE	22.37 MW	28.70 AEX	FLBLS	7/16-9/16
	Tampa-St. Petersburg-Clearwater MSA, FL	H	10.54 AE	20.86 MW	23.73 AEX	FLBLS	7/16-9/16
	Georgia	Y	33500 FQ	41470 MW	52630 TQ	USBLS	5/15
	Atlanta-Sandy Springs-Roswell MSA, GA	Y	34230 FQ	41810 MW	51400 TQ	USBLS	5/15
	Hawaii	Y	25000 FQ	28450 MW	40390 TQ	USBLS	5/15
	Urban Honolulu MSA, HI	Y	24660 FQ	28030 MW	38510 TQ	USBLS	5/15
	Idaho	Y	25400 FQ	41250 MW	51030 TQ	USBLS	5/15
	Boise City MSA, ID	Y	22020 FQ	35240 MW	46680 TQ	USBLS	5/15
	Illinois	Y	32010 FQ	43200 MW	56490 TQ	USBLS	5/15
	Chicago-Naperville-Arlington Heights PMSA, IL	Y	32170 FQ	43210 MW	56730 TQ	USBLS	5/15
	Indiana	Y	24540 FQ	36080 MW	47800 TQ	USBLS	5/15
	Gary PMSA, IN	Y	23390 FQ	34410 MW	46280 TQ	USBLS	5/15
	Indianapolis-Carmel-Anderson MSA, IN	Y	23260 FQ	34310 MW	45920 TQ	USBLS	5/15
	Iowa	Y	23550 FQ	41530 MW	51250 TQ	USBLS	5/15
	Des Moines-West Des Moines MSA, IA	Y	37000 FQ	45890 MW	55210 TQ	USBLS	5/15
	Kansas	Y	33170 FQ	41300 MW	60300 TQ	USBLS	5/15
	Wichita MSA, KS	Y	33120 FQ	38520 MW	57290 TQ	USBLS	5/15
	Kentucky	Y	30980 FQ	43310 MW	56200 TQ	USBLS	5/15
	Louisville-Jefferson County MSA, KY-IN	Y	33090 FQ	48720 MW	58130 TQ	USBLS	5/15
	Louisiana	Y	29000 FQ	36150 MW	49750 TQ	USBLS	5/15
	Baton Rouge MSA, LA	Y	38470 FQ	67120 MW	73600 TQ	USBLS	5/15
	New Orleans-Metairie MSA, LA	Y	28830 FQ	35020 MW	46110 TQ	USBLS	5/15
	Maine	Y	36950 FQ	52370 MW	59000 TQ	USBLS	5/15
	Maryland	Y	29109 AE	42582 MW	49319 AEX	MDBLS	4/16
	Baltimore-Columbia-Towson MSA, MD	Y	33000 FQ	42400 MW	50510 TQ	USBLS	5/15
	Massachusetts	Y	34450 FQ	43410 MW	57340 TQ	USBLS	5/15
	Boston-Cambridge-Newton NECTA, MA	Y	34860 FQ	44030 MW	58440 TQ	USBLS	5/15
	Worcester MSA, MA-CT	Y	32130 FQ	41840 MW	53040 TQ	USBLS	5/15
	Michigan	Y	32980 FQ	38240 MW	48390 TQ	USBLS	5/15
	Detroit-Dearborn-Livonia PMSA, MI	Y	32820 FQ	37930 MW	48720 TQ	USBLS	5/15
	Grand Rapids-Wyoming MSA, MI	Y	30010 FQ	42500 MW	48490 TQ	USBLS	5/15
	Minnesota	Y	32846 FQ	42999 MW	54477 TQ	MNBLS	1/16-3/16
	Minneapolis-St. Paul-Bloomington MSA, MN-WI	Y	32098 FQ	41310 MW	51818 TQ	MNBLS	1/16-3/16
	Mississippi	Y	35640 FQ	43560 MW	49450 TQ	USBLS	5/15
	Jackson MSA, MS	Y	35590 FQ	44830 MW	52060 TQ	USBLS	5/15
	Missouri	Y	30870 FQ	40970 MW	49720 TQ	USBLS	5/15
	Kansas City MSA, MO-KS	Y	33720 FQ	42730 MW	56930 TQ	USBLS	5/15

AE Average entry wage	**AWR** Average wage range	**H** Hourly	**LR** Low end range	**MTC** Median total compensation	**TCC** Total cash compensation
AEX Average experienced wage	**B** Biweekly	**HI** Highest wage paid	**M** Monthly	**MW** Median wage paid	**TQ** Third quartile wage
ATC Average total compensation	**D** Daily	**HR** High end range	**MCC** Median cash compensation	**MWR** Median wage range	**W** Weekly
AW Average wage paid	**FQ** First quartile wage	**LO** Lowest wage paid	**ME** Median entry wage	**S** See annotated source	**Y** Yearly

Occupation/Type/Industry	Location	Per	Low	Mid	High	Source	Date
Cargo and Freight Agent	St. Louis MSA, MO-IL	Y	30220 FQ	40960 MW	49450 TQ	USBLS	5/15
	Montana	Y	25980 FQ	33870 MW	39420 TQ	USBLS	5/15
	Billings MSA, MT	Y	30920 FQ	36060 MW	43040 TQ	USBLS	5/15
	Nebraska	Y	34835 FQ	43680 MW	56415 TQ	NEBLS	7/16-9/16
	Omaha-Council Bluffs MSA, NE-IA	Y	38225 FQ	47780 MW	62155 TQ	NEBLS	7/16-9/16
	Nevada	Y	23340 FQ	35690 MW	51220 TQ	USBLS	5/15
	Las Vegas-Henderson-Paradise MSA, NV	Y	22880 FQ	31850 MW	49990 TQ	USBLS	5/15
	New Hampshire	H	16.68 AE	23.02 MW	29.55 AEX	NHBLS	6/16
	Nashua NECTA, NH-MA	Y	34980 FQ	40970 MW	50860 TQ	USBLS	5/15
	New Jersey	Y	31630 FQ	43210 MW	60420 TQ	USBLS	5/15
	Camden PMSA, NJ	Y	47170 FQ	54000 MW	60680 TQ	USBLS	5/15
	Newark PMSA, NJ-PA	Y	20230 FQ	40790 MW	61540 TQ	USBLS	5/15
	New Mexico	Y	22210 FQ	24350 MW	46280 TQ	USBLS	5/15
	Albuquerque MSA, NM	Y	21570 FQ	23070 MW	24560 TQ	USBLS	5/15
	New York	Y	26720 AE	43660 MW	54330 AEX	NYBLS	1/16-3/16
	Buffalo-Cheektowaga-Niagara Falls MSA, NY	Y	32630 FQ	37860 MW	46280 TQ	USBLS	5/15
	Nassau County-Suffolk County PMSA, NY	Y	36510 FQ	47470 MW	59210 TQ	USBLS	5/15
	New York-Jersey City-White Plains PMSA, NY-NJ	Y	30670 FQ	41950 MW	53840 TQ	USBLS	5/15
	Rochester MSA, NY	Y	33850 FQ	44510 MW	56010 TQ	USBLS	5/15
	North Carolina	Y	28000 FQ	39550 MW	50460 TQ	USBLS	5/15
	Charlotte-Concord-Gastonia MSA, NC-SC	Y	24580 FQ	42150 MW	54030 TQ	USBLS	5/15
	Raleigh MSA, NC	Y	25480 FQ	30080 MW	47180 TQ	USBLS	5/15
	North Dakota	Y	33180 FQ	38220 MW	46010 TQ	USBLS	5/15
	Fargo MSA, ND-MN	Y	32140 FQ	37270 MW	46030 TQ	USBLS	5/15
	Ohio	Y	31960 FQ	37040 MW	46110 TQ	USBLS	5/15
	Cincinnati MSA, OH-KY-IN	Y	29580 FQ	36130 MW	46120 TQ	USBLS	5/15
	Cleveland-Elyria MSA, OH	Y	32670 FQ	37710 MW	46830 TQ	USBLS	5/15
	Columbus MSA, OH	Y	32710 FQ	36910 MW	43890 TQ	USBLS	5/15
	Oklahoma	Y	34280 FQ	47470 MW	56290 TQ	USBLS	5/15
	Oklahoma City MSA, OK	Y	36600 FQ	52280 MW	58000 TQ	USBLS	5/15
	Tulsa MSA, OK	Y	33610 FQ	41670 MW	50320 TQ	USBLS	5/15
	Oregon	H	16.89 FQ	21.02 MW	27.96 TQ	ORBLS	2016
	Portland-Vancouver-Hillsboro MSA, OR-WA	Y	35310 FQ	44950 MW	57830 TQ	USBLS	5/15
	Pennsylvania	Y	37040 FQ	45320 MW	54890 TQ	USBLS	5/15
	Allentown-Bethlehem-Easton MSA, PA-NJ	Y	40960 FQ	47590 MW	55310 TQ	USBLS	5/15
	Harrisburg-Carlisle MSA, PA	Y	31330 FQ	39520 MW	55430 TQ	USBLS	5/15
	Montgomery County-Bucks County-Chester County PMSA, PA	Y	40120 FQ	46720 MW	56510 TQ	USBLS	5/15
	Philadelphia PMSA, PA	Y	41040 FQ	46890 MW	55890 TQ	USBLS	5/15
	Pittsburgh MSA, PA	Y	34960 FQ	42780 MW	54190 TQ	USBLS	5/15
	Rhode Island	Y	30520 FQ	48240 MW	57690 TQ	USBLS	5/15
	Providence-Warwick MSA, RI-MA	Y	31350 FQ	49780 MW	58140 TQ	USBLS	5/15
	Columbia MSA, SC	Y	37060 FQ	44650 MW	52790 TQ	USBLS	5/15
	Greenville-Anderson-Mauldin MSA, SC	Y	30850 FQ	38690 MW	48370 TQ	USBLS	5/15
	South Dakota	Y	36480 FQ	43940 MW	50870 TQ	USBLS	5/15
	Sioux Falls MSA, SD	Y	38240 FQ	44520 MW	50350 TQ	USBLS	5/15
	Tennessee	Y	30810 FQ	38630 MW	48770 TQ	USBLS	5/15
	Knoxville MSA, TN	Y	29180 FQ	33780 MW	41990 TQ	USBLS	5/15
	Memphis MSA, TN-MS-AR	Y	30490 FQ	37430 MW	46850 TQ	USBLS	5/15
	Nashville-Davidson–Murfreesboro–Franklin MSA, TN	Y	39820 FQ	45770 MW	53490 TQ	USBLS	5/15
	Texas	Y	36410 FQ	44860 MW	51570 TQ	USBLS	5/15
	Austin-Round Rock MSA, TX	Y	33500 FQ	38160 MW	53540 TQ	USBLS	5/15
	Dallas-Plano-Irving PMSA, TX	Y	34370 FQ	43000 MW	54810 TQ	USBLS	5/15
	Fort Worth-Arlington PMSA, TX	Y	41230 FQ	45400 MW	49570 TQ	USBLS	5/15
	Houston-The Woodlands-Sugar Land MSA, TX	Y	37670 FQ	48500 MW	58940 TQ	USBLS	5/15
	San Antonio-New Braunfels MSA, TX	Y	40240 FQ	47150 MW	62980 TQ	USBLS	5/15

AE	Average entry wage	AWR	Average wage range	H	Hourly	LR	Low end range	MTC	Median total compensation	TCC	Total cash compensation
AEX	Average experienced wage	B	Biweekly	HI	Highest wage paid	M	Monthly	MW	Median wage paid	TQ	Third quartile wage
ATC	Average total compensation	D	Daily	HR	High end range	MCC	Median cash compensation	MWR	Median wage range	W	Weekly
AW	Average wage paid	FQ	First quartile wage	LO	Lowest wage paid	ME	Median entry wage	S	See annotated source	Y	Yearly

Occupation/Type/Industry	Location	Per	Low	Mid	High	Source	Date
Cargo and Freight Agent	Utah	Y	28140 FQ	37810 MW	49250 TQ	USBLS	5/15
	Provo-Orem MSA, UT	Y	19500 FQ	22970 MW	28000 TQ	USBLS	5/15
	Salt Lake City MSA, UT	Y	31110 FQ	41930 MW	52710 TQ	USBLS	5/15
	Vermont	Y	24600 FQ	32470 MW	42380 TQ	USBLS	5/15
	Virginia	Y	26560 FQ	37820 MW	53760 TQ	USBLS	5/15
	Richmond MSA, VA	Y	33500 FQ	38800 MW	45250 TQ	USBLS	5/15
	Virginia Beach-Norfolk-Newport News MSA, VA-NC	Y	36170 FQ	46600 MW	64020 TQ	USBLS	5/15
	Washington	H	17.79 FQ	22.06 MW	28.33 TQ	WABLS	3/16
	Seattle-Bellevue-Everett PMSA, WA	H	18.26 FQ	22.64 MW	29.27 TQ	WABLS	3/16
	Tacoma-Lakewood PMSA, WA	H	17.69 FQ	21.99 MW	29.72 TQ	WABLS	3/16
	West Virginia	Y	39520 FQ	53580 MW	58930 TQ	USBLS	5/15
	Wisconsin	Y	33320 FQ	42260 MW	55050 TQ	USBLS	5/15
	Madison MSA, WI	Y	36210 FQ	45980 MW	59820 TQ	USBLS	5/15
	Milwaukee-Waukesha-West Allis MSA, WI	Y	33760 FQ	45650 MW	66780 TQ	USBLS	5/15
	Wyoming	Y	33690 FQ	37160 MW	45870 TQ	USBLS	5/15
	Puerto Rico	Y	16680 FQ	18020 MW	19370 TQ	USBLS	5/15
	San Juan-Carolina-Caguas MSA, PR	Y	16610 FQ	17890 MW	19170 TQ	USBLS	5/15
	Guam	Y	21700 FQ	35520 MW	46230 TQ	USBLS	5/15
Carpenter	Alabama	Y	24935 AE	35963 AW	41477 AEX	ALBLS	6/16
	Birmingham-Hoover MSA, AL	Y	25326 AE	37866 AW	44141 AEX	ALBLS	6/16
	Alaska	Y	55670 FQ	67650 MW	78080 TQ	USBLS	5/15
	Anchorage MSA, AK	Y	56320 FQ	68700 MW	78870 TQ	USBLS	5/15
	Arizona	Y	30390 FQ	37990 MW	46990 TQ	USBLS	5/15
	Phoenix-Mesa-Scottsdale MSA, AZ	Y	30960 FQ	38830 MW	47720 TQ	USBLS	5/15
	Tucson MSA, AZ	Y	28070 FQ	35580 MW	44730 TQ	USBLS	5/15
	Arkansas	Y	26810 FQ	33400 MW	39420 TQ	USBLS	5/15
	Little Rock-North Little Rock-Conway MSA, AR	Y	27640 FQ	34140 MW	41770 TQ	USBLS	5/15
	California	H	18.26 FQ	24.73 MW	32.56 TQ	CABLS	1/16-3/16
	Anaheim-Santa Ana-Irvine PMSA, CA	H	17.66 FQ	23.85 MW	30.24 TQ	CABLS	1/16-3/16
	Los Angeles-Long Beach-Glendale PMSA, CA	H	16.52 FQ	24.19 MW	34.68 TQ	CABLS	1/16-3/16
	Oakland-Hayward-Berkeley PMSA, CA	H	22.78 FQ	30.12 MW	40.17 TQ	CABLS	1/16-3/16
	Riverside-San Bernardino-Ontario MSA, CA	H	17.15 FQ	21.91 MW	27.78 TQ	CABLS	1/16-3/16
	Sacramento–Roseville–Arden-Arcade MSA, CA	H	17.70 FQ	21.76 MW	26.98 TQ	CABLS	1/16-3/16
	San Diego-Carlsbad MSA, CA	H	17.28 FQ	22.35 MW	29.13 TQ	CABLS	1/16-3/16
	San Francisco-Redwood City-South San Francisco PMSA, CA	H	20.08 FQ	30.11 MW	44.29 TQ	CABLS	1/16-3/16
	Colorado	Y	32210 FQ	41870 MW	52390 TQ	USBLS	5/15
	Denver-Aurora-Lakewood MSA, CO	Y	33250 FQ	43220 MW	53540 TQ	USBLS	5/15
	Connecticut	Y		51785 MW		CTBLS	1/16-3/16
	Bridgeport-Stamford-Norwalk MSA, CT	Y	43190 FQ	53910 MW	63050 TQ	USBLS	5/15
	Hartford-West Hartford-East Hartford MSA, CT	Y	40600 FQ	50440 MW	59540 TQ	USBLS	5/15
	Delaware	Y	35430 FQ	43030 MW	51220 TQ	USBLS	5/15
	Wilmington PMSA, DE-MD-NJ	Y	39160 FQ	46440 MW	56230 TQ	USBLS	5/15
	District of Columbia	Y	40130 FQ	48090 MW	57400 TQ	USBLS	5/15
	Washington-Arlington-Alexandria PMSA, DC-VA-MD-WV	Y	36740 FQ	44640 MW	54040 TQ	USBLS	5/15
	Florida	H	12.25 AE	17.25 MW	20.80 AEX	FLBLS	7/16-9/16
	Fort Lauderdale-Pompano Beach-Deerfield Beach PMSA, FL	H	13.24 AE	18.22 MW	22.01 AEX	FLBLS	7/16-9/16
	Miami-Miami Beach-Kendall PMSA, FL	H	11.82 AE	16.85 MW	20.39 AEX	FLBLS	7/16-9/16
	Orlando-Kissimmee-Sanford MSA, FL	H	13.21 AE	17.76 MW	20.94 AEX	FLBLS	7/16-9/16

AE Average entry wage	**AWR** Average wage range	**H** Hourly	**LR** Low end range	**MTC** Median total compensation	**TCC** Total cash compensation
AEX Average experienced wage	**B** Biweekly	**HI** Highest wage paid	**M** Monthly	**MW** Median wage paid	**TQ** Third quartile wage
ATC Average total compensation	**D** Daily	**HR** High end range	**MCC** Median cash compensation	**MWR** Median wage range	**W** Weekly
AW Average wage paid	**FQ** First quartile wage	**LO** Lowest wage paid	**ME** Median entry wage	**S** See annotated source	**Y** Yearly

Occupation/Type/Industry	Location	Per	Low	Mid	High	Source	Date
Carpenter	Tampa-St. Petersburg-Clearwater MSA, FL	H	11.56 AE	16.76 MW	19.41 AEX	FLBLS	7/16-9/16
	Georgia	Y	27920 FQ	36030 MW	46700 TQ	USBLS	5/15
	Atlanta-Sandy Springs-Roswell MSA, GA	Y	30040 FQ	37500 MW	48240 TQ	USBLS	5/15
	Augusta-Richmond County MSA, GA-SC	Y	22940 FQ	33890 MW	47170 TQ	USBLS	5/15
	Hawaii	Y	48600 FQ	65990 MW	87660 TQ	USBLS	5/15
	Urban Honolulu MSA, HI	Y	50930 FQ	69130 MW	89210 TQ	USBLS	5/15
	Idaho	Y	27910 FQ	34900 MW	44450 TQ	USBLS	5/15
	Boise City MSA, ID	Y	27330 FQ	33210 MW	38890 TQ	USBLS	5/15
	Illinois	Y	33610 FQ	55210 MW	85560 TQ	USBLS	5/15
	Chicago-Naperville-Arlington Heights PMSA, IL	Y	36040 FQ	79020 MW	91130 TQ	USBLS	5/15
	Lake County-Kenosha County PMSA, IL-WI	Y	34520 FQ	54190 MW	85250 TQ	USBLS	5/15
	Indiana	Y	30760 FQ	38490 MW	51710 TQ	USBLS	5/15
	Gary PMSA, IN	Y	31370 FQ	40610 MW	65910 TQ	USBLS	5/15
	Indianapolis-Carmel-Anderson MSA, IN	Y	32920 FQ	42150 MW	55250 TQ	USBLS	5/15
	Iowa	Y	32130 FQ	39020 MW	50780 TQ	USBLS	5/15
	Des Moines-West Des Moines MSA, IA	Y	33580 FQ	40870 MW	56260 TQ	USBLS	5/15
	Kansas	Y	31400 FQ	37230 MW	46820 TQ	USBLS	5/15
	Wichita MSA, KS	Y	30940 FQ	36200 MW	42950 TQ	USBLS	5/15
	Kentucky	Y	31850 FQ	38160 MW	48250 TQ	USBLS	5/15
	Louisville-Jefferson County MSA, KY-IN	Y	30930 FQ	37910 MW	47760 TQ	USBLS	5/15
	Louisiana	Y	30780 FQ	36710 MW	45000 TQ	USBLS	5/15
	Baton Rouge MSA, LA	Y	32600 FQ	37780 MW	45550 TQ	USBLS	5/15
	New Orleans-Metairie MSA, LA	Y	32460 FQ	38050 MW	47260 TQ	USBLS	5/15
	Maine	Y	32820 FQ	37890 MW	45220 TQ	USBLS	5/15
	Portland-South Portland MSA, ME	Y	33070 FQ	39160 MW	45930 TQ	USBLS	5/15
	Maryland	Y	31121 AE	46652 MW	54417 AEX	MDBLS	4/16
	Baltimore-Columbia-Towson MSA, MD	Y	36420 FQ	44590 MW	54290 TQ	USBLS	5/15
	Salisbury MSA, MD-DE	Y	30190 FQ	35850 MW	42010 TQ	USBLS	5/15
	Massachusetts	Y	43380 FQ	55830 MW	72210 TQ	USBLS	5/15
	Boston-Cambridge-Newton NECTA, MA	Y	51000 FQ	63740 MW	82770 TQ	USBLS	5/15
	Worcester MSA, MA-CT	Y	38270 FQ	48130 MW	58730 TQ	USBLS	5/15
	Michigan	Y	34040 FQ	42440 MW	54910 TQ	USBLS	5/15
	Detroit-Dearborn-Livonia PMSA, MI	Y	41700 FQ	54900 MW	64020 TQ	USBLS	5/15
	Grand Rapids-Wyoming MSA, MI	Y	33290 FQ	39970 MW	49310 TQ	USBLS	5/15
	Minnesota	Y	36920 FQ	47151 MW	63114 TQ	MNBLS	1/16-3/16
	Minneapolis-St. Paul-Bloomington MSA, MN-WI	Y	42379 FQ	54134 MW	69400 TQ	MNBLS	1/16-3/16
	Mississippi	Y	27340 FQ	33700 MW	39950 TQ	USBLS	5/15
	Jackson MSA, MS	Y	28300 FQ	34100 MW	38100 TQ	USBLS	5/15
	Missouri	Y	37190 FQ	50710 MW	65760 TQ	USBLS	5/15
	Kansas City MSA, MO-KS	Y	34250 FQ	44600 MW	67380 TQ	USBLS	5/15
	St. Louis MSA, MO-IL	Y	43450 FQ	57650 MW	70310 TQ	USBLS	5/15
	Montana	Y	33010 FQ	40480 MW	48320 TQ	USBLS	5/15
	Billings MSA, MT	Y	35790 FQ	43220 MW	51200 TQ	USBLS	5/15
	Nebraska	Y	27390 FQ	33685 MW	41450 TQ	NEBLS	7/16-9/16
	Omaha-Council Bluffs MSA, NE-IA	Y	31440 FQ	38075 MW	47895 TQ	NEBLS	7/16-9/16
	Nevada	Y	31340 FQ	43740 MW	58510 TQ	USBLS	5/15
	Las Vegas-Henderson-Paradise MSA, NV	Y	30460 FQ	43660 MW	59580 TQ	USBLS	5/15
	New Hampshire	H	15.87 AE	21.33 MW	24.29 AEX	NHBLS	6/16
	Manchester NECTA, NH	H	15.81 AE	21.99 MW	24.96 AEX	NHBLS	6/16
	Nashua NECTA, NH-MA	Y	40920 FQ	48070 MW	56450 TQ	USBLS	5/15
	New Jersey	Y	40500 FQ	52490 MW	79100 TQ	USBLS	5/15
	Camden PMSA, NJ	Y	36510 FQ	45990 MW	59480 TQ	USBLS	5/15
	Newark PMSA, NJ-PA	Y	41520 FQ	61580 MW	89000 TQ	USBLS	5/15
	Trenton MSA, NJ	Y	43550 FQ	50220 MW	81840 TQ	USBLS	5/15
	New Mexico	Y	29380 FQ	36340 MW	45600 TQ	USBLS	5/15

AE	Average entry wage	AWR	Average wage range	H	Hourly
AEX	Average experienced wage	B	Biweekly	HI	Highest wage paid
ATC	Average total compensation	D	Daily	HR	High end range
AW	Average wage paid	FQ	First quartile wage	LO	Lowest wage paid

LR	Low end range	MTC	Median total compensation
M	Monthly	MW	Median wage paid
MCC	Median cash compensation	MWR	Median wage range
ME	Median entry wage	S	See annotated source

TCC	Total cash compensation		
TQ	Third quartile wage		
W	Weekly		
Y	Yearly		

Occupation/Type/Industry	Location	Per	Low	Mid	High	Source	Date
Carpenter	Albuquerque MSA, NM	Y	28520 FQ	34250 MW	42800 TQ	USBLS	5/15
	New York	Y	35370 AE	52870 MW	74860 AEX	NYBLS	1/16-3/16
	Buffalo-Cheektowaga-Niagara Falls MSA, NY	Y	33580 FQ	41100 MW	53620 TQ	USBLS	5/15
	Nassau County-Suffolk County PMSA, NY	Y	39760 FQ	53860 MW	84300 TQ	USBLS	5/15
	New York-Jersey City-White Plains PMSA, NY-NJ	Y	44700 FQ	60510 MW	91090 TQ	USBLS	5/15
	Rochester MSA, NY	Y	33230 FQ	40550 MW	50460 TQ	USBLS	5/15
	North Carolina	Y	28170 FQ	34390 MW	40170 TQ	USBLS	5/15
	Charlotte-Concord-Gastonia MSA, NC-SC	Y	29290 FQ	34920 MW	40440 TQ	USBLS	5/15
	Raleigh MSA, NC	Y	29480 FQ	35240 MW	40900 TQ	USBLS	5/15
	North Dakota	Y	33150 FQ	38450 MW	46170 TQ	USBLS	5/15
	Fargo MSA, ND-MN	Y	32800 FQ	39490 MW	46770 TQ	USBLS	5/15
	Ohio	Y	34500 FQ	43780 MW	55800 TQ	USBLS	5/15
	Cincinnati MSA, OH-KY-IN	Y	34290 FQ	42080 MW	51810 TQ	USBLS	5/15
	Cleveland-Elyria MSA, OH	Y	38540 FQ	53250 MW	66010 TQ	USBLS	5/15
	Columbus MSA, OH	Y	35440 FQ	43620 MW	54250 TQ	USBLS	5/15
	Oklahoma	Y	29340 FQ	35770 MW	43430 TQ	USBLS	5/15
	Oklahoma City MSA, OK	Y	30980 FQ	36490 MW	43780 TQ	USBLS	5/15
	Tulsa MSA, OK	Y	26260 FQ	34330 MW	42760 TQ	USBLS	5/15
	Oregon	H	16.54 FQ	21.04 MW	28.14 TQ	ORBLS	2016
	Portland-Vancouver-Hillsboro MSA, OR-WA	Y	33710 FQ	46480 MW	62700 TQ	USBLS	5/15
	Pennsylvania	Y	32610 FQ	42900 MW	59800 TQ	USBLS	5/15
	Allentown-Bethlehem-Easton MSA, PA-NJ	Y	32750 FQ	39460 MW	48730 TQ	USBLS	5/15
	Harrisburg-Carlisle MSA, PA	Y	35430 FQ	44810 MW	54870 TQ	USBLS	5/15
	Montgomery County-Bucks County-Chester County PMSA, PA	Y	35820 FQ	50940 MW	75390 TQ	USBLS	5/15
	Philadelphia PMSA, PA	Y	37040 FQ	54480 MW	85510 TQ	USBLS	5/15
	Pittsburgh MSA, PA	Y	34180 FQ	47010 MW	66740 TQ	USBLS	5/15
	Rhode Island	Y	35190 FQ	43770 MW	54230 TQ	USBLS	5/15
	Providence-Warwick MSA, RI-MA	Y	36490 FQ	44790 MW	55480 TQ	USBLS	5/15
	South Carolina	Y	29610 FQ	36570 MW	46430 TQ	USBLS	5/15
	Charleston-North Charleston MSA, SC	Y	32680 FQ	39010 MW	50310 TQ	USBLS	5/15
	Columbia MSA, SC	Y	30500 FQ	37010 MW	48990 TQ	USBLS	5/15
	Greenville-Anderson-Mauldin MSA, SC	Y	29690 FQ	35830 MW	43200 TQ	USBLS	5/15
	South Dakota	Y	28130 FQ	32680 MW	38550 TQ	USBLS	5/15
	Sioux Falls MSA, SD	Y	29830 FQ	35630 MW	42550 TQ	USBLS	5/15
	Tennessee	Y	30180 FQ	35910 MW	43050 TQ	USBLS	5/15
	Knoxville MSA, TN	Y	27280 FQ	33290 MW	39900 TQ	USBLS	5/15
	Memphis MSA, TN-MS-AR	Y	32820 FQ	36550 MW	42710 TQ	USBLS	5/15
	Nashville-Davidson–Murfreesboro–Franklin MSA, TN	Y	32600 FQ	38260 MW	45440 TQ	USBLS	5/15
	Texas	Y	28240 FQ	34530 MW	42180 TQ	USBLS	5/15
	Austin-Round Rock MSA, TX	Y	28520 FQ	35630 MW	44650 TQ	USBLS	5/15
	Dallas-Plano-Irving PMSA, TX	Y	27820 FQ	33810 MW	38730 TQ	USBLS	5/15
	Fort Worth-Arlington PMSA, TX	Y	27560 FQ	32590 MW	38000 TQ	USBLS	5/15
	Houston-The Woodlands-Sugar Land MSA, TX	Y	28840 FQ	35190 MW	44180 TQ	USBLS	5/15
	San Antonio-New Braunfels MSA, TX	Y	29520 FQ	35960 MW	43560 TQ	USBLS	5/15
	Utah	Y	29140 FQ	35600 MW	43730 TQ	USBLS	5/15
	Ogden-Clearfield MSA, UT	Y	27730 FQ	33610 MW	41760 TQ	USBLS	5/15
	Provo-Orem MSA, UT	Y	30680 FQ	35960 MW	43010 TQ	USBLS	5/15
	Salt Lake City MSA, UT	Y	29140 FQ	36560 MW	45860 TQ	USBLS	5/15
	Vermont	Y	35060 FQ	41830 MW	50640 TQ	USBLS	5/15
	Burlington-South Burlington MSA, VT	Y	35220 FQ	42340 MW	48690 TQ	USBLS	5/15
	Virginia	Y	32590 FQ	38810 MW	47640 TQ	USBLS	5/15
	Richmond MSA, VA	Y	32240 FQ	37360 MW	44520 TQ	USBLS	5/15
	Virginia Beach-Norfolk-Newport News MSA, VA-NC	Y	32580 FQ	37970 MW	46800 TQ	USBLS	5/15
	Washington	H	19.49 FQ	25.21 MW	31.85 TQ	WABLS	3/16

Occupation/Type/Industry	Location	Per	Low	Mid	High	Source	Date
Carpenter	Seattle-Bellevue-Everett PMSA, WA	H	20.64 FQ	26.59 MW	33.52 TQ	WABLS	3/16
	Tacoma-Lakewood PMSA, WA	H	19.04 FQ	23.20 MW	31.04 TQ	WABLS	3/16
	West Virginia	Y	30080 FQ	37360 MW	52180 TQ	USBLS	5/15
	Huntington-Ashland MSA, WV-KY-OH	Y	33500 FQ	43750 MW	57050 TQ	USBLS	5/15
	Wisconsin	Y	34430 FQ	44350 MW	63350 TQ	USBLS	5/15
	Madison MSA, WI	Y	43790 FQ	62720 MW	73880 TQ	USBLS	5/15
	Milwaukee-Waukesha-West Allis MSA, WI	Y	37050 FQ	47270 MW	68370 TQ	USBLS	5/15
	Wyoming	Y	35480 FQ	43680 MW	52480 TQ	USBLS	5/15
	Cheyenne MSA, WY	Y	33630 FQ	41500 MW	53170 TQ	USBLS	5/15
	Puerto Rico	Y	16870 FQ	18250 MW	19710 TQ	USBLS	5/15
	San Juan-Carolina-Caguas MSA, PR	Y	16950 FQ	18400 MW	20060 TQ	USBLS	5/15
	Virgin Islands	Y	37960 FQ	45670 MW	58490 TQ	USBLS	5/15
	Guam	Y	26840 FQ	28820 MW	30810 TQ	USBLS	5/15
Carpet Installer	Alabama	Y	24956 AE	38545 AW	45345 AEX	ALBLS	6/16
	Alaska	Y	36290 FQ	54350 MW	59620 TQ	USBLS	5/15
	Arizona	Y	28430 FQ	33770 MW	38380 TQ	USBLS	5/15
	Phoenix-Mesa-Scottsdale MSA, AZ	Y	29610 FQ	34170 MW	38000 TQ	USBLS	5/15
	Arkansas	Y	18520 FQ	21390 MW	24120 TQ	USBLS	5/15
	California	H	12.14 FQ	21.26 MW	31.47 TQ	CABLS	1/16-3/16
	Anaheim-Santa Ana-Irvine PMSA, CA	H	14.94 FQ	21.09 MW	27.76 TQ	CABLS	1/16-3/16
	Los Angeles-Long Beach-Glendale PMSA, CA	H	10.90 FQ	12.19 MW	28.55 TQ	CABLS	1/16-3/16
	Oakland-Hayward-Berkeley PMSA, CA	H	23.55 FQ	37.44 MW	44.53 TQ	CABLS	1/16-3/16
	Riverside-San Bernardino-Ontario MSA, CA	H	17.60 FQ	23.86 MW	29.42 TQ	CABLS	1/16-3/16
	Sacramento–Roseville–Arden-Arcade MSA, CA	H	25.40 FQ	28.27 MW	31.14 TQ	CABLS	1/16-3/16
	San Diego-Carlsbad MSA, CA	H	11.08 FQ	15.24 MW	26.37 TQ	CABLS	1/16-3/16
	San Francisco-Redwood City-South San Francisco PMSA, CA	H	14.63 FQ	26.84 MW	40.28 TQ	CABLS	1/16-3/16
	Colorado	Y	25660 FQ	35180 MW	47790 TQ	USBLS	5/15
	Denver-Aurora-Lakewood MSA, CO	Y	23600 FQ	41480 MW	47280 TQ	USBLS	5/15
	Connecticut	Y		37932 MW		CTBLS	1/16-3/16
	Hartford-West Hartford-East Hartford MSA, CT	Y	27430 FQ	34230 MW	40090 TQ	USBLS	5/15
	Delaware	Y	31660 FQ	39370 MW	45860 TQ	USBLS	5/15
	Wilmington PMSA, DE-MD-NJ	Y	30240 FQ	40570 MW	46620 TQ	USBLS	5/15
	Washington-Arlington-Alexandria PMSA, DC-VA-MD-WV	Y	26120 FQ	27910 MW	29700 TQ	USBLS	5/15
	Florida	H	8.95 AE	11.46 MW	15.07 AEX	FLBLS	7/16-9/16
	Fort Lauderdale-Pompano Beach-Deerfield Beach PMSA, FL	H	13.03 AE	22.23 MW	24.84 AEX	FLBLS	7/16-9/16
	Orlando-Kissimmee-Sanford MSA, FL	H	11.25 AE	13.65 MW	17.04 AEX	FLBLS	7/16-9/16
	Tampa-St. Petersburg-Clearwater MSA, FL	H	10.83 AE	11.41 MW	12.36 AEX	FLBLS	7/16-9/16
	Georgia	Y	26320 FQ	32020 MW	45410 TQ	USBLS	5/15
	Atlanta-Sandy Springs-Roswell MSA, GA	Y	28570 FQ	38670 MW	45610 TQ	USBLS	5/15
	Hawaii	Y	41430 FQ	55680 MW	66740 TQ	USBLS	5/15
	Urban Honolulu MSA, HI	Y	47820 FQ	59550 MW	69030 TQ	USBLS	5/15
	Idaho	Y	22040 FQ	31010 MW	36340 TQ	USBLS	5/15
	Boise City MSA, ID	Y	22600 FQ	30620 MW	35820 TQ	USBLS	5/15
	Illinois	Y	31420 FQ	44900 MW	79150 TQ	USBLS	5/15
	Chicago-Naperville-Arlington Heights PMSA, IL	Y	34700 FQ	51990 MW	90080 TQ	USBLS	5/15
	Lake County-Kenosha County PMSA, IL-WI	Y	30080 FQ	44020 MW	51580 TQ	USBLS	5/15
	Indiana	Y	28280 FQ	36630 MW	47310 TQ	USBLS	5/15

AE	Average entry wage	AWR	Average wage range	H	Hourly	LR	Low end range	MTC	Median total compensation	TCC	Total cash compensation
AEX	Average experienced wage	B	Biweekly	HI	Highest wage paid	M	Monthly	MW	Median wage paid	TQ	Third quartile wage
ATC	Average total compensation	D	Daily	HR	High end range	MCC	Median cash compensation	MWR	Median wage range	W	Weekly
AW	Average wage paid	FQ	First quartile wage	LO	Lowest wage paid	ME	Median entry wage	S	See annotated source	Y	Yearly

Occupation/Type/Industry	Location	Per	Low	Mid	High	Source	Date
Carpet Installer	Indianapolis-Carmel-Anderson MSA, IN	Y	31330 FQ	38290 MW	49500 TQ	USBLS	5/15
	Iowa	Y	29970 FQ	42970 MW	56020 TQ	USBLS	5/15
	Kansas	Y	22290 FQ	41400 MW	53970 TQ	USBLS	5/15
	Kentucky	Y	22550 FQ	29970 MW	37010 TQ	USBLS	5/15
	Louisville-Jefferson County MSA, KY-IN	Y	21210 FQ	27580 MW	35140 TQ	USBLS	5/15
	Louisiana	Y	27030 FQ	34760 MW	42100 TQ	USBLS	5/15
	Baton Rouge MSA, LA	Y	19330 FQ	36040 MW	45180 TQ	USBLS	5/15
	Maryland	Y	25544 AE	36549 MW	42051 AEX	MDBLS	4/16
	Baltimore-Columbia-Towson MSA, MD	Y	27060 FQ	34630 MW	52200 TQ	USBLS	5/15
	Salisbury MSA, MD-DE	Y	33870 FQ	36420 MW	38970 TQ	USBLS	5/15
	Massachusetts	Y	35830 FQ	48660 MW	62800 TQ	USBLS	5/15
	Boston-Cambridge-Newton NECTA, MA	Y	41760 FQ	55140 MW	75870 TQ	USBLS	5/15
	Worcester MSA, MA-CT	Y	35360 FQ	39630 MW	45390 TQ	USBLS	5/15
	Michigan	Y	25970 FQ	36140 MW	52070 TQ	USBLS	5/15
	Grand Rapids-Wyoming MSA, MI	Y	28850 FQ	36340 MW	46430 TQ	USBLS	5/15
	Minnesota	Y	26860 FQ	49270 MW	68865 TQ	MNBLS	1/16-3/16
	Minneapolis-St. Paul-Bloomington MSA, MN-WI	Y	23500 FQ	56576 MW	70793 TQ	MNBLS	1/16-3/16
	Mississippi	Y	17380 FQ	19500 MW	27350 TQ	USBLS	5/15
	Jackson MSA, MS	Y	19510 FQ	25660 MW	28630 TQ	USBLS	5/15
	Missouri	Y	33350 FQ	46940 MW	59600 TQ	USBLS	5/15
	Kansas City MSA, MO-KS	Y	32090 FQ	46350 MW	58610 TQ	USBLS	5/15
	St. Louis MSA, MO-IL	Y	44100 FQ	53390 MW	63210 TQ	USBLS	5/15
	Montana	Y	18870 FQ	22100 MW	25130 TQ	USBLS	5/15
	Nebraska	Y	18920 FQ	30170 MW	43770 TQ	NEBLS	7/16-9/16
	Omaha-Council Bluffs MSA, NE-IA	Y	19205 FQ	34160 MW	45020 TQ	NEBLS	7/16-9/16
	Nevada	Y	35760 FQ	47750 MW	59790 TQ	USBLS	5/15
	Las Vegas-Henderson-Paradise MSA, NV	Y	42790 FQ	49430 MW	61250 TQ	USBLS	5/15
	New Hampshire	H	14.68 AE	17.53 MW	19.44 AEX	NHBLS	6/16
	New Jersey	Y	33340 FQ	41770 MW	67150 TQ	USBLS	5/15
	Camden PMSA, NJ	Y	65550 FQ	70630 MW	75710 TQ	USBLS	5/15
	Trenton MSA, NJ	Y	41730 FQ	45850 MW	49970 TQ	USBLS	5/15
	New Mexico	Y	28780 FQ	35140 MW	42750 TQ	USBLS	5/15
	New York	Y	28000 AE	47870 MW	75180 AEX	NYBLS	1/16-3/16
	Nassau County-Suffolk County PMSA, NY	Y	66170 FQ	78980 MW	110590 TQ	USBLS	5/15
	New York-Jersey City-White Plains PMSA, NY-NJ	Y	34560 FQ	46070 MW	89950 TQ	USBLS	5/15
	North Carolina	Y	25600 FQ	29400 MW	35890 TQ	USBLS	5/15
	North Dakota	Y	19000 FQ	31370 MW	37530 TQ	USBLS	5/15
	Fargo MSA, ND-MN	Y	28970 FQ	34800 MW	39730 TQ	USBLS	5/15
	Ohio	Y	28410 FQ	39070 MW	52330 TQ	USBLS	5/15
	Cincinnati MSA, OH-KY-IN	Y	29480 FQ	34760 MW	42670 TQ	USBLS	5/15
	Cleveland-Elyria MSA, OH	Y	44450 FQ	55160 MW	65650 TQ	USBLS	5/15
	Columbus MSA, OH	Y	26800 FQ	29320 MW	35310 TQ	USBLS	5/15
	Oklahoma	Y	25730 FQ	28480 MW	31910 TQ	USBLS	5/15
	Oklahoma City MSA, OK	Y	25720 FQ	27900 MW	30090 TQ	USBLS	5/15
	Oregon	H	16.28 FQ	21.11 MW	26.46 TQ	ORBLS	2016
	Portland-Vancouver-Hillsboro MSA, OR-WA	Y	34760 FQ	45270 MW	55350 TQ	USBLS	5/15
	Pennsylvania	Y	26510 FQ	34480 MW	47530 TQ	USBLS	5/15
	Allentown-Bethlehem-Easton MSA, PA-NJ	Y	32220 FQ	39450 MW	46630 TQ	USBLS	5/15
	Harrisburg-Carlisle MSA, PA	Y	31680 FQ	35610 MW	39600 TQ	USBLS	5/15
	Montgomery County-Bucks County-Chester County PMSA, PA	Y	19500 FQ	31820 MW	64090 TQ	USBLS	5/15
	Pittsburgh MSA, PA	Y	27100 FQ	37000 MW	53570 TQ	USBLS	5/15
	Rhode Island	Y	43530 FQ	48390 MW	71300 TQ	USBLS	5/15
	Providence-Warwick MSA, RI-MA	Y	39210 FQ	47010 MW	64790 TQ	USBLS	5/15
	South Carolina	Y	24630 FQ	28640 MW	42420 TQ	USBLS	5/15
	Tennessee	Y	26210 FQ	32720 MW	39100 TQ	USBLS	5/15

AE	Average entry wage	AWR	Average wage range	H	Hourly
AEX	Average experienced wage	B	Biweekly	HI	Highest wage paid
ATC	Average total compensation	D	Daily	HR	High end range
AW	Average wage paid	FQ	First quartile wage	LO	Lowest wage paid

LR	Low end range	MTC	Median total compensation	TCC	Total cash compensation
M	Monthly	MW	Median wage paid	TQ	Third quartile wage
MCC	Median cash compensation	MWR	Median wage range	W	Weekly
ME	Median entry wage	S	See annotated source	Y	Yearly

Occupation/Type/Industry	Location	Per	Low	Mid	High	Source	Date
Carpet Installer	Nashville-Davidson–Murfreesboro–Franklin MSA, TN	Y	24640 FQ	35880 MW	62420 TQ	USBLS	5/15
	Texas	Y	25690 FQ	33250 MW	37520 TQ	USBLS	5/15
	Dallas-Plano-Irving PMSA, TX	Y	34130 FQ	37850 MW	46990 TQ	USBLS	5/15
	Fort Worth-Arlington PMSA, TX	Y	23440 FQ	30140 MW	35250 TQ	USBLS	5/15
	Utah	Y	26520 FQ	30190 MW	38130 TQ	USBLS	5/15
	Ogden-Clearfield MSA, UT	Y	27710 FQ	30330 MW	34910 TQ	USBLS	5/15
	Salt Lake City MSA, UT	Y	27380 FQ	31270 MW	40130 TQ	USBLS	5/15
	Vermont	Y	31180 FQ	37660 MW	45640 TQ	USBLS	5/15
	Burlington-South Burlington MSA, VT	Y	30970 FQ	37600 MW	45660 TQ	USBLS	5/15
	Virginia	Y	27010 FQ	29400 MW	34360 TQ	USBLS	5/15
	Virginia Beach-Norfolk-Newport News MSA, VA-NC	Y	27260 FQ	29590 MW	33870 TQ	USBLS	5/15
	Washington	H	14.61 FQ	20.64 MW	25.07 TQ	WABLS	3/16
	Seattle-Bellevue-Everett PMSA, WA	H	13.21 FQ	14.82 MW	18.24 TQ	WABLS	3/16
	Tacoma-Lakewood PMSA, WA	H	10.19 FQ	20.92 MW	24.40 TQ	WABLS	3/16
	West Virginia	Y	19900 FQ	23130 MW	33930 TQ	USBLS	5/15
	Wisconsin	Y	32470 FQ	39360 MW	47200 TQ	USBLS	5/15
	Madison MSA, WI	Y	34220 FQ	40650 MW	49910 TQ	USBLS	5/15
	Milwaukee-Waukesha-West Allis MSA, WI	Y	29250 FQ	34640 MW	38920 TQ	USBLS	5/15
	Wyoming	Y	20430 FQ	28110 MW	42470 TQ	USBLS	5/15
Cartographer and Photogrammetrist	Alabama	Y	45074 AE	62332 AW	70965 AEX	ALBLS	6/16
	Birmingham-Hoover MSA, AL	Y	40804 AE	60640 AW	70558 AEX	ALBLS	6/16
	Alaska	Y	56580 FQ	72210 MW	86690 TQ	USBLS	5/15
	Anchorage MSA, AK	Y	64740 FQ	77060 MW	86690 TQ	USBLS	5/15
	Arizona	Y	50990 FQ	63000 MW	73910 TQ	USBLS	5/15
	Phoenix-Mesa-Scottsdale MSA, AZ	Y	52330 FQ	61840 MW	74250 TQ	USBLS	5/15
	Tucson MSA, AZ	Y	46300 FQ	57890 MW	70260 TQ	USBLS	5/15
	Arkansas	Y	36970 FQ	56440 MW	71520 TQ	USBLS	5/15
	California	H	28.42 FQ	34.97 MW	42.92 TQ	CABLS	1/16-3/16
	Anaheim-Santa Ana-Irvine PMSA, CA	H	18.90 FQ	29.79 MW	37.42 TQ	CABLS	1/16-3/16
	Los Angeles-Long Beach-Glendale PMSA, CA	H	30.59 FQ	36.72 MW	45.18 TQ	CABLS	1/16-3/16
	Oakland-Hayward-Berkeley PMSA, CA	H	25.99 FQ	30.87 MW	43.02 TQ	CABLS	1/16-3/16
	Riverside-San Bernardino-Ontario MSA, CA	H	28.58 FQ	34.43 MW	38.46 TQ	CABLS	1/16-3/16
	Sacramento–Roseville–Arden-Arcade MSA, CA	H	32.31 FQ	36.11 MW	40.42 TQ	CABLS	1/16-3/16
	San Diego-Carlsbad MSA, CA	H	31.52 FQ	34.92 MW	38.27 TQ	CABLS	1/16-3/16
	San Francisco-Redwood City-South San Francisco PMSA, CA	H	30.29 FQ	38.86 MW	52.88 TQ	CABLS	1/16-3/16
	Colorado	Y	53670 FQ	67260 MW	79610 TQ	USBLS	5/15
	Denver-Aurora-Lakewood MSA, CO	Y	55050 FQ	68550 MW	81720 TQ	USBLS	5/15
	Connecticut	Y		60555 MW		CTBLS	1/16-3/16
	Washington-Arlington-Alexandria PMSA, DC-VA-MD-WV	Y	63950 FQ	81550 MW	101110 TQ	USBLS	5/15
	Florida	H	23.35 AE	36.43 MW	43.25 AEX	FLBLS	7/16-9/16
	Miami-Miami Beach-Kendall PMSA, FL	H	17.18 AE	25.42 MW	37.71 AEX	FLBLS	7/16-9/16
	Orlando-Kissimmee-Sanford MSA, FL	H	28.65 AE	35.85 MW	43.73 AEX	FLBLS	7/16-9/16
	Tampa-St. Petersburg-Clearwater MSA, FL	H	27.62 AE	40.10 MW	42.10 AEX	FLBLS	7/16-9/16
	Georgia	Y	40650 FQ	48060 MW	64630 TQ	USBLS	5/15
	Atlanta-Sandy Springs-Roswell MSA, GA	Y	42500 FQ	50480 MW	77390 TQ	USBLS	5/15
	Hawaii	Y	48660 FQ	57550 MW	68970 TQ	USBLS	5/15
	Idaho	Y	42670 FQ	50330 MW	60790 TQ	USBLS	5/15
	Boise City MSA, ID	Y	46500 FQ	54440 MW	65000 TQ	USBLS	5/15

AE Average entry wage	**AWR** Average wage range	**H** Hourly	**LR** Low end range	**MTC** Median total compensation	**TCC** Total cash compensation
AEX Average experienced wage	**B** Biweekly	**HI** Highest wage paid	**M** Monthly	**MW** Median wage paid	**TQ** Third quartile wage
ATC Average total compensation	**D** Daily	**HR** High end range	**MCC** Median cash compensation	**MWR** Median wage range	**W** Weekly
AW Average wage paid	**FQ** First quartile wage	**LO** Lowest wage paid	**ME** Median entry wage	**S** See annotated source	**Y** Yearly

Occupation/Type/Industry	Location	Per	Low	Mid	High	Source	Date
Cartographer and Photogrammetrist	Illinois	Y	50130 FQ	71190 MW	95220 TQ	USBLS	5/15
	Chicago-Naperville-Arlington Heights PMSA, IL	Y	46350 FQ	68750 MW	88880 TQ	USBLS	5/15
	Indiana	Y	40290 FQ	47200 MW	55550 TQ	USBLS	5/15
	Iowa	Y	46680 FQ	55600 MW	64550 TQ	USBLS	5/15
	Kansas	Y	41460 FQ	49930 MW	59800 TQ	USBLS	5/15
	Wichita MSA, KS	Y	37130 FQ	48150 MW	58770 TQ	USBLS	5/15
	Kentucky	Y	42400 FQ	49830 MW	60270 TQ	USBLS	5/15
	Maine	Y	46760 FQ	52890 MW	61660 TQ	USBLS	5/15
	Maryland	Y	47614 AE	75863 MW	89988 AEX	MDBLS	4/16
	Baltimore-Columbia-Towson MSA, MD	Y	46770 FQ	57160 MW	75910 TQ	USBLS	5/15
	Massachusetts	Y	53080 FQ	59120 MW	74380 TQ	USBLS	5/15
	Michigan	Y	50990 FQ	58470 MW	70090 TQ	USBLS	5/15
	Detroit-Dearborn-Livonia PMSA, MI	Y	58030 FQ	69790 MW	88260 TQ	USBLS	5/15
	Grand Rapids-Wyoming MSA, MI	Y	38170 FQ	48360 MW	58190 TQ	USBLS	5/15
	Minnesota	Y	52550 FQ	59959 MW	74999 TQ	MNBLS	1/16-3/16
	Minneapolis-St. Paul-Bloomington MSA, MN-WI	Y	55030 FQ	61703 MW	77862 TQ	MNBLS	1/16-3/16
	Missouri	Y	44370 FQ	58970 MW	81050 TQ	USBLS	5/15
	Kansas City MSA, MO-KS	Y	45060 FQ	53880 MW	63810 TQ	USBLS	5/15
	St. Louis MSA, MO-IL	Y	59630 FQ	74840 MW	91250 TQ	USBLS	5/15
	Montana	Y	41990 FQ	47770 MW	56460 TQ	USBLS	5/15
	Nebraska	Y	44360 FQ	55225 MW	70580 TQ	NEBLS	7/16-9/16
	Omaha-Council Bluffs MSA, NE-IA	Y	45120 FQ	55905 MW	74610 TQ	NEBLS	7/16-9/16
	Nevada	Y	62470 FQ	79930 MW	92520 TQ	USBLS	5/15
	Las Vegas-Henderson-Paradise MSA, NV	Y	72850 FQ	85950 MW	96240 TQ	USBLS	5/15
	New Hampshire	H	17.74 AE	22.65 MW	27.88 AEX	NHBLS	6/16
	New Jersey	Y	51220 FQ	71220 MW	89440 TQ	USBLS	5/15
	Camden PMSA, NJ	Y	56370 FQ	63910 MW	72010 TQ	USBLS	5/15
	Newark PMSA, NJ-PA	Y	38490 FQ	57350 MW	76770 TQ	USBLS	5/15
	Trenton MSA, NJ	Y	82060 FQ	89710 MW	97280 TQ	USBLS	5/15
	New Mexico	Y	41170 FQ	55070 MW	79540 TQ	USBLS	5/15
	Albuquerque MSA, NM	Y	43630 FQ	62290 MW	79550 TQ	USBLS	5/15
	New York	Y	56350 AE	72190 MW	87720 AEX	NYBLS	1/16-3/16
	New York-Jersey City-White Plains PMSA, NY-NJ	Y	56190 FQ	68330 MW	87800 TQ	USBLS	5/15
	North Carolina	Y	45600 FQ	56890 MW	71330 TQ	USBLS	5/15
	Charlotte-Concord-Gastonia MSA, NC-SC	Y	43720 FQ	51450 MW	61150 TQ	USBLS	5/15
	Raleigh MSA, NC	Y	53210 FQ	61140 MW	74220 TQ	USBLS	5/15
	North Dakota	Y	45000 FQ	51450 MW	65990 TQ	USBLS	5/15
	Ohio	Y	55480 FQ	64020 MW	78580 TQ	USBLS	5/15
	Oklahoma	Y	43790 FQ	55670 MW	64120 TQ	USBLS	5/15
	Oregon	H	23.41 FQ	28.34 MW	34.91 TQ	ORBLS	2016
	Portland-Vancouver-Hillsboro MSA, OR-WA	Y	51950 FQ	61480 MW	76740 TQ	USBLS	5/15
	Pennsylvania	Y	42410 FQ	51460 MW	69890 TQ	USBLS	5/15
	Montgomery County-Bucks County-Chester County PMSA, PA	Y	52240 FQ	62920 MW	87040 TQ	USBLS	5/15
	Pittsburgh MSA, PA	Y	39920 FQ	48110 MW	80010 TQ	USBLS	5/15
	South Carolina	Y	41560 FQ	48510 MW	57990 TQ	USBLS	5/15
	Charleston-North Charleston MSA, SC	Y	41970 FQ	47530 MW	61060 TQ	USBLS	5/15
	Columbia MSA, SC	Y	41350 FQ	50420 MW	62720 TQ	USBLS	5/15
	Greenville-Anderson-Mauldin MSA, SC	Y	40240 FQ	47660 MW	61970 TQ	USBLS	5/15
	South Dakota	Y	46400 FQ	56100 MW	70270 TQ	USBLS	5/15
	Tennessee	Y	41730 FQ	48860 MW	59860 TQ	USBLS	5/15
	Nashville-Davidson–Murfreesboro–Franklin MSA, TN	Y	42300 FQ	47520 MW	56130 TQ	USBLS	5/15
	Texas	Y	45220 FQ	58630 MW	76310 TQ	USBLS	5/15
	Austin-Round Rock MSA, TX	Y	45740 FQ	54750 MW	62790 TQ	USBLS	5/15
	Dallas-Plano-Irving PMSA, TX	Y	39630 FQ	53970 MW	70900 TQ	USBLS	5/15

AE	Average entry wage	AWR	Average wage range	H	Hourly	LR	Low end range	MTC	Median total compensation
AEX	Average experienced wage	B	Biweekly	HI	Highest wage paid	M	Monthly	MW	Median wage paid
ATC	Average total compensation	D	Daily	HR	High end range	MCC	Median cash compensation	MWR	Median wage range
AW	Average wage paid	FQ	First quartile wage	LO	Lowest wage paid	ME	Median entry wage	S	See annotated source

TCC	Total cash compensation
TQ	Third quartile wage
W	Weekly
Y	Yearly

Occupation/Type/Industry	Location	Per	Low	Mid	High	Source	Date
Cartographer and Photogrammetrist	Fort Worth-Arlington PMSA, TX	Y	57630 FQ	73680 MW	86520 TQ	USBLS	5/15
	Houston-The Woodlands-Sugar Land MSA, TX	Y	54870 FQ	69550 MW	97620 TQ	USBLS	5/15
	San Antonio-New Braunfels MSA, TX	Y	46550 FQ	54990 MW	68080 TQ	USBLS	5/15
	Utah	Y	47550 FQ	61510 MW	74440 TQ	USBLS	5/15
	Provo-Orem MSA, UT	Y	50920 FQ	66470 MW	75580 TQ	USBLS	5/15
	Salt Lake City MSA, UT	Y	52720 FQ	62930 MW	77770 TQ	USBLS	5/15
	Vermont	Y	37750 FQ	52220 MW	59950 TQ	USBLS	5/15
	Virginia	Y	53180 FQ	66050 MW	90130 TQ	USBLS	5/15
	Richmond MSA, VA	Y	52690 FQ	59220 MW	68960 TQ	USBLS	5/15
	Virginia Beach-Norfolk-Newport News MSA, VA-NC	Y	48470 FQ	61320 MW	76060 TQ	USBLS	5/15
	Washington	H	31.47 FQ	37.36 MW	44.15 TQ	WABLS	3/16
	Seattle-Bellevue-Everett PMSA, WA	H	33.82 FQ	40.44 MW	46.43 TQ	WABLS	3/16
	Tacoma-Lakewood PMSA, WA	H	33.71 FQ	37.25 MW	45.26 TQ	WABLS	3/16
	West Virginia	Y	40390 FQ	47840 MW	68540 TQ	USBLS	5/15
	Wisconsin	Y	51000 FQ	60120 MW	72300 TQ	USBLS	5/15
	Madison MSA, WI	Y	57160 FQ	71040 MW	81900 TQ	USBLS	5/15
	Milwaukee-Waukesha-West Allis MSA, WI	Y	48780 FQ	59900 MW	70750 TQ	USBLS	5/15
	Wyoming	Y	46790 FQ	54520 MW	61720 TQ	USBLS	5/15
Cartoonist	United States	Y		51000 AW		SKU01	2016
Case Management Analyst Medicaid, State Government	Ohio	H	24.47 LO		34.56 HI	OHGOV	2015
Cashier	Alabama	Y	17613 AE	19403 AW	20302 AEX	ALBLS	6/16
	Birmingham-Hoover MSA, AL	Y	17593 AE	19216 AW	20033 AEX	ALBLS	6/16
	Alaska	Y	20940 FQ	23670 MW	28340 TQ	USBLS	5/15
	Anchorage MSA, AK	Y	20860 FQ	23330 MW	27510 TQ	USBLS	5/15
	Arizona	Y	18010 FQ	19210 MW	23160 TQ	USBLS	5/15
	Phoenix-Mesa-Scottsdale MSA, AZ	Y	18040 FQ	19260 MW	23310 TQ	USBLS	5/15
	Tucson MSA, AZ	Y	18180 FQ	19610 MW	24160 TQ	USBLS	5/15
	Arkansas	Y	16940 FQ	18190 MW	19530 TQ	USBLS	5/15
	Little Rock-North Little Rock-Conway MSA, AR	Y	17060 FQ	18440 MW	20190 TQ	USBLS	5/15
	California	H	9.36 FQ	10.16 MW	12.17 TQ	CABLS	1/16-3/16
	Anaheim-Santa Ana-Irvine PMSA, CA	H	9.35 FQ	9.90 MW	11.75 TQ	CABLS	1/16-3/16
	Los Angeles-Long Beach-Glendale PMSA, CA	H	9.32 FQ	9.66 MW	11.53 TQ	CABLS	1/16-3/16
	Oakland-Hayward-Berkeley PMSA, CA	H	9.71 FQ	11.37 MW	14.40 TQ	CABLS	1/16-3/16
	Riverside-San Bernardino-Ontario MSA, CA	H	9.32 FQ	9.75 MW	11.69 TQ	CABLS	1/16-3/16
	Sacramento–Roseville–Arden-Arcade MSA, CA	H	9.29 FQ	9.84 MW	13.32 TQ	CABLS	1/16-3/16
	San Diego-Carlsbad MSA, CA	H	9.33 FQ	9.88 MW	11.75 TQ	CABLS	1/16-3/16
	San Francisco-Redwood City-South San Francisco PMSA, CA	H	10.56 FQ	12.10 MW	15.37 TQ	CABLS	1/16-3/16
	Colorado	Y	18460 FQ	20050 MW	24260 TQ	USBLS	5/15
	Denver-Aurora-Lakewood MSA, CO	Y	18420 FQ	19850 MW	23580 TQ	USBLS	5/15
	Connecticut	Y		21208 MW		CTBLS	1/16-3/16
	Bridgeport-Stamford-Norwalk MSA, CT	Y	19900 FQ	22310 MW	25310 TQ	USBLS	5/15
	Hartford-West Hartford-East Hartford MSA, CT	Y	19300 FQ	20390 MW	23840 TQ	USBLS	5/15
	Delaware	Y	17740 FQ	19140 MW	22670 TQ	USBLS	5/15
	Wilmington PMSA, DE-MD-NJ	Y	17850 FQ	19180 MW	22450 TQ	USBLS	5/15
	District of Columbia	Y	19960 FQ	21840 MW	24440 TQ	USBLS	5/15
	Washington-Arlington-Alexandria PMSA, DC-VA-MD-WV	Y	18190 FQ	20190 MW	24100 TQ	USBLS	5/15

AE	Average entry wage	**AWR**	Average wage range	**H**	Hourly	**LR** Low end range	**MTC** Median total compensation	**TCC** Total cash compensation
AEX	Average experienced wage	**B**	Biweekly	**HI**	Highest wage paid	**M** Monthly	**MW** Median wage paid	**TQ** Third quartile wage
ATC	Average total compensation	**D**	Daily	**HR**	High end range	**MCC** Median cash compensation	**MWR** Median wage range	**W** Weekly
AW	Average wage paid	**FQ**	First quartile wage	**LO**	Lowest wage paid	**ME** Median entry wage	**S** See annotated source	**Y** Yearly

Occupation/Type/Industry	Location	Per	Low	Mid	High	Source	Date
Cashier	Florida	H	8.89 AE	9.32 MW	10.35 AEX	FLBLS	7/16-9/16
	Fort Lauderdale-Pompano Beach-Deerfield Beach PMSA, FL	H	8.89 AE	9.39 MW	10.81 AEX	FLBLS	7/16-9/16
	Miami-Miami Beach-Kendall PMSA, FL	H	8.89 AE	9.29 MW	10.31 AEX	FLBLS	7/16-9/16
	Orlando-Kissimmee-Sanford MSA, FL	H	8.90 AE	9.51 MW	10.46 AEX	FLBLS	7/16-9/16
	Tampa-St. Petersburg-Clearwater MSA, FL	H	8.88 AE	9.23 MW	10.13 AEX	FLBLS	7/16-9/16
	Georgia	Y	16930 FQ	18410 MW	20400 TQ	USBLS	5/15
	Atlanta-Sandy Springs-Roswell MSA, GA	Y	17050 FQ	18640 MW	21400 TQ	USBLS	5/15
	Augusta-Richmond County MSA, GA-SC	Y	16830 FQ	18200 MW	19700 TQ	USBLS	5/15
	Hawaii	Y	18320 FQ	21440 MW	26710 TQ	USBLS	5/15
	Urban Honolulu MSA, HI	Y	17990 FQ	20390 MW	24710 TQ	USBLS	5/15
	Idaho	Y	17260 FQ	19030 MW	22570 TQ	USBLS	5/15
	Boise City MSA, ID	Y	17230 FQ	19020 MW	22850 TQ	USBLS	5/15
	Illinois	Y	18560 FQ	19530 MW	22640 TQ	USBLS	5/15
	Chicago-Naperville-Arlington Heights PMSA, IL	Y	18670 FQ	19750 MW	23180 TQ	USBLS	5/15
	Lake County-Kenosha County PMSA, IL-WI	Y	18360 FQ	19260 MW	21720 TQ	USBLS	5/15
	Indiana	Y	16950 FQ	18420 MW	20500 TQ	USBLS	5/15
	Gary PMSA, IN	Y	16810 FQ	18110 MW	19450 TQ	USBLS	5/15
	Indianapolis-Carmel-Anderson MSA, IN	Y	16980 FQ	18520 MW	21210 TQ	USBLS	5/15
	Iowa	Y	17080 FQ	18660 MW	21320 TQ	USBLS	5/15
	Des Moines-West Des Moines MSA, IA	Y	17400 FQ	19340 MW	23420 TQ	USBLS	5/15
	Kansas	Y	17020 FQ	18580 MW	21230 TQ	USBLS	5/15
	Wichita MSA, KS	Y	17090 FQ	18700 MW	21450 TQ	USBLS	5/15
	Kentucky	Y	16930 FQ	18370 MW	20160 TQ	USBLS	5/15
	Louisville-Jefferson County MSA, KY-IN	Y	17130 FQ	18770 MW	22070 TQ	USBLS	5/15
	Louisiana	Y	16860 FQ	18230 MW	19730 TQ	USBLS	5/15
	Baton Rouge MSA, LA	Y	16810 FQ	18120 MW	19490 TQ	USBLS	5/15
	New Orleans-Metairie MSA, LA	Y	16980 FQ	18450 MW	20400 TQ	USBLS	5/15
	Maine	Y	17670 FQ	19310 MW	22870 TQ	USBLS	5/15
	Portland-South Portland MSA, ME	Y	17930 FQ	19970 MW	23800 TQ	USBLS	5/15
	Maryland	Y	18066 AE	21688 MW	23499 AEX	MDBLS	4/16
	Baltimore-Columbia-Towson MSA, MD	Y	17810 FQ	18980 MW	22760 TQ	USBLS	5/15
	Salisbury MSA, MD-DE	Y	17840 FQ	19150 MW	22710 TQ	USBLS	5/15
	Massachusetts	Y	19250 FQ	20940 MW	24490 TQ	USBLS	5/15
	Boston-Cambridge-Newton NECTA, MA	Y	19270 FQ	21230 MW	25330 TQ	USBLS	5/15
	Worcester MSA, MA-CT	Y	19210 FQ	20380 MW	23700 TQ	USBLS	5/15
	Michigan	Y	18100 FQ	19220 MW	22830 TQ	USBLS	5/15
	Detroit-Dearborn-Livonia PMSA, MI	Y	18250 FQ	19610 MW	24230 TQ	USBLS	5/15
	Grand Rapids-Wyoming MSA, MI	Y	18020 FQ	19050 MW	21460 TQ	USBLS	5/15
	Minnesota	Y	18181 FQ	19592 MW	23323 TQ	MNBLS	1/16-3/16
	Minneapolis-St. Paul-Bloomington MSA, MN-WI	Y	18312 FQ	20026 MW	24180 TQ	MNBLS	1/16-3/16
	Mississippi	Y	16920 FQ	18340 MW	20030 TQ	USBLS	5/15
	Jackson MSA, MS	Y	17050 FQ	18650 MW	21410 TQ	USBLS	5/15
	Missouri	Y	17390 FQ	18830 MW	22040 TQ	USBLS	5/15
	Kansas City MSA, MO-KS	Y	17490 FQ	19210 MW	22840 TQ	USBLS	5/15
	St. Louis MSA, MO-IL	Y	17930 FQ	19270 MW	23310 TQ	USBLS	5/15
	Montana	Y	18230 FQ	19700 MW	23380 TQ	USBLS	5/15
	Billings MSA, MT	Y	18030 FQ	19210 MW	22040 TQ	USBLS	5/15
	Nebraska	Y	17740 FQ	18840 MW	21050 TQ	NEBLS	7/16-9/16
	Omaha-Council Bluffs MSA, NE-IA	Y	17630 FQ	18765 MW	20830 TQ	NEBLS	7/16-9/16
	Nevada	Y	17610 FQ	19970 MW	24530 TQ	USBLS	5/15
	Las Vegas-Henderson-Paradise MSA, NV	Y	17630 FQ	20060 MW	24580 TQ	USBLS	5/15

AE	Average entry wage	**AWR**	Average wage range	**H**	Hourly
AEX	Average experienced wage	**B**	Biweekly	**HI**	Highest wage paid
ATC	Average total compensation	**D**	Daily	**HR**	High end range
AW	Average wage paid	**FQ**	First quartile wage	**LO**	Lowest wage paid

LR	Low end range	**MTC**	Median total compensation	**TCC**	Total cash compensation
M	Monthly	**MW**	Median wage paid	**TQ**	Third quartile wage
MCC	Median cash compensation	**MWR**	Median wage range	**W**	Weekly
ME	Median entry wage	**S**	See annotated source	**Y**	Yearly

Cashier

Occupation/Type/Industry	Location	Per	Low	Mid	High	Source	Date
Cashier	New Hampshire	H	8.48 AE	9.58 MW	11.06 AEX	NHBLS	6/16
	Manchester NECTA, NH	H	8.47 AE	9.43 MW	10.81 AEX	NHBLS	6/16
	Nashua NECTA, NH-MA	Y	17590 FQ	19710 MW	23760 TQ	USBLS	5/15
	New Jersey	Y	18460 FQ	19480 MW	22860 TQ	USBLS	5/15
	Camden PMSA, NJ	Y	18480 FQ	19590 MW	23170 TQ	USBLS	5/15
	Newark PMSA, NJ-PA	Y	18420 FQ	19400 MW	22510 TQ	USBLS	5/15
	Trenton MSA, NJ	Y	18580 FQ	19670 MW	24050 TQ	USBLS	5/15
	New Mexico	Y	17500 FQ	19010 MW	22540 TQ	USBLS	5/15
	Albuquerque MSA, NM	Y	17520 FQ	19110 MW	22970 TQ	USBLS	5/15
	New York	Y	19110 AE	19750 MW	24100 AEX	NYBLS	1/16-3/16
	Buffalo-Cheektowaga-Niagara Falls MSA, NY	Y	18740 FQ	19300 MW	21360 TQ	USBLS	5/15
	Nassau County-Suffolk County PMSA, NY	Y	18930 FQ	19940 MW	23780 TQ	USBLS	5/15
	New York-Jersey City-White Plains PMSA, NY-NJ	Y	18740 FQ	19560 MW	23230 TQ	USBLS	5/15
	Rochester MSA, NY	Y	18740 FQ	19280 MW	21170 TQ	USBLS	5/15
	North Carolina	Y	16940 FQ	18420 MW	20540 TQ	USBLS	5/15
	Charlotte-Concord-Gastonia MSA, NC-SC	Y	17000 FQ	18510 MW	21020 TQ	USBLS	5/15
	Raleigh MSA, NC	Y	16980 FQ	18510 MW	21090 TQ	USBLS	5/15
	North Dakota	Y	18470 FQ	21370 MW	24680 TQ	USBLS	5/15
	Fargo MSA, ND-MN	Y	17760 FQ	19580 MW	22660 TQ	USBLS	5/15
	Ohio	Y	17960 FQ	18990 MW	21670 TQ	USBLS	5/15
	Cincinnati MSA, OH-KY-IN	Y	17780 FQ	18910 MW	21530 TQ	USBLS	5/15
	Cleveland-Elyria MSA, OH	Y	18130 FQ	19320 MW	23990 TQ	USBLS	5/15
	Columbus MSA, OH	Y	17920 FQ	18900 MW	20680 TQ	USBLS	5/15
	Oklahoma	Y	17060 FQ	18620 MW	21090 TQ	USBLS	5/15
	Oklahoma City MSA, OK	Y	17160 FQ	18790 MW	21700 TQ	USBLS	5/15
	Tulsa MSA, OK	Y	17320 FQ	19100 MW	22310 TQ	USBLS	5/15
	Oregon	H	9.64 FQ	10.74 MW	12.42 TQ	ORBLS	2016
	Portland-Vancouver-Hillsboro MSA, OR-WA	Y	20100 FQ	22780 MW	27670 TQ	USBLS	5/15
	Pennsylvania	Y	17090 FQ	18700 MW	21690 TQ	USBLS	5/15
	Allentown-Bethlehem-Easton MSA, PA-NJ	Y	17230 FQ	18740 MW	21410 TQ	USBLS	5/15
	Harrisburg-Carlisle MSA, PA	Y	17110 FQ	18760 MW	21670 TQ	USBLS	5/15
	Montgomery County-Bucks County-Chester County PMSA, PA	Y	17390 FQ	19320 MW	23330 TQ	USBLS	5/15
	Philadelphia PMSA, PA	Y	17350 FQ	19230 MW	23110 TQ	USBLS	5/15
	Pittsburgh MSA, PA	Y	16970 FQ	18480 MW	20850 TQ	USBLS	5/15
	Rhode Island	Y	19240 FQ	20090 MW	23950 TQ	USBLS	5/15
	Providence-Warwick MSA, RI-MA	Y	19230 FQ	20260 MW	24100 TQ	USBLS	5/15
	South Carolina	Y	16820 FQ	18170 MW	19640 TQ	USBLS	5/15
	Charleston-North Charleston MSA, SC	Y	16860 FQ	18270 MW	19930 TQ	USBLS	5/15
	Columbia MSA, SC	Y	16680 FQ	17950 MW	19220 TQ	USBLS	5/15
	Greenville-Anderson-Mauldin MSA, SC	Y	16810 FQ	18160 MW	19640 TQ	USBLS	5/15
	South Dakota	Y	18530 FQ	19410 MW	21970 TQ	USBLS	5/15
	Sioux Falls MSA, SD	Y	18640 FQ	19730 MW	23000 TQ	USBLS	5/15
	Tennessee	Y	16960 FQ	18440 MW	20610 TQ	USBLS	5/15
	Knoxville MSA, TN	Y	16980 FQ	18480 MW	20850 TQ	USBLS	5/15
	Memphis MSA, TN-MS-AR	Y	16920 FQ	18350 MW	20050 TQ	USBLS	5/15
	Nashville-Davidson–Murfreesboro–Franklin MSA, TN	Y	17080 FQ	18690 MW	22380 TQ	USBLS	5/15
	Texas	Y	17290 FQ	19070 MW	22550 TQ	USBLS	5/15
	Austin-Round Rock MSA, TX	Y	18300 FQ	21060 MW	23930 TQ	USBLS	5/15
	Dallas-Plano-Irving PMSA, TX	Y	17070 FQ	18670 MW	21930 TQ	USBLS	5/15
	Fort Worth-Arlington PMSA, TX	Y	17300 FQ	19050 MW	23110 TQ	USBLS	5/15
	Houston-The Woodlands-Sugar Land MSA, TX	Y	17390 FQ	19280 MW	22920 TQ	USBLS	5/15
	San Antonio-New Braunfels MSA, TX	Y	17550 FQ	19630 MW	23060 TQ	USBLS	5/15
	Utah	Y	17310 FQ	19060 MW	22700 TQ	USBLS	5/15
	Ogden-Clearfield MSA, UT	Y	17170 FQ	18820 MW	22500 TQ	USBLS	5/15
	Provo-Orem MSA, UT	Y	17090 FQ	18620 MW	21160 TQ	USBLS	5/15
	Salt Lake City MSA, UT	Y	17440 FQ	19300 MW	22920 TQ	USBLS	5/15

AE	Average entry wage	AWR	Average wage range	H	Hourly
AEX	Average experienced wage	B	Biweekly	HI	Highest wage paid
ATC	Average total compensation	D	Daily	HR	High end range
AW	Average wage paid	FQ	First quartile wage	LO	Lowest wage paid

LR	Low end range	MTC	Median total compensation
M	Monthly	MW	Median wage paid
MCC	Median cash compensation	MWR	Median wage range
ME	Median entry wage	S	See annotated source

TCC	Total cash compensation		
TQ	Third quartile wage		
W	Weekly		
Y	Yearly		

Cashier

Occupation/Type/Industry	Location	Per	Low	Mid	High	Source	Date
Cashier	Vermont	Y	19480 FQ	20940 MW	24040 TQ	USBLS	5/15
	Burlington-South Burlington MSA, VT	Y	19540 FQ	21170 MW	23920 TQ	USBLS	5/15
	Virginia	Y	17100 FQ	18740 MW	22000 TQ	USBLS	5/15
	Richmond MSA, VA	Y	16980 FQ	18540 MW	21250 TQ	USBLS	5/15
	Virginia Beach-Norfolk-Newport News MSA, VA-NC	Y	16880 FQ	18300 MW	19980 TQ	USBLS	5/15
	Washington	H	10.43 FQ	11.56 MW	14.17 TQ	WABLS	3/16
	Seattle-Bellevue-Everett PMSA, WA	H	10.75 FQ	12.00 MW	15.10 TQ	WABLS	3/16
	Tacoma-Lakewood PMSA, WA	H	10.34 FQ	11.60 MW	14.83 TQ	WABLS	3/16
	West Virginia	Y	17520 FQ	18410 MW	19310 TQ	USBLS	5/15
	Huntington-Ashland MSA, WV-KY-OH	Y	17380 FQ	18290 MW	19200 TQ	USBLS	5/15
	Wisconsin	Y	17050 FQ	18620 MW	21510 TQ	USBLS	5/15
	Madison MSA, WI	Y	17050 FQ	18650 MW	22340 TQ	USBLS	5/15
	Milwaukee-Waukesha-West Allis MSA, WI	Y	17230 FQ	19000 MW	23350 TQ	USBLS	5/15
	Wyoming	Y	17830 FQ	20540 MW	24140 TQ	USBLS	5/15
	Cheyenne MSA, WY	Y	17260 FQ	19120 MW	23650 TQ	USBLS	5/15
	Puerto Rico	Y	16580 FQ	17700 MW	18820 TQ	USBLS	5/15
	San Juan-Carolina-Caguas MSA, PR	Y	16580 FQ	17710 MW	18830 TQ	USBLS	5/15
	Virgin Islands	Y	16840 FQ	18260 MW	19900 TQ	USBLS	5/15
	Guam	Y	17960 FQ	18750 MW	19680 TQ	USBLS	5/15
CAT Scan Technologist							
State Government	North Carolina	Y	42667 LO		69177 HI	NCGOV	7/1/16
Category Manager							
Supermarket, Large Company	United States	Y		125000 AW		SN01	2015
Supermarket, Medium Company	United States	Y		115000 AW		SN01	2015
Supermarket, Small Company	United States	Y		100000 AW		SN01	2015
Cement Mason and Concrete Finisher	Alabama	Y	27476 AE	36189 AW	40551 AEX	ALBLS	6/16
	Birmingham-Hoover MSA, AL	Y	27312 AE	34163 AW	37578 AEX	ALBLS	6/16
	Alaska	Y	47990 FQ	61680 MW	75910 TQ	USBLS	5/15
	Anchorage MSA, AK	Y	38050 FQ	59750 MW	72730 TQ	USBLS	5/15
	Arizona	Y	31710 FQ	36540 MW	43250 TQ	USBLS	5/15
	Phoenix-Mesa-Scottsdale MSA, AZ	Y	32760 FQ	37130 MW	43840 TQ	USBLS	5/15
	Tucson MSA, AZ	Y	27880 FQ	32120 MW	38170 TQ	USBLS	5/15
	Arkansas	Y	28110 FQ	32730 MW	37140 TQ	USBLS	5/15
	Little Rock-North Little Rock-Conway MSA, AR	Y	31680 FQ	35210 MW	38730 TQ	USBLS	5/15
	California	H	17.28 FQ	23.26 MW	29.76 TQ	CABLS	1/16-3/16
	Anaheim-Santa Ana-Irvine PMSA, CA	H	17.73 FQ	26.92 MW	33.51 TQ	CABLS	1/16-3/16
	Los Angeles-Long Beach-Glendale PMSA, CA	H	17.14 FQ	25.19 MW	32.12 TQ	CABLS	1/16-3/16
	Oakland-Hayward-Berkeley PMSA, CA	H	20.27 FQ	25.00 MW	30.37 TQ	CABLS	1/16-3/16
	Riverside-San Bernardino-Ontario MSA, CA	H	17.55 FQ	22.71 MW	28.37 TQ	CABLS	1/16-3/16
	Sacramento–Roseville–Arden-Arcade MSA, CA	H	17.40 FQ	22.18 MW	28.56 TQ	CABLS	1/16-3/16
	San Diego-Carlsbad MSA, CA	H	18.58 FQ	24.47 MW	31.16 TQ	CABLS	1/16-3/16
	San Francisco-Redwood City-South San Francisco PMSA, CA	H	15.42 FQ	23.64 MW	34.58 TQ	CABLS	1/16-3/16
	Colorado	Y	29740 FQ	36880 MW	45510 TQ	USBLS	5/15
	Denver-Aurora-Lakewood MSA, CO	Y	28980 FQ	35730 MW	44870 TQ	USBLS	5/15
	Connecticut	Y		47953 MW		CTBLS	1/16-3/16
	Bridgeport-Stamford-Norwalk MSA, CT	Y	41450 FQ	48560 MW	58100 TQ	USBLS	5/15
	Hartford-West Hartford-East Hartford MSA, CT	Y	37640 FQ	45760 MW	58790 TQ	USBLS	5/15
	Delaware	Y	34340 FQ	40810 MW	48460 TQ	USBLS	5/15
	Wilmington PMSA, DE-MD-NJ	Y	34680 FQ	39700 MW	46450 TQ	USBLS	5/15

AE Average entry wage	**AWR** Average wage range	**H** Hourly	**LR** Low end range	**MTC** Median total compensation	**TCC** Total cash compensation
AEX Average experienced wage	**B** Biweekly	**HI** Highest wage paid	**M** Monthly	**MW** Median wage paid	**TQ** Third quartile wage
ATC Average total compensation	**D** Daily	**HR** High end range	**MCC** Median cash compensation	**MWR** Median wage range	**W** Weekly
AW Average wage paid	**FQ** First quartile wage	**LO** Lowest wage paid	**ME** Median entry wage	**S** See annotated source	**Y** Yearly

Occupation/Type/Industry	Location	Per	Low	Mid	High	Source	Date
Cement Mason and Concrete Finisher							
	District of Columbia	Y	41170 FQ	46710 MW	54940 TQ	USBLS	5/15
	Washington-Arlington-Alexandria PMSA, DC-VA-MD-WV	Y	36220 FQ	43080 MW	49810 TQ	USBLS	5/15
	Florida	H	12.31 AE	15.74 MW	19.19 AEX	FLBLS	7/16-9/16
	Fort Lauderdale-Pompano Beach-Deerfield Beach PMSA, FL	H	12.22 AE	16.48 MW	19.81 AEX	FLBLS	7/16-9/16
	Miami-Miami Beach-Kendall PMSA, FL	H	11.01 AE	14.96 MW	17.94 AEX	FLBLS	7/16-9/16
	Orlando-Kissimmee-Sanford MSA, FL	H	13.37 AE	17.40 MW	20.20 AEX	FLBLS	7/16-9/16
	Tampa-St. Petersburg-Clearwater MSA, FL	H	11.60 AE	14.53 MW	19.02 AEX	FLBLS	7/16-9/16
	Georgia	Y	26120 FQ	30590 MW	36220 TQ	USBLS	5/15
	Atlanta-Sandy Springs-Roswell MSA, GA	Y	25730 FQ	30180 MW	36210 TQ	USBLS	5/15
	Augusta-Richmond County MSA, GA-SC	Y	28080 FQ	33670 MW	38310 TQ	USBLS	5/15
	Hawaii	Y	54760 FQ	66520 MW	75770 TQ	USBLS	5/15
	Urban Honolulu MSA, HI	Y	60400 FQ	68890 MW	76310 TQ	USBLS	5/15
	Idaho	Y	28160 FQ	33810 MW	38280 TQ	USBLS	5/15
	Boise City MSA, ID	Y	27450 FQ	32740 MW	37930 TQ	USBLS	5/15
	Illinois	Y	37320 FQ	55890 MW	82360 TQ	USBLS	5/15
	Chicago-Naperville-Arlington Heights PMSA, IL	Y	39740 FQ	64750 MW	89400 TQ	USBLS	5/15
	Lake County-Kenosha County PMSA, IL-WI	Y	41690 FQ	54690 MW	71900 TQ	USBLS	5/15
	Indiana	Y	31390 FQ	39200 MW	49690 TQ	USBLS	5/15
	Gary PMSA, IN	Y	40810 FQ	56080 MW	68410 TQ	USBLS	5/15
	Indianapolis-Carmel-Anderson MSA, IN	Y	33300 FQ	41350 MW	47190 TQ	USBLS	5/15
	Iowa	Y	30050 FQ	35460 MW	42130 TQ	USBLS	5/15
	Des Moines-West Des Moines MSA, IA	Y	32790 FQ	36550 MW	42450 TQ	USBLS	5/15
	Kansas	Y	31680 FQ	39750 MW	48260 TQ	USBLS	5/15
	Wichita MSA, KS	Y	36300 FQ	44440 MW	58940 TQ	USBLS	5/15
	Kentucky	Y	28180 FQ	34880 MW	42490 TQ	USBLS	5/15
	Louisville-Jefferson County MSA, KY-IN	Y	31060 FQ	36070 MW	43020 TQ	USBLS	5/15
	Louisiana	Y	30730 FQ	38520 MW	49780 TQ	USBLS	5/15
	Baton Rouge MSA, LA	Y	33640 FQ	41380 MW	47530 TQ	USBLS	5/15
	New Orleans-Metairie MSA, LA	Y	28380 FQ	36800 MW	54460 TQ	USBLS	5/15
	Maine	Y	27770 FQ	31350 MW	36850 TQ	USBLS	5/15
	Portland-South Portland MSA, ME	Y	27330 FQ	32130 MW	38680 TQ	USBLS	5/15
	Maryland	Y	31545 AE	42487 MW	47957 AEX	MDBLS	4/16
	Baltimore-Columbia-Towson MSA, MD	Y	35120 FQ	42250 MW	49260 TQ	USBLS	5/15
	Salisbury MSA, MD-DE	Y	30190 FQ	34850 MW	39390 TQ	USBLS	5/15
	Massachusetts	Y	34670 FQ	43720 MW	55760 TQ	USBLS	5/15
	Boston-Cambridge-Newton NECTA, MA	Y	29880 FQ	43590 MW	53940 TQ	USBLS	5/15
	Worcester MSA, MA-CT	Y	41440 FQ	47330 MW	55640 TQ	USBLS	5/15
	Michigan	Y	33120 FQ	41620 MW	56380 TQ	USBLS	5/15
	Detroit-Dearborn-Livonia PMSA, MI	Y	49330 FQ	57240 MW	67050 TQ	USBLS	5/15
	Grand Rapids-Wyoming MSA, MI	Y	30220 FQ	39280 MW	52230 TQ	USBLS	5/15
	Minnesota	Y	37899 FQ	46899 MW	57827 TQ	MNBLS	1/16-3/16
	Minneapolis-St. Paul-Bloomington MSA, MN-WI	Y	38898 FQ	48140 MW	58866 TQ	MNBLS	1/16-3/16
	Mississippi	Y	21880 FQ	26900 MW	34030 TQ	USBLS	5/15
	Jackson MSA, MS	Y	20070 FQ	26320 MW	31740 TQ	USBLS	5/15
	Missouri	Y	31760 FQ	44120 MW	61090 TQ	USBLS	5/15
	Kansas City MSA, MO-KS	Y	30160 FQ	41340 MW	54300 TQ	USBLS	5/15
	St. Louis MSA, MO-IL	Y	41060 FQ	57530 MW	68850 TQ	USBLS	5/15
	Montana	Y	28490 FQ	37170 MW	49760 TQ	USBLS	5/15
	Billings MSA, MT	Y	34110 FQ	38330 MW	46410 TQ	USBLS	5/15
	Nebraska	Y	29205 FQ	35090 MW	41085 TQ	NEBLS	7/16-9/16

AE Average entry wage	**AWR** Average wage range	**H** Hourly	**LR** Low end range	**MTC** Median total compensation	**TCC** Total cash compensation
AEX Average experienced wage	**B** Biweekly	**HI** Highest wage paid	**M** Monthly	**MW** Median wage paid	**TQ** Third quartile wage
ATC Average total compensation	**D** Daily	**HR** High end range	**MCC** Median cash compensation	**MWR** Median wage range	**W** Weekly
AW Average wage paid	**FQ** First quartile wage	**LO** Lowest wage paid	**ME** Median entry wage	**S** See annotated source	**Y** Yearly

Occupation/Type/Industry	Location	Per	Low	Mid	High	Source	Date
Cement Mason and Concrete Finisher	Omaha-Council Bluffs MSA, NE-IA	Y	30765 FQ	36060 MW	42960 TQ	NEBLS	7/16-9/16
	Nevada	Y	34080 FQ	39630 MW	47710 TQ	USBLS	5/15
	Las Vegas-Henderson-Paradise MSA, NV	Y	33740 FQ	39290 MW	47310 TQ	USBLS	5/15
	New Hampshire	H	16.90 AE	22.14 MW	25.14 AEX	NHBLS	6/16
	New Jersey	Y	44290 FQ	54510 MW	62830 TQ	USBLS	5/15
	Camden PMSA, NJ	Y	35600 FQ	45840 MW	85660 TQ	USBLS	5/15
	Newark PMSA, NJ-PA	Y	44480 FQ	54750 MW	65960 TQ	USBLS	5/15
	Trenton MSA, NJ	Y	43940 FQ	53620 MW	62060 TQ	USBLS	5/15
	New Mexico	Y	29640 FQ	34750 MW	39400 TQ	USBLS	5/15
	Albuquerque MSA, NM	Y	32460 FQ	35460 MW	38460 TQ	USBLS	5/15
	New York	Y	38370 AE	62940 MW	80280 AEX	NYBLS	1/16-3/16
	Buffalo-Cheektowaga-Niagara Falls MSA, NY	Y	32740 FQ	40760 MW	55430 TQ	USBLS	5/15
	Nassau County-Suffolk County PMSA, NY	Y	49350 FQ	58610 MW	87640 TQ	USBLS	5/15
	New York-Jersey City-White Plains PMSA, NY-NJ	Y	50330 FQ	68350 MW	88790 TQ	USBLS	5/15
	Rochester MSA, NY	Y	34670 FQ	44050 MW	55990 TQ	USBLS	5/15
	North Carolina	Y	27540 FQ	32870 MW	37810 TQ	USBLS	5/15
	Charlotte-Concord-Gastonia MSA, NC-SC	Y	30130 FQ	34640 MW	38570 TQ	USBLS	5/15
	Raleigh MSA, NC	Y	29230 FQ	33820 MW	37970 TQ	USBLS	5/15
	North Dakota	Y	34060 FQ	38510 MW	45580 TQ	USBLS	5/15
	Fargo MSA, ND-MN	Y	33350 FQ	37340 MW	43800 TQ	USBLS	5/15
	Ohio	Y	32520 FQ	41120 MW	53290 TQ	USBLS	5/15
	Cincinnati MSA, OH-KY-IN	Y	31170 FQ	36760 MW	48200 TQ	USBLS	5/15
	Cleveland-Elyria MSA, OH	Y	39410 FQ	54740 MW	63580 TQ	USBLS	5/15
	Columbus MSA, OH	Y	34110 FQ	40280 MW	47470 TQ	USBLS	5/15
	Oklahoma	Y	27860 FQ	34380 MW	39220 TQ	USBLS	5/15
	Oklahoma City MSA, OK	Y	24940 FQ	33530 MW	38080 TQ	USBLS	5/15
	Tulsa MSA, OK	Y	30690 FQ	35840 MW	42660 TQ	USBLS	5/15
	Oregon	H	16.55 FQ	18.82 MW	26.32 TQ	ORBLS	2016
	Portland-Vancouver-Hillsboro MSA, OR-WA	Y	34730 FQ	41320 MW	58420 TQ	USBLS	5/15
	Pennsylvania	Y	33870 FQ	43450 MW	56780 TQ	USBLS	5/15
	Allentown-Bethlehem-Easton MSA, PA-NJ	Y	31970 FQ	36530 MW	44820 TQ	USBLS	5/15
	Harrisburg-Carlisle MSA, PA	Y	28550 FQ	34380 MW	40770 TQ	USBLS	5/15
	Montgomery County-Bucks County-Chester County PMSA, PA	Y	38930 FQ	45820 MW	59230 TQ	USBLS	5/15
	Philadelphia PMSA, PA	Y	49230 FQ	64060 MW	72710 TQ	USBLS	5/15
	Pittsburgh MSA, PA	Y	31150 FQ	50880 MW	58020 TQ	USBLS	5/15
	Rhode Island	Y	39010 FQ	50650 MW	60420 TQ	USBLS	5/15
	Providence-Warwick MSA, RI-MA	Y	38490 FQ	50600 MW	64680 TQ	USBLS	5/15
	South Carolina	Y	27100 FQ	32310 MW	37540 TQ	USBLS	5/15
	Charleston-North Charleston MSA, SC	Y	29320 FQ	33440 MW	37120 TQ	USBLS	5/15
	Columbia MSA, SC	Y	32540 FQ	36840 MW	53520 TQ	USBLS	5/15
	Greenville-Anderson-Mauldin MSA, SC	Y	24370 FQ	28880 MW	34310 TQ	USBLS	5/15
	South Dakota	Y	26930 FQ	30640 MW	37160 TQ	USBLS	5/15
	Sioux Falls MSA, SD	Y	26310 FQ	29940 MW	38290 TQ	USBLS	5/15
	Tennessee	Y	27620 FQ	33050 MW	38600 TQ	USBLS	5/15
	Knoxville MSA, TN	Y	29800 FQ	35740 MW	44010 TQ	USBLS	5/15
	Memphis MSA, TN-MS-AR	Y	28020 FQ	32530 MW	37720 TQ	USBLS	5/15
	Nashville-Davidson–Murfreesboro–Franklin MSA, TN	Y	30640 FQ	35280 MW	39750 TQ	USBLS	5/15
	Texas	Y	26480 FQ	30780 MW	36400 TQ	USBLS	5/15
	Austin-Round Rock MSA, TX	Y	26890 FQ	31110 MW	36400 TQ	USBLS	5/15
	Dallas-Plano-Irving PMSA, TX	Y	26440 FQ	30840 MW	36170 TQ	USBLS	5/15
	Fort Worth-Arlington PMSA, TX	Y	28520 FQ	34090 MW	39290 TQ	USBLS	5/15
	Houston-The Woodlands-Sugar Land MSA, TX	Y	26500 FQ	30000 MW	35210 TQ	USBLS	5/15
	San Antonio-New Braunfels MSA, TX	Y	26580 FQ	32630 MW	38210 TQ	USBLS	5/15

AE	Average entry wage	AWR	Average wage range	H	Hourly	LR	Low end range	MTC	Median total compensation	TCC	Total cash compensation
AEX	Average experienced wage	B	Biweekly	HI	Highest wage paid	M	Monthly	MW	Median wage paid	TQ	Third quartile wage
ATC	Average total compensation	D	Daily	HR	High end range	MCC	Median cash compensation	MWR	Median wage range	W	Weekly
AW	Average wage paid	FQ	First quartile wage	LO	Lowest wage paid	ME	Median entry wage	S	See annotated source	Y	Yearly

Occupation/Type/Industry	Location	Per	Low	Mid	High	Source	Date
Cement Mason and Concrete Finisher							
	Utah	Y	30670 FQ	35810 MW	42180 TQ	USBLS	5/15
	Ogden-Clearfield MSA, UT	Y	28880 FQ	34030 MW	38790 TQ	USBLS	5/15
	Provo-Orem MSA, UT	Y	29760 FQ	36380 MW	43600 TQ	USBLS	5/15
	Salt Lake City MSA, UT	Y	33790 FQ	38790 MW	47380 TQ	USBLS	5/15
	Vermont	Y	32180 FQ	35970 MW	40550 TQ	USBLS	5/15
	Burlington-South Burlington MSA, VT	Y	30750 FQ	34770 MW	38410 TQ	USBLS	5/15
	Virginia	Y	32500 FQ	38310 MW	46370 TQ	USBLS	5/15
	Richmond MSA, VA	Y	31590 FQ	35350 MW	39110 TQ	USBLS	5/15
	Virginia Beach-Norfolk- Newport News MSA, VA-NC	Y	29770 FQ	35360 MW	42990 TQ	USBLS	5/15
	Washington	H	17.61 FQ	22.16 MW	29.66 TQ	WABLS	3/16
	Seattle-Bellevue-Everett PMSA, WA	H	17.63 FQ	21.97 MW	31.14 TQ	WABLS	3/16
	Tacoma-Lakewood PMSA, WA	H	18.04 FQ	22.74 MW	33.09 TQ	WABLS	3/16
	West Virginia	Y	26360 FQ	33740 MW	51140 TQ	USBLS	5/15
	Huntington-Ashland MSA, WV-KY-OH	Y	25280 FQ	31110 MW	42570 TQ	USBLS	5/15
	Wisconsin	Y	37440 FQ	45700 MW	60150 TQ	USBLS	5/15
	Madison MSA, WI	Y	40000 FQ	48010 MW	66580 TQ	USBLS	5/15
	Milwaukee-Waukesha-West Allis MSA, WI	Y	39560 FQ	47290 MW	64610 TQ	USBLS	5/15
	Wyoming	Y	33360 FQ	39200 MW	46590 TQ	USBLS	5/15
	Cheyenne MSA, WY	Y	30140 FQ	39350 MW	47660 TQ	USBLS	5/15
	Puerto Rico	Y	16760 FQ	18080 MW	19420 TQ	USBLS	5/15
	San Juan-Carolina-Caguas MSA, PR	Y	16820 FQ	18200 MW	19680 TQ	USBLS	5/15
	Guam	Y	27090 FQ	29570 MW	33410 TQ	USBLS	5/15
Cemetery Specialist							
Municipal Government	Colorado Springs, CO	Y	43115 LO		59283 HI	COSPRS	2017
Certified Ethical Hacker	United States	Y		103297 AW		DATAM1	2016
Certified Information Security Manager	United States	Y		122291 AW		DATAM1	2016
Certified Medical Assistant							
Health Department, Municipal Government	Pasadena, CA	Y			39882 HI	CACIT	6/28/16
Certified Professional Organizer	United States	Y		30000 AW		SKU01	2016
Chaplain							
Corrections Department, State Government	Marenisco, MI	H	18.84 LO		29.12 HI	MIGOV	2016
Chaplaincy Services Assistant							
State Government	Texas	Y	29439 LO		46388 HI	TXGOV	9/1/15-8/31/17
Chauffeur							
Chauffeured Transportation Company	United States	H		16.75 AW		LCT01	2016
Chef and Head Cook							
	Alabama	Y	31537 AE	48937 AW	57637 AEX	ALBLS	6/16
	Birmingham-Hoover MSA, AL	Y	43233 AE	58863 AW	66667 AEX	ALBLS	6/16
	Alaska	Y	30280 FQ	37030 MW	52560 TQ	USBLS	5/15
	Anchorage MSA, AK	Y	26830 FQ	33980 MW	41880 TQ	USBLS	5/15
	Arizona	Y	30620 FQ	38070 MW	56380 TQ	USBLS	5/15
	Phoenix-Mesa-Scottsdale MSA, AZ	Y	32520 FQ	38990 MW	57840 TQ	USBLS	5/15
	Tucson MSA, AZ	Y	26200 FQ	30420 MW	46110 TQ	USBLS	5/15
	Arkansas	Y	27720 FQ	33480 MW	43770 TQ	USBLS	5/15
	Little Rock-North Little Rock- Conway MSA, AR	Y	31430 FQ	37970 MW	53220 TQ	USBLS	5/15
	California	H	15.29 FQ	20.22 MW	27.90 TQ	CABLS	1/16-3/16
	Anaheim-Santa Ana-Irvine PMSA, CA	H	15.07 FQ	21.61 MW	29.01 TQ	CABLS	1/16-3/16
	Los Angeles-Long Beach- Glendale PMSA, CA	H	12.97 FQ	17.68 MW	25.66 TQ	CABLS	1/16-3/16
	Oakland-Hayward-Berkeley PMSA, CA	H	13.80 FQ	18.38 MW	28.39 TQ	CABLS	1/16-3/16
	Riverside-San Bernardino- Ontario MSA, CA	H	13.66 FQ	22.72 MW	32.95 TQ	CABLS	1/16-3/16

AE	Average entry wage	AWR	Average wage range	H	Hourly
AEX	Average experienced wage	B	Biweekly	HI	Highest wage paid
ATC	Average total compensation	D	Daily	HR	High end range
AW	Average wage paid	FQ	First quartile wage	LO	Lowest wage paid

LR	Low end range	MTC	Median total compensation	TCC	Total cash compensation
M	Monthly	MW	Median wage paid	TQ	Third quartile wage
MCC	Median cash compensation	MWR	Median wage range	W	Weekly
ME	Median entry wage	S	See annotated source	Y	Yearly

Occupation/Type/Industry	Location	Per	Low	Mid	High	Source	Date
Chef and Head Cook	Sacramento–Roseville–Arden-Arcade MSA, CA	H	16.66 FQ	21.09 MW	25.87 TQ	CABLS	1/16-3/16
	San Diego-Carlsbad MSA, CA	H	16.91 FQ	20.36 MW	27.93 TQ	CABLS	1/16-3/16
	San Francisco-Redwood City-South San Francisco PMSA, CA	H	17.29 FQ	22.61 MW	28.71 TQ	CABLS	1/16-3/16
	Colorado	Y	34520 FQ	45180 MW	57010 TQ	USBLS	5/15
	Denver-Aurora-Lakewood MSA, CO	Y	30840 FQ	42760 MW	52040 TQ	USBLS	5/15
	Connecticut	Y		44603 MW		CTBLS	1/16-3/16
	Bridgeport-Stamford-Norwalk MSA, CT	Y	28900 FQ	38060 MW	49420 TQ	USBLS	5/15
	Hartford-West Hartford-East Hartford MSA, CT	Y	41560 FQ	47320 MW	54720 TQ	USBLS	5/15
	Delaware	Y	39890 FQ	45220 MW	52360 TQ	USBLS	5/15
	Wilmington PMSA, DE-MD-NJ	Y	40410 FQ	45730 MW	55100 TQ	USBLS	5/15
	District of Columbia	Y	38080 FQ	53210 MW	77760 TQ	USBLS	5/15
	Washington-Arlington-Alexandria PMSA, DC-VA-MD-WV	Y	37620 FQ	55220 MW	77340 TQ	USBLS	5/15
	Florida	H	16.98 AE	25.11 MW	32.60 AEX	FLBLS	7/16-9/16
	Fort Lauderdale-Pompano Beach-Deerfield Beach PMSA, FL	H	16.01 AE	22.51 MW	28.55 AEX	FLBLS	7/16-9/16
	Miami-Miami Beach-Kendall PMSA, FL	H	16.55 AE	26.16 MW	32.90 AEX	FLBLS	7/16-9/16
	Orlando-Kissimmee-Sanford MSA, FL	H	16.14 AE	25.40 MW	33.40 AEX	FLBLS	7/16-9/16
	Tampa-St. Petersburg-Clearwater MSA, FL	H	15.72 AE	21.80 MW	26.60 AEX	FLBLS	7/16-9/16
	Georgia	Y	23050 FQ	29680 MW	41050 TQ	USBLS	5/15
	Atlanta-Sandy Springs-Roswell MSA, GA	Y	23050 FQ	30270 MW	42300 TQ	USBLS	5/15
	Augusta-Richmond County MSA, GA-SC	Y	31040 FQ	43430 MW	51490 TQ	USBLS	5/15
	Hawaii	Y	27910 FQ	36980 MW	56450 TQ	USBLS	5/15
	Urban Honolulu MSA, HI	Y	26630 FQ	30670 MW	51110 TQ	USBLS	5/15
	Idaho	Y	25860 FQ	29970 MW	36670 TQ	USBLS	5/15
	Boise City MSA, ID	Y	26680 FQ	29740 MW	35730 TQ	USBLS	5/15
	Illinois	Y	29940 FQ	38160 MW	56140 TQ	USBLS	5/15
	Chicago-Naperville-Arlington Heights PMSA, IL	Y	33980 FQ	43490 MW	59650 TQ	USBLS	5/15
	Lake County-Kenosha County PMSA, IL-WI	Y	41990 FQ	55460 MW	62810 TQ	USBLS	5/15
	Indiana	Y	31680 FQ	36710 MW	45650 TQ	USBLS	5/15
	Gary PMSA, IN	Y	35350 FQ	41170 MW	50970 TQ	USBLS	5/15
	Indianapolis-Carmel-Anderson MSA, IN	Y	30810 FQ	35890 MW	42960 TQ	USBLS	5/15
	Iowa	Y	26170 FQ	32490 MW	42870 TQ	USBLS	5/15
	Des Moines-West Des Moines MSA, IA	Y	28690 FQ	34700 MW	46250 TQ	USBLS	5/15
	Kansas	Y	24500 FQ	32650 MW	40400 TQ	USBLS	5/15
	Wichita MSA, KS	Y	23750 FQ	29760 MW	36630 TQ	USBLS	5/15
	Kentucky	Y	34050 FQ	40450 MW	57570 TQ	USBLS	5/15
	Louisville-Jefferson County MSA, KY-IN	Y	33340 FQ	37960 MW	47070 TQ	USBLS	5/15
	Louisiana	Y	25710 FQ	34110 MW	49260 TQ	USBLS	5/15
	Alexandria MSA, LA	Y	42520 FQ	74400 MW	77150 TQ	USBLS	5/15
	Baton Rouge MSA, LA	Y	29560 FQ	39950 MW	51030 TQ	USBLS	5/15
	New Orleans-Metairie MSA, LA	Y	23620 FQ	30270 MW	50960 TQ	USBLS	5/15
	Maine	Y	30080 FQ	40310 MW	47770 TQ	USBLS	5/15
	Portland-South Portland MSA, ME	Y	30400 FQ	37190 MW	47910 TQ	USBLS	5/15
	Maryland	Y	30593 AE	52135 MW	62905 AEX	MDBLS	4/16
	Baltimore-Columbia-Towson MSA, MD	Y	34600 FQ	46540 MW	60950 TQ	USBLS	5/15
	Salisbury MSA, MD-DE	Y	37670 FQ	44260 MW	50790 TQ	USBLS	5/15
	Massachusetts	Y	40820 FQ	52580 MW	66420 TQ	USBLS	5/15
	Boston-Cambridge-Newton NECTA, MA	Y	42300 FQ	55570 MW	68770 TQ	USBLS	5/15

AE	Average entry wage	AWR	Average wage range	H	Hourly	LR	Low end range	MTC	Median total compensation	TCC	Total cash compensation
AEX	Average experienced wage	B	Biweekly	HI	Highest wage paid	M	Monthly	MW	Median wage paid	TQ	Third quartile wage
ATC	Average total compensation	D	Daily	HR	High end range	MCC	Median cash compensation	MWR	Median wage range	W	Weekly
AW	Average wage paid	FQ	First quartile wage	LO	Lowest wage paid	ME	Median entry wage	S	See annotated source	Y	Yearly

Occupation/Type/Industry	Location	Per	Low	Mid	High	Source	Date
Chef and Head Cook	Worcester MSA, MA-CT	Y	36310 FQ	44790 MW	60090 TQ	USBLS	5/15
	Michigan	Y	27970 FQ	38540 MW	56560 TQ	USBLS	5/15
	Detroit-Dearborn-Livonia PMSA, MI	Y	29210 FQ	37410 MW	54020 TQ	USBLS	5/15
	Grand Rapids-Wyoming MSA, MI	Y	26180 FQ	36750 MW	48950 TQ	USBLS	5/15
	Minnesota	Y	33861 FQ	41920 MW	60016 TQ	MNBLS	1/16-3/16
	Minneapolis-St. Paul-Bloomington MSA, MN-WI	Y	34113 FQ	42728 MW	60733 TQ	MNBLS	1/16-3/16
	Mississippi	Y	23900 FQ	35600 MW	50520 TQ	USBLS	5/15
	Jackson MSA, MS	Y	35750 FQ	51280 MW	59970 TQ	USBLS	5/15
	Missouri	Y	30500 FQ	41820 MW	52770 TQ	USBLS	5/15
	Kansas City MSA, MO-KS	Y	27970 FQ	39840 MW	55110 TQ	USBLS	5/15
	St. Louis MSA, MO-IL	Y	26570 FQ	37710 MW	49960 TQ	USBLS	5/15
	Montana	Y	28200 FQ	34820 MW	44690 TQ	USBLS	5/15
	Billings MSA, MT	Y	25310 FQ	39690 MW	53240 TQ	USBLS	5/15
	Nebraska	Y	26895 FQ	44520 MW	62950 TQ	NEBLS	7/16-9/16
	Omaha-Council Bluffs MSA, NE-IA	Y	23860 FQ	32455 MW	55010 TQ	NEBLS	7/16-9/16
	Nevada	Y	38610 FQ	47500 MW	59810 TQ	USBLS	5/15
	Las Vegas-Henderson-Paradise MSA, NV	Y	39920 FQ	48040 MW	60230 TQ	USBLS	5/15
	New Hampshire	H	15.61 AE	20.29 MW	24.44 AEX	NHBLS	6/16
	Manchester NECTA, NH	H	15.72 AE	23.42 MW	27.79 AEX	NHBLS	6/16
	Nashua NECTA, NH-MA	Y	34320 FQ	39760 MW	48830 TQ	USBLS	5/15
	New Jersey	Y	43520 FQ	56730 MW	69390 TQ	USBLS	5/15
	Camden PMSA, NJ	Y	38050 FQ	58100 MW	73230 TQ	USBLS	5/15
	Newark PMSA, NJ-PA	Y	51660 FQ	58430 MW	67230 TQ	USBLS	5/15
	Trenton MSA, NJ	Y	34240 FQ	39660 MW	58600 TQ	USBLS	5/15
	New Mexico	Y	27260 FQ	36260 MW	48890 TQ	USBLS	5/15
	Albuquerque MSA, NM	Y	26580 FQ	34600 MW	44120 TQ	USBLS	5/15
	New York	Y	23310 AE	42930 MW	59800 AEX	NYBLS	1/16-3/16
	Buffalo-Cheektowaga-Niagara Falls MSA, NY	Y	26170 FQ	31140 MW	45670 TQ	USBLS	5/15
	Nassau County-Suffolk County PMSA, NY	Y	32120 FQ	50920 MW	73320 TQ	USBLS	5/15
	New York-Jersey City-White Plains PMSA, NY-NJ	Y	26910 FQ	45000 MW	63500 TQ	USBLS	5/15
	Rochester MSA, NY	Y	28170 FQ	35500 MW	48960 TQ	USBLS	5/15
	North Carolina	Y	35810 FQ	45210 MW	57620 TQ	USBLS	5/15
	Charlotte-Concord-Gastonia MSA, NC-SC	Y	38580 FQ	47780 MW	61900 TQ	USBLS	5/15
	Raleigh MSA, NC	Y	37500 FQ	44680 MW	54730 TQ	USBLS	5/15
	North Dakota	Y	31930 FQ	40040 MW	50270 TQ	USBLS	5/15
	Fargo MSA, ND-MN	Y	32490 FQ	36530 MW	43630 TQ	USBLS	5/15
	Ohio	Y	33790 FQ	40120 MW	49850 TQ	USBLS	5/15
	Cincinnati MSA, OH-KY-IN	Y	35960 FQ	44090 MW	56330 TQ	USBLS	5/15
	Cleveland-Elyria MSA, OH	Y	34890 FQ	41030 MW	48810 TQ	USBLS	5/15
	Columbus MSA, OH	Y	34120 FQ	39250 MW	49340 TQ	USBLS	5/15
	Oklahoma	Y	23720 FQ	32220 MW	49880 TQ	USBLS	5/15
	Oklahoma City MSA, OK	Y	33610 FQ	45730 MW	56170 TQ	USBLS	5/15
	Tulsa MSA, OK	Y	24520 FQ	30650 MW	48610 TQ	USBLS	5/15
	Oregon	H	15.86 FQ	20.50 MW	26.82 TQ	ORBLS	2016
	Portland-Vancouver-Hillsboro MSA, OR-WA	Y	34900 FQ	45870 MW	58570 TQ	USBLS	5/15
	Pennsylvania	Y	34830 FQ	44240 MW	58010 TQ	USBLS	5/15
	Allentown-Bethlehem-Easton MSA, PA-NJ	Y	29950 FQ	45500 MW	67830 TQ	USBLS	5/15
	Harrisburg-Carlisle MSA, PA	Y	33740 FQ	39190 MW	49600 TQ	USBLS	5/15
	Montgomery County-Bucks County-Chester County PMSA, PA	Y	35970 FQ	51090 MW	61880 TQ	USBLS	5/15
	Philadelphia PMSA, PA	Y	42630 FQ	54640 MW	67840 TQ	USBLS	5/15
	Pittsburgh MSA, PA	Y	34970 FQ	40950 MW	47540 TQ	USBLS	5/15
	Rhode Island	Y	39310 FQ	52950 MW	63670 TQ	USBLS	5/15
	Providence-Warwick MSA, RI-MA	Y	39980 FQ	53470 MW	63680 TQ	USBLS	5/15
	South Carolina	Y	23900 FQ	31410 MW	44520 TQ	USBLS	5/15
	Charleston-North Charleston MSA, SC	Y	21450 FQ	26100 MW	37750 TQ	USBLS	5/15
	Columbia MSA, SC	Y	28320 FQ	34510 MW	40010 TQ	USBLS	5/15

AE	Average entry wage	AWR	Average wage range	H	Hourly	LR	Low end range	MTC	Median total compensation	TCC	Total cash compensation
AEX	Average experienced wage	B	Biweekly	HI	Highest wage paid	M	Monthly	MW	Median wage paid	TQ	Third quartile wage
ATC	Average total compensation	D	Daily	HR	High end range	MCC	Median cash compensation	MWR	Median wage range	W	Weekly
AW	Average wage paid	FQ	First quartile wage	LO	Lowest wage paid	ME	Median entry wage	S	See annotated source	Y	Yearly

Occupation/Type/Industry	Location	Per	Low	Mid	High	Source	Date
Chef and Head Cook	Greenville-Anderson-Mauldin						
	MSA, SC	Y	28080 FQ	35000 MW	47400 TQ	USBLS	5/15
	South Dakota	Y	32560 FQ	37950 MW	46540 TQ	USBLS	5/15
	Tennessee	Y	20470 FQ	24540 MW	38340 TQ	USBLS	5/15
	Knoxville MSA, TN	Y	18900 FQ	22400 MW	28410 TQ	USBLS	5/15
	Memphis MSA, TN-MS-AR	Y	19530 FQ	23670 MW	38770 TQ	USBLS	5/15
	Nashville-Davidson–						
	Murfreesboro–Franklin						
	MSA, TN	Y	24770 FQ	37620 MW	47640 TQ	USBLS	5/15
	Texas	Y	29960 FQ	38550 MW	53800 TQ	USBLS	5/15
	Austin-Round Rock MSA, TX	Y	31570 FQ	35940 MW	42290 TQ	USBLS	5/15
	Dallas-Plano-Irving PMSA, TX	Y	34680 FQ	46810 MW	62730 TQ	USBLS	5/15
	Fort Worth-Arlington PMSA,						
	TX	Y	27700 FQ	30790 MW	44210 TQ	USBLS	5/15
	Houston-The Woodlands-						
	Sugar Land MSA, TX	Y	32370 FQ	40080 MW	56080 TQ	USBLS	5/15
	San Antonio-New Braunfels						
	MSA, TX	Y	32140 FQ	46840 MW	57950 TQ	USBLS	5/15
	Utah	Y	28990 FQ	36120 MW	46180 TQ	USBLS	5/15
	Ogden-Clearfield MSA, UT	Y	26680 FQ	30770 MW	35980 TQ	USBLS	5/15
	Provo-Orem MSA, UT	Y	32420 FQ	37250 MW	51920 TQ	USBLS	5/15
	Salt Lake City MSA, UT	Y	33730 FQ	41470 MW	48150 TQ	USBLS	5/15
	Vermont	Y	35880 FQ	42030 MW	50000 TQ	USBLS	5/15
	Burlington-South Burlington						
	MSA, VT	Y	35610 FQ	41840 MW	56840 TQ	USBLS	5/15
	Virginia	Y	27360 FQ	38480 MW	58640 TQ	USBLS	5/15
	Richmond MSA, VA	Y	32130 FQ	36980 MW	49280 TQ	USBLS	5/15
	Virginia Beach-Norfolk-						
	Newport News MSA, VA-NC	Y	22960 FQ	30000 MW	41300 TQ	USBLS	5/15
	Washington	H	19.09 FQ	23.15 MW	29.18 TQ	WABLS	3/16
	Seattle-Bellevue-Everett						
	PMSA, WA	H	20.46 FQ	24.36 MW	30.41 TQ	WABLS	3/16
	Tacoma-Lakewood PMSA, WA	H	17.53 FQ	21.74 MW	24.72 TQ	WABLS	3/16
	West Virginia	Y	32040 FQ	45370 MW	66280 TQ	USBLS	5/15
	Huntington-Ashland MSA,						
	WV-KY-OH	Y	34540 FQ	41050 MW	68730 TQ	USBLS	5/15
	Wisconsin	Y	26460 FQ	36430 MW	47800 TQ	USBLS	5/15
	Madison MSA, WI	Y	31880 FQ	35820 MW	39920 TQ	USBLS	5/15
	Milwaukee-Waukesha-West						
	Allis MSA, WI	Y	22580 FQ	35580 MW	46060 TQ	USBLS	5/15
	Wyoming	Y	35660 FQ	43060 MW	52750 TQ	USBLS	5/15
	Puerto Rico	Y	23260 FQ	28740 MW	37050 TQ	USBLS	5/15
	San Juan-Carolina-Caguas						
	MSA, PR	Y	24530 FQ	29330 MW	37610 TQ	USBLS	5/15
	Virgin Islands	Y	23560 FQ	29090 MW	38920 TQ	USBLS	5/15
	Guam	Y	18800 FQ	22660 MW	35200 TQ	USBLS	5/15
Chef De Partie							
Cruise Ship	United States	M	3200 LO		4600 HI	CRU04	2016
Chemical Dependency Counselor							
Community Supervision and Corrections Department, County Government	Travis County, TX	Y		42732 MW		TTT	10/13/15
Chemical Engineer	United States	Y		123000 MW		CEN01	3/16-4/16
	Alabama	Y	73850 AE	101902 AW	115928 AEX	ALBLS	6/16
	Birmingham-Hoover MSA, AL	Y	61751 AE	95256 AW	112003 AEX	ALBLS	6/16
	Alaska	Y	84970 FQ	110800 MW	131390 TQ	USBLS	5/15
	Anchorage MSA, AK	Y	82940 FQ	109090 MW	129830 TQ	USBLS	5/15
	Arizona	Y	80910 FQ	100180 MW	120830 TQ	USBLS	5/15
	Phoenix-Mesa-Scottsdale						
	MSA, AZ	Y	83020 FQ	103570 MW	123260 TQ	USBLS	5/15
	Arkansas	Y	74280 FQ	85790 MW	94850 TQ	USBLS	5/15
	Little Rock-North Little Rock-						
	Conway MSA, AR	Y	70330 FQ	88830 MW	102950 TQ	USBLS	5/15
	California	H	38.31 FQ	49.02 MW	64.13 TQ	CABLS	1/16-3/16
	Anaheim-Santa Ana-Irvine						
	PMSA, CA	H	35.11 FQ	45.58 MW	61.18 TQ	CABLS	1/16-3/16
	Los Angeles-Long Beach-						
	Glendale PMSA, CA	H	37.98 FQ	47.18 MW	70.37 TQ	CABLS	1/16-3/16
	Oakland-Hayward-Berkeley						
	PMSA, CA	H	41.62 FQ	50.27 MW	69.54 TQ	CABLS	1/16-3/16

AE	Average entry wage	AWR	Average wage range	H	Hourly	LR	Low end range	MTC	Median total compensation	TCC	Total cash compensation
AEX	Average experienced wage	B	Biweekly	HI	Highest wage paid	M	Monthly	MCC	Median cash compensation	TQ	Third quartile wage
ATC	Average total compensation	D	Daily	HR	High end range	MCC	Median cash compensation	MWR	Median wage range	W	Weekly
AW	Average wage paid	FQ	First quartile wage	LO	Lowest wage paid	ME	Median entry wage	S	See annotated source	Y	Yearly

Occupation/Type/Industry	Location	Per	Low	Mid	High	Source	Date
Chemical Engineer	Riverside-San Bernardino-Ontario MSA, CA	H	39.92 FQ	50.32 MW	72.31 TQ	CABLS	1/16-3/16
	Sacramento–Roseville–Arden-Arcade MSA, CA	H	23.71 FQ	27.43 MW	34.67 TQ	CABLS	1/16-3/16
	San Diego-Carlsbad MSA, CA	H	43.59 FQ	54.21 MW	62.29 TQ	CABLS	1/16-3/16
	San Francisco-Redwood City-South San Francisco PMSA, CA	H	43.08 FQ	61.64 MW	71.83 TQ	CABLS	1/16-3/16
	Colorado	Y	65120 FQ	84190 MW	114460 TQ	USBLS	5/15
	Denver-Aurora-Lakewood MSA, CO	Y	68790 FQ	88630 MW	118700 TQ	USBLS	5/15
	Connecticut	Y		92725 MW		CTBLS	1/16-3/16
	Bridgeport-Stamford-Norwalk MSA, CT	Y	75950 FQ	94450 MW	112400 TQ	USBLS	5/15
	Hartford-West Hartford-East Hartford MSA, CT	Y	74180 FQ	89580 MW	106260 TQ	USBLS	5/15
	Delaware	Y	91270 FQ	120310 MW	151420 TQ	USBLS	5/15
	District of Columbia	Y	97450 FQ	110900 MW	118860 TQ	USBLS	5/15
	Washington-Arlington-Alexandria PMSA, DC-VA-MD-WV	Y	90570 FQ	112170 MW	135010 TQ	USBLS	5/15
	Florida	H	21.44 AE	36.75 MW	60.60 AEX	FLBLS	7/16-9/16
	Tampa-St. Petersburg-Clearwater MSA, FL	H	29.10 AE	45.59 MW	58.85 AEX	FLBLS	7/16-9/16
	Georgia	Y	57040 FQ	82490 MW	114820 TQ	USBLS	5/15
	Atlanta-Sandy Springs-Roswell MSA, GA	Y	52030 FQ	83630 MW	120830 TQ	USBLS	5/15
	Idaho	Y	83740 FQ	106280 MW	138700 TQ	USBLS	5/15
	Illinois	Y	73140 FQ	92030 MW	116990 TQ	USBLS	5/15
	Chicago-Naperville-Arlington Heights PMSA, IL	Y	73920 FQ	92190 MW	116280 TQ	USBLS	5/15
	Indiana	Y	83630 FQ	104760 MW	118330 TQ	USBLS	5/15
	Iowa	Y	67400 FQ	84540 MW	107600 TQ	USBLS	5/15
	Kansas	Y	87990 FQ	106410 MW	119650 TQ	USBLS	5/15
	Kentucky	Y	61090 FQ	83990 MW	107990 TQ	USBLS	5/15
	Louisville-Jefferson County MSA, KY-IN	Y	78610 FQ	89220 MW	102380 TQ	USBLS	5/15
	Louisiana	Y	84590 FQ	108740 MW	137420 TQ	USBLS	5/15
	Baton Rouge MSA, LA	Y	87230 FQ	111320 MW	140360 TQ	USBLS	5/15
	New Orleans-Metairie MSA, LA	Y	81180 FQ	104410 MW	128050 TQ	USBLS	5/15
	Maine	Y	84810 FQ	96640 MW	110570 TQ	USBLS	5/15
	Maryland	Y	79901 AE	107260 MW	120940 AEX	MDBLS	4/16
	Baltimore-Columbia-Towson MSA, MD	Y	93860 FQ	111260 MW	123080 TQ	USBLS	5/15
	Massachusetts	Y	77490 FQ	101500 MW	130280 TQ	USBLS	5/15
	Boston-Cambridge-Newton NECTA, MA	Y	76200 FQ	100950 MW	128190 TQ	USBLS	5/15
	Worcester MSA, MA-CT	Y	81960 FQ	95300 MW	126440 TQ	USBLS	5/15
	Michigan	Y	64050 FQ	81900 MW	103280 TQ	USBLS	5/15
	Detroit-Dearborn-Livonia PMSA, MI	Y	84590 FQ	100580 MW	120610 TQ	USBLS	5/15
	Grand Rapids-Wyoming MSA, MI	Y	34450 FQ	51160 MW	84220 TQ	USBLS	5/15
	Minnesota	Y	64858 FQ	79112 MW	99817 TQ	MNBLS	1/16-3/16
	Minneapolis-St. Paul-Bloomington MSA, MN-WI	Y	64203 FQ	78870 MW	99273 TQ	MNBLS	1/16-3/16
	Mississippi	Y	65320 FQ	81140 MW	101970 TQ	USBLS	5/15
	Missouri	Y	69650 FQ	88760 MW	111050 TQ	USBLS	5/15
	Kansas City MSA, MO-KS	Y	68580 FQ	86860 MW	119700 TQ	USBLS	5/15
	St. Louis MSA, MO-IL	Y	67580 FQ	86300 MW	110240 TQ	USBLS	5/15
	Montana	Y	70350 FQ	89420 MW	113020 TQ	USBLS	5/15
	Nebraska	Y	66720 FQ	74655 MW	91265 TQ	NEBLS	7/16-9/16
	Omaha-Council Bluffs MSA, NE-IA	Y	66485 FQ	73960 MW	88155 TQ	NEBLS	7/16-9/16
	Nevada	Y	76020 FQ	94210 MW	114140 TQ	USBLS	5/15
	New Hampshire	H	38.17 AE	46.07 MW	52.66 AEX	NHBLS	6/16
	Nashua NECTA, NH-MA	Y	86030 FQ	93350 MW	100670 TQ	USBLS	5/15
	New Jersey	Y	75610 FQ	95650 MW	119830 TQ	USBLS	5/15
	Newark PMSA, NJ-PA	Y	80430 FQ	98180 MW	122330 TQ	USBLS	5/15
	Trenton MSA, NJ	Y	78210 FQ	99720 MW	121480 TQ	USBLS	5/15
	New Mexico	Y	98840 FQ	116160 MW	136470 TQ	USBLS	5/15

AE	Average entry wage	**AWR**	Average wage range	**H**	Hourly	**LR**	Low end range	**MTC** Median total compensation **TCC** Total cash compensation
AEX	Average experienced wage	**B**	Biweekly	**HI**	Highest wage paid	**M**	Monthly	**MW** Median wage paid **TQ** Third quartile wage
ATC	Average total compensation	**D**	Daily	**HR**	High end range	**MCC**	Median cash compensation	**MWR** Median wage range **W** Weekly
AW	Average wage paid	**FQ**	First quartile wage	**LO**	Lowest wage paid	**ME**	Median entry wage	**S** See annotated source **Y** Yearly

Occupation/Type/Industry	Location	Per	Low	Mid	High	Source	Date
Chemical Engineer	Albuquerque MSA, NM	Y	101660 FQ	119850 MW	141330 TQ	USBLS	5/15
	New York	Y	61770 AE	92310 MW	112510 AEX	NYBLS	1/16-3/16
	Buffalo-Cheektowaga-Niagara Falls MSA, NY	Y	65300 FQ	81920 MW	110610 TQ	USBLS	5/15
	Nassau County-Suffolk County PMSA, NY	Y	74690 FQ	95310 MW	115210 TQ	USBLS	5/15
	New York-Jersey City-White Plains PMSA, NY-NJ	Y	61910 FQ	89170 MW	113390 TQ	USBLS	5/15
	Rochester MSA, NY	Y	70150 FQ	89470 MW	111330 TQ	USBLS	5/15
	North Carolina	Y	69650 FQ	83800 MW	100820 TQ	USBLS	5/15
	Charlotte-Concord-Gastonia MSA, NC-SC	Y	71370 FQ	89500 MW	106230 TQ	USBLS	5/15
	Raleigh MSA, NC	Y	67920 FQ	84490 MW	105270 TQ	USBLS	5/15
	Ohio	Y	68560 FQ	86110 MW	107490 TQ	USBLS	5/15
	Cincinnati MSA, OH-KY-IN	Y	62710 FQ	81970 MW	105830 TQ	USBLS	5/15
	Cleveland-Elyria MSA, OH	Y	74900 FQ	93010 MW	113870 TQ	USBLS	5/15
	Columbus MSA, OH	Y	69950 FQ	80150 MW	98450 TQ	USBLS	5/15
	Oklahoma	Y	69490 FQ	86250 MW	113290 TQ	USBLS	5/15
	Oklahoma City MSA, OK	Y	74870 FQ	89630 MW	106310 TQ	USBLS	5/15
	Tulsa MSA, OK	Y	69350 FQ	82970 MW	110700 TQ	USBLS	5/15
	Oregon	H	33.86 FQ	43.66 MW	53.17 TQ	ORBLS	2016
	Portland-Vancouver-Hillsboro MSA, OR-WA	Y	71100 FQ	95090 MW	117230 TQ	USBLS	5/15
	Pennsylvania	Y	73590 FQ	94580 MW	120450 TQ	USBLS	5/15
	Allentown-Bethlehem-Easton MSA, PA-NJ	Y	86760 FQ	109470 MW	136140 TQ	USBLS	5/15
	Montgomery County-Bucks County-Chester County PMSA, PA	Y	63960 FQ	83070 MW	101020 TQ	USBLS	5/15
	Philadelphia PMSA, PA	Y	82510 FQ	106640 MW	134990 TQ	USBLS	5/15
	Pittsburgh MSA, PA	Y	80070 FQ	96860 MW	119630 TQ	USBLS	5/15
	Providence-Warwick MSA, RI-MA	Y	79300 FQ	98870 MW	115700 TQ	USBLS	5/15
	South Carolina	Y	70470 FQ	87600 MW	110040 TQ	USBLS	5/15
	Greenville-Anderson-Mauldin MSA, SC	Y	69340 FQ	82010 MW	100050 TQ	USBLS	5/15
	Tennessee	Y	76480 FQ	89750 MW	112080 TQ	USBLS	5/15
	Knoxville MSA, TN	Y	72910 FQ	89420 MW	118470 TQ	USBLS	5/15
	Memphis MSA, TN-MS-AR	Y	76010 FQ	107690 MW	144620 TQ	USBLS	5/15
	Nashville-Davidson–Murfreesboro–Franklin MSA, TN	Y	70480 FQ	82590 MW	95030 TQ	USBLS	5/15
	Texas	Y	85380 FQ	113620 MW	149230 TQ	USBLS	5/15
	Austin-Round Rock MSA, TX	Y	68960 FQ	89140 MW	118520 TQ	USBLS	5/15
	Dallas-Plano-Irving PMSA, TX	Y	79860 FQ	102360 MW	144920 TQ	USBLS	5/15
	Fort Worth-Arlington PMSA, TX	Y	91330 FQ	116610 MW	150640 TQ	USBLS	5/15
	Houston-The Woodlands-Sugar Land MSA, TX	Y	86260 FQ	116200 MW	153120 TQ	USBLS	5/15
	San Antonio-New Braunfels MSA, TX	Y	83770 FQ	96100 MW	149200 TQ	USBLS	5/15
	Utah	Y	71590 FQ	83240 MW	95930 TQ	USBLS	5/15
	Ogden-Clearfield MSA, UT	Y	67260 FQ	86580 MW	105710 TQ	USBLS	5/15
	Provo-Orem MSA, UT	Y	71860 FQ	82460 MW	93680 TQ	USBLS	5/15
	Salt Lake City MSA, UT	Y	72980 FQ	88610 MW	103890 TQ	USBLS	5/15
	Virginia	Y	74260 FQ	99840 MW	121690 TQ	USBLS	5/15
	Richmond MSA, VA	Y	63760 FQ	83980 MW	112910 TQ	USBLS	5/15
	Washington	H	37.69 FQ	48.49 MW	59.33 TQ	WABLS	3/16
	Seattle-Bellevue-Everett PMSA, WA	H	27.91 FQ	41.23 MW	54.52 TQ	WABLS	3/16
	Tacoma-Lakewood PMSA, WA	H	45.44 FQ	54.33 MW	60.69 TQ	WABLS	3/16
	West Virginia	Y	72840 FQ	98320 MW	123890 TQ	USBLS	5/15
	Wisconsin	Y	68040 FQ	82330 MW	107800 TQ	USBLS	5/15
	Madison MSA, WI	Y	65350 FQ	87000 MW	115150 TQ	USBLS	5/15
	Milwaukee-Waukesha-West Allis MSA, WI	Y	73800 FQ	90790 MW	112070 TQ	USBLS	5/15
	Wyoming	Y	65020 FQ	91900 MW	114060 TQ	USBLS	5/15
	Puerto Rico	Y	38220 FQ	49270 MW	78520 TQ	USBLS	5/15
	San Juan-Carolina-Caguas MSA, PR	Y	37150 FQ	53050 MW	80030 TQ	USBLS	5/15

AE	Average entry wage	AWR	Average wage range	H	Hourly	LR	Low end range	MTC Median total compensation	TCC Total cash compensation
AEX	Average experienced wage	B	Biweekly	HI	Highest wage paid	M	Monthly	MW Median wage paid	TQ Third quartile wage
ATC	Average total compensation	D	Daily	HR	High end range	MCC Median cash compensation	MWR Median wage range	W Weekly
AW	Average wage paid	FQ	First quartile wage	LO	Lowest wage paid	ME Median entry wage	S See annotated source	Y Yearly

Occupation/Type/Industry	Location	Per	Low	Mid	High	Source	Date
Chemical Equipment Operator and Tender	Alabama	Y	32564 AE	53591 AW	64109 AEX	ALBLS	6/16
	Birmingham-Hoover MSA, AL	Y	32358 AE	50218 AW	59153 AEX	ALBLS	6/16
	Arizona	Y	24890 FQ	41090 MW	51490 TQ	USBLS	5/15
	Phoenix-Mesa-Scottsdale MSA, AZ	Y	24350 FQ	40630 MW	51260 TQ	USBLS	5/15
	Arkansas	Y	39700 FQ	46840 MW	55890 TQ	USBLS	5/15
	Little Rock-North Little Rock-Conway MSA, AR	Y	33380 FQ	37120 MW	44190 TQ	USBLS	5/15
	California	H	13.97 FQ	18.80 MW	26.36 TQ	CABLS	1/16-3/16
	Anaheim-Santa Ana-Irvine PMSA, CA	H	14.04 FQ	19.50 MW	27.37 TQ	CABLS	1/16-3/16
	Los Angeles-Long Beach-Glendale PMSA, CA	H	12.69 FQ	15.14 MW	21.15 TQ	CABLS	1/16-3/16
	Oakland-Hayward-Berkeley PMSA, CA	H	16.63 FQ	21.80 MW	29.19 TQ	CABLS	1/16-3/16
	Riverside-San Bernardino-Ontario MSA, CA	H	13.22 FQ	17.71 MW	21.84 TQ	CABLS	1/16-3/16
	Sacramento–Roseville–Arden-Arcade MSA, CA	H	21.87 FQ	32.10 MW	36.79 TQ	CABLS	1/16-3/16
	San Francisco-Redwood City-South San Francisco PMSA, CA	H	19.31 FQ	23.21 MW	33.03 TQ	CABLS	1/16-3/16
	Colorado	Y	28630 FQ	37500 MW	53630 TQ	USBLS	5/15
	Denver-Aurora-Lakewood MSA, CO	Y	26870 FQ	33240 MW	41620 TQ	USBLS	5/15
	Connecticut	Y		36961 MW		CTBLS	1/16-3/16
	Bridgeport-Stamford-Norwalk MSA, CT	Y	20730 FQ	26920 MW	41560 TQ	USBLS	5/15
	Hartford-West Hartford-East Hartford MSA, CT	Y	30960 FQ	37610 MW	46710 TQ	USBLS	5/15
	Delaware	Y	40780 FQ	52940 MW	64310 TQ	USBLS	5/15
	Wilmington PMSA, DE-MD-NJ	Y	41250 FQ	54040 MW	63770 TQ	USBLS	5/15
	Washington-Arlington-Alexandria PMSA, DC-VA-MD-WV	Y	27330 FQ	32240 MW	41350 TQ	USBLS	5/15
	Florida	H	14.97 AE	19.31 MW	22.98 AEX	FLBLS	7/16-9/16
	Fort Lauderdale-Pompano Beach-Deerfield Beach PMSA, FL	H	12.95 AE	16.86 MW	18.58 AEX	FLBLS	7/16-9/16
	Miami-Miami Beach-Kendall PMSA, FL	H	15.01 AE	18.62 MW	23.05 AEX	FLBLS	7/16-9/16
	Orlando-Kissimmee-Sanford MSA, FL	H	16.12 AE	21.20 MW	22.94 AEX	FLBLS	7/16-9/16
	Tampa-St. Petersburg-Clearwater MSA, FL	H	13.97 AE	18.24 MW	20.65 AEX	FLBLS	7/16-9/16
	Georgia	Y	34940 FQ	43150 MW	53290 TQ	USBLS	5/15
	Atlanta-Sandy Springs-Roswell MSA, GA	Y	35640 FQ	43680 MW	50070 TQ	USBLS	5/15
	Augusta-Richmond County MSA, GA-SC	Y	56610 FQ	67070 MW	73290 TQ	USBLS	5/15
	Illinois	Y	34430 FQ	44820 MW	58020 TQ	USBLS	5/15
	Chicago-Naperville-Arlington Heights PMSA, IL	Y	33190 FQ	41040 MW	55150 TQ	USBLS	5/15
	Lake County-Kenosha County PMSA, IL-WI	Y	31200 FQ	36800 MW	46620 TQ	USBLS	5/15
	Indiana	Y	42110 FQ	56840 MW	70160 TQ	USBLS	5/15
	Gary PMSA, IN	Y	39900 FQ	48240 MW	61310 TQ	USBLS	5/15
	Indianapolis-Carmel-Anderson MSA, IN	Y	40600 FQ	51930 MW	68100 TQ	USBLS	5/15
	Iowa	Y	33940 FQ	42130 MW	50590 TQ	USBLS	5/15
	Kansas	Y	35010 FQ	44970 MW	63930 TQ	USBLS	5/15
	Kentucky	Y	36250 FQ	50060 MW	62600 TQ	USBLS	5/15
	Louisville-Jefferson County MSA, KY-IN	Y	35790 FQ	46520 MW	60380 TQ	USBLS	5/15
	Louisiana	Y	44670 FQ	60240 MW	76530 TQ	USBLS	5/15
	Baton Rouge MSA, LA	Y	52020 FQ	67890 MW	81330 TQ	USBLS	5/15
	New Orleans-Metairie MSA, LA	Y	37050 FQ	51090 MW	77370 TQ	USBLS	5/15
	Maine	Y	37360 FQ	43310 MW	49400 TQ	USBLS	5/15
	Maryland	Y	26590 AE	41913 MW	49575 AEX	MDBLS	4/16

AE	Average entry wage	AWR	Average wage range	H	Hourly	LR	Low end range	MTC	Median total compensation	TCC	Total cash compensation
AEX	Average experienced wage	B	Biweekly	HI	Highest wage paid	M	Monthly	MCC	Median cash compensation	TQ	Third quartile wage
ATC	Average total compensation	D	Daily	HR	High end range	MCC	Median cash compensation	MWR	Median wage range	W	Weekly
AW	Average wage paid	FQ	First quartile wage	LO	Lowest wage paid	ME	Median entry wage	S	See annotated source	Y	Yearly

Occupation/Type/Industry	Location	Per	Low	Mid	High	Source	Date
Chemical Equipment Operator and Tender							
	Baltimore-Columbia-Towson MSA, MD	Y	33770 FQ	42460 MW	50510 TQ	USBLS	5/15
	Salisbury MSA, MD-DE	Y	29680 FQ	37980 MW	47740 TQ	USBLS	5/15
	Massachusetts	Y	40210 FQ	48000 MW	60240 TQ	USBLS	5/15
	Boston-Cambridge-Newton NECTA, MA	Y	42770 FQ	49560 MW	61630 TQ	USBLS	5/15
	Michigan	Y	34650 FQ	43890 MW	52260 TQ	USBLS	5/15
	Detroit-Dearborn-Livonia PMSA, MI	Y	41950 FQ	51910 MW	66650 TQ	USBLS	5/15
	Grand Rapids-Wyoming MSA, MI	Y	42440 FQ	46560 MW	50770 TQ	USBLS	5/15
	Minnesota	Y	34859 FQ	42624 MW	55796 TQ	MNBLS	1/16-3/16
	Minneapolis-St. Paul-Bloomington MSA, MN-WI	Y	35142 FQ	44193 MW	56515 TQ	MNBLS	1/16-3/16
	Mississippi	Y	43450 FQ	54230 MW	59780 TQ	USBLS	5/15
	Missouri	Y	32210 FQ	40190 MW	49440 TQ	USBLS	5/15
	Kansas City MSA, MO-KS	Y	31930 FQ	37310 MW	45760 TQ	USBLS	5/15
	St. Louis MSA, MO-IL	Y	34070 FQ	44970 MW	55840 TQ	USBLS	5/15
	Nebraska	Y	32210 FQ	37845 MW	48425 TQ	NEBLS	7/16-9/16
	Omaha-Council Bluffs MSA, NE-IA	Y	29675 FQ	41385 MW	52765 TQ	NEBLS	7/16-9/16
	Nevada	Y	37190 FQ	49940 MW	58660 TQ	USBLS	5/15
	New Hampshire	H	14.46 AE	19.58 MW	22.51 AEX	NHBLS	6/16
	New Jersey	Y	35960 FQ	46120 MW	58380 TQ	USBLS	5/15
	Camden PMSA, NJ	Y	35150 FQ	46300 MW	60400 TQ	USBLS	5/15
	Newark PMSA, NJ-PA	Y	39560 FQ	49460 MW	67310 TQ	USBLS	5/15
	Trenton MSA, NJ	Y	36000 FQ	42520 MW	49580 TQ	USBLS	5/15
	New Mexico	Y	32690 FQ	38680 MW	48250 TQ	USBLS	5/15
	New York	Y	32090 AE	45750 MW	53150 AEX	NYBLS	1/16-3/16
	Buffalo-Cheektowaga-Niagara Falls MSA, NY	Y	42510 FQ	52220 MW	58130 TQ	USBLS	5/15
	Nassau County-Suffolk County PMSA, NY	Y	36960 FQ	51780 MW	60030 TQ	USBLS	5/15
	New York-Jersey City-White Plains PMSA, NY-NJ	Y	31860 FQ	38750 MW	50130 TQ	USBLS	5/15
	Rochester MSA, NY	Y	33340 FQ	39700 MW	48950 TQ	USBLS	5/15
	North Carolina	Y	35860 FQ	44760 MW	53600 TQ	USBLS	5/15
	Charlotte-Concord-Gastonia MSA, NC-SC	Y	38240 FQ	45860 MW	53730 TQ	USBLS	5/15
	Ohio	Y	33770 FQ	44850 MW	58130 TQ	USBLS	5/15
	Cincinnati MSA, OH-KY-IN	Y	37160 FQ	46500 MW	57300 TQ	USBLS	5/15
	Cleveland-Elyria MSA, OH	Y	29320 FQ	42430 MW	55110 TQ	USBLS	5/15
	Columbus MSA, OH	Y	43780 FQ	52610 MW	58780 TQ	USBLS	5/15
	Oklahoma	Y	39100 FQ	45810 MW	57280 TQ	USBLS	5/15
	Oklahoma City MSA, OK	Y	33650 FQ	40100 MW	46790 TQ	USBLS	5/15
	Tulsa MSA, OK	Y	44010 FQ	51430 MW	68410 TQ	USBLS	5/15
	Oregon	H	18.44 FQ	24.42 MW	28.97 TQ	ORBLS	2016
	Portland-Vancouver-Hillsboro MSA, OR-WA	Y	27120 FQ	30140 MW	40220 TQ	USBLS	5/15
	Pennsylvania	Y	33440 FQ	43650 MW	55580 TQ	USBLS	5/15
	Allentown-Bethlehem-Easton MSA, PA-NJ	Y	32990 FQ	41810 MW	52310 TQ	USBLS	5/15
	Montgomery County-Bucks County-Chester County PMSA, PA	Y	32200 FQ	41960 MW	55030 TQ	USBLS	5/15
	Philadelphia PMSA, PA	Y	34870 FQ	46570 MW	59850 TQ	USBLS	5/15
	Pittsburgh MSA, PA	Y	39860 FQ	49630 MW	62630 TQ	USBLS	5/15
	Rhode Island	Y	30730 FQ	35050 MW	38970 TQ	USBLS	5/15
	Providence-Warwick MSA, RI-MA	Y	30730 FQ	35050 MW	38970 TQ	USBLS	5/15
	South Carolina	Y	35260 FQ	44330 MW	55400 TQ	USBLS	5/15
	Charleston-North Charleston MSA, SC	Y	43200 FQ	49120 MW	57420 TQ	USBLS	5/15
	Columbia MSA, SC	Y	37560 FQ	47090 MW	59920 TQ	USBLS	5/15
	Greenville-Anderson-Mauldin MSA, SC	Y	30780 FQ	38620 MW	46400 TQ	USBLS	5/15
	South Dakota	Y	32130 FQ	36020 MW	40450 TQ	USBLS	5/15
	Sioux Falls MSA, SD	Y	32090 FQ	34850 MW	37620 TQ	USBLS	5/15
	Tennessee	Y	34650 FQ	43690 MW	55850 TQ	USBLS	5/15
	Memphis MSA, TN-MS-AR	Y	28290 FQ	36630 MW	47010 TQ	USBLS	5/15

Occupation/Type/Industry	Location	Per	Low	Mid	High	Source	Date
Chemical Equipment Operator and Tender	Nashville-Davidson– Murfreesboro–Franklin						
	MSA, TN	Y	36700 FQ	42950 MW	47640 TQ	USBLS	5/15
	Texas	Y	42590 FQ	62250 MW	77720 TQ	USBLS	5/15
	Austin-Round Rock MSA, TX	Y	35670 FQ	47420 MW	62610 TQ	USBLS	5/15
	Fort Worth-Arlington PMSA, TX	Y	27220 FQ	37010 MW	48950 TQ	USBLS	5/15
	Houston-The Woodlands- Sugar Land MSA, TX	Y	50960 FQ	66670 MW	82330 TQ	USBLS	5/15
	San Antonio-New Braunfels MSA, TX	Y	29330 FQ	37840 MW	61460 TQ	USBLS	5/15
	Utah	Y	31080 FQ	41110 MW	50030 TQ	USBLS	5/15
	Ogden-Clearfield MSA, UT	Y	42020 FQ	48470 MW	56380 TQ	USBLS	5/15
	Salt Lake City MSA, UT	Y	29180 FQ	35620 MW	43350 TQ	USBLS	5/15
	Virginia	Y	36600 FQ	54450 MW	70530 TQ	USBLS	5/15
	Richmond MSA, VA	Y	50670 FQ	63140 MW	73400 TQ	USBLS	5/15
	Washington	H	15.06 FQ	24.14 MW	32.89 TQ	WABLS	3/16
	Seattle-Bellevue-Everett PMSA, WA	H	19.95 FQ	24.42 MW	29.46 TQ	WABLS	3/16
	West Virginia	Y	41450 FQ	56710 MW	67610 TQ	USBLS	5/15
	Huntington-Ashland MSA, WV-KY-OH	Y	32300 FQ	41800 MW	55840 TQ	USBLS	5/15
	Wisconsin	Y	35080 FQ	43030 MW	55710 TQ	USBLS	5/15
	Madison MSA, WI	Y	33260 FQ	36770 MW	42400 TQ	USBLS	5/15
	Milwaukee-Waukesha-West Allis MSA, WI	Y	34980 FQ	43970 MW	56630 TQ	USBLS	5/15
	Wyoming	Y	59090 FQ	74150 MW	88380 TQ	USBLS	5/15
	Puerto Rico	Y	26460 FQ	30810 MW	39900 TQ	USBLS	5/15
	San Juan-Carolina-Caguas MSA, PR	Y	27770 FQ	33830 MW	42260 TQ	USBLS	5/15
Chemical Plant and System Operator	Alabama	Y	53560 AE	64212 AW	69528 AEX	ALBLS	6/16
	Arizona	Y	37380 FQ	44320 MW	51330 TQ	USBLS	5/15
	Phoenix-Mesa-Scottsdale MSA, AZ	Y	38950 FQ	45000 MW	51000 TQ	USBLS	5/15
	Arkansas	Y	47750 FQ	54710 MW	60380 TQ	USBLS	5/15
	California	H	20.41 FQ	26.35 MW	31.04 TQ	CABLS	1/16-3/16
	Los Angeles-Long Beach- Glendale PMSA, CA	H	24.40 FQ	27.75 MW	31.36 TQ	CABLS	1/16-3/16
	Oakland-Hayward-Berkeley PMSA, CA	H	18.72 FQ	22.84 MW	27.09 TQ	CABLS	1/16-3/16
	Riverside-San Bernardino- Ontario MSA, CA	H	25.75 FQ	29.16 MW	33.83 TQ	CABLS	1/16-3/16
	San Diego-Carlsbad MSA, CA	H	22.50 FQ	26.53 MW	30.27 TQ	CABLS	1/16-3/16
	Colorado	Y	29880 FQ	45110 MW	59470 TQ	USBLS	5/15
	Connecticut	Y		63644 MW		CTBLS	1/16-3/16
	Delaware	Y	58940 FQ	67710 MW	74370 TQ	USBLS	5/15
	Wilmington PMSA, DE-MD-NJ	Y	56220 FQ	66580 MW	73770 TQ	USBLS	5/15
	Florida	H	23.26 AE	27.59 MW	29.52 AEX	FLBLS	7/16-9/16
	Georgia	Y	43470 FQ	52440 MW	67460 TQ	USBLS	5/15
	Atlanta-Sandy Springs- Roswell MSA, GA	Y	44350 FQ	56580 MW	72590 TQ	USBLS	5/15
	Idaho	Y	49120 FQ	56150 MW	61510 TQ	USBLS	5/15
	Illinois	Y	43860 FQ	55980 MW	67660 TQ	USBLS	5/15
	Chicago-Naperville-Arlington Heights PMSA, IL	Y	32330 FQ	54710 MW	67960 TQ	USBLS	5/15
	Lake County-Kenosha County PMSA, IL-WI	Y	44420 FQ	56500 MW	69970 TQ	USBLS	5/15
	Indiana	Y	42510 FQ	59310 MW	71590 TQ	USBLS	5/15
	Gary PMSA, IN	Y	60070 FQ	69300 MW	75960 TQ	USBLS	5/15
	Indianapolis-Carmel-Anderson MSA, IN	Y	37260 FQ	51600 MW	64090 TQ	USBLS	5/15
	Iowa	Y	41900 FQ	58670 MW	70570 TQ	USBLS	5/15
	Kansas	Y	44210 FQ	56480 MW	70280 TQ	USBLS	5/15
	Kentucky	Y	52820 FQ	66280 MW	74080 TQ	USBLS	5/15
	Louisiana	Y	64260 FQ	71610 MW	78940 TQ	USBLS	5/15
	Baton Rouge MSA, LA	Y	65260 FQ	72310 MW	79400 TQ	USBLS	5/15

AE	Average entry wage	AWR	Average wage range	H	Hourly	LR	Low end range	MTC	Median total compensation	TCC	Total cash compensation
AEX	Average experienced wage	B	Biweekly	HI	Highest wage paid	M	Monthly	MW	Median wage paid	TQ	Third quartile wage
ATC	Average total compensation	D	Daily	HR	High end range	MCC	Median cash compensation	MWR	Median wage range	W	Weekly
AW	Average wage paid	FQ	First quartile wage	LO	Lowest wage paid	ME	Median entry wage	S	See annotated source	Y	Yearly

Chemical Plant and System Operator

Occupation/Type/Industry	Location	Per	Low	Mid	High	Source	Date
Chemical Plant and System Operator	New Orleans-Metairie MSA, LA	Y	66050 FQ	72600 MW	80000 TQ	USBLS	5/15
	Maryland	Y	43950 AE	58749 MW	66148 AEX	MDBLS	4/16
	Baltimore-Columbia-Towson MSA, MD	Y	50260 FQ	61690 MW	71080 TQ	USBLS	5/15
	Massachusetts	Y	50030 FQ	58050 MW	68070 TQ	USBLS	5/15
	Boston-Cambridge-Newton NECTA, MA	Y	56260 FQ	64550 MW	73250 TQ	USBLS	5/15
	Michigan	Y	46040 FQ	55530 MW	62730 TQ	USBLS	5/15
	Detroit-Dearborn-Livonia PMSA, MI	Y	48520 FQ	63350 MW	74320 TQ	USBLS	5/15
	Grand Rapids-Wyoming MSA, MI	Y	45050 FQ	54420 MW	60460 TQ	USBLS	5/15
	Minnesota	Y	37440 FQ	46765 MW	59866 TQ	MNBLS	1/16-3/16
	Minneapolis-St. Paul-Bloomington MSA, MN-WI	Y	37582 FQ	45672 MW	60484 TQ	MNBLS	1/16-3/16
	Mississippi	Y	53010 FQ	60220 MW	68780 TQ	USBLS	5/15
	Missouri	Y	41860 FQ	58340 MW	71690 TQ	USBLS	5/15
	Kansas City MSA, MO-KS	Y	58330 FQ	67470 MW	76590 TQ	USBLS	5/15
	St. Louis MSA, MO-IL	Y	43410 FQ	57640 MW	71350 TQ	USBLS	5/15
	Nebraska	Y	52585 FQ	63175 MW	80670 TQ	NEBLS	7/16-9/16
	Omaha-Council Bluffs MSA, NE-IA	Y	53890 FQ	66640 MW	82875 TQ	NEBLS	7/16-9/16
	New Jersey	Y	41710 FQ	50830 MW	66060 TQ	USBLS	5/15
	Newark PMSA, NJ-PA	Y	37760 FQ	46870 MW	62070 TQ	USBLS	5/15
	New York	Y	39480 AE	53300 MW	61340 AEX	NYBLS	1/16-3/16
	Buffalo-Cheektowaga-Niagara Falls MSA, NY	Y	45700 FQ	55200 MW	61600 TQ	USBLS	5/15
	New York-Jersey City-White Plains PMSA, NY-NJ	Y	42610 FQ	48630 MW	59980 TQ	USBLS	5/15
	Rochester MSA, NY	Y	30100 FQ	34840 MW	39350 TQ	USBLS	5/15
	North Carolina	Y	40140 FQ	52240 MW	62870 TQ	USBLS	5/15
	Charlotte-Concord-Gastonia MSA, NC-SC	Y	35420 FQ	41420 MW	49200 TQ	USBLS	5/15
	North Dakota	Y	64290 FQ	72810 MW	85490 TQ	USBLS	5/15
	Ohio	Y	38250 FQ	47620 MW	57040 TQ	USBLS	5/15
	Cincinnati MSA, OH-KY-IN	Y	43350 FQ	53060 MW	59760 TQ	USBLS	5/15
	Cleveland-Elyria MSA, OH	Y	30430 FQ	44510 MW	54820 TQ	USBLS	5/15
	Columbus MSA, OH	Y	32930 FQ	45420 MW	53700 TQ	USBLS	5/15
	Oklahoma	Y	46940 FQ	59980 MW	69270 TQ	USBLS	5/15
	Oregon	H	25.88 FQ	32.31 MW	36.32 TQ	ORBLS	2016
	Portland-Vancouver-Hillsboro MSA, OR-WA	Y	53520 FQ	67270 MW	74780 TQ	USBLS	5/15
	Pennsylvania	Y	43470 FQ	55090 MW	63650 TQ	USBLS	5/15
	Allentown-Bethlehem-Easton MSA, PA-NJ	Y	51960 FQ	58900 MW	71140 TQ	USBLS	5/15
	Montgomery County-Bucks County-Chester County PMSA, PA	Y	32670 FQ	41680 MW	54560 TQ	USBLS	5/15
	Philadelphia PMSA, PA	Y	57830 FQ	68750 MW	77290 TQ	USBLS	5/15
	Pittsburgh MSA, PA	Y	51170 FQ	57950 MW	66150 TQ	USBLS	5/15
	Rhode Island	Y	34540 FQ	37310 MW	40050 TQ	USBLS	5/15
	Providence-Warwick MSA, RI-MA	Y	34540 FQ	37310 MW	40050 TQ	USBLS	5/15
	South Carolina	Y	35670 FQ	44190 MW	54160 TQ	USBLS	5/15
	Charleston-North Charleston MSA, SC	Y	48220 FQ	56450 MW	65000 TQ	USBLS	5/15
	Columbia MSA, SC	Y	33670 FQ	43020 MW	51890 TQ	USBLS	5/15
	Greenville-Anderson-Mauldin MSA, SC	Y	47420 FQ	54780 MW	59930 TQ	USBLS	5/15
	South Dakota	Y	39220 FQ	44540 MW	49320 TQ	USBLS	5/15
	Sioux Falls MSA, SD	Y	41410 FQ	45290 MW	49180 TQ	USBLS	5/15
	Tennessee	Y	42980 FQ	50330 MW	57670 TQ	USBLS	5/15
	Memphis MSA, TN-MS-AR	Y	48660 FQ	54500 MW	59750 TQ	USBLS	5/15
	Texas	Y	56720 FQ	70160 MW	80750 TQ	USBLS	5/15
	Houston-The Woodlands-Sugar Land MSA, TX	Y	54870 FQ	69020 MW	79070 TQ	USBLS	5/15
	Utah	Y	52190 FQ	63480 MW	71990 TQ	USBLS	5/15
	Virginia	Y	48150 FQ	58380 MW	68680 TQ	USBLS	5/15
	Richmond MSA, VA	Y	51230 FQ	64760 MW	73000 TQ	USBLS	5/15
	Washington	H	23.60 FQ	32.44 MW	37.43 TQ	WABLS	3/16

AE	Average entry wage	AWR	Average wage range	H	Hourly
AEX	Average experienced wage	B	Biweekly	HI	Highest wage paid
ATC	Average total compensation	D	Daily	HR	High end range
AW	Average wage paid	FQ	First quartile wage	LO	Lowest wage paid

LR	Low end range	MTC	Median total compensation	TCC	Total cash compensation
M	Monthly	MW	Median wage paid	TQ	Third quartile wage
MCC	Median cash compensation	MWR	Median wage range	W	Weekly
ME	Median entry wage	S	See annotated source	Y	Yearly

Occupation/Type/Industry	Location	Per	Low	Mid	High	Source	Date
Chemical Plant and System Operator							
	West Virginia	Y	48630 FQ	61130 MW	73180 TQ	USBLS	5/15
	Wisconsin	Y	50090 FQ	61960 MW	73880 TQ	USBLS	5/15
	Wyoming	Y	66500 FQ	71730 MW	76960 TQ	USBLS	5/15
	Puerto Rico	Y	19630 FQ	28820 MW	39740 TQ	USBLS	5/15
	San Juan-Carolina-Caguas MSA, PR	Y	17920 FQ	22150 MW	29070 TQ	USBLS	5/15
Chemical Safety Officer							
Michigan State University	East Lansing, MI	Y			96372 HI	MSUSAL	10/1/14-9/30/15
Chemical Sprayer							
Public Works Department, Municipal Government	Orange, CA	Y			57086 HI	CACIT	6/28/16
Chemical Technician							
	Alabama	Y	30406 AE	49692 AW	59345 AEX	ALBLS	6/16
	Birmingham-Hoover MSA, AL	Y	29530 AE	48153 AW	57469 AEX	ALBLS	6/16
	Alaska	Y	49520 FQ	59170 MW	72200 TQ	USBLS	5/15
	Arizona	Y	34950 FQ	42800 MW	50590 TQ	USBLS	5/15
	Phoenix-Mesa-Scottsdale MSA, AZ	Y	34790 FQ	42800 MW	50680 TQ	USBLS	5/15
	Tucson MSA, AZ	Y	33010 FQ	38010 MW	46030 TQ	USBLS	5/15
	Arkansas	Y	30980 FQ	37660 MW	45500 TQ	USBLS	5/15
	Little Rock-North Little Rock-Conway MSA, AR	Y	31260 FQ	41580 MW	47100 TQ	USBLS	5/15
	California	H	16.19 FQ	21.48 MW	29.26 TQ	CABLS	1/16-3/16
	Anaheim-Santa Ana-Irvine PMSA, CA	H	15.76 FQ	18.22 MW	25.38 TQ	CABLS	1/16-3/16
	Los Angeles-Long Beach-Glendale PMSA, CA	H	15.80 FQ	19.91 MW	28.58 TQ	CABLS	1/16-3/16
	Oakland-Hayward-Berkeley PMSA, CA	H	18.01 FQ	24.27 MW	32.12 TQ	CABLS	1/16-3/16
	Riverside-San Bernardino-Ontario MSA, CA	H	16.85 FQ	22.08 MW	28.49 TQ	CABLS	1/16-3/16
	Sacramento–Roseville–Arden-Arcade MSA, CA	H	16.31 FQ	20.57 MW	27.10 TQ	CABLS	1/16-3/16
	San Diego-Carlsbad MSA, CA	H	15.68 FQ	23.19 MW	29.24 TQ	CABLS	1/16-3/16
	San Francisco-Redwood City-South San Francisco PMSA, CA	H	18.65 FQ	25.91 MW	39.52 TQ	CABLS	1/16-3/16
	Colorado	Y	32600 FQ	44320 MW	58000 TQ	USBLS	5/15
	Denver-Aurora-Lakewood MSA, CO	Y	30840 FQ	40750 MW	53660 TQ	USBLS	5/15
	Connecticut	Y		48381 MW		CTBLS	1/16-3/16
	Bridgeport-Stamford-Norwalk MSA, CT	Y	43150 FQ	49840 MW	59780 TQ	USBLS	5/15
	Hartford-West Hartford-East Hartford MSA, CT	Y	39030 FQ	46870 MW	57050 TQ	USBLS	5/15
	Delaware	Y	51000 FQ	64960 MW	73420 TQ	USBLS	5/15
	Wilmington PMSA, DE-MD-NJ	Y	47950 FQ	64050 MW	73140 TQ	USBLS	5/15
	Washington-Arlington-Alexandria PMSA, DC-VA-MD-WV	Y	38910 FQ	49720 MW	63300 TQ	USBLS	5/15
	Florida	H	13.81 AE	19.02 MW	24.28 AEX	FLBLS	7/16-9/16
	Fort Lauderdale-Pompano Beach-Deerfield Beach PMSA, FL	H	15.20 AE	19.06 MW	21.81 AEX	FLBLS	7/16-9/16
	Miami-Miami Beach-Kendall PMSA, FL	H	13.99 AE	18.51 MW	22.89 AEX	FLBLS	7/16-9/16
	Orlando-Kissimmee-Sanford MSA, FL	H	12.99 AE	16.66 MW	21.22 AEX	FLBLS	7/16-9/16
	Tampa-St. Petersburg-Clearwater MSA, FL	H	14.43 AE	19.48 MW	24.96 AEX	FLBLS	7/16-9/16
	Georgia	Y	33860 FQ	43290 MW	52090 TQ	USBLS	5/15
	Atlanta-Sandy Springs-Roswell MSA, GA	Y	30920 FQ	38590 MW	48070 TQ	USBLS	5/15
	Augusta-Richmond County MSA, GA-SC	Y	43970 FQ	53990 MW	65280 TQ	USBLS	5/15
	Idaho	Y	27140 FQ	36830 MW	49290 TQ	USBLS	5/15
	Boise City MSA, ID	Y	32300 FQ	42990 MW	54910 TQ	USBLS	5/15
	Illinois	Y	34570 FQ	44980 MW	57810 TQ	USBLS	5/15

AE	Average entry wage	AWR	Average wage range	H	Hourly
AEX	Average experienced wage	B	Biweekly	HI	Highest wage paid
ATC	Average total compensation	D	Daily	HR	High end range
AW	Average wage paid	FQ	First quartile wage	LO	Lowest wage paid

LR	Low end range	MTC	Median total compensation	TCC	Total cash compensation
M	Monthly	MW	Median wage paid	TQ	Third quartile wage
MCC	Median cash compensation	MWR	Median wage range	W	Weekly
ME	Median entry wage	S	See annotated source	Y	Yearly

Occupation/Type/Industry	Location	Per	Low	Mid	High	Source	Date
Chemical Technician	Chicago-Naperville-Arlington Heights PMSA, IL	Y	33940 FQ	43020 MW	54750 TQ	USBLS	5/15
	Lake County-Kenosha County PMSA, IL-WI	Y	43770 FQ	56610 MW	70530 TQ	USBLS	5/15
	Indiana	Y	28630 FQ	37760 MW	49440 TQ	USBLS	5/15
	Gary PMSA, IN	Y	28180 FQ	40110 MW	52910 TQ	USBLS	5/15
	Indianapolis-Carmel-Anderson MSA, IN	Y	28120 FQ	36570 MW	47730 TQ	USBLS	5/15
	Iowa	Y	36160 FQ	43300 MW	51280 TQ	USBLS	5/15
	Des Moines-West Des Moines MSA, IA	Y	36150 FQ	44050 MW	55400 TQ	USBLS	5/15
	Kansas	Y	35230 FQ	43670 MW	54490 TQ	USBLS	5/15
	Wichita MSA, KS	Y	41900 FQ	51270 MW	57930 TQ	USBLS	5/15
	Kentucky	Y	28670 FQ	38920 MW	60050 TQ	USBLS	5/15
	Louisville-Jefferson County MSA, KY-IN	Y	29160 FQ	41510 MW	62340 TQ	USBLS	5/15
	Louisiana	Y	41900 FQ	58660 MW	71910 TQ	USBLS	5/15
	Baton Rouge MSA, LA	Y	53220 FQ	64540 MW	74300 TQ	USBLS	5/15
	New Orleans-Metairie MSA, LA	Y	37630 FQ	51840 MW	66680 TQ	USBLS	5/15
	Maine	Y	28210 FQ	40550 MW	50710 TQ	USBLS	5/15
	Portland-South Portland MSA, ME	Y	23280 FQ	31300 MW	45120 TQ	USBLS	5/15
	Maryland	Y	27710 AE	45825 MW	54883 AEX	MDBLS	4/16
	Baltimore-Columbia-Towson MSA, MD	Y	30310 FQ	42210 MW	52050 TQ	USBLS	5/15
	Massachusetts	Y	42360 FQ	51440 MW	62780 TQ	USBLS	5/15
	Boston-Cambridge-Newton NECTA, MA	Y	44640 FQ	54950 MW	67510 TQ	USBLS	5/15
	Worcester MSA, MA-CT	Y	38540 FQ	46590 MW	56100 TQ	USBLS	5/15
	Michigan	Y	31190 FQ	41510 MW	53450 TQ	USBLS	5/15
	Detroit-Dearborn-Livonia PMSA, MI	Y	32840 FQ	49040 MW	62630 TQ	USBLS	5/15
	Grand Rapids-Wyoming MSA, MI	Y	32270 FQ	38370 MW	46280 TQ	USBLS	5/15
	Minnesota	Y	38608 FQ	49536 MW	63406 TQ	MNBLS	1/16-3/16
	Minneapolis-St. Paul-Bloomington MSA, MN-WI	Y	40100 FQ	51048 MW	64394 TQ	MNBLS	1/16-3/16
	Mississippi	Y	32890 FQ	38910 MW	49030 TQ	USBLS	5/15
	Jackson MSA, MS	Y	24700 FQ	35630 MW	59760 TQ	USBLS	5/15
	Missouri	Y	33780 FQ	39850 MW	55650 TQ	USBLS	5/15
	Kansas City MSA, MO-KS	Y	33620 FQ	38980 MW	47800 TQ	USBLS	5/15
	St. Louis MSA, MO-IL	Y	33080 FQ	39010 MW	52840 TQ	USBLS	5/15
	Montana	Y	39930 FQ	50470 MW	68390 TQ	USBLS	5/15
	Nebraska	Y	37980 FQ	45050 MW	52690 TQ	NEBLS	7/16-9/16
	Omaha-Council Bluffs MSA, NE-IA	Y	40040 FQ	49190 MW	62070 TQ	NEBLS	7/16-9/16
	Nevada	Y	40040 FQ	50730 MW	62050 TQ	USBLS	5/15
	Las Vegas-Henderson-Paradise MSA, NV	Y	44840 FQ	53580 MW	61110 TQ	USBLS	5/15
	New Hampshire	H	14.38 AE	19.34 MW	23.73 AEX	NHBLS	6/16
	Nashua NECTA, NH-MA	Y	28280 FQ	34080 MW	39120 TQ	USBLS	5/15
	New Jersey	Y	39490 FQ	50230 MW	75530 TQ	USBLS	5/15
	Camden PMSA, NJ	Y	32060 FQ	39870 MW	50140 TQ	USBLS	5/15
	Trenton MSA, NJ	Y	43110 FQ	51780 MW	61710 TQ	USBLS	5/15
	New Mexico	Y	33190 FQ	37510 MW	52070 TQ	USBLS	5/15
	Albuquerque MSA, NM	Y	33450 FQ	37030 MW	43130 TQ	USBLS	5/15
	New York	Y	31940 AE	46510 MW	58290 AEX	NYBLS	1/16-3/16
	Buffalo-Cheektowaga-Niagara Falls MSA, NY	Y	34330 FQ	43210 MW	51920 TQ	USBLS	5/15
	Nassau County-Suffolk County PMSA, NY	Y	32320 FQ	44110 MW	58520 TQ	USBLS	5/15
	New York-Jersey City-White Plains PMSA, NY-NJ	Y	38310 FQ	46860 MW	59970 TQ	USBLS	5/15
	Rochester MSA, NY	Y	33890 FQ	44190 MW	59930 TQ	USBLS	5/15
	North Carolina	Y	35840 FQ	44910 MW	55790 TQ	USBLS	5/15
	Charlotte-Concord-Gastonia MSA, NC-SC	Y	31490 FQ	45090 MW	57100 TQ	USBLS	5/15
	North Dakota	Y	54970 FQ	80220 MW	91050 TQ	USBLS	5/15
	Ohio	Y	34370 FQ	42210 MW	53420 TQ	USBLS	5/15
	Cincinnati MSA, OH-KY-IN	Y	34770 FQ	43660 MW	54510 TQ	USBLS	5/15
	Cleveland-Elyria MSA, OH	Y	34720 FQ	40410 MW	50690 TQ	USBLS	5/15

AE	Average entry wage	AWR	Average wage range	H	Hourly	LR	Low end range	MTC	Median total compensation	TCC	Total cash compensation
AEX	Average experienced wage	B	Biweekly	HI	Highest wage paid	M	Monthly	MW	Median wage paid	TQ	Third quartile wage
ATC	Average total compensation	D	Daily	HR	High end range	MCC	Median cash compensation	MWR	Median wage range	W	Weekly
AW	Average wage paid	FQ	First quartile wage	LO	Lowest wage paid	ME	Median entry wage	S	See annotated source	Y	Yearly

Occupation/Type/Industry	Location	Per	Low	Mid	High	Source	Date
Chemical Technician	Columbus MSA, OH	Y	34950 FQ	42910 MW	53610 TQ	USBLS	5/15
	Oklahoma	Y	30100 FQ	37930 MW	48980 TQ	USBLS	5/15
	Oklahoma City MSA, OK	Y	27630 FQ	36070 MW	45750 TQ	USBLS	5/15
	Tulsa MSA, OK	Y	30540 FQ	37870 MW	58460 TQ	USBLS	5/15
	Oregon	H	15.86 FQ	18.33 MW	23.51 TQ	ORBLS	2016
	Portland-Vancouver-Hillsboro MSA, OR-WA	Y	33110 FQ	39480 MW	83820 TQ	USBLS	5/15
	Pennsylvania	Y	33010 FQ	43880 MW	56350 TQ	USBLS	5/15
	Allentown-Bethlehem-Easton MSA, PA-NJ	Y	37340 FQ	47300 MW	65010 TQ	USBLS	5/15
	Harrisburg-Carlisle MSA, PA	Y	34120 FQ	43810 MW	54960 TQ	USBLS	5/15
	Montgomery County-Bucks County-Chester County PMSA, PA	Y	33990 FQ	44310 MW	55770 TQ	USBLS	5/15
	Philadelphia PMSA, PA	Y	34270 FQ	44520 MW	55910 TQ	USBLS	5/15
	Pittsburgh MSA, PA	Y	34580 FQ	45160 MW	57920 TQ	USBLS	5/15
	Rhode Island	Y	37620 FQ	44020 MW	50420 TQ	USBLS	5/15
	Providence-Warwick MSA, RI-MA	Y	37950 FQ	44420 MW	51300 TQ	USBLS	5/15
	South Carolina	Y	33080 FQ	41500 MW	53970 TQ	USBLS	5/15
	Charleston-North Charleston MSA, SC	Y	34040 FQ	38900 MW	49210 TQ	USBLS	5/15
	Columbia MSA, SC	Y	33840 FQ	39600 MW	52670 TQ	USBLS	5/15
	Greenville-Anderson-Mauldin MSA, SC	Y	32290 FQ	42120 MW	54120 TQ	USBLS	5/15
	South Dakota	Y	30030 FQ	34390 MW	38590 TQ	USBLS	5/15
	Sioux Falls MSA, SD	Y	32250 FQ	35600 MW	38960 TQ	USBLS	5/15
	Tennessee	Y	34150 FQ	43940 MW	57740 TQ	USBLS	5/15
	Knoxville MSA, TN	Y	31440 FQ	42070 MW	59090 TQ	USBLS	5/15
	Memphis MSA, TN-MS-AR	Y	32770 FQ	43620 MW	54630 TQ	USBLS	5/15
	Nashville-Davidson–Murfreesboro–Franklin MSA, TN	Y	32010 FQ	36180 MW	42930 TQ	USBLS	5/15
	Texas	Y	33780 FQ	45890 MW	64700 TQ	USBLS	5/15
	Austin-Round Rock MSA, TX	Y	28600 FQ	33130 MW	40330 TQ	USBLS	5/15
	Dallas-Plano-Irving PMSA, TX	Y	30040 FQ	39850 MW	57110 TQ	USBLS	5/15
	Fort Worth-Arlington PMSA, TX	Y	33340 FQ	39150 MW	53520 TQ	USBLS	5/15
	Houston-The Woodlands-Sugar Land MSA, TX	Y	37730 FQ	51770 MW	71920 TQ	USBLS	5/15
	San Antonio-New Braunfels MSA, TX	Y	28280 FQ	36690 MW	47010 TQ	USBLS	5/15
	Utah	Y	31510 FQ	38440 MW	47130 TQ	USBLS	5/15
	Ogden-Clearfield MSA, UT	Y	35100 FQ	43190 MW	49350 TQ	USBLS	5/15
	Provo-Orem MSA, UT	Y	30220 FQ	39540 MW	46440 TQ	USBLS	5/15
	Salt Lake City MSA, UT	Y	31280 FQ	36840 MW	44780 TQ	USBLS	5/15
	Vermont	Y	37580 FQ	47870 MW	58500 TQ	USBLS	5/15
	Virginia	Y	34850 FQ	43890 MW	55990 TQ	USBLS	5/15
	Richmond MSA, VA	Y	34840 FQ	43670 MW	54070 TQ	USBLS	5/15
	Virginia Beach-Norfolk-Newport News MSA, VA-NC	Y	36750 FQ	45570 MW	57050 TQ	USBLS	5/15
	Washington	H	17.57 FQ	22.52 MW	32.56 TQ	WABLS	3/16
	Seattle-Bellevue-Everett PMSA, WA	H	18.61 FQ	21.48 MW	23.84 TQ	WABLS	3/16
	Tacoma-Lakewood PMSA, WA	H	14.33 FQ	21.06 MW	26.39 TQ	WABLS	3/16
	West Virginia	Y	27450 FQ	44340 MW	58800 TQ	USBLS	5/15
	Huntington-Ashland MSA, WV-KY-OH	Y	26190 FQ	29780 MW	38290 TQ	USBLS	5/15
	Wisconsin	Y	32610 FQ	39940 MW	52280 TQ	USBLS	5/15
	Madison MSA, WI	Y	34300 FQ	41590 MW	48550 TQ	USBLS	5/15
	Milwaukee-Waukesha-West Allis MSA, WI	Y	35680 FQ	43550 MW	55570 TQ	USBLS	5/15
	Wyoming	Y	32290 FQ	43750 MW	65590 TQ	USBLS	5/15
	Puerto Rico	Y	23380 FQ	32050 MW	40650 TQ	USBLS	5/15
	San Juan-Carolina-Caguas MSA, PR	Y	23710 FQ	32910 MW	42450 TQ	USBLS	5/15
Chemist	United States	Y		97630 MW		CEN01	3/16-4/16
	Alabama	Y	50579 AE	79966 AW	94665 AEX	ALBLS	6/16
	Birmingham-Hoover MSA, AL	Y	41650 AE	61791 AW	71852 AEX	ALBLS	6/16
	Alaska	Y	69720 FQ	81640 MW	103340 TQ	USBLS	5/15
	Anchorage MSA, AK	Y	73580 FQ	83740 MW	102170 TQ	USBLS	5/15

AE	Average entry wage	AWR	Average wage range	H	Hourly
AEX	Average experienced wage	B	Biweekly	HI	Highest wage paid
ATC	Average total compensation	D	Daily	HR	High end range
AW	Average wage paid	FQ	First quartile wage	LO	Lowest wage paid

LR	Low end range	MTC	Median total compensation
M	Monthly	MW	Median wage paid
MCC	Median cash compensation	MWR	Median wage range
ME	Median entry wage	S	See annotated source

TCC	Total cash compensation
TQ	Third quartile wage
W	Weekly
Y	Yearly

Occupation/Type/Industry	Location	Per	Low	Mid	High	Source	Date
Chemist	Arizona	Y	57510 FQ	73250 MW	96890 TQ	USBLS	5/15
	Phoenix-Mesa-Scottsdale MSA, AZ	Y	62450 FQ	75850 MW	101000 TQ	USBLS	5/15
	Tucson MSA, AZ	Y	49050 FQ	59880 MW	76240 TQ	USBLS	5/15
	Arkansas	Y	53550 FQ	65910 MW	90900 TQ	USBLS	5/15
	Little Rock-North Little Rock-Conway MSA, AR	Y	41370 FQ	54420 MW	62160 TQ	USBLS	.5/15
	California	H	27.21 FQ	37.41 MW	50.91 TQ	CABLS	1/16-3/16
	Anaheim-Santa Ana-Irvine PMSA, CA	H	26.05 FQ	37.43 MW	48.82 TQ	CABLS	1/16-3/16
	Los Angeles-Long Beach-Glendale PMSA, CA	H	24.37 FQ	31.40 MW	44.85 TQ	CABLS	1/16-3/16
	Oakland-Hayward-Berkeley PMSA, CA	H	32.75 FQ	43.78 MW	58.02 TQ	CABLS	1/16-3/16
	Riverside-San Bernardino-Ontario MSA, CA	H	21.06 FQ	30.77 MW	39.45 TQ	CABLS	1/16-3/16
	Sacramento–Roseville–Arden-Arcade MSA, CA	H	26.58 FQ	33.69 MW	45.59 TQ	CABLS	1/16-3/16
	San Diego-Carlsbad MSA, CA	H	27.57 FQ	35.04 MW	48.22 TQ	CABLS	1/16-3/16
	San Francisco-Redwood City-South San Francisco PMSA, CA	H	36.02 FQ	46.20 MW	63.97 TQ	CABLS	1/16-3/16
	Colorado	Y	52370 FQ	75060 MW	106740 TQ	USBLS	5/15
	Denver-Aurora-Lakewood MSA, CO	Y	54050 FQ	80290 MW	109840 TQ	USBLS	5/15
	Connecticut	Y		79506 MW		CTBLS	1/16-3/16
	Bridgeport-Stamford-Norwalk MSA, CT	Y	64640 FQ	80600 MW	97300 TQ	USBLS	5/15
	Hartford-West Hartford-East Hartford MSA, CT	Y	47050 FQ	57810 MW	77720 TQ	USBLS	5/15
	District of Columbia	Y	99920 FQ	118070 MW	139520 TQ	USBLS	5/15
	Washington-Arlington-Alexandria PMSA, DC-VA-MD-WV	Y	91410 FQ	118050 MW	139530 TQ	USBLS	5/15
	Florida	H	19.78 AE	29.28 MW	38.34 AEX	FLBLS	7/16-9/16
	Fort Lauderdale-Pompano Beach-Deerfield Beach PMSA, FL	H	22.87 AE	30.59 MW	36.09 AEX	FLBLS	7/16-9/16
	Miami-Miami Beach-Kendall PMSA, FL	H	18.83 AE	35.62 MW	42.97 AEX	FLBLS	7/16-9/16
	Orlando-Kissimmee-Sanford MSA, FL	H	19.80 AE	26.59 MW	34.51 AEX	FLBLS	7/16-9/16
	Tampa-St. Petersburg-Clearwater MSA, FL	H	21.62 AE	28.84 MW	36.96 AEX	FLBLS	7/16-9/16
	Georgia	Y	52950 FQ	75470 MW	98850 TQ	USBLS	5/15
	Atlanta-Sandy Springs-Roswell MSA, GA	Y	50880 FQ	74390 MW	97460 TQ	USBLS	5/15
	Augusta-Richmond County MSA, GA-SC	Y	55520 FQ	82840 MW	94940 TQ	USBLS	5/15
	Hawaii	Y	50180 FQ	60680 MW	75370 TQ	USBLS	5/15
	Urban Honolulu MSA, HI	Y	49780 FQ	60020 MW	74340 TQ	USBLS	5/15
	Idaho	Y	51740 FQ	74870 MW	103280 TQ	USBLS	5/15
	Illinois	Y	52170 FQ	75000 MW	102970 TQ	USBLS	5/15
	Chicago-Naperville-Arlington Heights PMSA, IL	Y	50820 FQ	71320 MW	100000 TQ	USBLS	5/15
	Indiana	Y	44860 FQ	57780 MW	82380 TQ	USBLS	5/15
	Gary PMSA, IN	Y	43930 FQ	57580 MW	75670 TQ	USBLS	5/15
	Indianapolis-Carmel-Anderson MSA, IN	Y	44090 FQ	52520 MW	69390 TQ	USBLS	5/15
	Iowa	Y	51580 FQ	64970 MW	80910 TQ	USBLS	5/15
	Des Moines-West Des Moines MSA, IA	Y	52540 FQ	59530 MW	67080 TQ	USBLS	5/15
	Kansas	Y	51550 FQ	67800 MW	87190 TQ	USBLS	5/15
	Wichita MSA, KS	Y	62440 FQ	77280 MW	96680 TQ	USBLS	5/15
	Kentucky	Y	46000 FQ	61980 MW	81530 TQ	USBLS	5/15
	Louisville-Jefferson County MSA, KY-IN	Y	50940 FQ	64270 MW	85070 TQ	USBLS	5/15
	Louisiana	Y	52890 FQ	70990 MW	91000 TQ	USBLS	5/15
	Baton Rouge MSA, LA	Y	53320 FQ	71400 MW	90890 TQ	USBLS	5/15
	New Orleans-Metairie MSA, LA	Y	52320 FQ	72080 MW	93700 TQ	USBLS	5/15
	Maine	Y	51380 FQ	57760 MW	68900 TQ	USBLS	5/15

AE	Average entry wage	AWR	Average wage range	H	Hourly
AEX	Average experienced wage	B	Biweekly	HI	Highest wage paid
ATC	Average total compensation	D	Daily	HR	High end range
AW	Average wage paid	FQ	First quartile wage	LO	Lowest wage paid

LR	Low end range	MTC	Median total compensation	TCC	Total cash compensation
M	Monthly	MW	Median wage paid	TQ	Third quartile wage
MCC	Median cash compensation	MWR	Median wage range	W	Weekly
ME	Median entry wage	S	See annotated source	Y	Yearly

Chemist

Occupation/Type/Industry	Location	Per	Low	Mid	High	Source	Date
Chemist	Portland-South Portland MSA, ME	Y	51960 FQ	59480 MW	73430 TQ	USBLS	5/15
	Maryland	Y	67410 AE	106701 MW	126346 AEX	MDBLS	4/16
	Baltimore-Columbia-Towson MSA, MD	Y	65560 FQ	86220 MW	112270 TQ	USBLS	5/15
	Salisbury MSA, MD-DE	Y	46620 FQ	62750 MW	78160 TQ	USBLS	5/15
	Massachusetts	Y	52530 FQ	72590 MW	99770 TQ	USBLS	5/15
	Boston-Cambridge-Newton NECTA, MA	Y	50220 FQ	73370 MW	104490 TQ	USBLS	5/15
	Worcester MSA, MA-CT	Y	44830 FQ	63150 MW	86880 TQ	USBLS	5/15
	Michigan	Y	52540 FQ	69710 MW	92970 TQ	USBLS	5/15
	Detroit-Dearborn-Livonia PMSA, MI	Y	49070 FQ	65810 MW	94970 TQ	USBLS	5/15
	Grand Rapids-Wyoming MSA, MI	Y	47940 FQ	66410 MW	79800 TQ	USBLS	5/15
	Minnesota	Y	58356 FQ	74989 MW	98497 TQ	MNBLS	1/16-3/16
	Minneapolis-St. Paul-Bloomington MSA, MN-WI	Y	59626 FQ	76945 MW	101702 TQ	MNBLS	1/16-3/16
	Mississippi	Y	32990 FQ	55500 MW	74960 TQ	USBLS	5/15
	Missouri	Y	49640 FQ	63180 MW	81890 TQ	USBLS	5/15
	Kansas City MSA, MO-KS	Y	50200 FQ	64860 MW	81900 TQ	USBLS	5/15
	St. Louis MSA, MO-IL	Y	50530 FQ	63660 MW	80410 TQ	USBLS	5/15
	Montana	Y	43480 FQ	51000 MW	72770 TQ	USBLS	5/15
	Nebraska	Y	43795 FQ	56180 MW	76005 TQ	NEBLS	7/16-9/16
	Omaha-Council Bluffs MSA, NE-IA	Y	43580 FQ	55550 MW	77250 TQ	NEBLS	7/16-9/16
	Nevada	Y	54650 FQ	83580 MW	108510 TQ	USBLS	5/15
	Las Vegas-Henderson-Paradise MSA, NV	Y	58410 FQ	98860 MW	118380 TQ	USBLS	5/15
	New Hampshire	H	16.44 AE	28.32 MW	38.30 AEX	NHBLS	6/16
	New Jersey	Y	60010 FQ	76270 MW	99520 TQ	USBLS	5/15
	Camden PMSA, NJ	Y	60020 FQ	70360 MW	78800 TQ	USBLS	5/15
	Newark PMSA, NJ-PA	Y	63080 FQ	78500 MW	101930 TQ	USBLS	5/15
	Trenton MSA, NJ	Y	77860 FQ	94380 MW	113940 TQ	USBLS	5/15
	New Mexico	Y	47080 FQ	72580 MW	115320 TQ	USBLS	5/15
	Albuquerque MSA, NM	Y	47020 FQ	87610 MW	124640 TQ	USBLS	5/15
	New York	Y	49370 AE	73630 MW	95490 AEX	NYBLS	1/16-3/16
	Buffalo-Cheektowaga-Niagara Falls MSA, NY	Y	42130 FQ	58430 MW	77800 TQ	USBLS	5/15
	Nassau County-Suffolk County PMSA, NY	Y	55270 FQ	72300 MW	98880 TQ	USBLS	5/15
	New York-Jersey City-White Plains PMSA, NY-NJ	Y	58260 FQ	75050 MW	100500 TQ	USBLS	5/15
	Rochester MSA, NY	Y	45450 FQ	55140 MW	67830 TQ	USBLS	5/15
	North Carolina	Y	51960 FQ	67410 MW	89730 TQ	USBLS	5/15
	Charlotte-Concord-Gastonia MSA, NC-SC	Y	57600 FQ	71880 MW	88080 TQ	USBLS	5/15
	Raleigh MSA, NC	Y	51310 FQ	63070 MW	80930 TQ	USBLS	5/15
	North Dakota	Y	51050 FQ	62930 MW	83670 TQ	USBLS	5/15
	Fargo MSA, ND-MN	Y	41860 FQ	56480 MW	86370 TQ	USBLS	5/15
	Ohio	Y	49710 FQ	67890 MW	89830 TQ	USBLS	5/15
	Cincinnati MSA, OH-KY-IN	Y	40010 FQ	64100 MW	91950 TQ	USBLS	5/15
	Cleveland-Elyria MSA, OH	Y	52630 FQ	69050 MW	88940 TQ	USBLS	5/15
	Columbus MSA, OH	Y	55490 FQ	73550 MW	94700 TQ	USBLS	5/15
	Oklahoma	Y	46960 FQ	63750 MW	87910 TQ	USBLS	5/15
	Oklahoma City MSA, OK	Y	47180 FQ	61590 MW	83190 TQ	USBLS	5/15
	Tulsa MSA, OK	Y	41220 FQ	53850 MW	77370 TQ	USBLS	5/15
	Oregon	H	24.63 FQ	30.35 MW	39.35 TQ	ORBLS	2016
	Portland-Vancouver-Hillsboro MSA, OR-WA	Y	52620 FQ	62280 MW	77820 TQ	USBLS	5/15
	Pennsylvania	Y	48550 FQ	65370 MW	89880 TQ	USBLS	5/15
	Allentown-Bethlehem-Easton MSA, PA-NJ	Y	63430 FQ	84750 MW	109480 TQ	USBLS	5/15
	Harrisburg-Carlisle MSA, PA	Y	44490 FQ	57310 MW	74720 TQ	USBLS	5/15
	Montgomery County-Bucks County-Chester County PMSA, PA	Y	51960 FQ	69740 MW	93340 TQ	USBLS	5/15
	Philadelphia PMSA, PA	Y	59830 FQ	82720 MW	109000 TQ	USBLS	5/15
	Pittsburgh MSA, PA	Y	43740 FQ	61750 MW	82960 TQ	USBLS	5/15
	Rhode Island	Y	60370 FQ	79670 MW	97740 TQ	USBLS	5/15
	Providence-Warwick MSA, RI-MA	Y	61810 FQ	81130 MW	100990 TQ	USBLS	5/15

AE	Average entry wage	AWR	Average wage range	H	Hourly
AEX	Average experienced wage	B	Biweekly	HI	Highest wage paid
ATC	Average total compensation	D	Daily	HR	High end range
AW	Average wage paid	FQ	First quartile wage	LO	Lowest wage paid

LR	Low end range	MTC	Median total compensation	TCC	Total cash compensation
M	Monthly	MW	Median wage paid	TQ	Third quartile wage
MCC	Median cash compensation	MWR	Median wage range	W	Weekly
ME	Median entry wage	S	See annotated source	Y	Yearly

Occupation/Type/Industry	Location	Per	Low	Mid	High	Source	Date
Chemist	South Carolina	Y	50290 FQ	70300 MW	92360 TQ	USBLS	5/15
	Charleston-North Charleston MSA, SC	Y	63610 FQ	81950 MW	105380 TQ	USBLS	5/15
	Columbia MSA, SC	Y	44620 FQ	57150 MW	78100 TQ	USBLS	5/15
	Greenville-Anderson-Mauldin MSA, SC	Y	45320 FQ	69520 MW	89560 TQ	USBLS	5/15
	South Dakota	Y	44350 FQ	50900 MW	62350 TQ	USBLS	5/15
	Tennessee	Y	43360 FQ	60200 MW	95680 TQ	USBLS	5/15
	Knoxville MSA, TN	Y	50270 FQ	75310 MW	105380 TQ	USBLS	5/15
	Memphis MSA, TN-MS-AR	Y	41540 FQ	53270 MW	83230 TQ	USBLS	5/15
	Nashville-Davidson– Murfreesboro–Franklin MSA, TN	Y	33620 FQ	43840 MW	61190 TQ	USBLS	5/15
	Texas	Y	45990 FQ	61390 MW	91580 TQ	USBLS	5/15
	Austin-Round Rock MSA, TX	Y	40460 FQ	52200 MW	67690 TQ	USBLS	5/15
	Dallas-Plano-Irving PMSA, TX	Y	46670 FQ	61920 MW	95050 TQ	USBLS	5/15
	Fort Worth-Arlington PMSA, TX	Y	58330 FQ	84330 MW	110890 TQ	USBLS	5/15
	Houston-The Woodlands- Sugar Land MSA, TX	Y	47490 FQ	63400 MW	93300 TQ	USBLS	5/15
	San Antonio-New Braunfels MSA, TX	Y	49360 FQ	67160 MW	92450 TQ	USBLS	5/15
	Utah	Y	50500 FQ	61830 MW	84230 TQ	USBLS	5/15
	Ogden-Clearfield MSA, UT	Y	52140 FQ	61740 MW	90690 TQ	USBLS	5/15
	Provo-Orem MSA, UT	Y	50400 FQ	62810 MW	85520 TQ	USBLS	5/15
	Salt Lake City MSA, UT	Y	50530 FQ	61300 MW	81770 TQ	USBLS	5/15
	Vermont	Y	50900 FQ	58340 MW	68880 TQ	USBLS	5/15
	Burlington-South Burlington MSA, VT	Y	48810 FQ	56480 MW	63940 TQ	USBLS	5/15
	Virginia	Y	57890 FQ	81270 MW	118060 TQ	USBLS	5/15
	Richmond MSA, VA	Y	47530 FQ	64520 MW	98980 TQ	USBLS	5/15
	Virginia Beach-Norfolk- Newport News MSA, VA-NC	Y	59790 FQ	72530 MW	91240 TQ	USBLS	5/15
	Washington	H	25.15 FQ	35.78 MW	48.60 TQ	WABLS	3/16
	Seattle-Bellevue-Everett PMSA, WA	H	23.19 FQ	30.99 MW	46.30 TQ	WABLS	3/16
	Tacoma-Lakewood PMSA, WA	H	22.94 FQ	31.38 MW	37.79 TQ	WABLS	3/16
	West Virginia	Y	42000 FQ	69390 MW	95890 TQ	USBLS	5/15
	Wisconsin	Y	49040 FQ	61390 MW	79890 TQ	USBLS	5/15
	Madison MSA, WI	Y	46500 FQ	59280 MW	81320 TQ	USBLS	5/15
	Milwaukee-Waukesha-West Allis MSA, WI	Y	50560 FQ	62040 MW	75470 TQ	USBLS	5/15
	Wyoming	Y	48770 FQ	62300 MW	85910 TQ	USBLS	5/15
	Puerto Rico	Y	38420 FQ	51480 MW	72250 TQ	USBLS	5/15
	San Juan-Carolina-Caguas MSA, PR	Y	39160 FQ	53620 MW	75560 TQ	USBLS	5/15
Department of Agriculture, State Government	Bozeman, MT	H	23.63 LO		30.41 HI	MTGOV	2016
Forensic Laboratory, County Government	Oakland County, MI	B	2507 LO		3263 HI	MIOAK2	10/1/16
Municipal Utilities	Stockton, CA	Y		58879 AW		CACIT	6/28/16
Chemistry Teacher							
Postsecondary	Alabama	Y	49590 AE	79008 AW	93717 AEX	ALBLS	6/16
Postsecondary	Birmingham-Hoover MSA, AL	Y	48775 AE	74207 AW	86918 AEX	ALBLS	6/16
Postsecondary	Arizona	Y	51500 FQ	70750 MW	96570 TQ	USBLS	5/15
Postsecondary	Phoenix-Mesa-Scottsdale MSA, AZ	Y	56320 FQ	73330 MW	97380 TQ	USBLS	5/15
Postsecondary	Arkansas	Y	52680 FQ	61620 MW	94510 TQ	USBLS	5/15
Postsecondary	Little Rock-North Little Rock- Conway MSA, AR	Y	50630 FQ	59300 MW	83400 TQ	USBLS	5/15
Postsecondary	California	Y		121820 AW		CABLS	1/16-3/16
Postsecondary	Anaheim-Santa Ana-Irvine PMSA, CA	Y		116261 AW		CABLS	1/16-3/16
Postsecondary	Los Angeles-Long Beach- Glendale PMSA, CA	Y		120988 AW		CABLS	1/16-3/16
Postsecondary	Riverside-San Bernardino- Ontario MSA, CA	Y		118249 AW		CABLS	1/16-3/16
Postsecondary	Sacramento–Roseville– Arden-Arcade MSA, CA	Y		106948 AW		CABLS	1/16-3/16
Postsecondary	San Diego-Carlsbad MSA, CA	Y		128922 AW		CABLS	1/16-3/16
Postsecondary	Colorado	Y	38670 FQ	62210 MW	93800 TQ	USBLS	5/15

AE Average entry wage	**AWR** Average wage range	**H** Hourly	**LR** Low end range	**MTC** Median total compensation	**TCC** Total cash compensation
AEX Average experienced wage	**B** Biweekly	**HI** Highest wage paid	**M** Monthly	**MW** Median wage paid	**TQ** Third quartile wage
ATC Average total compensation	**D** Daily	**HR** High end range	**MCC** Median cash compensation	**MWR** Median wage range	**W** Weekly
AW Average wage paid	**FQ** First quartile wage	**LO** Lowest wage paid	**ME** Median entry wage	**S** See annotated source	**Y** Yearly

Chemistry Teacher

Occupation/Type/Industry	Location	Per	Low	Mid	High	Source	Date
Chemistry Teacher							
Postsecondary	Denver-Aurora-Lakewood MSA, CO	Y	36270 FQ	56250 MW	82160 TQ	USBLS	5/15
Postsecondary	Connecticut	Y		80439 MW		CTBLS	1/16-3/16
Postsecondary	Bridgeport-Stamford-Norwalk MSA, CT	Y	68060 FQ	84460 MW	117500 TQ	USBLS	5/15
Postsecondary	Hartford-West Hartford-East Hartford MSA, CT	Y	65340 FQ	77700 MW	110450 TQ	USBLS	5/15
Postsecondary	Delaware	Y	60420 FQ	72240 MW	88670 TQ	USBLS	5/15
Postsecondary	Wilmington PMSA, DE-MD-NJ	Y	61490 FQ	72890 MW	90420 TQ	USBLS	5/15
Postsecondary	District of Columbia	Y	66240 FQ	90890 MW	133510 TQ	USBLS	5/15
Postsecondary	Washington-Arlington-Alexandria PMSA, DC-VA-MD-WV	Y	55170 FQ	68880 MW	96960 TQ	USBLS	5/15
Postsecondary	Florida	Y	48407 AE	78077 MW	101576 AEX	FLBLS	7/16-9/16
Postsecondary	Fort Lauderdale-Pompano Beach-Deerfield Beach PMSA, FL	Y	54053 AE	69455 MW	75569 AEX	FLBLS	7/16-9/16
Postsecondary	Miami-Miami Beach-Kendall PMSA, FL	Y	60298 AE	91813 MW	110807 AEX	FLBLS	7/16-9/16
Postsecondary	Orlando-Kissimmee-Sanford MSA, FL	Y	58249 AE	87540 MW	107451 AEX	FLBLS	7/16-9/16
Postsecondary	Tampa-St. Petersburg-Clearwater MSA, FL	Y	47108 AE	77173 MW	95431 AEX	FLBLS	7/16-9/16
Postsecondary	Georgia	Y	46770 FQ	60880 MW	79580 TQ	USBLS	5/15
Postsecondary	Atlanta-Sandy Springs-Roswell MSA, GA	Y	43470 FQ	58340 MW	77500 TQ	USBLS	5/15
Postsecondary	Hawaii	Y	53950 FQ	72170 MW	96030 TQ	USBLS	5/15
Postsecondary	Urban Honolulu MSA, HI	Y	53980 FQ	74390 MW	103330 TQ	USBLS	5/15
Postsecondary	Idaho	Y	39820 FQ	53970 MW	71820 TQ	USBLS	5/15
Postsecondary	Boise City MSA, ID	Y	19360 FQ	45760 MW	63190 TQ	USBLS	5/15
Postsecondary	Illinois	Y	59440 FQ	81710 MW	110640 TQ	USBLS	5/15
Postsecondary	Chicago-Naperville-Arlington Heights PMSA, IL	Y	57460 FQ	75400 MW	101750 TQ	USBLS	5/15
Postsecondary	Indiana	Y	58800 FQ	78640 MW	106350 TQ	USBLS	5/15
Postsecondary	Indianapolis-Carmel-Anderson MSA, IN	Y	51690 FQ	68300 MW	91040 TQ	USBLS	5/15
Postsecondary	Iowa	Y	59690 FQ	75580 MW	92620 TQ	USBLS	5/15
Postsecondary	Des Moines-West Des Moines MSA, IA	Y	46400 FQ	60600 MW	76740 TQ	USBLS	5/15
Postsecondary	Kansas	Y	50380 FQ	57820 MW	70380 TQ	USBLS	5/15
Postsecondary	Kentucky	Y	53220 FQ	61480 MW	82700 TQ	USBLS	5/15
Postsecondary	Louisville-Jefferson County MSA, KY-IN	Y	50430 FQ	60600 MW	100310 TQ	USBLS	5/15
Postsecondary	Louisiana	Y	47080 FQ	71050 MW	99990 TQ	USBLS	5/15
Postsecondary	Maine	Y	58710 FQ	73580 MW	94240 TQ	USBLS	5/15
Postsecondary	Maryland	Y	48821 AE	69392 MW	79678 AEX	MDBLS	4/16
Postsecondary	Baltimore-Columbia-Towson MSA, MD	Y	56030 FQ	66670 MW	81070 TQ	USBLS	5/15
Postsecondary	Massachusetts	Y	67250 FQ	92220 MW	133910 TQ	USBLS	5/15
Postsecondary	Boston-Cambridge-Newton NECTA, MA	Y	72570 FQ	104410 MW	150280 TQ	USBLS	5/15
Postsecondary	Worcester MSA, MA-CT	Y	62040 FQ	88330 MW	133430 TQ	USBLS	5/15
Postsecondary	Michigan	Y	57900 FQ	78730 MW	102110 TQ	USBLS	5/15
Postsecondary	Detroit-Dearborn-Livonia PMSA, MI	Y	76730 FQ	88380 MW	98620 TQ	USBLS	5/15
Postsecondary	Minnesota	Y	54203 FQ	69868 MW	98497 TQ	MNBLS	1/16-3/16
Postsecondary	Minneapolis-St. Paul-Bloomington MSA, MN-WI	Y	55271 FQ	73759 MW	113486 TQ	MNBLS	1/16-3/16
Postsecondary	Mississippi	Y	53800 FQ	65280 MW	78650 TQ	USBLS	5/15
Postsecondary	Missouri	Y	58970 FQ	75070 MW	99150 TQ	USBLS	5/15
Postsecondary	Kansas City MSA, MO-KS	Y	58730 FQ	75570 MW	100710 TQ	USBLS	5/15
Postsecondary	St. Louis MSA, MO-IL	Y	63780 FQ	82840 MW	113700 TQ	USBLS	5/15
Postsecondary	Montana	Y	43020 FQ	57380 MW	77680 TQ	USBLS	5/15
Postsecondary	Nebraska	Y	57265 FQ	72305 MW	94475 TQ	NEBLS	7/16-9/16
Postsecondary	Nevada	Y	39080 FQ	70060 MW	94340 TQ	USBLS	5/15
Postsecondary	New Hampshire	Y	55656 AE	83624 MW	112034 AEX	NHBLS	6/16
Postsecondary	New Jersey	Y	59420 FQ	78170 MW	109060 TQ	USBLS	5/15
Postsecondary	Camden PMSA, NJ	Y	55120 FQ	73760 MW	95970 TQ	USBLS	5/15
Postsecondary	Newark PMSA, NJ-PA	Y	63200 FQ	83880 MW	116700 TQ	USBLS	5/15
Postsecondary	New Mexico	Y	48870 FQ	69470 MW	96570 TQ	USBLS	5/15

AE	Average entry wage	AWR	Average wage range	H	Hourly	LR	Low end range	MTC	Median total compensation	TCC	Total cash compensation
AEX	Average experienced wage	B	Biweekly	HI	Highest wage paid	M	Monthly	MW	Median wage paid	TQ	Third quartile wage
ATC	Average total compensation	D	Daily	HR	High end range	MCC	Median cash compensation	MWR	Median wage range	W	Weekly
AW	Average wage paid	FQ	First quartile wage	LO	Lowest wage paid	ME	Median entry wage	S	See annotated source	Y	Yearly

Occupation/Type/Industry	Location	Per	Low	Mid	High	Source	Date
Chemistry Teacher							
Postsecondary	New York	Y	54440 AE	89940 MW	122010 AEX	NYBLS	1/16-3/16
Postsecondary	Buffalo-Cheektowaga-Niagara Falls MSA, NY	Y	65600 FQ	83380 MW	98710 TQ	USBLS	5/15
Postsecondary	Nassau County-Suffolk County PMSA, NY	Y	53040 FQ	70700 MW	102680 TQ	USBLS	5/15
Postsecondary	New York-Jersey City-White Plains PMSA, NY-NJ	Y	71640 FQ	99180 MW	137350 TQ	USBLS	5/15
Postsecondary	Rochester MSA, NY	Y	61600 FQ	83230 MW	116370 TQ	USBLS	5/15
Postsecondary	North Carolina	Y	51840 FQ	64330 MW	84230 TQ	USBLS	5/15
Postsecondary	Charlotte-Concord-Gastonia MSA, NC-SC	Y	51430 FQ	60700 MW	75710 TQ	USBLS	5/15
Postsecondary	Raleigh MSA, NC	Y	55240 FQ	69680 MW	96810 TQ	USBLS	5/15
Postsecondary	North Dakota	Y	65290 FQ	94260 MW	125140 TQ	USBLS	5/15
Postsecondary	Fargo MSA, ND-MN	Y	82940 FQ	96830 MW	122400 TQ	USBLS	5/15
Postsecondary	Ohio	Y	55960 FQ	75000 MW	103210 TQ	USBLS	5/15
Postsecondary	Cincinnati MSA, OH-KY-IN	Y	53500 FQ	71510 MW	96660 TQ	USBLS	5/15
Postsecondary	Cleveland-Elyria MSA, OH	Y	58260 FQ	82310 MW	109550 TQ	USBLS	5/15
Postsecondary	Columbus MSA, OH	Y	63970 FQ	86210 MW	109910 TQ	USBLS	5/15
Postsecondary	Oklahoma	Y	47910 FQ	60370 MW	79380 TQ	USBLS	5/15
Postsecondary	Oklahoma City MSA, OK	Y	43530 FQ	52570 MW	66480 TQ	USBLS	5/15
Postsecondary	Oregon	Y	69418 FQ	86934 MW	105747 TQ	ORBLS	2016
Postsecondary	Portland-Vancouver-Hillsboro MSA, OR-WA	Y	60250 FQ	77450 MW	99110 TQ	USBLS	5/15
Postsecondary	Pennsylvania	Y	59050 FQ	79850 MW	104720 TQ	USBLS	5/15
Postsecondary	Allentown-Bethlehem-Easton MSA, PA-NJ	Y	59820 FQ	87720 MW	117720 TQ	USBLS	5/15
Postsecondary	Harrisburg-Carlisle MSA, PA	Y	56590 FQ	74670 MW	94750 TQ	USBLS	5/15
Postsecondary	Montgomery County-Bucks County-Chester County PMSA, PA	Y	41900 FQ	66810 MW	90730 TQ	USBLS	5/15
Postsecondary	Philadelphia PMSA, PA	Y	69080 FQ	92660 MW	118640 TQ	USBLS	5/15
Postsecondary	Pittsburgh MSA, PA	Y	56600 FQ	74380 MW	98630 TQ	USBLS	5/15
Postsecondary	Rhode Island	Y	59120 FQ	87020 MW	115620 TQ	USBLS	5/15
Postsecondary	Providence-Warwick MSA, RI-MA	Y	59190 FQ	85090 MW	114220 TQ	USBLS	5/15
Postsecondary	South Carolina	Y	53420 FQ	66080 MW	85730 TQ	USBLS	5/15
Postsecondary	Columbia MSA, SC	Y	67080 FQ	87260 MW	112020 TQ	USBLS	5/15
Postsecondary	Greenville-Anderson-Mauldin MSA, SC	Y	53800 FQ	67910 MW	94690 TQ	USBLS	5/15
Postsecondary	South Dakota	Y	54740 FQ	63900 MW	81510 TQ	USBLS	5/15
Postsecondary	Tennessee	Y	47130 FQ	59990 MW	79290 TQ	USBLS	5/15
Postsecondary	Knoxville MSA, TN	Y	37080 FQ	54720 MW	85510 TQ	USBLS	5/15
Postsecondary	Memphis MSA, TN-MS-AR	Y	50160 FQ	60120 MW	77750 TQ	USBLS	5/15
Postsecondary	Nashville-Davidson–Murfreesboro–Franklin MSA, TN	Y	51760 FQ	63310 MW	85220 TQ	USBLS	5/15
Postsecondary	Texas	Y	47170 FQ	68750 MW	96600 TQ	USBLS	5/15
Postsecondary	Austin-Round Rock MSA, TX	Y	52270 FQ	71630 MW	98370 TQ	USBLS	5/15
Postsecondary	Dallas-Plano-Irving PMSA, TX	Y	54510 FQ	73970 MW	100810 TQ	USBLS	5/15
Postsecondary	Fort Worth-Arlington PMSA, TX	Y	27990 FQ	53780 MW	76660 TQ	USBLS	5/15
Postsecondary	Houston-The Woodlands-Sugar Land MSA, TX	Y	43870 FQ	69480 MW	101270 TQ	USBLS	5/15
Postsecondary	San Antonio-New Braunfels MSA, TX	Y	24470 FQ	54200 MW	86360 TQ	USBLS	5/15
Postsecondary	Utah	Y	66160 FQ	88180 MW	115820 TQ	USBLS	5/15
Postsecondary	Salt Lake City MSA, UT	Y	79650 FQ	103560 MW	135620 TQ	USBLS	5/15
Postsecondary	Vermont	Y	67030 FQ	78310 MW	96810 TQ	USBLS	5/15
Postsecondary	Virginia	Y	40340 FQ	58660 MW	80240 TQ	USBLS	5/15
Postsecondary	Richmond MSA, VA	Y	35840 FQ	47920 MW	75110 TQ	USBLS	5/15
Postsecondary	Virginia Beach-Norfolk-Newport News MSA, VA-NC	Y	42390 FQ	58980 MW	78600 TQ	USBLS	5/15
Postsecondary	Washington	Y		67372 AW		WABLS	3/16
Postsecondary	Seattle-Bellevue-Everett PMSA, WA	Y		81312 AW		WABLS	3/16
Postsecondary	Tacoma-Lakewood PMSA, WA	Y		58648 AW		WABLS	3/16
Postsecondary	West Virginia	Y	54880 FQ	71140 MW	94690 TQ	USBLS	5/15
Postsecondary	Wisconsin	Y	48380 FQ	62280 MW	85500 TQ	USBLS	5/15
Postsecondary	Milwaukee-Waukesha-West Allis MSA, WI	Y	48730 FQ	68720 MW	106120 TQ	USBLS	5/15
Postsecondary	Wyoming	Y	65220 FQ	73030 MW	82470 TQ	USBLS	5/15

AE	Average entry wage	AWR	Average wage range	H	Hourly	LR	Low end range	MTC	Median total compensation	TCC	Total cash compensation
AEX	Average experienced wage	B	Biweekly	HI	Highest wage paid	M	Monthly	MW	Median wage paid	TQ	Third quartile wage
ATC	Average total compensation	D	Daily	HR	High end range	MCC	Median cash compensation	MWR	Median wage range	W	Weekly
AW	Average wage paid	FQ	First quartile wage	LO	Lowest wage paid	ME	Median entry wage	S	See annotated source	Y	Yearly

Occupation/Type/Industry	Location	Per	Low	Mid	High	Source	Date
Chemistry Teacher							
Postsecondary	Puerto Rico	Y	51890 FQ	64870 MW	85440 TQ	USBLS	5/15
Postsecondary	San Juan-Carolina-Caguas MSA, PR	Y	51750 FQ	60500 MW	84000 TQ	USBLS	5/15
Chief Academic Affairs Officer/ Provost							
College and University	United States	Y		193136 AW		HED02	2015-2016
Chief Airport Safety Officer							
Municipal Government	Los Angeles, CA	Y			116934 HI	CACIT	6/23/16
Chief Appraiser							
County Government	Columbia County, GA	Y	64998 LO		97497 HI	GACTY04	2016
County Government	Grady County, GA	Y	36500 LO		60000 HI	GACTY04	2016
County Government	Tift County, GA	Y	58731 LO		89367 HI	GACTY04	2016
Chief Athletics Administrator							
College and University	United States	Y		120000 AW		HED02	2015-2016
Chief Campus Marketing Administrator	United States	Y		87662 MW		BMO01	2014-2015
Chief Executive	Alabama	Y	123426 AE	215785 AW	261959 AEX	ALBLS	6/16
	Birmingham-Hoover MSA, AL	Y		251228 AW		ALBLS	6/16
	Alaska	Y	112470 FQ	154110 MW		USBLS	5/15
	Anchorage MSA, AK	Y	114530 FQ	156430 MW		USBLS	5/15
	Arizona	Y	103480 FQ	160550 MW		USBLS	5/15
	Phoenix-Mesa-Scottsdale MSA, AZ	Y	116700 FQ	174290 MW		USBLS	5/15
	Tucson MSA, AZ	Y	80750 FQ	126770 MW		USBLS	5/15
	California	H	62.40 FQ	100.47 AW		CABLS	1/16-3/16
	Anaheim-Santa Ana-Irvine PMSA, CA	H	75.81 FQ	109.26 AW		CABLS	1/16-3/16
	Los Angeles-Long Beach-Glendale PMSA, CA	H	70.69 FQ	106.47 AW		CABLS	1/16-3/16
	Oakland-Hayward-Berkeley PMSA, CA	H	70.50 FQ	106.35 AW		CABLS	1/16-3/16
	Riverside-San Bernardino-Ontario MSA, CA	H	51.07 FQ	86.15 MW		CABLS	1/16-3/16
	Sacramento–Roseville–Arden-Arcade MSA, CA	H	50.24 FQ	61.46 MW	81.64 TQ	CABLS	1/16-3/16
	San Diego-Carlsbad MSA, CA	H	61.37 FQ	101.15 AW		CABLS	1/16-3/16
	San Francisco-Redwood City-South San Francisco PMSA, CA	H	74.42 FQ	111.47 AW		CABLS	1/16-3/16
	Colorado	Y	120830 FQ	199220 AW		USBLS	5/15
	Denver-Aurora-Lakewood MSA, CO	Y	149440 FQ	226930 AW		USBLS	5/15
	Connecticut	Y		232751 AW		CTBLS	1/16-3/16
	Bridgeport-Stamford-Norwalk MSA, CT	Y		244790 AW		USBLS	5/15
	Hartford-West Hartford-East Hartford MSA, CT	Y	157660 FQ	224040 AW		USBLS	5/15
	Wilmington PMSA, DE-MD-NJ	Y		253340 AW		USBLS	5/15
	District of Columbia	Y	137980 FQ	186370 MW		USBLS	5/15
	Washington-Arlington-Alexandria PMSA, DC-VA-MD-WV	Y	147130 FQ	207090 AW		USBLS	5/15
	Florida	H	50.83 AE	100.55 AW	125.41 AEX	FLBLS	7/16-9/16
	Fort Lauderdale-Pompano Beach-Deerfield Beach PMSA, FL	H	54.19 AE	104.20 AW	129.21 AEX	FLBLS	7/16-9/16
	Miami-Miami Beach-Kendall PMSA, FL	H	54.49 AE	105.11 AW	130.43 AEX	FLBLS	7/16-9/16
	Orlando-Kissimmee-Sanford MSA, FL	H	46.76 AE	83.82 MW	113.82 AEX	FLBLS	7/16-9/16
	Tampa-St. Petersburg-Clearwater MSA, FL	H	56.59 AE	103.57 AW	127.05 AEX	FLBLS	7/16-9/16
	Georgia	Y	106750 FQ	181380 MW		USBLS	5/15

AE	Average entry wage	AWR	Average wage range	H	Hourly	LR	Low end range	MTC	Median total compensation	TCC	Total cash compensation
AEX	Average experienced wage	B	Biweekly	HI	Highest wage paid	M	Monthly	MW	Median wage paid	TQ	Third quartile wage
ATC	Average total compensation	D	Daily	HR	High end range	MCC	Median cash compensation	MWR	Median wage range	W	Weekly
AW	Average wage paid	FQ	First quartile wage	LO	Lowest wage paid	ME	Median entry wage	S	See annotated source	Y	Yearly

Occupation/Type/Industry	Location	Per	Low	Mid	High	Source	Date
Chief Executive	Atlanta-Sandy Springs-Roswell MSA, GA	Y	125140 FQ	199950 AW		USBLS	5/15
	Augusta-Richmond County MSA, GA-SC	Y	79330 FQ	139130 MW		USBLS	5/15
	Hawaii	Y	91930 FQ	139200 MW		USBLS	5/15
	Urban Honolulu MSA, HI	Y	97140 FQ	142510 MW		USBLS	5/15
	Idaho	Y	46550 FQ	96990 MW	163330 TQ	USBLS	5/15
	Boise City MSA, ID	Y	70260 FQ	107200 MW	174270 TQ	USBLS	5/15
	Illinois	Y	100890 FQ	161810 MW		USBLS	5/15
	Chicago-Naperville-Arlington Heights PMSA, IL	Y	112690 FQ	181010 MW		USBLS	5/15
	Lake County-Kenosha County PMSA, IL-WI	Y	114010 FQ	191850 AW		USBLS	5/15
	Indiana	Y	92880 FQ	150500 MW		USBLS	5/15
	Gary PMSA, IN	Y	78260 FQ	123390 MW	184430 TQ	USBLS	5/15
	Indianapolis-Carmel-Anderson MSA, IN	Y	112620 FQ	185730 MW		USBLS	5/15
	Iowa	Y	95810 FQ	160930 MW		USBLS	5/15
	Des Moines-West Des Moines MSA, IA	Y	130670 FQ	202740 AW		USBLS	5/15
	Kansas	Y	101610 FQ	143380 MW		USBLS	5/15
	Wichita MSA, KS	Y	100600 FQ	129790 MW		USBLS	5/15
	Kentucky	Y	106660 FQ	145510 MW		USBLS	5/15
	Louisville-Jefferson County MSA, KY-IN	Y	109940 FQ	164440 MW		USBLS	5/15
	Louisiana	Y	103200 FQ	156910 MW		USBLS	5/15
	Baton Rouge MSA, LA	Y	79340 FQ	147290 MW		USBLS	5/15
	New Orleans-Metairie MSA, LA	Y	126330 FQ	159740 MW		USBLS	5/15
	Maine	Y	86160 FQ	129710 MW		USBLS	5/15
	Portland-South Portland MSA, ME	Y	87730 FQ	144230 MW		USBLS	5/15
	Maryland	Y	57263 AE	179115 MW	240041 AEX	MDBLS	4/16
	Baltimore-Columbia-Towson MSA, MD	Y	102960 FQ	182420 MW		USBLS	5/15
	Salisbury MSA, MD-DE	Y	53740 FQ	126780 MW		USBLS	5/15
	Massachusetts	Y	134130 FQ	207510 AW		USBLS	5/15
	Boston-Cambridge-Newton NECTA, MA	Y	151150 FQ	218090 AW		USBLS	5/15
	Worcester MSA, MA-CT	Y	108670 FQ	165630 MW		USBLS	5/15
	Michigan	Y	112520 FQ	164570 MW		USBLS	5/15
	Detroit-Dearborn-Livonia PMSA, MI	Y	136050 FQ	203090 AW		USBLS	5/15
	Grand Rapids-Wyoming MSA, MI	Y	107080 FQ	154800 MW		USBLS	5/15
	Minnesota	Y	116771 FQ	166610 MW		MNBLS	1/16-3/16
	Minneapolis-St. Paul-Bloomington MSA, MN-WI	Y	134949 FQ	188396 MW		MNBLS	1/16-3/16
	Mississippi	Y	53010 FQ	96680 MW	158220 TQ	USBLS	5/15
	Jackson MSA, MS	Y	100620 FQ	134370 MW		USBLS	5/15
	Missouri	Y	76050 FQ	133220 MW		USBLS	5/15
	Kansas City MSA, MO-KS	Y	115040 FQ	170090 MW		USBLS	5/15
	St. Louis MSA, MO-IL	Y	77920 FQ	139380 MW		USBLS	5/15
	Montana	Y	62850 FQ	103730 MW	155170 TQ	USBLS	5/15
	Billings MSA, MT	Y	92670 FQ	121250 MW	165380 TQ	USBLS	5/15
	Nebraska	Y	138735 FQ	193470 MW		NEBLS	7/16-9/16
	Omaha-Council Bluffs MSA, NE-IA	Y	132575 FQ	191770 MW		NEBLS	7/16-9/16
	Nevada	Y	96970 FQ	160930 MW		USBLS	5/15
	Las Vegas-Henderson-Paradise MSA, NV	Y	98390 FQ	170050 MW		USBLS	5/15
	New Hampshire	H	47.70 AE	77.84 MW	112.23 AEX	NHBLS	6/16
	Manchester NECTA, NH	H	39.67 AE	69.22 MW	102.63 AEX	NHBLS	6/16
	Nashua NECTA, NH-MA	Y	142190 FQ	216620 AW		USBLS	5/15
	New Jersey	Y	145320 FQ	217850 AW		USBLS	5/15
	Camden PMSA, NJ	Y	143200 FQ	219360 AW		USBLS	5/15
	Newark PMSA, NJ-PA	Y	164620 FQ	232340 AW		USBLS	5/15
	Trenton MSA, NJ	Y	120500 FQ	140080 MW	162810 TQ	USBLS	5/15
	New York	Y	115890 AE	216890 AW		NYBLS	1/16-3/16
	Buffalo-Cheektowaga-Niagara Falls MSA, NY	Y	112380 FQ	155760 MW		USBLS	5/15

AE	Average entry wage	AWR	Average wage range	H	Hourly	LR	Low end range	MTC	Median total compensation	TCC	Total cash compensation
AEX	Average experienced wage	B	Biweekly	HI	Highest wage paid	M	Monthly	MW	Median wage paid	TQ	Third quartile wage
ATC	Average total compensation	D	Daily	HR	High end range	MCC	Median cash compensation	MWR	Median wage range	W	Weekly
AW	Average wage paid	FQ	First quartile wage	LO	Lowest wage paid	ME	Median entry wage	S	See annotated source	Y	Yearly

Chief Executive

Occupation/Type/Industry	Location	Per	Low	Mid	High	Source	Date
Chief Executive	Nassau County-Suffolk County PMSA, NY	Y	150340 FQ	220160 AW		USBLS	5/15
	New York-Jersey City-White Plains PMSA, NY-NJ	Y	181030 FQ	240470 AW		USBLS	5/15
	Rochester MSA, NY	Y	107000 FQ	144020 MW		USBLS	5/15
	North Carolina	Y	152630 FQ	220460 AW		USBLS	5/15
	Charlotte-Concord-Gastonia MSA, NC-SC	Y	159370 FQ	222910 AW		USBLS	5/15
	Raleigh MSA, NC	Y	155400 FQ	222870 AW		USBLS	5/15
	North Dakota	Y	92770 FQ	135810 MW		USBLS	5/15
	Fargo MSA, ND-MN	Y	110180 FQ	155890 MW		USBLS	5/15
	Ohio	Y	120870 FQ	200680 AW		USBLS	5/15
	Cincinnati MSA, OH-KY-IN	Y	136060 FQ	206400 AW		USBLS	5/15
	Cleveland-Elyria MSA, OH	Y	141890 FQ	211820 AW		USBLS	5/15
	Columbus MSA, OH	Y	134870 FQ	206940 AW		USBLS	5/15
	Oklahoma	Y	82580 FQ	128710 MW		USBLS	5/15
	Oklahoma City MSA, OK	Y	103160 FQ	155240 MW		USBLS	5/15
	Tulsa MSA, OK	Y	78060 FQ	131560 MW		USBLS	5/15
	Oregon	H	49.19 FQ	72.89 MW		ORBLS	2016
	Portland-Vancouver-Hillsboro MSA, OR-WA	Y	116270 FQ	173280 MW		USBLS	5/15
	Pennsylvania	Y	126330 FQ	199920 AW		USBLS	5/15
	Allentown-Bethlehem-Easton MSA, PA-NJ	Y	111360 FQ	168910 MW		USBLS	5/15
	East Stroudsburg MSA, PA	Y	87210 FQ	132680 MW		USBLS	5/15
	Harrisburg-Carlisle MSA, PA	Y	110570 FQ	133310 MW		USBLS	5/15
	Montgomery County-Bucks County-Chester County PMSA, PA	Y	162580 FQ	223620 AW		USBLS	5/15
	Philadelphia PMSA, PA	Y	166160 FQ	224220 AW		USBLS	5/15
	Pittsburgh MSA, PA	Y	126320 FQ	196580 AW		USBLS	5/15
	Rhode Island	Y	146820 FQ	215280 AW		USBLS	5/15
	Providence-Warwick MSA, RI-MA	Y	136690 FQ	202680 AW		USBLS	5/15
	South Carolina	Y	89610 FQ	145290 MW		USBLS	5/15
	Charleston-North Charleston MSA, SC	Y	80750 FQ	146020 MW		USBLS	5/15
	Columbia MSA, SC	Y	107850 FQ	172040 MW		USBLS	5/15
	Greenville-Anderson-Mauldin MSA, SC	Y	107290 FQ	148970 MW		USBLS	5/15
	South Dakota	Y	126220 FQ	203340 AW		USBLS	5/15
	Sioux Falls MSA, SD	Y	169640 FQ	237390 AW		USBLS	5/15
	Tennessee	Y	88300 FQ	143780 MW		USBLS	5/15
	Knoxville MSA, TN	Y	89660 FQ	159500 MW		USBLS	5/15
	Memphis MSA, TN-MS-AR	Y	101540 FQ	146010 MW		USBLS	5/15
	Nashville-Davidson–Murfreesboro–Franklin MSA, TN	Y	86910 FQ	145510 MW		USBLS	5/15
	Texas	Y	126800 FQ	203200 AW		USBLS	5/15
	Austin-Round Rock MSA, TX	Y	113460 FQ	182490 MW		USBLS	5/15
	Dallas-Plano-Irving PMSA, TX	Y	165160 FQ	229250 AW		USBLS	5/15
	Fort Worth-Arlington PMSA, TX	Y	138730 FQ	180110 MW		USBLS	5/15
	Houston-The Woodlands-Sugar Land MSA, TX	Y	183250 FQ	241130 AW		USBLS	5/15
	San Antonio-New Braunfels MSA, TX	Y	121950 FQ	177340 MW		USBLS	5/15
	Utah	Y	87680 FQ	129260 MW		USBLS	5/15
	Ogden-Clearfield MSA, UT	Y	18890 FQ	106450 MW	155910 TQ	USBLS	5/15
	Provo-Orem MSA, UT	Y	106830 FQ	148020 MW		USBLS	5/15
	Salt Lake City MSA, UT	Y	91880 FQ	135570 MW		USBLS	5/15
	Vermont	Y	114810 FQ	182950 MW		USBLS	5/15
	Burlington-South Burlington MSA, VT	Y	116310 FQ	185990 MW		USBLS	5/15
	Virginia	Y	126310 FQ	197120 AW		USBLS	5/15
	Richmond MSA, VA	Y	126600 FQ	203560 AW		USBLS	5/15
	Virginia Beach-Norfolk-Newport News MSA, VA-NC	Y	118030 FQ	176350 MW		USBLS	5/15
	Washington	H	58.08 FQ	86.15 MW		WABLS	3/16
	Seattle-Bellevue-Everett PMSA, WA	H	70.08 FQ	105.00 AW		WABLS	3/16
	Tacoma-Lakewood PMSA, WA	H	59.09 FQ	79.68 MW		WABLS	3/16

AE	Average entry wage	AWR	Average wage range	H	Hourly
AEX	Average experienced wage	B	Biweekly	HI	Highest wage paid
ATC	Average total compensation	D	Daily	HR	High end range
AW	Average wage paid	FQ	First quartile wage	LO	Lowest wage paid

LR	Low end range	MTC	Median total compensation	TCC	Total cash compensation
M	Monthly	MW	Median wage paid	TQ	Third quartile wage
MCC	Median cash compensation	MWR	Median wage range	W	Weekly
ME	Median entry wage	S	See annotated source	Y	Yearly

Occupation/Type/Industry	Location	Per	Low	Mid	High	Source	Date
Chief Executive	West Virginia	Y	64020 FQ	102030 MW	174450 TQ	USBLS	5/15
	Huntington-Ashland MSA, WV-KY-OH	Y	86630 FQ	135080 MW		USBLS	5/15
	Wisconsin	Y	72250 FQ	129560 MW		USBLS	5/15
	Madison MSA, WI	Y	80530 FQ	139530 MW		USBLS	5/15
	Milwaukee-Waukesha-West Allis MSA, WI	Y	126360 FQ	192840 AW		USBLS	5/15
	Wyoming	Y	108030 FQ	134240 MW	171590 TQ	USBLS	5/15
	Puerto Rico	Y	56590 FQ	80730 MW	126200 TQ	USBLS	5/15
	San Juan-Carolina-Caguas MSA, PR	Y	56900 FQ	81560 MW	126430 TQ	USBLS	5/15
	Virgin Islands	Y	91320 FQ	110990 MW	142670 TQ	USBLS	5/15
	Guam	Y	42680 FQ	69080 MW	110850 TQ	USBLS	5/15
Chief Executive Officer							
Charity	United States	Y		150000 AW		CNAV01	2015
Credit Union	United States	Y		346143 MW		CUMGT	2016
East Detroit Public Schools	Eastpointe, MI	Y			160000 HI	LSJ04	2016
Large Cap Company	United States	Y		8695703 MTC		ERI01	2015
Mid Cap Company	United States	Y		3801650 MTC		ERI01	2015
Not-for-Profit Healthcare Organization, Female	United States	Y		368686 MW		MHLTH02	2013
Not-for-Profit Healthcare Organization, Male	United States	Y		738446 MW		MHLTH02	2013
Pharmaceutical, Medical Device, and Healthcare Industries	United States	Y		223000 AW		MMM01	7/16
Small Cap Company	United States	Y		1869511 MTC		ERI01	2015
Supermarket, Large Company	United States	Y		1500000 AW		SN01	2015
Supermarket, Medium Company	United States	Y		825000 AW		SN01	2015
Supermarket, Small Company	United States	Y		600000 AW		SN01	2015
Chief Financial Officer							
Large Cap Company	United States	Y		2749858 MTC		ERI01	2015
Mid Cap Company	United States	Y		1361543 MTC		ERI01	2015
S&P 500 Company	United States	Y		3570000 MW		WSJ02	2015
Small Cap Company	United States	Y		757725 MTC		ERI01	2015
Chief Forensic Pathologist							
County Government	Oakland County, MI	B	7667 LO		8629 HI	MIOAK2	10/1/16
Chief Health Affairs Officer							
College and University	United States	Y		368168 AW		HED02	2015-2016
Chief Human Resources Officer	United States	Y	85625 LO		234295 HI	WF01	7/15
Chief Information Officer							
County Government	Ingham County, MI	Y			110000 HI	TC03	2015
Municipal Government	Lansing, MI	Y			135000 HI	LSJ05	2016
Chief Institutional Research Officer							
College and University	United States	Y		94769 AW		HED02	2015-2016
Chief Investment Officer							
University of Michigan	Ann Arbor, MI	Y			690000 HI	MLV01	2016
Chief Jailer/Jail Administrator							
Municipal Government	Hartwell, GA	Y	25000 LO		39146 HI	GACTY01	2016
Municipal Government	Roswell, GA	Y	52463 LO		83941 HI	GACTY01	2016
Chief Justice							
United States Supreme Court	United States	Y			263300 HI	OPM01	2017
Chief Marketing Technologist	United States	Y	144000 LO		248000 HI	ADAGE02	2015
Chief Master Sergeant							
U.S. Air Force, Active Duty, Pay Grade E-9	United States	M	5053 LO		7845 HI	DOD1	2017
Chief Medical Officer							
Healthcare System	United States	Y		535100 MCC		MHLTH01	2015
Hospital	United States	Y		436600 MCC		MHLTH01	2015

AE	Average entry wage	**AWR**	Average wage range	**H**	Hourly	
AEX	Average experienced wage	**B**	Biweekly	**HI**	Highest wage paid	
ATC	Average total compensation	**D**	Daily	**HR**	High end range	
AW	Average wage paid	**FQ**	First quartile wage	**LO**	Lowest wage paid	

LR Low end range   **MTC** Median total compensation   **TCC** Total cash compensation
M Monthly   **MW** Median wage paid   **TQ** Third quartile wage
MCC Median cash compensation   **MWR** Median wage range   **W** Weekly
ME Median entry wage   **S** See annotated source   **Y** Yearly

Occupation/Type/Industry	Location	Per	Low	Mid	High	Source	Date
Chief Nursing Officer							
Hospital, Revenue > $1 Billion	United States	Y		389000 AW		NSI	2016
Hospital, Revenue > $250 Million	United States	Y		189000 AW		NSI	2016
Hospital, Revenue > $500 Million	United States	Y		277000 AW		NSI	2016
Chief of Mobility Innovation							
Municipal Government	Detroit, MI	M	8217 LO		10783 HI	DETGOV	2016
Chief Petty Officer							
U.S. Navy, Active Duty, Pay Grade E-7	United States	M	2875 LO		5168 HI	DOD1	2017
Chief Procurement Officer							
Healthcare	United States	Y		240000 AW		HPN02	2016
Chief Registrar							
County Government	Athens-Clarke County, GA	Y	63924 LO		102278 HI	GACTY04	2016
County Government	Habersham County, GA	Y	21920 LO		33354 HI	GACTY04	2016
County Government	Wilkes County, GA	Y	14500 LO		15700 HI	GACTY04	2016
Chief Security Officer							
Information Technology	United States	Y		137500 MW		INFOW02	10/15-2/16
Chief Technology Officer	United States	Y		136927 AW		CWRLD1	2016
Chief Wharfinger							
Harbor, Municipal Government	Long Beach, CA	Y			97703 HI	CACIT	6/28/16
Child, Family, and School Social Worker	Alabama	Y	28898 AE	41976 AW	48510 AEX	ALBLS	6/16
	Birmingham-Hoover MSA, AL	Y	27613 AE	38683 AW	44208 AEX	ALBLS	6/16
	Alaska	Y	38290 FQ	48650 MW	60610 TQ	USBLS	5/15
	Anchorage MSA, AK	Y	43090 FQ	52390 MW	61140 TQ	USBLS	5/15
	Arizona	Y	31660 FQ	36160 MW	42700 TQ	USBLS	5/15
	Phoenix-Mesa-Scottsdale MSA, AZ	Y	31660 FQ	36170 MW	42940 TQ	USBLS	5/15
	Tucson MSA, AZ	Y	30320 FQ	34830 MW	40880 TQ	USBLS	5/15
	Arkansas	Y	30360 FQ	32670 MW	40330 TQ	USBLS	5/15
	Little Rock-North Little Rock-Conway MSA, AR	Y	31370 FQ	35200 MW	42780 TQ	USBLS	5/15
	California	H	17.49 FQ	23.13 MW	31.82 TQ	CABLS	1/16-3/16
	Anaheim-Santa Ana-Irvine PMSA, CA	H	17.05 FQ	22.56 MW	40.55 TQ	CABLS	1/16-3/16
	Los Angeles-Long Beach-Glendale PMSA, CA	H	17.69 FQ	25.89 MW	38.68 TQ	CABLS	1/16-3/16
	Oakland-Hayward-Berkeley PMSA, CA	H	20.06 FQ	24.29 MW	31.50 TQ	CABLS	1/16-3/16
	Riverside-San Bernardino-Ontario MSA, CA	H	18.33 FQ	24.44 MW	29.21 TQ	CABLS	1/16-3/16
	Sacramento–Roseville–Arden-Arcade MSA, CA	H	14.64 FQ	21.30 MW	27.36 TQ	CABLS	1/16-3/16
	San Diego-Carlsbad MSA, CA	H	15.15 FQ	19.13 MW	23.37 TQ	CABLS	1/16-3/16
	San Francisco-Redwood City-South San Francisco PMSA, CA	H	19.31 FQ	24.58 MW	35.06 TQ	CABLS	1/16-3/16
	Colorado	Y	36200 FQ	44600 MW	56460 TQ	USBLS	5/15
	Denver-Aurora-Lakewood MSA, CO	Y	38020 FQ	45710 MW	57810 TQ	USBLS	5/15
	Connecticut	Y		68955 MW		CTBLS	1/16-3/16
	Bridgeport-Stamford-Norwalk MSA, CT	Y	47030 FQ	69050 MW	83460 TQ	USBLS	5/15
	Hartford-West Hartford-East Hartford MSA, CT	Y	55370 FQ	71330 MW	83460 TQ	USBLS	5/15
	Delaware	Y	33900 FQ	36320 MW	42180 TQ	USBLS	5/15
	Wilmington PMSA, DE-MD-NJ	Y	33910 FQ	37350 MW	45010 TQ	USBLS	5/15
	District of Columbia	Y	46790 FQ	58910 MW	75310 TQ	USBLS	5/15
	Washington-Arlington-Alexandria PMSA, DC-VA-MD-WV	Y	46170 FQ	58560 MW	74890 TQ	USBLS	5/15
	Florida	H	13.70 AE	18.62 MW	23.20 AEX	FLBLS	7/16-9/16

Occupation/Type/Industry	Location	Per	Low	Mid	High	Source	Date
Child, Family, and School Social Worker	Fort Lauderdale-Pompano Beach-Deerfield Beach PMSA, FL	H	15.26 AE	19.11 MW	25.62 AEX	FLBLS	7/16-9/16
	Miami-Miami Beach-Kendall PMSA, FL	H	15.87 AE	21.67 MW	27.29 AEX	FLBLS	7/16-9/16
	Orlando-Kissimmee-Sanford MSA, FL	H	13.79 AE	18.31 MW	22.71 AEX	FLBLS	7/16-9/16
	Tampa-St. Petersburg-Clearwater MSA, FL	H	12.74 AE	18.48 MW	24.08 AEX	FLBLS	7/16-9/16
	Georgia	Y	28880 FQ	34610 MW	40940 TQ	USBLS	5/15
	Atlanta-Sandy Springs-Roswell MSA, GA	Y	31310 FQ	36700 MW	46900 TQ	USBLS	5/15
	Augusta-Richmond County MSA, GA-SC	Y	23480 FQ	31950 MW	39420 TQ	USBLS	5/15
	Hawaii	Y	42550 FQ	52240 MW	62650 TQ	USBLS	5/15
	Urban Honolulu MSA, HI	Y	40840 FQ	51720 MW	62890 TQ	USBLS	5/15
	Idaho	Y	34090 FQ	40200 MW	47170 TQ	USBLS	5/15
	Boise City MSA, ID	Y	34190 FQ	38560 MW	44090 TQ	USBLS	5/15
	Illinois	Y	33930 FQ	51710 MW	80020 TQ	USBLS	5/15
	Chicago-Naperville-Arlington Heights PMSA, IL	Y	33220 FQ	48700 MW	77770 TQ	USBLS	5/15
	Lake County-Kenosha County PMSA, IL-WI	Y	34140 FQ	54900 MW	80190 TQ	USBLS	5/15
	Indiana	Y	33950 FQ	36420 MW	42620 TQ	USBLS	5/15
	Gary PMSA, IN	Y	34630 FQ	37260 MW	46350 TQ	USBLS	5/15
	Indianapolis-Carmel-Anderson MSA, IN	Y	36100 FQ	37430 MW	44700 TQ	USBLS	5/15
	Iowa	Y	30720 FQ	39680 MW	55890 TQ	USBLS	5/15
	Des Moines-West Des Moines MSA, IA	Y	35390 FQ	49760 MW	60530 TQ	USBLS	5/15
	Kansas	Y	30450 FQ	38610 MW	49690 TQ	USBLS	5/15
	Wichita MSA, KS	Y	32190 FQ	38430 MW	48840 TQ	USBLS	5/15
	Kentucky	Y	29980 FQ	36200 MW	44450 TQ	USBLS	5/15
	Louisville-Jefferson County MSA, KY-IN	Y	30770 FQ	36450 MW	44390 TQ	USBLS	5/15
	Louisiana	Y	41680 FQ	52840 MW	61190 TQ	USBLS	5/15
	Baton Rouge MSA, LA	Y	46980 FQ	56430 MW	65680 TQ	USBLS	5/15
	New Orleans-Metairie MSA, LA	Y	42860 FQ	52800 MW	59640 TQ	USBLS	5/15
	Maine	Y	39990 FQ	45790 MW	52470 TQ	USBLS	5/15
	Portland-South Portland MSA, ME	Y	40450 FQ	47690 MW	58760 TQ	USBLS	5/15
	Maryland	Y	28823 AE	47183 MW	56363 AEX	MDBLS	4/16
	Baltimore-Columbia-Towson MSA, MD	Y	29180 FQ	44590 MW	55050 TQ	USBLS	5/15
	Salisbury MSA, MD-DE	Y	34080 FQ	40010 MW	47540 TQ	USBLS	5/15
	Massachusetts	Y	33450 FQ	43340 MW	57810 TQ	USBLS	5/15
	Boston-Cambridge-Newton NECTA, MA	Y	35460 FQ	48090 MW	63850 TQ	USBLS	5/15
	Worcester MSA, MA-CT	Y	34550 FQ	43930 MW	53580 TQ	USBLS	5/15
	Michigan	Y	35260 FQ	46230 MW	55360 TQ	USBLS	5/15
	Detroit-Dearborn-Livonia PMSA, MI	Y	34950 FQ	43770 MW	55360 TQ	USBLS	5/15
	Grand Rapids-Wyoming MSA, MI	Y	34370 FQ	43500 MW	55350 TQ	USBLS	5/15
	Minnesota	Y	43266 FQ	56693 MW	71259 TQ	MNBLS	1/16-3/16
	Minneapolis-St. Paul-Bloomington MSA, MN-WI	Y	43266 FQ	58517 MW	74404 TQ	MNBLS	1/16-3/16
	Mississippi	Y	27930 FQ	32100 MW	38900 TQ	USBLS	5/15
	Jackson MSA, MS	Y	27920 FQ	32110 MW	40510 TQ	USBLS	5/15
	Missouri	Y	30030 FQ	33790 MW	38890 TQ	USBLS	5/15
	Kansas City MSA, MO-KS	Y	29180 FQ	33790 MW	40450 TQ	USBLS	5/15
	St. Louis MSA, MO-IL	Y	30020 FQ	34330 MW	42560 TQ	USBLS	5/15
	Montana	Y	27100 FQ	34030 MW	39420 TQ	USBLS	5/15
	Billings MSA, MT	Y	25000 FQ	35090 MW	44140 TQ	USBLS	5/15
	Omaha-Council Bluffs MSA, NE-IA	Y	33260 FQ	37310 MW	44425 TQ	NEBLS	7/16-9/16
	Nevada	Y	36470 FQ	44940 MW	57710 TQ	USBLS	5/15
	Las Vegas-Henderson-Paradise MSA, NV	Y	36360 FQ	45020 MW	57850 TQ	USBLS	5/15
	New Hampshire	H	15.83 AE	19.41 MW	23.34 AEX	NHBLS	6/16

AE	Average entry wage	AWR	Average wage range	H	Hourly	LR	Low end range	MTC	Median total compensation	TCC	Total cash compensation
AEX	Average experienced wage	B	Biweekly	HI	Highest wage paid	M	Monthly	MW	Median wage paid	TQ	Third quartile wage
ATC	Average total compensation	D	Daily	HR	High end range	MCC	Median cash compensation	MWR	Median wage range	W	Weekly
AW	Average wage paid	FQ	First quartile wage	LO	Lowest wage paid	ME	Median entry wage	S	See annotated source	Y	Yearly

Occupation/Type/Industry	Location	Per	Low	Mid	High	Source	Date
Child, Family, and School Social Worker							
	Manchester NECTA, NH	H	16.69 AE	22.18 MW	25.94 AEX	NHBLS	6/16
	Nashua NECTA, NH-MA	Y	34400 FQ	39760 MW	47870 TQ	USBLS	5/15
	New Jersey	Y	43600 FQ	57750 MW	77150 TQ	USBLS	5/15
	Camden PMSA, NJ	Y	43320 FQ	57260 MW	75120 TQ	USBLS	5/15
	Newark PMSA, NJ-PA	Y	43030 FQ	56200 MW	73730 TQ	USBLS	5/15
	Trenton MSA, NJ	Y	40490 FQ	48990 MW	67420 TQ	USBLS	5/15
	New Mexico	Y	29980 FQ	38200 MW	51160 TQ	USBLS	5/15
	Albuquerque MSA, NM	Y	31410 FQ	39870 MW	52300 TQ	USBLS	5/15
	New York	Y	37580 AE	52170 MW	66450 AEX	NYBLS	1/16-3/16
	Buffalo-Cheektowaga-Niagara Falls MSA, NY	Y	33520 FQ	40410 MW	57020 TQ	USBLS	5/15
	Nassau County-Suffolk County PMSA, NY	Y	45170 FQ	57900 MW	89070 TQ	USBLS	5/15
	New York-Jersey City-White Plains PMSA, NY-NJ	Y	42350 FQ	53360 MW	70420 TQ	USBLS	5/15
	Rochester MSA, NY	Y	36560 FQ	48390 MW	61300 TQ	USBLS	5/15
	North Carolina	Y	37970 FQ	44650 MW	52000 TQ	USBLS	5/15
	Charlotte-Concord-Gastonia MSA, NC-SC	Y	41720 FQ	47500 MW	56700 TQ	USBLS	5/15
	Raleigh MSA, NC	Y	39320 FQ	45550 MW	55010 TQ	USBLS	5/15
	North Dakota	Y	40210 FQ	48100 MW	59340 TQ	USBLS	5/15
	Fargo MSA, ND-MN	Y	37570 FQ	45860 MW	58130 TQ	USBLS	5/15
	Ohio	Y	32980 FQ	39010 MW	48830 TQ	USBLS	5/15
	Cincinnati MSA, OH-KY-IN	Y	33610 FQ	39090 MW	48440 TQ	USBLS	5/15
	Cleveland-Elyria MSA, OH	Y	36580 FQ	45580 MW	54970 TQ	USBLS	5/15
	Columbus MSA, OH	Y	32600 FQ	37820 MW	46440 TQ	USBLS	5/15
	Oklahoma	Y	27550 FQ	33250 MW	39240 TQ	USBLS	5/15
	Oklahoma City MSA, OK	Y	28590 FQ	34010 MW	39530 TQ	USBLS	5/15
	Tulsa MSA, OK	Y	29660 FQ	35290 MW	43480 TQ	USBLS	5/15
	Oregon	H	17.91 FQ	22.39 MW	27.05 TQ	ORBLS	2016
	Portland-Vancouver-Hillsboro MSA, OR-WA	Y	35800 FQ	46360 MW	55450 TQ	USBLS	5/15
	Pennsylvania	Y	31210 FQ	37580 MW	48140 TQ	USBLS	5/15
	Allentown-Bethlehem-Easton MSA, PA-NJ	Y	32400 FQ	43500 MW	56940 TQ	USBLS	5/15
	Harrisburg-Carlisle MSA, PA	Y	32750 FQ	43180 MW	53680 TQ	USBLS	5/15
	Montgomery County-Bucks County-Chester County PMSA, PA	Y	30180 FQ	36840 MW	46500 TQ	USBLS	5/15
	Philadelphia PMSA, PA	Y	34220 FQ	41170 MW	52250 TQ	USBLS	5/15
	Pittsburgh MSA, PA	Y	30600 FQ	37110 MW	48360 TQ	USBLS	5/15
	Rhode Island	Y	46210 FQ	62330 MW	75020 TQ	USBLS	5/15
	Providence-Warwick MSA, RI-MA	Y	43540 FQ	57160 MW	72580 TQ	USBLS	5/15
	South Carolina	Y	28830 FQ	35600 MW	45450 TQ	USBLS	5/15
	Charleston-North Charleston MSA, SC	Y	32100 FQ	36220 MW	42380 TQ	USBLS	5/15
	Columbia MSA, SC	Y	31760 FQ	35860 MW	40710 TQ	USBLS	5/15
	Greenville-Anderson-Mauldin MSA, SC	Y	31260 FQ	38040 MW	49600 TQ	USBLS	5/15
	South Dakota	Y	33190 FQ	38020 MW	44500 TQ	USBLS	5/15
	Sioux Falls MSA, SD	Y	34060 FQ	38060 MW	45700 TQ	USBLS	5/15
	Tennessee	Y	34390 FQ	42010 MW	47340 TQ	USBLS	5/15
	Knoxville MSA, TN	Y	35000 FQ	42240 MW	47280 TQ	USBLS	5/15
	Memphis MSA, TN-MS-AR	Y	31790 FQ	40730 MW	47320 TQ	USBLS	5/15
	Nashville-Davidson–Murfreesboro–Franklin MSA, TN	Y	34910 FQ	41950 MW	48090 TQ	USBLS	5/15
	Texas	Y	34610 FQ	39260 MW	46760 TQ	USBLS	5/15
	Austin-Round Rock MSA, TX	Y	35620 FQ	40640 MW	48730 TQ	USBLS	5/15
	Dallas-Plano-Irving PMSA, TX	Y	35620 FQ	40560 MW	49850 TQ	USBLS	5/15
	Fort Worth-Arlington PMSA, TX	Y	34020 FQ	39150 MW	45650 TQ	USBLS	5/15
	Houston-The Woodlands-Sugar Land MSA, TX	Y	34610 FQ	40300 MW	49400 TQ	USBLS	5/15
	San Antonio-New Braunfels MSA, TX	Y	34020 FQ	38730 MW	45980 TQ	USBLS	5/15
	Utah	Y	28130 FQ	38420 MW	52260 TQ	USBLS	5/15
	Ogden-Clearfield MSA, UT	Y	27520 FQ	32010 MW	44110 TQ	USBLS	5/15
	Provo-Orem MSA, UT	Y	33370 FQ	41240 MW	61180 TQ	USBLS	5/15
	Salt Lake City MSA, UT	Y	24260 FQ	40420 MW	55820 TQ	USBLS	5/15

AE	Average entry wage	AWR	Average wage range	H	Hourly	LR Low end range	MTC Median total compensation	TCC Total cash compensation
AEX	Average experienced wage	B	Biweekly	HI	Highest wage paid	M Monthly	MW Median wage paid	TQ Third quartile wage
ATC	Average total compensation	D	Daily	HR	High end range	MCC Median cash compensation	MWR Median wage range	W Weekly
AW	Average wage paid	FQ	First quartile wage	LO	Lowest wage paid	ME Median entry wage	S See annotated source	Y Yearly

Occupation/Type/Industry	Location	Per	Low	Mid	High	Source	Date
Child, Family, and School Social Worker	Vermont	Y	32910 FQ	38820 MW	49360 TQ	USBLS	5/15
	Burlington-South Burlington MSA, VT	Y	32510 FQ	39720 MW	50860 TQ	USBLS	5/15
	Virginia	Y	35860 FQ	44110 MW	56930 TQ	USBLS	5/15
	Richmond MSA, VA	Y	36170 FQ	43410 MW	52040 TQ	USBLS	5/15
	Virginia Beach-Norfolk-Newport News MSA, VA-NC	Y	37340 FQ	44090 MW	51210 TQ	USBLS	5/15
	Washington	H	20.11 FQ	24.36 MW	27.54 TQ	WABLS	3/16
	Seattle-Bellevue-Everett PMSA, WA	H	19.82 FQ	23.54 MW	27.43 TQ	WABLS	3/16
	Tacoma-Lakewood PMSA, WA	H	22.61 FQ	26.88 MW	28.86 TQ	WABLS	3/16
	West Virginia	Y	28520 FQ	33110 MW	37730 TQ	USBLS	5/15
	Huntington-Ashland MSA, WV-KY-OH	Y	28140 FQ	33090 MW	38650 TQ	USBLS	5/15
	Wisconsin	Y	34960 FQ	44430 MW	55240 TQ	USBLS	5/15
	Madison MSA, WI	Y	34310 FQ	45660 MW	56890 TQ	USBLS	5/15
	Milwaukee-Waukesha-West Allis MSA, WI	Y	34430 FQ	45170 MW	57140 TQ	USBLS	5/15
	Wyoming	Y	35590 FQ	45360 MW	52440 TQ	USBLS	5/15
	Cheyenne MSA, WY	Y	43300 FQ	50990 MW	64410 TQ	USBLS	5/15
	Puerto Rico	Y	25130 FQ	31830 MW	39290 TQ	USBLS	5/15
	San Juan-Carolina-Caguas MSA, PR	Y	24500 FQ	31670 MW	38690 TQ	USBLS	5/15
	Virgin Islands	Y	30060 FQ	35640 MW	44350 TQ	USBLS	5/15
	Guam	Y	27730 FQ	31580 MW	42370 TQ	USBLS	5/15
Childcare Teacher	San Francisco, CA	Y		36649 MW		NHC01	2016
	Sioux Falls, SD	Y		23025 MW		NHC01	2016
Childcare Worker	Alabama	Y	17493 AE	19243 AW	20118 AEX	ALBLS	6/16
	Birmingham-Hoover MSA, AL	Y	17472 AE	19387 AW	20345 AEX	ALBLS	6/16
	Alaska	Y	21530 FQ	24550 MW	28850 TQ	USBLS	5/15
	Anchorage MSA, AK	Y	21480 FQ	24230 MW	28350 TQ	USBLS	5/15
	Arizona	Y	18370 FQ	20070 MW	23480 TQ	USBLS	5/15
	Phoenix-Mesa-Scottsdale MSA, AZ	Y	18430 FQ	20230 MW	23570 TQ	USBLS	5/15
	Tucson MSA, AZ	Y	18340 FQ	19870 MW	23400 TQ	USBLS	5/15
	Arkansas	Y	16960 FQ	18290 MW	19720 TQ	USBLS	5/15
	Little Rock-North Little Rock-Conway MSA, AR	Y	17290 FQ	18940 MW	21460 TQ	USBLS	5/15
	California	H	9.96 FQ	11.84 MW	14.67 TQ	CABLS	1/16-3/16
	Anaheim-Santa Ana-Irvine PMSA, CA	H	10.54 FQ	12.71 MW	15.14 TQ	CABLS	1/16-3/16
	Los Angeles-Long Beach-Glendale PMSA, CA	H	9.77 FQ	11.57 MW	14.07 TQ	CABLS	1/16-3/16
	Oakland-Hayward-Berkeley PMSA, CA	H	9.99 FQ	12.40 MW	15.85 TQ	CABLS	1/16-3/16
	Riverside-San Bernardino-Ontario MSA, CA	H	9.70 FQ	11.42 MW	14.42 TQ	CABLS	1/16-3/16
	Sacramento–Roseville–Arden-Arcade MSA, CA	H	9.84 FQ	11.66 MW	14.12 TQ	CABLS	1/16-3/16
	San Diego-Carlsbad MSA, CA	H	10.54 FQ	12.11 MW	14.26 TQ	CABLS	1/16-3/16
	San Francisco-Redwood City-South San Francisco PMSA, CA	H	11.04 FQ	14.27 MW	17.51 TQ	CABLS	1/16-3/16
	Colorado	Y	19410 FQ	23870 MW	29010 TQ	USBLS	5/15
	Denver-Aurora-Lakewood MSA, CO	Y	19830 FQ	24970 MW	29700 TQ	USBLS	5/15
	Connecticut	Y		22852 MW		CTBLS	1/16-3/16
	Bridgeport-Stamford-Norwalk MSA, CT	Y	19790 FQ	22330 MW	25350 TQ	USBLS	5/15
	Hartford-West Hartford-East Hartford MSA, CT	Y	19560 FQ	22630 MW	27290 TQ	USBLS	5/15
	Delaware	Y	18310 FQ	20690 MW	24210 TQ	USBLS	5/15
	Wilmington PMSA, DE-MD-NJ	Y	18280 FQ	20390 MW	23870 TQ	USBLS	5/15
	District of Columbia	Y	19920 FQ	23010 MW	32520 TQ	USBLS	5/15
	Washington-Arlington-Alexandria PMSA, DC-VA-MD-WV	Y	18660 FQ	22980 MW	29680 TQ	USBLS	5/15
	Florida	H	9.00 AE	9.91 MW	11.38 AEX	FLBLS	7/16-9/16

AE	Average entry wage	AWR	Average wage range	H	Hourly	LR	Low end range	MTC	Median total compensation	TCC	Total cash compensation
AEX	Average experienced wage	B	Biweekly	HI	Highest wage paid	M	Monthly	MW	Median wage paid	TQ	Third quartile wage
ATC	Average total compensation	D	Daily	HR	High end range	MCC	Median cash compensation	MWR	Median wage range	W	Weekly
AW	Average wage paid	FQ	First quartile wage	LO	Lowest wage paid	ME	Median entry wage	S	See annotated source	Y	Yearly

Occupation/Type/Industry	Location	Per	Low	Mid	High	Source	Date
Childcare Worker	Fort Lauderdale-Pompano Beach-Deerfield Beach PMSA, FL	H	8.99 AE	9.66 MW	10.91 AEX	FLBLS	7/16-9/16
	Miami-Miami Beach-Kendall PMSA, FL	H	8.98 AE	9.69 MW	11.53 AEX	FLBLS	7/16-9/16
	Orlando-Kissimmee-Sanford MSA, FL	H	9.03 AE	9.99 MW	10.99 AEX	FLBLS	7/16-9/16
	Tampa-St. Petersburg-Clearwater MSA, FL	H	8.98 AE	9.89 MW	11.12 AEX	FLBLS	7/16-9/16
	Georgia	Y	17240 FQ	19050 MW	22930 TQ	USBLS	5/15
	Atlanta-Sandy Springs-Roswell MSA, GA	Y	17530 FQ	19670 MW	23890 TQ	USBLS	5/15
	Augusta-Richmond County MSA, GA-SC	Y	16900 FQ	18300 MW	19770 TQ	USBLS	5/15
	Hawaii	Y	17490 FQ	18860 MW	21620 TQ	USBLS	5/15
	Urban Honolulu MSA, HI	Y	17400 FQ	18680 MW	20680 TQ	USBLS	5/15
	Idaho	Y	16890 FQ	18280 MW	19740 TQ	USBLS	5/15
	Boise City MSA, ID	Y	16790 FQ	18030 MW	19270 TQ	USBLS	5/15
	Illinois	Y	19270 FQ	21830 MW	25410 TQ	USBLS	5/15
	Chicago-Naperville-Arlington Heights PMSA, IL	Y	19790 FQ	22720 MW	27360 TQ	USBLS	5/15
	Lake County-Kenosha County PMSA, IL-WI	Y	19050 FQ	21940 MW	25470 TQ	USBLS	5/15
	Indiana	Y	17460 FQ	19480 MW	22610 TQ	USBLS	5/15
	Gary PMSA, IN	Y	17160 FQ	18930 MW	22820 TQ	USBLS	5/15
	Indianapolis-Carmel-Anderson MSA, IN	Y	18230 FQ	20720 MW	23140 TQ	USBLS	5/15
	Iowa	Y	16950 FQ	18480 MW	20730 TQ	USBLS	5/15
	Des Moines-West Des Moines MSA, IA	Y	17820 FQ	20210 MW	22890 TQ	USBLS	5/15
	Kansas	Y	17140 FQ	18900 MW	22190 TQ	USBLS	5/15
	Wichita MSA, KS	Y	17570 FQ	20110 MW	23100 TQ	USBLS	5/15
	Kentucky	Y	17180 FQ	18910 MW	22490 TQ	USBLS	5/15
	Louisville-Jefferson County MSA, KY-IN	Y	17190 FQ	18930 MW	23710 TQ	USBLS	5/15
	Louisiana	Y	16890 FQ	18340 MW	20120 TQ	USBLS	5/15
	Baton Rouge MSA, LA	Y	16840 FQ	18250 MW	19790 TQ	USBLS	5/15
	New Orleans-Metairie MSA, LA	Y	17410 FQ	19500 MW	22770 TQ	USBLS	5/15
	Maine	Y	18740 FQ	21580 MW	24710 TQ	USBLS	5/15
	Portland-South Portland MSA, ME	Y	20600 FQ	23210 MW	26860 TQ	USBLS	5/15
	Maryland	Y	18080 AE	24439 MW	27618 AEX	MDBLS	4/16
	Baltimore-Columbia-Towson MSA, MD	Y	18400 FQ	21070 MW	26670 TQ	USBLS	5/15
	Salisbury MSA, MD-DE	Y	17820 FQ	19070 MW	22380 TQ	USBLS	5/15
	Massachusetts	Y	20640 FQ	24980 MW	30120 TQ	USBLS	5/15
	Boston-Cambridge-Newton NECTA, MA	Y	21270 FQ	26110 MW	31170 TQ	USBLS	5/15
	Worcester MSA, MA-CT	Y	19620 FQ	23210 MW	29530 TQ	USBLS	5/15
	Michigan	Y	18290 FQ	19620 MW	23530 TQ	USBLS	5/15
	Detroit-Dearborn-Livonia PMSA, MI	Y	18500 FQ	20200 MW	24650 TQ	USBLS	5/15
	Grand Rapids-Wyoming MSA, MI	Y	18880 FQ	22420 MW	32370 TQ	USBLS	5/15
	Minnesota	Y	19188 FQ	22692 MW	27347 TQ	MNBLS	1/16-3/16
	Minneapolis-St. Paul-Bloomington MSA, MN-WI	Y	19864 FQ	23742 MW	28196 TQ	MNBLS	1/16-3/16
	Mississippi	Y	16790 FQ	18140 MW	19560 TQ	USBLS	5/15
	Jackson MSA, MS	Y	16870 FQ	18330 MW	20300 TQ	USBLS	5/15
	Missouri	Y	17380 FQ	18840 MW	22030 TQ	USBLS	5/15
	Kansas City MSA, MO-KS	Y	17340 FQ	18930 MW	22130 TQ	USBLS	5/15
	St. Louis MSA, MO-IL	Y	18030 FQ	19750 MW	23710 TQ	USBLS	5/15
	Montana	Y	17940 FQ	19100 MW	22160 TQ	USBLS	5/15
	Billings MSA, MT	Y	18180 FQ	19610 MW	22900 TQ	USBLS	5/15
	Omaha-Council Bluffs MSA, NE-IA	Y	18475 FQ	20695 MW	23350 TQ	NEBLS	7/16-9/16
	Nevada	Y	17940 FQ	21120 MW	25750 TQ	USBLS	5/15
	Las Vegas-Henderson-Paradise MSA, NV	Y	17600 FQ	19950 MW	23850 TQ	USBLS	5/15
	New Hampshire	H	8.50 AE	10.78 MW	12.23 AEX	NHBLS	6/16
	Manchester NECTA, NH	H	9.10 AE	12.41 MW	13.44 AEX	NHBLS	6/16

AE Average entry wage	**AWR** Average wage range	**H** Hourly	**LR** Low end range	**MTC** Median total compensation	**TCC** Total cash compensation
AEX Average experienced wage	**B** Biweekly	**HI** Highest wage paid	**M** Monthly	**MW** Median wage paid	**TQ** Third quartile wage
ATC Average total compensation	**D** Daily	**HR** High end range	**MCC** Median cash compensation	**MWR** Median wage range	**W** Weekly
AW Average wage paid	**FQ** First quartile wage	**LO** Lowest wage paid	**ME** Median entry wage	**S** See annotated source	**Y** Yearly

Occupation/Type/Industry	Location	Per	Low	Mid	High	Source	Date
Childcare Worker	Nashua NECTA, NH-MA	Y	20200 FQ	22120 MW	24040 TQ	USBLS	5/15
	New Jersey	Y	19030 FQ	22070 MW	28070 TQ	USBLS	5/15
	Camden PMSA, NJ	Y	19460 FQ	23000 MW	27650 TQ	USBLS	5/15
	Newark PMSA, NJ-PA	Y	18860 FQ	21280 MW	27350 TQ	USBLS	5/15
	Trenton MSA, NJ	Y	18650 FQ	20360 MW	28320 TQ	USBLS	5/15
	New Mexico	Y	17470 FQ	18920 MW	21930 TQ	USBLS	5/15
	Albuquerque MSA, NM	Y	17620 FQ	19130 MW	22050 TQ	USBLS	5/15
	New York	Y	19960 AE	25960 MW	30220 AEX	NYBLS	1/16-3/16
	Buffalo-Cheektowaga-Niagara Falls MSA, NY	Y	18810 FQ	19450 MW	22970 TQ	USBLS	5/15
	Nassau County-Suffolk County PMSA, NY	Y	20720 FQ	27010 MW	32700 TQ	USBLS	5/15
	New York-Jersey City-White Plains PMSA, NY-NJ	Y	20530 FQ	26600 MW	31360 TQ	USBLS	5/15
	Rochester MSA, NY	Y	18990 FQ	20060 MW	23420 TQ	USBLS	5/15
	North Carolina	Y	17510 FQ	19650 MW	23670 TQ	USBLS	5/15
	Charlotte-Concord-Gastonia MSA, NC-SC	Y	18360 FQ	21550 MW	25030 TQ	USBLS	5/15
	Raleigh MSA, NC	Y	17600 FQ	19730 MW	23430 TQ	USBLS	5/15
	North Dakota	Y	17340 FQ	19200 MW	23030 TQ	USBLS	5/15
	Fargo MSA, ND-MN	Y	17080 FQ	18550 MW	21130 TQ	USBLS	5/15
	Ohio	Y	18300 FQ	19860 MW	23730 TQ	USBLS	5/15
	Cincinnati MSA, OH-KY-IN	Y	18550 FQ	21470 MW	25440 TQ	USBLS	5/15
	Cleveland-Elyria MSA, OH	Y	18200 FQ	19530 MW	23830 TQ	USBLS	5/15
	Columbus MSA, OH	Y	18870 FQ	21140 MW	23670 TQ	USBLS	5/15
	Oklahoma	Y	16950 FQ	18520 MW	21210 TQ	USBLS	5/15
	Oklahoma City MSA, OK	Y	16880 FQ	18430 MW	21150 TQ	USBLS	5/15
	Tulsa MSA, OK	Y	17040 FQ	18630 MW	21380 TQ	USBLS	5/15
	Oregon	H	9.70 FQ	10.90 MW	12.47 TQ	ORBLS	2016
	Portland-Vancouver-Hillsboro MSA, OR-WA	Y	20500 FQ	23050 MW	26850 TQ	USBLS	5/15
	Pennsylvania	Y	17480 FQ	19590 MW	23380 TQ	USBLS	5/15
	Allentown-Bethlehem-Easton MSA, PA-NJ	Y	17800 FQ	19220 MW	22820 TQ	USBLS	5/15
	Harrisburg-Carlisle MSA, PA	Y	18030 FQ	20960 MW	23830 TQ	USBLS	5/15
	Montgomery County-Bucks County-Chester County PMSA, PA	Y	17780 FQ	20720 MW	24520 TQ	USBLS	5/15
	Philadelphia PMSA, PA	Y	17900 FQ	20720 MW	23910 TQ	USBLS	5/15
	Pittsburgh MSA, PA	Y	17840 FQ	20130 MW	23520 TQ	USBLS	5/15
	Rhode Island	Y	19140 FQ	19720 MW	23310 TQ	USBLS	5/15
	Providence-Warwick MSA, RI-MA	Y	19200 FQ	20160 MW	24120 TQ	USBLS	5/15
	South Carolina	Y	16900 FQ	18370 MW	20510 TQ	USBLS	5/15
	Charleston-North Charleston MSA, SC	Y	16930 FQ	18440 MW	21610 TQ	USBLS	5/15
	Columbia MSA, SC	Y	16820 FQ	18220 MW	19740 TQ	USBLS	5/15
	Greenville-Anderson-Mauldin MSA, SC	Y	16440 FQ	17590 MW	18740 TQ	USBLS	5/15
	South Dakota	Y	18500 FQ	19340 MW	22030 TQ	USBLS	5/15
	Sioux Falls MSA, SD	Y	18520 FQ	19390 MW	22110 TQ	USBLS	5/15
	Tennessee	Y	16980 FQ	18560 MW	21720 TQ	USBLS	5/15
	Knoxville MSA, TN	Y	16610 FQ	17820 MW	19020 TQ	USBLS	5/15
	Memphis MSA, TN-MS-AR	Y	16870 FQ	18310 MW	20020 TQ	USBLS	5/15
	Nashville-Davidson–Murfreesboro–Franklin MSA, TN	Y	18090 FQ	21330 MW	25830 TQ	USBLS	5/15
	Texas	Y	17200 FQ	18970 MW	22620 TQ	USBLS	5/15
	Austin-Round Rock MSA, TX	Y	18100 FQ	21500 MW	26230 TQ	USBLS	5/15
	Dallas-Plano-Irving PMSA, TX	Y	17430 FQ	19490 MW	23800 TQ	USBLS	5/15
	Fort Worth-Arlington PMSA, TX	Y	17140 FQ	18850 MW	21710 TQ	USBLS	5/15
	Houston-The Woodlands-Sugar Land MSA, TX	Y	17240 FQ	19040 MW	22530 TQ	USBLS	5/15
	San Antonio-New Braunfels MSA, TX	Y	17530 FQ	19610 MW	23720 TQ	USBLS	5/15
	Utah	Y	17540 FQ	19700 MW	24040 TQ	USBLS	5/15
	Ogden-Clearfield MSA, UT	Y	16730 FQ	18000 MW	19270 TQ	USBLS	5/15
	Provo-Orem MSA, UT	Y	17290 FQ	19280 MW	22510 TQ	USBLS	5/15
	Salt Lake City MSA, UT	Y	18390 FQ	21670 MW	25890 TQ	USBLS	5/15
	Vermont	Y	20830 FQ	23400 MW	27990 TQ	USBLS	5/15

AE	Average entry wage	AWR	Average wage range	H	Hourly	LR	Low end range	MTC	Median total compensation	TCC	Total cash compensation
AEX	Average experienced wage	B	Biweekly	HI	Highest wage paid	M	Monthly	MW	Median wage paid	TQ	Third quartile wage
ATC	Average total compensation	D	Daily	HR	High end range	MCC	Median cash compensation	MWR	Median wage range	W	Weekly
AW	Average wage paid	FQ	First quartile wage	LO	Lowest wage paid	ME	Median entry wage	S	See annotated source	Y	Yearly

Occupation/Type/Industry	Location	Per	Low	Mid	High	Source	Date
Childcare Worker	Burlington-South Burlington						
	MSA, VT	Y	20710 FQ	22860 MW	25830 TQ	USBLS	5/15
	Virginia	Y	17460 FQ	19510 MW	26130 TQ	USBLS	5/15
	Richmond MSA, VA	Y	17000 FQ	18580 MW	21420 TQ	USBLS	5/15
	Virginia Beach-Norfolk-						
	Newport News MSA, VA-NC	Y	17120 FQ	18760 MW	21880 TQ	USBLS	5/15
	Washington	H	10.42 FQ	11.53 MW	13.72 TQ	WABLS	3/16
	Seattle-Bellevue-Everett						
	PMSA, WA	H	10.86 FQ	12.21 MW	14.74 TQ	WABLS	3/16
	Tacoma-Lakewood PMSA, WA	H	10.62 FQ	11.66 MW	13.85 TQ	WABLS	3/16
	West Virginia	Y	17760 FQ	18890 MW	21220 TQ	USBLS	5/15
	Huntington-Ashland MSA,						
	WV-KY-OH	Y	17470 FQ	18420 MW	19450 TQ	USBLS	5/15
	Wisconsin	Y	17780 FQ	20410 MW	23970 TQ	USBLS	5/15
	Eau Claire MSA, WI	Y	17990 FQ	20830 MW	23820 TQ	USBLS	5/15
	Madison MSA, WI	Y	19980 FQ	23180 MW	28740 TQ	USBLS	5/15
	Milwaukee-Waukesha-West						
	Allis MSA, WI	Y	18600 FQ	21620 MW	24440 TQ	USBLS	5/15
	Wyoming	Y	17900 FQ	20850 MW	24870 TQ	USBLS	5/15
	Cheyenne MSA, WY	Y	16650 FQ	17980 MW	19330 TQ	USBLS	5/15
	Puerto Rico	Y	16550 FQ	17650 MW	18740 TQ	USBLS	5/15
	San Juan-Carolina-Caguas						
	MSA, PR	Y	16570 FQ	17660 MW	18750 TQ	USBLS	5/15
	Virgin Islands	Y	16330 FQ	17420 MW	18510 TQ	USBLS	5/15
	Guam	Y	17920 FQ	18670 MW	19500 TQ	USBLS	5/15
Children's Librarian							
Public Library	Deerfield, MA	H			20.03 HI	FRCOG	2016
Public Library	Montague, MA	Y			39926 HI	FRCOG	2016
Children's Minister							
Church of Christ	United States	Y		45350 AW		ACU	2/16-3/16
Chiropractor	Alabama	Y	47786 AE	98436 AW	123766 AEX	ALBLS	6/16
	Alaska	Y	75930 FQ	98360 MW		USBLS	5/15
	Anchorage MSA, AK	Y	78660 FQ	99140 MW		USBLS	5/15
	Arizona	Y	42440 FQ	61630 MW	88210 TQ	USBLS	5/15
	Phoenix-Mesa-Scottsdale						
	MSA, AZ	Y	41910 FQ	61680 MW	88770 TQ	USBLS	5/15
	Tucson MSA, AZ	Y	54090 FQ	59430 MW	65050 TQ	USBLS	5/15
	Arkansas	Y	27770 FQ	44580 MW	79830 TQ	USBLS	5/15
	California	H	24.47 FQ	34.61 MW	52.96 TQ	CABLS	1/16-3/16
	Anaheim-Santa Ana-Irvine						
	PMSA, CA	H	16.31 FQ	28.73 MW	43.19 TQ	CABLS	1/16-3/16
	Los Angeles-Long Beach-						
	Glendale PMSA, CA	H	27.80 FQ	36.13 MW	62.45 TQ	CABLS	1/16-3/16
	Oakland-Hayward-Berkeley						
	PMSA, CA	H	19.21 FQ	33.68 MW	59.69 TQ	CABLS	1/16-3/16
	Riverside-San Bernardino-						
	Ontario MSA, CA	H	33.73 FQ	41.60 MW	62.13 TQ	CABLS	1/16-3/16
	Sacramento–Roseville–						
	Arden-Arcade MSA, CA	H	30.49 FQ	33.47 MW	36.14 TQ	CABLS	1/16-3/16
	San Diego-Carlsbad MSA, CA	H	25.06 FQ	30.85 MW	58.14 TQ	CABLS	1/16-3/16
	San Francisco-Redwood City-						
	South San Francisco PMSA,						
	CA	H	21.33 FQ	23.62 MW	35.49 TQ	CABLS	1/16-3/16
	Colorado	Y	39620 FQ	49410 MW	74720 TQ	USBLS	5/15
	Denver-Aurora-Lakewood						
	MSA, CO	Y	37820 FQ	45150 MW	55220 TQ	USBLS	5/15
	Connecticut	Y		71512 MW		CTBLS	1/16-3/16
	Bridgeport-Stamford-Norwalk						
	MSA, CT	Y	59450 FQ	158280 MW	180490 TQ	USBLS	5/15
	Hartford-West Hartford-East						
	Hartford MSA, CT	Y	67200 FQ	71820 MW	76450 TQ	USBLS	5/15
	Delaware	Y	106580 FQ	117600 MW	128740 TQ	USBLS	5/15
	Wilmington PMSA, DE-MD-						
	NJ	Y	106520 FQ	117270 MW	128570 TQ	USBLS	5/15
	Washington-Arlington-						
	Alexandria PMSA, DC-VA-						
	MD-WV	Y	61840 FQ	76650 MW	96750 TQ	USBLS	5/15
	Florida	H	19.65 AE	33.04 MW	54.93 AEX	FLBLS	7/16-9/16

AE Average entry wage	**AWR** Average wage range	**H** Hourly	**LR** Low end range	**MTC** Median total compensation	**TCC** Total cash compensation
AEX Average experienced wage	**B** Biweekly	**HI** Highest wage paid	**M** Monthly	**MW** Median wage paid	**TQ** Third quartile wage
ATC Average total compensation	**D** Daily	**HR** High end range	**MCC** Median cash compensation	**MWR** Median wage range	**W** Weekly
AW Average wage paid	**FQ** First quartile wage	**LO** Lowest wage paid	**ME** Median entry wage	**S** See annotated source	**Y** Yearly

Occupation/Type/Industry	Location	Per	Low	Mid	High	Source	Date
Chiropractor	Fort Lauderdale-Pompano Beach-Deerfield Beach PMSA, FL	H	20.05 AE	24.47 MW	46.44 AEX	FLBLS	7/16-9/16
	Miami-Miami Beach-Kendall PMSA, FL	H	27.12 AE	59.73 MW	111.62 AEX	FLBLS	7/16-9/16
	Orlando-Kissimmee-Sanford MSA, FL	H	16.30 AE	29.98 MW	45.86 AEX	FLBLS	7/16-9/16
	Tampa-St. Petersburg-Clearwater MSA, FL	H	28.07 AE	39.27 MW	56.32 AEX	FLBLS	7/16-9/16
	Georgia	Y	35120 FQ	53900 MW	95670 TQ	USBLS	5/15
	Augusta-Richmond County MSA, GA-SC	Y	33710 FQ	39730 MW	71040 TQ	USBLS	5/15
	Idaho	Y	41390 FQ	46800 MW	62930 TQ	USBLS	5/15
	Boise City MSA, ID	Y	42780 FQ	46710 MW	54100 TQ	USBLS	5/15
	Illinois	Y	29690 FQ	54030 MW	85950 TQ	USBLS	5/15
	Chicago-Naperville-Arlington Heights PMSA, IL	Y	26440 FQ	39510 MW	79220 TQ	USBLS	5/15
	Lake County-Kenosha County PMSA, IL-WI	Y	32480 FQ	54470 MW	61790 TQ	USBLS	5/15
	Indiana	Y	47940 FQ	64920 MW	106800 TQ	USBLS	5/15
	Iowa	Y	49020 FQ	65970 MW	86770 TQ	USBLS	5/15
	Des Moines-West Des Moines MSA, IA	Y	67630 FQ	74960 MW	134210 TQ	USBLS	5/15
	Kansas	Y	37730 FQ	52990 MW	76080 TQ	USBLS	5/15
	Kentucky	Y	43730 FQ	55970 MW	72710 TQ	USBLS	5/15
	Louisville-Jefferson County MSA, KY-IN	Y	44410 FQ	50410 MW	59700 TQ	USBLS	5/15
	Louisiana	Y	47440 FQ	67860 MW	92610 TQ	USBLS	5/15
	Baton Rouge MSA, LA	Y	36390 FQ	65300 MW	73970 TQ	USBLS	5/15
	New Orleans-Metairie MSA, LA	Y	58250 FQ	86260 MW	95720 TQ	USBLS	5/15
	Maine	Y	57780 FQ	72680 MW	89270 TQ	USBLS	5/15
	Portland-South Portland MSA, ME	Y	65970 FQ	78810 MW	92310 TQ	USBLS	5/15
	Maryland	Y	39911 AE	82081 MW	103167 AEX	MDBLS	4/16
	Baltimore-Columbia-Towson MSA, MD	Y	37030 FQ	65300 MW	85970 TQ	USBLS	5/15
	Salisbury MSA, MD-DE	Y	52180 FQ	88200 MW	134820 TQ	USBLS	5/15
	Massachusetts	Y	57580 FQ	86280 MW	103280 TQ	USBLS	5/15
	Boston-Cambridge-Newton NECTA, MA	Y	66720 FQ	87680 MW	101000 TQ	USBLS	5/15
	Worcester MSA, MA-CT	Y	50910 FQ	70180 MW	111190 TQ	USBLS	5/15
	Michigan	Y	47010 FQ	60680 MW	95300 TQ	USBLS	5/15
	Detroit-Dearborn-Livonia PMSA, MI	Y	55250 FQ	61390 MW	102670 TQ	USBLS	5/15
	Grand Rapids-Wyoming MSA, MI	Y	52400 FQ	60520 MW	84470 TQ	USBLS	5/15
	Minnesota	Y	44717 FQ	55786 MW	72741 TQ	MNBLS	1/16-3/16
	Minneapolis-St. Paul-Bloomington MSA, MN-WI	Y	44757 FQ	54798 MW	66733 TQ	MNBLS	1/16-3/16
	Mississippi	Y	56300 FQ	71280 MW	92960 TQ	USBLS	5/15
	Missouri	Y	27390 FQ	53450 MW	75940 TQ	USBLS	5/15
	Kansas City MSA, MO-KS	Y	31970 FQ	45600 MW	61290 TQ	USBLS	5/15
	St. Louis MSA, MO-IL	Y	34500 FQ	52660 MW	69920 TQ	USBLS	5/15
	Montana	Y	44550 FQ	57490 MW	73850 TQ	USBLS	5/15
	Billings MSA, MT	Y	47970 FQ	58780 MW	72880 TQ	USBLS	5/15
	Nebraska	Y	35610 FQ	59930 MW	110240 TQ	NEBLS	7/16-9/16
	Omaha-Council Bluffs MSA, NE-IA	Y	51750 FQ	59925 MW	105185 TQ	NEBLS	7/16-9/16
	Nevada	Y	43810 FQ	76200 MW	94760 TQ	USBLS	5/15
	Las Vegas-Henderson-Paradise MSA, NV	Y	39850 FQ	73080 MW	86770 TQ	USBLS	5/15
	New Hampshire	H	24.44 AE	37.88 MW	59.83 AEX	NHBLS	6/16
	New Jersey	Y	75360 FQ	105560 MW	170610 TQ	USBLS	5/15
	Camden PMSA, NJ	Y	88470 FQ	153160 MW		USBLS	5/15
	Newark PMSA, NJ-PA	Y	69750 FQ	104380 MW	182000 TQ	USBLS	5/15
	New Mexico	Y	54430 FQ	68610 MW	84180 TQ	USBLS	5/15
	New York	Y	57910 AE	76920 MW	110860 AEX	NYBLS	1/16-3/16
	Buffalo-Cheektowaga-Niagara Falls MSA, NY	Y	53970 FQ	58050 MW	62130 TQ	USBLS	5/15
	Nassau County-Suffolk County PMSA, NY	Y	83310 FQ	96100 MW	165450 TQ	USBLS	5/15

AE Average entry wage	**AWR** Average wage range	**H** Hourly	**LR** Low end range	**MTC** Median total compensation	**TCC** Total cash compensation
AEX Average experienced wage	**B** Biweekly	**HI** Highest wage paid	**M** Monthly	**MW** Median wage paid	**TQ** Third quartile wage
ATC Average total compensation	**D** Daily	**HR** High end range	**MCC** Median cash compensation	**MWR** Median wage range	**W** Weekly
AW Average wage paid	**FQ** First quartile wage	**LO** Lowest wage paid	**ME** Median entry wage	**S** See annotated source	**Y** Yearly

Occupation/Type/Industry	Location	Per	Low	Mid	High	Source	Date
Chiropractor	New York-Jersey City-White						
	Plains PMSA, NY-NJ	Y	65680 FQ	79650 MW	110580 TQ	USBLS	5/15
	Rochester MSA, NY	Y	53630 FQ	57650 MW	61670 TQ	USBLS	5/15
	North Carolina	Y	69680 FQ	77590 MW	101240 TQ	USBLS	5/15
	Charlotte-Concord-Gastonia						
	MSA, NC-SC	Y	65980 FQ	80430 MW	115270 TQ	USBLS	5/15
	Raleigh MSA, NC	Y	69470 FQ	74700 MW	79970 TQ	USBLS	5/15
	North Dakota	Y	35090 FQ	58350 MW	81630 TQ	USBLS	5/15
	Fargo MSA, ND-MN	Y	33190 FQ	51470 MW	63770 TQ	USBLS	5/15
	Ohio	Y	57790 FQ	86720 MW	116930 TQ	USBLS	5/15
	Cincinnati MSA, OH-KY-IN	Y	54270 FQ	82490 MW	168960 TQ	USBLS	5/15
	Cleveland-Elyria MSA, OH	Y	57870 FQ	85000 MW	114670 TQ	USBLS	5/15
	Columbus MSA, OH	Y	58590 FQ	84230 MW	94250 TQ	USBLS	5/15
	Oklahoma	Y	46620 FQ	62960 MW	93220 TQ	USBLS	5/15
	Oklahoma City MSA, OK	Y	48780 FQ	59960 MW	134410 TQ	USBLS	5/15
	Tulsa MSA, OK	Y	45010 FQ	69400 MW	96990 TQ	USBLS	5/15
	Oregon	H	18.29 FQ	28.90 MW	45.47 TQ	ORBLS	2016
	Portland-Vancouver-Hillsboro						
	MSA, OR-WA	Y	35400 FQ	40810 MW	62510 TQ	USBLS	5/15
	Pennsylvania	Y	39200 FQ	64470 MW	93160 TQ	USBLS	5/15
	Allentown-Bethlehem-Easton						
	MSA, PA-NJ	Y	68740 FQ	85530 MW	109100 TQ	USBLS	5/15
	Harrisburg-Carlisle MSA, PA	Y	44280 FQ	48970 MW	67410 TQ	USBLS	5/15
	Montgomery County-Bucks						
	County-Chester County						
	PMSA, PA	Y	27620 FQ	35000 MW	71030 TQ	USBLS	5/15
	Philadelphia PMSA, PA	Y	74920 FQ	85800 MW	95380 TQ	USBLS	5/15
	Pittsburgh MSA, PA	Y	40080 FQ	63390 MW	102960 TQ	USBLS	5/15
	Rhode Island	Y	51680 FQ	62150 MW	85620 TQ	USBLS	5/15
	Providence-Warwick MSA, RI-						
	MA	Y	49910 FQ	60630 MW	88230 TQ	USBLS	5/15
	South Carolina	Y	44320 FQ	61910 MW	92530 TQ	USBLS	5/15
	Charleston-North Charleston						
	MSA, SC	Y	52150 FQ	59980 MW	69330 TQ	USBLS	5/15
	Columbia MSA, SC	Y	53170 FQ	62230 MW	104170 TQ	USBLS	5/15
	South Dakota	Y	58040 FQ	70380 MW	87030 TQ	USBLS	5/15
	Sioux Falls MSA, SD	Y	67760 FQ	78280 MW	92220 TQ	USBLS	5/15
	Tennessee	Y	43230 FQ	54370 MW	105720 TQ	USBLS	5/15
	Knoxville MSA, TN	Y	46050 FQ	55150 MW	74150 TQ	USBLS	5/15
	Nashville-Davidson–						
	Murfreesboro–Franklin						
	MSA, TN	Y	41270 FQ	46860 MW	110520 TQ	USBLS	5/15
	Texas	Y	29480 FQ	54080 MW	72630 TQ	USBLS	5/15
	Austin-Round Rock MSA, TX	Y	44330 FQ	54160 MW	82620 TQ	USBLS	5/15
	Dallas-Plano-Irving PMSA, TX	Y	40360 FQ	56120 MW	67560 TQ	USBLS	5/15
	Fort Worth-Arlington PMSA,						
	TX	Y	47670 FQ	66050 MW	72800 TQ	USBLS	5/15
	Houston-The Woodlands-						
	Sugar Land MSA, TX	Y	22060 FQ	24290 MW	56270 TQ	USBLS	5/15
	Utah	Y	32750 FQ	55510 MW	73620 TQ	USBLS	5/15
	Ogden-Clearfield MSA, UT	Y	43550 FQ	62010 MW	76860 TQ	USBLS	5/15
	Provo-Orem MSA, UT	Y	53110 FQ	58290 MW	68250 TQ	USBLS	5/15
	Salt Lake City MSA, UT	Y	29000 FQ	57920 MW	79390 TQ	USBLS	5/15
	Vermont	Y	39360 FQ	48250 MW	86070 TQ	USBLS	5/15
	Virginia	Y	58300 FQ	73950 MW	99460 TQ	USBLS	5/15
	Richmond MSA, VA	Y	50980 FQ	59870 MW	74480 TQ	USBLS	5/15
	Washington	H	20.49 FQ	26.46 MW	33.77 TQ	WABLS	3/16
	Seattle-Bellevue-Everett						
	PMSA, WA	H	21.70 FQ	25.70 MW	29.26 TQ	WABLS	3/16
	Tacoma-Lakewood PMSA, WA	H	25.37 FQ	32.72 MW	39.21 TQ	WABLS	3/16
	West Virginia	Y	43320 FQ	53570 MW	83900 TQ	USBLS	5/15
	Wisconsin	Y	39740 FQ	62640 MW	85240 TQ	USBLS	5/15
	Madison MSA, WI	Y	52530 FQ	61500 MW	79670 TQ	USBLS	5/15
	Milwaukee-Waukesha-West						
	Allis MSA, WI	Y	25520 FQ	39910 MW	88430 TQ	USBLS	5/15
	Wyoming	Y	45490 FQ	55610 MW	71510 TQ	USBLS	5/15
	Puerto Rico	Y	39220 FQ	64750 MW	77550 TQ	USBLS	5/15
	San Juan-Carolina-Caguas						
	MSA, PR	Y	38830 FQ	49960 MW	73660 TQ	USBLS	5/15
Choreographer	Los Angeles-Long Beach-						
	Glendale PMSA, CA	H	13.78 FQ	20.06 MW	24.33 TQ	CABLS	1/16-3/16

AE	Average entry wage	AWR	Average wage range	H	Hourly	LR	Low end range	MTC	Median total compensation	TCC	Total cash compensation
AEX	Average experienced wage	B	Biweekly	HI	Highest wage paid	M	Monthly	MW	Median wage paid	TQ	Third quartile wage
ATC	Average total compensation	D	Daily	HR	High end range	MCC	Median cash compensation	MWR	Median wage range	W	Weekly
AW	Average wage paid	FQ	First quartile wage	LO	Lowest wage paid	ME	Median entry wage	S	See annotated source	Y	Yearly

Occupation/Type/Industry	Location	Per	Low	Mid	High	Source	Date
Choreographer	Riverside-San Bernardino-Ontario MSA, CA	H	21.61 FQ	23.87 MW	35.37 TQ	CABLS	1/16-3/16
	San Diego-Carlsbad MSA, CA	H	24.95 FQ	26.94 MW	28.94 TQ	CABLS	1/16-3/16
	San Francisco-Redwood City-South San Francisco PMSA, CA	H	38.16 FQ	48.54 MW	56.49 TQ	CABLS	1/16-3/16
	Colorado	Y	32280 FQ	46500 MW	63370 TQ	USBLS	5/15
	Connecticut	Y		56375 MW		CTBLS	1/16-3/16
	Hartford-West Hartford-East Hartford MSA, CT	Y	44600 FQ	49920 MW	63370 TQ	USBLS	5/15
	District of Columbia	Y	43240 FQ	46290 MW	49350 TQ	USBLS	5/15
	Washington-Arlington-Alexandria PMSA, DC-VA-MD-WV	Y	43820 FQ	48940 MW	55800 TQ	USBLS	5/15
	Florida	H	14.98 AE	18.16 MW	25.02 AEX	FLBLS	7/16-9/16
	Fort Lauderdale-Pompano Beach-Deerfield Beach PMSA, FL	H	13.76 AE	16.26 MW	20.69 AEX	FLBLS	7/16-9/16
	Orlando-Kissimmee-Sanford MSA, FL	H	16.61 AE	19.42 MW	25.60 AEX	FLBLS	7/16-9/16
	Georgia	Y	27020 FQ	30020 MW	38700 TQ	USBLS	5/15
	Atlanta-Sandy Springs-Roswell MSA, GA	Y	27100 FQ	29520 MW	33390 TQ	USBLS	5/15
	Urban Honolulu MSA, HI	Y	17160 FQ	18190 MW	19220 TQ	USBLS	5/15
	Illinois	Y	37010 FQ	43810 MW	48590 TQ	USBLS	5/15
	Chicago-Naperville-Arlington Heights PMSA, IL	Y	41150 FQ	45250 MW	49360 TQ	USBLS	5/15
	Iowa	Y	23530 FQ	41720 MW	46860 TQ	USBLS	5/15
	Louisiana	Y	18940 FQ	28090 MW	65690 TQ	USBLS	5/15
	Massachusetts	Y	31580 FQ	34920 MW	38260 TQ	USBLS	5/15
	Michigan	Y	30100 FQ	56160 MW	71950 TQ	USBLS	5/15
	Minnesota	Y	33800 FQ	50403 MW	62177 TQ	MNBLS	1/16-3/16
	Minneapolis-St. Paul-Bloomington MSA, MN-WI	Y	50352 FQ	57822 MW	70332 TQ	MNBLS	1/16-3/16
	Missouri	Y	36930 FQ	44860 MW	54970 TQ	USBLS	5/15
	Las Vegas-Henderson-Paradise MSA, NV	Y	51510 FQ	58940 MW	88570 TQ	USBLS	5/15
	New Jersey	Y	45880 FQ	64330 MW	97310 TQ	USBLS	5/15
	Newark PMSA, NJ-PA	Y	43780 FQ	71480 MW	110830 TQ	USBLS	5/15
	New York	Y	33270 AE	76460 MW	111090 AEX	NYBLS	1/16-3/16
	New York-Jersey City-White Plains PMSA, NY-NJ	Y	47450 FQ	67340 MW	102450 TQ	USBLS	5/15
	Oregon	H	11.60 FQ	23.66 MW	35.28 TQ	ORBLS	2016
	Portland-Vancouver-Hillsboro MSA, OR-WA	Y	23900 FQ	64750 MW	74080 TQ	USBLS	5/15
	Pennsylvania	Y	27200 FQ	31350 MW	39160 TQ	USBLS	5/15
	Montgomery County-Bucks County-Chester County PMSA, PA	Y	26830 FQ	28550 MW	30260 TQ	USBLS	5/15
	South Carolina	Y	24120 FQ	43170 MW	59910 TQ	USBLS	5/15
	Columbia MSA, SC	Y	30780 FQ	45090 MW	55030 TQ	USBLS	5/15
	South Dakota	Y	19240 FQ	27030 MW	32750 TQ	USBLS	5/15
	Utah	Y	41290 FQ	51820 MW	61150 TQ	USBLS	5/15
	Vermont	Y	42960 FQ	57970 MW	70450 TQ	USBLS	5/15
	Virginia	Y	45990 FQ	55950 MW	70300 TQ	USBLS	5/15
	Richmond MSA, VA	Y	58950 FQ	71140 MW	86820 TQ	USBLS	5/15
	Washington	H	27.43 FQ	35.34 MW	42.21 TQ	WABLS	3/16
	Seattle-Bellevue-Everett PMSA, WA	H	32.09 FQ	38.12 MW	44.20 TQ	WABLS	3/16
	Milwaukee-Waukesha-West Allis MSA, WI	Y	55160 FQ	62120 MW	73010 TQ	USBLS	5/15
	Wyoming	Y	29210 FQ	35750 MW	45280 TQ	USBLS	5/15
Cinematographer/Videographer							
Music Video	United States	Y		1000-100000 AWR		BBRD01	2014
Circuit Judge	United States	Y			217600 HI	OPM01	2017
Circulation Coordinator							
Public Library	Folsom, CA	Y			47595 HI	CACIT	6/28/16

AE	Average entry wage	AWR	Average wage range	H	Hourly	LR	Low end range	MTC	Median total compensation	TCC	Total cash compensation
AEX	Average experienced wage	B	Biweekly	HI	Highest wage paid	M	Monthly	MW	Median wage paid	TQ	Third quartile wage
ATC	Average total compensation	D	Daily	HR	High end range	MCC	Median cash compensation	MWR	Median wage range	W	Weekly
AW	Average wage paid	FQ	First quartile wage	LO	Lowest wage paid	ME	Median entry wage	S	See annotated source	Y	Yearly

Occupation/Type/Industry	Location	Per	Low	Mid	High	Source	Date
Circulation Supervisor							
Public Library	Brawley, CA	Y			38567 HI	CACIT	6/28/16
Public Library	Corona, CA	Y			69756 HI	CACIT	6/28/16
City Attorney	Anaheim, CA	Y			228370 HI	CACIT	6/28/16
	Inglewood, CA	Y			201431 HI	CACIT	7/18/16
	Santa Monica, CA	Y			316528 HI	CACIT	6/28/16
	Seattle, WA	H			77.59 HI	CSSS	1/13/16
City Auditor	Long Beach, CA	Y			209218 HI	CACIT	6/28/16
	Palo Alto, CA	Y			173945 HI	CACIT	6/28/16
City Clerk	Alameda, CA	Y			132833 HI	CACIT	6/28/16
	Brentwood, CA	Y			135481 HI	CACIT	6/28/16
	Fresno, CA	Y			102438 HI	CACIT	6/28/16
City Controller	Long Beach, CA	Y			152827 HI	CACIT	6/28/16
City Engineer	Arroyo Grande, CA	Y			122401 HI	CACIT	6/28/16
	Dixon, CA	Y			137519 HI	CACIT	6/28/16
	Fremont, CA	Y			117403 HI	CACIT	6/28/16
City Letter Carrier							
Hired On or After January 12, 2013	United States	H	17.70 LO		29.37 HI	NALC	2/19/16
Hired Prior to January 12, 2013	United States	H	22.70 LO		29.37 HI	NALC	2/19/16
City Manager	Bell, CA	Y			37019 HI	CACIT	6/28/16
	Torrance, CA	Y			268382 HI	CACIT	6/28/16
Civic Arts Coordinator							
Municipal Government	Berkeley, CA	Y			96338 HI	CACIT	6/28/16
Civil Engineer	Alabama	Y	51608 AE	79354 AW	93217 AEX	ALBLS	6/16
	Birmingham-Hoover MSA, AL	Y	54371 AE	83370 AW	97865 AEX	ALBLS	6/16
	Alaska	Y	85350 FQ	103640 MW	127060 TQ	USBLS	5/15
	Anchorage MSA, AK	Y	86640 FQ	108000 MW	132930 TQ	USBLS	5/15
	Arizona	Y	59800 FQ	75320 MW	95230 TQ	USBLS	5/15
	Phoenix-Mesa-Scottsdale MSA, AZ	Y	60500 FQ	76280 MW	96680 TQ	USBLS	5/15
	Tucson MSA, AZ	Y	58440 FQ	73610 MW	92760 TQ	USBLS	5/15
	Arkansas	Y	56020 FQ	72910 MW	91270 TQ	USBLS	5/15
	Little Rock-North Little Rock-Conway MSA, AR	Y	56510 FQ	76310 MW	94950 TQ	USBLS	5/15
	California	H	38.49 FQ	48.64 MW	58.90 TQ	CABLS	1/16-3/16
	Anaheim-Santa Ana-Irvine PMSA, CA	H	37.26 FQ	51.08 MW	60.25 TQ	CABLS	1/16-3/16
	Los Angeles-Long Beach-Glendale PMSA, CA	H	37.67 FQ	49.58 MW	59.44 TQ	CABLS	1/16-3/16
	Oakland-Hayward-Berkeley PMSA, CA	H	43.08 FQ	51.08 MW	60.18 TQ	CABLS	1/16-3/16
	Riverside-San Bernardino-Ontario MSA, CA	H	38.02 FQ	47.88 MW	56.92 TQ	CABLS	1/16-3/16
	Sacramento–Roseville–Arden-Arcade MSA, CA	H	40.83 FQ	49.63 MW	60.12 TQ	CABLS	1/16-3/16
	San Diego-Carlsbad MSA, CA	H	34.91 FQ	43.28 MW	52.69 TQ	CABLS	1/16-3/16
	San Francisco-Redwood City-South San Francisco PMSA, CA	H	39.68 FQ	50.23 MW	62.50 TQ	CABLS	1/16-3/16
	Colorado	Y	64610 FQ	80360 MW	101520 TQ	USBLS	5/15
	Denver-Aurora-Lakewood MSA, CO	Y	65250 FQ	80360 MW	104220 TQ	USBLS	5/15
	Connecticut	Y		88951 MW		CTBLS	1/16-3/16
	Bridgeport-Stamford-Norwalk MSA, CT	Y	73170 FQ	89750 MW	111620 TQ	USBLS	5/15
	Hartford-West Hartford-East Hartford MSA, CT	Y	70990 FQ	88190 MW	104710 TQ	USBLS	5/15
	Delaware	Y	69380 FQ	82390 MW	100000 TQ	USBLS	5/15
	Wilmington PMSA, DE-MD-NJ	Y	71790 FQ	87190 MW	109360 TQ	USBLS	5/15
	District of Columbia	Y	71680 FQ	91590 MW	114760 TQ	USBLS	5/15
	Washington-Arlington-Alexandria PMSA, DC-VA-MD-WV	Y	65660 FQ	85850 MW	112160 TQ	USBLS	5/15

AE	Average entry wage	AWR	Average wage range	H	Hourly	LR	Low end range	MTC	Median total compensation	TCC	Total cash compensation
AEX	Average experienced wage	B	Biweekly	HI	Highest wage paid	M	Monthly	MW	Median wage paid	TQ	Third quartile wage
ATC	Average total compensation	D	Daily	HR	High end range	MCC	Median cash compensation	MWR	Median wage range	W	Weekly
AW	Average wage paid	FQ	First quartile wage	LO	Lowest wage paid	ME	Median entry wage	S	See annotated source	Y	Yearly

Occupation/Type/Industry	Location	Per	Low	Mid	High	Source	Date
Civil Engineer	Florida	H	27.11 AE	38.70 MW	49.44 AEX	FLBLS	7/16-9/16
	Fort Lauderdale-Pompano Beach-Deerfield Beach PMSA, FL	H	25.14 AE	38.07 MW	46.82 AEX	FLBLS	7/16-9/16
	Miami-Miami Beach-Kendall PMSA, FL	H	27.43 AE	41.54 MW	52.43 AEX	FLBLS	7/16-9/16
	Orlando-Kissimmee-Sanford MSA, FL	H	29.92 AE	38.72 MW	49.14 AEX	FLBLS	7/16-9/16
	Tampa-St. Petersburg-Clearwater MSA, FL	H	26.11 AE	38.66 MW	49.77 AEX	FLBLS	7/16-9/16
	Georgia	Y	56780 FQ	77770 MW	112890 TQ	USBLS	5/15
	Atlanta-Sandy Springs-Roswell MSA, GA	Y	57770 FQ	80030 MW	117190 TQ	USBLS	5/15
	Augusta-Richmond County MSA, GA-SC	Y	73220 FQ	92650 MW	114710 TQ	USBLS	5/15
	Hawaii	Y	63870 FQ	78400 MW	94140 TQ	USBLS	5/15
	Urban Honolulu MSA, HI	Y	65300 FQ	79920 MW	94780 TQ	USBLS	5/15
	Idaho	Y	58830 FQ	73820 MW	91260 TQ	USBLS	5/15
	Boise City MSA, ID	Y	57080 FQ	73060 MW	89330 TQ	USBLS	5/15
	Illinois	Y	67060 FQ	84440 MW	103770 TQ	USBLS	5/15
	Chicago-Naperville-Arlington Heights PMSA, IL	Y	68230 FQ	87000 MW	108410 TQ	USBLS	5/15
	Lake County-Kenosha County PMSA, IL-WI	Y	68880 FQ	86070 MW	108650 TQ	USBLS	5/15
	Indiana	Y	56570 FQ	70210 MW	88360 TQ	USBLS	5/15
	Gary PMSA, IN	Y	60730 FQ	77440 MW	112330 TQ	USBLS	5/15
	Indianapolis-Carmel-Anderson MSA, IN	Y	56830 FQ	71630 MW	90120 TQ	USBLS	5/15
	Iowa	Y	59440 FQ	77150 MW	95230 TQ	USBLS	5/15
	Des Moines-West Des Moines MSA, IA	Y	59610 FQ	77880 MW	95510 TQ	USBLS	5/15
	Kansas	Y	63070 FQ	74770 MW	90720 TQ	USBLS	5/15
	Wichita MSA, KS	Y	63580 FQ	77590 MW	95480 TQ	USBLS	5/15
	Kentucky	Y	55480 FQ	72360 MW	92490 TQ	USBLS	5/15
	Louisville-Jefferson County MSA, KY-IN	Y	56490 FQ	72540 MW	92180 TQ	USBLS	5/15
	Louisiana	Y	68290 FQ	87890 MW	108510 TQ	USBLS	5/15
	Baton Rouge MSA, LA	Y	73880 FQ	92090 MW	114120 TQ	USBLS	5/15
	New Orleans-Metairie MSA, LA	Y	73600 FQ	92320 MW	113350 TQ	USBLS	5/15
	Maine	Y	59510 FQ	73960 MW	90160 TQ	USBLS	5/15
	Portland-South Portland MSA, ME	Y	62680 FQ	82220 MW	94630 TQ	USBLS	5/15
	Maryland	Y	58843 AE	85583 MW	98953 AEX	MDBLS	4/16
	Baltimore-Columbia-Towson MSA, MD	Y	62730 FQ	76660 MW	95630 TQ	USBLS	5/15
	Salisbury MSA, MD-DE	Y	57810 FQ	70800 MW	88940 TQ	USBLS	5/15
	Massachusetts	Y	64540 FQ	84030 MW	102650 TQ	USBLS	5/15
	Boston-Cambridge-Newton NECTA, MA	Y	64580 FQ	84470 MW	101770 TQ	USBLS	5/15
	Worcester MSA, MA-CT	Y	64000 FQ	74770 MW	88610 TQ	USBLS	5/15
	Michigan	Y	60430 FQ	72350 MW	83940 TQ	USBLS	5/15
	Detroit-Dearborn-Livonia PMSA, MI	Y	56340 FQ	70020 MW	86620 TQ	USBLS	5/15
	Grand Rapids-Wyoming MSA, MI	Y	59670 FQ	70860 MW	80800 TQ	USBLS	5/15
	Minnesota	Y	65806 FQ	83255 MW	100231 TQ	MNBLS	1/16-3/16
	Minneapolis-St. Paul-Bloomington MSA, MN-WI	Y	66400 FQ	84273 MW	101380 TQ	MNBLS	1/16-3/16
	Mississippi	Y	59790 FQ	76500 MW	96850 TQ	USBLS	5/15
	Jackson MSA, MS	Y	56070 FQ	72470 MW	82190 TQ	USBLS	5/15
	Missouri	Y	60320 FQ	72910 MW	89380 TQ	USBLS	5/15
	Kansas City MSA, MO-KS	Y	65410 FQ	78030 MW	94960 TQ	USBLS	5/15
	St. Louis MSA, MO-IL	Y	62470 FQ	74620 MW	91800 TQ	USBLS	5/15
	Montana	Y	57860 FQ	69260 MW	84240 TQ	USBLS	5/15
	Billings MSA, MT	Y	60530 FQ	75920 MW	93010 TQ	USBLS	5/15
	Nebraska	Y	61665 FQ	78295 MW	95810 TQ	NEBLS	7/16-9/16
	Omaha-Council Bluffs MSA, NE-IA	Y	62480 FQ	79560 MW	97385 TQ	NEBLS	7/16-9/16
	Nevada	Y	64690 FQ	83190 MW	103760 TQ	USBLS	5/15
	Las Vegas-Henderson-Paradise MSA, NV	Y	69250 FQ	88850 MW	109260 TQ	USBLS	5/15

Occupation/Type/Industry	Location	Per	Low	Mid	High	Source	Date
Civil Engineer	New Hampshire	H	24.03 AE	34.78 MW	42.38 AEX	NHBLS	6/16
	Manchester NECTA, NH	H	22.19 AE	32.98 MW	40.69 AEX	NHBLS	6/16
	Nashua NECTA, NH-MA	Y	56120 FQ	76100 MW	93780 TQ	USBLS	5/15
	New Jersey	Y	68440 FQ	89850 MW	116090 TQ	USBLS	5/15
	Camden PMSA, NJ	Y	62190 FQ	85240 MW	116390 TQ	USBLS	5/15
	Newark PMSA, NJ-PA	Y	70470 FQ	93040 MW	120530 TQ	USBLS	5/15
	Trenton MSA, NJ	Y	71290 FQ	91150 MW	116240 TQ	USBLS	5/15
	New Mexico	Y	65740 FQ	81940 MW	100170 TQ	USBLS	5/15
	Albuquerque MSA, NM	Y	67270 FQ	84350 MW	100090 TQ	USBLS	5/15
	New York	Y	63540 AE	86630 MW	106860 AEX	NYBLS	1/16-3/16
	Buffalo-Cheektowaga-Niagara Falls MSA, NY	Y	68360 FQ	79030 MW	94090 TQ	USBLS	5/15
	Nassau County-Suffolk County PMSA, NY	Y	66600 FQ	85920 MW	103490 TQ	USBLS	5/15
	New York-Jersey City-White Plains PMSA, NY-NJ	Y	69420 FQ	88480 MW	112250 TQ	USBLS	5/15
	Rochester MSA, NY	Y	65800 FQ	80870 MW	102610 TQ	USBLS	5/15
	North Carolina	Y	59770 FQ	72920 MW	89470 TQ	USBLS	5/15
	Charlotte-Concord-Gastonia MSA, NC-SC	Y	59640 FQ	73680 MW	93870 TQ	USBLS	5/15
	Raleigh MSA, NC	Y	59490 FQ	72830 MW	87520 TQ	USBLS	5/15
	North Dakota	Y	57000 FQ	70770 MW	88330 TQ	USBLS	5/15
	Fargo MSA, ND-MN	Y	56580 FQ	69020 MW	85520 TQ	USBLS	5/15
	Ohio	Y	59340 FQ	76190 MW	92660 TQ	USBLS	5/15
	Cincinnati MSA, OH-KY-IN	Y	57050 FQ	74530 MW	94730 TQ	USBLS	5/15
	Cleveland-Elyria MSA, OH	Y	61770 FQ	78510 MW	94880 TQ	USBLS	5/15
	Columbus MSA, OH	Y	60550 FQ	78560 MW	94850 TQ	USBLS	5/15
	Oklahoma	Y	54250 FQ	72960 MW	92670 TQ	USBLS	5/15
	Oklahoma City MSA, OK	Y	48650 FQ	67830 MW	91250 TQ	USBLS	5/15
	Tulsa MSA, OK	Y	61850 FQ	81600 MW	95970 TQ	USBLS	5/15
	Oregon	H	30.73 FQ	38.16 MW	47.83 TQ	ORBLS	2016
	Portland-Vancouver-Hillsboro MSA, OR-WA	Y	63930 FQ	79020 MW	98500 TQ	USBLS	5/15
	Pennsylvania	Y	62610 FQ	77940 MW	99780 TQ	USBLS	5/15
	Allentown-Bethlehem-Easton MSA, PA-NJ	Y	65500 FQ	78010 MW	101770 TQ	USBLS	5/15
	Harrisburg-Carlisle MSA, PA	Y	63960 FQ	77190 MW	95450 TQ	USBLS	5/15
	Montgomery County-Bucks County-Chester County PMSA, PA	Y	60010 FQ	77860 MW	104390 TQ	USBLS	5/15
	Philadelphia PMSA, PA	Y	64340 FQ	79980 MW	108880 TQ	USBLS	5/15
	Pittsburgh MSA, PA	Y	63400 FQ	80430 MW	101420 TQ	USBLS	5/15
	Rhode Island	Y	65880 FQ	82520 MW	101260 TQ	USBLS	5/15
	Providence-Warwick MSA, RI-MA	Y	65790 FQ	83190 MW	101160 TQ	USBLS	5/15
	South Carolina	Y	55910 FQ	72630 MW	95780 TQ	USBLS	5/15
	Charleston-North Charleston MSA, SC	Y	50280 FQ	69470 MW	88010 TQ	USBLS	5/15
	Columbia MSA, SC	Y	49810 FQ	60660 MW	78950 TQ	USBLS	5/15
	Greenville-Anderson-Mauldin MSA, SC	Y	65450 FQ	83680 MW	105180 TQ	USBLS	5/15
	South Dakota	Y	57280 FQ	67840 MW	80000 TQ	USBLS	5/15
	Sioux Falls MSA, SD	Y	66710 FQ	76570 MW	95290 TQ	USBLS	5/15
	Tennessee	Y	68060 FQ	86790 MW	109430 TQ	USBLS	5/15
	Knoxville MSA, TN	Y	69230 FQ	88580 MW	111100 TQ	USBLS	5/15
	Memphis MSA, TN-MS-AR	Y	70480 FQ	90760 MW	118780 TQ	USBLS	5/15
	Nashville-Davidson–Murfreesboro–Franklin MSA, TN	Y	66370 FQ	84080 MW	102950 TQ	USBLS	5/15
	Texas	Y	67960 FQ	87910 MW	120400 TQ	USBLS	5/15
	Austin-Round Rock MSA, TX	Y	64060 FQ	76710 MW	94090 TQ	USBLS	5/15
	Dallas-Plano-Irving PMSA, TX	Y	69260 FQ	83700 MW	111090 TQ	USBLS	5/15
	Fort Worth-Arlington PMSA, TX	Y	68850 FQ	86040 MW	102940 TQ	USBLS	5/15
	Houston-The Woodlands-Sugar Land MSA, TX	Y	72860 FQ	102880 MW	137510 TQ	USBLS	5/15
	San Antonio-New Braunfels MSA, TX	Y	60800 FQ	77770 MW	95960 TQ	USBLS	5/15
	Utah	Y	61820 FQ	75800 MW	95390 TQ	USBLS	5/15
	Ogden-Clearfield MSA, UT	Y	62220 FQ	79260 MW	95830 TQ	USBLS	5/15
	Provo-Orem MSA, UT	Y	64430 FQ	81390 MW	101480 TQ	USBLS	5/15
	Salt Lake City MSA, UT	Y	61380 FQ	74600 MW	93610 TQ	USBLS	5/15

AE	Average entry wage	AWR	Average wage range	H	Hourly	LR	Low end range	MTC	Median total compensation	TCC	Total cash compensation
AEX	Average experienced wage	B	Biweekly	HI	Highest wage paid	M	Monthly	MW	Median wage paid	TQ	Third quartile wage
ATC	Average total compensation	D	Daily	HR	High end range	MCC	Median cash compensation	MWR	Median wage range	W	Weekly
AW	Average wage paid	FQ	First quartile wage	LO	Lowest wage paid	ME	Median entry wage	S	See annotated source	Y	Yearly

Occupation/Type/Industry	Location	Per	Low	Mid	High	Source	Date
Civil Engineer	Vermont	Y	58880 FQ	70670 MW	82680 TQ	USBLS	5/15
	Burlington-South Burlington MSA, VT	Y	59240 FQ	69860 MW	79030 TQ	USBLS	5/15
	Virginia	Y	62720 FQ	80900 MW	104560 TQ	USBLS	5/15
	Richmond MSA, VA	Y	63040 FQ	78790 MW	98500 TQ	USBLS	5/15
	Virginia Beach-Norfolk-Newport News MSA, VA-NC	Y	67660 FQ	81900 MW	102940 TQ	USBLS	5/15
	Washington	H	33.30 FQ	41.29 MW	50.86 TQ	WABLS	3/16
	Seattle-Bellevue-Everett PMSA, WA	H	32.44 FQ	41.36 MW	51.02 TQ	WABLS	3/16
	Tacoma-Lakewood PMSA, WA	H	34.54 FQ	41.97 MW	47.51 TQ	WABLS	3/16
	West Virginia	Y	52020 FQ	68380 MW	83750 TQ	USBLS	5/15
	Huntington-Ashland MSA, WV-KY-OH	Y	59670 FQ	74860 MW	91830 TQ	USBLS	5/15
	Wisconsin	Y	59020 FQ	72710 MW	87850 TQ	USBLS	5/15
	Janesville-Beloit MSA, WI	Y	52920 FQ	71970 MW	87780 TQ	USBLS	5/15
	Madison MSA, WI	Y	62820 FQ	75480 MW	90950 TQ	USBLS	5/15
	Milwaukee-Waukesha-West Allis MSA, WI	Y	59440 FQ	72830 MW	88330 TQ	USBLS	5/15
	Wyoming	Y	58440 FQ	71140 MW	86060 TQ	USBLS	5/15
	Cheyenne MSA, WY	Y	60110 FQ	68030 MW	78830 TQ	USBLS	5/15
	Puerto Rico	Y	38560 FQ	49820 MW	68410 TQ	USBLS	5/15
	San Juan-Carolina-Caguas MSA, PR	Y	39220 FQ	50660 MW	69660 TQ	USBLS	5/15
	Virgin Islands	Y	54660 FQ	60000 MW	89100 TQ	USBLS	5/15
	Guam	Y	40340 FQ	52910 MW	74810 TQ	USBLS	5/15
Civil Engineering Technician	Alabama	Y	29265 AE	40885 AW	46695 AEX	ALBLS	6/16
	Birmingham-Hoover MSA, AL	Y	31446 AE	42924 AW	48652 AEX	ALBLS	6/16
	Alaska	Y	57240 FQ	69300 MW	82950 TQ	USBLS	5/15
	Anchorage MSA, AK	Y	55390 FQ	69290 MW	79970 TQ	USBLS	5/15
	Arizona	Y	40690 FQ	51530 MW	60990 TQ	USBLS	5/15
	Phoenix-Mesa-Scottsdale MSA, AZ	Y	41920 FQ	52310 MW	61250 TQ	USBLS	5/15
	Tucson MSA, AZ	Y	37600 FQ	52280 MW	61770 TQ	USBLS	5/15
	Arkansas	Y	37890 FQ	45410 MW	57920 TQ	USBLS	5/15
	Little Rock-North Little Rock-Conway MSA, AR	Y	36320 FQ	45820 MW	65690 TQ	USBLS	5/15
	California	H	25.30 FQ	31.70 MW	37.66 TQ	CABLS	1/16-3/16
	Anaheim-Santa Ana-Irvine PMSA, CA	H	24.62 FQ	31.38 MW	36.58 TQ	CABLS	1/16-3/16
	Los Angeles-Long Beach-Glendale PMSA, CA	H	30.41 FQ	38.67 MW	46.61 TQ	CABLS	1/16-3/16
	Oakland-Hayward-Berkeley PMSA, CA	H	26.61 FQ	32.16 MW	36.94 TQ	CABLS	1/16-3/16
	Riverside-San Bernardino-Ontario MSA, CA	H	25.27 FQ	29.82 MW	34.92 TQ	CABLS	1/16-3/16
	Sacramento–Roseville–Arden-Arcade MSA, CA	H	25.90 FQ	32.26 MW	37.21 TQ	CABLS	1/16-3/16
	San Diego-Carlsbad MSA, CA	H	24.09 FQ	28.19 MW	32.34 TQ	CABLS	1/16-3/16
	San Francisco-Redwood City-South San Francisco PMSA, CA	H	25.45 FQ	27.88 MW	30.31 TQ	CABLS	1/16-3/16
	Colorado	Y	34280 FQ	46700 MW	60670 TQ	USBLS	5/15
	Denver-Aurora-Lakewood MSA, CO	Y	36480 FQ	48530 MW	62120 TQ	USBLS	5/15
	Connecticut	Y		63426 MW		CTBLS	1/16-3/16
	Bridgeport-Stamford-Norwalk MSA, CT	Y	58000 FQ	71530 MW	86700 TQ	USBLS	5/15
	Hartford-West Hartford-East Hartford MSA, CT	Y	47050 FQ	66100 MW	79930 TQ	USBLS	5/15
	Delaware	Y	33920 FQ	43330 MW	52680 TQ	USBLS	5/15
	Wilmington PMSA, DE-MD-NJ	Y	35170 FQ	43270 MW	54980 TQ	USBLS	5/15
	District of Columbia	Y	56440 FQ	69950 MW	83790 TQ	USBLS	5/15
	Washington-Arlington-Alexandria PMSA, DC-VA-MD-WV	Y	28690 FQ	41750 MW	60550 TQ	USBLS	5/15
	Florida	H	16.55 AE	23.20 MW	27.84 AEX	FLBLS	7/16-9/16
	Fort Lauderdale-Pompano Beach-Deerfield Beach PMSA, FL	H	16.82 AE	23.45 MW	29.08 AEX	FLBLS	7/16-9/16

AE	Average entry wage	**AWR**	Average wage range	**H**	Hourly	**LR**	Low end range	**MTC** Median total compensation **TCC** Total cash compensation
AEX	Average experienced wage	**B**	Biweekly	**HI**	Highest wage paid	**M**	Monthly	**MW** Median wage paid **TQ** Third quartile wage
ATC	Average total compensation	**D**	Daily	**HR**	High end range	**MCC**	Median cash compensation	**MWR** Median wage range **W** Weekly
AW	Average wage paid	**FQ**	First quartile wage	**LO**	Lowest wage paid	**ME**	Median entry wage	**S** See annotated source **Y** Yearly

Occupation/Type/Industry	Location	Per	Low	Mid	High	Source	Date
Civil Engineering Technician	Miami-Miami Beach-Kendall PMSA, FL	H	17.11 AE	26.89 MW	30.93 AEX	FLBLS	7/16-9/16
	Orlando-Kissimmee-Sanford MSA, FL	H	17.32 AE	23.19 MW	27.65 AEX	FLBLS	7/16-9/16
	Tampa-St. Petersburg-Clearwater MSA, FL	H	17.40 AE	23.33 MW	27.91 AEX	FLBLS	7/16-9/16
	Georgia	Y	32840 FQ	39690 MW	50060 TQ	USBLS	5/15
	Atlanta-Sandy Springs-Roswell MSA, GA	Y	33450 FQ	39750 MW	49350 TQ	USBLS	5/15
	Hawaii	Y	37690 FQ	46970 MW	57970 TQ	USBLS	5/15
	Urban Honolulu MSA, HI	Y	36930 FQ	47080 MW	58570 TQ	USBLS	5/15
	Idaho	Y	43580 FQ	48310 MW	55480 TQ	USBLS	5/15
	Boise City MSA, ID	Y	43660 FQ	50310 MW	58740 TQ	USBLS	5/15
	Illinois	Y	41570 FQ	55040 MW	69020 TQ	USBLS	5/15
	Chicago-Naperville-Arlington Heights PMSA, IL	Y	39000 FQ	55370 MW	70240 TQ	USBLS	5/15
	Lake County-Kenosha County PMSA, IL-WI	Y	45050 FQ	57420 MW	72300 TQ	USBLS	5/15
	Indiana	Y	40650 FQ	50180 MW	63240 TQ	USBLS	5/15
	Gary PMSA, IN	Y	40110 FQ	64230 MW	79450 TQ	USBLS	5/15
	Indianapolis-Carmel-Anderson MSA, IN	Y	47920 FQ	58290 MW	69460 TQ	USBLS	5/15
	Iowa	Y	38890 FQ	52470 MW	66320 TQ	USBLS	5/15
	Des Moines-West Des Moines MSA, IA	Y	36810 FQ	52880 MW	66200 TQ	USBLS	5/15
	Kansas	Y	33450 FQ	41330 MW	50290 TQ	USBLS	5/15
	Wichita MSA, KS	Y	36240 FQ	44480 MW	57510 TQ	USBLS	5/15
	Kentucky	Y	35720 FQ	44620 MW	54300 TQ	USBLS	5/15
	Louisville-Jefferson County MSA, KY-IN	Y	32290 FQ	41650 MW	51930 TQ	USBLS	5/15
	Louisiana	Y	35330 FQ	45390 MW	56770 TQ	USBLS	5/15
	Baton Rouge MSA, LA	Y	35980 FQ	47200 MW	59820 TQ	USBLS	5/15
	New Orleans-Metairie MSA, LA	Y	34190 FQ	43040 MW	54210 TQ	USBLS	5/15
	Maine	Y	43710 FQ	50090 MW	57260 TQ	USBLS	5/15
	Portland-South Portland MSA, ME	Y	44630 FQ	52940 MW	62590 TQ	USBLS	5/15
	Maryland	Y	35434 AE	51032 MW	58832 AEX	MDBLS	4/16
	Baltimore-Columbia-Towson MSA, MD	Y	45350 FQ	56540 MW	63800 TQ	USBLS	5/15
	Salisbury MSA, MD-DE	Y	33910 FQ	43350 MW	51270 TQ	USBLS	5/15
	Massachusetts	Y	44090 FQ	55620 MW	79430 TQ	USBLS	5/15
	Michigan	Y	39970 FQ	50680 MW	57230 TQ	USBLS	5/15
	Detroit-Dearborn-Livonia PMSA, MI	Y	35990 FQ	45360 MW	54970 TQ	USBLS	5/15
	Grand Rapids-Wyoming MSA, MI	Y	43250 FQ	50160 MW	57230 TQ	USBLS	5/15
	Minnesota	Y	51007 FQ	59939 MW	70322 TQ	MNBLS	1/16-3/16
	Minneapolis-St. Paul-Bloomington MSA, MN-WI	Y	50251 FQ	59939 MW	73306 TQ	MNBLS	1/16-3/16
	Mississippi	Y	28760 FQ	34590 MW	40830 TQ	USBLS	5/15
	Jackson MSA, MS	Y	30830 FQ	36310 MW	43690 TQ	USBLS	5/15
	Missouri	Y	37070 FQ	46260 MW	57340 TQ	USBLS	5/15
	Kansas City MSA, MO-KS	Y	35790 FQ	45330 MW	56610 TQ	USBLS	5/15
	St. Louis MSA, MO-IL	Y	35280 FQ	48370 MW	59850 TQ	USBLS	5/15
	Montana	Y	33910 FQ	44570 MW	52060 TQ	USBLS	5/15
	Billings MSA, MT	Y	31660 FQ	33260 MW	50070 TQ	USBLS	5/15
	Nebraska	Y	33680 FQ	46925 MW	58290 TQ	NEBLS	7/16-9/16
	Omaha-Council Bluffs MSA, NE-IA	Y	30435 FQ	39590 MW	53280 TQ	NEBLS	7/16-9/16
	Nevada	Y	41230 FQ	54190 MW	67930 TQ	USBLS	5/15
	Las Vegas-Henderson-Paradise MSA, NV	Y	39720 FQ	57460 MW	73470 TQ	USBLS	5/15
	New Hampshire	H	14.69 AE	22.13 MW	26.40 AEX	NHBLS	6/16
	Manchester NECTA, NH	H	15.16 AE	21.73 MW	24.67 AEX	NHBLS	6/16
	New Jersey	Y	40880 FQ	54010 MW	65170 TQ	USBLS	5/15
	Camden PMSA, NJ	Y	49320 FQ	55200 MW	60860 TQ	USBLS	5/15
	Newark PMSA, NJ-PA	Y	36530 FQ	52780 MW	66130 TQ	USBLS	5/15
	Trenton MSA, NJ	Y	41750 FQ	51530 MW	66600 TQ	USBLS	5/15
	New Mexico	Y	34710 FQ	39880 MW	47290 TQ	USBLS	5/15
	Albuquerque MSA, NM	Y	35080 FQ	39970 MW	52360 TQ	USBLS	5/15
	New York	Y	34100 AE	55220 MW	65130 AEX	NYBLS	1/16-3/16

AE	Average entry wage	AWR	Average wage range	H	Hourly
AEX	Average experienced wage	B	Biweekly	HI	Highest wage paid
ATC	Average total compensation	D	Daily	HR	High end range
AW	Average wage paid	FQ	First quartile wage	LO	Lowest wage paid

LR	Low end range	MTC	Median total compensation	TCC	Total cash compensation
M	Monthly	MW	Median wage paid	TQ	Third quartile wage
MCC	Median cash compensation	MWR	Median wage range	W	Weekly
ME	Median entry wage	S	See annotated source	Y	Yearly

Occupation/Type/Industry	Location	Per	Low	Mid	High	Source	Date
Civil Engineering Technician	Buffalo-Cheektowaga-Niagara Falls MSA, NY	Y	37120 FQ	49160 MW	61210 TQ	USBLS	5/15
	Nassau County-Suffolk County PMSA, NY	Y	35340 FQ	50590 MW	69120 TQ	USBLS	5/15
	New York-Jersey City-White Plains PMSA, NY-NJ	Y	40210 FQ	57470 MW	69880 TQ	USBLS	5/15
	Rochester MSA, NY	Y	44230 FQ	56640 MW	68810 TQ	USBLS	5/15
	North Carolina	Y	37680 FQ	46130 MW	53890 TQ	USBLS	5/15
	Charlotte-Concord-Gastonia MSA, NC-SC	Y	38070 FQ	47040 MW	56800 TQ	USBLS	5/15
	Raleigh MSA, NC	Y	37780 FQ	47650 MW	55650 TQ	USBLS	5/15
	North Dakota	Y	41890 FQ	47960 MW	58760 TQ	USBLS	5/15
	Fargo MSA, ND-MN	Y	41690 FQ	48390 MW	59450 TQ	USBLS	5/15
	Ohio	Y	41480 FQ	51290 MW	61140 TQ	USBLS	5/15
	Cincinnati MSA, OH-KY-IN	Y	38800 FQ	47810 MW	57280 TQ	USBLS	5/15
	Cleveland-Elyria MSA, OH	Y	44090 FQ	54040 MW	66340 TQ	USBLS	5/15
	Columbus MSA, OH	Y	41830 FQ	53740 MW	68390 TQ	USBLS	5/15
	Oklahoma	Y	40930 FQ	51550 MW	62170 TQ	USBLS	5/15
	Oklahoma City MSA, OK	Y	45210 FQ	55470 MW	64800 TQ	USBLS	5/15
	Tulsa MSA, OK	Y	41130 FQ	48790 MW	61610 TQ	USBLS	5/15
	Oregon	H	25.66 FQ	30.14 MW	34.02 TQ	ORBLS	2016
	Portland-Vancouver-Hillsboro MSA, OR-WA	Y	53760 FQ	61120 MW	69920 TQ	USBLS	5/15
	Pennsylvania	Y	40930 FQ	49280 MW	60770 TQ	USBLS	5/15
	Allentown-Bethlehem-Easton MSA, PA-NJ	Y	36520 FQ	50760 MW	61830 TQ	USBLS	5/15
	Harrisburg-Carlisle MSA, PA	Y	44920 FQ	53890 MW	62640 TQ	USBLS	5/15
	Montgomery County-Bucks County-Chester County PMSA, PA	Y	40760 FQ	48170 MW	60130 TQ	USBLS	5/15
	Philadelphia PMSA, PA	Y	45420 FQ	54510 MW	64730 TQ	USBLS	5/15
	Pittsburgh MSA, PA	Y	40700 FQ	48340 MW	60040 TQ	USBLS	5/15
	Rhode Island	Y	42410 FQ	51870 MW	60910 TQ	USBLS	5/15
	Providence-Warwick MSA, RI-MA	Y	41980 FQ	51840 MW	60910 TQ	USBLS	5/15
	South Carolina	Y	32140 FQ	42460 MW	53400 TQ	USBLS	5/15
	Charleston-North Charleston MSA, SC	Y	33630 FQ	42940 MW	52510 TQ	USBLS	5/15
	Columbia MSA, SC	Y	41950 FQ	51320 MW	59580 TQ	USBLS	5/15
	Greenville-Anderson-Mauldin MSA, SC	Y	26880 FQ	35630 MW	44400 TQ	USBLS	5/15
	South Dakota	Y	35400 FQ	41350 MW	47770 TQ	USBLS	5/15
	Sioux Falls MSA, SD	Y	35020 FQ	42710 MW	50000 TQ	USBLS	5/15
	Tennessee	Y	42730 FQ	51150 MW	60310 TQ	USBLS	5/15
	Knoxville MSA, TN	Y	40170 FQ	48810 MW	60810 TQ	USBLS	5/15
	Memphis MSA, TN-MS-AR	Y	36600 FQ	50430 MW	57600 TQ	USBLS	5/15
	Nashville-Davidson–Murfreesboro–Franklin MSA, TN	Y	45000 FQ	53250 MW	61140 TQ	USBLS	5/15
	Texas	Y	35860 FQ	42330 MW	52640 TQ	USBLS	5/15
	Austin-Round Rock MSA, TX	Y	42450 FQ	49520 MW	58250 TQ	USBLS	5/15
	Dallas-Plano-Irving PMSA, TX	Y	39740 FQ	48110 MW	58890 TQ	USBLS	5/15
	Fort Worth-Arlington PMSA, TX	Y	36150 FQ	44550 MW	53750 TQ	USBLS	5/15
	Houston-The Woodlands-Sugar Land MSA, TX	Y	34950 FQ	44740 MW	59380 TQ	USBLS	5/15
	San Antonio-New Braunfels MSA, TX	Y	37320 FQ	43550 MW	52200 TQ	USBLS	5/15
	Utah	Y	38730 FQ	48990 MW	58670 TQ	USBLS	5/15
	Ogden-Clearfield MSA, UT	Y	45310 FQ	50570 MW	57500 TQ	USBLS	5/15
	Provo-Orem MSA, UT	Y	37710 FQ	49460 MW	58440 TQ	USBLS	5/15
	Salt Lake City MSA, UT	Y	38400 FQ	48310 MW	59270 TQ	USBLS	5/15
	Vermont	Y	38100 FQ	47360 MW	60210 TQ	USBLS	5/15
	Burlington-South Burlington MSA, VT	Y	34230 FQ	44330 MW	54220 TQ	USBLS	5/15
	Virginia	Y	29340 FQ	38910 MW	52180 TQ	USBLS	5/15
	Richmond MSA, VA	Y	27920 FQ	33920 MW	46260 TQ	USBLS	5/15
	Virginia Beach-Norfolk-Newport News MSA, VA-NC	Y	41230 FQ	49040 MW	57610 TQ	USBLS	5/15
	Washington	H	25.72 FQ	28.90 MW	34.22 TQ	WABLS	3/16
	Seattle-Bellevue-Everett PMSA, WA	H	26.47 FQ	30.11 MW	37.20 TQ	WABLS	3/16

AE	Average entry wage	AWR	Average wage range	H	Hourly
AEX	Average expreienced wage	B	Biweekly	HI	Highest wage paid
ATC	Average total compensation	D	Daily	HR	High end range
AW	Average wage paid	FQ	First quartile wage	LO	Lowest wage paid

LR	Low end range	MTC	Median total compensation	TCC	Total cash compensation
M	Monthly	MW	Median wage paid	TQ	Third quartile wage
MCC	Median cash compensation	MWR	Median wage range	W	Weekly
ME	Median entry wage	S	See annotated source	Y	Yearly

Occupation/Type/Industry	Location	Per	Low	Mid	High	Source	Date
Civil Engineering Technician	Tacoma-Lakewood PMSA, WA	H	27.53 FQ	32.09 MW	36.20 TQ	WABLS	3/16
	West Virginia	Y	32700 FQ	41760 MW	52930 TQ	USBLS	5/15
	Huntington-Ashland MSA, WV-KY-OH	Y	40370 FQ	48690 MW	57680 TQ	USBLS	5/15
	Wisconsin	Y	41770 FQ	51270 MW	59560 TQ	USBLS	5/15
	Madison MSA, WI	Y	41610 FQ	48260 MW	57390 TQ	USBLS	5/15
	Milwaukee-Waukesha-West Allis MSA, WI	Y	38680 FQ	52230 MW	64020 TQ	USBLS	5/15
	Wyoming	Y	36920 FQ	42750 MW	52220 TQ	USBLS	5/15
	Cheyenne MSA, WY	Y	37990 FQ	44030 MW	48390 TQ	USBLS	5/15
	Puerto Rico	Y	20700 FQ	24210 MW	30870 TQ	USBLS	5/15
	San Juan-Carolina-Caguas MSA, PR	Y	20700 FQ	24190 MW	30770 TQ	USBLS	5/15
Civil Liability Claims Administrator							
City Attorney's Office	Anaheim, CA	Y			90029 HI	CACIT	6/28/16
Civil Rights Analyst							
Municipal Government	Seattle, WA	H	30.59 LO		35.54 HI	CSSS	1/13/16
Civil Service Mariner							
U.S. Navy's Military Sealift Command	United States	D			600.44 HI	HCHRON3	2017
Claims Adjuster, Examiner, and Investigator	Alabama	Y	38180 AE	60995 AW	72403 AEX	ALBLS	6/16
	Birmingham-Hoover MSA, AL	Y	39748 AE	62031 AW	73172 AEX	ALBLS	6/16
	Alaska	Y	54380 FQ	72490 MW	89460 TQ	USBLS	5/15
	Anchorage MSA, AK	Y	54610 FQ	72210 MW	89040 TQ	USBLS	5/15
	Arizona	Y	43580 FQ	55640 MW	70790 TQ	USBLS	5/15
	Phoenix-Mesa-Scottsdale MSA, AZ	Y	44080 FQ	56330 MW	71740 TQ	USBLS	5/15
	Tucson MSA, AZ	Y	38920 FQ	45990 MW	56820 TQ	USBLS	5/15
	Arkansas	Y	47920 FQ	63270 MW	77210 TQ	USBLS	5/15
	Little Rock-North Little Rock-Conway MSA, AR	Y	47700 FQ	62270 MW	78300 TQ	USBLS	5/15
	California	H	26.47 FQ	33.91 MW	41.57 TQ	CABLS	1/16-3/16
	Anaheim-Santa Ana-Irvine PMSA, CA	H	26.70 FQ	37.07 MW	46.41 TQ	CABLS	1/16-3/16
	Los Angeles-Long Beach-Glendale PMSA, CA	H	26.66 FQ	33.59 MW	39.28 TQ	CABLS	1/16-3/16
	Oakland-Hayward-Berkeley PMSA, CA	H	29.46 FQ	37.01 MW	44.35 TQ	CABLS	1/16-3/16
	Riverside-San Bernardino-Ontario MSA, CA	H	25.00 FQ	32.10 MW	37.73 TQ	CABLS	1/16-3/16
	Sacramento–Roseville–Arden-Arcade MSA, CA	H	25.82 FQ	33.76 MW	42.71 TQ	CABLS	1/16-3/16
	San Diego-Carlsbad MSA, CA	H	24.19 FQ	31.05 MW	38.63 TQ	CABLS	1/16-3/16
	San Francisco-Redwood City-South San Francisco PMSA, CA	H	29.28 FQ	39.33 MW	49.43 TQ	CABLS	1/16-3/16
	Colorado	Y	53670 FQ	67710 MW	81080 TQ	USBLS	5/15
	Denver-Aurora-Lakewood MSA, CO	Y	54080 FQ	67670 MW	81710 TQ	USBLS	5/15
	Connecticut	Y		67162 MW		CTBLS	1/16-3/16
	Bridgeport-Stamford-Norwalk MSA, CT	Y	50980 FQ	61750 MW	82110 TQ	USBLS	5/15
	Hartford-West Hartford-East Hartford MSA, CT	Y	52070 FQ	64940 MW	83810 TQ	USBLS	5/15
	Delaware	Y	55130 FQ	68720 MW	81210 TQ	USBLS	5/15
	Wilmington PMSA, DE-MD-NJ	Y	54550 FQ	67710 MW	80420 TQ	USBLS	5/15
	District of Columbia	Y	58010 FQ	78920 MW	96870 TQ	USBLS	5/15
	Washington-Arlington-Alexandria PMSA, DC-VA-MD-WV	Y	59350 FQ	74350 MW	87830 TQ	USBLS	5/15
	Florida	H	19.67 AE	29.24 MW	34.82 AEX	FLBLS	7/16-9/16
	Fort Lauderdale-Pompano Beach-Deerfield Beach PMSA, FL	H	20.50 AE	32.80 MW	38.16 AEX	FLBLS	7/16-9/16
	Miami-Miami Beach-Kendall PMSA, FL	H	18.03 AE	28.04 MW	33.32 AEX	FLBLS	7/16-9/16

AE	Average entry wage	AWR	Average wage range	H	Hourly	LR	Low end range	MTC	Median total compensation	TCC	Total cash compensation
AEX	Average experienced wage	B	Biweekly	HI	Highest wage paid	M	Monthly	MW	Median wage paid	TQ	Third quartile wage
ATC	Average total compensation	D	Daily	HR	High end range	MCC	Median cash compensation	MWR	Median wage range	W	Weekly
AW	Average wage paid	FQ	First quartile wage	LO	Lowest wage paid	ME	Median entry wage	S	See annotated source	Y	Yearly

227

Occupation/Type/Industry	Location	Per	Low	Mid	High	Source	Date
Claims Adjuster, Examiner, and Investigator	Orlando-Kissimmee-Sanford MSA, FL	H	21.46 AE	30.94 MW	35.56 AEX	FLBLS	7/16-9/16
	Tampa-St. Petersburg-Clearwater MSA, FL	H	20.48 AE	29.77 MW	35.15 AEX	FLBLS	7/16-9/16
	Georgia	Y	44580 FQ	58880 MW	75090 TQ	USBLS	5/15
	Atlanta-Sandy Springs-Roswell MSA, GA	Y	44490 FQ	59200 MW	75480 TQ	USBLS	5/15
	Augusta-Richmond County MSA, GA-SC	Y	41520 FQ	58560 MW	72280 TQ	USBLS	5/15
	Hawaii	Y	45930 FQ	60060 MW	74690 TQ	USBLS	5/15
	Urban Honolulu MSA, HI	Y	45850 FQ	59700 MW	74610 TQ	USBLS	5/15
	Idaho	Y	43850 FQ	60520 MW	74180 TQ	USBLS	5/15
	Boise City MSA, ID	Y	41090 FQ	56850 MW	71760 TQ	USBLS	5/15
	Illinois	Y	46770 FQ	64180 MW	79860 TQ	USBLS	5/15
	Chicago-Naperville-Arlington Heights PMSA, IL	Y	49560 FQ	67890 MW	83420 TQ	USBLS	5/15
	Indiana	Y	42210 FQ	56460 MW	72560 TQ	USBLS	5/15
	Gary PMSA, IN	Y	67260 FQ	79150 MW	84610 TQ	USBLS	5/15
	Indianapolis-Carmel-Anderson MSA, IN	Y	41080 FQ	54060 MW	72070 TQ	USBLS	5/15
	Iowa	Y	42960 FQ	54160 MW	70280 TQ	USBLS	5/15
	Des Moines-West Des Moines MSA, IA	Y	43660 FQ	52980 MW	68640 TQ	USBLS	5/15
	Kansas	Y	45320 FQ	60720 MW	74620 TQ	USBLS	5/15
	Wichita MSA, KS	Y	62480 FQ	70340 MW	79190 TQ	USBLS	5/15
	Kentucky	Y	43220 FQ	56670 MW	72540 TQ	USBLS	5/15
	Louisville-Jefferson County MSA, KY-IN	Y	42620 FQ	54840 MW	71960 TQ	USBLS	5/15
	Louisiana	Y	52860 FQ	66740 MW	79230 TQ	USBLS	5/15
	Baton Rouge MSA, LA	Y	49710 FQ	60860 MW	72790 TQ	USBLS	5/15
	New Orleans-Metairie MSA, LA	Y	55180 FQ	68660 MW	84570 TQ	USBLS	5/15
	Maine	Y	45100 FQ	60750 MW	75630 TQ	USBLS	5/15
	Portland-South Portland MSA, ME	Y	44590 FQ	59170 MW	75820 TQ	USBLS	5/15
	Maryland	Y	46312 AE	69051 MW	80421 AEX	MDBLS	4/16
	Baltimore-Columbia-Towson MSA, MD	Y	52670 FQ	70090 MW	84020 TQ	USBLS	5/15
	Salisbury MSA, MD-DE	Y	46340 FQ	64430 MW	70730 TQ	USBLS	5/15
	Massachusetts	Y	53860 FQ	68750 MW	82350 TQ	USBLS	5/15
	Boston-Cambridge-Newton NECTA, MA	Y	53610 FQ	69380 MW	83260 TQ	USBLS	5/15
	Worcester MSA, MA-CT	Y	53680 FQ	63310 MW	76980 TQ	USBLS	5/15
	Michigan	Y	45860 FQ	61530 MW	76240 TQ	USBLS	5/15
	Detroit-Dearborn-Livonia PMSA, MI	Y	52500 FQ	69210 MW	81380 TQ	USBLS	5/15
	Minnesota	Y	49383 FQ	63700 MW	76320 TQ	MNBLS	1/16-3/16
	Minneapolis-St. Paul-Bloomington MSA, MN-WI	Y	51283 FQ	65051 MW	77610 TQ	MNBLS	1/16-3/16
	Mississippi	Y	51400 FQ	66870 MW	76570 TQ	USBLS	5/15
	Jackson MSA, MS	Y	44320 FQ	62820 MW	74870 TQ	USBLS	5/15
	Missouri	Y	42610 FQ	59520 MW	76640 TQ	USBLS	5/15
	Kansas City MSA, MO-KS	Y	47230 FQ	63870 MW	78720 TQ	USBLS	5/15
	St. Louis MSA, MO-IL	Y	44630 FQ	57840 MW	73900 TQ	USBLS	5/15
	Montana	Y	31810 FQ	40270 MW	58900 TQ	USBLS	5/15
	Billings MSA, MT	Y	33610 FQ	43800 MW	58980 TQ	USBLS	5/15
	Nebraska	Y	42315 FQ	55430 MW	70940 TQ	NEBLS	7/16-9/16
	Omaha-Council Bluffs MSA, NE-IA	Y	39580 FQ	51480 MW	66995 TQ	NEBLS	7/16-9/16
	Nevada	Y	52880 FQ	66360 MW	76140 TQ	USBLS	5/15
	Las Vegas-Henderson-Paradise MSA, NV	Y	53250 FQ	66430 MW	76150 TQ	USBLS	5/15
	New Hampshire	H	21.47 AE	32.39 MW	38.83 AEX	NHBLS	6/16
	Manchester NECTA, NH	H	18.81 AE	31.06 MW	36.05 AEX	NHBLS	6/16
	Nashua NECTA, NH-MA	Y	43010 FQ	61690 MW	74810 TQ	USBLS	5/15
	New Jersey	Y	54580 FQ	71520 MW	87440 TQ	USBLS	5/15
	Camden PMSA, NJ	Y	50560 FQ	64650 MW	77390 TQ	USBLS	5/15
	Newark PMSA, NJ-PA	Y	57820 FQ	74360 MW	91570 TQ	USBLS	5/15
	Trenton MSA, NJ	Y	63080 FQ	74900 MW	88340 TQ	USBLS	5/15
	New Mexico	Y	42210 FQ	58490 MW	72280 TQ	USBLS	5/15
	Albuquerque MSA, NM	Y	42050 FQ	57310 MW	72220 TQ	USBLS	5/15

AE	Average entry wage	AWR	Average wage range	H	Hourly	LR	Low end range	MTC	Median total compensation	TCC	Total cash compensation
AEX	Average experienced wage	B	Biweekly	HI	Highest wage paid	M	Monthly	MW	Median wage paid	TQ	Third quartile wage
ATC	Average total compensation	D	Daily	HR	High end range	MCC	Median cash compensation	MWR	Median wage range	W	Weekly
AW	Average wage paid	FQ	First quartile wage	LO	Lowest wage paid	ME	Median entry wage	S	See annotated source	Y	Yearly

Occupation/Type/Industry	Location	Per	Low	Mid	High	Source	Date
Claims Adjuster, Examiner, and Investigator	New York	Y	45010 AE	66010 MW	81320 AEX	NYBLS	1/16-3/16
	Buffalo-Cheektowaga-Niagara Falls MSA, NY	Y	48150 FQ	57730 MW	72010 TQ	USBLS	5/15
	Nassau County-Suffolk County PMSA, NY	Y	50620 FQ	62410 MW	79560 TQ	USBLS	5/15
	New York-Jersey City-White Plains PMSA, NY-NJ	Y	52750 FQ	70900 MW	88050 TQ	USBLS	5/15
	Rochester MSA, NY	Y	46650 FQ	62470 MW	79500 TQ	USBLS	5/15
	North Carolina	Y	46870 FQ	61090 MW	74760 TQ	USBLS	5/15
	Charlotte-Concord-Gastonia MSA, NC-SC	Y	53250 FQ	66360 MW	80350 TQ	USBLS	5/15
	Raleigh MSA, NC	Y	47800 FQ	60000 MW	75900 TQ	USBLS	5/15
	North Dakota	Y	30980 FQ	45630 MW	58770 TQ	USBLS	5/15
	Fargo MSA, ND-MN	Y	28760 FQ	37290 MW	55430 TQ	USBLS	5/15
	Ohio	Y	46950 FQ	62100 MW	77600 TQ	USBLS	5/15
	Cincinnati MSA, OH-KY-IN	Y	48330 FQ	62450 MW	75940 TQ	USBLS	5/15
	Cleveland-Elyria MSA, OH	Y	50330 FQ	67250 MW	82710 TQ	USBLS	5/15
	Columbus MSA, OH	Y	46680 FQ	60050 MW	77990 TQ	USBLS	5/15
	Oklahoma	Y	39340 FQ	53240 MW	68310 TQ	USBLS	5/15
	Oklahoma City MSA, OK	Y	29320 FQ	50970 MW	69470 TQ	USBLS	5/15
	Tulsa MSA, OK	Y	34330 FQ	46770 MW	65980 TQ	USBLS	5/15
	Oregon	H	26.69 FQ	33.35 MW	39.77 TQ	ORBLS	2016
	Portland-Vancouver-Hillsboro MSA, OR-WA	Y	56370 FQ	69410 MW	81720 TQ	USBLS	5/15
	Pennsylvania	Y	45580 FQ	59710 MW	74980 TQ	USBLS	5/15
	Allentown-Bethlehem-Easton MSA, PA-NJ	Y	50190 FQ	60530 MW	75660 TQ	USBLS	5/15
	Harrisburg-Carlisle MSA, PA	Y	43890 FQ	54580 MW	70910 TQ	USBLS	5/15
	Montgomery County-Bucks County-Chester County PMSA, PA	Y	47300 FQ	59830 MW	77460 TQ	USBLS	5/15
	Philadelphia PMSA, PA	Y	49370 FQ	62550 MW	76510 TQ	USBLS	5/15
	Pittsburgh MSA, PA	Y	41110 FQ	56870 MW	73930 TQ	USBLS	5/15
	Rhode Island	Y	53060 FQ	68890 MW	79300 TQ	USBLS	5/15
	Providence-Warwick MSA, RI-MA	Y	53590 FQ	69300 MW	79300 TQ	USBLS	5/15
	South Carolina	Y	37460 FQ	59870 MW	72540 TQ	USBLS	5/15
	Charleston-North Charleston MSA, SC	Y	43510 FQ	56160 MW	71530 TQ	USBLS	5/15
	Columbia MSA, SC	Y	42070 FQ	61780 MW	70360 TQ	USBLS	5/15
	Greenville-Anderson-Mauldin MSA, SC	Y	58560 FQ	68770 MW	78640 TQ	USBLS	5/15
	South Dakota	Y	49460 FQ	60910 MW	74180 TQ	USBLS	5/15
	Sioux Falls MSA, SD	Y	49330 FQ	60530 MW	74250 TQ	USBLS	5/15
	Tennessee	Y	43740 FQ	58540 MW	72240 TQ	USBLS	5/15
	Knoxville MSA, TN	Y	49810 FQ	62470 MW	77100 TQ	USBLS	5/15
	Memphis MSA, TN-MS-AR	Y	46280 FQ	62860 MW	73800 TQ	USBLS	5/15
	Nashville-Davidson–Murfreesboro–Franklin MSA, TN	Y	43030 FQ	55730 MW	70500 TQ	USBLS	5/15
	Texas	Y	48420 FQ	64100 MW	77980 TQ	USBLS	5/15
	Austin-Round Rock MSA, TX	Y	44250 FQ	54660 MW	69770 TQ	USBLS	5/15
	Dallas-Plano-Irving PMSA, TX	Y	50530 FQ	64350 MW	78970 TQ	USBLS	5/15
	Fort Worth-Arlington PMSA, TX	Y	43690 FQ	63980 MW	77700 TQ	USBLS	5/15
	Houston-The Woodlands-Sugar Land MSA, TX	Y	56610 FQ	73390 MW	89620 TQ	USBLS	5/15
	San Antonio-New Braunfels MSA, TX	Y	46600 FQ	60520 MW	76320 TQ	USBLS	5/15
	Utah	Y	41660 FQ	56800 MW	71810 TQ	USBLS	5/15
	Provo-Orem MSA, UT	Y	45360 FQ	56940 MW	69930 TQ	USBLS	5/15
	Salt Lake City MSA, UT	Y	40530 FQ	55960 MW	71350 TQ	USBLS	5/15
	Vermont	Y	50450 FQ	66360 MW	77570 TQ	USBLS	5/15
	Burlington-South Burlington MSA, VT	Y	50600 FQ	68650 MW	80710 TQ	USBLS	5/15
	Virginia	Y	49500 FQ	64430 MW	77230 TQ	USBLS	5/15
	Richmond MSA, VA	Y	51040 FQ	64640 MW	76720 TQ	USBLS	5/15
	Virginia Beach-Norfolk-Newport News MSA, VA-NC	Y	43450 FQ	53890 MW	66900 TQ	USBLS	5/15
	Washington	H	25.18 FQ	30.75 MW	39.96 TQ	WABLS	3/16

AE	Average entry wage	AWR	Average wage range	H	Hourly	LR	Low end range	MTC	Median total compensation	TCC	Total cash compensation
AEX	Average experienced wage	B	Biweekly	HI	Highest wage paid	M	Monthly	MW	Median wage paid	TQ	Third quartile wage
ATC	Average total compensation	D	Daily	HR	High end range	MCC	Median cash compensation	MWR	Median wage range	W	Weekly
AW	Average wage paid	FQ	First quartile wage	LO	Lowest wage paid	ME	Median entry wage	S	See annotated source	Y	Yearly

Occupation/Type/Industry	Location	Per	Low	Mid	High	Source	Date
Claims Adjuster, Examiner, and Investigator							
	Seattle-Bellevue-Everett PMSA, WA	H	26.65 FQ	34.85 MW	43.00 TQ	WABLS	3/16
	Tacoma-Lakewood PMSA, WA	H	23.66 FQ	31.67 MW	39.84 TQ	WABLS	3/16
	West Virginia	Y	45590 FQ	60890 MW	74630 TQ	USBLS	5/15
	Huntington-Ashland MSA, WV-KY-OH	Y	45780 FQ	64420 MW	77110 TQ	USBLS	5/15
	Wisconsin	Y	43670 FQ	60160 MW	75050 TQ	USBLS	5/15
	Madison MSA, WI	Y	43480 FQ	56890 MW	73260 TQ	USBLS	5/15
	Milwaukee-Waukesha-West Allis MSA, WI	Y	52020 FQ	64800 MW	77440 TQ	USBLS	5/15
	Wyoming	Y	36850 FQ	52590 MW	84220 TQ	USBLS	5/15
	Cheyenne MSA, WY	Y	31940 FQ	46730 MW	70000 TQ	USBLS	5/15
	Puerto Rico	Y	24590 FQ	35780 MW	51510 TQ	USBLS	5/15
	San Juan-Carolina-Caguas MSA, PR	Y	24380 FQ	34630 MW	50420 TQ	USBLS	5/15
	Guam	Y	29970 FQ	36570 MW	49460 TQ	USBLS	5/15
Cleaner of Vehicles and Equipment							
	Alabama	Y	17557 AE	22781 AW	25394 AEX	ALBLS	6/16
	Birmingham-Hoover MSA, AL	Y	17454 AE	22997 AW	25764 AEX	ALBLS	6/16
	Alaska	Y	21550 FQ	25560 MW	29990 TQ	USBLS	5/15
	Anchorage MSA, AK	Y	21750 FQ	25870 MW	30920 TQ	USBLS	5/15
	Arizona	Y	18160 FQ	19530 MW	23570 TQ	USBLS	5/15
	Phoenix-Mesa-Scottsdale MSA, AZ	Y	18180 FQ	19570 MW	23960 TQ	USBLS	5/15
	Tucson MSA, AZ	Y	18020 FQ	19180 MW	22190 TQ	USBLS	5/15
	Arkansas	Y	18480 FQ	21150 MW	24020 TQ	USBLS	5/15
	Little Rock-North Little Rock-Conway MSA, AR	Y	18240 FQ	20670 MW	23770 TQ	USBLS	5/15
	California	H	9.58 FQ	10.70 MW	12.92 TQ	CABLS	1/16-3/16
	Anaheim-Santa Ana-Irvine PMSA, CA	H	9.74 FQ	10.94 MW	12.50 TQ	CABLS	1/16-3/16
	Los Angeles-Long Beach-Glendale PMSA, CA	H	9.51 FQ	10.14 MW	12.23 TQ	CABLS	1/16-3/16
	Oakland-Hayward-Berkeley PMSA, CA	H	9.56 FQ	10.39 MW	13.35 TQ	CABLS	1/16-3/16
	Riverside-San Bernardino-Ontario MSA, CA	H	9.55 FQ	10.53 MW	12.81 TQ	CABLS	1/16-3/16
	Sacramento–Roseville–Arden-Arcade MSA, CA	H	9.60 FQ	11.10 MW	13.44 TQ	CABLS	1/16-3/16
	San Diego-Carlsbad MSA, CA	H	9.60 FQ	10.68 MW	12.40 TQ	CABLS	1/16-3/16
	San Francisco-Redwood City-South San Francisco PMSA, CA	H	10.95 FQ	12.38 MW	14.38 TQ	CABLS	1/16-3/16
	Colorado	Y	18910 FQ	21450 MW	25150 TQ	USBLS	5/15
	Denver-Aurora-Lakewood MSA, CO	Y	18590 FQ	20270 MW	24160 TQ	USBLS	5/15
	Connecticut	Y		23502 MW		CTBLS	1/16-3/16
	Bridgeport-Stamford-Norwalk MSA, CT	Y	19370 FQ	20120 MW	24800 TQ	USBLS	5/15
	Hartford-West Hartford-East Hartford MSA, CT	Y	21130 FQ	24950 MW	31210 TQ	USBLS	5/15
	Delaware	Y	18350 FQ	20760 MW	24780 TQ	USBLS	5/15
	Wilmington PMSA, DE-MD-NJ	Y	18750 FQ	21940 MW	25760 TQ	USBLS	5/15
	District of Columbia	Y	23970 FQ	40860 MW	45400 TQ	USBLS	5/15
	Washington-Arlington-Alexandria PMSA, DC-VA-MD-WV	Y	18330 FQ	21570 MW	27540 TQ	USBLS	5/15
	Florida	H	9.02 AE	9.82 MW	12.02 AEX	FLBLS	7/16-9/16
	Fort Lauderdale-Pompano Beach-Deerfield Beach PMSA, FL	H	8.98 AE	9.58 MW	11.44 AEX	FLBLS	7/16-9/16
	Miami-Miami Beach-Kendall PMSA, FL	H	9.06 AE	9.50 MW	11.86 AEX	FLBLS	7/16-9/16
	Orlando-Kissimmee-Sanford MSA, FL	H	9.04 AE	10.44 MW	12.42 AEX	FLBLS	7/16-9/16
	Tampa-St. Petersburg-Clearwater MSA, FL	H	8.98 AE	9.64 MW	11.69 AEX	FLBLS	7/16-9/16
	Georgia	Y	17540 FQ	19510 MW	24480 TQ	USBLS	5/15

Occupation/Type/Industry	Location	Per	Low	Mid	High	Source	Date
Cleaner of Vehicles and Equipment	Atlanta-Sandy Springs-Roswell MSA, GA	Y	17450 FQ	19310 MW	25540 TQ	USBLS	5/15
	Augusta-Richmond County MSA, GA-SC	Y	17600 FQ	19580 MW	23460 TQ	USBLS	5/15
	Hawaii	Y	20950 FQ	25820 MW	30520 TQ	USBLS	5/15
	Urban Honolulu MSA, HI	Y	21420 FQ	26280 MW	31030 TQ	USBLS	5/15
	Idaho	Y	18130 FQ	22430 MW	29540 TQ	USBLS	5/15
	Boise City MSA, ID	Y	18220 FQ	24270 MW	33110 TQ	USBLS	5/15
	Illinois	Y	18900 FQ	20440 MW	25200 TQ	USBLS	5/15
	Chicago-Naperville-Arlington Heights PMSA, IL	Y	18870 FQ	20070 MW	24340 TQ	USBLS	5/15
	Lake County-Kenosha County PMSA, IL-WI	Y	18990 FQ	21090 MW	25620 TQ	USBLS	5/15
	Indiana	Y	18020 FQ	21210 MW	27210 TQ	USBLS	5/15
	Gary PMSA, IN	Y	17360 FQ	19190 MW	24580 TQ	USBLS	5/15
	Indianapolis-Carmel-Anderson MSA, IN	Y	17730 FQ	20290 MW	25920 TQ	USBLS	5/15
	Iowa	Y	18680 FQ	22440 MW	27850 TQ	USBLS	5/15
	Des Moines-West Des Moines MSA, IA	Y	20880 FQ	25910 MW	29360 TQ	USBLS	5/15
	Kansas	Y	17880 FQ	20290 MW	25950 TQ	USBLS	5/15
	Wichita MSA, KS	Y	18040 FQ	20850 MW	25220 TQ	USBLS	5/15
	Kentucky	Y	17750 FQ	20100 MW	24490 TQ	USBLS	5/15
	Louisville-Jefferson County MSA, KY-IN	Y	17580 FQ	20010 MW	24770 TQ	USBLS	5/15
	Louisiana	Y	17640 FQ	20090 MW	26550 TQ	USBLS	5/15
	Baton Rouge MSA, LA	Y	18210 FQ	21650 MW	27690 TQ	USBLS	5/15
	New Orleans-Metairie MSA, LA	Y	17500 FQ	19850 MW	25110 TQ	USBLS	5/15
	Maine	Y	19460 FQ	23230 MW	27880 TQ	USBLS	5/15
	Portland-South Portland MSA, ME	Y	18750 FQ	23450 MW	28330 TQ	USBLS	5/15
	Maryland	Y	18139 AE	24398 MW	27528 AEX	MDBLS	4/16
	Baltimore-Columbia-Towson MSA, MD	Y	18940 FQ	22990 MW	29660 TQ	USBLS	5/15
	Salisbury MSA, MD-DE	Y	17910 FQ	19260 MW	24600 TQ	USBLS	5/15
	Massachusetts	Y	19780 FQ	23060 MW	28960 TQ	USBLS	5/15
	Boston-Cambridge-Newton NECTA, MA	Y	19480 FQ	22120 MW	28690 TQ	USBLS	5/15
	Worcester MSA, MA-CT	Y	20730 FQ	23570 MW	28040 TQ	USBLS	5/15
	Michigan	Y	18480 FQ	19930 MW	24120 TQ	USBLS	5/15
	Detroit-Dearborn-Livonia PMSA, MI	Y	18730 FQ	21250 MW	27980 TQ	USBLS	5/15
	Grand Rapids-Wyoming MSA, MI	Y	18560 FQ	20030 MW	23690 TQ	USBLS	5/15
	Minnesota	Y	18983 FQ	22955 MW	29327 TQ	MNBLS	1/16-3/16
	Minneapolis-St. Paul-Bloomington MSA, MN-WI	Y	19074 FQ	23661 MW	30275 TQ	MNBLS	1/16-3/16
	Mississippi	Y	18100 FQ	21220 MW	25960 TQ	USBLS	5/15
	Jackson MSA, MS	Y	18550 FQ	22390 MW	28560 TQ	USBLS	5/15
	Missouri	Y	17710 FQ	19450 MW	24080 TQ	USBLS	5/15
	Kansas City MSA, MO-KS	Y	17840 FQ	20000 MW	26190 TQ	USBLS	5/15
	St. Louis MSA, MO-IL	Y	17530 FQ	18940 MW	21800 TQ	USBLS	5/15
	Montana	Y	18840 FQ	21610 MW	25860 TQ	USBLS	5/15
	Billings MSA, MT	Y	19570 FQ	23060 MW	28920 TQ	USBLS	5/15
	Nebraska	Y	18800 FQ	22485 MW	29015 TQ	NEBLS	7/16-9/16
	Omaha-Council Bluffs MSA, NE-IA	Y	19695 FQ	25190 MW	30775 TQ	NEBLS	7/16-9/16
	Nevada	Y	17970 FQ	20830 MW	24810 TQ	USBLS	5/15
	Las Vegas-Henderson-Paradise MSA, NV	Y	17800 FQ	20460 MW	24620 TQ	USBLS	5/15
	New Hampshire	H	9.44 AE	11.70 MW	13.47 AEX	NHBLS	6/16
	Manchester NECTA, NH	H	9.53 AE	11.54 MW	13.87 AEX	NHBLS	6/16
	Nashua NECTA, NH-MA	Y	18710 FQ	21970 MW	26250 TQ	USBLS	5/15
	New Jersey	Y	18700 FQ	20450 MW	27970 TQ	USBLS	5/15
	Camden PMSA, NJ	Y	18600 FQ	19690 MW	25760 TQ	USBLS	5/15
	Newark PMSA, NJ-PA	Y	18480 FQ	19460 MW	23590 TQ	USBLS	5/15
	Trenton MSA, NJ	Y	19080 FQ	23120 MW	28350 TQ	USBLS	5/15
	New Mexico	Y	17840 FQ	19610 MW	23960 TQ	USBLS	5/15
	Albuquerque MSA, NM	Y	17790 FQ	19350 MW	22780 TQ	USBLS	5/15
	New York	Y	19400 AE	23380 MW	37470 AEX	NYBLS	1/16-3/16

AE	Average entry wage	AWR	Average wage range	H	Hourly	LR	Low end range	MTC	Median total compensation	TCC	Total cash compensation
AEX	Average experienced wage	B	Biweekly	HI	Highest wage paid	M	Monthly	MW	Median wage paid	TQ	Third quartile wage
ATC	Average total compensation	D	Daily	HR	High end range	MCC	Median cash compensation	MWR	Median wage range	W	Weekly
AW	Average wage paid	FQ	First quartile wage	LO	Lowest wage paid	ME	Median entry wage	S	See annotated source	Y	Yearly

Cleaner of Vehicles and Equipment

Occupation/Type/Industry	Location	Per	Low	Mid	High	Source	Date
	Buffalo-Cheektowaga-Niagara Falls MSA, NY	Y	19280 FQ	21070 MW	25210 TQ	USBLS	5/15
	Nassau County-Suffolk County PMSA, NY	Y	19080 FQ	20930 MW	27960 TQ	USBLS	5/15
	New York-Jersey City-White Plains PMSA, NY-NJ	Y	19220 FQ	25620 MW	54470 TQ	USBLS	5/15
	Rochester MSA, NY	Y	19130 FQ	20650 MW	23780 TQ	USBLS	5/15
	North Carolina	Y	17720 FQ	20010 MW	24300 TQ	USBLS	5/15
	Charlotte-Concord-Gastonia MSA, NC-SC	Y	17570 FQ	19510 MW	24390 TQ	USBLS	5/15
	Raleigh MSA, NC	Y	17360 FQ	19180 MW	23510 TQ	USBLS	5/15
	Fargo MSA, ND-MN	Y	17670 FQ	19700 MW	25230 TQ	USBLS	5/15
	Ohio	Y	18740 FQ	21630 MW	27930 TQ	USBLS	5/15
	Cincinnati MSA, OH-KY-IN	Y	18220 FQ	19760 MW	25470 TQ	USBLS	5/15
	Cleveland-Elyria MSA, OH	Y	18630 FQ	21010 MW	26130 TQ	USBLS	5/15
	Columbus MSA, OH	Y	20150 FQ	23240 MW	28640 TQ	USBLS	5/15
	Oklahoma	Y	18610 FQ	22020 MW	27530 TQ	USBLS	5/15
	Oklahoma City MSA, OK	Y	18620 FQ	22690 MW	29630 TQ	USBLS	5/15
	Tulsa MSA, OK	Y	18580 FQ	21560 MW	24730 TQ	USBLS	5/15
	Oregon	H	10.43 FQ	11.70 MW	13.82 TQ	ORBLS	2016
	Portland-Vancouver-Hillsboro MSA, OR-WA	Y	21840 FQ	24390 MW	28800 TQ	USBLS	5/15
	Pennsylvania	Y	17920 FQ	20700 MW	26280 TQ	USBLS	5/15
	Allentown-Bethlehem-Easton MSA, PA-NJ	Y	17530 FQ	19420 MW	23560 TQ	USBLS	5/15
	Harrisburg-Carlisle MSA, PA	Y	18990 FQ	22050 MW	27760 TQ	USBLS	5/15
	Montgomery County-Bucks County-Chester County PMSA, PA	Y	17410 FQ	19290 MW	23460 TQ	USBLS	5/15
	Philadelphia PMSA, PA	Y	17700 FQ	19740 MW	27260 TQ	USBLS	5/15
	Pittsburgh MSA, PA	Y	17560 FQ	19600 MW	23720 TQ	USBLS	5/15
	Rhode Island	Y	19620 FQ	23370 MW	29090 TQ	USBLS	5/15
	Providence-Warwick MSA, RI-MA	Y	19700 FQ	23550 MW	28970 TQ	USBLS	5/15
	South Carolina	Y	17730 FQ	19910 MW	24590 TQ	USBLS	5/15
	Charleston-North Charleston MSA, SC	Y	17760 FQ	19650 MW	23700 TQ	USBLS	5/15
	Columbia MSA, SC	Y	17590 FQ	19770 MW	24340 TQ	USBLS	5/15
	Greenville-Anderson-Mauldin MSA, SC	Y	18080 FQ	20620 MW	24570 TQ	USBLS	5/15
	South Dakota	Y	18940 FQ	20760 MW	23280 TQ	USBLS	5/15
	Sioux Falls MSA, SD	Y	18810 FQ	20600 MW	23160 TQ	USBLS	5/15
	Tennessee	Y	18270 FQ	21630 MW	27980 TQ	USBLS	5/15
	Knoxville MSA, TN	Y	18630 FQ	21800 MW	26560 TQ	USBLS	5/15
	Memphis MSA, TN-MS-AR	Y	19140 FQ	22170 MW	25830 TQ	USBLS	5/15
	Nashville-Davidson–Murfreesboro–Franklin MSA, TN	Y	18160 FQ	23030 MW	31110 TQ	USBLS	5/15
	Texas	Y	17970 FQ	20750 MW	25500 TQ	USBLS	5/15
	Austin-Round Rock MSA, TX	Y	18020 FQ	20680 MW	24400 TQ	USBLS	5/15
	Dallas-Plano-Irving PMSA, TX	Y	18480 FQ	21520 MW	25380 TQ	USBLS	5/15
	Fort Worth-Arlington PMSA, TX	Y	17330 FQ	19160 MW	22950 TQ	USBLS	5/15
	Houston-The Woodlands-Sugar Land MSA, TX	Y	17820 FQ	20510 MW	25540 TQ	USBLS	5/15
	San Antonio-New Braunfels MSA, TX	Y	19300 FQ	23310 MW	30740 TQ	USBLS	5/15
	Utah	Y	17690 FQ	20090 MW	24380 TQ	USBLS	5/15
	Logan MSA, UT-ID	Y	18410 FQ	22330 MW	28150 TQ	USBLS	5/15
	Ogden-Clearfield MSA, UT	Y	18260 FQ	21390 MW	27340 TQ	USBLS	5/15
	Provo-Orem MSA, UT	Y	17680 FQ	19700 MW	23210 TQ	USBLS	5/15
	Salt Lake City MSA, UT	Y	17480 FQ	19800 MW	23800 TQ	USBLS	5/15
	Vermont	Y	20270 FQ	24000 MW	28660 TQ	USBLS	5/15
	Burlington-South Burlington MSA, VT	Y	23200 FQ	27070 MW	30760 TQ	USBLS	5/15
	Virginia	Y	18140 FQ	21470 MW	27310 TQ	USBLS	5/15
	Richmond MSA, VA	Y	18800 FQ	22220 MW	29890 TQ	USBLS	5/15
	Virginia Beach-Norfolk-Newport News MSA, VA-NC	Y	18140 FQ	22220 MW	29990 TQ	USBLS	5/15
	Washington	H	10.92 FQ	12.56 MW	15.18 TQ	WABLS	3/16

AE Average entry wage	**AWR** Average wage range	**H** Hourly	**LR** Low end range	**MTC** Median total compensation	**TCC** Total cash compensation
AEX Average experienced wage	**B** Biweekly	**HI** Highest wage paid	**M** Monthly	**MW** Median wage paid	**TQ** Third quartile wage
ATC Average total compensation	**D** Daily	**HR** High end range	**MCC** Median cash compensation	**MWR** Median wage range	**W** Weekly
AW Average wage paid	**FQ** First quartile wage	**LO** Lowest wage paid	**ME** Median entry wage	**S** See annotated source	**Y** Yearly

Occupation/Type/Industry	Location	Per	Low	Mid	High	Source	Date
Cleaner of Vehicles and Equipment							
	Seattle-Bellevue-Everett PMSA, WA	H	11.68 FQ	13.80 MW	16.55 TQ	WABLS	3/16
	Tacoma-Lakewood PMSA, WA	H	10.82 FQ	12.01 MW	13.73 TQ	WABLS	3/16
	West Virginia	Y	17910 FQ	19190 MW	22680 TQ	USBLS	5/15
	Huntington-Ashland MSA, WV-KY-OH	Y	18120 FQ	19680 MW	24070 TQ	USBLS	5/15
	Wisconsin	Y	19000 FQ	23530 MW	30390 TQ	USBLS	5/15
	Madison MSA, WI	Y	22850 FQ	27740 MW	33990 TQ	USBLS	5/15
	Milwaukee-Waukesha-West Allis MSA, WI	Y	20380 FQ	24190 MW	30410 TQ	USBLS	5/15
	Wyoming	Y	19830 FQ	22910 MW	27420 TQ	USBLS	5/15
	Cheyenne MSA, WY	Y	19670 FQ	22390 MW	26600 TQ	USBLS	5/15
	Puerto Rico	Y	16750 FQ	17910 MW	19080 TQ	USBLS	5/15
	San Juan-Carolina-Caguas MSA, PR	Y	16770 FQ	17950 MW	19130 TQ	USBLS	5/15
	Virgin Islands	Y	17420 FQ	19410 MW	23110 TQ	USBLS	5/15
	Guam	Y	17940 FQ	18730 MW	19630 TQ	USBLS	5/15
Cleaning, Washing, and Metal Pickling Equipment Operator and Tender							
	Alabama	Y	21582 AE	30034 AW	34250 AEX	ALBLS	6/16
	Birmingham-Hoover MSA, AL	Y	21778 AE	28965 AW	32564 AEX	ALBLS	6/16
	Arizona	Y	21300 FQ	24340 MW	29680 TQ	USBLS	5/15
	Phoenix-Mesa-Scottsdale MSA, AZ	Y	21250 FQ	24280 MW	29580 TQ	USBLS	5/15
	Arkansas	Y	21560 FQ	24950 MW	30230 TQ	USBLS	5/15
	California	H	10.82 FQ	13.38 MW	17.40 TQ	CABLS	1/16-3/16
	Anaheim-Santa Ana-Irvine PMSA, CA	H	10.77 FQ	12.93 MW	15.21 TQ	CABLS	1/16-3/16
	Los Angeles-Long Beach-Glendale PMSA, CA	H	11.35 FQ	14.26 MW	18.16 TQ	CABLS	1/16-3/16
	Oakland-Hayward-Berkeley PMSA, CA	H	9.65 FQ	12.88 MW	17.02 TQ	CABLS	1/16-3/16
	Riverside-San Bernardino-Ontario MSA, CA	H	10.55 FQ	11.92 MW	14.40 TQ	CABLS	1/16-3/16
	San Diego-Carlsbad MSA, CA	H	12.62 FQ	14.32 MW	17.26 TQ	CABLS	1/16-3/16
	San Francisco-Redwood City-South San Francisco PMSA, CA	H	15.55 FQ	25.87 MW	28.31 TQ	CABLS	1/16-3/16
	Colorado	Y	23170 FQ	27910 MW	39110 TQ	USBLS	5/15
	Denver-Aurora-Lakewood MSA, CO	Y	22600 FQ	26220 MW	44070 TQ	USBLS	5/15
	Connecticut	Y		31296 MW		CTBLS	1/16-3/16
	Bridgeport-Stamford-Norwalk MSA, CT	Y	31590 FQ	34880 MW	38100 TQ	USBLS	5/15
	Hartford-West Hartford-East Hartford MSA, CT	Y	24280 FQ	28910 MW	35800 TQ	USBLS	5/15
	Delaware	Y	20440 FQ	22880 MW	25510 TQ	USBLS	5/15
	Florida	H	10.14 AE	12.62 MW	14.50 AEX	FLBLS	7/16-9/16
	Fort Lauderdale-Pompano Beach-Deerfield Beach PMSA, FL	H	11.03 AE	14.16 MW	15.52 AEX	FLBLS	7/16-9/16
	Orlando-Kissimmee-Sanford MSA, FL	H	9.08 AE	10.47 MW	13.27 AEX	FLBLS	7/16-9/16
	Tampa-St. Petersburg-Clearwater MSA, FL	H	9.22 AE	11.21 MW	13.04 AEX	FLBLS	7/16-9/16
	Georgia	Y	20680 FQ	25180 MW	29760 TQ	USBLS	5/15
	Atlanta-Sandy Springs-Roswell MSA, GA	Y	22000 FQ	27040 MW	30850 TQ	USBLS	5/15
	Hawaii	Y	22160 FQ	25330 MW	30240 TQ	USBLS	5/15
	Idaho	Y	27570 FQ	30760 MW	36600 TQ	USBLS	5/15
	Illinois	Y	25370 FQ	29790 MW	37040 TQ	USBLS	5/15
	Chicago-Naperville-Arlington Heights PMSA, IL	Y	26210 FQ	30100 MW	38220 TQ	USBLS	5/15
	Lake County-Kenosha County PMSA, IL-WI	Y	21250 FQ	23240 MW	30330 TQ	USBLS	5/15
	Indiana	Y	20250 FQ	22910 MW	27170 TQ	USBLS	5/15
	Gary PMSA, IN	Y	26140 FQ	29700 MW	34320 TQ	USBLS	5/15
	Indianapolis-Carmel-Anderson MSA, IN	Y	18670 FQ	22220 MW	27400 TQ	USBLS	5/15

AE Average entry wage	**AWR** Average wage range	**H** Hourly	**LR** Low end range	**MTC** Median total compensation	**TCC** Total cash compensation
AEX Average experienced wage	**B** Biweekly	**HI** Highest wage paid	**M** Monthly	**MW** Median wage paid	**TQ** Third quartile wage
ATC Average total compensation	**D** Daily	**HR** High end range	**MCC** Median cash compensation	**MWR** Median wage range	**W** Weekly
AW Average wage paid	**FQ** First quartile wage	**LO** Lowest wage paid	**ME** Median entry wage	**S** See annotated source	**Y** Yearly

Occupation/Type/Industry	Location	Per	Low	Mid	High	Source	Date
Cleaning, Washing, and Metal Pickling Equipment Operator and Tender							
	Iowa	Y	25200 FQ	28470 MW	33650 TQ	USBLS	5/15
	Kansas	Y	30540 FQ	35520 MW	39990 TQ	USBLS	5/15
	Kentucky	Y	23500 FQ	27990 MW	32460 TQ	USBLS	5/15
	Louisville-Jefferson County MSA, KY-IN	Y	22250 FQ	24540 MW	31990 TQ	USBLS	5/15
	Louisiana	Y	22950 FQ	27500 MW	37030 TQ	USBLS	5/15
	Maryland	Y	20553 AE	27420 MW	30853 AEX	MDBLS	4/16
	Baltimore-Columbia-Towson MSA, MD	Y	22950 FQ	31580 MW	36140 TQ	USBLS	5/15
	Salisbury MSA, MD-DE	Y	21170 FQ	23270 MW	25760 TQ	USBLS	5/15
	Massachusetts	Y	23470 FQ	29370 MW	39480 TQ	USBLS	5/15
	Boston-Cambridge-Newton NECTA, MA	Y	26110 FQ	32480 MW	46060 TQ	USBLS	5/15
	Michigan	Y	23650 FQ	29810 MW	37500 TQ	USBLS	5/15
	Detroit-Dearborn-Livonia PMSA, MI	Y	18750 FQ	22570 MW	30540 TQ	USBLS	5/15
	Grand Rapids-Wyoming MSA, MI	Y	24990 FQ	30800 MW	36590 TQ	USBLS	5/15
	Minnesota	Y	28440 FQ	34990 MW	42442 TQ	MNBLS	1/16-3/16
	Minneapolis-St. Paul-Bloomington MSA, MN-WI	Y	32581 FQ	38210 MW	44284 TQ	MNBLS	1/16-3/16
	Mississippi	Y	21560 FQ	26070 MW	29840 TQ	USBLS	5/15
	Jackson MSA, MS	Y	23700 FQ	27140 MW	29540 TQ	USBLS	5/15
	Missouri	Y	25180 FQ	28020 MW	31050 TQ	USBLS	5/15
	Kansas City MSA, MO-KS	Y	22070 FQ	29320 MW	36380 TQ	USBLS	5/15
	St. Louis MSA, MO-IL	Y	26410 FQ	29980 MW	35400 TQ	USBLS	5/15
	Nebraska	Y	26810 FQ	30240 MW	35435 TQ	NEBLS	7/16-9/16
	Omaha-Council Bluffs MSA, NE-IA	Y	25315 FQ	27905 MW	30495 TQ	NEBLS	7/16-9/16
	Nevada	Y	23910 FQ	28580 MW	34570 TQ	USBLS	5/15
	New Hampshire	H	11.95 AE	16.07 MW	18.05 AEX	NHBLS	6/16
	New Jersey	Y	21680 FQ	32080 MW	42290 TQ	USBLS	5/15
	Camden PMSA, NJ	Y	26590 FQ	37110 MW	43780 TQ	USBLS	5/15
	Newark PMSA, NJ-PA	Y	20040 FQ	30590 MW	43090 TQ	USBLS	5/15
	New York	Y	21740 AE	29310 MW	36820 AEX	NYBLS	1/16-3/16
	Nassau County-Suffolk County PMSA, NY	Y	23180 FQ	28570 MW	34440 TQ	USBLS	5/15
	New York-Jersey City-White Plains PMSA, NY-NJ	Y	21700 FQ	28940 MW	39200 TQ	USBLS	5/15
	Rochester MSA, NY	Y	22110 FQ	25530 MW	35590 TQ	USBLS	5/15
	North Carolina	Y	23540 FQ	28660 MW	35570 TQ	USBLS	5/15
	Charlotte-Concord-Gastonia MSA, NC-SC	Y	24000 FQ	29500 MW	36120 TQ	USBLS	5/15
	North Dakota	Y	20170 FQ	28330 MW	35350 TQ	USBLS	5/15
	Ohio	Y	24160 FQ	29270 MW	35910 TQ	USBLS	5/15
	Cincinnati MSA, OH-KY-IN	Y	26040 FQ	29580 MW	35500 TQ	USBLS	5/15
	Cleveland-Elyria MSA, OH	Y	22300 FQ	25210 MW	32760 TQ	USBLS	5/15
	Columbus MSA, OH	Y	21810 FQ	24070 MW	30640 TQ	USBLS	5/15
	Oklahoma	Y	21090 FQ	24180 MW	28910 TQ	USBLS	5/15
	Oklahoma City MSA, OK	Y	18200 FQ	21420 MW	23620 TQ	USBLS	5/15
	Tulsa MSA, OK	Y	26340 FQ	28770 MW	32450 TQ	USBLS	5/15
	Oregon	H	13.21 FQ	15.97 MW	19.95 TQ	ORBLS	2016
	Portland-Vancouver-Hillsboro MSA, OR-WA	Y	27170 FQ	34490 MW	43290 TQ	USBLS	5/15
	Pennsylvania	Y	24370 FQ	33420 MW	41800 TQ	USBLS	5/15
	Allentown-Bethlehem-Easton MSA, PA-NJ	Y	28090 FQ	32120 MW	37880 AEX	MDBLS	5/15
	Harrisburg-Carlisle MSA, PA	Y	32770 FQ	35900 MW	39040 TQ	USBLS	5/15
	Pittsburgh MSA, PA	Y	33470 FQ	38250 MW	44440 TQ	USBLS	5/15
	Providence-Warwick MSA, RI-MA	Y	25330 FQ	28580 MW	32510 TQ	USBLS	5/15
	South Carolina	Y	23270 FQ	31030 MW	36310 TQ	USBLS	5/15
	Greenville-Anderson-Mauldin MSA, SC	Y	22620 FQ	25590 MW	29340 TQ	USBLS	5/15
	South Dakota	Y	26430 FQ	29610 MW	33990 TQ	USBLS	5/15
	Tennessee	Y	21280 FQ	26350 MW	30570 TQ	USBLS	5/15
	Memphis MSA, TN-MS-AR	Y	23620 FQ	30290 MW	35330 TQ	USBLS	5/15

AE   Average entry wage   AWR   Average wage range   H   Hourly   LR   Low end range   MTC   Median total compensation   TCC   Total cash compensation
AEX   Average experienced wage   B   Biweekly   HI   Highest wage paid   M   Monthly   MW   Median wage paid   TQ   Third quartile wage
ATC   Average total compensation   D   Daily   HR   High end range   MCC   Median cash compensation   MWR   Median wage range   W   Weekly
AW   Average wage paid   FQ   First quartile wage   LO   Lowest wage paid   ME   Median entry wage   S   See annotated source   Y   Yearly

234

Occupation/Type/Industry	Location	Per	Low	Mid	High	Source	Date
Cleaning, Washing, and Metal Pickling Equipment Operator and Tender	Nashville-Davidson–Murfreesboro–Franklin MSA, TN	Y	23890 FQ	26900 MW	29690 TQ	USBLS	5/15
	Texas	Y	21840 FQ	26540 MW	31370 TQ	USBLS	5/15
	Austin-Round Rock MSA, TX	Y	22190 FQ	26360 MW	30790 TQ	USBLS	5/15
	Dallas-Plano-Irving PMSA, TX	Y	22770 FQ	27410 MW	33010 TQ	USBLS	5/15
	Fort Worth-Arlington PMSA, TX	Y	20320 FQ	25860 MW	34220 TQ	USBLS	5/15
	Houston-The Woodlands-Sugar Land MSA, TX	Y	21250 FQ	26820 MW	31750 TQ	USBLS	5/15
	Utah	Y	19550 FQ	28140 MW	34940 TQ	USBLS	5/15
	Ogden-Clearfield MSA, UT	Y	20040 FQ	25720 MW	28600 TQ	USBLS	5/15
	Salt Lake City MSA, UT	Y	18720 FQ	27620 MW	36170 TQ	USBLS	5/15
	Vermont	Y	22220 FQ	24640 MW	28840 TQ	USBLS	5/15
	Virginia	Y	23050 FQ	27920 MW	33110 TQ	USBLS	5/15
	Virginia Beach-Norfolk-Newport News MSA, VA-NC	Y	19160 FQ	24310 MW	29520 TQ	USBLS	5/15
	Washington	H	12.37 FQ	14.04 MW	16.27 TQ	WABLS	3/16
	Seattle-Bellevue-Everett PMSA, WA	H	12.74 FQ	14.64 MW	18.85 TQ	WABLS	3/16
	West Virginia	Y	28570 FQ	33170 MW	39870 TQ	USBLS	5/15
	Wisconsin	Y	30890 FQ	36950 MW	43610 TQ	USBLS	5/15
	Milwaukee-Waukesha-West Allis MSA, WI	Y	24700 FQ	31610 MW	36850 TQ	USBLS	5/15
	Puerto Rico	Y	17850 FQ	20230 MW	25420 TQ	USBLS	5/15
	San Juan-Carolina-Caguas MSA, PR	Y	17560 FQ	19530 MW	23650 TQ	USBLS	5/15
Clergy	Alabama	Y	27583 AE	43719 AW	51782 AEX	ALBLS	6/16
	Birmingham-Hoover MSA, AL	Y	24036 AE	43862 AW	53780 AEX	ALBLS	6/16
	Alaska	Y	31020 FQ	52020 MW	60410 TQ	USBLS	5/15
	Anchorage MSA, AK	Y	37670 FQ	55090 MW	61120 TQ	USBLS	5/15
	Arizona	Y	32420 FQ	39890 MW	55490 TQ	USBLS	5/15
	Phoenix-Mesa-Scottsdale MSA, AZ	Y	32010 FQ	38710 MW	56680 TQ	USBLS	5/15
	Tucson MSA, AZ	Y	41620 FQ	46280 MW	54380 TQ	USBLS	5/15
	Arkansas	Y	29880 FQ	38930 MW	57740 TQ	USBLS	5/15
	Little Rock-North Little Rock-Conway MSA, AR	Y	18060 FQ	29340 MW	38570 TQ	USBLS	5/15
	California	H	15.94 FQ	25.64 MW	34.28 TQ	CABLS	1/16-3/16
	Anaheim-Santa Ana-Irvine PMSA, CA	H	20.02 FQ	25.37 MW	36.43 TQ	CABLS	1/16-3/16
	Los Angeles-Long Beach-Glendale PMSA, CA	H	19.12 FQ	27.99 MW	36.49 TQ	CABLS	1/16-3/16
	Riverside-San Bernardino-Ontario MSA, CA	H	13.16 FQ	22.34 MW	31.47 TQ	CABLS	1/16-3/16
	Sacramento–Roseville–Arden-Arcade MSA, CA	H	15.94 FQ	23.99 MW	29.66 TQ	CABLS	1/16-3/16
	San Diego-Carlsbad MSA, CA	H	11.73 FQ	26.20 MW	33.64 TQ	CABLS	1/16-3/16
	San Francisco-Redwood City-South San Francisco PMSA, CA	H	18.26 FQ	30.40 MW	46.66 TQ	CABLS	1/16-3/16
	Colorado	Y	41950 FQ	51790 MW	61660 TQ	USBLS	5/15
	Denver-Aurora-Lakewood MSA, CO	Y	43510 FQ	51610 MW	60360 TQ	USBLS	5/15
	Connecticut	Y		54833 MW		CTBLS	1/16-3/16
	Bridgeport-Stamford-Norwalk MSA, CT	Y	38730 FQ	46430 MW	57790 TQ	USBLS	5/15
	Hartford-West Hartford-East Hartford MSA, CT	Y	42510 FQ	56480 MW	71200 TQ	USBLS	5/15
	Delaware	Y	43840 FQ	52030 MW	74060 TQ	USBLS	5/15
	Wilmington PMSA, DE-MD-NJ	Y	43420 FQ	50400 MW	77060 TQ	USBLS	5/15
	District of Columbia	Y	37390 FQ	62560 MW	74340 TQ	USBLS	5/15
	Washington-Arlington-Alexandria PMSA, DC-VA-MD-WV	Y	32520 FQ	47210 MW	67940 TQ	USBLS	5/15
	Florida	H	14.23 AE	21.11 MW	27.50 AEX	FLBLS	7/16-9/16

AE	Average entry wage	**AWR**	Average wage range	**H**	Hourly
AEX	Average experienced wage	**B**	Biweekly	**HI**	Highest wage paid
ATC	Average total compensation	**D**	Daily	**HR**	High end range
AW	Average wage paid	**FQ**	First quartile wage	**LO**	Lowest wage paid

LR	Low end range	**MTC**	Median total compensation	**TCC**	Total cash compensation
M	Monthly	**MW**	Median wage paid	**TQ**	Third quartile wage
MCC	Median cash compensation	**MWR**	Median wage range	**W**	Weekly
ME	Median entry wage	**S**	See annotated source	**Y**	Yearly

Occupation/Type/Industry	Location	Per	Low	Mid	High	Source	Date
Clergy	Fort Lauderdale-Pompano Beach-Deerfield Beach PMSA, FL	H	13.80 ᴀᴇ	22.82 ᴍᴡ	31.86 ᴀᴇx	FLBLS	7/16-9/16
	Miami-Miami Beach-Kendall PMSA, FL	H	14.08 ᴀᴇ	19.51 ᴍᴡ	27.40 ᴀᴇx	FLBLS	7/16-9/16
	Orlando-Kissimmee-Sanford MSA, FL	H	15.60 ᴀᴇ	22.03 ᴍᴡ	25.52 ᴀᴇx	FLBLS	7/16-9/16
	Tampa-St. Petersburg-Clearwater MSA, FL	H	12.84 ᴀᴇ	23.08 ᴍᴡ	29.27 ᴀᴇx	FLBLS	7/16-9/16
	Georgia	Y	34370 ꜰQ	44020 ᴍᴡ	55100 ᴛQ	USBLS	5/15
	Atlanta-Sandy Springs-Roswell MSA, GA	Y	36070 ꜰQ	45130 ᴍᴡ	57190 ᴛQ	USBLS	5/15
	Augusta-Richmond County MSA, GA-SC	Y	32210 ꜰQ	41030 ᴍᴡ	72540 ᴛQ	USBLS	5/15
	Hawaii	Y	31140 ꜰQ	49590 ᴍᴡ	71850 ᴛQ	USBLS	5/15
	Urban Honolulu MSA, HI	Y	31610 ꜰQ	51830 ᴍᴡ	74850 ᴛQ	USBLS	5/15
	Idaho	Y	29730 ꜰQ	39750 ᴍᴡ	48870 ᴛQ	USBLS	5/15
	Boise City MSA, ID	Y	29160 ꜰQ	39300 ᴍᴡ	48570 ᴛQ	USBLS	5/15
	Illinois	Y	28140 ꜰQ	41520 ᴍᴡ	56130 ᴛQ	USBLS	5/15
	Chicago-Naperville-Arlington Heights PMSA, IL	Y	27910 ꜰQ	41080 ᴍᴡ	50910 ᴛQ	USBLS	5/15
	Lake County-Kenosha County PMSA, IL-WI	Y	27790 ꜰQ	42430 ᴍᴡ	60440 ᴛQ	USBLS	5/15
	Indiana	Y	29790 ꜰQ	42280 ᴍᴡ	53450 ᴛQ	USBLS	5/15
	Gary PMSA, IN	Y	18760 ꜰQ	29730 ᴍᴡ	47200 ᴛQ	USBLS	5/15
	Indianapolis-Carmel-Anderson MSA, IN	Y	36040 ꜰQ	45650 ᴍᴡ	57300 ᴛQ	USBLS	5/15
	Iowa	Y	37680 ꜰQ	46320 ᴍᴡ	56780 ᴛQ	USBLS	5/15
	Des Moines-West Des Moines MSA, IA	Y	39260 ꜰQ	50390 ᴍᴡ	58970 ᴛQ	USBLS	5/15
	Kansas	Y	34830 ꜰQ	41580 ᴍᴡ	49570 ᴛQ	USBLS	5/15
	Wichita MSA, KS	Y	33830 ꜰQ	40600 ᴍᴡ	53010 ᴛQ	USBLS	5/15
	Kentucky	Y	40540 ꜰQ	48260 ᴍᴡ	58680 ᴛQ	USBLS	5/15
	Louisville-Jefferson County MSA, KY-IN	Y	37580 ꜰQ	47820 ᴍᴡ	56410 ᴛQ	USBLS	5/15
	Louisiana	Y	27560 ꜰQ	41560 ᴍᴡ	50020 ᴛQ	USBLS	5/15
	Baton Rouge MSA, LA	Y	40080 ꜰQ	45660 ᴍᴡ	52530 ᴛQ	USBLS	5/15
	New Orleans-Metairie MSA, LA	Y	26660 ꜰQ	30380 ᴍᴡ	44160 ᴛQ	USBLS	5/15
	Maine	Y	40970 ꜰQ	46750 ᴍᴡ	54810 ᴛQ	USBLS	5/15
	Maryland	Y	27925 ᴀᴇ	48587 ᴍᴡ	58917 ᴀᴇx	MDBLS	4/16
	Baltimore-Columbia-Towson MSA, MD	Y	32000 ꜰQ	40620 ᴍᴡ	54890 ᴛQ	USBLS	5/15
	Massachusetts	Y	30290 ꜰQ	47180 ᴍᴡ	61990 ᴛQ	USBLS	5/15
	Boston-Cambridge-Newton NECTA, MA	Y	28610 ꜰQ	36330 ᴍᴡ	59740 ᴛQ	USBLS	5/15
	Worcester MSA, MA-CT	Y	51020 ꜰQ	61480 ᴍᴡ	73120 ᴛQ	USBLS	5/15
	Michigan	Y	30000 ꜰQ	39530 ᴍᴡ	49300 ᴛQ	USBLS	5/15
	Detroit-Dearborn-Livonia PMSA, MI	Y	29370 ꜰQ	42700 ᴍᴡ	50840 ᴛQ	USBLS	5/15
	Grand Rapids-Wyoming MSA, MI	Y	30790 ꜰQ	38220 ᴍᴡ	48910 ᴛQ	USBLS	5/15
	Minnesota	Y	32651 ꜰQ	46179 ᴍᴡ	57177 ᴛQ	MNBLS	1/16-3/16
	Minneapolis-St. Paul-Bloomington MSA, MN-WI	Y	36743 ꜰQ	47157 ᴍᴡ	56975 ᴛQ	MNBLS	1/16-3/16
	Mississippi	Y	34320 ꜰQ	43860 ᴍᴡ	64580 ᴛQ	USBLS	5/15
	Jackson MSA, MS	Y	38990 ꜰQ	46620 ᴍᴡ	71210 ᴛQ	USBLS	5/15
	Missouri	Y	37200 ꜰQ	46740 ᴍᴡ	56860 ᴛQ	USBLS	5/15
	Kansas City MSA, MO-KS	Y	35490 ꜰQ	44360 ᴍᴡ	54990 ᴛQ	USBLS	5/15
	St. Louis MSA, MO-IL	Y	36190 ꜰQ	48520 ᴍᴡ	58560 ᴛQ	USBLS	5/15
	Montana	Y	23830 ꜰQ	35430 ᴍᴡ	50850 ᴛQ	USBLS	5/15
	Billings MSA, MT	Y	31130 ꜰQ	51200 ᴍᴡ	58170 ᴛQ	USBLS	5/15
	Omaha-Council Bluffs MSA, NE-IA	Y	36710 ꜰQ	47950 ᴍᴡ	58920 ᴛQ	NEBLS	7/16-9/16
	Nevada	Y	41670 ꜰQ	49100 ᴍᴡ	59910 ᴛQ	USBLS	5/15
	Las Vegas-Henderson-Paradise MSA, NV	Y	39370 ꜰQ	48050 ᴍᴡ	59360 ᴛQ	USBLS	5/15
	New Hampshire	H	22.70 ᴀᴇ	27.87 ᴍᴡ	31.61 ᴀᴇx	NHBLS	6/16
	New Jersey	Y	33530 ꜰQ	49900 ᴍᴡ	61590 ᴛQ	USBLS	5/15
	Camden PMSA, NJ	Y	52270 ꜰQ	59060 ᴍᴡ	72980 ᴛQ	USBLS	5/15
	Newark PMSA, NJ-PA	Y	29170 ꜰQ	46350 ᴍᴡ	59720 ᴛQ	USBLS	5/15
	Trenton MSA, NJ	Y	22870 ꜰQ	51140 ᴍᴡ	65260 ᴛQ	USBLS	5/15

AE Average entry wage	**AWR** Average wage range	**H** Hourly	**LR** Low end range	**MTC** Median total compensation	**TCC** Total cash compensation
AEX Average experienced wage	**B** Biweekly	**HI** Highest wage paid	**M** Monthly	**MW** Median wage paid	**TQ** Third quartile wage
ATC Average total compensation	**D** Daily	**HR** High end range	**MCC** Median cash compensation	**MWR** Median wage range	**W** Weekly
AW Average wage paid	**FQ** First quartile wage	**LO** Lowest wage paid	**ME** Median entry wage	**S** See annotated source	**Y** Yearly

Occupation/Type/Industry	Location	Per	Low	Mid	High	Source	Date
Clergy	New Mexico	Y	40380 FQ	46840 MW	57800 TQ	USBLS	5/15
	Albuquerque MSA, NM	Y	43810 FQ	49190 MW	61660 TQ	USBLS	5/15
	New York	Y	24820 AE	42730 MW	62950 AEX	NYBLS	1/16-3/16
	Buffalo-Cheektowaga-Niagara Falls MSA, NY	Y	33370 FQ	47770 MW	60640 TQ	USBLS	5/15
	Nassau County-Suffolk County PMSA, NY	Y	23190 FQ	46240 MW	60180 TQ	USBLS	5/15
	New York-Jersey City-White Plains PMSA, NY-NJ	Y	27630 FQ	40450 MW	64500 TQ	USBLS	5/15
	Rochester MSA, NY	Y	33950 FQ	44250 MW	55030 TQ	USBLS	5/15
	North Carolina	Y	36670 FQ	46980 MW	59120 TQ	USBLS	5/15
	Charlotte-Concord-Gastonia MSA, NC-SC	Y	34340 FQ	49010 MW	60170 TQ	USBLS	5/15
	Raleigh MSA, NC	Y	42150 FQ	49160 MW	58440 TQ	USBLS	5/15
	North Dakota	Y	42550 FQ	51990 MW	62910 TQ	USBLS	5/15
	Fargo MSA, ND-MN	Y	42930 FQ	59350 MW	72550 TQ	USBLS	5/15
	Ohio	Y	30290 FQ	39720 MW	51250 TQ	USBLS	5/15
	Cincinnati MSA, OH-KY-IN	Y	35850 FQ	46500 MW	62750 TQ	USBLS	5/15
	Cleveland-Elyria MSA, OH	Y	35540 FQ	47850 MW	71720 TQ	USBLS	5/15
	Columbus MSA, OH	Y	33060 FQ	39250 MW	49890 TQ	USBLS	5/15
	Oklahoma	Y	36490 FQ	43840 MW	50630 TQ	USBLS	5/15
	Oklahoma City MSA, OK	Y	39430 FQ	45690 MW	55360 TQ	USBLS	5/15
	Tulsa MSA, OK	Y	35220 FQ	42250 MW	48170 TQ	USBLS	5/15
	Oregon	H	15.68 FQ	21.18 MW	29.30 TQ	ORBLS	2016
	Portland-Vancouver-Hillsboro MSA, OR-WA	Y	34090 FQ	46940 MW	62970 TQ	USBLS	5/15
	Pennsylvania	Y	27920 FQ	41300 MW	54270 TQ	USBLS	5/15
	Allentown-Bethlehem-Easton MSA, PA-NJ	Y	32540 FQ	49230 MW	59970 TQ	USBLS	5/15
	Harrisburg-Carlisle MSA, PA	Y	31590 FQ	44210 MW	52900 TQ	USBLS	5/15
	Montgomery County-Bucks County-Chester County PMSA, PA	Y	35030 FQ	45370 MW	56210 TQ	USBLS	5/15
	Philadelphia PMSA, PA	Y	23840 FQ	41260 MW	54900 TQ	USBLS	5/15
	Pittsburgh MSA, PA	Y	25440 FQ	34740 MW	45100 TQ	USBLS	5/15
	Rhode Island	Y	33460 FQ	38210 MW	66840 TQ	USBLS	5/15
	Providence-Warwick MSA, RI-MA	Y	33650 FQ	38450 MW	66590 TQ	USBLS	5/15
	South Carolina	Y	33260 FQ	43300 MW	53990 TQ	USBLS	5/15
	Charleston-North Charleston MSA, SC	Y	43360 FQ	52580 MW	60260 TQ	USBLS	5/15
	Columbia MSA, SC	Y	31380 FQ	42300 MW	49470 TQ	USBLS	5/15
	Greenville-Anderson-Mauldin MSA, SC	Y	28590 FQ	34600 MW	44950 TQ	USBLS	5/15
	South Dakota	Y	33950 FQ	40150 MW	49260 TQ	USBLS	5/15
	Sioux Falls MSA, SD	Y	33270 FQ	39640 MW	47880 TQ	USBLS	5/15
	Tennessee	Y	32750 FQ	43300 MW	56260 TQ	USBLS	5/15
	Knoxville MSA, TN	Y	33440 FQ	42670 MW	51890 TQ	USBLS	5/15
	Memphis MSA, TN-MS-AR	Y	40600 FQ	49640 MW	65190 TQ	USBLS	5/15
	Nashville-Davidson–Murfreesboro–Franklin MSA, TN	Y	25440 FQ	40670 MW	53200 TQ	USBLS	5/15
	Texas	Y	38220 FQ	47360 MW	58570 TQ	USBLS	5/15
	Austin-Round Rock MSA, TX	Y	41410 FQ	47860 MW	59510 TQ	USBLS	5/15
	Dallas-Plano-Irving PMSA, TX	Y	36100 FQ	46920 MW	57720 TQ	USBLS	5/15
	Fort Worth-Arlington PMSA, TX	Y	40810 FQ	46770 MW	59630 TQ	USBLS	5/15
	Houston-The Woodlands-Sugar Land MSA, TX	Y	37390 FQ	53810 MW	62230 TQ	USBLS	5/15
	San Antonio-New Braunfels MSA, TX	Y	42540 FQ	49880 MW	61680 TQ	USBLS	5/15
	Salt Lake City MSA, UT	Y	42810 FQ	47540 MW	57410 TQ	USBLS	5/15
	Vermont	Y	37410 FQ	45140 MW	58670 TQ	USBLS	5/15
	Virginia	Y	29790 FQ	42720 MW	58390 TQ	USBLS	5/15
	Richmond MSA, VA	Y	32500 FQ	45590 MW	73990 TQ	USBLS	5/15
	Virginia Beach-Norfolk-Newport News MSA, VA-NC	Y	30400 FQ	45900 MW	57450 TQ	USBLS	5/15
	Washington	H	23.34 FQ	27.90 MW	33.75 TQ	WABLS	3/16
	Seattle-Bellevue-Everett PMSA, WA	H	25.57 FQ	29.17 MW	35.31 TQ	WABLS	3/16
	Tacoma-Lakewood PMSA, WA	H	22.06 FQ	25.93 MW	31.78 TQ	WABLS	3/16
	West Virginia	Y	30600 FQ	45020 MW	69170 TQ	USBLS	5/15

AE	Average entry wage	AWR	Average wage range	H	Hourly
AEX	Average experienced wage	B	Biweekly	HI	Highest wage paid
ATC	Average total compensation	D	Daily	HR	High end range
AW	Average wage paid	FQ	First quartile wage	LO	Lowest wage paid

LR	Low end range	MTC	Median total compensation
M	Monthly	MW	Median wage paid
MCC	Median cash compensation	MWR	Median wage range
ME	Median entry wage	S	See annotated source

TCC	Total cash compensation
TQ	Third quartile wage
W	Weekly
Y	Yearly

Occupation/Type/Industry	Location	Per	Low	Mid	High	Source	Date
Clergy	Wisconsin	Y	38710 FQ	46370 MW	56920 TQ	USBLS	5/15
	Madison MSA, WI	Y	28270 FQ	39780 MW	55810 TQ	USBLS	5/15
	Milwaukee-Waukesha-West						
	Allis MSA, WI	Y	43120 FQ	49300 MW	58880 TQ	USBLS	5/15
	Puerto Rico	Y	18790 FQ	27250 MW	39700 TQ	USBLS	5/15
	San Juan-Carolina-Caguas						
	MSA, PR	Y	25960 FQ	29620 MW	50100 TQ	USBLS	5/15
	Guam	Y	22930 FQ	41980 MW	47080 TQ	USBLS	5/15
Clerk							
Probate Court	Camden County, GA	H	11.11 LO		16.91 HI	GACTY04	2016
Probate Court	Coweta County, GA	H	15.85 LO		23.77 HI	GACTY04	2016
Probate Court	Haralson County, GA	H	10.75 LO		16.51 HI	GACTY04	2016
Clerk Stenographer							
United States Postal Service	United States	Y			56791 HI	APP02	1/16
Client Transporter							
County Government	Oakland County, MI	B	1180 LO		1537 HI	MIOAK2	10/1/16
Climate Change Analyst	United States	Y		74000 AW		SKU01	2016
Clinical, Counseling, and School							
Psychologist	Alabama	Y	43484 AE	79487 AW	97488 AEX	ALBLS	6/16
	Birmingham-Hoover MSA, AL	Y	42801 AE	75043 AW	91158 AEX	ALBLS	6/16
	Alaska	Y	58480 FQ	69390 MW	82930 TQ	USBLS	5/15
	Anchorage MSA, AK	Y	59240 FQ	74520 MW	96580 TQ	USBLS	5/15
	Arizona	Y	47970 FQ	57930 MW	70110 TQ	USBLS	5/15
	Phoenix-Mesa-Scottsdale						
	MSA, AZ	Y	52030 FQ	59580 MW	71350 TQ	USBLS	5/15
	Tucson MSA, AZ	Y	38310 FQ	46550 MW	59030 TQ	USBLS	5/15
	Arkansas	Y	44280 FQ	57520 MW	77760 TQ	USBLS	5/15
	Little Rock-North Little Rock-						
	Conway MSA, AR	Y	44290 FQ	58350 MW	72820 TQ	USBLS	5/15
	California	H	30.79 FQ	42.45 MW	53.28 TQ	CABLS	1/16-3/16
	Anaheim-Santa Ana-Irvine						
	PMSA, CA	H	28.77 FQ	44.67 MW	54.36 TQ	CABLS	1/16-3/16
	Los Angeles-Long Beach-						
	Glendale PMSA, CA	H	26.55 FQ	38.47 MW	48.13 TQ	CABLS	1/16-3/16
	Oakland-Hayward-Berkeley						
	PMSA, CA	H	33.51 FQ	43.66 MW	54.72 TQ	CABLS	1/16-3/16
	Riverside-San Bernardino-						
	Ontario MSA, CA	H	30.91 FQ	46.36 MW	56.34 TQ	CABLS	1/16-3/16
	Sacramento–Roseville–						
	Arden-Arcade MSA, CA	H	36.15 FQ	47.15 MW	56.36 TQ	CABLS	1/16-3/16
	San Diego-Carlsbad MSA, CA	H	32.91 FQ	39.02 MW	50.90 TQ	CABLS	1/16-3/16
	San Francisco-Redwood City-						
	South San Francisco PMSA,						
	CA	H	23.22 FQ	38.73 MW	51.02 TQ	CABLS	1/16-3/16
	Colorado	Y	56280 FQ	74230 MW	97790 TQ	USBLS	5/15
	Denver-Aurora-Lakewood						
	MSA, CO	Y	56170 FQ	76880 MW	104130 TQ	USBLS	5/15
	Connecticut	Y		87348 MW		CTBLS	1/16-3/16
	Bridgeport-Stamford-Norwalk						
	MSA, CT	Y	67600 FQ	86820 MW	104850 TQ	USBLS	5/15
	Hartford-West Hartford-East						
	Hartford MSA, CT	Y	69910 FQ	86040 MW	100950 TQ	USBLS	5/15
	Delaware	Y	62330 FQ	79490 MW	92170 TQ	USBLS	5/15
	Wilmington PMSA, DE-MD-						
	NJ	Y	59220 FQ	75020 MW	89220 TQ	USBLS	5/15
	District of Columbia	Y	62280 FQ	86720 MW	109970 TQ	USBLS	5/15
	Washington-Arlington-						
	Alexandria PMSA, DC-VA-						
	MD-WV	Y	60480 FQ	79500 MW	105260 TQ	USBLS	5/15
	Florida	H	21.86 AE	32.87 MW	42.10 AEX	FLBLS	7/16-9/16
	Fort Lauderdale-Pompano						
	Beach-Deerfield Beach						
	PMSA, FL	H	26.44 AE	36.85 MW	42.98 AEX	FLBLS	7/16-9/16
	Miami-Miami Beach-Kendall						
	PMSA, FL	H	26.76 AE	39.99 MW	46.47 AEX	FLBLS	7/16-9/16
	Orlando-Kissimmee-Sanford						
	MSA, FL	H	18.74 AE	29.41 MW	36.97 AEX	FLBLS	7/16-9/16

AE	Average entry wage	AWR	Average wage range	H	Hourly
AEX	Average experienced wage	B	Biweekly	HI	Highest wage paid
ATC	Average total compensation	D	Daily	HR	High end range
AW	Average wage paid	FQ	First quartile wage	LO	Lowest wage paid

LR	Low end range	MTC	Median total compensation	TCC	Total cash compensation
M	Monthly	MW	Median wage paid	TQ	Third quartile wage
MCC	Median cash compensation	MWR	Median wage range	W	Weekly
ME	Median entry wage	S	See annotated source	Y	Yearly

Occupation/Type/Industry	Location	Per	Low	Mid	High	Source	Date
Clinical, Counseling, and School Psychologist							
	Tampa-St. Petersburg-Clearwater MSA, FL	H	24.36 AE	34.90 MW	39.03 AEX	FLBLS	7/16-9/16
	Georgia	Y	53110 FQ	67630 MW	80410 TQ	USBLS	5/15
	Atlanta-Sandy Springs-Roswell MSA, GA	Y	51320 FQ	66250 MW	78900 TQ	USBLS	5/15
	Augusta-Richmond County MSA, GA-SC	Y	48980 FQ	60260 MW	76790 TQ	USBLS	5/15
	Hawaii	Y	52320 FQ	68800 MW	100880 TQ	USBLS	5/15
	Urban Honolulu MSA, HI	Y	53220 FQ	70910 MW	102750 TQ	USBLS	5/15
	Idaho	Y	44920 FQ	56440 MW	83460 TQ	USBLS	5/15
	Boise City MSA, ID	Y	43770 FQ	49760 MW	69880 TQ	USBLS	5/15
	Illinois	Y	46640 FQ	64950 MW	87720 TQ	USBLS	5/15
	Chicago-Naperville-Arlington Heights PMSA, IL	Y	46290 FQ	65400 MW	88780 TQ	USBLS	5/15
	Lake County-Kenosha County PMSA, IL-WI	Y	52430 FQ	69230 MW	92950 TQ	USBLS	5/15
	Indiana	Y	42770 FQ	58240 MW	77320 TQ	USBLS	5/15
	Gary PMSA, IN	Y	49790 FQ	59440 MW	75660 TQ	USBLS	5/15
	Indianapolis-Carmel-Anderson MSA, IN	Y	43090 FQ	64040 MW	81750 TQ	USBLS	5/15
	Iowa	Y	56000 FQ	70680 MW	88050 TQ	USBLS	5/15
	Des Moines-West Des Moines MSA, IA	Y	56020 FQ	70080 MW	97130 TQ	USBLS	5/15
	Kansas	Y	48580 FQ	58000 MW	72230 TQ	USBLS	5/15
	Wichita MSA, KS	Y	51960 FQ	59610 MW	71550 TQ	USBLS	5/15
	Kentucky	Y	52700 FQ	61310 MW	74020 TQ	USBLS	5/15
	Louisville-Jefferson County MSA, KY-IN	Y	55800 FQ	66980 MW	82960 TQ	USBLS	5/15
	Louisiana	Y	49750 FQ	69430 MW	105350 TQ	USBLS	5/15
	Baton Rouge MSA, LA	Y	66930 FQ	73320 MW	79660 TQ	USBLS	5/15
	New Orleans-Metairie MSA, LA	Y	70410 FQ	106690 MW	118150 TQ	USBLS	5/15
	Maine	Y	58140 FQ	75280 MW	101360 TQ	USBLS	5/15
	Portland-South Portland MSA, ME	Y	56860 FQ	63600 MW	89650 TQ	USBLS	5/15
	Maryland	Y	46428 AE	74430 MW	88430 AEX	MDBLS	4/16
	Baltimore-Columbia-Towson MSA, MD	Y	51570 FQ	67460 MW	89690 TQ	USBLS	5/15
	Salisbury MSA, MD-DE	Y	57930 FQ	80460 MW	102610 TQ	USBLS	5/15
	Massachusetts	Y	56310 FQ	73830 MW	93230 TQ	USBLS	5/15
	Boston-Cambridge-Newton NECTA, MA	Y	63910 FQ	76590 MW	93670 TQ	USBLS	5/15
	Worcester MSA, MA-CT	Y	59100 FQ	77590 MW	117330 TQ	USBLS	5/15
	Michigan	Y	52220 FQ	67940 MW	82460 TQ	USBLS	5/15
	Detroit-Dearborn-Livonia PMSA, MI	Y	47420 FQ	66850 MW	89300 TQ	USBLS	5/15
	Grand Rapids-Wyoming MSA, MI	Y	45980 FQ	61370 MW	76710 TQ	USBLS	5/15
	Minnesota	Y	53749 FQ	70080 MW	90473 TQ	MNBLS	1/16-3/16
	Minneapolis-St. Paul-Bloomington MSA, MN-WI	Y	55191 FQ	72721 MW	93023 TQ	MNBLS	1/16-3/16
	Missouri	Y	47220 FQ	62910 MW	82980 TQ	USBLS	5/15
	Kansas City MSA, MO-KS	Y	46870 FQ	61290 MW	84040 TQ	USBLS	5/15
	St. Louis MSA, MO-IL	Y	47560 FQ	62200 MW	81410 TQ	USBLS	5/15
	Montana	Y	34290 FQ	51640 MW	72480 TQ	USBLS	5/15
	Billings MSA, MT	Y	37690 FQ	70240 MW	108800 TQ	USBLS	5/15
	Nebraska	Y	49370 FQ	63020 MW	77145 TQ	NEBLS	7/16-9/16
	Omaha-Council Bluffs MSA, NE-IA	Y	49350 FQ	63215 MW	78395 TQ	NEBLS	7/16-9/16
	Nevada	Y	53520 FQ	68890 MW	85300 TQ	USBLS	5/15
	Las Vegas-Henderson-Paradise MSA, NV	Y	53210 FQ	64510 MW	79470 TQ	USBLS	5/15
	New Hampshire	H	23.59 AE	33.55 MW	41.52 AEX	NHBLS	6/16
	Manchester NECTA, NH	H	21.25 AE	30.60 MW	38.68 AEX	NHBLS	6/16
	Nashua NECTA, NH-MA	Y	49020 FQ	65070 MW	72770 TQ	USBLS	5/15
	New Jersey	Y	67540 FQ	82180 MW	104310 TQ	USBLS	5/15
	Camden PMSA, NJ	Y	64240 FQ	79820 MW	118820 TQ	USBLS	5/15
	Newark PMSA, NJ-PA	Y	63530 FQ	76160 MW	97000 TQ	USBLS	5/15
	Trenton MSA, NJ	Y	70910 FQ	88180 MW	115620 TQ	USBLS	5/15
	New Mexico	Y	47680 FQ	63850 MW	77990 TQ	USBLS	5/15
	Albuquerque MSA, NM	Y	45540 FQ	60910 MW	74550 TQ	USBLS	5/15

AE	Average entry wage	AWR	Average wage range	H	Hourly	LR	Low end range	MTC Median total compensation	TCC Total cash compensation
AEX	Average experienced wage	B	Biweekly	HI	Highest wage paid	M	Monthly	MW Median wage paid	TQ Third quartile wage
ATC	Average total compensation	D	Daily	HR	High end range	MCC	Median cash compensation	MWR Median wage range	W Weekly
AW	Average wage paid	FQ	First quartile wage	LO	Lowest wage paid	ME	Median entry wage	S See annotated source	Y Yearly

239

Occupation/Type/Industry	Location	Per	Low	Mid	High	Source	Date
Clinical, Counseling, and School Psychologist	New York	Y	54280 AE	84060 MW	104970 AEX	NYBLS	1/16-3/16
	Buffalo-Cheektowaga-Niagara Falls MSA, NY	Y	49840 FQ	66960 MW	83810 TQ	USBLS	5/15
	Nassau County-Suffolk County PMSA, NY	Y	78070 FQ	99020 MW	124770 TQ	USBLS	5/15
	New York-Jersey City-White Plains PMSA, NY-NJ	Y	68370 FQ	87370 MW	107280 TQ	USBLS	5/15
	Rochester MSA, NY	Y	53770 FQ	67030 MW	84160 TQ	USBLS	5/15
	North Carolina	Y	46320 FQ	57070 MW	74170 TQ	USBLS	5/15
	Charlotte-Concord-Gastonia MSA, NC-SC	Y	46540 FQ	58350 MW	72610 TQ	USBLS	5/15
	Raleigh MSA, NC	Y	45750 FQ	55890 MW	76320 TQ	USBLS	5/15
	North Dakota	Y	54060 FQ	77600 MW	100250 TQ	USBLS	5/15
	Fargo MSA, ND-MN	Y	51920 FQ	76820 MW	101140 TQ	USBLS	5/15
	Ohio	Y	53280 FQ	71000 MW	88050 TQ	USBLS	5/15
	Cincinnati MSA, OH-KY-IN	Y	54610 FQ	72360 MW	88440 TQ	USBLS	5/15
	Cleveland-Elyria MSA, OH	Y	48940 FQ	72710 MW	89720 TQ	USBLS	5/15
	Columbus MSA, OH	Y	51730 FQ	70350 MW	91030 TQ	USBLS	5/15
	Oklahoma	Y	38930 FQ	46800 MW	58750 TQ	USBLS	5/15
	Oklahoma City MSA, OK	Y	40470 FQ	46910 MW	58070 TQ	USBLS	5/15
	Tulsa MSA, OK	Y	38790 FQ	47150 MW	61040 TQ	USBLS	5/15
	Oregon	H	27.00 FQ	34.87 MW	44.11 TQ	ORBLS	2016
	Portland-Vancouver-Hillsboro MSA, OR-WA	Y	50670 FQ	69550 MW	93710 TQ	USBLS	5/15
	Pennsylvania	Y	51670 FQ	64420 MW	81560 TQ	USBLS	5/15
	Allentown-Bethlehem-Easton MSA, PA-NJ	Y	51620 FQ	77220 MW	92850 TQ	USBLS	5/15
	Harrisburg-Carlisle MSA, PA	Y	58900 FQ	71030 MW	85260 TQ	USBLS	5/15
	Montgomery County-Bucks County-Chester County PMSA, PA	Y	59420 FQ	71970 MW	86650 TQ	USBLS	5/15
	Philadelphia PMSA, PA	Y	50450 FQ	59480 MW	78270 TQ	USBLS	5/15
	Pittsburgh MSA, PA	Y	44430 FQ	56840 MW	76170 TQ	USBLS	5/15
	Rhode Island	Y	61650 FQ	74110 MW	91740 TQ	USBLS	5/15
	Providence-Warwick MSA, RI-MA	Y	60740 FQ	74250 MW	92320 TQ	USBLS	5/15
	South Carolina	Y	43920 FQ	56890 MW	71970 TQ	USBLS	5/15
	Charleston-North Charleston MSA, SC	Y	46150 FQ	57960 MW	71270 TQ	USBLS	5/15
	Columbia MSA, SC	Y	55370 FQ	65290 MW	78710 TQ	USBLS	5/15
	Greenville-Anderson-Mauldin MSA, SC	Y	39050 FQ	47060 MW	66960 TQ	USBLS	5/15
	South Dakota	Y	56550 FQ	71590 MW	91200 TQ	USBLS	5/15
	Sioux Falls MSA, SD	Y	63080 FQ	81810 MW	96610 TQ	USBLS	5/15
	Tennessee	Y	54790 FQ	66350 MW	80490 TQ	USBLS	5/15
	Knoxville MSA, TN	Y	55920 FQ	68490 MW	85170 TQ	USBLS	5/15
	Memphis MSA, TN-MS-AR	Y	59270 FQ	70120 MW	79900 TQ	USBLS	5/15
	Nashville-Davidson–Murfreesboro–Franklin MSA, TN	Y	54290 FQ	67160 MW	87050 TQ	USBLS	5/15
	Texas	Y	49730 FQ	59440 MW	73250 TQ	USBLS	5/15
	Austin-Round Rock MSA, TX	Y	47880 FQ	57660 MW	69770 TQ	USBLS	5/15
	Dallas-Plano-Irving PMSA, TX	Y	52190 FQ	60900 MW	74270 TQ	USBLS	5/15
	Fort Worth-Arlington PMSA, TX	Y	53970 FQ	68320 MW	86670 TQ	USBLS	5/15
	Houston-The Woodlands-Sugar Land MSA, TX	Y	52880 FQ	61670 MW	77630 TQ	USBLS	5/15
	San Antonio-New Braunfels MSA, TX	Y	47440 FQ	57500 MW	68860 TQ	USBLS	5/15
	Utah	Y	42570 FQ	59970 MW	78340 TQ	USBLS	5/15
	Ogden-Clearfield MSA, UT	Y	48220 FQ	61390 MW	77010 TQ	USBLS	5/15
	Provo-Orem MSA, UT	Y	43970 FQ	65540 MW	86410 TQ	USBLS	5/15
	Salt Lake City MSA, UT	Y	28990 FQ	57150 MW	75760 TQ	USBLS	5/15
	Vermont	Y	43280 FQ	54930 MW	68760 TQ	USBLS	5/15
	Burlington-South Burlington MSA, VT	Y	47960 FQ	66890 MW	85460 TQ	USBLS	5/15
	Virginia	Y	53800 FQ	68830 MW	91060 TQ	USBLS	5/15
	Richmond MSA, VA	Y	56080 FQ	64310 MW	75670 TQ	USBLS	5/15
	Virginia Beach-Norfolk-Newport News MSA, VA-NC	Y	45670 FQ	59900 MW	76550 TQ	USBLS	5/15
	Washington	H	27.41 FQ	32.34 MW	37.37 TQ	WABLS	3/16

AE	Average entry wage	AWR	Average wage range	H	Hourly	LR	Low end range	MTC	Median total compensation	TCC	Total cash compensation
AEX	Average experienced wage	B	Biweekly	HI	Highest wage paid	M	Monthly	MW	Median wage paid	TQ	Third quartile wage
ATC	Average total compensation	D	Daily	HR	High end range	MCC	Median cash compensation	MWR	Median wage range	W	Weekly
AW	Average wage paid	FQ	First quartile wage	LO	Lowest wage paid	ME	Median entry wage	S	See annotated source	Y	Yearly

Occupation/Type/Industry	Location	Per	Low	Mid	High	Source	Date
Clinical, Counseling, and School Psychologist	Seattle-Bellevue-Everett						
	PMSA, WA	H	28.48 FQ	33.43 MW	38.14 TQ	WABLS	3/16
	Tacoma-Lakewood PMSA, WA	H	26.88 FQ	32.76 MW	37.97 TQ	WABLS	3/16
	West Virginia	Y	38620 FQ	50500 MW	61940 TQ	USBLS	5/15
	Huntington-Ashland MSA, WV-KY-OH	Y	41180 FQ	53750 MW	66650 TQ	USBLS	5/15
	Wisconsin	Y	53030 FQ	71710 MW	91420 TQ	USBLS	5/15
	Madison MSA, WI	Y	47430 FQ	66530 MW	83650 TQ	USBLS	5/15
	Milwaukee-Waukesha-West Allis MSA, WI	Y	64420 FQ	79020 MW	102150 TQ	USBLS	5/15
	Wyoming	Y	54730 FQ	69050 MW	81930 TQ	USBLS	5/15
	Cheyenne MSA, WY	Y	68890 FQ	91030 MW	114420 TQ	USBLS	5/15
	Puerto Rico	Y	29450 FQ	38980 MW	64750 TQ	USBLS	5/15
	San Juan-Carolina-Caguas MSA, PR	Y	27880 FQ	40090 MW	66150 TQ	USBLS	5/15
	Virgin Islands	Y	43740 FQ	50080 MW	62910 TQ	USBLS	5/15
Clinical Consultant							
Adult Protective Services, State Government	New Mexico	H	17.01 LO		29.60 HI	NMGOV	7/30/16
Clinical Neuropsychologist							
First-Year	United States	Y		72500 MW		APAC01	2016
Clinical Nurse Educator							
Fire Department, Municipal Government	Fremont, CA	Y			130657 HI	CACIT	6/28/16
Clinical Nurse Specialist							
Michigan State University	East Lansing, MI	Y			65486 HI	MSUSAL	10/1/14-9/30/15
State Government	New Mexico	H	24.47 LO		42.56 HI	NMGOV	7/30/16
Clinical Pharmacist	United States	H		54.69-71.58 AWR		FORB03	2016
Clinical Podiatrist							
Veterans Health Administration	United States	Y	52329-103672 LO		68025-134776 HR	OPM01	2017
Clinical Psychologist Intern							
County Government	Oakland County, MI	H			10.41 HI	MIOAK2	10/1/16
Clinical Trial Nurse	United States	Y		92600 MW		FTIME	2016
Clothing Designer							
United States Coast Guard	Natick, MA	Y	94289 LO		118609 HI	APP01	2015
Cloud Specialist	United States	Y		107600 AW		CWRLD3	2016
Coach and Scout	Alabama	Y	17369 AE	38204 AW	48612 AEX	ALBLS	6/16
	Birmingham-Hoover MSA, AL	Y	17379 AE	26982 AW	31783 AEX	ALBLS	6/16
	Alaska	Y	40420 FQ	45980 AW	54260 TQ	USBLS	5/15
	Anchorage MSA, AK	Y	41040 FQ	46400 MW	54870 TQ	USBLS	5/15
	Arizona	Y	19010 FQ	27450 MW	39110 TQ	USBLS	5/15
	Phoenix-Mesa-Scottsdale MSA, AZ	Y	19050 FQ	27930 MW	39060 TQ	USBLS	5/15
	Tucson MSA, AZ	Y	18720 FQ	26250 MW	39460 TQ	USBLS	5/15
	Arkansas	Y	29070 FQ	45890 MW	61840 TQ	USBLS	5/15
	Little Rock-North Little Rock-Conway MSA, AR	Y	23460 FQ	33670 MW	59820 TQ	USBLS	5/15
	California	Y		41219 AW		CABLS	1/16-3/16
	Anaheim-Santa Ana-Irvine PMSA, CA	Y		37486 AW		CABLS	1/16-3/16
	Los Angeles-Long Beach-Glendale PMSA, CA	Y		48787 AW		CABLS	1/16-3/16
	Oakland-Hayward-Berkeley PMSA, CA	Y		35720 AW		CABLS	1/16-3/16
	Riverside-San Bernardino-Ontario MSA, CA	Y		35933 AW		CABLS	1/16-3/16
	Sacramento–Roseville–Arden-Arcade MSA, CA	Y		34290 AW		CABLS	1/16-3/16
	San Diego-Carlsbad MSA, CA	Y		44729 AW		CABLS	1/16-3/16

AE Average entry wage	**AWR** Average wage range	**H** Hourly	**LR** Low end range	**MTC** Median total compensation	**TCC** Total cash compensation
AEX Average experienced wage	**B** Biweekly	**HI** Highest wage paid	**M** Monthly	**MW** Median wage paid	**TQ** Third quartile wage
ATC Average total compensation	**D** Daily	**HR** High end range	**MCC** Median cash compensation	**MWR** Median wage range	**W** Weekly
AW Average wage paid	**FQ** First quartile wage	**LO** Lowest wage paid	**ME** Median entry wage	**S** See annotated source	**Y** Yearly

Occupation/Type/Industry	Location	Per	Low	Mid	High	Source	Date
Coach and Scout	San Francisco-Redwood City-South San Francisco PMSA, CA	Y		44567 AW		CABLS	1/16-3/16
	Colorado	Y	20380 FQ	26680 MW	38330 TQ	USBLS	5/15
	Denver-Aurora-Lakewood MSA, CO	Y	19430 FQ	26070 MW	37820 TQ	USBLS	5/15
	Connecticut	Y		41493 MW		CTBLS	1/16-3/16
	Bridgeport-Stamford-Norwalk MSA, CT	Y	29000 FQ	47420 MW	71980 TQ	USBLS	5/15
	Hartford-West Hartford-East Hartford MSA, CT	Y	20010 FQ	42790 MW	58860 TQ	USBLS	5/15
	Delaware	Y	20930 FQ	27620 MW	38310 TQ	USBLS	5/15
	Wilmington PMSA, DE-MD-NJ	Y	21200 FQ	28490 MW	42240 TQ	USBLS	5/15
	District of Columbia	Y	34950 FQ	47490 MW	69280 TQ	USBLS	5/15
	Washington-Arlington-Alexandria PMSA, DC-VA-MD-WV	Y	20080 FQ	35090 MW	49220 TQ	USBLS	5/15
	Florida	Y	23484 AE	40321 MW	65833 AEX	FLBLS	7/16-9/16
	Fort Lauderdale-Pompano Beach-Deerfield Beach PMSA, FL	Y	29031 AE	49360 MW	68204 AEX	FLBLS	7/16-9/16
	Miami-Miami Beach-Kendall PMSA, FL	Y	28648 AE	38079 MW	66420 AEX	FLBLS	7/16-9/16
	Orlando-Kissimmee-Sanford MSA, FL	Y	28250 AE	46263 MW	61017 AEX	FLBLS	7/16-9/16
	Tampa-St. Petersburg-Clearwater MSA, FL	Y	19919 AE	41398 MW	59083 AEX	FLBLS	7/16-9/16
	Georgia	Y	23040 FQ	36370 MW	56070 TQ	USBLS	5/15
	Atlanta-Sandy Springs-Roswell MSA, GA	Y	23160 FQ	35430 MW	54970 TQ	USBLS	5/15
	Augusta-Richmond County MSA, GA-SC	Y	19020 FQ	23400 MW	43630 TQ	USBLS	5/15
	Hawaii	Y	28080 FQ	51170 MW	62900 TQ	USBLS	5/15
	Urban Honolulu MSA, HI	Y	31480 FQ	52010 MW	61750 TQ	USBLS	5/15
	Idaho	Y	17230 FQ	18990 MW	24740 TQ	USBLS	5/15
	Boise City MSA, ID	Y	17190 FQ	18880 MW	24290 TQ	USBLS	5/15
	Illinois	Y	19140 FQ	26630 MW	54850 TQ	USBLS	5/15
	Chicago-Naperville-Arlington Heights PMSA, IL	Y	20890 FQ	37560 MW	63370 TQ	USBLS	5/15
	Lake County-Kenosha County PMSA, IL-WI	Y	21510 FQ	31180 MW	49630 TQ	USBLS	5/15
	Indiana	Y	17930 FQ	22110 MW	33980 TQ	USBLS	5/15
	Gary PMSA, IN	Y	20220 FQ	27120 MW	40420 TQ	USBLS	5/15
	Indianapolis-Carmel-Anderson MSA, IN	Y	18510 FQ	24140 MW	35050 TQ	USBLS	5/15
	Iowa	Y	17190 FQ	18950 MW	32730 TQ	USBLS	5/15
	Des Moines-West Des Moines MSA, IA	Y	17590 FQ	21870 MW	39890 TQ	USBLS	5/15
	Kansas	Y	17980 FQ	27580 MW	45230 TQ	USBLS	5/15
	Wichita MSA, KS	Y	18190 FQ	35540 MW	48670 TQ	USBLS	5/15
	Kentucky	Y	19100 FQ	26160 MW	44430 TQ	USBLS	5/15
	Louisville-Jefferson County MSA, KY-IN	Y	18630 FQ	22900 MW	31470 TQ	USBLS	5/15
	Louisiana	Y	26410 FQ	39130 MW	54860 TQ	USBLS	5/15
	Baton Rouge MSA, LA	Y	29120 FQ	39780 MW	65500 TQ	USBLS	5/15
	New Orleans-Metairie MSA, LA	Y	27940 FQ	36670 MW	47820 TQ	USBLS	5/15
	Maine	Y	17150 FQ	18290 MW	19460 TQ	USBLS	5/15
	Portland-South Portland MSA, ME	Y	17230 FQ	18360 MW	19490 TQ	USBLS	5/15
	Maryland	Y	20384 AE	45039 MW	57367 AEX	MDBLS	4/16
	Baltimore-Columbia-Towson MSA, MD	Y	28900 FQ	45490 MW	58440 TQ	USBLS	5/15
	Salisbury MSA, MD-DE	Y	20320 FQ	28320 MW	38090 TQ	USBLS	5/15
	Massachusetts	Y	20050 FQ	36650 MW	58330 TQ	USBLS	5/15
	Boston-Cambridge-Newton NECTA, MA	Y	26950 FQ	44760 MW	66040 TQ	USBLS	5/15
	Worcester MSA, MA-CT	Y	24360 FQ	34930 MW	53440 TQ	USBLS	5/15
	Michigan	Y	19240 FQ	25260 MW	39860 TQ	USBLS	5/15
	Detroit-Dearborn-Livonia PMSA, MI	Y	23630 FQ	30220 MW	42540 TQ	USBLS	5/15

AE	Average entry wage	AWR	Average wage range	H	Hourly	LR	Low end range	MTC	Median total compensation	TCC	Total cash compensation
AEX	Average experienced wage	B	Biweekly	HI	Highest wage paid	M	Monthly	MW	Median wage paid	TQ	Third quartile wage
ATC	Average total compensation	D	Daily	HR	High end range	MCC	Median cash compensation	MWR	Median wage range	W	Weekly
AW	Average wage paid	FQ	First quartile wage	LO	Lowest wage paid	ME	Median entry wage	S	See annotated source	Y	Yearly

Occupation/Type/Industry	Location	Per	Low	Mid	High	Source	Date
Coach and Scout	Grand Rapids-Wyoming MSA, MI	Y	19030 FQ	21590 MW	25560 TQ	USBLS	5/15
	Minnesota	Y	23084 FQ	35352 MW	49838 TQ	MNBLS	1/16-3/16
	Minneapolis-St. Paul-Bloomington MSA, MN-WI	Y	24385 FQ	35735 MW	49193 TQ	MNBLS	1/16-3/16
	Mississippi	Y	21260 FQ	39670 MW	58430 TQ	USBLS	5/15
	Jackson MSA, MS	Y	26800 FQ	43050 MW	60020 TQ	USBLS	5/15
	Missouri	Y	18230 FQ	22950 MW	44830 TQ	USBLS	5/15
	Kansas City MSA, MO-KS	Y	19560 FQ	32810 MW	46170 TQ	USBLS	5/15
	St. Louis MSA, MO-IL	Y	18350 FQ	21480 MW	40940 TQ	USBLS	5/15
	Montana	Y	18570 FQ	23260 MW	34170 TQ	USBLS	5/15
	Billings MSA, MT	Y	18770 FQ	24310 MW	40220 TQ	USBLS	5/15
	Nebraska	Y	18650 FQ	22290 MW	37025 TQ	NEBLS	7/16-9/16
	Omaha-Council Bluffs MSA, NE-IA	Y	18305 FQ	21270 MW	36515 TQ	NEBLS	7/16-9/16
	Nevada	Y	21920 FQ	24970 MW	33730 TQ	USBLS	5/15
	Las Vegas-Henderson-Paradise MSA, NV	Y	21600 FQ	24150 MW	30410 TQ	USBLS	5/15
	New Hampshire	Y	18393 AE	29052 MW	48410 AEX	NHBLS	6/16
	Manchester NECTA, NH	Y	20852 AE	28515 MW	43617 AEX	NHBLS	6/16
	Nashua NECTA, NH-MA	Y	17680 FQ	19590 MW	27850 TQ	USBLS	5/15
	New Jersey	Y	31660 FQ	46560 MW	60590 TQ	USBLS	5/15
	Camden PMSA, NJ	Y	32270 FQ	42030 MW	56960 TQ	USBLS	5/15
	Newark PMSA, NJ-PA	Y	31030 FQ	44950 MW	60090 TQ	USBLS	5/15
	Trenton MSA, NJ	Y	22360 FQ	40110 MW	55450 TQ	USBLS	5/15
	New Mexico	Y	18250 FQ	21330 MW	36210 TQ	USBLS	5/15
	Albuquerque MSA, NM	Y	17910 FQ	19980 MW	30670 TQ	USBLS	5/15
	New York	Y	23790 AE	37370 MW	58170 AEX	NYBLS	1/16-3/16
	Buffalo-Cheektowaga-Niagara Falls MSA, NY	Y	27080 FQ	34110 MW	45510 TQ	USBLS	5/15
	Nassau County-Suffolk County PMSA, NY	Y	29210 FQ	36790 MW	47230 TQ	USBLS	5/15
	New York-Jersey City-White Plains PMSA, NY-NJ	Y	29040 FQ	44060 MW	61690 TQ	USBLS	5/15
	Rochester MSA, NY	Y	24210 FQ	32460 MW	42170 TQ	USBLS	5/15
	North Carolina	Y	19500 FQ	30320 MW	45640 TQ	USBLS	5/15
	Charlotte-Concord-Gastonia MSA, NC-SC	Y	23280 FQ	29850 MW	43800 TQ	USBLS	5/15
	Raleigh MSA, NC	Y	18170 FQ	22520 MW	36750 TQ	USBLS	5/15
	North Dakota	Y	18980 FQ	27630 MW	45100 TQ	USBLS	5/15
	Fargo MSA, ND-MN	Y	19790 FQ	30790 MW	50040 TQ	USBLS	5/15
	Ohio	Y	18630 FQ	25230 MW	42610 TQ	USBLS	5/15
	Cincinnati MSA, OH-KY-IN	Y	18400 FQ	23070 MW	34950 TQ	USBLS	5/15
	Cleveland-Elyria MSA, OH	Y	18520 FQ	24560 MW	43550 TQ	USBLS	5/15
	Columbus MSA, OH	Y	22400 FQ	39190 MW	65900 TQ	USBLS	5/15
	Oklahoma	Y	18800 FQ	29070 MW	45550 TQ	USBLS	5/15
	Oklahoma City MSA, OK	Y	18230 FQ	25980 MW	38910 TQ	USBLS	5/15
	Tulsa MSA, OK	Y	21230 FQ	34490 MW	53060 TQ	USBLS	5/15
	Oregon	Y	22454 FQ	32693 MW	46711 TQ	ORBLS	2016
	Portland-Vancouver-Hillsboro MSA, OR-WA	Y	24750 FQ	35180 MW	48230 TQ	USBLS	5/15
	Pennsylvania	Y	19510 FQ	29140 MW	47740 TQ	USBLS	5/15
	Allentown-Bethlehem-Easton MSA, PA-NJ	Y	22720 FQ	36930 MW	55240 TQ	USBLS	5/15
	Harrisburg-Carlisle MSA, PA	Y	22900 FQ	35460 MW	64610 TQ	USBLS	5/15
	Montgomery County-Bucks County-Chester County PMSA, PA	Y	19050 FQ	23510 MW	32520 TQ	USBLS	5/15
	Philadelphia PMSA, PA	Y	25130 FQ	33600 MW	52830 TQ	USBLS	5/15
	Pittsburgh MSA, PA	Y	26210 FQ	39980 MW	59620 TQ	USBLS	5/15
	Rhode Island	Y	19870 FQ	34900 MW	55200 TQ	USBLS	5/15
	Providence-Warwick MSA, RI-MA	Y	20300 FQ	35440 MW	56390 TQ	USBLS	5/15
	South Carolina	Y	21660 FQ	33140 MW	53240 TQ	USBLS	5/15
	Charleston-North Charleston MSA, SC	Y	19020 FQ	30210 MW	50750 TQ	USBLS	5/15
	Columbia MSA, SC	Y	18240 FQ	25550 MW	44480 TQ	USBLS	5/15
	Greenville-Anderson-Mauldin MSA, SC	Y	38960 FQ	48930 MW	68470 TQ	USBLS	5/15
	South Dakota	Y	27330 FQ	30440 MW	37220 TQ	USBLS	5/15
	Sioux Falls MSA, SD	Y	27610 FQ	31450 MW	38060 TQ	USBLS	5/15
	Tennessee	Y	21870 FQ	34470 MW	50480 TQ	USBLS	5/15

AE	Average entry wage	AWR	Average wage range	H	Hourly
AEX	Average experienced wage	B	Biweekly	HI	Highest wage paid
ATC	Average total compensation	D	Daily	HR	High end range
AW	Average wage paid	FQ	First quartile wage	LO	Lowest wage paid

LR Low end range   MTC Median total compensation   TCC Total cash compensation
M Monthly   MW Median wage paid   TQ Third quartile wage
MCC Median cash compensation   MWR Median wage range   W Weekly
ME Median entry wage   S See annotated source   Y Yearly

Occupation/Type/Industry	Location	Per	Low	Mid	High	Source	Date
Coach and Scout	Knoxville MSA, TN	Y	23210 FQ	35740 MW	47840 TQ	USBLS	5/15
	Memphis MSA, TN-MS-AR	Y	22500 FQ	41470 MW	70850 TQ	USBLS	5/15
	Nashville-Davidson–						
	Murfreesboro–Franklin						
	MSA, TN	Y	22970 FQ	36660 MW	58110 TQ	USBLS	5/15
	Texas	Y	22120 FQ	35470 MW	57740 TQ	USBLS	5/15
	Austin-Round Rock MSA, TX	Y	25760 FQ	34180 MW	49950 TQ	USBLS	5/15
	Dallas-Plano-Irving PMSA, TX	Y	24330 FQ	35260 MW	59770 TQ	USBLS	5/15
	Fort Worth-Arlington PMSA,						
	TX	Y	25890 FQ	44640 MW	60220 TQ	USBLS	5/15
	Houston-The Woodlands-						
	Sugar Land MSA, TX	Y	21750 FQ	34360 MW	57570 TQ	USBLS	5/15
	San Antonio-New Braunfels						
	MSA, TX	Y	18930 FQ	24270 MW	39110 TQ	USBLS	5/15
	Utah	Y	18180 FQ	25100 MW	41280 TQ	USBLS	5/15
	Ogden-Clearfield MSA, UT	Y	17770 FQ	20070 MW	33520 TQ	USBLS	5/15
	Provo-Orem MSA, UT	Y	23910 FQ	37450 MW	44970 TQ	USBLS	5/15
	Salt Lake City MSA, UT	Y	17990 FQ	28730 MW	46150 TQ	USBLS	5/15
	Vermont	Y	23050 FQ	31310 MW	46060 TQ	USBLS	5/15
	Burlington-South Burlington						
	MSA, VT	Y	25460 FQ	38500 MW	58300 TQ	USBLS	5/15
	Virginia	Y	18900 FQ	29810 MW	45140 TQ	USBLS	5/15
	Richmond MSA, VA	Y	17860 FQ	22730 MW	39820 TQ	USBLS	5/15
	Virginia Beach-Norfolk-						
	Newport News MSA, VA-NC	Y	19340 FQ	26910 MW	39920 TQ	USBLS	5/15
	Washington	Y		42761 AW		WABLS	3/16
	Seattle-Bellevue-Everett						
	PMSA, WA	Y		46748 AW		WABLS	3/16
	Tacoma-Lakewood PMSA, WA	Y		37080 AW		WABLS	3/16
	West Virginia	Y	34360 FQ	45210 MW	57300 TQ	USBLS	5/15
	Huntington-Ashland MSA,						
	WV-KY-OH	Y	18080 FQ	20860 MW	43620 TQ	USBLS	5/15
	Wisconsin	Y	18610 FQ	24290 MW	38590 TQ	USBLS	5/15
	Madison MSA, WI	Y	20180 FQ	23710 MW	46680 TQ	USBLS	5/15
	Milwaukee-Waukesha-West						
	Allis MSA, WI	Y	19090 FQ	26310 MW	38520 TQ	USBLS	5/15
	Wyoming	Y	17660 FQ	20220 MW	33110 TQ	USBLS	5/15
	Cheyenne MSA, WY	Y	19420 FQ	26470 MW	38790 TQ	USBLS	5/15
	Puerto Rico	Y	17130 FQ	18760 MW	22850 TQ	USBLS	5/15
	San Juan-Carolina-Caguas						
	MSA, PR	Y	17040 FQ	18580 MW	21570 TQ	USBLS	5/15
	Virgin Islands	Y	18620 FQ	38030 MW	48270 TQ	USBLS	5/15
	Guam	Y	27310 FQ	31800 MW	41830 TQ	USBLS	5/15
Coating, Painting, and Spraying Machine Setter, Operator, and Tender	Alabama	Y	24235 AE	32913 AW	37252 AEX	ALBLS	6/16
	Birmingham-Hoover MSA, AL	Y	26209 AE	32019 AW	34918 AEX	ALBLS	6/16
	Arizona	Y	22410 FQ	27340 MW	34230 TQ	USBLS	5/15
	Phoenix-Mesa-Scottsdale						
	MSA, AZ	Y	22340 FQ	27110 MW	33750 TQ	USBLS	5/15
	Tucson MSA, AZ	Y	22710 FQ	29670 MW	35880 TQ	USBLS	5/15
	Arkansas	Y	25560 FQ	29870 MW	36440 TQ	USBLS	5/15
	Little Rock-North Little Rock-						
	Conway MSA, AR	Y	28570 FQ	32850 MW	37260 TQ	USBLS	5/15
	California	H	11.62 FQ	15.37 MW	20.03 TQ	CABLS	1/16-3/16
	Anaheim-Santa Ana-Irvine						
	PMSA, CA	H	11.35 FQ	14.47 MW	19.02 TQ	CABLS	1/16-3/16
	Los Angeles-Long Beach-						
	Glendale PMSA, CA	H	10.99 FQ	13.91 MW	18.50 TQ	CABLS	1/16-3/16
	Oakland-Hayward-Berkeley						
	PMSA, CA	H	15.98 FQ	21.13 MW	32.50 TQ	CABLS	1/16-3/16
	Riverside-San Bernardino-						
	Ontario MSA, CA	H	10.70 FQ	12.20 MW	16.26 TQ	CABLS	1/16-3/16
	Sacramento–Roseville–						
	Arden-Arcade MSA, CA	H	13.87 FQ	16.64 MW	22.03 TQ	CABLS	1/16-3/16
	San Diego-Carlsbad MSA, CA	H	11.45 FQ	17.85 MW	24.74 TQ	CABLS	1/16-3/16
	San Francisco-Redwood City-						
	South San Francisco PMSA,						
	CA	H	14.52 FQ	22.94 MW	26.85 TQ	CABLS	1/16-3/16
	Colorado	Y	26080 FQ	33110 MW	41990 TQ	USBLS	5/15

AE	Average entry wage	AWR	Average wage range	H	Hourly	LR	Low end range	MTC	Median total compensation	TCC	Total cash compensation
AEX	Average experienced wage	B	Biweekly	HI	Highest wage paid	M	Monthly	MW	Median wage paid	TQ	Third quartile wage
ATC	Average total compensation	D	Daily	HR	High end range	MCC	Median cash compensation	MWR	Median wage range	W	Weekly
AW	Average wage paid	FQ	First quartile wage	LO	Lowest wage paid	ME	Median entry wage	S	See annotated source	Y	Yearly

Occupation/Type/Industry	Location	Per	Low	Mid	High	Source	Date
Coating, Painting, and Spraying Machine Setter, Operator, and Tender							
	Denver-Aurora-Lakewood MSA, CO	Y	25980 FQ	34200 MW	42250 TQ	USBLS	5/15
	Connecticut	Y		35573 MW		CTBLS	1/16-3/16
	Bridgeport-Stamford-Norwalk MSA, CT	Y	26750 FQ	31050 MW	41230 TQ	USBLS	5/15
	Hartford-West Hartford-East Hartford MSA, CT	Y	31660 FQ	37760 MW	46440 TQ	USBLS	5/15
	Delaware	Y	21630 FQ	27010 MW	39230 TQ	USBLS	5/15
	Wilmington PMSA, DE-MD-NJ	Y	22060 FQ	28340 MW	61460 TQ	USBLS	5/15
	Washington-Arlington-Alexandria PMSA, DC-VA-MD-WV	Y	25310 FQ	30960 MW	39940 TQ	USBLS	5/15
	Florida	H	11.83 AE	15.88 MW	18.71 AEX	FLBLS	7/16-9/16
	Fort Lauderdale-Pompano Beach-Deerfield Beach PMSA, FL	H	13.77 AE	17.33 MW	19.43 AEX	FLBLS	7/16-9/16
	Miami-Miami Beach-Kendall PMSA, FL	H	10.27 AE	14.00 MW	17.46 AEX	FLBLS	7/16-9/16
	Orlando-Kissimmee-Sanford MSA, FL	H	11.53 AE	15.17 MW	17.88 AEX	FLBLS	7/16-9/16
	Panama City MSA, FL	Y	26190 FQ	33590 MW	39880 TQ	USBLS	5/15
	Tampa-St. Petersburg-Clearwater MSA, FL	H	12.54 AE	15.11 MW	17.57 AEX	FLBLS	7/16-9/16
	Georgia	Y	24010 FQ	29080 MW	35970 TQ	USBLS	5/15
	Atlanta-Sandy Springs-Roswell MSA, GA	Y	24380 FQ	29790 MW	37410 TQ	USBLS	5/15
	Augusta-Richmond County MSA, GA-SC	Y	26510 FQ	29000 MW	31650 TQ	USBLS	5/15
	Idaho	Y	22640 FQ	26690 MW	30390 TQ	USBLS	5/15
	Boise City MSA, ID	Y	20980 FQ	24150 MW	28170 TQ	USBLS	5/15
	Illinois	Y	26470 FQ	32350 MW	39230 TQ	USBLS	5/15
	Chicago-Naperville-Arlington Heights PMSA, IL	Y	27340 FQ	33860 MW	42000 TQ	USBLS	5/15
	Lake County-Kenosha County PMSA, IL-WI	Y	25370 FQ	30930 MW	37800 TQ	USBLS	5/15
	Indiana	Y	22720 FQ	28770 MW	36990 TQ	USBLS	5/15
	Gary PMSA, IN	Y	22720 FQ	29120 MW	34970 TQ	USBLS	5/15
	Indianapolis-Carmel-Anderson MSA, IN	Y	23780 FQ	29650 MW	36530 TQ	USBLS	5/15
	Iowa	Y	26770 FQ	31000 MW	37770 TQ	USBLS	5/15
	Des Moines-West Des Moines MSA, IA	Y	28260 FQ	32070 MW	36650 TQ	USBLS	5/15
	Kansas	Y	25520 FQ	29570 MW	35170 TQ	USBLS	5/15
	Wichita MSA, KS	Y	26280 FQ	30320 MW	35640 TQ	USBLS	5/15
	Kentucky	Y	24220 FQ	31090 MW	43910 TQ	USBLS	5/15
	Louisville-Jefferson County MSA, KY-IN	Y	27500 FQ	32990 MW	40580 TQ	USBLS	5/15
	Louisiana	Y	26320 FQ	32320 MW	40820 TQ	USBLS	5/15
	Baton Rouge MSA, LA	Y	29120 FQ	35530 MW	42990 TQ	USBLS	5/15
	Maine	Y	36230 FQ	53290 MW	60230 TQ	USBLS	5/15
	Maryland	Y	28484 AE	42759 MW	49896 AEX	MDBLS	4/16
	Baltimore-Columbia-Towson MSA, MD	Y	37690 FQ	47450 MW	58900 TQ	USBLS	5/15
	Salisbury MSA, MD-DE	Y	21390 FQ	29400 MW	35650 TQ	USBLS	5/15
	Massachusetts	Y	27920 FQ	34370 MW	43160 TQ	USBLS	5/15
	Boston-Cambridge-Newton NECTA, MA	Y	29170 FQ	35760 MW	44670 TQ	USBLS	5/15
	Worcester MSA, MA-CT	Y	27380 FQ	31180 MW	41050 TQ	USBLS	5/15
	Michigan	Y	22200 FQ	28270 MW	35970 TQ	USBLS	5/15
	Detroit-Dearborn-Livonia PMSA, MI	Y	25410 FQ	32570 MW	37000 TQ	USBLS	5/15
	Grand Rapids-Wyoming MSA, MI	Y	24970 FQ	31460 MW	40350 TQ	USBLS	5/15
	Minnesota	Y	29756 FQ	36033 MW	43799 TQ	MNBLS	1/16-3/16
	Minneapolis-St. Paul-Bloomington MSA, MN-WI	Y	29300 FQ	35010 MW	41601 TQ	MNBLS	1/16-3/16
	Mississippi	Y	26690 FQ	32760 MW	37620 TQ	USBLS	5/15
	Jackson MSA, MS	Y	26800 FQ	30700 MW	35540 TQ	USBLS	5/15

AE	Average entry wage	AWR	Average wage range	H	Hourly
AEX	Average experienced wage	B	Biweekly	HI	Highest wage paid
ATC	Average total compensation	D	Daily	HR	High end range
AW	Average wage paid	FQ	First quartile wage	LO	Lowest wage paid

LR	Low end range	MTC	Median total compensation
M	Monthly	MW	Median wage paid
MCC	Median cash compensation	MWR	Median wage range
ME	Median entry wage	S	See annotated source

TCC	Total cash compensation		
TQ	Third quartile wage		
W	Weekly		
Y	Yearly		

Occupation/Type/Industry	Location	Per	Low	Mid	High	Source	Date
Coating, Painting, and Spraying Machine Setter, Operator, and Tender							
	Missouri	Y	27490 FQ	33860 MW	40540 TQ	USBLS	5/15
	Kansas City MSA, MO-KS	Y	24070 FQ	29800 MW	37980 TQ	USBLS	5/15
	St. Louis MSA, MO-IL	Y	26170 FQ	32580 MW	38550 TQ	USBLS	5/15
	Montana	Y	25010 FQ	31720 MW	39490 TQ	USBLS	5/15
	Billings MSA, MT	Y	22020 FQ	24330 MW	31150 TQ	USBLS	5/15
	Nebraska	Y	28735 FQ	35020 MW	41935 TQ	NEBLS	7/16-9/16
	Omaha-Council Bluffs MSA, NE-IA	Y	27490 FQ	32785 MW	37490 TQ	NEBLS	7/16-9/16
	Nevada	Y	24310 FQ	28120 MW	31880 TQ	USBLS	5/15
	Las Vegas-Henderson-Paradise MSA, NV	Y	23170 FQ	26610 MW	30600 TQ	USBLS	5/15
	New Hampshire	H	12.85 AE	17.14 MW	19.53 AEX	NHBLS	6/16
	Manchester NECTA, NH	H	12.47 AE	15.87 MW	17.92 AEX	NHBLS	6/16
	Nashua NECTA, NH-MA	Y	27940 FQ	34170 MW	39480 TQ	USBLS	5/15
	New Jersey	Y	26130 FQ	34470 MW	43440 TQ	USBLS	5/15
	Camden PMSA, NJ	Y	32770 FQ	39760 MW	50530 TQ	USBLS	5/15
	Newark PMSA, NJ-PA	Y	25680 FQ	34780 MW	42760 TQ	USBLS	5/15
	New Mexico	Y	24860 FQ	30700 MW	36440 TQ	USBLS	5/15
	Albuquerque MSA, NM	Y	24530 FQ	30850 MW	36490 TQ	USBLS	5/15
	New York	Y	24500 AE	32880 MW	40210 AEX	NYBLS	1/16-3/16
	Buffalo-Cheektowaga-Niagara Falls MSA, NY	Y	26070 FQ	30520 MW	45620 TQ	USBLS	5/15
	Nassau County-Suffolk County PMSA, NY	Y	24570 FQ	32180 MW	40410 TQ	USBLS	5/15
	New York-Jersey City-White Plains PMSA, NY-NJ	Y	23700 FQ	30840 MW	40760 TQ	USBLS	5/15
	Rochester MSA, NY	Y	29010 FQ	34360 MW	42070 TQ	USBLS	5/15
	North Carolina	Y	25900 FQ	31050 MW	38890 TQ	USBLS	5/15
	Charlotte-Concord-Gastonia MSA, NC-SC	Y	31080 FQ	39670 MW	46300 TQ	USBLS	5/15
	Raleigh MSA, NC	Y	22560 FQ	25350 MW	30250 TQ	USBLS	5/15
	North Dakota	Y	30570 FQ	36090 MW	43080 TQ	USBLS	5/15
	Fargo MSA, ND-MN	Y	30560 FQ	37270 MW	44270 TQ	USBLS	5/15
	Ohio	Y	26110 FQ	32210 MW	38950 TQ	USBLS	5/15
	Cincinnati MSA, OH-KY-IN	Y	29610 FQ	35500 MW	42960 TQ	USBLS	5/15
	Cleveland-Elyria MSA, OH	Y	27610 FQ	33760 MW	39860 TQ	USBLS	5/15
	Columbus MSA, OH	Y	25040 FQ	32730 MW	38080 TQ	USBLS	5/15
	Oklahoma	Y	25980 FQ	31950 MW	38050 TQ	USBLS	5/15
	Oklahoma City MSA, OK	Y	24950 FQ	30230 MW	36290 TQ	USBLS	5/15
	Tulsa MSA, OK	Y	28070 FQ	34180 MW	39410 TQ	USBLS	5/15
	Oregon	H	13.14 FQ	16.03 MW	20.79 TQ	ORBLS	2016
	Portland-Vancouver-Hillsboro MSA, OR-WA	Y	26780 FQ	31920 MW	41690 TQ	USBLS	5/15
	Pennsylvania	Y	27300 FQ	33770 MW	40660 TQ	USBLS	5/15
	Allentown-Bethlehem-Easton MSA, PA-NJ	Y	28190 FQ	33450 MW	38040 TQ	USBLS	5/15
	Harrisburg-Carlisle MSA, PA	Y	21570 FQ	23920 MW	30280 TQ	USBLS	5/15
	Montgomery County-Bucks County-Chester County PMSA, PA	Y	29920 FQ	38310 MW	46090 TQ	USBLS	5/15
	Philadelphia PMSA, PA	Y	27620 FQ	33640 MW	40920 TQ	USBLS	5/15
	Pittsburgh MSA, PA	Y	29820 FQ	34520 MW	39240 TQ	USBLS	5/15
	Rhode Island	Y	22460 FQ	30240 MW	37520 TQ	USBLS	5/15
	Providence-Warwick MSA, RI-MA	Y	23410 FQ	29820 MW	36850 TQ	USBLS	5/15
	South Carolina	Y	26070 FQ	31250 MW	38790 TQ	USBLS	5/15
	Charleston-North Charleston MSA, SC	Y	26190 FQ	30260 MW	37000 TQ	USBLS	5/15
	Columbia MSA, SC	Y	31690 FQ	36000 MW	40370 TQ	USBLS	5/15
	Greenville-Anderson-Mauldin MSA, SC	Y	26310 FQ	30650 MW	40170 TQ	USBLS	5/15
	South Dakota	Y	27010 FQ	31510 MW	38280 TQ	USBLS	5/15
	Sioux Falls MSA, SD	Y	24460 FQ	28240 MW	31970 TQ	USBLS	5/15
	Tennessee	Y	26100 FQ	31790 MW	38530 TQ	USBLS	5/15
	Knoxville MSA, TN	Y	27390 FQ	32230 MW	41830 TQ	USBLS	5/15
	Memphis MSA, TN-MS-AR	Y	27250 FQ	32400 MW	38610 TQ	USBLS	5/15
	Nashville-Davidson–Murfreesboro–Franklin MSA, TN	Y	25910 FQ	31710 MW	36670 TQ	USBLS	5/15

AE Average entry wage	**AWR** Average wage range	**H** Hourly	**LR** Low end range	**MTC** Median total compensation	**TCC** Total cash compensation
AEX Average experienced wage	**B** Biweekly	**HI** Highest wage paid	**M** Monthly	**MW** Median wage paid	**TQ** Third quartile wage
ATC Average total compensation	**D** Daily	**HR** High end range	**MCC** Median cash compensation	**MWR** Median wage range	**W** Weekly
AW Average wage paid	**FQ** First quartile wage	**LO** Lowest wage paid	**ME** Median entry wage	**S** See annotated source	**Y** Yearly

Occupation/Type/Industry	Location	Per	Low	Mid	High	Source	Date
Coating, Painting, and Spraying Machine Setter, Operator, and Tender	Texas	Y	24490 FQ	31600 MW	38450 TQ	USBLS	5/15
	Austin-Round Rock MSA, TX	Y	22530 FQ	26960 MW	32230 TQ	USBLS	5/15
	Dallas-Plano-Irving PMSA, TX	Y	22930 FQ	29150 MW	40640 TQ	USBLS	5/15
	Fort Worth-Arlington PMSA, TX	Y	26470 FQ	31230 MW	38220 TQ	USBLS	5/15
	Houston-The Woodlands-Sugar Land MSA, TX	Y	26160 FQ	33790 MW	39940 TQ	USBLS	5/15
	San Antonio-New Braunfels MSA, TX	Y	22760 FQ	27740 MW	35000 TQ	USBLS	5/15
	Utah	Y	23630 FQ	29880 MW	36440 TQ	USBLS	5/15
	Ogden-Clearfield MSA, UT	Y	23280 FQ	31930 MW	38650 TQ	USBLS	5/15
	Provo-Orem MSA, UT	Y	24830 FQ	31250 MW	36040 TQ	USBLS	5/15
	Salt Lake City MSA, UT	Y	23410 FQ	29160 MW	35660 TQ	USBLS	5/15
	Vermont	Y	29340 FQ	36620 MW	44980 TQ	USBLS	5/15
	Burlington-South Burlington MSA, VT	Y	36670 FQ	42700 MW	47690 TQ	USBLS	5/15
	Virginia	Y	26370 FQ	33060 MW	41570 TQ	USBLS	5/15
	Richmond MSA, VA	Y	28930 FQ	35020 MW	42140 TQ	USBLS	5/15
	Virginia Beach-Norfolk-Newport News MSA, VA-NC	Y	33740 FQ	41840 MW	53790 TQ	USBLS	5/15
	Washington	H	13.72 FQ	16.60 MW	20.16 TQ	WABLS	3/16
	Seattle-Bellevue-Everett PMSA, WA	H	13.83 FQ	16.55 MW	20.75 TQ	WABLS	3/16
	Tacoma-Lakewood PMSA, WA	H	14.41 FQ	17.89 MW	22.23 TQ	WABLS	3/16
	West Virginia	Y	27640 FQ	32190 MW	39140 TQ	USBLS	5/15
	Wisconsin	Y	28320 FQ	34500 MW	41340 TQ	USBLS	5/15
	Madison MSA, WI	Y	27870 FQ	33430 MW	38460 TQ	USBLS	5/15
	Milwaukee-Waukesha-West Allis MSA, WI	Y	29300 FQ	35690 MW	43420 TQ	USBLS	5/15
	Wyoming	Y	33860 FQ	37650 MW	43890 TQ	USBLS	5/15
	Puerto Rico	Y	17420 FQ	19200 MW	22050 TQ	USBLS	5/15
	San Juan-Carolina-Caguas MSA, PR	Y	16870 FQ	18070 MW	19260 TQ	USBLS	5/15
Code Enforcement Officer							
Municipal Government	Atwater, CA	Y			5611 HI	CACIT	6/28/16
Municipal Government	Americus, GA	Y	25021 LO		35029 HI	GACTY01	2016
Municipal Government	Marietta, GA	Y	38314 LO		64034 HI	GACTY01	2016
Codifier of Rules							
State Government	North Carolina	Y	54887 LO		90780 HI	NCGOV	7/1/16
Cognitive Skills Facilitator							
Public Safety, County Government	Johnson County, KS	H	23.20 FQ	25.08 MW	26.96 TQ	JCOKS	2017
Coil Winder, Taper, and Finisher	Alabama	Y	26456 AE	38538 AW	44573 AEX	ALBLS	6/16
	Arizona	Y	20620 FQ	26760 MW	34640 TQ	USBLS	5/15
	Arkansas	Y	33380 FQ	36640 MW	41080 TQ	USBLS	5/15
	California	H	10.49 FQ	12.13 MW	17.19 TQ	CABLS	1/16-3/16
	Colorado	Y	24710 FQ	29810 MW	36540 TQ	USBLS	5/15
	Connecticut	Y		34654 MW		CTBLS	1/16-3/16
	Florida	H	12.76 AE	16.88 MW	19.46 AEX	FLBLS	7/16-9/16
	Georgia	Y	31590 FQ	36860 MW	42860 TQ	USBLS	5/15
	Idaho	Y	22770 FQ	27220 MW	31450 TQ	USBLS	5/15
	Illinois	Y	21220 FQ	26370 MW	31960 TQ	USBLS	5/15
	Indiana	Y	24200 FQ	34270 MW	42370 TQ	USBLS	5/15
	Kansas	Y	20380 FQ	26300 MW	30520 TQ	USBLS	5/15
	Kentucky	Y	24850 FQ	29360 MW	39500 TQ	USBLS	5/15
	Louisiana	Y	39580 FQ	44420 MW	49020 TQ	USBLS	5/15
	Maine	Y	22120 FQ	24380 MW	40090 TQ	USBLS	5/15
	Massachusetts	Y	28450 FQ	34460 MW	42860 TQ	USBLS	5/15
	Michigan	Y	28250 FQ	35060 MW	40180 TQ	USBLS	5/15
	Minnesota	Y	20927 FQ	31447 MW	39850 TQ	MNBLS	1/16-3/16
	Mississippi	Y	29060 FQ	34280 MW	39650 TQ	USBLS	5/15
	Missouri	Y	25310 FQ	32380 MW	38910 TQ	USBLS	5/15
	Nebraska	Y	26025 FQ	28830 MW	31875 TQ	NEBLS	7/16-9/16
	New Hampshire	H	13.62 AE	16.87 MW	18.00 AEX	NHBLS	6/16
	New Jersey	Y	27560 FQ	35390 MW	45130 TQ	USBLS	5/15
	New York	Y	21090 AE	26740 MW	32990 AEX	NYBLS	1/16-3/16
	North Carolina	Y	25650 FQ	30550 MW	40490 TQ	USBLS	5/15

AE Average entry wage	**AWR** Average wage range	**H** Hourly	**LR** Low end range	**MTC** Median total compensation	**TCC** Total cash compensation
AEX Average experienced wage	**B** Biweekly	**HI** Highest wage paid	**M** Monthly	**MW** Median wage paid	**TQ** Third quartile wage
ATC Average total compensation	**D** Daily	**HR** High end range	**MCC** Median cash compensation	**MWR** Median wage range	**W** Weekly
AW Average wage paid	**FQ** First quartile wage	**LO** Lowest wage paid	**ME** Median entry wage	**S** See annotated source	**Y** Yearly

Occupation/Type/Industry	Location	Per	Low	Mid	High	Source	Date
Coil Winder, Taper, and Finisher	Ohio	Y	27670 FQ	36220 MW	45290 TQ	USBLS	5/15
	Oklahoma	Y	26380 FQ	32880 MW	37930 TQ	USBLS	5/15
	Oregon	H	11.08 FQ	12.53 MW	14.84 TQ	ORBLS	2016
	Pennsylvania	Y	24590 FQ	36900 MW	46910 TQ	USBLS	5/15
	South Carolina	Y	18770 FQ	22050 MW	26670 TQ	USBLS	5/15
	Tennessee	Y	30040 FQ	35500 MW	41390 TQ	USBLS	5/15
	Texas	Y	26240 FQ	31380 MW	41590 TQ	USBLS	5/15
	Virginia	Y	19880 FQ	29340 MW	37470 TQ	USBLS	5/15
	Washington	H	14.11 FQ	16.75 MW	18.81 TQ	WABLS	3/16
	West Virginia	Y	25490 FQ	31220 MW	35800 TQ	USBLS	5/15
	Wisconsin	Y	28750 FQ	38270 MW	50340 TQ	USBLS	5/15
	Puerto Rico	Y	16700 FQ	17780 MW	18860 TQ	USBLS	5/15
Coin, Vending, and Amusement Machine Servicer and Repairer	Alabama	Y	23615 AE	33704 AW	38738 AEX	ALBLS	6/16
	Birmingham-Hoover MSA, AL	Y	29483 AE	38240 AW	42613 AEX	ALBLS	6/16
	Arizona	Y	24390 FQ	30480 MW	38200 TQ	USBLS	5/15
	Phoenix-Mesa-Scottsdale MSA, AZ	Y	25330 FQ	30680 MW	38910 TQ	USBLS	5/15
	Tucson MSA, AZ	Y	19890 FQ	29510 MW	37070 TQ	USBLS	5/15
	Arkansas	Y	25480 FQ	28480 MW	31510 TQ	USBLS	5/15
	Little Rock-North Little Rock-Conway MSA, AR	Y	24390 FQ	27860 MW	30900 TQ	USBLS	5/15
	California	H	11.85 FQ	15.48 MW	20.32 TQ	CABLS	1/16-3/16
	Anaheim-Santa Ana-Irvine PMSA, CA	H	10.86 FQ	14.41 MW	18.89 TQ	CABLS	1/16-3/16
	Los Angeles-Long Beach-Glendale PMSA, CA	H	13.45 FQ	15.91 MW	21.74 TQ	CABLS	1/16-3/16
	Oakland-Hayward-Berkeley PMSA, CA	H	15.82 FQ	17.23 MW	18.65 TQ	CABLS	1/16-3/16
	Riverside-San Bernardino-Ontario MSA, CA	H	11.67 FQ	18.14 MW	22.75 TQ	CABLS	1/16-3/16
	Sacramento–Roseville–Arden-Arcade MSA, CA	H	12.73 FQ	18.18 MW	23.43 TQ	CABLS	1/16-3/16
	San Diego-Carlsbad MSA, CA	H	9.68 FQ	13.81 MW	18.51 TQ	CABLS	1/16-3/16
	San Francisco-Redwood City-South San Francisco PMSA, CA	H	13.07 FQ	15.51 MW	17.75 TQ	CABLS	1/16-3/16
	Colorado	Y	31030 FQ	37770 MW	44770 TQ	USBLS	5/15
	Denver-Aurora-Lakewood MSA, CO	Y	32810 FQ	40880 MW	46330 TQ	USBLS	5/15
	Connecticut	Y		39382 MW		CTBLS	1/16-3/16
	Bridgeport-Stamford-Norwalk MSA, CT	Y	29900 FQ	38250 MW	46420 TQ	USBLS	5/15
	Hartford-West Hartford-East Hartford MSA, CT	Y	27960 FQ	40460 MW	47530 TQ	USBLS	5/15
	Delaware	Y	28170 FQ	36710 MW	53260 TQ	USBLS	5/15
	Wilmington PMSA, DE-MD-NJ	Y	23820 FQ	31540 MW	36820 TQ	USBLS	5/15
	Washington-Arlington-Alexandria PMSA, DC-VA-MD-WV	Y	33590 FQ	44040 MW	66540 TQ	USBLS	5/15
	Florida	H	9.57 AE	12.52 MW	15.83 AEX	FLBLS	7/16-9/16
	Fort Lauderdale-Pompano Beach-Deerfield Beach PMSA, FL	H	9.03 AE	10.54 MW	13.61 AEX	FLBLS	7/16-9/16
	Miami-Miami Beach-Kendall PMSA, FL	H	10.05 AE	13.21 MW	16.06 AEX	FLBLS	7/16-9/16
	Orlando-Kissimmee-Sanford MSA, FL	H	9.86 AE	13.24 MW	15.21 AEX	FLBLS	7/16-9/16
	Tampa-St. Petersburg-Clearwater MSA, FL	H	10.01 AE	12.58 MW	16.63 AEX	FLBLS	7/16-9/16
	Georgia	Y	25860 FQ	32160 MW	37920 TQ	USBLS	5/15
	Atlanta-Sandy Springs-Roswell MSA, GA	Y	26020 FQ	30560 MW	38520 TQ	USBLS	5/15
	Urban Honolulu MSA, HI	Y	18470 FQ	33000 MW	36270 TQ	USBLS	5/15
	Idaho	Y	29260 FQ	35980 MW	43610 TQ	USBLS	5/15
	Boise City MSA, ID	Y	31810 FQ	40770 MW	46340 TQ	USBLS	5/15
	Illinois	Y	24540 FQ	34250 MW	43320 TQ	USBLS	5/15
	Chicago-Naperville-Arlington Heights PMSA, IL	Y	20240 FQ	36270 MW	46100 TQ	USBLS	5/15

AE	Average entry wage	AWR	Average wage range	H	Hourly
AEX	Average experienced wage	B	Biweekly	HI	Highest wage paid
ATC	Average total compensation	D	Daily	HR	High range
AW	Average wage paid	FQ	First quartile wage	LO	Lowest wage paid

LR	Low end range	MTC	Median total compensation	TCC	Total cash compensation
M	Monthly	MW	Median wage paid	TQ	Third quartile wage
MCC	Median cash compensation	MWR	Median wage range	W	Weekly
ME	Median entry wage	S	See annotated source	Y	Yearly

Occupation/Type/Industry	Location	Per	Low	Mid	High	Source	Date
Coin, Vending, and Amusement Machine Servicer and Repairer	Lake County-Kenosha County						
	PMSA, IL-WI	Y	20120 FQ	23480 MW	29720 TQ	USBLS	5/15
	Indiana	Y	22000 FQ	26840 MW	34020 TQ	USBLS	5/15
	Gary PMSA, IN	Y	31390 FQ	35580 MW	40580 TQ	USBLS	5/15
	Indianapolis-Carmel-Anderson						
	MSA, IN	Y	22600 FQ	27620 MW	34820 TQ	USBLS	5/15
	Iowa	Y	24770 FQ	32380 MW	39390 TQ	USBLS	5/15
	Des Moines-West Des Moines						
	MSA, IA	Y	26490 FQ	30450 MW	38120 TQ	USBLS	5/15
	Kansas	Y	22700 FQ	27200 MW	40190 TQ	USBLS	5/15
	Wichita MSA, KS	Y	22700 FQ	25250 MW	29440 TQ	USBLS	5/15
	Kentucky	Y	23020 FQ	31160 MW	40050 TQ	USBLS	5/15
	Louisville-Jefferson County						
	MSA, KY-IN	Y	25810 FQ	34870 MW	42870 TQ	USBLS	5/15
	Louisiana	Y	21830 FQ	26390 MW	34020 TQ	USBLS	5/15
	Baton Rouge MSA, LA	Y	24220 FQ	30720 MW	39540 TQ	USBLS	5/15
	New Orleans-Metairie MSA,						
	LA	Y	21890 FQ	24910 MW	29560 TQ	USBLS	5/15
	Maine	Y	23420 FQ	27790 MW	31660 TQ	USBLS	5/15
	Maryland	Y	22478 AE	34372 MW	40318 AEX	MDBLS	4/16
	Baltimore-Columbia-Towson						
	MSA, MD	Y	25040 FQ	30310 MW	36760 TQ	USBLS	5/15
	Massachusetts	Y	32670 FQ	38230 MW	47460 TQ	USBLS	5/15
	Boston-Cambridge-Newton						
	NECTA, MA	Y	34190 FQ	38800 MW	85590 TQ	USBLS	5/15
	Worcester MSA, MA-CT	Y	32900 FQ	36280 MW	39660 TQ	USBLS	5/15
	Michigan	Y	25700 FQ	32040 MW	40270 TQ	USBLS	5/15
	Detroit-Dearborn-Livonia						
	PMSA, MI	Y	26630 FQ	31320 MW	46900 TQ	USBLS	5/15
	Grand Rapids-Wyoming MSA,						
	MI	Y	25960 FQ	34820 MW	44390 TQ	USBLS	5/15
	Minnesota	Y	30442 FQ	38869 MW	47548 TQ	MNBLS	1/16-3/16
	Minneapolis-St. Paul-						
	Bloomington MSA, MN-WI	Y	30381 FQ	39734 MW	50555 TQ	MNBLS	1/16-3/16
	Mississippi	Y	27580 FQ	33950 MW	39340 TQ	USBLS	5/15
	Jackson MSA, MS	Y	24140 FQ	30360 MW	38080 TQ	USBLS	5/15
	Missouri	Y	26050 FQ	34770 MW	41380 TQ	USBLS	5/15
	Kansas City MSA, MO-KS	Y	28020 FQ	38410 MW	45370 TQ	USBLS	5/15
	St. Louis MSA, MO-IL	Y	27190 FQ	34770 MW	40220 TQ	USBLS	5/15
	Montana	Y	28740 FQ	33280 MW	39210 TQ	USBLS	5/15
	Nebraska	Y	25900 FQ	33080 MW	38175 TQ	NEBLS	7/16-9/16
	Omaha-Council Bluffs MSA,						
	NE-IA	Y	29840 FQ	33885 MW	38005 TQ	NEBLS	7/16-9/16
	Nevada	Y	31640 FQ	41710 MW	53840 TQ	USBLS	5/15
	Las Vegas-Henderson-Paradise						
	MSA, NV	Y	33560 FQ	44650 MW	56430 TQ	USBLS	5/15
	New Hampshire	H	12.00 AE	19.63 MW	20.83 AEX	NHBLS	6/16
	New Jersey	Y	26970 FQ	35790 MW	43520 TQ	USBLS	5/15
	Camden PMSA, NJ	Y	27830 FQ	34920 MW	43520 TQ	USBLS	5/15
	Newark PMSA, NJ-PA	Y	21990 FQ	24430 MW	36740 TQ	USBLS	5/15
	Trenton MSA, NJ	Y	22060 FQ	24030 MW	52840 TQ	USBLS	5/15
	New Mexico	Y	27250 FQ	31380 MW	39840 TQ	USBLS	5/15
	Albuquerque MSA, NM	Y	27240 FQ	30820 MW	39520 TQ	USBLS	5/15
	New York	Y	23540 AE	36590 MW	52000 AEX	NYBLS	1/16-3/16
	Buffalo-Cheektowaga-Niagara						
	Falls MSA, NY	Y	27700 FQ	32970 MW	36170 TQ	USBLS	5/15
	Nassau County-Suffolk County						
	PMSA, NY	Y	25190 FQ	31070 MW	39700 TQ	USBLS	5/15
	New York-Jersey City-White						
	Plains PMSA, NY-NJ	Y	34440 FQ	43300 MW	70170 TQ	USBLS	5/15
	Rochester MSA, NY	Y	19510 FQ	28370 MW	34340 TQ	USBLS	5/15
	North Carolina	Y	24080 FQ	31090 MW	40820 TQ	USBLS	5/15
	Charlotte-Concord-Gastonia						
	MSA, NC-SC	Y	21860 FQ	27860 MW	34600 TQ	USBLS	5/15
	Raleigh MSA, NC	Y	27020 FQ	35710 MW	44680 TQ	USBLS	5/15
	North Dakota	Y	30690 FQ	36170 MW	42850 TQ	USBLS	5/15
	Ohio	Y	22550 FQ	29970 MW	37720 TQ	USBLS	5/15
	Cincinnati MSA, OH-KY-IN	Y	23990 FQ	31270 MW	36670 TQ	USBLS	5/15
	Cleveland-Elyria MSA, OH	Y	22690 FQ	27820 MW	37430 TQ	USBLS	5/15
	Columbus MSA, OH	Y	26680 FQ	34470 MW	42580 TQ	USBLS	5/15
	Oklahoma	Y	23100 FQ	28330 MW	34480 TQ	USBLS	5/15

AE	Average entry wage	AWR	Average wage range	H	Hourly
AEX	Average experienced wage	B	Biweekly	HI	Highest wage paid
ATC	Average total compensation	D	Daily	HR	High end range
AW	Average wage paid	FQ	First quartile wage	LO	Lowest wage paid

LR	Low end range	MTC	Median total compensation
M	Monthly	MW	Median wage paid
MCC	Median cash compensation	MWR	Median wage range
ME	Median entry wage	S	See annotated source

TCC	Total cash compensation
TQ	Third quartile wage
W	Weekly
Y	Yearly

Occupation/Type/Industry	Location	Per	Low	Mid	High	Source	Date
Coin, Vending, and Amusement Machine Servicer and Repairer	Oklahoma City MSA, OK	Y	23330 FQ	29070 MW	35160 TQ	USBLS	5/15
	Tulsa MSA, OK	Y	25970 FQ	30260 MW	37160 TQ	USBLS	5/15
	Oregon	H	12.80 FQ	15.81 MW	19.21 TQ	ORBLS	2016
	Portland-Vancouver-Hillsboro MSA, OR-WA	Y	25520 FQ	30520 MW	37960 TQ	USBLS	5/15
	Pennsylvania	Y	25520 FQ	33990 MW	39320 TQ	USBLS	5/15
	Harrisburg-Carlisle MSA, PA	Y	32620 FQ	37140 MW	43500 TQ	USBLS	5/15
	Montgomery County-Bucks County-Chester County PMSA, PA	Y	32600 FQ	35880 MW	39160 TQ	USBLS	5/15
	Philadelphia PMSA, PA	Y	37270 FQ	45320 MW	55270 TQ	USBLS	5/15
	Pittsburgh MSA, PA	Y	22740 FQ	32530 MW	41380 TQ	USBLS	5/15
	South Carolina	Y	19950 FQ	34100 MW	43440 TQ	USBLS	5/15
	Charleston-North Charleston MSA, SC	Y	17760 FQ	19560 MW	38670 TQ	USBLS	5/15
	Columbia MSA, SC	Y	24070 FQ	40660 MW	45980 TQ	USBLS	5/15
	Greenville-Anderson-Mauldin MSA, SC	Y	18750 FQ	24760 MW	41550 TQ	USBLS	5/15
	South Dakota	Y	28340 FQ	32750 MW	37000 TQ	USBLS	5/15
	Tennessee	Y	21240 FQ	29410 MW	37450 TQ	USBLS	5/15
	Knoxville MSA, TN	Y	22400 FQ	27190 MW	35150 TQ	USBLS	5/15
	Memphis MSA, TN-MS-AR	Y	25680 FQ	31540 MW	39120 TQ	USBLS	5/15
	Nashville-Davidson–Murfreesboro–Franklin MSA, TN	Y	27880 FQ	34860 MW	40490 TQ	USBLS	5/15
	Texas	Y	23220 FQ	30980 MW	42130 TQ	USBLS	5/15
	Austin-Round Rock MSA, TX	Y	23790 FQ	30800 MW	39000 TQ	USBLS	5/15
	Dallas-Plano-Irving PMSA, TX	Y	23670 FQ	35350 MW	59120 TQ	USBLS	5/15
	Fort Worth-Arlington PMSA, TX	Y	26980 FQ	33470 MW	41690 TQ	USBLS	5/15
	Houston-The Woodlands-Sugar Land MSA, TX	Y	23340 FQ	31660 MW	38770 TQ	USBLS	5/15
	San Antonio-New Braunfels MSA, TX	Y	24640 FQ	33180 MW	46110 TQ	USBLS	5/15
	Utah	Y	31310 FQ	39760 MW	48640 TQ	USBLS	5/15
	Ogden-Clearfield MSA, UT	Y	18710 FQ	29600 MW	43720 TQ	USBLS	5/15
	Salt Lake City MSA, UT	Y	34670 FQ	41870 MW	51250 TQ	USBLS	5/15
	Virginia	Y	22860 FQ	34730 MW	45200 TQ	USBLS	5/15
	Richmond MSA, VA	Y	26480 FQ	36250 MW	43670 TQ	USBLS	5/15
	Virginia Beach-Norfolk-Newport News MSA, VA-NC	Y	35940 FQ	41250 MW	46230 TQ	USBLS	5/15
	Washington	H	14.35 FQ	18.98 MW	22.69 TQ	WABLS	3/16
	Seattle-Bellevue-Everett PMSA, WA	H	12.68 FQ	19.47 MW	22.85 TQ	WABLS	3/16
	Tacoma-Lakewood PMSA, WA	H	17.30 FQ	19.76 MW	23.57 TQ	WABLS	3/16
	West Virginia	Y	23040 FQ	32550 MW	38040 TQ	USBLS	5/15
	Wisconsin	Y	28140 FQ	36400 MW	44860 TQ	USBLS	5/15
	Madison MSA, WI	Y	32630 FQ	40330 MW	48070 TQ	USBLS	5/15
	Milwaukee-Waukesha-West Allis MSA, WI	Y	33430 FQ	36790 MW	42990 TQ	USBLS	5/15
	Wyoming	Y	27830 FQ	32860 MW	38120 TQ	USBLS	5/15
	Puerto Rico	Y	16780 FQ	18170 MW	19590 TQ	USBLS	5/15
	San Juan-Carolina-Caguas MSA, PR	Y	16740 FQ	18070 MW	19420 TQ	USBLS	5/15
College Alumni Coordinator Michigan State University	East Lansing, MI	Y	52131 LO		68858 HI	MSUSAL	10/1/14-9/30/15
College Records Officer Michigan State University	East Lansing, MI	Y			59263 HI	MSUSAL	10/1/14-9/30/15
Combined DNA Index System Analyst State Government	Texas	Y	42244-48278 LR		68960-78953 HR	TXGOV	9/1/15-8/31/17
Combined Food Preparation and Serving Worker Including Fast Food	Alabama	Y	17472 AE	18265 AW	18656 AEX	ALBLS	6/16
Including Fast Food	Birmingham-Hoover MSA, AL	Y	17483 AE	18564 AW	19109 AEX	ALBLS	6/16

AE	Average entry wage	AWR	Average wage range	H	Hourly	LR	Low end range	MTC	Median total compensation	TCC	Total cash compensation
AEX	Average experienced wage	B	Biweekly	HI	Highest wage paid	M	Monthly	MW	Median wage paid	TQ	Third quartile wage
ATC	Average total compensation	D	Daily	HR	High end range	MCC	Median cash compensation	MWR	Median wage range	W	Weekly
AW	Average wage paid	FQ	First quartile wage	LO	Lowest wage paid	ME	Median entry wage	S	See annotated source	Y	Yearly

Occupation/Type/Industry	Location	Per	Low	Mid	High	Source	Date
Combined Food Preparation and Serving Worker							
Including Fast Food	Alaska	Y	18930 FQ	20350 MW	25430 TQ	USBLS	5/15
Including Fast Food	Anchorage MSA, AK	Y	18800 FQ	19500 MW	24690 TQ	USBLS	5/15
Including Fast Food	Arizona	Y	17720 FQ	18670 MW	19740 TQ	USBLS	5/15
Including Fast Food	Phoenix-Mesa-Scottsdale MSA, AZ	Y	17700 FQ	18640 MW	19660 TQ	USBLS	5/15
Including Fast Food	Tucson MSA, AZ	Y	17770 FQ	18770 MW	19960 TQ	USBLS	5/15
Including Fast Food	Arkansas	Y	16720 FQ	17820 MW	18910 TQ	USBLS	5/15
Including Fast Food	Little Rock-North Little Rock-Conway MSA, AR	Y	16740 FQ	17860 MW	18980 TQ	USBLS	5/15
Including Fast Food	California	H	9.41 FQ	9.69 MW	11.41 TQ	CABLS	1/16-3/16
Including Fast Food	Anaheim-Santa Ana-Irvine PMSA, CA	H	9.37 FQ	9.55 MW	10.61 TQ	CABLS	1/16-3/16
Including Fast Food	Los Angeles-Long Beach-Glendale PMSA, CA	H	9.40 FQ	9.64 MW	11.14 TQ	CABLS	1/16-3/16
Including Fast Food	Oakland-Hayward-Berkeley PMSA, CA	H	9.44 FQ	9.79 MW	12.08 TQ	CABLS	1/16-3/16
Including Fast Food	Riverside-San Bernardino-Ontario MSA, CA	H	9.41 FQ	9.65 MW	11.18 TQ	CABLS	1/16-3/16
Including Fast Food	Sacramento–Roseville–Arden-Arcade MSA, CA	H	9.39 FQ	9.59 MW	10.77 TQ	CABLS	1/16-3/16
Including Fast Food	San Diego-Carlsbad MSA, CA	H	9.44 FQ	9.78 MW	11.52 TQ	CABLS	1/16-3/16
Including Fast Food	San Francisco-Redwood City-South San Francisco PMSA, CA	H	10.21 FQ	11.45 MW	13.26 TQ	CABLS	1/16-3/16
Including Fast Food	Colorado	Y	18060 FQ	19000 MW	21260 TQ	USBLS	5/15
Including Fast Food	Denver-Aurora-Lakewood MSA, CO	Y	18050 FQ	18990 MW	20980 TQ	USBLS	5/15
Including Fast Food	Connecticut	Y		21374 MW		CTBLS	1/16-3/16
Including Fast Food	Bridgeport-Stamford-Norwalk MSA, CT	Y	19540 FQ	23280 MW	29270 TQ	USBLS	5/15
Including Fast Food	Hartford-West Hartford-East Hartford MSA, CT	Y	19330 FQ	19720 MW	22830 TQ	USBLS	5/15
Including Fast Food	Delaware	Y	17510 FQ	18620 MW	19950 TQ	USBLS	5/15
Including Fast Food	Wilmington PMSA, DE-MD-NJ	Y	17600 FQ	18740 MW	20620 TQ	USBLS	5/15
Including Fast Food	District of Columbia	Y	19920 FQ	21490 MW	25370 TQ	USBLS	5/15
Including Fast Food	Washington-Arlington-Alexandria PMSA, DC-VA-MD-WV	Y	17680 FQ	19580 MW	22930 TQ	USBLS	5/15
Including Fast Food	Florida	H	8.99 AE	9.33 MW	10.17 AEX	FLBLS	7/16-9/16
Including Fast Food	Fort Lauderdale-Pompano Beach-Deerfield Beach PMSA, FL	H	8.98 AE	9.30 MW	10.41 AEX	FLBLS	7/16-9/16
Including Fast Food	Miami-Miami Beach-Kendall PMSA, FL	H	9.00 AE	9.44 MW	10.52 AEX	FLBLS	7/16-9/16
Including Fast Food	Orlando-Kissimmee-Sanford MSA, FL	H	8.99 AE	9.33 MW	10.22 AEX	FLBLS	7/16-9/16
Including Fast Food	Tampa-St. Petersburg-Clearwater MSA, FL	H	8.99 AE	9.29 MW	9.86 AEX	FLBLS	7/16-9/16
Including Fast Food	Georgia	Y	16650 FQ	17910 MW	19160 TQ	USBLS	5/15
Including Fast Food	Atlanta-Sandy Springs-Roswell MSA, GA	Y	16680 FQ	17970 MW	19260 TQ	USBLS	5/15
Including Fast Food	Augusta-Richmond County MSA, GA-SC	Y	16590 FQ	17810 MW	19020 TQ	USBLS	5/15
Including Fast Food	Hawaii	Y	17610 FQ	19100 MW	24230 TQ	USBLS	5/15
Including Fast Food	Urban Honolulu MSA, HI	Y	17640 FQ	19160 MW	24110 TQ	USBLS	5/15
Including Fast Food	Idaho	Y	16710 FQ	18010 MW	19310 TQ	USBLS	5/15
Including Fast Food	Boise City MSA, ID	Y	16650 FQ	17970 MW	19300 TQ	USBLS	5/15
Including Fast Food	Lewiston MSA, ID-WA	Y	17320 FQ	19160 MW	21680 TQ	USBLS	5/15
Including Fast Food	Illinois	Y	18280 FQ	19020 MW	20370 TQ	USBLS	5/15
Including Fast Food	Chicago-Naperville-Arlington Heights PMSA, IL	Y	18320 FQ	19090 MW	20900 TQ	USBLS	5/15
Including Fast Food	Lake County-Kenosha County PMSA, IL-WI	Y	18080 FQ	18930 MW	20260 TQ	USBLS	5/15
Including Fast Food	Indiana	Y	16700 FQ	17960 MW	19220 TQ	USBLS	5/15
Including Fast Food	Gary PMSA, IN	Y	16760 FQ	18080 MW	19410 TQ	USBLS	5/15
Including Fast Food	Indianapolis-Carmel-Anderson MSA, IN	Y	16750 FQ	18030 MW	19320 TQ	USBLS	5/15
Including Fast Food	Iowa	Y	16770 FQ	18110 MW	19490 TQ	USBLS	5/15

AE	Average entry wage	AWR	Average wage range	H	Hourly	LR	Low end range	MTC	Median total compensation	TCC	Total cash compensation
AEX	Average experienced wage	B	Biweekly	HI	Highest wage paid	M	Monthly	MW	Median wage paid	TQ	Third quartile wage
ATC	Average total compensation	D	Daily	HR	High end range	MCC	Median cash compensation	MWR	Median wage range	W	Weekly
AW	Average wage paid	FQ	First quartile wage	LO	Lowest wage paid	ME	Median entry wage	S	See annotated source	Y	Yearly

251

Occupation/Type/Industry	Location	Per	Low	Mid	High	Source	Date
Combined Food Preparation and Serving Worker							
Including Fast Food	Des Moines-West Des Moines MSA, IA	Y	16820 FQ	18200 MW	19690 TQ	USBLS	5/15
Including Fast Food	Kansas	Y	16780 FQ	18180 MW	19680 TQ	USBLS	5/15
Including Fast Food	Wichita MSA, KS	Y	16770 FQ	18120 MW	19530 TQ	USBLS	5/15
Including Fast Food	Kentucky	Y	16590 FQ	17780 MW	18970 TQ	USBLS	5/15
Including Fast Food	Louisville-Jefferson County MSA, KY-IN	Y	16670 FQ	17930 MW	19190 TQ	USBLS	5/15
Including Fast Food	Louisiana	Y	16650 FQ	17890 MW	19120 TQ	USBLS	5/15
Including Fast Food	Baton Rouge MSA, LA	Y	16680 FQ	18000 MW	19330 TQ	USBLS	5/15
Including Fast Food	New Orleans-Metairie MSA, LA	Y	16760 FQ	18060 MW	19360 TQ	USBLS	5/15
Including Fast Food	Maine	Y	17250 FQ	18530 MW	20130 TQ	USBLS	5/15
Including Fast Food	Portland-South Portland MSA, ME	Y	17340 FQ	18710 MW	22220 TQ	USBLS	5/15
Including Fast Food	Maryland	Y	18030 AE	20058 MW	21072 AEX	MDBLS	4/16
Including Fast Food	Baltimore-Columbia-Towson MSA, MD	Y	17870 FQ	19100 MW	21800 TQ	USBLS	5/15
Including Fast Food	Salisbury MSA, MD-DE	Y	17500 FQ	18480 MW	19510 TQ	USBLS	5/15
Including Fast Food	Massachusetts	Y	19150 FQ	19760 MW	23450 TQ	USBLS	5/15
Including Fast Food	Boston-Cambridge-Newton NECTA, MA	Y	19230 FQ	20800 MW	25530 TQ	USBLS	5/15
Including Fast Food	Worcester MSA, MA-CT	Y	19170 FQ	19730 MW	22910 TQ	USBLS	5/15
Including Fast Food	Michigan	Y	17880 FQ	18700 MW	19620 TQ	USBLS	5/15
Including Fast Food	Detroit-Dearborn-Livonia PMSA, MI	Y	18040 FQ	19020 MW	21880 TQ	USBLS	5/15
Including Fast Food	Grand Rapids-Wyoming MSA, MI	Y	17820 FQ	18590 MW	19380 TQ	USBLS	5/15
Including Fast Food	Minnesota	Y	17905 FQ	18895 MW	20086 TQ	MNBLS	1/16-3/16
Including Fast Food	Minneapolis-St. Paul-Bloomington MSA, MN-WI	Y	17885 FQ	18895 MW	20187 TQ	MNBLS	1/16-3/16
Including Fast Food	Mississippi	Y	16730 FQ	18020 MW	19320 TQ	USBLS	5/15
Including Fast Food	Jackson MSA, MS	Y	16870 FQ	18230 MW	19650 TQ	USBLS	5/15
Including Fast Food	Missouri	Y	17120 FQ	18310 MW	19590 TQ	USBLS	5/15
Including Fast Food	Kansas City MSA, MO-KS	Y	17060 FQ	18330 MW	19720 TQ	USBLS	5/15
Including Fast Food	St. Louis MSA, MO-IL	Y	17500 FQ	18610 MW	20040 TQ	USBLS	5/15
Including Fast Food	Montana	Y	17840 FQ	18900 MW	21030 TQ	USBLS	5/15
Including Fast Food	Billings MSA, MT	Y	17790 FQ	18800 MW	20200 TQ	USBLS	5/15
Including Fast Food	Nebraska	Y	17630 FQ	18620 MW	19695 TQ	NEBLS	7/16-9/16
Including Fast Food	Omaha-Council Bluffs MSA, NE-IA	Y	17635 FQ	18785 MW	20615 TQ	NEBLS	7/16-9/16
Including Fast Food	Nevada	Y	17060 FQ	18740 MW	22270 TQ	USBLS	5/15
Including Fast Food	Las Vegas-Henderson-Paradise MSA, NV	Y	17010 FQ	18660 MW	21950 TQ	USBLS	5/15
Including Fast Food	New Hampshire	H	8.42 AE	9.19 MW	10.15 AEX	NHBLS	6/16
Including Fast Food	Manchester NECTA, NH	H	8.44 AE	10.15 MW	11.32 AEX	NHBLS	6/16
Including Fast Food	Nashua NECTA, NH-MA	Y	16860 FQ	18280 MW	19870 TQ	USBLS	5/15
Including Fast Food	New Jersey	Y	18490 FQ	19520 MW	23220 TQ	USBLS	5/15
Including Fast Food	Camden PMSA, NJ	Y	18450 FQ	19400 MW	22750 TQ	USBLS	5/15
Including Fast Food	Newark PMSA, NJ-PA	Y	18380 FQ	19260 MW	22070 TQ	USBLS	5/15
Including Fast Food	Trenton MSA, NJ	Y	18330 FQ	19180 MW	23110 TQ	USBLS	5/15
Including Fast Food	New Mexico	Y	17000 FQ	18050 MW	19090 TQ	USBLS	5/15
Including Fast Food	Albuquerque MSA, NM	Y	16990 FQ	18010 MW	19030 TQ	USBLS	5/15
Including Fast Food	New York	Y	19260 AE	19640 MW	23120 AEX	NYBLS	1/16-3/16
Including Fast Food	Buffalo-Cheektowaga-Niagara Falls MSA, NY	Y	18640 FQ	19090 MW	19770 TQ	USBLS	5/15
Including Fast Food	Nassau County-Suffolk County PMSA, NY	Y	18840 FQ	19570 MW	23270 TQ	USBLS	5/15
Including Fast Food	New York-Jersey City-White Plains PMSA, NY-NJ	Y	18730 FQ	19400 MW	22890 TQ	USBLS	5/15
Including Fast Food	Rochester MSA, NY	Y	18690 FQ	19180 MW	19980 TQ	USBLS	5/15
Including Fast Food	North Carolina	Y	16720 FQ	18010 MW	19310 TQ	USBLS	5/15
Including Fast Food	Charlotte-Concord-Gastonia MSA, NC-SC	Y	16720 FQ	18030 MW	19350 TQ	USBLS	5/15
Including Fast Food	Raleigh MSA, NC	Y	16880 FQ	18280 MW	19770 TQ	USBLS	5/15
Including Fast Food	North Dakota	Y	18140 FQ	20910 MW	24350 TQ	USBLS	5/15
Including Fast Food	Fargo MSA, ND-MN	Y	17730 FQ	19560 MW	22510 TQ	USBLS	5/15
Including Fast Food	Ohio	Y	17740 FQ	18600 MW	19530 TQ	USBLS	5/15
Including Fast Food	Cincinnati MSA, OH-KY-IN	Y	17540 FQ	18460 MW	19430 TQ	USBLS	5/15
Including Fast Food	Cleveland-Elyria MSA, OH	Y	17740 FQ	18600 MW	19550 TQ	USBLS	5/15
Including Fast Food	Columbus MSA, OH	Y	17810 FQ	18750 MW	19800 TQ	USBLS	5/15

Occupation/Type/Industry	Location	Per	Low	Mid	High	Source	Date
Combined Food Preparation and Serving Worker							
Including Fast Food	Oklahoma	Y	16640 FQ	17880 MW	19130 TQ	USBLS	5/15
Including Fast Food	Oklahoma City MSA, OK	Y	16630 FQ	17830 MW	19030 TQ	USBLS	5/15
Including Fast Food	Tulsa MSA, OK	Y	16710 FQ	18070 MW	19490 TQ	USBLS	5/15
Including Fast Food	Oregon	H	9.59 FQ	9.81 MW	11.33 TQ	ORBLS	2016
Including Fast Food	Portland-Vancouver-Hillsboro MSA, OR-WA	Y	19670 FQ	20960 MW	23730 TQ	USBLS	5/15
Including Fast Food	Pennsylvania	Y	16780 FQ	18180 MW	19720 TQ	USBLS	5/15
Including Fast Food	Allentown-Bethlehem-Easton MSA, PA-NJ	Y	16930 FQ	18320 MW	19790 TQ	USBLS	5/15
Including Fast Food	Harrisburg-Carlisle MSA, PA	Y	16970 FQ	18540 MW	21120 TQ	USBLS	5/15
Including Fast Food	Montgomery County-Bucks County-Chester County PMSA, PA	Y	16950 FQ	18530 MW	21870 TQ	USBLS	5/15
Including Fast Food	Philadelphia PMSA, PA	Y	16770 FQ	18120 MW	19540 TQ	USBLS	5/15
Including Fast Food	Pittsburgh MSA, PA	Y	16780 FQ	18180 MW	19690 TQ	USBLS	5/15
Including Fast Food	Rhode Island	Y	19020 FQ	19330 MW	19970 TQ	USBLS	5/15
Including Fast Food	Providence-Warwick MSA, RI-MA	Y	19010 FQ	19310 MW	19910 TQ	USBLS	5/15
Including Fast Food	South Carolina	Y	16600 FQ	17810 MW	19010 TQ	USBLS	5/15
Including Fast Food	Charleston-North Charleston MSA, SC	Y	16590 FQ	17780 MW	18970 TQ	USBLS	5/15
Including Fast Food	Columbia MSA, SC	Y	16480 FQ	17610 MW	18740 TQ	USBLS	5/15
Including Fast Food	Greenville-Anderson-Mauldin MSA, SC	Y	16560 FQ	17740 MW	18910 TQ	USBLS	5/15
Including Fast Food	South Dakota	Y	18310 FQ	18940 MW	19690 TQ	USBLS	5/15
Including Fast Food	Sioux Falls MSA, SD	Y	18310 FQ	18930 MW	19710 TQ	USBLS	5/15
Including Fast Food	Tennessee	Y	16710 FQ	18020 MW	19350 TQ	USBLS	5/15
Including Fast Food	Knoxville MSA, TN	Y	16810 FQ	18210 MW	19760 TQ	USBLS	5/15
Including Fast Food	Memphis MSA, TN-MS-AR	Y	16750 FQ	18080 MW	19420 TQ	USBLS	5/15
Including Fast Food	Nashville-Davidson–Murfreesboro–Franklin MSA, TN	Y	16820 FQ	18290 MW	20500 TQ	USBLS	5/15
Including Fast Food	Texas	Y	16820 FQ	18220 MW	19720 TQ	USBLS	5/15
Including Fast Food	Austin-Round Rock MSA, TX	Y	17000 FQ	18630 MW	21730 TQ	USBLS	5/15
Including Fast Food	Dallas-Plano-Irving PMSA, TX	Y	16820 FQ	18220 MW	19760 TQ	USBLS	5/15
Including Fast Food	Fort Worth-Arlington PMSA, TX	Y	16770 FQ	18140 MW	19580 TQ	USBLS	5/15
Including Fast Food	Houston-The Woodlands-Sugar Land MSA, TX	Y	16960 FQ	18450 MW	20400 TQ	USBLS	5/15
Including Fast Food	San Antonio-New Braunfels MSA, TX	Y	16700 FQ	18020 MW	19360 TQ	USBLS	5/15
Including Fast Food	Utah	Y	16800 FQ	18190 MW	19680 TQ	USBLS	5/15
Including Fast Food	Ogden-Clearfield MSA, UT	Y	16770 FQ	18120 MW	19520 TQ	USBLS	5/15
Including Fast Food	Provo-Orem MSA, UT	Y	16790 FQ	18160 MW	19640 TQ	USBLS	5/15
Including Fast Food	Salt Lake City MSA, UT	Y	16820 FQ	18240 MW	19770 TQ	USBLS	5/15
Including Fast Food	Vermont	Y	19440 FQ	21060 MW	24840 TQ	USBLS	5/15
Including Fast Food	Burlington-South Burlington MSA, VT	Y	19740 FQ	22530 MW	26630 TQ	USBLS	5/15
Including Fast Food	Virginia	Y	16930 FQ	18420 MW	20670 TQ	USBLS	5/15
Including Fast Food	Richmond MSA, VA	Y	17030 FQ	18680 MW	21660 TQ	USBLS	5/15
Including Fast Food	Virginia Beach-Norfolk-Newport News MSA, VA-NC	Y	16930 FQ	18420 MW	20610 TQ	USBLS	5/15
Including Fast Food	Washington	H	10.04 FQ	11.00 MW	11.95 TQ	WABLS	3/16
Including Fast Food	Seattle-Bellevue-Everett PMSA, WA	H	10.01 FQ	11.04 MW	12.11 TQ	WABLS	3/16
Including Fast Food	Tacoma-Lakewood PMSA, WA	H	10.03 FQ	10.93 MW	11.82 TQ	WABLS	3/16
Including Fast Food	West Virginia	Y	17480 FQ	18310 MW	19150 TQ	USBLS	5/15
Including Fast Food	Huntington-Ashland MSA, WV-KY-OH	Y	17190 FQ	18080 MW	18960 TQ	USBLS	5/15
Including Fast Food	Wisconsin	Y	16750 FQ	18100 MW	19490 TQ	USBLS	5/15
Including Fast Food	Madison MSA, WI	Y	16850 FQ	18250 MW	19750 TQ	USBLS	5/15
Including Fast Food	Milwaukee-Waukesha-West Allis MSA, WI	Y	16720 FQ	18030 MW	19350 TQ	USBLS	5/15
Including Fast Food	Wyoming	Y	16990 FQ	18490 MW	20700 TQ	USBLS	5/15
Including Fast Food	Cheyenne MSA, WY	Y	16870 FQ	18230 MW	19710 TQ	USBLS	5/15
Including Fast Food	Puerto Rico	Y	16460 FQ	17540 MW	18620 TQ	USBLS	5/15
Including Fast Food	San Juan-Carolina-Caguas MSA, PR	Y	16460 FQ	17550 MW	18630 TQ	USBLS	5/15
Including Fast Food	Virgin Islands	Y	17070 FQ	18790 MW	21790 TQ	USBLS	5/15
Including Fast Food	Guam	Y	17960 FQ	18770 MW	19660 TQ	USBLS	5/15

AE	Average entry wage	AWR	Average wage range	H	Hourly	LR	Low end range	MTC	Median total compensation
AEX	Average experienced wage	B	Biweekly	HI	Highest wage paid	M	Monthly	MW	Median wage paid
ATC	Average total compensation	D	Daily	HR	High end range	MCC	Median cash compensation	MWR	Median wage range
AW	Average wage paid	FQ	First quartile wage	LO	Lowest wage paid	ME	Median entry wage	S	See annotated source

TCC Total cash compensation
TQ Third quartile wage
W Weekly
Y Yearly

Occupation/Type/Industry	Location	Per	Low	Mid	High	Source	Date
Comfort Station Matron							
Municipal Government	Detroit, MI	M	1436 LO		2325 HI	DETGOV	2016
Command Sergeant Major							
U.S. Army, Active Duty, Pay Grade E-9	United States	M	5053 LO		7845 HI	DOD1	2017
Commercial and Industrial Designer							
	Alabama	Y	46675 AE	69661 AW	81148 AEX	ALBLS	6/16
	Birmingham-Hoover MSA, AL	Y	54146 AE	69946 AW	77856 AEX	ALBLS	6/16
	Arizona	Y	51010 FQ	66450 MW	84900 TQ	USBLS	5/15
	Phoenix-Mesa-Scottsdale MSA, AZ	Y	51750 FQ	67740 MW	86350 TQ	USBLS	5/15
	Arkansas	Y	59180 FQ	73130 MW	83560 TQ	USBLS	5/15
	California	H	25.94 FQ	33.85 MW	42.79 TQ	CABLS	1/16-3/16
	Anaheim-Santa Ana-Irvine PMSA, CA	H	19.67 FQ	31.80 MW	43.14 TQ	CABLS	1/16-3/16
	Los Angeles-Long Beach-Glendale PMSA, CA	H	25.22 FQ	31.27 MW	38.66 TQ	CABLS	1/16-3/16
	Oakland-Hayward-Berkeley PMSA, CA	H	18.22 FQ	32.02 MW	40.44 TQ	CABLS	1/16-3/16
	Riverside-San Bernardino-Ontario MSA, CA	H	28.12 FQ	38.70 MW	45.63 TQ	CABLS	1/16-3/16
	Sacramento–Roseville–Arden-Arcade MSA, CA	H	26.96 FQ	30.55 MW	37.67 TQ	CABLS	1/16-3/16
	San Diego-Carlsbad MSA, CA	H	34.67 FQ	45.09 MW	56.61 TQ	CABLS	1/16-3/16
	San Francisco-Redwood City-South San Francisco PMSA, CA	H	31.65 FQ	36.45 MW	44.46 TQ	CABLS	1/16-3/16
	Colorado	Y	50720 FQ	68070 MW	90890 TQ	USBLS	5/15
	Denver-Aurora-Lakewood MSA, CO	Y	55010 FQ	74860 MW	93820 TQ	USBLS	5/15
	Connecticut	Y		62533 MW		CTBLS	1/16-3/16
	Bridgeport-Stamford-Norwalk MSA, CT	Y	36800 FQ	50840 MW	64620 TQ	USBLS	5/15
	Hartford-West Hartford-East Hartford MSA, CT	Y	58770 FQ	69650 MW	80190 TQ	USBLS	5/15
	Washington-Arlington-Alexandria PMSA, DC-VA-MD-WV	Y	51040 FQ	60520 MW	76850 TQ	USBLS	5/15
	Florida	H	21.85 AE	29.86 MW	34.78 AEX	FLBLS	7/16-9/16
	Fort Lauderdale-Pompano Beach-Deerfield Beach PMSA, FL	H	24.09 AE	34.86 MW	41.81 AEX	FLBLS	7/16-9/16
	Miami-Miami Beach-Kendall PMSA, FL	H	25.40 AE	28.53 MW	31.57 AEX	FLBLS	7/16-9/16
	Orlando-Kissimmee-Sanford MSA, FL	H	27.29 AE	34.41 MW	35.74 AEX	FLBLS	7/16-9/16
	Tampa-St. Petersburg-Clearwater MSA, FL	H	20.94 AE	29.27 MW	32.70 AEX	FLBLS	7/16-9/16
	Georgia	Y	48700 FQ	66030 MW	84960 TQ	USBLS	5/15
	Atlanta-Sandy Springs-Roswell MSA, GA	Y	47870 FQ	64090 MW	84990 TQ	USBLS	5/15
	Idaho	Y	52470 FQ	64410 MW	95450 TQ	USBLS	5/15
	Boise City MSA, ID	Y	52970 FQ	64130 MW	103480 TQ	USBLS	5/15
	Illinois	Y	50160 FQ	63690 MW	77390 TQ	USBLS	5/15
	Chicago-Naperville-Arlington Heights PMSA, IL	Y	49600 FQ	63600 MW	79340 TQ	USBLS	5/15
	Lake County-Kenosha County PMSA, IL-WI	Y	55210 FQ	65870 MW	76310 TQ	USBLS	5/15
	Indiana	Y	42670 FQ	55670 MW	72320 TQ	USBLS	5/15
	Indianapolis-Carmel-Anderson MSA, IN	Y	43450 FQ	66730 MW	76110 TQ	USBLS	5/15
	Iowa	Y	39970 FQ	55370 MW	70280 TQ	USBLS	5/15
	Des Moines-West Des Moines MSA, IA	Y	50570 FQ	58830 MW	73590 TQ	USBLS	5/15
	Kansas	Y	43160 FQ	56650 MW	69440 TQ	USBLS	5/15
	Wichita MSA, KS	Y	42680 FQ	55980 MW	68420 TQ	USBLS	5/15
	Kentucky	Y	44720 FQ	57130 MW	74390 TQ	USBLS	5/15
	Louisville-Jefferson County MSA, KY-IN	Y	47780 FQ	59870 MW	85990 TQ	USBLS	5/15
	Louisiana	Y	53220 FQ	73230 MW	90340 TQ	USBLS	5/15
	Baton Rouge MSA, LA	Y	37030 FQ	62740 MW	88570 TQ	USBLS	5/15

AE	Average entry wage	AWR	Average wage range	H	Hourly	LR	Low end range	MTC	Median total compensation	TCC	Total cash compensation
AEX	Average experienced wage	B	Biweekly	HI	Highest wage paid	M	Monthly	MW	Median wage paid	TQ	Third quartile wage
ATC	Average total compensation	D	Daily	HR	High end range	MCC	Median cash compensation	MWR	Median wage range	W	Weekly
AW	Average wage paid	FQ	First quartile wage	LO	Lowest wage paid	ME	Median entry wage	S	See annotated source	Y	Yearly

Occupation/Type/Industry	Location	Per	Low	Mid	High	Source	Date
Commercial and Industrial Designer	New Orleans-Metairie MSA, LA	Y	61580 FQ	76010 MW	91560 TQ	USBLS	5/15
	Maine	Y	43550 FQ	52500 MW	73070 TQ	USBLS	5/15
	Portland-South Portland MSA, ME	Y	55160 FQ	65500 MW	87890 TQ	USBLS	5/15
	Maryland	Y	41893 AE	62527 MW	72844 AEX	MDBLS	4/16
	Baltimore-Columbia-Towson MSA, MD	Y	44170 FQ	55740 MW	70080 TQ	USBLS	5/15
	Massachusetts	Y	51320 FQ	71170 MW	94850 TQ	USBLS	5/15
	Boston-Cambridge-Newton NECTA, MA	Y	60560 FQ	80450 MW	98310 TQ	USBLS	5/15
	Michigan	Y	64220 FQ	79160 MW	94190 TQ	USBLS	5/15
	Detroit-Dearborn-Livonia PMSA, MI	Y	70950 FQ	84150 MW	99710 TQ	USBLS	5/15
	Grand Rapids-Wyoming MSA, MI	Y	44910 FQ	56680 MW	72800 TQ	USBLS	5/15
	Minnesota	Y	43921 FQ	57650 MW	71511 TQ	MNBLS	1/16-3/16
	Minneapolis-St. Paul-Bloomington MSA, MN-WI	Y	50403 FQ	60675 MW	75896 TQ	MNBLS	1/16-3/16
	Mississippi	Y	53020 FQ	64190 MW	78090 TQ	USBLS	5/15
	Missouri	Y	44660 FQ	57970 MW	72060 TQ	USBLS	5/15
	Kansas City MSA, MO-KS	Y	41250 FQ	60430 MW	73870 TQ	USBLS	5/15
	St. Louis MSA, MO-IL	Y	50140 FQ	60260 MW	75890 TQ	USBLS	5/15
	Montana	Y	43860 FQ	63350 MW	76690 TQ	USBLS	5/15
	Nebraska	Y	48865 FQ	67780 MW	81715 TQ	NEBLS	7/16-9/16
	Omaha-Council Bluffs MSA, NE-IA	Y	33755 FQ	41410 MW	62400 TQ	NEBLS	7/16-9/16
	Nevada	Y	66690 FQ	74920 MW	85400 TQ	USBLS	5/15
	Las Vegas-Henderson-Paradise MSA, NV	Y	67850 FQ	74120 MW	80370 TQ	USBLS	5/15
	New Hampshire	H	17.38 AE	38.06 MW	45.30 AEX	NHBLS	6/16
	New Jersey	Y	48160 FQ	67470 MW	91210 TQ	USBLS	5/15
	Camden PMSA, NJ	Y	52670 FQ	64400 MW	83580 TQ	USBLS	5/15
	Newark PMSA, NJ-PA	Y	48370 FQ	64430 MW	94340 TQ	USBLS	5/15
	Trenton MSA, NJ	Y	57660 FQ	70460 MW	80300 TQ	USBLS	5/15
	New Mexico	Y	42000 FQ	52130 MW	68680 TQ	USBLS	5/15
	Albuquerque MSA, NM	Y	42820 FQ	52860 MW	69100 TQ	USBLS	5/15
	New York	Y	45700 AE	70080 MW	88500 AEX	NYBLS	1/16-3/16
	Buffalo-Cheektowaga-Niagara Falls MSA, NY	Y	35360 FQ	44480 MW	64300 TQ	USBLS	5/15
	Nassau County-Suffolk County PMSA, NY	Y	56670 FQ	69580 MW	85200 TQ	USBLS	5/15
	New York-Jersey City-White Plains PMSA, NY-NJ	Y	52430 FQ	68840 MW	97700 TQ	USBLS	5/15
	Rochester MSA, NY	Y	62750 FQ	75590 MW	90570 TQ	USBLS	5/15
	North Carolina	Y	48570 FQ	67720 MW	83890 TQ	USBLS	5/15
	Charlotte-Concord-Gastonia MSA, NC-SC	Y	57070 FQ	70070 MW	82180 TQ	USBLS	5/15
	Raleigh MSA, NC	Y	42070 FQ	51770 MW	72860 TQ	USBLS	5/15
	Ohio	Y	46870 FQ	60410 MW	80720 TQ	USBLS	5/15
	Cincinnati MSA, OH-KY-IN	Y	50570 FQ	58440 MW	70970 TQ	USBLS	5/15
	Cleveland-Elyria MSA, OH	Y	48800 FQ	65930 MW	86680 TQ	USBLS	5/15
	Columbus MSA, OH	Y	49030 FQ	66140 MW	89170 TQ	USBLS	5/15
	Oklahoma	Y	42460 FQ	57640 MW	81780 TQ	USBLS	5/15
	Oklahoma City MSA, OK	Y	37580 FQ	52810 MW	61160 TQ	USBLS	5/15
	Tulsa MSA, OK	Y	52070 FQ	78280 MW	98970 TQ	USBLS	5/15
	Oregon	H	18.22 FQ	24.38 MW	35.90 TQ	ORBLS	2016
	Portland-Vancouver-Hillsboro MSA, OR-WA	Y	46120 FQ	62790 MW	85590 TQ	USBLS	5/15
	Pennsylvania	Y	45740 FQ	65840 MW	80820 TQ	USBLS	5/15
	Allentown-Bethlehem-Easton MSA, PA-NJ	Y	44410 FQ	57840 MW	72600 TQ	USBLS	5/15
	Harrisburg-Carlisle MSA, PA	Y	60530 FQ	70660 MW	79420 TQ	USBLS	5/15
	Montgomery County-Bucks County-Chester County PMSA, PA	Y	62350 FQ	72850 MW	94300 TQ	USBLS	5/15
	Philadelphia PMSA, PA	Y	60750 FQ	76370 MW	92410 TQ	USBLS	5/15
	Pittsburgh MSA, PA	Y	44730 FQ	68560 MW	81040 TQ	USBLS	5/15
	Rhode Island	Y	46010 FQ	59940 MW	77730 TQ	USBLS	5/15
	Providence-Warwick MSA, RI-MA	Y	46680 FQ	60470 MW	79190 TQ	USBLS	5/15

AE	Average entry wage	AWR	Average wage range	H	Hourly	LR	Low end range	MTC	Median total compensation	TCC	Total cash compensation
AEX	Average experienced wage	B	Biweekly	HI	Highest wage paid	M	Monthly	MW	Median wage paid	TQ	Third quartile wage
ATC	Average total compensation	D	Daily	HR	High end range	MCC	Median cash compensation	MWR	Median wage range	W	Weekly
AW	Average wage paid	FQ	First quartile wage	LO	Lowest wage paid	ME	Median entry wage	S	See annotated source	Y	Yearly

Occupation/Type/Industry	Location	Per	Low	Mid	High	Source	Date
Commercial and Industrial Designer	South Carolina	Y	57150 FQ	71730 MW	92510 TQ	USBLS	5/15
	Charleston-North Charleston MSA, SC	Y	41000 FQ	47720 MW	69570 TQ	USBLS	5/15
	Columbia MSA, SC	Y	62250 FQ	71330 MW	79260 TQ	USBLS	5/15
	Greenville-Anderson-Mauldin MSA, SC	Y	58570 FQ	79850 MW	105860 TQ	USBLS	5/15
	South Dakota	Y	31960 FQ	40510 MW	52130 TQ	USBLS	5/15
	Sioux Falls MSA, SD	Y	26510 FQ	31550 MW	38460 TQ	USBLS	5/15
	Tennessee	Y	35620 FQ	47840 MW	60550 TQ	USBLS	5/15
	Knoxville MSA, TN	Y	42430 FQ	57950 MW	109340 TQ	USBLS	5/15
	Memphis MSA, TN-MS-AR	Y	53780 FQ	60310 MW	75760 TQ	USBLS	5/15
	Nashville-Davidson– Murfreesboro–Franklin MSA, TN	Y	25370 FQ	42820 MW	55460 TQ	USBLS	5/15
	Texas	Y	45070 FQ	61310 MW	90270 TQ	USBLS	5/15
	Dallas-Plano-Irving PMSA, TX	Y	45140 FQ	59200 MW	84590 TQ	USBLS	5/15
	Fort Worth-Arlington PMSA, TX	Y	41910 FQ	53140 MW	72930 TQ	USBLS	5/15
	Houston-The Woodlands- Sugar Land MSA, TX	Y	55030 FQ	79290 MW	100930 TQ	USBLS	5/15
	Utah	Y	38060 FQ	49560 MW	70280 TQ	USBLS	5/15
	Provo-Orem MSA, UT	Y	41290 FQ	47090 MW	66250 TQ	USBLS	5/15
	Salt Lake City MSA, UT	Y	30510 FQ	51690 MW	65450 TQ	USBLS	5/15
	Vermont	Y	37250 FQ	51810 MW	62490 TQ	USBLS	5/15
	Burlington-South Burlington MSA, VT	Y	50560 FQ	55830 MW	61100 TQ	USBLS	5/15
	Virginia	Y	38150 FQ	49010 MW	63770 TQ	USBLS	5/15
	Richmond MSA, VA	Y	37270 FQ	46330 MW	68230 TQ	USBLS	5/15
	Virginia Beach-Norfolk- Newport News MSA, VA-NC	Y	32610 FQ	44650 MW	61190 TQ	USBLS	5/15
	Washington	H	24.91 FQ	33.99 MW	44.62 TQ	WABLS	3/16
	Seattle-Bellevue-Everett PMSA, WA	H	26.56 FQ	36.66 MW	45.75 TQ	WABLS	3/16
	West Virginia	Y	48580 FQ	58610 MW	78490 TQ	USBLS	5/15
	Wisconsin	Y	44640 FQ	56690 MW	72530 TQ	USBLS	5/15
	Madison MSA, WI	Y	44000 FQ	60270 MW	81750 TQ	USBLS	5/15
	Milwaukee-Waukesha-West Allis MSA, WI	Y	49040 FQ	59090 MW	74680 TQ	USBLS	5/15
	Puerto Rico	Y	32190 FQ	34790 MW	37390 TQ	USBLS	5/15
	San Juan-Carolina-Caguas MSA, PR	Y	32190 FQ	34790 MW	37390 TQ	USBLS	5/15
Commercial Building Inspector Municipal Government	Fresno, CA	Y			28837 HI	CACIT	6/28/16
Commercial Diver	Alabama	Y	35504 AE	47841 AW	54014 AEX	ALBLS	6/16
	Florida	H	15.35 AE	25.54 MW	32.69 AEX	FLBLS	7/16-9/16
	Hawaii	Y	32760 FQ	37600 MW	47120 TQ	USBLS	5/15
	Kentucky	Y	35980 FQ	45020 MW	59640 TQ	USBLS	5/15
	Louisiana	Y	40270 FQ	50620 MW	58960 TQ	USBLS	5/15
	Michigan	Y	39130 FQ	45440 MW	54480 TQ	USBLS	5/15
	Missouri	Y	34400 FQ	42160 MW	56010 TQ	USBLS	5/15
	New Jersey	Y	51540 FQ	80070 MW	117070 TQ	USBLS	5/15
	New York	Y	60430 AE	89550 MW	98640 AEX	NYBLS	1/16-3/16
	Pennsylvania	Y	33000 FQ	43980 MW	57510 TQ	USBLS	5/15
	Texas	Y	35330 FQ	44240 MW	55010 TQ	USBLS	5/15
	Vermont	Y	38050 FQ	53170 MW	62400 TQ	USBLS	5/15
	Virginia	Y	38760 FQ	52450 MW	69290 TQ	USBLS	5/15
	Puerto Rico	Y	20720 FQ	22360 MW	24000 TQ	USBLS	5/15
	Guam	Y	18150 FQ	19140 MW	20250 TQ	USBLS	5/15
Commercial Jet Mechanic	United States	H		22.50 AW		AVJOB06	2016
Commercial Pilot	Alabama	Y	58121 AE	88503 AW	103694 AEX	ALBLS	6/16
	Birmingham-Hoover MSA, AL	Y	70607 AE	97121 AW	110389 AEX	ALBLS	6/16
	Alaska	Y	49200 FQ	67990 MW	91400 TQ	USBLS	5/15
	Anchorage MSA, AK	Y	56860 FQ	78130 MW	139460 TQ	USBLS	5/15
	Arizona	Y	46540 FQ	66490 MW	83110 TQ	USBLS	5/15
	Phoenix-Mesa-Scottsdale MSA, AZ	Y	48470 FQ	66750 MW	79880 TQ	USBLS	5/15
	Arkansas	Y	32720 FQ	72900 MW	114780 TQ	USBLS	5/15

AE	Average entry wage	AWR	Average wage range	H	Hourly	LR	Low end range	MTC	Median total compensation	TCC	Total cash compensation
AEX	Average experienced wage	B	Biweekly	HI	Highest wage paid	M	Monthly	MW	Median wage paid	TQ	Third quartile wage
ATC	Average total compensation	D	Daily	HR	High end range	MCC	Median cash compensation	MWR	Median wage range	W	Weekly
AW	Average wage paid	FQ	First quartile wage	LO	Lowest wage paid	ME	Median entry wage	S	See annotated source	Y	Yearly

Commercial Pilot

Occupation/Type/Industry	Location	Per	Low	Mid	High	Source	Date
Commercial Pilot	Little Rock-North Little Rock-Conway MSA, AR	Y	69850 FQ	108250 MW	123210 TQ	USBLS	5/15
	California	Y		102107 AW		CABLS	1/16-3/16
	Anaheim-Santa Ana-Irvine PMSA, CA	Y		91237 AW		CABLS	1/16-3/16
	Los Angeles-Long Beach-Glendale PMSA, CA	Y		117531 AW		CABLS	1/16-3/16
	Oakland-Hayward-Berkeley PMSA, CA	Y		113670 AW		CABLS	1/16-3/16
	Riverside-San Bernardino-Ontario MSA, CA	Y		76721 AW		CABLS	1/16-3/16
	Sacramento–Roseville–Arden-Arcade MSA, CA	Y		113232 AW		CABLS	1/16-3/16
	San Diego-Carlsbad MSA, CA	Y		78167 AW		CABLS	1/16-3/16
	San Francisco-Redwood City-South San Francisco PMSA, CA	Y		99673 AW		CABLS	1/16-3/16
	Colorado	Y	52900 FQ	77140 MW	98920 TQ	USBLS	5/15
	Denver-Aurora-Lakewood MSA, CO	Y	49710 FQ	83460 MW	102790 TQ	USBLS	5/15
	Connecticut	Y		116227 MW		CTBLS	1/16-3/16
	Hartford-West Hartford-East Hartford MSA, CT	Y	67640 FQ	110530 MW	146310 TQ	USBLS	5/15
	Delaware	Y	81080 FQ	107790 MW	120010 TQ	USBLS	5/15
	Wilmington PMSA, DE-MD-NJ	Y	73180 FQ	100490 MW	119890 TQ	USBLS	5/15
	Washington-Arlington-Alexandria PMSA, DC-VA-MD-WV	Y	66720 FQ	75150 MW	135990 TQ	USBLS	5/15
	Florida	Y	41424 AE	77207 MW	110146 AEX	FLBLS	7/16-9/16
	Fort Lauderdale-Pompano Beach-Deerfield Beach PMSA, FL	Y	42446 AE	86622 MW	116374 AEX	FLBLS	7/16-9/16
	Miami-Miami Beach-Kendall PMSA, FL	Y	45298 AE	82226 MW	120996 AEX	FLBLS	7/16-9/16
	Orlando-Kissimmee-Sanford MSA, FL	Y	38536 AE	61668 MW	85579 AEX	FLBLS	7/16-9/16
	Tampa-St. Petersburg-Clearwater MSA, FL	Y	44182 AE	55594 MW	64667 AEX	FLBLS	7/16-9/16
	Georgia	Y	58210 FQ	75190 MW	116840 TQ	USBLS	5/15
	Atlanta-Sandy Springs-Roswell MSA, GA	Y	47990 FQ	74150 MW	114540 TQ	USBLS	5/15
	Augusta-Richmond County MSA, GA-SC	Y	64670 FQ	70470 MW	76230 TQ	USBLS	5/15
	Hawaii	Y	65440 FQ	83350 MW	96310 TQ	USBLS	5/15
	Urban Honolulu MSA, HI	Y	54260 FQ	75620 MW	90570 TQ	USBLS	5/15
	Idaho	Y	46970 FQ	64440 MW	109370 TQ	USBLS	5/15
	Boise City MSA, ID	Y	52800 FQ	64910 MW	129330 TQ	USBLS	5/15
	Illinois	Y	59380 FQ	94480 MW	139100 TQ	USBLS	5/15
	Chicago-Naperville-Arlington Heights PMSA, IL	Y	60190 FQ	99820 MW	147660 TQ	USBLS	5/15
	Lake County-Kenosha County PMSA, IL-WI	Y	65870 FQ	107990 MW	135360 TQ	USBLS	5/15
	Indiana	Y	50890 FQ	65330 MW	77560 TQ	USBLS	5/15
	Indianapolis-Carmel-Anderson MSA, IN	Y	55580 FQ	63170 MW	93260 TQ	USBLS	5/15
	Iowa	Y	42890 FQ	68320 MW	95720 TQ	USBLS	5/15
	Des Moines-West Des Moines MSA, IA	Y	53010 FQ	77170 MW	109020 TQ	USBLS	5/15
	Kansas	Y	46070 FQ	71360 MW	100450 TQ	USBLS	5/15
	Wichita MSA, KS	Y	54690 FQ	79140 MW	115230 TQ	USBLS	5/15
	Kentucky	Y	30250 FQ	65020 MW	79540 TQ	USBLS	5/15
	Louisville-Jefferson County MSA, KY-IN	Y	49110 FQ	73660 MW	88430 TQ	USBLS	5/15
	Louisiana	Y	63360 FQ	78960 MW	102320 TQ	USBLS	5/15
	New Orleans-Metairie MSA, LA	Y	58820 FQ	83080 MW	108450 TQ	USBLS	5/15
	Maine	Y	39060 FQ	52010 MW	71200 TQ	USBLS	5/15
	Maryland	Y	72334 AE	98389 MW	111416 AEX	MDBLS	4/16
	Baltimore-Columbia-Towson MSA, MD	Y	80430 FQ	94120 MW	110870 TQ	USBLS	5/15
	Massachusetts	Y	50650 FQ	58630 MW	79420 TQ	USBLS	5/15

AE	Average entry wage	AWR	Average wage range	H	Hourly	LR	Low end range	MTC	Median total compensation	TCC	Total cash compensation
AEX	Average experienced wage	B	Biweekly	HI	Highest wage paid	M	Monthly	MW	Median wage paid	TQ	Third quartile wage
ATC	Average total compensation	D	Daily	HR	High end range	MCC	Median cash compensation	MWR	Median wage range	W	Weekly
AW	Average wage paid	FQ	First quartile wage	LO	Lowest wage paid	ME	Median entry wage	S	See annotated source	Y	Yearly

Occupation/Type/Industry	Location	Per	Low	Mid	High	Source	Date
Commercial Pilot	Boston-Cambridge-Newton						
	NECTA, MA	Y	48980 FQ	56650 MW	75080 TQ	USBLS	5/15
	Worcester MSA, MA-CT	Y	55870 FQ	63630 MW	73710 TQ	USBLS	5/15
	Michigan	Y	52270 FQ	69350 MW	95410 TQ	USBLS	5/15
	Detroit-Dearborn-Livonia						
	PMSA, MI	Y	54220 FQ	65970 MW	87260 TQ	USBLS	5/15
	Grand Rapids-Wyoming MSA,						
	MI	Y	49950 FQ	57010 MW	66100 TQ	USBLS	5/15
	Minnesota	Y	39237 FQ	63100 MW	103748 TQ	MNBLS	1/16-3/16
	Minneapolis-St. Paul-						
	Bloomington MSA, MN-WI	Y	45739 FQ	70278 MW	124969 TQ	MNBLS	1/16-3/16
	Mississippi	Y	62580 FQ	76420 MW	98430 TQ	USBLS	5/15
	Jackson MSA, MS	Y	55850 FQ	61090 MW	76440 TQ	USBLS	5/15
	Missouri	Y	66880 FQ	78340 MW	98200 TQ	USBLS	5/15
	Kansas City MSA, MO-KS	Y	57730 FQ	70750 MW	81250 TQ	USBLS	5/15
	St. Louis MSA, MO-IL	Y	68550 FQ	80300 MW	99280 TQ	USBLS	5/15
	Montana	Y	43590 FQ	60770 MW	78170 TQ	USBLS	5/15
	Nebraska	Y	49790 FQ	71520 MW	100100 TQ	NEBLS	7/16-9/16
	Omaha-Council Bluffs MSA,						
	NE-IA	Y	39770 FQ	77790 MW	109800 TQ	NEBLS	7/16-9/16
	Nevada	Y	47870 FQ	68220 MW	92170 TQ	USBLS	5/15
	Las Vegas-Henderson-Paradise						
	MSA, NV	Y	47120 FQ	63140 MW	85980 TQ	USBLS	5/15
	New Hampshire	Y	45563 AE	73125 MW	85625 AEX	NHBLS	6/16
	New Jersey	Y	61000 FQ	95580 MW	127370 TQ	USBLS	5/15
	Newark PMSA, NJ-PA	Y	57690 FQ	81950 MW	114850 TQ	USBLS	5/15
	New Mexico	Y	65480 FQ	81660 MW	115180 TQ	USBLS	5/15
	New York	Y	61660 AE	80000 MW	114080 AEX	NYBLS	1/16-3/16
	Buffalo-Cheektowaga-Niagara						
	Falls MSA, NY	Y	60600 FQ	74620 MW	120250 TQ	USBLS	5/15
	Nassau County-Suffolk County						
	PMSA, NY	Y	66100 FQ	78570 MW	115640 TQ	USBLS	5/15
	New York-Jersey City-White						
	Plains PMSA, NY-NJ	Y	71490 FQ	99060 MW	121550 TQ	USBLS	5/15
	Rochester MSA, NY	Y	68260 FQ	78240 MW	105300 TQ	USBLS	5/15
	North Carolina	Y	56450 FQ	72580 MW	97460 TQ	USBLS	5/15
	Charlotte-Concord-Gastonia						
	MSA, NC-SC	Y	55740 FQ	81040 MW	131870 TQ	USBLS	5/15
	Raleigh MSA, NC	Y	57820 FQ	68690 MW	86510 TQ	USBLS	5/15
	North Dakota	Y	42110 FQ	56780 MW	71350 TQ	USBLS	5/15
	Fargo MSA, ND-MN	Y	51380 FQ	65730 MW	89150 TQ	USBLS	5/15
	Ohio	Y	28790 FQ	50920 MW	91390 TQ	USBLS	5/15
	Cincinnati MSA, OH-KY-IN	Y	50940 FQ	73450 MW	108000 TQ	USBLS	5/15
	Cleveland-Elyria MSA, OH	Y	71130 FQ	100800 MW	119780 TQ	USBLS	5/15
	Columbus MSA, OH	Y	27620 FQ	30000 MW	62300 TQ	USBLS	5/15
	Oklahoma	Y	58900 FQ	82460 MW	103110 TQ	USBLS	5/15
	Oklahoma City MSA, OK	Y	47310 FQ	64070 MW	87880 TQ	USBLS	5/15
	Tulsa MSA, OK	Y	69280 FQ	86720 MW	112450 TQ	USBLS	5/15
	Oregon	Y	38445 FQ	54129 MW	78317 TQ	ORBLS	2016
	Portland-Vancouver-Hillsboro						
	MSA, OR-WA	Y	35180 FQ	38980 MW	63250 TQ	USBLS	5/15
	Pennsylvania	Y	67070 FQ	89660 MW	137350 TQ	USBLS	5/15
	Allentown-Bethlehem-Easton						
	MSA, PA-NJ	Y	65940 FQ	72800 MW	79650 TQ	USBLS	5/15
	Montgomery County-Bucks						
	County-Chester County						
	PMSA, PA	Y	36100 FQ	52910 MW	73930 TQ	USBLS	5/15
	Philadelphia PMSA, PA	Y	82750 FQ	109880 MW	156670 TQ	USBLS	5/15
	Pittsburgh MSA, PA	Y	54930 FQ	68150 MW	100080 TQ	USBLS	5/15
	South Carolina	Y	69510 FQ	95530 MW	117170 TQ	USBLS	5/15
	Charleston-North Charleston						
	MSA, SC	Y	86520 FQ	113570 MW	139770 TQ	USBLS	5/15
	Greenville-Anderson-Mauldin						
	MSA, SC	Y	85890 FQ	98560 MW	116130 TQ	USBLS	5/15
	South Dakota	Y	51710 FQ	60690 MW	72870 TQ	USBLS	5/15
	Tennessee	Y	51000 FQ	75290 MW	92720 TQ	USBLS	5/15
	Knoxville MSA, TN	Y	64400 FQ	86460 MW	106270 TQ	USBLS	5/15
	Memphis MSA, TN-MS-AR	Y	40440 FQ	69070 MW	101740 TQ	USBLS	5/15
	Nashville-Davidson–						
	Murfreesboro–Franklin						
	MSA, TN	Y	33840 FQ	66920 MW	79380 TQ	USBLS	5/15
	Texas	Y	60780 FQ	85390 MW	120830 TQ	USBLS	5/15

AE	Average entry wage	AWR	Average wage range	H	Hourly	LR	Low end range	MTC	Median total compensation	TCC	Total cash compensation
AEX	Average experienced wage	B	Biweekly	HI	Highest wage paid	M	Monthly	MW	Median wage paid	TQ	Third quartile wage
ATC	Average total compensation	D	Daily	HR	High end range	MCC	Median cash compensation	MWR	Median wage range	W	Weekly
AW	Average wage paid	FQ	First quartile wage	LO	Lowest wage paid	ME	Median entry wage	S	See annotated source	Y	Yearly

Occupation/Type/Industry	Location	Per	Low	Mid	High	Source	Date
Commercial Pilot	Austin-Round Rock MSA, TX	Y	68710 FQ	82300 MW	101160 TQ	USBLS	5/15
	Dallas-Plano-Irving PMSA, TX	Y	49710 FQ	82980 MW	105440 TQ	USBLS	5/15
	Fort Worth-Arlington PMSA, TX	Y	48120 FQ	92610 MW	137080 TQ	USBLS	5/15
	Houston-The Woodlands-Sugar Land MSA, TX	Y	72170 FQ	99670 MW	167320 TQ	USBLS	5/15
	San Antonio-New Braunfels MSA, TX	Y	56460 FQ	72400 MW	94760 TQ	USBLS	5/15
	Tyler MSA, TX	Y	59430 FQ	70110 MW	79300 TQ	USBLS	5/15
	Utah	Y	29730 FQ	41890 MW	64040 TQ	USBLS	5/15
	Provo-Orem MSA, UT	Y	44150 FQ	55560 MW	107350 TQ	USBLS	5/15
	Vermont	Y	52530 FQ	56900 MW	61130 TQ	USBLS	5/15
	Burlington-South Burlington MSA, VT	Y	52990 FQ	57050 MW	61100 TQ	USBLS	5/15
	Virginia	Y	67040 FQ	92730 MW	128440 TQ	USBLS	5/15
	Richmond MSA, VA	Y	82460 FQ	97860 MW	136250 TQ	USBLS	5/15
	Virginia Beach-Norfolk-Newport News MSA, VA-NC	Y	77980 FQ	111890 MW	125280 TQ	USBLS	5/15
	Washington	Y		86612 AW		WABLS	3/16
	Seattle-Bellevue-Everett PMSA, WA	Y		102097 AW		WABLS	3/16
	Tacoma-Lakewood PMSA, WA	Y		65076 AW		WABLS	3/16
	Wisconsin	Y	48770 FQ	65490 MW	82560 TQ	USBLS	5/15
	Madison MSA, WI	Y	44680 FQ	56150 MW	74310 TQ	USBLS	5/15
	Milwaukee-Waukesha-West Allis MSA, WI	Y	51830 FQ	68600 MW	88450 TQ	USBLS	5/15
	Wyoming	Y	61830 FQ	70260 MW	79470 TQ	USBLS	5/15
	Puerto Rico	Y	31140 FQ	57070 MW	72080 TQ	USBLS	5/15
	San Juan-Carolina-Caguas MSA, PR	Y	31140 FQ	57070 MW	72080 TQ	USBLS	5/15
Commissioned Officer							
Military, Active Duty, Pay Grade O-1	United States	M	3035 LO		3819 HI	DOD1	2017
Military, Active Duty, Pay Grade O-10	United States	M		15583 AW		DOD1	2017
Military, Active Duty, Pay Grade O-1E	United States	M	3819 LO		4741 HI	DOD1	2017
Military, Active Duty, Pay Grade O-2	United States	M	3496 LO		4839 HI	DOD1	2017
Military, Active Duty, Pay Grade O-2E	United States	M	4741 LO		5604 HI	DOD1	2017
Military, Active Duty, Pay Grade O-3	United States	M	4047 LO		6584 HI	DOD1	2017
Military, Active Duty, Pay Grade O-3E	United States	M	5398 LO		7026 HI	DOD1	2017
Military, Active Duty, Pay Grade O-4	United States	M	4603 LO		7685 HI	DOD1	2017
Military, Active Duty, Pay Grade O-5	United States	M	5334 LO		9063 HI	DOD1	2017
Military, Active Duty, Pay Grade O-6	United States	M	6399 LO		11328 HI	DOD1	2017
Military, Active Duty, Pay Grade O-7	United States	M	8438 LO		12607 HI	DOD1	2017
Military, Active Duty, Pay Grade O-8	United States	M	10155 LO		14640 HI	DOD1	2017
Military, Active Duty, Pay Grade O-9	United States	M	14352 LO		15583 HI	DOD1	2017
Military, Reserve, 4-Drill Pay Grade O-1	United States	S	3035 LO		3819 HI	DOD1	2017
Military, Reserve, 4-Drill Pay Grade O-1E	United States	S	3819 LO		4741 HI	DOD1	2017
Military, Reserve, 4-Drill Pay Grade O-2	United States	S	3496 LO		4839 HI	DOD1	2017
Military, Reserve, 4-Drill Pay Grade O-2E	United States	S	4741 LO		5604 HI	DOD1	2017
Military, Reserve, 4-Drill Pay Grade O-3	United States	S	4047 LO		6584 HI	DOD1	2017
Military, Reserve, 4-Drill Pay Grade O-3E	United States	S	5398 LO		7026 HI	DOD1	2017
Military, Reserve, 4-Drill Pay Grade O-4	United States	S	4603 LO		7685 HI	DOD1	2017
Military, Reserve, 4-Drill Pay Grade O-5	United States	S	5334 LO		9063 HI	DOD1	2017
Military, Reserve, 4-Drill Pay Grade O-6	United States	S	6399 LO		11328 HI	DOD1	2017
Military, Reserve, 4-Drill Pay Grade O-7	United States	S	8438 LO		12607 HI	DOD1	2017
Communication Teacher							
Postsecondary	Alabama	Y	47174 AE	73840 AW	87173 AEX	ALBLS	6/16
Postsecondary	Alaska	Y	60980 FQ	76530 MW	91830 TQ	USBLS	5/15
Postsecondary	Arizona	Y	48160 FQ	67220 MW	90050 TQ	USBLS	5/15
Postsecondary	Arkansas	Y	42050 FQ	53110 MW	70150 TQ	USBLS	5/15
Postsecondary	California	Y		90614 AW		CABLS	1/16-3/16
Postsecondary	Colorado	Y	35030 FQ	47600 MW	69830 TQ	USBLS	5/15
Postsecondary	Connecticut	Y		68428 MW		CTBLS	1/16-3/16
Postsecondary	District of Columbia	Y	59200 FQ	73720 MW	95810 TQ	USBLS	5/15
Postsecondary	Florida	Y	46930 AE	69601 MW	88455 AEX	FLBLS	7/16-9/16
Postsecondary	Georgia	Y	50700 FQ	69470 MW	103080 TQ	USBLS	5/15
Postsecondary	Hawaii	Y	38370 FQ	59480 MW	78890 TQ	USBLS	5/15
Postsecondary	Idaho	Y	41000 FQ	49420 MW	61720 TQ	USBLS	5/15
Postsecondary	Illinois	Y	54640 FQ	78070 MW	109690 TQ	USBLS	5/15
Postsecondary	Indiana	Y	44070 FQ	57600 MW	76270 TQ	USBLS	5/15
Postsecondary	Iowa	Y	49140 FQ	62770 MW	81420 TQ	USBLS	5/15

AE	Average entry wage	AWR	Average wage range	H	Hourly	LR	Low end range	MTC	Median total compensation	TCC Total cash compensation
AEX	Average experienced wage	B	Biweekly	HI	Highest wage paid	M	Monthly	MW	Median wage paid	TQ Third quartile wage
ATC	Average total compensation	D	Daily	HR	High end range	MCC	Median cash compensation	MWR	Median wage range	W Weekly
AW	Average wage paid	FQ	First quartile wage	LO	Lowest wage paid	ME	Median entry wage	S	See annotated source	Y Yearly

Occupation/Type/Industry	Location	Per	Low	Mid	High	Source	Date
Communication Teacher							
Postsecondary	Kansas	Y	38140 FQ	54280 MW	65010 TQ	USBLS	5/15
Postsecondary	Kentucky	Y	42670 FQ	56790 MW	73570 TQ	USBLS	5/15
Postsecondary	Louisiana	Y	46860 FQ	62600 MW	84450 TQ	USBLS	5/15
Postsecondary	Maine	Y	45740 FQ	57980 MW	76340 TQ	USBLS	5/15
Postsecondary	Maryland	Y	45228 AE	72034 MW	85437 AEX	MDBLS	4/16
Postsecondary	Massachusetts	Y	56760 FQ	69910 MW	88060 TQ	USBLS	5/15
Postsecondary	Michigan	Y	43550 FQ	62320 MW	95390 TQ	USBLS	5/15
Postsecondary	Minnesota	Y	46280 FQ	60161 MW	77398 TQ	MNBLS	1/16-3/16
Postsecondary	Mississippi	Y	43960 FQ	56240 MW	70530 TQ	USBLS	5/15
Postsecondary	Missouri	Y	49780 FQ	62920 MW	83530 TQ	USBLS	5/15
Postsecondary	Montana	Y	36390 FQ	55340 MW	68500 TQ	USBLS	5/15
Postsecondary	Nebraska	Y	45090 FQ	60820 MW	78035 TQ	NEBLS	7/16-9/16
Postsecondary	New Hampshire	Y	54935 AE	73621 MW	88868 AEX	NHBLS	6/16
Postsecondary	New Jersey	Y	50580 FQ	68360 MW	91110 TQ	USBLS	5/15
Postsecondary	New Mexico	Y	56420 FQ	70180 MW	91220 TQ	USBLS	5/15
Postsecondary	New York	Y	39450 AE	66390 MW	100080 AEX	NYBLS	1/16-3/16
Postsecondary	North Carolina	Y	48480 FQ	61910 MW	77850 TQ	USBLS	5/15
Postsecondary	North Dakota	Y	39850 FQ	54830 MW	84880 TQ	USBLS	5/15
Postsecondary	Ohio	Y	31280 FQ	57290 MW	86780 TQ	USBLS	5/15
Postsecondary	Oklahoma	Y	38250 FQ	49090 MW	60780 TQ	USBLS	5/15
Postsecondary	Oregon	Y	48275 FQ	63967 MW	81339 TQ	ORBLS	2016
Postsecondary	Pennsylvania	Y	49040 FQ	66820 MW	88350 TQ	USBLS	5/15
Postsecondary	Rhode Island	Y	50400 FQ	69050 MW	80370 TQ	USBLS	5/15
Postsecondary	South Carolina	Y	36730 FQ	55180 MW	72010 TQ	USBLS	5/15
Postsecondary	South Dakota	Y	46540 FQ	55380 MW	68150 TQ	USBLS	5/15
Postsecondary	Tennessee	Y	35270 FQ	48970 MW	65790 TQ	USBLS	5/15
Postsecondary	Texas	Y	37540 FQ	57360 MW	74930 TQ	USBLS	5/15
Postsecondary	Utah	Y	46690 FQ	65110 MW	81680 TQ	USBLS	5/15
Postsecondary	Vermont	Y	44740 FQ	60850 MW	75080 TQ	USBLS	5/15
Postsecondary	Virginia	Y	43510 FQ	57210 MW	75420 TQ	USBLS	5/15
Postsecondary	Washington	Y		56203 AW		WABLS	3/16
Postsecondary	West Virginia	Y	43030 FQ	55000 MW	63390 TQ	USBLS	5/15
Postsecondary	Wisconsin	Y	49320 FQ	62730 MW	81840 TQ	USBLS	5/15
Postsecondary	Wyoming	Y	51810 FQ	58970 MW	71920 TQ	USBLS	5/15
Postsecondary	Puerto Rico	Y	38160 FQ	47660 MW	58950 TQ	USBLS	5/15
Communications Director							
Municipal Government	Elberton, GA	Y	49141 LO		71942 HI	GACTY01	2016
Municipal Government	Savannah, GA	Y	43192 LO		68064 HI	GACTY01	2016
Communications Manager							
State Government	Lansing, MI	Y	30000 LO		40000 HI	MIGOV	2016
Communications Specialist							
Baccalaureate Institution	United States	Y		37647 MW		CHE01	2015-2016
Master's Institution	United States	Y		38289 MW		CHE01	2015-2016
Research University	United States	Y		40793 MW		CHE01	2015-2016
Communications/Switchboard Operator							
College and University	United States	Y		31173 AW		HED03	2015-2016
Community Affairs Advocate							
Harbor, Municipal Government	Los Angeles, CA	Y			140560 HI	CACIT	6/23/16
Community Arts Director							
Cultural Affairs, Municipal Government	Los Angeles, CA	Y			115524 HI	CACIT	6/23/16
Community Behavioral Health Coordinator							
Municipal Government	Colorado Springs, CO	Y	50805 LO		69857 HI	COSPRS	2017
Community Engagement Specialist							
Police Department, Municipal Government	Albany, CA	Y			22121 HI	CACIT	6/28/16
Community Garden Coordinator							
Municipal Government	Seattle, WA	H	29.43 LO		34.30 HI	CSSS	1/13/16
Community Health Executive							
Healthcare System	United States	Y		250400 MCC		MHLTH01	2015

AE	Average entry wage	AWR	Average wage range	H	Hourly	LR	Low end range	MTC	Median total compensation	TCC	Total cash compensation
AEX	Average experienced wage	B	Biweekly	HI	Highest wage paid	M	Monthly	MW	Median wage paid	TQ	Third quartile wage
ATC	Average total compensation	D	Daily	HR	High end range	MCC	Median cash compensation	MWR	Median wage range	W	Weekly
AW	Average wage paid	FQ	First quartile wage	LO	Lowest wage paid	ME	Median entry wage	S	See annotated source	Y	Yearly

Occupation/Type/Industry	Location	Per	Low	Mid	High	Source	Date
Community Health Worker	Alabama	Y	21875 AE	42017 AW	52087 AEX	ALBLS	6/16
	Birmingham-Hoover MSA, AL	Y	27389 AE	38072 AW	43413 AEX	ALBLS	6/16
	Alaska	Y	33640 FQ	40860 MW	51960 TQ	USBLS	5/15
	Anchorage MSA, AK	Y	31140 MW	39970 MW	54270 TQ	USBLS	5/15
	Arizona	Y	27560 FQ	34690 MW	46170 TQ	USBLS	5/15
	Phoenix-Mesa-Scottsdale MSA, AZ	Y	29000 FQ	38930 MW	50440 TQ	USBLS	5/15
	Tucson MSA, AZ	Y	28780 FQ	33710 MW	40190 TQ	USBLS	5/15
	Arkansas	Y	28150 FQ	38290 MW	55560 TQ	USBLS	5/15
	Little Rock-North Little Rock-Conway MSA, AR	Y	36700 FQ	48330 MW	65230 TQ	USBLS	5/15
	California	H	14.94 FQ	19.14 MW	24.43 TQ	CABLS	1/16-3/16
	Anaheim-Santa Ana-Irvine PMSA, CA	H	13.71 FQ	19.24 MW	26.55 TQ	CABLS	1/16-3/16
	Los Angeles-Long Beach-Glendale PMSA, CA	H	16.43 FQ	19.53 MW	23.99 TQ	CABLS	1/16-3/16
	Oakland-Hayward-Berkeley PMSA, CA	H	14.40 FQ	18.56 MW	24.67 TQ	CABLS	1/16-3/16
	Riverside-San Bernardino-Ontario MSA, CA	H	16.64 FQ	22.10 MW	31.30 TQ	CABLS	1/16-3/16
	Sacramento–Roseville–Arden-Arcade MSA, CA	H	14.41 FQ	17.79 MW	27.28 TQ	CABLS	1/16-3/16
	San Diego-Carlsbad MSA, CA	H	15.10 FQ	18.31 MW	22.66 TQ	CABLS	1/16-3/16
	San Francisco-Redwood City-South San Francisco PMSA, CA	H	14.14 FQ	20.00 MW	23.54 TQ	CABLS	1/16-3/16
	Colorado	Y	29440 FQ	37620 MW	48970 TQ	USBLS	5/15
	Denver-Aurora-Lakewood MSA, CO	Y	33170 FQ	45040 MW	77430 TQ	USBLS	5/15
	Connecticut	Y		39433 MW		CTBLS	1/16-3/16
	Bridgeport-Stamford-Norwalk MSA, CT	Y	32370 FQ	37570 MW	48300 TQ	USBLS	5/15
	Hartford-West Hartford-East Hartford MSA, CT	Y	32260 FQ	38340 MW	45460 TQ	USBLS	5/15
	Delaware	Y	29070 FQ	33390 MW	38500 TQ	USBLS	5/15
	Wilmington PMSA, DE-MD-NJ	Y	30180 FQ	35450 MW	42140 TQ	USBLS	5/15
	District of Columbia	Y	43810 FQ	61150 MW	81290 TQ	USBLS	5/15
	Washington-Arlington-Alexandria PMSA, DC-VA-MD-WV	Y	40330 FQ	57210 MW	77690 TQ	USBLS	5/15
	Florida	H	11.60 AE	15.97 MW	19.68 AEX	FLBLS	7/16-9/16
	Fort Lauderdale-Pompano Beach-Deerfield Beach PMSA, FL	H	12.04 AE	17.09 MW	19.60 AEX	FLBLS	7/16-9/16
	Miami-Miami Beach-Kendall PMSA, FL	H	11.83 AE	14.79 MW	20.48 AEX	FLBLS	7/16-9/16
	Orlando-Kissimmee-Sanford MSA, FL	H	11.39 AE	14.79 MW	19.09 AEX	FLBLS	7/16-9/16
	Tampa-St. Petersburg-Clearwater MSA, FL	H	10.75 AE	16.88 MW	20.31 AEX	FLBLS	7/16-9/16
	Georgia	Y	25970 FQ	31720 MW	42190 TQ	USBLS	5/15
	Atlanta-Sandy Springs-Roswell MSA, GA	Y	28740 FQ	35190 MW	45210 TQ	USBLS	5/15
	Augusta-Richmond County MSA, GA-SC	Y	20800 FQ	22630 MW	24450 TQ	USBLS	5/15
	Hawaii	Y	27460 FQ	32900 MW	42570 TQ	USBLS	5/15
	Urban Honolulu MSA, HI	Y	27120 FQ	32170 MW	42990 TQ	USBLS	5/15
	Idaho	Y	17770 FQ	23040 MW	41380 TQ	USBLS	5/15
	Boise City MSA, ID	Y	18000 FQ	24590 MW	43440 TQ	USBLS	5/15
	Illinois	Y	25870 FQ	32770 MW	42360 TQ	USBLS	5/15
	Chicago-Naperville-Arlington Heights PMSA, IL	Y	29370 FQ	35480 MW	46080 TQ	USBLS	5/15
	Lake County-Kenosha County PMSA, IL-WI	Y	26570 FQ	32700 MW	41260 TQ	USBLS	5/15
	Indiana	Y	28100 FQ	36440 MW	49060 TQ	USBLS	5/15
	Gary PMSA, IN	Y	24560 FQ	36550 MW	60900 TQ	USBLS	5/15
	Indianapolis-Carmel-Anderson MSA, IN	Y	33040 FQ	42030 MW	54010 TQ	USBLS	5/15
	Iowa	Y	25620 FQ	34900 MW	44350 TQ	USBLS	5/15
	Kansas	Y	25800 FQ	30500 MW	38750 TQ	USBLS	5/15
	Wichita MSA, KS	Y	19340 FQ	28650 MW	35140 TQ	USBLS	5/15

AE Average entry wage	**AWR** Average wage range	**H** Hourly	**LR** Low end range	**MTC** Median total compensation	**TCC** Total cash compensation
AEX Average experienced wage	**B** Biweekly	**HI** Highest wage paid	**M** Monthly	**MW** Median wage paid	**TQ** Third quartile wage
ATC Average total compensation	**D** Daily	**HR** High end range	**MCC** Median cash compensation	**MWR** Median wage range	**W** Weekly
AW Average wage paid	**FQ** First quartile wage	**LO** Lowest wage paid	**ME** Median entry wage	**S** See annotated source	**Y** Yearly

Community Health Worker

Occupation/Type/Industry	Location	Per	Low	Mid	High	Source	Date
Community Health Worker	Kentucky	Y	23590 FQ	33330 MW	42890 TQ	USBLS	5/15
	Louisville-Jefferson County MSA, KY-IN	Y	33250 FQ	39220 MW	49300 TQ	USBLS	5/15
	Louisiana	Y	27200 FQ	33070 MW	43940 TQ	USBLS	5/15
	Baton Rouge MSA, LA	Y	24590 FQ	36340 MW	52910 TQ	USBLS	5/15
	New Orleans-Metairie MSA, LA	Y	27030 FQ	30700 MW	37210 TQ	USBLS	5/15
	Maine	Y	22900 FQ	33660 MW	39980 TQ	USBLS	5/15
	Portland-South Portland MSA, ME	Y	22360 FQ	31910 MW	39110 TQ	USBLS	5/15
	Maryland	Y	26189 AE	40831 MW	48152 AEX	MDBLS	4/16
	Baltimore-Columbia-Towson MSA, MD	Y	30380 FQ	40420 MW	54510 TQ	USBLS	5/15
	Salisbury MSA, MD-DE	Y	27700 FQ	34250 MW	51770 TQ	USBLS	5/15
	Massachusetts	Y	32840 FQ	39740 MW	52730 TQ	USBLS	5/15
	Boston-Cambridge-Newton NECTA, MA	Y	36460 FQ	45590 MW	56190 TQ	USBLS	5/15
	Worcester MSA, MA-CT	Y	31210 FQ	38300 MW	48680 TQ	USBLS	5/15
	Michigan	Y	25740 FQ	34520 MW	45650 TQ	USBLS	5/15
	Detroit-Dearborn-Livonia PMSA, MI	Y	29950 FQ	37490 MW	47550 TQ	USBLS	5/15
	Grand Rapids-Wyoming MSA, MI	Y	31070 FQ	37630 MW	47110 TQ	USBLS	5/15
	Minnesota	Y	29788 FQ	36804 MW	47671 TQ	MNBLS	1/16-3/16
	Minneapolis-St. Paul-Bloomington MSA, MN-WI	Y	30776 FQ	37540 MW	49001 TQ	MNBLS	1/16-3/16
	Mississippi	Y	23860 FQ	29510 MW	44150 TQ	USBLS	5/15
	Jackson MSA, MS	Y	23500 FQ	29690 MW	42720 TQ	USBLS	5/15
	Missouri	Y	27160 FQ	35420 MW	46460 TQ	USBLS	5/15
	Kansas City MSA, MO-KS	Y	26520 FQ	34390 MW	44670 TQ	USBLS	5/15
	St. Louis MSA, MO-IL	Y	26170 FQ	35800 MW	50500 TQ	USBLS	5/15
	Montana	Y	27070 FQ	32830 MW	39380 TQ	USBLS	5/15
	Omaha-Council Bluffs MSA, NE-IA	Y	27270 FQ	31710 MW	40730 TQ	NEBLS	7/16-9/16
	Nevada	Y	28900 FQ	35730 MW	56270 TQ	USBLS	5/15
	Las Vegas-Henderson-Paradise MSA, NV	Y	28570 FQ	35170 MW	63780 TQ	USBLS	5/15
	New Hampshire	H	12.35 AE	16.81 MW	21.79 AEX	NHBLS	6/16
	Manchester NECTA, NH	H	16.94 AE	24.82 MW	25.77 AEX	NHBLS	6/16
	Nashua NECTA, NH-MA	Y	22010 FQ	24200 MW	35200 TQ	USBLS	5/15
	New Jersey	Y	32870 FQ	40600 MW	50890 TQ	USBLS	5/15
	Camden PMSA, NJ	Y	33690 FQ	38680 MW	47670 TQ	USBLS	5/15
	Newark PMSA, NJ-PA	Y	32900 FQ	42180 MW	52940 TQ	USBLS	5/15
	Trenton MSA, NJ	Y	38450 FQ	48020 MW	59460 TQ	USBLS	5/15
	New Mexico	Y	23500 FQ	31350 MW	43440 TQ	USBLS	5/15
	Albuquerque MSA, NM	Y	20100 FQ	31690 MW	48600 TQ	USBLS	5/15
	New York	Y	27960 AE	39300 MW	53060 AEX	NYBLS	1/16-3/16
	Buffalo-Cheektowaga-Niagara Falls MSA, NY	Y	28160 FQ	36270 MW	55350 TQ	USBLS	5/15
	Nassau County-Suffolk County PMSA, NY	Y	32520 FQ	40620 MW	55680 TQ	USBLS	5/15
	New York-Jersey City-White Plains PMSA, NY-NJ	Y	30420 FQ	37550 MW	49550 TQ	USBLS	5/15
	Rochester MSA, NY	Y	32370 FQ	36690 MW	44950 TQ	USBLS	5/15
	North Carolina	Y	30140 FQ	36250 MW	46840 TQ	USBLS	5/15
	Charlotte-Concord-Gastonia MSA, NC-SC	Y	30160 FQ	36060 MW	45010 TQ	USBLS	5/15
	Raleigh MSA, NC	Y	32380 FQ	38140 MW	48590 TQ	USBLS	5/15
	North Dakota	Y	27140 FQ	30960 MW	41870 TQ	USBLS	5/15
	Fargo MSA, ND-MN	Y	29680 FQ	39900 MW	45730 TQ	USBLS	5/15
	Ohio	Y	30200 FQ	38640 MW	52930 TQ	USBLS	5/15
	Cincinnati MSA, OH-KY-IN	Y	33330 FQ	39700 MW	45110 TQ	USBLS	5/15
	Cleveland-Elyria MSA, OH	Y	35560 FQ	47870 MW	61720 TQ	USBLS	5/15
	Columbus MSA, OH	Y	26490 FQ	29520 MW	38710 TQ	USBLS	5/15
	Oklahoma	Y	24440 FQ	35460 MW	52640 TQ	USBLS	5/15
	Oklahoma City MSA, OK	Y	33750 FQ	39920 MW	58520 TQ	USBLS	5/15
	Tulsa MSA, OK	Y	22010 FQ	24440 MW	41930 TQ	USBLS	5/15
	Oregon	H	15.72 FQ	18.70 MW	23.67 TQ	ORBLS	2016
	Portland-Vancouver-Hillsboro MSA, OR-WA	Y	34750 FQ	43490 MW	53810 TQ	USBLS	5/15
	Pennsylvania	Y	29290 FQ	37310 MW	47810 TQ	USBLS	5/15

AE	Average entry wage	AWR	Average wage range	H	Hourly
AEX	Average experienced wage	B	Biweekly	HI	Highest wage paid
ATC	Average total compensation	D	Daily	HR	High end range
AW	Average wage paid	FQ	First quartile wage	LO	Lowest wage paid

LR	Low end range	MTC	Median total compensation	TCC	Total cash compensation
M	Monthly	MW	Median wage paid	TQ	Third quartile wage
MCC	Median cash compensation	MWR	Median wage range	W	Weekly
ME	Median entry wage	S	See annotated source	Y	Yearly

Occupation/Type/Industry	Location	Per	Low	Mid	High	Source	Date
Community Health Worker	Allentown-Bethlehem-Easton						
	MSA, PA-NJ	Y	23650 FQ	41030 MW	48890 TQ	USBLS	5/15
	Harrisburg-Carlisle MSA, PA	Y	35570 FQ	44260 MW	49760 TQ	USBLS	5/15
	Montgomery County-Bucks						
	County-Chester County						
	PMSA, PA	Y	32290 FQ	40130 MW	55980 TQ	USBLS	5/15
	Philadelphia PMSA, PA	Y	34020 FQ	39430 MW	46270 TQ	USBLS	5/15
	Pittsburgh MSA, PA	Y	29580 FQ	35210 MW	45750 TQ	USBLS	5/15
	Rhode Island	Y	35270 FQ	41860 MW	49180 TQ	USBLS	5/15
	Providence-Warwick MSA, RI-MA	Y	33830 FQ	40790 MW	49000 TQ	USBLS	5/15
	South Carolina	Y	31820 FQ	42440 MW	55390 TQ	USBLS	5/15
	Tennessee	Y	22960 FQ	28920 MW	37430 TQ	USBLS	5/15
	Knoxville MSA, TN	Y	26260 FQ	30090 MW	38340 TQ	USBLS	5/15
	Memphis MSA, TN-MS-AR	Y	29160 FQ	35070 MW	42880 TQ	USBLS	5/15
	Nashville-Davidson–Murfreesboro–Franklin						
	MSA, TN	Y	21050 FQ	28370 MW	43310 TQ	USBLS	5/15
	Texas	Y	29580 FQ	35830 MW	44600 TQ	USBLS	5/15
	Austin-Round Rock MSA, TX	Y	31810 FQ	37120 MW	42220 TQ	USBLS	5/15
	Dallas-Plano-Irving PMSA, TX	Y	29250 FQ	35880 MW	46510 TQ	USBLS	5/15
	Fort Worth-Arlington PMSA, TX	Y	29790 FQ	36610 MW	45510 TQ	USBLS	5/15
	Houston-The Woodlands-Sugar Land MSA, TX	Y	32730 FQ	38880 MW	50970 TQ	USBLS	5/15
	San Antonio-New Braunfels MSA, TX	Y	28390 FQ	32830 MW	38940 TQ	USBLS	5/15
	Utah	Y	31280 FQ	39860 MW	50210 TQ	USBLS	5/15
	Ogden-Clearfield MSA, UT	Y	29090 FQ	40960 MW	49530 TQ	USBLS	5/15
	Provo-Orem MSA, UT	Y	31170 FQ	36580 MW	43630 TQ	USBLS	5/15
	Salt Lake City MSA, UT	Y	35780 FQ	44870 MW	50910 TQ	USBLS	5/15
	Vermont	Y	26990 FQ	31390 MW	47440 TQ	USBLS	5/15
	Burlington-South Burlington MSA, VT	Y	27650 FQ	30780 MW	49510 TQ	USBLS	5/15
	Virginia	Y	35490 FQ	44150 MW	57460 TQ	USBLS	5/15
	Richmond MSA, VA	Y	40710 FQ	46550 MW	59500 TQ	USBLS	5/15
	Virginia Beach-Norfolk-Newport News MSA, VA-NC	Y	37000 FQ	44740 MW	57860 TQ	USBLS	5/15
	Washington	H	15.10 FQ	18.72 MW	27.01 TQ	WABLS	3/16
	Seattle-Bellevue-Everett PMSA, WA	H	15.95 FQ	19.10 MW	26.38 TQ	WABLS	3/16
	Tacoma-Lakewood PMSA, WA	H	19.48 FQ	29.24 MW	35.73 TQ	WABLS	3/16
	West Virginia	Y	19320 FQ	22850 MW	28110 TQ	USBLS	5/15
	Huntington-Ashland MSA, WV-KY-OH	Y	19600 FQ	22630 MW	26310 TQ	USBLS	5/15
	Wisconsin	Y	30410 FQ	36280 MW	46310 TQ	USBLS	5/15
	Madison MSA, WI	Y	33560 FQ	38520 MW	49740 TQ	USBLS	5/15
	Milwaukee-Waukesha-West Allis MSA, WI	Y	29420 FQ	34640 MW	40720 TQ	USBLS	5/15
	Wyoming	Y	27320 FQ	32270 MW	47410 TQ	USBLS	5/15
	Puerto Rico	Y	18360 FQ	22530 MW	28910 TQ	USBLS	5/15
	San Juan-Carolina-Caguas MSA, PR	Y	18360 FQ	23000 MW	29740 TQ	USBLS	5/15
	Guam	Y	26720 FQ	51280 MW	61820 TQ	USBLS	5/15
Community Manager for Brands or Businesses	United States	Y		48000 AW		LH03	2016
Community Outreach Coordinator							
Municipal Government	Buena Park, CA	Y			54101 HI	CACIT	6/28/16
Municipal Government	Santa Maria, CA	Y			33206 HI	CACIT	6/28/16
Community Preservation Officer							
Fire Department, Municipal Government	Benicia, CA	Y			54960 HI	CACIT	6/28/16
Community Relations Analyst							
Public Works Department, Municipal Government	Roseville, CA	Y			36782 HI	CACIT	6/28/16
Community Resource Specialist							
Police Department, Municipal Government	Visalia, CA	Y			53653 HI	CACIT	6/28/16

AE	Average entry wage	AWR	Average wage range	H	Hourly	LR	Low end range	MTC	Median total compensation	TCC	Total cash compensation
AEX	Average experienced wage	B	Biweekly	HI	Highest wage paid	M	Monthly	MW	Median wage paid	TQ	Third quartile wage
ATC	Average total compensation	D	Daily	HR	High end range	MCC	Median cash compensation	MWR	Median wage range	W	Weekly
AW	Average wage paid	FQ	First quartile wage	LO	Lowest wage paid	ME	Median entry wage	S	See annotated source	Y	Yearly

Occupation/Type/Industry	Location	Per	Low	Mid	High	Source	Date
Community Service Officer							
Municipal Government	Atwater, CA	Y			25241 HI	CACIT	6/28/16
Municipal Government	Gustine, CA	Y			39127 HI	CACIT	6/28/16
Municipal Government	Tulare, CA	Y			41650 HI	CACIT	6/28/16
Community Volunteer Coordinator							
Housing - Neighborhood Services, Municipal Government	Carlsbad, CA	Y			69199 HI	CACIT	6/28/16
Compensation, Benefits, and Job Analysis Specialist	Alabama	Y	42044 AE	60134 AW	69185 AEX	ALBLS	6/16
	Birmingham-Hoover MSA, AL	Y	48942 AE	65146 AW	73254 AEX	ALBLS	6/16
	Alaska	Y	55400 FQ	64270 MW	80870 TQ	USBLS	5/15
	Anchorage MSA, AK	Y	50160 FQ	62940 MW	83640 TQ	USBLS	5/15
	Arizona	Y	41190 FQ	53250 MW	69130 TQ	USBLS	5/15
	Phoenix-Mesa-Scottsdale MSA, AZ	Y	43020 FQ	55410 MW	71070 TQ	USBLS	5/15
	Tucson MSA, AZ	Y	36030 FQ	42750 MW	57410 TQ	USBLS	5/15
	Arkansas	Y	34150 FQ	41360 MW	57550 TQ	USBLS	5/15
	Little Rock-North Little Rock-Conway MSA, AR	Y	34590 FQ	40030 MW	50680 TQ	USBLS	5/15
	California	H	27.32 FQ	33.40 MW	40.60 TQ	CABLS	1/16-3/16
	Anaheim-Santa Ana-Irvine PMSA, CA	H	27.61 FQ	33.58 MW	38.30 TQ	CABLS	1/16-3/16
	Los Angeles-Long Beach-Glendale PMSA, CA	H	27.19 FQ	34.71 MW	44.82 TQ	CABLS	1/16-3/16
	Oakland-Hayward-Berkeley PMSA, CA	H	29.28 FQ	35.91 MW	45.46 TQ	CABLS	1/16-3/16
	Riverside-San Bernardino-Ontario MSA, CA	H	22.84 FQ	28.87 MW	35.40 TQ	CABLS	1/16-3/16
	Sacramento–Roseville–Arden-Arcade MSA, CA	H	26.83 FQ	30.82 MW	33.58 TQ	CABLS	1/16-3/16
	San Diego-Carlsbad MSA, CA	H	24.28 FQ	30.19 MW	38.88 TQ	CABLS	1/16-3/16
	San Francisco-Redwood City-South San Francisco PMSA, CA	H	31.69 FQ	37.66 MW	46.41 TQ	CABLS	1/16-3/16
	Colorado	Y	51010 FQ	65290 MW	82870 TQ	USBLS	5/15
	Denver-Aurora-Lakewood MSA, CO	Y	53070 FQ	67780 MW	86180 TQ	USBLS	5/15
	Connecticut	Y		71174 MW		CTBLS	1/16-3/16
	Bridgeport-Stamford-Norwalk MSA, CT	Y	51060 FQ	66610 MW	82480 TQ	USBLS	5/15
	Hartford-West Hartford-East Hartford MSA, CT	Y	53610 FQ	73040 MW	95020 TQ	USBLS	5/15
	Delaware	Y	54320 FQ	68930 MW	93580 TQ	USBLS	5/15
	Wilmington PMSA, DE-MD-NJ	Y	56100 FQ	72180 MW	99700 TQ	USBLS	5/15
	District of Columbia	Y	64910 FQ	76500 MW	93840 TQ	USBLS	5/15
	Washington-Arlington-Alexandria PMSA, DC-VA-MD-WV	Y	60340 FQ	73310 MW	91710 TQ	USBLS	5/15
	Florida	H	18.72 AE	26.77 MW	33.12 AEX	FLBLS	7/16-9/16
	Fort Lauderdale-Pompano Beach-Deerfield Beach PMSA, FL	H	18.89 AE	27.88 MW	33.27 AEX	FLBLS	7/16-9/16
	Miami-Miami Beach-Kendall PMSA, FL	H	17.83 AE	27.51 MW	34.42 AEX	FLBLS	7/16-9/16
	Orlando-Kissimmee-Sanford MSA, FL	H	18.66 AE	26.56 MW	34.30 AEX	FLBLS	7/16-9/16
	Tampa-St. Petersburg-Clearwater MSA, FL	H	20.10 AE	28.35 MW	34.31 AEX	FLBLS	7/16-9/16
	Georgia	Y	42890 FQ	58880 MW	80460 TQ	USBLS	5/15
	Atlanta-Sandy Springs-Roswell MSA, GA	Y	43130 FQ	60970 MW	83230 TQ	USBLS	5/15
	Augusta-Richmond County MSA, GA-SC	Y	43000 FQ	52170 MW	60870 TQ	USBLS	5/15
	Hawaii	Y	36340 FQ	47700 MW	61040 TQ	USBLS	5/15
	Urban Honolulu MSA, HI	Y	38250 FQ	49130 MW	61950 TQ	USBLS	5/15
	Idaho	Y	40590 FQ	53400 MW	66860 TQ	USBLS	5/15
	Boise City MSA, ID	Y	41330 FQ	54110 MW	65180 TQ	USBLS	5/15

AE	Average entry wage	AWR	Average wage range	H	Hourly
AEX	Average experienced wage	B	Biweekly	HI	Highest wage paid
ATC	Average total compensation	D	Daily	HR	High end range
AW	Average wage paid	FQ	First quartile wage	LO	Lowest wage paid

LR	Low end range	MTC	Median total compensation
M	Monthly	MW	Median wage paid
MCC	Median cash compensation	MWR	Median wage range
ME	Median entry wage	S	See annotated source

TCC	Total cash compensation
TQ	Third quartile wage
W	Weekly
Y	Yearly

Occupation/Type/Industry	Location	Per	Low	Mid	High	Source	Date
Compensation, Benefits, and Job Analysis Specialist	Illinois	Y	50400 FQ	62440 MW	78260 TQ	USBLS	5/15
	Chicago-Naperville-Arlington Heights PMSA, IL	Y	52390 FQ	64860 MW	80030 TQ	USBLS	5/15
	Lake County-Kenosha County PMSA, IL-WI	Y	44750 FQ	59030 MW	73480 TQ	USBLS	5/15
	Indiana	Y	41560 FQ	50220 MW	64320 TQ	USBLS	5/15
	Gary PMSA, IN	Y	43390 FQ	51650 MW	63970 TQ	USBLS	5/15
	Indianapolis-Carmel-Anderson MSA, IN	Y	42590 FQ	51670 MW	68190 TQ	USBLS	5/15
	Iowa	Y	50130 FQ	61850 MW	81020 TQ	USBLS	5/15
	Des Moines-West Des Moines MSA, IA	Y	58870 FQ	69550 MW	89060 TQ	USBLS	5/15
	Kansas	Y	48610 FQ	58080 MW	74630 TQ	USBLS	5/15
	Wichita MSA, KS	Y	39410 FQ	48840 MW	63630 TQ	USBLS	5/15
	Kentucky	Y	44910 FQ	55360 MW	67510 TQ	USBLS	5/15
	Louisville-Jefferson County MSA, KY-IN	Y	46680 FQ	58690 MW	73170 TQ	USBLS	5/15
	Louisiana	Y	34730 FQ	43250 MW	52460 TQ	USBLS	5/15
	Baton Rouge MSA, LA	Y	40850 FQ	47760 MW	58060 TQ	USBLS	5/15
	New Orleans-Metairie MSA, LA	Y	32640 FQ	38730 MW	47030 TQ	USBLS	5/15
	Maine	Y	45470 FQ	57750 MW	69820 TQ	USBLS	5/15
	Portland-South Portland MSA, ME	Y	46840 FQ	58340 MW	70100 TQ	USBLS	5/15
	Maryland	Y	46611 AE	66264 MW	76090 AEX	MDBLS	4/16
	Baltimore-Columbia-Towson MSA, MD	Y	47910 FQ	58300 MW	73610 TQ	USBLS	5/15
	Salisbury MSA, MD-DE	Y	53060 FQ	65420 MW	82550 TQ	USBLS	5/15
	Massachusetts	Y	52390 FQ	63900 MW	81330 TQ	USBLS	5/15
	Boston-Cambridge-Newton NECTA, MA	Y	52750 FQ	64060 MW	82940 TQ	USBLS	5/15
	Worcester MSA, MA-CT	Y	46970 FQ	60230 MW	77070 TQ	USBLS	5/15
	Michigan	Y	48010 FQ	59020 MW	74870 TQ	USBLS	5/15
	Detroit-Dearborn-Livonia PMSA, MI	Y	51240 FQ	61590 MW	77360 TQ	USBLS	5/15
	Grand Rapids-Wyoming MSA, MI	Y	42650 FQ	52820 MW	67320 TQ	USBLS	5/15
	Minnesota	Y	53315 FQ	65468 MW	80191 TQ	MNBLS	1/16-3/16
	Minneapolis-St. Paul-Bloomington MSA, MN-WI	Y	54067 FQ	65894 MW	81969 TQ	MNBLS	1/16-3/16
	Mississippi	Y	35690 FQ	42960 MW	58680 TQ	USBLS	5/15
	Jackson MSA, MS	Y	35690 FQ	42590 MW	58930 TQ	USBLS	5/15
	Missouri	Y	49040 FQ	60490 MW	77730 TQ	USBLS	5/15
	Kansas City MSA, MO-KS	Y	52810 FQ	61040 MW	78620 TQ	USBLS	5/15
	St. Louis MSA, MO-IL	Y	53210 FQ	64850 MW	84960 TQ	USBLS	5/15
	Montana	Y	42380 FQ	52110 MW	64140 TQ	USBLS	5/15
	Billings MSA, MT	Y	44770 FQ	57050 MW	75010 TQ	USBLS	5/15
	Nebraska	Y	46895 FQ	59040 MW	74875 TQ	NEBLS	7/16-9/16
	Omaha-Council Bluffs MSA, NE-IA	Y	46315 FQ	58810 MW	76800 TQ	NEBLS	7/16-9/16
	Nevada	Y	46120 FQ	56590 MW	73330 TQ	USBLS	5/15
	Las Vegas-Henderson-Paradise MSA, NV	Y	45400 FQ	56120 MW	73720 TQ	USBLS	5/15
	New Hampshire	H	20.80 AE	27.45 MW	35.06 AEX	NHBLS	6/16
	Manchester NECTA, NH	H	21.34 AE	23.07 MW	27.77 AEX	NHBLS	6/16
	Nashua NECTA, NH-MA	Y	49090 FQ	68250 MW	78970 TQ	USBLS	5/15
	New Jersey	Y	56930 FQ	70980 MW	89320 TQ	USBLS	5/15
	Camden PMSA, NJ	Y	52500 FQ	63760 MW	79850 TQ	USBLS	5/15
	Newark PMSA, NJ-PA	Y	63700 FQ	76970 MW	99010 TQ	USBLS	5/15
	Trenton MSA, NJ	Y	54500 FQ	66340 MW	77680 TQ	USBLS	5/15
	New Mexico	Y	39970 FQ	52210 MW	65320 TQ	USBLS	5/15
	Albuquerque MSA, NM	Y	36840 FQ	47530 MW	64310 TQ	USBLS	5/15
	New York	Y	48760 AE	69870 MW	84110 AEX	NYBLS	1/16-3/16
	Buffalo-Cheektowaga-Niagara Falls MSA, NY	Y	43900 FQ	52760 MW	64880 TQ	USBLS	5/15
	Nassau County-Suffolk County PMSA, NY	Y	47600 FQ	62000 MW	85660 TQ	USBLS	5/15
	New York-Jersey City-White Plains PMSA, NY-NJ	Y	59120 FQ	72070 MW	87590 TQ	USBLS	5/15
	Rochester MSA, NY	Y	44130 FQ	56350 MW	71370 TQ	USBLS	5/15
	North Carolina	Y	45380 FQ	56770 MW	74210 TQ	USBLS	5/15

AE Average entry wage	**AWR** Average wage range	**H** Hourly	**LR** Low end range	**MTC** Median total compensation	**TCC** Total cash compensation
AEX Average experienced wage	**B** Biweekly	**HI** Highest wage paid	**M** Monthly	**MW** Median wage paid	**TQ** Third quartile wage
ATC Average total compensation	**D** Daily	**HR** High end range	**MCC** Median cash compensation	**MWR** Median wage range	**W** Weekly
AW Average wage paid	**FQ** First quartile wage	**LO** Lowest wage paid	**ME** Median entry wage	**S** See annotated source	**Y** Yearly

Occupation/Type/Industry	Location	Per	Low	Mid	High	Source	Date
Compensation, Benefits, and Job Analysis Specialist	Charlotte-Concord-Gastonia MSA, NC-SC	Y	47950 FQ	63300 MW	80820 TQ	USBLS	5/15
	Raleigh MSA, NC	Y	45720 FQ	55810 MW	69970 TQ	USBLS	5/15
	North Dakota	Y	43130 FQ	55690 MW	70730 TQ	USBLS	5/15
	Fargo MSA, ND-MN	Y	39350 FQ	49060 MW	66040 TQ	USBLS	5/15
	Ohio	Y	46130 FQ	57040 MW	71300 TQ	USBLS	5/15
	Cincinnati MSA, OH-KY-IN	Y	46200 FQ	58170 MW	72900 TQ	USBLS	5/15
	Cleveland-Elyria MSA, OH	Y	44840 FQ	56150 MW	68120 TQ	USBLS	5/15
	Columbus MSA, OH	Y	52260 FQ	64310 MW	81220 TQ	USBLS	5/15
	Oklahoma	Y	40890 FQ	51010 MW	66060 TQ	USBLS	5/15
	Oklahoma City MSA, OK	Y	38710 FQ	46460 MW	58660 TQ	USBLS	5/15
	Tulsa MSA, OK	Y	46360 FQ	59610 MW	80710 TQ	USBLS	5/15
	Oregon	H	22.91 FQ	29.08 MW	38.26 TQ	ORBLS	2016
	Portland-Vancouver-Hillsboro MSA, OR-WA	Y	48640 FQ	61050 MW	79680 TQ	USBLS	5/15
	Pennsylvania	Y	46370 FQ	59470 MW	75690 TQ	USBLS	5/15
	Allentown-Bethlehem-Easton MSA, PA-NJ	Y	53470 FQ	68890 MW	87720 TQ	USBLS	5/15
	Harrisburg-Carlisle MSA, PA	Y	50290 FQ	58470 MW	71370 TQ	USBLS	5/15
	Montgomery County-Bucks County-Chester County PMSA, PA	Y	52260 FQ	67930 MW	83680 TQ	USBLS	5/15
	Philadelphia PMSA, PA	Y	51170 FQ	67540 MW	82070 TQ	USBLS	5/15
	Pittsburgh MSA, PA	Y	44760 FQ	55950 MW	72080 TQ	USBLS	5/15
	Rhode Island	Y	53800 FQ	68130 MW	79310 TQ	USBLS	5/15
	Providence-Warwick MSA, RI-MA	Y	54360 FQ	68210 MW	79500 TQ	USBLS	5/15
	South Carolina	Y	37700 FQ	46910 MW	60430 TQ	USBLS	5/15
	Charleston-North Charleston MSA, SC	Y	36770 FQ	46640 MW	66160 TQ	USBLS	5/15
	Columbia MSA, SC	Y	38390 FQ	44870 MW	55910 TQ	USBLS	5/15
	Greenville-Anderson-Mauldin MSA, SC	Y	42230 FQ	51330 MW	66980 TQ	USBLS	5/15
	South Dakota	Y	41960 FQ	48290 MW	58560 TQ	USBLS	5/15
	Sioux Falls MSA, SD	Y	43680 FQ	50330 MW	60410 TQ	USBLS	5/15
	Tennessee	Y	42070 FQ	53150 MW	64450 TQ	USBLS	5/15
	Knoxville MSA, TN	Y	39840 FQ	49510 MW	65260 TQ	USBLS	5/15
	Memphis MSA, TN-MS-AR	Y	46790 FQ	54740 MW	61600 TQ	USBLS	5/15
	Nashville-Davidson–Murfreesboro–Franklin MSA, TN	Y	43440 FQ	55120 MW	67250 TQ	USBLS	5/15
	Texas	Y	45300 FQ	60010 MW	79330 TQ	USBLS	5/15
	Austin-Round Rock MSA, TX	Y	39950 FQ	46560 MW	64720 TQ	USBLS	5/15
	Dallas-Plano-Irving PMSA, TX	Y	50590 FQ	65710 MW	84580 TQ	USBLS	5/15
	Fort Worth-Arlington PMSA, TX	Y	46880 FQ	61580 MW	90890 TQ	USBLS	5/15
	Houston-The Woodlands-Sugar Land MSA, TX	Y	48500 FQ	66260 MW	87190 TQ	USBLS	5/15
	San Antonio-New Braunfels MSA, TX	Y	44750 FQ	60460 MW	75230 TQ	USBLS	5/15
	Utah	Y	44140 FQ	55530 MW	68280 TQ	USBLS	5/15
	Ogden-Clearfield MSA, UT	Y	41820 FQ	50540 MW	61220 TQ	USBLS	5/15
	Provo-Orem MSA, UT	Y	46820 FQ	55630 MW	63000 TQ	USBLS	5/15
	Salt Lake City MSA, UT	Y	44870 FQ	56510 MW	69770 TQ	USBLS	5/15
	Vermont	Y	44650 FQ	56240 MW	71470 TQ	USBLS	5/15
	Burlington-South Burlington MSA, VT	Y	44200 FQ	56780 MW	71850 TQ	USBLS	5/15
	Virginia	Y	45680 FQ	60150 MW	77710 TQ	USBLS	5/15
	Richmond MSA, VA	Y	43060 FQ	57600 MW	74950 TQ	USBLS	5/15
	Virginia Beach-Norfolk-Newport News MSA, VA-NC	Y	36500 FQ	45450 MW	58970 TQ	USBLS	5/15
	Washington	H	26.90 FQ	34.33 MW	45.79 TQ	WABLS	3/16
	Seattle-Bellevue-Everett PMSA, WA	H	29.60 FQ	37.20 MW	49.32 TQ	WABLS	3/16
	Tacoma-Lakewood PMSA, WA	H	24.59 FQ	29.03 MW	34.45 TQ	WABLS	3/16
	West Virginia	Y	30960 FQ	46960 MW	71840 TQ	USBLS	5/15
	Huntington-Ashland MSA, WV-KY-OH	Y	40920 FQ	71090 MW	89090 TQ	USBLS	5/15
	Wisconsin	Y	42080 FQ	51510 MW	63570 TQ	USBLS	5/15
	Madison MSA, WI	Y	45610 FQ	52760 MW	63110 TQ	USBLS	5/15

AE	Average entry wage	AWR	Average wage range	H	Hourly	LR	Low end range	MTC	Median total compensation	TCC	Total cash compensation
AEX	Average experienced wage	B	Biweekly	HI	Highest wage paid	M	Monthly	MW	Median wage paid	TQ	Third quartile wage
ATC	Average total compensation	D	Daily	HR	High end range	MCC	Median cash compensation	MWR	Median wage range	W	Weekly
AW	Average wage paid	FQ	First quartile wage	LO	Lowest wage paid	ME	Median entry wage	S	See annotated source	Y	Yearly

Occupation/Type/Industry	Location	Per	Low	Mid	High	Source	Date
Compensation, Benefits, and Job Analysis Specialist	Milwaukee-Waukesha-West Allis MSA, WI	Y	46010 FQ	58720 MW	75780 TQ	USBLS	5/15
	Wyoming	Y	44470 FQ	55810 MW	66970 TQ	USBLS	5/15
	Puerto Rico	Y	26060 FQ	35030 MW	46870 TQ	USBLS	5/15
	San Juan-Carolina-Caguas MSA, PR	Y	26590 FQ	35970 MW	47480 TQ	USBLS	5/15
Compensation Analyst	United States	Y		70000 MW		TSTR	2017
Compensation and Benefits Manager	Alabama	Y	78061 AE	121130 AW	142674 AEX	ALBLS	6/16
	Birmingham-Hoover MSA, AL	Y	80060 AE	123128 AW	144653 AEX	ALBLS	6/16
	Arizona	Y	84310 FQ	105860 MW	138080 TQ	USBLS	5/15
	Phoenix-Mesa-Scottsdale MSA, AZ	Y	84710 FQ	107750 MW	138950 TQ	USBLS	5/15
	Tucson MSA, AZ	Y	82740 FQ	105230 MW	136060 TQ	USBLS	5/15
	Arkansas	Y	64620 FQ	108580 MW	165490 TQ	USBLS	5/15
	Little Rock-North Little Rock-Conway MSA, AR	Y	48080 FQ	65530 MW	83420 TQ	USBLS	5/15
	California	H	44.85 FQ	63.43 MW	85.97 TQ	CABLS	1/16-3/16
	Anaheim-Santa Ana-Irvine PMSA, CA	H	54.18 FQ	67.97 MW	85.11 TQ	CABLS	1/16-3/16
	Los Angeles-Long Beach-Glendale PMSA, CA	H	42.36 FQ	65.09 MW	87.67 TQ	CABLS	1/16-3/16
	Oakland-Hayward-Berkeley PMSA, CA	H	39.25 FQ	60.33 MW	86.03 TQ	CABLS	1/16-3/16
	Riverside-San Bernardino-Ontario MSA, CA	H	45.42 FQ	56.35 MW	74.16 TQ	CABLS	1/16-3/16
	Sacramento–Roseville–Arden-Arcade MSA, CA	H	45.54 FQ	58.83 MW	76.25 TQ	CABLS	1/16-3/16
	San Diego-Carlsbad MSA, CA	H	44.21 FQ	66.63 MW	86.64 TQ	CABLS	1/16-3/16
	San Francisco-Redwood City-South San Francisco PMSA, CA	H	46.25 FQ	62.27 MW	86.88 TQ	CABLS	1/16-3/16
	Colorado	Y	105680 FQ	137690 MW	163640 TQ	USBLS	5/15
	Denver-Aurora-Lakewood MSA, CO	Y	107460 FQ	139760 MW	163800 TQ	USBLS	5/15
	Connecticut	Y		125667 MW		CTBLS	1/16-3/16
	Bridgeport-Stamford-Norwalk MSA, CT	Y	105300 FQ	127380 MW	155490 TQ	USBLS	5/15
	Hartford-West Hartford-East Hartford MSA, CT	Y	109770 FQ	134190 MW	182380 TQ	USBLS	5/15
	Delaware	Y	105940 FQ	131860 MW	177780 TQ	USBLS	5/15
	Wilmington PMSA, DE-MD-NJ	Y	104690 FQ	130020 MW	175800 TQ	USBLS	5/15
	District of Columbia	Y	105100 FQ	121360 MW	146500 TQ	USBLS	5/15
	Washington-Arlington-Alexandria PMSA, DC-VA-MD-WV	Y	106940 FQ	127510 MW	160350 TQ	USBLS	5/15
	Florida	H	34.13 AE	47.51 MW	60.80 AEX	FLBLS	7/16-9/16
	Fort Lauderdale-Pompano Beach-Deerfield Beach PMSA, FL	H	37.29 AE	50.76 MW	59.87 AEX	FLBLS	7/16-9/16
	Miami-Miami Beach-Kendall PMSA, FL	H	32.63 AE	49.18 MW	62.14 AEX	FLBLS	7/16-9/16
	Orlando-Kissimmee-Sanford MSA, FL	H	34.30 AE	46.23 MW	54.43 AEX	FLBLS	7/16-9/16
	Tampa-St. Petersburg-Clearwater MSA, FL	H	32.95 AE	40.37 MW	54.68 AEX	FLBLS	7/16-9/16
	Georgia	Y	93100 FQ	119710 MW	168330 TQ	USBLS	5/15
	Atlanta-Sandy Springs-Roswell MSA, GA	Y	97590 FQ	122940 MW	175100 TQ	USBLS	5/15
	Hawaii	Y	58130 FQ	87560 MW	112710 TQ	USBLS	5/15
	Urban Honolulu MSA, HI	Y	58010 FQ	91380 MW	114570 TQ	USBLS	5/15
	Idaho	Y	56660 FQ	69600 MW	92150 TQ	USBLS	5/15
	Boise City MSA, ID	Y	61530 FQ	81970 MW	100300 TQ	USBLS	5/15
	Illinois	Y	72230 FQ	99080 MW	138930 TQ	USBLS	5/15
	Chicago-Naperville-Arlington Heights PMSA, IL	Y	73980 FQ	98100 MW	133730 TQ	USBLS	5/15
	Lake County-Kenosha County PMSA, IL-WI	Y	87880 FQ	130200 MW	181700 TQ	USBLS	5/15

AE	Average entry wage	**AWR**	Average wage range	**H**	Hourly
AEX	Average experienced wage	**B**	Biweekly	**HI**	Highest wage paid
ATC	Average total compensation	**D**	Daily	**HR**	High end range
AW	Average wage paid	**FQ**	First quartile wage	**LO**	Lowest wage paid

LR	Low end range	**MTC**	Median total compensation
M	Monthly	**MW**	Median wage paid
MCC	Median cash compensation	**MWR**	Median wage range
ME	Median entry wage	**S**	See annotated source

TCC	Total cash compensation
TQ	Third quartile wage
W	Weekly
Y	Yearly

Occupation/Type/Industry	Location	Per	Low	Mid	High	Source	Date
Compensation and Benefits							
Manager	Indiana	Y	72910 FQ	95320 MW	119950 TQ	USBLS	5/15
	Indianapolis-Carmel-Anderson						
	MSA, IN	Y	82360 FQ	101400 MW	122980 TQ	USBLS	5/15
	Iowa	Y	71770 FQ	91470 MW	124950 TQ	USBLS	5/15
	Des Moines-West Des Moines						
	MSA, IA	Y	81300 FQ	98300 MW	132930 TQ	USBLS	5/15
	Kansas	Y	60590 FQ	88740 MW	114930 TQ	USBLS	5/15
	Wichita MSA, KS	Y	57180 FQ	72240 MW	107990 TQ	USBLS	5/15
	Kentucky	Y	67460 FQ	92510 MW	121740 TQ	USBLS	5/15
	Louisville-Jefferson County						
	MSA, KY-IN	Y	70740 FQ	104900 MW	135000 TQ	USBLS	5/15
	Louisiana	Y	52360 FQ	67730 MW	86360 TQ	USBLS	5/15
	Baton Rouge MSA, LA	Y	64890 FQ	78570 MW	100240 TQ	USBLS	5/15
	New Orleans-Metairie MSA,						
	LA	Y	46730 FQ	57010 MW	85660 TQ	USBLS	5/15
	Maine	Y	79540 FQ	94360 MW	119930 TQ	USBLS	5/15
	Portland-South Portland MSA,						
	ME	Y	83600 FQ	97620 MW	138790 TQ	USBLS	5/15
	Maryland	Y	90351 AE	134938 MW	157231 AEX	MDBLS	4/16
	Baltimore-Columbia-Towson						
	MSA, MD	Y	100970 FQ	122570 MW	149060 TQ	USBLS	5/15
	Massachusetts	Y	94130 FQ	126200 MW	162750 TQ	USBLS	5/15
	Boston-Cambridge-Newton						
	NECTA, MA	Y	104560 FQ	132780 MW	173060 TQ	USBLS	5/15
	Worcester MSA, MA-CT	Y	83870 FQ	116330 MW	146050 TQ	USBLS	5/15
	Michigan	Y	65820 FQ	91310 MW	132070 TQ	USBLS	5/15
	Detroit-Dearborn-Livonia						
	PMSA, MI	Y	82150 FQ	116740 MW	163490 TQ	USBLS	5/15
	Grand Rapids-Wyoming MSA,						
	MI	Y	59120 FQ	80680 MW	107720 TQ	USBLS	5/15
	Minnesota	Y	94396 FQ	129777 MW	157821 TQ	MNBLS	1/16-3/16
	Minneapolis-St. Paul-						
	Bloomington MSA, MN-WI	Y	96946 FQ	133485 MW	159203 TQ	MNBLS	1/16-3/16
	Mississippi	Y	47420 FQ	57850 MW	78680 TQ	USBLS	5/15
	Jackson MSA, MS	Y	51550 FQ	62500 MW	103740 TQ	USBLS	5/15
	Missouri	Y	90030 FQ	110470 MW	140650 TQ	USBLS	5/15
	Kansas City MSA, MO-KS	Y	82710 FQ	102120 MW	128400 TQ	USBLS	5/15
	St. Louis MSA, MO-IL	Y	86700 FQ	111130 MW	143260 TQ	USBLS	5/15
	Nebraska	Y	70545 FQ	100495 MW	126740 TQ	NEBLS	7/16-9/16
	Omaha-Council Bluffs MSA,						
	NE-IA	Y	66410 FQ	98925 MW	126850 TQ	NEBLS	7/16-9/16
	Nevada	Y	70620 FQ	87450 MW	121810 TQ	USBLS	5/15
	Las Vegas-Henderson-Paradise						
	MSA, NV	Y	70090 FQ	89700 MW	122050 TQ	USBLS	5/15
	New Hampshire	H	36.79 AE	51.80 MW	60.35 AEX	NHBLS	6/16
	New Jersey	Y	111250 FQ	137380 MW	174750 TQ	USBLS	5/15
	Newark PMSA, NJ-PA	Y	113900 FQ	142210 MW		USBLS	5/15
	New Mexico	Y	65280 FQ	80070 MW	102570 TQ	USBLS	5/15
	Albuquerque MSA, NM	Y	73650 FQ	92080 MW	108600 TQ	USBLS	5/15
	New York	Y	93650 AE	139020 MW	183550 AEX	NYBLS	1/16-3/16
	Buffalo-Cheektowaga-Niagara						
	Falls MSA, NY	Y	103780 FQ	128560 MW	177280 TQ	USBLS	5/15
	Nassau County-Suffolk County						
	PMSA, NY	Y	102260 FQ	133900 MW	164620 TQ	USBLS	5/15
	New York-Jersey City-White						
	Plains PMSA, NY-NJ	Y	111290 FQ	143160 MW		USBLS	5/15
	Rochester MSA, NY	Y	83330 FQ	109270 MW	143210 TQ	USBLS	5/15
	North Carolina	Y	95490 FQ	124080 MW	161060 TQ	USBLS	5/15
	Charlotte-Concord-Gastonia						
	MSA, NC-SC	Y	103400 FQ	137600 MW	167210 TQ	USBLS	5/15
	Raleigh MSA, NC	Y	90950 FQ	107040 MW	140880 TQ	USBLS	5/15
	North Dakota	Y	69780 FQ	101480 MW	119570 TQ	USBLS	5/15
	Ohio	Y	79390 FQ	103550 MW	140870 TQ	USBLS	5/15
	Cincinnati MSA, OH-KY-IN	Y	82630 FQ	111510 MW	148620 TQ	USBLS	5/15
	Cleveland-Elyria MSA, OH	Y	77170 FQ	100200 MW	142240 TQ	USBLS	5/15
	Columbus MSA, OH	Y	86240 FQ	107650 MW	146550 TQ	USBLS	5/15
	Oklahoma	Y	65190 FQ	77370 MW	96270 TQ	USBLS	5/15
	Oklahoma City MSA, OK	Y	61480 FQ	77000 MW	94540 TQ	USBLS	5/15
	Tulsa MSA, OK	Y	67000 FQ	78070 MW	107830 TQ	USBLS	5/15
	Oregon	H	31.70 FQ	43.82 MW	54.18 TQ	ORBLS	2016

AE Average entry wage	**AWR** Average wage range	**H** Hourly	**LR** Low end range	**MTC** Median total compensation	**TCC** Total cash compensation
AEX Average experienced wage	**B** Biweekly	**HI** Highest wage paid	**M** Monthly	**MW** Median wage paid	**TQ** Third quartile wage
ATC Average total compensation	**D** Daily	**HR** High end range	**MCC** Median cash compensation	**MWR** Median wage range	**W** Weekly
AW Average wage paid	**FQ** First quartile wage	**LO** Lowest wage paid	**ME** Median entry wage	**S** See annotated source	**Y** Yearly

Occupation/Type/Industry	Location	Per	Low	Mid	High	Source	Date
Compensation and Benefits Manager	Portland-Vancouver-Hillsboro MSA, OR-WA	Y	81320 FQ	96890 MW	116720 TQ	USBLS	5/15
	Pennsylvania	Y	84420 FQ	108580 MW	149530 TQ	USBLS	5/15
	Allentown-Bethlehem-Easton MSA, PA-NJ	Y	88300 FQ	119970 MW	155850 TQ	USBLS	5/15
	Harrisburg-Carlisle MSA, PA	Y	72440 FQ	93920 MW	121640 TQ	USBLS	5/15
	Montgomery County-Bucks County-Chester County PMSA, PA	Y	85320 FQ	102410 MW	143750 TQ	USBLS	5/15
	Philadelphia PMSA, PA	Y	97880 FQ	128130 MW		USBLS	5/15
	Pittsburgh MSA, PA	Y	86890 FQ	107730 MW	139610 TQ	USBLS	5/15
	Rhode Island	Y	107710 FQ	127380 MW	163900 TQ	USBLS	5/15
	Providence-Warwick MSA, RI-MA	Y	108180 FQ	129720 MW	164430 TQ	USBLS	5/15
	South Carolina	Y	76450 FQ	96430 MW	120500 TQ	USBLS	5/15
	Columbia MSA, SC	Y	84300 FQ	106650 MW	123900 TQ	USBLS	5/15
	Greenville-Anderson-Mauldin MSA, SC	Y	73740 FQ	91280 MW	115940 TQ	USBLS	5/15
	Tennessee	Y	56280 FQ	80790 MW	107050 TQ	USBLS	5/15
	Knoxville MSA, TN	Y	69070 FQ	96390 MW	121600 TQ	USBLS	5/15
	Memphis MSA, TN-MS-AR	Y	48730 FQ	71430 MW	92410 TQ	USBLS	5/15
	Nashville-Davidson–Murfreesboro–Franklin MSA, TN	Y	67750 FQ	92520 MW	110880 TQ	USBLS	5/15
	Texas	Y	92670 FQ	124920 MW	163770 TQ	USBLS	5/15
	Austin-Round Rock MSA, TX	Y	89270 FQ	114370 MW		USBLS	5/15
	Dallas-Plano-Irving PMSA, TX	Y	102160 FQ	126030 MW	161630 TQ	USBLS	5/15
	Houston-The Woodlands-Sugar Land MSA, TX	Y	102000 FQ	139700 MW	175510 TQ	USBLS	5/15
	San Antonio-New Braunfels MSA, TX	Y	85670 FQ	107150 MW	130720 TQ	USBLS	5/15
	Utah	Y	68240 FQ	84220 MW	115030 TQ	USBLS	5/15
	Salt Lake City MSA, UT	Y	69860 FQ	87400 MW	119770 TQ	USBLS	5/15
	Virginia	Y	90570 FQ	118570 MW	153090 TQ	USBLS	5/15
	Richmond MSA, VA	Y	88500 FQ	109680 MW	134990 TQ	USBLS	5/15
	Virginia Beach-Norfolk-Newport News MSA, VA-NC	Y	58210 FQ	88480 MW	124090 TQ	USBLS	5/15
	Washington	H	43.47 FQ	56.11 MW	68.65 TQ	WABLS	3/16
	Seattle-Bellevue-Everett PMSA, WA	H	47.72 FQ	59.23 MW	72.15 TQ	WABLS	3/16
	Tacoma-Lakewood PMSA, WA	H	42.02 FQ	49.88 MW	58.14 TQ	WABLS	3/16
	West Virginia	Y	70830 FQ	86850 MW	97850 TQ	USBLS	5/15
	Wisconsin	Y	66860 FQ	90100 MW	125540 TQ	USBLS	5/15
	Madison MSA, WI	Y	49400 FQ	84890 MW	110610 TQ	USBLS	5/15
	Milwaukee-Waukesha-West Allis MSA, WI	Y	72700 FQ	97900 MW	129870 TQ	USBLS	5/15
	Puerto Rico	Y	55390 FQ	73550 MW	95600 TQ	USBLS	5/15
	San Juan-Carolina-Caguas MSA, PR	Y	60070 FQ	73740 MW	93320 TQ	USBLS	5/15
Complaint Investigator							
Municipal Government	Seattle, WA	H	28.86 LO		33.64 HI	CSSS	1/13/16
Compliance Officer	Alabama	Y	42649 AE	67719 AW	80265 AEX	ALBLS	6/16
	Birmingham-Hoover MSA, AL	Y	45375 AE	69257 AW	81197 AEX	ALBLS	6/16
	Alaska	Y	58620 FQ	72170 MW	86890 TQ	USBLS	5/15
	Anchorage MSA, AK	Y	58630 FQ	72190 MW	86900 TQ	USBLS	5/15
	Arizona	Y	47650 FQ	64310 MW	79540 TQ	USBLS	5/15
	Phoenix-Mesa-Scottsdale MSA, AZ	Y	46390 FQ	62150 MW	81370 TQ	USBLS	5/15
	Tucson MSA, AZ	Y	45790 FQ	61640 MW	78650 TQ	USBLS	5/15
	Arkansas	Y	36490 FQ	50520 MW	62930 TQ	USBLS	5/15
	Little Rock-North Little Rock-Conway MSA, AR	Y	36560 FQ	46860 MW	63580 TQ	USBLS	5/15
	California	H	28.51 FQ	37.35 MW	44.98 TQ	CABLS	1/16-3/16
	Anaheim-Santa Ana-Irvine PMSA, CA	H	29.19 FQ	38.46 MW	47.45 TQ	CABLS	1/16-3/16
	Los Angeles-Long Beach-Glendale PMSA, CA	H	27.89 FQ	36.65 MW	43.59 TQ	CABLS	1/16-3/16
	Oakland-Hayward-Berkeley PMSA, CA	H	32.11 FQ	41.88 MW	51.81 TQ	CABLS	1/16-3/16

AE Average entry wage	**AWR** Average wage range	**H** Hourly	**LR** Low end range	**MTC** Median total compensation	**TCC** Total cash compensation
AEX Average experienced wage	**B** Biweekly	**HI** Highest wage paid	**M** Monthly	**MW** Median wage paid	**TQ** Third quartile wage
ATC Average total compensation	**D** Daily	**HR** High end range	**MCC** Median cash compensation	**MWR** Median wage range	**W** Weekly
AW Average wage paid	**FQ** First quartile wage	**LO** Lowest wage paid	**ME** Median entry wage	**S** See annotated source	**Y** Yearly

Occupation/Type/Industry	Location	Per	Low	Mid	High	Source	Date
Compliance Officer	Riverside-San Bernardino-Ontario MSA, CA	H	26.87 FQ	33.20 MW	41.04 TQ	CABLS	1/16-3/16
	Sacramento–Roseville–Arden-Arcade MSA, CA	H	29.74 FQ	35.26 MW	42.23 TQ	CABLS	1/16-3/16
	San Diego-Carlsbad MSA, CA	H	28.06 FQ	38.23 MW	42.58 TQ	CABLS	1/16-3/16
	San Francisco-Redwood City-South San Francisco PMSA, CA	H	31.87 FQ	42.15 MW	48.48 TQ	CABLS	1/16-3/16
	Colorado	Y	51730 FQ	66380 MW	85300 TQ	USBLS	5/15
	Denver-Aurora-Lakewood MSA, CO	Y	53930 FQ	69020 MW	87750 TQ	USBLS	5/15
	Connecticut	Y		78256 MW		CTBLS	1/16-3/16
	Bridgeport-Stamford-Norwalk MSA, CT	Y	65580 FQ	83140 MW	101560 TQ	USBLS	5/15
	Hartford-West Hartford-East Hartford MSA, CT	Y	59960 FQ	75600 MW	95250 TQ	USBLS	5/15
	Delaware	Y	47610 FQ	65930 MW	94340 TQ	USBLS	5/15
	Wilmington PMSA, DE-MD-NJ	Y	52670 FQ	75300 MW	101260 TQ	USBLS	5/15
	District of Columbia	Y	63730 FQ	83880 MW	99920 TQ	USBLS	5/15
	Washington-Arlington-Alexandria PMSA, DC-VA-MD-WV	Y	61700 FQ	82260 MW	99900 TQ	USBLS	5/15
	Florida	H	17.84 AE	28.51 MW	36.10 AEX	FLBLS	7/16-9/16
	Fort Lauderdale-Pompano Beach-Deerfield Beach PMSA, FL	H	21.59 AE	32.94 MW	39.23 AEX	FLBLS	7/16-9/16
	Miami-Miami Beach-Kendall PMSA, FL	H	22.83 AE	39.37 MW	42.03 AEX	FLBLS	7/16-9/16
	Orlando-Kissimmee-Sanford MSA, FL	H	19.08 AE	28.14 MW	35.53 AEX	FLBLS	7/16-9/16
	Tampa-St. Petersburg-Clearwater MSA, FL	H	17.89 AE	28.26 MW	35.58 AEX	FLBLS	7/16-9/16
	Georgia	Y	40900 FQ	58030 MW	79900 TQ	USBLS	5/15
	Atlanta-Sandy Springs-Roswell MSA, GA	Y	41750 FQ	58140 MW	80660 TQ	USBLS	5/15
	Augusta-Richmond County MSA, GA-SC	Y	34200 FQ	46060 MW	64420 TQ	USBLS	5/15
	Hawaii	Y	50960 FQ	62700 MW	79030 TQ	USBLS	5/15
	Urban Honolulu MSA, HI	Y	52350 FQ	65060 MW	81190 TQ	USBLS	5/15
	Idaho	Y	37260 FQ	54980 MW	77090 TQ	USBLS	5/15
	Boise City MSA, ID	Y	36340 FQ	49680 MW	72060 TQ	USBLS	5/15
	Illinois	Y	53480 FQ	72230 MW	89660 TQ	USBLS	5/15
	Chicago-Naperville-Arlington Heights PMSA, IL	Y	56350 FQ	75570 MW	91240 TQ	USBLS	5/15
	Lake County-Kenosha County PMSA, IL-WI	Y	48570 FQ	67970 MW	89050 TQ	USBLS	5/15
	Indiana	Y	40260 FQ	55420 MW	78320 TQ	USBLS	5/15
	Gary PMSA, IN	Y	35660 FQ	50550 MW	62860 TQ	USBLS	5/15
	Indianapolis-Carmel-Anderson MSA, IN	Y	44040 FQ	62610 MW	90640 TQ	USBLS	5/15
	Iowa	Y	49070 FQ	58310 MW	71440 TQ	USBLS	5/15
	Des Moines-West Des Moines MSA, IA	Y	53620 FQ	65250 MW	77020 TQ	USBLS	5/15
	Kansas	Y	42380 FQ	53680 MW	70430 TQ	USBLS	5/15
	Wichita MSA, KS	Y	42450 FQ	58440 MW	75420 TQ	USBLS	5/15
	Kentucky	Y	41680 FQ	52160 MW	64330 TQ	USBLS	5/15
	Louisville-Jefferson County MSA, KY-IN	Y	42590 FQ	55300 MW	77210 TQ	USBLS	5/15
	Louisiana	Y	42850 FQ	56690 MW	75520 TQ	USBLS	5/15
	Baton Rouge MSA, LA	Y	39340 FQ	51420 MW	73190 TQ	USBLS	5/15
	New Orleans-Metairie MSA, LA	Y	44840 FQ	60910 MW	79750 TQ	USBLS	5/15
	Maine	Y	45460 FQ	63390 MW	77230 TQ	USBLS	5/15
	Portland-South Portland MSA, ME	Y	45990 FQ	61860 MW	81340 TQ	USBLS	5/15
	Maryland	Y	44639 AE	71208 MW	84492 AEX	MDBLS	4/16
	Baltimore-Columbia-Towson MSA, MD	Y	52040 FQ	66060 MW	84030 TQ	USBLS	5/15
	Salisbury MSA, MD-DE	Y	45250 FQ	54420 MW	70640 TQ	USBLS	5/15
	Massachusetts	Y	61180 FQ	78470 MW	99500 TQ	USBLS	5/15

AE	Average entry wage	AWR	Average wage range	H	Hourly	LR	Low end range	MTC	Median total compensation	TCC	Total cash compensation
AEX	Average experienced wage	B	Biweekly	HI	Highest wage paid	M	Monthly	MW	Median wage paid	TQ	Third quartile wage
ATC	Average total compensation	D	Daily	HR	High end range	MCC	Median cash compensation	MWR	Median wage range	W	Weekly
AW	Average wage paid	FQ	First quartile wage	LO	Lowest wage paid	ME	Median entry wage	S	See annotated source	Y	Yearly

Occupation/Type/Industry	Location	Per	Low	Mid	High	Source	Date
Compliance Officer	Boston-Cambridge-Newton NECTA, MA	Y	65260 FQ	83600 MW	102960 TQ	USBLS	5/15
	Worcester MSA, MA-CT	Y	53340 FQ	67510 MW	86500 TQ	USBLS	5/15
	Michigan	Y	51320 FQ	66760 MW	83940 TQ	USBLS	5/15
	Detroit-Dearborn-Livonia PMSA, MI	Y	62850 FQ	81380 MW	86470 TQ	USBLS	5/15
	Grand Rapids-Wyoming MSA, MI	Y	51540 FQ	63250 MW	76620 TQ	USBLS	5/15
	Muskegon MSA, MI	Y	44030 FQ	55520 MW	64370 TQ	USBLS	5/15
	Minnesota	Y	57166 FQ	71107 MW	85972 TQ	MNBLS	1/16-3/16
	Minneapolis-St. Paul-Bloomington MSA, MN-WI	Y	57898 FQ	72174 MW	88889 TQ	MNBLS	1/16-3/16
	Mississippi	Y	33190 FQ	47040 MW	67980 TQ	USBLS	5/15
	Jackson MSA, MS	Y	35860 FQ	48780 MW	73660 TQ	USBLS	5/15
	Missouri	Y	43700 FQ	58060 MW	74880 TQ	USBLS	5/15
	Kansas City MSA, MO-KS	Y	47820 FQ	58560 MW	77670 TQ	USBLS	5/15
	St. Louis MSA, MO-IL	Y	48980 FQ	62920 MW	79060 TQ	USBLS	5/15
	Montana	Y	43160 FQ	53020 MW	76330 TQ	USBLS	5/15
	Billings MSA, MT	Y	43790 FQ	48350 MW	68760 TQ	USBLS	5/15
	Nebraska	Y	45750 FQ	58555 MW	77210 TQ	NEBLS	7/16-9/16
	Omaha-Council Bluffs MSA, NE-IA	Y	46185 FQ	59145 MW	77165 TQ	NEBLS	7/16-9/16
	Nevada	Y	48730 FQ	60220 MW	76570 TQ	USBLS	5/15
	Las Vegas-Henderson-Paradise MSA, NV	Y	47880 FQ	58990 MW	74600 TQ	USBLS	5/15
	New Hampshire	H	22.09 AE	32.49 MW	39.62 AEX	NHBLS	6/16
	Manchester NECTA, NH	H	24.59 AE	39.64 MW	44.13 AEX	NHBLS	6/16
	Nashua NECTA, NH-MA	Y	61200 FQ	70970 MW	80690 TQ	USBLS	5/15
	New Jersey	Y	58150 FQ	75170 MW	90020 TQ	USBLS	5/15
	Camden PMSA, NJ	Y	54300 FQ	68500 MW	84590 TQ	USBLS	5/15
	Newark PMSA, NJ-PA	Y	59630 FQ	81000 MW	90970 TQ	USBLS	5/15
	Trenton MSA, NJ	Y	63220 FQ	76340 MW	92690 TQ	USBLS	5/15
	New Mexico	Y	42100 FQ	58570 MW	81380 TQ	USBLS	5/15
	Albuquerque MSA, NM	Y	43550 FQ	58540 MW	85090 TQ	USBLS	5/15
	New York	Y	49230 AE	73280 MW	95550 AEX	NYBLS	1/16-3/16
	Buffalo-Cheektowaga-Niagara Falls MSA, NY	Y	54190 FQ	71930 MW	79120 TQ	USBLS	5/15
	Nassau County-Suffolk County PMSA, NY	Y	55910 FQ	69150 MW	87690 TQ	USBLS	5/15
	New York-Jersey City-White Plains PMSA, NY-NJ	Y	58560 FQ	78410 MW	97920 TQ	USBLS	5/15
	Rochester MSA, NY	Y	43620 FQ	56030 MW	72580 TQ	USBLS	5/15
	North Carolina	Y	47010 FQ	63940 MW	85720 TQ	USBLS	5/15
	Charlotte-Concord-Gastonia MSA, NC-SC	Y	47980 FQ	64850 MW	82860 TQ	USBLS	5/15
	Raleigh MSA, NC	Y	52180 FQ	71920 MW	96440 TQ	USBLS	5/15
	North Dakota	Y	44750 FQ	59680 MW	76350 TQ	USBLS	5/15
	Fargo MSA, ND-MN	Y	28940 FQ	42720 MW	62370 TQ	USBLS	5/15
	Ohio	Y	44270 FQ	56470 MW	72890 TQ	USBLS	5/15
	Cincinnati MSA, OH-KY-IN	Y	48920 FQ	63370 MW	79310 TQ	USBLS	5/15
	Cleveland-Elyria MSA, OH	Y	44270 FQ	55450 MW	71930 TQ	USBLS	5/15
	Columbus MSA, OH	Y	46560 FQ	59270 MW	77020 TQ	USBLS	5/15
	Oklahoma	Y	33780 FQ	46000 MW	68320 TQ	USBLS	5/15
	Oklahoma City MSA, OK	Y	36150 FQ	52120 MW	75300 TQ	USBLS	5/15
	Tulsa MSA, OK	Y	33930 FQ	46160 MW	70930 TQ	USBLS	5/15
	Oregon	H	24.87 FQ	31.53 MW	37.65 TQ	ORBLS	2016
	Portland-Vancouver-Hillsboro MSA, OR-WA	Y	52940 FQ	67150 MW	83880 TQ	USBLS	5/15
	Pennsylvania	Y	48070 FQ	62860 MW	81090 TQ	USBLS	5/15
	Allentown-Bethlehem-Easton MSA, PA-NJ	Y	46010 FQ	58150 MW	73530 TQ	USBLS	5/15
	Harrisburg-Carlisle MSA, PA	Y	50000 FQ	61850 MW	74790 TQ	USBLS	5/15
	Montgomery County-Bucks County-Chester County PMSA, PA	Y	54170 FQ	72170 MW	97500 TQ	USBLS	5/15
	Philadelphia PMSA, PA	Y	53970 FQ	73150 MW	88740 TQ	USBLS	5/15
	Pittsburgh MSA, PA	Y	48070 FQ	62680 MW	78720 TQ	USBLS	5/15
	Rhode Island	Y	54560 FQ	68130 MW	90350 TQ	USBLS	5/15
	Providence-Warwick MSA, RI-MA	Y	53220 FQ	65920 MW	86990 TQ	USBLS	5/15
	South Carolina	Y	37220 FQ	49610 MW	70630 TQ	USBLS	5/15

AE	Average entry wage	AWR	Average wage range	H	Hourly	LR	Low end range	MTC	Median total compensation	TCC	Total cash compensation
AEX	Average experienced wage	B	Biweekly	HI	Highest wage paid	M	Monthly	MW	Median wage paid	TQ	Third quartile wage
ATC	Average total compensation	D	Daily	HR	High end range	MCC	Median cash compensation	MWR	Median wage range	W	Weekly
AW	Average wage paid	FQ	First quartile wage	LO	Lowest wage paid	ME	Median entry wage	S	See annotated source	Y	Yearly

Occupation/Type/Industry	Location	Per	Low	Mid	High	Source	Date
Compliance Officer	Charleston-North Charleston MSA, SC	Y	50120 FQ	72400 MW	81600 TQ	USBLS	5/15
	Columbia MSA, SC	Y	36010 FQ	45340 MW	60730 TQ	USBLS	5/15
	Greenville-Anderson-Mauldin MSA, SC	Y	40000 FQ	47810 MW	60770 TQ	USBLS	5/15
	South Dakota	Y	42170 FQ	49060 MW	61910 TQ	USBLS	5/15
	Sioux Falls MSA, SD	Y	44630 FQ	55090 MW	68990 TQ	USBLS	5/15
	Tennessee	Y	38850 FQ	53800 MW	76970 TQ	USBLS	5/15
	Knoxville MSA, TN	Y	40890 FQ	61290 MW	88390 TQ	USBLS	5/15
	Memphis MSA, TN-MS-AR	Y	36510 FQ	52300 MW	77220 TQ	USBLS	5/15
	Nashville-Davidson–Murfreesboro–Franklin MSA, TN	Y	40160 FQ	54070 MW	77220 TQ	USBLS	5/15
	Texas	Y	49690 FQ	70580 MW	86960 TQ	USBLS	5/15
	Austin-Round Rock MSA, TX	Y	46440 FQ	58960 MW	78890 TQ	USBLS	5/15
	Dallas-Plano-Irving PMSA, TX	Y	53360 FQ	73120 MW	91980 TQ	USBLS	5/15
	Fort Worth-Arlington PMSA, TX	Y	46230 FQ	61490 MW	84310 TQ	USBLS	5/15
	Houston-The Woodlands-Sugar Land MSA, TX	Y	55990 FQ	80850 MW	96110 TQ	USBLS	5/15
	San Antonio-New Braunfels MSA, TX	Y	46300 FQ	66360 MW	87770 TQ	USBLS	5/15
	Utah	Y	42790 FQ	56740 MW	77460 TQ	USBLS	5/15
	Ogden-Clearfield MSA, UT	Y	39890 FQ	47770 MW	69750 TQ	USBLS	5/15
	Provo-Orem MSA, UT	Y	36900 FQ	46370 MW	61850 TQ	USBLS	5/15
	Salt Lake City MSA, UT	Y	43770 FQ	59060 MW	79550 TQ	USBLS	5/15
	Vermont	Y	49140 FQ	62920 MW	79550 TQ	USBLS	5/15
	Burlington-South Burlington MSA, VT	Y	50010 FQ	62930 MW	79560 TQ	USBLS	5/15
	Virginia	Y	49960 FQ	67990 MW	89100 TQ	USBLS	5/15
	Richmond MSA, VA	Y	46880 FQ	61960 MW	79660 TQ	USBLS	5/15
	Virginia Beach-Norfolk-Newport News MSA, VA-NC	Y	45530 FQ	65390 MW	77270 TQ	USBLS	5/15
	Washington	H	27.15 FQ	33.93 MW	41.77 TQ	WABLS	3/16
	Seattle-Bellevue-Everett PMSA, WA	H	28.51 FQ	37.49 MW	45.20 TQ	WABLS	3/16
	Tacoma-Lakewood PMSA, WA	H	26.46 FQ	30.62 MW	38.95 TQ	WABLS	3/16
	West Virginia	Y	36050 FQ	50120 MW	68450 TQ	USBLS	5/15
	Huntington-Ashland MSA, WV-KY-OH	Y	35630 FQ	47250 MW	65480 TQ	USBLS	5/15
	Wisconsin	Y	46850 FQ	58100 MW	73950 TQ	USBLS	5/15
	Madison MSA, WI	Y	47320 FQ	57420 MW	70980 TQ	USBLS	5/15
	Milwaukee-Waukesha-West Allis MSA, WI	Y	50520 FQ	64430 MW	88830 TQ	USBLS	5/15
	Wyoming	Y	50020 FQ	60910 MW	78860 TQ	USBLS	5/15
	Cheyenne MSA, WY	Y	50610 FQ	60750 MW	80680 TQ	USBLS	5/15
	Puerto Rico	Y	27620 FQ	38150 MW	59570 TQ	USBLS	5/15
	San Juan-Carolina-Caguas MSA, PR	Y	27860 FQ	38250 MW	58170 TQ	USBLS	5/15
	Virgin Islands	Y	37030 FQ	63060 MW	77220 TQ	USBLS	5/15
	Guam	Y	39580 FQ	62130 MW	77230 TQ	USBLS	5/15
Computer, Automated Teller, and Office Machine Repairer	Alabama	Y	26168 AE	40223 AW	47251 AEX	ALBLS	6/16
	Birmingham-Hoover MSA, AL	Y	31050 AE	43915 AW	50342 AEX	ALBLS	6/16
	Alaska	Y	35850	42880 MW	51190 TQ	USBLS	5/15
	Anchorage MSA, AK	Y	35850 FQ	43270 MW	51730 TQ	USBLS	5/15
	Arizona	Y	26010 FQ	31090 MW	38830 TQ	USBLS	5/15
	Phoenix-Mesa-Scottsdale MSA, AZ	Y	26150 FQ	31130 MW	39210 TQ	USBLS	5/15
	Tucson MSA, AZ	Y	25280 FQ	30660 MW	38360 TQ	USBLS	5/15
	Arkansas	Y	26100 FQ	30750 MW	38330 TQ	USBLS	5/15
	Little Rock-North Little Rock-Conway MSA, AR	Y	24870 FQ	32370 MW	42120 TQ	USBLS	5/15
	California	H	15.05 FQ	19.43 MW	24.99 TQ	CABLS	1/16-3/16
	Anaheim-Santa Ana-Irvine PMSA, CA	H	14.77 FQ	19.04 MW	26.05 TQ	CABLS	1/16-3/16
	Los Angeles-Long Beach-Glendale PMSA, CA	H	16.21 FQ	19.62 MW	24.91 TQ	CABLS	1/16-3/16
	Oakland-Hayward-Berkeley PMSA, CA	H	13.19 FQ	17.76 MW	26.31 TQ	CABLS	1/16-3/16

AE	Average entry wage	AWR	Average wage range	H	Hourly	LR	Low end range	MTC	Median total compensation	TCC	Total cash compensation
AEX	Average experienced wage	B	Biweekly	HI	Highest wage paid	M	Monthly	MW	Median wage paid	TQ	Third quartile wage
ATC	Average total compensation	D	Daily	HR	High end range	MCC	Median cash compensation	MWR	Median wage range	W	Weekly
AW	Average wage paid	FQ	First quartile wage	LO	Lowest wage paid	ME	Median entry wage	S	See annotated source	Y	Yearly

Occupation/Type/Industry	Location	Per	Low	Mid	High	Source	Date
Computer, Automated Teller, and Office Machine Repairer							
	Riverside-San Bernardino-Ontario MSA, CA	H	13.12 FQ	15.17 MW	18.35 TQ	CABLS	1/16-3/16
	Sacramento–Roseville–Arden-Arcade MSA, CA	H	13.62 FQ	18.37 MW	23.05 TQ	CABLS	1/16-3/16
	San Diego-Carlsbad MSA, CA	H	13.88 FQ	18.66 MW	23.73 TQ	CABLS	1/16-3/16
	San Francisco-Redwood City-South San Francisco PMSA, CA	H	17.98 FQ	23.21 MW	32.38 TQ	CABLS	1/16-3/16
	Colorado	Y	29710 FQ	38940 MW	48310 TQ	USBLS	5/15
	Denver-Aurora-Lakewood MSA, CO	Y	29980 FQ	38340 MW	48010 TQ	USBLS	5/15
	Connecticut	Y		44267 MW		CTBLS	1/16-3/16
	Bridgeport-Stamford-Norwalk MSA, CT	Y	34830 FQ	44000 MW	53210 TQ	USBLS	5/15
	Hartford-West Hartford-East Hartford MSA, CT	Y	36010 FQ	45400 MW	54580 TQ	USBLS	5/15
	Delaware	Y	29470 FQ	35740 MW	43150 TQ	USBLS	5/15
	Wilmington PMSA, DE-MD-NJ	Y	29230 FQ	35680 MW	43250 TQ	USBLS	5/15
	District of Columbia	Y	39190 FQ	53500 MW	58830 TQ	USBLS	5/15
	Washington-Arlington-Alexandria PMSA, DC-VA-MD-WV	Y	29880 FQ	46720 MW	60940 TQ	USBLS	5/15
	Florida	H	11.69 AE	17.30 MW	21.97 AEX	FLBLS	7/16-9/16
	Fort Lauderdale-Pompano Beach-Deerfield Beach PMSA, FL	H	13.34 AE	19.61 MW	24.81 AEX	FLBLS	7/16-9/16
	Miami-Miami Beach-Kendall PMSA, FL	H	10.93 AE	16.89 MW	21.33 AEX	FLBLS	7/16-9/16
	Orlando-Kissimmee-Sanford MSA, FL	H	13.30 AE	18.81 MW	24.64 AEX	FLBLS	7/16-9/16
	Tampa-St. Petersburg-Clearwater MSA, FL	H	9.45 AE	13.56 MW	17.24 AEX	FLBLS	7/16-9/16
	Georgia	Y	23010 FQ	34370 MW	45790 TQ	USBLS	5/15
	Atlanta-Sandy Springs-Roswell MSA, GA	Y	21930 FQ	34690 MW	46860 TQ	USBLS	5/15
	Augusta-Richmond County MSA, GA-SC	Y	23050 FQ	28540 MW	37090 TQ	USBLS	5/15
	Hawaii	Y	25160 FQ	30250 MW	42110 TQ	USBLS	5/15
	Urban Honolulu MSA, HI	Y	25400 FQ	29990 MW	42060 TQ	USBLS	5/15
	Idaho	Y	24870 FQ	34060 MW	41550 TQ	USBLS	5/15
	Boise City MSA, ID	Y	32830 FQ	37680 MW	45920 TQ	USBLS	5/15
	Illinois	Y	31780 FQ	37740 MW	50210 TQ	USBLS	5/15
	Chicago-Naperville-Arlington Heights PMSA, IL	Y	32440 FQ	38620 MW	52270 TQ	USBLS	5/15
	Lake County-Kenosha County PMSA, IL-WI	Y	24980 FQ	35010 MW	46760 TQ	USBLS	5/15
	Indiana	Y	29380 FQ	39840 MW	47130 TQ	USBLS	5/15
	Gary PMSA, IN	Y	23020 FQ	34590 MW	48090 TQ	USBLS	5/15
	Indianapolis-Carmel-Anderson MSA, IN	Y	34120 FQ	42670 MW	47650 TQ	USBLS	5/15
	Iowa	Y	30730 FQ	37430 MW	45470 TQ	USBLS	5/15
	Des Moines-West Des Moines MSA, IA	Y	34090 FQ	41910 MW	48620 TQ	USBLS	5/15
	Kansas	Y	24160 FQ	31190 MW	44050 TQ	USBLS	5/15
	Wichita MSA, KS	Y	25560 FQ	33620 MW	45350 TQ	USBLS	5/15
	Kentucky	Y	23680 FQ	31120 MW	39750 TQ	USBLS	5/15
	Louisville-Jefferson County MSA, KY-IN	Y	25590 FQ	31940 MW	40000 TQ	USBLS	5/15
	Louisiana	Y	24920 FQ	33160 MW	45010 TQ	USBLS	5/15
	Baton Rouge MSA, LA	Y	29840 FQ	37780 MW	49650 TQ	USBLS	5/15
	New Orleans-Metairie MSA, LA	Y	24700 FQ	31880 MW	42050 TQ	USBLS	5/15
	Maine	Y	32220 FQ	40620 MW	48630 TQ	USBLS	5/15
	Portland-South Portland MSA, ME	Y	35130 FQ	41360 MW	46730 TQ	USBLS	5/15
	Maryland	Y	26415 AE	44531 MW	53589 AEX	MDBLS	4/16
	Baltimore-Columbia-Towson MSA, MD	Y	29490 FQ	42250 MW	54810 TQ	USBLS	5/15
	Salisbury MSA, MD-DE	Y	33630 FQ	43130 MW	52490 TQ	USBLS	5/15
	Massachusetts	Y	29500 FQ	44450 MW	57340 TQ	USBLS	5/15

AE	Average entry wage	AWR	Average wage range	H	Hourly	
AEX	Average experienced wage	B	Biweekly	HI	Highest wage paid	
ATC	Average total compensation	D	Daily	HR	High end range	
AW	Average wage paid	FQ	First quartile wage	LO	Lowest wage paid	
LR	Low end range	MTC	Median total compensation	TCC	Total cash compensation		
M	Monthly	MW	Median wage paid	TQ	Third quartile wage		
MCC	Median cash compensation	MWR	Median wage range	W	Weekly		
ME	Median entry wage	S	See annotated source	Y	Yearly		

Occupation/Type/Industry	Location	Per	Low	Mid	High	Source	Date
Computer, Automated Teller, and Office Machine Repairer							
	Boston-Cambridge-Newton NECTA, MA	Y	37900 FQ	53070 MW	60260 TQ	USBLS	5/15
	Worcester MSA, MA-CT	Y	35130 FQ	42410 MW	50320 TQ	USBLS	5/15
	Michigan	Y	25980 FQ	33270 MW	41600 TQ	USBLS	5/15
	Detroit-Dearborn-Livonia PMSA, MI	Y	28290 FQ	35720 MW	47120 TQ	USBLS	5/15
	Grand Rapids-Wyoming MSA, MI	Y	25450 FQ	29070 MW	34910 TQ	USBLS	5/15
	Minnesota	Y	33408 FQ	41866 MW	50243 TQ	MNBLS	1/16-3/16
	Minneapolis-St. Paul-Bloomington MSA, MN-WI	Y	33308 FQ	42258 MW	50485 TQ	MNBLS	1/16-3/16
	Mississippi	Y	25440 FQ	34040 MW	41170 TQ	USBLS	5/15
	Jackson MSA, MS	Y	21670 FQ	32220 MW	38670 TQ	USBLS	5/15
	Missouri	Y	25860 FQ	33880 MW	47020 TQ	USBLS	5/15
	Kansas City MSA, MO-KS	Y	23860 FQ	33260 MW	47390 TQ	USBLS	5/15
	St. Louis MSA, MO-IL	Y	27880 FQ	37760 MW	52400 TQ	USBLS	5/15
	Montana	Y	27090 FQ	35490 MW	44720 TQ	USBLS	5/15
	Billings MSA, MT	Y	24660 FQ	34030 MW	44690 TQ	USBLS	5/15
	Nebraska	Y	21020 FQ	30360 MW	43455 TQ	NEBLS	7/16-9/16
	Omaha-Council Bluffs MSA, NE-IA	Y	23330 FQ	36640 MW	51810 TQ	NEBLS	7/16-9/16
	Nevada	Y	29180 FQ	39030 MW	48150 TQ	USBLS	5/15
	Las Vegas-Henderson-Paradise MSA, NV	Y	29400 FQ	38650 MW	47730 TQ	USBLS	5/15
	New Hampshire	H	15.28 AE	21.10 MW	24.37 AEX	NHBLS	6/16
	Manchester NECTA, NH	H	15.64 AE	20.99 MW	23.58 AEX	NHBLS	6/16
	Nashua NECTA, NH-MA	Y	39700 FQ	45340 MW	51040 TQ	USBLS	5/15
	New Jersey	Y	32130 FQ	42330 MW	55230 TQ	USBLS	5/15
	Camden PMSA, NJ	Y	29680 FQ	40600 MW	59730 TQ	USBLS	5/15
	Newark PMSA, NJ-PA	Y	28720 FQ	39370 MW	54580 TQ	USBLS	5/15
	Trenton MSA, NJ	Y	32360 FQ	44210 MW	57460 TQ	USBLS	5/15
	New Mexico	Y	24140 FQ	31030 MW	38620 TQ	USBLS	5/15
	Albuquerque MSA, NM	Y	24620 FQ	29020 MW	37000 TQ	USBLS	5/15
	New York	Y	26460 AE	40450 MW	49740 AEX	NYBLS	1/16-3/16
	Buffalo-Cheektowaga-Niagara Falls MSA, NY	Y	30680 FQ	40230 MW	49070 TQ	USBLS	5/15
	Nassau County-Suffolk County PMSA, NY	Y	30940 FQ	40900 MW	54510 TQ	USBLS	5/15
	New York-Jersey City-White Plains PMSA, NY-NJ	Y	30000 FQ	39680 MW	52250 TQ	USBLS	5/15
	Rochester MSA, NY	Y	28410 FQ	39150 MW	51470 TQ	USBLS	5/15
	North Carolina	Y	28880 FQ	38500 MW	48540 TQ	USBLS	5/15
	Charlotte-Concord-Gastonia MSA, NC-SC	Y	28370 FQ	40370 MW	48980 TQ	USBLS	5/15
	Raleigh MSA, NC	Y	29780 FQ	37150 MW	47610 TQ	USBLS	5/15
	North Dakota	Y	28170 FQ	36840 MW	44920 TQ	USBLS	5/15
	Fargo MSA, ND-MN	Y	28790 FQ	38280 MW	45730 TQ	USBLS	5/15
	Ohio	Y	27430 FQ	34290 MW	41930 TQ	USBLS	5/15
	Cincinnati MSA, OH-KY-IN	Y	25710 FQ	32470 MW	41920 TQ	USBLS	5/15
	Cleveland-Elyria MSA, OH	Y	24760 FQ	32430 MW	41560 TQ	USBLS	5/15
	Columbus MSA, OH	Y	28470 FQ	34510 MW	39880 TQ	USBLS	5/15
	Oklahoma	Y	26400 FQ	33300 MW	42320 TQ	USBLS	5/15
	Oklahoma City MSA, OK	Y	29520 FQ	35500 MW	42680 TQ	USBLS	5/15
	Tulsa MSA, OK	Y	26110 FQ	31780 MW	44670 TQ	USBLS	5/15
	Oregon	H	12.83 FQ	16.14 MW	19.36 TQ	ORBLS	2016
	Portland-Vancouver-Hillsboro MSA, OR-WA	Y	27320 FQ	32970 MW	39800 TQ	USBLS	5/15
	Pennsylvania	Y	27870 FQ	36710 MW	46130 TQ	USBLS	5/15
	Allentown-Bethlehem-Easton MSA, PA-NJ	Y	33020 FQ	40820 MW	48730 TQ	USBLS	5/15
	Harrisburg-Carlisle MSA, PA	Y	26560 FQ	34410 MW	45800 TQ	USBLS	5/15
	Montgomery County-Bucks County-Chester County PMSA, PA	Y	31850 FQ	40970 MW	48950 TQ	USBLS	5/15
	Philadelphia PMSA, PA	Y	25190 FQ	36620 MW	45470 TQ	USBLS	5/15
	Pittsburgh MSA, PA	Y	25560 FQ	34470 MW	44240 TQ	USBLS	5/15
	Rhode Island	Y	31850 FQ	46280 MW	57110 TQ	USBLS	5/15
	Providence-Warwick MSA, RI-MA	Y	31550 FQ	45830 MW	56950 TQ	USBLS	5/15
	South Carolina	Y	29190 FQ	41660 MW	55560 TQ	USBLS	5/15

AE	Average entry wage	AWR	Average wage range	H	Hourly
AEX	Average experienced wage	B	Biweekly	HI	Highest wage paid
ATC	Average total compensation	D	Daily	HR	High end range
AW	Average wage paid	FQ	First quartile wage	LO	Lowest wage paid

LR	Low end range	MTC	Median total compensation	TCC	Total cash compensation
M	Monthly	MW	Median wage paid	TQ	Third quartile wage
MCC	Median cash compensation	MWR	Median wage range	W	Weekly
ME	Median entry wage	S	See annotated source	Y	Yearly

Occupation/Type/Industry	Location	Per	Low	Mid	High	Source	Date
Computer, Automated Teller, and Office Machine Repairer	Charleston-North Charleston MSA, SC	Y	25200 FQ	40440 MW	48670 TQ	USBLS	5/15
	Greenville-Anderson-Mauldin MSA, SC	Y	35150 FQ	43220 MW	48580 TQ	USBLS	5/15
	South Dakota	Y	33380 FQ	40890 MW	48160 TQ	USBLS	5/15
	Sioux Falls MSA, SD	Y	35370 FQ	46060 MW	56190 TQ	USBLS	5/15
	Tennessee	Y	28380 FQ	36760 MW	45820 TQ	USBLS	5/15
	Knoxville MSA, TN	Y	27860 FQ	34360 MW	38800 TQ	USBLS	5/15
	Memphis MSA, TN-MS-AR	Y	23680 FQ	30720 MW	40100 TQ	USBLS	5/15
	Nashville-Davidson– Murfreesboro–Franklin MSA, TN	Y	36630 FQ	44320 MW	54100 TQ	USBLS	5/15
	Texas	Y	25990 FQ	34340 MW	43670 TQ	USBLS	5/15
	Austin-Round Rock MSA, TX	Y	23660 FQ	28700 MW	36000 TQ	USBLS	5/15
	Dallas-Plano-Irving PMSA, TX	Y	28040 FQ	36830 MW	46030 TQ	USBLS	5/15
	Fort Worth-Arlington PMSA, TX	Y	23270 FQ	29900 MW	38790 TQ	USBLS	5/15
	Houston-The Woodlands- Sugar Land MSA, TX	Y	29750 FQ	37220 MW	45150 TQ	USBLS	5/15
	San Antonio-New Braunfels MSA, TX	Y	27200 FQ	35570 MW	44710 TQ	USBLS	5/15
	Utah	Y	31180 FQ	35400 MW	41120 TQ	USBLS	5/15
	Ogden-Clearfield MSA, UT	Y	28140 FQ	31370 MW	44400 TQ	USBLS	5/15
	Provo-Orem MSA, UT	Y	27250 FQ	33650 MW	39920 TQ	USBLS	5/15
	Salt Lake City MSA, UT	Y	31790 FQ	35560 MW	40090 TQ	USBLS	5/15
	Vermont	Y	31680 FQ	37520 MW	44580 TQ	USBLS	5/15
	Virginia	Y	27070 FQ	36670 MW	53220 TQ	USBLS	5/15
	Richmond MSA, VA	Y	27740 FQ	36560 MW	48670 TQ	USBLS	5/15
	Virginia Beach-Norfolk- Newport News MSA, VA-NC	Y	22650 FQ	30030 MW	42100 TQ	USBLS	5/15
	Washington	H	14.19 FQ	18.33 MW	26.20 TQ	WABLS	3/16
	Tacoma-Lakewood PMSA, WA	H	13.16 FQ	15.88 MW	19.50 TQ	WABLS	3/16
	West Virginia	Y	23240 FQ	30400 MW	39490 TQ	USBLS	5/15
	Huntington-Ashland MSA, WV-KY-OH	Y	20300 FQ	23840 MW	29790 TQ	USBLS	5/15
	Wisconsin	Y	25280 FQ	36280 MW	48750 TQ	USBLS	5/15
	Madison MSA, WI	Y	27260 FQ	34860 MW	45660 TQ	USBLS	5/15
	Milwaukee-Waukesha-West Allis MSA, WI	Y	31590 FQ	42030 MW	53000 TQ	USBLS	5/15
	Wyoming	Y	29610 FQ	35950 MW	44420 TQ	USBLS	5/15
	Cheyenne MSA, WY	Y	26840 FQ	34440 MW	37910 TQ	USBLS	5/15
	Puerto Rico	Y	19970 FQ	24430 MW	31440 TQ	USBLS	5/15
	San Juan-Carolina-Caguas MSA, PR	Y	20440 FQ	24900 MW	31890 TQ	USBLS	5/15
Computer and Information Research Scientist	Alabama	Y	73779 AE	109333 AW	127110 AEX	ALBLS	6/16
	Arizona	Y	97370 FQ	111800 MW	139230 TQ	USBLS	5/15
	Tucson MSA, AZ	Y	92560 FQ	116470 MW	138920 TQ	USBLS	5/15
	California	H	48.74 FQ	57.58 MW	74.05 TQ	CABLS	1/16-3/16
	Anaheim-Santa Ana-Irvine PMSA, CA	H	45.87 FQ	53.92 MW	62.02 TQ	CABLS	1/16-3/16
	Los Angeles-Long Beach- Glendale PMSA, CA	H	30.98 FQ	56.24 MW	73.90 TQ	CABLS	1/16-3/16
	Oakland-Hayward-Berkeley PMSA, CA	H	43.12 FQ	54.16 MW	68.78 TQ	CABLS	1/16-3/16
	Sacramento–Roseville– Arden-Arcade MSA, CA	H	51.71 FQ	60.91 MW		CABLS	1/16-3/16
	San Diego-Carlsbad MSA, CA	H	47.36 FQ	57.07 MW	57.58 TQ	CABLS	1/16-3/16
	San Francisco-Redwood City- South San Francisco PMSA, CA	H	51.49 FQ	59.73 MW	71.91 TQ	CABLS	1/16-3/16
	Colorado	Y	57110 FQ	88900 MW	131830 TQ	USBLS	5/15
	Denver-Aurora-Lakewood MSA, CO	Y	37460 FQ	57170 MW	100470 TQ	USBLS	5/15
	Connecticut	Y		110438 MW		CTBLS	1/16-3/16
	Hartford-West Hartford-East Hartford MSA, CT	Y	91000 FQ	109300 MW	127530 TQ	USBLS	5/15
	District of Columbia	Y	111020 FQ	120310 MW	132050 TQ	USBLS	5/15

Computer and Information Research Scientist

Occupation/Type/Industry	Location	Per	Low	Mid	High	Source	Date
	Washington-Arlington-Alexandria PMSA, DC-VA-MD-WV	Y	107690 FQ	127270 MW	154680 TQ	USBLS	5/15
	Florida	H	36.23 AE	45.22 MW	55.27 AEX	FLBLS	7/16-9/16
	Orlando-Kissimmee-Sanford MSA, FL	H	35.46 AE	44.94 MW	50.33 AEX	FLBLS	7/16-9/16
	Tampa-St. Petersburg-Clearwater MSA, FL	H	43.65 AE	53.42 MW	59.33 AEX	FLBLS	7/16-9/16
	Georgia	Y	66020 FQ	86580 MW	118470 TQ	USBLS	5/15
	Atlanta-Sandy Springs-Roswell MSA, GA	Y	64250 FQ	93820 MW	134150 TQ	USBLS	5/15
	Hawaii	Y	90050 FQ	110490 MW	123090 TQ	USBLS	5/15
	Urban Honolulu MSA, HI	Y	96540 FQ	110750 MW	124300 TQ	USBLS	5/15
	Illinois	Y	81120 FQ	99270 MW	120600 TQ	USBLS	5/15
	Chicago-Naperville-Arlington Heights PMSA, IL	Y	69220 FQ	93480 MW	115080 TQ	USBLS	5/15
	Lake County-Kenosha County PMSA, IL-WI	Y	91970 FQ	110110 MW	137720 TQ	USBLS	5/15
	Indiana	Y	79020 FQ	96910 MW	119430 TQ	USBLS	5/15
	Kansas	Y	76680 FQ	100160 MW	119670 TQ	USBLS	5/15
	Louisiana	Y	60550 FQ	70790 MW	86020 TQ	USBLS	5/15
	New Orleans-Metairie MSA, LA	Y	66600 FQ	76140 MW	88670 TQ	USBLS	5/15
	Maryland	Y	74269 AE	112199 MW	131164 AEX	MDBLS	4/16
	Baltimore-Columbia-Towson MSA, MD	Y	94990 FQ	112010 MW	128640 TQ	USBLS	5/15
	Massachusetts	Y	87300 FQ	112850 MW	148180 TQ	USBLS	5/15
	Boston-Cambridge-Newton NECTA, MA	Y	89560 FQ	114020 MW	149170 TQ	USBLS	5/15
	Worcester MSA, MA-CT	Y	68180 FQ	88800 MW	130110 TQ	USBLS	5/15
	Michigan	Y	81740 FQ	98370 MW	117950 TQ	USBLS	5/15
	Detroit-Dearborn-Livonia PMSA, MI	Y	95320 FQ	108190 MW	118290 TQ	USBLS	5/15
	Minnesota	Y	91541 FQ	115886 MW	148667 TQ	MNBLS	1/16-3/16
	Minneapolis-St. Paul-Bloomington MSA, MN-WI	Y	91813 FQ	115301 MW	148718 TQ	MNBLS	1/16-3/16
	Mississippi	Y	74870 FQ	91250 MW	108510 TQ	USBLS	5/15
	Missouri	Y	76160 FQ	92700 MW	113870 TQ	USBLS	5/15
	Kansas City MSA, MO-KS	Y	77160 FQ	101930 MW	121950 TQ	USBLS	5/15
	St. Louis MSA, MO-IL	Y	81390 FQ	97260 MW	118240 TQ	USBLS	5/15
	Omaha-Council Bluffs MSA, NE-IA	Y	53450 FQ	57280 MW	61115 TQ	NEBLS	7/16-9/16
	New Hampshire	H	47.12 AE	67.59 MW	74.25 AEX	NHBLS	6/16
	New Jersey	Y	96810 FQ	122200 MW	148280 TQ	USBLS	5/15
	Newark PMSA, NJ-PA	Y	92970 FQ	119270 MW	153200 TQ	USBLS	5/15
	Trenton MSA, NJ	Y	102180 FQ	124750 MW	149750 TQ	USBLS	5/15
	New Mexico	Y	62340 FQ	82670 MW	108190 TQ	USBLS	5/15
	Albuquerque MSA, NM	Y	53600 FQ	72580 MW	104980 TQ	USBLS	5/15
	New York-Jersey City-White Plains PMSA, NY-NJ	Y	103810 FQ	140950 MW	178550 TQ	USBLS	5/15
	North Carolina	Y	79620 FQ	96820 MW	119520 TQ	USBLS	5/15
	Raleigh MSA, NC	Y	73960 FQ	83660 MW	106180 TQ	USBLS	5/15
	Ohio	Y	82470 FQ	96810 MW	112880 TQ	USBLS	5/15
	Cincinnati MSA, OH-KY-IN	Y	87260 FQ	97660 MW	119530 TQ	USBLS	5/15
	Oklahoma	Y	74860 FQ	86570 MW	103090 TQ	USBLS	5/15
	Oklahoma City MSA, OK	Y	72550 FQ	83470 MW	96810 TQ	USBLS	5/15
	Oregon	H	53.22 FQ	64.00 MW	78.58 TQ	ORBLS	2016
	Portland-Vancouver-Hillsboro MSA, OR-WA	Y	111420 FQ	133230 MW	161850 TQ	USBLS	5/15
	Pennsylvania	Y	81940 FQ	102570 MW	132880 TQ	USBLS	5/15
	Montgomery County-Bucks County-Chester County PMSA, PA	Y	76720 FQ	107410 MW	135470 TQ	USBLS	5/15
	Pittsburgh MSA, PA	Y	70120 FQ	81150 MW	98640 TQ	USBLS	5/15
	Rhode Island	Y	98020 FQ	114000 MW	118610 TQ	USBLS	5/15
	Providence-Warwick MSA, RI-MA	Y	98020 FQ	114000 MW	118610 TQ	USBLS	5/15
	South Carolina	Y	77720 FQ	91600 MW	106520 TQ	USBLS	5/15
	Charleston-North Charleston MSA, SC	Y	77720 FQ	91820 MW	106430 TQ	USBLS	5/15
	Tennessee	Y	68230 FQ	86410 MW	101010 TQ	USBLS	5/15

AE	Average entry wage	AWR	Average wage range	H	Hourly	LR	Low end range	MTC	Median total compensation	TCC	Total cash compensation
AEX	Average experienced wage	B	Biweekly	HI	Highest wage paid	M	Monthly	MW	Median wage paid	TQ	Third quartile wage
ATC	Average total compensation	D	Daily	HR	High end range	MCC	Median cash compensation	MWR	Median wage range	W	Weekly
AW	Average wage paid	FQ	First quartile wage	LO	Lowest wage paid	ME	Median entry wage	S	See annotated source	Y	Yearly

Occupation/Type/Industry	Location	Per	Low	Mid	High	Source	Date
Computer and Information Research Scientist	Knoxville MSA, TN	Y	78510 FQ	87930 MW	97740 TQ	USBLS	5/15
	Nashville-Davidson–Murfreesboro–Franklin MSA, TN	Y	83760 FQ	95700 MW	111670 TQ	USBLS	5/15
	Texas	Y	57580 FQ	92390 MW	123330 TQ	USBLS	5/15
	Austin-Round Rock MSA, TX	Y	59480 FQ	90740 MW	126400 TQ	USBLS	5/15
	Dallas-Plano-Irving PMSA, TX	Y	18050 FQ	73350 MW	116500 TQ	USBLS	5/15
	Houston-The Woodlands-Sugar Land MSA, TX	Y	70090 FQ	97420 MW	126320 TQ	USBLS	5/15
	San Antonio-New Braunfels MSA, TX	Y	83460 FQ	97380 MW	108510 TQ	USBLS	5/15
	Utah	Y	77220 FQ	91260 MW	105710 TQ	USBLS	5/15
	Ogden-Clearfield MSA, UT	Y	70200 FQ	81900 MW	91270 TQ	USBLS	5/15
	Salt Lake City MSA, UT	Y	87940 FQ	104160 MW	129640 TQ	USBLS	5/15
	Virginia	Y	102480 FQ	118210 MW	150980 TQ	USBLS	5/15
	Virginia Beach-Norfolk-Newport News MSA, VA-NC	Y	85530 FQ	104220 MW	116720 TQ	USBLS	5/15
	Washington	H	50.59 FQ	63.88 MW	80.28 TQ	WABLS	3/16
	Seattle-Bellevue-Everett PMSA, WA	H	57.93 FQ	70.33 MW	85.87 TQ	WABLS	3/16
	Wisconsin	Y	64940 FQ	77230 MW	108760 TQ	USBLS	5/15
	Madison MSA, WI	Y	64840 FQ	77060 MW	107680 TQ	USBLS	5/15
Computer and Information Systems Manager	Alabama	Y	76226 AE	123005 AW	146395 AEX	ALBLS	6/16
	Birmingham-Hoover MSA, AL	Y	74361 AE	122103 AW	145975 AEX	ALBLS	6/16
	Alaska	Y	95990 FQ	112980 MW	130940 TQ	USBLS	5/15
	Anchorage MSA, AK	Y	95630 FQ	113440 MW	132890 TQ	USBLS	5/15
	Arizona	Y	94500 FQ	125130 MW	160510 TQ	USBLS	5/15
	Phoenix-Mesa-Scottsdale MSA, AZ	Y	102220 FQ	132500 MW	167970 TQ	USBLS	5/15
	Tucson MSA, AZ	Y	76650 FQ	99070 MW	123470 TQ	USBLS	5/15
	Arkansas	Y	76920 FQ	99240 MW	137860 TQ	USBLS	5/15
	Little Rock-North Little Rock-Conway MSA, AR	Y	80920 FQ	97110 MW	124250 TQ	USBLS	5/15
	California	H	58.73 FQ	75.68 MW		CABLS	1/16-3/16
	Anaheim-Santa Ana-Irvine PMSA, CA	H	49.37 FQ	65.58 MW	82.48 TQ	CABLS	1/16-3/16
	Los Angeles-Long Beach-Glendale PMSA, CA	H	55.95 FQ	70.48 MW	88.62 TQ	CABLS	1/16-3/16
	Oakland-Hayward-Berkeley PMSA, CA	H	58.38 FQ	74.25 MW		CABLS	1/16-3/16
	Riverside-San Bernardino-Ontario MSA, CA	H	45.45 FQ	56.40 MW	64.24 TQ	CABLS	1/16-3/16
	Sacramento–Roseville–Arden-Arcade MSA, CA	H	51.01 FQ	56.34 MW	72.37 TQ	CABLS	1/16-3/16
	San Diego-Carlsbad MSA, CA	H	60.34 FQ	74.17 MW		CABLS	1/16-3/16
	San Francisco-Redwood City-South San Francisco PMSA, CA	H	69.01 FQ	83.47 MW		CABLS	1/16-3/16
	Colorado	Y	118690 FQ	146480 MW	182890 TQ	USBLS	5/15
	Denver-Aurora-Lakewood MSA, CO	Y	123900 FQ	149060 MW		USBLS	5/15
	Connecticut	Y		132114 MW		CTBLS	1/16-3/16
	Bridgeport-Stamford-Norwalk MSA, CT	Y	115730 FQ	142700 MW	172970 TQ	USBLS	5/15
	Hartford-West Hartford-East Hartford MSA, CT	Y	107660 FQ	132200 MW	164430 TQ	USBLS	5/15
	Delaware	Y	121870 FQ	150130 MW	183400 TQ	USBLS	5/15
	Wilmington PMSA, DE-MD-NJ	Y	123050 FQ	151520 MW	184820 TQ	USBLS	5/15
	District of Columbia	Y	131940 FQ	151490 MW	163700 TQ	USBLS	5/15
	Washington-Arlington-Alexandria PMSA, DC-VA-MD-WV	Y	133370 FQ	155690 MW	184200 TQ	USBLS	5/15
	Florida	H	45.16 AE	63.65 MW	80.06 AEX	FLBLS	7/16-9/16
	Fort Lauderdale-Pompano Beach-Deerfield Beach PMSA, FL	H	46.42 AE	66.90 MW	82.24 AEX	FLBLS	7/16-9/16

AE	Average entry wage	AWR	Average wage range	H	Hourly	LR	Low end range	MTC	Median total compensation	TCC	Total cash compensation
AEX	Average experienced wage	B	Biweekly	HI	Highest wage paid	M	Monthly	MW	Median wage paid	TQ	Third quartile wage
ATC	Average total compensation	D	Daily	HR	High end range	MCC	Median cash compensation	MWR	Median wage range	W	Weekly
AW	Average wage paid	FQ	First quartile wage	LO	Lowest wage paid	ME	Median entry wage	S	See annotated source	Y	Yearly

Occupation/Type/Industry	Location	Per	Low	Mid	High	Source	Date
Computer and Information Systems Manager							
	Miami-Miami Beach-Kendall PMSA, FL	H	47.17 AE	64.78 MW	81.50 AEX	FLBLS	7/16-9/16
	Orlando-Kissimmee-Sanford MSA, FL	H	44.13 AE	64.70 MW	83.43 AEX	FLBLS	7/16-9/16
	Tampa-St. Petersburg-Clearwater MSA, FL	H	46.86 AE	65.68 MW	85.46 AEX	FLBLS	7/16-9/16
	Georgia	Y	98290 FQ	123830 MW	154320 TQ	USBLS	5/15
	Atlanta-Sandy Springs-Roswell MSA, GA	Y	102710 FQ	127730 MW	157810 TQ	USBLS	5/15
	Augusta-Richmond County MSA, GA-SC	Y	80610 FQ	107090 MW	127600 TQ	USBLS	5/15
	Hawaii	Y	79720 FQ	99450 MW	126160 TQ	USBLS	5/15
	Urban Honolulu MSA, HI	Y	82530 FQ	101720 MW	127580 TQ	USBLS	5/15
	Idaho	Y	75950 FQ	98800 MW	124240 TQ	USBLS	5/15
	Boise City MSA, ID	Y	81640 FQ	105400 MW	127900 TQ	USBLS	5/15
	Illinois	Y	92840 FQ	122220 MW	155260 TQ	USBLS	5/15
	Chicago-Naperville-Arlington Heights PMSA, IL	Y	97040 FQ	125810 MW	158180 TQ	USBLS	5/15
	Lake County-Kenosha County PMSA, IL-WI	Y	107060 FQ	131720 MW	161400 TQ	USBLS	5/15
	Indiana	Y	84790 FQ	102140 MW	125570 TQ	USBLS	5/15
	Gary PMSA, IN	Y	80040 FQ	96660 MW	122360 TQ	USBLS	5/15
	Indianapolis-Carmel-Anderson MSA, IN	Y	87760 FQ	104360 MW	127770 TQ	USBLS	5/15
	Iowa	Y	92480 FQ	114500 MW	138290 TQ	USBLS	5/15
	Des Moines-West Des Moines MSA, IA	Y	101770 FQ	120090 MW	145360 TQ	USBLS	5/15
	Kansas	Y	81520 FQ	103300 MW	129900 TQ	USBLS	5/15
	Wichita MSA, KS	Y	78010 FQ	94150 MW	118080 TQ	USBLS	5/15
	Kentucky	Y	78210 FQ	100450 MW	129690 TQ	USBLS	5/15
	Louisville-Jefferson County MSA, KY-IN	Y	85800 FQ	110650 MW	139720 TQ	USBLS	5/15
	Louisiana	Y	68300 FQ	89800 MW	113170 TQ	USBLS	5/15
	Baton Rouge MSA, LA	Y	82810 FQ	95960 MW	113340 TQ	USBLS	5/15
	New Orleans-Metairie MSA, LA	Y	65520 FQ	92910 MW	128240 TQ	USBLS	5/15
	Maine	Y	79150 FQ	101720 MW	130910 TQ	USBLS	5/15
	Portland-South Portland MSA, ME	Y	87960 FQ	107680 MW	131090 TQ	USBLS	5/15
	Maryland	Y	97876 AE	144344 MW	167578 AEX	MDBLS	4/16
	Baltimore-Columbia-Towson MSA, MD	Y	108650 FQ	136320 MW	160620 TQ	USBLS	5/15
	Salisbury MSA, MD-DE	Y	106850 FQ	130080 MW	151780 TQ	USBLS	5/15
	Massachusetts	Y	107290 FQ	136290 MW	170140 TQ	USBLS	5/15
	Boston-Cambridge-Newton NECTA, MA	Y	109590 FQ	138540 MW	173190 TQ	USBLS	5/15
	Worcester MSA, MA-CT	Y	86710 FQ	111930 MW	137540 TQ	USBLS	5/15
	Michigan	Y	88060 FQ	104290 MW	131980 TQ	USBLS	5/15
	Detroit-Dearborn-Livonia PMSA, MI	Y	94460 FQ	120550 MW	155530 TQ	USBLS	5/15
	Grand Rapids-Wyoming MSA, MI	Y	81730 FQ	98120 MW	118680 TQ	USBLS	5/15
	Minnesota	Y	104923 FQ	127440 MW	155748 TQ	MNBLS	1/16-3/16
	Minneapolis-St. Paul-Bloomington MSA, MN-WI	Y	109363 FQ	130955 MW	158299 TQ	MNBLS	1/16-3/16
	Mississippi	Y	65440 FQ	79920 MW	105790 TQ	USBLS	5/15
	Jackson MSA, MS	Y	64520 FQ	76430 MW	98350 TQ	USBLS	5/15
	Missouri	Y	94960 FQ	120260 MW	148630 TQ	USBLS	5/15
	Kansas City MSA, MO-KS	Y	98220 FQ	119570 MW	145770 TQ	USBLS	5/15
	St. Louis MSA, MO-IL	Y	104220 FQ	127130 MW	154850 TQ	USBLS	5/15
	Montana	Y	79450 FQ	96330 MW	124300 TQ	USBLS	5/15
	Billings MSA, MT	Y	78590 FQ	99820 MW	122370 TQ	USBLS	5/15
	Nebraska	Y	86575 FQ	111860 MW	141190 TQ	NEBLS	7/16-9/16
	Omaha-Council Bluffs MSA, NE-IA	Y	92845 FQ	118060 MW	147865 TQ	NEBLS	7/16-9/16
	Nevada	Y	88610 FQ	109070 MW	139200 TQ	USBLS	5/15
	Las Vegas-Henderson-Paradise MSA, NV	Y	90640 FQ	114780 MW	147300 TQ	USBLS	5/15
	New Hampshire	H	42.82 AE	60.09 MW	76.26 AEX	NHBLS	6/16
	Manchester NECTA, NH	H	38.13 AE	57.62 MW	73.22 AEX	NHBLS	6/16
	Nashua NECTA, NH-MA	Y	105370 FQ	136410 MW	170040 TQ	USBLS	5/15

AE	Average entry wage	AWR	Average wage range	H	Hourly	LR	Low end range	MTC	Median total compensation	TCC	Total cash compensation
AEX	Average experienced wage	B	Biweekly	HI	Highest wage paid	M	Monthly	MW	Median wage paid	TQ	Third quartile wage
ATC	Average total compensation	D	Daily	HR	High end range	MCC	Median cash compensation	MWR	Median wage range	W	Weekly
AW	Average wage paid	FQ	First quartile wage	LO	Lowest wage paid	ME	Median entry wage	S	See annotated source	Y	Yearly

Occupation/Type/Industry	Location	Per	Low	Mid	High	Source	Date
Computer and Information Systems Manager							
	New Jersey	Y	121370 FQ	149100 MW	185720 TQ	USBLS	5/15
	Camden PMSA, NJ	Y	105870 FQ	124960 MW	155440 TQ	USBLS	5/15
	Newark PMSA, NJ-PA	Y	127120 FQ	153430 MW		USBLS	5/15
	Trenton MSA, NJ	Y	107600 FQ	129410 MW	168390 TQ	USBLS	5/15
	New Mexico	Y	79630 FQ	96810 MW	125750 TQ	USBLS	5/15
	Albuquerque MSA, NM	Y	80320 FQ	103340 MW	131490 TQ	USBLS	5/15
	New York	Y	102420 AE	155860 MW		NYBLS	1/16-3/16
	Buffalo-Cheektowaga-Niagara Falls MSA, NY	Y	90580 FQ	110130 MW	129020 TQ	USBLS	5/15
	Nassau County-Suffolk County PMSA, NY	Y	119710 FQ	147690 MW	179870 TQ	USBLS	5/15
	New York-Jersey City-White Plains PMSA, NY-NJ	Y	126350 FQ	163190 MW		USBLS	5/15
	Rochester MSA, NY	Y	90940 FQ	113610 MW	147030 TQ	USBLS	5/15
	North Carolina	Y	101010 FQ	126380 MW	155140 TQ	USBLS	5/15
	Charlotte-Concord-Gastonia MSA, NC-SC	Y	107020 FQ	132990 MW	160840 TQ	USBLS	5/15
	Raleigh MSA, NC	Y	101350 FQ	125800 MW	154180 TQ	USBLS	5/15
	North Dakota	Y	83100 FQ	98020 MW	120260 TQ	USBLS	5/15
	Fargo MSA, ND-MN	Y	86020 FQ	102470 MW	133570 TQ	USBLS	5/15
	Ohio	Y	92540 FQ	118320 MW	150370 TQ	USBLS	5/15
	Cincinnati MSA, OH-KY-IN	Y	95270 FQ	119460 MW	148680 TQ	USBLS	5/15
	Cleveland-Elyria MSA, OH	Y	95400 FQ	120300 MW	151980 TQ	USBLS	5/15
	Columbus MSA, OH	Y	96760 FQ	124960 MW	158660 TQ	USBLS	5/15
	Oklahoma	Y	73710 FQ	95250 MW	119470 TQ	USBLS	5/15
	Oklahoma City MSA, OK	Y	75270 FQ	96770 MW	118960 TQ	USBLS	5/15
	Tulsa MSA, OK	Y	79090 FQ	101510 MW	126580 TQ	USBLS	5/15
	Oregon	H	43.01 FQ	55.32 MW	70.68 TQ	ORBLS	2016
	Portland-Vancouver-Hillsboro MSA, OR-WA	Y	92070 FQ	118110 MW	151070 TQ	USBLS	5/15
	Pennsylvania	Y	103940 FQ	128330 MW	163020 TQ	USBLS	5/15
	Allentown-Bethlehem-Easton MSA, PA-NJ	Y	91620 FQ	124630 MW	164190 TQ	USBLS	5/15
	Harrisburg-Carlisle MSA, PA	Y	93850 FQ	112020 MW	132010 TQ	USBLS	5/15
	Montgomery County-Bucks County-Chester County PMSA, PA	Y	122150 FQ	149220 MW	183400 TQ	USBLS	5/15
	Philadelphia PMSA, PA	Y	112100 FQ	139480 MW	180840 TQ	USBLS	5/15
	Pittsburgh MSA, PA	Y	95890 FQ	117850 MW	147810 TQ	USBLS	5/15
	Rhode Island	Y	108820 FQ	135860 MW	155870 TQ	USBLS	5/15
	Providence-Warwick MSA, RI-MA	Y	107860 FQ	135410 MW	156120 TQ	USBLS	5/15
	South Carolina	Y	84260 FQ	108510 MW	138590 TQ	USBLS	5/15
	Charleston-North Charleston MSA, SC	Y	97520 FQ	118960 MW	150040 TQ	USBLS	5/15
	Columbia MSA, SC	Y	79790 FQ	105110 MW	133320 TQ	USBLS	5/15
	Greenville-Anderson-Mauldin MSA, SC	Y	85530 FQ	100830 MW	129890 TQ	USBLS	5/15
	South Dakota	Y	98520 FQ	118010 MW	142580 TQ	USBLS	5/15
	Sioux Falls MSA, SD	Y	103110 FQ	122240 MW	149300 TQ	USBLS	5/15
	Tennessee	Y	71260 FQ	99100 MW	131110 TQ	USBLS	5/15
	Knoxville MSA, TN	Y	73380 FQ	94870 MW	120350 TQ	USBLS	5/15
	Memphis MSA, TN-MS-AR	Y	82990 FQ	112310 MW	140250 TQ	USBLS	5/15
	Nashville-Davidson–Murfreesboro–Franklin MSA, TN	Y	69560 FQ	98220 MW	131870 TQ	USBLS	5/15
	Texas	Y	111820 FQ	140960 MW	172880 TQ	USBLS	5/15
	Austin-Round Rock MSA, TX	Y	118410 FQ	146200 MW	179280 TQ	USBLS	5/15
	Dallas-Plano-Irving PMSA, TX	Y	112990 FQ	141310 MW	166860 TQ	USBLS	5/15
	Fort Worth-Arlington PMSA, TX	Y	109390 FQ	146900 MW		USBLS	5/15
	Houston-The Woodlands-Sugar Land MSA, TX	Y	115910 FQ	143010 MW	176980 TQ	USBLS	5/15
	San Antonio-New Braunfels MSA, TX	Y	108150 FQ	137420 MW	169930 TQ	USBLS	5/15
	Utah	Y	91520 FQ	117120 MW	147160 TQ	USBLS	5/15
	Ogden-Clearfield MSA, UT	Y	101500 FQ	120560 MW	142800 TQ	USBLS	5/15
	Provo-Orem MSA, UT	Y	93180 FQ	121190 MW	152560 TQ	USBLS	5/15
	Salt Lake City MSA, UT	Y	91900 FQ	117020 MW	147120 TQ	USBLS	5/15
	Vermont	Y	92460 FQ	126160 MW	157020 TQ	USBLS	5/15

AE	Average entry wage	**AWR**	Average wage range	**H**	Hourly	
AEX	Average experienced wage	**B**	Biweekly	**HI**	Highest wage paid	
ATC	Average total compensation	**D**	Daily	**HR**	High end range	
AW	Average wage paid	**FQ**	First quartile wage	**LO**	Lowest wage paid	

LR	Low end range	**MTC**	Median total compensation	**TCC**	Total cash compensation
M	Monthly	**MW**	Median wage paid	**TQ**	Third quartile wage
MCC	Median cash compensation	**MWR**	Median wage range	**W**	Weekly
ME	Median entry wage	**S**	See annotated source	**Y**	Yearly

Occupation/Type/Industry	Location	Per	Low	Mid	High	Source	Date
Computer and Information Systems Manager	Burlington-South Burlington MSA, VT	Y	101190 FQ	134410 MW	168950 TQ	USBLS	5/15
	Virginia	Y	123140 FQ	151850 MW	185710 TQ	USBLS	5/15
	Richmond MSA, VA	Y	111660 FQ	137300 MW	162900 TQ	USBLS	5/15
	Virginia Beach-Norfolk-Newport News MSA, VA-NC	Y	105110 FQ	129260 MW	159270 TQ	USBLS	5/15
	Washington	H	54.82 FQ	68.55 MW	83.80 TQ	WABLS	3/16
	Seattle-Bellevue-Everett PMSA, WA	H	58.76 FQ	71.92 MW	87.49 TQ	WABLS	3/16
	Tacoma-Lakewood PMSA, WA	H	41.76 FQ	50.81 MW	61.85 TQ	WABLS	3/16
	West Virginia	Y	75630 FQ	102300 MW	132380 TQ	USBLS	5/15
	Huntington-Ashland MSA, WV-KY-OH	Y	72640 FQ	93830 MW	120310 TQ	USBLS	5/15
	Wisconsin	Y	87390 FQ	107340 MW	129840 TQ	USBLS	5/15
	Madison MSA, WI	Y	90940 FQ	107310 MW	127020 TQ	USBLS	5/15
	Milwaukee-Waukesha-West Allis MSA, WI	Y	92580 FQ	113930 MW	138290 TQ	USBLS	5/15
	Wyoming	Y	73280 FQ	86420 MW	100640 TQ	USBLS	5/15
	Cheyenne MSA, WY	Y	73290 FQ	85890 MW	96030 TQ	USBLS	5/15
	Puerto Rico	Y	50960 FQ	67920 MW	95340 TQ	USBLS	5/15
	San Juan-Carolina-Caguas MSA, PR	Y	53140 FQ	69800 MW	96840 TQ	USBLS	5/15
	Virgin Islands	Y	52850 FQ	66980 MW	77560 TQ	USBLS	5/15
	Guam	Y	54500 FQ	64120 MW	76690 TQ	USBLS	5/15
Computer-Controlled Machine Tool Operator							
Metals and Plastics	Alabama	Y	25932 AE	36111 AW	41190 AEX	ALBLS	6/16
Metals and Plastics	Birmingham-Hoover MSA, AL	Y	25243 AE	34764 AW	39514 AEX	ALBLS	6/16
Metals and Plastics	Arizona	Y	32880 FQ	39690 MW	47640 TQ	USBLS	5/15
Metals and Plastics	Phoenix-Mesa-Scottsdale MSA, AZ	Y	33310 FQ	40800 MW	48460 TQ	USBLS	5/15
Metals and Plastics	Tucson MSA, AZ	Y	31500 FQ	35680 MW	40220 TQ	USBLS	5/15
Metals and Plastics	Arkansas	Y	26050 FQ	36310 MW	44950 TQ	USBLS	5/15
Metals and Plastics	Little Rock-North Little Rock-Conway MSA, AR	Y	25360 FQ	36140 MW	45710 TQ	USBLS	5/15
Metals and Plastics	California	H	14.10 FQ	18.27 MW	23.92 TQ	CABLS	1/16-3/16
Metals and Plastics	Anaheim-Santa Ana-Irvine PMSA, CA	H	13.84 FQ	17.64 MW	22.83 TQ	CABLS	1/16-3/16
Metals and Plastics	Los Angeles-Long Beach-Glendale PMSA, CA	H	13.26 FQ	17.16 MW	23.16 TQ	CABLS	1/16-3/16
Metals and Plastics	Oakland-Hayward-Berkeley PMSA, CA	H	15.06 FQ	20.06 MW	26.99 TQ	CABLS	1/16-3/16
Metals and Plastics	Riverside-San Bernardino-Ontario MSA, CA	H	13.50 FQ	17.76 MW	24.73 TQ	CABLS	1/16-3/16
Metals and Plastics	Sacramento–Roseville–Arden-Arcade MSA, CA	H	15.46 FQ	18.15 MW	22.77 TQ	CABLS	1/16-3/16
Metals and Plastics	San Diego-Carlsbad MSA, CA	H	16.42 FQ	21.21 MW	25.50 TQ	CABLS	1/16-3/16
Metals and Plastics	San Francisco-Redwood City-South San Francisco PMSA, CA	H	17.94 FQ	22.18 MW	26.58 TQ	CABLS	1/16-3/16
Metals and Plastics	Colorado	Y	26610 FQ	37040 MW	50110 TQ	USBLS	5/15
Metals and Plastics	Denver-Aurora-Lakewood MSA, CO	Y	27420 FQ	36940 MW	52490 TQ	USBLS	5/15
Metals and Plastics	Connecticut	Y		44852 MW		CTBLS	1/16-3/16
Metals and Plastics	Bridgeport-Stamford-Norwalk MSA, CT	Y	38800 FQ	55180 MW	61020 TQ	USBLS	5/15
Metals and Plastics	Hartford-West Hartford-East Hartford MSA, CT	Y	34340 FQ	42420 MW	51200 TQ	USBLS	5/15
Metals and Plastics	Wilmington PMSA, DE-MD-NJ	Y	35430 FQ	45780 MW	55520 TQ	USBLS	5/15
Metals and Plastics	Washington-Arlington-Alexandria PMSA, DC-VA-MD-WV	Y	36040 FQ	43360 MW	52470 TQ	USBLS	5/15
Metals and Plastics	Florida	H	12.88 AE	17.61 MW	20.57 AEX	FLBLS	7/16-9/16
Metals and Plastics	Fort Lauderdale-Pompano Beach-Deerfield Beach PMSA, FL	H	11.04 AE	16.59 MW	19.23 AEX	FLBLS	7/16-9/16
Metals and Plastics	Miami-Miami Beach-Kendall PMSA, FL	H	11.04 AE	16.09 MW	19.10 AEX	FLBLS	7/16-9/16

AE Average entry wage	**AWR** Average wage range	**H** Hourly	**LR** Low end range	**MTC** Median total compensation	**TCC** Total cash compensation
AEX Average experienced wage	**B** Biweekly	**HI** Highest wage paid	**M** Monthly	**MW** Median wage paid	**TQ** Third quartile wage
ATC Average total compensation	**D** Daily	**HR** High end range	**MCC** Median cash compensation	**MWR** Median wage range	**W** Weekly
AW Average wage paid	**FQ** First quartile wage	**LO** Lowest wage paid	**ME** Median entry wage	**S** See annotated source	**Y** Yearly

Occupation/Type/Industry	Location	Per	Low	Mid	High	Source	Date
Computer-Controlled Machine Tool Operator							
Metals and Plastics	Orlando-Kissimmee-Sanford MSA, FL	H	14.12 AE	18.47 MW	20.52 AEX	FLBLS	7/16-9/16
Metals and Plastics	Tampa-St. Petersburg-Clearwater MSA, FL	H	11.85 AE	16.07 MW	18.70 AEX	FLBLS	7/16-9/16
Metals and Plastics	Georgia	Y	27060 FQ	33390 MW	42790 TQ	USBLS	5/15
Metals and Plastics	Atlanta-Sandy Springs-Roswell MSA, GA	Y	27470 FQ	32590 MW	39990 TQ	USBLS	5/15
Metals and Plastics	Augusta-Richmond County MSA, GA-SC	Y	37050 FQ	42600 MW	46700 TQ	USBLS	5/15
Metals and Plastics	Idaho	Y	23590 FQ	28510 MW	35970 TQ	USBLS	5/15
Metals and Plastics	Boise City MSA, ID	Y	26880 FQ	32660 MW	43940 TQ	USBLS	5/15
Metals and Plastics	Illinois	Y	31010 FQ	37730 MW	47170 TQ	USBLS	5/15
Metals and Plastics	Chicago-Naperville-Arlington Heights PMSA, IL	Y	30720 FQ	36870 MW	45990 TQ	USBLS	5/15
Metals and Plastics	Lake County-Kenosha County PMSA, IL-WI	Y	31230 FQ	40390 MW	47170 TQ	USBLS	5/15
Metals and Plastics	Indiana	Y	27500 FQ	32290 MW	39310 TQ	USBLS	5/15
Metals and Plastics	Gary PMSA, IN	Y	32420 FQ	39470 MW	46950 TQ	USBLS	5/15
Metals and Plastics	Indianapolis-Carmel-Anderson MSA, IN	Y	29460 FQ	34610 MW	39680 TQ	USBLS	5/15
Metals and Plastics	Iowa	Y	31680 FQ	35560 MW	39620 TQ	USBLS	5/15
Metals and Plastics	Des Moines-West Des Moines MSA, IA	Y	27480 FQ	31080 MW	38070 TQ	USBLS	5/15
Metals and Plastics	Kansas	Y	28350 FQ	34180 MW	40310 TQ	USBLS	5/15
Metals and Plastics	Wichita MSA, KS	Y	29070 FQ	35020 MW	41560 TQ	USBLS	5/15
Metals and Plastics	Kentucky	Y	30110 FQ	37060 MW	45700 TQ	USBLS	5/15
Metals and Plastics	Louisville-Jefferson County MSA, KY-IN	Y	28250 FQ	34780 MW	41330 TQ	USBLS	5/15
Metals and Plastics	Louisiana	Y	31930 FQ	39710 MW	47430 TQ	USBLS	5/15
Metals and Plastics	Baton Rouge MSA, LA	Y	31650 FQ	39650 MW	46070 TQ	USBLS	5/15
Metals and Plastics	New Orleans-Metairie MSA, LA	Y	34050 FQ	44050 MW	60630 TQ	USBLS	5/15
Metals and Plastics	Maine	Y	33820 FQ	43880 MW	55050 TQ	USBLS	5/15
Metals and Plastics	Portland-South Portland MSA, ME	Y	33320 FQ	36920 MW	42330 TQ	USBLS	5/15
Metals and Plastics	Maryland	Y	29056 AE	43595 MW	50865 AEX	MDBLS	4/16
Metals and Plastics	Baltimore-Columbia-Towson MSA, MD	Y	33250 FQ	43870 MW	54430 TQ	USBLS	5/15
Metals and Plastics	Massachusetts	Y	35280 FQ	43450 MW	52760 TQ	USBLS	5/15
Metals and Plastics	Boston-Cambridge-Newton NECTA, MA	Y	38850 FQ	46270 MW	57040 TQ	USBLS	5/15
Metals and Plastics	Worcester MSA, MA-CT	Y	32260 FQ	38580 MW	49020 TQ	USBLS	5/15
Metals and Plastics	Michigan	Y	25530 FQ	34530 MW	45730 TQ	USBLS	5/15
Metals and Plastics	Detroit-Dearborn-Livonia PMSA, MI	Y	24420 FQ	32600 MW	46680 TQ	USBLS	5/15
Metals and Plastics	Grand Rapids-Wyoming MSA, MI	Y	26120 FQ	36560 MW	48030 TQ	USBLS	5/15
Metals and Plastics	Minnesota	Y	31902 FQ	38058 MW	48496 TQ	MNBLS	1/16-3/16
Metals and Plastics	Minneapolis-St. Paul-Bloomington MSA, MN-WI	Y	32783 FQ	40083 MW	51969 TQ	MNBLS	1/16-3/16
Metals and Plastics	Mississippi	Y	34340 FQ	39690 MW	46150 TQ	USBLS	5/15
Metals and Plastics	Jackson MSA, MS	Y	32620 FQ	35860 MW	39100 TQ	USBLS	5/15
Metals and Plastics	Missouri	Y	28560 FQ	34970 MW	44670 TQ	USBLS	5/15
Metals and Plastics	Kansas City MSA, MO-KS	Y	29840 FQ	37570 MW	48830 TQ	USBLS	5/15
Metals and Plastics	St. Louis MSA, MO-IL	Y	30810 FQ	39680 MW	48390 TQ	USBLS	5/15
Metals and Plastics	Montana	Y	32740 FQ	37590 MW	45530 TQ	USBLS	5/15
Metals and Plastics	Nebraska	Y	28620 FQ	34785 MW	41325 TQ	NEBLS	7/16-9/16
Metals and Plastics	Omaha-Council Bluffs MSA, NE-IA	Y	25010 FQ	30235 MW	36880 TQ	NEBLS	7/16-9/16
Metals and Plastics	Nevada	Y	25960 FQ	33260 MW	40790 TQ	USBLS	5/15
Metals and Plastics	Las Vegas-Henderson-Paradise MSA, NV	Y	23920 FQ	28880 MW	36050 TQ	USBLS	5/15
Metals and Plastics	New Hampshire	H	13.33 AE	17.82 MW	20.73 AEX	NHBLS	6/16
Metals and Plastics	Nashua NECTA, NH-MA	Y	30370 FQ	38560 MW	47710 TQ	USBLS	5/15
Metals and Plastics	New Jersey	Y	33430 FQ	42850 MW	53510 TQ	USBLS	5/15
Metals and Plastics	Camden PMSA, NJ	Y	38570 FQ	47290 MW	56420 TQ	USBLS	5/15
Metals and Plastics	Newark PMSA, NJ-PA	Y	31870 FQ	39070 MW	49810 TQ	USBLS	5/15
Metals and Plastics	New Mexico	Y	20180 FQ	24700 MW	31440 TQ	USBLS	5/15
Metals and Plastics	Albuquerque MSA, NM	Y	19790 FQ	25110 MW	32710 TQ	USBLS	5/15
Metals and Plastics	New York	Y	25860 AE	36020 MW	43570 AEX	NYBLS	1/16-3/16

AE	Average entry wage	AWR	Average wage range	H	Hourly
AEX	Average experienced wage	B	Biweekly	HI	Highest wage paid
ATC	Average total compensation	D	Daily	HR	High end range
AW	Average wage paid	FQ	First quartile wage	LO	Lowest wage paid

LR	Low end range	MTC	Median total compensation	TCC	Total cash compensation
M	Monthly	MW	Median wage paid	TQ	Third quartile wage
MCC	Median cash compensation	MWR	Median wage range	W	Weekly
ME	Median entry wage	S	See annotated source	Y	Yearly

Occupation/Type/Industry	Location	Per	Low	Mid	High	Source	Date
Computer-Controlled Machine Tool Operator							
Metals and Plastics	Buffalo-Cheektowaga-Niagara Falls MSA, NY	Y	27790 FQ	37530 MW	46950 TQ	USBLS	5/15
Metals and Plastics	Nassau County-Suffolk County PMSA, NY	Y	31290 FQ	36730 MW	46200 TQ	USBLS	5/15
Metals and Plastics	New York-Jersey City-White Plains PMSA, NY-NJ	Y	30670 FQ	43200 MW	55200 TQ	USBLS	5/15
Metals and Plastics	Rochester MSA, NY	Y	27470 FQ	34810 MW	47530 TQ	USBLS	5/15
Metals and Plastics	North Carolina	Y	30970 FQ	38690 MW	49370 TQ	USBLS	5/15
Metals and Plastics	Charlotte-Concord-Gastonia MSA, NC-SC	Y	28850 FQ	35540 MW	44660 TQ	USBLS	5/15
Metals and Plastics	Raleigh MSA, NC	Y	30370 FQ	38370 MW	45420 TQ	USBLS	5/15
Metals and Plastics	North Dakota	Y	41590 FQ	44940 MW	48290 TQ	USBLS	5/15
Metals and Plastics	Ohio	Y	29460 FQ	36830 MW	45190 TQ	USBLS	5/15
Metals and Plastics	Cincinnati MSA, OH-KY-IN	Y	31060 FQ	39840 MW	48910 TQ	USBLS	5/15
Metals and Plastics	Cleveland-Elyria MSA, OH	Y	28320 FQ	36460 MW	45530 TQ	USBLS	5/15
Metals and Plastics	Columbus MSA, OH	Y	33410 FQ	38290 MW	44140 TQ	USBLS	5/15
Metals and Plastics	Oklahoma	Y	31030 FQ	36940 MW	45210 TQ	USBLS	5/15
Metals and Plastics	Oklahoma City MSA, OK	Y	30220 FQ	35700 MW	42720 TQ	USBLS	5/15
Metals and Plastics	Tulsa MSA, OK	Y	32370 FQ	39920 MW	48980 TQ	USBLS	5/15
Metals and Plastics	Oregon	H	14.38 FQ	18.19 MW	22.97 TQ	ORBLS	2016
Metals and Plastics	Portland-Vancouver-Hillsboro MSA, OR-WA	Y	28620 FQ	37040 MW	46870 TQ	USBLS	5/15
Metals and Plastics	Pennsylvania	Y	30180 FQ	36900 MW	45040 TQ	USBLS	5/15
Metals and Plastics	Allentown-Bethlehem-Easton MSA, PA-NJ	Y	29320 FQ	38090 MW	45360 TQ	USBLS	5/15
Metals and Plastics	Harrisburg-Carlisle MSA, PA	Y	26700 FQ	30440 MW	36110 TQ	USBLS	5/15
Metals and Plastics	Montgomery County-Bucks County-Chester County PMSA, PA	Y	32600 FQ	42050 MW	49060 TQ	USBLS	5/15
Metals and Plastics	Philadelphia PMSA, PA	Y	31050 FQ	36530 MW	44170 TQ	USBLS	5/15
Metals and Plastics	Pittsburgh MSA, PA	Y	31670 FQ	36810 MW	44070 TQ	USBLS	5/15
Metals and Plastics	Rhode Island	Y	29970 FQ	38090 MW	49330 TQ	USBLS	5/15
Metals and Plastics	Providence-Warwick MSA, RI-MA	Y	28720 FQ	37810 MW	48370 TQ	USBLS	5/15
Metals and Plastics	South Carolina	Y	32340 FQ	37650 MW	44370 TQ	USBLS	5/15
Metals and Plastics	Charleston-North Charleston MSA, SC	Y	34570 FQ	39800 MW	45800 TQ	USBLS	5/15
Metals and Plastics	Columbia MSA, SC	Y	32000 FQ	35850 MW	39840 TQ	USBLS	5/15
Metals and Plastics	Greenville-Anderson-Mauldin MSA, SC	Y	29660 FQ	36930 MW	44060 TQ	USBLS	5/15
Metals and Plastics	South Dakota	Y	31710 FQ	36260 MW	41870 TQ	USBLS	5/15
Metals and Plastics	Sioux Falls MSA, SD	Y	34820 FQ	39220 MW	45000 TQ	USBLS	5/15
Metals and Plastics	Tennessee	Y	28130 FQ	36190 MW	46310 TQ	USBLS	5/15
Metals and Plastics	Knoxville MSA, TN	Y	29240 FQ	36460 MW	44750 TQ	USBLS	5/15
Metals and Plastics	Memphis MSA, TN-MS-AR	Y	34490 FQ	44780 MW	57420 TQ	USBLS	5/15
Metals and Plastics	Nashville-Davidson–Murfreesboro–Franklin MSA, TN	Y	28170 FQ	41710 MW	51460 TQ	USBLS	5/15
Metals and Plastics	Texas	Y	28880 FQ	37640 MW	48130 TQ	USBLS	5/15
Metals and Plastics	Austin-Round Rock MSA, TX	Y	27360 FQ	32320 MW	41010 TQ	USBLS	5/15
Metals and Plastics	Dallas-Plano-Irving PMSA, TX	Y	27460 FQ	35770 MW	48710 TQ	USBLS	5/15
Metals and Plastics	Fort Worth-Arlington PMSA, TX	Y	32910 FQ	40080 MW	47920 TQ	USBLS	5/15
Metals and Plastics	Houston-The Woodlands-Sugar Land MSA, TX	Y	29310 FQ	39830 MW	51320 TQ	USBLS	5/15
Metals and Plastics	San Antonio-New Braunfels MSA, TX	Y	25690 FQ	28950 MW	34300 TQ	USBLS	5/15
Metals and Plastics	Utah	Y	28920 FQ	34860 MW	42840 TQ	USBLS	5/15
Metals and Plastics	Ogden-Clearfield MSA, UT	Y	29020 FQ	36690 MW	47210 TQ	USBLS	5/15
Metals and Plastics	Provo-Orem MSA, UT	Y	33980 FQ	37620 MW	47870 TQ	USBLS	5/15
Metals and Plastics	Salt Lake City MSA, UT	Y	28790 FQ	34180 MW	40850 TQ	USBLS	5/15
Metals and Plastics	Vermont	Y	42050 FQ	55190 MW	60140 TQ	USBLS	5/15
Metals and Plastics	Burlington-South Burlington MSA, VT	Y	32320 FQ	38290 MW	47060 TQ	USBLS	5/15
Metals and Plastics	Virginia	Y	30490 FQ	38380 MW	46770 TQ	USBLS	5/15
Metals and Plastics	Richmond MSA, VA	Y	30920 FQ	37390 MW	46500 TQ	USBLS	5/15
Metals and Plastics	Virginia Beach-Norfolk-Newport News MSA, VA-NC	Y	25940 FQ	34580 MW	45380 TQ	USBLS	5/15
Metals and Plastics	Washington	H	17.82 FQ	26.42 MW	40.89 TQ	WABLS	3/16
Metals and Plastics	West Virginia	Y	33620 FQ	41660 MW	47420 TQ	USBLS	5/15

AE	Average entry wage	AWR	Average wage range	H	Hourly	LR	Low end range	MTC	Median total compensation	TCC	Total cash compensation
AEX	Average experienced wage	B	Biweekly	HI	Highest wage paid	M	Monthly	MW	Median wage paid	TQ	Third quartile wage
ATC	Average total compensation	D	Daily	HR	High end range	MCC	Median cash compensation	MWR	Median wage range	W	Weekly
AW	Average wage paid	FQ	First quartile wage	LO	Lowest wage paid	ME	Median entry wage	S	See annotated source	Y	Yearly

282

Occupation/Type/Industry	Location	Per	Low	Mid	High	Source	Date
Computer-Controlled Machine Tool Operator							
Metals and Plastics	Huntington-Ashland MSA, WV-KY-OH	Y	29700 FQ	36650 MW	44960 TQ	USBLS	5/15
Metals and Plastics	Wisconsin	Y	31760 FQ	38300 MW	46880 TQ	USBLS	5/15
Metals and Plastics	Madison MSA, WI	Y	28270 FQ	34010 MW	40550 TQ	USBLS	5/15
Metals and Plastics	Milwaukee-Waukesha-West Allis MSA, WI	Y	33640 FQ	40030 MW	48960 TQ	USBLS	5/15
Computer Forensic Examiner							
Police Department, Municipal Government	Bakersfield, CA	Y			46164 HI	CACIT	6/28/16
Computer Forensic Specialist							
Attorney General's Office, State Government	Ohio	H	23.31 LO		41.25 HI	OHGOV	2015
Computer Graphics Designer							
Cable TV, Municipal Government	El Segundo, CA	Y			74469 HI	CACIT	6/28/16
Computer Hardware Engineer	Alabama	Y	78417 AE	109863 AW	125591 AEX	ALBLS	6/16
	Birmingham-Hoover MSA, AL	Y	67112 AE	96785 AW	111626 AEX	ALBLS	6/16
	Alaska	Y	87700 FQ	105730 MW	119490 TQ	USBLS	5/15
	Anchorage MSA, AK	Y	87320 FQ	103620 MW	119730 TQ	USBLS	5/15
	Arizona	Y	85540 FQ	107120 MW	129530 TQ	USBLS	5/15
	Phoenix-Mesa-Scottsdale MSA, AZ	Y	88640 FQ	108910 MW	132280 TQ	USBLS	5/15
	Tucson MSA, AZ	Y	68190 FQ	74700 MW	90820 TQ	USBLS	5/15
	Arkansas	Y	54580 FQ	69880 MW	89760 TQ	USBLS	5/15
	Little Rock-North Little Rock-Conway MSA, AR	Y	57930 FQ	73690 MW	94640 TQ	USBLS	5/15
	California	H	50.27 FQ	63.40 MW	76.43 TQ	CABLS	1/16-3/16
	Anaheim-Santa Ana-Irvine PMSA, CA	H	49.05 FQ	61.70 MW	74.91 TQ	CABLS	1/16-3/16
	Los Angeles-Long Beach-Glendale PMSA, CA	H	40.10 FQ	53.34 MW	68.23 TQ	CABLS	1/16-3/16
	Oakland-Hayward-Berkeley PMSA, CA	H	37.97 FQ	53.96 MW	71.89 TQ	CABLS	1/16-3/16
	Riverside-San Bernardino-Ontario MSA, CA	H	41.69 FQ	48.80 MW	58.95 TQ	CABLS	1/16-3/16
	Sacramento–Roseville–Arden-Arcade MSA, CA	H	44.96 FQ	56.07 MW	68.59 TQ	CABLS	1/16-3/16
	San Diego-Carlsbad MSA, CA	H	45.06 FQ	55.42 MW	67.80 TQ	CABLS	1/16-3/16
	San Francisco-Redwood City-South San Francisco PMSA, CA	H	53.85 FQ	67.83 MW	79.26 TQ	CABLS	1/16-3/16
	Colorado	Y	84060 FQ	108120 MW	130300 TQ	USBLS	5/15
	Denver-Aurora-Lakewood MSA, CO	Y	75170 FQ	99010 MW	120330 TQ	USBLS	5/15
	Connecticut	Y		104472 MW		CTBLS	1/16-3/16
	Bridgeport-Stamford-Norwalk MSA, CT	Y	84610 FQ	102890 MW	123530 TQ	USBLS	5/15
	Hartford-West Hartford-East Hartford MSA, CT	Y	74290 FQ	106670 MW	132500 TQ	USBLS	5/15
	District of Columbia	Y	86790 FQ	111610 MW	126750 TQ	USBLS	5/15
	Washington-Arlington-Alexandria PMSA, DC-VA-MD-WV	Y	99870 FQ	118070 MW	139520 TQ	USBLS	5/15
	Florida	H	29.67 AE	45.23 MW	52.81 AEX	FLBLS	7/16-9/16
	Fort Lauderdale-Pompano Beach-Deerfield Beach PMSA, FL	H	41.37 AE	52.64 MW	65.47 AEX	FLBLS	7/16-9/16
	Miami-Miami Beach-Kendall PMSA, FL	H	33.63 AE	47.83 MW	57.53 AEX	FLBLS	7/16-9/16
	Orlando-Kissimmee-Sanford MSA, FL	H	36.69 AE	47.11 MW	53.45 AEX	FLBLS	7/16-9/16
	Tampa-St. Petersburg-Clearwater MSA, FL	H	34.89 AE	46.14 MW	51.37 AEX	FLBLS	7/16-9/16
	Georgia	Y	65420 FQ	97960 MW	118080 TQ	USBLS	5/15
	Atlanta-Sandy Springs-Roswell MSA, GA	Y	65410 FQ	98580 MW	118390 TQ	USBLS	5/15
	Hawaii	Y	57680 FQ	70780 MW	101830 TQ	USBLS	5/15
	Urban Honolulu MSA, HI	Y	57310 FQ	68840 MW	101000 TQ	USBLS	5/15

AE	Average entry wage	AWR	Average wage range	H	Hourly
AEX	Average experienced wage	B	Biweekly	HI	Highest wage paid
ATC	Average total compensation	D	Daily	HR	High end range
AW	Average wage paid	FQ	First quartile wage	LO	Lowest wage paid

LR	Low end range	MTC	Median total compensation
M	Monthly	MW	Median wage paid
MCC	Median cash compensation	MWR	Median wage range
ME	Median entry wage	S	See annotated source

TCC	Total cash compensation
TQ	Third quartile wage
W	Weekly
Y	Yearly

Occupation/Type/Industry	Location	Per	Low	Mid	High	Source	Date
Computer Hardware Engineer	Idaho	Y	81770 FQ	98110 MW	118780 TQ	USBLS	5/15
	Boise City MSA, ID	Y	82210 FQ	98620 MW	118850 TQ	USBLS	5/15
	Illinois	Y	68580 FQ	89420 MW	110890 TQ	USBLS	5/15
	Chicago-Naperville-Arlington Heights PMSA, IL	Y	76820 FQ	94860 MW	118460 TQ	USBLS	5/15
	Lake County-Kenosha County PMSA, IL-WI	Y	56320 FQ	64540 MW	93100 TQ	USBLS	5/15
	Indiana	Y	65610 FQ	79000 MW	98470 TQ	USBLS	5/15
	Indianapolis-Carmel-Anderson MSA, IN	Y	65930 FQ	76080 MW	104060 TQ	USBLS	5/15
	Iowa	Y	75560 FQ	97170 MW	122330 TQ	USBLS	5/15
	Des Moines-West Des Moines MSA, IA	Y	78940 FQ	111100 MW	138270 TQ	USBLS	5/15
	Kansas	Y	82690 FQ	94400 MW	110270 TQ	USBLS	5/15
	Kentucky	Y	74090 FQ	98890 MW	121290 TQ	USBLS	5/15
	Louisville-Jefferson County MSA, KY-IN	Y	37610 FQ	65970 MW	103830 TQ	USBLS	5/15
	Louisiana	Y	64600 FQ	80880 MW	101410 TQ	USBLS	5/15
	Baton Rouge MSA, LA	Y	70850 FQ	89000 MW	101560 TQ	USBLS	5/15
	New Orleans-Metairie MSA, LA	Y	69990 FQ	89300 MW	108810 TQ	USBLS	5/15
	Maryland	Y	82068 AE	118846 MW	137235 AEX	MDBLS	4/16
	Baltimore-Columbia-Towson MSA, MD	Y	97830 FQ	120430 MW	149670 TQ	USBLS	5/15
	Massachusetts	Y	87400 FQ	112470 MW	138050 TQ	USBLS	5/15
	Boston-Cambridge-Newton NECTA, MA	Y	89150 FQ	113820 MW	138730 TQ	USBLS	5/15
	Worcester MSA, MA-CT	Y	77240 FQ	119010 MW	138890 TQ	USBLS	5/15
	Michigan	Y	62190 FQ	88530 MW	112630 TQ	USBLS	5/15
	Detroit-Dearborn-Livonia PMSA, MI	Y	58420 FQ	83870 MW	99930 TQ	USBLS	5/15
	Grand Rapids-Wyoming MSA, MI	Y	81070 FQ	98790 MW	115360 TQ	USBLS	5/15
	Minnesota	Y	78467 FQ	104011 MW	124031 TQ	MNBLS	1/16-3/16
	Minneapolis-St. Paul-Bloomington MSA, MN-WI	Y	78467 FQ	106380 MW	125704 TQ	MNBLS	1/16-3/16
	Mississippi	Y	56600 FQ	79310 MW	124070 TQ	USBLS	5/15
	Jackson MSA, MS	Y	46290 FQ	77850 MW	137320 TQ	USBLS	5/15
	Missouri	Y	77990 FQ	102330 MW	116910 TQ	USBLS	5/15
	Kansas City MSA, MO-KS	Y	74740 FQ	94100 MW	120080 TQ	USBLS	5/15
	St. Louis MSA, MO-IL	Y	81900 FQ	102960 MW	113970 TQ	USBLS	5/15
	Nebraska	Y	66750 FQ	79015 MW	95625 TQ	NEBLS	7/16-9/16
	Omaha-Council Bluffs MSA, NE-IA	Y	67205 FQ	79680 MW	96305 TQ	NEBLS	7/16-9/16
	Nevada	Y	67170 FQ	76250 MW	109130 TQ	USBLS	5/15
	Las Vegas-Henderson-Paradise MSA, NV	Y	66360 FQ	74220 MW	83230 TQ	USBLS	5/15
	New Hampshire	H	37.18 AE	55.76 MW	72.80 AEX	NHBLS	6/16
	Nashua NECTA, NH-MA	Y	90330 FQ	115510 MW	141570 TQ	USBLS	5/15
	New Jersey	Y	86960 FQ	101400 MW	122370 TQ	USBLS	5/15
	Camden PMSA, NJ	Y	78070 FQ	95370 MW	132870 TQ	USBLS	5/15
	Newark PMSA, NJ-PA	Y	88360 FQ	102880 MW	121610 TQ	USBLS	5/15
	New Mexico	Y	77210 FQ	96150 MW	116630 TQ	USBLS	5/15
	Albuquerque MSA, NM	Y	76310 FQ	100150 MW	118940 TQ	USBLS	5/15
	New York	Y	72890 AE	106850 MW	126290 AEX	NYBLS	1/16-3/16
	Nassau County-Suffolk County PMSA, NY	Y	64300 FQ	90050 MW	118740 TQ	USBLS	5/15
	New York-Jersey City-White Plains PMSA, NY-NJ	Y	86500 FQ	109800 MW	135950 TQ	USBLS	5/15
	Rochester MSA, NY	Y	83280 FQ	101050 MW	122290 TQ	USBLS	5/15
	North Carolina	Y	66620 FQ	88800 MW	114700 TQ	USBLS	5/15
	Charlotte-Concord-Gastonia MSA, NC-SC	Y	72510 FQ	89990 MW	112170 TQ	USBLS	5/15
	Raleigh MSA, NC	Y	82300 FQ	100070 MW	120380 TQ	USBLS	5/15
	Ohio	Y	69550 FQ	88850 MW	102070 TQ	USBLS	5/15
	Cincinnati MSA, OH-KY-IN	Y	46780 FQ	61860 MW	94820 TQ	USBLS	5/15
	Cleveland-Elyria MSA, OH	Y	62490 FQ	88430 MW	99750 TQ	USBLS	5/15
	Columbus MSA, OH	Y	77610 FQ	94830 MW	138690 TQ	USBLS	5/15
	Oklahoma	Y	85270 FQ	105420 MW	121630 TQ	USBLS	5/15
	Oklahoma City MSA, OK	Y	99210 FQ	108650 MW	125550 TQ	USBLS	5/15
	Tulsa MSA, OK	Y	88030 FQ	99790 MW	117870 TQ	USBLS	5/15
	Pennsylvania	Y	56220 FQ	90310 MW	115770 TQ	USBLS	5/15

AE	Average entry wage	AWR	Average wage range	H	Hourly	LR	Low end range	MTC	Median total compensation	TCC	Total cash compensation
AEX	Average experienced wage	B	Biweekly	HI	Highest wage paid	M	Monthly	MW	Median wage paid	TQ	Third quartile wage
ATC	Average total compensation	D	Daily	HR	High end range	MCC	Median cash compensation	MWR	Median wage range	W	Weekly
AW	Average wage paid	FQ	First quartile wage	LO	Lowest wage paid	ME	Median entry wage	S	See annotated source	Y	Yearly

Occupation/Type/Industry	Location	Per	Low	Mid	High	Source	Date
Computer Hardware Engineer	Allentown-Bethlehem-Easton MSA, PA-NJ	Y	55860 FQ	75130 MW	141120 TQ	USBLS	5/15
	Montgomery County-Bucks County-Chester County PMSA, PA	Y	68990 FQ	99280 MW	118640 TQ	USBLS	5/15
	Philadelphia PMSA, PA	Y	82190 FQ	103890 MW	115760 TQ	USBLS	5/15
	Pittsburgh MSA, PA	Y	36730 FQ	57690 MW	107970 TQ	USBLS	5/15
	Rhode Island	Y	75900 FQ	93870 MW	112330 TQ	USBLS	5/15
	Providence-Warwick MSA, RI-MA	Y	72500 FQ	91150 MW	111230 TQ	USBLS	5/15
	South Carolina	Y	70590 FQ	87920 MW	106330 TQ	USBLS	5/15
	Columbia MSA, SC	Y	55640 FQ	68810 MW	95990 TQ	USBLS	5/15
	Tennessee	Y	68850 FQ	84720 MW	103720 TQ	USBLS	5/15
	Knoxville MSA, TN	Y	78610 FQ	95940 MW	124010 TQ	USBLS	5/15
	Nashville-Davidson–Murfreesboro–Franklin MSA, TN	Y	71210 FQ	84360 MW	99870 TQ	USBLS	5/15
	Texas	Y	84550 FQ	105890 MW	127730 TQ	USBLS	5/15
	Austin-Round Rock MSA, TX	Y	86180 FQ	103710 MW	127330 TQ	USBLS	5/15
	Dallas-Plano-Irving PMSA, TX	Y	81590 FQ	109570 MW	131090 TQ	USBLS	5/15
	Fort Worth-Arlington PMSA, TX	Y	86640 FQ	100610 MW	129430 TQ	USBLS	5/15
	San Antonio-New Braunfels MSA, TX	Y	87110 FQ	100250 MW	118360 TQ	USBLS	5/15
	Provo-Orem MSA, UT	Y	89180 FQ	108930 MW	129350 TQ	USBLS	5/15
	Vermont	Y	87690 FQ	107360 MW	127170 TQ	USBLS	5/15
	Burlington-South Burlington MSA, VT	Y	89570 FQ	108230 MW	130290 TQ	USBLS	5/15
	Virginia	Y	99460 FQ	117500 MW	137490 TQ	USBLS	5/15
	Richmond MSA, VA	Y	83800 FQ	107280 MW	123890 TQ	USBLS	5/15
	Virginia Beach-Norfolk-Newport News MSA, VA-NC	Y	93770 FQ	111780 MW	139220 TQ	USBLS	5/15
	Washington	H	35.65 FQ	50.36 MW	64.60 TQ	WABLS	3/16
	Seattle-Bellevue-Everett PMSA, WA	H	31.09 FQ	53.37 MW	69.45 TQ	WABLS	3/16
	Tacoma-Lakewood PMSA, WA	H	43.86 FQ	50.93 MW	57.55 TQ	WABLS	3/16
	West Virginia	Y	83460 FQ	95870 MW	113480 TQ	USBLS	5/15
	Madison MSA, WI	Y	48210 FQ	63630 MW	79770 TQ	USBLS	5/15
	Milwaukee-Waukesha-West Allis MSA, WI	Y	85660 FQ	109360 MW	133630 TQ	USBLS	5/15
	Puerto Rico	Y	49590 FQ	65330 MW	86030 TQ	USBLS	5/15
	San Juan-Carolina-Caguas MSA, PR	Y	50880 FQ	62950 MW	79070 TQ	USBLS	5/15
Computer Network Architect	Alabama	Y	67235 AE	96632 AW	111331 AEX	ALBLS	6/16
	Birmingham-Hoover MSA, AL	Y	79395 AE	103094 AW	114949 AEX	ALBLS	6/16
	Alaska	Y	89340 FQ	109740 MW	128930 TQ	USBLS	5/15
	Anchorage MSA, AK	Y	101400 FQ	116900 MW	131570 TQ	USBLS	5/15
	Arizona	Y	73310 FQ	93020 MW	116350 TQ	USBLS	5/15
	Phoenix-Mesa-Scottsdale MSA, AZ	Y	74270 FQ	94280 MW	117400 TQ	USBLS	5/15
	Tucson MSA, AZ	Y	64510 FQ	76460 MW	90550 TQ	USBLS	5/15
	Arkansas	Y	67110 FQ	84160 MW	106390 TQ	USBLS	5/15
	Little Rock-North Little Rock-Conway MSA, AR	Y	61070 FQ	79430 MW	104260 TQ	USBLS	5/15
	California	H	48.06 FQ	61.65 MW	75.31 TQ	CABLS	1/16-3/16
	Anaheim-Santa Ana-Irvine PMSA, CA	H	39.43 FQ	56.74 MW	70.14 TQ	CABLS	1/16-3/16
	Los Angeles-Long Beach-Glendale PMSA, CA	H	45.17 FQ	58.52 MW	72.23 TQ	CABLS	1/16-3/16
	Oakland-Hayward-Berkeley PMSA, CA	H	49.03 FQ	60.45 MW	78.30 TQ	CABLS	1/16-3/16
	Riverside-San Bernardino-Ontario MSA, CA	H	40.11 FQ	51.48 MW	67.02 TQ	CABLS	1/16-3/16
	Sacramento–Roseville–Arden-Arcade MSA, CA	H	51.30 FQ	61.49 MW	72.29 TQ	CABLS	1/16-3/16
	San Diego-Carlsbad MSA, CA	H	41.57 FQ	48.98 MW	61.24 TQ	CABLS	1/16-3/16
	San Francisco-Redwood City-South San Francisco PMSA, CA	H	55.11 FQ	67.61 MW	79.23 TQ	CABLS	1/16-3/16
	Colorado	Y	80440 FQ	105420 MW	125580 TQ	USBLS	5/15

AE	Average entry wage	AWR	Average wage range	H	Hourly	LR	Low end range	MTC	Median total compensation	TCC	Total cash compensation
AEX	Average experienced wage	B	Biweekly	HI	Highest wage paid	M	Monthly	MW	Median wage paid	TQ	Third quartile wage
ATC	Average total compensation	D	Daily	HR	High end range	MCC	Median cash compensation	MWR	Median wage range	W	Weekly
AW	Average wage paid	FQ	First quartile wage	LO	Lowest wage paid	ME	Median entry wage	S	See annotated source	Y	Yearly

Occupation/Type/Industry	Location	Per	Low	Mid	High	Source	Date
Computer Network Architect	Denver-Aurora-Lakewood MSA, CO	Y	83040 FQ	107810 MW	127130 TQ	USBLS	5/15
	Connecticut	Y		112041 MW		CTBLS	1/16-3/16
	Bridgeport-Stamford-Norwalk MSA, CT	Y	83650 FQ	107110 MW	131200 TQ	USBLS	5/15
	Hartford-West Hartford-East Hartford MSA, CT	Y	94850 FQ	114970 MW	138450 TQ	USBLS	5/15
	Delaware	Y	86340 FQ	110640 MW	140120 TQ	USBLS	5/15
	Wilmington PMSA, DE-MD-NJ	Y	89910 FQ	114650 MW	142360 TQ	USBLS	5/15
	District of Columbia	Y	80340 FQ	101470 MW	127570 TQ	USBLS	5/15
	Washington-Arlington-Alexandria PMSA, DC-VA-MD-WV	Y	88330 FQ	111890 MW	138410 TQ	USBLS	5/15
	Florida	H	22.85 AE	33.59 MW	43.39 AEX	FLBLS	7/16-9/16
	Fort Lauderdale-Pompano Beach-Deerfield Beach PMSA, FL	H	22.85 AE	33.81 MW	45.92 AEX	FLBLS	7/16-9/16
	Miami-Miami Beach-Kendall PMSA, FL	H	23.89 AE	34.16 MW	40.83 AEX	FLBLS	7/16-9/16
	Orlando-Kissimmee-Sanford MSA, FL	H	25.68 AE	37.93 MW	47.82 AEX	FLBLS	7/16-9/16
	Tampa-St. Petersburg-Clearwater MSA, FL	H	24.59 AE	37.49 MW	47.11 AEX	FLBLS	7/16-9/16
	Georgia	Y	85370 FQ	108610 MW	131290 TQ	USBLS	5/15
	Atlanta-Sandy Springs-Roswell MSA, GA	Y	86340 FQ	109260 MW	131850 TQ	USBLS	5/15
	Augusta-Richmond County MSA, GA-SC	Y	72210 FQ	92150 MW	113280 TQ	USBLS	5/15
	Urban Honolulu MSA, HI	Y	75580 FQ	92370 MW	113980 TQ	USBLS	5/15
	Idaho	Y	54610 FQ	66260 MW	97320 TQ	USBLS	5/15
	Boise City MSA, ID	Y	54240 FQ	65660 MW	89320 TQ	USBLS	5/15
	Illinois	Y	87520 FQ	112080 MW	133870 TQ	USBLS	5/15
	Chicago-Naperville-Arlington Heights PMSA, IL	Y	88840 FQ	112820 MW	134690 TQ	USBLS	5/15
	Lake County-Kenosha County PMSA, IL-WI	Y	99940 FQ	117940 MW	139020 TQ	USBLS	5/15
	Indiana	Y	61740 FQ	77060 MW	98670 TQ	USBLS	5/15
	Gary PMSA, IN	Y	83720 FQ	107640 MW	163450 TQ	USBLS	5/15
	Indianapolis-Carmel-Anderson MSA, IN	Y	61790 FQ	77450 MW	98720 TQ	USBLS	5/15
	Iowa	Y	69640 FQ	87420 MW	106400 TQ	USBLS	5/15
	Des Moines-West Des Moines MSA, IA	Y	72400 FQ	90020 MW	108090 TQ	USBLS	5/15
	Kansas	Y	70900 FQ	90710 MW	113820 TQ	USBLS	5/15
	Wichita MSA, KS	Y	69150 FQ	87600 MW	107670 TQ	USBLS	5/15
	Kentucky	Y	51450 FQ	72130 MW	99710 TQ	USBLS	5/15
	Louisville-Jefferson County MSA, KY-IN	Y	61110 FQ	87070 MW	113140 TQ	USBLS	5/15
	Louisiana	Y	64680 FQ	85230 MW	109630 TQ	USBLS	5/15
	Baton Rouge MSA, LA	Y	64110 FQ	73530 MW	91550 TQ	USBLS	5/15
	New Orleans-Metairie MSA, LA	Y	58190 FQ	84550 MW	104850 TQ	USBLS	5/15
	Maine	Y	71110 FQ	89910 MW	113140 TQ	USBLS	5/15
	Portland-South Portland MSA, ME	Y	67800 FQ	90760 MW	113400 TQ	USBLS	5/15
	Maryland	Y	60960 AE	105427 MW	127661 AEX	MDBLS	4/16
	Baltimore-Columbia-Towson MSA, MD	Y	67720 FQ	99330 MW	128210 TQ	USBLS	5/15
	Salisbury MSA, MD-DE	Y	76730 FQ	95590 MW	117620 TQ	USBLS	5/15
	Massachusetts	Y	87330 FQ	114400 MW	145710 TQ	USBLS	5/15
	Boston-Cambridge-Newton NECTA, MA	Y	88360 FQ	115270 MW	147150 TQ	USBLS	5/15
	Worcester MSA, MA-CT	Y	85840 FQ	104750 MW	126820 TQ	USBLS	5/15
	Michigan	Y	85650 FQ	105830 MW	124990 TQ	USBLS	5/15
	Detroit-Dearborn-Livonia PMSA, MI	Y	92220 FQ	110590 MW	127660 TQ	USBLS	5/15
	Grand Rapids-Wyoming MSA, MI	Y	63090 FQ	87900 MW	112990 TQ	USBLS	5/15
	Minnesota	Y	83709 FQ	102922 MW	121208 TQ	MNBLS	1/16-3/16
	Minneapolis-St. Paul-Bloomington MSA, MN-WI	Y	83880 FQ	103305 MW	121581 TQ	MNBLS	1/16-3/16

Occupation/Type/Industry	Location	Per	Low	Mid	High	Source	Date
Computer Network Architect	Mississippi	Y	56400 FQ	69240 MW	85660 TQ	USBLS	5/15
	Jackson MSA, MS	Y	79320 FQ	89650 MW	98400 TQ	USBLS	5/15
	Missouri	Y	80620 FQ	96280 MW	115200 TQ	USBLS	5/15
	Kansas City MSA, MO-KS	Y	79060 FQ	95840 MW	114830 TQ	USBLS	5/15
	St. Louis MSA, MO-IL	Y	80700 FQ	95980 MW	115230 TQ	USBLS	5/15
	Montana	Y	53040 FQ	62840 MW	79050 TQ	USBLS	5/15
	Nebraska	Y	67630 FQ	90985 MW	115890 TQ	NEBLS	7/16-9/16
	Omaha-Council Bluffs MSA, NE-IA	Y	72965 FQ	96235 MW	121470 TQ	NEBLS	7/16-9/16
	Nevada	Y	73430 FQ	91310 MW	111980 TQ	USBLS	5/15
	Las Vegas-Henderson-Paradise MSA, NV	Y	74580 FQ	95470 MW	115830 TQ	USBLS	5/15
	New Hampshire	H	29.88 AE	42.22 MW	54.11 AEX	NHBLS	6/16
	Manchester NECTA, NH	H	30.45 AE	45.16 MW	53.33 AEX	NHBLS	6/16
	Nashua NECTA, NH-MA	Y	68790 FQ	83350 MW	119550 TQ	USBLS	5/15
	New Jersey	Y	87080 FQ	114190 MW	145750 TQ	USBLS	5/15
	Camden PMSA, NJ	Y	72110 FQ	90840 MW	126160 TQ	USBLS	5/15
	Newark PMSA, NJ-PA	Y	81060 FQ	107910 MW	139320 TQ	USBLS	5/15
	Trenton MSA, NJ	Y	101120 FQ	129180 MW	151230 TQ	USBLS	5/15
	New Mexico	Y	83490 FQ	101480 MW	118640 TQ	USBLS	5/15
	Albuquerque MSA, NM	Y	88820 FQ	105150 MW	120360 TQ	USBLS	5/15
	New York	Y	71640 AE	110560 MW	138040 AEX	NYBLS	1/16-3/16
	Buffalo-Cheektowaga-Niagara Falls MSA, NY	Y	56540 FQ	80790 MW	105620 TQ	USBLS	5/15
	Nassau County-Suffolk County PMSA, NY	Y	88740 FQ	111630 MW	132910 TQ	USBLS	5/15
	New York-Jersey City-White Plains PMSA, NY-NJ	Y	91450 FQ	118070 MW	150560 TQ	USBLS	5/15
	Rochester MSA, NY	Y	60150 FQ	76690 MW	103360 TQ	USBLS	5/15
	North Carolina	Y	80590 FQ	102340 MW	126390 TQ	USBLS	5/15
	Charlotte-Concord-Gastonia MSA, NC-SC	Y	90140 FQ	112310 MW	134860 TQ	USBLS	5/15
	Raleigh MSA, NC	Y	83190 FQ	99490 MW	125210 TQ	USBLS	5/15
	North Dakota	Y	52910 FQ	70560 MW	90760 TQ	USBLS	5/15
	Fargo MSA, ND-MN	Y	50460 FQ	60870 MW	83010 TQ	USBLS	5/15
	Ohio	Y	75260 FQ	98740 MW	119420 TQ	USBLS	5/15
	Cincinnati MSA, OH-KY-IN	Y	83470 FQ	98570 MW	121210 TQ	USBLS	5/15
	Cleveland-Elyria MSA, OH	Y	73730 FQ	103530 MW	122050 TQ	USBLS	5/15
	Columbus MSA, OH	Y	76250 FQ	100200 MW	118080 TQ	USBLS	5/15
	Oklahoma	Y	56400 FQ	83220 MW	105490 TQ	USBLS	5/15
	Oklahoma City MSA, OK	Y	57480 FQ	78090 MW	104600 TQ	USBLS	5/15
	Tulsa MSA, OK	Y	49470 FQ	86300 MW	103790 TQ	USBLS	5/15
	Oregon	H	44.02 FQ	54.03 MW	67.62 TQ	ORBLS	2016
	Portland-Vancouver-Hillsboro MSA, OR-WA	Y	90300 FQ	112130 MW	141740 TQ	USBLS	5/15
	Pennsylvania	Y	75170 FQ	98220 MW	122260 TQ	USBLS	5/15
	Allentown-Bethlehem-Easton MSA, PA-NJ	Y	69960 FQ	97430 MW	123460 TQ	USBLS	5/15
	Harrisburg-Carlisle MSA, PA	Y	61780 FQ	84220 MW	108010 TQ	USBLS	5/15
	Philadelphia PMSA, PA	Y	79530 FQ	101340 MW	122200 TQ	USBLS	5/15
	Pittsburgh MSA, PA	Y	73320 FQ	92810 MW	115180 TQ	USBLS	5/15
	Rhode Island	Y	102420 FQ	111910 MW	121370 TQ	USBLS	5/15
	Providence-Warwick MSA, RI-MA	Y	102510 FQ	111970 MW	121400 TQ	USBLS	5/15
	South Carolina	Y	67860 FQ	88240 MW	115200 TQ	USBLS	5/15
	Charleston-North Charleston MSA, SC	Y	65630 FQ	83550 MW	106870 TQ	USBLS	5/15
	Columbia MSA, SC	Y	63100 FQ	80500 MW	102960 TQ	USBLS	5/15
	Greenville-Anderson-Mauldin MSA, SC	Y	91220 FQ	113230 MW	129680 TQ	USBLS	5/15
	South Dakota	Y	66290 FQ	84300 MW	100830 TQ	USBLS	5/15
	Sioux Falls MSA, SD	Y	62490 FQ	81250 MW	101000 TQ	USBLS	5/15
	Tennessee	Y	65330 FQ	96500 MW	121700 TQ	USBLS	5/15
	Knoxville MSA, TN	Y	62530 FQ	91850 MW	133370 TQ	USBLS	5/15
	Memphis MSA, TN-MS-AR	Y	78020 FQ	104370 MW	121980 TQ	USBLS	5/15
	Nashville-Davidson–Murfreesboro–Franklin MSA, TN	Y	80340 FQ	107080 MW	124040 TQ	USBLS	5/15
	Texas	Y	85270 FQ	108620 MW	132060 TQ	USBLS	5/15
	Austin-Round Rock MSA, TX	Y	95420 FQ	117150 MW	142640 TQ	USBLS	5/15
	Dallas-Plano-Irving PMSA, TX	Y	82530 FQ	104590 MW	125540 TQ	USBLS	5/15

AE	Average entry wage	AWR	Average wage range	H	Hourly	LR	Low end range	MTC	Median total compensation	TCC	Total cash compensation
AEX	Average experienced wage	B	Biweekly	HI	Highest wage paid	M	Monthly	MW	Median wage paid	TQ	Third quartile wage
ATC	Average total compensation	D	Daily	HR	High end range	MCC	Median cash compensation	MWR	Median wage range	W	Weekly
AW	Average wage paid	FQ	First quartile wage	LO	Lowest wage paid	ME	Median entry wage	S	See annotated source	Y	Yearly

Occupation/Type/Industry	Location	Per	Low	Mid	High	Source	Date
Computer Network Architect	Fort Worth-Arlington PMSA, TX	Y	87150 FQ	106370 MW	134500 TQ	USBLS	5/15
	Houston-The Woodlands-Sugar Land MSA, TX	Y	90480 FQ	114440 MW	139900 TQ	USBLS	5/15
	San Antonio-New Braunfels MSA, TX	Y	87650 FQ	112870 MW	142720 TQ	USBLS	5/15
	Utah	Y	70240 FQ	90810 MW	110960 TQ	USBLS	5/15
	Ogden-Clearfield MSA, UT	Y	62880 FQ	81190 MW	95310 TQ	USBLS	5/15
	Provo-Orem MSA, UT	Y	60390 FQ	88960 MW	102300 TQ	USBLS	5/15
	Salt Lake City MSA, UT	Y	71930 FQ	91950 MW	112240 TQ	USBLS	5/15
	Vermont	Y	58600 FQ	66660 MW	82580 TQ	USBLS	5/15
	Burlington-South Burlington MSA, VT	Y	58270 FQ	65840 MW	110680 TQ	USBLS	5/15
	Virginia	Y	85280 FQ	108860 MW	134340 TQ	USBLS	5/15
	Richmond MSA, VA	Y	85130 FQ	106500 MW	121350 TQ	USBLS	5/15
	Virginia Beach-Norfolk-Newport News MSA, VA-NC	Y	60370 FQ	77330 MW	101800 TQ	USBLS	5/15
	Washington	H	38.88 FQ	43.42 MW	58.92 TQ	WABLS	3/16
	Seattle-Bellevue-Everett PMSA, WA	H	38.21 FQ	52.45 MW	64.49 TQ	WABLS	3/16
	Tacoma-Lakewood PMSA, WA	H	38.75 FQ	41.50 MW	46.54 TQ	WABLS	3/16
	West Virginia	Y	56360 FQ	74320 MW	99890 TQ	USBLS	5/15
	Wisconsin	Y	73590 FQ	90270 MW	108060 TQ	USBLS	5/15
	Madison MSA, WI	Y	79470 FQ	88970 MW	98300 TQ	USBLS	5/15
	Milwaukee-Waukesha-West Allis MSA, WI	Y	79830 FQ	95530 MW	116190 TQ	USBLS	5/15
	Wyoming	Y	79880 FQ	87130 MW	94390 TQ	USBLS	5/15
	Cheyenne MSA, WY	Y	81750 FQ	87560 MW	93340 TQ	USBLS	5/15
	Puerto Rico	Y	34140 FQ	38090 MW	51890 TQ	USBLS	5/15
	San Juan-Carolina-Caguas MSA, PR	Y	36410 FQ	58580 MW	79190 TQ	USBLS	5/15
Computer Network Support Specialist	Alabama	Y	40151 AE	60680 AW	70935 AEX	ALBLS	6/16
	Birmingham-Hoover MSA, AL	Y	47847 AE	68172 AW	78335 AEX	ALBLS	6/16
	Alaska	Y	52940 FQ	63900 MW	84500 TQ	USBLS	5/15
	Anchorage MSA, AK	Y	56400 FQ	73820 MW	91550 TQ	USBLS	5/15
	Arizona	Y	44090 FQ	59490 MW	80150 TQ	USBLS	5/15
	Phoenix-Mesa-Scottsdale MSA, AZ	Y	45340 FQ	61610 MW	82240 TQ	USBLS	5/15
	Tucson MSA, AZ	Y	38700 FQ	48150 MW	62380 TQ	USBLS	5/15
	Arkansas	Y	36060 FQ	47730 MW	62880 TQ	USBLS	5/15
	Little Rock-North Little Rock-Conway MSA, AR	Y	38060 FQ	50420 MW	66060 TQ	USBLS	5/15
	California	H	27.89 FQ	36.38 MW	47.42 TQ	CABLS	1/16-3/16
	Anaheim-Santa Ana-Irvine PMSA, CA	H	22.78 FQ	32.34 MW	42.45 TQ	CABLS	1/16-3/16
	Los Angeles-Long Beach-Glendale PMSA, CA	H	27.26 FQ	34.76 MW	44.43 TQ	CABLS	1/16-3/16
	Oakland-Hayward-Berkeley PMSA, CA	H	28.53 FQ	37.91 MW	48.09 TQ	CABLS	1/16-3/16
	Riverside-San Bernardino-Ontario MSA, CA	H	26.08 FQ	30.30 MW	41.41 TQ	CABLS	1/16-3/16
	Sacramento–Roseville–Arden-Arcade MSA, CA	H	31.02 FQ	38.10 MW	49.07 TQ	CABLS	1/16-3/16
	San Diego-Carlsbad MSA, CA	H	27.49 FQ	34.70 MW	44.16 TQ	CABLS	1/16-3/16
	San Francisco-Redwood City-South San Francisco PMSA, CA	H	30.77 FQ	40.02 MW	50.51 TQ	CABLS	1/16-3/16
	Colorado	Y	51100 FQ	65360 MW	85120 TQ	USBLS	5/15
	Denver-Aurora-Lakewood MSA, CO	Y	51530 FQ	66290 MW	84320 TQ	USBLS	5/15
	Connecticut	Y		76858 MW		CTBLS	1/16-3/16
	Bridgeport-Stamford-Norwalk MSA, CT	Y	64230 FQ	81400 MW	102830 TQ	USBLS	5/15
	Hartford-West Hartford-East Hartford MSA, CT	Y	59030 FQ	73090 MW	91600 TQ	USBLS	5/15
	Delaware	Y	47710 FQ	62170 MW	90910 TQ	USBLS	5/15
	Wilmington PMSA, DE-MD-NJ	Y	48240 FQ	65620 MW	91380 TQ	USBLS	5/15
	District of Columbia	Y	67230 FQ	86470 MW	106360 TQ	USBLS	5/15

AE	Average entry wage	AWR	Average wage range	H	Hourly	LR	Low end range	MTC	Median total compensation	TCC	Total cash compensation
AEX	Average experienced wage	B	Biweekly	HI	Highest wage paid	M	Monthly	MW	Median wage paid	TQ	Third quartile wage
ATC	Average total compensation	D	Daily	HR	High end range	MCC	Median cash compensation	MWR	Median wage range	W	Weekly
AW	Average wage paid	FQ	First quartile wage	LO	Lowest wage paid	ME	Median entry wage	S	See annotated source	Y	Yearly

Occupation/Type/Industry	Location	Per	Low	Mid	High	Source	Date
Computer Network Support Specialist	Washington-Arlington-Alexandria PMSA, DC-VA-MD-WV	Y	57000 FQ	77520 MW	101440 TQ	USBLS	5/15
	Florida	H	17.49 AE	25.51 MW	33.65 AEX	FLBLS	7/16-9/16
	Fort Lauderdale-Pompano Beach-Deerfield Beach PMSA, FL	H	17.44 AE	26.80 MW	35.63 AEX	FLBLS	7/16-9/16
	Miami-Miami Beach-Kendall PMSA, FL	H	18.82 AE	24.57 MW	32.83 AEX	FLBLS	7/16-9/16
	Orlando-Kissimmee-Sanford MSA, FL	H	17.87 AE	24.93 MW	31.22 AEX	FLBLS	7/16-9/16
	Tampa-St. Petersburg-Clearwater MSA, FL	H	16.86 AE	27.78 MW	37.53 AEX	FLBLS	7/16-9/16
	Georgia	Y	50000 FQ	65910 MW	86330 TQ	USBLS	5/15
	Atlanta-Sandy Springs-Roswell MSA, GA	Y	51670 FQ	68710 MW	88780 TQ	USBLS	5/15
	Augusta-Richmond County MSA, GA-SC	Y	39890 FQ	52210 MW	79290 TQ	USBLS	5/15
	Hawaii	Y	49590 FQ	60140 MW	75760 TQ	USBLS	5/15
	Urban Honolulu MSA, HI	Y	51270 FQ	61080 MW	77020 TQ	USBLS	5/15
	Illinois	Y	51340 FQ	66040 MW	82110 TQ	USBLS	5/15
	Chicago-Naperville-Arlington Heights PMSA, IL	Y	54210 FQ	68780 MW	84800 TQ	USBLS	5/15
	Lake County-Kenosha County PMSA, IL-WI	Y	45440 FQ	57760 MW	72890 TQ	USBLS	5/15
	Indiana	Y	42970 FQ	56140 MW	75080 TQ	USBLS	5/15
	Indianapolis-Carmel-Anderson MSA, IN	Y	46110 FQ	60410 MW	83420 TQ	USBLS	5/15
	Iowa	Y	42150 FQ	50610 MW	62020 TQ	USBLS	5/15
	Des Moines-West Des Moines MSA, IA	Y	42800 FQ	51890 MW	69040 TQ	USBLS	5/15
	Kansas	Y	44520 FQ	54180 MW	64490 TQ	USBLS	5/15
	Wichita MSA, KS	Y	43100 FQ	50800 MW	58170 TQ	USBLS	5/15
	Kentucky	Y	41140 FQ	52640 MW	65790 TQ	USBLS	5/15
	Louisville-Jefferson County MSA, KY-IN	Y	40950 FQ	50340 MW	62360 TQ	USBLS	5/15
	Louisiana	Y	33510 FQ	40880 MW	55930 TQ	USBLS	5/15
	Baton Rouge MSA, LA	Y	34770 FQ	42000 MW	54110 TQ	USBLS	5/15
	New Orleans-Metairie MSA, LA	Y	36970 FQ	51550 MW	70840 TQ	USBLS	5/15
	Maine	Y	40570 FQ	50850 MW	62060 TQ	USBLS	5/15
	Portland-South Portland MSA, ME	Y	42830 FQ	53390 MW	62410 TQ	USBLS	5/15
	Maryland	Y	44769 AE	70651 MW	83592 AEX	MDBLS	4/16
	Baltimore-Columbia-Towson MSA, MD	Y	53450 FQ	66890 MW	90700 TQ	USBLS	5/15
	Salisbury MSA, MD-DE	Y	44300 FQ	54870 MW	69310 TQ	USBLS	5/15
	Massachusetts	Y	59270 FQ	78750 MW	107030 TQ	USBLS	5/15
	Boston-Cambridge-Newton NECTA, MA	Y	59730 FQ	80220 MW	109060 TQ	USBLS	5/15
	Worcester MSA, MA-CT	Y	60760 FQ	89450 MW	114300 TQ	USBLS	5/15
	Michigan	Y	40940 FQ	55110 MW	76270 TQ	USBLS	5/15
	Detroit-Dearborn-Livonia PMSA, MI	Y	49000 FQ	64040 MW	80760 TQ	USBLS	5/15
	Grand Rapids-Wyoming MSA, MI	Y	38810 FQ	49680 MW	64950 TQ	USBLS	5/15
	Minnesota	Y	52267 FQ	61552 MW	74334 TQ	MNBLS	1/16-3/16
	Minneapolis-St. Paul-Bloomington MSA, MN-WI	Y	53578 FQ	64021 MW	76451 TQ	MNBLS	1/16-3/16
	Mississippi	Y	33820 FQ	43530 MW	58760 TQ	USBLS	5/15
	Jackson MSA, MS	Y	33610 FQ	42540 MW	59740 TQ	USBLS	5/15
	Missouri	Y	43930 FQ	56180 MW	72380 TQ	USBLS	5/15
	Kansas City MSA, MO-KS	Y	48290 FQ	60850 MW	74160 TQ	USBLS	5/15
	St. Louis MSA, MO-IL	Y	47840 FQ	61550 MW	75570 TQ	USBLS	5/15
	Montana	Y	38260 FQ	53710 MW	78370 TQ	USBLS	5/15
	Billings MSA, MT	Y	53080 FQ	67170 MW	85320 TQ	USBLS	5/15
	Nebraska	Y	45715 FQ	57675 MW	73150 TQ	NEBLS	7/16-9/16
	Omaha-Council Bluffs MSA, NE-IA	Y	46630 FQ	58455 MW	74205 TQ	NEBLS	7/16-9/16
	Nevada	Y	45500 FQ	59100 MW	76040 TQ	USBLS	5/15

Occupation/Type/Industry	Location	Per	Low	Mid	High	Source	Date
Computer Network Support Specialist	Las Vegas-Henderson-Paradise						
	MSA, NV	Y	44380 FQ	58610 MW	78560 TQ	USBLS	5/15
	New Hampshire	H	21.28 AE	29.02 MW	34.79 AEX	NHBLS	6/16
	Manchester NECTA, NH	H	19.37 AE	30.04 MW	37.62 AEX	NHBLS	6/16
	Nashua NECTA, NH-MA	Y	54970 FQ	67710 MW	80240 TQ	USBLS	5/15
	New Jersey	Y	61370 FQ	82060 MW	103440 TQ	USBLS	5/15
	Camden PMSA, NJ	Y	57220 FQ	72130 MW	97170 TQ	USBLS	5/15
	Newark PMSA, NJ-PA	Y	62320 FQ	80770 MW	101860 TQ	USBLS	5/15
	Trenton MSA, NJ	Y	81710 FQ	90510 MW	99250 TQ	USBLS	5/15
	New Mexico	Y	39780 FQ	55180 MW	69280 TQ	USBLS	5/15
	Albuquerque MSA, NM	Y	36220 FQ	45960 MW	60550 TQ	USBLS	5/15
	New York	Y	44430 AE	72800 MW	95900 AEX	NYBLS	1/16-3/16
	Buffalo-Cheektowaga-Niagara Falls MSA, NY	Y	32560 FQ	47670 MW	67810 TQ	USBLS	5/15
	Nassau County-Suffolk County PMSA, NY	Y	53540 FQ	64820 MW	96170 TQ	USBLS	5/15
	New York-Jersey City-White Plains PMSA, NY-NJ	Y	61550 FQ	82070 MW	109670 TQ	USBLS	5/15
	Rochester MSA, NY	Y	41200 FQ	55220 MW	74610 TQ	USBLS	5/15
	North Carolina	Y	43030 FQ	58000 MW	78690 TQ	USBLS	5/15
	Charlotte-Concord-Gastonia MSA, NC-SC	Y	37430 FQ	50980 MW	73170 TQ	USBLS	5/15
	Raleigh MSA, NC	Y	50960 FQ	65300 MW	84230 TQ	USBLS	5/15
	North Dakota	Y	42370 FQ	50600 MW	63140 TQ	USBLS	5/15
	Fargo MSA, ND-MN	Y	43390 FQ	52640 MW	64560 TQ	USBLS	5/15
	Ohio	Y	40550 FQ	54470 MW	72570 TQ	USBLS	5/15
	Cincinnati MSA, OH-KY-IN	Y	45280 FQ	58220 MW	73330 TQ	USBLS	5/15
	Cleveland-Elyria MSA, OH	Y	36860 FQ	48600 MW	60830 TQ	USBLS	5/15
	Columbus MSA, OH	Y	45640 FQ	65770 MW	87930 TQ	USBLS	5/15
	Oklahoma	Y	38880 FQ	57630 MW	78500 TQ	USBLS	5/15
	Oklahoma City MSA, OK	Y	45900 FQ	58650 MW	78170 TQ	USBLS	5/15
	Tulsa MSA, OK	Y	38960 FQ	65420 MW	86800 TQ	USBLS	5/15
	Oregon	H	22.32 FQ	28.34 MW	35.19 TQ	ORBLS	2016
	Portland-Vancouver-Hillsboro MSA, OR-WA	Y	47160 FQ	58630 MW	73670 TQ	USBLS	5/15
	Pennsylvania	Y	49200 FQ	59900 MW	77240 TQ	USBLS	5/15
	Allentown-Bethlehem-Easton MSA, PA-NJ	Y	45810 FQ	55250 MW	66170 TQ	USBLS	5/15
	Harrisburg-Carlisle MSA, PA	Y	49120 FQ	59640 MW	72190 TQ	USBLS	5/15
	Montgomery County-Bucks County-Chester County PMSA, PA	Y	53260 FQ	65730 MW	86270 TQ	USBLS	5/15
	Philadelphia PMSA, PA	Y	53340 FQ	61210 MW	82000 TQ	USBLS	5/15
	Pittsburgh MSA, PA	Y	45410 FQ	57750 MW	73350 TQ	USBLS	5/15
	Rhode Island	Y	39070 FQ	47000 MW	56420 TQ	USBLS	5/15
	Providence-Warwick MSA, RI-MA	Y	39670 FQ	47420 MW	57250 TQ	USBLS	5/15
	South Carolina	Y	42740 FQ	52190 MW	66660 TQ	USBLS	5/15
	Charleston-North Charleston MSA, SC	Y	45500 FQ	55640 MW	69290 TQ	USBLS	5/15
	Columbia MSA, SC	Y	48160 FQ	62430 MW	76640 TQ	USBLS	5/15
	Greenville-Anderson-Mauldin MSA, SC	Y	41650 FQ	48500 MW	59340 TQ	USBLS	5/15
	South Dakota	Y	41610 FQ	47280 MW	56040 TQ	USBLS	5/15
	Sioux Falls MSA, SD	Y	41950 FQ	47460 MW	55490 TQ	USBLS	5/15
	Tennessee	Y	44830 FQ	55520 MW	70470 TQ	USBLS	5/15
	Knoxville MSA, TN	Y	43890 FQ	54590 MW	67890 TQ	USBLS	5/15
	Memphis MSA, TN-MS-AR	Y	43480 FQ	55690 MW	71780 TQ	USBLS	5/15
	Nashville-Davidson–Murfreesboro–Franklin MSA, TN	Y	47650 FQ	58580 MW	75790 TQ	USBLS	5/15
	Texas	Y	50220 FQ	66090 MW	85010 TQ	USBLS	5/15
	Austin-Round Rock MSA, TX	Y	45150 FQ	57330 MW	71380 TQ	USBLS	5/15
	Dallas-Plano-Irving PMSA, TX	Y	59670 FQ	75360 MW	93060 TQ	USBLS	5/15
	Fort Worth-Arlington PMSA, TX	Y	54770 FQ	70160 MW	82820 TQ	USBLS	5/15
	Houston-The Woodlands-Sugar Land MSA, TX	Y	50570 FQ	68210 MW	87600 TQ	USBLS	5/15
	San Antonio-New Braunfels MSA, TX	Y	45520 FQ	57930 MW	75660 TQ	USBLS	5/15
	Utah	Y	42190 FQ	55390 MW	73680 TQ	USBLS	5/15

AE	Average entry wage	**AWR**	Average wage range	**H**	Hourly
AEX	Average experienced wage	**B**	Biweekly	**HI**	Highest wage paid
ATC	Average total compensation	**D**	Daily	**HR**	High end range
AW	Average wage paid	**FQ**	First quartile wage	**LO**	Lowest wage paid

LR	Low end range	**MTC**	Median total compensation
M	Monthly	**MW**	Median wage paid
MCC	Median cash compensation	**MWR**	Median wage range
ME	Median entry wage	**S**	See annotated source

TCC	Total cash compensation
TQ	Third quartile wage
W	Weekly
Y	Yearly

Occupation/Type/Industry	Location	Per	Low	Mid	High	Source	Date
Computer Network Support Specialist	Ogden-Clearfield MSA, UT	Y	32160 FQ	42820 MW	60350 TQ	USBLS	5/15
	Provo-Orem MSA, UT	Y	33650 FQ	43580 MW	55160 TQ	USBLS	5/15
	Salt Lake City MSA, UT	Y	47660 FQ	61340 MW	77970 TQ	USBLS	5/15
	Vermont	Y	40850 FQ	53010 MW	67970 TQ	USBLS	5/15
	Burlington-South Burlington MSA, VT	Y	41480 FQ	51980 MW	66960 TQ	USBLS	5/15
	Virginia	Y	52160 FQ	71650 MW	96710 TQ	USBLS	5/15
	Richmond MSA, VA	Y	49760 FQ	64070 MW	80240 TQ	USBLS	5/15
	Virginia Beach-Norfolk-Newport News MSA, VA-NC	Y	40570 FQ	54260 MW	68860 TQ	USBLS	5/15
	Washington	H	27.37 FQ	33.84 MW	42.42 TQ	WABLS	3/16
	Seattle-Bellevue-Everett PMSA, WA	H	29.61 FQ	36.31 MW	46.35 TQ	WABLS	3/16
	Tacoma-Lakewood PMSA, WA	H	23.01 FQ	28.36 MW	34.51 TQ	WABLS	3/16
	West Virginia	Y	35410 FQ	45860 MW	56800 TQ	USBLS	5/15
	Huntington-Ashland MSA, WV-KY-OH	Y	39710 FQ	53790 MW	59930 TQ	USBLS	5/15
	Wisconsin	Y	44170 FQ	56840 MW	72400 TQ	USBLS	5/15
	Madison MSA, WI	Y	51510 FQ	67160 MW	83030 TQ	USBLS	5/15
	Milwaukee-Waukesha-West Allis MSA, WI	Y	42920 FQ	56650 MW	72260 TQ	USBLS	5/15
	Wyoming	Y	42350 FQ	55320 MW	66100 TQ	USBLS	5/15
	Cheyenne MSA, WY	Y	36740 FQ	58570 MW	68790 TQ	USBLS	5/15
	Puerto Rico	Y	27670 FQ	37230 MW	50480 TQ	USBLS	5/15
	San Juan-Carolina-Caguas MSA, PR	Y.	27680 FQ	37210 MW	52090 TQ	USBLS	5/15
Computer Numerically Controlled Machine Tool Programmer							
Metals and Plastics	Alabama	Y	28543 AE	40800 AW	46938 AEX	ALBLS	6/16
Metals and Plastics	Birmingham-Hoover MSA, AL	Y	36008 AE	40039 AW	42054 AEX	ALBLS	6/16
Metals and Plastics	Arizona	Y	36420 FQ	46840 MW	59660 TQ	USBLS	5/15
Metals and Plastics	Phoenix-Mesa-Scottsdale MSA, AZ	Y	40650 FQ	50520 MW	62750 TQ	USBLS	5/15
Metals and Plastics	Tucson MSA, AZ	Y	32490 FQ	39870 MW	51710 TQ	USBLS	5/15
Metals and Plastics	Arkansas	Y	31100 FQ	35910 MW	42310 TQ	USBLS	5/15
Metals and Plastics	Little Rock-North Little Rock-Conway MSA, AR	Y	32130 FQ	35660 MW	39180 TQ	USBLS	5/15
Metals and Plastics	California	H	23.16 FQ	28.58 MW	36.55 TQ	CABLS	1/16-3/16
Metals and Plastics	Anaheim-Santa Ana-Irvine PMSA, CA	H	20.54 FQ	26.58 MW	33.44 TQ	CABLS	1/16-3/16
Metals and Plastics	Los Angeles-Long Beach-Glendale PMSA, CA	H	22.44 FQ	28.81 MW	38.23 TQ	CABLS	1/16-3/16
Metals and Plastics	Oakland-Hayward-Berkeley PMSA, CA	H	29.82 FQ	34.87 MW	39.41 TQ	CABLS	1/16-3/16
Metals and Plastics	Riverside-San Bernardino-Ontario MSA, CA	H	22.48 FQ	27.71 MW	32.36 TQ	CABLS	1/16-3/16
Metals and Plastics	Sacramento–Roseville–Arden-Arcade MSA, CA	H	21.06 FQ	25.10 MW	28.43 TQ	CABLS	1/16-3/16
Metals and Plastics	San Diego-Carlsbad MSA, CA	H	25.88 FQ	32.40 MW	38.44 TQ	CABLS	1/16-3/16
Metals and Plastics	San Francisco-Redwood City-South San Francisco PMSA, CA	H	24.25 FQ	29.17 MW	43.07 TQ	CABLS	1/16-3/16
Metals and Plastics	Colorado	Y	45930 FQ	54540 MW	60580 TQ	USBLS	5/15
Metals and Plastics	Denver-Aurora-Lakewood MSA, CO	Y	48690 FQ	55350 MW	60950 TQ	USBLS	5/15
Metals and Plastics	Connecticut	Y		55845 MW		CTBLS	1/16-3/16
Metals and Plastics	Bridgeport-Stamford-Norwalk MSA, CT	Y	45280 FQ	53410 MW	60260 TQ	USBLS	5/15
Metals and Plastics	Hartford-West Hartford-East Hartford MSA, CT	Y	44920 FQ	57140 MW	73020 TQ	USBLS	5/15
Metals and Plastics	Wilmington PMSA, DE-MD-NJ	Y	41380 FQ	64450 MW	75130 TQ	USBLS	5/15
Metals and Plastics	Florida	H	15.73 AE	21.60 MW	25.05 AEX	FLBLS	7/16-9/16
Metals and Plastics	Fort Lauderdale-Pompano Beach-Deerfield Beach PMSA, FL	H	14.69 AE	24.58 MW	26.87 AEX	FLBLS	7/16-9/16
Metals and Plastics	Miami-Miami Beach-Kendall PMSA, FL	H	15.67 AE	22.59 MW	27.34 AEX	FLBLS	7/16-9/16

AE	Average entry wage	AWR	Average wage range	H	Hourly	LR	Low end range	MTC Median total compensation	TCC Total cash compensation
AEX	Average experienced wage	B	Biweekly	HI	Highest wage paid	M	Monthly	MW Median wage paid	TQ Third quartile wage
ATC	Average total compensation	D	Daily	HR	High end range	MCC Median cash compensation	MWR Median wage range	W Weekly
AW	Average wage paid	FQ	First quartile wage	LO	Lowest wage paid	ME Median entry wage	S See annotated source	Y Yearly

Occupation/Type/Industry	Location	Per	Low	Mid	High	Source	Date
Computer Numerically Controlled Machine Tool Programmer							
Metals and Plastics	Orlando-Kissimmee-Sanford MSA, FL	H	20.36 AE	25.77 MW	29.85 AEX	FLBLS	7/16-9/16
Metals and Plastics	Tampa-St. Petersburg-Clearwater MSA, FL	H	16.30 AE	20.22 MW	23.00 AEX	FLBLS	7/16-9/16
Metals and Plastics	Georgia	Y	35530 FQ	41860 MW	48690 TQ	USBLS	5/15
Metals and Plastics	Atlanta-Sandy Springs-Roswell MSA, GA	Y	36920 FQ	43170 MW	49220 TQ	USBLS	5/15
Metals and Plastics	Idaho	Y	23080 FQ	28740 MW	43660 TQ	USBLS	5/15
Metals and Plastics	Illinois	Y	38590 FQ	48590 MW	59250 TQ	USBLS	5/15
Metals and Plastics	Chicago-Naperville-Arlington Heights PMSA, IL	Y	46490 FQ	56070 MW	63510 TQ	USBLS	5/15
Metals and Plastics	Lake County-Kenosha County PMSA, IL-WI	Y	35150 FQ	43470 MW	52370 TQ	USBLS	5/15
Metals and Plastics	Indiana	Y	35420 FQ	41760 MW	48800 TQ	USBLS	5/15
Metals and Plastics	Gary PMSA, IN	Y	42470 FQ	45110 MW	47750 TQ	USBLS	5/15
Metals and Plastics	Indianapolis-Carmel-Anderson MSA, IN	Y	35980 FQ	42430 MW	55760 TQ	USBLS	5/15
Metals and Plastics	Iowa	Y	37570 FQ	44340 MW	51720 TQ	USBLS	5/15
Metals and Plastics	Kansas	Y	38920 FQ	52900 MW	73320 TQ	USBLS	5/15
Metals and Plastics	Wichita MSA, KS	Y	45800 FQ	62810 MW	83310 TQ	USBLS	5/15
Metals and Plastics	Kentucky	Y	29910 FQ	36730 MW	46240 TQ	USBLS	5/15
Metals and Plastics	Louisville-Jefferson County MSA, KY-IN	Y	28970 FQ	37770 MW	47620 TQ	USBLS	5/15
Metals and Plastics	Louisiana	Y	39380 FQ	46690 MW	56750 TQ	USBLS	5/15
Metals and Plastics	Maine	Y	44560 FQ	50150 MW	57510 TQ	USBLS	5/15
Metals and Plastics	Portland-South Portland MSA, ME	Y	42650 FQ	46080 MW	49510 TQ	USBLS	5/15
Metals and Plastics	Maryland	Y	30066 AE	50789 MW	61151 AEX	MDBLS	4/16
Metals and Plastics	Baltimore-Columbia-Towson MSA, MD	Y	33760 FQ	45090 MW	58650 TQ	USBLS	5/15
Metals and Plastics	Massachusetts	Y	43630 FQ	50860 MW	64360 TQ	USBLS	5/15
Metals and Plastics	Boston-Cambridge-Newton NECTA, MA	Y	43350 FQ	48850 MW	65760 TQ	USBLS	5/15
Metals and Plastics	Worcester MSA, MA-CT	Y	44490 FQ	53040 MW	67770 TQ	USBLS	5/15
Metals and Plastics	Michigan	Y	41110 FQ	49270 MW	58520 TQ	USBLS	5/15
Metals and Plastics	Detroit-Dearborn-Livonia PMSA, MI	Y	45320 FQ	54330 MW	60680 TQ	USBLS	5/15
Metals and Plastics	Grand Rapids-Wyoming MSA, MI	Y	38630 FQ	45410 MW	52100 TQ	USBLS	5/15
Metals and Plastics	Minnesota	Y	45722 FQ	54156 MW	61202 TQ	MNBLS	1/16-3/16
Metals and Plastics	Minneapolis-St. Paul-Bloomington MSA, MN-WI	Y	46795 FQ	55178 MW	61850 TQ	MNBLS	1/16-3/16
Metals and Plastics	Mississippi	Y	32120 FQ	39510 MW	55750 TQ	USBLS	5/15
Metals and Plastics	Missouri	Y	34550 FQ	38000 MW	48270 TQ	USBLS	5/15
Metals and Plastics	Kansas City MSA, MO-KS	Y	36140 FQ	44380 MW	58720 TQ	USBLS	5/15
Metals and Plastics	St. Louis MSA, MO-IL	Y	47810 FQ	58800 MW	71800 TQ	USBLS	5/15
Metals and Plastics	Nebraska	Y	40120 FQ	48535 MW	57775 TQ	NEBLS	7/16-9/16
Metals and Plastics	Omaha-Council Bluffs MSA, NE-IA	Y	37345 FQ	45690 MW	55530 TQ	NEBLS	7/16-9/16
Metals and Plastics	Nevada	Y	44340 FQ	50890 MW	60360 TQ	USBLS	5/15
Metals and Plastics	New Hampshire	H	21.73 AE	28.38 MW	32.43 AEX	NHBLS	6/16
Metals and Plastics	Manchester NECTA, NH	H	14.71 AE	18.65 MW	21.41 AEX	NHBLS	6/16
Metals and Plastics	Nashua NECTA, NH-MA	Y	52550 FQ	58490 MW	64550 TQ	USBLS	5/15
Metals and Plastics	New Jersey	Y	50520 FQ	61840 MW	74360 TQ	USBLS	5/15
Metals and Plastics	Camden PMSA, NJ	Y	44630 FQ	50600 MW	58830 TQ	USBLS	5/15
Metals and Plastics	Newark PMSA, NJ-PA	Y	55780 FQ	64530 MW	73490 TQ	USBLS	5/15
Metals and Plastics	New York	Y	33000 AE	46960 MW	54430 AEX	NYBLS	1/16-3/16
Metals and Plastics	Buffalo-Cheektowaga-Niagara Falls MSA, NY	Y	39910 FQ	47880 MW	57490 TQ	USBLS	5/15
Metals and Plastics	Nassau County-Suffolk County PMSA, NY	Y	51870 FQ	58350 MW	66480 TQ	USBLS	5/15
Metals and Plastics	New York-Jersey City-White Plains PMSA, NY-NJ	Y	30770 FQ	47990 MW	70250 TQ	USBLS	5/15
Metals and Plastics	Rochester MSA, NY	Y	39750 FQ	46350 MW	55860 TQ	USBLS	5/15
Metals and Plastics	North Carolina	Y	35700 FQ	43740 MW	52980 TQ	USBLS	5/15
Metals and Plastics	Charlotte-Concord-Gastonia MSA, NC-SC	Y	38730 FQ	45510 MW	54080 TQ	USBLS	5/15
Metals and Plastics	Raleigh MSA, NC	Y	33160 FQ	40160 MW	47360 TQ	USBLS	5/15
Metals and Plastics	Ohio	Y	39670 FQ	46620 MW	57470 TQ	USBLS	5/15
Metals and Plastics	Cincinnati MSA, OH-KY-IN	Y	39070 FQ	58190 MW	72250 TQ	USBLS	5/15

AE Average entry wage	**AWR** Average wage range	**H** Hourly	**LR** Low end range	**MTC** Median total compensation	**TCC** Total cash compensation
AEX Average experienced wage	**B** Biweekly	**HI** Highest wage paid	**M** Monthly	**MW** Median wage paid	**TQ** Third quartile wage
ATC Average total compensation	**D** Daily	**HR** High end range	**MCC** Median cash compensation	**MWR** Median wage range	**W** Weekly
AW Average wage paid	**FQ** First quartile wage	**LO** Lowest wage paid	**ME** Median entry wage	**S** See annotated source	**Y** Yearly

Occupation/Type/Industry	Location	Per	Low	Mid	High	Source	Date
Computer Numerically Controlled Machine Tool Programmer							
Metals and Plastics	Cleveland-Elyria MSA, OH	Y	42290 FQ	46770 MW	54540 TQ	USBLS	5/15
Metals and Plastics	Columbus MSA, OH	Y	37620 FQ	46340 MW	58460 TQ	USBLS	5/15
Metals and Plastics	Mansfield MSA, OH	Y	26550 FQ	35440 MW	48480 TQ	USBLS	5/15
Metals and Plastics	Oklahoma	Y	37470 FQ	46780 MW	62470 TQ	USBLS	5/15
Metals and Plastics	Tulsa MSA, OK	Y	43830 FQ	54310 MW	69270 TQ	USBLS	5/15
Metals and Plastics	Oregon	H	21.36 FQ	27.00 MW	30.85 TQ	ORBLS	2016
Metals and Plastics	Portland-Vancouver-Hillsboro MSA, OR-WA	Y	48070 FQ	56690 MW	64230 TQ	USBLS	5/15
Metals and Plastics	Pennsylvania	Y	40320 FQ	47050 MW	57170 TQ	USBLS	5/15
Metals and Plastics	Allentown-Bethlehem-Easton MSA, PA-NJ	Y	45910 FQ	54960 MW	63690 TQ	USBLS	5/15
Metals and Plastics	Montgomery County-Bucks County-Chester County PMSA, PA	Y	46090 FQ	54720 MW	65740 TQ	USBLS	5/15
Metals and Plastics	Pittsburgh MSA, PA	Y	41450 FQ	49420 MW	62610 TQ	USBLS	5/15
Metals and Plastics	Rhode Island	Y	40700 FQ	48330 MW	60470 TQ	USBLS	5/15
Metals and Plastics	Providence-Warwick MSA, RI-MA	Y	40690 FQ	48610 MW	61380 TQ	USBLS	5/15
Metals and Plastics	South Carolina	Y	40570 FQ	49050 MW	58030 TQ	USBLS	5/15
Metals and Plastics	Charleston-North Charleston MSA, SC	Y	44080 FQ	56250 MW	79670 TQ	USBLS	5/15
Metals and Plastics	Columbia MSA, SC	Y	36280 FQ	42190 MW	49350 TQ	USBLS	5/15
Metals and Plastics	Greenville-Anderson-Mauldin MSA, SC	Y	40830 FQ	47710 MW	55770 TQ	USBLS	5/15
Metals and Plastics	South Dakota	Y	36910 FQ	42660 MW	48880 TQ	USBLS	5/15
Metals and Plastics	Tennessee	Y	37490 FQ	47760 MW	57410 TQ	USBLS	5/15
Metals and Plastics	Knoxville MSA, TN	Y	35180 FQ	45030 MW	67640 TQ	USBLS	5/15
Metals and Plastics	Memphis MSA, TN-MS-AR	Y	40110 FQ	50170 MW	58940 TQ	USBLS	5/15
Metals and Plastics	Nashville-Davidson–Murfreesboro–Franklin MSA, TN	Y	47900 FQ	54580 MW	60760 TQ	USBLS	5/15
Metals and Plastics	Texas	Y	43580 FQ	55610 MW	70140 TQ	USBLS	5/15
Metals and Plastics	Austin-Round Rock MSA, TX	Y	44060 FQ	55460 MW	67040 TQ	USBLS	5/15
Metals and Plastics	Dallas-Plano-Irving PMSA, TX	Y	40800 FQ	48010 MW	59100 TQ	USBLS	5/15
Metals and Plastics	Fort Worth-Arlington PMSA, TX	Y	45190 FQ	56230 MW	78630 TQ	USBLS	5/15
Metals and Plastics	Houston-The Woodlands-Sugar Land MSA, TX	Y	51070 FQ	63650 MW	75150 TQ	USBLS	5/15
Metals and Plastics	San Antonio-New Braunfels MSA, TX	Y	37990 FQ	45930 MW	56120 TQ	USBLS	5/15
Metals and Plastics	Utah	Y	43610 FQ	52670 MW	59970 TQ	USBLS	5/15
Metals and Plastics	Salt Lake City MSA, UT	Y	49890 FQ	56390 MW	62400 TQ	USBLS	5/15
Metals and Plastics	Vermont	Y	29960 FQ	43580 MW	59450 TQ	USBLS	5/15
Metals and Plastics	Burlington-South Burlington MSA, VT	Y	31760 FQ	50610 MW	60280 TQ	USBLS	5/15
Metals and Plastics	Virginia	Y	43800 FQ	57090 MW	70620 TQ	USBLS	5/15
Metals and Plastics	Richmond MSA, VA	Y	53180 FQ	62760 MW	76580 TQ	USBLS	5/15
Metals and Plastics	Virginia Beach-Norfolk-Newport News MSA, VA-NC	Y	53270 FQ	61900 MW	72680 TQ	USBLS	5/15
Metals and Plastics	Washington	H	27.52 FQ	41.40 MW	50.39 TQ	WABLS	3/16
Metals and Plastics	Seattle-Bellevue-Everett PMSA, WA	H	18.32 FQ	27.91 MW	41.18 TQ	WABLS	3/16
Metals and Plastics	Tacoma-Lakewood PMSA, WA	H	23.32 FQ	27.62 MW	33.66 TQ	WABLS	3/16
Metals and Plastics	Wisconsin	Y	38370 FQ	47610 MW	57810 TQ	USBLS	5/15
Metals and Plastics	Milwaukee-Waukesha-West Allis MSA, WI	Y	43130 FQ	52690 MW	60800 TQ	USBLS	5/15
Computer Operator	Alabama	Y	24569 AE	38750 AW	45841 AEX	ALBLS	6/16
	Birmingham-Hoover MSA, AL	Y	30619 AE	41657 AW	47170 AEX	ALBLS	6/16
	Alaska	Y	45820 FQ	54320 MW	61010 TQ	USBLS	5/15
	Anchorage MSA, AK	Y	49230 FQ	55450 MW	60200 TQ	USBLS	5/15
	Arizona	Y	33670 FQ	38270 MW	48070 TQ	USBLS	5/15
	Phoenix-Mesa-Scottsdale MSA, AZ	Y	35340 FQ	44520 MW	54690 TQ	USBLS	5/15
	Tucson MSA, AZ	Y	32810 FQ	38470 MW	55010 TQ	USBLS	5/15
	Arkansas	Y	30970 FQ	35450 MW	40190 TQ	USBLS	5/15
	Little Rock-North Little Rock-Conway MSA, AR	Y	28730 FQ	34540 MW	43750 TQ	USBLS	5/15
	California	H	16.67 FQ	21.79 MW	27.52 TQ	CABLS	1/16-3/16

AE	Average entry wage	AWR	Average wage range	H	Hourly	LR	Low end range
AEX	Average experienced wage	B	Biweekly	HI	Highest wage paid	M	Monthly
ATC	Average total compensation	D	Daily	HR	High end range	MCC	Median cash compensation
AW	Average wage paid	FQ	First quartile wage	LO	Lowest wage paid	ME	Median entry wage

MTC	Median total compensation	TCC	Total cash compensation	
MW	Median wage paid	TQ	Third quartile wage	
MWR	Median wage range	W	Weekly	
S	See annotated source	Y	Yearly	

Occupation/Type/Industry	Location	Per	Low	Mid	High	Source	Date
Computer Operator	Anaheim-Santa Ana-Irvine PMSA, CA	H	14.07 FQ	19.39 MW	27.13 TQ	CABLS	1/16-3/16
	Los Angeles-Long Beach-Glendale PMSA, CA	H	15.37 FQ	21.06 MW	27.69 TQ	CABLS	1/16-3/16
	Oakland-Hayward-Berkeley PMSA, CA	H	17.44 FQ	19.35 MW	.25.50 TQ	CABLS	1/16-3/16
	Riverside-San Bernardino-Ontario MSA, CA	H	17.76 FQ	21.74 MW	25.13 TQ	CABLS	1/16-3/16
	Sacramento–Roseville–Arden-Arcade MSA, CA	H	19.42 FQ	23.02 MW	26.73 TQ	CABLS	1/16-3/16
	San Diego-Carlsbad MSA, CA	H	17.58 FQ	23.93 MW	28.25 TQ	CABLS	1/16-3/16
	San Francisco-Redwood City-South San Francisco PMSA, CA	H	17.65 FQ	23.00 MW	28.37 TQ	CABLS	1/16-3/16
	Colorado	Y	41500 FQ	51540 MW	62930 TQ	USBLS	5/15
	Denver-Aurora-Lakewood MSA, CO	Y	43490 FQ	53610 MW	67400 TQ	USBLS	5/15
	Connecticut	Y		46194 MW		CTBLS	1/16-3/16
	Bridgeport-Stamford-Norwalk MSA, CT	Y	35600 FQ	46040 MW	54550 TQ	USBLS	5/15
	Hartford-West Hartford-East Hartford MSA, CT	Y	32520 FQ	42100 MW	55130 TQ	USBLS	5/15
	Delaware	Y	35060 FQ	42590 MW	50380 TQ	USBLS	5/15
	Wilmington PMSA, DE-MD-NJ	Y	39920 FQ	52140 MW	58010 TQ	USBLS	5/15
	District of Columbia	Y	50230 FQ	56510 MW	60140 TQ	USBLS	5/15
	Washington-Arlington-Alexandria PMSA, DC-VA-MD-WV	Y	40960 FQ	49610 MW	57970 TQ	USBLS	5/15
	Florida	H	13.23 AE	18.60 MW	23.54 AEX	FLBLS	7/16-9/16
	Fort Lauderdale-Pompano Beach-Deerfield Beach PMSA, FL	H	13.26 AE	19.92 MW	25.14 AEX	FLBLS	7/16-9/16
	Miami-Miami Beach-Kendall PMSA, FL	H	13.18 AE	19.35 MW	23.56 AEX	FLBLS	7/16-9/16
	Orlando-Kissimmee-Sanford MSA, FL	H	14.48 AE	18.58 MW	22.70 AEX	FLBLS	7/16-9/16
	Tampa-St. Petersburg-Clearwater MSA, FL	H	13.20 AE	15.08 MW	19.29 AEX	FLBLS	7/16-9/16
	Georgia	Y	25500 FQ	33150 MW	47520 TQ	USBLS	5/15
	Atlanta-Sandy Springs-Roswell MSA, GA	Y	25330 FQ	32330 MW	45360 TQ	USBLS	5/15
	Augusta-Richmond County MSA, GA-SC	Y	44460 FQ	65720 MW	71900 TQ	USBLS	5/15
	Hawaii	Y	35170 FQ	46180 MW	57970 TQ	USBLS	5/15
	Urban Honolulu MSA, HI	Y	34900 FQ	45620 MW	57970 TQ	USBLS	5/15
	Idaho	Y	33190 FQ	37940 MW	45850 TQ	USBLS	5/15
	Boise City MSA, ID	Y	33480 FQ	37340 MW	43230 TQ	USBLS	5/15
	Illinois	Y	34990 FQ	49180 MW	59310 TQ	USBLS	5/15
	Chicago-Naperville-Arlington Heights PMSA, IL	Y	35630 FQ	49850 MW	59650 TQ	USBLS	5/15
	Lake County-Kenosha County PMSA, IL-WI	Y	31080 FQ	51080 MW	61910 TQ	USBLS	5/15
	Indiana	Y	30620 FQ	40170 MW	52510 TQ	USBLS	5/15
	Indianapolis-Carmel-Anderson MSA, IN	Y	34250 FQ	47260 MW	61390 TQ	USBLS	5/15
	Iowa	Y	27740 FQ	37460 MW	48810 TQ	USBLS	5/15
	Des Moines-West Des Moines MSA, IA	Y	33370 FQ	42540 MW	55010 TQ	USBLS	5/15
	Kansas	Y	28900 FQ	37160 MW	48380 TQ	USBLS	5/15
	Wichita MSA, KS	Y	37590 FQ	47090 MW	57970 TQ	USBLS	5/15
	Kentucky	Y	30430 FQ	37840 MW	47930 TQ	USBLS	5/15
	Louisville-Jefferson County MSA, KY-IN	Y	32940 FQ	38100 MW	46920 TQ	USBLS	5/15
	Louisiana	Y	31720 FQ	40250 MW	48850 TQ	USBLS	5/15
	Baton Rouge MSA, LA	Y	34640 FQ	42140 MW	48980 TQ	USBLS	5/15
	New Orleans-Metairie MSA, LA	Y	30500 FQ	39100 MW	49720 TQ	USBLS	5/15
	Maine	Y	23280 FQ	31010 MW	45000 TQ	USBLS	5/15
	Portland-South Portland MSA, ME	Y	34880 FQ	44540 MW	57970 TQ	USBLS	5/15
	Maryland	Y	22558 AE	39293 MW	47661 AEX	MDBLS	4/16

AE	Average entry wage	AWR	Average wage range	H	Hourly
AEX	Average experienced wage	B	Biweekly	HI	Highest wage paid
ATC	Average total compensation	D	Daily	HR	High end range
AW	Average wage paid	FQ	First quartile wage	LO	Lowest wage paid

LR	Low end range	MTC	Median total compensation
M	Monthly	MW	Median wage paid
MCC	Median cash compensation	MWR	Median wage range
ME	Median entry wage	S	See annotated source

TCC	Total cash compensation
TQ	Third quartile wage
W	Weekly
Y	Yearly

Computer Operator

Occupation/Type/Industry	Location	Per	Low	Mid	High	Source	Date
Computer Operator	Baltimore-Columbia-Towson MSA, MD	Y	22920 FQ	30380 MW	49700 TQ	USBLS	5/15
	Massachusetts	Y	40840 FQ	50890 MW	59000 TQ	USBLS	5/15
	Boston-Cambridge-Newton NECTA, MA	Y	44460 FQ	53710 MW	60570 TQ	USBLS	5/15
	Worcester MSA, MA-CT	Y	36280 FQ	44710 MW	53180 TQ	USBLS	5/15
	Michigan	Y	27410 FQ	38530 MW	51530 TQ	USBLS	5/15
	Detroit-Dearborn-Livonia PMSA, MI	Y	27370 FQ	38700 MW	52420 TQ	USBLS	5/15
	Grand Rapids-Wyoming MSA, MI	Y	29980 FQ	38850 MW	54860 TQ	USBLS	5/15
	Minnesota	Y	35930 FQ	43121 MW	53860 TQ	MNBLS	1/16-3/16
	Minneapolis-St. Paul-Bloomington MSA, MN-WI	Y	36527 FQ	44375 MW	56429 TQ	MNBLS	1/16-3/16
	Mississippi	Y	23950 FQ	31140 MW	44700 TQ	USBLS	5/15
	Jackson MSA, MS	Y	23220 FQ	28640 MW	42680 TQ	USBLS	5/15
	Missouri	Y	35000 FQ	43550 MW	57050 TQ	USBLS	5/15
	Kansas City MSA, MO-KS	Y	32280 FQ	41720 MW	54520 TQ	USBLS	5/15
	St. Louis MSA, MO-IL	Y	34870 FQ	42180 MW	56890 TQ	USBLS	5/15
	Montana	Y	31410 FQ	42950 MW	47920 TQ	USBLS	5/15
	Billings MSA, MT	Y	42290 FQ	45160 MW	48030 TQ	USBLS	5/15
	Nebraska	Y	25480 FQ	30560 MW	41825 TQ	NEBLS	7/16-9/16
	Omaha-Council Bluffs MSA, NE-IA	Y	25020 FQ	30810 MW	42635 TQ	NEBLS	7/16-9/16
	Nevada	Y	34650 FQ	43810 MW	56310 TQ	USBLS	5/15
	Las Vegas-Henderson-Paradise MSA, NV	Y	36400 FQ	45740 MW	57780 TQ	USBLS	5/15
	New Hampshire	H	14.70 AE	21.89 MW	25.24 AEX	NHBLS	6/16
	Manchester NECTA, NH	H	11.46 AE	18.39 MW	23.32 AEX	NHBLS	6/16
	Nashua NECTA, NH-MA	Y	43280 FQ	48970 MW	57990 TQ	USBLS	5/15
	New Jersey	Y	36120 FQ	46840 MW	57840 TQ	USBLS	5/15
	Camden PMSA, NJ	Y	32520 FQ	37530 MW	44510 TQ	USBLS	5/15
	Newark PMSA, NJ-PA	Y	41230 FQ	50910 MW	60320 TQ	USBLS	5/15
	Trenton MSA, NJ	Y	43340 FQ	51200 MW	62570 TQ	USBLS	5/15
	New Mexico	Y	25230 FQ	32920 MW	43470 TQ	USBLS	5/15
	Albuquerque MSA, NM	Y	29860 FQ	40460 MW	48530 TQ	USBLS	5/15
	New York	Y	23300 AE	39760 MW	50570 AEX	NYBLS	1/16-3/16
	Buffalo-Cheektowaga-Niagara Falls MSA, NY	Y	32720 FQ	44460 MW	56950 TQ	USBLS	6/15
	Nassau County-Suffolk County PMSA, NY	Y	22770 FQ	35830 MW	50990 TQ	USBLS	5/15
	New York-Jersey City-White Plains PMSA, NY-NJ	Y	26490 FQ	41930 MW	56080 TQ	USBLS	5/15
	Rochester MSA, NY	Y	33940 FQ	39170 MW	49770 TQ	USBLS	5/15
	North Carolina	Y	27170 FQ	35180 MW	44990 TQ	USBLS	5/15
	Charlotte-Concord-Gastonia MSA, NC-SC	Y	32710 FQ	38880 MW	47230 TQ	USBLS	5/15
	Raleigh MSA, NC	Y	28260 FQ	36790 MW	47060 TQ	USBLS	5/15
	North Dakota	Y	25720 FQ	32560 MW	40450 TQ	USBLS	5/15
	Fargo MSA, ND-MN	Y	29630 FQ	36420 MW	43760 TQ	USBLS	5/15
	Ohio	Y	28890 FQ	37850 MW	49880 TQ	USBLS	5/15
	Cincinnati MSA, OH-KY-IN	Y	34710 FQ	43650 MW	52990 TQ	USBLS	5/15
	Cleveland-Elyria MSA, OH	Y	25200 FQ	39950 MW	55130 TQ	USBLS	5/15
	Columbus MSA, OH	Y	28360 FQ	36340 MW	47440 TQ	USBLS	5/15
	Oklahoma	Y	24280 FQ	33090 MW	46020 TQ	USBLS	5/15
	Oklahoma City MSA, OK	Y	25130 FQ	36070 MW	48830 TQ	USBLS	5/15
	Tulsa MSA, OK	Y	26210 FQ	31050 MW	42510 TQ	USBLS	5/15
	Oregon	H	16.02 FQ	19.63 MW	24.26 TQ	ORBLS	2016
	Portland-Vancouver-Hillsboro MSA, OR-WA	Y	33850 FQ	40750 MW	50320 TQ	USBLS	5/15
	Pennsylvania	Y	28120 FQ	38760 MW	53560 TQ	USBLS	5/15
	Allentown-Bethlehem-Easton MSA, PA-NJ	Y	23080 FQ	36930 MW	47340 TQ	USBLS	5/15
	Harrisburg-Carlisle MSA, PA	Y	37760 FQ	45040 MW	53800 TQ	USBLS	5/15
	Montgomery County-Bucks County-Chester County PMSA, PA	Y	31270 FQ	41080 MW	54710 TQ	USBLS	5/15
	Philadelphia PMSA, PA	Y	30760 FQ	42220 MW	57980 TQ	USBLS	5/15
	Pittsburgh MSA, PA	Y	25510 FQ	35830 MW	53250 TQ	USBLS	5/15
	Rhode Island	Y	41940 FQ	49100 MW	57980 TQ	USBLS	5/15
	Providence-Warwick MSA, RI-MA	Y	39840 FQ	47230 MW	56740 TQ	USBLS	5/15

Occupation/Type/Industry	Location	Per	Low	Mid	High	Source	Date
Computer Operator	South Carolina	Y	29450 FQ	36090 MW	48790 TQ	USBLS	5/15
	Charleston-North Charleston MSA, SC	Y	28840 FQ	34450 MW	45670 TQ	USBLS	5/15
	Columbia MSA, SC	Y	29810 FQ	35260 MW	51610 TQ	USBLS	5/15
	Greenville-Anderson-Mauldin MSA, SC	Y	31760 FQ	38470 MW	48490 TQ	USBLS	5/15
	Tennessee	Y	31130 FQ	39870 MW	49170 TQ	USBLS	5/15
	Knoxville MSA, TN	Y	30380 FQ	36800 MW	45710 TQ	USBLS	5/15
	Memphis MSA, TN-MS-AR	Y	36130 FQ	43770 MW	51630 TQ	USBLS	5/15
	Nashville-Davidson–Murfreesboro–Franklin MSA, TN	Y	32440 FQ	42470 MW	51060 TQ	USBLS	5/15
	Texas	Y	28370 FQ	38290 MW	54650 TQ	USBLS	5/15
	Austin-Round Rock MSA, TX	Y	26190 FQ	36250 MW	48050 TQ	USBLS	5/15
	Dallas-Plano-Irving PMSA, TX	Y	31620 FQ	44980 MW	57530 TQ	USBLS	5/15
	Fort Worth-Arlington PMSA, TX	Y	35470 FQ	46410 MW	56180 TQ	USBLS	5/15
	Houston-The Woodlands-Sugar Land MSA, TX	Y	33460 FQ	41070 MW	58010 TQ	USBLS	5/15
	San Antonio-New Braunfels MSA, TX	Y	21570 FQ	29930 MW	41720 TQ	USBLS	5/15
	Utah	Y	31900 FQ	40880 MW	49220 TQ	USBLS	5/15
	Ogden-Clearfield MSA, UT	Y	34850 FQ	42210 MW	47480 TQ	USBLS	5/15
	Salt Lake City MSA, UT	Y	29830 FQ	39490 MW	49440 TQ	USBLS	5/15
	Vermont	Y	32370 FQ	39990 MW	50380 TQ	USBLS	5/15
	Virginia	Y	33980 FQ	44250 MW	54910 TQ	USBLS	5/15
	Richmond MSA, VA	Y	33700 FQ	43310 MW	52960 TQ	USBLS	5/15
	Virginia Beach-Norfolk-Newport News MSA, VA-NC	Y	26350 FQ	36160 MW	47210 TQ	USBLS	5/15
	Washington	H	17.38 FQ	22.02 MW	27.45 TQ	WABLS	3/16
	Seattle-Bellevue-Everett PMSA, WA	H	16.85 FQ	21.27 MW	26.48 TQ	WABLS	3/16
	Tacoma-Lakewood PMSA, WA	H	23.92 FQ	26.50 MW	28.53 TQ	WABLS	3/16
	West Virginia	Y	25300 FQ	38570 MW	46850 TQ	USBLS	5/15
	Wisconsin	Y	34280 FQ	41620 MW	50370 TQ	USBLS	5/15
	Madison MSA, WI	Y	26830 FQ	39240 MW	49100 TQ	USBLS	5/15
	Milwaukee-Waukesha-West Allis MSA, WI	Y	36370 FQ	43600 MW	52430 TQ	USBLS	5/15
	Wyoming	Y	29090 FQ	39850 MW	46630 TQ	USBLS	5/15
	Cheyenne MSA, WY	Y	28050 FQ	40210 MW	45320 TQ	USBLS	5/15
	Puerto Rico	Y	17710 FQ	20360 MW	25640 TQ	USBLS	5/15
	San Juan-Carolina-Caguas MSA, PR	Y	17680 FQ	20250 MW	25180 TQ	USBLS	5/15
	Guam	Y	26660 FQ	31520 MW	39960 TQ	USBLS	5/15
Computer Programmer	Alabama	Y	55584 AE	84798 AW	99415 AEX	ALBLS	6/16
	Birmingham-Hoover MSA, AL	Y	53800 AE	79956 AW	93034 AEX	ALBLS	6/16
	Daphne-Fairhope-Foley MSA, AL	Y	62430 FQ	77810 MW	91110 TQ	USBLS	5/15
	Alaska	Y	71820 FQ	85520 MW	101420 TQ	USBLS	5/15
	Anchorage MSA, AK	Y	69940 FQ	85510 MW	105910 TQ	USBLS	5/15
	Arizona	Y	63130 FQ	78660 MW	102600 TQ	USBLS	5/15
	Phoenix-Mesa-Scottsdale MSA, AZ	Y	64150 FQ	79420 MW	104070 TQ	USBLS	5/15
	Tucson MSA, AZ	Y	55960 FQ	70850 MW	87910 TQ	USBLS	5/15
	Arkansas	Y	58550 FQ	69370 MW	79920 TQ	USBLS	5/15
	Little Rock-North Little Rock-Conway MSA, AR	Y	56820 FQ	67040 MW	77100 TQ	USBLS	5/15
	California	H	32.75 FQ	43.58 MW	56.79 TQ	CABLS	1/16-3/16
	Anaheim-Santa Ana-Irvine PMSA, CA	H	25.58 FQ	41.27 MW	53.18 TQ	CABLS	1/16-3/16
	Los Angeles-Long Beach-Glendale PMSA, CA	H	36.20 FQ	45.75 MW	57.37 TQ	CABLS	1/16-3/16
	Oakland-Hayward-Berkeley PMSA, CA	H	32.35 FQ	42.21 MW	60.05 TQ	CABLS	1/16-3/16
	Riverside-San Bernardino-Ontario MSA, CA	H	26.99 FQ	35.22 MW	45.32 TQ	CABLS	1/16-3/16
	Sacramento–Roseville–Arden-Arcade MSA, CA	H	34.56 FQ	40.22 MW	44.21 TQ	CABLS	1/16-3/16
	San Diego-Carlsbad MSA, CA	H	30.24 FQ	38.61 MW	49.08 TQ	CABLS	1/16-3/16

AE	Average entry wage	AWR	Average wage range	H	Hourly	LR	Low end range	MTC	Median total compensation	TCC	Total cash compensation
AEX	Average experienced wage	B	Biweekly	HI	Highest wage paid	M	Monthly	MW	Median wage paid	TQ	Third quartile wage
ATC	Average total compensation	D	Daily	HR	High end range	MCC	Median cash compensation	MWR	Median wage range	W	Weekly
AW	Average wage paid	FQ	First quartile wage	LO	Lowest wage paid	ME	Median entry wage	S	See annotated source	Y	Yearly

Occupation/Type/Industry	Location	Per	Low	Mid	High	Source	Date
Computer Programmer	San Francisco-Redwood City-South San Francisco PMSA, CA	H	40.07 FQ	53.18 MW	67.57 TQ	CABLS	1/16-3/16
	Colorado	Y	65470 FQ	81290 MW	106350 TQ	USBLS	5/15
	Denver-Aurora-Lakewood MSA, CO	Y	67010 FQ	84130 MW	111140 TQ	USBLS	5/15
	Connecticut	Y		80835 MW		CTBLS	1/16-3/16
	Bridgeport-Stamford-Norwalk MSA, CT	Y	73150 FQ	88050 MW	101470 TQ	USBLS	5/15
	Hartford-West Hartford-East Hartford MSA, CT	Y	58870 FQ	73860 MW	91800 TQ	USBLS	5/15
	Delaware	Y	65010 FQ	76900 MW	93930 TQ	USBLS	5/15
	Wilmington PMSA, DE-MD-NJ	Y	65500 FQ	76230 MW	96340 TQ	USBLS	5/15
	District of Columbia	Y	70340 FQ	91100 MW	118040 TQ	USBLS	5/15
	Washington-Arlington-Alexandria PMSA, DC-VA-MD-WV	Y	79480 FQ	97130 MW	119780 TQ	USBLS	5/15
	Florida	H	22.97 AE	35.69 MW	44.57 AEX	FLBLS	7/16-9/16
	Fort Lauderdale-Pompano Beach-Deerfield Beach PMSA, FL	H	20.27 AE	35.78 MW	42.03 AEX	FLBLS	7/16-9/16
	Miami-Miami Beach-Kendall PMSA, FL	H	29.19 AE	43.69 MW	53.19 AEX	FLBLS	7/16-9/16
	Orlando-Kissimmee-Sanford MSA, FL	H	23.29 AE	34.47 MW	42.25 AEX	FLBLS	7/16-9/16
	Tampa-St. Petersburg-Clearwater MSA, FL	H	23.70 AE	38.00 MW	45.71 AEX	FLBLS	7/16-9/16
	Georgia	Y	61720 FQ	79620 MW	100320 TQ	USBLS	5/15
	Atlanta-Sandy Springs-Roswell MSA, GA	Y	63220 FQ	81030 MW	101590 TQ	USBLS	5/15
	Augusta-Richmond County MSA, GA-SC	Y	46560 FQ	56650 MW	69800 TQ	USBLS	5/15
	Hawaii	Y	56120 FQ	69660 MW	84710 TQ	USBLS	5/15
	Urban Honolulu MSA, HI	Y	56920 FQ	70020 MW	84040 TQ	USBLS	5/15
	Idaho	Y	51070 FQ	66890 MW	77610 TQ	USBLS	5/15
	Boise City MSA, ID	Y	52320 FQ	67330 MW	77880 TQ	USBLS	5/15
	Illinois	Y	54220 FQ	75130 MW	98930 TQ	USBLS	5/15
	Chicago-Naperville-Arlington Heights PMSA, IL	Y	53580 FQ	75560 MW	98340 TQ	USBLS	5/15
	Lake County-Kenosha County PMSA, IL-WI	Y	61890 FQ	96690 MW	113830 TQ	USBLS	5/15
	Indiana	Y	49840 FQ	65480 MW	80780 TQ	USBLS	5/15
	Gary PMSA, IN	Y	56370 FQ	67040 MW	91520 TQ	USBLS	5/15
	Indianapolis-Carmel-Anderson MSA, IN	Y	53410 FQ	68750 MW	84250 TQ	USBLS	5/15
	Iowa	Y	54280 FQ	66720 MW	79050 TQ	USBLS	5/15
	Des Moines-West Des Moines MSA, IA	Y	59500 FQ	71560 MW	88010 TQ	USBLS	5/15
	Kansas	Y	51340 FQ	67190 MW	87390 TQ	USBLS	5/15
	Wichita MSA, KS	Y	52590 FQ	62730 MW	88210 TQ	USBLS	5/15
	Kentucky	Y	51180 FQ	67720 MW	83440 TQ	USBLS	5/15
	Louisville-Jefferson County MSA, KY-IN	Y	45790 FQ	67430 MW	81760 TQ	USBLS	5/15
	Louisiana	Y	48720 FQ	63640 MW	82150 TQ	USBLS	5/15
	Baton Rouge MSA, LA	Y	48970 FQ	65880 MW	87490 TQ	USBLS	5/15
	New Orleans-Metairie MSA, LA	Y	55170 FQ	69250 MW	85930 TQ	USBLS	5/15
	Maine	Y	53150 FQ	67690 MW	77460 TQ	USBLS	5/15
	Portland-South Portland MSA, ME	Y	60580 FQ	70660 MW	79960 TQ	USBLS	5/15
	Maryland	Y	59584 AE	91463 MW	107402 AEX	MDBLS	4/16
	Baltimore-Columbia-Towson MSA, MD	Y	67270 FQ	80660 MW	109830 TQ	USBLS	5/15
	Massachusetts	Y	71370 FQ	93420 MW	117220 TQ	USBLS	5/15
	Boston-Cambridge-Newton NECTA, MA	Y	77770 FQ	99090 MW	121390 TQ	USBLS	5/15
	Worcester MSA, MA-CT	Y	59160 FQ	75070 MW	101250 TQ	USBLS	5/15
	Michigan	Y	55670 FQ	70860 MW	89380 TQ	USBLS	5/15
	Detroit-Dearborn-Livonia PMSA, MI	Y	53420 FQ	73850 MW	102560 TQ	USBLS	5/15

AE Average entry wage	**AWR** Average wage range	**H** Hourly	**LR** Low end range	**MTC** Median total compensation	**TCC** Total cash compensation
AEX Average experienced wage	**B** Biweekly	**HI** Highest wage paid	**M** Monthly	**MW** Median wage paid	**TQ** Third quartile wage
ATC Average total compensation	**D** Daily	**HR** High end range	**MCC** Median cash compensation	**MWR** Median wage range	**W** Weekly
AW Average wage paid	**FQ** First quartile wage	**LO** Lowest wage paid	**ME** Median entry wage	**S** See annotated source	**Y** Yearly

Occupation/Type/Industry	Location	Per	Low	Mid	High	Source	Date
Computer Programmer	Grand Rapids-Wyoming MSA, MI	Y	55410 FQ	68100 MW	84340 TQ	USBLS	5/15
	Minnesota	Y	64898 FQ	78436 MW	95735 TQ	MNBLS	1/16-3/16
	Minneapolis-St. Paul-Bloomington MSA, MN-WI	Y	65039 FQ	77428 MW	93063 TQ	MNBLS	1/16-3/16
	Mississippi	Y	48640 FQ	61020 MW	76080 TQ	USBLS	5/15
	Jackson MSA, MS	Y	55180 FQ	63320 MW	77890 TQ	USBLS	5/15
	Missouri	Y	58930 FQ	78310 MW	97520 TQ	USBLS	5/15
	Kansas City MSA, MO-KS	Y	52320 FQ	76060 MW	96340 TQ	USBLS	5/15
	St. Louis MSA, MO-IL	Y	67180 FQ	83900 MW	100320 TQ	USBLS	5/15
	Montana	Y	46410 FQ	60440 MW	75700 TQ	USBLS	5/15
	Billings MSA, MT	Y	44180 FQ	52840 MW	66460 TQ	USBLS	5/15
	Nebraska	Y	55540 FQ	72275 MW	91300 TQ	NEBLS	7/16-9/16
	Omaha-Council Bluffs MSA, NE-IA	Y	58810 FQ	75640 MW	94880 TQ	NEBLS	7/16-9/16
	Nevada	Y	52190 FQ	75920 MW	97730 TQ	USBLS	5/15
	Las Vegas-Henderson-Paradise MSA, NV	Y	49390 FQ	73020 MW	96130 TQ	USBLS	5/15
	New Hampshire	H	22.59 AE	34.36 MW	43.11 AEX	NHBLS	6/16
	Manchester NECTA, NH	H	23.17 AE	33.36 MW	38.61 AEX	NHBLS	6/16
	Nashua NECTA, NH-MA	Y	49910 FQ	72150 MW	91950 TQ	USBLS	5/15
	New Jersey	Y	65240 FQ	79190 MW	111390 TQ	USBLS	5/15
	Camden PMSA, NJ	Y	56560 FQ	68520 MW	81300 TQ	USBLS	5/15
	Newark PMSA, NJ-PA	Y	65120 FQ	80280 MW	114900 TQ	USBLS	5/15
	Trenton MSA, NJ	Y	71600 FQ	89440 MW	111890 TQ	USBLS	5/15
	New Mexico	Y	75680 FQ	103200 MW	122690 TQ	USBLS	5/15
	Albuquerque MSA, NM	Y	83500 FQ	107640 MW	126950 TQ	USBLS	5/15
	New York	Y	53170 AE	82780 MW	107350 AEX	NYBLS	1/16-3/16
	Buffalo-Cheektowaga-Niagara Falls MSA, NY	Y	50960 FQ	68780 MW	86940 TQ	USBLS	5/15
	Nassau County-Suffolk County PMSA, NY	Y	68210 FQ	92610 MW	118080 TQ	USBLS	5/15
	New York-Jersey City-White Plains PMSA, NY-NJ	Y	65700 FQ	85250 MW	121540 TQ	USBLS	5/15
	Rochester MSA, NY	Y	41340 FQ	61180 MW	80790 TQ	USBLS	5/15
	North Carolina	Y	63820 FQ	80800 MW	99920 TQ	USBLS	5/15
	Asheville MSA, NC	Y	47790 FQ	66430 MW	89840 TQ	USBLS	5/15
	Charlotte-Concord-Gastonia MSA, NC-SC	Y	66930 FQ	86700 MW	106790 TQ	USBLS	5/15
	Raleigh MSA, NC	Y	64090 FQ	80680 MW	99610 TQ	USBLS	5/15
	North Dakota	Y	43820 FQ	51700 MW	62790 TQ	USBLS	5/15
	Fargo MSA, ND-MN	Y	42620 FQ	48170 MW	59420 TQ	USBLS	5/15
	Ohio	Y	51920 FQ	68180 MW	84410 TQ	USBLS	5/15
	Cincinnati MSA, OH-KY-IN	Y	51070 FQ	64910 MW	84240 TQ	USBLS	5/15
	Cleveland-Elyria MSA, OH	Y	50380 FQ	65350 MW	78910 TQ	USBLS	5/15
	Columbus MSA, OH	Y	59140 FQ	73400 MW	88520 TQ	USBLS	5/15
	Oklahoma	Y	46360 FQ	64640 MW	87920 TQ	USBLS	5/15
	Oklahoma City MSA, OK	Y	49670 FQ	67550 MW	91330 TQ	USBLS	5/15
	Tulsa MSA, OK	Y	51710 FQ	68890 MW	90080 TQ	USBLS	5/15
	Oregon	H	28.69 FQ	37.25 MW	46.17 TQ	ORBLS	2016
	Portland-Vancouver-Hillsboro MSA, OR-WA	Y	62860 FQ	80530 MW	97920 TQ	USBLS	5/15
	Pennsylvania	Y	56980 FQ	74370 MW	96220 TQ	USBLS	5/15
	Allentown-Bethlehem-Easton MSA, PA-NJ	Y	54120 FQ	73440 MW	99550 TQ	USBLS	5/15
	Harrisburg-Carlisle MSA, PA	Y	59740 FQ	78290 MW	94700 TQ	USBLS	5/15
	Montgomery County-Bucks County-Chester County PMSA, PA	Y	63690 FQ	83080 MW	110310 TQ	USBLS	5/15
	Philadelphia PMSA, PA	Y	60310 FQ	76710 MW	102700 TQ	USBLS	5/15
	Pittsburgh MSA, PA	Y	51880 FQ	69730 MW	82530 TQ	USBLS	5/15
	Rhode Island	Y	58930 FQ	79040 MW	96050 TQ	USBLS	5/15
	Providence-Warwick MSA, RI-MA	Y	59450 FQ	79120 MW	96400 TQ	USBLS	5/15
	South Carolina	Y	51150 FQ	67610 MW	89850 TQ	USBLS	5/15
	Charleston-North Charleston MSA, SC	Y	59600 FQ	73520 MW	89610 TQ	USBLS	5/15
	Columbia MSA, SC	Y	51930 FQ	65480 MW	89880 TQ	USBLS	5/15
	Greenville-Anderson-Mauldin MSA, SC	Y	50700 FQ	67380 MW	84320 TQ	USBLS	5/15
	South Dakota	Y	43200 FQ	50060 MW	61430 TQ	USBLS	5/15
	Sioux Falls MSA, SD	Y	44550 FQ	52310 MW	64620 TQ	USBLS	5/15

AE Average entry wage	**AWR** Average wage range	**H** Hourly	**LR** Low end range	**MTC** Median total compensation	**TCC** Total cash compensation
AEX Average experienced wage	**B** Biweekly	**HI** Highest wage paid	**M** Monthly	**MW** Median wage paid	**TQ** Third quartile wage
ATC Average total compensation	**D** Daily	**HR** High end range	**MCC** Median cash compensation	**MWR** Median wage range	**W** Weekly
AW Average wage paid	**FQ** First quartile wage	**LO** Lowest wage paid	**ME** Median entry wage	**S** See annotated source	**Y** Yearly

Occupation/Type/Industry	Location	Per	Low	Mid	High	Source	Date
Computer Programmer	Tennessee	Y	54320 FQ	70270 MW	90650 TQ	USBLS	5/15
	Knoxville MSA, TN	Y	18660 FQ	51260 MW	87200 TQ	USBLS	5/15
	Memphis MSA, TN-MS-AR	Y	56770 FQ	69210 MW	85000 TQ	USBLS	5/15
	Nashville-Davidson–Murfreesboro–Franklin MSA, TN	Y	58480 FQ	74300 MW	94620 TQ	USBLS	5/15
	Texas	Y	58900 FQ	79480 MW	105690 TQ	USBLS	5/15
	Austin-Round Rock MSA, TX	Y	67650 FQ	82510 MW	112970 TQ	USBLS	5/15
	Dallas-Plano-Irving PMSA, TX	Y	57680 FQ	82580 MW	112230 TQ	USBLS	5/15
	Fort Worth-Arlington PMSA, TX	Y	55980 FQ	78870 MW	98310 TQ	USBLS	5/15
	Houston-The Woodlands-Sugar Land MSA, TX	Y	60600 FQ	84380 MW	106490 TQ	USBLS	5/15
	San Antonio-New Braunfels MSA, TX	Y	65720 FQ	78600 MW	102070 TQ	USBLS	5/15
	Utah	Y	55680 FQ	77540 MW	97670 TQ	USBLS	5/15
	Ogden-Clearfield MSA, UT	Y	44900 FQ	68450 MW	82430 TQ	USBLS	5/15
	Provo-Orem MSA, UT	Y	59290 FQ	76670 MW	96130 TQ	USBLS	5/15
	Salt Lake City MSA, UT	Y	56390 FQ	81430 MW	99040 TQ	USBLS	5/15
	Vermont	Y	40860 FQ	64300 MW	77610 TQ	USBLS	5/15
	Burlington-South Burlington MSA, VT	Y	46590 FQ	65600 MW	77520 TQ	USBLS	5/15
	Virginia	Y	68820 FQ	91460 MW	113620 TQ	USBLS	5/15
	Richmond MSA, VA	Y	59430 FQ	80740 MW	98480 TQ	USBLS	5/15
	Virginia Beach-Norfolk-Newport News MSA, VA-NC	Y	48610 FQ	62250 MW	80720 TQ	USBLS	5/15
	Washington	H	47.23 FQ	58.30 MW	70.29 TQ	WABLS	3/16
	Seattle-Bellevue-Everett PMSA, WA	H	49.78 FQ	60.00 MW	71.42 TQ	WABLS	3/16
	Tacoma-Lakewood PMSA, WA	H	27.47 FQ	34.48 MW	48.49 TQ	WABLS	3/16
	West Virginia	Y	46380 FQ	58020 MW	76520 TQ	USBLS	5/15
	Huntington-Ashland MSA, WV-KY-OH	Y	52810 FQ	74920 MW	90930 TQ	USBLS	5/15
	Wisconsin	Y	55310 FQ	72850 MW	90860 TQ	USBLS	5/15
	Madison MSA, WI	Y	66210 FQ	79260 MW	93200 TQ	USBLS	5/15
	Milwaukee-Waukesha-West Allis MSA, WI	Y	40290 FQ	62070 MW	85910 TQ	USBLS	5/15
	Wyoming	Y	51070 FQ	59010 MW	71240 TQ	USBLS	5/15
	Cheyenne MSA, WY	Y	39490 FQ	57020 MW	64060 TQ	USBLS	5/15
	Puerto Rico	Y	28800 FQ	41180 MW	57690 TQ	USBLS	5/15
	San Juan-Carolina-Caguas MSA, PR	Y	30200 FQ	43320 MW	59920 TQ	USBLS	5/15
Computer Science Teacher							
Postsecondary	Alabama	Y	53178 AE	94461 AW	115102 AEX	ALBLS	6/16
Postsecondary	Birmingham-Hoover MSA, AL	Y	58846 AE	105184 AW	128343 AEX	ALBLS	6/16
Postsecondary	Alaska	Y	84180 FQ	90980 MW	97770 TQ	USBLS	5/15
Postsecondary	Arizona	Y	53850 FQ	79580 MW	101640 TQ	USBLS	5/15
Postsecondary	Phoenix-Mesa-Scottsdale MSA, AZ	Y	63090 FQ	85060 MW	103980 TQ	USBLS	5/15
Postsecondary	Arkansas	Y	47600 FQ	61280 MW	105240 TQ	USBLS	5/15
Postsecondary	Little Rock-North Little Rock-Conway MSA, AR	Y	55420 FQ	87740 MW	126250 TQ	USBLS	5/15
Postsecondary	California	Y		98974 AW		CABLS	1/16-3/16
Postsecondary	Anaheim-Santa Ana-Irvine PMSA, CA	Y		114587 AW		CABLS	1/16-3/16
Postsecondary	Los Angeles-Long Beach-Glendale PMSA, CA	Y		101774 AW		CABLS	1/16-3/16
Postsecondary	Riverside-San Bernardino-Ontario MSA, CA	Y		99938 AW		CABLS	1/16-3/16
Postsecondary	Sacramento–Roseville–Arden-Arcade MSA, CA	Y		94886 AW		CABLS	1/16-3/16
Postsecondary	San Diego-Carlsbad MSA, CA	Y		91375 AW		CABLS	1/16-3/16
Postsecondary	San Francisco-Redwood City-South San Francisco PMSA, CA	Y		100414 AW		CABLS	1/16-3/16
Postsecondary	Colorado	Y	37610 FQ	64400 MW	101550 TQ	USBLS	5/15
Postsecondary	Denver-Aurora-Lakewood MSA, CO	Y	35890 FQ	57850 MW	92370 TQ	USBLS	5/15
Postsecondary	Connecticut	Y		80967 MW		CTBLS	1/16-3/16
Postsecondary	Bridgeport-Stamford-Norwalk MSA, CT	Y	56870 FQ	80140 MW	111420 TQ	USBLS	5/15

AE	Average entry wage	AWR	Average wage range	H	Hourly	LR	Low end range	MTC Median total compensation
AEX	Average experienced wage	B	Biweekly	HI	Highest wage paid	M	Monthly	MW Median wage paid
ATC	Average total compensation	D	Daily	HR	High end range	MCC	Median cash compensation	MWR Median wage range
AW	Average wage paid	FQ	First quartile wage	LO	Lowest wage paid	ME	Median entry wage	S See annotated source

TCC Total cash compensation
TQ Third quartile wage
W Weekly
Y Yearly

Computer Science Teacher

Occupation/Type/Industry	Location	Per	Low	Mid	High	Source	Date
Postsecondary	Hartford-West Hartford-East Hartford MSA, CT	Y	61560 FQ	79410 MW	97050 TQ	USBLS	5/15
Postsecondary	Delaware	Y	64200 FQ	76190 MW	96750 TQ	USBLS	5/15
Postsecondary	Wilmington PMSA, DE-MD-NJ	Y	54410 FQ	74820 MW	96540 TQ	USBLS	5/15
Postsecondary	District of Columbia	Y	56290 FQ	85230 MW	118950 TQ	USBLS	5/15
Postsecondary	Washington-Arlington-Alexandria PMSA, DC-VA-MD-WV	Y	53550 FQ	79250 MW	111870 TQ	USBLS	5/15
Postsecondary	Florida	Y	41639 AE	67360 MW	94726 AEX	FLBLS	7/16-9/16
Postsecondary	Fort Lauderdale-Pompano Beach-Deerfield Beach PMSA, FL	Y	52728 AE	75136 MW	86790 AEX	FLBLS	7/16-9/16
Postsecondary	Miami-Miami Beach-Kendall PMSA, FL	Y	46459 AE	77003 MW	100315 AEX	FLBLS	7/16-9/16
Postsecondary	Tampa-St. Petersburg-Clearwater MSA, FL	Y	40633 AE	58885 MW	73359 AEX	FLBLS	7/16-9/16
Postsecondary	Georgia	Y	48870 FQ	69620 MW	97280 TQ	USBLS	5/15
Postsecondary	Atlanta-Sandy Springs-Roswell MSA, GA	Y	49870 FQ	70900 MW	95470 TQ	USBLS	5/15
Postsecondary	Hawaii	Y	61790 FQ	82600 MW	101590 TQ	USBLS	5/15
Postsecondary	Urban Honolulu MSA, HI	Y	62460 FQ	85860 MW	104030 TQ	USBLS	5/15
Postsecondary	Idaho	Y	47700 FQ	67500 MW	109820 TQ	USBLS	5/15
Postsecondary	Boise City MSA, ID	Y	42370 FQ	51130 MW	108010 TQ	USBLS	5/15
Postsecondary	Illinois	Y	60120 FQ	86680 MW	120200 TQ	USBLS	5/15
Postsecondary	Chicago-Naperville-Arlington Heights PMSA, IL	Y	64390 FQ	88160 MW	116030 TQ	USBLS	5/15
Postsecondary	Indiana	Y	56980 FQ	80310 MW	111750 TQ	USBLS	5/15
Postsecondary	Indianapolis-Carmel-Anderson MSA, IN	Y	55890 FQ	80480 MW	104080 TQ	USBLS	5/15
Postsecondary	Iowa	Y	53740 FQ	75800 MW	100240 TQ	USBLS	5/15
Postsecondary	Des Moines-West Des Moines MSA, IA	Y	36360 FQ	56350 MW	88220 TQ	USBLS	5/15
Postsecondary	Kansas	Y	46200 FQ	58140 MW	71250 TQ	USBLS	5/15
Postsecondary	Kentucky	Y	52850 FQ	69690 MW	103370 TQ	USBLS	5/15
Postsecondary	Louisville-Jefferson County MSA, KY-IN	Y	56080 FQ	88600 MW	123760 TQ	USBLS	5/15
Postsecondary	Louisiana	Y	45900 FQ	66300 MW	89710 TQ	USBLS	5/15
Postsecondary	New Orleans-Metairie MSA, LA	Y	32600 FQ	49150 MW	81090 TQ	USBLS	5/15
Postsecondary	Maine	Y	50780 FQ	62790 MW	94340 TQ	USBLS	5/15
Postsecondary	Maryland	Y	54045 AE	97830 MW	119723 AEX	MDBLS	4/16
Postsecondary	Baltimore-Columbia-Towson MSA, MD	Y	64970 FQ	81630 MW	98160 TQ	USBLS	5/15
Postsecondary	Salisbury MSA, MD-DE	Y	37730 FQ	65950 MW	74100 TQ	USBLS	5/15
Postsecondary	Massachusetts	Y	64220 FQ	88540 MW	122410 TQ	USBLS	5/15
Postsecondary	Boston-Cambridge-Newton NECTA, MA	Y	69320 FQ	99760 MW	133200 TQ	USBLS	5/15
Postsecondary	Worcester MSA, MA-CT	Y	53700 FQ	70320 MW	97230 TQ	USBLS	5/15
Postsecondary	Michigan	Y	43340 FQ	81700 MW	102060 TQ	USBLS	5/15
Postsecondary	Detroit-Dearborn-Livonia PMSA, MI	Y	74140 FQ	88700 MW	99540 TQ	USBLS	5/15
Postsecondary	Grand Rapids-Wyoming MSA, MI	Y	38190 FQ	69580 MW	95250 TQ	USBLS	5/15
Postsecondary	Minnesota	Y	56773 FQ	71541 MW	97600 TQ	MNBLS	1/16-3/16
Postsecondary	Minneapolis-St. Paul-Bloomington MSA, MN-WI	Y	56733 FQ	71511 MW	96773 TQ	MNBLS	1/16-3/16
Postsecondary	Mississippi	Y	49130 FQ	66000 MW	87570 TQ	USBLS	5/15
Postsecondary	Jackson MSA, MS	Y	44210 FQ	55180 MW	70720 TQ	USBLS	5/15
Postsecondary	Missouri	Y	51220 FQ	74060 MW	97810 TQ	USBLS	5/15
Postsecondary	Kansas City MSA, MO-KS	Y	57900 FQ	74160 MW	93090 TQ	USBLS	5/15
Postsecondary	St. Louis MSA, MO-IL	Y	46230 FQ	66570 MW	94240 TQ	USBLS	5/15
Postsecondary	Montana	Y	42620 FQ	55680 MW	84140 TQ	USBLS	5/15
Postsecondary	Nebraska	Y	56730 FQ	72090 MW	103500 TQ	NEBLS	7/16-9/16
Postsecondary	Omaha-Council Bluffs MSA, NE-IA	Y	55200 FQ	69570 MW	103535 TQ	NEBLS	7/16-9/16
Postsecondary	Nevada	Y	37080 FQ	58400 MW	81120 TQ	USBLS	5/15
Postsecondary	Las Vegas-Henderson-Paradise MSA, NV	Y	36650 FQ	56520 MW	78720 TQ	USBLS	5/15
Postsecondary	New Hampshire	Y	58201 AE	90799 MW	114235 AEX	NHBLS	6/16
Postsecondary	Manchester NECTA, NH	Y	59715 AE	91781 MW	103482 AEX	NHBLS	6/16

AE	Average entry wage	AWR	Average wage range	H	Hourly
AEX	Average experienced wage	B	Biweekly	HI	Highest wage paid
ATC	Average total compensation	D	Daily	HR	High end range
AW	Average wage paid	FQ	First quartile wage	LO	Lowest wage paid

LR	Low end range	MTC	Median total compensation
M	Monthly	MW	Median wage paid
MCC	Median cash compensation	MWR	Median wage range
ME	Median entry wage	S	See annotated source

TCC	Total cash compensation
TQ	Third quartile wage
W	Weekly
Y	Yearly

Computer Science Teacher

Occupation/Type/Industry	Location	Per	Low	Mid	High	Source	Date
Computer Science Teacher							
Postsecondary	New Jersey	Y	59660 FQ	78490 MW	112210 TQ	USBLS	5/15
Postsecondary	Camden PMSA, NJ	Y	55890 FQ	79890 MW	106810 TQ	USBLS	5/15
Postsecondary	Newark PMSA, NJ-PA	Y	63120 FQ	80890 MW	117560 TQ	USBLS	5/15
Postsecondary	New Mexico	Y	54750 FQ	74300 MW	96960 TQ	USBLS	5/15
Postsecondary	Albuquerque MSA, NM	Y	57290 FQ	75650 MW	94580 TQ	USBLS	5/15
Postsecondary	New York	Y	45410 AE	87110 MW	127490 AEX	NYBLS	1/16-3/16
Postsecondary	Buffalo-Cheektowaga-Niagara Falls MSA, NY	Y	53560 FQ	84190 MW	106940 TQ	USBLS	5/15
Postsecondary	Nassau County-Suffolk County PMSA, NY	Y	40910 FQ	54530 MW	84430 TQ	USBLS	5/15
Postsecondary	New York-Jersey City-White Plains PMSA, NY-NJ	Y	59750 FQ	92340 MW	140890 TQ	USBLS	5/15
Postsecondary	Rochester MSA, NY	Y	73740 FQ	91450 MW	114440 TQ	USBLS	5/15
Postsecondary	North Carolina	Y	51280 FQ	64790 MW	86830 TQ	USBLS	5/15
Postsecondary	Charlotte-Concord-Gastonia MSA, NC-SC	Y	52910 FQ	68440 MW	95610 TQ	USBLS	5/15
Postsecondary	Raleigh MSA, NC	Y	50080 FQ	69860 MW	99530 TQ	USBLS	5/15
Postsecondary	North Dakota	Y	41830 FQ	64420 MW	113860 TQ	USBLS	5/15
Postsecondary	Ohio	Y	52440 FQ	76390 MW	110140 TQ	USBLS	5/15
Postsecondary	Cincinnati MSA, OH-KY-IN	Y	54910 FQ	79440 MW	117790 TQ	USBLS	5/15
Postsecondary	Cleveland-Elyria MSA, OH	Y	47600 FQ	70050 MW	99310 TQ	USBLS	5/15
Postsecondary	Columbus MSA, OH	Y	65980 FQ	99110 MW	118010 TQ	USBLS	5/15
Postsecondary	Oklahoma	Y	50400 FQ	66310 MW	84400 TQ	USBLS	5/15
Postsecondary	Oklahoma City MSA, OK	Y	47410 FQ	66030 MW	75080 TQ	USBLS	5/15
Postsecondary	Tulsa MSA, OK	Y	60690 FQ	86520 MW	97600 TQ	USBLS	5/15
Postsecondary	Oregon	Y	63626 FQ	86624 MW	114578 TQ	ORBLS	2016
Postsecondary	Portland-Vancouver-Hillsboro MSA, OR-WA	Y	55450 FQ	82100 MW	120960 TQ	USBLS	5/15
Postsecondary	Pennsylvania	Y	56000 FQ	80070 MW	105880 TQ	USBLS	5/15
Postsecondary	Allentown-Bethlehem-Easton MSA, PA-NJ	Y	57210 FQ	78220 MW	119500 TQ	USBLS	5/15
Postsecondary	Harrisburg-Carlisle MSA, PA	Y	50970 FQ	73150 MW	92050 TQ	USBLS	5/15
Postsecondary	Montgomery County-Bucks County-Chester County PMSA, PA	Y	23050 FQ	52210 MW	87600 TQ	USBLS	5/15
Postsecondary	Philadelphia PMSA, PA	Y	59980 FQ	88380 MW	116690 TQ	USBLS	5/15
Postsecondary	Pittsburgh MSA, PA	Y	57930 FQ	81560 MW	106140 TQ	USBLS	5/15
Postsecondary	Rhode Island	Y	60790 FQ	83920 MW	124800 TQ	USBLS	5/15
Postsecondary	Providence-Warwick MSA, RI-MA	Y	60120 FQ	82260 MW	120930 TQ	USBLS	5/15
Postsecondary	South Carolina	Y	56500 FQ	68970 MW	84150 TQ	USBLS	5/15
Postsecondary	Columbia MSA, SC	Y	51530 FQ	76310 MW	96100 TQ	USBLS	5/15
Postsecondary	Greenville-Anderson-Mauldin MSA, SC	Y	61710 FQ	76480 MW	108530 TQ	USBLS	5/15
Postsecondary	South Dakota	Y	49510 FQ	56900 MW	73660 TQ	USBLS	5/15
Postsecondary	Sioux Falls MSA, SD	Y	49530 FQ	61420 MW	84960 TQ	USBLS	5/15
Postsecondary	Tennessee	Per	46840 FQ	63920 MW	86410 TQ	USBLS	5/15
Postsecondary	Knoxville MSA, TN	Y	37440 FQ	57280 MW	73940 TQ	USBLS	5/15
Postsecondary	Memphis MSA, TN-MS-AR	Y	59120 FQ	79630 MW	98460 TQ	USBLS	5/15
Postsecondary	Nashville-Davidson–Murfreesboro–Franklin MSA, TN	Y	50490 FQ	65740 MW	82070 TQ	USBLS	5/15
Postsecondary	Texas	Y	48640 FQ	72250 MW	101700 TQ	USBLS	5/15
Postsecondary	Austin-Round Rock MSA, TX	Y	53170 FQ	71430 MW	99450 TQ	USBLS	5/15
Postsecondary	Dallas-Plano-Irving PMSA, TX	Y	52830 FQ	78040 MW	107450 TQ	USBLS	5/15
Postsecondary	Fort Worth-Arlington PMSA, TX	Y	39900 FQ	61860 MW	90500 TQ	USBLS	5/15
Postsecondary	Houston-The Woodlands-Sugar Land MSA, TX	Y	54470 FQ	78000 MW	121780 TQ	USBLS	5/15
Postsecondary	San Antonio-New Braunfels MSA, TX	Y	22610 FQ	51470 MW	94970 TQ	USBLS	5/15
Postsecondary	Utah	Y	48690 FQ	65430 MW	102540 TQ	USBLS	5/15
Postsecondary	Ogden-Clearfield MSA, UT	Y	41910 FQ	58720 MW	72750 TQ	USBLS	5/15
Postsecondary	Provo-Orem MSA, UT	Y	51250 FQ	81450 MW	102360 TQ	USBLS	5/15
Postsecondary	Salt Lake City MSA, UT	Y	48030 FQ	61430 MW	116770 TQ	USBLS	5/15
Postsecondary	Vermont	Y	39020 FQ	50020 MW	82310 TQ	USBLS	5/15
Postsecondary	Virginia	Y	39060 FQ	64760 MW	99000 TQ	USBLS	5/15
Postsecondary	Richmond MSA, VA	Y	36000 FQ	45320 MW	64990 TQ	USBLS	5/15
Postsecondary	Virginia Beach-Norfolk-Newport News MSA, VA-NC	Y	45350 FQ	69730 MW	102780 TQ	USBLS	5/15
Postsecondary	Washington	Y		70416 AW		WABLS	3/16

Computer Science Teacher

Occupation/Type/Industry	Location	Per	Low	Mid	High	Source	Date
Computer Science Teacher							
Postsecondary	Seattle-Bellevue-Everett PMSA, WA	Y		84964 AW		WABLS	3/16
Postsecondary	Tacoma-Lakewood PMSA, WA	Y		79506 AW		WABLS	3/16
Postsecondary	West Virginia	Y	32600 FQ	47740 MW	71600 TQ	USBLS	5/15
Postsecondary	Huntington-Ashland MSA, WV-KY-OH	Y	33320 FQ	44250 MW	59780 TQ	USBLS	5/15
Postsecondary	Wisconsin	Y	56170 FQ	74130 MW	99120 TQ	USBLS	5/15
Postsecondary	Madison MSA, WI	Y	63580 FQ	112220 MW	154380 TQ	USBLS	5/15
Postsecondary	Milwaukee-Waukesha-West Allis MSA, WI	Y	54110 FQ	80460 MW	105130 TQ	USBLS	5/15
Postsecondary	Wyoming	Y	59770 FQ	72600 MW	90130 TQ	USBLS	5/15
Postsecondary	Puerto Rico	Y	26790 FQ	42520 MW	59910 TQ	USBLS	5/15
Postsecondary	San Juan-Carolina-Caguas MSA, PR	Y	28470 FQ	45260 MW	60230 TQ	USBLS	5/15
Computer Systems Analyst	Alabama	Y	55614 AE	78427 AW	89833 AEX	ALBLS	6/16
	Birmingham-Hoover MSA, AL	Y	56471 AE	76093 AW	85898 AEX	ALBLS	6/16
	Alaska	Y	66980 FQ	82350 MW	95580 TQ	USBLS	5/15
	Anchorage MSA, AK	Y	69490 FQ	83670 MW	95940 TQ	USBLS	5/15
	Arizona	Y	66100 FQ	87640 MW	108000 TQ	USBLS	5/15
	Phoenix-Mesa-Scottsdale MSA, AZ	Y	68090 FQ	89660 MW	110100 TQ	USBLS	5/15
	Tucson MSA, AZ	Y	56610 FQ	74330 MW	93760 TQ	USBLS	5/15
	Arkansas	Y	49090 FQ	67650 MW	85980 TQ	USBLS	5/15
	Little Rock-North Little Rock-Conway MSA, AR	Y	49780 FQ	70380 MW	88850 TQ	USBLS	5/15
	California	H	36.35 FQ	46.17 MW	59.13 TQ	CABLS	1/16-3/16
	Anaheim-Santa Ana-Irvine PMSA, CA	H	35.62 FQ	46.31 MW	57.42 TQ	CABLS	1/16-3/16
	Los Angeles-Long Beach-Glendale PMSA, CA	H	34.86 FQ	45.43 MW	57.13 TQ	CABLS	1/16-3/16
	Oakland-Hayward-Berkeley PMSA, CA	H	34.37 FQ	44.76 MW	56.80 TQ	CABLS	1/16-3/16
	Riverside-San Bernardino-Ontario MSA, CA	H	30.72 FQ	36.97 MW	44.53 TQ	CABLS	1/16-3/16
	Sacramento–Roseville–Arden-Arcade MSA, CA	H	33.90 FQ	39.66 MW	44.21 TQ	CABLS	1/16-3/16
	San Diego-Carlsbad MSA, CA	H	34.64 FQ	45.18 MW	57.03 TQ	CABLS	1/16-3/16
	San Francisco-Redwood City-South San Francisco PMSA, CA	H	43.20 FQ	53.78 MW	67.13 TQ	CABLS	1/16-3/16
	San Luis Obispo-Paso Robles-Arroyo Grande MSA, CA	Y	60520 FQ	82460 MW	103330 TQ	USBLS	5/15
	Colorado	Y	70720 FQ	90020 MW	114270 TQ	USBLS	5/15
	Denver-Aurora-Lakewood MSA, CO	Y	71540 FQ	91060 MW	117280 TQ	USBLS	5/15
	Connecticut	Y		92278 MW		CTBLS	1/16-3/16
	Bridgeport-Stamford-Norwalk MSA, CT	Y	71360 FQ	92700 MW	115210 TQ	USBLS	5/15
	Hartford-West Hartford-East Hartford MSA, CT	Y	77260 FQ	91160 MW	106470 TQ	USBLS	5/15
	Delaware	Y	75370 FQ	93530 MW	114710 TQ	USBLS	5/15
	Wilmington PMSA, DE-MD-NJ	Y	74480 FQ	93370 MW	114620 TQ	USBLS	5/15
	District of Columbia	Y	74450 FQ	99350 MW	124020 TQ	USBLS	5/15
	Washington-Arlington-Alexandria PMSA, DC-VA-MD-WV	Y	76190 FQ	101780 MW	127800 TQ	USBLS	5/15
	Florida	H	26.25 AE	38.53 MW	47.53 AEX	FLBLS	7/16-9/16
	Fort Lauderdale-Pompano Beach-Deerfield Beach PMSA, FL	H	25.69 AE	37.04 MW	45.76 AEX	FLBLS	7/16-9/16
	Miami-Miami Beach-Kendall PMSA, FL	H	26.15 AE	41.32 MW	58.65 AEX	FLBLS	7/16-9/16
	Orlando-Kissimmee-Sanford MSA, FL	H	30.63 AE	39.61 MW	45.08 AEX	FLBLS	7/16-9/16
	Tampa-St. Petersburg-Clearwater MSA, FL	H	22.83 AE	38.75 MW	46.49 AEX	FLBLS	7/16-9/16
	Georgia	Y	56470 FQ	78310 MW	101210 TQ	USBLS	5/15
	Atlanta-Sandy Springs-Roswell MSA, GA	Y	56940 FQ	80270 MW	103720 TQ	USBLS	5/15

AE	Average entry wage	AWR	Average wage range	H	Hourly
AEX	Average experienced wage	B	Biweekly	HI	Highest paid
ATC	Average total compensation	D	Daily	HR	High end range
AW	Average wage paid	FQ	First quartile wage	LO	Lowest paid

AE Average entry wage · AWR Average wage range · H Hourly · LR Low end range · MTC Median total compensation · TCC Total cash compensation
AEX Average experienced wage · B Biweekly · HI Highest paid · M Monthly · MW Median wage paid · TQ Third quartile wage
ATC Average total compensation · D Daily · HR High end range · MCC Median cash compensation · MWR Median wage range · W Weekly
AW Average wage paid · FQ First quartile wage · LO Lowest paid · ME Median entry wage · S See annotated source · Y Yearly

Occupation/Type/Industry	Location	Per	Low	Mid	High	Source	Date
Computer Systems Analyst	Augusta-Richmond County MSA, GA-SC	Y	48390 FQ	61380 MW	79230 TQ	USBLS	5/15
	Hawaii	Y	58750 FQ	72110 MW	86850 TQ	USBLS	5/15
	Urban Honolulu MSA, HI	Y	60580 FQ	73790 MW	91620 TQ	USBLS	5/15
	Idaho	Y	59820 FQ	76760 MW	101050 TQ	USBLS	5/15
	Boise City MSA, ID	Y	59920 FQ	76530 MW	99520 TQ	USBLS	5/15
	Illinois	Y	67830 FQ	87780 MW	107530 TQ	USBLS	5/15
	Chicago-Naperville-Arlington Heights PMSA, IL	Y	67580 FQ	87250 MW	106470 TQ	USBLS	5/15
	Lake County-Kenosha County PMSA, IL-WI	Y	61520 FQ	87190 MW	108260 TQ	USBLS	5/15
	Indiana	Y	56910 FQ	71780 MW	89560 TQ	USBLS	5/15
	Gary PMSA, IN	Y	60500 FQ	80240 MW	99930 TQ	USBLS	5/15
	Indianapolis-Carmel-Anderson MSA, IN	Y	60870 FQ	75900 MW	93710 TQ	USBLS	5/15
	Iowa	Y	63230 FQ	78250 MW	96340 TQ	USBLS	5/15
	Des Moines-West Des Moines MSA, IA	Y	67260 FQ	83250 MW	99220 TQ	USBLS	5/15
	Kansas	Y	58300 FQ	75640 MW	93320 TQ	USBLS	5/15
	Wichita MSA, KS	Y	58210 FQ	73530 MW	90930 TQ	USBLS	5/15
	Kentucky	Y	55060 FQ	70250 MW	92230 TQ	USBLS	5/15
	Louisville-Jefferson County MSA, KY-IN	Y	54020 FQ	68380 MW	87640 TQ	USBLS	5/15
	Louisiana	Y	52460 FQ	65200 MW	86080 TQ	USBLS	5/15
	Baton Rouge MSA, LA	Y	54790 FQ	65290 MW	79490 TQ	USBLS	5/15
	New Orleans-Metairie MSA, LA	Y	51760 FQ	69420 MW	99350 TQ	USBLS	5/15
	Maine	Y	60160 FQ	73600 MW	93960 TQ	USBLS	5/15
	Portland-South Portland MSA, ME	Y	65170 FQ	80500 MW	97230 TQ	USBLS	5/15
	Maryland	Y	56448 AE	91263 MW	108671 AEX	MDBLS	4/16
	Baltimore-Columbia-Towson MSA, MD	Y	67080 FQ	89450 MW	112980 TQ	USBLS	5/15
	Salisbury MSA, MD-DE	Y	64760 FQ	90880 MW	121750 TQ	USBLS	5/15
	Massachusetts	Y	71340 FQ	88850 MW	112290 TQ	USBLS	5/15
	Boston-Cambridge-Newton NECTA, MA	Y	71740 FQ	89010 MW	113050 TQ	USBLS	5/15
	Haverhill-Newburyport-Amesbury Town NECTA, MA-NH	Y	78110 FQ	103700 MW	129120 TQ	USBLS	5/15
	Worcester MSA, MA-CT	Y	68490 FQ	85090 MW	110570 TQ	USBLS	5/15
	Michigan	Y	63130 FQ	84740 MW	105590 TQ	USBLS	5/15
	Detroit-Dearborn-Livonia PMSA, MI	Y	78660 FQ	94470 MW	114440 TQ	USBLS	5/15
	Grand Rapids-Wyoming MSA, MI	Y	50900 FQ	63460 MW	82010 TQ	USBLS	5/15
	Minnesota	Y	71642 FQ	88971 MW	103930 TQ	MNBLS	1/16-3/16
	Minneapolis-St. Paul-Bloomington MSA, MN-WI	Y	74233 FQ	90725 MW	105593 TQ	MNBLS	1/16-3/16
	Mississippi	Y	50670 FQ	61880 MW	79400 TQ	USBLS	5/15
	Jackson MSA, MS	Y	47970 FQ	57410 MW	72120 TQ	USBLS	5/15
	Missouri	Y	70380 FQ	87230 MW	103730 TQ	USBLS	5/15
	Kansas City MSA, MO-KS	Y	66230 FQ	84460 MW	99460 TQ	USBLS	5/15
	St. Louis MSA, MO-IL	Y	72060 FQ	87860 MW	105510 TQ	USBLS	5/15
	Montana	Y	53420 FQ	64330 MW	78060 TQ	USBLS	5/15
	Billings MSA, MT	Y	52700 FQ	69300 MW	86110 TQ	USBLS	5/15
	Nebraska	Y	57180 FQ	73435 MW	92755 TQ	NEBLS	7/16-9/16
	Omaha-Council Bluffs MSA, NE-IA	Y	59850 FQ	76080 MW	95000 TQ	NEBLS	7/16-9/16
	Nevada	Y	65600 FQ	85120 MW	100310 TQ	USBLS	5/15
	Las Vegas-Henderson-Paradise MSA, NV	Y	67230 FQ	86040 MW	100620 TQ	USBLS	5/15
	New Hampshire	H	28.10 AE	39.05 MW	51.35 AEX	NHBLS	6/16
	Manchester NECTA, NH	H	26.25 AE	40.39 MW	55.40 AEX	NHBLS	6/16
	Nashua NECTA, NH-MA	Y	68720 FQ	85250 MW	102550 TQ	USBLS	5/15
	New Jersey	Y	74180 FQ	94630 MW	119670 TQ	USBLS	5/15
	Camden PMSA, NJ	Y	67010 FQ	81810 MW	100330 TQ	USBLS	5/15
	Newark PMSA, NJ-PA	Y	73500 FQ	96020 MW	120270 TQ	USBLS	5/15
	Trenton MSA, NJ	Y	72530 FQ	90730 MW	110950 TQ	USBLS	5/15
	New Mexico	Y	51950 FQ	71040 MW	90090 TQ	USBLS	5/15
	Albuquerque MSA, NM	Y	53850 FQ	73630 MW	92340 TQ	USBLS	5/15
	New York	Y	59600 AE	91040 MW	117810 AEX	NYBLS	1/16-3/16

AE Average entry wage	**AWR** Average wage range	**H** Hourly	**LR** Low end range	**MTC** Median total compensation	**TCC** Total cash compensation
AEX Average experienced wage	**B** Biweekly	**HI** Highest wage paid	**M** Monthly	**MW** Median wage paid	**TQ** Third quartile wage
ATC Average total compensation	**D** Daily	**HR** High end range	**MCC** Median cash compensation	**MWR** Median wage range	**W** Weekly
AW Average wage paid	**FQ** First quartile wage	**LO** Lowest wage paid	**ME** Median entry wage	**S** See annotated source	**Y** Yearly

Occupation/Type/Industry	Location	Per	Low	Mid	High	Source	Date
Computer Systems Analyst	Buffalo-Cheektowaga-Niagara Falls MSA, NY	Y	53230 FQ	70990 MW	91790 TQ	USBLS	5/15
	Nassau County-Suffolk County PMSA, NY	Y	62520 FQ	86570 MW	112510 TQ	USBLS	5/15
	New York-Jersey City-White Plains PMSA, NY-NJ	Y	74980 FQ	97880 MW	127510 TQ	USBLS	5/15
	Rochester MSA, NY	Y	58570 FQ	75060 MW	97970 TQ	USBLS	5/15
	North Carolina	Y	69000 FQ	87870 MW	109550 TQ	USBLS	5/15
	Charlotte-Concord-Gastonia MSA, NC-SC	Y	72560 FQ	92350 MW	114170 TQ	USBLS	5/15
	Raleigh MSA, NC	Y	69100 FQ	85410 MW	104510 TQ	USBLS	5/15
	Ohio	Y	64880 FQ	82510 MW	101680 TQ	USBLS	5/15
	Cincinnati MSA, OH-KY-IN	Y	68350 FQ	86750 MW	108340 TQ	USBLS	5/15
	Cleveland-Elyria MSA, OH	Y	60870 FQ	76760 MW	98370 TQ	USBLS	5/15
	Columbus MSA, OH	Y	64850 FQ	82700 MW	99830 TQ	USBLS	5/15
	Oklahoma	Y	55420 FQ	72290 MW	92300 TQ	USBLS	5/15
	Oklahoma City MSA, OK	Y	54640 FQ	71960 MW	92180 TQ	USBLS	5/15
	Tulsa MSA, OK	Y	60900 FQ	78530 MW	98890 TQ	USBLS	5/15
	Oregon	H	32.84 FQ	40.96 MW	49.44 TQ	ORBLS	2016
	Portland-Vancouver-Hillsboro MSA, OR-WA	Y	70580 FQ	87280 MW	104940 TQ	USBLS	5/15
	Pennsylvania	Y	62880 FQ	80910 MW	102830 TQ	USBLS	5/15
	Allentown-Bethlehem-Easton MSA, PA-NJ	Y	60570 FQ	76550 MW	100810 TQ	USBLS	5/15
	Harrisburg-Carlisle MSA, PA	Y	59330 FQ	75860 MW	93520 TQ	USBLS	5/15
	Montgomery County-Bucks County-Chester County PMSA, PA	Y	69070 FQ	87590 MW	112020 TQ	USBLS	5/15
	Philadelphia PMSA, PA	Y	63940 FQ	86350 MW	113260 TQ	USBLS	5/15
	Pittsburgh MSA, PA	Y	57080 FQ	74880 MW	97550 TQ	USBLS	5/15
	Rhode Island	Y	65160 FQ	84850 MW	103570 TQ	USBLS	5/15
	Providence-Warwick MSA, RI-MA	Y	64140 FQ	82890 MW	100220 TQ	USBLS	5/15
	South Carolina	Y	55130 FQ	71800 MW	91290 TQ	USBLS	5/15
	Charleston-North Charleston MSA, SC	Y	55690 FQ	75630 MW	95170 TQ	USBLS	5/15
	Columbia MSA, SC	Y	51950 FQ	65100 MW	82020 TQ	USBLS	5/15
	Greenville-Anderson-Mauldin MSA, SC	Y	58210 FQ	73680 MW	92980 TQ	USBLS	5/15
	South Dakota	Y	58300 FQ	68970 MW	79340 TQ	USBLS	5/15
	Sioux Falls MSA, SD	Y	56670 FQ	67800 MW	78140 TQ	USBLS	5/15
	Tennessee	Y	57580 FQ	73530 MW	93410 TQ	USBLS	5/15
	Knoxville MSA, TN	Y	54800 FQ	74730 MW	98560 TQ	USBLS	5/15
	Memphis MSA, TN-MS-AR	Y	56530 FQ	70000 MW	87940 TQ	USBLS	5/15
	Nashville-Davidson–Murfreesboro–Franklin MSA, TN	Y	57000 FQ	72300 MW	89980 TQ	USBLS	5/15
	Texas	Y	68080 FQ	86950 MW	113560 TQ	USBLS	5/15
	Austin-Round Rock MSA, TX	Y	61730 FQ	79990 MW	101490 TQ	USBLS	5/15
	Dallas-Plano-Irving PMSA, TX	Y	70400 FQ	88450 MW	114870 TQ	USBLS	5/15
	Fort Worth-Arlington PMSA, TX	Y	68930 FQ	89030 MW	110930 TQ	USBLS	5/15
	Houston-The Woodlands-Sugar Land MSA, TX	Y	71500 FQ	93080 MW	122820 TQ	USBLS	5/15
	San Antonio-New Braunfels MSA, TX	Y	65780 FQ	82880 MW	110810 TQ	USBLS	5/15
	Utah	Y	53920 FQ	70610 MW	89710 TQ	USBLS	5/15
	Ogden-Clearfield MSA, UT	Y	63280 FQ	71050 MW	80120 TQ	USBLS	5/15
	Provo-Orem MSA, UT	Y	50110 FQ	75140 MW	106360 TQ	USBLS	5/15
	Salt Lake City MSA, UT	Y	53980 FQ	70720 MW	89310 TQ	USBLS	5/15
	Vermont	Y	55400 FQ	71450 MW	91240 TQ	USBLS	5/15
	Burlington-South Burlington MSA, VT	Y	54420 FQ	71020 MW	91440 TQ	USBLS	5/15
	Virginia	Y	70760 FQ	95370 MW	122810 TQ	USBLS	5/15
	Richmond MSA, VA	Y	69110 FQ	88940 MW	108560 TQ	USBLS	5/15
	Virginia Beach-Norfolk-Newport News MSA, VA-NC	Y	64400 FQ	78720 MW	101420 TQ	USBLS	5/15
	Washington	H	34.69 FQ	44.03 MW	55.88 TQ	WABLS	3/16
	Seattle-Bellevue-Everett PMSA, WA	H	37.60 FQ	47.82 MW	58.42 TQ	WABLS	3/16
	Tacoma-Lakewood PMSA, WA	H	32.32 FQ	37.43 MW	48.18 TQ	WABLS	3/16
	West Virginia	Y	49960 FQ	61580 MW	77080 TQ	USBLS	5/15

AE Average entry wage	**AWR** Average wage range	**H** Hourly	**LR** Low end range	**MTC** Median total compensation	**TCC** Total cash compensation
AEX Average experienced wage	**B** Biweekly	**HI** Highest wage paid	**M** Monthly	**MW** Median wage paid	**TQ** Third quartile wage
ATC Average total compensation	**D** Daily	**HR** High end range	**MCC** Median cash compensation	**MWR** Median wage range	**W** Weekly
AW Average wage paid	**FQ** First quartile wage	**LO** Lowest wage paid	**ME** Median entry wage	**S** See annotated source	**Y** Yearly

Occupation/Type/Industry	Location	Per	Low	Mid	High	Source	Date
Computer Systems Analyst	Huntington-Ashland MSA, WV-KY-OH	Y	44780 FQ	54970 MW	67910 TQ	USBLS	5/15
	Wisconsin	Y	57840 FQ	72910 MW	91390 TQ	USBLS	5/15
	Madison MSA, WI	Y	57340 FQ	71780 MW	88390 TQ	USBLS	5/15
	Milwaukee-Waukesha-West Allis MSA, WI	Y	63240 FQ	78360 MW	98320 TQ	USBLS	5/15
	Wyoming	Y	56170 FQ	68450 MW	79300 TQ	USBLS	5/15
	Cheyenne MSA, WY	Y	60440 FQ	71400 MW	85960 TQ	USBLS	5/15
	Puerto Rico	Y	34320 FQ	43730 MW	57400 TQ	USBLS	5/15
	San Juan-Carolina-Caguas MSA, PR	Y	34500 FQ	43710 MW	57300 TQ	USBLS	5/15
	Guam	Y	40910 FQ	46790 MW	57240 TQ	USBLS	5/15
Computer User Support Specialist	Alabama	Y	30213 AE	47929 AW	56797 AEX	ALBLS	6/16
	Birmingham-Hoover MSA, AL	Y	31426 AE	49437 AW	58438 AEX	ALBLS	6/16
	Alaska	Y	46410 FQ	56580 MW	67310 TQ	USBLS	5/15
	Anchorage MSA, AK	Y	44950 FQ	55150 MW	65310 TQ	USBLS	5/15
	Arizona	Y	35600 FQ	46570 MW	60090 TQ	USBLS	5/15
	Phoenix-Mesa-Scottsdale MSA, AZ	Y	36600 FQ	47500 MW	60910 TQ	USBLS	5/15
	Tucson MSA, AZ	Y	33960 FQ	45240 MW	58450 TQ	USBLS	5/15
	Arkansas	Y	29760 FQ	37410 MW	47310 TQ	USBLS	5/15
	Little Rock-North Little Rock-Conway MSA, AR	Y	34470 FQ	42620 MW	51700 TQ	USBLS	5/15
	California	H	21.60 FQ	28.15 MW	36.85 TQ	CABLS	1/16-3/16
	Anaheim-Santa Ana-Irvine PMSA, CA	H	21.27 FQ	27.69 MW	36.45 TQ	CABLS	1/16-3/16
	Los Angeles-Long Beach-Glendale PMSA, CA	H	20.44 FQ	26.93 MW	34.22 TQ	CABLS	1/16-3/16
	Oakland-Hayward-Berkeley PMSA, CA	H	23.36 FQ	29.96 MW	36.77 TQ	CABLS	1/16-3/16
	Riverside-San Bernardino-Ontario MSA, CA	H	20.51 FQ	25.25 MW	29.93 TQ	CABLS	1/16-3/16
	Sacramento–Roseville–Arden-Arcade MSA, CA	H	21.26 FQ	26.55 MW	33.22 TQ	CABLS	1/16-3/16
	San Diego-Carlsbad MSA, CA	H	21.44 FQ	27.02 MW	33.75 TQ	CABLS	1/16-3/16
	San Francisco-Redwood City-South San Francisco PMSA, CA	H	26.44 FQ	32.69 MW	45.89 TQ	CABLS	1/16-3/16
	Colorado	Y	41470 FQ	53020 MW	68390 TQ	USBLS	5/15
	Denver-Aurora-Lakewood MSA, CO	Y	43930 FQ	55380 MW	71940 TQ	USBLS	5/15
	Connecticut	Y		55523 MW		CTBLS	1/16-3/16
	Bridgeport-Stamford-Norwalk MSA, CT	Y	42880 FQ	55500 MW	69390 TQ	USBLS	5/15
	Hartford-West Hartford-East Hartford MSA, CT	Y	44520 FQ	56260 MW	70980 TQ	USBLS	5/15
	Delaware	Y	43340 FQ	52580 MW	65350 TQ	USBLS	5/15
	Wilmington PMSA, DE-MD-NJ	Y	44000 FQ	53290 MW	66670 TQ	USBLS	5/15
	District of Columbia	Y	46120 FQ	60470 MW	79690 TQ	USBLS	5/15
	Washington-Arlington-Alexandria PMSA, DC-VA-MD-WV	Y	44680 FQ	58920 MW	74700 TQ	USBLS	5/15
	Florida	H	14.19 AE	20.54 MW	26.01 AEX	FLBLS	7/16-9/16
	Fort Lauderdale-Pompano Beach-Deerfield Beach PMSA, FL	H	14.03 AE	20.52 MW	27.07 AEX	FLBLS	7/16-9/16
	Miami-Miami Beach-Kendall PMSA, FL	H	15.34 AE	22.53 MW	28.69 AEX	FLBLS	7/16-9/16
	Orlando-Kissimmee-Sanford MSA, FL	H	13.15 AE	19.30 MW	25.32 AEX	FLBLS	7/16-9/16
	Tampa-St. Petersburg-Clearwater MSA, FL	H	14.27 AE	20.85 MW	26.04 AEX	FLBLS	7/16-9/16
	Georgia	Y	35940 FQ	47590 MW	64100 TQ	USBLS	5/15
	Atlanta-Sandy Springs-Roswell MSA, GA	Y	36960 FQ	48990 MW	67850 TQ	USBLS	5/15
	Augusta-Richmond County MSA, GA-SC	Y	25680 FQ	38020 MW	53230 TQ	USBLS	5/15
	Hawaii	Y	37350 FQ	46930 MW	59130 TQ	USBLS	5/15
	Urban Honolulu MSA, HI	Y	37310 FQ	47700 MW	60140 TQ	USBLS	5/15
	Idaho	Y	30610 FQ	39800 MW	50080 TQ	USBLS	5/15

AE	Average entry wage	AWR	Average wage range	H	Hourly	LR	Low end range	MTC	Median total compensation
AEX	Average experienced wage	B	Biweekly	HI	Highest wage paid	M	Monthly	MW	Median wage paid
ATC	Average total compensation	D	Daily	HR	High end range	MCC	Median cash compensation	MWR	Median wage range
AW	Average wage paid	FQ	First quartile wage	LO	Lowest wage paid	ME	Median entry wage	S	See annotated source

TCC　Total cash compensation
TQ　Third quartile wage
W　Weekly
Y　Yearly

Occupation/Type/Industry	Location	Per	Low	Mid	High	Source	Date
Computer User Support Specialist	Boise City MSA, ID	Y	31110 FQ	40390 MW	49700 TQ	USBLS	5/15
	Illinois	Y	39980 FQ	51070 MW	66380 TQ	USBLS	5/15
	Chicago-Naperville-Arlington Heights PMSA, IL	Y	40940 FQ	52230 MW	67960 TQ	USBLS	5/15
	Lake County-Kenosha County PMSA, IL-WI	Y	41410 FQ	52260 MW	63820 TQ	USBLS	5/15
	Indiana	Y	33970 FQ	43360 MW	57340 TQ	USBLS	5/15
	Gary PMSA, IN	Y	27820 FQ	41610 MW	54950 TQ	USBLS	5/15
	Indianapolis-Carmel-Anderson MSA, IN	Y	35840 FQ	46540 MW	63210 TQ	USBLS	5/15
	Iowa	Y	33000 FQ	41760 MW	51630 TQ	USBLS	5/15
	Des Moines-West Des Moines MSA, IA	Y	36970 FQ	46080 MW	57030 TQ	USBLS	5/15
	Kansas	Y	33700 FQ	43820 MW	53400 TQ	USBLS	5/15
	Wichita MSA, KS	Y	26690 FQ	34810 MW	45970 TQ	USBLS	5/15
	Kentucky	Y	32690 FQ	41240 MW	52930 TQ	USBLS	5/15
	Louisville-Jefferson County MSA, KY-IN	Y	33620 FQ	42100 MW	53590 TQ	USBLS	5/15
	Louisiana	Y	33530 FQ	44080 MW	56150 TQ	USBLS	5/15
	Baton Rouge MSA, LA	Y	40200 FQ	50720 MW	64490 TQ	USBLS	5/15
	New Orleans-Metairie MSA, LA	Y	35610 FQ	44830 MW	54440 TQ	USBLS	5/15
	Maine	Y	35500 FQ	43650 MW	53350 TQ	USBLS	5/15
	Portland-South Portland MSA, ME	Y	41090 FQ	47720 MW	57580 TQ	USBLS	5/15
	Maryland	Y	34725 AE	54757 MW	64773 AEX	MDBLS	4/16
	Baltimore-Columbia-Towson MSA, MD	Y	41190 FQ	49920 MW	62270 TQ	USBLS	5/15
	Salisbury MSA, MD-DE	Y	32700 FQ	40760 MW	49350 TQ	USBLS	5/15
	Massachusetts	Y	46270 FQ	58920 MW	75440 TQ	USBLS	5/15
	Boston-Cambridge-Newton NECTA, MA	Y	48900 FQ	60770 MW	77980 TQ	USBLS	5/15
	Worcester MSA, MA-CT	Y	41360 FQ	51130 MW	63890 TQ	USBLS	5/15
	Michigan	Y	34570 FQ	45830 MW	60800 TQ	USBLS	5/15
	Detroit-Dearborn-Livonia PMSA, MI	Y	29630 FQ	41540 MW	55920 TQ	USBLS	5/15
	Grand Rapids-Wyoming MSA, MI	Y	35070 FQ	46690 MW	61440 TQ	USBLS	5/15
	Minnesota	Y	39747 FQ	51098 MW	64435 TQ	MNBLS	1/16-3/16
	Minneapolis-St. Paul-Bloomington MSA, MN-WI	Y	41128 FQ	53316 MW	67348 TQ	MNBLS	1/16-3/16
	Mississippi	Y	31960 FQ	41360 MW	51910 TQ	USBLS	5/15
	Jackson MSA, MS	Y	32800 FQ	41640 MW	50820 TQ	USBLS	5/15
	Missouri	Y	35940 FQ	46440 MW	59640 TQ	USBLS	5/15
	Kansas City MSA, MO-KS	Y	38320 FQ	46800 MW	58750 TQ	USBLS	5/15
	St. Louis MSA, MO-IL	Y	38330 FQ	49330 MW	62670 TQ	USBLS	5/15
	Montana	Y	32590 FQ	41180 MW	51530 TQ	USBLS	5/15
	Billings MSA, MT	Y	36050 FQ	43080 MW	53920 TQ	USBLS	5/15
	Nebraska	Y	33140 FQ	42315 MW	54935 TQ	NEBLS	7/16-9/16
	Omaha-Council Bluffs MSA, NE-IA	Y	36305 FQ	47050 MW	61700 TQ	NEBLS	7/16-9/16
	Nevada	Y	37060 FQ	46290 MW	59440 TQ	USBLS	5/15
	Las Vegas-Henderson-Paradise MSA, NV	Y	38250 FQ	47240 MW	60730 TQ	USBLS	5/15
	New Hampshire	H	17.73 AE	26.03 MW	32.09 AEX	NHBLS	6/16
	Manchester NECTA, NH	H	16.52 AE	26.24 MW	31.82 AEX	NHBLS	6/16
	Nashua NECTA, NH-MA	Y	43040 FQ	57200 MW	74160 TQ	USBLS	5/15
	New Jersey	Y	43780 FQ	54710 MW	68230 TQ	USBLS	5/15
	Camden PMSA, NJ	Y	38840 FQ	47190 MW	56920 TQ	USBLS	5/15
	Newark PMSA, NJ-PA	Y	44600 FQ	55680 MW	70880 TQ	USBLS	5/15
	Trenton MSA, NJ	Y	51080 FQ	64120 MW	75180 TQ	USBLS	5/15
	New Mexico	Y	34150 FQ	43220 MW	52690 TQ	USBLS	5/15
	Albuquerque MSA, NM	Y	34530 FQ	43150 MW	52180 TQ	USBLS	5/15
	New York	Y	35430 AE	52870 MW	66910 AEX	NYBLS	1/16-3/16
	Buffalo-Cheektowaga-Niagara Falls MSA, NY	Y	31230 FQ	40130 MW	52460 TQ	USBLS	5/15
	Nassau County-Suffolk County PMSA, NY	Y	41780 FQ	54310 MW	68950 TQ	USBLS	5/15
	New York-Jersey City-White Plains PMSA, NY-NJ	Y	43880 FQ	56180 MW	72740 TQ	USBLS	5/15
	Rochester MSA, NY	Y	36450 FQ	46580 MW	59090 TQ	USBLS	5/15
	North Carolina	Y	36680 FQ	47780 MW	61320 TQ	USBLS	5/15

AE	Average entry wage	AWR	Average wage range	H	Hourly	LR	Low end range	MTC	Median total compensation	TCC	Total cash compensation
AEX	Average experienced wage	B	Biweekly	HI	Highest wage paid	M	Monthly	MW	Median wage paid	TQ	Third quartile wage
ATC	Average total compensation	D	Daily	HR	High end range	MCC	Median cash compensation	MWR	Median wage range	W	Weekly
AW	Average wage paid	FQ	First quartile wage	LO	Lowest wage paid	ME	Median entry wage	S	See annotated source	Y	Yearly

Occupation/Type/Industry	Location	Per	Low	Mid	High	Source	Date
Computer User Support Specialist	Charlotte-Concord-Gastonia						
	MSA, NC-SC	Y	37610 FQ	49470 MW	62890 TQ	USBLS	5/15
	Raleigh MSA, NC	Y	41880 FQ	53420 MW	67550 TQ	USBLS	5/15
	North Dakota	Y	36440 FQ	45890 MW	56780 TQ	USBLS	5/15
	Fargo MSA, ND-MN	Y	34520 FQ	44490 MW	54840 TQ	USBLS	5/15
	Ohio	Y	34200 FQ	42960 MW	54920 TQ	USBLS	5/15
	Cincinnati MSA, OH-KY-IN	Y	36220 FQ	46950 MW	60000 TQ	USBLS	5/15
	Cleveland-Elyria MSA, OH	Y	35820 FQ	43860 MW	53880 TQ	USBLS	5/15
	Columbus MSA, OH	Y	34540 FQ	43570 MW	57700 TQ	USBLS	5/15
	Oklahoma	Y	31510 FQ	40410 MW	53620 TQ	USBLS	5/15
	Oklahoma City MSA, OK	Y	32630 FQ	40800 MW	52270 TQ	USBLS	5/15
	Tulsa MSA, OK	Y	34290 FQ	45570 MW	64000 TQ	USBLS	5/15
	Oregon	H	18.31 FQ	23.27 MW	29.52 TQ	ORBLS	2016
	Portland-Vancouver-Hillsboro						
	MSA, OR-WA	Y	38060 FQ	48470 MW	61590 TQ	USBLS	5/15
	Pennsylvania	Y	37180 FQ	47670 MW	61470 TQ	USBLS	5/15
	Allentown-Bethlehem-Easton						
	MSA, PA-NJ	Y	41300 FQ	50000 MW	62040 TQ	USBLS	5/15
	Harrisburg-Carlisle MSA, PA	Y	38610 FQ	46660 MW	58970 TQ	USBLS	5/15
	Montgomery County-Bucks						
	County-Chester County						
	PMSA, PA	Y	39570 FQ	51680 MW	71130 TQ	USBLS	5/15
	Philadelphia PMSA, PA	Y	41720 FQ	53390 MW	66150 TQ	USBLS	5/15
	Pittsburgh MSA, PA	Y	36630 FQ	46900 MW	60890 TQ	USBLS	5/15
	Rhode Island	Y	39410 FQ	48860 MW	60310 TQ	USBLS	5/15
	Providence-Warwick MSA, RI-						
	MA	Y	38760 FQ	48490 MW	60240 TQ	USBLS	5/15
	South Carolina	Y	33600 FQ	43450 MW	55250 TQ	USBLS	5/15
	Charleston-North Charleston						
	MSA, SC	Y	37940 FQ	46480 MW	59260 TQ	USBLS	5/15
	Columbia MSA, SC	Y	34480 FQ	45190 MW	57180 TQ	USBLS	5/15
	Greenville-Anderson-Mauldin						
	MSA, SC	Y	34430 FQ	42350 MW	52500 TQ	USBLS	5/15
	South Dakota	Y	31820 FQ	36760 MW	43480 TQ	USBLS	5/15
	Sioux Falls MSA, SD	Y	32580 FQ	37610 MW	44430 TQ	USBLS	5/15
	Tennessee	Y	34370 FQ	43420 MW	55180 TQ	USBLS	5/15
	Knoxville MSA, TN	Y	29060 FQ	38230 MW	48150 TQ	USBLS	5/15
	Memphis MSA, TN-MS-AR	Y	36150 FQ	47240 MW	60710 TQ	USBLS	5/15
	Nashville-Davidson–						
	Murfreesboro–Franklin						
	MSA, TN	Y	36960 FQ	45590 MW	57540 TQ	USBLS	5/15
	Texas	Y	36150 FQ	47670 MW	62300 TQ	USBLS	5/15
	Austin-Round Rock MSA, TX	Y	35830 FQ	47120 MW	61830 TQ	USBLS	5/15
	Dallas-Plano-Irving PMSA, TX	Y	37740 FQ	49560 MW	62500 TQ	USBLS	5/15
	Fort Worth-Arlington PMSA,						
	TX	Y	34200 FQ	45330 MW	61320 TQ	USBLS	5/15
	Houston-The Woodlands-						
	Sugar Land MSA, TX	Y	39550 FQ	53550 MW	71380 TQ	USBLS	5/15
	San Antonio-New Braunfels						
	MSA, TX	Y	36240 FQ	45890 MW	59320 TQ	USBLS	5/15
	Utah	Y	32020 FQ	42420 MW	55790 TQ	USBLS	5/15
	Ogden-Clearfield MSA, UT	Y	33590 FQ	42600 MW	53600 TQ	USBLS	5/15
	Provo-Orem MSA, UT	Y	28670 FQ	34980 MW	46140 TQ	USBLS	5/15
	Salt Lake City MSA, UT	Y	35410 FQ	46500 MW	59180 TQ	USBLS	5/15
	Vermont	Y	39680 FQ	49310 MW	62080 TQ	USBLS	5/15
	Burlington-South Burlington						
	MSA, VT	Y	42410 FQ	51110 MW	64130 TQ	USBLS	5/15
	Virginia	Y	40290 FQ	52730 MW	67460 TQ	USBLS	5/15
	Richmond MSA, VA	Y	40780 FQ	48690 MW	60560 TQ	USBLS	5/15
	Virginia Beach-Norfolk-						
	Newport News MSA, VA-NC	Y	38300 FQ	49090 MW	62490 TQ	USBLS	5/15
	Washington	H	20.70 FQ	25.51 MW	32.57 TQ	WABLS	3/16
	Seattle-Bellevue-Everett						
	PMSA, WA	H	21.69 FQ	27.10 MW	35.78 TQ	WABLS	3/16
	Tacoma-Lakewood PMSA, WA	H	20.26 FQ	24.35 MW	29.66 TQ	WABLS	3/16
	West Virginia	Y	32660 FQ	41290 MW	51050 TQ	USBLS	5/15
	Huntington-Ashland MSA,						
	WV-KY-OH	Y	32740 FQ	38980 MW	47900 TQ	USBLS	5/15
	Wisconsin	Y	36120 FQ	45690 MW	58050 TQ	USBLS	5/15
	Madison MSA, WI	Y	37070 FQ	45660 MW	57580 TQ	USBLS	5/15
	Milwaukee-Waukesha-West						
	Allis MSA, WI	Y	40280 FQ	50280 MW	64010 TQ	USBLS	5/15

AE Average entry wage	**AWR** Average wage range	**H** Hourly	**LR** Low end range	**MTC** Median total compensation	**TCC** Total cash compensation
AEX Average experienced wage	**B** Biweekly	**HI** Highest wage paid	**M** Monthly	**MW** Median wage paid	**TQ** Third quartile wage
ATC Average total compensation	**D** Daily	**HR** High end range	**MCC** Median cash compensation	**MWR** Median wage range	**W** Weekly
AW Average wage paid	**FQ** First quartile wage	**LO** Lowest wage paid	**ME** Median entry wage	**S** See annotated source	**Y** Yearly

Occupation/Type/Industry	Location	Per	Low	Mid	High	Source	Date
Computer User Support Specialist	Wyoming	Y	38130 FQ	46660 MW	56030 TQ	USBLS	5/15
	Cheyenne MSA, WY	Y	42360 FQ	48820 MW	56980 TQ	USBLS	5/15
	Puerto Rico	Y	21170 FQ	28380 MW	38120 TQ	USBLS	5/15
	San Juan-Carolina-Caguas MSA, PR	Y	22110 FQ	28810 MW	38480 TQ	USBLS	5/15
	Virgin Islands	Y	31210 FQ	36300 MW	44160 TQ	USBLS	5/15
	Guam	Y	26230 FQ	34540 MW	42100 TQ	USBLS	5/15
Concession Aide							
Recreation Department, Municipal Government	Carlsbad, CA	H	10.00 LO		11.25 HI	CCCA02	1/1/16
Concierge	Alabama	Y	19738 AE	24937 AW	27542 AEX	ALBLS	6/16
	Alaska	Y	24020 FQ	31460 MW	38140 TQ	USBLS	5/15
	Anchorage MSA, AK	Y	26230 FQ	32960 MW	38390 TQ	USBLS	5/15
	Arizona	Y	20900 FQ	25570 MW	29690 TQ	USBLS	5/15
	Phoenix-Mesa-Scottsdale MSA, AZ	Y	21640 FQ	26240 MW	30160 TQ	USBLS	5/15
	Tucson MSA, AZ	Y	20470 FQ	23930 MW	28390 TQ	USBLS	5/15
	California	H	12.30 FQ	15.64 MW	18.62 TQ	CABLS	1/16-3/16
	Anaheim-Santa Ana-Irvine PMSA, CA	H	12.23 FQ	14.18 MW	16.96 TQ	CABLS	1/16-3/16
	Los Angeles-Long Beach-Glendale PMSA, CA	H	13.52 FQ	16.15 MW	18.09 TQ	CABLS	1/16-3/16
	Oakland-Hayward-Berkeley PMSA, CA	H	10.53 FQ	11.43 MW	12.72 TQ	CABLS	1/16-3/16
	Riverside-San Bernardino-Ontario MSA, CA	H	11.45 FQ	13.89 MW	17.40 TQ	CABLS	1/16-3/16
	Sacramento–Roseville–Arden-Arcade MSA, CA	H	14.16 FQ	16.63 MW	18.83 TQ	CABLS	1/16-3/16
	San Diego-Carlsbad MSA, CA	H	12.28 FQ	15.77 MW	18.05 TQ	CABLS	1/16-3/16
	San Francisco-Redwood City-South San Francisco PMSA, CA	H	20.49 FQ	22.38 MW	24.30 TQ	CABLS	1/16-3/16
	Colorado	Y	25260 FQ	29080 MW	34690 TQ	USBLS	5/15
	Denver-Aurora-Lakewood MSA, CO	Y	24610 FQ	28600 MW	34170 TQ	USBLS	5/15
	Connecticut	Y		25473 MW		CTBLS	1/16-3/16
	Hartford-West Hartford-East Hartford MSA, CT	Y	22830 FQ	26440 MW	29180 TQ	USBLS	5/15
	District of Columbia	Y	27230 FQ	30850 MW	38640 TQ	USBLS	5/15
	Washington-Arlington-Alexandria PMSA, DC-VA-MD-WV	Y	28100 FQ	32980 MW	37840 TQ	USBLS	5/15
	Florida	H	10.11 AE	12.33 MW	14.76 AEX	FLBLS	7/16-9/16
	Fort Lauderdale-Pompano Beach-Deerfield Beach PMSA, FL	H	11.57 AE	14.47 MW	16.64 AEX	FLBLS	7/16-9/16
	Miami-Miami Beach-Kendall PMSA, FL	H	10.27 AE	13.62 MW	16.95 AEX	FLBLS	7/16-9/16
	Orlando-Kissimmee-Sanford MSA, FL	H	9.97 AE	11.55 MW	13.62 AEX	FLBLS	7/16-9/16
	Tampa-St. Petersburg-Clearwater MSA, FL	H	10.29 AE	12.28 MW	14.19 AEX	FLBLS	7/16-9/16
	Georgia	Y	22840 FQ	26410 MW	29680 TQ	USBLS	5/15
	Atlanta-Sandy Springs-Roswell MSA, GA	Y	23040 FQ	26460 MW	29610 TQ	USBLS	5/15
	Hawaii	Y	26560 FQ	41220 MW	45950 TQ	USBLS	5/15
	Urban Honolulu MSA, HI	Y	21080 FQ	32300 MW	43060 TQ	USBLS	5/15
	Idaho	Y	23020 FQ	27780 MW	36450 TQ	USBLS	5/15
	Illinois	Y	23830 FQ	30800 MW	36000 TQ	USBLS	5/15
	Chicago-Naperville-Arlington Heights PMSA, IL	Y	23840 FQ	31880 MW	36620 TQ	USBLS	5/15
	Indiana	Y	18360 FQ	21910 MW	26950 TQ	USBLS	5/15
	Indianapolis-Carmel-Anderson MSA, IN	Y	21100 FQ	26030 MW	32990 TQ	USBLS	5/15
	Iowa	Y	19760 FQ	22870 MW	27450 TQ	USBLS	5/15
	Kansas	Y	19000 FQ	26750 MW	29980 TQ	USBLS	5/15
	Kentucky	Y	21450 FQ	24240 MW	28980 TQ	USBLS	5/15
	Louisville-Jefferson County MSA, KY-IN	Y	19010 FQ	22210 MW	26420 TQ	USBLS	5/15
	Louisiana	Y	22470 FQ	25980 MW	29840 TQ	USBLS	5/15

AE Average entry wage	**AWR** Average wage range	**H** Hourly	**LR** Low end range	**MTC** Median total compensation	**TCC** Total cash compensation
AEX Average experienced wage	**B** Biweekly	**HI** Highest wage paid	**M** Monthly	**MW** Median wage paid	**TQ** Third quartile wage
ATC Average total compensation	**D** Daily	**HR** High end range	**MCC** Median cash compensation	**MWR** Median wage range	**W** Weekly
AW Average wage paid	**FQ** First quartile wage	**LO** Lowest wage paid	**ME** Median entry wage	**S** See annotated source	**Y** Yearly

Occupation/Type/Industry	Location	Per	Low	Mid	High	Source	Date
Concierge	Baton Rouge MSA, LA	Y	18450 FQ	21860 MW	25720 TQ	USBLS	5/15
	New Orleans-Metairie MSA, LA	Y	24220 FQ	27280 MW	30240 TQ	USBLS	5/15
	Maine	Y	19720 FQ	24150 MW	31500 TQ	USBLS	5/15
	Maryland	Y	24759 AE	30735 MW	33723 AEX	MDBLS	4/16
	Baltimore-Columbia-Towson MSA, MD	Y	24950 FQ	28930 MW	38400 TQ	USBLS	5/15
	Massachusetts	Y	25610 FQ	34190 MW	38850 TQ	USBLS	5/15
	Boston-Cambridge-Newton NECTA, MA	Y	31460 FQ	35510 MW	39740 TQ	USBLS	5/15
	Michigan	Y	18750 FQ	22820 MW	32750 TQ	USBLS	5/15
	Detroit-Dearborn-Livonia PMSA, MI	Y	28660 FQ	33680 MW	37990 TQ	USBLS	5/15
	Grand Rapids-Wyoming MSA, MI	Y	18000 FQ	18940 MW	22580 TQ	USBLS	5/15
	Minnesota	Y	22692 FQ	27347 MW	34467 TQ	MNBLS	1/16-3/16
	Minneapolis-St. Paul-Bloomington MSA, MN-WI	Y	22490 FQ	26650 MW	33649 TQ	MNBLS	1/16-3/16
	Mississippi	Y	18960 FQ	22100 MW	25050 TQ	USBLS	5/15
	Missouri	Y	20980 FQ	23640 MW	28430 TQ	USBLS	5/15
	Kansas City MSA, MO-KS	Y	22170 FQ	25910 MW	29160 TQ	USBLS	5/15
	St. Louis MSA, MO-IL	Y	21330 FQ	23900 MW	28310 TQ	USBLS	5/15
	Montana	Y	21430 FQ	23880 MW	27930 TQ	USBLS	5/15
	Omaha-Council Bluffs MSA, NE-IA	Y	21155 FQ	23235 MW	28595 TQ	NEBLS	7/16-9/16
	Nevada	Y	28310 FQ	33830 MW	37380 TQ	USBLS	5/15
	Las Vegas-Henderson-Paradise MSA, NV	Y	30820 FQ	34470 MW	37730 TQ	USBLS	5/15
	New Hampshire	H	10.69 AE	13.59 MW	15.34 AEX	NHBLS	6/16
	New Jersey	Y	25350 FQ	28410 MW	32620 TQ	USBLS	5/15
	Newark PMSA, NJ-PA	Y	26420 FQ	30090 MW	37460 TQ	USBLS	5/15
	Trenton MSA, NJ	Y	23640 FQ	28520 MW	36260 TQ	USBLS	5/15
	New Mexico	Y	22120 FQ	26450 MW	31200 TQ	USBLS	5/15
	New York	Y	30430 AE	43780 MW	48760 AEX	NYBLS	1/16-3/16
	Buffalo-Cheektowaga-Niagara Falls MSA, NY	Y	20380 FQ	22240 MW	24090 TQ	USBLS	5/15
	Nassau County-Suffolk County PMSA, NY	Y	27230 FQ	31980 MW	39540 TQ	USBLS	5/15
	New York-Jersey City-White Plains PMSA, NY-NJ	Y	34450 FQ	42750 MW	48200 TQ	USBLS	5/15
	Rochester MSA, NY	Y	21140 FQ	29420 MW	39590 TQ	USBLS	5/15
	North Carolina	Y	18040 FQ	20970 MW	24470 TQ	USBLS	5/15
	Charlotte-Concord-Gastonia MSA, NC-SC	Y	18390 FQ	21720 MW	26330 TQ	USBLS	5/15
	Raleigh MSA, NC	Y	18120 FQ	21290 MW	24840 TQ	USBLS	5/15
	Ohio	Y	20380 FQ	24480 MW	28720 TQ	USBLS	5/15
	Cincinnati MSA, OH-KY-IN	Y	19830 FQ	22480 MW	25860 TQ	USBLS	5/15
	Cleveland-Elyria MSA, OH	Y	20900 FQ	25370 MW	30050 TQ	USBLS	5/15
	Columbus MSA, OH	Y	20090 FQ	24740 MW	27770 TQ	USBLS	5/15
	Oklahoma	Y	21850 FQ	27190 MW	32270 TQ	USBLS	5/15
	Oklahoma City MSA, OK	Y	23170 FQ	27660 MW	32160 TQ	USBLS	5/15
	Tulsa MSA, OK	Y	25020 FQ	28910 MW	35360 TQ	USBLS	5/15
	Oregon	H	10.88 FQ	13.38 MW	17.08 TQ	ORBLS	2016
	Portland-Vancouver-Hillsboro MSA, OR-WA	Y	23110 FQ	28930 MW	35370 TQ	USBLS	5/15
	Pennsylvania	Y	23130 FQ	27510 MW	32830 TQ	USBLS	5/15
	Harrisburg-Carlisle MSA, PA	Y	19670 FQ	24040 MW	29650 TQ	USBLS	5/15
	Montgomery County-Bucks County-Chester County PMSA, PA	Y	22330 FQ	25590 MW	29730 TQ	USBLS	5/15
	Philadelphia PMSA, PA	Y	23130 FQ	28800 MW	35430 TQ	USBLS	5/15
	Pittsburgh MSA, PA	Y	26180 FQ	28850 MW	32010 TQ	USBLS	5/15
	Rhode Island	Y	25000 FQ	27320 MW	29650 TQ	USBLS	5/15
	Providence-Warwick MSA, RI-MA	Y	25000 FQ	27320 MW	29650 TQ	USBLS	5/15
	South Carolina	Y	22090 FQ	25390 MW	29290 TQ	USBLS	5/15
	Charleston-North Charleston MSA, SC	Y	23260 FQ	26460 MW	29380 TQ	USBLS	5/15
	Tennessee	Y	20140 FQ	22360 MW	24960 TQ	USBLS	5/15
	Memphis MSA, TN-MS-AR	Y	20390 FQ	21950 MW	23510 TQ	USBLS	5/15

AE	Average entry wage	**AWR** Average wage range	**H** Hourly	**LR** Low end range	**MTC** Median total compensation	**TCC** Total cash compensation
AEX	Average experienced wage	**B** Biweekly	**HI** Highest wage paid	**M** Monthly	**MW** Median wage paid	**TQ** Third quartile wage
ATC	Average total compensation	**D** Daily	**HR** High end range	**MCC** Median cash compensation	**MWR** Median wage range	**W** Weekly
AW	Average wage paid	**FQ** First quartile wage	**LO** Lowest wage paid	**ME** Median entry wage	**S** See annotated source	**Y** Yearly

Occupation/Type/Industry	Location	Per	Low	Mid	High	Source	Date
Concierge	Nashville-Davidson–Murfreesboro–Franklin MSA, TN	Y	21190 FQ	24050 MW	30010 TQ	USBLS	5/15
	Texas	Y	19580 FQ	22700 MW	27290 TQ	USBLS	5/15
	Austin-Round Rock MSA, TX	Y	20840 FQ	24610 MW	28820 TQ	USBLS	5/15
	Dallas-Plano-Irving PMSA, TX	Y	20620 FQ	23100 MW	27600 TQ	USBLS	5/15
	Fort Worth-Arlington PMSA, TX	Y	17730 FQ	19860 MW	23070 TQ	USBLS	5/15
	Houston-The Woodlands-Sugar Land MSA, TX	Y	19270 FQ	22420 MW	27360 TQ	USBLS	5/15
	San Antonio-New Braunfels MSA, TX	Y	19420 FQ	23640 MW	28240 TQ	USBLS	5/15
	Utah	Y	22800 FQ	27880 MW	34160 TQ	USBLS	5/15
	Salt Lake City MSA, UT	Y	23380 FQ	29830 MW	35920 TQ	USBLS	5/15
	Virginia	Y	27260 FQ	32250 MW	37170 TQ	USBLS	5/15
	Richmond MSA, VA	Y	25570 FQ	28690 MW	33650 TQ	USBLS	5/15
	Virginia Beach-Norfolk-Newport News MSA, VA-NC	Y	25910 FQ	28700 MW	31900 TQ	USBLS	5/15
	Washington	H	13.32 FQ	15.08 MW	17.59 TQ	WABLS	3/16
	Seattle-Bellevue-Everett PMSA, WA	H	13.56 FQ	15.23 MW	17.68 TQ	WABLS	3/16
	West Virginia	Y	21390 FQ	24850 MW	44060 TQ	USBLS	5/15
	Wisconsin	Y	20660 FQ	22820 MW	25620 TQ	USBLS	5/15
	Milwaukee-Waukesha-West Allis MSA, WI	Y	20620 FQ	22400 MW	24190 TQ	USBLS	5/15
	Wyoming	Y	27770 FQ	31940 MW	37050 TQ	USBLS	5/15
	Puerto Rico	Y	16690 FQ	18030 MW	19440 TQ	USBLS	5/15
	San Juan-Carolina-Caguas MSA, PR	Y	16820 FQ	18310 MW	21020 TQ	USBLS	5/15
	Virgin Islands	Y	27780 FQ	31290 MW	35420 TQ	USBLS	5/15
	Guam	Y	18160 FQ	19160 MW	22130 TQ	USBLS	5/15
Condemnation Award Specialist Municipal Government	Detroit, MI	M	2992 LO		3275 HI	DETGOV	2016
Conference Worker Michigan State University	East Lansing, MI	Y			31803 HI	MSUSAL	10/1/14-9/30/15
Conservation Policy Analyst Municipal Government	Seattle, WA	H	39.18 LO		45.66 HI	CSSS	1/13/16
Conservation Scientist	Alabama	Y	51629 AE	73167 AW	83931 AEX	ALBLS	6/16
	Birmingham-Hoover MSA, AL	Y	51038 AE	65706 AW	73035 AEX	ALBLS	6/16
	Alaska	Y	70350 FQ	86900 MW	109130 TQ	USBLS	5/15
	Anchorage MSA, AK	Y	63980 FQ	89460 MW	118500 TQ	USBLS	5/15
	Arizona	Y	54750 FQ	64780 MW	76510 TQ	USBLS	5/15
	Phoenix-Mesa-Scottsdale MSA, AZ	Y	62940 FQ	70350 MW	85710 TQ	USBLS	5/15
	Tucson MSA, AZ	Y	56470 FQ	65060 MW	77220 TQ	USBLS	5/15
	Arkansas	Y	27630 FQ	30530 MW	66360 TQ	USBLS	5/15
	California	H	29.12 FQ	36.18 MW	45.93 TQ	CABLS	1/16-3/16
	Anaheim-Santa Ana-Irvine PMSA, CA	H	30.32 FQ	34.79 MW	42.36 TQ	CABLS	1/16-3/16
	Los Angeles-Long Beach-Glendale PMSA, CA	H	26.42 FQ	43.50 MW	52.34 TQ	CABLS	1/16-3/16
	Oakland-Hayward-Berkeley PMSA, CA	H	39.23 FQ	43.73 MW	49.02 TQ	CABLS	1/16-3/16
	Riverside-San Bernardino-Ontario MSA, CA	H	27.41 FQ	34.59 MW	41.35 TQ	CABLS	1/16-3/16
	Sacramento–Roseville–Arden-Arcade MSA, CA	H	26.65 FQ	36.28 MW	47.65 TQ	CABLS	1/16-3/16
	San Diego-Carlsbad MSA, CA	H	31.36 FQ	46.48 MW	56.24 TQ	CABLS	1/16-3/16
	San Francisco-Redwood City-South San Francisco PMSA, CA	H	30.30 FQ	39.83 MW	49.81 TQ	CABLS	1/16-3/16
	Colorado	Y	51520 FQ	63480 MW	80120 TQ	USBLS	5/15
	Denver-Aurora-Lakewood MSA, CO	Y	51510 FQ	61870 MW	86380 TQ	USBLS	5/15
	Connecticut	Y		87784 MW		CTBLS	1/16-3/16
	Delaware	Y	44630 FQ	54860 MW	63120 TQ	USBLS	5/15
	Wilmington PMSA, DE-MD-NJ	Y	44620 FQ	54480 MW	65400 TQ	USBLS	5/15

AE Average entry wage	**AWR** Average wage range	**H** Hourly	**LR** Low end range	**MTC** Median total compensation	**TCC** Total cash compensation
AEX Average experienced wage	**B** Biweekly	**HI** Highest wage paid	**M** Monthly	**MW** Median wage paid	**TQ** Third quartile wage
ATC Average total compensation	**D** Daily	**HR** High end range	**MCC** Median cash compensation	**MWR** Median wage range	**W** Weekly
AW Average wage paid	**FQ** First quartile wage	**LO** Lowest wage paid	**ME** Median entry wage	**S** See annotated source	**Y** Yearly

Occupation/Type/Industry	Location	Per	Low	Mid	High	Source	Date
Conservation Scientist	Washington-Arlington-Alexandria PMSA, DC-VA-MD-WV	Y	56690 FQ	73790 MW	99450 TQ	USBLS	5/15
	Florida	H	22.21 AE	36.23 MW	43.67 AEX	FLBLS	7/16-9/16
	Fort Lauderdale-Pompano Beach-Deerfield Beach PMSA, FL	H	29.88 AE	36.62 MW	45.06 AEX	FLBLS	7/16-9/16
	Orlando-Kissimmee-Sanford MSA, FL	H	13.48 AE	18.10 MW	27.01 AEX	FLBLS	7/16-9/16
	Tampa-St. Petersburg-Clearwater MSA, FL	H	28.39 AE	42.63 MW	52.47 AEX	FLBLS	7/16-9/16
	Georgia	Y	45360 FQ	57920 MW	76150 TQ	USBLS	5/15
	Atlanta-Sandy Springs-Roswell MSA, GA	Y	44260 FQ	55870 MW	70770 TQ	USBLS	5/15
	Hawaii	Y	57170 FQ	71650 MW	88030 TQ	USBLS	5/15
	Urban Honolulu MSA, HI	Y	61100 FQ	77700 MW	100660 TQ	USBLS	5/15
	Idaho	Y	53240 FQ	62160 MW	72540 TQ	USBLS	5/15
	Boise City MSA, ID	Y	53240 FQ	69910 MW	81890 TQ	USBLS	5/15
	Illinois	Y	53230 FQ	69200 MW	81100 TQ	USBLS	5/15
	Chicago-Naperville-Arlington Heights PMSA, IL	Y	45590 FQ	65280 MW	87970 TQ	USBLS	5/15
	Indiana	Y	39570 FQ	62870 MW	79160 TQ	USBLS	5/15
	Indianapolis-Carmel-Anderson MSA, IN	Y	30420 FQ	47940 MW	76470 TQ	USBLS	5/15
	Iowa	Y	39870 FQ	52410 MW	72230 TQ	USBLS	5/15
	Kentucky	Y	32870 FQ	50010 MW	74190 TQ	USBLS	5/15
	Louisville-Jefferson County MSA, KY-IN	Y	63130 FQ	69890 MW	75830 TQ	USBLS	5/15
	Louisiana	Y	47400 FQ	58560 MW	74110 TQ	USBLS	5/15
	Baton Rouge MSA, LA	Y	46970 FQ	57370 MW	71840 TQ	USBLS	5/15
	New Orleans-Metairie MSA, LA	Y	45810 FQ	58950 MW	77230 TQ	USBLS	5/15
	Maine	Y	44180 FQ	53250 MW	62700 TQ	USBLS	5/15
	Portland-South Portland MSA, ME	Y	43950 FQ	53570 MW	61020 TQ	USBLS	5/15
	Maryland	Y	44077 AE	75462 MW	91155 AEX	MDBLS	4/16
	Baltimore-Columbia-Towson MSA, MD	Y	50460 FQ	60310 MW	71610 TQ	USBLS	5/15
	Salisbury MSA, MD-DE	Y	23610 FQ	42490 MW	67620 TQ	USBLS	5/15
	Massachusetts	Y	51060 FQ	62820 MW	82530 TQ	USBLS	5/15
	Boston-Cambridge-Newton NECTA, MA	Y	53750 FQ	71380 MW	88770 TQ	USBLS	5/15
	Worcester MSA, MA-CT	Y	36750 FQ	46240 MW	63490 TQ	USBLS	5/15
	Michigan	Y	39480 FQ	60520 MW	73390 TQ	USBLS	5/15
	Grand Rapids-Wyoming MSA, MI	Y	42660 FQ	46210 MW	50400 TQ	USBLS	5/15
	Minnesota	Y	51945 FQ	65554 MW	73215 TQ	MNBLS	1/16-3/16
	Minneapolis-St. Paul-Bloomington MSA, MN-WI	Y	47953 FQ	61118 MW	74001 TQ	MNBLS	1/16-3/16
	Mississippi	Y	42030 FQ	49520 MW	59070 TQ	USBLS	5/15
	Jackson MSA, MS	Y	43810 FQ	49640 MW	58250 TQ	USBLS	5/15
	Missouri	Y	42010 FQ	54860 MW	73540 TQ	USBLS	5/15
	St. Louis MSA, MO-IL	Y	36140 FQ	50000 MW	75470 TQ	USBLS	5/15
	Springfield MSA, MO	Y	43890 FQ	72220 MW	84220 TQ	USBLS	5/15
	Montana	Y	45090 FQ	58570 MW	72540 TQ	USBLS	5/15
	Nebraska	Y	47185 FQ	61315 MW	74180 TQ	NEBLS	7/16-9/16
	Nevada	Y	43920 FQ	60420 MW	76150 TQ	USBLS	5/15
	New Hampshire	H	26.22 AE	32.41 MW	43.09 AEX	NHBLS	6/16
	New Jersey	Y	58460 FQ	74990 MW	97730 TQ	USBLS	5/15
	Newark PMSA, NJ-PA	Y	61430 FQ	77600 MW	98950 TQ	USBLS	5/15
	Trenton MSA, NJ	Y	64920 FQ	88980 MW	107690 TQ	USBLS	5/15
	New Mexico	Y	56000 FQ	64440 MW	76140 TQ	USBLS	5/15
	Albuquerque MSA, NM	Y	64430 FQ	78790 MW	111780 TQ	USBLS	5/15
	New York	Y	48940 AE	68910 MW	82360 AEX	NYBLS	1/16-3/16
	New York-Jersey City-White Plains PMSA, NY-NJ	Y	57590 FQ	71110 MW	88780 TQ	USBLS	5/15
	North Carolina	Y	40550 FQ	54860 MW	75950 TQ	USBLS	5/15
	Charlotte-Concord-Gastonia MSA, NC-SC	Y	42130 FQ	53630 MW	66460 TQ	USBLS	5/15
	Raleigh MSA, NC	Y	56010 FQ	79570 MW	94040 TQ	USBLS	5/15
	North Dakota	Y	52710 FQ	62940 MW	76130 TQ	USBLS	5/15
	Ohio	Y	37740 FQ	53630 MW	79160 TQ	USBLS	5/15

AE	Average entry wage	AWR	Average wage range	H	Hourly
AEX	Average experienced wage	B	Biweekly	HI	Highest wage paid
ATC	Average total compensation	D	Daily	HR	High end range
AW	Average wage paid	FQ	First quartile wage	LO	Lowest wage paid

LR	Low end range	MTC	Median total compensation
M	Monthly	MW	Median wage paid
MCC	Median cash compensation	MWR	Median wage range
ME	Median entry wage	S	See annotated source

TCC	Total cash compensation
TQ	Third quartile wage
W	Weekly
Y	Yearly

311

Occupation/Type/Industry	Location	Per	Low	Mid	High	Source	Date
Conservation Scientist	Cincinnati MSA, OH-KY-IN	Y	40530 FQ	57610 MW	101070 TQ	USBLS	5/15
	Cleveland-Elyria MSA, OH	Y	34600 FQ	39060 MW	64900 TQ	USBLS	5/15
	Oklahoma	Y	40070 FQ	61260 MW	76130 TQ	USBLS	5/15
	Oklahoma City MSA, OK	Y	37420 FQ	61300 MW	86880 TQ	USBLS	5/15
	Tulsa MSA, OK	Y	33210 FQ	54590 MW	68330 TQ	USBLS	5/15
	Oregon	H	26.29 FQ	33.31 MW	40.90 TQ	ORBLS	2016
	Portland-Vancouver-Hillsboro MSA, OR-WA	Y	51450 FQ	69920 MW	88060 TQ	USBLS	5/15
	Pennsylvania	Y	34390 FQ	48410 MW	69030 TQ	USBLS	5/15
	Montgomery County-Bucks County-Chester County PMSA, PA	Y	41830 FQ	50150 MW	62520 TQ	USBLS	5/15
	Philadelphia PMSA, PA	Y	30780 FQ	64550 MW	77380 TQ	USBLS	5/15
	Pittsburgh MSA, PA	Y	40060 FQ	60480 MW	132790 TQ	USBLS	5/15
	Rhode Island	Y	52220 FQ	83160 MW	113900 TQ	USBLS	5/15
	Providence-Warwick MSA, RI-MA	Y	52090 FQ	72550 MW	107920 TQ	USBLS	5/15
	South Carolina	Y	31240 FQ	49770 MW	72230 TQ	USBLS	5/15
	Charleston-North Charleston MSA, SC	Y	48490 FQ	62470 MW	81900 TQ	USBLS	5/15
	Columbia MSA, SC	Y	27050 FQ	31340 MW	51060 TQ	USBLS	5/15
	South Dakota	Y	45420 FQ	58080 MW	70270 TQ	USBLS	5/15
	Tennessee	Y	53150 FQ	70190 MW	82690 TQ	USBLS	5/15
	Nashville-Davidson–Murfreesboro–Franklin MSA, TN	Y	47890 FQ	62990 MW	77230 TQ	USBLS	5/15
	Texas	Y	44320 FQ	54620 MW	64440 TQ	USBLS	5/15
	Austin-Round Rock MSA, TX	Y	43650 FQ	56190 MW	65670 TQ	USBLS	5/15
	Fort Worth-Arlington PMSA, TX	Y	37400 FQ	48830 MW	59200 TQ	USBLS	5/15
	Houston-The Woodlands-Sugar Land MSA, TX	Y	42710 FQ	52610 MW	60610 TQ	USBLS	5/15
	San Antonio-New Braunfels MSA, TX	Y	43530 FQ	54670 MW	62680 TQ	USBLS	5/15
	Utah	Y	50020 FQ	62930 MW	74880 TQ	USBLS	5/15
	Ogden-Clearfield MSA, UT	Y	49340 FQ	59690 MW	78330 TQ	USBLS	5/15
	Salt Lake City MSA, UT	Y	60510 FQ	66180 MW	74870 TQ	USBLS	5/15
	Vermont	Y	38510 FQ	52610 MW	75980 TQ	USBLS	5/15
	Virginia	Y	31950 FQ	52320 MW	75230 TQ	USBLS	5/15
	Washington	H	22.06 FQ	25.59 MW	33.52 TQ	WABLS	3/16
	Seattle-Bellevue-Everett PMSA, WA	H	24.96 FQ	32.50 MW	42.30 TQ	WABLS	3/16
	Tacoma-Lakewood PMSA, WA	H	22.72 FQ	27.31 MW	33.53 TQ	WABLS	3/16
	West Virginia	Y	52190 FQ	64430 MW	77630 TQ	USBLS	5/15
	Wisconsin	Y	52610 FQ	62620 MW	75540 TQ	USBLS	5/15
	Madison MSA, WI	Y	49820 FQ	62890 MW	78800 TQ	USBLS	5/15
	Milwaukee-Waukesha-West Allis MSA, WI	Y	47620 FQ	63160 MW	75490 TQ	USBLS	5/15
	Wyoming	Y	57750 FQ	64430 MW	74870 TQ	USBLS	5/15
	Puerto Rico	Y	55400 FQ	72220 MW	86580 TQ	USBLS	5/15
Conservation Technician							
Municipal Government	Visalia, CA	Y			59234 HI	CACIT	6/28/16
Conservationist	United States	Y		62242 MW		CCAST01	2016
Constituent Liaison Officer							
Attorney General's Office, State Government	Ohio	H			28.90 HI	OHGOV	2015
Constituent Service Representative							
Municipal Government	Detroit, MI	M	2292 LO		2600 HI	DETGOV	2016
Construction and Building Inspector							
	Alabama	Y	35644 AE	52751 AW	61300 AEX	ALBLS	6/16
	Birmingham-Hoover MSA, AL	Y	33762 AE	57041 AW	68675 AEX	ALBLS	6/16
	Alaska	Y	71510 FQ	84340 MW	95920 TQ	USBLS	5/15
	Anchorage MSA, AK	Y	73230 FQ	87320 MW	97670 TQ	USBLS	5/15
	Arizona	Y	41180 FQ	52300 MW	66230 TQ	USBLS	5/15
	Phoenix-Mesa-Scottsdale MSA, AZ	Y	43990 FQ	58090 MW	71180 TQ	USBLS	5/15

AE Average entry wage	**AWR** Average wage range	**H** Hourly	**LR** Low end range	**MTC** Median total compensation	**TCC** Total cash compensation
AEX Average experienced wage	**B** Biweekly	**HI** Highest wage paid	**M** Monthly	**MW** Median wage paid	**TQ** Third quartile wage
ATC Average total compensation	**D** Daily	**HR** High end range	**MCC** Median cash compensation	**MWR** Median wage range	**W** Weekly
AW Average wage paid	**FQ** First quartile wage	**LO** Lowest wage paid	**ME** Median entry wage	**S** See annotated source	**Y** Yearly

Occupation/Type/Industry	Location	Per	Low	Mid	High	Source	Date
Construction and Building Inspector							
	Tucson MSA, AZ	Y	38500 FQ	47210 MW	56990 TQ	USBLS	5/15
	Arkansas	Y	36180 FQ	45170 MW	55020 TQ	USBLS	5/15
	Little Rock-North Little Rock-Conway MSA, AR	Y	34010 FQ	39030 MW	48980 TQ	USBLS	5/15
	California	H	31.36 FQ	40.20 MW	47.66 TQ	CABLS	1/16-3/16
	Anaheim-Santa Ana-Irvine PMSA, CA	H	32.72 FQ	38.82 MW	47.28 TQ	CABLS	1/16-3/16
	Los Angeles-Long Beach-Glendale PMSA, CA	H	32.00 FQ	41.72 MW	46.93 TQ	CABLS	1/16-3/16
	Oakland-Hayward-Berkeley PMSA, CA	H	37.26 FQ	44.12 MW	49.81 TQ	CABLS	1/16-3/16
	Riverside-San Bernardino-Ontario MSA, CA	H	30.39 FQ	37.54 MW	47.57 TQ	CABLS	1/16-3/16
	Sacramento–Roseville–Arden-Arcade MSA, CA	H	31.67 FQ	37.72 MW	45.91 TQ	CABLS	1/16-3/16
	San Diego-Carlsbad MSA, CA	H	29.68 FQ	37.21 MW	45.62 TQ	CABLS	1/16-3/16
	San Francisco-Redwood City-South San Francisco PMSA, CA	H	40.40 FQ	48.02 MW	58.94 TQ	CABLS	1/16-3/16
	Colorado	Y	53090 FQ	65820 MW	80020 TQ	USBLS	5/15
	Denver-Aurora-Lakewood MSA, CO	Y	54890 FQ	67610 MW	78880 TQ	USBLS	5/15
	Connecticut	Y		72896 MW		CTBLS	1/16-3/16
	Bridgeport-Stamford-Norwalk MSA, CT	Y	52320 FQ	75110 MW	91030 TQ	USBLS	5/15
	Hartford-West Hartford-East Hartford MSA, CT	Y	61560 FQ	73780 MW	87370 TQ	USBLS	5/15
	Delaware	Y	46220 FQ	56430 MW	70500 TQ	USBLS	5/15
	Wilmington PMSA, DE-MD-NJ	Y	48070 FQ	60030 MW	76860 TQ	USBLS	5/15
	District of Columbia	Y	63370 FQ	76150 MW	93490 TQ	USBLS	5/15
	Washington-Arlington-Alexandria PMSA, DC-VA-MD-WV	Y	52140 FQ	63730 MW	75990 TQ	USBLS	5/15
	Florida	H	19.04 AE	27.73 MW	32.79 AEX	FLBLS	7/16-9/16
	Fort Lauderdale-Pompano Beach-Deerfield Beach PMSA, FL	H	19.09 AE	30.30 MW	35.13 AEX	FLBLS	7/16-9/16
	Miami-Miami Beach-Kendall PMSA, FL	H	20.73 AE	30.35 MW	35.84 AEX	FLBLS	7/16-9/16
	Orlando-Kissimmee-Sanford MSA, FL	H	22.69 AE	28.49 MW	31.51 AEX	FLBLS	7/16-9/16
	Tampa-St. Petersburg-Clearwater MSA, FL	H	17.66 AE	24.48 MW	29.42 AEX	FLBLS	7/16-9/16
	Georgia	Y	40140 FQ	49140 MW	62820 TQ	USBLS	5/15
	Atlanta-Sandy Springs-Roswell MSA, GA	Y	43160 FQ	52890 MW	67310 TQ	USBLS	5/15
	Augusta-Richmond County MSA, GA-SC	Y	36990 FQ	50900 MW	66840 TQ	USBLS	5/15
	Hawaii	Y	48130 FQ	60120 MW	73150 TQ	USBLS	5/15
	Urban Honolulu MSA, HI	Y	49750 FQ	62730 MW	75070 TQ	USBLS	5/15
	Idaho	Y	42040 FQ	47820 MW	55910 TQ	USBLS	5/15
	Boise City MSA, ID	Y	42710 FQ	48770 MW	57580 TQ	USBLS	5/15
	Illinois	Y	49710 FQ	66900 MW	85740 TQ	USBLS	5/15
	Chicago-Naperville-Arlington Heights PMSA, IL	Y	54530 FQ	73360 MW	90140 TQ	USBLS	5/15
	Lake County-Kenosha County PMSA, IL-WI	Y	54870 FQ	68590 MW	83320 TQ	USBLS	5/15
	Indiana	Y	39060 FQ	45920 MW	55700 TQ	USBLS	5/15
	Gary PMSA, IN	Y	41470 FQ	46840 MW	55450 TQ	USBLS	5/15
	Indianapolis-Carmel-Anderson MSA, IN	Y	40070 FQ	47120 MW	59930 TQ	USBLS	5/15
	Iowa	Y	45780 FQ	58550 MW	64760 TQ	USBLS	5/15
	Des Moines-West Des Moines MSA, IA	Y	51180 FQ	62660 MW	69570 TQ	USBLS	5/15
	Kansas	Y	43410 FQ	51970 MW	63030 TQ	USBLS	5/15
	Wichita MSA, KS	Y	41750 FQ	48800 MW	57530 TQ	USBLS	5/15
	Kentucky	Y	36500 FQ	44780 MW	56260 TQ	USBLS	5/15
	Louisville-Jefferson County MSA, KY-IN	Y	41820 FQ	48170 MW	61230 TQ	USBLS	5/15
	Louisiana	Y	43700 FQ	54870 MW	66350 TQ	USBLS	5/15

AE	Average entry wage	AWR	Average wage range	H	Hourly	LR	Low end range	MTC	Median total compensation	TCC	Total cash compensation
AEX	Average experienced wage	B	Biweekly	HI	Highest wage paid	M	Monthly	MW	Median wage paid	TQ	Third quartile wage
ATC	Average total compensation	D	Daily	HR	High end range	MCC	Median cash compensation	MWR	Median wage range	W	Weekly
AW	Average wage paid	FQ	First quartile wage	LO	Lowest wage paid	ME	Median entry wage	S	See annotated source	Y	Yearly

313

Occupation/Type/Industry	Location	Per	Low	Mid	High	Source	Date
Construction and Building Inspector	Baton Rouge MSA, LA	Y	45560 FQ	56220 MW	68890 TQ	USBLS	5/15
	New Orleans-Metairie MSA, LA	Y	43990 FQ	53660 MW	62270 TQ	USBLS	5/15
	Maine	Y	36430 FQ	46160 MW	56140 TQ	USBLS	5/15
	Portland-South Portland MSA, ME	Y	39590 FQ	49730 MW	57790 TQ	USBLS	5/15
	Maryland	Y	38999 AE	56118 MW	64677 AEX	MDBLS	4/16
	Baltimore-Columbia-Towson MSA, MD	Y	44560 FQ	54280 MW	63520 TQ	USBLS	5/15
	Salisbury MSA, MD-DE	Y	43880 FQ	54390 MW	65170 TQ	USBLS	5/15
	Massachusetts	Y	51040 FQ	62040 MW	75010 TQ	USBLS	5/15
	Boston-Cambridge-Newton NECTA, MA	Y	57150 FQ	67600 MW	77950 TQ	USBLS	5/15
	New Bedford MSA, MA	Y	51120 FQ	66020 MW	81080 TQ	USBLS	5/15
	Worcester MSA, MA-CT	Y	33880 FQ	43250 MW	59400 TQ	USBLS	5/15
	Michigan	Y	38880 FQ	53040 MW	62440 TQ	USBLS	5/15
	Detroit-Dearborn-Livonia PMSA, MI	Y	37410 FQ	52850 MW	62130 TQ	USBLS	5/15
	Grand Rapids-Wyoming MSA, MI	Y	38240 FQ	48520 MW	58520 TQ	USBLS	5/15
	Minnesota	Y	53851 FQ	65616 MW	77846 TQ	MNBLS	1/16-3/16
	Minneapolis-St. Paul-Bloomington MSA, MN-WI	Y	57696 FQ	68775 MW	79359 TQ	MNBLS	1/16-3/16
	Mississippi	Y	34060 FQ	43860 MW	54580 TQ	USBLS	5/15
	Jackson MSA, MS	Y	24450 FQ	41940 MW	51720 TQ	USBLS	5/15
	Missouri	Y	41210 FQ	49650 MW	58610 TQ	USBLS	5/15
	Kansas City MSA, MO-KS	Y	44700 FQ	52010 MW	61410 TQ	USBLS	5/15
	St. Louis MSA, MO-IL	Y	40860 FQ	51430 MW	64070 TQ	USBLS	5/15
	Montana	Y	35590 FQ	46160 MW	57640 TQ	USBLS	5/15
	Billings MSA, MT	Y	29900 FQ	48060 MW	57280 TQ	USBLS	5/15
	Nebraska	Y	40820 FQ	49455 MW	60630 TQ	NEBLS	7/16-9/16
	Omaha-Council Bluffs MSA, NE-IA	Y	44750 FQ	51730 MW	61300 TQ	NEBLS	7/16-9/16
	Nevada	Y	57360 FQ	73490 MW	89220 TQ	USBLS	5/15
	Las Vegas-Henderson-Paradise MSA, NV	Y	62130 FQ	77380 MW	91160 TQ	USBLS	5/15
	New Hampshire	H	18.19 AE	27.59 MW	32.38 AEX	NHBLS	6/16
	Manchester NECTA, NH	H	15.73 AE	26.22 MW	33.74 AEX	NHBLS	6/16
	Nashua NECTA, NH-MA	Y	43890 FQ	54420 MW	66530 TQ	USBLS	5/15
	New Jersey	Y	53110 FQ	67200 MW	82560 TQ	USBLS	5/15
	Camden PMSA, NJ	Y	47410 FQ	60490 MW	75520 TQ	USBLS	5/15
	Newark PMSA, NJ-PA	Y	53450 FQ	69390 MW	86590 TQ	USBLS	5/15
	Trenton MSA, NJ	Y	63040 FQ	73320 MW	86110 TQ	USBLS	5/15
	New Mexico	Y	41320 FQ	47910 MW	58430 TQ	USBLS	5/15
	Albuquerque MSA, NM	Y	37490 FQ	46510 MW	57610 TQ	USBLS	5/15
	New York	Y	42120 AE	61200 MW	75480 AEX	NYBLS	1/16-3/16
	Buffalo-Cheektowaga-Niagara Falls MSA, NY	Y	41550 FQ	54450 MW	65570 TQ	USBLS	5/15
	Nassau County-Suffolk County PMSA, NY	Y	51280 FQ	66400 MW	84120 TQ	USBLS	5/15
	New York-Jersey City-White Plains PMSA, NY-NJ	Y	53850 FQ	67650 MW	86390 TQ	USBLS	5/15
	Rochester MSA, NY	Y	46530 FQ	57420 MW	68660 TQ	USBLS	5/15
	North Carolina	Y	40310 FQ	49970 MW	60930 TQ	USBLS	5/15
	Charlotte-Concord-Gastonia MSA, NC-SC	Y	42040 FQ	53770 MW	61750 TQ	USBLS	5/15
	Raleigh MSA, NC	Y	43090 FQ	50160 MW	63190 TQ	USBLS	5/15
	North Dakota	Y	40480 FQ	54810 MW	78670 TQ	USBLS	5/15
	Ohio	Y	42630 FQ	53240 MW	61890 TQ	USBLS	5/15
	Cincinnati MSA, OH-KY-IN	Y	43900 FQ	52510 MW	59320 TQ	USBLS	5/15
	Cleveland-Elyria MSA, OH	Y	39060 FQ	49300 MW	60320 TQ	USBLS	5/15
	Columbus MSA, OH	Y	43610 FQ	55110 MW	67600 TQ	USBLS	5/15
	Oklahoma	Y	35250 FQ	45850 MW	57010 TQ	USBLS	5/15
	Oklahoma City MSA, OK	Y	31620 FQ	47560 MW	58960 TQ	USBLS	5/15
	Tulsa MSA, OK	Y	35080 FQ	42310 MW	48700 TQ	USBLS	5/15
	Oregon	H	24.82 FQ	30.73 MW	36.16 TQ	ORBLS	2016
	Portland-Vancouver-Hillsboro MSA, OR-WA	Y	55930 FQ	68520 MW	78350 TQ	USBLS	5/15
	Pennsylvania	Y	41280 FQ	50730 MW	61580 TQ	USBLS	5/15
	Allentown-Bethlehem-Easton MSA, PA-NJ	Y	38720 FQ	48290 MW	61430 TQ	USBLS	5/15

AE	Average entry wage	AWR	Average wage range	H	Hourly
AEX	Average experienced wage	B	Biweekly	HI	Highest wage paid
ATC	Average total compensation	D	Daily	HR	High end range
AW	Average wage paid	FQ	First quartile wage	LO	Lowest wage paid

LR	Low end range	MTC	Median total compensation
M	Monthly	MW	Median wage paid
MCC	Median cash compensation	MWR	Median wage range
ME	Median entry wage	S	See annotated source

TCC	Total cash compensation
TQ	Third quartile wage
W	Weekly
Y	Yearly

Occupation/Type/Industry	Location	Per	Low	Mid	High	Source	Date
Construction and Building Inspector	Harrisburg-Carlisle MSA, PA	Y	41180 FQ	49640 MW	61000 TQ	USBLS	5/15
	Montgomery County-Bucks County-Chester County PMSA, PA	Y	45730 FQ	56980 MW	70810 TQ	USBLS	5/15
	Philadelphia PMSA, PA	Y	43690 FQ	53140 MW	61460 TQ	USBLS	5/15
	Pittsburgh MSA, PA	Y	42180 FQ	50110 MW	62120 TQ	USBLS	5/15
	Rhode Island	Y	43710 FQ	51640 MW	62970 TQ	USBLS	5/15
	Providence-Warwick MSA, RI-MA	Y	44270 FQ	53510 MW	67580 TQ	USBLS	5/15
	South Carolina	Y	38340 FQ	48000 MW	59570 TQ	USBLS	5/15
	Charleston-North Charleston MSA, SC	Y	37600 FQ	47830 MW	63980 TQ	USBLS	5/15
	Columbia MSA, SC	Y	42650 FQ	50120 MW	64420 TQ	USBLS	5/15
	Greenville-Anderson-Mauldin MSA, SC	Y	31860 FQ	42920 MW	55600 TQ	USBLS	5/15
	South Dakota	Y	34160 FQ	39860 MW	55810 TQ	USBLS	5/15
	Sioux Falls MSA, SD	Y	33610 FQ	52070 MW	64490 TQ	USBLS	5/15
	Tennessee	Y	38020 FQ	46050 MW	55610 TQ	USBLS	5/15
	Knoxville MSA, TN	Y	40990 FQ	47740 MW	56770 TQ	USBLS	5/15
	Memphis MSA, TN-MS-AR	Y	39930 FQ	49530 MW	58320 TQ	USBLS	5/15
	Nashville-Davidson–Murfreesboro–Franklin MSA, TN	Y	41320 FQ	47110 MW	56010 TQ	USBLS	5/15
	Texas	Y	42680 FQ	53390 MW	64090 TQ	USBLS	5/15
	Austin-Round Rock MSA, TX	Y	47710 FQ	56560 MW	64410 TQ	USBLS	5/15
	Dallas-Plano-Irving PMSA, TX	Y	42410 FQ	50080 MW	60490 TQ	USBLS	5/15
	Fort Worth-Arlington PMSA, TX	Y	43620 FQ	51310 MW	64010 TQ	USBLS	5/15
	Houston-The Woodlands-Sugar Land MSA, TX	Y	48830 FQ	58350 MW	72000 TQ	USBLS	5/15
	San Antonio-New Braunfels MSA, TX	Y	43100 FQ	54230 MW	68000 TQ	USBLS	5/15
	Utah	Y	47920 FQ	58580 MW	76130 TQ	USBLS	5/15
	Provo-Orem MSA, UT	Y	50360 FQ	57140 MW	64380 TQ	USBLS	5/15
	Salt Lake City MSA, UT	Y	50750 FQ	60140 MW	85160 TQ	USBLS	5/15
	Vermont	Y	32820 FQ	40150 MW	55220 TQ	USBLS	5/15
	Burlington-South Burlington MSA, VT	Y	36650 FQ	46570 MW	59110 TQ	USBLS	5/15
	Virginia	Y	45150 FQ	56010 MW	68530 TQ	USBLS	5/15
	Richmond MSA, VA	Y	44790 FQ	53020 MW	61360 TQ	USBLS	5/15
	Virginia Beach-Norfolk-Newport News MSA, VA-NC	Y	41780 FQ	49410 MW	61800 TQ	USBLS	5/15
	Washington	H	27.83 FQ	33.60 MW	39.45 TQ	WABLS	3/16
	Seattle-Bellevue-Everett PMSA, WA	H	29.73 FQ	35.02 MW	41.00 TQ	WABLS	3/16
	Tacoma-Lakewood PMSA, WA	H	31.80 FQ	35.79 MW	41.59 TQ	WABLS	3/16
	West Virginia	Y	33820 FQ	41060 MW	50660 TQ	USBLS	5/15
	Huntington-Ashland MSA, WV-KY-OH	Y	33940 FQ	43050 MW	57040 TQ	USBLS	5/15
	Wisconsin	Y	43250 FQ	55580 MW	66280 TQ	USBLS	5/15
	Madison MSA, WI	Y	50510 FQ	57100 MW	65600 TQ	USBLS	5/15
	Milwaukee-Waukesha-West Allis MSA, WI	Y	48560 FQ	57720 MW	69260 TQ	USBLS	5/15
	Wyoming	Y	35420 FQ	46530 MW	59690 TQ	USBLS	5/15
	Cheyenne MSA, WY	Y	33250 FQ	40710 MW	53680 TQ	USBLS	5/15
	Puerto Rico	Y	18370 FQ	23410 MW	37620 TQ	USBLS	5/15
	San Juan-Carolina-Caguas MSA, PR	Y	19140 FQ	26730 MW	40570 TQ	USBLS	5/15
	Guam	Y	38130 FQ	49600 MW	58460 TQ	USBLS	5/15
Construction Contractor							
Residential	Grand Rapids, MI	H	75.00 LO		85.00 HI	HVACN01	2015
Construction Estimator							
Municipal Government	Los Angeles, CA	Y			101808 HI	CACIT	6/23/16
Construction Inspector							
Municipal Government	Detroit, MI	M	2783 LO		2992 HI	DETGOV	2016
Public Works Department, Municipal Government	Belmont, CA	Y			101718 HI	CACIT	6/28/16

AE	Average entry wage	AWR	Average wage range	H	Hourly	LR	Low end range	MTC	Median total compensation	TCC	Total cash compensation
AEX	Average experienced wage	B	Biweekly	HI	Highest wage paid	M	Monthly	MW	Median wage paid	TQ	Third quartile wage
ATC	Average total compensation	D	Daily	HR	High end range	MCC	Median cash compensation	MWR	Median wage range	W	Weekly
AW	Average wage paid	FQ	First quartile wage	LO	Lowest wage paid	ME	Median entry wage	S	See annotated source	Y	Yearly

Occupation/Type/Industry	Location	Per	Low	Mid	High	Source	Date
Construction Laborer	Alabama	Y	20646 AE	28248 AW	32054 AEX	ALBLS	6/16
	Birmingham-Hoover MSA, AL	Y	23300 AE	30748 AW	34461 AEX	ALBLS	6/16
	Alaska	Y	35210 FQ	46580 MW	57840 TQ	USBLS	5/15
	Anchorage MSA, AK	Y	31720 FQ	42940 MW	57340 TQ	USBLS	5/15
	Arizona	Y	24670 FQ	29480 MW	36070 TQ	USBLS	5/15
	Phoenix-Mesa-Scottsdale MSA, AZ	Y	24900 FQ	29640 MW	36230 TQ	USBLS	5/15
	Tucson MSA, AZ	Y	23470 FQ	28100 MW	34290 TQ	USBLS	5/15
	Arkansas	Y	19410 FQ	24100 MW	29260 TQ	USBLS	5/15
	Little Rock-North Little Rock-Conway MSA, AR	Y	18610 FQ	23640 MW	28940 TQ	USBLS	5/15
	California	H	14.31 FQ	18.46 MW	25.96 TQ	CABLS	1/16-3/16
	Anaheim-Santa Ana-Irvine PMSA, CA	H	12.83 FQ	16.13 MW	22.36 TQ	CABLS	1/16-3/16
	Los Angeles-Long Beach-Glendale PMSA, CA	H	13.80 FQ	18.66 MW	27.06 TQ	CABLS	1/16-3/16
	Oakland-Hayward-Berkeley PMSA, CA	H	17.40 FQ	22.69 MW	28.51 TQ	CABLS	1/16-3/16
	Riverside-San Bernardino-Ontario MSA, CA	H	13.26 FQ	17.10 MW	23.43 TQ	CABLS	1/16-3/16
	Sacramento–Roseville–Arden-Arcade MSA, CA	H	14.91 FQ	20.67 MW	25.74 TQ	CABLS	1/16-3/16
	San Diego-Carlsbad MSA, CA	H	13.61 FQ	17.31 MW	23.67 TQ	CABLS	1/16-3/16
	San Francisco-Redwood City-South San Francisco PMSA, CA	H	17.85 FQ	24.21 MW	30.22 TQ	CABLS	1/16-3/16
	Colorado	Y	25690 FQ	32090 MW	37860 TQ	USBLS	5/15
	Denver-Aurora-Lakewood MSA, CO	Y	26590 FQ	32700 MW	37780 TQ	USBLS	5/15
	Connecticut	Y		42221 MW		CTBLS	1/16-3/16
	Bridgeport-Stamford-Norwalk MSA, CT	Y	38520 FQ	45360 MW	53030 TQ	USBLS	5/15
	Hartford-West Hartford-East Hartford MSA, CT	Y	32670 FQ	40370 MW	53080 TQ	USBLS	5/15
	Delaware	Y	28220 FQ	33420 MW	37720 TQ	USBLS	5/15
	Wilmington PMSA, DE-MD-NJ	Y	28660 FQ	34250 MW	39080 TQ	USBLS	5/15
	District of Columbia	Y	31750 FQ	38300 MW	47510 TQ	USBLS	5/15
	Washington-Arlington-Alexandria PMSA, DC-VA-MD-WV	Y	27240 FQ	32900 MW	39040 TQ	USBLS	5/15
	Florida	H	10.16 AE	13.19 MW	15.73 AEX	FLBLS	7/16-9/16
	Fort Lauderdale-Pompano Beach-Deerfield Beach PMSA, FL	H	10.25 AE	13.71 MW	17.11 AEX	FLBLS	7/16-9/16
	Miami-Miami Beach-Kendall PMSA, FL	H	9.99 AE	13.35 MW	16.47 AEX	FLBLS	7/16-9/16
	Orlando-Kissimmee-Sanford MSA, FL	H	10.31 AE	13.17 MW	15.65 AEX	FLBLS	7/16-9/16
	Tampa-St. Petersburg-Clearwater MSA, FL	H	10.25 AE	13.21 MW	14.96 AEX	FLBLS	7/16-9/16
	Georgia	Y	20250 FQ	26520 MW	34050 TQ	USBLS	5/15
	Atlanta-Sandy Springs-Roswell MSA, GA	Y	20400 FQ	27120 MW	34830 TQ	USBLS	5/15
	Augusta-Richmond County MSA, GA-SC	Y	22020 FQ	29230 MW	37850 TQ	USBLS	5/15
	Hawaii	Y	35310 FQ	50050 MW	70070 TQ	USBLS	5/15
	Urban Honolulu MSA, HI	Y	35900 FQ	56030 MW	71990 TQ	USBLS	5/15
	Idaho	Y	22210 FQ	27570 MW	33880 TQ	USBLS	5/15
	Boise City MSA, ID	Y	21120 FQ	27030 MW	33230 TQ	USBLS	5/15
	Illinois	Y	31480 FQ	49770 MW	72030 TQ	USBLS	5/15
	Chicago-Naperville-Arlington Heights PMSA, IL	Y	33470 FQ	62580 MW	77710 TQ	USBLS	5/15
	Elgin PMSA, IL	Y	35330 FQ	53290 MW	70550 TQ	USBLS	5/15
	Lake County-Kenosha County PMSA, IL-WI	Y	32900 FQ	44990 MW	67120 TQ	USBLS	5/15
	Indiana	Y	28970 FQ	38370 MW	49510 TQ	USBLS	5/15
	Gary PMSA, IN	Y	36750 FQ	62870 MW	74970 TQ	USBLS	5/15
	Indianapolis-Carmel-Anderson MSA, IN	Y	29330 FQ	39790 MW	47660 TQ	USBLS	5/15
	Iowa	Y	26670 FQ	32390 MW	39250 TQ	USBLS	5/15

AE	Average entry wage	AWR	Average wage range	H	Hourly	LR	Low end range	MTC Median total compensation	TCC Total cash compensation
AEX	Average experienced wage	B	Biweekly	HI	Highest wage paid	M	Monthly	MW Median wage paid	TQ Third quartile wage
ATC	Average total compensation	D	Daily	HR	High end range	MCC Median cash compensation	MWR Median wage range	W Weekly
AW	Average wage paid	FQ	First quartile wage	LO	Lowest wage paid	ME Median entry wage	S See annotated source	Y Yearly

Construction Laborer

Occupation/Type/Industry	Location	Per	Low	Mid	High	Source	Date
Construction Laborer	Des Moines-West Des Moines MSA, IA	Y	28980 FQ	37180 MW	47090 TQ	USBLS	5/15
	Kansas	Y	25370 FQ	30390 MW	37320 TQ	USBLS	5/15
	Wichita MSA, KS	Y	22900 FQ	27070 MW	30760 TQ	USBLS	5/15
	Kentucky	Y	25730 FQ	31770 MW	39730 TQ	USBLS	5/15
	Louisville-Jefferson County MSA, KY-IN	Y	28080 FQ	34960 MW	43780 TQ	USBLS	5/15
	Louisiana	Y	23310 FQ	28520 MW	35840 TQ	USBLS	5/15
	Baton Rouge MSA, LA	Y	24810 FQ	29470 MW	36950 TQ	USBLS	5/15
	New Orleans-Metairie MSA, LA	Y	23010 FQ	28900 MW	36460 TQ	USBLS	5/15
	Maine	Y	24930 FQ	29160 MW	35030 TQ	USBLS	5/15
	Portland-South Portland MSA, ME	Y	27000 FQ	31900 MW	37270 TQ	USBLS	5/15
	Maryland	Y	23663 AE	32408 MW	36780 AEX	MDBLS	4/16
	Baltimore-Columbia-Towson MSA, MD	Y	26780 FQ	32140 MW	37490 TQ	USBLS	5/15
	Salisbury MSA, MD-DE	Y	24920 FQ	30310 MW	36010 TQ	USBLS	5/15
	Massachusetts	Y	35370 FQ	49230 MW	68570 TQ	USBLS	5/15
	Boston-Cambridge-Newton NECTA, MA	Y	38660 FQ	60800 MW	72880 TQ	USBLS	5/15
	Worcester MSA, MA-CT	Y	30150 FQ	36230 MW	45330 TQ	USBLS	5/15
	Michigan	Y	27490 FQ	35660 MW	46430 TQ	USBLS	5/15
	Detroit-Dearborn-Livonia PMSA, MI	Y	33400 FQ	48050 MW	56120 TQ	USBLS	5/15
	Grand Rapids-Wyoming MSA, MI	Y	23880 FQ	32520 MW	39720 TQ	USBLS	5/15
	Minnesota	Y	31390 FQ	40058 MW	58896 TQ	MNBLS	1/16-3/16
	Minneapolis-St. Paul-Bloomington MSA, MN-WI	Y	34307 FQ	47757 MW	65969 TQ	MNBLS	1/16-3/16
	Mississippi	Y	22160 FQ	26490 MW	32340 TQ	USBLS	5/15
	Jackson MSA, MS	Y	22080 FQ	25840 MW	31290 TQ	USBLS	5/15
	Missouri	Y	27960 FQ	37290 MW	53850 TQ	USBLS	5/15
	Kansas City MSA, MO-KS	Y	28930 FQ	36530 MW	51870 TQ	USBLS	5/15
	St. Louis MSA, MO-IL	Y	34200 FQ	48200 MW	61800 TQ	USBLS	5/15
	Montana	Y	26880 FQ	34310 MW	43110 TQ	USBLS	5/15
	Billings MSA, MT	Y	24900 FQ	33240 MW	40110 TQ	USBLS	5/15
	Nebraska	Y	23770 FQ	27925 MW	32545 TQ	NEBLS	7/16-9/16
	Omaha-Council Bluffs MSA, NE-IA	Y	25765 FQ	29480 MW	35370 TQ	NEBLS	7/16-9/16
	Nevada	Y	27930 FQ	36520 MW	51650 TQ	USBLS	5/15
	Las Vegas-Henderson-Paradise MSA, NV	Y	27130 FQ	36470 MW	54360 TQ	USBLS	5/15
	New Hampshire	H	12.25 AE	16.50 MW	18.67 AEX	NHBLS	6/16
	Manchester NECTA, NH	H	12.50 AE	16.75 MW	18.88 AEX	NHBLS	6/16
	Nashua NECTA, NH-MA	Y	31380 FQ	38840 MW	46290 TQ	USBLS	5/15
	New Jersey	Y	32950 FQ	45730 MW	67400 TQ	USBLS	5/15
	Camden PMSA, NJ	Y	33050 FQ	44850 MW	62070 TQ	USBLS	5/15
	Newark PMSA, NJ-PA	Y	35070 FQ	47380 MW	68320 TQ	USBLS	5/15
	Trenton MSA, NJ	Y	24460 FQ	35900 MW	62100 TQ	USBLS	5/15
	New Mexico	Y	22880 FQ	27390 MW	33140 TQ	USBLS	5/15
	Albuquerque MSA, NM	Y	22750 FQ	27710 MW	34310 TQ	USBLS	5/15
	New York	Y	25880 AE	39490 MW	59830 AEX	NYBLS	1/16-3/16
	Buffalo-Cheektowaga-Niagara Falls MSA, NY	Y	23350 FQ	30370 MW	48530 TQ	USBLS	5/15
	Nassau County-Suffolk County PMSA, NY	Y	31610 FQ	47550 MW	75080 TQ	USBLS	5/15
	New York-Jersey City-White Plains PMSA, NY-NJ	Y	30960 FQ	43920 MW	71580 TQ	USBLS	5/15
	Rochester MSA, NY	Y	27330 FQ	35420 MW	48050 TQ	USBLS	5/15
	North Carolina	Y	21440 FQ	26100 MW	30880 TQ	USBLS	5/15
	Charlotte-Concord-Gastonia MSA, NC-SC	Y	20070 FQ	25340 MW	30820 TQ	USBLS	5/15
	Raleigh MSA, NC	Y	24170 FQ	28210 MW	32790 TQ	USBLS	5/15
	North Dakota	Y	32140 FQ	37020 MW	46520 TQ	USBLS	5/15
	Fargo MSA, ND-MN	Y	28300 FQ	33360 MW	38090 TQ	USBLS	5/15
	Ohio	Y	28190 FQ	36730 MW	50600 TQ	USBLS	5/15
	Cincinnati MSA, OH-KY-IN	Y	30050 FQ	38590 MW	48160 TQ	USBLS	5/15
	Cleveland-Elyria MSA, OH	Y	31200 FQ	44030 MW	56250 TQ	USBLS	5/15
	Columbus MSA, OH	Y	27940 FQ	35490 MW	45880 TQ	USBLS	5/15
	Oklahoma	Y	24170 FQ	28700 MW	34370 TQ	USBLS	5/15
	Oklahoma City MSA, OK	Y	24700 FQ	28630 MW	33860 TQ	USBLS	5/15

AE	Average entry wage	AWR	Average wage range	H	Hourly
AEX	Average experienced wage	B	Biweekly	HI	Highest wage paid
ATC	Average total compensation	D	Daily	HR	High end range
AW	Average wage paid	FQ	First quartile wage	LO	Lowest wage paid

LR	Low end range	MTC	Median total compensation	TCC	Total cash compensation
M	Monthly	MW	Median wage paid	TQ	Third quartile wage
HR	High end range	MWR	Median wage range	W	Weekly
MCC	Median cash compensation				
ME	Median entry wage	S	See annotated source	Y	Yearly

Occupation/Type/Industry	Location	Per	Low	Mid	High	Source	Date
Construction Laborer	Tulsa MSA, OK	Y	25280 FQ	29620 MW	35010 TQ	USBLS	5/15
	Oregon	H	12.77 FQ	16.24 MW	21.60 TQ	ORBLS	2016
	Portland-Vancouver-Hillsboro MSA, OR-WA	Y	27570 FQ	35840 MW	50480 TQ	USBLS	5/15
	Pennsylvania	Y	26710 FQ	34620 MW	46610 TQ	USBLS	5/15
	Allentown-Bethlehem-Easton MSA, PA-NJ	Y	27920 FQ	34710 MW	44470 TQ	USBLS	5/15
	Harrisburg-Carlisle MSA, PA	Y	27200 FQ	31180 MW	42480 TQ	USBLS	5/15
	Montgomery County-Bucks County-Chester County PMSA, PA	Y	30550 FQ	39670 MW	54610 TQ	USBLS	5/15
	Philadelphia PMSA, PA	Y	28400 FQ	35580 MW	51870 TQ	USBLS	5/15
	Pittsburgh MSA, PA	Y	26780 FQ	36320 MW	48630 TQ	USBLS	5/15
	Rhode Island	Y	28300 FQ	38120 MW	53490 TQ	USBLS	5/15
	Providence-Warwick MSA, RI-MA	Y	29310 FQ	38880 MW	54690 TQ	USBLS	5/15
	South Carolina	Y	22400 FQ	27720 MW	35320 TQ	USBLS	5/15
	Charleston-North Charleston MSA, SC	Y	20220 FQ	26400 MW	33370 TQ	USBLS	5/15
	Columbia MSA, SC	Y	21710 FQ	25970 MW	36580 TQ	USBLS	5/15
	Greenville-Anderson-Mauldin MSA, SC	Y	23450 FQ	27940 MW	34560 TQ	USBLS	5/15
	South Dakota	Y	23230 FQ	27340 MW	31710 TQ	USBLS	5/15
	Sioux Falls MSA, SD	Y	22580 FQ	26260 MW	30580 TQ	USBLS	5/15
	Tennessee	Y	23740 FQ	28180 MW	33620 TQ	USBLS	5/15
	Knoxville MSA, TN	Y	23640 FQ	27800 MW	33430 TQ	USBLS	5/15
	Memphis MSA, TN-MS-AR	Y	24370 FQ	28380 MW	33200 TQ	USBLS	5/15
	Nashville-Davidson–Murfreesboro–Franklin MSA, TN	Y	25640 FQ	29470 MW	35190 TQ	USBLS	5/15
	Texas	Y	23230 FQ	27740 MW	33010 TQ	USBLS	5/15
	Austin-Round Rock MSA, TX	Y	22800 FQ	26990 MW	31270 TQ	USBLS	5/15
	Dallas-Plano-Irving PMSA, TX	Y	22150 FQ	26650 MW	30900 TQ	USBLS	5/15
	Fort Worth-Arlington PMSA, TX	Y	23370 FQ	27600 MW	32060 TQ	USBLS	5/15
	Houston-The Woodlands-Sugar Land MSA, TX	Y	24210 FQ	28510 MW	34870 TQ	USBLS	5/15
	San Antonio-New Braunfels MSA, TX	Y	22290 FQ	26630 MW	31010 TQ	USBLS	5/15
	Utah	Y	24420 FQ	29050 MW	34930 TQ	USBLS	5/15
	Ogden-Clearfield MSA, UT	Y	24070 FQ	28390 MW	33880 TQ	USBLS	5/15
	Provo-Orem MSA, UT	Y	24910 FQ	28680 MW	33820 TQ	USBLS	5/15
	Salt Lake City MSA, UT	Y	24100 FQ	28970 MW	34770 TQ	USBLS	5/15
	Vermont	Y	25730 FQ	30100 MW	37380 TQ	USBLS	5/15
	Burlington-South Burlington MSA, VT	Y	26280 FQ	30440 MW	37890 TQ	USBLS	5/15
	Virginia	Y	23290 FQ	28330 MW	34270 TQ	USBLS	5/15
	Richmond MSA, VA	Y	22490 FQ	27560 MW	33160 TQ	USBLS	5/15
	Virginia Beach-Norfolk-Newport News MSA, VA-NC	Y	21880 FQ	26830 MW	30880 TQ	USBLS	5/15
	Washington	H	15.24 FQ	19.23 MW	27.46 TQ	WABLS	3/16
	Seattle-Bellevue-Everett PMSA, WA	H	16.45 FQ	22.25 MW	32.70 TQ	WABLS	3/16
	Tacoma-Lakewood PMSA, WA	H	13.85 FQ	17.90 MW	24.11 TQ	WABLS	3/16
	West Virginia	Y	22230 FQ	28880 MW	38980 TQ	USBLS	5/15
	Huntington-Ashland MSA, WV-KY-OH	Y	21650 FQ	28170 MW	45310 TQ	USBLS	5/15
	Wisconsin	Y	28760 FQ	36960 MW	49320 TQ	USBLS	5/15
	Madison MSA, WI	Y	31650 FQ	41760 MW	50280 TQ	USBLS	5/15
	Milwaukee-Waukesha-West Allis MSA, WI	Y	30140 FQ	43280 MW	56610 TQ	USBLS	5/15
	Wyoming	Y	28110 FQ	33240 MW	37810 TQ	USBLS	5/15
	Cheyenne MSA, WY	Y	27810 FQ	31920 MW	37250 TQ	USBLS	5/15
	Puerto Rico	Y	16730 FQ	17950 MW	19180 TQ	USBLS	5/15
	San Juan-Carolina-Caguas MSA, PR	Y	16770 FQ	18060 MW	19360 TQ	USBLS	5/15
	Virgin Islands	Y	25130 FQ	29710 MW	38790 TQ	USBLS	5/15
	Guam	Y	18680 FQ	20960 MW	24940 TQ	USBLS	5/15
Construction Manager	Alabama	Y	60780 AE	91918 AW	107488 AEX	ALBLS	6/16
	Birmingham-Hoover MSA, AL	Y	64726 AE	103090 AW	122278 AEX	ALBLS	6/16
	Alaska	Y	84750 FQ	111370 MW	152820 TQ	USBLS	5/15

AE	Average entry wage	AWR	Average wage range	H	Hourly	LR	Low end range	MTC	Median total compensation	TCC	Total cash compensation
AEX	Average experienced wage	B	Biweekly	HI	Highest wage paid	M	Monthly	MW	Median wage paid	TQ	Third quartile wage
ATC	Average total compensation	D	Daily	HR	High end range	MCC	Median cash compensation	MWR	Median wage range	W	Weekly
AW	Average wage paid	FQ	First quartile wage	LO	Lowest wage paid	ME	Median entry wage	S	See annotated source	Y	Yearly

Occupation/Type/Industry	Location	Per	Low	Mid	High	Source	Date
Construction Manager	Anchorage MSA, AK	Y	88880 FQ	123990 MW	164480 TQ	USBLS	5/15
	Arizona	Y	58720 FQ	83280 MW	110700 TQ	USBLS	5/15
	Phoenix-Mesa-Scottsdale MSA, AZ	Y	61620 FQ	85720 MW	111540 TQ	USBLS	5/15
	Tucson MSA, AZ	Y	57060 FQ	82780 MW	116310 TQ	USBLS	5/15
	Arkansas	Y	51580 FQ	67940 MW	87120 TQ	USBLS	5/15
	Little Rock-North Little Rock-Conway MSA, AR	Y	55580 FQ	68960 MW	87140 TQ	USBLS	5/15
	California	H	35.13 FQ	47.90 MW	64.56 TQ	CABLS	1/16-3/16
	Anaheim-Santa Ana-Irvine PMSA, CA	H	40.07 FQ	51.30 MW	69.16 TQ	CABLS	1/16-3/16
	Los Angeles-Long Beach-Glendale PMSA, CA	H	32.62 FQ	42.01 MW	59.06 TQ	CABLS	1/16-3/16
	Oakland-Hayward-Berkeley PMSA, CA	H	40.09 FQ	53.76 MW	71.31 TQ	CABLS	1/16-3/16
	Riverside-San Bernardino-Ontario MSA, CA	H	33.99 FQ	44.67 MW	63.89 TQ	CABLS	1/16-3/16
	Sacramento–Roseville–Arden-Arcade MSA, CA	H	35.33 FQ	46.19 MW	59.59 TQ	CABLS	1/16-3/16
	San Diego-Carlsbad MSA, CA	H	33.85 FQ	43.19 MW	58.81 TQ	CABLS	1/16-3/16
	San Francisco-Redwood City-South San Francisco PMSA, CA	H	51.59 FQ	66.69 MW	82.65 TQ	CABLS	1/16-3/16
	Colorado	Y	64040 FQ	85880 MW	112550 TQ	USBLS	5/15
	Denver-Aurora-Lakewood MSA, CO	Y	66130 FQ	89940 MW	117050 TQ	USBLS	5/15
	Connecticut	Y		103563 MW		CTBLS	1/16-3/16
	Bridgeport-Stamford-Norwalk MSA, CT	Y	79630 FQ	113830 MW	145800 TQ	USBLS	5/15
	Hartford-West Hartford-East Hartford MSA, CT	Y	69240 FQ	93100 MW	115300 TQ	USBLS	5/15
	Delaware	Y	86400 FQ	104680 MW	123870 TQ	USBLS	5/15
	Wilmington PMSA, DE-MD-NJ	Y	84080 FQ	106080 MW	125860 TQ	USBLS	5/15
	District of Columbia	Y	81930 FQ	98280 MW	126720 TQ	USBLS	5/15
	Washington-Arlington-Alexandria PMSA, DC-VA-MD-WV	Y	83240 FQ	99920 MW	129130 TQ	USBLS	5/15
	Florida	H	25.60 AE	39.03 MW	54.53 AEX	FLBLS	7/16-9/16
	Fort Lauderdale-Pompano Beach-Deerfield Beach PMSA, FL	H	24.43 AE	40.82 MW	60.24 AEX	FLBLS	7/16-9/16
	Miami-Miami Beach-Kendall PMSA, FL	H	25.01 AE	39.51 MW	57.85 AEX	FLBLS	7/16-9/16
	Orlando-Kissimmee-Sanford MSA, FL	H	28.56 AE	39.00 MW	51.78 AEX	FLBLS	7/16-9/16
	Tampa-St. Petersburg-Clearwater MSA, FL	H	24.14 AE	36.71 MW	48.87 AEX	FLBLS	7/16-9/16
	Georgia	Y	66240 FQ	88170 MW	116560 TQ	USBLS	5/15
	Atlanta-Sandy Springs-Roswell MSA, GA	Y	69050 FQ	92380 MW	124990 TQ	USBLS	5/15
	Augusta-Richmond County MSA, GA-SC	Y	71400 FQ	88370 MW	113530 TQ	USBLS	5/15
	Hawaii	Y	68050 FQ	89450 MW	118060 TQ	USBLS	5/15
	Urban Honolulu MSA, HI	Y	70170 FQ	94750 MW	124450 TQ	USBLS	5/15
	Idaho	Y	56870 FQ	69680 MW	95750 TQ	USBLS	5/15
	Boise City MSA, ID	Y	57460 FQ	70270 MW	96670 TQ	USBLS	5/15
	Illinois	Y	69080 FQ	91630 MW	116290 TQ	USBLS	5/15
	Carbondale-Marion MSA, IL	Y	55320 FQ	70520 MW	77940 TQ	USBLS	5/15
	Chicago-Naperville-Arlington Heights PMSA, IL	Y	74080 FQ	99370 MW	120510 TQ	USBLS	5/15
	Lake County-Kenosha County PMSA, IL-WI	Y	55700 FQ	80480 MW	105960 TQ	USBLS	5/15
	Indiana	Y	56500 FQ	75160 MW	97150 TQ	USBLS	5/15
	Gary PMSA, IN	Y	58140 FQ	78000 MW	111100 TQ	USBLS	5/15
	Indianapolis-Carmel-Anderson MSA, IN	Y	61810 FQ	78280 MW	95850 TQ	USBLS	5/15
	Iowa	Y	50910 FQ	67470 MW	89460 TQ	USBLS	5/15
	Des Moines-West Des Moines MSA, IA	Y	56400 FQ	77960 MW	110960 TQ	USBLS	5/15
	Kansas	Y	57480 FQ	73400 MW	93660 TQ	USBLS	5/15
	Wichita MSA, KS	Y	56920 FQ	68620 MW	85240 TQ	USBLS	5/15

AE	Average entry wage	AWR	Average wage range	H	Hourly	LR	Low end range	MTC	Median total compensation	TCC	Total cash compensation
AEX	Average experienced wage	B	Biweekly	HI	Highest wage paid	M	Monthly	MW	Median wage paid	TQ	Third quartile wage
ATC	Average total compensation	D	Daily	HR	High end range	MCC	Median cash compensation	MWR	Median wage range	W	Weekly
AW	Average wage paid	FQ	First quartile wage	LO	Lowest wage paid	ME	Median entry wage	S	See annotated source	Y	Yearly

Occupation/Type/Industry	Location	Per	Low	Mid	High	Source	Date
Construction Manager	Kentucky	Y	59580 FQ	75290 MW	97760 TQ	USBLS	5/15
	Louisville-Jefferson County						
	MSA, KY-IN	Y	49760 FQ	69130 MW	95010 TQ	USBLS	5/15
	Louisiana	Y	62350 FQ	80140 MW	105870 TQ	USBLS	5/15
	Baton Rouge MSA, LA	Y	67140 FQ	83250 MW	101250 TQ	USBLS	5/15
	New Orleans-Metairie MSA,						
	LA	Y	65140 FQ	80120 MW	109820 TQ	USBLS	5/15
	Maine	Y	60140 FQ	75430 MW	99910 TQ	USBLS	5/15
	Portland-South Portland MSA,						
	ME	Y	64540 FQ	76990 MW	99270 TQ	USBLS	5/15
	Maryland	Y	64752 AE	103196 MW	122417 AEX	MDBLS	4/16
	Baltimore-Columbia-Towson						
	MSA, MD	Y	73620 FQ	92750 MW	120370 TQ	USBLS	5/15
	Salisbury MSA, MD-DE	Y	57980 FQ	77050 MW	95790 TQ	USBLS	5/15
	Massachusetts	Y	77830 FQ	102130 MW	132300 TQ	USBLS	5/15
	Boston-Cambridge-Newton						
	NECTA, MA	Y	83750 FQ	110810 MW	139560 TQ	USBLS	5/15
	Worcester MSA, MA-CT	Y	68520 FQ	83540 MW	109500 TQ	USBLS	5/15
	Michigan	Y	67920 FQ	81320 MW	100250 TQ	USBLS	5/15
	Detroit-Dearborn-Livonia						
	PMSA, MI	Y	75170 FQ	91120 MW	109420 TQ	USBLS	5/15
	Grand Rapids-Wyoming MSA,						
	MI	Y	61720 FQ	79310 MW	96900 TQ	USBLS	5/15
	Minnesota	Y	69725 FQ	86399 MW	105969 TQ	MNBLS	1/16-3/16
	Minneapolis-St. Paul-						
	Bloomington MSA, MN-WI	Y	71767 FQ	89549 MW	109861 TQ	MNBLS	1/16-3/16
	Mississippi	Y	45530 FQ	60090 MW	82190 TQ	USBLS	5/15
	Jackson MSA, MS	Y	49490 FQ	61450 MW	96780 TQ	USBLS	5/15
	Missouri	Y	65110 FQ	79450 MW	112060 TQ	USBLS	5/15
	Kansas City MSA, MO-KS	Y	66530 FQ	85080 MW	106190 TQ	USBLS	5/15
	St. Louis MSA, MO-IL	Y	70180 FQ	88030 MW	118250 TQ	USBLS	5/15
	Montana	Y	60260 FQ	73460 MW	91810 TQ	USBLS	5/15
	Billings MSA, MT	Y	63630 FQ	78300 MW	100390 TQ	USBLS	5/15
	Nebraska	Y	59605 FQ	76600 MW	99305 TQ	NEBLS	7/16-9/16
	Omaha-Council Bluffs MSA,						
	NE-IA	Y	61505 FQ	79210 MW	101205 TQ	NEBLS	7/16-9/16
	Nevada	Y	63300 FQ	76270 MW	97900 TQ	USBLS	5/15
	Las Vegas-Henderson-Paradise						
	MSA, NV	Y	63070 FQ	75910 MW	97540 TQ	USBLS	5/15
	New Hampshire	H	28.87 AE	42.71 MW	51.22 AEX	NHBLS	6/16
	Manchester NECTA, NH	H	32.91 AE	44.87 MW	52.18 AEX	NHBLS	6/16
	Nashua NECTA, NH-MA	Y	50700 FQ	87240 MW	113610 TQ	USBLS	5/15
	New Jersey	Y	96760 FQ	124140 MW	159510 TQ	USBLS	5/15
	Camden PMSA, NJ	Y	95290 FQ	116490 MW	142730 TQ	USBLS	5/15
	Newark PMSA, NJ-PA	Y	99510 FQ	131940 MW	159060 TQ	USBLS	5/15
	Trenton MSA, NJ	Y	105380 FQ	120480 MW	141460 TQ	USBLS	5/15
	New Mexico	Y	60990 FQ	80990 MW	103250 TQ	USBLS	5/15
	Albuquerque MSA, NM	Y	59920 FQ	77560 MW	94970 TQ	USBLS	5/15
	New York	Y	66050 AE	107220 MW	142470 AEX	NYBLS	1/16-3/16
	Buffalo-Cheektowaga-Niagara						
	Falls MSA, NY	Y	60510 FQ	76960 MW	96680 TQ	USBLS	5/15
	Nassau County-Suffolk County						
	PMSA, NY	Y	90450 FQ	118670 MW	153290 TQ	USBLS	5/15
	New York-Jersey City-White						
	Plains PMSA, NY-NJ	Y	83790 FQ	117320 MW	156180 TQ	USBLS	5/15
	Rochester MSA, NY	Y	58190 FQ	71530 MW	91460 TQ	USBLS	5/15
	North Carolina	Y	71220 FQ	87730 MW	111700 TQ	USBLS	5/15
	Charlotte-Concord-Gastonia						
	MSA, NC-SC	Y	73370 FQ	92170 MW	117140 TQ	USBLS	5/15
	Raleigh MSA, NC	Y	71970 FQ	88620 MW	112150 TQ	USBLS	5/15
	North Dakota	Y	64670 FQ	76330 MW	99400 TQ	USBLS	5/15
	Fargo MSA, ND-MN	Y	59420 FQ	73470 MW	91570 TQ	USBLS	5/15
	Ohio	Y	67490 FQ	84990 MW	111260 TQ	USBLS	5/15
	Cincinnati MSA, OH-KY-IN	Y	67410 FQ	85570 MW	109160 TQ	USBLS	5/15
	Cleveland-Elyria MSA, OH	Y	69150 FQ	85210 MW	109170 TQ	USBLS	5/15
	Columbus MSA, OH	Y	71480 FQ	91300 MW	119000 TQ	USBLS	5/15
	Oklahoma	Y	58120 FQ	71160 MW	90020 TQ	USBLS	5/15
	Oklahoma City MSA, OK	Y	58460 FQ	69180 MW	80750 TQ	USBLS	5/15
	Tulsa MSA, OK	Y	57710 FQ	71740 MW	91820 TQ	USBLS	5/15
	Oregon	H	33.70 FQ	42.90 MW	52.98 TQ	ORBLS	2016
	Portland-Vancouver-Hillsboro						
	MSA, OR-WA	Y	72050 FQ	90590 MW	112700 TQ	USBLS	5/15

AE	Average entry wage	AWR	Average wage range	H	Hourly	LR	Low end range	MTC Median total compensation TCC Total cash compensation
AEX	Average experienced wage	B	Biweekly	HI	Highest wage paid	M	Monthly	MW Median wage paid TQ Third quartile wage
ATC	Average total compensation	D	Daily	HR	High end range	MCC	Median cash compensation	MWR Median wage range W Weekly
AW	Average wage paid	FQ	First quartile wage	LO	Lowest wage paid	ME	Median entry wage	S See annotated source Y Yearly

Occupation/Type/Industry	Location	Per	Low	Mid	High	Source	Date
Construction Manager	Pennsylvania	Y	75230 FQ	99610 MW	138110 TQ	USBLS	5/15
	Allentown-Bethlehem-Easton MSA, PA-NJ	Y	80590 FQ	103860 MW	152180 TQ	USBLS	5/15
	Harrisburg-Carlisle MSA, PA	Y	70980 FQ	84090 MW	108780 TQ	USBLS	5/15
	Montgomery County-Bucks County-Chester County PMSA, PA	Y	91980 FQ	117620 MW	160730 TQ	USBLS	5/15
	Philadelphia PMSA, PA	Y	92960 FQ	121730 MW	165220 TQ	USBLS	5/15
	Pittsburgh MSA, PA	Y	73490 FQ	97320 MW	133860 TQ	USBLS	5/15
	Rhode Island	Y	89500 FQ	112680 MW	137420 TQ	USBLS	5/15
	Providence-Warwick MSA, RI-MA	Y	74840 FQ	97250 MW	127540 TQ	USBLS	5/15
	South Carolina	Y	59850 FQ	81000 MW	104090 TQ	USBLS	5/15
	Charleston-North Charleston MSA, SC	Y	69810 FQ	90930 MW	109350 TQ	USBLS	5/15
	Columbia MSA, SC	Y	59510 FQ	85400 MW	104800 TQ	USBLS	5/15
	Greenville-Anderson-Mauldin MSA, SC	Y	58350 FQ	73660 MW	95050 TQ	USBLS	5/15
	South Dakota	Y	74000 FQ	87180 MW	102080 TQ	USBLS	5/15
	Sioux Falls MSA, SD	Y	74110 FQ	86500 MW	98350 TQ	USBLS	5/15
	Tennessee	Y	59300 FQ	77060 MW	104190 TQ	USBLS	5/15
	Knoxville MSA, TN	Y	69250 FQ	88260 MW	131850 TQ	USBLS	5/15
	Memphis MSA, TN-MS-AR	Y	54520 FQ	74480 MW	101040 TQ	USBLS	5/15
	Nashville-Davidson–Murfreesboro–Franklin MSA, TN	Y	61600 FQ	79860 MW	103350 TQ	USBLS	5/15
	Texas	Y	64400 FQ	82280 MW	110810 TQ	USBLS	5/15
	Austin-Round Rock MSA, TX	Y	64400 FQ	87470 MW	116260 TQ	USBLS	5/15
	Dallas-Plano-Irving PMSA, TX	Y	65190 FQ	86380 MW	115050 TQ	USBLS	5/15
	Fort Worth-Arlington PMSA, TX	Y	51940 FQ	77430 MW	107640 TQ	USBLS	5/15
	Houston-The Woodlands-Sugar Land MSA, TX	Y	70760 FQ	85680 MW	115810 TQ	USBLS	5/15
	San Antonio-New Braunfels MSA, TX	Y	54450 FQ	76530 MW	97330 TQ	USBLS	5/15
	Utah	Y	59350 FQ	76170 MW	96420 TQ	USBLS	5/15
	Ogden-Clearfield MSA, UT	Y	57280 FQ	69600 MW	84680 TQ	USBLS	5/15
	Provo-Orem MSA, UT	Y	50070 FQ	72150 MW	90200 TQ	USBLS	5/15
	Salt Lake City MSA, UT	Y	68650 FQ	84540 MW	110370 TQ	USBLS	5/15
	Vermont	Y	68940 FQ	83130 MW	98670 TQ	USBLS	5/15
	Burlington-South Burlington MSA, VT	Y	67630 FQ	80510 MW	98130 TQ	USBLS	5/15
	Virginia	Y	75960 FQ	95760 MW	124260 TQ	USBLS	5/15
	Richmond MSA, VA	Y	71010 FQ	88920 MW	112770 TQ	USBLS	5/15
	Virginia Beach-Norfolk-Newport News MSA, VA-NC	Y	73150 FQ	97460 MW	122270 TQ	USBLS	5/15
	Washington	H	36.92 FQ	45.81 MW	56.34 TQ	WABLS	3/16
	Seattle-Bellevue-Everett PMSA, WA	H	38.36 FQ	47.26 MW	57.69 TQ	WABLS	3/16
	Tacoma-Lakewood PMSA, WA	H	35.93 FQ	45.74 MW	55.05 TQ	WABLS	3/16
	West Virginia	Y	66440 FQ	83030 MW	102280 TQ	USBLS	5/15
	Huntington-Ashland MSA, WV-KY-OH	Y	73080 FQ	90400 MW	116390 TQ	USBLS	5/15
	Wisconsin	Y	72520 FQ	93750 MW	126240 TQ	USBLS	5/15
	Madison MSA, WI	Y	65300 FQ	86180 MW	115590 TQ	USBLS	5/15
	Milwaukee-Waukesha-West Allis MSA, WI	Y	78310 FQ	101180 MW	131100 TQ	USBLS	5/15
	Wyoming	Y	68520 FQ	89840 MW	114370 TQ	USBLS	5/15
	Cheyenne MSA, WY	Y	77750 FQ	85880 MW	126290 TQ	USBLS	5/15
	Puerto Rico	Y	40540 FQ	55930 MW	76900 TQ	USBLS	5/15
	San Juan-Carolina-Caguas MSA, PR	Y	43330 FQ	57520 MW	79460 TQ	USBLS	5/15
	Guam	Y	54200 FQ	72700 MW	102740 TQ	USBLS	5/15
Construction Management Firm	United States	Y		147927 AW		ENR02	2015
General Contractor	United States	Y		138137 AW		ENR02	2015
Consumer Affairs Specialist							
City Attorney's Office	Santa Monica, CA	Y			110581 HI	CACIT	6/28/16
Consumer Protection Specialist							
State Government	North Carolina	Y	36761 LO		58006 HI	NCGOV	7/1/16

AE	Average entry wage	**AWR** Average wage range	**H** Hourly	**LR** Low end range	**MTC** Median total compensation	**TCC** Total cash compensation
AEX	Average experienced wage	**B** Biweekly	**HI** Highest wage paid	**M** Monthly	**MW** Median wage paid	**TQ** Third quartile wage
ATC	Average total compensation	**D** Daily	**HR** High end range	**MCC** Median cash compensation	**MWR** Median wage range	**W** Weekly
AW	Average wage paid	**FQ** First quartile wage	**LO** Lowest wage paid	**ME** Median entry wage	**S** See annotated source	**Y** Yearly

321

Occupation/Type/Industry	Location	Per	Low	Mid	High	Source	Date
Content Curator							
Digital/Streaming Music Firm	United States	Y		50000-70000 AWR		BBRD01	2014
Continuing Education Specialist							
College and University	United States	Y		55671 AW		HED01	2015-2016
Continuous Mining Machine Operator							
	Alabama	Y	48996 AE	55251 AW	58378 AEX	ALBLS	6/16
	Alaska	Y	49810 FQ	61250 MW	69940 TQ	USBLS	5/15
	Arizona	Y	36280 FQ	45260 MW	62720 TQ	USBLS	5/15
	Arkansas	Y	28300 FQ	32950 MW	37900 TQ	USBLS	5/15
	California	H	18.44 FQ	27.50 MW	39.18 TQ	CABLS	1/16-3/16
	Colorado	Y	50040 FQ	63010 MW	70890 TQ	USBLS	5/15
	Georgia	Y	35320 FQ	40650 MW	47640 TQ	USBLS	5/15
	Idaho	Y	45900 FQ	62920 MW	92360 TQ	USBLS	5/15
	Illinois	Y	40400 FQ	51320 MW	59580 TQ	USBLS	5/15
	Indiana	Y	42010 FQ	45810 MW	49690 TQ	USBLS	5/15
	Kentucky	Y	42570 FQ	47450 MW	55140 TQ	USBLS	5/15
	Maryland	Y	31234 AE	36596 MW	39277 AEX	MDBLS	4/16
	Michigan	Y	29930 FQ	39780 MW	45860 TQ	USBLS	5/15
	Missouri	Y	34960 FQ	40340 MW	46310 TQ	USBLS	5/15
	Montana	Y	61080 FQ	69450 MW	76930 TQ	USBLS	5/15
	Nevada	Y	55110 FQ	63980 MW	72180 TQ	USBLS	5/15
	New York	Y	31640 AE	36900 MW	43760 AEX	NYBLS	1/16-3/16
	Ohio	Y	35440 FQ	41700 MW	52030 TQ	USBLS	5/15
	Oklahoma	Y	33890 FQ	40880 MW	45200 TQ	USBLS	5/15
	Pennsylvania	Y	35130 FQ	42940 MW	52300 TQ	USBLS	5/15
	Tennessee	Y	33860 FQ	36840 MW	40010 TQ	USBLS	5/15
	Texas	Y	23430 FQ	28850 MW	37470 TQ	USBLS	5/15
	Virginia	Y	37630 FQ	43010 MW	47530 TQ	USBLS	5/15
	Washington	H	19.75 FQ	22.37 MW	26.70 TQ	WABLS	3/16
	West Virginia	Y	43740 FQ	51280 MW	60770 TQ	USBLS	5/15
	Wisconsin	Y	33150 FQ	35870 MW	38590 TQ	USBLS	5/15
	Wyoming	Y	67430 FQ	78590 MW	89440 TQ	USBLS	5/15
Contract Compliance Officer							
City Administration	San Francisco, CA	B	3217 LO		5126 HI	SFGOV	2016-2018
Control and Valve Installer and Repairer							
Except Mechanical Door	Alabama	Y	27297 AE	40345 AW	46874 AEX	ALBLS	6/16
Except Mechanical Door	Birmingham-Hoover MSA, AL	Y	27429 AE	40671 AW	47302 AEX	ALBLS	6/16
Except Mechanical Door	Alaska	Y	43430 FQ	47970 MW	72650 TQ	USBLS	5/15
Except Mechanical Door	Anchorage MSA, AK	Y	42840 FQ	86470 MW	102190 TQ	USBLS	5/15
Except Mechanical Door	Arizona	Y	37950 FQ	52160 MW	61820 TQ	USBLS	5/15
Except Mechanical Door	Phoenix-Mesa-Scottsdale MSA, AZ	Y	40460 FQ	54710 MW	63420 TQ	USBLS	5/15
Except Mechanical Door	Tucson MSA, AZ	Y	28080 FQ	37370 MW	48240 TQ	USBLS	5/15
Except Mechanical Door	Arkansas	Y	40670 FQ	47850 MW	63010 TQ	USBLS	5/15
Except Mechanical Door	Little Rock-North Little Rock-Conway MSA, AR	Y	42540 FQ	48010 MW	65810 TQ	USBLS	5/15
Except Mechanical Door	California	H	25.75 FQ	33.75 MW	39.97 TQ	CABLS	1/16-3/16
Except Mechanical Door	Anaheim-Santa Ana-Irvine PMSA, CA	H	23.59 FQ	34.65 MW	39.93 TQ	CABLS	1/16-3/16
Except Mechanical Door	Los Angeles-Long Beach-Glendale PMSA, CA	H	28.15 FQ	35.60 MW	42.56 TQ	CABLS	1/16-3/16
Except Mechanical Door	Oakland-Hayward-Berkeley PMSA, CA	H	32.34 FQ	38.38 MW	45.86 TQ	CABLS	1/16-3/16
Except Mechanical Door	Riverside-San Bernardino-Ontario MSA, CA	H	27.14 FQ	33.10 MW	38.13 TQ	CABLS	1/16-3/16
Except Mechanical Door	Sacramento–Roseville–Arden-Arcade MSA, CA	H	25.69 FQ	30.03 MW	38.65 TQ	CABLS	1/16-3/16
Except Mechanical Door	San Diego-Carlsbad MSA, CA	H	30.04 FQ	35.25 MW	39.54 TQ	CABLS	1/16-3/16
Except Mechanical Door	Colorado	Y	47080 FQ	63590 MW	81620 TQ	USBLS	5/15
Except Mechanical Door	Denver-Aurora-Lakewood MSA, CO	Y	43550 FQ	62700 MW	79180 TQ	USBLS	5/15
Except Mechanical Door	Connecticut	Y		70238 MW		CTBLS	1/16-3/16
Except Mechanical Door	Bridgeport-Stamford-Norwalk MSA, CT	Y	56350 FQ	68450 MW	78810 TQ	USBLS	5/15
Except Mechanical Door	Hartford-West Hartford-East Hartford MSA, CT	Y	65510 FQ	75480 MW	86960 TQ	USBLS	5/15

AE	Average entry wage	AWR	Average wage range	H	Hourly	LR	Low end range	MTC	Median total compensation	TCC	Total cash compensation
AEX	Average experienced wage	B	Biweekly	HI	Highest wage paid	M	Monthly	MCC	Median cash compensation	TQ	Third quartile wage
ATC	Average total compensation	D	Daily	HR	High end range	MCC	Median cash compensation	MWR	Median wage range	W	Weekly
AW	Average wage paid	FQ	First quartile wage	LO	Lowest wage paid	ME	Median entry wage	S	See annotated source	Y	Yearly

Occupation/Type/Industry	Location	Per	Low	Mid	High	Source	Date
Control and Valve Installer and Repairer							
Except Mechanical Door	Delaware	Y	50740 FQ	72090 MW	87510 TQ	USBLS	5/15
Except Mechanical Door	Wilmington PMSA, DE-MD-NJ	Y	44310 FQ	53590 MW	61460 TQ	USBLS	5/15
Except Mechanical Door	Washington-Arlington-Alexandria PMSA, DC-VA-MD-WV	Y	55070 FQ	65640 MW	75350 TQ	USBLS	5/15
Except Mechanical Door	Florida	H	14.60 AE	21.59 MW	26.54 AEX	FLBLS	7/16-9/16
Except Mechanical Door	Fort Lauderdale-Pompano Beach-Deerfield Beach PMSA, FL	H	14.73 AE	18.86 MW	22.01 AEX	FLBLS	7/16-9/16
Except Mechanical Door	Miami-Miami Beach-Kendall PMSA, FL	H	16.83 AE	23.18 MW	27.11 AEX	FLBLS	7/16-9/16
Except Mechanical Door	Orlando-Kissimmee-Sanford MSA, FL	H	10.79 AE	21.42 MW	26.51 AEX	FLBLS	7/16-9/16
Except Mechanical Door	Tampa-St. Petersburg-Clearwater MSA, FL	H	13.76 AE	19.95 MW	25.69 AEX	FLBLS	7/16-9/16
Except Mechanical Door	Georgia	Y	37140 FQ	46560 MW	57040 TQ	USBLS	5/15
Except Mechanical Door	Atlanta-Sandy Springs-Roswell MSA, GA	Y	36960 FQ	44520 MW	54120 TQ	USBLS	5/15
Except Mechanical Door	Hawaii	Y	45250 FQ	52160 MW	62880 TQ	USBLS	5/15
Except Mechanical Door	Idaho	Y	34520 FQ	43480 MW	51350 TQ	USBLS	5/15
Except Mechanical Door	Boise City MSA, ID	Y	35260 FQ	41930 MW	47400 TQ	USBLS	5/15
Except Mechanical Door	Illinois	Y	44530 FQ	59710 MW	72420 TQ	USBLS	5/15
Except Mechanical Door	Chicago-Naperville-Arlington Heights PMSA, IL	Y	53240 FQ	66270 MW	75230 TQ	USBLS	5/15
Except Mechanical Door	Indiana	Y	41920 FQ	51380 MW	60510 TQ	USBLS	5/15
Except Mechanical Door	Gary PMSA, IN	Y	45680 FQ	53220 MW	59140 TQ	USBLS	5/15
Except Mechanical Door	Indianapolis-Carmel-Anderson MSA, IN	Y	47100 FQ	56610 MW	63240 TQ	USBLS	5/15
Except Mechanical Door	Iowa	Y	43150 FQ	54350 MW	62720 TQ	USBLS	5/15
Except Mechanical Door	Des Moines-West Des Moines MSA, IA	Y	43270 FQ	52080 MW	61800 TQ	USBLS	5/15
Except Mechanical Door	Kansas	Y	43530 FQ	55480 MW	63020 TQ	USBLS	5/15
Except Mechanical Door	Kentucky	Y	29930 FQ	37820 MW	51260 TQ	USBLS	5/15
Except Mechanical Door	Louisville-Jefferson County MSA, KY-IN	Y	32030 FQ	44340 MW	60590 TQ	USBLS	5/15
Except Mechanical Door	Louisiana	Y	37400 FQ	45290 MW	57000 TQ	USBLS	5/15
Except Mechanical Door	Baton Rouge MSA, LA	Y	35360 FQ	43100 MW	50510 TQ	USBLS	5/15
Except Mechanical Door	New Orleans-Metairie MSA, LA	Y	39290 FQ	45400 MW	52910 TQ	USBLS	5/15
Except Mechanical Door	Maine	Y	48730 FQ	58750 MW	69180 TQ	USBLS	5/15
Except Mechanical Door	Portland-South Portland MSA, ME	Y	47270 FQ	60710 MW	70450 TQ	USBLS	5/15
Except Mechanical Door	Maryland	Y	33201 AE	50640 MW	59360 AEX	MDBLS	4/16
Except Mechanical Door	Baltimore-Columbia-Towson MSA, MD	Y	34830 FQ	42490 MW	56140 TQ	USBLS	5/15
Except Mechanical Door	Salisbury MSA, MD-DE	Y	41060 FQ	55160 MW	84040 TQ	USBLS	5/15
Except Mechanical Door	Massachusetts	Y	46350 FQ	59120 MW	71590 TQ	USBLS	5/15
Except Mechanical Door	Boston-Cambridge-Newton NECTA, MA	Y	50400 FQ	59150 MW	70730 TQ	USBLS	5/15
Except Mechanical Door	Worcester MSA, MA-CT	Y	39960 FQ	48150 MW	64910 TQ	USBLS	5/15
Except Mechanical Door	Michigan	Y	49390 FQ	66400 MW	76650 TQ	USBLS	5/15
Except Mechanical Door	Detroit-Dearborn-Livonia PMSA, MI	Y	59440 FQ	68410 MW	74970 TQ	USBLS	5/15
Except Mechanical Door	Grand Rapids-Wyoming MSA, MI	Y	43280 FQ	46870 MW	50550 TQ	USBLS	5/15
Except Mechanical Door	Minnesota	Y	57705 FQ	68325 MW	78774 TQ	MNBLS	1/16-3/16
Except Mechanical Door	Minneapolis-St. Paul-Bloomington MSA, MN-WI	Y	60491 FQ	71755 MW	84245 TQ	MNBLS	1/16-3/16
Except Mechanical Door	Mississippi	Y	24810 FQ	32780 MW	40590 TQ	USBLS	5/15
Except Mechanical Door	Jackson MSA, MS	Y	29070 FQ	34970 MW	41580 TQ	USBLS	5/15
Except Mechanical Door	Missouri	Y	47480 FQ	56940 MW	66790 TQ	USBLS	5/15
Except Mechanical Door	Kansas City MSA, MO-KS	Y	51090 FQ	56850 MW	62700 TQ	USBLS	5/15
Except Mechanical Door	St. Louis MSA, MO-IL	Y	51960 FQ	57800 MW	64850 TQ	USBLS	5/15
Except Mechanical Door	Montana	Y	40630 FQ	56120 MW	74390 TQ	USBLS	5/15
Except Mechanical Door	Nebraska	Y	34880 FQ	51645 MW	60965 TQ	NEBLS	7/16-9/16
Except Mechanical Door	Omaha-Council Bluffs MSA, NE-IA	Y	35960 FQ	42935 MW	57080 TQ	NEBLS	7/16-9/16
Except Mechanical Door	Nevada	Y	61250 FQ	70340 MW	77830 TQ	USBLS	5/15

AE	Average entry wage	AWR	Average wage range	H	Hourly	LR	Low end range	MTC	Median total compensation
AEX	Average experienced wage	B	Biweekly	HI	Highest wage paid	M	Monthly	MW	Median wage paid
ATC	Average total compensation	D	Daily	HR	High end range	MCC	Median cash compensation	MWR	Median wage range
AW	Average wage paid	FQ	First quartile wage	LO	Lowest wage paid	ME	Median entry wage	S	See annotated source

TCC	Total cash compensation
TQ	Third quartile wage
W	Weekly
Y	Yearly

Occupation/Type/Industry	Location	Per	Low	Mid	High	Source	Date
Control and Valve Installer and Repairer							
Except Mechanical Door	Las Vegas-Henderson-Paradise MSA, NV	Y	65210 FQ	70980 MW	76750 TQ	USBLS	5/15
Except Mechanical Door	New Hampshire	H	16.82 AE	23.96 MW	31.52 AEX	NHBLS	6/16
Except Mechanical Door	Nashua NECTA, NH-MA	Y	47650 FQ	63860 MW	71730 TQ	USBLS	5/15
Except Mechanical Door	New Jersey	Y	46870 FQ	61270 MW	74990 TQ	USBLS	5/15
Except Mechanical Door	Camden PMSA, NJ	Y	48150 FQ	59200 MW	68770 TQ	USBLS	5/15
Except Mechanical Door	Newark PMSA, NJ-PA	Y	44410 FQ	68390 MW	78350 TQ	USBLS	5/15
Except Mechanical Door	Trenton MSA, NJ	Y	41630 FQ	55580 MW	77210 TQ	USBLS	5/15
Except Mechanical Door	New Mexico	Y	44500 FQ	57140 MW	74260 TQ	USBLS	5/15
Except Mechanical Door	Albuquerque MSA, NM	Y	44110 FQ	51040 MW	65300 TQ	USBLS	5/15
Except Mechanical Door	New York	Y	56430 AE	81470 MW	90310 AEX	NYBLS	1/16-3/16
Except Mechanical Door	Buffalo-Cheektowaga-Niagara Falls MSA, NY	Y	63210 FQ	70980 MW	78530 TQ	USBLS	5/15
Except Mechanical Door	Nassau County-Suffolk County PMSA, NY	Y	67900 FQ	83280 MW	97940 TQ	USBLS	5/15
Except Mechanical Door	New York-Jersey City-White Plains PMSA, NY-NJ	Y	67990 FQ	84060 MW	96240 TQ	USBLS	5/15
Except Mechanical Door	Rochester MSA, NY	Y	52900 FQ	61860 MW	82020 TQ	USBLS	5/15
Except Mechanical Door	North Carolina	Y	34760 FQ	53380 MW	67650 TQ	USBLS	5/15
Except Mechanical Door	Charlotte-Concord-Gastonia MSA, NC-SC	Y	32450 FQ	52970 MW	67670 TQ	USBLS	5/15
Except Mechanical Door	Raleigh MSA, NC	Y	35330 FQ	53040 MW	70610 TQ	USBLS	5/15
Except Mechanical Door	North Dakota	Y	58510 FQ	69120 MW	77850 TQ	USBLS	5/15
Except Mechanical Door	Ohio	Y	46760 FQ	64950 MW	72660 TQ	USBLS	5/15
Except Mechanical Door	Cincinnati MSA, OH-KY-IN	Y	42980 FQ	55420 MW	68780 TQ	USBLS	5/15
Except Mechanical Door	Cleveland-Elyria MSA, OH	Y	48150 FQ	65440 MW	73070 TQ	USBLS	5/15
Except Mechanical Door	Columbus MSA, OH	Y	61230 FQ	68600 MW	74200 TQ	USBLS	5/15
Except Mechanical Door	Oklahoma	Y	39120 FQ	52430 MW	56390 TQ	USBLS	5/15
Except Mechanical Door	Oklahoma City MSA, OK	Y	47890 FQ	53860 MW	55860 TQ	USBLS	5/15
Except Mechanical Door	Tulsa MSA, OK	Y	37340 FQ	50450 MW	57600 TQ	USBLS	5/15
Except Mechanical Door	Oregon	H	20.40 FQ	24.46 MW	32.79 TQ	ORBLS	2016
Except Mechanical Door	Portland-Vancouver-Hillsboro MSA, OR-WA	Y	44630 FQ	54100 MW	66160 TQ	USBLS	5/15
Except Mechanical Door	Pennsylvania	Y	45120 FQ	55860 MW	67250 TQ	USBLS	5/15
Except Mechanical Door	Allentown-Bethlehem-Easton MSA, PA-NJ	Y	51560 FQ	60000 MW	70200 TQ	USBLS	5/15
Except Mechanical Door	Harrisburg-Carlisle MSA, PA	Y	47400 FQ	55800 MW	65260 TQ	USBLS	5/15
Except Mechanical Door	Montgomery County-Bucks County-Chester County PMSA, PA	Y	40320 FQ	45380 MW	50560 TQ	USBLS	5/15
Except Mechanical Door	Philadelphia PMSA, PA	Y	48140 FQ	54980 MW	60070 TQ	USBLS	5/15
Except Mechanical Door	Pittsburgh MSA, PA	Y	55800 FQ	63860 MW	71840 TQ	USBLS	5/15
Except Mechanical Door	Providence-Warwick MSA, RI-MA	Y	56870 FQ	69490 MW	80720 TQ	USBLS	5/15
Except Mechanical Door	South Carolina	Y	36190 FQ	48840 MW	59160 TQ	USBLS	5/15
Except Mechanical Door	Charleston-North Charleston MSA, SC	Y	40300 FQ	48000 MW	52220 TQ	USBLS	5/15
Except Mechanical Door	Columbia MSA, SC	Y	35150 FQ	75930 MW	88430 TQ	USBLS	5/15
Except Mechanical Door	Greenville-Anderson-Mauldin MSA, SC	Y	29250 FQ	35380 MW	42200 TQ	USBLS	5/15
Except Mechanical Door	South Dakota	Y	56390 FQ	70110 MW	80650 TQ	USBLS	5/15
Except Mechanical Door	Sioux Falls MSA, SD	Y	64240 AE	71820 MW	79240 TQ	USBLS	5/15
Except Mechanical Door	Tennessee	Y	36900 FQ	45990 MW	56900 TQ	USBLS	5/15
Except Mechanical Door	Knoxville MSA, TN	Y	43670 FQ	50480 MW	57650 TQ	USBLS	5/15
Except Mechanical Door	Memphis MSA, TN-MS-AR	Y	34610 FQ	46290 MW	63830 TQ	USBLS	5/15
Except Mechanical Door	Nashville-Davidson–Murfreesboro–Franklin MSA, TN	Y	45230 FQ	54030 MW	61770 TQ	USBLS	5/15
Except Mechanical Door	Texas	Y	32590 FQ	39730 MW	54670 TQ	USBLS	5/15
Except Mechanical Door	Austin-Round Rock MSA, TX	Y	33110 FQ	42210 MW	53920 TQ	USBLS	5/15
Except Mechanical Door	Dallas-Plano-Irving PMSA, TX	Y	31750 FQ	43920 MW	56980 TQ	USBLS	5/15
Except Mechanical Door	Fort Worth-Arlington PMSA, TX	Y	33500 FQ	40350 MW	63660 TQ	USBLS	5/15
Except Mechanical Door	Houston-The Woodlands-Sugar Land MSA, TX	Y	33090 FQ	38880 MW	54230 TQ	USBLS	5/15
Except Mechanical Door	San Antonio-New Braunfels MSA, TX	Y	29770 FQ	35100 MW	39530 TQ	USBLS	5/15
Except Mechanical Door	Utah	Y	44170 FQ	56540 MW	56550 TQ	USBLS	5/15
Except Mechanical Door	Ogden-Clearfield MSA, UT	Y	51070 FQ	56540 MW	56550 TQ	USBLS	5/15
Except Mechanical Door	Vermont	Y	33000 FQ	40250 MW	57070 TQ	USBLS	5/15

AE	Average entry wage	AWR	Average wage range	H	Hourly
AEX	Average experienced wage	B	Biweekly	HI	Highest wage paid
ATC	Average total compensation	D	Daily	HR	High end range
AW	Average wage paid	FQ	First quartile wage	LO	Lowest wage paid

LR	Low end range	MTC	Median total compensation
M	Monthly	MW	Median wage paid
MCC	Median cash compensation	MWR	Median wage range
ME	Median entry wage	S	See annotated source

TCC	Total cash compensation
TQ	Third quartile wage
W	Weekly
Y	Yearly

Occupation/Type/Industry	Location	Per	Low	Mid	High	Source	Date
Control and Valve Installer and Repairer							
Except Mechanical Door	Burlington-South Burlington MSA, VT	Y	41050 FQ	51500 MW	59350 TQ	USBLS	5/15
Except Mechanical Door	Virginia	Y	44140 FQ	55720 MW	68430 TQ	USBLS	5/15
Except Mechanical Door	Richmond MSA, VA	Y	51730 FQ	59060 MW	72730 TQ	USBLS	5/15
Except Mechanical Door	Virginia Beach-Norfolk-Newport News MSA, VA-NC	Y	41340 FQ	47260 MW	56130 TQ	USBLS	5/15
Except Mechanical Door	Washington	H	22.40 FQ	29.28 MW	37.96 TQ	WABLS	3/16
Except Mechanical Door	Seattle-Bellevue-Everett PMSA, WA	H	19.25 FQ	23.47 MW	31.34 TQ	WABLS	3/16
Except Mechanical Door	Tacoma-Lakewood PMSA, WA	H	31.67 FQ	36.16 MW	40.74 TQ	WABLS	3/16
Except Mechanical Door	West Virginia	Y	49660 FQ	65050 MW	72990 TQ	USBLS	5/15
Except Mechanical Door	Huntington-Ashland MSA, WV-KY-OH	Y	33670 FQ	45180 MW	59900 TQ	USBLS	5/15
Except Mechanical Door	Wisconsin	Y	56380 FQ	71770 MW	88750 TQ	USBLS	5/15
Except Mechanical Door	Madison MSA, WI	Y	64950 FQ	77750 MW	90140 TQ	USBLS	5/15
Except Mechanical Door	Milwaukee-Waukesha-West Allis MSA, WI	Y	60980 FQ	80040 MW	92410 TQ	USBLS	5/15
Except Mechanical Door	Wyoming	Y	43530 FQ	54790 MW	72040 TQ	USBLS	5/15
Except Mechanical Door	Puerto Rico	Y	23200 FQ	40750 MW	46250 TQ	USBLS	5/15
Except Mechanical Door	San Juan-Carolina-Caguas MSA, PR	Y	39990 FQ	43890 MW	47820 TQ	USBLS	5/15
Convention Center Manager							
Municipal Government	Anaheim, CA	Y			176459 HI	CACIT	6/28/16
Conveyor Operator and Tender	Alabama	Y	24735 AE	38898 AW	45984 AEX	ALBLS	6/16
	Birmingham-Hoover MSA, AL	Y	21506 AE	33930 AW	40142 AEX	ALBLS	6/16
	Alaska	Y	29800 FQ	44720 MW	56430 TQ	USBLS	5/15
	Arizona	Y	27670 FQ	35610 MW	55080 TQ	USBLS	5/15
	Phoenix-Mesa-Scottsdale MSA, AZ	Y	27690 FQ	36310 MW	55110 TQ	USBLS	5/15
	Arkansas	Y	27750 FQ	32560 MW	36460 TQ	USBLS	5/15
	Little Rock-North Little Rock-Conway MSA, AR	Y	27720 FQ	40640 MW	53350 TQ	USBLS	5/15
	California	H	12.39 FQ	16.77 MW	22.97 TQ	CABLS	1/16-3/16
	Anaheim-Santa Ana-Irvine PMSA, CA	H	9.55 FQ	13.49 MW	18.86 TQ	CABLS	1/16-3/16
	Los Angeles-Long Beach-Glendale PMSA, CA	H	11.97 FQ	16.00 MW	20.12 TQ	CABLS	1/16-3/16
	Oakland-Hayward-Berkeley PMSA, CA	H	14.40 FQ	19.60 MW	28.22 TQ	CABLS	1/16-3/16
	Riverside-San Bernardino-Ontario MSA, CA	H	13.22 FQ	16.33 MW	19.05 TQ	CABLS	1/16-3/16
	Sacramento–Roseville–Arden-Arcade MSA, CA	H	14.68 FQ	25.78 MW	28.71 TQ	CABLS	1/16-3/16
	Colorado	Y	30260 FQ	46520 MW	57490 TQ	USBLS	5/15
	Denver-Aurora-Lakewood MSA, CO	Y	40840 FQ	52210 MW	58580 TQ	USBLS	5/15
	Connecticut	Y		29207 MW		CTBLS	1/16-3/16
	Hartford-West Hartford-East Hartford MSA, CT	Y	19500 FQ	19960 MW	36130 TQ	USBLS	5/15
	Florida	H	10.58 AE	14.51 MW	19.50 AEX	FLBLS	7/16-9/16
	Fort Lauderdale-Pompano Beach-Deerfield Beach PMSA, FL	H	13.78 AE	14.54 MW	16.21 AEX	FLBLS	7/16-9/16
	Miami-Miami Beach-Kendall PMSA, FL	H	9.86 AE	13.95 MW	18.19 AEX	FLBLS	7/16-9/16
	Orlando-Kissimmee-Sanford MSA, FL	H	13.46 AE	15.62 MW	21.46 AEX	FLBLS	7/16-9/16
	Tampa-St. Petersburg-Clearwater MSA, FL	H	13.78 AE	14.72 MW	15.78 AEX	FLBLS	7/16-9/16
	Georgia	Y	23200 FQ	29280 MW	37520 TQ	USBLS	5/15
	Atlanta-Sandy Springs-Roswell MSA, GA	Y	27080 FQ	33290 MW	41280 TQ	USBLS	5/15
	Augusta-Richmond County MSA, GA-SC	Y	20910 FQ	26980 MW	31000 TQ	USBLS	5/15
	Hawaii	Y	24200 FQ	30350 MW	36370 TQ	USBLS	5/15
	Urban Honolulu MSA, HI	Y	23380 FQ	28780 MW	34840 TQ	USBLS	5/15
	Idaho	Y	25090 FQ	33000 MW	37770 TQ	USBLS	5/15
	Boise City MSA, ID	Y	28980 FQ	34320 MW	39680 TQ	USBLS	5/15

AE	Average entry wage	AWR	Average wage range	H	Hourly
AEX	Average experienced wage	B	Biweekly	HI	Highest wage paid
ATC	Average total compensation	D	Daily	HR	High end range
AW	Average wage paid	FQ	First quartile wage	LO	Lowest wage paid

LR	Low end range	MTC	Median total compensation	TCC	Total cash compensation
M	Monthly	MW	Median wage paid	TQ	Third quartile wage
MCC	Median cash compensation	MWR	Median wage range	W	Weekly
ME	Median entry wage	S	See annotated source	Y	Yearly

Occupation/Type/Industry	Location	Per	Low	Mid	High	Source	Date
Conveyor Operator and Tender	Illinois	Y	26170 FQ	32880 MW	42780 TQ	USBLS	5/15
	Chicago-Naperville-Arlington Heights PMSA, IL	Y	27450 FQ	33730 MW	44320 TQ	USBLS	5/15
	Indiana	Y	27640 FQ	32950 MW	41320 TQ	USBLS	5/15
	Gary PMSA, IN	Y	29260 FQ	34890 MW	47930 TQ	USBLS	5/15
	Indianapolis-Carmel-Anderson MSA, IN	Y	26570 FQ	31050 MW	37230 TQ	USBLS	5/15
	Iowa	Y	26620 FQ	30500 MW	35480 TQ	USBLS	5/15
	Des Moines-West Des Moines MSA, IA	Y	26390 FQ	28700 MW	30990 TQ	USBLS	5/15
	Kansas	Y	25670 FQ	29190 MW	34550 TQ	USBLS	5/15
	Wichita MSA, KS	Y	27840 FQ	31400 MW	36970 TQ	USBLS	5/15
	Kentucky	Y	36900 FQ	52540 MW	57830 TQ	USBLS	5/15
	Louisiana	Y	26550 FQ	31380 MW	39430 TQ	USBLS	5/15
	Baton Rouge MSA, LA	Y	28330 FQ	32180 MW	43480 TQ	USBLS	5/15
	New Orleans-Metairie MSA, LA	Y	28120 FQ	35250 MW	44820 TQ	USBLS	5/15
	Maine	Y	26220 FQ	34720 MW	45980 TQ	USBLS	5/15
	Portland-South Portland MSA, ME	Y	20570 FQ	23290 MW	32380 TQ	USBLS	5/15
	Maryland	Y	27047 AE	36270 MW	40881 AEX	MDBLS	4/16
	Baltimore-Columbia-Towson MSA, MD	Y	28910 FQ	38900 MW	46370 TQ	USBLS	5/15
	Massachusetts	Y	29680 FQ	36060 MW	41510 TQ	USBLS	5/15
	Boston-Cambridge-Newton NECTA, MA	Y	34510 FQ	39770 MW	45090 TQ	USBLS	5/15
	Michigan	Y	25130 FQ	31260 MW	41280 TQ	USBLS	5/15
	Detroit-Dearborn-Livonia PMSA, MI	Y	34970 FQ	40470 MW	45580 TQ	USBLS	5/15
	Grand Rapids-Wyoming MSA, MI	Y	28480 FQ	33830 MW	42270 TQ	USBLS	5/15
	Minnesota	Y	31968 FQ	36586 MW	42745 TQ	MNBLS	1/16-3/16
	Minneapolis-St. Paul-Bloomington MSA, MN-WI	Y	35557 FQ	43955 MW	51173 TQ	MNBLS	1/16-3/16
	Mississippi	Y	23540 FQ	27900 MW	33410 TQ	USBLS	5/15
	Jackson MSA, MS	Y	26620 FQ	30540 MW	37760 TQ	USBLS	5/15
	Missouri	Y	27590 FQ	32220 MW	39890 TQ	USBLS	5/15
	Kansas City MSA, MO-KS	Y	26330 FQ	29670 MW	35870 TQ	USBLS	5/15
	St. Louis MSA, MO-IL	Y	27180 FQ	31570 MW	44500 TQ	USBLS	5/15
	Montana	Y	26830 FQ	34270 MW	47800 TQ	USBLS	5/15
	Nebraska	Y	26540 FQ	29300 MW	33155 TQ	NEBLS	7/16-9/16
	Omaha-Council Bluffs MSA, NE-IA	Y	27620 FQ	30940 MW	36140 TQ	NEBLS	7/16-9/16
	Nevada	Y	27010 FQ	30250 MW	44820 TQ	USBLS	5/15
	Las Vegas-Henderson-Paradise MSA, NV	Y	27200 FQ	31890 MW	46340 TQ	USBLS	5/15
	New Hampshire	H	11.95 AE	15.77 MW	18.34 AEX	NHBLS	6/16
	New Jersey	Y	26360 FQ	31650 MW	42790 TQ	USBLS	5/15
	Newark PMSA, NJ-PA	Y	26060 FQ	28680 MW	31320 TQ	USBLS	5/15
	New Mexico	Y	28360 FQ	42330 MW	64930 TQ	USBLS	5/15
	New York	Y	26400 AE	40710 MW	44800 AEX	NYBLS	1/16-3/16
	Buffalo-Cheektowaga-Niagara Falls MSA, NY	Y	27350 FQ	30260 MW	36850 TQ	USBLS	5/15
	New York-Jersey City-White Plains PMSA, NY-NJ	Y	26010 FQ	33750 MW	46480 TQ	USBLS	5/15
	Rochester MSA, NY	Y	23210 FQ	30040 MW	41280 TQ	USBLS	5/15
	North Carolina	Y	24990 FQ	29700 MW	36190 TQ	USBLS	5/15
	Charlotte-Concord-Gastonia MSA, NC-SC	Y	29060 FQ	33790 MW	37770 TQ	USBLS	5/15
	Raleigh MSA, NC	Y	27300 FQ	30130 MW	34760 TQ	USBLS	5/15
	North Dakota	Y	27210 FQ	30810 MW	37460 TQ	USBLS	5/15
	Fargo MSA, ND-MN	Y	28000 FQ	33920 MW	38590 TQ	USBLS	5/15
	Ohio	Y	24490 FQ	30070 MW	37170 TQ	USBLS	5/15
	Cincinnati MSA, OH-KY-IN	Y	28410 FQ	33870 MW	40350 TQ	USBLS	5/15
	Cleveland-Elyria MSA, OH	Y	25720 FQ	29290 MW	43420 TQ	USBLS	5/15
	Columbus MSA, OH	Y	24950 FQ	29650 MW	35620 TQ	USBLS	5/15
	Oklahoma	Y	27440 FQ	32030 MW	38110 TQ	USBLS	5/15
	Tulsa MSA, OK	Y	28840 FQ	35870 MW	44140 TQ	USBLS	5/15
	Oregon	H	15.90 FQ	17.69 MW	19.49 TQ	ORBLS	2016
	Portland-Vancouver-Hillsboro MSA, OR-WA	Y	30540 FQ	39570 MW	54730 TQ	USBLS	5/15
	Pennsylvania	Y	32010 FQ	40170 MW	50430 TQ	USBLS	5/15

AE	Average entry wage	AWR	Average wage range	H	Hourly	LR	Low end range	MTC	Median total compensation	TCC	Total cash compensation
AEX	Average experienced wage	B	Biweekly	HI	Highest wage paid	M	Monthly	MW	Median wage paid	TQ	Third quartile wage
ATC	Average total compensation	D	Daily	HR	High end range	MCC	Median cash compensation	MWR	Median wage range	W	Weekly
AW	Average wage paid	FQ	First quartile wage	LO	Lowest wage paid	ME	Median entry wage	S	See annotated source	Y	Yearly

Occupation/Type/Industry	Location	Per	Low	Mid	High	Source	Date
Conveyor Operator and Tender	Allentown-Bethlehem-Easton MSA, PA-NJ	Y	27830 FQ	31350 MW	39290 TQ	USBLS	5/15
	Montgomery County-Bucks County-Chester County PMSA, PA	Y	34440 FQ	42340 MW	55680 TQ	USBLS	5/15
	Pittsburgh MSA, PA	Y	22270 FQ	29910 MW	37160 TQ	USBLS	5/15
	South Carolina	Y	24300 FQ	29490 MW	40340 TQ	USBLS	5/15
	Charleston-North Charleston MSA, SC	Y	22330 FQ	25400 MW	28640 TQ	USBLS	5/15
	Columbia MSA, SC	Y	26330 FQ	29270 MW	37390 TQ	USBLS	5/15
	South Dakota	Y	26260 FQ	28990 MW	32410 TQ	USBLS	5/15
	Sioux Falls MSA, SD	Y	25340 FQ	28280 MW	31320 TQ	USBLS	5/15
	Tennessee	Y	25190 FQ	30170 MW	52240 TQ	USBLS	5/15
	Knoxville MSA, TN	Y	50710 FQ	56190 MW	58680 TQ	USBLS	5/15
	Memphis MSA, TN-MS-AR	Y	23610 FQ	27860 MW	50080 TQ	USBLS	5/15
	Nashville-Davidson– Murfreesboro–Franklin MSA, TN	Y	28070 FQ	32190 MW	45920 TQ	USBLS	5/15
	Texas	Y	22950 FQ	28580 MW	39490 TQ	USBLS	5/15
	Austin-Round Rock MSA, TX	Y	24040 FQ	27120 MW	30120 TQ	USBLS	5/15
	Dallas-Plano-Irving PMSA, TX	Y	37650 FQ	54160 MW	59210 TQ	USBLS	5/15
	Fort Worth-Arlington PMSA, TX	Y	25370 FQ	30450 MW	46890 TQ	USBLS	5/15
	Houston-The Woodlands- Sugar Land MSA, TX	Y	22810 FQ	27920 MW	36170 TQ	USBLS	5/15
	San Antonio-New Braunfels MSA, TX	Y	25840 FQ	28340 MW	30830 TQ	USBLS	5/15
	Utah	Y	36030 FQ	42240 MW	46500 TQ	USBLS	5/15
	Virginia	Y	23230 FQ	29340 MW	37100 TQ	USBLS	5/15
	Richmond MSA, VA	Y	22550 FQ	25730 MW	35440 TQ	USBLS	5/15
	Virginia Beach-Norfolk- Newport News MSA, VA-NC	Y	23290 FQ	27980 MW	34560 TQ	USBLS	5/15
	Washington	H	12.60 FQ	14.64 MW	21.12 TQ	WABLS	3/16
	Seattle-Bellevue-Everett PMSA, WA	H	12.76 FQ	14.18 MW	17.21 TQ	WABLS	3/16
	Tacoma-Lakewood PMSA, WA	H	16.51 FQ	19.06 MW	23.39 TQ	WABLS	3/16
	West Virginia	Y	41310 FQ	52210 MW	59210 TQ	USBLS	5/15
	Wisconsin	Y	24990 FQ	30680 MW	36920 TQ	USBLS	5/15
	Madison MSA, WI	Y	19230 FQ	26760 MW	32240 TQ	USBLS	5/15
	Milwaukee-Waukesha-West Allis MSA, WI	Y	27260 FQ	30400 MW	44360 TQ	USBLS	5/15
	Wyoming	Y	29620 FQ	43500 MW	69300 TQ	USBLS	5/15
	Puerto Rico	Y	17090 FQ	18610 MW	20640 TQ	USBLS	5/15
	San Juan-Carolina-Caguas MSA, PR	Y	17030 FQ	18500 MW	20190 TQ	USBLS	5/15
Cook							
Fast Food	Alabama	Y	17534 AE	18162 AW	18481 AEX	ALBLS	6/16
Fast Food	Birmingham-Hoover MSA, AL	Y	17514 AE	18451 AW	18924 AEX	ALBLS	6/16
Fast Food	Alaska	Y	19490 FQ	22300 MW	27000 TQ	USBLS	5/15
Fast Food	Anchorage MSA, AK	Y	19540 FQ	22330 MW	27480 TQ	USBLS	5/15
Fast Food	Arizona	Y	18050 FQ	19360 MW	22300 TQ	USBLS	5/15
Fast Food	Phoenix-Mesa-Scottsdale MSA, AZ	Y	18290 FQ	20050 MW	22750 TQ	USBLS	5/15
Fast Food	Tucson MSA, AZ	Y	17630 FQ	18510 MW	19680 TQ	USBLS	5/15
Fast Food	Arkansas	Y	16680 FQ	17740 MW	18810 TQ	USBLS	5/15
Fast Food	Little Rock-North Little Rock- Conway MSA, AR	Y	16690 FQ	17780 MW	18860 TQ	USBLS	5/15
Fast Food	California	H	9.41 FQ	9.68 MW	11.18 TQ	CABLS	1/16-3/16
Fast Food	Anaheim-Santa Ana-Irvine PMSA, CA	H	9.42 FQ	9.70 MW	11.17 TQ	CABLS	1/16-3/16
Fast Food	Los Angeles-Long Beach- Glendale PMSA, CA	H	9.40 FQ	9.62 MW	10.90 TQ	CABLS	1/16-3/16
Fast Food	Oakland-Hayward-Berkeley PMSA, CA	H	9.48 FQ	9.94 MW	11.48 TQ	CABLS	1/16-3/16
Fast Food	Riverside-San Bernardino- Ontario MSA, CA	H	9.36 FQ	9.54 MW	10.68 TQ	CABLS	1/16-3/16
Fast Food	Sacramento–Roseville– Arden-Arcade MSA, CA	H	9.46 FQ	9.74 MW	10.92 TQ	CABLS	1/16-3/16
Fast Food	San Diego-Carlsbad MSA, CA	H	9.42 FQ	9.88 MW	11.44 TQ	CABLS	1/16-3/16

AE	Average entry wage	AWR	Average wage range	H	Hourly	LR	Low end range	MTC Median total compensation TCC Total cash compensation
AEX	Average experienced wage	B	Biweekly	HI	Highest wage paid	M	Monthly	MW Median wage paid TQ Third quartile wage
ATC	Average total compensation	D	Daily	HR	High end range	MCC	Median cash compensation	MWR Median wage range W Weekly
AW	Average wage paid	FQ	First quartile wage	LO	Lowest wage paid	ME	Median entry wage	S See annotated source Y Yearly

Cook

Occupation/Type/Industry	Location	Per	Low	Mid	High	Source	Date
Cook							
Fast Food	San Francisco-Redwood City-South San Francisco PMSA, CA	H	10.02 FQ	12.08 MW	13.78 TQ	CABLS	1/16-3/16
Fast Food	Santa Cruz-Watsonville MSA, CA	Y	19290 FQ	19800 MW	23770 TQ	USBLS	5/15
Fast Food	Colorado	Y	18200 FQ	19290 MW	22470 TQ	USBLS	5/15
Fast Food	Denver-Aurora-Lakewood MSA, CO	Y	18630 FQ	20670 MW	23140 TQ	USBLS	5/15
Fast Food	Connecticut	Y		20079 MW		CTBLS	1/16-3/16
Fast Food	Bridgeport-Stamford-Norwalk MSA, CT	Y	19250 FQ	19560 MW	22020 TQ	USBLS	5/15
Fast Food	Hartford-West Hartford-East Hartford MSA, CT	Y	19320 FQ	19630 MW	22940 TQ	USBLS	5/15
Fast Food	Delaware	Y	17430 FQ	18440 MW	19440 TQ	USBLS	5/15
Fast Food	Wilmington PMSA, DE-MD-NJ	Y	17760 FQ	18810 MW	20890 TQ	USBLS	5/15
Fast Food	District of Columbia	Y	19920 FQ	19950 MW	22520 TQ	USBLS	5/15
Fast Food	Washington-Arlington-Alexandria PMSA, DC-VA-MD-WV	Y	17830 FQ	19910 MW	22020 TQ	USBLS	5/15
Fast Food	Florida	H	9.00 AE	9.55 MW	11.12 AEX	FLBLS	7/16-9/16
Fast Food	Fort Lauderdale-Pompano Beach-Deerfield Beach PMSA, FL	H	9.01 AE	9.71 MW	12.65 AEX	FLBLS	7/16-9/16
Fast Food	Miami-Miami Beach-Kendall PMSA, FL	H	8.98 AE	9.39 MW	10.13 AEX	FLBLS	7/16-9/16
Fast Food	Ocala MSA, FL	Y	17560 FQ	18320 MW	19090 TQ	USBLS	5/15
Fast Food	Orlando-Kissimmee-Sanford MSA, FL	H	10.02 AE	11.33 MW	12.17 AEX	FLBLS	7/16-9/16
Fast Food	Tampa-St. Petersburg-Clearwater MSA, FL	H	9.01 AE	9.43 MW	10.71 AEX	FLBLS	7/16-9/16
Fast Food	Georgia	Y	16780 FQ	18130 MW	19510 TQ	USBLS	5/15
Fast Food	Atlanta-Sandy Springs-Roswell MSA, GA	Y	16870 FQ	18300 MW	19850 TQ	USBLS	5/15
Fast Food	Augusta-Richmond County MSA, GA-SC	Y	16710 FQ	17990 MW	19280 TQ	USBLS	5/15
Fast Food	Hawaii	Y	18700 FQ	21540 MW	24470 TQ	USBLS	5/15
Fast Food	Urban Honolulu MSA, HI	Y	20530 FQ	22690 MW	25930 TQ	USBLS	5/15
Fast Food	Idaho	Y	16540 FQ	17730 MW	18910 TQ	USBLS	5/15
Fast Food	Boise City MSA, ID	Y	16570 FQ	17790 MW	19000 TQ	USBLS	5/15
Fast Food	Illinois	Y	18340 FQ	19060 MW	19940 TQ	USBLS	5/15
Fast Food	Chicago-Naperville-Arlington Heights PMSA, IL	Y	18400 FQ	19130 MW	20030 TQ	USBLS	5/15
Fast Food	Lake County-Kenosha County PMSA, IL-WI	Y	18280 FQ	19290 MW	21690 TQ	USBLS	5/15
Fast Food	Indiana	Y	16750 FQ	18090 MW	19510 TQ	USBLS	5/15
Fast Food	Gary PMSA, IN	Y	16520 FQ	17690 MW	18850 TQ	USBLS	5/15
Fast Food	Indianapolis-Carmel-Anderson MSA, IN	Y	16800 FQ	18240 MW	20180 TQ	USBLS	5/15
Fast Food	Iowa	Y	16730 FQ	18080 MW	19490 TQ	USBLS	5/15
Fast Food	Des Moines-West Des Moines MSA, IA	Y	16940 FQ	18620 MW	24510 TQ	USBLS	5/15
Fast Food	Kansas	Y	16660 FQ	17870 MW	19070 TQ	USBLS	5/15
Fast Food	Wichita MSA, KS	Y	16720 FQ	17960 MW	19200 TQ	USBLS	5/15
Fast Food	Kentucky	Y	16720 FQ	18010 MW	19300 TQ	USBLS	5/15
Fast Food	Louisville-Jefferson County MSA, KY-IN	Y	16840 FQ	18300 MW	19990 TQ	USBLS	5/15
Fast Food	Louisiana	Y	16800 FQ	18110 MW	19430 TQ	USBLS	5/15
Fast Food	Baton Rouge MSA, LA	Y	16720 FQ	18000 MW	19280 TQ	USBLS	5/15
Fast Food	New Orleans-Metairie MSA, LA	Y	16770 FQ	18020 MW	19280 TQ	USBLS	5/15
Fast Food	Maine	Y	18040 FQ	20130 MW	23670 TQ	USBLS	5/15
Fast Food	Portland-South Portland MSA, ME	Y	19770 FQ	22990 MW	26780 TQ	USBLS	5/15
Fast Food	Maryland	Y	18007 AE	20797 MW	22192 AEX	MDBLS	4/16
Fast Food	Baltimore-Columbia-Towson MSA, MD	Y	18070 FQ	19620 MW	22840 TQ	USBLS	5/15
Fast Food	Salisbury MSA, MD-DE	Y	17490 FQ	18410 MW	19340 TQ	USBLS	5/15
Fast Food	Massachusetts	Y	19130 FQ	19690 MW	23460 TQ	USBLS	5/15
Fast Food	Boston-Cambridge-Newton NECTA, MA	Y	19120 FQ	19760 MW	24910 TQ	USBLS	5/15

AE Average entry wage	**AWR** Average wage range	**H** Hourly	**LR** Low end range	**MTC** Median total compensation	**TCC** Total cash compensation
AEX Average experienced wage	**B** Biweekly	**HI** Highest wage paid	**M** Monthly	**MW** Median wage paid	**TQ** Third quartile wage
ATC Average total compensation	**D** Daily	**HR** High end range	**MCC** Median cash compensation	**MWR** Median wage range	**W** Weekly
AW Average wage paid	**FQ** First quartile wage	**LO** Lowest wage paid	**ME** Median entry wage	**S** See annotated source	**Y** Yearly

Cook

Occupation/Type/Industry	Location	Per	Low	Mid	High	Source	Date
Fast Food	Worcester MSA, MA-CT	Y	19220 FQ	19730 MW	22850 TQ	USBLS	5/15
Fast Food	Michigan	Y	17860 FQ	18670 MW	19530 TQ	USBLS	5/15
Fast Food	Detroit-Dearborn-Livonia PMSA, MI	Y	17840 FQ	18620 MW	19450 TQ	USBLS	5/15
Fast Food	Grand Rapids-Wyoming MSA, MI	Y	17790 FQ	18500 MW	19210 TQ	USBLS	5/15
Fast Food	Minnesota	Y	17774 FQ	18622 MW	19470 TQ	MNBLS	1/16-3/16
Fast Food	Minneapolis-St. Paul-Bloomington MSA, MN-WI	Y	17723 FQ	18612 MW	19490 TQ	MNBLS	1/16-3/16
Fast Food	Mississippi	Y	16640 FQ	17840 MW	19050 TQ	USBLS	5/15
Fast Food	Jackson MSA, MS	Y	16590 FQ	17760 MW	18930 TQ	USBLS	5/15
Fast Food	Missouri	Y	17100 FQ	18270 MW	19470 TQ	USBLS	5/15
Fast Food	Kansas City MSA, MO-KS	Y	16830 FQ	18020 MW	19200 TQ	USBLS	5/15
Fast Food	St. Louis MSA, MO-IL	Y	17700 FQ	18730 MW	19800 TQ	USBLS	5/15
Fast Food	Montana	Y	17920 FQ	19080 MW	21880 TQ	USBLS	5/15
Fast Food	Billings MSA, MT	Y	18020 FQ	19260 MW	21950 TQ	USBLS	5/15
Fast Food	Nebraska	Y	17730 FQ	18820 MW	20560 TQ	NEBLS	7/16-9/16
Fast Food	Omaha-Council Bluffs MSA, NE-IA	Y	17795 FQ	19080 MW	21655 TQ	NEBLS	7/16-9/16
Fast Food	Nevada	Y	17130 FQ	18830 MW	21820 TQ	USBLS	5/15
Fast Food	Las Vegas-Henderson-Paradise MSA, NV	Y	17120 FQ	18790 MW	21870 TQ	USBLS	5/15
Fast Food	New Hampshire	H	8.40 AE	9.74 MW	11.39 AEX	NHBLS	6/16
Fast Food	Manchester NECTA, NH	H	8.41 AE	9.10 MW	10.29 AEX	NHBLS	6/16
Fast Food	Nashua NECTA, NH-MA	Y	17750 FQ	20630 MW	25460 TQ	USBLS	5/15
Fast Food	New Jersey	Y	18460 FQ	19600 MW	23970 TQ	USBLS	5/15
Fast Food	Camden PMSA, NJ	Y	18240 FQ	19000 MW	21180 TQ	USBLS	5/15
Fast Food	Newark PMSA, NJ-PA	Y	18490 FQ	19700 MW	25410 TQ	USBLS	5/15
Fast Food	Trenton MSA, NJ	Y	18050 FQ	18650 MW	19260 TQ	USBLS	5/15
Fast Food	New Mexico	Y	17130 FQ	18280 MW	19430 TQ	USBLS	5/15
Fast Food	Albuquerque MSA, NM	Y	17250 FQ	18460 MW	19660 TQ	USBLS	5/15
Fast Food	New York	Y	19250 AE	19720 MW	22240 AEX	NYBLS	1/16-3/16
Fast Food	Buffalo-Cheektowaga-Niagara Falls MSA, NY	Y	18920 FQ	19810 MW	22480 TQ	USBLS	5/15
Fast Food	Nassau County-Suffolk County PMSA, NY	Y	19370 FQ	21300 MW	24080 TQ	USBLS	5/15
Fast Food	New York-Jersey City-White Plains PMSA, NY-NJ	Y	18670 FQ	19200 MW	21420 TQ	USBLS	5/15
Fast Food	Rochester MSA, NY	Y	18750 FQ	19300 MW	22770 TQ	USBLS	5/15
Fast Food	North Carolina	Y	16610 FQ	17880 MW	19150 TQ	USBLS	5/15
Fast Food	Charlotte-Concord-Gastonia MSA, NC-SC	Y	16490 FQ	17670 MW	18840 TQ	USBLS	5/15
Fast Food	Raleigh MSA, NC	Y	17310 FQ	19230 MW	21980 TQ	USBLS	5/15
Fast Food	North Dakota	Y	19070 FQ	22560 MW	27390 TQ	USBLS	5/15
Fast Food	Fargo MSA, ND-MN	Y	17660 FQ	19800 MW	23080 TQ	USBLS	5/15
Fast Food	Ohio	Y	17760 FQ	18650 MW	19690 TQ	USBLS	5/15
Fast Food	Cincinnati MSA, OH-KY-IN	Y	17630 FQ	18670 MW	20680 TQ	USBLS	5/15
Fast Food	Cleveland-Elyria MSA, OH	Y	17710 FQ	18530 MW	19360 TQ	USBLS	5/15
Fast Food	Columbus MSA, OH	Y	18060 FQ	19240 MW	21860 TQ	USBLS	5/15
Fast Food	Oklahoma	Y	16700 FQ	17920 MW	19140 TQ	USBLS	5/15
Fast Food	Oklahoma City MSA, OK	Y	16750 FQ	18010 MW	19270 TQ	USBLS	5/15
Fast Food	Tulsa MSA, OK	Y	16640 FQ	17790 MW	18950 TQ	USBLS	5/15
Fast Food	Oregon	H	9.52 FQ	9.69 MW	10.98 TQ	ORBLS	2016
Fast Food	Portland-Vancouver-Hillsboro MSA, OR-WA	Y	19430 FQ	19980 MW	22630 TQ	USBLS	5/15
Fast Food	Pennsylvania	Y	16960 FQ	18430 MW	20380 TQ	USBLS	5/15
Fast Food	Allentown-Bethlehem-Easton MSA, PA-NJ	Y	18920 FQ	22110 MW	26760 TQ	USBLS	5/15
Fast Food	Harrisburg-Carlisle MSA, PA	Y	16570 FQ	17760 MW	18950 TQ	USBLS	5/15
Fast Food	Montgomery County-Bucks County-Chester County PMSA, PA	Y	17150 FQ	18850 MW	22260 TQ	USBLS	5/15
Fast Food	Philadelphia PMSA, PA	Y	18050 FQ	20940 MW	24340 TQ	USBLS	5/15
Fast Food	Pittsburgh MSA, PA	Y	16830 FQ	18210 MW	19680 TQ	USBLS	5/15
Fast Food	Rhode Island	Y	19100 FQ	19550 MW	23490 TQ	USBLS	5/15
Fast Food	Providence-Warwick MSA, RI-MA	Y	19130 FQ	19620 MW	23470 TQ	USBLS	5/15
Fast Food	South Carolina	Y	16590 FQ	17770 MW	18950 TQ	USBLS	5/15
Fast Food	Charleston-North Charleston MSA, SC	Y	16720 FQ	18090 MW	19520 TQ	USBLS	5/15
Fast Food	Columbia MSA, SC	Y	16470 FQ	17610 MW	18750 TQ	USBLS	5/15

AE Average entry wage	**AWR** Average wage range	**H** Hourly	**LR** Low end range	**MTC** Median total compensation	**TCC** Total cash compensation
AEX Average experienced wage	**B** Biweekly	**HI** Highest wage paid	**M** Monthly	**MW** Median wage paid	**TQ** Third quartile wage
ATC Average total compensation	**D** Daily	**HR** High end range	**MCC** Median cash compensation	**MWR** Median wage range	**W** Weekly
AW Average wage paid	**FQ** First quartile wage	**LO** Lowest wage paid	**ME** Median entry wage	**S** See annotated source	**Y** Yearly

Occupation/Type/Industry	Location	Per	Low	Mid	High	Source	Date
Cook							
Fast Food	Greenville-Anderson-Mauldin MSA, SC	Y	16570 FQ	17780 MW	18980 TQ	USBLS	5/15
Fast Food	South Dakota	Y	18440 FQ	19200 MW	20970 TQ	USBLS	5/15
Fast Food	Sioux Falls MSA, SD	Y	18470 FQ	19280 MW	21450 TQ	USBLS	5/15
Fast Food	Tennessee	Y	16600 FQ	17750 MW	18900 TQ	USBLS	5/15
Fast Food	Knoxville MSA, TN	Y	16650 FQ	17860 MW	19080 TQ	USBLS	5/15
Fast Food	Memphis MSA, TN-MS-AR	Y	16570 FQ	17760 MW	18950 TQ	USBLS	5/15
Fast Food	Nashville-Davidson–Murfreesboro–Franklin MSA, TN	Y	16590 FQ	17720 MW	18850 TQ	USBLS	5/15
Fast Food	Texas	Y	16860 FQ	18280 MW	19840 TQ	USBLS	5/15
Fast Food	Austin-Round Rock MSA, TX	Y	16850 FQ	18280 MW	19890 TQ	USBLS	5/15
Fast Food	Dallas-Plano-Irving PMSA, TX	Y	17160 FQ	18920 MW	21650 TQ	USBLS	5/15
Fast Food	Fort Worth-Arlington PMSA, TX	Y	16880 FQ	18300 MW	19870 TQ	USBLS	5/15
Fast Food	Houston-The Woodlands-Sugar Land MSA, TX	Y	16920 FQ	18400 MW	20230 TQ	USBLS	5/15
Fast Food	San Antonio-New Braunfels MSA, TX	Y	16770 FQ	18110 MW	19470 TQ	USBLS	5/15
Fast Food	Utah	Y	16970 FQ	18480 MW	20660 TQ	USBLS	5/15
Fast Food	Ogden-Clearfield MSA, UT	Y	17060 FQ	18640 MW	20970 TQ	USBLS	5/15
Fast Food	Provo-Orem MSA, UT	Y	17450 FQ	19410 MW	22160 TQ	USBLS	5/15
Fast Food	Salt Lake City MSA, UT	Y	17000 FQ	18500 MW	20770 TQ	USBLS	5/15
Fast Food	Vermont	Y	19380 FQ	19810 MW	24680 TQ	USBLS	5/15
Fast Food	Burlington-South Burlington MSA, VT	Y	19270 FQ	19500 MW	19830 TQ	USBLS	5/15
Fast Food	Virginia	Y	16730 FQ	18050 MW	19400 TQ	USBLS	5/15
Fast Food	Richmond MSA, VA	Y	16700 FQ	17930 MW	19170 TQ	USBLS	5/15
Fast Food	Virginia Beach-Norfolk-Newport News MSA, VA-NC	Y	16690 FQ	18070 MW	19580 TQ	USBLS	5/15
Fast Food	Washington	H	9.81 FQ	10.98 MW	12.28 TQ	WABLS	3/16
Fast Food	Seattle-Bellevue-Everett PMSA, WA	H	9.82 FQ	11.41 MW	13.21 TQ	WABLS	3/16
Fast Food	Tacoma-Lakewood PMSA, WA	H	9.78 FQ	11.18 MW	16.25 TQ	WABLS	3/16
Fast Food	West Virginia	Y	17480 FQ	18320 MW	19160 TQ	USBLS	5/15
Fast Food	Huntington-Ashland MSA, WV-KY-OH	Y	17370 FQ	18200 MW	19030 TQ	USBLS	5/15
Fast Food	Wisconsin	Y	17000 FQ	18480 MW	20250 TQ	USBLS	5/15
Fast Food	Madison MSA, WI	Y	18300 FQ	20940 MW	23250 TQ	USBLS	5/15
Fast Food	Milwaukee-Waukesha-West Allis MSA, WI	Y	17090 FQ	18660 MW	21030 TQ	USBLS	5/15
Fast Food	Wyoming	Y	17140 FQ	18910 MW	21640 TQ	USBLS	5/15
Fast Food	Cheyenne MSA, WY	Y	18610 FQ	20600 MW	22610 TQ	USBLS	5/15
Fast Food	Puerto Rico	Y	16570 FQ	17640 MW	18710 TQ	USBLS	5/15
Fast Food	San Juan-Carolina-Caguas MSA, PR	Y	16590 FQ	17660 MW	18730 TQ	USBLS	5/15
Fast Food	Virgin Islands	Y	16860 FQ	18170 MW	19480 TQ	USBLS	5/15
Fast Food	Guam	Y	18130 FQ	19090 MW	20500 TQ	USBLS	5/15
Institution and Cafeteria	Alabama	Y	17462 AE	19902 AW	21117 AEX	ALBLS	6/16
Institution and Cafeteria	Birmingham-Hoover MSA, AL	Y	17462 AE	20716 AW	22342 AEX	ALBLS	6/16
Institution and Cafeteria	Alaska	Y	31770 FQ	37750 MW	46250 TQ	USBLS	5/15
Institution and Cafeteria	Anchorage MSA, AK	Y	28990 FQ	34740 MW	39860 TQ	USBLS	5/15
Institution and Cafeteria	Arizona	Y	20910 FQ	24660 MW	29450 TQ	USBLS	5/15
Institution and Cafeteria	Phoenix-Mesa-Scottsdale MSA, AZ	Y	21140 FQ	25090 MW	29370 TQ	USBLS	5/15
Institution and Cafeteria	Tucson MSA, AZ	Y	21750 FQ	24530 MW	29060 TQ	USBLS	5/15
Institution and Cafeteria	Arkansas	Y	17030 FQ	18430 MW	20460 TQ	USBLS	5/15
Institution and Cafeteria	Little Rock-North Little Rock-Conway MSA, AR	Y	17200 FQ	18760 MW	21890 TQ	USBLS	5/15
Institution and Cafeteria	California	H	11.92 FQ	14.53 MW	17.84 TQ	CABLS	1/16-3/16
Institution and Cafeteria	Anaheim-Santa Ana-Irvine PMSA, CA	H	12.06 FQ	14.33 MW	17.20 TQ	CABLS	1/16-3/16
Institution and Cafeteria	Los Angeles-Long Beach-Glendale PMSA, CA	H	11.21 FQ	14.19 MW	17.65 TQ	CABLS	1/16-3/16
Institution and Cafeteria	Oakland-Hayward-Berkeley PMSA, CA	H	12.29 FQ	14.54 MW	18.31 TQ	CABLS	1/16-3/16
Institution and Cafeteria	Riverside-San Bernardino-Ontario MSA, CA	H	10.89 FQ	13.46 MW	16.50 TQ	CABLS	1/16-3/16
Institution and Cafeteria	Sacramento–Roseville–Arden-Arcade MSA, CA	H	12.11 FQ	14.66 MW	18.52 TQ	CABLS	1/16-3/16
Institution and Cafeteria	San Diego-Carlsbad MSA, CA	H	12.18 FQ	14.25 MW	17.21 TQ	CABLS	1/16-3/16

AE Average entry wage	**AWR** Average wage range	**H** Hourly	**LR** Low end range	**MTC** Median total compensation	**TCC** Total cash compensation
AEX Average experienced wage	**B** Biweekly	**HI** Highest wage paid	**M** Monthly	**MW** Median wage paid	**TQ** Third quartile wage
ATC Average total compensation	**D** Daily	**HR** High end range	**MCC** Median cash compensation	**MWR** Median wage range	**W** Weekly
AW Average wage paid	**FQ** First quartile wage	**LO** Lowest wage paid	**ME** Median entry wage	**S** See annotated source	**Y** Yearly

Occupation/Type/Industry	Location	Per	Low	Mid	High	Source	Date
Cook							
Institution and Cafeteria	San Francisco-Redwood City-South San Francisco PMSA, CA	H	14.83 FQ	17.14 MW	20.40 TQ	CABLS	1/16-3/16
Institution and Cafeteria	Colorado	Y	22270 FQ	26400 MW	32420 TQ	USBLS	5/15
Institution and Cafeteria	Denver-Aurora-Lakewood MSA, CO	Y	22730 FQ	26700 MW	31850 TQ	USBLS	5/15
Institution and Cafeteria	Connecticut	Y		33274 MW		CTBLS	1/16-3/16
Institution and Cafeteria	Bridgeport-Stamford-Norwalk MSA, CT	Y	28080 FQ	34670 MW	40630 TQ	USBLS	5/15
Institution and Cafeteria	Hartford-West Hartford-East Hartford MSA, CT	Y	27090 FQ	31340 MW	39910 TQ	USBLS	5/15
Institution and Cafeteria	Delaware	Y	26850 FQ	31100 MW	35920 TQ	USBLS	5/15
Institution and Cafeteria	Wilmington PMSA, DE-MD-NJ	Y	26730 FQ	31830 MW	36850 TQ	USBLS	5/15
Institution and Cafeteria	District of Columbia	Y	27980 FQ	32510 MW	37370 TQ	USBLS	5/15
Institution and Cafeteria	Washington-Arlington-Alexandria PMSA, DC-VA-MD-WV	Y	26320 FQ	30500 MW	36270 TQ	USBLS	5/15
Institution and Cafeteria	Florida	H	10.16 AE	12.36 MW	14.33 AEX	FLBLS	7/16-9/16
Institution and Cafeteria	Fort Lauderdale-Pompano Beach-Deerfield Beach PMSA, FL	H	10.92 AE	13.74 MW	15.20 AEX	FLBLS	7/16-9/16
Institution and Cafeteria	Miami-Miami Beach-Kendall PMSA, FL	H	10.59 AE	12.70 MW	15.94 AEX	FLBLS	7/16-9/16
Institution and Cafeteria	Orlando-Kissimmee-Sanford MSA, FL	H	10.71 AE	12.57 MW	14.06 AEX	FLBLS	7/16-9/16
Institution and Cafeteria	Tampa-St. Petersburg-Clearwater MSA, FL	H	10.27 AE	12.31 MW	14.23 AEX	FLBLS	7/16-9/16
Institution and Cafeteria	Georgia	Y	17450 FQ	19470 MW	24170 TQ	USBLS	5/15
Institution and Cafeteria	Atlanta-Sandy Springs-Roswell MSA, GA	Y	17760 FQ	20680 MW	25920 TQ	USBLS	5/15
Institution and Cafeteria	Augusta-Richmond County MSA, GA-SC	Y	17360 FQ	19290 MW	23900 TQ	USBLS	5/15
Institution and Cafeteria	Hawaii	Y	23950 FQ	32700 MW	43190 TQ	USBLS	5/15
Institution and Cafeteria	Urban Honolulu MSA, HI	Y	19970 FQ	28720 MW	38200 TQ	USBLS	5/15
Institution and Cafeteria	Idaho	Y	18000 FQ	21400 MW	26400 TQ	USBLS	5/15
Institution and Cafeteria	Boise City MSA, ID	Y	19430 FQ	24050 MW	28460 TQ	USBLS	5/15
Institution and Cafeteria	Illinois	Y	20340 FQ	24180 MW	30010 TQ	USBLS	5/15
Institution and Cafeteria	Chicago-Naperville-Arlington Heights PMSA, IL	Y	22110 FQ	26510 MW	32140 TQ	USBLS	5/15
Institution and Cafeteria	Lake County-Kenosha County PMSA, IL-WI	Y	22630 FQ	27200 MW	33330 TQ	USBLS	5/15
Institution and Cafeteria	Indiana	Y	19520 FQ	22430 MW	26080 TQ	USBLS	5/15
Institution and Cafeteria	Gary PMSA, IN	Y	19890 FQ	23710 MW	29690 TQ	USBLS	5/15
Institution and Cafeteria	Indianapolis-Carmel-Anderson MSA, IN	Y	18940 FQ	22030 MW	25620 TQ	USBLS	5/15
Institution and Cafeteria	Iowa	Y	19660 FQ	23140 MW	27600 TQ	USBLS	5/15
Institution and Cafeteria	Des Moines-West Des Moines MSA, IA	Y	21250 FQ	24850 MW	29280 TQ	USBLS	5/15
Institution and Cafeteria	Kansas	Y	19000 FQ	22060 MW	25120 TQ	USBLS	5/15
Institution and Cafeteria	Wichita MSA, KS	Y	20790 FQ	23230 MW	27050 TQ	USBLS	5/15
Institution and Cafeteria	Kentucky	Y	20370 FQ	23100 MW	27260 TQ	USBLS	5/15
Institution and Cafeteria	Louisville-Jefferson County MSA, KY-IN	Y	21720 FQ	26130 MW	30050 TQ	USBLS	5/15
Institution and Cafeteria	Louisiana	Y	17310 FQ	19090 MW	23030 TQ	USBLS	5/15
Institution and Cafeteria	Baton Rouge MSA, LA	Y	17670 FQ	19800 MW	23220 TQ	USBLS	5/15
Institution and Cafeteria	New Orleans-Metairie MSA, LA	Y	18660 FQ	22130 MW	26190 TQ	USBLS	5/15
Institution and Cafeteria	Maine	Y	22550 FQ	27010 MW	31360 TQ	USBLS	5/15
Institution and Cafeteria	Portland-South Portland MSA, ME	Y	24570 FQ	29490 MW	34800 TQ	USBLS	5/15
Institution and Cafeteria	Maryland	Y	23287 AE	31484 MW	35583 AEX	MDBLS	4/16
Institution and Cafeteria	Baltimore-Columbia-Towson MSA, MD	Y	26120 FQ	30760 MW	37250 TQ	USBLS	5/15
Institution and Cafeteria	Salisbury MSA, MD-DE	Y	26330 FQ	30650 MW	35710 TQ	USBLS	5/15
Institution and Cafeteria	Massachusetts	Y	27060 FQ	32710 MW	39670 TQ	USBLS	5/15
Institution and Cafeteria	Boston-Cambridge-Newton NECTA, MA	Y	28080 FQ	34680 MW	42770 TQ	USBLS	5/15
Institution and Cafeteria	Worcester MSA, MA-CT	Y	26650 FQ	31120 MW	36770 TQ	USBLS	5/15
Institution and Cafeteria	Michigan	Y	21640 FQ	25970 MW	29810 TQ	USBLS	5/15

AE	Average entry wage	AWR	Average wage range	H	Hourly
AEX	Average experienced wage	B	Biweekly	HI	Highest wage paid
ATC	Average total compensation	D	Daily	HR	High end range
AW	Average wage paid	FQ	First quartile wage	LO	Lowest wage paid

LR Low end range   MTC Median total compensation   TCC Total cash compensation
M Monthly   MW Median wage paid   TQ Third quartile wage
MCC Median cash compensation   MWR Median wage range   W Weekly
ME Median entry wage   S See annotated source   Y Yearly

Occupation/Type/Industry	Location	Per	Low	Mid	High	Source	Date
Cook							
Institution and Cafeteria	Detroit-Dearborn-Livonia PMSA, MI	Y	22010 FQ	26530 MW	30160 TQ	USBLS	5/15
Institution and Cafeteria	Grand Rapids-Wyoming MSA, MI	Y	21900 FQ	25910 MW	30650 TQ	USBLS	5/15
Institution and Cafeteria	Minnesota	Y	23510 FQ	28418 MW	34497 TQ	MNBLS	1/16-3/16
Institution and Cafeteria	Minneapolis-St. Paul-Bloomington MSA, MN-WI	Y	25822 FQ	30326 MW	36386 TQ	MNBLS	1/16-3/16
Institution and Cafeteria	Mississippi	Y	16860 FQ	18300 MW	20000 TQ	USBLS	5/15
Institution and Cafeteria	Jackson MSA, MS	Y	16710 FQ	18060 MW	19470 TQ	USBLS	5/15
Institution and Cafeteria	Missouri	Y	18110 FQ	20890 MW	24880 TQ	USBLS	5/15
Institution and Cafeteria	Kansas City MSA, MO-KS	Y	19010 FQ	22620 MW	27230 TQ	USBLS	5/15
Institution and Cafeteria	St. Louis MSA, MO-IL	Y	19320 FQ	22710 MW	27440 TQ	USBLS	5/15
Institution and Cafeteria	Montana	Y	21080 FQ	25070 MW	28950 TQ	USBLS	5/15
Institution and Cafeteria	Billings MSA, MT	Y	20370 FQ	24650 MW	30140 TQ	USBLS	5/15
Institution and Cafeteria	Nebraska	Y	20640 FQ	24140 MW	28285 TQ	NEBLS	7/16-9/16
Institution and Cafeteria	Omaha-Council Bluffs MSA, NE-IA	Y	21120 FQ	24855 MW	28870 TQ	NEBLS	7/16-9/16
Institution and Cafeteria	Nevada	Y	23350 FQ	28900 MW	37100 TQ	USBLS	5/15
Institution and Cafeteria	Las Vegas-Henderson-Paradise MSA, NV	Y	23850 FQ	29720 MW	38660 TQ	USBLS	5/15
Institution and Cafeteria	New Hampshire	H	11.88 AE	14.75 MW	16.93 AEX	NHBLS	6/16
Institution and Cafeteria	Manchester NECTA, NH	H	12.60 AE	14.53 MW	16.61 AEX	NHBLS	6/16
Institution and Cafeteria	Nashua NECTA, NH-MA	Y	28530 FQ	33310 MW	37020 TQ	USBLS	5/15
Institution and Cafeteria	New Jersey	Y	23690 FQ	28930 MW	35820 TQ	USBLS	5/15
Institution and Cafeteria	Camden PMSA, NJ	Y	22170 FQ	26370 MW	31040 TQ	USBLS	5/15
Institution and Cafeteria	Newark PMSA, NJ-PA	Y	23280 FQ	27630 MW	33330 TQ	USBLS	5/15
Institution and Cafeteria	Trenton MSA, NJ	Y	26800 FQ	32510 MW	39000 TQ	USBLS	5/15
Institution and Cafeteria	New Mexico	Y	18410 FQ	21270 MW	25800 TQ	USBLS	5/15
Institution and Cafeteria	Albuquerque MSA, NM	Y	18750 FQ	21550 MW	24710 TQ	USBLS	5/15
Institution and Cafeteria	New York	Y	22830 AE	30630 MW	36740 AEX	NYBLS	1/16-3/16
Institution and Cafeteria	Buffalo-Cheektowaga-Niagara Falls MSA, NY	Y	21760 FQ	26470 MW	32600 TQ	USBLS	5/15
Institution and Cafeteria	Nassau County-Suffolk County PMSA, NY	Y	25060 FQ	32420 MW	39420 TQ	USBLS	5/15
Institution and Cafeteria	New York-Jersey City-White Plains PMSA, NY-NJ	Y	26410 FQ	32810 MW	40070 TQ	USBLS	5/15
Institution and Cafeteria	Rochester MSA, NY	Y	23010 FQ	27510 MW	32410 TQ	USBLS	5/15
Institution and Cafeteria	North Carolina	Y	18970 FQ	22320 MW	26590 TQ	USBLS	5/15
Institution and Cafeteria	Charlotte-Concord-Gastonia MSA, NC-SC	Y	19560 FQ	23030 MW	27550 TQ	USBLS	5/15
Institution and Cafeteria	Raleigh MSA, NC	Y	20820 FQ	24280 MW	29300 TQ	USBLS	5/15
Institution and Cafeteria	North Dakota	Y	22780 FQ	27060 MW	31240 TQ	USBLS	5/15
Institution and Cafeteria	Fargo MSA, ND-MN	Y	23680 FQ	28240 MW	33340 TQ	USBLS	5/15
Institution and Cafeteria	Ohio	Y	19550 FQ	23770 MW	28880 TQ	USBLS	5/15
Institution and Cafeteria	Cincinnati MSA, OH-KY-IN	Y	21620 FQ	24950 MW	29120 TQ	USBLS	5/15
Institution and Cafeteria	Cleveland-Elyria MSA, OH	Y	19560 FQ	24790 MW	29610 TQ	USBLS	5/15
Institution and Cafeteria	Columbus MSA, OH	Y	21490 FQ	25320 MW	31110 TQ	USBLS	5/15
Institution and Cafeteria	Oklahoma	Y	17220 FQ	19030 MW	22690 TQ	USBLS	5/15
Institution and Cafeteria	Oklahoma City MSA, OK	Y	17140 FQ	18910 MW	22580 TQ	USBLS	5/15
Institution and Cafeteria	Tulsa MSA, OK	Y	18650 FQ	21830 MW	25040 TQ	USBLS	5/15
Institution and Cafeteria	Oregon	H	11.06 FQ	13.12 MW	15.53 TQ	ORBLS	2016
Institution and Cafeteria	Portland-Vancouver-Hillsboro MSA, OR-WA	Y	24720 FQ	29160 MW	35100 TQ	USBLS	5/15
Institution and Cafeteria	Pennsylvania	Y	21040 FQ	26040 MW	30850 TQ	USBLS	5/15
Institution and Cafeteria	Allentown-Bethlehem-Easton MSA, PA-NJ	Y	20750 FQ	26200 MW	33020 TQ	USBLS	5/15
Institution and Cafeteria	Harrisburg-Carlisle MSA, PA	Y	21250 FQ	26210 MW	31270 TQ	USBLS	5/15
Institution and Cafeteria	Montgomery County-Bucks County-Chester County PMSA, PA	Y	23370 FQ	28670 MW	34850 TQ	USBLS	5/15
Institution and Cafeteria	Philadelphia PMSA, PA	Y	22340 FQ	27940 MW	33980 TQ	USBLS	5/15
Institution and Cafeteria	Pittsburgh MSA, PA	Y	21160 FQ	25720 MW	29710 TQ	USBLS	5/15
Institution and Cafeteria	Rhode Island	Y	28500 FQ	33730 MW	39060 TQ	USBLS	5/15
Institution and Cafeteria	Providence-Warwick MSA, RI-MA	Y	27950 FQ	32860 MW	38550 TQ	USBLS	5/15
Institution and Cafeteria	South Carolina	Y	17620 FQ	19880 MW	24210 TQ	USBLS	5/15
Institution and Cafeteria	Charleston-North Charleston MSA, SC	Y	17660 FQ	20140 MW	26220 TQ	USBLS	5/15
Institution and Cafeteria	Columbia MSA, SC	Y	18120 FQ	21200 MW	24260 TQ	USBLS	5/15
Institution and Cafeteria	Greenville-Anderson-Mauldin MSA, SC	Y	18380 FQ	20990 MW	23890 TQ	USBLS	5/15

AE	Average entry wage	AWR	Average wage range	H	Hourly	LR	Low end range	MTC	Median total compensation	TCC	Total cash compensation
AEX	Average experienced wage	B	Biweekly	HI	Highest wage paid	M	Monthly	MW	Median wage paid	TQ	Third quartile wage
ATC	Average total compensation	D	Daily	HR	High end range	MCC	Median cash compensation	MWR	Median wage range	W	Weekly
AW	Average wage paid	FQ	First quartile wage	LO	Lowest wage paid	ME	Median entry wage	S	See annotated source	Y	Yearly

Occupation/Type/Industry	Location	Per	Low	Mid	High	Source	Date
Cook							
Institution and Cafeteria	South Dakota	Y	20630 FQ	23150 MW	26800 TQ	USBLS	5/15
Institution and Cafeteria	Sioux Falls MSA, SD	Y	20540 FQ	23270 MW	27210 TQ	USBLS	5/15
Institution and Cafeteria	Tennessee	Y	18010 FQ	20870 MW	24490 TQ	USBLS	5/15
Institution and Cafeteria	Knoxville MSA, TN	Y	18820 FQ	22410 MW	26420 TQ	USBLS	5/15
Institution and Cafeteria	Memphis MSA, TN-MS-AR	Y	18300 FQ	21760 MW	26710 TQ	USBLS	5/15
Institution and Cafeteria	Nashville-Davidson–Murfreesboro–Franklin MSA, TN	Y	19030 FQ	22510 MW	27070 TQ	USBLS	5/15
Institution and Cafeteria	Texas	Y	18740 FQ	22300 MW	26920 TQ	USBLS	5/15
Institution and Cafeteria	Austin-Round Rock MSA, TX	Y	18050 FQ	21700 MW	27100 TQ	USBLS	5/15
Institution and Cafeteria	Dallas-Plano-Irving PMSA, TX	Y	19320 FQ	23670 MW	28900 TQ	USBLS	5/15
Institution and Cafeteria	Fort Worth-Arlington PMSA, TX	Y	19770 FQ	23420 MW	28250 TQ	USBLS	5/15
Institution and Cafeteria	Houston-The Woodlands-Sugar Land MSA, TX	Y	20450 FQ	23760 MW	28390 TQ	USBLS	5/15
Institution and Cafeteria	San Antonio-New Braunfels MSA, TX	Y	20430 FQ	23750 MW	28210 TQ	USBLS	5/15
Institution and Cafeteria	Utah	Y	21060 FQ	24360 MW	28720 TQ	USBLS	5/15
Institution and Cafeteria	Ogden-Clearfield MSA, UT	Y	19770 FQ	22980 MW	27510 TQ	USBLS	5/15
Institution and Cafeteria	Provo-Orem MSA, UT	Y	20140 FQ	24190 MW	28450 TQ	USBLS	5/15
Institution and Cafeteria	Salt Lake City MSA, UT	Y	21550 FQ	24840 MW	28810 TQ	USBLS	5/15
Institution and Cafeteria	Vermont	Y	25360 FQ	28540 MW	32540 TQ	USBLS	5/15
Institution and Cafeteria	Burlington-South Burlington MSA, VT	Y	25850 FQ	29000 MW	33380 TQ	USBLS	5/15
Institution and Cafeteria	Virginia	Y	20350 FQ	25240 MW	30630 TQ	USBLS	5/15
Institution and Cafeteria	Richmond MSA, VA	Y	21040 FQ	25360 MW	29860 TQ	USBLS	5/15
Institution and Cafeteria	Virginia Beach-Norfolk-Newport News MSA, VA-NC	Y	21760 FQ	27140 MW	35840 TQ	USBLS	5/15
Institution and Cafeteria	Washington	H	12.76 FQ	15.16 MW	17.72 TQ	WABLS	3/16
Institution and Cafeteria	Seattle-Bellevue-Everett PMSA, WA	H	13.60 FQ	15.80 MW	18.16 TQ	WABLS	3/16
Institution and Cafeteria	Tacoma-Lakewood PMSA, WA	H	13.43 FQ	15.62 MW	17.78 TQ	WABLS	3/16
Institution and Cafeteria	West Virginia	Y	18670 FQ	21190 MW	24290 TQ	USBLS	5/15
Institution and Cafeteria	Huntington-Ashland MSA, WV-KY-OH	Y	18100 FQ	19730 MW	23060 TQ	USBLS	5/15
Institution and Cafeteria	Wisconsin	Y	21310 FQ	25610 MW	29960 TQ	USBLS	5/15
Institution and Cafeteria	Madison MSA, WI	Y	23160 FQ	28070 MW	33250 TQ	USBLS	5/15
Institution and Cafeteria	Milwaukee-Waukesha-West Allis MSA, WI	Y	19610 FQ	24430 MW	29280 TQ	USBLS	5/15
Institution and Cafeteria	Wyoming	Y	21810 FQ	26300 MW	31030 TQ	USBLS	5/15
Institution and Cafeteria	Cheyenne MSA, WY	Y	21030 FQ	24490 MW	29660 TQ	USBLS	5/15
Institution and Cafeteria	Puerto Rico	Y	16670 FQ	17920 MW	19170 TQ	USBLS	5/15
Institution and Cafeteria	San Juan-Carolina-Caguas MSA, PR	Y	16740 FQ	18080 MW	19490 TQ	USBLS	5/15
Institution and Cafeteria	Virgin Islands	Y	18310 FQ	21350 MW	24260 TQ	USBLS	5/15
Institution and Cafeteria	Guam	Y	19110 FQ	22080 MW	24760 TQ	USBLS	5/15
Private Household	California	H	11.81 FQ	17.96 MW	44.38 TQ	CABLS	1/16-3/16
Private Household	New York	Y	22010 AE	25810 MW	34350 AEX	NYBLS	1/16-3/16
Private Household	Oklahoma	Y	18100 FQ	20460 MW	22670 TQ	USBLS	5/15
Restaurant	Alabama	Y	17472 AE	21694 AW	23794 AEX	ALBLS	6/16
Restaurant	Birmingham-Hoover MSA, AL	Y	17483 AE	22476 AW	24978 AEX	ALBLS	6/16
Restaurant	Alaska	Y	23190 FQ	27570 MW	32540 TQ	USBLS	5/15
Restaurant	Anchorage MSA, AK	Y	24390 FQ	28130 MW	32460 TQ	USBLS	5/15
Restaurant	Arizona	Y	19770 FQ	22830 MW	26810 TQ	USBLS	5/15
Restaurant	Phoenix-Mesa-Scottsdale MSA, AZ	Y	19970 FQ	22990 MW	27070 TQ	USBLS	5/15
Restaurant	Tucson MSA, AZ	Y	19180 FQ	22170 MW	25590 TQ	USBLS	5/15
Restaurant	Yuma MSA, AZ	Y	18420 FQ	20510 MW	24260 TQ	USBLS	5/15
Restaurant	Arkansas	Y	17740 FQ	19910 MW	23820 TQ	USBLS	5/15
Restaurant	Little Rock-North Little Rock-Conway MSA, AR	Y	18560 FQ	21900 MW	25970 TQ	USBLS	5/15
Restaurant	California	H	10.36 FQ	12.12 MW	14.49 TQ	CABLS	1/16-3/16
Restaurant	Anaheim-Santa Ana-Irvine PMSA, CA	H	10.49 FQ	11.84 MW	14.08 TQ	CABLS	1/16-3/16
Restaurant	Los Angeles-Long Beach-Glendale PMSA, CA	H	10.01 FQ	11.71 MW	14.17 TQ	CABLS	1/16-3/16
Restaurant	Oakland-Hayward-Berkeley PMSA, CA	H	9.65 FQ	11.40 MW	13.73 TQ	CABLS	1/16-3/16
Restaurant	Riverside-San Bernardino-Ontario MSA, CA	H	10.06 FQ	11.53 MW	13.47 TQ	CABLS	1/16-3/16

AE Average entry wage	**AWR** Average wage range	**H** Hourly	**LR** Low end range	**MTC** Median total compensation	**TCC** Total cash compensation
AEX Average experienced wage	**B** Biweekly	**HI** Highest wage paid	**M** Monthly	**MW** Median wage paid	**TQ** Third quartile wage
ATC Average total compensation	**D** Daily	**HR** High end range	**MCC** Median cash compensation	**MWR** Median wage range	**W** Weekly
AW Average wage paid	**FQ** First quartile wage	**LO** Lowest wage paid	**ME** Median entry wage	**S** See annotated source	**Y** Yearly

Cook

Occupation/Type/Industry	Location	Per	Low	Mid	High	Source	Date
Cook							
Restaurant	Sacramento–Roseville–Arden-Arcade MSA, CA	H	10.15 FQ	12.37 MW	14.20 TQ	CABLS	1/16-3/16
Restaurant	San Diego-Carlsbad MSA, CA	H	10.64 FQ	12.09 MW	14.51 TQ	CABLS	1/16-3/16
Restaurant	San Francisco-Redwood City-South San Francisco PMSA, CA	H	12.37 FQ	14.22 MW	17.20 TQ	CABLS	1/16-3/16
Restaurant	Colorado	Y	20560 FQ	23530 MW	28270 TQ	USBLS	5/15
Restaurant	Denver-Aurora-Lakewood MSA, CO	Y	20410 FQ	23190 MW	27520 TQ	USBLS	5/15
Restaurant	Connecticut	Y		26523 MW	. .	CTBLS	1/16-3/16
Restaurant	Bridgeport-Stamford-Norwalk MSA, CT	Y	24620 FQ	28510 MW	34490 TQ	USBLS	5/15
Restaurant	Hartford-West Hartford-East Hartford MSA, CT	Y	20690 FQ	24280 MW	28810 TQ	USBLS	5/15
Restaurant	Delaware	Y	19920 FQ	24800 MW	29130 TQ	USBLS	5/15
Restaurant	Wilmington PMSA, DE-MD-NJ	Y	19650 FQ	25110 MW	29350 TQ	USBLS	5/15
Restaurant	District of Columbia	Y	22310 FQ	26410 MW	32810 TQ	USBLS	5/15
Restaurant	Washington-Arlington-Alexandria PMSA, DC-VA-MD-WV	Y	20260 FQ	24260 MW	30340 TQ	USBLS	5/15
Restaurant	Florida	H	9.83 AE	12.14 MW	14.06 AEX	FLBLS	7/16-9/16
Restaurant	Fort Lauderdale-Pompano Beach-Deerfield Beach PMSA, FL	H	10.90 AE	13.01 MW	14.57 AEX	FLBLS	7/16-9/16
Restaurant	Miami-Miami Beach-Kendall PMSA, FL	H	9.93 AE	12.95 MW	14.48 AEX	FLBLS	7/16-9/16
Restaurant	Orlando-Kissimmee-Sanford MSA, FL	H	9.44 AE	12.36 MW	14.19 AEX	FLBLS	7/16-9/16
Restaurant	Tampa-St. Petersburg-Clearwater MSA, FL	H	9.76 AE	11.71 MW	14.21 AEX	FLBLS	7/16-9/16
Restaurant	Georgia	Y	18500 FQ	21720 MW	25260 TQ	USBLS	5/15
Restaurant	Atlanta-Sandy Springs-Roswell MSA, GA	Y	19970 FQ	22900 MW	27160 TQ	USBLS	5/15
Restaurant	Augusta-Richmond County MSA, GA-SC	Y	17440 FQ	19700 MW	27470 TQ	USBLS	5/15
Restaurant	Hawaii	Y	22360 FQ	28010 MW	40540 TQ	USBLS	5/15
Restaurant	Urban Honolulu MSA, HI	Y	21140 FQ	24120 MW	30720 TQ	USBLS	5/15
Restaurant	Idaho	Y	18810 FQ	21670 MW	24500 TQ	USBLS	5/15
Restaurant	Boise City MSA, ID	Y	18190 FQ	21010 MW	24240 TQ	USBLS	5/15
Restaurant	Illinois	Y	19820 FQ	22550 MW	26520 TQ	USBLS	5/15
Restaurant	Chicago-Naperville-Arlington Heights PMSA, IL	Y	20100 FQ	22900 MW	27330 TQ	USBLS	5/15
Restaurant	Lake County-Kenosha County PMSA, IL-WI	Y	20930 FQ	24400 MW	30150 TQ	USBLS	5/15
Restaurant	Indiana	Y	17870 FQ	20600 MW	24210 TQ	USBLS	5/15
Restaurant	Gary PMSA, IN	Y	17340 FQ	19330 MW	23570 TQ	USBLS	5/15
Restaurant	Indianapolis-Carmel-Anderson MSA, IN	Y	19870 FQ	22790 MW	26450 TQ	USBLS	5/15
Restaurant	Iowa	Y	17490 FQ	19570 MW	23500 TQ	USBLS	5/15
Restaurant	Des Moines-West Des Moines MSA, IA	Y	18620 FQ	21730 MW	25420 TQ	USBLS	5/15
Restaurant	Kansas	Y	17780 FQ	20170 MW	23600 TQ	USBLS	5/15
Restaurant	Wichita MSA, KS	Y	17600 FQ	19770 MW	23590 TQ	USBLS	5/15
Restaurant	Kentucky	Y	17410 FQ	19360 MW	23650 TQ	USBLS	5/15
Restaurant	Louisville-Jefferson County MSA, KY-IN	Y	17580 FQ	19790 MW	25570 TQ	USBLS	5/15
Restaurant	Louisiana	Y	18160 FQ	21150 MW	24300 TQ	USBLS	5/15
Restaurant	Baton Rouge MSA, LA	Y	19800 FQ	22910 MW	27310 TQ	USBLS	5/15
Restaurant	New Orleans-Metairie MSA, LA	Y	18160 FQ	21260 MW	24590 TQ	USBLS	5/15
Restaurant	Maine	Y	21020 FQ	24510 MW	29200 TQ	USBLS	5/15
Restaurant	Portland-South Portland MSA, ME	Y	21010 FQ	24910 MW	28780 TQ	USBLS	5/15
Restaurant	Maryland	Y	19725 AE	25911 MW	29004 AEX	MDBLS	4/16
Restaurant	Baltimore-Columbia-Towson MSA, MD	Y	21090 FQ	25680 MW	29830 TQ	USBLS	5/15
Restaurant	Salisbury MSA, MD-DE	Y	20680 FQ	23980 MW	28340 TQ	USBLS	5/15
Restaurant	Massachusetts	Y	22780 FQ	27270 MW	32230 TQ	USBLS	5/15
Restaurant	Boston-Cambridge-Newton NECTA, MA	Y	23790 FQ	28350 MW	34190 TQ	USBLS	5/15

Cook

Occupation/Type/Industry	Location	Per	Low	Mid	High	Source	Date
Restaurant	Worcester MSA, MA-CT	Y	20680 FQ	25300 MW	30660 TQ	USBLS	5/15
Restaurant	Michigan	Y	18780 FQ	21480 MW	25690 TQ	USBLS	5/15
Restaurant	Detroit-Dearborn-Livonia PMSA, MI	Y	19540 FQ	23170 MW	28590 TQ	USBLS	5/15
Restaurant	Grand Rapids-Wyoming MSA, MI	Y	18490 FQ	20290 MW	23610 TQ	USBLS	5/15
Restaurant	Minnesota	Y	21106 FQ	24368 MW	28781 TQ	MNBLS	1/16-3/16
Restaurant	Minneapolis-St. Paul-Bloomington MSA, MN-WI	Y	21955 FQ	25186 MW	29428 TQ	MNBLS	1/16-3/16
Restaurant	Mississippi	Y	17720 FQ	20470 MW	24230 TQ	USBLS	5/15
Restaurant	Jackson MSA, MS	Y	17440 FQ	19600 MW	24340 TQ	USBLS	5/15
Restaurant	Missouri	Y	18660 FQ	21750 MW	25250 TQ	USBLS	5/15
Restaurant	Kansas City MSA, MO-KS	Y	18890 FQ	21830 MW	25090 TQ	USBLS	5/15
Restaurant	St. Louis MSA, MO-IL	Y	20320 FQ	23030 MW	27350 TQ	USBLS	5/15
Restaurant	Montana	Y	19370 FQ	22170 MW	25510 TQ	USBLS	5/15
Restaurant	Billings MSA, MT	Y	18420 FQ	20210 MW	23670 TQ	USBLS	5/15
Restaurant	Nebraska	Y	18995 FQ	21945 MW	25835 TQ	NEBLS	7/16-9/16
Restaurant	Omaha-Council Bluffs MSA, NE-IA	Y	19520 FQ	22675 MW	26980 TQ	NEBLS	7/16-9/16
Restaurant	Nevada	Y	22760 FQ	28720 MW	37220 TQ	USBLS	5/15
Restaurant	Las Vegas-Henderson-Paradise MSA, NV	Y	23840 FQ	30320 MW	39350 TQ	USBLS	5/15
Restaurant	New Hampshire	H	10.24 AE	13.25 MW	14.88 AEX	NHBLS	6/16
Restaurant	Manchester NECTA, NH	H	10.92 AE	13.65 MW	15.05 AEX	NHBLS	6/16
Restaurant	Nashua NECTA, NH-MA	Y	22280 FQ	25450 MW	29950 TQ	USBLS	5/15
Restaurant	New Jersey	Y	23410 FQ	27940 MW	34230 TQ	USBLS	5/15
Restaurant	Camden PMSA, NJ	Y	21630 FQ	24230 MW	28990 TQ	USBLS	5/15
Restaurant	Newark PMSA, NJ-PA	Y	24750 FQ	27890 MW	31050 TQ	USBLS	5/15
Restaurant	Trenton MSA, NJ	Y	21760 FQ	24510 MW	29820 TQ	USBLS	5/15
Restaurant	New Mexico	Y	18660 FQ	21690 MW	24910 TQ	USBLS	5/15
Restaurant	Albuquerque MSA, NM	Y	18920 FQ	21970 MW	25110 TQ	USBLS	5/15
Restaurant	New York	Y	20760 AE	26080 MW	31310 AEX	NYBLS	1/16-3/16
Restaurant	Buffalo-Cheektowaga-Niagara Falls MSA, NY	Y	21060 FQ	25870 MW	29860 TQ	USBLS	5/15
Restaurant	Nassau County-Suffolk County PMSA, NY	Y	21490 FQ	28930 MW	36400 TQ	USBLS	5/15
Restaurant	New York-Jersey City-White Plains PMSA, NY-NJ	Y	21680 FQ	26450 MW	31230 TQ	USBLS	5/15
Restaurant	Rochester MSA, NY	Y	20430 FQ	23110 MW	27000 TQ	USBLS	5/15
Restaurant	North Carolina	Y	18030 FQ	20960 MW	24350 TQ	USBLS	5/15
Restaurant	Charlotte-Concord-Gastonia MSA, NC-SC	Y	18690 FQ	21900 MW	25170 TQ	USBLS	5/15
Restaurant	Raleigh MSA, NC	Y	18860 FQ	22090 MW	25630 TQ	USBLS	5/15
Restaurant	North Dakota	Y	21130 FQ	24990 MW	32060 TQ	USBLS	5/15
Restaurant	Fargo MSA, ND-MN	Y	21050 FQ	24020 MW	30880 TQ	USBLS	5/15
Restaurant	Ohio	Y	18680 FQ	21310 MW	25360 TQ	USBLS	5/15
Restaurant	Cincinnati MSA, OH-KY-IN	Y	19340 FQ	22140 MW	25790 TQ	USBLS	5/15
Restaurant	Cleveland-Elyria MSA, OH	Y	18610 FQ	21190 MW	25120 TQ	USBLS	5/15
Restaurant	Columbus MSA, OH	Y	19550 FQ	23490 MW	28450 TQ	USBLS	5/15
Restaurant	Oklahoma	Y	18410 FQ	21350 MW	24240 TQ	USBLS	5/15
Restaurant	Oklahoma City MSA, OK	Y	20300 FQ	22800 MW	26690 TQ	USBLS	5/15
Restaurant	Tulsa MSA, OK	Y	18910 FQ	21820 MW	24260 TQ	USBLS	5/15
Restaurant	Oregon	H	10.03 FQ	11.50 MW	13.78 TQ	ORBLS	2016
Restaurant	Portland-Vancouver-Hillsboro MSA, OR-WA	Y	20670 FQ	23830 MW	28990 TQ	USBLS	5/15
Restaurant	Pennsylvania	Y	18760 FQ	22640 MW	27990 TQ	USBLS	5/15
Restaurant	Allentown-Bethlehem-Easton MSA, PA-NJ	Y	19810 FQ	24500 MW	31180 TQ	USBLS	5/15
Restaurant	Harrisburg-Carlisle MSA, PA	Y	19380 FQ	22420 MW	25780 TQ	USBLS	5/15
Restaurant	Montgomery County-Bucks County-Chester County PMSA, PA	Y	19480 FQ	24850 MW	30500 TQ	USBLS	5/15
Restaurant	Philadelphia PMSA, PA	Y	20820 FQ	25250 MW	29600 TQ	USBLS	5/15
Restaurant	Pittsburgh MSA, PA	Y	18350 FQ	21740 MW	26730 TQ	USBLS	5/15
Restaurant	Rhode Island	Y	20820 FQ	24320 MW	29310 TQ	USBLS	5/15
Restaurant	Providence-Warwick MSA, RI-MA	Y	20860 FQ	24100 MW	29040 TQ	USBLS	5/15
Restaurant	South Carolina	Y	17600 FQ	19900 MW	23870 TQ	USBLS	5/15
Restaurant	Charleston-North Charleston MSA, SC	Y	20000 FQ	22820 MW	26670 TQ	USBLS	5/15
Restaurant	Columbia MSA, SC	Y	17330 FQ	19210 MW	22280 TQ	USBLS	5/15

AE	Average entry wage	AWR	Average wage range	H	Hourly
AEX	Average experienced wage	B	Biweekly	HI	Highest wage paid
ATC	Average total compensation	D	Daily	HR	High end range
AW	Average wage paid	FQ	First quartile wage	LO	Lowest wage paid

LR	Low end range	MTC	Median total compensation	TCC Total cash compensation
M	Monthly	MW	Median wage paid	TQ Third quartile wage
MCC	Median cash compensation	MWR	Median wage range	W Weekly
ME	Median entry wage	S	See annotated source	Y Yearly

Occupation/Type/Industry	Location	Per	Low	Mid	High	Source	Date
Cook							
Restaurant	Greenville-Anderson-Mauldin MSA, SC	Y	17130 FQ	18810 MW	22360 TQ	USBLS	5/15
Restaurant	South Dakota	Y	20610 FQ	22730 MW	24910 TQ	USBLS	5/15
Restaurant	Sioux Falls MSA, SD	Y	21260 FQ	23220 MW	25710 TQ	USBLS	5/15
Restaurant	Tennessee	Y	18720 FQ	21770 MW	24870 TQ	USBLS	5/15
Restaurant	Knoxville MSA, TN	Y	19070 FQ	21700 MW	24150 TQ	USBLS	5/15
Restaurant	Memphis MSA, TN-MS-AR	Y	18430 FQ	21680 MW	25160 TQ	USBLS	5/15
Restaurant	Nashville-Davidson–Murfreesboro–Franklin MSA, TN	Y	19220 FQ	22490 MW	26730 TQ	USBLS	5/15
Restaurant	Texas	Y	18820 FQ	22090 MW	26060 TQ	USBLS	5/15
Restaurant	Austin-Round Rock MSA, TX	Y	20140 FQ	22660 MW	25760 TQ	USBLS	5/15
Restaurant	Dallas-Plano-Irving PMSA, TX	Y	20490 FQ	23970 MW	29310 TQ	USBLS	5/15
Restaurant	Fort Worth-Arlington PMSA, TX	Y	19960 FQ	22520 MW	25610 TQ	USBLS	5/15
Restaurant	Houston-The Woodlands-Sugar Land MSA, TX	Y	18500 FQ	21950 MW	26250 TQ	USBLS	5/15
Restaurant	San Antonio-New Braunfels MSA, TX	Y	19100 FQ	21840 MW	24580 TQ	USBLS	5/15
Restaurant	Utah	Y	19420 FQ	23680 MW	28870 TQ	USBLS	5/15
Restaurant	Ogden-Clearfield MSA, UT	Y	18510 FQ	22860 MW	28220 TQ	USBLS	5/15
Restaurant	Provo-Orem MSA, UT	Y	20170 FQ	24630 MW	29280 TQ	USBLS	5/15
Restaurant	Salt Lake City MSA, UT	Y	20620 FQ	24710 MW	29670 TQ	USBLS	5/15
Restaurant	Vermont	Y	23270 FQ	27300 MW	31150 TQ	USBLS	5/15
Restaurant	Burlington-South Burlington MSA, VT	Y	22000 FQ	25930 MW	29580 TQ	USBLS	5/15
Restaurant	Virginia	Y	19130 FQ	22840 MW	27790 TQ	USBLS	5/15
Restaurant	Richmond MSA, VA	Y	18840 FQ	22030 MW	24920 TQ	USBLS	5/15
Restaurant	Virginia Beach-Norfolk-Newport News MSA, VA-NC	Y	20630 FQ	23810 MW	27940 TQ	USBLS	5/15
Restaurant	Washington	H	11.24 FQ	13.11 MW	14.87 TQ	WABLS	3/16
Restaurant	Seattle-Bellevue-Everett PMSA, WA	H	12.00 FQ	13.75 MW	15.45 TQ	WABLS	3/16
Restaurant	Tacoma-Lakewood PMSA, WA	H	10.88 FQ	12.67 MW	14.45 TQ	WABLS	3/16
Restaurant	West Virginia	Y	18250 FQ	20040 MW	23470 TQ	USBLS	5/15
Restaurant	Huntington-Ashland MSA, WV-KY-OH	Y	17620 FQ	19230 MW	22470 TQ	USBLS	5/15
Restaurant	Wisconsin	Y	19260 FQ	22370 MW	26170 TQ	USBLS	5/15
Restaurant	Madison MSA, WI	Y	20600 FQ	22780 MW	25150 TQ	USBLS	5/15
Restaurant	Milwaukee-Waukesha-West Allis MSA, WI	Y	19770 FQ	23420 MW	27940 TQ	USBLS	5/15
Restaurant	Wyoming	Y	20530 FQ	24010 MW	28920 TQ	USBLS	5/15
Restaurant	Cheyenne MSA, WY	Y	21240 FQ	23640 MW	27180 TQ	USBLS	5/15
Restaurant	Puerto Rico	Y	16790 FQ	18140 MW	19560 TQ	USBLS	5/15
Restaurant	San Juan-Carolina-Caguas MSA, PR	Y	16890 FQ	18310 MW	19840 TQ	USBLS	5/15
Restaurant	Virgin Islands	Y	21250 FQ	25050 MW	30170 TQ	USBLS	5/15
Restaurant	Guam	Y	18090 FQ	19020 MW	21450 TQ	USBLS	5/15
Short Order	Alabama	Y	17524 AE	20376 AW	21807 AEX	ALBLS	6/16
Short Order	Birmingham-Hoover MSA, AL	Y	17678 AE	21189 AW	22950 AEX	ALBLS	6/16
Short Order	Alaska	Y	21930 FQ	24480 MW	32970 TQ	USBLS	5/15
Short Order	Anchorage MSA, AK	Y	22620 FQ	31290 MW	35980 TQ	USBLS	5/15
Short Order	Arizona	Y	20070 FQ	23010 MW	27140 TQ	USBLS	5/15
Short Order	Phoenix-Mesa-Scottsdale MSA, AZ	Y	20300 FQ	22790 MW	25970 TQ	USBLS	5/15
Short Order	Tucson MSA, AZ	Y	19360 FQ	22800 MW	26880 TQ	USBLS	5/15
Short Order	Arkansas	Y	16860 FQ	18080 MW	19320 TQ	USBLS	5/15
Short Order	Little Rock-North Little Rock-Conway MSA, AR	Y	16980 FQ	18250 MW	19530 TQ	USBLS	5/15
Short Order	California	H	10.39 FQ	11.50 MW	13.39 TQ	CABLS	1/16-3/16
Short Order	Anaheim-Santa Ana-Irvine PMSA, CA	H	10.62 FQ	11.71 MW	13.61 TQ	CABLS	1/16-3/16
Short Order	Los Angeles-Long Beach-Glendale PMSA, CA	H	10.30 FQ	11.32 MW	12.69 TQ	CABLS	1/16-3/16
Short Order	Oakland-Hayward-Berkeley PMSA, CA	H	10.78 FQ	11.91 MW	14.48 TQ	CABLS	1/16-3/16
Short Order	Riverside-San Bernardino-Ontario MSA, CA	H	10.33 FQ	11.51 MW	13.19 TQ	CABLS	1/16-3/16
Short Order	Sacramento–Roseville–Arden-Arcade MSA, CA	H	10.12 FQ	11.26 MW	13.05 TQ	CABLS	1/16-3/16
Short Order	San Diego-Carlsbad MSA, CA	H	10.36 FQ	11.21 MW	12.06 TQ	CABLS	1/16-3/16

AE Average entry wage	**AWR** Average wage range	**H** Hourly	**LR** Low end range	**MTC** Median total compensation	**TCC** Total cash compensation
AEX Average experienced wage	**B** Biweekly	**HI** Highest wage paid	**M** Monthly	**MW** Median wage paid	**TQ** Third quartile wage
ATC Average total compensation	**D** Daily	**HR** High end range	**MCC** Median cash compensation	**MWR** Median wage range	**W** Weekly
AW Average wage paid	**FQ** First quartile wage	**LO** Lowest wage paid	**ME** Median entry wage	**S** See annotated source	**Y** Yearly

Occupation/Type/Industry	Location	Per	Low	Mid	High	Source	Date
Cook							
Short Order	San Francisco-Redwood City-South San Francisco PMSA, CA	H	12.33 FQ	14.42 MW	17.16 TQ	CABLS	1/16-3/16
Short Order	Colorado	Y	19640 FQ	22430 MW	27610 TQ	USBLS	5/15
Short Order	Denver-Aurora-Lakewood MSA, CO	Y	20220 FQ	22390 MW	24560 TQ	USBLS	5/15
Short Order	Connecticut	Y		23536 MW		CTBLS	1/16-3/16
Short Order	Bridgeport-Stamford-Norwalk MSA, CT	Y	21140 FQ	24080 MW	29930 TQ	USBLS	5/15
Short Order	Hartford-West Hartford-East Hartford MSA, CT	Y	19510 FQ	20730 MW	23350 TQ	USBLS	5/15
Short Order	Delaware	Y	20740 FQ	22710 MW	24680 TQ	USBLS	5/15
Short Order	Wilmington PMSA, DE-MD-NJ	Y	20470 FQ	23030 MW	27370 TQ	USBLS	5/15
Short Order	District of Columbia	Y	21570 FQ	25990 MW	29880 TQ	USBLS	5/15
Short Order	Washington-Arlington-Alexandria PMSA, DC-VA-MD-WV	Y	21280 FQ	24060 MW	28490 TQ	USBLS	5/15
Short Order	Florida	H	9.04 AE	10.75 MW	12.37 AEX	FLBLS	7/16-9/16
Short Order	Fort Lauderdale-Pompano Beach-Deerfield Beach PMSA, FL	H	9.02 AE	10.97 MW	12.87 AEX	FLBLS	7/16-9/16
Short Order	Gainesville MSA, FL	H	9.53 AE	11.38 MW	12.97 AEX	FLBLS	7/16-9/16
Short Order	Miami-Miami Beach-Kendall PMSA, FL	H	8.95 AE	9.58 MW	12.04 AEX	FLBLS	7/16-9/16
Short Order	Orlando-Kissimmee-Sanford MSA, FL	H	9.62 AE	10.98 MW	11.94 AEX	FLBLS	7/16-9/16
Short Order	Tampa-St. Petersburg-Clearwater MSA, FL	H	9.14 AE	10.69 MW	11.63 AEX	FLBLS	7/16-9/16
Short Order	Georgia	Y	17350 FQ	19320 MW	23110 TQ	USBLS	5/15
Short Order	Atlanta-Sandy Springs-Roswell MSA, GA	Y	17660 FQ	20340 MW	23950 TQ	USBLS	5/15
Short Order	Augusta-Richmond County MSA, GA-SC	Y	17480 FQ	19530 MW	22940 TQ	USBLS	5/15
Short Order	Hawaii	Y	20440 FQ	24160 MW	34600 TQ	USBLS	5/15
Short Order	Urban Honolulu MSA, HI	Y	22560 FQ	27860 MW	35490 TQ	USBLS	5/15
Short Order	Idaho	Y	17410 FQ	19340 MW	23280 TQ	USBLS	5/15
Short Order	Boise City MSA, ID	Y	17910 FQ	20600 MW	24020 TQ	USBLS	5/15
Short Order	Illinois	Y	19840 FQ	21950 MW	24050 TQ	USBLS	5/15
Short Order	Chicago-Naperville-Arlington Heights PMSA, IL	Y	20800 FQ	22680 MW	24560 TQ	USBLS	5/15
Short Order	Lake County-Kenosha County PMSA, IL-WI	Y	20400 FQ	22070 MW	23740 TQ	USBLS	5/15
Short Order	Indiana	Y	17130 FQ	18850 MW	22520 TQ	USBLS	5/15
Short Order	Gary PMSA, IN	Y	16990 FQ	18490 MW	24560 TQ	USBLS	5/15
Short Order	Indianapolis-Carmel-Anderson MSA, IN	Y	17680 FQ	19900 MW	24520 TQ	USBLS	5/15
Short Order	Iowa	Y	17620 FQ	19990 MW	23470 TQ	USBLS	5/15
Short Order	Des Moines-West Des Moines MSA, IA	Y	20550 FQ	22770 MW	25330 TQ	USBLS	5/15
Short Order	Kansas	Y	16960 FQ	18460 MW	20520 TQ	USBLS	5/15
Short Order	Wichita MSA, KS	Y	16840 FQ	18240 MW	19750 TQ	CABLS	5/15
Short Order	Kentucky	Y	17310 FQ	19110 MW	22040 TQ	USBLS	5/15
Short Order	Louisville-Jefferson County MSA, KY-IN	Y	18590 FQ	21070 MW	23580 TQ	USBLS	5/15
Short Order	Louisiana	Y	17320 FQ	19180 MW	22390 TQ	USBLS	5/15
Short Order	Baton Rouge MSA, LA	Y	16940 FQ	18440 MW	20490 TQ	USBLS	5/15
Short Order	New Orleans-Metairie MSA, LA	Y	17820 FQ	20260 MW	23320 TQ	USBLS	5/15
Short Order	Maine	Y	18400 FQ	20780 MW	23600 TQ	USBLS	5/15
Short Order	Portland-South Portland MSA, ME	Y	17500 FQ	19050 MW	23400 TQ	USBLS	5/15
Short Order	Maryland	Y	18017 AE	23411 MW	26107 AEX	MDBLS	4/16
Short Order	Baltimore-Columbia-Towson MSA, MD	Y	18530 FQ	21840 MW	26180 TQ	USBLS	5/15
Short Order	Salisbury MSA, MD-DE	Y	18710 FQ	21260 MW	24560 TQ	USBLS	5/15
Short Order	Massachusetts	Y	21950 FQ	26300 MW	30110 TQ	USBLS	5/15
Short Order	Boston-Cambridge-Newton NECTA, MA	Y	24870 FQ	27490 MW	30040 TQ	USBLS	5/15
Short Order	Worcester MSA, MA-CT	Y	19760 FQ	23150 MW	28660 TQ	USBLS	5/15
Short Order	Michigan	Y	18180 FQ	19290 MW	22180 TQ	USBLS	5/15

AE	Average entry wage	AWR	Average wage range	H	Hourly	LR	Low end range	MTC	Median total compensation	TCC	Total cash compensation
AEX	Average experienced wage	B	Biweekly	HI	Highest wage paid	M	Monthly	MW	Median wage paid	TQ	Third quartile wage
ATC	Average total compensation	D	Daily	HR	High end range	MCC	Median cash compensation	MWR	Median wage range	W	Weekly
AW	Average wage paid	FQ	First quartile wage	LO	Lowest wage paid	ME	Median entry wage	S	See annotated source	Y	Yearly

Occupation/Type/Industry	Location	Per	Low	Mid	High	Source	Date
Cook							
Short Order	Detroit-Dearborn-Livonia PMSA, MI	Y	20250 FQ	22150 MW	24060 TQ	USBLS	5/15
Short Order	Grand Rapids-Wyoming MSA, MI	Y	18370 FQ	19640 MW	22410 TQ	USBLS	5/15
Short Order	Minnesota	Y	18874 FQ	21429 MW	25065 TQ	MNBLS	1/16-3/16
Short Order	Minneapolis-St. Paul-Bloomington MSA, MN-WI	Y	19157 FQ	22470 MW	27044 TQ	MNBLS	1/16-3/16
Short Order	Mississippi	Y	17190 FQ	18980 MW	22560 TQ	USBLS	5/15
Short Order	Jackson MSA, MS	Y	17670 FQ	20790 MW	26000 TQ	USBLS	5/15
Short Order	Missouri	Y	17420 FQ	18920 MW	22470 TQ	USBLS	5/15
Short Order	Kansas City MSA, MO-KS	Y	17420 FQ	19110 MW	22730 TQ	USBLS	5/15
Short Order	St. Louis MSA, MO-IL	Y	18890 FQ	21340 MW	23640 TQ	USBLS	5/15
Short Order	Montana	Y	18940 FQ	21110 MW	23280 TQ	USBLS	5/15
Short Order	Billings MSA, MT	Y	19500 FQ	21370 MW	23230 TQ	USBLS	5/15
Short Order	Nebraska	Y	18175 FQ	19705 MW	23740 TQ	NEBLS	7/16-9/16
Short Order	Omaha-Council Bluffs MSA, NE-IA	Y	18475 FQ	20745 MW	24330 TQ	NEBLS	7/16-9/16
Short Order	Nevada	Y	18840 FQ	23190 MW	34660 TQ	USBLS	5/15
Short Order	Las Vegas-Henderson-Paradise MSA, NV	Y	18850 FQ	23390 MW	39340 TQ	USBLS	5/15
Short Order	New Hampshire	H	8.42 AE	9.49 MW	10.75 AEX	NHBLS	6/16
Short Order	Manchester NECTA, NH	H	8.48 AE	9.97 MW	10.66 AEX	NHBLS	6/16
Short Order	Nashua NECTA, NH-MA	Y	17900 FQ	20670 MW	24510 TQ	USBLS	5/15
Short Order	New Jersey	Y	20220 FQ	23070 MW	27290 TQ	USBLS	5/15
Short Order	Camden PMSA, NJ	Y	19780 FQ	21930 MW	24050 TQ	USBLS	5/15
Short Order	Newark PMSA, NJ-PA	Y	20990 FQ	23010 MW	25470 TQ	USBLS	5/15
Short Order	Trenton MSA, NJ	Y	19150 FQ	22970 MW	34390 TQ	USBLS	5/15
Short Order	New Mexico	Y	17770 FQ	19480 MW	23940 TQ	USBLS	5/15
Short Order	Albuquerque MSA, NM	Y	17910 FQ	19770 MW	23190 TQ	USBLS	5/15
Short Order	New York	Y	19210 AE	20110 MW	25040 AEX	NYBLS	1/16-3/16
Short Order	Buffalo-Cheektowaga-Niagara Falls MSA, NY	Y	19000 FQ	20320 MW	24190 TQ	USBLS	5/15
Short Order	Nassau County-Suffolk County PMSA, NY	Y	21100 FQ	24920 MW	31120 TQ	USBLS	5/15
Short Order	New York-Jersey City-White Plains PMSA, NY-NJ	Y	18800 FQ	19510 MW	25920 TQ	USBLS	5/15
Short Order	Rochester MSA, NY	Y	18860 FQ	19880 MW	24470 TQ	USBLS	5/15
Short Order	North Carolina	Y	16910 FQ	18450 MW	21090 TQ	USBLS	5/15
Short Order	Charlotte-Concord-Gastonia MSA, NC-SC	Y	17760 FQ	19900 MW	23500 TQ	USBLS	5/15
Short Order	Raleigh MSA, NC	Y	16570 FQ	17850 MW	19130 TQ	USBLS	5/15
Short Order	North Dakota	Y	19310 FQ	22120 MW	24830 TQ	USBLS	5/15
Short Order	Fargo MSA, ND-MN	Y	20740 FQ	22880 MW	25060 TQ	USBLS	5/15
Short Order	Ohio	Y	18070 FQ	19280 MW	22720 TQ	USBLS	5/15
Short Order	Cincinnati MSA, OH-KY-IN	Y	18010 FQ	19210 MW	22260 TQ	USBLS	5/15
Short Order	Cleveland-Elyria MSA, OH	Y	18010 FQ	19160 MW	23020 TQ	USBLS	5/15
Short Order	Columbus MSA, OH	Y	18760 FQ	21350 MW	25160 TQ	USBLS	5/15
Short Order	Oklahoma	Y	16640 FQ	17990 MW	19340 TQ	USBLS	5/15
Short Order	Oklahoma City MSA, OK	Y	16420 FQ	17620 MW	18820 TQ	USBLS	5/15
Short Order	Tulsa MSA, OK	Y	17160 FQ	18950 MW	22250 TQ	USBLS	5/15
Short Order	Oregon	H	10.04 FQ	10.98 MW	11.91 TQ	ORBLS	2016
Short Order	Portland-Vancouver-Hillsboro MSA, OR-WA	Y	21130 FQ	22780 MW	24440 TQ	USBLS	5/15
Short Order	Pennsylvania	Y	17600 FQ	19740 MW	23760 TQ	USBLS	5/15
Short Order	Allentown-Bethlehem-Easton MSA, PA-NJ	Y	17600 FQ	20750 MW	26910 TQ	USBLS	5/15
Short Order	Harrisburg-Carlisle MSA, PA	Y	18300 FQ	21370 MW	25450 TQ	USBLS	5/15
Short Order	Montgomery County-Bucks County-Chester County PMSA, PA	Y	17190 FQ	18680 MW	20840 TQ	USBLS	5/15
Short Order	Philadelphia PMSA, PA	Y	20650 FQ	23690 MW	28070 TQ	USBLS	5/15
Short Order	Pittsburgh MSA, PA	Y	17120 FQ	18850 MW	22060 TQ	USBLS	5/15
Short Order	Rhode Island	Y	20030 FQ	22410 MW	24850 TQ	USBLS	5/15
Short Order	Providence-Warwick MSA, RI-MA	Y	20200 FQ	22550 MW	25090 TQ	USBLS	5/15
Short Order	South Carolina	Y	16930 FQ	18480 MW	21100 TQ	USBLS	5/15
Short Order	Charleston-North Charleston MSA, SC	Y	17330 FQ	19200 MW	22530 TQ	USBLS	5/15
Short Order	Columbia MSA, SC	Y	16540 FQ	17860 MW	19180 TQ	USBLS	5/15
Short Order	Greenville-Anderson-Mauldin MSA, SC	Y	17200 FQ	19020 MW	22140 TQ	USBLS	5/15

AE	Average entry wage	AWR	Average wage range	H	Hourly	LR	Low end range	MTC	Median total compensation	TCC	Total cash compensation
AEX	Average experienced wage	B	Biweekly	HI	Highest wage paid	M	Monthly	MW	Median wage paid	TQ	Third quartile wage
ATC	Average total compensation	D	Daily	HR	High end range	MCC	Median cash compensation	MWR	Median wage range	W	Weekly
AW	Average wage paid	FQ	First quartile wage	LO	Lowest wage paid	ME	Median entry wage	S	See annotated source	Y	Yearly

Occupation/Type/Industry	Location	Per	Low	Mid	High	Source	Date
Cook							
Short Order	South Dakota	Y	18660 FQ	19900 MW	22950 TQ	USBLS	5/15
Short Order	Sioux Falls MSA, SD	Y	18490 FQ	19290 MW	22220 TQ	USBLS	5/15
Short Order	Tennessee	Y	17150 FQ	18940 MW	22520 TQ	USBLS	5/15
Short Order	Knoxville MSA, TN	Y	17740 FQ	20400 MW	24110 TQ	USBLS	5/15
Short Order	Memphis MSA, TN-MS-AR	Y	17550 FQ	19520 MW	22380 TQ	USBLS	5/15
Short Order	Nashville-Davidson– Murfreesboro–Franklin MSA, TN	Y	17370 FQ	19540 MW	23740 TQ	USBLS	5/15
Short Order	Texas	Y	17430 FQ	19360 MW	22720 TQ	USBLS	5/15
Short Order	Austin-Round Rock MSA, TX	Y	17590 FQ	19630 MW	23300 TQ	USBLS	5/15
Short Order	Dallas-Plano-Irving PMSA, TX	Y	17900 FQ	20250 MW	23060 TQ	USBLS	5/15
Short Order	Fort Worth-Arlington PMSA, TX	Y	17750 FQ	20140 MW	23100 TQ	USBLS	5/15
Short Order	Houston-The Woodlands- Sugar Land MSA, TX	Y	17350 FQ	19210 MW	22920 TQ	USBLS	5/15
Short Order	San Antonio-New Braunfels MSA, TX	Y	17330 FQ	19150 MW	22470 TQ	USBLS	5/15
Short Order	Utah	Y	19740 FQ	22750 MW	26920 TQ	USBLS	5/15
Short Order	Ogden-Clearfield MSA, UT	Y	22040 FQ	26150 MW	30990 TQ	USBLS	5/15
Short Order	Salt Lake City MSA, UT	Y	19500 FQ	22350 MW	25490 TQ	USBLS	5/15
Short Order	Vermont	Y	22740 FQ	26160 MW	29340 TQ	USBLS	5/15
Short Order	Burlington-South Burlington MSA, VT	Y	22510 FQ	25490 MW	29170 TQ	USBLS	5/15
Short Order	Virginia	Y	17770 FQ	20700 MW	25190 TQ	USBLS	5/15
Short Order	Richmond MSA, VA	Y	16790 FQ	18330 MW	21640 TQ	USBLS	5/15
Short Order	Virginia Beach-Norfolk- Newport News MSA, VA-NC	Y	20130 FQ	23930 MW	29220 TQ	USBLS	5/15
Short Order	Washington	H	10.63 FQ	11.71 MW	13.92 TQ	WABLS	3/16
Short Order	Seattle-Bellevue-Everett PMSA, WA	H	10.86 FQ	12.05 MW	14.71 TQ	WABLS	3/16
Short Order	Tacoma-Lakewood PMSA, WA	H	10.68 FQ	11.76 MW	13.37 TQ	WABLS	3/16
Short Order	West Virginia	Y	18040 FQ	19480 MW	22620 TQ	USBLS	5/15
Short Order	Huntington-Ashland MSA, WV-KY-OH	Y	17540 FQ	18350 MW	19160 TQ	USBLS	5/15
Short Order	Wisconsin	Y	17620 FQ	19730 MW	23230 TQ	USBLS	5/15
Short Order	Madison MSA, WI	Y	18750 FQ	22690 MW	28010 TQ	USBLS	5/15
Short Order	Milwaukee-Waukesha-West Allis MSA, WI	Y	19000 FQ	21260 MW	23450 TQ	USBLS	5/15
Short Order	Wyoming	Y	17180 FQ	19080 MW	23090 TQ	USBLS	5/15
Short Order	Puerto Rico	Y	16390 FQ	17450 MW	18500 TQ	USBLS	5/15
Short Order	San Juan-Carolina-Caguas MSA, PR	Y	16310 FQ	17370 MW	18420 TQ	USBLS	5/15
Short Order	Virgin Islands	Y	19810 FQ	31530 MW	35590 TQ	USBLS	5/15
Short Order	Guam	Y	17740 FQ	18330 MW	18910 TQ	USBLS	5/15
Cooling and Freezing Equipment Operator and Tender							
	Alabama	Y	22096 AE	28296 AW	31391 AEX	ALBLS	6/16
	Arizona	Y	25260 FQ	28260 MW	33810 TQ	USBLS	5/15
	Arkansas	Y	20320 FQ	24640 MW	31100 TQ	USBLS	5/15
	California	H	11.26 FQ	13.61 MW	17.29 TQ	CABLS	1/16-3/16
	Connecticut	Y		37819 MW		CTBLS	1/16-3/16
	Florida	H	10.42 AE	13.19 MW	17.83 AEX	FLBLS	7/16-9/16
	Georgia	Y	22680 FQ	27080 MW	41100 TQ	USBLS	5/15
	Illinois	Y	29780 FQ	53840 MW	59040 TQ	USBLS	5/15
	Indiana	Y	21180 FQ	27870 MW	38600 TQ	USBLS	5/15
	Iowa	Y	27260 FQ	31150 MW	43420 TQ	USBLS	5/15
	Kansas	Y	26640 FQ	29520 MW	34970 TQ	USBLS	5/15
	Kentucky	Y	18440 FQ	21930 MW	30200 TQ	USBLS	5/15
	Louisiana	Y	20470 FQ	22660 MW	24830 TQ	USBLS	5/15
	Maryland	Y	22506 AE	33046 MW	38316 AEX	MDBLS	4/16
	Massachusetts	Y	20550 FQ	27010 MW	38720 TQ	USBLS	5/15
	Michigan	Y	23130 FQ	32430 MW	39440 TQ	USBLS	5/15
	Minnesota	Y	29341 FQ	34605 MW	38807 TQ	MNBLS	1/16-3/16
	Mississippi	Y	25460 FQ	27770 MW	30090 TQ	USBLS	5/15
	Missouri	Y	25830 FQ	31180 MW	45350 TQ	USBLS	5/15
	Nebraska	Y	27175 FQ	30240 MW	38510 TQ	NEBLS	7/16-9/16
	New Jersey	Y	19670 FQ	23490 MW	31680 TQ	USBLS	5/15
	New York	Y	21270 AE	28380 MW	35180 AEX	NYBLS	1/16-3/16
	North Carolina	Y	24950 FQ	28380 MW	33180 TQ	USBLS	5/15
	Ohio	Y	20350 FQ	25080 MW	29900 TQ	USBLS	5/15
	Oklahoma	Y	22210 FQ	27620 MW	34610 TQ	USBLS	5/15

AE	Average entry wage	**AWR**	Average wage range	**H**	Hourly	**LR**	Low end range	**MTC** Median total compensation	**TCC** Total cash compensation
AEX	Average experienced wage	**B**	Biweekly	**HI**	Highest wage paid	**M**	Monthly	**MW** Median wage paid	**TQ** Third quartile wage
ATC	Average total compensation	**D**	Daily	**HR**	High end range	**MCC**	Median cash compensation	**MWR** Median wage range	**W** Weekly
AW	Average wage paid	**FQ**	First quartile wage	**LO**	Lowest wage paid	**ME**	Median entry wage	**S** See annotated source	**Y** Yearly

Occupation/Type/Industry	Location	Per	Low	Mid	High	Source	Date
Cooling and Freezing Equipment Operator and Tender	Oregon	H	15.60 FQ	19.63 MW	22.64 TQ	ORBLS	2016
	Pennsylvania	Y	23740 FQ	30760 MW	43680 TQ	USBLS	5/15
	South Carolina	Y	28320 FQ	35250 MW	40100 TQ	USBLS	5/15
	Tennessee	Y	26300 FQ	28900 MW	31500 TQ	USBLS	5/15
	Texas	Y	22130 FQ	28120 MW	41440 TQ	USBLS	5/15
	Vermont	Y	22160 FQ	24310 MW	28150 TQ	USBLS	5/15
	Virginia	Y	20350 FQ	23640 MW	28610 TQ	USBLS	5/15
	Washington	H	12.91 FQ	15.28 MW	21.14 TQ	WABLS	3/16
	Wisconsin	Y	25870 FQ	31180 MW	42780 TQ	USBLS	5/15
Copywriter	United States	Y		60250 MW		MST03	5/15
Pharmaceutical, Medical Device, and Healthcare Industries	United States	Y		43800 AW		MMM01	7/16
Coroner							
County Government	Macon-Bibb County, GA	Y			73507 HI	GACTY03	2016
County Government	Pickens County, GA	Y			13246 HI	GACTY03	2016
County Government	Telfair County, GA	Y			3000 HI	GACTY03	2016
Corporate In-House Counsel							
Large Company, 0-3 Years Experience	United States	Y	128500 LO		166750 HI	RH01	2017
Large Company, 10+ Years Experience	United States	Y	190250 LO		269500 HI	RH01	2017
Midsize Company, 0-3 Years Experience	United States	Y	104750 LO		139250 HI	RH01	2017
Midsize Company, 10+ Years Experience	United States	Y	159750 LO		238250 HI	RH01	2017
Small Company, 0-3 Years Experience	United States	Y	87000 LO		114500 HI	RH01	2017
Small Company, 10+ Years Experience	United States	Y	137500 LO		192750 HI	RH01	2017
Corporate Jet Mechanic	United States	H		29.00 AW		AVJOB06	2016
Corporate Meeting Professional	United States	Y		81265 AW		CVENE	2016
Corporate Planner							
Meetings and Conventions	United States	Y		79231 AW		MANDC	2016
Corporate Recruiter	United States	Y		60000 MW		TSTR	2017
Correctional Officer and Jailer	Alabama	Y	27068 AE	36788 AW	41658 AEX	ALBLS	6/16
	Birmingham-Hoover MSA, AL	Y	31980 AE	41102 AW	45663 AEX	ALBLS	6/16
	Alaska	Y	49730 FQ	57700 MW	66320 TQ	USBLS	5/15
	Arizona	Y	35680 FQ	39960 MW	44990 TQ	USBLS	5/15
	Phoenix-Mesa-Scottsdale MSA, AZ	Y	36350 FQ	40050 MW	47420 TQ	USBLS	5/15
	Tucson MSA, AZ	Y	35830 FQ	39960 MW	42730 TQ	USBLS	5/15
	Arkansas	Y	28300 FQ	32480 MW	36750 TQ	USBLS	5/15
	Little Rock-North Little Rock-Conway MSA, AR	Y	28990 FQ	33920 MW	37080 TQ	USBLS	5/15
	California	H	28.55 FQ	37.20 MW	39.11 TQ	CABLS	1/16-3/16
	Anaheim-Santa Ana-Irvine PMSA, CA	H	27.00 FQ	31.00 MW	35.62 TQ	CABLS	1/16-3/16
	Los Angeles-Long Beach-Glendale PMSA, CA	H	26.40 FQ	29.18 MW	35.46 TQ	CABLS	1/16-3/16
	Oakland-Hayward-Berkeley PMSA, CA	H	27.55 FQ	32.09 MW	34.77 TQ	CABLS	1/16-3/16
	Riverside-San Bernardino-Ontario MSA, CA	H	28.94 FQ	37.86 MW	39.39 TQ	CABLS	1/16-3/16
	Sacramento–Roseville–Arden-Arcade MSA, CA	H	18.10 FQ	36.84 MW	39.44 TQ	CABLS	1/16-3/16
	San Diego-Carlsbad MSA, CA	H	34.11 FQ	38.63 MW	39.48 TQ	CABLS	1/16-3/16
	Colorado	Y	40680 FQ	43190 MW	53360 TQ	USBLS	5/15
	Denver-Aurora-Lakewood MSA, CO	Y	42280 FQ	46880 MW	59980 TQ	USBLS	5/15
	Connecticut	Y		54627 MW		CTBLS	1/16-3/16
	Wilmington PMSA, DE-MD-NJ	Y	32660 FQ	35360 MW	39640 TQ	USBLS	5/15
	Washington-Arlington-Alexandria PMSA, DC-VA-MD-WV	Y	38580 FQ	48990 MW	61110 TQ	USBLS	5/15
	Florida	H	16.04 AE	18.95 MW	24.46 AEX	FLBLS	7/16-9/16
	Fort Lauderdale-Pompano Beach-Deerfield Beach PMSA, FL	H	22.70 AE	32.90 MW	34.75 AEX	FLBLS	7/16-9/16

AE	Average entry wage	AWR	Average wage range	H	Hourly
AEX	Average experienced wage	B	Biweekly	HI	Highest wage paid
ATC	Average total compensation	D	Daily	HR	High end range
AW	Average wage paid	FQ	First quartile wage	LO	Lowest wage paid

LR	Low end range	MTC	Median total compensation	TCC	Total cash compensation
M	Monthly	MW	Median wage paid	TQ	Third quartile wage
MCC	Median cash compensation	MWR	Median wage range	W	Weekly
ME	Median entry wage	S	See annotated source	Y	Yearly

Occupation/Type/Industry	Location	Per	Low	Mid	High	Source	Date
Correctional Officer and Jailer	Miami-Miami Beach-Kendall						
	PMSA, FL	H	18.29 AE	29.34 MW	32.42 AEX	FLBLS	7/16-9/16
	Orlando-Kissimmee-Sanford						
	MSA, FL	H	16.65 AE	19.08 MW	21.75 AEX	FLBLS	7/16-9/16
	Georgia	Y	25340 FQ	28520 MW	33030 TQ	USBLS	5/15
	Atlanta-Sandy Springs-						
	Roswell MSA, GA	Y	26980 FQ	31040 MW	37230 TQ	USBLS	5/15
	Augusta-Richmond County						
	MSA, GA-SC	Y	25710 FQ	28720 MW	34070 TQ	USBLS	5/15
	Hawaii	Y	43960 FQ	48750 MW	56440 TQ	USBLS	5/15
	Boise City MSA, ID	Y	27830 FQ	29680 MW	33240 TQ	USBLS	5/15
	Illinois	Y	50140 FQ	57470 MW	66610 TQ	USBLS	5/15
	Chicago-Naperville-Arlington						
	Heights PMSA, IL	Y	53170 FQ	61100 MW	70890 TQ	USBLS	5/15
	Lake County-Kenosha County						
	PMSA, IL-WI	Y	55050 FQ	64800 MW	73350 TQ	USBLS	5/15
	Indiana	Y	27820 FQ	30410 MW	36360 TQ	USBLS	5/15
	Gary PMSA, IN	Y	25840 FQ	29320 MW	34050 TQ	USBLS	5/15
	Indianapolis-Carmel-Anderson						
	MSA, IN	Y	27830 FQ	31120 MW	37580 TQ	USBLS	5/15
	Iowa	Y	39080 FQ	49190 MW	55960 TQ	USBLS	5/15
	Des Moines-West Des Moines						
	MSA, IA	Y	43570 FQ	52030 MW	56120 TQ	USBLS	5/15
	Kansas	Y	28530 FQ	31510 MW	38280 TQ	USBLS	5/15
	Wichita MSA, KS	Y	28530 FQ	31330 MW	35050 TQ	USBLS	5/15
	Kentucky	Y	24930 FQ	29130 MW	39400 TQ	USBLS	5/15
	Louisville-Jefferson County						
	MSA, KY-IN	Y	26200 FQ	29900 MW	39630 TQ	USBLS	5/15
	Louisiana	Y	26210 FQ	31620 MW	41540 TQ	USBLS	5/15
	Baton Rouge MSA, LA	Y	26960 FQ	32650 MW	43210 TQ	USBLS	5/15
	New Orleans-Metairie MSA,						
	LA	Y	26590 FQ	28610 MW	30620 TQ	USBLS	5/15
	Maine	Y	30330 FQ	35620 MW	41230 TQ	USBLS	5/15
	Portland-South Portland MSA,						
	ME	Y	30350 FQ	36450 MW	44060 TQ	USBLS	5/15
	Maryland	Y	40318 AE	45518 MW	48118 AEX	MDBLS	4/16
	Baltimore-Columbia-Towson						
	MSA, MD	Y	41680 FQ	43200 MW	44820 TQ	USBLS	5/15
	Salisbury MSA, MD-DE	Y	37700 FQ	43180 MW	44810 TQ	USBLS	5/15
	Massachusetts	Y	62460 FQ	69260 MW	75530 TQ	USBLS	5/15
	Michigan	Y	42900 FQ	52400 MW	52410 TQ	USBLS	5/15
	Detroit-Dearborn-Livonia						
	PMSA, MI	Y	36730 FQ	46570 MW	52410 TQ	USBLS	5/15
	Grand Rapids-Wyoming MSA,						
	MI	Y	45080 FQ	52410 MW	63490 TQ	USBLS	5/15
	Minnesota	Y	41051 FQ	47343 MW	54553 TQ	MNBLS	1/16-3/16
	Minneapolis-St. Paul-						
	Bloomington MSA, MN-WI	Y	41728 FQ	48696 MW	55826 TQ	MNBLS	1/16-3/16
	Mississippi	Y	22170 FQ	24630 MW	29700 TQ	USBLS	5/15
	Jackson MSA, MS	Y	22530 FQ	24920 MW	30270 TQ	USBLS	5/15
	Missouri	Y	28820 FQ	29610 MW	31600 TQ	USBLS	5/15
	Kansas City MSA, MO-KS	Y	28630 FQ	31070 MW	38290 TQ	USBLS	5/15
	St. Louis MSA, MO-IL	Y	32320 FQ	38860 MW	54470 TQ	USBLS	5/15
	Montana	Y	30690 FQ	34980 MW	39570 TQ	USBLS	5/15
	Nebraska	Y	32210 FQ	36200 MW	42805 TQ	NEBLS	7/16-9/16
	Omaha-Council Bluffs MSA,						
	NE-IA	Y	35125 FQ	44055 MW	56610 TQ	NEBLS	7/16-9/16
	Nevada	Y	42580 FQ	50130 MW	71040 TQ	USBLS	5/15
	Las Vegas-Henderson-Paradise						
	MSA, NV	Y	44700 FQ	59470 MW	82790 TQ	USBLS	5/15
	New Hampshire	H	16.29 AE	21.15 MW	23.15 AEX	NHBLS	6/16
	New Jersey	Y	57700 FQ	73760 MW	83650 TQ	USBLS	5/15
	Camden PMSA, NJ	Y	59610 FQ	68380 MW	79030 TQ	USBLS	5/15
	Newark PMSA, NJ-PA	Y	47010 FQ	70700 MW	83650 TQ	USBLS	5/15
	New Mexico	Y	28020 FQ	31160 MW	37070 TQ	USBLS	5/15
	Albuquerque MSA, NM	Y	28480 FQ	32560 MW	38170 TQ	USBLS	5/15
	New York	Y	47700 AE	63650 MW	69700 AEX	NYBLS	1/16-3/16
	Buffalo-Cheektowaga-Niagara						
	Falls MSA, NY	Y	53010 FQ	61500 MW	70900 TQ	USBLS	5/15
	Nassau County-Suffolk County						
	PMSA, NY	Y	69310 FQ	84270 MW	93100 TQ	USBLS	5/15

AE	Average entry wage	AWR	Average wage range	H	Hourly	LR	Low end range	MTC	Median total compensation	TCC	Total cash compensation
AEX	Average experienced wage	B	Biweekly	HI	Highest wage paid	M	Monthly	MW	Median wage paid	TQ	Third quartile wage
ATC	Average total compensation	D	Daily	HR	High range	MCC	Median cash compensation	MWR	Median wage range	W	Weekly
AW	Average wage paid	FQ	First quartile wage	LO	Lowest wage paid	ME	Median entry wage	S	See annotated source	Y	Yearly

Occupation/Type/Industry	Location	Per	Low	Mid	High	Source	Date
Correctional Officer and Jailer	New York-Jersey City-White						
	Plains PMSA, NY-NJ	Y	53700 FQ	67900 MW	76560 TQ	USBLS	5/15
	Rochester MSA, NY	Y	51130 FQ	60580 MW	70410 TQ	USBLS	5/15
	North Carolina	Y	30050 FQ	31050 MW	35300 TQ	USBLS	5/15
	Charlotte-Concord-Gastonia						
	MSA, NC-SC	Y	31940 FQ	35980 MW	42380 TQ	USBLS	5/15
	Raleigh MSA, NC	Y	31040 FQ	31370 MW	34500 TQ	USBLS	5/15
	North Dakota	Y	34260 FQ	38170 MW	44310 TQ	USBLS	5/15
	Fargo MSA, ND-MN	Y	35680 FQ	41100 MW	47480 TQ	USBLS	5/15
	Ohio	Y	37130 FQ	43210 MW	45100 TQ	USBLS	5/15
	Cincinnati MSA, OH-KY-IN	Y	34140 FQ	40090 MW	44580 TQ	USBLS	5/15
	Cleveland-Elyria MSA, OH	Y	37280 FQ	43210 MW	45820 TQ	USBLS	5/15
	Columbus MSA, OH	Y	38490 FQ	43220 MW	44910 TQ	USBLS	5/15
	Oklahoma	Y	28010 FQ	33990 MW	39870 TQ	USBLS	5/15
	Oklahoma City MSA, OK	Y	33590 FQ	39000 MW	48520 TQ	USBLS	5/15
	Tulsa MSA, OK	Y	26660 FQ	30250 MW	35710 TQ	USBLS	5/15
	Oregon	H	23.23 FQ	27.54 MW	29.74 TQ	ORBLS	2016
	Portland-Vancouver-Hillsboro						
	MSA, OR-WA	Y	51230 FQ	61040 MW	71060 TQ	USBLS	5/15
	Pennsylvania	Y	38590 FQ	49670 MW	62330 TQ	USBLS	5/15
	Allentown-Bethlehem-Easton						
	MSA, PA-NJ	Y	39870 FQ	51560 MW	59530 TQ	USBLS	5/15
	Harrisburg-Carlisle MSA, PA	Y	42800 FQ	54950 MW	65170 TQ	USBLS	5/15
	Montgomery County-Bucks						
	County-Chester County						
	PMSA, PA	Y	38600 FQ	49980 MW	63130 TQ	USBLS	5/15
	Philadelphia PMSA, PA	Y	33510 FQ	36550 MW	41520 TQ	USBLS	5/15
	Pittsburgh MSA, PA	Y	43670 FQ	52560 MW	66440 TQ	USBLS	5/15
	South Carolina	Y	27870 FQ	30390 MW	36460 TQ	USBLS	5/15
	Charleston-North Charleston						
	MSA, SC	Y	29260 FQ	32900 MW	37000 TQ	USBLS	5/15
	Columbia MSA, SC	Y	27860 FQ	29260 MW	32890 TQ	USBLS	5/15
	Greenville-Anderson-Mauldin						
	MSA, SC	Y	28690 FQ	32480 MW	37000 TQ	USBLS	5/15
	South Dakota	Y	29370 FQ	34500 MW	39270 TQ	USBLS	5/15
	Tennessee	Y	26260 FQ	29510 MW	35740 TQ	USBLS	5/15
	Knoxville MSA, TN	Y	26570 FQ	28920 MW	31740 TQ	USBLS	5/15
	Nashville-Davidson–						
	Murfreesboro–Franklin						
	MSA, TN	Y	27080 FQ	29680 MW	34410 TQ	USBLS	5/15
	Texas	Y	33690 FQ	38020 MW	39180 TQ	USBLS	5/15
	Dallas-Plano-Irving PMSA, TX	Y	34650 FQ	38290 MW	46530 TQ	USBLS	5/15
	Fort Worth-Arlington PMSA,						
	TX	Y	33720 FQ	36710 MW	39200 TQ	USBLS	5/15
	Houston-The Woodlands-						
	Sugar Land MSA, TX	Y	35870 FQ	39180 MW	46770 TQ	USBLS	5/15
	San Antonio-New Braunfels						
	MSA, TX	Y	33910 FQ	38030 MW	42280 TQ	USBLS	5/15
	Utah	Y	34680 FQ	37900 MW	46300 TQ	USBLS	5/15
	Ogden-Clearfield MSA, UT	Y	36530 FQ	42610 MW	49360 TQ	USBLS	5/15
	Salt Lake City MSA, UT	Y	34360 FQ	37060 MW	45800 TQ	USBLS	5/15
	Virginia	Y	32570 FQ	35030 MW	39850 TQ	USBLS	5/15
	Richmond MSA, VA	Y	32630 FQ	35020 MW	40190 TQ	USBLS	5/15
	Virginia Beach-Norfolk-						
	Newport News MSA, VA-NC	Y	33440 FQ	37460 MW	43920 TQ	USBLS	5/15
	Washington	H	21.79 FQ	22.93 MW	28.63 TQ	WABLS	3/16
	Seattle-Bellevue-Everett						
	PMSA, WA	H	22.36 FQ	26.52 MW	33.29 TQ	WABLS	3/16
	Tacoma-Lakewood PMSA, WA	H	22.37 FQ	25.81 MW	34.37 TQ	WABLS	3/16
	West Virginia	Y	23160 FQ	28830 MW	42730 TQ	USBLS	5/15
	Huntington-Ashland MSA,						
	WV-KY-OH	Y	22760 FQ	28830 MW	50120 TQ	USBLS	5/15
	Wisconsin	Y	36740 FQ	41770 MW	47870 TQ	USBLS	5/15
	Madison MSA, WI	Y	34970 FQ	39980 MW	45610 TQ	USBLS	5/15
	Milwaukee-Waukesha-West						
	Allis MSA, WI	Y	36760 FQ	41550 MW	46960 TQ	USBLS	5/15
	Wyoming	Y	34360 FQ	39830 MW	47330 TQ	USBLS	5/15
	Puerto Rico	Y	22040 FQ	26490 MW	28930 TQ	USBLS	5/15
Correspondence Clerk	Alabama	Y	22580 AE	32093 AW	36854 AEX	ALBLS	6/16
	Birmingham-Hoover MSA, AL	Y	23054 AE	30557 AW	34309 AEX	ALBLS	6/16
	Arizona	Y	34080 FQ	41640 MW	48310 TQ	USBLS	5/15

AE Average entry wage	**AWR** Average wage range	**H** Hourly	**LR** Low end range	**MTC** Median total compensation	**TCC** Total cash compensation
AEX Average experienced wage	**B** Biweekly	**HI** Highest wage paid	**M** Monthly	**MW** Median wage paid	**TQ** Third quartile wage
ATC Average total compensation	**D** Daily	**HR** High end range	**MCC** Median cash compensation	**MWR** Median wage range	**W** Weekly
AW Average wage paid	**FQ** First quartile wage	**LO** Lowest wage paid	**ME** Median entry wage	**S** See annotated source	**Y** Yearly

Correspondence Clerk

Occupation/Type/Industry	Location	Per	Low	Mid	High	Source	Date
Correspondence Clerk	Phoenix-Mesa-Scottsdale						
	MSA, AZ	Y	34590 FQ	42360 MW	48670 TQ	USBLS	5/15
	Arkansas	Y	26900 FQ	29970 MW	35010 TQ	USBLS	5/15
	California	H	16.03 FQ	18.60 MW	22.26 TQ	CABLS	1/16-3/16
	Anaheim-Santa Ana-Irvine						
	PMSA, CA	H	16.60 FQ	19.01 MW	21.80 TQ	CABLS	1/16-3/16
	Los Angeles-Long Beach-						
	Glendale PMSA, CA	H	18.71 FQ	25.59 MW	28.75 TQ	CABLS	1/16-3/16
	Riverside-San Bernardino-						
	Ontario MSA, CA	H	11.31 FQ	12.94 MW	14.61 TQ	CABLS	1/16-3/16
	Sacramento–Roseville–						
	Arden-Arcade MSA, CA	H	14.58 FQ	16.66 MW	18.59 TQ	CABLS	1/16-3/16
	Colorado	Y	34150 FQ	39810 MW	47060 TQ	USBLS	5/15
	Denver-Aurora-Lakewood						
	MSA, CO	Y	37270 FQ	43990 MW	50220 TQ	USBLS	5/15
	Connecticut	Y		41394 MW		CTBLS	1/16-3/16
	Hartford-West Hartford-East						
	Hartford MSA, CT	Y	31220 FQ	41670 MW	47590 TQ	USBLS	5/15
	Washington-Arlington-						
	Alexandria PMSA, DC-VA-						
	MD-WV	Y	33260 FQ	39010 MW	55690 TQ	USBLS	5/15
	Florida	H	13.11 AE	16.83 MW	19.26 AEX	FLBLS	7/16-9/16
	Fort Lauderdale-Pompano						
	Beach-Deerfield Beach						
	PMSA, FL	H	16.12 AE	17.74 MW	18.54 AEX	FLBLS	7/16-9/16
	Orlando-Kissimmee-Sanford						
	MSA, FL	H	13.44 AE	14.90 MW	17.06 AEX	FLBLS	7/16-9/16
	Tampa-St. Petersburg-						
	Clearwater MSA, FL	H	11.89 AE	17.29 MW	19.90 AEX	FLBLS	7/16-9/16
	Georgia	Y	28450 FQ	36240 MW	45750 TQ	USBLS	5/15
	Atlanta-Sandy Springs-						
	Roswell MSA, GA	Y	35890 FQ	43630 MW	49130 TQ	USBLS	5/15
	Illinois	Y	31710 FQ	36640 MW	43780 TQ	USBLS	5/15
	Chicago-Naperville-Arlington						
	Heights PMSA, IL	Y	31710 FQ	36120 MW	43050 TQ	USBLS	5/15
	Indiana	Y	27800 FQ	31740 MW	37570 TQ	USBLS	5/15
	Indianapolis-Carmel-Anderson						
	MSA, IN	Y	31480 FQ	34750 MW	38120 TQ	USBLS	5/15
	Iowa	Y	26980 FQ	30190 MW	35990 TQ	USBLS	5/15
	Kansas	Y	28250 FQ	32780 MW	36680 TQ	USBLS	5/15
	Kentucky	Y	34140 FQ	40140 MW	47660 TQ	USBLS	5/15
	Louisville-Jefferson County						
	MSA, KY-IN	Y	33530 FQ	37860 MW	46020 TQ	USBLS	5/15
	Maryland	Y	23217 AE	33424 MW	38528 AEX	MDBLS	4/16
	Baltimore-Columbia-Towson						
	MSA, MD	Y	21870 FQ	27260 MW	36200 TQ	USBLS	5/15
	Massachusetts	Y	41490 FQ	46360 MW	52350 TQ	USBLS	5/15
	Boston-Cambridge-Newton						
	NECTA, MA	Y	42110 FQ	46230 MW	50750 TQ	USBLS	5/15
	Michigan	Y	28820 FQ	34660 MW	40850 TQ	USBLS	5/15
	Minnesota	Y	35506 FQ	42352 MW	58249 TQ	MNBLS	1/16-3/16
	Minneapolis-St. Paul-						
	Bloomington MSA, MN-WI	Y	33352 FQ	39753 MW	56935 TQ	MNBLS	1/16-3/16
	Missouri	Y	30850 FQ	35830 MW	42420 TQ	USBLS	5/15
	Kansas City MSA, MO-KS	Y	32460 FQ	35020 MW	37570 TQ	USBLS	5/15
	St. Louis MSA, MO-IL	Y	30790 FQ	36690 MW	44690 TQ	USBLS	5/15
	Nebraska	Y	33855 FQ	40905 MW	47380 TQ	NEBLS	7/16-9/16
	Omaha-Council Bluffs MSA,						
	NE-IA	Y	35830 FQ	42095 MW	47970 TQ	NEBLS	7/16-9/16
	New Jersey	Y	35670 FQ	41910 MW	47720 TQ	USBLS	5/15
	Camden PMSA, NJ	Y	29750 FQ	36840 MW	44270 TQ	USBLS	5/15
	Newark PMSA, NJ-PA	Y	36260 FQ	42280 MW	48310 TQ	USBLS	5/15
	New York	Y	32800 AE	41850 MW	47930 AEX	NYBLS	1/16-3/16
	Nassau County-Suffolk County						
	PMSA, NY	Y	39810 FQ	44200 MW	48590 TQ	USBLS	5/15
	New York-Jersey City-White						
	Plains PMSA, NY-NJ	Y	35380 FQ	41740 MW	48670 TQ	USBLS	5/15
	North Carolina	Y	29730 FQ	34150 MW	37880 TQ	USBLS	5/15
	Ohio	Y	29550 FQ	35230 MW	41870 TQ	USBLS	5/15
	Cincinnati MSA, OH-KY-IN	Y	35480 FQ	42800 MW	47970 TQ	USBLS	5/15
	Cleveland-Elyria MSA, OH	Y	28730 FQ	32680 MW	36680 TQ	USBLS	5/15
	Columbus MSA, OH	Y	27890 FQ	30810 MW	36720 TQ	USBLS	5/15

AE	Average entry wage	AWR	Average wage range	H	Hourly
AEX	Average experienced wage	B	Biweekly	HI	Highest wage paid
ATC	Average total compensation	D	Daily	HR	High end range
AW	Average wage paid	FQ	First quartile wage	LO	Lowest wage paid

LR	Low end range	MTC	Median total compensation
M	Monthly	MW	Median wage paid
MCC	Median cash compensation	MWR	Median wage range
ME	Median entry wage	S	See annotated source

TCC	Total cash compensation	
TQ	Third quartile wage	
W	Weekly	
Y	Yearly	

Occupation/Type/Industry	Location	Per	Low	Mid	High	Source	Date
Correspondence Clerk	Oklahoma	Y	26200 FQ	29390 MW	36030 TQ	USBLS	5/15
	Tulsa MSA, OK	Y	30340 FQ	35840 MW	42500 TQ	USBLS	5/15
	Oregon	H	16.25 FQ	17.61 MW	18.80 TQ	ORBLS	2016
	Portland-Vancouver-Hillsboro MSA, OR-WA	Y	32980 FQ	35580 MW	38180 TQ	USBLS	5/15
	Pennsylvania	Y	28000 FQ	33810 MW	39260 TQ	USBLS	5/15
	Harrisburg-Carlisle MSA, PA	Y	29560 FQ	35430 MW	40670 TQ	USBLS	5/15
	Montgomery County-Bucks County-Chester County PMSA, PA	Y	29230 FQ	34780 MW	40740 TQ	USBLS	5/15
	Philadelphia PMSA, PA	Y	27970 FQ	33940 MW	40370 TQ	USBLS	5/15
	Pittsburgh MSA, PA	Y	28570 FQ	33830 MW	38770 TQ	USBLS	5/15
	South Dakota	Y	24190 FQ	28160 MW	32900 TQ	USBLS	5/15
	Sioux Falls MSA, SD	Y	24300 FQ	28370 MW	33060 TQ	USBLS	5/15
	Knoxville MSA, TN	Y	23630 FQ	29660 MW	35540 TQ	USBLS	5/15
	Texas	Y	26020 FQ	32320 MW	37500 TQ	USBLS	5/15
	Austin-Round Rock MSA, TX	Y	17590 FQ	19550 MW	33930 TQ	USBLS	5/15
	Dallas-Plano-Irving PMSA, TX	Y	26230 FQ	32460 MW	37510 TQ	USBLS	5/15
	Fort Worth-Arlington PMSA, TX	Y	29970 FQ	35110 MW	39900 TQ	USBLS	5/15
	Houston-The Woodlands-Sugar Land MSA, TX	Y	25940 FQ	32120 MW	37660 TQ	USBLS	5/15
	San Antonio-New Braunfels MSA, TX	Y	25940 FQ	31040 MW	36530 TQ	USBLS	5/15
	Utah	Y	31660 FQ	35680 MW	40380 TQ	USBLS	5/15
	Salt Lake City MSA, UT	Y	32700 FQ	36160 MW	40280 TQ	USBLS	5/15
	Virginia	Y	29400 FQ	34210 MW	39150 TQ	USBLS	5/15
	Virginia Beach-Norfolk-Newport News MSA, VA-NC	Y	28200 FQ	31580 MW	36110 TQ	USBLS	5/15
	Washington	H	16.25 FQ	17.96 MW	19.31 TQ	WABLS	3/16
	Seattle-Bellevue-Everett PMSA, WA	H	16.36 FQ	17.76 MW	19.15 TQ	WABLS	3/16
	Wisconsin	Y	27700 FQ	34420 MW	41560 TQ	USBLS	5/15
Cosmetic Art Examiner							
State Government	North Carolina	Y	29826 LO		45099 HI	NCGOV	7/1/16
Cosmetology Inspector							
State Government	Ohio	H	17.65 LO		24.08 HI	OHGOV	2015
Cost Estimator	Alabama	Y	39533 AE	62307 AW	73695 AEX	ALBLS	6/16
	Birmingham-Hoover MSA, AL	Y	40281 AE	64900 AW	77200 AEX	ALBLS	6/16
	Alaska	Y	62350 FQ	82790 MW	109740 TQ	USBLS	5/15
	Anchorage MSA, AK	Y	66930 FQ	87000 MW	116190 TQ	USBLS	5/15
	Arizona	Y	45920 FQ	61590 MW	77580 TQ	USBLS	5/15
	Phoenix-Mesa-Scottsdale MSA, AZ	Y	46990 FQ	63560 MW	78300 TQ	USBLS	5/15
	Tucson MSA, AZ	Y	44720 FQ	55990 MW	71700 TQ	USBLS	5/15
	Arkansas	Y	42270 FQ	52700 MW	64200 TQ	USBLS	5/15
	Little Rock-North Little Rock-Conway MSA, AR	Y	43050 FQ	52960 MW	64620 TQ	USBLS	5/15
	California	H	23.52 FQ	31.97 MW	43.48 TQ	CABLS	1/16-3/16
	Anaheim-Santa Ana-Irvine PMSA, CA	H	24.02 FQ	30.96 MW	42.22 TQ	CABLS	1/16-3/16
	Los Angeles-Long Beach-Glendale PMSA, CA	H	20.24 FQ	29.76 MW	42.88 TQ	CABLS	1/16-3/16
	Oakland-Hayward-Berkeley PMSA, CA	H	26.86 FQ	36.14 MW	49.02 TQ	CABLS	1/16-3/16
	Riverside-San Bernardino-Ontario MSA, CA	H	23.66 FQ	30.20 MW	37.77 TQ	CABLS	1/16-3/16
	Sacramento–Roseville–Arden-Arcade MSA, CA	H	21.41 FQ	30.45 MW	42.10 TQ	CABLS	1/16-3/16
	San Diego-Carlsbad MSA, CA	H	24.39 FQ	32.77 MW	43.27 TQ	CABLS	1/16-3/16
	San Francisco-Redwood City-South San Francisco PMSA, CA	H	29.18 FQ	38.98 MW	54.79 TQ	CABLS	1/16-3/16
	Colorado	Y	46870 FQ	61910 MW	79460 TQ	USBLS	5/15
	Denver-Aurora-Lakewood MSA, CO	Y	48890 FQ	66240 MW	82970 TQ	USBLS	5/15
	Connecticut	Y		75298 MW		CTBLS	1/16-3/16
	Bridgeport-Stamford-Norwalk MSA, CT	Y	48770 FQ	66040 MW	82980 TQ	USBLS	5/15

AE	Average entry wage	AWR	Average wage range	H	Hourly
AEX	Average experienced wage	B	Biweekly	HI	Highest wage paid
ATC	Average total compensation	D	Daily	HR	High end range
AW	Average wage paid	FQ	First quartile wage	LO	Lowest wage paid

LR	Low end range	MTC	Median total compensation
M	Monthly	MW	Median wage paid
MCC	Median cash compensation	MWR	Median wage range
ME	Median entry wage	S	See annotated source

TCC	Total cash compensation
TQ	Third quartile wage
W	Weekly
Y	Yearly

Occupation/Type/Industry	Location	Per	Low	Mid	High	Source	Date
Cost Estimator	Hartford-West Hartford-East Hartford MSA, CT	Y	60240 FQ	79000 MW	98060 TQ	USBLS	5/15
	Delaware	Y	51010 FQ	65090 MW	84990 TQ	USBLS	5/15
	Wilmington PMSA, DE-MD-NJ	Y	56150 FQ	69540 MW	85830 TQ	USBLS	5/15
	District of Columbia	Y	57130 FQ	72850 MW	95100 TQ	USBLS	5/15
	Washington-Arlington-Alexandria PMSA, DC-VA-MD-WV	Y	53320 FQ	69950 MW	89350 TQ	USBLS	5/15
	Florida	H	17.63 AE	27.26 MW	34.07 AEX	FLBLS	7/16-9/16
	Fort Lauderdale-Pompano Beach-Deerfield Beach PMSA, FL	H	22.12 AE	30.00 MW	36.05 AEX	FLBLS	7/16-9/16
	Miami-Miami Beach-Kendall PMSA, FL	H	15.79 AE	22.25 MW	29.29 AEX	FLBLS	7/16-9/16
	Orlando-Kissimmee-Sanford MSA, FL	H	16.89 AE	28.77 MW	37.54 AEX	FLBLS	7/16-9/16
	Tampa-St. Petersburg-Clearwater MSA, FL	H	16.41 AE	27.16 MW	34.46 AEX	FLBLS	7/16-9/16
	Georgia	Y	41800 FQ	57340 MW	75620 TQ	USBLS	5/15
	Atlanta-Sandy Springs-Roswell MSA, GA	Y	43940 FQ	60170 MW	78820 TQ	USBLS	5/15
	Augusta-Richmond County MSA, GA-SC	Y	40820 FQ	55040 MW	72530 TQ	USBLS	5/15
	Hawaii	Y	45650 FQ	61400 MW	87170 TQ	USBLS	5/15
	Urban Honolulu MSA, HI	Y	45980 FQ	63440 MW	91860 TQ	USBLS	5/15
	Idaho	Y	37420 FQ	50530 MW	61130 TQ	USBLS	5/15
	Boise City MSA, ID	Y	42540 FQ	53470 MW	62160 TQ	USBLS	5/15
	Illinois	Y	49730 FQ	66340 MW	88170 TQ	USBLS	5/15
	Chicago-Naperville-Arlington Heights PMSA, IL	Y	51300 FQ	68440 MW	91660 TQ	USBLS	5/15
	Lake County-Kenosha County PMSA, IL-WI	Y	52570 FQ	68250 MW	89560 TQ	USBLS	5/15
	Indiana	Y	43700 FQ	58400 MW	76900 TQ	USBLS	5/15
	Gary PMSA, IN	Y	55730 FQ	74060 MW	99850 TQ	USBLS	5/15
	Indianapolis-Carmel-Anderson MSA, IN	Y	46420 FQ	61660 MW	80230 TQ	USBLS	5/15
	Iowa	Y	42550 FQ	54220 MW	70660 TQ	USBLS	5/15
	Des Moines-West Des Moines MSA, IA	Y	45340 FQ	54890 MW	70720 TQ	USBLS	5/15
	Kansas	Y	49610 FQ	61860 MW	76650 TQ	USBLS	5/15
	Wichita MSA, KS	Y	51860 FQ	60490 MW	75860 TQ	USBLS	5/15
	Kentucky	Y	43340 FQ	56790 MW	73850 TQ	USBLS	5/15
	Louisville-Jefferson County MSA, KY-IN	Y	47810 FQ	61250 MW	77780 TQ	USBLS	5/15
	Louisiana	Y	41440 FQ	52590 MW	68200 TQ	USBLS	5/15
	Baton Rouge MSA, LA	Y	41880 FQ	52290 MW	66740 TQ	USBLS	5/15
	New Orleans-Metairie MSA, LA	Y	38760 FQ	50460 MW	63410 TQ	USBLS	5/15
	Maine	Y	45660 FQ	58030 MW	72290 TQ	USBLS	5/15
	Portland-South Portland MSA, ME	Y	45270 FQ	56300 MW	71210 TQ	USBLS	5/15
	Maryland	Y	42856 AE	71196 MW	85365 AEX	MDBLS	4/16
	Baltimore-Columbia-Towson MSA, MD	Y	52130 FQ	67070 MW	86190 TQ	USBLS	5/15
	Salisbury MSA, MD-DE	Y	43770 FQ	50890 MW	70020 TQ	USBLS	5/15
	Massachusetts	Y	50580 FQ	65110 MW	89840 TQ	USBLS	5/15
	Boston-Cambridge-Newton NECTA, MA	Y	55110 FQ	71720 MW	96130 TQ	USBLS	5/15
	Worcester MSA, MA-CT	Y	42870 FQ	55100 MW	79150 TQ	USBLS	5/15
	Michigan	Y	44400 FQ	58470 MW	76160 TQ	USBLS	5/15
	Detroit-Dearborn-Livonia PMSA, MI	Y	48290 FQ	64450 MW	84560 TQ	USBLS	5/15
	Grand Rapids-Wyoming MSA, MI	Y	44030 FQ	58020 MW	73900 TQ	USBLS	5/15
	Minnesota	Y	47289 FQ	59544 MW	73617 TQ	MNBLS	1/16-3/16
	Minneapolis-St. Paul-Bloomington MSA, MN-WI	Y	51862 FQ	62094 MW	76218 TQ	MNBLS	1/16-3/16
	Mississippi	Y	42660 FQ	57320 MW	72950 TQ	USBLS	5/15
	Jackson MSA, MS	Y	43930 FQ	63060 MW	74380 TQ	USBLS	5/15
	Missouri	Y	47550 FQ	65150 MW	81980 TQ	USBLS	5/15
	Kansas City MSA, MO-KS	Y	49030 FQ	64760 MW	81620 TQ	USBLS	5/15

AE Average entry wage	**AWR** Average wage range	**H** Hourly	**LR** Low end range	**MTC** Median total compensation	**TCC** Total cash compensation
AEX Average experienced wage	**B** Biweekly	**HI** Highest wage paid	**M** Monthly	**MW** Median wage paid	**TQ** Third quartile wage
ATC Average total compensation	**D** Daily	**HR** High end range	**MCC** Median cash compensation	**MWR** Median wage range	**W** Weekly
AW Average wage paid	**FQ** First quartile wage	**LO** Lowest wage paid	**ME** Median entry wage	**S** See annotated source	**Y** Yearly

Occupation/Type/Industry	Location	Per	Low	Mid	High	Source	Date
Cost Estimator	St. Louis MSA, MO-IL	Y	52980 FQ	69790 MW	85710 TQ	USBLS	5/15
	Montana	Y	41280 FQ	51380 MW	62280 TQ	USBLS	5/15
	Billings MSA, MT	Y	41860 FQ	48890 MW	61780 TQ	USBLS	5/15
	Nebraska	Y	40810 FQ	53740 MW	68345 TQ	NEBLS	7/16-9/16
	Omaha-Council Bluffs MSA, NE-IA	Y	44310 FQ	56685 MW	73485 TQ	NEBLS	7/16-9/16
	Nevada	Y	44530 FQ	56300 MW	74790 TQ	USBLS	5/15
	Las Vegas-Henderson-Paradise MSA, NV	Y	46040 FQ	57410 MW	75540 TQ	USBLS	5/15
	New Hampshire	H	22.72 AE	30.89 MW	39.61 AEX	NHBLS	6/16
	Manchester NECTA, NH	H	24.99 AE	35.75 MW	41.70 AEX	NHBLS	6/16
	Nashua NECTA, NH-MA	Y	51330 FQ	59220 MW	72340 TQ	USBLS	5/15
	New Jersey	Y	54540 FQ	69590 MW	94960 TQ	USBLS	5/15
	Camden PMSA, NJ	Y	53230 FQ	67170 MW	87920 TQ	USBLS	5/15
	Newark PMSA, NJ-PA	Y	57190 FQ	75180 MW	100320 TQ	USBLS	5/15
	Trenton MSA, NJ	Y	53230 FQ	61550 MW	81060 TQ	USBLS	5/15
	New Mexico	Y	40770 FQ	50950 MW	69440 TQ	USBLS	5/15
	Albuquerque MSA, NM	Y	43070 FQ	51720 MW	68810 TQ	USBLS	5/15
	New York	Y	41680 AE	69800 MW	94570 AEX	NYBLS	1/16-3/16
	Buffalo-Cheektowaga-Niagara Falls MSA, NY	Y	44430 FQ	56190 MW	71230 TQ	USBLS	5/15
	Nassau County-Suffolk County PMSA, NY	Y	41070 FQ	66790 MW	92480 TQ	USBLS	5/15
	New York-Jersey City-White Plains PMSA, NY-NJ	Y	56920 FQ	77900 MW	102090 TQ	USBLS	5/15
	Rochester MSA, NY	Y	44750 FQ	56230 MW	72840 TQ	USBLS	5/15
	North Carolina	Y	42640 FQ	56780 MW	74850 TQ	USBLS	5/15
	Charlotte-Concord-Gastonia MSA, NC-SC	Y	45070 FQ	59870 MW	77860 TQ	USBLS	5/15
	Raleigh MSA, NC	Y	48510 FQ	61420 MW	75950 TQ	USBLS	5/15
	North Dakota	Y	41770 FQ	56410 MW	69140 TQ	USBLS	5/15
	Fargo MSA, ND-MN	Y	43410 FQ	54830 MW	62850 TQ	USBLS	5/15
	Ohio	Y	43040 FQ	56610 MW	71580 TQ	USBLS	5/15
	Cincinnati MSA, OH-KY-IN	Y	46620 FQ	60060 MW	75960 TQ	USBLS	5/15
	Cleveland-Elyria MSA, OH	Y	43850 FQ	57370 MW	72740 TQ	USBLS	5/15
	Columbus MSA, OH	Y	42380 FQ	58360 MW	73920 TQ	USBLS	5/15
	Oklahoma	Y	42620 FQ	55610 MW	69640 TQ	USBLS	5/15
	Oklahoma City MSA, OK	Y	42680 FQ	55930 MW	72020 TQ	USBLS	5/15
	Tulsa MSA, OK	Y	45720 FQ	57390 MW	71140 TQ	USBLS	5/15
	Oregon	H	21.35 FQ	28.77 MW	37.17 TQ	ORBLS	2016
	Portland-Vancouver-Hillsboro MSA, OR-WA	Y	43270 FQ	61590 MW	77070 TQ	USBLS	5/15
	Pennsylvania	Y	48230 FQ	60310 MW	76550 TQ	USBLS	5/15
	Allentown-Bethlehem-Easton MSA, PA-NJ	Y	46720 FQ	57660 MW	80570 TQ	USBLS	5/15
	Harrisburg-Carlisle MSA, PA	Y	48400 FQ	59040 MW	74750 TQ	USBLS	5/15
	Montgomery County-Bucks County-Chester County PMSA, PA	Y	52510 FQ	62910 MW	81600 TQ	USBLS	5/15
	Philadelphia PMSA, PA	Y	53700 FQ	70740 MW	90420 TQ	USBLS	5/15
	Pittsburgh MSA, PA	Y	51270 FQ	63710 MW	76190 TQ	USBLS	5/15
	Rhode Island	Y	48650 FQ	62000 MW	75190 TQ	USBLS	5/15
	Providence-Warwick MSA, RI-MA	Y	47560 FQ	61870 MW	75940 TQ	USBLS	5/15
	South Carolina	Y	40010 FQ	52970 MW	69260 TQ	USBLS	5/15
	Charleston-North Charleston MSA, SC	Y	44580 FQ	56120 MW	69940 TQ	USBLS	5/15
	Columbia MSA, SC	Y	40120 FQ	47870 MW	61060 TQ	USBLS	5/15
	Greenville-Anderson-Mauldin MSA, SC	Y	37820 FQ	49900 MW	70150 TQ	USBLS	5/15
	South Dakota	Y	41660 FQ	49930 MW	58780 TQ	USBLS	5/15
	Sioux Falls MSA, SD	Y	41700 FQ	51150 MW	59880 TQ	USBLS	5/15
	Tennessee	Y	41720 FQ	55800 MW	74770 TQ	USBLS	5/15
	Knoxville MSA, TN	Y	40140 FQ	56450 MW	75110 TQ	USBLS	5/15
	Memphis MSA, TN-MS-AR	Y	44240 FQ	58330 MW	83910 TQ	USBLS	5/15
	Nashville-Davidson–Murfreesboro–Franklin MSA, TN	Y	41910 FQ	55710 MW	74170 TQ	USBLS	5/15
	Texas	Y	45890 FQ	61050 MW	79210 TQ	USBLS	5/15
	Austin-Round Rock MSA, TX	Y	47310 FQ	59040 MW	72910 TQ	USBLS	5/15
	Dallas-Plano-Irving PMSA, TX	Y	46870 FQ	62290 MW	80910 TQ	USBLS	5/15

AE	Average entry wage	AWR	Average wage range		H	Hourly		LR	Low end range		MTC	Median total compensation		TCC	Total cash compensation
AEX	Average experienced wage	B	Biweekly		HI	Highest wage paid		M	Monthly		MW	Median wage paid		TQ	Third quartile wage
ATC	Average total compensation	D	Daily		HR	High end range		MCC	Median cash compensation		MWR	Median wage range		W	Weekly
AW	Average wage paid	FQ	First quartile wage		LO	Lowest wage paid		ME	Median entry wage		S	See annotated source		Y	Yearly

Occupation/Type/Industry	Location	Per	Low	Mid	High	Source	Date
Cost Estimator	Fort Worth-Arlington PMSA, TX	Y	46460 FQ	61050 MW	76530 TQ	USBLS	5/15
	Houston-The Woodlands-Sugar Land MSA, TX	Y	48660 FQ	67020 MW	91980 TQ	USBLS	5/15
	San Antonio-New Braunfels MSA, TX	Y	46360 FQ	60890 MW	76710 TQ	USBLS	5/15
	Utah	Y	45380 FQ	59430 MW	76190 TQ	USBLS	5/15
	Ogden-Clearfield MSA, UT	Y	43830 FQ	60570 MW	75890 TQ	USBLS	5/15
	Provo-Orem MSA, UT	Y	31850 FQ	49840 MW	60150 TQ	USBLS	5/15
	Salt Lake City MSA, UT	Y	52810 FQ	64850 MW	83430 TQ	USBLS	5/15
	Vermont	Y	52810 FQ	62650 MW	86350 TQ	USBLS	5/15
	Burlington-South Burlington MSA, VT	Y	59960 FQ	77750 MW	98470 TQ	USBLS	5/15
	Virginia	Y	47000 FQ	61340 MW	79810 TQ	USBLS	5/15
	Richmond MSA, VA	Y	46720 FQ	59200 MW	76160 TQ	USBLS	5/15
	Virginia Beach-Norfolk-Newport News MSA, VA-NC	Y	41380 FQ	55270 MW	73670 TQ	USBLS	5/15
	Washington	H	25.94 FQ	33.52 MW	42.36 TQ	WABLS	3/16
	Seattle-Bellevue-Everett PMSA, WA	H	28.20 FQ	35.59 MW	44.44 TQ	WABLS	3/16
	Tacoma-Lakewood PMSA, WA	H	26.97 FQ	35.61 MW	44.20 TQ	WABLS	3/16
	West Virginia	Y	42500 FQ	58060 MW	74680 TQ	USBLS	5/15
	Huntington-Ashland MSA, WV-KY-OH	Y	44080 FQ	61780 MW	89940 TQ	USBLS	5/15
	Wisconsin	Y	44960 FQ	57640 MW	72820 TQ	USBLS	5/15
	Madison MSA, WI	Y	48310 FQ	61630 MW	76650 TQ	USBLS	5/15
	Milwaukee-Waukesha-West Allis MSA, WI	Y	48340 FQ	62300 MW	77100 TQ	USBLS	5/15
	Wyoming	Y	47130 FQ	63740 MW	77790 TQ	USBLS	5/15
	Cheyenne MSA, WY	Y	40640 FQ	58090 MW	76190 TQ	USBLS	5/15
	Puerto Rico	Y	22950 FQ	31130 MW	44060 TQ	USBLS	5/15
	San Juan-Carolina-Caguas MSA, PR	Y	22860 FQ	30590 MW	43580 TQ	USBLS	5/15
	Guam	Y	41270 FQ	51790 MW	69630 TQ	USBLS	5/15
Costume Attendant	Alabama	Y	20170 AE	27017 AW	30445 AEX	ALBLS	6/16
	California	H	15.47 FQ	24.42 MW	34.75 TQ	CABLS	1/16-3/16
	Connecticut	Y		39739 MW		CTBLS	1/16-3/16
	District of Columbia	Y	31660 FQ	40270 MW	49050 TQ	USBLS	5/15
	Florida	H	9.06 AE	9.89 MW	15.12 AEX	FLBLS	7/16-9/16
	Georgia	Y	28610 FQ	53800 MW	59130 TQ	USBLS	5/15
	Illinois	Y	22770 FQ	31540 MW	43780 TQ	USBLS	5/15
	Indiana	Y	19960 FQ	24520 MW	33270 TQ	USBLS	5/15
	Louisiana	Y	19820 FQ	24020 MW	43120 TQ	USBLS	5/15
	Maryland	Y	25919 AE	39570 MW	46396 AEX	MDBLS	4/16
	Massachusetts	Y	22660 FQ	32400 MW	48610 TQ	USBLS	5/15
	Michigan	Y	19590 FQ	35340 MW	54310 TQ	USBLS	5/15
	Minnesota	Y	40253 FQ	45939 MW	54139 TQ	MNBLS	1/16-3/16
	Missouri	Y	26360 FQ	31970 MW	48420 TQ	USBLS	5/15
	Nevada	Y	40340 FQ	48210 MW	61640 TQ	USBLS	5/15
	New Jersey	Y	29110 FQ	51470 MW	57400 TQ	USBLS	5/15
	New York	Y	36300 AE	71730 MW	102130 AEX	NYBLS	1/16-3/16
	North Carolina	Y	32720 FQ	52720 MW	66990 TQ	USBLS	5/15
	Ohio	Y	23770 FQ	34430 MW	43140 TQ	USBLS	5/15
	Oklahoma	Y	20000 FQ	24290 MW	42880 TQ	USBLS	5/15
	Oregon	H	9.54 FQ	9.61 MW	11.73 TQ	ORBLS	2016
	Pennsylvania	Y	29680 FQ	41880 MW	51310 TQ	USBLS	5/15
	Tennessee	Y	27790 FQ	42120 MW	86110 TQ	USBLS	5/15
	Texas	Y	25900 FQ	36570 MW	49630 TQ	USBLS	5/15
	Utah	Y	19410 FQ	29000 MW	38450 TQ	USBLS	5/15
	Virginia	Y	18540 FQ	23400 MW	30360 TQ	USBLS	5/15
	Washington	H	16.52 FQ	20.31 MW	23.97 TQ	WABLS	3/16
	Wisconsin	Y	22100 FQ	26200 MW	31240 TQ	USBLS	5/15
Costumer							
Made for Television Motion Picture	United States	W	1087 LO			MPEG01	7/31/16-7/29/17
Council Member							
Municipal Government	Bakersfield, CA	Y			1200 HI	CACIT	6/28/16
Municipal Government	Carlsbad, CA	Y			21634 HI	CACIT	6/28/16
Municipal Government	Dos Palos, CA	Y			1800 HI	CACIT	6/28/16
Municipal Government	Detroit, MI	M			6776 HI	DETGOV	2016

AE	Average entry wage	AWR	Average wage range	H	Hourly	LR	Low end range	MTC	Median total compensation	TCC	Total cash compensation
AEX	Average experienced wage	B	Biweekly	HI	Highest wage paid	M	Monthly	MW	Median wage paid	TQ	Third quartile wage
ATC	Average total compensation	D	Daily	HR	High end range	MCC	Median cash compensation	MWR	Median wage range	W	Weekly
AW	Average wage paid	FQ	First quartile wage	LO	Lowest wage paid	ME	Median entry wage	S	See annotated source	Y	Yearly

Occupation/Type/Industry	Location	Per	Low	Mid	High	Source	Date
Council Member							
Municipal Government	Lansing, MI	Y			24240 HI	LSJ16	2017
Municipal Government	Seattle, WA	H			59.08 HI	CSSS	1/1/16
Counter and Rental Clerk	Alabama	Y	17758 AE	26498 AW	30862 AEX	ALBLS	6/16
	Birmingham-Hoover MSA, AL	Y	17831 AE	28018 AW	33117 AEX	ALBLS	6/16
	Alaska	Y	23200 FQ	28360 MW	34690 TQ	USBLS	5/15
	Anchorage MSA, AK	Y	22240 FQ	27440 MW	33200 TQ	USBLS	5/15
	Arizona	Y	19580 FQ	23700 MW	30680 TQ	USBLS	5/15
	Phoenix-Mesa-Scottsdale MSA, AZ	Y	19660 FQ	24090 MW	31110 TQ	USBLS	5/15
	Tucson MSA, AZ	Y	19180 FQ	23040 MW	29540 TQ	USBLS	5/15
	Arkansas	Y	17380 FQ	19070 MW	24110 TQ	USBLS	5/15
	Little Rock-North Little Rock-Conway MSA, AR	Y	17320 FQ	18930 MW	25140 TQ	USBLS	5/15
	California	H	9.97 FQ	12.70 MW	16.90 TQ	CABLS	1/16-3/16
	Anaheim-Santa Ana-Irvine PMSA, CA	H	10.59 FQ	13.81 MW	17.89 TQ	CABLS	1/16-3/16
	Los Angeles-Long Beach-Glendale PMSA, CA	H	9.49 FQ	11.67 MW	15.89 TQ	CABLS	1/16-3/16
	Oakland-Hayward-Berkeley PMSA, CA	H	11.52 FQ	14.02 MW	19.52 TQ	CABLS	1/16-3/16
	Riverside-San Bernardino-Ontario MSA, CA	H	9.66 FQ	12.90 MW	17.34 TQ	CABLS	1/16-3/16
	Sacramento–Roseville–Arden-Arcade MSA, CA	H	10.17 FQ	12.46 MW	16.13 TQ	CABLS	1/16-3/16
	San Diego-Carlsbad MSA, CA	H	10.55 FQ	12.91 MW	16.89 TQ	CABLS	1/16-3/16
	San Francisco-Redwood City-South San Francisco PMSA, CA	H	11.13 FQ	13.83 MW	17.89 TQ	CABLS	1/16-3/16
	Colorado	Y	19400 FQ	25210 MW	33710 TQ	USBLS	5/15
	Denver-Aurora-Lakewood MSA, CO	Y	19240 FQ	24630 MW	32680 TQ	USBLS	5/15
	Connecticut	Y		26121 MW		CTBLS	1/16-3/16
	Bridgeport-Stamford-Norwalk MSA, CT	Y	20020 FQ	26030 MW	40820 TQ	USBLS	5/15
	Hartford-West Hartford-East Hartford MSA, CT	Y	20510 FQ	27860 MW	41290 TQ	USBLS	5/15
	Delaware	Y	22360 FQ	28040 MW	37580 TQ	USBLS	5/15
	Wilmington PMSA, DE-MD-NJ	Y	23450 FQ	29580 MW	43480 TQ	USBLS	5/15
	District of Columbia	Y	23140 FQ	31080 MW	38090 TQ	USBLS	5/15
	Washington-Arlington-Alexandria PMSA, DC-VA-MD-WV	Y	21910 FQ	29740 MW	37610 TQ	USBLS	5/15
	Florida	H	9.34 AE	12.02 MW	15.06 AEX	FLBLS	7/16-9/16
	Fort Lauderdale-Pompano Beach-Deerfield Beach PMSA, FL	H	9.59 AE	12.72 MW	15.35 AEX	FLBLS	7/16-9/16
	Miami-Miami Beach-Kendall PMSA, FL	H	8.97 AE	11.01 MW	13.62 AEX	FLBLS	7/16-9/16
	Orlando-Kissimmee-Sanford MSA, FL	H	9.53 AE	12.14 MW	15.14 AEX	FLBLS	7/16-9/16
	Tampa-St. Petersburg-Clearwater MSA, FL	H	9.72 AE	12.44 MW	15.04 AEX	FLBLS	7/16-9/16
	Georgia	Y	19180 FQ	24640 MW	32150 TQ	USBLS	5/15
	Atlanta-Sandy Springs-Roswell MSA, GA	Y	20170 FQ	26230 MW	34750 TQ	USBLS	5/15
	Augusta-Richmond County MSA, GA-SC	Y	17850 FQ	21480 MW	28330 TQ	USBLS	5/15
	Hawaii	Y	20850 FQ	28370 MW	36430 TQ	USBLS	5/15
	Urban Honolulu MSA, HI	Y	20360 FQ	28960 MW	36790 TQ	USBLS	5/15
	Idaho	Y	18030 FQ	21730 MW	31170 TQ	USBLS	5/15
	Boise City MSA, ID	Y	17750 FQ	20050 MW	30210 TQ	USBLS	5/15
	Illinois	Y	19180 FQ	22110 MW	28790 TQ	USBLS	5/15
	Chicago-Naperville-Arlington Heights PMSA, IL	Y	19360 FQ	22510 MW	28880 TQ	USBLS	5/15
	Lake County-Kenosha County PMSA, IL-WI	Y	18690 FQ	21700 MW	30530 TQ	USBLS	5/15
	Indiana	Y	18780 FQ	24090 MW	33400 TQ	USBLS	5/15
	Gary PMSA, IN	Y	18140 FQ	21730 MW	33300 TQ	USBLS	5/15

AE	Average entry wage	AWR	Average wage range	H	Hourly	LR	Low end range	MTC	Median total compensation	TCC	Total cash compensation
AEX	Average experienced wage	B	Biweekly	HI	Highest wage paid	M	Monthly	MW	Median wage paid	TQ	Third quartile wage
ATC	Average total compensation	D	Daily	HR	High end range	MCC	Median cash compensation	MWR	Median wage range	W	Weekly
AW	Average wage paid	FQ	First quartile wage	LO	Lowest wage paid	ME	Median entry wage	S	See annotated source	Y	Yearly

Occupation/Type/Industry	Location	Per	Low	Mid	High	Source	Date
Counter and Rental Clerk	Indianapolis-Carmel-Anderson						
	MSA, IN	Y	20790 FQ	27090 MW	37910 TQ	USBLS	5/15
	Iowa	Y	18000 FQ	21850 MW	29080 TQ	USBLS	5/15
	Des Moines-West Des Moines						
	MSA, IA	Y	19630 FQ	26960 MW	35960 TQ	USBLS	5/15
	Kansas	Y	19130 FQ	25540 MW	34070 TQ	USBLS	5/15
	Wichita MSA, KS	Y	19260 FQ	26990 MW	34890 TQ	USBLS	5/15
	Kentucky	Y	17590 FQ	19730 MW	28000 TQ	USBLS	5/15
	Louisville-Jefferson County						
	MSA, KY-IN	Y	17800 FQ	20070 MW	28280 TQ	USBLS	5/15
	Louisiana	Y	18940 FQ	23280 MW	29250 TQ	USBLS	5/15
	Baton Rouge MSA, LA	Y	19370 FQ	23890 MW	29130 TQ	USBLS	5/15
	New Orleans-Metairie MSA,						
	LA	Y	18790 FQ	22520 MW	27840 TQ	USBLS	5/15
	Maine	Y	17950 FQ	20180 MW	25420 TQ	USBLS	5/15
	Portland-South Portland MSA,						
	ME	Y	18860 FQ	21770 MW	26280 TQ	USBLS	5/15
	Maryland	Y	19819 AE	31602 MW	37493 AEX	MDBLS	4/16
	Baltimore-Columbia-Towson						
	MSA, MD	Y	23090 FQ	30800 MW	38690 TQ	USBLS	5/15
	Salisbury MSA, MD-DE	Y	22100 FQ	28340 MW	36530 TQ	USBLS	5/15
	Massachusetts	Y	22690 FQ	29210 MW	41160 TQ	USBLS	5/15
	Boston-Cambridge-Newton						
	NECTA, MA	Y	23600 FQ	31990 MW	44170 TQ	USBLS	5/15
	Worcester MSA, MA-CT	Y	21900 FQ	29180 MW	44250 TQ	USBLS	5/15
	Michigan	Y	18870 FQ	22660 MW	30260 TQ	USBLS	5/15
	Detroit-Dearborn-Livonia						
	PMSA, MI	Y	19730 FQ	25250 MW	37560 TQ	USBLS	5/15
	Grand Rapids-Wyoming MSA,						
	MI	Y	19670 FQ	26240 MW	34990 TQ	USBLS	5/15
	Minnesota	Y	18957 FQ	22849 MW	30422 TQ	MNBLS	1/16-3/16
	Minneapolis-St. Paul-						
	Bloomington MSA, MN-WI	Y	19976 FQ	24543 MW	31642 TQ	MNBLS	1/16-3/16
	Mississippi	Y	18350 FQ	21910 MW	28610 TQ	USBLS	5/15
	Jackson MSA, MS	Y	19220 FQ	22710 MW	28950 TQ	USBLS	5/15
	Missouri	Y	18580 FQ	21850 MW	28680 TQ	USBLS	5/15
	Kansas City MSA, MO-KS	Y	18910 FQ	23240 MW	30460 TQ	USBLS	5/15
	St. Louis MSA, MO-IL	Y	18650 FQ	21870 MW	33230 TQ	USBLS	5/15
	Montana	Y	18950 FQ	22890 MW	30690 TQ	USBLS	5/15
	Billings MSA, MT	Y	20160 FQ	24650 MW	31500 TQ	USBLS	5/15
	Nebraska	Y	18735 FQ	22605 MW	30235 TQ	NEBLS	7/16-9/16
	Omaha-Council Bluffs MSA,						
	NE-IA	Y	19645 FQ	25020 MW	32830 TQ	NEBLS	7/16-9/16
	Nevada	Y	21440 FQ	26620 MW	34940 TQ	USBLS	5/15
	Las Vegas-Henderson-Paradise						
	MSA, NV	Y	21700 FQ	27090 MW	35140 TQ	USBLS	5/15
	New Hampshire	H	9.63 AE	14.29 MW	18.44 AEX	NHBLS	6/16
	Manchester NECTA, NH	H	10.54 AE	14.55 MW	18.01 AEX	NHBLS	6/16
	Nashua NECTA, NH-MA	Y	21570 FQ	26670 MW	37480 TQ	USBLS	5/15
	New Jersey	Y	20650 FQ	27040 MW	36300 TQ	USBLS	5/15
	Camden PMSA, NJ	Y	20280 FQ	25200 MW	35670 TQ	USBLS	5/15
	Newark PMSA, NJ-PA	Y	21130 FQ	27940 MW	38010 TQ	USBLS	5/15
	Trenton MSA, NJ	Y	19580 FQ	27670 MW	34170 TQ	USBLS	5/15
	New Mexico	Y	19340 FQ	22860 MW	29760 TQ	USBLS	5/15
	Albuquerque MSA, NM	Y	19510 FQ	23250 MW	31550 TQ	USBLS	5/15
	New York	Y	19360 AE	24170 MW	33120 AEX	NYBLS	1/16-3/16
	Buffalo-Cheektowaga-Niagara						
	Falls MSA, NY	Y	19120 FQ	22330 MW	29920 TQ	USBLS	5/15
	Nassau County-Suffolk County						
	PMSA, NY	Y	19470 FQ	22970 MW	32770 TQ	USBLS	5/15
	New York-Jersey City-White						
	Plains PMSA, NY-NJ	Y	19530 FQ	24630 MW	34720 TQ	USBLS	5/15
	Rochester MSA, NY	Y	19710 FQ	25940 MW	33040 TQ	USBLS	5/15
	North Carolina	Y	18650 FQ	22840 MW	29900 TQ	USBLS	5/15
	Charlotte-Concord-Gastonia						
	MSA, NC-SC	Y	19210 FQ	23790 MW	30510 TQ	USBLS	5/15
	Raleigh MSA, NC	Y	19540 FQ	23380 MW	30910 TQ	USBLS	5/15
	North Dakota	Y	21500 FQ	26840 MW	34810 TQ	USBLS	5/15
	Fargo MSA, ND-MN	Y	19340 FQ	22840 MW	27770 TQ	USBLS	5/15
	Ohio	Y	18550 FQ	21020 MW	27530 TQ	USBLS	5/15
	Cincinnati MSA, OH-KY-IN	Y	18950 FQ	22070 MW	28400 TQ	USBLS	5/15
	Cleveland-Elyria MSA, OH	Y	18560 FQ	21790 MW	29660 TQ	USBLS	5/15

AE	Average entry wage	AWR	Average wage range	H	Hourly	LR	Low end range	MTC	Median total compensation	TCC	Total cash compensation
AEX	Average experienced wage	B	Biweekly	HI	Highest wage paid	M	Monthly	MW	Median wage paid	TQ	Third quartile wage
ATC	Average total compensation	D	Daily	HR	High end range	MCC	Median cash compensation	MWR	Median wage range	W	Weekly
AW	Average wage paid	FQ	First quartile wage	LO	Lowest wage paid	ME	Median entry wage	S	See annotated source	Y	Yearly

Occupation/Type/Industry	Location	Per	Low	Mid	High	Source	Date
Counter and Rental Clerk	Columbus MSA, OH	Y	18870 FQ	22500 MW	29340 TQ	USBLS	5/15
	Oklahoma	Y	18370 FQ	22590 MW	30210 TQ	USBLS	5/15
	Oklahoma City MSA, OK	Y	18370 FQ	23530 MW	31260 TQ	USBLS	5/15
	Tulsa MSA, OK	Y	18140 FQ	21800 MW	29390 TQ	USBLS	5/15
	Oregon	H	9.80 FQ	11.97 MW	16.89 TQ	ORBLS	2016
	Portland-Vancouver-Hillsboro MSA, OR-WA	Y	20270 FQ	24620 MW	35260 TQ	USBLS	5/15
	Pennsylvania	Y	19170 FQ	24810 MW	35080 TQ	USBLS	5/15
	Allentown-Bethlehem-Easton MSA, PA-NJ	Y	21530 FQ	28730 MW	37130 TQ	USBLS	5/15
	Harrisburg-Carlisle MSA, PA	Y	18610 FQ	22470 MW	29330 TQ	USBLS	5/15
	Montgomery County-Bucks County-Chester County PMSA, PA	Y	25300 FQ	35520 MW	50210 TQ	USBLS	5/15
	Philadelphia PMSA, PA	Y	19990 FQ	26030 MW	39660 TQ	USBLS	5/15
	Pittsburgh MSA, PA	Y	18060 FQ	21560 MW	30010 TQ	USBLS	5/15
	Rhode Island	Y	20030 FQ	26490 MW	35660 TQ	USBLS	5/15
	Providence-Warwick MSA, RI-MA	Y	19980 FQ	26030 MW	35300 TQ	USBLS	5/15
	South Carolina	Y	18230 FQ	22380 MW	29980 TQ	USBLS	5/15
	Charleston-North Charleston MSA, SC	Y	18690 FQ	22900 MW	32080 TQ	USBLS	5/15
	Columbia MSA, SC	Y	19200 FQ	25840 MW	32090 TQ	USBLS	5/15
	Greenville-Anderson-Mauldin MSA, SC	Y	17450 FQ	19630 MW	25710 TQ	USBLS	5/15
	South Dakota	Y	19090 FQ	22980 MW	30400 TQ	USBLS	5/15
	Sioux Falls MSA, SD	Y	20020 FQ	24020 MW	34710 TQ	USBLS	5/15
	Tennessee	Y	18170 FQ	22060 MW	30370 TQ	USBLS	5/15
	Knoxville MSA, TN	Y	17810 FQ	20590 MW	28530 TQ	USBLS	5/15
	Memphis MSA, TN-MS-AR	Y	17990 FQ	22390 MW	31030 TQ	USBLS	5/15
	Nashville-Davidson–Murfreesboro–Franklin MSA, TN	Y	18630 FQ	22630 MW	31720 TQ	USBLS	5/15
	Texas	Y	18900 FQ	24180 MW	31040 TQ	USBLS	5/15
	Austin-Round Rock MSA, TX	Y	20530 FQ	26590 MW	34800 TQ	USBLS	5/15
	College Station-Bryan MSA, TX	Y	17770 FQ	20850 MW	27510 TQ	USBLS	5/15
	Dallas-Plano-Irving PMSA, TX	Y	19300 FQ	24660 MW	32570 TQ	USBLS	5/15
	Fort Worth-Arlington PMSA, TX	Y	18370 FQ	24670 MW	32380 TQ	USBLS	5/15
	Houston-The Woodlands-Sugar Land MSA, TX	Y	19490 FQ	24740 MW	30290 TQ	USBLS	5/15
	San Antonio-New Braunfels MSA, TX	Y	19020 FQ	24530 MW	31310 TQ	USBLS	5/15
	Utah	Y	18240 FQ	21750 MW	27500 TQ	USBLS	5/15
	Ogden-Clearfield MSA, UT	Y	17700 FQ	19920 MW	28440 TQ	USBLS	5/15
	Provo-Orem MSA, UT	Y	17570 FQ	20110 MW	23250 TQ	USBLS	5/15
	Salt Lake City MSA, UT	Y	19180 FQ	23090 MW	28660 TQ	USBLS	5/15
	Vermont	Y	23740 FQ	28670 MW	37240 TQ	USBLS	5/15
	Burlington-South Burlington MSA, VT	Y	23980 FQ	28350 MW	36030 TQ	USBLS	5/15
	Virginia	Y	21300 FQ	28070 MW	36620 TQ	USBLS	5/15
	Richmond MSA, VA	Y	21400 FQ	28460 MW	40230 TQ	USBLS	5/15
	Virginia Beach-Norfolk-Newport News MSA, VA-NC	Y	21560 FQ	27040 MW	34350 TQ	USBLS	5/15
	Washington	H	11.45 FQ	14.42 MW	18.36 TQ	WABLS	3/16
	Seattle-Bellevue-Everett PMSA, WA	H	11.98 FQ	15.27 MW	19.07 TQ	WABLS	3/16
	Tacoma-Lakewood PMSA, WA	H	12.00 FQ	14.22 MW	18.52 TQ	WABLS	3/16
	West Virginia	Y	18010 FQ	19460 MW	24730 TQ	USBLS	5/15
	Huntington-Ashland MSA, WV-KY-OH	Y	18170 FQ	19950 MW	25880 TQ	USBLS	5/15
	Wisconsin	Y	18290 FQ	22990 MW	32490 TQ	USBLS	5/15
	Madison MSA, WI	Y	17520 FQ	19610 MW	32550 TQ	USBLS	5/15
	Milwaukee-Waukesha-West Allis MSA, WI	Y	19270 FQ	24630 MW	33740 TQ	USBLS	5/15
	Wausau MSA, WI	Y	17290 FQ	19080 MW	33580 TQ	USBLS	5/15
	Wyoming	Y	19030 FQ	27340 MW	35170 TQ	USBLS	5/15
	Cheyenne MSA, WY	Y	19580 FQ	27790 MW	31400 TQ	USBLS	5/15
	Puerto Rico	Y	16930 FQ	18370 MW	20330 TQ	USBLS	5/15
	San Juan-Carolina-Caguas MSA, PR	Y	16910 FQ	18350 MW	20310 TQ	USBLS	5/15

AE	Average entry wage	AWR	Average wage range	H	Hourly
AEX	Average experienced wage	B	Biweekly	HI	Highest wage paid
ATC	Average total compensation	D	Daily	HR	High end range
AW	Average wage paid	FQ	First quartile wage	LO	Lowest wage paid

LR	Low end range	MTC	Median total compensation
M	Monthly	MW	Median wage paid
MCC	Median cash compensation	MWR	Median wage range
ME	Median entry wage	S	See annotated source

TCC	Total cash compensation		
TQ	Third quartile wage		
W	Weekly		
Y	Yearly		

Occupation/Type/Industry	Location	Per	Low	Mid	High	Source	Date
Counter and Rental Clerk	Virgin Islands	Y	19420 FQ	22610 MW	27290 TQ	USBLS	5/15
	Guam	Y	18140 FQ	19130 MW	22030 TQ	USBLS	5/15
Counter Attendant							
Cafeteria, Food, Coffee Shop	Alabama	Y	17472 AE	19264 AW	20160 AEX	ALBLS	6/16
Cafeteria, Food, Coffee Shop	Birmingham-Hoover MSA, AL	Y	17442 AE	20098 AW	21426 AEX	ALBLS	6/16
Cafeteria, Food, Coffee Shop	Alaska	Y	19060 FQ	20540 MW	24630 TQ	USBLS	5/15
Cafeteria, Food, Coffee Shop	Anchorage MSA, AK	Y	19040 FQ	20410 MW	24430 TQ	USBLS	5/15
Cafeteria, Food, Coffee Shop	Arizona	Y	17930 FQ	19100 MW	22310 TQ	USBLS	5/15
Cafeteria, Food, Coffee Shop	Phoenix-Mesa-Scottsdale MSA, AZ	Y	17970 FQ	19170 MW	22380 TQ	USBLS	5/15
Cafeteria, Food, Coffee Shop	Tucson MSA, AZ	Y	18100 FQ	19460 MW	26640 TQ	USBLS	5/15
Cafeteria, Food, Coffee Shop	Arkansas	Y	16730 FQ	17850 MW	18970 TQ	USBLS	5/15
Cafeteria, Food, Coffee Shop	Little Rock-North Little Rock-Conway MSA, AR	Y	16780 FQ	17940 MW	19110 TQ	USBLS	5/15
Cafeteria, Food, Coffee Shop	California	H	9.49 FQ	10.35 MW	12.69 TQ	CABLS	1/16-3/16
Cafeteria, Food, Coffee Shop	Anaheim-Santa Ana-Irvine PMSA, CA	H	9.55 FQ	10.52 MW	12.02 TQ	CABLS	1/16-3/16
Cafeteria, Food, Coffee Shop	Los Angeles-Long Beach-Glendale PMSA, CA	H	9.43 FQ	9.70 MW	12.42 TQ	CABLS	1/16-3/16
Cafeteria, Food, Coffee Shop	Oakland-Hayward-Berkeley PMSA, CA	H	9.52 FQ	10.71 MW	13.38 TQ	CABLS	1/16-3/16
Cafeteria, Food, Coffee Shop	Riverside-San Bernardino-Ontario MSA, CA	H	9.47 FQ	10.19 MW	12.06 TQ	CABLS	1/16-3/16
Cafeteria, Food, Coffee Shop	Sacramento–Roseville–Arden-Arcade MSA, CA	H	9.47 FQ	9.75 MW	11.92 TQ	CABLS	1/16-3/16
Cafeteria, Food, Coffee Shop	San Diego-Carlsbad MSA, CA	H	9.55 FQ	10.60 MW	12.40 TQ	CABLS	1/16-3/16
Cafeteria, Food, Coffee Shop	San Francisco-Redwood City-South San Francisco PMSA, CA	H	9.80 FQ	11.50 MW	14.24 TQ	CABLS	1/16-3/16
Cafeteria, Food, Coffee Shop	Colorado	Y	18540 FQ	20730 MW	25750 TQ	USBLS	5/15
Cafeteria, Food, Coffee Shop	Denver-Aurora-Lakewood MSA, CO	Y	18620 FQ	21530 MW	26850 TQ	USBLS	5/15
Cafeteria, Food, Coffee Shop	Connecticut	Y		20017 MW		CTBLS	1/16-3/16
Cafeteria, Food, Coffee Shop	Bridgeport-Stamford-Norwalk MSA, CT	Y	19250 FQ	19520 MW	19940 TQ	USBLS	5/15
Cafeteria, Food, Coffee Shop	Hartford-West Hartford-East Hartford MSA, CT	Y	19290 FQ	19570 MW	19910 TQ	USBLS	5/15
Cafeteria, Food, Coffee Shop	Delaware	Y	17640 FQ	18870 MW	21030 TQ	USBLS	5/15
Cafeteria, Food, Coffee Shop	Wilmington PMSA, DE-MD-NJ	Y	17880 FQ	19060 MW	21820 TQ	USBLS	5/15
Cafeteria, Food, Coffee Shop	District of Columbia	Y	20000 FQ	22400 MW	26240 TQ	USBLS	5/15
Cafeteria, Food, Coffee Shop	Washington-Arlington-Alexandria PMSA, DC-VA-MD-WV	Y	17660 FQ	19610 MW	24090 TQ	USBLS	5/15
Cafeteria, Food, Coffee Shop	Florida	H	9.00 AE	9.43 MW	10.36 AEX	FLBLS	7/16-9/16
Cafeteria, Food, Coffee Shop	Fort Lauderdale-Pompano Beach-Deerfield Beach PMSA, FL	H	9.01 AE	9.47 MW	10.58 AEX	FLBLS	7/16-9/16
Cafeteria, Food, Coffee Shop	Miami-Miami Beach-Kendall PMSA, FL	H	9.00 AE	9.32 MW	10.57 AEX	FLBLS	7/16-9/16
Cafeteria, Food, Coffee Shop	Orlando-Kissimmee-Sanford MSA, FL	H	8.99 AE	10.24 MW	11.17 AEX	FLBLS	7/16-9/16
Cafeteria, Food, Coffee Shop	Tampa-St. Petersburg-Clearwater MSA, FL	H	8.96 AE	9.17 MW	9.64 AEX	FLBLS	7/16-9/16
Cafeteria, Food, Coffee Shop	Georgia	Y	16760 FQ	18080 MW	19420 TQ	USBLS	5/15
Cafeteria, Food, Coffee Shop	Atlanta-Sandy Springs-Roswell MSA, GA	Y	16840 FQ	18200 MW	19580 TQ	USBLS	5/15
Cafeteria, Food, Coffee Shop	Augusta-Richmond County MSA, GA-SC	Y	16610 FQ	17860 MW	19100 TQ	USBLS	5/15
Cafeteria, Food, Coffee Shop	Hawaii	Y	18290 FQ	21370 MW	26540 TQ	USBLS	5/15
Cafeteria, Food, Coffee Shop	Urban Honolulu MSA, HI	Y	18300 FQ	21250 MW	25710 TQ	USBLS	5/15
Cafeteria, Food, Coffee Shop	Idaho	Y	16690 FQ	17960 MW	19220 TQ	USBLS	5/15
Cafeteria, Food, Coffee Shop	Boise City MSA, ID	Y	16670 FQ	17920 MW	19160 TQ	USBLS	5/15
Cafeteria, Food, Coffee Shop	Illinois	Y	18280 FQ	19020 MW	20320 TQ	USBLS	5/15
Cafeteria, Food, Coffee Shop	Chicago-Naperville-Arlington Heights PMSA, IL	Y	18280 FQ	19020 MW	20420 TQ	USBLS	5/15
Cafeteria, Food, Coffee Shop	Lake County-Kenosha County PMSA, IL-WI	Y	18410 FQ	19260 MW	21150 TQ	USBLS	5/15
Cafeteria, Food, Coffee Shop	Indiana	Y	16710 FQ	18010 MW	19320 TQ	USBLS	5/15
Cafeteria, Food, Coffee Shop	Gary PMSA, IN	Y	17280 FQ	19160 MW	23080 TQ	USBLS	5/15

AE	Average entry wage	AWR	Average wage range	H	Hourly	LR	Low end range	MTC	Median total compensation	TCC	Total cash compensation
AEX	Average experienced wage	B	Biweekly	HI	Highest wage paid	M	Monthly	MW	Median wage paid	TQ	Third quartile wage
ATC	Average total compensation	D	Daily	HR	High end range	MCC	Median cash compensation	MWR	Median wage range	W	Weekly
AW	Average wage paid	FQ	First quartile wage	LO	Lowest wage paid	ME	Median entry wage	S	See annotated source	Y	Yearly

351

Counter Attendant

Occupation/Type/Industry	Location	Per	Low	Mid	High	Source	Date
Cafeteria, Food, Coffee Shop	Indianapolis-Carmel-Anderson MSA, IN	Y	16620 FQ	17840 MW	19070 TQ	USBLS	5/15
Cafeteria, Food, Coffee Shop	Iowa	Y	16930 FQ	18470 MW	21210 TQ	USBLS	5/15
Cafeteria, Food, Coffee Shop	Des Moines-West Des Moines MSA, IA	Y	16990 FQ	18510 MW	20900 TQ	USBLS	5/15
Cafeteria, Food, Coffee Shop	Kansas	Y	16880 FQ	18380 MW	20680 TQ	USBLS	5/15
Cafeteria, Food, Coffee Shop	Wichita MSA, KS	Y	16810 FQ	18340 MW	20590 TQ	USBLS	5/15
Cafeteria, Food, Coffee Shop	Kentucky	Y	16790 FQ	18180 MW	19670 TQ	USBLS	5/15
Cafeteria, Food, Coffee Shop	Louisville-Jefferson County MSA, KY-IN	Y	17070 FQ	18800 MW	22060 TQ	USBLS	5/15
Cafeteria, Food, Coffee Shop	Louisiana	Y	16900 FQ	18350 MW	19960 TQ	USBLS	5/15
Cafeteria, Food, Coffee Shop	Baton Rouge MSA, LA	Y	16860 FQ	18210 MW	19560 TQ	USBLS	5/15
Cafeteria, Food, Coffee Shop	New Orleans-Metairie MSA, LA	Y	16910 FQ	18390 MW	20340 TQ	USBLS	5/15
Cafeteria, Food, Coffee Shop	Maine	Y	17150 FQ	18350 MW	19640 TQ	USBLS	5/15
Cafeteria, Food, Coffee Shop	Portland-South Portland MSA, ME	Y	17220 FQ	18510 MW	20300 TQ	USBLS	5/15
Cafeteria, Food, Coffee Shop	Maryland	Y	18018 AE	22874 MW	25303 AEX	MDBLS	4/16
Cafeteria, Food, Coffee Shop	Baltimore-Columbia-Towson MSA, MD	Y	17970 FQ	19320 MW	23260 TQ	USBLS	5/15
Cafeteria, Food, Coffee Shop	Salisbury MSA, MD-DE	Y	17550 FQ	18610 MW	19770 TQ	USBLS	5/15
Cafeteria, Food, Coffee Shop	Massachusetts	Y	19070 FQ	19470 MW	21250 TQ	USBLS	5/15
Cafeteria, Food, Coffee Shop	Boston-Cambridge-Newton NECTA, MA	Y	19060 FQ	19450 MW	20520 TQ	USBLS	5/15
Cafeteria, Food, Coffee Shop	Worcester MSA, MA-CT	Y	19020 FQ	19320 MW	19890 TQ	USBLS	5/15
Cafeteria, Food, Coffee Shop	Michigan	Y	17940 FQ	18820 MW	20020 TQ	USBLS	5/15
Cafeteria, Food, Coffee Shop	Detroit-Dearborn-Livonia PMSA, MI	Y	18090 FQ	19140 MW	23200 TQ	USBLS	5/15
Cafeteria, Food, Coffee Shop	Grand Rapids-Wyoming MSA, MI	Y	17960 FQ	18850 MW	20440 TQ	USBLS	5/15
Cafeteria, Food, Coffee Shop	Niles-Benton Harbor MSA, MI	Y	18160 FQ	19250 MW	21250 TQ	USBLS	5/15
Cafeteria, Food, Coffee Shop	Minnesota	Y	17935 FQ	18945 MW	20288 TQ	MNBLS	1/16-3/16
Cafeteria, Food, Coffee Shop	Minneapolis-St. Paul-Bloomington MSA, MN-WI	Y	17925 FQ	18935 MW	20197 TQ	MNBLS	1/16-3/16
Cafeteria, Food, Coffee Shop	Mississippi	Y	16770 FQ	18080 MW	19410 TQ	USBLS	5/15
Cafeteria, Food, Coffee Shop	Jackson MSA, MS	Y	16500 FQ	17650 MW	18800 TQ	USBLS	5/15
Cafeteria, Food, Coffee Shop	Missouri	Y	17170 FQ	18420 MW	19980 TQ	USBLS	5/15
Cafeteria, Food, Coffee Shop	Kansas City MSA, MO-KS	Y	17410 FQ	19040 MW	22760 TQ	USBLS	5/15
Cafeteria, Food, Coffee Shop	St. Louis MSA, MO-IL	Y	17350 FQ	18580 MW	20100 TQ	USBLS	5/15
Cafeteria, Food, Coffee Shop	Montana	Y	17670 FQ	18570 MW	19520 TQ	USBLS	5/15
Cafeteria, Food, Coffee Shop	Billings MSA, MT	Y	18050 FQ	19300 MW	22710 TQ	USBLS	5/15
Cafeteria, Food, Coffee Shop	Nebraska	Y	17650 FQ	18660 MW	20005 TQ	NEBLS	7/16-9/16
Cafeteria, Food, Coffee Shop	Omaha-Council Bluffs MSA, NE-IA	Y	17500 FQ	18415 MW	19385 TQ	NEBLS	7/16-9/16
Cafeteria, Food, Coffee Shop	Nevada	Y	19950 FQ	23240 MW	28770 TQ	USBLS	5/15
Cafeteria, Food, Coffee Shop	Las Vegas-Henderson-Paradise MSA, NV	Y	20800 FQ	23830 MW	29930 TQ	USBLS	5/15
Cafeteria, Food, Coffee Shop	New Hampshire	H	8.42 AE	9.49 MW	11.62 AEX	NHBLS	6/16
Cafeteria, Food, Coffee Shop	Manchester NECTA, NH	H	9.01 AE	11.28 MW	13.01 AEX	NHBLS	6/16
Cafeteria, Food, Coffee Shop	Nashua NECTA, NH-MA	Y	17380 FQ	19260 MW	24300 TQ	USBLS	5/15
Cafeteria, Food, Coffee Shop	New Jersey	Y	18240 FQ	18960 MW	19930 TQ	USBLS	5/15
Cafeteria, Food, Coffee Shop	Camden PMSA, NJ	Y	18330 FQ	19150 MW	20980 TQ	USBLS	5/15
Cafeteria, Food, Coffee Shop	Newark PMSA, NJ-PA	Y	18300 FQ	19080 MW	21040 TQ	USBLS	5/15
Cafeteria, Food, Coffee Shop	Trenton MSA, NJ	Y	18360 FQ	19210 MW	21290 TQ	USBLS	5/15
Cafeteria, Food, Coffee Shop	New Mexico	Y	17100 FQ	18220 MW	19370 TQ	USBLS	5/15
Cafeteria, Food, Coffee Shop	Albuquerque MSA, NM	Y	17140 FQ	18350 MW	19620 TQ	USBLS	5/15
Cafeteria, Food, Coffee Shop	New York	Y	19280 AE	20230 MW	25890 AEX	NYBLS	1/16-3/16
Cafeteria, Food, Coffee Shop	Buffalo-Cheektowaga-Niagara Falls MSA, NY	Y	18620 FQ	19040 MW	19710 TQ	USBLS	5/15
Cafeteria, Food, Coffee Shop	Nassau County-Suffolk County PMSA, NY	Y	18860 FQ	19580 MW	27740 TQ	USBLS	5/15
Cafeteria, Food, Coffee Shop	New York-Jersey City-White Plains PMSA, NY-NJ	Y	18630 FQ	19490 MW	23410 TQ	USBLS	5/15
Cafeteria, Food, Coffee Shop	Rochester MSA, NY	Y	18640 FQ	19090 MW	19640 TQ	USBLS	5/15
Cafeteria, Food, Coffee Shop	North Carolina	Y	16780 FQ	18110 MW	19490 TQ	USBLS	5/15
Cafeteria, Food, Coffee Shop	Charlotte-Concord-Gastonia MSA, NC-SC	Y	16770 FQ	18080 MW	19430 TQ	USBLS	5/15
Cafeteria, Food, Coffee Shop	Raleigh MSA, NC	Y	16770 FQ	18100 MW	19470 TQ	USBLS	5/15
Cafeteria, Food, Coffee Shop	North Dakota	Y	20060 FQ	23640 MW	27670 TQ	USBLS	5/15
Cafeteria, Food, Coffee Shop	Fargo MSA, ND-MN	Y	17680 FQ	19300 MW	22940 TQ	USBLS	5/15
Cafeteria, Food, Coffee Shop	Ohio	Y	17850 FQ	18810 MW	20520 TQ	USBLS	5/15

Counter Attendant

Occupation/Type/Industry	Location	Per	Low	Mid	High	Source	Date
Cafeteria, Food, Coffee Shop	Cincinnati MSA, OH-KY-IN	Y	17900 FQ	19090 MW	22460 TQ	USBLS	5/15
Cafeteria, Food, Coffee Shop	Cleveland-Elyria MSA, OH	Y	17990 FQ	19110 MW	22700 TQ	USBLS	5/15
Cafeteria, Food, Coffee Shop	Columbus MSA, OH	Y	17950 FQ	19020 MW	22240 TQ	USBLS	5/15
Cafeteria, Food, Coffee Shop	Oklahoma	Y	16710 FQ	17970 MW	19230 TQ	USBLS	5/15
Cafeteria, Food, Coffee Shop	Oklahoma City MSA, OK	Y	16680 FQ	17910 MW	19140 TQ	USBLS	5/15
Cafeteria, Food, Coffee Shop	Tulsa MSA, OK	Y	16700 FQ	17910 MW	19120 TQ	USBLS	5/15
Cafeteria, Food, Coffee Shop	Oregon	H	9.64 FQ	10.48 MW	11.57 TQ	ORBLS	2016
Cafeteria, Food, Coffee Shop	Portland-Vancouver-Hillsboro MSA, OR-WA	Y	19820 FQ	21670 MW	23650 TQ	USBLS	5/15
Cafeteria, Food, Coffee Shop	Pennsylvania	Y	16970 FQ	18460 MW	20730 TQ	USBLS	5/15
Cafeteria, Food, Coffee Shop	Allentown-Bethlehem-Easton MSA, PA-NJ	Y	17610 FQ	18580 MW	19600 TQ	USBLS	5/15
Cafeteria, Food, Coffee Shop	Harrisburg-Carlisle MSA, PA	Y	17390 FQ	19200 MW	21850 TQ	USBLS	5/15
Cafeteria, Food, Coffee Shop	Montgomery County-Bucks County-Chester County PMSA, PA	Y	16920 FQ	18310 MW	19780 TQ	USBLS	5/15
Cafeteria, Food, Coffee Shop	Philadelphia PMSA, PA	Y	18210 FQ	22700 MW	29350 TQ	USBLS	5/15
Cafeteria, Food, Coffee Shop	Pittsburgh MSA, PA	Y	16740 FQ	17990 MW	19240 TQ	USBLS	5/15
Cafeteria, Food, Coffee Shop	Rhode Island	Y	19090 FQ	19530 MW	23500 TQ	USBLS	5/15
Cafeteria, Food, Coffee Shop	Providence-Warwick MSA, RI-MA	Y	19100 FQ	19550 MW	22960 TQ	USBLS	5/15
Cafeteria, Food, Coffee Shop	South Carolina	Y	16740 FQ	17990 MW	19240 TQ	USBLS	5/15
Cafeteria, Food, Coffee Shop	Charleston-North Charleston MSA, SC	Y	16920 FQ	18250 MW	19590 TQ	USBLS	5/15
Cafeteria, Food, Coffee Shop	Columbia MSA, SC	Y	16570 FQ	17710 MW	18850 TQ	USBLS	5/15
Cafeteria, Food, Coffee Shop	Greenville-Anderson-Mauldin MSA, SC	Y	16770 FQ	18020 MW	19270 TQ	USBLS	5/15
Cafeteria, Food, Coffee Shop	South Dakota	Y	18540 FQ	19430 MW	22090 TQ	USBLS	5/15
Cafeteria, Food, Coffee Shop	Sioux Falls MSA, SD	Y	18660 FQ	19780 MW	22840 TQ	USBLS	5/15
Cafeteria, Food, Coffee Shop	Tennessee	Y	16700 FQ	17970 MW	19230 TQ	USBLS	5/15
Cafeteria, Food, Coffee Shop	Knoxville MSA, TN	Y	16630 FQ	17770 MW	18910 TQ	USBLS	5/15
Cafeteria, Food, Coffee Shop	Memphis MSA, TN-MS-AR	Y	16620 FQ	17820 MW	19020 TQ	USBLS	5/15
Cafeteria, Food, Coffee Shop	Nashville-Davidson–Murfreesboro–Franklin MSA, TN	Y	16740 FQ	17980 MW	19210 TQ	USBLS	5/15
Cafeteria, Food, Coffee Shop	Texas	Y	16740 FQ	18100 MW	19520 TQ	USBLS	5/15
Cafeteria, Food, Coffee Shop	Austin-Round Rock MSA, TX	Y	16940 FQ	18480 MW	21440 TQ	USBLS	5/15
Cafeteria, Food, Coffee Shop	Dallas-Plano-Irving PMSA, TX	Y	16940 FQ	18440 MW	20650 TQ	USBLS	5/15
Cafeteria, Food, Coffee Shop	Fort Worth-Arlington PMSA, TX	Y	16760 FQ	18130 MW	19560 TQ	USBLS	5/15
Cafeteria, Food, Coffee Shop	Houston-The Woodlands-Sugar Land MSA, TX	Y	16630 FQ	17940 MW	19250 TQ	USBLS	5/15
Cafeteria, Food, Coffee Shop	San Antonio-New Braunfels MSA, TX	Y	16860 FQ	18300 MW	19880 TQ	USBLS	5/15
Cafeteria, Food, Coffee Shop	Utah	Y	17030 FQ	18680 MW	22990 TQ	USBLS	5/15
Cafeteria, Food, Coffee Shop	Ogden-Clearfield MSA, UT	Y	16560 FQ	17690 MW	18810 TQ	USBLS	5/15
Cafeteria, Food, Coffee Shop	Provo-Orem MSA, UT	Y	16770 FQ	18300 MW	22640 TQ	USBLS	5/15
Cafeteria, Food, Coffee Shop	Salt Lake City MSA, UT	Y	17660 FQ	20330 MW	25700 TQ	USBLS	5/15
Cafeteria, Food, Coffee Shop	Vermont	Y	19310 FQ	19920 MW	23980 TQ	USBLS	5/15
Cafeteria, Food, Coffee Shop	Burlington-South Burlington MSA, VT	Y	19970 FQ	22820 MW	27220 TQ	USBLS	5/15
Cafeteria, Food, Coffee Shop	Virginia	Y	16990 FQ	18510 MW	21230 TQ	USBLS	5/15
Cafeteria, Food, Coffee Shop	Richmond MSA, VA	Y	17130 FQ	18670 MW	22310 TQ	USBLS	5/15
Cafeteria, Food, Coffee Shop	Virginia Beach-Norfolk-Newport News MSA, VA-NC	Y	16980 FQ	18460 MW	20410 TQ	USBLS	5/15
Cafeteria, Food, Coffee Shop	Washington	H	9.78 FQ	10.81 MW	11.88 TQ	WABLS	3/16
Cafeteria, Food, Coffee Shop	Seattle-Bellevue-Everett PMSA, WA	H	9.76 FQ	10.80 MW	11.99 TQ	WABLS	3/16
Cafeteria, Food, Coffee Shop	Tacoma-Lakewood PMSA, WA	H	10.32 FQ	11.06 MW	11.81 TQ	WABLS	3/16
Cafeteria, Food, Coffee Shop	West Virginia	Y	17490 FQ	18350 MW	19200 TQ	USBLS	5/15
Cafeteria, Food, Coffee Shop	Huntington-Ashland MSA, WV-KY-OH	Y	17410 FQ	18180 MW	18940 TQ	USBLS	5/15
Cafeteria, Food, Coffee Shop	Wisconsin	Y	17010 FQ	18590 MW	21580 TQ	USBLS	5/15
Cafeteria, Food, Coffee Shop	Madison MSA, WI	Y	17040 FQ	18680 MW	21840 TQ	USBLS	5/15
Cafeteria, Food, Coffee Shop	Milwaukee-Waukesha-West Allis MSA, WI	Y	17250 FQ	18960 MW	23010 TQ	USBLS	5/15
Cafeteria, Food, Coffee Shop	Wyoming	Y	17170 FQ	18940 MW	23270 TQ	USBLS	5/15
Cafeteria, Food, Coffee Shop	Cheyenne MSA, WY	Y	16800 FQ	17980 MW	19170 TQ	USBLS	5/15
Cafeteria, Food, Coffee Shop	Puerto Rico	Y	16600 FQ	17700 MW	18800 TQ	USBLS	5/15
Cafeteria, Food, Coffee Shop	San Juan-Carolina-Caguas MSA, PR	Y	16610 FQ	17710 MW	18820 TQ	USBLS	5/15

AE	Average entry wage	AWR	Average wage range	H	Hourly
AEX	Average experienced wage	B	Biweekly	HI	Highest wage paid
ATC	Average total compensation	D	Daily	HR	High end range
AW	Average wage paid	FQ	First quartile wage	LO	Lowest wage paid

LR	Low end range	MTC	Median total compensation
M	Monthly	MW	Median wage paid
MCC	Median cash compensation	MWR	Median wage range
ME	Median entry wage	S	See annotated source

TCC	Total cash compensation		
TQ	Third quartile wage		
W	Weekly		
Y	Yearly		

Occupation/Type/Industry	Location	Per	Low	Mid	High	Source	Date
Counter Attendant							
Cafeteria, Food, Coffee Shop	Virgin Islands	Y	17890 FQ	20600 MW	25010 TQ	USBLS	5/15
Cafeteria, Food, Coffee Shop	Guam	Y	17790 FQ	18410 MW	19040 TQ	USBLS	5/15
Counterintelligence Threat Analyst							
Central Intelligence Agency	District of Columbia	Y	51603 LO		76498 HI	CIA02	2016
County Attorney	Gordon County, GA	Y			102870 HI	GACTY04	2016
	Henry County, GA	Y	92680 LO		139019 HI	GACTY04	2016
County Clerk	Columbia County, GA	Y	40359 LO		60538 HI	GACTY04	2016
	Hancock County, GA	Y	48621 LO		68477 HI	GACTY04	2016
	Lumpkin County, GA	Y	44748 LO		68089 HI	GACTY04	2016
County Commission Chairperson							
Full-Time	Clayton County, GA	Y			154756 HI	GACTY03	2016
Full-Time	Mitchell County, GA	Y			8240 HI	GACTY03	2016
County Commissioner	Cherokee County, GA	Y			30000 HI	GACTY03	2016
	Crawford County, GA	Y			15780 HI	GACTY03	2016
	Rockdale County, GA	Y			25106 HI	GACTY03	2016
County Executive	Oakland County, MI	B			7325 HI	MIOAK1	10/1/16
County Manager/Administrator	Brooks County, GA	Y	55708 LO		70644 HI	GACTY04	2016
	Macon-Bibb County, GA	Y	124425 LO		207168 HI	GACTY04	2016
	Randolph County, GA	Y	47919 LO		70188 HI	GACTY04	2016
Courier and Messenger	Alabama	Y	18056 AE	26146 AW	30196 AEX	ALBLS	6/16
	Birmingham-Hoover MSA, AL	Y	20715 AE	28939 AW	33041 AEX	ALBLS	6/16
	Alaska	Y	19470 FQ	27520 MW	35420 TQ	USBLS	5/15
	Anchorage MSA, AK	Y	19300 FQ	25340 MW	33470 TQ	USBLS	5/15
	Arizona	Y	23610 FQ	27380 MW	30640 TQ	USBLS	5/15
	Phoenix-Mesa-Scottsdale MSA, AZ	Y	25330 FQ	28150 MW	30980 TQ	USBLS	5/15
	Tucson MSA, AZ	Y	18850 FQ	21820 MW	24840 TQ	USBLS	5/15
	Arkansas	Y	21580 FQ	24160 MW	28620 TQ	USBLS	5/15
	Little Rock-North Little Rock-Conway MSA, AR	Y	21740 FQ	24630 MW	29540 TQ	USBLS	5/15
	California	H	12.00 FQ	15.25 MW	19.01 TQ	CABLS	1/16-3/16
	Anaheim-Santa Ana-Irvine PMSA, CA	H	10.52 FQ	13.14 MW	15.44 TQ	CABLS	1/16-3/16
	Los Angeles-Long Beach-Glendale PMSA, CA	H	11.64 FQ	15.75 MW	18.94 TQ	CABLS	1/16-3/16
	Oakland-Hayward-Berkeley PMSA, CA	H	15.65 FQ	18.06 MW	21.22 TQ	CABLS	1/16-3/16
	Riverside-San Bernardino-Ontario MSA, CA	H	10.18 FQ	12.28 MW	14.57 TQ	CABLS	1/16-3/16
	Sacramento–Roseville–Arden-Arcade MSA, CA	H	10.77 FQ	14.19 MW	17.43 TQ	CABLS	1/16-3/16
	San Diego-Carlsbad MSA, CA	H	13.17 FQ	15.01 MW	17.95 TQ	CABLS	1/16-3/16
	San Francisco-Redwood City-South San Francisco PMSA, CA	H	14.76 FQ	19.48 MW	26.68 TQ	CABLS	1/16-3/16
	Colorado	Y	23730 FQ	27990 MW	33900 TQ	USBLS	5/15
	Denver-Aurora-Lakewood MSA, CO	Y	24230 FQ	28210 MW	34170 TQ	USBLS	5/15
	Connecticut	Y		32635 MW		CTBLS	1/16-3/16
	Bridgeport-Stamford-Norwalk MSA, CT	Y	23470 FQ	30900 MW	36280 TQ	USBLS	5/15
	Hartford-West Hartford-East Hartford MSA, CT	Y	20490 FQ	28230 MW	33630 TQ	USBLS	5/15
	District of Columbia	Y	25990 FQ	39990 MW	45740 TQ	USBLS	5/15
	Washington-Arlington-Alexandria PMSA, DC-VA-MD-WV	Y	28740 FQ	36690 MW	47890 TQ	USBLS	5/15
	Florida	H	10.49 AE	13.56 MW	15.99 AEX	FLBLS	7/16-9/16
	Fort Lauderdale-Pompano Beach-Deerfield Beach PMSA, FL	H	12.04 AE	14.77 MW	17.49 AEX	FLBLS	7/16-9/16
	Miami-Miami Beach-Kendall PMSA, FL	H	12.33 AE	15.25 MW	18.19 AEX	FLBLS	7/16-9/16

AE	Average entry wage	AWR	Average wage range	H	Hourly	LR	Low end range	MTC	Median total compensation	TCC	Total cash compensation
AEX	Average experienced wage	B	Biweekly	HI	Highest wage paid	M	Monthly	MW	Median wage paid	TQ	Third quartile wage
ATC	Average total compensation	D	Daily	HR	High end range	MCC	Median cash compensation	MWR	Median wage range	W	Weekly
AW	Average wage paid	FQ	First quartile wage	LO	Lowest wage paid	ME	Median entry wage	S	See annotated source	Y	Yearly

Occupation/Type/Industry	Location	Per	Low	Mid	High	Source	Date
Courier and Messenger	Orlando-Kissimmee-Sanford MSA, FL	H	10.58 AE	13.43 MW	15.95 AEX	FLBLS	7/16-9/16
	Tampa-St. Petersburg-Clearwater MSA, FL	H	10.32 AE	13.02 MW	15.49 AEX	FLBLS	7/16-9/16
	Georgia	Y	18770 FQ	23290 MW	29860 TQ	USBLS	5/15
	Atlanta-Sandy Springs-Roswell MSA, GA	Y	18500 FQ	23590 MW	32150 TQ	USBLS	5/15
	Augusta-Richmond County MSA, GA-SC	Y	20410 FQ	22440 MW	24480 TQ	USBLS	5/15
	Hawaii	Y	21690 FQ	26480 MW	31250 TQ	USBLS	5/15
	Urban Honolulu MSA, HI	Y	22140 FQ	26680 MW	30680 TQ	USBLS	5/15
	Idaho	Y	21050 FQ	23720 MW	28620 TQ	USBLS	5/15
	Boise City MSA, ID	Y	21680 FQ	23830 MW	27580 TQ	USBLS	5/15
	Illinois	Y	21070 FQ	26480 MW	36880 TQ	USBLS	5/15
	Chicago-Naperville-Arlington Heights PMSA, IL	Y	23440 FQ	30170 MW	41670 TQ	USBLS	5/15
	Indiana	Y	21950 FQ	25440 MW	31050 TQ	USBLS	5/15
	Gary PMSA, IN	Y	18650 FQ	24750 MW	32070 TQ	USBLS	5/15
	Indianapolis-Carmel-Anderson MSA, IN	Y	22690 FQ	25740 MW	32390 TQ	USBLS	5/15
	Iowa	Y	20100 FQ	24070 MW	28990 TQ	USBLS	5/15
	Des Moines-West Des Moines MSA, IA	Y	22220 FQ	28340 MW	35930 TQ	USBLS	5/15
	Kansas	Y	19460 FQ	22470 MW	26880 TQ	USBLS	5/15
	Wichita MSA, KS	Y	18070 FQ	20830 MW	24580 TQ	USBLS	5/15
	Kentucky	Y	18430 FQ	21960 MW	27350 TQ	USBLS	5/15
	Louisville-Jefferson County MSA, KY-IN	Y	18010 FQ	21150 MW	27820 TQ	USBLS	5/15
	Louisiana	Y	18640 FQ	22480 MW	28430 TQ	USBLS	5/15
	Baton Rouge MSA, LA	Y	18990 FQ	22610 MW	28320 TQ	USBLS	5/15
	New Orleans-Metairie MSA, LA	Y	21730 FQ	26980 MW	33470 TQ	USBLS	5/15
	Portland-South Portland MSA, ME	Y	24400 FQ	27630 MW	30750 TQ	USBLS	5/15
	Maryland	Y	22011 AE	30879 MW	35313 AEX	MDBLS	4/16
	Baltimore-Columbia-Towson MSA, MD	Y	23520 FQ	28590 MW	35270 TQ	USBLS	5/15
	Salisbury MSA, MD-DE	Y	18150 FQ	21080 MW	31000 TQ	USBLS	5/15
	Massachusetts	Y	26480 FQ	30940 MW	38060 TQ	USBLS	5/15
	Boston-Cambridge-Newton NECTA, MA	Y	26740 FQ	30740 MW	38080 TQ	USBLS	5/15
	Worcester MSA, MA-CT	Y	27750 FQ	31030 MW	36740 TQ	USBLS	5/15
	Michigan	Y	20090 FQ	23770 MW	29440 TQ	USBLS	5/15
	Detroit-Dearborn-Livonia PMSA, MI	Y	21600 FQ	27820 MW	31670 TQ	USBLS	5/15
	Grand Rapids-Wyoming MSA, MI	Y	19830 FQ	22620 MW	26610 TQ	USBLS	5/15
	Minnesota	Y	24999 FQ	32189 MW	40360 TQ	MNBLS	1/16-3/16
	Minneapolis-St. Paul-Bloomington MSA, MN-WI	Y	23613 FQ	34221 MW	44354 TQ	MNBLS	1/16-3/16
	Mississippi	Y	17640 FQ	19850 MW	24810 TQ	USBLS	5/15
	Jackson MSA, MS	Y	17910 FQ	20700 MW	25060 TQ	USBLS	5/15
	Missouri	Y	22060 FQ	27500 MW	33670 TQ	USBLS	5/15
	Kansas City MSA, MO-KS	Y	20060 FQ	23380 MW	29090 TQ	USBLS	5/15
	St. Louis MSA, MO-IL	Y	23460 FQ	29480 MW	37170 TQ	USBLS	5/15
	Montana	Y	25080 FQ	33260 MW	40010 TQ	USBLS	5/15
	Nebraska	Y	19760 FQ	23245 MW	30455 TQ	NEBLS	7/16-9/16
	Omaha-Council Bluffs MSA, NE-IA	Y	21980 FQ	25600 MW	31425 TQ	NEBLS	7/16-9/16
	Nevada	Y	20620 FQ	27740 MW	35310 TQ	USBLS	5/15
	Las Vegas-Henderson-Paradise MSA, NV	Y	19620 FQ	26760 MW	32270 TQ	USBLS	5/15
	New Hampshire	H	10.12 AE	11.27 MW	12.45 AEX	NHBLS	6/16
	Manchester NECTA, NH	H	8.97 AE	11.10 MW	13.49 AEX	NHBLS	6/16
	Nashua NECTA, NH-MA	Y	21030 FQ	26790 MW	29430 TQ	USBLS	5/15
	New Jersey	Y	26340 FQ	30100 MW	37130 TQ	USBLS	5/15
	Camden PMSA, NJ	Y	21540 FQ	27310 MW	30480 TQ	USBLS	5/15
	Newark PMSA, NJ-PA	Y	26220 FQ	31480 MW	40060 TQ	USBLS	5/15
	Trenton MSA, NJ	Y	25890 FQ	30980 MW	36200 TQ	USBLS	5/15
	New Mexico	Y	20800 FQ	23460 MW	28020 TQ	USBLS	5/15
	Albuquerque MSA, NM	Y	20600 FQ	22930 MW	26400 TQ	USBLS	5/15
	New York	Y	20080 AE	29030 MW	38500 AEX	NYBLS	1/16-3/16

AE	Average entry wage	AWR	Average wage range	H	Hourly	LR	Low end range	MTC	Median total compensation	TCC	Total cash compensation
AEX	Average experienced wage	B	Biweekly	HI	Highest wage paid	M	Monthly	MW	Median wage paid	TQ	Third quartile wage
ATC	Average total compensation	D	Daily	HR	High end range	MCC	Median cash compensation	MWR	Median wage range	W	Weekly
AW	Average wage paid	FQ	First quartile wage	LO	Lowest wage paid	ME	Median entry wage	S	See annotated source	Y	Yearly

Courier and Messenger

Occupation/Type/Industry	Location	Per	Low	Mid	High	Source	Date
Courier and Messenger	Buffalo-Cheektowaga-Niagara Falls MSA, NY	Y	22810 FQ	30030 MW	36520 TQ	USBLS	5/15
	Nassau County-Suffolk County PMSA, NY	Y	27190 FQ	35350 MW	43940 TQ	USBLS	5/15
	New York-Jersey City-White Plains PMSA, NY-NJ	Y	20530 FQ	29810 MW	40150 TQ	USBLS	5/15
	Rochester MSA, NY	Y	19410 FQ	23260 MW	28950 TQ	USBLS	5/15
	North Carolina	Y	21120 FQ	25880 MW	31200 TQ	USBLS	5/15
	Charlotte-Concord-Gastonia MSA, NC-SC	Y	22630 FQ	27740 MW	34020 TQ	USBLS	5/15
	Raleigh MSA, NC	Y	22560 FQ	26560 MW	30440 TQ	USBLS	5/15
	North Dakota	Y	19840 FQ	24470 MW	29330 TQ	USBLS	5/15
	Fargo MSA, ND-MN	Y	19050 FQ	23260 MW	27580 TQ	USBLS	5/15
	Ohio	Y	21310 FQ	24410 MW	29290 TQ	USBLS	5/15
	Cincinnati MSA, OH-KY-IN	Y	22500 FQ	26340 MW	30470 TQ	USBLS	5/15
	Cleveland-Elyria MSA, OH	Y	24140 FQ	28330 MW	32630 TQ	USBLS	5/15
	Columbus MSA, OH	Y	21370 FQ	25750 MW	33500 TQ	USBLS	5/15
	Oklahoma	Y	22520 FQ	27660 MW	34800 TQ	USBLS	5/15
	Oklahoma City MSA, OK	Y	24300 FQ	29960 MW	38110 TQ	USBLS	5/15
	Tulsa MSA, OK	Y	22370 FQ	26260 MW	30280 TQ	USBLS	5/15
	Oregon	H	13.55 FQ	16.29 MW	18.72 TQ	ORBLS	2016
	Portland-Vancouver-Hillsboro MSA, OR-WA	Y	31930 FQ	36080 MW	40980 TQ	USBLS	5/15
	Pennsylvania	Y	22820 FQ	26840 MW	30730 TQ	USBLS	5/15
	Allentown-Bethlehem-Easton MSA, PA-NJ	Y	22500 FQ	25400 MW	29500 TQ	USBLS	5/15
	Harrisburg-Carlisle MSA, PA	Y	20960 FQ	29780 MW	41300 TQ	USBLS	5/15
	Montgomery County-Bucks County-Chester County PMSA, PA	Y	25460 FQ	29010 MW	34270 TQ	USBLS	5/15
	Philadelphia PMSA, PA	Y	24830 FQ	27590 MW	30320 TQ	USBLS	5/15
	Pittsburgh MSA, PA	Y	23030 FQ	26890 MW	30410 TQ	USBLS	5/15
	Rhode Island	Y	25670 FQ	30680 MW	37330 TQ	USBLS	5/15
	Providence-Warwick MSA, RI-MA	Y	25800 FQ	31190 MW	37340 TQ	USBLS	5/15
	South Carolina	Y	19270 FQ	23080 MW	28030 TQ	USBLS	5/15
	Charleston-North Charleston MSA, SC	Y	20040 FQ	23080 MW	26820 TQ	USBLS	5/15
	Columbia MSA, SC	Y	18840 FQ	22190 MW	26300 TQ	USBLS	5/15
	Greenville-Anderson-Mauldin MSA, SC	Y	18650 FQ	22570 MW	29290 TQ	USBLS	5/15
	South Dakota	Y	21780 FQ	24100 MW	28420 TQ	USBLS	5/15
	Tennessee	Y	24800 FQ	30300 MW	37040 TQ	USBLS	5/15
	Knoxville MSA, TN	Y	20480 FQ	24660 MW	29650 TQ	USBLS	5/15
	Memphis MSA, TN-MS-AR	Y	27340 FQ	32550 MW	37880 TQ	USBLS	5/15
	Nashville-Davidson–Murfreesboro–Franklin MSA, TN	Y	24480 FQ	29100 MW	35960 TQ	USBLS	5/15
	Texas	Y	19900 FQ	25620 MW	30690 TQ	USBLS	5/15
	Austin-Round Rock MSA, TX	Y	21740 FQ	27350 MW	33330 TQ	USBLS	5/15
	Dallas-Plano-Irving PMSA, TX	Y	21770 FQ	27810 MW	35770 TQ	USBLS	5/15
	Fort Worth-Arlington PMSA, TX	Y	19620 FQ	26840 MW	29790 TQ	USBLS	5/15
	Houston-The Woodlands-Sugar Land MSA, TX	Y	21060 FQ	25160 MW	30750 TQ	USBLS	5/15
	San Antonio-New Braunfels MSA, TX	Y	25250 FQ	28460 MW	34690 TQ	USBLS	5/15
	Utah	Y	21650 FQ	24600 MW	29430 TQ	USBLS	5/15
	Ogden-Clearfield MSA, UT	Y	22860 FQ	26320 MW	28970 TQ	USBLS	5/15
	Provo-Orem MSA, UT	Y	21240 FQ	23160 MW	25200 TQ	USBLS	5/15
	Salt Lake City MSA, UT	Y	21680 FQ	24740 MW	30220 TQ	USBLS	5/15
	Vermont	Y	19850 FQ	22500 MW	26750 TQ	USBLS	5/15
	Burlington-South Burlington MSA, VT	Y	19670 FQ	23170 MW	33820 TQ	USBLS	5/15
	Virginia	Y	23750 FQ	29220 MW	36690 TQ	USBLS	5/15
	Richmond MSA, VA	Y	22870 FQ	27400 MW	33070 TQ	USBLS	5/15
	Virginia Beach-Norfolk-Newport News MSA, VA-NC	Y	21860 FQ	25900 MW	31590 TQ	USBLS	5/15
	Washington	H	12.60 FQ	14.70 MW	17.51 TQ	WABLS	3/16
	Seattle-Bellevue-Everett PMSA, WA	H	13.41 FQ	15.22 MW	17.86 TQ	WABLS	3/16
	Tacoma-Lakewood PMSA, WA	H	13.01 FQ	15.28 MW	18.56 TQ	WABLS	3/16

AE Average entry wage	**AWR** Average wage range	**H** Hourly	**LR** Low end range	**MTC** Median total compensation	**TCC** Total cash compensation
AEX Average experienced wage	**B** Biweekly	**HI** Highest wage paid	**M** Monthly	**MW** Median wage paid	**TQ** Third quartile wage
ATC Average total compensation	**D** Daily	**HR** High end range	**MCC** Median cash compensation	**MWR** Median wage range	**W** Weekly
AW Average wage paid	**FQ** First quartile wage	**LO** Lowest wage paid	**ME** Median entry wage	**S** See annotated source	**Y** Yearly

Occupation/Type/Industry	Location	Per	Low	Mid	High	Source	Date
Courier and Messenger	West Virginia	Y	20890 FQ	24450 MW	30070 TQ	USBLS	5/15
	Huntington-Ashland MSA, WV-KY-OH	Y	20680 FQ	24620 MW	28660 TQ	USBLS	5/15
	Wisconsin	Y	18730 FQ	23070 MW	28930 TQ	USBLS	5/15
	Madison MSA, WI	Y	21240 FQ	24540 MW	32080 TQ	USBLS	5/15
	Milwaukee-Waukesha-West Allis MSA, WI	Y	18520 FQ	22960 MW	28700 TQ	USBLS	5/15
	Wyoming	Y	20630 FQ	28560 MW	35130 TQ	USBLS	5/15
	Cheyenne MSA, WY	Y	18650 FQ	21710 MW	27210 TQ	USBLS	5/15
	Puerto Rico	Y	17180 FQ	18900 MW	23350 TQ	USBLS	5/15
	San Juan-Carolina-Caguas MSA, PR	Y	17110 FQ	18800 MW	23070 TQ	USBLS	5/15
	Virgin Islands	Y	18710 FQ	22800 MW	31020 TQ	USBLS	5/15
	Guam	Y	18620 FQ	21170 MW	27320 TQ	USBLS	5/15
Court, Municipal, and License Clerk	Alabama	Y	25229 AE	33154 AW	37112 AEX	ALBLS	6/16
	Birmingham-Hoover MSA, AL	Y	26105 AE	36153 AW	41183 AEX	ALBLS	6/16
	Alaska	Y	39480 FQ	45040 MW	52350 TQ	USBLS	5/15
	Anchorage MSA, AK	Y	36400 FQ	41840 MW	48050 TQ	USBLS	5/15
	Arizona	Y	28930 FQ	31950 MW	38160 TQ	USBLS	5/15
	Phoenix-Mesa-Scottsdale MSA, AZ	Y	29140 FQ	32730 MW	38800 TQ	USBLS	5/15
	Tucson MSA, AZ	Y	27880 FQ	30140 MW	35670 TQ	USBLS	5/15
	Arkansas	Y	22420 FQ	27480 MW	33680 TQ	USBLS	5/15
	Little Rock-North Little Rock-Conway MSA, AR	Y	25940 FQ	29670 MW	35860 TQ	USBLS	5/15
	California	H	18.85 FQ	21.68 MW	23.12 TQ	CABLS	1/16-3/16
	Anaheim-Santa Ana-Irvine PMSA, CA	H	15.72 FQ	21.68 MW	22.29 TQ	CABLS	1/16-3/16
	Los Angeles-Long Beach-Glendale PMSA, CA	H	18.80 FQ	21.70 MW	22.30 TQ	CABLS	1/16-3/16
	Oakland-Hayward-Berkeley PMSA, CA	H	21.54 FQ	21.70 MW	25.87 TQ	CABLS	1/16-3/16
	Riverside-San Bernardino-Ontario MSA, CA	H	19.62 FQ	21.68 MW	22.79 TQ	CABLS	1/16-3/16
	Sacramento–Roseville–Arden-Arcade MSA, CA	H	19.65 FQ	21.68 MW	23.02 TQ	CABLS	1/16-3/16
	San Diego-Carlsbad MSA, CA	H	17.71 FQ	21.45 MW	22.29 TQ	CABLS	1/16-3/16
	San Francisco-Redwood City-South San Francisco PMSA, CA	H	21.70 FQ	31.59 MW	37.74 TQ	CABLS	1/16-3/16
	Colorado	Y	33460 FQ	38910 MW	47030 TQ	USBLS	5/15
	Denver-Aurora-Lakewood MSA, CO	Y	35220 FQ	39980 MW	47060 TQ	USBLS	5/15
	Connecticut	Y		49029 MW		CTBLS	1/16-3/16
	Bridgeport-Stamford-Norwalk MSA, CT	Y	40140 FQ	49590 MW	60420 TQ	USBLS	5/15
	Hartford-West Hartford-East Hartford MSA, CT	Y	42160 FQ	49250 MW	57720 TQ	USBLS	5/15
	Delaware	Y	27770 FQ	34000 MW	38540 TQ	USBLS	5/15
	Wilmington PMSA, DE-MD-NJ	Y	28810 FQ	34000 MW	40080 TQ	USBLS	5/15
	Washington-Arlington-Alexandria PMSA, DC-VA-MD-WV	Y	34420 FQ	40340 MW	49690 TQ	USBLS	5/15
	Florida	H	13.17 AE	16.40 MW	19.12 AEX	FLBLS	7/16-9/16
	Fort Lauderdale-Pompano Beach-Deerfield Beach PMSA, FL	H	12.92 AE	15.05 MW	18.01 AEX	FLBLS	7/16-9/16
	Miami-Miami Beach-Kendall PMSA, FL	H	12.96 AE	17.74 MW	21.21 AEX	FLBLS	7/16-9/16
	Orlando-Kissimmee-Sanford MSA, FL	H	13.89 AE	16.06 MW	18.09 AEX	FLBLS	7/16-9/16
	Tampa-St. Petersburg-Clearwater MSA, FL	H	13.72 AE	17.07 MW	19.60 AEX	FLBLS	7/16-9/16
	Georgia	Y	26260 FQ	30330 MW	36720 TQ	USBLS	5/15
	Atlanta-Sandy Springs-Roswell MSA, GA	Y	27470 FQ	31930 MW	38160 TQ	USBLS	5/15
	Augusta-Richmond County MSA, GA-SC	Y	24460 FQ	29860 MW	36240 TQ	USBLS	5/15
	Hawaii	Y	35650 FQ	42190 MW	50750 TQ	USBLS	5/15

AE	Average entry wage	**AWR**	Average wage range	**H**	Hourly	**LR** Low end range	**MTC** Median total compensation	**TCC** Total cash compensation
AEX	Average experienced wage	**B**	Biweekly	**HI**	Highest wage paid	**M** Monthly	**MW** Median wage paid	**TQ** Third quartile wage
ATC	Average total compensation	**D**	Daily	**HR**	High end range	**MCC** Median cash compensation	**MWR** Median wage range	**W** Weekly
AW	Average wage paid	**FQ**	First quartile wage	**LO**	Lowest wage paid	**ME** Median entry wage	**S** See annotated source	**Y** Yearly

Occupation/Type/Industry	Location	Per	Low	Mid	High	Source	Date
Court, Municipal, and License Clerk	Idaho	Y	28070 FQ	32810 MW	37700 TQ	USBLS	5/15
	Boise City MSA, ID	Y	28070 FQ	32170 MW	37890 TQ	USBLS	5/15
	Illinois	Y	27870 FQ	41710 MW	49740 TQ	USBLS	5/15
	Chicago-Naperville-Arlington Heights PMSA, IL	Y	40160 FQ	46160 MW	55110 TQ	USBLS	5/15
	Lake County-Kenosha County PMSA, IL-WI	Y	37830 FQ	45620 MW	55160 TQ	USBLS	5/15
	Indiana	Y	26050 FQ	29990 MW	35760 TQ	USBLS	5/15
	Gary PMSA, IN	Y	22090 FQ	27550 MW	34670 TQ	USBLS	5/15
	Indianapolis-Carmel-Anderson MSA, IN	Y	26810 FQ	30440 MW	37450 TQ	USBLS	5/15
	Michigan City-La Porte MSA, IN	Y	25120 FQ	29730 MW	35370 TQ	USBLS	5/15
	Iowa	Y	28610 FQ	37350 MW	44570 TQ	USBLS	5/15
	Des Moines-West Des Moines MSA, IA	Y	37840 FQ	44560 MW	44570 TQ	USBLS	5/15
	Kansas	Y	26780 FQ	30960 MW	37070 TQ	USBLS	5/15
	Wichita MSA, KS	Y	27520 FQ	30960 MW	35450 TQ	USBLS	5/15
	Kentucky	Y	26410 FQ	29990 MW	37460 TQ	USBLS	5/15
	Louisville-Jefferson County MSA, KY-IN	Y	26490 FQ	29170 MW	34160 TQ	USBLS	5/15
	Louisiana	Y	26080 FQ	31910 MW	38740 TQ	USBLS	5/15
	Baton Rouge MSA, LA	Y	24860 FQ	30070 MW	36730 TQ	USBLS	5/15
	New Orleans-Metairie MSA, LA	Y	26830 FQ	33780 MW	38480 TQ	USBLS	5/15
	Maine	Y	27560 FQ	32650 MW	38430 TQ	USBLS	5/15
	Portland-South Portland MSA, ME	Y	29080 FQ	36240 MW	42300 TQ	USBLS	5/15
	Salisbury MSA, MD-DE	Y	29710 FQ	35530 MW	40460 TQ	USBLS	5/15
	Massachusetts	Y	38390 FQ	45410 MW	53230 TQ	USBLS	5/15
	Boston-Cambridge-Newton NECTA, MA	Y	40570 FQ	46100 MW	53050 TQ	USBLS	5/15
	Worcester MSA, MA-CT	Y	33860 FQ	41260 MW	48430 TQ	USBLS	5/15
	Michigan	Y	32720 FQ	38540 MW	46720 TQ	USBLS	5/15
	Detroit-Dearborn-Livonia PMSA, MI	Y	32180 FQ	38130 MW	46120 TQ	USBLS	5/15
	Grand Rapids-Wyoming MSA, MI	Y	34580 FQ	40410 MW	46790 TQ	USBLS	5/15
	Minnesota	Y	36911 FQ	43930 MW	51251 TQ	MNBLS	1/16-3/16
	Minneapolis-St. Paul-Bloomington MSA, MN-WI	Y	37447 FQ	43990 MW	50928 TQ	MNBLS	1/16-3/16
	Mississippi	Y	23120 FQ	28200 MW	33940 TQ	USBLS	5/15
	Jackson MSA, MS	Y	25030 FQ	28700 MW	34110 TQ	USBLS	5/15
	Missouri	Y	24620 FQ	26700 MW	32170 TQ	USBLS	5/15
	Kansas City MSA, MO-KS	Y	25150 FQ	28310 MW	35310 TQ	USBLS	5/15
	St. Louis MSA, MO-IL	Y	25510 FQ	29110 MW	36810 TQ	USBLS	5/15
	Montana	Y	24960 FQ	29450 MW	35480 TQ	USBLS	5/15
	Billings MSA, MT	Y	27070 FQ	29530 MW	34240 TQ	USBLS	5/15
	Nebraska	Y	27000 FQ	31450 MW	37925 TQ	NEBLS	7/16-9/16
	Omaha-Council Bluffs MSA, NE-IA	Y	29985 FQ	36680 MW	43340 TQ	NEBLS	7/16-9/16
	Nevada	Y	34130 FQ	41100 MW	50080 TQ	USBLS	5/15
	Las Vegas-Henderson-Paradise MSA, NV	Y	35150 FQ	43170 MW	53770 TQ	USBLS	5/15
	New Hampshire	H	13.70 AE	18.09 MW	21.35 AEX	NHBLS	6/16
	Manchester NECTA, NH	H	15.94 AE	20.90 MW	22.71 AEX	NHBLS	6/16
	Nashua NECTA, NH-MA	Y	30540 FQ	38420 MW	45450 TQ	USBLS	5/15
	New Jersey	Y	38660 FQ	46850 MW	56120 TQ	USBLS	5/15
	Camden PMSA, NJ	Y	35210 FQ	44830 MW	51990 TQ	USBLS	5/15
	Newark PMSA, NJ-PA	Y	39010 FQ	48570 MW	58130 TQ	USBLS	5/15
	Trenton MSA, NJ	Y	40990 FQ	47060 MW	55500 TQ	USBLS	5/15
	New Mexico	Y	27340 FQ	29520 MW	36880 TQ	USBLS	5/15
	Albuquerque MSA, NM	Y	27720 FQ	29170 MW	32230 TQ	USBLS	5/15
	New York	Y	32860 AE	49740 MW	67420 AEX	NYBLS	1/16-3/16
	Buffalo-Cheektowaga-Niagara Falls MSA, NY	Y	32980 FQ	40900 MW	56560 TQ	USBLS	5/15
	Nassau County-Suffolk County PMSA, NY	Y	43490 FQ	55780 MW	83240 TQ	USBLS	5/15
	New York-Jersey City-White Plains PMSA, NY-NJ	Y	43450 FQ	55720 MW	79530 TQ	USBLS	5/15
	Rochester MSA, NY	Y	30650 FQ	37260 MW	50330 TQ	USBLS	5/15

AE	Average entry wage	AWR	Average wage range	H	Hourly
AEX	Average experienced wage	B	Biweekly	HI	Highest wage paid
ATC	Average total compensation	D	Daily	HR	High end range
AW	Average wage paid	FQ	First quartile wage	LO	Lowest wage paid

LR	Low end range	MTC	Median total compensation	TCC	Total cash compensation
M	Monthly	MW	Median wage paid	TQ	Third quartile wage
MCC	Median cash compensation	MWR	Median wage range	W	Weekly
ME	Median entry wage	S	See annotated source	Y	Yearly

Occupation/Type/Industry	Location	Per	Low	Mid	High	Source	Date
Court, Municipal, and License Clerk	North Carolina	Y	28610 FQ	31210 MW	39080 TQ	USBLS	5/15
	Charlotte-Concord-Gastonia MSA, NC-SC	Y	28610 FQ	30740 MW	38320 TQ	USBLS	5/15
	Raleigh MSA, NC	Y	29650 FQ	33070 MW	41200 TQ	USBLS	5/15
	North Dakota	Y	35490 FQ	42750 MW	48080 TQ	USBLS	5/15
	Fargo MSA, ND-MN	Y	38710 FQ	46160 MW	49640 TQ	USBLS	5/15
	Ohio	Y	27070 FQ	33840 MW	41230 TQ	USBLS	5/15
	Cincinnati MSA, OH-KY-IN	Y	28210 FQ	33370 MW	40020 TQ	USBLS	5/15
	Cleveland-Elyria MSA, OH	Y	28360 FQ	34470 MW	41830 TQ	USBLS	5/15
	Columbus MSA, OH	Y	29310 FQ	36080 MW	44510 TQ	USBLS	5/15
	Oklahoma	Y	23830 FQ	30180 MW	37420 TQ	USBLS	5/15
	Oklahoma City MSA, OK	Y	23770 FQ	32280 MW	39090 TQ	USBLS	5/15
	Tulsa MSA, OK	Y	24290 FQ	29300 MW	37650 TQ	USBLS	5/15
	Oregon	H	17.19 FQ	20.36 MW	23.57 TQ	ORBLS	2016
	Portland-Vancouver-Hillsboro MSA, OR-WA	Y	35770 FQ	42640 MW	48350 TQ	USBLS	5/15
	Pennsylvania	Y	26350 FQ	34490 MW	43530 TQ	USBLS	5/15
	Allentown-Bethlehem-Easton MSA, PA-NJ	Y	33810 FQ	40000 MW	51320 TQ	USBLS	5/15
	Harrisburg-Carlisle MSA, PA	Y	26880 FQ	35950 MW	45050 TQ	USBLS	5/15
	Montgomery County-Bucks County-Chester County PMSA, PA	Y	29740 FQ	35000 MW	40870 TQ	USBLS	5/15
	Philadelphia PMSA, PA	Y	33190 FQ	40780 MW	46770 TQ	USBLS	5/15
	Pittsburgh MSA, PA	Y	22640 FQ	31170 MW	41420 TQ	USBLS	5/15
	Rhode Island	Y	41030 FQ	46760 MW	53480 TQ	USBLS	5/15
	Providence-Warwick MSA, RI-MA	Y	41170 FQ	47100 MW	53700 TQ	USBLS	5/15
	South Carolina	Y	26750 FQ	31750 MW	38300 TQ	USBLS	5/15
	Charleston-North Charleston MSA, SC	Y	26900 FQ	31770 MW	38140 TQ	USBLS	5/15
	Columbia MSA, SC	Y	28500 FQ	34200 MW	40000 TQ	USBLS	5/15
	Greenville-Anderson-Mauldin MSA, SC	Y	27700 FQ	32620 MW	37830 TQ	USBLS	5/15
	South Dakota	Y	25860 FQ	29560 MW	35410 TQ	USBLS	5/15
	Sioux Falls MSA, SD	Y	28060 FQ	32320 MW	38030 TQ	USBLS	5/15
	Tennessee	Y	27570 FQ	32630 MW	38540 TQ	USBLS	5/15
	Knoxville MSA, TN	Y	27020 FQ	33180 MW	38850 TQ	USBLS	5/15
	Memphis MSA, TN-MS-AR	Y	27540 FQ	31250 MW	36710 TQ	USBLS	5/15
	Nashville-Davidson–Murfreesboro–Franklin MSA, TN	Y	30760 FQ	36570 MW	45680 TQ	USBLS	5/15
	Texas	Y	26810 FQ	32770 MW	38880 TQ	USBLS	5/15
	Austin-Round Rock MSA, TX	Y	32820 FQ	36500 MW	41270 TQ	USBLS	5/15
	Dallas-Plano-Irving PMSA, TX	Y	29820 FQ	35590 MW	44100 TQ	USBLS	5/15
	Fort Worth-Arlington PMSA, TX	Y	31500 FQ	35310 MW	39140 TQ	USBLS	5/15
	Houston-The Woodlands-Sugar Land MSA, TX	Y	23440 FQ	31900 MW	43080 TQ	USBLS	5/15
	San Antonio-New Braunfels MSA, TX	Y	26840 FQ	31480 MW	37640 TQ	USBLS	5/15
	Utah	Y	27540 FQ	30820 MW	37750 TQ	USBLS	5/15
	Ogden-Clearfield MSA, UT	Y	27290 FQ	29780 MW	34640 TQ	USBLS	5/15
	Provo-Orem MSA, UT	Y	27910 FQ	31810 MW	40120 TQ	USBLS	5/15
	Salt Lake City MSA, UT	Y	27610 FQ	30790 MW	38890 TQ	USBLS	5/15
	Vermont	Y	29770 FQ	35820 MW	41840 TQ	USBLS	5/15
	Burlington-South Burlington MSA, VT	Y	34380 FQ	37960 MW	43460 TQ	USBLS	5/15
	Virginia	Y	29150 FQ	34000 MW	39910 TQ	USBLS	5/15
	Richmond MSA, VA	Y	29080 FQ	32660 MW	38860 TQ	USBLS	5/15
	Virginia Beach-Norfolk-Newport News MSA, VA-NC	Y	29090 FQ	31470 MW	38560 TQ	USBLS	5/15
	Washington	H	18.61 FQ	22.08 MW	26.28 TQ	WABLS	3/16
	Seattle-Bellevue-Everett PMSA, WA	H	20.70 FQ	25.37 MW	28.61 TQ	WABLS	3/16
	Tacoma-Lakewood PMSA, WA	H	20.89 FQ	26.48 MW	31.95 TQ	WABLS	3/16
	West Virginia	Y	23790 FQ	30910 MW	43260 TQ	USBLS	5/15
	Huntington-Ashland MSA, WV-KY-OH	Y	25320 FQ	29450 MW	36640 TQ	USBLS	5/15
	Wisconsin	Y	18590 FQ	24510 MW	38610 TQ	USBLS	5/15
	Madison MSA, WI	Y	25460 FQ	33650 MW	44930 TQ	USBLS	5/15

AE	Average entry wage	AWR	Average wage range	H	Hourly
AEX	Average experienced wage	B	Biweekly	HI	Highest wage paid
ATC	Average total compensation	D	Daily	HR	High end range
AW	Average wage paid	FQ	First quartile wage	LO	Lowest wage paid

LR	Low end range	MTC	Median total compensation
M	Monthly	MW	Median wage paid
MCC	Median cash compensation	MWR	Median wage range
ME	Median entry wage	S	See annotated source

TCC	Total cash compensation
TQ	Third quartile wage
W	Weekly
Y	Yearly

Occupation/Type/Industry	Location	Per	Low	Mid	High	Source	Date
Court, Municipal, and License Clerk	Milwaukee-Waukesha-West Allis MSA, WI	Y	22130 FQ	24330 MW	41340 TQ	USBLS	5/15
	Wyoming	Y	30370 FQ	35870 MW	43710 TQ	USBLS	5/15
	Cheyenne MSA, WY	Y	28120 FQ	30820 MW	34830 TQ	USBLS	5/15
Court Appointment Specialist							
County Government	Oakland County, MI	B	1439 LO		1874 HI	MIOAK2	10/1/16
Court Interpreter							
Municipal Government	Seattle, WA	H	29.43 LO		34.30 HI	CSSS	1/13/16
Court Liaison							
Police Department, Municipal Government	Costa Mesa, CA	Y			74902 HI	CACIT	6/28/16
Police Department, Municipal Government	Montebello, CA	Y			41891 HI	CACIT	6/28/16
Police Department, Municipal Government	Colorado Springs, CO	Y	46996 LO		64619 HI	COSPRS	2017
Court Referral Counselor							
Municipal Government	Nashville, TN	Y		54707 AW		NTNGOV	2017
Court Reporter	Alabama	Y	17971 AE	39081 AW	49631 AEX	ALBLS	6/16
	Birmingham-Hoover MSA, AL	Y	17848 AE	35391 AW	44167 AEX	ALBLS	6/16
	Montgomery MSA, AL	Y	17318 AE	32394 AW	39937 AEX	ALBLS	6/16
	Arizona	Y	52270 FQ	60630 MW	70410 TQ	USBLS	5/15
	Phoenix-Mesa-Scottsdale MSA, AZ	Y	53310 FQ	63640 MW	72240 TQ	USBLS	5/15
	Tucson MSA, AZ	Y	55970 FQ	62590 MW	71890 TQ	USBLS	5/15
	Arkansas	Y	30920 FQ	47030 MW	60620 TQ	USBLS	5/15
	Little Rock-North Little Rock-Conway MSA, AR	Y	25280 FQ	34600 MW	53830 TQ	USBLS	5/15
	California	H	25.27 FQ	36.07 MW	43.58 TQ	CABLS	1/16-3/16
	Anaheim-Santa Ana-Irvine PMSA, CA	H	20.98 FQ	22.55 MW	24.12 TQ	CABLS	1/16-3/16
	Los Angeles-Long Beach-Glendale PMSA, CA	H	36.06 FQ	36.07 MW	42.80 TQ	CABLS	1/16-3/16
	Oakland-Hayward-Berkeley PMSA, CA	H	38.08 FQ	41.29 MW	44.59 TQ	CABLS	1/16-3/16
	Riverside-San Bernardino-Ontario MSA, CA	H	35.32 FQ	40.76 MW	45.74 TQ	CABLS	1/16-3/16
	Sacramento–Roseville–Arden-Arcade MSA, CA	H	31.70 FQ	36.77 MW	44.42 TQ	CABLS	1/16-3/16
	San Diego-Carlsbad MSA, CA	H	20.08 FQ	23.29 MW	37.54 TQ	CABLS	1/16-3/16
	Colorado	Y	59870 FQ	72250 MW	89950 TQ	USBLS	5/15
	Denver-Aurora-Lakewood MSA, CO	Y	64810 FQ	83450 MW	95400 TQ	USBLS	5/15
	Connecticut	Y		51080 MW		CTBLS	1/16-3/16
	Bridgeport-Stamford-Norwalk MSA, CT	Y	45330 FQ	52340 MW	60320 TQ	USBLS	5/15
	Hartford-West Hartford-East Hartford MSA, CT	Y	19400 FQ	46690 MW	57540 TQ	USBLS	5/15
	Delaware	Y	29640 FQ	55870 MW	68360 TQ	USBLS	5/15
	Wilmington PMSA, DE-MD-NJ	Y	34830 FQ	40510 MW	60520 TQ	USBLS	5/15
	District of Columbia	Y	38770 FQ	47320 MW	58250 TQ	USBLS	5/15
	Washington-Arlington-Alexandria PMSA, DC-VA-MD-WV	Y	35830 FQ	39760 MW	48420 TQ	USBLS	5/15
	Florida	H	11.74 AE	17.72 MW	25.29 AEX	FLBLS	7/16-9/16
	Fort Lauderdale-Pompano Beach-Deerfield Beach PMSA, FL	H	13.93 AE	15.96 MW	18.34 AEX	FLBLS	7/16-9/16
	Orlando-Kissimmee-Sanford MSA, FL	H	16.98 AE	25.52 MW	28.19 AEX	FLBLS	7/16-9/16
	Tampa-St. Petersburg-Clearwater MSA, FL	H	9.05 AE	16.34 MW	18.95 AEX	FLBLS	7/16-9/16
	Georgia	Y	33080 FQ	52090 MW	59070 TQ	USBLS	5/15
	Atlanta-Sandy Springs-Roswell MSA, GA	Y	41090 FQ	54600 MW	59970 TQ	USBLS	5/15
	Hawaii	Y	38750 FQ	49340 MW	66460 TQ	USBLS	5/15
	Urban Honolulu MSA, HI	Y	37760 FQ	46780 MW	61910 TQ	USBLS	5/15
	Illinois	Y	45840 FQ	56560 MW	74290 TQ	USBLS	5/15
	Indiana	Y	31800 FQ	35830 MW	40200 TQ	USBLS	5/15

AE	Average entry wage	AWR	Average wage range	H	Hourly
AEX	Average experienced wage	B	Biweekly	HI	Highest wage paid
ATC	Average total compensation	D	Daily	HR	High end range
AW	Average wage paid	FQ	First quartile wage	LO	Lowest wage paid

LR	Low end range	MTC	Median total compensation	TCC	Total cash compensation
M	Monthly	MW	Median wage paid	TQ	Third quartile wage
MCC	Median cash compensation	MWR	Median wage range	W	Weekly
ME	Median entry wage	S	See annotated source	Y	Yearly

Occupation/Type/Industry	Location	Per	Low	Mid	High	Source	Date
Court Reporter	Gary PMSA, IN	Y	31620 FQ	34770 MW	37910 TQ	USBLS	5/15
	Indianapolis-Carmel-Anderson MSA, IN	Y	33660 FQ	37810 MW	45280 TQ	USBLS	5/15
	Iowa	Y	67250 FQ	76050 MW	76060 TQ	USBLS	5/15
	Kansas	Y	47880 FQ	55480 MW	55490 TQ	USBLS	5/15
	Kentucky	Y	25630 FQ	30610 MW	36790 TQ	USBLS	5/15
	Louisiana	Y	26760 FQ	42420 MW	53830 TQ	USBLS	5/15
	Baton Rouge MSA, LA	Y	35530 FQ	47250 MW	56730 TQ	USBLS	5/15
	New Orleans-Metairie MSA, LA	Y	40310 FQ	46390 MW	53930 TQ	USBLS	5/15
	Maryland	Y	33805 AE	42422 MW	46731 AEX	MDBLS	4/16
	Baltimore-Columbia-Towson MSA, MD	Y	36870 FQ	41050 MW	47920 TQ	USBLS	5/15
	Salisbury MSA, MD-DE	Y	19750 FQ	36860 MW	42300 TQ	USBLS	5/15
	Michigan	Y	33770 FQ	43040 MW	51230 TQ	USBLS	5/15
	Detroit-Dearborn-Livonia PMSA, MI	Y	29810 FQ	41960 MW	54240 TQ	USBLS	5/15
	Grand Rapids-Wyoming MSA, MI	Y	48070 FQ	55410 MW	61140 TQ	USBLS	5/15
	Minnesota	Y	50201 FQ	67449 MW	67469 TQ	MNBLS	1/16-3/16
	Minneapolis-St. Paul-Bloomington MSA, MN-WI	Y	49626 FQ	67459 MW	67469 TQ	MNBLS	1/16-3/16
	Mississippi	Y	19770 FQ	32310 MW	42310 TQ	USBLS	5/15
	Jackson MSA, MS	Y	30450 FQ	39140 MW	42350 TQ	USBLS	5/15
	Missouri	Y	57240 FQ	57250 MW	57260 TQ	USBLS	5/15
	St. Louis MSA, MO-IL	Y	57240 FQ	57250 MW	58570 TQ	USBLS	5/15
	Montana	Y	38950 FQ	43820 MW	51620 TQ	USBLS	5/15
	Nebraska	Y	27820 FQ	44450 MW	56160 TQ	NEBLS	7/16-9/16
	Omaha-Council Bluffs MSA, NE-IA	Y	23360 FQ	51775 MW	69620 TQ	NEBLS	7/16-9/16
	Nevada	Y	52480 FQ	57350 MW	62350 TQ	USBLS	5/15
	Las Vegas-Henderson-Paradise MSA, NV	Y	52250 FQ	56040 MW	59690 TQ	USBLS	5/15
	New Jersey	Y	36910 FQ	43000 MW	48750 TQ	USBLS	5/15
	Newark PMSA, NJ-PA	Y	40090 FQ	44700 MW	49430 TQ	USBLS	5/15
	New Mexico	Y	43820 FQ	68880 MW	75680 TQ	USBLS	5/15
	New York	Y	56640 AE	98420 MW	107970 AEX	NYBLS	1/16-3/16
	Buffalo-Cheektowaga-Niagara Falls MSA, NY	Y	64920 FQ	82720 MW	97450 TQ	USBLS	5/15
	Nassau County-Suffolk County PMSA, NY	Y	26150 FQ	68430 MW	93770 TQ	USBLS	5/15
	New York-Jersey City-White Plains PMSA, NY-NJ	Y	70310 FQ	97560 MW	114760 TQ	USBLS	5/15
	North Carolina	Y	31680 FQ	49910 MW	57490 TQ	USBLS	5/15
	Charlotte-Concord-Gastonia MSA, NC-SC	Y	30070 FQ	46000 MW	60670 TQ	USBLS	5/15
	North Dakota	Y	42480 FQ	47950 MW	55820 TQ	USBLS	5/15
	Ohio	Y	37880 FQ	47120 MW	57060 TQ	USBLS	5/15
	Cincinnati MSA, OH-KY-IN	Y	32680 FQ	45340 MW	56150 TQ	USBLS	5/15
	Cleveland-Elyria MSA, OH	Y	51960 FQ	56570 MW	61180 TQ	USBLS	5/15
	Columbus MSA, OH	Y	40060 FQ	47490 MW	57720 TQ	USBLS	5/15
	Oklahoma	Y	19930 FQ	52160 MW	60270 TQ	USBLS	5/15
	Oregon	H	13.81 FQ	15.23 MW	23.30 TQ	ORBLS	2016
	Pennsylvania	Y	30440 FQ	47170 MW	62240 TQ	USBLS	5/15
	Allentown-Bethlehem-Easton MSA, PA-NJ	Y	39230 FQ	53300 MW	61610 TQ	USBLS	5/15
	Harrisburg-Carlisle MSA, PA	Y	46130 FQ	62900 MW	76500 TQ	USBLS	5/15
	Montgomery County-Bucks County-Chester County PMSA, PA	Y	44860 FQ	58020 MW	85400 TQ	USBLS	5/15
	Philadelphia PMSA, PA	Y	45560 FQ	59550 MW	71760 TQ	USBLS	5/15
	Pittsburgh MSA, PA	Y	26530 FQ	30790 MW	51340 TQ	USBLS	5/15
	South Carolina	Y	37690 FQ	44010 MW	56980 TQ	USBLS	5/15
	Charleston-North Charleston MSA, SC	Y	38070 FQ	62940 MW	70340 TQ	USBLS	5/15
	South Dakota	Y	42170 FQ	46520 MW	50890 TQ	USBLS	5/15
	Tennessee	Y	46470 FQ	62180 MW	87530 TQ	USBLS	5/15
	Memphis MSA, TN-MS-AR	Y	42430 FQ	57770 MW	71800 TQ	USBLS	5/15
	Texas	Y	41090 FQ	68610 MW	80610 TQ	USBLS	5/15
	Austin-Round Rock MSA, TX	Y	59740 FQ	80910 MW	92030 TQ	USBLS	5/15
	Houston-The Woodlands-Sugar Land MSA, TX	Y	28680 FQ	61980 MW	73370 TQ	USBLS	5/15

AE	Average entry wage	AWR	Average wage range	H	Hourly	LR	Low end range	MTC	Median total compensation	TCC	Total cash compensation
AEX	Average experienced wage	B	Biweekly	HI	Highest wage paid	M	Monthly	MW	Median wage paid	TQ	Third quartile wage
ATC	Average total compensation	D	Daily	HR	High end range	MCC	Median cash compensation	MWR	Median wage range	W	Weekly
AW	Average wage paid	FQ	First quartile wage	LO	Lowest wage paid	ME	Median entry wage	S	See annotated source	Y	Yearly

361

Occupation/Type/Industry	Location	Per	Low	Mid	High	Source	Date
Court Reporter	San Antonio-New Braunfels						
	MSA, TX	Y	55720 FQ	74550 MW	90140 TQ	USBLS	5/15
	Utah	Y	16530 FQ	17950 MW	30980 TQ	USBLS	5/15
	Virginia	Y	36970 FQ	43580 MW	48920 TQ	USBLS	5/15
	Virginia Beach-Norfolk-						
	Newport News MSA, VA-NC	Y	42320 FQ	45290 MW	48250 TQ	USBLS	5/15
	Washington	H	22.03 FQ	30.56 MW	41.14 TQ	WABLS	3/16
	Seattle-Bellevue-Everett						
	PMSA, WA	H	19.23 FQ	27.80 MW	41.38 TQ	WABLS	3/16
	West Virginia	Y	42820 FQ	52290 MW	58120 TQ	USBLS	5/15
	Charleston MSA, WV	Y	43870 FQ	54350 MW	59060 TQ	USBLS	5/15
	Wisconsin	Y	43910 FQ	54070 MW	72040 TQ	USBLS	5/15
	Milwaukee-Waukesha-West						
	Allis MSA, WI	Y	44260 FQ	59500 MW	97000 TQ	USBLS	5/15
	Puerto Rico	Y	24250 FQ	27060 MW	29670 TQ	USBLS	5/15
	San Juan-Carolina-Caguas						
	MSA, PR	Y	24250 FQ	27060 MW	29670 TQ	USBLS	5/15
Courtroom Assistant							
Municipal Government	Colorado Springs, CO	Y	39555 LO		54388 HI	COSPRS	2017
Craft Artist	Alabama	Y	21171 AE	29438 AW	33577 AEX	ALBLS	6/16
	Arizona	Y	19190 FQ	24920 MW	38290 TQ	USBLS	5/15
	California	H	14.45 FQ	20.93 MW	32.74 TQ	CABLS	1/16-3/16
	Colorado	Y	19810 FQ	27780 MW	32990 TQ	USBLS	5/15
	Florida	H	9.00 AE	12.36 MW	15.30 AEX	FLBLS	7/16-9/16
	Georgia	Y	25230 FQ	31330 MW	53590 TQ	USBLS	5/15
	Hawaii	Y	41340 FQ	52270 MW	64030 TQ	USBLS	5/15
	Idaho	Y	24620 FQ	28910 MW	42510 TQ	USBLS	5/15
	Illinois	Y	23790 FQ	36620 MW	63320 TQ	USBLS	5/15
	Indiana	Y	24260 FQ	33410 MW	40150 TQ	USBLS	5/15
	Iowa	Y	26430 FQ	30490 MW	36540 TQ	USBLS	5/15
	Kansas	Y	27380 FQ	30580 MW	34990 TQ	USBLS	5/15
	Kentucky	Y	32930 FQ	35230 MW	37530 TQ	USBLS	5/15
	Maine	Y	19190 FQ	24610 MW	28430 TQ	USBLS	5/15
	Maryland	Y	18703 AE	37416 MW	46773 AEX	MDBLS	4/16
	Massachusetts	Y	23860 FQ	34440 MW	45710 TQ	USBLS	5/15
	Michigan	Y	22510 FQ	34200 MW	45200 TQ	USBLS	5/15
	Minnesota	Y	31602 FQ	48336 MW	57449 TQ	MNBLS	1/16-3/16
	Mississippi	Y	22700 FQ	27130 MW	32580 TQ	USBLS	5/15
	Missouri	Y	19270 FQ	25110 MW	29860 TQ	USBLS	5/15
	Nebraska	Y	18855 FQ	34015 MW	37960 TQ	NEBLS	7/16-9/16
	Nevada	Y	20490 FQ	29170 MW	37550 TQ	USBLS	5/15
	New Hampshire	H	9.17 AE	13.22 MW	14.36 AEX	NHBLS	6/16
	New Jersey	Y	19350 FQ	32360 MW	46860 TQ	USBLS	5/15
	New Mexico	Y	24980 FQ	27540 MW	30140 TQ	USBLS	5/15
	New York	Y	23330 AE	33670 MW	52830 AEX	NYBLS	1/16-3/16
	North Carolina	Y	26200 FQ	33130 MW	46650 TQ	USBLS	5/15
	Ohio	Y	19940 FQ	29010 MW	35610 TQ	USBLS	5/15
	Oklahoma	Y	17670 FQ	19910 MW	41180 TQ	USBLS	5/15
	Pennsylvania	Y	32370 FQ	40950 MW	45880 TQ	USBLS	5/15
	Tennessee	Y	28170 FQ	32310 MW	38300 TQ	USBLS	5/15
	Texas	Y	22230 FQ	29460 MW	41290 TQ	USBLS	5/15
	Utah	Y	33080 FQ	41360 MW	46660 TQ	USBLS	5/15
	Vermont	Y	22540 FQ	26520 MW	38720 TQ	USBLS	5/15
	Wisconsin	Y	21830 FQ	27190 MW	38210 TQ	USBLS	5/15
	Wyoming	Y	21080 FQ	24590 MW	29480 TQ	USBLS	5/15
Crafts Instructor							
Recreation and Park Commission,							
Municipal Government	San Francisco, CA	Y		31950 AW		CACIT	6/28/16
Crane and Tower Operator	Alabama	Y	31606 AE	51764 AW	61844 AEX	ALBLS	6/16
	Birmingham-Hoover MSA, AL	Y	29631 AE	42827 AW	49430 AEX	ALBLS	6/16
	Alaska	Y	58560 FQ	71180 MW	79970 TQ	USBLS	5/15
	Arizona	Y	32970 FQ	43380 MW	52730 TQ	USBLS	5/15
	Phoenix-Mesa-Scottsdale						
	MSA, AZ	Y	32010 FQ	43180 MW	52690 TQ	USBLS	5/15
	Arkansas	Y	35220 FQ	44390 MW	55180 TQ	USBLS	5/15
	Little Rock-North Little Rock-						
	Conway MSA, AR	Y	31140 FQ	47170 MW	66320 TQ	USBLS	5/15
	California	H	24.55 FQ	34.04 MW	43.40 TQ	CABLS	1/16-3/16

AE	Average entry wage	AWR	Average wage range	H	Hourly	LR	Low end range	MTC	Median total compensation	TCC	Total cash compensation
AEX	Average experienced wage	B	Biweekly	HI	Highest wage paid	M	Monthly	MW	Median wage paid	TQ	Third quartile wage
ATC	Average total compensation	D	Daily	HR	High end range	MCC	Median cash compensation	MWR	Median wage range	W	Weekly
AW	Average wage paid	FQ	First quartile wage	LO	Lowest wage paid	ME	Median entry wage	S	See annotated source	Y	Yearly

Occupation/Type/Industry	Location	Per	Low	Mid	High	Source	Date
Crane and Tower Operator	Anaheim-Santa Ana-Irvine PMSA, CA	H	24.16 FQ	30.85 MW	35.05 TQ	CABLS	1/16-3/16
	Oakland-Hayward-Berkeley PMSA, CA	H	22.60 FQ	29.83 MW	43.00 TQ	CABLS	1/16-3/16
	Riverside-San Bernardino-Ontario MSA, CA	H	19.90 FQ	22.69 MW	26.95 TQ	CABLS	1/16-3/16
	Sacramento–Roseville–Arden-Arcade MSA, CA	H	40.20 FQ	43.47 MW	46.67 TQ	CABLS	1/16-3/16
	San Diego-Carlsbad MSA, CA	H	25.83 FQ	28.41 MW	30.52 TQ	CABLS	1/16-3/16
	San Francisco-Redwood City-South San Francisco PMSA, CA	H	31.00 FQ	39.88 MW	44.40 TQ	CABLS	1/16-3/16
	Colorado	Y	37100 FQ	44480 MW	57420 TQ	USBLS	5/15
	Denver-Aurora-Lakewood MSA, CO	Y	31570 FQ	36530 MW	44480 TQ	USBLS	5/15
	Connecticut	Y		37499 MW		CTBLS	1/16-3/16
	Delaware	Y	37340 FQ	44580 MW	53090 TQ	USBLS	5/15
	Wilmington PMSA, DE-MD-NJ	Y	38590 FQ	47030 MW	59950 TQ	USBLS	5/15
	District of Columbia	Y	50420 FQ	65630 MW	75150 TQ	USBLS	5/15
	Washington-Arlington-Alexandria PMSA, DC-VA-MD-WV	Y	54660 FQ	66270 MW	76130 TQ	USBLS	5/15
	Florida	H	17.55 AE	24.93 MW	27.75 AEX	FLBLS	7/16-9/16
	Fort Lauderdale-Pompano Beach-Deerfield Beach PMSA, FL	H	18.60 AE	25.26 MW	28.11 AEX	FLBLS	7/16-9/16
	Miami-Miami Beach-Kendall PMSA, FL	H	19.14 AE	26.85 MW	29.98 AEX	FLBLS	7/16-9/16
	Orlando-Kissimmee-Sanford MSA, FL	H	15.74 AE	26.53 MW	28.06 AEX	FLBLS	7/16-9/16
	Tampa-St. Petersburg-Clearwater MSA, FL	H	18.99 AE	27.21 MW	29.96 AEX	FLBLS	7/16-9/16
	Georgia	Y	34720 FQ	44440 MW	55260 TQ	USBLS	5/15
	Atlanta-Sandy Springs-Roswell MSA, GA	Y	36110 FQ	45900 MW	55900 TQ	USBLS	5/15
	Augusta-Richmond County MSA, GA-SC	Y	35250 FQ	50750 MW	58910 TQ	USBLS	5/15
	Hawaii	Y	67460 FQ	74790 MW	82270 TQ	USBLS	5/15
	Urban Honolulu MSA, HI	Y	68810 FQ	74790 MW	82270 TQ	USBLS	5/15
	Idaho	Y	39520 FQ	53370 MW	62090 TQ	USBLS	5/15
	Illinois	Y	32160 FQ	39580 MW	61840 TQ	USBLS	5/15
	Indiana	Y	39260 FQ	59640 MW	75730 TQ	USBLS	5/15
	Gary PMSA, IN	Y	53510 FQ	75880 MW	100440 TQ	USBLS	5/15
	Indianapolis-Carmel-Anderson MSA, IN	Y	35540 FQ	42450 MW	55910 TQ	USBLS	5/15
	Iowa	Y	36930 FQ	44990 MW	52470 TQ	USBLS	5/15
	Des Moines-West Des Moines MSA, IA	Y	48120 FQ	58880 MW	68650 TQ	USBLS	5/15
	Kansas	Y	44830 FQ	56540 MW	71860 TQ	USBLS	5/15
	Wichita MSA, KS	Y	41630 FQ	46320 MW	52690 TQ	USBLS	5/15
	Kentucky	Y	38370 FQ	47600 MW	64680 TQ	USBLS	5/15
	Louisville-Jefferson County MSA, KY-IN	Y	32110 FQ	52490 MW	62760 TQ	USBLS	5/15
	Louisiana	Y	36520 FQ	46400 MW	60330 TQ	USBLS	5/15
	Baton Rouge MSA, LA	Y	33830 FQ	46460 MW	60010 TQ	USBLS	5/15
	New Orleans-Metairie MSA, LA	Y	36940 FQ	48170 MW	66270 TQ	USBLS	5/15
	Maine	Y	41250 FQ	48940 MW	56270 TQ	USBLS	5/15
	Portland-South Portland MSA, ME	Y	41560 FQ	49600 MW	57520 TQ	USBLS	5/15
	Maryland	Y	40046 AE	60211 MW	70294 AEX	MDBLS	4/16
	Baltimore-Columbia-Towson MSA, MD	Y	51100 FQ	63060 MW	72580 TQ	USBLS	5/15
	Massachusetts	Y	40950 FQ	49870 MW	60220 TQ	USBLS	5/15
	Boston-Cambridge-Newton NECTA, MA	Y	44040 FQ	49900 MW	57230 TQ	USBLS	5/15
	Worcester MSA, MA-CT	Y	39280 FQ	44470 MW	49460 TQ	USBLS	5/15
	Michigan	Y	40410 FQ	59100 MW	73050 TQ	USBLS	5/15
	Detroit-Dearborn-Livonia PMSA, MI	Y	36540 FQ	49110 MW	71940 TQ	USBLS	5/15

AE Average entry wage	**AWR** Average wage range	**H** Hourly	**LR** Low end range	**MTC** Median total compensation	**TCC** Total cash compensation
AEX Average experienced wage	**B** Biweekly	**HI** Highest wage paid	**M** Monthly	**MW** Median wage paid	**TQ** Third quartile wage
ATC Average total compensation	**D** Daily	**HR** High end range	**MCC** Median cash compensation	**MWR** Median wage range	**W** Weekly
AW Average wage paid	**FQ** First quartile wage	**LO** Lowest wage paid	**ME** Median entry wage	**S** See annotated source	**Y** Yearly

Occupation/Type/Industry	Location	Per	Low	Mid	High	Source	Date
Crane and Tower Operator	Grand Rapids-Wyoming MSA, MI	Y	34850 FQ	39260 MW	47750 TQ	USBLS	5/15
	Minnesota	Y	44762 FQ	67072 MW	75076 TQ	MNBLS*	1/16-3/16
	Minneapolis-St. Paul-Bloomington MSA, MN-WI	Y	49984 FQ	69411 MW	76276 TQ	MNBLS	1/16-3/16
	Mississippi	Y	31190 FQ	43920 MW	53550 TQ	USBLS	5/15
	Jackson MSA, MS	Y	40260 FQ	44450 MW	48660 TQ	USBLS	5/15
	Missouri	Y	40080 FQ	48520 MW	61080 TQ	USBLS	5/15
	Kansas City MSA, MO-KS	Y	55340 FQ	67820 MW	82770 TQ	USBLS	5/15
	St. Louis MSA, MO-IL	Y	38680 FQ	54680 MW	62990 TQ	USBLS	5/15
	Montana	Y	58430 FQ	68050 MW	75820 TQ	USBLS	5/15
	Nebraska	Y	36585 FQ	46210 MW	56240 TQ	NEBLS	7/16-9/16
	Omaha-Council Bluffs MSA, NE-IA	Y	43300 FQ	52260 MW	58845 TQ	NEBLS	7/16-9/16
	Nevada	Y	44480 FQ	56930 MW	80950 TQ	USBLS	5/15
	Las Vegas-Henderson-Paradise MSA, NV	Y	43690 FQ	56310 MW	83220 TQ	USBLS	5/15
	New Hampshire	H	18.61 AE	23.40 MW	27.66 AEX	NHBLS	6/16
	New Jersey	Y	53400 FQ	68490 MW	82010 TQ	USBLS	5/15
	Camden PMSA, NJ	Y	45520 FQ	57460 MW	77870 TQ	USBLS	5/15
	Newark PMSA, NJ-PA	Y	66800 FQ	75910 MW	94210 TQ	USBLS	5/15
	New Mexico	Y	52660 FQ	57270 MW	62570 TQ	USBLS	5/15
	New York	Y	44270 AE	69610 MW	98390 AEX	NYBLS	1/16-3/16
	Buffalo-Cheektowaga-Niagara Falls MSA, NY	Y	76110 FQ	90120 MW	103340 TQ	USBLS	5/15
	Nassau County-Suffolk County PMSA, NY	Y	40890 FQ	59610 MW	86550 TQ	USBLS	5/15
	New York-Jersey City-White Plains PMSA, NY-NJ	Y	64900 FQ	86800 MW	120650 TQ	USBLS	5/15
	Rochester MSA, NY	Y	40890 FQ	47980 MW	56860 TQ	USBLS	5/15
	North Carolina	Y	41610 FQ	48780 MW	57370 TQ	USBLS	5/15
	Charlotte-Concord-Gastonia MSA, NC-SC	Y	41240 FQ	47170 MW	54480 TQ	USBLS	5/15
	Raleigh MSA, NC	Y	52090 FQ	56990 MW	61880 TQ	USBLS	5/15
	North Dakota	Y	37230 FQ	53060 MW	63400 TQ	USBLS	5/15
	Ohio	Y	31970 FQ	37760 MW	49350 TQ	USBLS	5/15
	Cincinnati MSA, OH-KY-IN	Y	32900 FQ	43140 MW	67300 TQ	USBLS	5/15
	Cleveland-Elyria MSA, OH	Y	33510 FQ	39010 MW	56040 TQ	USBLS	5/15
	Columbus MSA, OH	Y	28850 FQ	33300 MW	37640 TQ	USBLS	5/15
	Oklahoma	Y	36600 FQ	52020 MW	59090 TQ	USBLS	5/15
	Oklahoma City MSA, OK	Y	50180 FQ	56260 MW	62160 TQ	USBLS	5/15
	Tulsa MSA, OK	Y	33420 FQ	39390 MW	55620 TQ	USBLS	5/15
	Oregon	H	21.10 FQ	25.24 MW	36.97 TQ	ORBLS	2016
	Portland-Vancouver-Hillsboro MSA, OR-WA	Y	45050 FQ	55190 MW	71200 TQ	USBLS	5/15
	Pennsylvania	Y	38010 FQ	46600 MW	59090 TQ	USBLS	5/15
	Allentown-Bethlehem-Easton MSA, PA-NJ	Y	42830 FQ	47490 MW	55890 TQ	USBLS	5/15
	Montgomery County-Bucks County-Chester County PMSA, PA	Y	42640 FQ	51310 MW	62100 TQ	USBLS	5/15
	Philadelphia PMSA, PA	Y	48640 FQ	59260 MW	76130 TQ	USBLS	5/15
	Pittsburgh MSA, PA	Y	35850 FQ	43420 MW	53710 TQ	USBLS	5/15
	Providence-Warwick MSA, RI-MA	Y	41470 FQ	46720 MW	56830 TQ	USBLS	5/15
	South Carolina	Y	37400 FQ	50380 MW	62830 TQ	USBLS	5/15
	Charleston-North Charleston MSA, SC	Y	37370 FQ	53450 MW	71230 TQ	USBLS	5/15
	Columbia MSA, SC	Y	44960 FQ	54090 MW	58740 TQ	USBLS	5/15
	Greenville-Anderson-Mauldin MSA, SC	Y	35600 FQ	40880 MW	46320 TQ	USBLS	5/15
	South Dakota	Y	36560 FQ	46790 MW	55630 TQ	USBLS	5/15
	Sioux Falls MSA, SD	Y	43360 FQ	52780 MW	59160 TQ	USBLS	5/15
	Tennessee	Y	35660 FQ	42510 MW	55360 TQ	USBLS	5/15
	Knoxville MSA, TN	Y	35100 FQ	42400 MW	56160 TQ	USBLS	5/15
	Memphis MSA, TN-MS-AR	Y	35100 FQ	48630 MW	58820 TQ	USBLS	5/15
	Nashville-Davidson–Murfreesboro–Franklin MSA, TN	Y	35890 FQ	43350 MW	55530 TQ	USBLS	5/15
	Texas	Y	40940 FQ	52630 MW	63330 TQ	USBLS	5/15
	Austin-Round Rock MSA, TX	Y	34540 FQ	43860 MW	56010 TQ	USBLS	5/15
	Dallas-Plano-Irving PMSA, TX	Y	40460 FQ	47080 MW	56280 TQ	USBLS	5/15

AE	Average entry wage	AWR	Average wage range	H	Hourly
AEX	Average experienced wage	B	Biweekly	HI	Highest wage paid
ATC	Average total compensation	D	Daily	HR	High end range
AW	Average wage paid	FQ	First quartile wage	LO	Lowest wage paid

LR	Low end range	MTC	Median total compensation
M	Monthly	MW	Median wage paid
MCC	Median cash compensation	MWR	Median wage range
ME	Median entry wage	S	See annotated source

TCC	Total cash compensation		
TQ	Third quartile wage		
W	Weekly		
Y	Yearly		

Occupation/Type/Industry	Location	Per	Low	Mid	High	Source	Date
Crane and Tower Operator	Fort Worth-Arlington PMSA, TX	Y	44330 FQ	52970 MW	61400 TQ	USBLS	5/15
	Houston-The Woodlands-Sugar Land MSA, TX	Y	42070 FQ	56050 MW	67160 TQ	USBLS	5/15
	San Antonio-New Braunfels MSA, TX	Y	38060 FQ	49760 MW	62180 TQ	USBLS	5/15
	Utah	Y	39410 FQ	51450 MW	58310 TQ	USBLS	5/15
	Salt Lake City MSA, UT	Y	47940 FQ	54000 MW	59130 TQ	USBLS	5/15
	Vermont	Y	43580 FQ	47330 MW	52750 TQ	USBLS	5/15
	Virginia	Y	48590 FQ	54470 MW	60040 TQ	USBLS	5/15
	Richmond MSA, VA	Y	51150 FQ	55350 MW	59580 TQ	USBLS	5/15
	Virginia Beach-Norfolk-Newport News MSA, VA-NC	Y	51200 FQ	55100 MW	59880 TQ	USBLS	5/15
	Washington	H	27.99 FQ	34.75 MW	42.56 TQ	WABLS	3/16
	Seattle-Bellevue-Everett PMSA, WA	H	27.99 FQ	36.36 MW	44.20 TQ	WABLS	3/16
	West Virginia	Y	38750 FQ	45920 MW	54410 TQ	USBLS	5/15
	Huntington-Ashland MSA, WV-KY-OH	Y	35190 FQ	40630 MW	48400 TQ	USBLS	5/15
	Wisconsin	Y	33930 FQ	47560 MW	68820 TQ	USBLS	5/15
	Milwaukee-Waukesha-West Allis MSA, WI	Y	33910 FQ	54380 MW	70270 TQ	USBLS	5/15
	Wyoming	Y	51910 FQ	59120 MW	69180 TQ	USBLS	5/15
	Puerto Rico	Y	19750 FQ	22940 MW	30630 TQ	USBLS	5/15
	San Juan-Carolina-Caguas MSA, PR	Y	20550 FQ	23610 MW	34430 TQ	USBLS	5/15
	Guam	Y	31030 FQ	42150 MW	48140 TQ	USBLS	5/15
Credential Analyst							
California State University	California	Y	35016 LO		65352 HI	CALST	2016-2017
Credential Specialist							
Baccalaureate Institution	United States	Y		39140 MW		CHE02	2015-2016
Master's Institution	United States	Y		47774 MW		CHE02	2015-2016
Research University	United States	Y		51981 MW		CHE02	2015-2016
Credit Analyst	Alabama	Y	37842 AE	61846 AW	73848 AEX	ALBLS	6/16
	Birmingham-Hoover MSA, AL	Y	42597 AE	66448 AW	78379 AEX	ALBLS	6/16
	Arizona	Y	53390 FQ	70770 MW	94760 TQ	USBLS	5/15
	Phoenix-Mesa-Scottsdale MSA, AZ	Y	53530 FQ	70640 MW	93440 TQ	USBLS	5/15
	Arkansas	Y	35950 FQ	48720 MW	72600 TQ	USBLS	5/15
	Little Rock-North Little Rock-Conway MSA, AR	Y	39110 FQ	65950 MW	79320 TQ	USBLS	5/15
	California	H	27.73 FQ	36.96 MW	51.84 TQ	CABLS	1/16-3/16
	Anaheim-Santa Ana-Irvine PMSA, CA	H	28.39 FQ	36.80 MW	50.58 TQ	CABLS	1/16-3/16
	Los Angeles-Long Beach-Glendale PMSA, CA	H	26.33 FQ	34.77 MW	46.52 TQ	CABLS	1/16-3/16
	Oakland-Hayward-Berkeley PMSA, CA	H	33.60 FQ	49.26 MW	69.69 TQ	CABLS	1/16-3/16
	Riverside-San Bernardino-Ontario MSA, CA	H	28.65 FQ	39.03 MW	54.78 TQ	CABLS	1/16-3/16
	Sacramento–Roseville–Arden-Arcade MSA, CA	H	15.22 FQ	27.47 MW	43.28 TQ	CABLS	1/16-3/16
	San Diego-Carlsbad MSA, CA	H	25.30 FQ	31.72 MW	45.78 TQ	CABLS	1/16-3/16
	San Francisco-Redwood City-South San Francisco PMSA, CA	H	35.73 FQ	53.47 MW	74.14 TQ	CABLS	1/16-3/16
	Colorado	Y	56330 FQ	70250 MW	96770 TQ	USBLS	5/15
	Denver-Aurora-Lakewood MSA, CO	Y	56690 FQ	70940 MW	101220 TQ	USBLS	5/15
	Connecticut	Y		88243 MW		CTBLS	1/16-3/16
	Bridgeport-Stamford-Norwalk MSA, CT	Y	65310 FQ	90040 MW	125320 TQ	USBLS	5/15
	Hartford-West Hartford-East Hartford MSA, CT	Y	66210 FQ	83880 MW	101520 TQ	USBLS	5/15
	Delaware	Y	43390 FQ	55090 MW	84650 TQ	USBLS	5/15
	Wilmington PMSA, DE-MD-NJ	Y	43120 FQ	54090 MW	80630 TQ	USBLS	5/15
	District of Columbia	Y	75460 FQ	109340 MW	141570 TQ	USBLS	5/15

AE	Average entry wage	AWR	Average wage range	H	Hourly
AEX	Average experienced wage	B	Biweekly	HI	Highest wage paid
ATC	Average total compensation	D	Daily	HR	High end range
AW	Average wage paid	FQ	First quartile wage	LO	Lowest wage paid

LR	Low end range	MTC	Median total compensation	TCC	Total cash compensation
M	Monthly	MW	Median wage paid	TQ	Third quartile wage
MCC	Median cash compensation	MWR	Median wage range	W	Weekly
ME	Median entry wage	S	See annotated source	Y	Yearly

Occupation/Type/Industry	Location	Per	Low	Mid	High	Source	Date
Credit Analyst	Washington-Arlington-Alexandria PMSA, DC-VA-MD-WV	Y	62860 FQ	80580 MW	108590 TQ	USBLS	5/15
	Florida	H	22.99 AE	34.31 MW	42.06 AEX	FLBLS	7/16-9/16
	Fort Lauderdale-Pompano Beach-Deerfield Beach PMSA, FL	H	22.49 AE	34.66 MW	40.43 AEX	FLBLS	7/16-9/16
	Miami-Miami Beach-Kendall PMSA, FL	H	23.03 AE	34.22 MW	43.27 AEX	FLBLS	7/16-9/16
	Orlando-Kissimmee-Sanford MSA, FL	H	21.93 AE	29.27 MW	37.93 AEX	FLBLS	7/16-9/16
	Tampa-St. Petersburg-Clearwater MSA, FL	H	24.62 AE	37.60 MW	43.77 AEX	FLBLS	7/16-9/16
	Georgia	Y	50170 FQ	63420 MW	82930 TQ	USBLS	5/15
	Atlanta-Sandy Springs-Roswell MSA, GA	Y	51240 FQ	64470 MW	86360 TQ	USBLS	5/15
	Augusta-Richmond County MSA, GA-SC	Y	51230 FQ	69590 MW	84930 TQ	USBLS	5/15
	Hawaii	Y	47690 FQ	60170 MW	80110 TQ	USBLS	5/15
	Urban Honolulu MSA, HI	Y	47920 FQ	60370 MW	80320 TQ	USBLS	5/15
	Idaho	Y	38810 FQ	57980 MW	77140 TQ	USBLS	5/15
	Boise City MSA, ID	Y	35840 FQ	44040 MW	66350 TQ	USBLS	5/15
	Illinois	Y	47060 FQ	63510 MW	80180 TQ	USBLS	5/15
	Chicago-Naperville-Arlington Heights PMSA, IL	Y	54140 FQ	68670 MW	87530 TQ	USBLS	5/15
	Lake County-Kenosha County PMSA, IL-WI	Y	45250 FQ	53530 MW	69270 TQ	USBLS	5/15
	Indiana	Y	44120 FQ	55870 MW	72630 TQ	USBLS	5/15
	Gary PMSA, IN	Y	41010 FQ	50200 MW	59250 TQ	USBLS	5/15
	Indianapolis-Carmel-Anderson MSA, IN	Y	46260 FQ	60440 MW	75710 TQ	USBLS	5/15
	Iowa	Y	47070 FQ	65320 MW	88070 TQ	USBLS	5/15
	Kansas	Y	43110 FQ	56580 MW	79290 TQ	USBLS	5/15
	Wichita MSA, KS	Y	44370 FQ	59950 MW	79730 TQ	USBLS	5/15
	Kentucky	Y	46910 FQ	59990 MW	87920 TQ	USBLS	5/15
	Louisville-Jefferson County MSA, KY-IN	Y	50460 FQ	69340 MW	109580 TQ	USBLS	5/15
	Louisiana	Y	46500 FQ	66610 MW	82920 TQ	USBLS	5/15
	Baton Rouge MSA, LA	Y	66180 FQ	73060 MW	79940 TQ	USBLS	5/15
	New Orleans-Metairie MSA, LA	Y	54620 FQ	71010 MW	93320 TQ	USBLS	5/15
	Maine	Y	51920 FQ	62900 MW	78450 TQ	USBLS	5/15
	Portland-South Portland MSA, ME	Y	55690 FQ	72570 MW	89910 TQ	USBLS	5/15
	Maryland	Y	40807 AE	66469 MW	79300 AEX	MDBLS	4/16
	Baltimore-Columbia-Towson MSA, MD	Y	46720 FQ	62300 MW	79140 TQ	USBLS	5/15
	Salisbury MSA, MD-DE	Y	48500 FQ	82710 MW	93990 TQ	USBLS	5/15
	Massachusetts	Y	56860 FQ	70310 MW	92510 TQ	USBLS	5/15
	Boston-Cambridge-Newton NECTA, MA	Y	59110 FQ	73120 MW	96530 TQ	USBLS	5/15
	Worcester MSA, MA-CT	Y	46680 FQ	63320 MW	79900 TQ	USBLS	5/15
	Michigan	Y	42100 FQ	51280 MW	70210 TQ	USBLS	5/15
	Detroit-Dearborn-Livonia PMSA, MI	Y	47320 FQ	68140 MW	75770 TQ	USBLS	5/15
	Grand Rapids-Wyoming MSA, MI	Y	41660 FQ	48160 MW	68760 TQ	USBLS	5/15
	Minnesota	Y	56871 FQ	72387 MW	93939 TQ	MNBLS	1/16-3/16
	Minneapolis-St. Paul-Bloomington MSA, MN-WI	Y	59036 FQ	74531 MW	96926 TQ	MNBLS	1/16-3/16
	Mississippi	Y	39980 FQ	52640 MW	71480 TQ	USBLS	5/15
	Jackson MSA, MS	Y	39560 FQ	53870 MW	72760 TQ	USBLS	5/15
	Missouri	Y	50440 FQ	64650 MW	87930 TQ	USBLS	5/15
	Kansas City MSA, MO-KS	Y	47110 FQ	61750 MW	85570 TQ	USBLS	5/15
	St. Louis MSA, MO-IL	Y	52890 FQ	68870 MW	89760 TQ	USBLS	5/15
	Montana	Y	43420 FQ	49990 MW	62460 TQ	USBLS	5/15
	Billings MSA, MT	Y	41930 FQ	48290 MW	59420 TQ	USBLS	5/15
	Nebraska	Y	48475 FQ	65570 MW	84895 TQ	NEBLS	7/16-9/16
	Omaha-Council Bluffs MSA, NE-IA	Y	49240 FQ	67260 MW	89160 TQ	NEBLS	7/16-9/16
	Nevada	Y	51880 FQ	64780 MW	88230 TQ	USBLS	5/15

AE	Average entry wage	AWR	Average wage range	H	Hourly	LR	Low end range	MTC Median total compensation	TCC Total cash compensation
AEX	Average experienced wage	B	Biweekly	HI	Highest wage paid	M	Monthly	MW Median wage paid	TQ Third quartile wage
ATC	Average total compensation	D	Daily	HR	High end range	MCC Median cash compensation	MWR Median wage range	W Weekly
AW	Average wage paid	FQ	First quartile wage	LO	Lowest wage paid	ME Median entry wage	S See annotated source	Y Yearly

Occupation/Type/Industry	Location	Per	Low	Mid	High	Source	Date
Credit Analyst	Las Vegas-Henderson-Paradise MSA, NV	Y	51880 FQ	64280 MW	87340 TQ	USBLS	5/15
	New Hampshire	H	25.37 AE	31.96 MW	36.84 AEX	NHBLS	6/16
	Manchester NECTA, NH	H	24.57 AE	32.16 MW	36.65 AEX	NHBLS	6/16
	New Jersey	Y	57610 FQ	71830 MW	90610 TQ	USBLS	5/15
	Camden PMSA, NJ	Y	58130 FQ	73260 MW	88620 TQ	USBLS	5/15
	Newark PMSA, NJ-PA	Y	59730 FQ	74030 MW	94680 TQ	USBLS	5/15
	Trenton MSA, NJ	Y	56870 FQ	68330 MW	94020 TQ	USBLS	5/15
	New Mexico	Y	37060 FQ	57750 MW	81570 TQ	USBLS	5/15
	Albuquerque MSA, NM	Y	54400 FQ	74310 MW	90480 TQ	USBLS	5/15
	New York	Y	60570 AE	102280 MW	152830 AEX	NYBLS	1/16-3/16
	Nassau County-Suffolk County PMSA, NY	Y	53650 FQ	70690 MW	99130 TQ	USBLS	5/15
	New York-Jersey City-White Plains PMSA, NY-NJ	Y	72200 FQ	99960 MW	153110 TQ	USBLS	5/15
	Rochester MSA, NY	Y	48100 FQ	64700 MW	87210 TQ	USBLS	5/15
	North Carolina	Y	56420 FQ	77910 MW	106020 TQ	USBLS	5/15
	Charlotte-Concord-Gastonia MSA, NC-SC	Y	60750 FQ	83400 MW	111500 TQ	USBLS	5/15
	Raleigh MSA, NC	Y	56540 FQ	73760 MW	100750 TQ	USBLS	5/15
	North Dakota	Y	38530 FQ	47720 MW	61480 TQ	USBLS	5/15
	Fargo MSA, ND-MN	Y	38330 FQ	48810 MW	68090 TQ	USBLS	5/15
	Ohio	Y	51390 FQ	65170 MW	85070 TQ	USBLS	5/15
	Cincinnati MSA, OH-KY-IN	Y	48240 FQ	63310 MW	83480 TQ	USBLS	5/15
	Cleveland-Elyria MSA, OH	Y	56530 FQ	70760 MW	89380 TQ	USBLS	5/15
	Columbus MSA, OH	Y	52410 FQ	68820 MW	90800 TQ	USBLS	5/15
	Oklahoma	Y	39520 FQ	53280 MW	70580 TQ	USBLS	5/15
	Oklahoma City MSA, OK	Y	43400 FQ	54770 MW	74420 TQ	USBLS	5/15
	Tulsa MSA, OK	Y	36670 FQ	51410 MW	68330 TQ	USBLS	5/15
	Oregon	H	27.19 FQ	34.21 MW	42.71 TQ	ORBLS	2016
	Portland-Vancouver-Hillsboro MSA, OR-WA	Y	56200 FQ	70630 MW	88640 TQ	USBLS	5/15
	Pennsylvania	Y	48730 FQ	62500 MW	83300 TQ	USBLS	5/15
	Allentown-Bethlehem-Easton MSA, PA-NJ	Y	50280 FQ	62260 MW	89230 TQ	USBLS	5/15
	Harrisburg-Carlisle MSA, PA	Y	40810 FQ	51780 MW	74350 TQ	USBLS	5/15
	Montgomery County-Bucks County-Chester County PMSA, PA	Y	52050 FQ	60570 MW	77500 TQ	USBLS	5/15
	Philadelphia PMSA, PA	Y	57150 FQ	73690 MW	92820 TQ	USBLS	5/15
	Pittsburgh MSA, PA	Y	48010 FQ	67500 MW	88260 TQ	USBLS	5/15
	Rhode Island	Y	47840 FQ	70600 MW	123640 TQ	USBLS	5/15
	Providence-Warwick MSA, RI-MA	Y	48810 FQ	68910 MW	113600 TQ	USBLS	5/15
	South Carolina	Y	45320 FQ	60110 MW	78970 TQ	USBLS	5/15
	Charleston-North Charleston MSA, SC	Y	45230 FQ	62460 MW	79880 TQ	USBLS	5/15
	Columbia MSA, SC	Y	41520 FQ	59560 MW	78290 TQ	USBLS	5/15
	Greenville-Anderson-Mauldin MSA, SC	Y	48090 FQ	62630 MW	90400 TQ	USBLS	5/15
	South Dakota	Y	45840 FQ	56770 MW	72580 TQ	USBLS	5/15
	Sioux Falls MSA, SD	Y	44650 FQ	56960 MW	79290 TQ	USBLS	5/15
	Tennessee	Y	42670 FQ	58870 MW	80850 TQ	USBLS	5/15
	Knoxville MSA, TN	Y	44470 FQ	63460 MW	74630 TQ	USBLS	5/15
	Memphis MSA, TN-MS-AR	Y	50430 FQ	60990 MW	92540 TQ	USBLS	5/15
	Nashville-Davidson–Murfreesboro–Franklin MSA, TN	Y	41730 FQ	61040 MW	83780 TQ	USBLS	5/15
	Texas	Y	51960 FQ	69490 MW	94760 TQ	USBLS	5/15
	Austin-Round Rock MSA, TX	Y	56110 FQ	70450 MW	93370 TQ	USBLS	5/15
	Dallas-Plano-Irving PMSA, TX	Y	57090 FQ	77870 MW	106200 TQ	USBLS	5/15
	Fort Worth-Arlington PMSA, TX	Y	58150 FQ	75500 MW	104640 TQ	USBLS	5/15
	Houston-The Woodlands-Sugar Land MSA, TX	Y	54070 FQ	68680 MW	90400 TQ	USBLS	5/15
	San Antonio-New Braunfels MSA, TX	Y	47890 FQ	65010 MW	90210 TQ	USBLS	5/15
	Utah	Y	33890 FQ	41840 MW	50330 TQ	USBLS	5/15
	Ogden-Clearfield MSA, UT	Y	36060 FQ	42510 MW	47980 TQ	USBLS	5/15
	Provo-Orem MSA, UT	Y	33430 FQ	38050 MW	51410 TQ	USBLS	5/15
	Salt Lake City MSA, UT	Y	33720 FQ	41940 MW	50770 TQ	USBLS	5/15
	Vermont	Y	42430 FQ	48560 MW	65180 TQ	USBLS	5/15

AE	Average entry wage	AWR	Average wage range	H	Hourly
AEX	Average experienced wage	B	Biweekly	HI	Highest wage paid
ATC	Average total compensation	D	Daily	HR	High end range
AW	Average wage paid	FQ	First quartile wage	LO	Lowest wage paid

LR	Low end range	MTC	Median total compensation	TCC	Total cash compensation
M	Monthly	MW	Median wage paid	TQ	Third quartile wage
MCC	Median cash compensation	MWR	Median wage range	W	Weekly
ME	Median entry wage	S	See annotated source	Y	Yearly

Occupation/Type/Industry	Location	Per	Low	Mid	High	Source	Date
Credit Analyst	Burlington-South Burlington MSA, VT	Y	42310 FQ	50450 MW	64270 TQ	USBLS	5/15
	Virginia	Y	52310 FQ	73870 MW	98450 TQ	USBLS	5/15
	Richmond MSA, VA	Y	55870 FQ	77360 MW	107180 TQ	USBLS	5/15
	Virginia Beach-Norfolk-Newport News MSA, VA-NC	Y	45230 FQ	58890 MW	82350 TQ	USBLS	5/15
	Washington	H	27.87 FQ	37.79 MW	52.18 TQ	WABLS	3/16
	Seattle-Bellevue-Everett PMSA, WA	H	31.65 FQ	40.93 MW	54.01 TQ	WABLS	3/16
	Tacoma-Lakewood PMSA, WA	H	30.94 FQ	43.89 MW	57.53 TQ	WABLS	3/16
	West Virginia	Y	42000 FQ	56800 MW	82040 TQ	USBLS	5/15
	Wisconsin	Y	44820 FQ	60050 MW	77580 TQ	USBLS	5/15
	Madison MSA, WI	Y	44960 FQ	55400 MW	69700 TQ	USBLS	5/15
	Milwaukee-Waukesha-West Allis MSA, WI	Y	52690 FQ	68640 MW	88150 TQ	USBLS	5/15
	Puerto Rico	Y	26890 FQ	35050 MW	47080 TQ	USBLS	5/15
	San Juan-Carolina-Caguas MSA, PR	Y	28430 FQ	36880 MW	49040 TQ	USBLS	5/15
	Guam	Y	41490 FQ	48630 MW	68990 TQ	USBLS	5/15
Credit Authorizer, Checker, and Clerk	Alabama	Y	26713 AE	35185 AW	39420 AEX	ALBLS	6/16
	Birmingham-Hoover MSA, AL	Y	28496 AE	37802 AW	42450 AEX	ALBLS	6/16
	Alaska	Y	30300 FQ	36190 MW	43980 TQ	USBLS	5/15
	Anchorage MSA, AK	Y	30580 FQ	36280 MW	43630 TQ	USBLS	5/15
	Arizona	Y	30870 FQ	38570 MW	53090 TQ	USBLS	5/15
	Phoenix-Mesa-Scottsdale MSA, AZ	Y	31450 FQ	39110 MW	53520 TQ	USBLS	5/15
	Tucson MSA, AZ	Y	27660 FQ	30300 MW	35620 TQ	USBLS	5/15
	Arkansas	Y	26780 FQ	31400 MW	36820 TQ	USBLS	5/15
	Little Rock-North Little Rock-Conway MSA, AR	Y	27560 FQ	31350 MW	36340 TQ	USBLS	5/15
	California	H	16.68 FQ	21.13 MW	27.89 TQ	CABLS	1/16-3/16
	Anaheim-Santa Ana-Irvine PMSA, CA	H	17.71 FQ	22.39 MW	29.35 TQ	CABLS	1/16-3/16
	Los Angeles-Long Beach-Glendale PMSA, CA	H	17.28 FQ	21.14 MW	28.59 TQ	CABLS	1/16-3/16
	Oakland-Hayward-Berkeley PMSA, CA	H	15.90 FQ	18.95 MW	24.71 TQ	CABLS	1/16-3/16
	Riverside-San Bernardino-Ontario MSA, CA	H	13.76 FQ	16.17 MW	20.69 TQ	CABLS	1/16-3/16
	Sacramento–Roseville–Arden-Arcade MSA, CA	H	16.72 FQ	19.28 MW	27.20 TQ	CABLS	1/16-3/16
	San Diego-Carlsbad MSA, CA	H	14.04 FQ	23.03 MW	28.15 TQ	CABLS	1/16-3/16
	San Francisco-Redwood City-South San Francisco PMSA, CA	H	15.86 FQ	21.58 MW	28.10 TQ	CABLS	1/16-3/16
	Colorado	Y	34680 FQ	44320 MW	56910 TQ	USBLS	5/15
	Denver-Aurora-Lakewood MSA, CO	Y	35320 FQ	43660 MW	57270 TQ	USBLS	5/15
	Connecticut	Y		40965 MW		CTBLS	1/16-3/16
	Bridgeport-Stamford-Norwalk MSA, CT	Y	31650 FQ	40400 MW	53520 TQ	USBLS	5/15
	Hartford-West Hartford-East Hartford MSA, CT	Y	35270 FQ	40500 MW	47220 TQ	USBLS	5/15
	Delaware	Y	34590 FQ	42940 MW	48590 TQ	USBLS	5/15
	Wilmington PMSA, DE-MD-NJ	Y	33740 FQ	42570 MW	48200 TQ	USBLS	5/15
	Washington-Arlington-Alexandria PMSA, DC-VA-MD-WV	Y	28190 FQ	33410 MW	37880 TQ	USBLS	5/15
	Florida	H	12.51 AE	17.00 MW	21.08 AEX	FLBLS	7/16-9/16
	Fort Lauderdale-Pompano Beach-Deerfield Beach PMSA, FL	H	12.90 AE	17.46 MW	21.97 AEX	FLBLS	7/16-9/16
	Miami-Miami Beach-Kendall PMSA, FL	H	11.19 AE	14.29 MW	18.05 AEX	FLBLS	7/16-9/16
	Orlando-Kissimmee-Sanford MSA, FL	H	12.95 AE	17.28 MW	22.72 AEX	FLBLS	7/16-9/16
	Tampa-St. Petersburg-Clearwater MSA, FL	H	12.84 AE	17.01 MW	20.46 AEX	FLBLS	7/16-9/16
	Georgia	Y	30860 FQ	37990 MW	48490 TQ	USBLS	5/15

AE	Average entry wage	AWR Average wage range	H Hourly	LR Low end range	MTC Median total compensation	TCC Total cash compensation
AEX	Average experienced wage	B Biweekly	HI Highest wage paid	M Monthly	MW Median wage paid	TQ Third quartile wage
ATC	Average total compensation	D Daily	HR High end range	MCC Median cash compensation	MWR Median wage range	W Weekly
AW	Average wage paid	FQ First quartile wage	LO Lowest wage paid	ME Median entry wage	S See annotated source	Y Yearly

Occupation/Type/Industry	Location	Per	Low	Mid	High	Source	Date
Credit Authorizer, Checker, and Clerk							
	Atlanta-Sandy Springs-Roswell MSA, GA	Y	34330 FQ	40470 MW	49490 TQ	USBLS	5/15
	Augusta-Richmond County MSA, GA-SC	Y	23990 FQ	27400 MW	30450 TQ	USBLS	5/15
	Hawaii	Y	31530 FQ	37540 MW	46990 TQ	USBLS	5/15
	Urban Honolulu MSA, HI	Y	31510 FQ	37020 MW	47400 TQ	USBLS	5/15
	Idaho	Y	29360 FQ	34740 MW	39940 TQ	USBLS	5/15
	Boise City MSA, ID	Y	28880 FQ	33950 MW	38210 TQ	USBLS	5/15
	Illinois	Y	32660 FQ	38630 MW	51640 TQ	USBLS	5/15
	Chicago-Naperville-Arlington Heights PMSA, IL	Y	33800 FQ	40340 MW	50930 TQ	USBLS	5/15
	Lake County-Kenosha County PMSA, IL-WI	Y	33150 FQ	37680 MW	48740 TQ	USBLS	5/15
	Indiana	Y	27910 FQ	32150 MW	38490 TQ	USBLS	5/15
	Gary PMSA, IN	Y	31700 FQ	35370 MW	39060 TQ	USBLS	5/15
	Indianapolis-Carmel-Anderson MSA, IN	Y	27300 FQ	30870 MW	37490 TQ	USBLS	5/15
	Iowa	Y	23530 FQ	32020 MW	44630 TQ	USBLS	5/15
	Des Moines-West Des Moines MSA, IA	Y	25730 FQ	33410 MW	45620 TQ	USBLS	5/15
	Kansas	Y	29410 FQ	36530 MW	45100 TQ	USBLS	5/15
	Wichita MSA, KS	Y	28400 FQ	34690 MW	39490 TQ	USBLS	5/15
	Kentucky	Y	29690 FQ	35730 MW	43990 TQ	USBLS	5/15
	Louisville-Jefferson County MSA, KY-IN	Y	31640 FQ	37720 MW	49460 TQ	USBLS	5/15
	Louisiana	Y	21180 FQ	26090 MW	30390 TQ	USBLS	5/15
	Baton Rouge MSA, LA	Y	20790 FQ	25390 MW	29870 TQ	USBLS	5/15
	New Orleans-Metairie MSA, LA	Y	21290 FQ	25050 MW	36260 TQ	USBLS	5/15
	Portland-South Portland MSA, ME	Y	31630 FQ	36200 MW	42050 TQ	USBLS	5/15
	Maryland	Y	26601 AE	33808 MW	37411 AEX	MDBLS	4/16
	Baltimore-Columbia-Towson MSA, MD	Y	32370 FQ	37870 MW	48700 TQ	USBLS	5/15
	Massachusetts	Y	33770 FQ	41060 MW	50470 TQ	USBLS	5/15
	Boston-Cambridge-Newton NECTA, MA	Y	33620 FQ	42370 MW	50250 TQ	USBLS	5/15
	Worcester MSA, MA-CT	Y	31950 FQ	35720 MW	39500 TQ	USBLS	5/15
	Michigan	Y	29290 FQ	35750 MW	45600 TQ	USBLS	5/15
	Detroit-Dearborn-Livonia PMSA, MI	Y	33080 FQ	47950 MW	57190 TQ	USBLS	5/15
	Grand Rapids-Wyoming MSA, MI	Y	31260 FQ	37200 MW	47040 TQ	USBLS	5/15
	Minnesota	Y	34282 FQ	41199 MW	47065 TQ	MNBLS	1/16-3/16
	Minneapolis-St. Paul-Bloomington MSA, MN-WI	Y	34950 FQ	41624 MW	47156 TQ	MNBLS	1/16-3/16
	Mississippi	Y	20960 FQ	27710 MW	35230 TQ	USBLS	5/15
	Jackson MSA, MS	Y	28640 FQ	35040 MW	39420 TQ	USBLS	5/15
	Missouri	Y	30690 FQ	35510 MW	42120 TQ	USBLS	5/15
	Kansas City MSA, MO-KS	Y	29010 FQ	34720 MW	43110 TQ	USBLS	5/15
	St. Louis MSA, MO-IL	Y	30330 FQ	36070 MW	45650 TQ	USBLS	5/15
	Nebraska	Y	28345 FQ	34670 MW	43945 TQ	NEBLS	7/16-9/16
	Omaha-Council Bluffs MSA, NE-IA	Y	29615 FQ	36320 MW	45380 TQ	NEBLS	7/16-9/16
	Nevada	Y	29570 FQ	34880 MW	41050 TQ	USBLS	5/15
	Las Vegas-Henderson-Paradise MSA, NV	Y	29640 FQ	34840 MW	40820 TQ	USBLS	5/15
	New Hampshire	H	14.14 AE	18.04 MW	21.91 AEX	NHBLS	6/16
	New Jersey	Y	33520 FQ	39820 MW	47190 TQ	USBLS	5/15
	Camden PMSA, NJ	Y	35130 FQ	42450 MW	48400 TQ	USBLS	5/15
	Newark PMSA, NJ-PA	Y	35290 FQ	42590 MW	48970 TQ	USBLS	5/15
	Trenton MSA, NJ	Y	34860 FQ	40250 MW	46520 TQ	USBLS	5/15
	New Mexico	Y	20810 FQ	24020 MW	33340 TQ	USBLS	5/15
	Albuquerque MSA, NM	Y	20400 FQ	23290 MW	31440 TQ	USBLS	5/15
	New York	Y	32320 AE	44670 MW	50900 AEX	NYBLS	1/16-3/16
	Buffalo-Cheektowaga-Niagara Falls MSA, NY	Y	31390 FQ	40620 MW	47640 TQ	USBLS	5/15
	Nassau County-Suffolk County PMSA, NY	Y	36200 FQ	42880 MW	48880 TQ	USBLS	5/15
	New York-Jersey City-White Plains PMSA, NY-NJ	Y	35970 FQ	43320 MW	48790 TQ	USBLS	5/15

AE	Average entry wage	AWR	Average wage range	H	Hourly	
AEX	Average experienced wage	B	Biweekly	HI	Highest wage paid	
ATC	Average total compensation	D	Daily	HR	High end range	
AW	Average wage paid	FQ	First quartile wage	LO	Lowest wage paid	

LR	Low end range	MTC	Median total compensation	TCC	Total cash compensation
M	Monthly	MW	Median wage paid	TQ	Third quartile wage
MCC	Median cash compensation	MWR	Median wage range	W	Weekly
ME	Median entry wage	S	See annotated source	Y	Yearly

Occupation/Type/Industry	Location	Per	Low	Mid	High	Source	Date
Credit Authorizer, Checker, and Clerk							
	Rochester MSA, NY	Y	30400 FQ	37580 MW	46610 TQ	USBLS	5/15
	North Carolina	Y	27240 FQ	36710 MW	47500 TQ	USBLS	5/15
	Raleigh MSA, NC	Y	39730 FQ	47060 MW	55590 TQ	USBLS	5/15
	North Dakota	Y	31620 FQ	36420 MW	42990 TQ	USBLS	5/15
	Fargo MSA, ND-MN	Y	32740 FQ	37380 MW	43870 TQ	USBLS	5/15
	Ohio	Y	28260 FQ	33070 MW	39580 TQ	USBLS	5/15
	Cincinnati MSA, OH-KY-IN	Y	31090 FQ	38160 MW	50010 TQ	USBLS	5/15
	Cleveland-Elyria MSA, OH	Y	27080 FQ	31260 MW	37130 TQ	USBLS	5/15
	Columbus MSA, OH	Y	28990 FQ	34680 MW	44010 TQ	USBLS	5/15
	Oklahoma	Y	26340 FQ	29360 MW	35420 TQ	USBLS	5/15
	Oklahoma City MSA, OK	Y	29020 FQ	36160 MW	45350 TQ	USBLS	5/15
	Tulsa MSA, OK	Y	26570 FQ	28760 MW	31530 TQ	USBLS	5/15
	Oregon	H	16.25 FQ	20.46 MW	24.20 TQ	ORBLS	2016
	Portland-Vancouver-Hillsboro MSA, OR-WA	Y	37550 FQ	43920 MW	49470 TQ	USBLS	5/15
	Pennsylvania	Y	28990 FQ	35040 MW	44010 TQ	USBLS	5/15
	Harrisburg-Carlisle MSA, PA	Y	29080 FQ	34160 MW	40810 TQ	USBLS	5/15
	Montgomery County-Bucks County-Chester County PMSA, PA	Y	30660 FQ	36580 MW	44230 TQ	USBLS	5/15
	Philadelphia PMSA, PA	Y	31370 FQ	37430 MW	44870 TQ	USBLS	5/15
	Pittsburgh MSA, PA	Y	28110 FQ	31670 MW	41220 TQ	USBLS	5/15
	Rhode Island	Y	32350 FQ	38260 MW	49050 TQ	USBLS	5/15
	Providence-Warwick MSA, RI-MA	Y	32920 FQ	38800 MW	49030 TQ	USBLS	5/15
	South Carolina	Y	26320 FQ	30160 MW	35880 TQ	USBLS	5/15
	Columbia MSA, SC	Y	27950 FQ	31270 MW	38480 TQ	USBLS	5/15
	Greenville-Anderson-Mauldin MSA, SC	Y	24950 FQ	28590 MW	32400 TQ	USBLS	5/15
	South Dakota	Y	25350 FQ	29440 MW	35260 TQ	USBLS	5/15
	Sioux Falls MSA, SD	Y	29260 FQ	34330 MW	38690 TQ	USBLS	5/15
	Tennessee	Y	27370 FQ	33500 MW	42660 TQ	USBLS	5/15
	Knoxville MSA, TN	Y	23970 FQ	30470 MW	38130 TQ	USBLS	5/15
	Memphis MSA, TN-MS-AR	Y	27550 FQ	35050 MW	47830 TQ	USBLS	5/15
	Nashville-Davidson–Murfreesboro–Franklin MSA, TN	Y	27770 FQ	33870 MW	46270 TQ	USBLS	5/15
	Texas	Y	27060 FQ	32270 MW	39910 TQ	USBLS	5/15
	Austin-Round Rock MSA, TX	Y	27550 FQ	30450 MW	38300 TQ	USBLS	5/15
	Dallas-Plano-Irving PMSA, TX	Y	29330 FQ	34710 MW	42840 TQ	USBLS	5/15
	Fort Worth-Arlington PMSA, TX	Y	27700 FQ	33180 MW	42180 TQ	USBLS	5/15
	Houston-The Woodlands-Sugar Land MSA, TX	Y	27990 FQ	33520 MW	43950 TQ	USBLS	5/15
	San Antonio-New Braunfels MSA, TX	Y	26120 FQ	31360 MW	38330 TQ	USBLS	5/15
	Utah	Y	28940 FQ	33690 MW	37840 TQ	USBLS	5/15
	Ogden-Clearfield MSA, UT	Y	26330 FQ	28780 MW	31270 TQ	USBLS	5/15
	Salt Lake City MSA, UT	Y	31660 FQ	35100 MW	38550 TQ	USBLS	5/15
	Virginia	Y	28040 FQ	31690 MW	37300 TQ	USBLS	5/15
	Richmond MSA, VA	Y	28220 FQ	31730 MW	37240 TQ	USBLS	5/15
	Virginia Beach-Norfolk-Newport News MSA, VA-NC	Y	27350 FQ	30260 MW	38250 TQ	USBLS	5/15
	Washington	H	17.21 FQ	20.20 MW	26.55 TQ	WABLS	3/16
	Tacoma-Lakewood PMSA, WA	H	19.67 FQ	22.27 MW	25.23 TQ	WABLS	3/16
	West Virginia	Y	28020 FQ	34410 MW	44510 TQ	USBLS	5/15
	Wisconsin	Y	34830 FQ	41850 MW	49630 TQ	USBLS	5/15
	Madison MSA, WI	Y	37800 FQ	43940 MW	49900 TQ	USBLS	5/15
	Milwaukee-Waukesha-West Allis MSA, WI	Y	35100 FQ	41200 MW	50140 TQ	USBLS	5/15
	Puerto Rico	Y	20200 FQ	23300 MW	29160 TQ	USBLS	5/15
	San Juan-Carolina-Caguas MSA, PR	Y	20310 FQ	23510 MW	30280 TQ	USBLS	5/15
Credit Counselor	Alabama	Y	33137 AE	52570 AW	62287 AEX	ALBLS	6/16
	Arizona	Y	35720 FQ	42510 MW	49390 TQ	USBLS	5/15
	Phoenix-Mesa-Scottsdale MSA, AZ	Y	35650 FQ	42150 MW	48920 TQ	USBLS	5/15
	Arkansas	Y	35670 FQ	44500 MW	58060 TQ	USBLS	5/15
	Little Rock-North Little Rock-Conway MSA, AR	Y	36050 FQ	44220 MW	50120 TQ	USBLS	5/15

AE	Average entry wage	AWR	Average wage range	H	Hourly
AEX	Average experienced wage	B	Biweekly	HI	Highest wage paid
ATC	Average total compensation	D	Daily	HR	High end range
AW	Average wage paid	FQ	First quartile wage	LO	Lowest wage paid

LR	Low end range	MTC	Median total compensation	TCC	Total cash compensation
M	Monthly	MW	Median wage paid	TQ	Third quartile wage
MCC	Median cash compensation	MWR	Median wage range	W	Weekly
ME	Median entry wage	S	See annotated source	Y	Yearly

Occupation/Type/Industry	Location	Per	Low	Mid	High	Source	Date
Credit Counselor	California	H	19.58 FQ	24.01 MW	29.84 TQ	CABLS	1/16-3/16
	Anaheim-Santa Ana-Irvine PMSA, CA	H	19.70 FQ	25.44 MW	37.25 TQ	CABLS	1/16-3/16
	Los Angeles-Long Beach-Glendale PMSA, CA	H	19.49 FQ	23.52 MW	28.42 TQ	CABLS	1/16-3/16
	Oakland-Hayward-Berkeley PMSA, CA	H	19.17 FQ	22.68 MW	27.97 TQ	CABLS	1/16-3/16
	Riverside-San Bernardino-Ontario MSA, CA	H	19.57 FQ	23.77 MW	28.95 TQ	CABLS	1/16-3/16
	Sacramento–Roseville–Arden-Arcade MSA, CA	H	18.89 FQ	24.97 MW	28.93 TQ	CABLS	1/16-3/16
	San Diego-Carlsbad MSA, CA	H	20.05 FQ	24.61 MW	40.96 TQ	CABLS	1/16-3/16
	San Francisco-Redwood City-South San Francisco PMSA, CA	H	20.02 FQ	24.52 MW	31.27 TQ	CABLS	1/16-3/16
	Colorado	Y	38270 FQ	58060 MW	88100 TQ	USBLS	5/15
	Denver-Aurora-Lakewood MSA, CO	Y	54360 FQ	81400 MW	93250 TQ	USBLS	5/15
	Connecticut	Y		44731 MW		CTBLS	1/16-3/16
	Hartford-West Hartford-East Hartford MSA, CT	Y	35140 FQ	39780 MW	48400 TQ	USBLS	5/15
	Delaware	Y	35710 FQ	40220 MW	47740 TQ	USBLS	5/15
	Wilmington PMSA, DE-MD-NJ	Y	36440 FQ	41990 MW	50560 TQ	USBLS	5/15
	District of Columbia	Y	42680 FQ	51580 MW	65970 TQ	USBLS	5/15
	Washington-Arlington-Alexandria PMSA, DC-VA-MD-WV	Y	39260 FQ	47690 MW	61160 TQ	USBLS	5/15
	Florida	H	16.03 AE	19.93 MW	23.90 AEX	FLBLS	7/16-9/16
	Fort Lauderdale-Pompano Beach-Deerfield Beach PMSA, FL	H	16.03 AE	20.12 MW	23.14 AEX	FLBLS	7/16-9/16
	Miami-Miami Beach-Kendall PMSA, FL	H	15.59 AE	20.41 MW	24.75 AEX	FLBLS	7/16-9/16
	Orlando-Kissimmee-Sanford MSA, FL	H	16.47 AE	20.52 MW	23.62 AEX	FLBLS	7/16-9/16
	Tampa-St. Petersburg-Clearwater MSA, FL	H	16.81 AE	21.01 MW	24.58 AEX	FLBLS	7/16-9/16
	Georgia	Y	35660 FQ	41760 MW	51700 TQ	USBLS	5/15
	Atlanta-Sandy Springs-Roswell MSA, GA	Y	36950 FQ	43000 MW	49580 TQ	USBLS	5/15
	Hawaii	Y	32380 FQ	37050 MW	44010 TQ	USBLS	5/15
	Idaho	Y	21110 FQ	33900 MW	49620 TQ	USBLS	5/15
	Boise City MSA, ID	Y	34000 FQ	45130 MW	82470 TQ	USBLS	5/15
	Illinois	Y	38890 FQ	45460 MW	53700 TQ	USBLS	5/15
	Chicago-Naperville-Arlington Heights PMSA, IL	Y	39880 FQ	46060 MW	54820 TQ	USBLS	5/15
	Lake County-Kenosha County PMSA, IL-WI	Y	40640 FQ	46320 MW	54680 TQ	USBLS	5/15
	Indiana	Y	33670 FQ	37310 MW	43580 TQ	USBLS	5/15
	Indianapolis-Carmel-Anderson MSA, IN	Y	34500 FQ	38350 MW	45830 TQ	USBLS	5/15
	Iowa	Y	33360 FQ	37540 MW	46510 TQ	USBLS	5/15
	Des Moines-West Des Moines MSA, IA	Y	34910 FQ	38580 MW	50310 TQ	USBLS	5/15
	Kansas	Y	31930 FQ	35700 MW	39640 TQ	USBLS	5/15
	Kentucky	Y	30410 FQ	36140 MW	45310 TQ	USBLS	5/15
	Louisville-Jefferson County MSA, KY-IN	Y	33070 FQ	39990 MW	51750 TQ	USBLS	5/15
	Louisiana	Y	32020 FQ	37360 MW	43930 TQ	USBLS	5/15
	Maine	Y	32870 FQ	37360 MW	44770 TQ	USBLS	5/15
	Portland-South Portland MSA, ME	Y	33660 FQ	37500 MW	42620 TQ	USBLS	5/15
	Maryland	Y	32580 AE	45327 MW	51700 AEX	MDBLS	4/16
	Baltimore-Columbia-Towson MSA, MD	Y	33060 FQ	39550 MW	47850 TQ	USBLS	5/15
	Salisbury MSA, MD-DE	Y	35260 FQ	39180 MW	47590 TQ	USBLS	5/15
	Massachusetts	Y	41670 FQ	50310 MW	62050 TQ	USBLS	5/15
	Boston-Cambridge-Newton NECTA, MA	Y	43320 FQ	51860 MW	61870 TQ	USBLS	5/15
	Worcester MSA, MA-CT	Y	40980 FQ	48800 MW	62290 TQ	USBLS	5/15
	Michigan	Y	39320 FQ	44170 MW	48940 TQ	USBLS	5/15

AE Average entry wage	**AWR** Average wage range	**H** Hourly	**LR** Low end range	**MTC** Median total compensation	**TCC** Total cash compensation
AEX Average experienced wage	**B** Biweekly	**HI** Highest wage paid	**M** Monthly	**MW** Median wage paid	**TQ** Third quartile wage
ATC Average total compensation	**D** Daily	**HR** High end range	**MCC** Median cash compensation	**MWR** Median wage range	**W** Weekly
AW Average wage paid	**FQ** First quartile wage	**LO** Lowest wage paid	**ME** Median entry wage	**S** See annotated source	**Y** Yearly

Credit Counselor

Occupation/Type/Industry	Location	Per	Low	Mid	High	Source	Date
	Grand Rapids-Wyoming MSA, MI	Y	34050 FQ	40810 MW	49130 TQ	USBLS	5/15
	Minnesota	Y	37575 FQ	43784 MW	50043 TQ	MNBLS	1/16-3/16
	Minneapolis-St. Paul-Bloomington MSA, MN-WI	Y	38145 FQ	44180 MW	50053 TQ	MNBLS	1/16-3/16
	Mississippi	Y	31550 FQ	37430 MW	45240 TQ	USBLS	5/15
	Jackson MSA, MS	Y	34930 FQ	41050 MW	46270 TQ	USBLS	5/15
	Missouri	Y	34890 FQ	43640 MW	70530 TQ	USBLS	5/15
	Kansas City MSA, MO-KS	Y	32440 FQ	37020 MW	53180 TQ	USBLS	5/15
	St. Louis MSA, MO-IL	Y	36850 FQ	46550 MW	82100 TQ	USBLS	5/15
	Montana	Y	30400 FQ	34150 MW	38270 TQ	USBLS	5/15
	Nebraska	Y	33495 FQ	37380 MW	47155 TQ	NEBLS	7/16-9/16
	Omaha-Council Bluffs MSA, NE-IA	Y	32690 FQ	37445 MW	46835 TQ	NEBLS	7/16-9/16
	Nevada	Y	37420 FQ	48020 MW	55780 TQ	USBLS	5/15
	New Hampshire	H	18.91 AE	23.35 MW	26.98 AEX	NHBLS	6/16
	New Jersey	Y	44800 FQ	53190 MW	64980 TQ	USBLS	5/15
	Newark PMSA, NJ-PA	Y	43840 FQ	50050 MW	58460 TQ	USBLS	5/15
	New Mexico	Y	34500 FQ	38810 MW	46300 TQ	USBLS	5/15
	Albuquerque MSA, NM	Y	35520 FQ	41040 MW	47950 TQ	USBLS	5/15
	New York	Y	38580 AE	50990 MW	65190 AEX	NYBLS	1/16-3/16
	Buffalo-Cheektowaga-Niagara Falls MSA, NY	Y	38970 FQ	47740 MW	58150 TQ	USBLS	5/15
	Nassau County-Suffolk County PMSA, NY	Y	38060 FQ	46920 MW	58910 TQ	USBLS	5/15
	New York-Jersey City-White Plains PMSA, NY-NJ	Y	43100 FQ	52260 MW	67420 TQ	USBLS	5/15
	Rochester MSA, NY	Y	34760 FQ	43270 MW	55020 TQ	USBLS	5/15
	North Carolina	Y	32140 FQ	38560 MW	62520 TQ	USBLS	5/15
	Charlotte-Concord-Gastonia MSA, NC-SC	Y	38270 FQ	51530 MW	69880 TQ	USBLS	5/15
	Raleigh MSA, NC	Y	29030 FQ	35160 MW	57480 TQ	USBLS	5/15
	North Dakota	Y	36940 FQ	45970 MW	61020 TQ	USBLS	5/15
	Ohio	Y	35890 FQ	42790 MW	50740 TQ	USBLS	5/15
	Cincinnati MSA, OH-KY-IN	Y	34440 FQ	40000 MW	50170 TQ	USBLS	5/15
	Cleveland-Elyria MSA, OH	Y	37400 FQ	43590 MW	48780 TQ	USBLS	5/15
	Columbus MSA, OH	Y	36140 FQ	43140 MW	54980 TQ	USBLS	5/15
	Oklahoma	Y	30030 FQ	37610 MW	46620 TQ	USBLS	5/15
	Oklahoma City MSA, OK	Y	29720 FQ	38810 MW	47970 TQ	USBLS	5/15
	Tulsa MSA, OK	Y	31620 FQ	36600 MW	44020 TQ	USBLS	5/15
	Oregon	H	18.10 FQ	21.96 MW	27.09 TQ	ORBLS	2016
	Portland-Vancouver-Hillsboro MSA, OR-WA	Y	38030 FQ	48630 MW	59100 TQ	USBLS	5/15
	Pennsylvania	Y	37620 FQ	47510 MW	60120 TQ	USBLS	5/15
	Allentown-Bethlehem-Easton MSA, PA-NJ	Y	36710 FQ	45050 MW	58360 TQ	USBLS	5/15
	Harrisburg-Carlisle MSA, PA	Y	37560 FQ	43910 MW	50080 TQ	USBLS	5/15
	Montgomery County-Bucks County-Chester County PMSA, PA	Y	48820 FQ	67900 MW	78390 TQ	USBLS	5/15
	Philadelphia PMSA, PA	Y	41590 FQ	48310 MW	57730 TQ	USBLS	5/15
	Pittsburgh MSA, PA	Y	34810 FQ	39600 MW	53830 TQ	USBLS	5/15
	Rhode Island	Y	44400 FQ	52680 MW	61410 TQ	USBLS	5/15
	Providence-Warwick MSA, RI-MA	Y	43970 FQ	52400 MW	62220 TQ	USBLS	5/15
	South Carolina	Y	32790 FQ	38210 MW	46950 TQ	USBLS	5/15
	Charleston-North Charleston MSA, SC	Y	33840 FQ	38530 MW	46210 TQ	USBLS	5/15
	Greenville-Anderson-Mauldin MSA, SC	Y	32390 FQ	39260 MW	47760 TQ	USBLS	5/15
	South Dakota	Y	27490 FQ	30630 MW	43460 TQ	USBLS	5/15
	Tennessee	Y	28960 FQ	39200 MW	60060 TQ	USBLS	5/15
	Knoxville MSA, TN	Y	27680 FQ	30230 MW	36280 TQ	USBLS	5/15
	Memphis MSA, TN-MS-AR	Y	37110 FQ	51460 MW	70130 TQ	USBLS	5/15
	Nashville-Davidson–Murfreesboro–Franklin MSA, TN	Y	25360 FQ	39830 MW	57690 TQ	USBLS	5/15
	Texas	Y	33780 FQ	41270 MW	53670 TQ	USBLS	5/15
	Austin-Round Rock MSA, TX	Y	35380 FQ	44990 MW	57070 TQ	USBLS	5/15
	Dallas-Plano-Irving PMSA, TX	Y	32000 FQ	39410 MW	52080 TQ	USBLS	5/15
	Fort Worth-Arlington PMSA, TX	Y	32700 FQ	37580 MW	46260 TQ	USBLS	5/15

AE	Average entry wage	AWR	Average wage range	
AEX	Average experienced wage	B	Biweekly	
ATC	Average total compensation	D	Daily	
AW	Average wage paid	FQ	First quartile wage	
H	Hourly	LR	Low end range	MTC Median total compensation
HI	Highest wage paid	M	Monthly	MW Median wage paid
HR	High end range	MCC	Median cash compensation	MWR Median wage range
LO	Lowest wage paid	ME	Median entry wage	S See annotated source
				TCC Total cash compensation
				TQ Third quartile wage
				W Weekly
				Y Yearly

Occupation/Type/Industry	Location	Per	Low	Mid	High	Source	Date
Credit Counselor	Houston-The Woodlands- Sugar Land MSA, TX	Y	34400 FQ	42290 MW	53280 TQ	USBLS	5/15
	Utah	Y	23440 FQ	28190 MW	38380 TQ	USBLS	5/15
	Ogden-Clearfield MSA, UT	Y	22780 FQ	25020 MW	35810 TQ	USBLS	5/15
	Provo-Orem MSA, UT	Y	29350 FQ	37060 MW	46710 TQ	USBLS	5/15
	Salt Lake City MSA, UT	Y	22870 FQ	26470 MW	34490 TQ	USBLS	5/15
	Virginia	Y	34500 FQ	40540 MW	51530 TQ	USBLS	5/15
	Richmond MSA, VA	Y	34760 FQ	38720 MW	48690 TQ	USBLS	5/15
	Virginia Beach-Norfolk- Newport News MSA, VA-NC	Y	29140 FQ	35030 MW	42460 TQ	USBLS	5/15
	Washington	H	19.76 FQ	22.83 MW	26.69 TQ	WABLS	3/16
	Seattle-Bellevue-Everett PMSA, WA	H	20.92 FQ	23.05 MW	25.63 TQ	WABLS	3/16
	West Virginia	Y	28010 FQ	33380 MW	44310 TQ	USBLS	5/15
	Wisconsin	Y	35370 FQ	42710 MW	56410 TQ	USBLS	5/15
	Madison MSA, WI	Y	35420 FQ	39540 MW	56140 TQ	USBLS	5/15
	Puerto Rico	Y	30040 FQ	38270 MW	49210 TQ	USBLS	5/15
	San Juan-Carolina-Caguas MSA, PR	Y	30600 FQ	39080 MW	49720 TQ	USBLS	5/15
Crew Leader							
Department of Public Works, Municipal Government	Albany, GA	H	13.22 LO		17.98 HI	GACTY02	2016
Department of Public Works, Municipal Government	Clarkesville, GA	H	11.00 LO		20.00 HI	GACTY02	2016
Department of Public Works, Municipal Government	Rome, GA	H	12.64 LO		20.53 HI	GACTY02	2016
Crime Analysis Supervisor							
Municipal Government	Anaheim, CA	Y			96574 HI	CACIT	6/28/16
Municipal Government	Colorado Springs, CO	Y	65794 LO		90467 HI	COSPRS	2017
Crime Analyst							
Department of Corrections, State Government	Helena, MT	H			26.99 HI	MTGOV	2016
Department of Justice, State Government	Helena, MT	H	19.88 LO		20.79 HI	MTGOV	2016
Michigan State University	East Lansing, MI	Y			66300 HI	MSUSAL	10/1/14-9/30/15
Municipal Government	Detroit, MI	M	3467 LO		3625 HI	DETGOV	2016
Police Department, Municipal Government	Elk Grove, CA	Y			81323 HI	CACIT	6/28/16
Police Department, Municipal Government	Escondido, CA	Y			63833 HI	CACIT	6/28/16
Police Department, Municipal Government	San Bernardino, CA	Y			61704 HI	CACIT	6/28/16
Police Special Operations, Municipal Government	Tustin, CA	Y			82927 HI	CACIT	8/16/16
Crime Intelligence Analyst							
Attorney General's Office, State Government	Ohio	H	21.12 LO		33.97 HI	OHGOV	2015
Crime Laboratory Manager							
Police Department, Municipal Government	San Diego, CA	Y			112676 HI	CACIT	6/28/16
Crime Laboratory Technician							
Sheriff's Department	Alameda County, CA	M	4860 LO		5838 HI	CAC	7/16
Sheriff's Department, Scientific Services Bureau	Los Angeles County, CA	M	3590 LO		4452 HI	CAC	10/15
Crime Prevention Specialist							
Municipal Government	Alhambra, CA	Y			70189 HI	CACIT	6/28/16
Municipal Government	Carlsbad, CA	H	22.76 LO	26.27 MW	29.78 HI	CCCA01	6/28/16
Municipal Government	Chino, CA	Y			58751 HI	CACIT	6/28/16
Municipal Government	Duarte, CA	Y			69527 HI	CACIT	6/28/16
Crime Prevention Supervisor							
Municipal Government	Seattle, WA	H	35.69 LO		41.52 HI	CSSS	1/13/16
Crime Scene Investigator							
Municipal Government	Desert Hot Springs, CA	Y			49367 HI	CACIT	6/28/16
Municipal Government	Newport Beach, CA	Y		79597 AW		CACIT	6/28/16
Municipal Government	Colorado Springs, CO	Y	46996 LO		64619 HI	COSPRS	2017
Crime Scene Specialist							
Municipal Government	Alameda, CA	Y		83671 AW		CACIT	6/28/16

AE	Average entry wage	**AWR**	Average wage range	**H**	Hourly
AEX	Average experienced wage	**B**	Biweekly	**HI**	Highest wage paid
ATC	Average total compensation	**D**	Daily	**HR**	High end range
AW	Average wage paid	**FQ**	First quartile wage	**LO**	Lowest wage paid

LR	Low end range	**MTC**	Median total compensation	**TCC**	Total cash compensation
M	Monthly	**MW**	Median wage paid	**TQ**	Third quartile wage
MCC	Median cash compensation	**MWR**	Median wage range	**W**	Weekly
ME	Median entry wage	**S**	See annotated source	**Y**	Yearly

Occupation/Type/Industry	Location	Per	Low	Mid	High	Source	Date
Crime Scene Technician							
Municipal Government	Hayward, CA	Y		67735 AW		CACIT	6/28/16
Municipal Government	Redding, CA	Y			47335 HI	CACIT	6/28/16
Municipal Government	Tracy, CA	Y			60783 HI	CACIT	6/28/16
Crime Specialist							
Police Department, Municipal Government	Clovis, CA	Y			67764 HI	CACIT	9/5/16
Crime Victims' Claims Investigator							
Attorney General's Office, State Government	Ohio	H	22.66 LO		28.90 HI	OHGOV	2015
Criminal Attorney							
Court-Appointed	Lansing, MI	S		560.00 AW		LSJ08	2015
Criminal Justice and Law Enforcement Teacher							
Postsecondary	Alabama	Y	48153 AE	74156 AW	87152 AEX	ALBLS	6/16
Postsecondary	Birmingham-Hoover MSA, AL	Y	48326 AE	72280 AW	84267 AEX	ALBLS	6/16
Postsecondary	Alaska	Y	55890 FQ	61770 MW	79020 TQ	USBLS	5/15
Postsecondary	Anchorage MSA, AK	Y	55080 FQ	60150 MW	67140 TQ	USBLS	5/15
Postsecondary	Arizona	Y	38640 FQ	60100 MW	86800 TQ	USBLS	5/15
Postsecondary	Phoenix-Mesa-Scottsdale MSA, AZ	Y	43780 FQ	61230 MW	89320 TQ	USBLS	5/15
Postsecondary	Arkansas	Y	47540 FQ	56110 MW	69000 TQ	USBLS	5/15
Postsecondary	Little Rock-North Little Rock-Conway MSA, AR	Y	49040 FQ	56870 MW	71320 TQ	USBLS	5/15
Postsecondary	California	Y		85075 AW		CABLS	1/16-3/16
Postsecondary	Anaheim-Santa Ana-Irvine PMSA, CA	Y		91406 AW		CABLS	1/16-3/16
Postsecondary	Los Angeles-Long Beach-Glendale PMSA, CA	Y		83757 AW		CABLS	1/16-3/16
Postsecondary	Riverside-San Bernardino-Ontario MSA, CA	Y		103813 AW		CABLS	1/16-3/16
Postsecondary	Sacramento–Roseville–Arden-Arcade MSA, CA	Y		56588 AW		CABLS	1/16-3/16
Postsecondary	Colorado	Y	33390 FQ	46390 MW	82900 TQ	USBLS	5/15
Postsecondary	Denver-Aurora-Lakewood MSA, CO	Y	34970 FQ	52880 MW	86700 TQ	USBLS	5/15
Postsecondary	Connecticut	Y		59662 MW		CTBLS	1/16-3/16
Postsecondary	Hartford-West Hartford-East Hartford MSA, CT	Y	49860 FQ	56320 MW	62410 TQ	USBLS	5/15
Postsecondary	Delaware	Y	66610 FQ	73020 MW	80180 TQ	USBLS	5/15
Postsecondary	District of Columbia	Y	54350 FQ	66420 MW	83270 TQ	USBLS	5/15
Postsecondary	Washington-Arlington-Alexandria PMSA, DC-VA-MD-WV	Y	48880 FQ	64640 MW	104810 TQ	USBLS	5/15
Postsecondary	Florida	Y	44191 AE	61816 MW	78296 AEX	FLBLS	7/16-9/16
Postsecondary	Miami-Miami Beach-Kendall PMSA, FL	Y	52803 AE	80511 MW	91959 AEX	FLBLS	7/16-9/16
Postsecondary	Orlando-Kissimmee-Sanford MSA, FL	Y	43134 AE	75637 MW	101081 AEX	FLBLS	7/16-9/16
Postsecondary	Tampa-St. Petersburg-Clearwater MSA, FL	Y	43433 AE	57873 MW	65653 AEX	FLBLS	7/16-9/16
Postsecondary	Georgia	Y	48940 FQ	58290 MW	71060 TQ	USBLS	5/15
Postsecondary	Atlanta-Sandy Springs-Roswell MSA, GA	Y	46790 FQ	57760 MW	68820 TQ	USBLS	5/15
Postsecondary	Hawaii	Y	37890 FQ	51390 MW	74010 TQ	USBLS	5/15
Postsecondary	Urban Honolulu MSA, HI	Y	37470 FQ	48970 MW	75070 TQ	USBLS	5/15
Postsecondary	Idaho	Y	40710 FQ	48660 MW	63790 TQ	USBLS	5/15
Postsecondary	Illinois	Y	52740 FQ	65810 MW	88370 TQ	USBLS	5/15
Postsecondary	Chicago-Naperville-Arlington Heights PMSA, IL	Y	50350 FQ	60090 MW	79380 TQ	USBLS	5/15
Postsecondary	Indiana	Y	38620 FQ	45860 MW	57400 TQ	USBLS	5/15
Postsecondary	Indianapolis-Carmel-Anderson MSA, IN	Y	32080 FQ	41820 MW	46140 TQ	USBLS	5/15
Postsecondary	Iowa	Y	53890 FQ	60560 MW	71950 TQ	USBLS	5/15
Postsecondary	Des Moines-West Des Moines MSA, IA	Y	54220 FQ	60160 MW	70930 TQ	USBLS	5/15
Postsecondary	Kansas	Y	28970 FQ	39320 MW	61940 TQ	USBLS	5/15
Postsecondary	Kentucky	Y	50880 FQ	67050 MW	100350 TQ	USBLS	5/15

AE	Average entry wage	AWR	Average wage range	H	Hourly	LR	Low end range	MTC	Median total compensation	TCC	Total cash compensation
AEX	Average experienced wage	B	Biweekly	HI	Highest wage paid	M	Monthly	MW	Median wage paid	TQ	Third quartile wage
ATC	Average total compensation	D	Daily	HR	High end range	MCC	Median cash compensation	MWR	Median wage range	W	Weekly
AW	Average wage paid	FQ	First quartile wage	LO	Lowest wage paid	ME	Median entry wage	S	See annotated source	Y	Yearly

Criminal Justice and Law Enforcement Teacher

Occupation/Type/Industry	Location	Per	Low	Mid	High	Source	Date
Postsecondary	Louisville-Jefferson County MSA, KY-IN	Y	42150 FQ	51170 MW	70620 TQ	USBLS	5/15
Postsecondary	Louisiana	Y	51240 FQ	66720 MW	78850 TQ	USBLS	5/15
Postsecondary	Maine	Y	37200 FQ	54650 MW	64490 TQ	USBLS	5/15
Postsecondary	Maryland	Y	42227 AE	72862 MW	88180 AEX	MDBLS	4/16
Postsecondary	Baltimore-Columbia-Towson MSA, MD	Y	54070 FQ	61820 MW	77710 TQ	USBLS	5/15
Postsecondary	Massachusetts	Y	49830 FQ	60780 MW	77110 TQ	USBLS	5/15
Postsecondary	Boston-Cambridge-Newton NECTA, MA	Y	53050 FQ	61990 MW	84060 TQ	USBLS	5/15
Postsecondary	Worcester MSA, MA-CT	Y	45300 FQ	51940 MW	66240 TQ	USBLS	5/15
Postsecondary	Michigan	Y	39060 FQ	63130 MW	78300 TQ	USBLS	5/15
Postsecondary	Detroit-Dearborn-Livonia PMSA, MI	Y	51380 FQ	65890 MW	74160 TQ	USBLS	5/15
Postsecondary	Grand Rapids-Wyoming MSA, MI	Y	36830 FQ	58580 MW	76920 TQ	USBLS	5/15
Postsecondary	Minnesota	Y	46552 FQ	59515 MW	73235 TQ	MNBLS	1/16-3/16
Postsecondary	Minneapolis-St. Paul-Bloomington MSA, MN-WI	Y	45534 FQ	58800 MW	71501 TQ	MNBLS	1/16-3/16
Postsecondary	Mississippi	Y	51720 FQ	60400 MW	71870 TQ	USBLS	5/15
Postsecondary	Missouri	Y	45000 FQ	60740 MW	83390 TQ	USBLS	5/15
Postsecondary	Kansas City MSA, MO-KS	Y	46330 FQ	66200 MW	92770 TQ	USBLS	5/15
Postsecondary	St. Louis MSA, MO-IL	Y	51140 FQ	67220 MW	84200 TQ	USBLS	5/15
Postsecondary	Nebraska	Y	36140 FQ	60510 MW	74830 TQ	NEBLS	7/16-9/16
Postsecondary	Omaha-Council Bluffs MSA, NE-IA	Y	30290 FQ	51785 MW	72965 TQ	NEBLS	7/16-9/16
Postsecondary	New Hampshire	Y	57093 AE	69175 MW	76551 AEX	NHBLS	6/16
Postsecondary	New Jersey	Y	50310 FQ	66710 MW	82160 TQ	USBLS	5/15
Postsecondary	Newark PMSA, NJ-PA	Y	63750 FQ	76790 MW	104900 TQ	USBLS	5/15
Postsecondary	New Mexico	Y	46240 FQ	56120 MW	72940 TQ	USBLS	5/15
Postsecondary	New York	Y	37850 AE	61930 MW	84090 AEX	NYBLS	1/16-3/16
Postsecondary	Buffalo-Cheektowaga-Niagara Falls MSA, NY	Y	47010 FQ	62350 MW	88250 TQ	USBLS	5/15
Postsecondary	Nassau County-Suffolk County PMSA, NY	Y	39690 FQ	54100 MW	70390 TQ	USBLS	5/15
Postsecondary	New York-Jersey City-White Plains PMSA, NY-NJ	Y	53140 FQ	69610 MW	93120 TQ	USBLS	5/15
Postsecondary	Rochester MSA, NY	Y	34450 FQ	37770 MW	45070 TQ	USBLS	5/15
Postsecondary	North Carolina	Y	48950 FQ	55650 MW	61410 TQ	USBLS	5/15
Postsecondary	Charlotte-Concord-Gastonia MSA, NC-SC	Y	52260 FQ	56870 MW	61480 TQ	USBLS	5/15
Postsecondary	North Dakota	Y	47720 FQ	68950 MW	87260 TQ	USBLS	5/15
Postsecondary	Ohio	Y	38740 FQ	56570 MW	78260 TQ	USBLS	5/15
Postsecondary	Cincinnati MSA, OH-KY-IN	Y	46830 FQ	64600 MW	85340 TQ	USBLS	5/15
Postsecondary	Cleveland-Elyria MSA, OH	Y	46360 FQ	59360 MW	90640 TQ	USBLS	5/15
Postsecondary	Columbus MSA, OH	Y	50830 FQ	68480 MW	108600 TQ	USBLS	5/15
Postsecondary	Oklahoma	Y	40040 FQ	49550 MW	70500 TQ	USBLS	5/15
Postsecondary	Oklahoma City MSA, OK	Y	37070 FQ	47280 MW	71710 TQ	USBLS	5/15
Postsecondary	Oregon	Y	46361 FQ	62225 MW	86508 TQ	ORBLS	2016
Postsecondary	Portland-Vancouver-Hillsboro MSA, OR-WA	Y	42800 FQ	52610 MW	74910 TQ	USBLS	5/15
Postsecondary	Pennsylvania	Y	50560 FQ	62500 MW	87680 TQ	USBLS	5/15
Postsecondary	Allentown-Bethlehem-Easton MSA, PA-NJ	Y	53320 FQ	63670 MW	79150 TQ	USBLS	5/15
Postsecondary	Harrisburg-Carlisle MSA, PA	Y	50880 FQ	64410 MW	77910 TQ	USBLS	5/15
Postsecondary	Montgomery County-Bucks County-Chester County PMSA, PA	Y	44610 FQ	57360 MW	72020 TQ	USBLS	5/15
Postsecondary	Philadelphia PMSA, PA	Y	52280 FQ	64000 MW	108030 TQ	USBLS	5/15
Postsecondary	Pittsburgh MSA, PA	Y	44660 FQ	61490 MW	80890 TQ	USBLS	5/15
Postsecondary	Rhode Island	Y	63750 FQ	96770 MW	148770 TQ	USBLS	5/15
Postsecondary	Providence-Warwick MSA, RI-MA	Y	59210 FQ	78440 MW	146090 TQ	USBLS	5/15
Postsecondary	South Carolina	Y	53970 FQ	69180 MW	85810 TQ	USBLS	5/15
Postsecondary	Columbia MSA, SC	Y	55220 FQ	79670 MW	92230 TQ	USBLS	5/15
Postsecondary	South Dakota	Y	52610 FQ	59890 MW	74320 TQ	USBLS	5/15
Postsecondary	Tennessee	Y	32900 FQ	47520 MW	60130 TQ	USBLS	5/15

AE	Average entry wage	AWR	Average wage range	H	Hourly
AEX	Average experienced wage	B	Biweekly	HI	Highest wage paid
ATC	Average total compensation	D	Daily	HR	High end range
AW	Average wage paid	FQ	First quartile wage	LO	Lowest wage paid

LR	Low end range	MTC	Median total compensation	TCC	Total cash compensation
M	Monthly	MW	Median wage paid
MCC	Median cash compensation	MWR	Median wage range	TQ	Third quartile wage
ME	Median entry wage	S	See annotated source	W	Weekly
			Y	Yearly

Occupation/Type/Industry	Location	Per	Low	Mid	High	Source	Date
Criminal Justice and Law Enforcement Teacher							
Postsecondary	Nashville-Davidson– Murfreesboro–Franklin MSA, TN	Y	44880 FQ	55940 MW	65130 TQ	USBLS	5/15
Postsecondary	Texas	Y	25010 FQ	52050 MW	67360 TQ	USBLS	5/15
Postsecondary	Austin-Round Rock MSA, TX	Y	19140 FQ	54660 MW	73740 TQ	USBLS	5/15
Postsecondary	Dallas-Plano-Irving PMSA, TX	Y	28430 FQ	51400 MW	65360 TQ	USBLS	5/15
Postsecondary	Fort Worth-Arlington PMSA, TX	Y	27480 FQ	49820 MW	59700 TQ	USBLS	5/15
Postsecondary	Houston-The Woodlands- Sugar Land MSA, TX	Y	51030 FQ	57910 MW	70010 TQ	USBLS	5/15
Postsecondary	San Antonio-New Braunfels MSA, TX	Y	22530 FQ	26780 MW	65900 TQ	USBLS	5/15
Postsecondary	Utah	Y	49250 FQ	58060 MW	72450 TQ	USBLS	5/15
Postsecondary	Ogden-Clearfield MSA, UT	Y	53190 FQ	57380 MW	61570 TQ	USBLS	5/15
Postsecondary	Provo-Orem MSA, UT	Y	53380 FQ	67140 MW	95410 TQ	USBLS	5/15
Postsecondary	Salt Lake City MSA, UT	Y	45750 FQ	56660 MW	72570 TQ	USBLS	5/15
Postsecondary	Virginia	Y	45510 FQ	59420 MW	95020 TQ	USBLS	5/15
Postsecondary	Virginia Beach-Norfolk- Newport News MSA, VA-NC	Y	44740 FQ	57090 MW	70840 TQ	USBLS	5/15
Postsecondary	Washington	Y		52307 AW		WABLS	3/16
Postsecondary	Seattle-Bellevue-Everett PMSA, WA	Y		58313 AW		WABLS	3/16
Postsecondary	West Virginia	Y	27680 FQ	44850 MW	58060 TQ	USBLS	5/15
Postsecondary	Wisconsin	Y	39740 FQ	57950 MW	78660 TQ	USBLS	5/15
Postsecondary	Milwaukee-Waukesha-West Allis MSA, WI	Y	38670 FQ	63750 MW	86240 TQ	USBLS	5/15
Postsecondary	Wyoming	Y	59250 FQ	66080 MW	75260 TQ	USBLS	5/15
Postsecondary	Puerto Rico	Y	17410 FQ	20380 MW	70350 TQ	USBLS	5/15
Postsecondary	San Juan-Carolina-Caguas MSA, PR	Y	16500 FQ	17780 MW	19060 TQ	USBLS	5/15
Criminal Research Specialist							
Police Department, Municipal Government	Anaheim, CA	Y			65519 HI	CACIT	6/28/16
Criminalist							
Sheriff's Department, Scientific Services Bureau	Los Angeles County, CA	M	5332 LO		6623 HI	CAC	10/15
Crossing Guard	Alabama	Y	17452 AE	20860 AW	22569 AEX	ALBLS	6/16
	Birmingham-Hoover MSA, AL	Y	20417 AE	22713 AW	23856 AEX	ALBLS	6/16
	Alaska	Y	21860 FQ	24340 MW	40970 TQ	USBLS	5/15
	Anchorage MSA, AK	Y	21190 FQ	22990 MW	41000 TQ	USBLS	5/15
	Arizona	Y	17680 FQ	18590 MW	19660 TQ	USBLS	5/15
	Phoenix-Mesa-Scottsdale MSA, AZ	Y	17710 FQ	18650 MW	19790 TQ	USBLS	5/15
	Tucson MSA, AZ	Y	17510 FQ	18270 MW	19030 TQ	USBLS	5/15
	Arkansas	Y	16980 FQ	18330 MW	19870 TQ	USBLS	5/15
	Little Rock-North Little Rock- Conway MSA, AR	Y	16680 FQ	17750 MW	18820 TQ	USBLS	5/15
	California	H	9.66 FQ	13.02 MW	16.54 TQ	CABLS	1/16-3/16
	Anaheim-Santa Ana-Irvine PMSA, CA	H	9.61 FQ	11.17 MW	15.10 TQ	CABLS	1/16-3/16
	Los Angeles-Long Beach- Glendale PMSA, CA	H	11.32 FQ	14.03 MW	16.81 TQ	CABLS	1/16-3/16
	Oakland-Hayward-Berkeley PMSA, CA	H	12.43 FQ	15.62 MW	17.97 TQ	CABLS	1/16-3/16
	Oxnard-Thousand Oaks- Ventura MSA, CA	Y	20680 FQ	23600 MW	27760 TQ	USBLS	5/15
	Riverside-San Bernardino- Ontario MSA, CA	H	9.42 FQ	9.62 MW	13.00 TQ	CABLS	1/16-3/16
	Sacramento–Roseville– Arden-Arcade MSA, CA	H	9.51 FQ	11.25 MW	14.59 TQ	CABLS	1/16-3/16
	San Diego-Carlsbad MSA, CA	H	15.52 FQ	16.96 MW	18.39 TQ	CABLS	1/16-3/16
	San Francisco-Redwood City- South San Francisco PMSA, CA	H	14.97 FQ	16.81 MW	18.52 TQ	CABLS	1/16-3/16
	Colorado	Y	21080 FQ	25590 MW	29970 TQ	USBLS	5/15
	Denver-Aurora-Lakewood MSA, CO	Y	20190 FQ	23720 MW	29120 TQ	USBLS	5/15
	Connecticut	Y		27778 MW		CTBLS	1/16-3/16

AE	Average entry wage	AWR	Average wage range	H	Hourly	LR	Low end range	MTC	Median total compensation	TCC	Total cash compensation
AEX	Average experienced wage	B	Biweekly	HI	Highest wage paid	M	Monthly	MW	Median wage paid	TQ	Third quartile wage
ATC	Average total compensation	D	Daily	HR	High end range	MCC	Median cash compensation	MWR	Median wage range	W	Weekly
AW	Average wage paid	FQ	First quartile wage	LO	Lowest wage paid	ME	Median entry wage	S	See annotated source	Y	Yearly

Crossing Guard

Occupation/Type/Industry	Location	Per	Low	Mid	High	Source	Date
Crossing Guard	Delaware	Y	24730 FQ	29480 MW	35540 TQ	USBLS	5/15
	Wilmington PMSA, DE-MD-NJ	Y	24520 FQ	29100 MW	34430 TQ	USBLS	5/15
	Washington-Arlington-Alexandria PMSA, DC-VA-MD-WV	Y	27380 FQ	32250 MW	37370 TQ	USBLS	5/15
	Florida	H	9.69 AE	11.29 MW	12.62 AEX	FLBLS	7/16-9/16
	Fort Lauderdale-Pompano Beach-Deerfield Beach PMSA, FL	H	10.19 AE	13.31 MW	15.20 AEX	FLBLS	7/16-9/16
	Miami-Miami Beach-Kendall PMSA, FL	H	10.10 AE	11.02 MW	11.42 AEX	FLBLS	7/16-9/16
	Orlando-Kissimmee-Sanford MSA, FL	H	10.38 AE	11.36 MW	12.68 AEX	FLBLS	7/16-9/16
	Tampa-St. Petersburg-Clearwater MSA, FL	H	9.60 AE	11.16 MW	12.39 AEX	FLBLS	7/16-9/16
	Georgia	Y	18050 FQ	21570 MW	27010 TQ	USBLS	5/15
	Atlanta-Sandy Springs-Roswell MSA, GA	Y	19810 FQ	23200 MW	29600 TQ	USBLS	5/15
	Augusta-Richmond County MSA, GA-SC	Y	20750 FQ	23960 MW	32290 TQ	USBLS	5/15
	Hawaii	Y	25750 FQ	27570 MW	29390 TQ	USBLS	5/15
	Idaho	Y	20490 FQ	23630 MW	29080 TQ	USBLS	5/15
	Boise City MSA, ID	Y	20120 FQ	22980 MW	26760 TQ	USBLS	5/15
	Illinois	Y	20360 FQ	28290 MW	36370 TQ	USBLS	5/15
	Chicago-Naperville-Arlington Heights PMSA, IL	Y	22320 FQ	31750 MW	37830 TQ	USBLS	5/15
	Lake County-Kenosha County PMSA, IL-WI	Y	24530 FQ	27920 MW	32380 TQ	USBLS	5/15
	Indiana	Y	18570 FQ	24300 MW	39100 TQ	USBLS	5/15
	Iowa	Y	25200 FQ	27740 MW	30280 TQ	USBLS	5/15
	Des Moines-West Des Moines MSA, IA	Y	26710 FQ	28560 MW	30410 TQ	USBLS	5/15
	Kansas	Y	19330 FQ	21530 MW	23880 TQ	USBLS	5/15
	Kentucky	Y	24660 FQ	27620 MW	30400 TQ	USBLS	5/15
	Louisville-Jefferson County MSA, KY-IN	Y	25630 FQ	27830 MW	30030 TQ	USBLS	5/15
	Louisiana	Y	16870 FQ	18410 MW	23560 TQ	USBLS	5/15
	Baton Rouge MSA, LA	Y	16810 FQ	18020 MW	19240 TQ	USBLS	5/15
	New Orleans-Metairie MSA, LA	Y	16890 FQ	18660 MW	27400 TQ	USBLS	5/15
	Maine	Y	19850 FQ	21670 MW	23510 TQ	USBLS	5/15
	Portland-South Portland MSA, ME	Y	19440 FQ	21320 MW	23210 TQ	USBLS	5/15
	Maryland	Y	21895 AE	26685 MW	29079 AEX	MDBLS	4/16
	Baltimore-Columbia-Towson MSA, MD	Y	26000 FQ	27690 MW	29370 TQ	USBLS	5/15
	Salisbury MSA, MD-DE	Y	21270 FQ	29730 MW	38470 TQ	USBLS	5/15
	Massachusetts	Y	19320 FQ	23790 MW	30990 TQ	USBLS	5/15
	Boston-Cambridge-Newton NECTA, MA	Y	19170 FQ	24110 MW	37220 TQ	USBLS	5/15
	Worcester MSA, MA-CT	Y	19190 FQ	19660 MW	24720 TQ	USBLS	5/15
	Michigan	Y	18590 FQ	20770 MW	24680 TQ	USBLS	5/15
	Detroit-Dearborn-Livonia PMSA, MI	Y	19560 FQ	21980 MW	24470 TQ	USBLS	5/15
	Minnesota	Y	23409 FQ	31750 MW	36052 TQ	MNBLS	1/16-3/16
	Minneapolis-St. Paul-Bloomington MSA, MN-WI	Y	27287 FQ	33103 MW	36699 TQ	MNBLS	1/16-3/16
	Mississippi	Y	17260 FQ	19040 MW	27260 TQ	USBLS	5/15
	Jackson MSA, MS	Y	17830 FQ	24840 MW	27960 TQ	USBLS	5/15
	Missouri	Y	18860 FQ	23940 MW	36370 TQ	USBLS	5/15
	Kansas City MSA, MO-KS	Y	20350 FQ	22190 MW	24030 TQ	USBLS	5/15
	St. Louis MSA, MO-IL	Y	19330 FQ	26670 MW	37700 TQ	USBLS	5/15
	Montana	Y	21520 FQ	24350 MW	27860 TQ	USBLS	5/15
	Billings MSA, MT	Y	22260 FQ	24660 MW	28010 TQ	USBLS	5/15
	Nebraska	Y	20040 FQ	23290 MW	27145 TQ	NEBLS	7/16-9/16
	Omaha-Council Bluffs MSA, NE-IA	Y	20945 FQ	23705 MW	27620 TQ	NEBLS	7/16-9/16
	Nevada	Y	20010 FQ	21790 MW	23570 TQ	USBLS	5/15
	Las Vegas-Henderson-Paradise MSA, NV	Y	19810 FQ	21560 MW	23360 TQ	USBLS	5/15
	New Hampshire	H	10.77 AE	13.07 MW	14.47 AEX	NHBLS	6/16

AE	Average entry wage	AWR	Average wage range	H	Hourly
AEX	Average experienced wage	B	Biweekly	HI	Highest wage paid
ATC	Average total compensation	D	Daily	HR	High end range
AW	Average wage paid	FQ	First quartile wage	LO	Lowest wage paid

LR	Low end range	MTC	Median total compensation	TCC	Total cash compensation
M	Monthly	MW	Median wage paid	TQ	Third quartile wage
MCC	Median cash compensation	MWR	Median wage range	W	Weekly
ME	Median entry wage	S	See annotated source	Y	Yearly

Occupation/Type/Industry	Location	Per	Low	Mid	High	Source	Date
Crossing Guard	Nashua NECTA, NH-MA	Y	26570 FQ	28290 MW	30010 TQ	USBLS	5/15
	New Jersey	Y	25640 FQ	30580 MW	37390 TQ	USBLS	5/15
	Camden PMSA, NJ	Y	20580 FQ	25090 MW	32910 TQ	USBLS	5/15
	Newark PMSA, NJ-PA	Y	27320 FQ	32340 MW	37730 TQ	USBLS	5/15
	Trenton MSA, NJ	Y	19200 FQ	29710 MW	36120 TQ	USBLS	5/15
	New Mexico	Y	20020 FQ	25930 MW	28370 TQ	USBLS	5/15
	New York	Y	22730 AE	32440 MW	35780 AEX	NYBLS	1/16-3/16
	Buffalo-Cheektowaga-Niagara Falls MSA, NY	Y	19530 FQ	21550 MW	23900 TQ	USBLS	5/15
	Nassau County-Suffolk County PMSA, NY	Y	19040 FQ	24710 MW	38250 TQ	USBLS	5/15
	New York-Jersey City-White Plains PMSA, NY-NJ	Y	27780 FQ	32730 MW	36770 TQ	USBLS	5/15
	Rochester MSA, NY	Y	21340 FQ	23310 MW	26660 TQ	USBLS	5/15
	North Carolina	Y	18820 FQ	22870 MW	33180 TQ	USBLS	5/15
	Charlotte-Concord-Gastonia MSA, NC-SC	Y	17400 FQ	19310 MW	22420 TQ	USBLS	5/15
	Raleigh MSA, NC	Y	22410 FQ	26400 MW	34300 TQ	USBLS	5/15
	Ohio	Y	19200 FQ	26070 MW	38440 TQ	USBLS	5/15
	Cincinnati MSA, OH-KY-IN	Y	17890 FQ	18890 MW	19970 TQ	USBLS	5/15
	Cleveland-Elyria MSA, OH	Y	22390 FQ	33770 MW	43850 TQ	USBLS	5/15
	Columbus MSA, OH	Y	19140 FQ	23490 MW	41820 TQ	USBLS	5/15
	Oklahoma	Y	16930 FQ	18560 MW	23080 TQ	USBLS	5/15
	Oklahoma City MSA, OK	Y	16680 FQ	17980 MW	19300 TQ	USBLS	5/15
	Tulsa MSA, OK	Y	17390 FQ	20010 MW	25980 TQ	USBLS	5/15
	Oregon	H	10.81 FQ	12.84 MW	19.87 TQ	ORBLS	2016
	Portland-Vancouver-Hillsboro MSA, OR-WA	Y	22340 FQ	25760 MW	39740 TQ	USBLS	5/15
	Pennsylvania	Y	17710 FQ	22670 MW	29740 TQ	USBLS	5/15
	Allentown-Bethlehem-Easton MSA, PA-NJ	Y	18260 FQ	22250 MW	27120 TQ	USBLS	5/15
	Harrisburg-Carlisle MSA, PA	Y	21090 FQ	26330 MW	30240 TQ	USBLS	5/15
	Montgomery County-Bucks County-Chester County PMSA, PA	Y	26270 FQ	29840 MW	35830 TQ	USBLS	5/15
	Philadelphia PMSA, PA	Y	16580 FQ	18060 MW	24750 TQ	USBLS	5/15
	Pittsburgh MSA, PA	Y	19850 FQ	25960 MW	31190 TQ	USBLS	5/15
	Rhode Island	Y	26070 FQ	28670 MW	40260 TQ	USBLS	5/15
	Providence-Warwick MSA, RI-MA	Y	25310 FQ	28140 MW	38480 TQ	USBLS	5/15
	South Carolina	Y	18290 FQ	21660 MW	29340 TQ	USBLS	5/15
	Charleston-North Charleston MSA, SC	Y	18180 FQ	22290 MW	54150 TQ	USBLS	5/15
	Columbia MSA, SC	Y	23870 FQ	43380 MW	47350 TQ	USBLS	5/15
	Greenville-Anderson-Mauldin MSA, SC	Y	20660 FQ	22070 MW	23470 TQ	USBLS	5/15
	South Dakota	Y	18990 FQ	21680 MW	25090 TQ	USBLS	5/15
	Tennessee	Y	21050 FQ	24650 MW	34400 TQ	USBLS	5/15
	Knoxville MSA, TN	Y	19260 FQ	26500 MW	42200 TQ	USBLS	5/15
	Memphis MSA, TN-MS-AR	Y	28940 FQ	33180 MW	36100 TQ	USBLS	5/15
	Nashville-Davidson–Murfreesboro–Franklin MSA, TN	Y	20480 FQ	22320 MW	24160 TQ	USBLS	5/15
	Texas	Y	18160 FQ	21360 MW	27030 TQ	USBLS	5/15
	Austin-Round Rock MSA, TX	Y	19940 FQ	22080 MW	24240 TQ	USBLS	5/15
	Dallas-Plano-Irving PMSA, TX	Y	17610 FQ	19690 MW	22990 TQ	USBLS	5/15
	Fort Worth-Arlington PMSA, TX	Y	17300 FQ	19760 MW	22610 TQ	USBLS	5/15
	Houston-The Woodlands-Sugar Land MSA, TX	Y	22880 FQ	31610 MW	36260 TQ	USBLS	5/15
	San Antonio-New Braunfels MSA, TX	Y	20740 FQ	22960 MW	26360 TQ	USBLS	5/15
	Utah	Y	17190 FQ	19050 MW	22960 TQ	USBLS	5/15
	Ogden-Clearfield MSA, UT	Y	16990 FQ	18680 MW	21840 TQ	USBLS	5/15
	Provo-Orem MSA, UT	Y	16760 FQ	18280 MW	20630 TQ	USBLS	5/15
	Salt Lake City MSA, UT	Y	17250 FQ	19160 MW	23640 TQ	USBLS	5/15
	Vermont	Y	22340 FQ	26380 MW	36340 TQ	USBLS	5/15
	Burlington-South Burlington MSA, VT	Y	22900 FQ	27200 MW	41800 TQ	USBLS	5/15
	Virginia	Y	21500 FQ	29960 MW	38670 TQ	USBLS	5/15
	Richmond MSA, VA	Y	18640 FQ	23800 MW	35390 TQ	USBLS	5/15

AE Average entry wage	**AWR** Average wage range	**H** Hourly	**LR** Low end range	**MTC** Median total compensation	**TCC** Total cash compensation
AEX Average experienced wage	**B** Biweekly	**HI** Highest wage paid	**M** Monthly	**MW** Median wage paid	**TQ** Third quartile wage
ATC Average total compensation	**D** Daily	**HR** High end range	**MCC** Median cash compensation	**MWR** Median wage range	**W** Weekly
AW Average wage paid	**FQ** First quartile wage	**LO** Lowest wage paid	**ME** Median entry wage	**S** See annotated source	**Y** Yearly

Occupation/Type/Industry	Location	Per	Low	Mid	High	Source	Date
Crossing Guard	Virginia Beach-Norfolk-Newport News MSA, VA-NC	Y	19590 FQ	31790 MW	39570 TQ	USBLS	5/15
	Washington	H	12.90 FQ	20.16 MW	27.44 TQ	WABLS	3/16
	Seattle-Bellevue-Everett PMSA, WA	H	11.64 FQ	17.39 MW	24.23 TQ	WABLS	3/16
	Tacoma-Lakewood PMSA, WA	H	14.34 FQ	20.14 MW	23.39 TQ	WABLS	3/16
	West Virginia	Y	25050 FQ	27470 MW	29860 TQ	USBLS	5/15
	Wisconsin	Y	20670 FQ	23700 MW	28530 TQ	USBLS	5/15
	Madison MSA, WI	Y	19200 FQ	28190 MW	34280 TQ	USBLS	5/15
	Milwaukee-Waukesha-West Allis MSA, WI	Y	21200 FQ	23200 MW	26700 TQ	USBLS	5/15
	Wyoming	Y	28220 FQ	38860 MW	44940 TQ	USBLS	5/15
Crushing, Grinding, and Polishing Machine Setter, Operator, and Tender	Alabama	Y	23495 AE	34538 AW	40059 AEX	ALBLS	6/16
	Birmingham-Hoover MSA, AL	Y	22405 AE	35103 AW	41447 AEX	ALBLS	6/16
	Alaska	Y	46150 FQ	55950 MW	69930 TQ	USBLS	5/15
	Arizona	Y	26550 FQ	30600 MW	38730 TQ	USBLS	5/15
	Phoenix-Mesa-Scottsdale MSA, AZ	Y	26000 FQ	29440 MW	35580 TQ	USBLS	5/15
	Tucson MSA, AZ	Y	36330 FQ	42380 MW	46320 TQ	USBLS	5/15
	Arkansas	Y	22080 FQ	28080 MW	35710 TQ	USBLS	5/15
	California	H	11.31 FQ	14.86 MW	19.83 TQ	CABLS	1/16-3/16
	Anaheim-Santa Ana-Irvine PMSA, CA	H	10.69 FQ	12.56 MW	16.39 TQ	CABLS	1/16-3/16
	Los Angeles-Long Beach-Glendale PMSA, CA	H	10.83 FQ	12.65 MW	15.88 TQ	CABLS	1/16-3/16
	Oakland-Hayward-Berkeley PMSA, CA	H	11.37 FQ	14.40 MW	21.09 TQ	CABLS	1/16-3/16
	Riverside-San Bernardino-Ontario MSA, CA	H	13.77 FQ	17.14 MW	21.08 TQ	CABLS	1/16-3/16
	Sacramento–Roseville–Arden-Arcade MSA, CA	H	13.00 FQ	17.74 MW	22.15 TQ	CABLS	1/16-3/16
	San Diego-Carlsbad MSA, CA	H	11.16 FQ	16.61 MW	26.08 TQ	CABLS	1/16-3/16
	Colorado	Y	33120 FQ	41430 MW	48970 TQ	USBLS	5/15
	Denver-Aurora-Lakewood MSA, CO	Y	31480 FQ	39830 MW	46810 TQ	USBLS	5/15
	Connecticut	Y		36584 MW		CTBLS	1/16-3/16
	Bridgeport-Stamford-Norwalk MSA, CT	Y	24180 FQ	30060 MW	38420 TQ	USBLS	5/15
	Hartford-West Hartford-East Hartford MSA, CT	Y	25840 FQ	32760 MW	40910 TQ	USBLS	5/15
	Delaware	Y	26450 FQ	32020 MW	38690 TQ	USBLS	5/15
	Wilmington PMSA, DE-MD-NJ	Y	30150 FQ	37110 MW	43910 TQ	USBLS	5/15
	Washington-Arlington-Alexandria PMSA, DC-VA-MD-WV	Y	30490 FQ	34660 MW	38410 TQ	USBLS	5/15
	Florida	H	11.79 AE	15.22 MW	17.58 AEX	FLBLS	7/16-9/16
	Fort Lauderdale-Pompano Beach-Deerfield Beach PMSA, FL	H	11.14 AE	12.61 MW	14.56 AEX	FLBLS	7/16-9/16
	Miami-Miami Beach-Kendall PMSA, FL	H	12.45 AE	15.63 MW	16.63 AEX	FLBLS	7/16-9/16
	Orlando-Kissimmee-Sanford MSA, FL	H	11.08 AE	11.85 MW	13.84 AEX	FLBLS	7/16-9/16
	Tampa-St. Petersburg-Clearwater MSA, FL	H	12.38 AE	14.14 MW	15.69 AEX	FLBLS	7/16-9/16
	Georgia	Y	26500 FQ	30540 MW	37490 TQ	USBLS	5/15
	Atlanta-Sandy Springs-Roswell MSA, GA	Y	26720 FQ	29500 MW	33990 TQ	USBLS	5/15
	Idaho	Y	31980 FQ	41590 MW	53110 TQ	USBLS	5/15
	Illinois	Y	27450 FQ	37900 MW	52990 TQ	USBLS	5/15
	Chicago-Naperville-Arlington Heights PMSA, IL	Y	28170 FQ	40140 MW	53970 TQ	USBLS	5/15
	Lake County-Kenosha County PMSA, IL-WI	Y	21860 FQ	24830 MW	33530 TQ	USBLS	5/15
	Indiana	Y	23630 FQ	30220 MW	39640 TQ	USBLS	5/15
	Gary PMSA, IN	Y	25240 FQ	30350 MW	42360 TQ	USBLS	5/15

AE	Average entry wage	AWR	Average wage range	H	Hourly
AEX	Average experienced wage	B	Biweekly	HI	Highest wage paid
ATC	Average total compensation	D	Daily	HR	High end range
AW	Average wage paid	FQ	First quartile wage	LO	Lowest wage paid

LR	Low end range	MTC	Median total compensation	TCC	Total cash compensation
M	Monthly	MW	Median wage paid	TQ	Third quartile wage
MCC	Median cash compensation	MWR	Median wage range	W	Weekly
ME	Median entry wage	S	See annotated source	Y	Yearly

Occupation/Type/Industry	Location	Per	Low	Mid	High	Source	Date
Crushing, Grinding, and Polishing Machine Setter, Operator, and Tender							
	Indianapolis-Carmel-Anderson MSA, IN	Y	22060 FQ	28070 MW	34700 TQ	USBLS	5/15
	Iowa	Y	29930 FQ	36410 MW	46410 TQ	USBLS	5/15
	Kansas	Y	29180 FQ	35150 MW	42570 TQ	USBLS	5/15
	Wichita MSA, KS	Y	27520 FQ	34500 MW	42710 TQ	USBLS	5/15
	Kentucky	Y	24420 FQ	32240 MW	42140 TQ	USBLS	5/15
	Louisville-Jefferson County MSA, KY-IN	Y	23140 FQ	32750 MW	39690 TQ	USBLS	5/15
	Louisiana	Y	24640 FQ	36480 MW	48600 TQ	USBLS	5/15
	Baton Rouge MSA, LA	Y	21190 FQ	25920 MW	35580 TQ	USBLS	5/15
	Maine	Y	30190 FQ	36530 MW	47510 TQ	USBLS	5/15
	Portland-South Portland MSA, ME	Y	31420 FQ	34770 MW	38080 TQ	USBLS	5/15
	Maryland	Y	25297 AE	34402 MW	38955 AEX	MDBLS	4/16
	Baltimore-Columbia-Towson MSA, MD	Y	26680 FQ	32820 MW	42960 TQ	USBLS	5/15
	Massachusetts	Y	32290 FQ	40000 MW	49230 TQ	USBLS	5/15
	Worcester MSA, MA-CT	Y	35670 FQ	43310 MW	51930 TQ	USBLS	5/15
	Michigan	Y	27880 FQ	35710 MW	42820 TQ	USBLS	5/15
	Detroit-Dearborn-Livonia PMSA, MI	Y	22480 FQ	26410 MW	30840 TQ	USBLS	5/15
	Grand Rapids-Wyoming MSA, MI	Y	31880 FQ	35610 MW	39330 TQ	USBLS	5/15
	Minnesota	Y	34454 FQ	40437 MW	48213 TQ	MNBLS	1/16-3/16
	Minneapolis-St. Paul-Bloomington MSA, MN-WI	Y	34535 FQ	43920 MW	54460 TQ	MNBLS	1/16-3/16
	Mississippi	Y	22400 FQ	27750 MW	33690 TQ	USBLS	5/15
	Missouri	Y	28300 FQ	36070 MW	44960 TQ	USBLS	5/15
	Kansas City MSA, MO-KS	Y	28290 FQ	35230 MW	43690 TQ	USBLS	5/15
	St. Louis MSA, MO-IL	Y	32380 FQ	39070 MW	49220 TQ	USBLS	5/15
	Montana	Y	32500 FQ	36860 MW	47860 TQ	USBLS	5/15
	Nebraska	Y	30475 FQ	36180 MW	44915 TQ	NEBLS	7/16-9/16
	Omaha-Council Bluffs MSA, NE-IA	Y	25915 FQ	31360 MW	45405 TQ	NEBLS	7/16-9/16
	Nevada	Y	31780 FQ	40750 MW	53960 TQ	USBLS	5/15
	Las Vegas-Henderson-Paradise MSA, NV	Y	26560 FQ	29600 MW	37570 TQ	USBLS	5/15
	New Hampshire	H	14.06 AE	18.34 MW	20.37 AEX	NHBLS	6/16
	Manchester NECTA, NH	H	15.13 AE	17.68 MW	19.10 AEX	NHBLS	6/16
	New Jersey	Y	21280 FQ	29540 MW	38880 TQ	USBLS	5/15
	Camden PMSA, NJ	Y	24070 FQ	34580 MW	43610 TQ	USBLS	5/15
	Newark PMSA, NJ-PA	Y	18820 FQ	21480 MW	37860 TQ	USBLS	5/15
	New Mexico	Y	26970 FQ	30120 MW	38920 TQ	USBLS	5/15
	New York	Y	24970 AE	36020 MW	43380 AEX	NYBLS	1/16-3/16
	Buffalo-Cheektowaga-Niagara Falls MSA, NY	Y	30410 FQ	41510 MW	51990 TQ	USBLS	5/15
	Nassau County-Suffolk County PMSA, NY	Y	28530 FQ	37340 MW	45390 TQ	USBLS	5/15
	New York-Jersey City-White Plains PMSA, NY-NJ	Y	24680 FQ	32050 MW	43290 TQ	USBLS	5/15
	Rochester MSA, NY	Y	29080 FQ	33800 MW	37550 TQ	USBLS	5/15
	North Carolina	Y	24100 FQ	30010 MW	37590 TQ	USBLS	5/15
	Charlotte-Concord-Gastonia MSA, NC-SC	Y	24180 FQ	29080 MW	36630 TQ	USBLS	5/15
	Raleigh MSA, NC	Y	27610 FQ	30580 MW	35340 TQ	USBLS	5/15
	North Dakota	Y	35500 FQ	43200 MW	61950 TQ	USBLS	5/15
	Ohio	Y	26310 FQ	33050 MW	38740 TQ	USBLS	5/15
	Cincinnati MSA, OH-KY-IN	Y	26580 FQ	33730 MW	37590 TQ	USBLS	5/15
	Cleveland-Elyria MSA, OH	Y	31390 FQ	36450 MW	44250 TQ	USBLS	5/15
	Columbus MSA, OH	Y	24330 FQ	30110 MW	42110 TQ	USBLS	5/15
	Oklahoma	Y	24450 FQ	32190 MW	39220 TQ	USBLS	5/15
	Oklahoma City MSA, OK	Y	31280 FQ	35380 MW	40070 TQ	USBLS	5/15
	Tulsa MSA, OK	Y	22300 FQ	24960 MW	30220 TQ	USBLS	5/15
	Oregon	H	14.74 FQ	17.80 MW	21.54 TQ	ORBLS	2016
	Portland-Vancouver-Hillsboro MSA, OR-WA	Y	29700 FQ	37280 MW	45630 TQ	USBLS	5/15
	Pennsylvania	Y	30950 FQ	36550 MW	44030 TQ	USBLS	5/15
	Allentown-Bethlehem-Easton MSA, PA-NJ	Y	32040 FQ	36340 MW	43110 TQ	USBLS	5/15

AE	Average entry wage	**AWR**	Average wage range	**H**	Hourly
AEX	Average experienced wage	**B**	Biweekly	**HI**	Highest wage paid
ATC	Average total compensation	**D**	Daily	**HR**	High end range
AW	Average wage paid	**FQ**	First quartile wage	**LO**	Lowest wage paid

LR	Low end range	**MTC**	Median total compensation	**TCC**	Total cash compensation
M	Monthly	**MW**	Median wage paid	**TQ**	Third quartile wage
MCC	Median cash compensation	**MWR**	Median wage range	**W**	Weekly
ME	Median entry wage	**S**	See annotated source	**Y**	Yearly

Occupation/Type/Industry	Location	Per	Low	Mid	High	Source	Date
Crushing, Grinding, and Polishing Machine Setter, Operator, and Tender							
	Harrisburg-Carlisle MSA, PA	Y	26180 FQ	30980 MW	41150 TQ	USBLS	5/15
	Montgomery County-Bucks County-Chester County PMSA, PA	Y	32450 FQ	38990 MW	46530 TQ	USBLS	5/15
	Philadelphia PMSA, PA	Y	37710 FQ	43010 MW	47360 TQ	USBLS	5/15
	Pittsburgh MSA, PA	Y	30890 FQ	35440 MW	39970 TQ	USBLS	5/15
	Rhode Island	Y	23210 FQ	27380 MW	34520 TQ	USBLS	5/15
	Providence-Warwick MSA, RI-MA	Y	23860 FQ	29420 MW	37340 TQ	USBLS	5/15
	South Carolina	Y	23700 FQ	37250 MW	44820 TQ	USBLS	5/15
	South Dakota	Y	26410 FQ	32030 MW	39080 TQ	USBLS	5/15
	Tennessee	Y	25960 FQ	31750 MW	38500 TQ	USBLS	5/15
	Knoxville MSA, TN	Y	26360 FQ	34290 MW	39850 TQ	USBLS	5/15
	Memphis MSA, TN-MS-AR	Y	26700 FQ	29290 MW	32320 TQ	USBLS	5/15
	Nashville-Davidson–Murfreesboro–Franklin MSA, TN	Y	27700 FQ	33290 MW	37710 TQ	USBLS	5/15
	Texas	Y	24260 FQ	29020 MW	36450 TQ	USBLS	5/15
	Austin-Round Rock MSA, TX	Y	21410 FQ	25480 MW	29020 TQ	USBLS	5/15
	Dallas-Plano-Irving PMSA, TX	Y	24730 FQ	28560 MW	34800 TQ	USBLS	5/15
	Fort Worth-Arlington PMSA, TX	Y	27960 FQ	35360 MW	42950 TQ	USBLS	5/15
	Houston-The Woodlands-Sugar Land MSA, TX	Y	25520 FQ	29800 MW	35930 TQ	USBLS	5/15
	San Antonio-New Braunfels MSA, TX	Y	27250 FQ	31160 MW	37190 TQ	USBLS	5/15
	Utah	Y	25790 FQ	30150 MW	38440 TQ	USBLS	5/15
	Ogden-Clearfield MSA, UT	Y	24050 FQ	26770 MW	29350 TQ	USBLS	5/15
	Salt Lake City MSA, UT	Y	28980 FQ	34260 MW	38650 TQ	USBLS	5/15
	Vermont	Y	40900 FQ	45960 MW	53260 TQ	USBLS	5/15
	Virginia	Y	23560 FQ	29840 MW	40190 TQ	USBLS	5/15
	Virginia Beach-Norfolk-Newport News MSA, VA-NC	Y	23460 FQ	39190 MW	48020 TQ	USBLS	5/15
	Washington	H	12.34 FQ	15.07 MW	18.73 TQ	WABLS	3/16
	Seattle-Bellevue-Everett PMSA, WA	H	13.20 FQ	16.37 MW	20.99 TQ	WABLS	3/16
	West Virginia	Y	26730 FQ	33500 MW	42650 TQ	USBLS	5/15
	Wisconsin	Y	27840 FQ	37170 MW	46720 TQ	USBLS	5/15
	Madison MSA, WI	Y	23960 FQ	37680 MW	47410 TQ	USBLS	5/15
	Milwaukee-Waukesha-West Allis MSA, WI	Y	29610 FQ	35740 MW	43500 TQ	USBLS	5/15
	Wyoming	Y	60630 FQ	70200 MW	76690 TQ	USBLS	5/15
	Puerto Rico	Y	17420 FQ	19280 MW	22040 TQ	USBLS	5/15
	San Juan-Carolina-Caguas MSA, PR	Y	17350 FQ	19260 MW	21600 TQ	USBLS	5/15
Cryptanalyst							
Federal Bureau of Investigation	District of Columbia, DC	Y	90823 LO		151496 HI	APP01	2015
Cultural Affairs Director							
Municipal Government	Thousand Oaks, CA	Y			171039 HI	CACIT	6/28/16
Municipal Government	Detroit, MI	M	6233 LO		10408 HI	DETGOV	2016
Cultural Arts Manager							
Municipal Government	Manhattan Beach, CA	Y			109404 HI	CACIT	6/28/16
Municipal Government	Rancho Cucamonga, CA	Y			81815 HI	CACIT	6/28/16
Cultural Arts Specialist							
Municipal Government	South San Francisco, CA	Y			46063 HI	CACIT	6/28/16
Cultural Event Coordinator							
Municipal Government	Agoura Hills, CA	Y			44975 HI	CACIT	6/28/16
Culture and History Specialist							
State Government	North Carolina	Y	31888 LO		70436 HI	NCGOV	7/1/16
Curator							
	Alabama	Y	34005 AE	52281 AW	61414 AEX	ALBLS	6/16
	Birmingham-Hoover MSA, AL	Y	38724 AE	54136 AW	61842 AEX	ALBLS	6/16
	Alaska	Y	42840 FQ	56760 MW	68550 TQ	USBLS	5/15
	Arizona	Y	37080 FQ	50160 MW	63990 TQ	USBLS	5/15

AE	Average entry wage	**AWR**	Average wage range	**H**	Hourly	**LR**	Low end range	**MTC**	Median total compensation	**TCC**	Total cash compensation
AEX	Average experienced wage	**B**	Biweekly	**HI**	Highest wage paid	**M**	Monthly	**MW**	Median wage paid	**TQ**	Third quartile wage
ATC	Average total compensation	**D**	Daily	**HR**	High end range	**MCC**	Median cash compensation	**MWR**	Median wage range	**W**	Weekly
AW	Average wage paid	**FQ**	First quartile wage	**LO**	Lowest wage paid	**ME**	Median entry wage	**S**	See annotated source	**Y**	Yearly

Occupation/Type/Industry	Location	Per	Low	Mid	High	Source	Date
Curator	Phoenix-Mesa-Scottsdale MSA, AZ	Y	36040 FQ	49010 MW	62510 TQ	USBLS	5/15
	Tucson MSA, AZ	Y	39280 FQ	50860 MW	63770 TQ	USBLS	5/15
	Arkansas	Y	34820 FQ	39520 MW	49570 TQ	USBLS	5/15
	California	H	24.54 FQ	31.60 MW	41.11 TQ	CABLS	1/16-3/16
	Anaheim-Santa Ana-Irvine PMSA, CA	H	21.95 FQ	31.56 MW	34.82 TQ	CABLS	1/16-3/16
	Los Angeles-Long Beach-Glendale PMSA, CA	H	26.13 FQ	32.90 MW	44.04 TQ	CABLS	1/16-3/16
	Oakland-Hayward-Berkeley PMSA, CA	H	17.63 FQ	22.90 MW	30.61 TQ	CABLS	1/16-3/16
	Riverside-San Bernardino-Ontario MSA, CA	H	15.65 FQ	20.06 MW	26.52 TQ	CABLS	1/16-3/16
	Sacramento–Roseville–Arden-Arcade MSA, CA	H	24.77 FQ	28.06 MW	32.43 TQ	CABLS	1/16-3/16
	San Diego-Carlsbad MSA, CA	H	18.26 FQ	23.42 MW	35.89 TQ	CABLS	1/16-3/16
	San Francisco-Redwood City-South San Francisco PMSA, CA	H	33.51 FQ	39.95 MW	49.42 TQ	CABLS	1/16-3/16
	Colorado	Y	33040 FQ	46130 MW	62770 TQ	USBLS	5/15
	Denver-Aurora-Lakewood MSA, CO	Y	43020 FQ	51050 MW	70270 TQ	USBLS	5/15
	Connecticut	Y		63314 MW		CTBLS	1/16-3/16
	Bridgeport-Stamford-Norwalk MSA, CT	Y	19630 FQ	53430 MW	63090 TQ	USBLS	5/15
	Hartford-West Hartford-East Hartford MSA, CT	Y	43490 FQ	63200 MW	86110 TQ	USBLS	5/15
	Delaware	Y	42770 FQ	52280 MW	67120 TQ	USBLS	5/15
	Wilmington PMSA, DE-MD-NJ	Y	41550 FQ	51850 MW	66470 TQ	USBLS	5/15
	District of Columbia	Y	67960 FQ	82830 MW	94190 TQ	USBLS	5/15
	Washington-Arlington-Alexandria PMSA, DC-VA-MD-WV	Y	62170 FQ	78930 MW	91660 TQ	USBLS	5/15
	Florida	H	17.53 AE	24.21 MW	33.90 AEX	FLBLS	7/16-9/16
	Fort Lauderdale-Pompano Beach-Deerfield Beach PMSA, FL	H	24.67 AE	34.63 MW	39.30 AEX	FLBLS	7/16-9/16
	Miami-Miami Beach-Kendall PMSA, FL	H	21.07 AE	25.81 MW	34.71 AEX	FLBLS	7/16-9/16
	Orlando-Kissimmee-Sanford MSA, FL	H	16.80 AE	26.20 MW	32.02 AEX	FLBLS	7/16-9/16
	Tampa-St. Petersburg-Clearwater MSA, FL	H	19.60 AE	23.01 MW	26.60 AEX	FLBLS	7/16-9/16
	Georgia	Y	34960 FQ	48420 MW	61220 TQ	USBLS	5/15
	Atlanta-Sandy Springs-Roswell MSA, GA	Y	39230 FQ	52520 MW	64340 TQ	USBLS	5/15
	Hawaii	Y	45320 FQ	64220 MW	71960 TQ	USBLS	5/15
	Idaho	Y	22950 FQ	34800 MW	45740 TQ	USBLS	5/15
	Illinois	Y	40420 FQ	62000 MW	88890 TQ	USBLS	5/15
	Chicago-Naperville-Arlington Heights PMSA, IL	Y	38470 FQ	55580 MW	79870 TQ	USBLS	5/15
	Indiana	Y	35380 FQ	44140 MW	56310 TQ	USBLS	5/15
	Indianapolis-Carmel-Anderson MSA, IN	Y	39450 FQ	46250 MW	68290 TQ	USBLS	5/15
	Iowa	Y	30790 FQ	42480 MW	53230 TQ	USBLS	5/15
	Kansas	Y	32030 FQ	41810 MW	53790 TQ	USBLS	5/15
	Kentucky	Y	28230 FQ	42830 MW	49710 TQ	USBLS	5/15
	Louisiana	Y	31280 FQ	37170 MW	45280 TQ	USBLS	5/15
	New Orleans-Metairie MSA, LA	Y	32690 FQ	37760 MW	45270 TQ	USBLS	5/15
	Maine	Y	37080 FQ	45680 MW	57830 TQ	USBLS	5/15
	Portland-South Portland MSA, ME	Y	34840 FQ	38390 MW	47880 TQ	USBLS	5/15
	Maryland	Y	25116 AE	52048 MW	65514 AEX	MDBLS	4/16
	Baltimore-Columbia-Towson MSA, MD	Y	24210 FQ	47700 MW	65840 TQ	USBLS	5/15
	Massachusetts	Y	40180 FQ	53570 MW	70690 TQ	USBLS	5/15
	Boston-Cambridge-Newton NECTA, MA	Y	42130 FQ	54540 MW	71130 TQ	USBLS	5/15
	Michigan	Y	34490 FQ	47890 MW	60640 TQ	USBLS	5/15

Curator

Occupation/Type/Industry	Location	Per	Low	Mid	High	Source	Date
Curator	Detroit-Dearborn-Livonia PMSA, MI	Y	34330 FQ	41060 MW	58740 TQ	USBLS	5/15
	Minnesota	Y	36723 FQ	47782 MW	62479 TQ	MNBLS	1/16-3/16
	Minneapolis-St. Paul-Bloomington MSA, MN-WI	Y	41743 FQ	51118 MW	67166 TQ	MNBLS	1/16-3/16
	Mississippi	Y	24520 FQ	38470 MW	63470 TQ	USBLS	5/15
	Missouri	Y	44860 FQ	55490 MW	70940 TQ	USBLS	5/15
	Kansas City MSA, MO-KS	Y	46730 FQ	59120 MW	72120 TQ	USBLS	5/15
	St. Louis MSA, MO-IL	Y	47320 FQ	61130 MW	83700 TQ	USBLS	5/15
	Montana	Y	26430 FQ	34790 MW	47010 TQ	USBLS	5/15
	Nebraska	Y	39445 FQ	48900 MW	59915 TQ	NEBLS	7/16-9/16
	Omaha-Council Bluffs MSA, NE-IA	Y	35765 FQ	52665 MW	62795 TQ	NEBLS	7/16-9/16
	Nevada	Y	37330 FQ	53700 MW	70240 TQ	USBLS	5/15
	Las Vegas-Henderson-Paradise MSA, NV	Y	42600 FQ	59380 MW	77120 TQ	USBLS	5/15
	New Hampshire	H	9.95 AE	19.75 MW	25.09 AEX	NHBLS	6/16
	Manchester NECTA, NH	H	18.09 AE	26.07 MW	27.50 AEX	NHBLS	6/16
	New Jersey	Y	38590 FQ	54320 MW	81170 TQ	USBLS	5/15
	Newark PMSA, NJ-PA	Y	35120 FQ	39360 MW	79710 TQ	USBLS	5/15
	New Mexico	Y	44670 FQ	50390 MW	59330 TQ	USBLS	5/15
	Albuquerque MSA, NM	Y	47050 FQ	54520 MW	65250 TQ	USBLS	5/15
	New York	Y	41010 AE	64430 MW	89790 AEX	NYBLS	1/16-3/16
	Buffalo-Cheektowaga-Niagara Falls MSA, NY	Y	21100 FQ	30240 MW	53040 TQ	USBLS	5/15
	Nassau County-Suffolk County PMSA, NY	Y	29150 FQ	43330 MW	57650 TQ	USBLS	5/15
	New York-Jersey City-White Plains PMSA, NY-NJ	Y	54740 FQ	71060 MW	93690 TQ	USBLS	5/15
	Rochester MSA, NY	Y	44190 FQ	60200 MW	71750 TQ	USBLS	5/15
	North Carolina	Y	34880 FQ	42450 MW	52480 TQ	USBLS	5/15
	Charlotte-Concord-Gastonia MSA, NC-SC	Y	40680 FQ	46440 MW	55950 TQ	USBLS	5/15
	Raleigh MSA, NC	Y	30170 FQ	41970 MW	51090 TQ	USBLS	5/15
	North Dakota	Y	32860 FQ	39080 MW	48580 TQ	USBLS	5/15
	Ohio	Y	33120 FQ	47080 MW	68940 TQ	USBLS	5/15
	Cincinnati MSA, OH-KY-IN	Y	43320 FQ	54590 MW	70460 TQ	USBLS	5/15
	Cleveland-Elyria MSA, OH	Y	34610 FQ	46590 MW	78320 TQ	USBLS	5/15
	Columbus MSA, OH	Y	27910 FQ	38770 MW	64000 TQ	USBLS	5/15
	Oklahoma	Y	32140 FQ	44810 MW	63600 TQ	USBLS	5/15
	Oklahoma City MSA, OK	Y	35020 FQ	44190 MW	59590 TQ	USBLS	5/15
	Oregon	H	17.82 FQ	23.60 MW	34.68 TQ	ORBLS	2016
	Portland-Vancouver-Hillsboro MSA, OR-WA	Y	47310 FQ	70590 MW	87430 TQ	USBLS	5/15
	Pennsylvania	Y	34720 FQ	45840 MW	62030 TQ	USBLS	5/15
	Harrisburg-Carlisle MSA, PA	Y	43060 FQ	48220 MW	66360 TQ	USBLS	5/15
	Montgomery County-Bucks County-Chester County PMSA, PA	Y	33370 FQ	44940 MW	64090 TQ	USBLS	5/15
	Philadelphia PMSA, PA	Y	43520 FQ	55860 MW	75250 TQ	USBLS	5/15
	Pittsburgh MSA, PA	Y	42600 FQ	47370 MW	55700 TQ	USBLS	5/15
	Rhode Island	Y	38850 FQ	55140 MW	64020 TQ	USBLS	5/15
	Providence-Warwick MSA, RI-MA	Y	37280 FQ	53090 MW	62640 TQ	USBLS	5/15
	South Carolina	Y	34010 FQ	41640 MW	51650 TQ	USBLS	5/15
	Columbia MSA, SC	Y	37120 FQ	42510 MW	54860 TQ	USBLS	5/15
	South Dakota	Y	30710 FQ	41760 MW	58150 TQ	USBLS	5/15
	Tennessee	Y	37380 FQ	48670 MW	63470 TQ	USBLS	5/15
	Memphis MSA, TN-MS-AR	Y	51380 FQ	62370 MW	70810 TQ	USBLS	5/15
	Nashville-Davidson–Murfreesboro–Franklin MSA, TN	Y	38760 FQ	45810 MW	55280 TQ	USBLS	5/15
	Texas	Y	37510 FQ	47960 MW	66540 TQ	USBLS	5/15
	Austin-Round Rock MSA, TX	Y	42650 FQ	48760 MW	79350 TQ	USBLS	5/15
	Dallas-Plano-Irving PMSA, TX	Y	42670 FQ	55010 MW	70890 TQ	USBLS	5/15
	Fort Worth-Arlington PMSA, TX	Y	44070 FQ	56800 MW	73280 TQ	USBLS	5/15
	Houston-The Woodlands-Sugar Land MSA, TX	Y	40450 FQ	47520 MW	66060 TQ	USBLS	5/15
	San Antonio-New Braunfels MSA, TX	Y	43320 FQ	59900 MW	74790 TQ	USBLS	5/15
	Utah	Y	37580 FQ	46810 MW	55950 TQ	USBLS	5/15

AE Average entry wage	**AWR** Average wage range	**H** Hourly	**LR** Low end range	**MTC** Median total compensation	**TCC** Total cash compensation
AEX Average experienced wage	**B** Biweekly	**HI** Highest wage paid	**M** Monthly	**MW** Median wage paid	**TQ** Third quartile wage
ATC Average total compensation	**D** Daily	**HR** High end range	**MCC** Median cash compensation	**MWR** Median wage range	**W** Weekly
AW Average wage paid	**FQ** First quartile wage	**LO** Lowest wage paid	**ME** Median entry wage	**S** See annotated source	**Y** Yearly

Occupation/Type/Industry	Location	Per	Low	Mid	High	Source	Date
Curator	Vermont	Y	43330 FQ	58710 MW	71270 TQ	USBLS	5/15
	Virginia	Y	39190 FQ	54260 MW	72230 TQ	USBLS	5/15
	Richmond MSA, VA	Y	46800 FQ	54630 MW	67930 TQ	USBLS	5/15
	Virginia Beach-Norfolk- Newport News MSA, VA-NC	Y	41800 FQ	53920 MW	68130 TQ	USBLS	5/15
	Washington	H	22.17 FQ	27.26 MW	34.96 TQ	WABLS	3/16
	Seattle-Bellevue-Everett PMSA, WA	H	22.73 FQ	28.31 MW	37.72 TQ	WABLS	3/16
	Tacoma-Lakewood PMSA, WA	H	24.35 FQ	29.38 MW	34.33 TQ	WABLS	3/16
	West Virginia	Y	22080 FQ	29760 MW	51830 TQ	USBLS	5/15
	Wisconsin	Y	31820 FQ	46660 MW	58460 TQ	USBLS	5/15
	Madison MSA, WI	Y	30060 FQ	49940 MW	58470 TQ	USBLS	5/15
	Milwaukee-Waukesha-West Allis MSA, WI	Y	38850 FQ	55540 MW	66480 TQ	USBLS	5/15
	Wyoming	Y	34150 FQ	37970 MW	53060 TQ	USBLS	5/15
Curriculum Writer	United States	H		50.00 AW		FORB03	2016
Customer Service Representative	Alabama	Y	20828 AE	32144 AW	37802 AEX	ALBLS	6/16
	Birmingham-Hoover MSA, AL	Y	23662 AE	34896 AW	40502 AEX	ALBLS	6/16
	Alaska	Y	27510 FQ	34410 MW	42390 TQ	USBLS	5/15
	Anchorage MSA, AK	Y	26520 FQ	33760 MW	42470 TQ	USBLS	5/15
	Arizona	Y	24440 FQ	30040 MW	37260 TQ	USBLS	5/15
	Phoenix-Mesa-Scottsdale MSA, AZ	Y	25640 FQ	31030 MW	38110 TQ	USBLS	5/15
	Tucson MSA, AZ	Y	22260 FQ	25110 MW	31690 TQ	USBLS	5/15
	Arkansas	Y	22670 FQ	28350 MW	36030 TQ	USBLS	5/15
	Little Rock-North Little Rock- Conway MSA, AR	Y	25160 FQ	30850 MW	37480 TQ	USBLS	5/15
	California	H	14.38 FQ	18.18 MW	23.62 TQ	CABLS	1/16-3/16
	Anaheim-Santa Ana-Irvine PMSA, CA	H	15.28 FQ	18.39 MW	23.24 TQ	CABLS	1/16-3/16
	Los Angeles-Long Beach- Glendale PMSA, CA	H	13.97 FQ	17.47 MW	22.52 TQ	CABLS	1/16-3/16
	Oakland-Hayward-Berkeley PMSA, CA	H	16.54 FQ	20.40 MW	25.76 TQ	CABLS	1/16-3/16
	Riverside-San Bernardino- Ontario MSA, CA	H	13.32 FQ	16.86 MW	22.01 TQ	CABLS	1/16-3/16
	Sacramento–Roseville– Arden-Arcade MSA, CA	H	13.67 FQ	17.71 MW	23.21 TQ	CABLS	1/16-3/16
	San Diego-Carlsbad MSA, CA	H	14.43 FQ	18.20 MW	22.94 TQ	CABLS	1/16-3/16
	San Francisco-Redwood City- South San Francisco PMSA, CA	H	17.63 FQ	22.47 MW	29.04 TQ	CABLS	1/16-3/16
	Colorado	Y	26550 FQ	33000 MW	40580 TQ	USBLS	5/15
	Denver-Aurora-Lakewood MSA, CO	Y	28430 FQ	34850 MW	43230 TQ	USBLS	5/15
	Connecticut	Y		38509 MW		CTBLS	1/16-3/16
	Bridgeport-Stamford-Norwalk MSA, CT	Y	28290 FQ	37990 MW	49640 TQ	USBLS	5/15
	Hartford-West Hartford-East Hartford MSA, CT	Y	30120 FQ	39500 MW	49340 TQ	USBLS	5/15
	Delaware	Y	25840 FQ	33480 MW	43210 TQ	USBLS	5/15
	Wilmington PMSA, DE-MD- NJ	Y	27600 FQ	35400 MW	45320 TQ	USBLS	5/15
	District of Columbia	Y	30650 FQ	39710 MW	50960 TQ	USBLS	5/15
	Washington-Arlington- Alexandria PMSA, DC-VA- MD-WV	Y	27400 FQ	37190 MW	48460 TQ	USBLS	5/15
	Florida	H	10.38 AE	14.22 MW	17.63 AEX	FLBLS	7/16-9/16
	Fort Lauderdale-Pompano Beach-Deerfield Beach PMSA, FL	H	10.11 AE	14.27 MW	18.11 AEX	FLBLS	7/16-9/16
	Miami-Miami Beach-Kendall PMSA, FL	H	10.71 AE	14.40 MW	17.63 AEX	FLBLS	7/16-9/16
	Naples-Immokalee-Marco Island MSA, FL	Y	25230 FQ	31010 MW	38310 TQ	USBLS	5/15
	Orlando-Kissimmee-Sanford MSA, FL	H	10.70 AE	14.29 MW	17.72 AEX	FLBLS	7/16-9/16
	Tampa-St. Petersburg- Clearwater MSA, FL	H	10.75 AE	14.75 MW	18.18 AEX	FLBLS	7/16-9/16
	Georgia	Y	24260 FQ	31090 MW	39710 TQ	USBLS	5/15

AE	Average entry wage	**AWR**	Average wage range	**H**	Hourly	**LR**	Low end range	**MTC** Median total compensation **TCC** Total cash compensation
AEX	Average experienced wage	**B**	Biweekly	**HI**	Highest wage paid	**M**	Monthly	**MW** Median wage paid **TQ** Third quartile wage
ATC	Average total compensation	**D**	Daily	**HR**	High end range	**MCC**	Median cash compensation	**MWR** Median wage range **W** Weekly
AW	Average wage paid	**FQ**	First quartile wage	**LO**	Lowest wage paid	**ME**	Median entry wage	**S** See annotated source **Y** Yearly

Occupation/Type/Industry	Location	Per	Low	Mid	High	Source	Date
Customer Service Representative	Atlanta-Sandy Springs-Roswell MSA, GA	Y	25910 FQ	32990 MW	42810 TQ	USBLS	5/15
	Augusta-Richmond County MSA, GA-SC	Y	20430 FQ	25540 MW	31780 TQ	USBLS	5/15
	Hawaii	Y	27860 FQ	35420 MW	44880 TQ	USBLS	5/15
	Urban Honolulu MSA, HI	Y	26930 FQ	35000 MW	44930 TQ	USBLS	5/15
	Idaho	Y	21750 FQ	26700 MW	32980 TQ	USBLS	5/15
	Boise City MSA, ID	Y	22160 FQ	27220 MW	33830 TQ	USBLS	5/15
	Illinois	Y	26080 FQ	33470 MW	44480 TQ	USBLS	5/15
	Chicago-Naperville-Arlington Heights PMSA, IL	Y	26750 FQ	34650 MW	45960 TQ	USBLS	5/15
	Lake County-Kenosha County PMSA, IL-WI	Y	29350 FQ	38330 MW	48290 TQ	USBLS	5/15
	Indiana	Y	25010 FQ	31480 MW	40670 TQ	USBLS	5/15
	Gary PMSA, IN	Y	23910 FQ	28860 MW	36840 TQ	USBLS	5/15
	Indianapolis-Carmel-Anderson MSA, IN	Y	25810 FQ	32960 MW	43640 TQ	USBLS	5/15
	Iowa	Y	24680 FQ	30970 MW	38450 TQ	USBLS	5/15
	Des Moines-West Des Moines MSA, IA	Y	27600 FQ	34640 MW	42730 TQ	USBLS	5/15
	Kansas	Y	25280 FQ	31420 MW	38460 TQ	USBLS	5/15
	Wichita MSA, KS	Y	23320 FQ	28740 MW	35970 TQ	USBLS	5/15
	Kentucky	Y	23260 FQ	29130 MW	37160 TQ	USBLS	5/15
	Louisville-Jefferson County MSA, KY-IN	Y	27090 FQ	32470 MW	38390 TQ	USBLS	5/15
	Louisiana	Y	22370 FQ	27670 MW	35330 TQ	USBLS	5/15
	Baton Rouge MSA, LA	Y	22690 FQ	28060 MW	35100 TQ	USBLS	5/15
	New Orleans-Metairie MSA, LA	Y	23580 FQ	28150 MW	34600 TQ	USBLS	5/15
	Maine	Y	26940 FQ	32100 MW	38960 TQ	USBLS	5/15
	Portland-South Portland MSA, ME	Y	27950 FQ	34370 MW	41030 TQ	USBLS	5/15
	Maryland	Y	23088 AE	36386 MW	43036 AEX	MDBLS	4/16
	Baltimore-Columbia-Towson MSA, MD	Y	27410 FQ	35290 MW	44920 TQ	USBLS	5/15
	Salisbury MSA, MD-DE	Y	22320 FQ	28150 MW	35970 TQ	USBLS	5/15
	Massachusetts	Y	30320 FQ	38490 MW	48960 TQ	USBLS	5/15
	Boston-Cambridge-Newton NECTA, MA	Y	32690 FQ	41170 MW	52130 TQ	USBLS	5/15
	Worcester MSA, MA-CT	Y	28720 FQ	36260 MW	46090 TQ	USBLS	5/15
	Michigan	Y	24220 FQ	31080 MW	40350 TQ	USBLS	5/15
	Detroit-Dearborn-Livonia PMSA, MI	Y	25490 FQ	32330 MW	41780 TQ	USBLS	5/15
	Grand Rapids-Wyoming MSA, MI	Y	26790 FQ	33800 MW	42610 TQ	USBLS	5/15
	Minnesota	Y	29195 FQ	36881 MW	46256 TQ	MNBLS	1/16-3/16
	Minneapolis-St. Paul-Bloomington MSA, MN-WI	Y	31380 FQ	38449 MW	47813 TQ	MNBLS	1/16-3/16
	Mississippi	Y	21250 FQ	26120 MW	33610 TQ	USBLS	5/15
	Jackson MSA, MS	Y	24730 FQ	29080 MW	37620 TQ	USBLS	5/15
	Missouri	Y	24480 FQ	30910 MW	39090 TQ	USBLS	5/15
	Kansas City MSA, MO-KS	Y	27040 FQ	33600 MW	41250 TQ	USBLS	5/15
	St. Louis MSA, MO-IL	Y	26190 FQ	33680 MW	41220 TQ	USBLS	5/15
	Montana	Y	22680 FQ	27940 MW	35630 TQ	USBLS	5/15
	Billings MSA, MT	Y	22120 FQ	27840 MW	34920 TQ	USBLS	5/15
	Nebraska	Y	24375 FQ	29955 MW	37585 TQ	NEBLS	7/16-9/16
	Omaha-Council Bluffs MSA, NE-IA	Y	25200 FQ	30730 MW	38110 TQ	NEBLS	7/16-9/16
	Nevada	Y	24210 FQ	29840 MW	38330 TQ	USBLS	5/15
	Las Vegas-Henderson-Paradise MSA, NV	Y	23450 FQ	29350 MW	38490 TQ	USBLS	5/15
	New Hampshire	H	11.79 AE	17.38 MW	21.37 AEX	NHBLS	6/16
	Manchester NECTA, NH	H	11.79 AE	17.51 MW	22.07 AEX	NHBLS	6/16
	Nashua NECTA, NH-MA	Y	25950 FQ	35110 MW	42600 TQ	USBLS	5/15
	New Jersey	Y	28950 FQ	36820 MW	47150 TQ	USBLS	5/15
	Camden PMSA, NJ	Y	28070 FQ	35520 MW	45260 TQ	USBLS	5/15
	Newark PMSA, NJ-PA	Y	29820 FQ	37610 MW	48730 TQ	USBLS	5/15
	Trenton MSA, NJ	Y	29260 FQ	36300 MW	45650 TQ	USBLS	5/15
	New Mexico	Y	23970 FQ	28660 MW	35060 TQ	USBLS	5/15
	Albuquerque MSA, NM	Y	25700 FQ	29720 MW	36070 TQ	USBLS	5/15
	New York	Y	24500 AE	36420 MW	47880 AEX	NYBLS	1/16-3/16

AE	Average entry wage	AWR	Average wage range	H	Hourly
AEX	Average experienced wage	B	Biweekly	HI	Highest wage paid
ATC	Average total compensation	D	Daily	HR	High end range
AW	Average wage paid	FQ	First quartile wage	LO	Lowest wage paid

LR	Low end range	MTC	Median total compensation
M	Monthly	MW	Median wage paid
MCC	Median cash compensation	MWR	Median wage range
ME	Median entry wage	S	See annotated source

TCC	Total cash compensation
TQ	Third quartile wage
W	Weekly
Y	Yearly

Occupation/Type/Industry	Location	Per	Low	Mid	High	Source	Date
Customer Service Representative	Buffalo-Cheektowaga-Niagara Falls MSA, NY	Y	26640 FQ	33600 MW	41560 TQ	USBLS	5/15
	Nassau County-Suffolk County PMSA, NY	Y	28750 FQ	38370 MW	50790 TQ	USBLS	5/15
	New York-Jersey City-White Plains PMSA, NY-NJ	Y	28720 FQ	37730 MW	49750 TQ	USBLS	5/15
	Rochester MSA, NY	Y	25580 FQ	31390 MW	42200 TQ	USBLS	5/15
	North Carolina	Y	23370 FQ	30740 MW	39460 TQ	USBLS	5/15
	Charlotte-Concord-Gastonia MSA, NC-SC	Y	26160 FQ	33630 MW	43690 TQ	USBLS	5/15
	Raleigh MSA, NC	Y	22170 FQ	28770 MW	38690 TQ	USBLS	5/15
	North Dakota	Y	26780 FQ	30410 MW	37530 TQ	USBLS	5/15
	Fargo MSA, ND-MN	Y	26480 FQ	29980 MW	36450 TQ	USBLS	5/15
	Ohio	Y	24870 FQ	30510 MW	38970 TQ	USBLS	5/15
	Cincinnati MSA, OH-KY-IN	Y	24910 FQ	30650 MW	40180 TQ	USBLS	5/15
	Cleveland-Elyria MSA, OH	Y	27130 FQ	34510 MW	43910 TQ	USBLS	5/15
	Columbus MSA, OH	Y	26050 FQ	30010 MW	37010 TQ	USBLS	5/15
	Oklahoma	Y	23130 FQ	28840 MW	36590 TQ	USBLS	5/15
	Oklahoma City MSA, OK	Y	23980 FQ	29840 MW	37660 TQ	USBLS	5/15
	Tulsa MSA, OK	Y	24200 FQ	29210 MW	36530 TQ	USBLS	5/15
	Oregon	H	12.92 FQ	16.15 MW	20.22 TQ	ORBLS	2016
	Portland-Vancouver-Hillsboro MSA, OR-WA	Y	28020 FQ	35000 MW	43990 TQ	USBLS	5/15
	Pennsylvania	Y	25810 FQ	32480 MW	40590 TQ	USBLS	5/15
	Allentown-Bethlehem-Easton MSA, PA-NJ	Y	25120 FQ	31430 MW	40170 TQ	USBLS	5/15
	Harrisburg-Carlisle MSA, PA	Y	25560 FQ	30880 MW	38840 TQ	USBLS	5/15
	Montgomery County-Bucks County-Chester County PMSA, PA	Y	28260 FQ	35170 MW	44120 TQ	USBLS	5/15
	Philadelphia PMSA, PA	Y	28350 FQ	35470 MW	44430 TQ	USBLS	5/15
	Pittsburgh MSA, PA	Y	25480 FQ	31360 MW	39780 TQ	USBLS	5/15
	Rhode Island	Y	27290 FQ	34470 MW	43320 TQ	USBLS	5/15
	Providence-Warwick MSA, RI-MA	Y	27280 FQ	34430 MW	43350 TQ	USBLS	5/15
	South Carolina	Y	22470 FQ	28530 MW	36880 TQ	USBLS	5/15
	Charleston-North Charleston MSA, SC	Y	25380 FQ	30190 MW	38130 TQ	USBLS	5/15
	Columbia MSA, SC	Y	25120 FQ	30630 MW	38710 TQ	USBLS	5/15
	Greenville-Anderson-Mauldin MSA, SC	Y	22990 FQ	29030 MW	38430 TQ	USBLS	5/15
	South Dakota	Y	23480 FQ	27740 MW	32520 TQ	USBLS	5/15
	Sioux Falls MSA, SD	Y	24260 FQ	28160 MW	32580 TQ	USBLS	5/15
	Tennessee	Y	22860 FQ	29100 MW	37480 TQ	USBLS	5/15
	Knoxville MSA, TN	Y	23390 FQ	28320 MW	34700 TQ	USBLS	5/15
	Memphis MSA, TN-MS-AR	Y	25170 FQ	31540 MW	40020 TQ	USBLS	5/15
	Nashville-Davidson–Murfreesboro–Franklin MSA, TN	Y	24660 FQ	30860 MW	40130 TQ	USBLS	5/15
	Texas	Y	23990 FQ	30040 MW	38160 TQ	USBLS	5/15
	Austin-Round Rock MSA, TX	Y	24290 FQ	29740 MW	37420 TQ	USBLS	5/15
	Dallas-Plano-Irving PMSA, TX	Y	27500 FQ	33960 MW	42680 TQ	USBLS	5/15
	Fort Worth-Arlington PMSA, TX	Y	25490 FQ	30910 MW	38030 TQ	USBLS	5/15
	Houston-The Woodlands-Sugar Land MSA, TX	Y	24450 FQ	31110 MW	41160 TQ	USBLS	5/15
	San Antonio-New Braunfels MSA, TX	Y	23690 FQ	28730 MW	35550 TQ	USBLS	5/15
	Utah	Y	23280 FQ	28150 MW	35470 TQ	USBLS	5/15
	Ogden-Clearfield MSA, UT	Y	21800 FQ	24650 MW	30050 TQ	USBLS	5/15
	Provo-Orem MSA, UT	Y	21790 FQ	24810 MW	30120 TQ	USBLS	5/15
	Salt Lake City MSA, UT	Y	25430 FQ	30170 MW	37880 TQ	USBLS	5/15
	Vermont	Y	24820 FQ	32090 MW	40450 TQ	USBLS	5/15
	Burlington-South Burlington MSA, VT	Y	27980 FQ	36400 MW	46300 TQ	USBLS	5/15
	Virginia	Y	23850 FQ	31740 MW	41130 TQ	USBLS	5/15
	Richmond MSA, VA	Y	26970 FQ	33940 MW	40100 TQ	USBLS	5/15
	Virginia Beach-Norfolk-Newport News MSA, VA-NC	Y	22960 FQ	29000 MW	36610 TQ	USBLS	5/15
	Washington	H	13.61 FQ	17.34 MW	21.51 TQ	WABLS	3/16
	Seattle-Bellevue-Everett PMSA, WA	H	14.66 FQ	18.16 MW	22.54 TQ	WABLS	3/16

AE	Average entry wage	AWR Average wage range	H Hourly	LR Low end range	MTC Median total compensation	TCC Total cash compensation
AEX	Average experienced wage	B Biweekly	HI Highest wage paid	M Monthly	MW Median wage paid	TQ Third quartile wage
ATC	Average total compensation	D Daily	HR High end range	MCC Median cash compensation	MWR Median wage range	W Weekly
AW	Average wage paid	FQ First quartile wage	LO Lowest wage paid	ME Median entry wage	S See annotated source	Y Yearly

Occupation/Type/Industry	Location	Per	Low	Mid	High	Source	Date
Customer Service Representative	Tacoma-Lakewood PMSA, WA	H	12.02 FQ	16.28 MW	20.63 TQ	WABLS	3/16
	West Virginia	Y	21410 FQ	25670 MW	32300 TQ	USBLS	5/15
	Huntington-Ashland MSA, WV-KY-OH	Y	21470 FQ	26200 MW	31040 TQ	USBLS	5/15
	Wisconsin	Y	27040 FQ	33970 MW	42480 TQ	USBLS	5/15
	Madison MSA, WI	Y	28120 FQ	35040 MW	43240 TQ	USBLS	5/15
	Milwaukee-Waukesha-West Allis MSA, WI	Y	28950 FQ	36030 MW	45690 TQ	USBLS	5/15
	Wyoming	Y	23820 FQ	29100 MW	37090 TQ	USBLS	5/15
	Cheyenne MSA, WY	Y	22400 FQ	27420 MW	41940 TQ	USBLS	5/15
	Puerto Rico	Y	17540 FQ	19560 MW	26210 TQ	USBLS	5/15
	San Juan-Carolina-Caguas MSA, PR	Y	17600 FQ	19670 MW	26320 TQ	USBLS	5/15
	Virgin Islands	Y	22750 FQ	27030 MW	33670 TQ	USBLS	5/15
	Guam	Y	18440 FQ	21070 MW	28950 TQ	USBLS	5/15
Customer Success Manager	United States	Y		72000 MW		HCHRON1	2017
Customer Support Professional							
Co-Located	United States	Y		65220 MW		HSCT	2016
Remote	United States	Y		65000 MW		HSCT	2016
Customs Broker	United States	Y		73000 AW		SKU01	2016
Cutter and Trimmer							
Hand	Alabama	Y	17459 AE	25767 AW	29921 AEX	ALBLS	6/16
Hand	Birmingham-Hoover MSA, AL	Y	17223 AE	25520 AW	29674 AEX	ALBLS	6/16
Hand	Arizona	Y	17820 FQ	18850 MW	22530 TQ	USBLS	5/15
Hand	Phoenix-Mesa-Scottsdale MSA, AZ	Y	17690 FQ	18590 MW	19560 TQ	USBLS	5/15
Hand	California	H	9.89 FQ	12.02 MW	14.62 TQ	CABLS	1/16-3/16
Hand	Anaheim-Santa Ana-Irvine PMSA, CA	H	9.60 FQ	10.57 MW	13.03 TQ	CABLS	1/16-3/16
Hand	Los Angeles-Long Beach-Glendale PMSA, CA	H	9.67 FQ	12.61 MW	14.96 TQ	CABLS	1/16-3/16
Hand	Oakland-Hayward-Berkeley PMSA, CA	H	11.15 FQ	13.29 MW	15.61 TQ	CABLS	1/16-3/16
Hand	Riverside-San Bernardino-Ontario MSA, CA	H	9.72 FQ	11.29 MW	13.43 TQ	CABLS	1/16-3/16
Hand	Sacramento–Roseville–Arden-Arcade MSA, CA	H	11.48 FQ	13.33 MW	14.93 TQ	CABLS	1/16-3/16
Hand	San Diego-Carlsbad MSA, CA	H	11.50 FQ	13.34 MW	14.60 TQ	CABLS	1/16-3/16
Hand	San Francisco-Redwood City-South San Francisco PMSA, CA	H	10.33 FQ	10.99 MW	11.66 TQ	CABLS	1/16-3/16
Hand	Colorado	Y	18510 FQ	22920 MW	34520 TQ	USBLS	5/15
Hand	Denver-Aurora-Lakewood MSA, CO	Y	18230 FQ	19430 MW	32830 TQ	USBLS	5/15
Hand	Connecticut	Y		28703 MW		CTBLS	1/16-3/16
Hand	Florida	H	9.02 AE	10.64 MW	13.35 AEX	FLBLS	7/16-9/16
Hand	Miami-Miami Beach-Kendall PMSA, FL	H	8.96 AE	9.17 MW	9.44 AEX	FLBLS	7/16-9/16
Hand	Tampa-St. Petersburg-Clearwater MSA, FL	H	10.31 AE	13.14 MW	15.97 AEX	FLBLS	7/16-9/16
Hand	Georgia	Y	19140 FQ	25250 MW	34030 TQ	USBLS	5/15
Hand	Atlanta-Sandy Springs-Roswell MSA, GA	Y	25000 FQ	29740 MW	48750 TQ	USBLS	5/15
Hand	Hawaii	Y	25060 FQ	27350 MW	29640 TQ	USBLS	5/15
Hand	Urban Honolulu MSA, HI	Y	24970 FQ	27310 MW	29660 TQ	USBLS	5/15
Hand	Idaho	Y	22750 FQ	25760 MW	28690 TQ	USBLS	5/15
Hand	Illinois	Y	22230 FQ	26650 MW	31470 TQ	USBLS	5/15
Hand	Chicago-Naperville-Arlington Heights PMSA, IL	Y	19760 FQ	24210 MW	34180 TQ	USBLS	5/15
Hand	Lake County-Kenosha County PMSA, IL-WI	Y	28670 FQ	43090 MW	65090 TQ	USBLS	5/15
Hand	Indiana	Y	22850 FQ	28120 MW	37270 TQ	USBLS	5/15
Hand	Gary PMSA, IN	Y	21880 FQ	23750 MW	28450 TQ	USBLS	5/15
Hand	Indianapolis-Carmel-Anderson MSA, IN	Y	19600 FQ	22120 MW	28300 TQ	USBLS	5/15
Hand	Iowa	Y	24450 FQ	29440 MW	33770 TQ	USBLS	5/15
Hand	Kansas	Y	24410 FQ	29940 MW	35710 TQ	USBLS	5/15
Hand	Wichita MSA, KS	Y	25700 FQ	29480 MW	34520 TQ	USBLS	5/15

AE	Average entry wage	AWR	Average wage range	H	Hourly
AEX	Average experienced wage	B	Biweekly	HI	Highest wage paid
ATC	Average total compensation	D	Daily	HR	High end range
AW	Average wage paid	FQ	First quartile wage	LO	Lowest wage paid

LR	Low end range	MTC	Median total compensation	TCC	Total cash compensation
M	Monthly	MW	Median wage paid	TQ	Third quartile wage
MCC	Median cash compensation	MWR	Median wage range	W	Weekly
ME	Median entry wage	S	See annotated source	Y	Yearly

Cutter and Trimmer

Occupation/Type/Industry	Location	Per	Low	Mid	High	Source	Date
Cutter and Trimmer							
Hand	Kentucky	Y	23210 FQ	27730 MW	33800 TQ	USBLS	5/15
Hand	Louisville-Jefferson County MSA, KY-IN	Y	23740 FQ	29330 MW	34750 TQ	USBLS	5/15
Hand	Louisiana	Y	21250 FQ	24400 MW	29580 TQ	USBLS	5/15
Hand	Maine	Y	33080 FQ	39170 MW	44400 TQ	USBLS	5/15
Hand	Maryland	Y	19044 AE	29480 MW	34698 AEX	MDBLS	4/16
Hand	Baltimore-Columbia-Towson MSA, MD	Y	19600 FQ	26880 MW	36850 TQ	USBLS	5/15
Hand	Massachusetts	Y	21600 FQ	24100 MW	31190 TQ	USBLS	5/15
Hand	Boston-Cambridge-Newton NECTA, MA	Y	21650 FQ	23530 MW	26690 TQ	USBLS	5/15
Hand	Worcester MSA, MA-CT	Y	21760 FQ	23570 MW	26400 TQ	USBLS	5/15
Hand	Michigan	Y	21370 FQ	23540 MW	29950 TQ	USBLS	5/15
Hand	Grand Rapids-Wyoming MSA, MI	Y	21750 FQ	23960 MW	33610 TQ	USBLS	5/15
Hand	Minnesota	Y	25169 FQ	30677 MW	36671 TQ	MNBLS	1/16-3/16
Hand	Minneapolis-St. Paul-Bloomington MSA, MN-WI	Y	27883 FQ	32712 MW	38017 TQ	MNBLS	1/16-3/16
Hand	Mississippi	Y	23120 FQ	30190 MW	35430 TQ	USBLS	5/15
Hand	Missouri	Y	25490 FQ	28690 MW	32720 TQ	USBLS	5/15
Hand	Kansas City MSA, MO-KS	Y	27540 FQ	31040 MW	38200 TQ	USBLS	5/15
Hand	St. Louis MSA, MO-IL	Y	28430 FQ	34430 MW	44300 TQ	USBLS	5/15
Hand	Nebraska	Y	20005 FQ	30450 MW	37935 TQ	NEBLS	7/16-9/16
Hand	Omaha-Council Bluffs MSA, NE-IA	Y	30180 FQ	35175 MW	39935 TQ	NEBLS	7/16-9/16
Hand	Nevada	Y	21810 FQ	30560 MW	35460 TQ	USBLS	5/15
Hand	Las Vegas-Henderson-Paradise MSA, NV	Y	21950 FQ	29460 MW	34840 TQ	USBLS	5/15
Hand	New Hampshire	H	12.55 AE	14.57 MW	17.96 AEX	NHBLS	6/16
Hand	New Jersey	Y	22490 FQ	27080 MW	37120 TQ	USBLS	5/15
Hand	Camden PMSA, NJ	Y	19320 FQ	22620 MW	26970 TQ	USBLS	5/15
Hand	Newark PMSA, NJ-PA	Y	23210 FQ	29040 MW	55230 TQ	USBLS	5/15
Hand	New York	Y	20060 AE	31700 MW	43520 AEX	NYBLS	1/16-3/16
Hand	Nassau County-Suffolk County PMSA, NY	Y	26540 FQ	35530 MW	49660 TQ	USBLS	5/15
Hand	New York-Jersey City-White Plains PMSA, NY-NJ	Y	19550 FQ	25840 MW	37530 TQ	USBLS	5/15
Hand	Rochester MSA, NY	Y	26170 FQ	33490 MW	38250 TQ	USBLS	5/15
Hand	North Carolina	Y	23160 FQ	29860 MW	38210 TQ	USBLS	5/15
Hand	Charlotte-Concord-Gastonia MSA, NC-SC	Y	22160 FQ	27160 MW	36640 TQ	USBLS	5/15
Hand	Ohio	Y	21420 FQ	24600 MW	29600 TQ	USBLS	5/15
Hand	Cincinnati MSA, OH-KY-IN	Y	22450 FQ	24800 MW	30270 TQ	USBLS	5/15
Hand	Cleveland-Elyria MSA, OH	Y	22180 FQ	27800 MW	32310 TQ	USBLS	5/15
Hand	Columbus MSA, OH	Y	19080 FQ	21640 MW	24670 TQ	USBLS	5/15
Hand	Oklahoma	Y	20870 FQ	24090 MW	30000 TQ	USBLS	5/15
Hand	Oregon	H	11.43 FQ	16.01 MW	21.23 TQ	ORBLS	2016
Hand	Portland-Vancouver-Hillsboro MSA, OR-WA	Y	24010 FQ	32310 MW	43140 TQ	USBLS	5/15
Hand	Pennsylvania	Y	24090 FQ	29230 MW	34580 TQ	USBLS	5/15
Hand	Philadelphia PMSA, PA	Y	27120 FQ	30090 MW	34310 TQ	USBLS	5/15
Hand	Pittsburgh MSA, PA	Y	31820 FQ	34420 MW	37010 TQ	USBLS	5/15
Hand	Rhode Island	Y	26380 FQ	31700 MW	36670 TQ	USBLS	5/15
Hand	Providence-Warwick MSA, RI-MA	Y	22360 FQ	26170 MW	33890 TQ	USBLS	5/15
Hand	South Carolina	Y	18810 FQ	22770 MW	27940 TQ	USBLS	5/15
Hand	Tennessee	Y	18690 FQ	22130 MW	27210 TQ	USBLS	5/15
Hand	Memphis MSA, TN-MS-AR	Y	23260 FQ	28780 MW	34590 TQ	USBLS	5/15
Hand	Nashville-Davidson–Murfreesboro–Franklin MSA, TN	Y	17630 FQ	19610 MW	23390 TQ	USBLS	5/15
Hand	Texas	Y	21300 FQ	26960 MW	34080 TQ	USBLS	5/15
Hand	Dallas-Plano-Irving PMSA, TX	Y	22210 FQ	27440 MW	33830 TQ	USBLS	5/15
Hand	Fort Worth-Arlington PMSA, TX	Y	24060 FQ	27330 MW	29900 TQ	USBLS	5/15
Hand	Houston-The Woodlands-Sugar Land MSA, TX	Y	21310 FQ	27240 MW	36220 TQ	USBLS	5/15
Hand	San Antonio-New Braunfels MSA, TX	Y	32020 FQ	34720 MW	37420 TQ	USBLS	5/15
Hand	Utah	Y	27140 FQ	30310 MW	34410 TQ	USBLS	5/15
Hand	Ogden-Clearfield MSA, UT	Y	24250 FQ	31160 MW	38380 TQ	USBLS	5/15

AE	Average entry wage	AWR	Average wage range	H	Hourly
AEX	Average experienced wage	B	Biweekly	HI	Highest wage paid
ATC	Average total compensation	D	Daily	HR	High end range
AW	Average wage paid	FQ	First quartile wage	LO	Lowest wage paid

LR	Low end range	MTC	Median total compensation	TCC	Total cash compensation
M	Monthly	MW	Median wage paid	TQ	Third quartile wage
MCC	Median cash compensation	MWR	Median wage range	W	Weekly
ME	Median entry wage	S	See annotated source	Y	Yearly

Occupation/Type/Industry	Location	Per	Low	Mid	High	Source	Date
Cutter and Trimmer							
Hand	Salt Lake City MSA, UT	Y	32140 FQ	34490 MW	36840 TQ	USBLS	5/15
Hand	Vermont	Y	25920 FQ	33350 MW	41300 TQ	USBLS	5/15
Hand	Virginia	Y	23640 FQ	28330 MW	38580 TQ	USBLS	5/15
Hand	Washington	H	13.05 FQ	15.27 MW	18.04 TQ	WABLS	3/16
Hand	Seattle-Bellevue-Everett PMSA, WA	H	13.31 FQ	15.64 MW	18.28 TQ	WABLS	3/16
Hand	Wisconsin	Y	23480 FQ	26860 MW	29840 TQ	USBLS	5/15
Hand	Milwaukee-Waukesha-West Allis MSA, WI	Y	21660 FQ	25390 MW	29950 TQ	USBLS	5/15
Hand	Puerto Rico	Y	16700 FQ	17800 MW	18900 TQ	USBLS	5/15
Hand	San Juan-Carolina-Caguas MSA, PR	Y	16760 FQ	17840 MW	18920 TQ	USBLS	5/15
Cutting, Punching, and Press Machine Setter, Operator, and Tender							
Metals and Plastics	Alabama	Y	21181 AE	31731 AW	37016 AEX	ALBLS	6/16
Metals and Plastics	Birmingham-Hoover MSA, AL	Y	25202 AE	33746 AW	38023 AEX	ALBLS	6/16
Metals and Plastics	Alaska	Y	26470 FQ	34570 MW	40810 TQ	USBLS	5/15
Metals and Plastics	Anchorage MSA, AK	Y	25110 FQ	34460 MW	42100 TQ	USBLS	5/15
Metals and Plastics	Arizona	Y	27950 FQ	34210 MW	41390 TQ	USBLS	5/15
Metals and Plastics	Phoenix-Mesa-Scottsdale MSA, AZ	Y	28300 FQ	34480 MW	41570 TQ	USBLS	5/15
Metals and Plastics	Tucson MSA, AZ	Y	26450 FQ	34460 MW	42400 TQ	USBLS	5/15
Metals and Plastics	Arkansas	Y	27240 FQ	32930 MW	38930 TQ	USBLS	5/15
Metals and Plastics	Little Rock-North Little Rock-Conway MSA, AR	Y	28960 FQ	33620 MW	37590 TQ	USBLS	5/15
Metals and Plastics	California	H	11.81 FQ	14.72 MW	18.76 TQ	CABLS	1/16-3/16
Metals and Plastics	Anaheim-Santa Ana-Irvine PMSA, CA	H	12.62 FQ	15.15 MW	19.74 TQ	CABLS	1/16-3/16
Metals and Plastics	Los Angeles-Long Beach-Glendale PMSA, CA	H	10.92 FQ	13.28 MW	16.87 TQ	CABLS	1/16-3/16
Metals and Plastics	Oakland-Hayward-Berkeley PMSA, CA	H	12.72 FQ	14.96 MW	19.04 TQ	CABLS	1/16-3/16
Metals and Plastics	Riverside-San Bernardino-Ontario MSA, CA	H	12.48 FQ	15.19 MW	18.70 TQ	CABLS	1/16-3/16
Metals and Plastics	Sacramento–Roseville–Arden-Arcade MSA, CA	H	13.09 FQ	14.72 MW	17.74 TQ	CABLS	1/16-3/16
Metals and Plastics	San Diego-Carlsbad MSA, CA	H	12.38 FQ	16.05 MW	19.77 TQ	CABLS	1/16-3/16
Metals and Plastics	San Francisco-Redwood City-South San Francisco PMSA, CA	H	11.59 FQ	19.84 MW	26.38 TQ	CABLS	1/16-3/16
Metals and Plastics	Colorado	Y	23860 FQ	32020 MW	39740 TQ	USBLS	5/15
Metals and Plastics	Denver-Aurora-Lakewood MSA, CO	Y	23280 FQ	30740 MW	38730 TQ	USBLS	5/15
Metals and Plastics	Connecticut	Y		34379 MW		CTBLS	1/16-3/16
Metals and Plastics	Bridgeport-Stamford-Norwalk MSA, CT	Y	28410 FQ	36510 MW	43810 TQ	USBLS	5/15
Metals and Plastics	Hartford-West Hartford-East Hartford MSA, CT	Y	28050 FQ	35760 MW	45150 TQ	USBLS	5/15
Metals and Plastics	Delaware	Y	26920 FQ	32560 MW	38010 TQ	USBLS	5/15
Metals and Plastics	Wilmington PMSA, DE-MD-NJ	Y	25620 FQ	30510 MW	36690 TQ	USBLS	5/15
Metals and Plastics	Washington-Arlington-Alexandria PMSA, DC-VA-MD-WV	Y	27310 FQ	32710 MW	36870 TQ	USBLS	5/15
Metals and Plastics	Florida	H	10.24 AE	13.88 MW	16.53 AEX	FLBLS	7/16-9/16
Metals and Plastics	Fort Lauderdale-Pompano Beach-Deerfield Beach PMSA, FL	H	10.49 AE	14.44 MW	16.94 AEX	FLBLS	7/16-9/16
Metals and Plastics	Miami-Miami Beach-Kendall PMSA, FL	H	8.87 AE	12.54 MW	14.05 AEX	FLBLS	7/16-9/16
Metals and Plastics	Orlando-Kissimmee-Sanford MSA, FL	H	11.30 AE	15.58 MW	19.04 AEX	FLBLS	7/16-9/16
Metals and Plastics	Tampa-St. Petersburg-Clearwater MSA, FL	H	10.18 AE	13.07 MW	15.35 AEX	FLBLS	7/16-9/16
Metals and Plastics	Georgia	Y	25360 FQ	30900 MW	37170 TQ	USBLS	5/15
Metals and Plastics	Atlanta-Sandy Springs-Roswell MSA, GA	Y	26750 FQ	31740 MW	37150 TQ	USBLS	5/15

AE Average entry wage	**AWR** Average wage range	**H** Hourly	**LR** Low end range	**MTC** Median total compensation	**TCC** Total cash compensation
AEX Average experienced wage	**B** Biweekly	**HI** Highest wage paid	**M** Monthly	**MW** Median wage paid	**TQ** Third quartile wage
ATC Average total compensation	**D** Daily	**HR** High end range	**MCC** Median cash compensation	**MWR** Median wage range	**W** Weekly
AW Average wage paid	**FQ** First quartile wage	**LO** Lowest wage paid	**ME** Median entry wage	**S** See annotated source	**Y** Yearly

Occupation/Type/Industry	Location	Per	Low	Mid	High	Source	Date
Cutting, Punching, and Press Machine Setter, Operator, and Tender							
Metals and Plastics	Augusta-Richmond County MSA, GA-SC	Y	26130 FQ	28460 MW	30800 TQ	USBLS	5/15
Metals and Plastics	Hawaii	Y	19540 FQ	22840 MW	26920 TQ	USBLS	5/15
Metals and Plastics	Idaho	Y	26210 FQ	31930 MW	37340 TQ	USBLS	5/15
Metals and Plastics	Boise City MSA, ID	Y	22080 FQ	27980 MW	34380 TQ	USBLS	5/15
Metals and Plastics	Illinois	Y	25390 FQ	31900 MW	41790 TQ	USBLS	5/15
Metals and Plastics	Chicago-Naperville-Arlington Heights PMSA, IL	Y	24720 FQ	32380 MW	43490 TQ	USBLS	5/15
Metals and Plastics	Lake County-Kenosha County PMSA, IL-WI	Y	24760 FQ	28990 MW	34920 TQ	USBLS	5/15
Metals and Plastics	Indiana	Y	24150 FQ	29140 MW	35880 TQ	USBLS	5/15
Metals and Plastics	Gary PMSA, IN	Y	26900 FQ	34800 MW	43840 TQ	USBLS	5/15
Metals and Plastics	Indianapolis-Carmel-Anderson MSA, IN	Y	22360 FQ	27970 MW	36160 TQ	USBLS	5/15
Metals and Plastics	Iowa	Y	27440 FQ	34000 MW	39720 TQ	USBLS	5/15
Metals and Plastics	Des Moines-West Des Moines MSA, IA	Y	31490 FQ	35690 MW	40200 TQ	USBLS	5/15
Metals and Plastics	Kansas	Y	26100 FQ	31250 MW	37880 TQ	USBLS	5/15
Metals and Plastics	Wichita MSA, KS	Y	26250 FQ	31470 MW	37120 TQ	USBLS	5/15
Metals and Plastics	Kentucky	Y	27810 FQ	35100 MW	52310 TQ	USBLS	5/15
Metals and Plastics	Louisville-Jefferson County MSA, KY-IN	Y	30680 FQ	52760 MW	58930 TQ	USBLS	5/15
Metals and Plastics	Louisiana	Y	28900 FQ	36170 MW	43880 TQ	USBLS	5/15
Metals and Plastics	Baton Rouge MSA, LA	Y	27730 FQ	30330 MW	38470 TQ	USBLS	5/15
Metals and Plastics	New Orleans-Metairie MSA, LA	Y	30070 FQ	36550 MW	44530 TQ	USBLS	5/15
Metals and Plastics	Maine	Y	23960 FQ	29560 MW	38040 TQ	USBLS	5/15
Metals and Plastics	Portland-South Portland MSA, ME	Y	33230 FQ	40680 MW	45550 TQ	USBLS	5/15
Metals and Plastics	Maryland	Y	26502 AE	36368 MW	41301 AEX	MDBLS	4/16
Metals and Plastics	Baltimore-Columbia-Towson MSA, MD	Y	31120 FQ	38090 MW	46180 TQ	USBLS	5/15
Metals and Plastics	Massachusetts	Y	28260 FQ	35570 MW	44510 TQ	USBLS	5/15
Metals and Plastics	Boston-Cambridge-Newton NECTA, MA	Y	28830 FQ	35620 MW	43910 TQ	USBLS	5/15
Metals and Plastics	Worcester MSA, MA-CT	Y	28460 FQ	34490 MW	41720 TQ	USBLS	5/15
Metals and Plastics	Michigan	Y	24710 FQ	30950 MW	43420 TQ	USBLS	5/15
Metals and Plastics	Detroit-Dearborn-Livonia PMSA, MI	Y	28490 FQ	38500 MW	54680 TQ	USBLS	5/15
Metals and Plastics	Grand Rapids-Wyoming MSA, MI	Y	26430 FQ	30720 MW	40790 TQ	USBLS	5/15
Metals and Plastics	Minnesota	Y	24258 FQ	32712 MW	41510 TQ	MNBLS	1/16-3/16
Metals and Plastics	Minneapolis-St. Paul-Bloomington MSA, MN-WI	Y	21940 FQ	29705 MW	40052 TQ	MNBLS	1/16-3/16
Metals and Plastics	Mississippi	Y	25930 FQ	30140 MW	36940 TQ	USBLS	5/15
Metals and Plastics	Jackson MSA, MS	Y	25680 FQ	29910 MW	35190 TQ	USBLS	5/15
Metals and Plastics	Missouri	Y	25110 FQ	29690 MW	36210 TQ	USBLS	5/15
Metals and Plastics	Kansas City MSA, MO-KS	Y	24500 FQ	29370 MW	35940 TQ	USBLS	5/15
Metals and Plastics	St. Louis MSA, MO-IL	Y	24560 FQ	29990 MW	36230 TQ	USBLS	5/15
Metals and Plastics	Montana	Y	24570 FQ	31220 MW	41440 TQ	USBLS	5/15
Metals and Plastics	Billings MSA, MT	Y	26990 FQ	30960 MW	37270 TQ	USBLS	5/15
Metals and Plastics	Nebraska	Y	28315 FQ	33020 MW	38020 TQ	NEBLS	7/16-9/16
Metals and Plastics	Omaha-Council Bluffs MSA, NE-IA	Y	32680 FQ	36810 MW	42460 TQ	NEBLS	7/16-9/16
Metals and Plastics	Nevada	Y	24300 FQ	30140 MW	37160 TQ	USBLS	5/15
Metals and Plastics	Las Vegas-Henderson-Paradise MSA, NV	Y	22170 FQ	28050 MW	35340 TQ	USBLS	5/15
Metals and Plastics	New Hampshire	H	12.35 AE	16.85 MW	19.58 AEX	NHBLS	6/16
Metals and Plastics	Manchester NECTA, NH	H	12.83 AE	16.19 MW	18.48 AEX	NHBLS	6/16
Metals and Plastics	Nashua NECTA, NH-MA	Y	29790 FQ	37180 MW	44670 TQ	USBLS	5/15
Metals and Plastics	New Jersey	Y	24690 FQ	31260 MW	40030 TQ	USBLS	5/15
Metals and Plastics	Camden PMSA, NJ	Y	26150 FQ	34410 MW	42570 TQ	USBLS	5/15
Metals and Plastics	Newark PMSA, NJ-PA	Y	23180 FQ	28800 MW	37300 TQ	USBLS	5/15
Metals and Plastics	Trenton MSA, NJ	Y	41220 FQ	44180 MW	47140 TQ	USBLS	5/15
Metals and Plastics	New Mexico	Y	21980 FQ	27140 MW	35030 TQ	USBLS	5/15
Metals and Plastics	Albuquerque MSA, NM	Y	22240 FQ	25830 MW	31660 TQ	USBLS	5/15
Metals and Plastics	New York	Y	24380 AE	33260 MW	39890 AEX	NYBLS	1/16-3/16

Occupation/Type/Industry	Location	Per	Low	Mid	High	Source	Date
Cutting, Punching, and Press Machine Setter, Operator, and Tender							
Metals and Plastics	Buffalo-Cheektowaga-Niagara Falls MSA, NY	Y	29520 FQ	34940 MW	39950 TQ	USBLS	5/15
Metals and Plastics	Nassau County-Suffolk County PMSA, NY	Y	24230 FQ	30940 MW	38220 TQ	USBLS	5/15
Metals and Plastics	New York-Jersey City-White Plains PMSA, NY-NJ	Y	25370 FQ	32440 MW	41680 TQ	USBLS	5/15
Metals and Plastics	Rochester MSA, NY	Y	28500 FQ	34400 MW	39820 TQ	USBLS	5/15
Metals and Plastics	North Carolina	Y	21880 FQ	26190 MW	33630 TQ	USBLS	5/15
Metals and Plastics	Charlotte-Concord-Gastonia MSA, NC-SC	Y	24470 FQ	31940 MW	41500 TQ	USBLS	5/15
Metals and Plastics	Raleigh MSA, NC	Y	21910 FQ	26120 MW	30260 TQ	USBLS	5/15
Metals and Plastics	North Dakota	Y	32090 FQ	35580 MW	39080 TQ	USBLS	5/15
Metals and Plastics	Fargo MSA, ND-MN	Y	31740 FQ	35950 MW	40660 TQ	USBLS	5/15
Metals and Plastics	Ohio	Y	25070 FQ	31400 MW	38490 TQ	USBLS	5/15
Metals and Plastics	Cincinnati MSA, OH-KY-IN	Y	27710 FQ	33470 MW	39880 TQ	USBLS	5/15
Metals and Plastics	Cleveland-Elyria MSA, OH	Y	24850 FQ	31050 MW	37230 TQ	USBLS	5/15
Metals and Plastics	Columbus MSA, OH	Y	25620 FQ	32840 MW	43060 TQ	USBLS	5/15
Metals and Plastics	Oklahoma	Y	24200 FQ	29310 MW	36160 TQ	USBLS	5/15
Metals and Plastics	Oklahoma City MSA, OK	Y	24290 FQ	28580 MW	34430 TQ	USBLS	5/15
Metals and Plastics	Tulsa MSA, OK	Y	25980 FQ	31990 MW	38220 TQ	USBLS	5/15
Metals and Plastics	Oregon	H	13.42 FQ	16.64 MW	19.86 TQ	ORBLS	2016
Metals and Plastics	Portland-Vancouver-Hillsboro MSA, OR-WA	Y	27790 FQ	34770 MW	43690 TQ	USBLS	5/15
Metals and Plastics	Pennsylvania	Y	28640 FQ	35140 MW	42300 TQ	USBLS	5/15
Metals and Plastics	Allentown-Bethlehem-Easton MSA, PA-NJ	Y	27660 FQ	32840 MW	40520 TQ	USBLS	5/15
Metals and Plastics	Harrisburg-Carlisle MSA, PA	Y	31270 FQ	38780 MW	47940 TQ	USBLS	5/15
Metals and Plastics	Montgomery County-Bucks County-Chester County PMSA, PA	Y	29500 FQ	35260 MW	41550 TQ	USBLS	5/15
Metals and Plastics	Philadelphia PMSA, PA	Y	28680 FQ	36160 MW	44350 TQ	USBLS	5/15
Metals and Plastics	Pittsburgh MSA, PA	Y	32510 FQ	37720 MW	44530 TQ	USBLS	5/15
Metals and Plastics	Rhode Island	Y	19930 FQ	23990 MW	31180 TQ	USBLS	5/15
Metals and Plastics	Providence-Warwick MSA, RI-MA	Y	20650 FQ	26480 MW	36380 TQ	USBLS	5/15
Metals and Plastics	South Carolina	Y	27920 FQ	35940 MW	47230 TQ	USBLS	5/15
Metals and Plastics	Charleston-North Charleston MSA, SC	Y	32320 FQ	35930 MW	40400 TQ	USBLS	5/15
Metals and Plastics	Columbia MSA, SC	Y	32650 FQ	48700 MW	57520 TQ	USBLS	5/15
Metals and Plastics	Greenville-Anderson-Mauldin MSA, SC	Y	25160 FQ	36230 MW	45030 TQ	USBLS	5/15
Metals and Plastics	South Dakota	Y	28280 FQ	32040 MW	37090 TQ	USBLS	5/15
Metals and Plastics	Sioux Falls MSA, SD	Y	29130 FQ	33480 MW	38270 TQ	USBLS	5/15
Metals and Plastics	Tennessee	Y	23280 FQ	30060 MW	36990 TQ	USBLS	5/15
Metals and Plastics	Knoxville MSA, TN	Y	30740 FQ	35360 MW	39920 TQ	USBLS	5/15
Metals and Plastics	Memphis MSA, TN-MS-AR	Y	25610 FQ	29410 MW	34740 TQ	USBLS	5/15
Metals and Plastics	Nashville-Davidson–Murfreesboro–Franklin MSA, TN	Y	22700 FQ	29140 MW	35510 TQ	USBLS	5/15
Metals and Plastics	Texas	Y	24540 FQ	29550 MW	36270 TQ	USBLS	5/15
Metals and Plastics	Austin-Round Rock MSA, TX	Y	23530 FQ	28920 MW	36560 TQ	USBLS	5/15
Metals and Plastics	Dallas-Plano-Irving PMSA, TX	Y	26250 FQ	30290 MW	35410 TQ	USBLS	5/15
Metals and Plastics	Fort Worth-Arlington PMSA, TX	Y	22670 FQ	27590 MW	34300 TQ	USBLS	5/15
Metals and Plastics	Houston-The Woodlands-Sugar Land MSA, TX	Y	25230 FQ	29710 MW	36280 TQ	USBLS	5/15
Metals and Plastics	San Antonio-New Braunfels MSA, TX	Y	22650 FQ	27370 MW	34090 TQ	USBLS	5/15
Metals and Plastics	Utah	Y	26260 FQ	32150 MW	37070 TQ	USBLS	5/15
Metals and Plastics	Ogden-Clearfield MSA, UT	Y	25240 FQ	33970 MW	38610 TQ	USBLS	5/15
Metals and Plastics	Provo-Orem MSA, UT	Y	26210 FQ	29850 MW	34990 TQ	USBLS	5/15
Metals and Plastics	Salt Lake City MSA, UT	Y	27110 FQ	33190 MW	37230 TQ	USBLS	5/15
Metals and Plastics	Vermont	Y	25650 FQ	29040 MW	33940 TQ	USBLS	5/15
Metals and Plastics	Virginia	Y	27890 FQ	34370 MW	42980 TQ	USBLS	5/15
Metals and Plastics	Richmond MSA, VA	Y	30140 FQ	35910 MW	46640 TQ	USBLS	5/15
Metals and Plastics	Virginia Beach-Norfolk-Newport News MSA, VA-NC	Y	23890 FQ	29190 MW	39450 TQ	USBLS	5/15
Metals and Plastics	Washington	H	14.72 FQ	17.82 MW	22.02 TQ	WABLS	3/16

AE	Average entry wage	AWR	Average wage range	H	Hourly
AEX	Average experienced wage	B	Biweekly	HI	Highest wage paid
ATC	Average total compensation	D	Daily	HR	High end range
AW	Average wage paid	FQ	First quartile wage	LO	Lowest wage paid

LR	Low end range	MTC	Median total compensation
M	Monthly	MW	Median wage paid
MCC	Median cash compensation	MWR	Median wage range
ME	Median entry wage	S	See annotated source

TCC	Total cash compensation
TQ	Third quartile wage
W	Weekly
Y	Yearly

Occupation/Type/Industry	Location	Per	Low	Mid	High	Source	Date
Cutting, Punching, and Press Machine Setter, Operator, and Tender							
Metals and Plastics	Seattle-Bellevue-Everett PMSA, WA	H	16.08 FQ	18.77 MW	23.56 TQ	WABLS	3/16
Metals and Plastics	Tacoma-Lakewood PMSA, WA	H	14.18 FQ	17.83 MW	23.09 TQ	WABLS	3/16
Metals and Plastics	West Virginia	Y	28950 FQ	35450 MW	42720 TQ	USBLS	5/15
Metals and Plastics	Huntington-Ashland MSA, WV-KY-OH	Y	27910 FQ	32650 MW	39570 TQ	USBLS	5/15
Metals and Plastics	Wisconsin	Y	27880 FQ	34140 MW	40640 TQ	USBLS	5/15
Metals and Plastics	Madison MSA, WI	Y	30660 FQ	37420 MW	44780 TQ	USBLS	5/15
Metals and Plastics	Milwaukee-Waukesha-West Allis MSA, WI	Y	27830 FQ	34930 MW	43410 TQ	USBLS	5/15
Metals and Plastics	Wyoming	Y	32420 FQ	36240 MW	40570 TQ	USBLS	5/15
Metals and Plastics	Puerto Rico	Y	16800 FQ	18270 MW	20560 TQ	USBLS	5/15
Metals and Plastics	San Juan-Carolina-Caguas MSA, PR	Y	16770 FQ	18220 MW	20390 TQ	USBLS	5/15
Cutting and Slicing Machine Setter, Operator, and Tender	Alabama	Y	22395 AE	36173 AW	43062 AEX	ALBLS	6/16
	Birmingham-Hoover MSA, AL	Y	22281 AE	28317 AW	31340 AEX	ALBLS	6/16
	Arizona	Y	26290 FQ	30280 MW	36510 TQ	USBLS	5/15
	Phoenix-Mesa-Scottsdale MSA, AZ	Y	26530 FQ	30220 MW	36350 TQ	USBLS	5/15
	Tucson MSA, AZ	Y	25410 FQ	32670 MW	37760 TQ	USBLS	5/15
	Arkansas	Y	25440 FQ	32930 MW	37470 TQ	USBLS	5/15
	Little Rock-North Little Rock-Conway MSA, AR	Y	24590 FQ	28460 MW	32280 TQ	USBLS	5/15
	California	H	11.54 FQ	14.56 MW	18.20 TQ	CABLS	1/16-3/16
	Anaheim-Santa Ana-Irvine PMSA, CA	H	13.00 FQ	15.73 MW	17.78 TQ	CABLS	1/16-3/16
	Los Angeles-Long Beach-Glendale PMSA, CA	H	11.38 FQ	14.07 MW	17.66 TQ	CABLS	1/16-3/16
	Oakland-Hayward-Berkeley PMSA, CA	H	12.52 FQ	14.63 MW	18.09 TQ	CABLS	1/16-3/16
	Riverside-San Bernardino-Ontario MSA, CA	H	10.27 FQ	11.91 MW	17.70 TQ	CABLS	1/16-3/16
	Sacramento-Roseville-Arden-Arcade MSA, CA	H	14.32 FQ	19.51 MW	22.69 TQ	CABLS	1/16-3/16
	San Diego-Carlsbad MSA, CA	H	13.62 FQ	16.20 MW	25.69 TQ	CABLS	1/16-3/16
	San Francisco-Redwood City-South San Francisco PMSA, CA	H	16.30 FQ	17.53 MW	18.75 TQ	CABLS	1/16-3/16
	Colorado	Y	27420 FQ	31660 MW	39100 TQ	USBLS	5/15
	Denver-Aurora-Lakewood MSA, CO	Y	27470 FQ	31360 MW	39360 TQ	USBLS	5/15
	Connecticut	Y		36584 MW		CTBLS	1/16-3/16
	Bridgeport-Stamford-Norwalk MSA, CT	Y	27490 FQ	33160 MW	39910 TQ	USBLS	5/15
	Hartford-West Hartford-East Hartford MSA, CT	Y	35980 FQ	49620 MW	55970 TQ	USBLS	5/15
	Delaware	Y	29430 FQ	36160 MW	43600 TQ	USBLS	5/15
	Wilmington PMSA, DE-MD-NJ	Y	30000 FQ	37420 MW	44620 TQ	USBLS	5/15
	Washington-Arlington-Alexandria PMSA, DC-VA-MD-WV	Y	29840 FQ	34590 MW	38680 TQ	USBLS	5/15
	Florida	H	10.47 AE	13.92 MW	17.05 AEX	FLBLS	7/16-9/16
	Fort Lauderdale-Pompano Beach-Deerfield Beach PMSA, FL	H	9.92 AE	13.27 MW	15.36 AEX	FLBLS	7/16-9/16
	Miami-Miami Beach-Kendall PMSA, FL	H	10.15 AE	12.11 MW	14.24 AEX	FLBLS	7/16-9/16
	Orlando-Kissimmee-Sanford MSA, FL	H	10.48 AE	13.62 MW	17.18 AEX	FLBLS	7/16-9/16
	Tampa-St. Petersburg-Clearwater MSA, FL	H	10.52 AE	13.82 MW	17.90 AEX	FLBLS	7/16-9/16
	Georgia	Y	23480 FQ	28870 MW	36660 TQ	USBLS	5/15
	Atlanta-Sandy Springs-Roswell MSA, GA	Y	25030 FQ	29370 MW	36130 TQ	USBLS	5/15

AE	Average entry wage	AWR	Average wage range	H	Hourly	LR	Low end range	MTC	Median total compensation	TCC	Total cash compensation
AEX	Average experienced wage	B	Biweekly	HI	Highest wage paid	M	Monthly	MW	Median wage paid	TQ	Third quartile wage
ATC	Average total compensation	D	Daily	HR	High end range	MCC	Median cash compensation	MWR	Median wage range	W	Weekly
AW	Average wage paid	FQ	First quartile wage	LO	Lowest wage paid	ME	Median entry wage	S	See annotated source	Y	Yearly

392

Occupation/Type/Industry	Location	Per	Low	Mid	High	Source	Date
Cutting and Slicing Machine Setter, Operator, and Tender	Augusta-Richmond County MSA, GA-SC	Y	40860 FQ	43890 MW	46910 TQ	USBLS	5/15
	Hawaii	Y	18280 FQ	21600 MW	36620 TQ	USBLS	5/15
	Urban Honolulu MSA, HI	Y	17840 FQ	19560 MW	31970 TQ	USBLS	5/15
	Idaho	Y	24710 FQ	29750 MW	37470 TQ	USBLS	5/15
	Illinois	Y	25480 FQ	32680 MW	38800 TQ	USBLS	5/15
	Chicago-Naperville-Arlington Heights PMSA, IL	Y	24710 FQ	31470 MW	37600 TQ	USBLS	5/15
	Lake County-Kenosha County PMSA, IL-WI	Y	30430 FQ	33830 MW	37130 TQ	USBLS	5/15
	Indiana	Y	27140 FQ	33080 MW	38390 TQ	USBLS	5/15
	Gary PMSA, IN	Y	22110 FQ	24960 MW	30330 TQ	USBLS	5/15
	Indianapolis-Carmel-Anderson MSA, IN	Y	28810 FQ	34210 MW	39150 TQ	USBLS	5/15
	Iowa	Y	28960 FQ	34890 MW	39650 TQ	USBLS	5/15
	Des Moines-West Des Moines MSA, IA	Y	22690 FQ	29840 MW	35470 TQ	USBLS	5/15
	Kansas	Y	25480 FQ	29420 MW	38530 TQ	USBLS	5/15
	Wichita MSA, KS	Y	25370 FQ	30990 MW	44090 TQ	USBLS	5/15
	Kentucky	Y	25930 FQ	33490 MW	39550 TQ	USBLS	5/15
	Louisville-Jefferson County MSA, KY-IN	Y	28440 FQ	34710 MW	39790 TQ	USBLS	5/15
	Louisiana	Y	40830 FQ	44800 MW	48780 TQ	USBLS	5/15
	Baton Rouge MSA, LA	Y	42990 FQ	46370 MW	49750 TQ	USBLS	5/15
	New Orleans-Metairie MSA, LA	Y	30430 FQ	41500 MW	46040 TQ	USBLS	5/15
	Maine	Y	27970 FQ	37920 MW	52160 TQ	USBLS	5/15
	Maryland	Y	28160 AE	38338 MW	43427 AEX	MDBLS	4/16
	Baltimore-Columbia-Towson MSA, MD	Y	33630 FQ	37860 MW	44510 TQ	USBLS	5/15
	Massachusetts	Y	30460 FQ	36370 MW	43270 TQ	USBLS	5/15
	Boston-Cambridge-Newton NECTA, MA	Y	34120 FQ	39770 MW	47490 TQ	USBLS	5/15
	Worcester MSA, MA-CT	Y	27900 FQ	33350 MW	40110 TQ	USBLS	5/15
	Michigan	Y	22980 FQ	29400 MW	37840 TQ	USBLS	5/15
	Detroit-Dearborn-Livonia PMSA, MI	Y	18700 FQ	22700 MW	30630 TQ	USBLS	5/15
	Grand Rapids-Wyoming MSA, MI	Y	25860 FQ	32530 MW	41370 TQ	USBLS	5/15
	Minnesota	Y	31740 FQ	40964 MW	46724 TQ	MNBLS	1/16-3/16
	Minneapolis-St. Paul-Bloomington MSA, MN-WI	Y	28835 FQ	36570 MW	44578 TQ	MNBLS	1/16-3/16
	Mississippi	Y	20730 FQ	23570 MW	29760 TQ	USBLS	5/15
	Jackson MSA, MS	Y	20470 FQ	22280 MW	24090 TQ	USBLS	5/15
	Missouri	Y	28410 FQ	34430 MW	40060 TQ	USBLS	5/15
	Kansas City MSA, MO-KS	Y	26040 FQ	31590 MW	40120 TQ	USBLS	5/15
	St. Louis MSA, MO-IL	Y	29230 FQ	35180 MW	41190 TQ	USBLS	5/15
	Montana	Y	25050 FQ	29460 MW	34270 TQ	USBLS	5/15
	Nebraska	Y	28725 FQ	34210 MW	39925 TQ	NEBLS	7/16-9/16
	Omaha-Council Bluffs MSA, NE-IA	Y	27050 FQ	30920 MW	37750 TQ	NEBLS	7/16-9/16
	Nevada	Y	28480 FQ	34570 MW	41510 TQ	USBLS	5/15
	Las Vegas-Henderson-Paradise MSA, NV	Y	31430 FQ	36100 MW	41930 TQ	USBLS	5/15
	New Hampshire	H	12.32 AE	18.52 MW	20.69 AEX	NHBLS	6/16
	Nashua NECTA, NH-MA	Y	36360 FQ	41390 MW	45790 TQ	USBLS	5/15
	New Jersey	Y	25920 FQ	33090 MW	39430 TQ	USBLS	5/15
	Camden PMSA, NJ	Y	27880 FQ	33670 MW	39350 TQ	USBLS	5/15
	Newark PMSA, NJ-PA	Y	29020 FQ	34590 MW	39030 TQ	USBLS	5/15
	Trenton MSA, NJ	Y	32710 FQ	36790 MW	41980 TQ	USBLS	5/15
	New Mexico	Y	21090 FQ	23130 MW	28800 TQ	USBLS	5/15
	Albuquerque MSA, NM	Y	21050 FQ	23150 MW	29360 TQ	USBLS	5/15
	New York	Y	22090 AE	32360 MW	39630 AEX	NYBLS	1/16-3/16
	Buffalo-Cheektowaga-Niagara Falls MSA, NY	Y	25250 FQ	31290 MW	39520 TQ	USBLS	5/15
	Nassau County-Suffolk County PMSA, NY	Y	23530 FQ	31880 MW	37920 TQ	USBLS	5/15
	New York-Jersey City-White Plains PMSA, NY-NJ	Y	22630 FQ	30510 MW	40240 TQ	USBLS	5/15
	Rochester MSA, NY	Y	23560 FQ	29620 MW	37770 TQ	USBLS	5/15
	North Carolina	Y	25020 FQ	30270 MW	38990 TQ	USBLS	5/15

AE	Average entry wage	**AWR**	Average wage range	**H**	Hourly
AEX	Average experienced wage	**B**	Biweekly	**HI**	Highest wage paid
ATC	Average total compensation	**D**	Daily	**HR**	High end range
AW	Average wage paid	**FQ**	First quartile wage	**LO**	Lowest wage paid

LR	Low end range	**MTC**	Median total compensation	**TCC**	Total cash compensation
M	Monthly	**MW**	Median wage paid	**TQ**	Third quartile wage
MCC	Median cash compensation	**MWR**	Median wage range	**W**	Weekly
ME	Median entry wage	**S**	See annotated source	**Y**	Yearly

Occupation/Type/Industry	Location	Per	Low	Mid	High	Source	Date
Cutting and Slicing Machine Setter, Operator, and Tender	Charlotte-Concord-Gastonia MSA, NC-SC	Y	24890 FQ	30140 MW	37260 TQ	USBLS	5/15
	Raleigh MSA, NC	Y	25130 FQ	28300 MW	32420 TQ	USBLS	5/15
	North Dakota	Y	26210 FQ	33270 MW	36710 TQ	USBLS	5/15
	Ohio	Y	24730 FQ	30500 MW	37440 TQ	USBLS	5/15
	Cincinnati MSA, OH-KY-IN	Y	26740 FQ	30650 MW	38800 TQ	USBLS	5/15
	Cleveland-Elyria MSA, OH	Y	23050 FQ	29440 MW	37120 TQ	USBLS	5/15
	Columbus MSA, OH	Y	28270 FQ	33400 MW	39340 TQ	USBLS	5/15
	Oklahoma	Y	24620 FQ	28610 MW	33940 TQ	USBLS	5/15
	Oklahoma City MSA, OK	Y	24410 FQ	27570 MW	30450 TQ	USBLS	5/15
	Tulsa MSA, OK	Y	24530 FQ	31380 MW	36580 TQ	USBLS	5/15
	Oregon	H	15.26 FQ	18.52 MW	22.06 TQ	ORBLS	2016
	Portland-Vancouver-Hillsboro MSA, OR-WA	Y	32620 FQ	38180 MW	45860 TQ	USBLS	5/15
	Pennsylvania	Y	28200 FQ	34040 MW	39830 TQ	USBLS	5/15
	Allentown-Bethlehem-Easton MSA, PA-NJ	Y	32470 FQ	35900 MW	39410 TQ	USBLS	5/15
	Harrisburg-Carlisle MSA, PA	Y	28840 FQ	35170 MW	41970 TQ	USBLS	5/15
	Montgomery County-Bucks County-Chester County PMSA, PA	Y	28810 FQ	33970 MW	39390 TQ	USBLS	5/15
	Philadelphia PMSA, PA	Y	31240 FQ	38530 MW	45080 TQ	USBLS	5/15
	Pittsburgh MSA, PA	Y	27320 FQ	34070 MW	40940 TQ	USBLS	5/15
	Rhode Island	Y	26010 FQ	31090 MW	37620 TQ	USBLS	5/15
	Providence-Warwick MSA, RI-MA	Y	26010 FQ	31450 MW	38070 TQ	USBLS	5/15
	South Carolina	Y	27050 FQ	36900 MW	45120 TQ	USBLS	5/15
	Columbia MSA, SC	Y	25080 FQ	34310 MW	39550 TQ	USBLS	5/15
	Greenville-Anderson-Mauldin MSA, SC	Y	24110 FQ	38220 MW	48160 TQ	USBLS	5/15
	South Dakota	Y	28860 FQ	34140 MW	39050 TQ	USBLS	5/15
	Sioux Falls MSA, SD	Y	28050 FQ	30900 MW	35690 TQ	USBLS	5/15
	Tennessee	Y	24360 FQ	31170 MW	36700 TQ	USBLS	5/15
	Knoxville MSA, TN	Y	17170 FQ	19380 MW	33240 TQ	USBLS	5/15
	Memphis MSA, TN-MS-AR	Y	25760 FQ	33690 MW	41750 TQ	USBLS	5/15
	Nashville-Davidson–Murfreesboro–Franklin MSA, TN	Y	23510 FQ	29760 MW	35420 TQ	USBLS	5/15
	Texas	Y	22260 FQ	27630 MW	34910 TQ	USBLS	5/15
	Austin-Round Rock MSA, TX	Y	19360 FQ	22520 MW	27680 TQ	USBLS	5/15
	Dallas-Plano-Irving PMSA, TX	Y	24640 FQ	29460 MW	36810 TQ	USBLS	5/15
	Fort Worth-Arlington PMSA, TX	Y	25070 FQ	31450 MW	40230 TQ	USBLS	5/15
	Houston-The Woodlands-Sugar Land MSA, TX	Y	19110 FQ	23280 MW	29180 TQ	USBLS	5/15
	San Antonio-New Braunfels MSA, TX	Y	22720 FQ	31100 MW	37290 TQ	USBLS	5/15
	Utah	Y	24200 FQ	29390 MW	35820 TQ	USBLS	5/15
	Ogden-Clearfield MSA, UT	Y	23110 FQ	31060 MW	36880 TQ	USBLS	5/15
	Provo-Orem MSA, UT	Y	18590 FQ	21840 MW	26580 TQ	USBLS	5/15
	Salt Lake City MSA, UT	Y	25530 FQ	28660 MW	32210 TQ	USBLS	5/15
	Vermont	Y	26490 FQ	31370 MW	38340 TQ	USBLS	5/15
	Virginia	Y	31770 FQ	49570 MW	56240 TQ	USBLS	5/15
	Richmond MSA, VA	Y	30470 FQ	37210 MW	47100 TQ	USBLS	5/15
	Virginia Beach-Norfolk-Newport News MSA, VA-NC	Y	22760 FQ	26770 MW	38690 TQ	USBLS	5/15
	Washington	H	13.70 FQ	16.52 MW	21.24 TQ	WABLS	3/16
	Seattle-Bellevue-Everett PMSA, WA	H	14.44 FQ	18.17 MW	22.37 TQ	WABLS	3/16
	Tacoma-Lakewood PMSA, WA	H	14.59 FQ	17.39 MW	21.34 TQ	WABLS	3/16
	West Virginia	Y	23650 FQ	30410 MW	38130 TQ	USBLS	5/15
	Huntington-Ashland MSA, WV-KY-OH	Y	36800 FQ	53360 MW	58240 TQ	USBLS	5/15
	Wisconsin	Y	28830 FQ	34410 MW	39310 TQ	USBLS	5/15
	Madison MSA, WI	Y	31960 FQ	34850 MW	37750 TQ	USBLS	5/15
	Milwaukee-Waukesha-West Allis MSA, WI	Y	29400 FQ	34240 MW	38470 TQ	USBLS	5/15
	Puerto Rico	Y	17860 FQ	20050 MW	24980 TQ	USBLS	5/15
	San Juan-Carolina-Caguas MSA, PR	Y	17750 FQ	19820 MW	24080 TQ	USBLS	5/15

AE	Average entry wage	AWR	Average wage range	H	Hourly
AEX	Average experienced wage	B	Biweekly	HI	Highest wage paid
ATC	Average total compensation	D	Daily	HR	High end range
AW	Average wage paid	FQ	First quartile wage	LO	Lowest wage paid

LR	Low end range	MTC	Median total compensation	TCC	Total cash compensation
M	Monthly	MW	Median wage paid	TQ	Third quartile wage
MCC	Median cash compensation	MWR	Median wage range	W	Weekly
ME	Median entry wage	S	See annotated source	Y	Yearly

Occupation/Type/Industry	Location	Per	Low	Mid	High	Source	Date
Cyber Threat Analyst							
Central Intelligence Agency	District of Columbia	Y	51603 LO		90216 HI	CIA04	2016
Cybersecurity Analyst							
State Government	Texas	Y	63104- 92390 LR		103491- 156256 HR	TXGOV	9/1/15-8/31/17
Cybersecurity Specialist	United States	Y		125000 MW		LH01	2016
Cytotechnologist							
State Government	North Carolina	Y	42667 LO		75719 HI	NCGOV	7/1/16
Dairy Herdsperson	United States	Y		25000 AW		SKU01	2016
Dairy Plant Manager							
Michigan State University	East Lansing, MI	Y			68939 HI	MSUSAL	10/1/14-9/30/15
Dam Safety Specialist							
Department of Natural Resources and Conservation, State Government	Helena, MT	H			22.68 HI	MTGOV	2016
Dance Therapist							
State Government	Maryland	Y	34390 LO		57808 HI	MDGOV	2016
Dancer	California	H	10.84 FQ	14.45 MW	22.71 TQ	CABLS	1/16-3/16
	Colorado	H	9.44 FQ	15.98 MW	18.33 TQ	USBLS	5/15
	Connecticut	H		21.58 MW		CTBLS	1/16-3/16
	District of Columbia	H	13.47 FQ	16.71 MW	24.15 TQ	USBLS	5/15
	Florida	H	9.46 AE	11.80 MW	16.49 AEX	FLBLS	7/16-9/16
	Hawaii	H	8.95 FQ	12.53 MW	20.63 TQ	USBLS	5/15
	Idaho	H	12.31 FQ	15.34 MW	20.56 TQ	USBLS	5/15
	Illinois	H	13.06 FQ	20.74 MW	26.54 TQ	USBLS	5/15
	Iowa	H	8.82 FQ	11.80 MW	17.95 TQ	USBLS	5/15
	Maryland	H	9.75 AE	18.25 MW	22.25 AEX	MDBLS	4/16
	Minnesota	H	9.11 FQ	17.64 MW	26.31 TQ	MNBLS	1/16-3/16
	Missouri	H	13.23 FQ	16.86 MW	20.15 TQ	USBLS	5/15
	New Jersey	H	16.65 FQ	20.63 MW	24.73 TQ	USBLS	5/15
	New Mexico	H	8.72 FQ	9.66 MW	22.13 TQ	USBLS	5/15
	Pennsylvania	H	13.37 FQ	16.82 MW	21.26 TQ	USBLS	5/15
	Rhode Island	H	10.69 FQ	12.96 MW	14.17 TQ	USBLS	5/15
	South Carolina	H	12.71 FQ	15.60 MW	17.82 TQ	USBLS	5/15
	Tennessee	H	11.75 FQ	15.03 MW	18.02 TQ	USBLS	5/15
	Texas	H	8.11 FQ	8.81 MW	12.14 TQ	USBLS	5/15
	Utah	H	13.53 FQ	17.05 MW	21.23 TQ	USBLS	5/15
	Virginia	H	12.57 FQ	16.99 MW	19.31 TQ	USBLS	5/15
	Wisconsin	H	8.52 FQ	12.87 MW	22.16 TQ	USBLS	5/15
Darkroom Technician							
Police Department, Municipal Government	San Jose, CA	Y			51532 HI	CACIT	6/28/16
Data Entry Keyer	Alabama	Y	21663 AE	28764 AW	32319 AEX	ALBLS	6/16
	Birmingham-Hoover MSA, AL	Y	24477 AE	31021 AW	34288 AEX	ALBLS	6/16
	Alaska	Y	30270 FQ	35010 MW	39210 TQ	USBLS	5/15
	Anchorage MSA, AK	Y	28770 FQ	34250 MW	38710 TQ	USBLS	5/15
	Arizona	Y	24030 FQ	28370 MW	33500 TQ	USBLS	5/15
	Phoenix-Mesa-Scottsdale MSA, AZ	Y	24380 FQ	28700 MW	33970 TQ	USBLS	5/15
	Tucson MSA, AZ	Y	22770 FQ	26150 MW	30020 TQ	USBLS	5/15
	Arkansas	Y	23350 FQ	27880 MW	32690 TQ	USBLS	5/15
	Little Rock-North Little Rock- Conway MSA, AR	Y	25150 FQ	29200 MW	34490 TQ	USBLS	5/15
	California	H	12.38 FQ	15.27 MW	18.69 TQ	CABLS	1/16-3/16
	Anaheim-Santa Ana-Irvine PMSA, CA	H	12.42 FQ	15.89 MW	19.00 TQ	CABLS	1/16-3/16
	Los Angeles-Long Beach- Glendale PMSA, CA	H	11.79 FQ	14.44 MW	17.85 TQ	CABLS	1/16-3/16
	Oakland-Hayward-Berkeley PMSA, CA	H	15.20 FQ	18.50 MW	22.76 TQ	CABLS	1/16-3/16
	Riverside-San Bernardino- Ontario MSA, CA	H	11.89 FQ	14.67 MW	18.13 TQ	CABLS	1/16-3/16
	Sacramento–Roseville– Arden-Arcade MSA, CA	H	14.95 FQ	17.32 MW	19.05 TQ	CABLS	1/16-3/16
	San Diego-Carlsbad MSA, CA	H	11.77 FQ	14.21 MW	17.43 TQ	CABLS	1/16-3/16

Occupation/Type/Industry	Location	Per	Low	Mid	High	Source	Date
Data Entry Keyer	San Francisco-Redwood City-South San Francisco PMSA, CA	H	14.46 FQ	17.91 MW	23.03 TQ	CABLS	1/16-3/16
	Colorado	Y	27110 FQ	34240 MW	39760 TQ	USBLS	5/15
	Denver-Aurora-Lakewood MSA, CO	Y	27380 FQ	34240 MW	39180 TQ	USBLS	5/15
	Connecticut	Y	.	35653 MW		CTBLS	1/16-3/16
	Bridgeport-Stamford-Norwalk MSA, CT	Y	27940 FQ	34660 MW	45860 TQ	USBLS	5/15
	Hartford-West Hartford-East Hartford MSA, CT	Y	27970 FQ	35170 MW	45520 TQ	USBLS	5/15
	Delaware	Y	24260 FQ	27780 MW	31610 TQ	USBLS	5/15
	Wilmington PMSA, DE-MD-NJ	Y	23770 FQ	28010 MW	32300 TQ	USBLS	5/15
	District of Columbia	Y	32660 FQ	38050 MW	46760 TQ	USBLS	5/15
	Washington-Arlington-Alexandria PMSA, DC-VA-MD-WV	Y	26120 FQ	32480 MW	39100 TQ	USBLS	5/15
	Florida	H	10.39 AE	13.73 MW	16.09 AEX	FLBLS	7/16-9/16
	Fort Lauderdale-Pompano Beach-Deerfield Beach PMSA, FL	H	10.34 AE	13.50 MW	15.96 AEX	FLBLS	7/16-9/16
	Miami-Miami Beach-Kendall PMSA, FL	H	10.32 AE	12.71 MW	15.48 AEX	FLBLS	7/16-9/16
	Orlando-Kissimmee-Sanford MSA, FL	H	11.08 AE	14.21 MW	16.15 AEX	FLBLS	7/16-9/16
	Tampa-St. Petersburg-Clearwater MSA, FL	H	10.36 AE	14.20 MW	16.34 AEX	FLBLS	7/16-9/16
	Georgia	Y	23370 FQ	28680 MW	34900 TQ	USBLS	5/15
	Atlanta-Sandy Springs-Roswell MSA, GA	Y	25210 FQ	29900 MW	36090 TQ	USBLS	5/15
	Augusta-Richmond County MSA, GA-SC	Y	22030 FQ	26010 MW	29780 TQ	USBLS	5/15
	Hawaii	Y	27610 FQ	33970 MW	40940 TQ	USBLS	5/15
	Urban Honolulu MSA, HI	Y	28010 FQ	34530 MW	41910 TQ	USBLS	5/15
	Idaho	Y	21270 FQ	26410 MW	32530 TQ	USBLS	5/15
	Boise City MSA, ID	Y	21220 FQ	26120 MW	31980 TQ	USBLS	5/15
	Illinois	Y	22760 FQ	28880 MW	37920 TQ	USBLS	5/15
	Chicago-Naperville-Arlington Heights PMSA, IL	Y	23000 FQ	29230 MW	38810 TQ	USBLS	5/15
	Lake County-Kenosha County PMSA, IL-WI	Y	24200 FQ	29320 MW	37150 TQ	USBLS	5/15
	Indiana	Y	19590 FQ	25890 MW	31950 TQ	USBLS	5/15
	Gary PMSA, IN	Y	24060 FQ	28920 MW	35100 TQ	USBLS	5/15
	Indianapolis-Carmel-Anderson MSA, IN	Y	18480 FQ	23700 MW	30220 TQ	USBLS	5/15
	Iowa	Y	23750 FQ	28290 MW	33490 TQ	USBLS	5/15
	Des Moines-West Des Moines MSA, IA	Y	21690 FQ	26140 MW	30820 TQ	USBLS	5/15
	Kansas	Y	24630 FQ	29660 MW	35710 TQ	USBLS	5/15
	Wichita MSA, KS	Y	24750 FQ	29110 MW	35870 TQ	USBLS	5/15
	Kentucky	Y	22840 FQ	29650 MW	35810 TQ	USBLS	5/15
	Louisville-Jefferson County MSA, KY-IN	Y	23460 FQ	31550 MW	39460 TQ	USBLS	5/15
	Louisiana	Y	22200 FQ	27810 MW	34210 TQ	USBLS	5/15
	Baton Rouge MSA, LA	Y	25040 FQ	31120 MW	38500 TQ	USBLS	5/15
	New Orleans-Metairie MSA, LA	Y	19450 FQ	25610 MW	31050 TQ	USBLS	5/15
	Maine	Y	24960 FQ	29150 MW	34570 TQ	USBLS	5/15
	Portland-South Portland MSA, ME	Y	24840 FQ	29230 MW	34900 TQ	USBLS	5/15
	Maryland	Y	21871 AE	32640 MW	38025 AEX	MDBLS	4/16
	Baltimore-Columbia-Towson MSA, MD	Y	28670 FQ	34470 MW	39100 TQ	USBLS	5/15
	Salisbury MSA, MD-DE	Y	24960 FQ	31750 MW	38170 TQ	USBLS	5/15
	Massachusetts	Y	30610 FQ	36220 MW	42960 TQ	USBLS	5/15
	Boston-Cambridge-Newton NECTA, MA	Y	32020 FQ	37480 MW	44400 TQ	USBLS	5/15
	Worcester MSA, MA-CT	Y	28660 FQ	33500 MW	38700 TQ	USBLS	5/15
	Michigan	Y	23130 FQ	28880 MW	35880 TQ	USBLS	5/15
	Detroit-Dearborn-Livonia PMSA, MI	Y	23300 FQ	31730 MW	37350 TQ	USBLS	5/15

AE	Average entry wage	AWR	Average wage range	H	Hourly	LR	Low end range
AEX	Average experienced wage	B	Biweekly	HI	Highest wage paid	M	Monthly
ATC	Average total compensation	D	Daily	HR	High end range	MCC	Median cash compensation
AW	Average wage paid	FQ	First quartile wage	LO	Lowest wage paid	ME	Median entry wage

MTC	Median total compensation	TCC	Total cash compensation
MW	Median wage paid	TQ	Third quartile wage
MWR	Median wage range	W	Weekly
S	See annotated source	Y	Yearly

Data Entry Keyer

Occupation/Type/Industry	Location	Per	Low	Mid	High	Source	Date
Data Entry Keyer	Grand Rapids-Wyoming MSA, MI	Y	20130 FQ	26170 MW	33140 TQ	USBLS	5/15
	Minnesota	Y	26809 FQ	31461 MW	38550 TQ	MNBLS	1/16-3/16
	Minneapolis-St. Paul-Bloomington MSA, MN-WI	Y	28083 FQ	33129 MW	39612 TQ	MNBLS	1/16-3/16
	Mississippi	Y	19930 FQ	24370 MW	29850 TQ	USBLS	5/15
	Jackson MSA, MS	Y	20340 FQ	24080 MW	30980 TQ	USBLS	5/15
	Missouri	Y	23410 FQ	28420 MW	32550 TQ	USBLS	5/15
	Kansas City MSA, MO-KS	Y	27210 FQ	30460 MW	35350 TQ	USBLS	5/15
	St. Louis MSA, MO-IL	Y	23150 FQ	27650 MW	34140 TQ	USBLS	5/15
	Montana	Y	22050 FQ	26950 MW	32790 TQ	USBLS	5/15
	Billings MSA, MT	Y	24770 FQ	30660 MW	35680 TQ	USBLS	5/15
	Nebraska	Y	24795 FQ	28300 MW	32360 TQ	NEBLS	7/16-9/16
	Omaha-Council Bluffs MSA, NE-IA	Y	25410 FQ	28430 MW	31675 TQ	NEBLS	7/16-9/16
	Nevada	Y	23190 FQ	27710 MW	32460 TQ	USBLS	5/15
	Las Vegas-Henderson-Paradise MSA, NV	Y	25720 FQ	29400 MW	34830 TQ	USBLS	5/15
	New Hampshire	H	10.87 AE	13.89 MW	16.19 AEX	NHBLS	6/16
	Manchester NECTA, NH	H	10.80 AE	14.54 MW	18.56 AEX	NHBLS	6/16
	Nashua NECTA, NH-MA	Y	21490 FQ	23310 MW	26740 TQ	USBLS	5/15
	New Jersey	Y	28600 FQ	35570 MW	44740 TQ	USBLS	5/15
	Camden PMSA, NJ	Y	25900 FQ	31210 MW	38690 TQ	USBLS	5/15
	Newark PMSA, NJ-PA	Y	30760 FQ	36760 MW	45330 TQ	USBLS	5/15
	Trenton MSA, NJ	Y	32180 FQ	39810 MW	47710 TQ	USBLS	5/15
	New Mexico	Y	21700 FQ	25930 MW	30330 TQ	USBLS	5/15
	Albuquerque MSA, NM	Y	22350 FQ	27280 MW	30980 TQ	USBLS	5/15
	New York	Y	23330 AE	32250 MW	39280 AEX	NYBLS	1/16-3/16
	Buffalo-Cheektowaga-Niagara Falls MSA, NY	Y	25450 FQ	31380 MW	37190 TQ	USBLS	5/15
	Nassau County-Suffolk County PMSA, NY	Y	25330 FQ	35160 MW	44120 TQ	USBLS	5/15
	New York-Jersey City-White Plains PMSA, NY-NJ	Y	26700 FQ	33500 MW	41940 TQ	USBLS	5/15
	Rochester MSA, NY	Y	24370 FQ	29320 MW	35380 TQ	USBLS	5/15
	North Carolina	Y	25270 FQ	30120 MW	35590 TQ	USBLS	5/15
	Charlotte-Concord-Gastonia MSA, NC-SC	Y	24080 FQ	28760 MW	34330 TQ	USBLS	5/15
	Raleigh MSA, NC	Y	27420 FQ	32430 MW	37320 TQ	USBLS	5/15
	North Dakota	Y	24210 FQ	29420 MW	35850 TQ	USBLS	5/15
	Fargo MSA, ND-MN	Y	24200 FQ	29190 MW	36000 TQ	USBLS	5/15
	Ohio	Y	24200 FQ	29060 MW	35260 TQ	USBLS	5/15
	Cincinnati MSA, OH-KY-IN	Y	27370 FQ	32150 MW	36660 TQ	USBLS	5/15
	Cleveland-Elyria MSA, OH	Y	24800 FQ	28720 MW	34490 TQ	USBLS	5/15
	Columbus MSA, OH	Y	25550 FQ	30930 MW	36260 TQ	USBLS	5/15
	Oklahoma	Y	22060 FQ	27460 MW	33380 TQ	USBLS	5/15
	Oklahoma City MSA, OK	Y	21450 FQ	27240 MW	33090 TQ	USBLS	5/15
	Tulsa MSA, OK	Y	21670 FQ	27950 MW	35560 TQ	USBLS	5/15
	Oregon	H	11.83 FQ	14.13 MW	17.19 TQ	ORBLS	2016
	Portland-Vancouver-Hillsboro MSA, OR-WA	Y	24190 FQ	29410 MW	35640 TQ	USBLS	5/15
	Pennsylvania	Y	23670 FQ	28810 MW	35190 TQ	USBLS	5/15
	Allentown-Bethlehem-Easton MSA, PA-NJ	Y	26100 FQ	31220 MW	35850 TQ	USBLS	5/15
	Harrisburg-Carlisle MSA, PA	Y	22520 FQ	26750 MW	34370 TQ	USBLS	5/15
	Montgomery County-Bucks County-Chester County PMSA, PA	Y	23900 FQ	29640 MW	36600 TQ	USBLS	5/15
	Philadelphia PMSA, PA	Y	25660 FQ	31180 MW	37880 TQ	USBLS	5/15
	Pittsburgh MSA, PA	Y	23400 FQ	27640 MW	31620 TQ	USBLS	5/15
	Rhode Island	Y	25330 FQ	33410 MW	39720 TQ	USBLS	5/15
	Providence-Warwick MSA, RI-MA	Y	25580 FQ	32520 MW	38870 TQ	USBLS	5/15
	South Carolina	Y	24470 FQ	29250 MW	35160 TQ	USBLS	5/15
	Charleston-North Charleston MSA, SC	Y	27180 FQ	31010 MW	35530 TQ	USBLS	5/15
	Columbia MSA, SC	Y	24120 FQ	28150 MW	32260 TQ	USBLS	5/15
	Greenville-Anderson-Mauldin MSA, SC	Y	23580 FQ	31560 MW	38330 TQ	USBLS	5/15
	South Dakota	Y	21750 FQ	24430 MW	28800 TQ	USBLS	5/15
	Sioux Falls MSA, SD	Y	22060 FQ	24620 MW	28760 TQ	USBLS	5/15
	Tennessee	Y	22290 FQ	26540 MW	31340 TQ	USBLS	5/15

AE Average entry wage	**AWR** Average wage range	**H** Hourly	**LR** Low end range	**MTC** Median total compensation	**TCC** Total cash compensation
AEX Average experienced wage	**B** Biweekly	**HI** Highest wage paid	**M** Monthly	**MW** Median wage paid	**TQ** Third quartile wage
ATC Average total compensation	**D** Daily	**HR** High end range	**MCC** Median cash compensation	**MWR** Median wage range	**W** Weekly
AW Average wage paid	**FQ** First quartile wage	**LO** Lowest wage paid	**ME** Median entry wage	**S** See annotated source	**Y** Yearly

Occupation/Type/Industry	Location	Per	Low	Mid	High	Source	Date
Data Entry Keyer	Knoxville MSA, TN	Y	22440 FQ	26790 MW	29690 TQ	USBLS	5/15
	Memphis MSA, TN-MS-AR	Y	21920 FQ	25540 MW	29410 TQ	USBLS	5/15
	Nashville-Davidson–Murfreesboro–Franklin MSA, TN	Y	24220 FQ	29060 MW	35850 TQ	USBLS	5/15
	Texas	Y	23290 FQ	28260 MW	33800 TQ	USBLS	5/15
	Austin-Round Rock MSA, TX	Y	25430 FQ	28550 MW	32220 TQ	USBLS	5/15
	Dallas-Plano-Irving PMSA, TX	Y	25650 FQ	29570 MW	35630 TQ	USBLS	5/15
	Fort Worth-Arlington PMSA, TX	Y	22280 FQ	27040 MW	31260 TQ	USBLS	5/15
	Houston-The Woodlands-Sugar Land MSA, TX	Y	24040 FQ	29580 MW	36020 TQ	USBLS	5/15
	San Antonio-New Braunfels MSA, TX	Y	24500 FQ	28940 MW	33310 TQ	USBLS	5/15
	Utah	Y	24210 FQ	30560 MW	36080 TQ	USBLS	5/15
	Ogden-Clearfield MSA, UT	Y	20200 FQ	29630 MW	35220 TQ	USBLS	5/15
	Provo-Orem MSA, UT	Y	19690 FQ	22980 MW	27200 TQ	USBLS	5/15
	Salt Lake City MSA, UT	Y	27470 FQ	30570 MW	37050 TQ	USBLS	5/15
	Vermont	Y	27210 FQ	31470 MW	36400 TQ	USBLS	5/15
	Burlington-South Burlington MSA, VT	Y	28320 FQ	32430 MW	36440 TQ	USBLS	5/15
	Virginia	Y	23640 FQ	29150 MW	36700 TQ	USBLS	5/15
	Richmond MSA, VA	Y	23960 FQ	29260 MW	36230 TQ	USBLS	5/15
	Virginia Beach-Norfolk-Newport News MSA, VA-NC	Y	25010 FQ	29030 MW	36230 TQ	USBLS	5/15
	Washington	H	13.29 FQ	16.69 MW	20.71 TQ	WABLS	3/16
	Seattle-Bellevue-Everett PMSA, WA	H	15.43 FQ	18.24 MW	22.49 TQ	WABLS	3/16
	Tacoma-Lakewood PMSA, WA	H	11.87 FQ	14.86 MW	18.98 TQ	WABLS	3/16
	West Virginia	Y	21870 FQ	26040 MW	33010 TQ	USBLS	5/15
	Huntington-Ashland MSA, WV-KY-OH	Y	23070 FQ	27630 MW	32890 TQ	USBLS	5/15
	Morgantown MSA, WV	Y	21350 FQ	23150 MW	25050 TQ	USBLS	5/15
	Wisconsin	Y	21760 FQ	27860 MW	34400 TQ	USBLS	5/15
	Madison MSA, WI	Y	19490 FQ	25080 MW	33780 TQ	USBLS	5/15
	Milwaukee-Waukesha-West Allis MSA, WI	Y	25210 FQ	30770 MW	36440 TQ	USBLS	5/15
	Wyoming	Y	21270 FQ	24920 MW	30960 TQ	USBLS	5/15
	Cheyenne MSA, WY	Y	18790 FQ	22550 MW	27510 TQ	USBLS	5/15
	Puerto Rico	Y	17260 FQ	19040 MW	23940 TQ	USBLS	5/15
	San Juan-Carolina-Caguas MSA, PR	Y	17310 FQ	19140 MW	24520 TQ	USBLS	5/15
	Virgin Islands	Y	22020 FQ	24260 MW	29800 TQ	USBLS	5/15
	Guam	Y	18580 FQ	20970 MW	25910 TQ	USBLS	5/15
Data-Reporting Specialist							
Baccalaureate Institution	United States	Y		32526 MW		CHE01	2015-2016
Master's Institution	United States	Y		36223 MW		CHE01	2015-2016
Research University	United States	Y		34820 MW		CHE01	2015-2016
Data Scientist	United States	Y		116840 MW		TDY01	2016
Central Intelligence Agency	District of Columbia	Y	62338 LO		160300 HI	CIA03	2016
Data Security Analyst	United States	Y	118250-169000 LR			INFOW01	2017
Data Technician							
Police Department, Municipal Government	Seattle, WA	H	23.80 LO		26.54 HI	CSSS	1/13/16
Database Administrator	Alabama	Y	50192 AE	77122 AW	90587 AEX	ALBLS	6/16
	Birmingham-Hoover MSA, AL	Y	59447 AE	85215 AW	98100 AEX	ALBLS	6/16
	Montgomery MSA, AL	Y	58091 AE	80802 AW	92157 AEX	ALBLS	6/16
	Alaska	Y	51490 FQ	77920 MW	102270 TQ	USBLS	5/15
	Anchorage MSA, AK	Y	48630 FQ	86690 MW	110590 TQ	USBLS	5/15
	Arizona	Y	57790 FQ	80960 MW	102230 TQ	USBLS	5/15
	Phoenix-Mesa-Scottsdale MSA, AZ	Y	59590 FQ	84000 MW	105510 TQ	USBLS	5/15
	Tucson MSA, AZ	Y	49830 FQ	66740 MW	80390 TQ	USBLS	5/15
	Arkansas	Y	55570 FQ	72160 MW	97070 TQ	USBLS	5/15
	Little Rock-North Little Rock-Conway MSA, AR	Y	56400 FQ	71740 MW	102610 TQ	USBLS	5/15
	California	H	32.71 FQ	45.88 MW	58.83 TQ	CABLS	1/16-3/16

AE	Average entry wage	AWR	Average wage range	H	Hourly
AEX	Average experienced wage	B	Biweekly	HI	Highest wage paid
ATC	Average total compensation	D	Daily	HR	High end range
AW	Average wage paid	FQ	First quartile wage	LO	Lowest wage paid

LR	Low end range	MTC	Median total compensation
M	Monthly	MW	Median wage paid
MCC	Median cash compensation	MWR	Median wage range
ME	Median entry wage	S	See annotated source

TCC	Total cash compensation
TQ	Third quartile wage
W	Weekly
Y	Yearly

Database Administrator

Occupation/Type/Industry	Location	Per	Low	Mid	High	Source	Date
Database Administrator	Anaheim-Santa Ana-Irvine PMSA, CA	H	28.36 FQ	43.32 MW	55.67 TQ	CABLS	1/16-3/16
	Los Angeles-Long Beach-Glendale PMSA, CA	H	33.85 FQ	47.63 MW	58.51 TQ	CABLS	1/16-3/16
	Oakland-Hayward-Berkeley PMSA, CA	H	32.71 FQ	48.23 MW	58.73 TQ	CABLS	1/16-3/16
	Riverside-San Bernardino-Ontario MSA, CA	H	27.93 FQ	38.28 MW	47.79 TQ	CABLS	1/16-3/16
	Sacramento–Roseville–Arden-Arcade MSA, CA	H	29.57 FQ	38.40 MW	50.47 TQ	CABLS	1/16-3/16
	San Diego-Carlsbad MSA, CA	H	33.77 FQ	46.67 MW	57.56 TQ	CABLS	1/16-3/16
	San Francisco-Redwood City-South San Francisco PMSA, CA	H	38.74 FQ	52.95 MW	66.01 TQ	CABLS	1/16-3/16
	Colorado	Y	75620 FQ	96790 MW	114780 TQ	USBLS	5/15
	Denver-Aurora-Lakewood MSA, CO	Y	81030 FQ	100070 MW	116800 TQ	USBLS	5/15
	Connecticut	Y		89103 MW		CTBLS	1/16-3/16
	Bridgeport-Stamford-Norwalk MSA, CT	Y	55450 FQ	84400 MW	105960 TQ	USBLS	5/15
	Hartford-West Hartford-East Hartford MSA, CT	Y	73160 FQ	96940 MW	117650 TQ	USBLS	5/15
	Delaware	Y	63570 FQ	83490 MW	109370 TQ	USBLS	5/15
	Wilmington PMSA, DE-MD-NJ	Y	65430 FQ	85980 MW	110610 TQ	USBLS	5/15
	District of Columbia	Y	77180 FQ	103180 MW	124230 TQ	USBLS	5/15
	Washington-Arlington-Alexandria PMSA, DC-VA-MD-WV	Y	74670 FQ	103190 MW	124740 TQ	USBLS	5/15
	Florida	H	25.68 AE	38.99 MW	47.11 AEX	FLBLS	7/16-9/16
	Fort Lauderdale-Pompano Beach-Deerfield Beach PMSA, FL	H	28.87 AE	39.27 MW	51.89 AEX	FLBLS	7/16-9/16
	Miami-Miami Beach-Kendall PMSA, FL	H	25.56 AE	40.90 MW	48.00 AEX	FLBLS	7/16-9/16
	Orlando-Kissimmee-Sanford MSA, FL	H	24.12 AE	37.43 MW	44.71 AEX	FLBLS	7/16-9/16
	Tampa-St. Petersburg-Clearwater MSA, FL	H	26.69 AE	42.37 MW	49.79 AEX	FLBLS	7/16-9/16
	Georgia	Y	64000 FQ	80020 MW	103820 TQ	USBLS	5/15
	Atlanta-Sandy Springs-Roswell MSA, GA	Y	65970 FQ	81970 MW	105290 TQ	USBLS	5/15
	Augusta-Richmond County MSA, GA-SC	Y	59130 FQ	74680 MW	94700 TQ	USBLS	5/15
	Hawaii	Y	51250 FQ	68170 MW	85060 TQ	USBLS	5/15
	Urban Honolulu MSA, HI	Y	51740 FQ	68070 MW	83280 TQ	USBLS	5/15
	Idaho	Y	43330 FQ	56800 MW	80540 TQ	USBLS	5/15
	Boise City MSA, ID	Y	42740 FQ	53930 MW	73740 TQ	USBLS	5/15
	Illinois	Y	59680 FQ	78720 MW	103940 TQ	USBLS	5/15
	Chicago-Naperville-Arlington Heights PMSA, IL	Y	60600 FQ	80860 MW	106260 TQ	USBLS	5/15
	Lake County-Kenosha County PMSA, IL-WI	Y	53420 FQ	72900 MW	100060 TQ	USBLS	5/15
	Indiana	Y	52410 FQ	69670 MW	89260 TQ	USBLS	5/15
	Gary PMSA, IN	Y	34180 FQ	38750 MW	73710 TQ	USBLS	5/15
	Indianapolis-Carmel-Anderson MSA, IN	Y	57440 FQ	76640 MW	94910 TQ	USBLS	5/15
	Iowa	Y	58360 FQ	82610 MW	99810 TQ	USBLS	5/15
	Des Moines-West Des Moines MSA, IA	Y	70400 FQ	90100 MW	104670 TQ	USBLS	5/15
	Kansas	Y	56770 FQ	74230 MW	97800 TQ	USBLS	5/15
	Wichita MSA, KS	Y	51720 FQ	73700 MW	95230 TQ	USBLS	5/15
	Kentucky	Y	47920 FQ	66200 MW	90980 TQ	USBLS	5/15
	Louisville-Jefferson County MSA, KY-IN	Y	51790 FQ	75780 MW	92250 TQ	USBLS	5/15
	Louisiana	Y	53330 FQ	64280 MW	82780 TQ	USBLS	5/15
	Baton Rouge MSA, LA	Y	53020 FQ	61630 MW	86780 TQ	USBLS	5/15
	New Orleans-Metairie MSA, LA	Y	56610 FQ	70670 MW	89350 TQ	USBLS	5/15
	Maine	Y	46090 FQ	62000 MW	78900 TQ	USBLS	5/15
	Portland-South Portland MSA, ME	Y	50530 FQ	61730 MW	92520 TQ	USBLS	5/15

AE	Average entry wage	AWR	Average wage range	H	Hourly
AEX	Average experienced wage	B	Biweekly	HI	Highest wage paid
ATC	Average total compensation	D	Daily	HR	High end range
AW	Average wage paid	FQ	First quartile wage	LO	Lowest wage paid

LR	Low end range	MTC	Median total compensation	TCC	Total cash compensation
M	Monthly	MW	Median wage paid	TQ	Third quartile wage
MCC	Median cash compensation	MWR	Median wage range	W	Weekly
ME	Median entry wage	S	See annotated source	Y	Yearly

Occupation/Type/Industry	Location	Per	Low	Mid	High	Source	Date
Database Administrator	Maryland	Y	54383 AE	89563 MW	107154 AEX	MDBLS	4/16
	Baltimore-Columbia-Towson MSA, MD	Y	68600 FQ	91480 MW	116900 TQ	USBLS	5/15
	Salisbury MSA, MD-DE	Y	45390 FQ	62160 MW	84110 TQ	USBLS	5/15
	Massachusetts	Y	62380 FQ	79520 MW	104180 TQ	USBLS	5/15
	Boston-Cambridge-Newton NECTA, MA	Y	63340 FQ	81150 MW	105540 TQ	USBLS	5/15
	Worcester MSA, MA-CT	Y	59330 FQ	79880 MW	106120 TQ	USBLS	5/15
	Michigan	Y	63820 FQ	85040 MW	103390 TQ	USBLS	5/15
	Detroit-Dearborn-Livonia PMSA, MI	Y	66560 FQ	90350 MW	108420 TQ	USBLS	5/15
	Grand Rapids-Wyoming MSA, MI	Y	61960 FQ	73430 MW	87670 TQ	USBLS	5/15
	Minnesota	Y	69576 FQ	92166 MW	109051 TQ	MNBLS	1/16-3/16
	Minneapolis-St. Paul-Bloomington MSA, MN-WI	Y	71884 FQ	93507 MW	110160 TQ	MNBLS	1/16-3/16
	Mississippi	Y	55620 FQ	66120 MW	81570 TQ	USBLS	5/15
	Jackson MSA, MS	Y	57420 FQ	66220 MW	83600 TQ	USBLS	5/15
	Missouri	Y	57000 FQ	79350 MW	98580 TQ	USBLS	5/15
	Kansas City MSA, MO-KS	Y	56430 FQ	74800 MW	96310 TQ	USBLS	5/15
	St. Louis MSA, MO-IL	Y	69730 FQ	89020 MW	105550 TQ	USBLS	5/15
	Montana	Y	43580 FQ	57060 MW	69550 TQ	USBLS	5/15
	Billings MSA, MT	Y	48360 FQ	58580 MW	73930 TQ	USBLS	5/15
	Nebraska	Y	56110 FQ	76880 MW	96250 TQ	NEBLS	7/16-9/16
	Omaha-Council Bluffs MSA, NE-IA	Y	59350 FQ	82975 MW	99090 TQ	NEBLS	7/16-9/16
	Nevada	Y	54380 FQ	77340 MW	101080 TQ	USBLS	5/15
	Las Vegas-Henderson-Paradise MSA, NV	Y	50810 FQ	78180 MW	105350 TQ	USBLS	5/15
	New Hampshire	H	25.91 AE	40.14 MW	48.90 AEX	NHBLS	6/16
	Nashua NECTA, NH-MA	Y	55480 FQ	61100 MW	90080 TQ	USBLS	5/15
	New Jersey	Y	81020 FQ	105640 MW	128570 TQ	USBLS	5/15
	Camden PMSA, NJ	Y	63520 FQ	89970 MW	109400 TQ	USBLS	5/15
	Newark PMSA, NJ-PA	Y	82630 FQ	107640 MW	130490 TQ	USBLS	5/15
	Trenton MSA, NJ	Y	85230 FQ	103600 MW	120440 TQ	USBLS	5/15
	New Mexico	Y	54100 FQ	69620 MW	90010 TQ	USBLS	5/15
	Albuquerque MSA, NM	Y	57350 FQ	73080 MW	91820 TQ	USBLS	5/15
	New York	Y	51100 AE	85210 MW	107780 AEX	NYBLS	1/16-3/16
	Buffalo-Cheektowaga-Niagara Falls MSA, NY	Y	47610 FQ	71280 MW	101920 TQ	USBLS	5/15
	Nassau County-Suffolk County PMSA, NY	Y	56160 FQ	83300 MW	104930 TQ	USBLS	5/15
	New York-Jersey City-White Plains PMSA, NY-NJ	Y	67980 FQ	94700 MW	125530 TQ	USBLS	5/15
	Rochester MSA, NY	Y	50670 FQ	73050 MW	99440 TQ	USBLS	5/15
	North Carolina	Y	59690 FQ	83540 MW	104940 TQ	USBLS	5/15
	Charlotte-Concord-Gastonia MSA, NC-SC	Y	66880 FQ	92790 MW	114630 TQ	USBLS	5/15
	Raleigh MSA, NC	Y	71310 FQ	90180 MW	108540 TQ	USBLS	5/15
	North Dakota	Y	57700 FQ	74220 MW	94340 TQ	USBLS	5/15
	Fargo MSA, ND-MN	Y	57950 FQ	73180 MW	95060 TQ	USBLS	5/15
	Ohio	Y	58220 FQ	75890 MW	97140 TQ	USBLS	5/15
	Cincinnati MSA, OH-KY-IN	Y	60990 FQ	77300 MW	101040 TQ	USBLS	5/15
	Cleveland-Elyria MSA, OH	Y	52370 FQ	61710 MW	84870 TQ	USBLS	5/15
	Columbus MSA, OH	Y	67520 FQ	87860 MW	105220 TQ	USBLS	5/15
	Oklahoma	Y	49990 FQ	67800 MW	89720 TQ	USBLS	5/15
	Oklahoma City MSA, OK	Y	52110 FQ	70900 MW	94000 TQ	USBLS	5/15
	Tulsa MSA, OK	Y	58980 FQ	75530 MW	94710 TQ	USBLS	5/15
	Oregon	H	32.18 FQ	42.07 MW	52.07 TQ	ORBLS	2016
	Portland-Vancouver-Hillsboro MSA, OR-WA	Y	65650 FQ	86820 MW	107220 TQ	USBLS	5/15
	Pennsylvania	Y	56770 FQ	73900 MW	97240 TQ	USBLS	5/15
	Allentown-Bethlehem-Easton MSA, PA-NJ	Y	58780 FQ	77230 MW	102710 TQ	USBLS	5/15
	Harrisburg-Carlisle MSA, PA	Y	62480 FQ	72210 MW	85340 TQ	USBLS	5/15
	Montgomery County-Bucks County-Chester County PMSA, PA	Y	59640 FQ	86500 MW	111750 TQ	USBLS	5/15
	Philadelphia PMSA, PA	Y	57650 FQ	75140 MW	97890 TQ	USBLS	5/15
	Pittsburgh MSA, PA	Y	55830 FQ	72470 MW	93830 TQ	USBLS	5/15
	Rhode Island	Y	66860 FQ	89700 MW	110700 TQ	USBLS	5/15

Occupation/Type/Industry	Location	Per	Low	Mid	High	Source	Date
Database Administrator	Providence-Warwick MSA, RI-MA	Y	67040 FQ	89510 MW	110370 TQ	USBLS	5/15
	South Carolina	Y	50070 FQ	66370 MW	93410 TQ	USBLS	5/15
	Charleston-North Charleston MSA, SC	Y	56390 FQ	78490 MW	100910 TQ	USBLS	5/15
	Columbia MSA, SC	Y	50750 FQ	64190 MW	87700 TQ	USBLS	5/15
	Greenville-Anderson-Mauldin MSA, SC	Y	49100 FQ	72050 MW	104360 TQ	USBLS	5/15
	South Dakota	Y	57970 FQ	70550 MW	84780 TQ	USBLS	5/15
	Sioux Falls MSA, SD	Y	57650 FQ	69500 MW	82930 TQ	USBLS	5/15
	Tennessee	Y	59960 FQ	81850 MW	101360 TQ	USBLS	5/15
	Knoxville MSA, TN	Y	53390 FQ	76300 MW	94540 TQ	USBLS	5/15
	Memphis MSA, TN-MS-AR	Y	61990 FQ	82580 MW	98110 TQ	USBLS	5/15
	Nashville-Davidson–Murfreesboro–Franklin MSA, TN	Y	66270 FQ	86500 MW	108530 TQ	USBLS	5/15
	Texas	Y	56830 FQ	75890 MW	100430 TQ	USBLS	5/15
	Austin-Round Rock MSA, TX	Y	59570 FQ	75780 MW	96350 TQ	USBLS	5/15
	Dallas-Plano-Irving PMSA, TX	Y	65160 FQ	85410 MW	110200 TQ	USBLS	5/15
	Fort Worth-Arlington PMSA, TX	Y	57990 FQ	78910 MW	102690 TQ	USBLS	5/15
	Houston-The Woodlands-Sugar Land MSA, TX	Y	56410 FQ	73460 MW	100790 TQ	USBLS	5/15
	San Antonio-New Braunfels MSA, TX	Y	52190 FQ	74800 MW	98000 TQ	USBLS	5/15
	Utah	Y	57980 FQ	82520 MW	103760 TQ	USBLS	5/15
	Ogden-Clearfield MSA, UT	Y	60600 FQ	84560 MW	97550 TQ	USBLS	5/15
	Provo-Orem MSA, UT	Y	45780 FQ	60670 MW	91540 TQ	USBLS	5/15
	Salt Lake City MSA, UT	Y	71260 FQ	90600 MW	110890 TQ	USBLS	5/15
	Vermont	Y	52600 FQ	64140 MW	81110 TQ	USBLS	5/15
	Burlington-South Burlington MSA, VT	Y	51150 FQ	69950 MW	96840 TQ	USBLS	5/15
	Virginia	Y	64870 FQ	91860 MW	118900 TQ	USBLS	5/15
	Richmond MSA, VA	Y	72280 FQ	92890 MW	111660 TQ	USBLS	5/15
	Virginia Beach-Norfolk-Newport News MSA, VA-NC	Y	47990 FQ	70140 MW	89730 TQ	USBLS	5/15
	Washington	H	33.05 FQ	45.01 MW	55.95 TQ	WABLS	3/16
	Seattle-Bellevue-Everett PMSA, WA	H	35.88 FQ	47.62 MW	57.33 TQ	WABLS	3/16
	Tacoma-Lakewood PMSA, WA	H	28.12 FQ	38.71 MW	51.74 TQ	WABLS	3/16
	West Virginia	Y	47960 FQ	61040 MW	75010 TQ	USBLS	5/15
	Huntington-Ashland MSA, WV-KY-OH	Y	45960 FQ	57820 MW	69020 TQ	USBLS	5/15
	Wisconsin	Y	58470 FQ	73980 MW	92130 TQ	USBLS	5/15
	Madison MSA, WI	Y	59970 FQ	72210 MW	87110 TQ	USBLS	5/15
	Milwaukee-Waukesha-West Allis MSA, WI	Y	64490 FQ	81180 MW	98710 TQ	USBLS	5/15
	Wyoming	Y	45500 FQ	56340 MW	70680 TQ	USBLS	5/15
	Cheyenne MSA, WY	Y	45010 FQ	52220 MW	61570 TQ	USBLS	5/15
	Puerto Rico	Y	36720 FQ	49500 MW	62000 TQ	USBLS	5/15
	San Juan-Carolina-Caguas MSA, PR	Y	38490 FQ	51080 MW	62880 TQ	USBLS	5/15
Dean of Academics Public Schools	Baldwin County, AL	Y			117000 HI	BCPSSS	2016-2017
Debt Analyst City Treasurer's Office	Sacramento, CA	Y		64791 AW		CACIT	6/28/16
Delegate United States House of Representatives	United States	Y			174000 HI	OPM01	2017
Delinquent Tax Supervisor County Government	Oakland County, MI	B	2014 LO		2628 HI	MIOAK2	10/1/16
Delivery Technician Home Healthcare	United States	H		14.00 AW		HCARE2	2015
Demand Planner	United States	Y	50649 LO		86160 HI	BHR01	2016
Demographer State Government	Ohio	H	34.89 LO		41.20 HI	OHGOV	2015

AE	Average entry wage	AWR	Average wage range	H	Hourly	LR	Low end range	MTC	Median total compensation	TCC	Total cash compensation
AEX	Average experienced wage	B	Biweekly	HI	Highest wage paid	M	Monthly	MW	Median wage paid	TQ	Third quartile wage
ATC	Average total compensation	D	Daily	HR	High end range	MCC	Median cash compensation	MWR	Median wage range	W	Weekly
AW	Average wage paid	FQ	First quartile wage	LO	Lowest wage paid	ME	Median entry wage	S	See annotated source	Y	Yearly

Occupation/Type/Industry	Location	Per	Low	Mid	High	Source	Date
Demonstrator and Product Promoter	Alabama	Y	17924 AE	28576 AW	33903 AEX	ALBLS	6/16
	Birmingham-Hoover MSA, AL	Y	23074 AE	31855 AW	36251 AEX	ALBLS	6/16
	Alaska	Y	21860 FQ	24180 MW	29200 TQ	USBLS	5/15
	Anchorage MSA, AK	Y	22320 FQ	25150 MW	30240 TQ	USBLS	5/15
	Arizona	Y	21720 FQ	24040 MW	28880 TQ	USBLS	5/15
	Phoenix-Mesa-Scottsdale MSA, AZ	Y	21960 FQ	24140 MW	29020 TQ	USBLS	5/15
	Tucson MSA, AZ	Y	18470 FQ	22230 MW	28300 TQ	USBLS	5/15
	Little Rock-North Little Rock-Conway MSA, AR	Y	17100 FQ	18570 MW	21350 TQ	USBLS	5/15
	California	H	10.79 FQ	13.07 MW	16.57 TQ	CABLS	1/16-3/16
	Anaheim-Santa Ana-Irvine PMSA, CA	H	10.58 FQ	12.51 MW	17.06 TQ	CABLS	1/16-3/16
	Los Angeles-Long Beach-Glendale PMSA, CA	H	10.18 FQ	12.05 MW	14.84 TQ	CABLS	1/16-3/16
	Oakland-Hayward-Berkeley PMSA, CA	H	10.66 FQ	12.36 MW	18.02 TQ	CABLS	1/16-3/16
	Riverside-San Bernardino-Ontario MSA, CA	H	10.86 FQ	12.88 MW	15.06 TQ	CABLS	1/16-3/16
	Sacramento–Roseville–Arden-Arcade MSA, CA	H	11.15 FQ	12.78 MW	14.28 TQ	CABLS	1/16-3/16
	San Diego-Carlsbad MSA, CA	H	10.46 FQ	11.58 MW	14.62 TQ	CABLS	1/16-3/16
	San Francisco-Redwood City-South San Francisco PMSA, CA	H	11.32 FQ	13.65 MW	16.68 TQ	CABLS	1/16-3/16
	Colorado	Y	24300 FQ	30780 MW	43490 TQ	USBLS	5/15
	Denver-Aurora-Lakewood MSA, CO	Y	26740 FQ	31450 MW	42320 TQ	USBLS	5/15
	Connecticut	Y		29264 MW		CTBLS	1/16-3/16
	Bridgeport-Stamford-Norwalk MSA, CT	Y	23640 FQ	32760 MW	41290 TQ	USBLS	5/15
	Hartford-West Hartford-East Hartford MSA, CT	Y	25330 FQ	29610 MW	39290 TQ	USBLS	5/15
	Delaware	Y	21520 FQ	27640 MW	35030 TQ	USBLS	5/15
	Wilmington PMSA, DE-MD-NJ	Y	23100 FQ	30800 MW	36830 TQ	USBLS	5/15
	District of Columbia	Y	23490 FQ	30760 MW	38600 TQ	USBLS	5/15
	Washington-Arlington-Alexandria PMSA, DC-VA-MD-WV	Y	25450 FQ	31060 MW	43830 TQ	USBLS	5/15
	Florida	H	9.77 AE	11.71 MW	16.88 AEX	FLBLS	7/16-9/16
	Fort Lauderdale-Pompano Beach-Deerfield Beach PMSA, FL	H	9.02 AE	10.22 MW	13.38 AEX	FLBLS	7/16-9/16
	Miami-Miami Beach-Kendall PMSA, FL	H	9.59 AE	11.91 MW	18.14 AEX	FLBLS	7/16-9/16
	Orlando-Kissimmee-Sanford MSA, FL	H	10.16 AE	11.50 MW	14.89 AEX	FLBLS	7/16-9/16
	Tampa-St. Petersburg-Clearwater MSA, FL	H	10.28 AE	14.79 MW	19.72 AEX	FLBLS	7/16-9/16
	Georgia	Y	17380 FQ	19580 MW	35690 TQ	USBLS	5/15
	Atlanta-Sandy Springs-Roswell MSA, GA	Y	17240 FQ	19240 MW	32370 TQ	USBLS	5/15
	Hawaii	Y	21510 FQ	23960 MW	29060 TQ	USBLS	5/15
	Urban Honolulu MSA, HI	Y	21960 FQ	24850 MW	29320 TQ	USBLS	5/15
	Idaho	Y	22920 FQ	26160 MW	29940 TQ	USBLS	5/15
	Boise City MSA, ID	Y	23370 FQ	26650 MW	30240 TQ	USBLS	5/15
	Illinois	Y	21900 FQ	24730 MW	36770 TQ	USBLS	5/15
	Chicago-Naperville-Arlington Heights PMSA, IL	Y	23300 FQ	31740 MW	41350 TQ	USBLS	5/15
	Lake County-Kenosha County PMSA, IL-WI	Y	25670 FQ	30530 MW	42890 TQ	USBLS	5/15
	Indiana	Y	19770 FQ	23920 MW	34070 TQ	USBLS	5/15
	Gary PMSA, IN	Y	19830 FQ	21950 MW	23940 TQ	USBLS	5/15
	Indianapolis-Carmel-Anderson MSA, IN	Y	22190 FQ	26920 MW	37590 TQ	USBLS	5/15
	Iowa	Y	19760 FQ	22570 MW	26320 TQ	USBLS	5/15
	Des Moines-West Des Moines MSA, IA	Y	19660 FQ	22150 MW	24380 TQ	USBLS	5/15
	Kansas	Y	17430 FQ	19410 MW	23870 TQ	USBLS	5/15
	Wichita MSA, KS	Y	16930 FQ	18300 MW	19680 TQ	USBLS	5/15

AE	Average entry wage	AWR	Average wage range	H	Hourly
AEX	Average experienced wage	B	Biweekly	HI	Highest wage paid
ATC	Average total compensation	D	Daily	HR	High end range
AW	Average wage paid	FQ	First quartile wage	LO	Lowest wage paid

LR	Low end range	MTC	Median total compensation
M	Monthly	MW	Median wage paid
MCC	Median cash compensation	MWR	Median wage range
ME	Median entry wage	S	See annotated source

TCC	Total cash compensation
TQ	Third quartile wage
W	Weekly
Y	Yearly

Occupation/Type/Industry	Location	Per	Low	Mid	High	Source	Date
Demonstrator and Product Promoter	Kentucky	Y	21100 FQ	24100 MW	30710 TQ	USBLS	5/15
	Louisville-Jefferson County MSA, KY-IN	Y	21480 FQ	24770 MW	31780 TQ	USBLS	5/15
	Louisiana	Y	20420 FQ	24020 MW	34960 TQ	USBLS	5/15
	New Orleans-Metairie MSA, LA	Y	20180 FQ	22190 MW	24210 TQ	USBLS	5/15
	Maine	Y	21560 FQ	23940 MW	33640 TQ	USBLS	5/15
	Portland-South Portland MSA, ME	Y	21270 FQ	23520 MW	43680 TQ	USBLS	5/15
	Maryland	Y	17815 AE	26646 MW	31061 AEX	MDBLS	4/16
	Baltimore-Columbia-Towson MSA, MD	Y	17660 FQ	18680 MW	28380 TQ	USBLS	5/15
	Salisbury MSA, MD-DE	Y	18960 FQ	22250 MW	29450 TQ	USBLS	5/15
	Massachusetts	Y	23680 FQ	32350 MW	50990 TQ	USBLS	5/15
	Boston-Cambridge-Newton NECTA, MA	Y	22660 FQ	30120 MW	47670 TQ	USBLS	5/15
	Worcester MSA, MA-CT	Y	25230 FQ	30300 MW	51030 TQ	USBLS	5/15
	Michigan	Y	20790 FQ	23510 MW	29950 TQ	USBLS	5/15
	Grand Rapids-Wyoming MSA, MI	Y	20930 FQ	23870 MW	29980 TQ	USBLS	5/15
	Minnesota	Y	19814 FQ	21901 MW	24069 TQ	MNBLS	1/16-3/16
	Minneapolis-St. Paul-Bloomington MSA, MN-WI	Y	19865 FQ	21760 MW	23797 TQ	MNBLS	1/16-3/16
	Mississippi	Y	19490 FQ	28320 MW	45370 TQ	USBLS	5/15
	Jackson MSA, MS	Y	25100 FQ	50470 MW	57550 TQ	USBLS	5/15
	Missouri	Y	18880 FQ	21580 MW	24120 TQ	USBLS	5/15
	Kansas City MSA, MO-KS	Y	17780 FQ	20410 MW	23760 TQ	USBLS	5/15
	St. Louis MSA, MO-IL	Y	18900 FQ	21580 MW	24070 TQ	USBLS	5/15
	Montana	Y	20720 FQ	23310 MW	27040 TQ	USBLS	5/15
	Nebraska	Y	19650 FQ	22555 MW	26300 TQ	NEBLS	7/16-9/16
	Omaha-Council Bluffs MSA, NE-IA	Y	19965 FQ	22745 MW	26935 TQ	NEBLS	7/16-9/16
	Nevada	Y	21750 FQ	24280 MW	29450 TQ	USBLS	5/15
	Las Vegas-Henderson-Paradise MSA, NV	Y	21280 FQ	23320 MW	27870 TQ	USBLS	5/15
	New Hampshire	H	10.41 AE	11.50 MW	14.14 AEX	NHBLS	6/16
	New Jersey	Y	19990 FQ	25110 MW	30340 TQ	USBLS	5/15
	Camden PMSA, NJ	Y	20810 FQ	25800 MW	28890 TQ	USBLS	5/15
	Newark PMSA, NJ-PA	Y	20220 FQ	29340 MW	44980 TQ	USBLS	5/15
	New Mexico	Y	24960 FQ	28710 MW	36060 TQ	USBLS	5/15
	Albuquerque MSA, NM	Y	24860 FQ	28590 MW	36020 TQ	USBLS	5/15
	New York	Y	21760 AE	28870 MW	42850 AEX	NYBLS	1/16-3/16
	Buffalo-Cheektowaga-Niagara Falls MSA, NY	Y	22590 FQ	31130 MW	45040 TQ	USBLS	5/15
	Nassau County-Suffolk County PMSA, NY	Y	21650 FQ	23960 MW	32580 TQ	USBLS	5/15
	New York-Jersey City-White Plains PMSA, NY-NJ	Y	22090 FQ	25670 MW	39440 TQ	USBLS	5/15
	Rochester MSA, NY	Y	19540 FQ	21630 MW	25950 TQ	USBLS	5/15
	North Carolina	Y	18180 FQ	22840 MW	28840 TQ	USBLS	5/15
	Charlotte-Concord-Gastonia MSA, NC-SC	Y	18020 FQ	21900 MW	29510 TQ	USBLS	5/15
	Raleigh MSA, NC	Y	18790 FQ	23560 MW	35100 TQ	USBLS	5/15
	North Dakota	Y	25270 FQ	28170 MW	31090 TQ	USBLS	5/15
	Fargo MSA, ND-MN	Y	26780 FQ	29030 MW	31310 TQ	USBLS	5/15
	Ohio	Y	20140 FQ	22710 MW	26680 TQ	USBLS	5/15
	Cincinnati MSA, OH-KY-IN	Y	19110 FQ	22210 MW	28100 TQ	USBLS	5/15
	Cleveland-Elyria MSA, OH	Y	18520 FQ	19970 MW	29170 TQ	USBLS	5/15
	Columbus MSA, OH	Y	20060 FQ	24630 MW	35430 TQ	USBLS	5/15
	Oklahoma	Y	23920 FQ	34380 MW	52490 TQ	USBLS	5/15
	Oklahoma City MSA, OK	Y	22900 FQ	50310 MW	74250 TQ	USBLS	5/15
	Tulsa MSA, OK	Y	24120 FQ	29010 MW	35600 TQ	USBLS	5/15
	Oregon	H	10.76 FQ	12.47 MW	14.63 TQ	ORBLS	2016
	Portland-Vancouver-Hillsboro MSA, OR-WA	Y	22240 FQ	25690 MW	29660 TQ	USBLS	5/15
	Pennsylvania	Y	21490 FQ	24950 MW	36970 TQ	USBLS	5/15
	Harrisburg-Carlisle MSA, PA	Y	20930 FQ	22580 MW	24220 TQ	USBLS	5/15
	Montgomery County-Bucks County-Chester County PMSA, PA	Y	22620 FQ	32820 MW	48130 TQ	USBLS	5/15
	Philadelphia PMSA, PA	Y	26720 FQ	30240 MW	35250 TQ	USBLS	5/15

AE	Average entry wage	AWR	Average wage range	H	Hourly
AEX	Average experienced wage	B	Biweekly	HI	Highest wage paid
ATC	Average total compensation	D	Daily	HR	High end range
AW	Average wage paid	FQ	First quartile wage	LO	Lowest wage paid

LR	Low end range	MTC	Median total compensation
M	Monthly	MCC	Median cash compensation
MCC	Median cash compensation	MWR	Median wage range
ME	Median entry wage	S	See annotated source

TCC	Total cash compensation		
TQ	Third quartile wage		
W	Weekly		
Y	Yearly		

Occupation/Type/Industry	Location	Per	Low	Mid	High	Source	Date
Demonstrator and Product Promoter	Pittsburgh MSA, PA	Y	20430 FQ	23360 MW	29610 TQ	USBLS	5/15
	Rhode Island	Y	28640 FQ	39180 MW	44570 TQ	USBLS	5/15
	Providence-Warwick MSA, RI-MA	Y	28740 FQ	39350 MW	44780 TQ	USBLS	5/15
	South Carolina	Y	19980 FQ	22690 MW	30570 TQ	USBLS	5/15
	Charleston-North Charleston MSA, SC	Y	18450 FQ	26810 MW	41490 TQ	USBLS	5/15
	Columbia MSA, SC	Y	20840 FQ	24010 MW	34490 TQ	USBLS	5/15
	Greenville-Anderson-Mauldin MSA, SC	Y	21960 FQ	27220 MW	39130 TQ	USBLS	5/15
	South Dakota	Y	19180 FQ	20970 MW	23450 TQ	USBLS	5/15
	Tennessee	Y	22100 FQ	33080 MW	38620 TQ	USBLS	5/15
	Memphis MSA, TN-MS-AR	Y	32490 FQ	38230 MW	44850 TQ	USBLS	5/15
	Nashville-Davidson–Murfreesboro–Franklin MSA, TN	Y	22700 FQ	33590 MW	38360 TQ	USBLS	5/15
	Texas	Y	22110 FQ	25060 MW	32030 TQ	USBLS	5/15
	Austin-Round Rock MSA, TX	Y	22730 FQ	26820 MW	34010 TQ	USBLS	5/15
	Dallas-Plano-Irving PMSA, TX	Y	22540 FQ	26310 MW	31340 TQ	USBLS	5/15
	Fort Worth-Arlington PMSA, TX	Y	20610 FQ	22720 MW	24970 TQ	USBLS	5/15
	Houston-The Woodlands-Sugar Land MSA, TX	Y	22280 FQ	24890 MW	35140 TQ	USBLS	5/15
	San Antonio-New Braunfels MSA, TX	Y	21970 FQ	24960 MW	28730 TQ	USBLS	5/15
	Utah	Y	21750 FQ	24090 MW	28290 TQ	USBLS	5/15
	Ogden-Clearfield MSA, UT	Y	22010 FQ	25660 MW	30600 TQ	USBLS	5/15
	Salt Lake City MSA, UT	Y	21910 FQ	24240 MW	28280 TQ	USBLS	5/15
	Vermont	Y	25540 FQ	29500 MW	36010 TQ	USBLS	5/15
	Burlington-South Burlington MSA, VT	Y	26520 FQ	30050 MW	36120 TQ	USBLS	5/15
	Virginia	Y	25380 FQ	30320 MW	43730 TQ	USBLS	5/15
	Richmond MSA, VA	Y	23700 FQ	29770 MW	44210 TQ	USBLS	5/15
	Virginia Beach-Norfolk-Newport News MSA, VA-NC	Y	22670 FQ	27270 MW	33700 TQ	USBLS	5/15
	Washington	H	11.18 FQ	12.65 MW	14.30 TQ	WABLS	3/16
	Seattle-Bellevue-Everett PMSA, WA	H	11.93 FQ	13.22 MW	14.56 TQ	WABLS	3/16
	Tacoma-Lakewood PMSA, WA	H	10.35 FQ	11.07 MW	11.79 TQ	WABLS	3/16
	West Virginia	Y	20930 FQ	24740 MW	34320 TQ	USBLS	5/15
	Wisconsin	Y	20140 FQ	22620 MW	27000 TQ	USBLS	5/15
	Madison MSA, WI	Y	21980 FQ	25280 MW	29380 TQ	USBLS	5/15
	Milwaukee-Waukesha-West Allis MSA, WI	Y	18700 FQ	22700 MW	30610 TQ	USBLS	5/15
	Puerto Rico	Y	17020 FQ	18460 MW	20110 TQ	USBLS	5/15
	San Juan-Carolina-Caguas MSA, PR	Y	17060 FQ	18550 MW	20510 TQ	USBLS	5/15
Dental Assistant	Alabama	Y	24649 AE	32165 AW	35933 AEX	ALBLS	6/16
	Birmingham-Hoover MSA, AL	Y	27388 AE	34070 AW	37406 AEX	ALBLS	6/16
	Alaska	Y	37760 FQ	44620 MW	51720 TQ	USBLS	5/15
	Anchorage MSA, AK	Y	40010 FQ	45660 MW	52090 TQ	USBLS	5/15
	Arizona	Y	30340 FQ	35940 MW	42970 TQ	USBLS	5/15
	Phoenix-Mesa-Scottsdale MSA, AZ	Y	31270 FQ	36630 MW	43970 TQ	USBLS	5/15
	Tucson MSA, AZ	Y	27800 FQ	33960 MW	40680 TQ	USBLS	5/15
	Arkansas	Y	27170 FQ	32720 MW	37630 TQ	USBLS	5/15
	Little Rock-North Little Rock-Conway MSA, AR	Y	29580 FQ	34800 MW	39550 TQ	USBLS	5/15
	California	H	14.71 FQ	18.18 MW	22.98 TQ	CABLS	1/16-3/16
	Anaheim-Santa Ana-Irvine PMSA, CA	H	13.08 FQ	16.29 MW	20.40 TQ	CABLS	1/16-3/16
	Los Angeles-Long Beach-Glendale PMSA, CA	H	14.31 FQ	17.81 MW	22.27 TQ	CABLS	1/16-3/16
	Oakland-Hayward-Berkeley PMSA, CA	H	16.95 FQ	19.05 MW	25.12 TQ	CABLS	1/16-3/16
	Riverside-San Bernardino-Ontario MSA, CA	H	12.01 FQ	15.85 MW	19.14 TQ	CABLS	1/16-3/16
	Sacramento–Roseville–Arden-Arcade MSA, CA	H	15.07 FQ	19.63 MW	24.53 TQ	CABLS	1/16-3/16
	San Diego-Carlsbad MSA, CA	H	16.25 FQ	19.15 MW	22.88 TQ	CABLS	1/16-3/16

AE	Average entry wage	**AWR** Average wage range	**H** Hourly	**LR** Low end range	**MTC** Median total compensation	**TCC** Total cash compensation
AEX	Average experienced wage	**B** Biweekly	**HI** Highest wage paid	**M** Monthly	**MW** Median wage paid	**TQ** Third quartile wage
ATC	Average total compensation	**D** Daily	**HR** High end range	**MCC** Median cash compensation	**MWR** Median wage range	**W** Weekly
AW	Average wage paid	**FQ** First quartile wage	**LO** Lowest wage paid	**ME** Median entry wage	**S** See annotated source	**Y** Yearly

Occupation/Type/Industry	Location	Per	Low	Mid	High	Source	Date
Dental Assistant	San Francisco-Redwood City-South San Francisco PMSA, CA	H	17.86 FQ	21.39 MW	25.99 TQ	CABLS	1/16-3/16
	Colorado	Y	31410 FQ	37340 MW	45680 TQ	USBLS	5/15
	Denver-Aurora-Lakewood MSA, CO	Y	33580 FQ	39310 MW	48360 TQ	USBLS	5/15
	Connecticut	Y		42288 MW		CTBLS	1/16-3/16
	Bridgeport-Stamford-Norwalk MSA, CT	Y	35360 FQ	42090 MW	48340 TQ	USBLS	5/15
	Hartford-West Hartford-East Hartford MSA, CT	Y	34780 FQ	42870 MW	48030 TQ	USBLS	5/15
	Delaware	Y	32340 FQ	37770 MW	44660 TQ	USBLS	5/15
	Wilmington PMSA, DE-MD-NJ	Y	32900 FQ	39110 MW	45680 TQ	USBLS	5/15
	District of Columbia	Y	30660 FQ	40680 MW	51630 TQ	USBLS	5/15
	Washington-Arlington-Alexandria PMSA, DC-VA-MD-WV	Y	33570 FQ	39020 MW	49240 TQ	USBLS	5/15
	Florida	H	13.05 AE	17.53 MW	20.29 AEX	FLBLS	7/16-9/16
	Fort Lauderdale-Pompano Beach-Deerfield Beach PMSA, FL	H	14.27 AE	17.68 MW	21.55 AEX	FLBLS	7/16-9/16
	Miami-Miami Beach-Kendall PMSA, FL	H	11.79 AE	15.38 MW	18.80 AEX	FLBLS	7/16-9/16
	Orlando-Kissimmee-Sanford MSA, FL	H	15.37 AE	17.84 MW	20.07 AEX	FLBLS	7/16-9/16
	Tampa-St. Petersburg-Clearwater MSA, FL	H	13.12 AE	17.48 MW	20.20 AEX	FLBLS	7/16-9/16
	Georgia	Y	29370 FQ	35750 MW	42850 TQ	USBLS	5/15
	Atlanta-Sandy Springs-Roswell MSA, GA	Y	31640 FQ	37610 MW	44750 TQ	USBLS	5/15
	Augusta-Richmond County MSA, GA-SC	Y	24600 FQ	30420 MW	36830 TQ	USBLS	5/15
	Hawaii	Y	29000 FQ	34450 MW	39000 TQ	USBLS	5/15
	Urban Honolulu MSA, HI	Y	28960 FQ	34070 MW	38160 TQ	USBLS	5/15
	Idaho	Y	29030 FQ	33790 MW	37820 TQ	USBLS	5/15
	Boise City MSA, ID	Y	31760 FQ	35370 MW	38970 TQ	USBLS	5/15
	Illinois	Y	30350 FQ	36620 MW	44000 TQ	USBLS	5/15
	Chicago-Naperville-Arlington Heights PMSA, IL	Y	30950 FQ	37650 MW	44730 TQ	USBLS	5/15
	Lake County-Kenosha County PMSA, IL-WI	Y	33700 FQ	38550 MW	45510 TQ	USBLS	5/15
	Indiana	Y	30640 FQ	35590 MW	41240 TQ	USBLS	5/15
	Gary PMSA, IN	Y	27770 FQ	34200 MW	38690 TQ	USBLS	5/15
	Indianapolis-Carmel-Anderson MSA, IN	Y	32780 FQ	36930 MW	43090 TQ	USBLS	5/15
	Iowa	Y	31450 FQ	37610 MW	44700 TQ	USBLS	5/15
	Des Moines-West Des Moines MSA, IA	Y	30810 FQ	40520 MW	47040 TQ	USBLS	5/15
	Kansas	Y	26890 FQ	33350 MW	40370 TQ	USBLS	5/15
	Wichita MSA, KS	Y	28450 FQ	33620 MW	41770 TQ	USBLS	5/15
	Kentucky	Y	26650 FQ	33470 MW	39740 TQ	USBLS	5/15
	Louisville-Jefferson County MSA, KY-IN	Y	31940 FQ	38610 MW	45240 TQ	USBLS	5/15
	Louisiana	Y	24060 FQ	28540 MW	34330 TQ	USBLS	5/15
	Baton Rouge MSA, LA	Y	25430 FQ	31370 MW	37560 TQ	USBLS	5/15
	New Orleans-Metairie MSA, LA	Y	25520 FQ	28770 MW	33550 TQ	USBLS	5/15
	Maine	Y	30570 FQ	36310 MW	44470 TQ	USBLS	5/15
	Portland-South Portland MSA, ME	Y	30720 FQ	40200 MW	52220 TQ	USBLS	5/15
	Maryland	Y	28602 AE	39262 MW	44593 AEX	MDBLS	4/16
	Baltimore-Columbia-Towson MSA, MD	Y	33520 FQ	40640 MW	47040 TQ	USBLS	5/15
	Salisbury MSA, MD-DE	Y	32270 FQ	36250 MW	42440 TQ	USBLS	5/15
	Massachusetts	Y	35210 FQ	42070 MW	48810 TQ	USBLS	5/15
	Boston-Cambridge-Newton NECTA, MA	Y	35600 FQ	42340 MW	49080 TQ	USBLS	5/15
	Worcester MSA, MA-CT	Y	37840 FQ	44000 MW	49360 TQ	USBLS	5/15
	Michigan	Y	28820 FQ	34740 MW	40590 TQ	USBLS	5/15
	Detroit-Dearborn-Livonia PMSA, MI	Y	26900 FQ	33090 MW	41960 TQ	USBLS	5/15

AE Average entry wage	**AWR** Average wage range	**H** Hourly	**LR** Low end range	**MTC** Median total compensation	**TCC** Total cash compensation
AEX Average experienced wage	**B** Biweekly	**HI** Highest wage paid	**M** Monthly	**MW** Median wage paid	**TQ** Third quartile wage
ATC Average total compensation	**D** Daily	**HR** High end range	**MCC** Median cash compensation	**MWR** Median wage range	**W** Weekly
AW Average wage paid	**FQ** First quartile wage	**LO** Lowest wage paid	**ME** Median entry wage	**S** See annotated source	**Y** Yearly

Dental Assistant

Occupation/Type/Industry	Location	Per	Low	Mid	High	Source	Date
Dental Assistant	Grand Rapids-Wyoming MSA, MI	Y	36090 FQ	41770 MW	46580 TQ	USBLS	5/15
	Minnesota	Y	38698 FQ	44465 MW	49968 TQ	MNBLS	1/16-3/16
	Minneapolis-St. Paul-Bloomington MSA, MN-WI	Y	39516 FQ	45101 MW	50897 TQ	MNBLS	1/16-3/16
	Mississippi	Y	25330 FQ	29200 MW	35750 TQ	USBLS	5/15
	Jackson MSA, MS	Y	27070 FQ	30870 MW	38630 TQ	USBLS	5/15
	Missouri	Y	27780 FQ	33170 MW	41130 TQ	USBLS	5/15
	Kansas City MSA, MO-KS	Y	27030 FQ	34330 MW	46080 TQ	USBLS	5/15
	St. Louis MSA, MO-IL	Y	27770 FQ	33460 MW	42230 TQ	USBLS	5/15
	Montana	Y	28900 FQ	34110 MW	39140 TQ	USBLS	5/15
	Billings MSA, MT	Y	31930 FQ	37850 MW	44240 TQ	USBLS	5/15
	Nebraska	Y	28895 FQ	33685 MW	37940 TQ	NEBLS	7/16-9/16
	Omaha-Council Bluffs MSA, NE-IA	Y	28710 FQ	33360 MW	37590 TQ	NEBLS	7/16-9/16
	Nevada	Y	28910 FQ	34560 MW	39920 TQ	USBLS	5/15
	Las Vegas-Henderson-Paradise MSA, NV	Y	28350 FQ	33960 MW	38810 TQ	USBLS	5/15
	New Hampshire	H	18.18 AE	22.18 MW	24.68 AEX	NHBLS	6/16
	Manchester NECTA, NH	H	21.34 AE	22.66 MW	25.59 AEX	NHBLS	6/16
	Nashua NECTA, NH-MA	Y	39980 FQ	45370 MW	52790 TQ	USBLS	5/15
	New Jersey	Y	32220 FQ	39670 MW	47800 TQ	USBLS	5/15
	Camden PMSA, NJ	Y	32480 FQ	38050 MW	45420 TQ	USBLS	5/15
	Newark PMSA, NJ-PA	Y	33230 FQ	41510 MW	49560 TQ	USBLS	5/15
	Trenton MSA, NJ	Y	25860 FQ	31120 MW	43550 TQ	USBLS	5/15
	New Mexico	Y	26570 FQ	32230 MW	37740 TQ	USBLS	5/15
	Albuquerque MSA, NM	Y	26780 FQ	31930 MW	36550 TQ	USBLS	5/15
	New York	Y	25470 AE	35750 MW	41980 AEX	NYBLS	1/16-3/16
	Buffalo-Cheektowaga-Niagara Falls MSA, NY	Y	31380 FQ	36620 MW	42790 TQ	USBLS	5/15
	Nassau County-Suffolk County PMSA, NY	Y	31570 FQ	40940 MW	47530 TQ	USBLS	5/15
	New York-Jersey City-White Plains PMSA, NY-NJ	Y	27160 FQ	35060 MW	44270 TQ	USBLS	5/15
	Rochester MSA, NY	Y	30030 FQ	34950 MW	40900 TQ	USBLS	5/15
	North Carolina	Y	32670 FQ	37750 MW	45020 TQ	USBLS	5/15
	Charlotte-Concord-Gastonia MSA, NC-SC	Y	32530 FQ	38420 MW	45330 TQ	USBLS	5/15
	Raleigh MSA, NC	Y	35760 FQ	41520 MW	48570 TQ	USBLS	5/15
	North Dakota	Y	35190 FQ	39890 MW	48050 TQ	USBLS	5/15
	Fargo MSA, ND-MN	Y	33840 FQ	37880 MW	49640 TQ	USBLS	5/15
	Ohio	Y	30440 FQ	35460 MW	41630 TQ	USBLS	5/15
	Cincinnati MSA, OH-KY-IN	Y	31740 FQ	35890 MW	41290 TQ	USBLS	5/15
	Cleveland-Elyria MSA, OH	Y	32710 FQ	36120 MW	40000 TQ	USBLS	5/15
	Columbus MSA, OH	Y	30260 FQ	36010 MW	44280 TQ	USBLS	5/15
	Springfield MSA, OH	Y	32550 FQ	35690 MW	38830 TQ	USBLS	5/15
	Oklahoma	Y	27130 FQ	32390 MW	38400 TQ	USBLS	5/15
	Oklahoma City MSA, OK	Y	27070 FQ	32850 MW	37460 TQ	USBLS	5/15
	Tulsa MSA, OK	Y	27520 FQ	33740 MW	42120 TQ	USBLS	5/15
	Oregon	H	17.37 FQ	20.46 MW	23.33 TQ	ORBLS	2016
	Portland-Vancouver-Hillsboro MSA, OR-WA	Y	36280 FQ	42460 MW	48320 TQ	USBLS	5/15
	Pennsylvania	Y	28030 FQ	33970 MW	39500 TQ	USBLS	5/15
	Allentown-Bethlehem-Easton MSA, PA-NJ	Y	27900 FQ	33180 MW	39090 TQ	USBLS	5/15
	Harrisburg-Carlisle MSA, PA	Y	29480 FQ	34690 MW	40020 TQ	USBLS	5/15
	Montgomery County-Bucks County-Chester County PMSA, PA	Y	28540 FQ	34690 MW	44450 TQ	USBLS	5/15
	Philadelphia PMSA, PA	Y	27710 FQ	36590 MW	45740 TQ	USBLS	5/15
	Pittsburgh MSA, PA	Y	29210 FQ	34280 MW	38520 TQ	USBLS	5/15
	Rhode Island	Y	33560 FQ	38390 MW	44420 TQ	USBLS	5/15
	Providence-Warwick MSA, RI-MA	Y	34210 FQ	39750 MW	45440 TQ	USBLS	5/15
	South Carolina	Y	29910 FQ	34480 MW	38670 TQ	USBLS	5/15
	Charleston-North Charleston MSA, SC	Y	32830 FQ	36280 MW	39870 TQ	USBLS	5/15
	Columbia MSA, SC	Y	29010 FQ	34540 MW	40360 TQ	USBLS	5/15
	Greenville-Anderson-Mauldin MSA, SC	Y	31950 FQ	35560 MW	39180 TQ	USBLS	5/15
	South Dakota	Y	28450 FQ	33370 MW	38850 TQ	USBLS	5/15
	Sioux Falls MSA, SD	Y	31100 FQ	37780 MW	45290 TQ	USBLS	5/15

AE Average entry wage	AWR Average wage range	H Hourly	LR Low end range	MTC Median total compensation	TCC Total cash compensation
AEX Average experienced wage	B Biweekly	HI Highest wage paid	M Monthly	MW Median wage paid	TQ Third quartile wage
ATC Average total compensation	D Daily	HR High end range	MCC Median cash compensation	MWR Median wage range	W Weekly
AW Average wage paid	FQ First quartile wage	LO Lowest wage paid	ME Median entry wage	S See annotated source	Y Yearly

Occupation/Type/Industry	Location	Per	Low	Mid	High	Source	Date
Dental Assistant	Tennessee	Y	29370 FQ	34990 MW	40710 TQ	USBLS	5/15
	Knoxville MSA, TN	Y	33090 FQ	37540 MW	43760 TQ	USBLS	5/15
	Memphis MSA, TN-MS-AR	Y	28070 FQ	34490 MW	39650 TQ	USBLS	5/15
	Nashville-Davidson– Murfreesboro–Franklin MSA, TN	Y	31240 FQ	35410 MW	40280 TQ	USBLS	5/15
	Texas	Y	27800 FQ	34390 MW	42000 TQ	USBLS	5/15
	Austin-Round Rock MSA, TX	Y	32990 FQ	39770 MW	46650 TQ	USBLS	5/15
	Dallas-Plano-Irving PMSA, TX	Y	29590 FQ	37190 MW	44900 TQ	USBLS	5/15
	Fort Worth-Arlington PMSA, TX	Y	27920 FQ	35440 MW	43210 TQ	USBLS	5/15
	Houston-The Woodlands- Sugar Land MSA, TX	Y	28570 FQ	35400 MW	42800 TQ	USBLS	5/15
	San Antonio-New Braunfels MSA, TX	Y	26300 FQ	30560 MW	37190 TQ	USBLS	5/15
	Utah	Y	25840 FQ	28900 MW	33210 TQ	USBLS	5/15
	Ogden-Clearfield MSA, UT	Y	25350 FQ	28080 MW	30810 TQ	USBLS	5/15
	Provo-Orem MSA, UT	Y	26860 FQ	30460 MW	35780 TQ	USBLS	5/15
	Salt Lake City MSA, UT	Y	26800 FQ	29720 MW	34310 TQ	USBLS	5/15
	Vermont	Y	33950 FQ	38740 MW	47540 TQ	USBLS	5/15
	Burlington-South Burlington MSA, VT	Y	34290 FQ	38540 MW	45900 TQ	USBLS	5/15
	Virginia	Y	31510 FQ	36840 MW	45050 TQ	USBLS	5/15
	Richmond MSA, VA	Y	33760 FQ	38570 MW	46110 TQ	USBLS	5/15
	Virginia Beach-Norfolk- Newport News MSA, VA-NC	Y	26540 FQ	31240 MW	36990 TQ	USBLS	5/15
	Washington	H	16.81 FQ	19.73 MW	23.07 TQ	WABLS	3/16
	Seattle-Bellevue-Everett PMSA, WA	H	17.72 FQ	20.69 MW	23.83 TQ	WABLS	3/16
	Tacoma-Lakewood PMSA, WA	H	14.71 FQ	18.13 MW	21.93 TQ	WABLS	3/16
	West Virginia	Y	22840 FQ	27750 MW	33550 TQ	USBLS	5/15
	Huntington-Ashland MSA, WV-KY-OH	Y	25870 FQ	30700 MW	35970 TQ	USBLS	5/15
	Wisconsin	Y	31570 FQ	36630 MW	42930 TQ	USBLS	5/15
	Madison MSA, WI	Y	32510 FQ	36190 MW	40690 TQ	USBLS	5/15
	Milwaukee-Waukesha-West Allis MSA, WI	Y	30910 FQ	37000 MW	43250 TQ	USBLS	5/15
	Wyoming	Y	27580 FQ	32870 MW	38020 TQ	USBLS	5/15
	Cheyenne MSA, WY	Y	28990 FQ	34150 MW	38420 TQ	USBLS	5/15
	Puerto Rico	Y	16800 FQ	18190 MW	19740 TQ	USBLS	5/15
	San Juan-Carolina-Caguas MSA, PR	Y	16830 FQ	18250 MW	19870 TQ	USBLS	5/15
	Virgin Islands	Y	25540 FQ	28750 MW	34300 TQ	USBLS	5/15
	Guam	Y	21310 FQ	27830 MW	37720 TQ	USBLS	5/15
Dental Hygienist	Alabama	Y	36543 AE	45258 AW	49610 AEX	ALBLS	6/16
	Birmingham-Hoover MSA, AL	Y	40131 AE	45207 AW	40131 AEX	ALBLS	6/16
	Alaska	Y	70670 FQ	86080 MW	98410 TQ	USBLS	5/15
	Anchorage MSA, AK	Y	74200 FQ	86640 MW	99910 TQ	USBLS	5/15
	Arizona	Y	78900 FQ	86660 MW	93870 TQ	USBLS	5/15
	Phoenix-Mesa-Scottsdale MSA, AZ	Y	80040 FQ	87320 MW	94310 TQ	USBLS	5/15
	Tucson MSA, AZ	Y	70820 FQ	84920 MW	92560 TQ	USBLS	5/15
	Arkansas	Y	47580 FQ	66350 MW	79410 TQ	USBLS	5/15
	Little Rock-North Little Rock- Conway MSA, AR	Y	45580 FQ	67830 MW	84550 TQ	USBLS	5/15
	California	H	40.85 FQ	47.12 MW	54.15 TQ	CABLS	1/16-3/16
	Anaheim-Santa Ana-Irvine PMSA, CA	H	40.28 FQ	46.50 MW	52.64 TQ	CABLS	1/16-3/16
	Los Angeles-Long Beach- Glendale PMSA, CA	H	43.26 FQ	50.65 MW	56.34 TQ	CABLS	1/16-3/16
	Oakland-Hayward-Berkeley PMSA, CA	H	44.63 FQ	50.87 MW	56.84 TQ	CABLS	1/16-3/16
	Riverside-San Bernardino- Ontario MSA, CA	H	38.41 FQ	43.76 MW	48.62 TQ	CABLS	1/16-3/16
	Sacramento–Roseville– Arden-Arcade MSA, CA	H	42.09 FQ	46.26 MW	50.85 TQ	CABLS	1/16-3/16
	San Diego-Carlsbad MSA, CA	H	37.15 FQ	42.55 MW	47.13 TQ	CABLS	1/16-3/16
	San Francisco-Redwood City- South San Francisco PMSA, CA	H	46.34 FQ	55.01 MW	61.32 TQ	CABLS	1/16-3/16
	Colorado	Y	70870 FQ	81410 MW	91180 TQ	USBLS	5/15

AE	Average entry wage	AWR	Average wage range	H	Hourly	LR	Low end range	MTC	Median total compensation	TCC	Total cash compensation
AEX	Average experienced wage	B	Biweekly	HI	Highest wage paid	M	Monthly	MW	Median wage paid	TQ	Third quartile wage
ATC	Average total compensation	D	Daily	HR	High end range	MCC	Median cash compensation	MWR	Median wage range	W	Weekly
AW	Average wage paid	FQ	First quartile wage	LO	Lowest wage paid	ME	Median entry wage	S	See annotated source	Y	Yearly

Occupation/Type/Industry	Location	Per	Low	Mid	High	Source	Date
Dental Hygienist	Denver-Aurora-Lakewood MSA, CO	Y	74190 FQ	84430 MW	92670 TQ	USBLS	5/15
	Connecticut	Y		82904 MW		CTBLS	1/16-3/16
	Bridgeport-Stamford-Norwalk MSA, CT	Y	70460 FQ	81980 MW	91930 TQ	USBLS	5/15
	Hartford-West Hartford-East Hartford MSA, CT	Y	73990 FQ	84540 MW	95480 TQ	USBLS	5/15
	Delaware	Y	63990 FQ	75140 MW	86320 TQ	USBLS	5/15
	Wilmington PMSA, DE-MD-NJ	Y	63920 FQ	77170 MW	87640 TQ	USBLS	5/15
	District of Columbia	Y	93460 FQ	105570 MW	115130 TQ	USBLS	5/15
	Washington-Arlington-Alexandria PMSA, DC-VA-MD-WV	Y	79470 FQ	93580 MW	106730 TQ	USBLS	5/15
	Florida	H	23.91 AE	32.14 MW	34.84 AEX	FLBLS	7/16-9/16
	Fort Lauderdale-Pompano Beach-Deerfield Beach PMSA, FL	H	22.39 AE	33.54 MW	35.45 AEX	FLBLS	7/16-9/16
	Miami-Miami Beach-Kendall PMSA, FL	H	21.53 AE	27.40 MW	31.24 AEX	FLBLS	7/16-9/16
	Orlando-Kissimmee-Sanford MSA, FL	H	27.05 AE	33.52 MW	35.93 AEX	FLBLS	7/16-9/16
	Tampa-St. Petersburg-Clearwater MSA, FL	H	25.29 AE	34.55 MW	36.65 AEX	FLBLS	7/16-9/16
	Georgia	Y	51900 FQ	64300 MW	75590 TQ	USBLS	5/15
	Atlanta-Sandy Springs-Roswell MSA, GA	Y	61450 FQ	70680 MW	78760 TQ	USBLS	5/15
	Augusta-Richmond County MSA, GA-SC	Y	52500 FQ	59050 MW	67250 TQ	USBLS	5/15
	Hawaii	Y	65830 FQ	72490 MW	79820 TQ	USBLS	5/15
	Urban Honolulu MSA, HI	Y	66980 FQ	73570 MW	81500 TQ	USBLS	5/15
	Idaho	Y	66680 FQ	73250 MW	79950 TQ	USBLS	5/15
	Boise City MSA, ID	Y	66900 FQ	72310 MW	77730 TQ	USBLS	5/15
	Illinois	Y	59580 FQ	70960 MW	81630 TQ	USBLS	5/15
	Chicago-Naperville-Arlington Heights PMSA, IL	Y	65980 FQ	74530 MW	85710 TQ	USBLS	5/15
	Lake County-Kenosha County PMSA, IL-WI	Y	62120 FQ	71660 MW	80650 TQ	USBLS	5/15
	Indiana	Y	61100 FQ	69330 MW	76140 TQ	USBLS	5/15
	Gary PMSA, IN	Y	66540 FQ	71250 MW	75970 TQ	USBLS	5/15
	Indianapolis-Carmel-Anderson MSA, IN	Y	63800 FQ	71110 MW	78350 TQ	USBLS	5/15
	Iowa	Y	63250 FQ	69640 MW	75830 TQ	USBLS	5/15
	Des Moines-West Des Moines MSA, IA	Y	65250 FQ	71060 MW	76870 TQ	USBLS	5/15
	Kansas	Y	58620 FQ	68780 MW	79010 TQ	USBLS	5/15
	Wichita MSA, KS	Y	59370 FQ	67790 MW	75780 TQ	USBLS	5/15
	Kentucky	Y	50140 FQ	56780 MW	63510 TQ	USBLS	5/15
	Louisville-Jefferson County MSA, KY-IN	Y	55700 FQ	62910 MW	72850 TQ	USBLS	5/15
	Louisiana	Y	41050 FQ	54850 MW	71960 TQ	USBLS	5/15
	Baton Rouge MSA, LA	Y	47190 FQ	65820 MW	73850 TQ	USBLS	5/15
	New Orleans-Metairie MSA, LA	Y	37270 FQ	58490 MW	77690 TQ	USBLS	5/15
	Maine	Y	55550 FQ	62190 MW	71610 TQ	USBLS	5/15
	Portland-South Portland MSA, ME	Y	56720 FQ	66070 MW	75170 TQ	USBLS	5/15
	Maryland	Y	63547 AE	81746 MW	90846 AEX	MDBLS	4/16
	Baltimore-Columbia-Towson MSA, MD	Y	78360 FQ	87030 MW	94760 TQ	USBLS	5/15
	Salisbury MSA, MD-DE	Y	67830 FQ	74220 MW	80220 TQ	USBLS	5/15
	Massachusetts	Y	71830 FQ	83730 MW	92970 TQ	USBLS	5/15
	Boston-Cambridge-Newton NECTA, MA	Y	73760 FQ	85520 MW	93750 TQ	USBLS	5/15
	Worcester MSA, MA-CT	Y	73030 FQ	83830 MW	92880 TQ	USBLS	5/15
	Michigan	Y	54510 FQ	61170 MW	70120 TQ	USBLS	5/15
	Detroit-Dearborn-Livonia PMSA, MI	Y	59800 FQ	67300 MW	74300 TQ	USBLS	5/15
	Grand Rapids-Wyoming MSA, MI	Y	54510 FQ	58860 MW	63850 TQ	USBLS	5/15
	Minnesota	Y	65493 FQ	72509 MW	79545 TQ	MNBLS	1/16-3/16

AE	Average entry wage	AWR	Average wage range	H	Hourly	LR	Low end range	MTC	Median total compensation	TCC	Total cash compensation
AEX	Average hexperienced wage	B	Biweekly	HI	Highest wage paid	M	Monthly	MW	Median wage paid	TQ	Third quartile wage
ATC	Average total compensation	D	Daily	HR	High end range	MCC	Median cash compensation	MWR	Median wage range	W	Weekly
AW	Average wage paid	FQ	First quartile wage	LO	Lowest wage paid	ME	Median entry wage	S	See annotated source	Y	Yearly

Occupation/Type/Industry	Location	Per	Low	Mid	High	Source	Date
Dental Hygienist	Minneapolis-St. Paul-Bloomington MSA, MN-WI	Y	67136 FQ	74072 MW	80947 TQ	MNBLS	1/16-3/16
	Mississippi	Y	47320 FQ	55550 MW	62540 TQ	USBLS	5/15
	Jackson MSA, MS	Y	53150 FQ	57840 MW	62460 TQ	USBLS	5/15
	Missouri	Y	60510 FQ	69180 MW	76130 TQ	USBLS	5/15
	Kansas City MSA, MO-KS	Y	63480 FQ	71190 MW	78770 TQ	USBLS	5/15
	St. Louis MSA, MO-IL	Y	52740 FQ	64190 MW	73130 TQ	USBLS	5/15
	Montana	Y	63590 FQ	69880 MW	76110 TQ	USBLS	5/15
	Billings MSA, MT	Y	61280 FQ	70010 MW	77670 TQ	USBLS	5/15
	Nebraska	Y	56670 FQ	66370 MW	74780 TQ	NEBLS	7/16-9/16
	Omaha-Council Bluffs MSA, NE-IA	Y	63425 FQ	69370 MW	75225 TQ	NEBLS	7/16-9/16
	Nevada	Y	76610 FQ	89110 MW	99250 TQ	USBLS	5/15
	Las Vegas-Henderson-Paradise MSA, NV	Y	70250 FQ	86130 MW	96470 TQ	USBLS	5/15
	New Hampshire	H	30.87 AE	39.03 MW	42.12 AEX	NHBLS	6/16
	Manchester NECTA, NH	H	34.10 AE	38.53 MW	40.80 AEX	NHBLS	6/16
	Nashua NECTA, NH-MA	Y	69990 FQ	83050 MW	93990 TQ	USBLS	5/15
	New Jersey	Y	75390 FQ	85530 MW	93510 TQ	USBLS	5/15
	Camden PMSA, NJ	Y	73060 FQ	81380 MW	90890 TQ	USBLS	5/15
	Newark PMSA, NJ-PA	Y	81380 FQ	87980 MW	94430 TQ	USBLS	5/15
	Trenton MSA, NJ	Y	63350 FQ	73520 MW	86980 TQ	USBLS	5/15
	New Mexico	Y	68110 FQ	84940 MW	96290 TQ	USBLS	5/15
	Albuquerque MSA, NM	Y	73650 FQ	87560 MW	96290 TQ	USBLS	5/15
	New York	Y	54940 AE	73140 MW	83500 AEX	NYBLS	1/16-3/16
	Buffalo-Cheektowaga-Niagara Falls MSA, NY	Y	52630 FQ	57310 MW	61970 TQ	USBLS	5/15
	Nassau County-Suffolk County PMSA, NY	Y	70540 FQ	80510 MW	90790 TQ	USBLS	5/15
	New York-Jersey City-White Plains PMSA, NY-NJ	Y	73500 FQ	86540 MW	95720 TQ	USBLS	5/15
	Rochester MSA, NY	Y	54950 FQ	61260 MW	68920 TQ	USBLS	5/15
	North Carolina	Y	58090 FQ	67750 MW	76080 TQ	USBLS	5/15
	Charlotte-Concord-Gastonia MSA, NC-SC	Y	63040 FQ	70920 MW	78540 TQ	USBLS	5/15
	Raleigh MSA, NC	Y	60860 FQ	69510 MW	77460 TQ	USBLS	5/15
	North Dakota	Y	56640 FQ	63350 MW	72820 TQ	USBLS	5/15
	Fargo MSA, ND-MN	Y	55470 FQ	60490 MW	68520 TQ	USBLS	5/15
	Ohio	Y	58550 FQ	67500 MW	75200 TQ	USBLS	5/15
	Cincinnati MSA, OH-KY-IN	Y	64740 FQ	71540 MW	78350 TQ	USBLS	5/15
	Cleveland-Elyria MSA, OH	Y	56730 FQ	65410 MW	72970 TQ	USBLS	5/15
	Columbus MSA, OH	Y	66110 FQ	71990 MW	77880 TQ	USBLS	5/15
	Oklahoma	Y	64690 FQ	74080 MW	85850 TQ	USBLS	5/15
	Oklahoma City MSA, OK	Y	61070 FQ	73240 MW	85130 TQ	USBLS	5/15
	Tulsa MSA, OK	Y	67550 FQ	75590 MW	91770 TQ	USBLS	5/15
	Oregon	H	33.81 FQ	37.37 MW	42.46 TQ	ORBLS	2016
	Portland-Vancouver-Hillsboro MSA, OR-WA	Y	68000 FQ	74570 MW	82200 TQ	USBLS	5/15
	Pennsylvania	Y	53340 FQ	61850 MW	74100 TQ	USBLS	5/15
	Allentown-Bethlehem-Easton MSA, PA-NJ	Y	56690 FQ	65410 MW	78430 TQ	USBLS	5/15
	Harrisburg-Carlisle MSA, PA	Y	55250 FQ	60550 MW	69290 TQ	USBLS	5/15
	Montgomery County-Bucks County-Chester County PMSA, PA	Y	56900 FQ	69110 MW	77210 TQ	USBLS	5/15
	Philadelphia PMSA, PA	Y	68310 FQ	80920 MW	91130 TQ	USBLS	5/15
	Pittsburgh MSA, PA	Y	50430 FQ	55800 MW	61060 TQ	USBLS	5/15
	Rhode Island	Y	67670 FQ	72400 MW	77160 TQ	USBLS	5/15
	Providence-Warwick MSA, RI-MA	Y	67910 FQ	73260 MW	78920 TQ	USBLS	5/15
	South Carolina	Y	49140 FQ	57270 MW	66110 TQ	USBLS	5/15
	Charleston-North Charleston MSA, SC	Y	54700 FQ	62360 MW	73980 TQ	USBLS	5/15
	Columbia MSA, SC	Y	45180 FQ	55700 MW	67780 TQ	USBLS	5/15
	Greenville-Anderson-Mauldin MSA, SC	Y	52050 FQ	58700 MW	66820 TQ	USBLS	5/15
	South Dakota	Y	49950 FQ	57790 MW	67370 TQ	USBLS	5/15
	Sioux Falls MSA, SD	Y	40180 FQ	54640 MW	63540 TQ	USBLS	5/15
	Tennessee	Y	56230 FQ	67160 MW	75750 TQ	USBLS	5/15
	Knoxville MSA, TN	Y	61970 FQ	71930 MW	81380 TQ	USBLS	5/15
	Memphis MSA, TN-MS-AR	Y	53240 FQ	64660 MW	73100 TQ	USBLS	5/15

AE	Average entry wage	**AWR**	Average wage range	**H**	Hourly	**LR**	Low end range	
AEX	Average experienced wage	**B**	Biweekly	**HI**	Highest wage paid	**M**	Monthly	
ATC	Average total compensation	**D**	Daily	**HR**	High end range	**MCC**	Median cash compensation	
AW	Average wage paid	**FQ**	First quartile wage	**LO**	Lowest wage paid	**ME**	Median entry wage	

MTC	Median total compensation	**TCC**	Total cash compensation
MW	Median wage paid	**TQ**	Third quartile wage
MWR	Median wage range	**W**	Weekly
S	See annotated source	**Y**	Yearly

Occupation/Type/Industry	Location	Per	Low	Mid	High	Source	Date
Dental Hygienist	Nashville-Davidson– Murfreesboro–Franklin MSA, TN	Y	62330 FQ	70090 MW	76930 TQ	USBLS	5/15
	Texas	Y	65630 FQ	72700 MW	80090 TQ	USBLS	5/15
	Austin-Round Rock MSA, TX	Y	66200 FQ	74910 MW	86000 TQ	USBLS	5/15
	Dallas-Plano-Irving PMSA, TX	Y	68710 FQ	75600 MW	84090 TQ	USBLS	5/15
	Fort Worth-Arlington PMSA, TX	Y	68730 FQ	75800 MW	86670 TQ	USBLS	5/15
	Houston-The Woodlands- Sugar Land MSA, TX	Y	67390 FQ	73890 MW	80200 TQ	USBLS	5/15
	San Antonio-New Braunfels MSA, TX	Y	64300 FQ	70310 MW	76320 TQ	USBLS	5/15
	Utah	Y	64940 FQ	71150 MW	77360 TQ	USBLS	5/15
	Ogden-Clearfield MSA, UT	Y	62270 FQ	68510 MW	74890 TQ	USBLS	5/15
	Provo-Orem MSA, UT	Y	67760 FQ	74570 MW	83400 TQ	USBLS	5/15
	Salt Lake City MSA, UT	Y	65200 FQ	70450 MW	75700 TQ	USBLS	5/15
	Vermont	Y	57420 FQ	66260 MW	73430 TQ	USBLS	5/15
	Burlington-South Burlington MSA, VT	Y	54290 FQ	63330 MW	72070 TQ	USBLS	5/15
	Virginia	Y	65330 FQ	80770 MW	96010 TQ	USBLS	5/15
	Richmond MSA, VA	Y	80580 FQ	87310 MW	93930 TQ	USBLS	5/15
	Virginia Beach-Norfolk- Newport News MSA, VA-NC	Y	56600 FQ	66980 MW	78110 TQ	USBLS	5/15
	Washington	H	39.80 FQ	44.30 MW	48.84 TQ	WABLS	3/16
	Seattle-Bellevue-Everett PMSA, WA	H	40.70 FQ	45.69 MW	50.89 TQ	WABLS	3/16
	Tacoma-Lakewood PMSA, WA	H	40.90 FQ	44.24 MW	47.58 TQ	WABLS	3/16
	West Virginia	Y	48050 FQ	54860 MW	60820 TQ	USBLS	5/15
	Huntington-Ashland MSA, WV-KY-OH	Y	45330 FQ	50540 MW	58730 TQ	USBLS	5/15
	Wisconsin	Y	56050 FQ	64030 MW	72700 TQ	USBLS	5/15
	Madison MSA, WI	Y	55370 FQ	62370 MW	71770 TQ	USBLS	5/15
	Milwaukee-Waukesha-West Allis MSA, WI	Y	57130 FQ	66150 MW	73910 TQ	USBLS	5/15
	Wyoming	Y	61390 FQ	69550 MW	77110 TQ	USBLS	5/15
	Cheyenne MSA, WY	Y	66600 FQ	72600 MW	78600 TQ	USBLS	5/15
	Guam	Y	21950 FQ	31160 MW	41460 TQ	USBLS	5/15
Dental Informaticist	United States	Y		85000- 110000 AWR		EXHC05	2016
Dental Laboratory Technician	Alabama	Y	22878 AE	35895 AW	42393 AEX	ALBLS	6/16
	Birmingham-Hoover MSA, AL	Y	21541 AE	38620 AW	47154 AEX	ALBLS	6/16
	Alaska	Y	41650 FQ	49570 MW	57520 TQ	USBLS	5/15
	Anchorage MSA, AK	Y	41140 FQ	48600 MW	57070 TQ	USBLS	5/15
	Arizona	Y	28330 FQ	37680 MW	51270 TQ	USBLS	5/15
	Phoenix-Mesa-Scottsdale MSA, AZ	Y	28840 FQ	38320 MW	51480 TQ	USBLS	5/15
	Tucson MSA, AZ	Y	28580 FQ	45620 MW	56010 TQ	USBLS	5/15
	Arkansas	Y	27550 FQ	35250 MW	46510 TQ	USBLS	5/15
	Little Rock-North Little Rock- Conway MSA, AR	Y	33360 FQ	38290 MW	55870 TQ	USBLS	5/15
	California	H	13.75 FQ	17.84 MW	23.61 TQ	CABLS	1/16-3/16
	Anaheim-Santa Ana-Irvine PMSA, CA	H	12.86 FQ	18.06 MW	23.55 TQ	CABLS	1/16-3/16
	Los Angeles-Long Beach- Glendale PMSA, CA	H	15.64 FQ	17.79 MW	20.97 TQ	CABLS	1/16-3/16
	Oakland-Hayward-Berkeley PMSA, CA	H	18.29 FQ	21.66 MW	24.26 TQ	CABLS	1/16-3/16
	Riverside-San Bernardino- Ontario MSA, CA	H	11.12 FQ	15.09 MW	19.56 TQ	CABLS	1/16-3/16
	Sacramento–Roseville– Arden-Arcade MSA, CA	H	15.25 FQ	19.56 MW	26.84 TQ	CABLS	1/16-3/16
	San Francisco-Redwood City- South San Francisco PMSA, CA	H	14.31 FQ	21.24 MW	25.31 TQ	CABLS	1/16-3/16
	Colorado	Y	23600 FQ	32840 MW	45610 TQ	USBLS	5/15
	Denver-Aurora-Lakewood MSA, CO	Y	22530 FQ	27780 MW	42150 TQ	USBLS	5/15
	Connecticut	Y		39840 MW		CTBLS	1/16-3/16
	Bridgeport-Stamford-Norwalk MSA, CT	Y	33350 FQ	43810 MW	59860 TQ	USBLS	5/15

AE Average entry wage	**AWR** Average wage range	**H** Hourly	**LR** Low end range	**MTC** Median total compensation **TCC** Total cash compensation
AEX Average experienced wage	**B** Biweekly	**HI** Highest wage paid	**M** Monthly	**MW** Median wage paid **TQ** Third quartile wage
ATC Average total compensation	**D** Daily	**HR** High end range	**MCC** Median cash compensation **MWR** Median wage range **W** Weekly
AW Average wage paid	**FQ** First quartile wage	**LO** Lowest wage paid	**ME** Median entry wage	**S** See annotated source **Y** Yearly

Occupation/Type/Industry	Location	Per	Low	Mid	High	Source	Date
Dental Laboratory Technician	Hartford-West Hartford-East Hartford MSA, CT	Y	27180 FQ	39570 MW	48960 TQ	USBLS	5/15
	Delaware	Y	22740 FQ	26340 MW	31580 TQ	USBLS	5/15
	Wilmington PMSA, DE-MD-NJ	Y	35240 FQ	43880 MW	62260 TQ	USBLS	5/15
	District of Columbia	Y	57240 FQ	71510 MW	92570 TQ	USBLS	5/15
	Washington-Arlington-Alexandria PMSA, DC-VA-MD-WV	Y	26650 FQ	33820 MW	47050 TQ	USBLS	5/15
	Florida	H	12.21 AE	17.64 MW	23.20 AEX	FLBLS	7/16-9/16
	Fort Lauderdale-Pompano Beach-Deerfield Beach PMSA, FL	H	14.24 AE	19.04 MW	23.08 AEX	FLBLS	7/16-9/16
	Miami-Miami Beach-Kendall PMSA, FL	H	12.40 AE	15.49 MW	20.06 AEX	FLBLS	7/16-9/16
	Orlando-Kissimmee-Sanford MSA, FL	H	12.38 AE	15.20 MW	17.58 AEX	FLBLS	7/16-9/16
	Tampa-St. Petersburg-Clearwater MSA, FL	H	11.11 AE	17.47 MW	24.96 AEX	FLBLS	7/16-9/16
	Georgia	Y	27160 FQ	33390 MW	40300 TQ	USBLS	5/15
	Atlanta-Sandy Springs-Roswell MSA, GA	Y	27410 FQ	32930 MW	38300 TQ	USBLS	5/15
	Augusta-Richmond County MSA, GA-SC	Y	35140 FQ	46750 MW	56600 TQ	USBLS	5/15
	Hawaii	Y	29150 FQ	34960 MW	46170 TQ	USBLS	5/15
	Urban Honolulu MSA, HI	Y	28730 FQ	34490 MW	52620 TQ	USBLS	5/15
	Idaho	Y	32880 FQ	40640 MW	49780 TQ	USBLS	5/15
	Boise City MSA, ID	Y	37580 FQ	42720 MW	47900 TQ	USBLS	5/15
	Illinois	Y	27460 FQ	38550 MW	53510 TQ	USBLS	5/15
	Chicago-Naperville-Arlington Heights PMSA, IL	Y	32180 FQ	40070 MW	54950 TQ	USBLS	5/15
	Indiana	Y	32130 FQ	36940 MW	46260 TQ	USBLS	5/15
	Gary PMSA, IN	Y	32580 FQ	37940 MW	52070 TQ	USBLS	5/15
	Indianapolis-Carmel-Anderson MSA, IN	Y	32370 FQ	36250 MW	42180 TQ	USBLS	5/15
	Iowa	Y	27430 FQ	33410 MW	43650 TQ	USBLS	5/15
	Des Moines-West Des Moines MSA, IA	Y	26120 FQ	30790 MW	44780 TQ	USBLS	5/15
	Kansas	Y	32070 FQ	40830 MW	47850 TQ	USBLS	5/15
	Wichita MSA, KS	Y	26130 FQ	30170 MW	38060 TQ	USBLS	5/15
	Kentucky	Y	25740 FQ	34040 MW	46590 TQ	USBLS	5/15
	Louisville-Jefferson County MSA, KY-IN	Y	24860 FQ	35670 MW	45570 TQ	USBLS	5/15
	Louisiana	Y	25260 FQ	31590 MW	40540 TQ	USBLS	5/15
	Baton Rouge MSA, LA	Y	26220 FQ	33700 MW	39870 TQ	USBLS	5/15
	New Orleans-Metairie MSA, LA	Y	27320 FQ	32410 MW	39430 TQ	USBLS	5/15
	Maine	Y	32570 FQ	43500 MW	54520 TQ	USBLS	5/15
	Portland-South Portland MSA, ME	Y	30210 FQ	40920 MW	53620 TQ	USBLS	5/15
	Maryland	Y	22424 AE	40820 MW	50018 AEX	MDBLS	4/16
	Baltimore-Columbia-Towson MSA, MD	Y	23850 FQ	32240 MW	50900 TQ	USBLS	5/15
	Salisbury MSA, MD-DE	Y	21990 FQ	24840 MW	29740 TQ	USBLS	5/15
	Massachusetts	Y	33930 FQ	45450 MW	56890 TQ	USBLS	5/15
	Boston-Cambridge-Newton NECTA, MA	Y	38160 FQ	53100 MW	60740 TQ	USBLS	5/15
	Michigan	Y	31950 FQ	39620 MW	54690 TQ	USBLS	5/15
	Detroit-Dearborn-Livonia PMSA, MI	Y	30130 FQ	37180 MW	51020 TQ	USBLS	5/15
	Grand Rapids-Wyoming MSA, MI	Y	35510 FQ	39670 MW	46150 TQ	USBLS	5/15
	Minnesota	Y	28622 FQ	35466 MW	45196 TQ	MNBLS	1/16-3/16
	Minneapolis-St. Paul-Bloomington MSA, MN-WI	Y	29209 FQ	35426 MW	44052 TQ	MNBLS	1/16-3/16
	Mississippi	Y	23490 FQ	29250 MW	37330 TQ	USBLS	5/15
	Jackson MSA, MS	Y	33670 FQ	43960 MW	51310 TQ	USBLS	5/15
	Missouri	Y	25560 FQ	36830 MW	46520 TQ	USBLS	5/15
	Kansas City MSA, MO-KS	Y	31640 FQ	40350 MW	48160 TQ	USBLS	5/15
	St. Louis MSA, MO-IL	Y	26940 FQ	37260 MW	48730 TQ	USBLS	5/15
	Montana	Y	27830 FQ	39790 MW	49970 TQ	USBLS	5/15
	Nebraska	Y	32860 FQ	42500 MW	50650 TQ	NEBLS	7/16-9/16

AE	Average entry wage	AWR	Average wage range	H	Hourly
AEX	Average experienced wage	B	Biweekly	HI	Highest wage paid
ATC	Average total compensation	D	Daily	HR	High end range
AW	Average wage paid	FQ	First quartile wage	LO	Lowest wage paid

LR	Low end range	MTC	Median total compensation	TCC	Total cash compensation
M	Monthly	MW	Median wage paid	TQ	Third quartile wage
MCC	Median cash compensation	MWR	Median wage range	W	Weekly
ME	Median entry wage	S	See annotated source	Y	Yearly

Occupation/Type/Industry	Location	Per	Low	Mid	High	Source	Date
Dental Laboratory Technician	Omaha-Council Bluffs MSA, NE-IA	Y	34000 FQ	42395 MW	48010 TQ	NEBLS	7/16-9/16
	Nevada	Y	28860 FQ	36110 MW	44980 TQ	USBLS	5/15
	Las Vegas-Henderson-Paradise MSA, NV	Y	28300 FQ	33680 MW	43330 TQ	USBLS	5/15
	New Hampshire	H	14.70 AE	19.67 MW	24.79 AEX	NHBLS	6/16
	Manchester NECTA, NH	H	15.89 AE	20.33 MW	23.94 AEX	NHBLS	6/16
	Nashua NECTA, NH-MA	Y	34220 FQ	47520 MW	67750 TQ	USBLS	5/15
	New Jersey	Y	28700 FQ	37430 MW	50450 TQ	USBLS	5/15
	Camden PMSA, NJ	Y	32100 FQ	38100 MW	48660 TQ	USBLS	5/15
	Newark PMSA, NJ-PA	Y	27180 FQ	35470 MW	48330 TQ	USBLS	5/15
	New Mexico	Y	28690 FQ	34350 MW	39650 TQ	USBLS	5/15
	Albuquerque MSA, NM	Y	29690 FQ	35100 MW	40020 TQ	USBLS	5/15
	New York	Y	28800 AE	44900 MW	64360 AEX	NYBLS	1/16-3/16
	Buffalo-Cheektowaga-Niagara Falls MSA, NY	Y	29540 FQ	40000 MW	56210 TQ	USBLS	5/15
	Nassau County-Suffolk County PMSA, NY	Y	39210 FQ	54400 MW	75060 TQ	USBLS	5/15
	New York-Jersey City-White Plains PMSA, NY-NJ	Y	33410 FQ	41820 MW	69520 TQ	USBLS	5/15
	Rochester MSA, NY	Y	38340 FQ	49500 MW	60980 TQ	USBLS	5/15
	North Carolina	Y	34140 FQ	41980 MW	54060 TQ	USBLS	5/15
	Charlotte-Concord-Gastonia MSA, NC-SC	Y	35380 FQ	43800 MW	57630 TQ	USBLS	5/15
	Raleigh MSA, NC	Y	37050 FQ	45100 MW	52880 TQ	USBLS	5/15
	North Dakota	Y	27070 FQ	34800 MW	40390 TQ	USBLS	5/15
	Fargo MSA, ND-MN	Y	27440 FQ	35090 MW	43510 TQ	USBLS	5/15
	Ohio	Y	29840 FQ	39950 MW	49000 TQ	USBLS	5/15
	Cincinnati MSA, OH-KY-IN	Y	28980 FQ	40290 MW	47610 TQ	USBLS	5/15
	Cleveland-Elyria MSA, OH	Y	28040 FQ	40140 MW	48690 TQ	USBLS	5/15
	Columbus MSA, OH	Y	28640 FQ	43810 MW	58690 TQ	USBLS	5/15
	Oklahoma	Y	29950 FQ	37260 MW	50140 TQ	USBLS	5/15
	Oklahoma City MSA, OK	Y	32420 FQ	42140 MW	54960 TQ	USBLS	5/15
	Tulsa MSA, OK	Y	28270 FQ	37910 MW	49700 TQ	USBLS	5/15
	Oregon	H	14.00 FQ	20.16 MW	25.47 TQ	ORBLS	2016
	Portland-Vancouver-Hillsboro MSA, OR-WA	Y	29700 FQ	43200 MW	53970 TQ	USBLS	5/15
	Pennsylvania	Y	28410 FQ	37200 MW	49890 TQ	USBLS	5/15
	Allentown-Bethlehem-Easton MSA, PA-NJ	Y	23090 FQ	31310 MW	41620 TQ	USBLS	5/15
	Harrisburg-Carlisle MSA, PA	Y	28050 FQ	34160 MW	41090 TQ	USBLS	5/15
	Montgomery County-Bucks County-Chester County PMSA, PA	Y	29670 FQ	39460 MW	53390 TQ	USBLS	5/15
	Pittsburgh MSA, PA	Y	26170 FQ	36820 MW	48910 TQ	USBLS	5/15
	Rhode Island	Y	28440 FQ	40090 MW	71750 TQ	USBLS	5/15
	Providence-Warwick MSA, RI-MA	Y	28170 FQ	36170 MW	69390 TQ	USBLS	5/15
	South Carolina	Y	29690 FQ	37890 MW	46760 TQ	USBLS	5/15
	Charleston-North Charleston MSA, SC	Y	31800 FQ	36130 MW	41910 TQ	USBLS	5/15
	South Dakota	Y	25930 FQ	30560 MW	38720 TQ	USBLS	5/15
	Tennessee	Y	23050 FQ	32390 MW	42250 TQ	USBLS	5/15
	Memphis MSA, TN-MS-AR	Y	27560 FQ	33900 MW	38520 TQ	USBLS	5/15
	Nashville-Davidson–Murfreesboro–Franklin MSA, TN	Y	23290 FQ	29930 MW	41940 TQ	USBLS	5/15
	Texas	Y	27430 FQ	35770 MW	48180 TQ	USBLS	5/15
	Austin-Round Rock MSA, TX	Y	27900 FQ	32010 MW	43210 TQ	USBLS	5/15
	Dallas-Plano-Irving PMSA, TX	Y	31650 FQ	41670 MW	52670 TQ	USBLS	5/15
	Fort Worth-Arlington PMSA, TX	Y	30960 FQ	39520 MW	53860 TQ	USBLS	5/15
	Houston-The Woodlands-Sugar Land MSA, TX	Y	23850 FQ	31470 MW	39220 TQ	USBLS	5/15
	San Antonio-New Braunfels MSA, TX	Y	30440 FQ	36540 MW	47470 TQ	USBLS	5/15
	Utah	Y	27040 FQ	34690 MW	55040 TQ	USBLS	5/15
	Ogden-Clearfield MSA, UT	Y	28810 FQ	35320 MW	66260 TQ	USBLS	5/15
	Provo-Orem MSA, UT	Y	26320 FQ	30970 MW	59800 TQ	USBLS	5/15
	Salt Lake City MSA, UT	Y	26450 FQ	34000 MW	46750 TQ	USBLS	5/15
	Vermont	Y	37780 FQ	45420 MW	52710 TQ	USBLS	5/15

AE Average entry wage	**AWR** Average wage range	**H** Hourly	**LR** Low end range	**MTC** Median total compensation	**TCC** Total cash compensation
AEX Average experienced wage	**B** Biweekly	**HI** Highest wage paid	**M** Monthly	**MW** Median wage paid	**TQ** Third quartile wage
ATC Average total compensation	**D** Daily	**HR** High end range	**MCC** Median cash compensation	**MWR** Median wage range	**W** Weekly
AW Average wage paid	**FQ** First quartile wage	**LO** Lowest wage paid	**ME** Median entry wage	**S** See annotated source	**Y** Yearly

Occupation/Type/Industry	Location	Per	Low	Mid	High	Source	Date
Dental Laboratory Technician	Burlington-South Burlington MSA, VT	Y	37940 FQ	44740 MW	50290 TQ	USBLS	5/15
	Virginia	Y	29750 FQ	37460 MW	49970 TQ	USBLS	5/15
	Richmond MSA, VA	Y	36790 FQ	43480 MW	49640 TQ	USBLS	5/15
	Virginia Beach-Norfolk-Newport News MSA, VA-NC	Y	33610 FQ	39190 MW	57040 TQ	USBLS	5/15
	Washington	H	17.28 FQ	21.90 MW	26.39 TQ	WABLS	3/16
	Seattle-Bellevue-Everett PMSA, WA	H	20.12 FQ	22.90 MW	26.88 TQ	WABLS	3/16
	Tacoma-Lakewood PMSA, WA	H	12.47 FQ	22.36 MW	31.87 TQ	WABLS	3/16
	West Virginia	Y	27340 FQ	36050 MW	44100 TQ	USBLS	5/15
	Huntington-Ashland MSA, WV-KY-OH	Y	27930 FQ	40330 MW	44980 TQ	USBLS	5/15
	Wisconsin	Y	25540 FQ	35930 MW	44380 TQ	USBLS	5/15
	Madison MSA, WI	Y	30510 FQ	37540 MW	49260 TQ	USBLS	5/15
	Milwaukee-Waukesha-West Allis MSA, WI	Y	34180 FQ	39880 MW	45790 TQ	USBLS	5/15
	Wyoming	Y	34920 FQ	40290 MW	46290 TQ	USBLS	5/15
	Puerto Rico	Y	16670 FQ	17760 MW	18850 TQ	USBLS	5/15
Dental Sleep Doctor	United States	Y		150000 MW		SLEEP	2015
Dentist	Alabama	Y	74166 AE	178249 AW	230296 AEX	ALBLS	6/16
	Birmingham-Hoover MSA, AL	Y	48764 AE	145937 AW	194518 AEX	ALBLS	6/16
	Alaska	Y	156510 FQ	217120 AW		USBLS	5/15
	Anchorage MSA, AK	Y	177250 FQ	234390 AW		USBLS	5/15
	Arizona	Y	80800 FQ	166710 MW		USBLS	5/15
	Phoenix-Mesa-Scottsdale MSA, AZ	Y	77370 FQ	173050 MW		USBLS	5/15
	Tucson MSA, AZ	Y	86990 FQ	108410 MW		USBLS	5/15
	Arkansas	Y	91710 FQ	150570 MW		USBLS	5/15
	Little Rock-North Little Rock-Conway MSA, AR	Y	139120 FQ	163160 MW		USBLS	5/15
	California	H	45.21 FQ	74.95 MW		CABLS	1/16-3/16
	Anaheim-Santa Ana-Irvine PMSA, CA	H	57.55 FQ	76.10 MW		CABLS	1/16-3/16
	Los Angeles-Long Beach-Glendale PMSA, CA	H	34.46 FQ	76.92 MW		CABLS	1/16-3/16
	Oakland-Hayward-Berkeley PMSA, CA	H	64.47 FQ	96.07 AW		CABLS	1/16-3/16
	Riverside-San Bernardino-Ontario MSA, CA	H	35.01 FQ	60.12 MW	73.28 TQ	CABLS	1/16-3/16
	Sacramento–Roseville–Arden-Arcade MSA, CA	H	43.03 FQ	77.31 MW		CABLS	1/16-3/16
	San Diego-Carlsbad MSA, CA	H	37.30 FQ	73.46 MW		CABLS	1/16-3/16
	San Francisco-Redwood City-South San Francisco PMSA, CA	H	78.00 FQ	88.30 MW		CABLS	1/16-3/16
	Colorado	Y	124580 FQ	158230 MW		USBLS	5/15
	Denver-Aurora-Lakewood MSA, CO	Y	132260 FQ	156190 MW		USBLS	5/15
	Connecticut	Y		170323 MW		CTBLS	1/16-3/16
	Bridgeport-Stamford-Norwalk MSA, CT	Y	139280 FQ	156550 MW		USBLS	5/15
	Hartford-West Hartford-East Hartford MSA, CT	Y	123710 FQ	183710 MW		USBLS	5/15
	Delaware	Y	172930 FQ	227160 AW		USBLS	5/15
	Wilmington PMSA, DE-MD-NJ	Y	176920 FQ	228660 AW		USBLS	5/15
	District of Columbia	Y	37130 FQ	90090 MW	130720 TQ	USBLS	5/15
	Washington-Arlington-Alexandria PMSA, DC-VA-MD-WV	Y	84500 FQ	133830 MW		USBLS	5/15
	Florida	H	40.67 AE	70.67 MW	105.43 AEX	FLBLS	7/16-9/16
	Fort Lauderdale-Pompano Beach-Deerfield Beach PMSA, FL	H	36.48 AE	57.60 MW	73.34 AEX	FLBLS	7/16-9/16
	Miami-Miami Beach-Kendall PMSA, FL	H	36.17 AE	74.38 MW	109.69 AEX	FLBLS	7/16-9/16
	Orlando-Kissimmee-Sanford MSA, FL	H	38.79 AE	66.19 MW	99.48 AEX	FLBLS	7/16-9/16

AE	Average entry wage	AWR	Average wage range	H	Hourly	LR	Low end range	MTC	Median total compensation	TCC	Total cash compensation
AEX	Average experienced wage	B	Biweekly	HI	Highest wage paid	M	Monthly	MW	Median wage paid	TQ	Third quartile wage
ATC	Average total compensation	D	Daily	HR	High end range	MCC	Median cash compensation	MWR	Median wage range	W	Weekly
AW	Average wage paid	FQ	First quartile wage	LO	Lowest wage paid	ME	Median entry wage	S	See annotated source	Y	Yearly

413

Occupation/Type/Industry	Location	Per	Low	Mid	High	Source	Date
Dentist	Tampa-St. Petersburg-Clearwater MSA, FL	H	48.20 AE	92.24 MW	121.53 AEX	FLBLS	7/16-9/16
	Georgia	Y	111960 FQ	157540 MW		USBLS	5/15
	Atlanta-Sandy Springs-Roswell MSA, GA	Y	111830 FQ	142050 MW		USBLS	5/15
	Augusta-Richmond County MSA, GA-SC	Y	164790 FQ	194900 AW		USBLS	5/15
	Hawaii	Y	98580 FQ	120900 MW		USBLS	5/15
	Urban Honolulu MSA, HI	Y	97540 FQ	117810 MW		USBLS	5/15
	Idaho	Y	105340 FQ	178190 MW		USBLS	5/15
	Boise City MSA, ID	Y	158050 FQ	224190 AW		USBLS	5/15
	Illinois	Y	76420 FQ	130910 MW		USBLS	5/15
	Chicago-Naperville-Arlington Heights PMSA, IL	Y	68670 FQ	122690 MW	154340 TQ	USBLS	5/15
	Lake County-Kenosha County PMSA, IL-WI	Y	135520 FQ	228270 AW		USBLS	5/15
	Indiana	Y	89300 FQ	127010 MW		USBLS	5/15
	Gary PMSA, IN	Y	106440 FQ	155610 MW	186430 TQ	USBLS	5/15
	Indianapolis-Carmel-Anderson MSA, IN	Y	63920 FQ	111220 MW	148360 TQ	USBLS	5/15
	Iowa	Y	109720 FQ	157500 MW		USBLS	5/15
	Des Moines-West Des Moines MSA, IA	Y	108320 FQ	129880 MW		USBLS	5/15
	Kansas	Y	121070 FQ	152490 MW		USBLS	5/15
	Wichita MSA, KS	Y	113210 FQ	163400 MW		USBLS	5/15
	Kentucky	Y	106170 FQ	142850 MW		USBLS	5/15
	Louisville-Jefferson County MSA, KY-IN	Y	113920 FQ	142600 MW		USBLS	5/15
	Louisiana	Y	70610 FQ	123840 MW		USBLS	5/15
	Baton Rouge MSA, LA	Y	121960 FQ	195950 AW		USBLS	5/15
	Maine	Y	119460 FQ	176610 MW		USBLS	5/15
	Portland-South Portland MSA, ME	Y	127830 FQ	183330 MW		USBLS	5/15
	Maryland	Y	67384 AE	158306 MW	203768 AEX	MDBLS	4/16
	Baltimore-Columbia-Towson MSA, MD	Y	130650 FQ	176990 MW		USBLS	5/15
	Salisbury MSA, MD-DE	Y	29670 FQ	132860 MW		USBLS	5/15
	Massachusetts	Y	113670 FQ	155060 MW		USBLS	5/15
	Boston-Cambridge-Newton NECTA, MA	Y	105590 FQ	153200 MW		USBLS	5/15
	Worcester MSA, MA-CT	Y	139270 FQ	222290 AW		USBLS	5/15
	Michigan	Y	88170 FQ	156210 MW		USBLS	5/15
	Detroit-Dearborn-Livonia PMSA, MI	Y	76720 FQ	118160 MW		USBLS	5/15
	Grand Rapids-Wyoming MSA, MI	Y	120530 FQ	205960 AW		USBLS	5/15
	Minnesota	Y	136672 FQ	167901 MW		MNBLS	1/16-3/16
	Minneapolis-St. Paul-Bloomington MSA, MN-WI	Y	137488 FQ	163829 MW		MNBLS	1/16-3/16
	Mississippi	Y	112830 FQ	155090 MW		USBLS	5/15
	Jackson MSA, MS	Y	119980 FQ	159830 MW		USBLS	5/15
	Missouri	Y	100840 FQ	145640 MW		USBLS	5/15
	Kansas City MSA, MO-KS	Y	97150 FQ	143470 MW		USBLS	5/15
	St. Louis MSA, MO-IL	Y	111120 FQ	152630 MW		USBLS	5/15
	Montana	Y	91810 FQ	129470 MW	180500 TQ	USBLS	5/15
	Billings MSA, MT	Y	89780 FQ	121500 MW		USBLS	5/15
	Nebraska	Y	87565 FQ	139800 MW	193850 TQ	NEBLS	7/16-9/16
	Omaha-Council Bluffs MSA, NE-IA	Y	98390 FQ	151615 MW		NEBLS	7/16-9/16
	Nevada	Y	131690 FQ	181280 MW		USBLS	5/15
	Las Vegas-Henderson-Paradise MSA, NV	Y	126860 FQ	169240 MW		USBLS	5/15
	New Hampshire	H	68.09 AE	106.73 AW	126.05 AEX	NHBLS	6/16
	Manchester NECTA, NH	H	74.38 AE	91.75 MW	107.11 AEX	NHBLS	6/16
	Nashua NECTA, NH-MA	Y	147180 FQ	216550 AW		USBLS	5/15
	New Jersey	Y	114890 FQ	146190 MW		USBLS	5/15
	Camden PMSA, NJ	Y	113710 FQ	140240 MW	160910 TQ	USBLS	5/15
	Newark PMSA, NJ-PA	Y	115570 FQ	137010 MW		USBLS	5/15
	Trenton MSA, NJ	Y	99520 FQ	149000 MW		USBLS	5/15
	New Mexico	Y	60050 FQ	163040 MW		USBLS	5/15
	Albuquerque MSA, NM	Y	46400 FQ	155790 MW		USBLS	5/15
	New York	Y	112540 AE	150970 MW		NYBLS	1/16-3/16

Occupation/Type/Industry	Location	Per	Low	Mid	High	Source	Date
Dentist	Buffalo-Cheektowaga-Niagara Falls MSA, NY	Y	153890 FQ	205080 AW		USBLS	5/15
	Nassau County-Suffolk County PMSA, NY	Y	141720 FQ	221560 AW		USBLS	5/15
	New York-Jersey City-White Plains PMSA, NY-NJ	Y	119850 FQ	142180 MW	178900 TQ	USBLS	5/15
	Rochester MSA, NY	Y	145030 FQ	217370 AW		USBLS	5/15
	North Carolina	Y	140710 FQ	211370 AW		USBLS	5/15
	Charlotte-Concord-Gastonia MSA, NC-SC	Y	140070 FQ	222440 AW		USBLS	5/15
	Raleigh MSA, NC	Y	136780 FQ	206870 AW		USBLS	5/15
	North Dakota	Y	140360 FQ	214450 AW		USBLS	5/15
	Fargo MSA, ND-MN	Y	143570 FQ	211360 AW		USBLS	5/15
	Ohio	Y	122580 FQ	171180 MW		USBLS	5/15
	Cincinnati MSA, OH-KY-IN	Y	110760 FQ	149980 MW		USBLS	5/15
	Cleveland-Elyria MSA, OH	Y	112420 FQ	164220 MW		USBLS	5/15
	Columbus MSA, OH	Y	127210 FQ	171170 MW		USBLS	5/15
	Oklahoma	Y	83750 FQ	125850 MW		USBLS	5/15
	Oklahoma City MSA, OK	Y	88260 FQ	104290 MW		USBLS	5/15
	Tulsa MSA, OK	Y	71120 FQ	95580 MW	147900 TQ	USBLS	5/15
	Oregon	H	68.11 FQ	86.71 MW		ORBLS	2016
	Portland-Vancouver-Hillsboro MSA, OR-WA	Y	130260 FQ	153600 MW		USBLS	5/15
	Pennsylvania	Y	86130 FQ	133170 MW		USBLS	5/15
	Allentown-Bethlehem-Easton MSA, PA-NJ	Y	146250 FQ	167840 MW		USBLS	5/15
	Harrisburg-Carlisle MSA, PA	Y	119130 FQ	156640 MW		USBLS	5/15
	Montgomery County-Bucks County-Chester County PMSA, PA	Y	120100 FQ	166550 MW		USBLS	5/15
	Philadelphia PMSA, PA	Y	90850 FQ	144400 MW		USBLS	5/15
	Pittsburgh MSA, PA	Y	56030 FQ	84380 MW	167450 TQ	USBLS	5/15
	Rhode Island	Y	137410 FQ	169270 MW		USBLS	5/15
	Providence-Warwick MSA, RI-MA	Y	136320 FQ	155350 MW		USBLS	5/15
	South Carolina	Y	126590 FQ	186780 MW		USBLS	5/15
	Charleston-North Charleston MSA, SC	Y	130380 FQ	210810 AW		USBLS	5/15
	Columbia MSA, SC	Y	115870 FQ	151910 MW		USBLS	5/15
	Greenville-Anderson-Mauldin MSA, SC	Y	149000 FQ	189470 AW		USBLS	5/15
	South Dakota	Y	99220 FQ	136240 MW	163570 TQ	USBLS	5/15
	Sioux Falls MSA, SD	Y	132570 FQ	149760 MW		USBLS	5/15
	Tennessee	Y	112560 FQ	150070 MW		USBLS	5/15
	Knoxville MSA, TN	Y	106380 FQ	136030 MW		USBLS	5/15
	Memphis MSA, TN-MS-AR	Y	109890 FQ	122130 MW	174000 TQ	USBLS	5/15
	Nashville-Davidson–Murfreesboro–Franklin MSA, TN	Y	108600 FQ	157880 MW		USBLS	5/15
	Texas	Y	126440 FQ	159230 MW		USBLS	5/15
	Austin-Round Rock MSA, TX	Y	133290 FQ	151600 MW	181480 TQ	USBLS	5/15
	Dallas-Plano-Irving PMSA, TX	Y	143530 FQ	195990 AW		USBLS	5/15
	Fort Worth-Arlington PMSA, TX	Y	127710 FQ	175590 MW		USBLS	5/15
	Houston-The Woodlands-Sugar Land MSA, TX	Y	119330 FQ	147360 MW		USBLS	5/15
	San Antonio-New Braunfels MSA, TX	Y	112640 FQ	149330 MW		USBLS	5/15
	Utah	Y	75350 FQ	107450 MW	143460 TQ	USBLS	5/15
	Ogden-Clearfield MSA, UT	Y	59060 FQ	81980 MW	108790 TQ	USBLS	5/15
	Provo-Orem MSA, UT	Y	99890 FQ	130590 MW		USBLS	5/15
	Salt Lake City MSA, UT	Y	109360 FQ	135850 MW	154050 TQ	USBLS	5/15
	Vermont	Y	119290 FQ	166320 MW		USBLS	5/15
	Burlington-South Burlington MSA, VT	Y	102910 FQ	170320 MW		USBLS	5/15
	Virginia	Y	96300 FQ	127980 MW		USBLS	5/15
	Richmond MSA, VA	Y	92100 FQ	112840 MW	144480 TQ	USBLS	5/15
	Virginia Beach-Norfolk-Newport News MSA, VA-NC	Y	61630 FQ	118760 MW		USBLS	5/15
	Washington	H	56.54 FQ	79.23 MW		WABLS	3/16
	Seattle-Bellevue-Everett PMSA, WA	H	63.77 FQ	96.33 AW		WABLS	3/16

AE	Average entry wage	AWR	Average wage range	H	Hourly
AEX	Average experienced wage	B	Biweekly	HI	Highest wage paid
ATC	Average total compensation	D	Daily	HR	High end range
AW	Average wage paid	FQ	First quartile wage	LO	Lowest wage paid

LR	Low end range	MTC	Median total compensation	TCC	Total cash compensation
M	Monthly	MW	Median wage paid	TQ	Third quartile wage
MCC	Median cash compensation	MWR	Median wage range	W	Weekly
ME	Median entry wage	S	See annotated source	Y	Yearly

Occupation/Type/Industry	Location	Per	Low	Mid	High	Source	Date
Dentist	Tacoma-Lakewood PMSA, WA	H	65.65 FQ	80.07 MW		WABLS	3/16
	West Virginia	Y	109090 FQ	138460 MW		USBLS	5/15
	Huntington-Ashland MSA, WV-KY-OH	Y	119640 FQ	172990 MW		USBLS	5/15
	Wisconsin	Y	132710 FQ	203570 AW		USBLS	5/15
	Madison MSA, WI	Y	142030 FQ	184940 MW		USBLS	5/15
	Milwaukee-Waukesha-West Allis MSA, WI	Y	137720 FQ	210260 AW		USBLS	5/15
	Wyoming	Y	110880 FQ	164160 MW		USBLS	5/15
	Cheyenne MSA, WY	Y	121920 FQ	202000 AW		USBLS	5/15
	Puerto Rico	Y	36950 FQ	57770 MW	81840 TQ	USBLS	5/15
	San Juan-Carolina-Caguas MSA, PR	Y	36720 FQ	54160 MW	81970 TQ	USBLS	5/15
	Guam	Y	78340 FQ	141180 MW		USBLS	5/15
Department Manager							
Apparel, Wal-Mart	United States	H	12.00 LO		20.71 HI	WSJ01	2016
Electronics, Wal-Mart	United States	H	15.00 LO		24.70 HI	WSJ01	2016
Departmental Audit Manager							
Airports, Municipal Government	Los Angeles, CA	Y			161947 HI	CACIT	6/23/16
Deputy							
Sheriff's Department, County Government	Wayne County, MI	Y	29000 LO			LSJ12	2016
Deputy Clerk							
Superior Court	Augusta/Richmond County, GA	Y	52599 LO		75393 HI	GACTY04	2016
Superior Court	Crisp County, GA	Y			40500 HI	GACTY04	2016
Superior Court	Glynn County, GA	Y	36728 LO		58763 HI	GACTY04	2016
Deputy Fire Chief							
Municipal Government	Arcadia, CA	Y			170965 HI	CACIT	6/28/16
Municipal Government	Ashfield, MA	H			11.19 HI	FRCOG	2016
Deputy Probation Officer							
Pre-Sentencing Investigation, Adult Probation Department	San Francisco, CA	B	2425 LO		3933 HI	SFGOV	2016-2018
Deputy Registrar							
County Government	Montgomery County, GA	Y	18700 LO		21485 HI	GACTY04	2016
County Government	Newton County, GA	Y	34362 LO		51626 HI	GACTY04	2016
County Government	Ware County, GA	Y	27418 LO		41802 HI	GACTY04	2016
Derrick Operator							
Oil and Gas	Alaska	Y	56130 FQ	69300 MW	78920 TQ	USBLS	5/15
Oil and Gas	Arkansas	Y	42170 FQ	49670 MW	66880 TQ	USBLS	5/15
Oil and Gas	California	H	22.74 FQ	27.20 MW	31.25 TQ	CABLS	1/16-3/16
Oil and Gas	Colorado	Y	35190 FQ	39650 MW	52300 TQ	USBLS	5/15
Oil and Gas	Illinois	Y	31870 FQ	37580 MW	46610 TQ	USBLS	5/15
Oil and Gas	Indiana	Y	36110 FQ	42290 MW	50760 TQ	USBLS	5/15
Oil and Gas	Kansas	Y	36430 FQ	45530 MW	56540 TQ	USBLS	5/15
Oil and Gas	Louisiana	Y	39440 FQ	46060 MW	55040 TQ	USBLS	5/15
Oil and Gas	Michigan	Y	34070 FQ	37510 MW	43570 TQ	USBLS	5/15
Oil and Gas	Mississippi	Y	42020 FQ	50970 MW	58730 TQ	USBLS	5/15
Oil and Gas	New Mexico	Y	37700 FQ	46290 MW	55200 TQ	USBLS	5/15
Oil and Gas	North Dakota	Y	43630 FQ	56230 MW	70960 TQ	USBLS	5/15
Oil and Gas	Ohio	Y	35170 FQ	40000 MW	53130 TQ	USBLS	5/15
Oil and Gas	Oklahoma	Y	40140 FQ	48910 MW	57050 TQ	USBLS	5/15
Oil and Gas	Pennsylvania	Y	36840 FQ	44140 MW	52700 TQ	USBLS	5/15
Oil and Gas	Texas	Y	38250 FQ	46900 MW	58100 TQ	USBLS	5/15
Oil and Gas	Utah	Y	44670 FQ	54170 MW	71270 TQ	USBLS	5/15
Oil and Gas	West Virginia	Y	34990 FQ	43670 MW	55800 TQ	USBLS	5/15
Oil and Gas	Wyoming	Y	43030 FQ	50810 MW	60270 TQ	USBLS	5/15
Desktop Publisher	Alabama	Y	21983 AE	32526 AW	37792 AEX	ALBLS	6/16
	Birmingham-Hoover MSA, AL	Y	22549 AE	36339 AW	43223 AEX	ALBLS	6/16
	Arizona	Y	29730 FQ	43360 MW	54420 TQ	USBLS	5/15
	Phoenix-Mesa-Scottsdale MSA, AZ	Y	29990 FQ	44050 MW	55720 TQ	USBLS	5/15
	Arkansas	Y	20950 FQ	33460 MW	41050 TQ	USBLS	5/15
	California	H	17.61 FQ	22.43 MW	28.82 TQ	CABLS	1/16-3/16

AE	Average entry wage	AWR	Average wage range	H	Hourly	LR	Low end range	MTC	Median total compensation	TCC Total cash compensation
AEX	Average experienced wage	B	Biweekly	HI	Highest wage paid	M	Monthly	MW	Median wage paid	TQ Third quartile wage
ATC	Average total compensation	D	Daily	HR	High end range	MCC	Median cash compensation	MWR	Median wage range	W Weekly
AW	Average wage paid	FQ	First quartile wage	LO	Lowest wage paid	ME	Median entry wage	S	See annotated source	Y Yearly

Occupation/Type/Industry	Location	Per	Low	Mid	High	Source	Date
Desktop Publisher	Anaheim-Santa Ana-Irvine PMSA, CA	H	21.97 FQ	26.82 MW	30.29 TQ	CABLS	1/16-3/16
	Los Angeles-Long Beach-Glendale PMSA, CA	H	18.33 FQ	21.96 MW	27.40 TQ	CABLS	1/16-3/16
	Oakland-Hayward-Berkeley PMSA, CA	H	15.80 FQ	19.70 MW	29.21 TQ	CABLS	1/16-3/16
	Riverside-San Bernardino-Ontario MSA, CA	H	14.91 FQ	17.48 MW	20.09 TQ	CABLS	1/16-3/16
	Sacramento–Roseville–Arden-Arcade MSA, CA	H	20.65 FQ	25.28 MW	29.60 TQ	CABLS	1/16-3/16
	San Diego-Carlsbad MSA, CA	H	13.14 FQ	20.68 MW	26.56 TQ	CABLS	1/16-3/16
	San Francisco-Redwood City-South San Francisco PMSA, CA	H	19.15 FQ	22.54 MW	27.51 TQ	CABLS	1/16-3/16
	Colorado	Y	29230 FQ	38820 MW	58150 TQ	USBLS	5/15
	Denver-Aurora-Lakewood MSA, CO	Y	47730 FQ	57210 MW	66170 TQ	USBLS	5/15
	Connecticut	Y		47770 MW		CTBLS	1/16-3/16
	Hartford-West Hartford-East Hartford MSA, CT	Y	34600 FQ	42310 MW	50270 TQ	USBLS	5/15
	Delaware	Y	27860 FQ	30720 MW	45340 TQ	USBLS	5/15
	Wilmington PMSA, DE-MD-NJ	Y	27800 FQ	30380 MW	44570 TQ	USBLS	5/15
	District of Columbia	Y	39580 FQ	53100 MW	61920 TQ	USBLS	5/15
	Washington-Arlington-Alexandria PMSA, DC-VA-MD-WV	Y	37040 FQ	50500 MW	60790 TQ	USBLS	5/15
	Florida	H	11.84 AE	16.06 MW	19.50 AEX	FLBLS	7/16-9/16
	Fort Lauderdale-Pompano Beach-Deerfield Beach PMSA, FL	H	12.01 AE	19.74 MW	22.58 AEX	FLBLS	7/16-9/16
	Miami-Miami Beach-Kendall PMSA, FL	H	13.11 AE	16.06 MW	18.22 AEX	FLBLS	7/16-9/16
	Orlando-Kissimmee-Sanford MSA, FL	H	9.60 AE	14.28 MW	17.91 AEX	FLBLS	7/16-9/16
	Tampa-St. Petersburg-Clearwater MSA, FL	H	12.30 AE	16.06 MW	19.61 AEX	FLBLS	7/16-9/16
	Georgia	Y	37730 FQ	52420 MW	59430 TQ	USBLS	5/15
	Atlanta-Sandy Springs-Roswell MSA, GA	Y	47570 FQ	55310 MW	60850 TQ	USBLS	5/15
	Hawaii	Y	25970 FQ	32580 MW	42460 TQ	USBLS	5/15
	Urban Honolulu MSA, HI	Y	26420 FQ	33480 MW	43300 TQ	USBLS	5/15
	Idaho	Y	22760 FQ	28900 MW	54330 TQ	USBLS	5/15
	Illinois	Y	33450 FQ	39300 MW	58470 TQ	USBLS	5/15
	Indiana	Y	27310 FQ	31130 MW	37950 TQ	USBLS	5/15
	Indianapolis-Carmel-Anderson MSA, IN	Y	27220 FQ	30550 MW	37430 TQ	USBLS	5/15
	Iowa	Y	32820 FQ	40720 MW	50970 TQ	USBLS	5/15
	Des Moines-West Des Moines MSA, IA	Y	35940 FQ	42700 MW	50040 TQ	USBLS	5/15
	Kansas	Y	27090 FQ	33750 MW	41090 TQ	USBLS	5/15
	Kentucky	Y	33600 FQ	37310 MW	42830 TQ	USBLS	5/15
	Louisiana	Y	30630 FQ	41140 MW	54790 TQ	USBLS	5/15
	Maine	Y	29980 FQ	35300 MW	39390 TQ	USBLS	5/15
	Portland-South Portland MSA, ME	Y	24030 FQ	33120 MW	37220 TQ	USBLS	5/15
	Maryland	Y	36145 AE	53403 MW	62032 AEX	MDBLS	4/16
	Baltimore-Columbia-Towson MSA, MD	Y	35210 FQ	45360 MW	58830 TQ	USBLS	5/15
	Massachusetts	Y	39110 FQ	48240 MW	60100 TQ	USBLS	5/15
	Boston-Cambridge-Newton NECTA, MA	Y	43260 FQ	48860 MW	62050 TQ	USBLS	5/15
	Worcester MSA, MA-CT	Y	52150 FQ	55630 MW	59120 TQ	USBLS	5/15
	Michigan	Y	33330 FQ	39270 MW	47550 TQ	USBLS	5/15
	Detroit-Dearborn-Livonia PMSA, MI	Y	33770 FQ	36610 MW	39460 TQ	USBLS	5/15
	Grand Rapids-Wyoming MSA, MI	Y	36830 FQ	41910 MW	46900 TQ	USBLS	5/15
	Minnesota	Y	33827 FQ	47843 MW	58836 TQ	MNBLS	1/16-3/16
	Minneapolis-St. Paul-Bloomington MSA, MN-WI	Y	36193 FQ	51514 MW	59918 TQ	MNBLS	1/16-3/16
	Mississippi	Y	28140 FQ	31620 MW	38930 TQ	USBLS	5/15

AE	Average entry wage	AWR	Average wage range	H	Hourly
AEX	Average experienced wage	B	Biweekly	HI	Highest wage paid
ATC	Average total compensation	D	Daily	HR	High end range
AW	Average wage paid	FQ	First quartile wage	LO	Lowest wage paid

LR	Low end range	MTC	Median total compensation	TCC	Total cash compensation
M	Monthly	MW	Median wage paid	TQ	Third quartile wage
MCC	Median cash compensation	MWR	Median wage range	W	Weekly
ME	Median entry wage	S	See annotated source	Y	Yearly

Occupation/Type/Industry	Location	Per	Low	Mid	High	Source	Date
Desktop Publisher	Missouri	Y	20060 FQ	26730 MW	46150 TQ	USBLS	5/15
	Kansas City MSA, MO-KS	Y	30190 FQ	36160 MW	44170 TQ	USBLS	5/15
	St. Louis MSA, MO-IL	Y	34910 FQ	48130 MW	60220 TQ	USBLS	5/15
	Nebraska	Y	30165 FQ	35940 MW	42205 TQ	NEBLS	7/16-9/16
	Omaha-Council Bluffs MSA, NE-IA	Y	40275 FQ	45410 MW	51165 TQ	NEBLS	7/16-9/16
	New Hampshire	H	18.35 AE	24.68 MW	27.14 AEX	NHBLS	6/16
	New Jersey	Y	30790 FQ	49880 MW	62820 TQ	USBLS	5/15
	Camden PMSA, NJ	Y	37070 FQ	49740 MW	57290 TQ	USBLS	5/15
	Newark PMSA, NJ-PA	Y	29120 FQ	52680 MW	59910 TQ	USBLS	5/15
	New Mexico	Y	21940 FQ	24630 MW	34630 TQ	USBLS	5/15
	Albuquerque MSA, NM	Y	21650 FQ	23930 MW	30370 TQ	USBLS	5/15
	New York	Y	37440 AE	51940 MW	63510 AEX	NYBLS	1/16-3/16
	Nassau County-Suffolk County PMSA, NY	Y	46540 FQ	55680 MW	64790 TQ	USBLS	5/15
	New York-Jersey City-White Plains PMSA, NY-NJ	Y	41060 FQ	51640 MW	69520 TQ	USBLS	5/15
	Rochester MSA, NY	Y	36320 FQ	42160 MW	56770 TQ	USBLS	5/15
	North Carolina	Y	28450 FQ	36420 MW	55660 TQ	USBLS	5/15
	Raleigh MSA, NC	Y	38700 FQ	58840 MW	69380 TQ	USBLS	5/15
	North Dakota	Y	21280 FQ	26980 MW	40600 TQ	USBLS	5/15
	Ohio	Y	25780 FQ	34700 MW	46710 TQ	USBLS	5/15
	Cincinnati MSA, OH-KY-IN	Y	23950 FQ	32150 MW	40030 TQ	USBLS	5/15
	Cleveland-Elyria MSA, OH	Y	28090 FQ	37610 MW	61250 TQ	USBLS	5/15
	Oklahoma	Y	22650 FQ	32220 MW	43410 TQ	USBLS	5/15
	Oklahoma City MSA, OK	Y	23780 FQ	33770 MW	56370 TQ	USBLS	5/15
	Oregon	H	17.26 FQ	21.42 MW	26.09 TQ	ORBLS	2016
	Portland-Vancouver-Hillsboro MSA, OR-WA	Y	32900 FQ	41650 MW	60900 TQ	USBLS	5/15
	Pennsylvania	Y	29720 FQ	37950 MW	49840 TQ	USBLS	5/15
	Allentown-Bethlehem-Easton MSA, PA-NJ	Y	28480 FQ	33510 MW	39750 TQ	USBLS	5/15
	Harrisburg-Carlisle MSA, PA	Y	32580 FQ	35890 MW	39210 TQ	USBLS	5/15
	Montgomery County-Bucks County-Chester County PMSA, PA	Y	31280 FQ	40560 MW	52530 TQ	USBLS	5/15
	Philadelphia PMSA, PA	Y	23290 FQ	45350 MW	62790 TQ	USBLS	5/15
	Pittsburgh MSA, PA	Y	35150 FQ	41540 MW	52480 TQ	USBLS	5/15
	South Carolina	Y	25200 FQ	31880 MW	45660 TQ	USBLS	5/15
	Charleston-North Charleston MSA, SC	Y	23740 FQ	30740 MW	45180 TQ	USBLS	5/15
	Tennessee	Y	25280 FQ	31230 MW	46330 TQ	USBLS	5/15
	Texas	Y	26890 FQ	34700 MW	41450 TQ	USBLS	5/15
	Austin-Round Rock MSA, TX	Y	24420 FQ	34790 MW	39380 TQ	USBLS	5/15
	Dallas-Plano-Irving PMSA, TX	Y	33050 FQ	37260 MW	51970 TQ	USBLS	5/15
	Fort Worth-Arlington PMSA, TX	Y	26340 FQ	33940 MW	39070 TQ	USBLS	5/15
	Houston-The Woodlands-Sugar Land MSA, TX	Y	31940 FQ	40200 MW	47090 TQ	USBLS	5/15
	Utah	Y	28570 FQ	40800 MW	47200 TQ	USBLS	5/15
	Vermont	Y	31590 FQ	36720 MW	45740 TQ	USBLS	5/15
	Virginia	Y	34510 FQ	48240 MW	61210 TQ	USBLS	5/15
	Washington	H	17.58 FQ	27.31 MW	33.72 TQ	WABLS	3/16
	Seattle-Bellevue-Everett PMSA, WA	H	19.92 FQ	28.83 MW	34.87 TQ	WABLS	3/16
	West Virginia	Y	24140 FQ	31030 MW	44930 TQ	USBLS	5/15
	Wisconsin	Y	34390 FQ	42690 MW	51590 TQ	USBLS	5/15
	Madison MSA, WI	Y	35770 FQ	44720 MW	60660 TQ	USBLS	5/15
	Milwaukee-Waukesha-West Allis MSA, WI	Y	39140 FQ	46210 MW	55540 TQ	USBLS	5/15
Detective and Criminal Investigator	Alabama	Y	36222 AE	62363 AW	75439 AEX	ALBLS	6/16
	Birmingham-Hoover MSA, AL	Y	44222 AE	76675 AW	92901 AEX	ALBLS	6/16
	Alaska	Y	92020 FQ	118190 MW	132940 TQ	USBLS	5/15
	Anchorage MSA, AK	Y	99660 FQ	121540 MW	132950 TQ	USBLS	5/15
	Arizona	Y	70190 FQ	77210 MW	78980 TQ	USBLS	5/15
	Phoenix-Mesa-Scottsdale MSA, AZ	Y	48850 FQ	73440 MW	86140 TQ	USBLS	5/15
	Tucson MSA, AZ	Y	70190 FQ	77210 MW	79550 TQ	USBLS	5/15
	Arkansas	Y	34760 FQ	41180 MW	67470 TQ	USBLS	5/15

AE	Average entry wage	AWR	Average wage range	H	Hourly	LR	Low end range	MTC	Median total compensation	TCC	Total cash compensation
AEX	Average experienced wage	B	Biweekly	HI	Highest wage paid	M	Monthly	MW	Median wage paid	TQ	Third quartile wage
ATC	Average total compensation	D	Daily	HR	High end range	MCC	Median cash compensation	MWR	Median wage range	W	Weekly
AW	Average wage paid	FQ	First quartile wage	LO	Lowest wage paid	ME	Median entry wage	S	See annotated source	Y	Yearly

418

Occupation/Type/Industry	Location	Per	Low	Mid	High	Source	Date
Detective and Criminal Investigator	Little Rock-North Little Rock-Conway MSA, AR	Y	36060 FQ	43740 MW	104340 TQ	USBLS	5/15
	California	H	38.47 FQ	43.44 MW	57.97 TQ	CABLS	1/16-3/16
	Anaheim-Santa Ana-Irvine PMSA, CA	H	40.35 FQ	49.82 MW	59.00 TQ	CABLS	1/16-3/16
	Los Angeles-Long Beach-Glendale PMSA, CA	H	48.56 FQ	56.87 MW	62.68 TQ	CABLS	1/16-3/16
	Oakland-Hayward-Berkeley PMSA, CA	H	41.27 FQ	53.28 MW	62.22 TQ	CABLS	1/16-3/16
	Riverside-San Bernardino-Ontario MSA, CA	H	40.89 FQ	43.02 MW	47.51 TQ	CABLS	1/16-3/16
	Sacramento–Roseville–Arden-Arcade MSA, CA	H	32.34 FQ	38.18 MW	50.45 TQ	CABLS	1/16-3/16
	San Diego-Carlsbad MSA, CA	H	39.33 FQ	41.19 MW	43.69 TQ	CABLS	1/16-3/16
	San Francisco-Redwood City-South San Francisco PMSA, CA	H	44.97 FQ	62.58 MW	70.66 TQ	CABLS	1/16-3/16
	Colorado	Y	61530 FQ	80350 MW	97940 TQ	USBLS	5/15
	Denver-Aurora-Lakewood MSA, CO	Y	71250 FQ	87180 MW	101420 TQ	USBLS	5/15
	Connecticut	Y		79825 MW		CTBLS	1/16-3/16
	Bridgeport-Stamford-Norwalk MSA, CT	Y	71530 FQ	84660 MW	95790 TQ	USBLS	5/15
	Hartford-West Hartford-East Hartford MSA, CT	Y	68970 FQ	78190 MW	95070 TQ	USBLS	5/15
	Delaware	Y	54810 FQ	93610 MW	133560 TQ	USBLS	5/15
	Wilmington PMSA, DE-MD-NJ	Y	54840 FQ	93600 MW	126150 TQ	USBLS	5/15
	District of Columbia	Y	96350 FQ	128650 MW	136230 TQ	USBLS	5/15
	Washington-Arlington-Alexandria PMSA, DC-VA-MD-WV	Y	90290 FQ	124880 MW	136240 TQ	USBLS	5/15
	Florida	H	21.45 AE	31.62 MW	45.76 AEX	FLBLS	7/16-9/16
	Fort Lauderdale-Pompano Beach-Deerfield Beach PMSA, FL	H	26.80 AE	47.65 MW	57.41 AEX	FLBLS	7/16-9/16
	Miami-Miami Beach-Kendall PMSA, FL	H	27.76 AE	55.18 MW	59.95 AEX	FLBLS	7/16-9/16
	Orlando-Kissimmee-Sanford MSA, FL	H	21.34 AE	27.33 MW	39.98 AEX	FLBLS	7/16-9/16
	Tampa-St. Petersburg-Clearwater MSA, FL	H	23.05 AE	33.80 MW	44.48 AEX	FLBLS	7/16-9/16
	Georgia	Y	39330 FQ	47480 MW	75180 TQ	USBLS	5/15
	Atlanta-Sandy Springs-Roswell MSA, GA	Y	41410 FQ	49050 MW	86680 TQ	USBLS	5/15
	Augusta-Richmond County MSA, GA-SC	Y	42390 FQ	54310 MW	79550 TQ	USBLS	5/15
	Hawaii	Y	83400 FQ	93560 MW	110440 TQ	USBLS	5/15
	Urban Honolulu MSA, HI	Y	85690 FQ	95530 MW	117140 TQ	USBLS	5/15
	Idaho	Y	47810 FQ	59540 MW	73300 TQ	USBLS	5/15
	Boise City MSA, ID	Y	48550 FQ	63100 MW	105300 TQ	USBLS	5/15
	Illinois	Y	69400 FQ	88310 MW	115870 TQ	USBLS	5/15
	Chicago-Naperville-Arlington Heights PMSA, IL	Y	73540 FQ	93140 MW	125770 TQ	USBLS	5/15
	Lake County-Kenosha County PMSA, IL-WI	Y	68500 FQ	77110 MW	91670 TQ	USBLS	5/15
	Indiana	Y	45350 FQ	58770 MW	72350 TQ	USBLS	5/15
	Gary PMSA, IN	Y	55440 FQ	96150 MW	129570 TQ	USBLS	5/15
	Indianapolis-Carmel-Anderson MSA, IN	Y	55670 FQ	68100 MW	75600 TQ	USBLS	5/15
	Iowa	Y	59940 FQ	74400 MW	89200 TQ	USBLS	5/15
	Des Moines-West Des Moines MSA, IA	Y	63630 FQ	74390 MW	97590 TQ	USBLS	5/15
	Kansas	Y	41790 FQ	50200 MW	69350 TQ	USBLS	5/15
	Wichita MSA, KS	Y	53820 FQ	68270 MW	78250 TQ	USBLS	5/15
	Kentucky	Y	40120 FQ	50650 MW	99290 TQ	USBLS	5/15
	Louisville-Jefferson County MSA, KY-IN	Y	41630 FQ	49320 MW	107810 TQ	USBLS	5/15
	Louisiana	Y	38060 FQ	48210 MW	79550 TQ	USBLS	5/15
	Baton Rouge MSA, LA	Y	40260 FQ	53160 MW	69430 TQ	USBLS	5/15

AE	Average entry wage	AWR	Average wage range	H	Hourly
AEX	Average experiened wage	B	Biweekly	HI	Highest wage paid
ATC	Average total compensation	D	Daily	HR	High end range
AW	Average wage paid	FQ	First quartile wage	LO	Lowest wage paid

LR	Low end range	MTC	Median total compensation	TCC	Total cash compensation
M	Monthly	MW	Median wage paid	TQ	Third quartile wage
MCC	Median cash compensation	MWR	Median wage range	W	Weekly
ME	Median entry wage	S	See annotated source	Y	Yearly

Occupation/Type/Industry	Location	Per	Low	Mid	High	Source	Date
Detective and Criminal Investigator	New Orleans-Metairie MSA, LA	Y	47020 FQ	88540 MW	118240 TQ	USBLS	5/15
	Maine	Y	46470 FQ	60060 MW	77230 TQ	USBLS	5/15
	Portland-South Portland MSA, ME	Y	51530 FQ	61810 MW	99280 TQ	USBLS	5/15
	Maryland	Y	50017 AE	96412 MW	119610 AEX	MDBLS	4/16
	Baltimore-Columbia-Towson MSA, MD	Y	53190 FQ	96760 MW	132440 TQ	USBLS	5/15
	Massachusetts	Y	61380 FQ	73420 MW	99770 TQ	USBLS	5/15
	Boston-Cambridge-Newton NECTA, MA	Y	63950 FQ	74740 MW	117860 TQ	USBLS	5/15
	Worcester MSA, MA-CT	Y	70930 FQ	84880 MW	97870 TQ	USBLS	5/15
	Michigan	Y	63110 FQ	75460 MW	99870 TQ	USBLS	5/15
	Detroit-Dearborn-Livonia PMSA, MI	Y	75440 FQ	86480 MW	128530 TQ	USBLS	5/15
	Grand Rapids-Wyoming MSA, MI	Y	65600 FQ	76170 MW	114770 TQ	USBLS	5/15
	Minnesota	Y	56078 FQ	70671 MW	81052 TQ	MNBLS	1/16-3/16
	Minneapolis-St. Paul-Bloomington MSA, MN-WI	Y	57482 FQ	72599 MW	90131 TQ	MNBLS	1/16-3/16
	Mississippi	Y	36740 FQ	45660 MW	59360 TQ	USBLS	5/15
	Jackson MSA, MS	Y	37490 FQ	44940 MW	56700 TQ	USBLS	5/15
	Missouri	Y	41020 FQ	65390 MW	92340 TQ	USBLS	5/15
	Kansas City MSA, MO-KS	Y	47960 FQ	70610 MW	96530 TQ	USBLS	5/15
	St. Louis MSA, MO-IL	Y	53840 FQ	73330 MW	101870 TQ	USBLS	5/15
	Montana	Y	54760 FQ	74870 MW	84220 TQ	USBLS	5/15
	Billings MSA, MT	Y	54760 FQ	77220 MW	121730 TQ	USBLS	5/15
	Nebraska	Y	48730 FQ	62455 MW	111140 TQ	NEBLS	7/16-9/16
	Omaha-Council Bluffs MSA, NE-IA	Y	57955 FQ	80765 MW	114765 TQ	NEBLS	7/16-9/16
	Nevada	Y	60180 FQ	77230 MW	99990 TQ	USBLS	5/15
	Las Vegas-Henderson-Paradise MSA, NV	Y	60080 FQ	81900 MW	109300 TQ	USBLS	5/15
	New Hampshire	H	25.03 AE	32.13 MW	42.82 AEX	NHBLS	6/16
	Manchester NECTA, NH	H	28.89 AE	41.37 MW	58.63 AEX	NHBLS	6/16
	Nashua NECTA, NH-MA	Y	63850 FQ	69050 MW	74620 TQ	USBLS	5/15
	New Jersey	Y	80100 FQ	100850 MW	122340 TQ	USBLS	5/15
	Camden PMSA, NJ	Y	76900 FQ	93700 MW	110020 TQ	USBLS	5/15
	Newark PMSA, NJ-PA	Y	87060 FQ	104910 MW	125780 TQ	USBLS	5/15
	Trenton MSA, NJ	Y	71920 FQ	91370 MW	112020 TQ	USBLS	5/15
	New Mexico	Y	72540 FQ	77220 MW	77230 TQ	USBLS	5/15
	New York	Y	50340 AE	83060 MW	106350 AEX	NYBLS	1/16-3/16
	Buffalo-Cheektowaga-Niagara Falls MSA, NY	Y	66880 FQ	79120 MW	98890 TQ	USBLS	5/15
	Nassau County-Suffolk County PMSA, NY	Y	106420 FQ	124730 MW	144150 TQ	USBLS	5/15
	New York-Jersey City-White Plains PMSA, NY-NJ	Y	52620 FQ	78220 MW	121200 TQ	USBLS	5/15
	Rochester MSA, NY	Y	66660 FQ	75940 MW	89740 TQ	USBLS	5/15
	North Carolina	Y	40880 FQ	47150 MW	58530 TQ	USBLS	5/15
	Charlotte-Concord-Gastonia MSA, NC-SC	Y	42200 FQ	48930 MW	66570 TQ	USBLS	5/15
	Raleigh MSA, NC	Y	46630 FQ	56390 MW	70340 TQ	USBLS	5/15
	North Dakota	Y	59500 FQ	77210 MW	91260 TQ	USBLS	5/15
	Fargo MSA, ND-MN	Y	64590 FQ	80320 MW	104340 TQ	USBLS	5/15
	Ohio	Y	50670 FQ	61420 MW	78400 TQ	USBLS	5/15
	Cincinnati MSA, OH-KY-IN	Y	53830 FQ	65350 MW	94140 TQ	USBLS	5/15
	Cleveland-Elyria MSA, OH	Y	53840 FQ	71350 MW	115700 TQ	USBLS	5/15
	Columbus MSA, OH	Y	51730 FQ	59050 MW	76100 TQ	USBLS	5/15
	Oklahoma	Y	46220 FQ	60490 MW	84620 TQ	USBLS	5/15
	Oklahoma City MSA, OK	Y	49300 FQ	64060 MW	96520 TQ	USBLS	5/15
	Tulsa MSA, OK	Y	49860 FQ	68650 MW	114740 TQ	USBLS	5/15
	Oregon	H	31.28 FQ	39.81 MW	49.24 TQ	ORBLS	2016
	Portland-Vancouver-Hillsboro MSA, OR-WA	Y	63800 FQ	83940 MW	101960 TQ	USBLS	5/15
	Pennsylvania	Y	64300 FQ	74870 MW	97340 TQ	USBLS	5/15
	Allentown-Bethlehem-Easton MSA, PA-NJ	Y	62990 FQ	73210 MW	102880 TQ	USBLS	5/15
	Harrisburg-Carlisle MSA, PA	Y	57420 FQ	71200 MW	85410 TQ	USBLS	5/15

AE	Average entry wage	AWR	Average wage range	H	Hourly	LR	Low end range	MTC	Median total compensation	TCC	Total cash compensation
AEX	Average experienced wage	B	Biweekly	HI	Highest wage paid	M	Monthly	MW	Median wage paid	TQ	Third quartile wage
ATC	Average total compensation	D	Daily	HR	High end range	MCC	Median cash compensation	MWR	Median wage range	W	Weekly
AW	Average wage paid	FQ	First quartile wage	LO	Lowest wage paid	ME	Median entry wage	S	See annotated source	Y	Yearly

420

Occupation/Type/Industry	Location	Per	Low	Mid	High	Source	Date
Detective and Criminal Investigator	Montgomery County-Bucks County-Chester County PMSA, PA	Y	64100 FQ	86120 MW	97050 TQ	USBLS	5/15
	Philadelphia PMSA, PA	Y	67160 FQ	76010 MW	115010 TQ	USBLS	5/15
	Pittsburgh MSA, PA	Y	64600 FQ	74900 MW	99270 TQ	USBLS	5/15
	Rhode Island	Y	64610 FQ	71570 MW	99120 TQ	USBLS	5/15
	Providence-Warwick MSA, RI-MA	Y	62950 FQ	71560 MW	91480 TQ	USBLS	5/15
	South Carolina	Y	38000 FQ	48110 MW	71030 TQ	USBLS	5/15
	Charleston-North Charleston MSA, SC	Y	55230 FQ	107810 MW	125210 TQ	USBLS	5/15
	Columbia MSA, SC	Y	39890 FQ	53830 MW	77210 TQ	USBLS	5/15
	Greenville-Anderson-Mauldin MSA, SC	Y	42580 FQ	48730 MW	73210 TQ	USBLS	5/15
	South Dakota	Y	46360 FQ	59100 MW	90650 TQ	USBLS	5/15
	Sioux Falls MSA, SD	Y	57860 FQ	87750 MW	118240 TQ	USBLS	5/15
	Tennessee	Y	42060 FQ	51180 MW	76560 TQ	USBLS	5/15
	Knoxville MSA, TN	Y	42260 FQ	60280 MW	99440 TQ	USBLS	5/15
	Memphis MSA, TN-MS-AR	Y	45930 FQ	56080 MW	90650 TQ	USBLS	5/15
	Nashville-Davidson–Murfreesboro–Franklin MSA, TN	Y	46220 FQ	57700 MW	90850 TQ	USBLS	5/15
	Texas	Y	52350 FQ	74880 MW	79550 TQ	USBLS	5/15
	Austin-Round Rock MSA, TX	Y	43790 FQ	58560 MW	86780 TQ	USBLS	5/15
	Dallas-Plano-Irving PMSA, TX	Y	54870 FQ	92730 MW	132330 TQ	USBLS	5/15
	Fort Worth-Arlington PMSA, TX	Y	42970 FQ	54930 MW	74900 TQ	USBLS	5/15
	Houston-The Woodlands-Sugar Land MSA, TX	Y	52350 FQ	71150 MW	133320 TQ	USBLS	5/15
	San Antonio-New Braunfels MSA, TX	Y	52340 FQ	68960 MW	78560 TQ	USBLS	5/15
	Utah	Y	46130 FQ	59500 MW	107810 TQ	USBLS	5/15
	Ogden-Clearfield MSA, UT	Y	48000 FQ	56050 MW	65540 TQ	USBLS	5/15
	Salt Lake City MSA, UT	Y	44830 FQ	71100 MW	114760 TQ	USBLS	5/15
	Vermont	Y	59320 FQ	77220 MW	84230 TQ	USBLS	5/15
	Burlington-South Burlington MSA, VT	Y	59690 FQ	77270 MW	104700 TQ	USBLS	5/15
	Virginia	Y	59150 FQ	86720 MW	125210 TQ	USBLS	5/15
	Richmond MSA, VA	Y	54970 FQ	66710 MW	90630 TQ	USBLS	5/15
	Virginia Beach-Norfolk-Newport News MSA, VA-NC	Y	55010 FQ	79540 MW	114770 TQ	USBLS	5/15
	Washington	H	26.26 FQ	38.99 MW	49.30 TQ	WABLS	3/16
	Seattle-Bellevue-Everett PMSA, WA	H	27.89 FQ	46.62 MW	60.03 TQ	WABLS	3/16
	Tacoma-Lakewood PMSA, WA	H	24.98 FQ	33.67 MW	47.73 TQ	WABLS	3/16
	West Virginia	Y	33960 FQ	41290 MW	90670 TQ	USBLS	5/15
	Huntington-Ashland MSA, WV-KY-OH	Y	45060 FQ	65690 MW	77280 TQ	USBLS	5/15
	Wisconsin	Y	58990 FQ	70150 MW	80520 TQ	USBLS	5/15
	Madison MSA, WI	Y	62660 FQ	74360 MW	89050 TQ	USBLS	5/15
	Milwaukee-Waukesha-West Allis MSA, WI	Y	66770 FQ	76560 MW	111550 TQ	USBLS	5/15
	Wyoming	Y	59780 FQ	69730 MW	82850 TQ	USBLS	5/15
	Cheyenne MSA, WY	Y	61230 FQ	73210 MW	99430 TQ	USBLS	5/15
	Puerto Rico	Y	33130 FQ	48370 MW	105710 TQ	USBLS	5/15
	San Juan-Carolina-Caguas MSA, PR	Y	31680 FQ	42740 MW	104350 TQ	USBLS	5/15
Detention Facility Officer							
Municipal Government	East Point, GA	Y	30603 LO		47731 HI	GACTY01	2016
Municipal Government	Powder Springs, GA	Y	27122 LO		42040 HI	GACTY01	2016
Municipal Government	Detroit, MI	M	2267 LO		2700 HI	DETGOV	2016
Detention Nurse							
County Government	Apache County, AZ	Y			50554 HI	AZGOV	2017
County Government	La Paz County, AZ	Y			48006 HI	AZGOV	2017
Developmental Psychologist							
First-Year	United States	Y		55000 MW		APAC01	2016
DevOps Engineer	United States	Y		110000 MW		CNBC08	2017

AE	Average entry wage	AWR	Average wage range	H	Hourly	LR	Low end range
AEX	Average experienced wage	B	Biweekly	HI	Highest wage paid	M	Monthly
ATC	Average total compensation	D	Daily	HR	High end range	MCC	Median cash compensation
AW	Average wage paid	FQ	First quartile wage	LO	Lowest wage paid	ME	Median entry wage

MTC Median total compensation TCC Total cash compensation
MW Median wage paid TQ Third quartile wage
MWR Median wage range W Weekly
S See annotated source Y Yearly

Occupation/Type/Industry	Location	Per	Low	Mid	High	Source	Date
DevOps Specialist							
Bachelor's Degree	United States	Y		105544 AW		FTUNE02	2015
Diagnostic Medical Sonographer	Alabama	Y	41609 AE	55523 AW	62485 AEX	ALBLS	6/16
	Birmingham-Hoover MSA, AL	Y	50854 AE	60731 AW	50854 AEX	ALBLS	6/16
	Alaska	Y	68170 FQ	82880 MW	92990 TQ	USBLS	5/15
	Anchorage MSA, AK	Y	66520 FQ	79950 MW	91250 TQ	USBLS	5/15
	Arizona	Y	70280 FQ	83030 MW	93810 TQ	USBLS	5/15
	Phoenix-Mesa-Scottsdale MSA, AZ	Y	71410 FQ	84340 MW	94610 TQ	USBLS	5/15
	Tucson MSA, AZ	Y	69290 FQ	77980 MW	90610 TQ	USBLS	5/15
	Arkansas	Y	46910 FQ	58470 MW	70640 TQ	USBLS	5/15
	Little Rock-North Little Rock-Conway MSA, AR	Y	38910 FQ	58830 MW	71170 TQ	USBLS	5/15
	California	H	36.89 FQ	47.05 MW	57.54 TQ	CABLS	1/16-3/16
	Anaheim-Santa Ana-Irvine PMSA, CA	H	33.53 FQ	39.53 MW	52.46 TQ	CABLS	1/16-3/16
	Los Angeles-Long Beach-Glendale PMSA, CA	H	35.44 FQ	43.07 MW	50.80 TQ	CABLS	1/16-3/16
	Oakland-Hayward-Berkeley PMSA, CA	H	48.26 FQ	57.15 MW	67.56 TQ	CABLS	1/16-3/16
	Riverside-San Bernardino-Ontario MSA, CA	H	27.44 FQ	35.49 MW	44.74 TQ	CABLS	1/16-3/16
	Sacramento–Roseville–Arden-Arcade MSA, CA	H	46.38 FQ	53.95 MW	59.45 TQ	CABLS	1/16-3/16
	San Diego-Carlsbad MSA, CA	H	39.41 FQ	44.99 MW	51.26 TQ	CABLS	1/16-3/16
	San Francisco-Redwood City-South San Francisco PMSA, CA	H	51.65 FQ	58.99 MW	68.35 TQ	CABLS	1/16-3/16
	Colorado	Y	69820 FQ	79850 MW	92200 TQ	USBLS	5/15
	Denver-Aurora-Lakewood MSA, CO	Y	70810 FQ	81050 MW	93310 TQ	USBLS	5/15
	Connecticut	Y		75793 MW		CTBLS	1/16-3/16
	Bridgeport-Stamford-Norwalk MSA, CT	Y	58170 FQ	64750 MW	81730 TQ	USBLS	5/15
	Hartford-West Hartford-East Hartford MSA, CT	Y	59830 FQ	74170 MW	88830 TQ	USBLS	5/15
	Delaware	Y	64440 FQ	71640 MW	79270 TQ	USBLS	5/15
	Wilmington PMSA, DE-MD-NJ	Y	63950 FQ	71370 MW	79230 TQ	USBLS	5/15
	District of Columbia	Y	77300 FQ	89240 MW	99380 TQ	USBLS	5/15
	Washington-Arlington-Alexandria PMSA, DC-VA-MD-WV	Y	63780 FQ	78460 MW	92460 TQ	USBLS	5/15
	Florida	H	23.97 AE	30.45 MW	33.93 AEX	FLBLS	7/16-9/16
	Fort Lauderdale-Pompano Beach-Deerfield Beach PMSA, FL	H	27.12 AE	32.76 MW	35.99 AEX	FLBLS	7/16-9/16
	Miami-Miami Beach-Kendall PMSA, FL	H	21.53 AE	30.04 MW	33.18 AEX	FLBLS	7/16-9/16
	Orlando-Kissimmee-Sanford MSA, FL	H	23.95 AE	30.87 MW	34.62 AEX	FLBLS	7/16-9/16
	Tampa-St. Petersburg-Clearwater MSA, FL	H	23.78 AE	31.20 MW	34.30 AEX	FLBLS	7/16-9/16
	Georgia	Y	52370 FQ	61070 MW	71940 TQ	USBLS	5/15
	Atlanta-Sandy Springs-Roswell MSA, GA	Y	54960 FQ	63340 MW	73560 TQ	USBLS	5/15
	Augusta-Richmond County MSA, GA-SC	Y	56740 FQ	65560 MW	73360 TQ	USBLS	5/15
	Hawaii	Y	60390 FQ	79890 MW	92570 TQ	USBLS	5/15
	Urban Honolulu MSA, HI	Y	70740 FQ	86840 MW	96120 TQ	USBLS	5/15
	Idaho	Y	58220 FQ	67380 MW	74950 TQ	USBLS	5/15
	Boise City MSA, ID	Y	56620 FQ	65000 MW	73790 TQ	USBLS	5/15
	Illinois	Y	64370 FQ	75490 MW	88560 TQ	USBLS	5/15
	Chicago-Naperville-Arlington Heights PMSA, IL	Y	66440 FQ	77730 MW	91140 TQ	USBLS	5/15
	Lake County-Kenosha County PMSA, IL-WI	Y	60300 FQ	72620 MW	86160 TQ	USBLS	5/15
	Indiana	Y	55290 FQ	63750 MW	74070 TQ	USBLS	5/15
	Gary PMSA, IN	Y	58120 FQ	70640 MW	83750 TQ	USBLS	5/15
	Indianapolis-Carmel-Anderson MSA, IN	Y	59350 FQ	68260 MW	76370 TQ	USBLS	5/15

AE	Average entry wage	AWR	Average wage range	H	Hourly
AEX	Average experienced wage	B	Biweekly	HI	Highest wage paid
ATC	Average total compensation	D	Daily	HR	High end range
AW	Average wage paid	FQ	First quartile wage	LO	Lowest wage paid

LR	Low end range	MTC	Median total compensation
M	Monthly	MW	Median wage paid
MCC	Median cash compensation	MWR	Median wage range
ME	Median entry wage	S	See annotated source

TCC	Total cash compensation		
TQ	Third quartile wage		
W	Weekly		
Y	Yearly		

Occupation/Type/Industry	Location	Per	Low	Mid	High	Source	Date
Diagnostic Medical Sonographer	Iowa	Y	54240 FQ	61460 MW	71870 TQ	USBLS	5/15
	Des Moines-West Des Moines MSA, IA	Y	55500 FQ	64160 MW	73370 TQ	USBLS	5/15
	Kansas	Y	55670 FQ	66100 MW	78200 TQ	USBLS	5/15
	Wichita MSA, KS	Y	57380 FQ	66570 MW	78350 TQ	USBLS	5/15
	Kentucky	Y	51560 FQ	60030 MW	70730 TQ	USBLS	5/15
	Louisville-Jefferson County MSA, KY-IN	Y	50530 FQ	58920 MW	69190 TQ	USBLS	5/15
	Louisiana	Y	50470 FQ	58420 MW	68750 TQ	USBLS	5/15
	Baton Rouge MSA, LA	Y	49670 FQ	58740 MW	71510 TQ	USBLS	5/15
	New Orleans-Metairie MSA, LA	Y	52000 FQ	60640 MW	70710 TQ	USBLS	5/15
	Maine	Y	59980 FQ	73680 MW	88750 TQ	USBLS	5/15
	Portland-South Portland MSA, ME	Y	61870 FQ	79960 MW	97700 TQ	USBLS	5/15
	Maryland	Y	59005 AE	72758 MW	79635 AEX	MDBLS	4/16
	Baltimore-Columbia-Towson MSA, MD	Y	63640 FQ	72060 MW	81460 TQ	USBLS	5/15
	Salisbury MSA, MD-DE	Y	60580 FQ	71800 MW	81820 TQ	USBLS	5/15
	Massachusetts	Y	69130 FQ	83460 MW	95630 TQ	USBLS	5/15
	Boston-Cambridge-Newton NECTA, MA	Y	69140 FQ	85280 MW	96940 TQ	USBLS	5/15
	Worcester MSA, MA-CT	Y	68150 FQ	76090 MW	90120 TQ	USBLS	5/15
	Michigan	Y	52670 FQ	59710 MW	68840 TQ	USBLS	5/15
	Detroit-Dearborn-Livonia PMSA, MI	Y	51690 FQ	59120 MW	68240 TQ	USBLS	5/15
	Grand Rapids-Wyoming MSA, MI	Y	51710 FQ	57900 MW	64600 TQ	USBLS	5/15
	Minnesota	Y	66914 FQ	75937 MW	87569 TQ	MNBLS	1/16-3/16
	Minneapolis-St. Paul-Bloomington MSA, MN-WI	Y	66733 FQ	75755 MW	87196 TQ	MNBLS	1/16-3/16
	Mississippi	Y	53090 FQ	61050 MW	71500 TQ	USBLS	5/15
	Jackson MSA, MS	Y	55700 FQ	64110 MW	72880 TQ	USBLS	5/15
	Missouri	Y	57070 FQ	66290 MW	75570 TQ	USBLS	5/15
	Kansas City MSA, MO-KS	Y	63050 FQ	71280 MW	80110 TQ	USBLS	5/15
	St. Louis MSA, MO-IL	Y	55310 FQ	63960 MW	74950 TQ	USBLS	5/15
	Montana	Y	58250 FQ	69350 MW	79940 TQ	USBLS	5/15
	Billings MSA, MT	Y	57380 FQ	65700 MW	75370 TQ	USBLS	5/15
	Nebraska	Y	55605 FQ	63450 MW	73400 TQ	NEBLS	7/16-9/16
	Omaha-Council Bluffs MSA, NE-IA	Y	56580 FQ	64780 MW	73785 TQ	NEBLS	7/16-9/16
	Nevada	Y	66700 FQ	75760 MW	88140 TQ	USBLS	5/15
	Las Vegas-Henderson-Paradise MSA, NV	Y	66480 FQ	75620 MW	88280 TQ	USBLS	5/15
	New Hampshire	H	30.22 AE	37.61 MW	40.66 AEX	NHBLS	6/16
	Manchester NECTA, NH	H	31.32 AE	39.39 MW	42.13 AEX	NHBLS	6/16
	New Jersey	Y	64080 FQ	73300 MW	84830 TQ	USBLS	5/15
	Camden PMSA, NJ	Y	65670 FQ	74360 MW	86050 TQ	USBLS	5/15
	Newark PMSA, NJ-PA	Y	64820 FQ	73720 MW	85580 TQ	USBLS	5/15
	Trenton MSA, NJ	Y	64260 FQ	74080 MW	86310 TQ	USBLS	5/15
	New Mexico	Y	55770 FQ	65340 MW	75490 TQ	USBLS	5/15
	Albuquerque MSA, NM	Y	58550 FQ	67020 MW	75160 TQ	USBLS	5/15
	New York	Y	52510 AE	70190 MW	78720 AEX	NYBLS	1/16-3/16
	Buffalo-Cheektowaga-Niagara Falls MSA, NY	Y	58330 FQ	66860 MW	74380 TQ	USBLS	5/15
	Nassau County-Suffolk County PMSA, NY	Y	56880 FQ	67250 MW	77410 TQ	USBLS	5/15
	New York-Jersey City-White Plains PMSA, NY-NJ	Y	61130 FQ	71800 MW	82410 TQ	USBLS	5/15
	Rochester MSA, NY	Y	58570 FQ	68510 MW	76930 TQ	USBLS	5/15
	North Carolina	Y	56020 FQ	64370 MW	74180 TQ	USBLS	5/15
	Charlotte-Concord-Gastonia MSA, NC-SC	Y	55630 FQ	62680 MW	72490 TQ	USBLS	5/15
	Raleigh MSA, NC	Y	57190 FQ	65170 MW	73810 TQ	USBLS	5/15
	North Dakota	Y	57100 FQ	66590 MW	73820 TQ	USBLS	5/15
	Ohio	Y	54410 FQ	62650 MW	72390 TQ	USBLS	5/15
	Cincinnati MSA, OH-KY-IN	Y	58790 FQ	68550 MW	76330 TQ	USBLS	5/15
	Cleveland-Elyria MSA, OH	Y	55160 FQ	62800 MW	74200 TQ	USBLS	5/15
	Columbus MSA, OH	Y	54690 FQ	62470 MW	72190 TQ	USBLS	5/15
	Oklahoma	Y	55720 FQ	65060 MW	77590 TQ	USBLS	5/15
	Oklahoma City MSA, OK	Y	55860 FQ	65460 MW	80630 TQ	USBLS	5/15
	Tulsa MSA, OK	Y	56840 FQ	65350 MW	74440 TQ	USBLS	5/15

AE	Average entry wage	AWR	Average wage range		
AEX	Average experienced wage	B	Biweekly		
ATC	Average total compensation	D	Daily		
AW	Average wage paid	FQ	First quartile wage		

H	Hourly	LR	Low end range	
HI	Highest wage paid	M	Monthly	
HR	High end range	MCC	Median cash compensation	
LO	Lowest wage paid	ME	Median entry wage	

MTC	Median total compensation	TCC	Total cash compensation
MW	Median wage paid	TQ	Third quartile wage
MWR	Median wage range	W	Weekly
S	See annotated source	Y	Yearly

Occupation/Type/Industry	Location	Per	Low	Mid	High	Source	Date
Diagnostic Medical Sonographer	Oregon	H	37.60 FQ	42.90 MW	47.42 TQ	ORBLS	2016
	Portland-Vancouver-Hillsboro MSA, OR-WA	Y	81460 FQ	89940 MW	98260 TQ	USBLS	5/15
	Pennsylvania	Y	53220 FQ	63300 MW	75970 TQ	USBLS	5/15
	Allentown-Bethlehem-Easton MSA, PA-NJ	Y	52550 FQ	62130 MW	74690 TQ	USBLS	5/15
	Harrisburg-Carlisle MSA, PA	Y	56520 FQ	64560 MW	73110 TQ	USBLS	5/15
	Montgomery County-Bucks County-Chester County PMSA, PA	Y	60180 FQ	70660 MW	81240 TQ	USBLS	5/15
	Philadelphia PMSA, PA	Y	62980 FQ	73230 MW	85210 TQ	USBLS	5/15
	Pittsburgh MSA, PA	Y	48340 FQ	55810 MW	63130 TQ	USBLS	5/15
	Rhode Island	Y	56150 FQ	70450 MW	85170 TQ	USBLS	5/15
	Providence-Warwick MSA, RI-MA	Y	57370 FQ	71580 MW	86020 TQ	USBLS	5/15
	South Carolina	Y	51520 FQ	59630 MW	70710 TQ	USBLS	5/15
	Charleston-North Charleston MSA, SC	Y	56490 FQ	63690 MW	75350 TQ	USBLS	5/15
	Columbia MSA, SC	Y	47920 FQ	57850 MW	69420 TQ	USBLS	5/15
	Greenville-Anderson-Mauldin MSA, SC	Y	55380 FQ	64360 MW	73830 TQ	USBLS	5/15
	South Dakota	Y	51920 FQ	60600 MW	69940 TQ	USBLS	5/15
	Sioux Falls MSA, SD	Y	49090 FQ	57510 MW	67800 TQ	USBLS	5/15
	Tennessee	Y	50300 FQ	59430 MW	70640 TQ	USBLS	5/15
	Knoxville MSA, TN	Y	49280 FQ	58240 MW	69020 TQ	USBLS	5/15
	Memphis MSA, TN-MS-AR	Y	49710 FQ	60080 MW	72440 TQ	USBLS	5/15
	Nashville-Davidson–Murfreesboro–Franklin MSA, TN	Y	54180 FQ	64280 MW	74160 TQ	USBLS	5/15
	Texas	Y	57620 FQ	68240 MW	78540 TQ	USBLS	5/15
	Austin-Round Rock MSA, TX	Y	59430 FQ	69310 MW	79330 TQ	USBLS	5/15
	Dallas-Plano-Irving PMSA, TX	Y	64290 FQ	72660 MW	83090 TQ	USBLS	5/15
	Fort Worth-Arlington PMSA, TX	Y	55510 FQ	65190 MW	77780 TQ	USBLS	5/15
	Houston-The Woodlands-Sugar Land MSA, TX	Y	61990 FQ	71380 MW	81890 TQ	USBLS	5/15
	San Antonio-New Braunfels MSA, TX	Y	54760 FQ	64580 MW	78770 TQ	USBLS	5/15
	Utah	Y	62570 FQ	73610 MW	86400 TQ	USBLS	5/15
	Ogden-Clearfield MSA, UT	Y	65550 FQ	77250 MW	94110 TQ	USBLS	5/15
	Provo-Orem MSA, UT	Y	64360 FQ	72540 MW	81670 TQ	USBLS	5/15
	Salt Lake City MSA, UT	Y	62240 FQ	73480 MW	85620 TQ	USBLS	5/15
	Vermont	Y	60680 FQ	72340 MW	84550 TQ	USBLS	5/15
	Virginia	Y	58030 FQ	69850 MW	82550 TQ	USBLS	5/15
	Richmond MSA, VA	Y	57450 FQ	67450 MW	76310 TQ	USBLS	5/15
	Virginia Beach-Norfolk-Newport News MSA, VA-NC	Y	56280 FQ	65550 MW	74220 TQ	USBLS	5/15
	Washington	H	35.86 FQ	41.77 MW	46.65 TQ	WABLS	3/16
	Seattle-Bellevue-Everett PMSA, WA	H	37.37 FQ	42.60 MW	47.20 TQ	WABLS	3/16
	Tacoma-Lakewood PMSA, WA	H	35.21 FQ	41.24 MW	47.03 TQ	WABLS	3/16
	West Virginia	Y	48040 FQ	56340 MW	65200 TQ	USBLS	5/15
	Huntington-Ashland MSA, WV-KY-OH	Y	52390 FQ	62180 MW	72560 TQ	USBLS	5/15
	Wisconsin	Y	62510 FQ	75860 MW	88750 TQ	USBLS	5/15
	Madison MSA, WI	Y	70950 FQ	80710 MW	90300 TQ	USBLS	5/15
	Milwaukee-Waukesha-West Allis MSA, WI	Y	65130 FQ	81370 MW	92750 TQ	USBLS	5/15
	Wyoming	Y	55500 FQ	61840 MW	72400 TQ	USBLS	5/15
	Puerto Rico	Y	20180 FQ	24440 MW	28700 TQ	USBLS	5/15
	San Juan-Carolina-Caguas MSA, PR	Y	19880 FQ	24120 MW	28740 TQ	USBLS	5/15
Dietetic Technician	Alabama	Y	21120 AE	38510 AW	47195 AEX	ALBLS	6/16
	Birmingham-Hoover MSA, AL	Y	24260 AE	42598 AW	24260 AEX	ALBLS	6/16
	Arizona	Y	21000 FQ	25780 MW	33390 TQ	USBLS	5/15
	Phoenix-Mesa-Scottsdale MSA, AZ	Y	20810 FQ	25690 MW	34410 TQ	USBLS	5/15
	Tucson MSA, AZ	Y	18700 FQ	21410 MW	26230 TQ	USBLS	5/15
	Arkansas	Y	18540 FQ	22790 MW	30640 TQ	USBLS	5/15
	Little Rock-North Little Rock-Conway MSA, AR	Y	17630 FQ	19410 MW	24690 TQ	USBLS	5/15

AE	Average entry wage	AWR	Average wage range	H	Hourly	LR	Low end range	MTC	Median total compensation	TCC	Total cash compensation
AEX	Average experienced wage	B	Biweekly	HI	Highest wage paid	M	Monthly	MW	Median wage paid	TQ	Third quartile wage
ATC	Average total compensation	D	Daily	HR	High end range	MCC	Median cash compensation	MWR	Median wage range	W	Weekly
AW	Average wage paid	FQ	First quartile wage	LO	Lowest wage paid	ME	Median entry wage	S	See annotated source	Y	Yearly

Occupation/Type/Industry	Location	Per	Low	Mid	High	Source	Date
Dietetic Technician	California	H	11.65 FQ	17.17 MW	22.72 TQ	CABLS	1/16-3/16
	Anaheim-Santa Ana-Irvine PMSA, CA	H	15.92 FQ	22.14 MW	26.33 TQ	CABLS	1/16-3/16
	Los Angeles-Long Beach-Glendale PMSA, CA	H	10.96 FQ	15.92 MW	20.00 TQ	CABLS	1/16-3/16
	Oakland-Hayward-Berkeley PMSA, CA	H	15.18 FQ	18.36 MW	25.28 TQ	CABLS	1/16-3/16
	Riverside-San Bernardino-Ontario MSA, CA	H	11.23 FQ	13.44 MW	17.96 TQ	CABLS	1/16-3/16
	Sacramento–Roseville–Arden-Arcade MSA, CA	H	12.64 FQ	17.64 MW	24.36 TQ	CABLS	1/16-3/16
	San Diego-Carlsbad MSA, CA	H	11.84 FQ	16.11 MW	23.17 TQ	CABLS	1/16-3/16
	San Francisco-Redwood City-South San Francisco PMSA, CA	H	21.62 FQ	25.22 MW	28.29 TQ	CABLS	1/16-3/16
	Colorado	Y	25400 FQ	31740 MW	36750 TQ	USBLS	5/15
	Denver-Aurora-Lakewood MSA, CO	Y	30400 FQ	34430 MW	38080 TQ	USBLS	5/15
	Connecticut	Y		34249 MW		CTBLS	1/16-3/16
	Bridgeport-Stamford-Norwalk MSA, CT	Y	31810 FQ	42270 MW	48470 TQ	USBLS	5/15
	Hartford-West Hartford-East Hartford MSA, CT	Y	24840 FQ	32100 MW	37770 TQ	USBLS	5/15
	Delaware	Y	25220 FQ	30200 MW	36700 TQ	USBLS	5/15
	Wilmington PMSA, DE-MD-NJ	Y	30760 FQ	34810 MW	40060 TQ	USBLS	5/15
	Washington-Arlington-Alexandria PMSA, DC-VA-MD-WV	Y	27920 FQ	33770 MW	39290 TQ	USBLS	5/15
	Florida	H	9.97 AE	11.93 MW	14.92 AEX	FLBLS	7/16-9/16
	Fort Lauderdale-Pompano Beach-Deerfield Beach PMSA, FL	H	10.96 AE	13.50 MW	15.29 AEX	FLBLS	7/16-9/16
	Miami-Miami Beach-Kendall PMSA, FL	H	10.33 AE	13.02 MW	18.51 AEX	FLBLS	7/16-9/16
	Orlando-Kissimmee-Sanford MSA, FL	H	10.77 AE	11.53 MW	12.32 AEX	FLBLS	7/16-9/16
	Tampa-St. Petersburg-Clearwater MSA, FL	H	9.78 AE	11.38 MW	13.16 AEX	FLBLS	7/16-9/16
	Georgia	Y	19340 FQ	23610 MW	29830 TQ	USBLS	5/15
	Atlanta-Sandy Springs-Roswell MSA, GA	Y	20890 FQ	25270 MW	30890 TQ	USBLS	5/15
	Hawaii	Y	26420 FQ	34080 MW	41040 TQ	USBLS	5/15
	Urban Honolulu MSA, HI	Y	25620 FQ	33760 MW	41770 TQ	USBLS	5/15
	Idaho	Y	18860 FQ	23670 MW	29750 TQ	USBLS	5/15
	Illinois	Y	18840 FQ	21260 MW	26820 TQ	USBLS	5/15
	Chicago-Naperville-Arlington Heights PMSA, IL	Y	19130 FQ	22650 MW	29320 TQ	USBLS	5/15
	Lake County-Kenosha County PMSA, IL-WI	Y	20130 FQ	22420 MW	25210 TQ	USBLS	5/15
	Indiana	Y	22420 FQ	26860 MW	33060 TQ	USBLS	5/15
	Gary PMSA, IN	Y	19460 FQ	24660 MW	30760 TQ	USBLS	5/15
	Indianapolis-Carmel-Anderson MSA, IN	Y	25510 FQ	32100 MW	36720 TQ	USBLS	5/15
	Iowa	Y	18700 FQ	23370 MW	31870 TQ	USBLS	5/15
	Des Moines-West Des Moines MSA, IA	Y	18370 FQ	23260 MW	29840 TQ	USBLS	5/15
	Kansas	Y	23520 FQ	31690 MW	41090 TQ	USBLS	5/15
	Kentucky	Y	22520 FQ	26280 MW	30740 TQ	USBLS	5/15
	Louisville-Jefferson County MSA, KY-IN	Y	23020 FQ	26030 MW	29380 TQ	USBLS	5/15
	Louisiana	Y	18700 FQ	22590 MW	27840 TQ	USBLS	5/15
	Baton Rouge MSA, LA	Y	16640 FQ	18030 MW	19420 TQ	USBLS	5/15
	New Orleans-Metairie MSA, LA	Y	20300 FQ	22630 MW	25820 TQ	USBLS	5/15
	Maine	Y	22810 FQ	28310 MW	36160 TQ	USBLS	5/15
	Maryland	Y	22907 AE	34629 MW	40490 AEX	MDBLS	4/16
	Baltimore-Columbia-Towson MSA, MD	Y	27540 FQ	33530 MW	42530 TQ	USBLS	5/15
	Massachusetts	Y	21250 FQ	27560 MW	36280 TQ	USBLS	5/15
	Boston-Cambridge-Newton NECTA, MA	Y	27090 FQ	33800 MW	41420 TQ	USBLS	5/15

AE	Average entry wage	AWR	Average wage range	H	Hourly	LR	Low end range	MTC	Median total compensation	TCC	Total cash compensation
AEX	Average experienced wage	B	Biweekly	HI	Highest wage paid	M	Monthly	MW	Median wage paid	TQ	Third quartile wage
ATC	Average total compensation	D	Daily	HR	High end range	MCC	Median cash compensation	MWR	Median wage range	W	Weekly
AW	Average wage paid	FQ	First quartile wage	LO	Lowest wage paid	ME	Median entry wage	S	See annotated source	Y	Yearly

Occupation/Type/Industry	Location	Per	Low	Mid	High	Source	Date
Dietetic Technician	Worcester MSA, MA-CT	Y	20850 FQ	28020 MW	34760 TQ	USBLS	5/15
	Michigan	Y	22640 FQ	28350 MW	34900 TQ	USBLS	5/15
	Detroit-Dearborn-Livonia PMSA, MI	Y	23290 FQ	29100 MW	34310 TQ	USBLS	5/15
	Grand Rapids-Wyoming MSA, MI	Y	22740 FQ	27010 MW	30940 TQ	USBLS	5/15
	Minnesota	Y	22893 FQ	27651 MW	35564 TQ	MNBLS	1/16-3/16
	Minneapolis-St. Paul-Bloomington MSA, MN-WI	Y	23649 FQ	29647 MW	36955 TQ	MNBLS	1/16-3/16
	Mississippi	Y	18410 FQ	21490 MW	24790 TQ	USBLS	5/15
	Jackson MSA, MS	Y	19500 FQ	21870 MW	24450 TQ	USBLS	5/15
	Missouri	Y	19800 FQ	22460 MW	26140 TQ	USBLS	5/15
	Kansas City MSA, MO-KS	Y	21330 FQ	23300 MW	27320 TQ	USBLS	5/15
	St. Louis MSA, MO-IL	Y	18780 FQ	21300 MW	26810 TQ	USBLS	5/15
	Montana	Y	21720 FQ	24490 MW	29730 TQ	USBLS	5/15
	Nebraska	Y	25110 FQ	29420 MW	35705 TQ	NEBLS	7/16-9/16
	Nevada	Y	24910 FQ	31920 MW	39740 TQ	USBLS	5/15
	New Hampshire	H	13.21 AE	16.54 MW	18.48 AEX	NHBLS	6/16
	New Jersey	Y	27980 FQ	33430 MW	39320 TQ	USBLS	5/15
	Camden PMSA, NJ	Y	26380 FQ	31300 MW	37580 TQ	USBLS	5/15
	Newark PMSA, NJ-PA	Y	30620 FQ	35590 MW	41500 TQ	USBLS	5/15
	New Mexico	Y	18730 FQ	21570 MW	24760 TQ	USBLS	5/15
	Albuquerque MSA, NM	Y	17570 FQ	19060 MW	22690 TQ	USBLS	5/15
	New York	Y	29870 AE	42740 MW	46940 AEX	NYBLS	1/16-3/16
	Buffalo-Cheektowaga-Niagara Falls MSA, NY	Y	25530 FQ	37270 MW	45810 TQ	USBLS	5/15
	Nassau County-Suffolk County PMSA, NY	Y	41600 FQ	45930 MW	50410 TQ	USBLS	5/15
	New York-Jersey City-White Plains PMSA, NY-NJ	Y	34720 FQ	41590 MW	47160 TQ	USBLS	5/15
	Rochester MSA, NY	Y	19470 FQ	24090 MW	37700 TQ	USBLS	5/15
	North Carolina	Y	24430 FQ	27310 MW	29910 TQ	USBLS	5/15
	Charlotte-Concord-Gastonia MSA, NC-SC	Y	18470 FQ	21370 MW	25970 TQ	USBLS	5/15
	North Dakota	Y	25360 FQ	28310 MW	31740 TQ	USBLS	5/15
	Ohio	Y	32920 FQ	36840 MW	42680 TQ	USBLS	5/15
	Cincinnati MSA, OH-KY-IN	Y	38650 FQ	44990 MW	52030 TQ	USBLS	5/15
	Cleveland-Elyria MSA, OH	Y	32920 FQ	35990 MW	39060 TQ	USBLS	5/15
	Columbus MSA, OH	Y	32190 FQ	37230 MW	43320 TQ	USBLS	5/15
	Oklahoma	Y	18200 FQ	21440 MW	25810 TQ	USBLS	5/15
	Oklahoma City MSA, OK	Y	18120 FQ	21670 MW	27960 TQ	USBLS	5/15
	Tulsa MSA, OK	Y	20420 FQ	23080 MW	26610 TQ	USBLS	5/15
	Oregon	H	11.04 FQ	15.08 MW	20.44 TQ	ORBLS	2016
	Portland-Vancouver-Hillsboro MSA, OR-WA	Y	22720 FQ	35060 MW	44770 TQ	USBLS	5/15
	Pennsylvania	Y	18930 FQ	23210 MW	31670 TQ	USBLS	5/15
	Allentown-Bethlehem-Easton MSA, PA-NJ	Y	18400 FQ	24670 MW	34150 TQ	USBLS	5/15
	Harrisburg-Carlisle MSA, PA	Y	21530 FQ	23300 MW	25120 TQ	USBLS	5/15
	Montgomery County-Bucks County-Chester County PMSA, PA	Y	21340 FQ	24500 MW	34440 TQ	USBLS	5/15
	Philadelphia PMSA, PA	Y	23830 FQ	31210 MW	42630 TQ	USBLS	5/15
	Pittsburgh MSA, PA	Y	18050 FQ	20930 MW	28510 TQ	USBLS	5/15
	Rhode Island	Y	34170 FQ	38200 MW	49320 TQ	USBLS	5/15
	Providence-Warwick MSA, RI-MA	Y	22820 FQ	33820 MW	39960 TQ	USBLS	5/15
	South Carolina	Y	18720 FQ	22420 MW	26940 TQ	USBLS	5/15
	Charleston-North Charleston MSA, SC	Y	17980 FQ	20750 MW	23740 TQ	USBLS	5/15
	Columbia MSA, SC	Y	19780 FQ	23440 MW	27530 TQ	USBLS	5/15
	Greenville-Anderson-Mauldin MSA, SC	Y	19620 FQ	25350 MW	28510 TQ	USBLS	5/15
	Tennessee	Y	17930 FQ	21040 MW	26500 TQ	USBLS	5/15
	Memphis MSA, TN-MS-AR	Y	18830 FQ	22450 MW	27250 TQ	USBLS	5/15
	Nashville-Davidson–Murfreesboro–Franklin MSA, TN	Y	20510 FQ	26880 MW	34560 TQ	USBLS	5/15
	Texas	Y	19850 FQ	23290 MW	29850 TQ	USBLS	5/15
	Austin-Round Rock MSA, TX	Y	25790 FQ	33960 MW	45810 TQ	USBLS	5/15
	Dallas-Plano-Irving PMSA, TX	Y	21550 FQ	25440 MW	33370 TQ	USBLS	5/15

AE	Average entry wage	AWR	Average wage range	H	Hourly
AEX	Average experienced wage	B	Biweekly	HI	Highest wage paid
ATC	Average total compensation	D	Daily	HR	High end range
AW	Average wage paid	FQ	First quartile wage	LO	Lowest wage paid

LR	Low end range	MTC	Median total compensation
		MW	Median wage paid
M	Monthly	MWR	Median wage range
MCC	Median cash compensation		
ME	Median entry wage	S	See annotated source

TCC	Total cash compensation
TQ	Third quartile wage
W	Weekly
Y	Yearly

Occupation/Type/Industry	Location	Per	Low	Mid	High	Source	Date
Dietetic Technician	Fort Worth-Arlington PMSA, TX	Y	20200 FQ	23080 MW	28360 TQ	USBLS	5/15
	Houston-The Woodlands-Sugar Land MSA, TX	Y	20460 FQ	22920 MW	26720 TQ	USBLS	5/15
	San Antonio-New Braunfels MSA, TX	Y	17910 FQ	21110 MW	26290 TQ	USBLS	5/15
	Utah	Y	21210 FQ	24620 MW	28890 TQ	USBLS	5/15
	Ogden-Clearfield MSA, UT	Y	21530 FQ	24820 MW	28840 TQ	USBLS	5/15
	Provo-Orem MSA, UT	Y	21830 FQ	25490 MW	28890 TQ	USBLS	5/15
	Salt Lake City MSA, UT	Y	22080 FQ	26070 MW	29870 TQ	USBLS	5/15
	Vermont	Y	27250 FQ	33530 MW	40390 TQ	USBLS	5/15
	Virginia	Y	18270 FQ	24300 MW	30850 TQ	USBLS	5/15
	Richmond MSA, VA	Y	21070 FQ	27160 MW	30980 TQ	USBLS	5/15
	Virginia Beach-Norfolk-Newport News MSA, VA-NC	Y	18770 FQ	23410 MW	27710 TQ	USBLS	5/15
	Washington	H	12.59 FQ	15.85 MW	19.26 TQ	WABLS	3/16
	Bremerton-Silverdale MSA, WA	Y	20800 FQ	24300 MW	34770 TQ	USBLS	5/15
	Seattle-Bellevue-Everett PMSA, WA	H	15.08 FQ	18.25 MW	22.49 TQ	WABLS	3/16
	West Virginia	Y	20190 FQ	23040 MW	27190 TQ	USBLS	5/15
	Wisconsin	Y	20380 FQ	23800 MW	31720 TQ	USBLS	5/15
	Milwaukee-Waukesha-West Allis MSA, WI	Y	25850 FQ	31780 MW	39380 TQ	USBLS	5/15
	Puerto Rico	Y	17450 FQ	19460 MW	35820 TQ	USBLS	5/15
	San Juan-Carolina-Caguas MSA, PR	Y	17460 FQ	19780 MW	33840 TQ	USBLS	5/15
Dietitian and Nutritionist	Alabama	Y	34137 AE	51588 AW	60313 AEX	ALBLS	6/16
	Birmingham-Hoover MSA, AL	Y	30814 AE	47786 AW	56267 AEX	ALBLS	6/16
	Alaska	Y	58850 FQ	68940 MW	77570 TQ	USBLS	5/15
	Anchorage MSA, AK	Y	58390 FQ	69850 MW	84710 TQ	USBLS	5/15
	Arizona	Y	38860 FQ	53130 MW	64440 TQ	USBLS	5/15
	Phoenix-Mesa-Scottsdale MSA, AZ	Y	36590 FQ	52480 MW	63510 TQ	USBLS	5/15
	Tucson MSA, AZ	Y	45240 FQ	55820 MW	68700 TQ	USBLS	5/15
	Arkansas	Y	40190 FQ	51160 MW	61090 TQ	USBLS	5/15
	Little Rock-North Little Rock-Conway MSA, AR	Y	39700 FQ	51020 MW	61640 TQ	USBLS	5/15
	California	H	30.77 FQ	35.51 MW	41.11 TQ	CABLS	1/16-3/16
	Anaheim-Santa Ana-Irvine PMSA, CA	H	32.30 FQ	36.55 MW	42.92 TQ	CABLS	1/16-3/16
	Los Angeles-Long Beach-Glendale PMSA, CA	H	31.38 FQ	35.51 MW	40.15 TQ	CABLS	1/16-3/16
	Oakland-Hayward-Berkeley PMSA, CA	H	33.82 FQ	39.85 MW	49.08 TQ	CABLS	1/16-3/16
	Riverside-San Bernardino-Ontario MSA, CA	H	29.34 FQ	33.88 MW	37.60 TQ	CABLS	1/16-3/16
	Sacramento–Roseville–Arden-Arcade MSA, CA	H	32.62 FQ	36.22 MW	41.29 TQ	CABLS	1/16-3/16
	San Diego-Carlsbad MSA, CA	H	27.64 FQ	33.15 MW	37.55 TQ	CABLS	1/16-3/16
	San Francisco-Redwood City-South San Francisco PMSA, CA	H	31.71 FQ	41.15 MW	47.64 TQ	CABLS	1/16-3/16
	Colorado	Y	49550 FQ	58100 MW	68900 TQ	USBLS	5/15
	Denver-Aurora-Lakewood MSA, CO	Y	51620 FQ	59500 MW	71990 TQ	USBLS	5/15
	Connecticut	Y		65090 MW		CTBLS	1/16-3/16
	Bridgeport-Stamford-Norwalk MSA, CT	Y	42960 FQ	65840 MW	75730 TQ	USBLS	5/15
	Hartford-West Hartford-East Hartford MSA, CT	Y	49240 FQ	60720 MW	72300 TQ	USBLS	5/15
	Delaware	Y	50950 FQ	61350 MW	73280 TQ	USBLS	5/15
	Wilmington PMSA, DE-MD-NJ	Y	49140 FQ	59880 MW	72710 TQ	USBLS	5/15
	District of Columbia	Y	42410 FQ	60240 MW	74360 TQ	USBLS	5/15
	Washington-Arlington-Alexandria PMSA, DC-VA-MD-WV	Y	41660 FQ	59750 MW	75360 TQ	USBLS	5/15
	Florida	H	18.66 AE	27.21 MW	31.97 AEX	FLBLS	7/16-9/16

AE	Average entry wage	AWR	Average wage range	H	Hourly
AEX	Average experienced wage	B	Biweekly	HI	Highest wage paid
ATC	Average total compensation	D	Daily	HR	High end range
AW	Average wage paid	FQ	First quartile wage	LO	Lowest wage paid

LR	Low end range	MTC	Median total compensation	TCC	Total cash compensation
M	Monthly	MW	Median wage paid	TQ	Third quartile wage
MCC	Median cash compensation	MWR	Median wage range	W	Weekly
ME	Median entry wage	S	See annotated source	Y	Yearly

Occupation/Type/Industry	Location	Per	Low	Mid	High	Source	Date
Dietitian and Nutritionist	Fort Lauderdale-Pompano Beach-Deerfield Beach PMSA, FL	H	18.55 AE	27.86 MW	33.31 AEX	FLBLS	7/16-9/16
	Miami-Miami Beach-Kendall PMSA, FL	H	21.49 AE	28.83 MW	34.26 AEX	FLBLS	7/16-9/16
	Orlando-Kissimmee-Sanford MSA, FL	H	17.93 AE	26.28 MW	30.06 AEX	FLBLS	7/16-9/16
	Tampa-St. Petersburg-Clearwater MSA, FL	H	19.57 AE	27.22 MW	32.17 AEX	FLBLS	7/16-9/16
	Georgia	Y	36780 FQ	50880 MW	65110 TQ	USBLS	5/15
	Atlanta-Sandy Springs-Roswell MSA, GA	Y	43120 FQ	55020 MW	67330 TQ	USBLS	5/15
	Augusta-Richmond County MSA, GA-SC	Y	17590 FQ	21170 MW	55040 TQ	USBLS	5/15
	Hawaii	Y	54780 FQ	65370 MW	74830 TQ	USBLS	5/15
	Urban Honolulu MSA, HI	Y	54760 FQ	65680 MW	75320 TQ	USBLS	5/15
	Idaho	Y	42870 FQ	51340 MW	61750 TQ	USBLS	5/15
	Boise City MSA, ID	Y	42660 FQ	51070 MW	62230 TQ	USBLS	5/15
	Illinois	Y	45930 FQ	57310 MW	68790 TQ	USBLS	5/15
	Chicago-Naperville-Arlington Heights PMSA, IL	Y	50710 FQ	59320 MW	70680 TQ	USBLS	5/15
	Lake County-Kenosha County PMSA, IL-WI	Y	51970 FQ	60460 MW	75810 TQ	USBLS	5/15
	Indiana	Y	43320 FQ	53700 MW	63270 TQ	USBLS	5/15
	Gary PMSA, IN	Y	45120 FQ	56240 MW	65490 TQ	USBLS	5/15
	Indianapolis-Carmel-Anderson MSA, IN	Y	42860 FQ	54650 MW	64830 TQ	USBLS	5/15
	Iowa	Y	45050 FQ	53400 MW	62480 TQ	USBLS	5/15
	Des Moines-West Des Moines MSA, IA	Y	43690 FQ	49580 MW	62480 TQ	USBLS	5/15
	Kansas	Y	44130 FQ	54670 MW	63730 TQ	USBLS	5/15
	Wichita MSA, KS	Y	42870 FQ	57240 MW	73100 TQ	USBLS	5/15
	Kentucky	Y	45430 FQ	53860 MW	60870 TQ	USBLS	5/15
	Louisville-Jefferson County MSA, KY-IN	Y	46770 FQ	54150 MW	60490 TQ	USBLS	5/15
	Louisiana	Y	38550 FQ	49280 MW	60770 TQ	USBLS	5/15
	Baton Rouge MSA, LA	Y	33700 FQ	44130 MW	57750 TQ	USBLS	5/15
	New Orleans-Metairie MSA, LA	Y	45970 FQ	55890 MW	64820 TQ	USBLS	5/15
	Maine	Y	46280 FQ	56950 MW	67290 TQ	USBLS	5/15
	Portland-South Portland MSA, ME	Y	47640 FQ	57670 MW	68570 TQ	USBLS	5/15
	Maryland	Y	42124 AE	64380 MW	75508 AEX	MDBLS	4/16
	Baltimore-Columbia-Towson MSA, MD	Y	51830 FQ	64780 MW	76080 TQ	USBLS	5/15
	Salisbury MSA, MD-DE	Y	48920 FQ	58900 MW	69840 TQ	USBLS	5/15
	Massachusetts	Y	49180 FQ	59630 MW	73730 TQ	USBLS	5/15
	Boston-Cambridge-Newton NECTA, MA	Y	51730 FQ	61070 MW	75330 TQ	USBLS	5/15
	Worcester MSA, MA-CT	Y	43190 FQ	54250 MW	65600 TQ	USBLS	5/15
	Michigan	Y	46300 FQ	54760 MW	61570 TQ	USBLS	5/15
	Detroit-Dearborn-Livonia PMSA, MI	Y	43770 FQ	50990 MW	59650 TQ	USBLS	5/15
	Grand Rapids-Wyoming MSA, MI	Y	47520 FQ	55490 MW	62180 TQ	USBLS	5/15
	Minnesota	Y	51118 FQ	58890 MW	68860 TQ	MNBLS	1/16-3/16
	Minneapolis-St. Paul-Bloomington MSA, MN-WI	Y	50020 FQ	58064 MW	67993 TQ	MNBLS	1/16-3/16
	Mississippi	Y	35510 FQ	44180 MW	57820 TQ	USBLS	5/15
	Jackson MSA, MS	Y	37460 FQ	48760 MW	59240 TQ	USBLS	5/15
	Missouri	Y	38130 FQ	47610 MW	59120 TQ	USBLS	5/15
	Kansas City MSA, MO-KS	Y	43490 FQ	52750 MW	62890 TQ	USBLS	5/15
	St. Louis MSA, MO-IL	Y	34510 FQ	47920 MW	62150 TQ	USBLS	5/15
	Montana	Y	37470 FQ	46180 MW	58560 TQ	USBLS	5/15
	Nebraska	Y	44515 FQ	53225 MW	61540 TQ	NEBLS	7/16-9/16
	Omaha-Council Bluffs MSA, NE-IA	Y	47615 FQ	56100 MW	64190 TQ	NEBLS	7/16-9/16
	Nevada	Y	51590 FQ	64420 MW	74000 TQ	USBLS	5/15
	Las Vegas-Henderson-Paradise MSA, NV	Y	53390 FQ	64640 MW	74570 TQ	USBLS	5/15
	New Hampshire	H	24.86 AE	32.39 MW	34.87 AEX	NHBLS	6/16
	Manchester NECTA, NH	H	29.45 AE	34.24 MW	35.89 AEX	NHBLS	6/16

AE	Average entry wage	AWR	Average wage range	H	Hourly	LR	Low end range	MTC	Median total compensation	TCC	Total cash compensation
AEX	Average experienced wage	B	Biweekly	HI	Highest wage paid	M	Monthly	MW	Median wage paid	TQ	Third quartile wage
ATC	Average total compensation	D	Daily	HR	High end range	MCC	Median cash compensation	MWR	Median wage range	W	Weekly
AW	Average wage paid	FQ	First quartile wage	LO	Lowest wage paid	ME	Median entry wage	S	See annotated source	Y	Yearly

Dietitian and Nutritionist

Occupation/Type/Industry	Location	Per	Low	Mid	High	Source	Date
Dietitian and Nutritionist	Nashua NECTA, NH-MA	Y	45930 FQ	55460 MW	67640 TQ	USBLS	5/15
	New Jersey	Y	55340 FQ	65910 MW	75380 TQ	USBLS	5/15
	Camden PMSA, NJ	Y	55950 FQ	65510 MW	74840 TQ	USBLS	5/15
	Newark PMSA, NJ-PA	Y	58160 FQ	67620 MW	75700 TQ	USBLS	5/15
	Trenton MSA, NJ	Y	54930 FQ	68260 MW	79160 TQ	USBLS	5/15
	New Mexico	Y	40500 FQ	49460 MW	65500 TQ	USBLS	5/15
	Albuquerque MSA, NM	Y	45430 FQ	56220 MW	69050 TQ	USBLS	5/15
	New York	Y	47040 AE	62450 MW	72290 AEX	NYBLS	1/16-3/16
	Buffalo-Cheektowaga-Niagara Falls MSA, NY	Y	51650 FQ	59070 MW	68490 TQ	USBLS	5/15
	Nassau County-Suffolk County PMSA, NY	Y	49510 FQ	63810 MW	75300 TQ	USBLS	5/15
	New York-Jersey City-White Plains PMSA, NY-NJ	Y	53560 FQ	64120 MW	76230 TQ	USBLS	5/15
	Rochester MSA, NY	Y	47560 FQ	56230 MW	64380 TQ	USBLS	5/15
	North Carolina	Y	42480 FQ	51550 MW	60820 TQ	USBLS	5/15
	Charlotte-Concord-Gastonia MSA, NC-SC	Y	41350 FQ	48750 MW	57560 TQ	USBLS	5/15
	Raleigh MSA, NC	Y	46180 FQ	55280 MW	63120 TQ	USBLS	5/15
	North Dakota	Y	43710 FQ	51880 MW	59900 TQ	USBLS	5/15
	Fargo MSA, ND-MN	Y	41160 FQ	48880 MW	58570 TQ	USBLS	5/15
	Ohio	Y	47500 FQ	56120 MW	64160 TQ	USBLS	5/15
	Cincinnati MSA, OH-KY-IN	Y	48270 FQ	57080 MW	68070 TQ	USBLS	5/15
	Cleveland-Elyria MSA, OH	Y	48060 FQ	56970 MW	65190 TQ	USBLS	5/15
	Columbus MSA, OH	Y	47520 FQ	55310 MW	62350 TQ	USBLS	5/15
	Oklahoma	Y	41450 FQ	52820 MW	62380 TQ	USBLS	5/15
	Oklahoma City MSA, OK	Y	44900 FQ	54990 MW	63190 TQ	USBLS	5/15
	Tulsa MSA, OK	Y	43960 FQ	52140 MW	62340 TQ	USBLS	5/15
	Oregon	H	26.91 FQ	32.31 MW	36.98 TQ	ORBLS	2016
	Portland-Vancouver-Hillsboro MSA, OR-WA	Y	59430 FQ	69770 MW	78240 TQ	USBLS	5/15
	Pennsylvania	Y	43200 FQ	55780 MW	67080 TQ	USBLS	5/15
	Allentown-Bethlehem-Easton MSA, PA-NJ	Y	51780 FQ	58910 MW	68970 TQ	USBLS	5/15
	Harrisburg-Carlisle MSA, PA	Y	42680 FQ	54060 MW	63360 TQ	USBLS	5/15
	Montgomery County-Bucks County-Chester County PMSA, PA	Y	50640 FQ	62790 MW	73380 TQ	USBLS	5/15
	Philadelphia PMSA, PA	Y	36590 FQ	58560 MW	72090 TQ	USBLS	5/15
	Pittsburgh MSA, PA	Y	43490 FQ	50700 MW	60070 TQ	USBLS	5/15
	Rhode Island	Y	54210 FQ	65130 MW	74630 TQ	USBLS	5/15
	Providence-Warwick MSA, RI-MA	Y	52370 FQ	63880 MW	74280 TQ	USBLS	5/15
	South Carolina	Y	31980 FQ	47540 MW	58620 TQ	USBLS	5/15
	Charleston-North Charleston MSA, SC	Y	27080 FQ	44350 MW	58560 TQ	USBLS	5/15
	Columbia MSA, SC	Y	44590 FQ	53650 MW	60520 TQ	USBLS	5/15
	Greenville-Anderson-Mauldin MSA, SC	Y	36050 FQ	46760 MW	58140 TQ	USBLS	5/15
	South Dakota	Y	44890 FQ	52870 MW	60820 TQ	USBLS	5/15
	Tennessee	Y	43930 FQ	52380 MW	62530 TQ	USBLS	5/15
	Knoxville MSA, TN	Y	44200 FQ	52570 MW	61980 TQ	USBLS	5/15
	Memphis MSA, TN-MS-AR	Y	45980 FQ	55500 MW	68260 TQ	USBLS	5/15
	Nashville-Davidson–Murfreesboro–Franklin MSA, TN	Y	44360 FQ	50980 MW	60740 TQ	USBLS	5/15
	Texas	Y	45910 FQ	56650 MW	66890 TQ	USBLS	5/15
	Austin-Round Rock MSA, TX	Y	40710 FQ	54570 MW	62150 TQ	USBLS	5/15
	Dallas-Plano-Irving PMSA, TX	Y	50770 FQ	57020 MW	63500 TQ	USBLS	5/15
	Fort Worth-Arlington PMSA, TX	Y	48230 FQ	56980 MW	67360 TQ	USBLS	5/15
	Houston-The Woodlands-Sugar Land MSA, TX	Y	50980 FQ	58720 MW	69050 TQ	USBLS	5/15
	San Antonio-New Braunfels MSA, TX	Y	40110 FQ	57010 MW	66670 TQ	USBLS	5/15
	Utah	Y	35100 FQ	45470 MW	58500 TQ	USBLS	5/15
	Ogden-Clearfield MSA, UT	Y	33900 FQ	41580 MW	57080 TQ	USBLS	5/15
	Provo-Orem MSA, UT	Y	28500 FQ	41230 MW	50390 TQ	USBLS	5/15
	Salt Lake City MSA, UT	Y	36070 FQ	46340 MW	58900 TQ	USBLS	5/15
	Burlington-South Burlington MSA, VT	Y	52100 FQ	59470 MW	69440 TQ	USBLS	5/15
	Virginia	Y	40080 FQ	54460 MW	66150 TQ	USBLS	5/15

AE	Average entry wage	AWR	Average wage range	H	Hourly	LR	Low end range	MTC	Median total compensation	TCC	Total cash compensation
AEX	Average experienced wage	B	Biweekly	HI	Highest wage paid	M	Monthly	MW	Median wage paid	TQ	Third quartile wage
ATC	Average total compensation	D	Daily	HR	High end range	MCC	Median cash compensation	MWR	Median wage range	W	Weekly
AW	Average wage paid	FQ	First quartile wage	LO	Lowest wage paid	ME	Median entry wage	S	See annotated source	Y	Yearly

Occupation/Type/Industry	Location	Per	Low	Mid	High	Source	Date
Dietitian and Nutritionist	Richmond MSA, VA	Y	48650 FQ	63140 MW	73000 TQ	USBLS	5/15
	Virginia Beach-Norfolk- Newport News MSA, VA-NC	Y	33310 FQ	50730 MW	58900 TQ	USBLS	5/15
	Washington	H	26.40 FQ	31.58 MW	36.60 TQ	WABLS	3/16
	Seattle-Bellevue-Everett PMSA, WA	H	27.52 FQ	32.83 MW	37.56 TQ	WABLS	3/16
	Tacoma-Lakewood PMSA, WA	H	27.51 FQ	31.90 MW	36.58 TQ	WABLS	3/16
	West Virginia	Y	40750 FQ	55570 MW	70280 TQ	USBLS	5/15
	Huntington-Ashland MSA, WV-KY-OH	Y	37880 FQ	54480 MW	67750 TQ	USBLS	5/15
	Wisconsin	Y	46620 FQ	55520 MW	64000 TQ	USBLS	5/15
	Madison MSA, WI	Y	45140 FQ	55950 MW	68330 TQ	USBLS	5/15
	Milwaukee-Waukesha-West Allis MSA, WI	Y	50070 FQ	57610 MW	66290 TQ	USBLS	5/15
	Wyoming	Y	46180 FQ	60070 MW	70270 TQ	USBLS	5/15
	Puerto Rico	Y	26960 FQ	33610 MW	37990 TQ	USBLS	5/15
	San Juan-Carolina-Caguas MSA, PR	Y	26630 FQ	33390 MW	37810 TQ	USBLS	5/15
	Guam	Y	22990 FQ	32470 MW	44260 TQ	USBLS	5/15

**Digital Communication
  Coordinator**
Administrative Services, Municipal
  Government
	Laguna Beach, CA	Y			21984 HI	CACIT	6/28/16

Digital Media Influencer Facebook	United States	S		1000- 187500 AWR		CNBC01	2016
Twitter	United States	S		320- 60000 AWR		CNBC01	2016
YouTube	United States	S		2000- 300000 AWR		CNBC01	2016
Digital Media Specialist Finance Department, Municipal Government	Glendora, CA	Y			45753 HI	CACIT	6/28/16
Digital Remastering Engineer	United States	Y		57000 AW		SKU01	2016
Dining Room and Cafeteria Attendant and Bartender Helper	Alabama	Y	17555 AE	19192 AW	20016 AEX	ALBLS	6/16
	Birmingham-Hoover MSA, AL	Y	17575 AE	20582 AW	22095 AEX	ALBLS	6/16
	Alaska	Y	18860 FQ	19710 MW	28220 TQ	USBLS	5/15
	Anchorage MSA, AK	Y	18910 FQ	19900 MW	32910 TQ	USBLS	5/15
	Arizona	Y	17800 FQ	18830 MW	21270 TQ	USBLS	5/15
	Phoenix-Mesa-Scottsdale MSA, AZ	Y	17830 FQ	18890 MW	21770 TQ	USBLS	5/15
	Tucson MSA, AZ	Y	17830 FQ	18890 MW	22600 TQ	USBLS	5/15
	Arkansas	Y	16820 FQ	18030 MW	19230 TQ	USBLS	5/15
	Little Rock-North Little Rock- Conway MSA, AR	Y	16630 FQ	17650 MW	18660 TQ	USBLS	5/15
	California	H	9.42 FQ	9.69 MW	11.68 TQ	CABLS	1/16-3/16
	Anaheim-Santa Ana-Irvine PMSA, CA	H	9.40 FQ	9.66 MW	11.91 TQ	CABLS	1/16-3/16
	Los Angeles-Long Beach- Glendale PMSA, CA	H	9.41 FQ	9.64 MW	11.17 TQ	CABLS	1/16-3/16
	Oakland-Hayward-Berkeley PMSA, CA	H	9.48 FQ	10.17 MW	11.69 TQ	CABLS	1/16-3/16
	Riverside-San Bernardino- Ontario MSA, CA	H	9.36 FQ	9.50 MW	10.10 TQ	CABLS	1/16-3/16
	Sacramento–Roseville– Arden-Arcade MSA, CA	H	9.37 FQ	9.51 MW	10.21 TQ	CABLS	1/16-3/16
	San Diego-Carlsbad MSA, CA	H	9.41 FQ	9.66 MW	12.29 TQ	CABLS	1/16-3/16
	San Francisco-Redwood City- South San Francisco PMSA, CA	H	9.79 FQ	11.31 MW	14.17 TQ	CABLS	1/16-3/16
	Colorado	Y	17970 FQ	18820 MW	19860 TQ	USBLS	5/15
	Denver-Aurora-Lakewood MSA, CO	Y	17980 FQ	18830 MW	20010 TQ	USBLS	5/15
	Connecticut	Y		19864 MW		CTBLS	1/16-3/16
	Bridgeport-Stamford-Norwalk MSA, CT	Y	19210 FQ	19430 MW	19780 TQ	USBLS	5/15

AE Average entry wage	**AWR** Average wage range	**H** Hourly	**LR** Low end range	**MTC** Median total compensation	**TCC** Total cash compensation
AEX Average experienced wage	**B** Biweekly	**HI** Highest wage paid	**M** Monthly	**MW** Median wage paid	**TQ** Third quartile wage
ATC Average total compensation	**D** Daily	**HR** High end range	**MCC** Median cash compensation	**MWR** Median wage range	**W** Weekly
AW Average wage paid	**FQ** First quartile wage	**LO** Lowest wage paid	**ME** Median entry wage	**S** See annotated source	**Y** Yearly

Occupation/Type/Industry	Location	Per	Low	Mid	High	Source	Date
Dining Room and Cafeteria Attendant and Bartender Helper	Hartford-West Hartford-East Hartford MSA, CT	Y	19230 FQ	19450 MW	19770 TQ	USBLS	5/15
	Delaware	Y	17210 FQ	18120 MW	19030 TQ	USBLS	5/15
	Wilmington PMSA, DE-MD-NJ	Y	17440 FQ	18470 MW	19630 TQ	USBLS	5/15
	District of Columbia	Y	19920 FQ	20140 MW	26330 TQ	USBLS	5/15
	Washington-Arlington-Alexandria PMSA, DC-VA-MD-WV	Y	18530 FQ	19920 MW	24590 TQ	USBLS	5/15
	Florida	H	8.99 AE	9.49 MW	11.94 AEX	FLBLS	7/16-9/16
	Fort Lauderdale-Pompano Beach-Deerfield Beach PMSA, FL	H	8.99 AE	9.63 MW	11.86 AEX	FLBLS	7/16-9/16
	Miami-Miami Beach-Kendall PMSA, FL	H	9.02 AE	9.54 MW	12.90 AEX	FLBLS	7/16-9/16
	Orlando-Kissimmee-Sanford MSA, FL	H	8.97 AE	9.59 MW	14.08 AEX	FLBLS	7/16-9/16
	Tampa-St. Petersburg-Clearwater MSA, FL	H	9.00 AE	9.39 MW	10.28 AEX	FLBLS	7/16-9/16
	Georgia	Y	16950 FQ	18500 MW	21140 TQ	USBLS	5/15
	Atlanta-Sandy Springs-Roswell MSA, GA	Y	16930 FQ	18460 MW	21160 TQ	USBLS	5/15
	Augusta-Richmond County MSA, GA-SC	Y	17420 FQ	19310 MW	21840 TQ	USBLS	5/15
	Hawaii	Y	18810 FQ	26360 MW	39760 TQ	USBLS	5/15
	Urban Honolulu MSA, HI	Y	18370 FQ	23390 MW	31490 TQ	USBLS	5/15
	Idaho	Y	16970 FQ	18550 MW	21030 TQ	USBLS	5/15
	Boise City MSA, ID	Y	16950 FQ	18540 MW	21090 TQ	USBLS	5/15
	Illinois	Y	18320 FQ	19130 MW	22330 TQ	USBLS	5/15
	Chicago-Naperville-Arlington Heights PMSA, IL	Y	18350 FQ	19190 MW	22660 TQ	USBLS	5/15
	Lake County-Kenosha County PMSA, IL-WI	Y	18320 FQ	19470 MW	26160 TQ	USBLS	5/15
	Indiana	Y	16820 FQ	18230 MW	19850 TQ	USBLS	5/15
	Gary PMSA, IN	Y	17410 FQ	19480 MW	23240 TQ	USBLS	5/15
	Indianapolis-Carmel-Anderson MSA, IN	Y	16860 FQ	18330 MW	20480 TQ	USBLS	5/15
	Iowa	Y	16940 FQ	18500 MW	20990 TQ	USBLS	5/15
	Des Moines-West Des Moines MSA, IA	Y	17540 FQ	19760 MW	23000 TQ	USBLS	5/15
	Kansas	Y	16920 FQ	18400 MW	20500 TQ	USBLS	5/15
	Wichita MSA, KS	Y	16840 FQ	18100 MW	19350 TQ	USBLS	5/15
	Kentucky	Y	16890 FQ	18410 MW	20790 TQ	USBLS	5/15
	Louisville-Jefferson County MSA, KY-IN	Y	17300 FQ	19200 MW	22860 TQ	USBLS	5/15
	Louisiana	Y	16800 FQ	18190 MW	19670 TQ	USBLS	5/15
	Baton Rouge MSA, LA	Y	16850 FQ	18310 MW	19970 TQ	USBLS	5/15
	New Orleans-Metairie MSA, LA	Y	17180 FQ	18920 MW	22540 TQ	USBLS	5/15
	Maine	Y	17600 FQ	19160 MW	22710 TQ	USBLS	5/15
	Portland-South Portland MSA, ME	Y	17460 FQ	18880 MW	20850 TQ	USBLS	5/15
	Maryland	Y	18065 AE	21220 MW	22798 AEX	MDBLS	4/16
	Baltimore-Columbia-Towson MSA, MD	Y	17830 FQ	19030 MW	22450 TQ	USBLS	5/15
	Salisbury MSA, MD-DE	Y	17430 FQ	18390 MW	19400 TQ	USBLS	5/15
	Massachusetts	Y	19230 FQ	20870 MW	26510 TQ	USBLS	5/15
	Boston-Cambridge-Newton NECTA, MA	Y	19290 FQ	22060 MW	28130 TQ	USBLS	5/15
	Worcester MSA, MA-CT	Y	19290 FQ	21430 MW	25660 TQ	USBLS	5/15
	Michigan	Y	18070 FQ	19090 MW	21840 TQ	USBLS	5/15
	Detroit-Dearborn-Livonia PMSA, MI	Y	18310 FQ	19620 MW	25320 TQ	USBLS	5/15
	Grand Rapids-Wyoming MSA, MI	Y	18270 FQ	19510 MW	22790 TQ	USBLS	5/15
	Minnesota	Y	18006 FQ	19107 MW	22874 TQ	MNBLS	1/16-3/16
	Minneapolis-St. Paul-Bloomington MSA, MN-WI	Y	18026 FQ	19157 MW	23328 TQ	MNBLS	1/16-3/16
	Mississippi	Y	16830 FQ	18190 MW	19600 TQ	USBLS	5/15
	Jackson MSA, MS	Y	17060 FQ	18580 MW	21100 TQ	USBLS	5/15
	Missouri	Y	17260 FQ	18590 MW	21000 TQ	USBLS	5/15

AE	Average entry wage	**AWR**	Average wage range	**H**	Hourly
AEX	Average experienced wage	**B**	Biweekly	**HI**	Highest wage paid
ATC	Average total compensation	**D**	Daily	**HR**	High end range
AW	Average wage paid	**FQ**	First quartile wage	**LO**	Lowest wage paid

LR	Low end range	**MTC**	Median total compensation
M	Monthly	**MW**	Median wage paid
MCC	Median cash compensation	**MWR**	Median wage range
ME	Median entry wage	**S**	See annotated source

TCC	Total cash compensation
TQ	Third quartile wage
W	Weekly
Y	Yearly

Occupation/Type/Industry	Location	Per	Low	Mid	High	Source	Date
Dining Room and Cafeteria Attendant and Bartender Helper	Kansas City MSA, MO-KS	Y	17350 FQ	18910 MW	22320 TQ	USBLS	5/15
	St. Louis MSA, MO-IL	Y	17270 FQ	18490 MW	19810 TQ	USBLS	5/15
	Montana	Y	17710 FQ	18650 MW	19680 TQ	USBLS	5/15
	Billings MSA, MT	Y	17980 FQ	19180 MW	23020 TQ	USBLS	5/15
	Nebraska	Y	17750 FQ	18855 MW	20815 TQ	NEBLS	7/16-9/16
	Omaha-Council Bluffs MSA, NE-IA	Y	17750 FQ	18945 MW	21300 TQ	NEBLS	7/16-9/16
	Nevada	Y	17990 FQ	22020 MW	28430 TQ	USBLS	5/15
	Las Vegas-Henderson-Paradise MSA, NV	Y	18590 FQ	24200 MW	29160 TQ	USBLS	5/15
	New Hampshire	H	8.43 AE	9.04 MW	9.69 AEX	NHBLS	6/16
	Manchester NECTA, NH	H	8.44 AE	8.94 MW	9.10 AEX	NHBLS	6/16
	Nashua NECTA, NH-MA	Y	16720 FQ	17900 MW	19090 TQ	USBLS	5/15
	New Jersey	Y	18430 FQ	19370 MW	22660 TQ	USBLS	5/15
	Camden PMSA, NJ	Y	18330 FQ	19160 MW	21250 TQ	USBLS	5/15
	Newark PMSA, NJ-PA	Y	18470 FQ	19450 MW	22500 TQ	USBLS	5/15
	Trenton MSA, NJ	Y	18460 FQ	19580 MW	22710 TQ	USBLS	5/15
	New Mexico	Y	17300 FQ	18610 MW	21600 TQ	USBLS	5/15
	Albuquerque MSA, NM	Y	17040 FQ	18090 MW	19150 TQ	USBLS	5/15
	New York	Y	19290 AE	19940 MW	27870 AEX	NYBLS	1/16-3/16
	Buffalo-Cheektowaga-Niagara Falls MSA, NY	Y	19020 FQ	20300 MW	23450 TQ	USBLS	5/15
	Nassau County-Suffolk County PMSA, NY	Y	18740 FQ	19280 MW	21380 TQ	USBLS	5/15
	New York-Jersey City-White Plains PMSA, NY-NJ	Y	18830 FQ	19610 MW	25430 TQ	USBLS	5/15
	Rochester MSA, NY	Y	18720 FQ	19240 MW	24190 TQ	USBLS	5/15
	North Carolina	Y	16930 FQ	18430 MW	20870 TQ	USBLS	5/15
	Charlotte-Concord-Gastonia MSA, NC-SC	Y	17050 FQ	18610 MW	22310 TQ	USBLS	5/15
	Raleigh MSA, NC	Y	16690 FQ	18040 MW	19480 TQ	USBLS	5/15
	North Dakota	Y	17140 FQ	18790 MW	22420 TQ	USBLS	5/15
	Fargo MSA, ND-MN	Y	17270 FQ	19020 MW	22440 TQ	USBLS	5/15
	Ohio	Y	17710 FQ	18540 MW	19420 TQ	USBLS	5/15
	Cincinnati MSA, OH-KY-IN	Y	17630 FQ	18670 MW	20060 TQ	USBLS	5/15
	Cleveland-Elyria MSA, OH	Y	17660 FQ	18440 MW	19230 TQ	USBLS	5/15
	Columbus MSA, OH	Y	17790 FQ	18700 MW	19770 TQ	USBLS	5/15
	Oklahoma	Y	16800 FQ	18190 MW	19740 TQ	USBLS	5/15
	Oklahoma City MSA, OK	Y	16830 FQ	18260 MW	20270 TQ	USBLS	5/15
	Tulsa MSA, OK	Y	16970 FQ	18550 MW	21200 TQ	USBLS	5/15
	Oregon	H	9.50 FQ	9.62 MW	10.13 TQ	ORBLS	2016
	Portland-Vancouver-Hillsboro MSA, OR-WA	Y	19380 FQ	19660 MW	21450 TQ	USBLS	5/15
	Pennsylvania	Y	16900 FQ	18350 MW	20020 TQ	USBLS	5/15
	Allentown-Bethlehem-Easton MSA, PA-NJ	Y	16760 FQ	18060 MW	19310 TQ	USBLS	5/15
	Harrisburg-Carlisle MSA, PA	Y	16970 FQ	18500 MW	20780 TQ	USBLS	5/15
	Montgomery County-Bucks County-Chester County PMSA, PA	Y	16830 FQ	18160 MW	19540 TQ	USBLS	5/15
	Philadelphia PMSA, PA	Y	17170 FQ	18830 MW	21750 TQ	USBLS	5/15
	Pittsburgh MSA, PA	Y	16790 FQ	18150 MW	19600 TQ	USBLS	5/15
	Rhode Island	Y	19090 FQ	19560 MW	23110 TQ	USBLS	5/15
	Providence-Warwick MSA, RI-MA	Y	19080 FQ	19540 MW	23080 TQ	USBLS	5/15
	South Carolina	Y	17110 FQ	18790 MW	21590 TQ	USBLS	5/15
	Charleston-North Charleston MSA, SC	Y	16980 FQ	18560 MW	21340 TQ	USBLS	5/15
	Columbia MSA, SC	Y	18080 FQ	20550 MW	22740 TQ	USBLS	5/15
	Greenville-Anderson-Mauldin MSA, SC	Y	16640 FQ	17850 MW	19050 TQ	USBLS	5/15
	South Dakota	Y	18470 FQ	19250 MW	21450 TQ	USBLS	5/15
	Sioux Falls MSA, SD	Y	18630 FQ	19660 MW	22560 TQ	USBLS	5/15
	Tennessee	Y	16860 FQ	18260 MW	19750 TQ	USBLS	5/15
	Knoxville MSA, TN	Y	16770 FQ	18090 MW	19410 TQ	USBLS	5/15
	Memphis MSA, TN-MS-AR	Y	16720 FQ	18030 MW	19350 TQ	USBLS	5/15
	Nashville-Davidson–Murfreesboro–Franklin MSA, TN	Y	17030 FQ	18580 MW	21660 TQ	USBLS	5/15
	Texas	Y	16890 FQ	18360 MW	20400 TQ	USBLS	5/15
	Austin-Round Rock MSA, TX	Y	16850 FQ	18270 MW	19930 TQ	USBLS	5/15

AE	Average entry wage	AWR	Average wage range	H	Hourly	LR	Low end range	MTC	Median total compensation	TCC	Total cash compensation
AEX	Average experienced wage	B	Biweekly	HI	Highest wage paid	M	Monthly	MW	Median wage paid	TQ	Third quartile wage
ATC	Average total compensation	D	Daily	HR	High end range	MCC	Median cash compensation	MWR	Median wage range	W	Weekly
AW	Average wage paid	FQ	First quartile wage	LO	Lowest wage paid	ME	Median entry wage	S	See annotated source	Y	Yearly

Occupation/Type/Industry	Location	Per	Low	Mid	High	Source	Date
Dining Room and Cafeteria							
Attendant and Bartender Helper	Dallas-Plano-Irving PMSA, TX	Y	17310 FQ	19190 MW	24350 TQ	USBLS	5/15
	Fort Worth-Arlington PMSA, TX	Y	16880 FQ	18330 MW	20030 TQ	USBLS	5/15
	Houston-The Woodlands-Sugar Land MSA, TX	Y	16850 FQ	18260 MW	19820 TQ	USBLS	5/15
	San Antonio-New Braunfels MSA, TX	Y	16830 FQ	18270 MW	19980 TQ	USBLS	5/15
	Utah	Y	17030 FQ	18560 MW	21350 TQ	USBLS	5/15
	Ogden-Clearfield MSA, UT	Y	16780 FQ	18090 MW	19400 TQ	USBLS	5/15
	Provo-Orem MSA, UT	Y	17280 FQ	18910 MW	26410 TQ	USBLS	5/15
	Salt Lake City MSA, UT	Y	17000 FQ	18530 MW	21030 TQ	USBLS	5/15
	Vermont	Y	19480 FQ	20680 MW	23760 TQ	USBLS	5/15
	Burlington-South Burlington MSA, VT	Y	19520 FQ	20840 MW	23960 TQ	USBLS	5/15
	Virginia	Y	17150 FQ	18860 MW	22570 TQ	USBLS	5/15
	Richmond MSA, VA	Y	17380 FQ	19380 MW	22730 TQ	USBLS	5/15
	Virginia Beach-Norfolk-Newport News MSA, VA-NC	Y	17230 FQ	18970 MW	21950 TQ	USBLS	5/15
	Washington	H	9.76 FQ	10.67 MW	11.87 TQ	WABLS	3/16
	Seattle-Bellevue-Everett PMSA, WA	H	9.76 FQ	10.86 MW	12.65 TQ	WABLS	3/16
	Tacoma-Lakewood PMSA, WA	H	9.84 FQ	10.75 MW	11.66 TQ	WABLS	3/16
	West Virginia	Y	17740 FQ	18850 MW	22180 TQ	USBLS	5/15
	Huntington-Ashland MSA, WV-KY-OH	Y	17800 FQ	18930 MW	21600 TQ	USBLS	5/15
	Wisconsin	Y	16720 FQ	17970 MW	19220 TQ	USBLS	5/15
	Madison MSA, WI	Y	17000 FQ	18480 MW	20580 TQ	USBLS	5/15
	Milwaukee-Waukesha-West Allis MSA, WI	Y	16740 FQ	18010 MW	19280 TQ	USBLS	5/15
	Wyoming	Y	16990 FQ	18520 MW	20730 TQ	USBLS	5/15
	Cheyenne MSA, WY	Y	16900 FQ	18270 MW	19670 TQ	USBLS	5/15
	Puerto Rico	Y	16640 FQ	18040 MW	19820 TQ	USBLS	5/15
	San Juan-Carolina-Caguas MSA, PR	Y	16690 FQ	18130 MW	20800 TQ	USBLS	5/15
	Virgin Islands	Y	17900 FQ	21030 MW	28790 TQ	USBLS	5/15
	Guam	Y	17810 FQ	18460 MW	19110 TQ	USBLS	5/15
Director							
Admissions and Financial Aid, College and University	United States	Y		83726 MW		BMO01	2014-2015
Film Industry Development, State Government	North Carolina	Y	68528 LO		114340 HI	NCGOV	7/1/16
Geopsychiatry Unit, State Government	North Carolina	Y	46206 LO		75719 HI	NCGOV	7/1/16
Religious Activities and Education	Alabama	Y	22048 AE	42190 AW	52271 AEX	ALBLS	6/16
Religious Activities and Education	Alaska	Y	35880 FQ	42850 MW	58680 TQ	USBLS	5/15
Religious Activities and Education	Arkansas	Y	28160 FQ	35030 MW	57910 TQ	USBLS	5/15
Religious Activities and Education	California	H	14.26 FQ	20.80 MW	32.85 TQ	CABLS	1/16-3/16
Religious Activities and Education	Anaheim-Santa Ana-Irvine PMSA, CA	H	16.30 FQ	21.11 MW	27.64 TQ	CABLS	1/16-3/16
Religious Activities and Education	Los Angeles-Long Beach-Glendale PMSA, CA	H	15.18 FQ	23.26 MW	41.31 TQ	CABLS	1/16-3/16
Religious Activities and Education	Oakland-Hayward-Berkeley PMSA, CA	H	17.83 FQ	25.54 MW	30.43 TQ	CABLS	1/16-3/16
Religious Activities and Education	Riverside-San Bernardino-Ontario MSA, CA	H	14.00 FQ	17.88 MW	22.55 TQ	CABLS	1/16-3/16
Religious Activities and Education	San Diego-Carlsbad MSA, CA	H	15.84 FQ	28.00 MW	36.66 TQ	CABLS	1/16-3/16
Religious Activities and Education	San Francisco-Redwood City-South San Francisco PMSA, CA	H	25.76 FQ	34.49 MW	49.61 TQ	CABLS	1/16-3/16
Religious Activities and Education	Colorado	Y	39490 FQ	56700 MW	73180 TQ	USBLS	5/15
Religious Activities and Education	Denver-Aurora-Lakewood MSA, CO	Y	36100 FQ	55730 MW	73140 TQ	USBLS	5/15
Religious Activities and Education	Connecticut	Y		59703 MW		CTBLS	1/16-3/16
Religious Activities and Education	District of Columbia	Y	38040 FQ	53830 MW	59510 TQ	USBLS	5/15
Religious Activities and Education	Washington-Arlington-Alexandria PMSA, DC-VA-MD-WV	Y	32770 FQ	50570 MW	60510 TQ	USBLS	5/15
Religious Activities and Education	Florida	H	12.41 AE	18.51 MW	23.68 AEX	FLBLS	7/16-9/16
Religious Activities and Education	Fort Lauderdale-Pompano Beach-Deerfield Beach PMSA, FL	H	13.97 AE	18.76 MW	21.24 AEX	FLBLS	7/16-9/16

AE Average entry wage	**AWR** Average wage range	**H** Hourly	**LR** Low end range	**MTC** Median total compensation	**TCC** Total cash compensation
AEX Average experienced wage	**B** Biweekly	**HI** Highest wage paid	**M** Monthly	**MW** Median wage paid	**TQ** Third quartile wage
ATC Average total compensation	**D** Daily	**HR** High end range	**MCC** Median cash compensation	**MWR** Median wage range	**W** Weekly
AW Average wage paid	**FQ** First quartile wage	**LO** Lowest wage paid	**ME** Median entry wage	**S** See annotated source	**Y** Yearly

Occupation/Type/Industry	Location	Per	Low	Mid	High	Source	Date
Director							
Religious Activities and Education	Miami-Miami Beach-Kendall PMSA, FL	H	10.86 AE	16.64 MW	25.58 AEX	FLBLS	7/16-9/16
Religious Activities and Education	Orlando-Kissimmee-Sanford MSA, FL	H	10.95 AE	18.79 MW	21.01 AEX	FLBLS	7/16-9/16
Religious Activities and Education	Tampa-St. Petersburg-Clearwater MSA, FL	H	14.59 AE	19.33 MW	25.68 AEX	FLBLS	7/16-9/16
Religious Activities and Education	Georgia	Y	22000 FQ	36300 MW	49460 TQ	USBLS	5/15
Religious Activities and Education	Atlanta-Sandy Springs-Roswell MSA, GA	Y	19920 FQ	33980 MW	51440 TQ	USBLS	5/15
Religious Activities and Education	Hawaii	Y	37440 FQ	48050 MW	69720 TQ	USBLS	5/15
Religious Activities and Education	Urban Honolulu MSA, HI	Y	38680 FQ	50610 MW	71390 TQ	USBLS	5/15
Religious Activities and Education	Illinois	Y	26670 FQ	36460 MW	51100 TQ	USBLS	5/15
Religious Activities and Education	Chicago-Naperville-Arlington Heights PMSA, IL	Y	28820 FQ	37560 MW	53160 TQ	USBLS	5/15
Religious Activities and Education	Lake County-Kenosha County PMSA, IL-WI	Y	30860 FQ	43210 MW	48110 TQ	USBLS	5/15
Religious Activities and Education	Indiana	Y	35240 FQ	48140 MW	80350 TQ	USBLS	5/15
Religious Activities and Education	Indianapolis-Carmel-Anderson MSA, IN	Y	48750 FQ	62880 MW	91590 TQ	USBLS	5/15
Religious Activities and Education	Iowa	Y	24710 FQ	39460 MW	86350 TQ	USBLS	5/15
Religious Activities and Education	Kansas	Y	44270 FQ	63070 MW	72080 TQ	USBLS	5/15
Religious Activities and Education	Kentucky	Y	30520 FQ	53240 MW	75900 TQ	USBLS	5/15
Religious Activities and Education	Louisville-Jefferson County MSA, KY-IN	Y	43040 FQ	54530 MW	62490 TQ	USBLS	5/15
Religious Activities and Education	Maryland	Y	24974 AE	46411 MW	57130 AEX	MDBLS	4/16
Religious Activities and Education	Massachusetts	Y	23560 FQ	32260 MW	74140 TQ	USBLS	5/15
Religious Activities and Education	Boston-Cambridge-Newton NECTA, MA	Y	23160 FQ	30470 MW	74030 TQ	USBLS	5/15
Religious Activities and Education	Michigan	Y	23240 FQ	32010 MW	42230 TQ	USBLS	5/15
Religious Activities and Education	Detroit-Dearborn-Livonia PMSA, MI	Y	24800 FQ	41190 MW	47860 TQ	USBLS	5/15
Religious Activities and Education	Grand Rapids-Wyoming MSA, MI	Y	20630 FQ	32010 MW	42330 TQ	USBLS	5/15
Religious Activities and Education	Minnesota	Y	31270 FQ	43891 MW	57691 TQ	MNBLS	1/16-3/16
Religious Activities and Education	Minneapolis-St. Paul-Bloomington MSA, MN-WI	Y	38931 FQ	50241 MW	62479 TQ	MNBLS	1/16-3/16
Religious Activities and Education	Mississippi	Y	25290 FQ	28800 MW	40800 TQ	USBLS	5/15
Religious Activities and Education	Jackson MSA, MS	Y	25010 FQ	28050 MW	31130 TQ	USBLS	5/15
Religious Activities and Education	Missouri	Y	37490 FQ	55720 MW	71730 TQ	USBLS	5/15
Religious Activities and Education	St. Louis MSA, MO-IL	Y	19280 FQ	33130 MW	46650 TQ	USBLS	5/15
Religious Activities and Education	Montana	Y	19510 FQ	26960 MW	34830 TQ	USBLS	5/15
Religious Activities and Education	Billings MSA, MT	Y	23050 FQ	31150 MW	35510 TQ	USBLS	5/15
Religious Activities and Education	Omaha-Council Bluffs MSA, NE-IA	Y	52010 FQ	56605 MW	61200 TQ	NEBLS	7/16-9/16
Religious Activities and Education	New Jersey	Y	36410 FQ	45440 MW	65760 TQ	USBLS	5/15
Religious Activities and Education	Newark PMSA, NJ-PA	Y	36890 FQ	43930 MW	58070 TQ	USBLS	5/15
Religious Activities and Education	New York	Y	20990 AE	36620 MW	53000 AEX	NYBLS	1/16-3/16
Religious Activities and Education	Buffalo-Cheektowaga-Niagara Falls MSA, NY	Y	19560 FQ	23370 MW	35880 TQ	USBLS	5/15
Religious Activities and Education	Nassau County-Suffolk County PMSA, NY	Y	19450 FQ	28440 MW	46620 TQ	USBLS	5/15
Religious Activities and Education	New York-Jersey City-White Plains PMSA, NY-NJ	Y	28320 FQ	43750 MW	61540 TQ	USBLS	5/15
Religious Activities and Education	Rochester MSA, NY	Y	30540 FQ	35650 MW	42440 TQ	USBLS	5/15
Religious Activities and Education	Syracuse MSA, NY	Y	39240 FQ	43430 MW	47270 TQ	USBLS	5/15
Religious Activities and Education	North Carolina	Y	67650 FQ	79620 MW	106110 TQ	USBLS	5/15
Religious Activities and Education	Ohio	Y	29360 FQ	41770 MW	60690 TQ	USBLS	5/15
Religious Activities and Education	Cincinnati MSA, OH-KY-IN	Y	51950 FQ	56110 MW	60270 TQ	USBLS	5/15
Religious Activities and Education	Oklahoma	Y	30050 FQ	58570 MW	74660 TQ	USBLS	5/15
Religious Activities and Education	Oregon	H	9.67 FQ	15.76 MW	23.39 TQ	ORBLS	2016
Religious Activities and Education	Portland-Vancouver-Hillsboro MSA, OR-WA	Y	19650 FQ	24770 MW	48600 TQ	USBLS	5/15
Religious Activities and Education	Pennsylvania	Y	23710 FQ	31610 MW	47400 TQ	USBLS	5/15
Religious Activities and Education	Allentown-Bethlehem-Easton MSA, PA-NJ	Y	26350 FQ	28410 MW	30480 TQ	USBLS	5/15
Religious Activities and Education	Harrisburg-Carlisle MSA, PA	Y	20430 FQ	28160 MW	37140 TQ	USBLS	5/15
Religious Activities and Education	Montgomery County-Bucks County-Chester County PMSA, PA	Y	30420 FQ	46740 MW	62740 TQ	USBLS	5/15
Religious Activities and Education	Philadelphia PMSA, PA	Y	26360 FQ	40490 MW	49150 TQ	USBLS	5/15
Religious Activities and Education	Pittsburgh MSA, PA	Y	22900 FQ	29470 MW	39250 TQ	USBLS	5/15

Occupation/Type/Industry	Location	Per	Low	Mid	High	Source	Date
Director							
Religious Activities and Education	Rhode Island	Y	20980 FQ	36020 MW	49530 TQ	USBLS	5/15
Religious Activities and Education	Providence-Warwick MSA, RI-MA	Y	21190 FQ	36180 MW	49870 TQ	USBLS	5/15
Religious Activities and Education	South Carolina	Y	49450 FQ	61460 MW	84220 TQ	USBLS	5/15
Religious Activities and Education	South Dakota	Y	34290 FQ	40480 MW	48500 TQ	USBLS	5/15
Religious Activities and Education	Tennessee	Y	41200 FQ	45870 MW	51950 TQ	USBLS	5/15
Religious Activities and Education	Knoxville MSA, TN	Y	41650 FQ	45830 MW	50580 TQ	USBLS	5/15
Religious Activities and Education	Texas	Y	47840 FQ	69490 MW	80330 TQ	USBLS	5/15
Religious Activities and Education	Dallas-Plano-Irving PMSA, TX	Y	65580 FQ	75550 MW	91580 TQ	USBLS	5/15
Religious Activities and Education	Fort Worth-Arlington PMSA, TX	Y	64650 FQ	73750 MW	84140 TQ	USBLS	5/15
Religious Activities and Education	Houston-The Woodlands-Sugar Land MSA, TX	Y	65850 FQ	72640 MW	79470 TQ	USBLS	5/15
Religious Activities and Education	San Antonio-New Braunfels MSA, TX	Y	39770 FQ	59920 MW	77420 TQ	USBLS	5/15
Religious Activities and Education	Virginia	Y	29410 FQ	38330 MW	61140 TQ	USBLS	5/15
Religious Activities and Education	Richmond MSA, VA	Y	35040 FQ	46620 MW	66510 TQ	USBLS	5/15
Religious Activities and Education	Virginia Beach-Norfolk-Newport News MSA, VA-NC	Y	31080 FQ	36380 MW	45310 TQ	USBLS	5/15
Religious Activities and Education	Washington	H	18.19 FQ	24.18 MW	36.62 TQ	WABLS	3/16
Religious Activities and Education	Seattle-Bellevue-Everett PMSA, WA	H	19.80 FQ	32.83 MW	43.80 TQ	WABLS	3/16
Religious Activities and Education	West Virginia	Y	27210 FQ	43340 MW	70190 TQ	USBLS	5/15
Religious Activities and Education	Wisconsin	Y	32590 FQ	38740 MW	58030 TQ	USBLS	5/15
Religious Activities and Education	Madison MSA, WI	Y	31700 FQ	35760 MW	40110 TQ	USBLS	5/15
Religious Activities and Education	Milwaukee-Waukesha-West Allis MSA, WI	Y	33530 FQ	48400 MW	62340 TQ	USBLS	5/15
Director of Advertising							
Supermarket, Large Company	United States	Y		180000 AW		SN01	2015
Supermarket, Medium Company	United States	Y		160000 AW		SN01	2015
Supermarket, Small Company	United States	Y		140000 AW		SN01	2015
Director of E-Commerce	United States	Y	115000 LO		173000 HI	ADAGE02	2015
Director of Elections							
County Government	Oakland County, MI	B	2646 LO		3443 HI	MIOAK2	10/1/16
Municipal Government	Detroit, MI	M	5833 LO		7917 HI	DETGOV	2016
Director of Nursing	United States	Y		90003 AW		MLTCN01	2016
Life Plan Community	United States	Y		92680 AW		MLTCN04	2016
Disability Access Coordinator							
Department of Public Works	San Francisco, CA	B	5018 LO		6099 HI	SFGOV	2016-2018
Disaster Housing Inspector	United States	H		35.00-45.00 AWR		MST02	2017
Disaster Medical Specialist	United States	Y		45000-150000 AWR		EXHC08	2016
Disaster Preparedness Coordinator							
Fire Department, Municipal Government	Oxnard, CA	Y			92221 HI	CACIT	6/28/16
Disbursement Specialist							
Finance Department, Municipal Government	Folsom, CA	Y		70489 AW		CACIT	6/28/16
Disc Jockey	United States	Y		29010 MW		FTUNE01	2016
Disease Control Investigator							
Public Health Department, Municipal Government	San Francisco, CA	Y		58383 AW		CACIT	6/28/16
Dishwasher	Alabama	Y	17462 AE	18615 AW	19202 AEX	ALBLS	6/16
	Birmingham-Hoover MSA, AL	Y	17462 AE	18986 AW	19748 AEX	ALBLS	6/16
	Alaska	Y	18880 FQ	19640 MW	22800 TQ	USBLS	5/15
	Anchorage MSA, AK	Y	18880 FQ	19640 MW	23300 TQ	USBLS	5/15
	Arizona	Y	17850 FQ	18930 MW	21000 TQ	USBLS	5/15
	Phoenix-Mesa-Scottsdale MSA, AZ	Y	17930 FQ	19090 MW	21470 TQ	USBLS	5/15

AE	Average entry wage	**AWR**	Average wage range	**H**	Hourly	**LR**	Low end range	**MTC**	Median total compensation
AEX	Average experienced wage	**B**	Biweekly	**HI**	Highest wage paid	**M**	Monthly	**MW**	Median wage paid
ATC	Average total compensation	**D**	Daily	**HR**	High end range	**MCC**	Median cash compensation	**MWR**	Median wage range
AW	Average wage paid	**FQ**	First quartile wage	**LO**	Lowest wage paid	**ME**	Median entry wage	**S**	See annotated source

TCC Total cash compensation
TQ Third quartile wage
W Weekly
Y Yearly

Occupation/Type/Industry	Location	Per	Low	Mid	High	Source	Date
Dishwasher	Tucson MSA, AZ	Y	17650 FQ	18540 MW	19540 TQ	USBLS	5/15
	Arkansas	Y	16870 FQ	18120 MW	19420 TQ	USBLS	5/15
	Little Rock-North Little Rock-Conway MSA, AR	Y	17160 FQ	18720 MW	21260 TQ	USBLS	5/15
	California	H	9.42 FQ	9.73 MW	11.16 TQ	CABLS	1/16-3/16
	Anaheim-Santa Ana-Irvine PMSA, CA	H	9.44 FQ	9.89 MW	11.32 TQ	CABLS	1/16-3/16
	Los Angeles-Long Beach-Glendale PMSA, CA	H	9.42 FQ	9.64 MW	10.74 TQ	CABLS	1/16-3/16
	Oakland-Hayward-Berkeley PMSA, CA	H	9.45 FQ	9.80 MW	11.79 TQ	CABLS	1/16-3/16
	Riverside-San Bernardino-Ontario MSA, CA	H	9.37 FQ	9.59 MW	10.60 TQ	CABLS	1/16-3/16
	Sacramento–Roseville–Arden-Arcade MSA, CA	H	9.37 FQ	9.58 MW	10.69 TQ	CABLS	1/16-3/16
	San Diego-Carlsbad MSA, CA	H	9.39 FQ	9.64 MW	11.06 TQ	CABLS	1/16-3/16
	San Francisco-Redwood City-South San Francisco PMSA, CA	H	10.11 FQ	11.14 MW	12.22 TQ	CABLS	1/16-3/16
	Colorado	Y	18460 FQ	20010 MW	23050 TQ	USBLS	5/15
	Denver-Aurora-Lakewood MSA, CO	Y	18620 FQ	20370 MW	22840 TQ	USBLS	5/15
	Connecticut	Y		20405 MW		CTBLS	1/16-3/16
	Bridgeport-Stamford-Norwalk MSA, CT	Y	19320 FQ	19670 MW	22510 TQ	USBLS	5/15
	Hartford-West Hartford-East Hartford MSA, CT	Y	19460 FQ	20980 MW	23800 TQ	USBLS	5/15
	Delaware	Y	17860 FQ	19370 MW	22430 TQ	USBLS	5/15
	Wilmington PMSA, DE-MD-NJ	Y	17840 FQ	19110 MW	22070 TQ	USBLS	5/15
	District of Columbia	Y	19990 FQ	22900 MW	29170 TQ	USBLS	5/15
	Washington-Arlington-Alexandria PMSA, DC-VA-MD-WV	Y	18870 FQ	20730 MW	24110 TQ	USBLS	5/15
	Florida	H	9.01 AE	9.56 MW	10.51 AEX	FLBLS	7/16-9/16
	Fort Lauderdale-Pompano Beach-Deerfield Beach PMSA, FL	H	8.98 AE	9.94 MW	11.37 AEX	FLBLS	7/16-9/16
	Miami-Miami Beach-Kendall PMSA, FL	H	9.01 AE	9.54 MW	10.38 AEX	FLBLS	7/16-9/16
	Orlando-Kissimmee-Sanford MSA, FL	H	9.01 AE	9.76 MW	11.05 AEX	FLBLS	7/16-9/16
	Tampa-St. Petersburg-Clearwater MSA, FL	H	9.00 AE	9.32 MW	9.73 AEX	FLBLS	7/16-9/16
	Georgia	Y	16770 FQ	18120 MW	19500 TQ	USBLS	5/15
	Atlanta-Sandy Springs-Roswell MSA, GA	Y	16830 FQ	18220 MW	19680 TQ	USBLS	5/15
	Augusta-Richmond County MSA, GA-SC	Y	17090 FQ	18720 MW	21110 TQ	USBLS	5/15
	Hawaii	Y	18160 FQ	21020 MW	32710 TQ	USBLS	5/15
	Urban Honolulu MSA, HI	Y	17680 FQ	19240 MW	29950 TQ	USBLS	5/15
	Idaho	Y	16640 FQ	17900 MW	19160 TQ	USBLS	5/15
	Boise City MSA, ID	Y	16550 FQ	17830 MW	19100 TQ	USBLS	5/15
	Illinois	Y	18440 FQ	19260 MW	21640 TQ	USBLS	5/15
	Chicago-Naperville-Arlington Heights PMSA, IL	Y	18530 FQ	19470 MW	22700 TQ	USBLS	5/15
	Lake County-Kenosha County PMSA, IL-WI	Y	18310 FQ	19190 MW	20640 TQ	USBLS	5/15
	Indiana	Y	16840 FQ	18250 MW	19820 TQ	USBLS	5/15
	Gary PMSA, IN	Y	16710 FQ	18020 MW	19370 TQ	USBLS	5/15
	Indianapolis-Carmel-Anderson MSA, IN	Y	16950 FQ	18460 MW	20550 TQ	USBLS	5/15
	Iowa	Y	16840 FQ	18260 MW	19850 TQ	USBLS	5/15
	Des Moines-West Des Moines MSA, IA	Y	17040 FQ	18650 MW	21010 TQ	USBLS	5/15
	Kansas	Y	16850 FQ	18260 MW	19810 TQ	USBLS	5/15
	Wichita MSA, KS	Y	16830 FQ	18140 MW	19470 TQ	USBLS	5/15
	Kentucky	Y	16870 FQ	18300 MW	19910 TQ	USBLS	5/15
	Louisville-Jefferson County MSA, KY-IN	Y	17050 FQ	18700 MW	21440 TQ	USBLS	5/15
	Louisiana	Y	16720 FQ	18040 MW	19370 TQ	USBLS	5/15
	Baton Rouge MSA, LA	Y	17050 FQ	18670 MW	21050 TQ	USBLS	5/15

AE	Average entry wage	AWR	Average wage range	
AEX	Average experienced wage	B	Biweekly	
ATC	Average total compensation	D	Daily	
AW	Average wage paid	FQ	First quartile wage	

H	Hourly	LR	Low end range	
HI	Highest wage paid	M	Monthly	
HR	High end range	MCC	Median cash compensation	
LO	Lowest wage paid	ME	Median entry wage	

MTC	Median total compensation	TCC	Total cash compensation	
MW	Median wage paid	TQ	Third quartile wage	
MWR	Median wage range	W	Weekly	
S	See annotated source	Y	Yearly	

Occupation/Type/Industry	Location	Per	Low	Mid	High	Source	Date
Dishwasher	New Orleans-Metairie MSA, LA	Y	16620 FQ	17870 MW	19120 TQ	USBLS	5/15
	Maine	Y	17540 FQ	19080 MW	21610 TQ	USBLS	5/15
	Portland-South Portland MSA, ME	Y	17610 FQ	19210 MW	21870 TQ	USBLS	5/15
	Maryland	Y	18064 AE	19974 MW	20930 AEX	MDBLS	4/16
	Baltimore-Columbia-Towson MSA, MD	Y	17850 FQ	19060 MW	22620 TQ	USBLS	5/15
	Salisbury MSA, MD-DE	Y	17760 FQ	19000 MW	21550 TQ	USBLS	5/15
	Massachusetts	Y	19340 FQ	21110 MW	24150 TQ	USBLS	5/15
	Boston-Cambridge-Newton NECTA, MA	Y	19520 FQ	21960 MW	25500 TQ	USBLS	5/15
	Worcester MSA, MA-CT	Y	19280 FQ	20490 MW	23280 TQ	USBLS	5/15
	Michigan	Y	17970 FQ	18880 MW	20430 TQ	USBLS	5/15
	Detroit-Dearborn-Livonia PMSA, MI	Y	18100 FQ	19150 MW	22320 TQ	USBLS	5/15
	Grand Rapids-Wyoming MSA, MI	Y	17920 FQ	18790 MW	19780 TQ	USBLS	5/15
	Minnesota	Y	18117 FQ	19309 MW	21874 TQ	MNBLS	1/16-3/16
	Minneapolis-St. Paul-Bloomington MSA, MN-WI	Y	18309 FQ	19763 MW	22651 TQ	MNBLS	1/16-3/16
	Mississippi	Y	16770 FQ	18120 MW	19530 TQ	USBLS	5/15
	Jackson MSA, MS	Y	16810 FQ	18190 MW	19610 TQ	USBLS	5/15
	Missouri	Y	17160 FQ	18390 MW	19690 TQ	USBLS	5/15
	Kansas City MSA, MO-KS	Y	17260 FQ	18790 MW	21390 TQ	USBLS	5/15
	St. Louis MSA, MO-IL	Y	17470 FQ	18640 MW	19800 TQ	USBLS	5/15
	Montana	Y	17720 FQ	18660 MW	19670 TQ	USBLS	5/15
	Billings MSA, MT	Y	17650 FQ	18520 MW	19420 TQ	USBLS	5/15
	Nebraska	Y	17685 FQ	18725 MW	20070 TQ	NEBLS	7/16-9/16
	Omaha-Council Bluffs MSA, NE-IA	Y	17595 FQ	18665 MW	19965 TQ	NEBLS	7/16-9/16
	Nevada	Y	18670 FQ	24760 MW	34380 TQ	USBLS	5/15
	Las Vegas-Henderson-Paradise MSA, NV	Y	19340 FQ	28850 MW	35140 TQ	USBLS	5/15
	New Hampshire	H	8.42 AE	9.39 MW	10.29 AEX	NHBLS	6/16
	Manchester NECTA, NH	H	8.39 AE	10.09 MW	11.02 AEX	NHBLS	6/16
	Nashua NECTA, NH-MA	Y	17220 FQ	18960 MW	21980 TQ	USBLS	5/15
	New Jersey	Y	18490 FQ	19520 MW	22650 TQ	USBLS	5/15
	Camden PMSA, NJ	Y	18410 FQ	19310 MW	21680 TQ	USBLS	5/15
	Newark PMSA, NJ-PA	Y	18470 FQ	19550 MW	22990 TQ	USBLS	5/15
	Trenton MSA, NJ	Y	18760 FQ	20180 MW	22990 TQ	USBLS	5/15
	New Mexico	Y	17430 FQ	18890 MW	21440 TQ	USBLS	5/15
	Albuquerque MSA, NM	Y	17480 FQ	18940 MW	21190 TQ	USBLS	5/15
	New York	Y	19240 AE	19960 MW	24260 AEX	NYBLS	1/16-3/16
	Buffalo-Cheektowaga-Niagara Falls MSA, NY	Y	18770 FQ	19350 MW	21730 TQ	USBLS	5/15
	Nassau County-Suffolk County PMSA, NY	Y	19070 FQ	20460 MW	23110 TQ	USBLS	5/15
	New York-Jersey City-White Plains PMSA, NY-NJ	Y	18860 FQ	20070 MW	23980 TQ	USBLS	5/15
	Rochester MSA, NY	Y	18690 FQ	19180 MW	19880 TQ	USBLS	5/15
	North Carolina	Y	16770 FQ	18140 MW	19590 TQ	USBLS	5/15
	Charlotte-Concord-Gastonia MSA, NC-SC	Y	16750 FQ	18140 MW	19620 TQ	USBLS	5/15
	Raleigh MSA, NC	Y	16930 FQ	18500 MW	21070 TQ	USBLS	5/15
	North Dakota	Y	17500 FQ	19440 MW	22470 TQ	USBLS	5/15
	Fargo MSA, ND-MN	Y	17300 FQ	18810 MW	20880 TQ	USBLS	5/15
	Ohio	Y	17780 FQ	18690 MW	19750 TQ	USBLS	5/15
	Cincinnati MSA, OH-KY-IN	Y	17590 FQ	18540 MW	19570 TQ	USBLS	5/15
	Cleveland-Elyria MSA, OH	Y	17770 FQ	18670 MW	19760 TQ	USBLS	5/15
	Columbus MSA, OH	Y	18360 FQ	20120 MW	22580 TQ	USBLS	5/15
	Oklahoma	Y	16990 FQ	18560 MW	20960 TQ	USBLS	5/15
	Oklahoma City MSA, OK	Y	17150 FQ	18920 MW	21810 TQ	USBLS	5/15
	Tulsa MSA, OK	Y	17330 FQ	19200 MW	22110 TQ	USBLS	5/15
	Oregon	H	9.60 FQ	9.96 MW	11.14 TQ	ORBLS	2016
	Portland-Vancouver-Hillsboro MSA, OR-WA	Y	19660 FQ	20650 MW	22950 TQ	USBLS	5/15
	Pennsylvania	Y	17010 FQ	18600 MW	21410 TQ	USBLS	5/15
	Allentown-Bethlehem-Easton MSA, PA-NJ	Y	17060 FQ	18440 MW	20190 TQ	USBLS	5/15
	Harrisburg-Carlisle MSA, PA	Y	16840 FQ	18300 MW	20160 TQ	USBLS	5/15

AE	Average entry wage	AWR	Average wage range	H	Hourly	LR	Low end range	MTC	Median total compensation	TCC	Total cash compensation
AEX	Average experienced wage	B	Biweekly	HI	Highest wage paid	M	Monthly	MW	Median wage paid	TQ	Third quartile wage
ATC	Average total compensation	D	Daily	HR	High end range	MCC	Median cash compensation	MWR	Median wage range	W	Weekly
AW	Average wage paid	FQ	First quartile wage	LO	Lowest wage paid	ME	Median entry wage	S	See annotated source	Y	Yearly

Occupation/Type/Industry	Location	Per	Low	Mid	High	Source	Date
Dishwasher	Montgomery County-Bucks County-Chester County						
	PMSA, PA	Y	17590 FQ	19740 MW	23880 TQ	USBLS	5/15
	Philadelphia PMSA, PA	Y	17620 FQ	20370 MW	24440 TQ	USBLS	5/15
	Pittsburgh MSA, PA	Y	17070 FQ	18730 MW	21510 TQ	USBLS	5/15
	Rhode Island	Y	19140 FQ	19850 MW	22700 TQ	USBLS	5/15
	Providence-Warwick MSA, RI-MA	Y	19130 FQ	19770 MW	22600 TQ	USBLS	5/15
	South Carolina	Y	16850 FQ	18260 MW	19750 TQ	USBLS	5/15
	Charleston-North Charleston MSA, SC	Y	16970 FQ	18520 MW	20590 TQ	USBLS	5/15
	Columbia MSA, SC	Y	16810 FQ	18090 MW	19370 TQ	USBLS	5/15
	Greenville-Anderson-Mauldin MSA, SC	Y	16920 FQ	18290 MW	19670 TQ	USBLS	5/15
	South Dakota	Y	18340 FQ	18990 MW	19750 TQ	USBLS	5/15
	Sioux Falls MSA, SD	Y	18390 FQ	19100 MW	20620 TQ	USBLS	5/15
	Tennessee	Y	17020 FQ	18570 MW	20670 TQ	USBLS	5/15
	Knoxville MSA, TN	Y	16990 FQ	18470 MW	20210 TQ	USBLS	5/15
	Memphis MSA, TN-MS-AR	Y	16900 FQ	18340 MW	19940 TQ	USBLS	5/15
	Nashville-Davidson–Murfreesboro–Franklin MSA, TN	Y	17430 FQ	19360 MW	21930 TQ	USBLS	5/15
	Texas	Y	17080 FQ	18690 MW	21140 TQ	USBLS	5/15
	Austin-Round Rock MSA, TX	Y	17440 FQ	19470 MW	22260 TQ	USBLS	5/15
	Dallas-Plano-Irving PMSA, TX	Y	17080 FQ	18680 MW	21090 TQ	USBLS	5/15
	Fort Worth-Arlington PMSA, TX	Y	17490 FQ	19440 MW	22670 TQ	USBLS	5/15
	Houston-The Woodlands-Sugar Land MSA, TX	Y	17280 FQ	19070 MW	21820 TQ	USBLS	5/15
	San Antonio-New Braunfels MSA, TX	Y	17060 FQ	18640 MW	20830 TQ	USBLS	5/15
	Utah	Y	16990 FQ	18520 MW	20930 TQ	USBLS	5/15
	Ogden-Clearfield MSA, UT	Y	16750 FQ	18060 MW	19380 TQ	USBLS	5/15
	Provo-Orem MSA, UT	Y	16860 FQ	18230 MW	19660 TQ	USBLS	5/15
	Salt Lake City MSA, UT	Y	17290 FQ	19160 MW	22530 TQ	USBLS	5/15
	Vermont	Y	19460 FQ	20850 MW	23380 TQ	USBLS	5/15
	Burlington-South Burlington MSA, VT	Y	19340 FQ	19970 MW	23300 TQ	USBLS	5/15
	Virginia	Y	17180 FQ	18910 MW	21850 TQ	USBLS	5/15
	Richmond MSA, VA	Y	17160 FQ	18820 MW	21470 TQ	USBLS	5/15
	Virginia Beach-Norfolk-Newport News MSA, VA-NC	Y	16940 FQ	18410 MW	20250 TQ	USBLS	5/15
	Washington	H	10.13 FQ	11.05 MW	11.97 TQ	WABLS	3/16
	Seattle-Bellevue-Everett PMSA, WA	H	10.45 FQ	11.42 MW	12.65 TQ	WABLS	3/16
	Tacoma-Lakewood PMSA, WA	H	10.37 FQ	11.10 MW	11.85 TQ	WABLS	3/16
	West Virginia	Y	17500 FQ	18360 MW	19220 TQ	USBLS	5/15
	Huntington-Ashland MSA, WV-KY-OH	Y	17410 FQ	18290 MW	19170 TQ	USBLS	5/15
	Wisconsin	Y	16780 FQ	18160 MW	19630 TQ	USBLS	5/15
	Madison MSA, WI	Y	17140 FQ	18860 MW	21750 TQ	USBLS	5/15
	Milwaukee-Waukesha-West Allis MSA, WI	Y	16720 FQ	18120 MW	19660 TQ	USBLS	5/15
	Wyoming	Y	17270 FQ	19130 MW	22610 TQ	USBLS	5/15
	Cheyenne MSA, WY	Y	16890 FQ	18360 MW	20380 TQ	USBLS*	5/15
	Puerto Rico	Y	16500 FQ	17630 MW	18750 TQ	USBLS	5/15
	San Juan-Carolina-Caguas MSA, PR	Y	16520 FQ	17650 MW	18780 TQ	USBLS	5/15
	Virgin Islands	Y	17300 FQ	19180 MW	24560 TQ	USBLS	5/15
	Guam	Y	17810 FQ	18460 MW	19100 TQ	USBLS	5/15
Dispatcher							
Except Police, Fire, and Ambulance	Alabama	Y	24796 AE	43275 AW	52509 AEX	ALBLS	6/16
Except Police, Fire, and Ambulance	Birmingham-Hoover MSA, AL	Y	25744 AE	46511 AW	56889 AEX	ALBLS	6/16
Except Police, Fire, and Ambulance	Alaska	Y	34500 FQ	44320 MW	59150 TQ	USBLS	5/15
Except Police, Fire, and Ambulance	Anchorage MSA, AK	Y	36420 FQ	50110 MW	62360 TQ	USBLS	5/15
Except Police, Fire, and Ambulance	Arizona	Y	26450 FQ	33290 MW	42910 TQ	USBLS	5/15
Except Police, Fire, and Ambulance	Phoenix-Mesa-Scottsdale MSA, AZ	Y	26890 FQ	33870 MW	43560 TQ	USBLS	5/15
Except Police, Fire, and Ambulance	Tucson MSA, AZ	Y	26270 FQ	31390 MW	42620 TQ	USBLS	5/15
Except Police, Fire, and Ambulance	Arkansas	Y	26690 FQ	33390 MW	42970 TQ	USBLS	5/15

AE	Average entry wage	AWR	Average wage range	H	Hourly	LR	Low end range	MTC	Median total compensation	TCC	Total cash compensation
AEX	Average experienced wage	B	Biweekly	HI	Highest wage paid	M	Monthly	MW	Median wage paid	TQ	Third quartile wage
ATC	Average total compensation	D	Daily	HR	High end range	MCC	Median cash compensation	MWR	Median wage range	W	Weekly
AW	Average wage paid	FQ	First quartile wage	LO	Lowest wage paid	ME	Median entry wage	S	See annotated source	Y	Yearly

Dispatcher

Occupation/Type/Industry	Location	Per	Low	Mid	High	Source	Date
Except Police, Fire, and Ambulance	Little Rock-North Little Rock-Conway MSA, AR	Y	26270 FQ	33480 MW	44300 TQ	USBLS	5/15
Except Police, Fire, and Ambulance	California	H	14.39 FQ	18.45 MW	24.29 TQ	CABLS	1/16-3/16
Except Police, Fire, and Ambulance	Anaheim-Santa Ana-Irvine PMSA, CA	H	14.13 FQ	17.90 MW	23.38 TQ	CABLS	1/16-3/16
Except Police, Fire, and Ambulance	Los Angeles-Long Beach-Glendale PMSA, CA	H	13.47 FQ	17.44 MW	23.16 TQ	CABLS	1/16-3/16
Except Police, Fire, and Ambulance	Oakland-Hayward-Berkeley PMSA, CA	H	14.84 FQ	21.18 MW	28.90 TQ	CABLS	1/16-3/16
Except Police, Fire, and Ambulance	Riverside-San Bernardino-Ontario MSA, CA	H	15.47 FQ	18.88 MW	24.65 TQ	CABLS	1/16-3/16
Except Police, Fire, and Ambulance	Sacramento–Roseville–Arden-Arcade MSA, CA	H	14.32 FQ	17.62 MW	22.10 TQ	CABLS	1/16-3/16
Except Police, Fire, and Ambulance	San Diego-Carlsbad MSA, CA	H	14.09 FQ	17.67 MW	21.73 TQ	CABLS	1/16-3/16
Except Police, Fire, and Ambulance	San Francisco-Redwood City-South San Francisco PMSA, CA	H	17.50 FQ	21.75 MW	30.58 TQ	CABLS	1/16-3/16
Except Police, Fire, and Ambulance	Colorado	Y	33340 FQ	41630 MW	50160 TQ	USBLS	5/15
Except Police, Fire, and Ambulance	Denver-Aurora-Lakewood MSA, CO	Y	35420 FQ	43920 MW	53970 TQ	USBLS	5/15
Except Police, Fire, and Ambulance	Connecticut	Y		39911 MW		CTBLS	1/16-3/16
Except Police, Fire, and Ambulance	Bridgeport-Stamford-Norwalk MSA, CT	Y	33080 FQ	39520 MW	53820 TQ	USBLS	5/15
Except Police, Fire, and Ambulance	Hartford-West Hartford-East Hartford MSA, CT	Y	31600 FQ	39270 MW	49850 TQ	USBLS	5/15
Except Police, Fire, and Ambulance	Delaware	Y	33150 FQ	37920 MW	45170 TQ	USBLS	5/15
Except Police, Fire, and Ambulance	Wilmington PMSA, DE-MD-NJ	Y	33540 FQ	38110 MW	45130 TQ	USBLS	5/15
Except Police, Fire, and Ambulance	District of Columbia	Y	30000 FQ	39570 MW	50790 TQ	USBLS	5/15
Except Police, Fire, and Ambulance	Washington-Arlington-Alexandria PMSA, DC-VA-MD-WV	Y	29690 FQ	38310 MW	48720 TQ	USBLS	5/15
Except Police, Fire, and Ambulance	Florida	H	11.70 AE	16.30 MW	20.51 AEX	FLBLS	7/16-9/16
Except Police, Fire, and Ambulance	Fort Lauderdale-Pompano Beach-Deerfield Beach PMSA, FL	H	13.23 AE	16.01 MW	20.08 AEX	FLBLS	7/16-9/16
Except Police, Fire, and Ambulance	Miami-Miami Beach-Kendall PMSA, FL	H	11.06 AE	14.86 MW	19.28 AEX	FLBLS	7/16-9/16
Except Police, Fire, and Ambulance	Orlando-Kissimmee-Sanford MSA, FL	H	10.26 AE	14.48 MW	18.76 AEX	FLBLS	7/16-9/16
Except Police, Fire, and Ambulance	Tampa-St. Petersburg-Clearwater MSA, FL	H	13.60 AE	18.67 MW	22.90 AEX	FLBLS	7/16-9/16
Except Police, Fire, and Ambulance	Georgia	Y	27020 FQ	34810 MW	46270 TQ	USBLS	5/15
Except Police, Fire, and Ambulance	Atlanta-Sandy Springs-Roswell MSA, GA	Y	28680 FQ	36840 MW	46670 TQ	USBLS	5/15
Except Police, Fire, and Ambulance	Augusta-Richmond County MSA, GA-SC	Y	27870 FQ	36570 MW	51630 TQ	USBLS	5/15
Except Police, Fire, and Ambulance	Hawaii	Y	32940 FQ	40930 MW	49460 TQ	USBLS	5/15
Except Police, Fire, and Ambulance	Urban Honolulu MSA, HI	Y	34870 FQ	43460 MW	52650 TQ	USBLS	5/15
Except Police, Fire, and Ambulance	Idaho	Y	27870 FQ	37440 MW	54810 TQ	USBLS	5/15
Except Police, Fire, and Ambulance	Boise City MSA, ID	Y	27240 FQ	37870 MW	64560 TQ	USBLS	5/15
Except Police, Fire, and Ambulance	Illinois	Y	28610 FQ	40160 MW	55530 TQ	USBLS	5/15
Except Police, Fire, and Ambulance	Chicago-Naperville-Arlington Heights PMSA, IL	Y	29450 FQ	43530 MW	58390 TQ	USBLS	5/15
Except Police, Fire, and Ambulance	Lake County-Kenosha County PMSA, IL-WI	Y	32470 FQ	38990 MW	56040 TQ	USBLS	5/15
Except Police, Fire, and Ambulance	Indiana	Y	28540 FQ	38030 MW	47580 TQ	USBLS	5/15
Except Police, Fire, and Ambulance	Gary PMSA, IN	Y	28790 FQ	40310 MW	54170 TQ	USBLS	5/15
Except Police, Fire, and Ambulance	Indianapolis-Carmel-Anderson MSA, IN	Y	25800 FQ	34910 MW	44450 TQ	USBLS	5/15
Except Police, Fire, and Ambulance	Iowa	Y	32090 FQ	39120 MW	47980 TQ	USBLS	5/15
Except Police, Fire, and Ambulance	Des Moines-West Des Moines MSA, IA	Y	32180 FQ	41890 MW	48210 TQ	USBLS	5/15
Except Police, Fire, and Ambulance	Kansas	Y	27700 FQ	38150 MW	49220 TQ	USBLS	5/15
Except Police, Fire, and Ambulance	Wichita MSA, KS	Y	25050 FQ	30520 MW	42120 TQ	USBLS	5/15
Except Police, Fire, and Ambulance	Kentucky	Y	25050 FQ	33790 MW	44200 TQ	USBLS	5/15
Except Police, Fire, and Ambulance	Louisville-Jefferson County MSA, KY-IN	Y	31290 FQ	38580 MW	47620 TQ	USBLS	5/15
Except Police, Fire, and Ambulance	Louisiana	Y	26730 FQ	34820 MW	47060 TQ	USBLS	5/15
Except Police, Fire, and Ambulance	Baton Rouge MSA, LA	Y	27790 FQ	38970 MW	50920 TQ	USBLS	5/15

AE	Average entry wage	AWR	Average wage range	H	Hourly
AEX	Average experienced wage	B	Biweekly	HI	Highest wage paid
ATC	Average total compensation	D	Daily	HR	High wage paid
AW	Average wage paid	FQ	First quartile wage	LO	Lowest wage paid

LR	Low end range	MTC	Median total compensation	TCC	Total cash compensation
M	Monthly	MW	Median wage paid	TQ	Third quartile wage
MCC	Median cash compensation	MWR	Median wage range	W	Weekly
ME	Median entry wage	S	See annotated source	Y	Yearly

Occupation/Type/Industry	Location	Per	Low	Mid	High	Source	Date

Dispatcher

Occupation/Type/Industry	Location	Per	Low	Mid	High	Source	Date
Except Police, Fire, and Ambulance	New Orleans-Metairie MSA, LA	Y	26870 FQ	34650 MW	47630 TQ	USBLS	5/15
Except Police, Fire, and Ambulance	Maine	Y	29720 FQ	37050 MW	48540 TQ	USBLS	5/15
Except Police, Fire, and Ambulance	Portland-South Portland MSA, ME	Y	32240 FQ	40230 MW	49700 TQ	USBLS	5/15
Except Police, Fire, and Ambulance	Maryland	Y	26270 AE	40840 MW	48125 AEX	MDBLS	4/16
Except Police, Fire, and Ambulance	Baltimore-Columbia-Towson MSA, MD	Y	28000 FQ	36620 MW	46810 TQ	USBLS	5/15
Except Police, Fire, and Ambulance	Salisbury MSA, MD-DE	Y	30260 FQ	35930 MW	42620 TQ	USBLS	5/15
Except Police, Fire, and Ambulance	Massachusetts	Y	31650 FQ	39410 MW	50910 TQ	USBLS	5/15
Except Police, Fire, and Ambulance	Boston-Cambridge-Newton NECTA, MA	Y	35280 FQ	44090 MW	56480 TQ	USBLS	5/15
Except Police, Fire, and Ambulance	Worcester MSA, MA-CT	Y	30560 FQ	36700 MW	46870 TQ	USBLS	5/15
Except Police, Fire, and Ambulance	Michigan	Y	27880 FQ	36810 MW	46290 TQ	USBLS	5/15
Except Police, Fire, and Ambulance	Detroit-Dearborn-Livonia PMSA, MI	Y	29040 FQ	40150 MW	49100 TQ	USBLS	5/15
Except Police, Fire, and Ambulance	Grand Rapids-Wyoming MSA, MI	Y	30120 FQ	40310 MW	49460 TQ	USBLS	5/15
Except Police, Fire, and Ambulance	Minnesota	Y	32432 FQ	40239 MW	50553 TQ	MNBLS	1/16-3/16
Except Police, Fire, and Ambulance	Minneapolis-St. Paul-Bloomington MSA, MN-WI	Y	33443 FQ	41381 MW	50432 TQ	MNBLS	1/16-3/16
Except Police, Fire, and Ambulance	Mississippi	Y	25760 FQ	35330 MW	45900 TQ	USBLS	5/15
Except Police, Fire, and Ambulance	Jackson MSA, MS	Y	28440 FQ	36530 MW	46770 TQ	USBLS	5/15
Except Police, Fire, and Ambulance	Missouri	Y	29310 FQ	37930 MW	49800 TQ	USBLS	5/15
Except Police, Fire, and Ambulance	Kansas City MSA, MO-KS	Y	31700 FQ	41550 MW	52870 TQ	USBLS	5/15
Except Police, Fire, and Ambulance	St. Louis MSA, MO-IL	Y	31580 FQ	38630 MW	49470 TQ	USBLS	5/15
Except Police, Fire, and Ambulance	Montana	Y	31020 FQ	41970 MW	53120 TQ	USBLS	5/15
Except Police, Fire, and Ambulance	Billings MSA, MT	Y	36720 FQ	46130 MW	57210 TQ	USBLS	5/15
Except Police, Fire, and Ambulance	Nebraska	Y	31945 FQ	38775 MW	50325 TQ	NEBLS	7/16-9/16
Except Police, Fire, and Ambulance	Omaha-Council Bluffs MSA, NE-IA	Y	33575 FQ	40525 MW	51640 TQ	NEBLS	7/16-9/16
Except Police, Fire, and Ambulance	Nevada	Y	26690 FQ	33630 MW	40100 TQ	USBLS	5/15
Except Police, Fire, and Ambulance	Las Vegas-Henderson-Paradise MSA, NV	Y	26390 FQ	33030 MW	38580 TQ	USBLS	5/15
Except Police, Fire, and Ambulance	New Hampshire	H	14.11 AE	19.46 MW	23.17 AEX	NHBLS	6/16
Except Police, Fire, and Ambulance	Manchester NECTA, NH	H	11.12 AE	17.65 MW	21.32 AEX	NHBLS	6/16
Except Police, Fire, and Ambulance	Nashua NECTA, NH-MA	Y	38250 FQ	51150 MW	59070 TQ	USBLS	5/15
Except Police, Fire, and Ambulance	New Jersey	Y	30620 FQ	38190 MW	49900 TQ	USBLS	5/15
Except Police, Fire, and Ambulance	Camden PMSA, NJ	Y	32840 FQ	38750 MW	46360 TQ	USBLS	5/15
Except Police, Fire, and Ambulance	Newark PMSA, NJ-PA	Y	34030 FQ	38900 MW	54970 TQ	USBLS	5/15
Except Police, Fire, and Ambulance	Trenton MSA, NJ	Y	35090 FQ	43700 MW	53810 TQ	USBLS	5/15
Except Police, Fire, and Ambulance	New Mexico	Y	27260 FQ	37270 MW	54590 TQ	USBLS	5/15
Except Police, Fire, and Ambulance	Albuquerque MSA, NM	Y	26850 FQ	31070 MW	44830 TQ	USBLS	5/15
Except Police, Fire, and Ambulance	New York	Y	27010 AE	40210 MW	57760 AEX	NYBLS	1/16-3/16
Except Police, Fire, and Ambulance	Buffalo-Cheektowaga-Niagara Falls MSA, NY	Y	21500 FQ	30780 MW	40970 TQ	USBLS	5/15
Except Police, Fire, and Ambulance	Nassau County-Suffolk County PMSA, NY	Y	30850 FQ	43640 MW	58820 TQ	USBLS	5/15
Except Police, Fire, and Ambulance	New York-Jersey City-White Plains PMSA, NY-NJ	Y	29570 FQ	39580 MW	61780 TQ	USBLS	5/15
Except Police, Fire, and Ambulance	Rochester MSA, NY	Y	27370 FQ	35340 MW	47950 TQ	USBLS	5/15
Except Police, Fire, and Ambulance	North Carolina	Y	25170 FQ	35080 MW	45890 TQ	USBLS	5/15
Except Police, Fire, and Ambulance	Charlotte-Concord-Gastonia MSA, NC-SC	Y	27860 FQ	37510 MW	48050 TQ	USBLS	5/15
Except Police, Fire, and Ambulance	Raleigh MSA, NC	Y	21970 FQ	30370 MW	38060 TQ	USBLS	5/15
Except Police, Fire, and Ambulance	North Dakota	Y	35150 FQ	42900 MW	58870 TQ	USBLS	5/15
Except Police, Fire, and Ambulance	Fargo MSA, ND-MN	Y	34830 FQ	44090 MW	55490 TQ	USBLS	5/15
Except Police, Fire, and Ambulance	Ohio	Y	28630 FQ	38520 MW	47640 TQ	USBLS	5/15
Except Police, Fire, and Ambulance	Cincinnati MSA, OH-KY-IN	Y	24530 FQ	34730 MW	46120 TQ	USBLS	5/15
Except Police, Fire, and Ambulance	Cleveland-Elyria MSA, OH	Y	34760 FQ	43360 MW	49560 TQ	USBLS	5/15
Except Police, Fire, and Ambulance	Columbus MSA, OH	Y	29480 FQ	36650 MW	46480 TQ	USBLS	5/15
Except Police, Fire, and Ambulance	Oklahoma	Y	26690 FQ	35080 MW	45800 TQ	USBLS	5/15
Except Police, Fire, and Ambulance	Oklahoma City MSA, OK	Y	27990 FQ	37760 MW	46320 TQ	USBLS	5/15
Except Police, Fire, and Ambulance	Tulsa MSA, OK	Y	27180 FQ	34340 MW	46830 TQ	USBLS	5/15
Except Police, Fire, and Ambulance	Oregon	H	13.50 FQ	17.33 MW	22.38 TQ	ORBLS	2016
Except Police, Fire, and Ambulance	Portland-Vancouver-Hillsboro MSA, OR-WA	Y	27150 FQ	35160 MW	46250 TQ	USBLS	5/15
Except Police, Fire, and Ambulance	Pennsylvania	Y	29580 FQ	38050 MW	47840 TQ	USBLS	5/15
Except Police, Fire, and Ambulance	Allentown-Bethlehem-Easton MSA, PA-NJ	Y	29360 FQ	36570 MW	45450 TQ	USBLS	5/15
Except Police, Fire, and Ambulance	Harrisburg-Carlisle MSA, PA	Y	28690 FQ	36390 MW	46580 TQ	USBLS	5/15

AE	Average entry wage	AWR	Average wage range	H	Hourly	LR	Low end range	MTC	Median total compensation
AEX	Average experienced wage	B	Biweekly	HI	Highest wage paid	M	Monthly	MW	Median wage paid
ATC	Average total compensation	D	Daily	HR	High end range	MCC	Median cash compensation	MWR	Median wage range
AW	Average wage paid	FQ	First quartile wage	LO	Lowest wage paid	ME	Median entry wage	S	See annotated source

(continued) TCC Total cash compensation, TQ Third quartile wage, W Weekly, Y Yearly

Occupation/Type/Industry	Location	Per	Low	Mid	High	Source	Date
Dispatcher							
Except Police, Fire, and Ambulance	Montgomery County-Bucks County-Chester County PMSA, PA	Y	30470 FQ	38900 MW	49770 TQ	USBLS	5/15
Except Police, Fire, and Ambulance	Philadelphia PMSA, PA	Y	29780 FQ	35230 MW	40990 TQ	USBLS	5/15
Except Police, Fire, and Ambulance	Pittsburgh MSA, PA	Y	32890 FQ	41050 MW	48170 TQ	USBLS	5/15
Except Police, Fire, and Ambulance	Rhode Island	Y	31650 FQ	38150 MW	45750 TQ	USBLS	5/15
Except Police, Fire, and Ambulance	Providence-Warwick MSA, RI-MA	Y	31400 FQ	37340 MW	45240 TQ	USBLS	5/15
Except Police, Fire, and Ambulance	South Carolina	Y	28160 FQ	36200 MW	45040 TQ	USBLS	5/15
Except Police, Fire, and Ambulance	Charleston-North Charleston MSA, SC	Y	27860 FQ	33950 MW	39720 TQ	USBLS	5/15
Except Police, Fire, and Ambulance	Columbia MSA, SC	Y	30370 FQ	37920 MW	50970 TQ	USBLS	5/15
Except Police, Fire, and Ambulance	Greenville-Anderson-Mauldin MSA, SC	Y	24100 FQ	33710 MW	42960 TQ	USBLS	5/15
Except Police, Fire, and Ambulance	South Dakota	Y	23030 FQ	27740 MW	33990 TQ	USBLS	5/15
Except Police, Fire, and Ambulance	Sioux Falls MSA, SD	Y	21850 FQ	24410 MW	30760 TQ	USBLS	5/15
Except Police, Fire, and Ambulance	Tennessee	Y	27580 FQ	38510 MW	50560 TQ	USBLS	5/15
Except Police, Fire, and Ambulance	Knoxville MSA, TN	Y	30770 FQ	38330 MW	49910 TQ	USBLS	5/15
Except Police, Fire, and Ambulance	Memphis MSA, TN-MS-AR	Y	33340 FQ	44330 MW	55180 TQ	USBLS	5/15
Except Police, Fire, and Ambulance	Nashville-Davidson–Murfreesboro–Franklin MSA, TN	Y	26530 FQ	33410 MW	49850 TQ	USBLS	5/15
Except Police, Fire, and Ambulance	Texas	Y	28390 FQ	36410 MW	47320 TQ	USBLS	5/15
Except Police, Fire, and Ambulance	Austin-Round Rock MSA, TX	Y	31800 FQ	37470 MW	46290 TQ	USBLS	5/15
Except Police, Fire, and Ambulance	Dallas-Plano-Irving PMSA, TX	Y	27540 FQ	35810 MW	45380 TQ	USBLS	5/15
Except Police, Fire, and Ambulance	Fort Worth-Arlington PMSA, TX	Y	30440 FQ	38110 MW	49490 TQ	USBLS	5/15
Except Police, Fire, and Ambulance	Houston-The Woodlands-Sugar Land MSA, TX	Y	30040 FQ	36870 MW	46920 TQ	USBLS	5/15
Except Police, Fire, and Ambulance	San Antonio-New Braunfels MSA, TX	Y	27720 FQ	36040 MW	47660 TQ	USBLS	5/15
Except Police, Fire, and Ambulance	Utah	Y	30090 FQ	38540 MW	48520 TQ	USBLS	5/15
Except Police, Fire, and Ambulance	Ogden-Clearfield MSA, UT	Y	34530 FQ	43450 MW	51580 TQ	USBLS	5/15
Except Police, Fire, and Ambulance	Provo-Orem MSA, UT	Y	32170 FQ	42480 MW	48060 TQ	USBLS	5/15
Except Police, Fire, and Ambulance	Salt Lake City MSA, UT	Y	27970 FQ	35650 MW	45950 TQ	USBLS	5/15
Except Police, Fire, and Ambulance	Vermont	Y	29500 FQ	35920 MW	44830 TQ	USBLS	5/15
Except Police, Fire, and Ambulance	Burlington-South Burlington MSA, VT	Y	29560 FQ	38120 MW	49060 TQ	USBLS	5/15
Except Police, Fire, and Ambulance	Virginia	Y	25700 FQ	34200 MW	44280 TQ	USBLS	5/15
Except Police, Fire, and Ambulance	Richmond MSA, VA	Y	25370 FQ	33050 MW	41350 TQ	USBLS	5/15
Except Police, Fire, and Ambulance	Virginia Beach-Norfolk-Newport News MSA, VA-NC	Y	23810 FQ	33010 MW	43920 TQ	USBLS	5/15
Except Police, Fire, and Ambulance	Washington	H	16.03 FQ	20.02 MW	27.24 TQ	WABLS	3/16
Except Police, Fire, and Ambulance	Seattle-Bellevue-Everett PMSA, WA	H	16.67 FQ	21.21 MW	29.35 TQ	WABLS	3/16
Except Police, Fire, and Ambulance	Tacoma-Lakewood PMSA, WA	H	16.77 FQ	21.09 MW	26.86 TQ	WABLS	3/16
Except Police, Fire, and Ambulance	West Virginia	Y	25970 FQ	31190 MW	41220 TQ	USBLS	5/15
Except Police, Fire, and Ambulance	Huntington-Ashland MSA, WV-KY-OH	Y	26630 FQ	35260 MW	44890 TQ	USBLS	5/15
Except Police, Fire, and Ambulance	Wisconsin	Y	30550 FQ	39080 MW	48030 TQ	USBLS	5/15
Except Police, Fire, and Ambulance	Madison MSA, WI	Y	31760 FQ	35060 MW	50770 TQ	USBLS	5/15
Except Police, Fire, and Ambulance	Milwaukee-Waukesha-West Allis MSA, WI	Y	33560 FQ	39900 MW	46590 TQ	USBLS	5/15
Except Police, Fire, and Ambulance	Wyoming	Y	27260 FQ	39480 MW	55510 TQ	USBLS	5/15
Except Police, Fire, and Ambulance	Cheyenne MSA, WY	Y	24720 FQ	35440 MW	43920 TQ	USBLS	5/15
Except Police, Fire, and Ambulance	Puerto Rico	Y	17180 FQ	18900 MW	26590 TQ	USBLS	5/15
Except Police, Fire, and Ambulance	San Juan-Carolina-Caguas MSA, PR	Y	17390 FQ	19330 MW	34980 TQ	USBLS	5/15
Except Police, Fire, and Ambulance	Virgin Islands	Y	22590 FQ	27530 MW	36110 TQ	USBLS	5/15
Except Police, Fire, and Ambulance	Guam	Y	19790 FQ	30020 MW	38230 TQ	USBLS	5/15
Dispatcher/Reservationist							
Chauffeured Transportation Company	United States	H		14.15 AW		LCT01	2016
Dispute Resolution Mediator							
Municipal Government	Seattle, WA	H	35.05 LO		40.75 HI	CSSS	1/13/16
District Attorney							
	San Francisco, CA	Y			255329 HI	CACIT	6/28/16
	Atkinson County, GA	Y			36108 HI	GACTY03	2016
	Gwinnett County, GA	Y			52670 HI	GACTY03	2016
	Peach County, GA	Y			1343 HI	GACTY03	2016

AE	Average entry wage	**AWR**	Average wage range	**H**	Hourly	
AEX	Average experienced wage	**B**	Biweekly	**HI**	Highest wage paid	
ATC	Average total compensation	**D**	Daily	**HR**	High end range	
AW	Average wage paid	**FQ**	First quartile wage	**LO**	Lowest wage paid	
LR	Low end range	**MTC**	Median total compensation	**TCC**	Total cash compensation
M	Monthly	**MW**	Median wage paid	**TQ**	Third quartile wage
MCC	Median cash compensation	**MWR**	Median wage range	**W**	Weekly
ME	Median entry wage	**S**	See annotated source	**Y**	Yearly

Occupation/Type/Industry	Location	Per	Low	Mid	High	Source	Date
District Judge	United States	Y			205100 HI	OPM01	2017
Division Chief Fire Department, Municipal Government	San Marcos, CA	Y		124237 AW		CACIT	6/28/16
DNA Analyst Municipal Government	Colorado Springs, CO	Y	62111 LO		85402 HI	COSPRS	2017
DNA Specialist Municipal Government	Glendale, CA	Y			56314 HI	CACIT	6/28/16
DNA Technical Leader Municipal Government	Colorado Springs, CO	Y	67700 LO		93088 HI	COSPRS	2017
DNA Technical Manager Municipal Government	San Diego, CA	Y			89477 HI	CACIT	6/28/16
DNA Technician County Government	Oakland County, MI	B	2014 LO		2628 HI	MIOAK2	10/1/16
Dock Attendant Municipal Government	Poway, CA	Y		8817 AW		CACIT	6/28/16
Docket/Calendar Clerk	United States	Y	36000 LO		52750 HI	RH01	2017
Document Examiner Technician Sheriff's Office, Municipal Government	San Francisco, CA	Y			71311 HI	CACIT	6/28/16
Document Imaging Operator Department of Administration, State Government	Helena, MT	H			14.41 HI	MTGOV	2016
Documentation Technician Department of Water and Power, Municipal Government	Los Angeles, CA	Y			78998 HI	CACIT	6/23/16
Dog Walker	United States	H	15.00 LO		75.00 HI	TJN01	2015
Children's Chore	United States	S		2.66 AW		LSJ06	2016
Dolly Grip Made for Television Motion Picture	United States	H	34.06 LO			MPEG01	7/31/16-7/29/17
Domestic Support Specialist County Government	Oakland County, MI	B	1583 LO		2060 HI	MIOAK2	10/1/16
Door-to-Door Sales Worker, News and Street Vendor, and Related Worker							
	Alaska	Y	19000 FQ	32870 MW	55870 TQ	USBLS	5/15
	California	H	9.85 FQ	11.74 MW	16.10 TQ	CABLS	1/16-3/16
	Colorado	Y	17940 FQ	18760 MW	21170 TQ	USBLS	5/15
	Florida	H	8.89 AE	9.15 MW	10.29 AEX	FLBLS	7/16-9/16
	Idaho	Y	17730 FQ	19720 MW	34800 TQ	USBLS	5/15
	Illinois	Y	18390 FQ	19210 MW	23510 TQ	USBLS	5/15
	Indiana	Y	19450 FQ	22690 MW	27070 TQ	USBLS	5/15
	Kentucky	Y	21310 FQ	23160 MW	25010 TQ	USBLS	5/15
	Massachusetts	Y	22210 FQ	27110 MW	33270 TQ	USBLS	5/15
	Michigan	Y	18260 FQ	19730 MW	30200 TQ	USBLS	5/15
	Minnesota	Y	17858 FQ	18886 MW	19915 TQ	MNBLS	1/16-3/16
	Mississippi	Y	18540 FQ	23980 MW	34580 TQ	USBLS	5/15
	Missouri	Y	17560 FQ	19170 MW	22390 TQ	USBLS	5/15
	Montana	Y	20770 FQ	23030 MW	27410 TQ	USBLS	5/15
	Nevada	Y	18180 FQ	21970 MW	28350 TQ	USBLS	5/15
	New Hampshire	H	8.70 AE	9.83 MW	12.44 AEX	NHBLS	6/16
	New York	Y	19400 AE	22090 MW	34850 AEX	NYBLS	1/16-3/16
	North Carolina	Y	21200 FQ	22690 MW	24170 TQ	USBLS	5/15
	Ohio	Y	19340 FQ	21360 MW	23350 TQ	USBLS	5/15
	Oregon	H	9.67 FQ	11.69 MW	14.24 TQ	ORBLS	2016
	Pennsylvania	Y	23970 FQ	30180 MW	47590 TQ	USBLS	5/15
	Tennessee	Y	17220 FQ	18950 MW	40850 TQ	USBLS	5/15
	Texas	Y	21170 FQ	23730 MW	27300 TQ	USBLS	5/15
	Virginia	Y	18630 FQ	22520 MW	30010 TQ	USBLS	5/15
	Wisconsin	Y	16570 FQ	17990 MW	21650 TQ	USBLS	5/15
	Puerto Rico	Y	17230 FQ	18950 MW	21660 TQ	USBLS	5/15

AE Average entry wage	**AWR** Average wage range	**H** Hourly	**LR** Low end range	**MTC** Median total compensation	**TCC** Total cash compensation
AEX Average experienced wage	**B** Biweekly	**HI** Highest wage paid	**M** Monthly	**MW** Median wage paid	**TQ** Third quartile wage
ATC Average total compensation	**D** Daily	**HR** High end range	**MCC** Median cash compensation	**MWR** Median wage range	**W** Weekly
AW Average wage paid	**FQ** First quartile wage	**LO** Lowest wage paid	**ME** Median entry wage	**S** See annotated source	**Y** Yearly

Occupation/Type/Industry	Location	Per	Low	Mid	High	Source	Date
Dormitory Supervisor							
California State University	California	Y	22704 LO		44208 HI	CALST	2016-2017
Drafting Aide							
Fire Department, Municipal Government	Los Angeles, CA	Y			15397 HI	CACIT	6/23/16
Drain Commissioner							
County Government	Ingham County, MI	Y			86588 HI	LSJ14	2017
Dredge Operator	California	H	22.52 FQ	29.65 MW	42.02 TQ	CABLS	1/16-3/16
	Florida	H	9.83 AE	18.79 MW	26.25 AEX	FLBLS	7/16-9/16
	Georgia	Y	39700 FQ	45160 MW	50850 TQ	USBLS	5/15
	Idaho	Y	37970 FQ	52140 MW	64150 TQ	USBLS	5/15
	Illinois	Y	33900 FQ	36390 MW	38890 TQ	USBLS	5/15
	Indiana	Y	33610 FQ	36470 MW	39330 TQ	USBLS	5/15
	Iowa	Y	30920 FQ	41900 MW	46460 TQ	USBLS	5/15
	Louisiana	Y	34370 FQ	40530 MW	50400 TQ	USBLS	5/15
	Maryland	Y	33755 AE	49108 MW	56784 AEX	MDBLS	4/16
	Massachusetts	Y	39450 FQ	44850 MW	50850 TQ	USBLS	5/15
	Missouri	Y	35580 FQ	47590 MW	59050 TQ	USBLS	5/15
	Nebraska	Y	29675 FQ	35450 MW	43840 TQ	NEBLS	7/16-9/16
	New Jersey	Y	37890 FQ	49870 MW	65630 TQ	USBLS	5/15
	Ohio	Y	32840 FQ	36200 MW	40490 TQ	USBLS	5/15
	South Carolina	Y	42590 FQ	45740 MW	48880 TQ	USBLS	5/15
	Tennessee	Y	28480 FQ	36650 MW	46790 TQ	USBLS	5/15
	Texas	Y	31330 FQ	38070 MW	51020 TQ	USBLS	5/15
Drill Rig Operator							
General Services, Municipal Government	Los Angeles, CA	Y		85514 AW		CACIT	6/23/16
Drilling and Boring Machine Tool Setter, Operator, and Tender							
Metals and Plastics	Alabama	Y	31402 AE	47267 AW	55195 AEX	ALBLS	6/16
Metals and Plastics	Birmingham-Hoover MSA, AL	Y	28266 AE	33273 AW	35782 AEX	ALBLS	6/16
Metals and Plastics	Arizona	Y	24050 FQ	32080 MW	37530 TQ	USBLS	5/15
Metals and Plastics	Phoenix-Mesa-Scottsdale MSA, AZ	Y	24190 FQ	31920 MW	37940 TQ	USBLS	5/15
Metals and Plastics	Arkansas	Y	26320 FQ	30760 MW	37920 TQ	USBLS	5/15
Metals and Plastics	California	H	12.21 FQ	14.71 MW	18.35 TQ	CABLS	1/16-3/16
Metals and Plastics	Anaheim-Santa Ana-Irvine PMSA, CA	H	12.97 FQ	14.74 MW	17.79 TQ	CABLS	1/16-3/16
Metals and Plastics	Los Angeles-Long Beach-Glendale PMSA, CA	H	12.62 FQ	15.12 MW	19.06 TQ	CABLS	1/16-3/16
Metals and Plastics	Oakland-Hayward-Berkeley PMSA, CA	H	11.54 FQ	14.88 MW	18.24 TQ	CABLS	1/16-3/16
Metals and Plastics	Riverside-San Bernardino-Ontario MSA, CA	H	11.04 FQ	13.33 MW	17.03 TQ	CABLS	1/16-3/16
Metals and Plastics	Sacramento–Roseville–Arden-Arcade MSA, CA	H	10.31 FQ	11.17 MW	12.62 TQ	CABLS	1/16-3/16
Metals and Plastics	San Diego-Carlsbad MSA, CA	H	11.58 FQ	14.44 MW	18.21 TQ	CABLS	1/16-3/16
Metals and Plastics	Colorado	Y	23290 FQ	28110 MW	37570 TQ	USBLS	5/15
Metals and Plastics	Denver-Aurora-Lakewood MSA, CO	Y	22670 FQ	27740 MW	36670 TQ	USBLS	5/15
Metals and Plastics	Connecticut	Y		32133 MW		CTBLS	1/16-3/16
Metals and Plastics	Bridgeport-Stamford-Norwalk MSA, CT	Y	25540 FQ	29820 MW	40150 TQ	USBLS	5/15
Metals and Plastics	Hartford-West Hartford-East Hartford MSA, CT	Y	26700 FQ	32520 MW	39670 TQ	USBLS	5/15
Metals and Plastics	Florida	H	10.34 AE	13.15 MW	19.33 AEX	FLBLS	7/16-9/16
Metals and Plastics	Tampa-St. Petersburg-Clearwater MSA, FL	H	10.89 AE	12.67 MW	20.42 AEX	FLBLS	7/16-9/16
Metals and Plastics	Georgia	Y	29980 FQ	35270 MW	40020 TQ	USBLS	5/15
Metals and Plastics	Atlanta-Sandy Springs-Roswell MSA, GA	Y	29600 FQ	35580 MW	41710 TQ	USBLS	5/15
Metals and Plastics	Illinois	Y	25980 FQ	35890 MW	45330 TQ	USBLS	5/15
Metals and Plastics	Chicago-Naperville-Arlington Heights PMSA, IL	Y	23010 FQ	30160 MW	41800 TQ	USBLS	5/15
Metals and Plastics	Lake County-Kenosha County PMSA, IL-WI	Y	28730 FQ	39640 MW	49290 TQ	USBLS	5/15
Metals and Plastics	Indiana	Y	28530 FQ	35860 MW	44010 TQ	USBLS	5/15
Metals and Plastics	Gary PMSA, IN	Y	34320 FQ	37820 MW	44180 TQ	USBLS	5/15

Drilling and Boring Machine Tool Setter, Operator, and Tender

Occupation/Type/Industry	Location	Per	Low	Mid	High	Source	Date
Metals and Plastics	Indianapolis-Carmel-Anderson MSA, IN	Y	26640 FQ	34520 MW	39330 TQ	USBLS	5/15
Metals and Plastics	Iowa	Y	34180 FQ	39230 MW	44790 TQ	USBLS	5/15
Metals and Plastics	Kansas	Y	28750 FQ	33620 MW	37680 TQ	USBLS	5/15
Metals and Plastics	Wichita MSA, KS	Y	28270 FQ	32920 MW	37510 TQ	USBLS	5/15
Metals and Plastics	Kentucky	Y	26020 FQ	33880 MW	43310 TQ	USBLS	5/15
Metals and Plastics	Louisville-Jefferson County MSA, KY-IN	Y	32540 FQ	41720 MW	46140 TQ	USBLS	5/15
Metals and Plastics	Louisiana	Y	30310 FQ	38490 MW	49090 TQ	USBLS	5/15
Metals and Plastics	Maine	Y	34380 FQ	39920 MW	45700 TQ	USBLS	5/15
Metals and Plastics	Maryland	Y	29563 AE	37311 MW	41184 AEX	MDBLS	4/16
Metals and Plastics	Massachusetts	Y	33920 FQ	40350 MW	47490 TQ	USBLS	5/15
Metals and Plastics	Boston-Cambridge-Newton NECTA, MA	Y	28430 FQ	41860 MW	50220 TQ	USBLS	5/15
Metals and Plastics	Michigan	Y	35240 FQ	44690 MW	52480 TQ	USBLS	5/15
Metals and Plastics	Detroit-Dearborn-Livonia PMSA, MI	Y	31170 FQ	45820 MW	54880 TQ	USBLS	5/15
Metals and Plastics	Grand Rapids-Wyoming MSA, MI	Y	40820 FQ	44840 MW	48860 TQ	USBLS	5/15
Metals and Plastics	Minnesota	Y	27123 FQ	32469 MW	39617 TQ	MNBLS	1/16-3/16
Metals and Plastics	Minneapolis-St. Paul-Bloomington MSA, MN-WI	Y	29219 FQ	34737 MW	42604 TQ	MNBLS	1/16-3/16
Metals and Plastics	Mississippi	Y	30620 FQ	34760 MW	38500 TQ	USBLS	5/15
Metals and Plastics	Missouri	Y	24190 FQ	30200 MW	37270 TQ	USBLS	5/15
Metals and Plastics	Kansas City MSA, MO-KS	Y	30670 FQ	34510 MW	37670 TQ	USBLS	5/15
Metals and Plastics	St. Louis MSA, MO-IL	Y	23580 FQ	29750 MW	37610 TQ	USBLS	5/15
Metals and Plastics	Nebraska	Y	30470 FQ	38635 MW	45485 TQ	NEBLS	7/16-9/16
Metals and Plastics	Nevada	Y	27730 FQ	36050 MW	55680 TQ	USBLS	5/15
Metals and Plastics	New Hampshire	H	10.03 AE	15.41 MW	22.19 AEX	NHBLS	6/16
Metals and Plastics	New Jersey	Y	23890 FQ	29490 MW	36670 TQ	USBLS	5/15
Metals and Plastics	Camden PMSA, NJ	Y	25590 FQ	30310 MW	35350 TQ	USBLS	5/15
Metals and Plastics	Newark PMSA, NJ-PA	Y	21460 FQ	26400 MW	34710 TQ	USBLS	5/15
Metals and Plastics	New York	Y	24660 AE	35990 MW	43270 AEX	NYBLS	1/16-3/16
Metals and Plastics	Nassau County-Suffolk County PMSA, NY	Y	25270 FQ	30710 MW	41190 TQ	USBLS	5/15
Metals and Plastics	New York-Jersey City-White Plains PMSA, NY-NJ	Y	25230 FQ	30690 MW	38590 TQ	USBLS	5/15
Metals and Plastics	Rochester MSA, NY	Y	36320 FQ	42840 MW	47410 TQ	USBLS	5/15
Metals and Plastics	North Carolina	Y	30520 FQ	37230 MW	51910 TQ	USBLS	5/15
Metals and Plastics	Charlotte-Concord-Gastonia MSA, NC-SC	Y	24380 FQ	31890 MW	51560 TQ	USBLS	5/15
Metals and Plastics	North Dakota	Y	30870 FQ	37530 MW	45900 TQ	USBLS	5/15
Metals and Plastics	Ohio	Y	31210 FQ	36210 MW	43130 TQ	USBLS	5/15
Metals and Plastics	Cincinnati MSA, OH-KY-IN	Y	28310 FQ	36300 MW	47860 TQ	USBLS	5/15
Metals and Plastics	Cleveland-Elyria MSA, OH	Y	32630 FQ	37770 MW	45230 TQ	USBLS	5/15
Metals and Plastics	Columbus MSA, OH	Y	18770 FQ	26580 MW	35110 TQ	USBLS	5/15
Metals and Plastics	Oklahoma	Y	33840 FQ	37950 MW	43400 TQ	USBLS	5/15
Metals and Plastics	Oklahoma City MSA, OK	Y	32640 FQ	35220 MW	37800 TQ	USBLS	5/15
Metals and Plastics	Tulsa MSA, OK	Y	35070 FQ	39780 MW	45160 TQ	USBLS	5/15
Metals and Plastics	Oregon	H	14.73 FQ	17.31 MW	19.65 TQ	ORBLS	2016
Metals and Plastics	Portland-Vancouver-Hillsboro MSA, OR-WA	Y	29680 FQ	35110 MW	39920 TQ	USBLS	5/15
Metals and Plastics	Pennsylvania	Y	31720 FQ	39560 MW	48750 TQ	USBLS	5/15
Metals and Plastics	Montgomery County-Bucks County-Chester County PMSA, PA	Y	38740 FQ	43780 MW	48390 TQ	USBLS	5/15
Metals and Plastics	Pittsburgh MSA, PA	Y	39860 FQ	48150 MW	68240 TQ	USBLS	5/15
Metals and Plastics	Rhode Island	Y	27320 FQ	32700 MW	39420 TQ	USBLS	5/15
Metals and Plastics	Providence-Warwick MSA, RI-MA	Y	26800 FQ	32690 MW	39050 TQ	USBLS	5/15
Metals and Plastics	South Carolina	Y	28110 FQ	33140 MW	37760 TQ	USBLS	5/15
Metals and Plastics	South Dakota	Y	30160 FQ	34760 MW	38900 TQ	USBLS	5/15
Metals and Plastics	Tennessee	Y	28730 FQ	34120 MW	38920 TQ	USBLS	5/15
Metals and Plastics	Nashville-Davidson–Murfreesboro–Franklin MSA, TN	Y	31300 FQ	35900 MW	41340 TQ	USBLS	5/15
Metals and Plastics	Texas	Y	26690 FQ	34230 MW	51740 TQ	USBLS	5/15
Metals and Plastics	Dallas-Plano-Irving PMSA, TX	Y	25580 FQ	32430 MW	51080 TQ	USBLS	5/15

AE	Average entry wage	AWR	Average wage range	H	Hourly	LR	Low end range	MTC	Median total compensation	TCC	Total cash compensation
AEX	Average experienced wage	B	Biweekly	HI	Highest wage paid	M	Monthly	MW	Median wage paid	TQ	Third quartile wage
ATC	Average total compensation	D	Daily	HR	High end range	MCC	Median cash compensation	MWR	Median wage range	W	Weekly
AW	Average wage paid	FQ	First quartile wage	LO	Lowest wage paid	ME	Median entry wage	S	See annotated source	Y	Yearly

444

Occupation/Type/Industry	Location	Per	Low	Mid	High	Source	Date
Drilling and Boring Machine Tool Setter, Operator, and Tender							
Metals and Plastics	Fort Worth-Arlington PMSA, TX	Y	31070 FQ	59450 MW	88270 TQ	USBLS	5/15
Metals and Plastics	Houston-The Woodlands-Sugar Land MSA, TX	Y	25850 FQ	32150 MW	51970 TQ	USBLS	5/15
Metals and Plastics	San Antonio-New Braunfels MSA, TX	Y	25540 FQ	30670 MW	37880 TQ	USBLS	5/15
Metals and Plastics	Utah	Y	27450 FQ	33050 MW	38640 TQ	USBLS	5/15
Metals and Plastics	Vermont	Y	25190 FQ	31780 MW	35870 TQ	USBLS	5/15
Metals and Plastics	Virginia	Y	28830 FQ	37510 MW	46600 TQ	USBLS	5/15
Metals and Plastics	Virginia Beach-Norfolk-Newport News MSA, VA-NC	Y	32440 FQ	37890 MW	54190 TQ	USBLS	5/15
Metals and Plastics	Washington	H	13.24 FQ	15.79 MW	20.80 TQ	WABLS	3/16
Metals and Plastics	Seattle-Bellevue-Everett PMSA, WA	H	13.48 FQ	16.13 MW	24.12 TQ	WABLS	3/16
Metals and Plastics	Wisconsin	Y	33780 FQ	42080 MW	58100 TQ	USBLS	5/15
Metals and Plastics	Milwaukee-Waukesha-West Allis MSA, WI	Y	39270 FQ	55850 MW	73140 TQ	USBLS	5/15
Driver/Sales Worker	Alabama	Y	17752 AE	30032 AW	36172 AEX	ALBLS	6/16
	Birmingham-Hoover MSA, AL	Y	17721 AE	29312 AW	35103 AEX	ALBLS	6/16
	Alaska	Y	23070 FQ	27560 MW	34540 TQ	USBLS	5/15
	Anchorage MSA, AK	Y	23270 FQ	27350 MW	33330 TQ	USBLS	5/15
	Arizona	Y	18110 FQ	19370 MW	24980 TQ	USBLS	5/15
	Phoenix-Mesa-Scottsdale MSA, AZ	Y	18470 FQ	20780 MW	29250 TQ	USBLS	5/15
	Tucson MSA, AZ	Y	17620 FQ	18420 MW	19210 TQ	USBLS	5/15
	Arkansas	Y	19110 FQ	24420 MW	33450 TQ	USBLS	5/15
	Little Rock-North Little Rock-Conway MSA, AR	Y	23640 FQ	30360 MW	36210 TQ	USBLS	5/15
	California	H	9.83 FQ	13.21 MW	18.51 TQ	CABLS	1/16-3/16
	Anaheim-Santa Ana-Irvine PMSA, CA	H	9.60 FQ	11.29 MW	19.02 TQ	CABLS	1/16-3/16
	Los Angeles-Long Beach-Glendale PMSA, CA	H	9.67 FQ	11.90 MW	17.49 TQ	CABLS	1/16-3/16
	Oakland-Hayward-Berkeley PMSA, CA	H	9.75 FQ	14.57 MW	20.00 TQ	CABLS	1/16-3/16
	Riverside-San Bernardino-Ontario MSA, CA	H	9.87 FQ	11.48 MW	15.25 TQ	CABLS	1/16-3/16
	Sacramento–Roseville–Arden-Arcade MSA, CA	H	12.72 FQ	17.53 MW	22.72 TQ	CABLS	1/16-3/16
	San Diego-Carlsbad MSA, CA	H	9.98 FQ	13.62 MW	18.26 TQ	CABLS	1/16-3/16
	San Francisco-Redwood City-South San Francisco PMSA, CA	H	12.62 FQ	15.53 MW	18.90 TQ	CABLS	1/16-3/16
	Colorado	Y	18440 FQ	19940 MW	31200 TQ	USBLS	5/15
	Denver-Aurora-Lakewood MSA, CO	Y	18430 FQ	19890 MW	31790 TQ	USBLS	5/15
	Connecticut	Y		26619 MW		CTBLS	1/16-3/16
	Bridgeport-Stamford-Norwalk MSA, CT	Y	21020 FQ	28580 MW	45080 TQ	USBLS	5/15
	Hartford-West Hartford-East Hartford MSA, CT	Y	19330 FQ	23400 MW	31420 TQ	USBLS	5/15
	Delaware	Y	18780 FQ	22600 MW	31230 TQ	USBLS	5/15
	Wilmington PMSA, DE-MD-NJ	Y	18640 FQ	21260 MW	24760 TQ	USBLS	5/15
	District of Columbia	Y	20090 FQ	23680 MW	39070 TQ	USBLS	5/15
	Washington-Arlington-Alexandria PMSA, DC-VA-MD-WV	Y	19170 FQ	28900 MW	41840 TQ	USBLS	5/15
	Florida	H	9.04 AE	9.72 MW	13.50 AEX	FLBLS	7/16-9/16
	Fort Lauderdale-Pompano Beach-Deerfield Beach PMSA, FL	H	9.07 AE	10.03 MW	14.30 AEX	FLBLS	7/16-9/16
	Miami-Miami Beach-Kendall PMSA, FL	H	9.02 AE	9.61 MW	12.21 AEX	FLBLS	7/16-9/16
	Orlando-Kissimmee-Sanford MSA, FL	H	9.00 AE	9.72 MW	14.51 AEX	FLBLS	7/16-9/16
	Tampa-St. Petersburg-Clearwater MSA, FL	H	9.09 AE	9.67 MW	13.30 AEX	FLBLS	7/16-9/16
	Georgia	Y	17990 FQ	21610 MW	34700 TQ	USBLS	5/15

AE	Average entry wage	**AWR**	Average wage range	**H**	Hourly
AEX	Average experienced wage	**B**	Biweekly	**HI**	Highest wage paid
ATC	Average total compensation	**D**	Daily	**HR**	High end range
AW	Average wage paid	**FQ**	First quartile wage	**LO**	Lowest wage paid

LR	Low end range	**MTC**	Median total compensation	**TCC**	Total cash compensation
M	Monthly	**MW**	Median wage paid	**TQ**	Third quartile wage
MCC	Median cash compensation	**MWR**	Median wage range	**W**	Weekly
ME	Median entry wage	**S**	See annotated source	**Y**	Yearly

Occupation/Type/Industry	Location	Per	Low	Mid	High	Source	Date
Driver/Sales Worker	Atlanta-Sandy Springs- Roswell MSA, GA	Y	18450 FQ	23410 MW	37470 TQ	USBLS	5/15
	Augusta-Richmond County MSA, GA-SC	Y	16960 FQ	18440 MW	25350 TQ	USBLS	5/15
	Hawaii	Y	22810 FQ	28330 MW	37480 TQ	USBLS	5/15
	Urban Honolulu MSA, HI	Y	22760 FQ	27470 MW	35870 TQ	USBLS	5/15
	Idaho	Y	21670 FQ	27470 MW	42340 TQ	USBLS	5/15
	Boise City MSA, ID	Y	21630 FQ	28010 MW	44680 TQ	USBLS	5/15
	Illinois	Y	18850 FQ	23140 MW	39010 TQ	USBLS	5/15
	Chicago-Naperville-Arlington Heights PMSA, IL	Y	19060 FQ	30730 MW	41170 TQ	USBLS	5/15
	Lake County-Kenosha County PMSA, IL-WI	Y	19020 FQ	22080 MW	33230 TQ	USBLS	5/15
	Indiana	Y	17300 FQ	19050 MW	27500 TQ	USBLS	5/15
	Gary PMSA, IN	Y	18200 FQ	23130 MW	48590 TQ	USBLS	5/15
	Indianapolis-Carmel-Anderson MSA, IN	Y	17040 FQ	18520 MW	22240 TQ	USBLS	5/15
	Iowa	Y	17530 FQ	19520 MW	34930 TQ	USBLS	5/15
	Des Moines-West Des Moines MSA, IA	Y	17390 FQ	19190 MW	25300 TQ	USBLS	5/15
	Kansas	Y	19310 FQ	24890 MW	37090 TQ	USBLS	5/15
	Wichita MSA, KS	Y	18630 FQ	21920 MW	26910 TQ	USBLS	5/15
	Kentucky	Y	17820 FQ	20230 MW	29790 TQ	USBLS	5/15
	Louisville-Jefferson County MSA, KY-IN	Y	17820 FQ	20420 MW	32080 TQ	USBLS	5/15
	Louisiana	Y	20000 FQ	25860 MW	36860 TQ	USBLS	5/15
	Baton Rouge MSA, LA	Y	19610 FQ	27840 MW	42750 TQ	USBLS	5/15
	New Orleans-Metairie MSA, LA	Y	19440 FQ	24500 MW	32770 TQ	USBLS	5/15
	Maine	Y	22040 FQ	28310 MW	37680 TQ	USBLS	5/15
	Portland-South Portland MSA, ME	Y	22860 FQ	28870 MW	39200 TQ	USBLS	5/15
	Maryland	Y	18174 AE	31272 MW	37821 AEX	MDBLS	4/16
	Baltimore-Columbia-Towson MSA, MD	Y	18820 FQ	29120 MW	49430 TQ	USBLS	5/15
	Salisbury MSA, MD-DE	Y	18360 FQ	24410 MW	45660 TQ	USBLS	5/15
	Massachusetts	Y	20120 FQ	25320 MW	38870 TQ	USBLS	5/15
	Boston-Cambridge-Newton NECTA, MA	Y	21580 FQ	27870 MW	42660 TQ	USBLS	5/15
	Worcester MSA, MA-CT	Y	23550 FQ	30120 MW	50410 TQ	USBLS	5/15
	Michigan	Y	18590 FQ	20920 MW	32960 TQ	USBLS	5/15
	Detroit-Dearborn-Livonia PMSA, MI	Y	18300 FQ	19510 MW	25060 TQ	USBLS	5/15
	Grand Rapids-Wyoming MSA, MI	Y	18380 FQ	19660 MW	32490 TQ	USBLS	5/15
	Minnesota	Y	18570 FQ	21302 MW	35275 TQ	MNBLS	1/16-3/16
	Minneapolis-St. Paul- Bloomington MSA, MN-WI	Y	18449 FQ	20022 MW	34751 TQ	MNBLS	1/16-3/16
	Mississippi	Y	17730 FQ	20930 MW	30130 TQ	USBLS	5/15
	Jackson MSA, MS	Y	20790 FQ	26970 MW	31570 TQ	USBLS	5/15
	Missouri	Y	17810 FQ	19700 MW	29570 TQ	USBLS	5/15
	Kansas City MSA, MO-KS	Y	18080 FQ	22290 MW	30890 TQ	USBLS	5/15
	St. Louis MSA, MO-IL	Y	18610 FQ	22650 MW	37530 TQ	USBLS	5/15
	Montana	Y	18680 FQ	23650 MW	37340 TQ	USBLS	5/15
	Billings MSA, MT	Y	18590 FQ	34530 MW	44410 TQ	USBLS	5/15
	Nebraska	Y	18525 FQ	21820 MW	30280 TQ	NEBLS	7/16-9/16
	Omaha-Council Bluffs MSA, NE-IA	Y	18455 FQ	21695 MW	30570 TQ	NEBLS	7/16-9/16
	Nevada	Y	18750 FQ	27250 MW	39700 TQ	USBLS	5/15
	Las Vegas-Henderson-Paradise MSA, NV	Y	18230 FQ	24870 MW	36350 TQ	USBLS	5/15
	New Hampshire	H	8.47 AE	10.89 MW	18.27 AEX	NHBLS	6/16
	Manchester NECTA, NH	H	8.42 AE	9.98 MW	17.97 AEX	NHBLS	6/16
	Nashua NECTA, NH-MA	Y	17000 FQ	18450 MW	21120 TQ	USBLS	5/15
	New Jersey	Y	20090 FQ	32150 MW	44710 TQ	USBLS	5/15
	Camden PMSA, NJ	Y	25080 FQ	35590 MW	47650 TQ	USBLS	5/15
	Newark PMSA, NJ-PA	Y	18880 FQ	21860 MW	39250 TQ	USBLS	5/15
	Trenton MSA, NJ	Y	20410 FQ	26590 MW	29300 TQ	USBLS	5/15
	New Mexico	Y	18500 FQ	23900 MW	34750 TQ	USBLS	5/15
	Albuquerque MSA, NM	Y	21150 FQ	29280 MW	37160 TQ	USBLS	5/15
	New York	Y	19230 AE	21550 MW	32860 AEX	NYBLS	1/16-3/16

AE	Average entry wage	AWR	Average wage range	H	Hourly	LR	Low end range	MTC	Median total compensation	TCC	Total cash compensation
AEX	Average experienced wage	B	Biweekly	HI	Highest wage paid	M	Monthly	MW	Median wage paid	TQ	Third quartile wage
ATC	Average total compensation	D	Daily	HR	High end range	MCC	Median cash compensation	MWR	Median wage range	W	Weekly
AW	Average wage paid	FQ	First quartile wage	LO	Lowest wage paid	ME	Median entry wage	S	See annotated source	Y	Yearly

Occupation/Type/Industry	Location	Per	Low	Mid	High	Source	Date
Driver/Sales Worker	Buffalo-Cheektowaga-Niagara Falls MSA, NY	Y	18790 FQ	19490 MW	28410 TQ	USBLS	5/15
	Nassau County-Suffolk County PMSA, NY	Y	18910 FQ	20050 MW	35800 TQ	USBLS	5/15
	New York-Jersey City-White Plains PMSA, NY-NJ	Y	19010 FQ	23500 MW	36780 TQ	USBLS	5/15
	Rochester MSA, NY	Y	18850 FQ	19540 MW	24410 TQ	USBLS	5/15
	North Carolina	Y	18300 FQ	22940 MW	32890 TQ	USBLS	5/15
	Charlotte-Concord-Gastonia MSA, NC-SC	Y	18370 FQ	26160 MW	36430 TQ	USBLS	5/15
	Raleigh MSA, NC	Y	17630 FQ	21120 MW	31110 TQ	USBLS	5/15
	North Dakota	Y	18520 FQ	23290 MW	36470 TQ	USBLS	5/15
	Fargo MSA, ND-MN	Y	20470 FQ	31690 MW	37060 TQ	USBLS	5/15
	Ohio	Y	18020 FQ	19070 MW	25180 TQ	USBLS	5/15
	Cincinnati MSA, OH-KY-IN	Y	17830 FQ	18820 MW	22000 TQ	USBLS	5/15
	Cleveland-Elyria MSA, OH	Y	18000 FQ	18990 MW	21230 TQ	USBLS	5/15
	Columbus MSA, OH	Y	17940 FQ	18900 MW	20270 TQ	USBLS	5/15
	Oklahoma	Y	18620 FQ	23660 MW	34630 TQ	USBLS	5/15
	Oklahoma City MSA, OK	Y	17950 FQ	20920 MW	32940 TQ	USBLS	5/15
	Tulsa MSA, OK	Y	18870 FQ	23710 MW	35690 TQ	USBLS	5/15
	Oregon	H	10.19 FQ	13.39 MW	18.21 TQ	ORBLS	2016
	Portland-Vancouver-Hillsboro MSA, OR-WA	Y	19870 FQ	28090 MW	37370 TQ	USBLS	5/15
	Pennsylvania	Y	17860 FQ	21290 MW	35580 TQ	USBLS	5/15
	Allentown-Bethlehem-Easton MSA, PA-NJ	Y	17730 FQ	19890 MW	25380 TQ	USBLS	5/15
	Harrisburg-Carlisle MSA, PA	Y	17170 FQ	18800 MW	22380 TQ	USBLS	5/15
	Montgomery County-Bucks County-Chester County PMSA, PA	Y	17810 FQ	20290 MW	35940 TQ	USBLS	5/15
	Philadelphia PMSA, PA	Y	27050 FQ	36820 MW	47240 TQ	USBLS	5/15
	Pittsburgh MSA, PA	Y	17520 FQ	19840 MW	35050 TQ	USBLS	5/15
	Rhode Island	Y	19190 FQ	23820 MW	45070 TQ	USBLS	5/15
	Providence-Warwick MSA, RI-MA	Y	19250 FQ	23590 MW	42500 TQ	USBLS	5/15
	South Carolina	Y	17560 FQ	19560 MW	33300 TQ	USBLS	5/15
	Charleston-North Charleston MSA, SC	Y	17180 FQ	18670 MW	22560 TQ	USBLS	5/15
	Columbia MSA, SC	Y	18050 FQ	25870 MW	41400 TQ	USBLS	5/15
	Greenville-Anderson-Mauldin MSA, SC	Y	17450 FQ	19300 MW	35200 TQ	USBLS	5/15
	South Dakota	Y	21590 FQ	26800 MW	36240 TQ	USBLS	5/15
	Sioux Falls MSA, SD	Y	20280 FQ	27150 MW	36250 TQ	USBLS	5/15
	Tennessee	Y	18070 FQ	23090 MW	37560 TQ	USBLS	5/15
	Knoxville MSA, TN	Y	17080 FQ	18710 MW	29910 TQ	USBLS	5/15
	Memphis MSA, TN-MS-AR	Y	17780 FQ	21810 MW	36580 TQ	USBLS	5/15
	Nashville-Davidson– Murfreesboro–Franklin MSA, TN	Y	21940 FQ	36590 MW	49010 TQ	USBLS	5/15
	Texas	Y	18360 FQ	22570 MW	33280 TQ	USBLS	5/15
	Austin-Round Rock MSA, TX	Y	17470 FQ	19390 MW	26840 TQ	USBLS	5/15
	Dallas-Plano-Irving PMSA, TX	Y	19540 FQ	24560 MW	33850 TQ	USBLS	5/15
	Fort Worth-Arlington PMSA, TX	Y	17090 FQ	18700 MW	25310 TQ	USBLS	5/15
	Houston-The Woodlands-Sugar Land MSA, TX	Y	19150 FQ	23540 MW	38950 TQ	USBLS	5/15
	San Antonio-New Braunfels MSA, TX	Y	18360 FQ	21960 MW	29260 TQ	USBLS	5/15
	Utah	Y	18410 FQ	26520 MW	33210 TQ	USBLS	5/15
	Ogden-Clearfield MSA, UT	Y	19000 FQ	26740 MW	29520 TQ	USBLS	5/15
	Provo-Orem MSA, UT	Y	18100 FQ	20230 MW	28280 TQ	USBLS	5/15
	Salt Lake City MSA, UT	Y	17900 FQ	25240 MW	43940 TQ	USBLS	5/15
	Vermont	Y	22490 FQ	26910 MW	39410 TQ	USBLS	5/15
	Burlington-South Burlington MSA, VT	Y	22100 FQ	24850 MW	31410 TQ	USBLS	5/15
	Virginia	Y	18310 FQ	23120 MW	35890 TQ	USBLS	5/15
	Richmond MSA, VA	Y	18750 FQ	23220 MW	35560 TQ	USBLS	5/15
	Virginia Beach-Norfolk-Newport News MSA, VA-NC	Y	17380 FQ	19450 MW	24820 TQ	USBLS	5/15
	Washington	H	10.48 FQ	12.03 MW	15.61 TQ	WABLS	3/16
	Seattle-Bellevue-Everett PMSA, WA	H	10.30 FQ	12.00 MW	14.89 TQ	WABLS	3/16

AE	Average entry wage	AWR	Average wage range	H	Hourly	LR	Low end range	MTC	Median total compensation	TCC	Total cash compensation
AEX	Average experienced wage	B	Biweekly	HI	Highest wage paid	M	Monthly	MW	Median wage paid	TQ	Third quartile wage
ATC	Average total compensation	D	Daily	HR	High end range	MCC	Median cash compensation	MWR	Median wage range	W	Weekly
AW	Average wage paid	FQ	First quartile wage	LO	Lowest wage paid	ME	Median entry wage	S	See annotated source	Y	Yearly

Occupation/Type/Industry	Location	Per	Low	Mid	High	Source	Date
Driver/Sales Worker	Tacoma-Lakewood PMSA, WA	H	10.51 FQ	11.81 MW	17.28 TQ	WABLS	3/16
	West Virginia	Y	18420 FQ	21310 MW	30440 TQ	USBLS	5/15
	Huntington-Ashland MSA, WV-KY-OH	Y	18410 FQ	21540 MW	29870 TQ	USBLS	5/15
	Wisconsin	Y	18200 FQ	22110 MW	34930 TQ	USBLS	5/15
	Madison MSA, WI	Y	18160 FQ	21350 MW	34510 TQ	USBLS	5/15
	Milwaukee-Waukesha-West Allis MSA, WI	Y	17570 FQ	19310 MW	25340 TQ	USBLS	5/15
	Wyoming	Y	17370 FQ	19280 MW	31520 TQ	USBLS	5/15
	Cheyenne MSA, WY	Y	17010 FQ	18570 MW	24200 TQ	USBLS	5/15
	Puerto Rico	Y	16810 FQ	18100 MW	19440 TQ	USBLS	5/15
	San Juan-Carolina-Caguas MSA, PR	Y	16780 FQ	18050 MW	19330 TQ	USBLS	5/15
	Virgin Islands	Y	17090 FQ	18650 MW	21530 TQ	USBLS	5/15
	Guam	Y	18070 FQ	18980 MW	21960 TQ	USBLS	5/15
Drug Court Coordinator Judicial Branch, State Government	Helena, MT	H			26.31 HI	MTGOV	2016
Drug Rebate Specialist Department of Public Health and Human Services, State Government	Helena, MT	H	18.75 LO		18.80 HI	MTGOV	2016
Drywall and Ceiling Tile Installer	Alabama	Y	24246 AE	34307 AW	39337 AEX	ALBLS	6/16
	Birmingham-Hoover MSA, AL	Y	31797 AE	38895 AW	42444 AEX	ALBLS	6/16
	Alaska	Y	61140 FQ	74090 MW	88300 TQ	USBLS	5/15
	Arizona	Y	32050 FQ	36280 MW	42070 TQ	USBLS	5/15
	Phoenix-Mesa-Scottsdale MSA, AZ	Y	32430 FQ	36600 MW	42500 TQ	USBLS	5/15
	Tucson MSA, AZ	Y	29090 FQ	34190 MW	39010 TQ	USBLS	5/15
	Arkansas	Y	25480 FQ	29150 MW	34700 TQ	USBLS	5/15
	California	H	18.42 FQ	24.80 MW	37.60 TQ	CABLS	1/16-3/16
	Anaheim-Santa Ana-Irvine PMSA, CA	H	17.26 FQ	22.35 MW	33.90 TQ	CABLS	1/16-3/16
	Los Angeles-Long Beach-Glendale PMSA, CA	H	19.92 FQ	25.00 MW	35.61 TQ	CABLS	1/16-3/16
	Oakland-Hayward-Berkeley PMSA, CA	H	24.70 FQ	40.77 MW	47.95 TQ	CABLS	1/16-3/16
	Riverside-San Bernardino-Ontario MSA, CA	H	18.09 FQ	24.33 MW	36.03 TQ	CABLS	1/16-3/16
	Sacramento–Roseville–Arden-Arcade MSA, CA	H	18.20 FQ	23.35 MW	37.20 TQ	CABLS	1/16-3/16
	San Diego-Carlsbad MSA, CA	H	17.52 FQ	23.64 MW	30.98 TQ	CABLS	1/16-3/16
	San Francisco-Redwood City-South San Francisco PMSA, CA	H	19.91 FQ	27.46 MW	43.77 TQ	CABLS	1/16-3/16
	Colorado	Y	34700 FQ	40700 MW	46650 TQ	USBLS	5/15
	Denver-Aurora-Lakewood MSA, CO	Y	36610 FQ	42150 MW	47250 TQ	USBLS	5/15
	Connecticut	Y		53137 MW		CTBLS	1/16-3/16
	Hartford-West Hartford-East Hartford MSA, CT	Y	52280 FQ	58720 MW	66580 TQ	USBLS	5/15
	Delaware	Y	34150 FQ	39760 MW	53540 TQ	USBLS	5/15
	Wilmington PMSA, DE-MD-NJ	Y	34520 FQ	44740 MW	57810 TQ	USBLS	5/15
	Washington-Arlington-Alexandria PMSA, DC-VA-MD-WV	Y	33920 FQ	39150 MW	46880 TQ	USBLS	5/15
	Florida	H	10.54 AE	14.74 MW	17.40 AEX	FLBLS	7/16-9/16
	Fort Lauderdale-Pompano Beach-Deerfield Beach PMSA, FL	H	11.71 AE	14.80 MW	17.93 AEX	FLBLS	7/16-9/16
	Miami-Miami Beach-Kendall PMSA, FL	H	9.83 AE	12.14 MW	15.28 AEX	FLBLS	7/16-9/16
	Orlando-Kissimmee-Sanford MSA, FL	H	13.54 AE	16.85 MW	17.76 AEX	FLBLS	7/16-9/16
	Tampa-St. Petersburg-Clearwater MSA, FL	H	10.93 AE	14.32 MW	16.47 AEX	FLBLS	7/16-9/16
	Georgia	Y	32040 FQ	38060 MW	45750 TQ	USBLS	5/15
	Atlanta-Sandy Springs-Roswell MSA, GA	Y	34310 FQ	39620 MW	46550 TQ	USBLS	5/15

AE	Average entry wage	AWR	Average wage range	H	Hourly
AEX	Average experienced wage	B	Biweekly	HI	Highest wage paid
ATC	Average total compensation	D	Daily	HR	High end range
AW	Average wage paid	FQ	First quartile wage	LO	Lowest wage paid

LR	Low end range	MTC	Median total compensation	TCC	Total cash compensation
M	Monthly	MW	Median wage paid	TQ	Third quartile wage
MCC	Median cash compensation	MWR	Median wage range	W	Weekly
ME	Median entry wage	S	See annotated source	Y	Yearly

Occupation/Type/Industry	Location	Per	Low	Mid	High	Source	Date
Drywall and Ceiling Tile Installer	Augusta-Richmond County						
	MSA, GA-SC	Y	31640 FQ	36110 MW	44210 TQ	USBLS	5/15
	Hawaii	Y	37370 FQ	54770 MW	73780 TQ	USBLS	5/15
	Urban Honolulu MSA, HI	Y	36970 FQ	53110 MW	70310 TQ	USBLS	5/15
	Idaho	Y	30840 FQ	34740 MW	38480 TQ	USBLS	5/15
	Boise City MSA, ID	Y	31710 FQ	34820 MW	37920 TQ	USBLS	5/15
	Illinois	Y	35770 FQ	53790 MW	78410 TQ	USBLS	5/15
	Chicago-Naperville-Arlington						
	Heights PMSA, IL	Y	42080 FQ	60790 MW	82020 TQ	USBLS	5/15
	Indiana	Y	31420 FQ	40390 MW	54150 TQ	USBLS	5/15
	Gary PMSA, IN	Y	51410 FQ	55630 MW	59860 TQ	USBLS	5/15
	Indianapolis-Carmel-Anderson						
	MSA, IN	Y	41530 FQ	47890 MW	56100 TQ	USBLS	5/15
	Iowa	Y	30440 FQ	37190 MW	45500 TQ	USBLS	5/15
	Des Moines-West Des Moines						
	MSA, IA	Y	25730 FQ	33340 MW	38860 TQ	USBLS	5/15
	Kansas	Y	28320 FQ	36620 MW	49380 TQ	USBLS	5/15
	Wichita MSA, KS	Y	27160 FQ	29870 MW	43540 TQ	USBLS	5/15
	Kentucky	Y	28070 FQ	34220 MW	42580 TQ	USBLS	5/15
	Louisville-Jefferson County						
	MSA, KY-IN	Y	27580 FQ	30980 MW	44840 TQ	USBLS	5/15
	Louisiana	Y	31830 FQ	38050 MW	49670 TQ	USBLS	5/15
	Baton Rouge MSA, LA	Y	33060 FQ	39880 MW	55300 TQ	USBLS	5/15
	New Orleans-Metairie MSA,						
	LA	Y	29760 FQ	34820 MW	40340 TQ	USBLS	5/15
	Maine	Y	39370 FQ	45220 MW	55590 TQ	USBLS	5/15
	Portland-South Portland MSA,						
	ME	Y	40940 FQ	45030 MW	49130 TQ	USBLS	5/15
	Maryland	Y	31942 AE	39702 MW	43581 AEX	MDBLS	4/16
	Baltimore-Columbia-Towson						
	MSA, MD	Y	34340 FQ	39600 MW	45320 TQ	USBLS	5/15
	Salisbury MSA, MD-DE	Y	33660 FQ	36540 MW	39420 TQ	USBLS	5/15
	Massachusetts	Y	33150 FQ	47370 MW	59940 TQ	USBLS	5/15
	Boston-Cambridge-Newton						
	NECTA, MA	Y	35340 FQ	52580 MW	61670 TQ	USBLS	5/15
	Worcester MSA, MA-CT	Y	29660 FQ	34510 MW	39110 TQ	USBLS	5/15
	Michigan	Y	34870 FQ	44380 MW	57110 TQ	USBLS	5/15
	Grand Rapids-Wyoming MSA,						
	MI	Y	32830 FQ	41540 MW	47830 TQ	USBLS	5/15
	Minnesota	Y	41763 FQ	53266 MW	68764 TQ	MNBLS	1/16-3/16
	Minneapolis-St. Paul-						
	Bloomington MSA, MN-WI	Y	44175 FQ	55314 MW	69511 TQ	MNBLS	1/16-3/16
	Mississippi	Y	26700 FQ	33670 MW	37930 TQ	USBLS	5/15
	Jackson MSA, MS	Y	33560 FQ	35970 MW	38380 TQ	USBLS	5/15
	Missouri	Y	32930 FQ	40510 MW	57800 TQ	USBLS	5/15
	Kansas City MSA, MO-KS	Y	34340 FQ	47030 MW	71060 TQ	USBLS	5/15
	St. Louis MSA, MO-IL	Y	35060 FQ	43990 MW	55050 TQ	USBLS	5/15
	Montana	Y	31810 FQ	38280 MW	46160 TQ	USBLS	5/15
	Billings MSA, MT	Y	33420 FQ	38070 MW	44830 TQ	USBLS	5/15
	Nebraska	Y	24625 FQ	34480 MW	46955 TQ	NEBLS	7/16-9/16
	Omaha-Council Bluffs MSA,						
	NE-IA	Y	23070 FQ	35060 MW	48915 TQ	NEBLS	7/16-9/16
	Nevada	Y	30680 FQ	39930 MW	46600 TQ	USBLS	5/15
	Las Vegas-Henderson-Paradise						
	MSA, NV	Y	29880 FQ	38100 MW	44970 TQ	USBLS	5/15
	New Hampshire	H	16.94 AE	22.27 MW	24.38 AEX	NHBLS	6/16
	Manchester NECTA, NH	H	16.15 AE	21.01 MW	23.31 AEX	NHBLS	6/16
	Nashua NECTA, NH-MA	Y	43090 FQ	47670 MW	52540 TQ	USBLS	5/15
	New Jersey	Y	38450 FQ	59900 MW	86450 TQ	USBLS	5/15
	Camden PMSA, NJ	Y	37310 FQ	77420 MW	91350 TQ	USBLS	5/15
	Newark PMSA, NJ-PA	Y	53240 FQ	62470 MW	74480 TQ	USBLS	5/15
	New Mexico	Y	28300 FQ	33320 MW	43360 TQ	USBLS	5/15
	Albuquerque MSA, NM	Y	28180 FQ	32010 MW	44630 TQ	USBLS	5/15
	New York	Y	35280 AE	57210 MW	84200 AEX	NYBLS	1/16-3/16
	Buffalo-Cheektowaga-Niagara						
	Falls MSA, NY	Y	34500 FQ	38470 MW	46020 TQ	USBLS	5/15
	Nassau County-Suffolk County						
	PMSA, NY	Y	43590 FQ	81730 MW	107160 TQ	USBLS	5/15
	New York-Jersey City-White						
	Plains PMSA, NY-NJ	Y	47380 FQ	77040 MW	99400 TQ	USBLS	5/15
	Rochester MSA, NY	Y	36790 FQ	43560 MW	48490 TQ	USBLS	5/15
	North Carolina	Y	28910 FQ	33920 MW	38590 TQ	USBLS	5/15

AE	Average entry wage	AWR	Average wage range	H	Hourly	LR	Low end range	MTC	Median total compensation	TCC	Total cash compensation
AEX	Average experienced wage	B	Biweekly	HI	Highest wage paid	M	Monthly	MW	Median wage paid	TQ	Third quartile wage
ATC	Average total compensation	D	Daily	HR	High end range	MCC	Median cash compensation	MWR	Median wage range	W	Weekly
AW	Average wage paid	FQ	First quartile wage	LO	Lowest wage paid	ME	Median entry wage	S	See annotated source	Y	Yearly

Occupation/Type/Industry	Location	Per	Low	Mid	High	Source	Date
Drywall and Ceiling Tile Installer	Charlotte-Concord-Gastonia						
	MSA, NC-SC	Y	30910 FQ	34880 MW	38600 TQ	USBLS	5/15
	Raleigh MSA, NC	Y	29670 FQ	34450 MW	39170 TQ	USBLS	5/15
	North Dakota	Y	33470 FQ	37020 MW	42660 TQ	USBLS	5/15
	Fargo MSA, ND-MN	Y	33590 FQ	37210 MW	42010 TQ	USBLS	5/15
	Ohio	Y	29300 FQ	36100 MW	47660 TQ	USBLS	5/15
	Cincinnati MSA, OH-KY-IN	Y	28310 FQ	32550 MW	41270 TQ	USBLS	5/15
	Cleveland-Elyria MSA, OH	Y	23650 FQ	44040 MW	66320 TQ	USBLS	5/15
	Columbus MSA, OH	Y	31850 FQ	35420 MW	38980 TQ	USBLS	5/15
	Oklahoma	Y	32010 FQ	36210 MW	41470 TQ	USBLS	5/15
	Oklahoma City MSA, OK	Y	31160 FQ	36220 MW	42450 TQ	USBLS	5/15
	Tulsa MSA, OK	Y	32940 FQ	36390 MW	40530 TQ	USBLS	5/15
	Oregon	H	16.27 FQ	20.12 MW	26.52 TQ	ORBLS	2016
	Portland-Vancouver-Hillsboro						
	MSA, OR-WA	Y	34080 FQ	42690 MW	57390 TQ	USBLS	5/15
	Pennsylvania	Y	33960 FQ	43890 MW	57040 TQ	USBLS	5/15
	Allentown-Bethlehem-Easton						
	MSA, PA-NJ	Y	30780 FQ	38350 MW	46070 TQ	USBLS	5/15
	Harrisburg-Carlisle MSA, PA	Y	35710 FQ	42650 MW	52180 TQ	USBLS	5/15
	Montgomery County-Bucks						
	County-Chester County						
	PMSA, PA	Y	48890 FQ	55060 MW	60900 TQ	USBLS	5/15
	Philadelphia PMSA, PA	Y	35670 FQ	41860 MW	59450 TQ	USBLS	5/15
	Pittsburgh MSA, PA	Y	33980 FQ	53140 MW	68060 TQ	USBLS	5/15
	Providence-Warwick MSA, RI-						
	MA	Y	36430 FQ	45830 MW	67300 TQ	USBLS	5/15
	South Carolina	Y	26810 FQ	30970 MW	36180 TQ	USBLS	5/15
	Charleston-North Charleston						
	MSA, SC	Y	28930 FQ	33630 MW	37730 TQ	USBLS	5/15
	Columbia MSA, SC	Y	29070 FQ	33550 MW	37970 TQ	USBLS	5/15
	Greenville-Anderson-Mauldin						
	MSA, SC	Y	26550 FQ	28520 MW	30490 TQ	USBLS	5/15
	South Dakota	Y	27260 FQ	32050 MW	39270 TQ	USBLS	5/15
	Sioux Falls MSA, SD	Y	27880 FQ	33500 MW	42840 TQ	USBLS	5/15
	Tennessee	Y	31230 FQ	34910 MW	38540 TQ	USBLS	5/15
	Knoxville MSA, TN	Y	31350 FQ	36170 MW	42430 TQ	USBLS	5/15
	Memphis MSA, TN-MS-AR	Y	31330 FQ	35730 MW	41150 TQ	USBLS	5/15
	Nashville-Davidson–						
	Murfreesboro–Franklin						
	MSA, TN	Y	31320 FQ	34360 MW	37370 TQ	USBLS	5/15
	Texas	Y	28560 FQ	33590 MW	37900 TQ	USBLS	5/15
	Austin-Round Rock MSA, TX	Y	29430 FQ	34600 MW	39240 TQ	USBLS	5/15
	Dallas-Plano-Irving PMSA, TX	Y	29540 FQ	34060 MW	38060 TQ	USBLS	5/15
	Fort Worth-Arlington PMSA,						
	TX	Y	29550 FQ	33870 MW	37270 TQ	USBLS	5/15
	Houston-The Woodlands-						
	Sugar Land MSA, TX	Y	28310 FQ	33680 MW	38140 TQ	USBLS	5/15
	San Antonio-New Braunfels						
	MSA, TX	Y	29230 FQ	34110 MW	38260 TQ	USBLS	5/15
	Utah	Y	32400 FQ	36530 MW	42110 TQ	USBLS	5/15
	Ogden-Clearfield MSA, UT	Y	30530 FQ	35760 MW	41360 TQ	USBLS	5/15
	Provo-Orem MSA, UT	Y	26520 FQ	38040 MW	44690 TQ	USBLS	5/15
	Salt Lake City MSA, UT	Y	33780 FQ	36960 MW	41260 TQ	USBLS	5/15
	Vermont	Y	36440 FQ	44040 MW	51230 TQ	USBLS	5/15
	Burlington-South Burlington						
	MSA, VT	Y	39520 FQ	45390 MW	52500 TQ	USBLS	5/15
	Virginia	Y	32560 FQ	38200 MW	46830 TQ	USBLS	5/15
	Richmond MSA, VA	Y	33820 FQ	40720 MW	49470 TQ	USBLS	5/15
	Virginia Beach-Norfolk-						
	Newport News MSA, VA-NC	Y	33340 FQ	37480 MW	44010 TQ	USBLS	5/15
	Washington	H	20.74 FQ	24.01 MW	31.45 TQ	WABLS	3/16
	Seattle-Bellevue-Everett						
	PMSA, WA	H	21.18 FQ	23.97 MW	33.67 TQ	WABLS	3/16
	Tacoma-Lakewood PMSA, WA	H	19.54 FQ	24.41 MW	33.55 TQ	WABLS	3/16
	West Virginia	Y	30940 FQ	35730 MW	43510 TQ	USBLS	5/15
	Huntington-Ashland MSA,						
	WV-KY-OH	Y	29930 FQ	35430 MW	42780 TQ	USBLS	5/15
	Wisconsin	Y	34100 FQ	42840 MW	50050 TQ	USBLS	5/15
	Madison MSA, WI	Y	44510 FQ	56080 MW	72580 TQ	USBLS	5/15
	Milwaukee-Waukesha-West						
	Allis MSA, WI	Y	39790 FQ	44360 MW	48890 TQ	USBLS	5/15
	Wyoming	Y	34670 FQ	38480 MW	45540 TQ	USBLS	5/15

Occupation/Type/Industry	Location	Per	Low	Mid	High	Source	Date
Drywall and Ceiling Tile Installer	Puerto Rico	Y	17400 FQ	19440 MW	23950 TQ	USBLS	5/15
	San Juan-Carolina-Caguas MSA, PR	Y	17530 FQ	19820 MW	24240 TQ	USBLS	5/15
DUI Victims Assistant							
Municipal Government	Louisville, KY	Y			46197 HI	LKY01	2017
Duplicating Devices Operator							
Municipal Government	Detroit, MI	M	2292 LO		2642 HI	DETGOV	2016
E-911 Operator							
Municipal Government	Albany, GA	H	14.81 LO		20.43 HI	GACTY01	2016
Municipal Government	Forest Park, GA	H	14.33 LO		24.07 HI	GACTY01	2016
E-Government Business Analyst							
Municipal Government	North Myrtle Beach, SC	Y			57009 HI	WMBFN	2017
E-Learning Specialist							
Department of Corrections, State Government	Helena, MT	H	26.41 LO		27.49 HI	MTGOV	2016
Early Intervention Specialist							
Department of Developmental Disabilities, State Government	Ohio	H	35.14 LO		38.25 HI	OHGOV	2015
Earth Driller							
Except Oil and Gas	Alabama	Y	27744 AE	38854 AW	44408 AEX	ALBLS	6/16
Except Oil and Gas	Birmingham-Hoover MSA, AL	Y	27857 AE	37527 AW	42361 AEX	ALBLS	6/16
Except Oil and Gas	Alaska	Y	49560 FQ	54900 MW	59810 TQ	USBLS	5/15
Except Oil and Gas	Anchorage MSA, AK	Y	51130 FQ	55460 MW	59790 TQ	USBLS	5/15
Except Oil and Gas	Arizona	Y	38590 FQ	44460 MW	50300 TQ	USBLS	5/15
Except Oil and Gas	Phoenix-Mesa-Scottsdale MSA, AZ	Y	39360 FQ	44060 MW	48670 TQ	USBLS	5/15
Except Oil and Gas	Tucson MSA, AZ	Y	37180 FQ	42510 MW	46810 TQ	USBLS	5/15
Except Oil and Gas	California	H	22.19 FQ	29.47 MW	36.49 TQ	CABLS	1/16-3/16
Except Oil and Gas	Anaheim-Santa Ana-Irvine PMSA, CA	H	27.10 FQ	32.03 MW	36.96 TQ	CABLS	1/16-3/16
Except Oil and Gas	Los Angeles-Long Beach-Glendale PMSA, CA	H	30.39 FQ	34.14 MW	37.16 TQ	CABLS	1/16-3/16
Except Oil and Gas	Riverside-San Bernardino-Ontario MSA, CA	H	33.13 FQ	41.16 MW	45.14 TQ	CABLS	1/16-3/16
Except Oil and Gas	Sacramento–Roseville–Arden-Arcade MSA, CA	H	23.65 FQ	32.18 MW	35.81 TQ	CABLS	1/16-3/16
Except Oil and Gas	San Diego-Carlsbad MSA, CA	H	26.06 FQ	28.24 MW	30.41 TQ	CABLS	1/16-3/16
Except Oil and Gas	Colorado	Y	38730 FQ	46470 MW	54980 TQ	USBLS	5/15
Except Oil and Gas	Denver-Aurora-Lakewood MSA, CO	Y	36350 FQ	42120 MW	48010 TQ	USBLS	5/15
Except Oil and Gas	Connecticut	Y		41245 MW		CTBLS	1/16-3/16
Except Oil and Gas	Delaware	Y	39650 FQ	43990 MW	48290 TQ	USBLS	5/15
Except Oil and Gas	Washington-Arlington-Alexandria PMSA, DC-VA-MD-WV	Y	31900 FQ	41020 MW	50780 TQ	USBLS	5/15
Except Oil and Gas	Florida	H	13.27 AE	17.17 MW	20.07 AEX	FLBLS	7/16-9/16
Except Oil and Gas	Fort Lauderdale-Pompano Beach-Deerfield Beach PMSA, FL	H	11.18 AE	18.11 MW	20.26 AEX	FLBLS	7/16-9/16
Except Oil and Gas	Orlando-Kissimmee-Sanford MSA, FL	H	15.15 AE	18.17 MW	21.06 AEX	FLBLS	7/16-9/16
Except Oil and Gas	Tampa-St. Petersburg-Clearwater MSA, FL	H	13.44 AE	17.26 MW	20.14 AEX	FLBLS	7/16-9/16
Except Oil and Gas	Georgia	Y	32690 FQ	37780 MW	47150 TQ	USBLS	5/15
Except Oil and Gas	Atlanta-Sandy Springs-Roswell MSA, GA	Y	34640 FQ	39510 MW	50240 TQ	USBLS	5/15
Except Oil and Gas	Hawaii	Y	47760 FQ	55000 MW	63330 TQ	USBLS	5/15
Except Oil and Gas	Idaho	Y	29010 FQ	43540 MW	60300 TQ	USBLS	5/15
Except Oil and Gas	Illinois	Y	49120 FQ	68290 MW	90160 TQ	USBLS	5/15
Except Oil and Gas	Chicago-Naperville-Arlington Heights PMSA, IL	Y	66950 FQ	86780 MW	95100 TQ	USBLS	5/15
Except Oil and Gas	Indiana	Y	37840 FQ	44360 MW	50710 TQ	USBLS	5/15
Except Oil and Gas	Gary PMSA, IN	Y	40090 FQ	84930 MW	93320 TQ	USBLS	5/15
Except Oil and Gas	Iowa	Y	33620 FQ	37970 MW	46560 TQ	USBLS	5/15
Except Oil and Gas	Kansas	Y	31160 FQ	36400 MW	43100 TQ	USBLS	5/15
Except Oil and Gas	Kentucky	Y	34880 FQ	41650 MW	50520 TQ	USBLS	5/15

AE	Average entry wage	AWR	Average wage range	H	Hourly	LR	Low end range	MTC	Median total compensation	TCC	Total cash compensation
AEX	Average experienced wage	B	Biweekly	HI	Highest wage paid	M	Monthly	MW	Median wage paid	TQ	Third quartile wage
ATC	Average total compensation	D	Daily	HR	High end range	MCC	Median cash compensation	MWR	Median wage range	W	Weekly
AW	Average wage paid	FQ	First quartile wage	LO	Lowest wage paid	ME	Median entry wage	S	See annotated source	Y	Yearly

451

Earth Driller

Occupation/Type/Industry	Location	Per	Low	Mid	High	Source	Date
Except Oil and Gas	Louisville-Jefferson County MSA, KY-IN	Y	40300 FQ	45930 MW	53210 TQ	USBLS	5/15
Except Oil and Gas	Louisiana	Y	43690 FQ	52120 MW	64690 TQ	USBLS	5/15
Except Oil and Gas	Maine	Y	35290 FQ	39190 MW	44410 TQ	USBLS	5/15
Except Oil and Gas	Salisbury MSA, MD-DE	Y	34190 FQ	42380 MW	47430 TQ	USBLS	5/15
Except Oil and Gas	Massachusetts	Y	33690 FQ	51620 MW	61790 TQ	USBLS	5/15
Except Oil and Gas	Michigan	Y	29990 FQ	36570 MW	50510 TQ	USBLS	5/15
Except Oil and Gas	Grand Rapids-Wyoming MSA, MI	Y	32820 FQ	36750 MW	42310 TQ	USBLS	5/15
Except Oil and Gas	Minnesota	Y	34064 FQ	43216 MW	55587 TQ	MNBLS	1/16-3/16
Except Oil and Gas	Minneapolis-St. Paul-Bloomington MSA, MN-WI	Y	43368 FQ	49290 MW	58805 TQ	MNBLS	1/16-3/16
Except Oil and Gas	Mississippi	Y	28100 FQ	31550 MW	42080 TQ	USBLS	5/15
Except Oil and Gas	Missouri	Y	30310 FQ	36040 MW	47090 TQ	USBLS	5/15
Except Oil and Gas	Kansas City MSA, MO-KS	Y	28080 FQ	31270 MW	36250 TQ	USBLS	5/15
Except Oil and Gas	St. Louis MSA, MO-IL	Y	40130 FQ	48450 MW	58820 TQ	USBLS	5/15
Except Oil and Gas	Montana	Y	38700 FQ	47120 MW	60420 TQ	USBLS	5/15
Except Oil and Gas	Nebraska	Y	25620 FQ	30740 MW	36160 TQ	NEBLS	7/16-9/16
Except Oil and Gas	Omaha-Council Bluffs MSA, NE-IA	Y	23590 FQ	33140 MW	37370 TQ	NEBLS	7/16-9/16
Except Oil and Gas	Nevada	Y	47130 FQ	60620 MW	72310 TQ	USBLS	5/15
Except Oil and Gas	New Hampshire	H	16.73 AE	21.30 MW	23.74 AEX	NHBLS	6/16
Except Oil and Gas	Manchester NECTA, NH	H	17.26 AE	21.94 MW	24.46 AEX	NHBLS	6/16
Except Oil and Gas	New Jersey	Y	37950 FQ	54740 MW	66600 TQ	USBLS	5/15
Except Oil and Gas	Camden PMSA, NJ	Y	31160 FQ	39190 MW	52120 TQ	USBLS	5/15
Except Oil and Gas	Newark PMSA, NJ-PA	Y	47760 FQ	57760 MW	67680 TQ	USBLS	5/15
Except Oil and Gas	New Mexico	Y	32230 FQ	42280 MW	48330 TQ	USBLS	5/15
Except Oil and Gas	New York	Y	37860 AE	52860 MW	67200 AEX	NYBLS	1/16-3/16
Except Oil and Gas	Nassau County-Suffolk County PMSA, NY	Y	51310 FQ	59320 MW	87520 TQ	USBLS	5/15
Except Oil and Gas	New York-Jersey City-White Plains PMSA, NY-NJ	Y	33310 FQ	50840 MW	67460 TQ	USBLS	5/15
Except Oil and Gas	North Carolina	Y	35520 FQ	41530 MW	47150 TQ	USBLS	5/15
Except Oil and Gas	Charlotte-Concord-Gastonia MSA, NC-SC	Y	33110 FQ	36130 MW	39160 TQ	USBLS	5/15
Except Oil and Gas	Raleigh MSA, NC	Y	42460 FQ	46580 MW	50130 TQ	USBLS	5/15
Except Oil and Gas	Ohio	Y	36460 FQ	44120 MW	52320 TQ	USBLS	5/15
Except Oil and Gas	Cincinnati MSA, OH-KY-IN	Y	35300 FQ	41370 MW	47540 TQ	USBLS	5/15
Except Oil and Gas	Columbus MSA, OH	Y	41050 FQ	45630 MW	51420 TQ	USBLS	5/15
Except Oil and Gas	Oklahoma	Y	32040 FQ	39000 MW	49650 TQ	USBLS	5/15
Except Oil and Gas	Oklahoma City MSA, OK	Y	28960 FQ	35520 MW	43640 TQ	USBLS	5/15
Except Oil and Gas	Tulsa MSA, OK	Y	36870 FQ	42810 MW	47430 TQ	USBLS	5/15
Except Oil and Gas	Oregon	H	18.17 FQ	22.43 MW	37.70 TQ	ORBLS	2016
Except Oil and Gas	Portland-Vancouver-Hillsboro MSA, OR-WA	Y	43600 FQ	51170 MW	68540 TQ	USBLS	5/15
Except Oil and Gas	Pennsylvania	Y	35790 FQ	42710 MW	50690 TQ	USBLS	5/15
Except Oil and Gas	Allentown-Bethlehem-Easton MSA, PA-NJ	Y	40750 FQ	46420 MW	61490 TQ	USBLS	5/15
Except Oil and Gas	Harrisburg-Carlisle MSA, PA	Y	40400 FQ	44940 MW	50030 TQ	USBLS	5/15
Except Oil and Gas	Montgomery County-Bucks County-Chester County PMSA, PA	Y	53930 FQ	93620 MW	118940 TQ	USBLS	5/15
Except Oil and Gas	Pittsburgh MSA, PA	Y	34940 FQ	40250 MW	47180 TQ	USBLS	5/15
Except Oil and Gas	South Carolina	Y	26980 FQ	35540 MW	43080 TQ	USBLS	5/15
Except Oil and Gas	Columbia MSA, SC	Y	34880 FQ	38160 MW	43080 TQ	USBLS	5/15
Except Oil and Gas	South Dakota	Y	28650 FQ	35610 MW	44810 TQ	USBLS	5/15
Except Oil and Gas	Tennessee	Y	34020 FQ	42900 MW	55910 TQ	USBLS	5/15
Except Oil and Gas	Knoxville MSA, TN	Y	34060 FQ	39880 MW	50830 TQ	USBLS	5/15
Except Oil and Gas	Memphis MSA, TN-MS-AR	Y	38200 FQ	47760 MW	57690 TQ	USBLS	5/15
Except Oil and Gas	Nashville-Davidson–Murfreesboro–Franklin MSA, TN	Y	37860 FQ	46600 MW	69570 TQ	USBLS	5/15
Except Oil and Gas	Texas	Y	33340 FQ	42290 MW	57970 TQ	USBLS	5/15
Except Oil and Gas	Austin-Round Rock MSA, TX	Y	37120 FQ	52170 MW	61240 TQ	USBLS	5/15
Except Oil and Gas	Fort Worth-Arlington PMSA, TX	Y	32150 FQ	35510 MW	38870 TQ	USBLS	5/15
Except Oil and Gas	San Antonio-New Braunfels MSA, TX	Y	33140 FQ	39060 MW	54040 TQ	USBLS	5/15
Except Oil and Gas	Utah	Y	41910 FQ	48380 MW	56710 TQ	USBLS	5/15
Except Oil and Gas	Vermont	Y	35360 FQ	40370 MW	46420 TQ	USBLS	5/15
Except Oil and Gas	Virginia	Y	30510 FQ	44720 MW	57430 TQ	USBLS	5/15

AE	Average entry wage	AWR	Average wage range	H	Hourly
AEX	Average experienced wage	B	Biweekly	HI	Highest wage paid
ATC	Average total compensation	D	Daily	HR	High end range
AW	Average wage paid	FQ	First quartile wage	LO	Lowest wage paid

LR	Low end range	MTC	Median total compensation	TCC	Total cash compensation
M	Monthly	MW	Median wage paid	TQ	Third quartile wage
MCC	Median cash compensation	MWR	Median wage range	W	Weekly
ME	Median entry wage	S	See annotated source	Y	Yearly

Occupation/Type/Industry	Location	Per	Low	Mid	High	Source	Date
Earth Driller							
Except Oil and Gas	Richmond MSA, VA	Y	26960 FQ	29230 MW	32760 TQ	USBLS	5/15
Except Oil and Gas	Virginia Beach-Norfolk- Newport News MSA, VA-NC	Y	51300 FQ	57880 MW	65810 TQ	USBLS	5/15
Except Oil and Gas	Washington	H	19.19 FQ	28.29 MW	37.89 TQ	WABLS	3/16
Except Oil and Gas	Seattle-Bellevue-Everett PMSA, WA	H	29.30 FQ	35.99 MW	41.02 TQ	WABLS	3/16
Except Oil and Gas	West Virginia	Y	33750 FQ	39330 MW	47250 TQ	USBLS	5/15
Except Oil and Gas	Wisconsin	Y	32070 FQ	43620 MW	56000 TQ	USBLS	5/15
Except Oil and Gas	Wyoming	Y	42560 FQ	47890 MW	56230 TQ	USBLS	5/15
Earth Science Specialist							
State Government	Texas	Y	36976- 55184 LR		58399- 90393 HR	TXGOV	9/1/15-8/31/17
Economic Development Director							
County Government	Fannin County, GA	Y	30000 LO		32000 HI	GACTY04	2016
County Government	Gwinnett County, GA	Y	75576 LO		128479 HI	GACTY04	2016
Economic Planner							
Airport	San Francisco, CA	B	4067 LO		4943 HI	SFGOV	2016-2018
Economics Teacher							
Postsecondary	Alabama	Y	47837 AE	116244 AW	150442 AEX	ALBLS	6/16
Postsecondary	Birmingham-Hoover MSA, AL	Y	68600 AE	111932 AW	133593 AEX	ALBLS	6/16
Postsecondary	Arizona	Y	61810 FQ	92930 MW	129680 TQ	USBLS	5/15
Postsecondary	Arkansas	Y	68170 FQ	87730 MW	115550 TQ	USBLS	5/15
Postsecondary	Little Rock-North Little Rock- Conway MSA, AR	Y	69450 FQ	87630 MW	108540 TQ	USBLS	5/15
Postsecondary	California	Y		117965 AW		CABLS	1/16-3/16
Postsecondary	Anaheim-Santa Ana-Irvine PMSA, CA	Y		114191 AW		CABLS	1/16-3/16
Postsecondary	Los Angeles-Long Beach- Glendale PMSA, CA	Y		135729 AW		CABLS	1/16-3/16
Postsecondary	Riverside-San Bernardino- Ontario MSA, CA	Y		111574 AW		CABLS	1/16-3/16
Postsecondary	Sacramento–Roseville– Arden-Arcade MSA, CA	Y		126122 AW		CABLS	1/16-3/16
Postsecondary	San Diego-Carlsbad MSA, CA	Y		139787 AW		CABLS	1/16-3/16
Postsecondary	San Francisco-Redwood City- South San Francisco PMSA, CA	Y		110904 AW		CABLS	1/16-3/16
Postsecondary	Colorado	Y	45930 FQ	79780 MW	109070 TQ	USBLS	5/15
Postsecondary	Denver-Aurora-Lakewood MSA, CO	Y	50140 FQ	75720 MW	101430 TQ	USBLS	5/15
Postsecondary	Connecticut	Y		94825 MW		CTBLS	1/16-3/16
Postsecondary	Bridgeport-Stamford-Norwalk MSA, CT	Y	69860 FQ	89190 MW	119110 TQ	USBLS	5/15
Postsecondary	Hartford-West Hartford-East Hartford MSA, CT	Y	70840 FQ	91730 MW	117950 TQ	USBLS	5/15
Postsecondary	District of Columbia	Y	54860 FQ	97730 MW	142330 TQ	USBLS	5/15
Postsecondary	Washington-Arlington- Alexandria PMSA, DC-VA- MD-WV	Y	58110 FQ	99420 MW	147450 TQ	USBLS	5/15
Postsecondary	Florida	Y	56267 AE	94958 MW	140306 AEX	FLBLS	7/16-9/16
Postsecondary	Georgia	Y	57780 FQ	81790 MW	103720 TQ	USBLS	5/15
Postsecondary	Atlanta-Sandy Springs- Roswell MSA, GA	Y	59500 FQ	85300 MW	102250 TQ	USBLS	5/15
Postsecondary	Hawaii	Y	62880 FQ	90600 MW	113790 TQ	USBLS	5/15
Postsecondary	Urban Honolulu MSA, HI	Y	59740 FQ	89150 MW	114440 TQ	USBLS	5/15
Postsecondary	Idaho	Y	46230 FQ	68320 MW	98470 TQ	USBLS	5/15
Postsecondary	Illinois	Y	74330 FQ	111320 MW	146240 TQ	USBLS	5/15
Postsecondary	Indiana	Y	76760 FQ	108900 MW	143180 TQ	USBLS	5/15
Postsecondary	Indianapolis-Carmel-Anderson MSA, IN	Y	65350 FQ	84660 MW	107560 TQ	USBLS	5/15
Postsecondary	Iowa	Y	78920 FQ	99320 MW	126840 TQ	USBLS	5/15
Postsecondary	Kansas	Y	39000 FQ	70500 MW	91410 TQ	USBLS	5/15
Postsecondary	Kentucky	Y	63990 FQ	91170 MW	122150 TQ	USBLS	5/15
Postsecondary	Louisiana	Y	47290 FQ	78100 MW	108820 TQ	USBLS	5/15
Postsecondary	New Orleans-Metairie MSA, LA	Y	39590 FQ	90390 MW	122790 TQ	USBLS	5/15
Postsecondary	Maine	Y	76560 FQ	97430 MW	121140 TQ	USBLS	5/15

AE	Average entry wage	AWR	Average wage range	H	Hourly	LR	Low end range	MTC	Median total compensation	TCC	Total cash compensation
AEX	Average experienced wage	B	Biweekly	HI	Highest wage paid	M	Monthly	MW	Median wage paid	TQ	Third quartile wage
ATC	Average total compensation	D	Daily	HR	High end range	MCC	Median cash compensation	MWR	Median wage range	W	Weekly
AW	Average wage paid	FQ	First quartile wage	LO	Lowest wage paid	ME	Median entry wage	S	See annotated source	Y	Yearly

Occupation/Type/Industry	Location	Per	Low	Mid	High	Source	Date

Economics Teacher

Occupation/Type/Industry	Location	Per	Low	Mid	High	Source	Date
Postsecondary	Maryland	Y	47283 AE	96692 MW	121397 AEX	MDBLS	4/16
Postsecondary	Baltimore-Columbia-Towson MSA, MD	Y	57160 FQ	87250 MW	103570 TQ	USBLS	5/15
Postsecondary	Massachusetts	Y	71630 FQ	104110 MW	167450 TQ	USBLS	5/15
Postsecondary	Boston-Cambridge-Newton NECTA, MA	Y	84070 FQ	138890 MW		USBLS	5/15
Postsecondary	Worcester MSA, MA-CT	Y	62000 FQ	78050 MW	98940 TQ	USBLS	5/15
Postsecondary	Michigan	Y	85880 FQ	110110 MW	149010 TQ	USBLS	5/15
Postsecondary	Minnesota	Y	65765 FQ	98346 MW	132135 TQ	MNBLS	1/16-3/16
Postsecondary	Minneapolis-St. Paul-Bloomington MSA, MN-WI	Y	69314 FQ	105039 MW	145835 TQ	MNBLS	1/16-3/16
Postsecondary	Mississippi	Y	68500 FQ	88930 MW	108180 TQ	USBLS	5/15
Postsecondary	Missouri	Y	64860 FQ	89660 MW	117780 TQ	USBLS	5/15
Postsecondary	St. Louis MSA, MO-IL	Y	57340 FQ	84790 MW	117130 TQ	USBLS	5/15
Postsecondary	Nevada	Y	36560 FQ	69980 MW	96870 TQ	USBLS	5/15
Postsecondary	New Hampshire	Y	83524 AE	115635 MW	151448 AEX	NHBLS	6/16
Postsecondary	Manchester NECTA, NH	Y	72552 AE	90790 MW	98605 AEX	NHBLS	6/16
Postsecondary	New Jersey	Y	79540 FQ	109910 MW	153110 TQ	USBLS	5/15
Postsecondary	Camden PMSA, NJ	Y	66270 FQ	90600 MW	118860 TQ	USBLS	5/15
Postsecondary	Newark PMSA, NJ-PA	Y	87790 FQ	121670 MW	171220 TQ	USBLS	5/15
Postsecondary	New Mexico	Y	80310 FQ	106210 MW	124360 TQ	USBLS	5/15
Postsecondary	New York	Y	55550 AE	106170 MW	150180 AEX	NYBLS	1/16-3/16
Postsecondary	Buffalo-Cheektowaga-Niagara Falls MSA, NY	Y	50150 FQ	83440 MW	105240 TQ	USBLS	5/15
Postsecondary	Nassau County-Suffolk County PMSA, NY	Y	59150 FQ	77460 MW	111970 TQ	USBLS	5/15
Postsecondary	New York-Jersey City-White Plains PMSA, NY-NJ	Y	75790 FQ	122090 MW	161560 TQ	USBLS	5/15
Postsecondary	Rochester MSA, NY	Y	84680 FQ	125890 MW		USBLS	5/15
Postsecondary	North Carolina	Y	72500 FQ	99970 MW	137550 TQ	USBLS	5/15
Postsecondary	Charlotte-Concord-Gastonia MSA, NC-SC	Y	59130 FQ	77740 MW	114460 TQ	USBLS	5/15
Postsecondary	Raleigh MSA, NC	Y	91270 FQ	119510 MW	149160 TQ	USBLS	5/15
Postsecondary	North Dakota	Y	78930 FQ	108830 MW	129160 TQ	USBLS	5/15
Postsecondary	Ohio	Y	69040 FQ	93760 MW	130350 TQ	USBLS	5/15
Postsecondary	Cincinnati MSA, OH-KY-IN	Y	70670 FQ	101400 MW	134150 TQ	USBLS	5/15
Postsecondary	Columbus MSA, OH	Y	84290 FQ	113940 MW	150440 TQ	USBLS	5/15
Postsecondary	Oklahoma	Y	48920 FQ	69880 MW	89610 TQ	USBLS	5/15
Postsecondary	Oregon	Y	80565 FQ	111485 MW	138931 TQ	ORBLS	2016
Postsecondary	Portland-Vancouver-Hillsboro MSA, OR-WA	Y	64600 FQ	96920 MW	127210 TQ	USBLS	5/15
Postsecondary	Pennsylvania	Y	60380 FQ	87410 MW	121410 TQ	USBLS	5/15
Postsecondary	Allentown-Bethlehem-Easton MSA, PA-NJ	Y	74370 FQ	112320 MW	163230 TQ	USBLS	5/15
Postsecondary	Montgomery County-Bucks County-Chester County PMSA, PA	Y	47530 FQ	78780 MW	112500 TQ	USBLS	5/15
Postsecondary	Philadelphia PMSA, PA	Y	59900 FQ	91340 MW	139850 TQ	USBLS	5/15
Postsecondary	Pittsburgh MSA, PA	Y	61500 FQ	88140 MW	120950 TQ	USBLS	5/15
Postsecondary	Providence-Warwick MSA, RI-MA	Y	75290 FQ	98480 MW	139980 TQ	USBLS	5/15
Postsecondary	South Carolina	Y	54340 FQ	75690 MW	109230 TQ	USBLS	5/15
Postsecondary	Columbia MSA, SC	Y	52620 FQ	66810 MW	94040 TQ	USBLS	5/15
Postsecondary	Greenville-Anderson-Mauldin MSA, SC	Y	74870 FQ	111110 MW	144580 TQ	USBLS	5/15
Postsecondary	South Dakota	Y	59150 FQ	77330 MW	95390 TQ	USBLS	5/15
Postsecondary	Tennessee	Y	59820 FQ	75820 MW	103020 TQ	USBLS	5/15
Postsecondary	Knoxville MSA, TN	Y	79090 FQ	98960 MW	115830 TQ	USBLS	5/15
Postsecondary	Memphis MSA, TN-MS-AR	Y	59440 FQ	72660 MW	88200 TQ	USBLS	5/15
Postsecondary	Nashville-Davidson–Murfreesboro–Franklin MSA, TN	Y	67350 FQ	97880 MW	145890 TQ	USBLS	5/15
Postsecondary	Texas	Y	63890 FQ	91190 MW	125680 TQ	USBLS	5/15
Postsecondary	Austin-Round Rock MSA, TX	Y	67870 FQ	101000 MW	129520 TQ	USBLS	5/15
Postsecondary	Houston-The Woodlands-Sugar Land MSA, TX	Y	61740 FQ	91470 MW	135590 TQ	USBLS	5/15
Postsecondary	San Antonio-New Braunfels MSA, TX	Y	33010 FQ	85110 MW	104260 TQ	USBLS	5/15
Postsecondary	Utah	Y	82910 FQ	107910 MW	138150 TQ	USBLS	5/15
Postsecondary	Salt Lake City MSA, UT	Y	64370 FQ	93320 MW	118820 TQ	USBLS	5/15
Postsecondary	Vermont	Y	44990 FQ	51320 MW	93020 TQ	USBLS	5/15

AE	Average entry wage	AWR	Average wage range	H	Hourly	LR	Low end range	MTC	Median total compensation	TCC	Total cash compensation
AEX	Average experienced wage	B	Biweekly	HI	Highest wage paid	M	Monthly	MW	Median wage paid	TQ	Third quartile wage
ATC	Average total compensation	D	Daily	HR	High end range	MCC	Median cash compensation	MWR	Median wage range	W	Weekly
AW	Average wage paid	FQ	First quartile wage	LO	Lowest wage paid	ME	Median entry wage	S	See annotated source	Y	Yearly

Occupation/Type/Industry	Location	Per	Low	Mid	High	Source	Date
Economics Teacher							
Postsecondary	Virginia	Y	60700 FQ	91890 MW	125730 TQ	USBLS	5/15
Postsecondary	Virginia Beach-Norfolk-Newport News MSA, VA-NC	Y	54760 FQ	80000 MW	114410 TQ	USBLS	5/15
Postsecondary	Washington	Y		72486 AW		WABLS	3/16
Postsecondary	Seattle-Bellevue-Everett PMSA, WA	Y		82194 AW		WABLS	3/16
Postsecondary	Tacoma-Lakewood PMSA, WA	Y		88170 AW		WABLS	3/16
Postsecondary	West Virginia	Y	48160 FQ	71810 MW	114630 TQ	USBLS	5/15
Postsecondary	Wisconsin	Y	69920 FQ	89950 MW	124740 TQ	USBLS	5/15
Postsecondary	Milwaukee-Waukesha-West Allis MSA, WI	Y	82360 FQ	105560 MW	141190 TQ	USBLS	5/15
Postsecondary	Wyoming	Y	77530 FQ	97060 MW	122560 TQ	USBLS	5/15
Economist	Alabama	Y	55971 AE	97243 AW	117885 AEX	ALBLS	6/16
	Birmingham-Hoover MSA, AL	Y	91199 AE	129617 AW	148831 AEX	ALBLS	6/16
	Alaska	Y	67160 FQ	78580 MW	92690 TQ	USBLS	5/15
	Arizona	Y	56900 FQ	70920 MW	90290 TQ	USBLS	5/15
	Phoenix-Mesa-Scottsdale MSA, AZ	Y	57510 FQ	70990 MW	89470 TQ	USBLS	5/15
	Arkansas	Y	46760 FQ	62540 MW	87050 TQ	USBLS	5/15
	Little Rock-North Little Rock-Conway MSA, AR	Y	45880 FQ	56280 MW	87060 TQ	USBLS	5/15
	California	H	35.56 FQ	51.42 MW	66.44 TQ	CABLS	1/16-3/16
	Anaheim-Santa Ana-Irvine PMSA, CA	H	33.00 FQ	47.72 MW	57.57 TQ	CABLS	1/16-3/16
	Los Angeles-Long Beach-Glendale PMSA, CA	H	43.26 FQ	65.92 MW		CABLS	1/16-3/16
	Oakland-Hayward-Berkeley PMSA, CA	H	51.58 FQ	57.92 MW	66.58 TQ	CABLS	1/16-3/16
	Riverside-San Bernardino-Ontario MSA, CA	H	39.41 FQ	48.60 MW	58.60 TQ	CABLS	1/16-3/16
	Sacramento–Roseville–Arden-Arcade MSA, CA	H	22.58 FQ	34.92 MW	42.94 TQ	CABLS	1/16-3/16
	San Diego-Carlsbad MSA, CA	H	29.35 FQ	39.21 MW	49.91 TQ	CABLS	1/16-3/16
	San Francisco-Redwood City-South San Francisco PMSA, CA	H	42.59 FQ	52.69 MW	64.57 TQ	CABLS	1/16-3/16
	Colorado	Y	62520 FQ	89570 MW	111250 TQ	USBLS	5/15
	Denver-Aurora-Lakewood MSA, CO	Y	62850 FQ	89570 MW	112910 TQ	USBLS	5/15
	Connecticut	Y		91801 MW		CTBLS	1/16-3/16
	Bridgeport-Stamford-Norwalk MSA, CT	Y	93630 FQ	153380 MW		USBLS	5/15
	Hartford-West Hartford-East Hartford MSA, CT	Y	74600 FQ	87070 MW	97680 TQ	USBLS	5/15
	Delaware	Y	61210 FQ	67490 MW	83410 TQ	USBLS	5/15
	District of Columbia	Y	84300 FQ	113230 MW	148840 TQ	USBLS	5/15
	Washington-Arlington-Alexandria PMSA, DC-VA-MD-WV	Y	86560 FQ	115030 MW	149710 TQ	USBLS	5/15
	Florida	H	25.61 AE	39.94 MW	53.44 AEX	FLBLS	7/16-9/16
	Miami-Miami Beach-Kendall PMSA, FL	H	35.77 AE	50.09 MW	63.25 AEX	FLBLS	7/16-9/16
	Orlando-Kissimmee-Sanford MSA, FL	H	21.90 AE	28.09 MW	37.17 AEX	FLBLS	7/16-9/16
	Tampa-St. Petersburg-Clearwater MSA, FL	H	38.04 AE	47.69 MW	78.12 AEX	FLBLS	7/16-9/16
	Georgia	Y	75780 FQ	92910 MW	113360 TQ	USBLS	5/15
	Atlanta-Sandy Springs-Roswell MSA, GA	Y	78230 FQ	95350 MW	114350 TQ	USBLS	5/15
	Hawaii	Y	54100 FQ	69410 MW	89630 TQ	USBLS	5/15
	Urban Honolulu MSA, HI	Y	54540 FQ	77800 MW	96540 TQ	USBLS	5/15
	Idaho	Y	58950 FQ	107460 MW	120660 TQ	USBLS	5/15
	Illinois	Y	71660 FQ	94880 MW	119830 TQ	USBLS	5/15
	Chicago-Naperville-Arlington Heights PMSA, IL	Y	66910 FQ	92840 MW	122130 TQ	USBLS	5/15
	Indiana	Y	86490 FQ	179220 AW		USBLS	5/15
	Kansas	Y	54890 FQ	60860 MW	83530 TQ	USBLS	5/15
	Kentucky	Y	55040 FQ	66820 MW	82110 TQ	USBLS	5/15
	Louisiana	Y	59710 FQ	87150 MW	125850 TQ	USBLS	5/15
	Maryland	Y	79049 AE	114790 MW	132660 AEX	MDBLS	4/16

AE	Average entry wage	AWR	Average wage range	H	Hourly	
AEX	Average experienced wage	B	Biweekly	HI	Highest wage paid	
ATC	Average total compensation	D	Daily	HR	High end range	
AW	Average wage paid	FQ	First quartile wage	LO	Lowest wage paid	

LR	Low end range	MTC	Median total compensation	TCC	Total cash compensation
M	Monthly	MW	Median wage paid	TQ	Third quartile wage
MCC	Median cash compensation	MWR	Median wage range	W	Weekly
ME	Median entry wage	S	See annotated source	Y	Yearly

Occupation/Type/Industry	Location	Per	Low	Mid	High	Source	Date
Economist	Baltimore-Columbia-Towson MSA, MD	Y	77230 FQ	102940 MW	128720 TQ	USBLS	5/15
	Massachusetts	Y	58770 FQ	80440 MW	118490 TQ	USBLS	5/15
	Boston-Cambridge-Newton NECTA, MA	Y	58190 FQ	80680 MW	119170 TQ	USBLS	5/15
	Michigan	Y	54050 FQ	73350 MW	94100 TQ	USBLS	5/15
	Detroit-Dearborn-Livonia PMSA, MI	Y	56080 FQ	67830 MW	85060 TQ	USBLS	5/15
	Minnesota	Y	52600 FQ	59415 MW	74999 TQ	MNBLS	1/16-3/16
	Minneapolis-St. Paul-Bloomington MSA, MN-WI	Y	51007 FQ	65070 MW	75019 TQ	MNBLS	1/16-3/16
	Missouri	Y	69550 FQ	88380 MW	102520 TQ	USBLS	5/15
	Kansas City MSA, MO-KS	Y	70180 FQ	89130 MW	100170 TQ	USBLS	5/15
	St. Louis MSA, MO-IL	Y	74980 FQ	106870 MW		USBLS	5/15
	Montana	Y	67670 FQ	82840 MW	96140 TQ	USBLS	5/15
	Nebraska	Y	60520 FQ	81120 MW	106560 TQ	NEBLS	7/16-9/16
	Omaha-Council Bluffs MSA, NE-IA	Y	64425 FQ	94560 MW	105890 TQ	NEBLS	7/16-9/16
	Nevada	Y	63500 FQ	75120 MW	98780 TQ	USBLS	5/15
	Las Vegas-Henderson-Paradise MSA, NV	Y	73000 FQ	82780 MW	114190 TQ	USBLS	5/15
	New Hampshire	H	25.79 AE	37.34 MW	46.82 AEX	NHBLS	6/16
	New Jersey	Y	62140 FQ	89710 MW	110170 TQ	USBLS	5/15
	New Mexico	Y	54980 FQ	60580 MW	65810 TQ	USBLS	5/15
	New York	Y	69380 AE	108130 MW	151400 AEX	NYBLS	1/16-3/16
	Buffalo-Cheektowaga-Niagara Falls MSA, NY	Y	74330 FQ	91190 MW	110160 TQ	USBLS	5/15
	New York-Jersey City-White Plains PMSA, NY-NJ	Y	92240 FQ	125070 MW	175140 TQ	USBLS	5/15
	North Carolina	Y	61280 FQ	97490 MW	137870 TQ	USBLS	5/15
	Charlotte-Concord-Gastonia MSA, NC-SC	Y	66530 FQ	96560 MW	142960 TQ	USBLS	5/15
	Ohio	Y	77780 FQ	92350 MW	119640 TQ	USBLS	5/15
	Cleveland-Elyria MSA, OH	Y	48380 FQ	82920 MW	93000 TQ	USBLS	5/15
	Columbus MSA, OH	Y	101230 FQ	200790 AW		USBLS	5/15
	Oklahoma	Y	61560 FQ	80040 MW	103950 TQ	USBLS	5/15
	Oregon	H	32.74 FQ	39.62 MW	47.86 TQ	ORBLS	2016
	Portland-Vancouver-Hillsboro MSA, OR-WA	Y	67000 FQ	88000 MW	108340 TQ	USBLS	5/15
	Pennsylvania	Y	54930 FQ	76950 MW	100910 TQ	USBLS	5/15
	Harrisburg-Carlisle MSA, PA	Y	54920 FQ	65460 MW	80810 TQ	USBLS	5/15
	Philadelphia PMSA, PA	Y	70130 FQ	94860 MW	119420 TQ	USBLS	5/15
	Pittsburgh MSA, PA	Y	49560 FQ	64430 MW	110250 TQ	USBLS	5/15
	South Carolina	Y	49340 FQ	58770 MW	86590 TQ	USBLS	5/15
	Columbia MSA, SC	Y	47450 FQ	55430 MW	82540 TQ	USBLS	5/15
	Tennessee	Y	61680 FQ	81220 MW	111780 TQ	USBLS	5/15
	Nashville-Davidson–Murfreesboro–Franklin MSA, TN	Y	59290 FQ	80360 MW	108500 TQ	USBLS	5/15
	Texas	Y	81220 FQ	102240 MW	149980 TQ	USBLS	5/15
	Austin-Round Rock MSA, TX	Y	48490 FQ	80180 MW	122070 TQ	USBLS	5/15
	Dallas-Plano-Irving PMSA, TX	Y	87130 FQ	101320 MW	139080 TQ	USBLS	5/15
	Fort Worth-Arlington PMSA, TX	Y	34350 FQ	37360 MW	78410 TQ	USBLS	5/15
	Houston-The Woodlands-Sugar Land MSA, TX	Y	93000 FQ	119330 MW	180050 TQ	USBLS	5/15
	Utah	Y	63140 FQ	78110 MW	98730 TQ	USBLS	5/15
	Salt Lake City MSA, UT	Y	68600 FQ	82970 MW	100160 TQ	USBLS	5/15
	Vermont	Y	65320 FQ	71850 MW	80010 TQ	USBLS	5/15
	Virginia	Y	91290 FQ	119870 MW	150570 TQ	USBLS	5/15
	Richmond MSA, VA	Y	70170 FQ	84850 MW	113340 TQ	USBLS	5/15
	Washington	H	34.41 FQ	40.50 MW	47.89 TQ	WABLS	3/16
	Seattle-Bellevue-Everett PMSA, WA	H	38.67 FQ	45.35 MW	55.74 TQ	WABLS	3/16
	West Virginia	Y	32380 FQ	37790 MW	49610 TQ	USBLS	5/15
	Wisconsin	Y	47280 FQ	56810 MW	83970 TQ	USBLS	5/15
	Madison MSA, WI	Y	55490 FQ	69520 MW	111520 TQ	USBLS	5/15
	Milwaukee-Waukesha-West Allis MSA, WI	Y	44150 FQ	48190 MW	60480 TQ	USBLS	5/15
	Wyoming	Y	61450 FQ	71150 MW	86580 TQ	USBLS	5/15
	Cheyenne MSA, WY	Y	62050 FQ	72050 MW	80990 TQ	USBLS	5/15
	Puerto Rico	Y	29130 FQ	35370 MW	45950 TQ	USBLS	5/15

AE	Average entry wage	**AWR**	Average wage range	**H**	Hourly	**LR**	Low end range	**MTC**	Median total compensation	**TCC**	Total cash compensation
AEX	Average experienced wage	**B**	Biweekly	**HI**	Highest wage paid	**M**	Monthly	**MW**	Median wage paid	**TQ**	Third quartile wage
ATC	Average total compensation	**D**	Daily	**HR**	High end range	**MCC**	Median cash compensation	**MWR**	Median wage range	**W**	Weekly
AW	Average wage paid	**FQ**	First quartile wage	**LO**	Lowest wage paid	**ME**	Median entry wage	**S**	See annotated source	**Y**	Yearly

Occupation/Type/Industry	Location	Per	Low	Mid	High	Source	Date
Economist	San Juan-Carolina-Caguas MSA, PR	Y	29060 FQ	35350 MW	46170 TQ	USBLS	5/15
Editor	Alabama	Y	28256 AE	49396 AW	59957 AEX	ALBLS	6/16
	Birmingham-Hoover MSA, AL	Y	30223 AE	47399 AW	55981 AEX	ALBLS	6/16
	Alaska	Y	41130 FQ	56010 MW	67320 TQ	USBLS	5/15
	Anchorage MSA, AK	Y	36760 FQ	51550 MW	63920 TQ	USBLS	5/15
	Arizona	Y	35950 FQ	44470 MW	58130 TQ	USBLS	5/15
	Phoenix-Mesa-Scottsdale MSA, AZ	Y	35690 FQ	44770 MW	59460 TQ	USBLS	5/15
	Tucson MSA, AZ	Y	36570 FQ	42920 MW	49100 TQ	USBLS	5/15
	Arkansas	Y	31240 FQ	39130 MW	48630 TQ	USBLS	5/15
	Little Rock-North Little Rock-Conway MSA, AR	Y	38190 FQ	46380 MW	57900 TQ	USBLS	5/15
	California	H	21.04 FQ	30.88 MW	43.06 TQ	CABLS	1/16-3/16
	Anaheim-Santa Ana-Irvine PMSA, CA	H	17.24 FQ	26.97 MW	39.08 TQ	CABLS	1/16-3/16
	Los Angeles-Long Beach-Glendale PMSA, CA	H	21.86 FQ	31.33 MW	44.38 TQ	CABLS	1/16-3/16
	Oakland-Hayward-Berkeley PMSA, CA	H	17.28 FQ	25.27 MW	37.38 TQ	CABLS	1/16-3/16
	Riverside-San Bernardino-Ontario MSA, CA	H	12.55 FQ	21.36 MW	30.49 TQ	CABLS	1/16-3/16
	Sacramento–Roseville–Arden-Arcade MSA, CA	H	23.21 FQ	33.06 MW	43.34 TQ	CABLS	1/16-3/16
	San Diego-Carlsbad MSA, CA	H	19.59 FQ	28.86 MW	40.33 TQ	CABLS	1/16-3/16
	San Francisco-Redwood City-South San Francisco PMSA, CA	H	23.30 FQ	33.47 MW	46.22 TQ	CABLS	1/16-3/16
	Colorado	Y	40000 FQ	55590 MW	73340 TQ	USBLS	5/15
	Denver-Aurora-Lakewood MSA, CO	Y	41230 FQ	56840 MW	73630 TQ	USBLS	5/15
	Connecticut	Y		56670 MW		CTBLS	1/16-3/16
	Bridgeport-Stamford-Norwalk MSA, CT	Y	37180 FQ	51810 MW	73370 TQ	USBLS	5/15
	Hartford-West Hartford-East Hartford MSA, CT	Y	42540 FQ	64020 MW	75140 TQ	USBLS	5/15
	Delaware	Y	40510 FQ	52020 MW	75520 TQ	USBLS	5/15
	Wilmington PMSA, DE-MD-NJ	Y	41530 FQ	53380 MW	74400 TQ	USBLS	5/15
	District of Columbia	Y	54940 FQ	74650 MW	101330 TQ	USBLS	5/15
	Washington-Arlington-Alexandria PMSA, DC-VA-MD-WV	Y	56840 FQ	74130 MW	97000 TQ	USBLS	5/15
	Florida	H	17.56 AE	26.97 MW	39.47 AEX	FLBLS	7/16-9/16
	Fort Lauderdale-Pompano Beach-Deerfield Beach PMSA, FL	H	15.94 AE	25.79 MW	34.88 AEX	FLBLS	7/16-9/16
	Miami-Miami Beach-Kendall PMSA, FL	H	18.54 AE	27.36 MW	38.77 AEX	FLBLS	7/16-9/16
	Orlando-Kissimmee-Sanford MSA, FL	H	18.84 AE	29.36 MW	39.89 AEX	FLBLS	7/16-9/16
	Georgia	Y	30730 FQ	42950 MW	61200 TQ	USBLS	5/15
	Atlanta-Sandy Springs-Roswell MSA, GA	Y	30410 FQ	42460 MW	60330 TQ	USBLS	5/15
	Augusta-Richmond County MSA, GA-SC	Y	27790 FQ	39210 MW	48800 TQ	USBLS	5/15
	Hawaii	Y	41260 FQ	51280 MW	71530 TQ	USBLS	5/15
	Urban Honolulu MSA, HI	Y	38720 FQ	48660 MW	63930 TQ	USBLS	5/15
	Idaho	Y	25850 FQ	34100 MW	50280 TQ	USBLS	5/15
	Boise City MSA, ID	Y	31760 FQ	43810 MW	56970 TQ	USBLS	5/15
	Illinois	Y	39960 FQ	53430 MW	68160 TQ	USBLS	5/15
	Chicago-Naperville-Arlington Heights PMSA, IL	Y	40890 FQ	54060 MW	69150 TQ	USBLS	5/15
	Lake County-Kenosha County PMSA, IL-WI	Y	50950 FQ	67460 MW	86260 TQ	USBLS	5/15
	Indiana	Y	31980 FQ	43300 MW	58550 TQ	USBLS	5/15
	Gary PMSA, IN	Y	31340 FQ	38000 MW	58580 TQ	USBLS	5/15
	Indianapolis-Carmel-Anderson MSA, IN	Y	32560 FQ	46370 MW	66480 TQ	USBLS	5/15
	Iowa	Y	30730 FQ	39130 MW	52950 TQ	USBLS	5/15

AE	Average entry wage	AWR	Average wage range	H	Hourly	LR	Low end range	MTC	Median total compensation	TCC	Total cash compensation
AEX	Average experienced wage	B	Biweekly	HI	Highest wage paid	M	Monthly	MW	Median wage paid	TQ	Third quartile wage
ATC	Average total compensation	D	Daily	HR	High end range	MCC	Median cash compensation	MWR	Median wage range	W	Weekly
AW	Average wage paid	FQ	First quartile wage	LO	Lowest wage paid	ME	Median entry wage	S	See annotated source	Y	Yearly

457

Editor

Occupation/Type/Industry	Location	Per	Low	Mid	High	Source	Date
Editor	Des Moines-West Des Moines MSA, IA	Y	37350 FQ	46550 MW	67710 TQ	USBLS	5/15
	Kansas	Y	31910 FQ	42640 MW	63920 TQ	USBLS	5/15
	Wichita MSA, KS	Y	28920 FQ	39340 MW	52350 TQ	USBLS	5/15
	Kentucky	Y	31360 FQ	39310 MW	53490 TQ	USBLS	5/15
	Louisville-Jefferson County MSA, KY-IN	Y	35530 FQ	43770 MW	61380 TQ	USBLS	5/15
	Louisiana	Y	37340 FQ	46160 MW	58200 TQ	USBLS	5/15
	Baton Rouge MSA, LA	Y	35130 FQ	43720 MW	57420 TQ	USBLS	5/15
	New Orleans-Metairie MSA, LA	Y	42670 FQ	49290 MW	61580 TQ	USBLS	5/15
	Maine	Y	31760 FQ	40150 MW	56680 TQ	USBLS	5/15
	Portland-South Portland MSA, ME	Y	28730 FQ	39070 MW	49620 TQ	USBLS	5/15
	Maryland	Y	37589 AE	63836 MW	76959 AEX	MDBLS	4/16
	Baltimore-Columbia-Towson MSA, MD	Y	42750 FQ	55940 MW	70940 TQ	USBLS	5/15
	Salisbury MSA, MD-DE	Y	38290 FQ	48540 MW	123900 TQ	USBLS	5/15
	Massachusetts	Y	44860 FQ	63610 MW	86840 TQ	USBLS	5/15
	Boston-Cambridge-Newton NECTA, MA	Y	45240 FQ	66020 MW	90290 TQ	USBLS	5/15
	Worcester MSA, MA-CT	Y	33720 FQ	50780 MW	61450 TQ	USBLS	5/15
	Michigan	Y	36340 FQ	49130 MW	68510 TQ	USBLS	5/15
	Detroit-Dearborn-Livonia PMSA, MI	Y	51480 FQ	68830 MW	88380 TQ	USBLS	5/15
	Grand Rapids-Wyoming MSA, MI	Y	28160 FQ	42500 MW	58780 TQ	USBLS	5/15
	Minnesota	Y	39667 FQ	53729 MW	72187 TQ	MNBLS	1/16-3/16
	Minneapolis-St. Paul-Bloomington MSA, MN-WI	Y	42227 FQ	56098 MW	73769 TQ	MNBLS	1/16-3/16
	Mississippi	Y	24480 FQ	34510 MW	48780 TQ	USBLS	5/15
	Jackson MSA, MS	Y	27160 FQ	33740 MW	45640 TQ	USBLS	5/15
	Missouri	Y	39460 FQ	52590 MW	71160 TQ	USBLS	5/15
	Kansas City MSA, MO-KS	Y	43200 FQ	63800 MW	86780 TQ	USBLS	5/15
	St. Louis MSA, MO-IL	Y	44390 FQ	56910 MW	73470 TQ	USBLS	5/15
	Montana	Y	28170 FQ	38760 MW	46720 TQ	USBLS	5/15
	Billings MSA, MT	Y	23260 FQ	35070 MW	51400 TQ	USBLS	5/15
	Nebraska	Y	28280 FQ	39215 MW	55660 TQ	NEBLS	7/16-9/16
	Omaha-Council Bluffs MSA, NE-IA	Y	30185 FQ	47145 MW	58270 TQ	NEBLS	7/16-9/16
	Nevada	Y	36580 FQ	47580 MW	61070 TQ	USBLS	5/15
	Las Vegas-Henderson-Paradise MSA, NV	Y	35480 FQ	45700 MW	59710 TQ	USBLS	5/15
	New Hampshire	H	16.36 AE	20.35 MW	27.44 AEX	NHBLS	6/16
	Manchester NECTA, NH	H	13.23 AE	28.27 MW	31.94 AEX	NHBLS	6/16
	Nashua NECTA, NH-MA	Y	52010 FQ	61240 MW	105860 TQ	USBLS	5/15
	New Jersey	Y	54230 FQ	71710 MW	93990 TQ	USBLS	5/15
	Camden PMSA, NJ	Y	56080 FQ	68350 MW	79060 TQ	USBLS	5/15
	Newark PMSA, NJ-PA	Y	61250 FQ	77680 MW	108490 TQ	USBLS	5/15
	Trenton MSA, NJ	Y	56190 FQ	69870 MW	79460 TQ	USBLS	5/15
	New Mexico	Y	33220 FQ	44360 MW	57300 TQ	USBLS	5/15
	Albuquerque MSA, NM	Y	33050 FQ	43610 MW	58260 TQ	USBLS	5/15
	Santa Fe MSA, NM	Y	43650 FQ	48660 MW	56770 TQ	USBLS	5/15
	New York	Y	42410 AE	69350 MW	101050 AEX	NYBLS	1/16-3/16
	Buffalo-Cheektowaga-Niagara Falls MSA, NY	Y	35150 FQ	65110 MW	76070 TQ	USBLS	5/15
	Nassau County-Suffolk County PMSA, NY	Y	47750 FQ	64110 MW	87980 TQ	USBLS	5/15
	New York-Jersey City-White Plains PMSA, NY-NJ	Y	52130 FQ	71210 MW	99580 TQ	USBLS	5/15
	Rochester MSA, NY	Y	39030 FQ	60330 MW	89620 TQ	USBLS	5/15
	North Carolina	Y	35270 FQ	47140 MW	64810 TQ	USBLS	5/15
	Charlotte-Concord-Gastonia MSA, NC-SC	Y	39580 FQ	53470 MW	75260 TQ	USBLS	5/15
	Raleigh MSA, NC	Y	32570 FQ	44090 MW	63530 TQ	USBLS	5/15
	North Dakota	Y	25060 FQ	30240 MW	43420 TQ	USBLS	5/15
	Fargo MSA, ND-MN	Y	23430 FQ	35280 MW	55540 TQ	USBLS	5/15
	Ohio	Y	31980 FQ	44170 MW	61110 TQ	USBLS	5/15
	Cincinnati MSA, OH-KY-IN	Y	27090 FQ	39230 MW	53230 TQ	USBLS	5/15
	Cleveland-Elyria MSA, OH	Y	34690 FQ	51000 MW	67890 TQ	USBLS	5/15
	Columbus MSA, OH	Y	31890 FQ	44750 MW	64390 TQ	USBLS	5/15
	Oklahoma	Y	28530 FQ	40710 MW	65390 TQ	USBLS	5/15

Occupation/Type/Industry	Location	Per	Low	Mid	High	Source	Date
Editor	Oklahoma City MSA, OK	Y	25850 FQ	38310 MW	52710 TQ	USBLS	5/15
	Tulsa MSA, OK	Y	35530 FQ	53640 MW	77720 TQ	USBLS	5/15
	Oregon	H	16.13 FQ	21.96 MW	29.00 TQ	ORBLS	2016
	Portland-Vancouver-Hillsboro MSA, OR-WA	Y	33930 FQ	44240 MW	58830 TQ	USBLS	5/15
	Pennsylvania	Y	38120 FQ	53250 MW	73520 TQ	USBLS	5/15
	Harrisburg-Carlisle MSA, PA	Y	33700 FQ	48640 MW	61780 TQ	USBLS	5/15
	Montgomery County-Bucks County-Chester County PMSA, PA	Y	41790 FQ	62670 MW	84820 TQ	USBLS	5/15
	Philadelphia PMSA, PA	Y	40120 FQ	58790 MW	77660 TQ	USBLS	5/15
	Pittsburgh MSA, PA	Y	41950 FQ	50570 MW	64070 TQ	USBLS	5/15
	Rhode Island	Y	38630 FQ	62080 MW	83700 TQ	USBLS	5/15
	Providence-Warwick MSA, RI-MA	Y	37800 FQ	55930 MW	83750 TQ	USBLS	5/15
	South Carolina	Y	28470 FQ	41580 MW	59910 TQ	USBLS	5/15
	Charleston-North Charleston MSA, SC	Y	22700 FQ	34980 MW	49470 TQ	USBLS	5/15
	Columbia MSA, SC	Y	42130 FQ	52870 MW	60450 TQ	USBLS	5/15
	Greenville-Anderson-Mauldin MSA, SC	Y	34100 FQ	48700 MW	71720 TQ	USBLS	5/15
	South Dakota	Y	37500 FQ	45750 MW	56720 TQ	USBLS	5/15
	Sioux Falls MSA, SD	Y	48580 FQ	57600 MW	81660 TQ	USBLS	5/15
	Tennessee	Y	32890 FQ	43740 MW	61470 TQ	USBLS	5/15
	Knoxville MSA, TN	Y	30870 FQ	48860 MW	66850 TQ	USBLS	5/15
	Memphis MSA, TN-MS-AR	Y	33290 FQ	43980 MW	56630 TQ	USBLS	5/15
	Nashville-Davidson–Murfreesboro–Franklin MSA, TN	Y	37420 FQ	50640 MW	70510 TQ	USBLS	5/15
	Texas	Y	37100 FQ	50120 MW	66040 TQ	USBLS	5/15
	Austin-Round Rock MSA, TX	Y	38150 FQ	49610 MW	62420 TQ	USBLS	5/15
	Dallas-Plano-Irving PMSA, TX	Y	42100 FQ	53810 MW	68000 TQ	USBLS	5/15
	Fort Worth-Arlington PMSA, TX	Y	42850 FQ	55100 MW	72480 TQ	USBLS	5/15
	Houston-The Woodlands-Sugar Land MSA, TX	Y	44880 FQ	60480 MW	78060 TQ	USBLS	5/15
	San Antonio-New Braunfels MSA, TX	Y	37890 FQ	51620 MW	61190 TQ	USBLS	5/15
	Utah	Y	29590 FQ	44680 MW	60910 TQ	USBLS	5/15
	Ogden-Clearfield MSA, UT	Y	47360 FQ	54330 MW	60890 TQ	USBLS	5/15
	Provo-Orem MSA, UT	Y	23790 FQ	38330 MW	49680 TQ	USBLS	5/15
	Salt Lake City MSA, UT	Y	32540 FQ	47700 MW	68100 TQ	USBLS	5/15
	Vermont	Y	35660 FQ	45830 MW	63180 TQ	USBLS	5/15
	Burlington-South Burlington MSA, VT	Y	38600 FQ	49000 MW	69630 TQ	USBLS	5/15
	Virginia	Y	51930 FQ	66870 MW	87450 TQ	USBLS	5/15
	Richmond MSA, VA	Y	44780 FQ	57980 MW	74170 TQ	USBLS	5/15
	Virginia Beach-Norfolk-Newport News MSA, VA-NC	Y	36770 FQ	46400 MW	57670 TQ	USBLS	5/15
	Washington	H	20.28 FQ	29.07 MW	38.42 TQ	WABLS	3/16
	Seattle-Bellevue-Everett PMSA, WA	H	21.52 FQ	30.68 MW	42.80 TQ	WABLS	3/16
	Tacoma-Lakewood PMSA, WA	H	17.59 FQ	25.87 MW	34.33 TQ	WABLS	3/16
	West Virginia	Y	30320 FQ	41580 MW	55760 TQ	USBLS	5/15
	Wisconsin	Y	32650 FQ	42880 MW	58180 TQ	USBLS	5/15
	Madison MSA, WI	Y	33170 FQ	45020 MW	56990 TQ	USBLS	5/15
	Milwaukee-Waukesha-West Allis MSA, WI	Y	35800 FQ	48580 MW	61180 TQ	USBLS	5/15
	Wyoming	Y	28340 FQ	40390 MW	46970 TQ	USBLS	5/15
	Puerto Rico	Y	30480 FQ	44190 MW	63000 TQ	USBLS	5/15
	San Juan-Carolina-Caguas MSA, PR	Y	31560 FQ	44850 MW	63530 TQ	USBLS	5/15
Education Administrator							
Elementary and Secondary School	Alabama	Y	63968 AE	81700 AW	90565 AEX	ALBLS	6/16
Elementary and Secondary School	Birmingham-Hoover MSA, AL	Y	62236 AE	82028 AW	91929 AEX	ALBLS	6/16
Elementary and Secondary School	Alaska	Y	96690 FQ	111230 MW	123220 TQ	USBLS	5/15
Elementary and Secondary School	Anchorage MSA, AK	Y	107220 FQ	117030 MW	126840 TQ	USBLS	5/15
Elementary and Secondary School	Arizona	Y	63920 FQ	75920 MW	90630 TQ	USBLS	5/15
Elementary and Secondary School	Phoenix-Mesa-Scottsdale MSA, AZ	Y	65900 FQ	78960 MW	93240 TQ	USBLS	5/15
Elementary and Secondary School	Tucson MSA, AZ	Y	59650 FQ	71870 MW	82320 TQ	USBLS	5/15

AE	Average entry wage	AWR	Average wage range	H	Hourly	LR	Low end range	MTC Median total compensation	TCC Total cash compensation
AEX	Average experienced wage	B	Biweekly	HI	Highest wage paid	M	Monthly	MW Median wage paid	TQ Third quartile wage
ATC	Average total compensation	D	Daily	HR	High end range	MCC Median cash compensation	MWR Median wage range	W Weekly
AW	Average wage paid	FQ	First quartile wage	LO	Lowest wage paid	ME Median entry wage	S See annotated source	Y Yearly

Education Administrator

Occupation/Type/Industry	Location	Per	Low	Mid	High	Source	Date
Elementary and Secondary School	Arkansas	Y	66180 FQ	75100 MW	87830 TQ	USBLS	5/15
Elementary and Secondary School	Little Rock-North Little Rock-Conway MSA, AR	Y	64710 FQ	74020 MW	86500 TQ	USBLS	5/15
Elementary and Secondary School	California	Y		111760 AW		CABLS	1/16-3/16
Elementary and Secondary School	Anaheim-Santa Ana-Irvine PMSA, CA	Y		124316 AW		CABLS	1/16-3/16
Elementary and Secondary School	Los Angeles-Long Beach-Glendale PMSA, CA	Y		109836 AW		CABLS	1/16-3/16
Elementary and Secondary School	Oakland-Hayward-Berkeley PMSA, CA	Y		112630 AW		CABLS	1/16-3/16
Elementary and Secondary School	Riverside-San Bernardino-Ontario MSA, CA	Y		114349 AW		CABLS	1/16-3/16
Elementary and Secondary School	Sacramento–Roseville–Arden-Arcade MSA, CA	Y		102007 AW		CABLS	1/16-3/16
Elementary and Secondary School	San Diego-Carlsbad MSA, CA	Y		119578 AW		CABLS	1/16-3/16
Elementary and Secondary School	San Francisco-Redwood City-South San Francisco PMSA, CA	Y		112568 AW		CABLS	1/16-3/16
Elementary and Secondary School	Colorado	Y	72420 FQ	86430 MW	98890 TQ	USBLS	5/15
Elementary and Secondary School	Denver-Aurora-Lakewood MSA, CO	Y	75570 FQ	88950 MW	100470 TQ	USBLS	5/15
Elementary and Secondary School	Connecticut	Y		131193 MW		CTBLS	1/16-3/16
Elementary and Secondary School	Bridgeport-Stamford-Norwalk MSA, CT	Y	115130 FQ	139240 MW	156850 TQ	USBLS	5/15
Elementary and Secondary School	Hartford-West Hartford-East Hartford MSA, CT	Y	106580 FQ	124960 MW	144280 TQ	USBLS	5/15
Elementary and Secondary School	Delaware	Y	95960 FQ	110280 MW	122060 TQ	USBLS	5/15
Elementary and Secondary School	Wilmington PMSA, DE-MD-NJ	Y	95300 FQ	111680 MW	124770 TQ	USBLS	5/15
Elementary and Secondary School	District of Columbia	Y	67990 FQ	94440 MW	118890 TQ	USBLS	5/15
Elementary and Secondary School	Washington-Arlington-Alexandria PMSA, DC-VA-MD-WV	Y	84570 FQ	107150 MW	125690 TQ	USBLS	5/15
Elementary and Secondary School	Florida	Y	71521 AE	93301 MW	105403 AEX	FLBLS	7/16-9/16
Elementary and Secondary School	Fort Lauderdale-Pompano Beach-Deerfield Beach PMSA, FL	Y	76987 AE	115949 MW	128304 AEX	FLBLS	7/16-9/16
Elementary and Secondary School	Miami-Miami Beach-Kendall PMSA, FL	Y	68666 AE	92271 MW	110962 AEX	FLBLS	7/16-9/16
Elementary and Secondary School	Orlando-Kissimmee-Sanford MSA, FL	Y	72401 AE	92528 MW	100333 AEX	FLBLS	7/16-9/16
Elementary and Secondary School	Tampa-St. Petersburg-Clearwater MSA, FL	Y	79885 AE	93636 MW	100393 AEX	FLBLS	7/16-9/16
Elementary and Secondary School	Georgia	Y	72260 FQ	85860 MW	99720 TQ	USBLS	5/15
Elementary and Secondary School	Atlanta-Sandy Springs-Roswell MSA, GA	Y	71730 FQ	85900 MW	101290 TQ	USBLS	5/15
Elementary and Secondary School	Augusta-Richmond County MSA, GA-SC	Y	71730 FQ	85060 MW	95630 TQ	USBLS	5/15
Elementary and Secondary School	Hawaii	Y	72710 FQ	84040 MW	104750 TQ	USBLS	5/15
Elementary and Secondary School	Urban Honolulu MSA, HI	Y	73110 FQ	83930 MW	103370 TQ	USBLS	5/15
Elementary and Secondary School	Idaho	Y	68060 FQ	79250 MW	92790 TQ	USBLS	5/15
Elementary and Secondary School	Boise City MSA, ID	Y	73280 FQ	85060 MW	94400 TQ	USBLS	5/15
Elementary and Secondary School	Illinois	Y	77390 FQ	98870 MW	121150 TQ	USBLS	5/15
Elementary and Secondary School	Chicago-Naperville-Arlington Heights PMSA, IL	Y	86240 FQ	109750 MW	128160 TQ	USBLS	5/15
Elementary and Secondary School	Lake County-Kenosha County PMSA, IL-WI	Y	77130 FQ	94130 MW	115780 TQ	USBLS	5/15
Elementary and Secondary School	Indiana	Y	69830 FQ	82500 MW	96360 TQ	USBLS	5/15
Elementary and Secondary School	Gary PMSA, IN	Y	72840 FQ	86510 MW	97550 TQ	USBLS	5/15
Elementary and Secondary School	Indianapolis-Carmel-Anderson MSA, IN	Y	72970 FQ	88840 MW	104590 TQ	USBLS	5/15
Elementary and Secondary School	Iowa	Y	81520 FQ	94130 MW	109940 TQ	USBLS	5/15
Elementary and Secondary School	Des Moines-West Des Moines MSA, IA	Y	84100 FQ	100090 MW	117620 TQ	USBLS	5/15
Elementary and Secondary School	Kansas	Y	69740 FQ	81290 MW	95060 TQ	USBLS	5/15
Elementary and Secondary School	Wichita MSA, KS	Y	69810 FQ	79830 MW	93470 TQ	USBLS	5/15
Elementary and Secondary School	Kentucky	Y	69760 FQ	81600 MW	95770 TQ	USBLS	5/15
Elementary and Secondary School	Louisville-Jefferson County MSA, KY-IN	Y	78980 FQ	94130 MW	111070 TQ	USBLS	5/15
Elementary and Secondary School	Louisiana	Y	62920 FQ	72500 MW	83140 TQ	USBLS	5/15
Elementary and Secondary School	Baton Rouge MSA, LA	Y	66680 FQ	74940 MW	86090 TQ	USBLS	5/15

AE	Average entry wage	AWR	Average wage range	H	Hourly
AEX	Average experienced wage	B	Biweekly	HI	Highest wage paid
ATC	Average total compensation	D	Daily	HR	High end range
AW	Average wage paid	FQ	First quartile wage	LO	Lowest wage paid

LR	Low end range	MTC	Median total compensation	TCC	Total cash compensation
M	Monthly	MW	Median wage paid	TQ	Third quartile wage
MCC	Median cash compensation	MWR	Median wage range	W	Weekly
ME	Median entry wage	S	See annotated source	Y	Yearly

Education Administrator

Occupation/Type/Industry	Location	Per	Low	Mid	High	Source	Date
Elementary and Secondary School	New Orleans-Metairie MSA, LA	Y	64110 FQ	77000 MW	92190 TQ	USBLS	5/15
Elementary and Secondary School	Maine	Y	65600 FQ	78540 MW	92260 TQ	USBLS	5/15
Elementary and Secondary School	Portland-South Portland MSA, ME	Y	82300 FQ	90910 MW	99690 TQ	USBLS	5/15
Elementary and Secondary School	Maryland	Y	70207 AE	102389 MW	118480 AEX	MDBLS	4/16
Elementary and Secondary School	Baltimore-Columbia-Towson MSA, MD	Y	73640 FQ	99440 MW	118520 TQ	USBLS	5/15
Elementary and Secondary School	Salisbury MSA, MD-DE	Y	83960 FQ	95180 MW	109710 TQ	USBLS	5/15
Elementary and Secondary School	Massachusetts	Y	85720 FQ	102010 MW	118780 TQ	USBLS	5/15
Elementary and Secondary School	Boston-Cambridge-Newton NECTA, MA	Y	89970 FQ	106860 MW	121880 TQ	USBLS	5/15
Elementary and Secondary School	Worcester MSA, MA-CT	Y	84290 FQ	101090 MW	123660 TQ	USBLS	5/15
Elementary and Secondary School	Michigan	Y	74180 FQ	90800 MW	106950 TQ	USBLS	5/15
Elementary and Secondary School	Detroit-Dearborn-Livonia PMSA, MI	Y	80630 FQ	95940 MW	112550 TQ	USBLS	5/15
Elementary and Secondary School	Grand Rapids-Wyoming MSA, MI	Y	67640 FQ	85080 MW	98720 TQ	USBLS	5/15
Elementary and Secondary School	Minnesota	Y	84906 FQ	102870 MW	121932 TQ	MNBLS	1/16-3/16
Elementary and Secondary School	Minneapolis-St. Paul-Bloomington MSA, MN-WI	Y	91795 FQ	112401 MW	127379 TQ	MNBLS	1/16-3/16
Elementary and Secondary School	Mississippi	Y	62080 FQ	72790 MW	84490 TQ	USBLS	5/15
Elementary and Secondary School	Jackson MSA, MS	Y	56250 FQ	67110 MW	80450 TQ	USBLS	5/15
Elementary and Secondary School	Missouri	Y	72990 FQ	90200 MW	113420 TQ	USBLS	5/15
Elementary and Secondary School	Kansas City MSA, MO-KS	Y	73730 FQ	89760 MW	109290 TQ	USBLS	5/15
Elementary and Secondary School	St. Louis MSA, MO-IL	Y	82050 FQ	100420 MW	119910 TQ	USBLS	5/15
Elementary and Secondary School	Montana	Y	61390 FQ	76720 MW	92030 TQ	USBLS	5/15
Elementary and Secondary School	Billings MSA, MT	Y	61270 FQ	79510 MW	92120 TQ	USBLS	5/15
Elementary and Secondary School	Nebraska	Y	78410 FQ	90055 MW	102295 TQ	NEBLS	7/16-9/16
Elementary and Secondary School	Omaha-Council Bluffs MSA, NE-IA	Y	76475 FQ	88925 MW	101395 TQ	NEBLS	7/16-9/16
Elementary and Secondary School	Nevada	Y	77290 FQ	89940 MW	101620 TQ	USBLS	5/15
Elementary and Secondary School	Las Vegas-Henderson-Paradise MSA, NV	Y	77150 FQ	89220 MW	100140 TQ	USBLS	5/15
Elementary and Secondary School	New Hampshire	Y	66995 AE	87385 MW	98095 AEX	NHBLS	6/16
Elementary and Secondary School	Manchester NECTA, NH	Y	64922 AE	85170 MW	92824 AEX	NHBLS	6/16
Elementary and Secondary School	Nashua NECTA, NH-MA	Y	74350 FQ	85520 MW	96800 TQ	USBLS	5/15
Elementary and Secondary School	New Jersey	Y	105760 FQ	123780 MW	146410 TQ	USBLS	5/15
Elementary and Secondary School	Camden PMSA, NJ	Y	101740 FQ	116830 MW	135570 TQ	USBLS	5/15
Elementary and Secondary School	Newark PMSA, NJ-PA	Y	106600 FQ	124450 MW	146660 TQ	USBLS	5/15
Elementary and Secondary School	Trenton MSA, NJ	Y	108740 FQ	126950 MW	149570 TQ	USBLS	5/15
Elementary and Secondary School	New Mexico	Y	68840 FQ	79450 MW	92560 TQ	USBLS	5/15
Elementary and Secondary School	Albuquerque MSA, NM	Y	67240 FQ	75990 MW	87990 TQ	USBLS	5/15
Elementary and Secondary School	New York	Y	76600 AE	114450 MW	136830 AEX	NYBLS	1/16-3/16
Elementary and Secondary School	Buffalo-Cheektowaga-Niagara Falls MSA, NY	Y	76860 FQ	92260 MW	108510 TQ	USBLS	5/15
Elementary and Secondary School	Nassau County-Suffolk County PMSA, NY	Y	121720 FQ	144970 MW	168280 TQ	USBLS	5/15
Elementary and Secondary School	New York-Jersey City-White Plains PMSA, NY-NJ	Y	96620 FQ	119200 MW	144420 TQ	USBLS	5/15
Elementary and Secondary School	Rochester MSA, NY	Y	82870 FQ	97890 MW	117200 TQ	USBLS	5/15
Elementary and Secondary School	North Carolina	Y	53920 FQ	63720 MW	77670 TQ	USBLS	5/15
Elementary and Secondary School	Charlotte-Concord-Gastonia MSA, NC-SC	Y	54150 FQ	65420 MW	84080 TQ	USBLS	5/15
Elementary and Secondary School	Raleigh MSA, NC	Y	58680 FQ	71370 MW	88630 TQ	USBLS	5/15
Elementary and Secondary School	North Dakota	Y	69210 FQ	85740 MW	104380 TQ	USBLS	5/15
Elementary and Secondary School	Fargo MSA, ND-MN	Y	81050 FQ	92300 MW	105010 TQ	USBLS	5/15
Elementary and Secondary School	Ohio	Y	70520 FQ	84480 MW	96860 TQ	USBLS	5/15
Elementary and Secondary School	Cincinnati MSA, OH-KY-IN	Y	71400 FQ	85790 MW	98660 TQ	USBLS	5/15
Elementary and Secondary School	Cleveland-Elyria MSA, OH	Y	70010 FQ	85580 MW	98090 TQ	USBLS	5/15
Elementary and Secondary School	Columbus MSA, OH	Y	77140 FQ	89560 MW	100160 TQ	USBLS	5/15
Elementary and Secondary School	Oklahoma	Y	60340 FQ	71040 MW	81250 TQ	USBLS	5/15
Elementary and Secondary School	Oklahoma City MSA, OK	Y	59760 FQ	69930 MW	78830 TQ	USBLS	5/15
Elementary and Secondary School	Tulsa MSA, OK	Y	63370 FQ	74080 MW	88400 TQ	USBLS	5/15
Elementary and Secondary School	Oregon	Y	86014 FQ	100772 MW	116743 TQ	ORBLS	2016
Elementary and Secondary School	Portland-Vancouver-Hillsboro MSA, OR-WA	Y	87080 FQ	103850 MW	117800 TQ	USBLS	5/15
Elementary and Secondary School	Pennsylvania	Y	79970 FQ	95500 MW	116290 TQ	USBLS	5/15
Elementary and Secondary School	Allentown-Bethlehem-Easton MSA, PA-NJ	Y	79440 FQ	96110 MW	114320 TQ	USBLS	5/15
Elementary and Secondary School	Harrisburg-Carlisle MSA, PA	Y	79660 FQ	94010 MW	109230 TQ	USBLS	5/15

AE	Average entry wage	AWR	Average wage range	H	Hourly
AEX	Average experienced wage	B	Biweekly	HI	Highest wage paid
ATC	Average total compensation	D	Daily	HR	High end range
AW	Average wage paid	FQ	First quartile wage	LO	Lowest wage paid

LR	Low end range	MTC	Median total compensation
M	Monthly	MW	Median wage paid
MCC	Median cash compensation	MWR	Median wage range
ME	Median entry wage	S	See annotated source

TCC	Total cash compensation
TQ	Third quartile wage
W	Weekly
Y	Yearly

Education Administrator

Occupation/Type/Industry	Location	Per	Low	Mid	High	Source	Date
Elementary and Secondary School	Montgomery County-Bucks County-Chester County PMSA, PA	Y	94930 FQ	116510 MW	138770 TQ	USBLS	5/15
Elementary and Secondary School	Philadelphia PMSA, PA	Y	76090 FQ	102720 MW	127080 TQ	USBLS	5/15
Elementary and Secondary School	Pittsburgh MSA, PA	Y	83600 FQ	96500 MW	114690 TQ	USBLS	5/15
Elementary and Secondary School	Scranton–Wilkes-Barre–Hazleton MSA, PA	Y	75990 FQ	91580 MW	109070 TQ	USBLS	5/15
Elementary and Secondary School	Rhode Island	Y	86780 FQ	101380 MW	117810 TQ	USBLS	5/15
Elementary and Secondary School	Providence-Warwick MSA, RI-MA	Y	87230 FQ	101180 MW	116750 TQ	USBLS	5/15
Elementary and Secondary School	South Carolina	Y	68010 FQ	81660 MW	95270 TQ	USBLS	5/15
Elementary and Secondary School	Charleston-North Charleston MSA, SC	Y	70230 FQ	82350 MW	95120 TQ	USBLS	5/15
Elementary and Secondary School	Columbia MSA, SC	Y	71210 FQ	83970 MW	95890 TQ	USBLS	5/15
Elementary and Secondary School	Greenville-Anderson-Mauldin MSA, SC	Y	63370 FQ	78500 MW	94830 TQ	USBLS	5/15
Elementary and Secondary School	South Dakota	Y	66120 FQ	77050 MW	92860 TQ	USBLS	5/15
Elementary and Secondary School	Sioux Falls MSA, SD	Y	81160 FQ	94900 MW	111700 TQ	USBLS	5/15
Elementary and Secondary School	Tennessee	Y	61220 FQ	74490 MW	90860 TQ	USBLS	5/15
Elementary and Secondary School	Knoxville MSA, TN	Y	64900 FQ	75250 MW	89110 TQ	USBLS	5/15
Elementary and Secondary School	Memphis MSA, TN-MS-AR	Y	67590 FQ	84230 MW	99970 TQ	USBLS	5/15
Elementary and Secondary School	Nashville-Davidson–Murfreesboro–Franklin MSA, TN	Y	61710 FQ	77620 MW	92970 TQ	USBLS	5/15
Elementary and Secondary School	Texas	Y	66670 FQ	76890 MW	91840 TQ	USBLS	5/15
Elementary and Secondary School	Austin-Round Rock MSA, TX	Y	64230 FQ	75440 MW	91560 TQ	USBLS	5/15
Elementary and Secondary School	Dallas-Plano-Irving PMSA, TX	Y	68770 FQ	81240 MW	96100 TQ	USBLS	5/15
Elementary and Secondary School	Fort Worth-Arlington PMSA, TX	Y	68220 FQ	78070 MW	93380 TQ	USBLS	5/15
Elementary and Secondary School	Houston-The Woodlands-Sugar Land MSA, TX	Y	69270 FQ	80070 MW	95430 TQ	USBLS	5/15
Elementary and Secondary School	San Antonio-New Braunfels MSA, TX	Y	67420 FQ	77500 MW	91440 TQ	USBLS	5/15
Elementary and Secondary School	Utah	Y	72910 FQ	86390 MW	98180 TQ	USBLS	5/15
Elementary and Secondary School	Ogden-Clearfield MSA, UT	Y	73240 FQ	88800 MW	105450 TQ	USBLS	5/15
Elementary and Secondary School	Provo-Orem MSA, UT	Y	73890 FQ	86830 MW	97370 TQ	USBLS	5/15
Elementary and Secondary School	Salt Lake City MSA, UT	Y	73590 FQ	87870 MW	99730 TQ	USBLS	5/15
Elementary and Secondary School	Vermont	Y	67430 FQ	85050 MW	100400 TQ	USBLS	5/15
Elementary and Secondary School	Burlington-South Burlington MSA, VT	Y	84070 FQ	98530 MW	116230 TQ	USBLS	5/15
Elementary and Secondary School	Virginia	Y	72040 FQ	88470 MW	110390 TQ	USBLS	5/15
Elementary and Secondary School	Richmond MSA, VA	Y	71220 FQ	83760 MW	98530 TQ	USBLS	5/15
Elementary and Secondary School	Virginia Beach-Norfolk-Newport News MSA, VA-NC	Y	67660 FQ	79770 MW	96070 TQ	USBLS	5/15
Elementary and Secondary School	Washington	Y		107810 AW		WABLS	3/16
Elementary and Secondary School	Seattle-Bellevue-Everett PMSA, WA	Y		114851 AW		WABLS	3/16
Elementary and Secondary School	Tacoma-Lakewood PMSA, WA	Y		112210 AW		WABLS	3/16
Elementary and Secondary School	West Virginia	Y	57590 FQ	68960 MW	78880 TQ	USBLS	5/15
Elementary and Secondary School	Huntington-Ashland MSA, WV-KY-OH	Y	57090 FQ	70290 MW	79580 TQ	USBLS	5/15
Elementary and Secondary School	Wisconsin	Y	81700 FQ	94290 MW	111500 TQ	USBLS	5/15
Elementary and Secondary School	Madison MSA, WI	Y	82420 FQ	90930 MW	100610 TQ	USBLS	5/15
Elementary and Secondary School	Milwaukee-Waukesha-West Allis MSA, WI	Y	83850 FQ	100040 MW	119870 TQ	USBLS	5/15
Elementary and Secondary School	Wyoming	Y	85100 FQ	93900 MW	103880 TQ	USBLS	5/15
Elementary and Secondary School	Puerto Rico	Y	40590 FQ	49040 MW	57200 TQ	USBLS	5/15
Elementary and Secondary School	San Juan-Carolina-Caguas MSA, PR	Y	39930 FQ	49030 MW	57590 TQ	USBLS	5/15
Elementary and Secondary School	Virgin Islands	Y	50550 FQ	61090 MW	73730 TQ	USBLS	5/15
Elementary and Secondary School	Guam	Y	58910 FQ	69190 MW	77150 TQ	USBLS	5/15
Postsecondary	Alabama	Y	58433 AE	100559 AW	121622 AEX	ALBLS	6/16
Postsecondary	Birmingham-Hoover MSA, AL	Y	60165 AE	97135 AW	115615 AEX	ALBLS	6/16
Postsecondary	Alaska	Y	78340 FQ	112010 MW	142570 TQ	USBLS	5/15
Postsecondary	Anchorage MSA, AK	Y	81630 FQ	112620 MW	152600 TQ	USBLS	5/15
Postsecondary	Arizona	Y	69280 FQ	91910 MW	122810 TQ	USBLS	5/15
Postsecondary	Phoenix-Mesa-Scottsdale MSA, AZ	Y	71990 FQ	93160 MW	121510 TQ	USBLS	5/15
Postsecondary	Tucson MSA, AZ	Y	62180 FQ	88490 MW	138580 TQ	USBLS	5/15
Postsecondary	Arkansas	Y	55180 FQ	74650 MW	102230 TQ	USBLS	5/15

AE	Average entry wage	AWR	Average wage range	H	Hourly	LR	Low end range	MTC	Median total compensation	TCC	Total cash compensation
AEX	Average experienced wage	B	Biweekly	HI	Highest wage paid	M	Monthly	MW	Median wage paid	TQ	Third quartile wage
ATC	Average total compensation	D	Daily	HR	High end range	MCC	Median cash compensation	MWR	Median wage range	W	Weekly
AW	Average wage paid	FQ	First quartile wage	LO	Lowest wage paid	ME	Median entry wage	S	See annotated source	Y	Yearly

Occupation/Type/Industry	Location	Per	Low	Mid	High	Source	Date
Education Administrator							
Postsecondary	Little Rock-North Little Rock-Conway MSA, AR	Y	53460 FQ	73960 MW	105370 TQ	USBLS	5/15
Postsecondary	California	H	38.69 FQ	50.69 MW	69.30 TQ	CABLS	1/16-3/16
Postsecondary	Anaheim-Santa Ana-Irvine PMSA, CA	H	37.12 FQ	47.39 MW	64.04 TQ	CABLS	1/16-3/16
Postsecondary	Los Angeles-Long Beach-Glendale PMSA, CA	H	38.08 FQ	50.71 MW	69.71 TQ	CABLS	1/16-3/16
Postsecondary	Oakland-Hayward-Berkeley PMSA, CA	H	40.18 FQ	51.53 MW	71.33 TQ	CABLS	1/16-3/16
Postsecondary	Riverside-San Bernardino-Ontario MSA, CA	H	42.17 FQ	54.66 MW	69.28 TQ	CABLS	1/16-3/16
Postsecondary	Sacramento–Roseville–Arden-Arcade MSA, CA	H	46.42 FQ	58.53 MW	74.08 TQ	CABLS	1/16-3/16
Postsecondary	San Diego-Carlsbad MSA, CA	H	35.60 FQ	48.03 MW	65.66 TQ	CABLS	1/16-3/16
Postsecondary	San Francisco-Redwood City-South San Francisco PMSA, CA	H	39.86 FQ	50.64 MW	69.33 TQ	CABLS	1/16-3/16
Postsecondary	Colorado	Y	56650 FQ	77140 MW	103210 TQ	USBLS	5/15
Postsecondary	Denver-Aurora-Lakewood MSA, CO	Y	59300 FQ	80460 MW	108460 TQ	USBLS	5/15
Postsecondary	Connecticut	Y		78982 MW		CTBLS	1/16-3/16
Postsecondary	Bridgeport-Stamford-Norwalk MSA, CT	Y	85920 FQ	107820 MW	131620 TQ	USBLS	5/15
Postsecondary	Hartford-West Hartford-East Hartford MSA, CT	Y	71460 FQ	104670 MW	137010 TQ	USBLS	5/15
Postsecondary	Delaware	Y	95880 FQ	122630 MW	180890 TQ	USBLS	5/15
Postsecondary	Wilmington PMSA, DE-MD-NJ	Y	91640 FQ	118730 MW	173550 TQ	USBLS	5/15
Postsecondary	District of Columbia	Y	60510 FQ	85040 MW	123630 TQ	USBLS	5/15
Postsecondary	Washington-Arlington-Alexandria PMSA, DC-VA-MD-WV	Y	66070 FQ	90900 MW	127210 TQ	USBLS	5/15
Postsecondary	Florida	H	38.99 AE	54.58 MW	70.95 AEX	FLBLS	7/16-9/16
Postsecondary	Fort Lauderdale-Pompano Beach-Deerfield Beach PMSA, FL	H	43.22 AE	66.08 MW	90.32 AEX	FLBLS	7/16-9/16
Postsecondary	Miami-Miami Beach-Kendall PMSA, FL	H	42.47 AE	56.46 MW	73.94 AEX	FLBLS	7/16-9/16
Postsecondary	Orlando-Kissimmee-Sanford MSA, FL	H	37.02 AE	49.03 MW	61.64 AEX	FLBLS	7/16-9/16
Postsecondary	Tampa-St. Petersburg-Clearwater MSA, FL	H	38.71 AE	47.73 MW	60.28 AEX	FLBLS	7/16-9/16
Postsecondary	Georgia	Y	69220 FQ	91710 MW	126250 TQ	USBLS	5/15
Postsecondary	Atlanta-Sandy Springs-Roswell MSA, GA	Y	69160 FQ	88830 MW	119420 TQ	USBLS	5/15
Postsecondary	Augusta-Richmond County MSA, GA-SC	Y	96320 FQ	152260 MW		USBLS	5/15
Postsecondary	Hawaii	Y	78530 FQ	110570 MW	162550 TQ	USBLS	5/15
Postsecondary	Urban Honolulu MSA, HI	Y	78770 FQ	111630 MW	164220 TQ	USBLS	5/15
Postsecondary	Idaho	Y	59480 FQ	78400 MW	112640 TQ	USBLS	5/15
Postsecondary	Boise City MSA, ID	Y	54180 FQ	69490 MW	94320 TQ	USBLS	5/15
Postsecondary	Illinois	Y	60600 FQ	81530 MW	114460 TQ	USBLS	5/15
Postsecondary	Chicago-Naperville-Arlington Heights PMSA, IL	Y	65810 FQ	86150 MW	118640 TQ	USBLS	5/15
Postsecondary	Lake County-Kenosha County PMSA, IL-WI	Y	65580 FQ	90550 MW	118610 TQ	USBLS	5/15
Postsecondary	Indiana	Y	55610 FQ	76740 MW	119910 TQ	USBLS	5/15
Postsecondary	Gary PMSA, IN	Y	54660 FQ	78460 MW	120130 TQ	USBLS	5/15
Postsecondary	Indianapolis-Carmel-Anderson MSA, IN	Y	54430 FQ	71030 MW	99530 TQ	USBLS	5/15
Postsecondary	Iowa	Y	63150 FQ	84480 MW	117280 TQ	USBLS	5/15
Postsecondary	Des Moines-West Des Moines MSA, IA	Y	58730 FQ	87420 MW	125090 TQ	USBLS	5/15
Postsecondary	Kansas	Y	56060 FQ	73750 MW	97070 TQ	USBLS	5/15
Postsecondary	Wichita MSA, KS	Y	54390 FQ	70530 MW	95790 TQ	USBLS	5/15
Postsecondary	Kentucky	Y	43050 FQ	65530 MW	97570 TQ	USBLS	5/15
Postsecondary	Louisville-Jefferson County MSA, KY-IN	Y	49680 FQ	65950 MW	101630 TQ	USBLS	5/15
Postsecondary	Louisiana	Y	61510 FQ	78580 MW	106380 TQ	USBLS	5/15
Postsecondary	Baton Rouge MSA, LA	Y	69750 FQ	86240 MW	126690 TQ	USBLS	5/15

AE	Average entry wage	AWR	Average wage range	H	Hourly	LR	Low end range	MTC	Median total compensation	TCC	Total cash compensation
AEX	Average experienced wage	B	Biweekly	HI	Highest wage paid	M	Monthly	MW	Median wage paid	TQ	Third quartile wage
ATC	Average total compensation	D	Daily	HR	High end range	MCC	Median cash compensation	MWR	Median wage range	W	Weekly
AW	Average wage paid	FQ	First quartile wage	LO	Lowest wage paid	ME	Median entry wage	S	See annotated source	Y	Yearly

Education Administrator

Occupation/Type/Industry	Location	Per	Low	Mid	High	Source	Date
Postsecondary	New Orleans-Metairie MSA, LA	Y	59310 FQ	75930 MW	100300 TQ	USBLS	5/15
Postsecondary	Maine	Y	55160 FQ	73790 MW	102750 TQ	USBLS	5/15
Postsecondary	Portland-South Portland MSA, ME	Y	53450 FQ	71990 MW	104550 TQ	USBLS	5/15
Postsecondary	Maryland	Y	67185 AE	119677 MW	145923 AEX	MDBLS	4/16
Postsecondary	Baltimore-Columbia-Towson MSA, MD	Y	83510 FQ	108430 MW	161560 TQ	USBLS	5/15
Postsecondary	Salisbury MSA, MD-DE	Y	89780 FQ	116070 MW	144140 TQ	USBLS	5/15
Postsecondary	Massachusetts	Y	66050 FQ	84170 MW	115390 TQ	USBLS	5/15
Postsecondary	Boston-Cambridge-Newton NECTA, MA	Y	67140 FQ	85900 MW	119930 TQ	USBLS	5/15
Postsecondary	Worcester MSA, MA-CT	Y	62890 FQ	81340 MW	102440 TQ	USBLS	5/15
Postsecondary	Michigan	Y	64710 FQ	89620 MW	133310 TQ	USBLS	5/15
Postsecondary	Detroit-Dearborn-Livonia PMSA, MI	Y	57500 FQ	76690 MW	108650 TQ	USBLS	5/15
Postsecondary	Grand Rapids-Wyoming MSA, MI	Y	59710 FQ	75170 MW	100250 TQ	USBLS	5/15
Postsecondary	Minnesota	Y	61931 FQ	79419 MW	97749 TQ	MNBLS	1/16-3/16
Postsecondary	Minneapolis-St. Paul-Bloomington MSA, MN-WI	Y	60336 FQ	77386 MW	95351 TQ	MNBLS	1/16-3/16
Postsecondary	Mississippi	Y	57160 FQ	75360 MW	101080 TQ	USBLS	5/15
Postsecondary	Jackson MSA, MS	Y	55190 FQ	69970 MW	96290 TQ	USBLS	5/15
Postsecondary	Missouri	Y	61630 FQ	86490 MW	120860 TQ	USBLS	5/15
Postsecondary	Kansas City MSA, MO-KS	Y	55490 FQ	77650 MW	102990 TQ	USBLS	5/15
Postsecondary	St. Louis MSA, MO-IL	Y	50200 FQ	75350 MW	107240 TQ	USBLS	5/15
Postsecondary	Montana	Y	52620 FQ	75780 MW	108340 TQ	USBLS	5/15
Postsecondary	Nebraska	Y	60180 FQ	80500 MW	125315 TQ	NEBLS	7/16-9/16
Postsecondary	Omaha-Council Bluffs MSA, NE-IA	Y	65380 FQ	82835 MW	116305 TQ	NEBLS	7/16-9/16
Postsecondary	Nevada	Y	72080 FQ	96480 MW	134000 TQ	USBLS	5/15
Postsecondary	Las Vegas-Henderson-Paradise MSA, NV	Y	70000 FQ	92590 MW	126410 TQ	USBLS	5/15
Postsecondary	New Hampshire	H	27.44 AE	38.76 MW	56.74 AEX	NHBLS	6/16
Postsecondary	Manchester NECTA, NH	H	28.43 AE	36.59 MW	45.63 AEX	NHBLS	6/16
Postsecondary	New Jersey	Y	98270 FQ	120650 MW	157440 TQ	USBLS	5/15
Postsecondary	Camden PMSA, NJ	Y	100060 FQ	122150 MW	171200 TQ	USBLS	5/15
Postsecondary	Newark PMSA, NJ-PA	Y	101770 FQ	125230 MW	178850 TQ	USBLS	5/15
Postsecondary	Trenton MSA, NJ	Y	99100 FQ	119610 MW	151280 TQ	USBLS	5/15
Postsecondary	New Mexico	Y	63010 FQ	80890 MW	102660 TQ	USBLS	5/15
Postsecondary	Albuquerque MSA, NM	Y	72150 FQ	91770 MW	128640 TQ	USBLS	5/15
Postsecondary	New York	Y	64650 AE	101950 MW	144140 AEX	NYBLS	1/16-3/16
Postsecondary	Buffalo-Cheektowaga-Niagara Falls MSA, NY	Y	59020 FQ	76610 MW	109780 TQ	USBLS	5/15
Postsecondary	Nassau County-Suffolk County PMSA, NY	Y	61330 FQ	88870 MW	133720 TQ	USBLS	5/15
Postsecondary	New York-Jersey City-White Plains PMSA, NY-NJ	Y	83680 FQ	108420 MW	146740 TQ	USBLS	5/15
Postsecondary	Rochester MSA, NY	Y	73550 FQ	103540 MW	155360 TQ	USBLS	5/15
Postsecondary	North Carolina	Y	62970 FQ	84450 MW	120570 TQ	USBLS	5/15
Postsecondary	Charlotte-Concord-Gastonia MSA, NC-SC	Y	59040 FQ	81760 MW	112410 TQ	USBLS	5/15
Postsecondary	Raleigh MSA, NC	Y	70340 FQ	93050 MW	133230 TQ	USBLS	5/15
Postsecondary	North Dakota	Y	74890 FQ	105770 MW	146350 TQ	USBLS	5/15
Postsecondary	Fargo MSA, ND-MN	Y	81080 FQ	120370 MW	169020 TQ	USBLS	5/15
Postsecondary	Ohio	Y	62970 FQ	81120 MW	114930 TQ	USBLS	5/15
Postsecondary	Cincinnati MSA, OH-KY-IN	Y	67060 FQ	86350 MW	126200 TQ	USBLS	5/15
Postsecondary	Cleveland-Elyria MSA, OH	Y	58090 FQ	73370 MW	96010 TQ	USBLS	5/15
Postsecondary	Columbus MSA, OH	Y	67130 FQ	88550 MW	128140 TQ	USBLS	5/15
Postsecondary	Oklahoma	Y	55060 FQ	72350 MW	97500 TQ	USBLS	5/15
Postsecondary	Oklahoma City MSA, OK	Y	52180 FQ	72600 MW	101840 TQ	USBLS	5/15
Postsecondary	Tulsa MSA, OK	Y	53030 FQ	68400 MW	79780 TQ	USBLS	5/15
Postsecondary	Oregon	H	34.92 FQ	45.90 MW	61.74 TQ	ORBLS	2016
Postsecondary	Portland-Vancouver-Hillsboro MSA, OR-WA	Y	68500 FQ	91120 MW	119530 TQ	USBLS	5/15
Postsecondary	Pennsylvania	Y	67190 FQ	91700 MW	127720 TQ	USBLS	5/15
Postsecondary	Allentown-Bethlehem-Easton MSA, PA-NJ	Y	62600 FQ	77980 MW	113810 TQ	USBLS	5/15
Postsecondary	Harrisburg-Carlisle MSA, PA	Y	75700 FQ	92040 MW	122740 TQ	USBLS	5/15

AE	Average entry wage	AWR	Average wage range	H	Hourly	LR	Low end range	MTC	Median total compensation	TCC	Total cash compensation
AEX	Average experienced wage	B	Biweekly	HI	Highest wage paid	M	Monthly	MW	Median wage paid	TQ	Third quartile wage
ATC	Average total compensation	D	Daily	HR	High end range	MCC	Median cash compensation	MWR	Median wage range	W	Weekly
AW	Average wage paid	FQ	First quartile wage	LO	Lowest wage paid	ME	Median entry wage	S	See annotated source	Y	Yearly

Occupation/Type/Industry	Location	Per	Low	Mid	High	Source	Date
Education Administrator							
Postsecondary	Montgomery County-Bucks County-Chester County PMSA, PA	Y	61790 FQ	86460 MW	114530 TQ	USBLS	5/15
Postsecondary	Philadelphia PMSA, PA	Y	71540 FQ	101590 MW	138630 TQ	USBLS	5/15
Postsecondary	Pittsburgh MSA, PA	Y	63260 FQ	86500 MW	131320 TQ	USBLS	5/15
Postsecondary	Rhode Island	Y	77630 FQ	97720 MW	126870 TQ	USBLS	5/15
Postsecondary	Providence-Warwick MSA, RI-MA	Y	74620 FQ	92980 MW	121630 TQ	USBLS	5/15
Postsecondary	South Carolina	Y	53560 FQ	71690 MW	104420 TQ	USBLS	5/15
Postsecondary	Charleston-North Charleston MSA, SC	Y	56930 FQ	78380 MW	130240 TQ	USBLS	5/15
Postsecondary	Columbia MSA, SC	Y	62760 FQ	97070 MW	161640 TQ	USBLS	5/15
Postsecondary	Greenville-Anderson-Mauldin MSA, SC	Y	52190 FQ	68910 MW	105980 TQ	USBLS	5/15
Postsecondary	South Dakota	Y	76230 FQ	95740 MW	133650 TQ	USBLS	5/15
Postsecondary	Tennessee	Y	49010 FQ	67230 MW	100110 TQ	USBLS	5/15
Postsecondary	Knoxville MSA, TN	Y	53050 FQ	70940 MW	114710 TQ	USBLS	5/15
Postsecondary	Memphis MSA, TN-MS-AR	Y	52450 FQ	74770 MW	104180 TQ	USBLS	5/15
Postsecondary	Nashville-Davidson–Murfreesboro–Franklin MSA, TN	Y	54060 FQ	74640 MW	106520 TQ	USBLS	5/15
Postsecondary	Texas	Y	73310 FQ	100350 MW	137250 TQ	USBLS	5/15
Postsecondary	Austin-Round Rock MSA, TX	Y	79860 FQ	110370 MW	152980 TQ	USBLS	5/15
Postsecondary	Dallas-Plano-Irving PMSA, TX	Y	78730 FQ	107640 MW	147530 TQ	USBLS	5/15
Postsecondary	Fort Worth-Arlington PMSA, TX	Y	62810 FQ	84400 MW	118480 TQ	USBLS	5/15
Postsecondary	Houston-The Woodlands-Sugar Land MSA, TX	Y	79160 FQ	104330 MW	135760 TQ	USBLS	5/15
Postsecondary	San Antonio-New Braunfels MSA, TX	Y	75950 FQ	97850 MW	132830 TQ	USBLS	5/15
Postsecondary	Utah	Y	60490 FQ	81580 MW	120470 TQ	USBLS	5/15
Postsecondary	Ogden-Clearfield MSA, UT	Y	58990 FQ	72430 MW	104170 TQ	USBLS	5/15
Postsecondary	Provo-Orem MSA, UT	Y	59450 FQ	78840 MW	110220 TQ	USBLS	5/15
Postsecondary	Salt Lake City MSA, UT	Y	60290 FQ	87130 MW	133740 TQ	USBLS	5/15
Postsecondary	Vermont	Y	51030 FQ	74870 MW	104870 TQ	USBLS	5/15
Postsecondary	Burlington-South Burlington MSA, VT	Y	49970 FQ	76160 MW	101500 TQ	USBLS	5/15
Postsecondary	Virginia	Y	65650 FQ	87710 MW	120710 TQ	USBLS	5/15
Postsecondary	Richmond MSA, VA	Y	66710 FQ	89050 MW	117770 TQ	USBLS	5/15
Postsecondary	Virginia Beach-Norfolk-Newport News MSA, VA-NC	Y	65820 FQ	84690 MW	115830 TQ	USBLS	5/15
Postsecondary	Washington	H	35.42 FQ	43.11 MW	53.94 TQ	WABLS	3/16
Postsecondary	Seattle-Bellevue-Everett PMSA, WA	H	36.78 FQ	45.11 MW	59.86 TQ	WABLS	3/16
Postsecondary	Tacoma-Lakewood PMSA, WA	H	36.52 FQ	43.82 MW	51.75 TQ	WABLS	3/16
Postsecondary	West Virginia	Y	63750 FQ	85460 MW	114620 TQ	USBLS	5/15
Postsecondary	Huntington-Ashland MSA, WV-KY-OH	Y	62800 FQ	80920 MW	98440 TQ	USBLS	5/15
Postsecondary	Wisconsin	Y	69980 FQ	91860 MW	120640 TQ	USBLS	5/15
Postsecondary	Madison MSA, WI	Y	81210 FQ	101900 MW	132700 TQ	USBLS	5/15
Postsecondary	Milwaukee-Waukesha-West Allis MSA, WI	Y	73550 FQ	96110 MW	128830 TQ	USBLS	5/15
Postsecondary	Wyoming	Y	80250 FQ	95410 MW	124710 TQ	USBLS	5/15
Postsecondary	Puerto Rico	Y	37330 FQ	48990 MW	67200 TQ	USBLS	5/15
Postsecondary	San Juan-Carolina-Caguas MSA, PR	Y	37730 FQ	49430 MW	67570 TQ	USBLS	5/15
Preschool and Childcare Center/Program	Alabama	Y	25030 AE	51248 AW	64367 AEX	ALBLS	6/16
Preschool and Childcare Center/Program	Alaska	Y	50230 FQ	56520 MW	63330 TQ	USBLS	5/15
Preschool and Childcare Center/Program	Anchorage MSA, AK	Y	51980 FQ	56900 MW	61810 TQ	USBLS	5/15
Preschool and Childcare Center/Program	Arizona	Y	31680 FQ	38380 MW	46550 TQ	USBLS	5/15
Preschool and Childcare Center/Program	Phoenix-Mesa-Scottsdale MSA, AZ	Y	30760 FQ	36790 MW	44600 TQ	USBLS	5/15
Preschool and Childcare Center/Program	Tucson MSA, AZ	Y	34340 FQ	41990 MW	48610 TQ	USBLS	5/15
Preschool and Childcare Center/Program	Arkansas	Y	33100 FQ	44580 MW	59560 TQ	USBLS	5/15
Preschool and Childcare Center/Program	Little Rock-North Little Rock-Conway MSA, AR	Y	41110 FQ	54750 MW	75610 TQ	USBLS	5/15
Preschool and Childcare Center/Program	California	H	20.00 FQ	25.37 MW	34.22 TQ	CABLS	1/16-3/16
Preschool and Childcare Center/Program	Anaheim-Santa Ana-Irvine PMSA, CA	H	24.96 FQ	32.78 MW	43.86 TQ	CABLS	1/16-3/16
Preschool and Childcare Center/Program	Los Angeles-Long Beach-Glendale PMSA, CA	H	19.05 FQ	24.50 MW	35.33 TQ	CABLS	1/16-3/16

AE	Average entry wage	**AWR**	Average wage range	**H**	Hourly	**LR**	Low end range	**MTC** Median total compensation	**TCC** Total cash compensation
AEX	Average experienced wage	**B**	Biweekly	**HI**	Highest wage paid	**M**	Monthly	**MW** Median wage paid	**TQ** Third quartile wage
ATC	Average total compensation	**D**	Daily	**HR**	High end range	**MCC**	Median cash compensation	**MWR** Median wage range	**W** Weekly
AW	Average wage paid	**FQ**	First quartile wage	**LO**	Lowest wage paid	**ME**	Median entry wage	**S** See annotated source	**Y** Yearly

Occupation/Type/Industry	Location	Per	Low	Mid	High	Source	Date
Education Administrator							
Preschool and Childcare Center/Program	Modesto MSA, CA	Y	36780 FQ	46150 MW	80080 TQ	USBLS	5/15
Preschool and Childcare Center/Program	Oakland-Hayward-Berkeley PMSA, CA	H	22.63 FQ	28.64 MW	34.54 TQ	CABLS	1/16-3/16
Preschool and Childcare Center/Program	Riverside-San Bernardino-Ontario MSA, CA	H	17.44 FQ	21.55 MW	31.89 TQ	CABLS	1/16-3/16
. Preschool and Childcare Center/Program	Sacramento–Roseville–Arden-Arcade MSA, CA	H	14.09 FQ	17.71 MW	23.51 TQ	CABLS	1/16-3/16
Preschool and Childcare Center/Program	San Diego-Carlsbad MSA, CA	H	21.19 FQ	28.85 MW	37.94 TQ	CABLS	1/16-3/16
Preschool and Childcare Center/Program	San Francisco-Redwood City-South San Francisco PMSA, CA	H	22.52 FQ	25.32 MW	31.22 TQ	CABLS	1/16-3/16
Preschool and Childcare Center/Program	Colorado	Y	32530 FQ	43190 MW	56970 TQ	USBLS	5/15
Preschool and Childcare Center/Program	Colorado Springs MSA, CO	Y	42940 FQ	48540 MW	55830 TQ	USBLS	5/15
Preschool and Childcare Center/Program	Denver-Aurora-Lakewood MSA, CO	Y	30890 FQ	39550 MW	55730 TQ	USBLS	5/15
Preschool and Childcare Center/Program	Connecticut	Y		52140 MW		CTBLS	1/16-3/16
Preschool and Childcare Center/Program	Bridgeport-Stamford-Norwalk MSA, CT	Y	55070 FQ	73510 MW	107230 TQ	USBLS	5/15
Preschool and Childcare Center/Program	Hartford-West Hartford-East Hartford MSA, CT	Y	30500 FQ	44520 MW	60370 TQ	USBLS	5/15
Preschool and Childcare Center/Program	Delaware	Y	40340 FQ	48190 MW	59370 TQ	USBLS	5/15
Preschool and Childcare Center/Program	Wilmington PMSA, DE-MD-NJ	Y	37900 FQ	47610 MW	58410 TQ	USBLS	5/15
Preschool and Childcare Center/Program	District of Columbia	Y	45680 FQ	60330 MW	77480 TQ	USBLS	5/15
Preschool and Childcare Center/Program	Washington-Arlington-Alexandria PMSA, DC-VA-MD-WV	Y	43490 FQ	55630 MW	70560 TQ	USBLS	5/15
Preschool and Childcare Center/Program	Florida	H	19.03 AE	28.81 MW	37.25 AEX	FLBLS	7/16-9/16
Preschool and Childcare Center/Program	Fort Lauderdale-Pompano Beach-Deerfield Beach PMSA, FL	H	16.99 AE	22.91 MW	26.66 AEX	FLBLS	7/16-9/16
Preschool and Childcare Center/Program	Miami-Miami Beach-Kendall PMSA, FL	H	21.24 AE	28.82 MW	34.71 AEX	FLBLS	7/16-9/16
Preschool and Childcare Center/Program	Tampa-St. Petersburg-Clearwater MSA, FL	H	16.91 AE	19.26 MW	28.02 AEX	FLBLS	7/16-9/16
Preschool and Childcare Center/Program	Georgia	Y	30740 FQ	37470 MW	56660 TQ	USBLS	5/15
Preschool and Childcare Center/Program	Atlanta-Sandy Springs-Roswell MSA, GA	Y	29950 FQ	35770 MW	47910 TQ	USBLS	5/15
Preschool and Childcare Center/Program	Augusta-Richmond County MSA, GA-SC	Y	30160 FQ	50650 MW	65090 TQ	USBLS	5/15
Preschool and Childcare Center/Program	Hawaii	Y	37400 FQ	45480 MW	61120 TQ	USBLS	5/15
Preschool and Childcare Center/Program	Urban Honolulu MSA, HI	Y	38500 FQ	46140 MW	60520 TQ	USBLS	5/15
Preschool and Childcare Center/Program	Idaho	Y	29220 FQ	37550 MW	65920 TQ	USBLS	5/15
Education Administrator	Boise City MSA, ID	Y	24690 FQ	38660 MW	85350 TQ	USBLS	5/15
Preschool and Childcare Center/Program	Illinois	Y	36630 FQ	47010 MW	61490 TQ	USBLS	5/15
Preschool and Childcare Center/Program	Chicago-Naperville-Arlington Heights PMSA, IL	Y	38890 FQ	49760 MW	62380 TQ	USBLS	5/15
Preschool and Childcare Center/Program	Indiana	Y	31450 FQ	37090 MW	50870 TQ	USBLS	5/15
Preschool and Childcare Center/Program	Gary PMSA, IN	Y	32940 FQ	38620 MW	55650 TQ	USBLS	5/15
Preschool and Childcare Center/Program	Indianapolis-Carmel-Anderson MSA, IN	Y	30770 FQ	35800 MW	48100 TQ	USBLS	5/15
Preschool and Childcare Center/Program	Iowa	Y	29430 FQ	36360 MW	45630 TQ	USBLS	5/15
Preschool and Childcare Center/Program	Des Moines-West Des Moines MSA, IA	Y	33790 FQ	37630 MW	48060 TQ	USBLS	5/15
Preschool and Childcare Center/Program	Kansas	Y	33050 FQ	38940 MW	55060 TQ	USBLS	5/15
Preschool and Childcare Center/Program	Wichita MSA, KS	Y	33950 FQ	38130 MW	46920 TQ	USBLS	5/15
Preschool and Childcare Center/Program	Kentucky	Y	31320 FQ	38910 MW	49400 TQ	USBLS	5/15
Preschool and Childcare Center/Program	Louisville-Jefferson County MSA, KY-IN	Y	38300 FQ	45010 MW	58090 TQ	USBLS	5/15
Preschool and Childcare Center/Program	Louisiana	Y	31350 FQ	39570 MW	52630 TQ	USBLS	5/15
Preschool and Childcare Center/Program	Baton Rouge MSA, LA	Y	31800 FQ	38030 MW	52920 TQ	USBLS	5/15
Preschool and Childcare Center/Program	New Orleans-Metairie MSA, LA	Y	39270 FQ	44970 MW	50360 TQ	USBLS	5/15
Preschool and Childcare Center/Program	Maine	Y	31480 FQ	37440 MW	47090 TQ	USBLS	5/15
Preschool and Childcare Center/Program	Portland-South Portland MSA, ME	Y	29860 FQ	35870 MW	48400 TQ	USBLS	5/15
Preschool and Childcare Center/Program	Maryland	Y	34038 AE	54867 MW	65282 AEX	MDBLS	4/16
Preschool and Childcare Center/Program	Baltimore-Columbia-Towson MSA, MD	Y	41870 FQ	49990 MW	73020 TQ	USBLS	5/15
Preschool and Childcare Center/Program	Salisbury MSA, MD-DE	Y	42050 FQ	46150 MW	50300 TQ	USBLS	5/15
Preschool and Childcare Center/Program	Massachusetts	Y	41020 FQ	57780 MW	75130 TQ	USBLS	5/15

AE	Average entry wage	AWR	Average wage range	H	Hourly	LR	Low end range	MTC	Median total compensation	TCC	Total cash compensation
AEX	Average experienced wage	B	Biweekly	HI	Highest wage paid	M	Monthly	MW	Median wage paid	TQ	Third quartile wage
ATC	Average total compensation	D	Daily	HR	High end range	MCC	Median cash compensation	MWR	Median wage range	W	Weekly
AW	Average wage paid	FQ	First quartile wage	LO	Lowest wage paid	ME	Median entry wage	S	See annotated source	Y	Yearly

Occupation/Type/Industry	Location	Per	Low	Mid	High	Source	Date
Education Administrator							
Preschool and Childcare Center/Program	Boston-Cambridge-Newton NECTA, MA	Y	50110 FQ	69460 MW	80200 TQ	USBLS	5/15
Preschool and Childcare Center/Program	Worcester MSA, MA-CT	Y	41810 FQ	54950 MW	72140 TQ	USBLS	5/15
Preschool and Childcare Center/Program	Michigan	Y	32600 FQ	41070 MW	52880 TQ	USBLS	5/15
Preschool and Childcare Center/Program	Detroit-Dearborn-Livonia PMSA, MI	Y	30350 FQ	42610 MW	50470 TQ	USBLS	5/15
Preschool and Childcare Center/Program	Grand Rapids-Wyoming MSA, MI	Y	31870 FQ	40480 MW	55500 TQ	USBLS	5/15
Preschool and Childcare Center/Program	Minnesota	Y	40776 FQ	52512 MW	61860 TQ	MNBLS	1/16-3/16
Preschool and Childcare Center/Program	Minneapolis-St. Paul-Bloomington MSA, MN-WI	Y	42788 FQ	53640 MW	61850 TQ	MNBLS	1/16-3/16
Preschool and Childcare Center/Program	Mississippi	Y	27940 FQ	39800 MW	55400 TQ	USBLS	5/15
Preschool and Childcare Center/Program	Jackson MSA, MS	Y	24630 FQ	39630 MW	54560 TQ	USBLS	5/15
Preschool and Childcare Center/Program	Missouri	Y	34670 FQ	41180 MW	59320 TQ	USBLS	5/15
Preschool and Childcare Center/Program	Kansas City MSA, MO-KS	Y	30750 FQ	39270 MW	63240 TQ	USBLS	5/15
Preschool and Childcare Center/Program	St. Louis MSA, MO-IL	Y	34220 FQ	38960 MW	52490 TQ	USBLS	5/15
Preschool and Childcare Center/Program	Montana	Y	32250 FQ	36700 MW	44870 TQ	USBLS	5/15
Preschool and Childcare Center/Program	Nebraska	Y	35945 FQ	45305 MW	59300 TQ	NEBLS	7/16-9/16
Preschool and Childcare Center/Program	Omaha-Council Bluffs MSA, NE-IA	Y	34755 FQ	42640 MW	55085 TQ	NEBLS	7/16-9/16
Preschool and Childcare Center/Program	Nevada	Y	38130 FQ	43990 MW	48970 TQ	USBLS	5/15
Preschool and Childcare Center/Program	Las Vegas-Henderson-Paradise MSA, NV	Y	40670 FQ	45200 MW	50060 TQ	USBLS	5/15
Preschool and Childcare Center/Program	New Hampshire	H	16.21 AE	20.44 MW	24.71 AEX	NHBLS	6/16
Preschool and Childcare Center/Program	Manchester NECTA, NH	H	17.44 AE	18.66 MW	24.96 AEX	NHBLS	6/16
Preschool and Childcare Center/Program	Nashua NECTA, NH-MA	Y	39730 FQ	44130 MW	48530 TQ	USBLS	5/15
Preschool and Childcare Center/Program	New Jersey	Y	40620 FQ	49210 MW	74350 TQ	USBLS	5/15
Preschool and Childcare Center/Program	Camden PMSA, NJ	Y	39530 FQ	46130 MW	66420 TQ	USBLS	5/15
Preschool and Childcare Center/Program	Newark PMSA, NJ-PA	Y	43490 FQ	59630 MW	90990 TQ	USBLS	5/15
Preschool and Childcare Center/Program	Trenton MSA, NJ	Y	49580 FQ	57530 MW	68290 TQ	USBLS	5/15
Preschool and Childcare Center/Program	New Mexico	Y	33370 FQ	41080 MW	66610 TQ	USBLS	5/15
Preschool and Childcare Center/Program	Albuquerque MSA, NM	Y	33340 FQ	39170 MW	61200 TQ	USBLS	5/15
Preschool and Childcare Center/Program	New York	Y	36480 AE	57960 MW	80810 AEX	NYBLS	1/16-3/16
Preschool and Childcare Center/Program	Buffalo-Cheektowaga-Niagara Falls MSA, NY	Y	32150 FQ	37710 MW	46230 TQ	USBLS	5/15
Preschool and Childcare Center/Program	Nassau County-Suffolk County PMSA, NY	Y	35890 FQ	52600 MW	80840 TQ	USBLS	5/15
Preschool and Childcare Center/Program	New York-Jersey City-White Plains PMSA, NY-NJ	Y	46460 FQ	61160 MW	85360 TQ	USBLS	5/15
Preschool and Childcare Center/Program	Rochester MSA, NY	Y	35350 FQ	50530 MW	63600 TQ	USBLS	5/15
Preschool and Childcare Center/Program	North Carolina	Y	35940 FQ	44770 MW	56030 TQ	USBLS	5/15
Preschool and Childcare Center/Program	Charlotte-Concord-Gastonia MSA, NC-SC	Y	38150 FQ	49000 MW	58840 TQ	USBLS	5/15
Preschool and Childcare Center/Program	Raleigh MSA, NC	Y	38120 FQ	44910 MW	53060 TQ	USBLS	5/15
Preschool and Childcare Center/Program	North Dakota	Y	33900 FQ	37620 MW	44560 TQ	USBLS	5/15
Preschool and Childcare Center/Program	Fargo MSA, ND-MN	Y	34450 FQ	38550 MW	45990 TQ	USBLS	5/15
Preschool and Childcare Center/Program	Ohio	Y	30660 FQ	36970 MW	44830 TQ	USBLS	5/15
Preschool and Childcare Center/Program	Cincinnati MSA, OH-KY-IN	Y	29620 FQ	36410 MW	44260 TQ	USBLS	5/15
Preschool and Childcare Center/Program	Cleveland-Elyria MSA, OH	Y	30390 FQ	38580 MW	46110 TQ	USBLS	5/15
Preschool and Childcare Center/Program	Columbus MSA, OH	Y	32340 FQ	36620 MW	42830 TQ	USBLS	5/15
Preschool and Childcare Center/Program	Oklahoma	Y	28880 FQ	40120 MW	56580 TQ	USBLS	5/15
Preschool and Childcare Center/Program	Oklahoma City MSA, OK	Y	29240 FQ	42120 MW	60420 TQ	USBLS	5/15
Preschool and Childcare Center/Program	Tulsa MSA, OK	Y	27620 FQ	41370 MW	51360 TQ	USBLS	5/15
Preschool and Childcare Center/Program	Oregon	H	14.70 FQ	18.31 MW	23.26 TQ	ORBLS	2016
Preschool and Childcare Center/Program	Portland-Vancouver-Hillsboro MSA, OR-WA	Y	31850 FQ	37940 MW	46460 TQ	USBLS	5/15
Preschool and Childcare Center/Program	Pennsylvania	Y	34160 FQ	42490 MW	54300 TQ	USBLS	5/15
Preschool and Childcare Center/Program	Allentown-Bethlehem-Easton MSA, PA-NJ	Y	30160 FQ	41650 MW	47610 TQ	USBLS	5/15
Preschool and Childcare Center/Program	Harrisburg-Carlisle MSA, PA	Y	25910 FQ	32160 MW	37240 TQ	USBLS	5/15
Preschool and Childcare Center/Program	Montgomery County-Bucks County-Chester County PMSA, PA	Y	35030 FQ	39560 MW	47730 TQ	USBLS	5/15
Preschool and Childcare Center/Program	Philadelphia PMSA, PA	Y	44870 FQ	54270 MW	62020 TQ	USBLS	5/15
Preschool and Childcare Center/Program	Pittsburgh MSA, PA	Y	36670 FQ	46370 MW	59330 TQ	USBLS	5/15
Preschool and Childcare Center/Program	State College MSA, PA	Y	37000 FQ	44410 MW	56130 TQ	USBLS	5/15
Preschool and Childcare Center/Program	Rhode Island	Y	46080 FQ	58990 MW	92010 TQ	USBLS	5/15
Preschool and Childcare Center/Program	Providence-Warwick MSA, RI-MA	Y	38450 FQ	52920 MW	85780 TQ	USBLS	5/15
Preschool and Childcare Center/Program	South Carolina	Y	27000 FQ	37820 MW	70560 TQ	USBLS	5/15

AE	Average entry wage	AWR	Average wage range	H	Hourly
AEX	Average experienced wage	B	Biweekly	HI	Highest wage paid
ATC	Average total compensation	D	Daily	HR	High end wage paid
AW	Average wage paid	FQ	First quartile wage	LO	Lowest wage paid

LR	Low end range	MTC	Median total compensation	TCC	Total cash compensation
M	Monthly	MW	Median wage paid	TQ	Third quartile wage
MCC	Median cash compensation	MWR	Median wage range	W	Weekly
ME	Median entry wage	S	See annotated source	Y	Yearly

Occupation/Type/Industry	Location	Per	Low	Mid	High	Source	Date
Education Administrator							
Preschool and Childcare Center/Program	Charleston-North Charleston MSA, SC	Y	21290 FQ	27530 MW	49290 TQ	USBLS	5/15
Preschool and Childcare Center/Program	Columbia MSA, SC	Y	19320 FQ	30690 MW	68500 TQ	USBLS	5/15
Preschool and Childcare Center/Program	Greenville-Anderson-Mauldin MSA, SC	Y	31980 FQ	65070 MW	72830 TQ	USBLS	5/15
Preschool and Childcare Center/Program	South Dakota	Y	45320 FQ	53940 MW	60060 TQ	USBLS	5/15
Preschool and Childcare Center/Program	Tennessee	Y	29890 FQ	36780 MW	46190 TQ	USBLS	5/15
Preschool and Childcare Center/Program	Knoxville MSA, TN	Y	34180 FQ	38000 MW	43700 TQ	USBLS	5/15
Preschool and Childcare Center/Program	Memphis MSA, TN-MS-AR	Y	33950 FQ	40460 MW	51410 TQ	USBLS	5/15
Preschool and Childcare Center/Program	Nashville-Davidson–Murfreesboro–Franklin MSA, TN	Y	23590 FQ	31400 MW	48170 TQ	USBLS	5/15
Preschool and Childcare Center/Program	Texas	Y	35070 FQ	45200 MW	60610 TQ	USBLS	5/15
Preschool and Childcare Center/Program	Austin-Round Rock MSA, TX	Y	37340 FQ	45670 MW	55530 TQ	USBLS	5/15
Preschool and Childcare Center/Program	Dallas-Plano-Irving PMSA, TX	Y	31450 FQ	40240 MW	57360 TQ	USBLS	5/15
Preschool and Childcare Center/Program	Fort Worth-Arlington PMSA, TX	Y	40930 FQ	59140 MW	163340 TQ	USBLS	5/15
Preschool and Childcare Center/Program	Houston-The Woodlands-Sugar Land MSA, TX	Y	37860 FQ	45940 MW	65950 TQ	USBLS	5/15
Preschool and Childcare Center/Program	San Antonio-New Braunfels MSA, TX	Y	31650 FQ	37800 MW	50810 TQ	USBLS	5/15
Preschool and Childcare Center/Program	Utah	Y	26830 FQ	37780 MW	51240 TQ	USBLS	5/15
Preschool and Childcare Center/Program	Ogden-Clearfield MSA, UT	Y	24890 FQ	34260 MW	46650 TQ	USBLS	5/15
Preschool and Childcare Center/Program	Salt Lake City MSA, UT	Y	24900 FQ	34030 MW	46000 TQ	USBLS	5/15
Preschool and Childcare Center/Program	Vermont	Y	36160 FQ	43990 MW	50070 TQ	USBLS	5/15
Preschool and Childcare Center/Program	Burlington-South Burlington MSA, VT	Y	28460 FQ	41230 MW	48630 TQ	USBLS	5/15
Preschool and Childcare Center/Program	Virginia	Y	39300 FQ	54280 MW	69950 TQ	USBLS	5/15
Preschool and Childcare Center/Program	Richmond MSA, VA	Y	50070 FQ	61950 MW	74110 TQ	USBLS	5/15
Preschool and Childcare Center/Program	Virginia Beach-Norfolk-Newport News MSA, VA-NC	Y	34060 FQ	37230 MW	45160 TQ	USBLS	5/15
Preschool and Childcare Center/Program	Washington	H	16.79 FQ	19.68 MW	26.72 TQ	WABLS	3/16
Preschool and Childcare Center/Program	Seattle-Bellevue-Everett PMSA, WA	H	16.70 FQ	19.20 MW	27.27 TQ	WABLS	3/16
Preschool and Childcare Center/Program	Tacoma-Lakewood PMSA, WA	H	15.65 FQ	17.37 MW	19.08 TQ	WABLS	3/16
Preschool and Childcare Center/Program	West Virginia	Y	32320 FQ	37360 MW	50200 TQ	USBLS	5/15
Preschool and Childcare Center/Program	Huntington-Ashland MSA, WV-KY-OH	Y	32230 FQ	37170 MW	45850 TQ	USBLS	5/15
Preschool and Childcare Center/Program	Wisconsin	Y	33160 FQ	42780 MW	54710 TQ	USBLS	5/15
Preschool and Childcare Center/Program	Madison MSA, WI	Y	32720 FQ	38560 MW	51820 TQ	USBLS	5/15
Preschool and Childcare Center/Program	Milwaukee-Waukesha-West Allis MSA, WI	Y	31970 FQ	48650 MW	57730 TQ	USBLS	5/15
Preschool and Childcare Center/Program	Wyoming	Y	32830 FQ	49580 MW	61400 TQ	USBLS	5/15
Preschool and Childcare Center/Program	Puerto Rico	Y	20390 FQ	29840 MW	43360 TQ	USBLS	5/15
Preschool and Childcare Center/Program	San Juan-Carolina-Caguas MSA, PR	Y	21100 FQ	35860 MW	46120 TQ	USBLS	5/15
Education Services Worker	United States	Y		69965 AW		IWRLD	2016
Education Teacher							
Postsecondary	Alabama	Y	44840 AE	75440 AW	90740 AEX	ALBLS	6/16
Postsecondary	Birmingham-Hoover MSA, AL	Y	51027 AE	73779 AW	85154 AEX	ALBLS	6/16
Postsecondary	Alaska	Y	66600 FQ	79440 MW	94160 TQ	USBLS	5/15
Postsecondary	Arizona	Y	43010 FQ	60490 MW	82730 TQ	USBLS	5/15
Postsecondary	Phoenix-Mesa-Scottsdale MSA, AZ	Y	43120 FQ	60050 MW	81880 TQ	USBLS	5/15
Postsecondary	Arkansas	Y	43790 FQ	57310 MW	75050 TQ	USBLS	5/15
Postsecondary	Little Rock-North Little Rock-Conway MSA, AR	Y	41770 FQ	55990 MW	73160 TQ	USBLS	5/15
Postsecondary	California	Y		78877 AW		CABLS	1/16-3/16
Postsecondary	Anaheim-Santa Ana-Irvine PMSA, CA	Y		81545 AW		CABLS	1/16-3/16
Postsecondary	Los Angeles-Long Beach-Glendale PMSA, CA	Y		78126 AW		CABLS	1/16-3/16
Postsecondary	Riverside-San Bernardino-Ontario MSA, CA	Y		79536 AW		CABLS	1/16-3/16
Postsecondary	Sacramento–Roseville–Arden-Arcade MSA, CA	Y		75154 AW		CABLS	1/16-3/16
Postsecondary	San Diego-Carlsbad MSA, CA	Y		81819 AW		CABLS	1/16-3/16

AE	Average entry wage	AWR	Average wage range	H	Hourly	LR	Low end range	MTC	Median total compensation
AEX	Average experienced wage	B	Biweekly	HI	Highest wage paid	M	Monthly	MCC	Median cash compensation
ATC	Average total compensation	D	Daily	HR	High end range	MCC	Median cash compensation	MWR	Median wage range
AW	Average wage paid	FQ	First quartile wage	LO	Lowest wage paid	ME	Median entry wage	S	See annotated source

TCC Total cash compensation
TQ Third quartile wage
W Weekly
Y Yearly

Occupation/Type/Industry	Location	Per	Low	Mid	High	Source	Date
Education Teacher							
Postsecondary	San Francisco-Redwood City-South San Francisco PMSA, CA	Y		75062 AW		CABLS	1/16-3/16
Postsecondary	Colorado	Y	34410 FQ	54350 MW	77500 TQ	USBLS	5/15
Postsecondary	Denver-Aurora-Lakewood MSA, CO	Y	25890 FQ	52160 MW	81090 TQ	USBLS	5/15
Postsecondary	Connecticut	Y		64217 MW		CTBLS	1/16-3/16
Postsecondary	Bridgeport-Stamford-Norwalk MSA, CT	Y	56570 FQ	68490 MW	87510 TQ	USBLS	5/15
Postsecondary	Hartford-West Hartford-East Hartford MSA, CT	Y	54940 FQ	61320 MW	75080 TQ	USBLS	5/15
Postsecondary	Delaware	Y	50320 FQ	69290 MW	89250 TQ	USBLS	5/15
Postsecondary	Wilmington PMSA, DE-MD-NJ	Y	52110 FQ	70970 MW	90790 TQ	USBLS	5/15
Postsecondary	District of Columbia	Y	43890 FQ	56960 MW	74600 TQ	USBLS	5/15
Postsecondary	Washington-Arlington-Alexandria PMSA, DC-VA-MD-WV	Y	48130 FQ	62750 MW	84780 TQ	USBLS	5/15
Postsecondary	Florida	Y	37841 AE	70564 MW	92815 AEX	FLBLS	7/16-9/16
Postsecondary	Miami-Miami Beach-Kendall PMSA, FL	Y	28956 AE	63269 MW	82092 AEX	FLBLS	7/16-9/16
Postsecondary	Orlando-Kissimmee-Sanford MSA, FL	Y	29583 AE	67001 MW	90964 AEX	FLBLS	7/16-9/16
Postsecondary	Tampa-St. Petersburg-Clearwater MSA, FL	Y	44732 AE	72479 MW	90013 AEX	FLBLS	7/16-9/16
Postsecondary	Georgia	Y	38460 FQ	52670 MW	70320 TQ	USBLS	5/15
Postsecondary	Atlanta-Sandy Springs-Roswell MSA, GA	Y	35640 FQ	43760 MW	60160 TQ	USBLS	5/15
Postsecondary	Hawaii	Y	54750 FQ	67550 MW	80170 TQ	USBLS	5/15
Postsecondary	Urban Honolulu MSA, HI	Y	54650 FQ	67820 MW	80900 TQ	USBLS	5/15
Postsecondary	Idaho	Y	42800 FQ	54760 MW	68050 FQ	USBLS	5/15
Postsecondary	Boise City MSA, ID	Y	40920 FQ	52220 MW	63280 TQ	USBLS	5/15
Postsecondary	Illinois	Y	47250 FQ	61540 MW	86560 TQ	USBLS	5/15
Postsecondary	Chicago-Naperville-Arlington Heights PMSA, IL	Y	47990 FQ	59520 MW	77090 TQ	USBLS	5/15
Postsecondary	Lake County-Kenosha County PMSA, IL-WI	Y	42150 FQ	53430 MW	84120 TQ	USBLS	5/15
Postsecondary	Indiana	Y	43880 FQ	58550 MW	77480 TQ	USBLS	5/15
Postsecondary	Indianapolis-Carmel-Anderson MSA, IN	Y	44030 FQ	56040 MW	76030 TQ	USBLS	5/15
Postsecondary	Iowa	Y	52640 FQ	65700 MW	80280 TQ	USBLS	5/15
Postsecondary	Des Moines-West Des Moines MSA, IA	Y	55280 FQ	65560 MW	77470 TQ	USBLS	5/15
Postsecondary	Kansas	Y	30530 FQ	45410 MW	61400 TQ	USBLS	5/15
Postsecondary	Kentucky	Y	50150 FQ	65270 MW	80400 TQ	USBLS	5/15
Postsecondary	Louisville-Jefferson County MSA, KY-IN	Y	47850 FQ	63920 MW	79300 TQ	USBLS	5/15
Postsecondary	Louisiana	Y	48440 FQ	59240 MW	72260 TQ	USBLS	5/15
Postsecondary	New Orleans-Metairie MSA, LA	Y	18510 FQ	50800 MW	60190 TQ	USBLS	5/15
Postsecondary	Maine	Y	45860 FQ	58400 MW	73900 TQ	USBLS	5/15
Postsecondary	Portland-South Portland MSA, ME	Y	46340 FQ	58380 MW	76380 TQ	USBLS	5/15
Postsecondary	Maryland	Y	39375 AE	67704 MW	81869 AEX	MDBLS	4/16
Postsecondary	Baltimore-Columbia-Towson MSA, MD	Y	45370 FQ	59660 MW	87840 TQ	USBLS	5/15
Postsecondary	Salisbury MSA, MD-DE	Y	36530 FQ	57030 MW	72670 TQ	USBLS	5/15
Postsecondary	Massachusetts	Y	46190 FQ	64910 MW	93010 TQ	USBLS	5/15
Postsecondary	Boston-Cambridge-Newton NECTA, MA	Y	52020 FQ	73460 MW	112690 TQ	USBLS	5/15
Postsecondary	Worcester MSA, MA-CT	Y	55740 FQ	66490 MW	78650 TQ	USBLS	5/15
Postsecondary	Michigan	Y	47050 FQ	66530 MW	88680 TQ	USBLS	5/15
Postsecondary	Detroit-Dearborn-Livonia PMSA, MI	Y	49320 FQ	62760 MW	78720 TQ	USBLS	5/15
Postsecondary	Grand Rapids-Wyoming MSA, MI	Y	40200 FQ	55160 MW	72050 TQ	USBLS	5/15
Postsecondary	Minnesota	Y	37752 FQ	55019 MW	71189 TQ	MNBLS	1/16-3/16
Postsecondary	Minneapolis-St. Paul-Bloomington MSA, MN-WI	Y	40645 FQ	55352 MW	71007 TQ	MNBLS	1/16-3/16
Postsecondary	Mississippi	Y	50600 FQ	59420 MW	75650 TQ	USBLS	5/15
Postsecondary	Jackson MSA, MS	Y	33790 FQ	47440 MW	76770 TQ	USBLS	5/15

AE	Average entry wage	AWR	Average wage range	H	Hourly	LR	Low end range	MTC	Median total compensation	TCC	Total cash compensation
AEX	Average experienced wage	B	Biweekly	HI	Highest wage paid	M	Monthly	MW	Median wage paid	TQ	Third quartile wage
ATC	Average total compensation	D	Daily	HR	High end range	MCC	Median cash compensation	*MWR	Median wage range	W	Weekly
AW	Average wage paid	FQ	First quartile wage	LO	Lowest wage paid	ME	Median entry wage	S	See annotated source	Y	Yearly

Education Teacher

Occupation/Type/Industry	Location	Per	Low	Mid	High	Source	Date
Postsecondary	Missouri	Y	39560 FQ	59210 MW	80330 TQ	USBLS	5/15
Postsecondary	Kansas City MSA, MO-KS	Y	48160 FQ	78450 MW	102630 TQ	USBLS	5/15
Postsecondary	St. Louis MSA, MO-IL	Y	29960 FQ	51110 MW	73650 TQ	USBLS	5/15
Postsecondary	Montana	Y	31270 FQ	45460 MW	59410 TQ	USBLS	5/15
Postsecondary	Nebraska	Y	44330 FQ	58565 MW	78235 TQ	NEBLS	7/16-9/16
Postsecondary	Omaha-Council Bluffs MSA, NE-IA	Y	31090 FQ	53285 MW	68165 TQ	NEBLS	7/16-9/16
Postsecondary	Nevada	Y	36930 FQ	56630 MW	80630 TQ	USBLS	5/15
Postsecondary	Las Vegas-Henderson-Paradise MSA, NV	Y	56450 FQ	70830 MW	93100 TQ	USBLS	5/15
Postsecondary	New Hampshire	Y	52435 FQ	68827 MW	81524 AEX	NHBLS	6/16
Postsecondary	Manchester NECTA, NH	Y	50377 AE	59464 MW	65920 AEX	NHBLS	6/16
Postsecondary	New Jersey	Y	49110 FQ	67430 MW	90920 TQ	USBLS	5/15
Postsecondary	Newark PMSA, NJ-PA	Y	54150 FQ	73500 MW	98360 TQ	USBLS	5/15
Postsecondary	New Mexico	Y	50200 FQ	64430 MW	80650 TQ	USBLS	5/15
Postsecondary	Albuquerque MSA, NM	Y	65500 FQ	80190 MW	93110 TQ	USBLS	5/15
Postsecondary	New York	Y	41220 AE	64630 MW	99980 AEX	NYBLS	1/16-3/16
Postsecondary	Buffalo-Cheektowaga-Niagara Falls MSA, NY	Y	36960 FQ	52250 MW	71770 TQ	USBLS	5/15
Postsecondary	Nassau County-Suffolk County PMSA, NY	Y	48140 FQ	57680 MW	79010 TQ	USBLS	5/15
Postsecondary	New York-Jersey City-White Plains PMSA, NY-NJ	Y	51190 FQ	78360 MW	136160 TQ	USBLS	5/15
Postsecondary	Rochester MSA, NY	Y	49390 FQ	76030 MW	110370 TQ	USBLS	5/15
Postsecondary	North Carolina	Y	50140 FQ	61810 MW	76880 TQ	USBLS	5/15
Postsecondary	Charlotte-Concord-Gastonia MSA, NC-SC	Y	50410 FQ	61280 MW	75520 TQ	USBLS	5/15
Postsecondary	Raleigh MSA, NC	Y	50600 FQ	64000 MW	81580 TQ	USBLS	5/15
Postsecondary	North Dakota	Y	52290 FQ	77990 MW	97980 TQ	USBLS	5/15
Postsecondary	Fargo MSA, ND-MN	Y	54730 FQ	75950 MW	94810 TQ	USBLS	5/15
Postsecondary	Ohio	Y	41870 FQ	61020 MW	89090 TQ	USBLS	5/15
Postsecondary	Cincinnati MSA, OH-KY-IN	Y	48680 FQ	69380 MW	93530 TQ	USBLS	5/15
Postsecondary	Cleveland-Elyria MSA, OH	Y	45320 FQ	67840 MW	93510 TQ	USBLS	5/15
Postsecondary	Columbus MSA, OH	Y	50150 FQ	68750 MW	99930 TQ	USBLS	5/15
Postsecondary	Oklahoma	Y	39710 FQ	50980 MW	64710 TQ	USBLS	5/15
Postsecondary	Oklahoma City MSA, OK	Y	37100 FQ	48160 MW	64770 TQ	USBLS	5/15
Postsecondary	Tulsa MSA, OK	Y	49050 FQ	57740 MW	66670 TQ	USBLS	5/15
Postsecondary	Oregon	Y	52511 FQ	67178 MW	82853 TQ	ORBLS	2016
Postsecondary	Portland-Vancouver-Hillsboro MSA, OR-WA	Y	55220 FQ	67850 MW	82320 TQ	USBLS	5/15
Postsecondary	Pennsylvania	Y	47840 FQ	62520 MW	84270 TQ	USBLS	5/15
Postsecondary	Allentown-Bethlehem-Easton MSA, PA-NJ	Y	43760 FQ	62610 MW	99700 TQ	USBLS	5/15
Postsecondary	Harrisburg-Carlisle MSA, PA	Y	53620 FQ	63210 MW	77380 TQ	USBLS	5/15
Postsecondary	Montgomery County-Bucks County-Chester County PMSA, PA	Y	40540 FQ	53330 MW	75190 TQ	USBLS	5/15
Postsecondary	Philadelphia PMSA, PA	Y	51540 FQ	67510 MW	92210 TQ	USBLS	5/15
Postsecondary	Pittsburgh MSA, PA	Y	45040 FQ	58220 MW	76060 TQ	USBLS	5/15
Postsecondary	Rhode Island	Y	57570 FQ	74130 MW	94800 TQ	USBLS	5/15
Postsecondary	Providence-Warwick MSA, RI-MA	Y	57460 FQ	73310 MW	93630 TQ	USBLS	5/15
Postsecondary	South Carolina	Y	41130 FQ	56870 MW	72910 TQ	USBLS	5/15
Postsecondary	Columbia MSA, SC	Y	36170 FQ	53750 MW	73750 TQ	USBLS	5/15
Postsecondary	Greenville-Anderson-Mauldin MSA, SC	Y	53300 FQ	63940 MW	77970 TQ	USBLS	5/15
Postsecondary	South Dakota	Y	49790 FQ	59420 MW	73820 TQ	USBLS	5/15
Postsecondary	Sioux Falls MSA, SD	Y	50770 FQ	58980 MW	70850 TQ	USBLS	5/15
Postsecondary	Tennessee	Y	34570 FQ	54740 MW	73850 TQ	USBLS	5/15
Postsecondary	Knoxville MSA, TN	Y	38890 FQ	53400 MW	84990 TQ	USBLS	5/15
Postsecondary	Memphis MSA, TN-MS-AR	Y	32730 FQ	58680 MW	76830 TQ	USBLS	5/15
Postsecondary	Nashville-Davidson–Murfreesboro–Franklin MSA, TN	Y	37390 FQ	57090 MW	75260 TQ	USBLS	5/15
Postsecondary	Texas	Y	27720 FQ	59990 MW	78020 TQ	USBLS	5/15
Postsecondary	Austin-Round Rock MSA, TX	Y	29850 FQ	59020 MW	75870 TQ	USBLS	5/15
Postsecondary	Dallas-Plano-Irving PMSA, TX	Y	18570 FQ	54560 MW	72710 TQ	USBLS	5/15
Postsecondary	Fort Worth-Arlington PMSA, TX	Y	49580 FQ	58070 MW	72630 TQ	USBLS	5/15
Postsecondary	Houston-The Woodlands-Sugar Land MSA, TX	Y	31650 FQ	64020 MW	77590 TQ	USBLS	5/15

AE	Average entry wage	AWR	Average wage range	H	Hourly
AEX	Average experienced wage	B	Biweekly	HI	Highest wage paid
ATC	Average total compensation	D	Daily	HR	High end range
AW	Average wage paid	FQ	First quartile wage	LO	Lowest wage paid

LR	Low end range	MTC	Median total compensation	TCC	Total cash compensation
M	Monthly	MW	Median wage paid	TQ	Third quartile wage
MCC	Median cash compensation	MWR	Median wage range	W	Weekly
ME	Median entry wage	S	See annotated source	Y	Yearly

Occupation/Type/Industry	Location	Per	Low	Mid	High	Source	Date
Education Teacher							
Postsecondary	San Antonio-New Braunfels MSA, TX	Y	19760 FQ	43610 MW	74000 TQ	USBLS	5/15
Postsecondary	Utah	Y	50350 FQ	63240 MW	84350 TQ	USBLS	5/15
Postsecondary	Salt Lake City MSA, UT	Y	48250 FQ	60320 MW	76290 TQ	USBLS	5/15
Postsecondary	Vermont	Y	43130 FQ	53710 MW	73490 TQ	USBLS	5/15
Postsecondary	Burlington-South Burlington MSA, VT	Y	45290 FQ	57900 MW	81100 TQ	USBLS	5/15
Postsecondary	Virginia	Y	38680 FQ	57480 MW	76530 TQ	USBLS	5/15
Postsecondary	Virginia Beach-Norfolk-Newport News MSA, VA-NC	Y	41670 FQ	57220 MW	74200 TQ	USBLS	5/15
Postsecondary	Washington	Y		69513 AW		WABLS	3/16
Postsecondary	Seattle-Bellevue-Everett PMSA, WA	Y		83909 AW		WABLS	3/16
Postsecondary	Tacoma-Lakewood PMSA, WA	Y		64420 AW		WABLS	3/16
Postsecondary	West Virginia	Y	39030 FQ	52300 MW	68500 TQ	USBLS	5/15
Postsecondary	Huntington-Ashland MSA, WV-KY-OH	Y	40060 FQ	49730 MW	69790 TQ	USBLS	5/15
Postsecondary	Wisconsin	Y	40620 FQ	58850 MW	80560 TQ	USBLS	5/15
Postsecondary	Madison MSA, WI	Y	59690 FQ	78290 MW	99690 TQ	USBLS	5/15
Postsecondary	Wyoming	Y	53240 FQ	61340 MW	72300 TQ	USBLS	5/15
Postsecondary	Puerto Rico	Y	19150 FQ	38370 MW	64260 TQ	USBLS	5/15
Postsecondary	San Juan-Carolina-Caguas MSA, PR	Y	19120 FQ	38890 MW	66670 TQ	USBLS	5/15
Educational, Guidance, School, and Vocational Counselor	Alabama	Y	37236 AE	52872 AW	60701 AEX	ALBLS	6/16
	Birmingham-Hoover MSA, AL	Y	35156 AE	52505 AW	61180 AEX	ALBLS	6/16
	Alaska	Y	55100 FQ	70010 MW	87090 TQ	USBLS	5/15
	Anchorage MSA, AK	Y	53820 FQ	68760 MW	87130 TQ	USBLS	5/15
	Arizona	Y	36760 FQ	44430 MW	52460 TQ	USBLS	5/15
	Phoenix-Mesa-Scottsdale MSA, AZ	Y	40120 FQ	46020 MW	54710 TQ	USBLS	5/15
	Tucson MSA, AZ	Y	31680 FQ	37640 MW	45780 TQ	USBLS	5/15
	Arkansas	Y	41580 FQ	51780 MW	61200 TQ	USBLS	5/15
	Little Rock-North Little Rock-Conway MSA, AR	Y	39780 FQ	49130 MW	62020 TQ	USBLS	5/15
	California	H	21.32 FQ	29.03 MW	40.76 TQ	CABLS	1/16-3/16
	Anaheim-Santa Ana-Irvine PMSA, CA	H	22.27 FQ	28.91 MW	43.50 TQ	CABLS	1/16-3/16
	Los Angeles-Long Beach-Glendale PMSA, CA	H	21.42 FQ	30.62 MW	42.03 TQ	CABLS	1/16-3/16
	Oakland-Hayward-Berkeley PMSA, CA	H	22.57 FQ	27.24 MW	34.94 TQ	CABLS	1/16-3/16
	Riverside-San Bernardino-Ontario MSA, CA	H	22.35 FQ	34.52 MW	43.80 TQ	CABLS	1/16-3/16
	Sacramento–Roseville–Arden-Arcade MSA, CA	H	20.80 FQ	30.56 MW	39.68 TQ	CABLS	1/16-3/16
	San Diego-Carlsbad MSA, CA	H	21.29 FQ	27.79 MW	39.90 TQ	CABLS	1/16-3/16
	San Francisco-Redwood City-South San Francisco PMSA, CA	H	24.21 FQ	29.29 MW	40.62 TQ	CABLS	1/16-3/16
	Yuba City MSA, CA	H	27.33 FQ	32.48 MW	37.13 TQ	CABLS	1/16-3/16
	Colorado	Y	38230 FQ	46690 MW	58670 TQ	USBLS	5/15
	Denver-Aurora-Lakewood MSA, CO	Y	36580 FQ	46810 MW	61830 TQ	USBLS	5/15
	Connecticut	Y		57968 MW		CTBLS	1/16-3/16
	Bridgeport-Stamford-Norwalk MSA, CT	Y	28370 FQ	51710 MW	80560 TQ	USBLS	5/15
	Hartford-West Hartford-East Hartford MSA, CT	Y	41950 FQ	57120 MW	77090 TQ	USBLS	5/15
	Delaware	Y	46480 FQ	64010 MW	75390 TQ	USBLS	5/15
	Wilmington PMSA, DE-MD-NJ	Y	45320 FQ	61940 MW	75240 TQ	USBLS	5/15
	District of Columbia	Y	49090 FQ	59370 MW	75840 TQ	USBLS	5/15
	Washington-Arlington-Alexandria PMSA, DC-VA-MD-WV	Y	50920 FQ	64030 MW	84350 TQ	USBLS	5/15
	Florida	H	16.00 AE	25.82 MW	32.17 AEX	FLBLS	7/16-9/16
	Fort Lauderdale-Pompano Beach-Deerfield Beach PMSA, FL	H	8.79 AE	19.19 MW	28.59 AEX	FLBLS	7/16-9/16

AE Average entry wage	**AWR** Average wage range	**H** Hourly	**LR** Low end range	**MTC** Median total compensation	**TCC** Total cash compensation
AEX Average experienced wage	**B** Biweekly	**HI** Highest wage paid	**M** Monthly	**MW** Median wage paid	**TQ** Third quartile wage
ATC Average total compensation	**D** Daily	**HR** High end range	**MCC** Median cash compensation	**MWR** Median wage range	**W** Weekly
AW Average wage paid	**FQ** First quartile wage	**LO** Lowest wage paid	**ME** Median entry wage	**S** See annotated source	**Y** Yearly

Occupation/Type/Industry	Location	Per	Low	Mid	High	Source	Date
Educational, Guidance, School, and Vocational Counselor	Miami-Miami Beach-Kendall PMSA, FL	H	15.73 AE	26.71 MW	34.99 AEX	FLBLS	7/16-9/16
	Orlando-Kissimmee-Sanford MSA, FL	H	18.84 AE	24.99 MW	30.62 AEX	FLBLS	7/16-9/16
	Tampa-St. Petersburg-Clearwater MSA, FL	H	17.84 AE	26.49 MW	32.50 AEX	FLBLS	7/16-9/16
	Georgia	Y	41820 FQ	54990 MW	69810 TQ	USBLS	5/15
	Atlanta-Sandy Springs-Roswell MSA, GA	Y	43670 FQ	57030 MW	72390 TQ	USBLS	5/15
	Augusta-Richmond County MSA, GA-SC	Y	38120 FQ	50320 MW	68720 TQ	USBLS	5/15
	Hawaii	Y	41720 FQ	53210 MW	62530 TQ	USBLS	5/15
	Urban Honolulu MSA, HI	Y	42360 FQ	53980 MW	62900 TQ	USBLS	5/15
	Idaho	Y	33540 FQ	37820 MW	51870 TQ	USBLS	5/15
	Boise City MSA, ID	Y	34320 FQ	41680 MW	58620 TQ	USBLS	5/15
	Illinois	Y	38030 FQ	53180 MW	75420 TQ	USBLS	5/15
	Chicago-Naperville-Arlington Heights PMSA, IL	Y	40270 FQ	55880 MW	79230 TQ	USBLS	5/15
	Lake County-Kenosha County PMSA, IL-WI	Y	24680 FQ	48640 MW	78730 TQ	USBLS	5/15
	Indiana	Y	39550 FQ	48960 MW	62590 TQ	USBLS	5/15
	Gary PMSA, IN	Y	39790 FQ	47820 MW	61940 TQ	USBLS	5/15
	Indianapolis-Carmel-Anderson MSA, IN	Y	42230 FQ	52150 MW	65240 TQ	USBLS	5/15
	Iowa	Y	38790 FQ	49310 MW	60070 TQ	USBLS	5/15
	Des Moines-West Des Moines MSA, IA	Y	42490 FQ	50320 MW	63140 TQ	USBLS	5/15
	Kansas	Y	38720 FQ	49200 MW	59740 TQ	USBLS	5/15
	Wichita MSA, KS	Y	38730 FQ	50810 MW	59230 TQ	USBLS	5/15
	Kentucky	Y	39030 FQ	55920 MW	69180 TQ	USBLS	5/15
	Louisville-Jefferson County MSA, KY-IN	Y	35800 FQ	50680 MW	76070 TQ	USBLS	5/15
	Louisiana	Y	44110 FQ	53650 MW	61670 TQ	USBLS	5/15
	Baton Rouge MSA, LA	Y	40240 FQ	50510 MW	61680 TQ	USBLS	5/15
	Maine	Y	38460 FQ	46220 MW	58690 TQ	USBLS	5/15
	Portland-South Portland MSA, ME	Y	40730 FQ	47950 MW	63360 TQ	USBLS	5/15
	Maryland	Y	38734 AE	62396 MW	74227 AEX	MDBLS	4/16
	Baltimore-Columbia-Towson MSA, MD	Y	42940 FQ	54550 MW	71010 TQ	USBLS	5/15
	Salisbury MSA, MD-DE	Y	48590 FQ	65550 MW	74920 TQ	USBLS	5/15
	Massachusetts	Y	44770 FQ	60920 MW	77770 TQ	USBLS	5/15
	Boston-Cambridge-Newton NECTA, MA	Y	43970 FQ	58270 MW	77460 TQ	USBLS	5/15
	Taunton-Middleborough-Norton NECTA, MA	Y	59660 FQ	76010 MW	89680 TQ	USBLS	5/15
	Worcester MSA, MA-CT	Y	44890 FQ	62650 MW	74140 TQ	USBLS	5/15
	Michigan	Y	40310 FQ	51370 MW	69030 TQ	USBLS	5/15
	Detroit-Dearborn-Livonia PMSA, MI	Y	40290 FQ	48160 MW	63670 TQ	USBLS	5/15
	Grand Rapids-Wyoming MSA, MI	Y	36630 FQ	46780 MW	67890 TQ	USBLS	5/15
	Minnesota	Y	41935 FQ	51229 MW	65402 TQ	MNBLS	1/16-3/16
	Minneapolis-St. Paul-Bloomington MSA, MN-WI	Y	43699 FQ	54405 MW	69435 TQ	MNBLS	1/16-3/16
	Mississippi	Y	39830 FQ	48510 MW	58770 TQ	USBLS	5/15
	Jackson MSA, MS	Y	32720 FQ	43730 MW	50640 TQ	USBLS	5/15
	Missouri	Y	33650 FQ	43460 MW	56610 TQ	USBLS	5/15
	Kansas City MSA, MO-KS	Y	38090 FQ	47630 MW	61890 TQ	USBLS	5/15
	St. Louis MSA, MO-IL	Y	33060 FQ	44500 MW	60150 TQ	USBLS	5/15
	Montana	Y	32470 FQ	46810 MW	59960 TQ	USBLS	5/15
	Billings MSA, MT	Y	33220 FQ	38740 MW	61280 TQ	USBLS	5/15
	Omaha-Council Bluffs MSA, NE-IA	Y	38820 FQ	48155 MW	57670 TQ	NEBLS	7/16-9/16
	Nevada	Y	44930 FQ	55240 MW	67640 TQ	USBLS	5/15
	Las Vegas-Henderson-Paradise MSA, NV	Y	45340 FQ	55490 MW	68170 TQ	USBLS	5/15
	New Hampshire	H	19.76 AE	27.51 MW	32.01 AEX	NHBLS	6/16
	Manchester NECTA, NH	H	19.30 AE	27.64 MW	31.21 AEX	NHBLS	6/16
	Nashua NECTA, NH-MA	Y	46780 FQ	56570 MW	68070 TQ	USBLS	5/15
	New Jersey	Y	56500 FQ	70000 MW	88250 TQ	USBLS	5/15

Occupation/Type/Industry	Location	Per	Low	Mid	High	Source	Date
Educational, Guidance, School, and Vocational Counselor	Camden PMSA, NJ	Y	55560 FQ	70600 MW	89010 TQ	USBLS	5/15
	Newark PMSA, NJ-PA	Y	54730 FQ	66380 MW	84280 TQ	USBLS	5/15
	Trenton MSA, NJ	Y	57540 FQ	71760 MW	86640 TQ	USBLS	5/15
	New Mexico	Y	34600 FQ	50070 MW	63570 TQ	USBLS	5/15
	Albuquerque MSA, NM	Y	29480 FQ	50730 MW	60870 TQ	USBLS	5/15
	New York	Y	38300 AE	60280 MW	79370 AEX	NYBLS	1/16-3/16
	Buffalo-Cheektowaga-Niagara Falls MSA, NY	Y	39110 FQ	50320 MW	63580 TQ	USBLS	5/15
	Nassau County-Suffolk County PMSA, NY	Y	52960 FQ	85640 MW	112700 TQ	USBLS	5/15
	New York-Jersey City-White Plains PMSA, NY-NJ	Y	46830 FQ	64650 MW	88840 TQ	USBLS	5/15
	Rochester MSA, NY	Y	41210 FQ	51980 MW	65470 TQ	USBLS	5/15
	North Carolina	Y	39880 FQ	47010 MW	56270 TQ	USBLS	5/15
	Charlotte-Concord-Gastonia MSA, NC-SC	Y	39630 FQ	47280 MW	57140 TQ	USBLS	5/15
	Raleigh MSA, NC	Y	43220 FQ	49690 MW	60600 TQ	USBLS	5/15
	North Dakota	Y	43820 FQ	53000 MW	64360 TQ	USBLS	5/15
	Fargo MSA, ND-MN	Y	40230 FQ	46830 MW	56100 TQ	USBLS	5/15
	Ohio	Y	41200 FQ	51960 MW	70580 TQ	USBLS	5/15
	Cincinnati MSA, OH-KY-IN	Y	44120 FQ	54210 MW	69860 TQ	USBLS	5/15
	Cleveland-Elyria MSA, OH	Y	43510 FQ	61290 MW	83290 TQ	USBLS	5/15
	Columbus MSA, OH	Y	40790 FQ	51830 MW	79130 TQ	USBLS	5/15
	Oklahoma	Y	33730 FQ	41640 MW	52630 TQ	USBLS	5/15
	Oklahoma City MSA, OK	Y	33830 FQ	40280 MW	51460 TQ	USBLS	5/15
	Tulsa MSA, OK	Y	35530 FQ	44940 MW	59990 TQ	USBLS	5/15
	Oregon	H	21.11 FQ	26.02 MW	31.44 TQ	ORBLS	2016
	Portland-Vancouver-Hillsboro MSA, OR-WA	Y	44650 FQ	56540 MW	69780 TQ	USBLS	5/15
	Pennsylvania	Y	42850 FQ	54840 MW	71170 TQ	USBLS	5/15
	Allentown-Bethlehem-Easton MSA, PA-NJ	Y	47170 FQ	57450 MW	72280 TQ	USBLS	5/15
	Harrisburg-Carlisle MSA, PA	Y	41060 FQ	51820 MW	61140 TQ	USBLS	5/15
	Montgomery County-Bucks County-Chester County PMSA, PA	Y	51380 FQ	68190 MW	88940 TQ	USBLS	5/15
	Philadelphia PMSA, PA	Y	41910 FQ	53650 MW	72540 TQ	USBLS	5/15
	Pittsburgh MSA, PA	Y	40620 FQ	50850 MW	63630 TQ	USBLS	5/15
	Rhode Island	Y	47070 FQ	60490 MW	75460 TQ	USBLS	5/15
	Providence-Warwick MSA, RI-MA	Y	47270 FQ	62940 MW	77440 TQ	USBLS	5/15
	South Carolina	Y	37610 FQ	49010 MW	61970 TQ	USBLS	5/15
	Charleston-North Charleston MSA, SC	Y	45000 FQ	55260 MW	63270 TQ	USBLS	5/15
	Columbia MSA, SC	Y	35870 FQ	45920 MW	60390 TQ	USBLS	5/15
	Greenville-Anderson-Mauldin MSA, SC	Y	37610 FQ	47910 MW	62490 TQ	USBLS	5/15
	South Dakota	Y	33420 FQ	38990 MW	48820 TQ	USBLS	5/15
	Sioux Falls MSA, SD	Y	36120 FQ	42870 MW	52420 TQ	USBLS	5/15
	Tennessee	Y	37320 FQ	46420 MW	57790 TQ	USBLS	5/15
	Knoxville MSA, TN	Y	39060 FQ	45990 MW	54890 TQ	USBLS	5/15
	Memphis MSA, TN-MS-AR	Y	39100 FQ	49540 MW	60860 TQ	USBLS	5/15
	Nashville-Davidson–Murfreesboro–Franklin MSA, TN	Y	38420 FQ	49380 MW	63290 TQ	USBLS	5/15
	Texas	Y	46240 FQ	57350 MW	68030 TQ	USBLS	5/15
	Austin-Round Rock MSA, TX	Y	39840 FQ	55630 MW	68300 TQ	USBLS	5/15
	Dallas-Plano-Irving PMSA, TX	Y	53160 FQ	62210 MW	72860 TQ	USBLS	5/15
	Fort Worth-Arlington PMSA, TX	Y	52030 FQ	60970 MW	71390 TQ	USBLS	5/15
	Houston-The Woodlands-Sugar Land MSA, TX	Y	49380 FQ	59070 MW	70440 TQ	USBLS	5/15
	San Antonio-New Braunfels MSA, TX	Y	47580 FQ	56410 MW	64410 TQ	USBLS	5/15
	Utah	Y	34000 FQ	44760 MW	59150 TQ	USBLS	5/15
	Ogden-Clearfield MSA, UT	Y	33460 FQ	42260 MW	52600 TQ	USBLS	5/15
	Provo-Orem MSA, UT	Y	29140 FQ	41620 MW	57210 TQ	USBLS	5/15
	Salt Lake City MSA, UT	Y	38180 FQ	51480 MW	67850 TQ	USBLS	5/15
	Vermont	Y	41140 FQ	51740 MW	63800 TQ	USBLS	5/15
	Burlington-South Burlington MSA, VT	Y	38370 FQ	53330 MW	71570 TQ	USBLS	5/15

AE	Average entry wage	AWR	Average wage range	H	Hourly	LR	Low end range
AEX	Average experienced wage	B	Biweekly	HI	Highest wage paid	M	Monthly
ATC	Average total compensation	D	Daily	HR	High end range	MCC	Median cash compensation
AW	Average wage paid	FQ	First quartile wage	LO	Lowest wage paid	ME	Median entry wage

MTC Median total compensation TCC Total cash compensation
MW Median wage paid TQ Third quartile wage
MWR Median wage range W Weekly
S See annotated source Y Yearly

Occupation/Type/Industry	Location	Per	Low	Mid	High	Source	Date
Educational, Guidance, School, and Vocational Counselor	Virginia	Y	44440 FQ	56220 MW	72770 TQ	USBLS	5/15
	Richmond MSA, VA	Y	45670 FQ	56380 MW	65760 TQ	USBLS	5/15
	Virginia Beach-Norfolk-Newport News MSA, VA-NC	Y	40970 FQ	51780 MW	66550 TQ	USBLS	5/15
	Washington	H	23.43 FQ	28.73 MW	34.21 TQ	WABLS	3/16
	Seattle-Bellevue-Everett PMSA, WA	H	23.85 FQ	28.27 MW	33.50 TQ	WABLS	3/16
	Tacoma-Lakewood PMSA, WA	H	19.15 FQ	28.13 MW	34.02 TQ	WABLS	3/16
	West Virginia	Y	32840 FQ	43430 MW	51930 TQ	USBLS	5/15
	Huntington-Ashland MSA, WV-KY-OH	Y	32190 FQ	41000 MW	52940 TQ	USBLS	5/15
	Wisconsin	Y	37820 FQ	48500 MW	62110 TQ	USBLS	5/15
	Madison MSA, WI	Y	28650 FQ	42460 MW	53500 TQ	USBLS	5/15
	Milwaukee-Waukesha-West Allis MSA, WI	Y	43600 FQ	57630 MW	75140 TQ	USBLS	5/15
	Wyoming	Y	44340 FQ	54730 MW	67440 TQ	USBLS	5/15
	Cheyenne MSA, WY	Y	45860 FQ	56690 MW	70190 TQ	USBLS	5/15
	Puerto Rico	Y	26850 FQ	34710 MW	45110 TQ	USBLS	5/15
	San Juan-Carolina-Caguas MSA, PR	Y	26080 FQ	31660 MW	44700 TQ	USBLS	5/15
	Virgin Islands	Y	34310 FQ	41570 MW	49360 TQ	USBLS	5/15
	Guam	Y	41880 FQ	49630 MW	58810 TQ	USBLS	5/15
Educational Resource Specialist County Government	Oakland County, MI	B	1913 LO		2490 HI	MIOAK2	10/1/16
Educational Television Program Director California State University	California	Y	62280 LO		107040 HI	CALST	2016-2017
Educational Therapist Department of Public Health and Human Services, State Government	Warm Springs, MT	H			27.97 HI	MTGOV	2016
Election Recount Worker	Ingham County, MI	D			125 HI	TC08	2016
Election Worker	Lansing, MI	H	10.00 LO		13.50 HI	TC07	2016
Elections Clerk	San Francisco, CA	B	1946 LO		2365 HI	SFGOV	2016-2018
Elections Specialist County Government	Oakland County, MI	B	1913 LO		2490 HI	MIOAK2	10/1/16
Municipal Government	Detroit, MI	M	3967 LO		4658 HI	DETGOV	2016
State Government	North Carolina	Y	36761 LO		72346 HI	NCGOV	7/1/16
Elections Supervisor/Coordinator County Government	Columbia County, GA	Y	53718 LO		80576 HI	GACTY04	2016
County Government	Jefferson County, GA	Y	18720 LO		36050 HI	GACTY04	2016
County Government	Spalding County, GA	Y	33909 LO		52886 HI	GACTY04	2016
Electric Motor, Power Tool, and Related Repairer	Alabama	Y	30897 AE	44149 AW	50780 AEX	ALBLS	6/16
	Birmingham-Hoover MSA, AL	Y	32199 AE	47780 AW	55570 AEX	ALBLS	6/16
	Arizona	Y	32550 FQ	36970 MW	46520 TQ	USBLS	5/15
	Phoenix-Mesa-Scottsdale MSA, AZ	Y	32700 FQ	36970 MW	45440 TQ	USBLS	5/15
	Arkansas	Y	27390 FQ	36380 MW	59600 TQ	USBLS	5/15
	Little Rock-North Little Rock-Conway MSA, AR	Y	25830 FQ	32770 MW	37660 TQ	USBLS	5/15
	California	H	19.27 FQ	25.14 MW	40.63 TQ	CABLS	1/16-3/16
	Anaheim-Santa Ana-Irvine PMSA, CA	H	24.09 FQ	28.79 MW	33.71 TQ	CABLS	1/16-3/16
	Los Angeles-Long Beach-Glendale PMSA, CA	H	18.79 FQ	22.46 MW	29.22 TQ	CABLS	1/16-3/16
	Riverside-San Bernardino-Ontario MSA, CA	H	18.76 FQ	25.14 MW	34.69 TQ	CABLS	1/16-3/16
	Sacramento–Roseville–Arden-Arcade MSA, CA	H	13.78 FQ	23.08 MW	28.09 TQ	CABLS	1/16-3/16
	Colorado	Y	35680 FQ	43180 MW	49270 TQ	USBLS	5/15
	Denver-Aurora-Lakewood MSA, CO	Y	38650 FQ	44270 MW	49540 TQ	USBLS	5/15

AE	Average entry wage	AWR	Average wage range	H	Hourly	LR	Low end range	MTC	Median total compensation	TCC	Total cash compensation
AEX	Average experienced wage	B	Biweekly	HI	Highest wage paid	M	Monthly	MW	Median wage paid	TQ	Third quartile wage
ATC	Average total compensation	D	Daily	HR	High end range	MCC	Median cash compensation	MWR	Median wage range	W	Weekly
AW	Average wage paid	FQ	First quartile wage	LO	Lowest wage paid	ME	Median entry wage	S	See annotated source	Y	Yearly

Occupation/Type/Industry	Location	Per	Low	Mid	High	Source	Date
Electric Motor, Power Tool, and Related Repairer	Connecticut	Y		55664 MW		CTBLS	1/16-3/16
	Hartford-West Hartford-East Hartford MSA, CT	Y	38600 FQ	47700 MW	60590 TQ	USBLS	5/15
	Washington-Arlington-Alexandria PMSA, DC-VA-MD-WV	Y	29110 FQ	39370 MW	54880 TQ	USBLS	5/15
	Florida	H	11.86 AE	17.50 MW	21.62 AEX	FLBLS	7/16-9/16
	Fort Lauderdale-Pompano Beach-Deerfield Beach PMSA, FL	H	10.89 AE	13.53 MW	17.41 AEX	FLBLS	7/16-9/16
	Orlando-Kissimmee-Sanford MSA, FL	H	17.07 AE	23.17 MW	26.07 AEX	FLBLS	7/16-9/16
	Tampa-St. Petersburg-Clearwater MSA, FL	H	10.84 AE	14.64 MW	17.98 AEX	FLBLS	7/16-9/16
	Georgia	Y	27970 FQ	34780 MW	42850 TQ	USBLS	5/15
	Atlanta-Sandy Springs-Roswell MSA, GA	Y	28490 FQ	33370 MW	38230 TQ	USBLS	5/15
	Idaho	Y	31550 FQ	36130 MW	45710 TQ	USBLS	5/15
	Boise City MSA, ID	Y	31870 FQ	37770 MW	53070 TQ	USBLS	5/15
	Illinois	Y	27290 FQ	47890 MW	88340 TQ	USBLS	5/15
	Indiana	Y	32580 FQ	39820 MW	49980 TQ	USBLS	5/15
	Gary PMSA, IN	Y	39700 FQ	44860 MW	50550 TQ	USBLS	5/15
	Indianapolis-Carmel-Anderson MSA, IN	Y	33180 FQ	37090 MW	49290 TQ	USBLS	5/15
	Iowa	Y	30180 FQ	39660 MW	46970 TQ	USBLS	5/15
	Kansas	Y	29950 FQ	37370 MW	45140 TQ	USBLS	5/15
	Wichita MSA, KS	Y	43030 FQ	46930 MW	50850 TQ	USBLS	5/15
	Kentucky	Y	32000 FQ	40330 MW	47120 TQ	USBLS	5/15
	Louisville-Jefferson County MSA, KY-IN	Y	33550 FQ	41440 MW	48010 TQ	USBLS	5/15
	Louisiana	Y	28200 FQ	36760 MW	47540 TQ	USBLS	5/15
	Baton Rouge MSA, LA	Y	32650 FQ	41590 MW	58950 TQ	USBLS	5/15
	New Orleans-Metairie MSA, LA	Y	25460 FQ	32690 MW	41870 TQ	USBLS	5/15
	Maine	Y	32870 FQ	36540 MW	41600 TQ	USBLS	5/15
	Baltimore-Columbia-Towson MSA, MD	Y	26770 FQ	28560 MW	30350 TQ	USBLS	5/15
	Massachusetts	Y	31720 FQ	38150 MW	45160 TQ	USBLS	5/15
	Boston-Cambridge-Newton NECTA, MA	Y	34130 FQ	37870 MW	44200 TQ	USBLS	5/15
	Worcester MSA, MA-CT	Y	27140 FQ	34360 MW	44960 TQ	USBLS	5/15
	Detroit-Dearborn-Livonia PMSA, MI	Y	39550 FQ	56320 MW	73510 TQ	USBLS	5/15
	Grand Rapids-Wyoming MSA, MI	Y	40410 FQ	44460 MW	48520 TQ	USBLS	5/15
	Minnesota	Y	32242 FQ	39563 MW	55473 TQ	MNBLS	1/16-3/16
	Minneapolis-St. Paul-Bloomington MSA, MN-WI	Y	33489 FQ	39493 MW	56740 TQ	MNBLS	1/16-3/16
	Mississippi	Y	22930 FQ	29430 MW	44870 TQ	USBLS	5/15
	Missouri	Y	29650 FQ	38080 MW	50300 TQ	USBLS	5/15
	Kansas City MSA, MO-KS	Y	40390 FQ	46210 MW	54350 TQ	USBLS	5/15
	St. Louis MSA, MO-IL	Y	29120 FQ	36730 MW	49860 TQ	USBLS	5/15
	Montana	Y	26470 FQ	30460 MW	38600 TQ	USBLS	5/15
	Nebraska	Y	30010 FQ	34815 MW	39345 TQ	NEBLS	7/16-9/16
	Nevada	Y	20730 FQ	36850 MW	51940 TQ	USBLS	5/15
	Las Vegas-Henderson-Paradise MSA, NV	Y	18950 FQ	33800 MW	54310 TQ	USBLS	5/15
	New Hampshire	H	20.57 AE	26.90 MW	30.31 AEX	NHBLS	6/16
	New Jersey	Y	41270 FQ	45500 MW	49730 TQ	USBLS	5/15
	Camden PMSA, NJ	Y	37290 FQ	44390 MW	52740 TQ	USBLS	5/15
	Newark PMSA, NJ-PA	Y	39140 FQ	49590 MW	70610 TQ	USBLS	5/15
	New York	Y	30610 AE	43410 MW	53210 AEX	NYBLS	1/16-3/16
	Buffalo-Cheektowaga-Niagara Falls MSA, NY	Y	34570 FQ	38980 MW	54640 TQ	USBLS	5/15
	Nassau County-Suffolk County PMSA, NY	Y	38820 FQ	47870 MW	60630 TQ	USBLS	5/15
	New York-Jersey City-White Plains PMSA, NY-NJ	Y	43100 FQ	47370 MW	53670 TQ	USBLS	5/15
	North Carolina	Y	31850 FQ	36860 MW	44520 TQ	USBLS	5/15
	Charlotte-Concord-Gastonia MSA, NC-SC	Y	33650 FQ	40980 MW	47220 TQ	USBLS	5/15

AE	Average entry wage	AWR	Average wage range	H	Hourly	LR	Low end range	MTC	Median total compensation	TCC	Total cash compensation
AEX	Average experienced wage	B	Biweekly	HI	Highest wage paid	M	Monthly	MW	Median wage paid	TQ	Third quartile wage
ATC	Average total compensation	D	Daily	HR	High end range	MCC	Median cash compensation	MWR	Median wage range	W	Weekly
AW	Average wage paid	FQ	First quartile wage	LO	Lowest wage paid	ME	Median entry wage	S	See annotated source	Y	Yearly

Occupation/Type/Industry	Location	Per	Low	Mid	High	Source	Date
Electric Motor, Power Tool, and Related Repairer	Raleigh MSA, NC	Y	42920 FQ	48650 MW	56730 TQ	USBLS	5/15
	North Dakota	Y	34000 FQ	37840 MW	49620 TQ	USBLS	5/15
	Ohio	Y	34270 FQ	45970 MW	62470 TQ	USBLS	5/15
	Cincinnati MSA, OH-KY-IN	Y	44440 FQ	66850 MW	76320 TQ	USBLS	5/15
	Cleveland-Elyria MSA, OH	Y	35630 FQ	43990 MW	52570 TQ	USBLS	5/15
	Columbus MSA, OH	Y	43850 FQ	50060 MW	57000 TQ	USBLS	5/15
	Oklahoma	Y	32050 FQ	42300 MW	52010 TQ	USBLS	5/15
	Oklahoma City MSA, OK	Y	34050 FQ	45060 MW	56330 TQ	USBLS	5/15
	Oregon	H	11.16 FQ	14.34 MW	20.11 TQ	ORBLS	2016
	Portland-Vancouver-Hillsboro MSA, OR-WA	Y	22420 FQ	28950 MW	41900 TQ	USBLS	5/15
	Pennsylvania	Y	33830 FQ	40310 MW	48730 TQ	USBLS	5/15
	Allentown-Bethlehem-Easton MSA, PA-NJ	Y	30800 FQ	37320 MW	45610 TQ	USBLS	5/15
	Montgomery County-Bucks County-Chester County PMSA, PA	Y	35380 FQ	40150 MW	47670 TQ	USBLS	5/15
	Pittsburgh MSA, PA	Y	33770 FQ	38880 MW	45700 TQ	USBLS	5/15
	Rhode Island	Y	36420 FQ	42070 MW	48200 TQ	USBLS	5/15
	Providence-Warwick MSA, RI-MA	Y	36420 FQ	42070 MW	48200 TQ	USBLS	5/15
	South Carolina	Y	23880 FQ	32510 MW	40860 TQ	USBLS	5/15
	Charleston-North Charleston MSA, SC	Y	19490 FQ	28270 MW	43030 TQ	USBLS	5/15
	Greenville-Anderson-Mauldin MSA, SC	Y	25380 FQ	31080 MW	39790 TQ	USBLS	5/15
	South Dakota	Y	33460 FQ	37330 MW	42990 TQ	USBLS	5/15
	Tennessee	Y	29370 FQ	36740 MW	48160 TQ	USBLS	5/15
	Knoxville MSA, TN	Y	32030 FQ	38010 MW	45020 TQ	USBLS	5/15
	Memphis MSA, TN-MS-AR	Y	28600 FQ	32730 MW	40780 TQ	USBLS	5/15
	Nashville-Davidson–Murfreesboro–Franklin MSA, TN	Y	30250 FQ	40800 MW	54190 TQ	USBLS	5/15
	Texas	Y	29820 FQ	38050 MW	48560 TQ	USBLS	5/15
	Austin-Round Rock MSA, TX	Y	27450 FQ	29670 MW	34140 TQ	USBLS	5/15
	Dallas-Plano-Irving PMSA, TX	Y	35010 FQ	42170 MW	49520 TQ	USBLS	5/15
	Fort Worth-Arlington PMSA, TX	Y	27620 FQ	35330 MW	44040 TQ	USBLS	5/15
	Houston-The Woodlands-Sugar Land MSA, TX	Y	29390 FQ	39870 MW	52880 TQ	USBLS	5/15
	San Antonio-New Braunfels MSA, TX	Y	23720 FQ	29220 MW	39460 TQ	USBLS	5/15
	Utah	Y	19280 FQ	24720 MW	40370 TQ	USBLS	5/15
	Salt Lake City MSA, UT	Y	31830 FQ	42440 MW	55490 TQ	USBLS	5/15
	Virginia	Y	33910 FQ	42540 MW	52810 TQ	USBLS	5/15
	Richmond MSA, VA	Y	40170 FQ	50300 MW	58860 TQ	USBLS	5/15
	Virginia Beach-Norfolk-Newport News MSA, VA-NC	Y	32460 FQ	37200 MW	43770 TQ	USBLS	5/15
	Washington	H	17.69 FQ	22.80 MW	34.27 TQ	WABLS	3/16
	Tacoma-Lakewood PMSA, WA	H	23.47 FQ	29.18 MW	40.47 TQ	WABLS	3/16
	West Virginia	Y	30170 FQ	39600 MW	48790 TQ	USBLS	5/15
	Huntington-Ashland MSA, WV-KY-OH	Y	35420 FQ	43940 MW	54190 TQ	USBLS	5/15
	Wisconsin	Y	35040 FQ	42800 MW	48960 TQ	USBLS	5/15
	Madison MSA, WI	Y	33380 FQ	40520 MW	47230 TQ	USBLS	5/15
	Milwaukee-Waukesha-West Allis MSA, WI	Y	31270 FQ	40490 MW	47700 TQ	USBLS	5/15
	Wyoming	Y	38940 FQ	46800 MW	55690 TQ	USBLS	5/15
	Puerto Rico	Y	17770 FQ	19910 MW	24400 TQ	USBLS	5/15
	San Juan-Carolina-Caguas MSA, PR	Y	17910 FQ	20190 MW	24640 TQ	USBLS	5/15
Electrical and Electronic Engineering Technician	Alabama	Y	39631 AE	60854 AW	71465 AEX	ALBLS	6/16
	Birmingham-Hoover MSA, AL	Y	40467 AE	58540 AW	67581 AEX	ALBLS	6/16
	Alaska	Y	68500 FQ	83150 MW	100090 TQ	USBLS	5/15
	Anchorage MSA, AK	Y	66210 FQ	80460 MW	98030 TQ	USBLS	5/15
	Arizona	Y	46900 FQ	59140 MW	71510 TQ	USBLS	5/15
	Phoenix-Mesa-Scottsdale MSA, AZ	Y	47090 FQ	59100 MW	71080 TQ	USBLS	5/15

AE	Average entry wage	AWR	Average wage range	H	Hourly
AEX	Average experienced wage	B	Biweekly	HI	Highest wage paid
ATC	Average total compensation	D	Daily	HR	High end range
AW	Average wage paid	FQ	First quartile wage	LO	Lowest wage paid

LR	Low end range	MTC	Median total compensation	TCC	Total cash compensation
M	Monthly	MW	Median wage paid	TQ	Third quartile wage
MCC	Median cash compensation	MWR	Median wage range	W	Weekly
ME	Median entry wage	S	See annotated source	Y	Yearly

Occupation/Type/Industry	Location	Per	Low	Mid	High	Source	Date
Electrical and Electronic Engineering Technician	Tucson MSA, AZ	Y	50020 FQ	60250 MW	72040 TQ	USBLS	5/15
	Arkansas	Y	43480 FQ	59140 MW	70650 TQ	USBLS	5/15
	Little Rock-North Little Rock-Conway MSA, AR	Y	40290 FQ	60160 MW	70080 TQ	USBLS	5/15
	California	H	24.94 FQ	31.80 MW	38.90 TQ	CABLS	1/16-3/16
	Anaheim-Santa Ana-Irvine PMSA, CA	H	22.44 FQ	28.81 MW	35.46 TQ	CABLS	1/16-3/16
	Los Angeles-Long Beach-Glendale PMSA, CA	H	24.43 FQ	30.46 MW	37.51 TQ	CABLS	1/16-3/16
	Oakland-Hayward-Berkeley PMSA, CA	H	27.33 FQ	37.17 MW	49.89 TQ	CABLS	1/16-3/16
	Riverside-San Bernardino-Ontario MSA, CA	H	25.57 FQ	32.28 MW	38.47 TQ	CABLS	1/16-3/16
	Sacramento–Roseville–Arden-Arcade MSA, CA	H	24.04 FQ	31.78 MW	35.44 TQ	CABLS	1/16-3/16
	San Diego-Carlsbad MSA, CA	H	24.02 FQ	30.82 MW	39.29 TQ	CABLS	1/16-3/16
	San Francisco-Redwood City-South San Francisco PMSA, CA	H	25.99 FQ	32.29 MW	37.78 TQ	CABLS	1/16-3/16
	Colorado	Y	49190 FQ	65830 MW	76260 TQ	USBLS	5/15
	Denver-Aurora-Lakewood MSA, CO	Y	54800 FQ	67040 MW	78090 TQ	USBLS	5/15
	Connecticut	Y		63213 MW		CTBLS	1/16-3/16
	Bridgeport-Stamford-Norwalk MSA, CT	Y	49090 FQ	65140 MW	73940 TQ	USBLS	5/15
	Hartford-West Hartford-East Hartford MSA, CT	Y	45910 FQ	59120 MW	68600 TQ	USBLS	5/15
	Delaware	Y	42860 FQ	55150 MW	66200 TQ	USBLS	5/15
	Wilmington PMSA, DE-MD-NJ	Y	47080 FQ	62750 MW	68340 TQ	USBLS	5/15
	District of Columbia	Y	66200 FQ	79000 MW	93570 TQ	USBLS	5/15
	Washington-Arlington-Alexandria PMSA, DC-VA-MD-WV	Y	58510 FQ	69360 MW	84030 TQ	USBLS	5/15
	Florida	H	15.38 AE	24.72 MW	30.00 AEX	FLBLS	7/16-9/16
	Fort Lauderdale-Pompano Beach-Deerfield Beach PMSA, FL	H	15.94 AE	21.91 MW	26.62 AEX	FLBLS	7/16-9/16
	Miami-Miami Beach-Kendall PMSA, FL	H	20.80 AE	32.06 MW	34.42 AEX	FLBLS	7/16-9/16
	Orlando-Kissimmee-Sanford MSA, FL	H	17.63 AE	25.09 MW	29.41 AEX	FLBLS	7/16-9/16
	Tampa-St. Petersburg-Clearwater MSA, FL	H	14.46 AE	22.24 MW	28.45 AEX	FLBLS	7/16-9/16
	Georgia	Y	43630 FQ	59580 MW	72940 TQ	USBLS	5/15
	Atlanta-Sandy Springs-Roswell MSA, GA	Y	40410 FQ	57590 MW	71000 TQ	USBLS	5/15
	Augusta-Richmond County MSA, GA-SC	Y	54850 FQ	71030 MW	84210 TQ	USBLS	5/15
	Hawaii	Y	57320 FQ	68070 MW	81130 TQ	USBLS	5/15
	Urban Honolulu MSA, HI	Y	55850 FQ	66720 MW	81200 TQ	USBLS	5/15
	Idaho	Y	44290 FQ	55680 MW	66200 TQ	USBLS	5/15
	Illinois	Y	50680 FQ	65150 MW	75370 TQ	USBLS	5/15
	Chicago-Naperville-Arlington Heights PMSA, IL	Y	53020 FQ	66200 MW	77920 TQ	USBLS	5/15
	Lake County-Kenosha County PMSA, IL-WI	Y	47770 FQ	59520 MW	72710 TQ	USBLS	5/15
	Indiana	Y	43090 FQ	58600 MW	73370 TQ	USBLS	5/15
	Gary PMSA, IN	Y	45590 FQ	66190 MW	66930 TQ	USBLS	5/15
	Indianapolis-Carmel-Anderson MSA, IN	Y	36810 FQ	52660 MW	66210 TQ	USBLS	5/15
	Iowa	Y	48090 FQ	62300 MW	71480 TQ	USBLS	5/15
	Des Moines-West Des Moines MSA, IA	Y	54500 FQ	66190 MW	73660 TQ	USBLS	5/15
	Kansas	Y	45650 FQ	57010 MW	68880 TQ	USBLS	5/15
	Wichita MSA, KS	Y	43270 FQ	52990 MW	66190 TQ	USBLS	5/15
	Kentucky	Y	37780 FQ	59590 MW	74480 TQ	USBLS	5/15
	Louisville-Jefferson County MSA, KY-IN	Y	31860 FQ	46500 MW	66200 TQ	USBLS	5/15
	Louisiana	Y	41150 FQ	54380 MW	68160 TQ	USBLS	5/15
	Baton Rouge MSA, LA	Y	46840 FQ	67200 MW	80870 TQ	USBLS	5/15

Occupation/Type/Industry	Location	Per	Low	Mid	High	Source	Date
Electrical and Electronic Engineering Technician	New Orleans-Metairie MSA, LA	Y	44300 FQ	55830 MW	66210 TQ	USBLS	5/15
	Maine	Y	57200 FQ	66200 MW	74870 TQ	USBLS	5/15
	Portland-South Portland MSA, ME	Y	51090 FQ	66190 MW	72390 TQ	USBLS	5/15
	Maryland	Y	47212 AE	69434 MW	80545 AEX	MDBLS	4/16
	Baltimore-Columbia-Towson MSA, MD	Y	53580 FQ	66200 MW	78610 TQ	USBLS	5/15
	Salisbury MSA, MD-DE	Y	38620 FQ	49380 MW	72990 TQ	USBLS	5/15
	Massachusetts	Y	52350 FQ	65260 MW	75100 TQ	USBLS	5/15
	Boston-Cambridge-Newton NECTA, MA	Y	58280 FQ	68080 MW	77070 TQ	USBLS	5/15
	Worcester MSA, MA-CT	Y	38810 FQ	58700 MW	70640 TQ	USBLS	5/15
	Michigan	Y	40970 FQ	54360 MW	67170 TQ	USBLS	5/15
	Detroit-Dearborn-Livonia PMSA, MI	Y	51150 FQ	65140 MW	72120 TQ	USBLS	5/15
	Grand Rapids-Wyoming MSA, MI	Y	46670 FQ	62470 MW	69790 TQ	USBLS	5/15
	Minnesota	Y	46542 FQ	58044 MW	68961 TQ	MNBLS	1/16-3/16
	Minneapolis-St. Paul-Bloomington MSA, MN-WI	Y	48003 FQ	58951 MW	69324 TQ	MNBLS	1/16-3/16
	Mississippi	Y	40960 FQ	53600 MW	66200 TQ	USBLS	5/15
	Jackson MSA, MS	Y	34330 FQ	39870 MW	66190 TQ	USBLS	5/15
	Missouri	Y	47650 FQ	64430 MW	73220 TQ	USBLS	5/15
	Kansas City MSA, MO-KS	Y	52870 FQ	65320 MW	74500 TQ	USBLS	5/15
	St. Louis MSA, MO-IL	Y	44650 FQ	64370 MW	73760 TQ	USBLS	5/15
	Montana	Y	53350 FQ	66200 MW	77070 TQ	USBLS	5/15
	Billings MSA, MT	Y	63360 FQ	66210 MW	72890 TQ	USBLS	5/15
	Nebraska	Y	48300 FQ	58130 MW	66200 TQ	NEBLS	7/16-9/16
	Omaha-Council Bluffs MSA, NE-IA	Y	51210 FQ	58750 MW	66195 TQ	NEBLS	7/16-9/16
	Nevada	Y	58560 FQ	69090 MW	84010 TQ	USBLS	5/15
	Las Vegas-Henderson-Paradise MSA, NV	Y	59030 FQ	69660 MW	86350 TQ	USBLS	5/15
	New Hampshire	H	19.20 AE	27.09 MW	30.71 AEX	NHBLS	6/16
	Manchester NECTA, NH	H	17.07 AE	29.52 MW	33.82 AEX	NHBLS	6/16
	Nashua NECTA, NH-MA	Y	46690 FQ	55590 MW	62740 TQ	USBLS	5/15
	New Jersey	Y	46180 FQ	62090 MW	74180 TQ	USBLS	5/15
	Camden PMSA, NJ	Y	50580 FQ	66190 MW	73780 TQ	USBLS	5/15
	Newark PMSA, NJ-PA	Y	46180 FQ	57380 MW	73710 TQ	USBLS	5/15
	Trenton MSA, NJ	Y	41370 FQ	65040 MW	67290 TQ	USBLS	5/15
	New Mexico	Y	51850 FQ	65640 MW	75730 TQ	USBLS	5/15
	Albuquerque MSA, NM	Y	49280 FQ	63610 MW	74190 TQ	USBLS	5/15
	New York	Y	42290 AE	64710 MW	75060 AEX	NYBLS	1/16-3/16
	Buffalo-Cheektowaga-Niagara Falls MSA, NY	Y	40280 FQ	53720 MW	66200 TQ	USBLS	5/15
	Nassau County-Suffolk County PMSA, NY	Y	50750 FQ	63840 MW	74140 TQ	USBLS	5/15
	New York-Jersey City-White Plains PMSA, NY-NJ	Y	57000 FQ	66470 MW	81370 TQ	USBLS	5/15
	Rochester MSA, NY	Y	41150 FQ	50820 MW	63130 TQ	USBLS	5/15
	North Carolina	Y	46600 FQ	58560 MW	70450 TQ	USBLS	5/15
	Charlotte-Concord-Gastonia MSA, NC-SC	Y	43130 FQ	50340 MW	62530 TQ	USBLS	5/15
	Raleigh MSA, NC	Y	41740 FQ	52040 MW	66190 TQ	USBLS	5/15
	North Dakota	Y	48890 FQ	59960 MW	70510 TQ	USBLS	5/15
	Fargo MSA, ND-MN	Y	46690 FQ	57120 MW	66200 TQ	USBLS	5/15
	Ohio	Y	43800 FQ	59680 MW	69460 TQ	USBLS	5/15
	Cincinnati MSA, OH-KY-IN	Y	48370 FQ	61800 MW	69880 TQ	USBLS	5/15
	Cleveland-Elyria MSA, OH	Y	47420 FQ	64470 MW	71980 TQ	USBLS	5/15
	Columbus MSA, OH	Y	48560 FQ	66080 MW	73260 TQ	USBLS	5/15
	Oklahoma	Y	46590 FQ	61390 MW	74890 TQ	USBLS	5/15
	Oklahoma City MSA, OK	Y	56160 FQ	68490 MW	89030 TQ	USBLS	5/15
	Tulsa MSA, OK	Y	40690 FQ	52160 MW	66200 TQ	USBLS	5/15
	Pennsylvania	Y	43260 FQ	55380 MW	66200 TQ	USBLS	5/15
	Allentown-Bethlehem-Easton MSA, PA-NJ	Y	47470 FQ	58210 MW	66300 TQ	USBLS	5/15
	Harrisburg-Carlisle MSA, PA	Y	51680 FQ	59450 MW	66200 TQ	USBLS	5/15
	Lancaster MSA, PA	Y	39950 FQ	50610 MW	66190 TQ	USBLS	5/15

AE	Average entry wage	AWR	Average wage range	H	Hourly	LR	Low end range	MTC	Median total compensation	TCC	Total cash compensation
AEX	Average experienced wage	B	Biweekly	HI	Highest wage paid	M	Monthly	MW	Median wage paid	TQ	Third quartile wage
ATC	Average total compensation	D	Daily	HR	High end range	MCC	Median cash compensation	MWR	Median wage range	W	Weekly
AW	Average wage paid	FQ	First quartile wage	LO	Lowest wage paid	ME	Median entry wage	S	See annotated source	Y	Yearly

Occupation/Type/Industry	Location	Per	Low	Mid	High	Source	Date
Electrical and Electronic Engineering Technician	Montgomery County-Bucks County-Chester County						
	PMSA, PA	Y	43940 FQ	56560 MW	71370 TQ	USBLS	5/15
	Philadelphia PMSA, PA	Y	54300 FQ	66190 MW	72440 TQ	USBLS	5/15
	Pittsburgh MSA, PA	Y	41190 FQ	52020 MW	66190 TQ	USBLS	5/15
	Rhode Island	Y	41450 FQ	58960 MW	75120 TQ	USBLS	5/15
	Providence-Warwick MSA, RI-MA	Y	41420 FQ	57260 MW	74300 TQ	USBLS	5/15
	South Carolina	Y	46400 FQ	59350 MW	74920 TQ	USBLS	5/15
	Charleston-North Charleston MSA, SC	Y	56170 FQ	76170 MW	91250 TQ	USBLS	5/15
	Columbia MSA, SC	Y	51670 FQ	62190 MW	69690 TQ	USBLS	5/15
	Greenville-Anderson-Mauldin MSA, SC	Y	44230 FQ	52370 MW	63160 TQ	USBLS	5/15
	South Dakota	Y	38150 FQ	47150 MW	61480 TQ	USBLS	5/15
	Sioux Falls MSA, SD	Y	36490 FQ	44650 MW	66190 TQ	USBLS	5/15
	Tennessee	Y	41410 FQ	52610 MW	66190 TQ	USBLS	5/15
	Knoxville MSA, TN	Y	43110 FQ	56760 MW	71720 TQ	USBLS	5/15
	Memphis MSA, TN-MS-AR	Y	37550 FQ	55390 MW	67130 TQ	USBLS	5/15
	Nashville-Davidson–Murfreesboro–Franklin MSA, TN	Y	42600 FQ	50990 MW	66190 TQ	USBLS	5/15
	Texas	Y	46290 FQ	60860 MW	76680 TQ	USBLS	5/15
	Austin-Round Rock MSA, TX	Y	53030 FQ	67750 MW	87570 TQ	USBLS	5/15
	Dallas-Plano-Irving PMSA, TX	Y	44230 FQ	57530 MW	70500 TQ	USBLS	5/15
	Fort Worth-Arlington PMSA, TX	Y	48550 FQ	60110 MW	71160 TQ	USBLS	5/15
	Houston-The Woodlands-Sugar Land MSA, TX	Y	43300 FQ	60120 MW	79490 TQ	USBLS	5/15
	San Antonio-New Braunfels MSA, TX	Y	46500 FQ	60410 MW	72230 TQ	USBLS	5/15
	Utah	Y	44860 FQ	58410 MW	69710 TQ	USBLS	5/15
	Ogden-Clearfield MSA, UT	Y	58570 FQ	68310 MW	76130 TQ	USBLS	5/15
	Provo-Orem MSA, UT	Y	38860 FQ	47490 MW	58170 TQ	USBLS	5/15
	Salt Lake City MSA, UT	Y	47900 FQ	58570 MW	66500 TQ	USBLS	5/15
	Vermont	Y	54050 FQ	66190 MW	73820 TQ	USBLS	5/15
	Burlington-South Burlington MSA, VT	Y	58260 FQ	67220 MW	74690 TQ	USBLS	5/15
	Virginia	Y	51700 FQ	64020 MW	78430 TQ	USBLS	5/15
	Richmond MSA, VA	Y	40870 FQ	56290 MW	66200 TQ	USBLS	5/15
	Virginia Beach-Norfolk-Newport News MSA, VA-NC	Y	47890 FQ	61140 MW	79230 TQ	USBLS	5/15
	Washington	H	25.45 FQ	32.17 MW	37.75 TQ	WABLS	3/16
	Seattle-Bellevue-Everett PMSA, WA	H	25.87 FQ	31.51 MW	37.41 TQ	WABLS	3/16
	Tacoma-Lakewood PMSA, WA	H	31.86 FQ	33.54 MW	36.80 TQ	WABLS	3/16
	West Virginia	Y	37440 FQ	51850 MW	66200 TQ	USBLS	5/15
	Huntington-Ashland MSA, WV-KY-OH	Y	45490 FQ	58660 MW	69620 TQ	USBLS	5/15
	Wisconsin	Y	42700 FQ	54080 MW	66190 TQ	USBLS	5/15
	Madison MSA, WI	Y	41610 FQ	52760 MW	66190 TQ	USBLS	5/15
	Milwaukee-Waukesha-West Allis MSA, WI	Y	41530 FQ	52690 MW	61680 TQ	USBLS	5/15
	Wyoming	Y	42550 FQ	50980 MW	66190 TQ	USBLS	5/15
	Puerto Rico	Y	30760 FQ	41680 MW	50970 TQ	USBLS	5/15
	San Juan-Carolina-Caguas MSA, PR	Y	30850 FQ	43390 MW	52590 TQ	USBLS	5/15
	Guam	Y	37340 FQ	53240 MW	66190 TQ	USBLS	5/15
Electrical and Electronic Equipment Assembler	Alabama	Y	20523 AE	31371 AW	36800 AEX	ALBLS	6/16
	Birmingham-Hoover MSA, AL	Y	23114 AE	33366 AW	38486 AEX	ALBLS	6/16
	Arizona	Y	27980 FQ	35200 MW	43900 TQ	USBLS	5/15
	Phoenix-Mesa-Scottsdale MSA, AZ	Y	29320 FQ	36150 MW	44820 TQ	USBLS	5/15
	Tucson MSA, AZ	Y	22880 FQ	30040 MW	39060 TQ	USBLS	5/15
	Arkansas	Y	25010 FQ	34190 MW	43180 TQ	USBLS	5/15
	Little Rock-North Little Rock-Conway MSA, AR	Y	23840 FQ	28190 MW	34970 TQ	USBLS	5/15
	California	H	12.25 FQ	15.87 MW	20.76 TQ	CABLS	1/16-3/16

AE Average entry wage	**AWR** Average wage range	**H** Hourly	**LR** Low end range	**MTC** Median total compensation	**TCC** Total cash compensation
AEX Average experienced wage	**B** Biweekly	**HI** Highest wage paid	**M** Monthly	**MW** Median wage paid	**TQ** Third quartile wage
ATC Average total compensation	**D** Daily	**HR** High end range	**MCC** Median cash compensation	**MWR** Median wage range	**W** Weekly
AW Average wage paid	**FQ** First quartile wage	**LO** Lowest wage paid	**ME** Median entry	**S** See annotated source	**Y** Yearly

Occupation/Type/Industry	Location	Per	Low	Mid	High	Source	Date
Electrical and Electronic Equipment Assembler	Anaheim-Santa Ana-Irvine PMSA, CA	H	10.51 FQ	13.42 MW	17.02 TQ	CABLS	1/16-3/16
	Los Angeles-Long Beach-Glendale PMSA, CA	H	11.81 FQ	15.12 MW	19.11 TQ	CABLS	1/16-3/16
	Oakland-Hayward-Berkeley PMSA, CA	H	13.90 FQ	18.92 MW	23.97 TQ	CABLS	1/16-3/16
	Riverside-San Bernardino-Ontario MSA, CA	H	12.26 FQ	15.77 MW	19.83 TQ	CABLS	1/16-3/16
	Sacramento–Roseville–Arden-Arcade MSA, CA	H	12.29 FQ	16.30 MW	22.27 TQ	CABLS	1/16-3/16
	San Diego-Carlsbad MSA, CA	H	13.81 FQ	17.71 MW	22.50 TQ	CABLS	1/16-3/16
	San Francisco-Redwood City-South San Francisco PMSA, CA	H	13.69 FQ	18.02 MW	23.83 TQ	CABLS	1/16-3/16
	Colorado	Y	25650 FQ	32450 MW	42470 TQ	USBLS	5/15
	Denver-Aurora-Lakewood MSA, CO	Y	21980 FQ	30380 MW	43130 TQ	USBLS	5/15
	Connecticut	Y		34440 MW		CTBLS	1/16-3/16
	Bridgeport-Stamford-Norwalk MSA, CT	Y	28040 FQ	35990 MW	48600 TQ	USBLS	5/15
	Hartford-West Hartford-East Hartford MSA, CT	Y	29240 FQ	35770 MW	45330 TQ	USBLS	5/15
	Delaware	Y	27910 FQ	33440 MW	39440 TQ	USBLS	5/15
	Wilmington PMSA, DE-MD-NJ	Y	27080 FQ	32850 MW	39040 TQ	USBLS	5/15
	Washington-Arlington-Alexandria PMSA, DC-VA-MD-WV	Y	30250 FQ	36840 MW	47160 TQ	USBLS	5/15
	Florida	H	10.75 AE	14.69 MW	19.08 AEX	FLBLS	7/16-9/16
	Fort Lauderdale-Pompano Beach-Deerfield Beach PMSA, FL	H	10.33 AE	14.81 MW	17.66 AEX	FLBLS	7/16-9/16
	Miami-Miami Beach-Kendall PMSA, FL	H	11.78 AE	14.14 MW	16.13 AEX	FLBLS	7/16-9/16
	Orlando-Kissimmee-Sanford MSA, FL	H	9.97 AE	14.01 MW	17.78 AEX	FLBLS	7/16-9/16
	Tampa-St. Petersburg-Clearwater MSA, FL	H	12.44 AE	16.73 MW	22.88 AEX	FLBLS	7/16-9/16
	Georgia	Y	23150 FQ	29570 MW	38480 TQ	USBLS	5/15
	Atlanta-Sandy Springs-Roswell MSA, GA	Y	22210 FQ	27400 MW	35350 TQ	USBLS	5/15
	Idaho	Y	21570 FQ	24610 MW	29610 TQ	USBLS	5/15
	Boise City MSA, ID	Y	21120 FQ	23900 MW	28610 TQ	USBLS	5/15
	Illinois	Y	22640 FQ	29540 MW	37880 TQ	USBLS	5/15
	Chicago-Naperville-Arlington Heights PMSA, IL	Y	22270 FQ	29070 MW	37520 TQ	USBLS	5/15
	Lake County-Kenosha County PMSA, IL-WI	Y	23640 FQ	30520 MW	37790 TQ	USBLS	5/15
	Indiana	Y	21730 FQ	26410 MW	34130 TQ	USBLS	5/15
	Indianapolis-Carmel-Anderson MSA, IN	Y	22090 FQ	27350 MW	35320 TQ	USBLS	5/15
	Iowa	Y	31090 FQ	37860 MW	45440 TQ	USBLS	5/15
	Des Moines-West Des Moines MSA, IA	Y	25250 FQ	29700 MW	35680 TQ	USBLS	5/15
	Kansas	Y	25860 FQ	29770 MW	35700 TQ	USBLS	5/15
	Wichita MSA, KS	Y	27300 FQ	34770 MW	44180 TQ	USBLS	5/15
	Kentucky	Y	24420 FQ	32850 MW	38100 TQ	USBLS	5/15
	Louisville-Jefferson County MSA, KY-IN	Y	21980 FQ	24630 MW	33540 TQ	USBLS	5/15
	Louisiana	Y	29710 FQ	36780 MW	46460 TQ	USBLS	5/15
	New Orleans-Metairie MSA, LA	Y	30790 FQ	37550 MW	48780 TQ	USBLS	5/15
	Maine	Y	25110 FQ	29450 MW	36940 TQ	USBLS	5/15
	Portland-South Portland MSA, ME	Y	25110 FQ	29110 MW	36550 TQ	USBLS	5/15
	Maryland	Y	21861 AE	34642 MW	41032 AEX	MDBLS	4/16
	Baltimore-Columbia-Towson MSA, MD	Y	21130 FQ	32880 MW	41950 TQ	USBLS	5/15
	Massachusetts	Y	29060 FQ	36300 MW	46470 TQ	USBLS	5/15
	Boston-Cambridge-Newton NECTA, MA	Y	29750 FQ	37580 MW	47900 TQ	USBLS	5/15

AE	Average entry wage	AWR	Average wage range	H	Hourly	LR	Low end range	MTC	Median total compensation
AEX	Average experienced wage	B	Biweekly	HI	Highest wage paid	M	Monthly	MW	Median wage paid
ATC	Average total compensation	D	Daily	HR	High end range	MCC	Median cash compensation	MWR	Median wage range
AW	Average wage paid	FQ	First quartile wage	LO	Lowest wage paid	ME	Median entry wage	S	See annotated source

TCC Total cash compensation
TQ Third quartile wage
W Weekly
Y Yearly

Occupation/Type/Industry	Location	Per	Low	Mid	High	Source	Date
Electrical and Electronic Equipment Assembler	Worcester MSA, MA-CT	Y	25220 FQ	33870 MW	43160 TQ	USBLS	5/15
	Michigan	Y	23940 FQ	29720 MW	37970 TQ	USBLS	5/15
	Detroit-Dearborn-Livonia PMSA, MI	Y	23090 FQ	28960 MW	35570 TQ	USBLS	5/15
	Grand Rapids-Wyoming MSA, MI	Y	25700 FQ	30070 MW	40250 TQ	USBLS	5/15
	Minnesota	Y	27792 FQ	32489 MW	37967 TQ	MNBLS	1/16-3/16
	Minneapolis-St. Paul-Bloomington MSA, MN-WI	Y	28349 FQ	33289 MW	38412 TQ	MNBLS	1/16-3/16
	Mississippi	Y	19260 FQ	24210 MW	36180 TQ	USBLS	5/15
	Missouri	Y	26400 FQ	33400 MW	40210 TQ	USBLS	5/15
	Kansas City MSA, MO-KS	Y	23780 FQ	27900 MW	31850 TQ	USBLS	5/15
	St. Louis MSA, MO-IL	Y	28380 FQ	36790 MW	44370 TQ	USBLS	5/15
	Montana	Y	25250 FQ	33370 MW	40360 TQ	USBLS	5/15
	Nebraska	Y	26460 FQ	31330 MW	36250 TQ	NEBLS	7/16-9/16
	Omaha-Council Bluffs MSA, NE-IA	Y	27860 FQ	33525 MW	38265 TQ	NEBLS	7/16-9/16
	Nevada	Y	24240 FQ	29670 MW	36990 TQ	USBLS	5/15
	Las Vegas-Henderson-Paradise MSA, NV	Y	23390 FQ	28480 MW	37750 TQ	USBLS	5/15
	New Hampshire	H	10.81 AE	15.09 MW	18.52 AEX	NHBLS	6/16
	Manchester NECTA, NH	H	11.60 AE	15.59 MW	16.93 AEX	NHBLS	6/16
	Nashua NECTA, NH-MA	Y	25750 FQ	34010 MW	42170 TQ	USBLS	5/15
	New Jersey	Y	24700 FQ	30700 MW	40110 TQ	USBLS	5/15
	Camden PMSA, NJ	Y	25140 FQ	32260 MW	43030 TQ	USBLS	5/15
	Newark PMSA, NJ-PA	Y	22800 FQ	28950 MW	37210 TQ	USBLS	5/15
	Trenton MSA, NJ	Y	24170 FQ	34350 MW	44140 TQ	USBLS	5/15
	New Mexico	Y	22350 FQ	27580 MW	35640 TQ	USBLS	5/15
	Albuquerque MSA, NM	Y	24130 FQ	30170 MW	37240 TQ	USBLS	5/15
	New York	Y	22090 AE	29940 MW	39250 AEX	NYBLS	1/16-3/16
	Buffalo-Cheektowaga-Niagara Falls MSA, NY	Y	24000 FQ	28250 MW	33650 TQ	USBLS	5/15
	Nassau County-Suffolk County PMSA, NY	Y	26650 FQ	37440 MW	48010 TQ	USBLS	5/15
	New York-Jersey City-White Plains PMSA, NY-NJ	Y	24730 FQ	31170 MW	41870 TQ	USBLS	5/15
	Rochester MSA, NY	Y	24130 FQ	28630 MW	35620 TQ	USBLS	5/15
	North Carolina	Y	22030 FQ	27800 MW	34650 TQ	USBLS	5/15
	Charlotte-Concord-Gastonia MSA, NC-SC	Y	21770 FQ	28480 MW	38340 TQ	USBLS	5/15
	Raleigh MSA, NC	Y	20080 FQ	24740 MW	30710 TQ	USBLS	5/15
	North Dakota	Y	22730 FQ	28020 MW	36610 TQ	USBLS	5/15
	Fargo MSA, ND-MN	Y	21790 FQ	26400 MW	30640 TQ	USBLS	5/15
	Ohio	Y	23530 FQ	29520 MW	37660 TQ	USBLS	5/15
	Cincinnati MSA, OH-KY-IN	Y	27540 FQ	33750 MW	40580 TQ	USBLS	5/15
	Cleveland-Elyria MSA, OH	Y	22220 FQ	28230 MW	36900 TQ	USBLS	5/15
	Columbus MSA, OH	Y	25820 FQ	30770 MW	38590 TQ	USBLS	5/15
	Oklahoma	Y	24290 FQ	29050 MW	35260 TQ	USBLS	5/15
	Oklahoma City MSA, OK	Y	23500 FQ	28280 MW	33760 TQ	USBLS	5/15
	Tulsa MSA, OK	Y	25800 FQ	28600 MW	32830 TQ	USBLS	5/15
	Oregon	H	12.99 FQ	16.51 MW	20.10 TQ	ORBLS	2016
	Portland-Vancouver-Hillsboro MSA, OR-WA	Y	26120 FQ	32380 MW	38430 TQ	USBLS	5/15
	Pennsylvania	Y	27020 FQ	35250 MW	44330 TQ	USBLS	5/15
	Allentown-Bethlehem-Easton MSA, PA-NJ	Y	27680 FQ	32740 MW	37670 TQ	USBLS	5/15
	Harrisburg-Carlisle MSA, PA	Y	22710 FQ	27970 MW	36930 TQ	USBLS	5/15
	Montgomery County-Bucks County-Chester County PMSA, PA	Y	26900 FQ	33590 MW	43260 TQ	USBLS	5/15
	Philadelphia PMSA, PA	Y	25410 FQ	31340 MW	43030 TQ	USBLS	5/15
	Pittsburgh MSA, PA	Y	26750 FQ	33540 MW	39510 TQ	USBLS	5/15
	Rhode Island	Y	28450 FQ	39110 MW	47950 TQ	USBLS	5/15
	Providence-Warwick MSA, RI-MA	Y	26880 FQ	37310 MW	47020 TQ	USBLS	5/15
	South Carolina	Y	28630 FQ	35670 MW	43470 TQ	USBLS	5/15
	Charleston-North Charleston MSA, SC	Y	27080 FQ	40530 MW	51980 TQ	USBLS	5/15
	Columbia MSA, SC	Y	32700 FQ	35500 MW	38300 TQ	USBLS	5/15
	Greenville-Anderson-Mauldin MSA, SC	Y	23890 FQ	30340 MW	36560 TQ	USBLS	5/15

AE	Average entry wage	AWR	Average wage range	H Hourly
AEX	Average experienced wage	B	Biweekly	HI Highest wage paid
ATC	Average total compensation	D	Daily	HR High end range
AW	Average wage paid	FQ	First quartile wage	LO Lowest wage paid

LR Low end range   MTC Median total compensation   TCC Total cash compensation
M Monthly   MW Median wage paid   TQ Third quartile wage
MCC Median cash compensation   MWR Median wage range   W Weekly
ME Median entry wage   S See annotated source   Y Yearly

Occupation/Type/Industry	Location	Per	Low	Mid	High	Source	Date
Electrical and Electronic Equipment Assembler							
	South Dakota	Y	22930 FQ	26610 MW	29750 TQ	USBLS	5/15
	Sioux Falls MSA, SD	Y	23680 FQ	27080 MW	30190 TQ	USBLS	5/15
	Tennessee	Y	20900 FQ	26910 MW	33490 TQ	USBLS	5/15
	Knoxville MSA, TN	Y	25680 FQ	31330 MW	39330 TQ	USBLS	5/15
	Memphis MSA, TN-MS-AR	Y	17840 FQ	19910 MW	22880 TQ	USBLS	5/15
	Nashville-Davidson–Murfreesboro–Franklin MSA, TN	Y	27090 FQ	32620 MW	36370 TQ	USBLS	5/15
	Texas	Y	22350 FQ	27930 MW	35550 TQ	USBLS	5/15
	Austin-Round Rock MSA, TX	Y	26250 FQ	31230 MW	38070 TQ	USBLS	5/15
	Dallas-Plano-Irving PMSA, TX	Y	21010 FQ	24930 MW	30710 TQ	USBLS	5/15
	Fort Worth-Arlington PMSA, TX	Y	21110 FQ	27300 MW	31080 TQ	USBLS	5/15
	Houston-The Woodlands-Sugar Land MSA, TX	Y	22040 FQ	27790 MW	35800 TQ	USBLS	5/15
	San Antonio-New Braunfels MSA, TX	Y	23740 FQ	29830 MW	38820 TQ	USBLS	5/15
	Utah	Y	26600 FQ	33300 MW	39760 TQ	USBLS	5/15
	Ogden-Clearfield MSA, UT	Y	22300 FQ	33390 MW	37610 TQ	USBLS	5/15
	Provo-Orem MSA, UT	Y	31890 FQ	34730 MW	37580 TQ	USBLS	5/15
	Salt Lake City MSA, UT	Y	28480 FQ	35700 MW	46050 TQ	USBLS	5/15
	Vermont	Y	32210 FQ	45010 MW	54050 TQ	USBLS	5/15
	Burlington-South Burlington MSA, VT	Y	39370 FQ	48290 MW	55450 TQ	USBLS	5/15
	Virginia	Y	27510 FQ	33720 MW	39190 TQ	USBLS	5/15
	Richmond MSA, VA	Y	24380 FQ	29530 MW	39090 TQ	USBLS	5/15
	Virginia Beach-Norfolk-Newport News MSA, VA-NC	Y	27630 FQ	32150 MW	38150 TQ	USBLS	5/15
	Washington	H	14.24 FQ	17.07 MW	20.58 TQ	WABLS	3/16
	Olympia-Tumwater MSA, WA	Y	23760 FQ	32210 MW	40880 TQ	USBLS	5/15
	Seattle-Bellevue-Everett PMSA, WA	H	14.36 FQ	17.05 MW	20.06 TQ	WABLS	3/16
	Tacoma-Lakewood PMSA, WA	H	19.19 FQ	22.03 MW	24.67 TQ	WABLS	3/16
	West Virginia	Y	25030 FQ	34540 MW	43070 TQ	USBLS	5/15
	Huntington-Ashland MSA, WV-KY-OH	Y	27490 FQ	34490 MW	38450 TQ	USBLS	5/15
	Wisconsin	Y	24280 FQ	28930 MW	36350 TQ	USBLS	5/15
	Madison MSA, WI	Y	25840 FQ	29990 MW	38760 TQ	USBLS	5/15
	Milwaukee-Waukesha-West Allis MSA, WI	Y	26050 FQ	30180 MW	38200 TQ	USBLS	5/15
	Wyoming	Y	27200 FQ	30470 MW	37620 TQ	USBLS	5/15
	Puerto Rico	Y	17360 FQ	19080 MW	23450 TQ	USBLS	5/15
	San Juan-Carolina-Caguas MSA, PR	Y	17110 FQ	18580 MW	20830 TQ	USBLS	5/15
Electrical and Electronics Drafter	Alabama	Y	40885 AE	64513 AW	76317 AEX	ALBLS	6/16
	Birmingham-Hoover MSA, AL	Y	41884 AE	54513 AW	60823 AEX	ALBLS	6/16
	Alaska	Y	52510 FQ	67860 MW	78040 TQ	USBLS	5/15
	Anchorage MSA, AK	Y	50080 FQ	69350 MW	80060 TQ	USBLS	5/15
	Arizona	Y	43140 FQ	52220 MW	70500 TQ	USBLS	5/15
	Phoenix-Mesa-Scottsdale MSA, AZ	Y	43550 FQ	52860 MW	70990 TQ	USBLS	5/15
	Tucson MSA, AZ	Y	41090 FQ	47510 MW	68160 TQ	USBLS	5/15
	Arkansas	Y	50040 FQ	58620 MW	69290 TQ	USBLS	5/15
	Little Rock-North Little Rock-Conway MSA, AR	Y	56720 FQ	65070 MW	73350 TQ	USBLS	5/15
	California	H	23.34 FQ	28.88 MW	35.94 TQ	CABLS	1/16-3/16
	Anaheim-Santa Ana-Irvine PMSA, CA	H	23.33 FQ	29.66 MW	36.00 TQ	CABLS	1/16-3/16
	Los Angeles-Long Beach-Glendale PMSA, CA	H	21.99 FQ	27.47 MW	35.65 TQ	CABLS	1/16-3/16
	Oakland-Hayward-Berkeley PMSA, CA	H	27.63 FQ	35.64 MW	42.51 TQ	CABLS	1/16-3/16
	Riverside-San Bernardino-Ontario MSA, CA	H	25.20 FQ	29.83 MW	36.58 TQ	CABLS	1/16-3/16
	Sacramento–Roseville–Arden-Arcade MSA, CA	H	24.88 FQ	29.96 MW	37.55 TQ	CABLS	1/16-3/16
	San Diego-Carlsbad MSA, CA	H	23.92 FQ	27.33 MW	30.44 TQ	CABLS	1/16-3/16
	San Francisco-Redwood City-South San Francisco PMSA, CA	H	25.40 FQ	28.88 MW	35.55 TQ	CABLS	1/16-3/16

AE Average entry wage	**AWR** Average wage range	**H** Hourly	**LR** Low end range	**MTC** Median total compensation	**TCC** Total cash compensation
AEX Average experienced wage	**B** Biweekly	**HI** Highest wage paid	**M** Monthly	**MW** Median wage paid	**TQ** Third quartile wage
ATC Average total compensation	**D** Daily	**HR** High end range	**MCC** Median cash compensation	**MWR** Median wage range	**W** Weekly
AW Average wage paid	**FQ** First quartile wage	**LO** Lowest wage paid	**ME** Median entry wage	**S** See annotated source	**Y** Yearly

Occupation/Type/Industry	Location	Per	Low	Mid	High	Source	Date
Electrical and Electronics Drafter	Colorado	Y	53300 FQ	63780 MW	85230 TQ	USBLS	5/15
	Denver-Aurora-Lakewood MSA, CO	Y	54030 FQ	65600 MW	88630 TQ	USBLS	5/15
	Connecticut	Y		67920 MW		CTBLS	1/16-3/16
	Bridgeport-Stamford-Norwalk MSA, CT	Y	54840 FQ	66710 MW	76950 TQ	USBLS	5/15
	Hartford-West Hartford-East Hartford MSA, CT	Y	50010 FQ	60930 MW	76990 TQ	USBLS	5/15
	Delaware	Y	44520 FQ	63800 MW	74540 TQ	USBLS	5/15
	Wilmington PMSA, DE-MD-NJ	Y	45230 FQ	62830 MW	75450 TQ	USBLS	5/15
	Washington-Arlington-Alexandria PMSA, DC-VA-MD-WV	Y	46550 FQ	68640 MW	86680 TQ	USBLS	5/15
	Florida	H	14.60 AE	23.54 MW	27.68 AEX	FLBLS	7/16-9/16
	Fort Lauderdale-Pompano Beach-Deerfield Beach PMSA, FL	H	15.84 AE	18.45 MW	22.22 AEX	FLBLS	7/16-9/16
	Miami-Miami Beach-Kendall PMSA, FL	H	14.36 AE	23.42 MW	26.74 AEX	FLBLS	7/16-9/16
	Orlando-Kissimmee-Sanford MSA, FL	H	15.33 AE	23.29 MW	26.52 AEX	FLBLS	7/16-9/16
	Tampa-St. Petersburg-Clearwater MSA, FL	H	13.45 AE	24.63 MW	30.31 AEX	FLBLS	7/16-9/16
	Georgia	Y	50100 FQ	63120 MW	85990 TQ	USBLS	5/15
	Atlanta-Sandy Springs-Roswell MSA, GA	Y	52440 FQ	67510 MW	88770 TQ	USBLS	5/15
	Augusta-Richmond County MSA, GA-SC	Y	51550 FQ	60300 MW	74660 TQ	USBLS	5/15
	Hawaii	Y	44510 FQ	58070 MW	75350 TQ	USBLS	5/15
	Urban Honolulu MSA, HI	Y	45320 FQ	58730 MW	75060 TQ	USBLS	5/15
	Idaho	Y	44110 FQ	55700 MW	77810 TQ	USBLS	5/15
	Boise City MSA, ID	Y	54800 FQ	76880 MW	118980 TQ	USBLS	5/15
	Illinois	Y	51950 FQ	68080 MW	87610 TQ	USBLS	5/15
	Chicago-Naperville-Arlington Heights PMSA, IL	Y	54590 FQ	74750 MW	91320 TQ	USBLS	5/15
	Indiana	Y	44660 FQ	59690 MW	72510 TQ	USBLS	5/15
	Indianapolis-Carmel-Anderson MSA, IN	Y	52010 FQ	65570 MW	75100 TQ	USBLS	5/15
	Iowa	Y	35840 FQ	49290 MW	67670 TQ	USBLS	5/15
	Des Moines-West Des Moines MSA, IA	Y	33950 FQ	40190 MW	58110 TQ	USBLS	5/15
	Kansas	Y	41100 FQ	50640 MW	64560 TQ	USBLS	5/15
	Wichita MSA, KS	Y	37820 FQ	53760 MW	61910 TQ	USBLS	5/15
	Kentucky	Y	42810 FQ	54990 MW	71670 TQ	USBLS	5/15
	Louisville-Jefferson County MSA, KY-IN	Y	45010 FQ	57380 MW	79130 TQ	USBLS	5/15
	Louisiana	Y	47850 FQ	59990 MW	79000 TQ	USBLS	5/15
	Baton Rouge MSA, LA	Y	45650 FQ	63100 MW	95410 TQ	USBLS	5/15
	New Orleans-Metairie MSA, LA	Y	50340 FQ	61860 MW	80860 TQ	USBLS	5/15
	Maine	Y	61420 FQ	68640 MW	75010 TQ	USBLS	5/15
	Maryland	Y	38343 AE	61142 MW	72541 AEX	MDBLS	4/16
	Baltimore-Columbia-Towson MSA, MD	Y	45590 FQ	58580 MW	74350 TQ	USBLS	5/15
	Massachusetts	Y	47920 FQ	62330 MW	84560 TQ	USBLS	5/15
	Boston-Cambridge-Newton NECTA, MA	Y	51790 FQ	61450 MW	76730 TQ	USBLS	5/15
	Worcester MSA, MA-CT	Y	41140 FQ	50980 MW	64200 TQ	USBLS	5/15
	Michigan	Y	38790 FQ	51890 MW	68020 TQ	USBLS	5/15
	Detroit-Dearborn-Livonia PMSA, MI	Y	38080 FQ	51950 MW	63540 TQ	USBLS	5/15
	Grand Rapids-Wyoming MSA, MI	Y	40990 FQ	53270 MW	62370 TQ	USBLS	5/15
	Minnesota	Y	43165 FQ	49999 MW	63931 TQ	MNBLS	1/16-3/16
	Minneapolis-St. Paul-Bloomington MSA, MN-WI	Y	43941 FQ	50221 MW	63114 TQ	MNBLS	1/16-3/16
	Mississippi	Y	35900 FQ	48550 MW	62370 TQ	USBLS	5/15
	Jackson MSA, MS	Y	34980 FQ	39370 MW	57140 TQ	USBLS	5/15
	Missouri	Y	49350 FQ	59050 MW	73160 TQ	USBLS	5/15
	Kansas City MSA, MO-KS	Y	45050 FQ	55820 MW	68720 TQ	USBLS	5/15
	St. Louis MSA, MO-IL	Y	51720 FQ	61530 MW	77290 TQ	USBLS	5/15

AE	Average entry wage	**AWR**	Average wage range	**H**	Hourly
AEX	Average experienced wage	**B**	Biweekly	**HI**	Highest wage paid
ATC	Average total compensation	**D**	Daily	**HR**	High end range
AW	Average wage paid	**FQ**	First quartile wage	**LO**	Lowest wage paid

LR	Low end range	**MTC**	Median total compensation	**TCC** Total cash compensation
M	Monthly	**MW**	Median wage paid	**TQ** Third quartile wage
MCC	Median cash compensation	**MWR**	Median wage range	**W** Weekly
ME	Median entry wage	**S**	See annotated source	**Y** Yearly

Occupation/Type/Industry	Location	Per	Low	Mid	High	Source	Date
Electrical and Electronics Drafter	Montana	Y	38890 FQ	52120 MW	62050 TQ	USBLS	5/15
	Billings MSA, MT	Y	40470 FQ	52750 MW	61700 TQ	USBLS	5/15
	Nebraska	Y	40020 FQ	47150 MW	57740 TQ	NEBLS	7/16-9/16
	Omaha-Council Bluffs MSA, NE-IA	Y	40305 FQ	49980 MW	59605 TQ	NEBLS	7/16-9/16
	Nevada	Y	51590 FQ	60540 MW	71140 TQ	USBLS	5/15
	Las Vegas-Henderson-Paradise MSA, NV	Y	52800 FQ	61400 MW	71680 TQ	USBLS	5/15
	New Hampshire	H	21.27 AE	30.66 MW	36.24 AEX	NHBLS	6/16
	Manchester NECTA, NH	H	25.15 AE	30.51 MW	32.59 AEX	NHBLS	6/16
	Nashua NECTA, NH-MA	Y	50800 FQ	69610 MW	84690 TQ	USBLS	5/15
	New Jersey	Y	48090 FQ	64460 MW	78760 TQ	USBLS	5/15
	Camden PMSA, NJ	Y	43210 FQ	50500 MW	66770 TQ	USBLS	5/15
	Newark PMSA, NJ-PA	Y	52040 FQ	64590 MW	78450 TQ	USBLS	5/15
	New Mexico	Y	36150 FQ	47170 MW	61810 TQ	USBLS	5/15
	Albuquerque MSA, NM	Y	35890 FQ	44800 MW	63310 TQ	USBLS	5/15
	New York	Y	46880 AE	70410 MW	84030 AEX	NYBLS	1/16-3/16
	Buffalo-Cheektowaga-Niagara Falls MSA, NY	Y	43430 FQ	54760 MW	61040 TQ	USBLS	5/15
	Nassau County-Suffolk County PMSA, NY	Y	54880 FQ	69260 MW	82950 TQ	USBLS	5/15
	New York-Jersey City-White Plains PMSA, NY-NJ	Y	58700 FQ	77770 MW	92560 TQ	USBLS	5/15
	Rochester MSA, NY	Y	46660 FQ	61440 MW	83520 TQ	USBLS	5/15
	North Carolina	Y	42440 FQ	52520 MW	65400 TQ	USBLS	5/15
	Charlotte-Concord-Gastonia MSA, NC-SC	Y	38940 FQ	52680 MW	63410 TQ	USBLS	5/15
	Raleigh MSA, NC	Y	42650 FQ	48650 MW	61480 TQ	USBLS	5/15
	North Dakota	Y	41330 FQ	50380 MW	59970 TQ	USBLS	5/15
	Ohio	Y	41310 FQ	51010 MW	63920 TQ	USBLS	5/15
	Cincinnati MSA, OH-KY-IN	Y	41530 FQ	51950 MW	66520 TQ	USBLS	5/15
	Cleveland-Elyria MSA, OH	Y	45000 FQ	54290 MW	69080 TQ	USBLS	5/15
	Columbus MSA, OH	Y	44230 FQ	51970 MW	66610 TQ	USBLS	5/15
	Oklahoma	Y	48700 FQ	56410 MW	63540 TQ	USBLS	5/15
	Oklahoma City MSA, OK	Y	53110 FQ	58340 MW	63930 TQ	USBLS	5/15
	Tulsa MSA, OK	Y	47750 FQ	55620 MW	62660 TQ	USBLS	5/15
	Oregon	H	21.11 FQ	25.34 MW	29.85 TQ	ORBLS	2016
	Portland-Vancouver-Hillsboro MSA, OR-WA	Y	43060 FQ	51680 MW	60510 TQ	USBLS	5/15
	Pennsylvania	Y	43170 FQ	56350 MW	73900 TQ	USBLS	5/15
	Allentown-Bethlehem-Easton MSA, PA-NJ	Y	40720 FQ	58650 MW	74450 TQ	USBLS	5/15
	Harrisburg-Carlisle MSA, PA	Y	36500 FQ	45150 MW	58680 TQ	USBLS	5/15
	Montgomery County-Bucks County-Chester County PMSA, PA	Y	43500 FQ	56760 MW	80060 TQ	USBLS	5/15
	Philadelphia PMSA, PA	Y	53630 FQ	69100 MW	97120 TQ	USBLS	5/15
	Pittsburgh MSA, PA	Y	43140 FQ	54700 MW	67980 TQ	USBLS	5/15
	Rhode Island	Y	40910 FQ	52580 MW	71040 TQ	USBLS	5/15
	Providence-Warwick MSA, RI-MA	Y	41960 FQ	56200 MW	75250 TQ	USBLS	5/15
	South Carolina	Y	48070 FQ	58580 MW	76330 TQ	USBLS	5/15
	Charleston-North Charleston MSA, SC	Y	44660 FQ	52320 MW	61560 TQ	USBLS	5/15
	Columbia MSA, SC	Y	52150 FQ	60240 MW	73300 TQ	USBLS	5/15
	Greenville-Anderson-Mauldin MSA, SC	Y	47270 FQ	61800 MW	103860 TQ	USBLS	5/15
	Tennessee	Y	42410 FQ	53980 MW	64910 TQ	USBLS	5/15
	Knoxville MSA, TN	Y	50320 FQ	58320 MW	68910 TQ	USBLS	5/15
	Memphis MSA, TN-MS-AR	Y	43510 FQ	49790 MW	58170 TQ	USBLS	5/15
	Nashville-Davidson–Murfreesboro–Franklin MSA, TN	Y	46900 FQ	57810 MW	71350 TQ	USBLS	5/15
	Texas	Y	54940 FQ	71650 MW	92480 TQ	USBLS	5/15
	Austin-Round Rock MSA, TX	Y	59710 FQ	80040 MW	99760 TQ	USBLS	5/15
	Dallas-Plano-Irving PMSA, TX	Y	53450 FQ	66220 MW	84870 TQ	USBLS	5/15
	Fort Worth-Arlington PMSA, TX	Y	54860 FQ	63050 MW	77740 TQ	USBLS	5/15
	Houston-The Woodlands-Sugar Land MSA, TX	Y	58840 FQ	81290 MW	98510 TQ	USBLS	5/15
	San Antonio-New Braunfels MSA, TX	Y	45270 FQ	56500 MW	71620 TQ	USBLS	5/15

AE	Average entry wage	AWR	Average wage range	H	Hourly
AEX	Average experienced wage	B	Biweekly	HI	Highest wage paid
ATC	Average total compensation	D	Daily	HR	High end range
AW	Average wage paid	FQ	First quartile wage	LO	Lowest wage paid

LR	Low end range	MTC	Median total compensation
M	Monthly	MW	Median wage paid
MCC	Median cash compensation	MWR	Median wage range
ME	Median entry wage	S	See annotated source

TCC	Total cash compensation		
TQ	Third quartile wage		
W	Weekly		
Y	Yearly		

Occupation/Type/Industry	Location	Per	Low	Mid	High	Source	Date
Electrical and Electronics Drafter	Utah	Y	41210 FQ	60300 MW	79090 TQ	USBLS	5/15
	Salt Lake City MSA, UT	Y	51680 FQ	69230 MW	87690 TQ	USBLS	5/15
	Vermont	Y	53510 FQ	76350 MW	94900 TQ	USBLS	5/15
	Burlington-South Burlington MSA, VT	Y	58970 FQ	84890 MW	98510 TQ	USBLS	5/15
	Virginia	Y	38110 FQ	53670 MW	77080 TQ	USBLS	5/15
	Richmond MSA, VA	Y	37230 FQ	50410 MW	86160 TQ	USBLS	5/15
	Virginia Beach-Norfolk-Newport News MSA, VA-NC	Y	32180 FQ	46500 MW	61410 TQ	USBLS	5/15
	Washington	H	30.51 FQ	39.44 MW	47.57 TQ	WABLS	3/16
	Seattle-Bellevue-Everett PMSA, WA	H	34.27 FQ	42.66 MW	49.18 TQ	WABLS	3/16
	Tacoma-Lakewood PMSA, WA	H	22.19 FQ	32.83 MW	36.26 TQ	WABLS	3/16
	West Virginia	Y	43830 FQ	48930 MW	59060 TQ	USBLS	5/15
	Wisconsin	Y	43390 FQ	53370 MW	61690 TQ	USBLS	5/15
	Madison MSA, WI	Y	47130 FQ	54100 MW	59790 TQ	USBLS	5/15
	Milwaukee-Waukesha-West Allis MSA, WI	Y	46030 FQ	56210 MW	68940 TQ	USBLS	5/15
	Puerto Rico	Y	28950 FQ	41310 MW	56340 TQ	USBLS	5/15
	San Juan-Carolina-Caguas MSA, PR	Y	32770 FQ	42330 MW	58730 TQ	USBLS	5/15
Electrical and Electronics Installer and Repairer							
Transportation Equipment	Alabama	Y	50831 AE	58306 AW	62038 AEX	ALBLS	6/16
Transportation Equipment	Birmingham-Hoover MSA, AL	Y	40304 AE	53485 AW	60075 AEX	ALBLS	6/16
Transportation Equipment	Alaska	Y	63280 FQ	69030 MW	74240 TQ	USBLS	5/15
Transportation Equipment	Arizona	Y	46750 FQ	54510 MW	63880 TQ	USBLS	5/15
Transportation Equipment	California	H	27.44 FQ	32.60 MW	41.59 TQ	CABLS	1/16-3/16
Transportation Equipment	Anaheim-Santa Ana-Irvine PMSA, CA	H	20.02 FQ	22.75 MW	27.61 TQ	CABLS	1/16-3/16
Transportation Equipment	Los Angeles-Long Beach-Glendale PMSA, CA	H	29.19 FQ	35.56 MW	41.33 TQ	CABLS	1/16-3/16
Transportation Equipment	Oakland-Hayward-Berkeley PMSA, CA	H	31.04 FQ	38.08 MW	44.07 TQ	CABLS	1/16-3/16
Transportation Equipment	Riverside-San Bernardino-Ontario MSA, CA	H	19.44 FQ	26.02 MW	29.24 TQ	CABLS	1/16-3/16
Transportation Equipment	Sacramento–Roseville–Arden-Arcade MSA, CA	H	18.89 FQ	35.52 MW	43.07 TQ	CABLS	1/16-3/16
Transportation Equipment	San Diego-Carlsbad MSA, CA	H	26.01 FQ	28.26 MW	30.51 TQ	CABLS	1/16-3/16
Transportation Equipment	San Francisco-Redwood City-South San Francisco PMSA, CA	H	26.41 FQ	29.27 MW	34.91 TQ	CABLS	1/16-3/16
Transportation Equipment	Colorado	Y	53630 FQ	59570 MW	67520 TQ	USBLS	5/15
Transportation Equipment	Connecticut	Y		58951 MW		CTBLS	1/16-3/16
Transportation Equipment	Hartford-West Hartford-East Hartford MSA, CT	Y	46390 FQ	60040 MW	71600 TQ	USBLS	5/15
Transportation Equipment	Washington-Arlington-Alexandria PMSA, DC-VA-MD-WV	Y	55140 FQ	64840 MW	75800 TQ	USBLS	5/15
Transportation Equipment	Florida	H	17.81 AE	26.17 MW	30.87 AEX	FLBLS	7/16-9/16
Transportation Equipment	Fort Lauderdale-Pompano Beach-Deerfield Beach PMSA, FL	H	17.59 AE	24.00 MW	29.64 AEX	FLBLS	7/16-9/16
Transportation Equipment	Miami-Miami Beach-Kendall PMSA, FL	H	21.06 AE	31.40 MW	34.38 AEX	FLBLS	7/16-9/16
Transportation Equipment	Orlando-Kissimmee-Sanford MSA, FL	H	16.79 AE	22.77 MW	26.84 AEX	FLBLS	7/16-9/16
Transportation Equipment	Georgia	Y	41460 FQ	47710 MW	63550 TQ	USBLS	5/15
Transportation Equipment	Illinois	Y	44940 FQ	56820 MW	64310 TQ	USBLS	5/15
Transportation Equipment	Chicago-Naperville-Arlington Heights PMSA, IL	Y	50680 FQ	65990 MW	78330 TQ	USBLS	5/15
Transportation Equipment	Indiana	Y	42440 FQ	54890 MW	62670 TQ	USBLS	5/15
Transportation Equipment	Iowa	Y	43800 FQ	50980 MW	58570 TQ	USBLS	5/15
Transportation Equipment	Kansas	Y	29640 FQ	45130 MW	59570 TQ	USBLS	5/15
Transportation Equipment	Kentucky	Y	53620 FQ	57330 MW	61040 TQ	USBLS	5/15
Transportation Equipment	Louisiana	Y	39390 FQ	50090 MW	58990 TQ	USBLS	5/15
Transportation Equipment	Baton Rouge MSA, LA	Y	43810 FQ	52440 MW	59590 TQ	USBLS	5/15
Transportation Equipment	New Orleans-Metairie MSA, LA	Y	42030 FQ	52610 MW	61950 TQ	USBLS	5/15
Transportation Equipment	Maine	Y	34700 FQ	42290 MW	55370 TQ	USBLS	5/15
Transportation Equipment	Maryland	Y	47598 AE	64621 MW	73132 AEX	MDBLS	4/16

Occupation/Type/Industry	Location	Per	Low	Mid	High	Source	Date
Electrical and Electronics Installer and Repairer							
Transportation Equipment	Baltimore-Columbia-Towson MSA, MD	Y	54900 FQ	64470 MW	73050 TQ	USBLS	5/15
Transportation Equipment	Massachusetts	Y	50610 FQ	61570 MW	76130 TQ	USBLS	5/15
Transportation Equipment	Boston-Cambridge-Newton NECTA, MA	Y	57720 FQ	69130 MW	81380 TQ	USBLS	5/15
Transportation Equipment	Michigan	Y	37730 FQ	49180 MW	56990 TQ	USBLS	5/15
Transportation Equipment	Minnesota	Y	51018 FQ	58621 MW	61688 TQ	MNBLS	1/16-3/16
Transportation Equipment	Minneapolis-St. Paul-Bloomington MSA, MN-WI	Y	55674 FQ	58259 MW	59526 TQ	MNBLS	1/16-3/16
Transportation Equipment	Mississippi	Y	31020 FQ	43120 MW	49120 TQ	USBLS	5/15
Transportation Equipment	Missouri	Y	50950 FQ	58670 MW	67030 TQ	USBLS	5/15
Transportation Equipment	Kansas City MSA, MO-KS	Y	35500 FQ	47750 MW	61580 TQ	USBLS	5/15
Transportation Equipment	St. Louis MSA, MO-IL	Y	36300 FQ	43650 MW	51590 TQ	USBLS	5/15
Transportation Equipment	Montana	Y	56950 FQ	83000 MW	91450 TQ	USBLS	5/15
Transportation Equipment	Nevada	Y	53900 FQ	72310 MW	87820 TQ	USBLS	5/15
Transportation Equipment	New Jersey	Y	51920 FQ	57370 MW	62820 TQ	USBLS	5/15
Transportation Equipment	Camden PMSA, NJ	Y	53160 FQ	58030 MW	62900 TQ	USBLS	5/15
Transportation Equipment	Newark PMSA, NJ-PA	Y	35600 FQ	48580 MW	63050 TQ	USBLS	5/15
Transportation Equipment	New York	Y	62370 AE	72370 MW	73710 AEX	NYBLS	1/16-3/16
Transportation Equipment	New York-Jersey City-White Plains PMSA, NY-NJ	Y	67860 FQ	72800 MW	77740 TQ	USBLS	5/15
Transportation Equipment	North Carolina	Y	50380 FQ	58140 MW	67070 TQ	USBLS	5/15
Transportation Equipment	North Dakota	Y	38610 FQ	52290 MW	66070 TQ	USBLS	5/15
Transportation Equipment	Ohio	Y	45830 FQ	58100 MW	68950 TQ	USBLS	5/15
Transportation Equipment	Cleveland-Elyria MSA, OH	Y	45890 FQ	53180 MW	58700 TQ	USBLS	5/15
Transportation Equipment	Columbus MSA, OH	Y	39330 FQ	47670 MW	53780 TQ	USBLS	5/15
Transportation Equipment	Oklahoma	Y	52200 FQ	55990 MW	59830 TQ	USBLS	5/15
Transportation Equipment	Oklahoma City MSA, OK	Y	53090 FQ	56470 MW	59850 TQ	USBLS	5/15
Transportation Equipment	Oregon	H	13.38 FQ	21.63 MW	34.16 TQ	ORBLS	2016
Transportation Equipment	Pennsylvania	Y	49280 FQ	58970 MW	70410 TQ	USBLS	5/15
Transportation Equipment	South Carolina	Y	41050 FQ	51080 MW	61770 TQ	USBLS	5/15
Transportation Equipment	South Dakota	Y	27480 FQ	29960 MW	34040 TQ	USBLS	5/15
Transportation Equipment	Tennessee	Y	42920 FQ	47310 MW	56340 TQ	USBLS	5/15
Transportation Equipment	Nashville-Davidson–Murfreesboro–Franklin MSA, TN	Y	44410 FQ	48700 MW	61640 TQ	USBLS	5/15
Transportation Equipment	Texas	Y	46730 FQ	56720 MW	67940 TQ	USBLS	5/15
Transportation Equipment	Austin-Round Rock MSA, TX	Y	41440 FQ	45730 MW	49650 TQ	USBLS	5/15
Transportation Equipment	Dallas-Plano-Irving PMSA, TX	Y	50690 FQ	55590 MW	60470 TQ	USBLS	5/15
Transportation Equipment	Fort Worth-Arlington PMSA, TX	Y	40810 FQ	56800 MW	70820 TQ	USBLS	5/15
Transportation Equipment	Houston-The Woodlands-Sugar Land MSA, TX	Y	48160 FQ	59100 MW	76660 TQ	USBLS	5/15
Transportation Equipment	San Antonio-New Braunfels MSA, TX	Y	51610 FQ	65800 MW	73830 TQ	USBLS	5/15
Transportation Equipment	Virginia	Y	46340 FQ	59920 MW	69760 TQ	USBLS	5/15
Transportation Equipment	Virginia Beach-Norfolk-Newport News MSA, VA-NC	Y	46800 FQ	59680 MW	69540 TQ	USBLS	5/15
Transportation Equipment	Washington	H	24.10 FQ	31.15 MW	36.82 TQ	WABLS	3/16
Transportation Equipment	Seattle-Bellevue-Everett PMSA, WA	H	26.27 FQ	31.86 MW	35.92 TQ	WABLS	3/16
Transportation Equipment	West Virginia	Y	55890 FQ	64870 MW	71860 TQ	USBLS	5/15
Transportation Equipment	Wisconsin	Y	38190 FQ	51230 MW	62140 TQ	USBLS	5/15
Transportation Equipment	Milwaukee-Waukesha-West Allis MSA, WI	Y	35350 FQ	40470 MW	50430 TQ	USBLS	5/15
Transportation Equipment	Wyoming	Y	53460 FQ	58740 MW	64000 TQ	USBLS	5/15
Transportation Equipment	Puerto Rico	Y	17720 FQ	20330 MW	28830 TQ	USBLS	5/15
Transportation Equipment	San Juan-Carolina-Caguas MSA, PR	Y	17730 FQ	20730 MW	28800 TQ	USBLS	5/15
Electrical and Electronics Repairer							
Commercial and Industrial Equipment	Alabama	Y	41159 AE	56577 AW	64286 AEX	ALBLS	6/16
Commercial and Industrial Equipment	Alaska	Y	72630 FQ	81380 MW	89380 TQ	USBLS	5/15
Commercial and Industrial Equipment	Anchorage MSA, AK	Y	77090 FQ	83420 MW	91310 TQ	USBLS	5/15
Commercial and Industrial Equipment	Arizona	Y	42110 FQ	52010 MW	64840 TQ	USBLS	5/15
Commercial and Industrial Equipment	Phoenix-Mesa-Scottsdale MSA, AZ	Y	40450 FQ	47810 MW	63230 TQ	USBLS	5/15
Commercial and Industrial Equipment	Tucson MSA, AZ	Y	54230 FQ	61700 MW	66440 TQ	USBLS	5/15

AE	Average entry wage	AWR	Average wage range	H	Hourly
AEX	Average experienced wage	B	Biweekly	HI	Highest wage paid
ATC	Average total compensation	D	Daily	HR	High wage paid
AW	Average wage paid	FQ	First quartile wage	LO	Lowest wage paid

LR	Low end range	MTC	Median total compensation	TCC	Total cash compensation
M	Monthly	MW	Median wage paid	TQ	Third quartile wage
MCC	Median cash compensation	MWR	Median wage range	W	Weekly
ME	Median entry wage	S	See annotated source	Y	Yearly

Occupation/Type/Industry	Location	Per	Low	Mid	High	Source	Date

Electrical and Electronics Repairer

Occupation/Type/Industry	Location	Per	Low	Mid	High	Source	Date
Commercial and Industrial Equipment	Arkansas	Y	36750 FQ	47160 MW	55480 TQ	USBLS	5/15
Commercial and Industrial Equipment	Little Rock-North Little Rock-Conway MSA, AR	Y	46960 FQ	51530 MW	55490 TQ	USBLS	5/15
Commercial and Industrial Equipment	California	H	21.62 FQ	28.64 MW	36.04 TQ	CABLS	1/16-3/16
Commercial and Industrial Equipment	Anaheim-Santa Ana-Irvine PMSA, CA	H	19.81 FQ	24.58 MW	32.89 TQ	CABLS	1/16-3/16
Commercial and Industrial Equipment	Los Angeles-Long Beach-Glendale PMSA, CA	H	20.91 FQ	26.96 MW	36.55 TQ	CABLS	1/16-3/16
Commercial and Industrial Equipment	Oakland-Hayward-Berkeley PMSA, CA	H	28.99 FQ	36.75 MW	43.91 TQ	CABLS	1/16-3/16
Commercial and Industrial Equipment	Riverside-San Bernardino-Ontario MSA, CA	H	24.38 FQ	29.48 MW	34.66 TQ	CABLS	1/16-3/16
Commercial and Industrial Equipment	Sacramento–Roseville–Arden-Arcade MSA, CA	H	26.13 FQ	34.80 MW	43.19 TQ	CABLS	1/16-3/16
Commercial and Industrial Equipment	San Diego-Carlsbad MSA, CA	H	25.06 FQ	29.23 MW	35.89 TQ	CABLS	1/16-3/16
Commercial and Industrial Equipment	San Francisco-Redwood City-South San Francisco PMSA, CA	H	25.75 FQ	32.97 MW	36.76 TQ	CABLS	1/16-3/16
Commercial and Industrial Equipment	Colorado	Y	48180 FQ	59000 MW	72590 TQ	USBLS	5/15
Commercial and Industrial Equipment	Denver-Aurora-Lakewood MSA, CO	Y	48140 FQ	59800 MW	71860 TQ	USBLS	5/15
Commercial and Industrial Equipment	Connecticut	Y		66466 MW		CTBLS	1/16-3/16
Commercial and Industrial Equipment	Bridgeport-Stamford-Norwalk MSA, CT	Y	49920 FQ	66750 MW	77490 TQ	USBLS	5/15
Commercial and Industrial Equipment	Hartford-West Hartford-East Hartford MSA, CT	Y	55780 FQ	66930 MW	79570 TQ	USBLS	5/15
Commercial and Industrial Equipment	Delaware	Y	56210 FQ	65630 MW	72640 TQ	USBLS	5/15
Commercial and Industrial Equipment	Wilmington PMSA, DE-MD-NJ	Y	64130 FQ	69560 MW	75400 TQ	USBLS	5/15
Commercial and Industrial Equipment	District of Columbia	Y	63970 FQ	82560 MW	100100 TQ	USBLS	5/15
Commercial and Industrial Equipment	Washington-Arlington-Alexandria PMSA, DC-VA-MD-WV	Y	57220 FQ	69260 MW	79920 TQ	USBLS	5/15
Commercial and Industrial Equipment	Florida	H	17.43 AE	25.66 MW	28.84 AEX	FLBLS	7/16-9/16
Commercial and Industrial Equipment	Fort Lauderdale-Pompano Beach-Deerfield Beach PMSA, FL	H	15.84 AE	22.30 MW	27.52 AEX	FLBLS	7/16-9/16
Commercial and Industrial Equipment	Miami-Miami Beach-Kendall PMSA, FL	H	11.86 AE	20.28 MW	27.67 AEX	FLBLS	7/16-9/16
Commercial and Industrial Equipment	Orlando-Kissimmee-Sanford MSA, FL	H	19.29 AE	25.64 MW	28.71 AEX	FLBLS	7/16-9/16
Commercial and Industrial Equipment	Tampa-St. Petersburg-Clearwater MSA, FL	H	16.09 AE	21.99 MW	26.78 AEX	FLBLS	7/16-9/16
Commercial and Industrial Equipment	Georgia	Y	47580 FQ	54730 MW	59150 TQ	USBLS	5/15
Commercial and Industrial Equipment	Atlanta-Sandy Springs-Roswell MSA, GA	Y	37050 FQ	51680 MW	69170 TQ	USBLS	5/15
Commercial and Industrial Equipment	Augusta-Richmond County MSA, GA-SC	Y	38980 FQ	53700 MW	68710 TQ	USBLS	5/15
Commercial and Industrial Equipment	Hawaii	Y	53210 FQ	66780 MW	74790 TQ	USBLS	5/15
Commercial and Industrial Equipment	Urban Honolulu MSA, HI	Y	54260 FQ	67490 MW	74800 TQ	USBLS	5/15
Commercial and Industrial Equipment	Idaho	Y	49890 FQ	56370 MW	62130 TQ	USBLS	5/15
Commercial and Industrial Equipment	Illinois	Y	40480 FQ	52930 MW	66240 TQ	USBLS	5/15
Commercial and Industrial Equipment	Chicago-Naperville-Arlington Heights PMSA, IL	Y	40970 FQ	50810 MW	69660 TQ	USBLS	5/15
Commercial and Industrial Equipment	Lake County-Kenosha County PMSA, IL-WI	Y	40140 FQ	56920 MW	65580 TQ	USBLS	5/15
Commercial and Industrial Equipment	Indiana	Y	41020 FQ	53830 MW	63820 TQ	USBLS	5/15
Commercial and Industrial Equipment	Gary PMSA, IN	Y	44680 FQ	62000 MW	81870 TQ	USBLS	5/15
Commercial and Industrial Equipment	Indianapolis-Carmel-Anderson MSA, IN	Y	37350 FQ	54290 MW	65070 TQ	USBLS	5/15
Commercial and Industrial Equipment	Iowa	Y	38500 FQ	50240 MW	58780 TQ	USBLS	5/15
Commercial and Industrial Equipment	Des Moines-West Des Moines MSA, IA	Y	36780 FQ	49770 MW	58420 TQ	USBLS	5/15
Commercial and Industrial Equipment	Kansas	Y	41610 FQ	53600 MW	64200 TQ	USBLS	5/15
Commercial and Industrial Equipment	Wichita MSA, KS	Y	35270 FQ	43400 MW	52090 TQ	USBLS	5/15
Commercial and Industrial Equipment	Kentucky	Y	44310 FQ	54730 MW	63110 TQ	USBLS	5/15
Commercial and Industrial Equipment	Louisville-Jefferson County MSA, KY-IN	Y	38900 FQ	52980 MW	62090 TQ	USBLS	5/15
Commercial and Industrial Equipment	Louisiana	Y	46590 FQ	62500 MW	74350 TQ	USBLS	5/15
Commercial and Industrial Equipment	Baton Rouge MSA, LA	Y	55730 FQ	69200 MW	79350 TQ	USBLS	5/15

AE Average entry wage	**AWR** Average wage range	**H** Hourly	**LR** Low end range	**MTC** Median total compensation	**TCC** Total cash compensation
AEX Average experienced wage	**B** Biweekly	**HI** Highest wage paid	**M** Monthly	**MW** Median wage paid	**TQ** Third quartile wage
ATC Average total compensation	**D** Daily	**HR** High end range	**MCC** Median cash compensation	**MWR** Median wage range	**W** Weekly
AW Average wage paid	**FQ** First quartile wage	**LO** Lowest wage paid	**ME** Median entry wage	**S** See annotated source	**Y** Yearly

Occupation/Type/Industry	Location	Per	Low	Mid	High	Source	Date
Electrical and Electronics Repairer							
Commercial and Industrial Equipment	New Orleans-Metairie MSA, LA	Y	51790 FQ	70510 MW	80010 TQ	USBLS	5/15
Commercial and Industrial Equipment	Maine	Y	52940 FQ	59680 MW	68730 TQ	USBLS	5/15
Commercial and Industrial Equipment	Portland-South Portland MSA, ME	Y	58650 FQ	66880 MW	72840 TQ	USBLS	5/15
Commercial and Industrial Equipment	Maryland	Y	45231 AE	66913 MW	77754 AEX	MDBLS	4/16
Commercial and Industrial Equipment	Baltimore-Columbia-Towson MSA, MD	Y	48920 FQ	69170 MW	84950 TQ	USBLS	5/15
Commercial and Industrial Equipment	Salisbury MSA, MD-DE	Y	41280 FQ	45940 MW	51810 TQ	USBLS	5/15
Commercial and Industrial Equipment	Massachusetts	Y	50400 FQ	59340 MW	70730 TQ	USBLS	5/15
Commercial and Industrial Equipment	Boston-Cambridge-Newton NECTA, MA	Y	51920 FQ	59220 MW	68950 TQ	USBLS	5/15
Commercial and Industrial Equipment	Worcester MSA, MA-CT	Y	57310 FQ	68350 MW	76210 TQ	USBLS	5/15
Commercial and Industrial Equipment	Michigan	Y	46070 FQ	57340 MW	68710 TQ	USBLS	5/15
Commercial and Industrial Equipment	Detroit-Dearborn-Livonia PMSA, MI	Y	48540 FQ	56350 MW	65990 TQ	USBLS	5/15
Commercial and Industrial Equipment	Grand Rapids-Wyoming MSA, MI	Y	42550 FQ	52770 MW	59050 TQ	USBLS	5/15
Commercial and Industrial Equipment	Minnesota	Y	52426 FQ	60491 MW	70156 TQ	MNBLS	1/16-3/16
Commercial and Industrial Equipment	Minneapolis-St. Paul-Bloomington MSA, MN-WI	Y	53391 FQ	61316 MW	71413 TQ	MNBLS	1/16-3/16
Commercial and Industrial Equipment	Mississippi	Y	41410 FQ	50450 MW	60030 TQ	USBLS	5/15
Commercial and Industrial Equipment	Jackson MSA, MS	Y	44410 FQ	55060 MW	60840 TQ	USBLS	5/15
Commercial and Industrial Equipment	Missouri	Y	41020 FQ	53580 MW	63310 TQ	USBLS	5/15
Commercial and Industrial Equipment	Kansas City MSA, MO-KS	Y	42850 FQ	54900 MW	66300 TQ	USBLS	5/15
Commercial and Industrial Equipment	St. Louis MSA, MO-IL	Y	45750 FQ	56360 MW	63820 TQ	USBLS	5/15
Commercial and Industrial Equipment	Montana	Y	50280 FQ	58910 MW	69780 TQ	USBLS	5/15
Commercial and Industrial Equipment	Nebraska	Y	37610 FQ	48690 MW	54885 TQ	NEBLS	7/16-9/16
Commercial and Industrial Equipment	Omaha-Council Bluffs MSA, NE-IA	Y	36120 FQ	50525 MW	55015 TQ	NEBLS	7/16-9/16
Commercial and Industrial Equipment	Nevada	Y	44920 FQ	60540 MW	71530 TQ	USBLS	5/15
Commercial and Industrial Equipment	Las Vegas-Henderson-Paradise MSA, NV	Y	44810 FQ	62040 MW	72780 TQ	USBLS	5/15
Commercial and Industrial Equipment	New Hampshire	H	18.66 AE	28.65 MW	32.40 AEX	NHBLS	6/16
Commercial and Industrial Equipment	Nashua NECTA, NH-MA	Y	45270 FQ	63700 MW	72320 TQ	USBLS	5/15
Commercial and Industrial Equipment	New Jersey	Y	46230 FQ	57720 MW	68000 TQ	USBLS	5/15
Commercial and Industrial Equipment	Camden PMSA, NJ	Y	41180 FQ	53100 MW	64080 TQ	USBLS	5/15
Commercial and Industrial Equipment	Newark PMSA, NJ-PA	Y	45340 FQ	57810 MW	70580 TQ	USBLS	5/15
Commercial and Industrial Equipment	Trenton MSA, NJ	Y	33650 FQ	50670 MW	57580 TQ	USBLS	5/15
Commercial and Industrial Equipment	New Mexico	Y	44890 FQ	55860 MW	67060 TQ	USBLS	5/15
Commercial and Industrial Equipment	Albuquerque MSA, NM	Y	50780 FQ	58030 MW	65850 TQ	USBLS	5/15
Commercial and Industrial Equipment	New York	Y	37600 AE	54840 MW	63060 AEX	NYBLS	1/16-3/16
Commercial and Industrial Equipment	Buffalo-Cheektowaga-Niagara Falls MSA, NY	Y	44010 FQ	54770 MW	65520 TQ	USBLS	5/15
Commercial and Industrial Equipment	Nassau County-Suffolk County PMSA, NY	Y	46320 FQ	59840 MW	74150 TQ	USBLS	5/15
Commercial and Industrial Equipment	New York-Jersey City-White Plains PMSA, NY-NJ	Y	43170 FQ	56140 MW	65590 TQ	USBLS	5/15
Commercial and Industrial Equipment	Rochester MSA, NY	Y	40060 FQ	49250 MW	60000 TQ	USBLS	5/15
Commercial and Industrial Equipment	North Carolina	Y	41340 FQ	52370 MW	62830 TQ	USBLS	5/15
Commercial and Industrial Equipment	Charlotte-Concord-Gastonia MSA, NC-SC	Y	44230 FQ	56830 MW	69090 TQ	USBLS	5/15
Commercial and Industrial Equipment	Raleigh MSA, NC	Y	33750 FQ	45730 MW	57660 TQ	USBLS	5/15
Commercial and Industrial Equipment	North Dakota	Y	53610 FQ	65120 MW	77460 TQ	USBLS	5/15
Commercial and Industrial Equipment	Ohio	Y	43160 FQ	54420 MW	64860 TQ	USBLS	5/15
Commercial and Industrial Equipment	Cincinnati MSA, OH-KY-IN	Y	46460 FQ	56780 MW	66140 TQ	USBLS	5/15
Commercial and Industrial Equipment	Cleveland-Elyria MSA, OH	Y	43870 FQ	58980 MW	69700 TQ	USBLS	5/15
Commercial and Industrial Equipment	Columbus MSA, OH	Y	43510 FQ	56820 MW	66970 TQ	USBLS	5/15
Commercial and Industrial Equipment	Oklahoma	Y	46220 FQ	55870 MW	61370 TQ	USBLS	5/15
Commercial and Industrial Equipment	Oklahoma City MSA, OK	Y	52100 FQ	56420 MW	60760 TQ	USBLS	5/15
Commercial and Industrial Equipment	Tulsa MSA, OK	Y	36030 FQ	47230 MW	67480 TQ	USBLS	5/15
Commercial and Industrial Equipment	Oregon	H	25.70 FQ	30.65 MW	36.03 TQ	ORBLS	2016
Commercial and Industrial Equipment	Portland-Vancouver-Hillsboro MSA, OR-WA	Y	52030 FQ	63640 MW	78270 TQ	USBLS	5/15
Commercial and Industrial Equipment	Pennsylvania	Y	45280 FQ	52000 MW	57450 TQ	USBLS	5/15
Commercial and Industrial Equipment	Allentown-Bethlehem-Easton MSA, PA-NJ	Y	41810 FQ	51260 MW	59230 TQ	USBLS	5/15
Commercial and Industrial Equipment	Harrisburg-Carlisle MSA, PA	Y	38320 FQ	46110 MW	53290 TQ	USBLS	5/15

AE Average entry wage	**AWR** Average wage range	**H** Hourly	**LR** Low end range	**MTC** Median total compensation	**TCC** Total cash compensation
AEX Average experienced wage	**B** Biweekly	**HI** Highest wage paid	**M** Monthly	**MW** Median wage paid	**TQ** Third quartile wage
ATC Average total compensation	**D** Daily	**HR** High end range	**MCC** Median cash compensation	**MWR** Median wage range	**W** Weekly
AW Average wage paid	**FQ** First quartile wage	**LO** Lowest wage paid	**ME** Median entry wage	**S** See annotated source	**Y** Yearly

Occupation/Type/Industry	Location	Per	Low	Mid	High	Source	Date
Electrical and Electronics Repairer							
Commercial and Industrial Equipment	Montgomery County-Bucks County-Chester County PMSA, PA	Y	46720 FQ	56590 MW	63730 TQ	USBLS	5/15
Commercial and Industrial Equipment	Philadelphia PMSA, PA	Y	38710 FQ	43940 MW	49120 TQ	USBLS	5/15
Commercial and Industrial Equipment	Pittsburgh MSA, PA	Y	38440 FQ	52820 MW	59890 TQ	USBLS	5/15
Commercial and Industrial Equipment	Rhode Island	Y	36910 FQ	47450 MW	55280 TQ	USBLS	5/15
Commercial and Industrial Equipment	Providence-Warwick MSA, RI-MA	Y	37590 FQ	48810 MW	57060 TQ	USBLS	5/15
Commercial and Industrial Equipment	South Carolina	Y	27690 FQ	48520 MW	59200 TQ	USBLS	5/15
Commercial and Industrial Equipment	Charleston-North Charleston MSA, SC	Y	45100 FQ	53620 MW	58280 TQ	USBLS	5/15
Commercial and Industrial Equipment	Columbia MSA, SC	Y	51860 FQ	55220 MW	61070 TQ	USBLS	5/15
Commercial and Industrial Equipment	Greenville-Anderson-Mauldin MSA, SC	Y	38730 FQ	51360 MW	58500 TQ	USBLS	5/15
Commercial and Industrial Equipment	South Dakota	Y	36350 FQ	44520 MW	52600 TQ	USBLS	5/15
Commercial and Industrial Equipment	Sioux Falls MSA, SD	Y	37120 FQ	45090 MW	52590 TQ	USBLS	5/15
Commercial and Industrial Equipment	Tennessee	Y	44120 FQ	54750 MW	62730 TQ	USBLS	5/15
Commercial and Industrial Equipment	Knoxville MSA, TN	Y	44900 FQ	53610 MW	61470 TQ	USBLS	5/15
Commercial and Industrial Equipment	Memphis MSA, TN-MS-AR	Y	33330 FQ	52630 MW	66080 TQ	USBLS	5/15
Commercial and Industrial Equipment	Nashville-Davidson–Murfreesboro–Franklin MSA, TN	Y	45770 FQ	53630 MW	59700 TQ	USBLS	5/15
Commercial and Industrial Equipment	Texas	Y	41540 FQ	54110 MW	67460 TQ	USBLS	5/15
Commercial and Industrial Equipment	Austin-Round Rock MSA, TX	Y	31410 FQ	38540 MW	51750 TQ	USBLS	5/15
Commercial and Industrial Equipment	Dallas-Plano-Irving PMSA, TX	Y	43100 FQ	53680 MW	64460 TQ	USBLS	5/15
Commercial and Industrial Equipment	Fort Worth-Arlington PMSA, TX	Y	39240 FQ	52520 MW	63800 TQ	USBLS	5/15
Commercial and Industrial Equipment	Houston-The Woodlands-Sugar Land MSA, TX	Y	40340 FQ	54960 MW	75730 TQ	USBLS	5/15
Commercial and Industrial Equipment	San Antonio-New Braunfels MSA, TX	Y	46670 FQ	53160 MW	60250 TQ	USBLS	5/15
Commercial and Industrial Equipment	Utah	Y	54530 FQ	59910 MW	62930 TQ	USBLS	5/15
Commercial and Industrial Equipment	Ogden-Clearfield MSA, UT	Y	56540 FQ	59910 MW	62930 TQ	USBLS	5/15
Commercial and Industrial Equipment	Provo-Orem MSA, UT	Y	53750 FQ	63220 MW	70910 TQ	USBLS	5/15
Commercial and Industrial Equipment	Salt Lake City MSA, UT	Y	51200 FQ	58080 MW	63400 TQ	USBLS	5/15
Commercial and Industrial Equipment	Vermont	Y	46240 FQ	61880 MW	72030 TQ	USBLS	5/15
Commercial and Industrial Equipment	Burlington-South Burlington MSA, VT	Y	46090 FQ	61230 MW	71760 TQ	USBLS	5/15
Commercial and Industrial Equipment	Virginia	Y	44620 FQ	54300 MW	67040 TQ	USBLS	5/15
Commercial and Industrial Equipment	Richmond MSA, VA	Y	46960 FQ	56560 MW	64270 TQ	USBLS	5/15
Commercial and Industrial Equipment	Virginia Beach-Norfolk-Newport News MSA, VA-NC	Y	41720 FQ	51150 MW	57420 TQ	USBLS	5/15
Commercial and Industrial Equipment	Washington	H	28.07 FQ	33.42 MW	40.81 TQ	WABLS	3/16
Commercial and Industrial Equipment	Seattle-Bellevue-Everett PMSA, WA	H	27.27 FQ	34.39 MW	43.35 TQ	WABLS	3/16
Commercial and Industrial Equipment	Tacoma-Lakewood PMSA, WA	H	31.66 FQ	33.73 MW	35.82 TQ	WABLS	3/16
Commercial and Industrial Equipment	West Virginia	Y	39560 FQ	52020 MW	63700 TQ	USBLS	5/15
Commercial and Industrial Equipment	Huntington-Ashland MSA, WV-KY-OH	Y	48010 FQ	56920 MW	64580 TQ	USBLS	5/15
Commercial and Industrial Equipment	Wisconsin	Y	46350 FQ	55640 MW	63540 TQ	USBLS	5/15
Commercial and Industrial Equipment	Madison MSA, WI	Y	52570 FQ	59200 MW	69710 TQ	USBLS	5/15
Commercial and Industrial Equipment	Milwaukee-Waukesha-West Allis MSA, WI	Y	43400 FQ	54890 MW	63060 TQ	USBLS	5/15
Commercial and Industrial Equipment	Wyoming	Y	53200 FQ	61470 MW	77760 TQ	USBLS	5/15
Commercial and Industrial Equipment	Puerto Rico	Y	19690 FQ	24290 MW	36850 TQ	USBLS	5/15
Commercial and Industrial Equipment	San Juan-Carolina-Caguas MSA, PR	Y	18940 FQ	23330 MW	34700 TQ	USBLS	5/15
Powerhouse, Substation, and Relay	Alabama	Y	62903 AE	74883 AW	80873 AEX	ALBLS	6/16
Powerhouse, Substation, and Relay	Birmingham-Hoover MSA, AL	Y	63289 AE	76612 AW	83273 AEX	ALBLS	6/16
Powerhouse, Substation, and Relay	Alaska	Y	69730 FQ	88160 MW	96170 TQ	USBLS	5/15
Powerhouse, Substation, and Relay	Arizona	Y	75630 FQ	85730 MW	93470 TQ	USBLS	5/15
Powerhouse, Substation, and Relay	Phoenix-Mesa-Scottsdale MSA, AZ	Y	79590 FQ	86720 MW	93870 TQ	USBLS	5/15
Powerhouse, Substation, and Relay	Arkansas	Y	67560 FQ	75380 MW	87090 TQ	USBLS	5/15
Powerhouse, Substation, and Relay	California	H	35.70 FQ	41.01 MW	46.30 TQ	CABLS	1/16-3/16
Powerhouse, Substation, and Relay	Los Angeles-Long Beach-Glendale PMSA, CA	H	36.07 FQ	40.36 MW	45.87 TQ	CABLS	1/16-3/16
Powerhouse, Substation, and Relay	Oakland-Hayward-Berkeley PMSA, CA	H	39.51 FQ	42.93 MW	46.00 TQ	CABLS	1/16-3/16

AE	Average entry wage	AWR	Average wage range	H	Hourly	LR	Low end range	MTC	Median total compensation	TCC	Total cash compensation
AEX	Average experienced wage	B	Biweekly	HI	Highest wage paid	M	Monthly	MW	Median wage paid	TQ	Third quartile wage
ATC	Average total compensation	D	Daily	HR	High end range	MCC	Median cash compensation	MWR	Median wage range	W	Weekly
AW	Average wage paid	FQ	First quartile wage	LO	Lowest wage paid	ME	Median entry wage	S	See annotated source	Y	Yearly

Occupation/Type/Industry	Location	Per	Low	Mid	High	Source	Date
Electrical and Electronics Repairer							
Powerhouse, Substation, and Relay	Riverside-San Bernardino-Ontario MSA, CA	H	33.49 FQ	37.53 MW	48.82 TQ	CABLS	1/16-3/16
Powerhouse, Substation, and Relay	Colorado	Y	69810 FQ	80670 MW	90810 TQ	USBLS	5/15
Powerhouse, Substation, and Relay	Denver-Aurora-Lakewood MSA, CO	Y	69800 FQ	81060 MW	90620 TQ	USBLS	5/15
Powerhouse, Substation, and Relay	Connecticut	Y		85287 MW		CTBLS	1/16-3/16
Powerhouse, Substation, and Relay	Bridgeport-Stamford-Norwalk MSA, CT	Y	68670 FQ	76160 MW	84580 TQ	USBLS	5/15
Powerhouse, Substation, and Relay	Delaware	Y	67070 FQ	74290 MW	81320 TQ	USBLS	5/15
Powerhouse, Substation, and Relay	Wilmington PMSA, DE-MD-NJ	Y	67440 FQ	74520 MW	81390 TQ	USBLS	5/15
Powerhouse, Substation, and Relay	District of Columbia	Y	67810 FQ	81500 MW	90190 TQ	USBLS	5/15
Powerhouse, Substation, and Relay	Washington-Arlington-Alexandria PMSA, DC-VA-MD-WV	Y	64290 FQ	75990 MW	87200 TQ	USBLS	5/15
Powerhouse, Substation, and Relay	Florida	H	19.68 AE	29.32 MW	33.87 AEX	FLBLS	7/16-9/16
Powerhouse, Substation, and Relay	Orlando-Kissimmee-Sanford MSA, FL	H	19.75 AE	25.97 MW	31.75 AEX	FLBLS	7/16-9/16
Powerhouse, Substation, and Relay	Georgia	Y	65350 FQ	73630 MW	86140 TQ	USBLS	5/15
Powerhouse, Substation, and Relay	Atlanta-Sandy Springs-Roswell MSA, GA	Y	63160 FQ	71330 MW	82310 TQ	USBLS	5/15
Powerhouse, Substation, and Relay	Hawaii	Y	75020 FQ	85980 MW	94870 TQ	USBLS	5/15
Powerhouse, Substation, and Relay	Urban Honolulu MSA, HI	Y	73450 FQ	83800 MW	93310 TQ	USBLS	5/15
Powerhouse, Substation, and Relay	Idaho	Y	61190 FQ	81760 MW	91960 TQ	USBLS	5/15
Powerhouse, Substation, and Relay	Illinois	Y	60640 FQ	71810 MW	82550 TQ	USBLS	5/15
Powerhouse, Substation, and Relay	Indiana	Y	62920 FQ	71900 MW	79830 TQ	USBLS	5/15
Powerhouse, Substation, and Relay	Indianapolis-Carmel-Anderson MSA, IN	Y	64250 FQ	70760 MW	77300 TQ	USBLS	5/15
Powerhouse, Substation, and Relay	Iowa	Y	66490 FQ	75730 MW	86900 TQ	USBLS	5/15
Powerhouse, Substation, and Relay	Kansas	Y	65590 FQ	71620 MW	77650 TQ	USBLS	5/15
Powerhouse, Substation, and Relay	Kentucky	Y	56210 FQ	69570 MW	76000 TQ	USBLS	5/15
Powerhouse, Substation, and Relay	Louisville-Jefferson County MSA, KY-IN	Y	48100 FQ	63640 MW	71620 TQ	USBLS	5/15
Powerhouse, Substation, and Relay	Louisiana	Y	46870 FQ	62380 MW	77140 TQ	USBLS	5/15
Powerhouse, Substation, and Relay	Maine	Y	56690 FQ	65380 MW	77940 TQ	USBLS	5/15
Powerhouse, Substation, and Relay	Maryland	Y	52983 AE	70382 MW	79081 AEX	MDBLS	4/16
Powerhouse, Substation, and Relay	Baltimore-Columbia-Towson MSA, MD	Y	60900 FQ	71180 MW	79830 TQ	USBLS	5/15
Powerhouse, Substation, and Relay	Massachusetts	Y	70520 FQ	80120 MW	91870 TQ	USBLS	5/15
Powerhouse, Substation, and Relay	Boston-Cambridge-Newton NECTA, MA	Y	67670 FQ	77630 MW	90450 TQ	USBLS	5/15
Powerhouse, Substation, and Relay	Michigan	Y	69450 FQ	77680 MW	88330 TQ	USBLS	5/15
Powerhouse, Substation, and Relay	Detroit-Dearborn-Livonia PMSA, MI	Y	65020 FQ	71270 MW	77450 TQ	USBLS	5/15
Powerhouse, Substation, and Relay	Minnesota	Y	67199 FQ	73806 MW	81248 TQ	MNBLS	1/16-3/16
Powerhouse, Substation, and Relay	Minneapolis-St. Paul-Bloomington MSA, MN-WI	Y	66666 FQ	73203 MW	79961 TQ	MNBLS	1/16-3/16
Powerhouse, Substation, and Relay	Mississippi	Y	60430 FQ	68880 MW	74590 TQ	USBLS	5/15
Powerhouse, Substation, and Relay	Missouri	Y	67690 FQ	75620 MW	85540 TQ	USBLS	5/15
Powerhouse, Substation, and Relay	Kansas City MSA, MO-KS	Y	64910 FQ	70870 MW	76830 TQ	USBLS	5/15
Powerhouse, Substation, and Relay	St. Louis MSA, MO-IL	Y	60020 FQ	72170 MW	83490 TQ	USBLS	5/15
Powerhouse, Substation, and Relay	Montana	Y	73180 FQ	87080 MW	98010 TQ	USBLS	5/15
Powerhouse, Substation, and Relay	Nebraska	Y	69520 FQ	78105 MW	88575 TQ	NEBLS	7/16-9/16
Powerhouse, Substation, and Relay	Nevada	Y	66710 FQ	74670 MW	82890 TQ	USBLS	5/15
Powerhouse, Substation, and Relay	Las Vegas-Henderson-Paradise MSA, NV	Y	65320 FQ	73020 MW	80690 TQ	USBLS	5/15
Powerhouse, Substation, and Relay	New Hampshire	H	26.67 AE	36.08 MW	39.96 AEX	NHBLS	6/16
Powerhouse, Substation, and Relay	New Jersey	Y	68510 FQ	83480 MW	93180 TQ	USBLS	5/15
Powerhouse, Substation, and Relay	Camden PMSA, NJ	Y	66830 FQ	80130 MW	91540 TQ	USBLS	5/15
Powerhouse, Substation, and Relay	Newark PMSA, NJ-PA	Y	67070 FQ	78650 MW	90310 TQ	USBLS	5/15
Powerhouse, Substation, and Relay	New Mexico	Y	79110 FQ	86370 MW	93710 TQ	USBLS	5/15
Powerhouse, Substation, and Relay	New York	Y	69700 AE	78330 MW	83400 AEX	NYBLS	1/16-3/16
Powerhouse, Substation, and Relay	New York-Jersey City-White Plains PMSA, NY-NJ	Y	70270 FQ	77100 MW	85330 TQ	USBLS	5/15
Powerhouse, Substation, and Relay	North Carolina	Y	60500 FQ	71350 MW	81790 TQ	USBLS	5/15
Powerhouse, Substation, and Relay	Charlotte-Concord-Gastonia MSA, NC-SC	Y	56330 FQ	69770 MW	79920 TQ	USBLS	5/15
Powerhouse, Substation, and Relay	Raleigh MSA, NC	Y	56780 FQ	67910 MW	74830 TQ	USBLS	5/15
Powerhouse, Substation, and Relay	North Dakota	Y	81510 FQ	87430 MW	93230 TQ	USBLS	5/15
Powerhouse, Substation, and Relay	Ohio	Y	64430 FQ	70480 MW	76380 TQ	USBLS	5/15

AE	Average entry wage	AWR	Average wage range	H	Hourly	LR	Low end range	MTC	Median total compensation	TCC	Total cash compensation
AEX	Average experienced wage	B	Biweekly	HI	Highest wage paid	M	Monthly	MW	Median wage paid	TQ	Third quartile wage
ATC	Average total compensation	D	Daily	HR	High end range	MCC	Median cash compensation	MWR	Median wage range	W	Weekly
AW	Average wage paid	FQ	First quartile wage	LO	Lowest wage paid	ME	Median entry wage	S	See annotated source	Y	Yearly

Occupation/Type/Industry	Location	Per	Low	Mid	High	Source	Date
Electrical and Electronics Repairer							
Powerhouse, Substation, and Relay	Cincinnati MSA, OH-KY-IN	Y	57180 FQ	65660 MW	72850 TQ	USBLS	5/15
Powerhouse, Substation, and Relay	Cleveland-Elyria MSA, OH	Y	67060 FQ	71990 MW	76910 TQ	USBLS	5/15
Powerhouse, Substation, and Relay	Columbus MSA, OH	Y	68890 FQ	75320 MW	83010 TQ	USBLS	5/15
Powerhouse, Substation, and Relay	Oklahoma	Y	52520 FQ	67050 MW	80480 TQ	USBLS	5/15
Powerhouse, Substation, and Relay	Oregon	H	38.76 FQ	43.31 MW	47.11 TQ	ORBLS	2016
Powerhouse, Substation, and Relay	Portland-Vancouver-Hillsboro MSA, OR-WA	Y	83270 FQ	90350 MW	97430 TQ	USBLS	5/15
Powerhouse, Substation, and Relay	Pennsylvania	Y	60330 FQ	68320 MW	75650 TQ	USBLS	5/15
Powerhouse, Substation, and Relay	Montgomery County-Bucks County-Chester County PMSA, PA	Y	60160 FQ	67280 MW	74330 TQ	USBLS	5/15
Powerhouse, Substation, and Relay	Pittsburgh MSA, PA	Y	60580 FQ	68300 MW	75530 TQ	USBLS	5/15
Powerhouse, Substation, and Relay	South Carolina	Y	58170 FQ	65730 MW	70190 TQ	USBLS	5/15
Powerhouse, Substation, and Relay	Charleston-North Charleston MSA, SC	Y	62490 FQ	66870 MW	68930 TQ	USBLS	5/15
Powerhouse, Substation, and Relay	Tennessee	Y	63240 FQ	74410 MW	78130 TQ	USBLS	5/15
Powerhouse, Substation, and Relay	Knoxville MSA, TN	Y	74410 FQ	78130 MW	78140 TQ	USBLS	5/15
Powerhouse, Substation, and Relay	Memphis MSA, TN-MS-AR	Y	58600 FQ	69800 MW	74890 TQ	USBLS	5/15
Powerhouse, Substation, and Relay	Nashville-Davidson–Murfreesboro–Franklin MSA, TN	Y	57740 FQ	69740 MW	74420 TQ	USBLS	5/15
Powerhouse, Substation, and Relay	Texas	Y	42210 FQ	56050 MW	71980 TQ	USBLS	5/15
Powerhouse, Substation, and Relay	Austin-Round Rock MSA, TX	Y	49920 FQ	63690 MW	82520 TQ	USBLS	5/15
Powerhouse, Substation, and Relay	Dallas-Plano-Irving PMSA, TX	Y	36410 FQ	47410 MW	61260 TQ	USBLS	5/15
Powerhouse, Substation, and Relay	Fort Worth-Arlington PMSA, TX	Y	36030 FQ	48880 MW	69980 TQ	USBLS	5/15
Powerhouse, Substation, and Relay	Houston-The Woodlands-Sugar Land MSA, TX	Y	45820 FQ	59510 MW	75660 TQ	USBLS	5/15
Powerhouse, Substation, and Relay	San Antonio-New Braunfels MSA, TX	Y	41020 FQ	45840 MW	54770 TQ	USBLS	5/15
Powerhouse, Substation, and Relay	Utah	Y	78830 FQ	89390 MW	97200 TQ	USBLS	5/15
Powerhouse, Substation, and Relay	Vermont	Y	73320 FQ	87580 MW	98650 TQ	USBLS	5/15
Powerhouse, Substation, and Relay	Virginia	Y	63320 FQ	72950 MW	83920 TQ	USBLS	5/15
Powerhouse, Substation, and Relay	Richmond MSA, VA	Y	65940 FQ	73360 MW	82930 TQ	USBLS	5/15
Powerhouse, Substation, and Relay	Virginia Beach-Norfolk-Newport News MSA, VA-NC	Y	53890 FQ	65220 MW	86500 TQ	USBLS	5/15
Powerhouse, Substation, and Relay	Washington	H	40.75 FQ	45.12 MW	49.73 TQ	WABLS	3/16
Powerhouse, Substation, and Relay	West Virginia	Y	67400 FQ	74140 MW	82470 TQ	USBLS	5/15
Powerhouse, Substation, and Relay	Wisconsin	Y	65730 FQ	78510 MW	89260 TQ	USBLS	5/15
Powerhouse, Substation, and Relay	Milwaukee-Waukesha-West Allis MSA, WI	Y	75690 FQ	84660 MW	92050 TQ	USBLS	5/15
Powerhouse, Substation, and Relay	Wyoming	Y	73110 FQ	84300 MW	93170 TQ	USBLS	5/15
Powerhouse, Substation, and Relay	Puerto Rico	Y	23280 FQ	30370 MW	42970 TQ	USBLS	5/15
Powerhouse, Substation, and Relay	San Juan-Carolina-Caguas MSA, PR	Y	23270 FQ	30320 MW	42920 TQ	USBLS	5/15
Electrical Craft Helper							
Harbor, Municipal Government	Los Angeles, CA	Y		59887 AW		CACIT	6/23/16
Electrical Engineer	United States	Y		106250 AW		EDES	2016
	Alabama	Y	63963 AE	97621 AW	114450 AEX	ALBLS	6/16
	Birmingham-Hoover MSA, AL	Y	66440 AE	95398 AW	109883 AEX	ALBLS	6/16
	Alaska	Y	90490 FQ	112960 MW	140390 TQ	USBLS	5/15
	Anchorage MSA, AK	Y	86870 FQ	113130 MW	142170 TQ	USBLS	5/15
	Arizona	Y	75260 FQ	98330 MW	122640 TQ	USBLS	5/15
	Phoenix-Mesa-Scottsdale MSA, AZ	Y	80860 FQ	104470 MW	127230 TQ	USBLS	5/15
	Tucson MSA, AZ	Y	58550 FQ	75980 MW	95960 TQ	USBLS	5/15
	Arkansas	Y	66510 FQ	81810 MW	99930 TQ	USBLS	5/15
	Little Rock-North Little Rock-Conway MSA, AR	Y	72460 FQ	86350 MW	104280 TQ	USBLS	5/15
	California	H	42.79 FQ	55.68 MW	70.41 TQ	CABLS	1/16-3/16
	Anaheim-Santa Ana-Irvine PMSA, CA	H	40.42 FQ	53.54 MW	66.25 TQ	CABLS	1/16-3/16
	Los Angeles-Long Beach-Glendale PMSA, CA	H	37.41 FQ	49.66 MW	65.84 TQ	CABLS	1/16-3/16
	Oakland-Hayward-Berkeley PMSA, CA	H	43.80 FQ	53.14 MW	64.17 TQ	CABLS	1/16-3/16
	Riverside-San Bernardino-Ontario MSA, CA	H	35.97 FQ	46.28 MW	54.03 TQ	CABLS	1/16-3/16

AE	Average entry wage	AWR	Average wage range	H	Hourly
AEX	Average experienced wage	B	Biweekly	HI	Highest wage paid
ATC	Average total compensation	D	Daily	HR	High end range
AW	Average wage paid	FQ	First quartile wage	LO	Lowest wage paid

LR	Low end range	MTC	Median total compensation	TCC	Total cash compensation
M	Monthly	MW	Median wage paid	TQ	Third quartile wage
MCC	Median cash compensation	MWR	Median wage range	W	Weekly
ME	Median entry wage	S	See annotated source	Y	Yearly

Electrical Engineer

Occupation/Type/Industry	Location	Per	Low	Mid	High	Source	Date
Electrical Engineer	Sacramento–Roseville–Arden-Arcade MSA, CA	H	30.54 FQ	45.22 MW	56.66 TQ	CABLS	1/16-3/16
	San Diego-Carlsbad MSA, CA	H	44.61 FQ	56.86 MW	71.04 TQ	CABLS	1/16-3/16
	San Francisco-Redwood City-South San Francisco PMSA, CA	H	44.89 FQ	56.64 MW	67.84 TQ	CABLS	1/16-3/16
	Colorado	Y	73760 FQ	93620 MW	116380 TQ	USBLS	5/15
	Denver-Aurora-Lakewood MSA, CO	Y	73300 FQ	92560 MW	115830 TQ	USBLS	5/15
	Connecticut	Y		92116 MW		CTBLS	1/16-3/16
	Bridgeport-Stamford-Norwalk MSA, CT	Y	76920 FQ	91110 MW	107120 TQ	USBLS	5/15
	Hartford-West Hartford-East Hartford MSA, CT	Y	75990 FQ	91310 MW	106770 TQ	USBLS	5/15
	Delaware	Y	80840 FQ	95910 MW	115620 TQ	USBLS	5/15
	Wilmington PMSA, DE-MD-NJ	Y	83620 FQ	98770 MW	119770 TQ	USBLS	5/15
	District of Columbia	Y	88760 FQ	105010 MW	118310 TQ	USBLS	5/15
	Washington-Arlington-Alexandria PMSA, DC-VA-MD-WV	Y	85210 FQ	108890 MW	146100 TQ	USBLS	5/15
	Florida	H	27.54 AE	40.59 MW	49.87 AEX	FLBLS	7/16-9/16
	Fort Lauderdale-Pompano Beach-Deerfield Beach PMSA, FL	H	27.60 AE	41.30 MW	52.54 AEX	FLBLS	7/16-9/16
	Miami-Miami Beach-Kendall PMSA, FL	H	27.30 AE	36.75 MW	44.47 AEX	FLBLS	7/16-9/16
	Orlando-Kissimmee-Sanford MSA, FL	H	28.45 AE	40.57 MW	50.91 AEX	FLBLS	7/16-9/16
	Tampa-St. Petersburg-Clearwater MSA, FL	H	29.62 AE	40.18 MW	49.62 AEX	FLBLS	7/16-9/16
	Georgia	Y	69450 FQ	86580 MW	106520 TQ	USBLS	5/15
	Atlanta-Sandy Springs-Roswell MSA, GA	Y	69960 FQ	86860 MW	106980 TQ	USBLS	5/15
	Augusta-Richmond County MSA, GA-SC	Y	68600 FQ	82130 MW	98180 TQ	USBLS	5/15
	Hawaii	Y	69040 FQ	85820 MW	99290 TQ	USBLS	5/15
	Urban Honolulu MSA, HI	Y	70320 FQ	86320 MW	99290 TQ	USBLS	5/15
	Idaho	Y	70060 FQ	88160 MW	107900 TQ	USBLS	5/15
	Boise City MSA, ID	Y	68280 FQ	85670 MW	104230 TQ	USBLS	5/15
	Illinois	Y	74600 FQ	92040 MW	112630 TQ	USBLS	5/15
	Chicago-Naperville-Arlington Heights PMSA, IL	Y	75900 FQ	92490 MW	112680 TQ	USBLS	5/15
	Lake County-Kenosha County PMSA, IL-WI	Y	63030 FQ	78900 MW	98540 TQ	USBLS	5/15
	Indiana	Y	62810 FQ	77040 MW	93600 TQ	USBLS	5/15
	Gary PMSA, IN	Y	59240 FQ	77450 MW	96030 TQ	USBLS	5/15
	Indianapolis-Carmel-Anderson MSA, IN	Y	62240 FQ	81750 MW	97150 TQ	USBLS	5/15
	Iowa	Y	67910 FQ	81980 MW	97890 TQ	USBLS	5/15
	Des Moines-West Des Moines MSA, IA	Y	55620 FQ	72140 MW	91080 TQ	USBLS	5/15
	Kansas	Y	68620 FQ	81430 MW	99860 TQ	USBLS	5/15
	Wichita MSA, KS	Y	58880 FQ	73970 MW	94310 TQ	USBLS	5/15
	Kentucky	Y	67500 FQ	82270 MW	99670 TQ	USBLS	5/15
	Louisville-Jefferson County MSA, KY-IN	Y	69320 FQ	84060 MW	97680 TQ	USBLS	5/15
	Louisiana	Y	71580 FQ	91510 MW	117820 TQ	USBLS	5/15
	Baton Rouge MSA, LA	Y	68680 FQ	88690 MW	112800 TQ	USBLS	5/15
	New Orleans-Metairie MSA, LA	Y	76070 FQ	95280 MW	118410 TQ	USBLS	5/15
	Maine	Y	68040 FQ	83150 MW	95660 TQ	USBLS	5/15
	Portland-South Portland MSA, ME	Y	74080 FQ	88590 MW	101000 TQ	USBLS	5/15
	Maryland	Y	66302 AE	99349 MW	115873 AEX	MDBLS	4/16
	Baltimore-Columbia-Towson MSA, MD	Y	73520 FQ	91770 MW	116430 TQ	USBLS	5/15
	Salisbury MSA, MD-DE	Y	60580 FQ	87190 MW	103950 TQ	USBLS	5/15
	Massachusetts	Y	81670 FQ	103090 MW	130650 TQ	USBLS	5/15
	Boston-Cambridge-Newton NECTA, MA	Y	82250 FQ	106030 MW	131930 TQ	USBLS	5/15
	Worcester MSA, MA-CT	Y	82120 FQ	93440 MW	111290 TQ	USBLS	5/15

AE	Average entry wage	AWR	Average wage range	H	Hourly
AEX	Average experienced wage	B	Biweekly	HI	Highest wage paid
ATC	Average total compensation	D	Daily	HR	High end range
AW	Average wage paid	FQ	First quartile wage	LO	Lowest wage paid

LR	Low end range	MTC	Median total compensation	TCC	Total cash compensation
M	Monthly	MW	Median wage paid	TQ	Third quartile wage
MCC	Median cash compensation	MWR	Median wage range	W	Weekly
ME	Median entry wage	S	See annotated source	Y	Yearly

Occupation/Type/Industry	Location	Per	Low	Mid	High	Source	Date
Electrical Engineer	Michigan	Y	69650 FQ	86130 MW	102580 TQ	USBLS	5/15
	Detroit-Dearborn-Livonia PMSA, MI	Y	76770 FQ	93850 MW	113250 TQ	USBLS	5/15
	Grand Rapids-Wyoming MSA, MI	Y	61100 FQ	74980 MW	94400 TQ	USBLS	5/15
	Minnesota	Y	72560 FQ	89807 MW	111632 TQ	MNBLS	1/16-3/16
	Minneapolis-St. Paul-Bloomington MSA, MN-WI	Y	72902 FQ	90533 MW	112801 TQ	MNBLS	1/16-3/16
	Mississippi	Y	71390 FQ	89820 MW	111630 TQ	USBLS	5/15
	Jackson MSA, MS	Y	68030 FQ	87800 MW	107720 TQ	USBLS	5/15
	Missouri	Y	76720 FQ	94130 MW	114390 TQ	USBLS	5/15
	Kansas City MSA, MO-KS	Y	74870 FQ	89570 MW	103900 TQ	USBLS	5/15
	St. Louis MSA, MO-IL	Y	79830 FQ	99700 MW	120870 TQ	USBLS	5/15
	Montana	Y	63230 FQ	74040 MW	88850 TQ	USBLS	5/15
	Billings MSA, MT	Y	71720 FQ	82320 MW	93820 TQ	USBLS	5/15
	Nebraska	Y	64775 FQ	78250 MW	95625 TQ	NEBLS	7/16-9/16
	Omaha-Council Bluffs MSA, NE-IA	Y	59625 FQ	74720 MW	93605 TQ	NEBLS	7/16-9/16
	Nevada	Y	70410 FQ	85430 MW	109900 TQ	USBLS	5/15
	Las Vegas-Henderson-Paradise MSA, NV	Y	72680 FQ	89310 MW	113290 TQ	USBLS	5/15
	New Hampshire	H	32.85 AE	45.94 MW	55.73 AEX	NHBLS	6/16
	Manchester NECTA, NH	H	37.39 AE	46.00 MW	51.38 AEX	NHBLS	6/16
	Nashua NECTA, NH-MA	Y	76960 FQ	100280 MW	125900 TQ	USBLS	5/15
	New Jersey	Y	80530 FQ	99420 MW	122360 TQ	USBLS	5/15
	Camden PMSA, NJ	Y	75160 FQ	100890 MW	130110 TQ	USBLS	5/15
	Newark PMSA, NJ-PA	Y	81600 FQ	97020 MW	116410 TQ	USBLS	5/15
	Trenton MSA, NJ	Y	83840 FQ	110340 MW	139470 TQ	USBLS	5/15
	New Mexico	Y	60150 FQ	91480 MW	119630 TQ	USBLS	5/15
	Albuquerque MSA, NM	Y	55940 FQ	93410 MW	120960 TQ	USBLS	5/15
	New York	Y	69530 AE	96480 MW	115020 AEX	NYBLS	1/16-3/16
	Buffalo-Cheektowaga-Niagara Falls MSA, NY	Y	66180 FQ	77320 MW	95390 TQ	USBLS	5/15
	Nassau County-Suffolk County PMSA, NY	Y	83880 FQ	105180 MW	128260 TQ	USBLS	5/15
	New York-Jersey City-White Plains PMSA, NY-NJ	Y	78320 FQ	98820 MW	121420 TQ	USBLS	5/15
	Rochester MSA, NY	Y	73130 FQ	88460 MW	107120 TQ	USBLS	5/15
	North Carolina	Y	73180 FQ	93060 MW	121320 TQ	USBLS	5/15
	Charlotte-Concord-Gastonia MSA, NC-SC	Y	75370 FQ	96590 MW	128220 TQ	USBLS	5/15
	Raleigh MSA, NC	Y	74070 FQ	95930 MW	126600 TQ	USBLS	5/15
	North Dakota	Y	71560 FQ	88740 MW	104770 TQ	USBLS	5/15
	Fargo MSA, ND-MN	Y	70450 FQ	87810 MW	102260 TQ	USBLS	5/15
	Ohio	Y	63720 FQ	77220 MW	94380 TQ	USBLS	5/15
	Cincinnati MSA, OH-KY-IN	Y	63120 FQ	74950 MW	91240 TQ	USBLS	5/15
	Cleveland-Elyria MSA, OH	Y	59960 FQ	77770 MW	94850 TQ	USBLS	5/15
	Columbus MSA, OH	Y	67520 FQ	77510 MW	93110 TQ	USBLS	5/15
	Oklahoma	Y	67960 FQ	83080 MW	104180 TQ	USBLS	5/15
	Oklahoma City MSA, OK	Y	66660 FQ	82320 MW	108570 TQ	USBLS	5/15
	Tulsa MSA, OK	Y	72230 FQ	87440 MW	107120 TQ	USBLS	5/15
	Oregon	H	33.64 FQ	41.33 MW	51.73 TQ	ORBLS	2016
	Portland-Vancouver-Hillsboro MSA, OR-WA	Y	70150 FQ	87200 MW	107820 TQ	USBLS	5/15
	Pennsylvania	Y	71840 FQ	89660 MW	108460 TQ	USBLS	5/15
	Allentown-Bethlehem-Easton MSA, PA-NJ	Y	71180 FQ	85380 MW	102990 TQ	USBLS	5/15
	Harrisburg-Carlisle MSA, PA	Y	71530 FQ	85890 MW	99050 TQ	USBLS	5/15
	Montgomery County-Bucks County-Chester County PMSA, PA	Y	74870 FQ	94210 MW	116840 TQ	USBLS	5/15
	Philadelphia PMSA, PA	Y	85440 FQ	99640 MW	115760 TQ	USBLS	5/15
	Pittsburgh MSA, PA	Y	70940 FQ	88130 MW	104890 TQ	USBLS	5/15
	Rhode Island	Y	79800 FQ	104800 MW	123120 TQ	USBLS	5/15
	Providence-Warwick MSA, RI-MA	Y	77220 FQ	100660 MW	121730 TQ	USBLS	5/15
	South Carolina	Y	65610 FQ	80190 MW	99200 TQ	USBLS	5/15
	Charleston-North Charleston MSA, SC	Y	61720 FQ	79100 MW	95980 TQ	USBLS	5/15
	Columbia MSA, SC	Y	68760 FQ	82240 MW	98540 TQ	USBLS	5/15
	Greenville-Anderson-Mauldin MSA, SC	Y	64210 FQ	80140 MW	97120 TQ	USBLS	5/15

AE Average entry wage	**AWR** Average wage range	**H** Hourly	**LR** Low end range	**MTC** Median total compensation	**TCC** Total cash compensation
AEX Average experienced wage	**B** Biweekly	**HI** Highest wage paid	**M** Monthly	**MW** Median wage paid	**TQ** Third quartile wage
ATC Average total compensation	**D** Daily	**HR** High end range	**MCC** Median cash compensation	**MWR** Median wage range	**W** Weekly
AW Average wage paid	**FQ** First quartile wage	**LO** Lowest wage paid	**ME** Median entry wage	**S** See annotated source	**Y** Yearly

Occupation/Type/Industry	Location	Per	Low	Mid	High	Source	Date
Electrical Engineer	South Dakota	Y	61500 FQ	77800 MW	91810 TQ	USBLS	5/15
	Sioux Falls MSA, SD	Y	60620 FQ	82400 MW	91830 TQ	USBLS	5/15
	Tennessee	Y	66450 FQ	85130 MW	106150 TQ	USBLS	5/15
	Knoxville MSA, TN	Y	68860 FQ	89930 MW	116350 TQ	USBLS	5/15
	Memphis MSA, TN-MS-AR	Y	58200 FQ	72520 MW	94910 TQ	USBLS	5/15
	Nashville-Davidson–Murfreesboro–Franklin MSA, TN	Y	63340 FQ	74900 MW	93680 TQ	USBLS	5/15
	Texas	Y	77940 FQ	98630 MW	124560 TQ	USBLS	5/15
	Austin-Round Rock MSA, TX	Y	87970 FQ	111140 MW	139690 TQ	USBLS	5/15
	Dallas-Plano-Irving PMSA, TX	Y	75660 FQ	92480 MW	115930 TQ	USBLS	5/15
	Fort Worth-Arlington PMSA, TX	Y	68920 FQ	92690 MW	123410 TQ	USBLS	5/15
	Houston-The Woodlands-Sugar Land MSA, TX	Y	80420 FQ	104220 MW	127870 TQ	USBLS	5/15
	San Antonio-New Braunfels MSA, TX	Y	76410 FQ	92180 MW	112850 TQ	USBLS	5/15
	Utah	Y	68560 FQ	89360 MW	112810 TQ	USBLS	5/15
	Ogden-Clearfield MSA, UT	Y	74370 FQ	99450 MW	116770 TQ	USBLS	5/15
	Provo-Orem MSA, UT	Y	66880 FQ	84290 MW	106740 TQ	USBLS	5/15
	Salt Lake City MSA, UT	Y	69290 FQ	90780 MW	114330 TQ	USBLS	5/15
	Vermont	Y	68730 FQ	85050 MW	114330 TQ	USBLS	5/15
	Burlington-South Burlington MSA, VT	Y	69540 FQ	86820 MW	118250 TQ	USBLS	5/15
	Virginia	Y	72590 FQ	92310 MW	121250 TQ	USBLS	5/15
	Richmond MSA, VA	Y	70590 FQ	87700 MW	112430 TQ	USBLS	5/15
	Virginia Beach-Norfolk-Newport News MSA, VA-NC	Y	66040 FQ	80650 MW	96380 TQ	USBLS	5/15
	Washington	H	39.96 FQ	49.45 MW	61.02 TQ	WABLS	3/16
	Seattle-Bellevue-Everett PMSA, WA	H	40.85 FQ	51.42 MW	63.32 TQ	WABLS	3/16
	Tacoma-Lakewood PMSA, WA	H	38.60 FQ	47.87 MW	55.83 TQ	WABLS	3/16
	West Virginia	Y	69620 FQ	86970 MW	102450 TQ	USBLS	5/15
	Huntington-Ashland MSA, WV-KY-OH	Y	69980 FQ	86570 MW	107690 TQ	USBLS	5/15
	Wisconsin	Y	64590 FQ	81800 MW	98350 TQ	USBLS	5/15
	Madison MSA, WI	Y	69030 FQ	86300 MW	105620 TQ	USBLS	5/15
	Milwaukee-Waukesha-West Allis MSA, WI	Y	68570 FQ	85980 MW	100820 TQ	USBLS	5/15
	Wyoming	Y	58290 FQ	75310 MW	97620 TQ	USBLS	5/15
	Cheyenne MSA, WY	Y	69680 FQ	82310 MW	98490 TQ	USBLS	5/15
	Puerto Rico	Y	53340 FQ	68210 MW	78700 TQ	USBLS	5/15
	San Juan-Carolina-Caguas MSA, PR	Y	54090 FQ	68680 MW	78880 TQ	USBLS	5/15
	Guam	Y	36690 FQ	46040 MW	65910 TQ	USBLS	5/15
Electrical Power-Line Installer and Repairer	Alabama	Y	46559 AE	65455 AW	74903 AEX	ALBLS	6/16
	Birmingham-Hoover MSA, AL	Y	55041 AE	71527 AW	79775 AEX	ALBLS	6/16
	Alaska	Y	80970 FQ	90350 MW	99120 TQ	USBLS	5/15
	Anchorage MSA, AK	Y	82990 FQ	90660 MW	98330 TQ	USBLS	5/15
	Arizona	Y	55180 FQ	81910 MW	92220 TQ	USBLS	5/15
	Phoenix-Mesa-Scottsdale MSA, AZ	Y	50320 FQ	83430 MW	92810 TQ	USBLS	5/15
	Arkansas	Y	52570 FQ	65120 MW	73310 TQ	USBLS	5/15
	Little Rock-North Little Rock-Conway MSA, AR	Y	36030 FQ	54420 MW	68750 TQ	USBLS	5/15
	California	H	38.22 FQ	50.80 MW	56.66 TQ	CABLS	1/16-3/16
	Anaheim-Santa Ana-Irvine PMSA, CA	H	39.48 FQ	52.06 MW	57.47 TQ	CABLS	1/16-3/16
	Los Angeles-Long Beach-Glendale PMSA, CA	H	42.25 FQ	50.42 MW	56.14 TQ	CABLS	1/16-3/16
	Oakland-Hayward-Berkeley PMSA, CA	H	41.83 FQ	51.20 MW	56.69 TQ	CABLS	1/16-3/16
	Riverside-San Bernardino-Ontario MSA, CA	H	30.30 FQ	43.11 MW	53.77 TQ	CABLS	1/16-3/16
	Sacramento–Roseville–Arden-Arcade MSA, CA	H	44.70 FQ	52.05 MW	58.23 TQ	CABLS	1/16-3/16
	San Diego-Carlsbad MSA, CA	H	32.61 FQ	52.34 MW	57.88 TQ	CABLS	1/16-3/16
	Colorado	Y	51870 FQ	71700 MW	87780 TQ	USBLS	5/15
	Denver-Aurora-Lakewood MSA, CO	Y	51620 FQ	70840 MW	88570 TQ	USBLS	5/15

AE	Average entry wage	AWR	Average wage range	H	Hourly
AEX	Average experienced wage	B	Biweekly	HI	Highest wage paid
ATC	Average total compensation	D	Daily	HR	High end range
AW	Average wage paid	FQ	First quartile wage	LO	Lowest wage paid

LR	Low end range	MTC	Median total compensation	TCC	Total cash compensation
M	Monthly	MW	Median wage paid	TQ	Third quartile wage
MCC	Median cash compensation	MWR	Median wage range	W	Weekly
ME	Median entry wage	S	See annotated source	Y	Yearly

Occupation/Type/Industry	Location	Per	Low	Mid	High	Source	Date
Electrical Power-Line Installer and Repairer	Connecticut	Y		89990 MW		CTBLS	1/16-3/16
	Bridgeport-Stamford-Norwalk MSA, CT	Y	62520 FQ	87120 MW	94890 TQ	USBLS	5/15
	Hartford-West Hartford-East Hartford MSA, CT	Y	85480 FQ	91440 MW	97400 TQ	USBLS	5/15
	Delaware	Y	61410 FQ	78760 MW	91360 TQ	USBLS	5/15
	Wilmington PMSA, DE-MD-NJ	Y	65340 FQ	83810 MW	92870 TQ	USBLS	5/15
	District of Columbia	Y	58500 FQ	70540 MW	84840 TQ	USBLS	5/15
	Washington-Arlington-Alexandria PMSA, DC-VA-MD-WV	Y	52310 FQ	66550 MW	75790 TQ	USBLS	5/15
	Florida	H	17.39 AE	25.05 MW	29.54 AEX	FLBLS	7/16-9/16
	Fort Lauderdale-Pompano Beach-Deerfield Beach PMSA, FL	H	16.84 AE	22.44 MW	27.05 AEX	FLBLS	7/16-9/16
	Miami-Miami Beach-Kendall PMSA, FL	H	16.58 AE	25.65 MW	30.06 AEX	FLBLS	7/16-9/16
	Orlando-Kissimmee-Sanford MSA, FL	H	16.43 AE	24.66 MW	29.52 AEX	FLBLS	7/16-9/16
	Tampa-St. Petersburg-Clearwater MSA, FL	H	15.53 AE	24.81 MW	29.72 AEX	FLBLS	7/16-9/16
	Georgia	Y	32550 FQ	47090 MW	61870 TQ	USBLS	5/15
	Atlanta-Sandy Springs-Roswell MSA, GA	Y	30120 FQ	45220 MW	59870 TQ	USBLS	5/15
	Augusta-Richmond County MSA, GA-SC	Y	51770 FQ	63840 MW	72150 TQ	USBLS	5/15
	Hawaii	Y	62290 FQ	79660 MW	91730 TQ	USBLS	5/15
	Urban Honolulu MSA, HI	Y	60280 FQ	79000 MW	91690 TQ	USBLS	5/15
	Idaho	Y	70100 FQ	85010 MW	93310 TQ	USBLS	5/15
	Boise City MSA, ID	Y	46670 FQ	70410 MW	86540 TQ	USBLS	5/15
	Illinois	Y	62090 FQ	76020 MW	88840 TQ	USBLS	5/15
	Chicago-Naperville-Arlington Heights PMSA, IL	Y	57790 FQ	72490 MW	86950 TQ	USBLS	5/15
	Lake County-Kenosha County PMSA, IL-WI	Y	54650 FQ	64280 MW	76480 TQ	USBLS	5/15
	Indiana	Y	53520 FQ	67770 MW	75970 TQ	USBLS	5/15
	Gary PMSA, IN	Y	57790 FQ	69230 MW	76850 TQ	USBLS	5/15
	Indianapolis-Carmel-Anderson MSA, IN	Y	60300 FQ	70940 MW	78920 TQ	USBLS	5/15
	Iowa	Y	50130 FQ	65720 MW	74320 TQ	USBLS	5/15
	Des Moines-West Des Moines MSA, IA	Y	48200 FQ	66840 MW	77740 TQ	USBLS	5/15
	Kansas	Y	53440 FQ	68430 MW	79740 TQ	USBLS	5/15
	Wichita MSA, KS	Y	62280 FQ	70940 MW	78360 TQ	USBLS	5/15
	Kentucky	Y	48570 FQ	59110 MW	71240 TQ	USBLS	5/15
	Louisville-Jefferson County MSA, KY-IN	Y	44590 FQ	55160 MW	64950 TQ	USBLS	5/15
	Louisiana	Y	37290 FQ	50030 MW	64500 TQ	USBLS	5/15
	Baton Rouge MSA, LA	Y	43140 FQ	54890 MW	64600 TQ	USBLS	5/15
	New Orleans-Metairie MSA, LA	Y	34390 FQ	40740 MW	56570 TQ	USBLS	5/15
	Maine	Y	51100 FQ	59120 MW	67970 TQ	USBLS	5/15
	Portland-South Portland MSA, ME	Y	49480 FQ	61110 MW	71700 TQ	USBLS	5/15
	Maryland	Y	50920 AE	65032 MW	72088 AEX	MDBLS	4/16
	Baltimore-Columbia-Towson MSA, MD	Y	53530 FQ	59480 MW	68130 TQ	USBLS	5/15
	Salisbury MSA, MD-DE	Y	69060 FQ	83950 MW	93610 TQ	USBLS	5/15
	Massachusetts	Y	77650 FQ	86930 MW	94400 TQ	USBLS	5/15
	Boston-Cambridge-Newton NECTA, MA	Y	75460 FQ	85820 MW	93470 TQ	USBLS	5/15
	Worcester MSA, MA-CT	Y	69160 FQ	85650 MW	94370 TQ	USBLS	5/15
	Michigan	Y	60590 FQ	73150 MW	86110 TQ	USBLS	5/15
	Detroit-Dearborn-Livonia PMSA, MI	Y	63430 FQ	73140 MW	87440 TQ	USBLS	5/15
	Grand Rapids-Wyoming MSA, MI	Y	52770 FQ	64410 MW	80830 TQ	USBLS	5/15
	Minnesota	Y	64262 FQ	76421 MW	89434 TQ	MNBLS	1/16-3/16
	Minneapolis-St. Paul-Bloomington MSA, MN-WI	Y	65369 FQ	81077 MW	92301 TQ	MNBLS	1/16-3/16

AE Average entry wage	**AWR** Average wage range	**H** Hourly	**LR** Low end range	**MTC** Median total compensation	**TCC** Total cash compensation
AEX Average experienced wage	**B** Biweekly	**HI** Highest wage paid	**M** Monthly	**MW** Median wage paid	**TQ** Third quartile wage
ATC Average total compensation	**D** Daily	**HR** High end range	**MCC** Median cash compensation	**MWR** Median wage range	**W** Weekly
AW Average wage paid	**FQ** First quartile wage	**LO** Lowest wage paid	**ME** Median entry wage	**S** See annotated source	**Y** Yearly

Occupation/Type/Industry	Location	Per	Low	Mid	High	Source	Date
Electrical Power-Line Installer and Repairer							
	Mississippi	Y	47410 FQ	57820 MW	68300 TQ	USBLS	5/15
	Jackson MSA, MS	Y	52140 FQ	61050 MW	70310 TQ	USBLS	5/15
	Missouri	Y	60800 FQ	73570 MW	85900 TQ	USBLS	5/15
	Kansas City MSA, MO-KS	Y	65180 FQ	80180 MW	90400 TQ	USBLS	5/15
	St. Louis MSA, MO-IL	Y	64200 FQ	76360 MW	89330 TQ	USBLS	5/15
	Montana	Y	68670 FQ	79360 MW	89940 TQ	USBLS	5/15
	Billings MSA, MT	Y	73810 FQ	85870 MW	94370 TQ	USBLS	5/15
	Nebraska	Y	46310 FQ	59595 MW	74555 TQ	NEBLS	7/16-9/16
	Omaha-Council Bluffs MSA, NE-IA	Y	41390 FQ	50540 MW	59540 TQ	NEBLS	7/16-9/16
	Nevada	Y	58490 FQ	78040 MW	92620 TQ	USBLS	5/15
	Las Vegas-Henderson-Paradise MSA, NV	Y	50100 FQ	72840 MW	91970 TQ	USBLS	5/15
	New Hampshire	H	29.56 AE	37.24 MW	40.35 AEX	NHBLS	6/16
	New Jersey	Y	63910 FQ	83910 MW	93990 TQ	USBLS	5/15
	Camden PMSA, NJ	Y	60850 FQ	83750 MW	95730 TQ	USBLS	5/15
	Newark PMSA, NJ-PA	Y	79730 FQ	88140 MW	95560 TQ	USBLS	5/15
	New Mexico	Y	46030 FQ	58790 MW	74080 TQ	USBLS	5/15
	Albuquerque MSA, NM	Y	41900 FQ	63170 MW	83770 TQ	USBLS	5/15
	New York	Y	54250 AE	80140 MW	89800 AEX	NYBLS	1/16-3/16
	Buffalo-Cheektowaga-Niagara Falls MSA, NY	Y	70900 FQ	85510 MW	96190 TQ	USBLS	5/15
	Nassau County-Suffolk County PMSA, NY	Y	58640 FQ	74190 MW	87330 TQ	USBLS	5/15
	New York-Jersey City-White Plains PMSA, NY-NJ	Y	61750 FQ	78570 MW	94500 TQ	USBLS	5/15
	Rochester MSA, NY	Y	75510 FQ	87960 MW	96110 TQ	USBLS	5/15
	North Carolina	Y	39010 FQ	53240 MW	67240 TQ	USBLS	5/15
	Charlotte-Concord-Gastonia MSA, NC-SC	Y	40900 FQ	52540 MW	62430 TQ	USBLS	5/15
	Raleigh MSA, NC	Y	38160 FQ	59820 MW	76270 TQ	USBLS	5/15
	North Dakota	Y	53540 FQ	64820 MW	77120 TQ	USBLS	5/15
	Fargo MSA, ND-MN	Y	37060 FQ	66780 MW	89690 TQ	USBLS	5/15
	Ohio	Y	54340 FQ	67040 MW	74940 TQ	USBLS	5/15
	Cincinnati MSA, OH-KY-IN	Y	56450 FQ	66650 MW	74000 TQ	USBLS	5/15
	Cleveland-Elyria MSA, OH	Y	54250 FQ	66930 MW	73930 TQ	USBLS	5/15
	Columbus MSA, OH	Y	52110 FQ	64630 MW	77380 TQ	USBLS	5/15
	Oklahoma	Y	37920 FQ	53200 MW	65920 TQ	USBLS	5/15
	Oklahoma City MSA, OK	Y	46270 FQ	64010 MW	73310 TQ	USBLS	5/15
	Tulsa MSA, OK	Y	40220 FQ	55360 MW	69040 TQ	USBLS	5/15
	Oregon	H	39.15 FQ	43.10 MW	47.21 TQ	ORBLS	2016
	Portland-Vancouver-Hillsboro MSA, OR-WA	Y	84740 FQ	88660 MW	96120 TQ	USBLS	5/15
	Pennsylvania	Y	59710 FQ	70040 MW	78920 TQ	USBLS	5/15
	Allentown-Bethlehem-Easton MSA, PA-NJ	Y	54850 FQ	65900 MW	78960 TQ	USBLS	5/15
	Harrisburg-Carlisle MSA, PA	Y	66070 FQ	73690 MW	81580 TQ	USBLS	5/15
	Montgomery County-Bucks County-Chester County PMSA, PA	Y	58880 FQ	68890 MW	77240 TQ	USBLS	5/15
	Pittsburgh MSA, PA	Y	57960 FQ	68110 MW	76640 TQ	USBLS	5/15
	Rhode Island	Y	53920 FQ	60710 MW	87280 TQ	USBLS	5/15
	Providence-Warwick MSA, RI-MA	Y	54980 FQ	63570 MW	89090 TQ	USBLS	5/15
	South Carolina	Y	40030 FQ	53260 MW	65610 TQ	USBLS	5/15
	Charleston-North Charleston MSA, SC	Y	37620 FQ	50200 MW	65090 TQ	USBLS	5/15
	Columbia MSA, SC	Y	29950 FQ	49180 MW	64580 TQ	USBLS	5/15
	Greenville-Anderson-Mauldin MSA, SC	Y	46370 FQ	57780 MW	70170 TQ	USBLS	5/15
	South Dakota	Y	58740 FQ	68480 MW	75300 TQ	USBLS	5/15
	Sioux Falls MSA, SD	Y	61290 FQ	70030 MW	78830 TQ	USBLS	5/15
	Tennessee	Y	57110 FQ	68310 MW	76320 TQ	USBLS	5/15
	Knoxville MSA, TN	Y	52170 FQ	63120 MW	72350 TQ	USBLS	5/15
	Memphis MSA, TN-MS-AR	Y	52070 FQ	66680 MW	73570 TQ	USBLS	5/15
	Nashville-Davidson–Murfreesboro–Franklin MSA, TN	Y	66490 FQ	74780 MW	85380 TQ	USBLS	5/15
	Texas	Y	40040 FQ	53810 MW	67690 TQ	USBLS	5/15
	Austin-Round Rock MSA, TX	Y	42220 FQ	58900 MW	75290 TQ	USBLS	5/15
	Dallas-Plano-Irving PMSA, TX	Y	41560 FQ	54500 MW	67400 TQ	USBLS	5/15

Occupation/Type/Industry	Location	Per	Low	Mid	High	Source	Date
Electrical Power-Line Installer and Repairer	Fort Worth-Arlington PMSA, TX	Y	44540 FQ	56410 MW	65140 TQ	USBLS	5/15
	Houston-The Woodlands-Sugar Land MSA, TX	Y	41450 FQ	58190 MW	72220 TQ	USBLS	5/15
	San Antonio-New Braunfels MSA, TX	Y	35940 FQ	49590 MW	72080 TQ	USBLS	5/15
	Utah	Y	51560 FQ	68350 MW	85940 TQ	USBLS	5/15
	Ogden-Clearfield MSA, UT	Y	44200 FQ	64370 MW	89470 TQ	USBLS	5/15
	Provo-Orem MSA, UT	Y	43110 FQ	64300 MW	83930 TQ	USBLS	5/15
	Vermont	Y	57510 FQ	69670 MW	78110 TQ	USBLS	5/15
	Burlington-South Burlington MSA, VT	Y	66620 FQ	72320 MW	78030 TQ	USBLS	5/15
	Virginia	Y	44790 FQ	60920 MW	73240 TQ	USBLS	5/15
	Richmond MSA, VA	Y	43970 FQ	61300 MW	73440 TQ	USBLS	5/15
	Virginia Beach-Norfolk-Newport News MSA, VA-NC	Y	45260 FQ	53660 MW	69810 TQ	USBLS	5/15
	Washington	H	38.07 FQ	43.10 MW	46.35 TQ	WABLS	3/16
	Seattle-Bellevue-Everett PMSA, WA	H	39.57 FQ	43.11 MW	46.85 TQ	WABLS	3/16
	Tacoma-Lakewood PMSA, WA	H	17.55 FQ	32.04 MW	40.95 TQ	WABLS	3/16
	West Virginia	Y	47630 FQ	66350 MW	74540 TQ	USBLS	5/15
	Wisconsin	Y	63860 FQ	72620 MW	81190 TQ	USBLS	5/15
	Madison MSA, WI	Y	56070 FQ	67620 MW	79970 TQ	USBLS	5/15
	Milwaukee-Waukesha-West Allis MSA, WI	Y	65130 FQ	76920 MW	88440 TQ	USBLS	5/15
	Wyoming	Y	49670 FQ	66220 MW	82400 TQ	USBLS	5/15
	Cheyenne MSA, WY	Y	30490 FQ	70540 MW	86680 TQ	USBLS	5/15
	Puerto Rico	Y	41970 FQ	44850 MW	47740 TQ	USBLS	5/15
	San Juan-Carolina-Caguas MSA, PR	Y	41970 FQ	44850 MW	47740 TQ	USBLS	5/15
Electrical Quality Assurance Specialist Municipal Government	Seattle, WA	H	37.92 LO		44.25 HI	CSSS	1/13/16
Electrician	Alabama	Y	32949 AE	46651 AW	53502 AEX	ALBLS	6/16
	Birmingham-Hoover MSA, AL	Y	37074 AE	49058 AW	55055 AEX	ALBLS	6/16
	Alaska	Y	66700 FQ	79820 MW	93470 TQ	USBLS	5/15
	Anchorage MSA, AK	Y	60980 FQ	77870 MW	90150 TQ	USBLS	5/15
	Arizona	Y	35600 FQ	46310 MW	60130 TQ	USBLS	5/15
	Phoenix-Mesa-Scottsdale MSA, AZ	Y	35220 FQ	45940 MW	60220 TQ	USBLS	5/15
	Tucson MSA, AZ	Y	35990 FQ	44490 MW	55820 TQ	USBLS	5/15
	Arkansas	Y	32280 FQ	41480 MW	50030 TQ	USBLS	5/15
	Little Rock-North Little Rock-Conway MSA, AR	Y	34510 FQ	43020 MW	48860 TQ	USBLS	5/15
	California	H	23.69 FQ	30.65 MW	41.75 TQ	CABLS	1/16-3/16
	Anaheim-Santa Ana-Irvine PMSA, CA	H	19.36 FQ	25.45 MW	31.76 TQ	CABLS	1/16-3/16
	Los Angeles-Long Beach-Glendale PMSA, CA	H	22.23 FQ	30.56 MW	38.23 TQ	CABLS	1/16-3/16
	Oakland-Hayward-Berkeley PMSA, CA	H	29.01 FQ	38.54 MW	48.25 TQ	CABLS	1/16-3/16
	Riverside-San Bernardino-Ontario MSA, CA	H	21.33 FQ	27.22 MW	33.20 TQ	CABLS	1/16-3/16
	Sacramento–Roseville–Arden-Arcade MSA, CA	H	25.54 FQ	32.87 MW	43.81 TQ	CABLS	1/16-3/16
	San Diego-Carlsbad MSA, CA	H	25.12 FQ	30.21 MW	43.36 TQ	CABLS	1/16-3/16
	San Francisco-Redwood City-South San Francisco PMSA, CA	H	31.10 FQ	47.42 MW	58.14 TQ	CABLS	1/16-3/16
	Colorado	Y	34960 FQ	46220 MW	59730 TQ	USBLS	5/15
	Denver-Aurora-Lakewood MSA, CO	Y	33870 FQ	44400 MW	59720 TQ	USBLS	5/15
	Connecticut	Y		56623 MW		CTBLS	1/16-3/16
	Bridgeport-Stamford-Norwalk MSA, CT	Y	53940 FQ	59610 MW	70160 TQ	USBLS	5/15
	Hartford-West Hartford-East Hartford MSA, CT	Y	39890 FQ	54480 MW	61320 TQ	USBLS	5/15
	Delaware	Y	37880 FQ	49090 MW	62720 TQ	USBLS	5/15

AE	Average entry wage	**AWR**	Average wage range	**H**	Hourly	**LR**	Low end range	**MTC**	Median total compensation
AEX	Average experienced wage	**B**	Biweekly	**HI**	Highest wage paid	**M**	Monthly	**MW**	Median wage paid
ATC	Average total compensation	**D**	Daily	**HR**	High end range	**MCC**	Median cash compensation	**MWR**	Median wage range
AW	Average wage paid	**FQ**	First quartile wage	**LO**	Lowest wage paid	**ME**	Median entry wage	**S**	See annotated source

TCC Total cash compensation
TQ Third quartile wage
W Weekly
Y Yearly

Occupation/Type/Industry	Location	Per	Low	Mid	High	Source	Date
Electrician	Wilmington PMSA, DE-MD-NJ	Y	39170 FQ	50950 MW	67110 TQ	USBLS	5/15
	District of Columbia	Y	53690 FQ	62640 MW	81750 TQ	USBLS	5/15
	Washington-Arlington-Alexandria PMSA, DC-VA-MD-WV	Y	40220 FQ	53800 MW	70090 TQ	USBLS	5/15
	Florida	H	14.51 AE	19.85 MW	24.38 AEX	FLBLS	7/16-9/16
	Fort Lauderdale-Pompano Beach-Deerfield Beach PMSA, FL	H	14.90 AE	19.30 MW	22.60 AEX	FLBLS	7/16-9/16
	Miami-Miami Beach-Kendall PMSA, FL	H	12.14 AE	22.32 MW	31.08 AEX	FLBLS	7/16-9/16
	Orlando-Kissimmee-Sanford MSA, FL	H	14.03 AE	18.18 MW	21.93 AEX	FLBLS	7/16-9/16
	Tampa-St. Petersburg-Clearwater MSA, FL	H	15.16 AE	19.88 MW	23.27 AEX	FLBLS	7/16-9/16
	Georgia	Y	34940 FQ	43580 MW	54430 TQ	USBLS	5/15
	Atlanta-Sandy Springs-Roswell MSA, GA	Y	35650 FQ	44360 MW	56310 TQ	USBLS	5/15
	Augusta-Richmond County MSA, GA-SC	Y	34310 FQ	41750 MW	51030 TQ	USBLS	5/15
	Hawaii	Y	54100 FQ	70320 MW	86970 TQ	USBLS	5/15
	Urban Honolulu MSA, HI	Y	55030 FQ	70740 MW	87650 TQ	USBLS	5/15
	Idaho	Y	33410 FQ	46190 MW	58100 TQ	USBLS	5/15
	Boise City MSA, ID	Y	30680 FQ	46590 MW	58270 TQ	USBLS	5/15
	Illinois	Y	50870 FQ	74060 MW	89300 TQ	USBLS	5/15
	Chicago-Naperville-Arlington Heights PMSA, IL	Y	55140 FQ	81330 MW	92050 TQ	USBLS	5/15
	Lake County-Kenosha County PMSA, IL-WI	Y	53360 FQ	68910 MW	84720 TQ	USBLS	5/15
	Indiana	Y	44530 FQ	60210 MW	73810 TQ	USBLS	5/15
	Gary PMSA, IN	Y	56930 FQ	74690 MW	88370 TQ	USBLS	5/15
	Indianapolis-Carmel-Anderson MSA, IN	Y	42850 FQ	57480 MW	71080 TQ	USBLS	5/15
	Iowa	Y	40050 FQ	52400 MW	65900 TQ	USBLS	5/15
	Des Moines-West Des Moines MSA, IA	Y	49390 FQ	58880 MW	68800 TQ	USBLS	5/15
	Kansas	Y	40970 FQ	50680 MW	63250 TQ	USBLS	5/15
	Wichita MSA, KS	Y	42240 FQ	48890 MW	60470 TQ	USBLS	5/15
	Kentucky	Y	37630 FQ	48140 MW	62860 TQ	USBLS	5/15
	Louisville-Jefferson County MSA, KY-IN	Y	40310 FQ	54030 MW	68990 TQ	USBLS	5/15
	Louisiana	Y	37780 FQ	46940 MW	58010 TQ	USBLS	5/15
	Baton Rouge MSA, LA	Y	39490 FQ	47710 MW	61240 TQ	USBLS	5/15
	New Orleans-Metairie MSA, LA	Y	38630 FQ	47970 MW	58040 TQ	USBLS	5/15
	Maine	Y	40410 FQ	47530 MW	56100 TQ	USBLS	5/15
	Portland-South Portland MSA, ME	Y	41980 FQ	51030 MW	58540 TQ	USBLS	5/15
	Maryland	Y	34825 AE	54868 MW	64890 AEX	MDBLS	4/16
	Baltimore-Columbia-Towson MSA, MD	Y	40520 FQ	52230 MW	64550 TQ	USBLS	5/15
	Salisbury MSA, MD-DE	Y	35090 FQ	44220 MW	54860 TQ	USBLS	5/15
	Massachusetts	Y	49160 FQ	62800 MW	83820 TQ	USBLS	5/15
	Boston-Cambridge-Newton NECTA, MA	Y	51440 FQ	69810 MW	89540 TQ	USBLS	5/15
	Worcester MSA, MA-CT	Y	54520 FQ	72860 MW	89970 TQ	USBLS	5/15
	Michigan	Y	43560 FQ	59030 MW	71400 TQ	USBLS	5/15
	Detroit-Dearborn-Livonia PMSA, MI	Y	56250 FQ	67160 MW	74970 TQ	USBLS	5/15
	Grand Rapids-Wyoming MSA, MI	Y	39980 FQ	49330 MW	57970 TQ	USBLS	5/15
	Minnesota	Y	40613 FQ	60672 MW	74839 TQ	MNBLS	1/16-3/16
	Minneapolis-St. Paul-Bloomington MSA, MN-WI	Y	44861 FQ	66413 MW	78451 TQ	MNBLS	1/16-3/16
	Mississippi	Y	38410 FQ	46680 MW	54780 TQ	USBLS	5/15
	Jackson MSA, MS	Y	33210 FQ	42970 MW	50820 TQ	USBLS	5/15
	Missouri	Y	43470 FQ	60460 MW	71960 TQ	USBLS	5/15
	Kansas City MSA, MO-KS	Y	44070 FQ	63300 MW	73550 TQ	USBLS	5/15
	St. Louis MSA, MO-IL	Y	52990 FQ	65450 MW	74120 TQ	USBLS	5/15
	Montana	Y	50780 FQ	59980 MW	70630 TQ	USBLS	5/15
	Billings MSA, MT	Y	51530 FQ	62110 MW	70200 TQ	USBLS	5/15

AE Average entry wage	**AWR** Average wage range	**H** Hourly	**LR** Low end range	**MTC** Median total compensation	**TCC** Total cash compensation
AEX Average experienced wage	**B** Biweekly	**HI** Highest wage paid	**M** Monthly	**MW** Median wage paid	**TQ** Third quartile wage
ATC Average total compensation	**D** Daily	**HR** High end range	**MCC** Median cash compensation	**MWR** Median wage range	**W** Weekly
AW Average wage paid	**FQ** First quartile wage	**LO** Lowest wage paid	**ME** Median entry wage	**S** See annotated source	**Y** Yearly

Occupation/Type/Industry	Location	Per	Low	Mid	High	Source	Date
Electrician	Nebraska	Y	33525 FQ	44140 MW	57170 TQ	NEBLS	7/16-9/16
	Grand Island MSA, NE	Y	22220 FQ	24405 MW	39425 TQ	NEBLS	7/16-9/16
	Omaha-Council Bluffs MSA, NE-IA	Y	35710 FQ	51670 MW	68430 TQ	NEBLS	7/16-9/16
	Nevada	Y	45250 FQ	59760 MW	74120 TQ	USBLS	5/15
	Las Vegas-Henderson-Paradise MSA, NV	Y	43060 FQ	59770 MW	74840 TQ	USBLS	5/15
	New Hampshire	H	17.13 AE	24.48 MW	27.28 AEX	NHBLS	6/16
	Manchester NECTA, NH	H	18.87 AE	26.02 MW	28.83 AEX	NHBLS	6/16
	Nashua NECTA, NH-MA	Y	34960 FQ	49350 MW	56710 TQ	USBLS	5/15
	New Jersey	Y.	46300 FQ	60460 MW	93800 TQ	USBLS	5/15
	Camden PMSA, NJ	Y	46330 FQ	57780 MW	89510 TQ	USBLS	5/15
	Newark PMSA, NJ-PA	Y	48550 FQ	64870 MW	103730 TQ	USBLS	5/15
	Trenton MSA, NJ	Y	51330 FQ	59700 MW	81050 TQ	USBLS	5/45
	New Mexico	Y	36550 FQ	46250 MW	61390 TQ	USBLS	5/15
	Albuquerque MSA, NM	Y	34580 FQ	43170 MW	52990 TQ	USBLS	5/15
	New York	Y	41350 AE	68770 MW	89920 AEX	NYBLS	1/16-3/16
	Buffalo-Cheektowaga-Niagara Falls MSA, NY	Y	42070 FQ	64100 MW	73240 TQ	USBLS	5/15
	Nassau County-Suffolk County PMSA, NY	Y	45130 FQ	60890 MW	97980 TQ	USBLS	5/15
	New York-Jersey City-White Plains PMSA, NY-NJ	Y	49110 FQ	76090 MW	107910 TQ	USBLS	5/15
	Rochester MSA, NY	Y	50180 FQ	66230 MW	74710 TQ	USBLS	5/15
	North Carolina	Y	34310 FQ	39790 MW	47540 TQ	USBLS	5/15
	Charlotte-Concord-Gastonia MSA, NC-SC	Y	35060 FQ	40260 MW	47840 TQ	USBLS	5/15
	Raleigh MSA, NC	Y	33270 FQ	38120 MW	44930 TQ	USBLS	5/15
	North Dakota	Y	44140 FQ	56470 MW	74620 TQ	USBLS	5/15
	Fargo MSA, ND-MN	Y	40140 FQ	50560 MW	62640 TQ	USBLS	5/15
	Ohio	Y	37650 FQ	49670 MW	64510 TQ	USBLS	5/15
	Cincinnati MSA, OH-KY-IN	Y	36320 FQ	48100 MW	59190 TQ	USBLS	5/15
	Cleveland-Elyria MSA, OH	Y	43900 FQ	59660 MW	75090 TQ	USBLS	5/15
	Columbus MSA, OH	Y	33100 FQ	43170 MW	55990 TQ	USBLS	5/15
	Oklahoma	Y	36640 FQ	47450 MW	56380 TQ	USBLS	5/15
	Oklahoma City MSA, OK	Y	37170 FQ	48720 MW	56210 TQ	USBLS	5/15
	Tulsa MSA, OK	Y	36570 FQ	49920 MW	57320 TQ	USBLS	5/15
	Oregon	H	26.81 FQ	32.79 MW	39.28 TQ	ORBLS	2016
	Portland-Vancouver-Hillsboro MSA, OR-WA	Y	57110 FQ	72950 MW	87140 TQ	USBLS	5/15
	Pennsylvania	Y	41690 FQ	53670 MW	70960 TQ	USBLS	5/15
	Allentown-Bethlehem-Easton MSA, PA-NJ	Y	38210 FQ	48030 MW	61000 TQ	USBLS	5/15
	Harrisburg-Carlisle MSA, PA	Y	43740 FQ	52890 MW	60160 TQ	USBLS	5/15
	Montgomery County-Bucks County-Chester County PMSA, PA	Y	45830 FQ	60330 MW	88450 TQ	USBLS	5/15
	Philadelphia PMSA, PA	Y	48580 FQ	62310 MW	92040 TQ	USBLS	5/15
	Pittsburgh MSA, PA	Y	39340 FQ	50220 MW	66770 TQ	USBLS	5/15
	Rhode Island	Y	39820 FQ	51720 MW	63370 TQ	USBLS	5/15
	Providence-Warwick MSA, RI-MA	Y	39680 FQ	51380 MW	64710 TQ	USBLS	5/15
	South Carolina	Y	34790 FQ	41950 MW	51160 TQ	USBLS	5/15
	Charleston-North Charleston MSA, SC	Y	36610 FQ	44430 MW	53140 TQ	USBLS	5/15
	Columbia MSA, SC	Y	34870 FQ	42990 MW	50780 TQ	USBLS	5/15
	Greenville-Anderson-Mauldin MSA, SC	Y	34670 FQ	40830 MW	53620 TQ	USBLS	5/15
	South Dakota	Y	36820 FQ	46180 MW	55830 TQ	USBLS	5/15
	Sioux Falls MSA, SD	Y	35770 FQ	45450 MW	55100 TQ	USBLS	5/15
	Tennessee	Y	36800 FQ	46060 MW	56850 TQ	USBLS	5/15
	Knoxville MSA, TN	Y	36870 FQ	44690 MW	56670 TQ	USBLS	5/15
	Memphis MSA, TN-MS-AR	Y	39160 FQ	51470 MW	59190 TQ	USBLS	5/15
	Nashville-Davidson–Murfreesboro–Franklin MSA, TN	Y	38630 FQ	46600 MW	57410 TQ	USBLS	5/15
	Texas	Y	34450 FQ	43670 MW	55320 TQ	USBLS	5/15
	Austin-Round Rock MSA, TX	Y	37590 FQ	45880 MW	56030 TQ	USBLS	5/15
	Dallas-Plano-Irving PMSA, TX	Y	33980 FQ	41870 MW	53360 TQ	USBLS	5/15
	Fort Worth-Arlington PMSA, TX	Y	31910 FQ	41290 MW	52530 TQ	USBLS	5/15

AE	Average entry wage	AWR	Average wage range	H	Hourly	LR	Low end range	MTC	Median total compensation	TCC	Total cash compensation
AEX	Average experienced wage	B	Biweekly	HI	Highest wage paid	M	Monthly	MW	Median wage paid	TQ	Third quartile wage
ATC	Average total compensation	D	Daily	HR	High end range	MCC	Median cash compensation	MWR	Median wage range	W	Weekly
AW	Average wage paid	FQ	First quartile wage	LO	Lowest wage paid	ME	Median entry wage	S	See annotated source	Y	Yearly

Occupation/Type/Industry	Location	Per	Low	Mid	High	Source	Date
Electrician	Houston-The Woodlands-Sugar Land MSA, TX	Y	35780 FQ	46160 MW	58280 TQ	USBLS	5/15
	San Antonio-New Braunfels MSA, TX	Y	34080 FQ	44090 MW	53890 TQ	USBLS	5/15
	Utah	Y	40170 FQ	49440 MW	58570 TQ	USBLS	5/15
	Ogden-Clearfield MSA, UT	Y	36430 FQ	47990 MW	58390 TQ	USBLS	5/15
	Provo-Orem MSA, UT	Y	40420 FQ	47120 MW	55920 TQ	USBLS	5/15
	Salt Lake City MSA, UT	Y	41930 FQ	51320 MW	59390 TQ	USBLS	5/15
	Vermont	Y	38560 FQ	45430 MW	53170 TQ	USBLS	5/15
	Burlington-South Burlington MSA, VT	Y	38770 FQ	45410 MW	53520 TQ	USBLS	5/15
	Virginia	Y	37280 FQ	47020 MW	57540 TQ	USBLS	5/15
	Richmond MSA, VA	Y	35760 FQ	45620 MW	58020 TQ	USBLS	5/15
	Virginia Beach-Norfolk-Newport News MSA, VA-NC	Y	40610 FQ	48030 MW	55440 TQ	USBLS	5/15
	Washington	H	23.15 FQ	30.96 MW	40.73 TQ	WABLS	3/16
	Seattle-Bellevue-Everett PMSA, WA	H	26.33 FQ	35.53 MW	44.10 TQ	WABLS	3/16
	Tacoma-Lakewood PMSA, WA	H	20.91 FQ	28.80 MW	37.79 TQ	WABLS	3/16
	West Virginia	Y	38250 FQ	51800 MW	68930 TQ	USBLS	5/15
	Huntington-Ashland MSA, WV-KY-OH	Y	41130 FQ	55710 MW	70890 TQ	USBLS	5/15
	Wisconsin	Y	45270 FQ	58160 MW	69840 TQ	USBLS	5/15
	Madison MSA, WI	Y	46850 FQ	57680 MW	69400 TQ	USBLS	5/15
	Milwaukee-Waukesha-West Allis MSA, WI	Y	54070 FQ	65610 MW	73550 TQ	USBLS	5/15
	Wyoming	Y	47940 FQ	57490 MW	68540 TQ	USBLS	5/15
	Cheyenne MSA, WY	Y	43710 FQ	52930 MW	59270 TQ	USBLS	5/15
	Puerto Rico	Y	18690 FQ	22890 MW	31590 TQ	USBLS	5/15
	San Juan-Carolina-Caguas MSA, PR	Y	19060 FQ	23570 MW	34410 TQ	USBLS	5/15
	Virgin Islands	Y	33430 FQ	41160 MW	47270 TQ	USBLS	5/15
	Guam	Y	32790 FQ	36810 MW	42890 TQ	USBLS	5/15
Electro-Mechanical Technician	Alabama	Y	42088 AE	52893 AW	58295 AEX	ALBLS	6/16
	Arizona	Y	43970 FQ	54980 MW	69590 TQ	USBLS	5/15
	Phoenix-Mesa-Scottsdale MSA, AZ	Y	43050 FQ	54250 MW	68750 TQ	USBLS	5/15
	Tucson MSA, AZ	Y	43490 FQ	67990 MW	76580 TQ	USBLS	5/15
	California	H	19.35 FQ	25.27 MW	31.23 TQ	CABLS	1/16-3/16
	Anaheim-Santa Ana-Irvine PMSA, CA	H	18.17 FQ	24.27 MW	30.30 TQ	CABLS	1/16-3/16
	Los Angeles-Long Beach-Glendale PMSA, CA	H	17.26 FQ	20.27 MW	29.06 TQ	CABLS	1/16-3/16
	Oakland-Hayward-Berkeley PMSA, CA	H	20.45 FQ	24.35 MW	29.65 TQ	CABLS	1/16-3/16
	Riverside-San Bernardino-Ontario MSA, CA	H	19.85 FQ	28.56 MW	33.98 TQ	CABLS	1/16-3/16
	Sacramento–Roseville–Arden-Arcade MSA, CA	H	26.24 FQ	29.31 MW	33.94 TQ	CABLS	1/16-3/16
	San Diego-Carlsbad MSA, CA	H	22.04 FQ	29.19 MW	36.29 TQ	CABLS	1/16-3/16
	Colorado	Y	51930 FQ	62210 MW	71590 TQ	USBLS	5/15
	Connecticut	Y		64623 MW		CTBLS	1/16-3/16
	Washington-Arlington-Alexandria PMSA, DC-VA-MD-WV	Y	43060 FQ	51630 MW	61540 TQ	USBLS	5/15
	Florida	H	16.15 AE	18.74 MW	24.12 AEX	FLBLS	7/16-9/16
	Fort Lauderdale-Pompano Beach-Deerfield Beach PMSA, FL	H	17.19 AE	19.10 MW	23.78 AEX	FLBLS	7/16-9/16
	Orlando-Kissimmee-Sanford MSA, FL	H	14.08 AE	17.56 MW	19.93 AEX	FLBLS	7/16-9/16
	Tampa-St. Petersburg-Clearwater MSA, FL	H	19.40 AE	28.41 MW	32.18 AEX	FLBLS	7/16-9/16
	Georgia	Y	58220 FQ	71950 MW	83300 TQ	USBLS	5/15
	Atlanta-Sandy Springs-Roswell MSA, GA	Y	48490 FQ	67030 MW	77260 TQ	USBLS	5/15
	Illinois	Y	41240 FQ	49490 MW	62760 TQ	USBLS	5/15
	Chicago-Naperville-Arlington Heights PMSA, IL	Y	41890 FQ	49830 MW	63260 TQ	USBLS	5/15
	Indiana	Y	43210 FQ	50440 MW	60970 TQ	USBLS	5/15

AE	Average entry wage	**AWR**	Average wage range	**H**	Hourly	**LR**	Low end range	**MTC**	Median total compensation	**TCC**	Total cash compensation
AEX	Average experienced wage	**B**	Biweekly	**HI**	Highest wage paid	**M**	Monthly	**MCC**	Median cash compensation	**MWR**	Median wage range	**TQ**	Third quartile wage
ATC	Average total compensation	**D**	Daily	**HR**	High end range	**MCC**	Median cash compensation	**MWR**	Median wage range	**W**	Weekly
AW	Average wage paid	**FQ**	First quartile wage	**LO**	Lowest wage paid	**ME**	Median entry wage	**S**	See annotated source	**Y**	Yearly

Occupation/Type/Industry	Location	Per	Low	Mid	High	Source	Date
Electro-Mechanical Technician	Indianapolis-Carmel-Anderson						
	MSA, IN	Y	46410 FQ	55770 MW	68850 TQ	USBLS	5/15
	Iowa	Y	45910 FQ	62240 MW	72340 TQ	USBLS	5/15
	Kentucky	Y	31580 FQ	43660 MW	52120 TQ	USBLS	5/15
	Louisville-Jefferson County						
	MSA, KY-IN	Y	34070 FQ	42360 MW	54040 TQ	USBLS	5/15
	Louisiana	Y	31260 FQ	38180 MW	52380 TQ	USBLS	5/15
	Massachusetts	Y	43930 FQ	52440 MW	64470 TQ	USBLS	5/15
	Boston-Cambridge-Newton						
	NECTA, MA	Y	45900 FQ	56230 MW	68120 TQ	USBLS	5/15
	Worcester MSA, MA-CT	Y	43370 FQ	54620 MW	64750 TQ	USBLS	5/15
	Michigan	Y	47500 FQ	64730 MW	75620 TQ	USBLS	5/15
	Minnesota	Y	47530 FQ	56794 MW	65614 TQ	MNBLS	1/16-3/16
	Minneapolis-St. Paul-						
	Bloomington MSA, MN-WI	Y	49757 FQ	57933 MW	67177 TQ	MNBLS	1/16-3/16
	Mississippi	Y	52150 FQ	56410 MW	60680 TQ	USBLS	5/15
	Missouri	Y	39130 FQ	52400 MW	61330 TQ	USBLS	5/15
	Nebraska	Y	35915 FQ	47370 MW	63730 TQ	NEBLS	7/16-9/16
	Nevada	Y	33730 FQ	48990 MW	62490 TQ	USBLS	5/15
	Las Vegas-Henderson-Paradise						
	MSA, NV	Y	39180 FQ	47470 MW	58570 TQ	USBLS	5/15
	New Hampshire	H	19.94 AE	24.26 MW	28.85 AEX	NHBLS	6/16
	Manchester NECTA, NH	H	24.71 AE	33.77 MW	36.96 AEX	NHBLS	6/16
	Nashua NECTA, NH-MA	Y	43020 FQ	48560 MW	57340 TQ	USBLS	5/15
	New Jersey	Y	45290 FQ	57510 MW	81260 TQ	USBLS	5/15
	Camden PMSA, NJ	Y	50770 FQ	71990 MW	96270 TQ	USBLS	5/15
	Newark PMSA, NJ-PA	Y	42900 FQ	53540 MW	67400 TQ	USBLS	5/15
	New Mexico	Y	62750 FQ	70980 MW	80510 TQ	USBLS	5/15
	Albuquerque MSA, NM	Y	63050 FQ	71140 MW	80560 TQ	USBLS	5/15
	New York	Y	39500 AE	60960 MW	74390 AEX	NYBLS	1/16-3/16
	Nassau County-Suffolk County						
	PMSA, NY	Y	57130 FQ	73280 MW	89120 TQ	USBLS	5/15
	New York-Jersey City-White						
	Plains PMSA, NY-NJ	Y	43510 FQ	57320 MW	76630 TQ	USBLS	5/15
	Rochester MSA, NY	Y	42990 FQ	50970 MW	61280 TQ	USBLS	5/15
	North Carolina	Y	50120 FQ	60010 MW	86330 TQ	USBLS	5/15
	Charlotte-Concord-Gastonia						
	MSA, NC-SC	Y	42590 FQ	51760 MW	59320 TQ	USBLS	5/15
	Ohio	Y	43110 FQ	54460 MW	68750 TQ	USBLS	5/15
	Cincinnati MSA, OH-KY-IN	Y	52310 FQ	64610 MW	73220 TQ	USBLS	5/15
	Cleveland-Elyria MSA, OH	Y	43020 FQ	52410 MW	66730 TQ	USBLS	5/15
	Columbus MSA, OH	Y	41040 FQ	46140 MW	54800 TQ	USBLS	5/15
	Oklahoma	Y	34150 FQ	42890 MW	51530 TQ	USBLS	5/15
	Oklahoma City MSA, OK	Y	30590 FQ	38890 MW	47190 TQ	USBLS	5/15
	Tulsa MSA, OK	Y	51610 FQ	63200 MW	78900 TQ	USBLS	5/15
	Oregon	H	25.90 FQ	30.86 MW	35.87 TQ	ORBLS	2016
	Portland-Vancouver-Hillsboro						
	MSA, OR-WA	Y	53660 FQ	63740 MW	73880 TQ	USBLS	5/15
	Pennsylvania	Y	37390 FQ	45900 MW	57330 TQ	USBLS	5/15
	Montgomery County-Bucks						
	County-Chester County						
	PMSA, PA	Y	41320 FQ	48290 MW	58410 TQ	USBLS	5/15
	Pittsburgh MSA, PA	Y	33770 FQ	39410 MW	53880 TQ	USBLS	5/15
	Providence-Warwick MSA, RI-						
	MA	Y	24090 FQ	35790 MW	49140 TQ	USBLS	5/15
	South Carolina	Y	33480 FQ	37750 MW	48160 TQ	USBLS	5/15
	Tennessee	Y	41570 FQ	56210 MW	70770 TQ	USBLS	5/15
	Knoxville MSA, TN	Y	48710 FQ	59080 MW	89310 TQ	USBLS	5/15
	Memphis MSA, TN-MS-AR	Y	32640 FQ	35960 MW	44210 TQ	USBLS	5/15
	Nashville-Davidson–						
	Murfreesboro–Franklin						
	MSA, TN	Y	46060 FQ	54690 MW	63440 TQ	USBLS	5/15
	Texas	Y	43910 FQ	56590 MW	72610 TQ	USBLS	5/15
	Austin-Round Rock MSA, TX	Y	45090 FQ	55250 MW	63180 TQ	USBLS	5/15
	Dallas-Plano-Irving PMSA, TX	Y	41900 FQ	53580 MW	65710 TQ	USBLS	5/15
	Fort Worth-Arlington PMSA,						
	TX	Y	54000 FQ	67470 MW	79270 TQ	USBLS	5/15
	Houston-The Woodlands-						
	Sugar Land MSA, TX	Y	45050 FQ	65220 MW	85020 TQ	USBLS	5/15
	San Antonio-New Braunfels						
	MSA, TX	Y	53490 FQ	58890 MW	67370 TQ	USBLS	5/15
	Utah	Y	38190 FQ	54950 MW	61930 TQ	USBLS	5/15

AE	Average entry wage	AWR	Average wage range	H	Hourly	LR	Low end range	MTC	Median total compensation
AEX	Average experienced wage	B	Biweekly	HI	Highest wage paid	M	Monthly	MW	Median wage paid
ATC	Average total compensation	D	Daily	HR	High end range	MCC	Median cash compensation	MWR	Median wage range
AW	Average wage paid	FQ	First quartile wage	LO	Lowest wage paid	ME	Median entry wage	S	See annotated source

TCC	Total cash compensation	
TQ	Third quartile wage	
W	Weekly	
Y	Yearly	

Occupation/Type/Industry	Location	Per	Low	Mid	High	Source	Date
Electro-Mechanical Technician	Ogden-Clearfield MSA, UT	Y	35730 FQ	43790 MW	64440 TQ	USBLS	5/15
	Salt Lake City MSA, UT	Y	52910 FQ	57020 MW	61120 TQ	USBLS	5/15
	Vermont	Y	58890 FQ	71690 MW	82020 TQ	USBLS	5/15
	Virginia	Y	42740 FQ	50390 MW	60150 TQ	USBLS	5/15
	Virginia Beach-Norfolk- Newport News MSA, VA-NC	Y	42500 FQ	49750 MW	60590 TQ	USBLS	5/15
	Washington	H	28.98 FQ	42.71 MW	47.57 TQ	WABLS	3/16
	Wisconsin	Y	43790 FQ	51830 MW	60960 TQ	USBLS	5/15
	Milwaukee-Waukesha-West Allis MSA, WI	Y	49740 FQ	58290 MW	67460 TQ	USBLS	5/15
	Wyoming	Y	44060 FQ	52310 MW	64890 TQ	USBLS	5/15
	Puerto Rico	Y	41990 FQ	50490 MW	57710 TQ	USBLS	5/15
	San Juan-Carolina-Caguas MSA, PR	Y	44010 FQ	51660 MW	58300 TQ	USBLS	5/15
Electroencephalograph Technician Department of Public Health, Acute Care, Hospital	San Francisco, CA	B	2360 LO		2868 HI	SFGOV	2016-2018
Electromechanical Equipment Assembler	Alabama	Y	24862 AE	32636 AW	36512 AEX	ALBLS	6/16
	Birmingham-Hoover MSA, AL	Y	32769 AE	41550 AW	45941 AEX	ALBLS	6/16
	Arizona	Y	28690 FQ	36300 MW	45830 TQ	USBLS	5/15
	Phoenix-Mesa-Scottsdale MSA, AZ	Y	29200 FQ	39230 MW	47980 TQ	USBLS	5/15
	Tucson MSA, AZ	Y	27260 FQ	33140 MW	38870 TQ	USBLS	5/15
	Arkansas	Y	25230 FQ	29120 MW	39570 TQ	USBLS	5/15
	California	H	11.32 FQ	14.24 MW	18.65 TQ	CABLS	1/16-3/16
	Anaheim-Santa Ana-Irvine PMSA, CA	H	10.91 FQ	13.51 MW	17.43 TQ	CABLS	1/16-3/16
	Los Angeles-Long Beach- Glendale PMSA, CA	H	10.81 FQ	13.21 MW	17.12 TQ	CABLS	1/16-3/16
	Oakland-Hayward-Berkeley PMSA, CA	H	14.34 FQ	17.77 MW	21.38 TQ	CABLS	1/16-3/16
	Riverside-San Bernardino- Ontario MSA, CA	H	10.41 FQ	12.02 MW	15.11 TQ	CABLS	1/16-3/16
	Sacramento–Roseville– Arden-Arcade MSA, CA	H	10.63 FQ	11.71 MW	14.46 TQ	CABLS	1/16-3/16
	San Diego-Carlsbad MSA, CA	H	12.58 FQ	14.84 MW	19.19 TQ	CABLS	1/16-3/16

	San Francisco-Redwood City-
	  South San Francisco PMSA,
	  CA
		H	13.91 FQ	19.97 MW	22.91 TQ	CABLS	1/16-3/16

	Colorado	Y	29230 FQ	34990 MW	39530 TQ	USBLS	5/15
	Denver-Aurora-Lakewood MSA, CO	Y	32380 FQ	35060 MW	37740 TQ	USBLS	5/15
	Connecticut	Y		37900 MW		CTBLS	1/16-3/16
	Bridgeport-Stamford-Norwalk MSA, CT	Y	28180 FQ	40730 MW	47070 TQ	USBLS	5/15
	Hartford-West Hartford-East Hartford MSA, CT	Y	19650 FQ	28250 MW	46220 TQ	USBLS	5/15

	Washington-Arlington-
	  Alexandria PMSA, DC-VA-
	  MD-WV
		Y	28620 FQ	35890 MW	43430 TQ	USBLS	5/15

	Florida	H	10.89 AE	14.54 MW	18.26 AEX	FLBLS	7/16-9/16

	Fort Lauderdale-Pompano
	  Beach-Deerfield Beach
	  PMSA, FL
		H	12.55 AE	16.55 MW	17.41 AEX	FLBLS	7/16-9/16

	Orlando-Kissimmee-Sanford MSA, FL	H	14.71 AE	19.15 MW	23.31 AEX	FLBLS	7/16-9/16
	Tampa-St. Petersburg- Clearwater MSA, FL	H	14.73 AE	18.75 MW	21.99 AEX	FLBLS	7/16-9/16
	Georgia	Y	23290 FQ	37330 MW	44280 TQ	USBLS	5/15
	Atlanta-Sandy Springs- Roswell MSA, GA	Y	30470 FQ	35960 MW	42480 TQ	USBLS	5/15
	Illinois	Y	27290 FQ	35160 MW	42060 TQ	USBLS	5/15
	Chicago-Naperville-Arlington Heights PMSA, IL	Y	26840 FQ	35690 MW	42990 TQ	USBLS	5/15
	Lake County-Kenosha County PMSA, IL-WI	Y	24660 FQ	33760 MW	37750 TQ	USBLS	5/15
	Indiana	Y	27090 FQ	33110 MW	39320 TQ	USBLS	5/15

Occupation/Type/Industry	Location	Per	Low	Mid	High	Source	Date
Electromechanical Equipment Assembler							
	Indianapolis-Carmel-Anderson MSA, IN	Y	25000 FQ	30690 MW	37680 TQ	USBLS	5/15
	Iowa	Y	27010 FQ	31550 MW	42350 TQ	USBLS	5/15
	Kansas	Y	28310 FQ	33710 MW	38720 TQ	USBLS	5/15
	Wichita MSA, KS	Y	27710 FQ	32890 MW	37900 TQ	USBLS	5/15
	Kentucky	Y	38410 FQ	44990 MW	50430 TQ	USBLS	5/15
	Louisville-Jefferson County MSA, KY-IN	Y	30520 FQ	35720 MW	42680 TQ	USBLS	5/15
	Maryland	Y	25529 AE	37952 MW	44163 AEX	MDBLS	4/16
	Baltimore-Columbia-Towson MSA, MD	Y	28990 FQ	35430 MW	44000 TQ	USBLS	5/15
	Massachusetts	Y	31970 FQ	40080 MW	48380 TQ	USBLS	5/15
	Boston-Cambridge-Newton NECTA, MA	Y	32260 FQ	40470 MW	49080 TQ	USBLS	5/15
	Worcester MSA, MA-CT	Y	32320 FQ	37500 MW	44490 TQ	USBLS	5/15
	Michigan	Y	25490 FQ	31680 MW	42810 TQ	USBLS	5/15
	Grand Rapids-Wyoming MSA, MI	Y	25970 FQ	32520 MW	43280 TQ	USBLS	5/15
	Minnesota	Y	28338 FQ	34008 MW	40579 TQ	MNBLS	1/16-3/16
	Minneapolis-St. Paul-Bloomington MSA, MN-WI	Y	28602 FQ	34251 MW	41369 TQ	MNBLS	1/16-3/16
	Mississippi	Y	25710 FQ	29940 MW	37170 TQ	USBLS	5/15
	Missouri	Y	22070 FQ	27770 MW	39600 TQ	USBLS	5/15
	Kansas City MSA, MO-KS	Y	21570 FQ	24560 MW	29110 TQ	USBLS	5/15
	Nebraska	Y	36430 FQ	42530 MW	46410 TQ	NEBLS	7/16-9/16
	Omaha-Council Bluffs MSA, NE-IA	Y	36670 FQ	42730 MW	46505 TQ	NEBLS	7/16-9/16
	Nevada	Y	20960 FQ	26380 MW	34470 TQ	USBLS	5/15
	New Hampshire	H	12.90 AE	16.93 MW	20.36 AEX	NHBLS	6/16
	Manchester NECTA, NH	H	12.93 AE	19.98 MW	22.48 AEX	NHBLS	6/16
	Nashua NECTA, NH-MA	Y	33160 FQ	39250 MW	48230 TQ	USBLS	5/15
	New Jersey	Y	26100 FQ	34270 MW	43970 TQ	USBLS	5/15
	Camden PMSA, NJ	Y	27770 FQ	35740 MW	43710 TQ	USBLS	5/15
	Newark PMSA, NJ-PA	Y	27670 FQ	33790 MW	43860 TQ	USBLS	5/15
	Trenton MSA, NJ	Y	23470 FQ	37060 MW	45180 TQ	USBLS	5/15
	New Mexico	Y	30830 FQ	37420 MW	57630 TQ	USBLS	5/15
	Albuquerque MSA, NM	Y	31560 FQ	37920 MW	60350 TQ	USBLS	5/15
	New York	Y	26950 AE	35670 MW	43350 AEX	NYBLS	1/16-3/16
	Buffalo-Cheektowaga-Niagara Falls MSA, NY	Y	30760 FQ	38970 MW	48480 TQ	USBLS	5/15
	Nassau County-Suffolk County PMSA, NY	Y	31780 FQ	37440 MW	44750 TQ	USBLS	5/15
	New York-Jersey City-White Plains PMSA, NY-NJ	Y	25760 FQ	32650 MW	42790 TQ	USBLS	5/15
	Rochester MSA, NY	Y	33440 FQ	38990 MW	54430 TQ	USBLS	5/15
	North Carolina	Y	27040 FQ	33290 MW	40270 TQ	USBLS	5/15
	Charlotte-Concord-Gastonia MSA, NC-SC	Y	31640 FQ	35930 MW	41160 TQ	USBLS	5/15
	Raleigh MSA, NC	Y	24650 FQ	29770 MW	37900 TQ	USBLS	5/15
	Ohio	Y	28860 FQ	35450 MW	42960 TQ	USBLS	5/15
	Cincinnati MSA, OH-KY-IN	Y	33190 FQ	39670 MW	46330 TQ	USBLS	5/15
	Cleveland-Elyria MSA, OH	Y	26610 FQ	31070 MW	36670 TQ	USBLS	5/15
	Columbus MSA, OH	Y	32660 FQ	37400 MW	43780 TQ	USBLS	5/15
	Oklahoma	Y	27760 FQ	33950 MW	39490 TQ	USBLS	5/15
	Oklahoma City MSA, OK	Y	23220 FQ	27150 MW	32040 TQ	USBLS	5/15
	Tulsa MSA, OK	Y	31570 FQ	36010 MW	42020 TQ	USBLS	5/15
	Oregon	H	12.46 FQ	15.91 MW	18.61 TQ	ORBLS	2016
	Portland-Vancouver-Hillsboro MSA, OR-WA	Y	25490 FQ	32380 MW	37650 TQ	USBLS	5/15
	Pennsylvania	Y	27400 FQ	32980 MW	40050 TQ	USBLS	5/15
	Allentown-Bethlehem-Easton MSA, PA-NJ	Y	27980 FQ	32820 MW	38490 TQ	USBLS	5/15
	Montgomery County-Bucks County-Chester County PMSA, PA	Y	28500 FQ	33530 MW	39550 TQ	USBLS	5/15
	Pittsburgh MSA, PA	Y	28170 FQ	33700 MW	43670 TQ	USBLS	5/15
	Rhode Island	Y	32390 FQ	36230 MW	40320 TQ	USBLS	5/15
	Providence-Warwick MSA, RI-MA	Y	31970 FQ	35940 MW	39970 TQ	USBLS	5/15
	South Carolina	Y	27220 FQ	31050 MW	36390 TQ	USBLS	5/15
	South Dakota	Y	25040 FQ	30650 MW	35900 TQ	USBLS	5/15

AE	Average entry wage	AWR	Average wage range	H	Hourly	LR	Low end range	MTC	Median total compensation	TCC	Total cash compensation
AEX	Average experienced wage	B	Biweekly	HI	Highest wage paid	M	Monthly	MW	Median wage paid	TQ	Third quartile wage
ATC	Average total compensation	D	Daily	HR	High end range	MCC	Median cash compensation	MWR	Median wage range	W	Weekly
AW	Average wage paid	FQ	First quartile wage	LO	Lowest wage paid	ME	Median entry wage	S	See annotated source	Y	Yearly

Occupation/Type/Industry	Location	Per	Low	Mid	High	Source	Date
Electromechanical Equipment Assembler	Tennessee	Y	30200 FQ	34720 MW	38770 TQ	USBLS	5/15
	Texas	Y	24300 FQ	31400 MW	40550 TQ	USBLS	5/15
	Austin-Round Rock MSA, TX	Y	32730 FQ	38480 MW	48520 TQ	USBLS	5/15
	Dallas-Plano-Irving PMSA, TX	Y	23440 FQ	29600 MW	40260 TQ	USBLS	5/15
	Fort Worth-Arlington PMSA, TX	Y	19850 FQ	23500 MW	29170 TQ	USBLS	5/15
	Houston-The Woodlands-Sugar Land MSA, TX	Y	25350 FQ	32690 MW	41770 TQ	USBLS	5/15
	San Antonio-New Braunfels MSA, TX	Y	17220 FQ	19670 MW	29450 TQ	USBLS	5/15
	Utah	Y	33510 FQ	38620 MW	48840 TQ	USBLS	5/15
	Virginia	Y	27730 FQ	33810 MW	41820 TQ	USBLS	5/15
	Richmond MSA, VA	Y	25540 FQ	28990 MW	34550 TQ	USBLS	5/15
	Virginia Beach-Norfolk-Newport News MSA, VA-NC	Y	32520 FQ	38880 MW	46600 TQ	USBLS	5/15
	Washington	H	14.47 FQ	17.45 MW	21.21 TQ	WABLS	3/16
	Seattle-Bellevue-Everett PMSA, WA	H	14.30 FQ	17.32 MW	20.95 TQ	WABLS	3/16
	West Virginia	Y	24720 FQ	31650 MW	37720 TQ	USBLS	5/15
	Wisconsin	Y	30630 FQ	37430 MW	47000 TQ	USBLS	5/15
	Madison MSA, WI	Y	28650 FQ	33240 MW	38400 TQ	USBLS	5/15
	Milwaukee-Waukesha-West Allis MSA, WI	Y	30760 FQ	38440 MW	51600 TQ	USBLS	5/15
Electron Microscopist Michigan State University	East Lansing, MI	Y	44585 LO		51064 HI	MSUSAL	10/1/14-9/30/15
Electronic Equipment Installer and Repairer Motor Vehicles	Alabama	Y	21835 AE	26758 AW	29229 AEX	ALBLS	6/16
Motor Vehicles	Arizona	Y	20360 FQ	27490 MW	35210 TQ	USBLS	5/15
Motor Vehicles	Phoenix-Mesa-Scottsdale MSA, AZ	Y	19540 FQ	25860 MW	34600 TQ	USBLS	5/15
Motor Vehicles	Arkansas	Y	21340 FQ	27650 MW	34150 TQ	USBLS	5/15
Motor Vehicles	California	H	10.93 FQ	14.10 MW	18.06 TQ	CABLS	1/16-3/16
Motor Vehicles	Anaheim-Santa Ana-Irvine PMSA, CA	H	10.94 FQ	13.14 MW	16.60 TQ	CABLS	1/16-3/16
Motor Vehicles	Los Angeles-Long Beach-Glendale PMSA, CA	H	13.40 FQ	17.15 MW	22.59 TQ	CABLS	1/16-3/16
Motor Vehicles	Oakland-Hayward-Berkeley PMSA, CA	H	10.38 FQ	11.50 MW	20.18 TQ	CABLS	1/16-3/16
Motor Vehicles	Riverside-San Bernardino-Ontario MSA, CA	H	12.87 FQ	16.28 MW	19.13 TQ	CABLS	1/16-3/16
Motor Vehicles	Sacramento–Roseville–Arden-Arcade MSA, CA	H	13.26 FQ	15.26 MW	20.62 TQ	CABLS	1/16-3/16
Motor Vehicles	San Diego-Carlsbad MSA, CA	H	10.57 FQ	16.59 MW	18.72 TQ	CABLS	1/16-3/16
Motor Vehicles	San Francisco-Redwood City-South San Francisco PMSA, CA	H	15.64 FQ	19.16 MW	21.90 TQ	CABLS	1/16-3/16
Motor Vehicles	Colorado	Y	25280 FQ	30600 MW	37440 TQ	USBLS	5/15
Motor Vehicles	Denver-Aurora-Lakewood MSA, CO	Y	25250 FQ	31260 MW	38260 TQ	USBLS	5/15
Motor Vehicles	Connecticut	Y		30674 MW		CTBLS	1/16-3/16
Motor Vehicles	Hartford-West Hartford-East Hartford MSA, CT	Y	27080 FQ	29440 MW	32880 TQ	USBLS	5/15
Motor Vehicles	Delaware	Y	27770 FQ	30930 MW	43430 TQ	USBLS	5/15
Motor Vehicles	Wilmington PMSA, DE-MD-NJ	Y	27770 FQ	30930 MW	43430 TQ	USBLS	5/15
Motor Vehicles	District of Columbia	Y	40870 FQ	44120 MW	47380 TQ	USBLS	5/15
Motor Vehicles	Washington-Arlington-Alexandria PMSA, DC-VA-MD-WV	Y	26640 FQ	34740 MW	43720 TQ	USBLS	5/15
Motor Vehicles	Florida	H	10.25 AE	15.61 MW	18.59 AEX	FLBLS	7/16-9/16
Motor Vehicles	Fort Lauderdale-Pompano Beach-Deerfield Beach PMSA, FL	H	14.07 AE	17.46 MW	20.56 AEX	FLBLS	7/16-9/16
Motor Vehicles	Miami-Miami Beach-Kendall PMSA, FL	H	11.31 AE	15.70 MW	18.12 AEX	FLBLS	7/16-9/16
Motor Vehicles	Orlando-Kissimmee-Sanford MSA, FL	H	14.37 AE	18.19 MW	21.90 AEX	FLBLS	7/16-9/16

AE	Average entry wage	AWR	Average wage range	H	Hourly	LR	Low end range	MTC	Median total compensation	TCC	Total cash compensation
AEX	Average experienced wage	B	Biweekly	HI	Highest wage paid	M	Monthly	MW	Median wage paid	TQ	Third quartile wage
ATC	Average total compensation	D	Daily	HR	High end range	MCC	Median cash compensation	MWR	Median wage range	W	Weekly
AW	Average wage paid	FQ	First quartile wage	LO	Lowest wage paid	ME	Median entry wage	S	See annotated source	Y	Yearly

Occupation/Type/Industry	Location	Per	Low	Mid	High	Source	Date
Electronic Equipment Installer and Repairer							
Motor Vehicles	Tampa-St. Petersburg-Clearwater MSA, FL	H	12.79 AE	16.46 MW	19.09 AEX	FLBLS	7/16-9/16
Motor Vehicles	Georgia	Y	22330 FQ	27960 MW	35440 TQ	USBLS	5/15
Motor Vehicles	Atlanta-Sandy Springs-Roswell MSA, GA	Y	23460 FQ	29000 MW	36110 TQ	USBLS	5/15
Motor Vehicles	Hawaii	Y	21470 FQ	24730 MW	28890 TQ	USBLS	5/15
Motor Vehicles	Urban Honolulu MSA, HI	Y	21410 FQ	24590 MW	28630 TQ	USBLS	5/15
Motor Vehicles	Illinois	Y	28500 FQ	36800 MW	50610 TQ	USBLS	5/15
Motor Vehicles	Chicago-Naperville-Arlington Heights PMSA, IL	Y	33640 FQ	39940 MW	54080 TQ	USBLS	5/15
Motor Vehicles	Indiana	Y	18180 FQ	27990 MW	37120 TQ	USBLS	5/15
Motor Vehicles	Indianapolis-Carmel-Anderson MSA, IN	Y	24020 FQ	29510 MW	36560 TQ	USBLS	5/15
Motor Vehicles	Kansas	Y	27410 FQ	34590 MW	51970 TQ	USBLS	5/15
Motor Vehicles	Kentucky	Y	26460 FQ	29580 MW	34700 TQ	USBLS	5/15
Motor Vehicles	Louisiana	Y	23830 FQ	27960 MW	33350 TQ	USBLS	5/15
Motor Vehicles	Maine	Y	27890 FQ	30820 MW	35350 TQ	USBLS	5/15
Motor Vehicles	Maryland	Y	25513 AE	32506 MW	36003 AEX	MDBLS	4/16
Motor Vehicles	Baltimore-Columbia-Towson MSA, MD	Y	25410 FQ	33450 MW	37140 TQ	USBLS	5/15
Motor Vehicles	Massachusetts	Y	33610 FQ	42570 MW	48270 TQ	USBLS	5/15
Motor Vehicles	Boston-Cambridge-Newton NECTA, MA	Y	32210 FQ	39710 MW	74570 TQ	USBLS	5/15
Motor Vehicles	Michigan	Y	26250 FQ	32200 MW	39180 TQ	USBLS	5/15
Motor Vehicles	Minnesota	Y	25504 FQ	33549 MW	39553 TQ	MNBLS	1/16-3/16
Motor Vehicles	Minneapolis-St. Paul-Bloomington MSA, MN-WI	Y	30120 FQ	35470 MW	41615 TQ	MNBLS	1/16-3/16
Motor Vehicles	Mississippi	Y	20040 FQ	41840 MW	55780 TQ	USBLS	5/15
Motor Vehicles	Missouri	Y	26400 FQ	32480 MW	43440 TQ	USBLS	5/15
Motor Vehicles	St. Louis MSA, MO-IL	Y	26540 FQ	30680 MW	36490 TQ	USBLS	5/15
Motor Vehicles	Nebraska	Y	24670 FQ	32365 MW	42650 TQ	NEBLS	7/16-9/16
Motor Vehicles	Omaha-Council Bluffs MSA, NE-IA	Y	22655 FQ	25935 MW	30805 TQ	NEBLS	7/16-9/16
Motor Vehicles	Nevada	Y	30430 FQ	36970 MW	45390 TQ	USBLS	5/15
Motor Vehicles	New Hampshire	H	12.00 AE	17.55 MW	20.18 AEX	NHBLS	6/16
Motor Vehicles	New Jersey	Y	22680 FQ	28270 MW	36790 TQ	USBLS	5/15
Motor Vehicles	Camden PMSA, NJ	Y	30540 FQ	43440 MW	55400 TQ	USBLS	5/15
Motor Vehicles	New York	Y	25500 AE	38840 MW	49260 AEX	NYBLS	1/16-3/16
Motor Vehicles	Nassau County-Suffolk County PMSA, NY	Y	35440 FQ	45360 MW	55170 TQ	USBLS	5/15
Motor Vehicles	New York-Jersey City-White Plains PMSA, NY-NJ	Y	21950 FQ	25000 MW	37660 TQ	USBLS	5/15
Motor Vehicles	Rochester MSA, NY	Y	29070 FQ	36690 MW	52460 TQ	USBLS	5/15
Motor Vehicles	North Carolina	Y	19870 FQ	27900 MW	38580 TQ	USBLS	5/15
Motor Vehicles	Charlotte-Concord-Gastonia MSA, NC-SC	Y	24430 FQ	32320 MW	38120 TQ	USBLS	5/15
Motor Vehicles	Raleigh MSA, NC	Y	29290 FQ	35000 MW	42100 TQ	USBLS	5/15
Motor Vehicles	North Dakota	Y	25860 FQ	32210 MW	50560 TQ	USBLS	5/15
Motor Vehicles	Ohio	Y	29130 FQ	35190 MW	42110 TQ	USBLS	5/15
Motor Vehicles	Cincinnati MSA, OH-KY-IN	Y	23080 FQ	28660 MW	34240 TQ	USBLS	5/15
Motor Vehicles	Cleveland-Elyria MSA, OH	Y	34070 FQ	38620 MW	46390 TQ	USBLS	5/15
Motor Vehicles	Columbus MSA, OH	Y	28120 FQ	34990 MW	45570 TQ	USBLS	5/15
Motor Vehicles	Oklahoma	Y	26900 FQ	30670 MW	36030 TQ	USBLS	5/15
Motor Vehicles	Tulsa MSA, OK	Y	25640 FQ	28200 MW	30750 TQ	USBLS	5/15
Motor Vehicles	Oregon	H	12.90 FQ	14.83 MW	17.98 TQ	ORBLS	2016
Motor Vehicles	Pennsylvania	Y	25950 FQ	30790 MW	35910 TQ	USBLS	5/15
Motor Vehicles	Allentown-Bethlehem-Easton MSA, PA-NJ	Y	32220 FQ	34520 MW	36820 TQ	USBLS	5/15
Motor Vehicles	Pittsburgh MSA, PA	Y	28800 FQ	33800 MW	38200 TQ	USBLS	5/15
Motor Vehicles	South Carolina	Y	26860 FQ	32810 MW	36710 TQ	USBLS	5/15
Motor Vehicles	Columbia MSA, SC	Y	32140 FQ	34740 MW	37330 TQ	USBLS	5/15
Motor Vehicles	Tennessee	Y	22070 FQ	32720 MW	39130 TQ	USBLS	5/15
Motor Vehicles	Memphis MSA, TN-MS-AR	Y	37630 FQ	52640 MW	61740 TQ	USBLS	5/15
Motor Vehicles	Texas	Y	24410 FQ	31690 MW	39820 TQ	USBLS	5/15
Motor Vehicles	Austin-Round Rock MSA, TX	Y	27120 FQ	30070 MW	35830 TQ	USBLS	5/15
Motor Vehicles	Dallas-Plano-Irving PMSA, TX	Y	25280 FQ	33450 MW	39910 TQ	USBLS	5/15
Motor Vehicles	Fort Worth-Arlington PMSA, TX	Y	22100 FQ	29130 MW	35520 TQ	USBLS	5/15

AE	Average entry wage	AWR	Average wage range	H	Hourly	LR	Low end range	MTC	Median total compensation	TCC	Total cash compensation
AEX	Average experienced wage	B	Biweekly	HI	Highest wage paid	M	Monthly	MW	Median wage paid	TQ	Third quartile wage
ATC	Average total compensation	D	Daily	HR	High end range	MCC	Median cash compensation	MWR	Median wage range	W	Weekly
AW	Average wage paid	FQ	First quartile wage	LO	Lowest wage paid	ME	Median entry wage	S	See annotated source	Y	Yearly

Occupation/Type/Industry	Location	Per	Low	Mid	High	Source	Date
Electronic Equipment Installer and Repairer							
Motor Vehicles	Houston-The Woodlands-Sugar Land MSA, TX	Y	24970 FQ	31380 MW	38750 TQ	USBLS	5/15
Motor Vehicles	San Antonio-New Braunfels MSA, TX	Y	18760 FQ	33880 MW	38360 TQ	USBLS	5/15
Motor Vehicles	Virginia	Y	26160 FQ	31180 MW	37210 TQ	USBLS	5/15
Motor Vehicles	Richmond MSA, VA	Y	27200 FQ	31380 MW	36030 TQ	USBLS	5/15
Motor Vehicles	Virginia Beach-Norfolk-Newport News MSA, VA-NC	Y	28340 FQ	33320 MW	37170 TQ	USBLS	5/15
Motor Vehicles	Washington	H	16.44 FQ	25.01 MW	27.98 TQ	WABLS	3/16
Motor Vehicles	Wisconsin	Y	27420 FQ	31360 MW	38060 TQ	USBLS	5/15
Motor Vehicles	Milwaukee-Waukesha-West Allis MSA, WI	Y	27310 FQ	29580 MW	34950 TQ	USBLS	5/15
Motor Vehicles	Puerto Rico	Y	25620 FQ	35420 MW	81370 TQ	USBLS	5/15
Motor Vehicles	San Juan-Carolina-Caguas MSA, PR	Y	31460 FQ	37900 MW	84180 TQ	USBLS	5/15
Electronic Home Entertainment Equipment Installer and Repairer	Alabama	Y	22690 AE	44261 AW	55041 AEX	ALBLS	6/16
	Birmingham-Hoover MSA, AL	Y	19262 AE	33236 AW	40223 AEX	ALBLS	6/16
	Alaska	Y	44140 FQ	50820 MW	69750 TQ	USBLS	5/15
	Arizona	Y	36680 FQ	45200 MW	54630 TQ	USBLS	5/15
	Phoenix-Mesa-Scottsdale MSA, AZ	Y	39530 FQ	46420 MW	56120 TQ	USBLS	5/15
	Tucson MSA, AZ	Y	30800 FQ	40480 MW	47770 TQ	USBLS	5/15
	Arkansas	Y	21370 FQ	26750 MW	36810 TQ	USBLS	5/15
	California	H	15.50 FQ	19.49 MW	23.44 TQ	CABLS	1/16-3/16
	Los Angeles-Long Beach-Glendale PMSA, CA	H	16.28 FQ	20.57 MW	23.24 TQ	CABLS	1/16-3/16
	Oakland-Hayward-Berkeley PMSA, CA	H	10.98 FQ	15.96 MW	19.86 TQ	CABLS	1/16-3/16
	Riverside-San Bernardino-Ontario MSA, CA	H	18.94 FQ	22.10 MW	25.64 TQ	CABLS	1/16-3/16
	Sacramento–Roseville–Arden-Arcade MSA, CA	H	16.25 FQ	18.23 MW	22.10 TQ	CABLS	1/16-3/16
	San Diego-Carlsbad MSA, CA	H	16.23 FQ	18.93 MW	22.92 TQ	CABLS	1/16-3/16
	San Francisco-Redwood City-South San Francisco PMSA, CA	H	15.02 FQ	18.19 MW	26.70 TQ	CABLS	1/16-3/16
	Colorado	Y	38240 FQ	47730 MW	61430 TQ	USBLS	5/15
	Denver-Aurora-Lakewood MSA, CO	Y	42990 FQ	50290 MW	62530 TQ	USBLS	5/15
	Connecticut	Y		44631 MW		CTBLS	1/16-3/16
	Bridgeport-Stamford-Norwalk MSA, CT	Y	33770 FQ	41600 MW	48000 TQ	USBLS	5/15
	Wilmington PMSA, DE-MD-NJ	Y	32250 FQ	36510 MW	44300 TQ	USBLS	5/15
	Florida	H	12.50 AE	18.72 MW	23.48 AEX	FLBLS	7/16-9/16
	Fort Lauderdale-Pompano Beach-Deerfield Beach PMSA, FL	H	18.23 AE	23.12 MW	26.12 AEX	FLBLS	7/16-9/16
	Miami-Miami Beach-Kendall PMSA, FL	H	11.05 AE	17.99 MW	22.42 AEX	FLBLS	7/16-9/16
	Orlando-Kissimmee-Sanford MSA, FL	H	11.82 AE	21.19 MW	26.12 AEX	FLBLS	7/16-9/16
	Tampa-St. Petersburg-Clearwater MSA, FL	H	12.47 AE	17.16 MW	19.45 AEX	FLBLS	7/16-9/16
	Georgia	Y	21360 FQ	37680 MW	47470 TQ	USBLS	5/15
	Atlanta-Sandy Springs-Roswell MSA, GA	Y	22290 FQ	40660 MW	48350 TQ	USBLS	5/15
	Idaho	Y	27770 FQ	32170 MW	37690 TQ	USBLS	5/15
	Boise City MSA, ID	Y	28460 FQ	33700 MW	40520 TQ	USBLS	5/15
	Illinois	Y	34120 FQ	50020 MW	64040 TQ	USBLS	5/15
	Chicago-Naperville-Arlington Heights PMSA, IL	Y	43110 FQ	57670 MW	70300 TQ	USBLS	5/15
	Lake County-Kenosha County PMSA, IL-WI	Y	32300 FQ	50040 MW	60270 TQ	USBLS	5/15
	Indiana	Y	26710 FQ	31540 MW	38770 TQ	USBLS	5/15
	Gary PMSA, IN	Y	27360 FQ	29900 MW	34450 TQ	USBLS	5/15

AE Average entry wage	**AWR** Average wage range	**H** Hourly	**LR** Low end range	**MTC** Median total compensation	**TCC** Total cash compensation
AEX Average experienced wage	**B** Biweekly	**HI** Highest wage paid	**M** Monthly	**MW** Median wage paid	**TQ** Third quartile wage
ATC Average total compensation	**D** Daily	**HR** High end range	**MCC** Median cash compensation	**MWR** Median wage range	**W** Weekly
AW Average wage paid	**FQ** First quartile wage	**LO** Lowest wage paid	**ME** Median entry wage	**S** See annotated source	**Y** Yearly

Occupation/Type/Industry	Location	Per	Low	Mid	High	Source	Date
Electronic Home Entertainment Equipment Installer and Repairer	Indianapolis-Carmel-Anderson MSA, IN	Y	26360 FQ	31910 MW	38390 TQ	USBLS	5/15
	Iowa	Y	32420 FQ	39720 MW	47610 TQ	USBLS	5/15
	Kansas	Y	22680 FQ	35890 MW	55550 TQ	USBLS	5/15
	Kentucky	Y	26820 FQ	33390 MW	42410 TQ	USBLS	5/15
	Louisville-Jefferson County MSA, KY-IN	Y	30320 FQ	37100 MW	47590 TQ	USBLS	5/15
	Louisiana	Y	26930 FQ	35520 MW	51770 TQ	USBLS	5/15
	Baton Rouge MSA, LA	Y	33120 FQ	35640 MW	38160 TQ	USBLS	5/15
	Maine	Y	34120 FQ	38910 MW	45360 TQ	USBLS	5/15
	Maryland	Y	25943 AE	42459 MW	50717 AEX	MDBLS	4/16
	Baltimore-Columbia-Towson MSA, MD	Y	33010 FQ	42210 MW	53530 TQ	USBLS	5/15
	Massachusetts	Y	24400 FQ	34850 MW	44350 TQ	USBLS	5/15
	Michigan	Y	28750 FQ	35470 MW	47000 TQ	USBLS	5/15
	Grand Rapids-Wyoming MSA, MI	Y	27250 FQ	30090 MW	37730 TQ	USBLS	5/15
	Minnesota	Y	29285 FQ	39432 MW	52013 TQ	MNBLS	1/16-3/16
	Minneapolis-St. Paul-Bloomington MSA, MN-WI	Y	29617 FQ	42268 MW	53884 TQ	MNBLS	1/16-3/16
	Mississippi	Y	19350 FQ	31140 MW	38260 TQ	USBLS	5/15
	Missouri	Y	29590 FQ	36210 MW	50260 TQ	USBLS	5/15
	Kansas City MSA, MO-KS	Y	32030 FQ	37420 MW	47390 TQ	USBLS	5/15
	St. Louis MSA, MO-IL	Y	29250 FQ	35440 MW	48080 TQ	USBLS	5/15
	Montana	Y	26430 FQ	28810 MW	31670 TQ	USBLS	5/15
	Nebraska	Y	32635 FQ	42055 MW	53125 TQ	NEBLS	7/16-9/16
	Omaha-Council Bluffs MSA, NE-IA	Y	30530 FQ	39355 MW	45425 TQ	NEBLS	7/16-9/16
	Nevada	Y	34590 FQ	46800 MW	57900 TQ	USBLS	5/15
	Las Vegas-Henderson-Paradise MSA, NV	Y	34880 FQ	47300 MW	58360 TQ	USBLS	5/15
	New Hampshire	H	14.33 AE	22.54 MW	27.71 AEX	NHBLS	6/16
	Manchester NECTA, NH	H	13.86 AE	17.35 MW	23.91 AEX	NHBLS	6/16
	New Jersey	Y	36800 FQ	47040 MW	57110 TQ	USBLS	5/15
	Camden PMSA, NJ	Y	32600 FQ	37560 MW	60480 TQ	USBLS	5/15
	New Mexico	Y	33360 FQ	36230 MW	39100 TQ	USBLS	5/15
	Albuquerque MSA, NM	Y	33650 FQ	35910 MW	38170 TQ	USBLS	5/15
	New York	Y	24880 AE	38730 MW	47840 AEX	NYBLS	1/16-3/16
	Buffalo-Cheektowaga-Niagara Falls MSA, NY	Y	29330 FQ	34720 MW	42840 TQ	USBLS	5/15
	Nassau County-Suffolk County PMSA, NY	Y	23500 FQ	31540 MW	38200 TQ	USBLS	5/15
	New York-Jersey City-White Plains PMSA, NY-NJ	Y	32490 FQ	42980 MW	53460 TQ	USBLS	5/15
	North Carolina	Y	27840 FQ	30720 MW	38520 TQ	USBLS	5/15
	Charlotte-Concord-Gastonia MSA, NC-SC	Y	37400 FQ	43620 MW	48750 TQ	USBLS	5/15
	Raleigh MSA, NC	Y	27490 FQ	29860 MW	34900 TQ	USBLS	5/15
	North Dakota	Y	31460 FQ	38610 MW	52170 TQ	USBLS	5/15
	Ohio	Y	24760 FQ	34000 MW	39120 TQ	USBLS	5/15
	Cincinnati MSA, OH-KY-IN	Y	26320 FQ	33790 MW	38620 TQ	USBLS	5/15
	Cleveland-Elyria MSA, OH	Y	33680 FQ	36550 MW	39400 TQ	USBLS	5/15
	Columbus MSA, OH	Y	32590 FQ	39090 MW	44260 TQ	USBLS	5/15
	Oklahoma	Y	27820 FQ	32510 MW	41560 TQ	USBLS	5/15
	Oklahoma City MSA, OK	Y	28020 FQ	34170 MW	43980 TQ	USBLS	5/15
	Oregon	H	15.81 FQ	19.23 MW	24.18 TQ	ORBLS	2016
	Portland-Vancouver-Hillsboro MSA, OR-WA	Y	33400 FQ	39830 MW	55770 TQ	USBLS	5/15
	Pennsylvania	Y	27320 FQ	31270 MW	40470 TQ	USBLS	5/15
	Harrisburg-Carlisle MSA, PA	Y	26370 FQ	28730 MW	31090 TQ	USBLS	5/15
	Pittsburgh MSA, PA	Y	19240 FQ	29590 MW	40280 TQ	USBLS	5/15
	Providence-Warwick MSA, RI-MA	Y	30230 FQ	36140 MW	44180 TQ	USBLS	5/15
	South Carolina	Y	24140 FQ	29670 MW	41010 TQ	USBLS	5/15
	South Dakota	Y	26320 FQ	30790 MW	36700 TQ	USBLS	5/15
	Sioux Falls MSA, SD	Y	28000 FQ	31810 MW	37780 TQ	USBLS	5/15
	Tennessee	Y	27790 FQ	31580 MW	42290 TQ	USBLS	5/15

AE	Average entry wage	AWR	Average wage range	H	Hourly	LR	Low end range	MTC	Median total compensation	TCC	Total cash compensation
AEX	Average experienced wage	B	Biweekly	HI	Highest wage paid	M	Monthly	MW	Median wage paid	TQ	Third quartile wage
ATC	Average total compensation	D	Daily	HR	High end range	MCC	Median cash compensation	MWR	Median wage range	W	Weekly
AW	Average wage paid	FQ	First quartile wage	LO	Lowest wage paid	ME	Median entry wage	S	See annotated source	Y	Yearly

Occupation/Type/Industry	Location	Per	Low	Mid	High	Source	Date
Electronic Home Entertainment Equipment Installer and Repairer	Nashville-Davidson–Murfreesboro–Franklin MSA, TN	Y	29410 FQ	39940 MW	48470 TQ	USBLS	5/15
	Texas	Y	23510 FQ	33970 MW	44350 TQ	USBLS	5/15
	Austin-Round Rock MSA, TX	Y	25710 FQ	31930 MW	51270 TQ	USBLS	5/15
	Dallas-Plano-Irving PMSA, TX	Y	27150 FQ	37860 MW	46320 TQ	USBLS	5/15
	Houston-The Woodlands-Sugar Land MSA, TX	Y	27530 FQ	35720 MW	45590 TQ	USBLS	5/15
	San Antonio-New Braunfels MSA, TX	Y	31020 FQ	45740 MW	56910 TQ	USBLS	5/15
	Utah	Y	30580 FQ	38360 MW	46000 TQ	USBLS	5/15
	Salt Lake City MSA, UT	Y	34460 FQ	38650 MW	44670 TQ	USBLS	5/15
	Vermont	Y	29400 FQ	39530 MW	47100 TQ	USBLS	5/15
	Burlington-South Burlington MSA, VT	Y	29750 FQ	39630 MW	47790 TQ	USBLS	5/15
	Virginia	Y	35270 FQ	47700 MW	59740 TQ	USBLS	5/15
	Virginia Beach-Norfolk-Newport News MSA, VA-NC	Y	30680 FQ	36140 MW	44240 TQ	USBLS	5/15
	Washington	H	17.01 FQ	23.28 MW	27.85 TQ	WABLS	3/16
	Seattle-Bellevue-Everett PMSA, WA	H	15.77 FQ	24.03 MW	27.91 TQ	WABLS	3/16
	West Virginia	Y	24300 FQ	31510 MW	37840 TQ	USBLS	5/15
	Wisconsin	Y	29000 FQ	33860 MW	37830 TQ	USBLS	5/15
	Madison MSA, WI	Y	32130 FQ	37760 MW	47790 TQ	USBLS	5/15
	Milwaukee-Waukesha-West Allis MSA, WI	Y	31880 FQ	34840 MW	37790 TQ	USBLS	5/15
	Wyoming	Y	30180 FQ	36700 MW	43920 TQ	USBLS	5/15
	Puerto Rico	Y	17060 FQ	18520 MW	20360 TQ	USBLS	5/15
	San Juan-Carolina-Caguas MSA, PR	Y	17110 FQ	18640 MW	21380 TQ	USBLS	5/15
	Guam	Y	18260 FQ	19400 MW	22760 TQ	USBLS	5/15
Electronics Engineer							
Except Computer	Alabama	Y	68753 AE	106856 AW	125897 AEX	ALBLS	6/16
Except Computer	Birmingham-Hoover MSA, AL	Y	66796 AE	102177 AW	119862 AEX	ALBLS	6/16
Except Computer	Alaska	Y	81400 FQ	96440 MW	113910 TQ	USBLS	5/15
Except Computer	Anchorage MSA, AK	Y	82320 FQ	97070 MW	114070 TQ	USBLS	5/15
Except Computer	Arizona	Y	71900 FQ	91260 MW	114210 TQ	USBLS	5/15
Except Computer	Phoenix-Mesa-Scottsdale MSA, AZ	Y	69070 FQ	87710 MW	112910 TQ	USBLS	5/15
Except Computer	Tucson MSA, AZ	Y	83360 FQ	100850 MW	122810 TQ	USBLS	5/15
Except Computer	Arkansas	Y	55340 FQ	71250 MW	86270 TQ	USBLS	5/15
Except Computer	Little Rock-North Little Rock-Conway MSA, AR	Y	44450 FQ	61150 MW	76340 TQ	USBLS	5/15
Except Computer	California	H	43.04 FQ	54.38 MW	68.37 TQ	CABLS	1/16-3/16
Except Computer	Anaheim-Santa Ana-Irvine PMSA, CA	H	36.48 FQ	48.60 MW	66.52 TQ	CABLS	1/16-3/16
Except Computer	Los Angeles-Long Beach-Glendale PMSA, CA	H	44.32 FQ	57.64 MW	73.03 TQ	CABLS	1/16-3/16
Except Computer	Oakland-Hayward-Berkeley PMSA, CA	H	42.78 FQ	50.98 MW	59.94 TQ	CABLS	1/16-3/16
Except Computer	Riverside-San Bernardino-Ontario MSA, CA	H	40.05 FQ	49.42 MW	57.47 TQ	CABLS	1/16-3/16
Except Computer	Sacramento–Roseville–Arden-Arcade MSA, CA	H	39.63 FQ	52.02 MW	57.94 TQ	CABLS	1/16-3/16
Except Computer	San Diego-Carlsbad MSA, CA	H	44.64 FQ	54.74 MW	64.06 TQ	CABLS	1/16-3/16
Except Computer	San Francisco-Redwood City-South San Francisco PMSA, CA	H	44.82 FQ	55.36 MW	67.82 TQ	CABLS	1/16-3/16
Except Computer	Colorado	Y	77800 FQ	96950 MW	125170 TQ	USBLS	5/15
Except Computer	Denver-Aurora-Lakewood MSA, CO	Y	75770 FQ	93280 MW	118460 TQ	USBLS	5/15
Except Computer	Connecticut	Y		99430 MW		CTBLS	1/16-3/16
Except Computer	Bridgeport-Stamford-Norwalk MSA, CT	Y	85840 FQ	103270 MW	121510 TQ	USBLS	5/15
Except Computer	Hartford-West Hartford-East Hartford MSA, CT	Y	83950 FQ	99020 MW	119370 TQ	USBLS	5/15
Except Computer	District of Columbia	Y	99920 FQ	118100 MW	148720 TQ	USBLS	5/15

Occupation/Type/Industry	Location	Per	Low	Mid	High	Source	Date
Electronics Engineer							
Except Computer	Washington-Arlington-Alexandria PMSA, DC-VA-MD-WV	Y	97190 FQ	118070 MW	143680 TQ	USBLS	5/15
Except Computer	Florida	H	29.76 AE	43.84 MW	51.06 AEX	FLBLS	7/16-9/16
Except Computer	Fort Lauderdale-Pompano Beach-Deerfield Beach PMSA, FL	H	24.29 AE	39.68 MW	47.26 AEX	FLBLS	7/16-9/16
Except Computer	Miami-Miami Beach-Kendall PMSA, FL	H	23.12 AE	36.82 MW	45.11 AEX	FLBLS	7/16-9/16
Except Computer	Orlando-Kissimmee-Sanford MSA, FL	H	28.35 AE	44.81 MW	51.69 AEX	FLBLS	7/16-9/16
Except Computer	Tampa-St. Petersburg-Clearwater MSA, FL	H	29.01 AE	38.60 MW	48.10 AEX	FLBLS	7/16-9/16
Except Computer	Georgia	Y	73670 FQ	89030 MW	107140 TQ	USBLS	5/15
Except Computer	Atlanta-Sandy Springs-Roswell MSA, GA	Y	70650 FQ	89090 MW	110770 TQ	USBLS	5/15
Except Computer	Augusta-Richmond County MSA, GA-SC	Y	88570 FQ	107870 MW	129120 TQ	USBLS	5/15
Except Computer	Hawaii	Y	77700 FQ	96280 MW	110750 TQ	USBLS	5/15
Except Computer	Urban Honolulu MSA, HI	Y	77270 FQ	95430 MW	110750 TQ	USBLS	5/15
Except Computer	Illinois	Y	78480 FQ	97770 MW	120730 TQ	USBLS	5/15
Except Computer	Chicago-Naperville-Arlington Heights PMSA, IL	Y	82100 FQ	100690 MW	124780 TQ	USBLS	5/15
Except Computer	Lake County-Kenosha County PMSA, IL-WI	Y	71160 FQ	84970 MW	106950 TQ	USBLS	5/15
Except Computer	Indiana	Y	64870 FQ	79950 MW	99100 TQ	USBLS	5/15
Except Computer	Gary PMSA, IN	Y	62700 FQ	83250 MW	93040 TQ	USBLS	5/15
Except Computer	Indianapolis-Carmel-Anderson MSA, IN	Y	41440 FQ	70970 MW	94840 TQ	USBLS	5/15
Except Computer	Iowa	Y	61810 FQ	74700 MW	91040 TQ	USBLS	5/15
Except Computer	Des Moines-West Des Moines MSA, IA	Y	65080 FQ	75880 MW	91610 TQ	USBLS	5/15
Except Computer	Kansas	Y	63880 FQ	78300 MW	98620 TQ	USBLS	5/15
Except Computer	Wichita MSA, KS	Y	70490 FQ	82570 MW	97220 TQ	USBLS	5/15
Except Computer	Kentucky	Y	63710 FQ	75790 MW	100410 TQ	USBLS	5/15
Except Computer	Louisville-Jefferson County MSA, KY-IN	Y	66080 FQ	75450 MW	95360 TQ	USBLS	5/15
Except Computer	Louisiana	Y	62690 FQ	77230 MW	97610 TQ	USBLS	5/15
Except Computer	Baton Rouge MSA, LA	Y	63900 FQ	76080 MW	94450 TQ	USBLS	5/15
Except Computer	New Orleans-Metairie MSA, LA	Y	85860 FQ	102340 MW	121610 TQ	USBLS	5/15
Except Computer	Maine	Y	69810 FQ	82750 MW	108050 TQ	USBLS	5/15
Except Computer	Portland-South Portland MSA, ME	Y	70390 FQ	85060 MW	112030 TQ	USBLS	5/15
Except Computer	Maryland	Y	80441 AE	116497 MW	134524 AEX	MDBLS	4/16
Except Computer	Baltimore-Columbia-Towson MSA, MD	Y	95640 FQ	118070 MW	145110 TQ	USBLS	5/15
Except Computer	Salisbury MSA, MD-DE	Y	66440 FQ	71130 MW	75810 TQ	USBLS	5/15
Except Computer	Massachusetts	Y	77890 FQ	100290 MW	127380 TQ	USBLS	5/15
Except Computer	Boston-Cambridge-Newton NECTA, MA	Y	76180 FQ	98050 MW	123760 TQ	USBLS	5/15
Except Computer	Worcester MSA, MA-CT	Y	72300 FQ	98570 MW	112610 TQ	USBLS	5/15
Except Computer	Michigan	Y	70630 FQ	86400 MW	100520 TQ	USBLS	5/15
Except Computer	Detroit-Dearborn-Livonia PMSA, MI	Y	51170 FQ	76480 MW	92480 TQ	USBLS	5/15
Except Computer	Grand Rapids-Wyoming MSA, MI	Y	72830 FQ	86410 MW	96600 TQ	USBLS	5/15
Except Computer	Minnesota	Y	73930 FQ	89182 MW	111077 TQ	MNBLS	1/16-3/16
Except Computer	Minneapolis-St. Paul-Bloomington MSA, MN-WI	Y	74253 FQ	89918 MW	110986 TQ	MNBLS	1/16-3/16
Except Computer	Mississippi	Y	66670 FQ	81900 MW	106770 TQ	USBLS	5/15
Except Computer	Jackson MSA, MS	Y	64850 FQ	79860 MW	104790 TQ	USBLS	5/15
Except Computer	Missouri	Y	80520 FQ	99580 MW	117480 TQ	USBLS	5/15
Except Computer	Kansas City MSA, MO-KS	Y	70110 FQ	87180 MW	108260 TQ	USBLS	5/15
Except Computer	St. Louis MSA, MO-IL	Y	79110 FQ	97970 MW	118990 TQ	USBLS	5/15
Except Computer	Montana	Y	67500 FQ	83290 MW	98200 TQ	USBLS	5/15
Except Computer	Billings MSA, MT	Y	74310 FQ	93740 MW	118880 TQ	USBLS	5/15
Except Computer	Nebraska	Y	63065 FQ	74315 MW	90280 TQ	NEBLS	7/16-9/16
Except Computer	Omaha-Council Bluffs MSA, NE-IA	Y	66845 FQ	76950 MW	94350 TQ	NEBLS	7/16-9/16
Except Computer	Nevada	Y	75290 FQ	93260 MW	115270 TQ	USBLS	5/15

AE	Average entry wage	AWR	Average wage range	H	Hourly	LR	Low end range
AEX	Average experienced wage	B	Biweekly	HI	Highest wage paid	M	Monthly
ATC	Average total compensation	D	Daily	HR	High end range	MCC	Median cash compensation
AW	Average wage paid	FQ	First quartile wage	LO	Lowest wage paid	ME	Median entry wage

MTC	Median total compensation	TCC	Total cash compensation
MW	Median wage paid	TQ	Third quartile wage
MWR	Median wage range	W	Weekly
S	See annotated source	Y	Yearly

Occupation/Type/Industry	Location	Per	Low	Mid	High	Source	Date
Electronics Engineer							
Except Computer	Las Vegas-Henderson-Paradise MSA, NV	Y	74840 FQ	90600 MW	109200 TQ	USBLS	
Except Computer	New Hampshire	H	32.19 AE	45.29 MW	54.96 AEX	NHBLS	6/16
Except Computer	Manchester NECTA, NH	H	34.82 AE	47.32 MW	58.55 AEX	NHBLS	6/16
Except Computer	Nashua NECTA, NH-MA	Y	77550 FQ	104390 MW	132380 TQ	USBLS	5/15
Except Computer	New Jersey	Y	82070 FQ	104850 MW	124480 TQ	USBLS	5/15
Except Computer	Camden PMSA, NJ	Y	81820 FQ	105430 MW	121990 TQ	USBLS	5/15
Except Computer	Newark PMSA, NJ-PA	Y	87050 FQ	104610 MW	122350 TQ	USBLS	5/15
Except Computer	New Mexico	Y	78150 FQ	99400 MW	122200 TQ	USBLS	5/15
Except Computer	Albuquerque MSA, NM	Y	84270 FQ	105390 MW	130970 TQ	USBLS	5/15
Except Computer	New York	Y	63770 AE	99680 MW	119410 AEX	NYBLS	1/16-3/16
Except Computer	Buffalo-Cheektowaga-Niagara Falls MSA, NY	Y	67180 FQ	81590 MW	102130 TQ	USBLS	5/15
Except Computer	Nassau County-Suffolk County PMSA, NY	Y	62980 FQ	83810 MW	114240 TQ	USBLS	5/15
Except Computer	New York-Jersey City-White Plains PMSA, NY-NJ	Y	85390 FQ	111770 MW	137700 TQ	USBLS	5/15
Except Computer	Rochester MSA, NY	Y	74670 FQ	96710 MW	112560 TQ	USBLS	5/15
Except Computer	North Carolina	Y	74680 FQ	91260 MW	110100 TQ	USBLS	5/15
Except Computer	Charlotte-Concord-Gastonia MSA, NC-SC	Y	78410 FQ	92760 MW	109900 TQ	USBLS	5/15
Except Computer	Raleigh MSA, NC	Y	75910 FQ	92590 MW	112770 TQ	USBLS	5/15
Except Computer	North Dakota	Y	54720 FQ	67840 MW	80270 TQ	USBLS	5/15
Except Computer	Fargo MSA, ND-MN	Y	54260 FQ	62600 MW	74520 TQ	USBLS	5/15
Except Computer	Ohio	Y	72030 FQ	89260 MW	107500 TQ	USBLS	5/15
Except Computer	Cincinnati MSA, OH-KY-IN	Y	80690 FQ	95150 MW	113480 TQ	USBLS	5/15
Except Computer	Cleveland-Elyria MSA, OH	Y	72260 FQ	88250 MW	104180 TQ	USBLS	5/15
Except Computer	Columbus MSA, OH	Y	64400 FQ	79280 MW	93650 TQ	USBLS	5/15
Except Computer	Oklahoma	Y	70960 FQ	86570 MW	100170 TQ	USBLS	5/15
Except Computer	Oklahoma City MSA, OK	Y	72540 FQ	89030 MW	105720 TQ	USBLS	5/15
Except Computer	Tulsa MSA, OK	Y	72290 FQ	82580 MW	92450 TQ	USBLS	5/15
Except Computer	Oregon	H	34.09 FQ	44.89 MW	57.23 TQ	ORBLS	2016
Except Computer	Portland-Vancouver-Hillsboro MSA, OR-WA	Y	73050 FQ	95060 MW	118000 TQ	USBLS	5/15
Except Computer	Pennsylvania	Y	66900 FQ	89390 MW	113040 TQ	USBLS	5/15
Except Computer	Harrisburg-Carlisle MSA, PA	Y	44190 FQ	65740 MW	91260 TQ	USBLS	5/15
Except Computer	Montgomery County-Bucks County-Chester County PMSA, PA	Y	71480 FQ	90280 MW	113180 TQ	USBLS	5/15
Except Computer	Philadelphia PMSA, PA	Y	73520 FQ	99480 MW	117340 TQ	USBLS	5/15
Except Computer	Pittsburgh MSA, PA	Y	61610 FQ	83340 MW	103580 TQ	USBLS	5/15
Except Computer	Rhode Island	Y	104900 FQ	118600 MW	129570 TQ	USBLS	5/15
Except Computer	Providence-Warwick MSA, RI-MA	Y	104430 FQ	118600 MW	128180 TQ	USBLS	5/15
Except Computer	South Carolina	Y	75890 FQ	95890 MW	110640 TQ	USBLS	5/15
Except Computer	Charleston-North Charleston MSA, SC	Y	87110 FQ	104960 MW	108510 TQ	USBLS	5/15
Except Computer	Columbia MSA, SC	Y	64460 FQ	75500 MW	94620 TQ	USBLS	5/15
Except Computer	Greenville-Anderson-Mauldin MSA, SC	Y	66650 FQ	82740 MW	101190 TQ	USBLS	5/15
Except Computer	South Dakota	Y	67270 FQ	76720 MW	89980 TQ	USBLS	5/15
Except Computer	Sioux Falls MSA, SD	Y	69160 FQ	79310 MW	94520 TQ	USBLS	5/15
Except Computer	Tennessee	Y	71710 FQ	88420 MW	108500 TQ	USBLS	5/15
Except Computer	Knoxville MSA, TN	Y	72750 FQ	92780 MW	118040 TQ	USBLS	5/15
Except Computer	Memphis MSA, TN-MS-AR	Y	58330 FQ	70850 MW	93010 TQ	USBLS	5/15
Except Computer	Nashville-Davidson–Murfreesboro–Franklin MSA, TN	Y	73190 FQ	88710 MW	108320 TQ	USBLS	5/15
Except Computer	Texas	Y	79510 FQ	100000 MW	125880 TQ	USBLS	5/15
Except Computer	Austin-Round Rock MSA, TX	Y	77140 FQ	101400 MW	133180 TQ	USBLS	5/15
Except Computer	Dallas-Plano-Irving PMSA, TX	Y	80090 FQ	101630 MW	125500 TQ	USBLS	5/15
Except Computer	Fort Worth-Arlington PMSA, TX	Y	80930 FQ	94600 MW	114730 TQ	USBLS	5/15
Except Computer	Houston-The Woodlands-Sugar Land MSA, TX	Y	83190 FQ	105960 MW	135570 TQ	USBLS	5/15
Except Computer	San Antonio-New Braunfels MSA, TX	Y	72690 FQ	92720 MW	108510 TQ	USBLS	5/15
Except Computer	Utah	Y	70180 FQ	84230 MW	96320 TQ	USBLS	5/15
Except Computer	Ogden-Clearfield MSA, UT	Y	74860 FQ	89030 MW	97380 TQ	USBLS	5/15
Except Computer	Provo-Orem MSA, UT	Y	70260 FQ	81010 MW	95180 TQ	USBLS	5/15
Except Computer	Salt Lake City MSA, UT	Y	61570 FQ	77280 MW	93820 TQ	USBLS	5/15

AE	Average entry wage	AWR	Average wage range	H	Hourly	LR	Low end range	MTC	Median total compensation	TCC	Total cash compensation
AEX	Average experienced wage	B	Biweekly	HI	Highest wage paid	M	Monthly	MW	Median wage paid	TQ	Third quartile wage
ATC	Average total compensation	D	Daily	HR	High end range	MCC	Median cash compensation	MWR	Median wage range	W	Weekly
AW	Average wage paid	FQ	First quartile wage	LO	Lowest wage paid	ME	Median entry wage	S	See annotated source	Y	Yearly

Occupation/Type/Industry	Location	Per	Low	Mid	High	Source	Date
Electronics Engineer							
Except Computer	Vermont	Y	73780 FQ	91000 MW	113900 TQ	USBLS	5/15
Except Computer	Burlington-South Burlington MSA, VT	Y	76790 FQ	94650 MW	117590 TQ	USBLS	5/15
Except Computer	Virginia	Y	83350 FQ	108360 MW	130490 TQ	USBLS	5/15
Except Computer	Richmond MSA, VA	Y	65640 FQ	76280 MW	97230 TQ	USBLS	5/15
Except Computer	Virginia Beach-Norfolk-Newport News MSA, VA-NC	Y	71980 FQ	89850 MW	108500 TQ	USBLS	5/15
Except Computer	Washington	H	42.71 FQ	53.31 MW	62.53 TQ	WABLS	3/16
Except Computer	Seattle-Bellevue-Everett PMSA, WA	H	45.18 FQ	55.30 MW	64.29 TQ	WABLS	3/16
Except Computer	Tacoma-Lakewood PMSA, WA	H	35.04 FQ	42.97 MW	47.98 TQ	WABLS	3/16
Except Computer	West Virginia	Y	81490 FQ	90510 MW	99490 TQ	USBLS	5/15
Except Computer	Huntington-Ashland MSA, WV-KY-OH	Y	70680 FQ	82620 MW	93580 TQ	USBLS	5/15
Except Computer	Wisconsin	Y	64920 FQ	77940 MW	97550 TQ	USBLS	5/15
Except Computer	Madison MSA, WI	Y	62550 FQ	75100 MW	91360 TQ	USBLS	5/15
Except Computer	Milwaukee-Waukesha-West Allis MSA, WI	Y	65260 FQ	81530 MW	111730 TQ	USBLS	5/15
Except Computer	Wyoming	Y	66350 FQ	76970 MW	97050 TQ	USBLS	5/15
Except Computer	Cheyenne MSA, WY	Y	67500 FQ	87190 MW	107520 TQ	USBLS	5/15
Except Computer	Puerto Rico	Y	54990 FQ	73600 MW	92820 TQ	USBLS	5/15
Except Computer	San Juan-Carolina-Caguas MSA, PR	Y	57030 FQ	75360 MW	93540 TQ	USBLS	5/15
Elementary School Teacher							
Except Special Education	Alabama	Y	41527 AE	50660 AW	55237 AEX	ALBLS	6/16
Except Special Education	Birmingham-Hoover MSA, AL	Y	42598 AE	52424 AW	57347 AEX	ALBLS	6/16
Except Special Education	Alaska	Y	60690 FQ	71490 MW	83880 TQ	USBLS	5/15
Except Special Education	Anchorage MSA, AK	Y	62830 FQ	73530 MW	86630 TQ	USBLS	5/15
Except Special Education	Arizona	Y	34610 FQ	39300 MW	47640 TQ	USBLS	5/15
Except Special Education	Phoenix-Mesa-Scottsdale MSA, AZ	Y	34970 FQ	39990 MW	48370 TQ	USBLS	5/15
Except Special Education	Tucson MSA, AZ	Y	33400 FQ	37160 MW	43240 TQ	USBLS	5/15
Except Special Education	Arkansas	Y	38550 FQ	44570 MW	50590 TQ	USBLS	5/15
Except Special Education	Little Rock-North Little Rock-Conway MSA, AR	Y	38800 FQ	44650 MW	50840 TQ	USBLS	5/15
Except Special Education	California	Y		73409 AW		CABLS	1/16-3/16
Except Special Education	Anaheim-Santa Ana-Irvine PMSA, CA	Y		77355 AW		CABLS	1/16-3/16
Except Special Education	Los Angeles-Long Beach-Glendale PMSA, CA	Y		74494 AW		CABLS	1/16-3/16
Except Special Education	Oakland-Hayward-Berkeley PMSA, CA	Y		75519 AW		CABLS	1/16-3/16
Except Special Education	Riverside-San Bernardino-Ontario MSA, CA	Y		77051 AW		CABLS	1/16-3/16
Except Special Education	Sacramento–Roseville–Arden-Arcade MSA, CA	Y		70071 AW		CABLS	1/16-3/16
Except Special Education	San Diego-Carlsbad MSA, CA	Y		70416 AW		CABLS	1/16-3/16
Except Special Education	San Francisco-Redwood City-South San Francisco PMSA, CA	Y		70487 AW		CABLS	1/16-3/16
Except Special Education	Colorado	Y	39140 FQ	48130 MW	60590 TQ	USBLS	5/15
Except Special Education	Denver-Aurora-Lakewood MSA, CO	Y	40980 FQ	50880 MW	65150 TQ	USBLS	5/15
Except Special Education	Connecticut	Y		77030 MW		CTBLS	1/16-3/16
Except Special Education	Bridgeport-Stamford-Norwalk MSA, CT	Y	61490 FQ	79120 MW	95350 TQ	USBLS	5/15
Except Special Education	Hartford-West Hartford-East Hartford MSA, CT	Y	58390 FQ	76150 MW	91110 TQ	USBLS	5/15
Except Special Education	Delaware	Y	47280 FQ	58860 MW	73320 TQ	USBLS	5/15
Except Special Education	Wilmington PMSA, DE-MD-NJ	Y	48880 FQ	60830 MW	74290 TQ	USBLS	5/15
Except Special Education	District of Columbia	Y	54450 FQ	67090 MW	86050 TQ	USBLS	5/15
Except Special Education	Washington-Arlington-Alexandria PMSA, DC-VA-MD-WV	Y	53330 FQ	68120 MW	84780 TQ	USBLS	5/15
Except Special Education	Florida	Y	37856 AE	47175 MW	54243 AEX	FLBLS	7/16-9/16
Except Special Education	Fort Lauderdale-Pompano Beach-Deerfield Beach PMSA, FL	Y	37171 AE	49297 MW	57742 AEX	FLBLS	7/16-9/16

AE	Average entry wage	AWR	Average wage range	H
AEX	Average experienced wage	B	Biweekly	HI
ATC	Average total compensation	D	Daily	HR
AW	Average wage paid	FQ	First quartile wage	LO

AE Average entry wage AWR Average wage range H Hourly LR Low end range MTC Median total compensation TCC Total cash compensation
AEX Average experienced wage B Biweekly HI Highest wage paid M Monthly MW Median wage paid TQ Third quartile wage
ATC Average total compensation D Daily HR High end range MCC Median cash compensation MWR Median wage range W Weekly
AW Average wage paid FQ First quartile wage LO Lowest wage paid ME Median entry wage S See annotated source Y Yearly

Elementary School Teacher

Occupation/Type/Industry	Location	Per	Low	Mid	High	Source	Date
Elementary School Teacher							
Except Special Education	Miami-Miami Beach-Kendall PMSA, FL	Y	40903 AE	49067 MW	57828 AEX	FLBLS	7/16-9/16
Except Special Education	Orlando-Kissimmee-Sanford MSA, FL	Y	40423 AE	47304 MW	53008 AEX	FLBLS	7/16-9/16
Except Special Education	Tampa-St. Petersburg-Clearwater MSA, FL	Y	34397 AE	44634 MW	50896 AEX	FLBLS	7/16-9/16
Except Special Education	Georgia	Y	44310 FQ	53790 MW	62370 TQ	USBLS	5/15
Except Special Education	Atlanta-Sandy Springs-Roswell MSA, GA	Y	45050 FQ	53870 MW	62490 TQ	USBLS	5/15
Except Special Education	Augusta-Richmond County MSA, GA-SC	Y	44440 FQ	54560 MW	63930 TQ	USBLS	5/15
Except Special Education	Hawaii	Y	46890 FQ	56020 MW	65640 TQ	USBLS	5/15
Except Special Education	Urban Honolulu MSA, HI	Y	46780 FQ	55940 MW	65700 TQ	USBLS	5/15
Except Special Education	Idaho	Y	37000 FQ	44940 MW	55940 TQ	USBLS	5/15
Except Special Education	Boise City MSA, ID	Y	38180 FQ	45860 MW	57920 TQ	USBLS	5/15
Except Special Education	Idaho Falls MSA, ID	Y	34820 FQ	39810 MW	46450 TQ	USBLS	5/15
Except Special Education	Illinois	Y	43170 FQ	55320 MW	72690 TQ	USBLS	5/15
Except Special Education	Chicago-Naperville-Arlington Heights PMSA, IL	Y	47010 FQ	59210 MW	77590 TQ	USBLS	5/15
Except Special Education	Lake County-Kenosha County PMSA, IL-WI	Y	44740 FQ	59020 MW	76750 TQ	USBLS	5/15
Except Special Education	Indiana	Y	39170 FQ	48710 MW	60040 TQ	USBLS	5/15
Except Special Education	Gary PMSA, IN	Y	40650 FQ	50380 MW	61490 TQ	USBLS	5/15
Except Special Education	Indianapolis-Carmel-Anderson MSA, IN	Y	39480 FQ	48640 MW	60210 TQ	USBLS	5/15
Except Special Education	Iowa	Y	41760 FQ	51150 MW	60470 TQ	USBLS	5/15
Except Special Education	Des Moines-West Des Moines MSA, IA	Y	44240 FQ	54010 MW	63830 TQ	USBLS	5/15
Except Special Education	Kansas	Y	39210 FQ	45110 MW	51500 TQ	USBLS	5/15
Except Special Education	Wichita MSA, KS	Y	38150 FQ	44370 MW	50380 TQ	USBLS	5/15
Except Special Education	Kentucky	Y	43970 FQ	51850 MW	59440 TQ	USBLS	5/15
Except Special Education	Louisville-Jefferson County MSA, KY-IN	Y	46470 FQ	56850 MW	68740 TQ	USBLS	5/15
Except Special Education	Louisiana	Y	42890 FQ	47460 MW	54050 TQ	USBLS	5/15
Except Special Education	Baton Rouge MSA, LA	Y	43970 FQ	48950 MW	56510 TQ	USBLS	5/15
Except Special Education	New Orleans-Metairie MSA, LA	Y	42810 FQ	48110 MW	55470 TQ	USBLS	5/15
Except Special Education	Maine	Y	40570 FQ	51170 MW	60550 TQ	USBLS	5/15
Except Special Education	Portland-South Portland MSA, ME	Y	47450 FQ	57600 MW	67800 TQ	USBLS	5/15
Except Special Education	Maryland	Y	44783 AE	63750 MW	73234 AEX	MDBLS	4/16
Except Special Education	Baltimore-Columbia-Towson MSA, MD	Y	49840 FQ	60520 MW	74840 TQ	USBLS	5/15
Except Special Education	Salisbury MSA, MD-DE	Y	46710 FQ	56110 MW	67990 TQ	USBLS	5/15
Except Special Education	Massachusetts	Y	57600 FQ	71240 MW	84720 TQ	USBLS	5/15
Except Special Education	Boston-Cambridge-Newton NECTA, MA	Y	60430 FQ	74490 MW	88840 TQ	USBLS	5/15
Except Special Education	Worcester MSA, MA-CT	Y	56610 FQ	69460 MW	78980 TQ	USBLS	5/15
Except Special Education	Michigan	Y	47210 FQ	63530 MW	76500 TQ	USBLS	5/15
Except Special Education	Detroit-Dearborn-Livonia PMSA, MI	Y	44450 FQ	62830 MW	77070 TQ	USBLS	5/15
Except Special Education	Grand Rapids-Wyoming MSA, MI	Y	49520 FQ	65690 MW	75570 TQ	USBLS	5/15
Except Special Education	Minnesota	Y	44536 FQ	58023 MW	73094 TQ	MNBLS	1/16-3/16
Except Special Education	Minneapolis-St. Paul-Bloomington MSA, MN-WI	Y	47026 FQ	63003 MW	76945 TQ	MNBLS	1/16-3/16
Except Special Education	Mississippi	Y	35520 FQ	40810 MW	47580 TQ	USBLS	5/15
Except Special Education	Jackson MSA, MS	Y	34950 FQ	39300 MW	46360 TQ	USBLS	5/15
Except Special Education	Missouri	Y	39270 FQ	48030 MW	62700 TQ	USBLS	5/15
Except Special Education	Kansas City MSA, MO-KS	Y	40630 FQ	46950 MW	56970 TQ	USBLS	5/15
Except Special Education	St. Louis MSA, MO-IL	Y	43190 FQ	53880 MW	69840 TQ	USBLS	5/15
Except Special Education	Montana	Y	36310 FQ	48550 MW	61110 TQ	USBLS	5/15
Except Special Education	Billings MSA, MT	Y	32110 FQ	43430 MW	54980 TQ	USBLS	5/15
Except Special Education	Nebraska	Y	42615 FQ	50600 MW	58855 TQ	NEBLS	7/16-9/16
Except Special Education	Omaha-Council Bluffs MSA, NE-IA	Y	41275 FQ	47990 MW	55980 TQ	NEBLS	7/16-9/16
Except Special Education	Nevada	Y	44410 FQ	53010 MW	63450 TQ	USBLS	5/15
Except Special Education	Las Vegas-Henderson-Paradise MSA, NV	Y	43940 FQ	51800 MW	63030 TQ	USBLS	5/15
Except Special Education	New Hampshire	Y	42077 AE	56762 MW	64044 AEX	NHBLS	6/16
Except Special Education	Manchester NECTA, NH	Y	43488 AE	58204 MW	64436 AEX	NHBLS	6/16

Occupation/Type/Industry	Location	Per	Low	Mid	High	Source	Date
Elementary School Teacher							
Except Special Education	Nashua NECTA, NH-MA	Y	45450 FQ	54740 MW	65060 TQ	USBLS	5/15
Except Special Education	New Jersey	Y	55200 FQ	63960 MW	81420 TQ	USBLS	5/15
Except Special Education	Camden PMSA, NJ	Y	55400 FQ	62450 MW	77900 TQ	USBLS	5/15
Except Special Education	Newark PMSA, NJ-PA	Y	56440 FQ	65920 MW	81330 TQ	USBLS	5/15
Except Special Education	Trenton MSA, NJ	Y	53520 FQ	63510 MW	83130 TQ	USBLS	5/15
Except Special Education	New Mexico	Y	44410 FQ	56750 MW	72480 TQ	USBLS	5/15
Except Special Education	Albuquerque MSA, NM	Y	41990 FQ	51160 MW	66510 TQ	USBLS	5/15
Except Special Education	New York	Y	47220 AE	69530 MW	87370 AEX	NYBLS	1/16-3/16
Except Special Education	Buffalo-Cheektowaga-Niagara Falls MSA, NY	Y	48020 FQ	60050 MW	76390 TQ	USBLS	5/15
Except Special Education	Nassau County-Suffolk County PMSA, NY	Y	83260 FQ	105500 MW	120050 TQ	USBLS	5/15
Except Special Education	New York-Jersey City-White Plains PMSA, NY-NJ	Y	54550 FQ	67230 MW	88670 TQ	USBLS	5/15
Except Special Education	Rochester MSA, NY	Y	49040 FQ	57420 MW	69170 TQ	USBLS	5/15
Except Special Education	North Carolina	Y	36210 FQ	42170 MW	48880 TQ	USBLS	5/15
Except Special Education	Charlotte-Concord-Gastonia MSA, NC-SC	Y	36880 FQ	43190 MW	49980 TQ	USBLS	5/15
Except Special Education	Raleigh MSA, NC	Y	38060 FQ	45230 MW	54430 TQ	USBLS	5/15
Except Special Education	North Dakota	Y	39320 FQ	46180 MW	54860 TQ	USBLS	5/15
Except Special Education	Fargo MSA, ND-MN	Y	38560 FQ	46490 MW	57380 TQ	USBLS	5/15
Except Special Education	Ohio	Y	45590 FQ	59620 MW	71900 TQ	USBLS	5/15
Except Special Education	Cincinnati MSA, OH-KY-IN	Y	45040 FQ	57650 MW	70220 TQ	USBLS	5/15
Except Special Education	Cleveland-Elyria MSA, OH	Y	43970 FQ	65110 MW	74490 TQ	USBLS	5/15
Except Special Education	Columbus MSA, OH	Y	44600 FQ	61730 MW	75240 TQ	USBLS	5/15
Except Special Education	Oklahoma	Y	34810 FQ	39270 MW	47070 TQ	USBLS	5/15
Except Special Education	Oklahoma City MSA, OK	Y	34430 FQ	38160 MW	44740 TQ	USBLS	5/15
Except Special Education	Tulsa MSA, OK	Y	36100 FQ	43660 MW	56120 TQ	USBLS	5/15
Except Special Education	Oregon	Y	46957 FQ	58656 MW	71450 TQ	ORBLS	2016
Except Special Education	Portland-Vancouver-Hillsboro MSA, OR-WA	Y	47890 FQ	60860 MW	73000 TQ	USBLS	5/15
Except Special Education	Pennsylvania	Y	47300 FQ	59780 MW	75030 TQ	USBLS	5/15
Except Special Education	Allentown-Bethlehem-Easton MSA, PA-NJ	Y	49200 FQ	59910 MW	76200 TQ	USBLS	5/15
Except Special Education	Harrisburg-Carlisle MSA, PA	Y	48780 FQ	58070 MW	68960 TQ	USBLS	5/15
Except Special Education	Montgomery County-Bucks County-Chester County PMSA, PA	Y	51040 FQ	71280 MW	94350 TQ	USBLS	5/15
Except Special Education	Philadelphia PMSA, PA	Y	47630 FQ	62430 MW	80200 TQ	USBLS	5/15
Except Special Education	Pittsburgh MSA, PA	Y	46100 FQ	56840 MW	71180 TQ	USBLS	5/15
Except Special Education	Rhode Island	Y	58910 FQ	71220 MW	80650 TQ	USBLS	5/15
Except Special Education	Providence-Warwick MSA, RI-MA	Y	59320 FQ	71600 MW	81670 TQ	USBLS	5/15
Except Special Education	South Carolina	Y	40180 FQ	48660 MW	58380 TQ	USBLS	5/15
Except Special Education	Charleston-North Charleston MSA, SC	Y	38630 FQ	47990 MW	58350 TQ	USBLS	5/15
Except Special Education	Columbia MSA, SC	Y	39970 FQ	47960 MW	57280 TQ	USBLS	5/15
Except Special Education	Greenville-Anderson-Mauldin MSA, SC	Y	40980 FQ	48600 MW	57840 TQ	USBLS	5/15
Except Special Education	South Dakota	Y	34820 FQ	40690 MW	48870 TQ	USBLS	5/15
Except Special Education	Sioux Falls MSA, SD	Y	35580 FQ	42960 MW	52620 TQ	USBLS	5/15
Except Special Education	Tennessee	Y	41180 FQ	47980 MW	57690 TQ	USBLS	5/15
Except Special Education	Knoxville MSA, TN	Y	40730 FQ	47000 MW	55410 TQ	USBLS	5/15
Except Special Education	Memphis MSA, TN-MS-AR	Y	42200 FQ	51170 MW	61030 TQ	USBLS	5/15
Except Special Education	Nashville-Davidson–Murfreesboro–Franklin MSA, TN	Y	41920 FQ	50060 MW	60740 TQ	USBLS	5/15
Except Special Education	Texas	Y	45130 FQ	52410 MW	59720 TQ	USBLS	5/15
Except Special Education	Austin-Round Rock MSA, TX	Y	44600 FQ	50940 MW	60010 TQ	USBLS	5/15
Except Special Education	Dallas-Plano-Irving PMSA, TX	Y	46890 FQ	53980 MW	60510 TQ	USBLS	5/15
Except Special Education	Fort Worth-Arlington PMSA, TX	Y	48670 FQ	54740 MW	60240 TQ	USBLS	5/15
Except Special Education	Houston-The Woodlands-Sugar Land MSA, TX	Y	49800 FQ	56550 MW	63210 TQ	USBLS	5/15
Except Special Education	San Antonio-New Braunfels MSA, TX	Y	49790 FQ	54450 MW	59090 TQ	USBLS	5/15
Except Special Education	Utah	Y	40110 FQ	51890 MW	63750 TQ	USBLS	5/15
Except Special Education	Ogden-Clearfield MSA, UT	Y	40160 FQ	51490 MW	60590 TQ	USBLS	5/15
Except Special Education	Provo-Orem MSA, UT	Y	41250 FQ	53230 MW	67480 TQ	USBLS	5/15
Except Special Education	Salt Lake City MSA, UT	Y	41890 FQ	55920 MW	72630 TQ	USBLS	5/15
Except Special Education	Vermont	Y	43090 FQ	53360 MW	63930 TQ	USBLS	5/15

AE	Average entry wage	AWR	Average wage range	H	Hourly	LR	Low end range	MTC	Median total compensation	TCC Total cash compensation
AEX	Average experienced wage	B	Biweekly	HI	Highest wage paid	M	Monthly	MW	Median wage paid	TQ Third quartile wage
ATC	Average total compensation	D	Daily	HR	High end range	MCC	Median cash compensation	MWR	Median wage range	W Weekly
AW	Average wage paid	FQ	First quartile wage	LO	Lowest wage paid	ME	Median entry wage	S	See annotated source	Y Yearly

Occupation/Type/Industry	Location	Per	Low	Mid	High	Source	Date
Elementary School Teacher							
Except Special Education	Burlington-South Burlington MSA, VT	Y	50180 FQ	64710 MW	77640 TQ	USBLS	5/15
Except Special Education	Virginia	Y	46800 FQ	59190 MW	75720 TQ	USBLS	5/15
Except Special Education	Richmond MSA, VA	Y	47690 FQ	56240 MW	63520 TQ	USBLS	5/15
Except Special Education	Virginia Beach-Norfolk-Newport News MSA, VA-NC	Y	47510 FQ	58220 MW	72460 TQ	USBLS	5/15
Except Special Education	Washington	Y		61012 AW		WABLS	3/16
Except Special Education	Seattle-Bellevue-Everett PMSA, WA	Y		62016 AW		WABLS	3/16
Except Special Education	Tacoma-Lakewood PMSA, WA	Y		62452 AW		WABLS	3/16
Except Special Education	West Virginia	Y	38970 FQ	45740 MW	53720 TQ	USBLS	5/15
Except Special Education	Huntington-Ashland MSA, WV-KY-OH	Y	39240 FQ	47950 MW	56430 TQ	USBLS	5/15
Except Special Education	Wisconsin	Y	43330 FQ	54120 MW	64840 TQ	USBLS	5/15
Except Special Education	Madison MSA, WI	Y	41630 FQ	52690 MW	61190 TQ	USBLS	5/15
Except Special Education	Milwaukee-Waukesha-West Allis MSA, WI	Y	46140 FQ	58400 MW	71610 TQ	USBLS	5/15
Except Special Education	Wyoming	Y	49870 FQ	57550 MW.	67110 TQ	USBLS	5/15
Except Special Education	Puerto Rico	Y	28870 FQ	36290 MW	43430 TQ	USBLS	5/15
Except Special Education	San Juan-Carolina-Caguas MSA, PR	Y	28040 FQ	35740 MW	43190 TQ	USBLS	5/15
Except Special Education	Virgin Islands	Y	31490 FQ	40560 MW	49000 TQ	USBLS	5/15
Except Special Education	Guam	Y	33970 FQ	44560 MW	55010 TQ	USBLS	5/15
Elevator Installer and Repairer	Alabama	Y	51476 AE	74693 AW	86297 AEX	ALBLS	6/16
	Arizona	Y	56600 FQ	68960 MW	89530 TQ	USBLS	5/15
	Phoenix-Mesa-Scottsdale MSA, AZ	Y	56660 FQ	69100 MW	89600 TQ	USBLS	5/15
	Arkansas	Y	43330 FQ	70500 MW	85910 TQ	USBLS	5/15
	Little Rock-North Little Rock-Conway MSA, AR	Y	70130 FQ	77540 MW	90670 TQ	USBLS	5/15
	California	H	37.94 FQ	46.68 MW	56.52 TQ	CABLS	1/16-3/16
	Anaheim-Santa Ana-Irvine PMSA, CA	H	43.76 FQ	48.87 MW	56.03 TQ	CABLS	1/16-3/16
	Los Angeles-Long Beach-Glendale PMSA, CA	H	19.01 FQ	42.66 MW	49.82 TQ	CABLS	1/16-3/16
	Sacramento–Roseville–Arden-Arcade MSA, CA	H	48.63 FQ	58.03 MW	65.30 TQ	CABLS	1/16-3/16
	San Diego-Carlsbad MSA, CA	H	24.40 FQ	31.35 MW	43.91 TQ	CABLS	1/16-3/16
	Colorado	Y	53300 FQ	83870 MW	93170 TQ	USBLS	5/15
	Denver-Aurora-Lakewood MSA, CO	Y	65540 FQ	85590 MW	94030 TQ	USBLS	5/15
	Connecticut	Y		99617 MW		CTBLS	1/16-3/16
	Hartford-West Hartford-East Hartford MSA, CT	Y	76170 FQ	103360 MW	115250 TQ	USBLS	5/15
	Delaware	Y	56920 FQ	68060 MW	86320 TQ	USBLS	5/15
	Wilmington PMSA, DE-MD-NJ	Y	56920 FQ	68060 MW	86320 TQ	USBLS	5/15
	Washington-Arlington-Alexandria PMSA, DC-VA-MD-WV	Y	70430 FQ	82840 MW	92800 TQ	USBLS	5/15
	Florida	H	16.19 AE	31.16 MW	37.23 AEX	FLBLS	7/16-9/16
	Fort Lauderdale-Pompano Beach-Deerfield Beach PMSA, FL	H	23.67 AE	40.17 MW	42.64 AEX	FLBLS	7/16-9/16
	Miami-Miami Beach-Kendall PMSA, FL	H	14.17 AE	19.09 MW	30.36 AEX	FLBLS	7/16-9/16
	Orlando-Kissimmee-Sanford MSA, FL	H	15.15 AE	33.29 MW	38.06 AEX	FLBLS	7/16-9/16
	Tampa-St. Petersburg-Clearwater MSA, FL	H	15.30 AE	26.16 MW	34.36 AEX	FLBLS	7/16-9/16
	Georgia	Y	45270 FQ	61540 MW	77540 TQ	USBLS	5/15
	Atlanta-Sandy Springs-Roswell MSA, GA	Y	50010 FQ	63730 MW	79710 TQ	USBLS	5/15
	Hawaii	Y	68270 FQ	85070 MW	103870 TQ	USBLS	5/15
	Urban Honolulu MSA, HI	Y	68270 FQ	85070 MW	103870 TQ	USBLS	5/15
	Illinois	Y	64220 FQ	82770 MW	99800 TQ	USBLS	5/15
	Chicago-Naperville-Arlington Heights PMSA, IL	Y	63130 FQ	81970 MW	105110 TQ	USBLS	5/15
	Lake County-Kenosha County PMSA, IL-WI	Y	52420 FQ	74360 MW	92360 TQ	USBLS	5/15

Occupation/Type/Industry	Location	Per	Low	Mid	High	Source	Date
Elevator Installer and Repairer	Indiana	Y	72370 FQ	82600 MW	91430 TQ	USBLS	5/15
	Indianapolis-Carmel-Anderson MSA, IN	Y	76130 FQ	82880 MW	90540 TQ	USBLS	5/15
	Iowa	Y	82490 FQ	88660 MW	94830 TQ	USBLS	5/15
	Kansas	Y	61380 FQ	87250 MW	99080 TQ	USBLS	5/15
	Kentucky	Y	56590 FQ	66950 MW	80690 TQ	USBLS	5/15
	Louisville-Jefferson County MSA, KY-IN	Y	54780 FQ	63190 MW	74910 TQ	USBLS	5/15
	Louisiana	Y	30170 FQ	35720 MW	51660 TQ	USBLS	5/15
	New Orleans-Metairie MSA, LA	Y	28640 FQ	33310 MW	39090 TQ	USBLS	5/15
	Maryland	Y	61362 AE	78746 MW	87438 AEX	MDBLS	4/16
	Baltimore-Columbia-Towson MSA, MD	Y	67630 FQ	79890 MW	91360 TQ	USBLS	5/15
	Massachusetts	Y	64230 FQ	86210 MW	101560 TQ	USBLS	5/15
	Boston-Cambridge-Newton NECTA, MA	Y	49070 FQ	81460 MW	97010 TQ	USBLS	5/15
	Michigan	Y	44380 FQ	80180 MW	99240 TQ	USBLS	5/15
	Detroit-Dearborn-Livonia PMSA, MI	Y	29950 FQ	81640 MW	92160 TQ	USBLS	5/15
	Minnesota	Y	73799 FQ	85121 MW	93132 TQ	MNBLS	1/16-3/16
	Minneapolis-St. Paul-Bloomington MSA, MN-WI	Y	74677 FQ	85373 MW	93284 TQ	MNBLS	1/16-3/16
	Missouri	Y	74190 FQ	86500 MW	94770 TQ	USBLS	5/15
	Kansas City MSA, MO-KS	Y	72610 FQ	88110 MW	99370 TQ	USBLS	5/15
	St. Louis MSA, MO-IL	Y	79800 FQ	88060 MW	95960 TQ	USBLS	5/15
	New Jersey	Y	65860 FQ	87910 MW	111840 TQ	USBLS	5/15
	New York	Y	59300 AE	87400 MW	98230 AEX	NYBLS	1/16-3/16
	Buffalo-Cheektowaga-Niagara Falls MSA, NY	Y	61540 FQ	83730 MW	93500 TQ	USBLS	5/15
	Nassau County-Suffolk County PMSA, NY	Y	71960 FQ	87080 MW	95830 TQ	USBLS	5/15
	New York-Jersey City-White Plains PMSA, NY-NJ	Y	68410 FQ	86090 MW	100040 TQ	USBLS	5/15
	North Carolina	Y	44650 FQ	72400 MW	88510 TQ	USBLS	5/15
	Ohio	Y	67670 FQ	82730 MW	93410 TQ	USBLS	5/15
	Cincinnati MSA, OH-KY-IN	Y	81710 FQ	89740 MW	97520 TQ	USBLS	5/15
	Oregon	H	44.60 FQ	51.67 MW	58.17 TQ	ORBLS	2016
	Portland-Vancouver-Hillsboro MSA, OR-WA	Y	94520 FQ	107810 MW	120070 TQ	USBLS	5/15
	Pennsylvania	Y	44770 FQ	58590 MW	80380 TQ	USBLS	5/15
	Allentown-Bethlehem-Easton MSA, PA-NJ	Y	53970 FQ	87460 MW	108310 TQ	USBLS	5/15
	Montgomery County-Bucks County-Chester County PMSA, PA	Y	42020 FQ	51940 MW	63240 TQ	USBLS	5/15
	Pittsburgh MSA, PA	Y	42410 FQ	50460 MW	73150 TQ	USBLS	5/15
	South Carolina	Y	43120 FQ	66490 MW	80920 TQ	USBLS	5/15
	South Dakota	Y	82240 FQ	88610 MW	94980 TQ	USBLS	5/15
	Tennessee	Y	41310 FQ	54310 MW	71400 TQ	USBLS	5/15
	Texas	Y	57370 FQ	74330 MW	87760 TQ	USBLS	5/15
	Austin-Round Rock MSA, TX	Y	53140 FQ	72030 MW	84400 TQ	USBLS	5/15
	Dallas-Plano-Irving PMSA, TX	Y	59520 FQ	77950 MW	88970 TQ	USBLS	5/15
	Fort Worth-Arlington PMSA, TX	Y	60910 FQ	71850 MW	82270 TQ	USBLS	5/15
	Houston-The Woodlands-Sugar Land MSA, TX	Y	59530 FQ	74690 MW	88880 TQ	USBLS	5/15
	San Antonio-New Braunfels MSA, TX	Y	59630 FQ	72310 MW	86680 TQ	USBLS	5/15
	Utah	Y	43190 FQ	79410 MW	90400 TQ	USBLS	5/15
	Salt Lake City MSA, UT	Y	39190 FQ	78790 MW	89220 TQ	USBLS	5/15
	Virginia	Y	54290 FQ	71940 MW	91170 TQ	USBLS	5/15
	Washington	H	34.56 FQ	52.71 MW	58.12 TQ	WABLS	3/16
	Seattle-Bellevue-Everett PMSA, WA	H	36.38 FQ	53.24 MW	58.40 TQ	WABLS	3/16
	West Virginia	Y	43700 FQ	53400 MW	60400 TQ	USBLS	5/15
	Wisconsin	Y	65530 FQ	81790 MW	93970 TQ	USBLS	5/15
	Milwaukee-Waukesha-West Allis MSA, WI	Y	73660 FQ	86330 MW	97310 TQ	USBLS	5/15
	Puerto Rico	Y	22440 FQ	28610 MW	36540 TQ	USBLS	5/15
	San Juan-Carolina-Caguas MSA, PR	Y	22050 FQ	28250 MW	35250 TQ	USBLS	5/15

AE	Average entry wage	AWR	Average wage range	H	Hourly
AEX	Average experienced wage	B	Biweekly	HI	Highest wage paid
ATC	Average total compensation	D	Daily	HR	High end range
AW	Average wage paid	FQ	First quartile wage	LO	Lowest wage paid

LR	Low end range	MTC	Median total compensation
M	Monthly	MW	Median wage paid
MCC	Median cash compensation	MWR	Median wage range
ME	Median entry wage	S	See annotated source

TCC	Total cash compensation
TQ	Third quartile wage
W	Weekly
Y	Yearly

Eligibility Interviewer

Occupation/Type/Industry	Location	Per	Low	Mid	High	Source	Date
Government Programs	Alabama	Y	33783 AE	42151 AW	46325 AEX	ALBLS	6/16
Government Programs	Birmingham-Hoover MSA, AL	Y	35288 AE	45130 AW	50056 AEX	ALBLS	6/16
Government Programs	Alaska	Y	44140 FQ	49230 MW	56710 TQ	USBLS	5/15
Government Programs	Anchorage MSA, AK	Y	44310 FQ	49230 MW	56700 TQ	USBLS	5/15
Government Programs	Arizona	Y	29370 FQ	35690 MW	45140 TQ	USBLS	5/15
Government Programs	Phoenix-Mesa-Scottsdale MSA, AZ	Y	29370 FQ	35690 MW	44410 TQ	USBLS	5/15
Government Programs	Tucson MSA, AZ	Y	30000 FQ	35690 MW	45920 TQ	USBLS	5/15
Government Programs	Arkansas	Y	29110 FQ	30160 MW	35570 TQ	USBLS	5/15
Government Programs	Little Rock-North Little Rock-Conway MSA, AR	Y	29860 FQ	30990 MW	44500 TQ	USBLS	5/15
Government Programs	California	H	20.41 FQ	23.55 MW	26.78 TQ	CABLS	1/16-3/16
Government Programs	Anaheim-Santa Ana-Irvine PMSA, CA	H	25.47 FQ	27.14 MW	28.85 TQ	CABLS	1/16-3/16
Government Programs	Los Angeles-Long Beach-Glendale PMSA, CA	H	20.77 FQ	22.62 MW	24.39 TQ	CABLS	1/16-3/16
Government Programs	Oakland-Hayward-Berkeley PMSA, CA	H	25.90 FQ	27.67 MW	30.18 TQ	CABLS	1/16-3/16
Government Programs	Riverside-San Bernardino-Ontario MSA, CA	H	17.50 FQ	20.41 MW	23.59 TQ	CABLS	1/16-3/16
Government Programs	Sacramento–Roseville–Arden-Arcade MSA, CA	H	21.75 FQ	25.01 MW	26.97 TQ	CABLS	1/16-3/16
Government Programs	San Diego-Carlsbad MSA, CA	H	23.59 FQ	26.32 MW	27.36 TQ	CABLS	1/16-3/16
Government Programs	San Francisco-Redwood City-South San Francisco PMSA, CA	H	24.19 FQ	26.78 MW	28.45 TQ	CABLS	1/16-3/16
Government Programs	Colorado	Y	36300 FQ	42410 MW	50170 TQ	USBLS	5/15
Government Programs	Denver-Aurora-Lakewood MSA, CO	Y	39300 FQ	47030 MW	53080 TQ	USBLS	5/15
Government Programs	Connecticut	Y		57717 MW		CTBLS	1/16-3/16
Government Programs	Bridgeport-Stamford-Norwalk MSA, CT	Y	48020 FQ	55280 MW	61660 TQ	USBLS	5/15
Government Programs	Hartford-West Hartford-East Hartford MSA, CT	Y	51060 FQ	57090 MW	63050 TQ	USBLS	5/15
Government Programs	Delaware	Y	27750 FQ	33830 MW	43260 TQ	USBLS	5/15
Government Programs	Wilmington PMSA, DE-MD-NJ	Y	27020 FQ	32590 MW	43830 TQ	USBLS	5/15
Government Programs	District of Columbia	Y	50230 FQ	56570 MW	62550 TQ	USBLS	5/15
Government Programs	Washington-Arlington-Alexandria PMSA, DC-VA-MD-WV	Y	45490 FQ	53460 MW	61240 TQ	USBLS	5/15
Government Programs	Florida	H	12.18 AE	18.14 MW	21.66 AEX	FLBLS	7/16-9/16
Government Programs	Fort Lauderdale-Pompano Beach-Deerfield Beach PMSA, FL	H	14.27 AE	19.64 MW	23.40 AEX	FLBLS	7/16-9/16
Government Programs	Miami-Miami Beach-Kendall PMSA, FL	H	12.21 AE	15.94 MW	19.40 AEX	FLBLS	7/16-9/16
Government Programs	Orlando-Kissimmee-Sanford MSA, FL	H	12.33 AE	18.20 MW	21.24 AEX	FLBLS	7/16-9/16
Government Programs	Tampa-St. Petersburg-Clearwater MSA, FL	H	12.05 AE	16.83 MW	19.60 AEX	FLBLS	7/16-9/16
Government Programs	Georgia	Y	37210 FQ	47300 MW	53230 TQ	USBLS	5/15
Government Programs	Atlanta-Sandy Springs-Roswell MSA, GA	Y	41340 FQ	47320 MW	54940 TQ	USBLS	5/15
Government Programs	Augusta-Richmond County MSA, GA-SC	Y	33000 FQ	40370 MW	43530 TQ	USBLS	5/15
Government Programs	Hawaii	Y	36890 FQ	44060 MW	50700 TQ	USBLS	5/15
Government Programs	Urban Honolulu MSA, HI	Y	37700 FQ	45010 MW	52500 TQ	USBLS	5/15
Government Programs	Idaho	Y	31590 FQ	36630 MW	40880 TQ	USBLS	5/15
Government Programs	Illinois	Y	39250 FQ	48020 MW	57610 TQ	USBLS	5/15
Government Programs	Chicago-Naperville-Arlington Heights PMSA, IL	Y	41350 FQ	48010 MW	56020 TQ	USBLS	5/15
Government Programs	Lake County-Kenosha County PMSA, IL-WI	Y	37890 FQ	49630 MW	59230 TQ	USBLS	5/15
Government Programs	Indiana	Y	30500 FQ	33030 MW	39700 TQ	USBLS	5/15
Government Programs	Gary PMSA, IN	Y	30510 FQ	33840 MW	40520 TQ	USBLS	5/15
Government Programs	Indianapolis-Carmel-Anderson MSA, IN	Y	30500 FQ	34070 MW	46050 TQ	USBLS	5/15
Government Programs	Iowa	Y	29330 FQ	48510 MW	57810 TQ	USBLS	5/15
Government Programs	Des Moines-West Des Moines MSA, IA	Y	45300 FQ	53710 MW	60680 TQ	USBLS	5/15

Occupation/Type/Industry	Location	Per	Low	Mid	High	Source	Date
Eligibility Interviewer							
Government Programs	Kansas	Y	31930 FQ	36800 MW	44830 TQ	USBLS	5/15
Government Programs	Kentucky	Y	36370 FQ	46170 MW	51580 TQ	USBLS	5/15
Government Programs	Louisville-Jefferson County MSA, KY-IN	Y	31940 FQ	36470 MW	43590 TQ	USBLS	5/15
Government Programs	Louisiana	Y	31940 FQ	39410 MW	48200 TQ	USBLS	5/15
Government Programs	Baton Rouge MSA, LA	Y	33810 FQ	39290 MW	48200 TQ	USBLS	5/15
Government Programs	New Orleans-Metairie MSA, LA	Y	31940 FQ	36710 MW	46760 TQ	USBLS	5/15
Government Programs	Maine	Y	32410 FQ	35500 MW	41510 TQ	USBLS	5/15
Government Programs	Portland-South Portland MSA, ME	Y	32410 FQ	35810 MW	41510 TQ	USBLS	5/15
Government Programs	Maryland	Y	36615 AE	49129 MW	55386 AEX	MDBLS	4/16
Government Programs	Baltimore-Columbia-Towson MSA, MD	Y	43070 FQ	52440 MW	57240 TQ	USBLS	5/15
Government Programs	Massachusetts	Y	44330 FQ	51610 MW	59270 TQ	USBLS	5/15
Government Programs	Boston-Cambridge-Newton NECTA, MA	Y	47510 FQ	52710 MW	60670 TQ	USBLS	5/15
Government Programs	Worcester MSA, MA-CT	Y	39760 FQ	51090 MW	60090 TQ	USBLS	5/15
Government Programs	Michigan	Y	48820 FQ	51440 MW	51450 TQ	USBLS	5/15
Government Programs	Detroit-Dearborn-Livonia PMSA, MI	Y	47900 FQ	51370 MW	51450 TQ	USBLS	5/15
Government Programs	Grand Rapids-Wyoming MSA, MI	Y	48830 FQ	51370 MW	51450 TQ	USBLS	5/15
Government Programs	Minnesota	Y	40481 FQ	46690 MW	54002 TQ	MNBLS	1/16-3/16
Government Programs	Minneapolis-St. Paul-Bloomington MSA, MN-WI	Y	41806 FQ	48157 MW	55580 TQ	MNBLS	1/16-3/16
Government Programs	Mississippi	Y	26650 FQ	29500 MW	34440 TQ	USBLS	5/15
Government Programs	Jackson MSA, MS	Y	26830 FQ	29510 MW	37610 TQ	USBLS	5/15
Government Programs	Missouri	Y	30110 FQ	35600 MW	48200 TQ	USBLS	5/15
Government Programs	Kansas City MSA, MO-KS	Y	35950 FQ	46740 MW	51140 TQ	USBLS	5/15
Government Programs	St. Louis MSA, MO-IL	Y	30110 FQ	35600 MW	49650 TQ	USBLS	5/15
Government Programs	Montana	Y	30620 FQ	32790 MW	37990 TQ	USBLS	5/15
Government Programs	Nebraska	Y	30555 FQ	35645 MW	43525 TQ	NEBLS	7/16-9/16
Government Programs	Omaha-Council Bluffs MSA, NE-IA	Y	35920 FQ	45075 MW	52600 TQ	NEBLS	7/16-9/16
Government Programs	Nevada	Y	34950 FQ	41380 MW	48460 TQ	USBLS	5/15
Government Programs	Las Vegas-Henderson-Paradise MSA, NV	Y	36390 FQ	42870 MW	49150 TQ	USBLS	5/15
Government Programs	New Hampshire	H	15.40 AE	18.92 MW	21.86 AEX	NHBLS	6/16
Government Programs	Manchester NECTA, NH	H	14.62 AE	18.17 MW	22.28 AEX	NHBLS	6/16
Government Programs	Nashua NECTA, NH-MA	Y	36060 FQ	38220 MW	47600 TQ	USBLS	5/15
Government Programs	New Jersey	Y	33220 FQ	46680 MW	54660 TQ	USBLS	5/15
Government Programs	Camden PMSA, NJ	Y	41780 FQ	49860 MW	56530 TQ	USBLS	5/15
Government Programs	Newark PMSA, NJ-PA	Y	34290 FQ	52000 MW	59280 TQ	USBLS	5/15
Government Programs	Trenton MSA, NJ	Y	43580 FQ	52040 MW	59820 TQ	USBLS	5/15
Government Programs	New Mexico	Y	34120 FQ	44350 MW	51130 TQ	USBLS	5/15
Government Programs	Albuquerque MSA, NM	Y	39570 FQ	48200 MW	52590 TQ	USBLS	5/15
Government Programs	New York	Y	36990 AE	47590 MW	53860 AEX	NYBLS	1/16-3/16
Government Programs	Buffalo-Cheektowaga-Niagara Falls MSA, NY	Y	46390 FQ	50980 MW	56880 TQ	USBLS	5/15
Government Programs	Nassau County-Suffolk County PMSA, NY	Y	46690 FQ	52700 MW	59100 TQ	USBLS	5/15
Government Programs	New York-Jersey City-White Plains PMSA, NY-NJ	Y	37050 FQ	45790 MW	56180 TQ	USBLS	5/15
Government Programs	Rochester MSA, NY	Y	35690 FQ	41710 MW	46840 TQ	USBLS	5/15
Government Programs	North Carolina	Y	31500 FQ	35780 MW	41400 TQ	USBLS	5/15
Government Programs	Charlotte-Concord-Gastonia MSA, NC-SC	Y	33610 FQ	37000 MW	42410 TQ	USBLS	5/15
Government Programs	Raleigh MSA, NC	Y	34850 FQ	38790 MW	44600 TQ	USBLS	5/15
Government Programs	North Dakota	Y	37190 FQ	43420 MW	49060 TQ	USBLS	5/15
Government Programs	Fargo MSA, ND-MN	Y	40390 FQ	44970 MW	49740 TQ	USBLS	5/15
Government Programs	Ohio	Y	33710 FQ	40320 MW	48830 TQ	USBLS	5/15
Government Programs	Cincinnati MSA, OH-KY-IN	Y	36980 FQ	48370 MW	54610 TQ	USBLS	5/15
Government Programs	Cleveland-Elyria MSA, OH	Y	34800 FQ	41970 MW	49040 TQ	USBLS	5/15
Government Programs	Columbus MSA, OH	Y	35650 FQ	43830 MW	49550 TQ	USBLS	5/15
Government Programs	Oklahoma	Y	29520 FQ	36220 MW	47680 TQ	USBLS	5/15
Government Programs	Oklahoma City MSA, OK	Y	31980 FQ	36720 MW	47820 TQ	USBLS	5/15
Government Programs	Tulsa MSA, OK	Y	33460 FQ	46290 MW	49650 TQ	USBLS	5/15
Government Programs	Oregon	H	15.65 FQ	18.47 MW	22.73 TQ	ORBLS	2016
Government Programs	Portland-Vancouver-Hillsboro MSA, OR-WA	Y	33530 FQ	40030 MW	50050 TQ	USBLS	5/15

AE	Average entry wage	AWR	Average wage range	H	Hourly
AEX	Average experienced wage	B	Biweekly	HI	Highest wage paid
ATC	Average total compensation	D	Daily	HR	High end range
AW	Average wage paid	FQ	First quartile wage	LO	Lowest wage paid

LR	Low end range	MTC	Median total compensation	TCC	Total cash compensation
M	Monthly	MW	Median wage paid	TQ	Third quartile wage
HI		MWR	Median wage range	W	Weekly
MCC	Median cash compensation	MWR	Median wage range		
ME	Median entry wage	S	See annotated source	Y	Yearly

Occupation/Type/Industry	Location	Per	Low	Mid	High	Source	Date
Eligibility Interviewer							
Government Programs	Pennsylvania	Y	43160 FQ	46110 MW	52310 TQ	USBLS	5/15
Government Programs	Allentown-Bethlehem-Easton MSA, PA-NJ	Y	39710 FQ	45050 MW	51480 TQ	USBLS	5/15
Government Programs	Harrisburg-Carlisle MSA, PA	Y	39710 FQ	43170 MW	47160 TQ	USBLS	5/15
Government Programs	Montgomery County-Bucks County-Chester County PMSA, PA	Y	44100 FQ	46110 MW	51480 TQ	USBLS	5/15
Government Programs	Philadelphia PMSA, PA	Y	43180 FQ	48320 MW	56110 TQ	USBLS	5/15
Government Programs	Pittsburgh MSA, PA	Y	40550 FQ	45040 MW	51100 TQ	USBLS	5/15
Government Programs	Rhode Island	Y	51570 FQ	56330 MW	60830 TQ	USBLS	5/15
Government Programs	Providence-Warwick MSA, RI-MA	Y	51350 FQ	56330 MW	60830 TQ	USBLS	5/15
Government Programs	South Carolina	Y	29500 FQ	35590 MW	43810 TQ	USBLS	5/15
Government Programs	Charleston-North Charleston MSA, SC	Y	27840 FQ	38810 MW	46160 TQ	USBLS	5/15
Government Programs	Columbia MSA, SC	Y	37880 FQ	41540 MW	46930 TQ	USBLS	5/15
Government Programs	Greenville-Anderson-Mauldin MSA, SC	Y	27980 FQ	31220 MW	38240 TQ	USBLS	5/15
Government Programs	South Dakota	Y	29360 FQ	34390 MW	38860 TQ	USBLS	5/15
Government Programs	Sioux Falls MSA, SD	Y	30690 FQ	34040 MW	37900 TQ	USBLS	5/15
Government Programs	Tennessee	Y	31950 FQ	36140 MW	43810 TQ	USBLS	5/15
Government Programs	Knoxville MSA, TN	Y	29370 FQ	34340 MW	38290 TQ	USBLS	5/15
Government Programs	Memphis MSA, TN-MS-AR	Y	32870 FQ	38120 MW	46740 TQ	USBLS	5/15
Government Programs	Nashville-Davidson–Murfreesboro–Franklin MSA, TN	Y	31790 FQ	36700 MW	46750 TQ	USBLS	5/15
Government Programs	Texas	Y	29200 FQ	32240 MW	37910 TQ	USBLS	5/15
Government Programs	Dallas-Plano-Irving PMSA, TX	Y	31210 FQ	36550 MW	50950 TQ	USBLS	5/15
Government Programs	Fort Worth-Arlington PMSA, TX	Y	31160 FQ	32260 MW	35890 TQ	USBLS	5/15
Government Programs	Houston-The Woodlands-Sugar Land MSA, TX	Y	31170 FQ	32690 MW	38730 TQ	USBLS	5/15
Government Programs	San Antonio-New Braunfels MSA, TX	Y	29870 FQ	31260 MW	34890 TQ	USBLS	5/15
Government Programs	Sherman-Denison MSA, TX	Y	30190 FQ	33760 MW	46330 TQ	USBLS	5/15
Government Programs	Utah	Y	35610 FQ	38860 MW	47020 TQ	USBLS	5/15
Government Programs	Ogden-Clearfield MSA, UT	Y	37700 FQ	45300 MW	52590 TQ	USBLS	5/15
Government Programs	Provo-Orem MSA, UT	Y	33600 FQ	36730 MW	40360 TQ	USBLS	5/15
Government Programs	Salt Lake City MSA, UT	Y	35520 FQ	37580 MW	41480 TQ	USBLS	5/15
Government Programs	Vermont	Y	39430 FQ	45470 MW	50880 TQ	USBLS	5/15
Government Programs	Burlington-South Burlington MSA, VT	Y	41950 FQ	49110 MW	56570 TQ	USBLS	5/15
Government Programs	Virginia	Y	33110 FQ	38890 MW	48510 TQ	USBLS	5/15
Government Programs	Richmond MSA, VA	Y	36190 FQ	42320 MW	49880 TQ	USBLS	5/15
Government Programs	Virginia Beach-Norfolk-Newport News MSA, VA-NC	Y	33440 FQ	39160 MW	47050 TQ	USBLS	5/15
Government Programs	Washington	H	18.76 FQ	23.46 MW	25.24 TQ	WABLS	3/16
Government Programs	Seattle-Bellevue-Everett PMSA, WA	H	18.77 FQ	24.03 MW	26.21 TQ	WABLS	3/16
Government Programs	Tacoma-Lakewood PMSA, WA	H	18.77 FQ	23.44 MW	24.63 TQ	WABLS	3/16
Government Programs	West Virginia	Y	24970 FQ	28260 MW	32270 TQ	USBLS	5/15
Government Programs	Huntington-Ashland MSA, WV-KY-OH	Y	25160 FQ	29010 MW	36760 TQ	USBLS	5/15
Government Programs	Wisconsin	Y	35940 FQ	42320 MW	47470 TQ	USBLS	5/15
Government Programs	Madison MSA, WI	Y	38200 FQ	43440 MW	48370 TQ	USBLS	5/15
Government Programs	Milwaukee-Waukesha-West Allis MSA, WI	Y	39630 FQ	44670 MW	49880 TQ	USBLS	5/15
Government Programs	Wyoming	Y	40090 FQ	41880 MW	49510 TQ	USBLS	5/15
Government Programs	Cheyenne MSA, WY	Y	40370 FQ	43070 MW	49520 TQ	USBLS	5/15
Government Programs	Puerto Rico	Y	19800 FQ	31040 MW	48200 TQ	USBLS	5/15
Government Programs	San German MSA, PR	Y	17040 FQ	18190 MW	19340 TQ	USBLS	5/15
Government Programs	San Juan-Carolina-Caguas MSA, PR	Y	22000 FQ	35600 MW	48210 TQ	USBLS	5/15
Embalmer	Alabama	Y	29272 AE	43635 AW	50821 AEX	ALBLS	6/16
	Birmingham-Hoover MSA, AL	Y	30590 AE	53570 AW	65050 AEX	ALBLS	6/16
	Arizona	Y	25690 FQ	31540 MW	38360 TQ	USBLS	5/15
	Phoenix-Mesa-Scottsdale MSA, AZ	Y	25930 FQ	30880 MW	36700 TQ	USBLS	5/15
	Arkansas	Y	37040 FQ	45040 MW	55720 TQ	USBLS	5/15
	California	H	15.01 FQ	22.09 MW	27.97 TQ	CABLS	1/16-3/16

AE	Average entry wage	AWR	Average wage range	H	Hourly
AEX	Average experienced wage	B	Biweekly	HI	Highest wage paid
ATC	Average total compensation	D	Daily	HR	High end range
AW	Average wage paid	FQ	First quartile wage	LO	Lowest wage paid

LR	Low end range	MTC	Median total compensation	TCC	Total cash compensation
M	Monthly	MW	Median wage paid	TQ	Third quartile wage
MCC	Median cash compensation	MWR	Median wage range	W	Weekly
ME	Median entry wage	S	See annotated source	Y	Yearly

Occupation/Type/Industry	Location	Per	Low	Mid	High	Source	Date
Embalmer	Los Angeles-Long Beach-Glendale PMSA, CA	H	16.87 FQ	22.83 MW	27.67 TQ	CABLS	1/16-3/16
	Oakland-Hayward-Berkeley PMSA, CA	H	13.22 FQ	14.46 MW	26.49 TQ	CABLS	1/16-3/16
	San Diego-Carlsbad MSA, CA	H	17.70 FQ	21.50 MW	26.47 TQ	CABLS	1/16-3/16
	San Francisco-Redwood City-South San Francisco PMSA, CA	H	22.24 FQ	25.65 MW	28.40 TQ	CABLS	1/16-3/16
	Colorado	Y	24240 FQ	38770 MW	45260 TQ	USBLS	5/15
	Denver-Aurora-Lakewood MSA, CO	Y	31430 FQ	39730 MW	45850 TQ	USBLS	5/15
	Connecticut	Y		68088 MW		CTBLS	1/16-3/16
	Florida	H	16.42 AE	21.40 MW	23.46 AEX	FLBLS	7/16-9/16
	Tampa-St. Petersburg-Clearwater MSA, FL	H	20.85 AE	22.24 MW	24.01 AEX	FLBLS	7/16-9/16
	Georgia	Y	25820 FQ	30480 MW	47240 TQ	USBLS	5/15
	Atlanta-Sandy Springs-Roswell MSA, GA	Y	24290 FQ	35210 MW	52250 TQ	USBLS	5/15
	Illinois	Y	24020 FQ	35360 MW	47230 TQ	USBLS	5/15
	Chicago-Naperville-Arlington Heights PMSA, IL	Y	19670 FQ	27760 MW	39540 TQ	USBLS	5/15
	Lake County-Kenosha County PMSA, IL-WI	Y	29170 FQ	34030 MW	39620 TQ	USBLS	5/15
	Indiana	Y	28530 FQ	34240 MW	39710 TQ	USBLS	5/15
	Kansas	Y	35540 FQ	48830 MW	57280 TQ	USBLS	5/15
	Kentucky	Y	29070 FQ	36470 MW	48630 TQ	USBLS	5/15
	Louisville-Jefferson County MSA, KY-IN	Y	27020 FQ	32390 MW	37620 TQ	USBLS	5/15
	Louisiana	Y	33060 FQ	39360 MW	49870 TQ	USBLS	5/15
	New Orleans-Metairie MSA, LA	Y	32280 FQ	35820 MW	39420 TQ	USBLS	5/15
	Michigan	Y	40640 FQ	43520 MW	46400 TQ	USBLS	5/15
	Mississippi	Y	21030 FQ	30400 MW	36350 TQ	USBLS	5/15
	Missouri	Y	41470 FQ	51550 MW	59130 TQ	USBLS	5/15
	Kansas City MSA, MO-KS	Y	32580 FQ	42960 MW	53070 TQ	USBLS	5/15
	New York	Y	28060 AE	29950 MW	38250 AEX	NYBLS	1/16-3/16
	North Carolina	Y	28710 FQ	36890 MW	48570 TQ	USBLS	5/15
	Charlotte-Concord-Gastonia MSA, NC-SC	Y	36430 FQ	42070 MW	46660 TQ	USBLS	5/15
	Oklahoma	Y	24370 FQ	42770 MW	47660 TQ	USBLS	5/15
	Oklahoma City MSA, OK	Y	34630 FQ	44740 MW	52800 TQ	USBLS	5/15
	Oregon	H	13.77 FQ	16.92 MW	22.89 TQ	ORBLS	2016
	Rhode Island	Y	50920 FQ	54590 MW	58260 TQ	USBLS	5/15
	Providence-Warwick MSA, RI-MA	Y	49230 FQ	53580 MW	57800 TQ	USBLS	5/15
	South Carolina	Y	26570 FQ	41580 MW	50260 TQ	USBLS	5/15
	Greenville-Anderson-Mauldin MSA, SC	Y	30130 FQ	51230 MW	58590 TQ	USBLS	5/15
	Tennessee	Y	28490 FQ	39980 MW	48610 TQ	USBLS	5/15
	Knoxville MSA, TN	Y	41780 FQ	47370 MW	59800 TQ	USBLS	5/15
	Texas	Y	33350 FQ	37280 MW	44220 TQ	USBLS	5/15
	Virginia	Y	40880 FQ	44910 MW	48940 TQ	USBLS	5/15
	Washington	H	16.64 FQ	24.11 MW	28.63 TQ	WABLS	3/16
	Seattle-Bellevue-Everett PMSA, WA	H	16.49 FQ	26.33 MW	30.41 TQ	WABLS	3/16
Embedded Application Developer	United States	Y		110899 AW		STOF2	2016
Emergency Management Director	Alabama	Y	40137 AE	69882 AW	84754 AEX	ALBLS	6/16
	Alaska	Y	56640 FQ	63500 MW	83000 TQ	USBLS	5/15
	Anchorage MSA, AK	Y	56630 FQ	60870 MW	75400 TQ	USBLS	5/15
	Arizona	Y	55290 FQ	69060 MW	93470 TQ	USBLS	5/15
	Phoenix-Mesa-Scottsdale MSA, AZ	Y	55450 FQ	71450 MW	100890 TQ	USBLS	5/15
	Arkansas	Y	27770 FQ	37900 MW	52150 TQ	USBLS	5/15
	California	H	40.81 FQ	52.72 MW	69.17 TQ	CABLS	1/16-3/16
	Anaheim-Santa Ana-Irvine PMSA, CA	H	41.00 FQ	50.52 MW	68.44 TQ	CABLS	1/16-3/16
	Los Angeles-Long Beach-Glendale PMSA, CA	H	45.00 FQ	55.79 MW	68.28 TQ	CABLS	1/16-3/16
	Oakland-Hayward-Berkeley PMSA, CA	H	45.40 FQ	56.85 MW	72.75 TQ	CABLS	1/16-3/16

AE Average entry wage	**AWR** Average wage range	**H** Hourly	**LR** Low end range	**MTC** Median total compensation	**TCC** Total cash compensation
AEX Average experienced wage	**B** Biweekly	**HI** Highest wage paid	**M** Monthly	**MW** Median wage paid	**TQ** Third quartile wage
ATC Average total compensation	**D** Daily	**HR** High end range	**MCC** Median cash compensation	**MWR** Median wage range	**W** Weekly
AW Average wage paid	**FQ** First quartile wage	**LO** Lowest wage paid	**ME** Median entry wage	**S** See annotated source	**Y** Yearly

Emergency Management Director

Occupation/Type/Industry	Location	Per	Low	Mid	High	Source	Date
Emergency Management Director	Sacramento–Roseville– Arden-Arcade MSA, CA	H	36.85 FQ	43.38 MW	57.04 TQ	CABLS	1/16-3/16
	San Diego-Carlsbad MSA, CA	H	37.13 FQ	44.29 MW	54.81 TQ	CABLS	1/16-3/16
	San Francisco-Redwood City-South San Francisco PMSA, CA	H	47.71 FQ	64.12 MW	77.57 TQ	CABLS	1/16-3/16
	Colorado	Y	57230 FQ	75560 MW	97480 TQ	USBLS	5/15
	Denver-Aurora-Lakewood MSA, CO	Y	70770 FQ	88250 MW	107750 TQ	USBLS	5/15
	Connecticut	Y		80476 MW		CTBLS	1/16-3/16
	Hartford-West Hartford-East Hartford MSA, CT	Y	67690 FQ	75990 MW	90560 TQ	USBLS	5/15
	Wilmington PMSA, DE-MD-NJ	Y	49460 FQ	74310 MW	94650 TQ	USBLS	5/15
	District of Columbia	Y	105550 FQ	138870 MW	151500 TQ	USBLS	5/15
	Washington-Arlington-Alexandria PMSA, DC-VA-MD-WV	Y	73290 FQ	105310 MW	146720 TQ	USBLS	5/15
	Florida	H	30.40 AE	42.68 MW	51.24 AEX	FLBLS	7/16-9/16
	Fort Lauderdale-Pompano Beach-Deerfield Beach PMSA, FL	H	31.42 AE	38.68 MW	52.95 AEX	FLBLS	7/16-9/16
	Miami-Miami Beach-Kendall PMSA, FL	H	27.88 AE	46.55 MW	55.77 AEX	FLBLS	7/16-9/16
	Orlando-Kissimmee-Sanford MSA, FL	H	38.11 AE	46.80 MW	53.47 AEX	FLBLS	7/16-9/16
	Tampa-St. Petersburg-Clearwater MSA, FL	H	36.20 AE	45.27 MW	50.40 AEX	FLBLS	7/16-9/16
	Georgia	Y	46250 FQ	63730 MW	81270 TQ	USBLS	5/15
	Atlanta-Sandy Springs-Roswell MSA, GA	Y	60310 FQ	74640 MW	96510 TQ	USBLS	5/15
	Augusta-Richmond County MSA, GA-SC	Y	44560 FQ	57340 MW	78870 TQ	USBLS	5/15
	Hawaii	Y	52570 FQ	59810 MW	86710 TQ	USBLS	5/15
	Urban Honolulu MSA, HI	Y	51730 FQ	58080 MW	69070 TQ	USBLS	5/15
	Idaho	Y	53580 FQ	72680 MW	94160 TQ	USBLS	5/15
	Illinois	Y	19300 FQ	44500 MW	78320 TQ	USBLS	5/15
	Indiana	Y	31970 FQ	38750 MW	55240 TQ	USBLS	5/15
	Indianapolis-Carmel-Anderson MSA, IN	Y	31320 FQ	39830 MW	56890 TQ	USBLS	5/15
	Iowa	Y	42890 FQ	53390 MW	67080 TQ	USBLS	5/15
	Des Moines-West Des Moines MSA, IA	Y	53380 FQ	58600 MW	62980 TQ	USBLS	5/15
	Kansas	Y	38440 FQ	48220 MW	67270 TQ	USBLS	5/15
	Kentucky	Y	30050 FQ	41080 MW	52780 TQ	USBLS	5/15
	Louisville-Jefferson County MSA, KY-IN	Y	29300 FQ	37480 MW	51830 TQ	USBLS	5/15
	Louisiana	Y	51880 FQ	70300 MW	93320 TQ	USBLS	5/15
	New Orleans-Metairie MSA, LA	Y	71180 FQ	96670 MW	133120 TQ	USBLS	5/15
	Maine	Y	38190 FQ	56100 MW	72830 TQ	USBLS	5/15
	Maryland	Y	59681 AE	91011 MW	106676 AEX	MDBLS	4/16
	Baltimore-Columbia-Towson MSA, MD	Y	67660 FQ	89210 MW	110220 TQ	USBLS	5/15
	Massachusetts	Y	39820 FQ	66720 MW	104690 TQ	USBLS	5/15
	Boston-Cambridge-Newton NECTA, MA	Y	57430 FQ	79430 MW	123900 TQ	USBLS	5/15
	Michigan	Y	50980 FQ	60140 MW	76220 TQ	USBLS	5/15
	Minnesota	Y	58558 FQ	77752 MW	101692 TQ	MNBLS	1/16-3/16
	Minneapolis-St. Paul-Bloomington MSA, MN-WI	Y	69288 FQ	92293 MW	113986 TQ	MNBLS	1/16-3/16
	Mississippi	Y	36620 FQ	40780 MW	66280 TQ	USBLS	5/15
	Missouri	Y	30910 FQ	47220 MW	69360 TQ	USBLS	5/15
	Kansas City MSA, MO-KS	Y	37580 FQ	67130 MW	97450 TQ	USBLS	5/15
	St. Louis MSA, MO-IL	Y	40520 FQ	70710 MW	90360 TQ	USBLS	5/15
	Montana	Y	33420 FQ	40280 MW	50150 TQ	USBLS	5/15
	Nebraska	Y	38945 FQ	47670 MW	60890 TQ	NEBLS	7/16-9/16
	Omaha-Council Bluffs MSA, NE-IA	Y	44130 FQ	56755 MW	99440 TQ	NEBLS	7/16-9/16
	Nevada	Y	55280 FQ	81750 MW	96310 TQ	USBLS	5/15
	New Hampshire	H	14.93 AE	23.91 MW	39.61 AEX	NHBLS	6/16
	New Jersey	Y	54430 FQ	88620 MW	115170 TQ	USBLS	5/15

AE	Average entry wage	AWR	Average wage range	H	Hourly	LR	Low end range	MTC	Median total compensation	TCC	Total cash compensation
AEX	Average experienced wage	B	Biweekly	HI	Highest wage paid	M	Monthly	MW	Median wage paid	TQ	Third quartile wage
ATC	Average total compensation	D	Daily	HR	High end range	MCC	Median cash compensation	MWR	Median wage range	W	Weekly
AW	Average wage paid	FQ	First quartile wage	LO	Lowest wage paid	ME	Median entry wage	S	See annotated source	Y	Yearly

Occupation/Type/Industry	Location	Per	Low	Mid	High	Source	Date
Emergency Management Director	Camden PMSA, NJ	Y	44190 FQ	83650 MW	123820 TQ	USBLS	5/15
	Newark PMSA, NJ-PA	Y	43420 FQ	91310 MW	119630 TQ	USBLS	5/15
	New Mexico	Y	50530 FQ	71910 MW	107750 TQ	USBLS	5/15
	New York	Y	60000 AE	86010 MW	108950 AEX	NYBLS	1/16-3/16
	Nassau County-Suffolk County PMSA, NY	Y	73620 FQ	89020 MW	104380 TQ	USBLS	5/15
	New York-Jersey City-White Plains PMSA, NY-NJ	Y	73020 FQ	95950 MW	124590 TQ	USBLS	5/15
	Rochester MSA, NY	Y	61900 FQ	83890 MW	104670 TQ	USBLS	5/15
	North Carolina	Y	55790 FQ	69550 MW	86850 TQ	USBLS	5/15
	Charlotte-Concord-Gastonia MSA, NC-SC	Y	65560 FQ	81300 MW	103460 TQ	USBLS	5/15
	North Dakota	Y	44660 FQ	56960 MW	70300 TQ	USBLS	5/15
	Ohio	Y	48880 FQ	67170 MW	84870 TQ	USBLS	5/15
	Cincinnati MSA, OH-KY-IN	Y	41320 FQ	53830 MW	72960 TQ	USBLS	5/15
	Cleveland-Elyria MSA, OH	Y	53110 FQ	68700 MW	89600 TQ	USBLS	5/15
	Columbus MSA, OH	Y	64280 FQ	71700 MW	87870 TQ	USBLS	5/15
	Oklahoma	Y	33690 FQ	47350 MW	66980 TQ	USBLS	5/15
	Oklahoma City MSA, OK	Y	42380 FQ	59820 MW	76440 TQ	USBLS	5/15
	Oregon	H	28.79 FQ	36.84 MW	47.76 TQ	ORBLS	2016
	Portland-Vancouver-Hillsboro MSA, OR-WA	Y	60610 FQ	84220 MW	102120 TQ	USBLS	5/15
	Pennsylvania	Y	49180 FQ	58730 MW	75530 TQ	USBLS	5/15
	Harrisburg-Carlisle MSA, PA	Y	51410 FQ	58730 MW	73140 TQ	USBLS	5/15
	Montgomery County-Bucks County-Chester County PMSA, PA	Y	51220 FQ	64860 MW	85290 TQ	USBLS	5/15
	Philadelphia PMSA, PA	Y	47070 FQ	64390 MW	80980 TQ	USBLS	5/15
	Pittsburgh MSA, PA	Y	43610 FQ	61760 MW	112610 TQ	USBLS	5/15
	South Carolina	Y	46270 FQ	56390 MW	75290 TQ	USBLS	5/15
	Columbia MSA, SC	Y	43170 FQ	46460 MW	52650 TQ	USBLS	5/15
	Greenville-Anderson-Mauldin MSA, SC	Y	57120 FQ	64910 MW	76400 TQ	USBLS	5/15
	South Dakota	Y	35310 FQ	40620 MW	49220 TQ	USBLS	5/15
	Tennessee	Y	44560 FQ	65390 MW	102490 TQ	USBLS	5/15
	Knoxville MSA, TN	Y	60500 FQ	78140 MW	122880 TQ	USBLS	5/15
	Texas	Y	48690 FQ	65080 MW	89110 TQ	USBLS	5/15
	Austin-Round Rock MSA, TX	Y	55050 FQ	67110 MW	83630 TQ	USBLS	5/15
	Dallas-Plano-Irving PMSA, TX	Y	57500 FQ	73170 MW	99080 TQ	USBLS	5/15
	Fort Worth-Arlington PMSA, TX	Y	79260 FQ	96190 MW	114390 TQ	USBLS	5/15
	Houston-The Woodlands-Sugar Land MSA, TX	Y	54120 FQ	79030 MW	101160 TQ	USBLS	5/15
	San Antonio-New Braunfels MSA, TX	Y	51980 FQ	56840 MW	61700 TQ	USBLS	5/15
	Utah	Y	52470 FQ	64190 MW	77700 TQ	USBLS	5/15
	Salt Lake City MSA, UT	Y	52440 FQ	64400 MW	77870 TQ	USBLS	5/15
	Vermont	Y	47750 FQ	58140 MW	73170 TQ	USBLS	5/15
	Virginia	Y	63720 FQ	74550 MW	102390 TQ	USBLS	5/15
	Richmond MSA, VA	Y	52410 FQ	64860 MW	79490 TQ	USBLS	5/15
	Virginia Beach-Norfolk-Newport News MSA, VA-NC	Y	65220 FQ	72980 MW	87100 TQ	USBLS	5/15
	Washington	H	30.51 FQ	38.93 MW	49.89 TQ	WABLS	3/16
	Seattle-Bellevue-Everett PMSA, WA	H	37.77 FQ	44.79 MW	53.63 TQ	WABLS	3/16
	West Virginia	Y	44380 FQ	59120 MW	76890 TQ	USBLS	5/15
	Wisconsin	Y	53970 FQ	63510 MW	75100 TQ	USBLS	5/15
	Wyoming	Y	44340 FQ	58350 MW	72730 TQ	USBLS	5/15
	Puerto Rico	Y	25670 FQ	32100 MW	43460 TQ	USBLS	5/15
	San Juan-Carolina-Caguas MSA, PR	Y	26890 FQ	35350 MW	46760 TQ	USBLS	5/15
Emergency Management Specialist							
State Government	Helena, MT	H	35.84 LO		38.36 HI	MTGOV	2016
State Government	New Mexico	H	15.28 LO		26.59 HI	NMGOV	7/30/16
Emergency Medical Educator							
Fire Department, Municipal Government	Long Beach, CA	Y		106040 AW		CACIT	6/28/16
Emergency Medical Technician							
Basic	United States	Y	27000 FQ	33000 MW	43348 TQ	JEMS	2014

AE	Average entry wage	AWR	Average wage range	H	Hourly
AEX	Average experienced wage	B	Biweekly	HI	Highest wage paid
ATC	Average total compensation	D	Daily	HR	High end range
AW	Average wage paid	FQ	First quartile wage	LO	Lowest wage paid

LR	Low end range	MTC	Median total compensation	TCC	Total cash compensation
M	Monthly	MW	Median wage paid	TQ	Third quartile wage
MCC	Median cash compensation	MWR	Median wage range	W	Weekly
ME	Median entry wage	S	See annotated source	Y	Yearly

Occupation/Type/Industry	Location	Per	Low	Mid	High	Source	Date
Emergency Medical Technician							
Intermediate	United States	Y	29204 FQ	34500 MW	44100 TQ	JEMS	2014
Paramedic	United States	Y	36500 FQ	43711 MW	54960 TQ	JEMS	2014
Emergency Medical Technician and Paramedic							
	Alabama	Y	20111 AE	29469 AW	34147 AEX	ALBLS	6/16
	Birmingham-Hoover MSA, AL	Y	20223 AE	28490 AW	20223 AEX	ALBLS	6/16
	Alaska	Y	42750 FQ	54160 MW	65370 TQ	USBLS	5/15
	Anchorage MSA, AK	Y	37390 FQ	56010 MW	69340 TQ	USBLS	5/15
	Arizona	Y	28390 FQ	33460 MW	44030 TQ	USBLS	5/15
	Phoenix-Mesa-Scottsdale MSA, AZ	Y	28160 FQ	31350 MW	42930 TQ	USBLS	5/15
	Tucson MSA, AZ	Y	37890 FQ	43760 MW	48750 TQ	USBLS	5/15
	Arkansas	Y	21200 FQ	26900 MW	35800 TQ	USBLS	5/15
	Little Rock-North Little Rock-Conway MSA, AR	Y	20280 FQ	26510 MW	37130 TQ	USBLS	5/15
	California	H	12.06 FQ	16.21 MW	23.40 TQ	CABLS	1/16-3/16
	Anaheim-Santa Ana-Irvine PMSA, CA	H	11.97 FQ	14.74 MW	20.46 TQ	CABLS	1/16-3/16
	Los Angeles-Long Beach-Glendale PMSA, CA	H	11.26 FQ	14.53 MW	23.95 TQ	CABLS	1/16-3/16
	Oakland-Hayward-Berkeley PMSA, CA	H	12.26 FQ	17.99 MW	25.00 TQ	CABLS	1/16-3/16
	Riverside-San Bernardino-Ontario MSA, CA	H	12.73 FQ	15.39 MW	18.77 TQ	CABLS	1/16-3/16
	Sacramento–Roseville–Arden-Arcade MSA, CA	H	13.88 FQ	19.40 MW	25.45 TQ	CABLS	1/16-3/16
	San Diego-Carlsbad MSA, CA	H	10.44 FQ	13.09 MW	20.17 TQ	CABLS	1/16-3/16
	San Francisco-Redwood City-South San Francisco PMSA, CA	H	18.99 FQ	23.46 MW	29.04 TQ	CABLS	1/16-3/16
	Colorado	Y	26610 FQ	36300 MW	50550 TQ	USBLS	5/15
	Denver-Aurora-Lakewood MSA, CO	Y	32250 FQ	41610 MW	62410 TQ	USBLS	5/15
	Connecticut	Y		44800 MW		CTBLS	1/16-3/16
	Bridgeport-Stamford-Norwalk MSA, CT	Y	45100 FQ	54020 MW	61460 TQ	USBLS	5/15
	Hartford-West Hartford-East Hartford MSA, CT	Y	35020 FQ	43370 MW	50630 TQ	USBLS	5/15
	Delaware	Y	28810 FQ	34790 MW	42600 TQ	USBLS	5/15
	Wilmington PMSA, DE-MD-NJ	Y	34170 FQ	38230 MW	47160 TQ	USBLS	5/15
	District of Columbia	Y	50860 FQ	59790 MW	66400 TQ	USBLS	5/15
	Washington-Arlington-Alexandria PMSA, DC-VA-MD-WV	Y	31120 FQ	46050 MW	59790 TQ	USBLS	5/15
	Florida	H	11.15 AE	14.52 MW	17.38 AEX	FLBLS	7/16-9/16
	Fort Lauderdale-Pompano Beach-Deerfield Beach PMSA, FL	H	10.43 AE	13.53 MW	16.67 AEX	FLBLS	7/16-9/16
	Miami-Miami Beach-Kendall PMSA, FL	H	12.39 AE	14.64 MW	16.67 AEX	FLBLS	7/16-9/16
	Orlando-Kissimmee-Sanford MSA, FL	H	14.50 AE	18.29 MW	21.71 AEX	FLBLS	7/16-9/16
	Tampa-St. Petersburg-Clearwater MSA, FL	H	10.76 AE	13.91 MW	16.02 AEX	FLBLS	7/16-9/16
	Georgia	Y	25940 FQ	30610 MW	38590 TQ	USBLS	5/15
	Atlanta-Sandy Springs-Roswell MSA, GA	Y	27670 FQ	34010 MW	42110 TQ	USBLS	5/15
	Augusta-Richmond County MSA, GA-SC	Y	26760 FQ	30350 MW	37000 TQ	USBLS	5/15
	Idaho	Y	25740 FQ	33300 MW	41220 TQ	USBLS	5/15
	Boise City MSA, ID	Y	27110 FQ	34490 MW	42460 TQ	USBLS	5/15
	Illinois	Y	23280 FQ	32180 MW	49930 TQ	USBLS	5/15
	Chicago-Naperville-Arlington Heights PMSA, IL	Y	24440 FQ	37970 MW	75020 TQ	USBLS	5/15
	Lake County-Kenosha County PMSA, IL-WI	Y	19750 FQ	29830 MW	39130 TQ	USBLS	5/15
	Indiana	Y	23750 FQ	30580 MW	38200 TQ	USBLS	5/15
	Gary PMSA, IN	Y	31820 FQ	39600 MW	46960 TQ	USBLS	5/15
	Indianapolis-Carmel-Anderson MSA, IN	Y	23110 FQ	29320 MW	37350 TQ	USBLS	5/15

AE	Average entry wage	AWR	Average wage range	H	Hourly
AEX	Average experienced wage	B	Biweekly	HI	Highest wage paid
ATC	Average total compensation	D	Daily	HR	High end range
AW	Average wage paid	FQ	First quartile wage	LO	Lowest wage paid

LR	Low end range	MTC	Median total compensation	TCC	Total cash compensation
M	Monthly	MW	Median wage paid	TQ	Third quartile wage
MCC	Median cash compensation	MWR	Median wage range	W	Weekly
ME	Median entry wage	S	See annotated source	Y	Yearly

Occupation/Type/Industry	Location	Per	Low	Mid	High	Source	Date
Emergency Medical Technician and Paramedic	Iowa	Y	24950 FQ	31000 MW	39450 TQ	USBLS	5/15
	Des Moines-West Des Moines MSA, IA	Y	29160 FQ	36620 MW	48890 TQ	USBLS	5/15
	Kansas	Y	21100 FQ	27480 MW	36110 TQ	USBLS	5/15
	Wichita MSA, KS	Y	23100 FQ	32840 MW	39520 TQ	USBLS	5/15
	Kentucky	Y	22940 FQ	28690 MW	36330 TQ	USBLS	5/15
	Louisville-Jefferson County MSA, KY-IN	Y	23730 FQ	29000 MW	38380 TQ	USBLS	5/15
	Louisiana	Y	26440 FQ	36810 MW	46570 TQ	USBLS	5/15
	New Orleans-Metairie MSA, LA	Y	27560 FQ	39250 MW	47230 TQ	USBLS	5/15
	Maine	Y	26010 FQ	32940 MW	38730 TQ	USBLS	5/15
	Portland-South Portland MSA, ME	Y	26590 FQ	30920 MW	36430 TQ	USBLS	5/15
	Maryland	Y	25589 AE	40741 MW	48316 AEX	MDBLS	4/16
	Baltimore-Columbia-Towson MSA, MD	Y	29170 FQ	42850 MW	55540 TQ	USBLS	5/15
	Salisbury MSA, MD-DE	Y	26150 FQ	30820 MW	40060 TQ	USBLS	5/15
	Massachusetts	Y	30430 FQ	37690 MW	46880 TQ	USBLS	5/15
	Boston-Cambridge-Newton NECTA, MA	Y	29740 FQ	35940 MW	44780 TQ	USBLS	5/15
	Worcester MSA, MA-CT	Y	30500 FQ	36880 MW	46120 TQ	USBLS	5/15
	Michigan	Y	23120 FQ	29650 MW	37510 TQ	USBLS	5/15
	Detroit-Dearborn-Livonia PMSA, MI	Y	22110 FQ	26350 MW	35190 TQ	USBLS	5/15
	Grand Rapids-Wyoming MSA, MI	Y	26300 FQ	33910 MW	40720 TQ	USBLS	5/15
	Minnesota	Y	28246 FQ	35937 MW	46663 TQ	MNBLS	1/16-3/16
	Minneapolis-St. Paul-Bloomington MSA, MN-WI	Y	33296 FQ	43508 MW	56189 TQ	MNBLS	1/16-3/16
	St. Cloud MSA, MN	Y	27390 FQ	30560 MW	35450 TQ	USBLS	5/15
	Mississippi	Y	24570 FQ	33850 MW	44620 TQ	USBLS	5/15
	Jackson MSA, MS	Y	26920 FQ	30270 MW	35530 TQ	USBLS	5/15
	Missouri	Y	24560 FQ	31860 MW	40150 TQ	USBLS	5/15
	Kansas City MSA, MO-KS	Y	29010 FQ	36760 MW	46740 TQ	USBLS	5/15
	St. Louis MSA, MO-IL	Y	25800 FQ	34150 MW	42110 TQ	USBLS	5/15
	Montana	Y	23710 FQ	29060 MW	36520 TQ	USBLS	5/15
	Billings MSA, MT	Y	36170 FQ	41420 MW	46120 TQ	USBLS	5/15
	Nebraska	Y	25175 FQ	31875 MW	37770 TQ	NEBLS	7/16-9/16
	Omaha-Council Bluffs MSA, NE-IA	Y	24770 FQ	31795 MW	37025 TQ	NEBLS	7/16-9/16
	Nevada	Y	31520 FQ	41580 MW	56320 TQ	USBLS	5/15
	Las Vegas-Henderson-Paradise MSA, NV	Y	30360 FQ	43310 MW	59060 TQ	USBLS	5/15
	New Hampshire	H	10.87 AE	18.11 MW	21.56 AEX	NHBLS	6/16
	Manchester NECTA, NH	H	11.79 AE	17.76 MW	19.71 AEX	NHBLS	6/16
	Nashua NECTA, NH-MA	Y	25790 FQ	34670 MW	44510 TQ	USBLS	5/15
	New Jersey	Y	27050 FQ	30560 MW	41030 TQ	USBLS	5/15
	Camden PMSA, NJ	Y	26260 FQ	29430 MW	40220 TQ	USBLS	5/15
	Newark PMSA, NJ-PA	Y	27510 FQ	31810 MW	45130 TQ	USBLS	5/15
	New Mexico	Y	25570 FQ	32380 MW	41570 TQ	USBLS	5/15
	Albuquerque MSA, NM	Y	23950 FQ	30700 MW	40240 TQ	USBLS	5/15
	New York	Y	25450 AE	37640 MW	46530 AEX	NYBLS	1/16-3/16
	Buffalo-Cheektowaga-Niagara Falls MSA, NY	Y	22430 FQ	27380 MW	37820 TQ	USBLS	5/15
	Nassau County-Suffolk County PMSA, NY	Y	30700 FQ	45650 MW	57570 TQ	USBLS	5/15
	New York-Jersey City-White Plains PMSA, NY-NJ	Y	28440 FQ	35350 MW	47420 TQ	USBLS	5/15
	Rochester MSA, NY	Y	26870 FQ	34010 MW	39880 TQ	USBLS	5/15
	North Carolina	Y	26640 FQ	32500 MW	38350 TQ	USBLS	5/15
	Charlotte-Concord-Gastonia MSA, NC-SC	Y	29260 FQ	35220 MW	42010 TQ	USBLS	5/15
	Raleigh MSA, NC	Y	27070 FQ	33390 MW	38480 TQ	USBLS	5/15
	North Dakota	Y	19500 FQ	30890 MW	38280 TQ	USBLS	5/15
	Ohio	Y	23600 FQ	28820 MW	36060 TQ	USBLS	5/15
	Cincinnati MSA, OH-KY-IN	Y	24490 FQ	31940 MW	38190 TQ	USBLS	5/15
	Cleveland-Elyria MSA, OH	Y	25670 FQ	30970 MW	38910 TQ	USBLS	5/15
	Columbus MSA, OH	Y	21910 FQ	25370 MW	32210 TQ	USBLS	5/15
	Oklahoma	Y	21760 FQ	28160 MW	35300 TQ	USBLS	5/15
	Oklahoma City MSA, OK	Y	23710 FQ	31610 MW	38770 TQ	USBLS	5/15

AE	Average entry wage	AWR	Average wage range	H	Hourly	LR	Low end range	MTC	Median total compensation	TCC	Total cash compensation
AEX	Average experienced wage	B	Biweekly	HI	Highest wage paid	M	Monthly	MW	Median wage paid	TQ	Third quartile wage
ATC	Average total compensation	D	Daily	HR	High end range	MCC	Median cash compensation	MWR	Median wage range	W	Weekly
AW	Average wage paid	FQ	First quartile wage	LO	Lowest wage paid	ME	Median entry wage	S	See annotated source	Y	Yearly

Occupation/Type/Industry	Location	Per	Low	Mid	High	Source	Date
Emergency Medical Technician and Paramedic	Tulsa MSA, OK	Y	26450 FQ	31390 MW	36200 TQ	USBLS	5/15
	Oregon	H	14.42 FQ	18.03 MW	22.90 TQ	ORBLS	2016
	Portland-Vancouver-Hillsboro MSA, OR-WA	Y	31900 FQ	42820 MW	53910 TQ	USBLS	5/15
	Pennsylvania	Y	24610 FQ	29850 MW	38500 TQ	USBLS	5/15
	Allentown-Bethlehem-Easton MSA, PA-NJ	Y	28650 FQ	37050 MW	46080 TQ	USBLS	5/15
	Harrisburg-Carlisle MSA, PA	Y	24340 FQ	28780 MW	36450 TQ	USBLS	5/15
	Montgomery County-Bucks County-Chester County PMSA, PA	Y	28060 FQ	32590 MW	41430 TQ	USBLS	5/15
	Philadelphia PMSA, PA	Y	27510 FQ	35840 MW	55010 TQ	USBLS	5/15
	Pittsburgh MSA, PA	Y	25620 FQ	30680 MW	37900 TQ	USBLS	5/15
	Rhode Island	Y	28650 FQ	34130 MW	41090 TQ	USBLS	5/15
	Providence-Warwick MSA, RI-MA	Y	28850 FQ	34820 MW	43720 TQ	USBLS	5/15
	South Carolina	Y	25240 FQ	29950 MW	37340 TQ	USBLS	5/15
	Charleston-North Charleston MSA, SC	Y	26890 FQ	32210 MW	40050 TQ	USBLS	5/15
	Columbia MSA, SC	Y	24960 FQ	31030 MW	39220 TQ	USBLS	5/15
	Greenville-Anderson-Mauldin MSA, SC	Y	26240 FQ	30380 MW	36910 TQ	USBLS	5/15
	South Dakota	Y	23450 FQ	27390 MW	31440 TQ	USBLS	5/15
	Sioux Falls MSA, SD	Y	23470 FQ	27640 MW	32970 TQ	USBLS	5/15
	Tennessee	Y	26060 FQ	31590 MW	38850 TQ	USBLS	5/15
	Knoxville MSA, TN	Y	22050 FQ	25300 MW	33310 TQ	USBLS	5/15
	Memphis MSA, TN-MS-AR	Y	32120 FQ	36340 MW	50170 TQ	USBLS	5/15
	Nashville-Davidson–Murfreesboro–Franklin MSA, TN	Y	26780 FQ	30840 MW	42590 TQ	USBLS	5/15
	Texas	Y	26910 FQ	33790 MW	42720 TQ	USBLS	5/15
	Austin-Round Rock MSA, TX	Y	32180 FQ	39840 MW	53870 TQ	USBLS	5/15
	Dallas-Plano-Irving PMSA, TX	Y	34220 FQ	40330 MW	51460 TQ	USBLS	5/15
	Fort Worth-Arlington PMSA, TX	Y	27020 FQ	34840 MW	47610 TQ	USBLS	5/15
	Houston-The Woodlands-Sugar Land MSA, TX	Y	27380 FQ	31820 MW	38940 TQ	USBLS	5/15
	San Antonio-New Braunfels MSA, TX	Y	24510 FQ	29860 MW	36590 TQ	USBLS	5/15
	Utah	Y	23680 FQ	30210 MW	39640 TQ	USBLS	5/15
	Ogden-Clearfield MSA, UT	Y	24950 FQ	34810 MW	40350 TQ	USBLS	5/15
	Provo-Orem MSA, UT	Y	17720 FQ	20750 MW	26010 TQ	USBLS	5/15
	Salt Lake City MSA, UT	Y	27040 FQ	36630 MW	45090 TQ	USBLS	5/15
	Vermont	Y	24800 FQ	30940 MW	36020 TQ	USBLS	5/15
	Burlington-South Burlington MSA, VT	Y	25120 FQ	29440 MW	34870 TQ	USBLS	5/15
	Virginia	Y	24920 FQ	30370 MW	37940 TQ	USBLS	5/15
	Richmond MSA, VA	Y	24600 FQ	29900 MW	37430 TQ	USBLS	5/15
	Virginia Beach-Norfolk-Newport News MSA, VA-NC	Y	27350 FQ	32950 MW	41700 TQ	USBLS	5/15
	Washington	H	16.92 FQ	25.88 MW	42.13 TQ	WABLS	3/16
	Seattle-Bellevue-Everett PMSA, WA	H	19.13 FQ	32.04 MW	44.59 TQ	WABLS	3/16
	Tacoma-Lakewood PMSA, WA	H	26.79 FQ	40.46 MW	47.22 TQ	WABLS	3/16
	West Virginia	Y	19770 FQ	24000 MW	30910 TQ	USBLS	5/15
	Huntington-Ashland MSA, WV-KY-OH	Y	21440 FQ	27670 MW	36170 TQ	USBLS	5/15
	Wisconsin	Y	21150 FQ	28760 MW	36500 TQ	USBLS	5/15
	Madison MSA, WI	Y	17650 FQ	19840 MW	34420 TQ	USBLS	5/15
	Milwaukee-Waukesha-West Allis MSA, WI	Y	23590 FQ	29270 MW	37080 TQ	USBLS	5/15
	Wyoming	Y	23780 FQ	33400 MW	41190 TQ	USBLS	5/15
	Cheyenne MSA, WY	Y	31620 FQ	34960 MW	38300 TQ	USBLS	5/15
	Puerto Rico	Y	17830 FQ	20540 MW	25320 TQ	USBLS	5/15
	San Juan-Carolina-Caguas MSA, PR	Y	18430 FQ	21920 MW	26440 TQ	USBLS	5/15
Emergency Mobile Medical Technician							
Municipal Government	Detroit, MI	M	2260 LO		3073 HI	DETGOV	2016

AE	Average entry wage	AWR	Average wage range	H	Hourly	LR	Low end range	MTC	Median total compensation	TCC	Total cash compensation
AEX	Average experienced wage	B	Biweekly	HI	Highest wage paid	M	Monthly	MW	Median wage paid	TQ	Third quartile wage
ATC	Average total compensation	D	Daily	HR	High end range	MCC	Median cash compensation	MWR	Median wage range	W	Weekly
AW	Average wage paid	FQ	First quartile wage	LO	Lowest wage paid	ME	Median entry wage	S	See annotated source	Y	Yearly

Occupation/Type/Industry	Location	Per	Low	Mid	High	Source	Date
Emergency Planning Coordinator							
Airport	San Francisco, CA	B	3162 LO		3844 HI	SFGOV	2016-2018
Emergency Preparedness Coordinator							
Fire Department, Municipal Government	Carlsbad, CA	Y			96200 HI	CACIT	6/28/16
Fire Department, Municipal Government	Santa Rosa, CA	Y			74852 HI	CACIT	6/28/16
Fire Prevention, Municipal Government	Downey, CA	Y			77458 HI	CACIT	6/28/16
Employee Relations Manager							
Human Resources Department, Municipal Government	Anaheim, CA	Y			136561 HI	CACIT	6/28/16
EMS Coordinator							
Fire Department, Municipal Government	Anaheim, CA	Y			82314 HI	CACIT	6/28/16
Fire Department, Municipal Government	Huntington Beach, CA	Y			118471 HI	CACIT	6/28/16
Fire Department, Municipal Government	Murrieta, CA	Y			83801 HI	CACIT	6/28/16
Fire Department, Municipal Government	Santa Monica, CA	Y			123267 HI	CACIT	6/28/16
EMS Director							
Municipal Government	Cedartown, GA	Y	38000 LO		46000 HI	GACTY01	2016
EMS Exercise Training Planner							
Department of Public Health and Human Services, State Government	Helena, MT	H			21.62 HI	MTGOV	2016
EMS Illustrator							
State Government	Maryland	Y	36557 LO		57808 HI	MDGOV	2016
EMS Nurse Specialist							
Fire Department, Municipal Government	Burbank, CA	Y			107729 HI	CACIT	6/28/16
Endocrinologist	United States	Y		206000 AW		TIME01	2016
Endoscopy Technician	United States	Y		37000 AW		SKU01	2016
Energy Marketer-Trader							
Municipal Government	Glendale, CA	Y			117113 HI	CACIT	6/28/16
Energy Specialist							
Public Utility Commission, State Government	Ohio	H			46.55 HI	OHGOV	2015
Energy Trader-Scheduler							
Municipal Government	Burbank, CA	Y		157769 AW		CACIT	6/28/16
Engagement Manager	United States	Y		120000 MW		CNBC02	2016
Engine and Other Machine Assembler	Alabama	Y	26847 AE	38753 AW	44717 AEX	ALBLS	6/16
	Arizona	Y	25430 FQ	32110 MW	40820 TQ	USBLS	5/15
	Phoenix-Mesa-Scottsdale MSA, AZ	Y	25370 FQ	31690 MW	38660 TQ	USBLS	5/15
	Arkansas	Y	19260 FQ	24320 MW	42490 TQ	USBLS	5/15
	California	H	16.12 FQ	21.09 MW	27.67 TQ	CABLS	1/16-3/16
	Anaheim-Santa Ana-Irvine PMSA, CA	H	13.39 FQ	24.07 MW	30.85 TQ	CABLS	1/16-3/16
	Los Angeles-Long Beach-Glendale PMSA, CA	H	14.73 FQ	18.44 MW	27.56 TQ	CABLS	1/16-3/16
	Oakland-Hayward-Berkeley PMSA, CA	H	19.84 FQ	23.85 MW	27.81 TQ	CABLS	1/16-3/16
	Sacramento–Roseville–Arden-Arcade MSA, CA	H	11.33 FQ	14.69 MW	18.44 TQ	CABLS	1/16-3/16
	Colorado	Y	32910 FQ	36990 MW	42550 TQ	USBLS	5/15
	Denver-Aurora-Lakewood MSA, CO	Y	33440 FQ	36910 MW	40800 TQ	USBLS	5/15
	Connecticut	Y		39309 MW		CTBLS	1/16-3/16
	Hartford-West Hartford-East Hartford MSA, CT	Y	32980 FQ	38080 MW	49060 TQ	USBLS	5/15
	Fort Lauderdale-Pompano Beach-Deerfield Beach PMSA, FL	H	11.39 AE	14.92 MW	20.72 AEX	FLBLS	7/16-9/16
	Georgia	Y	31250 FQ	41070 MW	49440 TQ	USBLS	5/15

AE	Average entry wage	AWR	Average wage range	H	Hourly	LR	Low end range	MTC	Median total compensation	TCC	Total cash compensation
AEX	Average experienced wage	B	Biweekly	HI	Highest wage paid	M	Monthly	MW	Median wage paid	TQ	Third quartile wage
ATC	Average total compensation	D	Daily	HR	High end range	MCC	Median cash compensation	MWR	Median wage range	W	Weekly
AW	Average wage paid	FQ	First quartile wage	LO	Lowest wage paid	ME	Median entry wage	S	See annotated source	Y	Yearly

Occupation/Type/Industry	Location	Per	Low	Mid	High	Source	Date
Engine and Other Machine Assembler							
	Atlanta-Sandy Springs-Roswell MSA, GA	Y	29490 FQ	37960 MW	47890 TQ	USBLS	5/15
	Illinois	Y	34570 FQ	40700 MW	47750 TQ	USBLS	5/15
	Chicago-Naperville-Arlington Heights PMSA, IL	Y	35240 FQ	39340 MW	54860 TQ	USBLS	5/15
	Lake County-Kenosha County PMSA, IL-WI	Y	26760 FQ	29060 MW	31350 TQ	USBLS	5/15
	Gary PMSA, IN	Y	27810 FQ	32990 MW	39220 TQ	USBLS	5/15
	Iowa	Y	33030 FQ	37930 MW	45620 TQ	USBLS	5/15
	Kansas	Y	30860 FQ	36500 MW	42920 TQ	USBLS	5/15
	Kentucky	Y	28050 FQ	34410 MW	53980 TQ	USBLS	5/15
	Louisville-Jefferson County MSA, KY-IN	Y	25530 FQ	29180 MW	34060 TQ	USBLS	5/15
	Louisiana	Y	29470 FQ	40500 MW	49830 TQ	USBLS	5/15
	Maryland	Y	34383 AE	45677 MW	51325 AEX	MDBLS	4/16
	Baltimore-Columbia-Towson MSA, MD	Y	36390 FQ	44570 MW	53570 TQ	USBLS	5/15
	Massachusetts	Y	32640 FQ	48460 MW	57490 TQ	USBLS	5/15
	Michigan	Y	37590 FQ	52750 MW	58830 TQ	USBLS	5/15
	Detroit-Dearborn-Livonia PMSA, MI	Y	53010 FQ	56740 MW	60470 TQ	USBLS	5/15
	Minnesota	Y	29766 FQ	37015 MW	46957 TQ	MNBLS	1/16-3/16
	Minneapolis-St. Paul-Bloomington MSA, MN-WI	Y	34433 FQ	39253 MW	46279 TQ	MNBLS	1/16-3/16
	Mississippi	Y	31040 FQ	39350 MW	44820 TQ	USBLS	5/15
	Missouri	Y	32330 FQ	36780 MW	50080 TQ	USBLS	5/15
	Kansas City MSA, MO-KS	Y	40970 FQ	45950 MW	51730 TQ	USBLS	5/15
	St. Louis MSA, MO-IL	Y	20780 FQ	24460 MW	41710 TQ	USBLS	5/15
	Nebraska	Y	29090 FQ	34020 MW	40570 TQ	NEBLS	7/16-9/16
	Nevada	Y	38720 FQ	49800 MW	56430 TQ	USBLS	5/15
	Las Vegas-Henderson-Paradise MSA, NV	Y	50980 FQ	55090 MW	59190 TQ	USBLS	5/15
	New Hampshire	H	16.27 AE	22.66 MW	25.57 AEX	NHBLS	6/16
	New Jersey	Y	32580 FQ	36840 MW	44130 TQ	USBLS	5/15
	Newark PMSA, NJ-PA	Y	31750 FQ	35050 MW	38340 TQ	USBLS	5/15
	New Mexico	Y	28740 FQ	32660 MW	39270 TQ	USBLS	5/15
	New York	Y	34010 AE	45890 MW	49860 AEX	NYBLS	1/16-3/16
	New York-Jersey City-White Plains PMSA, NY-NJ	Y	32490 FQ	42680 MW	52660 TQ	USBLS	5/15
	Rochester MSA, NY	Y	34650 FQ	42750 MW	50820 TQ	USBLS	5/15
	North Carolina	Y	31640 FQ	36060 MW	43680 TQ	USBLS	5/15
	Charlotte-Concord-Gastonia MSA, NC-SC	Y	31390 FQ	36480 MW	46060 TQ	USBLS	5/15
	North Dakota	Y	31540 FQ	42320 MW	50410 TQ	USBLS	5/15
	Fargo MSA, ND-MN	Y	31690 FQ	43610 MW	51770 TQ	USBLS	5/15
	Ohio	Y	35140 FQ	47240 MW	57130 TQ	USBLS	5/15
	Cincinnati MSA, OH-KY-IN	Y	36470 FQ	52510 MW	65070 TQ	USBLS	5/15
	Columbus MSA, OH	Y	33580 FQ	38830 MW	50490 TQ	USBLS	5/15
	Oklahoma	Y	31860 FQ	37470 MW	44110 TQ	USBLS	5/15
	Oklahoma City MSA, OK	Y	33980 FQ	40410 MW	45900 TQ	USBLS	5/15
	Tulsa MSA, OK	Y	27770 FQ	31660 MW	36780 TQ	USBLS	5/15
	Oregon	H	16.44 FQ	18.67 MW	22.32 TQ	ORBLS	2016
	Portland-Vancouver-Hillsboro MSA, OR-WA	Y	33080 FQ	37670 MW	46500 TQ	USBLS	5/15
	Pennsylvania	Y	26630 FQ	30980 MW	38490 TQ	USBLS	5/15
	Allentown-Bethlehem-Easton MSA, PA-NJ	Y	36780 FQ	46280 MW	60170 TQ	USBLS	5/15
	Montgomery County-Bucks County-Chester County PMSA, PA	Y	29480 FQ	35280 MW	47150 TQ	USBLS	5/15
	Pittsburgh MSA, PA	Y	28300 FQ	34810 MW	42910 TQ	USBLS	5/15
	South Carolina	Y	30380 FQ	41330 MW	49200 TQ	USBLS	5/15
	Greenville-Anderson-Mauldin MSA, SC	Y	29510 FQ	40000 MW	52640 TQ	USBLS	5/15
	South Dakota	Y	28460 FQ	32520 MW	36630 TQ	USBLS	5/15
	Tennessee	Y	27180 FQ	32000 MW	44370 TQ	USBLS	5/15
	Texas	Y	27600 FQ	35470 MW	45310 TQ	USBLS	5/15
	Dallas-Plano-Irving PMSA, TX	Y	33640 FQ	43300 MW	51890 TQ	USBLS	5/15
	Fort Worth-Arlington PMSA, TX	Y	28640 FQ	36700 MW	47550 TQ	USBLS	5/15

AE	Average entry wage	AWR	Average wage range	
AEX	Average experienced wage	B	Biweekly	
ATC	Average total compensation	D	Daily	
AW	Average wage paid	FQ	First quartile wage	

H	Hourly	
HI	Highest wage paid	
HR	High end range	
LO	Lowest wage paid	

LR	Low end range	
M	Monthly	
MCC	Median cash compensation	
ME	Median entry wage	

MTC	Median total compensation	
MW	Median wage paid	
MWR	Median wage range	
S	See annotated source	

TCC	Total cash compensation	
TQ	Third quartile wage	
W	Weekly	
Y	Yearly	

Occupation/Type/Industry	Location	Per	Low	Mid	High	Source	Date
Engine and Other Machine Assembler	Houston-The Woodlands-Sugar Land MSA, TX	Y	27690 FQ	35450 MW	44290 TQ	USBLS	5/15
	San Antonio-New Braunfels MSA, TX	Y	29590 FQ	40630 MW	47750 TQ	USBLS	5/15
	Utah	Y	28970 FQ	33990 MW	38450 TQ	USBLS	5/15
	Salt Lake City MSA, UT	Y	27710 FQ	32290 MW	36420 TQ	USBLS	5/15
	Vermont	Y	32920 FQ	36230 MW	39540 TQ	USBLS	5/15
	Virginia	Y	32310 FQ	38970 MW	49250 TQ	USBLS	5/15
	Virginia Beach-Norfolk-Newport News MSA, VA-NC	Y	38230 FQ	44870 MW	51360 TQ	USBLS	5/15
	Washington	H	18.09 FQ	20.75 MW	23.55 TQ	WABLS	3/16
	Seattle-Bellevue-Everett PMSA, WA	H	18.13 FQ	20.74 MW	23.48 TQ	WABLS	3/16
	West Virginia	Y	35520 FQ	52320 MW	58760 TQ	USBLS	5/15
	Wisconsin	Y	30260 FQ	39890 MW	52070 TQ	USBLS	5/15
	Milwaukee-Waukesha-West Allis MSA, WI	Y	32380 FQ	40570 MW	46760 TQ	USBLS	5/15
Engineer	Silicon Valley, CA	Y	105000 LO			FORB02	2016
Engineering Aide							
Municipal Government	Seattle, WA	H	24.48 LO		28.50 HI	CSSS	1/13/16
Engineering Geologist							
Department of Water and Power, Municipal Government	Los Angeles, CA	Y			145205 HI	CACIT	6/23/16
Engineering Teacher							
Postsecondary	Alabama	Y	75471 AE	131065 AW	158862 AEX	ALBLS	6/16
Postsecondary	Arizona	Y	71980 FQ	93730 MW	124260 TQ	USBLS	5/15
Postsecondary	Arkansas	Y	45380 FQ	79210 MW	100490 TQ	USBLS	5/15
Postsecondary	California	Y		120045 AW		CABLS	1/16-3/16
Postsecondary	Colorado	Y	43680 FQ	80520 MW	116300 TQ	USBLS	5/15
Postsecondary	Connecticut	Y		89357 AW		CTBLS	1/16-3/16
Postsecondary	Florida	Y	64412 AE	112039 MW	149337 AEX	FLBLS	7/16-9/16
Postsecondary	Georgia	Y	54310 FQ	82170 MW	110510 TQ	USBLS	5/15
Postsecondary	Idaho	Y	53630 FQ	79690 MW	103790 TQ	USBLS	5/15
Postsecondary	Illinois	Y	62930 FQ	92970 MW	124620 TQ	USBLS	5/15
Postsecondary	Indiana	Y	74520 FQ	99750 MW	130920 TQ	USBLS	5/15
Postsecondary	Iowa	Y	74840 FQ	94950 MW	124810 TQ	USBLS	5/15
Postsecondary	Kansas	Y	51260 FQ	63020 MW	75310 TQ	USBLS	5/15
Postsecondary	Kentucky	Y	95490 FQ	116220 MW	143700 TQ	USBLS	5/15
Postsecondary	Louisiana	Y	51690 FQ	73960 MW	101140 TQ	USBLS	5/15
Postsecondary	Maine	Y	72670 FQ	93600 MW	116670 TQ	USBLS	5/15
Postsecondary	Massachusetts	Y	84130 FQ	115160 MW	150440 TQ	USBLS	5/15
Postsecondary	Michigan	Y	82070 FQ	103410 MW	133920 TQ	USBLS	5/15
Postsecondary	Minnesota	Y	61592 FQ	69435 MW	76098 TQ	MNBLS	1/16-3/16
Postsecondary	Mississippi	Y	82500 FQ	96100 MW	121260 TQ	USBLS	5/15
Postsecondary	Missouri	Y	64470 FQ	90200 MW	121270 TQ	USBLS	5/15
Postsecondary	Montana	Y	59240 FQ	71090 MW	83860 TQ	USBLS	5/15
Postsecondary	Nebraska	Y	73760 FQ	92650 MW	127520 TQ	NEBLS	7/16-9/16
Postsecondary	New Hampshire	Y	72243 AE	111000 MW	141850 AEX	NHBLS	6/16
Postsecondary	New Jersey	Y	76890 FQ	104590 MW	140660 TQ	USBLS	5/15
Postsecondary	New Mexico	Y	80950 FQ	110550 MW	131790 TQ	USBLS	5/15
Postsecondary	New York	Y	60620 AE	101980 MW	137510 AEX	NYBLS	1/16-3/16
Postsecondary	North Carolina	Y	62640 FQ	89720 MW	119220 TQ	USBLS	5/15
Postsecondary	Ohio	Y	62830 FQ	91780 MW	124510 TQ	USBLS	5/15
Postsecondary	Oklahoma	Y	66630 FQ	85730 MW	101010 TQ	USBLS	5/15
Postsecondary	Oregon	Y	79573 FQ	100561 MW	128268 TQ	ORBLS	2016
Postsecondary	Pennsylvania	Y	68190 FQ	98180 MW	139340 TQ	USBLS	5/15
Postsecondary	Rhode Island	Y	76760 FQ	98180 MW	125160 TQ	USBLS	5/15
Postsecondary	South Carolina	Y	59670 FQ	83360 MW	103630 TQ	USBLS	5/15
Postsecondary	South Dakota	Y	65050 FQ	77660 MW	96360 TQ	USBLS	5/15
Postsecondary	Tennessee	Y	69160 FQ	92680 MW	122150 TQ	USBLS	5/15
Postsecondary	Texas	Y	68390 FQ	97590 MW	136630 TQ	USBLS	5/15
Postsecondary	Utah	Y	70300 FQ	100870 MW	131710 TQ	USBLS	5/15
Postsecondary	Virginia	Y	52700 FQ	76310 MW	104090 TQ	USBLS	5/15
Postsecondary	Washington	Y		92491 AW		WABLS	3/16
Postsecondary	West Virginia	Y	57930 FQ	84040 MW	107140 TQ	USBLS	5/15
Postsecondary	Wisconsin	Y	74820 FQ	95340 MW	126370 TQ	USBLS	5/15
Postsecondary	Wyoming	Y	70640 FQ	89180 MW	107170 TQ	USBLS	5/15

AE Average entry wage	**AWR** Average wage range	**H** Hourly	**LR** Low end range	**MTC** Median total compensation	**TCC** Total cash compensation
AEX Average experienced wage	**B** Biweekly	**HI** Highest wage paid	**M** Monthly	**MW** Median wage paid	**TQ** Third quartile wage
ATC Average total compensation	**D** Daily	**HR** High end range	**MCC** Median cash compensation	**MWR** Median wage range	**W** Weekly
AW Average wage paid	**FQ** First quartile wage	**LO** Lowest wage paid	**ME** Median entry wage	**S** See annotated source	**Y** Yearly

Occupation/Type/Industry	Location	Per	Low	Mid	High	Source	Date
Engineering Teacher							
Postsecondary	Puerto Rico	Y	45050 FQ	64770 MW	82890 TQ	USBLS	5/15
English Language and Literature Teacher							
Postsecondary	Alabama	Y	38908 AE	58968 AW	68988 AEX	ALBLS	6/16
Postsecondary	Birmingham-Hoover MSA, AL	Y	43474 AE	62209 AW	71567 AEX	ALBLS	6/16
Postsecondary	Alaska	Y	79550 FQ	88530 MW	97560 TQ	USBLS	5/15
Postsecondary	Arizona	Y	42520 FQ	59250 MW	80690 TQ	USBLS	5/15
Postsecondary	Phoenix-Mesa-Scottsdale MSA, AZ	Y	46340 FQ	61350 MW	84900 TQ	USBLS	5/15
Postsecondary	Arkansas	Y	43370 FQ	51430 MW	64050 TQ	USBLS	5/15
Postsecondary	Little Rock-North Little Rock-Conway MSA, AR	Y	42030 FQ	55550 MW	71700 TQ	USBLS	5/15
Postsecondary	California	Y		92086 AW		CABLS	1/16-3/16
Postsecondary	Anaheim-Santa Ana-Irvine PMSA, CA	Y		121384 AW		CABLS	1/16-3/16
Postsecondary	Los Angeles-Long Beach-Glendale PMSA, CA	Y		92187 AW		CABLS	1/16-3/16
Postsecondary	Riverside-San Bernardino-Ontario MSA, CA	Y		99999 AW		CABLS	1/16-3/16
Postsecondary	Sacramento–Roseville–Arden-Arcade MSA, CA	Y		76026 AW		CABLS	1/16-3/16
Postsecondary	San Diego-Carlsbad MSA, CA	Y		94348 AW		CABLS	1/16-3/16
Postsecondary	San Francisco-Redwood City-South San Francisco PMSA, CA	Y		81748 AW		CABLS	1/16-3/16
Postsecondary	Colorado	Y	35080 FQ	44620 MW	60830 TQ	USBLS	5/15
Postsecondary	Denver-Aurora-Lakewood MSA, CO	Y	34910 FQ	42470 MW	58780 TQ	USBLS	5/15
Postsecondary	Connecticut	Y		73896 MW		CTBLS	1/16-3/16
Postsecondary	Bridgeport-Stamford-Norwalk MSA, CT	Y	60450 FQ	77110 MW	97040 TQ	USBLS	5/15
Postsecondary	Hartford-West Hartford-East Hartford MSA, CT	Y	58370 FQ	74030 MW	91140 TQ	USBLS	5/15
Postsecondary	Delaware	Y	60150 FQ	68380 MW	74460 TQ	USBLS	5/15
Postsecondary	Wilmington PMSA, DE-MD-NJ	Y	56340 FQ	67640 MW	74460 TQ	USBLS	5/15
Postsecondary	District of Columbia	Y	53320 FQ	65160 MW	92750 TQ	USBLS	5/15
Postsecondary	Washington-Arlington-Alexandria PMSA, DC-VA-MD-WV	Y	45150 FQ	57050 MW	77980 TQ	USBLS	5/15
Postsecondary	Florida	Y	41805 AE	65095 MW	83028 AEX	FLBLS	7/16-9/16
Postsecondary	Fort Lauderdale-Pompano Beach-Deerfield Beach PMSA, FL	Y	52065 AE	68716 MW	74691 AEX	FLBLS	7/16-9/16
Postsecondary	Miami-Miami Beach-Kendall PMSA, FL	Y	52733 AE	84302 MW	91316 AEX	FLBLS	7/16-9/16
Postsecondary	Tampa-St. Petersburg-Clearwater MSA, FL	Y	42585 AE	72103 MW	97707 AEX	FLBLS	7/16-9/16
Postsecondary	Georgia	Y	45590 FQ	58840 MW	80750 TQ	USBLS	5/15
Postsecondary	Atlanta-Sandy Springs-Roswell MSA, GA	Y	41540 FQ	49070 MW	62420 TQ	USBLS	5/15
Postsecondary	Hawaii	Y	34720 FQ	57140 MW	75350 TQ	USBLS	5/15
Postsecondary	Urban Honolulu MSA, HI	Y	34280 FQ	57460 MW	77180 TQ	USBLS	5/15
Postsecondary	Idaho	Y	33280 FQ	45360 MW	56270 TQ	USBLS	5/15
Postsecondary	Boise City MSA, ID	Y	19260 FQ	42810 MW	49550 TQ	USBLS	5/15
Postsecondary	Illinois	Y	49930 FQ	67970 MW	96640 TQ	USBLS	5/15
Postsecondary	Chicago-Naperville-Arlington Heights PMSA, IL	Y	48210 FQ	63380 MW	89700 TQ	USBLS	5/15
Postsecondary	Lake County-Kenosha County PMSA, IL-WI	Y	44400 FQ	58500 MW	79940 TQ	USBLS	5/15
Postsecondary	Indiana	Y	44980 FQ	58200 MW	74990 TQ	USBLS	5/15
Postsecondary	Indianapolis-Carmel-Anderson MSA, IN	Y	47820 FQ	62850 MW	76760 TQ	USBLS	5/15
Postsecondary	Iowa	Y	42520 FQ	59090 MW	77240 TQ	USBLS	5/15
Postsecondary	Des Moines-West Des Moines MSA, IA	Y	36960 FQ	54420 MW	69240 TQ	USBLS	5/15
Postsecondary	Kansas	Y	40820 FQ	50720 MW	64750 TQ	USBLS	5/15
Postsecondary	Kentucky	Y	43870 FQ	57490 MW	75310 TQ	USBLS	5/15
Postsecondary	Louisville-Jefferson County MSA, KY-IN	Y	46720 FQ	61720 MW	84510 TQ	USBLS	5/15

AE	Average entry wage	AWR	Average wage range	H	Hourly	LR	Low end range	MTC	Median total compensation	TCC	Total cash compensation
AEX	Average experienced wage	B	Biweekly	HI	Highest wage paid	M	Monthly	MW	Median wage paid	TQ	Third quartile wage
ATC	Average total compensation	D	Daily	HR	High end range	MCC	Median cash compensation	MWR	Median wage range	W	Weekly
AW	Average wage paid	FQ	First quartile wage	LO	Lowest wage paid	ME	Median entry wage	S	See annotated source	Y	Yearly

Occupation/Type/Industry	Location	Per	Low	Mid	High	Source	Date
English Language and Literature Teacher							
Postsecondary	Louisiana	Y	33300 FQ	46360 MW	69770 TQ	USBLS	5/15
Postsecondary	Maine	Y	41620 FQ	54360 MW	76060 TQ	USBLS	5/15
Postsecondary	Portland-South Portland MSA, ME	Y	31210 FQ	44240 MW	72470 TQ	USBLS	5/15
Postsecondary	Maryland	Y	41417 AE	70503 MW	85046 AEX	MDBLS	4/16
Postsecondary	Baltimore-Columbia-Towson MSA, MD	Y	53050 FQ	65230 MW	86370 TQ	USBLS	5/15
Postsecondary	Salisbury MSA, MD-DE	Y	45290 FQ	58440 MW	70230 TQ	USBLS	5/15
Postsecondary	Massachusetts	Y	52960 FQ	67500 MW	86040 TQ	USBLS	5/15
Postsecondary	Boston-Cambridge-Newton NECTA, MA	Y	53730 FQ	69420 MW	92140 TQ	USBLS	5/15
Postsecondary	Worcester MSA, MA-CT	Y	48570 FQ	58070 MW	71400 TQ	USBLS	5/15
Postsecondary	Michigan	Y	47090 FQ	65470 MW	89030 TQ	USBLS	5/15
Postsecondary	Detroit-Dearborn-Livonia PMSA, MI	Y	55280 FQ	68600 MW	86290 TQ	USBLS	5/15
Postsecondary	Grand Rapids-Wyoming MSA, MI	Y	36410 FQ	50070 MW	71360 TQ	USBLS	5/15
Postsecondary	Minnesota	Y	44979 FQ	58094 MW	76965 TQ	MNBLS	1/16-3/16
Postsecondary	Minneapolis-St. Paul-Bloomington MSA, MN-WI	Y	42610 FQ	54485 MW	71310 TQ	MNBLS	1/16-3/16
Postsecondary	Mississippi	Y	44310 FQ	54670 MW	67380 TQ	USBLS	5/15
Postsecondary	Jackson MSA, MS	Y	43210 FQ	52770 MW	70120 TQ	USBLS	5/15
Postsecondary	Missouri	Y	42460 FQ	57760 MW	77720 TQ	USBLS	5/15
Postsecondary	Kansas City MSA, MO-KS	Y	51920 FQ	66180 MW	77790 TQ	USBLS	5/15
Postsecondary	St. Louis MSA, MO-IL	Y	40870 FQ	59660 MW	83660 TQ	USBLS	5/15
Postsecondary	Montana	Y	32870 FQ	50630 MW	63070 TQ	USBLS	5/15
Postsecondary	Nebraska	Y	50240 FQ	61395 MW	78505 TQ	NEBLS	7/16-9/16
Postsecondary	Nevada	Y	36940 FQ	52270 MW	70300 TQ	USBLS	5/15
Postsecondary	New Hampshire	Y	55824 AE	76512 MW	92098 AEX	NHBLS	6/16
Postsecondary	New Jersey	Y	50690 FQ	69150 MW	95830 TQ	USBLS	5/15
Postsecondary	Newark PMSA, NJ-PA	Y	53280 FQ	72670 MW	104400 TQ	USBLS	5/15
Postsecondary	New Mexico	Y	52440 FQ	65050 MW	87100 TQ	USBLS	5/15
Postsecondary	New York	Y	46080 AE	76640 MW	115540 AEX	NYBLS	1/16-3/16
Postsecondary	Buffalo-Cheektowaga-Niagara Falls MSA, NY	Y	39840 FQ	60440 MW	86990 TQ	USBLS	5/15
Postsecondary	Nassau County-Suffolk County PMSA, NY	Y	48430 FQ	64800 MW	90590 TQ	USBLS	5/15
Postsecondary	New York-Jersey City-White Plains PMSA, NY-NJ	Y	57720 FQ	84020 MW	136140 TQ	USBLS	5/15
Postsecondary	Rochester MSA, NY	Y	50360 FQ	69290 MW	91900 TQ	USBLS	5/15
Postsecondary	North Carolina	Y	45370 FQ	56550 MW	70470 TQ	USBLS	5/15
Postsecondary	Charlotte-Concord-Gastonia MSA, NC-SC	Y	45760 FQ	55620 MW	68350 TQ	USBLS	5/15
Postsecondary	Raleigh MSA, NC	Y	41220 FQ	50130 MW	63030 TQ	USBLS	5/15
Postsecondary	North Dakota	Y	43500 FQ	59770 MW	80540 TQ	USBLS	5/15
Postsecondary	Fargo MSA, ND-MN	Y	53630 FQ	66220 MW	84870 TQ	USBLS	5/15
Postsecondary	Ohio	Y	44200 FQ	61160 MW	86400 TQ	USBLS	5/15
Postsecondary	Cincinnati MSA, OH-KY-IN	Y	44690 FQ	59370 MW	80170 TQ	USBLS	5/15
Postsecondary	Cleveland-Elyria MSA, OH	Y	46750 FQ	65440 MW	91560 TQ	USBLS	5/15
Postsecondary	Columbus MSA, OH	Y	48500 FQ	67850 MW	103780 TQ	USBLS	5/15
Postsecondary	Oklahoma	Y	40770 FQ	53470 MW	78770 TQ	USBLS	5/15
Postsecondary	Oklahoma City MSA, OK	Y	32690 FQ	43710 MW	59890 TQ	USBLS	5/15
Postsecondary	Tulsa MSA, OK	Y	59240 FQ	87120 MW	96570 TQ	USBLS	5/15
Postsecondary	Oregon	Y	48945 FQ	67022 MW	84990 TQ	ORBLS	2016
Postsecondary	Portland-Vancouver-Hillsboro MSA, OR-WA	Y	42160 FQ	60310 MW	81460 TQ	USBLS	5/15
Postsecondary	Pennsylvania	Y	49810 FQ	64430 MW	86710 TQ	USBLS	5/15
Postsecondary	Allentown-Bethlehem-Easton MSA, PA-NJ	Y	52950 FQ	70670 MW	96680 TQ	USBLS	5/15
Postsecondary	Harrisburg-Carlisle MSA, PA	Y	52130 FQ	68230 MW	89120 TQ	USBLS	5/15
Postsecondary	Montgomery County-Bucks County-Chester County PMSA, PA	Y	51670 FQ	59890 MW	78040 TQ	USBLS	5/15
Postsecondary	Philadelphia PMSA, PA	Y	49550 FQ	65000 MW	86070 TQ	USBLS	5/15
Postsecondary	Pittsburgh MSA, PA	Y	40250 FQ	59190 MW	78810 TQ	USBLS	5/15
Postsecondary	Rhode Island	Y	53320 FQ	67160 MW	86100 TQ	USBLS	5/15
Postsecondary	Providence-Warwick MSA, RI-MA	Y	53890 FQ	66930 MW	83950 TQ	USBLS	5/15
Postsecondary	South Carolina	Y	45790 FQ	58330 MW	73520 TQ	USBLS	5/15
Postsecondary	Columbia MSA, SC	Y	45410 FQ	59450 MW	75910 TQ	USBLS	5/15

AE	Average entry wage	AWR	Average wage range	H	Hourly
AEX	Average experienced wage	B	Biweekly	HI	Highest wage paid
ATC	Average total compensation	D	Daily	HR	High end range
AW	Average wage paid	FQ	First quartile wage	LO	Lowest wage paid

LR	Low end range	MTC	Median total compensation
M	Monthly	MW	Median wage paid
MCC	Median cash compensation	MWR	Median wage range
ME	Median entry wage	S	See annotated source

TCC	Total cash compensation		
TQ	Third quartile wage		
W	Weekly		
Y	Yearly		

529

Occupation/Type/Industry	Location	Per	Low	Mid	High	Source	Date
English Language and Literature Teacher							
Postsecondary	Greenville-Anderson-Mauldin MSA, SC	Y	42660 FQ	54550 MW	71930 TQ	USBLS	5/15
Postsecondary	South Dakota	Y	46640 FQ	55580 MW	66120 TQ	USBLS	5/15
Postsecondary	Sioux Falls MSA, SD	Y	47740 FQ	56400 MW	67120 TQ	USBLS	5/15
Postsecondary	Tennessee	Y	28920 FQ	39840 MW	58310 TQ	USBLS	5/15
Postsecondary	Knoxville MSA, TN	Y	32130 FQ	37760 MW	52080 TQ	USBLS	5/15
Postsecondary	Memphis MSA, TN-MS-AR	Y	33800 FQ	47320 MW	69640 TQ	USBLS	5/15
Postsecondary	Nashville-Davidson– Murfreesboro–Franklin MSA, TN	Y	26410 FQ	42540 MW	58860 TQ	USBLS	5/15
Postsecondary	Texas	Y	40030 FQ	58020 MW	78430 TQ	USBLS	5/15
Postsecondary	Austin-Round Rock MSA, TX	Y	40500 FQ	55600 MW	75120 TQ	USBLS	5/15
Postsecondary	Dallas-Plano-Irving PMSA, TX	Y	40600 FQ	57730 MW	75500 TQ	USBLS	5/15
Postsecondary	Fort Worth-Arlington PMSA, TX	Y	26640 FQ	49750 MW	64590 TQ	USBLS	5/15
Postsecondary	Houston-The Woodlands- Sugar Land MSA, TX	Y	48570 FQ	71890 MW	103860 TQ	USBLS	5/15
Postsecondary	San Antonio-New Braunfels MSA, TX	Y	23130 FQ	42680 MW	81270 TQ	USBLS	5/15
Postsecondary	Utah	Y	48460 FQ	63180 MW	86140 TQ	USBLS	5/15
Postsecondary	Ogden-Clearfield MSA, UT	Y	43420 FQ	56590 MW	70700 TQ	USBLS	5/15
Postsecondary	Provo-Orem MSA, UT	Y	55490 FQ	75790 MW	95250 TQ	USBLS	5/15
Postsecondary	Salt Lake City MSA, UT	Y	45950 FQ	58670 MW	76900 TQ	USBLS	5/15
Postsecondary	Vermont	Y	38080 FQ	46320 MW	68880 TQ	USBLS	5/15
Postsecondary	Burlington-South Burlington MSA, VT	Y	35260 FQ	44680 MW	61660 TQ	USBLS	5/15
Postsecondary	Virginia	Y	38370 FQ	50060 MW	66730 TQ	USBLS	5/15
Postsecondary	Richmond MSA, VA	Y	33330 FQ	42750 MW	59190 TQ	USBLS	5/15
Postsecondary	Virginia Beach-Norfolk- Newport News MSA, VA-NC	Y	37930 FQ	47490 MW	61970 TQ	USBLS	5/15
Postsecondary	Washington	Y		56233 AW		WABLS	3/16
Postsecondary	Seattle-Bellevue-Everett PMSA, WA	Y		63396 AW		WABLS	3/16
Postsecondary	Tacoma-Lakewood PMSA, WA	Y		58080 AW		WABLS	3/16
Postsecondary	West Virginia	Y	41430 FQ	54950 MW	68320 TQ	USBLS	5/15
Postsecondary	Wisconsin	Y	43500 FQ	56840 MW	77630 TQ	USBLS	5/15
Postsecondary	Milwaukee-Waukesha-West Allis MSA, WI	Y	45740 FQ	59730 MW	83570 TQ	USBLS	5/15
Postsecondary	Wyoming	Y	52290 FQ	59580 MW	70570 TQ	USBLS	5/15
Postsecondary	Puerto Rico	Y	38530 FQ	59830 MW	77270 TQ	USBLS	5/15
Postsecondary	San Juan-Carolina-Caguas MSA, PR	Y	30520 FQ	62300 MW	83760 TQ	USBLS	5/15
Enlisted Member							
Military, Active Duty, Pay Grade E-1 < 4 Months	United States	M		1600 AW		DOD1	2017
Military, Active Duty, Pay Grade E-1 > 4 Months	United States	M		1479 AW		DOD1	2017
Military, Active Duty, Pay Grade E-2	United States	M		1793 AW		DOD1	2017
Military, Active Duty, Pay Grade E-3	United States	M	1886 LO		2126 HI	DOD1	2017
Military, Active Duty, Pay Grade E-4	United States	M	2089 LO		2354 HI	DOD1	2017
Military, Active Duty, Pay Grade E-5	United States	M	2278 LO		3233 HI	DOD1	2017
Military, Active Duty, Pay Grade E-6	United States	M	2487 LO		3852 HI	DOD1	2017
Military, Active Duty, Pay Grade E-7	United States	M	2875 LO		5168 HI	DOD1	2017
Military, Active Duty, Pay Grade E-8	United States	M	4136 LO		5899 HI	DOD1	2017
Military, Active Duty, Pay Grade E-9	United States	M	5053 LO		7845 HI	DOD1	2017
Military, Reserve, 4-Drill Pay Grade E-1	United States	S		1600 AW		DOD1	2017
Military, Reserve, 4-Drill Pay Grade E-2	United States	S		1793 AW		DOD1	2017
Military, Reserve, 4-Drill Pay Grade E-3	United States	S	1886 LO		2126 HI	DOD1	2017
Military, Reserve, 4-Drill Pay Grade E-4	United States	S	2089 LO		2536 HI	DOD1	2017
Military, Reserve, 4-Drill Pay Grade E-5	United States	S	2278 LO		3233 HI	DOD1	2017
Military, Reserve, 4-Drill Pay Grade E-6	United States	S	2487 LO		3852 HI	DOD1	2017
Military, Reserve, 4-Drill Pay Grade E-7	United States	S	2875 LO		5168 HI	DOD1	2017
Military, Reserve, 4-Drill Pay Grade E-8	United States	S	4136 LO		5899 HI	DOD1	2017
Military, Reserve, 4-Drill Pay Grade E-9	United States	S	5052 LO		7845 HI	DOD1	2017
Enologist	United States	Y		59970 AW		WBM	2/1/16
Enterostomal Therapist	United States	Y		74639 MW		FPAT	2015

AE	Average entry wage	AWR	Average wage range	H	Hourly	LR	Low end range	MTC	Median total compensation	TCC	Total cash compensation
AEX	Average experienced wage	B	Biweekly	HI	Highest wage paid	M	Monthly	MW	Median wage paid	TQ	Third quartile wage
ATC	Average total compensation	D	Daily	HR	High end range	MCC	Median cash compensation	MWR	Median wage range	W	Weekly
AW	Average wage paid	FQ	First quartile wage	LO	Lowest wage paid	ME	Median entry wage	S	See annotated source	Y	Yearly

Occupation/Type/Industry	Location	Per	Low	Mid	High	Source	Date
Enterprise Architect	United States	Y		120759 AW		CWRLD3	2016
Entry-Level Assembler							
Automotive Cameras, Magna Electronics	Holly, MI	H			14.00 HI	LSJ10	2016
Environmental Analyst							
Water Pollution Control Pit, Municipal Government	Pinole, CA	Y			77132 HI	CACIT	6/28/16
Environmental Chemist							
State Government	North Carolina	Y	44347 LO		72346 HI	NCGOV	7/1/16
Environmental Compliance Coordinator							
Public Works Department, Municipal Government	Fort Bragg, CA	Y			54663 HI	CACIT	6/28/16
Environmental Engineer	Alabama	Y	49488 AE	82239 AW	98620 AEX	ALBLS	6/16
	Birmingham-Hoover MSA, AL	Y	43556 AE	65695 AW	76765 AEX	ALBLS	6/16
	Alaska	Y	86390 FQ	107400 MW	138470 TQ	USBLS	5/15
	Anchorage MSA, AK	Y	94990 FQ	116700 MW	159410 TQ	USBLS	5/15
	Arizona	Y	58180 FQ	76360 MW	98090 TQ	USBLS	5/15
	Phoenix-Mesa-Scottsdale MSA, AZ	Y	57590 FQ	75020 MW	97570 TQ	USBLS	5/15
	Tucson MSA, AZ	Y	65810 FQ	87340 MW	125770 TQ	USBLS	5/15
	Arkansas	Y	58150 FQ	73800 MW	93630 TQ	USBLS	5/15
	Little Rock-North Little Rock-Conway MSA, AR	Y	54550 FQ	64600 MW	79140 TQ	USBLS	5/15
	California	H	39.97 FQ	49.29 MW	59.87 TQ	CABLS	1/16-3/16
	Anaheim-Santa Ana-Irvine PMSA, CA	H	40.40 FQ	53.72 MW	70.29 TQ	CABLS	1/16-3/16
	Los Angeles-Long Beach-Glendale PMSA, CA	H	45.20 FQ	52.24 MW	60.83 TQ	CABLS	1/16-3/16
	Oakland-Hayward-Berkeley PMSA, CA	H	40.48 FQ	50.27 MW	60.60 TQ	CABLS	1/16-3/16
	Riverside-San Bernardino-Ontario MSA, CA	H	21.65 FQ	36.77 MW	48.07 TQ	CABLS	1/16-3/16
	Sacramento–Roseville–Arden-Arcade MSA, CA	H	44.59 FQ	51.08 MW	60.18 TQ	CABLS	1/16-3/16
	San Diego-Carlsbad MSA, CA	H	36.48 FQ	44.74 MW	51.96 TQ	CABLS	1/16-3/16
	San Francisco-Redwood City-South San Francisco PMSA, CA	H	46.20 FQ	56.21 MW	62.64 TQ	CABLS	1/16-3/16
	Colorado	Y	70540 FQ	90390 MW	112740 TQ	USBLS	5/15
	Denver-Aurora-Lakewood MSA, CO	Y	73380 FQ	92280 MW	113470 TQ	USBLS	5/15
	Connecticut	Y		92877 MW		CTBLS	1/16-3/16
	Bridgeport-Stamford-Norwalk MSA, CT	Y	79370 FQ	91190 MW	102820 TQ	USBLS	5/15
	Hartford-West Hartford-East Hartford MSA, CT	Y	77680 FQ	93720 MW	107700 TQ	USBLS	5/15
	Delaware	Y	67210 FQ	84870 MW	131000 TQ	USBLS	5/15
	District of Columbia	Y	80400 FQ	99300 MW	112030 TQ	USBLS	5/15
	Washington-Arlington-Alexandria PMSA, DC-VA-MD-WV	Y	72900 FQ	98560 MW	118080 TQ	USBLS	5/15
	Florida	H	20.57 AE	30.62 MW	42.26 AEX	FLBLS	7/16-9/16
	Fort Lauderdale-Pompano Beach-Deerfield Beach PMSA, FL	H	21.92 AE	27.12 MW	41.49 AEX	FLBLS	7/16-9/16
	Miami-Miami Beach-Kendall PMSA, FL	H	23.06 AE	32.49 MW	44.08 AEX	FLBLS	7/16-9/16
	Orlando-Kissimmee-Sanford MSA, FL	H	23.42 AE	36.19 MW	48.01 AEX	FLBLS	7/16-9/16
	Tampa-St. Petersburg-Clearwater MSA, FL	H	17.49 AE	27.65 MW	36.55 AEX	FLBLS	7/16-9/16
	Georgia	Y	46110 FQ	63410 MW	90630 TQ	USBLS	5/15
	Atlanta-Sandy Springs-Roswell MSA, GA	Y	48160 FQ	68490 MW	93920 TQ	USBLS	5/15
	Augusta-Richmond County MSA, GA-SC	Y	67640 FQ	77840 MW	109610 TQ	USBLS	5/15
	Hawaii	Y	67910 FQ	85630 MW	95200 TQ	USBLS	5/15

AE Average entry wage	**AWR** Average wage range	**H** Hourly	**LR** Low end range	**MTC** Median total compensation	**TCC** Total cash compensation
AEX Average experienced wage	**B** Biweekly	**HI** Highest wage paid	**M** Monthly	**MW** Median wage paid	**TQ** Third quartile wage
ATC Average total compensation	**D** Daily	**HR** High end range	**MCC** Median cash compensation	**MWR** Median wage range	**W** Weekly
AW Average wage paid	**FQ** First quartile wage	**LO** Lowest wage paid	**ME** Median entry wage	**S** See annotated source	**Y** Yearly

Occupation/Type/Industry	Location	Per	Low	Mid	High	Source	Date
Environmental Engineer	Urban Honolulu MSA, HI	Y	67350 FQ	87420 MW	95200 TQ	USBLS	5/15
	Idaho	Y	69430 FQ	88510 MW	108490 TQ	USBLS	5/15
	Boise City MSA, ID	Y	70190 FQ	89340 MW	104400 TQ	USBLS	5/15
	Illinois	Y	61200 FQ	84610 MW	100470 TQ	USBLS	5/15
	Chicago-Naperville-Arlington Heights PMSA, IL	Y	56600 FQ	84700 MW	104120 TQ	USBLS	5/15
	Lake County-Kenosha County PMSA, IL-WI	Y	69770 FQ	82040 MW	99930 TQ	USBLS	5/15
	Indiana	Y	60540 FQ	72380 MW	91970 TQ	USBLS	5/15
	Gary PMSA, IN	Y	46100 FQ	56690 MW	82640 TQ	USBLS	5/15
	Indianapolis-Carmel-Anderson MSA, IN	Y	58640 FQ	72560 MW	95940 TQ	USBLS	5/15
	Iowa	Y	65580 FQ	76250 MW	91820 TQ	USBLS	5/15
	Des Moines-West Des Moines MSA, IA	Y	66090 FQ	76060 MW	91810 TQ	USBLS	5/15
	Kansas	Y	72760 FQ	90000 MW	108510 TQ	USBLS	5/15
	Wichita MSA, KS	Y	77300 FQ	96340 MW	114910 TQ	USBLS	5/15
	Kentucky	Y	60880 FQ	73150 MW	91260 TQ	USBLS	5/15
	Louisville-Jefferson County MSA, KY-IN	Y	56820 FQ	70180 MW	80000 TQ	USBLS	5/15
	Louisiana	Y	64690 FQ	86580 MW	113520 TQ	USBLS	5/15
	Baton Rouge MSA, LA	Y	59590 FQ	78490 MW	115960 TQ	USBLS	5/15
	New Orleans-Metairie MSA, LA	Y	85680 FQ	102840 MW	128830 TQ	USBLS	5/15
	Maine	Y	47450 FQ	70820 MW	90320 TQ	USBLS	5/15
	Portland-South Portland MSA, ME	Y	72590 FQ	87110 MW	101390 TQ	USBLS	5/15
	Maryland	Y	62266 AE	91652 MW	106345 AEX	MDBLS	4/16
	Baltimore-Columbia-Towson MSA, MD	Y	67730 FQ	86560 MW	106160 TQ	USBLS	5/15
	Salisbury MSA, MD-DE	Y	73950 FQ	86940 MW	97640 TQ	USBLS	5/15
	Massachusetts	Y	68130 FQ	81740 MW	98980 TQ	USBLS	5/15
	Boston-Cambridge-Newton NECTA, MA	Y	71400 FQ	84820 MW	100000 TQ	USBLS	5/15
	Worcester MSA, MA-CT	Y	63180 FQ	72010 MW	83400 TQ	USBLS	5/15
	Michigan	Y	69720 FQ	83870 MW	102290 TQ	USBLS	5/15
	Detroit-Dearborn-Livonia PMSA, MI	Y	77280 FQ	95180 MW	114410 TQ	USBLS	5/15
	Grand Rapids-Wyoming MSA, MI	Y	66120 FQ	75440 MW	94260 TQ	USBLS	5/15
	Minnesota	Y	60533 FQ	75947 MW	94354 TQ	MNBLS	1/16-3/16
	Minneapolis-St. Paul-Bloomington MSA, MN-WI	Y	60463 FQ	75715 MW	94706 TQ	MNBLS	1/16-3/16
	Mississippi	Y	56570 FQ	67430 MW	82950 TQ	USBLS	5/15
	Jackson MSA, MS	Y	54780 FQ	63670 MW	74320 TQ	USBLS	5/15
	Missouri	Y	55550 FQ	74460 MW	99190 TQ	USBLS	5/15
	Kansas City MSA, MO-KS	Y	64030 FQ	89450 MW	108500 TQ	USBLS	5/15
	St. Louis MSA, MO-IL	Y	63760 FQ	81620 MW	100510 TQ	USBLS	5/15
	Montana	Y	53260 FQ	72780 MW	88680 TQ	USBLS	5/15
	Billings MSA, MT	Y	30150 FQ	60910 MW	81700 TQ	USBLS	5/15
	Nebraska	Y	60710 FQ	77075 MW	95500 TQ	NEBLS	7/16-9/16
	Omaha-Council Bluffs MSA, NE-IA	Y	62310 FQ	77340 MW	96435 TQ	NEBLS	7/16-9/16
	Nevada	Y	64690 FQ	76160 MW	95570 TQ	USBLS	5/15
	Las Vegas-Henderson-Paradise MSA, NV	Y	67710 FQ	77110 MW	95010 TQ	USBLS	5/15
	New Hampshire	H	28.56 AE	41.18 MW	49.04 AEX	NHBLS	6/16
	Manchester NECTA, NH	H	28.54 AE	39.10 MW	45.62 AEX	NHBLS	6/16
	New Jersey	Y	70100 FQ	88650 MW	106230 TQ	USBLS	5/15
	Camden PMSA, NJ	Y	77300 FQ	90490 MW	112150 TQ	USBLS	5/15
	Newark PMSA, NJ-PA	Y	66190 FQ	87670 MW	113040 TQ	USBLS	5/15
	Trenton MSA, NJ	Y	77340 FQ	89440 MW	99320 TQ	USBLS	5/15
	New Mexico	Y	72120 FQ	104860 MW	139100 TQ	USBLS	5/15
	Albuquerque MSA, NM	Y	61760 FQ	83150 MW	110010 TQ	USBLS	5/15
	New York	Y	63090 AE	89160 MW	105750 AEX	NYBLS	1/16-3/16
	Buffalo-Cheektowaga-Niagara Falls MSA, NY	Y	68540 FQ	81760 MW	94090 TQ	USBLS	5/15
	Nassau County-Suffolk County PMSA, NY	Y	65610 FQ	87580 MW	110330 TQ	USBLS	5/15
	New York-Jersey City-White Plains PMSA, NY-NJ	Y	74430 FQ	94410 MW	117830 TQ	USBLS	5/15
	Rochester MSA, NY	Y	70270 FQ	85130 MW	98920 TQ	USBLS	5/15

AE	Average entry wage	AWR	Average wage range	H	Hourly
AEX	Average experienced wage	B	Biweekly	HI	Highest wage paid
ATC	Average total compensation	D	Daily	HR	High end range
AW	Average wage paid	FQ	First quartile wage	LO	Lowest wage paid

LR	Low end range	MTC	Median total compensation	TCC	Total cash compensation
M	Monthly	MW	Median wage paid	TQ	Third quartile wage
MCC	Median cash compensation	MWR	Median wage range	W	Weekly
ME	Median entry wage	S	See annotated source	Y	Yearly

Occupation/Type/Industry	Location	Per	Low	Mid	High	Source	Date
Environmental Engineer	North Carolina	Y	59590 FQ	72910 MW	94600 TQ	USBLS	5/15
	Charlotte-Concord-Gastonia MSA, NC-SC	Y	61340 FQ	74240 MW	96840 TQ	USBLS	5/15
	Raleigh MSA, NC	Y	58200 FQ	68650 MW	87390 TQ	USBLS	5/15
	North Dakota	Y	60250 FQ	77750 MW	93220 TQ	USBLS	5/15
	Ohio	Y	71650 FQ	88410 MW	101490 TQ	USBLS	5/15
	Cincinnati MSA, OH-KY-IN	Y	75110 FQ	95180 MW	116010 TQ	USBLS	5/15
	Columbus MSA, OH	Y	62360 FQ	79240 MW	95440 TQ	USBLS	5/15
	Oklahoma	Y	60390 FQ	79930 MW	104730 TQ	USBLS	5/15
	Oklahoma City MSA, OK	Y	69330 FQ	89360 MW	115560 TQ	USBLS	5/15
	Tulsa MSA, OK	Y	66470 FQ	83060 MW	103230 TQ	USBLS	5/15
	Oregon	H	31.67 FQ	43.14 MW	50.76 TQ	ORBLS	2016
	Portland-Vancouver-Hillsboro MSA, OR-WA	Y	62730 FQ	87370 MW	105030 TQ	USBLS	5/15
	Pennsylvania	Y	60370 FQ	80680 MW	103320 TQ	USBLS	5/15
	Allentown-Bethlehem-Easton MSA, PA-NJ	Y	69860 FQ	86300 MW	102770 TQ	USBLS	5/15
	Harrisburg-Carlisle MSA, PA	Y	60020 FQ	73040 MW	85250 TQ	USBLS	5/15
	Montgomery County-Bucks County-Chester County PMSA, PA	Y	63900 FQ	85250 MW	107180 TQ	USBLS	5/15
	Philadelphia PMSA, PA	Y	62480 FQ	90390 MW	115750 TQ	USBLS	5/15
	Pittsburgh MSA, PA	Y	65800 FQ	82820 MW	103790 TQ	USBLS	5/15
	Rhode Island	Y	63180 FQ	86150 MW	106410 TQ	USBLS	5/15
	Providence-Warwick MSA, RI-MA	Y	62580 FQ	83630 MW	104930 TQ	USBLS	5/15
	South Carolina	Y	57120 FQ	72080 MW	94290 TQ	USBLS	5/15
	Charleston-North Charleston MSA, SC	Y	56550 FQ	71450 MW	91070 TQ	USBLS	5/15
	Columbia MSA, SC	Y	50480 FQ	60080 MW	75190 TQ	USBLS	5/15
	Greenville-Anderson-Mauldin MSA, SC	Y	48480 FQ	65250 MW	81440 TQ	USBLS	5/15
	South Dakota	Y	57930 FQ	70230 MW	91380 TQ	USBLS	5/15
	Sioux Falls MSA, SD	Y	72410 FQ	84780 MW	96060 TQ	USBLS	5/15
	Tennessee	Y	66400 FQ	88330 MW	114340 TQ	USBLS	5/15
	Knoxville MSA, TN	Y	72260 FQ	97970 MW	123030 TQ	USBLS	5/15
	Memphis MSA, TN-MS-AR	Y	67680 FQ	85590 MW	115200 TQ	USBLS	5/15
	Nashville-Davidson–Murfreesboro–Franklin MSA, TN	Y	69620 FQ	87980 MW	106560 TQ	USBLS	5/15
	Texas	Y	70180 FQ	92270 MW	114730 TQ	USBLS	5/15
	Dallas-Plano-Irving PMSA, TX	Y	74290 FQ	93290 MW	113690 TQ	USBLS	5/15
	Fort Worth-Arlington PMSA, TX	Y	71560 FQ	88470 MW	108810 TQ	USBLS	5/15
	Houston-The Woodlands-Sugar Land MSA, TX	Y	63590 FQ	83950 MW	116750 TQ	USBLS	5/15
	San Antonio-New Braunfels MSA, TX	Y	72240 FQ	91240 MW	103800 TQ	USBLS	5/15
	Utah	Y	64480 FQ	79310 MW	96320 TQ	USBLS	5/15
	Ogden-Clearfield MSA, UT	Y	66880 FQ	86580 MW	96690 TQ	USBLS	5/15
	Salt Lake City MSA, UT	Y	64640 FQ	76460 MW	96290 TQ	USBLS	5/15
	Vermont	Y	52270 FQ	67610 MW	85380 TQ	USBLS	5/15
	Burlington-South Burlington MSA, VT	Y	47540 FQ	65290 MW	81600 TQ	USBLS	5/15
	Virginia	Y	63710 FQ	86590 MW	110510 TQ	USBLS	5/15
	Richmond MSA, VA	Y	59770 FQ	84770 MW	117420 TQ	USBLS	5/15
	Virginia Beach-Norfolk-Newport News MSA, VA-NC	Y	66210 FQ	85920 MW	101820 TQ	USBLS	5/15
	Washington	H	37.05 FQ	45.14 MW	54.73 TQ	WABLS	3/16
	Seattle-Bellevue-Everett PMSA, WA	H	37.19 FQ	46.19 MW	56.47 TQ	WABLS	3/16
	Tacoma-Lakewood PMSA, WA	H	33.76 FQ	39.51 MW	49.66 TQ	WABLS	3/16
	West Virginia	Y	54790 FQ	73710 MW	93510 TQ	USBLS	5/15
	Huntington-Ashland MSA, WV-KY-OH	Y	53370 FQ	66500 MW	84860 TQ	USBLS	5/15
	Wisconsin	Y	64390 FQ	77190 MW	89450 TQ	USBLS	5/15
	Madison MSA, WI	Y	66140 FQ	79110 MW	89300 TQ	USBLS	5/15
	Milwaukee-Waukesha-West Allis MSA, WI	Y	64190 FQ	79610 MW	94740 TQ	USBLS	5/15
	Wyoming	Y	65000 FQ	80780 MW	103510 TQ	USBLS	5/15
	Cheyenne MSA, WY	Y	58560 FQ	79790 MW	97750 TQ	USBLS	5/15
	Puerto Rico	Y	41700 FQ	52880 MW	82210 TQ	USBLS	5/15

AE	Average entry wage	AWR	Average wage range	H	Hourly	LR	Low end range	MTC Median total compensation TCC Total cash compensation
AEX	Average experienced wage	B	Biweekly	HI	Highest wage paid	M	Monthly	MW Median wage paid TQ Third quartile wage
ATC	Average total compensation	D	Daily	HR	High end range	MCC Median cash compensation	MWR Median wage range W Weekly
AW	Average wage paid	FQ	First quartile wage	LO	Lowest wage paid	ME Median entry wage	S See annotated source Y Yearly

Occupation/Type/Industry	Location	Per	Low	Mid	High	Source	Date
Environmental Engineer	San Juan-Carolina-Caguas MSA, PR	Y	41310 FQ	50010 MW	87900 TQ	USBLS	5/15
Environmental Engineering Technician							
	Alabama	Y	35982 AE	57480 AW	68223 AEX	ALBLS	6/16
	Birmingham-Hoover MSA, AL	Y	36247 AE	57857 AW	68662 AEX	ALBLS	6/16
	Alaska	Y	52630 FQ	59210 MW	67940 TQ	USBLS	5/15
	Anchorage MSA, AK	Y	51180 FQ	57510 MW	64550 TQ	USBLS	5/15
	Arizona	Y	33040 FQ	47950 MW	60320 TQ	USBLS	5/15
	Phoenix-Mesa-Scottsdale MSA, AZ	Y	29820 FQ	39300 MW	56980 TQ	USBLS	5/15
	Tucson MSA, AZ	Y	37950 FQ	52660 MW	58600 TQ	USBLS	5/15
	Arkansas	Y	35290 FQ	39970 MW	56370 TQ	USBLS	5/15
	Little Rock-North Little Rock-Conway MSA, AR	Y	35280 FQ	37790 MW	45530 TQ	USBLS	5/15
	California	H	22.72 FQ	29.14 MW	37.16 TQ	CABLS	1/16-3/16
	Anaheim-Santa Ana-Irvine PMSA, CA	H	26.03 FQ	29.46 MW	36.44 TQ	CABLS	1/16-3/16
	Los Angeles-Long Beach-Glendale PMSA, CA	H	24.32 FQ	29.68 MW	43.23 TQ	CABLS	1/16-3/16
	Oakland-Hayward-Berkeley PMSA, CA	H	24.87 FQ	32.16 MW	38.13 TQ	CABLS	1/16-3/16
	Riverside-San Bernardino-Ontario MSA, CA	H	26.12 FQ	31.94 MW	36.45 TQ	CABLS	1/16-3/16
	Sacramento–Roseville–Arden-Arcade MSA, CA	H	22.34 FQ	26.70 MW	30.67 TQ	CABLS	1/16-3/16
	San Diego-Carlsbad MSA, CA	H	23.07 FQ	32.94 MW	38.52 TQ	CABLS	1/16-3/16
	San Francisco-Redwood City-South San Francisco PMSA, CA	H	28.13 FQ	32.99 MW	38.81 TQ	CABLS	1/16-3/16
	Colorado	Y	40720 FQ	55490 MW	62850 TQ	USBLS	5/15
	Denver-Aurora-Lakewood MSA, CO	Y	42630 FQ	57100 MW	79800 TQ	USBLS	5/15
	Connecticut	Y		48462 MW		CTBLS	1/16-3/16
	Hartford-West Hartford-East Hartford MSA, CT	Y	39880 FQ	48770 MW	59640 TQ	USBLS	5/15
	Delaware	Y	37920 FQ	43660 MW	56750 TQ	USBLS	5/15
	Washington-Arlington-Alexandria PMSA, DC-VA-MD-WV	Y	42580 FQ	55910 MW	71640 TQ	USBLS	5/15
	Florida	H	14.23 AE	19.34 MW	25.05 AEX	FLBLS	7/16-9/16
	Fort Lauderdale-Pompano Beach-Deerfield Beach PMSA, FL	H	12.79 AE	14.46 MW	18.79 AEX	FLBLS	7/16-9/16
	Miami-Miami Beach-Kendall PMSA, FL	H	13.98 AE	19.20 MW	25.46 AEX	FLBLS	7/16-9/16
	Orlando-Kissimmee-Sanford MSA, FL	H	13.80 AE	17.97 MW	21.94 AEX	FLBLS	7/16-9/16
	Tampa-St. Petersburg-Clearwater MSA, FL	H	17.38 AE	24.97 MW	28.41 AEX	FLBLS	7/16-9/16
	Georgia	Y	35510 FQ	45610 MW	57240 TQ	USBLS	5/15
	Atlanta-Sandy Springs-Roswell MSA, GA	Y	35370 FQ	44810 MW	56620 TQ	USBLS	5/15
	Augusta-Richmond County MSA, GA-SC	Y	42850 FQ	64030 MW	81840 TQ	USBLS	5/15
	Illinois	Y	23370 FQ	40330 MW	56750 TQ	USBLS	5/15
	Chicago-Naperville-Arlington Heights PMSA, IL	Y	31800 FQ	45530 MW	59580 TQ	USBLS	5/15
	Indiana	Y	40580 FQ	47430 MW	58020 TQ	USBLS	5/15
	Indianapolis-Carmel-Anderson MSA, IN	Y	43140 FQ	50110 MW	60190 TQ	USBLS	5/15
	Iowa	Y	35130 FQ	39760 MW	56800 TQ	USBLS	5/15
	Kansas	Y	32640 FQ	42670 MW	48960 TQ	USBLS	5/15
	Kentucky	Y	37250 FQ	45430 MW	55990 TQ	USBLS	5/15
	Louisville-Jefferson County MSA, KY-IN	Y	39740 FQ	46250 MW	62440 TQ	USBLS	5/15
	Louisiana	Y	29270 FQ	40590 MW	54760 TQ	USBLS	5/15
	Baton Rouge MSA, LA	Y	38270 FQ	46710 MW	56200 TQ	USBLS	5/15
	New Orleans-Metairie MSA, LA	Y	21510 FQ	23780 MW	55820 TQ	USBLS	5/15
	Maine	Y	36860 FQ	48650 MW	60180 TQ	USBLS	5/15
	Maryland	Y	36253 AE	62082 MW	74997 AEX	MDBLS	4/16

AE	Average entry wage	AWR	Average wage range	H	Hourly
AEX	Average experienced wage	B	Biweekly	HI	Highest wage paid
ATC	Average total compensation	D	Daily	HR	High end range
AW	Average wage paid	FQ	First quartile wage	LO	Lowest wage paid

LR	Low end range	MTC	Median total compensation	TCC	Total cash compensation
M	Monthly	MW	Median wage paid	TQ	Third quartile wage
MCC	Median cash compensation	MWR	Median wage range	W	Weekly
ME	Median entry wage	S	See annotated source	Y	Yearly

Occupation/Type/Industry	Location	Per	Low	Mid	High	Source	Date
Environmental Engineering Technician	Baltimore-Columbia-Towson MSA, MD	Y	36670 FQ	63910 MW	82870 TQ	USBLS	5/15
	Massachusetts	Y	37470 FQ	44780 MW	55570 TQ	USBLS	5/15
	Boston-Cambridge-Newton NECTA, MA	Y	36860 FQ	43650 MW	54060 TQ	USBLS	5/15
	Worcester MSA, MA-CT	Y	31510 FQ	52260 MW	63530 TQ	USBLS	5/15
	Michigan	Y	36430 FQ	45220 MW	56300 TQ	USBLS	5/15
	Detroit-Dearborn-Livonia PMSA, MI	Y	31410 FQ	43130 MW	50830 TQ	USBLS	5/15
	Grand Rapids-Wyoming MSA, MI	Y	39900 FQ	52190 MW	59670 TQ	USBLS	5/15
	Minnesota	Y	36673 FQ	46471 MW	58417 TQ	MNBLS	1/16-3/16
	Minneapolis-St. Paul-Bloomington MSA, MN-WI	Y	37399 FQ	48245 MW	58709 TQ	MNBLS	1/16-3/16
	Mississippi	Y	27580 FQ	32170 MW	41420 TQ	USBLS	5/15
	Jackson MSA, MS	Y	28130 FQ	34460 MW	44070 TQ	USBLS	5/15
	Missouri	Y	32840 FQ	41960 MW	49830 TQ	USBLS	5/15
	Kansas City MSA, MO-KS	Y	29340 FQ	41870 MW	50430 TQ	USBLS	5/15
	St. Louis MSA, MO-IL	Y	31580 FQ	39130 MW	51540 TQ	USBLS	5/15
	Montana	Y	39220 FQ	52410 MW	60840 TQ	USBLS	5/15
	Nebraska	Y	29455 FQ	39000 MW	51095 TQ	NEBLS	7/16-9/16
	Omaha-Council Bluffs MSA, NE-IA	Y	28520 FQ	42845 MW	54930 TQ	NEBLS	7/16-9/16
	Nevada	Y	41060 FQ	55610 MW	72020 TQ	USBLS	5/15
	Las Vegas-Henderson-Paradise MSA, NV	Y	36320 FQ	47270 MW	65520 TQ	USBLS	5/15
	New Jersey	Y	39420 FQ	46820 MW	58440 TQ	USBLS	5/15
	Camden PMSA, NJ	Y	41150 FQ	47090 MW	59610 TQ	USBLS	5/15
	Newark PMSA, NJ-PA	Y	43070 FQ	49060 MW	59750 TQ	USBLS	5/15
	New Mexico	Y	38610 FQ	54330 MW	74880 TQ	USBLS	5/15
	Albuquerque MSA, NM	Y	34190 FQ	39820 MW	59350 TQ	USBLS	5/15
	New York	Y	30390 AE	46200 MW	58540 AEX	NYBLS	1/16-3/16
	Buffalo-Cheektowaga-Niagara Falls MSA, NY	Y	33530 FQ	40740 MW	47830 TQ	USBLS	5/15
	Nassau County-Suffolk County PMSA, NY	Y	25750 FQ	50870 MW	71300 TQ	USBLS	5/15
	New York-Jersey City-White Plains PMSA, NY-NJ	Y	37040 FQ	47360 MW	59070 TQ	USBLS	5/15
	Rochester MSA, NY	Y	36960 FQ	47310 MW	57190 TQ	USBLS	5/15
	North Carolina	Y	38530 FQ	47380 MW	57590 TQ	USBLS	5/15
	Charlotte-Concord-Gastonia MSA, NC-SC	Y	39890 FQ	47990 MW	57490 TQ	USBLS	5/15
	Raleigh MSA, NC	Y	45050 FQ	54380 MW	62250 TQ	USBLS	5/15
	Ohio	Y	48710 FQ	57450 MW	67970 TQ	USBLS	5/15
	Cincinnati MSA, OH-KY-IN	Y	51540 FQ	59590 MW	70560 TQ	USBLS	5/15
	Cleveland-Elyria MSA, OH	Y	49320 FQ	56790 MW	65650 TQ	USBLS	5/15
	Columbus MSA, OH	Y	46190 FQ	54550 MW	62270 TQ	USBLS	5/15
	Oklahoma	Y	23540 FQ	29250 MW	43780 TQ	USBLS	5/15
	Oklahoma City MSA, OK	Y	22890 FQ	27730 MW	44550 TQ	USBLS	5/15
	Tulsa MSA, OK	Y	33110 FQ	40130 MW	48420 TQ	USBLS	5/15
	Oregon	H	21.96 FQ	27.40 MW	34.35 TQ	ORBLS	2016
	Portland-Vancouver-Hillsboro MSA, OR-WA	Y	46370 FQ	59940 MW	72300 TQ	USBLS	5/15
	Pennsylvania	Y	35840 FQ	48860 MW	61220 TQ	USBLS	5/15
	Allentown-Bethlehem-Easton MSA, PA-NJ	Y	33210 FQ	40550 MW	47950 TQ	USBLS	5/15
	Harrisburg-Carlisle MSA, PA	Y	38390 FQ	50340 MW	63770 TQ	USBLS	5/15
	Montgomery County-Bucks County-Chester County PMSA, PA	Y	39190 FQ	55020 MW	62390 TQ	USBLS	5/15
	Philadelphia PMSA, PA	Y	37800 FQ	53410 MW	61050 TQ	USBLS	5/15
	Pittsburgh MSA, PA	Y	38640 FQ	47320 MW	59280 TQ	USBLS	5/15
	Rhode Island	Y	33580 FQ	37040 MW	54430 TQ	USBLS	5/15
	Providence-Warwick MSA, RI-MA	Y	35770 FQ	42840 MW	49770 TQ	USBLS	5/15
	South Carolina	Y	37470 FQ	56460 MW	74760 TQ	USBLS	5/15
	Columbia MSA, SC	Y	35210 FQ	42000 MW	57490 TQ	USBLS	5/15
	Greenville-Anderson-Mauldin MSA, SC	Y	28350 FQ	38410 MW	62830 TQ	USBLS	5/15
	Tennessee	Y	34940 FQ	45860 MW	57730 TQ	USBLS	5/15
	Knoxville MSA, TN	Y	37230 FQ	50620 MW	72410 TQ	USBLS	5/15

Occupation/Type/Industry	Location	Per	Low	Mid	High	Source	Date
Environmental Engineering Technician	Memphis MSA, TN-MS-AR	Y	28970 FQ	34900 MW	43390 TQ	USBLS	5/15
	Nashville-Davidson–Murfreesboro–Franklin MSA, TN	Y	34950 FQ	44540 MW	55150 TQ	USBLS	5/15
	Texas	Y	43680 FQ	58630 MW	73490 TQ	USBLS	5/15
	Austin-Round Rock MSA, TX	Y	43740 FQ	52310 MW	59820 TQ	USBLS	5/15
	Dallas-Plano-Irving PMSA, TX	Y	52900 FQ	68350 MW	77730 TQ	USBLS	5/15
	Houston-The Woodlands-Sugar Land MSA, TX	Y	52020 FQ	70390 MW	88010 TQ	USBLS	5/15
	Utah	Y	36820 FQ	41910 MW	48670 TQ	USBLS	5/15
	Ogden-Clearfield MSA, UT	Y	37880 FQ	42740 MW	48350 TQ	USBLS	5/15
	Salt Lake City MSA, UT	Y	36320 FQ	41120 MW	47940 TQ	USBLS	5/15
	Vermont	Y	35780 FQ	43960 MW	52450 TQ	USBLS	5/15
	Burlington-South Burlington MSA, VT	Y	33920 FQ	37990 MW	48870 TQ	USBLS	5/15
	Virginia	Y	38130 FQ	48310 MW	57420 TQ	USBLS	5/15
	Richmond MSA, VA	Y	44830 FQ	53700 MW	60100 TQ	USBLS	5/15
	Virginia Beach-Norfolk-Newport News MSA, VA-NC	Y	32280 FQ	44090 MW	54330 TQ	USBLS	5/15
	Washington	H	20.31 FQ	28.57 MW	34.71 TQ	WABLS	3/16
	Seattle-Bellevue-Everett PMSA, WA	H	17.82 FQ	25.86 MW	32.56 TQ	WABLS	3/16
	Tacoma-Lakewood PMSA, WA	H	21.42 FQ	23.59 MW	27.58 TQ	WABLS	3/16
	West Virginia	Y	38470 FQ	44890 MW	51490 TQ	USBLS	5/15
	Huntington-Ashland MSA, WV-KY-OH	Y	26770 FQ	31330 MW	37150 TQ	USBLS	5/15
	Wisconsin	Y	40950 FQ	53570 MW	65120 TQ	USBLS	5/15
	Milwaukee-Waukesha-West Allis MSA, WI	Y	47270 FQ	56170 MW	64730 TQ	USBLS	5/15
	Wyoming	Y	39870 FQ	47990 MW	61800 TQ	USBLS	5/15
	Puerto Rico	Y	28350 FQ	52220 MW	58620 TQ	USBLS	5/15
	San Juan-Carolina-Caguas MSA, PR	Y	23270 FQ	27980 MW	39920 TQ	USBLS	5/15
Environmental Planner							
Municipal Government	Vista, CA	Y			94569 HI	CACIT	6/28/16
Environmental Science and Protection Technician							
Including Health	Alabama	Y	29387 AE	48010 AW	57327 AEX	ALBLS	6/16
Including Health	Birmingham-Hoover MSA, AL	Y	37909 AE	60140 AW	71261 AEX	ALBLS	6/16
Including Health	Alaska	Y	41850 FQ	46780 MW	63210 TQ	USBLS	5/15
Including Health	Anchorage MSA, AK	Y	41310 FQ	51710 MW	67340 TQ	USBLS	5/15
Including Health	Arizona	Y	32330 FQ	39440 MW	51900 TQ	USBLS	5/15
Including Health	Phoenix-Mesa-Scottsdale MSA, AZ	Y	32120 FQ	38890 MW	51580 TQ	USBLS	5/15
Including Health	Tucson MSA, AZ	Y	35110 FQ	43450 MW	55820 TQ	USBLS	5/15
Including Health	Arkansas	Y	33200 FQ	38170 MW	54630 TQ	USBLS	5/15
Including Health	Little Rock-North Little Rock-Conway MSA, AR	Y	32710 FQ	36800 MW	52260 TQ	USBLS	5/15
Including Health	California	H	16.98 FQ	22.21 MW	29.25 TQ	CABLS	1/16-3/16
Including Health	Anaheim-Santa Ana-Irvine PMSA, CA	H	18.37 FQ	23.34 MW	30.20 TQ	CABLS	1/16-3/16
Including Health	Los Angeles-Long Beach-Glendale PMSA, CA	H	16.91 FQ	22.18 MW	28.54 TQ	CABLS	1/16-3/16
Including Health	Oakland-Hayward-Berkeley PMSA, CA	H	18.45 FQ	24.12 MW	30.61 TQ	CABLS	1/16-3/16
Including Health	Riverside-San Bernardino-Ontario MSA, CA	H	18.56 FQ	25.82 MW	32.23 TQ	CABLS	1/16-3/16
Including Health	Sacramento–Roseville–Arden-Arcade MSA, CA	H	14.77 FQ	17.11 MW	21.01 TQ	CABLS	1/16-3/16
Including Health	San Diego-Carlsbad MSA, CA	H	17.02 FQ	21.57 MW	26.38 TQ	CABLS	1/16-3/16
Including Health	San Francisco-Redwood City-South San Francisco PMSA, CA	H	18.79 FQ	28.80 MW	39.11 TQ	CABLS	1/16-3/16
Including Health	Colorado	Y	33660 FQ	43110 MW	55240 TQ	USBLS	5/15
Including Health	Denver-Aurora-Lakewood MSA, CO	Y	33950 FQ	42040 MW	56330 TQ	USBLS	5/15
Including Health	Connecticut	Y		39738 MW		CTBLS	1/16-3/16

AE	Average entry wage	AWR	Average wage range	H	Hourly
AEX	Average experienced wage	B	Biweekly	HI	Highest wage paid
ATC	Average total compensation	D	Daily	HR	High end range
AW	Average wage paid	FQ	First quartile wage	LO	Lowest wage paid

LR	Low end range	MTC	Median total compensation	TCC	Total cash compensation
M	Monthly	MW	Median wage paid	TQ	Third quartile wage
MCC	Median cash compensation	MWR	Median wage range	W	Weekly
ME	Median entry wage	S	See annotated source	Y	Yearly

Occupation/Type/Industry	Location	Per	Low	Mid	High	Source	Date
Environmental Science and Protection Technician							
Including Health	Hartford-West Hartford-East Hartford MSA, CT	Y	32850 FQ	39510 MW	53340 TQ	USBLS	5/15
Including Health	Delaware	Y	32010 FQ	37200 MW	44190 TQ	USBLS	5/15
Including Health	Wilmington PMSA, DE-MD-NJ	Y	32650 FQ	37860 MW	44600 TQ	USBLS	5/15
Including Health	District of Columbia	Y	61650 FQ	78580 MW	88300 TQ	USBLS	5/15
Including Health	Washington-Arlington-Alexandria PMSA, DC-VA-MD-WV	Y	46680 FQ	56580 MW	72920 TQ	USBLS	5/15
Including Health	Florida	H	15.34 AE	18.41 MW	24.83 AEX	FLBLS	7/16-9/16
Including Health	Fort Lauderdale-Pompano Beach-Deerfield Beach PMSA, FL	H	16.36 AE	17.78 MW	19.01 AEX	FLBLS	7/16-9/16
Including Health	Miami-Miami Beach-Kendall PMSA, FL	H	14.85 AE	18.05 MW	21.95 AEX	FLBLS	7/16-9/16
Including Health	Orlando-Kissimmee-Sanford MSA, FL	H	12.47 AE	17.15 MW	20.46 AEX	FLBLS	7/16-9/16
Including Health	Georgia	Y	35060 FQ	45510 MW	59030 TQ	USBLS	5/15
Including Health	Atlanta-Sandy Springs-Roswell MSA, GA	Y	38500 FQ	50180 MW	61350 TQ	USBLS	5/15
Including Health	Augusta-Richmond County MSA, GA-SC	Y	64890 FQ	69490 MW	74090 TQ	USBLS	5/15
Including Health	Hawaii	Y	33210 FQ	44410 MW	53730 TQ	USBLS	5/15
Including Health	Urban Honolulu MSA, HI	Y	35700 FQ	46470 MW	55600 TQ	USBLS	5/15
Including Health	Idaho	Y	34660 FQ	43760 MW	52430 TQ	USBLS	5/15
Including Health	Boise City MSA, ID	Y	43010 FQ	49970 MW	57080 TQ	USBLS	5/15
Including Health	Illinois	Y	25840 FQ	36310 MW	46750 TQ	USBLS	5/15
Including Health	Chicago-Naperville-Arlington Heights PMSA, IL	Y	27280 FQ	38440 MW	46340 TQ	USBLS	5/15
Including Health	Lake County-Kenosha County PMSA, IL-WI	Y	26280 FQ	33020 MW	37210 TQ	USBLS	5/15
Including Health	Indiana	Y	32640 FQ	39370 MW	54980 TQ	USBLS	5/15
Including Health	Gary PMSA, IN	Y	31550 FQ	35770 MW	43910 TQ	USBLS	5/15
Including Health	Indianapolis-Carmel-Anderson MSA, IN	Y	34610 FQ	43360 MW	58360 TQ	USBLS	5/15
Including Health	Iowa	Y	34390 FQ	43020 MW	55750 TQ	USBLS	5/15
Including Health	Kansas	Y	31590 FQ	43620 MW	59640 TQ	USBLS	5/15
Including Health	Kentucky	Y	32240 FQ	41600 MW	54070 TQ	USBLS	5/15
Including Health	Louisville-Jefferson County MSA, KY-IN	Y	32530 FQ	45070 MW	67850 TQ	USBLS	5/15
Including Health	Louisiana	Y	32670 FQ	41310 MW	57090 TQ	USBLS	5/15
Including Health	Baton Rouge MSA, LA	Y	37740 FQ	48140 MW	63410 TQ	USBLS	5/15
Including Health	New Orleans-Metairie MSA, LA	Y	23870 FQ	31850 MW	37770 TQ	USBLS	5/15
Including Health	Maine	Y	34130 FQ	40450 MW	47530 TQ	USBLS	5/15
Including Health	Portland-South Portland MSA, ME	Y	39340 FQ	45080 MW	53160 TQ	USBLS	5/15
Including Health	Maryland	Y	34920 AE	53347 MW	62561 AEX	MDBLS	4/16
Including Health	Baltimore-Columbia-Towson MSA, MD	Y	39210 FQ	52010 MW	67060 TQ	USBLS	5/15
Including Health	Massachusetts	Y	37510 FQ	47110 MW	58520 TQ	USBLS	5/15
Including Health	Boston-Cambridge-Newton NECTA, MA	Y	39920 FQ	47830 MW	58640 TQ	USBLS	5/15
Including Health	Worcester MSA, MA-CT	Y	44470 FQ	52570 MW	58330 TQ	USBLS	5/15
Including Health	Michigan	Y	34320 FQ	41250 MW	50960 TQ	USBLS	5/15
Including Health	Detroit-Dearborn-Livonia PMSA, MI	Y	34410 FQ	41560 MW	51070 TQ	USBLS	5/15
Including Health	Grand Rapids-Wyoming MSA, MI	Y	34160 FQ	38270 MW	50680 TQ	USBLS	5/15
Including Health	Minnesota	Y	38346 FQ	47227 MW	57459 TQ	MNBLS	1/16-3/16
Including Health	Minneapolis-St. Paul-Bloomington MSA, MN-WI	Y	38679 FQ	49294 MW	60100 TQ	MNBLS	1/16-3/16
Including Health	Mississippi	Y	26620 FQ	36220 MW	47870 TQ	USBLS	5/15
Including Health	Jackson MSA, MS	Y	30130 FQ	35680 MW	41850 TQ	USBLS	5/15
Including Health	Missouri	Y	29770 FQ	36910 MW	45810 TQ	USBLS	5/15
Including Health	Kansas City MSA, MO-KS	Y	32550 FQ	38750 MW	48190 TQ	USBLS	5/15
Including Health	St. Louis MSA, MO-IL	Y	34610 FQ	40660 MW	47870 TQ	USBLS	5/15
Including Health	Montana	Y	33260 FQ	41170 MW	49210 TQ	USBLS	5/15
Including Health	Nebraska	Y	35810 FQ	46385 MW	63990 TQ	NEBLS	7/16-9/16

AE	Average entry wage	AWR	Average wage range	H	Hourly
AEX	Average experienced wage	B	Biweekly	HI	Highest wage paid
ATC	Average total compensation	D	Daily	HR	High end range
AW	Average wage paid	FQ	First quartile wage	LO	Lowest wage paid

LR	Low end range	MTC	Median total compensation
M	Monthly	MW	Median wage paid
MCC	Median cash compensation	MWR	Median wage range
ME	Median entry wage	S	See annotated source

TCC	Total cash compensation		
TQ	Third quartile wage		
W	Weekly		
Y	Yearly		

Occupation/Type/Industry	Location	Per	Low	Mid	High	Source	Date
Environmental Science and							
Protection Technician							
Including Health	Omaha-Council Bluffs MSA, NE-IA	Y	39645 FQ	48055 MW	66400 TQ	NEBLS	7/16-9/16
Including Health	Nevada	Y	44540 FQ	61120 MW	78430 TQ	USBLS	5/15
Including Health	Las Vegas-Henderson-Paradise MSA, NV	Y	34060 FQ	60200 MW	75600 TQ	USBLS	5/15
Including Health	New Hampshire	H	15.07 AE	19.31 MW	23.39 AEX	NHBLS	6/16
Including Health	Manchester NECTA, NH	H	17.38 AE	25.26 MW	28.16 AEX	NHBLS	6/16
Including Health	New Jersey	Y	34690 FQ	44070 MW	53590 TQ	USBLS	5/15
Including Health	Camden PMSA, NJ	Y	34700 FQ	38550 MW	51340 TQ	USBLS	5/15
Including Health	Newark PMSA, NJ-PA	Y	35370 FQ	44720 MW	56520 TQ	USBLS	5/15
Including Health	Trenton MSA, NJ	Y	32660 FQ	39470 MW	53060 TQ	USBLS	5/15
Including Health	New Mexico	Y	30370 FQ	41810 MW	48980 TQ	USBLS	5/15
Including Health	Albuquerque MSA, NM	Y	37450 FQ	44250 MW	52070 TQ	USBLS	5/15
Including Health	New York	Y	32740 AE	46790 MW	57530 AEX	NYBLS	1/16-3/16
Including Health	Buffalo-Cheektowaga-Niagara Falls MSA, NY	Y	31680 FQ	37000 MW	50310 TQ	USBLS	5/15
Including Health	Nassau County-Suffolk County PMSA, NY	Y	36250 FQ	47840 MW	61070 TQ	USBLS	5/15
Including Health	New York-Jersey City-White Plains PMSA, NY-NJ	Y	42580 FQ	48720 MW	58860 TQ	USBLS	5/15
Including Health	Rochester MSA, NY	Y	31030 FQ	35260 MW	39360 TQ	USBLS	5/15
Including Health	North Carolina	Y	33020 FQ	39800 MW	49360 TQ	USBLS	5/15
Including Health	Charlotte-Concord-Gastonia MSA, NC-SC	Y	42370 FQ	50580 MW	62470 TQ	USBLS	5/15
Including Health	Raleigh MSA, NC	Y	34110 FQ	38230 MW	48000 TQ	USBLS	5/15
Including Health	North Dakota	Y	38430 FQ	46000 MW	57610 TQ	USBLS	5/15
Including Health	Ohio	Y	31070 FQ	39520 MW	48560 TQ	USBLS	5/15
Including Health	Cincinnati MSA, OH-KY-IN	Y	33110 FQ	38950 MW	46190 TQ	USBLS	5/15
Including Health	Cleveland-Elyria MSA, OH	Y	34440 FQ	43810 MW	56630 TQ	USBLS	5/15
Including Health	Columbus MSA, OH	Y	26760 FQ	35130 MW	44500 TQ	USBLS	5/15
Including Health	Oklahoma	Y	23880 FQ	40720 MW	50490 TQ	USBLS	5/15
Including Health	Oklahoma City MSA, OK	Y	42170 FQ	49090 MW	58790 TQ	USBLS	5/15
Including Health	Tulsa MSA, OK	Y	22980 FQ	38820 MW	46660 TQ	USBLS	5/15
Including Health	Oregon	H	20.69 FQ	25.60 MW	29.34 TQ	ORBLS	2016
Including Health	Portland-Vancouver-Hillsboro MSA, OR-WA	Y	47030 FQ	55670 MW	62780 TQ	USBLS	5/15
Including Health	Pennsylvania	Y	33750 FQ	42320 MW	53680 TQ	USBLS	5/15
Including Health	Allentown-Bethlehem-Easton MSA, PA-NJ	Y	27710 FQ	46010 MW	58630 TQ	USBLS	5/15
Including Health	Harrisburg-Carlisle MSA, PA	Y	40120 FQ	46740 MW	56130 TQ	USBLS	5/15
Including Health	Montgomery County-Bucks County-Chester County PMSA, PA	Y	41100 FQ	46160 MW	55790 TQ	USBLS	5/15
Including Health	Philadelphia PMSA, PA	Y	42060 FQ	52020 MW	65370 TQ	USBLS	5/15
Including Health	Pittsburgh MSA, PA	Y	34180 FQ	39230 MW	53850 TQ	USBLS	5/15
Including Health	Rhode Island	Y	39770 FQ	51970 MW	60690 TQ	USBLS	5/15
Including Health	Providence-Warwick MSA, RI-MA	Y	30580 FQ	46810 MW	59120 TQ	USBLS	5/15
Including Health	South Carolina	Y	59840 FQ	67810 MW	73500 TQ	USBLS	5/15
Including Health	Charleston-North Charleston MSA, SC	Y	37140 FQ	47500 MW	59500 TQ	USBLS	5/15
Including Health	Greenville-Anderson-Mauldin MSA, SC	Y	50620 FQ	63140 MW	74840 TQ	USBLS	5/15
Including Health	South Dakota	Y	24930 FQ	27500 MW	30070 TQ	USBLS	5/15
Including Health	Tennessee	Y	34040 FQ	44190 MW	55120 TQ	USBLS	5/15
Including Health	Knoxville MSA, TN	Y	32680 FQ	50460 MW	59650 TQ	USBLS	5/15
Including Health	Memphis MSA, TN-MS-AR	Y	37550 FQ	44680 MW	52330 TQ	USBLS	5/15
Including Health	Nashville-Davidson–Murfreesboro–Franklin MSA, TN	Y	35440 FQ	42870 MW	48450 TQ	USBLS	5/15
Including Health	Texas	Y	32930 FQ	40680 MW	52970 TQ	USBLS	5/15
Including Health	Austin-Round Rock MSA, TX	Y	31000 FQ	39160 MW	45720 TQ	USBLS	5/15
Including Health	Dallas-Plano-Irving PMSA, TX	Y	38420 FQ	46430 MW	60270 TQ	USBLS	5/15
Including Health	Fort Worth-Arlington PMSA, TX	Y	35300 FQ	46020 MW	60530 TQ	USBLS	5/15
Including Health	Houston-The Woodlands-Sugar Land MSA, TX	Y	32850 FQ	40410 MW	61110 TQ	USBLS	5/15
Including Health	San Antonio-New Braunfels MSA, TX	Y	35150 FQ	44260 MW	50870 TQ	USBLS	5/15
Including Health	Utah	Y	33310 FQ	43310 MW	59240 TQ	USBLS	5/15

AE	Average entry wage	AWR	Average wage range	H	Hourly
AEX	Average experienced wage	B	Biweekly	HI	Highest wage paid
ATC	Average total compensation	D	Daily	HR	High end range
AW	Average wage paid	FQ	First quartile wage	LO	Lowest wage paid

LR	Low end range	MTC	Median total compensation	TCC	Total cash compensation
M	Monthly	MW	Median wage paid	TQ	Third quartile wage
MCC	Median cash compensation	MWR	Median wage range	W	Weekly
ME	Median entry wage	S	See annotated source	Y	Yearly

Occupation/Type/Industry	Location	Per	Low	Mid	High	Source	Date
Environmental Science and Protection Technician							
Including Health	Provo-Orem MSA, UT	Y	45590 FQ	61590 MW	71520 TQ	USBLS	5/15
Including Health	Salt Lake City MSA, UT	Y	32440 FQ	41600 MW	48930 TQ	USBLS	5/15
Including Health	Vermont	Y	34700 FQ	46500 MW	54980 TQ	USBLS	5/15
Including Health	Virginia	Y	35920 FQ	46420 MW	58600 TQ	USBLS	5/15
Including Health	Richmond MSA, VA	Y	35650 FQ	42980 MW	49860 TQ	USBLS	5/15
Including Health	Virginia Beach-Norfolk-Newport News MSA, VA-NC	Y	33050 FQ	48210 MW	57720 TQ	USBLS	5/15
Including Health	Washington	H	16.79 FQ	22.31 MW	28.32 TQ	WABLS	3/16
Including Health	Seattle-Bellevue-Everett PMSA, WA	H	20.63 FQ	23.31 MW	28.15 TQ	WABLS	3/16
Including Health	Tacoma-Lakewood PMSA, WA	H	13.96 FQ	22.84 MW	31.44 TQ	WABLS	3/16
Including Health	West Virginia	Y	29180 FQ	36860 MW	48370 TQ	USBLS	5/15
Including Health	Huntington-Ashland MSA, WV-KY-OH	Y	41480 FQ	49810 MW	57190 TQ	USBLS	5/15
Including Health	Wisconsin	Y	32560 FQ	39650 MW	55480 TQ	USBLS	5/15
Including Health	Madison MSA, WI	Y	34130 FQ	38630 MW	55080 TQ	USBLS	5/15
Including Health	Milwaukee-Waukesha-West Allis MSA, WI	Y	38410 FQ	54520 MW	64970 TQ	USBLS	5/15
Including Health	Wyoming	Y	36830 FQ	42840 MW	49860 TQ	USBLS	5/15
Including Health	Puerto Rico	Y	22340 FQ	30250 MW	47430 TQ	USBLS	5/15
Including Health	San Juan-Carolina-Caguas MSA, PR	Y	27460 FQ	39890 MW	50060 TQ	USBLS	5/15
Environmental Science Teacher							
Postsecondary	Alabama	Y	46879 AE	76979 AW	92025 AEX	ALBLS	6/16
Postsecondary	Arizona	Y	71930 FQ	93170 MW	121240 TQ	USBLS	5/15
Postsecondary	Arkansas	Y	51690 FQ	82290 MW	114590 TQ	USBLS	5/15
Postsecondary	California	Y		104777 AW		CABLS	1/16-3/16
Postsecondary	Colorado	Y	38200 FQ	62880 MW	82810 TQ	USBLS	5/15
Postsecondary	Connecticut	Y		73297 MW		CTBLS	1/16-3/16
Postsecondary	Florida	Y	46893 AE	70544 MW	90084 AEX	FLBLS	7/16-9/16
Postsecondary	Georgia	Y	51330 FQ	70500 MW	94680 TQ	USBLS	5/15
Postsecondary	Illinois	Y	52170 FQ	85690 MW	120250 TQ	USBLS	5/15
Postsecondary	Indiana	Y	59180 FQ	82180 MW	104760 TQ	USBLS	5/15
Postsecondary	Iowa	Y	61280 FQ	80920 MW	110380 TQ	USBLS	5/15
Postsecondary	Louisiana	Y	57690 FQ	77000 MW	100410 TQ	USBLS	5/15
Postsecondary	Maine	Y	56990 FQ	69640 MW	81330 TQ	USBLS	5/15
Postsecondary	Maryland	Y	55329 AE	96290 MW	116771 AEX	MDBLS	4/16
Postsecondary	Massachusetts	Y	65820 FQ	85280 MW	115800 TQ	USBLS	5/15
Postsecondary	Michigan	Y	85850 FQ	109420 MW	147800 TQ	USBLS	5/15
Postsecondary	Minnesota	Y	56723 FQ	74364 MW	95120 TQ	MNBLS	1/16-3/16
Postsecondary	Mississippi	Y	61530 FQ	82160 MW	104600 TQ	USBLS	5/15
Postsecondary	Missouri	Y	62420 FQ	84950 MW	111940 TQ	USBLS	5/15
Postsecondary	Montana	Y	51880 FQ	64280 MW	77500 TQ	USBLS	5/15
Postsecondary	Nevada	Y	38510 FQ	64760 MW	95000 TQ	USBLS	5/15
Postsecondary	New Hampshire	Y	53909 AE	74177 MW	96095 AEX	NHBLS	6/16
Postsecondary	New Jersey	Y	64850 FQ	92240 MW	122560 TQ	USBLS	5/15
Postsecondary	New Mexico	Y	51810 FQ	71950 MW	98350 TQ	USBLS	5/15
Postsecondary	New York	Y	53320 AE	77510 MW	112220 AEX	NYBLS	1/16-3/16
Postsecondary	North Carolina	Y	53960 FQ	73830 MW	97050 TQ	USBLS	5/15
Postsecondary	Ohio	Y	58330 FQ	79070 MW	103390 TQ	USBLS	5/15
Postsecondary	Oregon	Y	59222 FQ	79535 MW	104010 TQ	ORBLS	2016
Postsecondary	Pennsylvania	Y	58610 FQ	76140 MW	110260 TQ	USBLS	5/15
Postsecondary	South Carolina	Y	58180 FQ	80730 MW	105810 TQ	USBLS	5/15
Postsecondary	Tennessee	Y	59150 FQ	78150 MW	94200 TQ	USBLS	5/15
Postsecondary	Texas	Y	48170 FQ	69250 MW	102550 TQ	USBLS	5/15
Postsecondary	Utah	Y	62080 FQ	91130 MW	119490 TQ	USBLS	5/15
Postsecondary	Vermont	Y	43370 FQ	54850 MW	77720 TQ	USBLS	5/15
Postsecondary	Virginia	Y	51280 FQ	68280 MW	91790 TQ	USBLS	5/15
Postsecondary	Washington	Y		107303 AW		WABLS	3/16
Postsecondary	Wisconsin	Y	63930 FQ	75440 MW	102960 TQ	USBLS	5/15
Environmental Scientist and Specialist							
Including Health	Alabama	Y	40783 AE	62270 AW	73014 AEX	ALBLS	6/16
Including Health	Birmingham-Hoover MSA, AL	Y	40080 AE	68346 AW	82473 AEX	ALBLS	6/16
Including Health	Alaska	Y	60380 FQ	75490 MW	97650 TQ	USBLS	5/15
Including Health	Anchorage MSA, AK	Y	61250 FQ	80260 MW	103110 TQ	USBLS	5/15
Including Health	Arizona	Y	45530 FQ	54700 MW	71860 TQ	USBLS	5/15

AE	Average entry wage	AWR	Average wage range	H	Hourly	LR	Low end range	MTC	Median total compensation
AEX	Average experienced wage	B	Biweekly	HI	Highest wage paid	M	Monthly	MW	Median wage paid
ATC	Average total compensation	D	Daily	HR	High end range	MCC	Median cash compensation	MWR	Median wage range
AW	Average wage paid	FQ	First quartile wage	LO	Lowest wage paid	ME	Median entry wage	S	See annotated source

TCC	Total cash compensation
TQ	Third quartile wage
W	Weekly
Y	Yearly

Occupation/Type/Industry	Location	Per	Low	Mid	High	Source	Date
Environmental Scientist and Specialist							
Including Health	Phoenix-Mesa-Scottsdale MSA, AZ	Y	45900 FQ	55210 MW	73810 TQ	USBLS	5/15
Including Health	Tucson MSA, AZ	Y	43780 FQ	49970 MW	64210 TQ	USBLS	5/15
Including Health	Arkansas	Y	43370 FQ	59670 MW	78370 TQ	USBLS	5/15
Including Health	Little Rock-North Little Rock-Conway MSA, AR	Y	47810 FQ	61970 MW	78930 TQ	USBLS	5/15
Including Health	California	H	31.33 FQ	38.79 MW	50.21 TQ	CABLS	1/16-3/16
Including Health	Anaheim-Santa Ana-Irvine PMSA, CA	H	29.41 FQ	37.74 MW	50.64 TQ	CABLS	1/16-3/16
Including Health	Los Angeles-Long Beach-Glendale PMSA, CA	H	34.02 FQ	41.28 MW	51.72 TQ	CABLS	1/16-3/16
Including Health	Oakland-Hayward-Berkeley PMSA, CA	H	32.06 FQ	43.29 MW	57.60 TQ	CABLS	1/16-3/16
Including Health	Riverside-San Bernardino-Ontario MSA, CA	H	31.77 FQ	37.73 MW	49.57 TQ	CABLS	1/16-3/16
Including Health	Sacramento–Roseville–Arden-Arcade MSA, CA	H	30.19 FQ	37.14 MW	48.16 TQ	CABLS	1/16-3/16
Including Health	San Diego-Carlsbad MSA, CA	H	32.08 FQ	38.35 MW	48.41 TQ	CABLS	1/16-3/16
Including Health	San Francisco-Redwood City-South San Francisco PMSA, CA	H	33.33 FQ	50.90 MW	61.85 TQ	CABLS	1/16-3/16
Including Health	Colorado	Y	59890 FQ	75440 MW	98540 TQ	USBLS	5/15
Including Health	Denver-Aurora-Lakewood MSA, CO	Y	61780 FQ	76050 MW	98990 TQ	USBLS	5/15
Including Health	Connecticut	Y		70061 MW		CTBLS	1/16-3/16
Including Health	Bridgeport-Stamford-Norwalk MSA, CT	Y	52140 FQ	71770 MW	87430 TQ	USBLS	5/15
Including Health	Hartford-West Hartford-East Hartford MSA, CT	Y	53950 FQ	65910 MW	82490 TQ	USBLS	5/15
Including Health	District of Columbia	Y	80870 FQ	107330 MW	135930 TQ	USBLS	5/15
Including Health	Washington-Arlington-Alexandria PMSA, DC-VA-MD-WV	Y	74320 FQ	102930 MW	128940 TQ	USBLS	5/15
Including Health	Florida	H	17.82 AE	24.42 MW	32.78 AEX	FLBLS	7/16-9/16
Including Health	Fort Lauderdale-Pompano Beach-Deerfield Beach PMSA, FL	H	14.25 AE	22.78 MW	28.53 AEX	FLBLS	7/16-9/16
Including Health	Miami-Miami Beach-Kendall PMSA, FL	H	17.92 AE	27.69 MW	37.08 AEX	FLBLS	7/16-9/16
Including Health	Orlando-Kissimmee-Sanford MSA, FL	H	17.97 AE	23.84 MW	30.92 AEX	FLBLS	7/16-9/16
Including Health	Tampa-St. Petersburg-Clearwater MSA, FL	H	18.31 AE	29.18 MW	37.53 AEX	FLBLS	7/16-9/16
Including Health	Georgia	Y	40460 FQ	50050 MW	71800 TQ	USBLS	5/15
Including Health	Atlanta-Sandy Springs-Roswell MSA, GA	Y	41110 FQ	53330 MW	75480 TQ	USBLS	5/15
Including Health	Augusta-Richmond County MSA, GA-SC	Y	46380 FQ	79590 MW	107820 TQ	USBLS	5/15
Including Health	Hawaii	Y	49120 FQ	61720 MW	76540 TQ	USBLS	5/15
Including Health	Urban Honolulu MSA, HI	Y	49900 FQ	62800 MW	77700 TQ	USBLS	5/15
Including Health	Idaho	Y	49770 FQ	54710 MW	63670 TQ	USBLS	5/15
Including Health	Boise City MSA, ID	Y	51080 FQ	56120 MW	63060 TQ	USBLS	5/15
Including Health	Illinois	Y	65750 FQ	83720 MW	103070 TQ	USBLS	5/15
Including Health	Chicago-Naperville-Arlington Heights PMSA, IL	Y	67830 FQ	87340 MW	111680 TQ	USBLS	5/15
Including Health	Lake County-Kenosha County PMSA, IL-WI	Y	43330 FQ	55510 MW	71980 TQ	USBLS	5/15
Including Health	Indiana	Y	41900 FQ	54320 MW	74860 TQ	USBLS	5/15
Including Health	Gary PMSA, IN	Y	43600 FQ	59460 MW	77360 TQ	USBLS	5/15
Including Health	Indianapolis-Carmel-Anderson MSA, IN	Y	42380 FQ	56020 MW	75740 TQ	USBLS	5/15
Including Health	Iowa	Y	48140 FQ	66460 MW	76820 TQ	USBLS	5/15
Including Health	Des Moines-West Des Moines MSA, IA	Y	48900 FQ	66470 MW	76820 TQ	USBLS	5/15
Including Health	Kansas	Y	49060 FQ	55330 MW	79690 TQ	USBLS	5/15
Including Health	Wichita MSA, KS	Y	49060 FQ	54030 MW	71590 TQ	USBLS	5/15
Including Health	Kentucky	Y	40710 FQ	47340 MW	59140 TQ	USBLS	5/15
Including Health	Louisville-Jefferson County MSA, KY-IN	Y	44250 FQ	56420 MW	77490 TQ	USBLS	5/15
Including Health	Louisiana	Y	41310 FQ	54150 MW	78520 TQ	USBLS	5/15

AE	Average entry wage	AWR	Average wage range	H	Hourly	LR	Low end range	MTC	Median total compensation	TCC	Total cash compensation
AEX	Average experienced wage	B	Biweekly	HI	Highest wage paid	M	Monthly	MW	Median wage paid	TQ	Third quartile wage
ATC	Average total compensation	D	Daily	HR	High end range	MCC	Median cash compensation	MWR	Median wage range	W	Weekly
AW	Average wage paid	FQ	First quartile wage	LO	Lowest wage paid	ME	Median entry wage	S	See annotated source	Y	Yearly

Occupation/Type/Industry	Location	Per	Low	Mid	High	Source	Date
Environmental Scientist and Specialist							
Including Health	Baton Rouge MSA, LA	Y	44380 FQ	57110 MW	73570 TQ	USBLS	5/15
Including Health	New Orleans-Metairie MSA, LA	Y	41480 FQ	55010 MW	92220 TQ	USBLS	5/15
Including Health	Maine	Y	46300 FQ	51430 MW	66160 TQ	USBLS	5/15
Including Health	Portland-South Portland MSA, ME	Y	50080 FQ	66390 MW	78690 TQ	USBLS	5/15
Including Health	Maryland	Y	45486 AE	78132 MW	94455 AEX	MDBLS	4/16
Including Health	Baltimore-Columbia-Towson MSA, MD	Y	51580 FQ	69980 MW	99910 TQ	USBLS	5/15
Including Health	Salisbury MSA, MD-DE	Y	49180 FQ	54960 MW	62500 TQ	USBLS	5/15
Including Health	Massachusetts	Y	55380 FQ	71830 MW	95540 TQ	USBLS	5/15
Including Health	Boston-Cambridge-Newton NECTA, MA	Y	59760 FQ	75280 MW	99640 TQ	USBLS	5/15
Including Health	Worcester MSA, MA-CT	Y	30390 FQ	60610 MW	88990 TQ	USBLS	5/15
Including Health	Michigan	Y	50100 FQ	63560 MW	74270 TQ	USBLS	5/15
Including Health	Detroit-Dearborn-Livonia PMSA, MI	Y	51450 FQ	59040 MW	71100 TQ	USBLS	5/15
Including Health	Grand Rapids-Wyoming MSA, MI	Y	46120 FQ	59450 MW	71110 TQ	USBLS	5/15
Including Health	Minnesota	Y	53396 FQ	65080 MW	78356 TQ	MNBLS	1/16-3/16
Including Health	Minneapolis-St. Paul-Bloomington MSA, MN-WI	Y	58800 FQ	71481 MW	81844 TQ	MNBLS	1/16-3/16
Including Health	Mississippi	Y	35830 FQ	43160 MW	67670 TQ	USBLS	5/15
Including Health	Jackson MSA, MS	Y	34670 FQ	39920 MW	49460 TQ	USBLS	5/15
Including Health	Missouri	Y	36270 FQ	42860 MW	53640 TQ	USBLS	5/15
Including Health	Kansas City MSA, MO-KS	Y	47360 FQ	69020 MW	91820 TQ	USBLS	5/15
Including Health	St. Louis MSA, MO-IL	Y	31340 FQ	42030 MW	58370 TQ	USBLS	5/15
Including Health	Montana	Y	47010 FQ	55480 MW	66230 TQ	USBLS	5/15
Including Health	Nebraska	Y	44680 FQ	55320 MW	72015 TQ	NEBLS	7/16-9/16
Including Health	Omaha-Council Bluffs MSA, NE-IA	Y	40555 FQ	50860 MW	67760 TQ	NEBLS	7/16-9/16
Including Health	Nevada	Y	49070 FQ	67350 MW	80170 TQ	USBLS	5/15
Including Health	Las Vegas-Henderson-Paradise MSA, NV	Y	61040 FQ	73890 MW	88300 TQ	USBLS	5/15
Including Health	New Hampshire	H	23.36 AE	31.79 MW	41.90 AEX	NHBLS	6/16
Including Health	Manchester NECTA, NH	H	26.17 AE	34.22 MW	40.60 AEX	NHBLS	6/16
Including Health	Nashua NECTA, NH-MA	Y	54700 FQ	63320 MW	77300 TQ	USBLS	5/15
Including Health	New Jersey	Y	57940 FQ	81270 MW	95820 TQ	USBLS	5/15
Including Health	Camden PMSA, NJ	Y	55390 FQ	75860 MW	88830 TQ	USBLS	5/15
Including Health	Newark PMSA, NJ-PA	Y	56910 FQ	83280 MW	102180 TQ	USBLS	5/15
Including Health	Trenton MSA, NJ	Y	70960 FQ	86140 MW	96480 TQ	USBLS	5/15
Including Health	New Mexico	Y	52900 FQ	63530 MW	81190 TQ	USBLS	5/15
Including Health	Albuquerque MSA, NM	Y	49760 FQ	62150 MW	76130 TQ	USBLS	5/15
Including Health	New York	Y	47650 AE	72750 MW	91490 AEX	NYBLS	1/16-3/16
Including Health	Buffalo-Cheektowaga-Niagara Falls MSA, NY	Y	53670 FQ	63060 MW	78090 TQ	USBLS	5/15
Including Health	Nassau County-Suffolk County PMSA, NY	Y	48810 FQ	68630 MW	88020 TQ	USBLS	5/15
Including Health	New York-Jersey City-White Plains PMSA, NY-NJ	Y	54990 FQ	73950 MW	95280 TQ	USBLS	5/15
Including Health	Rochester MSA, NY	Y	50390 FQ	62760 MW	90340 TQ	USBLS	5/15
Including Health	North Carolina	Y	47100 FQ	56800 MW	70830 TQ	USBLS	5/15
Including Health	Charlotte-Concord-Gastonia MSA, NC-SC	Y	44540 FQ	55930 MW	72470 TQ	USBLS	5/15
Including Health	Raleigh MSA, NC	Y	51440 FQ	58620 MW	69990 TQ	USBLS	5/15
Including Health	North Dakota	Y	46240 FQ	54360 MW	67800 TQ	USBLS	5/15
Including Health	Fargo MSA, ND-MN	Y	46130 FQ	53500 MW	62030 TQ	USBLS	5/15
Including Health	Ohio	Y	52520 FQ	65920 MW	75970 TQ	USBLS	5/15
Including Health	Cincinnati MSA, OH-KY-IN	Y	48870 FQ	65590 MW	90810 TQ	USBLS	5/15
Including Health	Cleveland-Elyria MSA, OH	Y	52940 FQ	62190 MW	76090 TQ	USBLS	5/15
Including Health	Columbus MSA, OH	Y	56930 FQ	70920 MW	75820 TQ	USBLS	5/15
Including Health	Oklahoma	Y	46370 FQ	62130 MW	80010 TQ	USBLS	5/15
Including Health	Oklahoma City MSA, OK	Y	45970 FQ	56970 MW	72290 TQ	USBLS	5/15
Including Health	Tulsa MSA, OK	Y	58840 FQ	80290 MW	110050 TQ	USBLS	5/15
Including Health	Oregon	H	28.38 FQ	34.96 MW	40.39 TQ	ORBLS	2016
Including Health	Portland-Vancouver-Hillsboro MSA, OR-WA	Y	60060 FQ	74970 MW	87470 TQ	USBLS	5/15
Including Health	Pennsylvania	Y	51810 FQ	67680 MW	89110 TQ	USBLS	5/15

AE	Average entry wage	AWR	Average wage range	H	Hourly
AEX	Average experienced wage	B	Biweekly	HI	Highest wage paid
ATC	Average total compensation	D	Daily	HR	High end range
AW	Average wage paid	FQ	First quartile wage	LO	Lowest wage paid

LR	Low end range	MTC	Median total compensation	TCC	Total cash compensation
M	Monthly	MW	Median wage paid	TQ	Third quartile wage
MCC	Median cash compensation	MWR	Median wage range	W	Weekly
ME	Median entry wage	S	See annotated source	Y	Yearly

Occupation/Type/Industry	Location	Per	Low	Mid	High	Source	Date
Environmental Scientist and Specialist							
Including Health	Allentown-Bethlehem-Easton MSA, PA-NJ	Y	44590 FQ	54190 MW	74150 TQ	USBLS	5/15
Including Health	Harrisburg-Carlisle MSA, PA	Y	54590 FQ	61030 MW	73290 TQ	USBLS	5/15
Including Health	Montgomery County-Bucks County-Chester County PMSA, PA	Y	50600 FQ	62320 MW	81360 TQ	USBLS	5/15
Including Health	Philadelphia PMSA, PA	Y	67310 FQ	80310 MW	109350 TQ	USBLS	5/15
Including Health	Pittsburgh MSA, PA	Y	56180 FQ	74600 MW	96470 TQ	USBLS	5/15
Including Health	Rhode Island	Y	67050 FQ	86530 MW	97380 TQ	USBLS	5/15
Including Health	Providence-Warwick MSA, RI-MA	Y	65650 FQ	85010 MW	97340 TQ	USBLS	5/15
Including Health	South Carolina	Y	40390 FQ	59350 MW	81260 TQ	USBLS	5/15
Including Health	Charleston-North Charleston MSA, SC	Y	32290 FQ	55160 MW	63640 TQ	USBLS	5/15
Including Health	Columbia MSA, SC	Y	49920 FQ	67310 MW	85580 TQ	USBLS	5/15
Including Health	Greenville-Anderson-Mauldin MSA, SC	Y	30830 FQ	83270 MW	102240 TQ	USBLS	5/15
Including Health	South Dakota	Y	44720 FQ	55650 MW	74450 TQ	USBLS	5/15
Including Health	Sioux Falls MSA, SD	Y	51440 FQ	62890 MW	96770 TQ	USBLS	5/15
Including Health	Tennessee	Y	47030 FQ	63460 MW	82470 TQ	USBLS	5/15
Including Health	Knoxville MSA, TN	Y	51480 FQ	74830 MW	116540 TQ	USBLS	5/15
Including Health	Memphis MSA, TN-MS-AR	Y	44410 FQ	58060 MW	72880 TQ	USBLS	5/15
Including Health	Nashville-Davidson–Murfreesboro–Franklin MSA, TN	Y	48180 FQ	64220 MW	77540 TQ	USBLS	5/15
Including Health	Texas	Y	52190 FQ	73290 MW	108290 TQ	USBLS	5/15
Including Health	Austin-Round Rock MSA, TX	Y	46260 FQ	58290 MW	74620 TQ	USBLS	5/15
Including Health	Dallas-Plano-Irving PMSA, TX	Y	61390 FQ	82550 MW	111750 TQ	USBLS	5/15
Including Health	Houston-The Woodlands-Sugar Land MSA, TX	Y	56550 FQ	86900 MW	125540 TQ	USBLS	5/15
Including Health	San Antonio-New Braunfels MSA, TX	Y	45970 FQ	62710 MW	86030 TQ	USBLS	5/15
Including Health	Utah	Y	53780 FQ	64980 MW	76500 TQ	USBLS	5/15
Including Health	Ogden-Clearfield MSA, UT	Y	53240 FQ	63830 MW	77140 TQ	USBLS	5/15
Including Health	Salt Lake City MSA, UT	Y	59890 FQ	66760 MW	79520 TQ	USBLS	5/15
Including Health	Vermont	Y	46570 FQ	57240 MW	69060 TQ	USBLS	5/15
Including Health	Burlington-South Burlington MSA, VT	Y	45130 FQ	53000 MW	66970 TQ	USBLS	5/15
Including Health	Virginia	Y	54850 FQ	70300 MW	105970 TQ	USBLS	5/15
Including Health	Richmond MSA, VA	Y	48730 FQ	58980 MW	69800 TQ	USBLS	5/15
Including Health	Virginia Beach-Norfolk-Newport News MSA, VA-NC	Y	56460 FQ	70220 MW	91270 TQ	USBLS	5/15
Including Health	Washington	H	26.21 FQ	32.76 MW	43.85 TQ	WABLS	3/16
Including Health	Seattle-Bellevue-Everett PMSA, WA	H	26.30 FQ	34.87 MW	46.96 TQ	WABLS	3/16
Including Health	Tacoma-Lakewood PMSA, WA	H	28.85 FQ	33.80 MW	39.80 TQ	WABLS	3/16
Including Health	West Virginia	Y	37300 FQ	45720 MW	58940 TQ	USBLS	5/15
Including Health	Huntington-Ashland MSA, WV-KY-OH	Y	36260 FQ	55930 MW	89810 TQ	USBLS	5/15
Including Health	Wisconsin	Y	49090 FQ	59090 MW	79410 TQ	USBLS	5/15
Including Health	Madison MSA, WI	Y	51620 FQ	60500 MW	76300 TQ	USBLS	5/15
Including Health	Milwaukee-Waukesha-West Allis MSA, WI	Y	46640 FQ	59050 MW	90530 TQ	USBLS	5/15
Including Health	Wyoming	Y	52090 FQ	58710 MW	72560 TQ	USBLS	5/15
Including Health	Cheyenne MSA, WY	Y	56170 FQ	66430 MW	73560 TQ	USBLS	5/15
Including Health	Puerto Rico	Y	24520 FQ	32650 MW	62520 TQ	USBLS	5/15
Including Health	San Juan-Carolina-Caguas MSA, PR	Y	25410 FQ	33750 MW	63540 TQ	USBLS	5/15
Including Health	Virgin Islands	Y	30330 FQ	42990 MW	58070 TQ	USBLS	5/15
Including Health	Guam	Y	48440 FQ	57060 MW	79550 TQ	USBLS	5/15
Environmental Services Officer							
Public Works Department, Municipal Government	Arcadia, CA	Y			98970 HI	CACIT	6/28/16
Epidemiologist	Alabama	Y	51863 AE	64778 AW	71230 AEX	ALBLS	6/16
	Arizona	Y	45780 FQ	50030 MW	64710 TQ	USBLS	5/15
	Arkansas	Y	49940 FQ	58420 MW	70540 TQ	USBLS	5/15
	California	H	32.54 FQ	42.11 MW	55.81 TQ	CABLS	1/16-3/16
	Colorado	Y	57020 FQ	64690 MW	71360 TQ	USBLS	5/15

AE Average entry wage	AWR Average wage range	H Hourly	LR Low end range	MTC Median total compensation	TCC Total cash compensation
AEX Average experienced wage	B Biweekly	HI Highest wage paid	M Monthly	MCC Median cash compensation	TQ Third quartile wage
ATC Average total compensation	D Daily	HR High end range	MCC Median cash compensation	MWR Median wage range	W Weekly
AW Average wage paid	FQ First quartile wage	LO Lowest wage paid	ME Median entry wage	S See annotated source	Y Yearly

Occupation/Type/Industry	Location	Per	Low	Mid	High	Source	Date
Epidemiologist	Connecticut	Y		86607 MW		CTBLS	1/16-3/16
	District of Columbia	Y	74590 FQ	91910 MW	118380 TQ	USBLS	5/15
	Florida	H	21.93 AE	39.53 MW	42.54 AEX	FLBLS	7/16-9/16
	Georgia	Y	50380 FQ	59660 MW	71660 TQ	USBLS	5/15
	Illinois	Y	61660 FQ	73160 MW	88280 TQ	USBLS	5/15
	Indiana	Y	66570 FQ	74630 MW	86790 TQ	USBLS	5/15
	Iowa	Y	54110 FQ	64710 MW	76400 TQ	USBLS	5/15
	Kentucky	Y	41790 FQ	53000 MW	62930 TQ	USBLS	5/15
	Louisiana	Y	44120 FQ	55220 MW	75180 TQ	USBLS	5/15
	Maine	Y	49070 FQ	57520 MW	70790 TQ	USBLS	5/15
	Maryland	Y	58043 AE	78430 MW	88624 AEX	MDBLS	4/16
	Massachusetts	Y	62270 FQ	74190 MW	96320 TQ	USBLS	5/15
	Michigan	Y	58930 FQ	69720 MW	77400 TQ	USBLS	5/15
	Minnesota	Y	56481 FQ	74404 MW	89061 TQ	MNBLS	1/16-3/16
	Missouri	Y	47960 FQ	55610 MW	74400 TQ	USBLS	5/15
	Nebraska	Y	52005 FQ	59350 MW	73635 TQ	NEBLS	7/16-9/16
	New Jersey	Y	84080 FQ	97790 MW	117200 TQ	USBLS	5/15
	New York	Y	55370 AE	75370 MW	97500 AEX	NYBLS	1/16-3/16
	North Carolina	Y	59730 FQ	98850 MW	138480 TQ	USBLS	5/15
	Ohio	Y	47970 FQ	56620 MW	72450 TQ	USBLS	5/15
	Oklahoma	Y	46710 FQ	55470 MW	63540 TQ	USBLS	5/15
	Pennsylvania	Y	56470 FQ	67860 MW	78500 TQ	USBLS	5/15
	Tennessee	Y	64180 FQ	71000 MW	77810 TQ	USBLS	5/15
	Texas	Y	51810 FQ	61450 MW	76880 TQ	USBLS	5/15
	Virginia	Y	57270 FQ	66640 MW	83580 TQ	USBLS	5/15
	Washington	H	32.56 FQ	39.90 MW	46.67 TQ	WABLS	3/16
	West Virginia	Y	41630 FQ	49910 MW	58820 TQ	USBLS	5/15
	Wisconsin	Y	55820 FQ	62880 MW	74820 TQ	USBLS	5/15
	Puerto Rico	Y	34280 FQ	37490 MW	42660 TQ	USBLS	5/15
Epidemiology Specialist Public Health, County Government	Tarrant County, TX	Y		50708 MW		TTT	6/23/16
Equal Employment Coordinator Municipal Government	Seattle, WA	H	35.69 LO		41.52 HI	CSSS	1/13/16
Equal Opportunity Specialist Department of Labor and Industry, State Government	Billings, MT	H			27.96 HI	MTGOV	2016
Equine Dental Technician	United States	Y	69000 LO		76000 HI	BAL02	9/11
Equipment Keeper Police Department, Municipal Government	Los Angeles, CA	Y			58629 HI	CACIT	6/23/16
Equity Research Associate	United States	Y		100000 MW		CNBC05	2016
Ergonomist United States Postal Service	District of Columbia	Y	101000 LO		105000 HI	APP02	1/16
ERP Manager County Government	Douglas County, CO	Y			58168 HI	DCOGOV	2016
ESL Liaison Public Schools	Baldwin County, AL	Y	29202 LO		38329 HI	BCPSSS	2016-2017
ESL Translator Public Schools	Baldwin County, AL	Y	22766 LO		29779 HI	BCPSSS	2016-2017
Etcher and Engraver	Alabama	Y	22868 AE	30487 AW	34301 AEX	ALBLS	6/16
	Arizona	Y	18170 FQ	19440 MW	23780 TQ	USBLS	5/15
	Phoenix-Mesa-Scottsdale MSA, AZ	Y	18150 FQ	19370 MW	23130 TQ	USBLS	5/15
	California	H	12.42 FQ	16.54 MW	21.71 TQ	CABLS	1/16-3/16
	Los Angeles-Long Beach-Glendale PMSA, CA	H	12.89 FQ	17.80 MW	22.29 TQ	CABLS	1/16-3/16
	Oakland-Hayward-Berkeley PMSA, CA	H	16.30 FQ	17.44 MW	18.58 TQ	CABLS	1/16-3/16
	Riverside-San Bernardino-Ontario MSA, CA	H	10.01 FQ	11.23 MW	12.74 TQ	CABLS	1/16-3/16
	Sacramento-Roseville-Arden-Arcade MSA, CA	H	12.26 FQ	17.15 MW	21.69 TQ	CABLS	1/16-3/16

AE	Average entry wage	**AWR**	Average wage range	**H**	Hourly	**LR** Low end range	**MTC** Median total compensation	**TCC** Total cash compensation
AEX	Average experienced wage	**B**	Biweekly	**HI**	Highest wage paid	**M** Monthly	**MW** Median wage paid	**TQ** Third quartile wage
ATC	Average total compensation	**D**	Daily	**HR**	High end range	**MCC** Median cash compensation	**MWR** Median wage range	**W** Weekly
AW	Average wage paid	**FQ**	First quartile wage	**LO**	Lowest wage paid	**ME** Median entry wage	**S** See annotated source	**Y** Yearly

Occupation/Type/Industry	Location	Per	Low	Mid	High	Source	Date
Etcher and Engraver	San Francisco-Redwood City- South San Francisco PMSA, CA	H	12.81 FQ	14.31 MW	16.87 TQ	CABLS	1/16-3/16
	Colorado	Y	18760 FQ	20710 MW	27170 TQ	USBLS	5/15
	Denver-Aurora-Lakewood MSA, CO	Y	19380 FQ	23420 MW	28670 TQ	USBLS	5/15
	Connecticut	Y		31949 MW		CTBLS	1/16-3/16
	Bridgeport-Stamford-Norwalk MSA, CT	Y	27680 FQ	32120 MW	37810 TQ	USBLS	5/15
	Washington-Arlington- Alexandria PMSA, DC-VA- MD-WV	Y	26650 FQ	29700 MW	35640 TQ	USBLS	5/15
	Florida	H	10.54 AE	14.68 MW	17.48 AEX	FLBLS	7/16-9/16
	Fort Lauderdale-Pompano Beach-Deerfield Beach PMSA, FL	H	12.00 AE	16.87 MW	19.80 AEX	FLBLS	7/16-9/16
	Tampa-St. Petersburg- Clearwater MSA, FL	H	12.30 AE	16.19 MW	17.45 AEX	FLBLS	7/16-9/16
	Georgia	Y	22070 FQ	26170 MW	35330 TQ	USBLS	5/15
	Atlanta-Sandy Springs- Roswell MSA, GA	Y	22630 FQ	26720 MW	36830 TQ	USBLS	5/15
	Idaho	Y	22710 FQ	26400 MW	29450 TQ	USBLS	5/15
	Illinois	Y	25290 FQ	31030 MW	50000 TQ	USBLS	5/15
	Chicago-Naperville-Arlington Heights PMSA, IL	Y	37340 FQ	54000 MW	59450 TQ	USBLS	5/15
	Lake County-Kenosha County PMSA, IL-WI	Y	22840 FQ	29090 MW	43040 TQ	USBLS	5/15
	Indiana	Y	21450 FQ	24530 MW	30370 TQ	USBLS	5/15
	Gary PMSA, IN	Y	20850 FQ	22910 MW	26010 TQ	USBLS	5/15
	Iowa	Y	22290 FQ	29130 MW	35170 TQ	USBLS	5/15
	Kansas	Y	22040 FQ	26570 MW	29580 TQ	USBLS	5/15
	Wichita MSA, KS	Y	22100 FQ	26850 MW	29250 TQ	USBLS	5/15
	Kentucky	Y	21650 FQ	26160 MW	30260 TQ	USBLS	5/15
	Louisiana	Y	21400 FQ	24660 MW	30460 TQ	USBLS	5/15
	Maryland	Y	24856 AE	28988 MW	31054 AEX	MDBLS	4/16
	Massachusetts	Y	29010 FQ	36210 MW	44360 TQ	USBLS	5/15
	Boston-Cambridge-Newton NECTA, MA	Y	29860 FQ	37800 MW	46140 TQ	USBLS	5/15
	Michigan	Y	25830 FQ	30790 MW	37820 TQ	USBLS	5/15
	Grand Rapids-Wyoming MSA, MI	Y	32600 FQ	36010 MW	39420 TQ	USBLS	5/15
	Minnesota	Y	30718 FQ	34808 MW	38929 TQ	MNBLS	1/16-3/16
	Minneapolis-St. Paul- Bloomington MSA, MN-WI	Y	30262 FQ	34211 MW	37936 TQ	MNBLS	1/16-3/16
	Mississippi	Y	25400 FQ	28050 MW	30690 TQ	USBLS	5/15
	Missouri	Y	24070 FQ	30850 MW	40340 TQ	USBLS	5/15
	St. Louis MSA, MO-IL	Y	22630 FQ	32950 MW	39330 TQ	USBLS	5/15
	Nebraska	Y	23525 FQ	28895 MW	34980 TQ	NEBLS	7/16-9/16
	Omaha-Council Bluffs MSA, NE-IA	Y	23550 FQ	31995 MW	35825 TQ	NEBLS	7/16-9/16
	Nevada	Y	20110 FQ	23260 MW	27840 TQ	USBLS	5/15
	New Hampshire	H	10.70 AE	13.77 MW	15.68 AEX	NHBLS	6/16
	New Jersey	Y	29800 FQ	36500 MW	43750 TQ	USBLS	5/15
	Camden PMSA, NJ	Y	25040 FQ	30710 MW	41600 TQ	USBLS	5/15
	Newark PMSA, NJ-PA	Y	30430 FQ	38960 MW	47140 TQ	USBLS	5/15
	New York	Y	24330 AE	34790 MW	40980 AEX	NYBLS	1/16-3/16
	Nassau County-Suffolk County PMSA, NY	Y	24830 FQ	36900 MW	44000 TQ	USBLS	5/15
	New York-Jersey City-White Plains PMSA, NY-NJ	Y	32440 FQ	37350 MW	43910 TQ	USBLS	5/15
	Rochester MSA, NY	Y	33430 FQ	36540 MW	39640 TQ	USBLS	5/15
	North Carolina	Y	27900 FQ	37000 MW	44790 TQ	USBLS	5/15
	North Dakota	Y	32350 FQ	34890 MW	37440 TQ	USBLS	5/15
	Ohio	Y	27110 FQ	32500 MW	41040 TQ	USBLS	5/15
	Cincinnati MSA, OH-KY-IN	Y	24260 FQ	27250 MW	30120 TQ	USBLS	5/15
	Cleveland-Elyria MSA, OH	Y	28650 FQ	35650 MW	44830 TQ	USBLS	5/15
	Oklahoma	Y	23070 FQ	27530 MW	31280 TQ	USBLS	5/15
	Oregon	H	10.90 FQ	12.04 MW	16.55 TQ	ORBLS	2016
	Portland-Vancouver-Hillsboro MSA, OR-WA	Y	24130 FQ	30880 MW	38480 TQ	USBLS	5/15
	Pennsylvania	Y	27170 FQ	34770 MW	41780 TQ	USBLS	5/15

AE	Average entry wage	AWR	Average wage range	H	Hourly	LR	Low end range	MTC	Median total compensation	TCC	Total cash compensation
AEX	Average experienced wage	B	Biweekly	HI	Highest wage paid	M	Monthly	MW	Median wage paid	TQ	Third quartile wage
ATC	Average total compensation	D	Daily	HR	High end range	MCC	Median cash compensation	MWR	Median wage range	W	Weekly
AW	Average wage paid	FQ	First quartile wage	LO	Lowest wage paid	ME	Median entry wage	S	See annotated source	Y	Yearly

544

Occupation/Type/Industry	Location	Per	Low	Mid	High	Source	Date
Etcher and Engraver	Allentown-Bethlehem-Easton						
	MSA, PA-NJ	Y	34000 FQ	39250 MW	44620 TQ	USBLS	5/15
	Harrisburg-Carlisle MSA, PA	Y	27150 FQ	32620 MW	36370 TQ	USBLS	5/15
	Montgomery County-Bucks County-Chester County						
	PMSA, PA	Y	26560 FQ	32230 MW	42260 TQ	USBLS	5/15
	Pittsburgh MSA, PA	Y	37320 FQ	42850 MW	46510 TQ	USBLS	5/15
	Rhode Island	Y	29980 FQ	35810 MW	42170 TQ	USBLS	5/15
	Providence-Warwick MSA, RI-MA	Y	29420 FQ	35090 MW	40990 TQ	USBLS	5/15
	South Dakota	Y	21550 FQ	25470 MW	29070 TQ	USBLS	5/15
	Tennessee	Y	22870 FQ	31220 MW	42500 TQ	USBLS	5/15
	Texas	Y	19650 FQ	25430 MW	33600 TQ	USBLS	5/15
	Austin-Round Rock MSA, TX	Y	24100 FQ	27330 MW	30140 TQ	USBLS	5/15
	Dallas-Plano-Irving PMSA, TX	Y	19660 FQ	25600 MW	35390 TQ	USBLS	5/15
	Houston-The Woodlands-Sugar Land MSA, TX	Y	18210 FQ	20990 MW	28000 TQ	USBLS	5/15
	San Antonio-New Braunfels MSA, TX	Y	18960 FQ	26510 MW	32530 TQ	USBLS	5/15
	Utah	Y	26080 FQ	30420 MW	35530 TQ	USBLS	5/15
	Salt Lake City MSA, UT	Y	28480 FQ	32560 MW	36640 TQ	USBLS	5/15
	Virginia	Y	27110 FQ	31110 MW	37670 TQ	USBLS	5/15
	Richmond MSA, VA	Y	26790 FQ	30440 MW	39390 TQ	USBLS	5/15
	Virginia Beach-Norfolk-Newport News MSA, VA-NC	Y	26690 FQ	29140 MW	32250 TQ	USBLS	5/15
	Washington	H	14.19 FQ	21.83 MW	27.68 TQ	WABLS	3/16
	Seattle-Bellevue-Everett PMSA, WA	H	21.93 FQ	25.25 MW	29.23 TQ	WABLS	3/16
	Tacoma-Lakewood PMSA, WA	H	13.71 FQ	15.17 MW	18.62 TQ	WABLS	3/16
	West Virginia	Y	21850 FQ	23680 MW	26830 TQ	USBLS	5/15
	Huntington-Ashland MSA, WV-KY-OH	Y	20760 FQ	23840 MW	27390 TQ	USBLS	5/15
	Wisconsin	Y	23420 FQ	29710 MW	37220 TQ	USBLS	5/15
	Milwaukee-Waukesha-West Allis MSA, WI	Y	24070 FQ	33260 MW	40440 TQ	USBLS	5/15
	Wyoming	Y	23920 FQ	37450 MW	45530 TQ	USBLS	5/15
Event Coordinator	United States	Y		46490 MW		CBS04	2016
Baccalaureate Institution	United States	Y		44726 MW		CHE02	2015-2016
Master's Institution	United States	Y		48688 MW		CHE02	2015-2016
Research University	United States	Y		48905 MW		CHE02	2015-2016
Event Crowd Control Supervisor							
Municipal Government	Anaheim, CA	Y			63272 HI	CACIT	6/28/16
Event-Planning Assistant							
Baccalaureate Institution	United States	Y		36400 MW		CHE01	2015-2016
Master's Institution	United States	Y		33619 MW		CHE01	2015-2016
Research University	United States	Y		38348 MW		CHE01	2015-2016
Events Booking Representative							
Municipal Government	Seattle, WA	H	29.43 LO		34.30 HI	CSSS	1/13/16
Evidence Supervisor							
Police Department, Municipal Government	Colorado Springs, CO	Y	60361 LO		82997 HI	COSPRS	2017
Evidence Technician							
Police Department, Municipal Government	Arcata, CA	Y			46948 HI	CACIT	6/28/16
Police Department, Municipal Government	Dinuba, CA	Y			32661 HI	CACIT	6/28/16
Police Department, Municipal Government	Novato, CA	Y			64506 HI	CACIT	6/28/16
Police Investigations, Municipal Government	Tulare, CA	Y			51726 HI	CACIT	6/28/16
Public Safety Department, Municipal Government	Dunwoody, GA	H	15.87 LO		27.12 HI	GACTY01	2016
Public Safety Department, Municipal Government	Johns Creek City, GA	H	19.43 LO		26.03 HI	GACTY01	2016
Public Safety Department, Municipal Government	Suwanee, GA	H	18.04 LO		23.85 HI	GACTY01	2016
Evidence Warehouser							
Municipal Government	Seattle, WA	H	23.61 LO		25.48 HI	CSSS	6/4/14

AE	Average entry wage	**AWR**	Average wage range	**H**	Hourly	**LR**	Low end range	**MTC**	Median total compensation	**TCC**	Total cash compensation
AEX	Average experienced wage	**B**	Biweekly	**HI**	Highest wage paid	**M**	Monthly	**MW**	Median wage paid	**TQ**	Third quartile wage
ATC	Average total compensation	**D**	Daily	**HR**	High end range	**MCC**	Median cash compensation	**MWR**	Median wage range	**W**	Weekly
AW	Average wage paid	**FQ**	First quartile wage	**LO**	Lowest wage paid	**ME**	Median entry wage	**S**	See annotated source	**Y**	Yearly

Excavating and Loading Machine and Dragline Operator

Occupation/Type/Industry	Location	Per	Low	Mid	High	Source	Date
Excavating and Loading Machine and Dragline Operator	Alabama	Y	27214 AE	40616 AW	47321 AEX	ALBLS	6/16
	Birmingham-Hoover MSA, AL	Y	33797 AE	46889 AW	53431 AEX	ALBLS	6/16
	Alaska	Y	44260 FQ	52450 MW	71700 TQ	USBLS	5/15
	Anchorage MSA, AK	Y	42040 FQ	47060 MW	55320 TQ	USBLS	5/15
	Arizona	Y	31520 FQ	38730 MW	45740 TQ	USBLS	5/15
	Phoenix-Mesa-Scottsdale MSA, AZ	Y	31490 FQ	37870 MW	45250 TQ	USBLS	5/15
	Tucson MSA, AZ	Y	40550 FQ	44840 MW	49130 TQ	USBLS	5/15
	Arkansas	Y	27230 FQ	30670 MW	34380 TQ	USBLS	5/15
	Little Rock-North Little Rock-Conway MSA, AR	Y	28260 FQ	30680 MW	34710 TQ	USBLS	5/15
	California	H	22.33 FQ	27.95 MW	35.35 TQ	CABLS	1/16-3/16
	Los Angeles-Long Beach-Glendale PMSA, CA	H	16.30 FQ	19.25 MW	23.58 TQ	CABLS	1/16-3/16
	Oakland-Hayward-Berkeley PMSA, CA	H	27.67 FQ	30.37 MW	44.49 TQ	CABLS	1/16-3/16
	Riverside-San Bernardino-Ontario MSA, CA	H	25.06 FQ	27.50 MW	29.74 TQ	CABLS	1/16-3/16
	Sacramento–Roseville–Arden-Arcade MSA, CA	H	26.77 FQ	29.55 MW	35.47 TQ	CABLS	1/16-3/16
	San Diego-Carlsbad MSA, CA	H	25.31 FQ	27.37 MW	29.45 TQ	CABLS	1/16-3/16
	San Francisco-Redwood City-South San Francisco PMSA, CA	H	33.30 FQ	37.40 MW	46.91 TQ	CABLS	1/16-3/16
	Colorado	Y	35430 FQ	43140 MW	52570 TQ	USBLS	5/15
	Denver-Aurora-Lakewood MSA, CO	Y	35690 FQ	43110 MW	49400 TQ	USBLS	5/15
	Connecticut	Y		46138 MW		CTBLS	1/16-3/16
	Hartford-West Hartford-East Hartford MSA, CT	Y	26370 FQ	35320 MW	46970 TQ	USBLS	5/15
	Delaware	Y	38200 FQ	44880 MW	52420 TQ	USBLS	5/15
	Wilmington PMSA, DE-MD-NJ	Y	39690 FQ	48570 MW	57190 TQ	USBLS	5/15
	District of Columbia	Y	53140 FQ	56780 MW	60420 TQ	USBLS	5/15
	Washington-Arlington-Alexandria PMSA, DC-VA-MD-WV	Y	39860 FQ	47730 MW	56160 TQ	USBLS	5/15
	Florida	H	13.45 AE	18.14 MW	22.02 AEX	FLBLS	7/16-9/16
	Fort Lauderdale-Pompano Beach-Deerfield Beach PMSA, FL	H	11.48 AE	17.05 MW	19.53 AEX	FLBLS	7/16-9/16
	Miami-Miami Beach-Kendall PMSA, FL	H	15.01 AE	18.16 MW	22.55 AEX	FLBLS	7/16-9/16
	Orlando-Kissimmee-Sanford MSA, FL	H	12.94 AE	17.37 MW	20.54 AEX	FLBLS	7/16-9/16
	Tampa-St. Petersburg-Clearwater MSA, FL	H	16.55 AE	18.15 MW	19.73 AEX	FLBLS	7/16-9/16
	Georgia	Y	34660 FQ	41690 MW	48200 TQ	USBLS	5/15
	Atlanta-Sandy Springs-Roswell MSA, GA	Y	34900 FQ	41290 MW	46970 TQ	USBLS	5/15
	Augusta-Richmond County MSA, GA-SC	Y	55760 FQ	66200 MW	72630 TQ	USBLS	5/15
	Hawaii	Y	32710 FQ	41520 MW	56470 TQ	USBLS	5/15
	Urban Honolulu MSA, HI	Y	35180 FQ	47770 MW	61860 TQ	USBLS	5/15
	Idaho	Y	29280 FQ	35260 MW	45100 TQ	USBLS	5/15
	Illinois	Y	39390 FQ	54490 MW	67850 TQ	USBLS	5/15
	Chicago-Naperville-Arlington Heights PMSA, IL	Y	36600 FQ	53780 MW	64940 TQ	USBLS	5/15
	Indiana	Y	34130 FQ	41220 MW	67000 TQ	USBLS	5/15
	Gary PMSA, IN	Y	82410 FQ	90400 MW	97710 TQ	USBLS	5/15
	Indianapolis-Carmel-Anderson MSA, IN	Y	36530 FQ	48570 MW	71030 TQ	USBLS	5/15
	Iowa	Y	29760 FQ	35340 MW	40670 TQ	USBLS	5/15
	Des Moines-West Des Moines MSA, IA	Y	34560 FQ	43900 MW	48460 TQ	USBLS	5/15
	Kansas	Y	33500 FQ	38390 MW	48500 TQ	USBLS	5/15
	Wichita MSA, KS	Y	33850 FQ	38880 MW	45640 TQ	USBLS	5/15
	Kentucky	Y	31560 FQ	39820 MW	48300 TQ	USBLS	5/15
	Louisville-Jefferson County MSA, KY-IN	Y	30330 FQ	38090 MW	45770 TQ	USBLS	5/15
	Louisiana	Y	33620 FQ	38250 MW	47700 TQ	USBLS	5/15

AE	Average entry wage	AWR	Average wage range	H	Hourly	LR	Low end range	MTC	Median total compensation	TCC	Total cash compensation
AEX	Average experienced wage	B	Biweekly	HI	Highest wage paid	M	Monthly	MW	Median wage paid	TQ	Third quartile wage
ATC	Average total compensation	D	Daily	HR	High end range	MCC	Median cash compensation	MWR	Median wage range	W	Weekly
AW	Average wage paid	FQ	First quartile wage	LO	Lowest wage paid	ME	Median entry wage	S	See annotated source	Y	Yearly

Occupation/Type/Industry	Location	Per	Low	Mid	High	Source	Date
Excavating and Loading Machine and Dragline Operator	Baton Rouge MSA, LA	Y	33570 FQ	37200 MW	42790 TQ	USBLS	5/15
	New Orleans-Metairie MSA, LA	Y	35610 FQ	44050 MW	52570 TQ	USBLS	5/15
	Maine	Y	33510 FQ	38420 MW	46820 TQ	USBLS	5/15
	Portland-South Portland MSA, ME	Y	33730 FQ	38040 MW	48630 TQ	USBLS	5/15
	Maryland	Y	35366 AE	47293 MW	53256 AEX	MDBLS	4/16
	Baltimore-Columbia-Towson MSA, MD	Y	40500 FQ	46540 MW	55040 TQ	USBLS	5/15
	Salisbury MSA, MD-DE	Y	35870 FQ	41280 MW	47150 TQ	USBLS	5/15
	Massachusetts	Y	44090 FQ	59550 MW	104160 TQ	USBLS	5/15
	Worcester MSA, MA-CT	Y	49960 FQ	57040 MW	67070 TQ	USBLS	5/15
	Michigan	Y	34190 FQ	40570 MW	48780 TQ	USBLS	5/15
	Grand Rapids-Wyoming MSA, MI	Y	33220 FQ	42000 MW	55280 TQ	USBLS	5/15
	Minnesota	Y	39943 FQ	46617 MW	59702 TQ	MNBLS	1/16-3/16
	Minneapolis-St. Paul-Bloomington MSA, MN-WI	Y	43007 FQ	47756 MW	61608 TQ	MNBLS	1/16-3/16
	Mississippi	Y	29610 FQ	35030 MW	42230 TQ	USBLS	5/15
	Jackson MSA, MS	Y	27010 FQ	30890 MW	38720 TQ	USBLS	5/15
	Missouri	Y	28290 FQ	37620 MW	48330 TQ	USBLS	5/15
	Kansas City MSA, MO-KS	Y	32880 FQ	35790 MW	38700 TQ	USBLS	5/15
	St. Louis MSA, MO-IL	Y	23010 FQ	37390 MW	48160 TQ	USBLS	5/15
	Montana	Y	34170 FQ	39280 MW	51860 TQ	USBLS	5/15
	Nebraska	Y	29310 FQ	36230 MW	47610 TQ	NEBLS	7/16-9/16
	Omaha-Council Bluffs MSA, NE-IA	Y	27730 FQ	30710 MW	41495 TQ	NEBLS	7/16-9/16
	Nevada	Y	39890 FQ	51440 MW	65760 TQ	USBLS	5/15
	Las Vegas-Henderson-Paradise MSA, NV	Y	37390 FQ	46950 MW	83190 TQ	USBLS	5/15
	New Hampshire	H	16.89 AE	20.92 MW	24.09 AEX	NHBLS	6/16
	Manchester NECTA, NH	H	18.41 AE	25.67 MW	27.66 AEX	NHBLS	6/16
	Nashua NECTA, NH-MA	Y	40530 FQ	47770 MW	56170 TQ	USBLS	5/15
	New Jersey	Y	40060 FQ	51390 MW	62100 TQ	USBLS	5/15
	Camden PMSA, NJ	Y	42880 FQ	51010 MW	76580 TQ	USBLS	5/15
	Newark PMSA, NJ-PA	Y	37170 FQ	50650 MW	62270 TQ	USBLS	5/15
	New Mexico	Y	33430 FQ	41360 MW	50690 TQ	USBLS	5/15
	Albuquerque MSA, NM	Y	35920 FQ	42380 MW	47130 TQ	USBLS	5/15
	New York	Y	36320 AE	54290 MW	74330 AEX	NYBLS	1/16-3/16
	Nassau County-Suffolk County PMSA, NY	Y	34910 FQ	46510 MW	59260 TQ	USBLS	5/15
	New York-Jersey City-White Plains PMSA, NY-NJ	Y	53560 FQ	78470 MW	89470 TQ	USBLS	5/15
	Rochester MSA, NY	Y	30380 FQ	38880 MW	46250 TQ	USBLS	5/15
	North Carolina	Y	30510 FQ	35670 MW	41670 TQ	USBLS	5/15
	Charlotte-Concord-Gastonia MSA, NC-SC	Y	32050 FQ	36350 MW	41740 TQ	USBLS	5/15
	Raleigh MSA, NC	Y	33720 FQ	37010 MW	41750 TQ	USBLS	5/15
	North Dakota	Y	41460 FQ	48660 MW	62240 TQ	USBLS	5/15
	Fargo MSA, ND-MN	Y	39500 FQ	45090 MW	50200 TQ	USBLS	5/15
	Ohio	Y	30050 FQ	40420 MW	48870 TQ	USBLS	5/15
	Cincinnati MSA, OH-KY-IN	Y	33910 FQ	38970 MW	47240 TQ	USBLS	5/15
	Cleveland-Elyria MSA, OH	Y	27090 FQ	36480 MW	59140 TQ	USBLS	5/15
	Columbus MSA, OH	Y	30990 FQ	36250 MW	46820 TQ	USBLS	5/15
	Oklahoma	Y	31810 FQ	38190 MW	47080 TQ	USBLS	5/15
	Oklahoma City MSA, OK	Y	31900 FQ	38740 MW	45790 TQ	USBLS	5/15
	Tulsa MSA, OK	Y	31430 FQ	36280 MW	42980 TQ	USBLS	5/15
	Oregon	H	16.53 FQ	19.21 MW	24.82 TQ	ORBLS	2016
	Portland-Vancouver-Hillsboro MSA, OR-WA	Y	43450 FQ	58170 MW	73940 TQ	USBLS	5/15
	Pennsylvania	Y	34490 FQ	42220 MW	50560 TQ	USBLS	5/15
	Allentown-Bethlehem-Easton MSA, PA-NJ	Y	34960 FQ	39690 MW	46250 TQ	USBLS	5/15
	Harrisburg-Carlisle MSA, PA	Y	33510 FQ	36510 MW	39510 TQ	USBLS	5/15
	Montgomery County-Bucks County-Chester County PMSA, PA	Y	39310 FQ	44400 MW	49480 TQ	USBLS	5/15
	Pittsburgh MSA, PA	Y	37020 FQ	44450 MW	54790 TQ	USBLS	5/15
	Rhode Island	Y	44380 FQ	52570 MW	58690 TQ	USBLS	5/15
	Providence-Warwick MSA, RI-MA	Y	42950 FQ	53090 MW	59840 TQ	USBLS	5/15

AE Average entry wage	**AWR** Average wage range	**H** Hourly	**LR** Low end range	**MTC** Median total compensation	**TCC** Total cash compensation
AEX Average experienced wage	**B** Biweekly	**HI** Highest wage paid	**M** Monthly	**MW** Median wage paid	**TQ** Third quartile wage
ATC Average total compensation	**D** Daily	**HR** High end range	**MCC** Median cash compensation	**MWR** Median wage range	**W** Weekly
AW Average wage paid	**FQ** First quartile wage	**LO** Lowest wage paid	**ME** Median entry wage	**S** See annotated source	**Y** Yearly

Occupation/Type/Industry	Location	Per	Low	Mid	High	Source	Date
Excavating and Loading Machine and Dragline Operator	South Carolina	Y	41720 FQ	63480 MW	71070 TQ	USBLS	5/15
	Charleston-North Charleston MSA, SC	Y	38030 FQ	43120 MW	47350 TQ	USBLS	5/15
	Columbia MSA, SC	Y	29830 FQ	38550 MW	45340 TQ	USBLS	5/15
	Greenville-Anderson-Mauldin MSA, SC	Y	30860 FQ	34890 MW	38830 TQ	USBLS	5/15
	South Dakota	Y	29790 FQ	34610 MW	39350 TQ	USBLS	5/15
	Sioux Falls MSA, SD	Y	32810 FQ	36200 MW	39530 TQ	USBLS	5/15
	Tennessee	Y	31020 FQ	35150 MW	39020 TQ	USBLS	5/15
	Knoxville MSA, TN	Y	29060 FQ	34760 MW	40170 TQ	USBLS	5/15
	Memphis MSA, TN-MS-AR	Y	27840 FQ	33580 MW	37510 TQ	USBLS	5/15
	Nashville-Davidson–Murfreesboro–Franklin MSA, TN	Y	33630 FQ	36640 MW	39730 TQ	USBLS	5/15
	Texas	Y	28240 FQ	33970 MW	39100 TQ	USBLS	5/15
	Austin-Round Rock MSA, TX	Y	27530 FQ	32130 MW	37790 TQ	USBLS	5/15
	Dallas-Plano-Irving PMSA, TX	Y	24890 FQ	30820 MW	36990 TQ	USBLS	5/15
	Fort Worth-Arlington PMSA, TX	Y	30190 FQ	36620 MW	45220 TQ	USBLS	5/15
	Houston-The Woodlands-Sugar Land MSA, TX	Y	27990 FQ	32440 MW	37200 TQ	USBLS	5/15
	San Antonio-New Braunfels MSA, TX	Y	32830 FQ	35390 MW	37940 TQ	USBLS	5/15
	Utah	Y	32230 FQ	39740 MW	48310 TQ	USBLS	5/15
	Ogden-Clearfield MSA, UT	Y	39440 FQ	44270 MW	48920 TQ	USBLS	5/15
	Salt Lake City MSA, UT	Y	18410 FQ	34840 MW	44850 TQ	USBLS	5/15
	Vermont	Y	33620 FQ	36600 MW	39610 TQ	USBLS	5/15
	Burlington-South Burlington MSA, VT	Y	32720 FQ	35500 MW	38280 TQ	USBLS	5/15
	Virginia	Y	32340 FQ	37590 MW	45110 TQ	USBLS	5/15
	Richmond MSA, VA	Y	31150 FQ	36850 MW	43250 TQ	USBLS	5/15
	Virginia Beach-Norfolk-Newport News MSA, VA-NC	Y	34160 FQ	38280 MW	45060 TQ	USBLS	5/15
	Washington	H	25.68 FQ	30.57 MW	35.99 TQ	WABLS	3/16
	Seattle-Bellevue-Everett PMSA, WA	H	27.96 FQ	31.90 MW	35.93 TQ	WABLS	3/16
	Tacoma-Lakewood PMSA, WA	H	20.22 FQ	25.92 MW	30.38 TQ	WABLS	3/16
	West Virginia	Y	32360 FQ	42360 MW	51990 TQ	USBLS	5/15
	Huntington-Ashland MSA, WV-KY-OH	Y	30360 FQ	36800 MW	48450 TQ	USBLS	5/15
	Wisconsin	Y	38120 FQ	45870 MW	59730 TQ	USBLS	5/15
	Madison MSA, WI	Y	39760 FQ	47180 MW	57020 TQ	USBLS	5/15
	Milwaukee-Waukesha-West Allis MSA, WI	Y	41100 FQ	46360 MW	58010 TQ	USBLS	5/15
	Wyoming	Y	62200 FQ	69940 MW	75820 TQ	USBLS	5/15
	Puerto Rico	Y	17470 FQ	19220 MW	22520 TQ	USBLS	5/15
	San Juan-Carolina-Caguas MSA, PR	Y	17570 FQ	19350 MW	22870 TQ	USBLS	5/15
	Guam	Y	21570 FQ	23220 MW	24910 TQ	USBLS	5/15
Executive Director							
Life Plan Community	United States	Y		159922 AW		MLTCN04	2016
Nonprofit Organization	Maine	Y		52000-135096 MWR		MENP	2016
Executive Pastry Chef	Chicago, IL	Y		35000-60000 AWR		NYT04	2016
Executive Secretary and Executive Administrative Assistant	Alabama	Y	41883 AE	56590 AW	63938 AEX	ALBLS	6/16
	Birmingham-Hoover MSA, AL	Y	43986 AE	58971 AW	66463 AEX	ALBLS	6/16
	Alaska	Y	46540 FQ	55750 MW	66130 TQ	USBLS	5/15
	Anchorage MSA, AK	Y	45340 FQ	54640 MW	65770 TQ	USBLS	5/15
	Arizona	Y	40990 FQ	49520 MW	59920 TQ	USBLS	5/15
	Phoenix-Mesa-Scottsdale MSA, AZ	Y	41460 FQ	50230 MW	60730 TQ	USBLS	5/15
	Tucson MSA, AZ	Y	40960 FQ	50890 MW	59000 TQ	USBLS	5/15
	Arkansas	Y	34990 FQ	43340 MW	51810 TQ	USBLS	5/15
	Little Rock-North Little Rock-Conway MSA, AR	Y	36270 FQ	45080 MW	56050 TQ	USBLS	5/15
	California	H	23.23 FQ	29.37 MW	36.26 TQ	CABLS	1/16-3/16

AE	Average entry wage	**AWR**	Average wage range	**H**	Hourly	**LR** Low end range
AEX	Average experienced wage	**B**	Biweekly	**HI**	Highest wage paid	**M** Monthly
ATC	Average total compensation	**D**	Daily	**HR**	High end range	**MCC** Median cash compensation
AW	Average wage paid	**FQ**	First quartile wage	**LO**	Lowest wage paid	**ME** Median entry wage

MTC Median total compensation   TCC Total cash compensation
MW Median wage paid   TQ Third quartile wage
MWR Median wage range   W Weekly
S See annotated source   Y Yearly

Occupation/Type/Industry	Location	Per	Low	Mid	High	Source	Date
Executive Secretary and Executive Administrative Assistant							
	Anaheim-Santa Ana-Irvine PMSA, CA	H	22.15 FQ	28.34 MW	34.65 TQ	CABLS	1/16-3/16
	Los Angeles-Long Beach-Glendale PMSA, CA	H	22.96 FQ	29.13 MW	36.05 TQ	CABLS	1/16-3/16
	Oakland-Hayward-Berkeley PMSA, CA	H	25.49 FQ	32.13 MW	37.87 TQ	CABLS	1/16-3/16
	Riverside-San Bernardino-Ontario MSA, CA	H	21.21 FQ	26.01 MW	30.96 TQ	CABLS	1/16-3/16
	Sacramento–Roseville–Arden-Arcade MSA, CA	H	22.14 FQ	26.02 MW	31.66 TQ	CABLS	1/16-3/16
	San Diego-Carlsbad MSA, CA	H	22.89 FQ	28.38 MW	34.53 TQ	CABLS	1/16-3/16
	San Francisco-Redwood City-South San Francisco PMSA, CA	H	28.33 FQ	34.61 MW	40.88 TQ	CABLS	1/16-3/16
	Colorado	Y	42460 FQ	50870 MW	61000 TQ	USBLS	5/15
	Denver-Aurora-Lakewood MSA, CO	Y	44880 FQ	53590 MW	62880 TQ	USBLS	5/15
	Connecticut	Y		68462 MW		CTBLS	1/16-3/16
	Bridgeport-Stamford-Norwalk MSA, CT	Y	62500 FQ	73500 MW	87740 TQ	USBLS	5/15
	Hartford-West Hartford-East Hartford MSA, CT	Y	54050 FQ	65120 MW	74560 TQ	USBLS	5/15
	Delaware	Y	48760 FQ	57660 MW	68350 TQ	USBLS	5/15
	Wilmington PMSA, DE-MD-NJ	Y	50770 FQ	59920 MW	70990 TQ	USBLS	5/15
	District of Columbia	Y	48920 FQ	61930 MW	75430 TQ	USBLS	5/15
	Washington-Arlington-Alexandria PMSA, DC-VA-MD-WV	Y	50360 FQ	63360 MW	76370 TQ	USBLS	5/15
	Florida	H	16.82 AE	23.44 MW	28.30 AEX	FLBLS	7/16-9/16
	Fort Lauderdale-Pompano Beach-Deerfield Beach PMSA, FL	H	18.64 AE	25.21 MW	30.70 AEX	FLBLS	7/16-9/16
	Miami-Miami Beach-Kendall PMSA, FL	H	18.70 AE	25.01 MW	30.16 AEX	FLBLS	7/16-9/16
	Orlando-Kissimmee-Sanford MSA, FL	H	16.03 AE	22.22 MW	26.47 AEX	FLBLS	7/16-9/16
	Tampa-St. Petersburg-Clearwater MSA, FL	H	17.91 AE	23.86 MW	28.38 AEX	FLBLS	7/16-9/16
	Georgia	Y	38740 FQ	48570 MW	63520 TQ	USBLS	5/15
	Atlanta-Sandy Springs-Roswell MSA, GA	Y	41450 FQ	51590 MW	66520 TQ	USBLS	5/15
	Augusta-Richmond County MSA, GA-SC	Y	32830 FQ	38830 MW	50500 TQ	USBLS	5/15
	Hawaii	Y	42790 FQ	51290 MW	60230 TQ	USBLS	5/15
	Urban Honolulu MSA, HI	Y	43420 FQ	52390 MW	60730 TQ	USBLS	5/15
	Idaho	Y	30990 FQ	39660 MW	52600 TQ	USBLS	5/15
	Boise City MSA, ID	Y	32640 FQ	42610 MW	55020 TQ	USBLS	5/15
	Illinois	Y	39020 FQ	50270 MW	62510 TQ	USBLS	5/15
	Chicago-Naperville-Arlington Heights PMSA, IL	Y	42300 FQ	53440 MW	64390 TQ	USBLS	5/15
	Lake County-Kenosha County PMSA, IL-WI	Y	44290 FQ	55180 MW	67990 TQ	USBLS	5/15
	Indiana	Y	35530 FQ	44060 MW	55460 TQ	USBLS	5/15
	Gary PMSA, IN	Y	34140 FQ	42470 MW	52670 TQ	USBLS	5/15
	Indianapolis-Carmel-Anderson MSA, IN	Y	37440 FQ	47610 MW	60240 TQ	USBLS	5/15
	Iowa	Y	34100 FQ	42070 MW	51860 TQ	USBLS	5/15
	Des Moines-West Des Moines MSA, IA	Y	37860 FQ	47110 MW	57250 TQ	USBLS	5/15
	Kansas	Y	35330 FQ	44040 MW	56080 TQ	USBLS	5/15
	Wichita MSA, KS	Y	37830 FQ	47280 MW	60030 TQ	USBLS	5/15
	Kentucky	Y	34830 FQ	43120 MW	51900 TQ	USBLS	5/15
	Louisville-Jefferson County MSA, KY-IN	Y	38330 FQ	45320 MW	53560 TQ	USBLS	5/15
	Louisiana	Y	30760 FQ	38050 MW	48010 TQ	USBLS	5/15
	Baton Rouge MSA, LA	Y	31760 FQ	39640 MW	49740 TQ	USBLS	5/15
	New Orleans-Metairie MSA, LA	Y	32670 FQ	39800 MW	50670 TQ	USBLS	5/15
	Maine	Y	39460 FQ	46290 MW	56320 TQ	USBLS	5/15

AE	Average entry wage	AWR	Average wage range	H	Hourly
AEX	Average experienced wage	B	Biweekly	HI	Highest wage paid
ATC	Average total compensation	D	Daily	HR	High end range
AW	Average wage paid	FQ	First quartile wage	LO	Lowest wage paid

LR	Low end range	MTC	Median total compensation	TCC	Total cash compensation
M	Monthly	MW	Median wage paid	TQ	Third quartile wage
MCC	Median cash compensation	MWR	Median wage range	W	Weekly
ME	Median entry wage	S	See annotated source	Y	Yearly

Occupation/Type/Industry	Location	Per	Low	Mid	High	Source	Date
Executive Secretary and Executive Administrative Assistant	Portland-South Portland MSA, ME	Y	41110 FQ	48690 MW	58560 TQ	USBLS	5/15
	Maryland	Y	46872 AE	64818 MW	73791 AEX	MDBLS	4/16
	Baltimore-Columbia-Towson MSA, MD	Y	50090 FQ	61180 MW	73940 TQ	USBLS	5/15
	Salisbury MSA, MD-DE	Y	42770 FQ	51930 MW	65270 TQ	USBLS	5/15
	Massachusetts	Y	45720 FQ	56790 MW	69380 TQ	USBLS	5/15
	Boston-Cambridge-Newton NECTA, MA	Y	48980 FQ	60370 MW	73070 TQ	USBLS	5/15
	Worcester MSA, MA-CT	Y	42000 FQ	48410 MW	57850 TQ	USBLS	5/15
	Michigan	Y	41360 FQ	50570 MW	60410 TQ	USBLS	5/15
	Detroit-Dearborn-Livonia PMSA, MI	Y	44860 FQ	54740 MW	64270 TQ	USBLS	5/15
	Grand Rapids-Wyoming MSA, MI	Y	41120 FQ	48180 MW	56780 TQ	USBLS	5/15
	Minnesota	Y	42069 FQ	50371 MW	60474 TQ	MNBLS	1/16-3/16
	Minneapolis-St. Paul-Bloomington MSA, MN-WI	Y	43950 FQ	52910 MW	62173 TQ	MNBLS	1/16-3/16
	Mississippi	Y	29140 FQ	38300 MW	53060 TQ	USBLS	5/15
	Jackson MSA, MS	Y	28510 FQ	36500 MW	54040 TQ	USBLS	5/15
	Missouri	Y	39010 FQ	49150 MW	62280 TQ	USBLS	5/15
	Kansas City MSA, MO-KS	Y	40870 FQ	49250 MW	61870 TQ	USBLS	5/15
	St. Louis MSA, MO-IL	Y	39920 FQ	49940 MW	62140 TQ	USBLS	5/15
	Montana	Y	35230 FQ	43340 MW	51890 TQ	USBLS	5/15
	Billings MSA, MT	Y	38440 FQ	48360 MW	59550 TQ	USBLS	5/15
	Nebraska	Y	35090 FQ	42190 MW	50185 TQ	NEBLS	7/16-9/16
	Omaha-Council Bluffs MSA, NE-IA	Y	36500 FQ	44290 MW	53140 TQ	NEBLS	7/16-9/16
	Nevada	Y	44490 FQ	53280 MW	62400 TQ	USBLS	5/15
	Las Vegas-Henderson-Paradise MSA, NV	Y	45150 FQ	54550 MW	63400 TQ	USBLS	5/15
	New Hampshire	H	20.11 AE	26.73 MW	30.97 AEX	NHBLS	6/16
	Manchester NECTA, NH	H	21.12 AE	28.16 MW	32.39 AEX	NHBLS	6/16
	Nashua NECTA, NH-MA	Y	44980 FQ	55060 MW	67960 TQ	USBLS	5/15
	New Jersey	Y	52790 FQ	61910 MW	73570 TQ	USBLS	5/15
	Camden PMSA, NJ	Y	48300 FQ	56750 MW	66040 TQ	USBLS	5/15
	Newark PMSA, NJ-PA	Y	53930 FQ	64670 MW	75200 TQ	USBLS	5/15
	Trenton MSA, NJ	Y	53410 FQ	60550 MW	71350 TQ	USBLS	5/15
	New Mexico	Y	40790 FQ	52680 MW	61660 TQ	USBLS	5/15
	Albuquerque MSA, NM	Y	40920 FQ	52240 MW	59800 TQ	USBLS	5/15
	New York	Y	50810 AE	69140 MW	79140 AEX	NYBLS	1/16-3/16
	Buffalo-Cheektowaga-Niagara Falls MSA, NY	Y	44330 FQ	55360 MW	66640 TQ	USBLS	5/15
	Nassau County-Suffolk County PMSA, NY	Y	57280 FQ	67780 MW	77600 TQ	USBLS	5/15
	New York-Jersey City-White Plains PMSA, NY-NJ	Y	57510 FQ	69020 MW	80080 TQ	USBLS	5/15
	Rochester MSA, NY	Y	46720 FQ	59850 MW	70980 TQ	USBLS	5/15
	North Carolina	Y	41240 FQ	48410 MW	58590 TQ	USBLS	5/15
	Charlotte-Concord-Gastonia MSA, NC-SC	Y	43830 FQ	52470 MW	61540 TQ	USBLS	5/15
	Raleigh MSA, NC	Y	40070 FQ	46680 MW	56540 TQ	USBLS	5/15
	North Dakota	Y	35700 FQ	43030 MW	56800 TQ	USBLS	5/15
	Fargo MSA, ND-MN	Y	37410 FQ	45910 MW	58690 TQ	USBLS	5/15
	Ohio	Y	40650 FQ	49010 MW	59370 TQ	USBLS	5/15
	Cincinnati MSA, OH-KY-IN	Y	41600 FQ	50630 MW	60620 TQ	USBLS	5/15
	Cleveland-Elyria MSA, OH	Y	41600 FQ	50480 MW	60440 TQ	USBLS	5/15
	Columbus MSA, OH	Y	43240 FQ	51740 MW	61830 TQ	USBLS	5/15
	Oklahoma	Y	34480 FQ	42650 MW	53600 TQ	USBLS	5/15
	Oklahoma City MSA, OK	Y	34920 FQ	42640 MW	52920 TQ	USBLS	5/15
	Tulsa MSA, OK	Y	36240 FQ	45470 MW	57700 TQ	USBLS	5/15
	Oregon	H	20.70 FQ	24.69 MW	29.90 TQ	ORBLS	2016
	Portland-Vancouver-Hillsboro MSA, OR-WA	Y	44190 FQ	53390 MW	62720 TQ	USBLS	5/15
	Pennsylvania	Y	43150 FQ	53530 MW	66350 TQ	USBLS	5/15
	Allentown-Bethlehem-Easton MSA, PA-NJ	Y	41630 FQ	50230 MW	65340 TQ	USBLS	5/15
	Harrisburg-Carlisle MSA, PA	Y	42110 FQ	49090 MW	61100 TQ	USBLS	5/15

AE Average entry wage	**AWR** Average wage range	**H** Hourly	**LR** Low end range	**MTC** Median total compensation	**TCC** Total cash compensation
AEX Average experienced wage	**B** Biweekly	**HI** Highest wage paid	**M** Monthly	**MW** Median wage paid	**TQ** Third quartile wage
ATC Average total compensation	**D** Daily	**HR** High end range	**MCC** Median cash compensation	**MWR** Median wage range	**W** Weekly
AW Average wage paid	**FQ** First quartile wage	**LO** Lowest wage paid	**ME** Median entry wage	**S** See annotated source	**Y** Yearly

Occupation/Type/Industry	Location	Per	Low	Mid	High	Source	Date
Executive Secretary and Executive Administrative Assistant	Montgomery County-Bucks County-Chester County PMSA, PA	Y	47670 FQ	58910 MW	72690 TQ	USBLS	5/15
	Philadelphia PMSA, PA	Y	46210 FQ	57130 MW	69720 TQ	USBLS	5/15
	Pittsburgh MSA, PA	Y	41670 FQ	51350 MW	62010 TQ	USBLS	5/15
	Rhode Island	Y	49000 FQ	57700 MW	69750 TQ	USBLS	5/15
	Providence-Warwick MSA, RI-MA	Y	46480 FQ	55850 MW	67470 TQ	USBLS	5/15
	South Carolina	Y	37840 FQ	45580 MW	55650 TQ	USBLS	5/15
	Charleston-North Charleston MSA, SC	Y	39590 FQ	46900 MW	56190 TQ	USBLS	5/15
	Columbia MSA, SC	Y	39170 FQ	45680 MW	54560 TQ	USBLS	5/15
	Greenville-Anderson-Mauldin MSA, SC	Y	38810 FQ	46230 MW	57260 TQ	USBLS	5/15
	South Dakota	Y	32530 FQ	36670 MW	42170 TQ	USBLS	5/15
	Sioux Falls MSA, SD	Y	33840 FQ	37770 MW	43930 TQ	USBLS	5/15
	Tennessee	Y	35260 FQ	43940 MW	54590 TQ	USBLS	5/15
	Knoxville MSA, TN	Y	38170 FQ	46020 MW	55290 TQ	USBLS	5/15
	Memphis MSA, TN-MS-AR	Y	37350 FQ	45730 MW	56200 TQ	USBLS	5/15
	Nashville-Davidson–Murfreesboro–Franklin MSA, TN	Y	35760 FQ	44550 MW	56320 TQ	USBLS	5/15
	Texas	Y	43480 FQ	53560 MW	64470 TQ	USBLS	5/15
	Austin-Round Rock MSA, TX	Y	46520 FQ	55150 MW	65080 TQ	USBLS	5/15
	Dallas-Plano-Irving PMSA, TX	Y	47250 FQ	57390 MW	68190 TQ	USBLS	5/15
	Fort Worth-Arlington PMSA, TX	Y	42320 FQ	51600 MW	62720 TQ	USBLS	5/15
	Houston-The Woodlands-Sugar Land MSA, TX	Y	45300 FQ	56280 MW	68430 TQ	USBLS	5/15
	San Antonio-New Braunfels MSA, TX	Y	41210 FQ	51570 MW	61820 TQ	USBLS	5/15
	Utah	Y	37180 FQ	44970 MW	55120 TQ	USBLS	5/15
	Ogden-Clearfield MSA, UT	Y	37720 FQ	47300 MW	58270 TQ	USBLS	5/15
	Provo-Orem MSA, UT	Y	35820 FQ	43940 MW	53610 TQ	USBLS	5/15
	Salt Lake City MSA, UT	Y	37540 FQ	45080 MW	55250 TQ	USBLS	5/15
	Vermont	Y	40320 FQ	47330 MW	56780 TQ	USBLS	5/15
	Burlington-South Burlington MSA, VT	Y	41140 FQ	48190 MW	59180 TQ	USBLS	5/15
	Virginia	Y	44170 FQ	55670 MW	70270 TQ	USBLS	5/15
	Richmond MSA, VA	Y	42330 FQ	51420 MW	60620 TQ	USBLS	5/15
	Virginia Beach-Norfolk-Newport News MSA, VA-NC	Y	40920 FQ	49180 MW	60860 TQ	USBLS	5/15
	Washington	H	23.13 FQ	27.97 MW	33.26 TQ	WABLS	3/16
	Seattle-Bellevue-Everett PMSA, WA	H	24.23 FQ	28.93 MW	34.57 TQ	WABLS	3/16
	Tacoma-Lakewood PMSA, WA	H	22.16 FQ	27.40 MW	31.79 TQ	WABLS	3/16
	West Virginia	Y	35710 FQ	42780 MW	49900 TQ	USBLS	5/15
	Huntington-Ashland MSA, WV-KY-OH	Y	34100 FQ	42110 MW	49090 TQ	USBLS	5/15
	Wisconsin	Y	39750 FQ	47170 MW	56910 TQ	USBLS	5/15
	Madison MSA, WI	Y	37770 FQ	46410 MW	55700 TQ	USBLS	5/15
	Milwaukee-Waukesha-West Allis MSA, WI	Y	42950 FQ	50560 MW	60630 TQ	USBLS	5/15
	Wyoming	Y	40090 FQ	43460 MW	49810 TQ	USBLS	5/15
	Cheyenne MSA, WY	Y	40080 FQ	40880 MW	45360 TQ	USBLS	5/15
	Puerto Rico	Y	21130 FQ	28270 MW	37090 TQ	USBLS	5/15
	San Juan-Carolina-Caguas MSA, PR	Y	22110 FQ	29580 MW	38080 TQ	USBLS	5/15
	Virgin Islands	Y	34660 FQ	44500 MW	54230 TQ	USBLS	5/15
	Guam	Y	23360 FQ	29030 MW	36980 TQ	USBLS	5/15
Executive Sous Chef							
Cruise Ship	United States	M	3800 LO		6500 HI	CRU04	2016
Michigan State University	East Lansing, MI	Y	55140 LO		67563 HI	MSUSAL	10/1/14-9/30/15
Exercise Physiologist	Alabama	Y	32343 AE	44636 AW	50783 AEX	ALBLS	6/16
	Arizona	Y	44690 FQ	54010 MW	64470 TQ	USBLS	5/15
	Phoenix-Mesa-Scottsdale MSA, AZ	Y	44850 FQ	53210 MW	63320 TQ	USBLS	5/15
	Arkansas	Y	49020 FQ	59870 MW	71660 TQ	USBLS	5/15
	California	H	24.97 FQ	32.84 MW	40.62 TQ	CABLS	1/16-3/16

AE	Average entry wage	AWR	Average wage range	H	Hourly	LR	Low end range	MTC	Median total compensation	TCC	Total cash compensation
AEX	Average experienced wage	B	Biweekly	HI	Highest wage paid	M	Monthly	MW	Median wage paid	TQ	Third quartile wage
ATC	Average total compensation	D	Daily	HR	High end range	MCC	Median cash compensation	MWR	Median wage range	W	Weekly
AW	Average wage paid	FQ	First quartile wage	LO	Lowest wage paid	ME	Median entry wage	S	See annotated source	Y	Yearly

Occupation/Type/Industry	Location	Per	Low	Mid	High	Source	Date
Exercise Physiologist	Anaheim-Santa Ana-Irvine PMSA, CA	H	19.39 FQ	23.57 MW	40.96 TQ	CABLS	1/16-3/16
	Los Angeles-Long Beach-Glendale PMSA, CA	H	32.80 FQ	36.72 MW	41.43 TQ	CABLS	1/16-3/16
	Oakland-Hayward-Berkeley PMSA, CA	H	13.95 FQ	31.33 MW	39.84 TQ	CABLS	1/16-3/16
	Riverside-San Bernardino-Ontario MSA, CA	H	14.84 FQ	41.46 MW	47.49 TQ	CABLS	1/16-3/16
	Sacramento–Roseville–Arden-Arcade MSA, CA	H	24.73 FQ	31.50 MW	38.08 TQ	CABLS	1/16-3/16
	San Diego-Carlsbad MSA, CA	H	27.17 FQ	33.56 MW	44.24 TQ	CABLS	1/16-3/16
	San Francisco-Redwood City-South San Francisco PMSA, CA	H	26.57 FQ	29.44 MW	34.24 TQ	CABLS	1/16-3/16
	Colorado	Y	33640 FQ	39550 MW	50860 TQ	USBLS	5/15
	Denver-Aurora-Lakewood MSA, CO	Y	32610 FQ	39130 MW	53220 TQ	USBLS	5/15
	Connecticut	Y		57846 MW		CTBLS	1/16-3/16
	Washington-Arlington-Alexandria PMSA, DC-VA-MD-WV	Y	18630 FQ	29510 MW	44340 TQ	USBLS	5/15
	Florida	H	17.11 AE	22.89 MW	27.57 AEX	FLBLS	7/16-9/16
	Fort Lauderdale-Pompano Beach-Deerfield Beach PMSA, FL	H	19.28 AE	22.90 MW	25.16 AEX	FLBLS	7/16-9/16
	Miami-Miami Beach-Kendall PMSA, FL	H	19.22 AE	22.45 MW	27.34 AEX	FLBLS	7/16-9/16
	Orlando-Kissimmee-Sanford MSA, FL	H	13.23 AE	20.32 MW	22.01 AEX	FLBLS	7/16-9/16
	Tampa-St. Petersburg-Clearwater MSA, FL	H	19.59 AE	23.46 MW	27.69 AEX	FLBLS	7/16-9/16
	Georgia	Y	37550 FQ	43560 MW	48850 TQ	USBLS	5/15
	Atlanta-Sandy Springs-Roswell MSA, GA	Y	37030 FQ	43580 MW	49510 TQ	USBLS	5/15
	Illinois	Y	46620 FQ	56710 MW	67500 TQ	USBLS	5/15
	Chicago-Naperville-Arlington Heights PMSA, IL	Y	50080 FQ	58230 MW	70970 TQ	USBLS	5/15
	Indiana	Y	38860 FQ	45430 MW	54640 TQ	USBLS	5/15
	Indianapolis-Carmel-Anderson MSA, IN	Y	40850 FQ	46460 MW	55780 TQ	USBLS	5/15
	Iowa	Y	38940 FQ	44630 MW	50970 TQ	USBLS	5/15
	Kansas	Y	50270 FQ	56030 MW	61020 TQ	USBLS	5/15
	Kentucky	Y	36030 FQ	43720 MW	48720 TQ	USBLS	5/15
	Louisiana	Y	39580 FQ	45980 MW	57890 TQ	USBLS	5/15
	Maryland	Y	40927 AE	54130 MW	60732 AEX	MDBLS	4/16
	Baltimore-Columbia-Towson MSA, MD	Y	44030 FQ	49890 MW	57350 TQ	USBLS	5/15
	Massachusetts	Y	48080 FQ	56370 MW	65500 TQ	USBLS	5/15
	Boston-Cambridge-Newton NECTA, MA	Y	51070 FQ	57820 MW	71310 TQ	USBLS	5/15
	Michigan	Y	40140 FQ	45900 MW	53150 TQ	USBLS	5/15
	Detroit-Dearborn-Livonia PMSA, MI	Y	37070 FQ	44340 MW	50640 TQ	USBLS	5/15
	Minnesota	Y	51088 FQ	58386 MW	67267 TQ	MNBLS	1/16-3/16
	Minneapolis-St. Paul-Bloomington MSA, MN-WI	Y	53588 FQ	59939 MW	69656 TQ	MNBLS	1/16-3/16
	Mississippi	Y	29970 FQ	35870 MW	50700 TQ	USBLS	5/15
	Missouri	Y	36830 FQ	43730 MW	54040 TQ	USBLS	5/15
	Kansas City MSA, MO-KS	Y	41540 FQ	51070 MW	58230 TQ	USBLS	5/15
	St. Louis MSA, MO-IL	Y	37730 FQ	48490 MW	61110 TQ	USBLS	5/15
	Nebraska	Y	40115 FQ	45525 MW	51850 TQ	NEBLS	7/16-9/16
	Omaha-Council Bluffs MSA, NE-IA	Y	42640 FQ	47015 MW	53205 TQ	NEBLS	7/16-9/16
	New Hampshire	H	17.84 AE	22.33 MW	25.03 AEX	NHBLS	6/16
	New Jersey	Y	42130 FQ	50890 MW	61790 TQ	USBLS	5/15
	Newark PMSA, NJ-PA	Y	37420 FQ	48260 MW	58440 TQ	USBLS	5/15
	New York	Y	39210 AE	60630 MW	72870 AEX	NYBLS	1/16-3/16
	Nassau County-Suffolk County PMSA, NY	Y	36390 FQ	60340 MW	76210 TQ	USBLS	5/15
	New York-Jersey City-White Plains PMSA, NY-NJ	Y	53090 FQ	64470 MW	78150 TQ	USBLS	5/15
	North Carolina	Y	40600 FQ	47120 MW	57290 TQ	USBLS	5/15

AE	Average entry wage	AWR	Average wage range	H	Hourly	LR	Low end range	MTC	Median total compensation	TCC	Total cash compensation
AEX	Average experienced wage	B	Biweekly	HI	Highest wage paid	M	Monthly	MW	Median wage paid	TQ	Third quartile wage
ATC	Average total compensation	D	Daily	HR	High end range	MCC	Median cash compensation	MWR	Median wage range	W	Weekly
AW	Average wage paid	FQ	First quartile wage	LO	Lowest wage paid	ME	Median entry wage	S	See annotated source	Y	Yearly

Occupation/Type/Industry	Location	Per	Low	Mid	High	Source	Date
Exercise Physiologist	Charlotte-Concord-Gastonia MSA, NC-SC	Y	40530 FQ	48080 MW	60440 TQ	USBLS	5/15
	Ohio	Y	39060 FQ	50160 MW	59540 TQ	USBLS	5/15
	Cincinnati MSA, OH-KY-IN	Y	42750 FQ	49580 MW	58130 TQ	USBLS	5/15
	Cleveland-Elyria MSA, OH	Y	33950 FQ	40490 MW	56490 TQ	USBLS	5/15
	Columbus MSA, OH	Y	45890 FQ	55070 MW	60950 TQ	USBLS	5/15
	Oklahoma	Y	36110 FQ	45360 MW	55530 TQ	USBLS	5/15
	Oregon	H	21.76 FQ	26.21 MW	29.54 TQ	ORBLS	2016
	Portland-Vancouver-Hillsboro MSA, OR-WA	Y	48700 FQ	56160 MW	62300 TQ	USBLS	5/15
	Pennsylvania	Y	33160 FQ	39010 MW	48780 TQ	USBLS	5/15
	Allentown-Bethlehem-Easton MSA, PA-NJ	Y	35840 FQ	40790 MW	47260 TQ	USBLS	5/15
	Montgomery County-Bucks County-Chester County PMSA, PA	Y	32190 FQ	36590 MW	53850 TQ	USBLS	5/15
	Philadelphia PMSA, PA	Y	31870 FQ	37250 MW	45590 TQ	USBLS	5/15
	Pittsburgh MSA, PA	Y	39930 FQ	48580 MW	66640 TQ	USBLS	5/15
	South Carolina	Y	26590 FQ	35990 MW	45880 TQ	USBLS	5/15
	Tennessee	Y	34310 FQ	40580 MW	55090 TQ	USBLS	5/15
	Nashville-Davidson– Murfreesboro–Franklin MSA, TN	Y	35740 FQ	44980 MW	64420 TQ	USBLS	5/15
	Texas	Y	36900 FQ	44280 MW	54830 TQ	USBLS	5/15
	Austin-Round Rock MSA, TX	Y	41650 FQ	48340 MW	55770 TQ	USBLS	5/15
	Dallas-Plano-Irving PMSA, TX	Y	34120 FQ	37250 MW	45190 TQ	USBLS	5/15
	Fort Worth-Arlington PMSA, TX	Y	40260 FQ	46240 MW	60580 TQ	USBLS	5/15
	Houston-The Woodlands- Sugar Land MSA, TX	Y	40720 FQ	47540 MW	59490 TQ	USBLS	5/15
	Virginia	Y	25990 FQ	36860 MW	48120 TQ	USBLS	5/15
	Richmond MSA, VA	Y	49820 FQ	59810 MW	71700 TQ	USBLS	5/15
	Virginia Beach-Norfolk- Newport News MSA, VA-NC	Y	31970 FQ	39350 MW	49040 TQ	USBLS	5/15
	Washington	H	14.76 FQ	17.97 MW	23.43 TQ	WABLS	3/16
	Seattle-Bellevue-Everett PMSA, WA	H	15.18 FQ	17.64 MW	21.65 TQ	WABLS	3/16
	Wisconsin	Y	46640 FQ	56090 MW	69300 TQ	USBLS	5/15
	Madison MSA, WI	Y	49380 FQ	57260 MW	68440 TQ	USBLS	5/15
	Milwaukee-Waukesha-West Allis MSA, WI	Y	43710 FQ	53120 MW	73400 TQ	USBLS	5/15
Public Safety Department, State Government	Ohio	H			33.57 HI	OHGOV	2015
Exhibits Technician							
Municipal Government	Seattle, WA	H	27.53 LO		29.68 HI	CSSS	3/9/16
Explosives Specialist							
State Government	North Carolina	Y	28875 LO		43422 HI	NCGOV	7/1/16
Explosives Worker, Ordnance Handling Expert, and Blaster	Alabama	Y	31519 AE	51702 AW	61804 AEX	ALBLS	6/16
	Alaska	Y	63590 FQ	69910 MW	76590 TQ	USBLS	5/15
	Arizona	Y	30940 FQ	42190 MW	53840 TQ	USBLS	5/15
	Arkansas	Y	37260 FQ	38640 MW	42450 TQ	USBLS	5/15
	California	H	25.12 AE	29.63 MW	33.25 TQ	CABLS	1/16-3/16
	Colorado	Y	34920 FQ	44250 MW	52020 TQ	USBLS	5/15
	Florida	H	21.51 AE	23.98 MW	25.43 AEX	FLBLS	7/16-9/16
	Hawaii	Y	57450 FQ	66810 MW	74060 TQ	USBLS	5/15
	Idaho	Y	48130 FQ	55550 MW	61550 TQ	USBLS	5/15
	Illinois	Y	68060 FQ	73270 MW	78520 TQ	USBLS	5/15
	Indiana	Y	37710 FQ	42230 MW	44910 TQ	USBLS	5/15
	Iowa	Y	42210 FQ	52010 MW	60190 TQ	USBLS	5/15
	Kentucky	Y	40920 FQ	42410 MW	48270 TQ	USBLS	5/15
	Louisiana	Y	39780 FQ	49530 MW	72340 TQ	USBLS	5/15
	Maryland	Y	49563 AE	54947 MW	57640 AEX	MDBLS	4/16
	Massachusetts	Y	51580 FQ	58700 MW	69820 TQ	USBLS	5/15
	Michigan	Y	49680 FQ	65460 MW	71670 TQ	USBLS	5/15
	Minnesota	Y	45840 FQ	54830 MW	63064 TQ	MNBLS	1/16-3/16
	Missouri	Y	19490 FQ	40600 MW	49130 TQ	USBLS	5/15
	Nevada	Y	56150 FQ	66760 MW	74230 TQ	USBLS	5/15
	New Hampshire	H	22.67 AE	28.74 MW	32.67 AEX	NHBLS	6/16

AE	Average entry wage	**AWR**	Average wage range	**H**	Hourly	**LR** Low end range	**MTC** Median total compensation	**TCC** Total cash compensation
AEX	Average experienced wage	**B**	Biweekly	**HI**	Highest wage paid	**M** Monthly	**MW** Median wage paid	**TQ** Third quartile wage
ATC	Average total compensation	**D**	Daily	**HR**	High end range	**MCC** Median cash compensation	**MWR** Median wage range	**W** Weekly
AW	Average wage paid	**FQ**	First quartile wage	**LO**	Lowest wage paid	**ME** Median entry wage	**S** See annotated source	**Y** Yearly

Occupation/Type/Industry	Location	Per	Low	Mid	High	Source	Date
Explosives Worker, Ordnance Handling Expert, and Blaster	New Mexico	Y	39440 FQ	47920 MW	66380 TQ	USBLS	5/15
	New York	Y	46380 AE	53460 MW	59930 AEX	NYBLS	1/16-3/16
	North Carolina	Y	43760 FQ	49130 MW	60720 TQ	USBLS	5/15
	Ohio	Y	35650 FQ	40280 MW	47260 TQ	USBLS	5/15
	Oklahoma	Y	35800 FQ	41050 MW	49570 TQ	USBLS	5/15
	Pennsylvania	Y	44540 FQ	50780 MW	65970 TQ	USBLS	5/15
	Tennessee	Y	38650 FQ	58980 MW	76440 TQ	USBLS	5/15
	Texas	Y	32390 FQ	38230 MW	45670 TQ	USBLS	5/15
	Utah	Y	44700 FQ	49790 MW	53160 TQ	USBLS	5/15
	Virginia	Y	51270 FQ	56930 MW	62610 TQ	USBLS	5/15
	Washington	H	33.31 FQ	36.74 MW	46.79 TQ	WABLS	3/16
	West Virginia	Y	50260 FQ	57520 MW	64600 TQ	USBLS	5/15
	Wisconsin	Y	33680 FQ	39430 MW	76620 TQ	USBLS	5/15
	Wyoming	Y	63060 FQ	69850 MW	75580 TQ	USBLS	5/15
External Affairs Manager Fire Department, Municipal Government	Anaheim, CA	Y			144979 HI	CACIT	6/28/16
Extruding, Forming, Pressing, and Compacting Machine Setter, Operator, and Tender	Alabama	Y	24729 AE	41941 AW	50547 AEX	ALBLS	6/16
	Birmingham-Hoover MSA, AL	Y	22281 AE	28656 AW	31844 AEX	ALBLS	6/16
	Arizona	Y	22980 FQ	28320 MW	35060 TQ	USBLS	5/15
	Phoenix-Mesa-Scottsdale MSA, AZ	Y	24540 FQ	29760 MW	35760 TQ	USBLS	5/15
	Tucson MSA, AZ	Y	28840 FQ	33870 MW	37890 TQ	USBLS	5/15
	Arkansas	Y	27080 FQ	35620 MW	45750 TQ	USBLS	5/15
	Little Rock-North Little Rock-Conway MSA, AR	Y	24870 FQ	32870 MW	43910 TQ	USBLS	5/15
	California	H	10.81 FQ	13.47 MW	17.35 TQ	CABLS	1/16-3/16
	Anaheim-Santa Ana-Irvine PMSA, CA	H	10.34 FQ	12.26 MW	15.71 TQ	CABLS	1/16-3/16
	Los Angeles-Long Beach-Glendale PMSA, CA	H	10.94 FQ	13.30 MW	15.97 TQ	CABLS	1/16-3/16
	Oakland-Hayward-Berkeley PMSA, CA	H	9.84 FQ	11.70 MW	14.96 TQ	CABLS	1/16-3/16
	Riverside-San Bernardino-Ontario MSA, CA	H	10.76 FQ	13.85 MW	19.18 TQ	CABLS	1/16-3/16
	Sacramento–Roseville–Arden-Arcade MSA, CA	H	10.87 FQ	14.00 MW	18.98 TQ	CABLS	1/16-3/16
	San Diego-Carlsbad MSA, CA	H	11.61 FQ	14.67 MW	20.83 TQ	CABLS	1/16-3/16
	Colorado	Y	26060 FQ	28960 MW	32840 TQ	USBLS	5/15
	Connecticut	Y		33685 MW		CTBLS	1/16-3/16
	Bridgeport-Stamford-Norwalk MSA, CT	Y	24090 FQ	34810 MW	55540 TQ	USBLS	5/15
	Hartford-West Hartford-East Hartford MSA, CT	Y	22810 FQ	32670 MW	45700 TQ	USBLS	5/15
	Delaware	Y	35480 FQ	40290 MW	47060 TQ	USBLS	5/15
	Wilmington PMSA, DE-MD-NJ	Y	34830 FQ	39270 MW	45870 TQ	USBLS	5/15
	Florida	H	10.57 AE	14.36 MW	17.01 AEX	FLBLS	7/16-9/16
	Fort Lauderdale-Pompano Beach-Deerfield Beach PMSA, FL	H	9.59 AE	16.04 MW	19.27 AEX	FLBLS	7/16-9/16
	Miami-Miami Beach-Kendall PMSA, FL	H	10.14 AE	13.03 MW	15.17 AEX	FLBLS	7/16-9/16
	Orlando-Kissimmee-Sanford MSA, FL	H	10.19 AE	13.64 MW	16.76 AEX	FLBLS	7/16-9/16
	Tampa-St. Petersburg-Clearwater MSA, FL	H	10.62 AE	13.74 MW	15.67 AEX	FLBLS	7/16-9/16
	Georgia	Y	25910 FQ	33330 MW	43160 TQ	USBLS	5/15
	Atlanta-Sandy Springs-Roswell MSA, GA	Y	24730 FQ	30310 MW	38740 TQ	USBLS	5/15
	Augusta-Richmond County MSA, GA-SC	Y	35460 FQ	41020 MW	45890 TQ	USBLS	5/15
	Hawaii	Y	20230 FQ	29490 MW	36780 TQ	USBLS	5/15
	Urban Honolulu MSA, HI	Y	19790 FQ	24410 MW	37630 TQ	USBLS	5/15
	Idaho	Y	23230 FQ	30610 MW	37360 TQ	USBLS	5/15
	Boise City MSA, ID	Y	27780 FQ	33540 MW	37340 TQ	USBLS	5/15
	Illinois	Y	26490 FQ	33680 MW	38930 TQ	USBLS	5/15

AE Average entry wage	**AWR** Average wage range	**H** Hourly	**LR** Low end range	**MTC** Median total compensation	**TCC** Total cash compensation
AEX Average experienced wage	**B** Biweekly	**HI** Highest wage paid	**M** Monthly	**MW** Median wage paid	**TQ** Third quartile wage
ATC Average total compensation	**D** Daily	**HR** High end range	**MCC** Median cash compensation	**MWR** Median wage range	**W** Weekly
AW Average wage paid	**FQ** First quartile wage	**LO** Lowest wage paid	**ME** Median entry wage	**S** See annotated source	**Y** Yearly

Occupation/Type/Industry	Location	Per	Low	Mid	High	Source	Date
Extruding, Forming, Pressing, and Compacting Machine Setter, Operator, and Tender	Chicago-Naperville-Arlington Heights PMSA, IL	Y	29250 FQ	35780 MW	42030 TQ	USBLS	5/15
	Lake County-Kenosha County PMSA, IL-WI	Y	22720 FQ	27680 MW	33730 TQ	USBLS	5/15
	Indiana	Y	24420 FQ	33140 MW	43850 TQ	USBLS	5/15
	Gary PMSA, IN	Y	29690 FQ	39260 MW	46640 TQ	USBLS	5/15
	Indianapolis-Carmel-Anderson MSA, IN	Y	23500 FQ	33860 MW	44260 TQ	USBLS	5/15
	Iowa	Y	28240 FQ	36800 MW	44840 TQ	USBLS	5/15
	Des Moines-West Des Moines MSA, IA	Y	28220 FQ	33090 MW	37900 TQ	USBLS	5/15
	Kansas	Y	27780 FQ	33440 MW	38590 TQ	USBLS	5/15
	Kentucky	Y	25840 FQ	31970 MW	37740 TQ	USBLS	5/15
	Louisville-Jefferson County MSA, KY-IN	Y	18490 FQ	23790 MW	33470 TQ	USBLS	5/15
	Louisiana	Y	34370 FQ	38950 MW	47740 TQ	USBLS	5/15
	Maine	Y	27180 FQ	31130 MW	38660 TQ	USBLS	5/15
	Maryland	Y	20155 AE	31109 MW	36585 AEX	MDBLS	4/16
	Baltimore-Columbia-Towson MSA, MD	Y	30030 FQ	34930 MW	39380 TQ	USBLS	5/15
	Massachusetts	Y	26220 FQ	33430 MW	40340 TQ	USBLS	5/15
	Boston-Cambridge-Newton NECTA, MA	Y	32170 FQ	41220 MW	47020 TQ	USBLS	5/15
	Worcester MSA, MA-CT	Y	29540 FQ	34020 MW	37920 TQ	USBLS	5/15
	Michigan	Y	21150 FQ	25430 MW	35880 TQ	USBLS	5/15
	Detroit-Dearborn-Livonia PMSA, MI	Y	25590 FQ	30000 MW	35750 TQ	USBLS	5/15
	Grand Rapids-Wyoming MSA, MI	Y	21260 FQ	25710 MW	36290 TQ	USBLS	5/15
	Minnesota	Y	29219 FQ	35709 MW	44193 TQ	MNBLS	1/16-3/16
	Minneapolis-St. Paul-Bloomington MSA, MN-WI	Y	29908 FQ	36367 MW	43839 TQ	MNBLS	1/16-3/16
	Mississippi	Y	24020 FQ	30560 MW	36340 TQ	USBLS	5/15
	Missouri	Y	26530 FQ	30810 MW	37680 TQ	USBLS	5/15
	Kansas City MSA, MO-KS	Y	19940 FQ	26530 MW	35380 TQ	USBLS	5/15
	St. Louis MSA, MO-IL	Y	26540 FQ	30480 MW	35680 TQ	USBLS	5/15
	Montana	Y	27490 FQ	33930 MW	40990 TQ	USBLS	5/15
	Nebraska	Y	32280 FQ	40240 MW	45675 TQ	NEBLS	7/16-9/16
	Omaha-Council Bluffs MSA, NE-IA	Y	26775 FQ	31855 MW	38865 TQ	NEBLS	7/16-9/16
	Nevada	Y	27110 FQ	32640 MW	38820 TQ	USBLS	5/15
	Las Vegas-Henderson-Paradise MSA, NV	Y	28340 FQ	32210 MW	36710 TQ	USBLS	5/15
	New Hampshire	H	12.39 AE	15.76 MW	17.47 AEX	NHBLS	6/16
	Nashua NECTA, NH-MA	Y	27300 FQ	31310 MW	35730 TQ	USBLS	5/15
	New Jersey	Y	25410 FQ	33070 MW	45260 TQ	USBLS	5/15
	Camden PMSA, NJ	Y	23430 FQ	34570 MW	49170 TQ	USBLS	5/15
	Newark PMSA, NJ-PA	Y	26160 FQ	32430 MW	45510 TQ	USBLS	5/15
	Trenton MSA, NJ	Y	22980 FQ	29940 MW	35860 TQ	USBLS	5/15
	New Mexico	Y	17290 FQ	18620 MW	21620 TQ	USBLS	5/15
	New York	Y	21900 AE	32580 MW	42110 AEX	NYBLS	1/16-3/16
	Buffalo-Cheektowaga-Niagara Falls MSA, NY	Y	29170 FQ	40890 MW	53640 TQ	USBLS	5/15
	Nassau County-Suffolk County PMSA, NY	Y	19120 FQ	24140 MW	36460 TQ	USBLS	5/15
	New York-Jersey City-White Plains PMSA, NY-NJ	Y	22510 FQ	28290 MW	38060 TQ	USBLS	5/15
	Rochester MSA, NY	Y	28410 FQ	35080 MW	40230 TQ	USBLS	5/15
	North Carolina	Y	26640 FQ	34400 MW	44070 TQ	USBLS	5/15
	Charlotte-Concord-Gastonia MSA, NC-SC	Y	26390 FQ	30020 MW	36680 TQ	USBLS	5/15
	North Dakota	Y	33180 FQ	37720 MW	55140 TQ	USBLS	5/15
	Ohio	Y	25550 FQ	29610 MW	36500 TQ	USBLS	5/15
	Cincinnati MSA, OH-KY-IN	Y	29010 FQ	35500 MW	46250 TQ	USBLS	5/15
	Cleveland-Elyria MSA, OH	Y	23620 FQ	28740 MW	35510 TQ	USBLS	5/15
	Columbus MSA, OH	Y	25580 FQ	29610 MW	41640 TQ	USBLS	5/15
	Oklahoma	Y	25730 FQ	33700 MW	47820 TQ	USBLS	5/15
	Oklahoma City MSA, OK	Y	32550 FQ	37020 MW	43330 TQ	USBLS	5/15
	Tulsa MSA, OK	Y	25300 FQ	28570 MW	33650 TQ	USBLS	5/15

AE	Average entry wage	AWR	Average wage range	H	Hourly
AEX	Average experienced wage	B	Biweekly	HI	Highest wage paid
ATC	Average total compensation	D	Daily	HR	High end range
AW	Average wage paid	FQ	First quartile wage	LO	Lowest wage paid

LR	Low end range	MTC	Median total compensation	TCC	Total cash compensation
M	Monthly	MW	Median wage paid	TQ	Third quartile wage
MCC	Median cash compensation	MWR	Median wage range	W	Weekly
ME	Median entry wage	S	See annotated source	Y	Yearly

Occupation/Type/Industry	Location	Per	Low	Mid	High	Source	Date
Extruding, Forming, Pressing, and Compacting Machine Setter, Operator, and Tender	Oregon	H	12.86 FQ	15.29 MW	21.04 TQ	ORBLS	2016
	Portland-Vancouver-Hillsboro MSA, OR-WA	Y	26320 FQ	30440 MW	43400 TQ	USBLS	5/15
	Pennsylvania	Y	28180 FQ	35160 MW	43410 TQ	USBLS	5/15
	Allentown-Bethlehem-Easton MSA, PA-NJ	Y	26870 FQ	32130 MW	38830 TQ	USBLS	5/15
	Montgomery County-Bucks County-Chester County PMSA, PA	Y	26810 FQ	33160 MW	41740 TQ	USBLS	5/15
	Philadelphia PMSA, PA	Y	31550 FQ	41220 MW	47250 TQ	USBLS	5/15
	Pittsburgh MSA, PA	Y	27730 FQ	33400 MW	39350 TQ	USBLS	5/15
	Rhode Island	Y	32230 FQ	36940 MW	44270 TQ	USBLS	5/15
	Providence-Warwick MSA, RI-MA	Y	32170 FQ	36830 MW	43990 TQ	USBLS	5/15
	South Carolina	Y	30220 FQ	37260 MW	44590 TQ	USBLS	5/15
	Charleston-North Charleston MSA, SC	Y	28810 FQ	35590 MW	42580 TQ	USBLS	5/15
	Columbia MSA, SC	Y	33990 FQ	37830 MW	45630 TQ	USBLS	5/15
	Greenville-Anderson-Mauldin MSA, SC	Y	33230 FQ	42000 MW	48540 TQ	USBLS	5/15
	South Dakota	Y	28090 FQ	32580 MW	38700 TQ	USBLS	5/15
	Sioux Falls MSA, SD	Y	27080 FQ	30110 MW	35000 TQ	USBLS	5/15
	Tennessee	Y	26070 FQ	30900 MW	36420 TQ	USBLS	5/15
	Nashville-Davidson–Murfreesboro–Franklin MSA, TN	Y	27810 FQ	31150 MW	36570 TQ	USBLS	5/15
	Texas	Y	23330 FQ	29570 MW	36790 TQ	USBLS	5/15
	Austin-Round Rock MSA, TX	Y	25530 FQ	29800 MW	35160 TQ	USBLS	5/15
	Dallas-Plano-Irving PMSA, TX	Y	22200 FQ	28190 MW	34510 TQ	USBLS	5/15
	Fort Worth-Arlington PMSA, TX	Y	29490 FQ	35020 MW	39350 TQ	USBLS	5/15
	Houston-The Woodlands-Sugar Land MSA, TX	Y	21580 FQ	26010 MW	31150 TQ	USBLS	5/15
	San Antonio-New Braunfels MSA, TX	Y	22660 FQ	28310 MW	36340 TQ	USBLS	5/15
	Utah	Y	27140 FQ	32090 MW	37660 TQ	USBLS	5/15
	Ogden-Clearfield MSA, UT	Y	26670 FQ	30640 MW	43940 TQ	USBLS	5/15
	Provo-Orem MSA, UT	Y	26110 FQ	33200 MW	37690 TQ	USBLS	5/15
	Salt Lake City MSA, UT	Y	27780 FQ	32030 MW	37670 TQ	USBLS	5/15
	Vermont	Y	25570 FQ	31390 MW	36180 TQ	USBLS	5/15
	Burlington-South Burlington MSA, VT	Y	25150 FQ	30950 MW	35810 TQ	USBLS	5/15
	Virginia	Y	28520 FQ	34290 MW	43020 TQ	USBLS	5/15
	Richmond MSA, VA	Y	29600 FQ	34410 MW	38290 TQ	USBLS	5/15
	Virginia Beach-Norfolk-Newport News MSA, VA-NC	Y	28450 FQ	39170 MW	60080 TQ	USBLS	5/15
	Washington	H	11.90 FQ	14.91 MW	18.90 TQ	WABLS	3/16
	Seattle-Bellevue-Everett PMSA, WA	H	11.16 FQ	13.12 MW	16.18 TQ	WABLS	3/16
	Tacoma-Lakewood PMSA, WA	H	17.86 FQ	20.67 MW	22.71 TQ	WABLS	3/16
	West Virginia	Y	32310 FQ	40480 MW	57120 TQ	USBLS	5/15
	Huntington-Ashland MSA, WV-KY-OH	Y	22060 FQ	26730 MW	31840 TQ	USBLS	5/15
	Wisconsin	Y	25850 FQ	34450 MW	42350 TQ	USBLS	5/15
	Madison MSA, WI	Y	31500 FQ	35990 MW	40950 TQ	USBLS	5/15
	Milwaukee-Waukesha-West Allis MSA, WI	Y	18870 FQ	23070 MW	35070 TQ	USBLS	5/15
	Puerto Rico	Y	17800 FQ	20220 MW	23340 TQ	USBLS	5/15
	San Juan-Carolina-Caguas MSA, PR	Y	18480 FQ	20960 MW	23730 TQ	USBLS	5/15
Extruding and Drawing Machine Setter, Operator, and Tender							
Metals and Plastics	Alabama	Y	22086 AE	34075 AW	40070 AEX	ALBLS	6/16
Metals and Plastics	Birmingham-Hoover MSA, AL	Y	20564 AE	33654 AW	40203 AEX	ALBLS	6/16
Metals and Plastics	Arizona	Y	22800 FQ	29130 MW	37360 TQ	USBLS	5/15
Metals and Plastics	Phoenix-Mesa-Scottsdale MSA, AZ	Y	22970 FQ	31800 MW	38970 TQ	USBLS	5/15
Metals and Plastics	Tucson MSA, AZ	Y	21570 FQ	23450 MW	28340 TQ	USBLS	5/15

AE	Average entry wage	AWR	Average wage range	H	Hourly	LR	Low end range	MTC	Median total compensation
AEX	Average experienced wage	B	Biweekly	HI	Highest wage paid	M	Monthly	MW	Median wage paid
ATC	Average total compensation	D	Daily	HR	High end range	MCC	Median cash compensation	MWR	Median wage range
AW	Average wage paid	FQ	First quartile wage	LO	Lowest wage paid	ME	Median entry wage	S	See annotated source

TCC   Total cash compensation
TQ   Third quartile wage
W   Weekly
Y   Yearly

Occupation/Type/Industry	Location	Per	Low	Mid	High	Source	Date
Extruding and Drawing Machine Setter, Operator, and Tender							
Metals and Plastics	Arkansas	Y	27780 FQ	34730 MW	39510 TQ	USBLS	5/15
Metals and Plastics	Little Rock-North Little Rock-Conway MSA, AR	Y	33340 FQ	35840 MW	38350 TQ	USBLS	5/15
Metals and Plastics	California	H	10.63 FQ	14.95 MW	21.33 TQ	CABLS	1/16-3/16
Metals and Plastics	Anaheim-Santa Ana-Irvine PMSA, CA	H	12.01 FQ	15.68 MW	21.20 TQ	CABLS	1/16-3/16
Metals and Plastics	Los Angeles-Long Beach-Glendale PMSA, CA	H	10.62 FQ	14.20 MW	21.29 TQ	CABLS	1/16-3/16
Metals and Plastics	Oakland-Hayward-Berkeley PMSA, CA	H	18.14 FQ	22.25 MW	27.05 TQ	CABLS	1/16-3/16
Metals and Plastics	Riverside-San Bernardino-Ontario MSA, CA	H	9.41 FQ	10.26 MW	12.60 TQ	CABLS	1/16-3/16
Metals and Plastics	San Diego-Carlsbad MSA, CA	H	9.51 FQ	14.23 MW	19.66 TQ	CABLS	1/16-3/16
Metals and Plastics	Colorado	Y	28170 FQ	33090 MW	40620 TQ	USBLS	5/15
Metals and Plastics	Denver-Aurora-Lakewood MSA, CO	Y	27350 FQ	30680 MW	37320 TQ	USBLS	5/15
Metals and Plastics	Connecticut	Y		39054 MW		CTBLS	1/16-3/16
Metals and Plastics	Bridgeport-Stamford-Norwalk MSA, CT	Y	36750 FQ	42740 MW	48570 TQ	USBLS	5/15
Metals and Plastics	Hartford-West Hartford-East Hartford MSA, CT	Y	29100 FQ	36360 MW	44610 TQ	USBLS	5/15
Metals and Plastics	Delaware	Y	26240 FQ	34480 MW	44720 TQ	USBLS	5/15
Metals and Plastics	Wilmington PMSA, DE-MD-NJ	Y	27230 FQ	33800 MW	42660 TQ	USBLS	5/15
Metals and Plastics	Florida	H	10.77 AE	13.98 MW	16.61 AEX	FLBLS	7/16-9/16
Metals and Plastics	Fort Lauderdale-Pompano Beach-Deerfield Beach PMSA, FL	H	12.22 AE	15.79 MW	18.28 AEX	FLBLS	7/16-9/16
Metals and Plastics	Miami-Miami Beach-Kendall PMSA, FL	H	9.57 AE	11.86 MW	14.64 AEX	FLBLS	7/16-9/16
Metals and Plastics	Orlando-Kissimmee-Sanford MSA, FL	H	10.92 AE	13.53 MW	16.95 AEX	FLBLS	7/16-9/16
Metals and Plastics	Tampa-St. Petersburg-Clearwater MSA, FL	H	12.84 AE	15.58 MW	18.03 AEX	FLBLS	7/16-9/16
Metals and Plastics	Georgia	Y	26600 FQ	33590 MW	40730 TQ	USBLS	5/15
Metals and Plastics	Atlanta-Sandy Springs-Roswell MSA, GA	Y	27850 FQ	36240 MW	44260 TQ	USBLS	5/15
Metals and Plastics	Idaho	Y	27380 FQ	34110 MW	39740 TQ	USBLS	5/15
Metals and Plastics	Boise City MSA, ID	Y	22820 FQ	29100 MW	38060 TQ	USBLS	5/15
Metals and Plastics	Illinois	Y	26810 FQ	31970 MW	39520 TQ	USBLS	5/15
Metals and Plastics	Chicago-Naperville-Arlington Heights PMSA, IL	Y	27120 FQ	32910 MW	40320 TQ	USBLS	5/15
Metals and Plastics	Lake County-Kenosha County PMSA, IL-WI	Y	22540 FQ	27930 MW	33590 TQ	USBLS	5/15
Metals and Plastics	Indiana	Y	26510 FQ	32800 MW	41090 TQ	USBLS	5/15
Metals and Plastics	Gary PMSA, IN	Y	26710 FQ	33270 MW	40090 TQ	USBLS	5/15
Metals and Plastics	Indianapolis-Carmel-Anderson MSA, IN	Y	22070 FQ	27970 MW	36810 TQ	USBLS	5/15
Metals and Plastics	Iowa	Y	29210 FQ	35200 MW	42380 TQ	USBLS	5/15
Metals and Plastics	Kansas	Y	30160 FQ	34420 MW	37960 TQ	USBLS	5/15
Metals and Plastics	Wichita MSA, KS	Y	28870 FQ	34150 MW	37920 TQ	USBLS	5/15
Metals and Plastics	Kentucky	Y	29030 FQ	36910 MW	47020 TQ	USBLS	5/15
Metals and Plastics	Louisville-Jefferson County MSA, KY-IN	Y	22510 FQ	35190 MW	44680 TQ	USBLS	5/15
Metals and Plastics	Louisiana	Y	27110 FQ	33080 MW	38010 TQ	USBLS	5/15
Metals and Plastics	New Orleans-Metairie MSA, LA	Y	21320 FQ	26690 MW	34240 TQ	USBLS	5/15
Metals and Plastics	Maine	Y	24550 FQ	32340 MW	38700 TQ	USBLS	5/15
Metals and Plastics	Salisbury MSA, MD-DE	Y	18910 FQ	23000 MW	28890 TQ	USBLS	5/15
Metals and Plastics	Massachusetts	Y	30810 FQ	38330 MW	45840 TQ	USBLS	5/15
Metals and Plastics	Boston-Cambridge-Newton NECTA, MA	Y	34430 FQ	43190 MW	49660 TQ	USBLS	5/15
Metals and Plastics	Worcester MSA, MA-CT	Y	30060 FQ	35970 MW	44440 TQ	USBLS	5/15
Metals and Plastics	Michigan	Y	26270 FQ	30910 MW	39360 TQ	USBLS	5/15
Metals and Plastics	Detroit-Dearborn-Livonia PMSA, MI	Y	28280 FQ	34920 MW	43070 TQ	USBLS	5/15
Metals and Plastics	Grand Rapids-Wyoming MSA, MI	Y	24400 FQ	32980 MW	42600 TQ	USBLS	5/15
Metals and Plastics	Minnesota	Y	31477 FQ	37440 MW	44224 TQ	MNBLS	1/16-3/16

AE	Average entry wage	AWR	Average wage range	H	Hourly
AEX	Average experienced wage	B	Biweekly	HI	Highest wage paid
ATC	Average total compensation	D	Daily	HR	High end range
AW	Average wage paid	FQ	First quartile wage	LO	Lowest wage paid

LR	Low end range	MTC	Median total compensation	TCC	Total cash compensation
M	Monthly	MW	Median wage paid	TQ	Third quartile wage
MCC	Median cash compensation	MWR	Median wage range	W	Weekly
ME	Median entry wage	S	See annotated source	Y	Yearly

Occupation/Type/Industry	Location	Per	Low	Mid	High	Source	Date
Extruding and Drawing Machine Setter, Operator, and Tender							
Metals and Plastics	Minneapolis-St. Paul-Bloomington MSA, MN-WI	Y	31052 FQ	38969 MW	45661 TQ	MNBLS	1/16-3/16
Metals and Plastics	Mississippi	Y	25390 FQ	31560 MW	37400 TQ	USBLS	5/15
Metals and Plastics	Missouri	Y	23740 FQ	29740 MW	37620 TQ	USBLS	5/15
Metals and Plastics	Kansas City MSA, MO-KS	Y	25340 FQ	31860 MW	38530 TQ	USBLS	5/15
Metals and Plastics	St. Louis MSA, MO-IL	Y	23420 FQ	27470 MW	33150 TQ	USBLS	5/15
Metals and Plastics	Nebraska	Y	31025 FQ	37000 MW	44230 TQ	NEBLS	7/16-9/16
Metals and Plastics	Omaha-Council Bluffs MSA, NE-IA	Y	35320 FQ	42015 MW	45975 TQ	NEBLS	7/16-9/16
Metals and Plastics	Nevada	Y	23450 FQ	30380 MW	37350 TQ	USBLS	5/15
Metals and Plastics	Las Vegas-Henderson-Paradise MSA, NV	Y	26070 FQ	32860 MW	38620 TQ	USBLS	5/15
Metals and Plastics	New Hampshire	H	13.26 AE	16.85 MW	19.31 AEX	NHBLS	6/16
Metals and Plastics	Manchester NECTA, NH	H	12.31 AE	18.68 MW	24.73 AEX	NHBLS	6/16
Metals and Plastics	New Jersey	Y	23300 FQ	28520 MW	35920 TQ	USBLS	5/15
Metals and Plastics	Camden PMSA, NJ	Y	26100 FQ	30940 MW	37150 TQ	USBLS	5/15
Metals and Plastics	Newark PMSA, NJ-PA	Y	26640 FQ	29650 MW	36430 TQ	USBLS	5/15
Metals and Plastics	New Mexico	Y	24750 FQ	30400 MW	37260 TQ	USBLS	5/15
Metals and Plastics	New York	Y	26150 AE	37520 MW	43100 AEX	NYBLS	1/16-3/16
Metals and Plastics	Buffalo-Cheektowaga-Niagara Falls MSA, NY	Y	29940 FQ	37430 MW	45140 TQ	USBLS	5/15
Metals and Plastics	Nassau County-Suffolk County PMSA, NY	Y	27750 FQ	32010 MW	43070 TQ	USBLS	5/15
Metals and Plastics	New York-Jersey City-White Plains PMSA, NY-NJ	Y	22160 FQ	28030 MW	36760 TQ	USBLS	5/15
Metals and Plastics	Rochester MSA, NY	Y	29880 FQ	34820 MW	38960 TQ	USBLS	5/15
Metals and Plastics	North Carolina	Y	28280 FQ	34690 MW	41690 TQ	USBLS	5/15
Metals and Plastics	Charlotte-Concord-Gastonia MSA, NC-SC	Y	30760 FQ	36360 MW	44040 TQ	USBLS	5/15
Metals and Plastics	Raleigh MSA, NC	Y	26400 FQ	34940 MW	42440 TQ	USBLS	5/15
Metals and Plastics	North Dakota	Y	23940 FQ	30630 MW	39680 TQ	USBLS	5/15
Metals and Plastics	Ohio	Y	26570 FQ	33250 MW	39820 TQ	USBLS	5/15
Metals and Plastics	Cincinnati MSA, OH-KY-IN	Y	27150 FQ	34180 MW	43230 TQ	USBLS	5/15
Metals and Plastics	Cleveland-Elyria MSA, OH	Y	27740 FQ	34670 MW	40250 TQ	USBLS	5/15
Metals and Plastics	Columbus MSA, OH	Y	22890 FQ	27860 MW	35810 TQ	USBLS	5/15
Metals and Plastics	Oklahoma	Y	31140 FQ	37290 MW	45660 TQ	USBLS	5/15
Metals and Plastics	Oklahoma City MSA, OK	Y	24270 FQ	31340 MW	44280 TQ	USBLS	5/15
Metals and Plastics	Tulsa MSA, OK	Y	31570 FQ	36380 MW	43060 TQ	USBLS	5/15
Metals and Plastics	Oregon	H	12.59 FQ	16.04 MW	19.28 TQ	ORBLS	2016
Metals and Plastics	Portland-Vancouver-Hillsboro MSA, OR-WA	Y	24900 FQ	32340 MW	38780 TQ	USBLS	5/15
Metals and Plastics	Pennsylvania	Y	28110 FQ	35470 MW	44090 TQ	USBLS	5/15
Metals and Plastics	Allentown-Bethlehem-Easton MSA, PA-NJ	Y	28740 FQ	36990 MW	48870 TQ	USBLS	5/15
Metals and Plastics	Harrisburg-Carlisle MSA, PA	Y	33880 FQ	42340 MW	48170 TQ	USBLS	5/15
Metals and Plastics	Montgomery County-Bucks County-Chester County PMSA, PA	Y	31800 FQ	38610 MW	47010 TQ	USBLS	5/15
Metals and Plastics	Philadelphia PMSA, PA	Y	28980 FQ	33460 MW	40550 TQ	USBLS	5/15
Metals and Plastics	Pittsburgh MSA, PA	Y	26230 FQ	33710 MW	43110 TQ	USBLS	5/15
Metals and Plastics	Rhode Island	Y	28920 FQ	35600 MW	42530 TQ	USBLS	5/15
Metals and Plastics	Providence-Warwick MSA, RI-MA	Y	30360 FQ	35860 MW	42330 TQ	USBLS	5/15
Metals and Plastics	South Carolina	Y	39980 FQ	48410 MW	57320 TQ	USBLS	5/15
Metals and Plastics	Charleston-North Charleston MSA, SC	Y	45880 FQ	73630 MW	92150 TQ	USBLS	5/15
Metals and Plastics	Greenville-Anderson-Mauldin MSA, SC	Y	42660 FQ	50610 MW	57240 TQ	USBLS	5/15
Metals and Plastics	South Dakota	Y	23450 FQ	28600 MW	36760 TQ	USBLS	5/15
Metals and Plastics	Sioux Falls MSA, SD	Y	22490 FQ	24670 MW	32030 TQ	USBLS	5/15
Metals and Plastics	Tennessee	Y	23120 FQ	29490 MW	36200 TQ	USBLS	5/15
Metals and Plastics	Knoxville MSA, TN	Y	25650 FQ	28680 MW	32060 TQ	USBLS	5/15
Metals and Plastics	Memphis MSA, TN-MS-AR	Y	25240 FQ	33980 MW	40460 TQ	USBLS	5/15
Metals and Plastics	Nashville-Davidson–Murfreesboro–Franklin MSA, TN	Y	19300 FQ	28800 MW	36650 TQ	USBLS	5/15
Metals and Plastics	Texas	Y	23520 FQ	28520 MW	36620 TQ	USBLS	5/15
Metals and Plastics	Austin-Round Rock MSA, TX	Y	24650 FQ	29720 MW	36600 TQ	USBLS	5/15
Metals and Plastics	Dallas-Plano-Irving PMSA, TX	Y	23280 FQ	28150 MW	36250 TQ	USBLS	5/15

AE	Average entry wage	AWR	Average wage range	H	Hourly	LR	Low end range	MTC	Median total compensation	TCC	Total cash compensation
AEX	Average experienced wage	B	Biweekly	HI	Highest wage paid	M	Monthly	MW	Median wage paid	TQ	Third quartile wage
ATC	Average total compensation	D	Daily	HR	High end range	MCC	Median cash compensation	MWR	Median wage range	W	Weekly
AW	Average wage paid	FQ	First quartile wage	LO	Lowest wage paid	ME	Median entry wage	S	See annotated source	Y	Yearly

Occupation/Type/Industry	Location	Per	Low	Mid	High	Source	Date
Extruding and Drawing Machine Setter, Operator, and Tender							
Metals and Plastics	Fort Worth-Arlington PMSA, TX	Y	24140 FQ	29250 MW	44070 TQ	USBLS	5/15
Metals and Plastics	Houston-The Woodlands-Sugar Land MSA, TX	Y	24090 FQ	29430 MW	40100 TQ	USBLS	5/15
Metals and Plastics	San Antonio-New Braunfels MSA, TX	Y	23380 FQ	27020 MW	30330 TQ	USBLS	5/15
Metals and Plastics	Utah	Y	28150 FQ	32380 MW	37810 TQ	USBLS	5/15
Metals and Plastics	Ogden-Clearfield MSA, UT	Y	32810 FQ	41090 MW	45760 TQ	USBLS	5/15
Metals and Plastics	Salt Lake City MSA, UT	Y	28850 FQ	33620 MW	38810 TQ	USBLS	5/15
Metals and Plastics	Vermont	Y	28560 FQ	34080 MW	39470 TQ	USBLS	5/15
Metals and Plastics	Virginia	Y	29050 FQ	34090 MW	39280 TQ	USBLS	5/15
Metals and Plastics	Richmond MSA, VA	Y	28270 FQ	31980 MW	37350 TQ	USBLS	5/15
Metals and Plastics	Virginia Beach-Norfolk-Newport News MSA, VA-NC	Y	28550 FQ	33310 MW	37940 TQ	USBLS	5/15
Metals and Plastics	Washington	H	14.45 FQ	18.43 MW	23.67 TQ	WABLS	3/16
Metals and Plastics	Seattle-Bellevue-Everett PMSA, WA	H	16.30 FQ	20.50 MW	25.89 TQ	WABLS	3/16
Metals and Plastics	Tacoma-Lakewood PMSA, WA	H	13.28 FQ	16.07 MW	18.63 TQ	WABLS	3/16
Metals and Plastics	West Virginia	Y	28820 FQ	40280 MW	48750 TQ	USBLS	5/15
Metals and Plastics	Wisconsin	Y	26220 FQ	31010 MW	37550 TQ	USBLS	5/15
Metals and Plastics	Madison MSA, WI	Y	25620 FQ	33660 MW	39800 TQ	USBLS	5/15
Metals and Plastics	Milwaukee-Waukesha-West Allis MSA, WI	Y	27210 FQ	30750 MW	36720 TQ	USBLS	5/15
Metals and Plastics	Puerto Rico	Y	17340 FQ	18940 MW	23980 TQ	USBLS	5/15
Metals and Plastics	San Juan-Carolina-Caguas MSA, PR	Y	19710 FQ	26020 MW	34680 TQ	USBLS	5/15
Extruding and Forming Machine Setter, Operator, and Tender							
Synthetic and Glass Fibers	Alabama	Y	30929 AE	37921 AW	41417 AEX	ALBLS	6/16
Synthetic and Glass Fibers	Arkansas	Y	23830 FQ	29880 MW	37670 TQ	USBLS	5/15
Synthetic and Glass Fibers	California	H	11.72 FQ	15.44 MW	19.22 TQ	CABLS	1/16-3/16
Synthetic and Glass Fibers	Anaheim-Santa Ana-Irvine PMSA, CA	H	12.58 FQ	16.39 MW	20.82 TQ	CABLS	1/16-3/16
Synthetic and Glass Fibers	Los Angeles-Long Beach-Glendale PMSA, CA	H	13.86 FQ	16.92 MW	19.26 TQ	CABLS	1/16-3/16
Synthetic and Glass Fibers	Connecticut	Y		41738 MW		CTBLS	1/16-3/16
Synthetic and Glass Fibers	Delaware	Y	33010 FQ	39330 MW	45310 TQ	USBLS	5/15
Synthetic and Glass Fibers	Wilmington PMSA, DE-MD-NJ	Y	33010 FQ	39330 MW	45310 TQ	USBLS	5/15
Synthetic and Glass Fibers	Florida	H	10.23 AE	18.75 MW	22.92 AEX	FLBLS	7/16-9/16
Synthetic and Glass Fibers	Georgia	Y	27320 FQ	32670 MW	37390 TQ	USBLS	5/15
Synthetic and Glass Fibers	Atlanta-Sandy Springs-Roswell MSA, GA	Y	21310 FQ	27390 MW	36300 TQ	USBLS	5/15
Synthetic and Glass Fibers	Augusta-Richmond County MSA, GA-SC	Y	24690 FQ	28340 MW	33420 TQ	USBLS	5/15
Synthetic and Glass Fibers	Illinois	Y	29580 FQ	38000 MW	44760 TQ	USBLS	5/15
Synthetic and Glass Fibers	Chicago-Naperville-Arlington Heights PMSA, IL	Y	31130 FQ	38720 MW	45000 TQ	USBLS	5/15
Synthetic and Glass Fibers	Indiana	Y	24360 FQ	29330 MW	35170 TQ	USBLS	5/15
Synthetic and Glass Fibers	Gary PMSA, IN	Y	26220 FQ	29280 MW	33330 TQ	USBLS	5/15
Synthetic and Glass Fibers	Kansas	Y	28720 FQ	35450 MW	48820 TQ	USBLS	5/15
Synthetic and Glass Fibers	Wichita MSA, KS	Y	33840 FQ	36970 MW	40310 TQ	USBLS	5/15
Synthetic and Glass Fibers	Kentucky	Y	22440 FQ	27500 MW	34710 TQ	USBLS	5/15
Synthetic and Glass Fibers	Louisville-Jefferson County MSA, KY-IN	Y	30500 FQ	35870 MW	40700 TQ	USBLS	5/15
Synthetic and Glass Fibers	Maine	Y	28830 FQ	34560 MW	42200 TQ	USBLS	5/15
Synthetic and Glass Fibers	Maryland	Y	20195 AE	28746 MW	33021 AEX	MDBLS	4/16
Synthetic and Glass Fibers	Massachusetts	Y	27950 FQ	33800 MW	38750 TQ	USBLS	5/15
Synthetic and Glass Fibers	Michigan	Y	22150 FQ	26460 MW	32500 TQ	USBLS	5/15
Synthetic and Glass Fibers	Grand Rapids-Wyoming MSA, MI	Y	21300 FQ	30360 MW	35420 TQ	USBLS	5/15
Synthetic and Glass Fibers	Minnesota	Y	31194 FQ	40579 MW	45641 TQ	MNBLS	1/16-3/16
Synthetic and Glass Fibers	Minneapolis-St. Paul-Bloomington MSA, MN-WI	Y	31072 FQ	41065 MW	45834 TQ	MNBLS	1/16-3/16
Synthetic and Glass Fibers	Mississippi	Y	25740 FQ	43800 MW	51490 TQ	USBLS	5/15
Synthetic and Glass Fibers	Kansas City MSA, MO-KS	Y	36720 FQ	49250 MW	56480 TQ	USBLS	5/15
Synthetic and Glass Fibers	Nebraska	Y	41125 FQ	44060 MW	46990 TQ	NEBLS	7/16-9/16
Synthetic and Glass Fibers	Nevada	Y	23360 FQ	26320 MW	29710 TQ	USBLS	5/15

AE	Average entry wage	AWR	Average wage range	H	Hourly
AEX	Average experienced wage	B	Biweekly	HI	Highest wage paid
ATC	Average total compensation	D	Daily	HR	High end range
AW	Average wage paid	FQ	First quartile wage	LO	Lowest wage paid

LR	Low end range	MTC	Median total compensation	TCC	Total cash compensation
M	Monthly	MW	Median wage paid	TQ	Third quartile wage
MCC	Median cash compensation	MWR	Median wage range	W	Weekly
ME	Median entry wage	S	See annotated source	Y	Yearly

Occupation/Type/Industry	Location	Per	Low	Mid	High	Source	Date
Extruding and Forming Machine Setter, Operator, and Tender							
Synthetic and Glass Fibers	Las Vegas-Henderson-Paradise MSA, NV	Y	23360 FQ	26320 MW	29710 TQ	USBLS	5/15
Synthetic and Glass Fibers	New Hampshire	H	13.42 AE	18.00 MW	19.99 AEX	NHBLS	6/16
Synthetic and Glass Fibers	New Jersey	Y	21420 FQ	23290 MW	26190 TQ	USBLS	5/15
Synthetic and Glass Fibers	New York	Y	29870 AE	37750 MW	42080 AEX	NYBLS	1/16-3/16
Synthetic and Glass Fibers	North Carolina	Y	28690 FQ	34330 MW	38640 TQ	USBLS	5/15
Synthetic and Glass Fibers	Charlotte-Concord-Gastonia MSA, NC-SC	Y	31450 FQ	35790 MW	41630 TQ	USBLS	5/15
Synthetic and Glass Fibers	Ohio	Y	26960 FQ	30950 MW	37900 TQ	USBLS	5/15
Synthetic and Glass Fibers	Cincinnati MSA, OH-KY-IN	Y	27050 FQ	31320 MW	35950 TQ	USBLS	5/15
Synthetic and Glass Fibers	Cleveland-Elyria MSA, OH	Y	23550 FQ	29510 MW	53430 TQ	USBLS	5/15
Synthetic and Glass Fibers	Oklahoma	Y	26800 FQ	39480 MW	47400 TQ	USBLS	5/15
Synthetic and Glass Fibers	Pennsylvania	Y	26150 FQ	34440 MW	43490 TQ	USBLS	5/15
Synthetic and Glass Fibers	Allentown-Bethlehem-Easton MSA, PA-NJ	Y	28420 FQ	35060 MW	42610 TQ	USBLS	5/15
Synthetic and Glass Fibers	Pittsburgh MSA, PA	Y	21260 FQ	23050 MW	25970 TQ	USBLS	5/15
Synthetic and Glass Fibers	Rhode Island	Y	27520 FQ	31370 MW	37760 TQ	USBLS	5/15
Synthetic and Glass Fibers	Providence-Warwick MSA, RI-MA	Y	30120 FQ	34540 MW	38090 TQ	USBLS	5/15
Synthetic and Glass Fibers	South Carolina	Y	23940 FQ	31840 MW	43590 TQ	USBLS	5/15
Synthetic and Glass Fibers	Columbia MSA, SC	Y	22320 FQ	24670 MW	43180 TQ	USBLS	5/15
Synthetic and Glass Fibers	Greenville-Anderson-Mauldin MSA, SC	Y	27190 FQ	34380 MW	39280 TQ	USBLS	5/15
Synthetic and Glass Fibers	Tennessee	Y	23490 FQ	38500 MW	45850 TQ	USBLS	5/15
Synthetic and Glass Fibers	Texas	Y	20830 FQ	27560 MW	36770 TQ	USBLS	5/15
Synthetic and Glass Fibers	Dallas-Plano-Irving PMSA, TX	Y	21110 FQ	24880 MW	29970 TQ	USBLS	5/15
Synthetic and Glass Fibers	Fort Worth-Arlington PMSA, TX	Y	18150 FQ	27710 MW	39650 TQ	USBLS	5/15
Synthetic and Glass Fibers	Houston-The Woodlands-Sugar Land MSA, TX	Y	21640 FQ	26640 MW	33920 TQ	USBLS	5/15
Synthetic and Glass Fibers	Utah	Y	26770 FQ	29070 MW	32650 TQ	USBLS	5/15
Synthetic and Glass Fibers	Vermont	Y	31060 FQ	36060 MW	41860 TQ	USBLS	5/15
Synthetic and Glass Fibers	Virginia	Y	28120 FQ	38430 MW	71880 TQ	USBLS	5/15
Synthetic and Glass Fibers	Washington	H	14.70 FQ	16.90 MW	19.11 TQ	WABLS	3/16
Synthetic and Glass Fibers	Seattle-Bellevue-Everett PMSA, WA	H	12.85 FQ	14.72 MW	17.41 TQ	WABLS	3/16
Synthetic and Glass Fibers	West Virginia	Y	26770 FQ	29740 MW	35900 TQ	USBLS	5/15
Synthetic and Glass Fibers	Wisconsin	Y	30820 FQ	41590 MW	46340 TQ	USBLS	5/15
Fabric and Apparel Patternmaker	Alabama	Y	27690 AE	43812 AW	51873 AEX	ALBLS	6/16
	California	H	15.30 FQ	23.98 MW	38.44 TQ	CABLS	1/16-3/16
	Colorado	Y	19820 FQ	24420 MW	30360 TQ	USBLS	5/15
	Florida	H	13.78 AE	17.96 MW	25.02 AEX	FLBLS	7/16-9/16
	Georgia	Y	26770 FQ	33070 MW	39410 TQ	USBLS	5/15
	Illinois	Y	21720 FQ	24080 MW	31290 TQ	USBLS	5/15
	Indiana	Y	31720 FQ	39070 MW	48700 TQ	USBLS	5/15
	Louisiana	Y	21860 FQ	24070 MW	27620 TQ	USBLS	5/15
	Massachusetts	Y	21080 FQ	30970 MW	37440 TQ	USBLS	5/15
	Minnesota	Y	23853 FQ	31275 MW	46917 TQ	MNBLS	1/16-3/16
	Mississippi	Y	28250 FQ	33890 MW	41960 TQ	USBLS	5/15
	New Jersey	Y	30510 FQ	54380 MW	76710 TQ	USBLS	5/15
	New York	Y	41400 AE	65390 MW	76570 AEX	NYBLS	1/16-3/16
	North Carolina	Y	32450 FQ	39970 MW	50490 TQ	USBLS	5/15
	Oregon	H	11.66 FQ	19.64 MW	33.08 TQ	ORBLS	2016
	Pennsylvania	Y	30170 FQ	41600 MW	50180 TQ	USBLS	5/15
	South Carolina	Y	26890 FQ	29150 MW	31390 TQ	USBLS	5/15
	Texas	Y	28250 FQ	35480 MW	49850 TQ	USBLS	5/15
	Washington	H	13.77 FQ	20.39 MW	24.83 TQ	WABLS	3/16
	Puerto Rico	Y	17590 FQ	19510 MW	22270 TQ	USBLS	5/15
Fabric Mender							
Except Garment	California	H	9.62 FQ	11.68 MW	13.37 TQ	CABLS	1/16-3/16
Except Garment	Florida	H	9.85 AE	12.15 MW	15.31 AEX	FLBLS	7/16-9/16
Except Garment	Georgia	Y	25440 FQ	27590 MW	29750 TQ	USBLS	5/15
Except Garment	Illinois	Y	24140 FQ	30810 MW	36030 TQ	USBLS	5/15
Except Garment	Michigan	Y	21370 FQ	22760 MW	24140 TQ	USBLS	5/15
Except Garment	North Carolina	Y	22130 FQ	24740 MW	28830 TQ	USBLS	5/15
Except Garment	South Carolina	Y	22130 FQ	24670 MW	27960 TQ	USBLS	5/15
Except Garment	Texas	Y	17580 FQ	19350 MW	22540 TQ	USBLS	5/15

AE Average entry wage	**AWR** Average wage range	**H** Hourly	**LR** Low end range	**MTC** Median total compensation	**TCC** Total cash compensation
AEX Average experienced wage	**B** Biweekly	**HI** Highest wage paid	**M** Monthly	**MW** Median wage paid	**TQ** Third quartile wage
ATC Average total compensation	**D** Daily	**HR** High end range	**MCC** Median cash compensation	**MWR** Median wage range	**W** Weekly
AW Average wage paid	**FQ** First quartile wage	**LO** Lowest wage paid	**ME** Median entry wage	**S** See annotated source	**Y** Yearly

Occupation/Type/Industry	Location	Per	Low	Mid	High	Source	Date
Fair Hearing Coordinator							
Municipal Government	Seattle, WA	H	31.65 LO		36.83 HI	CSSS	1/13/16
Faller	Alabama	Y	20810 AE	39203 AW	48400 AEX	ALBLS	6/16
	Alaska	Y	51980 FQ	56090 MW	60200 TQ	USBLS	5/15
	Arkansas	Y	22130 FQ	24380 MW	33560 TQ	USBLS	5/15
	California	H	18.92 FQ	31.68 MW	36.00 TQ	CABLS	1/16-3/16
	Florida	H	10.49 AE	26.03 MW	26.49 AEX	FLBLS	7/16-9/16
	Georgia	Y	26960 FQ	30340 MW	38530 TQ	USBLS	5/15
	Idaho	Y	43430 FQ	64970 MW	72020 TQ	USBLS	5/15
	Indiana	Y	23760 FQ	34350 MW	55020 TQ	USBLS	5/15
	Kentucky	Y	26160 FQ	33010 MW	37410 TQ	USBLS	5/15
	Louisiana	Y	20210 FQ	24210 MW	42880 TQ	USBLS	5/15
	Michigan	Y	26570 FQ	28600 MW	30630 TQ	USBLS	5/15
	Minnesota	Y	36839 FQ	44165 MW	52075 TQ	MNBLS	1/16-3/16
	Missouri	Y	17850 FQ	19770 MW	40620 TQ	USBLS	5/15
	Montana	Y	41460 FQ	45340 MW	49220 TQ	USBLS	5/15
	New York	Y	24730 AE	29510 MW	43330 AEX	NYBLS	1/16-3/16
	North Carolina	Y	29820 FQ	34970 MW	39910 TQ	USBLS	5/15
	Ohio	Y	22150 FQ	33770 MW	62770 TQ	USBLS	5/15
	Oregon	H	24.52 FQ	30.50 MW	35.69 TQ	ORBLS	2016
	Pennsylvania	Y	24580 FQ	26570 MW	28640 TQ	USBLS	5/15
	South Carolina	Y	23510 FQ	28050 MW	40930 TQ	USBLS	5/15
	Tennessee	Y	25550 FQ	28200 MW	30840 TQ	USBLS	5/15
	Texas	Y	30940 FQ	36660 MW	53390 TQ	USBLS	5/15
	Virginia	Y	28030 FQ	34490 MW	38980 TQ	USBLS	5/15
	Washington	H	21.02 FQ	25.20 MW	35.89 TQ	WABLS	3/16
	West Virginia	Y	25040 FQ	27930 MW	30950 TQ	USBLS	5/15
	Wisconsin	Y	17160 FQ	18550 MW	19940 TQ	USBLS	5/15*
Family and General Practitioner	Alabama	Y	131248 AE	202733 AW	238481 AEX	ALBLS	6/16
	Birmingham-Hoover MSA, AL	Y	115469 AE	171043 AW	198839 AEX	ALBLS	6/16
	Alaska	Y	176500 FQ	235600 AW		USBLS	5/15
	Anchorage MSA, AK	Y	164700 FQ	215340 AW		USBLS	5/15
	Arizona	Y	112240 FQ	156030 MW		USBLS	5/15
	Phoenix-Mesa-Scottsdale MSA, AZ	Y	110710 FQ	146220 MW		USBLS	5/15
	Tucson MSA, AZ	Y	123970 FQ	198570 AW		USBLS	5/15
	Arkansas	Y	144350 FQ	211410 AW		USBLS	5/15
	Little Rock-North Little Rock-Conway MSA, AR	Y	179540 FQ	234060 AW		USBLS	5/15
	California	H	68.52 FQ	96.75 AW		CABLS	1/16-3/16
	Anaheim-Santa Ana-Irvine PMSA, CA	H	85.65 FQ	113.16 AW		CABLS	1/16-3/16
	Los Angeles-Long Beach-Glendale PMSA, CA	H	55.35 FQ	80.67 MW		CABLS	1/16-3/16
	Oakland-Hayward-Berkeley PMSA, CA	H	74.44 FQ	97.97 AW		CABLS	1/16-3/16
	Riverside-San Bernardino-Ontario MSA, CA	H	79.68 FQ	110.04 AW		CABLS	1/16-3/16
	Sacramento–Roseville–Arden-Arcade MSA, CA	H	37.30 FQ	85.95 MW		CABLS	1/16-3/16
	San Diego-Carlsbad MSA, CA	H	70.16 FQ	97.12 AW		CABLS	1/16-3/16
	San Francisco-Redwood City-South San Francisco PMSA, CA	H	72.22 FQ	94.52 AW		CABLS	1/16-3/16
	Colorado	Y	142530 FQ	202780 AW		USBLS	5/15
	Denver-Aurora-Lakewood MSA, CO	Y	151480 FQ	221520 AW		USBLS	5/15
	Connecticut	Y		199581 AW		CTBLS	1/16-3/16
	Bridgeport-Stamford-Norwalk MSA, CT	Y	147210 FQ	167450 MW		USBLS	5/15
	Hartford-West Hartford-East Hartford MSA, CT	Y	120920 FQ	191590 AW		USBLS	5/15
	Delaware	Y	133710 FQ	164630 MW		USBLS	5/15
	Wilmington PMSA, DE-MD-NJ	Y	137640 FQ	167680 MW		USBLS	5/15
	Washington-Arlington-Alexandria PMSA, DC-VA-MD-WV	Y	115850 FQ	151590 MW		USBLS	5/15
	Florida	H	50.90 AE	93.76 MW	120.11 AEX	FLBLS	7/16-9/16

AE   Average entry wage   AWR   Average wage range   H   Hourly   LR   Low end range   MTC   Median total compensation   TCC   Total cash compensation
AEX   Average experienced wage   B   Biweekly   HI   Highest wage paid   M   Monthly   MW   Median wage paid   TQ   Third quartile wage
ATC   Average total compensation   D   Daily   HR   High end range   MCC   Median cash compensation   MWR   Median wage range   W   Weekly
AW   Average wage paid   FQ   First quartile wage   LO   Lowest wage paid   ME   Median entry wage   S   See annotated source   Y   Yearly

Occupation/Type/Industry	Location	Per	Low	Mid	High	Source	Date
Family and General Practitioner	Fort Lauderdale-Pompano Beach-Deerfield Beach PMSA, FL	H	55.32 AE	92.37 MW	111.92 AEX	FLBLS	7/16-9/16
	Miami-Miami Beach-Kendall PMSA, FL	H	51.73 AE	95.74 MW	118.64 AEX	FLBLS	7/16-9/16
	Orlando-Kissimmee-Sanford MSA, FL	H	30.86 AE	72.09 MW	92.99 AEX	FLBLS	7/16-9/16
	Tampa-St. Petersburg-Clearwater MSA, FL	H	66.88 AE	113.83 AW	137.31 AEX	FLBLS	7/16-9/16
	Georgia	Y	139950 FQ	207770 AW		USBLS	5/15
	Atlanta-Sandy Springs-Roswell MSA, GA	Y	129430 FQ	210290 AW		USBLS	5/15
	Augusta-Richmond County MSA, GA-SC	Y	158260 FQ	227620 AW		USBLS	5/15
	Hawaii	Y		228220 AW		USBLS	5/15
	Urban Honolulu MSA, HI	Y		240010 AW		USBLS	5/15
	Idaho	Y	130330 FQ	182020 MW		USBLS	5/15
	Boise City MSA, ID	Y	144470 FQ	186130 MW		USBLS	5/15
	Illinois	Y	92310 FQ	182150 MW		USBLS	5/15
	Chicago-Naperville-Arlington Heights PMSA, IL	Y	73650 FQ	162470 MW		USBLS	5/15
	Lake County-Kenosha County PMSA, IL-WI	Y	117770 FQ	161850 MW		USBLS	5/15
	Indiana	Y	124150 FQ	172390 MW		USBLS	5/15
	Gary PMSA, IN	Y	110460 FQ	156210 MW		USBLS	5/15
	Indianapolis-Carmel-Anderson MSA, IN	Y	122260 FQ	164580 MW		USBLS	5/15
	Iowa	Y	181050 FQ	234600 AW		USBLS	5/15
	Des Moines-West Des Moines MSA, IA	Y	175880 FQ	235260 AW		USBLS	5/15
	Kansas	Y	171840 FQ	228590 AW		USBLS	5/15
	Wichita MSA, KS	Y	166950 FQ	229870 AW		USBLS	5/15
	Kentucky	Y	140390 FQ	177720 MW		USBLS	5/15
	Louisville-Jefferson County MSA, KY-IN	Y	161060 FQ	183760 MW		USBLS	5/15
	Louisiana	Y	146460 FQ	206440 AW		USBLS	5/15
	Baton Rouge MSA, LA	Y	145830 FQ	201320 AW		USBLS	5/15
	New Orleans-Metairie MSA, LA	Y	144110 FQ	161900 MW		USBLS	5/15
	Maine	Y	136460 FQ	168410 MW		USBLS	5/15
	Portland-South Portland MSA, ME	Y	128160 FQ	160380 MW		USBLS	5/15
	Maryland	Y	89879 AE	179411 MW	224176 AEX	MDBLS	4/16
	Baltimore-Columbia-Towson MSA, MD	Y	112900 FQ	163060 MW		USBLS	5/15
	Salisbury MSA, MD-DE	Y	99710 FQ	142190 MW		USBLS	5/15
	Massachusetts	Y	154960 FQ	212210 AW		USBLS	5/15
	Boston-Cambridge-Newton NECTA, MA	Y	155120 FQ	210330 AW		USBLS	5/15
	Worcester MSA, MA-CT	Y	162490 FQ	209710 AW		USBLS	5/15
	Michigan	Y	94960 FQ	170040 MW		USBLS	5/15
	Detroit-Dearborn-Livonia PMSA, MI	Y	71890 FQ	155500 MW		USBLS	5/15
	Grand Rapids-Wyoming MSA, MI	Y	49850 FQ	111650 MW		USBLS	5/15
	Minnesota	Y	151843 FQ	181359 MW		MNBLS	1/16-3/16
	Minneapolis-St. Paul-Bloomington MSA, MN-WI	Y	150563 FQ	179867 MW		MNBLS	1/16-3/16
	Mississippi	Y	173280 FQ	223250 AW		USBLS	5/15
	Jackson MSA, MS	Y	163730 FQ	215860 AW		USBLS	5/15
	Missouri	Y	58390 FQ	151730 MW		USBLS	5/15
	Kansas City MSA, MO-KS	Y	62060 FQ	176210 MW		USBLS	5/15
	St. Louis MSA, MO-IL	Y	55910 FQ	62850 MW		USBLS	5/15
	Montana	Y	147420 FQ	181320 MW		USBLS	5/15
	Nevada	Y	97430 FQ	154680 MW		USBLS	5/15
	Las Vegas-Henderson-Paradise MSA, NV	Y	90170 FQ	110980 MW	174510 TQ	USBLS	5/15
	New Hampshire	H	74.07 AE	104.89 AW	120.29 AEX	NHBLS	6/16
	Manchester NECTA, NH	H	75.18 AE	96.24 MW	119.35 AEX	NHBLS	6/16
	Nashua NECTA, NH-MA	Y	178510 FQ	235250 AW		USBLS	5/15
	New Jersey	Y	124180 FQ	153620 MW		USBLS	5/15
	Camden PMSA, NJ	Y	136280 FQ	180140 MW		USBLS	5/15

AE	Average entry wage	AWR	Average wage range	H	Hourly	LR	Low end range	MTC	Median total compensation	TCC	Total cash compensation
AEX	Average experienced wage	B	Biweekly	HI	Highest wage paid	M	Monthly	MW	Median wage paid	TQ	Third quartile wage
ATC	Average total compensation	D	Daily	HR	High end range	MCC	Median cash compensation	MWR	Median wage range	W	Weekly
AW	Average wage paid	FQ	First quartile wage	LO	Lowest wage paid	ME	Median entry wage	S	See annotated source	Y	Yearly

Occupation/Type/Industry	Location	Per	Low	Mid	High	Source	Date
Family and General Practitioner	Trenton MSA, NJ	Y	136550 FQ	158040 MW	177940 TQ	USBLS	5/15
	New Mexico	Y	115750 FQ	153550 MW		USBLS	5/15
	Albuquerque MSA, NM	Y	116180 FQ	143250 MW	185390 TQ	USBLS	5/15
	New York	Y	104840 AE	171430 MW		NYBLS	1/16-3/16
	Nassau County-Suffolk County PMSA, NY	Y	170230 FQ	230770 AW		USBLS	5/15
	New York-Jersey City-White Plains PMSA, NY-NJ	Y	127690 FQ	154680 MW		USBLS	5/15
	North Carolina	Y	138080 FQ	183400 MW		USBLS	5/15
	Charlotte-Concord-Gastonia MSA, NC-SC	Y	166360 FQ	233500 AW		USBLS	5/15
	Raleigh MSA, NC	Y	132520 FQ	165100 MW		USBLS	5/15
	North Dakota	Y	106870 FQ	191930 AW		USBLS	5/15
	Fargo MSA, ND-MN	Y	178260 FQ	204120 AW		USBLS	5/15
	Ohio	Y	144850 FQ	180220 MW		USBLS	5/15
	Cincinnati MSA, OH-KY-IN	Y	149580 FQ	186950 MW		USBLS	5/15
	Cleveland-Elyria MSA, OH	Y	152660 FQ	180870 MW		USBLS	5/15
	Columbus MSA, OH	Y	124410 FQ	162870 MW		USBLS	5/15
	Oklahoma	Y	56440 FQ	105060 MW		USBLS	5/15
	Oklahoma City MSA, OK	Y	54520 FQ	62100 MW		USBLS	5/15
	Tulsa MSA, OK	Y	113800 FQ	193600 AW		USBLS	5/15
	Oregon	H	68.20 FQ	85.27 MW		ORBLS	2016
	Portland-Vancouver-Hillsboro MSA, OR-WA	Y	133630 FQ	161400 MW		USBLS	5/15
	Pennsylvania	Y	146740 FQ	205310 AW		USBLS	5/15
	Allentown-Bethlehem-Easton MSA, PA-NJ	Y	161120 FQ	210080 AW		USBLS	5/15
	Harrisburg-Carlisle MSA, PA	Y	120750 FQ	158070 MW		USBLS	5/15
	Montgomery County-Bucks County-Chester County PMSA, PA	Y	165140 FQ	218060 AW		USBLS	5/15
	Philadelphia PMSA, PA	Y	151980 FQ	212460 AW		USBLS	5/15
	Pittsburgh MSA, PA	Y	145700 FQ	186100 MW		USBLS	5/15
	Rhode Island	Y	137150 FQ	155550 MW		USBLS	5/15
	Providence-Warwick MSA, RI-MA	Y	140820 FQ	186590 MW		USBLS	5/15
	South Carolina	Y	139580 FQ	202120 AW		USBLS	5/15
	Charleston-North Charleston MSA, SC	Y	84330 FQ	119210 MW	186310 TQ	USBLS	5/15
	Columbia MSA, SC	Y	60990 FQ	173130 MW		USBLS	5/15
	Greenville-Anderson-Mauldin MSA, SC	Y	179710 FQ	240140 AW		USBLS	5/15
	South Dakota	Y	157450 FQ	210150 AW		USBLS	5/15
	Sioux Falls MSA, SD	Y	137980 FQ	188740 AW		USBLS	5/15
	Tennessee	Y	115510 FQ	170910 MW		USBLS	5/15
	Knoxville MSA, TN	Y	141280 FQ	170930 MW		USBLS	5/15
	Memphis MSA, TN-MS-AR	Y	117170 FQ	146180 MW	181480 TQ	USBLS	5/15
	Nashville-Davidson–Murfreesboro–Franklin MSA, TN	Y	109930 FQ	184330 MW		USBLS	5/15
	Texas	Y	137970 FQ	198430 AW		USBLS	5/15
	Austin-Round Rock MSA, TX	Y	89660 FQ	131500 MW	177020 TQ	USBLS	5/15
	Dallas-Plano-Irving PMSA, TX	Y	145850 FQ	171780 MW		USBLS	5/15
	Fort Worth-Arlington PMSA, TX	Y	97810 FQ	205930 AW		USBLS	5/15
	Houston-The Woodlands-Sugar Land MSA, TX	Y	138870 FQ	201340 AW		USBLS	5/15
	San Antonio-New Braunfels MSA, TX	Y	158510 FQ	204200 AW		USBLS	5/15
	Utah	Y	123910 FQ	205720 AW		USBLS	5/15
	Ogden-Clearfield MSA, UT	Y	161760 FQ	227750 AW		USBLS	5/15
	Provo-Orem MSA, UT	Y	185930 FQ	245060 AW		USBLS	5/15
	Salt Lake City MSA, UT	Y	118250 FQ	205290 AW		USBLS	5/15
	Vermont	Y	133680 FQ	150160 MW		USBLS	5/15
	Burlington-South Burlington MSA, VT	Y	128210 FQ	138900 MW	149600 TQ	USBLS	5/15
	Virginia	Y	117510 FQ	168630 MW		USBLS	5/15
	Richmond MSA, VA	Y	161780 FQ	216020 AW		USBLS	5/15
	Virginia Beach-Norfolk-Newport News MSA, VA-NC	Y	80310 FQ	149760 MW		USBLS	5/15
	Washington	H	65.31 FQ	100.60 AW		WABLS	3/16

AE	Average entry wage	AWR	Average wage range	H	Hourly	LR	Low end range	MTC	Median total compensation
AEX	Average experienced wage	B	Biweekly	HI	Highest wage paid	M	Monthly	MW	Median wage paid
ATC	Average total compensation	D	Daily	HR	High end range	MCC	Median cash compensation	MWR	Median wage range
AW	Average wage paid	FQ	First quartile wage	LO	Lowest wage paid	ME	Median entry wage	S	See annotated source

TCC Total cash compensation
TQ Third quartile wage
W Weekly
Y Yearly

Occupation/Type/Industry	Location	Per	Low	Mid	High	Source	Date
Family and General Practitioner	Seattle-Bellevue-Everett						
	PMSA, WA	H	63.42 FQ	98.79 AW		WABLS	3/16
	Tacoma-Lakewood PMSA, WA	H	70.53 FQ	112.59 AW		WABLS	3/16
	West Virginia	Y	135600 FQ	164920 MW		USBLS	5/15
	Huntington-Ashland MSA,						
	WV-KY-OH	Y	134840 FQ	160480 MW		USBLS	5/15
	Wisconsin	Y	159360 FQ	218480 AW		USBLS	5/15
	Madison MSA, WI	Y	158630 FQ	208200 AW		USBLS	5/15
	Milwaukee-Waukesha-West						
	Allis MSA, WI	Y	147530 FQ	210530 AW		USBLS	5/15
	Wyoming	Y	146700 FQ	200260 AW		USBLS	5/15
	Puerto Rico	Y	54570 FQ	69660 MW	92040 TQ	USBLS	5/15
	San Juan-Carolina-Caguas						
	MSA, PR	Y	57500 FQ	79830 MW	97390 TQ	USBLS	5/15
	Guam	Y	90370 FQ	151710 MW		USBLS	5/15
Family Counselor							
Friend of the Court, County Government	Oakland County, MI	B	2351 LO		3092 HI	MIOAK2	10/1/16
Family Literacy Specialist							
Public Library	Richmond, CA	Y			64100 HI	CACIT	6/28/16
Family Violence Coordinator							
Manager							
Police Services, Municipal Government	South Gate, CA	Y			71854 HI	CACIT	6/28/16
F&I Manager							
Automotive Dealership	United States	Y		135710 AW		AUTON	2015
Fare Collections Receiver							
Municipal Transportation Agency	San Francisco, CA	B	2038 LO		2478 HI	SFGOV	2016-2018
Farm, Ranch, and Other							
Agricultural Manager	Alabama	Y	64685 AE	83534 AW	92964 AEX	ALBLS	6/16
	Arizona	Y	45180 FQ	58510 MW	72260 TQ	USBLS	5/15
	Arkansas	Y	56820 FQ	67070 MW	83420 TQ	USBLS	5/15
	California	H	24.82 FQ	34.75 MW	44.36 TQ	CABLS	1/16-3/16
	Colorado	Y	34310 FQ	41860 MW	48540 TQ	USBLS	5/15
	Florida	H	30.71 AE	43.98 MW	56.21 AEX	FLBLS	7/16-9/16
	Idaho	Y	49520 FQ	61360 MW	81640 TQ	USBLS	5/15
	Illinois	Y	44390 FQ	67930 MW	82720 TQ	USBLS	5/15
	Indiana	Y	52800 FQ	61450 MW	77660 TQ	USBLS	5/15
	Iowa	Y	56360 FQ	70990 MW	92050 TQ	USBLS	5/15
	Kentucky	Y	47830 FQ	64800 MW	79110 TQ	USBLS	5/15
	Louisiana	Y	53080 FQ	63940 MW	78530 TQ	USBLS	5/15
	Michigan	Y	52720 FQ	61020 MW	71910 TQ	USBLS	5/15
	Minnesota	Y	49423 FQ	73708 MW	92537 TQ	MNBLS	1/16-3/16
	Mississippi	Y	41030 FQ	45970 MW	50200 TQ	USBLS	5/15
	Missouri	Y	35350 FQ	45990 MW	63930 TQ	USBLS	5/15
	New Jersey	Y	59430 FQ	90460 MW	105530 TQ	USBLS	5/15
	New Mexico	Y	38450 FQ	45190 MW	52960 TQ	USBLS	5/15
	New York	Y	39690 AE	73100 MW	85220 AEX	NYBLS	1/16-3/16
	North Carolina	Y	44630 FQ	49470 MW	62870 TQ	USBLS	5/15
	North Dakota	Y	67360 FQ	72260 MW	77160 TQ	USBLS	5/15
	Ohio	Y	47490 FQ	56480 MW	78270 TQ	USBLS	5/15
	Oklahoma	Y	39490 FQ	52190 MW	63800 TQ	USBLS	5/15
	Oregon	H	17.22 FQ	29.51 MW	37.51 TQ	ORBLS	2016
	Pennsylvania	Y	71730 FQ	87280 MW	105610 TQ	USBLS	5/15
	South Carolina	Y	46310 FQ	74800 MW	97010 TQ	USBLS	5/15
	Tennessee	Y	30960 FQ	44020 MW	55600 TQ	USBLS	5/15
	Texas	Y	30980 FQ	44220 MW	65580 TQ	USBLS	5/15
	Washington	H	28.68 FQ	34.03 MW	38.60 TQ	WABLS	3/16
	Wisconsin	Y	46490 FQ	67780 MW	76750 TQ	USBLS	5/15
Farm and Home Management							
Advisor	Alabama	Y	33169 AE	53484 AW	63647 AEX	ALBLS	6/16
	Arizona	Y	28440 FQ	51800 MW	67270 TQ	USBLS	5/15
	Arkansas	Y	41000 FQ	50050 MW	62610 TQ	USBLS	5/15
	Colorado	Y	43690 FQ	53460 MW	65290 TQ	USBLS	5/15
	Delaware	Y	50000 FQ	57520 MW	64880 TQ	USBLS	5/15
	Florida	H	11.92 AE	20.86 MW	27.55 AEX	FLBLS	7/16-9/16
	Georgia	Y	17750 FQ	21080 MW	50570 TQ	USBLS	5/15

AE	Average entry wage	AWR	Average wage range	H	Hourly
AEX	Average experienced wage	B	Biweekly	HI	Highest wage paid
ATC	Average total compensation	D	Daily	HR	High end range
AW	Average wage paid	FQ	First quartile wage	LO	Lowest wage paid

LR	Low end range	MTC	Median total compensation	TCC	Total cash compensation
M	Monthly	MW	Median wage paid	TQ	Third quartile wage
MCC	Median cash compensation	MWR	Median wage range	W	Weekly
ME	Median entry wage	S	See annotated source	Y	Yearly

Occupation/Type/Industry	Location	Per	Low	Mid	High	Source	Date
Farm and Home Management Advisor	Hawaii	Y	56610 FQ	67280 MW	82980 TQ	USBLS	5/15
	Idaho	Y	40820 FQ	50510 MW	59150 TQ	USBLS	5/15
	Illinois	Y	36480 FQ	45210 MW	62190 TQ	USBLS	5/15
	Indiana	Y	41110 FQ	48830 MW	61030 TQ	USBLS	5/15
	Iowa	Y	28210 FQ	33070 MW	54290 TQ	USBLS	5/15
	Kansas	Y	43480 FQ	51780 MW	59780 TQ	USBLS	5/15
	Kentucky	Y	35310 FQ	46060 MW	56960 TQ	USBLS	5/15
	Massachusetts	Y	52150 FQ	56440 MW	60740 TQ	USBLS	5/15
	Michigan	Y	28800 FQ	42760 MW	61010 TQ	USBLS	5/15
	Minnesota	Y	46391 FQ	60372 MW	77932 TQ	MNBLS	1/16-3/16
	Mississippi	Y	34100 FQ	46930 MW	58730 TQ	USBLS	5/15
	Montana	Y	43660 FQ	51160 MW	58910 TQ	USBLS	5/15
	Nebraska	Y	67825 FQ	87590 MW	100260 TQ	NEBLS	7/16-9/16
	Nevada	Y	56190 FQ	76710 MW	104260 TQ	USBLS	5/15
	New Jersey	Y	38410 FQ	71470 MW	92420 TQ	USBLS	5/15
	New York	Y	28810 AE	37480 MW	47580 AEX	NYBLS	1/16-3/16
	North Carolina	Y	34320 FQ	46280 MW	57620 TQ	USBLS	5/15
	North Dakota	Y	45130 FQ	53160 MW	69330 TQ	USBLS	5/15
	Oklahoma	Y	51580 FQ	61900 MW	75400 TQ	USBLS	5/15
	Oregon	H	21.52 FQ	29.60 MW	37.12 TQ	ORBLS	2016
	South Dakota	Y	36050 FQ	43620 MW	52260 TQ	USBLS	5/15
	Texas	Y	19010 FQ	25170 MW	40390 TQ	USBLS	5/15
	Virginia	Y	29340 FQ	41680 MW	55940 TQ	USBLS	5/15
	Washington	H	22.57 FQ	26.92 MW	29.52 TQ	WABLS	3/16
	West Virginia	Y	44570 FQ	53400 MW	68350 TQ	USBLS	5/15
	Wisconsin	Y	44670 FQ	51280 MW	68930 TQ	USBLS	5/15
	Wyoming	Y	44760 FQ	52840 MW	67190 TQ	USBLS	5/15
	Puerto Rico	Y	28270 FQ	34150 MW	42430 TQ	USBLS	5/15
Farm Equipment Mechanic and Service Technician	Alabama	Y	27104 AE	37019 AW	41972 AEX	ALBLS	6/16
	Birmingham-Hoover MSA, AL	Y	27348 AE	32565 AW	35179 AEX	ALBLS	6/16
	Arizona	Y	28110 FQ	35490 MW	44160 TQ	USBLS	5/15
	Phoenix-Mesa-Scottsdale MSA, AZ	Y	26810 FQ	33760 MW	42090 TQ	USBLS	5/15
	Arkansas	Y	24670 FQ	34010 MW	42860 TQ	USBLS	5/15
	Little Rock-North Little Rock-Conway MSA, AR	Y	26800 FQ	34970 MW	41030 TQ	USBLS	5/15
	California	H	14.82 FQ	18.67 MW	24.75 TQ	CABLS	1/16-3/16
	Anaheim-Santa Ana-Irvine PMSA, CA	H	19.71 FQ	24.55 MW	28.31 TQ	CABLS	1/16-3/16
	Bakersfield MSA, CA	Y	32310 FQ	35790 MW	39280 TQ	USBLS	5/15
	Los Angeles-Long Beach-Glendale PMSA, CA	H	17.08 FQ	21.23 MW	27.11 TQ	CABLS	1/16-3/16
	Oakland-Hayward-Berkeley PMSA, CA	H	18.49 FQ	26.82 MW	30.11 TQ	CABLS	1/16-3/16
	Riverside-San Bernardino-Ontario MSA, CA	H	14.33 FQ	24.27 MW	28.03 TQ	CABLS	1/16-3/16
	Sacramento–Roseville–Arden-Arcade MSA, CA	H	17.98 FQ	24.18 MW	29.79 TQ	CABLS	1/16-3/16
	San Diego-Carlsbad MSA, CA	H	15.58 FQ	22.01 MW	27.44 TQ	CABLS	1/16-3/16
	Colorado	Y	33190 FQ	39520 MW	48050 TQ	USBLS	5/15
	Denver-Aurora-Lakewood MSA, CO	Y	30410 FQ	33810 MW	36870 TQ	USBLS	5/15
	Connecticut	Y		40039 MW		CTBLS	1/16-3/16
	Delaware	Y	28340 FQ	35850 MW	44040 TQ	USBLS	5/15
	Wilmington PMSA, DE-MD-NJ	Y	29580 FQ	35010 MW	39720 TQ	USBLS	5/15
	Washington-Arlington-Alexandria PMSA, DC-VA-MD-WV	Y	28260 FQ	33950 MW	46430 TQ	USBLS	5/15
	Florida	H	12.54 AE	17.33 MW	20.50 AEX	FLBLS	7/16-9/16
	Miami-Miami Beach-Kendall PMSA, FL	H	12.37 AE	17.86 MW	21.81 AEX	FLBLS	7/16-9/16
	Orlando-Kissimmee-Sanford MSA, FL	H	15.61 AE	20.92 MW	23.24 AEX	FLBLS	7/16-9/16
	Georgia	Y	26800 FQ	31340 MW	39670 TQ	USBLS	5/15
	Atlanta-Sandy Springs-Roswell MSA, GA	Y	27730 FQ	30190 MW	37570 TQ	USBLS	5/15
	Idaho	Y	33000 FQ	40030 MW	47890 TQ	USBLS	5/15

AE	Average entry wage	AWR	Average wage range	H	Hourly
AEX	Average experienced wage	B	Biweekly	HI	Highest wage paid
ATC	Average total compensation	D	Daily	HR	High end range
AW	Average wage paid	FQ	First quartile wage	LO	Lowest wage paid

LR	Low end range	MTC	Median total compensation
M	Monthly	MW	Median wage paid
MCC	Median cash compensation	MWR	Median wage range
ME	Median entry wage	S	See annotated source

TCC	Total cash compensation
TQ	Third quartile wage
W	Weekly
Y	Yearly

Occupation/Type/Industry	Location	Per	Low	Mid	High	Source	Date
Farm Equipment Mechanic and Service Technician	Boise City MSA, ID	Y	33010 FQ	38640 MW	46680 TQ	USBLS	5/15
	Illinois	Y	29600 FQ	37640 MW	46370 TQ	USBLS	5/15
	Chicago-Naperville-Arlington Heights PMSA, IL	Y	43310 FQ	53320 MW	69170 TQ	USBLS	5/15
	Lake County-Kenosha County PMSA, IL-WI	Y	30470 FQ	36000 MW	42130 TQ	USBLS	5/15
	Indiana	Y	30100 FQ	36310 MW	44220 TQ	USBLS	5/15
	Indianapolis-Carmel-Anderson MSA, IN	Y	28880 FQ	33690 MW	38040 TQ	USBLS	5/15
	Iowa	Y	32470 FQ	37780 MW	45240 TQ	USBLS	5/15
	Cedar Rapids MSA, IA	Y	27580 FQ	32730 MW	38800 TQ	USBLS	5/15
	Des Moines-West Des Moines MSA, IA	Y	28160 FQ	38100 MW	44390 TQ	USBLS	5/15
	Kansas	Y	32700 FQ	39550 MW	54270 TQ	USBLS	5/15
	Kentucky	Y	24590 FQ	30000 MW	37610 TQ	USBLS	5/15
	Louisville-Jefferson County MSA, KY-IN	Y	22990 FQ	28480 MW	35800 TQ	USBLS	5/15
	Louisiana	Y	27400 FQ	34630 MW	44440 TQ	USBLS	5/15
	Maine	Y	23470 FQ	29830 MW	38520 TQ	USBLS	5/15
	Maryland	Y	26863 AE	38794 MW	44760 AEX	MDBLS	4/16
	Baltimore-Columbia-Towson MSA, MD	Y	28090 FQ	32970 MW	42560 TQ	USBLS	5/15
	Salisbury MSA, MD-DE	Y	30600 FQ	37600 MW	45440 TQ	USBLS	5/15
	Massachusetts	Y	35230 FQ	39020 MW	45020 TQ	USBLS	5/15
	Worcester MSA, MA-CT	Y	39960 FQ	44250 MW	48380 TQ	USBLS	5/15
	Michigan	Y	30450 FQ	37050 MW	46290 TQ	USBLS	5/15
	Grand Rapids-Wyoming MSA, MI	Y	30340 FQ	36630 MW	45380 TQ	USBLS	5/15
	Minnesota	Y	31819 FQ	40599 MW	50344 TQ	MNBLS	1/16-3/16
	Minneapolis-St. Paul-Bloomington MSA, MN-WI	Y	31407 FQ	42278 MW	53411 TQ	MNBLS	1/16-3/16
	Mississippi	Y	25420 FQ	33620 MW	41790 TQ	USBLS	5/15
	Jackson MSA, MS	Y	27120 FQ	32730 MW	38080 TQ	USBLS	5/15
	Missouri	Y	27050 FQ	33700 MW	38660 TQ	USBLS	5/15
	Kansas City MSA, MO-KS	Y	28570 FQ	33760 MW	37490 TQ	USBLS	5/15
	St. Louis MSA, MO-IL	Y	23350 FQ	33900 MW	38450 TQ	USBLS	5/15
	Montana	Y	32470 FQ	41550 MW	50940 TQ	USBLS	5/15
	Billings MSA, MT	Y	40130 FQ	49280 MW	64630 TQ	USBLS	5/15
	Nebraska	Y	29815 FQ	37290 MW	47995 TQ	NEBLS	7/16-9/16
	Omaha-Council Bluffs MSA, NE-IA	Y	33035 FQ	42685 MW	54630 TQ	NEBLS	7/16-9/16
	Nevada	Y	34370 FQ	42530 MW	48170 TQ	USBLS	5/15
	New Hampshire	H	16.24 AE	19.66 MW	25.97 AEX	NHBLS	6/16
	New Jersey	Y	30890 FQ	36180 MW	41880 TQ	USBLS	5/15
	New Mexico	Y	34880 FQ	42730 MW	57850 TQ	USBLS	5/15
	New York	Y	28190 AE	38810 MW	48220 AEX	NYBLS	1/16-3/16
	Buffalo-Cheektowaga-Niagara Falls MSA, NY	Y	27350 FQ	32920 MW	43810 TQ	USBLS	5/15
	New York-Jersey City-White Plains PMSA, NY-NJ	Y	47030 FQ	55290 MW	62280 TQ	USBLS	5/15
	Rochester MSA, NY	Y	30690 FQ	38560 MW	45570 TQ	USBLS	5/15
	North Carolina	Y	27580 FQ	34260 MW	41520 TQ	USBLS	5/15
	Charlotte-Concord-Gastonia MSA, NC-SC	Y	32120 FQ	36490 MW	42820 TQ	USBLS	5/15
	Raleigh MSA, NC	Y	30410 FQ	36730 MW	43760 TQ	USBLS	5/15
	North Dakota	Y	41580 FQ	47030 MW	55240 TQ	USBLS	5/15
	Fargo MSA, ND-MN	Y	40750 FQ	47050 MW	56390 TQ	USBLS	5/15
	Ohio	Y	28510 FQ	34780 MW	41560 TQ	USBLS	5/15
	Cincinnati MSA, OH-KY-IN	Y	29910 FQ	36730 MW	45890 TQ	USBLS	5/15
	Cleveland-Elyria MSA, OH	Y	26160 FQ	29050 MW	34470 TQ	USBLS	5/15
	Columbus MSA, OH	Y	28430 FQ	37630 MW	45150 TQ	USBLS	5/15
	Oklahoma	Y	27680 FQ	35680 MW	51260 TQ	USBLS	5/15
	Oklahoma City MSA, OK	Y	29210 FQ	38250 MW	55480 TQ	USBLS	5/15
	Tulsa MSA, OK	Y	23360 FQ	35180 MW	47210 TQ	USBLS	5/15
	Oregon	H	15.38 FQ	17.94 MW	23.12 TQ	ORBLS	2016
	Portland-Vancouver-Hillsboro MSA, OR-WA	Y	33080 FQ	37010 MW	44710 TQ	USBLS	5/15
	Pennsylvania	Y	28920 FQ	35300 MW	43460 TQ	USBLS	5/15
	Allentown-Bethlehem-Easton MSA, PA-NJ	Y	32900 FQ	35820 MW	38740 TQ	USBLS	5/15
	Harrisburg-Carlisle MSA, PA	Y	28760 FQ	36020 MW	47580 TQ	USBLS	5/15

AE	Average entry wage	AWR	Average wage range	H	Hourly	LR	Low end range	MTC	Median total compensation	TCC	Total cash compensation
AEX	Average experienced wage	B	Biweekly	HI	Highest wage paid	M	Monthly	MW	Median wage paid	TQ	Third quartile wage
ATC	Average total compensation	D	Daily	HR	High end range	MCC	Median cash compensation	MWR	Median wage range	W	Weekly
AW	Average wage paid	FQ	First quartile wage	LO	Lowest wage paid	ME	Median entry wage	S	See annotated source	Y	Yearly

Occupation/Type/Industry	Location	Per	Low	Mid	High	Source	Date
Farm Equipment Mechanic and Service Technician	Montgomery County-Bucks County-Chester County						
	PMSA, PA	Y	40840 FQ	48000 MW	55410 TQ	USBLS	5/15
	Pittsburgh MSA, PA	Y	31560 FQ	36090 MW	41320 TQ	USBLS	5/15
	South Carolina	Y	28760 FQ	35080 MW	42310 TQ	USBLS	5/15
	Columbia MSA, SC	Y	27420 FQ	33500 MW	43700 TQ	USBLS	5/15
	Greenville-Anderson-Mauldin MSA, SC	Y	30560 FQ	35790 MW	41230 TQ	USBLS	5/15
	South Dakota	Y	31740 FQ	37810 MW	46270 TQ	USBLS	5/15
	Sioux Falls MSA, SD	Y	34490 FQ	41110 MW	47220 TQ	USBLS	5/15
	Tennessee	Y	23720 FQ	31220 MW	37090 TQ	USBLS	5/15
	Memphis MSA, TN-MS-AR	Y	27640 FQ	35070 MW	39380 TQ	USBLS	5/15
	Nashville-Davidson–Murfreesboro–Franklin MSA, TN	Y	29720 FQ	34960 MW	39020 TQ	USBLS	5/15
	Texas	Y	27160 FQ	36170 MW	45470 TQ	USBLS	5/15
	Austin-Round Rock MSA, TX	Y	23160 FQ	25810 MW	28770 TQ	USBLS	5/15
	Fort Worth-Arlington PMSA, TX	Y	30850 FQ	39110 MW	47220 TQ	USBLS	5/15
	Houston-The Woodlands-Sugar Land MSA, TX	Y	35230 FQ	42770 MW	49720 TQ	USBLS	5/15
	San Antonio-New Braunfels MSA, TX	Y	28110 FQ	31670 MW	41920 TQ	USBLS	5/15
	Utah	Y	31580 FQ	38600 MW	46620 TQ	USBLS	5/15
	Provo-Orem MSA, UT	Y	24260 FQ	41790 MW	47910 TQ	USBLS	5/15
	Salt Lake City MSA, UT	Y	31710 FQ	38780 MW	49690 TQ	USBLS	5/15
	Vermont	Y	34770 FQ	43770 MW	53900 TQ	USBLS	5/15
	Burlington-South Burlington MSA, VT	Y	35240 FQ	40880 MW	46130 TQ	USBLS	5/15
	Virginia	Y	27660 FQ	33340 MW	43430 TQ	USBLS	5/15
	Richmond MSA, VA	Y	28210 FQ	31110 MW	44110 TQ	USBLS	5/15
	Washington	H	15.92 FQ	19.31 MW	23.11 TQ	WABLS	3/16
	Seattle-Bellevue-Everett PMSA, WA	H	16.56 FQ	20.27 MW	23.02 TQ	WABLS	3/16
	Tacoma-Lakewood PMSA, WA	H	15.41 FQ	19.63 MW	22.10 TQ	WABLS	3/16
	West Virginia	Y	21350 FQ	24270 MW	28770 TQ	USBLS	5/15
	Wisconsin	Y	31770 FQ	37570 MW	45490 TQ	USBLS	5/15
	Madison MSA, WI	Y	35310 FQ	40080 MW	47720 TQ	USBLS	5/15
	Milwaukee-Waukesha-West Allis MSA, WI	Y	32920 FQ	36560 MW	40320 TQ	USBLS	5/15
	Wyoming	Y	36180 FQ	43140 MW	49080 TQ	USBLS	5/15
	Puerto Rico	Y	17130 FQ	18830 MW	21490 TQ	USBLS	5/15
Farm Labor Contractor	California	H	16.13 FQ	25.80 MW	36.62 TQ	CABLS	1/16-3/16
	Bakersfield MSA, CA	H	17.10 FQ	21.84 MW	36.88 TQ	CABLS	1/16-3/16
	Riverside-San Bernardino-Ontario MSA, CA	H	16.38 FQ	18.11 MW	28.13 TQ	CABLS	1/16-3/16
	Salinas MSA, CA	H	14.84 FQ	24.84 MW	29.86 TQ	CABLS	1/16-3/16
	Florida	H	9.15 AE	15.97 MW	26.85 AEX	FLBLS	7/16-9/16
	Sebring MSA, FL	H	19.62 AE	38.66 MW	40.00 AEX	FLBLS	7/16-9/16
Farmer							
Sheriff's Department	San Francisco, CA	B	2145 LO		2607 HI	SFGOV	2016-2018
Farmers' Market Manager							
Municipal Government	Torrance, CA	Y			75226 HI	CACIT	6/28/16
Farmworker							
Farm, Ranch, and Aquacultural Animals	Alabama	Y	17560 AE	23999 AW	27219 AEX	ALBLS	6/16
Farm, Ranch, and Aquacultural Animals	Birmingham-Hoover MSA, AL	Y	19360 AE	26201 AW	29616 AEX	ALBLS	6/16
Farm, Ranch, and Aquacultural Animals	Arizona	Y	19390 FQ	24110 MW	29840 TQ	USBLS	5/15
Farm, Ranch, and Aquacultural Animals	Phoenix-Mesa-Scottsdale MSA, AZ	Y	18180 FQ	19580 MW	24000 TQ	USBLS	5/15
Farm, Ranch, and Aquacultural Animals	Tucson MSA, AZ	Y	19910 FQ	25070 MW	30210 TQ	USBLS	5/15
Farm, Ranch, and Aquacultural Animals	Arkansas	Y	19270 FQ	22780 MW	27230 TQ	USBLS	5/15
Farm, Ranch, and Aquacultural Animals	California	H	10.70 FQ	13.55 MW	17.66 TQ	CABLS	1/16-3/16
Farm, Ranch, and Aquacultural Animals	Anaheim-Santa Ana-Irvine PMSA, CA	H	9.50 FQ	11.50 MW	16.68 TQ	CABLS	1/16-3/16
Farm, Ranch, and Aquacultural Animals	Los Angeles-Long Beach-Glendale PMSA, CA	H	11.18 FQ	15.40 MW	18.69 TQ	CABLS	1/16-3/16

AE	Average entry wage	AWR	Average wage range	H	Hourly	LR	Low end range	MTC	Median total compensation	TCC	Total cash compensation
AEX	Average experienced wage	B	Biweekly	HI	Highest wage paid	M	Monthly	MW	Median wage paid	TQ	Third quartile wage
ATC	Average total compensation	D	Daily	HR	High end range	MCC	Median cash compensation	MWR	Median wage range	W	Weekly
AW	Average wage paid	FQ	First quartile wage	LO	Lowest wage paid	ME	Median entry wage	S	See annotated source	Y	Yearly

Occupation/Type/Industry	Location	Per	Low	Mid	High	Source	Date
Farmworker							
Farm, Ranch, and Aquacultural Animals	Oakland-Hayward-Berkeley PMSA, CA	H	10.87 FQ	13.45 MW	15.73 TQ	CABLS	1/16-3/16
Farm, Ranch, and Aquacultural Animals	Riverside-San Bernardino-Ontario MSA, CA	H	10.82 FQ	12.91 MW	20.36 TQ	CABLS	1/16-3/16
Farm, Ranch, and Aquacultural Animals	Sacramento–Roseville–Arden-Arcade MSA, CA	H	9.99 FQ	10.90 MW	11.79 TQ	CABLS	1/16-3/16
Farm, Ranch, and Aquacultural Animals	San Diego-Carlsbad MSA, CA	H	12.76 FQ	16.34 MW	18.07 TQ	CABLS	1/16-3/16
Farm, Ranch, and Aquacultural Animals	San Francisco-Redwood City-South San Francisco PMSA, CA	H	10.89 FQ	14.15 MW	17.48 TQ	CABLS	1/16-3/16
Farm, Ranch, and Aquacultural Animals	Colorado	Y	18660 FQ	21780 MW	30250 TQ	USBLS	5/15
Farm, Ranch, and Aquacultural Animals	Denver-Aurora-Lakewood MSA, CO	Y	18340 FQ	19540 MW	27980 TQ	USBLS	5/15
Farm, Ranch, and Aquacultural Animals	Connecticut	Y		32311 MW		CTBLS	1/16-3/16
Farm, Ranch, and Aquacultural Animals	Hartford-West Hartford-East Hartford MSA, CT	Y	21870 FQ	24920 MW	30070 TQ	USBLS	5/15
Farm, Ranch, and Aquacultural Animals	Delaware	Y	21120 FQ	23620 MW	27420 TQ	USBLS	5/15
Farm, Ranch, and Aquacultural Animals	Wilmington PMSA, DE-MD-NJ	Y	20050 FQ	22960 MW	28460 TQ	USBLS	5/15
Farm, Ranch, and Aquacultural Animals	Washington-Arlington-Alexandria PMSA, DC-VA-MD-WV	Y	26690 FQ	30840 MW	40970 TQ	USBLS	5/15
Farm, Ranch, and Aquacultural Animals	Florida	H	9.02 AE	11.38 MW	13.53 AEX	FLBLS	7/16-9/16
Farm, Ranch, and Aquacultural Animals	Fort Lauderdale-Pompano Beach-Deerfield Beach PMSA, FL	H	12.00 AE	13.47 MW	13.74 AEX	FLBLS	7/16-9/16
Farm, Ranch, and Aquacultural Animals	Tampa-St. Petersburg-Clearwater MSA, FL	H	13.04 AE	14.12 MW	15.03 AEX	FLBLS	7/16-9/16
Farm, Ranch, and Aquacultural Animals	Georgia	Y	18160 FQ	21940 MW	27820 TQ	USBLS	5/15
Farm, Ranch, and Aquacultural Animals	Atlanta-Sandy Springs-Roswell MSA, GA	Y	17660 FQ	19540 MW	28110 TQ	USBLS	5/15
Farm, Ranch, and Aquacultural Animals	Augusta-Richmond County MSA, GA-SC	Y	28590 FQ	34030 MW	37790 TQ	USBLS	5/15
Farm, Ranch, and Aquacultural Animals	Hawaii	Y	24390 FQ	32450 MW	38150 TQ	USBLS	5/15
Farm, Ranch, and Aquacultural Animals	Urban Honolulu MSA, HI	Y	22760 FQ	28470 MW	36660 TQ	USBLS	5/15
Farm, Ranch, and Aquacultural Animals	Idaho	Y	18880 FQ	22730 MW	34640 TQ	USBLS	5/15
Farm, Ranch, and Aquacultural Animals	Boise City MSA, ID	Y	20830 FQ	23460 MW	36820 TQ	USBLS	5/15
Farm, Ranch, and Aquacultural Animals	Illinois	Y	19670 FQ	23290 MW	28150 TQ	USBLS	5/15
Farm, Ranch, and Aquacultural Animals	Chicago-Naperville-Arlington Heights PMSA, IL	Y	19290 FQ	21130 MW	23670 TQ	USBLS	5/15
Farm, Ranch, and Aquacultural Animals	Lake County-Kenosha County PMSA, IL-WI	Y	19920 FQ	22470 MW	25290 TQ	USBLS	5/15
Farm, Ranch, and Aquacultural Animals	Indiana	Y	21460 FQ	25000 MW	30740 TQ	USBLS	5/15
Farm, Ranch, and Aquacultural Animals	Indianapolis-Carmel-Anderson MSA, IN	Y	26080 FQ	28020 MW	29950 TQ	USBLS	5/15
Farm, Ranch, and Aquacultural Animals	Iowa	Y	22230 FQ	25640 MW	31950 TQ	USBLS	5/15
Farm, Ranch, and Aquacultural Animals	Kansas	Y	18890 FQ	21950 MW	24610 TQ	USBLS	5/15
Farm, Ranch, and Aquacultural Animals	Wichita MSA, KS	Y	21420 FQ	22960 MW	24510 TQ	USBLS	5/15
Farm, Ranch, and Aquacultural Animals	Kentucky	Y	19160 FQ	22680 MW	28850 TQ	USBLS	5/15
Farm, Ranch, and Aquacultural Animals	Louisville-Jefferson County MSA, KY-IN	Y	20620 FQ	24230 MW	29680 TQ	USBLS	5/15
Farm, Ranch, and Aquacultural Animals	Louisiana	Y	18650 FQ	22450 MW	26720 TQ	USBLS	5/15
Farm, Ranch, and Aquacultural Animals	New Orleans-Metairie MSA, LA	Y	18560 FQ	21550 MW	24490 TQ	USBLS	5/15
Farm, Ranch, and Aquacultural Animals	Maine	Y	20930 FQ	24680 MW	32410 TQ	USBLS	5/15
Farm, Ranch, and Aquacultural Animals	Portland-South Portland MSA, ME	Y	20540 FQ	23060 MW	28710 TQ	USBLS	5/15
Farm, Ranch, and Aquacultural Animals	Maryland	Y	20224 AE	29329 MW	33882 AEX	MDBLS	4/16
Farm, Ranch, and Aquacultural Animals	Salisbury MSA, MD-DE	Y	21040 FQ	23450 MW	26690 TQ	USBLS	5/15
Farm, Ranch, and Aquacultural Animals	Massachusetts	Y	20490 FQ	24090 MW	29360 TQ	USBLS	5/15
Farm, Ranch, and Aquacultural Animals	Michigan	Y	19180 FQ	21690 MW	25410 TQ	USBLS	5/15
Farm, Ranch, and Aquacultural Animals	Grand Rapids-Wyoming MSA, MI	Y	18010 FQ	18950 MW	20880 TQ	USBLS	5/15
Farm, Ranch, and Aquacultural Animals	Minnesota	Y	19020 FQ	23016 MW	28010 TQ	MNBLS	1/16-3/16
Farm, Ranch, and Aquacultural Animals	Minneapolis-St. Paul-Bloomington MSA, MN-WI	Y	18788 FQ	21573 MW	26729 TQ	MNBLS	1/16-3/16
Farm, Ranch, and Aquacultural Animals	Mississippi	Y	17510 FQ	20110 MW	28780 TQ	USBLS	5/15
Farm, Ranch, and Aquacultural Animals	Missouri	Y	19390 FQ	23340 MW	29720 TQ	USBLS	5/15
Farm, Ranch, and Aquacultural Animals	St. Louis MSA, MO-IL	Y	19330 FQ	23150 MW	28720 TQ	USBLS	5/15
Farm, Ranch, and Aquacultural Animals	Montana	Y	19240 FQ	23450 MW	29980 TQ	USBLS	5/15
Farm, Ranch, and Aquacultural Animals	Billings MSA, MT	Y	18960 FQ	22380 MW	29400 TQ	USBLS	5/15

AE	Average entry wage	AWR	Average wage range	H	Hourly
AEX	Average experienced wage	B	Biweekly	HI	Highest wage paid
ATC	Average total compensation	D	Daily	HR	High end range
AW	Average wage paid	FQ	First quartile wage	LO	Lowest wage paid

LR	Low end range	MTC	Median total compensation	TCC	Total cash compensation
M	Monthly	MW	Median wage paid	TQ	Third quartile wage
MCC	Median cash compensation	MWR	Median wage range	W	Weekly
ME	Median entry wage	S	See annotated source	Y	Yearly

Occupation/Type/Industry	Location	Per	Low	Mid	High	Source	Date
Farmworker							
Farm, Ranch, and Aquacultural Animals	Nebraska	Y	21640 FQ	26765 MW	31480 TQ	NEBLS	7/16-9/16
Farm, Ranch, and Aquacultural Animals	Omaha-Council Bluffs MSA, NE-IA	Y	20120 FQ	27220 MW	30845 TQ	NEBLS	7/16-9/16
Farm, Ranch, and Aquacultural Animals	Nevada	Y	27710 FQ	38010 MW	45930 TQ	USBLS	5/15
Farm, Ranch, and Aquacultural Animals	New Hampshire	H	10.67 AE	11.82 M	14.41 AEX	NHBLS	6/16
Farm, Ranch, and Aquacultural Animals	New Jersey	Y	21970 FQ	27260 MW	32800 TQ	USBLS	5/15
Farm, Ranch, and Aquacultural Animals	Newark PMSA, NJ-PA	Y	24430 FQ	27880 MW	31520 TQ	USBLS	5/15
Farm, Ranch, and Aquacultural Animals	New Mexico	Y	18830 FQ	27870 MW	35660 TQ	USBLS	5/15
Farm, Ranch, and Aquacultural Animals	New York	Y	19870 AE	28180 MW	37970 AEX	NYBLS	1/16-3/16
Farm, Ranch, and Aquacultural Animals	New York-Jersey City-White Plains PMSA, NY-NJ	Y	19660 FQ	25640 MW	34400 TQ	USBLS	5/15
Farm, Ranch, and Aquacultural Animals	North Carolina	Y	20920 FQ	24150 MW	31150 TQ	USBLS	5/15
Farm, Ranch, and Aquacultural Animals	Charlotte-Concord-Gastonia MSA, NC-SC	Y	21060 FQ	23450 MW	32870 TQ	USBLS	5/15
Farm, Ranch, and Aquacultural Animals	Raleigh MSA, NC	Y	24590 FQ	27240 MW	29830 TQ	USBLS	5/15
Farm, Ranch, and Aquacultural Animals	North Dakota	Y	20560 FQ	23780 MW	32720 TQ	USBLS	5/15
Farm, Ranch, and Aquacultural Animals	Ohio	Y	18730 FQ	22920 MW	31860 TQ	USBLS	5/15
Farm, Ranch, and Aquacultural Animals	Cincinnati MSA, OH-KY-IN	Y	18480 FQ	24220 MW	35870 TQ	USBLS	5/15
Farm, Ranch, and Aquacultural Animals	Cleveland-Elyria MSA, OH	Y	18730 FQ	21430 MW	24720 TQ	USBLS	5/15
Farm, Ranch, and Aquacultural Animals	Columbus MSA, OH	Y	19050 FQ	24250 MW	30650 TQ	USBLS	5/15
Farm, Ranch, and Aquacultural Animals	Oklahoma	Y	18610 FQ	22650 MW	29270 TQ	USBLS	5/15
Farm, Ranch, and Aquacultural Animals	Oklahoma City MSA, OK	Y	18070 FQ	20650 MW	26710 TQ	USBLS	5/15
Farm, Ranch, and Aquacultural Animals	Tulsa MSA, OK	Y	18420 FQ	21770 MW	26840 TQ	USBLS	5/15
Farm, Ranch, and Aquacultural Animals	Oregon	H	10.56 FQ	12.29 MW	16.14 TQ	ORBLS	2016
Farm, Ranch, and Aquacultural Animals	Portland-Vancouver-Hillsboro MSA, OR-WA	Y	29080 FQ	35380 MW	39750 TQ	USBLS	5/15
Farm, Ranch, and Aquacultural Animals	Pennsylvania	Y	20410 FQ	26650 MW	34990 TQ	USBLS	5/15
Farm, Ranch, and Aquacultural Animals	Harrisburg-Carlisle MSA, PA	Y	25230 FQ	33530 MW	38300 TQ	USBLS	5/15
Farm, Ranch, and Aquacultural Animals	Montgomery County-Bucks County-Chester County PMSA, PA	Y	18850 FQ	23680 MW	29830 TQ	USBLS	5/15
Farm, Ranch, and Aquacultural Animals	Pittsburgh MSA, PA	Y	21730 FQ	25410 MW	29290 TQ	USBLS	5/15
Farm, Ranch, and Aquacultural Animals	South Carolina	Y	20600 FQ	23610 MW	29140 TQ	USBLS	5/15
Farm, Ranch, and Aquacultural Animals	Columbia MSA, SC	Y	21390 FQ	23740 MW	28220 TQ	USBLS	5/15
Farm, Ranch, and Aquacultural Animals	Greenville-Anderson-Mauldin MSA, SC	Y	21350 FQ	23150 MW	24970 TQ	USBLS	5/15
Farm, Ranch, and Aquacultural Animals	South Dakota	Y	22420 FQ	24860 MW	28470 TQ	USBLS	5/15
Farm, Ranch, and Aquacultural Animals	Tennessee	Y	17840 FQ	20460 MW	24250 TQ	USBLS	5/15
Farm, Ranch, and Aquacultural Animals	Knoxville MSA, TN	Y	17260 FQ	19120 MW	24750 TQ	USBLS	5/15
Farm, Ranch, and Aquacultural Animals	Memphis MSA, TN-MS-AR	Y	21740 FQ	23720 MW	27010 TQ	USBLS	5/15
Farm, Ranch, and Aquacultural Animals	Nashville-Davidson–Murfreesboro–Franklin MSA, TN	Y	18880 FQ	22260 MW	27370 TQ	USBLS	5/15
Farm, Ranch, and Aquacultural Animals	Texas	Y	18240 FQ	21490 MW	28100 TQ	USBLS	5/15
Farm, Ranch, and Aquacultural Animals	Austin-Round Rock MSA, TX	Y	17510 FQ	19560 MW	22480 TQ	USBLS	5/15
Farm, Ranch, and Aquacultural Animals	Dallas-Plano-Irving PMSA, TX	Y	18030 FQ	21100 MW	26550 TQ	USBLS	5/15
Farm, Ranch, and Aquacultural Animals	Fort Worth-Arlington PMSA, TX	Y	18400 FQ	21750 MW	25750 TQ	USBLS	5/15
Farm, Ranch, and Aquacultural Animals	Houston-The Woodlands-Sugar Land MSA, TX	Y	19330 FQ	22850 MW	31370 TQ	USBLS	5/15
Farm, Ranch, and Aquacultural Animals	San Antonio-New Braunfels MSA, TX	Y	20670 FQ	24050 MW	29950 TQ	USBLS	5/15
Farm, Ranch, and Aquacultural Animals	Utah	Y	18150 FQ	23980 MW	30740 TQ	USBLS	5/15
Farm, Ranch, and Aquacultural Animals	Salt Lake City MSA, UT	Y	17440 FQ	19420 MW	26750 TQ	USBLS	5/15
Farm, Ranch, and Aquacultural Animals	Vermont	Y	22370 FQ	29230 MW	38620 TQ	USBLS	5/15
Farm, Ranch, and Aquacultural Animals	Virginia	Y	18570 FQ	24820 MW	30320 TQ	USBLS	5/15
Farm, Ranch, and Aquacultural Animals	Richmond MSA, VA	Y	16980 FQ	18780 MW	22150 TQ	USBLS	5/15
Farm, Ranch, and Aquacultural Animals	Virginia Beach-Norfolk-Newport News MSA, VA-NC	Y	17420 FQ	19520 MW	28270 TQ	USBLS	5/15
Farm, Ranch, and Aquacultural Animals	Washington	H	11.91 FQ	14.67 MW	18.98 TQ	WABLS	3/16
Farm, Ranch, and Aquacultural Animals	Seattle-Bellevue-Everett PMSA, WA	H	13.61 FQ	16.25 MW	19.26 TQ	WABLS	3/16
Farm, Ranch, and Aquacultural Animals	Tacoma-Lakewood PMSA, WA	H	13.44 FQ	14.91 MW	21.57 TQ	WABLS	3/16
Farm, Ranch, and Aquacultural Animals	West Virginia	Y	18660 FQ	25310 MW	30510 TQ	USBLS	5/15
Farm, Ranch, and Aquacultural Animals	Wisconsin	Y	20610 FQ	26130 MW	30480 TQ	USBLS	5/15
Farm, Ranch, and Aquacultural Animals	Madison MSA, WI	Y	25530 FQ	28920 MW	33700 TQ	USBLS	5/15
Farm, Ranch, and Aquacultural Animals	Milwaukee-Waukesha-West Allis MSA, WI	Y	19040 FQ	26160 MW	28660 TQ	USBLS	5/15
Farm, Ranch, and Aquacultural Animals	Wyoming	Y	22130 FQ	27260 MW	30170 TQ	USBLS	5/15

AE	Average entry wage	AWR	Average wage range	H	Hourly	LR	Low end range	MTC	Median total compensation	TCC	Total cash compensation
AEX	Average experienced wage	B	Biweekly	HI	Highest wage paid	M	Monthly	MW	Median wage paid	TQ	Third quartile wage
ATC	Average total compensation	D	Daily	HR	High end range	MCC	Median cash compensation	MWR	Median wage range	W	Weekly
AW	Average wage paid	FQ	First quartile wage	LO	Lowest wage paid	ME	Median entry wage	S	See annotated source	Y	Yearly

Occupation/Type/Industry	Location	Per	Low	Mid	High	Source	Date
Farmworker and Laborer							
Crop, Nursery, and Greenhouse	Alabama	Y	17467 AE	22158 AW	24503 AEX	ALBLS	6/16
Crop, Nursery, and Greenhouse	Birmingham-Hoover MSA, AL	Y	19432 AE	26016 AW	29297 AEX	ALBLS	6/16
Crop, Nursery, and Greenhouse	Alaska	Y	20330 FQ	24810 MW	30180 TQ	USBLS	5/15
Crop, Nursery, and Greenhouse	Arizona	Y	17690 FQ	18580 MW	19480 TQ	USBLS	5/15
Crop, Nursery, and Greenhouse	Phoenix-Mesa-Scottsdale MSA, AZ	Y	17790 FQ	18790 MW	20080 TQ	USBLS	5/15
Crop, Nursery, and Greenhouse	Tucson MSA, AZ	Y	17670 FQ	18590 MW	19600 TQ	USBLS	5/15
Crop, Nursery, and Greenhouse	Arkansas	Y	18030 FQ	21550 MW	26990 TQ	USBLS	5/15
Crop, Nursery, and Greenhouse	Little Rock-North Little Rock-Conway MSA, AR	Y	17340 FQ	19070 MW	26010 TQ	USBLS	5/15
Crop, Nursery, and Greenhouse	California	H	9.38 FQ	9.62 MW	10.98 TQ	CABLS	1/16-3/16
Crop, Nursery, and Greenhouse	Anaheim-Santa Ana-Irvine PMSA, CA	H	9.37 FQ	9.51 MW	9.75 TQ	CABLS	1/16-3/16
Crop, Nursery, and Greenhouse	Los Angeles-Long Beach-Glendale PMSA, CA	H	9.52 FQ	10.49 MW	11.73 TQ	CABLS	1/16-3/16
Crop, Nursery, and Greenhouse	Madera MSA, CA	H	9.37 FQ	9.53 MW	9.73 TQ	CABLS	1/16-3/16
Crop, Nursery, and Greenhouse	Oakland-Hayward-Berkeley PMSA, CA	H	9.55 FQ	11.10 MW	15.74 TQ	CABLS	1/16-3/16
Crop, Nursery, and Greenhouse	Riverside-San Bernardino-Ontario MSA, CA	H	9.33 FQ	9.57 MW	10.73 TQ	CABLS	1/16-3/16
Crop, Nursery, and Greenhouse	Sacramento–Roseville–Arden-Arcade MSA, CA	H	9.44 FQ	9.74 MW	11.17 TQ	CABLS	1/16-3/16
Crop, Nursery, and Greenhouse	San Diego-Carlsbad MSA, CA	H	9.75 FQ	11.73 MW	15.13 TQ	CABLS	1/16-3/16
Crop, Nursery, and Greenhouse	San Francisco-Redwood City-South San Francisco PMSA, CA	H	11.42 FQ	13.16 MW	14.72 TQ	CABLS	1/16-3/16
Crop, Nursery, and Greenhouse	Colorado	Y	19390 FQ	23930 MW	29170 TQ	USBLS	5/15
Crop, Nursery, and Greenhouse	Denver-Aurora-Lakewood MSA, CO	Y	19160 FQ	25520 MW	30020 TQ	USBLS	5/15
Crop, Nursery, and Greenhouse	Connecticut	Y		22198 MW		CTBLS	1/16-3/16
Crop, Nursery, and Greenhouse	Bridgeport-Stamford-Norwalk MSA, CT	Y	23970 FQ	26840 MW	29430 TQ	USBLS	5/15
Crop, Nursery, and Greenhouse	Hartford-West Hartford-East Hartford MSA, CT	Y	19230 FQ	19870 MW	27470 TQ	USBLS	5/15
Crop, Nursery, and Greenhouse	Delaware	Y	23240 FQ	28480 MW	35290 TQ	USBLS	5/15
Crop, Nursery, and Greenhouse	Wilmington PMSA, DE-MD-NJ	Y	18290 FQ	19650 MW	23770 TQ	USBLS	5/15
Crop, Nursery, and Greenhouse	Washington-Arlington-Alexandria PMSA, DC-VA-MD-WV	Y	24450 FQ	32600 MW	36790 TQ	USBLS	5/15
Crop, Nursery, and Greenhouse	Florida	H	8.93 AE	9.40 MW	10.90 AEX	FLBLS	7/16-9/16
Crop, Nursery, and Greenhouse	Fort Lauderdale-Pompano Beach-Deerfield Beach PMSA, FL	H	9.53 AE	12.81 MW	16.02 AEX	FLBLS	7/16-9/16
Crop, Nursery, and Greenhouse	Miami-Miami Beach-Kendall PMSA, FL	H	8.95 AE	9.33 MW	10.28 AEX	FLBLS	7/16-9/16
Crop, Nursery, and Greenhouse	Orlando-Kissimmee-Sanford MSA, FL	H	8.95 AE	10.24 MW	11.68 AEX	FLBLS	7/16-9/16
Crop, Nursery, and Greenhouse	Tampa-St. Petersburg-Clearwater MSA, FL	H	8.85 AE	9.17 MW	10.88 AEX	FLBLS	7/16-9/16
Crop, Nursery, and Greenhouse	Georgia	Y	17240 FQ	18960 MW	24270 TQ	USBLS	5/15
Crop, Nursery, and Greenhouse	Augusta-Richmond County MSA, GA-SC	Y	19360 FQ	24100 MW	32840 TQ	USBLS	5/15
Crop, Nursery, and Greenhouse	Hawaii	Y	19210 FQ	22670 MW	32260 TQ	USBLS	5/15
Crop, Nursery, and Greenhouse	Urban Honolulu MSA, HI	Y	20960 FQ	36950 MW	44110 TQ	USBLS	5/15
Crop, Nursery, and Greenhouse	Idaho	Y	17640 FQ	19930 MW	24570 TQ	USBLS	5/15
Crop, Nursery, and Greenhouse	Boise City MSA, ID	Y	17330 FQ	19150 MW	23790 TQ	USBLS	5/15
Crop, Nursery, and Greenhouse	Illinois	Y	22220 FQ	27910 MW	35650 TQ	USBLS	5/15
Crop, Nursery, and Greenhouse	Chicago-Naperville-Arlington Heights PMSA, IL	Y	20630 FQ	28400 MW	35400 TQ	USBLS	5/15
Crop, Nursery, and Greenhouse	Lake County-Kenosha County PMSA, IL-WI	Y	19470 FQ	22620 MW	28470 TQ	USBLS	5/15
Crop, Nursery, and Greenhouse	Indiana	Y	18680 FQ	22430 MW	29510 TQ	USBLS	5/15
Crop, Nursery, and Greenhouse	Gary PMSA, IN	Y	17440 FQ	19210 MW	26350 TQ	USBLS	5/15
Crop, Nursery, and Greenhouse	Indianapolis-Carmel-Anderson MSA, IN	Y	18590 FQ	23060 MW	34150 TQ	USBLS	5/15
Crop, Nursery, and Greenhouse	Iowa	Y	22650 FQ	27490 MW	32010 TQ	USBLS	5/15
Crop, Nursery, and Greenhouse	Des Moines-West Des Moines MSA, IA	Y	25170 FQ	28250 MW	31280 TQ	USBLS	5/15
Crop, Nursery, and Greenhouse	Kansas	Y	20720 FQ	23610 MW	28340 TQ	USBLS	5/15
Crop, Nursery, and Greenhouse	Wichita MSA, KS	Y	21440 FQ	23600 MW	27550 TQ	USBLS	5/15

AE	Average entry wage	AWR	Average wage range	H	Hourly	LR	Low end range	MTC	Median total compensation	TCC	Total cash compensation
AEX	Average experienced wage	B	Biweekly	HI	Highest wage paid	M	Monthly	MW	Median wage paid	TQ	Third quartile wage
ATC	Average total compensation	D	Daily	HR	High end range	MCC	Median cash compensation	MWR	Median wage range	W	Weekly
AW	Average wage paid	FQ	First quartile wage	LO	Lowest wage paid	ME	Median entry wage	S	See annotated source	Y	Yearly

Occupation/Type/Industry	Location	Per	Low	Mid	High	Source	Date
Farmworker and Laborer							
Crop, Nursery, and Greenhouse	Kentucky	Y	22100 FQ	27440 MW	31170 TQ	USBLS	5/15
Crop, Nursery, and Greenhouse	Louisville-Jefferson County MSA, KY-IN	Y	20440 FQ	27150 MW	31300 TQ	USBLS	5/15
Crop, Nursery, and Greenhouse	Louisiana	Y	19590 FQ	22510 MW	29410 TQ	USBLS	5/15
Crop, Nursery, and Greenhouse	Baton Rouge MSA, LA	Y	17680 FQ	21060 MW	32120 TQ	USBLS	5/15
Crop, Nursery, and Greenhouse	New Orleans-Metairie MSA, LA	Y	19380 FQ	23150 MW	31500 TQ	USBLS	5/15
Crop, Nursery, and Greenhouse	Maine	Y	21100 FQ	25320 MW	31700 TQ	USBLS	5/15
Crop, Nursery, and Greenhouse	Portland-South Portland MSA, ME	Y	21760 FQ	24830 MW	30080 TQ	USBLS	5/15
Crop, Nursery, and Greenhouse	Maryland	Y	20137 AE	28313 MW	32401 AEX	MDBLS	4/16
Crop, Nursery, and Greenhouse	Baltimore-Columbia-Towson MSA, MD	Y	22250 FQ	27940 MW	36300 TQ	USBLS	5/15
Crop, Nursery, and Greenhouse	Salisbury MSA, MD-DE	Y	21560 FQ	26220 MW	34450 TQ	USBLS	5/15
Crop, Nursery, and Greenhouse	Massachusetts	Y	21300 FQ	24900 MW	30450 TQ	USBLS	5/15
Crop, Nursery, and Greenhouse	Boston-Cambridge-Newton NECTA, MA	Y	21510 FQ	27520 MW	35120 TQ	USBLS	5/15
Crop, Nursery, and Greenhouse	Worcester MSA, MA-CT	Y	25430 FQ	28880 MW	33530 TQ	USBLS	5/15
Crop, Nursery, and Greenhouse	Michigan	Y	20090 FQ	23910 MW	31150 TQ	USBLS	5/15
Crop, Nursery, and Greenhouse	Detroit-Dearborn-Livonia PMSA, MI	Y	21830 FQ	24870 MW	29500 TQ	USBLS	5/15
Crop, Nursery, and Greenhouse	Grand Rapids-Wyoming MSA, MI	Y	19860 FQ	22530 MW	25550 TQ	USBLS	5/15
Crop, Nursery, and Greenhouse	Minnesota	Y	20382 FQ	24620 MW	29534 TQ	MNBLS	1/16-3/16
Crop, Nursery, and Greenhouse	Minneapolis-St. Paul-Bloomington MSA, MN-WI	Y	21310 FQ	24812 MW	29110 TQ	MNBLS	1/16-3/16
Crop, Nursery, and Greenhouse	Mississippi	Y	17040 FQ	18430 MW	19850 TQ	USBLS	5/15
Crop, Nursery, and Greenhouse	Jackson MSA, MS	Y	16930 FQ	18370 MW	20170 TQ	USBLS	5/15
Crop, Nursery, and Greenhouse	Missouri	Y	17980 FQ	20010 MW	25570 TQ	USBLS	5/15
Crop, Nursery, and Greenhouse	Kansas City MSA, MO-KS	Y	18530 FQ	22180 MW	27820 TQ	USBLS	5/15
Crop, Nursery, and Greenhouse	St. Louis MSA, MO-IL	Y	18840 FQ	22160 MW	28180 TQ	USBLS	5/15
Crop, Nursery, and Greenhouse	Montana	Y	19420 FQ	22760 MW	28920 TQ	USBLS	5/15
Crop, Nursery, and Greenhouse	Nebraska	Y	22915 FQ	29550 MW	40340 TQ	NEBLS	7/16-9/16
Crop, Nursery, and Greenhouse	Omaha-Council Bluffs MSA, NE-IA	Y	23030 FQ	27965 MW	34965 TQ	NEBLS	7/16-9/16
Crop, Nursery, and Greenhouse	Nevada	Y	22650 FQ	29080 MW	36090 TQ	USBLS	5/15
Crop, Nursery, and Greenhouse	Las Vegas-Henderson-Paradise MSA, NV	Y	20130 FQ	25280 MW	29350 TQ	USBLS	5/15
Crop, Nursery, and Greenhouse	New Hampshire	H	9.73 AE	12.32 MW	15.43 AEX	NHBLS	6/16
Crop, Nursery, and Greenhouse	Nashua NECTA, NH-MA	Y	18770 FQ	26570 MW	34310 TQ	USBLS	5/15
Crop, Nursery, and Greenhouse	New Jersey	Y	20200 FQ	23480 MW	28910 TQ	USBLS	5/15
Crop, Nursery, and Greenhouse	Camden PMSA, NJ	Y	18920 FQ	21850 MW	30010 TQ	USBLS	5/15
Crop, Nursery, and Greenhouse	Newark PMSA, NJ-PA	Y	18840 FQ	20920 MW	27760 TQ	USBLS	5/15
Crop, Nursery, and Greenhouse	Trenton MSA, NJ	Y	18360 FQ	19280 MW	22970 TQ	USBLS	5/15
Crop, Nursery, and Greenhouse	New Mexico	Y	17280 FQ	18590 MW	20830 TQ	USBLS	5/15
Crop, Nursery, and Greenhouse	Albuquerque MSA, NM	Y	17350 FQ	19010 MW	23070 TQ	USBLS	5/15
Crop, Nursery, and Greenhouse	New York	Y	19470 AE	23750 MW	30090 AEX	NYBLS	1/16-3/16
Crop, Nursery, and Greenhouse	Buffalo-Cheektowaga-Niagara Falls MSA, NY	Y	20400 FQ	22350 MW	24310 TQ	USBLS	5/15
Crop, Nursery, and Greenhouse	Nassau County-Suffolk County PMSA, NY	Y	19090 FQ	20280 MW	24290 TQ	USBLS	5/15
Crop, Nursery, and Greenhouse	New York-Jersey City-White Plains PMSA, NY-NJ	Y	21830 FQ	24870 MW	34520 TQ	USBLS	5/15
Crop, Nursery, and Greenhouse	Rochester MSA, NY	Y	19970 FQ	23240 MW	30230 TQ	USBLS	5/15
Crop, Nursery, and Greenhouse	North Carolina	Y	17430 FQ	19530 MW	24700 TQ	USBLS	5/15
Crop, Nursery, and Greenhouse	Charlotte-Concord-Gastonia MSA, NC-SC	Y	18760 FQ	22910 MW	30310 TQ	USBLS	5/15
Crop, Nursery, and Greenhouse	Raleigh MSA, NC	Y	17550 FQ	20400 MW	24840 TQ	USBLS	5/15
Crop, Nursery, and Greenhouse	North Dakota	Y	19330 FQ	23150 MW	30550 TQ	USBLS	5/15
Crop, Nursery, and Greenhouse	Fargo MSA, ND-MN	Y	20100 FQ	23920 MW	31450 TQ	USBLS	5/15
Crop, Nursery, and Greenhouse	Ohio	Y	19120 FQ	24040 MW	30530 TQ	USBLS	5/15
Crop, Nursery, and Greenhouse	Cincinnati MSA, OH-KY-IN	Y	18900 FQ	22070 MW	25570 TQ	USBLS	5/15
Crop, Nursery, and Greenhouse	Cleveland-Elyria MSA, OH	Y	21100 FQ	24420 MW	28710 TQ	USBLS	5/15
Crop, Nursery, and Greenhouse	Columbus MSA, OH	Y	20580 FQ	25550 MW	29490 TQ	USBLS	5/15
Crop, Nursery, and Greenhouse	Oklahoma	Y	20440 FQ	23450 MW	27840 TQ	USBLS	5/15
Crop, Nursery, and Greenhouse	Oklahoma City MSA, OK	Y	19210 FQ	22500 MW	26980 TQ	USBLS	5/15
Crop, Nursery, and Greenhouse	Tulsa MSA, OK	Y	20120 FQ	23620 MW	27550 TQ	USBLS	5/15
Crop, Nursery, and Greenhouse	Oregon	H	9.64 FQ	10.47 MW	12.40 TQ	ORBLS	2016
Crop, Nursery, and Greenhouse	Portland-Vancouver-Hillsboro MSA, OR-WA	Y	19820 FQ	22270 MW	26320 TQ	USBLS	5/15
Crop, Nursery, and Greenhouse	Pennsylvania	Y	18430 FQ	22100 MW	27580 TQ	USBLS	5/15

AE	Average entry wage	AWR	Average wage range	H	Hourly
AEX	Average experienced wage	B	Biweekly	HI	Highest wage paid
ATC	Average total compensation	D	Daily	HR	High end range
AW	Average wage paid	FQ	First quartile wage	LO	Lowest wage paid

LR	Low end range	MTC	Median total compensation
M	Monthly	MW	Median wage paid
MCC	Median cash compensation	MWR	Median wage range
ME	Median entry wage	S	See annotated source

TCC	Total cash compensation
TQ	Third quartile wage
W	Weekly
Y	Yearly

Occupation/Type/Industry	Location	Per	Low	Mid	High	Source	Date
Farmworker and Laborer							
Crop, Nursery, and Greenhouse	Allentown-Bethlehem-Easton MSA, PA-NJ	Y	18960 FQ	21960 MW	25770 TQ	USBLS	5/15
Crop, Nursery, and Greenhouse	Harrisburg-Carlisle MSA, PA	Y	17540 FQ	20010 MW	24130 TQ	USBLS	5/15
Crop, Nursery, and Greenhouse	Montgomery County-Bucks County-Chester County PMSA, PA	Y	18940 FQ	23230 MW	29870 TQ	USBLS	5/15
Crop, Nursery, and Greenhouse	Philadelphia PMSA, PA	Y	17510 FQ	20740 MW	26840 TQ	USBLS	5/15
Crop, Nursery, and Greenhouse	Pittsburgh MSA, PA	Y	17330 FQ	19450 MW	24730 TQ	USBLS	5/15
Crop, Nursery, and Greenhouse	Rhode Island	Y	19510 FQ	22190 MW	31070 TQ	USBLS	5/15
Crop, Nursery, and Greenhouse	Providence-Warwick MSA, RI-MA	Y	19580 FQ	25310 MW	35460 TQ	USBLS	5/15
Crop, Nursery, and Greenhouse	South Carolina	Y	18260 FQ	21890 MW	28790 TQ	USBLS	5/15
Crop, Nursery, and Greenhouse	Charleston-North Charleston MSA, SC	Y	22060 FQ	26500 MW	34120 TQ	USBLS	5/15
Crop, Nursery, and Greenhouse	Columbia MSA, SC	Y	18070 FQ	20590 MW	24160 TQ	USBLS	5/15
Crop, Nursery, and Greenhouse	Greenville-Anderson-Mauldin MSA, SC	Y	17680 FQ	19610 MW	25540 TQ	USBLS	5/15
Crop, Nursery, and Greenhouse	South Dakota	Y	18840 FQ	20770 MW	25870 TQ	USBLS	5/15
Crop, Nursery, and Greenhouse	Tennessee	Y	17310 FQ	19450 MW	24240 TQ	USBLS	5/15
Crop, Nursery, and Greenhouse	Knoxville MSA, TN	Y	16770 FQ	18440 MW	24170 TQ	USBLS	5/15
Crop, Nursery, and Greenhouse	Memphis MSA, TN-MS-AR	Y	17220 FQ	18900 MW	23960 TQ	USBLS	5/15
Crop, Nursery, and Greenhouse	Nashville-Davidson–Murfreesboro–Franklin MSA, TN	Y	20340 FQ	22770 MW	25470 TQ	USBLS	5/15
Crop, Nursery, and Greenhouse	Texas	Y	17100 FQ	18740 MW	21780 TQ	USBLS	5/15
Crop, Nursery, and Greenhouse	Austin-Round Rock MSA, TX	Y	18660 FQ	22280 MW	26780 TQ	USBLS	5/15
Crop, Nursery, and Greenhouse	Dallas-Plano-Irving PMSA, TX	Y	16900 FQ	18450 MW	21200 TQ	USBLS	5/15
Crop, Nursery, and Greenhouse	Fort Worth-Arlington PMSA, TX	Y	17000 FQ	18470 MW	20300 TQ	USBLS	5/15
Crop, Nursery, and Greenhouse	Houston-The Woodlands-Sugar Land MSA, TX	Y	16900 FQ	18420 MW	20660 TQ	USBLS	5/15
Crop, Nursery, and Greenhouse	San Antonio-New Braunfels MSA, TX	Y	17490 FQ	19600 MW	23800 TQ	USBLS	5/15
Crop, Nursery, and Greenhouse	Utah	Y	20170 FQ	22900 MW	26720 TQ	USBLS	5/15
Crop, Nursery, and Greenhouse	Ogden-Clearfield MSA, UT	Y	19710 FQ	22520 MW	26430 TQ	USBLS	5/15
Crop, Nursery, and Greenhouse	Provo-Orem MSA, UT	Y	20290 FQ	23070 MW	26920 TQ	USBLS	5/15
Crop, Nursery, and Greenhouse	Salt Lake City MSA, UT	Y	21430 FQ	23140 MW	24850 TQ	USBLS	5/15
Crop, Nursery, and Greenhouse	Vermont	Y	22950 FQ	26910 MW	31630 TQ	USBLS	5/15
Crop, Nursery, and Greenhouse	Burlington-South Burlington MSA, VT	Y	22250 FQ	25230 MW	30070 TQ	USBLS	5/15
Crop, Nursery, and Greenhouse	Virginia	Y	19050 FQ	23400 MW	29830 TQ	USBLS	5/15
Crop, Nursery, and Greenhouse	Richmond MSA, VA	Y	20220 FQ	25140 MW	30550 TQ	USBLS	5/15
Crop, Nursery, and Greenhouse	Virginia Beach-Norfolk-Newport News MSA, VA-NC	Y	16700 FQ	18180 MW	21150 TQ	USBLS	5/15
Crop, Nursery, and Greenhouse	Washington	H	10.51 FQ	11.79 MW	14.40 TQ	WABLS	3/16
Crop, Nursery, and Greenhouse	Seattle-Bellevue-Everett PMSA, WA	H	9.98 FQ	11.20 MW	12.95 TQ	WABLS	3/16
Crop, Nursery, and Greenhouse	Tacoma-Lakewood PMSA, WA	H	11.88 FQ	16.52 MW	23.20 TQ	WABLS	3/16
Crop, Nursery, and Greenhouse	West Virginia	Y	17670 FQ	18700 MW	22350 TQ	USBLS	5/15
Crop, Nursery, and Greenhouse	Wisconsin	Y	18500 FQ	22560 MW	28590 TQ	USBLS	5/15
Crop, Nursery, and Greenhouse	Madison MSA, WI	Y	18480 FQ	22640 MW	31230 TQ	USBLS	5/15
Crop, Nursery, and Greenhouse	Milwaukee-Waukesha-West Allis MSA, WI	Y	20780 FQ	23910 MW	31020 TQ	USBLS	5/15
Crop, Nursery, and Greenhouse	Wyoming	Y	18930 FQ	22240 MW	31640 TQ	USBLS	5/15
Crop, Nursery, and Greenhouse	Puerto Rico	Y	16740 FQ	17960 MW	19180 TQ	USBLS	5/15
Crop, Nursery, and Greenhouse	San Juan-Carolina-Caguas MSA, PR	Y	16750 FQ	17960 MW	19180 TQ	USBLS	5/15
Fashion Designer	California	H	21.06 FQ	31.73 MW	45.01 TQ	CABLS	1/16-3/16
	Anaheim-Santa Ana-Irvine PMSA, CA	H	20.76 FQ	28.70 MW	38.64 TQ	CABLS	1/16-3/16
	Los Angeles-Long Beach-Glendale PMSA, CA	H	21.81 FQ	33.43 MW	46.44 TQ	CABLS	1/16-3/16
	Oakland-Hayward-Berkeley PMSA, CA	H	23.19 FQ	34.96 MW	52.87 TQ	CABLS	1/16-3/16
	Riverside-San Bernardino-Ontario MSA, CA	H	14.36 FQ	21.11 MW	28.26 TQ	CABLS	1/16-3/16
	Sacramento–Roseville–Arden-Arcade MSA, CA	H	20.78 FQ	30.19 MW	38.47 TQ	CABLS	1/16-3/16
	San Diego-Carlsbad MSA, CA	H	18.95 FQ	31.44 MW	47.38 TQ	CABLS	1/16-3/16

AE Average entry wage	**AWR** Average wage range	**H** Hourly	**LR** Low end range	**MTC** Median total compensation	**TCC** Total cash compensation
AEX Average experienced wage	**B** Biweekly	**HI** Highest wage paid	**M** Monthly	**MW** Median wage paid	**TQ** Third quartile wage
ATC Average total compensation	**D** Daily	**HR** High end range	**MCC** Median cash compensation	**MWR** Median wage range	**W** Weekly
AW Average wage paid	**FQ** First quartile wage	**LO** Lowest wage paid	**ME** Median entry wage	**S** See annotated source	**Y** Yearly

Fashion Designer

Occupation/Type/Industry	Location	Per	Low	Mid	High	Source	Date
Fashion Designer	San Francisco-Redwood City-South San Francisco PMSA, CA	H	19.73 FQ	24.91 MW	39.66 TQ	CABLS	1/16-3/16
	Colorado	Y	42950 FQ	51980 MW	69100 TQ	USBLS	5/15
	Denver-Aurora-Lakewood MSA, CO	Y	41510 FQ	51790 MW	63580 TQ	USBLS	5/15
	Bridgeport-Stamford-Norwalk MSA, CT	Y	49510 FQ	73520 MW	99630 TQ	USBLS	5/15
	Washington-Arlington-Alexandria PMSA, DC-VA-MD-WV	Y	36490 FQ	45480 MW	61820 TQ	USBLS	5/15
	Florida	H	17.44 AE	26.71 MW	33.83 AEX	FLBLS	7/16-9/16
	Miami-Miami Beach-Kendall PMSA, FL	H	22.98 AE	28.91 MW	31.10 AEX	FLBLS	7/16-9/16
	Orlando-Kissimmee-Sanford MSA, FL	H	17.08 AE	25.54 MW	31.31 AEX	FLBLS	7/16-9/16
	Tampa-St. Petersburg-Clearwater MSA, FL	H	18.31 AE	25.46 MW	30.33 AEX	FLBLS	7/16-9/16
	Georgia	Y	54390 FQ	86880 MW	120600 TQ	USBLS	5/15
	Hawaii	Y	35220 FQ	43750 MW	54940 TQ	USBLS	5/15
	Urban Honolulu MSA, HI	Y	35740 FQ	44170 MW	55290 TQ	USBLS	5/15
	Illinois	Y	41430 FQ	64700 MW	101680 TQ	USBLS	5/15
	Chicago-Naperville-Arlington Heights PMSA, IL	Y	47490 FQ	69520 MW	105100 TQ	USBLS	5/15
	Indiana	Y	46290 FQ	66220 MW	79110 TQ	USBLS	5/15
	Kansas	Y	42390 FQ	56420 MW	75630 TQ	USBLS	5/15
	Kentucky	Y	39620 FQ	58320 MW	77590 TQ	USBLS	5/15
	Maine	Y	45090 FQ	62980 MW	93030 TQ	USBLS	5/15
	Portland-South Portland MSA, ME	Y	47320 FQ	70360 MW	93820 TQ	USBLS	5/15
	Baltimore-Columbia-Towson MSA, MD	Y	29360 FQ	34060 MW	39320 TQ	USBLS	5/15
	Massachusetts	Y	60380 FQ	78520 MW	103270 TQ	USBLS	5/15
	Boston-Cambridge-Newton NECTA, MA	Y	60150 FQ	81470 MW	108580 TQ	USBLS	5/15
	Michigan	Y	46840 FQ	59000 MW	81700 TQ	USBLS	5/15
	Minnesota	Y	36431 FQ	47157 MW	62469 TQ	MNBLS	1/16-3/16
	Minneapolis-St. Paul-Bloomington MSA, MN-WI	Y	36048 FQ	45796 MW	60019 TQ	MNBLS	1/16-3/16
	Missouri	Y	18840 FQ	47890 MW	102820 TQ	USBLS	5/15
	Kansas City MSA, MO-KS	Y	34890 FQ	50590 MW	72400 TQ	USBLS	5/15
	St. Louis MSA, MO-IL	Y	46980 FQ	74980 MW	128100 TQ	USBLS	5/15
	New Jersey	Y	30340 FQ	52100 MW	74130 TQ	USBLS	5/15
	Newark PMSA, NJ-PA	Y	36780 FQ	70760 MW	112480 TQ	USBLS	5/15
	New York	Y	43950 AE	69510 MW	99170 AEX	NYBLS	1/16-3/16
	Nassau County-Suffolk County PMSA, NY	Y	39900 FQ	57150 MW	81310 TQ	USBLS	5/15
	New York-Jersey City-White Plains PMSA, NY-NJ	Y	49490 FQ	68220 MW	92930 TQ	USBLS	5/15
	North Carolina	Y	38400 FQ	51460 MW	62460 TQ	USBLS	5/15
	Charlotte-Concord-Gastonia MSA, NC-SC	Y	39260 FQ	50330 MW	60200 TQ	USBLS	5/15
	Ohio	Y	54470 FQ	69970 MW	90130 TQ	USBLS	5/15
	Cincinnati MSA, OH-KY-IN	Y	46760 FQ	58080 MW	74230 TQ	USBLS	5/15
	Columbus MSA, OH	Y	56680 FQ	71940 MW	91520 TQ	USBLS	5/15
	Oregon	H	20.39 FQ	26.57 MW	35.61 TQ	ORBLS	2016
	Portland-Vancouver-Hillsboro MSA, OR-WA	Y	41090 FQ	52620 MW	66110 TQ	USBLS	5/15
	Pennsylvania	Y	37720 FQ	47410 MW	64230 TQ	USBLS	5/15
	Allentown-Bethlehem-Easton MSA, PA-NJ	Y	35420 FQ	40850 MW	53680 TQ	USBLS	5/15
	Philadelphia PMSA, PA	Y	45200 FQ	56660 MW	73000 TQ	USBLS	5/15
	South Carolina	Y	40300 FQ	47070 MW	78840 TQ	USBLS	5/15
	Nashville-Davidson–Murfreesboro–Franklin MSA, TN	Y	37690 FQ	59560 MW	72210 TQ	USBLS	5/15
	Texas	Y	41820 FQ	51850 MW	67490 TQ	USBLS	5/15
	Austin-Round Rock MSA, TX	Y	35320 FQ	56780 MW	71690 TQ	USBLS	5/15
	Dallas-Plano-Irving PMSA, TX	Y	43060 FQ	53630 MW	67130 TQ	USBLS	5/15
	Houston-The Woodlands-Sugar Land MSA, TX	Y	46870 FQ	66270 MW	75150 TQ	USBLS	5/15
	Utah	Y	36220 FQ	46680 MW	75460 TQ	USBLS	5/15

AE Average entry wage	**AWR** Average wage range	**H** Hourly	**LR** Low end range	**MTC** Median total compensation	**TCC** Total cash compensation
AEX Average experienced wage	**B** Biweekly	**HI** Highest wage paid	**M** Monthly	**MW** Median wage paid	**TQ** Third quartile wage
ATC Average total compensation	**D** Daily	**HR** High end range	**MCC** Median cash compensation	**MWR** Median wage range	**W** Weekly
AW Average wage paid	**FQ** First quartile wage	**LO** Lowest wage paid	**ME** Median entry wage	**S** See annotated source	**Y** Yearly

Occupation/Type/Industry	Location	Per	Low	Mid	High	Source	Date
Fashion Designer	Salt Lake City MSA, UT	Y	39890 FQ	48260 MW	77260 TQ	USBLS	5/15
	Virginia	Y	35710 FQ	40380 MW	48950 TQ	USBLS	5/15
	Seattle-Bellevue-Everett PMSA, WA	H	29.85 FQ	37.42 MW	54.89 TQ	WABLS	3/16
	Milwaukee-Waukesha-West Allis MSA, WI	Y	46750 FQ	67440 MW	102160 TQ	USBLS	5/15
Feasibility Analyst							
Port, Municipal Government	San Francisco, CA	Y			108920 HI	CACIT	6/28/16
Federal Programs Coordinator							
California State University	California	Y	39516 LO		76980 HI	CALST	2016-2017
Feed Mill Operator							
California State University	California	Y	35220 LO		68628 HI	CALST	2016-2017
Fellow							
Detroit Revitalization	Detroit, MI	Y	50000 LO		60000 HI	STHE	2015
Fence Erector	Alabama	Y	19710 AE	27517 AW	31416 AEX	ALBLS	6/16
	Arizona	Y	25600 FQ	30560 MW	50690 TQ	USBLS	5/15
	Arkansas	Y	21150 FQ	26150 MW	39430 TQ	USBLS	5/15
	California	H	14.02 FQ	17.38 MW	21.75 TQ	CABLS	1/16-3/16
	Colorado	Y	27890 FQ	33100 MW	38550 TQ	USBLS	5/15
	Connecticut	Y		40310 MW		CTBLS	1/16-3/16
	Florida	H	11.81 AE	14.94 MW	19.02 AEX	FLBLS	7/16-9/16
	Georgia	Y	25350 FQ	31400 MW	38350 TQ	USBLS	5/15
	Hawaii	Y	32100 FQ	38330 MW	50640 TQ	USBLS	5/15
	Idaho	Y	21890 FQ	28510 MW	35900 TQ	USBLS	5/15
	Illinois	Y	26830 FQ	51070 MW	71400 TQ	USBLS	5/15
	Indiana	Y	22550 FQ	27390 MW	32390 TQ	USBLS	5/15
	Iowa	Y	25140 FQ	31450 MW	38470 TQ	USBLS	5/15
	Kansas	Y	23190 FQ	31930 MW	37720 TQ	USBLS	5/15
	Kentucky	Y	22830 FQ	26590 MW	29610 TQ	USBLS	5/15
	Louisiana	Y	26120 FQ	33700 MW	38470 TQ	USBLS	5/15
	Maine	Y	24510 FQ	28280 MW	32700 TQ	USBLS	5/15
	Maryland	Y	21550 AE	30823 MW	35460 AEX	MDBLS	4/16
	Massachusetts	Y	29630 FQ	35750 MW	43830 TQ	USBLS	5/15
	Michigan	Y	23760 FQ	30340 MW	38610 TQ	USBLS	5/15
	Minnesota	Y	29917 FQ	34801 MW	39473 TQ	MNBLS	1/16-3/16
	Mississippi	Y	24000 FQ	30470 MW	36410 TQ	USBLS	5/15
	Missouri	Y	22440 FQ	27050 MW	34400 TQ	USBLS	5/15
	Montana	Y	26680 FQ	29680 MW	35060 TQ	USBLS	5/15
	Nebraska	Y	26625 FQ	29370 MW	33275 TQ	NEBLS	7/16-9/16
	Nevada	Y	30730 FQ	38980 MW	56090 TQ	USBLS	5/15
	New Jersey	Y	26550 FQ	35260 MW	43560 TQ	USBLS	5/15
	New Mexico	Y	26370 FQ	28670 MW	31000 TQ	USBLS	5/15
	New York	Y	30750 AE	39080 MW	55920 AEX	NYBLS	1/16-3/16
	North Carolina	Y	21960 FQ	29800 MW	35480 TQ	USBLS	5/15
	North Dakota	Y	33080 FQ	41220 MW	48300 TQ	USBLS	5/15
	Ohio	Y	25000 FQ	30090 MW	36920 TQ	USBLS	5/15
	Oklahoma	Y	23270 FQ	27340 MW	30740 TQ	USBLS	5/15
	Oregon	H	11.39 FQ	14.03 MW	18.12 TQ	ORBLS	2016
	Pennsylvania	Y	28480 FQ	35890 MW	44420 TQ	USBLS	5/15
	South Carolina	Y	21230 FQ	23080 MW	25880 TQ	USBLS	5/15
	South Dakota	Y	27110 FQ	30440 MW	34610 TQ	USBLS	5/15
	Tennessee	Y	26410 FQ	30890 MW	35450 TQ	USBLS	5/15
	Texas	Y	19220 FQ	28770 MW	35930 TQ	USBLS	5/15
	Utah	Y	26700 FQ	30570 MW	40820 TQ	USBLS	5/15
	Virginia	Y	25310 FQ	32380 MW	38650 TQ	USBLS	5/15
	Washington	H	14.23 FQ	16.96 MW	19.27 TQ	WABLS	3/16
	Wisconsin	Y	24270 FQ	32290 MW	39580 TQ	USBLS	5/15
	Wyoming	Y	24750 FQ	33020 MW	38440 TQ	USBLS	5/15
Ferry Oiler							
State Government	North Carolina	Y	27903 LO		41789 HI	NCGOV	7/1/16
Fiber Splicing Technician							
Electric Utility, Municipal Government	Santa Clara, CA	Y			66216 HI	CACIT	6/28/16
Fiberglass Laminator and Fabricator	Alabama	Y	26723 AE	32132 AW	34846 AEX	ALBLS	6/16

Occupation/Type/Industry	Location	Per	Low	Mid	High	Source	Date
Fiberglass Laminator and Fabricator	Alaska	Y	43490 FQ	52280 MW	58310 TQ	USBLS	5/15
	Arizona	Y	27580 FQ	32770 MW	40920 TQ	USBLS	5/15
	Phoenix-Mesa-Scottsdale MSA, AZ	Y	27530 FQ	31760 MW	39280 TQ	USBLS	5/15
	Arkansas	Y	21480 FQ	26420 MW	30770 TQ	USBLS	5/15
	Little Rock-North Little Rock-Conway MSA, AR	Y	23480 FQ	28200 MW	33510 TQ	USBLS	5/15
	California	H	11.91 FQ	14.56 MW	18.66 TQ	CABLS	1/16-3/16
	Anaheim-Santa Ana-Irvine PMSA, CA	H	12.85 FQ	15.25 MW	24.31 TQ	CABLS	1/16-3/16
	Los Angeles-Long Beach-Glendale PMSA, CA	H	12.46 FQ	15.78 MW	20.29 TQ	CABLS	1/16-3/16
	Oakland-Hayward-Berkeley PMSA, CA	H	13.18 FQ	17.20 MW	24.20 TQ	CABLS	1/16-3/16
	Riverside-San Bernardino-Ontario MSA, CA	H	11.14 FQ	12.88 MW	17.33 TQ	CABLS	1/16-3/16
	San Diego-Carlsbad MSA, CA	H	12.52 FQ	14.13 MW	16.06 TQ	CABLS	1/16-3/16
	Colorado	Y	21630 FQ	24100 MW	29250 TQ	USBLS	5/15
	Connecticut	Y		36083 MW		CTBLS	1/16-3/16
	Washington-Arlington-Alexandria PMSA, DC-VA-MD-WV	Y	22550 FQ	30670 MW	43570 TQ	USBLS	5/15
	Florida	H	11.93 AE	15.21 MW	17.64 AEX	FLBLS	7/16-9/16
	Fort Lauderdale-Pompano Beach-Deerfield Beach PMSA, FL	H	11.49 AE	15.76 MW	18.50 AEX	FLBLS	7/16-9/16
	Miami-Miami Beach-Kendall PMSA, FL	H	9.32 AE	11.88 MW	16.12 AEX	FLBLS	7/16-9/16
	Orlando-Kissimmee-Sanford MSA, FL	H	13.78 AE	16.67 MW	18.30 AEX	FLBLS	7/16-9/16
	Tampa-St. Petersburg-Clearwater MSA, FL	H	11.27 AE	14.58 MW	17.01 AEX	FLBLS	7/16-9/16
	Georgia	Y	21610 FQ	26210 MW	30030 TQ	USBLS	5/15
	Atlanta-Sandy Springs-Roswell MSA, GA	Y	25910 FQ	28090 MW	30270 TQ	USBLS	5/15
	Idaho	Y	23460 FQ	27610 MW	32180 TQ	USBLS	5/15
	Illinois	Y	23950 FQ	27740 MW	32450 TQ	USBLS	5/15
	Chicago-Naperville-Arlington Heights PMSA, IL	Y	24170 FQ	27380 MW	30450 TQ	USBLS	5/15
	Lake County-Kenosha County PMSA, IL-WI	Y	25410 FQ	30370 MW	38420 TQ	USBLS	5/15
	Indiana	Y	21980 FQ	27810 MW	34980 TQ	USBLS	5/15
	Indianapolis-Carmel-Anderson MSA, IN	Y	24490 FQ	32300 MW	36930 TQ	USBLS	5/15
	Iowa	Y	27510 FQ	30680 MW	35340 TQ	USBLS	5/15
	Kansas	Y	23460 FQ	27830 MW	33770 TQ	USBLS	5/15
	Kentucky	Y	25660 FQ	31710 MW	37390 TQ	USBLS	5/15
	Louisiana	Y	25200 FQ	33560 MW	42490 TQ	USBLS	5/15
	Baton Rouge MSA, LA	Y	23650 FQ	31920 MW	37690 TQ	USBLS	5/15
	Maine	Y	29330 FQ	34130 MW	38570 TQ	USBLS	5/15
	Maryland	Y	29574 AE	37368 MW	41265 AEX	MDBLS	4/16
	Massachusetts	Y	32220 FQ	36850 MW	45190 TQ	USBLS	5/15
	Michigan	Y	26820 FQ	31830 MW	36830 TQ	USBLS	5/15
	Grand Rapids-Wyoming MSA, MI	Y	27730 FQ	32770 MW	36830 TQ	USBLS	5/15
	Minnesota	Y	28217 FQ	31538 MW	36418 TQ	MNBLS	1/16-3/16
	Minneapolis-St. Paul-Bloomington MSA, MN-WI	Y	27326 FQ	30637 MW	35334 TQ	MNBLS	1/16-3/16
	Mississippi	Y	24900 FQ	29350 MW	35000 TQ	USBLS	5/15
	Missouri	Y	23060 FQ	27750 MW	34210 TQ	USBLS	5/15
	Kansas City MSA, MO-KS	Y	23120 FQ	28670 MW	39440 TQ	USBLS	5/15
	New Hampshire	H	10.86 AE	14.33 MW	17.38 AEX	NHBLS	6/16
	New York	Y	23960 AE	35020 MW	42980 AEX	NYBLS	1/16-3/16
	Buffalo-Cheektowaga-Niagara Falls MSA, NY	Y	24140 FQ	28710 MW	37930 TQ	USBLS	5/15
	Nassau County-Suffolk County PMSA, NY	Y	24850 FQ	32430 MW	47360 TQ	USBLS	5/15
	North Carolina	Y	24610 FQ	30860 MW	36280 TQ	USBLS	5/15
	North Dakota	Y	32470 FQ	36700 MW	43390 TQ	USBLS	5/15
	Ohio	Y	23040 FQ	27940 MW	34700 TQ	USBLS	5/15
	Cincinnati MSA, OH-KY-IN	Y	23010 FQ	27520 MW	33320 TQ	USBLS	5/15

AE	Average entry wage	AWR	Average wage range	H	Hourly	LR	Low end range	MTC	Median total compensation	TCC	Total cash compensation
AEX	Average experienced wage	B	Biweekly	HI	Highest wage paid	M	Monthly	MW	Median wage paid	TQ	Third quartile wage
ATC	Average total compensation	D	Daily	HR	High end range	MCC	Median cash compensation	MWR	Median wage range	W	Weekly
AW	Average wage paid	FQ	First quartile wage	LO	Lowest wage paid	ME	Median entry wage	S	See annotated source	Y	Yearly

Occupation/Type/Industry	Location	Per	Low	Mid	High	Source	Date
Fiberglass Laminator and Fabricator	Cleveland-Elyria MSA, OH	Y	23630 FQ	29800 MW	36780 TQ	USBLS	5/15
	Oklahoma	Y	23950 FQ	27940 MW	32050 TQ	USBLS	5/15
	Oregon	H	12.20 FQ	13.86 MW	16.07 TQ	ORBLS	2016
	Portland-Vancouver-Hillsboro MSA, OR-WA	Y	26000 FQ	33100 MW	43190 TQ	USBLS	5/15
	Pennsylvania	Y	26770 FQ	31190 MW	37970 TQ	USBLS	5/15
	Montgomery County-Bucks County-Chester County PMSA, PA	Y	27800 FQ	31690 MW	35900 TQ	USBLS	5/15
	Rhode Island	Y	25070 FQ	31300 MW	37480 TQ	USBLS	5/15
	Providence-Warwick MSA, RI-MA	Y	26770 FQ	33700 MW	39600 TQ	USBLS	5/15
	South Carolina	Y	24430 FQ	28380 MW	33970 TQ	USBLS	5/15
	Charleston-North Charleston MSA, SC	Y	23700 FQ	27850 MW	33600 TQ	USBLS	5/15
	Columbia MSA, SC	Y	23000 FQ	27150 MW	32700 TQ	USBLS	5/15
	Greenville-Anderson-Mauldin MSA, SC	Y	26340 FQ	28590 MW	30840 TQ	USBLS	5/15
	South Dakota	Y	22330 FQ	24430 MW	27940 TQ	USBLS	5/15
	Tennessee	Y	23680 FQ	29730 MW	35790 TQ	USBLS	5/15
	Knoxville MSA, TN	Y	25170 FQ	32930 MW	37370 TQ	USBLS	5/15
	Texas	Y	20590 FQ	25040 MW	34540 TQ	USBLS	5/15
	Dallas-Plano-Irving PMSA, TX	Y	20200 FQ	25550 MW	35130 TQ	USBLS	5/15
	Houston-The Woodlands-Sugar Land MSA, TX	Y	21100 FQ	24380 MW	34550 TQ	USBLS	5/15
	Utah	Y	24870 FQ	31080 MW	40800 TQ	USBLS	5/15
	Virginia	Y	20040 FQ	23490 MW	35300 TQ	USBLS	5/15
	Washington	H	11.59 FQ	14.74 MW	18.69 TQ	WABLS	3/16
	Seattle-Bellevue-Everett PMSA, WA	H	11.83 FQ	15.03 MW	18.95 TQ	WABLS	3/16
	West Virginia	Y	25420 FQ	51440 MW	57390 TQ	USBLS	5/15
	Wisconsin	Y	24000 FQ	28930 MW	35260 TQ	USBLS	5/15
	Wyoming	Y	34190 FQ	36550 MW	38910 TQ	USBLS	5/15
Field Engineer							
Construction Management Firm	United States	Y	61158 AE		73982 AEX	ENR02	2015
General Contractor	United States	Y	60540 AE		71241 AEX	ENR02	2015
Fighter							
Entry-Level, Ultimate Fighting Championship	United States	S			12000 HI	NYT01	2016
Title Bout, Ultimate Fighting Championship	United States	S	300000 LO		500000 HI	NYT01	2016
File Clerk	Alabama	Y	17840 AE	26105 AW	30238 AEX	ALBLS	6/16
	Birmingham-Hoover MSA, AL	Y	18798 AE	28846 AW	33865 AEX	ALBLS	6/16
	Alaska	Y	23250 FQ	33550 MW	38480 TQ	USBLS	5/15
	Anchorage MSA, AK	Y	31290 FQ	35170 MW	38770 TQ	USBLS	5/15
	Arizona	Y	24160 FQ	30590 MW	39210 TQ	USBLS	5/15
	Phoenix-Mesa-Scottsdale MSA, AZ	Y	24500 FQ	31300 MW	41300 TQ	USBLS	5/15
	Tucson MSA, AZ	Y	23320 FQ	28870 MW	35390 TQ	USBLS	5/15
	Arkansas	Y	18800 FQ	23060 MW	28520 TQ	USBLS	5/15
	Little Rock-North Little Rock-Conway MSA, AR	Y	19710 FQ	25170 MW	29730 TQ	USBLS	5/15
	California	H	11.09 FQ	14.03 MW	18.35 TQ	CABLS	1/16-3/16
	Anaheim-Santa Ana-Irvine PMSA, CA	H	11.14 FQ	14.26 MW	18.82 TQ	CABLS	1/16-3/16
	Los Angeles-Long Beach-Glendale PMSA, CA	H	11.48 FQ	14.47 MW	18.48 TQ	CABLS	1/16-3/16
	Oakland-Hayward-Berkeley PMSA, CA	H	13.16 FQ	16.71 MW	23.16 TQ	CABLS	1/16-3/16
	Riverside-San Bernardino-Ontario MSA, CA	H	11.17 FQ	13.92 MW	18.64 TQ	CABLS	1/16-3/16
	Sacramento–Roseville–Arden-Arcade MSA, CA	H	10.96 FQ	14.18 MW	18.93 TQ	CABLS	1/16-3/16
	San Diego-Carlsbad MSA, CA	H	10.91 FQ	13.56 MW	16.83 TQ	CABLS	1/16-3/16
	San Francisco-Redwood City-South San Francisco PMSA, CA	H	12.40 FQ	15.25 MW	21.40 TQ	CABLS	1/16-3/16
	Colorado	Y	25750 FQ	30160 MW	37860 TQ	USBLS	5/15

AE	Average entry wage	AWR	Average wage range	H	Hourly
AEX	Average experienced wage	B	Biweekly	HI	Highest wage paid
ATC	Average total compensation	D	Daily	HR	High end range
AW	Average wage paid	FQ	First quartile wage	LO	Lowest wage paid

LR	Low end range	MTC	Median total compensation	TCC	Total cash compensation
M	Monthly	MW	Median wage paid	TQ	Third quartile wage
MCC	Median cash compensation	MWR	Median wage range	W	Weekly
ME	Median entry wage	S	See annotated source	Y	Yearly

File Clerk

Occupation/Type/Industry	Location	Per	Low	Mid	High	Source	Date
File Clerk	Denver-Aurora-Lakewood MSA, CO	Y	27270 FQ	31120 MW	40690 TQ	USBLS	5/15
	Connecticut	Y		30250 MW		CTBLS	1/16-3/16
	Bridgeport-Stamford-Norwalk MSA, CT	Y	21280 FQ	27930 MW	39820 TQ	USBLS	5/15
	Hartford-West Hartford-East Hartford MSA, CT	Y	22580 FQ	32380 MW	40940 TQ	USBLS	5/15
	Delaware	Y	23250 FQ	28970 MW	35330 TQ	USBLS	5/15
	Wilmington PMSA, DE-MD-NJ	Y	22120 FQ	27540 MW	35020 TQ	USBLS	5/15
	District of Columbia	Y	35840 FQ	44070 MW	53050 TQ	USBLS	5/15
	Washington-Arlington-Alexandria PMSA, DC-VA-MD-WV	Y	22780 FQ	33010 MW	44100 TQ	USBLS	5/15
	Florida	H	10.41 AE	13.80 MW	16.37 AEX	FLBLS	7/16-9/16
	Fort Lauderdale-Pompano Beach-Deerfield Beach PMSA, FL	H	10.59 AE	13.36 MW	15.84 AEX	FLBLS	7/16-9/16
	Miami-Miami Beach-Kendall PMSA, FL	H	10.64 AE	15.03 MW	18.01 AEX	FLBLS	7/16-9/16
	Orlando-Kissimmee-Sanford MSA, FL	H	10.34 AE	13.53 MW	15.98 AEX	FLBLS	7/16-9/16
	Tampa-St. Petersburg-Clearwater MSA, FL	H	10.62 AE	13.85 MW	16.11 AEX	FLBLS	7/16-9/16
	Georgia	Y	21450 FQ	26780 MW	33120 TQ	USBLS	5/15
	Atlanta-Sandy Springs-Roswell MSA, GA	Y	23710 FQ	28670 MW	35140 TQ	USBLS	5/15
	Augusta-Richmond County MSA, GA-SC	Y	19730 FQ	25550 MW	29970 TQ	USBLS	5/15
	Hawaii	Y	17750 FQ	19390 MW	29140 TQ	USBLS	5/15
	Kahului-Wailuku-Lahaina MSA, HI	Y	17130 FQ	18130 MW	19140 TQ	USBLS	5/15
	Urban Honolulu MSA, HI	Y	18010 FQ	21280 MW	30320 TQ	USBLS	5/15
	Idaho	Y	21070 FQ	27010 MW	33720 TQ	USBLS	5/15
	Boise City MSA, ID	Y	24450 FQ	28760 MW	34950 TQ	USBLS	5/15
	Illinois	Y	23580 FQ	28730 MW	36550 TQ	USBLS	5/15
	Chicago-Naperville-Arlington Heights PMSA, IL	Y	25300 FQ	29890 MW	38490 TQ	USBLS	5/15
	Lake County-Kenosha County PMSA, IL-WI	Y	23440 FQ	29700 MW	38010 TQ	USBLS	5/15
	Indiana	Y	22110 FQ	27510 MW	32650 TQ	USBLS	5/15
	Gary PMSA, IN	Y	18780 FQ	22730 MW	27490 TQ	USBLS	5/15
	Indianapolis-Carmel-Anderson MSA, IN	Y	25070 FQ	29070 MW	35020 TQ	USBLS	5/15
	Iowa	Y	24570 FQ	28870 MW	36020 TQ	USBLS	5/15
	Des Moines-West Des Moines MSA, IA	Y	24770 FQ	29350 MW	35670 TQ	USBLS	5/15
	Kansas	Y	19740 FQ	25490 MW	31260 TQ	USBLS	5/15
	Wichita MSA, KS	Y	18050 FQ	20910 MW	28690 TQ	USBLS	5/15
	Kentucky	Y	18990 FQ	22810 MW	29310 TQ	USBLS	5/15
	Louisville-Jefferson County MSA, KY-IN	Y	19260 FQ	24120 MW	29690 TQ	USBLS	5/15
	Louisiana	Y	19650 FQ	22650 MW	26770 TQ	USBLS	5/15
	Baton Rouge MSA, LA	Y	17860 FQ	20760 MW	27080 TQ	USBLS	5/15
	New Orleans-Metairie MSA, LA	Y	21040 FQ	23570 MW	27830 TQ	USBLS	5/15
	Maine	Y	24160 FQ	28350 MW	34230 TQ	USBLS	5/15
	Portland-South Portland MSA, ME	Y	25420 FQ	28980 MW	36010 TQ	USBLS	5/15
	Maryland	Y	21462 AE	31920 MW	37149 AEX	MDBLS	4/16
	Baltimore-Columbia-Towson MSA, MD	Y	23370 FQ	29520 MW	38030 TQ	USBLS	5/15
	Salisbury MSA, MD-DE	Y	21990 FQ	26540 MW	33270 TQ	USBLS	5/15
	Massachusetts	Y	22620 FQ	29130 MW	39110 TQ	USBLS	5/15
	Boston-Cambridge-Newton NECTA, MA	Y	22520 FQ	30230 MW	40200 TQ	USBLS	5/15
	Worcester MSA, MA-CT	Y	22090 FQ	32730 MW	40960 TQ	USBLS	5/15
	Michigan	Y	21310 FQ	27030 MW	34270 TQ	USBLS	5/15
	Detroit-Dearborn-Livonia PMSA, MI	Y	22130 FQ	27530 MW	34800 TQ	USBLS	5/15
	Grand Rapids-Wyoming MSA, MI	Y	22700 FQ	30550 MW	41810 TQ	USBLS	5/15

AE	Average entry wage	AWR	Average wage range	H	Hourly	LR	Low end range	MTC	Median total compensation	TCC	Total cash compensation
AEX	Average experienced wage	B	Biweekly	HI	Highest wage paid	M	Monthly	MW	Median wage paid	TQ	Third quartile wage
ATC	Average total compensation	D	Daily	HR	High end range	MCC	Median cash compensation	MWR	Median wage range	W	Weekly
AW	Average wage paid	FQ	First quartile wage	LO	Lowest wage paid	ME	Median entry wage	S	See annotated source	Y	Yearly

File Clerk

Occupation/Type/Industry	Location	Per	Low	Mid	High	Source	Date
File Clerk	Minnesota	Y	27031 FQ	31299 MW	38408 TQ	MNBLS	1/16-3/16
	Minneapolis-St. Paul-Bloomington MSA, MN-WI	Y	27132 FQ	31188 MW	39298 TQ	MNBLS	1/16-3/16
	Mississippi	Y	18170 FQ	22570 MW	28420 TQ	USBLS	5/15
	Jackson MSA, MS	Y	17220 FQ	19100 MW	24960 TQ	USBLS	5/15
	Missouri	Y	22950 FQ	30410 MW	40820 TQ	USBLS	5/15
	St. Louis MSA, MO-IL	Y	22660 FQ	29440 MW	46520 TQ	USBLS	5/15
	Montana	Y	20750 FQ	25220 MW	29670 TQ	USBLS	5/15
	Billings MSA, MT	Y	18820 FQ	24500 MW	29120 TQ	USBLS	5/15
	Nebraska	Y	21515 FQ	26710 MW	32600 TQ	NEBLS	7/16-9/16
	Omaha-Council Bluffs MSA, NE-IA	Y	23175 FQ	28955 MW	37650 TQ	NEBLS	7/16-9/16
	Nevada	Y	20250 FQ	26110 MW	34240 TQ	USBLS	5/15
	Las Vegas-Henderson-Paradise MSA, NV	Y	20140 FQ	26260 MW	35420 TQ	USBLS	5/15
	New Hampshire	H	8.95 AE	11.65 MW	14.40 AEX	NHBLS	6/16
	Manchester NECTA, NH	H	8.38 AE	10.91 MW	13.36 AEX	NHBLS	6/16
	Nashua NECTA, NH-MA	Y	21480 FQ	24500 MW	31420 TQ	USBLS	5/15
	New Jersey	Y	21270 FQ	26480 MW	34030 TQ	USBLS	5/15
	Camden PMSA, NJ	Y	20650 FQ	26410 MW	31110 TQ	USBLS	5/15
	Newark PMSA, NJ-PA	Y	22180 FQ	28390 MW	35900 TQ	USBLS	5/15
	Trenton MSA, NJ	Y	24390 FQ	30230 MW	38310 TQ	USBLS	5/15
	New Mexico	Y	22100 FQ	26730 MW	31140 TQ	USBLS	5/15
	Albuquerque MSA, NM	Y	21310 FQ	25720 MW	30160 TQ	USBLS	5/15
	New York	Y	20860 AE	27200 MW	34650 AEX	NYBLS	1/16-3/16
	Buffalo-Cheektowaga-Niagara Falls MSA, NY	Y	20750 FQ	24930 MW	32770 TQ	USBLS	5/15
	Nassau County-Suffolk County PMSA, NY	Y	22320 FQ	27250 MW	33030 TQ	USBLS	5/15
	New York-Jersey City-White Plains PMSA, NY-NJ	Y	20850 FQ	26050 MW	35860 TQ	USBLS	5/15
	Rochester MSA, NY	Y	19290 FQ	25300 MW	30080 TQ	USBLS	5/15
	North Carolina	Y	21730 FQ	27450 MW	33160 TQ	USBLS	5/15
	Charlotte-Concord-Gastonia MSA, NC-SC	Y	23440 FQ	29260 MW	37070 TQ	USBLS	5/15
	Raleigh MSA, NC	Y	25710 FQ	29070 MW	34640 TQ	USBLS	5/15
	North Dakota	Y	23180 FQ	28180 MW	34060 TQ	USBLS	5/15
	Fargo MSA, ND-MN	Y	22040 FQ	26930 MW	33030 TQ	USBLS	5/15
	Ohio	Y	23500 FQ	29330 MW	36620 TQ	USBLS	5/15
	Cincinnati MSA, OH-KY-IN	Y	21910 FQ	27670 MW	34100 TQ	USBLS	5/15
	Cleveland-Elyria MSA, OH	Y	24310 FQ	30770 MW	36570 TQ	USBLS	5/15
	Columbus MSA, OH	Y	27680 FQ	33640 MW	39480 TQ	USBLS	5/15
	Oklahoma	Y	22130 FQ	26830 MW	31230 TQ	USBLS	5/15
	Oklahoma City MSA, OK	Y	22930 FQ	27130 MW	32090 TQ	USBLS	5/15
	Tulsa MSA, OK	Y	23240 FQ	27980 MW	32520 TQ	USBLS	5/15
	Oregon	H	13.11 FQ	16.48 MW	19.52 TQ	ORBLS	2016
	Portland-Vancouver-Hillsboro MSA, OR-WA	Y	27690 FQ	34600 MW	42380 TQ	USBLS	5/15
	Pennsylvania	Y	22160 FQ	27400 MW	33930 TQ	USBLS	5/15
	Allentown-Bethlehem-Easton MSA, PA-NJ	Y	23110 FQ	27360 MW	31440 TQ	USBLS	5/15
	Harrisburg-Carlisle MSA, PA	Y	25350 FQ	32340 MW	41420 TQ	USBLS	5/15
	Montgomery County-Bucks County-Chester County PMSA, PA	Y	21030 FQ	27510 MW	34560 TQ	USBLS	5/15
	Philadelphia PMSA, PA	Y	21790 FQ	28050 MW	36100 TQ	USBLS	5/15
	Pittsburgh MSA, PA	Y	23570 FQ	27620 MW	31370 TQ	USBLS	5/15
	Rhode Island	Y	24180 FQ	32260 MW	45090 TQ	USBLS	5/15
	Providence-Warwick MSA, RI-MA	Y	24930 FQ	31720 MW	44750 TQ	USBLS	5/15
	South Carolina	Y	21930 FQ	27490 MW	33620 TQ	USBLS	5/15
	Charleston-North Charleston MSA, SC	Y	26560 FQ	31130 MW	35960 TQ	USBLS	5/15
	Columbia MSA, SC	Y	21050 FQ	26480 MW	34370 TQ	USBLS	5/15
	Greenville-Anderson-Mauldin MSA, SC	Y	22880 FQ	26460 MW	30710 TQ	USBLS	5/15
	South Dakota	Y	20990 FQ	23910 MW	28770 TQ	USBLS	5/15
	Sioux Falls MSA, SD	Y	23040 FQ	28320 MW	34180 TQ	USBLS	5/15
	Tennessee	Y	21470 FQ	25930 MW	32140 TQ	USBLS	5/15
	Knoxville MSA, TN	Y	21590 FQ	23580 MW	27070 TQ	USBLS	5/15
	Memphis MSA, TN-MS-AR	Y	22930 FQ	29010 MW	34590 TQ	USBLS	5/15

AE	Average entry wage	AWR	Average wage range	H	Hourly	LR	Low end range	MTC	Median total compensation	TCC	Total cash compensation
AEX	Average experienced wage	B	Biweekly	HI	Highest wage paid	M	Monthly	MW	Median wage paid	TQ	Third quartile wage
ATC	Average total compensation	D	Daily	HR	High end range	MCC	Median cash compensation	MWR	Median wage range	W	Weekly
AW	Average wage paid	FQ	First quartile wage	LO	Lowest wage paid	ME	Median entry wage	S	See annotated source	Y	Yearly

Occupation/Type/Industry	Location	Per	Low	Mid	High	Source	Date
File Clerk	Nashville-Davidson–Murfreesboro–Franklin MSA, TN	Y	22630 FQ	28260 MW	34360 TQ	USBLS	5/15
	Texas	Y	21500 FQ	28200 MW	37290 TQ	USBLS	5/15
	Austin-Round Rock MSA, TX	Y	24950 FQ	30410 MW	39430 TQ	USBLS	5/15
	Dallas-Plano-Irving PMSA, TX	Y	23730 FQ	32160 MW	42780 TQ	USBLS	5/15
	Fort Worth-Arlington PMSA, TX	Y	21750 FQ	29400 MW	38190 TQ	USBLS	5/15
	Houston-The Woodlands-Sugar Land MSA, TX	Y	24410 FQ	31260 MW	39380 TQ	USBLS	5/15
	San Antonio-New Braunfels MSA, TX	Y	22630 FQ	27680 MW	36430 TQ	USBLS	5/15
	Utah	Y	22140 FQ	27880 MW	33320 TQ	USBLS	5/15
	Ogden-Clearfield MSA, UT	Y	22710 FQ	28010 MW	34120 TQ	USBLS	5/15
	Provo-Orem MSA, UT	Y	21360 FQ	25040 MW	33920 TQ	USBLS	5/15
	Salt Lake City MSA, UT	Y	22170 FQ	28430 MW	33550 TQ	USBLS	5/15
	Vermont	Y	27710 FQ	34060 MW	37910 TQ	USBLS	5/15
	Burlington-South Burlington MSA, VT	Y	32910 FQ	35880 MW	38840 TQ	USBLS	5/15
	Virginia	Y	20930 FQ	26640 MW	32310 TQ	USBLS	5/15
	Richmond MSA, VA	Y	24270 FQ	27950 MW	31760 TQ	USBLS	5/15
	Virginia Beach-Norfolk-Newport News MSA, VA-NC	Y	20380 FQ	24920 MW	29380 TQ	USBLS	5/15
	Washington	H	11.65 FQ	14.46 MW	19.47 TQ	WABLS	3/16
	Seattle-Bellevue-Everett PMSA, WA	H	12.33 FQ	16.03 MW	21.22 TQ	WABLS	3/16
	Tacoma-Lakewood PMSA, WA	H	11.08 FQ	12.27 MW	17.29 TQ	WABLS	3/16
	West Virginia	Y	22820 FQ	27990 MW	36970 TQ	USBLS	5/15
	Huntington-Ashland MSA, WV-KY-OH	Y	18750 FQ	22360 MW	27270 TQ	USBLS	5/15
	Wisconsin	Y	25840 FQ	30270 MW	36290 TQ	USBLS	5/15
	Madison MSA, WI	Y	27960 FQ	32370 MW	37210 TQ	USBLS	5/15
	Milwaukee-Waukesha-West Allis MSA, WI	Y	28870 FQ	34750 MW	43570 TQ	USBLS	5/15
	Wyoming	Y	19930 FQ	24010 MW	29850 TQ	USBLS	5/15
	Cheyenne MSA, WY	Y	17910 FQ	19810 MW	22920 TQ	USBLS	5/15
	Puerto Rico	Y	17660 FQ	20000 MW	25780 TQ	USBLS	5/15
	San Juan-Carolina-Caguas MSA, PR	Y	17840 FQ	20780 MW	26620 TQ	USBLS	5/15
	Virgin Islands	Y	21820 FQ	24480 MW	29050 TQ	USBLS	5/15
	Guam	Y	18100 FQ	19030 MW	20670 TQ	USBLS	5/15
Film and Video Editor	Alabama	Y	28928 AE	51639 AW	62994 AEX	ALBLS	6/16
	Birmingham-Hoover MSA, AL	Y	32129 AE	58000 AW	70935 AEX	ALBLS	6/16
	Alaska	Y	34030 FQ	36540 MW	39060 TQ	USBLS	5/15
	Anchorage MSA, AK	Y	33970 FQ	36360 MW	38740 TQ	USBLS	5/15
	Arizona	Y	27190 FQ	37320 MW	50880 TQ	USBLS	5/15
	Phoenix-Mesa-Scottsdale MSA, AZ	Y	27660 FQ	39650 MW	52260 TQ	USBLS	5/15
	Arkansas	Y	28010 FQ	34760 MW	46010 TQ	USBLS	5/15
	Little Rock-North Little Rock-Conway MSA, AR	Y	27190 FQ	33450 MW	43720 TQ	USBLS	5/15
	California	H	26.13 FQ	43.00 MW	68.99 TQ	CABLS	1/16-3/16
	Anaheim-Santa Ana-Irvine PMSA, CA	H	12.29 FQ	14.56 MW	23.69 TQ	CABLS	1/16-3/16
	Los Angeles-Long Beach-Glendale PMSA, CA	H	27.25 FQ	45.92 MW	71.81 TQ	CABLS	1/16-3/16
	Oakland-Hayward-Berkeley PMSA, CA	H	21.72 FQ	29.25 MW	43.34 TQ	CABLS	1/16-3/16
	San Francisco-Redwood City-South San Francisco PMSA, CA	H	26.17 FQ	32.41 MW	43.86 TQ	CABLS	1/16-3/16
	Colorado	Y	31130 FQ	37810 MW	65780 TQ	USBLS	5/15
	Denver-Aurora-Lakewood MSA, CO	Y	34430 FQ	45560 MW	89510 TQ	USBLS	5/15
	Hartford-West Hartford-East Hartford MSA, CT	Y	43030 FQ	57600 MW	87730 TQ	USBLS	5/15
	District of Columbia	Y	48580 FQ	76290 MW	97860 TQ	USBLS	5/15
	Washington-Arlington-Alexandria PMSA, DC-VA-MD-WV	Y	47760 FQ	75410 MW	94940 TQ	USBLS	5/15
	Florida	H	11.89 AE	18.48 MW	25.78 AEX	FLBLS	7/16-9/16

AE	Average entry wage	AWR	Average wage range	H	Hourly	LR Low end range	MTC Median total compensation	TCC Total cash compensation
AEX	Average experienced wage	B	Biweekly	HI	Highest wage paid	M Monthly	MW Median wage paid	TQ Third quartile wage
ATC	Average total compensation	D	Daily	HR	High end range	MCC Median cash compensation	MWR Median wage range	W Weekly
AW	Average wage paid	FQ	First quartile wage	LO	Lowest wage paid	ME Median entry wage	S See annotated source	Y Yearly

Occupation/Type/Industry	Location	Per	Low	Mid	High	Source	Date
Film and Video Editor	Fort Lauderdale-Pompano Beach-Deerfield Beach PMSA, FL	H	14.00 AE	20.90 MW	31.51 AEX	FLBLS	7/16-9/16
	Miami-Miami Beach-Kendall PMSA, FL	H	11.28 AE	19.10 MW	26.94 AEX	FLBLS	7/16-9/16
	Orlando-Kissimmee-Sanford MSA, FL	H	12.12 AE	17.52 MW	23.26 AEX	FLBLS	7/16-9/16
	Tampa-St. Petersburg-Clearwater MSA, FL	H	13.69 AE	18.37 MW	23.77 AEX	FLBLS	7/16-9/16
	Georgia	Y	41260 FQ	48180 MW	63670 TQ	USBLS	5/15
	Atlanta-Sandy Springs-Roswell MSA, GA	Y	41140 FQ	47690 MW	61650 TQ	USBLS	5/15
	Urban Honolulu MSA, HI	Y	34300 FQ	44270 MW	60560 TQ	USBLS	5/15
	Idaho	Y	19430 FQ	32750 MW	43710 TQ	USBLS	5/15
	Boise City MSA, ID	Y	21610 FQ	35800 MW	46160 TQ	USBLS	5/15
	Illinois	Y	35150 FQ	54640 MW	74180 TQ	USBLS	5/15
	Chicago-Naperville-Arlington Heights PMSA, IL	Y	41580 FQ	57360 MW	78080 TQ	USBLS	5/15
	Indiana	Y	32400 FQ	37790 MW	53380 TQ	USBLS	5/15
	Indianapolis-Carmel-Anderson MSA, IN	Y	31240 FQ	37050 MW	54810 TQ	USBLS	5/15
	Iowa	Y	32920 FQ	42960 MW	50890 TQ	USBLS	5/15
	Kansas	Y	24600 FQ	33640 MW	52800 TQ	USBLS	5/15
	Kentucky	Y	29310 FQ	40010 MW	56840 TQ	USBLS	5/15
	Louisville-Jefferson County MSA, KY-IN	Y	26610 FQ	35670 MW	66200 TQ	USBLS	5/15
	Baton Rouge MSA, LA	Y	48340 FQ	56040 MW	65810 TQ	USBLS	5/15
	Maine	Y	27690 FQ	34350 MW	37870 TQ	USBLS	5/15
	Portland-South Portland MSA, ME	Y	32130 FQ	35110 MW	38080 TQ	USBLS	5/15
	Maryland	Y	32011 AE	51294 MW	60935 AEX	MDBLS	4/16
	Baltimore-Columbia-Towson MSA, MD	Y	32060 FQ	40230 MW	56990 TQ	USBLS	5/15
	Massachusetts	Y	31290 FQ	41380 MW	66740 TQ	USBLS	5/15
	Boston-Cambridge-Newton NECTA, MA	Y	31820 FQ	41930 MW	66730 TQ	USBLS	5/15
	Michigan	Y	35060 FQ	52590 MW	74430 TQ	USBLS	5/15
	Detroit-Dearborn-Livonia PMSA, MI	Y	36390 FQ	47900 MW	57780 TQ	USBLS	5/15
	Minnesota	Y	32560 FQ	41995 MW	63185 TQ	MNBLS	1/16-3/16
	Minneapolis-St. Paul-Bloomington MSA, MN-WI	Y	32681 FQ	41794 MW	65906 TQ	MNBLS	1/16-3/16
	Missouri	Y	31020 FQ	46480 MW	66910 TQ	USBLS	5/15
	Kansas City MSA, MO-KS	Y	29730 FQ	44890 MW	70970 TQ	USBLS	5/15
	St. Louis MSA, MO-IL	Y	38120 FQ	47300 MW	66750 TQ	USBLS	5/15
	Montana	Y	32080 FQ	45090 MW	58370 TQ	USBLS	5/15
	Nebraska	Y	33525 FQ	40590 MW	58035 TQ	NEBLS	7/16-9/16
	Omaha-Council Bluffs MSA, NE-IA	Y	33525 FQ	39850 MW	54270 TQ	NEBLS	7/16-9/16
	Nevada	Y	33250 FQ	44280 MW	59910 TQ	USBLS	5/15
	Las Vegas-Henderson-Paradise MSA, NV	Y	33280 FQ	44110 MW	60190 TQ	USBLS	5/15
	New Jersey	Y	40190 FQ	55080 MW	93320 TQ	USBLS	5/15
	Camden PMSA, NJ	Y	48260 FQ	77000 MW	116120 TQ	USBLS	5/15
	Newark PMSA, NJ-PA	Y	40510 FQ	74760 MW	91700 TQ	USBLS	5/15
	New York	Y	36210 AE	71140 MW	100620 AEX	NYBLS	1/16-3/16
	Nassau County-Suffolk County PMSA, NY	Y	19880 FQ	57090 MW	87220 TQ	USBLS	5/15
	New York-Jersey City-White Plains PMSA, NY-NJ	Y	47760 FQ	71250 MW	107590 TQ	USBLS	5/15
	Rochester MSA, NY	Y	21210 FQ	23180 MW	30530 TQ	USBLS	5/15
	North Carolina	Y	27830 FQ	34410 MW	47150 TQ	USBLS	5/15
	Charlotte-Concord-Gastonia MSA, NC-SC	Y	26620 FQ	36150 MW	53580 TQ	USBLS	5/15
	Raleigh MSA, NC	Y	27760 FQ	31300 MW	39640 TQ	USBLS	5/15
	North Dakota	Y	46650 FQ	56450 MW	70850 TQ	USBLS	5/15
	Ohio	Y	32610 FQ	43630 MW	66420 TQ	USBLS	5/15
	Cincinnati MSA, OH-KY-IN	Y	27640 FQ	42060 MW	57800 TQ	USBLS	5/15
	Cleveland-Elyria MSA, OH	Y	37730 FQ	65340 MW	81260 TQ	USBLS	5/15
	Columbus MSA, OH	Y	37220 FQ	48500 MW	68800 TQ	USBLS	5/15
	Oklahoma	Y	23050 FQ	32610 MW	39150 TQ	USBLS	5/15
	Oklahoma City MSA, OK	Y	26540 FQ	34010 MW	39480 TQ	USBLS	5/15

AE	Average entry wage	AWR	Average wage range	H	Hourly	LR	Low end range	MTC	Median total compensation	TCC	Total cash compensation
AEX	Average experienced wage	B	Biweekly	HI	Highest wage paid	M	Monthly	MCC	Median cash compensation	MWR	Median wage range	TQ	Third quartile wage
ATC	Average total compensation	D	Daily	HR	High end range	MCC	Median cash compensation	MW	Median wage paid	W	Weekly
AW	Average wage paid	FQ	First quartile wage	LO	Lowest wage paid	ME	Median entry wage	S	See annotated source	Y	Yearly

Occupation/Type/Industry	Location	Per	Low	Mid	High	Source	Date
Film and Video Editor	Tulsa MSA, OK	Y	19650 FQ	28880 MW	38400 TQ	USBLS	5/15
	Oregon	H	15.51 FQ	23.07 MW	31.49 TQ	ORBLS	2016
	Portland-Vancouver-Hillsboro MSA, OR-WA	Y	40510 FQ	49580 MW	68150 TQ	USBLS	5/15
	Pennsylvania	Y	29600 FQ	41920 MW	59300 TQ	USBLS	5/15
	Montgomery County-Bucks County-Chester County PMSA, PA	Y	39130 FQ	44370 MW	49530 TQ	USBLS	5/15
	Philadelphia PMSA, PA	Y	30690 FQ	51840 MW	67550 TQ	USBLS	5/15
	Pittsburgh MSA, PA	Y	30860 FQ	47600 MW	67700 TQ	USBLS	5/15
	South Carolina	Y	25060 FQ	34260 MW	41900 TQ	USBLS	5/15
	Tennessee	Y	35850 FQ	54300 MW	80590 TQ	USBLS	5/15
	Knoxville MSA, TN	Y	28270 FQ	33450 MW	47810 TQ	USBLS	5/15
	Nashville-Davidson–Murfreesboro–Franklin MSA, TN	Y	41390 FQ	63460 MW	96480 TQ	USBLS	5/15
	Texas	Y	25090 FQ	42770 MW	62800 TQ	USBLS	5/15
	Austin-Round Rock MSA, TX	Y	38090 FQ	51770 MW	65770 TQ	USBLS	5/15
	Dallas-Plano-Irving PMSA, TX	Y	35250 FQ	48970 MW	87000 TQ	USBLS	5/15
	Houston-The Woodlands-Sugar Land MSA, TX	Y	17820 FQ	29160 MW	53450 TQ	USBLS	5/15
	San Antonio-New Braunfels MSA, TX	Y	35270 FQ	47240 MW	83020 TQ	USBLS	5/15
	Utah	Y	22720 FQ	46070 MW	70060 TQ	USBLS	5/15
	Salt Lake City MSA, UT	Y	30610 FQ	52180 MW	73110 TQ	USBLS	5/15
	Virginia	Y	37270 FQ	57500 MW	81040 TQ	USBLS	5/15
	Richmond MSA, VA	Y	31960 FQ	53450 MW	60910 TQ	USBLS	5/15
	Virginia Beach-Norfolk-Newport News MSA, VA-NC	Y	40200 FQ	56040 MW	62470 TQ	USBLS	5/15
	Washington	H	16.89 FQ	23.69 MW	33.92 TQ	WABLS	3/16
	Seattle-Bellevue-Everett PMSA, WA	H	17.49 FQ	24.84 MW	34.50 TQ	WABLS	3/16
	Wisconsin	Y	40420 FQ	45570 MW	51460 TQ	USBLS	5/15
	Madison MSA, WI	Y	40500 FQ	45360 MW	50310 TQ	USBLS	5/15
	Milwaukee-Waukesha-West Allis MSA, WI	Y	42240 FQ	47090 MW	55000 TQ	USBLS	5/15
	Puerto Rico	Y	23950 FQ	39730 MW	45040 TQ	USBLS	5/15
Film Coordinator							
Communications Department, Municipal Government	West Hollywood, CA	Y			95499 HI	CACIT	6/28/16
Film Loader							
Made for Television Motion Picture	United States	W	1282 LO			MPEG01	7/31/16-7/29/17
Finance Director							
County Government	Coweta County, GA	Y	65856 LO		101805 HI	GACTY04	2016
County Government	Miller County, GA	Y			46000 HI	GACTY04	2016
County Government	Oconee County, GA	Y	76644 LO		111132 HI	GACTY04	2016
Municipal Government	Bakersfield, CA	Y			155099 HI	CACIT	6/28/16
Municipal Government	Dos Palos, CA	Y			58232 HI	CACIT	6/28/16
Financial Advisor	United States	Y		34453-195955 AWR		IBD02	2015
Financial Analyst	Alabama	Y	47435 AE	91652 AW	113760 AEX	ALBLS	6/16
	Birmingham-Hoover MSA, AL	Y	44606 AE	94891 AW	120033 AEX	ALBLS	6/16
	Alaska	Y	76230 FQ	96750 MW	119400 TQ	USBLS	5/15
	Anchorage MSA, AK	Y	72390 FQ	91780 MW	116500 TQ	USBLS	5/15
	Arizona	Y	54760 FQ	66640 MW	83970 TQ	USBLS	5/15
	Phoenix-Mesa-Scottsdale MSA, AZ	Y	54940 FQ	67870 MW	84910 TQ	USBLS	5/15
	Tucson MSA, AZ	Y	54170 FQ	60350 MW	76360 TQ	USBLS	5/15
	Arkansas	Y	48260 FQ	62470 MW	82480 TQ	USBLS	5/15
	Little Rock-North Little Rock-Conway MSA, AR	Y	47600 FQ	59730 MW	78820 TQ	USBLS	5/15
	California	H	35.53 FQ	46.53 MW	61.29 TQ	CABLS	1/16-3/16
	Anaheim-Santa Ana-Irvine PMSA, CA	H	32.87 FQ	42.89 MW	56.11 TQ	CABLS	1/16-3/16
	Los Angeles-Long Beach-Glendale PMSA, CA	H	33.81 FQ	42.50 MW	54.42 TQ	CABLS	1/16-3/16

Occupation/Type/Industry	Location	Per	Low	Mid	High	Source	Date
Financial Analyst	Oakland-Hayward-Berkeley PMSA, CA	H	39.44 FQ	49.15 MW	61.76 TQ	CABLS	1/16-3/16
	Riverside-San Bernardino-Ontario MSA, CA	H	29.48 FQ	36.88 MW	46.87 TQ	CABLS	1/16-3/16
	Sacramento–Roseville–Arden-Arcade MSA, CA	H	32.86 FQ	41.17 MW	49.90 TQ	CABLS	1/16-3/16
	San Diego-Carlsbad MSA, CA	H	31.93 FQ	41.66 MW	56.25 TQ	CABLS	1/16-3/16
	San Francisco-Redwood City-South San Francisco PMSA, CA	H	41.63 FQ	57.91 MW	81.99 TQ	CABLS	1/16-3/16
	Colorado	Y	60910 FQ	76510 MW	124500 TQ	USBLS	5/15
	Denver-Aurora-Lakewood MSA, CO	Y	62090 FQ	75820 MW	125880 TQ	USBLS	5/15
	Connecticut	Y		82154 MW		CTBLS	1/16-3/16
	Bridgeport-Stamford-Norwalk MSA, CT	Y	63740 FQ	83060 MW	125910 TQ	USBLS	5/15
	Hartford-West Hartford-East Hartford MSA, CT	Y	63860 FQ	79960 MW	98480 TQ	USBLS	5/15
	Delaware	Y	55760 FQ	70640 MW	106020 TQ	USBLS	5/15
	Wilmington PMSA, DE-MD-NJ	Y	56000 FQ	70950 MW	106470 TQ	USBLS	5/15
	District of Columbia	Y	69860 FQ	86420 MW	116590 TQ	USBLS	5/15
	Washington-Arlington-Alexandria PMSA, DC-VA-MD-WV	Y	68450 FQ	89320 MW	116810 TQ	USBLS	5/15
	Florida	H	24.50 AE	34.48 MW	45.17 AEX	FLBLS	7/16-9/16
	Fort Lauderdale-Pompano Beach-Deerfield Beach PMSA, FL	H	23.93 AE	35.21 MW	45.35 AEX	FLBLS	7/16-9/16
	Miami-Miami Beach-Kendall PMSA, FL	H	24.26 AE	37.43 MW	50.05 AEX	FLBLS	7/16-9/16
	Orlando-Kissimmee-Sanford MSA, FL	H	25.32 AE	33.25 MW	44.56 AEX	FLBLS	7/16-9/16
	Tampa-St. Petersburg-Clearwater MSA, FL	H	25.55 AE	34.73 MW	42.93 AEX	FLBLS	7/16-9/16
	Georgia	Y	55380 FQ	71070 MW	92140 TQ	USBLS	5/15
	Atlanta-Sandy Springs-Roswell MSA, GA	Y	56560 FQ	72620 MW	93990 TQ	USBLS	5/15
	Augusta-Richmond County MSA, GA-SC	Y	46270 FQ	59050 MW	72790 TQ	USBLS	5/15
	Hawaii	Y	50940 FQ	64260 MW	78910 TQ	USBLS	5/15
	Urban Honolulu MSA, HI	Y	50200 FQ	63710 MW	78020 TQ	USBLS	5/15
	Idaho	Y	56980 FQ	72020 MW	88530 TQ	USBLS	5/15
	Boise City MSA, ID	Y	58390 FQ	73690 MW	90570 TQ	USBLS	5/15
	Illinois	Y	60010 FQ	79750 MW	101350 TQ	USBLS	5/15
	Chicago-Naperville-Arlington Heights PMSA, IL	Y	60760 FQ	80390 MW	101840 TQ	USBLS	5/15
	Indiana	Y	53820 FQ	66310 MW	84780 TQ	USBLS	5/15
	Gary PMSA, IN	Y	53240 FQ	72880 MW	94970 TQ	USBLS	5/15
	Indianapolis-Carmel-Anderson MSA, IN	Y	54040 FQ	66280 MW	82610 TQ	USBLS	5/15
	Iowa	Y	55120 FQ	70980 MW	91930 TQ	USBLS	5/15
	Kansas	Y	58580 FQ	73210 MW	94380 TQ	USBLS	5/15
	Wichita MSA, KS	Y	61950 FQ	73860 MW	86320 TQ	USBLS	5/15
	Kentucky	Y	52130 FQ	65630 MW	88430 TQ	USBLS	5/15
	Louisville-Jefferson County MSA, KY-IN	Y	51850 FQ	66430 MW	92520 TQ	USBLS	5/15
	Louisiana	Y	51510 FQ	65290 MW	89710 TQ	USBLS	5/15
	New Orleans-Metairie MSA, LA	Y	51940 FQ	67990 MW	91070 TQ	USBLS	5/15
	Maine	Y	57740 FQ	69760 MW	84370 TQ	USBLS	5/15
	Portland-South Portland MSA, ME	Y	55680 FQ	65760 MW	79120 TQ	USBLS	5/15
	Maryland	Y	54036 AE	94756 MW	115116 AEX	MDBLS	4/16
	Baltimore-Columbia-Towson MSA, MD	Y	61500 FQ	77860 MW	112700 TQ	USBLS	5/15
	Salisbury MSA, MD-DE	Y	56600 FQ	73970 MW	104450 TQ	USBLS	5/15
	Massachusetts	Y	68490 FQ	88740 MW	121150 TQ	USBLS	5/15
	Boston-Cambridge-Newton NECTA, MA	Y	69360 FQ	90950 MW	128310 TQ	USBLS	5/15
	Worcester MSA, MA-CT	Y	67450 FQ	86230 MW	101650 TQ	USBLS	5/15
	Michigan	Y	59060 FQ	75410 MW	95350 TQ	USBLS	5/15

AE	Average entry wage	AWR	Average wage range	H	Hourly
AEX	Average experienced wage	B	Biweekly	HI	Highest wage paid
ATC	Average total compensation	D	Daily	HR	High end range
AW	Average wage paid	FQ	First quartile wage	LO	Lowest wage paid

LR	Low end range	MTC	Median total compensation
M	Monthly	MW	Median wage paid
MCC	Median cash compensation	MWR	Median wage range
ME	Median entry wage	S	See annotated source

TCC	Total cash compensation
TQ	Third quartile wage
W	Weekly
Y	Yearly

Occupation/Type/Industry	Location	Per	Low	Mid	High	Source	Date
Financial Analyst	Detroit-Dearborn-Livonia PMSA, MI	Y	66860 FQ	86230 MW	103490 TQ	USBLS	5/15
	Grand Rapids-Wyoming MSA, MI	Y	56430 FQ	70880 MW	82740 TQ	USBLS	5/15
	Minnesota	Y	62815 FQ	81227 MW	103267 TQ	MNBLS	1/16-3/16
	Minneapolis-St. Paul-Bloomington MSA, MN-WI	Y	63334 FQ	82162 MW	104496 TQ	MNBLS	1/16-3/16
	Mississippi	Y	52830 FQ	61730 MW	78430 TQ	USBLS	5/15
	Jackson MSA, MS	Y	51400 FQ	66070 MW	80310 TQ	USBLS	5/15
	Missouri	Y	56160 FQ	75080 MW	95840 TQ	USBLS	5/15
	Kansas City MSA, MO-KS	Y	56900 FQ	73840 MW	93730 TQ	USBLS	5/15
	St. Louis MSA, MO-IL	Y	60430 FQ	79170 MW	102090 TQ	USBLS	5/15
	Montana	Y	55650 FQ	71270 MW	92330 TQ	USBLS	5/15
	Billings MSA, MT	Y	52220 FQ	85490 MW	107620 TQ	USBLS	5/15
	Nebraska	Y	53830 FQ	66420 MW	82555 TQ	NEBLS	7/16-9/16
	Omaha-Council Bluffs MSA, NE-IA	Y	53965 FQ	66965 MW	83190 TQ	NEBLS	7/16-9/16
	Nevada	Y	50630 FQ	69030 MW	84240 TQ	USBLS	5/15
	Las Vegas-Henderson-Paradise MSA, NV	Y	51810 FQ	69280 MW	83900 TQ	USBLS	5/15
	New Hampshire	H	20.96 AE	30.42 MW	40.79 AEX	NHBLS	6/16
	Manchester NECTA, NH	H	25.40 AE	34.86 MW	41.67 AEX	NHBLS	6/16
	Nashua NECTA, NH-MA	Y	46420 FQ	58930 MW	77720 TQ	USBLS	5/15
	New Jersey	Y	64440 FQ	80840 MW	106470 TQ	USBLS	5/15
	Camden PMSA, NJ	Y	65120 FQ	75240 MW	94060 TQ	USBLS	5/15
	Newark PMSA, NJ-PA	Y	69980 FQ	89140 MW	114820 TQ	USBLS	5/15
	Trenton MSA, NJ	Y	58010 FQ	74940 MW	97810 TQ	USBLS	5/15
	New Mexico	Y	55360 FQ	71640 MW	91140 TQ	USBLS	5/15
	Albuquerque MSA, NM	Y	59040 FQ	75530 MW	93840 TQ	USBLS	5/15
	New York	Y	65650 AE	102400 MW	154710 AEX	NYBLS	1/16-3/16
	Buffalo-Cheektowaga-Niagara Falls MSA, NY	Y	54160 FQ	66210 MW	84260 TQ	USBLS	5/15
	Nassau County-Suffolk County PMSA, NY	Y	59290 FQ	74690 MW	98750 TQ	USBLS	5/15
	New York-Jersey City-White Plains PMSA, NY-NJ	Y	74960 FQ	102260 MW	158150 TQ	USBLS	5/15
	Rochester MSA, NY	Y	58470 FQ	73080 MW	93830 TQ	USBLS	5/15
	North Carolina	Y	59520 FQ	76930 MW	100590 TQ	USBLS	5/15
	Charlotte-Concord-Gastonia MSA, NC-SC	Y	59720 FQ	78870 MW	104000 TQ	USBLS	5/15
	Raleigh MSA, NC	Y	61310 FQ	77430 MW	98780 TQ	USBLS	5/15
	North Dakota	Y	56890 FQ	68740 MW	79140 TQ	USBLS	5/15
	Fargo MSA, ND-MN	Y	57220 FQ	67640 MW	76720 TQ	USBLS	5/15
	Ohio	Y	54650 FQ	69580 MW	89360 TQ	USBLS	5/15
	Cincinnati MSA, OH-KY-IN	Y	56080 FQ	70870 MW	90060 TQ	USBLS	5/15
	Cleveland-Elyria MSA, OH	Y	57710 FQ	72490 MW	96010 TQ	USBLS	5/15
	Columbus MSA, OH	Y	51180 FQ	66720 MW	87600 TQ	USBLS	5/15
	Oklahoma	Y	51770 FQ	65680 MW	91820 TQ	USBLS	5/15
	Oklahoma City MSA, OK	Y	51180 FQ	62100 MW	81920 TQ	USBLS	5/15
	Tulsa MSA, OK	Y	57520 FQ	74050 MW	100830 TQ	USBLS	5/15
	Oregon	H	31.93 FQ	39.64 MW	51.13 TQ	ORBLS	2016
	Portland-Vancouver-Hillsboro MSA, OR-WA	Y	65400 FQ	80700 MW	103470 TQ	USBLS	5/15
	Pennsylvania	Y	55630 FQ	71800 MW	95260 TQ	USBLS	5/15
	Allentown-Bethlehem-Easton MSA, PA-NJ	Y	64930 FQ	82870 MW	103960 TQ	USBLS	5/15
	Harrisburg-Carlisle MSA, PA	Y	51510 FQ	66550 MW	87740 TQ	USBLS	5/15
	Montgomery County-Bucks County-Chester County PMSA, PA	Y	57260 FQ	73160 MW	99910 TQ	USBLS	5/15
	Philadelphia PMSA, PA	Y	59060 FQ	75390 MW	103450 TQ	USBLS	5/15
	Pittsburgh MSA, PA	Y	54940 FQ	71550 MW	93120 TQ	USBLS	5/15
	Rhode Island	Y	58910 FQ	72150 MW	88420 TQ	USBLS	5/15
	Providence-Warwick MSA, RI-MA	Y	58740 FQ	72060 MW	88270 TQ	USBLS	5/15
	South Carolina	Y	49690 FQ	63370 MW	79830 TQ	USBLS	5/15
	Charleston-North Charleston MSA, SC	Y	48910 FQ	60760 MW	79840 TQ	USBLS	5/15
	Columbia MSA, SC	Y	40100 FQ	59190 MW	74360 TQ	USBLS	5/15
	Greenville-Anderson-Mauldin MSA, SC	Y	55620 FQ	66660 MW	80270 TQ	USBLS	5/15
	South Dakota	Y	52570 FQ	65950 MW	81470 TQ	USBLS	5/15

AE	Average entry wage	AWR	Average wage range	H	Hourly	LR	Low end range	MTC Median total compensation	TCC Total cash compensation
AEX	Average experienced wage	B	Biweekly	HI	Highest wage paid	M	Monthly	MW Median wage paid	TQ Third quartile wage
ATC	Average total compensation	D	Daily	HR	High end range	MCC Median cash compensation	MWR Median wage range	W Weekly
AW	Average wage paid	FQ	First quartile wage	LO	Lowest wage paid	ME Median entry wage	S See annotated source	Y Yearly

Occupation/Type/Industry	Location	Per	Low	Mid	High	Source	Date
Financial Analyst	Sioux Falls MSA, SD	Y	53400 FQ	68270 MW	87180 TQ	USBLS	5/15
	Tennessee	Y	54740 FQ	69560 MW	88600 TQ	USBLS	5/15
	Knoxville MSA, TN	Y	51030 FQ	61440 MW	83030 TQ	USBLS	5/15
	Memphis MSA, TN-MS-AR	Y	52290 FQ	64200 MW	83180 TQ	USBLS	5/15
	Nashville-Davidson–Murfreesboro–Franklin MSA, TN	Y	57020 FQ	70910 MW	87270 TQ	USBLS	5/15
	Texas	Y	59740 FQ	79550 MW	110730 TQ	USBLS	5/15
	Austin-Round Rock MSA, TX	Y	61820 FQ	82620 MW	114390 TQ	USBLS	5/15
	Dallas-Plano-Irving PMSA, TX	Y	60770 FQ	81500 MW	110380 TQ	USBLS	5/15
	Fort Worth-Arlington PMSA, TX	Y	55120 FQ	69850 MW	92210 TQ	USBLS	5/15
	Houston-The Woodlands-Sugar Land MSA, TX	Y	63210 FQ	84740 MW	124730 TQ	USBLS	5/15
	San Antonio-New Braunfels MSA, TX	Y	57640 FQ	76920 MW	106850 TQ	USBLS	5/15
	Utah	Y	52780 FQ	72510 MW	92940 TQ	USBLS	5/15
	Ogden-Clearfield MSA, UT	Y	65730 FQ	80240 MW	90880 TQ	USBLS	5/15
	Provo-Orem MSA, UT	Y	51570 FQ	68750 MW	90710 TQ	USBLS	5/15
	Salt Lake City MSA, UT	Y	54330 FQ	74110 MW	94530 TQ	USBLS	5/15
	Vermont	Y	59060 FQ	78300 MW	125370 TQ	USBLS	5/15
	Burlington-South Burlington MSA, VT	Y	57280 FQ	74770 MW	120990 TQ	USBLS	5/15
	Virginia	Y	64040 FQ	87370 MW	113230 TQ	USBLS	5/15
	Richmond MSA, VA	Y	63020 FQ	82980 MW	109610 TQ	USBLS	5/15
	Virginia Beach-Norfolk-Newport News MSA, VA-NC	Y	52100 FQ	68990 MW	89680 TQ	USBLS	5/15
	Washington	H	26.58 FQ	34.88 MW	45.93 TQ	WABLS	3/16
	Seattle-Bellevue-Everett PMSA, WA	H	31.73 FQ	39.21 MW	49.59 TQ	WABLS	3/16
	Tacoma-Lakewood PMSA, WA	H	24.58 FQ	30.73 MW	42.17 TQ	WABLS	3/16
	West Virginia	Y	43930 FQ	56050 MW	70330 TQ	USBLS	5/15
	Huntington-Ashland MSA, WV-KY-OH	Y	52840 FQ	58250 MW	63700 TQ	USBLS	5/15
	Wisconsin	Y	55890 FQ	70500 MW	90560 TQ	USBLS	5/15
	Madison MSA, WI	Y	57430 FQ	74570 MW	93540 TQ	USBLS	5/15
	Milwaukee-Waukesha-West Allis MSA, WI	Y	59170 FQ	73920 MW	94030 TQ	USBLS	5/15
	Wyoming	Y	54790 FQ	72400 MW	91110 TQ	USBLS	5/15
	Puerto Rico	Y	39120 FQ	53320 MW	71980 TQ	USBLS	5/15
	San Juan-Carolina-Caguas MSA, PR	Y	39490 FQ	55440 MW	73720 TQ	USBLS	5/15
	Virgin Islands	Y	48650 FQ	57040 MW	70540 TQ	USBLS	5/15
Financial Examiner	Alabama	Y	42075 AE	66192 AW	78245 AEX	ALBLS	6/16
	Birmingham-Hoover MSA, AL	Y	42218 AE	64654 AW	75878 AEX	ALBLS	6/16
	Alaska	Y	49980 FQ	58230 MW	68560 TQ	USBLS	5/15
	Anchorage MSA, AK	Y	50960 FQ	59060 MW	69350 TQ	USBLS	5/15
	Arizona	Y	56590 FQ	72230 MW	94600 TQ	USBLS	5/15
	Phoenix-Mesa-Scottsdale MSA, AZ	Y	56720 FQ	72190 MW	94140 TQ	USBLS	5/15
	Arkansas	Y	53710 FQ	73800 MW	87630 TQ	USBLS	5/15
	Little Rock-North Little Rock-Conway MSA, AR	Y	59840 FQ	78500 MW	90910 TQ	USBLS	5/15
	California	H	34.26 FQ	43.66 MW	59.59 TQ	CABLS	1/16-3/16
	Anaheim-Santa Ana-Irvine PMSA, CA	H	33.79 FQ	42.40 MW	55.74 TQ	CABLS	1/16-3/16
	Los Angeles-Long Beach-Glendale PMSA, CA	H	31.37 FQ	40.83 MW	51.69 TQ	CABLS	1/16-3/16
	Oakland-Hayward-Berkeley PMSA, CA	H	37.48 FQ	45.85 MW	57.04 TQ	CABLS	1/16-3/16
	Riverside-San Bernardino-Ontario MSA, CA	H	18.20 FQ	26.66 MW	47.62 TQ	CABLS	1/16-3/16
	Sacramento–Roseville–Arden-Arcade MSA, CA	H	29.88 FQ	38.44 MW	49.05 TQ	CABLS	1/16-3/16
	San Diego-Carlsbad MSA, CA	H	33.86 FQ	39.31 MW	49.72 TQ	CABLS	1/16-3/16
	San Francisco-Redwood City-South San Francisco PMSA, CA	H	43.92 FQ	60.83 MW	83.12 TQ	CABLS	1/16-3/16
	Colorado	Y	57210 FQ	69510 MW	91760 TQ	USBLS	5/15
	Denver-Aurora-Lakewood MSA, CO	Y	57660 FQ	69990 MW	92910 TQ	USBLS	5/15

AE	Average entry wage	AWR	Average wage range	H	Hourly	LR	Low end range	MTC	Median total compensation	TCC	Total cash compensation
AEX	Average experienced wage	B	Biweekly	HI	Highest wage paid	M	Monthly	MW	Median wage paid	TQ	Third quartile wage
ATC	Average total compensation	D	Daily	HR	High end range	MCC	Median cash compensation	MWR	Median wage range	W	Weekly
AW	Average wage paid	FQ	First quartile wage	LO	Lowest wage paid	ME	Median entry wage	S	See annotated source	Y	Yearly

584

Occupation/Type/Industry	Location	Per	Low	Mid	High	Source	Date
Financial Examiner	Connecticut	Y		83945 MW		CTBLS	1/16-3/16
	Bridgeport-Stamford-Norwalk MSA, CT	Y	67320 FQ	91870 MW	135010 TQ	USBLS	5/15
	Hartford-West Hartford-East Hartford MSA, CT	Y	65530 FQ	81210 MW	97200 TQ	USBLS	5/15
	Delaware	Y	61190 FQ	76750 MW	107200 TQ	USBLS	5/15
	Wilmington PMSA, DE-MD-NJ	Y	61360 FQ	77140 MW	109110 TQ	USBLS	5/15
	District of Columbia	Y	107780 FQ	155160 MW		USBLS	5/15
	Washington-Arlington-Alexandria PMSA, DC-VA-MD-WV	Y	63050 FQ	113510 MW	164540 TQ	USBLS	5/15
	Florida	H	24.78 AE	34.38 MW	45.37 AEX	FLBLS	7/16-9/16
	Fort Lauderdale-Pompano Beach-Deerfield Beach PMSA, FL	H	30.34 AE	37.64 MW	50.06 AEX	FLBLS	7/16-9/16
	Miami-Miami Beach-Kendall PMSA, FL	H	23.99 AE	38.36 MW	49.69 AEX	FLBLS	7/16-9/16
	Orlando-Kissimmee-Sanford MSA, FL	H	21.90 AE	28.41 MW	33.70 AEX	FLBLS	7/16-9/16
	Tampa-St. Petersburg-Clearwater MSA, FL	H	25.41 AE	34.44 MW	46.10 AEX	FLBLS	7/16-9/16
	Georgia	Y	38660 FQ	67460 MW	114940 TQ	USBLS	5/15
	Atlanta-Sandy Springs-Roswell MSA, GA	Y	38500 FQ	71810 MW	123080 TQ	USBLS	5/15
	Hawaii	Y	57510 FQ	67280 MW	76690 TQ	USBLS	5/15
	Urban Honolulu MSA, HI	Y	57510 FQ	67280 MW	76690 TQ	USBLS	5/15
	Idaho	Y	56890 FQ	73890 MW	87870 TQ	USBLS	5/15
	Boise City MSA, ID	Y	54780 FQ	62250 MW	80460 TQ	USBLS	5/15
	Illinois	Y	71820 FQ	99590 MW	126560 TQ	USBLS	5/15
	Chicago-Naperville-Arlington Heights PMSA, IL	Y	76890 FQ	102360 MW	132570 TQ	USBLS	5/15
	Lake County-Kenosha County PMSA, IL-WI	Y	68170 FQ	81390 MW	103760 TQ	USBLS	5/15
	Indiana	Y	52010 FQ	65690 MW	93510 TQ	USBLS	5/15
	Indianapolis-Carmel-Anderson MSA, IN	Y	51980 FQ	68250 MW	94930 TQ	USBLS	5/15
	Iowa	Y	49440 FQ	64480 MW	89160 TQ	USBLS	5/15
	Kansas	Y	60490 FQ	72310 MW	97120 TQ	USBLS	5/15
	Wichita MSA, KS	Y	61220 FQ	70500 MW	115010 TQ	USBLS	5/15
	Kentucky	Y	44530 FQ	57830 MW	75860 TQ	USBLS	5/15
	Louisville-Jefferson County MSA, KY-IN	Y	47620 FQ	58820 MW	74600 TQ	USBLS	5/15
	Louisiana	Y	49990 FQ	69140 MW	106370 TQ	USBLS	5/15
	Baton Rouge MSA, LA	Y	47780 FQ	64660 MW	99890 TQ	USBLS	5/15
	New Orleans-Metairie MSA, LA	Y	49980 FQ	64020 MW	116320 TQ	USBLS	5/15
	Maine	Y	43000 FQ	63070 MW	75320 TQ	USBLS	5/15
	Portland-South Portland MSA, ME	Y	63600 FQ	71390 MW	78150 TQ	USBLS	5/15
	Maryland	Y	41422 AE	78442 MW	96952 AEX	MDBLS	4/16
	Baltimore-Columbia-Towson MSA, MD	Y	50110 FQ	67440 MW	93060 TQ	USBLS	5/15
	Massachusetts	Y	66580 FQ	89950 MW	132220 TQ	USBLS	5/15
	Boston-Cambridge-Newton NECTA, MA	Y	66620 FQ	91610 MW	136010 TQ	USBLS	5/15
	Michigan	Y	48040 FQ	64270 MW	81510 TQ	USBLS	5/15
	Detroit-Dearborn-Livonia PMSA, MI	Y	62140 FQ	88770 MW	118980 TQ	USBLS	5/15
	Grand Rapids-Wyoming MSA, MI	Y	55990 FQ	79710 MW	112060 TQ	USBLS	5/15
	Minnesota	Y	61403 FQ	82680 MW	110328 TQ	MNBLS	1/16-3/16
	Minneapolis-St. Paul-Bloomington MSA, MN-WI	Y	65661 FQ	85922 MW	114251 TQ	MNBLS	1/16-3/16
	Mississippi	Y	53590 FQ	71720 MW	97130 TQ	USBLS	5/15
	Jackson MSA, MS	Y	53590 FQ	72850 MW	97120 TQ	USBLS	5/15
	Missouri	Y	59320 FQ	77330 MW	99290 TQ	USBLS	5/15
	Kansas City MSA, MO-KS	Y	65490 FQ	83560 MW	122950 TQ	USBLS	5/15
	St. Louis MSA, MO-IL	Y	60700 FQ	77870 MW	97610 TQ	USBLS	5/15
	Montana	Y	51380 FQ	63490 MW	79320 TQ	USBLS	5/15
	Billings MSA, MT	Y	56860 FQ	69540 MW	91560 TQ	USBLS	5/15
	Nebraska	Y	53205 FQ	62410 MW	85980 TQ	NEBLS	7/16-9/16

AE	Average entry wage	AWR	Average wage range	H	Hourly	LR	Low end range	MTC	Median total compensation	TCC	Total cash compensation
AEX	Average experienced wage	B	Biweekly	HI	Highest wage paid	M	Monthly	MW	Median wage paid	TQ	Third quartile wage
ATC	Average total compensation	D	Daily	HR	High end range	MCC	Median cash compensation	MWR	Median wage range	W	Weekly
AW	Average wage paid	FQ	First quartile wage	LO	Lowest wage paid	ME	Median entry wage	S	See annotated source	Y	Yearly

Occupation/Type/Industry	Location	Per	Low	Mid	High	Source	Date
Financial Examiner	Omaha-Council Bluffs MSA, NE-IA	Y	53570 FQ	62165 MW	92990 TQ	NEBLS	7/16-9/16
	Nevada	Y	51350 FQ	69140 MW	88820 TQ	USBLS	5/15
	Las Vegas-Henderson-Paradise MSA, NV	Y	51390 FQ	68900 MW	88240 TQ	USBLS	5/15
	New Hampshire	H	25.62 AE	36.24 MW	48.17 AEX	NHBLS	6/16
	New Jersey	Y	69730 FQ	93200 MW	124140 TQ	USBLS	5/15
	Newark PMSA, NJ-PA	Y	66420 FQ	84720 MW	115850 TQ	USBLS	5/15
	Trenton MSA, NJ	Y	69240 FQ	94060 MW	126260 TQ	USBLS	5/15
	New Mexico	Y	44880 FQ	56430 MW	84440 TQ	USBLS	5/15
	Albuquerque MSA, NM	Y	45200 FQ	57180 MW	86800 TQ	USBLS	5/15
	New York	Y	62300 AE	103220 MW	144720 AEX	NYBLS	1/16-3/16
	Nassau County-Suffolk County PMSA, NY	Y	59030 FQ	82820 MW	105280 TQ	USBLS	5/15
	New York-Jersey City-White Plains PMSA, NY-NJ	Y	77080 FQ	103510 MW	147600 TQ	USBLS	5/15
	Rochester MSA, NY	Y	45450 FQ	55190 MW	61920 TQ	USBLS	5/15
	North Carolina	Y	60960 FQ	79170 MW	103210 TQ	USBLS	5/15
	Charlotte-Concord-Gastonia MSA, NC-SC	Y	65690 FQ	82630 MW	108400 TQ	USBLS	5/15
	Raleigh MSA, NC	Y	51960 FQ	69900 MW	95060 TQ	USBLS	5/15
	North Dakota	Y	53370 FQ	64800 MW	88170 TQ	USBLS	5/15
	Fargo MSA, ND-MN	Y	52560 FQ	67820 MW	90730 TQ	USBLS	5/15
	Ohio	Y	51300 FQ	62460 MW	82800 TQ	USBLS	5/15
	Cincinnati MSA, OH-KY-IN	Y	53520 FQ	61810 MW	79020 TQ	USBLS	5/15
	Cleveland-Elyria MSA, OH	Y	47020 FQ	59340 MW	80640 TQ	USBLS	5/15
	Columbus MSA, OH	Y	51920 FQ	63450 MW	81150 TQ	USBLS	5/15
	Oklahoma	Y	56620 FQ	76130 MW	102580 TQ	USBLS	5/15
	Oklahoma City MSA, OK	Y	62390 FQ	80400 MW	117640 TQ	USBLS	5/15
	Tulsa MSA, OK	Y	50000 FQ	65440 MW	111390 TQ	USBLS	5/15
	Oregon	H	26.61 FQ	34.67 MW	43.49 TQ	ORBLS	2016
	Portland-Vancouver-Hillsboro MSA, OR-WA	Y	56560 FQ	74330 MW	95350 TQ	USBLS	5/15
	Pennsylvania	Y	60050 FQ	77590 MW	108090 TQ	USBLS	5/15
	Allentown-Bethlehem-Easton MSA, PA-NJ	Y	53950 FQ	61440 MW	78140 TQ	USBLS	5/15
	Harrisburg-Carlisle MSA, PA	Y	52710 FQ	63230 MW	82390 TQ	USBLS	5/15
	Montgomery County-Bucks County-Chester County PMSA, PA	Y	68970 FQ	87140 MW	116510 TQ	USBLS	5/15
	Philadelphia PMSA, PA	Y	60730 FQ	83570 MW	107010 TQ	USBLS	5/15
	Pittsburgh MSA, PA	Y	60680 FQ	82600 MW	121560 TQ	USBLS	5/15
	Rhode Island	Y	61340 FQ	75870 MW	93750 TQ	USBLS	5/15
	Providence-Warwick MSA, RI-MA	Y	62390 FQ	76650 MW	94130 TQ	USBLS	5/15
	South Carolina	Y	45300 FQ	59520 MW	79400 TQ	USBLS	5/15
	Columbia MSA, SC	Y	45010 FQ	58990 MW	76630 TQ	USBLS	5/15
	Greenville-Anderson-Mauldin MSA, SC	Y	47390 FQ	67880 MW	91930 TQ	USBLS	5/15
	South Dakota	Y	42400 FQ	62100 MW	106180 TQ	USBLS	5/15
	Tennessee	Y	59120 FQ	83480 MW	105400 TQ	USBLS	5/15
	Knoxville MSA, TN	Y	48950 FQ	73880 MW	110870 TQ	USBLS	5/15
	Memphis MSA, TN-MS-AR	Y	66890 FQ	109220 MW	141340 TQ	USBLS	5/15
	Nashville-Davidson–Murfreesboro–Franklin MSA, TN	Y	57430 FQ	82460 MW	103540 TQ	USBLS	5/15
	Texas	Y	57900 FQ	77010 MW	107440 TQ	USBLS	5/15
	Austin-Round Rock MSA, TX	Y	58880 FQ	73890 MW	100140 TQ	USBLS	5/15
	Dallas-Plano-Irving PMSA, TX	Y	61210 FQ	81520 MW	120000 TQ	USBLS	5/15
	Fort Worth-Arlington PMSA, TX	Y	58180 FQ	79120 MW	109400 TQ	USBLS	5/15
	Houston-The Woodlands-Sugar Land MSA, TX	Y	54670 FQ	73480 MW	103250 TQ	USBLS	5/15
	San Antonio-New Braunfels MSA, TX	Y	55170 FQ	72570 MW	94610 TQ	USBLS	5/15
	Utah	Y	42370 FQ	68640 MW	96860 TQ	USBLS	5/15
	Provo-Orem MSA, UT	Y	33130 FQ	36070 MW	39000 TQ	USBLS	5/15
	Salt Lake City MSA, UT	Y	48910 FQ	70790 MW	101420 TQ	USBLS	5/15
	Vermont	Y	53860 FQ	67960 MW	76980 TQ	USBLS	5/15
	Virginia	Y	52200 FQ	75050 MW	110740 TQ	USBLS	5/15
	Richmond MSA, VA	Y	48610 FQ	75440 MW	98680 TQ	USBLS	5/15

AE	Average entry wage	AWR	Average wage range	H	Hourly	LR	Low end range	MTC	Median total compensation	TCC	Total cash compensation
AEX	Average experienced wage	B	Biweekly	HI	Highest wage paid	M	Monthly	MW	Median wage paid	TQ	Third quartile wage
ATC	Average total compensation	D	Daily	HR	High end range	MCC	Median cash compensation	MWR	Median wage range	W	Weekly
AW	Average wage paid	FQ	First quartile wage	LO	Lowest wage paid	ME	Median entry wage	S	See annotated source	Y	Yearly

Occupation/Type/Industry	Location	Per	Low	Mid	High	Source	Date
Financial Examiner	Virginia Beach-Norfolk- Newport News MSA, VA-NC	Y	68660 FQ	76400 MW	94040 TQ	USBLS	5/15
	Washington	H	32.24 FQ	40.97 MW	50.97 TQ	WABLS	3/16
	Seattle-Bellevue-Everett PMSA, WA	H	33.32 FQ	42.77 MW	61.92 TQ	WABLS	3/16
	Tacoma-Lakewood PMSA, WA	H	28.28 FQ	32.25 MW	42.32 TQ	WABLS	3/16
	West Virginia	Y	52050 FQ	66070 MW	105960 TQ	USBLS	5/15
	Wisconsin	Y	56110 FQ	70160 MW	93110 TQ	USBLS	5/15
	Madison MSA, WI	Y	58210 FQ	68020 MW	87110 TQ	USBLS	5/15
	Milwaukee-Waukesha-West Allis MSA, WI	Y	58670 FQ	71970 MW	95470 TQ	USBLS	5/15
	Puerto Rico	Y	24880 FQ	33170 MW	49810 TQ	USBLS	5/15
	San Juan-Carolina-Caguas MSA, PR	Y	24520 FQ	32340 MW	48130 TQ	USBLS	5/15
Financial Investigator Municipal Government	Bakersfield, CA	Y		45442 AW		CACIT	6/28/16
Financial Manager	Alabama	Y	77477 AE	128735 AW	154369 AEX	ALBLS	6/16
	Birmingham-Hoover MSA, AL	Y	82069 AE	138769 AW	167109 AEX	ALBLS	6/16
	Alaska	Y	77140 FQ	100900 MW	138030 TQ	USBLS	5/15
	Anchorage MSA, AK	Y	80340 FQ	108500 MW	152110 TQ	USBLS	5/15
	Arizona	Y	78080 FQ	98950 MW	138150 TQ	USBLS	5/15
	Phoenix-Mesa-Scottsdale MSA, AZ	Y	82970 FQ	103520 MW	145330 TQ	USBLS	5/15
	Tucson MSA, AZ	Y	67860 FQ	83390 MW	107150 TQ	USBLS	5/15
	Arkansas	Y	53440 FQ	84740 MW	124800 TQ	USBLS	5/15
	Little Rock-North Little Rock- Conway MSA, AR	Y	50310 FQ	83000 MW	119350 TQ	USBLS	5/15
	California	H	46.08 FQ	63.73 MW	89.30 TQ	CABLS	1/16-3/16
	Anaheim-Santa Ana-Irvine PMSA, CA	H	45.04 FQ	62.68 MW	85.53 TQ	CABLS	1/16-3/16
	Los Angeles-Long Beach- Glendale PMSA, CA	H	49.67 FQ	66.60 MW		CABLS	1/16-3/16
	Oakland-Hayward-Berkeley PMSA, CA	H	47.03 FQ	66.61 MW		CABLS	1/16-3/16
	Riverside-San Bernardino- Ontario MSA, CA	H	39.83 FQ	53.21 MW	66.66 TQ	CABLS	1/16-3/16
	Sacramento–Roseville– Arden-Arcade MSA, CA	H	39.69 FQ	52.41 MW	71.95 TQ	CABLS	1/16-3/16
	San Diego-Carlsbad MSA, CA	H	45.50 FQ	62.16 MW	86.19 TQ	CABLS	1/16-3/16

	San Francisco-Redwood City-
	  South San Francisco PMSA,
	  CA
		H	59.53 FQ	84.18 MW		CABLS	1/16-3/16

	Colorado	Y	107790 FQ	136980 MW	181280 TQ	USBLS	5/15
	Denver-Aurora-Lakewood MSA, CO	Y	112680 FQ	142620 MW		USBLS	5/15
	Connecticut	Y		128952 MW		CTBLS	1/16-3/16
	Bridgeport-Stamford-Norwalk MSA, CT	Y	97070 FQ	131750 MW		USBLS	5/15
	Hartford-West Hartford-East Hartford MSA, CT	Y	100550 FQ	130590 MW	166000 TQ	USBLS	5/15
	Delaware	Y	113970 FQ	142000 MW		USBLS	5/15
	Wilmington PMSA, DE-MD- NJ	Y	114400 FQ	142960 MW	186010 TQ	USBLS	5/15
	District of Columbia	Y	118050 FQ	139510 MW	163840 TQ	USBLS	5/15

	Washington-Arlington-
	  Alexandria PMSA, DC-VA-
	  MD-WV
		Y	116510 FQ	139520 MW	174340 TQ	USBLS	5/15

	Florida	H	38.14 AE	59.69 MW	82.89 AEX	FLBLS	7/16-9/16

	Fort Lauderdale-Pompano
	  Beach-Deerfield Beach
	  PMSA, FL
		H	38.56 AE	60.51 MW	84.13 AEX	FLBLS	7/16-9/16

	Miami-Miami Beach-Kendall PMSA, FL	H	44.40 AE	69.78 MW	92.10 AEX	FLBLS	7/16-9/16
	Orlando-Kissimmee-Sanford MSA, FL	H	36.17 AE	57.48 MW	78.36 AEX	FLBLS	7/16-9/16
	Tampa-St. Petersburg- Clearwater MSA, FL	H	38.71 AE	60.19 MW	84.27 AEX	FLBLS	7/16-9/16
	Georgia	Y	88560 FQ	122220 MW	162880 TQ	USBLS	5/15
	Atlanta-Sandy Springs- Roswell MSA, GA	Y	96400 FQ	129660 MW	169400 TQ	USBLS	5/15

AE	Average entry wage	AWR	Average wage range	H	Hourly	LR	Low end range	MTC	Median total compensation	TCC	Total cash compensation
AEX	Average experienced wage	B	Biweekly	HI	Highest wage paid	M	Monthly	MW	Median wage paid	TQ	Third quartile wage
ATC	Average total compensation	D	Daily	HR	High end range	MCC	Median cash compensation	MWR	Median wage range	W	Weekly
AW	Average wage paid	FQ	First quartile wage	LO	Lowest wage paid	ME	Median entry wage	S	See annotated source	Y	Yearly

Occupation/Type/Industry	Location	Per	Low	Mid	High	Source	Date
Financial Manager	Augusta-Richmond County						
	MSA, GA-SC	Y	64950 FQ	84490 MW	119870 TQ	USBLS	5/15
	Hawaii	Y	66590 FQ	87870 MW	117440 TQ	USBLS	5/15
	Urban Honolulu MSA, HI	Y	69040 FQ	91560 MW	122360 TQ	USBLS	5/15
	Idaho	Y	58060 FQ	81080 MW	107750 TQ	USBLS	5/15
	Boise City MSA, ID	Y	58880 FQ	86560 MW	114590 TQ	USBLS	5/15
	Illinois	Y	76110 FQ	109700 MW	156940 TQ	USBLS	5/15
	Chicago-Naperville-Arlington						
	Heights PMSA, IL	Y	81590 FQ	115860 MW	165810 TQ	USBLS	5/15
	Lake County-Kenosha County						
	PMSA, IL-WI	Y	86270 FQ	122320 MW	164980 TQ	USBLS	5/15
	Indiana	Y	64070 FQ	94010 MW	129040 TQ	USBLS	5/15
	Gary PMSA, IN	Y	58420 FQ	82080 MW	109560 TQ	USBLS	5/15
	Indianapolis-Carmel-Anderson						
	MSA, IN	Y	75780 FQ	104720 MW	139000 TQ	USBLS	5/15
	Iowa	Y	70370 FQ	96350 MW	128250 TQ	USBLS	5/15
	Des Moines-West Des Moines						
	MSA, IA	Y	80820 FQ	108220 MW	148800 TQ	USBLS	5/15
	Kansas	Y	75010 FQ	98980 MW	132890 TQ	USBLS	5/15
	Wichita MSA, KS	Y	64200 FQ	91380 MW	119760 TQ	USBLS	5/15
	Kentucky	Y	62280 FQ	87260 MW	120380 TQ	USBLS	5/15
	Louisville-Jefferson County						
	MSA, KY-IN	Y	64500 FQ	92960 MW	133760 TQ	USBLS	5/15
	Louisiana	Y	64440 FQ	84010 MW	117640 TQ	USBLS	5/15
	Baton Rouge MSA, LA	Y	72560 FQ	92880 MW	122600 TQ	USBLS	5/15
	Lake Charles MSA, LA	Y	60020 FQ	73700 MW	100170 TQ	USBLS	5/15
	New Orleans-Metairie MSA,						
	LA	Y	66590 FQ	89000 MW	122700 TQ	USBLS	5/15
	Maine	Y	70470 FQ	90070 MW	116320 TQ	USBLS	5/15
	Portland-South Portland MSA,						
	ME	Y	79460 FQ	94540 MW	123810 TQ	USBLS	5/15
	Maryland	Y	76825 AE	135857 MW	165373 AEX	MDBLS	4/16
	Baltimore-Columbia-Towson						
	MSA, MD	Y	89820 FQ	120350 MW	157750 TQ	USBLS	5/15
	Salisbury MSA, MD-DE	Y	79820 FQ	106910 MW	137360 TQ	USBLS	5/15
	Massachusetts	Y	82250 FQ	115870 MW	162420 TQ	USBLS	5/15
	Boston-Cambridge-Newton						
	NECTA, MA	Y	91060 FQ	125790 MW	174880 TQ	USBLS	5/15
	Lawrence-Methuen Town-						
	Salem NECTA, MA-NH	Y	70230 FQ	94070 MW	134290 TQ	USBLS	5/15
	Worcester MSA, MA-CT	Y	65730 FQ	88930 MW	130450 TQ	USBLS	5/15
	Michigan	Y	77620 FQ	101530 MW	137270 TQ	USBLS	5/15
	Detroit-Dearborn-Livonia						
	PMSA, MI	Y	80060 FQ	107740 MW	153740 TQ	USBLS	5/15
	Grand Rapids-Wyoming MSA,						
	MI	Y	77050 FQ	99180 MW	126510 TQ	USBLS	5/15
	Minnesota	Y	91754 FQ	119717 MW	158624 TQ	MNBLS	1/16-3/16
	Minneapolis-St. Paul-						
	Bloomington MSA, MN-WI	Y	97932 FQ	126383 MW	166041 TQ	MNBLS	1/16-3/16
	Mississippi	Y	55370 FQ	79630 MW	110820 TQ	USBLS	5/15
	Jackson MSA, MS	Y	58390 FQ	81050 MW	116930 TQ	USBLS	5/15
	Missouri	Y	82090 FQ	112760 MW	152360 TQ	USBLS	5/15
	Kansas City MSA, MO-KS	Y	89520 FQ	115180 MW	153840 TQ	USBLS	5/15
	St. Louis MSA, MO-IL	Y	85680 FQ	119170 MW	160450 TQ	USBLS	5/15
	Montana	Y	71620 FQ	92140 MW	119910 TQ	USBLS	5/15
	Billings MSA, MT	Y	72510 FQ	103170 MW	144870 TQ	USBLS	5/15
	Nebraska	Y	86645 FQ	115245 MW	164775 TQ	NEBLS	7/16-9/16
	Omaha-Council Bluffs MSA,						
	NE-IA	Y	90005 FQ	118380 MW	172780 TQ	NEBLS	7/16-9/16
	Nevada	Y	64760 FQ	86800 MW	119310 TQ	USBLS	5/15
	Las Vegas-Henderson-Paradise						
	MSA, NV	Y	66600 FQ	88350 MW	120270 TQ	USBLS	5/15
	New Hampshire	H	32.10 AE	49.25 MW	70.74 AEX	NHBLS	6/16
	Manchester NECTA, NH	H	36.28 AE	48.71 MW	74.16 AEX	NHBLS	6/16
	Nashua NECTA, NH-MA	Y	84250 FQ	108100 MW	150930 TQ	USBLS	5/15
	New Jersey	Y	110160 FQ	143840 MW		USBLS	5/15
	Camden PMSA, NJ	Y	104370 FQ	135950 MW	181410 TQ	USBLS	5/15
	Newark PMSA, NJ-PA	Y	116350 FQ	153060 MW		USBLS	5/15
	Trenton MSA, NJ	Y	113160 FQ	141410 MW		USBLS	5/15
	New Mexico	Y	66270 FQ	88100 MW	116300 TQ	USBLS	5/15
	Albuquerque MSA, NM	Y	71980 FQ	93570 MW	120580 TQ	USBLS	5/15
	New York	Y	95410 AE	169500 MW		NYBLS	1/16-3/16

AE	Average entry wage	AWR	Average wage range	H	Hourly
AEX	Average experienced wage	B	Biweekly	HI	Highest wage paid
ATC	Average total compensation	D	Daily	HR	High end range
AW	Average wage paid	FQ	First quartile wage	LO	Lowest wage paid

LR	Low end range	
M	Monthly	
MCC	Median cash compensation	
ME	Median entry wage	

MTC	Median total compensation	
MW	Median wage paid	
MWR	Median wage range	
S	See annotated source	

TCC	Total cash compensation
TQ	Third quartile wage
W	Weekly
Y	Yearly

Occupation/Type/Industry	Location	Per	Low	Mid	High	Source	Date
Financial Manager	Buffalo-Cheektowaga-Niagara Falls MSA, NY	Y	84090 FQ	112470 MW	145750 TQ	USBLS	5/15
	Nassau County-Suffolk County PMSA, NY	Y	100020 FQ	140170 MW		USBLS	5/15
	New York-Jersey City-White Plains PMSA, NY-NJ	Y	122960 FQ	175980 MW		USBLS	5/15
	Rochester MSA, NY	Y	85980 FQ	117530 MW	155120 TQ	USBLS	5/15
	North Carolina	Y	92480 FQ	121370 MW	162430 TQ	USBLS	5/15
	Charlotte-Concord-Gastonia MSA, NC-SC	Y	106190 FQ	138360 MW	182370 TQ	USBLS	5/15
	Raleigh MSA, NC	Y	89990 FQ	110130 MW	147260 TQ	USBLS	5/15
	North Dakota	Y	79050 FQ	98750 MW	125450 TQ	USBLS	5/15
	Fargo MSA, ND-MN	Y	80080 FQ	102070 MW	130320 TQ	USBLS	5/15
	Ohio	Y	76670 FQ	106320 MW	144630 TQ	USBLS	5/15
	Cincinnati MSA, OH-KY-IN	Y	87270 FQ	114740 MW	152090 TQ	USBLS	5/15
	Cleveland-Elyria MSA, OH	Y	76610 FQ	108890 MW	147530 TQ	USBLS	5/15
	Columbus MSA, OH	Y	87330 FQ	116870 MW	160150 TQ	USBLS	5/15
	Oklahoma	Y	59730 FQ	85670 MW	120330 TQ	USBLS	5/15
	Oklahoma City MSA, OK	Y	64510 FQ	87390 MW	125970 TQ	USBLS	5/15
	Tulsa MSA, OK	Y	77310 FQ	104560 MW	137330 TQ	USBLS	5/15
	Oregon	H	35.62 FQ	48.55 MW	65.15 TQ	ORBLS	2016
	Portland-Vancouver-Hillsboro MSA, OR-WA	Y	76430 FQ	105760 MW	138670 TQ	USBLS	5/15
	Pennsylvania	Y	97440 FQ	131020 MW	174980 TQ	USBLS	5/15
	Allentown-Bethlehem-Easton MSA, PA-NJ	Y	92390 FQ	121110 MW	157620 TQ	USBLS	5/15
	Harrisburg-Carlisle MSA, PA	Y	84170 FQ	111300 MW	147500 TQ	USBLS	5/15
	Montgomery County-Bucks County-Chester County PMSA, PA	Y	109800 FQ	145230 MW		USBLS	5/15
	Philadelphia PMSA, PA	Y	113450 FQ	150560 MW		USBLS	5/15
	Pittsburgh MSA, PA	Y	104010 FQ	130690 MW	169230 TQ	USBLS	5/15
	Rhode Island	Y	99640 FQ	126600 MW	161110 TQ	USBLS	5/15
	Providence-Warwick MSA, RI-MA	Y	93750 FQ	121750 MW	157000 TQ	USBLS	5/15
	South Carolina	Y	74270 FQ	98760 MW	137470 TQ	USBLS	5/15
	Charleston-North Charleston MSA, SC	Y	76810 FQ	103080 MW	128230 TQ	USBLS	5/15
	Columbia MSA, SC	Y	71170 FQ	92970 MW	136210 TQ	USBLS	5/15
	Greenville-Anderson-Mauldin MSA, SC	Y	80780 FQ	105580 MW	148980 TQ	USBLS	5/15
	South Dakota	Y	98790 FQ	118140 MW	148100 TQ	USBLS	5/15
	Sioux Falls MSA, SD	Y	108610 FQ	128720 MW	157550 TQ	USBLS	5/15
	Tennessee	Y	61220 FQ	88280 MW	126290 TQ	USBLS	5/15
	Knoxville MSA, TN	Y	64870 FQ	94200 MW	137730 TQ	USBLS	5/15
	Memphis MSA, TN-MS-AR	Y	63000 FQ	95240 MW	134140 TQ	USBLS	5/15
	Nashville-Davidson–Murfreesboro–Franklin MSA, TN	Y	66260 FQ	92800 MW	128430 TQ	USBLS	5/15
	Texas	Y	95560 FQ	128870 MW	175760 TQ	USBLS	5/15
	Austin-Round Rock MSA, TX	Y	85580 FQ	125570 MW	169250 TQ	USBLS	5/15
	Dallas-Plano-Irving PMSA, TX	Y	103930 FQ	134710 MW	180250 TQ	USBLS	5/15
	Fort Worth-Arlington PMSA, TX	Y	83840 FQ	112280 MW	152170 TQ	USBLS	5/15
	Houston-The Woodlands-Sugar Land MSA, TX	Y	105860 FQ	139610 MW		USBLS	5/15
	San Antonio-New Braunfels MSA, TX	Y	101360 FQ	135950 MW		USBLS	5/15
	Utah	Y	71120 FQ	97680 MW	135930 TQ	USBLS	5/15
	Ogden-Clearfield MSA, UT	Y	66670 FQ	98640 MW	123750 TQ	USBLS	5/15
	Provo-Orem MSA, UT	Y	73170 FQ	99040 MW	126260 TQ	USBLS	5/15
	Salt Lake City MSA, UT	Y	74990 FQ	102610 MW	146260 TQ	USBLS	5/15
	Vermont	Y	82260 FQ	106140 MW	144840 TQ	USBLS	5/15
	Burlington-South Burlington MSA, VT	Y	96480 FQ	121920 MW	165290 TQ	USBLS	5/15
	Virginia	Y	99320 FQ	132370 MW	174860 TQ	USBLS	5/15
	Richmond MSA, VA	Y	91900 FQ	126330 MW	173450 TQ	USBLS	5/15
	Virginia Beach-Norfolk-Newport News MSA, VA-NC	Y	90820 FQ	116900 MW	145710 TQ	USBLS	5/15
	Washington	H	38.31 FQ	52.73 MW	69.86 TQ	WABLS	3/16
	Seattle-Bellevue-Everett PMSA, WA	H	45.40 FQ	59.40 MW	76.69 TQ	WABLS	3/16

AE Average entry wage	**AWR** Average wage range	**H** Hourly	**LR** Low end range	**MTC** Median total compensation	**TCC** Total cash compensation
AEX Average experienced wage	**B** Biweekly	**HI** Highest wage paid	**M** Monthly	**MW** Median wage paid	**TQ** Third quartile wage
ATC Average total compensation	**D** Daily	**HR** High end range	**MCC** Median cash compensation	**MWR** Median wage range	**W** Weekly
AW Average wage paid	**FQ** First quartile wage	**LO** Lowest wage paid	**ME** Median entry wage	**S** See annotated source	**Y** Yearly

Occupation/Type/Industry	Location	Per	Low	Mid	High	Source	Date
Financial Manager	Tacoma-Lakewood PMSA, WA	H	33.27 FQ	43.67 MW	58.37 TQ	WABLS	3/16
	West Virginia	Y	56160 FQ	79710 MW	112780 TQ	USBLS	5/15
	Huntington-Ashland MSA, WV-KY-OH	Y	57560 FQ	78060 MW	116240 TQ	USBLS	5/15
	Wisconsin	Y	78710 FQ	103540 MW	142700 TQ	USBLS	5/15
	Madison MSA, WI	Y	84480 FQ	104860 MW	145600 TQ	USBLS	5/15
	Milwaukee-Waukesha-West Allis MSA, WI	Y	84460 FQ	116830 MW	156500 TQ	USBLS	5/15
	Wyoming	Y	75390 FQ	91210 MW	118200 TQ	USBLS	5/15
	Cheyenne MSA, WY	Y	74440 FQ	83180 MW	101420 TQ	USBLS	5/15
	Puerto Rico	Y	48140 FQ	68980 MW	99070 TQ	USBLS	5/15
	San Juan-Carolina-Caguas MSA, PR	Y	50590 FQ	71060 MW	102570 TQ	USBLS	5/15
	Virgin Islands	Y	63860 FQ	74310 MW	88200 TQ	USBLS	5/15
	Guam	Y	48810 FQ	61550 MW	90450 TQ	USBLS	5/15
Financial Quantitative Analyst	United States	Y		72000 AW		SKU01	2016
Fine Artist, Including Painter, Sculptor, and Illustrator	Alabama	Y	31212 AE	53097 AW	64034 AEX	ALBLS	6/16
	Phoenix-Mesa-Scottsdale MSA, AZ	Y	23470 FQ	39400 MW	66530 TQ	USBLS	5/15
	Arkansas	Y	17530 FQ	19350 MW	71030 TQ	USBLS	5/15
	Little Rock-North Little Rock-Conway MSA, AR	Y	17510 FQ	19430 MW	50980 TQ	USBLS	5/15
	California	H	19.63 FQ	29.81 MW	42.40 TQ	CABLS	1/16-3/16
	Anaheim-Santa Ana-Irvine PMSA, CA	H	16.74 FQ	28.12 MW	41.87 TQ	CABLS	1/16-3/16
	Los Angeles-Long Beach-Glendale PMSA, CA	H	21.62 FQ	30.05 MW	49.78 TQ	CABLS	1/16-3/16
	Oakland-Hayward-Berkeley PMSA, CA	H	17.14 FQ	19.01 MW	36.91 TQ	CABLS	1/16-3/16
	Riverside-San Bernardino-Ontario MSA, CA	H	35.27 FQ	39.69 MW	45.58 TQ	CABLS	1/16-3/16
	Sacramento–Roseville–Arden-Arcade MSA, CA	H	22.43 FQ	27.88 MW	31.17 TQ	CABLS	1/16-3/16
	San Diego-Carlsbad MSA, CA	H	9.54 FQ	24.92 MW	29.57 TQ	CABLS	1/16-3/16
	Colorado	Y	23240 FQ	30380 MW	42530 TQ	USBLS	5/15
	Denver-Aurora-Lakewood MSA, CO	Y	28050 FQ	30920 MW	35960 TQ	USBLS	5/15
	Connecticut	Y		53017 MW		CTBLS	1/16-3/16
	Washington-Arlington-Alexandria PMSA, DC-VA-MD-WV	Y	40740 FQ	53630 MW	74930 TQ	USBLS	5/15
	Florida	H	12.76 AE	21.02 MW	32.95 AEX	FLBLS	7/16-9/16
	Orlando-Kissimmee-Sanford MSA, FL	H	15.86 AE	22.50 MW	29.58 AEX	FLBLS	7/16-9/16
	Georgia	Y	23400 FQ	43280 MW	57120 TQ	USBLS	5/15
	Atlanta-Sandy Springs-Roswell MSA, GA	Y	23430 FQ	44230 MW	57960 TQ	USBLS	5/15
	Illinois	Y	33530 FQ	48660 MW	62930 TQ	USBLS	5/15
	Chicago-Naperville-Arlington Heights PMSA, IL	Y	36300 FQ	50840 MW	63940 TQ	USBLS	5/15
	Indiana	Y	30230 FQ	35900 MW	46560 TQ	USBLS	5/15
	Indianapolis-Carmel-Anderson MSA, IN	Y	18710 FQ	35220 MW	40680 TQ	USBLS	5/15
	Iowa	Y	35180 FQ	44420 MW	52690 TQ	USBLS	5/15
	Kansas	Y	29750 FQ	44390 MW	54610 TQ	USBLS	5/15
	Kentucky	Y	19850 FQ	32480 MW	51480 TQ	USBLS	5/15
	Louisiana	Y	25630 FQ	28640 MW	41650 TQ	USBLS	5/15
	Maryland	Y	27263 AE	41542 MW	48682 AEX	MDBLS	4/16
	Baltimore-Columbia-Towson MSA, MD	Y	27340 FQ	30980 MW	51770 TQ	USBLS	5/15
	Massachusetts	Y	28860 FQ	40510 MW	56950 TQ	USBLS	5/15
	Boston-Cambridge-Newton NECTA, MA	Y	29710 FQ	40490 MW	55660 TQ	USBLS	5/15
	Detroit-Dearborn-Livonia PMSA, MI	Y	31240 FQ	36850 MW	47420 TQ	USBLS	5/15
	Minnesota	Y	42852 FQ	52368 MW	67630 TQ	MNBLS	1/16-3/16
	Minneapolis-St. Paul-Bloomington MSA, MN-WI	Y	43135 FQ	52399 MW	67358 TQ	MNBLS	1/16-3/16
	Missouri	Y	21280 FQ	28000 MW	38190 TQ	USBLS	5/15

AE	Average entry wage	AWR	Average wage range	H	Hourly	LR	Low end range	MTC	Median total compensation	TCC	Total cash compensation
AEX	Average experienced wage	B	Biweekly	HI	Highest wage paid	M	Monthly	MW	Median wage paid	TQ	Third quartile wage
ATC	Average total compensation	D	Daily	HR	High end range	MCC	Median cash compensation	MWR	Median wage range	W	Weekly
AW	Average wage paid	FQ	First quartile wage	LO	Lowest wage paid	ME	Median entry wage	S	See annotated source	Y	Yearly

590

Occupation/Type/Industry	Location	Per	Low	Mid	High	Source	Date
Fine Artist, Including Painter, Sculptor, and Illustrator	St. Louis MSA, MO-IL	Y	21210 FQ	27960 MW	51900 TQ	USBLS	5/15
	Nebraska	Y	26640 FQ	33075 MW	38910 TQ	NEBLS	7/16-9/16
	Omaha-Council Bluffs MSA, NE-IA	Y	24430 FQ	29430 MW	37965 TQ	NEBLS	7/16-9/16
	Nevada	Y	37070 FQ	42710 MW	46770 TQ	USBLS	5/15
	Las Vegas-Henderson-Paradise MSA, NV	Y	37780 FQ	42820 MW	46690 TQ	USBLS	5/15
	Newark PMSA, NJ-PA	Y	30120 FQ	44170 MW	58680 TQ	USBLS	5/15
	Albuquerque MSA, NM	Y	27100 FQ	29440 MW	33010 TQ	USBLS	5/15
	New York	Y	38310 AE	61310 MW	92640 AEX	NYBLS	1/16-3/16
	Nassau County-Suffolk County PMSA, NY	Y	54700 FQ	64400 MW	72700 TQ	USBLS	5/15
	New York-Jersey City-White Plains PMSA, NY-NJ	Y	43200 FQ	55050 MW	75670 TQ	USBLS	5/15
	North Carolina	Y	37910 FQ	45030 MW	55930 TQ	USBLS	5/15
	Raleigh MSA, NC	Y	40340 FQ	47490 MW	57920 TQ	USBLS	5/15
	Ohio	Y	17940 FQ	18980 MW	29790 TQ	USBLS	5/15
	Cincinnati MSA, OH-KY-IN	Y	17810 FQ	18670 MW	19520 TQ	USBLS	5/15
	Cleveland-Elyria MSA, OH	Y	17700 FQ	18540 MW	19370 TQ	USBLS	5/15
	Columbus MSA, OH	Y	17800 FQ	18730 MW	19660 TQ	USBLS	5/15
	Dayton MSA, OH	Y	26020 FQ	33090 MW	44640 TQ	USBLS	5/15
	Oklahoma	Y	34230 FQ	46640 MW	59670 TQ	USBLS	5/15
	Oklahoma City MSA, OK	Y	47660 FQ	56210 MW	64430 TQ	USBLS	5/15
	Oregon	H	16.72 FQ	20.13 MW	27.33 TQ	ORBLS	2016
	Portland-Vancouver-Hillsboro MSA, OR-WA	Y	36590 FQ	45510 MW	58780 TQ	USBLS	5/15
	Pennsylvania	Y	29890 FQ	36840 MW	54570 TQ	USBLS	5/15
	Harrisburg-Carlisle MSA, PA	Y	32580 FQ	35690 MW	38800 TQ	USBLS	5/15
	Montgomery County-Bucks County-Chester County PMSA, PA	Y	35510 FQ	46010 MW	82320 TQ	USBLS	5/15
	Philadelphia PMSA, PA	Y	29740 FQ	38750 MW	57340 TQ	USBLS	5/15
	Pittsburgh MSA, PA	Y	25200 FQ	32850 MW	48430 TQ	USBLS	5/15
	South Carolina	Y	17600 FQ	19500 MW	29170 TQ	USBLS	5/15
	Tennessee	Y	18360 FQ	31450 MW	39940 TQ	USBLS	5/15
	Nashville-Davidson–Murfreesboro–Franklin MSA, TN	Y	18630 FQ	31820 MW	38910 TQ	USBLS	5/15
	Texas	Y	19400 FQ	44100 MW	61320 TQ	USBLS	5/15
	Austin-Round Rock MSA, TX	Y	44500 FQ	50840 MW	57410 TQ	USBLS	5/15
	Dallas-Plano-Irving PMSA, TX	Y	48940 FQ	63160 MW	79820 TQ	USBLS	5/15
	Fort Worth-Arlington PMSA, TX	Y	45540 FQ	59110 MW	73730 TQ	USBLS	5/15
	Houston-The Woodlands-Sugar Land MSA, TX	Y	18610 FQ	29410 MW	44010 TQ	USBLS	5/15
	San Antonio-New Braunfels MSA, TX	Y	16280 FQ	17470 MW	18670 TQ	USBLS	5/15
	Utah	Y	26090 FQ	43130 MW	60290 TQ	USBLS	5/15
	Ogden-Clearfield MSA, UT	Y	41880 FQ	46020 MW	54960 TQ	USBLS	5/15
	Provo-Orem MSA, UT	Y	25340 FQ	30030 MW	43620 TQ	USBLS	5/15
	Salt Lake City MSA, UT	Y	17650 FQ	19500 MW	50240 TQ	USBLS	5/15
	Virginia	Y	36880 FQ	49360 MW	64660 TQ	USBLS	5/15
	Richmond MSA, VA	Y	23410 FQ	33100 MW	66900 TQ	USBLS	5/15
	Virginia Beach-Norfolk-Newport News MSA, VA-NC	Y	46430 FQ	55070 MW	64760 TQ	USBLS	5/15
	Washington	H	24.38 FQ	34.63 MW	44.37 TQ	WABLS	3/16
	Seattle-Bellevue-Everett PMSA, WA	H	27.84 FQ	37.53 MW	45.80 TQ	WABLS	3/16
	Wisconsin	Y	29100 FQ	35980 MW	47010 TQ	USBLS	5/15
	Madison MSA, WI	Y	29630 FQ	35440 MW	45210 TQ	USBLS	5/15
	Milwaukee-Waukesha-West Allis MSA, WI	Y	30620 FQ	37530 MW	47590 TQ	USBLS	5/15
Fingerprint and Evidence Technician							
Department of Justice, State Government	Billings, MT	H			14.69 HI	MTGOV	2016
Fingerprint Classifier							
Police Department, Municipal Government	Long Beach, CA	Y		46477 AW		CACIT	6/28/16

AE	Average entry wage	AWR	Average wage range	H	Hourly	
AEX	Average experienced wage	B	Biweekly	HI	Highest wage paid	
ATC	Average total compensation	D	Daily	HR	High end range	
AW	Average wage paid	FQ	First quartile wage	LO	Lowest wage paid	

LR	Low end range	MTC	Median total compensation	TCC	Total cash compensation
M	Monthly	MW	Median wage paid	TQ	Third quartile wage
MCC	Median cash compensation	MWR	Median wage range	W	Weekly
ME	Median entry wage	S	See annotated source	Y	Yearly

Occupation/Type/Industry	Location	Per	Low	Mid	High	Source	Date
Fingerprint Examiner							
Attorney General's Office, State Government	Ohio	H	22.13 LO		25.36 HI	OHGOV	2015
Fingerprint Technician							
Municipal Government	Colorado Springs, CO	Y	39085 LO		53742 HI	COSPRS	2017
Fire Apparatus Mechanic							
Public Works Department, Municipal Government	Garden Grove, CA	Y			68590 HI	CACIT	6/28/16
Fire Apparatus Operator							
Municipal Government	Alameda, CA	Y		103861 AW		CACIT	6/28/16
Fire Boat Mechanic							
Municipal Government	Detroit, MI	M	3592 LO		3625 HI	DETGOV	2016
Fire Boat Pilot							
Municipal Government	Los Angeles, CA	Y		109255 AW		CACIT	6/23/16
Municipal Government	Seattle, WA	H	42.47 LO		50.20 HI	CSSS	1/1/14
Fire Chief							
Municipal Government	Canyon Lake, CA	Y			36020 HI	CACIT	6/28/16
Municipal Government	Carlsbad, CA	Y			189308 HI	CACIT	6/28/16
Municipal Government	Fremont, CA	Y			226907 HI	CACIT	6/28/16
Municipal Government	San Francisco, CA	B			11734 HI	SFGOV	2016-2018
Municipal Government	Colorado Springs, CO	Y	128188 LO		176258 HI	COSPRS	2017
Municipal Government	Pembroke, GA	Y	31175 LO		43906 HI	GACTY01	2016
Municipal Government	Sandy Springs, GA	Y	108475 LO		166532 HI	GACTY01	2016
Municipal Government	Waycross, GA	Y	59342 LO		90293 HI	GACTY01	2016
Municipal Government	Ashfield, MA	Y			7500 HI	FRCOG	2016
Municipal Government	Conway, MA	Y			6873 HI	FRCOG	2016
Municipal Government	Greenfield, MA	Y			98000 HI	FRCOG	2016
Municipal Government	New Salem, MA	Y			24510 HI	FRCOG	2016
Municipal Government	Detroit, MI	M	6233 LO		10408 HI	DETGOV	2016
Municipal Government	Lyon Township, MI	Y			75000 HI	HTL01	2015
Fire Code Inspector							
Fire Department, Municipal Government	Vernon, CA	Y			64747 HI	CACIT	6/28/16
Fire Engineer							
Municipal Government	Arcadia, CA	Y		102623 AW		CACIT	6/28/16
Municipal Government	Carlsbad, CA	Y		79204 AW		CACIT	6/28/16
Municipal Government	Gonzales, CA	Y			82431 HI	CACIT	7/5/16
Fire Equipment Technician							
Municipal Government	Seattle, WA	H	26.78 LO		28.86 HI	CSSS	3/9/16
Fire Inspector							
Hazardous Materials, Municipal Government	Downey, CA	Y			96223 HI	CACIT	6/28/16
Fire Inspector and Investigator	Alabama	Y	40206 AE	56402 AW	64494 AEX	ALBLS	6/16
	Birmingham-Hoover MSA, AL	Y	49493 AE	62034 AW	68304 AEX	ALBLS	6/16
	Arizona	Y	48160 FQ	59410 MW	71660 TQ	USBLS	5/15
	Phoenix-Mesa-Scottsdale MSA, AZ	Y	54910 FQ	67090 MW	75900 TQ	USBLS	5/15
	Tucson MSA, AZ	Y	46600 FQ	53730 MW	58940 TQ	USBLS	5/15
	Arkansas	Y	37120 FQ	47530 MW	55210 TQ	USBLS	5/15
	California	H	32.09 FQ	40.60 MW	52.34 TQ	CABLS	1/16-3/16
	Anaheim-Santa Ana-Irvine PMSA, CA	H	34.62 FQ	40.63 MW	49.46 TQ	CABLS	1/16-3/16
	Los Angeles-Long Beach-Glendale PMSA, CA	H	39.14 FQ	50.63 MW	56.98 TQ	CABLS	1/16-3/16
	Oakland-Hayward-Berkeley PMSA, CA	H	29.60 FQ	43.01 MW	54.42 TQ	CABLS	1/16-3/16
	Riverside-San Bernardino-Ontario MSA, CA	H	30.21 FQ	34.51 MW	41.25 TQ	CABLS	1/16-3/16
	Sacramento–Roseville–Arden-Arcade MSA, CA	H	27.66 FQ	39.29 MW	46.04 TQ	CABLS	1/16-3/16
	San Diego-Carlsbad MSA, CA	H	29.98 FQ	35.17 MW	39.43 TQ	CABLS	1/16-3/16

AE	Average entry wage	AWR	Average wage range	H	Hourly	LR	Low end range	MTC	Median total compensation	TCC	Total cash compensation
AEX	Average experienced wage	B	Biweekly	HI	Highest wage paid	M	Monthly	MW	Median wage paid	TQ	Third quartile wage
ATC	Average total compensation	D	Daily	HR	High end range	MCC	Median cash compensation	MWR	Median wage range	W	Weekly
AW	Average wage paid	FQ	First quartile wage	LO	Lowest wage paid	ME	Median entry wage	S	See annotated source	Y	Yearly

Occupation/Type/Industry	Location	Per	Low	Mid	High	Source	Date
Fire Inspector and Investigator	San Francisco-Redwood City-South San Francisco PMSA, CA	H	48.45 FQ	66.67 MW	73.79 TQ	CABLS	1/16-3/16
	Colorado	Y	54520 FQ	61400 MW	78610 TQ	USBLS	5/15
	Denver-Aurora-Lakewood MSA, CO	Y	54220 FQ	58700 MW	63150 TQ	USBLS	5/15
	Connecticut	Y		65253 MW		CTBLS	1/16-3/16
	Bridgeport-Stamford-Norwalk MSA, CT	Y	45430 FQ	80610 MW	92030 TQ	USBLS	5/15
	Hartford-West Hartford-East Hartford MSA, CT	Y	44140 FQ	62220 MW	81670 TQ	USBLS	5/15
	Delaware	Y	33680 FQ	45150 MW	57440 TQ	USBLS	5/15
	Wilmington PMSA, DE-MD-NJ	Y	31610 FQ	37720 MW	57020 TQ	USBLS	5/15
	Washington-Arlington-Alexandria PMSA, DC-VA-MD-WV	Y	53660 FQ	61360 MW	79020 TQ	USBLS	5/15
	Florida	H	20.32 AE	28.71 MW	35.13 AEX	FLBLS	7/16-9/16
	Fort Lauderdale-Pompano Beach-Deerfield Beach PMSA, FL	H	24.05 AE	33.73 MW	39.80 AEX	FLBLS	7/16-9/16
	Miami-Miami Beach-Kendall PMSA, FL	H	22.41 AE	28.60 MW	35.31 AEX	FLBLS	7/16-9/16
	Orlando-Kissimmee-Sanford MSA, FL	H	19.65 AE	24.04 MW	28.96 AEX	FLBLS	7/16-9/16
	Tampa-St. Petersburg-Clearwater MSA, FL	H	21.43 AE	28.98 MW	33.32 AEX	FLBLS	7/16-9/16
	Georgia	Y	37550 FQ	46090 MW	62210 TQ	USBLS	5/15
	Atlanta-Sandy Springs-Roswell MSA, GA	Y	45020 FQ	58350 MW	79040 TQ	USBLS	5/15
	Augusta-Richmond County MSA, GA-SC	Y	37870 FQ	45310 MW	54410 TQ	USBLS	5/15
	Idaho	Y	53540 FQ	64800 MW	73400 TQ	USBLS	5/15
	Illinois	Y	31240 FQ	58270 MW	82630 TQ	USBLS	5/15
	Indiana	Y	36400 FQ	48010 MW	62070 TQ	USBLS	5/15
	Gary PMSA, IN	Y	31060 FQ	46380 MW	62200 TQ	USBLS	5/15
	Indianapolis-Carmel-Anderson MSA, IN	Y	36860 FQ	44830 MW	62240 TQ	USBLS	5/15
	Kansas	Y	40490 FQ	50040 MW	69570 TQ	USBLS	5/15
	Kentucky	Y	36700 FQ	44970 MW	56780 TQ	USBLS	5/15
	Louisville-Jefferson County MSA, KY-IN	Y	51350 FQ	57180 MW	62940 TQ	USBLS	5/15
	Louisiana	Y	42230 FQ	53590 MW	68490 TQ	USBLS	5/15
	Baton Rouge MSA, LA	Y	53840 FQ	67540 MW	80060 TQ	USBLS	5/15
	New Orleans-Metairie MSA, LA	Y	37680 FQ	46360 MW	60980 TQ	USBLS	5/15
	Maine	Y	39710 FQ	43360 MW	48610 TQ	USBLS	5/15
	Maryland	Y	39426 AE	57648 MW	66759 AEX	MDBLS	4/16
	Baltimore-Columbia-Towson MSA, MD	Y	44100 FQ	58100 MW	71670 TQ	USBLS	5/15
	Massachusetts	Y	50680 FQ	77950 MW	90470 TQ	USBLS	5/15
	Boston-Cambridge-Newton NECTA, MA	Y	73770 FQ	86610 MW	94510 TQ	USBLS	5/15
	Michigan	Y	52050 FQ	63950 MW	74390 TQ	USBLS	5/15
	Detroit-Dearborn-Livonia PMSA, MI	Y	42680 FQ	46100 MW	65980 TQ	USBLS	5/15
	Minnesota	Y	55916 FQ	66682 MW	74589 TQ	MNBLS	1/16-3/16
	Minneapolis-St. Paul-Bloomington MSA, MN-WI	Y	58906 FQ	68520 MW	75558 TQ	MNBLS	1/16-3/16
	Mississippi	Y	30080 FQ	39690 MW	47400 TQ	USBLS	5/15
	Missouri	Y	37980 FQ	49810 MW	64840 TQ	USBLS	5/15
	Kansas City MSA, MO-KS	Y	58330 FQ	67730 MW	74490 TQ	USBLS	5/15
	St. Louis MSA, MO-IL	Y	49720 FQ	66020 MW	84050 TQ	USBLS	5/15
	Nevada	Y	69590 FQ	84110 MW	94510 TQ	USBLS	5/15
	Las Vegas-Henderson-Paradise MSA, NV	Y	78530 FQ	88340 MW	96460 TQ	USBLS	5/15
	New Hampshire	H	18.35 AE	27.24 MW	30.89 AEX	NHBLS	6/16
	New Jersey	Y	40690 FQ	51890 MW	68300 TQ	USBLS	5/15
	Camden PMSA, NJ	Y	38210 FQ	53210 MW	68200 TQ	USBLS	5/15
	Newark PMSA, NJ-PA	Y	44300 FQ	53680 MW	72490 TQ	USBLS	5/15
	Trenton MSA, NJ	Y	47600 FQ	63520 MW	78580 TQ	USBLS	5/15
	New York	Y	41910 AE	58730 MW	71490 AEX	NYBLS	1/16-3/16

AE	Average entry wage	AWR	Average wage range	H	Hourly	LR	Low end range	MTC	Median total compensation	TCC	Total cash compensation
AEX	Average experienced wage	B	Biweekly	HI	Highest wage paid	M	Monthly	MW	Median wage paid	TQ	Third quartile wage
ATC	Average total compensation	D	Daily	HR	High end range	MCC	Median cash compensation	MWR	Median wage range	W	Weekly
AW	Average wage paid	FQ	First quartile wage	LO	Lowest wage paid	ME	Median entry wage	S	See annotated source	Y	Yearly

Occupation/Type/Industry	Location	Per	Low	Mid	High	Source	Date
Fire Inspector and Investigator	Nassau County-Suffolk County PMSA, NY	Y	52200 FQ	58960 MW	67770 TQ	USBLS	5/15
	New York-Jersey City-White Plains PMSA, NY-NJ	Y	41480 FQ	50760 MW	67810 TQ	USBLS	5/15
	Rochester MSA, NY	Y	40230 FQ	56050 MW	69120 TQ	USBLS	5/15
	North Carolina	Y	40780 FQ	51410 MW	58610 TQ	USBLS	5/15
	Charlotte-Concord-Gastonia MSA, NC-SC	Y	46050 FQ	53670 MW	59110 TQ	USBLS	5/15
	Ohio	Y	43630 FQ	53800 MW	70980 TQ	USBLS	5/15
	Cincinnati MSA, OH-KY-IN	Y	37560 FQ	47580 MW	70210 TQ	USBLS	5/15
	Cleveland-Elyria MSA, OH	Y	41090 FQ	47770 MW	61010 TQ	USBLS	5/15
	Columbus MSA, OH	Y	45920 FQ	53680 MW	81120 TQ	USBLS	5/15
	Oklahoma	Y	46970 FQ	67450 MW	83330 TQ	USBLS	5/15
	Oklahoma City MSA, OK	Y	45450 FQ	59910 MW	81090 TQ	USBLS	5/15
	Tulsa MSA, OK	Y	58910 FQ	77270 MW	90260 TQ	USBLS	5/15
	Oregon	H	39.52 FQ	43.43 MW	47.75 TQ	ORBLS	2016
	Portland-Vancouver-Hillsboro MSA, OR-WA	Y	81630 FQ	89900 MW	98210 TQ	USBLS	5/15
	Pennsylvania	Y	39920 FQ	46550 MW	60500 TQ	USBLS	5/15
	Allentown-Bethlehem-Easton MSA, PA-NJ	Y	31960 FQ	38470 MW	47980 TQ	USBLS	5/15
	Montgomery County-Bucks County-Chester County PMSA, PA	Y	40370 FQ	47000 MW	67180 TQ	USBLS	5/15
	Pittsburgh MSA, PA	Y	39620 FQ	49600 MW	58430 TQ	USBLS	5/15
	Rhode Island	Y	48480 FQ	58530 MW	68040 TQ	USBLS	5/15
	Providence-Warwick MSA, RI-MA	Y	49420 FQ	59330 MW	68150 TQ	USBLS	5/15
	South Carolina	Y	34720 FQ	40160 MW	49140 TQ	USBLS	5/15
	Greenville-Anderson-Mauldin MSA, SC	Y	34730 FQ	38760 MW	45600 TQ	USBLS	5/15
	Tennessee	Y	39740 FQ	51760 MW	59680 TQ	USBLS	5/15
	Memphis MSA, TN-MS-AR	Y	51360 FQ	56420 MW	61480 TQ	USBLS	5/15
	Nashville-Davidson– Murfreesboro–Franklin MSA, TN	Y	39130 FQ	50400 MW	60150 TQ	USBLS	5/15
	Texas	Y	44140 FQ	55730 MW	71400 TQ	USBLS	5/15
	Austin-Round Rock MSA, TX	Y	65520 FQ	72720 MW	79960 TQ	USBLS	5/15
	Dallas-Plano-Irving PMSA, TX	Y	47400 FQ	58100 MW	73280 TQ	USBLS	5/15
	Fort Worth-Arlington PMSA, TX	Y	52700 FQ	65550 MW	74770 TQ	USBLS	5/15
	Houston-The Woodlands- Sugar Land MSA, TX	Y	52380 FQ	67420 MW	75800 TQ	USBLS	5/15
	San Antonio-New Braunfels MSA, TX	Y	44880 FQ	53340 MW	61920 TQ	USBLS	5/15
	Utah	Y	52870 FQ	63840 MW	73000 TQ	USBLS	5/15
	Salt Lake City MSA, UT	Y	56620 FQ	66800 MW	74530 TQ	USBLS	5/15
	Virginia	Y	45830 FQ	54410 MW	61420 TQ	USBLS	5/15
	Virginia Beach-Norfolk- Newport News MSA, VA-NC	Y	42540 FQ	51740 MW	58980 TQ	USBLS	5/15
	Washington	H	36.04 FQ	43.75 MW	49.65 TQ	WABLS	3/16
	Seattle-Bellevue-Everett PMSA, WA	H	40.34 FQ	44.85 MW	49.43 TQ	WABLS	3/16
	Tacoma-Lakewood PMSA, WA	H	32.82 FQ	36.26 MW	41.44 TQ	WABLS	3/16
	West Virginia	Y	26940 FQ	29340 MW	35240 TQ	USBLS	5/15
	Huntington-Ashland MSA, WV-KY-OH	Y	26960 FQ	29470 MW	36000 TQ	USBLS	5/15
	Wisconsin	Y	39340 FQ	57240 MW	70920 TQ	USBLS	5/15
	Milwaukee-Waukesha-West Allis MSA, WI	Y	44350 FQ	62650 MW	72390 TQ	USBLS	5/15
Fire Marshal							
Municipal Government	Berkeley, CA	Y			74725 HI	CACIT	6/28/16
Municipal Government	Escondido, CA	Y			62256 HI	CACIT	6/28/16
Municipal Government	Hollister, CA	Y			112964 HI	CACIT	6/28/16
Municipal Government	Manteca, CA	Y			102362 HI	CACIT	7/4/16
Municipal Government	Visalia, CA	Y			90725 HI	CACIT	6/28/16
Municipal Government	Colorado Springs, CO	Y	90178 LO		123992 HI	COSPRS	2017
Municipal Government	Hephzibah, GA	Y	32000 LO		39000 HI	GACTY01	2016
Municipal Government	Peachtree City, GA	Y	69220 LO		103829 HI	GACTY01	2016

AE	Average entry wage	AWR	Average wage range	H	Hourly	LR	Low end range	MTC	Median total compensation	TCC	Total cash compensation
AEX	Average experienced wage	B	Biweekly	HI	Highest wage paid	M	Monthly	MW	Median wage paid	TQ	Third quartile wage
ATC	Average total compensation	D	Daily	HR	High end range	MCC	Median cash compensation	MWR	Median wage range	W	Weekly
AW	Average wage paid	FQ	First quartile wage	LO	Lowest wage paid	ME	Median entry wage	S	See annotated source	Y	Yearly

Occupation/Type/Industry	Location	Per	Low	Mid	High	Source	Date
Fire Photographer							
Municipal Government	Detroit, MI	M	3533 LO		3800 HI	DETGOV	2016
Fire Plan Check Engineer							
Municipal Government	Riverside, CA	Y		85502 AW		CACIT	7/6/16
Fire Plan Draftsperson							
Municipal Government	Santa Clara, CA	Y			81576 HI	CACIT	6/28/16
Fire Plans Examiner							
Municipal Government	Bakersfield, CA	Y			68694 HI	CACIT	6/28/16
Fire Prevention Analyst							
Municipal Government	Fountain Valley, CA	Y			82660 HI	CACIT	6/28/16
Fire Prevention Coordinator							
Municipal Government	Glendale, CA	Y			110466 HI	CACIT	6/28/16
Fire Prevention Inspector							
Municipal Government	Burbank, CA	Y		58207 AW		CACIT	6/28/16
Fire Prevention Instructor							
Municipal Government	Detroit, MI	M	5324 LO		5501 HI	DETGOV	2016
Fire Protection Analyst							
Municipal Government	Costa Mesa, CA	Y			85200 HI	CACIT	6/28/16
Fire Protection Engineer	United States	Y	65000 LO			FPE	2016
Municipal Government	Milpitas, CA	Y			130283 HI	CACIT	6/28/16
Municipal Government	Oakland, CA	Y		94074 AW		CACIT	6/28/16
Municipal Government	Seattle, WA	H	38.99 LO		45.55 HI	CSSS	1/13/16
Fire Safety Inspector							
State Government	North Carolina	Y	36761 LO		58006 HI	NCGOV	7/1/16
Fire Sprinkler Inspector							
Building and Safety Department, Municipal Government	Los Angeles, CA	Y		81407 AW		CACIT	6/23/16
Fire Trainee							
Municipal Government	Colorado Springs, CO	M			3856 HI	COSPRS	2017
Firearms Examiner							
Police Department, Municipal Government	Los Angeles, CA	Y			116386 HI	CACIT	6/23/16
Firefighter	Alabama	Y	27429 AE	40958 AW	47722 AEX	ALBLS	6/16
	Birmingham-Hoover MSA, AL	Y	27635 AE	42039 AW	49236 AEX	ALBLS	6/16
	Alaska	Y	48970 FQ	57860 MW	69520 TQ	USBLS	5/15
	Anchorage MSA, AK	Y	53240 FQ	65090 MW	73870 TQ	USBLS	5/15
	Arizona	Y	33970 FQ	45700 MW	56470 TQ	USBLS	5/15
	Phoenix-Mesa-Scottsdale MSA, AZ	Y	42400 FQ	51510 MW	59490 TQ	USBLS	5/15
	Tucson MSA, AZ	Y	33120 FQ	40790 MW	48430 TQ	USBLS	5/15
	Arkansas	Y	23290 FQ	30620 MW	42550 TQ	USBLS	5/15
	Little Rock-North Little Rock-Conway MSA, AR	Y	28240 FQ	40410 MW	51960 TQ	USBLS	5/15
	California	H	24.39 FQ	32.48 MW	41.53 TQ	CABLS	1/16-3/16
	Anaheim-Santa Ana-Irvine PMSA, CA	H	31.42 FQ	37.18 MW	43.78 TQ	CABLS	1/16-3/16
	El Centro MSA, CA	H	16.00 FQ	21.33 MW	26.19 TQ	CABLS	1/16-3/16
	Los Angeles-Long Beach-Glendale PMSA, CA	H	32.50 FQ	36.93 MW	44.54 TQ	CABLS	1/16-3/16
	Oakland-Hayward-Berkeley PMSA, CA	H	36.45 FQ	43.68 MW	50.18 TQ	CABLS	1/16-3/16
	Riverside-San Bernardino-Ontario MSA, CA	H	21.25 FQ	25.84 MW	31.76 TQ	CABLS	1/16-3/16
	Sacramento–Roseville–Arden-Arcade MSA, CA	H	23.19 FQ	30.35 MW	38.94 TQ	CABLS	1/16-3/16
	San Diego-Carlsbad MSA, CA	H	24.78 FQ	30.14 MW	38.69 TQ	CABLS	1/16-3/16
	San Francisco-Redwood City-South San Francisco PMSA, CA	H	37.10 FQ	43.34 MW	48.18 TQ	CABLS	1/16-3/16
	Colorado	Y	36410 FQ	50950 MW	65820 TQ	USBLS	5/15

Occupation/Type/Industry	Location	Per	Low	Mid	High	Source	Date
Firefighter	Denver-Aurora-Lakewood MSA, CO	Y	47380 FQ	63580 MW	73360 TQ	USBLS	5/15
	Connecticut	Y		64662 MW		CTBLS	1/16-3/16
	Bridgeport-Stamford-Norwalk MSA, CT	Y	56180 FQ	66750 MW	74000 TQ	USBLS	5/15
	Hartford-West Hartford-East Hartford MSA, CT	Y	52850 FQ	64920 MW	72680 TQ	USBLS	5/15
	Delaware	Y	33820 FQ	43750 MW	55260 TQ	USBLS	5/15
	Wilmington PMSA, DE-MD-NJ	Y	33880 FQ	44060 MW	55810 TQ	USBLS	5/15
	Washington-Arlington-Alexandria PMSA, DC-VA-MD-WV	Y	47370 FQ	56920 MW	68980 TQ	USBLS	5/15
	Florida	H	15.69 AE	23.75 MW	30.78 AEX	FLBLS	7/16-9/16
	Fort Lauderdale-Pompano Beach-Deerfield Beach PMSA, FL	H	22.82 AE	30.59 MW	34.84 AEX	FLBLS	7/16-9/16
	Miami-Miami Beach-Kendall PMSA, FL	H	27.03 AE	40.07 MW	42.51 AEX	FLBLS	7/16-9/16
	Orlando-Kissimmee-Sanford MSA, FL	H	15.12 AE	19.73 MW	24.66 AEX	FLBLS	7/16-9/16
	Tampa-St. Petersburg-Clearwater MSA, FL	H	17.16 AE	22.50 MW	26.30 AEX	FLBLS	7/16-9/16
	Georgia	Y	26470 FQ	33710 MW	40470 TQ	USBLS	5/15
	Atlanta-Sandy Springs-Roswell MSA, GA	Y	31200 FQ	36010 MW	43060 TQ	USBLS	5/15
	Hawaii	Y	45940 FQ	54280 MW	61970 TQ	USBLS	5/15
	Urban Honolulu MSA, HI	Y	52320 FQ	58320 MW	66830 TQ	USBLS	5/15
	Idaho	Y	21390 FQ	36200 MW	48900 TQ	USBLS	5/15
	Boise City MSA, ID	Y	33340 FQ	44210 MW	52230 TQ	USBLS	5/15
	Illinois	Y	24260 FQ	48090 MW	75790 TQ	USBLS	5/15
	Chicago-Naperville-Arlington Heights PMSA, IL	Y	33250 FQ	65270 MW	85050 TQ	USBLS	5/15
	Lake County-Kenosha County PMSA, IL-WI	Y	26440 FQ	30800 MW	69930 TQ	USBLS	5/15
	Indiana	Y	38060 FQ	47180 MW	55310 TQ	USBLS	5/15
	Gary PMSA, IN	Y	29200 FQ	42390 MW	50890 TQ	USBLS	5/15
	Indianapolis-Carmel-Anderson MSA, IN	Y	40740 FQ	50190 MW	57450 TQ	USBLS	5/15
	Iowa	Y	25290 FQ	40500 MW	48620 TQ	USBLS	5/15
	Des Moines-West Des Moines MSA, IA	Y	25000 FQ	32720 MW	46120 TQ	USBLS	5/15
	Kansas	Y	28650 FQ	35500 MW	44380 TQ	USBLS	5/15
	Wichita MSA, KS	Y	29180 FQ	35210 MW	41820 TQ	USBLS	5/15
	Kentucky	Y	23890 FQ	31570 MW	38350 TQ	USBLS	5/15
	Louisville-Jefferson County MSA, KY-IN	Y	31550 FQ	37040 MW	45460 TQ	USBLS	5/15
	Louisiana	Y	23340 FQ	30270 MW	41060 TQ	USBLS	5/15
	Baton Rouge MSA, LA	Y	23860 FQ	28820 MW	36830 TQ	USBLS	5/15
	New Orleans-Metairie MSA, LA	Y	25050 FQ	34650 MW	50740 TQ	USBLS	5/15
	Maine	Y	25700 FQ	29760 MW	39880 TQ	USBLS	5/15
	Portland-South Portland MSA, ME	Y	26010 FQ	29460 MW	37440 TQ	USBLS	5/15
	Maryland	Y	41302 AE	56528 MW	64142 AEX	MDBLS	4/16
	Baltimore-Columbia-Towson MSA, MD	Y	47630 FQ	56410 MW	67310 TQ	USBLS	5/15
	Salisbury MSA, MD-DE	Y	35890 FQ	42340 MW	47980 TQ	USBLS	5/15
	Massachusetts	Y	45960 FQ	57320 MW	70450 TQ	USBLS	5/15
	Boston-Cambridge-Newton NECTA, MA	Y	52790 FQ	62450 MW	78520 TQ	USBLS	5/15
	Peabody-Salem-Beverly NECTA, MA	Y	53320 FQ	57090 MW	60870 TQ	USBLS	5/15
	Worcester MSA, MA-CT	Y	37450 FQ	52580 MW	65040 TQ	USBLS	5/15
	Michigan	Y	30060 FQ	43840 MW	56190 TQ	USBLS	5/15
	Detroit-Dearborn-Livonia PMSA, MI	Y	37930 FQ	47980 MW	57590 TQ	USBLS	5/15
	Grand Rapids-Wyoming MSA, MI	Y	39330 FQ	49410 MW	55820 TQ	USBLS	5/15
	Minnesota	Y	23055 FQ	30023 MW	38900 TQ	MNBLS	1/16-3/16
	Minneapolis-St. Paul-Bloomington MSA, MN-WI	Y	24045 FQ	29801 MW	38425 TQ	MNBLS	1/16-3/16

AE	Average entry wage	AWR	Average wage range	H	Hourly	LR	Low end range	MTC	Median total compensation	TCC	Total cash compensation
AEX	Average experienced wage	B	Biweekly	HI	Highest wage paid	M	Monthly	MW	Median wage paid	TQ	Third quartile wage
ATC	Average total compensation	D	Daily	HR	High end range	MCC	Median cash compensation	MWR	Median wage range	W	Weekly
AW	Average wage paid	FQ	First quartile wage	LO	Lowest wage paid	ME	Median entry wage	S	See annotated source	Y	Yearly

Occupation/Type/Industry	Location	Per	Low	Mid	High	Source	Date
Firefighter	Mississippi	Y	22880 FQ	29170 MW	37160 TQ	USBLS	5/15
	Jackson MSA, MS	Y	22240 FQ	25940 MW	30410 TQ	USBLS	5/15
	Missouri	Y	30390 FQ	46170 MW	59460 TQ	USBLS	5/15
	Kansas City MSA, MO-KS	Y	30420 FQ	44830 MW	57400 TQ	USBLS	5/15
	St. Louis MSA, MO-IL	Y	41140 FQ	54760 MW	69970 TQ	USBLS	5/15
	Montana	Y	41040 FQ	47180 MW	55020 TQ	USBLS	5/15
	Nebraska	Y	43395 FQ	52295 MW	59465 TQ	NEBLS	7/16-9/16
	Omaha-Council Bluffs MSA, NE-IA	Y	51050 FQ	56205 MW	61380 TQ	NEBLS	7/16-9/16
	Nevada	Y	47330 FQ	58910 MW	73060 TQ	USBLS	5/15
	Las Vegas-Henderson-Paradise MSA, NV	Y	55670 FQ	65780 MW	77970 TQ	USBLS	5/15
	New Hampshire	H	12.62 AE	21.01 MW	25.02 AEX	NHBLS	6/16
	Manchester NECTA, NH	H	20.41 AE	26.72 MW	29.57 AEX	NHBLS	6/16
	Nashua NECTA, NH-MA	Y	50250 FQ	55720 MW	61280 TQ	USBLS	5/15
	New Jersey	Y	61670 FQ	85770 MW	99450 TQ	USBLS	5/15
	Camden PMSA, NJ	Y	63190 FQ	72380 MW	83720 TQ	USBLS	5/15
	Newark PMSA, NJ-PA	Y	78730 FQ	90310 MW	99620 TQ	USBLS	5/15
	Trenton MSA, NJ	Y	66810 FQ	83490 MW	96020 TQ	USBLS	5/15
	New Mexico	Y	29850 FQ	34960 MW	40890 TQ	USBLS	5/15
	New York	Y	52220 AE	70770 MW	76270 AEX	NYBLS	1/16-3/16
	Buffalo-Cheektowaga-Niagara Falls MSA, NY	Y	57040 FQ	65980 MW	73480 TQ	USBLS	5/15
	Nassau County-Suffolk County PMSA, NY	Y	55600 FQ	83690 MW	103760 TQ	USBLS	5/15
	New York-Jersey City-White Plains PMSA, NY-NJ	Y	64930 FQ	72510 MW	79950 TQ	USBLS	5/15
	Rochester MSA, NY	Y	60060 FQ	70440 MW	77350 TQ	USBLS	5/15
	North Carolina	Y	24010 FQ	31190 MW	41150 TQ	USBLS	5/15
	Charlotte-Concord-Gastonia MSA, NC-SC	Y	25470 FQ	32780 MW	43240 TQ	USBLS	5/15
	Raleigh MSA, NC	Y	27270 FQ	34680 MW	44030 TQ	USBLS	5/15
	North Dakota	Y	34460 FQ	42500 MW	51130 TQ	USBLS	5/15
	Fargo MSA, ND-MN	Y	34840 FQ	38990 MW	44560 TQ	USBLS	5/15
	Ohio	Y	27640 FQ	43010 MW	60140 TQ	USBLS	5/15
	Cincinnati MSA, OH-KY-IN	Y	27350 FQ	35700 MW	56340 TQ	USBLS	5/15
	Cleveland-Elyria MSA, OH	Y	32280 FQ	50070 MW	59340 TQ	USBLS	5/15
	Columbus MSA, OH	Y	31170 FQ	58600 MW	70480 TQ	USBLS	5/15
	Oklahoma	Y	30740 FQ	41520 MW	54680 TQ	USBLS	5/15
	Oklahoma City MSA, OK	Y	42800 FQ	54890 MW	68860 TQ	USBLS	5/15
	Tulsa MSA, OK	Y	31660 FQ	38490 MW	48520 TQ	USBLS	5/15
	Oregon	H	25.34 FQ	32.25 MW	37.05 TQ	ORBLS	2016
	Portland-Vancouver-Hillsboro MSA, OR-WA	Y	64270 FQ	72480 MW	80620 TQ	USBLS	5/15
	Pennsylvania	Y	43600 FQ	56580 MW	67700 TQ	USBLS	5/15
	Allentown-Bethlehem-Easton MSA, PA-NJ	Y	37060 FQ	52030 MW	58010 TQ	USBLS	5/15
	Harrisburg-Carlisle MSA, PA	Y	39780 FQ	45820 MW	55450 TQ	USBLS	5/15
	Montgomery County-Bucks County-Chester County PMSA, PA	Y	35390 FQ	49030 MW	57670 TQ	USBLS	5/15
	Philadelphia PMSA, PA	Y	55840 FQ	67930 MW	74710 TQ	USBLS	5/15
	Pittsburgh MSA, PA	Y	49060 FQ	56730 MW	63990 TQ	USBLS	5/15
	Rhode Island	Y	47580 FQ	54730 MW	60100 TQ	USBLS	5/15
	Providence-Warwick MSA, RI-MA	Y	47520 FQ	54960 MW	60590 TQ	USBLS	5/15
	South Carolina	Y	26580 FQ	32260 MW	40440 TQ	USBLS	5/15
	Charleston-North Charleston MSA, SC	Y	27330 FQ	34820 MW	41910 TQ	USBLS	5/15
	Columbia MSA, SC	Y	26380 FQ	30780 MW	41080 TQ	USBLS	5/15
	Greenville-Anderson-Mauldin MSA, SC	Y	27590 FQ	32010 MW	40320 TQ	USBLS	5/15
	South Dakota	Y	32670 FQ	39900 MW	50510 TQ	USBLS	5/15
	Rapid City MSA, SD	Y	30110 FQ	34360 MW	38420 TQ	USBLS	5/15
	Sioux Falls MSA, SD	Y	40830 FQ	51600 MW	58900 TQ	USBLS	5/15
	Tennessee	Y	27490 FQ	37930 MW	49850 TQ	USBLS	5/15
	Knoxville MSA, TN	Y	22620 FQ	33470 MW	46110 TQ	USBLS	5/15
	Memphis MSA, TN-MS-AR	Y	34660 FQ	50410 MW	56690 TQ	USBLS	5/15
	Nashville-Davidson–Murfreesboro–Franklin MSA, TN	Y	34530 FQ	41010 MW	47470 TQ	USBLS	5/15
	Texas	Y	36530 FQ	48690 MW	60780 TQ	USBLS	5/15

AE Average entry wage	**AWR** Average wage range	**LR** Low end range	**MTC** Median total compensation	**TCC** Total cash compensation
AEX Average experienced wage	**B** Biweekly	**HI** Highest wage paid	**M** Monthly	**MW** Median wage paid	**TQ** Third quartile wage
ATC Average total compensation	**D** Daily	**HR** High end range	**MCC** Median cash compensation	**MWR** Median wage range	**W** Weekly
AW Average wage paid	**FQ** First quartile wage	**LO** Lowest wage paid	**ME** Median entry wage	**S** See annotated source	**Y** Yearly

Occupation/Type/Industry	Location	Per	Low	Mid	High	Source	Date
Firefighter	Austin-Round Rock MSA, TX	Y	38220 FQ	51120 MW	64880 TQ	USBLS	5/15
	Dallas-Plano-Irving PMSA, TX	Y	39080 FQ	51080 MW	61740 TQ	USBLS	5/15
	Fort Worth-Arlington PMSA, TX	Y	45720 FQ	60390 MW	73870 TQ	USBLS	5/15
	Houston-The Woodlands-Sugar Land MSA, TX	Y	32860 FQ	46190 MW	57160 TQ	USBLS	5/15
	San Antonio-New Braunfels MSA, TX	Y	46280 FQ	59460 MW	71560 TQ	USBLS	5/15
	Utah	Y	22370 FQ	31130 MW	44970 TQ	USBLS	5/15
	Ogden-Clearfield MSA, UT	Y	24980 FQ	30310 MW	44250 TQ	USBLS	5/15
	Provo-Orem MSA, UT	Y	19010 FQ	25850 MW	33950 TQ	USBLS	5/15
	Salt Lake City MSA, UT	Y	29380 FQ	40850 MW	51220 TQ	USBLS	5/15
	Vermont	Y	28090 FQ	38020 MW	48730 TQ	USBLS	5/15
	Burlington-South Burlington MSA, VT	Y	39920 FQ	44280 MW	51290 TQ	USBLS	5/15
	Virginia	Y	41340 FQ	48730 MW	58920 TQ	USBLS	5/15
	Richmond MSA, VA	Y	44020 FQ	52530 MW	62550 TQ	USBLS	5/15
	Washington	H	25.53 FQ	34.98 MW	42.48 TQ	WABLS	3/16
	Seattle-Bellevue-Everett PMSA, WA	H	33.57 FQ	39.25 MW	44.58 TQ	WABLS	3/16
	Tacoma-Lakewood PMSA, WA	H	31.22 FQ	38.24 MW	47.38 TQ	WABLS	3/16
	West Virginia	Y	21410 FQ	29620 MW	39400 TQ	USBLS	5/15
	Huntington-Ashland MSA, WV-KY-OH	Y	28030 FQ	33990 MW	39650 TQ	USBLS	5/15
	Wisconsin	Y	20560 FQ	28250 MW	46180 TQ	USBLS	5/15
	Madison MSA, WI	Y	22150 FQ	28010 MW	51550 TQ	USBLS	5/15
	Wyoming	Y	35210 FQ	42480 MW	49400 TQ	USBLS	5/15
	Cheyenne MSA, WY	Y	38900 FQ	44730 MW	53260 TQ	USBLS	5/15
	Puerto Rico	Y	22540 FQ	25720 MW	28420 TQ	USBLS	5/15
	San Juan-Carolina-Caguas MSA, PR	Y	22670 FQ	25780 MW	28430 TQ	USBLS	5/15
First Aid Station Nurse							
Municipal Government	Detroit, MI	M	2358 LO		2717 HI	DETGOV	2016
First-Line Supervisor							
Construction Trade and Extraction Workers	Alabama	Y	39049 AE	58851 AW	68747 AEX	ALBLS	6/16
Construction Trade and Extraction Workers	Birmingham-Hoover MSA, AL	Y	40654 AE	62215 AW	72985 AEX	ALBLS	6/16
Construction Trade and Extraction Workers	Alaska	Y	69850 FQ	88650 MW	113500 TQ	USBLS	5/15
Construction Trade and Extraction Workers	Anchorage MSA, AK	Y	61610 FQ	89790 MW	120650 TQ	USBLS	5/15
Construction Trade and Extraction Workers	Arizona	Y	44830 FQ	57950 MW	76730 TQ	USBLS	5/15
Construction Trade and Extraction Workers	Phoenix-Mesa-Scottsdale MSA, AZ	Y	45600 FQ	59530 MW	80190 TQ	USBLS	5/15
Construction Trade and Extraction Workers	Tucson MSA, AZ	Y	41240 FQ	54460 MW	66740 TQ	USBLS	5/15
Construction Trade and Extraction Workers	Arkansas	Y	39640 FQ	48420 MW	61470 TQ	USBLS	5/15
Construction Trade and Extraction Workers	Little Rock-North Little Rock-Conway MSA, AR	Y	42910 FQ	51600 MW	63540 TQ	USBLS	5/15
Construction Trade and Extraction Workers	California	H	28.68 FQ	36.35 MW	46.36 TQ	CABLS	1/16-3/16
Construction Trade and Extraction Workers	Anaheim-Santa Ana-Irvine PMSA, CA	H	28.76 FQ	35.71 MW	45.85 TQ	CABLS	1/16-3/16
Construction Trade and Extraction Workers	Los Angeles-Long Beach-Glendale PMSA, CA	H	29.14 FQ	36.43 MW	45.17 TQ	CABLS	1/16-3/16
Construction Trade and Extraction Workers	Oakland-Hayward-Berkeley PMSA, CA	H	31.50 FQ	39.54 MW	47.69 TQ	CABLS	1/16-3/16
Construction Trade and Extraction Workers	Riverside-San Bernardino-Ontario MSA, CA	H	26.25 FQ	32.47 MW	41.81 TQ	CABLS	1/16-3/16
Construction Trade and Extraction Workers	Sacramento–Roseville–Arden-Arcade MSA, CA	H	30.10 FQ	36.17 MW	45.64 TQ	CABLS	1/16-3/16
Construction Trade and Extraction Workers	San Diego-Carlsbad MSA, CA	H	28.78 FQ	37.64 MW	45.92 TQ	CABLS	1/16-3/16
Construction Trade and Extraction Workers	San Francisco-Redwood City-South San Francisco PMSA, CA	H	34.45 FQ	46.73 MW	58.29 TQ	CABLS	1/16-3/16
Construction Trade and Extraction Workers	Colorado	Y	52190 FQ	64460 MW	79820 TQ	USBLS	5/15
Construction Trade and Extraction Workers	Denver-Aurora-Lakewood MSA, CO	Y	52850 FQ	65670 MW	81350 TQ	USBLS	5/15
Construction Trade and Extraction Workers	Connecticut	Y		73058 MW		CTBLS	1/16-3/16
Construction Trade and Extraction Workers	Bridgeport-Stamford-Norwalk MSA, CT	Y	60480 FQ	74680 MW	93550 TQ	USBLS	5/15
Construction Trade and Extraction Workers	Hartford-West Hartford-East Hartford MSA, CT	Y	56730 FQ	69870 MW	84960 TQ	USBLS	5/15
Construction Trade and Extraction Workers	Delaware	Y	56610 FQ	68190 MW	82590 TQ	USBLS	5/15

AE	Average entry wage	AWR	Average wage range	H	Hourly	LR Low end range	MTC Median total compensation	TCC Total cash compensation
AEX	Average experienced wage	B	Biweekly	HI	Highest wage paid	M Monthly	MW Median wage paid	TQ Third quartile wage
ATC	Average total compensation	D	Daily	HR	High end range	MCC Median cash compensation	MWR Median wage range	W Weekly
AW	Average wage paid	FQ	First quartile wage	LO	Lowest wage paid	ME Median entry wage	S See annotated source	Y Yearly

Occupation/Type/Industry	Location	Per	Low	Mid	High	Source	Date
First-Line Supervisor							
Construction Trade and Extraction Workers	Wilmington PMSA, DE-MD-NJ	Y	58110 FQ	70750 MW	87740 TQ	USBLS	5/15
Construction Trade and Extraction Workers	District of Columbia	Y	60460 FQ	75620 MW	92510 TQ	USBLS	5/15
Construction Trade and Extraction Workers	Washington-Arlington-Alexandria PMSA, DC-VA-MD-WV	Y	55120 FQ	68310 MW	85260 TQ	USBLS	5/15
Construction Trade and Extraction Workers	Florida	H	19.39 AE	27.24 MW	33.17 AEX	FLBLS	7/16-9/16
Construction Trade and Extraction Workers	Fort Lauderdale-Pompano Beach-Deerfield Beach PMSA, FL	H	22.87 AE	30.00 MW	37.10 AEX	FLBLS	7/16-9/16
Construction Trade and Extraction Workers	Miami-Miami Beach-Kendall PMSA, FL	H	20.56 AE	29.70 MW	36.19 AEX	FLBLS	7/16-9/16
Construction Trade and Extraction Workers	Orlando-Kissimmee-Sanford MSA, FL	H	19.50 AE	26.42 MW	31.70 AEX	FLBLS	7/16-9/16
Construction Trade and Extraction Workers	Tampa-St. Petersburg-Clearwater MSA, FL	H	18.86 AE	25.96 MW	31.17 AEX	FLBLS	7/16-9/16
Construction Trade and Extraction Workers	Georgia	Y	43030 FQ	55410 MW	70310 TQ	USBLS	5/15
Construction Trade and Extraction Workers	Atlanta-Sandy Springs-Roswell MSA, GA	Y	45700 FQ	58490 MW	73930 TQ	USBLS	5/15
Construction Trade and Extraction Workers	Augusta-Richmond County MSA, GA-SC	Y	44250 FQ	56400 MW	68740 TQ	USBLS	5/15
Construction Trade and Extraction Workers	Hawaii	Y	56320 FQ	74710 MW	92930 TQ	USBLS	5/15
Construction Trade and Extraction Workers	Urban Honolulu MSA, HI	Y	55530 FQ	76240 MW	92240 TQ	USBLS	5/15
Construction Trade and Extraction Workers	Idaho	Y	40110 FQ	52270 MW	63870 TQ	USBLS	5/15
Construction Trade and Extraction Workers	Boise City MSA, ID	Y	37470 FQ	48560 MW	61750 TQ	USBLS	5/15
Construction Trade and Extraction Workers	Illinois	Y	56540 FQ	76410 MW	94750 TQ	USBLS	5/15
Construction Trade and Extraction Workers	Chicago-Naperville-Arlington Heights PMSA, IL	Y	62560 FQ	85050 MW	99530 TQ	USBLS	5/15
Construction Trade and Extraction Workers	Lake County-Kenosha County PMSA, IL-WI	Y	53330 FQ	69700 MW	83780 TQ	USBLS	5/15
Construction Trade and Extraction Workers	Indiana	Y	48940 FQ	60750 MW	75940 TQ	USBLS	5/15
Construction Trade and Extraction Workers	Gary PMSA, IN	Y	58530 FQ	72280 MW	87810 TQ	USBLS	5/15
Construction Trade and Extraction Workers	Indianapolis-Carmel-Anderson MSA, IN	Y	51590 FQ	61720 MW	77810 TQ	USBLS	5/15
Construction Trade and Extraction Workers	Iowa	Y	44640 FQ	56560 MW	70190 TQ	USBLS	5/15
Construction Trade and Extraction Workers	Des Moines-West Des Moines MSA, IA	Y	45130 FQ	57920 MW	73560 TQ	USBLS	5/15
Construction Trade and Extraction Workers	Kansas	Y	44090 FQ	56570 MW	74980 TQ	USBLS	5/15
Construction Trade and Extraction Workers	Wichita MSA, KS	Y	40920 FQ	50790 MW	65290 TQ	USBLS	5/15
Construction Trade and Extraction Workers	Kentucky	Y	45200 FQ	57110 MW	71870 TQ	USBLS	5/15
Construction Trade and Extraction Workers	Louisville-Jefferson County MSA, KY-IN	Y	45910 FQ	58000 MW	72210 TQ	USBLS	5/15
Construction Trade and Extraction Workers	Louisiana	Y	47230 FQ	58420 MW	73270 TQ	USBLS	5/15
Construction Trade and Extraction Workers	Baton Rouge MSA, LA	Y	51580 FQ	60920 MW	75430 TQ	USBLS	5/15
Construction Trade and Extraction Workers	New Orleans-Metairie MSA, LA	Y	47530 FQ	58240 MW	72200 TQ	USBLS	5/15
Construction Trade and Extraction Workers	Maine	Y	42670 FQ	52870 MW	63000 TQ	USBLS	5/15
Construction Trade and Extraction Workers	Portland-South Portland MSA, ME	Y	43070 FQ	55310 MW	71220 TQ	USBLS	5/15
Construction Trade and Extraction Workers	Maryland	Y	48356 AE	68748 MW	78944 AEX	MDBLS	4/16
Construction Trade and Extraction Workers	Baltimore-Columbia-Towson MSA, MD	Y	53850 FQ	64120 MW	81450 TQ	USBLS	5/15
Construction Trade and Extraction Workers	Salisbury MSA, MD-DE	Y	49490 FQ	57380 MW	67870 TQ	USBLS	5/15
Construction Trade and Extraction Workers	Massachusetts	Y	59170 FQ	74450 MW	94190 TQ	USBLS	5/15
Construction Trade and Extraction Workers	Boston-Cambridge-Newton NECTA, MA	Y	64510 FQ	81680 MW	100620 TQ	USBLS	5/15
Construction Trade and Extraction Workers	Worcester MSA, MA-CT	Y	56140 FQ	65730 MW	78810 TQ	USBLS	5/15
Construction Trade and Extraction Workers	Michigan	Y	49390 FQ	59620 MW	76010 TQ	USBLS	5/15
Construction Trade and Extraction Workers	Detroit-Dearborn-Livonia PMSA, MI	Y	54100 FQ	63210 MW	78270 TQ	USBLS	5/15
Construction Trade and Extraction Workers	Grand Rapids-Wyoming MSA, MI	Y	51710 FQ	59250 MW	76070 TQ	USBLS	5/15
Construction Trade and Extraction Workers	Minnesota	Y	57342 FQ	69995 MW	81993 TQ	MNBLS	1/16-3/16
Construction Trade and Extraction Workers	Minneapolis-St. Paul-Bloomington MSA, MN-WI	Y	60501 FQ	72518 MW	86140 TQ	MNBLS	1/16-3/16
Construction Trade and Extraction Workers	Mississippi	Y	41110 FQ	50880 MW	64390 TQ	USBLS	5/15
Construction Trade and Extraction Workers	Jackson MSA, MS	Y	35890 FQ	46290 MW	60170 TQ	USBLS	5/15
Construction Trade and Extraction Workers	Missouri	Y	48030 FQ	64000 MW	79540 TQ	USBLS	5/15
Construction Trade and Extraction Workers	Kansas City MSA, MO-KS	Y	52340 FQ	68300 MW	86460 TQ	USBLS	5/15
Construction Trade and Extraction Workers	St. Louis MSA, MO-IL	Y	58820 FQ	72460 MW	91010 TQ	USBLS	5/15
Construction Trade and Extraction Workers	Montana	Y	48610 FQ	59920 MW	74840 TQ	USBLS	5/15

AE	Average entry wage	AWR	Average wage range	H	Hourly
AEX	Average experienced wage	B	Biweekly	HI	Highest wage paid
ATC	Average total compensation	D	Daily	HR	High end range
AW	Average wage paid	FQ	First quartile wage	LO	Lowest wage paid

LR	Low end range	MTC	Median total compensation	TCC	Total cash compensation
M	Monthly	MW	Median wage paid	TQ	Third quartile wage
MCC	Median cash compensation	MWR	Median wage range	W	Weekly
ME	Median entry wage	S	See annotated source	Y	Yearly

Occupation/Type/Industry	Location	Per	Low	Mid	High	Source	Date
First-Line Supervisor							
Construction Trade and Extraction Workers	Billings MSA, MT	Y	51870 FQ	62070 MW	81010 TQ	USBLS	5/15
Construction Trade and Extraction Workers	Nebraska	Y	44220 FQ	56020 MW	70035 TQ	NEBLS	7/16-9/16
Construction Trade and Extraction Workers	Omaha-Council Bluffs MSA, NE-IA	Y	51565 FQ	62960 MW	76320 TQ	NEBLS	7/16-9/16
Construction Trade and Extraction Workers	Nevada	Y	48860 FQ	66780 MW	85590 TQ	USBLS	5/15
Construction Trade and Extraction Workers	Las Vegas-Henderson-Paradise MSA, NV	Y	45970 FQ	64450 MW	84040 TQ	USBLS	5/15
Construction Trade and Extraction Workers	New Hampshire	H	20.91 AE	28.09 MW	34.80 AEX	NHBLS	6/16
Construction Trade and Extraction Workers	Manchester NECTA, NH	H	22.04 AE	30.80 MW	37.02 AEX	NHBLS	6/16
Construction Trade and Extraction Workers	Nashua NECTA, NH-MA	Y	46370 FQ	58830 MW	80330 TQ	USBLS	5/15
Construction Trade and Extraction Workers	New Jersey	Y	58590 FQ	73720 MW	94090 TQ	USBLS	5/15
Construction Trade and Extraction Workers	Camden PMSA, NJ	Y	57100 FQ	68890 MW	80290 TQ	USBLS	5/15
Construction Trade and Extraction Workers	Newark PMSA, NJ-PA	Y	59640 FQ	77270 MW	99020 TQ	USBLS	5/15
Construction Trade and Extraction Workers	Trenton MSA, NJ	Y	59930 FQ	74800 MW	93120 TQ	USBLS	5/15
Construction Trade and Extraction Workers	New Mexico	Y	42340 FQ	55480 MW	72680 TQ	USBLS	5/15
Construction Trade and Extraction Workers	Albuquerque MSA, NM	Y	38640 FQ	51090 MW	63870 TQ	USBLS	5/15
Construction Trade and Extraction Workers	New York	Y	55120 AE	81340 MW	101700 AEX	NYBLS	1/16-3/16
Construction Trade and Extraction Workers	Buffalo-Cheektowaga-Niagara Falls MSA, NY	Y	51270 FQ	64490 MW	77110 TQ	USBLS	5/15
Construction Trade and Extraction Workers	Nassau County-Suffolk County PMSA, NY	Y	66580 FQ	86440 MW	106790 TQ	USBLS	5/15
Construction Trade and Extraction Workers	New York-Jersey City-White Plains PMSA, NY-NJ	Y	68280 FQ	88310 MW	112840 TQ	USBLS	5/15
Construction Trade and Extraction Workers	Rochester MSA, NY	Y	54090 FQ	63690 MW	74910 TQ	USBLS	5/15
Construction Trade and Extraction Workers	North Carolina	Y	44940 FQ	55310 MW	66600 TQ	USBLS	5/15
Construction Trade and Extraction Workers	Charlotte-Concord-Gastonia MSA, NC-SC	Y	46380 FQ	56770 MW	69760 TQ	USBLS	5/15
Construction Trade and Extraction Workers	Raleigh MSA, NC	Y	46410 FQ	56880 MW	68490 TQ	USBLS	5/15
Construction Trade and Extraction Workers	North Dakota	Y	54400 FQ	70870 MW	91590 TQ	USBLS	5/15
Construction Trade and Extraction Workers	Fargo MSA, ND-MN	Y	47510 FQ	57890 MW	71240 TQ	USBLS	5/15
Construction Trade and Extraction Workers	Ohio	Y	50170 FQ	59710 MW	73410 TQ	USBLS	5/15
Construction Trade and Extraction Workers	Cincinnati MSA, OH-KY-IN	Y	51060 FQ	59990 MW	71420 TQ	USBLS	5/15
Construction Trade and Extraction Workers	Cleveland-Elyria MSA, OH	Y	51430 FQ	61220 MW	75370 TQ	USBLS	5/15
Construction Trade and Extraction Workers	Columbus MSA, OH	Y	52940 FQ	60320 MW	72100 TQ	USBLS	5/15
Construction Trade and Extraction Workers	Oklahoma	Y	44670 FQ	58610 MW	76270 TQ	USBLS	5/15
Construction Trade and Extraction Workers	Oklahoma City MSA, OK	Y	46330 FQ	58750 MW	72300 TQ	USBLS	5/15
Construction Trade and Extraction Workers	Tulsa MSA, OK	Y	45810 FQ	58240 MW	77070 TQ	USBLS	5/15
Construction Trade and Extraction Workers	Oregon	H	24.78 FQ	30.51 MW	38.17 TQ	ORBLS	2016
Construction Trade and Extraction Workers	Portland-Vancouver-Hillsboro MSA, OR-WA	Y	53710 FQ	67250 MW	81940 TQ	USBLS	5/15
Construction Trade and Extraction Workers	Pennsylvania	Y	52590 FQ	66710 MW	86410 TQ	USBLS	5/15
Construction Trade and Extraction Workers	Allentown-Bethlehem-Easton MSA, PA-NJ	Y	54540 FQ	67180 MW	85530 TQ	USBLS	5/15
Construction Trade and Extraction Workers	Harrisburg-Carlisle MSA, PA	Y	49450 FQ	62020 MW	76830 TQ	USBLS	5/15
Construction Trade and Extraction Workers	Montgomery County-Bucks County-Chester County PMSA, PA	Y	62580 FQ	79260 MW	100260 TQ	USBLS	5/15
Construction Trade and Extraction Workers	Philadelphia PMSA, PA	Y	70840 FQ	88510 MW	104520 TQ	USBLS	5/15
Construction Trade and Extraction Workers	Pittsburgh MSA, PA	Y	52890 FQ	65790 MW	81150 TQ	USBLS	5/15
Construction Trade and Extraction Workers	Rhode Island	Y	53770 FQ	67390 MW	85060 TQ	USBLS	5/15
Construction Trade and Extraction Workers	Providence-Warwick MSA, RI-MA	Y	53560 FQ	66060 MW	82150 TQ	USBLS	5/15
Construction Trade and Extraction Workers	South Carolina	Y	42360 FQ	53860 MW	66850 TQ	USBLS	5/15
Construction Trade and Extraction Workers	Charleston-North Charleston MSA, SC	Y	45470 FQ	57360 MW	70720 TQ	USBLS	5/15
Construction Trade and Extraction Workers	Columbia MSA, SC	Y	39130 FQ	50540 MW	64680 TQ	USBLS	5/15
Construction Trade and Extraction Workers	Greenville-Anderson-Mauldin MSA, SC	Y	40460 FQ	52970 MW	66770 TQ	USBLS	5/15
Construction Trade and Extraction Workers	South Dakota	Y	50230 FQ	58180 MW	68910 TQ	USBLS	5/15
Construction Trade and Extraction Workers	Sioux Falls MSA, SD	Y	52950 FQ	60550 MW	72930 TQ	USBLS	5/15
Construction Trade and Extraction Workers	Tennessee	Y	41570 FQ	52690 MW	69670 TQ	USBLS	5/15
Construction Trade and Extraction Workers	Knoxville MSA, TN	Y	40630 FQ	49310 MW	64590 TQ	USBLS	5/15
Construction Trade and Extraction Workers	Memphis MSA, TN-MS-AR	Y	41190 FQ	53480 MW	68000 TQ	USBLS	5/15
Construction Trade and Extraction Workers	Nashville-Davidson–Murfreesboro–Franklin MSA, TN	Y	44260 FQ	56140 MW	76840 TQ	USBLS	5/15
Construction Trade and Extraction Workers	Texas	Y	48300 FQ	62500 MW	79350 TQ	USBLS	5/15
Construction Trade and Extraction Workers	Austin-Round Rock MSA, TX	Y	49240 FQ	61450 MW	76320 TQ	USBLS	5/15
Construction Trade and Extraction Workers	Dallas-Plano-Irving PMSA, TX	Y	47450 FQ	61260 MW	75360 TQ	USBLS	5/15
Construction Trade and Extraction Workers	Fort Worth-Arlington PMSA, TX	Y	51000 FQ	64150 MW	79980 TQ	USBLS	5/15

AE	Average entry wage	AWR	Average wage range	H	Hourly
AEX	Average experienced wage	B	Biweekly	HI	Highest wage paid
ATC	Average total compensation	D	Daily	HR	High end range
AW	Average wage paid	FQ	First quartile wage	LO	Lowest wage paid

LR	Low end range	MTC	Median total compensation
M	Monthly	MW	Median wage paid
MCC	Median cash compensation	MWR	Median wage range
ME	Median entry wage	S	See annotated source

TCC	Total cash compensation		
TQ	Third quartile wage		
W	Weekly		
Y	Yearly		

Occupation/Type/Industry	Location	Per	Low	Mid	High	Source	Date
First-Line Supervisor							
Construction Trade and Extraction Workers	Houston-The Woodlands-Sugar Land MSA, TX	Y	51040 FQ	65250 MW	85750 TQ	USBLS	5/15
Construction Trade and Extraction Workers	San Antonio-New Braunfels MSA, TX	Y	51470 FQ	64290 MW	75690 TQ	USBLS	5/15
Construction Trade and Extraction Workers	Utah	Y	42530 FQ	54870 MW	70550 TQ	USBLS	5/15
Construction Trade and Extraction Workers	Ogden-Clearfield MSA, UT	Y	45550 FQ	57510 MW	70300 TQ	USBLS	5/15
Construction Trade and Extraction Workers	Provo-Orem MSA, UT	Y	39890 FQ	48510 MW	64040 TQ	USBLS	5/15
Construction Trade and Extraction Workers	Salt Lake City MSA, UT	Y	44290 FQ	56310 MW	71630 TQ	USBLS	5/15
Construction Trade and Extraction Workers	Vermont	Y	45670 FQ	57120 MW	72810 TQ	USBLS	5/15
Construction Trade and Extraction Workers	Burlington-South Burlington MSA, VT	Y	49170 FQ	61140 MW	78640 TQ	USBLS	5/15
Construction Trade and Extraction Workers	Virginia	Y	47430 FQ	59680 MW	75840 TQ	USBLS	5/15
Construction Trade and Extraction Workers	Richmond MSA, VA	Y	44590 FQ	54830 MW	68930 TQ	USBLS	5/15
Construction Trade and Extraction Workers	Virginia Beach-Norfolk-Newport News MSA, VA-NC	Y	46880 FQ	60050 MW	75330 TQ	USBLS	5/15
Construction Trade and Extraction Workers	Washington	H	28.62 FQ	36.29 MW	45.04 TQ	WABLS	3/16
Construction Trade and Extraction Workers	Seattle-Bellevue-Everett PMSA, WA	H	30.74 FQ	39.53 MW	47.11 TQ	WABLS	3/16
Construction Trade and Extraction Workers	Tacoma-Lakewood PMSA, WA	H	26.83 FQ	33.40 MW	42.81 TQ	WABLS	3/16
Construction Trade and Extraction Workers	West Virginia	Y	44550 FQ	64630 MW	83750 TQ	USBLS	5/15
Construction Trade and Extraction Workers	Huntington-Ashland MSA, WV-KY-OH	Y	44430 FQ	61680 MW	79490 TQ	USBLS	5/15
Construction Trade and Extraction Workers	Wisconsin	Y	51520 FQ	62950 MW	80310 TQ	USBLS	5/15
Construction Trade and Extraction Workers	Madison MSA, WI	Y	52600 FQ	63190 MW	79680 TQ	USBLS	5/15
Construction Trade and Extraction Workers	Milwaukee-Waukesha-West Allis MSA, WI	Y	58330 FQ	74560 MW	92610 TQ	USBLS	5/15
Construction Trade and Extraction Workers	Wyoming	Y	50690 FQ	67020 MW	90840 TQ	USBLS	5/15
Construction Trade and Extraction Workers	Cheyenne MSA, WY	Y	46120 FQ	59090 MW	81560 TQ	USBLS	5/15
Construction Trade and Extraction Workers	Puerto Rico	Y	21170 FQ	26970 MW	36000 TQ	USBLS	5/15
Construction Trade and Extraction Workers	San Juan-Carolina-Caguas MSA, PR	Y	22400 FQ	28280 MW	38160 TQ	USBLS	5/15
Construction Trade and Extraction Workers	Virgin Islands	Y	48410 FQ	57110 MW	65250 TQ	USBLS	5/15
Construction Trade and Extraction Workers	Guam	Y	32840 FQ	41580 MW	57630 TQ	USBLS	5/15
Correctional Officers	Alabama	Y	40381 AE	57483 AW	66039 AEX	ALBLS	6/16
Correctional Officers	Birmingham-Hoover MSA, AL	Y	51501 AE	61467 AW	66451 AEX	ALBLS	6/16
Correctional Officers	Alaska	Y	75050 FQ	86750 MW	95600 TQ	USBLS	5/15
Correctional Officers	Arizona	Y	45680 FQ	50360 MW	58970 TQ	USBLS	5/15
Correctional Officers	Phoenix-Mesa-Scottsdale MSA, AZ	Y	47610 FQ	53680 MW	65150 TQ	USBLS	5/15
Correctional Officers	Tucson MSA, AZ	Y	45680 FQ	50130 MW	57850 TQ	USBLS	5/15
Correctional Officers	Arkansas	Y	34410 FQ	46310 MW	56460 TQ	USBLS	5/15
Correctional Officers	Little Rock-North Little Rock-Conway MSA, AR	Y	28790 FQ	37800 MW	50440 TQ	USBLS	5/15
Correctional Officers	California	H	41.13 FQ	43.68 MW	46.04 TQ	CABLS	1/16-3/16
Correctional Officers	Los Angeles-Long Beach-Glendale PMSA, CA	H	40.34 FQ	43.26 MW	46.22 TQ	CABLS	1/16-3/16
Correctional Officers	Oakland-Hayward-Berkeley PMSA, CA	H	36.81 FQ	40.79 MW	44.81 TQ	CABLS	1/16-3/16
Correctional Officers	Riverside-San Bernardino-Ontario MSA, CA	H	41.12 FQ	43.68 MW	45.82 TQ	CABLS	1/16-3/16
Correctional Officers	San Diego-Carlsbad MSA, CA	H	42.49 FQ	43.86 MW	46.26 TQ	CABLS	1/16-3/16
Correctional Officers	Denver-Aurora-Lakewood MSA, CO	Y	61660 FQ	73340 MW	90750 TQ	USBLS	5/15
Correctional Officers	Connecticut	Y		79336 MW		CTBLS	1/16-3/16
Correctional Officers	Wilmington PMSA, DE-MD-NJ	Y	41410 FQ	45730 MW	53760 TQ	USBLS	5/15
Correctional Officers	Washington-Arlington-Alexandria PMSA, DC-VA-MD-WV	Y	51950 FQ	74420 MW	93940 TQ	USBLS	5/15
Correctional Officers	Florida	H	20.89 AE	27.53 MW	36.00 AEX	FLBLS	7/16-9/16
Correctional Officers	Fort Lauderdale-Pompano Beach-Deerfield Beach PMSA, FL	H	35.28 AE	47.24 MW	51.79 AEX	FLBLS	7/16-9/16
Correctional Officers	Miami-Miami Beach-Kendall PMSA, FL	H	21.81 AE	36.13 MW	46.68 AEX	FLBLS	7/16-9/16
Correctional Officers	Orlando-Kissimmee-Sanford MSA, FL	H	20.92 AE	28.41 MW	32.81 AEX	FLBLS	7/16-9/16
Correctional Officers	Tampa-St. Petersburg-Clearwater MSA, FL	H	23.18 AE	40.24 MW	44.22 AEX	FLBLS	7/16-9/16
Correctional Officers	Georgia	Y	30480 FQ	36020 MW	44910 TQ	USBLS	5/15

Occupation/Type/Industry	Location	Per	Low	Mid	High	Source	Date
First-Line Supervisor							
Correctional Officers	Augusta-Richmond County MSA, GA-SC	Y	35790 FQ	45350 MW	68320 TQ	USBLS	5/15
Correctional Officers	Idaho	Y	39110 FQ	47490 MW	53840 TQ	USBLS	5/15
Correctional Officers	Boise City MSA, ID	Y	37890 FQ	46240 MW	50950 TQ	USBLS	5/15
Correctional Officers	Illinois	Y	64390 FQ	75510 MW	92190 TQ	USBLS	5/15
Correctional Officers	Chicago-Naperville-Arlington Heights PMSA, IL	Y	65410 FQ	80200 MW	96230 TQ	USBLS	5/15
Correctional Officers	Lake County-Kenosha County PMSA, IL-WI	Y	68430 FQ	80270 MW	92430 TQ	USBLS	5/15
Correctional Officers	Indiana	Y	33420 FQ	37910 MW	44760 TQ	USBLS	5/15
Correctional Officers	Gary PMSA, IN	Y	37690 FQ	50100 MW	58210 TQ	USBLS	5/15
Correctional Officers	Indianapolis-Carmel-Anderson MSA, IN	Y	32960 FQ	37660 MW	44630 TQ	USBLS	5/15
Correctional Officers	Iowa	Y	54200 FQ	65550 MW	72210 TQ	USBLS	5/15
Correctional Officers	Kansas	Y	37930 FQ	49290 MW	62650 TQ	USBLS	5/15
Correctional Officers	Wichita MSA, KS	Y	37110 FQ	46020 MW	59890 TQ	USBLS	5/15
Correctional Officers	Kentucky	Y	31080 FQ	38770 MW	52840 TQ	USBLS	5/15
Correctional Officers	Louisville-Jefferson County MSA, KY-IN	Y	31700 FQ	40760 MW	50000 TQ	USBLS	5/15
Correctional Officers	Louisiana	Y	41350 FQ	52700 MW	61900 TQ	USBLS	5/15
Correctional Officers	Baton Rouge MSA, LA	Y	44510 FQ	54000 MW	61290 TQ	USBLS	5/15
Correctional Officers	New Orleans-Metairie MSA, LA	Y	32330 FQ	36850 MW	45020 TQ	USBLS	5/15
Correctional Officers	Maine	Y	38620 FQ	42640 MW	47980 TQ	USBLS	5/15
Correctional Officers	Portland-South Portland MSA, ME	Y	38620 FQ	42640 MW	47980 TQ	USBLS	5/15
Correctional Officers	Maryland	Y	48241 AE	59906 MW	65738 AEX	MDBLS	4/16
Correctional Officers	Baltimore-Columbia-Towson MSA, MD	Y	49510 FQ	56480 MW	64820 TQ	USBLS	5/15
Correctional Officers	Salisbury MSA, MD-DE	Y	47700 FQ	53750 MW	58670 TQ	USBLS	5/15
Correctional Officers	Michigan	Y	59740 FQ	63530 MW	65240 TQ	USBLS	5/15
Correctional Officers	Detroit-Dearborn-Livonia PMSA, MI	Y	53570 FQ	59750 MW	65230 TQ	USBLS	5/15
Correctional Officers	Grand Rapids-Wyoming MSA, MI	Y	59740 FQ	63530 MW	66810 TQ	USBLS	5/15
Correctional Officers	Minnesota	Y	62632 FQ	72882 MW	79992 TQ	MNBLS	1/16-3/16
Correctional Officers	Minneapolis-St. Paul-Bloomington MSA, MN-WI	Y	66025 FQ	77406 MW	86031 TQ	MNBLS	1/16-3/16
Correctional Officers	Mississippi	Y	33190 FQ	37800 MW	45830 TQ	USBLS	5/15
Correctional Officers	Jackson MSA, MS	Y	33900 FQ	38090 MW	60470 TQ	USBLS	5/15
Correctional Officers	Missouri	Y	38170 FQ	48500 MW	60520 TQ	USBLS	5/15
Correctional Officers	Kansas City MSA, MO-KS	Y	54840 FQ	61940 MW	70480 TQ	USBLS	5/15
Correctional Officers	St. Louis MSA, MO-IL	Y	55170 FQ	67010 MW	79380 TQ	USBLS	5/15
Correctional Officers	Montana	Y	45510 FQ	47280 MW	53100 TQ	USBLS	5/15
Correctional Officers	Nebraska	Y	38505 FQ	45295 MW	56490 TQ	NEBLS	7/16-9/16
Correctional Officers	Omaha-Council Bluffs MSA, NE-IA	Y	46210 FQ	71385 MW	88680 TQ	NEBLS	7/16-9/16
Correctional Officers	Nevada	Y	56970 FQ	73400 MW	106440 TQ	USBLS	5/15
Correctional Officers	Las Vegas-Henderson-Paradise MSA, NV	Y	64990 FQ	97060 MW	117900 TQ	USBLS	5/15
Correctional Officers	New Hampshire	H	23.10 AE	29.97 MW	32.19 AEX	NHBLS	6/16
Correctional Officers	New Jersey	Y	99510 FQ	107630 MW	115160 TQ	USBLS	5/15
Correctional Officers	Camden PMSA, NJ	Y	84400 FQ	103270 MW	110850 TQ	USBLS	5/15
Correctional Officers	Newark PMSA, NJ-PA	Y	93760 FQ	107050 MW	113610 TQ	USBLS	5/15
Correctional Officers	New Mexico	Y	37780 FQ	47240 MW	56480 TQ	USBLS	5/15
Correctional Officers	Albuquerque MSA, NM	Y	43570 FQ	49120 MW	56750 TQ	USBLS	5/15
Correctional Officers	New York	Y	68300 AE	84120 MW	92720 AEX	NYBLS	1/16-3/16
Correctional Officers	Buffalo-Cheektowaga-Niagara Falls MSA, NY	Y	67680 FQ	77820 MW	90670 TQ	USBLS	5/15
Correctional Officers	New York-Jersey City-White Plains PMSA, NY-NJ	Y	76030 FQ	88270 MW	101100 TQ	USBLS	5/15
Correctional Officers	Rochester MSA, NY	Y	67850 FQ	76110 MW	88010 TQ	USBLS	5/15
Correctional Officers	North Carolina	Y	39000 FQ	42940 MW	53240 TQ	USBLS	5/15
Correctional Officers	Charlotte-Concord-Gastonia MSA, NC-SC	Y	47990 FQ	63180 MW	81540 TQ	USBLS	5/15
Correctional Officers	Raleigh MSA, NC	Y	38790 FQ	42000 MW	46440 TQ	USBLS	5/15
Correctional Officers	North Dakota	Y	42880 FQ	47980 MW	60890 TQ	USBLS	5/15
Correctional Officers	Ohio	Y	50910 FQ	61300 MW	68300 TQ	USBLS	5/15
Correctional Officers	Cincinnati MSA, OH-KY-IN	Y	55060 FQ	62580 MW	71220 TQ	USBLS	5/15
Correctional Officers	Cleveland-Elyria MSA, OH	Y	51110 FQ	59010 MW	67810 TQ	USBLS	5/15
Correctional Officers	Columbus MSA, OH	Y	55940 FQ	66780 MW	70440 TQ	USBLS	5/15

AE	Average entry wage	AWR	Average wage range	H	Hourly	LR	Low end range	MTC	Median total compensation	TCC	Total cash compensation
AEX	Average experienced wage	B	Biweekly	HI	Highest wage paid	M	Monthly	MW	Median wage paid	TQ	Third quartile wage
ATC	Average total compensation	D	Daily	HR	High end range	MCC	Median cash compensation	MWR	Median wage range	W	Weekly
AW	Average wage paid	FQ	First quartile wage	LO	Lowest wage paid	ME	Median entry wage	S	See annotated source	Y	Yearly

Occupation/Type/Industry	Location	Per	Low	Mid	High	Source	Date
First-Line Supervisor							
Correctional Officers	Oklahoma	Y	42160 FQ	49500 MW	61470 TQ	USBLS	5/15
Correctional Officers	Oklahoma City MSA, OK	Y	43130 FQ	50820 MW	64780 TQ	USBLS	5/15
Correctional Officers	Tulsa MSA, OK	Y	40740 FQ	47180 MW	57050 TQ	USBLS	5/15
Correctional Officers	Oregon	H	34.16 FQ	37.64 MW	43.52 TQ	ORBLS	2016
Correctional Officers	Portland-Vancouver-Hillsboro MSA, OR-WA	Y	71490 FQ	82060 MW	94150 TQ	USBLS	5/15
Correctional Officers	Pennsylvania	Y	63660 FQ	73510 MW	81190 TQ	USBLS	5/15
Correctional Officers	Harrisburg-Carlisle MSA, PA	Y	70890 FQ	76020 MW	85510 TQ	USBLS	5/15
Correctional Officers	Montgomery County-Bucks County-Chester County PMSA, PA	Y	69510 FQ	74770 MW	80410 TQ	USBLS	5/15
Correctional Officers	Philadelphia PMSA, PA	Y	67130 FQ	74970 MW	88290 TQ	USBLS	5/15
Correctional Officers	Pittsburgh MSA, PA	Y	62980 FQ	73490 MW	81960 TQ	USBLS	5/15
Correctional Officers	South Carolina	Y	43000 FQ	55390 MW	65370 TQ	USBLS	5/15
Correctional Officers	Greenville-Anderson-Mauldin MSA, SC	Y	38730 FQ	44720 MW	52830 TQ	USBLS	5/15
Correctional Officers	South Dakota	Y	46860 FQ	56570 MW	67140 TQ	USBLS	5/15
Correctional Officers	Tennessee	Y	37000 FQ	44330 MW	53240 TQ	USBLS	5/15
Correctional Officers	Knoxville MSA, TN	Y	37430 FQ	43150 MW	48800 TQ	USBLS	5/15
Correctional Officers	Nashville-Davidson–Murfreesboro–Franklin MSA, TN	Y	37320 FQ	44010 MW	51210 TQ	USBLS	5/15
Correctional Officers	Texas	Y	41150 FQ	43180 MW	45360 TQ	USBLS	5/15
Correctional Officers	Austin-Round Rock MSA, TX	Y	41150 FQ	47240 MW	79550 TQ	USBLS	5/15
Correctional Officers	Dallas-Plano-Irving PMSA, TX	Y	43200 FQ	58960 MW	80460 TQ	USBLS	5/15
Correctional Officers	Fort Worth-Arlington PMSA, TX	Y	44450 FQ	55720 MW	71420 TQ	USBLS	5/15
Correctional Officers	Houston-The Woodlands-Sugar Land MSA, TX	Y	41150 FQ	41160 MW	45350 TQ	USBLS	5/15
Correctional Officers	San Antonio-New Braunfels MSA, TX	Y	41160 FQ	43510 MW	59960 TQ	USBLS	5/15
Correctional Officers	Utah	Y	55660 FQ	60380 MW	69330 TQ	USBLS	5/15
Correctional Officers	Ogden-Clearfield MSA, UT	Y	54760 FQ	61210 MW	63310 TQ	USBLS	5/15
Correctional Officers	Salt Lake City MSA, UT	Y	56770 FQ	62880 MW	72730 TQ	USBLS	5/15
Correctional Officers	Virginia	Y	41360 FQ	46140 MW	57320 TQ	USBLS	5/15
Correctional Officers	Richmond MSA, VA	Y	41420 FQ	47000 MW	57250 TQ	USBLS	5/15
Correctional Officers	Virginia Beach-Norfolk-Newport News MSA, VA-NC	Y	41700 FQ	48410 MW	60060 TQ	USBLS	5/15
Correctional Officers	Washington	H	24.71 FQ	25.30 MW	36.92 TQ	WABLS	3/16
Correctional Officers	Seattle-Bellevue-Everett PMSA, WA	H	25.30 FQ	33.48 MW	40.11 TQ	WABLS	3/16
Correctional Officers	Tacoma-Lakewood PMSA, WA	H	25.29 FQ	35.59 MW	46.27 TQ	WABLS	3/16
Correctional Officers	West Virginia	Y	35920 FQ	50230 MW	64440 TQ	USBLS	5/15
Correctional Officers	Wisconsin	Y	57670 FQ	62540 MW	67940 TQ	USBLS	5/15
Correctional Officers	Madison MSA, WI	Y	59630 FQ	63650 MW	76230 TQ	USBLS	5/15
Correctional Officers	Milwaukee-Waukesha-West Allis MSA, WI	Y	59660 FQ	64610 MW	70710 TQ	USBLS	5/15
Correctional Officers	Wyoming	Y	53770 FQ	56370 MW	67380 TQ	USBLS	5/15
Correctional Officers	Puerto Rico	Y	26780 FQ	29100 MW	33420 TQ	USBLS	5/15
Farming, Fishing, and Forestry Workers	Alabama	Y	31149 AE	49696 AW	58975 AEX	ALBLS	6/16
Farming, Fishing, and Forestry Workers	Birmingham-Hoover MSA, AL	Y	32815 AE	40407 AW	44213 AEX	ALBLS	6/16
Farming, Fishing, and Forestry Workers	Alaska	Y	46490 FQ	55540 MW	64070 TQ	USBLS	5/15
Farming, Fishing, and Forestry Workers	Arizona	Y	33520 FQ	43690 MW	54350 TQ	USBLS	5/15
Farming, Fishing, and Forestry Workers	Phoenix-Mesa-Scottsdale MSA, AZ	Y	40100 FQ	50390 MW	59540 TQ	USBLS	5/15
Farming, Fishing, and Forestry Workers	Tucson MSA, AZ	Y	39830 FQ	45890 MW	55010 TQ	USBLS	5/15
Farming, Fishing, and Forestry Workers	Arkansas	Y	31600 FQ	39260 MW	55350 TQ	USBLS	5/15
Farming, Fishing, and Forestry Workers	Little Rock-North Little Rock-Conway MSA, AR	Y	35420 FQ	41710 MW	86790 TQ	USBLS	5/15
Farming, Fishing, and Forestry Workers	California	H	13.81 FQ	18.18 MW	26.25 TQ	CABLS	1/16-3/16
Farming, Fishing, and Forestry Workers	Anaheim-Santa Ana-Irvine PMSA, CA	H	17.97 FQ	25.48 MW	28.69 TQ	CABLS	1/16-3/16
Farming, Fishing, and Forestry Workers	Los Angeles-Long Beach-Glendale PMSA, CA	H	22.00 FQ	25.40 MW	28.42 TQ	CABLS	1/16-3/16
Farming, Fishing, and Forestry Workers	Oakland-Hayward-Berkeley PMSA, CA	H	16.81 FQ	18.87 MW	22.96 TQ	CABLS	1/16-3/16
Farming, Fishing, and Forestry Workers	Riverside-San Bernardino-Ontario MSA, CA	H	14.12 FQ	20.29 MW	26.71 TQ	CABLS	1/16-3/16
Farming, Fishing, and Forestry Workers	Sacramento–Roseville–Arden-Arcade MSA, CA	H	14.20 FQ	25.32 MW	32.51 TQ	CABLS	1/16-3/16
Farming, Fishing, and Forestry Workers	San Diego-Carlsbad MSA, CA	H	18.43 FQ	24.80 MW	29.12 TQ	CABLS	1/16-3/16

AE	Average entry wage	AWR	Average wage range	H	Hourly
AEX	Average experienced wage	B	Biweekly	HI	Highest wage paid
ATC	Average total compensation	D	Daily	HR	High end range
AW	Average wage paid	FQ	First quartile wage	LO	Lowest wage paid

LR	Low end range	MTC	Median total compensation
M	Monthly	MW	Median wage paid
MCC	Median cash compensation	MWR	Median wage range
ME	Median entry wage	S	See annotated source

TCC	Total cash compensation		
TQ	Third quartile wage		
W	Weekly		
Y	Yearly		

First-Line Supervisor

Occupation/Type/Industry	Location	Per	Low	Mid	High	Source	Date
Farming, Fishing, and Forestry Workers	San Francisco-Redwood City-South San Francisco PMSA, CA	H	17.21 FQ	19.55 MW	54.20 TQ	CABLS	1/16-3/16
Farming, Fishing, and Forestry Workers	Colorado	Y	40410 FQ	53160 MW	69210 TQ	USBLS	5/15
Farming, Fishing, and Forestry Workers	Denver-Aurora-Lakewood MSA, CO	Y	37480 FQ	45440 MW	60720 TQ	USBLS	5/15
Farming, Fishing, and Forestry Workers	Connecticut	Y		40615 MW		CTBLS	1/16-3/16
Farming, Fishing, and Forestry Workers	Delaware	Y	44010 FQ	52870 MW	60350 TQ	USBLS	5/15
Farming, Fishing, and Forestry Workers	Wilmington PMSA, DE-MD-NJ	Y	36160 FQ	49760 MW	56750 TQ	USBLS	5/15
Farming, Fishing, and Forestry Workers	Washington-Arlington-Alexandria PMSA, DC-VA-MD-WV	Y	49000 FQ	65490 MW	80590 TQ	USBLS	5/15
Farming, Fishing, and Forestry Workers	Florida	H	14.88 AE	22.77 MW	27.58 AEX	FLBLS	7/16-9/16
Farming, Fishing, and Forestry Workers	Miami-Miami Beach-Kendall PMSA, FL	H	14.50 AE	18.91 MW	26.13 AEX	FLBLS	7/16-9/16
Farming, Fishing, and Forestry Workers	Orlando-Kissimmee-Sanford MSA, FL	H	15.97 AE	19.83 MW	24.10 AEX	FLBLS	7/16-9/16
Farming, Fishing, and Forestry Workers	Tampa-St. Petersburg-Clearwater MSA, FL	H	19.84 AE	27.35 MW	28.59 AEX	FLBLS	7/16-9/16
Farming, Fishing, and Forestry Workers	Georgia	Y	36450 FQ	49980 MW	59700 TQ	USBLS	5/15
Farming, Fishing, and Forestry Workers	Atlanta-Sandy Springs-Roswell MSA, GA	Y	35790 FQ	45310 MW	55360 TQ	USBLS	5/15
Farming, Fishing, and Forestry Workers	Augusta-Richmond County MSA, GA-SC	Y	42990 FQ	54540 MW	66170 TQ	USBLS	5/15
Farming, Fishing, and Forestry Workers	Hawaii	Y	29280 FQ	42240 MW	54830 TQ	USBLS	5/15
Farming, Fishing, and Forestry Workers	Idaho	Y	33090 FQ	39620 MW	48190 TQ	USBLS	5/15
Farming, Fishing, and Forestry Workers	Boise City MSA, ID	Y	40470 FQ	45900 MW	51200 TQ	USBLS	5/15
Farming, Fishing, and Forestry Workers	Illinois	Y	31410 FQ	41890 MW	58230 TQ	USBLS	5/15
Farming, Fishing, and Forestry Workers	Chicago-Naperville-Arlington Heights PMSA, IL	Y	35480 FQ	45710 MW	55840 TQ	USBLS	5/15
Farming, Fishing, and Forestry Workers	Indiana	Y	31540 FQ	42280 MW	53500 TQ	USBLS	5/15
Farming, Fishing, and Forestry Workers	Gary PMSA, IN	Y	25240 FQ	28670 MW	45740 TQ	USBLS	5/15
Farming, Fishing, and Forestry Workers	Iowa	Y	43970 FQ	54610 MW	62290 TQ	USBLS	5/15
Farming, Fishing, and Forestry Workers	Kansas	Y	35560 FQ	44430 MW	64630 TQ	USBLS	5/15
Farming, Fishing, and Forestry Workers	Kentucky	Y	32350 FQ	42220 MW	50100 TQ	USBLS	5/15
Farming, Fishing, and Forestry Workers	Louisville-Jefferson County MSA, KY-IN	Y	29600 FQ	42340 MW	50770 TQ	USBLS	5/15
Farming, Fishing, and Forestry Workers	Louisiana	Y	38360 FQ	51860 MW	68240 TQ	USBLS	5/15
Farming, Fishing, and Forestry Workers	Baton Rouge MSA, LA	Y	49830 FQ	59060 MW	69650 TQ	USBLS	5/15
Farming, Fishing, and Forestry Workers	Maine	Y	35030 FQ	39460 MW	49770 TQ	USBLS	5/15
Farming, Fishing, and Forestry Workers	Maryland	Y	32538 AE	51904 MW	61588 AEX	MDBLS	4/16
Farming, Fishing, and Forestry Workers	Baltimore-Columbia-Towson MSA, MD	Y	49120 FQ	56530 MW	71320 TQ	USBLS	5/15
Farming, Fishing, and Forestry Workers	Massachusetts	Y	42240 FQ	51810 MW	68690 TQ	USBLS	5/15
Farming, Fishing, and Forestry Workers	Boston-Cambridge-Newton NECTA, MA	Y	48330 FQ	67390 MW	73950 TQ	USBLS	5/15
Farming, Fishing, and Forestry Workers	Michigan	Y	29630 FQ	46030 MW	71130 TQ	USBLS	5/15
Farming, Fishing, and Forestry Workers	Grand Rapids-Wyoming MSA, MI	Y	37630 FQ	45950 MW	56770 TQ	USBLS	5/15
Farming, Fishing, and Forestry Workers	Minnesota	Y	39907 FQ	50077 MW	61217 TQ	MNBLS	1/16-3/16
Farming, Fishing, and Forestry Workers	Minneapolis-St. Paul-Bloomington MSA, MN-WI	Y	39614 FQ	53791 MW	64385 TQ	MNBLS	1/16-3/16
Farming, Fishing, and Forestry Workers	Mississippi	Y	34010 FQ	49230 MW	57430 TQ	USBLS	5/15
Farming, Fishing, and Forestry Workers	Missouri	Y	36270 FQ	44140 MW	51150 TQ	USBLS	5/15
Farming, Fishing, and Forestry Workers	Kansas City MSA, MO-KS	Y	35180 FQ	44220 MW	54560 TQ	USBLS	5/15
Farming, Fishing, and Forestry Workers	St. Louis MSA, MO-IL	Y	38710 FQ	43710 MW	47840 TQ	USBLS	5/15
Farming, Fishing, and Forestry Workers	Montana	Y	28070 FQ	34860 MW	43910 TQ	USBLS	5/15
Farming, Fishing, and Forestry Workers	Nebraska	Y	42700 FQ	49595 MW	58050 TQ	NEBLS	7/16-9/16
Farming, Fishing, and Forestry Workers	Omaha-Council Bluffs MSA, NE-IA	Y	48815 FQ	54955 MW	61075 TQ	NEBLS	7/16-9/16
Farming, Fishing, and Forestry Workers	Nevada	Y	38400 FQ	45200 MW	53530 TQ	USBLS	5/15
Farming, Fishing, and Forestry Workers	New Hampshire	H	20.55 AE	23.70 MW	27.96 AEX	NHBLS	6/16
Farming, Fishing, and Forestry Workers	New Jersey	Y	27180 FQ	37890 MW	60240 TQ	USBLS	5/15
Farming, Fishing, and Forestry Workers	New Mexico	Y	30830 FQ	37170 MW	46750 TQ	USBLS	5/15
Farming, Fishing, and Forestry Workers	New York	Y	37630 AE	58270 MW	68500 AEX	NYBLS	1/16-3/16
Farming, Fishing, and Forestry Workers	New York-Jersey City-White Plains PMSA, NY-NJ	Y	36990 FQ	57440 MW	71480 TQ	USBLS	5/15
Farming, Fishing, and Forestry Workers	North Carolina	Y	38740 FQ	48650 MW	66640 TQ	USBLS	5/15
Farming, Fishing, and Forestry Workers	Charlotte-Concord-Gastonia MSA, NC-SC	Y	42750 FQ	51120 MW	59980 TQ	USBLS	5/15

AE	Average entry wage	AWR	Average wage range	H	Hourly	LR	Low end range	MTC	Median total compensation	TCC	Total cash compensation
AEX	Average experienced wage	B	Biweekly	HI	Highest wage paid	M	Monthly	MW	Median wage paid	TQ	Third quartile wage
ATC	Average total compensation	D	Daily	HR	High end range	MCC	Median cash compensation	MWR	Median wage range	W	Weekly
AW	Average wage paid	FQ	First quartile wage	LO	Lowest wage paid	ME	Median entry wage	S	See annotated source	Y	Yearly

Occupation/Type/Industry	Location	Per	Low	Mid	High	Source	Date
First-Line Supervisor							
Farming, Fishing, and Forestry Workers	North Dakota	Y	41810 FQ	52990 MW	60510 TQ	USBLS	5/15
Farming, Fishing, and Forestry Workers	Ohio	Y	37380 FQ	53920 MW	62380 TQ	USBLS	5/15
Farming, Fishing, and Forestry Workers	Columbus MSA, OH	Y	51930 FQ	65620 MW	74810 TQ	USBLS	5/15
Farming, Fishing, and Forestry Workers	Oklahoma	Y	35980 FQ	54640 MW	73410 TQ	USBLS	5/15
Farming, Fishing, and Forestry Workers	Oklahoma City MSA, OK	Y	36040 FQ	47750 MW	64930 TQ	USBLS	5/15
Farming, Fishing, and Forestry Workers	Oregon	H	21.10 FQ	26.56 MW	33.11 TQ	ORBLS	2016
Farming, Fishing, and Forestry Workers	Portland-Vancouver-Hillsboro MSA, OR-WA	Y	36250 FQ	50110 MW	70230 TQ	USBLS	5/15
Farming, Fishing, and Forestry Workers	Pennsylvania	Y	38580 FQ	55110 MW	65360 TQ	USBLS	5/15
Farming, Fishing, and Forestry Workers	Montgomery County-Bucks County-Chester County PMSA, PA	Y	27810 FQ	30700 MW	62220 TQ	USBLS	5/15
Farming, Fishing, and Forestry Workers	Pittsburgh MSA, PA	Y	33640 FQ	51830 MW	65370 TQ	USBLS	5/15
Farming, Fishing, and Forestry Workers	South Carolina	Y	41610 FQ	54210 MW	62140 TQ	USBLS	5/15
Farming, Fishing, and Forestry Workers	Columbia MSA, SC	Y	30880 FQ	43160 MW	54090 TQ	USBLS	5/15
Farming, Fishing, and Forestry Workers	Tennessee	Y	33900 FQ	44710 MW	62790 TQ	USBLS	5/15
Farming, Fishing, and Forestry Workers	Memphis MSA, TN-MS-AR	Y	36670 FQ	55070 MW	67300 TQ	USBLS	5/15
Farming, Fishing, and Forestry Workers	Nashville-Davidson–Murfreesboro–Franklin MSA, TN	Y	29760 FQ	37290 MW	53470 TQ	USBLS	5/15
Farming, Fishing, and Forestry Workers	Texas	Y	33980 FQ	45420 MW	60100 TQ	USBLS	5/15
Farming, Fishing, and Forestry Workers	Austin-Round Rock MSA, TX	Y	40750 FQ	46960 MW	58640 TQ	USBLS	5/15
Farming, Fishing, and Forestry Workers	Dallas-Plano-Irving PMSA, TX	Y	37440 FQ	47030 MW	69630 TQ	USBLS	5/15
Farming, Fishing, and Forestry Workers	Fort Worth-Arlington PMSA, TX	Y	35140 FQ	42680 MW	48650 TQ	USBLS	5/15
Farming, Fishing, and Forestry Workers	Houston-The Woodlands-Sugar Land MSA, TX	Y	35700 FQ	48010 MW	58290 TQ	USBLS	5/15
Farming, Fishing, and Forestry Workers	Utah	Y	34330 FQ	45460 MW	56470 TQ	USBLS	5/15
Farming, Fishing, and Forestry Workers	Vermont	Y	38400 FQ	44350 MW	49600 TQ	USBLS	5/15
Farming, Fishing, and Forestry Workers	Burlington-South Burlington MSA, VT	Y	40530 FQ	44390 MW	48250 TQ	USBLS	5/15
Farming, Fishing, and Forestry Workers	Virginia	Y	40870 FQ	50140 MW	70780 TQ	USBLS	5/15
Farming, Fishing, and Forestry Workers	Richmond MSA, VA	Y	34250 FQ	41730 MW	54250 TQ	USBLS	5/15
Farming, Fishing, and Forestry Workers	Virginia Beach-Norfolk-Newport News MSA, VA-NC	Y	40910 FQ	45670 MW	51630 TQ	USBLS	5/15
Farming, Fishing, and Forestry Workers	Washington	H	15.15 FQ	23.83 MW	33.10 TQ	WABLS	3/16
Farming, Fishing, and Forestry Workers	Seattle-Bellevue-Everett PMSA, WA	H	15.66 FQ	28.11 MW	37.28 TQ	WABLS	3/16
Farming, Fishing, and Forestry Workers	Tacoma-Lakewood PMSA, WA	H	11.99 FQ	17.94 MW	25.89 TQ	WABLS	3/16
Farming, Fishing, and Forestry Workers	West Virginia	Y	36310 FQ	44730 MW	56800 TQ	USBLS	5/15
Farming, Fishing, and Forestry Workers	Wisconsin	Y	38590 FQ	52950 MW	58990 TQ	USBLS	5/15
Farming, Fishing, and Forestry Workers	Madison MSA, WI	Y	41610 FQ	47760 MW	55560 TQ	USBLS	5/15
Farming, Fishing, and Forestry Workers	Puerto Rico	Y	22290 FQ	26270 MW	30660 TQ	USBLS	5/15
Farming, Fishing, and Forestry Workers	San Juan-Carolina-Caguas MSA, PR	Y	26150 FQ	29050 MW	39760 TQ	USBLS	5/15
Fire Fighting and Prevention Workers	Alabama	Y	44108 AE	62528 AW	71733 AEX	ALBLS	6/16
Fire Fighting and Prevention Workers	Birmingham-Hoover MSA, AL	Y	55053 AE	75645 AW	85941 AEX	ALBLS	6/16
Fire Fighting and Prevention Workers	Alaska	Y	68230 FQ	81000 MW	95250 TQ	USBLS	5/15
Fire Fighting and Prevention Workers	Anchorage MSA, AK	Y	80820 FQ	89010 MW	99710 TQ	USBLS	5/15
Fire Fighting and Prevention Workers	Arizona	Y	54600 FQ	67730 MW	86630 TQ	USBLS	5/15
Fire Fighting and Prevention Workers	Phoenix-Mesa-Scottsdale MSA, AZ	Y	57010 FQ	69280 MW	88660 TQ	USBLS	5/15
Fire Fighting and Prevention Workers	Tucson MSA, AZ	Y	46270 FQ	60670 MW	77780 TQ	USBLS	5/15
Fire Fighting and Prevention Workers	Arkansas	Y	41680 FQ	51430 MW	64670 TQ	USBLS	5/15
Fire Fighting and Prevention Workers	Little Rock-North Little Rock-Conway MSA, AR	Y	47210 FQ	60340 MW	70980 TQ	USBLS	5/15
Fire Fighting and Prevention Workers	California	H	35.59 FQ	48.25 MW	67.14 TQ	CABLS	1/16-3/16
Fire Fighting and Prevention Workers	Anaheim-Santa Ana-Irvine PMSA, CA	H	52.11 FQ	63.35 MW	81.84 TQ	CABLS	1/16-3/16
Fire Fighting and Prevention Workers	Los Angeles-Long Beach-Glendale PMSA, CA	H	54.96 FQ	70.06 MW	88.31 TQ	CABLS	1/16-3/16
Fire Fighting and Prevention Workers	Oakland-Hayward-Berkeley PMSA, CA	H	55.72 FQ	69.35 MW	83.42 TQ	CABLS	1/16-3/16
Fire Fighting and Prevention Workers	Riverside-San Bernardino-Ontario MSA, CA	H	35.06 FQ	38.87 MW	62.36 TQ	CABLS	1/16-3/16
Fire Fighting and Prevention Workers	Sacramento–Roseville–Arden-Arcade MSA, CA	H	36.58 FQ	45.57 MW	59.32 TQ	CABLS	1/16-3/16
Fire Fighting and Prevention Workers	San Diego-Carlsbad MSA, CA	H	40.70 FQ	47.09 MW	59.61 TQ	CABLS	1/16-3/16
Fire Fighting and Prevention Workers	San Francisco-Redwood City-South San Francisco PMSA, CA	H	59.30 FQ	71.15 MW	81.28 TQ	CABLS	1/16-3/16

AE	Average entry wage	AWR	Average wage range	H	Hourly
AEX	Average experienced wage	B	Biweekly	HI	Highest wage paid
ATC	Average total compensation	D	Daily	HR	High end range
AW	Average wage paid	FQ	First quartile wage	LO	Lowest wage paid

LR	Low end range	MTC	Median total compensation	TCC	Total cash compensation
M	Monthly	MW	Median wage paid	TQ	Third quartile wage
MCC	Median cash compensation	MWR	Median wage range	W	Weekly
ME	Median entry wage	S	See annotated source	Y	Yearly

Occupation/Type/Industry	Location	Per	Low	Mid	High	Source	Date
First-Line Supervisor							
Fire Fighting and Prevention Workers	Colorado	Y	65120 FQ	77670 MW	93070 TQ	USBLS	5/15
Fire Fighting and Prevention Workers	Denver-Aurora-Lakewood MSA, CO	Y	72290 FQ	84610 MW	96700 TQ	USBLS	5/15
Fire Fighting and Prevention Workers	Connecticut	Y		79152 MW		CTBLS	1/16-3/16
Fire Fighting and Prevention Workers	Bridgeport-Stamford-Norwalk MSA, CT	Y	73720 FQ	84630 MW	95810 TQ	USBLS	5/15
Fire Fighting and Prevention Workers	Hartford-West Hartford-East Hartford MSA, CT	Y	66210 FQ	75280 MW	87710 TQ	USBLS	5/15
Fire Fighting and Prevention Workers	Delaware	Y	63730 FQ	75070 MW	88870 TQ	USBLS	5/15
Fire Fighting and Prevention Workers	Wilmington PMSA, DE-MD-NJ	Y	61110 FQ	72530 MW	86970 TQ	USBLS	5/15
Fire Fighting and Prevention Workers	Washington-Arlington-Alexandria PMSA, DC-VA-MD-WV	Y	77720 FQ	90700 MW	104700 TQ	USBLS	5/15
Fire Fighting and Prevention Workers	Florida	H	28.59 AE	39.83 MW	47.88 AEX	FLBLS	7/16-9/16
Fire Fighting and Prevention Workers	Fort Lauderdale-Pompano Beach-Deerfield Beach PMSA, FL	H	35.28 AE	43.30 MW	47.49 AEX	FLBLS	7/16-9/16
Fire Fighting and Prevention Workers	Miami-Miami Beach-Kendall PMSA, FL	H	46.14 AE	56.37 MW	61.09 AEX	FLBLS	7/16-9/16
Fire Fighting and Prevention Workers	Orlando-Kissimmee-Sanford MSA, FL	H	26.66 AE	36.33 MW	41.65 AEX	FLBLS	7/16-9/16
Fire Fighting and Prevention Workers	Tampa-St. Petersburg-Clearwater MSA, FL	H	26.82 AE	34.73 MW	39.71 AEX	FLBLS	7/16-9/16
Fire Fighting and Prevention Workers	Georgia	Y	44290 FQ	56430 MW	69970 TQ	USBLS	5/15
Fire Fighting and Prevention Workers	Atlanta-Sandy Springs-Roswell MSA, GA	Y	51590 FQ	62780 MW	77150 TQ	USBLS	5/15
Fire Fighting and Prevention Workers	Augusta-Richmond County MSA, GA-SC	Y	56670 FQ	63150 MW	74150 TQ	USBLS	5/15
Fire Fighting and Prevention Workers	Hawaii	Y	74820 FQ	86380 MW	95630 TQ	USBLS	5/15
Fire Fighting and Prevention Workers	Urban Honolulu MSA, HI	Y	83890 FQ	90750 MW	97710 TQ	USBLS	5/15
Fire Fighting and Prevention Workers	Idaho	Y	42820 FQ	55210 MW	70280 TQ	USBLS	5/15
Fire Fighting and Prevention Workers	Boise City MSA, ID	Y	45300 FQ	53770 MW	69730 TQ	USBLS	5/15
Fire Fighting and Prevention Workers	Illinois	Y	71310 FQ	93830 MW	114970 TQ	USBLS	5/15
Fire Fighting and Prevention Workers	Chicago-Naperville-Arlington Heights PMSA, IL	Y	85070 FQ	106060 MW	120650 TQ	USBLS	5/15
Fire Fighting and Prevention Workers	Lake County-Kenosha County PMSA, IL-WI	Y	52050 FQ	86960 MW	110890 TQ	USBLS	5/15
Fire Fighting and Prevention Workers	Indiana	Y	51790 FQ	58920 MW	68660 TQ	USBLS	5/15
Fire Fighting and Prevention Workers	Gary PMSA, IN	Y	48680 FQ	58850 MW	70300 TQ	USBLS	5/15
Fire Fighting and Prevention Workers	Indianapolis-Carmel-Anderson MSA, IN	Y	55020 FQ	62340 MW	72430 TQ	USBLS	5/15
Fire Fighting and Prevention Workers	Iowa	Y	53940 FQ	62350 MW	76650 TQ	USBLS	5/15
Fire Fighting and Prevention Workers	Des Moines-West Des Moines MSA, IA	Y	56530 FQ	63430 MW	84020 TQ	USBLS	5/15
Fire Fighting and Prevention Workers	Kansas	Y	46840 FQ	62130 MW	76340 TQ	USBLS	5/15
Fire Fighting and Prevention Workers	Wichita MSA, KS	Y	45230 FQ	57350 MW	69390 TQ	USBLS	5/15
Fire Fighting and Prevention Workers	Kentucky	Y	31530 FQ	44880 MW	62740 TQ	USBLS	5/15
Fire Fighting and Prevention Workers	Louisville-Jefferson County MSA, KY-IN	Y	36090 FQ	50660 MW	63420 TQ	USBLS	5/15
Fire Fighting and Prevention Workers	Louisiana	Y	43000 FQ	52530 MW	64300 TQ	USBLS	5/15
Fire Fighting and Prevention Workers	Baton Rouge MSA, LA	Y	46930 FQ	54950 MW	61670 TQ	USBLS	5/15
Fire Fighting and Prevention Workers	New Orleans-Metairie MSA, LA	Y	43130 FQ	48360 MW	59040 TQ	USBLS	5/15
Fire Fighting and Prevention Workers	Maine	Y	45870 FQ	55160 MW	62210 TQ	USBLS	5/15
Fire Fighting and Prevention Workers	Portland-South Portland MSA, ME	Y	52760 FQ	58230 MW	64820 TQ	USBLS	5/15
Fire Fighting and Prevention Workers	Maryland	Y	63317 AE	85368 MW	96394 AEX	MDBLS	4/16
Fire Fighting and Prevention Workers	Baltimore-Columbia-Towson MSA, MD	Y	66160 FQ	79100 MW	98190 TQ	USBLS	5/15
Fire Fighting and Prevention Workers	Salisbury MSA, MD-DE	Y	63260 FQ	73540 MW	87220 TQ	USBLS	5/15
Fire Fighting and Prevention Workers	Massachusetts	Y	66080 FQ	78220 MW	102410 TQ	USBLS	5/15
Fire Fighting and Prevention Workers	Boston-Cambridge-Newton NECTA, MA	Y	70840 FQ	93710 MW	115710 TQ	USBLS	5/15
Fire Fighting and Prevention Workers	Worcester MSA, MA-CT	Y	58050 FQ	75780 MW	89940 TQ	USBLS	5/15
Fire Fighting and Prevention Workers	Michigan	Y	51350 FQ	62250 MW	74120 TQ	USBLS	5/15
Fire Fighting and Prevention Workers	Detroit-Dearborn-Livonia PMSA, MI	Y	55750 FQ	63750 MW	74300 TQ	USBLS	5/15
Fire Fighting and Prevention Workers	Minnesota	Y	53735 FQ	69378 MW	90504 TQ	MNBLS	1/16-3/16
Fire Fighting and Prevention Workers	Minneapolis-St. Paul-Bloomington MSA, MN-WI	Y	54371 FQ	69762 MW	93302 TQ	MNBLS	1/16-3/16

AE	Average entry wage	AWR	Average wage range	H	Hourly	LR	Low end range	MTC	Median total compensation	TCC	Total cash compensation
AEX	Average experienced wage	B	Biweekly	HI	Highest wage paid	M	Monthly	MW	Median wage paid	TQ	Third quartile wage
ATC	Average total compensation	D	Daily	HR	High end range	MCC	Median cash compensation	MWR	Median wage range	W	Weekly
AW	Average wage paid	FQ	First quartile wage	LO	Lowest wage paid	ME	Median entry wage	S	See annotated source	Y	Yearly

Occupation/Type/Industry	Location	Per	Low	Mid	High	Source	Date
First-Line Supervisor							
Fire Fighting and Prevention Workers	Mississippi	Y	36360 FQ	43170 MW	49440 TQ	USBLS	5/15
Fire Fighting and Prevention Workers	Jackson MSA, MS	Y	34980 FQ	40200 MW	48800 TQ	USBLS	5/15
Fire Fighting and Prevention Workers	Missouri	Y	50390 FQ	70340 MW	85520 TQ	USBLS	5/15
Fire Fighting and Prevention Workers	Kansas City MSA, MO-KS	Y	58400 FQ	71890 MW	86380 TQ	USBLS	5/15
Fire Fighting and Prevention Workers	St. Louis MSA, MO-IL	Y	66140 FQ	78090 MW	94770 TQ	USBLS	5/15
Fire Fighting and Prevention Workers	Montana	Y	54620 FQ	62350 MW	77120 TQ	USBLS	5/15
Fire Fighting and Prevention Workers	Nebraska	Y	54860 FQ	63965 MW	88800 TQ	NEBLS	7/16-9/16
Fire Fighting and Prevention Workers	Omaha-Council Bluffs MSA, NE-IA	Y	58085 FQ	80650 MW	92110 TQ	NEBLS	7/16-9/16
Fire Fighting and Prevention Workers	Nevada	Y	63970 FQ	76390 MW	91420 TQ	USBLS	5/15
Fire Fighting and Prevention Workers	Las Vegas-Henderson-Paradise MSA, NV	Y	71640 FQ	80930 MW	93900 TQ	USBLS	5/15
Fire Fighting and Prevention Workers	New Hampshire	H	22.23 AE	32.83 MW	36.74 AEX	NHBLS	6/16
Fire Fighting and Prevention Workers	Manchester NECTA, NH	H	31.18 AE	38.04 MW	40.77 AEX	NHBLS	6/16
Fire Fighting and Prevention Workers	Nashua NECTA, NH-MA	Y	63570 FQ	69680 MW	75770 TQ	USBLS	5/15
Fire Fighting and Prevention Workers	New Jersey	Y	96480 FQ	116080 MW	133100 TQ	USBLS	5/15
Fire Fighting and Prevention Workers	Camden PMSA, NJ	Y	83680 FQ	102770 MW	119550 TQ	USBLS	5/15
Fire Fighting and Prevention Workers	Newark PMSA, NJ-PA	Y	104560 FQ	116400 MW	128270 TQ	USBLS	5/15
Fire Fighting and Prevention Workers	Trenton MSA, NJ	Y	85350 FQ	93590 MW	111140 TQ	USBLS	5/15
Fire Fighting and Prevention Workers	New Mexico	Y	43670 FQ	49670 MW	61880 TQ	USBLS	5/15
Fire Fighting and Prevention Workers	Albuquerque MSA, NM	Y	43080 FQ	47590 MW	57110 TQ	USBLS	5/15
Fire Fighting and Prevention Workers	New York	Y	75400 AE	95030 MW	107670 AEX	NYBLS	1/16-3/16
Fire Fighting and Prevention Workers	Buffalo-Cheektowaga-Niagara Falls MSA, NY	Y	68620 FQ	73990 MW	79280 TQ	USBLS	5/15
Fire Fighting and Prevention Workers	Nassau County-Suffolk County PMSA, NY	Y	69250 FQ	94540 MW	116380 TQ	USBLS	5/15
Fire Fighting and Prevention Workers	New York-Jersey City-White Plains PMSA, NY-NJ	Y	90360 FQ	101130 MW	123410 TQ	USBLS	5/15
Fire Fighting and Prevention Workers	Rochester MSA, NY	Y	73530 FQ	83380 MW	94040 TQ	USBLS	5/15
Fire Fighting and Prevention Workers	North Carolina	Y	46880 FQ	59980 MW	72410 TQ	USBLS	5/15
Fire Fighting and Prevention Workers	Charlotte-Concord-Gastonia MSA, NC-SC	Y	42550 FQ	57840 MW	71580 TQ	USBLS	5/15
Fire Fighting and Prevention Workers	Raleigh MSA, NC	Y	48680 FQ	58610 MW	71130 TQ	USBLS	5/15
Fire Fighting and Prevention Workers	North Dakota	Y	45380 FQ	57560 MW	70020 TQ	USBLS	5/15
Fire Fighting and Prevention Workers	Fargo MSA, ND-MN	Y	44340 FQ	50400 MW	60700 TQ	USBLS	5/15
Fire Fighting and Prevention Workers	Ohio	Y	56290 FQ	69810 MW	83200 TQ	USBLS	5/15
Fire Fighting and Prevention Workers	Cincinnati MSA, OH-KY-IN	Y	56180 FQ	67140 MW	75340 TQ	USBLS	5/15
Fire Fighting and Prevention Workers	Cleveland-Elyria MSA, OH	Y	60570 FQ	71790 MW	83670 TQ	USBLS	5/15
Fire Fighting and Prevention Workers	Columbus MSA, OH	Y	72600 FQ	85840 MW	94010 TQ	USBLS	5/15
Fire Fighting and Prevention Workers	Oklahoma	Y	51260 FQ	63980 MW	79770 TQ	USBLS	5/15
Fire Fighting and Prevention Workers	Oklahoma City MSA, OK	Y	66080 FQ	76340 MW	90120 TQ	USBLS	5/15
Fire Fighting and Prevention Workers	Tulsa MSA, OK	Y	52090 FQ	57320 MW	62560 TQ	USBLS	5/15
Fire Fighting and Prevention Workers	Oregon	H	31.10 FQ	41.88 MW	49.15 TQ	ORBLS	2016
Fire Fighting and Prevention Workers	Portland-Vancouver-Hillsboro MSA, OR-WA	Y	84860 FQ	93880 MW	103300 TQ	USBLS	5/15
Fire Fighting and Prevention Workers	Pennsylvania	Y	59940 FQ	70090 MW	78840 TQ	USBLS	5/15
Fire Fighting and Prevention Workers	Allentown-Bethlehem-Easton MSA, PA-NJ	Y	53230 FQ	63360 MW	80720 TQ	USBLS	5/15
Fire Fighting and Prevention Workers	Harrisburg-Carlisle MSA, PA	Y	44150 FQ	56850 MW	65070 TQ	USBLS	5/15
Fire Fighting and Prevention Workers	Montgomery County-Bucks County-Chester County PMSA, PA	Y	54660 FQ	62680 MW	105530 TQ	USBLS	5/15
Fire Fighting and Prevention Workers	Philadelphia PMSA, PA	Y	67260 FQ	72980 MW	78710 TQ	USBLS	5/15
Fire Fighting and Prevention Workers	Pittsburgh MSA, PA	Y	63770 FQ	71200 MW	78980 TQ	USBLS	5/15
Fire Fighting and Prevention Workers	Rhode Island	Y	63070 FQ	70380 MW	77300 TQ	USBLS	5/15
Fire Fighting and Prevention Workers	Providence-Warwick MSA, RI-MA	Y	63830 FQ	70740 MW	77480 TQ	USBLS	5/15
Fire Fighting and Prevention Workers	South Carolina	Y	41930 FQ	50940 MW	61250 TQ	USBLS	5/15
Fire Fighting and Prevention Workers	Charleston-North Charleston MSA, SC	Y	46890 FQ	56130 MW	65970 TQ	USBLS	5/15
Fire Fighting and Prevention Workers	Columbia MSA, SC	Y	40280 FQ	45930 MW	56460 TQ	USBLS	5/15
Fire Fighting and Prevention Workers	Greenville-Anderson-Mauldin MSA, SC	Y	46210 FQ	54430 MW	62020 TQ	USBLS	5/15
Fire Fighting and Prevention Workers	South Dakota	Y	64780 FQ	72190 MW	78980 TQ	USBLS	5/15
Fire Fighting and Prevention Workers	Tennessee	Y	39170 FQ	52180 MW	60520 TQ	USBLS	5/15
Fire Fighting and Prevention Workers	Knoxville MSA, TN	Y	36430 FQ	49850 MW	61840 TQ	USBLS	5/15
Fire Fighting and Prevention Workers	Nashville-Davidson–Murfreesboro–Franklin MSA, TN	Y	51060 FQ	57100 MW	65250 TQ	USBLS	5/15
Fire Fighting and Prevention Workers	Texas	Y	55560 FQ	72310 MW	91690 TQ	USBLS	5/15
Fire Fighting and Prevention Workers	Austin-Round Rock MSA, TX	Y	58450 FQ	79130 MW	99490 TQ	USBLS	5/15

AE	Average entry wage	AWR	Average wage range	
AEX	Average experienced wage	B	Biweekly	
ATC	Average total compensation	D	Daily	
AW	Average wage paid	FQ	First quartile wage	
H	Hourly	LR	Low end range	MTC Median total compensation	TCC Total cash compensation
HI	Highest wage paid	M	Monthly	MW Median wage paid	TQ Third quartile wage
HR	High end range	MCC	Median cash compensation	MWR Median wage range	W Weekly
LO	Lowest wage paid	ME	Median entry wage	S See annotated source	Y Yearly

Occupation/Type/Industry	Location	Per	Low	Mid	High	Source	Date
First-Line Supervisor							
Fire Fighting and Prevention Workers	Dallas-Plano-Irving PMSA, TX	Y	63060 FQ	77340 MW	106380 TQ	USBLS	5/15
Fire Fighting and Prevention Workers	Fort Worth-Arlington PMSA, TX	Y	71200 FQ	89740 MW	109440 TQ	USBLS	5/15
Fire Fighting and Prevention Workers	Houston-The Woodlands-Sugar Land MSA, TX	Y	54360 FQ	82010 MW	93740 TQ	USBLS	5/15
Fire Fighting and Prevention Workers	San Antonio-New Braunfels MSA, TX	Y	56460 FQ	68310 MW	77970 TQ	USBLS	5/15
Fire Fighting and Prevention Workers	Utah	Y	51630 FQ	69440 MW	86080 TQ	USBLS	5/15
Fire Fighting and Prevention Workers	Ogden-Clearfield MSA, UT	Y	46800 FQ	64750 MW	76140 TQ	USBLS	5/15
Fire Fighting and Prevention Workers	Provo-Orem MSA, UT	Y	35570 FQ	45990 MW	61230 TQ	USBLS	5/15
Fire Fighting and Prevention Workers	Salt Lake City MSA, UT	Y	67970 FQ	79550 MW	93340 TQ	USBLS	5/15
Fire Fighting and Prevention Workers	Vermont	Y	53310 FQ	62900 MW	77660 TQ	USBLS	5/15
Fire Fighting and Prevention Workers	Virginia	Y	64610 FQ	77130 MW	94570 TQ	USBLS	5/15
Fire Fighting and Prevention Workers	Richmond MSA, VA	Y	68570 FQ	79240 MW	93120 TQ	USBLS	5/15
Fire Fighting and Prevention Workers	Virginia Beach-Norfolk-Newport News MSA, VA-NC	Y	61620 FQ	71190 MW	81450 TQ	USBLS	5/15
Fire Fighting and Prevention Workers	Washington	H	38.56 FQ	45.06 MW	52.15 TQ	WABLS	3/16
Fire Fighting and Prevention Workers	Seattle-Bellevue-Everett PMSA, WA	H	42.02 FQ	47.63 MW	54.56 TQ	WABLS	3/16
Fire Fighting and Prevention Workers	Tacoma-Lakewood PMSA, WA	H	43.18 FQ	49.21 MW	57.13 TQ	WABLS	3/16
Fire Fighting and Prevention Workers	West Virginia	Y	35410 FQ	53440 MW	60780 TQ	USBLS	5/15
Fire Fighting and Prevention Workers	Huntington-Ashland MSA, WV-KY-OH	Y	48430 FQ	58940 MW	71620 TQ	USBLS	5/15
Fire Fighting and Prevention Workers	Wisconsin	Y	47680 FQ	69210 MW	87980 TQ	USBLS	5/15
Fire Fighting and Prevention Workers	Madison MSA, WI	Y	46580 FQ	60640 MW	89040 TQ	USBLS	5/15
Fire Fighting and Prevention Workers	Milwaukee-Waukesha-West Allis MSA, WI	Y	60060 FQ	84540 MW	95960 TQ	USBLS	5/15
Fire Fighting and Prevention Workers	Wyoming	Y	53860 FQ	60750 MW	76420 TQ	USBLS	5/15
Fire Fighting and Prevention Workers	Puerto Rico	Y	27340 FQ	30230 MW	35560 TQ	USBLS	5/15
Fire Fighting and Prevention Workers	San Juan-Carolina-Caguas MSA, PR	Y	27320 FQ	30200 MW	35470 TQ	USBLS	5/15
Food Preparation and Serving Workers	Alabama	Y	21014 AE	31557 AW	36819 AEX	ALBLS	6/16
Food Preparation and Serving Workers	Birmingham-Hoover MSA, AL	Y	22497 AE	34162 AW	40000 AEX	ALBLS	6/16
Food Preparation and Serving Workers	Alaska	Y	25580 FQ	35150 MW	48810 TQ	USBLS	5/15
Food Preparation and Serving Workers	Anchorage MSA, AK	Y	25540 FQ	32910 MW	45220 TQ	USBLS	5/15
Food Preparation and Serving Workers	Arizona	Y	23310 FQ	30840 MW	40520 TQ	USBLS	5/15
Food Preparation and Serving Workers	Phoenix-Mesa-Scottsdale MSA, AZ	Y	23980 FQ	31760 MW	41540 TQ	USBLS	5/15
Food Preparation and Serving Workers	Tucson MSA, AZ	Y	21730 FQ	29280 MW	38230 TQ	USBLS	5/15
Food Preparation and Serving Workers	Arkansas	Y	20120 FQ	24580 MW	31450 TQ	USBLS	5/15
Food Preparation and Serving Workers	Little Rock-North Little Rock-Conway MSA, AR	Y	21510 FQ	25770 MW	34390 TQ	USBLS	5/15
Food Preparation and Serving Workers	California	H	11.77 FQ	15.17 MW	21.25 TQ	CABLS	1/16-3/16
Food Preparation and Serving Workers	Anaheim-Santa Ana-Irvine PMSA, CA	H	11.83 FQ	15.15 MW	21.28 TQ	CABLS	1/16-3/16
Food Preparation and Serving Workers	Los Angeles-Long Beach-Glendale PMSA, CA	H	11.86 FQ	15.49 MW	20.27 TQ	CABLS	1/16-3/16
Food Preparation and Serving Workers	Oakland-Hayward-Berkeley PMSA, CA	H	12.08 FQ	15.10 MW	24.65 TQ	CABLS	1/16-3/16
Food Preparation and Serving Workers	Riverside-San Bernardino-Ontario MSA, CA	H	10.87 FQ	13.72 MW	19.32 TQ	CABLS	1/16-3/16
Food Preparation and Serving Workers	Sacramento–Roseville–Arden-Arcade MSA, CA	H	11.30 FQ	13.71 MW	18.03 TQ	CABLS	1/16-3/16
Food Preparation and Serving Workers	San Diego-Carlsbad MSA, CA	H	11.70 FQ	14.76 MW	21.62 TQ	CABLS	1/16-3/16
Food Preparation and Serving Workers	San Francisco-Redwood City-South San Francisco PMSA, CA	H	14.54 FQ	19.73 MW	26.29 TQ	CABLS	1/16-3/16
Food Preparation and Serving Workers	Colorado	Y	25950 FQ	34920 MW	44820 TQ	USBLS	5/15
Food Preparation and Serving Workers	Denver-Aurora-Lakewood MSA, CO	Y	27120 FQ	36530 MW	45470 TQ	USBLS	5/15
Food Preparation and Serving Workers	Connecticut	Y		33672 MW		CTBLS	1/16-3/16
Food Preparation and Serving Workers	Bridgeport-Stamford-Norwalk MSA, CT	Y	22680 FQ	35750 MW	50860 TQ	USBLS	5/15
Food Preparation and Serving Workers	Hartford-West Hartford-East Hartford MSA, CT	Y	23580 FQ	30410 MW	39360 TQ	USBLS	5/15
Food Preparation and Serving Workers	Delaware	Y	29550 FQ	37330 MW	45990 TQ	USBLS	5/15
Food Preparation and Serving Workers	Wilmington PMSA, DE-MD-NJ	Y	30240 FQ	37700 MW	46200 TQ	USBLS	5/15
Food Preparation and Serving Workers	District of Columbia	Y	30060 FQ	40760 MW	52820 TQ	USBLS	5/15

AE	Average entry wage	AWR	Average wage range	H	Hourly	LR	Low end range	MTC	Median total compensation	TCC	Total cash compensation
AEX	Average experienced wage	B	Biweekly	HI	Highest wage paid	M	Monthly	MW	Median wage paid	TQ	Third quartile wage
ATC	Average total compensation	D	Daily	HR	High end range	MCC	Median cash compensation	MWR	Median wage range	W	Weekly
AW	Average wage paid	FQ	First quartile wage	LO	Lowest wage paid	ME	Median entry wage	S	See annotated source	Y	Yearly

First-Line Supervisor

Occupation/Type/Industry	Location	Per	Low	Mid	High	Source	Date
Food Preparation and Serving Workers	Washington-Arlington-Alexandria PMSA, DC-VA-MD-WV	Y	28000 FQ	36980 MW	48410 TQ	USBLS	5/15
Food Preparation and Serving Workers	Florida	H	11.18 AE	15.63 MW	20.16 AEX	FLBLS	7/16-9/16
Food Preparation and Serving Workers	Fort Lauderdale-Pompano Beach-Deerfield Beach PMSA, FL	H	11.88 AE	15.43 MW	20.75 AEX	FLBLS	7/16-9/16
Food Preparation and Serving Workers	Miami-Miami Beach-Kendall PMSA, FL	H	11.54 AE	15.71 MW	19.71 AEX	FLBLS	7/16-9/16
Food Preparation and Serving Workers	Orlando-Kissimmee-Sanford MSA, FL	H	10.73 AE	16.22 MW	21.36 AEX	FLBLS	7/16-9/16
Food Preparation and Serving Workers	Tampa-St. Petersburg-Clearwater MSA, FL	H	11.40 AE	15.37 MW	20.08 AEX	FLBLS	7/16-9/16
Food Preparation and Serving Workers	Georgia	Y	21880 FQ	27950 MW	37150 TQ	USBLS	5/15
Food Preparation and Serving Workers	Atlanta-Sandy Springs-Roswell MSA, GA	Y	22700 FQ	29980 MW	39630 TQ	USBLS	5/15
Food Preparation and Serving Workers	Augusta-Richmond County MSA, GA-SC	Y	20550 FQ	25260 MW	32990 TQ	USBLS	5/15
Food Preparation and Serving Workers	Hawaii	Y	24850 FQ	34540 MW	47360 TQ	USBLS	5/15
Food Preparation and Serving Workers	Urban Honolulu MSA, HI	Y	26170 FQ	35370 MW	48380 TQ	USBLS	5/15
Food Preparation and Serving Workers	Idaho	Y	20860 FQ	25110 MW	33050 TQ	USBLS	5/15
Food Preparation and Serving Workers	Boise City MSA, ID	Y	22340 FQ	29180 MW	35840 TQ	USBLS	5/15
Food Preparation and Serving Workers	Illinois	Y	22560 FQ	28280 MW	38740 TQ	USBLS	5/15
Food Preparation and Serving Workers	Chicago-Naperville-Arlington Heights PMSA, IL	Y	23260 FQ	30210 MW	40360 TQ	USBLS	5/15
Food Preparation and Serving Workers	Lake County-Kenosha County PMSA, IL-WI	Y	24150 FQ	31140 MW	43330 TQ	USBLS	5/15
Food Preparation and Serving Workers	Indiana	Y	22140 FQ	28300 MW	36820 TQ	USBLS	5/15
Food Preparation and Serving Workers	Gary PMSA, IN	Y	20730 FQ	27710 MW	35710 TQ	USBLS	5/15
Food Preparation and Serving Workers	Indianapolis-Carmel-Anderson MSA, IN	Y	24180 FQ	29870 MW	37950 TQ	USBLS	5/15
Food Preparation and Serving Workers	Iowa	Y	21570 FQ	25890 MW	34680 TQ	USBLS	5/15
Food Preparation and Serving Workers	Des Moines-West Des Moines MSA, IA	Y	23740 FQ	30900 MW	37090 TQ	USBLS	5/15
Food Preparation and Serving Workers	Kansas	Y	21340 FQ	26520 MW	33380 TQ	USBLS	5/15
Food Preparation and Serving Workers	Wichita MSA, KS	Y	22290 FQ	27290 MW	34570 TQ	USBLS	5/15
Food Preparation and Serving Workers	Kentucky	Y	21440 FQ	25500 MW	34010 TQ	USBLS	5/15
Food Preparation and Serving Workers	Louisville-Jefferson County MSA, KY-IN	Y	21690 FQ	26600 MW	36640 TQ	USBLS	5/15
Food Preparation and Serving Workers	Louisiana	Y	23530 FQ	27930 MW	33490 TQ	USBLS	5/15
Food Preparation and Serving Workers	Baton Rouge MSA, LA	Y	23840 FQ	28280 MW	34230 TQ	USBLS	5/15
Food Preparation and Serving Workers	New Orleans-Metairie MSA, LA	Y	24870 FQ	28710 MW	34520 TQ	USBLS	5/15
Food Preparation and Serving Workers	Maine	Y	23830 FQ	30080 MW	38440 TQ	USBLS	5/15
Food Preparation and Serving Workers	Portland-South Portland MSA, ME	Y	23640 FQ	29440 MW	40120 TQ	USBLS	5/15
Food Preparation and Serving Workers	Maryland	Y	23264 AE	37729 MW	44962 AEX	MDBLS	4/16
Food Preparation and Serving Workers	Baltimore-Columbia-Towson MSA, MD	Y	28360 FQ	36550 MW	46220 TQ	USBLS	5/15
Food Preparation and Serving Workers	Salisbury MSA, MD-DE	Y	23390 FQ	31320 MW	39250 TQ	USBLS	5/15
Food Preparation and Serving Workers	Massachusetts	Y	27370 FQ	34850 MW	44730 TQ	USBLS	5/15
Food Preparation and Serving Workers	Boston-Cambridge-Newton NECTA, MA	Y	27480 FQ	36000 MW	46800 TQ	USBLS	5/15
Food Preparation and Serving Workers	Worcester MSA, MA-CT	Y	26900 FQ	34310 MW	42890 TQ	USBLS	5/15
Food Preparation and Serving Workers	Michigan	Y	22110 FQ	28860 MW	38720 TQ	USBLS	5/15
Food Preparation and Serving Workers	Detroit-Dearborn-Livonia PMSA, MI	Y	23580 FQ	31130 MW	45780 TQ	USBLS	5/15
Food Preparation and Serving Workers	Flint MSA, MI	Y	22000 FQ	31550 MW	37260 TQ	USBLS	5/15
Food Preparation and Serving Workers	Grand Rapids-Wyoming MSA, MI	Y	21850 FQ	27780 MW	36170 TQ	USBLS	5/15
Food Preparation and Serving Workers	Minnesota	Y	24358 FQ	29751 MW	37527 TQ	MNBLS	1/16-3/16
Food Preparation and Serving Workers	Minneapolis-St. Paul-Bloomington MSA, MN-WI	Y	24621 FQ	30074 MW	38011 TQ	MNBLS	1/16-3/16
Food Preparation and Serving Workers	Mississippi	Y	19450 FQ	24330 MW	31950 TQ	USBLS	5/15
Food Preparation and Serving Workers	Jackson MSA, MS	Y	23290 FQ	29340 MW	39320 TQ	USBLS	5/15
Food Preparation and Serving Workers	Missouri	Y	21820 FQ	26790 MW	35420 TQ	USBLS	5/15
Food Preparation and Serving Workers	Kansas City MSA, MO-KS	Y	22810 FQ	28000 MW	34900 TQ	USBLS	5/15
Food Preparation and Serving Workers	St. Louis MSA, MO-IL	Y	21800 FQ	26940 MW	37770 TQ	USBLS	5/15
Food Preparation and Serving Workers	Montana	Y	23380 FQ	29540 MW	37060 TQ	USBLS	5/15
Food Preparation and Serving Workers	Billings MSA, MT	Y	23960 FQ	30250 MW	37720 TQ	USBLS	5/15
Food Preparation and Serving Workers	Nebraska	Y	22200 FQ	27745 MW	35890 TQ	NEBLS	7/16-9/16

AE	Average entry wage	AWR	Average wage range	H	Hourly
AEX	Average experienced wage	B	Biweekly	HI	Highest wage paid
ATC	Average total compensation	D	Daily	HR	High end range
AW	Average wage paid	FQ	First quartile wage	LO	Lowest wage paid

LR	Low end range	MTC	Median total compensation
M	Monthly	MW	Median wage paid
MCC	Median cash compensation	MWR	Median wage range
ME	Median entry wage	S	See annotated source

TCC	Total cash compensation
TQ	Third quartile wage
W	Weekly
Y	Yearly

Occupation/Type/Industry	Location	Per	Low	Mid	High	Source	Date
First-Line Supervisor							
Food Preparation and Serving Workers	Omaha-Council Bluffs MSA, NE-IA	Y	22535 FQ	27885 MW	36830 TQ	NEBLS	7/16-9/16
Food Preparation and Serving Workers	Nevada	Y	26080 FQ	33700 MW	42580 TQ	USBLS	5/15
Food Preparation and Serving Workers	Las Vegas-Henderson-Paradise MSA, NV	Y	26180 FQ	34250 MW	43340 TQ	USBLS	5/15
Food Preparation and Serving Workers	New Hampshire	H	12.15 AE	17.59 MW	20.96 AEX	NHBLS	6/16
Food Preparation and Serving Workers	Manchester NECTA, NH	H	11.99 AE	17.65 MW	21.20 AEX	NHBLS	6/16
Food Preparation and Serving Workers	Nashua NECTA, NH-MA	Y	36550 FQ	43530 MW	49990 TQ	USBLS	5/15
Food Preparation and Serving Workers	New Jersey	Y	29110 FQ	37690 MW	48990 TQ	USBLS	5/15
Food Preparation and Serving Workers	Camden PMSA, NJ	Y	27180 FQ	33300 MW	41770 TQ	USBLS	5/15
Food Preparation and Serving Workers	Newark PMSA, NJ-PA	Y	27900 FQ	41240 MW	54180 TQ	USBLS	5/15
Food Preparation and Serving Workers	Trenton MSA, NJ	Y	28570 FQ	37770 MW	52730 TQ	USBLS	5/15
Food Preparation and Serving Workers	New Mexico	Y	21300 FQ	25060 MW	32740 TQ	USBLS	5/15
Food Preparation and Serving Workers	Albuquerque MSA, NM	Y	21700 FQ	24940 MW	33000 TQ	USBLS	5/15
Food Preparation and Serving Workers	New York	Y	23730 AE	34990 MW	45800 AEX	NYBLS	1/16-3/16
Food Preparation and Serving Workers	Buffalo-Cheektowaga-Niagara Falls MSA, NY	Y	23760 FQ	29080 MW	38540 TQ	USBLS	5/15
Food Preparation and Serving Workers	Nassau County-Suffolk County PMSA, NY	Y	26110 FQ	36230 MW	53240 TQ	USBLS	5/15
Food Preparation and Serving Workers	New York-Jersey City-White Plains PMSA, NY-NJ	Y	29000 FQ	38550 MW	50430 TQ	USBLS	5/15
Food Preparation and Serving Workers	Rochester MSA, NY	Y	23610 FQ	28790 MW	38180 TQ	USBLS	5/15
Food Preparation and Serving Workers	North Carolina	Y	24110 FQ	30530 MW	38460 TQ	USBLS	5/15
Food Preparation and Serving Workers	Charlotte-Concord-Gastonia MSA, NC-SC	Y	24970 FQ	32810 MW	41070 TQ	USBLS	5/15
Food Preparation and Serving Workers	Raleigh MSA, NC	Y	26010 FQ	33930 MW	42860 TQ	USBLS	5/15
Food Preparation and Serving Workers	North Dakota	Y	26150 FQ	32020 MW	39340 TQ	USBLS	5/15
Food Preparation and Serving Workers	Fargo MSA, ND-MN	Y	25000 FQ	32240 MW	39170 TQ	USBLS	5/15
Food Preparation and Serving Workers	Ohio	Y	22710 FQ	29100 MW	38410 TQ	USBLS	5/15
Food Preparation and Serving Workers	Cincinnati MSA, OH-KY-IN	Y	22830 FQ	29200 MW	40270 TQ	USBLS	5/15
Food Preparation and Serving Workers	Cleveland-Elyria MSA, OH	Y	22550 FQ	28040 MW	35420 TQ	USBLS	5/15
Food Preparation and Serving Workers	Columbus MSA, OH	Y	25660 FQ	33540 MW	43020 TQ	USBLS	5/15
Food Preparation and Serving Workers	Oklahoma	Y	20140 FQ	24320 MW	32620 TQ	USBLS	5/15
Food Preparation and Serving Workers	Oklahoma City MSA, OK	Y	19060 FQ	23960 MW	32610 TQ	USBLS	5/15
Food Preparation and Serving Workers	Tulsa MSA, OK	Y	20620 FQ	24050 MW	34560 TQ	USBLS	5/15
Food Preparation and Serving Workers	Oregon	H	11.22 FQ	13.49 MW	17.78 TQ	ORBLS	2016
Food Preparation and Serving Workers	Portland-Vancouver-Hillsboro MSA, OR-WA	Y	23380 FQ	28160 MW	38030 TQ	USBLS	5/15
Food Preparation and Serving Workers	Pennsylvania	Y	24440 FQ	33080 MW	43960 TQ	USBLS	5/15
Food Preparation and Serving Workers	Allentown-Bethlehem-Easton MSA, PA-NJ	Y	23910 FQ	30150 MW	43560 TQ	USBLS	5/15
Food Preparation and Serving Workers	Harrisburg-Carlisle MSA, PA	Y	23700 FQ	33070 MW	42850 TQ	USBLS	5/15
Food Preparation and Serving Workers	Montgomery County-Bucks County-Chester County PMSA, PA	Y	28580 FQ	37990 MW	48450 TQ	USBLS	5/15
Food Preparation and Serving Workers	Philadelphia PMSA, PA	Y	27600 FQ	38150 MW	48700 TQ	USBLS	5/15
Food Preparation and Serving Workers	Pittsburgh MSA, PA	Y	24300 FQ	31400 MW	42300 TQ	USBLS	5/15
Food Preparation and Serving Workers	Rhode Island	Y	28330 FQ	36740 MW	47920 TQ	USBLS	5/15
Food Preparation and Serving Workers	Providence-Warwick MSA, RI-MA	Y	27640 FQ	35360 MW	46450 TQ	USBLS	5/15
Food Preparation and Serving Workers	South Carolina	Y	21910 FQ	27660 MW	36040 TQ	USBLS	5/15
Food Preparation and Serving Workers	Charleston-North Charleston MSA, SC	Y	25600 FQ	31860 MW	38460 TQ	USBLS	5/15
Food Preparation and Serving Workers	Columbia MSA, SC	Y	21400 FQ	26250 MW	34680 TQ	USBLS	5/15
Food Preparation and Serving Workers	Greenville-Anderson-Mauldin MSA, SC	Y	21070 FQ	26020 MW	33660 TQ	USBLS	5/15
Food Preparation and Serving Workers	South Dakota	Y	27490 FQ	31130 MW	35900 TQ	USBLS	5/15
Food Preparation and Serving Workers	Sioux Falls MSA, SD	Y	27130 FQ	30540 MW	35670 TQ	USBLS	5/15
Food Preparation and Serving Workers	Tennessee	Y	21960 FQ	27130 MW	34800 TQ	USBLS	5/15
Food Preparation and Serving Workers	Knoxville MSA, TN	Y	22510 FQ	27100 MW	36030 TQ	USBLS	5/15
Food Preparation and Serving Workers	Memphis MSA, TN-MS-AR	Y	21060 FQ	26070 MW	32970 TQ	USBLS	5/15
Food Preparation and Serving Workers	Nashville-Davidson–Murfreesboro–Franklin MSA, TN	Y	24060 FQ	29750 MW	38200 TQ	USBLS	5/15
Food Preparation and Serving Workers	Texas	Y	23660 FQ	33690 MW	44650 TQ	USBLS	5/15
Food Preparation and Serving Workers	Austin-Round Rock MSA, TX	Y	26420 FQ	36310 MW	45930 TQ	USBLS	5/15
Food Preparation and Serving Workers	Dallas-Plano-Irving PMSA, TX	Y	23700 FQ	35740 MW	47660 TQ	USBLS	5/15
Food Preparation and Serving Workers	El Paso MSA, TX	Y	23060 FQ	29160 MW	39440 TQ	USBLS	5/15
Food Preparation and Serving Workers	Fort Worth-Arlington PMSA, TX	Y	23230 FQ	35230 MW	44820 TQ	USBLS	5/15

AE	Average entry wage	AWR	Average wage range	H	Hourly
AEX	Average experienced wage	B	Biweekly	HI	Highest wage paid
ATC	Average total compensation	D	Daily	HR	High end range
AW	Average wage paid	FQ	First quartile wage	LO	Lowest wage paid

LR	Low end range	MTC	Median total compensation	TCC	Total cash compensation
M	Monthly	MW	Median wage paid	TQ	Third quartile wage
MCC	Median cash compensation	MWR	Median wage range	W	Weekly
ME	Median entry wage	S	See annotated source	Y	Yearly

Occupation/Type/Industry	Location	Per	Low	Mid	High	Source	Date
First-Line Supervisor							
Food Preparation and Serving Workers	Houston-The Woodlands-Sugar Land MSA, TX	Y	23100 FQ	34910 MW	46750 TQ	USBLS	5/15
Food Preparation and Serving Workers	San Antonio-New Braunfels MSA, TX	Y	24110 FQ	32420 MW	41350 TQ	USBLS	5/15
Food Preparation and Serving Workers	Utah	Y	22070 FQ	26280 MW	34820 TQ	USBLS	5/15
Food Preparation and Serving Workers	Ogden-Clearfield MSA, UT	Y	20750 FQ	23140 MW	27060 TQ	USBLS	5/15
Food Preparation and Serving Workers	Provo-Orem MSA, UT	Y	22710 FQ	26800 MW	30820 TQ	USBLS	5/15
Food Preparation and Serving Workers	Salt Lake City MSA, UT	Y	22830 FQ	28910 MW	42450 TQ	USBLS	5/15
Food Preparation and Serving Workers	Vermont	Y	28570 FQ	35820 MW	45070 TQ	USBLS	5/15
Food Preparation and Serving Workers	Burlington-South Burlington MSA, VT	Y	26630 FQ	33590 MW	43930 TQ	USBLS	5/15
Food Preparation and Serving Workers	Virginia	Y	26150 FQ	33140 MW	41270 TQ	USBLS	5/15
Food Preparation and Serving Workers	Richmond MSA, VA	Y	23860 FQ	32020 MW	38420 TQ	USBLS	5/15
Food Preparation and Serving Workers	Virginia Beach-Norfolk-Newport News MSA, VA-NC	Y	28970 FQ	34480 MW	39820 TQ	USBLS	5/15
Food Preparation and Serving Workers	Washington	H	13.10 FQ	17.25 MW	22.33 TQ	WABLS	3/16
Food Preparation and Serving Workers	Seattle-Bellevue-Everett PMSA, WA	H	15.45 FQ	19.99 MW	24.30 TQ	WABLS	3/16
Food Preparation and Serving Workers	Tacoma-Lakewood PMSA, WA	H	11.10 FQ	13.53 MW	18.38 TQ	WABLS	3/16
Food Preparation and Serving Workers	West Virginia	Y	20670 FQ	24350 MW	30140 TQ	USBLS	5/15
Food Preparation and Serving Workers	Huntington-Ashland MSA, WV-KY-OH	Y	19810 FQ	23440 MW	29220 TQ	USBLS	5/15
Food Preparation and Serving Workers	Wisconsin	Y	22140 FQ	27620 MW	35030 TQ	USBLS	5/15
Food Preparation and Serving Workers	Madison MSA, WI	Y	24730 FQ	30000 MW	37840 TQ	USBLS.	5/15
Food Preparation and Serving Workers	Milwaukee-Waukesha-West Allis MSA, WI	Y	23090 FQ	28660 MW	36050 TQ	USBLS	5/15
Food Preparation and Serving Workers	Wyoming	Y	23270 FQ	29340 MW	38270 TQ	USBLS	5/15
Food Preparation and Serving Workers	Cheyenne MSA, WY	Y	19990 FQ	25430 MW	33810 TQ	USBLS	5/15
Food Preparation and Serving Workers	Puerto Rico	Y	18250 FQ	22460 MW	27970 TQ	USBLS	5/15
Food Preparation and Serving Workers	San Juan-Carolina-Caguas MSA, PR	Y	18230 FQ	22170 MW	27640 TQ	USBLS	5/15
Food Preparation and Serving Workers	Virgin Islands	Y	23880 FQ	28800 MW	37340 TQ	USBLS	5/15
Food Preparation and Serving Workers	Guam	Y	18820 FQ	21160 MW	24400 TQ	USBLS	5/15
Helpers, Laborers, and Material Movers	Alabama	Y	32418 AE	48144 AW	56002 AEX	ALBLS	6/16
Helpers, Laborers, and Material Movers	Birmingham-Hoover MSA, AL	Y	32521 AE	47075 AW	54356 AEX	ALBLS	6/16
Helpers, Laborers, and Material Movers	Alaska	Y	37320 FQ	45880 MW	70670 TQ	USBLS	5/15
Helpers, Laborers, and Material Movers	Anchorage MSA, AK	Y	38170 FQ	46570 MW	69120 TQ	USBLS	5/15
Helpers, Laborers, and Material Movers	Arizona	Y	35030 FQ	45900 MW	60570 TQ	USBLS	5/15
Helpers, Laborers, and Material Movers	Phoenix-Mesa-Scottsdale MSA, AZ	Y	35390 FQ	46050 MW	60820 TQ	USBLS	5/15
Helpers, Laborers, and Material Movers	Tucson MSA, AZ	Y	33370 FQ	47700 MW	65410 TQ	USBLS	5/15
Helpers, Laborers, and Material Movers	Arkansas	Y	34470 FQ	43650 MW	56520 TQ	USBLS	5/15
Helpers, Laborers, and Material Movers	Little Rock-North Little Rock-Conway MSA, AR	Y	35970 FQ	43960 MW	66080 TQ	USBLS	5/15
Helpers, Laborers, and Material Movers	California	H	17.81 FQ	23.51 MW	30.12 TQ	CABLS	1/16-3/16
Helpers, Laborers, and Material Movers	Anaheim-Santa Ana-Irvine PMSA, CA	H	17.17 FQ	21.57 MW	28.91 TQ	CABLS	1/16-3/16
Helpers, Laborers, and Material Movers	Los Angeles-Long Beach-Glendale PMSA, CA	H	16.71 FQ	21.97 MW	30.85 TQ	CABLS	1/16-3/16
Helpers, Laborers, and Material Movers	Oakland-Hayward-Berkeley PMSA, CA	H	20.09 FQ	28.68 MW	37.41 TQ	CABLS	1/16-3/16
Helpers, Laborers, and Material Movers	Riverside-San Bernardino-Ontario MSA, CA	H	19.61 FQ	25.47 MW	30.06 TQ	CABLS	1/16-3/16
Helpers, Laborers, and Material Movers	Sacramento–Roseville–Arden-Arcade MSA, CA	H	17.67 FQ	21.92 MW	27.68 TQ	CABLS	1/16-3/16
Helpers, Laborers, and Material Movers	San Diego-Carlsbad MSA, CA	H	17.31 FQ	21.46 MW	28.64 TQ	CABLS	1/16-3/16
Helpers, Laborers, and Material Movers	San Francisco-Redwood City-South San Francisco PMSA, CA	H	20.26 FQ	24.61 MW	30.35 TQ	CABLS	1/16-3/16
Helpers, Laborers, and Material Movers	Colorado	Y	35360 FQ	46320 MW	61150 TQ	USBLS	5/15
Helpers, Laborers, and Material Movers	Denver-Aurora-Lakewood MSA, CO	Y	35200 FQ	46180 MW	60720 TQ	USBLS	5/15
Helpers, Laborers, and Material Movers	Connecticut	Y		53544 MW		CTBLS	1/16-3/16
Helpers, Laborers, and Material Movers	Bridgeport-Stamford-Norwalk MSA, CT	Y	47340 FQ	57320 MW	67980 TQ	USBLS	5/15
Helpers, Laborers, and Material Movers	Hartford-West Hartford-East Hartford MSA, CT	Y	35680 FQ	50250 MW	65970 TQ	USBLS	5/15
Helpers, Laborers, and Material Movers	Delaware	Y	41170 FQ	55160 MW	69380 TQ	USBLS	5/15
Helpers, Laborers, and Material Movers	Wilmington PMSA, DE-MD-NJ	Y	37360 FQ	56500 MW	71220 TQ	USBLS	5/15
Helpers, Laborers, and Material Movers	District of Columbia	Y	47910 FQ	67760 MW	82170 TQ	USBLS	5/15

AE Average entry wage	**AWR** Average wage range	**H** Hourly	**LR** Low end range	**MTC** Median total compensation	**TCC** Total cash compensation
AEX Average experienced wage	**B** Biweekly	**HI** Highest wage paid	**M** Monthly	**MW** Median wage paid	**TQ** Third quartile wage
ATC Average total compensation	**D** Daily	**HR** High end range	**MCC** Median cash compensation	**MWR** Median wage range	**W** Weekly
AW Average wage paid	**FQ** First quartile wage	**LO** Lowest wage paid	**ME** Median entry wage	**S** See annotated source	**Y** Yearly

First-Line Supervisor

Occupation/Type/Industry	Location	Per	Low	Mid	High	Source	Date
Helpers, Laborers, and Material Movers	Washington-Arlington-Alexandria PMSA, DC-VA-MD-WV	Y	42260 FQ	51060 MW	68790 TQ	USBLS	5/15
Helpers, Laborers, and Material Movers	Florida	H	15.26 AE	21.71 MW	27.52 AEX	FLBLS	7/16-9/16
Helpers, Laborers, and Material Movers	Fort Lauderdale-Pompano Beach-Deerfield Beach PMSA, FL	H	15.20 AE	23.84 MW	28.70 AEX	FLBLS	7/16-9/16
Helpers, Laborers, and Material Movers	Miami-Miami Beach-Kendall PMSA, FL	H	14.92 AE	20.93 MW	26.40 AEX	FLBLS	7/16-9/16
Helpers, Laborers, and Material Movers	Orlando-Kissimmee-Sanford MSA, FL	H	13.84 AE	20.60 MW	26.29 AEX	FLBLS	7/16-9/16
Helpers, Laborers, and Material Movers	Tampa-St. Petersburg-Clearwater MSA, FL	H	15.99 AE	22.31 MW	27.27 AEX	FLBLS	7/16-9/16
Helpers, Laborers, and Material Movers	Georgia	Y	36240 FQ	47680 MW	61800 TQ	USBLS	5/15
Helpers, Laborers, and Material Movers	Atlanta-Sandy Springs-Roswell MSA, GA	Y	36950 FQ	49060 MW	62990 TQ	USBLS	5/15
Helpers, Laborers, and Material Movers	Augusta-Richmond County MSA, GA-SC	Y	37570 FQ	45540 MW	56830 TQ	USBLS	5/15
Helpers, Laborers, and Material Movers	Hawaii	Y	35030 FQ	45590 MW	59150 TQ	USBLS	5/15
Helpers, Laborers, and Material Movers	Urban Honolulu MSA, HI	Y	33870 FQ	44810 MW	58190 TQ	USBLS	5/15
Helpers, Laborers, and Material Movers	Idaho	Y	32600 FQ	40980 MW	50950 TQ	USBLS	5/15
Helpers, Laborers, and Material Movers	Boise City MSA, ID	Y	33060 FQ	41730 MW	49300 TQ	USBLS	5/15
Helpers, Laborers, and Material Movers	Illinois	Y	36370 FQ	49630 MW	65390 TQ	USBLS	5/15
Helpers, Laborers, and Material Movers	Chicago-Naperville-Arlington Heights PMSA, IL	Y	36400 FQ	50340 MW	67440 TQ	USBLS	5/15
Helpers, Laborers, and Material Movers	Lake County-Kenosha County PMSA, IL-WI	Y	37370 FQ	51180 MW	68820 TQ	USBLS	5/15
Helpers, Laborers, and Material Movers	Indiana	Y	34750 FQ	46630 MW	60780 TQ	USBLS	5/15
Helpers, Laborers, and Material Movers	Gary PMSA, IN	Y	34700 FQ	52650 MW	61840 TQ	USBLS	5/15
Helpers, Laborers, and Material Movers	Indianapolis-Carmel-Anderson MSA, IN	Y	36560 FQ	48230 MW	62250 TQ	USBLS	5/15
Helpers, Laborers, and Material Movers	Iowa	Y	35130 FQ	45790 MW	59610 TQ	USBLS	5/15
Helpers, Laborers, and Material Movers	Des Moines-West Des Moines MSA, IA	Y	40800 FQ	51680 MW	62400 TQ	USBLS	5/15
Helpers, Laborers, and Material Movers	Kansas	Y	35980 FQ	46150 MW	58270 TQ	USBLS	5/15
Helpers, Laborers, and Material Movers	Wichita MSA, KS	Y	32970 FQ	38630 MW	48690 TQ	USBLS	5/15
Helpers, Laborers, and Material Movers	Kentucky	Y	33480 FQ	43810 MW	57280 TQ	USBLS	5/15
Helpers, Laborers, and Material Movers	Louisville-Jefferson County MSA, KY-IN	Y	35770 FQ	46570 MW	62650 TQ	USBLS	5/15
Helpers, Laborers, and Material Movers	Louisiana	Y	35660 FQ	44270 MW	56280 TQ	USBLS	5/15
Helpers, Laborers, and Material Movers	Baton Rouge MSA, LA	Y	34910 FQ	41970 MW	52270 TQ	USBLS	5/15
Helpers, Laborers, and Material Movers	New Orleans-Metairie MSA, LA	Y	37340 FQ	45630 MW	61090 TQ	USBLS	5/15
Helpers, Laborers, and Material Movers	Maine	Y	38890 FQ	52670 MW	61830 TQ	USBLS	5/15
Helpers, Laborers, and Material Movers	Portland-South Portland MSA, ME	Y	41890 FQ	56190 MW	67030 TQ	USBLS	5/15
Helpers, Laborers, and Material Movers	Maryland	Y	32265 AE	50451 MW	59543 AEX	MDBLS	4/16
Helpers, Laborers, and Material Movers	Baltimore-Columbia-Towson MSA, MD	Y	34610 FQ	44190 MW	59500 TQ	USBLS	5/15
Helpers, Laborers, and Material Movers	Salisbury MSA, MD-DE	Y	37360 FQ	47920 MW	60700 TQ	USBLS	5/15
Helpers, Laborers, and Material Movers	Massachusetts	Y	37890 FQ	48520 MW	61670 TQ	USBLS	5/15
Helpers, Laborers, and Material Movers	Boston-Cambridge-Newton NECTA, MA	Y	41170 FQ	48980 MW	62310 TQ	USBLS	5/15
Helpers, Laborers, and Material Movers	Worcester MSA, MA-CT	Y	35280 FQ	47660 MW	59730 TQ	USBLS	5/15
Helpers, Laborers, and Material Movers	Michigan	Y	33740 FQ	45670 MW	61500 TQ	USBLS	5/15
Helpers, Laborers, and Material Movers	Detroit-Dearborn-Livonia PMSA, MI	Y	30660 FQ	45830 MW	64190 TQ	USBLS	5/15
Helpers, Laborers, and Material Movers	Grand Rapids-Wyoming MSA, MI	Y	35520 FQ	45810 MW	58280 TQ	USBLS	5/15
Helpers, Laborers, and Material Movers	Minnesota	Y	39721 FQ	50730 MW	62192 TQ	MNBLS	1/16-3/16
Helpers, Laborers, and Material Movers	Minneapolis-St. Paul-Bloomington MSA, MN-WI	Y	39922 FQ	51496 MW	63594 TQ	MNBLS	1/16-3/16
Helpers, Laborers, and Material Movers	Mississippi	Y	33600 FQ	44850 MW	58960 TQ	USBLS	5/15
Helpers, Laborers, and Material Movers	Jackson MSA, MS	Y	43120 FQ	53820 MW	62350 TQ	USBLS	5/15
Helpers, Laborers, and Material Movers	Missouri	Y	38220 FQ	47730 MW	58420 TQ	USBLS	5/15
Helpers, Laborers, and Material Movers	Kansas City MSA, MO-KS	Y	38370 FQ	47660 MW	58970 TQ	USBLS	5/15
Helpers, Laborers, and Material Movers	St. Louis MSA, MO-IL	Y	40350 FQ	48950 MW	59800 TQ	USBLS	5/15
Helpers, Laborers, and Material Movers	Montana	Y	35460 FQ	45130 MW	58610 TQ	USBLS	5/15
Helpers, Laborers, and Material Movers	Billings MSA, MT	Y	35180 FQ	42730 MW	49910 TQ	USBLS	5/15
Helpers, Laborers, and Material Movers	Nebraska	Y	38825 FQ	49510 MW	65265 TQ	NEBLS	7/16-9/16

AE	Average entry wage	AWR	Average wage range	H	Hourly
AEX	Average experienced wage	B	Biweekly	HI	Highest wage paid
ATC	Average total compensation	D	Daily	HR	High end range
AW	Average wage paid	FQ	First quartile wage	LO	Lowest wage paid

LR	Low end range	MTC	Median total compensation
M	Monthly	MW	Median wage paid
MCC	Median cash compensation	MWR	Median wage range
ME	Median entry wage	S	See annotated source

TCC	Total cash compensation		
TQ	Third quartile wage		
W	Weekly		
Y	Yearly		

First-Line Supervisor

Occupation/Type/Industry	Location	Per	Low	Mid	High	Source	Date
Helpers, Laborers, and Material Movers	Omaha-Council Bluffs MSA, NE-IA	Y	40845 FQ	49465 MW	64655 TQ	NEBLS	7/16-9/16
Helpers, Laborers, and Material Movers	Nevada	Y	33070 FQ	43690 MW	57150 TQ	USBLS	5/15
Helpers, Laborers, and Material Movers	Las Vegas-Henderson-Paradise MSA, NV	Y	30930 FQ	43190 MW	57480 TQ	USBLS	5/15
Helpers, Laborers, and Material Movers	New Hampshire	H	14.51 AE	21.46 MW	26.45 AEX	NHBLS	6/16
Helpers, Laborers, and Material Movers	Manchester NECTA, NH	H	14.41 AE	19.23 MW	25.49 AEX	NHBLS	6/16
Helpers, Laborers, and Material Movers	Nashua NECTA, NH-MA	Y	29080 FQ	44320 MW	58300 TQ	USBLS	5/15
Helpers, Laborers, and Material Movers	New Jersey	Y	40360 FQ	51540 MW	64930 TQ	USBLS	5/15
Helpers, Laborers, and Material Movers	Camden PMSA, NJ	Y	39260 FQ	51470 MW	62090 TQ	USBLS	5/15
Helpers, Laborers, and Material Movers	Newark PMSA, NJ-PA	Y	40040 FQ	51090 MW	63720 TQ	USBLS	5/15
Helpers, Laborers, and Material Movers	Trenton MSA, NJ	Y	45040 FQ	54760 MW	63730 TQ	USBLS	5/15
Helpers, Laborers, and Material Movers	New Mexico	Y	32470 FQ	40000 MW	53020 TQ	USBLS	5/15
Helpers, Laborers, and Material Movers	Albuquerque MSA, NM	Y	33840 FQ	43240 MW	54360 TQ	USBLS	5/15
Helpers, Laborers, and Material Movers	New York	Y	33290 AE	51080 MW	64920 AEX	NYBLS	1/16-3/16
Helpers, Laborers, and Material Movers	Buffalo-Cheektowaga-Niagara Falls MSA, NY	Y	34090 FQ	45400 MW	58050 TQ	USBLS	5/15
Helpers, Laborers, and Material Movers	Nassau County-Suffolk County PMSA, NY	Y	37880 FQ	57990 MW	74080 TQ	USBLS	5/15
Helpers, Laborers, and Material Movers	New York-Jersey City-White Plains PMSA, NY-NJ	Y	39710 FQ	51730 MW	69070 TQ	USBLS	5/15
Helpers, Laborers, and Material Movers	Rochester MSA, NY	Y	35800 FQ	47470 MW	59820 TQ	USBLS	5/15
Helpers, Laborers, and Material Movers	North Carolina	Y	36210 FQ	45480 MW	56980 TQ	USBLS	5/15
Helpers, Laborers, and Material Movers	Charlotte-Concord-Gastonia MSA, NC-SC	Y	37280 FQ	47020 MW	58110 TQ	USBLS	5/15
Helpers, Laborers, and Material Movers	Raleigh MSA, NC	Y	36130 FQ	45620 MW	56880 TQ	USBLS	5/15
Helpers, Laborers, and Material Movers	North Dakota	Y	37300 FQ	46750 MW	62510 TQ	USBLS	5/15
Helpers, Laborers, and Material Movers	Fargo MSA, ND-MN	Y	35860 FQ	47080 MW	68550 TQ	USBLS	5/15
Helpers, Laborers, and Material Movers	Ohio	Y	35080 FQ	45650 MW	58060 TQ	USBLS	5/15
Helpers, Laborers, and Material Movers	Cincinnati MSA, OH-KY-IN	Y	38050 FQ	49720 MW	59530 TQ	USBLS	5/15
Helpers, Laborers, and Material Movers	Cleveland-Elyria MSA, OH	Y	33270 FQ	47710 MW	60600 TQ	USBLS	5/15
Helpers, Laborers, and Material Movers	Columbus MSA, OH	Y	36570 FQ	46930 MW	58230 TQ	USBLS	5/15
Helpers, Laborers, and Material Movers	Oklahoma	Y	37720 FQ	46830 MW	59160 TQ	USBLS	5/15
Helpers, Laborers, and Material Movers	Oklahoma City MSA, OK	Y	36960 FQ	46680 MW	58580 TQ	USBLS	5/15
Helpers, Laborers, and Material Movers	Tulsa MSA, OK	Y	36680 FQ	44890 MW	56830 TQ	USBLS	5/15
Helpers, Laborers, and Material Movers	Oregon	H	16.56 FQ	19.41 MW	26.32 TQ	ORBLS	2016
Helpers, Laborers, and Material Movers	Portland-Vancouver-Hillsboro MSA, OR-WA	Y	36140 FQ	44240 MW	57440 TQ	USBLS	5/15
Helpers, Laborers, and Material Movers	Pennsylvania	Y	40440 FQ	51640 MW	62510 TQ	USBLS	5/15
Helpers, Laborers, and Material Movers	Allentown-Bethlehem-Easton MSA, PA-NJ	Y	43350 FQ	54180 MW	62400 TQ	USBLS	5/15
Helpers, Laborers, and Material Movers	Harrisburg-Carlisle MSA, PA	Y	39940 FQ	54690 MW	62330 TQ	USBLS	5/15
Helpers, Laborers, and Material Movers	Montgomery County-Bucks County-Chester County PMSA, PA	Y	39560 FQ	54530 MW	69960 TQ	USBLS	5/15
Helpers, Laborers, and Material Movers	Philadelphia PMSA, PA	Y	42810 FQ	55320 MW	67650 TQ	USBLS	5/15
Helpers, Laborers, and Material Movers	Pittsburgh MSA, PA	Y	40180 FQ	49460 MW	61180 TQ	USBLS	5/15
Helpers, Laborers, and Material Movers	Rhode Island	Y	38380 FQ	48150 MW	61230 TQ	USBLS	5/15
Helpers, Laborers, and Material Movers	Providence-Warwick MSA, RI-MA	Y	37750 FQ	48020 MW	61630 TQ	USBLS	5/15
Helpers, Laborers, and Material Movers	South Carolina	Y	35720 FQ	46420 MW	58610 TQ	USBLS	5/15
Helpers, Laborers, and Material Movers	Charleston-North Charleston MSA, SC	Y	29240 FQ	43440 MW	55950 TQ	USBLS	5/15
Helpers, Laborers, and Material Movers	Columbia MSA, SC	Y	37510 FQ	51010 MW	63130 TQ	USBLS	5/15
Helpers, Laborers, and Material Movers	Greenville-Anderson-Mauldin MSA, SC	Y	35870 FQ	44080 MW	56760 TQ	USBLS	5/15
Helpers, Laborers, and Material Movers	South Dakota	Y	37150 FQ	44800 MW	56020 TQ	USBLS	5/15
Helpers, Laborers, and Material Movers	Sioux Falls MSA, SD	Y	36410 FQ	43400 MW	55380 TQ	USBLS	5/15
Helpers, Laborers, and Material Movers	Tennessee	Y	33840 FQ	43560 MW	56880 TQ	USBLS	5/15
Helpers, Laborers, and Material Movers	Knoxville MSA, TN	Y	31270 FQ	40690 MW	55160 TQ	USBLS	5/15
Helpers, Laborers, and Material Movers	Memphis MSA, TN-MS-AR	Y	40100 FQ	50370 MW	63410 TQ	USBLS	5/15
Helpers, Laborers, and Material Movers	Nashville-Davidson–Murfreesboro–Franklin MSA, TN	Y	34140 FQ	42890 MW	55820 TQ	USBLS	5/15
Helpers, Laborers, and Material Movers	Texas	Y	34890 FQ	46430 MW	60160 TQ	USBLS	5/15
Helpers, Laborers, and Material Movers	Austin-Round Rock MSA, TX	Y	32630 FQ	45690 MW	58990 TQ	USBLS	5/15
Helpers, Laborers, and Material Movers	Dallas-Plano-Irving PMSA, TX	Y	34030 FQ	47450 MW	60330 TQ	USBLS	5/15
Helpers, Laborers, and Material Movers	Fort Worth-Arlington PMSA, TX	Y	36950 FQ	47600 MW	60800 TQ	USBLS	5/15
Helpers, Laborers, and Material Movers	Houston-The Woodlands-Sugar Land MSA, TX	Y	36400 FQ	47160 MW	61120 TQ	USBLS	5/15

AE	Average entry wage	AWR	Average wage range	H	Hourly
AEX	Average experienced wage	B	Biweekly	HI	Highest wage paid
ATC	Average total compensation	D	Daily	HR	High end range
AW	Average wage paid	FQ	First quartile wage	LO	Lowest wage paid

LR	Low end range	MTC	Median total compensation
M	Monthly	MW	Median wage paid
MCC	Median cash compensation	MWR	Median wage range
ME	Median entry wage	S	See annotated source

TCC	Total cash compensation
TQ	Third quartile wage
W	Weekly
Y	Yearly

Occupation/Type/Industry	Location	Per	Low	Mid	High	Source	Date
First-Line Supervisor							
Helpers, Laborers, and Material Movers	San Antonio-New Braunfels MSA, TX	Y	31800 FQ	44730 MW	58410 TQ	USBLS	5/15
Helpers, Laborers, and Material Movers	Utah	Y	32840 FQ	41250 MW	58480 TQ	USBLS	5/15
Helpers, Laborers, and Material Movers	Ogden-Clearfield MSA, UT	Y	37510 FQ	47910 MW	61470 TQ	USBLS	5/15
Helpers, Laborers, and Material Movers	Provo-Orem MSA, UT	Y	33730 FQ	40050 MW	55060 TQ	USBLS	5/15
Helpers, Laborers, and Material Movers	Salt Lake City MSA, UT	Y	31730 FQ	39240 MW	56790 TQ	USBLS	5/15
Helpers, Laborers, and Material Movers	Burlington-South Burlington MSA, VT	Y	42400 FQ	47940 MW	60300 TQ	USBLS	5/15
Helpers, Laborers, and Material Movers	Virginia	Y	37400 FQ	46860 MW	58670 TQ	USBLS	5/15
Helpers, Laborers, and Material Movers	Richmond MSA, VA	Y	36000 FQ	43430 MW	52850 TQ	USBLS	5/15
Helpers, Laborers, and Material Movers	Virginia Beach-Norfolk-Newport News MSA, VA-NC	Y	39060 FQ	47680 MW	59270 TQ	USBLS	5/15
Helpers, Laborers, and Material Movers	Washington	H	19.49 FQ	25.08 MW	33.80 TQ	WABLS	3/16
Helpers, Laborers, and Material Movers	Seattle-Bellevue-Everett PMSA, WA	H	19.49 FQ	26.84 MW	34.62 TQ	WABLS	3/16
Helpers, Laborers, and Material Movers	Tacoma-Lakewood PMSA, WA	H	21.59 FQ	27.82 MW	36.14 TQ	WABLS	3/16
Helpers, Laborers, and Material Movers	West Virginia	Y	32360 FQ	41980 MW	56520 TQ	USBLS	5/15
Helpers, Laborers, and Material Movers	Huntington-Ashland MSA, WV-KY-OH	Y	28120 FQ	34540 MW	48480 TQ	USBLS	5/15
Helpers, Laborers, and Material Movers	Wisconsin	Y	34450 FQ	44640 MW	58280 TQ	USBLS	5/15
Helpers, Laborers, and Material Movers	Madison MSA, WI	Y	33860 FQ	43980 MW	59900 TQ	USBLS	5/15
Helpers, Laborers, and Material Movers	Milwaukee-Waukesha-West Allis MSA, WI	Y	35720 FQ	45660 MW	61980 TQ	USBLS	5/15
Helpers, Laborers, and Material Movers	Sheboygan MSA, WI	Y	47270 FQ	56730 MW	63540 TQ	USBLS	5/15
Helpers, Laborers, and Material Movers	Wyoming	Y	40170 FQ	47940 MW	61210 TQ	USBLS	5/15
Helpers, Laborers, and Material Movers	Cheyenne MSA, WY	Y	42370 FQ	47100 MW	54260 TQ	USBLS	5/15
Helpers, Laborers, and Material Movers	Puerto Rico	Y	19090 FQ	25900 MW	37760 TQ	USBLS	5/15
Helpers, Laborers, and Material Movers	San Juan-Carolina-Caguas MSA, PR	Y	19040 FQ	26500 MW	37980 TQ	USBLS	5/15
Helpers, Laborers, and Material Movers	Guam	Y	29310 FQ	42600 MW	59940 TQ	USBLS	5/15
Housekeeping and Janitorial Workers	Alabama	Y	24525 AE	37292 AW	43676 AEX	ALBLS	6/16
Housekeeping and Janitorial Workers	Birmingham-Hoover MSA, AL	Y	27655 AE	42646 AW	50142 AEX	ALBLS	6/16
Housekeeping and Janitorial Workers	Alaska	Y	33620 FQ	37310 MW	46410 TQ	USBLS	5/15
Housekeeping and Janitorial Workers	Anchorage MSA, AK	Y	32940 FQ	36090 MW	39440 TQ	USBLS	5/15
Housekeeping and Janitorial Workers	Arizona	Y	27170 FQ	33300 MW	43040 TQ	USBLS	5/15
Housekeeping and Janitorial Workers	Phoenix-Mesa-Scottsdale MSA, AZ	Y	27690 FQ	34460 MW	45340 TQ	USBLS	5/15
Housekeeping and Janitorial Workers	Tucson MSA, AZ	Y	26320 FQ	31080 MW	40030 TQ	USBLS	5/15
Housekeeping and Janitorial Workers	Arkansas	Y	23000 FQ	28870 MW	36760 TQ	USBLS	5/15
Housekeeping and Janitorial Workers	Little Rock-North Little Rock-Conway MSA, AR	Y	20870 FQ	27580 MW	34730 TQ	USBLS	5/15
Housekeeping and Janitorial Workers	California	H	16.27 FQ	21.27 MW	27.75 TQ	CABLS	1/16-3/16
Housekeeping and Janitorial Workers	Anaheim-Santa Ana-Irvine PMSA, CA	H	13.33 FQ	22.09 MW	28.86 TQ	CABLS	1/16-3/16
Housekeeping and Janitorial Workers	Los Angeles-Long Beach-Glendale PMSA, CA	H	16.22 FQ	21.18 MW	26.52 TQ	CABLS	1/16-3/16
Housekeeping and Janitorial Workers	Oakland-Hayward-Berkeley PMSA, CA	H	17.90 FQ	21.46 MW	25.12 TQ	CABLS	1/16-3/16
Housekeeping and Janitorial Workers	Riverside-San Bernardino-Ontario MSA, CA	H	14.57 FQ	18.17 MW	22.78 TQ	CABLS	1/16-3/16
Housekeeping and Janitorial Workers	Sacramento–Roseville–Arden-Arcade MSA, CA	H	16.96 FQ	20.52 MW	25.05 TQ	CABLS	1/16-3/16
Housekeeping and Janitorial Workers	San Diego-Carlsbad MSA, CA	H	16.98 FQ	24.87 MW	32.66 TQ	CABLS	1/16-3/16
Housekeeping and Janitorial Workers	San Francisco-Redwood City-South San Francisco PMSA, CA	H	21.08 FQ	26.77 MW	31.64 TQ	CABLS	1/16-3/16
Housekeeping and Janitorial Workers	Colorado	Y	28830 FQ	36600 MW	47890 TQ	USBLS	5/15
Housekeeping and Janitorial Workers	Denver-Aurora-Lakewood MSA, CO	Y	28410 FQ	35930 MW	46930 TQ	USBLS	5/15
Housekeeping and Janitorial Workers	Connecticut	Y		52180 MW		CTBLS	1/16-3/16
Housekeeping and Janitorial Workers	Bridgeport-Stamford-Norwalk MSA, CT	Y	30320 FQ	52780 MW	61860 TQ	USBLS	5/15
Housekeeping and Janitorial Workers	Hartford-West Hartford-East Hartford MSA, CT	Y	37950 FQ	50550 MW	58090 TQ	USBLS	5/15
Housekeeping and Janitorial Workers	Delaware	Y	33380 FQ	42530 MW	49830 TQ	USBLS	5/15
Housekeeping and Janitorial Workers	Wilmington PMSA, DE-MD-NJ	Y	34940 FQ	44970 MW	54510 TQ	USBLS	5/15
Housekeeping and Janitorial Workers	District of Columbia	Y	33390 FQ	42980 MW	53250 TQ	USBLS	5/15
Housekeeping and Janitorial Workers	Washington-Arlington-Alexandria PMSA, DC-VA-MD-WV	Y	28550 FQ	37710 MW	48400 TQ	USBLS	5/15

AE	Average entry wage	**AWR**	Average wage range	**H**	Hourly
AEX	Average experienced wage	**B**	Biweekly	**HI**	Highest wage paid
ATC	Average total compensation	**D**	Daily	**HR**	High end range
AW	Average wage paid	**FQ**	First quartile wage	**LO**	Lowest wage paid

LR	Low end range	**MTC**	Median total compensation	**TCC**	Total cash compensation
M	Monthly	**MW**	Median wage paid	**TQ**	Third quartile wage
MCC	Median cash compensation	**MWR**	Median wage range	**W**	Weekly
ME	Median entry wage	**S**	See annotated source	**Y**	Yearly

Occupation/Type/Industry	Location	Per	Low	Mid	High	Source	Date
First-Line Supervisor							
Housekeeping and Janitorial Workers	Florida	H	12.23 AE	16.18 MW	20.89 AEX	FLBLS	7/16-9/16
Housekeeping and Janitorial Workers	Fort Lauderdale-Pompano Beach-Deerfield Beach PMSA, FL	H	11.09 AE	14.42 MW	18.59 AEX	FLBLS	7/16-9/16
Housekeeping and Janitorial Workers	Miami-Miami Beach-Kendall PMSA, FL	H	11.49 AE	15.08 MW	18.95 AEX	FLBLS	7/16-9/16
Housekeeping and Janitorial Workers	Orlando-Kissimmee-Sanford MSA, FL	H	12.31 AE	15.99 MW	21.45 AEX	FLBLS	7/16-9/16
Housekeeping and Janitorial Workers	Tampa-St. Petersburg-Clearwater MSA, FL	H	13.17 AE	17.20 MW	21.67 AEX	FLBLS	7/16-9/16
Housekeeping and Janitorial Workers	Georgia	Y	26970 FQ	34010 MW	40420 TQ	USBLS	5/15
Housekeeping and Janitorial Workers	Atlanta-Sandy Springs-Roswell MSA, GA	Y	29420 FQ	35200 MW	41950 TQ	USBLS	5/15
Housekeeping and Janitorial Workers	Augusta-Richmond County MSA, GA-SC	Y	25170 FQ	28800 MW	35400 TQ	USBLS	5/15
Housekeeping and Janitorial Workers	Hawaii	Y	34070 FQ	41060 MW	49170 TQ	USBLS	5/15
Housekeeping and Janitorial Workers	Urban Honolulu MSA, HI	Y	33370 FQ	40070 MW	49490 TQ	USBLS	5/15
Housekeeping and Janitorial Workers	Idaho	Y	27320 FQ	33730 MW	39490 TQ	USBLS	5/15
Housekeeping and Janitorial Workers	Boise City MSA, ID	Y	29080 FQ	34550 MW	40320 TQ	USBLS	5/15
Housekeeping and Janitorial Workers	Illinois	Y	29980 FQ	37310 MW	49430 TQ	USBLS	5/15
Housekeeping and Janitorial Workers	Chicago-Naperville-Arlington Heights PMSA, IL	Y	32360 FQ	39250 MW	53180 TQ	USBLS	5/15
Housekeeping and Janitorial Workers	Lake County-Kenosha County PMSA, IL-WI	Y	29650 FQ	35720 MW	43210 TQ	USBLS	5/15
Housekeeping and Janitorial Workers	Indiana	Y	25060 FQ	32190 MW	41800 TQ	USBLS	5/15
Housekeeping and Janitorial Workers	Gary PMSA, IN	Y	27700 FQ	37330 MW	46080 TQ	USBLS	5/15
Housekeeping and Janitorial Workers	Indianapolis-Carmel-Anderson MSA, IN	Y	24270 FQ	29480 MW	37400 TQ	USBLS	5/15
Housekeeping and Janitorial Workers	Iowa	Y	26350 FQ	35110 MW	41990 TQ	USBLS	5/15
Housekeeping and Janitorial Workers	Des Moines-West Des Moines MSA, IA	Y	30810 FQ	35380 MW	39420 TQ	USBLS	5/15
Housekeeping and Janitorial Workers	Kansas	Y	28400 FQ	34940 MW	43800 TQ	USBLS	5/15
Housekeeping and Janitorial Workers	Wichita MSA, KS	Y	27270 FQ	36170 MW	44920 TQ	USBLS	5/15
Housekeeping and Janitorial Workers	Kentucky	Y	25650 FQ	30610 MW	39260 TQ	USBLS	5/15
Housekeeping and Janitorial Workers	Louisville-Jefferson County MSA, KY-IN	Y	27490 FQ	35960 MW	46930 TQ	USBLS	5/15
Housekeeping and Janitorial Workers	Louisiana	Y	23960 FQ	28750 MW	36470 TQ	USBLS	5/15
Housekeeping and Janitorial Workers	Baton Rouge MSA, LA	Y	22650 FQ	27380 MW	35500 TQ	USBLS	5/15
Housekeeping and Janitorial Workers	New Orleans-Metairie MSA, LA	Y	25720 FQ	30380 MW	40560 TQ	USBLS	5/15
Housekeeping and Janitorial Workers	Maine	Y	29450 FQ	38250 MW	48370 TQ	USBLS	5/15
Housekeeping and Janitorial Workers	Portland-South Portland MSA, ME	Y	28120 FQ	37850 MW	45820 TQ	USBLS	5/15
Housekeeping and Janitorial Workers	Maryland	Y	24264 AE	39584 MW	47244 AEX	MDBLS	4/16
Housekeeping and Janitorial Workers	Baltimore-Columbia-Towson MSA, MD	Y	27800 FQ	35980 MW	45700 TQ	USBLS	5/15
Housekeeping and Janitorial Workers	Salisbury MSA, MD-DE	Y	25140 FQ	36520 MW	44470 TQ	USBLS	5/15
Housekeeping and Janitorial Workers	Massachusetts	Y	36410 FQ	45760 MW	57630 TQ	USBLS	5/15
Housekeeping and Janitorial Workers	Boston-Cambridge-Newton NECTA, MA	Y	38900 FQ	47740 MW	59680 TQ	USBLS	5/15
Housekeeping and Janitorial Workers	Worcester MSA, MA-CT	Y	39000 FQ	48210 MW	58730 TQ	USBLS	5/15
Housekeeping and Janitorial Workers	Michigan	Y	25950 FQ	33100 MW	42950 TQ	USBLS	5/15
Housekeeping and Janitorial Workers	Detroit-Dearborn-Livonia PMSA, MI	Y	25380 FQ	33370 MW	44030 TQ	USBLS	5/15
Housekeeping and Janitorial Workers	Grand Rapids-Wyoming MSA, MI	Y	28620 FQ	34260 MW	41140 TQ	USBLS	5/15
Housekeeping and Janitorial Workers	Minnesota	Y	30498 FQ	39779 MW	48312 TQ	MNBLS	1/16-3/16
Housekeeping and Janitorial Workers	Minneapolis-St. Paul-Bloomington MSA, MN-WI	Y	30872 FQ	40869 MW	48948 TQ	MNBLS	1/16-3/16
Housekeeping and Janitorial Workers	Mississippi	Y	20840 FQ	27280 MW	35290 TQ	USBLS	5/15
Housekeeping and Janitorial Workers	Jackson MSA, MS	Y	20150 FQ	24430 MW	34390 TQ	USBLS	5/15
Housekeeping and Janitorial Workers	Missouri	Y	27730 FQ	35760 MW	45030 TQ	USBLS	5/15
Housekeeping and Janitorial Workers	Kansas City MSA, MO-KS	Y	28890 FQ	36470 MW	45890 TQ	USBLS	5/15
Housekeeping and Janitorial Workers	St. Louis MSA, MO-IL	Y	31130 FQ	37670 MW	47650 TQ	USBLS	5/15
Housekeeping and Janitorial Workers	Montana	Y	24090 FQ	32840 MW	42260 TQ	USBLS	5/15
Housekeeping and Janitorial Workers	Billings MSA, MT	Y	24500 FQ	31510 MW	37740 TQ	USBLS	5/15
Housekeeping and Janitorial Workers	Nebraska	Y	26350 FQ	33505 MW	39410 TQ	NEBLS	7/16-9/16
Housekeeping and Janitorial Workers	Omaha-Council Bluffs MSA, NE-IA	Y	27980 FQ	34670 MW	39765 TQ	NEBLS	7/16-9/16
Housekeeping and Janitorial Workers	Nevada	Y	32350 FQ	37690 MW	44700 TQ	USBLS	5/15

AE	Average entry wage	AWR	Average wage range	H	Hourly
AEX	Average experienced wage	B	Biweekly	HI	Highest wage paid
ATC	Average total compensation	D	Daily	HR	High end range
AW	Average wage paid	FQ	First quartile wage	LO	Lowest wage paid

LR	Low end range	MTC	Median total compensation	TCC	Total cash compensation
M	Monthly	MW	Median wage paid	TQ	Third quartile wage
MCC	Median cash compensation	MWR	Median wage range	W	Weekly
ME	Median entry wage	S	See annotated source	Y	Yearly

First-Line Supervisor

Occupation/Type/Industry	Location	Per	Low	Mid	High	Source	Date
First-Line Supervisor							
Housekeeping and Janitorial Workers	Las Vegas-Henderson-Paradise MSA, NV	Y	33170 FQ	38200 MW	44790 TQ	USBLS	5/15
Housekeeping and Janitorial Workers	New Hampshire	H	14.28 AE	19.47 MW	22.61 AEX	NHBLS	6/16
Housekeeping and Janitorial Workers	Manchester NECTA, NH	H	13.60 AE	16.95 MW	21.46 AEX	NHBLS	6/16
Housekeeping and Janitorial Workers	Nashua NECTA, NH-MA	Y	34670 FQ	41840 MW	48850 TQ	USBLS	5/15
Housekeeping and Janitorial Workers	New Jersey	Y	33070 FQ	43200 MW	56880 TQ	USBLS	5/15
Housekeeping and Janitorial Workers	Camden PMSA, NJ	Y	32670 FQ	39670 MW	54860 TQ	USBLS	5/15
Housekeeping and Janitorial Workers	Newark PMSA, NJ-PA	Y	35420 FQ	44630 MW	60120 TQ	USBLS	5/15
Housekeeping and Janitorial Workers	Trenton MSA, NJ	Y	32810 FQ	46500 MW	62320 TQ	USBLS	5/15
Housekeeping and Janitorial Workers	New Mexico	Y	24890 FQ	30440 MW	38820 TQ	USBLS	5/15
Housekeeping and Janitorial Workers	Albuquerque MSA, NM	Y	25370 FQ	31570 MW	39350 TQ	USBLS	5/15
Housekeeping and Janitorial Workers	New York	Y	33220 AE	50600 MW	60650 AEX	NYBLS	1/16-3/16
Housekeeping and Janitorial Workers	Buffalo-Cheektowaga-Niagara Falls MSA, NY	Y	33510 FQ	45120 MW	55600 TQ	USBLS	5/15
Housekeeping and Janitorial Workers	Nassau County-Suffolk County PMSA, NY	Y	43700 FQ	59030 MW	71920 TQ	USBLS	5/15
Housekeeping and Janitorial Workers	New York-Jersey City-White Plains PMSA, NY-NJ	Y	38140 FQ	51980 MW	64210 TQ	USBLS	5/15
Housekeeping and Janitorial Workers	Rochester MSA, NY	Y	33170 FQ	42200 MW	51460 TQ	USBLS	5/15
Housekeeping and Janitorial Workers	North Carolina	Y	26950 FQ	33300 MW	43710 TQ	USBLS	5/15
Housekeeping and Janitorial Workers	Charlotte-Concord-Gastonia MSA, NC-SC	Y	25600 FQ	33090 MW	47330 TQ	USBLS	5/15
Housekeeping and Janitorial Workers	Raleigh MSA, NC	Y	27440 FQ	33090 MW	44500 TQ	USBLS	5/15
Housekeeping and Janitorial Workers	Winston-Salem MSA, NC	Y	27180 FQ	34010 MW	50280 TQ	USBLS	5/15
Housekeeping and Janitorial Workers	North Dakota	Y	28550 FQ	36060 MW	45940 TQ	USBLS	5/15
Housekeeping and Janitorial Workers	Fargo MSA, ND-MN	Y	24940 FQ	34410 MW	46850 TQ	USBLS	5/15
Housekeeping and Janitorial Workers	Ohio	Y	27250 FQ	36600 MW	46880 TQ	USBLS	5/15
Housekeeping and Janitorial Workers	Cincinnati MSA, OH-KY-IN	Y	29370 FQ	35830 MW	43890 TQ	USBLS	5/15
Housekeeping and Janitorial Workers	Cleveland-Elyria MSA, OH	Y	24690 FQ	35470 MW	47160 TQ	USBLS	5/15
Housekeeping and Janitorial Workers	Columbus MSA, OH	Y	28670 FQ	39590 MW	49330 TQ	USBLS	5/15
Housekeeping and Janitorial Workers	Oklahoma	Y	24130 FQ	29660 MW	39180 TQ	USBLS	5/15
Housekeeping and Janitorial Workers	Oklahoma City MSA, OK	Y	26350 FQ	32310 MW	41190 TQ	USBLS	5/15
Housekeeping and Janitorial Workers	Tulsa MSA, OK	Y	23730 FQ	32130 MW	41480 TQ	USBLS	5/15
Housekeeping and Janitorial Workers	Oregon	H	15.01 FQ	20.75 MW	26.73 TQ	ORBLS	2016
Housekeeping and Janitorial Workers	Portland-Vancouver-Hillsboro MSA, OR-WA	Y	32730 FQ	45410 MW	64010 TQ	USBLS	5/15
Housekeeping and Janitorial Workers	Pennsylvania	Y	31690 FQ	40220 MW	50290 TQ	USBLS	5/15
Housekeeping and Janitorial Workers	Allentown-Bethlehem-Easton MSA, PA-NJ	Y	29460 FQ	37080 MW	49210 TQ	USBLS	5/15
Housekeeping and Janitorial Workers	Harrisburg-Carlisle MSA, PA	Y	28690 FQ	37690 MW	45440 TQ	USBLS	5/15
Housekeeping and Janitorial Workers	Montgomery County-Bucks County-Chester County PMSA, PA	Y	37090 FQ	46270 MW	57470 TQ	USBLS	5/15
Housekeeping and Janitorial Workers	Philadelphia PMSA, PA	Y	34370 FQ	43290 MW	54260 TQ	USBLS	5/15
Housekeeping and Janitorial Workers	Pittsburgh MSA, PA	Y	33530 FQ	43890 MW	54090 TQ	USBLS	5/15
Housekeeping and Janitorial Workers	Rhode Island	Y	27320 FQ	30870 MW	44680 TQ	USBLS	5/15
Housekeeping and Janitorial Workers	Providence-Warwick MSA, RI-MA	Y	27350 FQ	31830 MW	46420 TQ	USBLS	5/15
Housekeeping and Janitorial Workers	South Carolina	Y	23720 FQ	30330 MW	38880 TQ	USBLS	5/15
Housekeeping and Janitorial Workers	Charleston-North Charleston MSA, SC	Y	25420 FQ	31010 MW	38450 TQ	USBLS	5/15
Housekeeping and Janitorial Workers	Columbia MSA, SC	Y	25330 FQ	33640 MW	42120 TQ	USBLS	5/15
Housekeeping and Janitorial Workers	Greenville-Anderson-Mauldin MSA, SC	Y	20670 FQ	26720 MW	37130 TQ	NHBLS	5/15
Housekeeping and Janitorial Workers	South Dakota	Y	31300 FQ	36950 MW	44310 TQ	USBLS	5/15
Housekeeping and Janitorial Workers	Sioux Falls MSA, SD	Y	34010 FQ	40930 MW	47000 TQ	USBLS	5/15
Housekeeping and Janitorial Workers	Tennessee	Y	22380 FQ	29080 MW	38530 TQ	USBLS	5/15
Housekeeping and Janitorial Workers	Cleveland MSA, TN	Y	26540 FQ	34120 MW	44570 TQ	USBLS	5/15
Housekeeping and Janitorial Workers	Knoxville MSA, TN	Y	25700 FQ	29490 MW	37370 TQ	USBLS	5/15
Housekeeping and Janitorial Workers	Memphis MSA, TN-MS-AR	Y	23090 FQ	29420 MW	39630 TQ	USBLS	5/15
Housekeeping and Janitorial Workers	Nashville-Davidson–Murfreesboro–Franklin MSA, TN	Y	19400 FQ	27410 MW	37090 TQ	USBLS	5/15
Housekeeping and Janitorial Workers	Texas	Y	25600 FQ	32480 MW	44960 TQ	USBLS	5/15
Housekeeping and Janitorial Workers	Austin-Round Rock MSA, TX	Y	31330 FQ	40020 MW	47810 TQ	USBLS	5/15
Housekeeping and Janitorial Workers	Dallas-Plano-Irving PMSA, TX	Y	25060 FQ	31140 MW	40490 TQ	USBLS	5/15
Housekeeping and Janitorial Workers	Fort Worth-Arlington PMSA, TX	Y	27570 FQ	33540 MW	41300 TQ	USBLS	5/15
Housekeeping and Janitorial Workers	Houston-The Woodlands-Sugar Land MSA, TX	Y	25310 FQ	33600 MW	49800 TQ	USBLS	5/15

First-Line Supervisor

Occupation/Type/Industry	Location	Per	Low	Mid	High	Source	Date
Housekeeping and Janitorial Workers	San Antonio-New Braunfels MSA, TX	Y	26110 FQ	30180 MW	41680 TQ	USBLS	5/15
Housekeeping and Janitorial Workers	Utah	Y	30180 FQ	39550 MW	46830 TQ	USBLS	5/15
Housekeeping and Janitorial Workers	Ogden-Clearfield MSA, UT	Y	28770 FQ	40000 MW	47720 TQ	USBLS	5/15
Housekeeping and Janitorial Workers	Provo-Orem MSA, UT	Y	38460 FQ	43610 MW	48040 TQ	USBLS	5/15
Housekeeping and Janitorial Workers	Salt Lake City MSA, UT	Y	29520 FQ	38660 MW	47440 TQ	USBLS	5/15
Housekeeping and Janitorial Workers	Virginia	Y	27330 FQ	34750 MW	44610 TQ	USBLS	5/15
Housekeeping and Janitorial Workers	Richmond MSA, VA	Y	26940 FQ	31580 MW	39770 TQ	USBLS	5/15
Housekeeping and Janitorial Workers	Virginia Beach-Norfolk-Newport News MSA, VA-NC	Y	27270 FQ	35790 MW	46470 TQ	USBLS	5/15
Housekeeping and Janitorial Workers	Washington	H	14.24 FQ	18.79 MW	23.23 TQ	WABLS	3/16
Housekeeping and Janitorial Workers	Seattle-Bellevue-Everett PMSA, WA	H	15.93 FQ	20.68 MW	24.33 TQ	WABLS	3/16
Housekeeping and Janitorial Workers	Tacoma-Lakewood PMSA, WA	H	14.78 FQ	18.95 MW	22.78 TQ	WABLS	3/16
Housekeeping and Janitorial Workers	West Virginia	Y	24440 FQ	30040 MW	37140 TQ	USBLS	5/15
Housekeeping and Janitorial Workers	Huntington-Ashland MSA, WV-KY-OH	Y	23080 FQ	28900 MW	38640 TQ	USBLS	5/15
Housekeeping and Janitorial Workers	Wisconsin	Y	28880 FQ	36910 MW	47840 TQ	USBLS	5/15
Housekeeping and Janitorial Workers	Madison MSA, WI	Y	31510 FQ	36500 MW	44190 TQ	USBLS	5/15
Housekeeping and Janitorial Workers	Milwaukee-Waukesha-West Allis MSA, WI	Y	26330 FQ	36600 MW	52350 TQ	USBLS	5/15
Housekeeping and Janitorial Workers	Wyoming	Y	28910 FQ	37240 MW	46530 TQ	USBLS	5/15
Housekeeping and Janitorial Workers	Cheyenne MSA, WY	Y	34110 FQ	43250 MW	50590 TQ	USBLS	5/15
Housekeeping and Janitorial Workers	Puerto Rico	Y	18470 FQ	22630 MW	28650 TQ	USBLS	5/15
Housekeeping and Janitorial Workers	San Juan-Carolina-Caguas MSA, PR	Y	18700 FQ	22940 MW	28900 TQ	USBLS	5/15
Housekeeping and Janitorial Workers	Virgin Islands	Y	26920 FQ	33570 MW	37920 TQ	USBLS	5/15
Housekeeping and Janitorial Workers	Guam	Y	18700 FQ	22010 MW	28900 TQ	USBLS	5/15
Landscaping, Lawn, Grounds	Alabama	Y	26008 AE	41678 AW	49503 AEX	ALBLS	6/16
Landscaping, Lawn, Grounds	Birmingham-Hoover MSA, AL	Y	29786 AE	40319 AW	45591 AEX	ALBLS	6/16
Landscaping, Lawn, Grounds	Alaska	Y	37560 FQ	44430 MW	51080 TQ	USBLS	5/15
Landscaping, Lawn, Grounds	Anchorage MSA, AK	Y	40980 FQ	45390 MW	49750 TQ	USBLS	5/15
Landscaping, Lawn, Grounds	Arizona	Y	25950 FQ	35060 MW	48230 TQ	USBLS	5/15
Landscaping, Lawn, Grounds	Phoenix-Mesa-Scottsdale MSA, AZ	Y	25230 FQ	35090 MW	47840 TQ	USBLS	5/15
Landscaping, Lawn, Grounds	Tucson MSA, AZ	Y	28010 FQ	33950 MW	50130 TQ	USBLS	5/15
Landscaping, Lawn, Grounds	Arkansas	Y	29000 FQ	35280 MW	43280 TQ	USBLS	5/15
Landscaping, Lawn, Grounds	Little Rock-North Little Rock-Conway MSA, AR	Y	27460 FQ	34380 MW	42090 TQ	USBLS	5/15
Landscaping, Lawn, Grounds	California	H	17.77 FQ	22.91 MW	29.64 TQ	CABLS	1/16-3/16
Landscaping, Lawn, Grounds	Anaheim-Santa Ana-Irvine PMSA, CA	H	19.66 FQ	23.65 MW	29.94 TQ	CABLS	1/16-3/16
Landscaping, Lawn, Grounds	Los Angeles-Long Beach-Glendale PMSA, CA	H	16.44 FQ	21.52 MW	28.69 TQ	CABLS	1/16-3/16
Landscaping, Lawn, Grounds	Oakland-Hayward-Berkeley PMSA, CA	H	16.77 FQ	24.30 MW	33.73 TQ	CABLS	1/16-3/16
Landscaping, Lawn, Grounds	Riverside-San Bernardino-Ontario MSA, CA	H	17.76 FQ	21.35 MW	26.68 TQ	CABLS	1/16-3/16
Landscaping, Lawn, Grounds	Sacramento-Roseville-Arden-Arcade MSA, CA	H	21.22 FQ	24.92 MW	33.34 TQ	CABLS	1/16-3/16
Landscaping, Lawn, Grounds	San Diego-Carlsbad MSA, CA	H	20.14 FQ	24.99 MW	32.31 TQ	CABLS	1/16-3/16
Landscaping, Lawn, Grounds	San Francisco-Redwood City-South San Francisco PMSA, CA	H	21.14 FQ	27.41 MW	36.62 TQ	CABLS	1/16-3/16
Landscaping, Lawn, Grounds	Colorado	Y	40760 FQ	53360 MW	66060 TQ	USBLS	5/15
Landscaping, Lawn, Grounds	Denver-Aurora-Lakewood MSA, CO	Y	42090 FQ	54220 MW	67320 TQ	USBLS	5/15
Landscaping, Lawn, Grounds	Connecticut	Y		54250 MW		CTBLS	1/16-3/16
Landscaping, Lawn, Grounds	Bridgeport-Stamford-Norwalk MSA, CT	Y	46510 FQ	63350 MW	86440 TQ	USBLS	5/15
Landscaping, Lawn, Grounds	Hartford-West Hartford-East Hartford MSA, CT	Y	43240 FQ	49940 MW	63080 TQ	USBLS	5/15
Landscaping, Lawn, Grounds	Delaware	Y	43500 FQ	51360 MW	63930 TQ	USBLS	5/15
Landscaping, Lawn, Grounds	Wilmington PMSA, DE-MD-NJ	Y	39820 FQ	54010 MW	65710 TQ	USBLS	5/15
Landscaping, Lawn, Grounds	District of Columbia	Y	65500 FQ	73900 MW	88280 TQ	USBLS	5/15
Landscaping, Lawn, Grounds	Washington-Arlington-Alexandria PMSA, DC-VA-MD-WV	Y	38160 FQ	50970 MW	69180 TQ	USBLS	5/15
Landscaping, Lawn, Grounds	Florida	H	13.99 AE	19.25 MW	25.34 AEX	FLBLS	7/16-9/16

AE	Average entry wage	AWR	Average wage range	H	Hourly	LR Low end range	MTC Median total compensation	TCC Total cash compensation
AEX	Average experienced wage	B	Biweekly	HI	Highest wage paid	M Monthly	MW Median wage paid	TQ Third quartile wage
ATC	Average total compensation	D	Daily	HR	High end range	MCC Median cash compensation	MWR Median wage range	W Weekly
AW	Average wage paid	FQ	First quartile wage	LO	Lowest wage paid	ME Median entry wage	S See annotated source	Y Yearly

Occupation/Type/Industry	Location	Per	Low	Mid	High	Source	Date
First-Line Supervisor							
Landscaping, Lawn, Grounds	Fort Lauderdale-Pompano Beach-Deerfield Beach PMSA, FL	H	15.85 AE	20.80 MW	25.54 AEX	FLBLS	7/16-9/16
Landscaping, Lawn, Grounds	Miami-Miami Beach-Kendall PMSA, FL	H	15.56 AE	21.05 MW	24.09 AEX	FLBLS	7/16-9/16
Landscaping, Lawn, Grounds	Orlando-Kissimmee-Sanford MSA, FL	H	12.27 AE	17.23 MW	22.55 AEX	FLBLS	7/16-9/16
Landscaping, Lawn, Grounds	Tampa-St. Petersburg-Clearwater MSA, FL	H	13.60 AE	18.27 MW	23.34 AEX	FLBLS	7/16-9/16
Landscaping, Lawn, Grounds	Georgia	Y	34260 FQ	43170 MW	52700 TQ	USBLS	5/15
Landscaping, Lawn, Grounds	Atlanta-Sandy Springs-Roswell MSA, GA	Y	37480 FQ	44890 MW	53670 TQ	USBLS	5/15
Landscaping, Lawn, Grounds	Augusta-Richmond County MSA, GA-SC	Y	30970 FQ	36700 MW	47050 TQ	USBLS	5/15
Landscaping, Lawn, Grounds	Hawaii	Y	41410 FQ	47360 MW	59070 TQ	USBLS	5/15
Landscaping, Lawn, Grounds	Urban Honolulu MSA, HI	Y	42180 FQ	47880 MW	62370 TQ	USBLS	5/15
Landscaping, Lawn, Grounds	Idaho	Y	33600 FQ	39550 MW	50070 TQ	USBLS	5/15
Landscaping, Lawn, Grounds	Boise City MSA, ID	Y	30570 FQ	35880 MW	42930 TQ	USBLS	5/15
Landscaping, Lawn, Grounds	Illinois	Y	28530 FQ	37870 MW	58860 TQ	USBLS	5/15
Landscaping, Lawn, Grounds	Chicago-Naperville-Arlington Heights PMSA, IL	Y	27850 FQ	42720 MW	62550 TQ	USBLS	5/15
Landscaping, Lawn, Grounds	Lake County-Kenosha County PMSA, IL-WI	Y	30490 FQ	37530 MW	59390 TQ	USBLS	5/15
Landscaping, Lawn, Grounds	Indiana	Y	33530 FQ	42500 MW	49210 TQ	USBLS	5/15
Landscaping, Lawn, Grounds	Gary PMSA, IN	Y	40400 FQ	44650 MW	48890 TQ	USBLS	5/15
Landscaping, Lawn, Grounds	Indianapolis-Carmel-Anderson MSA, IN	Y	36460 FQ	44040 MW	52950 TQ	USBLS	5/15
Landscaping, Lawn, Grounds	Iowa	Y	30330 FQ	36120 MW	46590 TQ	USBLS	5/15
Landscaping, Lawn, Grounds	Des Moines-West Des Moines MSA, IA	Y	35100 FQ	39900 MW	54580 TQ	USBLS	5/15
Landscaping, Lawn, Grounds	Kansas	Y	33440 FQ	40120 MW	50630 TQ	USBLS	5/15
Landscaping, Lawn, Grounds	Wichita MSA, KS	Y	34450 FQ	44950 MW	55600 TQ	USBLS	5/15
Landscaping, Lawn, Grounds	Kentucky	Y	30470 FQ	38090 MW	46550 TQ	USBLS	5/15
Landscaping, Lawn, Grounds	Louisville-Jefferson County MSA, KY-IN	Y	30810 FQ	42200 MW	47500 TQ	USBLS	5/15
Landscaping, Lawn, Grounds	Louisiana	Y	32920 FQ	40880 MW	49650 TQ	USBLS	5/15
Landscaping, Lawn, Grounds	Baton Rouge MSA, LA	Y	32470 FQ	38890 MW	49110 TQ	USBLS	5/15
Landscaping, Lawn, Grounds	New Orleans-Metairie MSA, LA	Y	35420 FQ	44120 MW	53150 TQ	USBLS	5/15
Landscaping, Lawn, Grounds	Maine	Y	39930 FQ	46270 MW	54550 TQ	USBLS	5/15
Landscaping, Lawn, Grounds	Portland-South Portland MSA, ME	Y	41590 FQ	52300 MW	59920 TQ	USBLS	5/15
Landscaping, Lawn, Grounds	Maryland	Y	34290 AE	51580 MW	60226 AEX	MDBLS	4/16
Landscaping, Lawn, Grounds	Baltimore-Columbia-Towson MSA, MD	Y	42250 FQ	52710 MW	66880 TQ	USBLS	5/15
Landscaping, Lawn, Grounds	Salisbury MSA, MD-DE	Y	36280 FQ	43560 MW	49910 TQ	USBLS	5/15
Landscaping, Lawn, Grounds	Massachusetts	Y	41320 FQ	50960 MW	61750 TQ	USBLS	5/15
Landscaping, Lawn, Grounds	Boston-Cambridge-Newton NECTA, MA	Y	41890 FQ	53460 MW	65140 TQ	USBLS	5/15
Landscaping, Lawn, Grounds	Worcester MSA, MA-CT	Y	41320 FQ	48370 MW	55610 TQ	USBLS	5/15
Landscaping, Lawn, Grounds	Michigan	Y	32090 FQ	40950 MW	51620 TQ	USBLS	5/15
Landscaping, Lawn, Grounds	Detroit-Dearborn-Livonia PMSA, MI	Y	33510 FQ	39330 MW	56950 TQ	USBLS	5/15
Landscaping, Lawn, Grounds	Grand Rapids-Wyoming MSA, MI	Y	29750 FQ	37760 MW	46340 TQ	USBLS	5/15
Landscaping, Lawn, Grounds	Minnesota	Y	34901 FQ	45151 MW	58401 TQ	MNBLS	1/16-3/16
Landscaping, Lawn, Grounds	Minneapolis-St. Paul-Bloomington MSA, MN-WI	Y	34638 FQ	44081 MW	57795 TQ	MNBLS	1/16-3/16
Landscaping, Lawn, Grounds	Mississippi	Y	26710 FQ	31720 MW	45310 TQ	USBLS	5/15
Landscaping, Lawn, Grounds	Jackson MSA, MS	Y	28160 FQ	33100 MW	50070 TQ	USBLS	5/15
Landscaping, Lawn, Grounds	Missouri	Y	35940 FQ	47390 MW	58390 TQ	USBLS	5/15
Landscaping, Lawn, Grounds	Kansas City MSA, MO-KS	Y	34220 FQ	39000 MW	53800 TQ	USBLS	5/15
Landscaping, Lawn, Grounds	St. Louis MSA, MO-IL	Y	34770 FQ	46750 MW	58830 TQ	USBLS	5/15
Landscaping, Lawn, Grounds	Montana	Y	31990 FQ	38430 MW	45940 TQ	USBLS	5/15
Landscaping, Lawn, Grounds	Billings MSA, MT	Y	33940 FQ	37130 MW	45360 TQ	USBLS	5/15
Landscaping, Lawn, Grounds	Nebraska	Y	34625 FQ	42385 MW	56350 TQ	NEBLS	7/16-9/16
Landscaping, Lawn, Grounds	Omaha-Council Bluffs MSA, NE-IA	Y	35265 FQ	43630 MW	57185 TQ	NEBLS	7/16-9/16
Landscaping, Lawn, Grounds	Nevada	Y	42620 FQ	51600 MW	62900 TQ	USBLS	5/15
Landscaping, Lawn, Grounds	Las Vegas-Henderson-Paradise MSA, NV	Y	42650 FQ	53880 MW	68090 TQ	USBLS	5/15

AE	Average entry wage	AWR	Average wage range	H	Hourly
AEX	Average experienced wage	B	Biweekly	HI	Highest wage paid
ATC	Average total compensation	D	Daily	HR	High end range
AW	Average wage paid	FQ	First quartile wage	LO	Lowest wage paid

LR	Low end range	MTC	Median total compensation	TCC	Total cash compensation
M	Monthly	MW	Median wage paid	TQ	Third quartile wage
MCC	Median cash compensation	MWR	Median wage range	W	Weekly
ME	Median entry wage	S	See annotated source	Y	Yearly

Occupation/Type/Industry	Location	Per	Low	Mid	High	Source	Date
First-Line Supervisor							
Landscaping, Lawn, Grounds	New Hampshire	H	16.60 AE	21.63 MW	25.96 AEX	NHBLS	6/16
Landscaping, Lawn, Grounds	Manchester NECTA, NH	H	16.98 AE	18.96 MW	23.24 AEX	NHBLS	6/16
Landscaping, Lawn, Grounds	Nashua NECTA, NH-MA	Y	42680 FQ	48050 MW	55480 TQ	USBLS	5/15
Landscaping, Lawn, Grounds	New Jersey	Y	40960 FQ	52230 MW	63280 TQ	USBLS	5/15
Landscaping, Lawn, Grounds	Camden PMSA, NJ	Y	43630 FQ	55290 MW	68890 TQ	USBLS	5/15
Landscaping, Lawn, Grounds	Newark PMSA, NJ-PA	Y	37090 FQ	45650 MW	59650 TQ	USBLS	5/15
Landscaping, Lawn, Grounds	Trenton MSA, NJ	Y	42620 FQ	53490 MW	67180 TQ	USBLS	5/15
Landscaping, Lawn, Grounds	New Mexico	Y	30380 FQ	36590 MW	47860 TQ	USBLS	5/15
Landscaping, Lawn, Grounds	Albuquerque MSA, NM	Y	29860 FQ	37170 MW	51790 TQ	USBLS	5/15
Landscaping, Lawn, Grounds	New York	Y	34970 AE	50310 MW	62290 AEX	NYBLS	1/16-3/16
Landscaping, Lawn, Grounds	Buffalo-Cheektowaga-Niagara Falls MSA, NY	Y	36170 FQ	43950 MW	55480 TQ	USBLS	5/15
Landscaping, Lawn, Grounds	Nassau County-Suffolk County PMSA, NY	Y	35390 FQ	49020 MW	63630 TQ	USBLS	5/15
Landscaping, Lawn, Grounds	New York-Jersey City-White Plains PMSA, NY-NJ	Y	45920 FQ	56570 MW	69280 TQ	USBLS	5/15
Landscaping, Lawn, Grounds	Rochester MSA, NY	Y	41610 FQ	46430 MW	53620 TQ	USBLS	5/15
Landscaping, Lawn, Grounds	North Carolina	Y	36260 FQ	46170 MW	58310 TQ	USBLS	5/15
Landscaping, Lawn, Grounds	Charlotte-Concord-Gastonia MSA, NC-SC	Y	38640 FQ	46830 MW	58720 TQ	USBLS	5/15
Landscaping, Lawn, Grounds	Raleigh MSA, NC	Y	31570 FQ	47820 MW	59190 TQ	USBLS	5/15
Landscaping, Lawn, Grounds	North Dakota	Y	34100 FQ	45380 MW	60000 TQ	USBLS	5/15
Landscaping, Lawn, Grounds	Fargo MSA, ND-MN	Y	37770 FQ	47340 MW	77200 TQ	USBLS	5/15
Landscaping, Lawn, Grounds	Ohio	Y	33670 FQ	42360 MW	55200 TQ	USBLS	5/15
Landscaping, Lawn, Grounds	Cincinnati MSA, OH-KY-IN	Y	33110 FQ	38520 MW	49040 TQ	USBLS	5/15
Landscaping, Lawn, Grounds	Cleveland-Elyria MSA, OH	Y	31810 FQ	36600 MW	48790 TQ	USBLS	5/15
Landscaping, Lawn, Grounds	Columbus MSA, OH	Y	41050 FQ	48460 MW	67250 TQ	USBLS	5/15
Landscaping, Lawn, Grounds	Oklahoma	Y	27000 FQ	38050 MW	48080 TQ	USBLS	5/15
Landscaping, Lawn, Grounds	Oklahoma City MSA, OK	Y	26130 FQ	33640 MW	43950 TQ	USBLS	5/15
Landscaping, Lawn, Grounds	Tulsa MSA, OK	Y	39630 FQ	46300 MW	60320 TQ	USBLS	5/15
Landscaping, Lawn, Grounds	Oregon	H	19.91 FQ	23.93 MW	31.91 TQ	ORBLS	2016
Landscaping, Lawn, Grounds	Portland-Vancouver-Hillsboro MSA, OR-WA	Y	41590 FQ	47680 MW	61760 TQ	USBLS	5/15
Landscaping, Lawn, Grounds	Pennsylvania	Y	38760 FQ	50090 MW	60500 TQ	USBLS	5/15
Landscaping, Lawn, Grounds	Allentown-Bethlehem-Easton MSA, PA-NJ	Y	35290 FQ	44230 MW	57810 TQ	USBLS	5/15
Landscaping, Lawn, Grounds	Harrisburg-Carlisle MSA, PA	Y	39440 FQ	46360 MW	54240 TQ	USBLS	5/15
Landscaping, Lawn, Grounds	Montgomery County-Bucks County-Chester County PMSA, PA	Y	48990 FQ	56300 MW	63760 TQ	USBLS	5/15
Landscaping, Lawn, Grounds	Philadelphia PMSA, PA	Y	44290 FQ	53210 MW	65990 TQ	USBLS	5/15
Landscaping, Lawn, Grounds	Pittsburgh MSA, PA	Y	34580 FQ	47720 MW	58290 TQ	USBLS	5/15
Landscaping, Lawn, Grounds	Rhode Island	Y	41720 FQ	48020 MW	65490 TQ	USBLS	5/15
Landscaping, Lawn, Grounds	Providence-Warwick MSA, RI-MA	Y	41480 FQ	47320 MW	64540 TQ	USBLS	5/15
Landscaping, Lawn, Grounds	South Carolina	Y	31850 FQ	39230 MW	51380 TQ	USBLS	5/15
Landscaping, Lawn, Grounds	Charleston-North Charleston MSA, SC	Y	34170 FQ	40130 MW	59320 TQ	USBLS	5/15
Landscaping, Lawn, Grounds	Columbia MSA, SC	Y	28020 FQ	34310 MW	47060 TQ	USBLS	5/15
Landscaping, Lawn, Grounds	Greenville-Anderson-Mauldin MSA, SC	Y	31650 FQ	36700 MW	44270 TQ	USBLS	5/15
Landscaping, Lawn, Grounds	South Dakota	Y	40350 FQ	45500 MW	52630 TQ	USBLS	5/15
Landscaping, Lawn, Grounds	Sioux Falls MSA, SD	Y	42380 FQ	48430 MW	57600 TQ	USBLS	5/15
Landscaping, Lawn, Grounds	Tennessee	Y	30960 FQ	38800 MW	49410 TQ	USBLS	5/15
Landscaping, Lawn, Grounds	Knoxville MSA, TN	Y	29180 FQ	39140 MW	47080 TQ	USBLS	5/15
Landscaping, Lawn, Grounds	Memphis MSA, TN-MS-AR	Y	31430 FQ	42140 MW	56460 TQ	USBLS	5/15
Landscaping, Lawn, Grounds	Nashville-Davidson–Murfreesboro–Franklin MSA, TN	Y	32020 FQ	37910 MW	47860 TQ	USBLS	5/15
Landscaping, Lawn, Grounds	Texas	Y	30980 FQ	43580 MW	57870 TQ	USBLS	5/15
Landscaping, Lawn, Grounds	Austin-Round Rock MSA, TX	Y	34520 FQ	43440 MW	54830 TQ	USBLS	5/15
Landscaping, Lawn, Grounds	Dallas-Plano-Irving PMSA, TX	Y	39060 FQ	53140 MW	66020 TQ	USBLS	5/15
Landscaping, Lawn, Grounds	Fort Worth-Arlington PMSA, TX	Y	30630 FQ	50380 MW	59840 TQ	USBLS	5/15
Landscaping, Lawn, Grounds	Houston-The Woodlands-Sugar Land MSA, TX	Y	27260 FQ	34140 MW	52750 TQ	USBLS	5/15
Landscaping, Lawn, Grounds	San Antonio-New Braunfels MSA, TX	Y	27600 FQ	39560 MW	48900 TQ	USBLS	5/15
Landscaping, Lawn, Grounds	Utah	Y	37500 FQ	45230 MW	54230 TQ	USBLS	5/15
Landscaping, Lawn, Grounds	Ogden-Clearfield MSA, UT	Y	30740 FQ	41940 MW	47760 TQ	USBLS	5/15
Landscaping, Lawn, Grounds	Provo-Orem MSA, UT	Y	34850 FQ	45310 MW	56740 TQ	USBLS	5/15

AE Average entry wage	**AWR** Average wage range	**H** Hourly	**LR** Low end range	**MTC** Median total compensation	**TCC** Total cash compensation
AEX Average experienced wage	**B** Biweekly	**HI** Highest wage paid	**M** Monthly	**MW** Median wage paid	**TQ** Third quartile wage
ATC Average total compensation	**D** Daily	**HR** High end range	**MCC** Median cash compensation	**MWR** Median wage range	**W** Weekly
AW Average wage paid	**FQ** First quartile wage	**LO** Lowest wage paid	**ME** Median entry wage	**S** See annotated source	**Y** Yearly

Occupation/Type/Industry	Location	Per	Low	Mid	High	Source	Date
First-Line Supervisor							
Landscaping, Lawn, Grounds	Salt Lake City MSA, UT	Y	40700 FQ	46880 MW	54540 TQ	USBLS	5/15
Landscaping, Lawn, Grounds	Vermont	Y	37940 FQ	44880 MW	54650 TQ	USBLS	5/15
Landscaping, Lawn, Grounds	Burlington-South Burlington MSA, VT	Y	35550 FQ	40800 MW	49020 TQ	USBLS	5/15
Landscaping, Lawn, Grounds	Virginia	Y	33920 FQ	43010 MW	58480 TQ	USBLS	5/15
Landscaping, Lawn, Grounds	Richmond MSA, VA	Y	31970 FQ	40170 MW	49240 TQ	USBLS	5/15
Landscaping, Lawn, Grounds	Virginia Beach-Norfolk-Newport News MSA, VA-NC	Y	30120 FQ	36440 MW	50100 TQ	USBLS	5/15
Landscaping, Lawn, Grounds	Washington	H	20.17 FQ	23.25 MW	28.15 TQ	WABLS	3/16
Landscaping, Lawn, Grounds	Seattle-Bellevue-Everett PMSA, WA	H	21.31 FQ	23.91 MW	28.35 TQ	WABLS	3/16
Landscaping, Lawn, Grounds	Tacoma-Lakewood PMSA, WA	H	17.74 FQ	22.47 MW	32.46 TQ	WABLS	3/16
Landscaping, Lawn, Grounds	West Virginia	Y	23620 FQ	30740 MW	42150 TQ	USBLS	5/15
Landscaping, Lawn, Grounds	Huntington-Ashland MSA, WV-KY-OH	Y	21600 FQ	28570 MW	45270 TQ	USBLS	5/15
Landscaping, Lawn, Grounds	Wisconsin	Y	36980 FQ	45740 MW	58300 TQ	USBLS	5/15
Landscaping, Lawn, Grounds	Madison MSA, WI	Y	35860 FQ	41640 MW	50630 TQ	USBLS	5/15
Landscaping, Lawn, Grounds	Milwaukee-Waukesha-West Allis MSA, WI	Y	42940 FQ	50330 MW	65850 TQ	USBLS	5/15
Landscaping, Lawn, Grounds	Wyoming	Y	43120 FQ	52980 MW	61170 TQ	USBLS	5/15
Landscaping, Lawn, Grounds	Cheyenne MSA, WY	Y	34700 FQ	46090 MW	55240 TQ	USBLS	5/15
Landscaping, Lawn, Grounds	Puerto Rico	Y	18270 FQ	23220 MW	36650 TQ	USBLS	5/15
Landscaping, Lawn, Grounds	San Juan-Carolina-Caguas MSA, PR	Y	20430 FQ	29730 MW	41300 TQ	USBLS	5/15
Landscaping, Lawn, Grounds	Virgin Islands	Y	29900 FQ	35110 MW	44110 TQ	USBLS	5/15
Landscaping, Lawn, Grounds	Guam	Y	21700 FQ	24990 MW	35070 TQ	USBLS	5/15
Mechanics, Installers, and Repairers	Alabama	Y	40223 AE	64204 AW	76195 AEX	ALBLS	6/16
Mechanics, Installers, and Repairers	Birmingham-Hoover MSA, AL	Y	45522 AE	70327 AW	82734 AEX	ALBLS	6/16
Mechanics, Installers, and Repairers	Alaska	Y	67190 FQ	84690 MW	96870 TQ	USBLS	5/15
Mechanics, Installers, and Repairers	Anchorage MSA, AK	Y	69500 FQ	85230 MW	97610 TQ	USBLS	5/15
Mechanics, Installers, and Repairers	Arizona	Y	43520 FQ	54560 MW	71760 TQ	USBLS	5/15
Mechanics, Installers, and Repairers	Phoenix-Mesa-Scottsdale MSA, AZ	Y	43470 FQ	53290 MW	70450 TQ	USBLS	5/15
Mechanics, Installers, and Repairers	Tucson MSA, AZ	Y	46780 FQ	61710 MW	74710 TQ	USBLS	5/15
Mechanics, Installers, and Repairers	Arkansas	Y	40950 FQ	53250 MW	67230 TQ	USBLS	5/15
Mechanics, Installers, and Repairers	Little Rock-North Little Rock-Conway MSA, AR	Y	42560 FQ	54750 MW	64680 TQ	USBLS	5/15
Mechanics, Installers, and Repairers	California	H	26.89 FQ	34.73 MW	44.03 TQ	CABLS	1/16-3/16
Mechanics, Installers, and Repairers	Anaheim-Santa Ana-Irvine PMSA, CA	H	26.41 FQ	35.28 MW	43.14 TQ	CABLS	1/16-3/16
Mechanics, Installers, and Repairers	Los Angeles-Long Beach-Glendale PMSA, CA	H	27.09 FQ	35.35 MW	45.34 TQ	CABLS	1/16-3/16
Mechanics, Installers, and Repairers	Oakland-Hayward-Berkeley PMSA, CA	H	29.79 FQ	37.00 MW	48.43 TQ	CABLS	1/16-3/16
Mechanics, Installers, and Repairers	Riverside-San Bernardino-Ontario MSA, CA	H	26.42 FQ	33.32 MW	41.87 TQ	CABLS	1/16-3/16
Mechanics, Installers, and Repairers	Sacramento–Roseville–Arden-Arcade MSA, CA	H	26.90 FQ	33.73 MW	39.83 TQ	CABLS	1/16-3/16
Mechanics, Installers, and Repairers	San Diego-Carlsbad MSA, CA	H	24.46 FQ	31.77 MW	37.54 TQ	CABLS	1/16-3/16
Mechanics, Installers, and Repairers	San Francisco-Redwood City-South San Francisco PMSA, CA	H	29.36 FQ	39.41 MW	50.27 TQ	CABLS	1/16-3/16
Mechanics, Installers, and Repairers	Colorado	Y	52690 FQ	67260 MW	82560 TQ	USBLS	5/15
Mechanics, Installers, and Repairers	Denver-Aurora-Lakewood MSA, CO	Y	52650 FQ	68360 MW	82830 TQ	USBLS	5/15
Mechanics, Installers, and Repairers	Connecticut	Y		69651 MW		CTBLS	1/16-3/16
Mechanics, Installers, and Repairers	Bridgeport-Stamford-Norwalk MSA, CT	Y	55570 FQ	69670 MW	80580 TQ	USBLS	5/15
Mechanics, Installers, and Repairers	Hartford-West Hartford-East Hartford MSA, CT	Y	54690 FQ	69280 MW	85690 TQ	USBLS	5/15
Mechanics, Installers, and Repairers	Delaware	Y	57190 FQ	71490 MW	86400 TQ	USBLS	5/15
Mechanics, Installers, and Repairers	Wilmington PMSA, DE-MD-NJ	Y	58090 FQ	73210 MW	91210 TQ	USBLS	5/15
Mechanics, Installers, and Repairers	District of Columbia	Y	63500 FQ	73070 MW	83590 TQ	USBLS	5/15
Mechanics, Installers, and Repairers	Washington-Arlington-Alexandria PMSA, DC-VA-MD-WV	Y	56250 FQ	71920 MW	88650 TQ	USBLS	5/15
Mechanics, Installers, and Repairers	Florida	H	19.71 AE	29.19 MW	35.32 AEX	FLBLS	7/16-9/16
Mechanics, Installers, and Repairers	Fort Lauderdale-Pompano Beach-Deerfield Beach PMSA, FL	H	20.91 AE	31.00 MW	37.19 AEX	FLBLS	7/16-9/16

AE	Average entry wage	AWR	Average wage range	H	Hourly
AEX	Average experienced wage	B	Biweekly	HI	Highest wage paid
ATC	Average total compensation	D	Daily	HR	High end range
AW	Average wage paid	FQ	First quartile wage	LO	Lowest wage paid

LR	Low end range	MTC	Median total compensation
M	Monthly	MW	Median wage paid
MCC	Median cash compensation	MWR	Median wage range
ME	Median entry wage	S	See annotated source

TCC	Total cash compensation		
TQ	Third quartile wage		
W	Weekly		
Y	Yearly		

Occupation/Type/Industry	Location	Per	Low	Mid	High	Source	Date
First-Line Supervisor							
Mechanics, Installers, and Repairers	Miami-Miami Beach-Kendall PMSA, FL	H	18.81 AE	28.43 MW	35.25 AEX	FLBLS	7/16-9/16
Mechanics, Installers, and Repairers	Orlando-Kissimmee-Sanford MSA, FL	H	20.29 AE	29.49 MW	35.58 AEX	FLBLS	7/16-9/16
Mechanics, Installers, and Repairers	Tampa-St. Petersburg-Clearwater MSA, FL	H	20.06 AE	29.40 MW	35.24 AEX	FLBLS	7/16-9/16
Mechanics, Installers, and Repairers	Georgia	Y	45720 FQ	58830 MW	74540 TQ	USBLS	5/15
Mechanics, Installers, and Repairers	Atlanta-Sandy Springs-Roswell MSA, GA	Y	46970 FQ	59770 MW	76660 TQ	USBLS	5/15
Mechanics, Installers, and Repairers	Augusta-Richmond County MSA, GA-SC	Y	47590 FQ	59040 MW	78980 TQ	USBLS	5/15
Mechanics, Installers, and Repairers	Hawaii	Y	55620 FQ	73300 MW	91380 TQ	USBLS	5/15
Mechanics, Installers, and Repairers	Urban Honolulu MSA, HI	Y	61870 FQ	81600 MW	92730 TQ	USBLS	5/15
Mechanics, Installers, and Repairers	Idaho	Y	45260 FQ	57180 MW	70720 TQ	USBLS	5/15
Mechanics, Installers, and Repairers	Boise City MSA, ID	Y	47140 FQ	59690 MW	73260 TQ	USBLS	5/15
Mechanics, Installers, and Repairers	Illinois	Y	47910 FQ	65090 MW	81940 TQ	USBLS	5/15
Mechanics, Installers, and Repairers	Chicago-Naperville-Arlington Heights PMSA, IL	Y	49520 FQ	67850 MW	86890 TQ	USBLS	5/15
Mechanics, Installers, and Repairers	Lake County-Kenosha County PMSA, IL-WI	Y	41670 FQ	62590 MW	84300 TQ	USBLS	5/15
Mechanics, Installers, and Repairers	Indiana	Y	45190 FQ	58540 MW	74640 TQ	USBLS	5/15
Mechanics, Installers, and Repairers	Gary PMSA, IN	Y	47270 FQ	64510 MW	78850 TQ	USBLS	5/15
Mechanics, Installers, and Repairers	Indianapolis-Carmel-Anderson MSA, IN	Y	44670 FQ	57570 MW	72500 TQ	USBLS	5/15
Mechanics, Installers, and Repairers	Iowa	Y	45550 FQ	58360 MW	72480 TQ	USBLS	5/15
Mechanics, Installers, and Repairers	Des Moines-West Des Moines MSA, IA	Y	45760 FQ	58270 MW	71740 TQ	USBLS	5/15
Mechanics, Installers, and Repairers	Kansas	Y	43420 FQ	56340 MW	73200 TQ	USBLS	5/15
Mechanics, Installers, and Repairers	Wichita MSA, KS	Y	46530 FQ	59080 MW	76540 TQ	USBLS	5/15
Mechanics, Installers, and Repairers	Kentucky	Y	41530 FQ	56000 MW	74700 TQ	USBLS	5/15
Mechanics, Installers, and Repairers	Louisville-Jefferson County MSA, KY-IN	Y	43700 FQ	59360 MW	77550 TQ	USBLS	5/15
Mechanics, Installers, and Repairers	Louisiana	Y	45350 FQ	59250 MW	77140 TQ	USBLS	5/15
Mechanics, Installers, and Repairers	Baton Rouge MSA, LA	Y	46360 FQ	62230 MW	83720 TQ	USBLS	5/15
Mechanics, Installers, and Repairers	New Orleans-Metairie MSA, LA	Y	48070 FQ	60300 MW	80440 TQ	USBLS	5/15
Mechanics, Installers, and Repairers	Maine	Y	46940 FQ	58640 MW	72800 TQ	USBLS	5/15
Mechanics, Installers, and Repairers	Portland-South Portland MSA, ME	Y	45330 FQ	57770 MW	75440 TQ	USBLS	5/15
Mechanics, Installers, and Repairers	Maryland	Y	43570 AE	67532 MW	79513 AEX	MDBLS	4/16
Mechanics, Installers, and Repairers	Baltimore-Columbia-Towson MSA, MD	Y	49940 FQ	63220 MW	79790 TQ	USBLS	5/15
Mechanics, Installers, and Repairers	Salisbury MSA, MD-DE	Y	47940 FQ	63410 MW	82930 TQ	USBLS	5/15
Mechanics, Installers, and Repairers	Massachusetts	Y	55220 FQ	70050 MW	88780 TQ	USBLS	5/15
Mechanics, Installers, and Repairers	Boston-Cambridge-Newton NECTA, MA	Y	58990 FQ	74200 MW	92810 TQ	USBLS	5/15
Mechanics, Installers, and Repairers	Worcester MSA, MA-CT	Y	54700 FQ	67970 MW	89870 TQ	USBLS	5/15
Mechanics, Installers, and Repairers	Michigan	Y	47880 FQ	62420 MW	79280 TQ	USBLS	5/15
Mechanics, Installers, and Repairers	Detroit-Dearborn-Livonia PMSA, MI	Y	48650 FQ	65960 MW	86380 TQ	USBLS	5/15
Mechanics, Installers, and Repairers	Grand Rapids-Wyoming MSA, MI	Y	45730 FQ	60170 MW	76110 TQ	USBLS	5/15
Mechanics, Installers, and Repairers	Minnesota	Y	50998 FQ	62141 MW	76974 TQ	MNBLS	1/16-3/16
Mechanics, Installers, and Repairers	Minneapolis-St. Paul-Bloomington MSA, MN-WI	Y	52044 FQ	63106 MW	78141 TQ	MNBLS	1/16-3/16
Mechanics, Installers, and Repairers	Mississippi	Y	38450 FQ	52840 MW	71040 TQ	USBLS	5/15
Mechanics, Installers, and Repairers	Jackson MSA, MS	Y	39820 FQ	58680 MW	76980 TQ	USBLS	5/15
Mechanics, Installers, and Repairers	Missouri	Y	42530 FQ	55310 MW	72090 TQ	USBLS	5/15
Mechanics, Installers, and Repairers	Kansas City MSA, MO-KS	Y	44590 FQ	57110 MW	73010 TQ	USBLS	5/15
Mechanics, Installers, and Repairers	St. Louis MSA, MO-IL	Y	45750 FQ	60870 MW	76670 TQ	USBLS	5/15
Mechanics, Installers, and Repairers	Montana	Y	42320 FQ	59040 MW	77660 TQ	USBLS	5/15
Mechanics, Installers, and Repairers	Billings MSA, MT	Y	37020 FQ	56520 MW	76610 TQ	USBLS	5/15
Mechanics, Installers, and Repairers	Nebraska	Y	47160 FQ	60015 MW	75935 TQ	NEBLS	7/16-9/16
Mechanics, Installers, and Repairers	Omaha-Council Bluffs MSA, NE-IA	Y	48685 FQ	62240 MW	78140 TQ	NEBLS	7/16-9/16
Mechanics, Installers, and Repairers	Nevada	Y	51570 FQ	68270 MW	83670 TQ	USBLS	5/15
Mechanics, Installers, and Repairers	Las Vegas-Henderson-Paradise MSA, NV	Y	50260 FQ	67680 MW	80440 TQ	USBLS	5/15
Mechanics, Installers, and Repairers	New Hampshire	H	23.72 AE	33.50 MW	39.53 AEX	NHBLS	6/16
Mechanics, Installers, and Repairers	Manchester NECTA, NH	H	22.75 AE	33.75 MW	39.50 AEX	NHBLS	6/16
Mechanics, Installers, and Repairers	Nashua NECTA, NH-MA	Y	62210 FQ	75920 MW	90030 TQ	USBLS	5/15

AE	Average entry wage	AWR	Average wage range	H	Hourly	LR	Low end range	MTC	Median total compensation	TCC	Total cash compensation
AEX	Average experienced wage	B	Biweekly	HI	Highest wage paid	M	Monthly	MW	Median wage paid	TQ	Third quartile wage
ATC	Average total compensation	D	Daily	HR	High end range	MCC	Median cash compensation	MWR	Median wage range	W	Weekly
AW	Average wage paid	FQ	First quartile wage	LO	Lowest wage paid	ME	Median entry wage	S	See annotated source	Y	Yearly

First-Line Supervisor

Occupation/Type/Industry	Location	Per	Low	Mid	High	Source	Date
Mechanics, Installers, and Repairers	New Jersey	Y	58570 FQ	73400 MW	90410 TQ	USBLS	5/15
Mechanics, Installers, and Repairers	Camden PMSA, NJ	Y	60560 FQ	73210 MW	86270 TQ	USBLS	5/15
Mechanics, Installers, and Repairers	Newark PMSA, NJ-PA	Y	58870 FQ	75740 MW	93250 TQ	USBLS	5/15
Mechanics, Installers, and Repairers	Trenton MSA, NJ	Y	59610 FQ	72650 MW	87290 TQ	USBLS	5/15
Mechanics, Installers, and Repairers	New Mexico	Y	42570 FQ	57370 MW	76090 TQ	USBLS	5/15
Mechanics, Installers, and Repairers	Albuquerque MSA, NM	Y	40140 FQ	51770 MW	71650 TQ	USBLS	5/15
Mechanics, Installers, and Repairers	New York	Y	50050 AE	73940 MW	90190 AEX	NYBLS	1/16-3/16
Mechanics, Installers, and Repairers	Buffalo-Cheektowaga-Niagara Falls MSA, NY	Y	50370 FQ	61760 MW	77320 TQ	USBLS	5/15
Mechanics, Installers, and Repairers	Nassau County-Suffolk County PMSA, NY	Y	64030 FQ	80640 MW	99650 TQ	USBLS	5/15
Mechanics, Installers, and Repairers	New York-Jersey City-White Plains PMSA, NY-NJ	Y	60630 FQ	78380 MW	98080 TQ	USBLS	5/15
Mechanics, Installers, and Repairers	Rochester MSA, NY	Y	49820 FQ	61310 MW	74670 TQ	USBLS	5/15
Mechanics, Installers, and Repairers	North Carolina	Y	48430 FQ	61060 MW	77170 TQ	USBLS	5/15
Mechanics, Installers, and Repairers	Charlotte-Concord-Gastonia MSA, NC-SC	Y	50630 FQ	64800 MW	82970 TQ	USBLS	5/15
Mechanics, Installers, and Repairers	Raleigh MSA, NC	Y	47850 FQ	59250 MW	75300 TQ	USBLS	5/15
Mechanics, Installers, and Repairers	North Dakota	Y	50080 FQ	64050 MW	79890 TQ	USBLS	5/15
Mechanics, Installers, and Repairers	Fargo MSA, ND-MN	Y	48530 FQ	58940 MW	71600 TQ	USBLS	5/15
Mechanics, Installers, and Repairers	Ohio	Y	47170 FQ	60240 MW	75530 TQ	USBLS	5/15
Mechanics, Installers, and Repairers	Cincinnati MSA, OH-KY-IN	Y	45400 FQ	60240 MW	75720 TQ	USBLS	5/15
Mechanics, Installers, and Repairers	Cleveland-Elyria MSA, OH	Y	51120 FQ	62030 MW	78310 TQ	USBLS	5/15
Mechanics, Installers, and Repairers	Columbus MSA, OH	Y	48680 FQ	61190 MW	74470 TQ	USBLS	5/15
Mechanics, Installers, and Repairers	Oklahoma	Y	45440 FQ	60870 MW	74950 TQ	USBLS	5/15
Mechanics, Installers, and Repairers	Oklahoma City MSA, OK	Y	50680 FQ	64810 MW	75990 TQ	USBLS	5/15
Mechanics, Installers, and Repairers	Tulsa MSA, OK	Y	46340 FQ	60610 MW	75440 TQ	USBLS	5/15
Mechanics, Installers, and Repairers	Oregon	H	25.18 FQ	31.76 MW	37.60 TQ	ORBLS	2016
Mechanics, Installers, and Repairers	Portland-Vancouver-Hillsboro MSA, OR-WA	Y	53900 FQ	67880 MW	79050 TQ	USBLS	5/15
Mechanics, Installers, and Repairers	Pennsylvania	Y	51430 FQ	64510 MW	78650 TQ	USBLS	5/15
Mechanics, Installers, and Repairers	Allentown-Bethlehem-Easton MSA, PA-NJ	Y	55190 FQ	67540 MW	83280 TQ	USBLS	5/15
Mechanics, Installers, and Repairers	Harrisburg-Carlisle MSA, PA	Y	46070 FQ	58480 MW	73680 TQ	USBLS	5/15
Mechanics, Installers, and Repairers	Montgomery County-Bucks County-Chester County PMSA, PA	Y	54770 FQ	68020 MW	82910 TQ	USBLS	5/15
Mechanics, Installers, and Repairers	Philadelphia PMSA, PA	Y	57120 FQ	70070 MW	83090 TQ	USBLS	5/15
Mechanics, Installers, and Repairers	Pittsburgh MSA, PA	Y	51500 FQ	66080 MW	80380 TQ	USBLS	5/15
Mechanics, Installers, and Repairers	Rhode Island	Y	49910 FQ	61990 MW	76280 TQ	USBLS	5/15
Mechanics, Installers, and Repairers	Providence-Warwick MSA, RI-MA	Y	50540 FQ	63040 MW	78270 TQ	USBLS	5/15
Mechanics, Installers, and Repairers	South Carolina	Y	42710 FQ	54470 MW	71330 TQ	USBLS	5/15
Mechanics, Installers, and Repairers	Charleston-North Charleston MSA, SC	Y	44050 FQ	55760 MW	70890 TQ	USBLS	5/15
Mechanics, Installers, and Repairers	Columbia MSA, SC	Y	42150 FQ	54640 MW	71720 TQ	USBLS	5/15
Mechanics, Installers, and Repairers	Greenville-Anderson-Mauldin MSA, SC	Y	42290 FQ	53580 MW	68950 TQ	USBLS	5/15
Mechanics, Installers, and Repairers	South Dakota	Y	57310 FQ	68420 MW	81680 TQ	USBLS	5/15
Mechanics, Installers, and Repairers	Sioux Falls MSA, SD	Y	60360 FQ	72190 MW	85730 TQ	USBLS	5/15
Mechanics, Installers, and Repairers	Tennessee	Y	44080 FQ	56450 MW	72860 TQ	USBLS	5/15
Mechanics, Installers, and Repairers	Knoxville MSA, TN	Y	41730 FQ	51340 MW	68510 TQ	USBLS	5/15
Mechanics, Installers, and Repairers	Memphis MSA, TN-MS-AR	Y	46230 FQ	60570 MW	75960 TQ	USBLS	5/15
Mechanics, Installers, and Repairers	Nashville-Davidson–Murfreesboro–Franklin MSA, TN	Y	45490 FQ	56820 MW	70730 TQ	USBLS	5/15
Mechanics, Installers, and Repairers	Texas	Y	46830 FQ	62580 MW	80710 TQ	USBLS	5/15
Mechanics, Installers, and Repairers	Austin-Round Rock MSA, TX	Y	46620 FQ	59250 MW	75100 TQ	USBLS	5/15
Mechanics, Installers, and Repairers	Dallas-Plano-Irving PMSA, TX	Y	50470 FQ	64880 MW	88290 TQ	USBLS	5/15
Mechanics, Installers, and Repairers	Fort Worth-Arlington PMSA, TX	Y	51630 FQ	65680 MW	81460 TQ	USBLS	5/15
Mechanics, Installers, and Repairers	Houston-The Woodlands-Sugar Land MSA, TX	Y	48980 FQ	66880 MW	87180 TQ	USBLS	5/15
Mechanics, Installers, and Repairers	San Antonio-New Braunfels MSA, TX	Y	47280 FQ	62330 MW	76650 TQ	USBLS	5/15
Mechanics, Installers, and Repairers	Utah	Y	46780 FQ	62150 MW	76710 TQ	USBLS	5/15
Mechanics, Installers, and Repairers	Ogden-Clearfield MSA, UT	Y	55500 FQ	69790 MW	79530 TQ	USBLS	5/15
Mechanics, Installers, and Repairers	Provo-Orem MSA, UT	Y	42610 FQ	59460 MW	75850 TQ	USBLS	5/15
Mechanics, Installers, and Repairers	Salt Lake City MSA, UT	Y	45640 FQ	59880 MW	75870 TQ	USBLS	5/15
Mechanics, Installers, and Repairers	Vermont	Y	46480 FQ	60490 MW	74520 TQ	USBLS	5/15

AE	Average entry wage	AWR	Average wage range	H	Hourly	LR	Low end range	MTC	Median total compensation	TCC	Total cash compensation
AEX	Average experienced wage	B	Biweekly	HI	Highest wage paid	M	Monthly	MW	Median wage paid	TQ	Third quartile wage
ATC	Average total compensation	D	Daily	HR	High end range	MCC	Median cash compensation	MWR	Median wage range	W	Weekly
AW	Average wage paid	FQ	First quartile wage	LO	Lowest wage paid	ME	Median entry wage	S	See annotated source	Y	Yearly

First-Line Supervisor

Occupation/Type/Industry	Location	Per	Low	Mid	High	Source	Date
Mechanics, Installers, and Repairers	Burlington-South Burlington MSA, VT	Y	46790 FQ	64920 MW	76830 TQ	USBLS	5/15
Mechanics, Installers, and Repairers	Virginia	Y	50980 FQ	64840 MW	79660 TQ	USBLS	5/15
Mechanics, Installers, and Repairers	Richmond MSA, VA	Y	53850 FQ	66710 MW	78360 TQ	USBLS	5/15
Mechanics, Installers, and Repairers	Virginia Beach-Norfolk-Newport News MSA, VA-NC	Y	49740 FQ	61940 MW	74260 TQ	USBLS	5/15
Mechanics, Installers, and Repairers	Washington	H	26.91 FQ	33.72 MW	40.81 TQ	WABLS	3/16
Mechanics, Installers, and Repairers	Seattle-Bellevue-Everett PMSA, WA	H	27.24 FQ	34.41 MW	41.44 TQ	WABLS	3/16
Mechanics, Installers, and Repairers	Tacoma-Lakewood PMSA, WA	H	28.58 FQ	35.45 MW	42.32 TQ	WABLS	3/16
Mechanics, Installers, and Repairers	West Virginia	Y	37780 FQ	50170 MW	69120 TQ	USBLS	5/15
Mechanics, Installers, and Repairers	Huntington-Ashland MSA, WV-KY-OH	Y	39720 FQ	52040 MW	70510 TQ	USBLS	5/15
Mechanics, Installers, and Repairers	Wisconsin	Y	50240 FQ	61920 MW	76770 TQ	USBLS	5/15
Mechanics, Installers, and Repairers	Madison MSA, WI	Y	51230 FQ	65110 MW	81800 TQ	USBLS	5/15
Mechanics, Installers, and Repairers	Milwaukee-Waukesha-West Allis MSA, WI	Y	54510 FQ	67130 MW	80450 TQ	USBLS	5/15
Mechanics, Installers, and Repairers	Wyoming	Y	58840 FQ	74400 MW	91920 TQ	USBLS	5/15
Mechanics, Installers, and Repairers	Cheyenne MSA, WY	Y	45620 FQ	62210 MW	74810 TQ	USBLS	5/15
Mechanics, Installers, and Repairers	Puerto Rico	Y	27170 FQ	38670 MW	49660 TQ	USBLS	5/15
Mechanics, Installers, and Repairers	San Juan-Carolina-Caguas MSA, PR	Y	27710 FQ	39300 MW	49610 TQ	USBLS	5/15
Mechanics, Installers, and Repairers	Virgin Islands	Y	37780 FQ	46680 MW	58800 TQ	USBLS	5/15
Mechanics, Installers, and Repairers	Guam	Y	33790 FQ	45990 MW	65390 TQ	USBLS	5/15
Non-Retail Sales Workers	Alabama	Y	45941 AE	80682 AW	98047 AEX	ALBLS	6/16
Non-Retail Sales Workers	Birmingham-Hoover MSA, AL	Y	48351 AE	87136 AW	106538 AEX	ALBLS	6/16
Non-Retail Sales Workers	Alaska	Y	38960 FQ	54690 MW	81140 TQ	USBLS	5/15
Non-Retail Sales Workers	Anchorage MSA, AK	Y	41320 FQ	58390 MW	104120 TQ	USBLS	5/15
Non-Retail Sales Workers	Arizona	Y	43860 FQ	61840 MW	90920 TQ	USBLS	5/15
Non-Retail Sales Workers	Phoenix-Mesa-Scottsdale MSA, AZ	Y	45640 FQ	64100 MW	94400 TQ	USBLS	5/15
Non-Retail Sales Workers	Tucson MSA, AZ	Y	34350 FQ	49830 MW	64590 TQ	USBLS	5/15
Non-Retail Sales Workers	Arkansas	Y	40900 FQ	61170 MW	91820 TQ	USBLS	5/15
Non-Retail Sales Workers	Little Rock-North Little Rock-Conway MSA, AR	Y	51830 FQ	67980 MW	89740 TQ	USBLS	5/15
Non-Retail Sales Workers	California	H	22.16 FQ	30.56 MW	44.00 TQ	CABLS	1/16-3/16
Non-Retail Sales Workers	Anaheim-Santa Ana-Irvine PMSA, CA	H	23.20 FQ	31.06 MW	41.95 TQ	CABLS	1/16-3/16
Non-Retail Sales Workers	Los Angeles-Long Beach-Glendale PMSA, CA	H	20.30 FQ	27.55 MW	38.77 TQ	CABLS	1/16-3/16
Non-Retail Sales Workers	Oakland-Hayward-Berkeley PMSA, CA	H	24.82 FQ	34.35 MW	49.50 TQ	CABLS	1/16-3/16
Non-Retail Sales Workers	Riverside-San Bernardino-Ontario MSA, CA	H	21.26 FQ	28.94 MW	37.73 TQ	CABLS	1/16-3/16
Non-Retail Sales Workers	Sacramento–Roseville–Arden-Arcade MSA, CA	H	22.95 FQ	30.89 MW	41.31 TQ	CABLS	1/16-3/16
Non-Retail Sales Workers	San Diego-Carlsbad MSA, CA	H	23.46 FQ	30.57 MW	40.19 TQ	CABLS	1/16-3/16
Non-Retail Sales Workers	San Francisco-Redwood City-South San Francisco PMSA, CA	H	26.11 FQ	43.56 MW	63.27 TQ	CABLS	1/16-3/16
Non-Retail Sales Workers	Colorado	Y	53730 FQ	74460 MW	101150 TQ	USBLS	5/15
Non-Retail Sales Workers	Denver-Aurora-Lakewood MSA, CO	Y	61320 FQ	82500 MW	105770 TQ	USBLS	5/15
Non-Retail Sales Workers	Connecticut	Y		78119 MW		CTBLS	1/16-3/16
Non-Retail Sales Workers	Bridgeport-Stamford-Norwalk MSA, CT	Y	64360 FQ	83500 MW	98070 TQ	USBLS	5/15
Non-Retail Sales Workers	Hartford-West Hartford-East Hartford MSA, CT	Y	60470 FQ	77890 MW	97790 TQ	USBLS	5/15
Non-Retail Sales Workers	Delaware	Y	64600 FQ	78770 MW	103080 TQ	USBLS	5/15
Non-Retail Sales Workers	Wilmington PMSA, DE-MD-NJ	Y	65370 FQ	80840 MW	109520 TQ	USBLS	5/15
Non-Retail Sales Workers	District of Columbia	Y	47920 FQ	78110 MW	107740 TQ	USBLS	5/15
Non-Retail Sales Workers	Washington-Arlington-Alexandria PMSA, DC-VA-MD-WV	Y	59630 FQ	86300 MW	122950 TQ	USBLS	5/15
Non-Retail Sales Workers	Florida	H	22.26 AE	37.56 MW	56.09 AEX	FLBLS	7/16-9/16
Non-Retail Sales Workers	Fort Lauderdale-Pompano Beach-Deerfield Beach PMSA, FL	H	23.62 AE	37.91 MW	59.04 AEX	FLBLS	7/16-9/16
Non-Retail Sales Workers	Miami-Miami Beach-Kendall PMSA, FL	H	23.90 AE	42.56 MW	62.44 AEX	FLBLS	7/16-9/16

Occupation/Type/Industry	Location	Per	Low	Mid	High	Source	Date
First-Line Supervisor							
Non-Retail Sales Workers	Orlando-Kissimmee-Sanford MSA, FL	H	21.66 AE	36.96 MW	53.29 AEX	FLBLS	7/16-9/16
Non-Retail Sales Workers	Tampa-St. Petersburg-Clearwater MSA, FL	H	24.05 AE	40.47 MW	59.69 AEX	FLBLS	7/16-9/16
Non-Retail Sales Workers	Georgia	Y	48440 FQ	64970 MW	90650 TQ	USBLS	5/15
Non-Retail Sales Workers	Atlanta-Sandy Springs-Roswell MSA, GA	Y	50090 FQ	66700 MW	95070 TQ	USBLS	5/15
Non-Retail Sales Workers	Augusta-Richmond County MSA, GA-SC	Y	39750 FQ	54820 MW	68910 TQ	USBLS	5/15
Non-Retail Sales Workers	Hawaii	Y	43320 FQ	52040 MW	75110 TQ	USBLS	5/15
Non-Retail Sales Workers	Urban Honolulu MSA, HI	Y	43670 FQ	53300 MW	78310 TQ	USBLS	5/15
Non-Retail Sales Workers	Idaho	Y	46410 FQ	61390 MW	86410 TQ	USBLS	5/15
Non-Retail Sales Workers	Boise City MSA, ID	Y	55240 FQ	71470 MW	92500 TQ	USBLS	5/15
Non-Retail Sales Workers	Illinois	Y	47630 FQ	67650 MW	98970 TQ	USBLS	5/15
Non-Retail Sales Workers	Chicago-Naperville-Arlington Heights PMSA, IL	Y	50600 FQ	69710 MW	100570 TQ	USBLS	5/15
Non-Retail Sales Workers	Lake County-Kenosha County PMSA, IL-WI	Y	59880 FQ	83310 MW	115650 TQ	USBLS	5/15
Non-Retail Sales Workers	Indiana	Y	46270 FQ	67600 MW	101960 TQ	USBLS	5/15
Non-Retail Sales Workers	Gary PMSA, IN	Y	35980 FQ	73890 MW	118200 TQ	USBLS	5/15
Non-Retail Sales Workers	Indianapolis-Carmel-Anderson MSA, IN	Y	48120 FQ	68330 MW	105730 TQ	USBLS	5/15
Non-Retail Sales Workers	Iowa	Y	43600 FQ	58330 MW	75120 TQ	USBLS	5/15
Non-Retail Sales Workers	Des Moines-West Des Moines MSA, IA	Y	49440 FQ	61520 MW	84390 TQ	USBLS	5/15
Non-Retail Sales Workers	Kansas	Y	50850 FQ	66950 MW	94830 TQ	USBLS	5/15
Non-Retail Sales Workers	Wichita MSA, KS	Y	46270 FQ	61390 MW	89370 TQ	USBLS	5/15
Non-Retail Sales Workers	Kentucky	Y	42810 FQ	60050 MW	80650 TQ	USBLS	5/15
Non-Retail Sales Workers	Louisville-Jefferson County MSA, KY-IN	Y	43120 FQ	64570 MW	92410 TQ	USBLS	5/15
Non-Retail Sales Workers	Louisiana	Y	39200 FQ	56510 MW	76520 TQ	USBLS	5/15
Non-Retail Sales Workers	Baton Rouge MSA, LA	Y	43580 FQ	58370 MW	76760 TQ	USBLS	5/15
Non-Retail Sales Workers	New Orleans-Metairie MSA, LA	Y	39400 FQ	55680 MW	80040 TQ	USBLS	5/15
Non-Retail Sales Workers	Maine	Y	46910 FQ	65160 MW	88270 TQ	USBLS	5/15
Non-Retail Sales Workers	Portland-South Portland MSA, ME	Y	57760 FQ	73720 MW	94850 TQ	USBLS	5/15
Non-Retail Sales Workers	Maryland	Y	45557 AE	85409 MW	105335 AEX	MDBLS	4/16
Non-Retail Sales Workers	Baltimore-Columbia-Towson MSA, MD	Y	57610 FQ	79550 MW	108350 TQ	USBLS	5/15
Non-Retail Sales Workers	Salisbury MSA, MD-DE	Y	50590 FQ	65880 MW	85810 TQ	USBLS	5/15
Non-Retail Sales Workers	Massachusetts	Y	64740 FQ	89540 MW	117740 TQ	USBLS	5/15
Non-Retail Sales Workers	Boston-Cambridge-Newton NECTA, MA	Y	68080 FQ	93190 MW	122970 TQ	USBLS	5/15
Non-Retail Sales Workers	Worcester MSA, MA-CT	Y	57120 FQ	84710 MW	103060 TQ	USBLS	5/15
Non-Retail Sales Workers	Michigan	Y	48370 FQ	64600 MW	92910 TQ	USBLS	5/15
Non-Retail Sales Workers	Detroit-Dearborn-Livonia PMSA, MI	Y	45840 FQ	64280 MW	83610 TQ	USBLS	5/15
Non-Retail Sales Workers	Grand Rapids-Wyoming MSA, MI	Y	45730 FQ	57480 MW	80140 TQ	USBLS	5/15
Non-Retail Sales Workers	Minnesota	Y	52092 FQ	70212 MW	93948 TQ	MNBLS	1/16-3/16
Non-Retail Sales Workers	Minneapolis-St. Paul-Bloomington MSA, MN-WI	Y	52989 FQ	73045 MW	96994 TQ	MNBLS	1/16-3/16
Non-Retail Sales Workers	Mississippi	Y	38630 FQ	55570 MW	78750 TQ	USBLS	5/15
Non-Retail Sales Workers	Jackson MSA, MS	Y	56150 FQ	78460 MW	95170 TQ	USBLS	5/15
Non-Retail Sales Workers	Missouri	Y	43420 FQ	58260 MW	79120 TQ	USBLS	5/15
Non-Retail Sales Workers	Kansas City MSA, MO-KS	Y	48110 FQ	65290 MW	92440 TQ	USBLS	5/15
Non-Retail Sales Workers	St. Louis MSA, MO-IL	Y	46300 FQ	60900 MW	91180 TQ	USBLS	5/15
Non-Retail Sales Workers	Montana	Y	42320 FQ	59770 MW	79340 TQ	USBLS	5/15
Non-Retail Sales Workers	Billings MSA, MT	Y	43850 FQ	64190 MW	89830 TQ	USBLS	5/15
Non-Retail Sales Workers	Nebraska	Y	42495 FQ	64665 MW	84910 TQ	NEBLS	7/16-9/16
Non-Retail Sales Workers	Omaha-Council Bluffs MSA, NE-IA	Y	36700 FQ	62805 MW	85275 TQ	NEBLS	7/16-9/16
Non-Retail Sales Workers	Nevada	Y	36220 FQ	50250 MW	68790 TQ	USBLS	5/15
Non-Retail Sales Workers	Las Vegas-Henderson-Paradise MSA, NV	Y	33610 FQ	47600 MW	62980 TQ	USBLS	5/15
Non-Retail Sales Workers	New Hampshire	H	29.75 AE	44.38 MW	63.60 AEX	NHBLS	6/16
Non-Retail Sales Workers	Manchester NECTA, NH	H	30.56 AE	43.49 MW	54.72 AEX	NHBLS	6/16
Non-Retail Sales Workers	Nashua NECTA, NH-MA	Y	71020 FQ	92950 MW	140450 TQ	USBLS	5/15
Non-Retail Sales Workers	New Jersey	Y	56680 FQ	78460 MW	103770 TQ	USBLS	5/15
Non-Retail Sales Workers	Camden PMSA, NJ	Y	54820 FQ	73180 MW	92780 TQ	USBLS	5/15

AE	Average entry wage	AWR	Average wage range	H	Hourly
AEX	Average experienced wage	B	Biweekly	HI	Highest wage paid
ATC	Average total compensation	D	Daily	HR	High end range
AW	Average wage paid	FQ	First quartile wage	LO	Lowest wage paid

LR	Low end range	MTC	Median total compensation
M	Monthly	MW	Median wage paid
MCC	Median cash compensation	MWR	Median wage range
ME	Median entry wage	S	See annotated source

TCC	Total cash compensation
TQ	Third quartile wage
W	Weekly
Y	Yearly

Occupation/Type/Industry	Location	Per	Low	Mid	High	Source	Date
First-Line Supervisor							
Non-Retail Sales Workers	Newark PMSA, NJ-PA	Y	57770 FQ	80700 MW	111090 TQ	USBLS	5/15
Non-Retail Sales Workers	Trenton MSA, NJ	Y	65600 FQ	81120 MW	104790 TQ	USBLS	5/15
Non-Retail Sales Workers	New Mexico	Y	41560 FQ	60530 MW	84960 TQ	USBLS	5/15
Non-Retail Sales Workers	Albuquerque MSA, NM	Y	41660 FQ	61560 MW	81890 TQ	USBLS	5/15
Non-Retail Sales Workers	New York	Y	57280 AE	104030 MW	148730 AEX	NYBLS	1/16-3/16
Non-Retail Sales Workers	Buffalo-Cheektowaga-Niagara Falls MSA, NY	Y	57160 FQ	75330 MW	110460 TQ	USBLS	5/15
Non-Retail Sales Workers	Nassau County-Suffolk County PMSA, NY	Y	67110 FQ	97150 MW	143130 TQ	USBLS	5/15
Non-Retail Sales Workers	New York-Jersey City-White Plains PMSA, NY-NJ	Y	71360 FQ	104500 MW	152810 TQ	USBLS	5/15
Non-Retail Sales Workers	Rochester MSA, NY	Y	56850 FQ	80860 MW	112710 TQ	USBLS	5/15
Non-Retail Sales Workers	North Carolina	Y	60160 FQ	83300 MW	120490 TQ	USBLS	5/15
Non-Retail Sales Workers	Charlotte-Concord-Gastonia MSA, NC-SC	Y	59170 FQ	86100 MW	118120 TQ	USBLS	5/15
Non-Retail Sales Workers	Raleigh MSA, NC	Y	67970 FQ	94070 MW	137110 TQ	USBLS	5/15
Non-Retail Sales Workers	North Dakota	Y	45700 FQ	61080 MW	82040 TQ	USBLS	5/15
Non-Retail Sales Workers	Fargo MSA, ND-MN	Y	43400 FQ	53230 MW	69280 TQ	USBLS	5/15
Non-Retail Sales Workers	Ohio	Y	51650 FQ	71210 MW	97540 TQ	USBLS	5/15
Non-Retail Sales Workers	Cincinnati MSA, OH-KY-IN	Y	52660 FQ	72550 MW	101330 TQ	USBLS	5/15
Non-Retail Sales Workers	Cleveland-Elyria MSA, OH	Y	55090 FQ	72700 MW	98150 TQ	USBLS	5/15
Non-Retail Sales Workers	Columbus MSA, OH	Y	55980 FQ	78040 MW	103450 TQ	USBLS	5/15
Non-Retail Sales Workers	Oklahoma	Y	40060 FQ	57010 MW	81850 TQ	USBLS	5/15
Non-Retail Sales Workers	Oklahoma City MSA, OK	Y	38720 FQ	53840 MW	80940 TQ	USBLS	5/15
Non-Retail Sales Workers	Tulsa MSA, OK	Y	46910 FQ	67310 MW	92360 TQ	USBLS	5/15
Non-Retail Sales Workers	Oregon	H	20.98 FQ	28.16 MW	37.33 TQ	ORBLS	2016
Non-Retail Sales Workers	Portland-Vancouver-Hillsboro MSA, OR-WA	Y	43980 FQ	57920 MW	81260 TQ	USBLS	5/15
Non-Retail Sales Workers	Pennsylvania	Y	62080 FQ	88570 MW	125190 TQ	USBLS	5/15
Non-Retail Sales Workers	Allentown-Bethlehem-Easton MSA, PA-NJ	Y	54500 FQ	74730 MW	98850 TQ	USBLS	5/15
Non-Retail Sales Workers	Harrisburg-Carlisle MSA, PA	Y	46620 FQ	60820 MW	87150 TQ	USBLS	5/15
Non-Retail Sales Workers	Montgomery County-Bucks County-Chester County PMSA, PA	Y	69920 FQ	100420 MW	139490 TQ	USBLS	5/15
Non-Retail Sales Workers	Philadelphia PMSA, PA	Y	76540 FQ	107650 MW	159570 TQ	USBLS	5/15
Non-Retail Sales Workers	Pittsburgh MSA, PA	Y	63320 FQ	89620 MW	118060 TQ	USBLS	5/15
Non-Retail Sales Workers	Rhode Island	Y	66430 FQ	84560 MW	113560 TQ	USBLS	5/15
Non-Retail Sales Workers	Providence-Warwick MSA, RI-MA	Y	64980 FQ	82660 MW	111750 TQ	USBLS	5/15
Non-Retail Sales Workers	South Carolina	Y	44760 FQ	60290 MW	80590 TQ	USBLS	5/15
Non-Retail Sales Workers	Charleston-North Charleston MSA, SC	Y	45460 FQ	65620 MW	81480 TQ	USBLS	5/15
Non-Retail Sales Workers	Columbia MSA, SC	Y	46920 FQ	61020 MW	84720 TQ	USBLS	5/15
Non-Retail Sales Workers	Greenville-Anderson-Mauldin MSA, SC	Y	39250 FQ	59140 MW	79850 TQ	USBLS	5/15
Non-Retail Sales Workers	South Dakota	Y	68800 FQ	88200 MW	108890 TQ	USBLS	5/15
Non-Retail Sales Workers	Sioux Falls MSA, SD	Y	69020 FQ	88550 MW	107130 TQ	USBLS	5/15
Non-Retail Sales Workers	Tennessee	Y	50900 FQ	72120 MW	99200 TQ	USBLS	5/15
Non-Retail Sales Workers	Clarksville MSA, TN-KY	Y	49880 FQ	61070 MW	87640 TQ	USBLS	5/15
Non-Retail Sales Workers	Knoxville MSA, TN	Y	45410 FQ	65960 MW	87870 TQ	USBLS	5/15
Non-Retail Sales Workers	Memphis MSA, TN-MS-AR	Y	53070 FQ	70940 MW	106370 TQ	USBLS	5/15
Non-Retail Sales Workers	Nashville-Davidson–Murfreesboro–Franklin MSA, TN	Y	55020 FQ	76850 MW	104130 TQ	USBLS	5/15
Non-Retail Sales Workers	Texas	Y	50650 FQ	71220 MW	104660 TQ	USBLS	5/15
Non-Retail Sales Workers	Austin-Round Rock MSA, TX	Y	56140 FQ	74850 MW	115870 TQ	USBLS	5/15
Non-Retail Sales Workers	Dallas-Plano-Irving PMSA, TX	Y	48780 FQ	72030 MW	106490 TQ	USBLS	5/15
Non-Retail Sales Workers	Fort Worth-Arlington PMSA, TX	Y	50880 FQ	68050 MW	100890 TQ	USBLS	5/15
Non-Retail Sales Workers	Houston-The Woodlands-Sugar Land MSA, TX	Y	55410 FQ	79570 MW	116310 TQ	USBLS	5/15
Non-Retail Sales Workers	San Antonio-New Braunfels MSA, TX	Y	47330 FQ	68150 MW	98660 TQ	USBLS	5/15
Non-Retail Sales Workers	Utah	Y	44400 FQ	66860 MW	95680 TQ	USBLS	5/15
Non-Retail Sales Workers	Ogden-Clearfield MSA, UT	Y	51600 FQ	64750 MW	138320 TQ	USBLS	5/15
Non-Retail Sales Workers	Provo-Orem MSA, UT	Y	42640 FQ	61620 MW	82110 TQ	USBLS	5/15
Non-Retail Sales Workers	Salt Lake City MSA, UT	Y	43710 FQ	68910 MW	96920 TQ	USBLS	5/15
Non-Retail Sales Workers	Vermont	Y	47990 FQ	66880 MW	98110 TQ	USBLS	5/15
Non-Retail Sales Workers	Burlington-South Burlington MSA, VT	Y	53940 FQ	75320 MW	107130 TQ	USBLS	5/15

AE Average entry wage	**AWR** Average wage range	**H** Hourly	**LR** Low end range	**MTC** Median total compensation	**TCC** Total cash compensation
AEX Average experienced wage	**B** Biweekly	**HI** Highest wage paid	**M** Monthly	**MW** Median wage paid	**TQ** Third quartile wage
ATC Average total compensation	**D** Daily	**HR** High end range	**MCC** Median cash compensation	**MWR** Median wage range	**W** Weekly
AW Average wage paid	**FQ** First quartile wage	**LO** Lowest wage paid	**ME** Median entry wage	**S** See annotated source	**Y** Yearly

Occupation/Type/Industry	Location	Per	Low	Mid	High	Source	Date
First-Line Supervisor							
Non-Retail Sales Workers	Virginia	Y	58130 FQ	82600 MW	119240 TQ	USBLS	5/15
Non-Retail Sales Workers	Richmond MSA, VA	Y	61400 FQ	89200 MW	121190 TQ	USBLS	5/15
Non-Retail Sales Workers	Virginia Beach-Norfolk-Newport News MSA, VA-NC	Y	52820 FQ	72550 MW	104100 TQ	USBLS	5/15
Non-Retail Sales Workers	Washington	H	25.34 FQ	33.80 MW	48.33 TQ	WABLS	3/16
Non-Retail Sales Workers	Seattle-Bellevue-Everett PMSA, WA	H	27.84 FQ	37.38 MW	55.56 TQ	WABLS	3/16
Non-Retail Sales Workers	Tacoma-Lakewood PMSA, WA	H	25.07 FQ	29.36 MW	38.84 TQ	WABLS	3/16
Non-Retail Sales Workers	West Virginia	Y	39310 FQ	59030 MW	85150 TQ	USBLS	5/15
Non-Retail Sales Workers	Huntington-Ashland MSA, WV-KY-OH	Y	37990 FQ	49570 MW	76640 TQ	USBLS	5/15
Non-Retail Sales Workers	Wisconsin	Y	53980 FQ	74100 MW	100440 TQ	USBLS	5/15
Non-Retail Sales Workers	Madison MSA, WI	Y	55010 FQ	71600 MW	95230 TQ	USBLS	5/15
Non-Retail Sales Workers	Milwaukee-Waukesha-West Allis MSA, WI	Y	58800 FQ	83420 MW	117360 TQ	USBLS	5/15
Non-Retail Sales Workers	Wyoming	Y	47030 FQ	60160 MW	75630 TQ	USBLS	5/15
Non-Retail Sales Workers	Cheyenne MSA, WY	Y	41580 FQ	52300 MW	67810 TQ	USBLS	5/15
Non-Retail Sales Workers	Puerto Rico	Y	27400 FQ	37000 MW	51410 TQ	USBLS	5/15
Non-Retail Sales Workers	San Juan-Carolina-Caguas MSA, PR	Y	28570 FQ	37940 MW	53890 TQ	USBLS	5/15
Non-Retail Sales Workers	Guam	Y	23090 FQ	31570 MW	45000 TQ	USBLS	5/15
Office and Administrative Support Workers	Alabama	Y	33752 AE	53138 MW	62835 AEX	ALBLS	6/16
Office and Administrative Support Workers	Birmingham-Hoover MSA, AL	Y	38204 AE	58414 AW	68514 AEX	ALBLS	6/16
Office and Administrative Support Workers	Alaska	Y	47970 FQ	59420 MW	74590 TQ	USBLS	5/15
Office and Administrative Support Workers	Anchorage MSA, AK	Y	49550 FQ	59700 MW	74990 TQ	USBLS	5/15
Office and Administrative Support Workers	Arizona	Y	36290 FQ	47140 MW	60880 TQ	USBLS	5/15
Office and Administrative Support Workers	Phoenix-Mesa-Scottsdale MSA, AZ	Y	37090 FQ	48100 MW	62180 TQ	USBLS	5/15
Office and Administrative Support Workers	Tucson MSA, AZ	Y	34800 FQ	45220 MW	58190 TQ	USBLS	5/15
Office and Administrative Support Workers	Arkansas	Y	33110 FQ	42290 MW	55270 TQ	USBLS	5/15
Office and Administrative Support Workers	Little Rock-North Little Rock-Conway MSA, AR	Y	35880 FQ	45250 MW	57650 TQ	USBLS	5/15
Office and Administrative Support Workers	California	H	21.77 FQ	27.98 MW	35.77 TQ	CABLS	1/16-3/16
Office and Administrative Support Workers	Anaheim-Santa Ana-Irvine PMSA, CA	H	23.14 FQ	28.68 MW	35.54 TQ	CABLS	1/16-3/16
Office and Administrative Support Workers	Los Angeles-Long Beach-Glendale PMSA, CA	H	21.20 FQ	27.80 MW	35.49 TQ	CABLS	1/16-3/16
Office and Administrative Support Workers	Oakland-Hayward-Berkeley PMSA, CA	H	23.64 FQ	29.62 MW	36.81 TQ	CABLS	1/16-3/16
Office and Administrative Support Workers	Riverside-San Bernardino-Ontario MSA, CA	H	20.70 FQ	25.71 MW	31.18 TQ	CABLS	1/16-3/16
Office and Administrative Support Workers	Sacramento–Roseville–Arden-Arcade MSA, CA	H	23.10 FQ	30.77 MW	38.22 TQ	CABLS	1/16-3/16
Office and Administrative Support Workers	San Diego-Carlsbad MSA, CA	H	21.00 FQ	26.51 MW	34.01 TQ	CABLS	1/16-3/16
Office and Administrative Support Workers	San Francisco-Redwood City-South San Francisco PMSA, CA	H	25.73 FQ	31.31 MW	39.98 TQ	CABLS	1/16-3/16
Office and Administrative Support Workers	Colorado	Y	42770 FQ	55200 MW	69970 TQ	USBLS	5/15
Office and Administrative Support Workers	Denver-Aurora-Lakewood MSA, CO	Y	45020 FQ	57870 MW	73320 TQ	USBLS	5/15
Office and Administrative Support Workers	Connecticut	Y		60674 MW		CTBLS	1/16-3/16
Office and Administrative Support Workers	Bridgeport-Stamford-Norwalk MSA, CT	Y	51720 FQ	61540 MW	77220 TQ	USBLS	5/15
Office and Administrative Support Workers	Hartford-West Hartford-East Hartford MSA, CT	Y	48880 FQ	60290 MW	74660 TQ	USBLS	5/15
Office and Administrative Support Workers	Delaware	Y	43280 FQ	54190 MW	66980 TQ	USBLS	5/15
Office and Administrative Support Workers	Wilmington PMSA, DE-MD-NJ	Y	45710 FQ	56800 MW	70270 TQ	USBLS	5/15
Office and Administrative Support Workers	District of Columbia	Y	54690 FQ	71270 MW	93900 TQ	USBLS	5/15
Office and Administrative Support Workers	Washington-Arlington-Alexandria PMSA, DC-VA-MD-WV	Y	48620 FQ	61570 MW	79160 TQ	USBLS	5/15
Office and Administrative Support Workers	Florida	H	17.28 AE	24.73 MW	30.72 AEX	FLBLS	7/16-9/16
Office and Administrative Support Workers	Fort Lauderdale-Pompano Beach-Deerfield Beach PMSA, FL	H	18.02 AE	25.04 MW	31.43 AEX	FLBLS	7/16-9/16
Office and Administrative Support Workers	Miami-Miami Beach-Kendall PMSA, FL	H	18.18 AE	26.10 MW	32.26 AEX	FLBLS	7/16-9/16
Office and Administrative Support Workers	Orlando-Kissimmee-Sanford MSA, FL	H	16.92 AE	24.28 MW	30.07 AEX	FLBLS	7/16-9/16

Occupation/Type/Industry	Location	Per	Low	Mid	High	Source	Date
First-Line Supervisor							
Office and Administrative Support Workers	Tampa-St. Petersburg-Clearwater MSA, FL	H	17.65 AE	25.50 MW	31.71 AEX	FLBLS	7/16-9/16
Office and Administrative Support Workers	Georgia	Y	38810 FQ	51400 MW	66810 TQ	USBLS	5/15
Office and Administrative Support Workers	Atlanta-Sandy Springs-Roswell MSA, GA	Y	42280 FQ	55150 MW	71150 TQ	USBLS	5/15
Office and Administrative Support Workers	Augusta-Richmond County MSA, GA-SC	Y	34250 FQ	43790 MW	59130 TQ	USBLS	5/15
Office and Administrative Support Workers	Hawaii	Y	40870 FQ	49260 MW	62180 TQ	USBLS	5/15
Office and Administrative Support Workers	Urban Honolulu MSA, HI	Y	41140 FQ	50030 MW	63400 TQ	USBLS	5/15
Office and Administrative Support Workers	Idaho	Y	34040 FQ	43800 MW	54920 TQ	USBLS	5/15
Office and Administrative Support Workers	Boise City MSA, ID	Y	35960 FQ	45020 MW	56280 TQ	USBLS	5/15
Office and Administrative Support Workers	Illinois	Y	39380 FQ	52370 MW	68940 TQ	USBLS	5/15
Office and Administrative Support Workers	Chicago-Naperville-Arlington Heights PMSA, IL	Y	41750 FQ	55360 MW	72000 TQ	USBLS	5/15
Office and Administrative Support Workers	Lake County-Kenosha County PMSA, IL-WI	Y	41430 FQ	53210 MW	69660 TQ	USBLS	5/15
Office and Administrative Support Workers	Indiana	Y	36170 FQ	47460 MW	61400 TQ	USBLS	5/15
Office and Administrative Support Workers	Gary PMSA, IN	Y	35880 FQ	47790 MW	61770 TQ	USBLS	5/15
Office and Administrative Support Workers	Indianapolis-Carmel-Anderson MSA, IN	Y	40910 FQ	50790 MW	65800 TQ	USBLS	5/15
Office and Administrative Support Workers	Iowa	Y	35310 FQ	45570 MW	58680 TQ	USBLS	5/15
Office and Administrative Support Workers	Des Moines-West Des Moines MSA, IA	Y	40280 FQ	50070 MW	61820 TQ	USBLS	5/15
Office and Administrative Support Workers	Kansas	Y	36050 FQ	46710 MW	60550 TQ	USBLS	5/15
Office and Administrative Support Workers	Wichita MSA, KS	Y	36020 FQ	46320 MW	60300 TQ	USBLS	5/15
Office and Administrative Support Workers	Kentucky	Y	35230 FQ	44420 MW	56840 TQ	USBLS	5/15
Office and Administrative Support Workers	Louisville-Jefferson County MSA, KY-IN	Y	39190 FQ	47970 MW	60620 TQ	USBLS	5/15
Office and Administrative Support Workers	Louisiana	Y	34750 FQ	43750 MW	56650 TQ	USBLS	5/15
Office and Administrative Support Workers	Baton Rouge MSA, LA	Y	35920 FQ	46270 MW	59470 TQ	USBLS	5/15
Office and Administrative Support Workers	New Orleans-Metairie MSA, LA	Y	36370 FQ	45580 MW	57550 TQ	USBLS	5/15
Office and Administrative Support Workers	Maine	Y	38550 FQ	46850 MW	57740 TQ	USBLS	5/15
Office and Administrative Support Workers	Portland-South Portland MSA, ME	Y	41920 FQ	50130 MW	60860 TQ	USBLS	5/15
Office and Administrative Support Workers	Maryland	Y	39117 AE	59434 MW	69593 AEX	MDBLS	4/16
Office and Administrative Support Workers	Baltimore-Columbia-Towson MSA, MD	Y	45470 FQ	56710 MW	70230 TQ	USBLS	5/15
Office and Administrative Support Workers	Salisbury MSA, MD-DE	Y	36770 FQ	47350 MW	59510 TQ	USBLS	5/15
Office and Administrative Support Workers	Massachusetts	Y	46140 FQ	58540 MW	73890 TQ	USBLS	5/15
Office and Administrative Support Workers	Boston-Cambridge-Newton NECTA, MA	Y	49170 FQ	62290 MW	77670 TQ	USBLS	5/15
Office and Administrative Support Workers	Worcester MSA, MA-CT	Y	44180 FQ	53630 MW	64190 TQ	USBLS	5/15
Office and Administrative Support Workers	Michigan	Y	38510 FQ	49240 MW	62530 TQ	USBLS	5/15
Office and Administrative Support Workers	Detroit-Dearborn-Livonia PMSA, MI	Y	41330 FQ	49450 MW	62990 TQ	USBLS	5/15
Office and Administrative Support Workers	Grand Rapids-Wyoming MSA, MI	Y	39450 FQ	50160 MW	62550 TQ	USBLS	5/15
Office and Administrative Support Workers	Minnesota	Y	43798 FQ	55347 MW	67381 TQ	MNBLS	1/16-3/16
Office and Administrative Support Workers	Minneapolis-St. Paul-Bloomington MSA, MN-WI	Y	46165 FQ	57845 MW	71012 TQ	MNBLS	1/16-3/16
Office and Administrative Support Workers	Mississippi	Y	30580 FQ	40850 MW	54850 TQ	USBLS	5/15
Office and Administrative Support Workers	Jackson MSA, MS	Y	32990 FQ	44460 MW	58090 TQ	USBLS	5/15
Office and Administrative Support Workers	Missouri	Y	39080 FQ	50660 MW	64260 TQ	USBLS	5/15
Office and Administrative Support Workers	Kansas City MSA, MO-KS	Y	40950 FQ	52490 MW	67380 TQ	USBLS	5/15
Office and Administrative Support Workers	St. Louis MSA, MO-IL	Y	41590 FQ	53700 MW	68200 TQ	USBLS	5/15
Office and Administrative Support Workers	Montana	Y	34290 FQ	43630 MW	59540 TQ	USBLS	5/15
Office and Administrative Support Workers	Billings MSA, MT	Y	37310 FQ	47870 MW	65020 TQ	USBLS	5/15
Office and Administrative Support Workers	Nebraska	Y	37200 FQ	47560 MW	61190 TQ	NEBLS	7/16-9/16
Office and Administrative Support Workers	Omaha-Council Bluffs MSA, NE-IA	Y	41465 FQ	51480 MW	66710 TQ	NEBLS	7/16-9/16
Office and Administrative Support Workers	Nevada	Y	38010 FQ	47360 MW	59860 TQ	USBLS	5/15
Office and Administrative Support Workers	Las Vegas-Henderson-Paradise MSA, NV	Y	38560 FQ	47230 MW	59840 TQ	USBLS	5/15
Office and Administrative Support Workers	New Hampshire	H	18.29 AE	25.54 MW	31.47 AEX	NHBLS	6/16
Office and Administrative Support Workers	Manchester NECTA, NH	H	19.09 AE	25.53 MW	30.93 AEX	NHBLS	6/16
Office and Administrative Support Workers	Nashua NECTA, NH-MA	Y	44010 FQ	57850 MW	72110 TQ	USBLS	5/15
Office and Administrative Support Workers	New Jersey	Y	46820 FQ	57960 MW	71380 TQ	USBLS	5/15
Office and Administrative Support Workers	Camden PMSA, NJ	Y	44180 FQ	54930 MW	67310 TQ	USBLS	5/15
Office and Administrative Support Workers	Newark PMSA, NJ-PA	Y	47820 FQ	59150 MW	72560 TQ	USBLS	5/15
Office and Administrative Support Workers	Trenton MSA, NJ	Y	49370 FQ	61320 MW	73650 TQ	USBLS	5/15

AE Average entry wage	**AWR** Average wage range	**H** Hourly	**LR** Low end range	**MTC** Median total compensation	**TCC** Total cash compensation
AEX Average experienced wage	**B** Biweekly	**HI** Highest wage paid	**M** Monthly	**MW** Median wage paid	**TQ** Third quartile wage
ATC Average total compensation	**D** Daily	**HR** High end range	**MCC** Median cash compensation	**MWR** Median wage range	**W** Weekly
AW Average wage paid	**FQ** First quartile wage	**LO** Lowest wage paid	**ME** Median entry wage	**S** See annotated source	**Y** Yearly

First-Line Supervisor

Occupation/Type/Industry	Location	Per	Low	Mid	High	Source	Date
Office and Administrative Support Workers	New Mexico	Y	35320 FQ	45310 MW	58500 TQ	USBLS	5/15
Office and Administrative Support Workers	Albuquerque MSA, NM	Y	36860 FQ	46760 MW	59930 TQ	USBLS	5/15
Office and Administrative Support Workers	New York	Y	41570 AE	61700 MW	79870 AEX	NYBLS	1/16-3/16
Office and Administrative Support Workers	Buffalo-Cheektowaga-Niagara Falls MSA, NY	Y	39050 FQ	51960 MW	64360 TQ	USBLS	5/15
Office and Administrative Support Workers	Nassau County-Suffolk County PMSA, NY	Y	49710 FQ	61690 MW	78410 TQ	USBLS	5/15
Office and Administrative Support Workers	New York-Jersey City-White Plains PMSA, NY-NJ	Y	50640 FQ	62530 MW	81420 TQ	USBLS	5/15
Office and Administrative Support Workers	Rochester MSA, NY	Y	43720 FQ	55410 MW	69720 TQ	USBLS	5/15
Office and Administrative Support Workers	North Carolina	Y	38050 FQ	49230 MW	61620 TQ	USBLS	5/15
Office and Administrative Support Workers	Charlotte-Concord-Gastonia MSA, NC-SC	Y	40000 FQ	51780 MW	66290 TQ	USBLS	5/15
Office and Administrative Support Workers	Raleigh MSA, NC	Y	39210 FQ	51170 MW	62120 TQ	USBLS	5/15
Office and Administrative Support Workers	North Dakota	Y	40170 FQ	49910 MW	63660 TQ	USBLS	5/15
Office and Administrative Support Workers	Fargo MSA, ND-MN	Y	41020 FQ	50720 MW	63380 TQ	USBLS	5/15
Office and Administrative Support Workers	Ohio	Y	38890 FQ	49410 MW	61850 TQ	USBLS	5/15
Office and Administrative Support Workers	Cincinnati MSA, OH-KY-IN	Y	39830 FQ	50130 MW	62900 TQ	USBLS	5/15
Office and Administrative Support Workers	Cleveland-Elyria MSA, OH	Y	41220 FQ	51810 MW	64680 TQ	USBLS	5/15
Office and Administrative Support Workers	Columbus MSA, OH	Y	40510 FQ	50400 MW	62220 TQ	USBLS	5/15
Office and Administrative Support Workers	Oklahoma	Y	33890 FQ	45190 MW	60370 TQ	USBLS	5/15
Office and Administrative Support Workers	Oklahoma City MSA, OK	Y	36940 FQ	49530 MW	64710 TQ	USBLS	5/15
Office and Administrative Support Workers	Tulsa MSA, OK	Y	35820 FQ	47840 MW	62300 TQ	USBLS	5/15
Office and Administrative Support Workers	Oregon	H	19.70 FQ	24.96 MW	30.77 TQ	ORBLS	2016
Office and Administrative Support Workers	Portland-Vancouver-Hillsboro MSA, OR-WA	Y	42240 FQ	53080 MW	65940 TQ	USBLS	5/15
Office and Administrative Support Workers	Pennsylvania	Y	42490 FQ	54440 MW	69210 TQ	USBLS	5/15
Office and Administrative Support Workers	Allentown-Bethlehem-Easton MSA, PA-NJ	Y	42690 FQ	53740 MW	67420 TQ	USBLS	5/15
Office and Administrative Support Workers	Harrisburg-Carlisle MSA, PA	Y	43980 FQ	52850 MW	65470 TQ	USBLS	5/15
Office and Administrative Support Workers	Montgomery County-Bucks County-Chester County PMSA, PA	Y	45670 FQ	58600 MW	74700 TQ	USBLS	5/15
Office and Administrative Support Workers	Philadelphia PMSA, PA	Y	47080 FQ	59490 MW	74670 TQ	USBLS	5/15
Office and Administrative Support Workers	Pittsburgh MSA, PA	Y	41840 FQ	53700 MW	67560 TQ	USBLS	5/15
Office and Administrative Support Workers	Rhode Island	Y	45140 FQ	56200 MW	67320 TQ	USBLS	5/15
Office and Administrative Support Workers	Providence-Warwick MSA, RI-MA	Y	44200 FQ	55290 MW	66330 TQ	USBLS	5/15
Office and Administrative Support Workers	South Carolina	Y	35740 FQ	45660 MW	58540 TQ	USBLS	5/15
Office and Administrative Support Workers	Charleston-North Charleston MSA, SC	Y	38510 FQ	48850 MW	60710 TQ	USBLS	5/15
Office and Administrative Support Workers	Columbia MSA, SC	Y	37380 FQ	45950 MW	57200 TQ	USBLS	5/15
Office and Administrative Support Workers	Greenville-Anderson-Mauldin MSA, SC	Y	35990 FQ	45360 MW	58220 TQ	USBLS	5/15
Office and Administrative Support Workers	South Dakota	Y	37980 FQ	45710 MW	55130 TQ	USBLS	5/15
Office and Administrative Support Workers	Sioux Falls MSA, SD	Y	40810 FQ	47650 MW	57330 TQ	USBLS	5/15
Office and Administrative Support Workers	Tennessee	Y	36170 FQ	47520 MW	63440 TQ	USBLS	5/15
Office and Administrative Support Workers	Knoxville MSA, TN	Y	35980 FQ	47140 MW	62420 TQ	USBLS	5/15
Office and Administrative Support Workers	Memphis MSA, TN-MS-AR	Y	39000 FQ	50080 MW	66200 TQ	USBLS	5/15
Office and Administrative Support Workers	Nashville-Davidson–Murfreesboro–Franklin MSA, TN	Y	39410 FQ	51630 MW	69010 TQ	USBLS	5/15
Office and Administrative Support Workers	Texas	Y	42120 FQ	55540 MW	71870 TQ	USBLS	5/15
Office and Administrative Support Workers	Austin-Round Rock MSA, TX	Y	45040 FQ	60130 MW	78140 TQ	USBLS	5/15
Office and Administrative Support Workers	Dallas-Plano-Irving PMSA, TX	Y	45580 FQ	59110 MW	76450 TQ	USBLS	5/15
Office and Administrative Support Workers	Fort Worth-Arlington PMSA, TX	Y	41450 FQ	53730 MW	68340 TQ	USBLS	5/15
Office and Administrative Support Workers	Houston-The Woodlands-Sugar Land MSA, TX	Y	46140 FQ	58490 MW	75060 TQ	USBLS	5/15
Office and Administrative Support Workers	San Antonio-New Braunfels MSA, TX	Y	41550 FQ	51700 MW	65950 TQ	USBLS	5/15
Office and Administrative Support Workers	Utah	Y	36810 FQ	46450 MW	60060 TQ	USBLS	5/15
Office and Administrative Support Workers	Ogden-Clearfield MSA, UT	Y	36720 FQ	46050 MW	59380 TQ	USBLS	5/15
Office and Administrative Support Workers	Provo-Orem MSA, UT	Y	34790 FQ	44290 MW	57950 TQ	USBLS	5/15
Office and Administrative Support Workers	Salt Lake City MSA, UT	Y	38610 FQ	48080 MW	61550 TQ	USBLS	5/15
Office and Administrative Support Workers	Vermont	Y	42460 FQ	53060 MW	64140 TQ	USBLS	5/15
Office and Administrative Support Workers	Burlington-South Burlington MSA, VT	Y	44570 FQ	55570 MW	67750 TQ	USBLS	5/15
Office and Administrative Support Workers	Virginia	Y	40720 FQ	53280 MW	69210 TQ	USBLS	5/15
Office and Administrative Support Workers	Richmond MSA, VA	Y	41640 FQ	53150 MW	67280 TQ	USBLS	5/15

First-Line Supervisor

Occupation/Type/Industry	Location	Per	Low	Mid	High	Source	Date
First-Line Supervisor							
Office and Administrative Support Workers	Virginia Beach-Norfolk-Newport News MSA, VA-NC	Y	37140 FQ	48530 MW	66000 TQ	USBLS	5/15
Office and Administrative Support Workers	Washington	H	21.06 FQ	26.32 MW	33.62 TQ	WABLS	3/16
Office and Administrative Support Workers	Seattle-Bellevue-Everett PMSA, WA	H	22.31 FQ	28.10 MW	36.11 TQ	WABLS	3/16
Office and Administrative Support Workers	Tacoma-Lakewood PMSA, WA	H	20.95 FQ	25.30 MW	31.50 TQ	WABLS	3/16
Office and Administrative Support Workers	West Virginia	Y	31790 FQ	40120 MW	53010 TQ	USBLS	5/15
Office and Administrative Support Workers	Huntington-Ashland MSA, WV-KY-OH	Y	33520 FQ	41460 MW	54160 TQ	USBLS	5/15
Office and Administrative Support Workers	Wisconsin	Y	38730 FQ	49670 MW	63840 TQ	USBLS	5/15
Office and Administrative Support Workers	Madison MSA, WI	Y	41880 FQ	51540 MW	65970 TQ	USBLS	5/15
Office and Administrative Support Workers	Milwaukee-Waukesha-West Allis MSA, WI	Y	41130 FQ	53310 MW	68890 TQ	USBLS	5/15
Office and Administrative Support Workers	Wyoming	Y	35090 FQ	45220 MW	57660 TQ	USBLS	5/15
Office and Administrative Support Workers	Cheyenne MSA, WY	Y	39330 FQ	49390 MW	59200 TQ	USBLS	5/15
Office and Administrative Support Workers	Puerto Rico	Y	24730 FQ	30770 MW	41440 TQ	USBLS	5/15
Office and Administrative Support Workers	San Juan-Carolina-Caguas MSA, PR	Y	25560 FQ	31330 MW	42900 TQ	USBLS	5/15
Office and Administrative Support Workers	Virgin Islands	Y	36310 FQ	45110 MW	57160 TQ	USBLS	5/15
Office and Administrative Support Workers	Guam	Y	29830 FQ	39560 MW	49310 TQ	USBLS	5/15
Personal Service Workers	Alabama	Y	20469 AE	34203 AW	41071 AEX	ALBLS	6/16
Personal Service Workers	Birmingham-Hoover MSA, AL	Y	24463 AE	37529 AW	44057 AEX	ALBLS	6/16
Personal Service Workers	Alaska	Y	31960 FQ	38640 MW	47420 TQ	USBLS	5/15
Personal Service Workers	Anchorage MSA, AK	Y	31800 FQ	38960 MW	47980 TQ	USBLS	5/15
Personal Service Workers	Arizona	Y	25700 FQ	31500 MW	40960 TQ	USBLS	5/15
Personal Service Workers	Phoenix-Mesa-Scottsdale MSA, AZ	Y	25920 FQ	33120 MW	42940 TQ	USBLS	5/15
Personal Service Workers	Tucson MSA, AZ	Y	25380 FQ	29420 MW	37240 TQ	USBLS	5/15
Personal Service Workers	Arkansas	Y	23930 FQ	29080 MW	36800 TQ	USBLS	5/15
Personal Service Workers	Little Rock-North Little Rock-Conway MSA, AR	Y	24840 FQ	30050 MW	37510 TQ	USBLS	5/15
Personal Service Workers	California	H	15.09 FQ	19.01 MW	24.69 TQ	CABLS	1/16-3/16
Personal Service Workers	Anaheim-Santa Ana-Irvine PMSA, CA	H	14.62 FQ	19.11 MW	25.14 TQ	CABLS	1/16-3/16
Personal Service Workers	Los Angeles-Long Beach-Glendale PMSA, CA	H	16.75 FQ	20.78 MW	26.71 TQ	CABLS	1/16-3/16
Personal Service Workers	Oakland-Hayward-Berkeley PMSA, CA	H	15.02 FQ	20.54 MW	27.86 TQ	CABLS	1/16-3/16
Personal Service Workers	Riverside-San Bernardino-Ontario MSA, CA	H	14.91 FQ	18.21 MW	23.93 TQ	CABLS	1/16-3/16
Personal Service Workers	Sacramento–Roseville–Arden-Arcade MSA, CA	H	12.70 FQ	15.02 MW	21.45 TQ	CABLS	1/16-3/16
Personal Service Workers	San Diego-Carlsbad MSA, CA	H	14.69 FQ	19.00 MW	23.25 TQ	CABLS	1/16-3/16
Personal Service Workers	San Francisco-Redwood City-South San Francisco PMSA, CA	H	15.83 FQ	18.84 MW	27.29 TQ	CABLS	1/16-3/16
Personal Service Workers	Colorado	Y	26950 FQ	36210 MW	47910 TQ	USBLS	5/15
Personal Service Workers	Denver-Aurora-Lakewood MSA, CO	Y	26080 FQ	34850 MW	46090 TQ	USBLS	5/15
Personal Service Workers	Connecticut	Y		41361 MW		CTBLS	1/16-3/16
Personal Service Workers	Bridgeport-Stamford-Norwalk MSA, CT	Y	34890 FQ	43090 MW	53030 TQ	USBLS	5/15
Personal Service Workers	Hartford-West Hartford-East Hartford MSA, CT	Y	34030 FQ	40890 MW	53430 TQ	USBLS	5/15
Personal Service Workers	Delaware	Y	33190 FQ	42790 MW	56760 TQ	USBLS	5/15
Personal Service Workers	Wilmington PMSA, DE-MD-NJ	Y	32220 FQ	43320 MW	57370 TQ	USBLS	5/15
Personal Service Workers	District of Columbia	Y	35140 FQ	43860 MW	60570 TQ	USBLS	5/15
Personal Service Workers	Washington-Arlington-Alexandria PMSA, DC-VA-MD-WV	Y	30590 FQ	40620 MW	56020 TQ	USBLS	5/15
Personal Service Workers	Florida	H	12.58 AE	18.58 MW	23.59 AEX	FLBLS	7/16-9/16
Personal Service Workers	Fort Lauderdale-Pompano Beach-Deerfield Beach PMSA, FL	H	12.55 AE	17.81 MW	22.90 AEX	FLBLS	7/16-9/16
Personal Service Workers	Miami-Miami Beach-Kendall PMSA, FL	H	12.81 AE	18.92 MW	25.23 AEX	FLBLS	7/16-9/16
Personal Service Workers	Orlando-Kissimmee-Sanford MSA, FL	H	13.43 AE	20.16 MW	25.02 AEX	FLBLS	7/16-9/16
Personal Service Workers	Tampa-St. Petersburg-Clearwater MSA, FL	H	12.60 AE	17.95 MW	21.74 AEX	FLBLS	7/16-9/16

AE Average entry wage	AWR Average wage range	H Hourly	LR Low end range	MTC Median total compensation	TCC Total cash compensation
AEX Average experienced wage	B Biweekly	HI Highest wage paid	M Monthly	MW Median wage paid	TQ Third quartile wage
ATC Average total compensation	D Daily	HR High end range	MCC Median cash compensation	MWR Median wage range	W Weekly
AW Average wage paid	FQ First quartile wage	LO Lowest wage paid	ME Median entry wage	S See annotated source	Y Yearly

Occupation/Type/Industry	Location	Per	Low	Mid	High	Source	Date
First-Line Supervisor							
Personal Service Workers	Georgia	Y	25800 FQ	33900 MW	47410 TQ	USBLS	5/15
Personal Service Workers	Atlanta-Sandy Springs-Roswell MSA, GA	Y	26990 FQ	35520 MW	50860 TQ	USBLS	5/15
Personal Service Workers	Augusta-Richmond County MSA, GA-SC	Y	21230 FQ	29660 MW	42590 TQ	USBLS	5/15
Personal Service Workers	Hawaii	Y	29940 FQ	41570 MW	51590 TQ	USBLS	5/15
Personal Service Workers	Urban Honolulu MSA, HI	Y	30360 FQ	40820 MW	49680 TQ	USBLS	5/15
Personal Service Workers	Idaho	Y	22240 FQ	26930 MW	34090 TQ	USBLS	5/15
Personal Service Workers	Boise City MSA, ID	Y	22280 FQ	26130 MW	30820 TQ	USBLS	5/15
Personal Service Workers	Illinois	Y	27270 FQ	37590 MW	47410 TQ	USBLS	5/15
Personal Service Workers	Chicago-Naperville-Arlington Heights PMSA, IL	Y	28780 FQ	40220 MW	48160 TQ	USBLS	5/15
Personal Service Workers	Lake County-Kenosha County PMSA, IL-WI	Y	21730 FQ	31010 MW	43160 TQ	USBLS	5/15
Personal Service Workers	Indiana	Y	26350 FQ	31910 MW	39160 TQ	USBLS	5/15
Personal Service Workers	Gary PMSA, IN	Y	21390 FQ	26470 MW	34810 TQ	USBLS	5/15
Personal Service Workers	Indianapolis-Carmel-Anderson MSA, IN	Y	28530 FQ	34660 MW	43140 TQ	USBLS	5/15
Personal Service Workers	Iowa	Y	25270 FQ	30710 MW	39220 TQ	USBLS	5/15
Personal Service Workers	Des Moines-West Des Moines MSA, IA	Y	29210 FQ	35960 MW	44690 TQ	USBLS	5/15
Personal Service Workers	Kansas	Y	27050 FQ	34260 MW	44650 TQ	USBLS	5/15
Personal Service Workers	Wichita MSA, KS	Y	32800 FQ	41540 MW	49350 TQ	USBLS	5/15
Personal Service Workers	Kentucky	Y	23450 FQ	28820 MW	36120 TQ	USBLS	5/15
Personal Service Workers	Louisville-Jefferson County MSA, KY-IN	Y	25000 FQ	32720 MW	41020 TQ	USBLS	5/15
Personal Service Workers	Louisiana	Y	25460 FQ	29690 MW	35950 TQ	USBLS	5/15
Personal Service Workers	Baton Rouge MSA, LA	Y	25620 FQ	30430 MW	36950 TQ	USBLS	5/15
Personal Service Workers	New Orleans-Metairie MSA, LA	Y	26550 FQ	30490 MW	36660 TQ	USBLS	5/15
Personal Service Workers	Maine	Y	28290 FQ	33610 MW	38930 TQ	USBLS	5/15
Personal Service Workers	Portland-South Portland MSA, ME	Y	27410 FQ	31340 MW	37890 TQ	USBLS	5/15
Personal Service Workers	Maryland	Y	24721 AE	40415 MW	48262 AEX	MDBLS	4/16
Personal Service Workers	Baltimore-Columbia-Towson MSA, MD	Y	28290 FQ	37340 MW	48300 TQ	USBLS	5/15
Personal Service Workers	Salisbury MSA, MD-DE	Y	30530 FQ	38400 MW	53800 TQ	USBLS	5/15
Personal Service Workers	Massachusetts	Y	33890 FQ	41560 MW	50270 TQ	USBLS	5/15
Personal Service Workers	Boston-Cambridge-Newton NECTA, MA	Y	35390 FQ	42990 MW	50620 TQ	USBLS	5/15
Personal Service Workers	Worcester MSA, MA-CT	Y	33470 FQ	40700 MW	54380 TQ	USBLS	5/15
Personal Service Workers	Michigan	Y	25000 FQ	33590 MW	43820 TQ	USBLS	5/15
Personal Service Workers	Detroit-Dearborn-Livonia PMSA, MI	Y	23620 FQ	32180 MW	43890 TQ	USBLS	5/15
Personal Service Workers	Grand Rapids-Wyoming MSA, MI	Y	31070 FQ	38710 MW	50750 TQ	USBLS	5/15
Personal Service Workers	Minnesota	Y	27448 FQ	35113 MW	43414 TQ	MNBLS	1/16-3/16
Personal Service Workers	Minneapolis-St. Paul-Bloomington MSA, MN-WI	Y	30750 FQ	37012 MW	46100 TQ	MNBLS	1/16-3/16
Personal Service Workers	Mississippi	Y	22070 FQ	28650 MW	39400 TQ	USBLS	5/15
Personal Service Workers	Jackson MSA, MS	Y	22860 FQ	28830 MW	36660 TQ	USBLS	5/15
Personal Service Workers	Missouri	Y	24540 FQ	30820 MW	38960 TQ	USBLS	5/15
Personal Service Workers	Kansas City MSA, MO-KS	Y	25570 FQ	33700 MW	43430 TQ	USBLS	5/15
Personal Service Workers	St. Louis MSA, MO-IL	Y	24010 FQ	29570 MW	39430 TQ	USBLS	5/15
Personal Service Workers	Montana	Y	24780 FQ	29900 MW	37060 TQ	USBLS	5/15
Personal Service Workers	Billings MSA, MT	Y	24410 FQ	29950 MW	36000 TQ	USBLS	5/15
Personal Service Workers	Omaha-Council Bluffs MSA, NE-IA	Y	26970 FQ	32555 MW	38775 TQ	NEBLS	7/16-9/16
Personal Service Workers	Nevada	Y	28070 FQ	35870 MW	44850 TQ	USBLS	5/15
Personal Service Workers	Las Vegas-Henderson-Paradise MSA, NV	Y	28950 FQ	36650 MW	45070 TQ	USBLS	5/15
Personal Service Workers	New Hampshire	H	12.44 AE	17.42 MW	20.86 AEX	NHBLS	6/16
Personal Service Workers	Manchester NECTA, NH	H	12.34 AE	17.30 MW	19.68 AEX	NHBLS	6/16
Personal Service Workers	Nashua NECTA, NH-MA	Y	30720 FQ	38820 MW	46020 TQ	USBLS	5/15
Personal Service Workers	New Jersey	Y	36060 FQ	46850 MW	58110 TQ	USBLS	5/15
Personal Service Workers	Camden PMSA, NJ	Y	32880 FQ	42330 MW	53370 TQ	USBLS	5/15
Personal Service Workers	Newark PMSA, NJ-PA	Y	37420 FQ	47150 MW	56720 TQ	USBLS	5/15
Personal Service Workers	Trenton MSA, NJ	Y	39400 FQ	48760 MW	59640 TQ	USBLS	5/15
Personal Service Workers	New Mexico	Y	25120 FQ	30610 MW	40890 TQ	USBLS	5/15
Personal Service Workers	Albuquerque MSA, NM	Y	25770 FQ	30560 MW	41470 TQ	USBLS	5/15
Personal Service Workers	New York	Y	28850 AE	39460 MW	49160 AEX	NYBLS	1/16-3/16

AE Average entry wage	**AWR** Average wage range	**H** Hourly	**LR** Low end range	**MTC** Median total compensation	**TCC** Total cash compensation
AEX Average experienced wage	**B** Biweekly	**HI** Highest wage paid	**M** Monthly	**MCC** Median cash compensation	**TQ** Third quartile wage
ATC Average total compensation	**D** Daily	**HR** High end range	**MCC** Median cash compensation	**MWR** Median wage range	**W** Weekly
AW Average wage paid	**FQ** First quartile wage	**LO** Lowest wage paid	**ME** Median entry wage	**S** See annotated source	**Y** Yearly

Occupation/Type/Industry	Location	Per	Low	Mid	High	Source	Date

First-Line Supervisor

Occupation/Type/Industry	Location	Per	Low	Mid	High	Source	Date
Personal Service Workers	Buffalo-Cheektowaga-Niagara Falls MSA, NY	Y	30520 FQ	37550 MW	48370 TQ	USBLS	5/15
Personal Service Workers	Nassau County-Suffolk County PMSA, NY	Y	34750 FQ	43860 MW	54050 TQ	USBLS	5/15
Personal Service Workers	New York-Jersey City-White Plains PMSA, NY-NJ	Y	32220 FQ	40650 MW	52940 TQ	USBLS	5/15
Personal Service Workers	Rochester MSA, NY	Y	31900 FQ	38150 MW	46760 TQ	USBLS	5/15
Personal Service Workers	North Carolina	Y	27650 FQ	34740 MW	45570 TQ	USBLS	5/15
Personal Service Workers	Charlotte-Concord-Gastonia MSA, NC-SC	Y	28390 FQ	35470 MW	45840 TQ	USBLS	5/15
Personal Service Workers	Raleigh MSA, NC	Y	28250 FQ	35470 MW	50200 TQ	USBLS	5/15
Personal Service Workers	North Dakota	Y	31980 FQ	37570 MW	45720 TQ	USBLS	5/15
Personal Service Workers	Fargo MSA, ND-MN	Y	29220 FQ	35880 MW	45150 TQ	USBLS	5/15
Personal Service Workers	Ohio	Y	25960 FQ	33090 MW	43970 TQ	USBLS	5/15
Personal Service Workers	Cincinnati MSA, OH-KY-IN	Y	26260 FQ	32780 MW	40930 TQ	USBLS	5/15
Personal Service Workers	Cleveland-Elyria MSA, OH	Y	24990 FQ	32830 MW	45290 TQ	USBLS	5/15
Personal Service Workers	Columbus MSA, OH	Y	28000 FQ	35840 MW	47250 TQ	USBLS	5/15
Personal Service Workers	Oklahoma	Y	21570 FQ	27440 MW	36990 TQ	USBLS	5/15
Personal Service Workers	Oklahoma City MSA, OK	Y	24870 FQ	31090 MW	42260 TQ	USBLS	5/15
Personal Service Workers	Tulsa MSA, OK	Y	19710 FQ	28530 MW	42700 TQ	USBLS	5/15
Personal Service Workers	Oregon	H	13.82 FQ	16.98 MW	20.63 TQ	ORBLS	2016
Personal Service Workers	Portland-Vancouver-Hillsboro MSA, OR-WA	Y	28710 FQ	35430 MW	45570 TQ	USBLS	5/15
Personal Service Workers	Pennsylvania	Y	28100 FQ	34970 MW	44440 TQ	USBLS	5/15
Personal Service Workers	Allentown-Bethlehem-Easton MSA, PA-NJ	Y	24380 FQ	33060 MW	45490 TQ	USBLS	5/15
Personal Service Workers	Harrisburg-Carlisle MSA, PA	Y	28740 FQ	34190 MW	40940 TQ	USBLS	5/15
Personal Service Workers	Lebanon MSA, PA	Y	26070 FQ	32000 MW	44230 TQ	USBLS	5/15
Personal Service Workers	Montgomery County-Bucks County-Chester County PMSA, PA	Y	28520 FQ	36580 MW	48610 TQ	USBLS	5/15
Personal Service Workers	Philadelphia PMSA, PA	Y	29030 FQ	34620 MW	42390 TQ	USBLS	5/15
Personal Service Workers	Pittsburgh MSA, PA	Y	30760 FQ	37510 MW	46000 TQ	USBLS	5/15
Personal Service Workers	Rhode Island	Y	28510 FQ	39480 MW	48290 TQ	USBLS	5/15
Personal Service Workers	Providence-Warwick MSA, RI-MA	Y	28470 FQ	38660 MW	47920 TQ	USBLS	5/15
Personal Service Workers	South Carolina	Y	23780 FQ	29830 MW	41610 TQ	USBLS	5/15
Personal Service Workers	Charleston-North Charleston MSA, SC	Y	22230 FQ	29950 MW	42900 TQ	USBLS	5/15
Personal Service Workers	Columbia MSA, SC	Y	25270 FQ	28780 MW	35950 TQ	USBLS	5/15
Personal Service Workers	Greenville-Anderson-Mauldin MSA, SC	Y	24770 FQ	30970 MW	45570 TQ	USBLS	5/15
Personal Service Workers	South Dakota	Y	30810 FQ	35420 MW	40490 TQ	USBLS	5/15
Personal Service Workers	Sioux Falls MSA, SD	Y	32220 FQ	36530 MW	42210 TQ	USBLS	5/15
Personal Service Workers	Tennessee	Y	23990 FQ	29730 MW	39210 TQ	USBLS	5/15
Personal Service Workers	Knoxville MSA, TN	Y	22910 FQ	27500 MW	36800 TQ	USBLS	5/15
Personal Service Workers	Memphis MSA, TN-MS-AR	Y	23630 FQ	28650 MW	38310 TQ	USBLS	5/15
Personal Service Workers	Nashville-Davidson–Murfreesboro–Franklin MSA, TN	Y	24850 FQ	30760 MW	39330 TQ	USBLS	5/15
Personal Service Workers	Texas	Y	26950 FQ	35330 MW	46580 TQ	USBLS	5/15
Personal Service Workers	Austin-Round Rock MSA, TX	Y	29300 FQ	41890 MW	51090 TQ	USBLS	5/15
Personal Service Workers	Dallas-Plano-Irving PMSA, TX	Y	27160 FQ	36860 MW	48400 TQ	USBLS	5/15
Personal Service Workers	Fort Worth-Arlington PMSA, TX	Y	27880 FQ	35050 MW	46470 TQ	USBLS	5/15
Personal Service Workers	Houston-The Woodlands-Sugar Land MSA, TX	Y	26650 FQ	33770 MW	43170 TQ	USBLS	5/15
Personal Service Workers	San Antonio-New Braunfels MSA, TX	Y	28620 FQ	37310 MW	48030 TQ	USBLS	5/15
Personal Service Workers	Utah	Y	24200 FQ	29930 MW	38680 TQ	USBLS	5/15
Personal Service Workers	Ogden-Clearfield MSA, UT	Y	21320 FQ	28720 MW	36680 TQ	USBLS	5/15
Personal Service Workers	Provo-Orem MSA, UT	Y	22780 FQ	27590 MW	35270 TQ	USBLS	5/15
Personal Service Workers	Salt Lake City MSA, UT	Y	25530 FQ	30690 MW	39130 TQ	USBLS	5/15
Personal Service Workers	Vermont	Y	33460 FQ	42040 MW	52410 TQ	USBLS	5/15
Personal Service Workers	Burlington-South Burlington MSA, VT	Y	35210 FQ	44240 MW	58140 TQ	USBLS	5/15
Personal Service Workers	Virginia	Y	28960 FQ	37580 MW	51570 TQ	USBLS	5/15
Personal Service Workers	Richmond MSA, VA	Y	29370 FQ	38610 MW	51190 TQ	USBLS	5/15
Personal Service Workers	Virginia Beach-Norfolk-Newport News MSA, VA-NC	Y	28800 FQ	36950 MW	47980 TQ	USBLS	5/15
Personal Service Workers	Washington	H	14.86 FQ	19.10 MW	25.83 TQ	WABLS	3/16

AE	Average entry wage	AWR	Average wage range	H	Hourly	LR	Low end range	MTC	Median total compensation	TCC	Total cash compensation
AEX	Average experienced wage	B	Biweekly	HI	Highest wage paid	M	Monthly	MW	Median wage paid	TQ	Third quartile wage
ATC	Average total compensation	D	Daily	HR	High end range	MCC	Median cash compensation	MWR	Median wage range	W	Weekly
AW	Average wage paid	FQ	First quartile wage	LO	Lowest wage paid	ME	Median entry wage	S	See annotated source	Y	Yearly

First-Line Supervisor

Occupation/Type/Industry	Location	Per	Low	Mid	High	Source	Date
Personal Service Workers	Seattle-Bellevue-Everett PMSA, WA	H	16.70 FQ	21.56 MW	29.12 TQ	WABLS	3/16
Personal Service Workers	Tacoma-Lakewood PMSA, WA	H	16.05 FQ	20.12 MW	23.80 TQ	WABLS	3/16
Personal Service Workers	West Virginia	Y	21610 FQ	26590 MW	35450 TQ	USBLS	5/15
Personal Service Workers	Huntington-Ashland MSA, WV-KY-OH	Y	19830 FQ	26820 MW	37510 TQ	USBLS	5/15
Personal Service Workers	Wisconsin	Y	27460 FQ	33960 MW	43000 TQ	USBLS	5/15
Personal Service Workers	Madison MSA, WI	Y	27980 FQ	36440 MW	52450 TQ	USBLS	5/15
Personal Service Workers	Milwaukee-Waukesha-West Allis MSA, WI	Y	27240 FQ	33360 MW	43480 TQ	USBLS	5/15
Personal Service Workers	Wyoming	Y	26270 FQ	32800 MW	42830 TQ	USBLS	5/15
Personal Service Workers	Cheyenne MSA, WY	Y	25620 FQ	34040 MW	40590 TQ	USBLS	5/15
Personal Service Workers	Puerto Rico	Y	18090 FQ	22660 MW	30550 TQ	USBLS	5/15
Personal Service Workers	San Juan-Carolina-Caguas MSA, PR	Y	18250 FQ	23380 MW	32200 TQ	USBLS	5/15
Police and Detectives	Alabama	Y	44232 AE	65267 AW	75789 AEX	ALBLS	6/16
Police and Detectives	Birmingham-Hoover MSA, AL	Y	45859 AE	76438 AW	91728 AEX	ALBLS	6/16
Police and Detectives	Alaska	Y	89630 FQ	104900 MW	117860 TQ	USBLS	5/15
Police and Detectives	Anchorage MSA, AK	Y	94870 FQ	108490 MW	120650 TQ	USBLS	5/15
Police and Detectives	Arizona	Y	70840 FQ	86410 MW	100510 TQ	USBLS	5/15
Police and Detectives	Phoenix-Mesa-Scottsdale MSA, AZ	Y	79020 FQ	89330 MW	100460 TQ	USBLS	5/15
Police and Detectives	Tucson MSA, AZ	Y	71540 FQ	93370 MW	123110 TQ	USBLS	5/15
Police and Detectives	Arkansas	Y	39320 FQ	49240 MW	63410 TQ	USBLS	5/15
Police and Detectives	Little Rock-North Little Rock-Conway MSA, AR	Y	45410 FQ	58820 MW	71910 TQ	USBLS	5/15
Police and Detectives	California	H	48.78 FQ	64.72 MW	75.74 TQ	CABLS	1/16-3/16
Police and Detectives	Anaheim-Santa Ana-Irvine PMSA, CA	H	57.12 FQ	69.09 MW	78.07 TQ	CABLS	1/16-3/16
Police and Detectives	Los Angeles-Long Beach-Glendale PMSA, CA	H	51.15 FQ	67.33 MW	77.81 TQ	CABLS	1/16-3/16
Police and Detectives	Oakland-Hayward-Berkeley PMSA, CA	H	59.41 FQ	71.43 MW	84.38 TQ	CABLS	1/16-3/16
Police and Detectives	Riverside-San Bernardino-Ontario MSA, CA	H	48.57 FQ	64.72 MW	76.39 TQ	CABLS	1/16-3/16
Police and Detectives	Sacramento–Roseville–Arden-Arcade MSA, CA	H	49.39 FQ	64.47 MW	69.18 TQ	CABLS	1/16-3/16
Police and Detectives	San Diego-Carlsbad MSA, CA	H	52.63 FQ	64.43 MW	74.52 TQ	CABLS	1/16-3/16
Police and Detectives	San Francisco-Redwood City-South San Francisco PMSA, CA	H	51.16 FQ	67.91 MW	77.81 TQ	CABLS	1/16-3/16
Police and Detectives	Santa Maria-Santa Barbara MSA, CA	Y	131430 FQ	146170 MW	176330 TQ	USBLS	5/15
Police and Detectives	Colorado	Y	80780 FQ	92500 MW	103060 TQ	USBLS	5/15
Police and Detectives	Denver-Aurora-Lakewood MSA, CO	Y	87090 FQ	95980 MW	107870 TQ	USBLS	5/15
Police and Detectives	Connecticut	Y		91277 MW		CTBLS	1/16-3/16
Police and Detectives	Bridgeport-Stamford-Norwalk MSA, CT	Y	83360 FQ	91890 MW	100530 TQ	USBLS	5/15
Police and Detectives	Hartford-West Hartford-East Hartford MSA, CT	Y	83400 FQ	91800 MW	100420 TQ	USBLS	5/15
Police and Detectives	Delaware	Y	85460 FQ	97140 MW	112320 TQ	USBLS	5/15
Police and Detectives	Wilmington PMSA, DE-MD-NJ	Y	78750 FQ	92560 MW	109330 TQ	USBLS	5/15
Police and Detectives	Washington-Arlington-Alexandria PMSA, DC-VA-MD-WV	Y	86290 FQ	105190 MW	147570 TQ	USBLS	5/15
Police and Detectives	Florida	H	31.40 AE	44.78 MW	53.04 AEX	FLBLS	7/16-9/16
Police and Detectives	Fort Lauderdale-Pompano Beach-Deerfield Beach PMSA, FL	H	41.86 AE	56.62 MW	62.26 AEX	FLBLS	7/16-9/16
Police and Detectives	Miami-Miami Beach-Kendall PMSA, FL	H	44.36 AE	56.04 MW	61.38 AEX	FLBLS	7/16-9/16
Police and Detectives	Orlando-Kissimmee-Sanford MSA, FL	H	31.92 AE	42.29 MW	47.39 AEX	FLBLS	7/16-9/16
Police and Detectives	Tampa-St. Petersburg-Clearwater MSA, FL	H	32.70 AE	44.38 MW	51.92 AEX	FLBLS	7/16-9/16
Police and Detectives	Georgia	Y	44990 FQ	56940 MW	72310 TQ	USBLS	5/15
Police and Detectives	Atlanta-Sandy Springs-Roswell MSA, GA	Y	52010 FQ	64630 MW	78490 TQ	USBLS	5/15

AE	Average entry wage	AWR	Average wage range	H	Hourly	LR	Low end range	MTC	Median total compensation	TCC	Total cash compensation
AEX	Average experienced wage	B	Biweekly	HI	Highest wage paid	M	Monthly	MW	Median wage paid	TQ	Third quartile wage
ATC	Average total compensation	D	Daily	HR	High end range	MCC	Median cash compensation	MWR	Median wage range	W	Weekly
AW	Average wage paid	FQ	First quartile wage	LO	Lowest wage paid	ME	Median entry wage	S	See annotated source	Y	Yearly

Occupation/Type/Industry	Location	Per	Low	Mid	High	Source	Date
First-Line Supervisor							
Police and Detectives	Augusta-Richmond County MSA, GA-SC	Y	41350 FQ	51940 MW	61470 TQ	USBLS	5/15
Police and Detectives	Hawaii	Y	83650 FQ	92570 MW	101480 TQ	USBLS	5/15
Police and Detectives	Idaho	Y	57650 FQ	69710 MW	84740 TQ	USBLS	5/15
Police and Detectives	Boise City MSA, ID	Y	70600 FQ	85520 MW	98230 TQ	USBLS	5/15
Police and Detectives	Illinois	Y	81390 FQ	102880 MW	119050 TQ	USBLS	5/15
Police and Detectives	Chicago-Naperville-Arlington Heights PMSA, IL	Y	89640 FQ	107980 MW	121710 TQ	USBLS	5/15
Police and Detectives	Lake County-Kenosha County PMSA, IL-WI	Y	88120 FQ	101810 MW	117040 TQ	USBLS	5/15
Police and Detectives	Indiana	Y	53480 FQ	64270 MW	72030 TQ	USBLS	5/15
Police and Detectives	Gary PMSA, IN	Y	56380 FQ	65990 MW	73410 TQ	USBLS	5/15
Police and Detectives	Indianapolis-Carmel-Anderson MSA, IN	Y	59070 FQ	67010 MW	75550 TQ	USBLS	5/15
Police and Detectives	Iowa	Y	55980 FQ	68090 MW	85330 TQ	USBLS	5/15
Police and Detectives	Des Moines-West Des Moines MSA, IA	Y	73100 FQ	87190 MW	96130 TQ	USBLS	5/15
Police and Detectives	Kansas	Y	48730 FQ	63200 MW	77800 TQ	USBLS	5/15
Police and Detectives	Wichita MSA, KS	Y	52350 FQ	67160 MW	76820 TQ	USBLS	5/15
Police and Detectives	Kentucky	Y	50000 FQ	59820 MW	75560 TQ	USBLS	5/15
Police and Detectives	Louisville-Jefferson County MSA, KY-IN	Y	55580 FQ	67670 MW	79890 TQ	USBLS	5/15
Police and Detectives	Louisiana	Y	46010 FQ	57470 MW	71850 TQ	USBLS	5/15
Police and Detectives	Baton Rouge MSA, LA	Y	50940 FQ	63320 MW	73360 TQ	USBLS	5/15
Police and Detectives	New Orleans-Metairie MSA, LA	Y	51930 FQ	58850 MW	72680 TQ	USBLS	5/15
Police and Detectives	Maine	Y	52360 FQ	60070 MW	71670 TQ	USBLS	5/15
Police and Detectives	Portland-South Portland MSA, ME	Y	58700 FQ	70690 MW	86380 TQ	USBLS	5/15
Police and Detectives	Maryland	Y	63312 AE	90363 MW	103888 AEX	MDBLS	4/16
Police and Detectives	Baltimore-Columbia-Towson MSA, MD	Y	72210 FQ	88210 MW	101880 TQ	USBLS	5/15
Police and Detectives	Salisbury MSA, MD-DE	Y	55310 FQ	74880 MW	92550 TQ	USBLS	5/15
Police and Detectives	Massachusetts	Y	75300 FQ	90840 MW	111180 TQ	USBLS	5/15
Police and Detectives	Boston-Cambridge-Newton NECTA, MA	Y	80000 FQ	95360 MW	120780 TQ	USBLS	5/15
Police and Detectives	Worcester MSA, MA-CT	Y	68850 FQ	86030 MW	98090 TQ	USBLS	5/15
Police and Detectives	Michigan	Y	63210 FQ	77290 MW	91560 TQ	USBLS	5/15
Police and Detectives	Detroit-Dearborn-Livonia PMSA, MI	Y	74190 FQ	86650 MW	99380 TQ	USBLS	5/15
Police and Detectives	Grand Rapids-Wyoming MSA, MI	Y	64140 FQ	72600 MW	82640 TQ	USBLS	5/15
Police and Detectives	Minnesota	Y	73084 FQ	86485 MW	96412 TQ	MNBLS	1/16-3/16
Police and Detectives	Minneapolis-St. Paul-Bloomington MSA, MN-WI	Y	83627 FQ	91282 MW	99331 TQ	MNBLS	1/16-3/16
Police and Detectives	Mississippi	Y	42350 FQ	49180 MW	59970 TQ	USBLS	5/15
Police and Detectives	Jackson MSA, MS	Y	42430 FQ	49050 MW	62820 TQ	USBLS	5/15
Police and Detectives	Missouri	Y	60300 FQ	74500 MW	85020 TQ	USBLS	5/15
First-Line Detectives	Kansas City MSA, MO-KS	Y	61120 FQ	76400 MW	95030 TQ	USBLS	5/15
Police and Detectives	St. Louis MSA, MO-IL	Y	66250 FQ	75270 MW	89490 TQ	USBLS	5/15
Police and Detectives	Montana	Y	55200 FQ	64370 MW	76210 TQ	USBLS	5/15
Police and Detectives	Billings MSA, MT	Y	68570 FQ	96230 MW	135620 TQ	USBLS	5/15
Police and Detectives	Nebraska	Y	58075 FQ	71580 MW	85355 TQ	NEBLS	7/16-9/16
Police and Detectives	Omaha-Council Bluffs MSA, NE-IA	Y	68290 FQ	76860 MW	91300 TQ	NEBLS	7/16-9/16
Police and Detectives	Nevada	Y	84710 FQ	105230 MW	121820 TQ	USBLS	5/15
Police and Detectives	Las Vegas-Henderson-Paradise MSA, NV	Y	100450 FQ	113950 MW	126920 TQ	USBLS	5/15
Police and Detectives	New Hampshire	H	29.71 AE	37.64 MW	42.77 AEX	NHBLS	6/16
Police and Detectives	Nashua NECTA, NH-MA	Y	78080 FQ	85660 MW	93180 TQ	USBLS	5/15
Police and Detectives	New Jersey	Y	113280 FQ	126900 MW	148470 TQ	USBLS	5/15
Police and Detectives	Camden PMSA, NJ	Y	92370 FQ	109800 MW	125800 TQ	USBLS	5/15
Police and Detectives	Newark PMSA, NJ-PA	Y	109590 FQ	125540 MW	145550 TQ	USBLS	5/15
Police and Detectives	Trenton MSA, NJ	Y	104940 FQ	122840 MW	144080 TQ	USBLS	5/15
Police and Detectives	New Mexico	Y	54990 FQ	69640 MW	88220 TQ	USBLS	5/15
Police and Detectives	Albuquerque MSA, NM	Y	63780 FQ	74630 MW	101100 TQ	USBLS	5/15
Police and Detectives	New York	Y	78400 AE	100670 MW	118590 AEX	NYBLS	1/16-3/16
Police and Detectives	Buffalo-Cheektowaga-Niagara Falls MSA, NY	Y	70050 FQ	80440 MW	97080 TQ	USBLS	5/15
Police and Detectives	Nassau County-Suffolk County PMSA, NY	Y	131430 FQ	145290 MW	158740 TQ	USBLS	5/15

AE	Average entry wage	AWR	Average wage range	H	Hourly
AEX	Average experienced wage	B	Biweekly	HI	Highest wage paid
ATC	Average total compensation	D	Daily	HR	High end range
AW	Average wage paid	FQ	First quartile wage	LO	Lowest wage paid

LR	Low end range	MTC	Median total compensation	TCC	Total cash compensation
M	Monthly	MW	Median wage paid	TQ	Third quartile wage
MCC	Median cash compensation	MWR	Median wage range	W	Weekly
ME	Median entry wage	S	See annotated source	Y	Yearly

Occupation/Type/Industry	Location	Per	Low	Mid	High	Source	Date
First-Line Supervisor							
Police and Detectives	New York-Jersey City-White Plains PMSA, NY-NJ	Y	88880 FQ	103480 MW	125530 TQ	USBLS	5/15
Police and Detectives	Rochester MSA, NY	Y	71500 FQ	83940 MW	97300 TQ	USBLS	5/15
Police and Detectives	North Carolina	Y	52860 FQ	64360 MW	76680 TQ	USBLS	5/15
Police and Detectives	Charlotte-Concord-Gastonia MSA, NC-SC	Y	59310 FQ	73390 MW	87530 TQ	USBLS	5/15
Police and Detectives	Raleigh MSA, NC	Y	61180 FQ	72880 MW	87010 TQ	USBLS	5/15
Police and Detectives	North Dakota	Y	54030 FQ	64780 MW	77050 TQ	USBLS	5/15
Police and Detectives	Fargo MSA, ND-MN	Y	65210 FQ	77260 MW	95810 TQ	USBLS	5/15
Police and Detectives	Ohio	Y	64330 FQ	76430 MW	90740 TQ	USBLS	5/15
Police and Detectives	Cincinnati MSA, OH-KY-IN	Y	66580 FQ	77670 MW	89880 TQ	USBLS	5/15
Police and Detectives	Cleveland-Elyria MSA, OH	Y	68540 FQ	77820 MW	91040 TQ	USBLS	5/15
Police and Detectives	Columbus MSA, OH	Y	73390 FQ	90710 MW	103920 TQ	USBLS	5/15
Police and Detectives	Oklahoma	Y	55300 FQ	69820 MW	84810 TQ	USBLS	5/15
Police and Detectives	Oklahoma City MSA, OK	Y	65490 FQ	76720 MW	90530 TQ	USBLS	5/15
Police and Detectives	Tulsa MSA, OK	Y	51860 FQ	65400 MW	77110 TQ	USBLS	5/15
Police and Detectives	Oregon	H	40.13 FQ	45.23 MW	50.36 TQ	ORBLS	2016
Police and Detectives	Portland-Vancouver-Hillsboro MSA, OR-WA	Y	86290 FQ	95130 MW	107400 TQ	USBLS	5/15
Police and Detectives	Pennsylvania	Y	66870 FQ	79360 MW	99070 TQ	USBLS	5/15
Police and Detectives	Allentown-Bethlehem-Easton MSA, PA-NJ	Y	73510 FQ	91310 MW	106950 TQ	USBLS	5/15
Police and Detectives	Harrisburg-Carlisle MSA, PA	Y	72100 FQ	100450 MW	114670 TQ	USBLS	5/15
Police and Detectives	Montgomery County-Bucks County-Chester County PMSA, PA	Y	86430 FQ	96560 MW	109850 TQ	USBLS	5/15
Police and Detectives	Philadelphia PMSA, PA	Y	70480 FQ	78860 MW	93830 TQ	USBLS	5/15
Police and Detectives	Pittsburgh MSA, PA	Y	59550 FQ	74180 MW	96370 TQ	USBLS	5/15
Police and Detectives	Rhode Island	Y	65230 FQ	76360 MW	92510 TQ	USBLS	5/15
Police and Detectives	Providence-Warwick MSA, RI-MA	Y	66490 FQ	77180 MW	92810 TQ	USBLS	5/15
Police and Detectives	South Carolina	Y	43040 FQ	52040 MW	64190 TQ	USBLS	5/15
Police and Detectives	Charleston-North Charleston MSA, SC	Y	46910 FQ	55760 MW	70850 TQ	USBLS	5/15
Police and Detectives	Columbia MSA, SC	Y	45350 FQ	56100 MW	70930 TQ	USBLS	5/15
Police and Detectives	Greenville-Anderson-Mauldin MSA, SC	Y	43120 FQ	52980 MW	62270 TQ	USBLS	5/15
Police and Detectives	South Dakota	Y	52090 FQ	65160 MW	81310 TQ	USBLS	5/15
Police and Detectives	Tennessee	Y	47000 FQ	56700 MW	68110 TQ	USBLS	5/15
Police and Detectives	Knoxville MSA, TN	Y	49690 FQ	56830 MW	66590 TQ	USBLS	5/15
Police and Detectives	Memphis MSA, TN-MS-AR	Y	54490 FQ	62060 MW	72410 TQ	USBLS	5/15
Police and Detectives	Nashville-Davidson–Murfreesboro–Franklin MSA, TN	Y	47220 FQ	57100 MW	71500 TQ	USBLS	5/15
Police and Detectives	Texas	Y	58840 FQ	85720 MW	114670 TQ	USBLS	5/15
Police and Detectives	Austin-Round Rock MSA, TX	Y	87540 FQ	96070 MW	105590 TQ	USBLS	5/15
Police and Detectives	Dallas-Plano-Irving PMSA, TX	Y	74080 FQ	106140 MW	146350 TQ	USBLS	5/15
Police and Detectives	Fort Worth-Arlington PMSA, TX	Y	72760 FQ	90390 MW	105830 TQ	USBLS	5/15
Police and Detectives	Houston-The Woodlands-Sugar Land MSA, TX	Y	71460 FQ	93560 MW	138990 TQ	USBLS	5/15
Police and Detectives	San Antonio-New Braunfels MSA, TX	Y	58570 FQ	80630 MW	101450 TQ	USBLS	5/15
Police and Detectives	Utah	Y	59600 FQ	68570 MW	79040 TQ	USBLS	5/15
Police and Detectives	Ogden-Clearfield MSA, UT	Y	56180 FQ	65070 MW	78420 TQ	USBLS	5/15
Police and Detectives	Provo-Orem MSA, UT	Y	63660 FQ	72300 MW	82130 TQ	USBLS	5/15
Police and Detectives	Salt Lake City MSA, UT	Y	64560 FQ	72040 MW	82590 TQ	USBLS	5/15
Police and Detectives	Vermont	Y	61520 FQ	73200 MW	84800 TQ	USBLS	5/15
Police and Detectives	Burlington-South Burlington MSA, VT	Y	69310 FQ	84800 MW	138450 TQ	USBLS	5/15
Police and Detectives	Virginia	Y	62460 FQ	81270 MW	110920 TQ	USBLS	5/15
Police and Detectives	Richmond MSA, VA	Y	64380 FQ	76560 MW	92730 TQ	USBLS	5/15
Police and Detectives	Virginia Beach-Norfolk-Newport News MSA, VA-NC	Y	53850 FQ	64710 MW	80510 TQ	USBLS	5/15
Police and Detectives	Washington	H	40.36 FQ	47.33 MW	56.18 TQ	WABLS	3/16
Police and Detectives	Seattle-Bellevue-Everett PMSA, WA	H	45.37 FQ	53.11 MW	59.86 TQ	WABLS	3/16
Police and Detectives	Tacoma-Lakewood PMSA, WA	H	40.69 FQ	47.17 MW	54.44 TQ	WABLS	3/16
Police and Detectives	West Virginia	Y	43190 FQ	53500 MW	64140 TQ	USBLS	5/15
Police and Detectives	Huntington-Ashland MSA, WV-KY-OH	Y	50140 FQ	59950 MW	73080 TQ	USBLS	5/15

AE	Average entry wage	AWR	Average wage range	H	Hourly
AEX	Average experienced wage	B	Biweekly	HI	Highest wage paid
ATC	Average total compensation	D	Daily	HR	High end range
AW	Average wage paid	FQ	First quartile wage	LO	Lowest wage paid

LR	Low end range	MTC	Median total compensation
M	Monthly	MW	Median wage paid
MCC	Median cash compensation	MWR	Median wage range
ME	Median entry wage	S	See annotated source

TCC	Total cash compensation
TQ	Third quartile wage
W	Weekly
Y	Yearly

Occupation/Type/Industry	Location	Per	Low	Mid	High	Source	Date
First-Line Supervisor							
Police and Detectives	Wisconsin	Y	64680 FQ	73880 MW	86980 TQ	USBLS	5/15
Police and Detectives	Madison MSA, WI	Y	67370 FQ	81200 MW	94070 TQ	USBLS	5/15
Police and Detectives	Milwaukee-Waukesha-West Allis MSA, WI	Y	70520 FQ	83040 MW	94410 TQ	USBLS	5/15
Police and Detectives	Wyoming	Y	60210 FQ	71980 MW	82860 TQ	USBLS	5/15
Police and Detectives	Cheyenne MSA, WY	Y	65040 FQ	73820 MW	86070 TQ	USBLS	5/15
Police and Detectives	Puerto Rico	Y	31690 FQ	34910 MW	38120 TQ	USBLS	5/15
Police and Detectives	San Juan-Carolina-Caguas MSA, PR	Y	32490 FQ	35430 MW	38360 TQ	USBLS	5/15
Production and Operating Workers	Alabama	Y	36934 AE	59266 AW	70433 AEX	ALBLS	6/16
Production and Operating Workers	Birmingham-Hoover MSA, AL	Y	38034 AE	61117 AW	72654 AEX	ALBLS	6/16
Production and Operating Workers	Alaska	Y	39170 FQ	63650 MW	94260 TQ	USBLS	5/15
Production and Operating Workers	Anchorage MSA, AK	Y	39740 FQ	55670 MW	85810 TQ	USBLS	5/15
Production and Operating Workers	Arizona	Y	39140 FQ	51660 MW	70680 TQ	USBLS	5/15
Production and Operating Workers	Phoenix-Mesa-Scottsdale MSA, AZ	Y	38780 FQ	51280 MW	70730 TQ	USBLS	5/15
Production and Operating Workers	Tucson MSA, AZ	Y	40180 FQ	50470 MW	67510 TQ	USBLS	5/15
Production and Operating Workers	Arkansas	Y	36980 FQ	47530 MW	61640 TQ	USBLS	5/15
Production and Operating Workers	Little Rock-North Little Rock-Conway MSA, AR	Y	37810 FQ	50280 MW	66680 TQ	USBLS	5/15
Production and Operating Workers	California	H	19.73 FQ	27.08 MW	37.16 TQ	CABLS	1/16-3/16
Production and Operating Workers	Anaheim-Santa Ana-Irvine PMSA, CA	H	19.62 FQ	25.35 MW	34.55 TQ	CABLS	1/16-3/16
Production and Operating Workers	Los Angeles-Long Beach-Glendale PMSA, CA	H	18.10 FQ	25.89 MW	36.37 TQ	CABLS	1/16-3/16
Production and Operating Workers	Oakland-Hayward-Berkeley PMSA, CA	H	21.72 FQ	29.74 MW	43.23 TQ	CABLS	1/16-3/16
Production and Operating Workers	Riverside-San Bernardino-Ontario MSA, CA	H	19.45 FQ	24.99 MW	33.84 TQ	CABLS	1/16-3/16
Production and Operating Workers	Sacramento–Roseville–Arden-Arcade MSA, CA	H	20.64 FQ	27.32 MW	36.23 TQ	CABLS	1/16-3/16
Production and Operating Workers	San Diego-Carlsbad MSA, CA	H	21.01 FQ	29.43 MW	37.77 TQ	CABLS	1/16-3/16
Production and Operating Workers	San Francisco-Redwood City-South San Francisco PMSA, CA	H	23.72 FQ	34.00 MW	48.19 TQ	CABLS	1/16-3/16
Production and Operating Workers	Colorado	Y	47200 FQ	60300 MW	76420 TQ	USBLS	5/15
Production and Operating Workers	Denver-Aurora-Lakewood MSA, CO	Y	46180 FQ	59180 MW	75300 TQ	USBLS	5/15
Production and Operating Workers	Connecticut	Y		64440 MW		CTBLS	1/16-3/16
Production and Operating Workers	Bridgeport-Stamford-Norwalk MSA, CT	Y	51540 FQ	64060 MW	82520 TQ	USBLS	5/15
Production and Operating Workers	Hartford-West Hartford-East Hartford MSA, CT	Y	47330 FQ	61080 MW	79500 TQ	USBLS	5/15
Production and Operating Workers	Delaware	Y	48990 FQ	61900 MW	78790 TQ	USBLS	5/15
Production and Operating Workers	Wilmington PMSA, DE-MD-NJ	Y	54640 FQ	71640 MW	93530 TQ	USBLS	5/15
Production and Operating Workers	District of Columbia	Y	58150 FQ	74670 MW	85420 TQ	USBLS	5/15
Production and Operating Workers	Washington-Arlington-Alexandria PMSA, DC-VA-MD-WV	Y	48890 FQ	65850 MW	83240 TQ	USBLS	5/15
Production and Operating Workers	Florida	H	18.38 AE	26.18 MW	32.47 AEX	FLBLS	7/16-9/16
Production and Operating Workers	Fort Lauderdale-Pompano Beach-Deerfield Beach PMSA, FL	H	17.98 AE	24.67 MW	30.53 AEX	FLBLS	7/16-9/16
Production and Operating Workers	Miami-Miami Beach-Kendall PMSA, FL	H	17.88 AE	25.59 MW	31.69 AEX	FLBLS	7/16-9/16
Production and Operating Workers	Orlando-Kissimmee-Sanford MSA, FL	H	17.53 AE	24.72 MW	31.99 AEX	FLBLS	7/16-9/16
Production and Operating Workers	Tampa-St. Petersburg-Clearwater MSA, FL	H	18.44 AE	26.83 MW	32.52 AEX	FLBLS	7/16-9/16
Production and Operating Workers	West Palm Beach-Boca Raton-Delray Beach PMSA, FL	Y	42000 FQ	51910 MW	67640 TQ	USBLS	5/15
Production and Operating Workers	Georgia	Y	41310 FQ	53040 MW	68770 TQ	USBLS	5/15
Production and Operating Workers	Atlanta-Sandy Springs-Roswell MSA, GA	Y	41590 FQ	54280 MW	69630 TQ	USBLS	5/15
Production and Operating Workers	Augusta-Richmond County MSA, GA-SC	Y	44980 FQ	57770 MW	79530 TQ	USBLS	5/15
Production and Operating Workers	Hawaii	Y	38290 FQ	51360 MW	78430 TQ	USBLS	5/15
Production and Operating Workers	Urban Honolulu MSA, HI	Y	38580 FQ	56670 MW	82850 TQ	USBLS	5/15
Production and Operating Workers	Idaho	Y	37310 FQ	49570 MW	63470 TQ	USBLS	5/15
Production and Operating Workers	Boise City MSA, ID	Y	35630 FQ	48790 MW	61770 TQ	USBLS	5/15

AE Average entry wage	**AWR** Average wage range	**H** Hourly	**LR** Low end range	**MTC** Median total compensation	**TCC** Total cash compensation
AEX Average experienced wage	**B** Biweekly	**HI** Highest wage paid	**M** Monthly	**MW** Median wage paid	**TQ** Third quartile wage
ATC Average total compensation	**D** Daily	**HR** High end range	**MCC** Median cash compensation	**MWR** Median wage range	**W** Weekly
AW Average wage paid	**FQ** First quartile wage	**LO** Lowest wage paid	**ME** Median entry wage	**S** See annotated source	**Y** Yearly

First-Line Supervisor

Occupation/Type/Industry	Location	Per	Low	Mid	High	Source	Date
Production and Operating Workers	Illinois	Y	43280 FQ	58010 MW	74500 TQ	USBLS	5/15
Production and Operating Workers	Chicago-Naperville-Arlington Heights PMSA, IL	Y	43020 FQ	57280 MW	73090 TQ	USBLS	5/15
Production and Operating Workers	Lake County-Kenosha County PMSA, IL-WI	Y	42520 FQ	58550 MW	76190 TQ	USBLS	5/15
Production and Operating Workers	Indiana	Y	41770 FQ	53600 MW	67880 TQ	USBLS	5/15
Production and Operating Workers	Gary PMSA, IN	Y	50250 FQ	61880 MW	76900 TQ	USBLS	5/15
Production and Operating Workers	Indianapolis-Carmel-Anderson MSA, IN	Y	41990 FQ	55390 MW	71640 TQ	USBLS	5/15
Production and Operating Workers	Iowa	Y	41090 FQ	50310 MW	64120 TQ	USBLS	5/15
Production and Operating Workers	Des Moines-West Des Moines MSA, IA	Y	40850 FQ	50660 MW	62910 TQ	USBLS	5/15
Production and Operating Workers	Kansas	Y	42390 FQ	54020 MW	67260 TQ	USBLS	5/15
Production and Operating Workers	Wichita MSA, KS	Y	44380 FQ	55670 MW	72770 TQ	USBLS	5/15
Production and Operating Workers	Kentucky	Y	40050 FQ	52390 MW	66270 TQ	USBLS	5/15
Production and Operating Workers	Louisville-Jefferson County MSA, KY-IN	Y	41170 FQ	53320 MW	65870 TQ	USBLS	5/15
Production and Operating Workers	Louisiana	Y	44610 FQ	62270 MW	89500 TQ	USBLS	5/15
Production and Operating Workers	Baton Rouge MSA, LA	Y	49890 FQ	77360 MW	118230 TQ	USBLS	5/15
Production and Operating Workers	New Orleans-Metairie MSA, LA	Y	43400 FQ	63350 MW	92560 TQ	USBLS	5/15
Production and Operating Workers	Maine	Y	43800 FQ	57080 MW	69720 TQ	USBLS	5/15
Production and Operating Workers	Portland-South Portland MSA, ME	Y	43100 FQ	54340 MW	65010 TQ	USBLS	5/15
Production and Operating Workers	Maryland	Y	40258 AE	64218 MW	76197 AEX	MDBLS	4/16
Production and Operating Workers	Baltimore-Columbia-Towson MSA, MD	Y	47900 FQ	63380 MW	81030 TQ	USBLS	5/15
Production and Operating Workers	Salisbury MSA, MD-DE	Y	44800 FQ	55570 MW	67980 TQ	USBLS	5/15
Production and Operating Workers	Massachusetts	Y	49290 FQ	62000 MW	78090 TQ	USBLS	5/15
Production and Operating Workers	Boston-Cambridge-Newton NECTA, MA	Y	52410 FQ	64790 MW	83120 TQ	USBLS	5/15
Production and Operating Workers	Worcester MSA, MA-CT	Y	46690 FQ	58820 MW	73220 TQ	USBLS	5/15
Production and Operating Workers	Michigan	Y	44110 FQ	57710 MW	75670 TQ	USBLS	5/15
Production and Operating Workers	Detroit-Dearborn-Livonia PMSA, MI	Y	47280 FQ	64070 MW	87340 TQ	USBLS	5/15
Production and Operating Workers	Grand Rapids-Wyoming MSA, MI	Y	42570 FQ	55090 MW	70700 TQ	USBLS	5/15
Production and Operating Workers	Minnesota	Y	46137 FQ	57355 MW	70851 TQ	MNBLS	1/16-3/16
Production and Operating Workers	Minneapolis-St. Paul-Bloomington MSA, MN-WI	Y	48871 FQ	60170 MW	74496 TQ	MNBLS	1/16-3/16
Production and Operating Workers	Mississippi	Y	37700 FQ	50130 MW	65360 TQ	USBLS	5/15
Production and Operating Workers	Jackson MSA, MS	Y	39190 FQ	52960 MW	69280 TQ	USBLS	5/15
Production and Operating Workers	Missouri	Y	38700 FQ	51030 MW	67860 TQ	USBLS	5/15
Production and Operating Workers	Kansas City MSA, MO-KS	Y	41940 FQ	54620 MW	70440 TQ	USBLS	5/15
Production and Operating Workers	St. Louis MSA, MO-IL	Y	45350 FQ	59150 MW	76390 TQ	USBLS	5/15
Production and Operating Workers	Montana	Y	39320 FQ	55310 MW	74280 TQ	USBLS	5/15
Production and Operating Workers	Billings MSA, MT	Y	38100 FQ	50300 MW	67200 TQ	USBLS	5/15
Production and Operating Workers	Nebraska	Y	42390 FQ	54440 MW	67265 TQ	NEBLS	7/16-9/16
Production and Operating Workers	Omaha-Council Bluffs MSA, NE-IA	Y	43465 FQ	55325 MW	68855 TQ	NEBLS	7/16-9/16
Production and Operating Workers	Nevada	Y	39420 FQ	51760 MW	72670 TQ	USBLS	5/15
Production and Operating Workers	Las Vegas-Henderson-Paradise MSA, NV	Y	37700 FQ	47200 MW	68650 TQ	USBLS	5/15
Production and Operating Workers	New Hampshire	H	20.37 AE	29.17 MW	35.77 AEX	NHBLS	6/16
Production and Operating Workers	Manchester NECTA, NH	H	16.98 AE	24.15 MW	31.33 AEX	NHBLS	6/16
Production and Operating Workers	Nashua NECTA, NH-MA	Y	52390 FQ	61060 MW	75850 TQ	USBLS	5/15
Production and Operating Workers	New Jersey	Y	50230 FQ	62820 MW	78260 TQ	USBLS	5/15
Production and Operating Workers	Camden PMSA, NJ	Y	52430 FQ	63080 MW	75650 TQ	USBLS	5/15
Production and Operating Workers	Newark PMSA, NJ-PA	Y	50500 FQ	63920 MW	80290 TQ	USBLS	5/15
Production and Operating Workers	Trenton MSA, NJ	Y	53530 FQ	61600 MW	77560 TQ	USBLS	5/15
Production and Operating Workers	Vineland-Bridgeton MSA, NJ	Y	51800 FQ	64340 MW	79560 TQ	USBLS	5/15
Production and Operating Workers	New Mexico	Y	39710 FQ	53120 MW	78530 TQ	USBLS	5/15
Production and Operating Workers	Albuquerque MSA, NM	Y	38370 FQ	50330 MW	70640 TQ	USBLS	5/15
Production and Operating Workers	New York	Y	38960 AE	61840 MW	79310 AEX	NYBLS	1/16-3/16
Production and Operating Workers	Buffalo-Cheektowaga-Niagara Falls MSA, NY	Y	46490 FQ	60120 MW	76170 TQ	USBLS	5/15
Production and Operating Workers	Nassau County-Suffolk County PMSA, NY	Y	51510 FQ	68000 MW	87990 TQ	USBLS	5/15
Production and Operating Workers	New York-Jersey City-White Plains PMSA, NY-NJ	Y	45320 FQ	61730 MW	82350 TQ	USBLS	5/15
Production and Operating Workers	Rochester MSA, NY	Y	46590 FQ	57880 MW	72080 TQ	USBLS	5/15

AE	Average entry wage	AWR	Average wage range	H	Hourly	LR	Low end range	MTC	Median total compensation	TCC	Total cash compensation
AEX	Average experienced wage	B	Biweekly	HI	Highest wage paid	M	Monthly	MW	Median wage paid	TQ	Third quartile wage
ATC	Average total compensation	D	Daily	HR	High end range	MCC	Median cash compensation	MWR	Median wage range	W	Weekly
AW	Average wage paid	FQ	First quartile wage	LO	Lowest wage paid	ME	Median entry wage	S	See annotated source	Y	Yearly

First-Line Supervisor

Occupation/Type/Industry	Location	Per	Low	Mid	High	Source	Date
Production and Operating Workers	North Carolina	Y	42550 FQ	54690 MW	69380 TQ	USBLS	5/15
Production and Operating Workers	Charlotte-Concord-Gastonia MSA, NC-SC	Y	44960 FQ	56960 MW	71280 TQ	USBLS	5/15
Production and Operating Workers	Raleigh MSA, NC	Y	44710 FQ	58250 MW	73720 TQ	USBLS	5/15
Production and Operating Workers	North Dakota	Y	43510 FQ	56180 MW	74740 TQ	USBLS	5/15
Production and Operating Workers	Fargo MSA, ND-MN	Y	39000 FQ	46600 MW	56480 TQ	USBLS	5/15
Production and Operating Workers	Ohio	Y	43220 FQ	55490 MW	69640 TQ	USBLS	5/15
Production and Operating Workers	Cincinnati MSA, OH-KY-IN	Y	46660 FQ	59240 MW	74130 TQ	USBLS	5/15
Production and Operating Workers	Cleveland-Elyria MSA, OH	Y	45300 FQ	57690 MW	72230 TQ	USBLS	5/15
Production and Operating Workers	Columbus MSA, OH	Y	44440 FQ	58530 MW	71500 TQ	USBLS	5/15
Production and Operating Workers	Oklahoma	Y	39160 FQ	52650 MW	69490 TQ	USBLS	5/15
Production and Operating Workers	Lawton MSA, OK	Y	35580 FQ	51820 MW	58920 TQ	USBLS	5/15
Production and Operating Workers	Oklahoma City MSA, OK	Y	38250 FQ	53450 MW	72090 TQ	USBLS	5/15
Production and Operating Workers	Tulsa MSA, OK	Y	42310 FQ	53900 MW	67950 TQ	USBLS	5/15
Production and Operating Workers	Oregon	H	20.30 FQ	26.23 MW	32.92 TQ	ORBLS	2016
Production and Operating Workers	Portland-Vancouver-Hillsboro MSA, OR-WA	Y	44450 FQ	56380 MW	70500 TQ	USBLS	5/15
Production and Operating Workers	Pennsylvania	Y	44740 FQ	56790 MW	71740 TQ	USBLS	5/15
Production and Operating Workers	Allentown-Bethlehem-Easton MSA, PA-NJ	Y	47440 FQ	59120 MW	74730 TQ	USBLS	5/15
Production and Operating Workers	Harrisburg-Carlisle MSA, PA	Y	45320 FQ	56480 MW	69530 TQ	USBLS	5/15
Production and Operating Workers	Montgomery County-Bucks County-Chester County PMSA, PA	Y	51150 FQ	63620 MW	77770 TQ	USBLS	5/15
Production and Operating Workers	Philadelphia PMSA, PA	Y	50900 FQ	65770 MW	78850 TQ	USBLS	5/15
Production and Operating Workers	Pittsburgh MSA, PA	Y	45860 FQ	58970 MW	74400 TQ	USBLS	5/15
Production and Operating Workers	Rhode Island	Y	49380 FQ	62250 MW	78940 TQ	USBLS	5/15
Production and Operating Workers	Providence-Warwick MSA, RI-MA	Y	48810 FQ	61420 MW	77530 TQ	USBLS	5/15
Production and Operating Workers	South Carolina	Y	44420 FQ	59200 MW	77180 TQ	USBLS	5/15
Production and Operating Workers	Charleston-North Charleston MSA, SC	Y	49610 FQ	64930 MW	86450 TQ	USBLS	5/15
Production and Operating Workers	Columbia MSA, SC	Y	44230 FQ	59910 MW	75090 TQ	USBLS	5/15
Production and Operating Workers	Greenville-Anderson-Mauldin MSA, SC	Y	41220 FQ	55060 MW	75710 TQ	USBLS	5/15
Production and Operating Workers	South Dakota	Y	47820 FQ	56650 MW	66170 TQ	USBLS	5/15
Production and Operating Workers	Sioux Falls MSA, SD	Y	47250 FQ	55220 MW	62810 TQ	USBLS	5/15
Production and Operating Workers	Tennessee	Y	39010 FQ	50970 MW	66490 TQ	USBLS	5/15
Production and Operating Workers	Knoxville MSA, TN	Y	37330 FQ	51210 MW	71190 TQ	USBLS	5/15
Production and Operating Workers	Memphis MSA, TN-MS-AR	Y	40530 FQ	51870 MW	67270 TQ	USBLS	5/15
Production and Operating Workers	Nashville-Davidson–Murfreesboro–Franklin MSA, TN	Y	40930 FQ	55690 MW	72010 TQ	USBLS	5/15
Production and Operating Workers	Texas	Y	44000 FQ	60440 MW	80430 TQ	USBLS	5/15
Production and Operating Workers	Austin-Round Rock MSA, TX	Y	41580 FQ	57540 MW	75180 TQ	USBLS	5/15
Production and Operating Workers	Dallas-Plano-Irving PMSA, TX	Y	43050 FQ	58360 MW	75890 TQ	USBLS	5/15
Production and Operating Workers	Fort Worth-Arlington PMSA, TX	Y	45440 FQ	58400 MW	74360 TQ	USBLS	5/15
Production and Operating Workers	Houston-The Woodlands-Sugar Land MSA, TX	Y	49930 FQ	68800 MW	91450 TQ	USBLS	5/15
Production and Operating Workers	San Antonio-New Braunfels MSA, TX	Y	38570 FQ	50760 MW	69920 TQ	USBLS	5/15
Production and Operating Workers	Utah	Y	41090 FQ	54610 MW	70560 TQ	USBLS	5/15
Production and Operating Workers	Ogden-Clearfield MSA, UT	Y	42960 FQ	57780 MW	72500 TQ	USBLS	5/15
Production and Operating Workers	Provo-Orem MSA, UT	Y	39000 FQ	50170 MW	63760 TQ	USBLS	5/15
Production and Operating Workers	Salt Lake City MSA, UT	Y	41730 FQ	55850 MW	72030 TQ	USBLS	5/15
Production and Operating Workers	Vermont	Y	41900 FQ	56280 MW	72370 TQ	USBLS	5/15
Production and Operating Workers	Burlington-South Burlington MSA, VT	Y	45830 FQ	60960 MW	77720 TQ	USBLS	5/15
Production and Operating Workers	Virginia	Y	45680 FQ	60480 MW	75500 TQ	USBLS	5/15
Production and Operating Workers	Richmond MSA, VA	Y	50870 FQ	64620 MW	84030 TQ	USBLS	5/15
Production and Operating Workers	Virginia Beach-Norfolk-Newport News MSA, VA-NC	Y	55130 FQ	67260 MW	76300 TQ	USBLS	5/15
Production and Operating Workers	Washington	H	23.47 FQ	31.90 MW	42.84 TQ	WABLS	3/16
Production and Operating Workers	Seattle-Bellevue-Everett PMSA, WA	H	25.74 FQ	35.74 MW	46.88 TQ	WABLS	3/16
Production and Operating Workers	Tacoma-Lakewood PMSA, WA	H	22.82 FQ	28.63 MW	36.68 TQ	WABLS	3/16
Production and Operating Workers	West Virginia	Y	41470 FQ	56320 MW	72760 TQ	USBLS	5/15
Production and Operating Workers	Huntington-Ashland MSA, WV-KY-OH	Y	51570 FQ	59440 MW	73680 TQ	USBLS	5/15
Production and Operating Workers	Wisconsin	Y	43470 FQ	54940 MW	69020 TQ	USBLS	5/15

AE	Average entry wage	AWR	Average wage range	H	Hourly
AEX	Average experienced wage	B	Biweekly	HI	Highest wage paid
ATC	Average total compensation	D	Daily	HR	High end range
AW	Average wage paid	FQ	First quartile wage	LO	Lowest wage paid

LR	Low end range	MTC	Median total compensation	TCC	Total cash compensation
M	Monthly	MW	Median wage paid	TQ	Third quartile wage
MCC	Median cash compensation	MWR	Median wage range	W	Weekly
ME	Median entry wage	S	See annotated source	Y	Yearly

Occupation/Type/Industry	Location	Per	Low	Mid	High	Source	Date
First-Line Supervisor							
Production and Operating Workers	Madison MSA, WI	Y	44610 FQ	55510 MW	68490 TQ	USBLS	5/15
Production and Operating Workers	Milwaukee-Waukesha-West Allis MSA, WI	Y	47340 FQ	59260 MW	73960 TQ	USBLS	5/15
Production and Operating Workers	Wyoming	Y	54660 FQ	79430 MW	100000 TQ	USBLS	5/15
Production and Operating Workers	Cheyenne MSA, WY	Y	42950 FQ	56280 MW	74050 TQ	USBLS	5/15
Production and Operating Workers	Puerto Rico	Y	25770 FQ	36030 MW	52740 TQ	USBLS	5/15
Production and Operating Workers	San Juan-Carolina-Caguas MSA, PR	Y	27310 FQ	38170 MW	54550 TQ	USBLS	5/15
Production and Operating Workers	Virgin Islands	Y	22220 FQ	28530 MW	42860 TQ	USBLS	5/15
Production and Operating Workers	Guam	Y	32120 FQ	50220 MW	61210 TQ	USBLS	5/15
Retail Sales Workers	Alabama	Y	25494 AE	42477 AW	50958 AEX	ALBLS	6/16
Retail Sales Workers	Birmingham-Hoover MSA, AL	Y	27263 AE	46955 AW	56801 AEX	ALBLS	6/16
Retail Sales Workers	Alaska	Y	32750 FQ	39470 MW	51000 TQ	USBLS	5/15
Retail Sales Workers	Anchorage MSA, AK	Y	32810 FQ	39130 MW	51690 TQ	USBLS	5/15
Retail Sales Workers	Arizona	Y	28850 FQ	37610 MW	48460 TQ	USBLS	5/15
Retail Sales Workers	Phoenix-Mesa-Scottsdale MSA, AZ	Y	29740 FQ	38560 MW	49060 TQ	USBLS	5/15
Retail Sales Workers	Tucson MSA, AZ	Y	28380 FQ	37280 MW	48790 TQ	USBLS	5/15
Retail Sales Workers	Arkansas	Y	24080 FQ	30480 MW	39070 TQ	USBLS	5/15
Retail Sales Workers	Little Rock-North Little Rock-Conway MSA, AR	Y	25450 FQ	32690 MW	41770 TQ	USBLS	5/15
Retail Sales Workers	California	H	14.98 FQ	18.97 MW	25.04 TQ	CABLS	1/16-3/16
Retail Sales Workers	Anaheim-Santa Ana-Irvine PMSA, CA	H	14.79 FQ	18.66 MW	25.45 TQ	CABLS	1/16-3/16
Retail Sales Workers	Los Angeles-Long Beach-Glendale PMSA, CA	H	14.74 FQ	18.56 MW	25.23 TQ	CABLS	1/16-3/16
Retail Sales Workers	Oakland-Hayward-Berkeley PMSA, CA	H	15.06 FQ	19.25 MW	24.99 TQ	CABLS	1/16-3/16
Retail Sales Workers	Riverside-San Bernardino-Ontario MSA, CA	H	14.30 FQ	18.44 MW	23.31 TQ	CABLS	1/16-3/16
Retail Sales Workers	Sacramento–Roseville–Arden-Arcade MSA, CA	H	14.70 FQ	18.46 MW	23.74 TQ	CABLS	1/16-3/16
Retail Sales Workers	San Diego-Carlsbad MSA, CA	H	15.18 FQ	19.61 MW	26.76 TQ	CABLS	1/16-3/16
Retail Sales Workers	San Francisco-Redwood City-South San Francisco PMSA, CA	H	17.94 FQ	22.03 MW	27.73 TQ	CABLS	1/16-3/16
Retail Sales Workers	Colorado	Y	31040 FQ	40190 MW	53770 TQ	USBLS	5/15
Retail Sales Workers	Denver-Aurora-Lakewood MSA, CO	Y	31670 FQ	41270 MW	55480 TQ	USBLS	5/15
Retail Sales Workers	Connecticut	Y		44215 MW		CTBLS	1/16-3/16
Retail Sales Workers	Bridgeport-Stamford-Norwalk MSA, CT	Y	33280 FQ	44610 MW	58430 TQ	USBLS	5/15
Retail Sales Workers	Hartford-West Hartford-East Hartford MSA, CT	Y	35000 FQ	45090 MW	58270 TQ	USBLS	5/15
Retail Sales Workers	Delaware	Y	35410 FQ	44600 MW	56160 TQ	USBLS	5/15
Retail Sales Workers	Wilmington PMSA, DE-MD-NJ	Y	34280 FQ	43710 MW	55060 TQ	USBLS	5/15
Retail Sales Workers	District of Columbia	Y	35420 FQ	43650 MW	52890 TQ	USBLS	5/15
Retail Sales Workers	Washington-Arlington-Alexandria PMSA, DC-VA-MD-WV	Y	33890 FQ	43280 MW	55130 TQ	USBLS	5/15
Retail Sales Workers	Florida	H	14.19 AE	19.59 MW	25.46 AEX	FLBLS	7/16-9/16
Retail Sales Workers	Fort Lauderdale-Pompano Beach-Deerfield Beach PMSA, FL	H	14.77 AE	20.48 MW	28.15 AEX	FLBLS	7/16-9/16
Retail Sales Workers	Miami-Miami Beach-Kendall PMSA, FL	H	14.90 AE	19.46 MW	25.39 AEX	FLBLS	7/16-9/16
Retail Sales Workers	Orlando-Kissimmee-Sanford MSA, FL	H	13.58 AE	19.92 MW	25.07 AEX	FLBLS	7/16-9/16
Retail Sales Workers	Tampa-St. Petersburg-Clearwater MSA, FL	H	14.50 AE	20.06 MW	26.01 AEX	FLBLS	7/16-9/16
Retail Sales Workers	Georgia	Y	26010 FQ	34870 MW	46110 TQ	USBLS	5/15
Retail Sales Workers	Atlanta-Sandy Springs-Roswell MSA, GA	Y	27340 FQ	36460 MW	48260 TQ	USBLS	5/15
Retail Sales Workers	Augusta-Richmond County MSA, GA-SC	Y	28290 FQ	37740 MW	49070 TQ	USBLS	5/15
Retail Sales Workers	Hawaii	Y	33200 FQ	41660 MW	50620 TQ	USBLS	5/15
Retail Sales Workers	Urban Honolulu MSA, HI	Y	34060 FQ	42550 MW	56110 TQ	USBLS	5/15
Retail Sales Workers	Idaho	Y	26950 FQ	34720 MW	45330 TQ	USBLS	5/15
Retail Sales Workers	Boise City MSA, ID	Y	28520 FQ	36050 MW	46020 TQ	USBLS	5/15
Retail Sales Workers	Illinois	Y	28940 FQ	37930 MW	50320 TQ	USBLS	5/15

AE	Average entry wage	AWR	Average wage range	H	Hourly
AEX	Average experienced wage	B	Biweekly	HI	Highest wage paid
ATC	Average total compensation	D	Daily	HR	High end range
AW	Average wage paid	FQ	First quartile wage	LO	Lowest wage paid

LR	Low end range	MTC	Median total compensation	TCC	Total cash compensation
M	Monthly	MW	Median wage paid	TQ	Third quartile wage
MCC	Median cash compensation	MWR	Median wage range	W	Weekly
ME	Median entry wage	S	See annotated source	Y	Yearly

Occupation/Type/Industry	Location	Per	Low	Mid	High	Source	Date
First-Line Supervisor							
Retail Sales Workers	Chicago-Naperville-Arlington Heights PMSA, IL	Y	31050 FQ	40360 MW	54190 TQ	USBLS	5/15
Retail Sales Workers	Lake County-Kenosha County PMSA, IL-WI	Y	30050 FQ	37630 MW	49340 TQ	USBLS	5/15
Retail Sales Workers	Indiana	Y	26300 FQ	35000 MW	46880 TQ	USBLS	5/15
Retail Sales Workers	Gary PMSA, IN	Y	26240 FQ	34500 MW	49140 TQ	USBLS	5/15
Retail Sales Workers	Indianapolis-Carmel-Anderson MSA, IN	Y	25910 FQ	37290 MW	49450 TQ	USBLS	5/15
Retail Sales Workers	Iowa	Y	26170 FQ	32960 MW	44430 TQ	USBLS	5/15
Retail Sales Workers	Des Moines-West Des Moines MSA, IA	Y	28360 FQ	36540 MW	48060 TQ	USBLS	5/15
Retail Sales Workers	Kansas	Y	26610 FQ	35640 MW	46590 TQ	USBLS	5/15
Retail Sales Workers	Wichita MSA, KS	Y	27460 FQ	36630 MW	47330 TQ	USBLS	5/15
Retail Sales Workers	Kentucky	Y	25210 FQ	33220 MW	43550 TQ	USBLS	5/15
Retail Sales Workers	Louisville-Jefferson County MSA, KY-IN	Y	25460 FQ	34200 MW	45390 TQ	USBLS	5/15
Retail Sales Workers	Louisiana	Y	27590 FQ	34310 MW	43130 TQ	USBLS	5/15
Retail Sales Workers	Baton Rouge MSA, LA	Y	29060 FQ	36450 MW	45290 TQ	USBLS	5/15
Retail Sales Workers	New Orleans-Metairie MSA, LA	Y	29730 FQ	36640 MW	46230 TQ	USBLS	5/15
Retail Sales Workers	Maine	Y	29880 FQ	38660 MW	47810 TQ	USBLS	5/15
Retail Sales Workers	Portland-South Portland MSA, ME	Y	33330 FQ	41980 MW	50380 TQ	USBLS	5/15
Retail Sales Workers	Maryland	Y	29009 AE	45149 MW	53218 AEX	MDBLS	4/16
Retail Sales Workers	Baltimore-Columbia-Towson MSA, MD	Y	33060 FQ	41590 MW	51780 TQ	USBLS	5/15
Retail Sales Workers	Salisbury MSA, MD-DE	Y	31770 FQ	41470 MW	51350 TQ	USBLS	5/15
Retail Sales Workers	Massachusetts	Y	32410 FQ	42220 MW	56010 TQ	USBLS	5/15
Retail Sales Workers	Boston-Cambridge-Newton NECTA, MA	Y	32280 FQ	43410 MW	57000 TQ	USBLS	5/15
Retail Sales Workers	Worcester MSA, MA-CT	Y	32420 FQ	39930 MW	52810 TQ	USBLS	5/15
Retail Sales Workers	Michigan	Y	29320 FQ	37510 MW	48790 TQ	USBLS	5/15
Retail Sales Workers	Detroit-Dearborn-Livonia PMSA, MI	Y	26210 FQ	34950 MW	46130 TQ	USBLS	5/15
Retail Sales Workers	Grand Rapids-Wyoming MSA, MI	Y	27820 FQ	35420 MW	49720 TQ	USBLS	5/15
Retail Sales Workers	Minnesota	Y	30503 FQ	38519 MW	49077 TQ	MNBLS	1/16-3/16
Retail Sales Workers	Minneapolis-St. Paul-Bloomington MSA, MN-WI	Y	32993 FQ	41927 MW	51608 TQ	MNBLS	1/16-3/16
Retail Sales Workers	Mississippi	Y	24590 FQ	34120 MW	45520 TQ	USBLS	5/15
Retail Sales Workers	Jackson MSA, MS	Y	26970 FQ	39550 MW	49950 TQ	USBLS	5/15
Retail Sales Workers	Missouri	Y	27550 FQ	35890 MW	46130 TQ	USBLS	5/15
Retail Sales Workers	Kansas City MSA, MO-KS	Y	28010 FQ	36290 MW	47250 TQ	USBLS	5/15
Retail Sales Workers	St. Louis MSA, MO-IL	Y	30270 FQ	38540 MW	48870 TQ	USBLS	5/15
Retail Sales Workers	Montana	Y	27460 FQ	36380 MW	48920 TQ	USBLS	5/15
Retail Sales Workers	Billings MSA, MT	Y	28930 FQ	38050 MW	49870 TQ	USBLS	5/15
Retail Sales Workers	Nebraska	Y	28360 FQ	36695 MW	49020 TQ	NEBLS	7/16-9/16
Retail Sales Workers	Omaha-Council Bluffs MSA, NE-IA	Y	30525 FQ	39335 MW	56215 TQ	NEBLS	7/16-9/16
Retail Sales Workers	Nevada	Y	31780 FQ	38090 MW	49160 TQ	USBLS	5/15
Retail Sales Workers	Las Vegas-Henderson-Paradise MSA, NV	Y	32620 FQ	38400 MW	49050 TQ	USBLS	5/15
Retail Sales Workers	New Hampshire	H	14.49 AE	21.05 MW	27.98 AEX	NHBLS	6/16
Retail Sales Workers	Manchester NECTA, NH	H	14.98 AE	21.38 MW	27.74 AEX	NHBLS	6/16
Retail Sales Workers	Nashua NECTA, NH-MA	Y	34210 FQ	44570 MW	59800 TQ	USBLS	5/15
Retail Sales Workers	New Jersey	Y	34590 FQ	44170 MW	57260 TQ	USBLS	5/15
Retail Sales Workers	Camden PMSA, NJ	Y	33350 FQ	40890 MW	50430 TQ	USBLS	5/15
Retail Sales Workers	Newark PMSA, NJ-PA	Y	34880 FQ	45000 MW	58510 TQ	USBLS	5/15
Retail Sales Workers	Trenton MSA, NJ	Y	34360 FQ	43600 MW	54650 TQ	USBLS	5/15
Retail Sales Workers	New Mexico	Y	26770 FQ	34410 MW	45860 TQ	USBLS	5/15
Retail Sales Workers	Albuquerque MSA, NM	Y	27680 FQ	35560 MW	46430 TQ	USBLS	5/15
Retail Sales Workers	New York	Y	30530 AE	44930 MW	60650 AEX	NYBLS	1/16-3/16
Retail Sales Workers	Buffalo-Cheektowaga-Niagara Falls MSA, NY	Y	29700 FQ	36900 MW	47830 TQ	USBLS	5/15
Retail Sales Workers	Nassau County-Suffolk County PMSA, NY	Y	39210 FQ	51110 MW	63310 TQ	USBLS	5/15
Retail Sales Workers	New York-Jersey City-White Plains PMSA, NY-NJ	Y	35660 FQ	46890 MW	61280 TQ	USBLS	5/15
Retail Sales Workers	Rochester MSA, NY	Y	31310 FQ	39810 MW	53320 TQ	USBLS	5/15
Retail Sales Workers	North Carolina	Y	29540 FQ	38080 MW	49030 TQ	USBLS	5/15

AE Average entry wage	**AWR** Average wage range	**H** Hourly	**LR** Low end range	**MTC** Median total compensation	**TCC** Total cash compensation
AEX Average experienced wage	**B** Biweekly	**HI** Highest wage paid	**M** Monthly	**MW** Median wage paid	**TQ** Third quartile wage
ATC Average total compensation	**D** Daily	**HR** High end range	**MCC** Median cash compensation	**MWR** Median wage range	**W** Weekly
AW Average wage paid	**FQ** First quartile wage	**LO** Lowest wage paid	**ME** Median entry wage	**S** See annotated source	**Y** Yearly

Occupation/Type/Industry	Location	Per	Low	Mid	High	Source	Date
First-Line Supervisor							
Retail Sales Workers	Charlotte-Concord-Gastonia MSA, NC-SC	Y	30910 FQ	39500 MW	51540 TQ	USBLS	5/15
Retail Sales Workers	Raleigh MSA, NC	Y	31740 FQ	40440 MW	50120 TQ	USBLS	5/15
Retail Sales Workers	North Dakota	Y	32380 FQ	39980 MW	50370 TQ	USBLS	5/15
Retail Sales Workers	Fargo MSA, ND-MN	Y	31140 FQ	38000 MW	46990 TQ	USBLS	5/15
Retail Sales Workers	Ohio	Y	26990 FQ	35510 MW	45870 TQ	USBLS	5/15
Retail Sales Workers	Cincinnati MSA, OH-KY-IN	Y	28200 FQ	36400 MW	46620 TQ	USBLS	5/15
Retail Sales Workers	Cleveland-Elyria MSA, OH	Y	27670 FQ	36070 MW	46430 TQ	USBLS	5/15
Retail Sales Workers	Columbus MSA, OH	Y	28520 FQ	37690 MW	48230 TQ	USBLS	5/15
Retail Sales Workers	Oklahoma	Y	26140 FQ	32840 MW	42400 TQ	USBLS	5/15
Retail Sales Workers	Oklahoma City MSA, OK	Y ·	26730 FQ	33070 MW	44310 TQ	USBLS	5/15
Retail Sales Workers	Tulsa MSA, OK	Y	25850 FQ	32260 MW	41880 TQ	USBLS	5/15
Retail Sales Workers	Oregon	H	14.16 FQ	17.72 MW	22.58 TQ	ORBLS	2016
Retail Sales Workers	Portland-Vancouver-Hillsboro MSA, OR-WA	Y	30910 FQ	38200 MW	48320 TQ	USBLS	5/15
Retail Sales Workers	Pennsylvania	Y	32070 FQ	40820 MW	53380 TQ	USBLS	5/15
Retail Sales Workers	Allentown-Bethlehem-Easton MSA, PA-NJ	Y	33000 FQ	43020 MW	59000 TQ	USBLS	5/15
Retail Sales Workers	Harrisburg-Carlisle MSA, PA	Y	32740 FQ	39440 MW	56260 TQ	USBLS	5/15
Retail Sales Workers	Montgomery County-Bucks County-Chester County PMSA, PA	Y	35010 FQ	44790 MW	57850 TQ	USBLS	5/15
Retail Sales Workers	Philadelphia PMSA, PA	Y	34810 FQ	44770 MW	56120 TQ	USBLS	5/15
Retail Sales Workers	Pittsburgh MSA, PA	Y	31780 FQ	39570 MW	52090 TQ	USBLS	5/15
Retail Sales Workers	Rhode Island	Y	35390 FQ	46080 MW	58250 TQ	USBLS	5/15
Retail Sales Workers	Providence-Warwick MSA, RI-MA	Y	35020 FQ	45530 MW	57750 TQ	USBLS	5/15
Retail Sales Workers	South Carolina	Y	27700 FQ	35620 MW	46010 TQ	USBLS	5/15
Retail Sales Workers	Charleston-North Charleston MSA, SC	Y	28800 FQ	36370 MW	48000 TQ	USBLS	5/15
Retail Sales Workers	Columbia MSA, SC	Y	27440 FQ	36050 MW	47150 TQ	USBLS	5/15
Retail Sales Workers	Greenville-Anderson-Mauldin MSA, SC	Y	26420 FQ	34330 MW	43790 TQ	USBLS	5/15
Retail Sales Workers	South Dakota	Y	34710 FQ	41750 MW	52180 TQ	USBLS	5/15
Retail Sales Workers	Sioux Falls MSA, SD	Y	34910 FQ	43500 MW	58560 TQ	USBLS	5/15
Retail Sales Workers	Tennessee	Y	28200 FQ	36540 MW	44750 TQ	USBLS	5/15
Retail Sales Workers	Knoxville MSA, TN	Y	28130 FQ	37050 MW	47700 TQ	USBLS	5/15
Retail Sales Workers	Memphis MSA, TN-MS-AR	Y	28250 FQ	37760 MW	49890 TQ	USBLS	5/15
Retail Sales Workers	Nashville-Davidson–Murfreesboro–Franklin MSA, TN	Y	29580 FQ	37440 MW	48530 TQ	USBLS	5/15
Retail Sales Workers	Texas	Y	30700 FQ	39790 MW	53320 TQ	USBLS	5/15
Retail Sales Workers	Austin-Round Rock MSA, TX	Y	31420 FQ	40150 MW	52440 TQ	USBLS	5/15
Retail Sales Workers	Dallas-Plano-Irving PMSA, TX	Y	30450 FQ	38800 MW	54360 TQ	USBLS	5/15
Retail Sales Workers	Fort Worth-Arlington PMSA, TX	Y	33720 FQ	42910 MW	59080 TQ	USBLS	5/15
Retail Sales Workers	Houston-The Woodlands-Sugar Land MSA, TX	Y	32650 FQ	42800 MW	55130 TQ	USBLS	5/15
Retail Sales Workers	San Antonio-New Braunfels MSA, TX	Y	32390 FQ	41160 MW	55530 TQ	USBLS	5/15
Retail Sales Workers	Utah	Y	27590 FQ	35060 MW	45730 TQ	USBLS	5/15
Retail Sales Workers	Ogden-Clearfield MSA, UT	Y	26980 FQ	36140 MW	47960 TQ	USBLS	5/15
Retail Sales Workers	Provo-Orem MSA, UT	Y	26850 FQ	33830 MW	44050 TQ	USBLS	5/15
Retail Sales Workers	Salt Lake City MSA, UT	Y	28560 FQ	35790 MW	47110 TQ	USBLS	5/15
Retail Sales Workers	Vermont	Y	33790 FQ	42830 MW	52990 TQ	USBLS	5/15
Retail Sales Workers	Burlington-South Burlington MSA, VT	Y	34250 FQ	42640 MW	52520 TQ	USBLS	5/15
Retail Sales Workers	Virginia	Y	31370 FQ	39660 MW	52330 TQ	USBLS	5/15
Retail Sales Workers	Richmond MSA, VA	Y	30360 FQ	40380 MW	54290 TQ	USBLS	5/15
Retail Sales Workers	Virginia Beach-Norfolk-Newport News MSA, VA-NC	Y	30060 FQ	37500 MW	48650 TQ	USBLS	5/15
Retail Sales Workers	Washington	H	16.38 FQ	20.55 MW	25.87 TQ	WABLS	3/16
Retail Sales Workers	Seattle-Bellevue-Everett PMSA, WA	H	17.44 FQ	21.62 MW	26.89 TQ	WABLS	3/16
Retail Sales Workers	Tacoma-Lakewood PMSA, WA	H	16.61 FQ	20.55 MW	24.91 TQ	WABLS	3/16
Retail Sales Workers	West Virginia	Y	24350 FQ	31740 MW	41110 TQ	USBLS	
Retail Sales Workers	Huntington-Ashland MSA, WV-KY-OH	Y	24300 FQ	31830 MW	42780 TQ	USBLS	5/15
Retail Sales Workers	Wisconsin	Y	27580 FQ	35320 MW	45740 TQ	USBLS	5/15
Retail Sales Workers	Madison MSA, WI	Y	28170 FQ	35500 MW	44900 TQ	USBLS	5/15

AE	Average entry wage	AWR	Average wage range	H	Hourly	LR	Low end range	MTC	Median total compensation	TCC	Total cash compensation
AEX	Average experienced wage	B	Biweekly	HI	Highest wage paid	M	Monthly	MW	Median wage paid	TQ	Third quartile wage
ATC	Average total compensation	D	Daily	HR	High end range	MCC	Median cash compensation	MWR	Median wage range	W	Weekly
AW	Average wage paid	FQ	First quartile wage	LO	Lowest wage paid	ME	Median entry wage	S	See annotated source	Y	Yearly

Occupation/Type/Industry	Location	Per	Low	Mid	High	Source	Date
First-Line Supervisor							
Retail Sales Workers	Milwaukee-Waukesha-West Allis MSA, WI	Y	29250 FQ	37320 MW	48200 TQ	USBLS	5/15
Retail Sales Workers	Wyoming	Y	28520 FQ	36190 MW	46490 TQ	USBLS	5/15
Retail Sales Workers	Cheyenne MSA, WY	Y	28560 FQ	35960 MW	47100 TQ	USBLS	5/15
Retail Sales Workers	Puerto Rico	Y	19650 FQ	25440 MW	33340 TQ	USBLS	5/15
Retail Sales Workers	San Juan-Carolina-Caguas MSA, PR	Y	20710 FQ	26610 MW	35520 TQ	USBLS	5/15
Retail Sales Workers	Virgin Islands	Y	29590 FQ	36560 MW	47550 TQ	USBLS	5/15
Retail Sales Workers	Guam	Y	21750 FQ	26740 MW	31390 TQ	USBLS	5/15
Transportation, Movers, Drivers	Alabama	Y	38610 AE	56784 AW	65865 AEX	ALBLS	6/16
Transportation, Movers, Drivers	Birmingham-Hoover MSA, AL	Y	39844 AE	58470 AW	67778 AEX	ALBLS	6/16
Transportation, Movers, Drivers	Alaska	Y	53720 FQ	69490 MW	86980 TQ	USBLS	5/15
Transportation, Movers, Drivers	Anchorage MSA, AK	Y	52720 FQ	70090 MW	88090 TQ	USBLS	5/15
Transportation, Movers, Drivers	Arizona	Y	40410 FQ	49620 MW	62700 TQ	USBLS	5/15
Transportation, Movers, Drivers	Phoenix-Mesa-Scottsdale MSA, AZ	Y	41270 FQ	50220 MW	62960 TQ	USBLS	5/15
Transportation, Movers, Drivers	Tucson MSA, AZ	Y	37220 FQ	48730 MW	61370 TQ	USBLS	5/15
Transportation, Movers, Drivers	Arkansas	Y	36320 FQ	46660 MW	59400 TQ	USBLS	5/15
Transportation, Movers, Drivers	Little Rock-North Little Rock-Conway MSA, AR	Y	40220 FQ	51420 MW	61500 TQ	USBLS	5/15
Transportation, Movers, Drivers	California	H	21.54 FQ	29.20 MW	37.15 TQ	CABLS	1/16-3/16
Transportation, Movers, Drivers	Anaheim-Santa Ana-Irvine PMSA, CA	H	19.17 FQ	27.87 MW	36.30 TQ	CABLS	1/16-3/16
Transportation, Movers, Drivers	Los Angeles-Long Beach-Glendale PMSA, CA	H	22.79 FQ	30.56 MW	38.34 TQ	CABLS	1/16-3/16
Transportation, Movers, Drivers	Oakland-Hayward-Berkeley PMSA, CA	H	23.39 FQ	31.50 MW	39.51 TQ	CABLS	1/16-3/16
Transportation, Movers, Drivers	Riverside-San Bernardino-Ontario MSA, CA	H	21.27 FQ	26.88 MW	34.40 TQ	CABLS	1/16-3/16
Transportation, Movers, Drivers	Sacramento–Roseville–Arden-Arcade MSA, CA	H	21.07 FQ	28.67 MW	35.87 TQ	CABLS	1/16-3/16
Transportation, Movers, Drivers	San Diego-Carlsbad MSA, CA	H	18.06 FQ	26.99 MW	35.31 TQ	CABLS	1/16-3/16
Transportation, Movers, Drivers	San Francisco-Redwood City-South San Francisco PMSA, CA	H	24.61 FQ	33.47 MW	40.68 TQ	CABLS	1/16-3/16
Transportation, Movers, Drivers	Colorado	Y	44990 FQ	59620 MW	74420 TQ	USBLS	5/15
Transportation, Movers, Drivers	Denver-Aurora-Lakewood MSA, CO	Y	47000 FQ	59940 MW	73480 TQ	USBLS	5/15
Transportation, Movers, Drivers	Connecticut	Y		63355 MW		CTBLS	1/16-3/16
Transportation, Movers, Drivers	Bridgeport-Stamford-Norwalk MSA, CT	Y	63930 FQ	72760 MW	80890 TQ	USBLS	5/15
Transportation, Movers, Drivers	Hartford-West Hartford-East Hartford MSA, CT	Y	48550 FQ	61880 MW	76860 TQ	USBLS	5/15
Transportation, Movers, Drivers	Delaware	Y	48550 FQ	60320 MW	75030 TQ	USBLS	5/15
Transportation, Movers, Drivers	Wilmington PMSA, DE-MD-NJ	Y	48220 FQ	60920 MW	75940 TQ	USBLS	5/15
Transportation, Movers, Drivers	District of Columbia	Y	54820 FQ	63680 MW	79640 TQ	USBLS	5/15
Transportation, Movers, Drivers	Washington-Arlington-Alexandria PMSA, DC-VA-MD-WV	Y	50710 FQ	64220 MW	78100 TQ	USBLS	5/15
Transportation, Movers, Drivers	Florida	H	17.72 AE	27.10 MW	33.47 AEX	FLBLS	7/16-9/16
Transportation, Movers, Drivers	Fort Lauderdale-Pompano Beach-Deerfield Beach PMSA, FL	H	18.51 AE	27.40 MW	35.31 AEX	FLBLS	7/16-9/16
Transportation, Movers, Drivers	Miami-Miami Beach-Kendall PMSA, FL	H	15.86 AE	27.20 MW	34.48 AEX	FLBLS	7/16-9/16
Transportation, Movers, Drivers	Orlando-Kissimmee-Sanford MSA, FL	H	18.66 AE	27.05 MW	32.49 AEX	FLBLS	7/16-9/16
Transportation, Movers, Drivers	Tampa-St. Petersburg-Clearwater MSA, FL	H	17.03 AE	27.78 MW	34.91 AEX	FLBLS	7/16-9/16
Transportation, Movers, Drivers	Georgia	Y	43330 FQ	54370 MW	67320 TQ	USBLS	5/15
Transportation, Movers, Drivers	Atlanta-Sandy Springs-Roswell MSA, GA	Y	46000 FQ	56900 MW	69680 TQ	USBLS	5/15
Transportation, Movers, Drivers	Augusta-Richmond County MSA, GA-SC	Y	41030 FQ	53260 MW	72460 TQ	USBLS	5/15
Transportation, Movers, Drivers	Hawaii	Y	42090 FQ	49790 MW	64130 TQ	USBLS	5/15
Transportation, Movers, Drivers	Urban Honolulu MSA, HI	Y	41120 FQ	50280 MW	69500 TQ	USBLS	5/15
Transportation, Movers, Drivers	Idaho	Y	39140 FQ	48040 MW	60770 TQ	USBLS	5/15
Transportation, Movers, Drivers	Boise City MSA, ID	Y	38740 FQ	49080 MW	61300 TQ	USBLS	5/15
Transportation, Movers, Drivers	Illinois	Y	42280 FQ	58250 MW	73790 TQ	USBLS	5/15

AE	Average entry wage	AWR	Average wage range	H	Hourly	LR	Low end range	MTC	Median total compensation	TCC	Total cash compensation
AEX	Average experienced wage	B	Biweekly	HI	Highest wage paid	M	Monthly	MW	Median wage paid	TQ	Third quartile wage
ATC	Average total compensation	D	Daily	HR	High end range	MCC	Median cash compensation	MWR	Median wage range	W	Weekly
AW	Average wage paid	FQ	First quartile wage	LO	Lowest wage paid	ME	Median entry wage	S	See annotated source	Y	Yearly

Occupation/Type/Industry	Location	Per	Low	Mid	High	Source	Date
First-Line Supervisor							
Transportation, Movers, Drivers	Chicago-Naperville-Arlington Heights PMSA, IL	Y	46920 FQ	62750 MW	76030 TQ	USBLS	5/15
Transportation, Movers, Drivers	Lake County-Kenosha County PMSA, IL-WI	Y	25490 FQ	50670 MW	72940 TQ	USBLS	5/15
Transportation, Movers, Drivers	Indiana	Y	41350 FQ	51360 MW	64450 TQ	USBLS	5/15
Transportation, Movers, Drivers	Gary PMSA, IN	Y	39690 FQ	52450 MW	73510 TQ	USBLS	5/15
Transportation, Movers, Drivers	Indianapolis-Carmel-Anderson MSA, IN	Y	43160 FQ	51450 MW	62480 TQ	USBLS	5/15
Transportation, Movers, Drivers	Iowa	Y	42940 FQ	54160 MW	63450 TQ	USBLS	5/15
Transportation, Movers, Drivers	Des Moines-West Des Moines MSA, IA	Y	45060 FQ	60430 MW	76210 TQ	USBLS	5/15
Transportation, Movers, Drivers	Kansas	Y	41240 FQ	52600 MW	65610 TQ	USBLS	5/15
Transportation, Movers, Drivers	Wichita MSA, KS	Y	40670 FQ	54040 MW	67270 TQ	USBLS	5/15
Transportation, Movers, Drivers	Kentucky	Y	40290 FQ	50880 MW	67010 TQ	USBLS	5/15
Transportation, Movers, Drivers	Louisville-Jefferson County MSA, KY-IN	Y	42440 FQ	53030 MW	67980 TQ	USBLS	5/15
Transportation, Movers, Drivers	Louisiana	Y	43650 FQ	56370 MW	74570 TQ	USBLS	5/15
Transportation, Movers, Drivers	Baton Rouge MSA, LA	Y	45450 FQ	57140 MW	75200 TQ	USBLS	5/15
Transportation, Movers, Drivers	New Orleans-Metairie MSA, LA	Y	44020 FQ	57650 MW	74490 TQ	USBLS	5/15
Transportation, Movers, Drivers	Maine	Y	36280 FQ	48430 MW	60430 TQ	USBLS	5/15
Transportation, Movers, Drivers	Portland-South Portland MSA, ME	Y	39800 FQ	51490 MW	62440 TQ	USBLS	5/15
Transportation, Movers, Drivers	Maryland	Y	40429 AE	60506 MW	70545 AEX	MDBLS	4/16
Transportation, Movers, Drivers	Baltimore-Columbia-Towson MSA, MD	Y	44870 FQ	55450 MW	68850 TQ	USBLS	5/15
Transportation, Movers, Drivers	Salisbury MSA, MD-DE	Y	45440 FQ	54320 MW	61900 TQ	USBLS	5/15
Transportation, Movers, Drivers	Massachusetts	Y	43770 FQ	57350 MW	74320 TQ	USBLS	5/15
Transportation, Movers, Drivers	Boston-Cambridge-Newton NECTA, MA	Y	42410 FQ	58090 MW	77570 TQ	USBLS	5/15
Transportation, Movers, Drivers	Worcester MSA, MA-CT	Y	47480 FQ	57320 MW	70090 TQ	USBLS	5/15
Transportation, Movers, Drivers	Michigan	Y	40160 FQ	53030 MW	68040 TQ	USBLS	5/15
Transportation, Movers, Drivers	Detroit-Dearborn-Livonia PMSA, MI	Y	38440 FQ	50430 MW	67560 TQ	USBLS	5/15
Transportation, Movers, Drivers	Grand Rapids-Wyoming MSA, MI	Y	37690 FQ	53270 MW	64050 TQ	USBLS	5/15
Transportation, Movers, Drivers	Minnesota	Y	44268 FQ	55135 MW	68644 TQ	MNBLS	1/16-3/16
Transportation, Movers, Drivers	Minneapolis-St. Paul-Bloomington MSA, MN-WI	Y	44731 FQ	56496 MW	70449 TQ	MNBLS	1/16-3/16
Transportation, Movers, Drivers	Mississippi	Y	35860 FQ	46670 MW	59640 TQ	USBLS	5/15
Transportation, Movers, Drivers	Jackson MSA, MS	Y	38140 FQ	50360 MW	62240 TQ	USBLS	5/15
Transportation, Movers, Drivers	Missouri	Y	37760 FQ	48770 MW	64540 TQ	USBLS	5/15
Transportation, Movers, Drivers	Kansas City MSA, MO-KS	Y	42700 FQ	56300 MW	70130 TQ	USBLS	5/15
Transportation, Movers, Drivers	St. Louis MSA, MO-IL	Y	41490 FQ	51430 MW	64910 TQ	USBLS	5/15
Transportation, Movers, Drivers	Montana	Y	40680 FQ	56500 MW	73570 TQ	USBLS	5/15
Transportation, Movers, Drivers	Billings MSA, MT	Y	50200 FQ	60030 MW	72930 TQ	USBLS	5/15
Transportation, Movers, Drivers	Nebraska	Y	40680 FQ	52395 MW	62700 TQ	NEBLS	7/16-9/16
Transportation, Movers, Drivers	Omaha-Council Bluffs MSA, NE-IA	Y	41630 FQ	53075 MW	62020 TQ	NEBLS	7/16-9/16
Transportation, Movers, Drivers	Nevada	Y	39490 FQ	51390 MW	64860 TQ	USBLS	5/15
Transportation, Movers, Drivers	Las Vegas-Henderson-Paradise MSA, NV	Y	39520 FQ	50240 MW	63180 TQ	USBLS	5/15
Transportation, Movers, Drivers	New Hampshire	H	19.71 AE	28.20 MW	33.46 AEX	NHBLS	6/16
Transportation, Movers, Drivers	Manchester NECTA, NH	H	20.88 AE	31.24 MW	35.40 AEX	NHBLS	6/16
Transportation, Movers, Drivers	Nashua NECTA, NH-MA	Y	45000 FQ	53740 MW	68660 TQ	USBLS	5/15
Transportation, Movers, Drivers	New Jersey	Y	42790 FQ	57890 MW	72870 TQ	USBLS	5/15
Transportation, Movers, Drivers	Camden PMSA, NJ	Y	44880 FQ	56810 MW	71220 TQ	USBLS	5/15
Transportation, Movers, Drivers	Newark PMSA, NJ-PA	Y	47040 FQ	62800 MW	74800 TQ	USBLS	5/15
Transportation, Movers, Drivers	Trenton MSA, NJ	Y	42110 FQ	59670 MW	74110 TQ	USBLS	5/15
Transportation, Movers, Drivers	New Mexico	Y	40290 FQ	56820 MW	80960 TQ	USBLS	5/15
Transportation, Movers, Drivers	Albuquerque MSA, NM	Y	36830 FQ	47300 MW	66750 TQ	USBLS	5/15
Transportation, Movers, Drivers	New York	Y	40580 AE	67190 MW	82050 AEX	NYBLS	1/16-3/16
Transportation, Movers, Drivers	Buffalo-Cheektowaga-Niagara Falls MSA, NY	Y	40670 FQ	53410 MW	67450 TQ	USBLS	5/15
Transportation, Movers, Drivers	Nassau County-Suffolk County PMSA, NY	Y	53250 FQ	67320 MW	84280 TQ	USBLS	5/15
Transportation, Movers, Drivers	New York-Jersey City-White Plains PMSA, NY-NJ	Y	45850 FQ	67010 MW	85360 TQ	USBLS	5/15
Transportation, Movers, Drivers	Rochester MSA, NY	Y	47100 FQ	59730 MW	72170 TQ	USBLS	5/15
Transportation, Movers, Drivers	North Carolina	Y	41910 FQ	51290 MW	63110 TQ	USBLS	5/15

AE	Average entry wage	AWR	Average wage range	H	Hourly	LR	Low end range	MTC	Median total compensation	TCC	Total cash compensation
AEX	Average experienced wage	B	Biweekly	HI	Highest wage paid	M	Monthly	MW	Median wage paid	TQ	Third quartile wage
ATC	Average total compensation	D	Daily	HR	High end range	MCC	Median cash compensation	MWR	Median wage range	W	Weekly
AW	Average wage paid	FQ	First quartile wage	LO	Lowest wage paid	ME	Median entry wage	S	See annotated source	Y	Yearly

Occupation/Type/Industry	Location	Per	Low	Mid	High	Source	Date

First-Line Supervisor

Occupation/Type/Industry	Location	Per	Low	Mid	High	Source	Date
Transportation, Movers, Drivers	Charlotte-Concord-Gastonia MSA, NC-SC	Y	43720 FQ	54760 MW	69410 TQ	USBLS	5/15
Transportation, Movers, Drivers	Raleigh MSA, NC	Y	41490 FQ	52560 MW	65090 TQ	USBLS	5/15
Transportation, Movers, Drivers	North Dakota	Y	47580 FQ	60620 MW	84550 TQ	USBLS	5/15
Transportation, Movers, Drivers	Fargo MSA, ND-MN	Y	41800 FQ	51620 MW	62230 TQ	USBLS	5/15
Transportation, Movers, Drivers	Ohio	Y	41970 FQ	54980 MW	67260 TQ	USBLS	5/15
Transportation, Movers, Drivers	Cincinnati MSA, OH-KY-IN	Y	43270 FQ	54760 MW	66200 TQ	USBLS	5/15
Transportation, Movers, Drivers	Cleveland-Elyria MSA, OH	Y	42480 FQ	58160 MW	71160 TQ	USBLS	5/15
Transportation, Movers, Drivers	Columbus MSA, OH	Y	38900 FQ	53570 MW	63020 TQ	USBLS	5/15
Transportation, Movers, Drivers	Oklahoma	Y	40090 FQ	53520 MW	71610 TQ	USBLS	5/15
Transportation, Movers, Drivers	Oklahoma City MSA, OK	Y	39080 FQ	51750 MW	66180 TQ	USBLS	5/15
Transportation, Movers, Drivers	Tulsa MSA, OK	Y	38240 FQ	53890 MW	73390 TQ	USBLS	5/15
Transportation, Movers, Drivers	Oregon	H	19.37 FQ	25.68 MW	32.80 TQ	ORBLS	2016
Transportation, Movers, Drivers	Portland-Vancouver-Hillsboro MSA, OR-WA	Y	40900 FQ	54970 MW	70180 TQ	USBLS	5/15
Transportation, Movers, Drivers	Pennsylvania	Y	48570 FQ	59790 MW	73640 TQ	USBLS	5/15
Transportation, Movers, Drivers	Allentown-Bethlehem-Easton MSA, PA-NJ	Y	50780 FQ	60140 MW	72090 TQ	USBLS	5/15
Transportation, Movers, Drivers	Harrisburg-Carlisle MSA, PA	Y	48580 FQ	60360 MW	73480 TQ	USBLS	5/15
Transportation, Movers, Drivers	Montgomery County-Bucks County-Chester County PMSA, PA	Y	51310 FQ	62410 MW	76620 TQ	USBLS	5/15
Transportation, Movers, Drivers	Philadelphia PMSA, PA	Y	44040 FQ	58080 MW	73450 TQ	USBLS	5/15
Transportation, Movers, Drivers	Pittsburgh MSA, PA	Y	44380 FQ	57030 MW	70450 TQ	USBLS	5/15
Transportation, Movers, Drivers	Rhode Island	Y	42540 FQ	57060 MW	68990 TQ	USBLS	5/15
Transportation, Movers, Drivers	Providence-Warwick MSA, RI-MA	Y	41990 FQ	56620 MW	69080 TQ	USBLS	5/15
Transportation, Movers, Drivers	South Carolina	Y	42610 FQ	55270 MW	70030 TQ	USBLS	5/15
Transportation, Movers, Drivers	Charleston-North Charleston MSA, SC	Y	40060 FQ	52070 MW	65750 TQ	USBLS	5/15
Transportation, Movers, Drivers	Columbia MSA, SC	Y	45180 FQ	59150 MW	75460 TQ	USBLS	5/15
Transportation, Movers, Drivers	Greenville-Anderson-Mauldin MSA, SC	Y	43940 FQ	54400 MW	64410 TQ	USBLS	5/15
Transportation, Movers, Drivers	South Dakota	Y	51410 FQ	60640 MW	71530 TQ	USBLS	5/15
Transportation, Movers, Drivers	Sioux Falls MSA, SD	Y	53080 FQ	60210 MW	70090 TQ	USBLS	5/15
Transportation, Movers, Drivers	Tennessee	Y	41230 FQ	53850 MW	68890 TQ	USBLS	5/15
Transportation, Movers, Drivers	Knoxville MSA, TN	Y	36980 FQ	48520 MW	64830 TQ	USBLS	5/15
Transportation, Movers, Drivers	Memphis MSA, TN-MS-AR	Y	44870 FQ	56380 MW	69510 TQ	USBLS	5/15
Transportation, Movers, Drivers	Nashville-Davidson–Murfreesboro–Franklin MSA, TN	Y	41930 FQ	55010 MW	69580 TQ	USBLS	5/15
Transportation, Movers, Drivers	Texas	Y	42660 FQ	55850 MW	72300 TQ	USBLS	5/15
Transportation, Movers, Drivers	Austin-Round Rock MSA, TX	Y	43490 FQ	56290 MW	70770 TQ	USBLS	5/15
Transportation, Movers, Drivers	Dallas-Plano-Irving PMSA, TX	Y	44710 FQ	55020 MW	68450 TQ	USBLS	5/15
Transportation, Movers, Drivers	Fort Worth-Arlington PMSA, TX	Y	39340 FQ	53110 MW	74960 TQ	USBLS	5/15
Transportation, Movers, Drivers	Houston-The Woodlands-Sugar Land MSA, TX	Y	46140 FQ	61020 MW	76900 TQ	USBLS	5/15
Transportation, Movers, Drivers	San Antonio-New Braunfels MSA, TX	Y	38000 FQ	50560 MW	64050 TQ	USBLS	5/15
Transportation, Movers, Drivers	Utah	Y	46940 FQ	57790 MW	68960 TQ	USBLS	5/15
Transportation, Movers, Drivers	Ogden-Clearfield MSA, UT	Y	38290 FQ	56040 MW	75100 TQ	USBLS	5/15
Transportation, Movers, Drivers	Provo-Orem MSA, UT	Y	34410 FQ	51880 MW	72450 TQ	USBLS	5/15
Transportation, Movers, Drivers	Salt Lake City MSA, UT	Y	51260 FQ	58590 MW	66550 TQ	USBLS	5/15
Transportation, Movers, Drivers	Vermont	Y	43870 FQ	59900 MW	73560 TQ	USBLS	5/15
Transportation, Movers, Drivers	Burlington-South Burlington MSA, VT	Y	50900 FQ	60510 MW	78210 TQ	USBLS	5/15
Transportation, Movers, Drivers	Virginia	Y	44460 FQ	57560 MW	71890 TQ	USBLS	5/15
Transportation, Movers, Drivers	Richmond MSA, VA	Y	45260 FQ	57080 MW	70200 TQ	USBLS	5/15
Transportation, Movers, Drivers	Virginia Beach-Norfolk-Newport News MSA, VA-NC	Y	43940 FQ	56900 MW	72380 TQ	USBLS	5/15
Transportation, Movers, Drivers	Washington	H	22.73 FQ	30.14 MW	38.95 TQ	WABLS	3/16
Transportation, Movers, Drivers	Seattle-Bellevue-Everett PMSA, WA	H	22.35 FQ	31.91 MW	40.00 TQ	WABLS	3/16
Transportation, Movers, Drivers	Tacoma-Lakewood PMSA, WA	H	25.92 FQ	31.67 MW	42.25 TQ	WABLS	3/16
Transportation, Movers, Drivers	West Virginia	Y	32730 FQ	39180 MW	55500 TQ	USBLS	5/15
Transportation, Movers, Drivers	Huntington-Ashland MSA, WV-KY-OH	Y	34860 FQ	45810 MW	67230 TQ	USBLS	5/15
Transportation, Movers, Drivers	Wisconsin	Y	40140 FQ	52200 MW	67410 TQ	USBLS	5/15
Transportation, Movers, Drivers	Madison MSA, WI	Y	42070 FQ	50820 MW	67120 TQ	USBLS	5/15

AE	Average entry wage	AWR	Average wage range	H	Hourly	LR	Low end range	MTC	Median total compensation	TCC	Total cash compensation
AEX	Average experienced wage	B	Biweekly	HI	Highest wage paid	M	Monthly	MW	Median wage paid	TQ	Third quartile wage
ATC	Average total compensation	D	Daily	HR	High end range	MCC	Median cash compensation	MWR	Median wage range	W	Weekly
AW	Average wage paid	FQ	First quartile wage	LO	Lowest wage paid	ME	Median entry wage	S	See annotated source	Y	Yearly

Occupation/Type/Industry	Location	Per	Low	Mid	High	Source	Date
First-Line Supervisor							
Transportation, Movers, Drivers	Milwaukee-Waukesha-West Allis MSA, WI	Y	42020 FQ	57530 MW	73020 TQ	USBLS	5/15
Transportation, Movers, Drivers	Wyoming	Y	51780 FQ	62340 MW	83230 TQ	USBLS	5/15
Transportation, Movers, Drivers	Cheyenne MSA, WY	Y	47890 FQ	55020 MW	61110 TQ	USBLS	5/15
Transportation, Movers, Drivers	Puerto Rico	Y	20060 FQ	26140 MW	36830 TQ	USBLS	5/15
Transportation, Movers, Drivers	San Juan-Carolina-Caguas MSA, PR	Y	21280 FQ	28310 MW	37900 TQ	USBLS	5/15
Transportation, Movers, Drivers	Virgin Islands	Y	37960 FQ	43860 MW	48850 TQ	USBLS	5/15
Transportation, Movers, Drivers	Guam	Y	27140 FQ	31160 MW	51700 TQ	USBLS	5/15
First-Year Associate Lawyer							
Law Firm With 50 or Fewer Lawyers	United States	Y		121500 MW		NALP	4/1/15
Law Firm With 51-100 Lawyers	United States	Y		111250 MW		NALP	4/1/15
Law Firm With 101-250 Lawyers	United States	Y		115000 MW		NALP	4/1/15
Law Firm With 251-500 Lawyers	United States	Y		145000 MW		NALP	4/1/15
Law Firm With 501-700 Lawyers	United States	Y		125000 MW		NALP	4/1/15
Law Firm With More Than 700 Lawyers	United States	Y		145000 MW		NALP	4/1/15
Fiscal Analyst							
Municipal Government	East Palo Alto, CA	Y			102850 HI	CACIT	6/28/16
Fiscal Officer							
Township Government	Ohio	Y	10918 LO		31064 HI	OHGOV1	2017
Fiscal Services Manager							
Municipal Government	El Segundo, CA	Y			53026 HI	CACIT	6/28/16
Municipal Government	Fullerton, CA	Y			87428 HI	CACIT	6/28/16
Fiscal Specialist							
Municipal Government	Brea, CA	Y		62134 AW		CACIT	6/28/16
Municipal Government	Newport Beach, CA	Y			78365 HI	CACIT	6/28/16
Fish and Game Warden	Alabama	Y	43676 AE	54343 AW	59676 AEX	ALBLS	6/16
	Arizona	Y	39440 FQ	45500 MW	53950 TQ	USBLS	5/15
	Arkansas	Y	42810 FQ	47870 MW	53470 TQ	USBLS	5/15
	California	H	30.93 FQ	35.73 MW	38.13 TQ	CABLS	1/16-3/16
	Connecticut	Y		56249 MW		CTBLS	1/16-3/16
	Georgia	Y	28420 FQ	35760 MW	46040 TQ	USBLS	5/15
	Hawaii	Y	50060 FQ	55950 MW	61730 TQ	USBLS	5/15
	Idaho	Y	44970 FQ	47740 MW	50810 TQ	USBLS	5/15
	Illinois	Y	75010 FQ	91540 MW	101290 TQ	USBLS	5/15
	Indiana	Y	42490 FQ	47750 MW	59390 TQ	USBLS	5/15
	Iowa	Y	53070 FQ	62300 MW	71190 TQ	USBLS	5/15
	Kansas	Y	40160 FQ	41200 MW	46450 TQ	USBLS	5/15
	Maine	Y	38810 FQ	49590 MW	49610 TQ	USBLS	5/15
	Maryland	Y	57303 AE	74619 MW	83277 AEX	MDBLS	4/16
	Massachusetts	Y	28810 FQ	40730 MW	57390 TQ	USBLS	5/15
	Michigan	Y	59700 FQ	59710 MW	59710 TQ	USBLS	5/15
	Montana	Y	40280 FQ	42510 MW	46860 TQ	USBLS	5/15
	Nevada	Y	50010 FQ	58590 MW	70080 TQ	USBLS	5/15
	New Jersey	Y	77320 FQ	87510 MW	91670 TQ	USBLS	5/15
	New Mexico	Y	40890 FQ	40910 MW	44640 TQ	USBLS	5/15
	New York	Y	54800 AE	70280 MW	76190 AEX	NYBLS	1/16-3/16
	North Carolina	Y	33860 FQ	37650 MW	46090 TQ	USBLS	5/15
	North Dakota	Y	53250 FQ	65600 MW	80910 TQ	USBLS	5/15
	Ohio	Y	49650 FQ	58040 MW	59790 TQ	USBLS	5/15
	Oklahoma	Y	43870 FQ	48910 MW	58600 TQ	USBLS	5/15
	South Dakota	Y	34450 FQ	41390 MW	46550 TQ	USBLS	5/15
	Tennessee	Y	56830 FQ	68950 MW	79290 TQ	USBLS	5/15
	Texas	Y	63820 FQ	63830 MW	71380 TQ	USBLS	5/15
	Vermont	Y	46330 FQ	54010 MW	59560 TQ	USBLS	5/15
	Virginia	Y	40230 FQ	43740 MW	52750 TQ	USBLS	5/15
	Washington	H	27.57 FQ	32.80 MW	33.61 TQ	WABLS	3/16
	Wisconsin	Y	46230 FQ	51430 MW	61110 TQ	USBLS	5/15
	Wyoming	Y	46130 FQ	60640 MW	61220 TQ	USBLS	5/15
Fish Culture Specialist							
State Government	Eureka, MT	H	19.74 LO		24.53 HI	MTGOV	2016
Fish Wildlife Biologist							
State Government	Kalispell, MT	H			26.45 HI	MTGOV	2016

AE	Average entry wage	AWR Average wage range	H Hourly	LR Low end range	MTC Median total compensation	TCC Total cash compensation
AEX	Average experienced wage	B Biweekly	HI Highest wage paid	M Monthly	MW Median wage paid	TQ Third quartile wage
ATC	Average total compensation	D Daily	HR High end range	MCC Median cash compensation	MWR Median wage range	W Weekly
AW	Average wage paid	FQ First quartile wage	LO Lowest wage paid	ME Median entry wage	S See annotated source	Y Yearly

Occupation/Type/Industry	Location	Per	Low	Mid	High	Source	Date
Fisher and Related Fishing Worker							
	Alaska	Y	27650 FQ	30460 MW	36850 TQ	USBLS	5/15
	California	H	12.52 FQ	14.49 MW	17.98 TQ	CABLS	1/16-3/16
	Florida	H	12.48 AE	13.52 MW	14.81 AEX	FLBLS	7/16-9/16
	Mississippi	Y	27170 FQ	29500 MW	39510 TQ	USBLS	5/15
	Washington	H	12.27 FQ	14.93 MW	22.50 TQ	WABLS	3/16
Fitness Trainer and Aerobics Instructor							
	Alabama	Y	22682 AE	37457 AW	44850 AEX	ALBLS	6/16
	Birmingham-Hoover MSA, AL	Y	26976 AE	41225 AW	48350 AEX	ALBLS	6/16
	Alaska	Y	29730 FQ	36450 MW	48960 TQ	USBLS	5/15
	Anchorage MSA, AK	Y	28960 FQ	35390 MW	44110 TQ	USBLS	5/15
	Arizona	Y	24810 FQ	40050 MW	49790 TQ	USBLS	5/15
	Phoenix-Mesa-Scottsdale MSA, AZ	Y	25910 FQ	40450 MW	50900 TQ	USBLS	5/15
	Tucson MSA, AZ	Y	23000 FQ	41210 MW	47540 TQ	USBLS	5/15
	Arkansas	Y	17530 FQ	19450 MW	28680 TQ	USBLS	5/15
	Little Rock-North Little Rock-Conway MSA, AR	Y	17510 FQ	19400 MW	28110 TQ	USBLS	5/15
	California	H	13.88 FQ	22.77 MW	31.92 TQ	CABLS	1/16-3/16
	Anaheim-Santa Ana-Irvine PMSA, CA	H	13.93 FQ	20.68 MW	28.81 TQ	CABLS	1/16-3/16
	Los Angeles-Long Beach-Glendale PMSA, CA	H	13.90 FQ	24.46 MW	32.53 TQ	CABLS	1/16-3/16
	Oakland-Hayward-Berkeley PMSA, CA	H	15.67 FQ	26.00 MW	33.73 TQ	CABLS	1/16-3/16
	Riverside-San Bernardino-Ontario MSA, CA	H	11.25 FQ	17.16 MW	27.90 TQ	CABLS	1/16-3/16
	Sacramento–Roseville–Arden-Arcade MSA, CA	H	17.25 FQ	24.00 MW	30.02 TQ	CABLS	1/16-3/16
	San Diego-Carlsbad MSA, CA	H	13.79 FQ	20.73 MW	31.53 TQ	CABLS	1/16-3/16
	San Francisco-Redwood City-South San Francisco PMSA, CA	H	13.24 FQ	23.40 MW	38.65 TQ	CABLS	1/16-3/16
	Colorado	Y	26190 FQ	40250 MW	54340 TQ	USBLS	5/15
	Denver-Aurora-Lakewood MSA, CO	Y	25050 FQ	40000 MW	52710 TQ	USBLS	5/15
	Connecticut	Y		44124 MW		CTBLS	1/16-3/16
	Bridgeport-Stamford-Norwalk MSA, CT	Y	27740 FQ	57840 MW	78170 TQ	USBLS	5/15
	Hartford-West Hartford-East Hartford MSA, CT	Y	27100 FQ	35590 MW	48960 TQ	USBLS	5/15
	Delaware	Y	21720 FQ	30050 MW	44700 TQ	USBLS	5/15
	Wilmington PMSA, DE-MD-NJ	Y	21520 FQ	31170 MW	45890 TQ	USBLS	5/15
	District of Columbia	Y	21780 FQ	37030 MW	60680 TQ	USBLS	5/15
	Washington-Arlington-Alexandria PMSA, DC-VA-MD-WV	Y	28270 FQ	44000 MW	59490 TQ	USBLS	5/15
	Florida	H	9.77 AE	16.32 MW	22.45 AEX	FLBLS	7/16-9/16
	Fort Lauderdale-Pompano Beach-Deerfield Beach PMSA, FL	H	9.87 AE	17.95 MW	27.58 AEX	FLBLS	7/16-9/16
	Miami-Miami Beach-Kendall PMSA, FL	H	9.82 AE	16.09 MW	22.88 AEX	FLBLS	7/16-9/16
	Orlando-Kissimmee-Sanford MSA, FL	H	9.83 AE	15.25 MW	21.60 AEX	FLBLS	7/16-9/16
	Tampa-St. Petersburg-Clearwater MSA, FL	H	9.74 AE	15.47 MW	20.59 AEX	FLBLS	7/16-9/16
	Georgia	Y	26250 FQ	38220 MW	52190 TQ	USBLS	5/15
	Atlanta-Sandy Springs-Roswell MSA, GA	Y	29680 FQ	41650 MW	56030 TQ	USBLS	5/15
	Augusta-Richmond County MSA, GA-SC	Y	18090 FQ	30930 MW	38950 TQ	USBLS	5/15
	Hawaii	Y	23690 FQ	36450 MW	55960 TQ	USBLS	5/15
	Urban Honolulu MSA, HI	Y	22660 FQ	34710 MW	53210 TQ	USBLS	5/15
	Idaho	Y	21350 FQ	29290 MW	37290 TQ	USBLS	5/15
	Boise City MSA, ID	Y	19720 FQ	30400 MW	37430 TQ	USBLS	5/15
	Illinois	Y	22700 FQ	30330 MW	51080 TQ	USBLS	5/15
	Chicago-Naperville-Arlington Heights PMSA, IL	Y	23720 FQ	30730 MW	54040 TQ	USBLS	5/15

AE	Average entry wage	**AWR**	Average wage range	**H**	Hourly
AEX	Average experienced wage	**B**	Biweekly	**HI**	Highest wage paid
ATC	Average total compensation	**D**	Daily	**HR**	High end range
AW	Average wage paid	**FQ**	First quartile wage	**LO**	Lowest wage paid

LR	Low end range	**MTC**	Median total compensation	**TCC**	Total cash compensation
M	Monthly	**MW**	Median wage paid	**TQ**	Third quartile wage
MCC	Median cash compensation	**MWR**	Median wage range	**W**	Weekly
ME	Median entry wage	**S**	See annotated source	**Y**	Yearly

Occupation/Type/Industry	Location	Per	Low	Mid	High	Source	Date
Fitness Trainer and Aerobics Instructor	Kankakee MSA, IL	Y	19990 FQ	31440 MW	37640 TQ	USBLS	5/15
	Lake County-Kenosha County PMSA, IL-WI	Y	25690 FQ	45750 MW	63240 TQ	USBLS	5/15
	Indiana	Y	20770 FQ	28380 MW	41570 TQ	USBLS	5/15
	Gary PMSA, IN	Y	26020 FQ	38070 MW	47920 TQ	USBLS	5/15
	Indianapolis-Carmel-Anderson MSA, IN	Y	22380 FQ	29670 MW	43910 TQ	USBLS	5/15
	Kokomo MSA, IN	Y	23740 FQ	28260 MW	31520 TQ	USBLS	5/15
	Iowa	Y	18360 FQ	23230 MW	32650 TQ	USBLS	5/15
	Des Moines-West Des Moines MSA, IA	Y	18700 FQ	22840 MW	30630 TQ	USBLS	5/15
	Kansas	Y	20160 FQ	35730 MW	52860 TQ	USBLS	5/15
	Wichita MSA, KS	Y	21200 FQ	43080 MW	56190 TQ	USBLS	5/15
	Kentucky	Y	19880 FQ	30450 MW	39900 TQ	USBLS	5/15
	Louisville-Jefferson County MSA, KY-IN	Y	22120 FQ	31210 MW	39890 TQ	USBLS	5/15
	Louisiana	Y	18840 FQ	26250 MW	37230 TQ	USBLS	5/15
	Baton Rouge MSA, LA	Y	18410 FQ	31980 MW	40410 TQ	USBLS	5/15
	New Orleans-Metairie MSA, LA	Y	22610 FQ	27560 MW	34010 TQ	USBLS	5/15
	Maine	Y	21120 FQ	32790 MW	52640 TQ	USBLS	5/15
	Portland-South Portland MSA, ME	Y	21310 FQ	41870 MW	59540 TQ	USBLS	5/15
	Maryland	Y	20051 AE	45666 MW	58473 AEX	MDBLS	4/16
	Baltimore-Columbia-Towson MSA, MD	Y	19560 FQ	38520 MW	56480 TQ	USBLS	5/15
	Salisbury MSA, MD-DE	Y	20990 FQ	29300 MW	47960 TQ	USBLS	5/15
	Massachusetts	Y	26330 FQ	40210 MW	58010 TQ	USBLS	5/15
	Boston-Cambridge-Newton NECTA, MA	Y	27010 FQ	39790 MW	59320 TQ	USBLS	5/15
	Worcester MSA, MA-CT	Y	34090 FQ	47370 MW	57880 TQ	USBLS	5/15
	Michigan	Y	21180 FQ	32230 MW	43640 TQ	USBLS	5/15
	Detroit-Dearborn-Livonia PMSA, MI	Y	23940 FQ	36000 MW	44040 TQ	USBLS	5/15
	Grand Rapids-Wyoming MSA, MI	Y	19600 FQ	29410 MW	42480 TQ	USBLS	5/15
	Minnesota	Y	26307 FQ	36123 MW	46949 TQ	MNBLS	1/16-3/16
	Minneapolis-St. Paul-Bloomington MSA, MN-WI	Y	28165 FQ	37517 MW	48120 TQ	MNBLS	1/16-3/16
	Mississippi	Y	18210 FQ	23000 MW	37660 TQ	USBLS	5/15
	Jackson MSA, MS	Y	17620 FQ	19740 MW	27200 TQ	USBLS	5/15
	Missouri	Y	18730 FQ	25990 MW	38810 TQ	USBLS	5/15
	Kansas City MSA, MO-KS	Y	24840 FQ	41420 MW	56950 TQ	USBLS	5/15
	St. Louis MSA, MO-IL	Y	18750 FQ	26320 MW	42650 TQ	USBLS	5/15
	Montana	Y	19710 FQ	32120 MW	39840 TQ	USBLS	5/15
	Billings MSA, MT	Y	25270 FQ	38320 MW	46160 TQ	USBLS	5/15
	Omaha-Council Bluffs MSA, NE-IA	Y	29070 FQ	38795 MW	55400 TQ	NEBLS	7/16-9/16
	Nevada	Y	19920 FQ	29890 MW	37360 TQ	USBLS	5/15
	Las Vegas-Henderson-Paradise MSA, NV	Y	22060 FQ	30630 MW	36210 TQ	USBLS	5/15
	New Hampshire	H	10.45 AE	16.94 MW	21.33 AEX	NHBLS	6/16
	Manchester NECTA, NH	H	11.50 AE	18.06 MW	22.32 AEX	NHBLS	6/16
	Nashua NECTA, NH-MA	Y	24470 FQ	33490 MW	45800 TQ	USBLS	5/15
	New Jersey	Y	30970 FQ	49270 MW	63110 TQ	USBLS	5/15
	Camden PMSA, NJ	Y	30300 FQ	46760 MW	59210 TQ	USBLS	5/15
	Newark PMSA, NJ-PA	Y	34680 FQ	49260 MW	63620 TQ	USBLS	5/15
	Trenton MSA, NJ	Y	29480 FQ	52200 MW	61050 TQ	USBLS	5/15
	New Mexico	Y	23940 FQ	34890 MW	45660 TQ	USBLS	5/15
	Albuquerque MSA, NM	Y	30070 FQ	39530 MW	46810 TQ	USBLS	5/15
	New York	Y	25590 AE	55980 MW	78710 AEX	NYBLS	1/16-3/16
	Buffalo-Cheektowaga-Niagara Falls MSA, NY	Y	24780 FQ	40060 MW	46640 TQ	USBLS	5/15
	Nassau County-Suffolk County PMSA, NY	Y	40040 FQ	54240 MW	63680 TQ	USBLS	5/15
	New York-Jersey City-White Plains PMSA, NY-NJ	Y	37770 FQ	60420 MW	89620 TQ	USBLS	5/15
	Rochester MSA, NY	Y	20010 FQ	28390 MW	48480 TQ	USBLS	5/15
	North Carolina	Y	22620 FQ	32790 MW	43550 TQ	USBLS	5/15
	Charlotte-Concord-Gastonia MSA, NC-SC	Y	21610 FQ	29930 MW	41360 TQ	USBLS	5/15

AE	Average entry wage	AWR	Average wage range	H	Hourly	LR	Low end range
AEX	Average experienced wage	B	Biweekly	HI	Highest wage paid	M	Monthly
ATC	Average total compensation	D	Daily	HR	High end range	MCC	Median cash compensation
AW	Average wage paid	FQ	First quartile wage	LO	Lowest wage paid	ME	Median entry wage

MTC	Median total compensation	TCC	Total cash compensation
MW	Median wage paid	TQ	Third quartile wage
MWR	Median wage range	W	Weekly
S	See annotated source	Y	Yearly

Occupation/Type/Industry	Location	Per	Low	Mid	High	Source	Date
Fitness Trainer and Aerobics Instructor	Raleigh MSA, NC	Y	34020 FQ	43260 MW	52330 TQ	USBLS	5/15
	North Dakota	Y	21160 FQ	25690 MW	34470 TQ	USBLS	5/15
	Fargo MSA, ND-MN	Y	20900 FQ	24620 MW	33170 TQ	USBLS	5/15
	Ohio	Y	18470 FQ	21690 MW	33980 TQ	USBLS	5/15
	Cincinnati MSA, OH-KY-IN	Y	19410 FQ	27350 MW	37350 TQ	USBLS	5/15
	Cleveland-Elyria MSA, OH	Y	19290 FQ	32720 MW	46590 TQ	USBLS	5/15
	Columbus MSA, OH	Y	18610 FQ	22950 MW	33700 TQ	USBLS	5/15
	Oklahoma	Y	20410 FQ	32640 MW	42750 TQ	USBLS	5/15
	Oklahoma City MSA, OK	Y	18920 FQ	31620 MW	39320 TQ	USBLS	5/15
	Tulsa MSA, OK	Y	23040 FQ	37790 MW	47840 TQ	USBLS	5/15
	Oregon	H	13.86 FQ	19.70 MW	25.93 TQ	ORBLS	2016
	Portland-Vancouver-Hillsboro MSA, OR-WA	Y	31350 FQ	45090 MW	58350 TQ	USBLS	5/15
	Pennsylvania	Y	20140 FQ	29630 MW	41140 TQ	USBLS	5/15
	Allentown-Bethlehem-Easton MSA, PA-NJ	Y	22530 FQ	31330 MW	37920 TQ	USBLS	5/15
	Harrisburg-Carlisle MSA, PA	Y	28830 FQ	34680 MW	39100 TQ	USBLS	5/15
	Montgomery County-Bucks County-Chester County PMSA, PA	Y	21570 FQ	30860 MW	46110 TQ	USBLS	5/15
	Philadelphia PMSA, PA	Y	22820 FQ	30330 MW	45670 TQ	USBLS	5/15
	Pittsburgh MSA, PA	Y	18720 FQ	28020 MW	39020 TQ	USBLS	5/15
	Rhode Island	Y	25890 FQ	38130 MW	49760 TQ	USBLS	5/15
	Providence-Warwick MSA, RI-MA	Y	30350 FQ	44020 MW	55520 TQ	USBLS	5/15
	South Carolina	Y	19340 FQ	31890 MW	43430 TQ	USBLS	5/15
	Charleston-North Charleston MSA, SC	Y	20730 FQ	30550 MW	38280 TQ	USBLS	5/15
	Columbia MSA, SC	Y	30960 FQ	37430 MW	44440 TQ	USBLS	5/15
	Greenville-Anderson-Mauldin MSA, SC	Y	19160 FQ	32070 MW	45260 TQ	USBLS	5/15
	South Dakota	Y	21890 FQ	26110 MW	32740 TQ	USBLS	5/15
	Sioux Falls MSA, SD	Y	22690 FQ	27790 MW	36490 TQ	USBLS	5/15
	Tennessee	Y	21400 FQ	34540 MW	45950 TQ	USBLS	5/15
	Knoxville MSA, TN	Y	29200 FQ	35010 MW	39500 TQ	USBLS	5/15
	Memphis MSA, TN-MS-AR	Y	18190 FQ	26300 MW	46980 TQ	USBLS	5/15
	Nashville-Davidson–Murfreesboro–Franklin MSA, TN	Y	28120 FQ	41430 MW	54000 TQ	USBLS	5/15
	Texas	Y	26970 FQ	41640 MW	55800 TQ	USBLS	5/15
	Austin-Round Rock MSA, TX	Y	30940 FQ	43820 MW	55320 TQ	USBLS	5/15
	Dallas-Plano-Irving PMSA, TX	Y	36430 FQ	48270 MW	61060 TQ	USBLS	5/15
	Fort Worth-Arlington PMSA, TX	Y	27770 FQ	38100 MW	55870 TQ	USBLS	5/15
	Houston-The Woodlands-Sugar Land MSA, TX	Y	28220 FQ	43210 MW	57590 TQ	USBLS	5/15
	San Antonio-New Braunfels MSA, TX	Y	19320 FQ	37020 MW	48630 TQ	USBLS	5/15
	Utah	Y	25990 FQ	36060 MW	51040 TQ	USBLS	5/15
	Ogden-Clearfield MSA, UT	Y	30600 FQ	35490 MW	41030 TQ	USBLS	5/15
	Provo-Orem MSA, UT	Y	22470 FQ	36110 MW	50970 TQ	USBLS	5/15
	Salt Lake City MSA, UT	Y	26780 FQ	38300 MW	55050 TQ	USBLS	5/15
	Vermont	Y	29860 FQ	40620 MW	48240 TQ	USBLS	5/15
	Burlington-South Burlington MSA, VT	Y	31300 FQ	40170 MW	52080 TQ	USBLS	5/15
	Virginia	Y	25630 FQ	38040 MW	52860 TQ	USBLS	5/15
	Richmond MSA, VA	Y	23820 FQ	40910 MW	50550 TQ	USBLS	5/15
	Virginia Beach-Norfolk-Newport News MSA, VA-NC	Y	21650 FQ	30280 MW	38210 TQ	USBLS	5/15
	Washington	H	14.11 FQ	20.15 MW	28.98 TQ	WABLS	3/16
	Seattle-Bellevue-Everett PMSA, WA	H	14.33 FQ	20.10 MW	30.14 TQ	WABLS	3/16
	Tacoma-Lakewood PMSA, WA	H	17.88 FQ	24.71 MW	32.84 TQ	WABLS	3/16
	West Virginia	Y	18200 FQ	19830 MW	28490 TQ	USBLS	5/15
	Huntington-Ashland MSA, WV-KY-OH	Y	18120 FQ	19790 MW	26240 TQ	USBLS	5/15
	Wisconsin	Y	19490 FQ	28480 MW	43150 TQ	USBLS	5/15
	Madison MSA, WI	Y	30150 FQ	38720 MW	48160 TQ	USBLS	5/15
	Milwaukee-Waukesha-West Allis MSA, WI	Y	20500 FQ	31130 MW	49310 TQ	USBLS	5/15
	Wyoming	Y	18980 FQ	29250 MW	39820 TQ	USBLS	5/15

AE	Average entry wage	AWR	Average wage range	H	Hourly	LR	Low end range	MTC	Median total compensation	TCC	Total cash compensation
AEX	Average experienced wage	B	Biweekly	HI	Highest wage paid	M	Monthly	MW	Median wage paid	TQ	Third quartile wage
ATC	Average total compensation	D	Daily	HR	High end range	MCC	Median cash compensation	MWR	Median wage range	W	Weekly
AW	Average wage paid	FQ	First quartile wage	LO	Lowest wage paid	ME	Median entry wage	S	See annotated source	Y	Yearly

647

Occupation/Type/Industry	Location	Per	Low	Mid	High	Source	Date
Fitness Trainer and Aerobics Instructor	Cheyenne MSA, WY	Y	17610 FQ	32640 MW	41500 TQ	USBLS	5/15
	Puerto Rico	Y	17600 FQ	22230 MW	55160 TQ	USBLS	5/15
	Guam	Y	37260 FQ	55220 MW	60820 TQ	USBLS	5/15
Flash Animator	United States	Y	29000 LO		99000 HI	LP01	7/15
Fleet Management Analyst							
Municipal Government	Seattle, WA	H	33.00 LO		38.44 HI	CSSS	1/13/16
Fleet Manager							
Female	United States	Y		83500 AW		AUTOF	2014
Male	United States	Y		87500 AW		AUTOF	2014
Fleet Services Writer							
Fleet Management, Municipal Government	Santa Monica, CA	Y			50837 HI	CACIT	6/28/16
Flight Attendant	Alaska	Y	25200 FQ	36580 MW	45940 TQ	USBLS	5/15
	Arizona	Y	33120 FQ	37660 MW	63770 TQ	USBLS	5/15
	California	Y		48379 AW		CABLS	1/16-3/16
	Colorado	Y	39150 FQ	44220 MW	48960 TQ	USBLS	5/15
	Florida	Y	36696 AE	50103 MW	60535 AEX	FLBLS	7/16-9/16
	Illinois	Y	29530 FQ	42720 MW	53950 TQ	USBLS	5/15
	Massachusetts	Y	35510 FQ	44230 MW	55250 TQ	USBLS	5/15
	Michigan	Y	40870 FQ	46290 MW	53870 TQ	USBLS	5/15
	Minnesota	Y	40013 FQ	44439 MW	48804 TQ	MNBLS	1/16-3/16
	New Jersey	Y	39960 FQ	43740 MW	47530 TQ	USBLS	5/15
	New York	Y	25350 AE	39730 MW	49490 AEX	NYBLS	1/16-3/16
	North Carolina	Y	24450 FQ	42490 MW	46890 TQ	USBLS	5/15
	Ohio	Y	28830 FQ	38000 MW	53500 TQ	USBLS	5/15
	Tennessee	Y	36140 FQ	44580 MW	56830 TQ	USBLS	5/15
	Texas	Y	41750 FQ	51260 MW	67380 TQ	USBLS	5/15
	Virginia	Y	40100 FQ	44150 MW	48160 TQ	USBLS	5/15
	Washington	Y		39690 AW		WABLS	3/16
	Wisconsin	Y	33070 FQ	38660 MW	48140 TQ	USBLS	5/15
Floor Layer							
Except Carpet, Wood, and Hard Tiles	Alabama	Y	21325 AE	30490 AW	35068 AEX	ALBLS	6/16
Except Carpet, Wood, and Hard Tiles	Birmingham-Hoover MSA, AL	Y	23063 AE	27764 AW	30120 AEX	ALBLS	6/16
Except Carpet, Wood, and Hard Tiles	California	H	16.41 FQ	21.18 MW	28.72 TQ	CABLS	1/16-3/16
Except Carpet, Wood, and Hard Tiles	Anaheim-Santa Ana-Irvine PMSA, CA	H	14.10 FQ	16.39 MW	19.31 TQ	CABLS	1/16-3/16
Except Carpet, Wood, and Hard Tiles	Los Angeles-Long Beach-Glendale PMSA, CA	H	21.53 FQ	26.45 MW	29.53 TQ	CABLS	1/16-3/16
Except Carpet, Wood, and Hard Tiles	Oakland-Hayward-Berkeley PMSA, CA	H	17.80 FQ	21.34 MW	31.74 TQ	CABLS	1/16-3/16
Except Carpet, Wood, and Hard Tiles	Riverside-San Bernardino-Ontario MSA, CA	H	16.00 FQ	18.46 MW	21.60 TQ	CABLS	1/16-3/16
Except Carpet, Wood, and Hard Tiles	Sacramento–Roseville–Arden-Arcade MSA, CA	H	13.65 FQ	19.17 MW	26.43 TQ	CABLS	1/16-3/16
Except Carpet, Wood, and Hard Tiles	San Francisco-Redwood City-South San Francisco PMSA, CA	H	16.58 FQ	18.77 MW	29.74 TQ	CABLS	1/16-3/16
Except Carpet, Wood, and Hard Tiles	Colorado	Y	31460 FQ	39610 MW	45330 TQ	USBLS	5/15
Except Carpet, Wood, and Hard Tiles	Connecticut	Y		59906 MW		CTBLS	1/16-3/16
Except Carpet, Wood, and Hard Tiles	Washington-Arlington-Alexandria PMSA, DC-VA-MD-WV	Y	28400 FQ	37210 MW	52660 TQ	USBLS	5/15
Except Carpet, Wood, and Hard Tiles	Florida	H	9.92 AE	15.69 MW	18.73 AEX	FLBLS	7/16-9/16
Except Carpet, Wood, and Hard Tiles	Georgia	Y	25470 FQ	30320 MW	38110 TQ	USBLS	5/15
Except Carpet, Wood, and Hard Tiles	Hawaii	Y	46650 FQ	59110 MW	69620 TQ	USBLS	5/15
Except Carpet, Wood, and Hard Tiles	Urban Honolulu MSA, HI	Y	46650 FQ	59110 MW	69620 TQ	USBLS	5/15
Except Carpet, Wood, and Hard Tiles	Idaho	Y	28580 FQ	38160 MW	48860 TQ	USBLS	5/15
Except Carpet, Wood, and Hard Tiles	Illinois	Y	35060 FQ	68750 MW	90630 TQ	USBLS	5/15
Except Carpet, Wood, and Hard Tiles	Chicago-Naperville-Arlington Heights PMSA, IL	Y	50930 FQ	83880 MW	94030 TQ	USBLS	5/15
Except Carpet, Wood, and Hard Tiles	Lake County-Kenosha County PMSA, IL-WI	Y	58000 FQ	86600 MW	95530 TQ	USBLS	5/15
Except Carpet, Wood, and Hard Tiles	Indiana	Y	24620 FQ	32250 MW	36570 TQ	USBLS	5/15
Except Carpet, Wood, and Hard Tiles	Indianapolis-Carmel-Anderson MSA, IN	Y	23430 FQ	31080 MW	35620 TQ	USBLS	5/15
Except Carpet, Wood, and Hard Tiles	Iowa	Y	25990 FQ	36260 MW	50760 TQ	USBLS	5/15

AE	Average entry wage	AWR	Average wage range	H	Hourly	
AEX	Average experienced wage	B	Biweekly	HI	Highest wage paid	
ATC	Average total compensation	D	Daily	HR	High end range	
AW	Average wage paid	FQ	First quartile wage	LO	Lowest wage paid	

LR	Low end range	MTC	Median total compensation	TCC	Total cash compensation
M	Monthly	MW	Median wage paid	TQ	Third quartile wage
MCC	Median cash compensation	MWR	Median wage range	W	Weekly
ME	Median entry wage	S	See annotated source	Y	Yearly

Occupation/Type/Industry	Location	Per	Low	Mid	High	Source	Date
Floor Layer							
Except Carpet, Wood, and Hard Tiles	Kansas	Y	27380 FQ	30380 MW	40550 TQ	USBLS	5/15
Except Carpet, Wood, and Hard Tiles	Louisiana	Y	24390 FQ	29540 MW	36530 TQ	USBLS	5/15
Except Carpet, Wood, and Hard Tiles	Maine	Y	28120 FQ	33860 MW	38360 TQ	USBLS	5/15
Except Carpet, Wood, and Hard Tiles	Maryland	Y	27638 AE	40130 MW	46376 AEX	MDBLS	4/16
Except Carpet, Wood, and Hard Tiles	Baltimore-Columbia-Towson MSA, MD	Y	32210 FQ	40260 MW	46250 TQ	USBLS	5/15
Except Carpet, Wood, and Hard Tiles	Massachusetts	Y	27210 FQ	35310 MW	55690 TQ	USBLS	5/15
Except Carpet, Wood, and Hard Tiles	Michigan	Y	28250 FQ	38580 MW	50300 TQ	USBLS	5/15
Except Carpet, Wood, and Hard Tiles	Grand Rapids-Wyoming MSA, MI	Y	23870 FQ	39200 MW	45680 TQ	USBLS	5/15
Except Carpet, Wood, and Hard Tiles	Minnesota	Y	30735 FQ	37838 MW	64971 TQ	MNBLS	1/16-3/16
Except Carpet, Wood, and Hard Tiles	Mississippi	Y	21870 FQ	32700 MW	42060 TQ	USBLS	5/15
Except Carpet, Wood, and Hard Tiles	Missouri	Y	37850 FQ	62250 MW	70430 TQ	USBLS	5/15
Except Carpet, Wood, and Hard Tiles	Kansas City MSA, MO-KS	Y	28320 FQ	33290 MW	45520 TQ	USBLS	5/15
Except Carpet, Wood, and Hard Tiles	St. Louis MSA, MO-IL	Y	43130 FQ	64100 MW	71310 TQ	USBLS	5/15
Except Carpet, Wood, and Hard Tiles	Montana	Y	22040 FQ	23980 MW	27570 TQ	USBLS	5/15
Except Carpet, Wood, and Hard Tiles	Nebraska	Y	19280 FQ	28385 MW	42625 TQ	NEBLS	7/16-9/16
Except Carpet, Wood, and Hard Tiles	Omaha-Council Bluffs MSA, NE-IA	Y	18935 FQ	32675 MW	46060 TQ	NEBLS	7/16-9/16
Except Carpet, Wood, and Hard Tiles	New Jersey	Y	33730 FQ	39040 MW	46200 TQ	USBLS	5/15
Except Carpet, Wood, and Hard Tiles	New Mexico	Y	32210 FQ	35010 MW	37800 TQ	USBLS	5/15
Except Carpet, Wood, and Hard Tiles	New York	Y	30910 AE	39080 MW	48920 AEX	NYBLS	1/16-3/16
Except Carpet, Wood, and Hard Tiles	Buffalo-Cheektowaga-Niagara Falls MSA, NY	Y	33070 FQ	35330 MW	37580 TQ	USBLS	5/15
Except Carpet, Wood, and Hard Tiles	New York-Jersey City-White Plains PMSA, NY-NJ	Y	31530 FQ	39470 MW	51030 TQ	USBLS	5/15
Except Carpet, Wood, and Hard Tiles	Rochester MSA, NY	Y	25900 FQ	30160 MW	34930 TQ	USBLS	5/15
Except Carpet, Wood, and Hard Tiles	North Carolina	Y	23770 FQ	30980 MW	39530 TQ	USBLS	5/15
Except Carpet, Wood, and Hard Tiles	North Dakota	Y	32040 FQ	35790 MW	39610 TQ	USBLS	5/15
Except Carpet, Wood, and Hard Tiles	Ohio	Y	34700 FQ	46070 MW	63640 TQ	USBLS	5/15
Except Carpet, Wood, and Hard Tiles	Cleveland-Elyria MSA, OH	Y	41600 FQ	65170 MW	71970 TQ	USBLS	5/15
Except Carpet, Wood, and Hard Tiles	Oklahoma	Y	30690 FQ	35380 MW	40090 TQ	USBLS	5/15
Except Carpet, Wood, and Hard Tiles	Oklahoma City MSA, OK	Y	32780 FQ	36610 MW	44440 TQ	USBLS	5/15
Except Carpet, Wood, and Hard Tiles	Oregon	H	14.73 FQ	17.66 MW	22.98 TQ	ORBLS	2016
Except Carpet, Wood, and Hard Tiles	Portland-Vancouver-Hillsboro MSA, OR-WA	Y	32180 FQ	38770 MW	56220 TQ	USBLS	5/15
Except Carpet, Wood, and Hard Tiles	Pittsburgh MSA, PA	Y	21370 FQ	23490 MW	34320 TQ	USBLS	5/15
Except Carpet, Wood, and Hard Tiles	South Carolina	Y	26580 FQ	28400 MW	30220 TQ	USBLS	5/15
Except Carpet, Wood, and Hard Tiles	South Dakota	Y	28770 FQ	33000 MW	36960 TQ	USBLS	5/15
Except Carpet, Wood, and Hard Tiles	Sioux Falls MSA, SD	Y	29150 FQ	33320 MW	37170 TQ	USBLS	5/15
Except Carpet, Wood, and Hard Tiles	Tennessee	Y	27030 FQ	36240 MW	44560 TQ	USBLS	5/15
Except Carpet, Wood, and Hard Tiles	Knoxville MSA, TN	Y	21720 FQ	26870 MW	30810 TQ	USBLS	5/15
Except Carpet, Wood, and Hard Tiles	Texas	Y	29470 FQ	33420 MW	36990 TQ	USBLS	5/15
Except Carpet, Wood, and Hard Tiles	Austin-Round Rock MSA, TX	Y	26750 FQ	29490 MW	33820 TQ	USBLS	5/15
Except Carpet, Wood, and Hard Tiles	Dallas-Plano-Irving PMSA, TX	Y	27620 FQ	30160 MW	34050 TQ	USBLS	5/15
Except Carpet, Wood, and Hard Tiles	San Antonio-New Braunfels MSA, TX	Y	31870 FQ	37570 MW	43500 TQ	USBLS	5/15
Except Carpet, Wood, and Hard Tiles	Utah	Y	18700 FQ	33620 MW	45100 TQ	USBLS	5/15
Except Carpet, Wood, and Hard Tiles	Salt Lake City MSA, UT	Y	17900 FQ	36600 MW	45500 TQ	USBLS	5/15
Except Carpet, Wood, and Hard Tiles	Virginia	Y	29130 FQ	34340 MW	39250 TQ	USBLS	5/15
Except Carpet, Wood, and Hard Tiles	Washington	H	11.36 FQ	16.17 MW	20.67 TQ	WABLS	3/16
Except Carpet, Wood, and Hard Tiles	Wisconsin	Y	32730 FQ	49420 MW	70790 TQ	USBLS	5/15
Except Carpet, Wood, and Hard Tiles	Madison MSA, WI	Y	30420 FQ	36890 MW	44330 TQ	USBLS	5/15
Except Carpet, Wood, and Hard Tiles	Milwaukee-Waukesha-West Allis MSA, WI	Y	43480 FQ	67520 MW	74100 TQ	USBLS	5/15
Floor Sander and Finisher	Alabama	Y	21932 AE	28186 AW	31313 AEX	ALBLS	6/16
	Arizona	Y	51180 FQ	56380 MW	61530 TQ	USBLS	5/15
	Arkansas	Y	20790 FQ	22620 MW	24530 TQ	USBLS	5/15
	California	H	17.70 FQ	20.99 MW	25.58 TQ	CABLS	1/16-3/16
	Colorado	Y	32140 FQ	35920 MW	41380 TQ	USBLS	5/15
	Connecticut	Y		41194 MW		CTBLS	1/16-3/16
	Florida	H	14.37 AE	17.22 MW	19.63 AEX	FLBLS	7/16-9/16
	Illinois	Y	23760 FQ	55030 MW	67930 TQ	USBLS	5/15
	Kentucky	Y	27780 FQ	34050 MW	41640 TQ	USBLS	5/15
	Maine	Y	27650 FQ	30430 MW	43700 TQ	USBLS	5/15
	Maryland	Y	30975 AE	40414 MW	45134 AEX	MDBLS	4/16
	Massachusetts	Y	37420 FQ	51510 MW	57850 TQ	USBLS	5/15
	Minnesota	Y	28596 FQ	36587 MW	44720 TQ	MNBLS	1/16-3/16
	Missouri	Y	51340 FQ	55070 MW	58800 TQ	USBLS	5/15
	New Jersey	Y	22820 FQ	41250 MW	46310 TQ	USBLS	5/15

AE	Average entry wage	AWR	Average wage range	H	Hourly	LR	Low end range	MTC	Median total compensation	TCC	Total cash compensation
AEX	Average experienced wage	B	Biweekly	HI	Highest wage paid	M	Monthly	MW	Median wage paid	TQ	Third quartile wage
ATC	Average total compensation	D	Daily	HR	High end range	MCC	Median cash compensation	MWR	Median wage range	W	Weekly
AW	Average wage paid	FQ	First quartile wage	LO	Lowest wage paid	ME	Median entry wage	S	See annotated source	Y	Yearly

Occupation/Type/Industry	Location	Per	Low	Mid	High	Source	Date
Floor Sander and Finisher	New York	Y	22130 AE	53500 MW	55130 AEX	NYBLS	1/16-3/16
	North Carolina	Y	25460 FQ	31730 MW	38500 TQ	USBLS	5/15
	Ohio	Y	23280 FQ	31640 MW	40980 TQ	USBLS	5/15
	South Carolina	Y	29920 FQ	36040 MW	49090 TQ	USBLS	5/15
	Tennessee	Y	20120 FQ	23710 MW	30280 TQ	USBLS	5/15
	Texas	Y	25780 FQ	31690 MW	37360 TQ	USBLS	5/15
	Vermont	Y	37580 FQ	44480 MW	50610 TQ	USBLS	5/15
	Virginia	Y	34320 FQ	40210 MW	45310 TQ	USBLS	5/15
	Washington	H	19.44 FQ	21.41 MW	23.38 TQ	WABLS	3/16
	Wisconsin	Y	26270 FQ	34350 MW	42200 TQ	USBLS	5/15
Floral Designer	Alabama	Y	17390 AE	24158 AW	27542 AEX	ALBLS	6/16
	Birmingham-Hoover MSA, AL	Y	17257 AE	27471 AW	32588 AEX	ALBLS	6/16
	Alaska	Y	26700 FQ	31690 MW	39890 TQ	USBLS	5/15
	Anchorage MSA, AK	Y	26820 FQ	32500 MW	41130 TQ	USBLS	5/15
	Arizona	Y	22190 FQ	24880 MW	28880 TQ	USBLS	5/15
	Phoenix-Mesa-Scottsdale MSA, AZ	Y	22470 FQ	25430 MW	29190 TQ	USBLS	5/15
	Tucson MSA, AZ	Y	22190 FQ	24980 MW	28360 TQ	USBLS	5/15
	Arkansas	Y	18570 FQ	22320 MW	28070 TQ	USBLS	5/15
	Little Rock-North Little Rock-Conway MSA, AR	Y	18230 FQ	22630 MW	30640 TQ	USBLS	5/15
	California	H	11.82 FQ	14.50 MW	17.93 TQ	CABLS	1/16-3/16
	Anaheim-Santa Ana-Irvine PMSA, CA	H	12.85 FQ	15.76 MW	18.98 TQ	CABLS	1/16-3/16
	Los Angeles-Long Beach-Glendale PMSA, CA	H	11.40 FQ	13.80 MW	18.94 TQ	CABLS	1/16-3/16
	Oakland-Hayward-Berkeley PMSA, CA	H	15.40 FQ	16.85 MW	18.30 TQ	CABLS	1/16-3/16
	Riverside-San Bernardino-Ontario MSA, CA	H	13.70 FQ	15.72 MW	17.90 TQ	CABLS	1/16-3/16
	Sacramento–Roseville–Arden-Arcade MSA, CA	H	9.87 FQ	13.58 MW	16.08 TQ	CABLS	1/16-3/16
	San Diego-Carlsbad MSA, CA	H	11.66 FQ	14.42 MW	17.59 TQ	CABLS	1/16-3/16
	San Francisco-Redwood City-South San Francisco PMSA, CA	H	15.15 FQ	18.05 MW	21.44 TQ	CABLS	1/16-3/16
	Colorado	Y	19530 FQ	25520 MW	30020 TQ	USBLS	5/15
	Denver-Aurora-Lakewood MSA, CO	Y	19670 FQ	25710 MW	29580 TQ	USBLS	5/15
	Connecticut	Y		35142 MW		CTBLS	1/16-3/16
	Bridgeport-Stamford-Norwalk MSA, CT	Y	34150 FQ	41980 MW	50330 TQ	USBLS	5/15
	Hartford-West Hartford-East Hartford MSA, CT	Y	26100 FQ	33630 MW	37970 TQ	USBLS	5/15
	Delaware	Y	19540 FQ	23090 MW	29280 TQ	USBLS	5/15
	Wilmington PMSA, DE-MD-NJ	Y	20780 FQ	23600 MW	28250 TQ	USBLS	5/15
	District of Columbia	Y	25900 FQ	29550 MW	37750 TQ	USBLS	5/15
	Washington-Arlington-Alexandria PMSA, DC-VA-MD-WV	Y	23620 FQ	30190 MW	38590 TQ	USBLS	5/15
	Florida	H	10.23 AE	11.83 MW	14.09 AEX	FLBLS	7/16-9/16
	Fort Lauderdale-Pompano Beach-Deerfield Beach PMSA, FL	H	9.05 AE	10.83 MW	12.95 AEX	FLBLS	7/16-9/16
	Miami-Miami Beach-Kendall PMSA, FL	H	10.91 AE	14.35 MW	16.02 AEX	FLBLS	7/16-9/16
	Orlando-Kissimmee-Sanford MSA, FL	H	9.78 AE	11.02 MW	12.01 AEX	FLBLS	7/16-9/16
	Tampa-St. Petersburg-Clearwater MSA, FL	H	10.59 AE	11.53 MW	13.49 AEX	FLBLS	7/16-9/16
	Georgia	Y	21520 FQ	24640 MW	29740 TQ	USBLS	5/15
	Atlanta-Sandy Springs-Roswell MSA, GA	Y	22250 FQ	25700 MW	31410 TQ	USBLS	5/15
	Augusta-Richmond County MSA, GA-SC	Y	18770 FQ	23240 MW	28180 TQ	USBLS	5/15
	Hawaii	Y	21800 FQ	28940 MW	35660 TQ	USBLS	5/15
	Urban Honolulu MSA, HI	Y	21430 FQ	28310 MW	35180 TQ	USBLS	5/15
	Idaho	Y	20550 FQ	24150 MW	29000 TQ	USBLS	5/15
	Boise City MSA, ID	Y	22630 FQ	26200 MW	30410 TQ	USBLS	5/15
	Illinois	Y	21120 FQ	26440 MW	31180 TQ	USBLS	5/15

AE	Average entry wage	AWR	Average wage range	H	Hourly
AEX	Average experienced wage	B	Biweekly	HI	Highest wage paid
ATC	Average total compensation	D	Daily	HR	High end range
AW	Average wage paid	FQ	First quartile wage	LO	Lowest wage paid

LR	Low end range	MTC	Median total compensation
M	Monthly	MW	Median wage paid
MCC	Median cash compensation	MWR	Median wage range
ME	Median entry wage	S	See annotated source

TCC	Total cash compensation
TQ	Third quartile wage
W	Weekly
Y	Yearly

Occupation/Type/Industry	Location	Per	Low	Mid	High	Source	Date
Floral Designer	Chicago-Naperville-Arlington Heights PMSA, IL	Y	22850 FQ	27920 MW	33390 TQ	USBLS	5/15
	Lake County-Kenosha County PMSA, IL-WI	Y	22340 FQ	26660 MW	34650 TQ	USBLS	5/15
	Indiana	Y	21100 FQ	23880 MW	28160 TQ	USBLS	5/15
	Gary PMSA, IN	Y	22080 FQ	26030 MW	29960 TQ	USBLS	5/15
	Indianapolis-Carmel-Anderson MSA, IN	Y	22110 FQ	24530 MW	28540 TQ	USBLS	5/15
	Iowa	Y	21770 FQ	26310 MW	30640 TQ	USBLS	5/15
	Des Moines-West Des Moines MSA, IA	Y	25590 FQ	28980 MW	33890 TQ	USBLS	5/15
	Kansas	Y	19530 FQ	23420 MW	28800 TQ	USBLS	5/15
	Wichita MSA, KS	Y	19210 FQ	22760 MW	27280 TQ	USBLS	5/15
	Kentucky	Y	18200 FQ	22140 MW	27230 TQ	USBLS	5/15
	Louisville-Jefferson County MSA, KY-IN	Y	24170 FQ	27320 MW	30240 TQ	USBLS	5/15
	Louisiana	Y	18800 FQ	22770 MW	27780 TQ	USBLS	5/15
	Baton Rouge MSA, LA	Y	22580 FQ	27390 MW	30730 TQ	USBLS	5/15
	New Orleans-Metairie MSA, LA	Y	22150 FQ	25330 MW	28850 TQ	USBLS	5/15
	Maine	Y	19790 FQ	25480 MW	29210 TQ	USBLS	5/15
	Portland-South Portland MSA, ME	Y	18800 FQ	24790 MW	27950 TQ	USBLS	5/15
	Maryland	Y	22607 AE	30523 MW	34481 AEX	MDBLS	4/16
	Baltimore-Columbia-Towson MSA, MD	Y	27110 FQ	29960 MW	34090 TQ	USBLS	5/15
	Salisbury MSA, MD-DE	Y	21840 FQ	28040 MW	33850 TQ	USBLS	5/15
	Massachusetts	Y	25490 FQ	31130 MW	37330 TQ	USBLS	5/15
	Boston-Cambridge-Newton NECTA, MA	Y	29430 FQ	34790 MW	40390 TQ	USBLS	5/15
	Worcester MSA, MA-CT	Y	25890 FQ	30210 MW	35550 TQ	USBLS	5/15
	Michigan	Y	19390 FQ	24200 MW	31050 TQ	USBLS	5/15
	Detroit-Dearborn-Livonia PMSA, MI	Y	18670 FQ	24760 MW	34170 TQ	USBLS	5/15
	Grand Rapids-Wyoming MSA, MI	Y	18380 FQ	19670 MW	25970 TQ	USBLS	5/15
	Minnesota	Y	21068 FQ	24707 MW	29939 TQ	MNBLS	1/16-3/16
	Minneapolis-St. Paul-Bloomington MSA, MN-WI	Y	22469 FQ	26885 MW	31108 TQ	MNBLS	1/16-3/16
	Mississippi	Y	17450 FQ	19410 MW	24380 TQ	USBLS	5/15
	Jackson MSA, MS	Y	17350 FQ	19060 MW	27110 TQ	USBLS	5/15
	Missouri	Y	18860 FQ	22950 MW	28730 TQ	USBLS	5/15
	Kansas City MSA, MO-KS	Y	21690 FQ	26540 MW	31300 TQ	USBLS	5/15
	St. Louis MSA, MO-IL	Y	19130 FQ	25230 MW	30980 TQ	USBLS	5/15
	Montana	Y	18480 FQ	21040 MW	26850 TQ	USBLS	5/15
	Billings MSA, MT	Y	22320 FQ	25760 MW	29760 TQ	USBLS	5/15
	Nebraska	Y	19060 FQ	23015 MW	28555 TQ	NEBLS	7/16-9/16
	Omaha-Council Bluffs MSA, NE-IA	Y	25240 FQ	28625 MW	33215 TQ	NEBLS	7/16-9/16
	Nevada	Y	24340 FQ	28530 MW	35810 TQ	USBLS	5/15
	Las Vegas-Henderson-Paradise MSA, NV	Y	25940 FQ	29870 MW	39900 TQ	USBLS	5/15
	New Hampshire	H	10.17 AE	12.44 MW	14.37 AEX	NHBLS	6/16
	Manchester NECTA, NH	H	9.78 AE	11.23 MW	12.78 AEX	NHBLS	6/16
	Nashua NECTA, NH-MA	Y	23770 FQ	28100 MW	33210 TQ	USBLS	5/15
	New Jersey	Y	19400 FQ	27190 MW	36130 TQ	USBLS	5/15
	Camden PMSA, NJ	Y	21230 FQ	27900 MW	35670 TQ	USBLS	5/15
	Newark PMSA, NJ-PA	Y	18620 FQ	19780 MW	30680 TQ	USBLS	5/15
	Trenton MSA, NJ	Y	29460 FQ	34780 MW	40720 TQ	USBLS	5/15
	New Mexico	Y	18970 FQ	22270 MW	26050 TQ	USBLS	5/15
	Albuquerque MSA, NM	Y	20980 FQ	22630 MW	24270 TQ	USBLS	5/15
	New York	Y	20620 AE	28560 MW	35550 AEX	NYBLS	1/16-3/16
	Buffalo-Cheektowaga-Niagara Falls MSA, NY	Y	20940 FQ	24050 MW	29870 TQ	USBLS	5/15
	Nassau County-Suffolk County PMSA, NY	Y	24770 FQ	30450 MW	36210 TQ	USBLS	5/15
	New York-Jersey City-White Plains PMSA, NY-NJ	Y	19720 FQ	29980 MW	44490 TQ	USBLS	5/15
	Rochester MSA, NY	Y	22740 FQ	27520 MW	33330 TQ	USBLS	5/15
	North Carolina	Y	20880 FQ	25990 MW	33260 TQ	USBLS	5/15
	Charlotte-Concord-Gastonia MSA, NC-SC	Y	21250 FQ	25590 MW	38790 TQ	USBLS	5/15

AE	Average entry wage	AWR	Average wage range	H	Hourly	LR	Low end range	MTC	Median total compensation
AEX	Average experienced wage	B	Biweekly	HI	Highest wage paid	M	Monthly	MW	Median wage paid
ATC	Average total compensation	D	Daily	HR	High end range	MCC	Median cash compensation	MWR	Median wage range
AW	Average wage paid	FQ	First quartile wage	LO	Lowest wage paid	ME	Median entry wage	S	See annotated source

TCC Total cash compensation
TQ Third quartile wage
W Weekly
Y Yearly

Occupation/Type/Industry	Location	Per	Low	Mid	High	Source	Date
Floral Designer	Raleigh MSA, NC	Y	31510 FQ	36940 MW	42920 TQ	USBLS	5/15
	North Dakota	Y	19810 FQ	23300 MW	28270 TQ	USBLS	5/15
	Fargo MSA, ND-MN	Y	20410 FQ	22540 MW	24670 TQ	USBLS	5/15
	Ohio	Y	19800 FQ	22800 MW	27400 TQ	USBLS	5/15
	Cincinnati MSA, OH-KY-IN	Y	18520 FQ	22160 MW	31680 TQ	USBLS	5/15
	Cleveland-Elyria MSA, OH	Y	20730 FQ	23550 MW	27880 TQ	USBLS	5/15
	Columbus MSA, OH	Y	19450 FQ	24280 MW	29560 TQ	USBLS	5/15
	Oklahoma	Y	20100 FQ	23830 MW	29080 TQ	USBLS	5/15
	Oklahoma City MSA, OK	Y	22440 FQ	27130 MW	32200 TQ	USBLS	5/15
	Tulsa MSA, OK	Y	20630 FQ	24170 MW	29750 TQ	USBLS	5/15
	Oregon	H	9.70 FQ	11.19 MW	13.64 TQ	ORBLS	2016
	Portland-Vancouver-Hillsboro MSA, OR-WA	Y	19760 FQ	22380 MW	28160 TQ	USBLS	5/15
	Pennsylvania	Y	21640 FQ	26160 MW	32820 TQ	USBLS	5/15
	Allentown-Bethlehem-Easton MSA, PA-NJ	Y	20610 FQ	23280 MW	29450 TQ	USBLS	5/15
	Harrisburg-Carlisle MSA, PA	Y	21480 FQ	25410 MW	29330 TQ	USBLS	5/15
	Montgomery County-Bucks County-Chester County PMSA, PA	Y	22290 FQ	26120 MW	31300 TQ	USBLS	5/15
	Philadelphia PMSA, PA	Y	30420 FQ	34280 MW	37580 TQ	USBLS	5/15
	Pittsburgh MSA, PA	Y	24160 FQ	29060 MW	34610 TQ	USBLS	5/15
	Rhode Island	Y	21440 FQ	24230 MW	41410 TQ	USBLS	5/15
	Providence-Warwick MSA, RI-MA	Y	21620 FQ	24680 MW	40000 TQ	USBLS	5/15
	South Carolina	Y	21250 FQ	24320 MW	28260 TQ	USBLS	5/15
	Charleston-North Charleston MSA, SC	Y	21170 FQ	24450 MW	29100 TQ	USBLS	5/15
	Columbia MSA, SC	Y	22540 FQ	25090 MW	28510 TQ	USBLS	5/15
	Greenville-Anderson-Mauldin MSA, SC	Y	21560 FQ	24580 MW	28340 TQ	USBLS	5/15
	South Dakota	Y	21440 FQ	25150 MW	28990 TQ	USBLS	5/15
	Sioux Falls MSA, SD	Y	22690 FQ	25610 MW	28910 TQ	USBLS	5/15
	Tennessee	Y	20430 FQ	23790 MW	30290 TQ	USBLS	5/15
	Knoxville MSA, TN	Y	20800 FQ	23600 MW	27750 TQ	USBLS	5/15
	Memphis MSA, TN-MS-AR	Y	21130 FQ	23120 MW	26760 TQ	USBLS	5/15
	Nashville-Davidson–Murfreesboro–Franklin MSA, TN	Y	22520 FQ	30840 MW	36640 TQ	USBLS	5/15
	Texas	Y	19760 FQ	23480 MW	29420 TQ	USBLS	5/15
	Austin-Round Rock MSA, TX	Y	25390 FQ	28840 MW	32470 TQ	USBLS	5/15
	Dallas-Plano-Irving PMSA, TX	Y	20870 FQ	26210 MW	31670 TQ	USBLS	5/15
	Fort Worth-Arlington PMSA, TX	Y	20690 FQ	24660 MW	32920 TQ	USBLS	5/15
	Houston-The Woodlands-Sugar Land MSA, TX	Y	19780 FQ	24340 MW	31060 TQ	USBLS	5/15
	San Antonio-New Braunfels MSA, TX	Y	20940 FQ	24030 MW	28610 TQ	USBLS	5/15
	Utah	Y	19430 FQ	22170 MW	25500 TQ	USBLS	5/15
	Ogden-Clearfield MSA, UT	Y	19480 FQ	22700 MW	28070 TQ	USBLS	5/15
	Provo-Orem MSA, UT	Y	18210 FQ	20610 MW	23560 TQ	USBLS	5/15
	Salt Lake City MSA, UT	Y	20560 FQ	22980 MW	27130 TQ	USBLS	5/15
	Vermont	Y	21400 FQ	24450 MW	30490 TQ	USBLS	5/15
	Burlington-South Burlington MSA, VT	Y	21830 FQ	23970 MW	30090 TQ	USBLS	5/15
	Virginia	Y	20680 FQ	23740 MW	30690 TQ	USBLS	5/15
	Richmond MSA, VA	Y	21870 FQ	24280 MW	30210 TQ	USBLS	5/15
	Virginia Beach-Norfolk-Newport News MSA, VA-NC	Y	19460 FQ	23210 MW	29190 TQ	USBLS	5/15
	Washington	H	11.10 FQ	13.94 MW	17.74 TQ	WABLS	3/16
	Seattle-Bellevue-Everett PMSA, WA	H	12.15 FQ	15.09 MW	19.27 TQ	WABLS	3/16
	Tacoma-Lakewood PMSA, WA	H	12.20 FQ	14.27 MW	17.78 TQ	WABLS	3/16
	West Virginia	Y	17760 FQ	18870 MW	21420 TQ	USBLS	5/15
	Huntington-Ashland MSA, WV-KY-OH	Y	17820 FQ	19120 MW	22900 TQ	USBLS	5/15
	Wisconsin	Y	21310 FQ	25200 MW	29970 TQ	USBLS	5/15
	Madison MSA, WI	Y	21690 FQ	26860 MW	32150 TQ	USBLS	5/15
	Milwaukee-Waukesha-West Allis MSA, WI	Y	23250 FQ	27140 MW	31110 TQ	USBLS	5/15
	Wyoming	Y	20860 FQ	27240 MW	33380 TQ	USBLS	5/15
	Puerto Rico	Y	17860 FQ	20070 MW	25890 TQ	USBLS	5/15

AE	Average entry wage	AWR	Average wage range	H	Hourly
AEX	Average experienced wage	B	Biweekly	HI	Highest wage paid
ATC	Average total compensation	D	Daily	HR	High end range
AW	Average wage paid	FQ	First quartile wage	LO	Lowest wage paid

LR	Low end range	MTC	Median total compensation	TCC	Total cash compensation
M	Monthly	MW	Median wage paid	TQ	Third quartile wage
MCC	Median cash compensation	MWR	Median wage range	W	Weekly
ME	Median entry wage	S	See annotated source	Y	Yearly

Occupation/Type/Industry	Location	Per	Low	Mid	High	Source	Date
Floral Designer	San Juan-Carolina-Caguas MSA, PR	Y	18210 FQ	21190 MW	28510 TQ	USBLS	5/15
Floriculture Supervisor							
Municipal Government	Detroit, MI	M	3608 LO		4108 HI	DETGOV	2016
FOIA Specialist							
United States Postal Service	District of Columbia	Y			56910 HI	APP02	1/16
Food and Beverage Professional	United States	Y		85000 MW		FOODP	2016
Food and Tobacco Roasting, Baking, and Drying Machine Operator and Tender							
	Alabama	Y	20009 AE	28266 AW	32399 AEX	ALBLS	6/16
	Birmingham-Hoover MSA, AL	Y	25818 AE	31165 AW	33839 AEX	ALBLS	6/16
	Alaska	Y	25710 FQ	29930 MW	39620 TQ	USBLS	5/15
	Arizona	Y	24990 FQ	28760 MW	34600 TQ	USBLS	5/15
	Phoenix-Mesa-Scottsdale MSA, AZ	Y	25210 FQ	28840 MW	37430 TQ	USBLS	5/15
	Arkansas	Y	17930 FQ	20290 MW	30960 TQ	USBLS	5/15
	California	H	10.33 FQ	12.69 MW	17.35 TQ	CABLS	1/16-3/16
	Anaheim-Santa Ana-Irvine PMSA, CA	H	11.98 FQ	13.85 MW	16.90 TQ	CABLS	1/16-3/16
	Los Angeles-Long Beach-Glendale PMSA, CA	H	10.93 FQ	13.28 MW	17.41 TQ	CABLS	1/16-3/16
	Oakland-Hayward-Berkeley PMSA, CA	H	13.43 FQ	14.89 MW	19.87 TQ	CABLS	1/16-3/16
	Riverside-San Bernardino-Ontario MSA, CA	H	10.72 FQ	12.17 MW	17.14 TQ	CABLS	1/16-3/16
	San Diego-Carlsbad MSA, CA	H	9.97 FQ	11.08 MW	14.70 TQ	CABLS	1/16-3/16
	Colorado	Y	23300 FQ	32110 MW	46340 TQ	USBLS	5/15
	Denver-Aurora-Lakewood MSA, CO	Y	27040 FQ	38990 MW	66040 TQ	USBLS	5/15
	Connecticut	Y		31133 MW		CTBLS	1/16-3/16
	Hartford-West Hartford-East Hartford MSA, CT	Y	23070 FQ	29770 MW	35680 TQ	USBLS	5/15
	Florida	H	9.75 AE	13.96 MW	18.36 AEX	FLBLS	7/16-9/16
	Miami-Miami Beach-Kendall PMSA, FL	H	9.20 AE	12.47 MW	18.12 AEX	FLBLS	7/16-9/16
	Orlando-Kissimmee-Sanford MSA, FL	H	9.12 AE	16.43 MW	18.44 AEX	FLBLS	7/16-9/16
	Tampa-St. Petersburg-Clearwater MSA, FL	H	9.15 AE	11.93 MW	15.50 AEX	FLBLS	7/16-9/16
	Georgia	Y	21900 FQ	26180 MW	30750 TQ	USBLS	5/15
	Atlanta-Sandy Springs-Roswell MSA, GA	Y	22380 FQ	26630 MW	31020 TQ	USBLS	5/15
	Hawaii	Y	27040 FQ	33870 MW	42130 TQ	USBLS	5/15
	Urban Honolulu MSA, HI	Y	23980 FQ	29970 MW	36380 TQ	USBLS	5/15
	Idaho	Y	23450 FQ	28880 MW	35390 TQ	USBLS	5/15
	Boise City MSA, ID	Y	24330 FQ	32000 MW	41010 TQ	USBLS	5/15
	Illinois	Y	20360 FQ	26860 MW	34100 TQ	USBLS	5/15
	Chicago-Naperville-Arlington Heights PMSA, IL	Y	19740 FQ	26640 MW	33300 TQ	USBLS	5/15
	Indiana	Y	25180 FQ	27900 MW	30590 TQ	USBLS	5/15
	Gary PMSA, IN	Y	19430 FQ	24980 MW	31310 TQ	USBLS	5/15
	Indianapolis-Carmel-Anderson MSA, IN	Y	26340 FQ	29000 MW	31640 TQ	USBLS	5/15
	Iowa	Y	26910 FQ	31430 MW	41670 TQ	USBLS	5/15
	Kansas	Y	21700 FQ	28600 MW	34930 TQ	USBLS	5/15
	Kentucky	Y	26600 FQ	29800 MW	35300 TQ	USBLS	5/15
	Louisville-Jefferson County MSA, KY-IN	Y	27150 FQ	29190 MW	31230 TQ	USBLS	5/15
	Louisiana	Y	24890 FQ	28560 MW	33740 TQ	USBLS	5/15
	Maine	Y	21890 FQ	25560 MW	30510 TQ	USBLS	5/15
	Massachusetts	Y	23140 FQ	28370 MW	34250 TQ	USBLS	5/15
	Boston-Cambridge-Newton NECTA, MA	Y	24110 FQ	28220 MW	32530 TQ	USBLS	5/15
	Michigan	Y	21560 FQ	26450 MW	30570 TQ	USBLS	5/15
	Grand Rapids-Wyoming MSA, MI	Y	19680 FQ	25230 MW	30420 TQ	USBLS	5/15
	Minnesota	Y	29604 FQ	34848 MW	40022 TQ	MNBLS	1/16-3/16

Occupation/Type/Industry	Location	Per	Low	Mid	High	Source	Date
Food and Tobacco Roasting, Baking, and Drying Machine Operator and Tender	Minneapolis-St. Paul-Bloomington MSA, MN-WI	Y	23428 FQ	28642 MW	35820 TQ	MNBLS	1/16-3/16
	Mississippi	Y	20760 FQ	23430 MW	33260 TQ	USBLS	5/15
	Missouri	Y	22000 FQ	25670 MW	31600 TQ	USBLS	5/15
	Kansas City MSA, MO-KS	Y	19570 FQ	23790 MW	31030 TQ	USBLS	5/15
	St. Louis MSA, MO-IL	Y	21560 FQ	24320 MW	31320 TQ	USBLS	5/15
	Montana	Y	22150 FQ	26640 MW	34470 TQ	USBLS	5/15
	Nebraska	Y	28690 FQ	36385 MW	46665 TQ	NEBLS	7/16-9/16
	Omaha-Council Bluffs MSA, NE-IA	Y	27785 FQ	52495 MW	58430 TQ	NEBLS	7/16-9/16
	Nevada	Y	21930 FQ	23900 MW	30940 TQ	USBLS	5/15
	New Jersey	Y	21110 FQ	26450 MW	35300 TQ	USBLS	5/15
	Camden PMSA, NJ	Y	19500 FQ	22160 MW	27190 TQ	USBLS	5/15
	Newark PMSA, NJ-PA	Y	25040 FQ	29310 MW	41180 TQ	USBLS	5/15
	New Mexico	Y	21920 FQ	25570 MW	36300 TQ	USBLS	5/15
	New York	Y	21920 AE	30390 MW	39370 AEX	NYBLS	1/16-3/16
	Nassau County-Suffolk County PMSA, NY	Y	29550 FQ	35170 MW	42240 TQ	USBLS	5/15
	New York-Jersey City-White Plains PMSA, NY-NJ	Y	25010 FQ	30040 MW	41410 TQ	USBLS	5/15
	North Carolina	Y	36540 FQ	50700 MW	56980 TQ	USBLS	5/15
	North Dakota	Y	25440 FQ	28510 MW	32380 TQ	USBLS	5/15
	Ohio	Y	23150 FQ	27510 MW	31440 TQ	USBLS	5/15
	Cincinnati MSA, OH-KY-IN	Y	22560 FQ	25820 MW	29130 TQ	USBLS	5/15
	Cleveland-Elyria MSA, OH	Y	25720 FQ	29470 MW	35110 TQ	USBLS	5/15
	Columbus MSA, OH	Y	25710 FQ	28920 MW	33710 TQ	USBLS	5/15
	Oklahoma	Y	22180 FQ	26550 MW	30860 TQ	USBLS	5/15
	Tulsa MSA, OK	Y	20570 FQ	24200 MW	35800 TQ	USBLS	5/15
	Oregon	H	13.60 FQ	15.49 MW	20.44 TQ	ORBLS	2016
	Portland-Vancouver-Hillsboro MSA, OR-WA	Y	27940 FQ	31670 MW	43250 TQ	USBLS	5/15
	Pennsylvania	Y	22620 FQ	28500 MW	37560 TQ	USBLS	5/15
	Montgomery County-Bucks County-Chester County PMSA, PA	Y	25790 FQ	31610 MW	35950 TQ	USBLS	5/15
	Philadelphia PMSA, PA	Y	23520 FQ	33740 MW	43440 TQ	USBLS	5/15
	Pittsburgh MSA, PA	Y	22680 FQ	25550 MW	29770 TQ	USBLS	5/15
	Providence-Warwick MSA, RI-MA	Y	23310 FQ	26840 MW	29680 TQ	USBLS	5/15
	South Carolina	Y	31790 FQ	41720 MW	46270 TQ	USBLS	5/15
	South Dakota	Y	23680 FQ	28130 MW	32710 TQ	USBLS	5/15
	Tennessee	Y	27010 FQ	37250 MW	44610 TQ	USBLS	5/15
	Knoxville MSA, TN	Y	27120 FQ	30350 MW	36430 TQ	USBLS	5/15
	Memphis MSA, TN-MS-AR	Y	22070 FQ	44180 MW	50250 TQ	USBLS	5/15
	Nashville-Davidson–Murfreesboro–Franklin MSA, TN	Y	29240 FQ	42230 MW	45810 TQ	USBLS	5/15
	Texas	Y	19140 FQ	23360 MW	30480 TQ	USBLS	5/15
	Austin-Round Rock MSA, TX	Y	20830 FQ	23740 MW	31620 TQ	USBLS	5/15
	Dallas-Plano-Irving PMSA, TX	Y	18850 FQ	23080 MW	29610 TQ	USBLS	5/15
	Fort Worth-Arlington PMSA, TX	Y	19740 FQ	23350 MW	29340 TQ	USBLS	5/15
	Houston-The Woodlands-Sugar Land MSA, TX	Y	18810 FQ	24930 MW	32110 TQ	USBLS	5/15
	San Antonio-New Braunfels MSA, TX	Y	19460 FQ	23490 MW	32920 TQ	USBLS	5/15
	Utah	Y	25370 FQ	32090 MW	37310 TQ	USBLS	5/15
	Provo-Orem MSA, UT	Y	22920 FQ	25980 MW	30140 TQ	USBLS	5/15
	Vermont	Y	32970 FQ	37860 MW	43930 TQ	USBLS	5/15
	Virginia	Y	19400 FQ	24070 MW	29520 TQ	USBLS	5/15
	Richmond MSA, VA	Y	21640 FQ	24310 MW	27970 TQ	USBLS	5/15
	Virginia Beach-Norfolk-Newport News MSA, VA-NC	Y	17050 FQ	18450 MW	19860 TQ	USBLS	5/15
	Washington	H	13.59 FQ	15.75 MW	19.04 TQ	WABLS	3/16
	Seattle-Bellevue-Everett PMSA, WA	H	13.57 FQ	15.15 MW	19.63 TQ	WABLS	3/16
	Tacoma-Lakewood PMSA, WA	H	15.76 FQ	18.62 MW	22.05 TQ	WABLS	3/16
	West Virginia	Y	20600 FQ	25460 MW	29980 TQ	USBLS	5/15
	Wisconsin	Y	18970 FQ	26230 MW	37020 TQ	USBLS	5/15

AE	Average entry wage	AWR	Average wage range	H	Hourly
AEX	Average experienced wage	B	Biweekly	HI	Highest wage paid
ATC	Average total compensation	D	Daily	HR	High end range
AW	Average wage paid	FQ	First quartile wage	LO	Lowest wage paid

LR	Low end range	MTC	Median total compensation
M	Monthly	MW	Median wage paid
MCC	Median cash compensation	MWR	Median wage range
ME	Median entry wage	S	See annotated source

TCC	Total cash compensation	
TQ	Third quartile wage	
W	Weekly	
Y	Yearly	

Occupation/Type/Industry	Location	Per	Low	Mid	High	Source	Date
Food and Tobacco Roasting, Baking, and Drying Machine Operator and Tender	Madison MSA, WI	Y	19870 FQ	27590 MW	33730 TQ	USBLS	5/15
	Milwaukee-Waukesha-West Allis MSA, WI	Y	21670 FQ	28800 MW	40780 TQ	USBLS	5/15
	Puerto Rico	Y	17780 FQ	19890 MW	23170 TQ	USBLS	5/15
	San Juan-Carolina-Caguas MSA, PR	Y	18390 FQ	20930 MW	23750 TQ	USBLS	5/15
Food Batchmaker	Alabama	Y	20739 AE	27248 AW	30507 AEX	ALBLS	6/16
	Birmingham-Hoover MSA, AL	Y	20081 AE	27782 AW	31628 AEX	ALBLS	6/16
	Mobile MSA, AL	Y	22580 AE	27052 AW	29294 AEX	ALBLS	6/16
	Alaska	Y	19020 FQ	20890 MW	24820 TQ	USBLS	5/15
	Anchorage MSA, AK	Y	19700 FQ	23540 MW	31300 TQ	USBLS	5/15
	Arizona	Y	20300 FQ	23200 MW	29680 TQ	USBLS	5/15
	Phoenix-Mesa-Scottsdale MSA, AZ	Y	20770 FQ	23620 MW	30630 TQ	USBLS	5/15
	Tucson MSA, AZ	Y	19170 FQ	22210 MW	30130 TQ	USBLS	5/15
	Arkansas	Y	20560 FQ	23180 MW	27930 TQ	USBLS	5/15
	Little Rock-North Little Rock-Conway MSA, AR	Y	19180 FQ	22490 MW	27880 TQ	USBLS	5/15
	California	H	9.89 FQ	11.85 MW	14.77 TQ	CABLS	1/16-3/16
	Anaheim-Santa Ana-Irvine PMSA, CA	H	9.67 FQ	11.18 MW	14.65 TQ	CABLS	1/16-3/16
	Los Angeles-Long Beach-Glendale PMSA, CA	H	9.56 FQ	10.88 MW	13.88 TQ	CABLS	1/16-3/16
	Oakland-Hayward-Berkeley PMSA, CA	H	10.86 FQ	12.68 MW	14.83 TQ	CABLS	1/16-3/16
	Riverside-San Bernardino-Ontario MSA, CA	H	10.27 FQ	12.54 MW	14.26 TQ	CABLS	1/16-3/16
	Sacramento–Roseville–Arden-Arcade MSA, CA	H	11.27 FQ	13.18 MW	14.57 TQ	CABLS	1/16-3/16
	San Diego-Carlsbad MSA, CA	H	9.64 FQ	10.84 MW	12.66 TQ	CABLS	1/16-3/16
	San Francisco-Redwood City-South San Francisco PMSA, CA	H	10.66 FQ	12.01 MW	14.29 TQ	CABLS	1/16-3/16
	Colorado	Y	20710 FQ	25340 MW	31470 TQ	USBLS	5/15
	Denver-Aurora-Lakewood MSA, CO	Y	21070 FQ	25290 MW	30340 TQ	USBLS	5/15
	Connecticut	Y		26274 MW		CTBLS	1/16-3/16
	Bridgeport-Stamford-Norwalk MSA, CT	Y	24080 FQ	34160 MW	49730 TQ	USBLS	5/15
	Hartford-West Hartford-East Hartford MSA, CT	Y	19170 FQ	21660 MW	27350 TQ	USBLS	5/15
	Delaware	Y	20980 FQ	22820 MW	24660 TQ	USBLS	5/15
	Washington-Arlington-Alexandria PMSA, DC-VA-MD-WV	Y	20330 FQ	24220 MW	31160 TQ	USBLS	5/15
	Florida	H	9.47 AE	11.59 MW	14.02 AEX	FLBLS	7/16-9/16
	Fort Lauderdale-Pompano Beach-Deerfield Beach PMSA, FL	H	9.48 AE	11.91 MW	14.30 AEX	FLBLS	7/16-9/16
	Miami-Miami Beach-Kendall PMSA, FL	H	9.16 AE	10.83 MW	13.07 AEX	FLBLS	7/16-9/16
	Orlando-Kissimmee-Sanford MSA, FL	H	9.00 AE	10.42 MW	12.64 AEX	FLBLS	7/16-9/16
	Tampa-St. Petersburg-Clearwater MSA, FL	H	9.20 AE	12.40 MW	14.81 AEX	FLBLS	7/16-9/16
	Georgia	Y	20580 FQ	26760 MW	31680 TQ	USBLS	5/15
	Atlanta-Sandy Springs-Roswell MSA, GA	Y	19590 FQ	25720 MW	31020 TQ	USBLS	5/15
	Augusta-Richmond County MSA, GA-SC	Y	19440 FQ	32480 MW	38850 TQ	USBLS	5/15
	Hawaii	Y	18470 FQ	21900 MW	27980 TQ	USBLS	5/15
	Urban Honolulu MSA, HI	Y	18250 FQ	21040 MW	27130 TQ	USBLS	5/15
	Idaho	Y	23570 FQ	28160 MW	33200 TQ	USBLS	5/15
	Boise City MSA, ID	Y	22200 FQ	26040 MW	30030 TQ	USBLS	5/15
	Illinois	Y	22290 FQ	28730 MW	38300 TQ	USBLS	5/15
	Chicago-Naperville-Arlington Heights PMSA, IL	Y	21770 FQ	28220 MW	38530 TQ	USBLS	5/15

AE	Average entry wage	AWR	Average wage range	H	Hourly
AEX	Average experienced wage	B	Biweekly	HI	Highest wage paid
ATC	Average total compensation	D	Daily	HR	High end range
AW	Average wage paid	FQ	First quartile wage	LO	Lowest wage paid

LR	Low end range	MTC	Median total compensation	TCC	Total cash compensation
M	Monthly	MW	Median wage paid	TQ	Third quartile wage
MCC	Median cash compensation	MWR	Median wage range	W	Weekly
ME	Median entry wage	S	See annotated source	Y	Yearly

Occupation/Type/Industry	Location	Per	Low	Mid	High	Source	Date
Food Batchmaker	Lake County-Kenosha County						
	PMSA, IL-WI	Y	17060 FQ	18600 MW	22250 TQ	USBLS	5/15
	Indiana	Y	21330 FQ	24910 MW	30960 TQ	USBLS	5/15
	Gary PMSA, IN	Y	21650 FQ	24270 MW	32610 TQ	USBLS	5/15
	Indianapolis-Carmel-Anderson						
	MSA, IN	Y	22190 FQ	27110 MW	34610 TQ	USBLS	5/15
	Iowa	Y	27330 FQ	38340 MW	49650 TQ	USBLS	5/15
	Des Moines-West Des Moines						
	MSA, IA	Y	23960 FQ	34390 MW	42810 TQ	USBLS	5/15
	Kansas	Y	21870 FQ	29660 MW	36910 TQ	USBLS	5/15
	Wichita MSA, KS	Y	25180 FQ	32710 MW	36490 TQ	USBLS	5/15
	Kentucky	Y	22850 FQ	28880 MW	38130 TQ	USBLS	5/15
	Louisville-Jefferson County						
	MSA, KY-IN	Y	21960 FQ	25790 MW	32310 TQ	USBLS	5/15
	Louisiana	Y	18660 FQ	22840 MW	29540 TQ	USBLS	5/15
	Baton Rouge MSA, LA	Y	20070 FQ	25360 MW	32970 TQ	USBLS	5/15
	New Orleans-Metairie MSA,						
	LA	Y	19700 FQ	24880 MW	29760 TQ	USBLS	5/15
	Maine	Y	25870 FQ	31420 MW	38070 TQ	USBLS	5/15
	Portland-South Portland MSA,						
	ME	Y	23200 FQ	27220 MW	31600 TQ	USBLS	5/15
	Maryland	Y	20915 AE	33620 MW	39973 AEX	MDBLS	4/16
	Baltimore-Columbia-Towson						
	MSA, MD	Y	25990 FQ	36490 MW	45090 TQ	USBLS	5/15
	Salisbury MSA, MD-DE	Y	20080 FQ	22750 MW	25530 TQ	USBLS	5/15
	Massachusetts	Y	22080 FQ	26710 MW	31810 TQ	USBLS	5/15
	Boston-Cambridge-Newton						
	NECTA, MA	Y	23710 FQ	28210 MW	33830 TQ	USBLS	5/15
	Worcester MSA, MA-CT	Y	22690 FQ	26470 MW	39350 TQ	USBLS	5/15
	Michigan	Y	23970 FQ	30950 MW	37880 TQ	USBLS	5/15
	Detroit-Dearborn-Livonia						
	PMSA, MI	Y	24880 FQ	33230 MW	45120 TQ	USBLS	5/15
	Grand Rapids-Wyoming MSA,						
	MI	Y	24640 FQ	32290 MW	37190 TQ	USBLS	5/15
	Minnesota	Y	25868 FQ	30819 MW	43444 TQ	MNBLS	1/16-3/16
	Minneapolis-St. Paul-						
	Bloomington MSA, MN-WI	Y	24896 FQ	29240 MW	40721 TQ	MNBLS	1/16-3/16
	Mississippi	Y	20710 FQ	26070 MW	33670 TQ	USBLS	5/15
	Jackson MSA, MS	Y	20760 FQ	24590 MW	28400 TQ	USBLS	5/15
	Missouri	Y	23140 FQ	32320 MW	38340 TQ	USBLS	5/15
	Kansas City MSA, MO-KS	Y	19660 FQ	25760 MW	32430 TQ	USBLS	5/15
	St. Louis MSA, MO-IL	Y	20980 FQ	27980 MW	37110 TQ	USBLS	5/15
	Montana	Y	21520 FQ	24350 MW	29330 TQ	USBLS	5/15
	Billings MSA, MT	Y	21970 FQ	24480 MW	30780 TQ	USBLS	5/15
	Nebraska	Y	22145 FQ	26075 MW	29900 TQ	NEBLS	7/16-9/16
	Omaha-Council Bluffs MSA,						
	NE-IA	Y	22545 FQ	27280 MW	35115 TQ	NEBLS	7/16-9/16
	Nevada	Y	21170 FQ	25560 MW	32950 TQ	USBLS	5/15
	Las Vegas-Henderson-Paradise						
	MSA, NV	Y	21510 FQ	25960 MW	33500 TQ	USBLS	5/15
	New Hampshire	H	10.03 AE	12.22 MW	14.77 AEX	NHBLS	6/16
	Manchester NECTA, NH	H	10.34 AE	11.37 MW	12.56 AEX	NHBLS	6/16
	Nashua NECTA, NH-MA	Y	20710 FQ	24180 MW	28330 TQ	USBLS	5/15
	New Jersey	Y	20850 FQ	26530 MW	36920 TQ	USBLS	5/15
	Camden PMSA, NJ	Y	21930 FQ	24330 MW	30760 TQ	USBLS	5/15
	Newark PMSA, NJ-PA	Y	19200 FQ	22530 MW	29770 TQ	USBLS	5/15
	Trenton MSA, NJ	Y	26330 FQ	33660 MW	39620 TQ	USBLS	5/15
	New Mexico	Y	18700 FQ	23690 MW	31470 TQ	USBLS	5/15
	Albuquerque MSA, NM	Y	22230 FQ	27190 MW	32490 TQ	USBLS	5/15
	New York	Y	19750 AE	24590 MW	30980 AEX	NYBLS	1/16-3/16
	Buffalo-Cheektowaga-Niagara						
	Falls MSA, NY	Y	22740 FQ	32730 MW	40430 TQ	USBLS	5/15
	Nassau County-Suffolk County						
	PMSA, NY	Y	19580 FQ	23300 MW	29000 TQ	USBLS	5/15
	New York-Jersey City-White						
	Plains PMSA, NY-NJ	Y	19220 FQ	22200 MW	29070 TQ	USBLS	5/15
	Rochester MSA, NY	Y	23800 FQ	30790 MW	38300 TQ	USBLS	5/15
	North Carolina	Y	19270 FQ	23900 MW	29910 TQ	USBLS	5/15
	Charlotte-Concord-Gastonia						
	MSA, NC-SC	Y	19310 FQ	23450 MW	29740 TQ	USBLS	5/15
	Raleigh MSA, NC	Y	19000 FQ	30640 MW	37100 TQ	USBLS	5/15
	North Dakota	Y	21640 FQ	26990 MW	32220 TQ	USBLS	5/15

AE	Average entry wage	AWR	Average wage range	
AEX	Average experienced wage	B	Biweekly	
ATC	Average total compensation	D	Daily	
AW	Average wage paid	FQ	First quartile wage	

H	Hourly
HI	Highest wage paid
HR	High end range
LO	Lowest wage paid

LR	Low end range
M	Monthly
MCC	Median cash compensation
ME	Median entry wage

MTC	Median total compensation
MW	Median wage paid
MWR	Median wage range
S	See annotated source

TCC	Total cash compensation
TQ	Third quartile wage
W	Weekly
Y	Yearly

Occupation/Type/Industry	Location	Per	Low	Mid	High	Source	Date
Food Batchmaker	Fargo MSA, ND-MN	Y	19600 FQ	24760 MW	33930 TQ	USBLS	5/15
	Ohio	Y	23820 FQ	29300 MW	37760 TQ	USBLS	5/15
	Cincinnati MSA, OH-KY-IN	Y	23860 FQ	28350 MW	34460 TQ	USBLS	5/15
	Cleveland-Elyria MSA, OH	Y	22260 FQ	26140 MW	30500 TQ	USBLS	5/15
	Columbus MSA, OH	Y	25630 FQ	30250 MW	38100 TQ	USBLS	5/15
	Oklahoma	Y	20830 FQ	24040 MW	28160 TQ	USBLS	5/15
	Oklahoma City MSA, OK	Y	17840 FQ	22420 MW	28180 TQ	USBLS	5/15
	Tulsa MSA, OK	Y	22000 FQ	24540 MW	28500 TQ	USBLS	5/15
	Oregon	H	10.38 FQ	12.96 MW	17.31 TQ	ORBLS	2016
	Portland-Vancouver-Hillsboro MSA, OR-WA	Y	22610 FQ	26760 MW	32990 TQ	USBLS	5/15
	Pennsylvania	Y	23140 FQ	31760 MW	40130 TQ	USBLS	5/15
	Allentown-Bethlehem-Easton MSA, PA-NJ	Y	33220 FQ	40290 MW	47050 TQ	USBLS	5/15
	Harrisburg-Carlisle MSA, PA	Y	29720 FQ	34610 MW	38550 TQ	USBLS	5/15
	Montgomery County-Bucks County-Chester County PMSA, PA	Y	25550 FQ	32180 MW	40220 TQ	USBLS	5/15
	Philadelphia PMSA, PA	Y	20420 FQ	27500 MW	37750 TQ	USBLS	5/15
	Pittsburgh MSA, PA	Y	20100 FQ	24280 MW	33110 TQ	USBLS	5/15
	Rhode Island	Y	21510 FQ	26420 MW	31260 TQ	USBLS	5/15
	Providence-Warwick MSA, RI-MA	Y	21410 FQ	26270 MW	31480 TQ	USBLS	5/15
	South Carolina	Y	26100 FQ	28120 MW	30150 TQ	USBLS	5/15
	Charleston-North Charleston MSA, SC	Y	23520 FQ	32760 MW	36480 TQ	USBLS	5/15
	Columbia MSA, SC	Y	21820 FQ	26330 MW	29970 TQ	USBLS	5/15
	Greenville-Anderson-Mauldin MSA, SC	Y	20600 FQ	25240 MW	29730 TQ	USBLS	5/15
	South Dakota	Y	24030 FQ	31480 MW	35820 TQ	USBLS	5/15
	Tennessee	Y	20510 FQ	29540 MW	40310 TQ	USBLS	5/15
	Knoxville MSA, TN	Y	16950 FQ	18820 MW	26550 TQ	USBLS	5/15
	Memphis MSA, TN-MS-AR	Y	28530 FQ	33770 MW	37290 TQ	USBLS	5/15
	Nashville-Davidson–Murfreesboro–Franklin MSA, TN	Y	25690 FQ	40940 MW	46390 TQ	USBLS	5/15
	Texas	Y	18630 FQ	22630 MW	29560 TQ	USBLS	5/15
	Austin-Round Rock MSA, TX	Y	19450 FQ	24940 MW	32550 TQ	USBLS	5/15
	Dallas-Plano-Irving PMSA, TX	Y	18650 FQ	22090 MW	28340 TQ	USBLS	5/15
	Fort Worth-Arlington PMSA, TX	Y	19430 FQ	24490 MW	30550 TQ	USBLS	5/15
	Houston-The Woodlands-Sugar Land MSA, TX	Y	18810 FQ	24640 MW	31200 TQ	USBLS	5/15
	San Antonio-New Braunfels MSA, TX	Y	18640 FQ	22960 MW	31750 TQ	USBLS	5/15
	Utah	Y	20970 FQ	27030 MW	39120 TQ	USBLS	5/15
	Ogden-Clearfield MSA, UT	Y	24790 FQ	33220 MW	39140 TQ	USBLS	5/15
	Provo-Orem MSA, UT	Y	21540 FQ	27070 MW	34450 TQ	USBLS	5/15
	Salt Lake City MSA, UT	Y	18470 FQ	22260 MW	33940 TQ	USBLS	5/15
	Vermont	Y	27470 FQ	33060 MW	42240 TQ	USBLS	5/15
	Burlington-South Burlington MSA, VT	Y	27560 FQ	34040 MW	45320 TQ	USBLS	5/15
	Virginia	Y	20580 FQ	24330 MW	29750 TQ	USBLS	5/15
	Richmond MSA, VA	Y	19770 FQ	24060 MW	30150 TQ	USBLS	5/15
	Virginia Beach-Norfolk-Newport News MSA, VA-NC	Y	22430 FQ	25630 MW	29210 TQ	USBLS	5/15
	Washington	H	11.13 FQ	13.75 MW	17.80 TQ	WABLS	3/16
	Seattle-Bellevue-Everett PMSA, WA	H	10.63 FQ	12.02 MW	16.00 TQ	WABLS	3/16
	Tacoma-Lakewood PMSA, WA	H	12.37 FQ	14.55 MW	17.30 TQ	WABLS	3/16
	West Virginia	Y	17630 FQ	18630 MW	19620 TQ	USBLS	5/15
	Wisconsin	Y	22860 FQ	32170 MW	39390 TQ	USBLS	5/15
	Milwaukee-Waukesha-West Allis MSA, WI	Y	21780 FQ	27770 MW	35640 TQ	USBLS	5/15
	Wyoming	Y	18670 FQ	25440 MW	30140 TQ	USBLS	5/15
	Puerto Rico	Y	16620 FQ	17770 MW	18920 TQ	USBLS	5/15
	San Juan-Carolina-Caguas MSA, PR	Y	16610 FQ	17780 MW	18950 TQ	USBLS	5/15
Food Cooking Machine Operator and Tender	Alabama	Y	20924 AE	27782 AW	31206 AEX	ALBLS	6/16
	Alaska	Y	25440 FQ	31560 MW	36040 TQ	USBLS	5/15

AE	Average entry wage	AWR	Average wage range	H	Hourly	LR	Low end range	MTC	Median total compensation	TCC	Total cash compensation
AEX	Average experienced wage	B	Biweekly	HI	Highest wage paid	M	Monthly	MW	Median wage paid	TQ	Third quartile wage
ATC	Average total compensation	D	Daily	HR	High end range	MCC	Median cash compensation	MWR	Median wage range	W	Weekly
AW	Average wage paid	FQ	First quartile wage	LO	Lowest wage paid	ME	Median entry wage	S	See annotated source	Y	Yearly

657

Occupation/Type/Industry	Location	Per	Low	Mid	High	Source	Date
Food Cooking Machine Operator and Tender	Arizona	Y	23990 FQ	27710 MW	33650 TQ	USBLS	5/15
	Phoenix-Mesa-Scottsdale MSA, AZ	Y	23880 FQ	27590 MW	32530 TQ	USBLS	5/15
	Arkansas	Y	22100 FQ	30250 MW	35630 TQ	USBLS	5/15
	California	H	9.65 FQ	12.02 MW	17.28 TQ	CABLS	1/16-3/16
	Anaheim-Santa Ana-Irvine PMSA, CA	H	9.41 FQ	11.04 MW	17.00 TQ	CABLS	1/16-3/16
	Los Angeles-Long Beach-Glendale PMSA, CA	H	9.42 FQ	10.26 MW	13.72 TQ	CABLS	1/16-3/16
	Oakland-Hayward-Berkeley PMSA, CA	H	9.67 FQ	11.51 MW	13.92 TQ	CABLS	1/16-3/16
	Riverside-San Bernardino-Ontario MSA, CA	H	9.53 FQ	10.44 MW	15.04 TQ	CABLS	1/16-3/16
	Sacramento–Roseville–Arden-Arcade MSA, CA	H	10.83 FQ	15.87 MW	20.60 TQ	CABLS	1/16-3/16
	San Diego-Carlsbad MSA, CA	H	9.38 FQ	11.40 MW	13.85 TQ	CABLS	1/16-3/16
	San Francisco-Redwood City-South San Francisco PMSA, CA	H	19.10 FQ	25.71 MW	28.94 TQ	CABLS	1/16-3/16
	Colorado	Y	19850 FQ	28350 MW	45320 TQ	USBLS	5/15
	Denver-Aurora-Lakewood MSA, CO	Y	22100 FQ	35900 MW	50700 TQ	USBLS	5/15
	Connecticut	Y		28458 MW		CTBLS	1/16-3/16
	Delaware	Y	24790 FQ	27970 MW	31100 TQ	USBLS	5/15
	Florida	H	9.02 AE	9.78 MW	15.32 AEX	FLBLS	7/16-9/16
	Miami-Miami Beach-Kendall PMSA, FL	H	9.11 AE	9.87 MW	12.96 AEX	FLBLS	7/16-9/16
	Orlando-Kissimmee-Sanford MSA, FL	H	10.38 AE	14.49 MW	18.20 AEX	FLBLS	7/16-9/16
	Tampa-St. Petersburg-Clearwater MSA, FL	H	8.99 AE	9.03 MW	9.08 AEX	FLBLS	7/16-9/16
	Georgia	Y	31440 FQ	38600 MW	45590 TQ	USBLS	5/15
	Atlanta-Sandy Springs-Roswell MSA, GA	Y	31260 FQ	38230 MW	45610 TQ	USBLS	5/15
	Hawaii	Y	18320 FQ	21050 MW	24810 TQ	USBLS	5/15
	Urban Honolulu MSA, HI	Y	18320 FQ	21050 MW	24810 TQ	USBLS	5/15
	Idaho	Y	18380 FQ	24040 MW	39660 TQ	USBLS	5/15
	Boise City MSA, ID	Y	19390 FQ	23130 MW	36280 TQ	USBLS	5/15
	Illinois	Y	20960 FQ	26570 MW	31650 TQ	USBLS	5/15
	Chicago-Naperville-Arlington Heights PMSA, IL	Y	19920 FQ	25800 MW	32750 TQ	USBLS	5/15
	Lake County-Kenosha County PMSA, IL-WI	Y	28750 FQ	34350 MW	37980 TQ	USBLS	5/15
	Indiana	Y	25490 FQ	30450 MW	41740 TQ	USBLS	5/15
	Indianapolis-Carmel-Anderson MSA, IN	Y	28100 FQ	38310 MW	53860 TQ	USBLS	5/15
	Iowa	Y	23030 FQ	29770 MW	37150 TQ	USBLS	5/15
	Des Moines-West Des Moines MSA, IA	Y	30100 FQ	34540 MW	38710 TQ	USBLS	5/15
	Kansas	Y	26440 FQ	29090 MW	32360 TQ	USBLS	5/15
	Kentucky	Y	25270 FQ	31830 MW	38000 TQ	USBLS	5/15
	Louisville-Jefferson County MSA, KY-IN	Y	30540 FQ	35720 MW	40970 TQ	USBLS	5/15
	Louisiana	Y	18370 FQ	21530 MW	25990 TQ	USBLS	5/15
	New Orleans-Metairie MSA, LA	Y	25050 FQ	28330 MW	31370 TQ	USBLS	5/15
	Maine	Y	21170 FQ	23160 MW	30860 TQ	USBLS	5/15
	Maryland	Y	19036 AE	26000 MW	29481 AEX	MDBLS	4/16
	Baltimore-Columbia-Towson MSA, MD	Y	19580 FQ	26120 MW	29210 TQ	USBLS	5/15
	Salisbury MSA, MD-DE	Y	24690 FQ	27810 MW	30800 TQ	USBLS	5/15
	Massachusetts	Y	26700 FQ	34730 MW	42250 TQ	USBLS	5/15
	Boston-Cambridge-Newton NECTA, MA	Y	24150 FQ	30080 MW	37240 TQ	USBLS	5/15
	Michigan	Y	19190 FQ	22620 MW	29850 TQ	USBLS	5/15
	Detroit-Dearborn-Livonia PMSA, MI	Y	20660 FQ	23040 MW	26410 TQ	USBLS	5/15
	Grand Rapids-Wyoming MSA, MI	Y	22520 FQ	26860 MW	34260 TQ	USBLS	5/15
	Minnesota	Y	27053 FQ	29553 MW	33087 TQ	MNBLS	1/16-3/16

AE	Average entry wage	AWR	Average wage range	H	Hourly	LR	Low end range
AEX	Average experienced wage	B	Biweekly	HI	Highest wage paid	M	Monthly
ATC	Average total compensation	D	Daily	HR	High end range	MCC	Median cash compensation
AW	Average wage paid	FQ	First quartile wage	LO	Lowest wage paid	ME	Median entry wage

MTC Median total compensation TCC Total cash compensation
MW Median wage paid TQ Third quartile wage
MWR Median wage range W Weekly
S See annotated source Y Yearly

Occupation/Type/Industry	Location	Per	Low	Mid	High	Source	Date
Food Cooking Machine Operator and Tender	Minneapolis-St. Paul-Bloomington MSA, MN-WI	Y	27933 FQ	36853 MW	46461 TQ	MNBLS	1/16-3/16
	Missouri	Y	28180 FQ	33660 MW	37100 TQ	USBLS	5/15
	St. Louis MSA, MO-IL	Y	23840 FQ	32390 MW	36340 TQ	USBLS	5/15
	Nebraska	Y	26435 FQ	29370 MW	35380 TQ	NEBLS	7/16-9/16
	Omaha-Council Bluffs MSA, NE-IA	Y	26745 FQ	31055 MW	42595 TQ	NEBLS	7/16-9/16
	Nevada	Y	21100 FQ	23830 MW	28590 TQ	USBLS	5/15
	Las Vegas-Henderson-Paradise MSA, NV	Y	21010 FQ	23320 MW	27020 TQ	USBLS	5/15
	New Hampshire	H	13.26 AE	15.24 MW	16.90 AEX	NHBLS	6/16
	New Jersey	Y	19870 FQ	23750 MW	30660 TQ	USBLS	5/15
	Camden PMSA, NJ	Y	19100 FQ	26360 MW	32760 TQ	USBLS	5/15
	Newark PMSA, NJ-PA	Y	20040 FQ	24490 MW	28900 TQ	USBLS	5/15
	New Mexico	Y	18610 FQ	21550 MW	24270 TQ	USBLS	5/15
	New York	Y	19800 AE	24590 MW	31220 AEX	NYBLS	1/16-3/16
	Buffalo-Cheektowaga-Niagara Falls MSA, NY	Y	23190 FQ	30710 MW	36730 TQ	USBLS	5/15
	Nassau County-Suffolk County PMSA, NY	Y	23500 FQ	27580 MW	30580 TQ	USBLS	5/15
	New York-Jersey City-White Plains PMSA, NY-NJ	Y	18930 FQ	20180 MW	23390 TQ	USBLS	5/15
	Rochester MSA, NY	Y	31570 FQ	35240 MW	38920 TQ	USBLS	5/15
	North Carolina	Y	17170 FQ	18820 MW	24950 TQ	USBLS	5/15
	Charlotte-Concord-Gastonia MSA, NC-SC	Y	17440 FQ	19020 MW	23360 TQ	USBLS	5/15
	North Dakota	Y	20730 FQ	27710 MW	33620 TQ	USBLS	5/15
	Ohio	Y	21960 FQ	26450 MW	30990 TQ	USBLS	5/15
	Cincinnati MSA, OH-KY-IN	Y	18700 FQ	26490 MW	32420 TQ	USBLS	5/15
	Cleveland-Elyria MSA, OH	Y	21300 FQ	23860 MW	28110 TQ	USBLS	5/15
	Columbus MSA, OH	Y	19960 FQ	26580 MW	41460 TQ	USBLS	5/15
	Oklahoma	Y	22420 FQ	26870 MW	35590 TQ	USBLS	5/15
	Tulsa MSA, OK	Y	22770 FQ	30000 MW	40870 TQ	USBLS	5/15
	Oregon	H	10.45 FQ	11.37 MW	13.01 TQ	ORBLS	2016
	Portland-Vancouver-Hillsboro MSA, OR-WA	Y	23430 FQ	28010 MW	33900 TQ	USBLS	5/15
	Pennsylvania	Y	30590 FQ	35840 MW	41720 TQ	USBLS	5/15
	Allentown-Bethlehem-Easton MSA, PA-NJ	Y	32470 FQ	35060 MW	37660 TQ	USBLS	5/15
	Montgomery County-Bucks County-Chester County PMSA, PA	Y	32510 FQ	36140 MW	39910 TQ	USBLS	5/15
	Philadelphia PMSA, PA	Y	18020 FQ	20200 MW	22860 TQ	USBLS	5/15
	Pittsburgh MSA, PA	Y	33800 FQ	37200 MW	42310 TQ	USBLS	5/15
	Rhode Island	Y	25060 FQ	29090 MW	34710 TQ	USBLS	5/15
	Providence-Warwick MSA, RI-MA	Y	29200 FQ	35020 MW	40950 TQ	USBLS	5/15
	South Carolina	Y	23370 FQ	27640 MW	33460 TQ	USBLS	5/15
	South Dakota	Y	24710 FQ	28520 MW	32880 TQ	USBLS	5/15
	Tennessee	Y	24280 FQ	30020 MW	38880 TQ	USBLS	5/15
	Knoxville MSA, TN	Y	17350 FQ	18830 MW	20190 TQ	USBLS	5/15
	Nashville-Davidson–Murfreesboro–Franklin MSA, TN	Y	24750 FQ	27540 MW	30200 TQ	USBLS	5/15
	Texas	Y	18540 FQ	22970 MW	29080 TQ	USBLS	5/15
	Austin-Round Rock MSA, TX	Y	19150 FQ	24170 MW	28350 TQ	USBLS	5/15
	Dallas-Plano-Irving PMSA, TX	Y	17700 FQ	20090 MW	27670 TQ	USBLS	5/15
	Fort Worth-Arlington PMSA, TX	Y	20700 FQ	24530 MW	28190 TQ	USBLS	5/15
	Houston-The Woodlands-Sugar Land MSA, TX	Y	19280 FQ	25360 MW	29840 TQ	USBLS	5/15
	San Antonio-New Braunfels MSA, TX	Y	19650 FQ	21860 MW	24090 TQ	USBLS	5/15
	Utah	Y	21450 FQ	27750 MW	34680 TQ	USBLS	5/15
	Salt Lake City MSA, UT	Y	24510 FQ	29640 MW	35690 TQ	USBLS	5/15
	Vermont	Y	26540 FQ	28600 MW	30650 TQ	USBLS	5/15
	Virginia	Y	18050 FQ	20250 MW	28590 TQ	USBLS	5/15
	Washington	H	13.42 FQ	16.25 MW	18.11 TQ	WABLS	3/16
	Seattle-Bellevue-Everett PMSA, WA	H	11.59 FQ	13.85 MW	16.20 TQ	WABLS	3/16
	Wisconsin	Y	26960 FQ	32790 MW	39620 TQ	USBLS	5/15

AE	Average entry wage	AWR	Average wage range	H	Hourly	LR	Low end range	MTC Median total compensation	TCC Total cash compensation
AEX	Average experienced wage	B	Biweekly	HI	Highest wage paid	M	Monthly	MW Median wage paid	TQ Third quartile wage
ATC	Average total compensation	D	Daily	HR	High end range	MCC Median cash compensation	MWR Median wage range	W Weekly
AW	Average wage paid	FQ	First quartile wage	LO	Lowest wage paid	ME Median entry wage	S See annotated source	Y Yearly

Occupation/Type/Industry	Location	Per	Low	Mid	High	Source	Date
Food Cooking Machine Operator and Tender	Milwaukee-Waukesha-West Allis MSA, WI	Y	24790 FQ	30410 MW	40390 TQ	USBLS	5/15
	Puerto Rico	Y	17550 FQ	19600 MW	24490 TQ	USBLS	5/15
	San Juan-Carolina-Caguas MSA, PR	Y	17690 FQ	20090 MW	24790 TQ	USBLS	5/15
Food Preparation Worker	Alabama	Y	17534 AE	20180 AW	21508 AEX	ALBLS	6/16
	Birmingham-Hoover MSA, AL	Y	17555 AE	20263 AW	21622 AEX	ALBLS	6/16
	Alaska	Y	20940 FQ	25250 MW	32260 TQ	USBLS	5/15
	Anchorage MSA, AK	Y	20490 FQ	24070 MW	29490 TQ	USBLS	5/15
	Arizona	Y	18290 FQ	20200 MW	23940 TQ	USBLS	5/15
	Phoenix-Mesa-Scottsdale MSA, AZ	Y	18330 FQ	20370 MW	24140 TQ	USBLS	5/15
	Tucson MSA, AZ	Y	18980 FQ	21730 MW	24380 TQ	USBLS	5/15
	Arkansas	Y	16840 FQ	18090 MW	19360 TQ	USBLS	5/15
	Little Rock-North Little Rock-Conway MSA, AR	Y	16960 FQ	18380 MW	20600 TQ	USBLS	5/15
	California	H	9.55 FQ	10.56 MW	12.29 TQ	CABLS	1/16-3/16
	Anaheim-Santa Ana-Irvine PMSA, CA	H	9.52 FQ	10.21 MW	11.92 TQ	CABLS	1/16-3/16
	Los Angeles-Long Beach-Glendale PMSA, CA	H	9.57 FQ	10.65 MW	12.42 TQ	CABLS	1/16-3/16
	Oakland-Hayward-Berkeley PMSA, CA	H	9.61 FQ	10.96 MW	13.08 TQ	CABLS	1/16-3/16
	Riverside-San Bernardino-Ontario MSA, CA	H	9.44 FQ	9.71 MW	11.54 TQ	CABLS	1/16-3/16
	Sacramento–Roseville–Arden-Arcade MSA, CA	H	9.44 FQ	9.83 MW	11.55 TQ	CABLS	1/16-3/16
	San Diego-Carlsbad MSA, CA	H	9.53 FQ	10.36 MW	11.88 TQ	CABLS	1/16-3/16
	San Francisco-Redwood City-South San Francisco PMSA, CA	H	10.48 FQ	11.57 MW	13.85 TQ	CABLS	1/16-3/16
	Colorado	Y	18570 FQ	20710 MW	24810 TQ	USBLS	5/15
	Denver-Aurora-Lakewood MSA, CO	Y	18330 FQ	19640 MW	24060 TQ	USBLS	5/15
	Connecticut	Y		22638 MW		CTBLS	1/16-3/16
	Bridgeport-Stamford-Norwalk MSA, CT	Y	19890 FQ	23700 MW	31000 TQ	USBLS	5/15
	Hartford-West Hartford-East Hartford MSA, CT	Y	19620 FQ	21420 MW	24200 TQ	USBLS	5/15
	Delaware	Y	18640 FQ	21600 MW	25920 TQ	USBLS	5/15
	Wilmington PMSA, DE-MD-NJ	Y	18280 FQ	20520 MW	25120 TQ	USBLS	5/15
	District of Columbia	Y	19920 FQ	22880 MW	29720 TQ	USBLS	5/15
	Washington-Arlington-Alexandria PMSA, DC-VA-MD-WV	Y	19910 FQ	22300 MW	27480 TQ	USBLS	5/15
	Florida	H	9.00 AE	10.53 MW	12.18 AEX	FLBLS	7/16-9/16
	Fort Lauderdale-Pompano Beach-Deerfield Beach PMSA, FL	H	9.02 AE	10.07 MW	11.87 AEX	FLBLS	7/16-9/16
	Miami-Miami Beach-Kendall PMSA, FL	H	9.24 AE	11.20 MW	13.00 AEX	FLBLS	7/16-9/16
	Orlando-Kissimmee-Sanford MSA, FL	H	9.03 AE	10.62 MW	12.15 AEX	FLBLS	7/16-9/16
	Tampa-St. Petersburg-Clearwater MSA, FL	H	9.00 AE	9.97 MW	11.70 AEX	FLBLS	7/16-9/16
	Georgia	Y	17110 FQ	18870 MW	22430 TQ	USBLS	5/15
	Atlanta-Sandy Springs-Roswell MSA, GA	Y	17360 FQ	19370 MW	23220 TQ	USBLS	5/15
	Augusta-Richmond County MSA, GA-SC	Y	16990 FQ	18490 MW	20410 TQ	USBLS	5/15
	Hawaii	Y	18530 FQ	22150 MW	28930 TQ	USBLS	5/15
	Urban Honolulu MSA, HI	Y	18100 FQ	20720 MW	24980 TQ	USBLS	5/15
	Idaho	Y	17110 FQ	18810 MW	22100 TQ	USBLS	5/15
	Boise City MSA, ID	Y	17220 FQ	18980 MW	22380 TQ	USBLS	5/15
	Illinois	Y	18650 FQ	19700 MW	23140 TQ	USBLS	5/15
	Chicago-Naperville-Arlington Heights PMSA, IL	Y	18780 FQ	19970 MW	23560 TQ	USBLS	5/15
	Lake County-Kenosha County PMSA, IL-WI	Y	18430 FQ	19380 MW	23320 TQ	USBLS	5/15

AE	Average entry wage	AWR	Average wage range	H	Hourly
AEX	Average experienced wage	B	Biweekly	HI	Highest wage paid
ATC	Average total compensation	D	Daily	HR	High end range
AW	Average wage paid	FQ	First quartile wage	LO	Lowest wage paid

LR	Low end range	MTC	Median total compensation
M	Monthly	MW	Median wage paid
MCC	Median cash compensation	MWR	Median wage range
ME	Median entry wage	S	See annotated source

TCC	Total cash compensation
TQ	Third quartile wage
W	Weekly
Y	Yearly

Occupation/Type/Industry	Location	Per	Low	Mid	High	Source	Date
Food Preparation Worker	Indiana	Y	17210 FQ	18980 MW	22660 TQ	USBLS	5/15
	Gary PMSA, IN	Y	16950 FQ	18580 MW	21800 TQ	USBLS	5/15
	Indianapolis-Carmel-Anderson MSA, IN	Y	17280 FQ	19060 MW	22450 TQ	USBLS	5/15
	Iowa	Y	17370 FQ	19310 MW	22930 TQ	USBLS	5/15
	Des Moines-West Des Moines MSA, IA	Y	17180 FQ	18910 MW	22650 TQ	USBLS	5/15
	Kansas	Y	17070 FQ	18680 MW	21300 TQ	USBLS	5/15
	Wichita MSA, KS	Y	16690 FQ	18010 MW	19350 TQ	USBLS	5/15
	Kentucky	Y	17310 FQ	19150 MW	22920 TQ	USBLS	5/15
	Louisville-Jefferson County MSA, KY-IN	Y	17560 FQ	19650 MW	23300 TQ	USBLS	5/15
	Louisiana	Y	16640 FQ	17880 MW	19110 TQ	USBLS	5/15
	Baton Rouge MSA, LA	Y	16610 FQ	17820 MW	19040 TQ	USBLS	5/15
	New Orleans-Metairie MSA, LA	Y	16680 FQ	17940 MW	19190 TQ	USBLS	5/15
	Maine	Y	18750 FQ	21930 MW	25860 TQ	USBLS	5/15
	Portland-South Portland MSA, ME	Y	18970 FQ	22080 MW	25980 TQ	USBLS	5/15
	Maryland	Y	18017 AE	23223 MW	25826 AEX	MDBLS	4/16
	Baltimore-Columbia-Towson MSA, MD	Y	18370 FQ	21460 MW	27580 TQ	USBLS	5/15
	Salisbury MSA, MD-DE	Y	18800 FQ	21320 MW	24120 TQ	USBLS	5/15
	Massachusetts	Y	19820 FQ	23430 MW	28650 TQ	USBLS	5/15
	Boston-Cambridge-Newton NECTA, MA	Y	21460 FQ	25300 MW	30240 TQ	USBLS	5/15
	Worcester MSA, MA-CT	Y	19320 FQ	21320 MW	24450 TQ	USBLS	5/15
	Michigan	Y	18980 FQ	22380 MW	28120 TQ	USBLS	5/15
	Detroit-Dearborn-Livonia PMSA, MI	Y	20140 FQ	23980 MW	30950 TQ	USBLS	5/15
	Grand Rapids-Wyoming MSA, MI	Y	18890 FQ	21800 MW	27540 TQ	USBLS	5/15
	Minnesota	Y	19612 FQ	23540 MW	28741 TQ	MNBLS	1/16-3/16
	Minneapolis-St. Paul-Bloomington MSA, MN-WI	Y	21227 FQ	25560 MW	30134 TQ	MNBLS	1/16-3/16
	Mississippi	Y	16780 FQ	18120 MW	19490 TQ	USBLS	5/15
	Jackson MSA, MS	Y	16850 FQ	18300 MW	19970 TQ	USBLS	5/15
	Missouri	Y	17470 FQ	19000 MW	22850 TQ	USBLS	5/15
	Kansas City MSA, MO-KS	Y	17900 FQ	20280 MW	23620 TQ	USBLS	5/15
	St. Louis MSA, MO-IL	Y	17980 FQ	19490 MW	23660 TQ	USBLS	5/15
	Montana	Y	18090 FQ	19450 MW	23000 TQ	USBLS	5/15
	Billings MSA, MT	Y	18200 FQ	19890 MW	24180 TQ	USBLS	5/15
	Nebraska	Y	17895 FQ	19155 MW	22255 TQ	NEBLS	7/16-9/16
	Omaha-Council Bluffs MSA, NE-IA	Y	17850 FQ	19165 MW	22335 TQ	NEBLS	7/16-9/16
	Nevada	Y	17920 FQ	22450 MW	33710 TQ	USBLS	5/15
	Las Vegas-Henderson-Paradise MSA, NV	Y	18180 FQ	24840 MW	35170 TQ	USBLS	5/15
	New Hampshire	H	8.73 AE	10.95 MW	12.26 AEX	NHBLS	6/16
	Manchester NECTA, NH	H	9.45 AE	11.21 MW	12.59 AEX	NHBLS	6/16
	Nashua NECTA, NH-MA	Y	18010 FQ	20750 MW	23900 TQ	USBLS	5/15
	New Jersey	Y	18690 FQ	20610 MW	24340 TQ	USBLS	5/15
	Camden PMSA, NJ	Y	18430 FQ	19380 MW	22810 TQ	USBLS	5/15
	Newark PMSA, NJ-PA	Y	18540 FQ	19890 MW	24030 TQ	USBLS	5/15
	Trenton MSA, NJ	Y	19050 FQ	21140 MW	23780 TQ	USBLS	5/15
	New Mexico	Y	18050 FQ	20240 MW	23700 TQ	USBLS	5/15
	Albuquerque MSA, NM	Y	18070 FQ	20350 MW	23920 TQ	USBLS	5/15
	New York	Y	19250 AE	21280 MW	26860 AEX	NYBLS	1/16-3/16
	Buffalo-Cheektowaga-Niagara Falls MSA, NY	Y	18850 FQ	19680 MW	25740 TQ	USBLS	5/15
	Nassau County-Suffolk County PMSA, NY	Y	19330 FQ	24200 MW	31310 TQ	USBLS	5/15
	New York-Jersey City-White Plains PMSA, NY-NJ	Y	18980 FQ	21380 MW	27310 TQ	USBLS	5/15
	Rochester MSA, NY	Y	18810 FQ	19460 MW	22620 TQ	USBLS	5/15
	North Carolina	Y	17320 FQ	19210 MW	22880 TQ	USBLS	5/15
	Charlotte-Concord-Gastonia MSA, NC-SC	Y	17650 FQ	19970 MW	23710 TQ	USBLS	5/15
	Raleigh MSA, NC	Y	17370 FQ	19380 MW	23400 TQ	USBLS	5/15
	North Dakota	Y	19870 FQ	24420 MW	29110 TQ	USBLS	5/15
	Fargo MSA, ND-MN	Y	21670 FQ	25150 MW	30130 TQ	USBLS	5/15
	Ohio	Y	18270 FQ	19800 MW	24310 TQ	USBLS	5/15

AE	Average entry wage	AWR	Average wage range	H	Hourly	LR	Low end range	MTC	Median total compensation	TCC	Total cash compensation
AEX	Average experienced wage	B	Biweekly	HI	Highest wage paid	M	Monthly	MW	Median wage paid	TQ	Third quartile wage
ATC	Average total compensation	D	Daily	HR	High end range	MCC	Median cash compensation	MWR	Median wage range	W	Weekly
AW	Average wage paid	FQ	First quartile wage	LO	Lowest wage paid	ME	Median entry wage	S	See annotated source	Y	Yearly

Occupation/Type/Industry	Location	Per	Low	Mid	High	Source	Date
Food Preparation Worker	Cincinnati MSA, OH-KY-IN	Y	18420 FQ	21080 MW	26410 TQ	USBLS	5/15
	Cleveland-Elyria MSA, OH	Y	18630 FQ	21000 MW	24690 TQ	USBLS	5/15
	Columbus MSA, OH	Y	18190 FQ	19610 MW	24420 TQ	USBLS	5/15
	Oklahoma	Y	17080 FQ	18820 MW	21960 TQ	USBLS	5/15
	Oklahoma City MSA, OK	Y	17210 FQ	19110 MW	23240 TQ	USBLS	5/15
	Tulsa MSA, OK	Y	17240 FQ	19170 MW	22050 TQ	USBLS	5/15
	Oregon	H	9.73 FQ	10.91 MW	12.30 TQ	ORBLS	2016
	Portland-Vancouver-Hillsboro MSA, OR-WA	Y	20580 FQ	23000 MW	26810 TQ	USBLS	5/15
	Pennsylvania	Y	17820 FQ	20490 MW	24440 TQ	USBLS	5/15
	Allentown-Bethlehem-Easton MSA, PA-NJ	Y	18470 FQ	21570 MW	26010 TQ	USBLS	5/15
	Harrisburg-Carlisle MSA, PA	Y	17860 FQ	20630 MW	24100 TQ	USBLS	5/15
	Montgomery County-Bucks County-Chester County PMSA, PA	Y	18730 FQ	23140 MW	28170 TQ	USBLS	5/15
	Philadelphia PMSA, PA	Y	17670 FQ	19930 MW	24320 TQ	USBLS	5/15
	Pittsburgh MSA, PA	Y	18200 FQ	21140 MW	24390 TQ	USBLS	5/15
	Rhode Island	Y	19200 FQ	20720 MW	26350 TQ	USBLS	5/15
	Providence-Warwick MSA, RI-MA	Y	19220 FQ	20760 MW	26150 TQ	USBLS	5/15
	South Carolina	Y	17160 FQ	18890 MW	22430 TQ	USBLS	5/15
	Charleston-North Charleston MSA, SC	Y	18410 FQ	21660 MW	25820 TQ	USBLS	5/15
	Columbia MSA, SC	Y	17100 FQ	18730 MW	21480 TQ	USBLS	5/15
	Greenville-Anderson-Mauldin MSA, SC	Y	16930 FQ	18550 MW	21490 TQ	USBLS	5/15
	South Dakota	Y	18610 FQ	19580 MW	22440 TQ	USBLS	5/15
	Sioux Falls MSA, SD	Y	18750 FQ	19910 MW	23160 TQ	USBLS	5/15
	Tennessee	Y	17100 FQ	18720 MW	21950 TQ	USBLS	5/15
	Knoxville MSA, TN	Y	17180 FQ	18860 MW	21960 TQ	USBLS	5/15
	Memphis MSA, TN-MS-AR	Y	16900 FQ	18410 MW	20850 TQ	USBLS	5/15
	Nashville-Davidson–Murfreesboro–Franklin MSA, TN	Y	17420 FQ	19250 MW	23280 TQ	USBLS	5/15
	Texas	Y	17660 FQ	19890 MW	23970 TQ	USBLS	5/15
	Austin-Round Rock MSA, TX	Y	19240 FQ	22370 MW	26530 TQ	USBLS	5/15
	Dallas-Plano-Irving PMSA, TX	Y	17330 FQ	19240 MW	23820 TQ	USBLS	5/15
	Fort Worth-Arlington PMSA, TX	Y	18790 FQ	21650 MW	24320 TQ	USBLS	5/15
	Houston-The Woodlands-Sugar Land MSA, TX	Y	18220 FQ	21190 MW	25010 TQ	USBLS	5/15
	San Antonio-New Braunfels MSA, TX	Y	17950 FQ	20540 MW	24700 TQ	USBLS	5/15
	Utah	Y	17270 FQ	19040 MW	22580 TQ	USBLS	5/15
	Ogden-Clearfield MSA, UT	Y	17870 FQ	20580 MW	23310 TQ	USBLS	5/15
	Provo-Orem MSA, UT	Y	17490 FQ	19460 MW	22860 TQ	USBLS	5/15
	Salt Lake City MSA, UT	Y	17210 FQ	18900 MW	22470 TQ	USBLS	5/15
	Vermont	Y	20130 FQ	22360 MW	24620 TQ	USBLS	5/15
	Burlington-South Burlington MSA, VT	Y	20830 FQ	22910 MW	25200 TQ	USBLS	5/15
	Virginia	Y	18010 FQ	20860 MW	24210 TQ	USBLS	5/15
	Richmond MSA, VA	Y	17760 FQ	20150 MW	23720 TQ	USBLS	5/15
	Virginia Beach-Norfolk-Newport News MSA, VA-NC	Y	18520 FQ	21320 MW	23920 TQ	USBLS	5/15
	Washington	H	10.38 FQ	11.70 MW	14.95 TQ	WABLS	3/16
	Seattle-Bellevue-Everett PMSA, WA	H	10.68 FQ	12.00 MW	15.06 TQ	WABLS	3/16
	Tacoma-Lakewood PMSA, WA	H	10.20 FQ	11.75 MW	15.88 TQ	WABLS	3/16
	West Virginia	Y	17820 FQ	18990 MW	21900 TQ	USBLS	5/15
	Huntington-Ashland MSA, WV-KY-OH	Y	17670 FQ	18740 MW	20020 TQ	USBLS	5/15
	Wisconsin	Y	17320 FQ	19180 MW	23020 TQ	USBLS	5/15
	Madison MSA, WI	Y	18010 FQ	20380 MW	23350 TQ	USBLS	5/15
	Milwaukee-Waukesha-West Allis MSA, WI	Y	17390 FQ	19340 MW	23690 TQ	USBLS	5/15
	Wyoming	Y	18370 FQ	21500 MW	25030 TQ	USBLS	5/15
	Cheyenne MSA, WY	Y	17200 FQ	18860 MW	21620 TQ	USBLS	5/15
	Puerto Rico	Y	16480 FQ	17590 MW	18690 TQ	USBLS	5/15
	San Juan-Carolina-Caguas MSA, PR	Y	16490 FQ	17620 MW	18750 TQ	USBLS	5/15
	Virgin Islands	Y	17460 FQ	19340 MW	22140 TQ	USBLS	5/15

AE	Average entry wage	AWR	Average wage range	H	Hourly
AEX	Average experienced wage	B	Biweekly	HI	Highest wage paid
ATC	Average total compensation	D	Daily	HR	High end range
AW	Average wage paid	FQ	First quartile wage	LO	Lowest wage paid

LR	Low end range	MTC	Median total compensation
M	Monthly	MW	Median wage paid
MCC	Median cash compensation	MWR	Median wage range
ME	Median entry wage	S	See annotated source

TCC	Total cash compensation
TQ	Third quartile wage
W	Weekly
Y	Yearly

Occupation/Type/Industry	Location	Per	Low	Mid	High	Source	Date
Food Preparation Worker	Guam	Y	17830 FQ	18500 MW	19170 TQ	USBLS	5/15
Food Safety Specialist	United States	Y		35000-70000 AWR		EXHC04	2016
Food Scientist and Technologist	Alabama	Y	38000 AE	66633 AW	80955 AEX	ALBLS	6/16
	Arizona	Y	52610 FQ	73040 MW	94220 TQ	USBLS	5/15
	Arkansas	Y	53590 FQ	67780 MW	77420 TQ	USBLS	5/15
	California	H	24.18 FQ	33.94 MW	45.83 TQ	CABLS	1/16-3/16
	Anaheim-Santa Ana-Irvine PMSA, CA	H	24.53 FQ	31.89 MW	43.35 TQ	CABLS	1/16-3/16
	Los Angeles-Long Beach-Glendale PMSA, CA	H	26.71 FQ	34.27 MW	43.04 TQ	CABLS	1/16-3/16
	Oakland-Hayward-Berkeley PMSA, CA	H	24.67 FQ	35.60 MW	47.19 TQ	CABLS	1/16-3/16
	Riverside-San Bernardino-Ontario MSA, CA	H	19.68 FQ	27.47 MW	43.01 TQ	CABLS	1/16-3/16
	Sacramento–Roseville–Arden-Arcade MSA, CA	H	22.24 FQ	26.57 MW	36.84 TQ	CABLS	1/16-3/16
	San Diego-Carlsbad MSA, CA	H	17.55 FQ	27.56 MW	38.70 TQ	CABLS	1/16-3/16
	San Francisco-Redwood City-South San Francisco PMSA, CA	H	31.69 FQ	42.74 MW	57.47 TQ	CABLS	1/16-3/16
	Colorado	Y	52990 FQ	71860 MW	96380 TQ	USBLS	5/15
	Denver-Aurora-Lakewood MSA, CO	Y	53480 FQ	74320 MW	98400 TQ	USBLS	5/15
	Connecticut	Y		37587 MW		CTBLS	1/16-3/16
	Washington-Arlington-Alexandria PMSA, DC-VA-MD-WV	Y	66020 FQ	84660 MW	108090 TQ	USBLS	5/15
	Florida	H	16.08 AE	22.60 MW	30.35 AEX	FLBLS	7/16-9/16
	Fort Lauderdale-Pompano Beach-Deerfield Beach PMSA, FL	H	30.44 AE	34.83 MW	35.27 AEX	FLBLS	7/16-9/16
	Orlando-Kissimmee-Sanford MSA, FL	H	14.49 AE	18.78 MW	23.84 AEX	FLBLS	7/16-9/16
	Tampa-St. Petersburg-Clearwater MSA, FL	H	14.83 AE	21.25 MW	28.37 AEX	FLBLS	7/16-9/16
	Georgia	Y	50770 FQ	57230 MW	64000 TQ	USBLS	5/15
	Atlanta-Sandy Springs-Roswell MSA, GA	Y	51820 FQ	57210 MW	62610 TQ	USBLS	5/15
	Idaho	Y	38960 FQ	57600 MW	78450 TQ	USBLS	5/15
	Boise City MSA, ID	Y	35980 FQ	53870 MW	81940 TQ	USBLS	5/15
	Illinois	Y	46160 FQ	61490 MW	79890 TQ	USBLS	5/15
	Chicago-Naperville-Arlington Heights PMSA, IL	Y	48750 FQ	63200 MW	82100 TQ	USBLS	5/15
	Indiana	Y	40050 FQ	60140 MW	84840 TQ	USBLS	5/15
	Indianapolis-Carmel-Anderson MSA, IN	Y	35560 FQ	46270 MW	67120 TQ	USBLS	5/15
	Iowa	Y	50920 FQ	64000 MW	82380 TQ	USBLS	5/15
	Des Moines-West Des Moines MSA, IA	Y	54720 FQ	65090 MW	83120 TQ	USBLS	5/15
	Kansas	Y	45300 FQ	57790 MW	75540 TQ	USBLS	5/15
	Kentucky	Y	43640 FQ	59760 MW	73690 TQ	USBLS	5/15
	Maryland	Y	42857 AE	72276 MW	86986 AEX	MDBLS	4/16
	Baltimore-Columbia-Towson MSA, MD	Y	52340 FQ	71630 MW	91750 TQ	USBLS	5/15
	Massachusetts	Y	58500 FQ	75310 MW	102370 TQ	USBLS	5/15
	Boston-Cambridge-Newton NECTA, MA	Y	57530 FQ	70960 MW	88420 TQ	USBLS	5/15
	Grand Rapids-Wyoming MSA, MI	Y	46960 FQ	55760 MW	63710 TQ	USBLS	5/15
	Minnesota	Y	62630 FQ	79918 MW	101632 TQ	MNBLS	1/16-3/16
	Minneapolis-St. Paul-Bloomington MSA, MN-WI	Y	64011 FQ	82045 MW	105593 TQ	MNBLS	1/16-3/16
	Missouri	Y	48450 FQ	63220 MW	79490 TQ	USBLS	5/15
	Kansas City MSA, MO-KS	Y	55320 FQ	67240 MW	78830 TQ	USBLS	5/15
	St. Louis MSA, MO-IL	Y	51740 FQ	70000 MW	93320 TQ	USBLS	5/15
	New Jersey	Y	50110 FQ	70380 MW	100690 TQ	USBLS	5/15
	Camden PMSA, NJ	Y	41710 FQ	50290 MW	82090 TQ	USBLS	5/15
	Newark PMSA, NJ-PA	Y	48850 FQ	77920 MW	113030 TQ	USBLS	5/15
	New Mexico	Y	51810 FQ	67730 MW	74550 TQ	USBLS	5/15

AE Average entry wage	**AWR** Average wage range	**H** Hourly	**LR** Low end range	**MTC** Median total compensation	**TCC** Total cash compensation
AEX Average experienced wage	**B** Biweekly	**HI** Highest wage paid	**M** Monthly	**MW** Median wage paid	**TQ** Third quartile wage
ATC Average total compensation	**D** Daily	**HR** High end range	**MCC** Median cash compensation	**MWR** Median wage range	**W** Weekly
AW Average wage paid	**FQ** First quartile wage	**LO** Lowest wage paid	**ME** Median entry wage	**S** See annotated source	**Y** Yearly

Occupation/Type/Industry	Location	Per	Low	Mid	High	Source	Date
Food Scientist and Technologist	New York	Y	37950 AE	57190 MW	76670 AEX	NYBLS	1/16-3/16
	Buffalo-Cheektowaga-Niagara Falls MSA, NY	Y	39850 FQ	46720 MW	86730 TQ	USBLS	5/15
	Nassau County-Suffolk County PMSA, NY	Y	42520 FQ	52570 MW	73440 TQ	USBLS	5/15
	New York-Jersey City-White Plains PMSA, NY-NJ	Y	55640 FQ	72820 MW	98580 TQ	USBLS	5/15
	Rochester MSA, NY	Y	35840 FQ	44140 MW	77750 TQ	USBLS	5/15
	North Carolina	Y	44440 FQ	63490 MW	83780 TQ	USBLS	5/15
	Charlotte-Concord-Gastonia MSA, NC-SC	Y	39940 FQ	66090 MW	89730 TQ	USBLS	5/15
	North Dakota	Y	35300 FQ	43620 MW	54750 TQ	USBLS	5/15
	Ohio	Y	44210 FQ	54540 MW	76220 TQ	USBLS	5/15
	Cincinnati MSA, OH-KY-IN	Y	43760 FQ	52690 MW	77480 TQ	USBLS	5/15
	Cleveland-Elyria MSA, OH	Y	47500 FQ	58940 MW	73050 TQ	USBLS	5/15
	Columbus MSA, OH	Y	44230 FQ	51750 MW	62290 TQ	USBLS	5/15
	Oklahoma	Y	37930 FQ	53710 MW	71610 TQ	USBLS	5/15
	Oklahoma City MSA, OK	Y	43180 FQ	53460 MW	61280 TQ	USBLS	5/15
	Oregon	H	20.83 FQ	31.24 MW	42.73 TQ	ORBLS	2016
	Portland-Vancouver-Hillsboro MSA, OR-WA	Y	45370 FQ	73790 MW	95540 TQ	USBLS	5/15
	Pennsylvania	Y	45230 FQ	60760 MW	82320 TQ	USBLS	5/15
	Allentown-Bethlehem-Easton MSA, PA-NJ	Y	52610 FQ	59430 MW	72750 TQ	USBLS	5/15
	Philadelphia PMSA, PA	Y	49030 FQ	76590 MW	97360 TQ	USBLS	5/15
	Pittsburgh MSA, PA	Y	38880 FQ	57430 MW	77110 TQ	USBLS	5/15
	Rhode Island	Y	54820 FQ	61750 MW	77210 TQ	USBLS	5/15
	Providence-Warwick MSA, RI-MA	Y	51440 FQ	61740 MW	75990 TQ	USBLS	5/15
	South Carolina	Y	34160 FQ	39090 MW	67820 TQ	USBLS	5/15
	South Dakota	Y	41250 FQ	51650 MW	61640 TQ	USBLS	5/15
	Tennessee	Y	36690 FQ	51880 MW	62320 TQ	USBLS	5/15
	Memphis MSA, TN-MS-AR	Y	36340 FQ	51130 MW	61230 TQ	USBLS	5/15
	Texas	Y	45740 FQ	59620 MW	80270 TQ	USBLS	5/15
	Dallas-Plano-Irving PMSA, TX	Y	48890 FQ	67800 MW	102580 TQ	USBLS	5/15
	Fort Worth-Arlington PMSA, TX	Y	40010 FQ	48550 MW	59980 TQ	USBLS	5/15
	Houston-The Woodlands-Sugar Land MSA, TX	Y	48900 FQ	70560 MW	82900 TQ	USBLS	5/15
	San Antonio-New Braunfels MSA, TX	Y	43170 FQ	51390 MW	71440 TQ	USBLS	5/15
	Utah	Y	35780 FQ	48810 MW	63260 TQ	USBLS	5/15
	Provo-Orem MSA, UT	Y	37660 FQ	56830 MW	75760 TQ	USBLS	5/15
	Vermont	Y	46240 FQ	58480 MW	76020 TQ	USBLS	5/15
	Burlington-South Burlington MSA, VT	Y	43530 FQ	53480 MW	72240 TQ	USBLS	5/15
	Virginia	Y	42380 FQ	54220 MW	74570 TQ	USBLS	5/15
	Washington	H	22.55 FQ	32.28 MW	41.39 TQ	WABLS	3/16
	Seattle-Bellevue-Everett PMSA, WA	H	30.14 FQ	35.99 MW	45.77 TQ	WABLS	3/16
	Tacoma-Lakewood PMSA, WA	H	18.56 FQ	23.04 MW	28.97 TQ	WABLS	3/16
	Wisconsin	Y	49140 FQ	62900 MW	81250 TQ	USBLS	5/15
	Madison MSA, WI	Y	46340 FQ	58000 MW	84960 TQ	USBLS	5/15
	Milwaukee-Waukesha-West Allis MSA, WI	Y	43040 FQ	50770 MW	63600 TQ	USBLS	5/15
Food Server							
Nonrestaurant	Alabama	Y	17462 AE	21097 AW	22919 AEX	ALBLS	6/16
Nonrestaurant	Birmingham-Hoover MSA, AL	Y	17390 AE	19789 AW	20994 AEX	ALBLS	6/16
Nonrestaurant	Alaska	Y	18800 FQ	19460 MW	28060 TQ	USBLS	5/15
Nonrestaurant	Anchorage MSA, AK	Y	19240 FQ	25810 MW	33970 TQ	USBLS	5/15
Nonrestaurant	Arizona	Y	18010 FQ	19250 MW	24590 TQ	USBLS	5/15
Nonrestaurant	Phoenix-Mesa-Scottsdale MSA, AZ	Y	18010 FQ	19230 MW	24780 TQ	USBLS	5/15
Nonrestaurant	Tucson MSA, AZ	Y	18120 FQ	19610 MW	23590 TQ	USBLS	5/15
Nonrestaurant	Arkansas	Y	16860 FQ	18110 MW	19350 TQ	USBLS	5/15
Nonrestaurant	Little Rock-North Little Rock-Conway MSA, AR	Y	16990 FQ	18360 MW	20010 TQ	USBLS	5/15
Nonrestaurant	California	H	9.82 FQ	11.88 MW	16.16 TQ	CABLS	1/16-3/16
Nonrestaurant	Anaheim-Santa Ana-Irvine PMSA, CA	H	9.84 FQ	11.89 MW	14.97 TQ	CABLS	1/16-3/16

AE	Average entry wage	AWR	Average wage range	H	Hourly
AEX	Average experienced wage	B	Biweekly	HI	Highest wage paid
ATC	Average total compensation	D	Daily	HR	High end range
AW	Average wage paid	FQ	First quartile wage	LO	Lowest wage paid

LR,	Low end range	MTC	Median total compensation
M	Monthly	MW	Median wage paid
MCC	Median cash compensation	MWR	Median wage range
ME	Median entry wage	S	See annotated source

TCC	Total cash compensation		
TQ	Third quartile wage		
W	Weekly		
Y	Yearly		

Occupation/Type/Industry	Location	Per	Low	Mid	High	Source	Date
Food Server							
Nonrestaurant	Los Angeles-Long Beach-Glendale PMSA, CA	H	9.74 FQ	12.05 MW	15.36 TQ	CABLS	1/16-3/16
Nonrestaurant	Oakland-Hayward-Berkeley PMSA, CA	H	10.21 FQ	11.70 MW	17.20 TQ	CABLS	1/16-3/16
Nonrestaurant	Riverside-San Bernardino-Ontario MSA, CA	H	9.55 FQ	10.66 MW	12.86 TQ	CABLS	1/16-3/16
Nonrestaurant	Sacramento–Roseville–Arden-Arcade MSA, CA	H	9.52 FQ	10.90 MW	16.15 TQ	CABLS	1/16-3/16
Nonrestaurant	San Diego-Carlsbad MSA, CA	H	9.65 FQ	11.02 MW	15.62 TQ	CABLS	1/16-3/16
Nonrestaurant	San Francisco-Redwood City-South San Francisco PMSA, CA	H	11.46 FQ	15.39 MW	21.02 TQ	CABLS	1/16-3/16
Nonrestaurant	Colorado	Y	18710 FQ	21250 MW	25260 TQ	USBLS	5/15
Nonrestaurant	Denver-Aurora-Lakewood MSA, CO	Y	18860 FQ	21570 MW	25080 TQ	USBLS	5/15
Nonrestaurant	Connecticut	Y		26238 MW		CTBLS	1/16-3/16
Nonrestaurant	Bridgeport-Stamford-Norwalk MSA, CT	Y	22920 FQ	27520 MW	35270 TQ	USBLS	5/15
Nonrestaurant	Hartford-West Hartford-East Hartford MSA, CT	Y	21450 FQ	24390 MW	30070 TQ	USBLS	5/15
Nonrestaurant	Delaware	Y	18080 FQ	19840 MW	24740 TQ	USBLS	5/15
Nonrestaurant	Wilmington PMSA, DE-MD-NJ	Y	18160 FQ	20290 MW	25480 TQ	USBLS	5/15
Nonrestaurant	District of Columbia	Y	19930 FQ	26060 MW	36030 TQ	USBLS	5/15
Nonrestaurant	Washington-Arlington-Alexandria PMSA, DC-VA-MD-WV	Y	19770 FQ	22530 MW	29680 TQ	USBLS	5/15
Nonrestaurant	Florida	H	9.01 AE	9.63 MW	11.70 AEX	FLBLS	7/16-9/16
Nonrestaurant	Fort Lauderdale-Pompano Beach-Deerfield Beach PMSA, FL	H	9.00 AE	9.66 MW	13.66 AEX	FLBLS	7/16-9/16
Nonrestaurant	Miami-Miami Beach-Kendall PMSA, FL	H	9.01 AE	9.87 MW	12.13 AEX	FLBLS	7/16-9/16
Nonrestaurant	Orlando-Kissimmee-Sanford MSA, FL	H	8.97 AE	9.74 MW	11.94 AEX	FLBLS	7/16-9/16
Nonrestaurant	Tampa-St. Petersburg-Clearwater MSA, FL	H	9.00 AE	9.41 MW	11.26 AEX	FLBLS	7/16-9/16
Nonrestaurant	Georgia	Y	17320 FQ	19210 MW	23910 TQ	USBLS	5/15
Nonrestaurant	Atlanta-Sandy Springs-Roswell MSA, GA	Y	17470 FQ	19530 MW	26060 TQ	USBLS	5/15
Nonrestaurant	Augusta-Richmond County MSA, GA-SC	Y	16930 FQ	18550 MW	22280 TQ	USBLS	5/15
Nonrestaurant	Hawaii	Y	17880 FQ	19790 MW	30680 TQ	USBLS	5/15
Nonrestaurant	Urban Honolulu MSA, HI	Y	18410 FQ	21830 MW	31170 TQ	USBLS	5/15
Nonrestaurant	Idaho	Y	18350 FQ	21000 MW	23650 TQ	USBLS	5/15
Nonrestaurant	Boise City MSA, ID	Y	18540 FQ	21250 MW	23920 TQ	USBLS	5/15
Nonrestaurant	Illinois	Y	18770 FQ	20640 MW	24920 TQ	USBLS	5/15
Nonrestaurant	Chicago-Naperville-Arlington Heights PMSA, IL	Y	18920 FQ	21170 MW	25260 TQ	USBLS	5/15
Nonrestaurant	Lake County-Kenosha County PMSA, IL-WI	Y	19190 FQ	24090 MW	28220 TQ	USBLS	5/15
Nonrestaurant	Indiana	Y	17420 FQ	19450 MW	22760 TQ	USBLS	5/15
Nonrestaurant	Gary PMSA, IN	Y	17160 FQ	19040 MW	23280 TQ	USBLS	5/15
Nonrestaurant	Indianapolis-Carmel-Anderson MSA, IN	Y	17740 FQ	20080 MW	23040 TQ	USBLS	5/15
Nonrestaurant	Iowa	Y	17620 FQ	20090 MW	23950 TQ	USBLS	5/15
Nonrestaurant	Des Moines-West Des Moines MSA, IA	Y	17840 FQ	20900 MW	24980 TQ	USBLS	5/15
Nonrestaurant	Kansas	Y	16860 FQ	18330 MW	20180 TQ	USBLS	5/15
Nonrestaurant	Wichita MSA, KS	Y	17170 FQ	18800 MW	23940 TQ	USBLS	5/15
Nonrestaurant	Kentucky	Y	17570 FQ	19730 MW	23960 TQ	USBLS	5/15
Nonrestaurant	Louisville-Jefferson County MSA, KY-IN	Y	17390 FQ	19180 MW	22260 TQ	USBLS	5/15
Nonrestaurant	Louisiana	Y	16870 FQ	18320 MW	20110 TQ	USBLS	5/15
Nonrestaurant	Baton Rouge MSA, LA	Y	16700 FQ	17950 MW	19210 TQ	USBLS	5/15
Nonrestaurant	New Orleans-Metairie MSA, LA	Y	17350 FQ	19370 MW	23050 TQ	USBLS	5/15
Nonrestaurant	Maine	Y	18370 FQ	20880 MW	23860 TQ	USBLS	5/15
Nonrestaurant	Portland-South Portland MSA, ME	Y	18270 FQ	20800 MW	24270 TQ	USBLS	5/15
Nonrestaurant	Maryland	Y	17971 AE	22587 MW	24894 AEX	MDBLS	4/16

AE	Average entry wage	AWR	Average wage range	H	Hourly	LR	Low end range	MTC	Median total compensation	TCC	Total cash compensation
AEX	Average experienced wage	B	Biweekly	HI	Highest wage paid	M	Monthly	MW	Median wage paid	TQ	Third quartile wage
ATC	Average total compensation	D	Daily	HR	High end range	MCC	Median cash compensation	MWR	Median wage range	W	Weekly
AW	Average wage paid	FQ	First quartile wage	LO	Lowest wage paid	ME	Median entry wage	S	See annotated source	Y	Yearly

Occupation/Type/Industry	Location	Per	Low	Mid	High	Source	Date
Food Server							
Nonrestaurant	Baltimore-Columbia-Towson MSA, MD	Y	18080 FQ	19720 MW	23710 TQ	USBLS	5/15
Nonrestaurant	Salisbury MSA, MD-DE	Y	18550 FQ	21300 MW	26450 TQ	USBLS	5/15
Nonrestaurant	Massachusetts	Y	19530 FQ	22330 MW	27730 TQ	USBLS	5/15
Nonrestaurant	Boston-Cambridge-Newton NECTA, MA	Y	19550 FQ	22580 MW	28730 TQ	USBLS	5/15
Nonrestaurant	Worcester MSA, MA-CT	Y	19320 FQ	22300 MW	28430 TQ	USBLS	5/15
Nonrestaurant	Michigan	Y	18830 FQ	21920 MW	27460 TQ	USBLS	5/15
Nonrestaurant	Bay City MSA, MI	Y	18700 FQ	20260 MW	22480 TQ	USBLS	5/15
Nonrestaurant	Detroit-Dearborn-Livonia PMSA, MI	Y	18510 FQ	20830 MW	28780 TQ	USBLS	5/15
Nonrestaurant	Grand Rapids-Wyoming MSA, MI	Y	19770 FQ	22300 MW	24950 TQ	USBLS	5/15
Nonrestaurant	Minnesota	Y	19824 FQ	23257 MW	28993 TQ	MNBLS	1/16-3/16
Nonrestaurant	Minneapolis-St. Paul-Bloomington MSA, MN-WI	Y	19642 FQ	23429 MW	30336 TQ	MNBLS	1/16-3/16
Nonrestaurant	Mississippi	Y	16880 FQ	18230 MW	19580 TQ	USBLS	5/15
Nonrestaurant	Jackson MSA, MS	Y	16800 FQ	18040 MW	19300 TQ	USBLS	5/15
Nonrestaurant	Missouri	Y	17260 FQ	18600 MW	20590 TQ	USBLS	5/15
Nonrestaurant	Kansas City MSA, MO-KS	Y	17390 FQ	19120 MW	22200 TQ	USBLS	5/15
Nonrestaurant	St. Louis MSA, MO-IL	Y	17410 FQ	18710 MW	20780 TQ	USBLS	5/15
Nonrestaurant	Montana	Y	18210 FQ	19620 MW	22780 TQ	USBLS	5/15
Nonrestaurant	Billings MSA, MT	Y	17740 FQ	18710 MW	19920 TQ	USBLS	5/15
Nonrestaurant	Nebraska	Y	18055 FQ	19460 MW	22605 TQ	NEBLS	7/16-9/16
Nonrestaurant	Omaha-Council Bluffs MSA, NE-IA	Y	18020 FQ	19475 MW	22920 TQ	NEBLS	7/16-9/16
Nonrestaurant	Nevada	Y	18190 FQ	22030 MW	27930 TQ	USBLS	5/15
Nonrestaurant	Las Vegas-Henderson-Paradise MSA, NV	Y	18500 FQ	22890 MW	28280 TQ	USBLS	5/15
Nonrestaurant	New Hampshire	H	8.44 AE	10.05 MW	11.87 AEX	NHBLS	6/16
Nonrestaurant	Manchester NECTA, NH	H	8.45 AE	9.40 MW	10.66 AEX	NHBLS	6/16
Nonrestaurant	Nashua NECTA, NH-MA	Y	18880 FQ	23360 MW	27790 TQ	USBLS	5/15
Nonrestaurant	New Jersey	Y	19720 FQ	22830 MW	27040 TQ	USBLS	5/15
Nonrestaurant	Camden PMSA, NJ	Y	18810 FQ	20680 MW	23890 TQ	USBLS	5/15
Nonrestaurant	Newark PMSA, NJ-PA	Y	21730 FQ	25160 MW	29210 TQ	USBLS	5/15
Nonrestaurant	Trenton MSA, NJ	Y	20700 FQ	23510 MW	28370 TQ	USBLS	5/15
Nonrestaurant	New Mexico	Y	17230 FQ	18510 MW	19950 TQ	USBLS	5/15
Nonrestaurant	Albuquerque MSA, NM	Y	17410 FQ	18810 MW	21240 TQ	USBLS	5/15
Nonrestaurant	New York	Y	20370 AE	29750 MW	35280 AEX	NYBLS	1/16-3/16
Nonrestaurant	Buffalo-Cheektowaga-Niagara Falls MSA, NY	Y	19390 FQ	23440 MW	29260 TQ	USBLS	5/15
Nonrestaurant	Nassau County-Suffolk County PMSA, NY	Y	23840 FQ	33200 MW	38070 TQ	USBLS	5/15
Nonrestaurant	New York-Jersey City-White Plains PMSA, NY-NJ	Y	21810 FQ	28720 MW	35500 TQ	USBLS	5/15
Nonrestaurant	Rochester MSA, NY	Y	19020 FQ	20960 MW	25250 TQ	USBLS	5/15
Nonrestaurant	North Carolina	Y	17090 FQ	18750 MW	21720 TQ	USBLS	5/15
Nonrestaurant	Charlotte-Concord-Gastonia MSA, NC-SC	Y	17030 FQ	18590 MW	21490 TQ	USBLS	5/15
Nonrestaurant	Raleigh MSA, NC	Y	18650 FQ	21080 MW	23160 TQ	USBLS	5/15
Nonrestaurant	North Dakota	Y	20750 FQ	22870 MW	25300 TQ	USBLS	5/15
Nonrestaurant	Fargo MSA, ND-MN	Y	20250 FQ	22380 MW	24540 TQ	USBLS	5/15
Nonrestaurant	Ohio	Y	18110 FQ	19360 MW	23130 TQ	USBLS	5/15
Nonrestaurant	Cincinnati MSA, OH-KY-IN	Y	18180 FQ	19600 MW	23660 TQ	USBLS	5/15
Nonrestaurant	Cleveland-Elyria MSA, OH	Y	18300 FQ	20070 MW	24290 TQ	USBLS	5/15
Nonrestaurant	Columbus MSA, OH	Y	17880 FQ	18880 MW	21120 TQ	USBLS	5/15
Nonrestaurant	Oklahoma	Y	17030 FQ	18720 MW	22400 TQ	USBLS	5/15
Nonrestaurant	Oklahoma City MSA, OK	Y	17610 FQ	20370 MW	24310 TQ	USBLS	5/15
Nonrestaurant	Tulsa MSA, OK	Y	16990 FQ	18580 MW	21570 TQ	USBLS	5/15
Nonrestaurant	Oregon	H	9.85 FQ	11.26 MW	13.65 TQ	ORBLS	2016
Nonrestaurant	Portland-Vancouver-Hillsboro MSA, OR-WA	Y	20200 FQ	23130 MW	28660 TQ	USBLS	5/15
Nonrestaurant	Pennsylvania	Y	17500 FQ	19630 MW	23650 TQ	USBLS	5/15
Nonrestaurant	Allentown-Bethlehem-Easton MSA, PA-NJ	Y	17660 FQ	19570 MW	23750 TQ	USBLS	5/15
Nonrestaurant	Harrisburg-Carlisle MSA, PA	Y	17000 FQ	18430 MW	19900 TQ	USBLS	5/15
Nonrestaurant	Montgomery County-Bucks County-Chester County PMSA, PA	Y	17680 FQ	20040 MW	23370 TQ	USBLS	5/15
Nonrestaurant	Philadelphia PMSA, PA	Y	17880 FQ	20790 MW	26680 TQ	USBLS	5/15
Nonrestaurant	Pittsburgh MSA, PA	Y	18080 FQ	21280 MW	25690 TQ	USBLS	5/15

AE	Average entry wage	AWR	Average wage range	H	Hourly	LR	Low end range	MTC	Median total compensation	TCC	Total cash compensation
AEX	Average experienced wage	B	Biweekly	HI	Highest wage paid	M	Monthly	MW	Median wage paid	TQ	Third quartile wage
ATC	Average total compensation	D	Daily	HR	High end range	MCC	Median cash compensation	MWR	Median wage range	W	Weekly
AW	Average wage paid	FQ	First quartile wage	LO	Lowest wage paid	ME	Median entry wage	S	See annotated source	Y	Yearly

Occupation/Type/Industry	Location	Per	Low	Mid	High	Source	Date
Food Server							
Nonrestaurant	Rhode Island	Y	19230 FQ	22070 MW	27810 TQ	USBLS	5/15
Nonrestaurant	Providence-Warwick MSA, RI-MA	Y	19250 FQ	21850 MW	27350 TQ	USBLS	5/15
Nonrestaurant	South Carolina	Y	17070 FQ	18710 MW	21700 TQ	USBLS	5/15
Nonrestaurant	Charleston-North Charleston MSA, SC	Y	17300 FQ	19060 MW	21770 TQ	USBLS	5/15
Nonrestaurant	Columbia MSA, SC	Y	17460 FQ	19430 MW	22260 TQ	USBLS	5/15
Nonrestaurant	Greenville-Anderson-Mauldin MSA, SC	Y	17250 FQ	19180 MW	23290 TQ	USBLS	5/15
Nonrestaurant	South Dakota	Y	19370 FQ	23300 MW	27870 TQ	USBLS	5/15
Nonrestaurant	Tennessee	Y	17020 FQ	18620 MW	21830 TQ	USBLS	5/15
Nonrestaurant	Knoxville MSA, TN	Y	17130 FQ	18840 MW	21930 TQ	USBLS	5/15
Nonrestaurant	Memphis MSA, TN-MS-AR	Y	17020 FQ	18570 MW	21780 TQ	USBLS	5/15
Nonrestaurant	Nashville-Davidson–Murfreesboro–Franklin MSA, TN	Y	16980 FQ	18610 MW	22810 TQ	USBLS	5/15
Nonrestaurant	Texas	Y	16910 FQ	18480 MW	21350 TQ	USBLS	5/15
Nonrestaurant	Austin-Round Rock MSA, TX	Y	16800 FQ	18410 MW	24090 TQ	USBLS	5/15
Nonrestaurant	Dallas-Plano-Irving PMSA, TX	Y	17110 FQ	18900 MW	22390 TQ	USBLS	5/15
Nonrestaurant	Fort Worth-Arlington PMSA, TX	Y	16670 FQ	18120 MW	20420 TQ	USBLS	5/15
Nonrestaurant	Houston-The Woodlands-Sugar Land MSA, TX	Y	17120 FQ	18770 MW	21860 TQ	USBLS	5/15
Nonrestaurant	San Antonio-New Braunfels MSA, TX	Y	17490 FQ	19510 MW	22840 TQ	USBLS	5/15
Nonrestaurant	Utah	Y	17210 FQ	19030 MW	23080 TQ	USBLS	5/15
Nonrestaurant	Ogden-Clearfield MSA, UT	Y	16870 FQ	18200 MW	19530 TQ	USBLS	5/15
Nonrestaurant	Provo-Orem MSA, UT	Y	17420 FQ	19810 MW	22880 TQ	USBLS	5/15
Nonrestaurant	Salt Lake City MSA, UT	Y	17390 FQ	19440 MW	23820 TQ	USBLS	5/15
Nonrestaurant	Vermont	Y	19480 FQ	21110 MW	23390 TQ	USBLS	5/15
Nonrestaurant	Burlington-South Burlington MSA, VT	Y	19380 FQ	21190 MW	23700 TQ	USBLS	5/15
Nonrestaurant	Virginia	Y	17480 FQ	19540 MW	23240 TQ	USBLS	5/15
Nonrestaurant	Richmond MSA, VA	Y	16910 FQ	18430 MW	20600 TQ	USBLS	5/15
Nonrestaurant	Virginia Beach-Norfolk-Newport News MSA, VA-NC	Y	18040 FQ	20520 MW	23380 TQ	USBLS	5/15
Nonrestaurant	Washington	H	9.80 FQ	10.91 MW	12.06 TQ	WABLS	3/16
Nonrestaurant	Seattle-Bellevue-Everett PMSA, WA	H	9.80 FQ	11.14 MW	13.63 TQ	WABLS	3/16
Nonrestaurant	Tacoma-Lakewood PMSA, WA	H	9.85 FQ	10.80 MW	11.72 TQ	WABLS	3/16
Nonrestaurant	West Virginia	Y	18080 FQ	19550 MW	24370 TQ	USBLS	5/15
Nonrestaurant	Huntington-Ashland MSA, WV-KY-OH	Y	18150 FQ	21000 MW	28870 TQ	USBLS	5/15
Nonrestaurant	Wisconsin	Y	17600 FQ	19980 MW	23840 TQ	USBLS	5/15
Nonrestaurant	Madison MSA, WI	Y	19370 FQ	23400 MW	28270 TQ	USBLS	5/15
Nonrestaurant	Milwaukee-Waukesha-West Allis MSA, WI	Y	17110 FQ	18900 MW	22270 TQ	USBLS	5/15
Nonrestaurant	Wyoming	Y	18240 FQ	21480 MW	24580 TQ	USBLS	5/15
Nonrestaurant	Cheyenne MSA, WY	Y	20070 FQ	22840 MW	27280 TQ	USBLS	5/15
Nonrestaurant	Puerto Rico	Y	16560 FQ	17630 MW	18700 TQ	USBLS	5/15
Nonrestaurant	Virgin Islands	Y	17050 FQ	18640 MW	24670 TQ	USBLS	5/15
Nonrestaurant	Guam	Y	17860 FQ	18550 MW	19270 TQ	USBLS	5/15
Food Service Manager	Alabama	Y	41675 AE	63404 AW	74279 AEX	ALBLS	6/16
	Birmingham-Hoover MSA, AL	Y	44309 AE	69585 AW	82233 AEX	ALBLS	6/16
	Alaska	Y	41890 FQ	49710 MW	59890 TQ	USBLS	5/15
	Anchorage MSA, AK	Y	43210 FQ	49410 MW	60200 TQ	USBLS	5/15
	Arizona	Y	40080 FQ	51130 MW	64100 TQ	USBLS	5/15
	Phoenix-Mesa-Scottsdale MSA, AZ	Y	39790 FQ	50770 MW	65560 TQ	USBLS	5/15
	Tucson MSA, AZ	Y	42040 FQ	53620 MW	62950 TQ	USBLS	5/15
	Arkansas	Y	33120 FQ	43090 MW	56960 TQ	USBLS	5/15
	Little Rock-North Little Rock-Conway MSA, AR	Y	38040 FQ	45410 MW	56550 TQ	USBLS	5/15
	California	H	17.15 FQ	22.52 MW	29.87 TQ	CABLS	1/16-3/16
	Anaheim-Santa Ana-Irvine PMSA, CA	H	18.99 FQ	24.07 MW	30.49 TQ	CABLS	1/16-3/16
	Los Angeles-Long Beach-Glendale PMSA, CA	H	16.79 FQ	21.10 MW	29.65 TQ	CABLS	1/16-3/16
	Merced MSA, CA	H	18.37 FQ	21.46 MW	24.41 TQ	CABLS	1/16-3/16

AE	Average entry wage	AWR	Average wage range	H	Hourly	LR	Low end range	MTC	Median total compensation	TCC	Total cash compensation
AEX	Average experienced wage	B	Biweekly	HI	Highest wage paid	M	Monthly	MW	Median wage paid	TQ	Third quartile wage
ATC	Average total compensation	D	Daily	HR	High end range	MCC	Median cash compensation	MWR	Median wage range	W	Weekly
AW	Average wage paid	FQ	First quartile wage	LO	Lowest wage paid	ME	Median entry wage	S	See annotated source	Y	Yearly

Food Service Manager

Occupation/Type/Industry	Location	Per	Low	Mid	High	Source	Date
Food Service Manager	Oakland-Hayward-Berkeley PMSA, CA	H	16.91 FQ	20.36 MW	28.13 TQ	CABLS	1/16-3/16
	Riverside-San Bernardino-Ontario MSA, CA	H	15.34 FQ	23.25 MW	28.37 TQ	CABLS	1/16-3/16
	Sacramento–Roseville–Arden-Arcade MSA, CA	H	15.78 FQ	22.15 MW	27.64 TQ	CABLS	1/16-3/16
	San Diego-Carlsbad MSA, CA	H	17.48 FQ	22.75 MW	32.95 TQ	CABLS	1/16-3/16
	San Francisco-Redwood City-South San Francisco PMSA, CA	H	20.92 FQ	26.21 MW	33.10 TQ	CABLS	1/16-3/16
	Colorado	Y	43860 FQ	58290 MW	74120 TQ	USBLS	5/15
	Denver-Aurora-Lakewood MSA, CO	Y	40580 FQ	58650 MW	74660 TQ	USBLS	5/15
	Connecticut	Y		54811 MW		CTBLS	1/16-3/16
	Bridgeport-Stamford-Norwalk MSA, CT	Y	45070 FQ	53760 MW	77830 TQ	USBLS	5/15
	Hartford-West Hartford-East Hartford MSA, CT	Y	41220 FQ	51110 MW	69010 TQ	USBLS	5/15
	Delaware	Y	49030 FQ	62310 MW	92670 TQ	USBLS	5/15
	Wilmington PMSA, DE-MD-NJ	Y	53090 FQ	72870 MW	110380 TQ	USBLS	5/15
	District of Columbia	Y	51660 FQ	59940 MW	78600 TQ	USBLS	5/15
	Washington-Arlington-Alexandria PMSA, DC-VA-MD-WV	Y	50360 FQ	58810 MW	75020 TQ	USBLS	5/15
	Florida	H	21.34 AE	30.06 MW	39.64 AEX	FLBLS	7/16-9/16
	Fort Lauderdale-Pompano Beach-Deerfield Beach PMSA, FL	H	17.37 AE	26.37 MW	33.29 AEX	FLBLS	7/16-9/16
	Miami-Miami Beach-Kendall PMSA, FL	H	25.28 AE	34.12 MW	43.53 AEX	FLBLS	7/16-9/16
	Orlando-Kissimmee-Sanford MSA, FL	H	22.61 AE	32.63 MW	43.12 AEX	FLBLS	7/16-9/16
	Tampa-St. Petersburg-Clearwater MSA, FL	H	21.24 AE	29.31 MW	41.68 AEX	FLBLS	7/16-9/16
	Georgia	Y	32140 FQ	43790 MW	57410 TQ	USBLS	5/15
	Atlanta-Sandy Springs-Roswell MSA, GA	Y	32410 FQ	45470 MW	58470 TQ	USBLS	5/15
	Augusta-Richmond County MSA, GA-SC	Y	36850 FQ	46250 MW	58320 TQ	USBLS	5/15
	Hawaii	Y	43910 FQ	54230 MW	67880 TQ	USBLS	5/15
	Urban Honolulu MSA, HI	Y	43410 FQ	54040 MW	69740 TQ	USBLS	5/15
	Idaho	Y	26570 FQ	33380 MW	45420 TQ	USBLS	5/15
	Boise City MSA, ID	Y	25860 FQ	30950 MW	45320 TQ	USBLS	5/15
	Illinois	Y	35750 FQ	46240 MW	62330 TQ	USBLS	5/15
	Chicago-Naperville-Arlington Heights PMSA, IL	Y	41530 FQ	51830 MW	68890 TQ	USBLS	5/15
	Lake County-Kenosha County PMSA, IL-WI	Y	30870 FQ	43810 MW	59530 TQ	USBLS	5/15
	Indiana	Y	38170 FQ	46980 MW	59330 TQ	USBLS	5/15
	Gary PMSA, IN	Y	26850 FQ	39970 MW	63050 TQ	USBLS	5/15
	Indianapolis-Carmel-Anderson MSA, IN	Y	42200 FQ	49690 MW	60860 TQ	USBLS	5/15
	Iowa	Y	29730 FQ	38450 MW	47670 TQ	USBLS	5/15
	Des Moines-West Des Moines MSA, IA	Y	34380 FQ	41720 MW	48990 TQ	USBLS	5/15
	Kansas	Y	35020 FQ	44030 MW	61790 TQ	USBLS	5/15
	Wichita MSA, KS	Y	35990 FQ	42330 MW	66110 TQ	USBLS	5/15
	Kentucky	Y	36580 FQ	45070 MW	55450 TQ	USBLS	5/15
	Louisville-Jefferson County MSA, KY-IN	Y	39740 FQ	46200 MW	54740 TQ	USBLS	5/15
	Louisiana	Y	36780 FQ	47230 MW	59110 TQ	USBLS	5/15
	Baton Rouge MSA, LA	Y	36020 FQ	47390 MW	59450 TQ	USBLS	5/15
	New Orleans-Metairie MSA, LA	Y	37890 FQ	48510 MW	60990 TQ	USBLS	5/15
	Maine	Y	40440 FQ	48560 MW	58420 TQ	USBLS	5/15
	Portland-South Portland MSA, ME	Y	43310 FQ	49440 MW	59470 TQ	USBLS	5/15
	Maryland	Y	41711 AE	61491 MW	71381 AEX	MDBLS	4/16
	Baltimore-Columbia-Towson MSA, MD	Y	45890 FQ	57540 MW	72100 TQ	USBLS	5/15
	Salisbury MSA, MD-DE	Y	43830 FQ	55630 MW	74060 TQ	USBLS	5/15

AE	Average entry wage	AWR	Average wage range	H	Hourly
AEX	Average experienced wage	B	Biweekly	HI	Highest wage paid
ATC	Average total compensation	D	Daily	HR	High end range
AW	Average wage paid	FQ	First quartile wage	LO	Lowest wage paid

LR	Low end range	MTC	Median total compensation	TCC	Total cash compensation
M	Monthly	MW	Median wage paid	TQ	Third quartile wage
MCC	Median cash compensation	MWR	Median wage range	W	Weekly
ME	Median entry wage	S	See annotated source	Y	Yearly

Occupation/Type/Industry	Location	Per	Low	Mid	High	Source	Date
Food Service Manager	Massachusetts	Y	45390 FQ	56650 MW	71420 TQ	USBLS	5/15
	Boston-Cambridge-Newton NECTA, MA	Y	47850 FQ	59340 MW	74550 TQ	USBLS	5/15
	Worcester MSA, MA-CT	Y	35790 FQ	48010 MW	62890 TQ	USBLS	5/15
	Michigan	Y	35900 FQ	45920 MW	61480 TQ	USBLS	5/15
	Detroit-Dearborn-Livonia PMSA, MI	Y	41800 FQ	48560 MW	63650 TQ	USBLS	5/15
	Grand Rapids-Wyoming MSA, MI	Y	34110 FQ	44250 MW	58600 TQ	USBLS	5/15
	Minnesota	Y	41498 FQ	48123 MW	58751 TQ	MNBLS	1/16-3/16
	Minneapolis-St. Paul-Bloomington MSA, MN-WI	Y	41091 FQ	48773 MW	60417 TQ	MNBLS	1/16-3/16
	Mississippi	Y	33660 FQ	43720 MW	56180 TQ	USBLS	5/15
	Jackson MSA, MS	Y	35030 FQ	42360 MW	52730 TQ	USBLS	5/15
	Missouri	Y	32350 FQ	44300 MW	57260 TQ	USBLS	5/15
	Kansas City MSA, MO-KS	Y	34180 FQ	45630 MW	61820 TQ	USBLS	5/15
	St. Louis MSA, MO-IL	Y	31950 FQ	45350 MW	57910 TQ	USBLS	5/15
	Montana	Y	37110 FQ	47030 MW	63690 TQ	USBLS	5/15
	Billings MSA, MT	Y	39920 FQ	52000 MW	72180 TQ	USBLS	5/15
	Nebraska	Y	39580 FQ	49560 MW	61085 TQ	NEBLS	7/16-9/16
	Omaha-Council Bluffs MSA, NE-IA	Y	38920 FQ	49315 MW	61050 TQ	NEBLS	7/16-9/16
	Nevada	Y	44270 FQ	54800 MW	74250 TQ	USBLS	5/15
	Las Vegas-Henderson-Paradise MSA, NV	Y	44520 FQ	54780 MW	76330 TQ	USBLS	5/15
	New Hampshire	H	19.28 AE	25.90 MW	30.68 AEX	NHBLS	6/16
	Manchester NECTA, NH	H	20.88 AE	30.08 MW	34.28 AEX	NHBLS	6/16
	Nashua NECTA, NH-MA	Y	40980 FQ	48180 MW	68310 TQ	USBLS	5/15
	New Jersey	Y	55490 FQ	68400 MW	83780 TQ	USBLS	5/15
	Camden PMSA, NJ	Y	55610 FQ	64610 MW	73450 TQ	USBLS	5/15
	Newark PMSA, NJ-PA	Y	56010 FQ	73120 MW	90300 TQ	USBLS	5/15
	Trenton MSA, NJ	Y	54010 FQ	66790 MW	76970 TQ	USBLS	5/15
	New Mexico	Y	34290 FQ	40560 MW	56830 TQ	USBLS	5/15
	Albuquerque MSA, NM	Y	35050 FQ	39880 MW	61120 TQ	USBLS	5/15
	New York	Y	41030 AE	61630 MW	83400 AEX	NYBLS	1/16-3/16
	Buffalo-Cheektowaga-Niagara Falls MSA, NY	Y	36620 FQ	48490 MW	65160 TQ	USBLS	5/15
	Nassau County-Suffolk County PMSA, NY	Y	52410 FQ	61210 MW	81220 TQ	USBLS	5/15
	New York-Jersey City-White Plains PMSA, NY-NJ	Y	53200 FQ	68780 MW	90860 TQ	USBLS	5/15
	Rochester MSA, NY	Y	39080 FQ	49070 MW	61820 TQ	USBLS	5/15
	North Carolina	Y	44700 FQ	56500 MW	72950 TQ	USBLS	5/15
	Charlotte-Concord-Gastonia MSA, NC-SC	Y	42430 FQ	54050 MW	69360 TQ	USBLS	5/15
	Raleigh MSA, NC	Y	52270 FQ	60470 MW	73630 TQ	USBLS	5/15
	North Dakota	Y	43620 FQ	48960 MW	59440 TQ	USBLS	5/15
	Fargo MSA, ND-MN	Y	42500 FQ	49100 MW	63170 TQ	USBLS	5/15
	Ohio	Y	38440 FQ	49590 MW	61950 TQ	USBLS	5/15
	Cincinnati MSA, OH-KY-IN	Y	40210 FQ	50790 MW	59870 TQ	USBLS	5/15
	Cleveland-Elyria MSA, OH	Y	39890 FQ	48000 MW	60990 TQ	USBLS	5/15
	Columbus MSA, OH	Y	48160 FQ	58780 MW	76650 TQ	USBLS	5/15
	Oklahoma	Y	32130 FQ	44410 MW	57100 TQ	USBLS	5/15
	Oklahoma City MSA, OK	Y	30970 FQ	42970 MW	54860 TQ	USBLS	5/15
	Tulsa MSA, OK	Y	40310 FQ	48230 MW	60010 TQ	USBLS	5/15
	Oregon	H	15.74 FQ	22.14 MW	28.82 TQ	ORBLS	2016
	Portland-Vancouver-Hillsboro MSA, OR-WA	Y	34450 FQ	48630 MW	60350 TQ	USBLS	5/15
	Pennsylvania	Y	40480 FQ	50300 MW	69340 TQ	USBLS	5/15
	Allentown-Bethlehem-Easton MSA, PA-NJ	Y	41490 FQ	61400 MW	88930 TQ	USBLS	5/15
	Harrisburg-Carlisle MSA, PA	Y	41640 FQ	49220 MW	58580 TQ	USBLS	5/15
	Montgomery County-Bucks County-Chester County PMSA, PA	Y	43490 FQ	55370 MW	72180 TQ	USBLS	5/15
	Philadelphia PMSA, PA	Y	45420 FQ	59030 MW	83430 TQ	USBLS	5/15
	Pittsburgh MSA, PA	Y	36710 FQ	46770 MW	64040 TQ	USBLS	5/15
	Rhode Island	Y	58370 FQ	69300 MW	77010 TQ	USBLS	5/15
	Providence-Warwick MSA, RI-MA	Y	52690 FQ	64040 MW	74750 TQ	USBLS	5/15
	South Carolina	Y	32340 FQ	41730 MW	51860 TQ	USBLS	5/15

AE	Average entry wage	AWR	Average wage range	H	Hourly
AEX	Average experienced wage	B	Biweekly	HI	Highest wage paid
ATC	Average total compensation	D	Daily	HR	High end range
AW	Average wage paid	FQ	First quartile wage	LO	Lowest wage paid

LR	Low end range	MTC	Median total compensation	TCC	Total cash compensation
M	Monthly	MW	Median wage paid	TQ	Third quartile wage
MCC	Median cash compensation	MWR	Median wage range	W	Weekly
ME	Median entry wage	S	See annotated source	Y	Yearly

Occupation/Type/Industry	Location	Per	Low	Mid	High	Source	Date
Food Service Manager	Charleston-North Charleston MSA, SC	Y	30530 FQ	40050 MW	47570 TQ	USBLS	5/15
	Columbia MSA, SC	Y	34950 FQ	42470 MW	55390 TQ	USBLS	5/15
	Greenville-Anderson-Mauldin MSA, SC	Y	28670 FQ	39980 MW	51590 TQ	USBLS	5/15
	South Dakota	Y	43990 FQ	48840 MW	56800 TQ	USBLS	5/15
	Sioux Falls MSA, SD	Y	44390 FQ	50240 MW	58060 TQ	USBLS	5/15
	Tennessee	Y	27050 FQ	36990 MW	48440 TQ	USBLS	5/15
	Knoxville MSA, TN	Y	28830 FQ	37420 MW	48190 TQ	USBLS	5/15
	Memphis MSA, TN-MS-AR	Y	25420 FQ	35630 MW	45310 TQ	USBLS	5/15
	Nashville-Davidson–Murfreesboro–Franklin MSA, TN	Y	29470 FQ	43060 MW	55330 TQ	USBLS	5/15
	Texas	Y	41980 FQ	52710 MW	68320 TQ	USBLS	5/15
	Austin-Round Rock MSA, TX	Y	39520 FQ	50300 MW	62900 TQ	USBLS	5/15
	Dallas-Plano-Irving PMSA, TX	Y	40200 FQ	48960 MW	73650 TQ	USBLS	5/15
	Fort Worth-Arlington PMSA, TX	Y	50760 FQ	63360 MW	77110 TQ	USBLS	5/15
	Houston-The Woodlands-Sugar Land MSA, TX	Y	44530 FQ	53550 MW	63340 TQ	USBLS	5/15
	San Antonio-New Braunfels MSA, TX	Y	48670 FQ	57060 MW	74800 TQ	USBLS	5/15
	Utah	Y	36240 FQ	44990 MW	57600 TQ	USBLS	5/15
	Ogden-Clearfield MSA, UT	Y	37900 FQ	44700 MW	52590 TQ	USBLS	5/15
	Provo-Orem MSA, UT	Y	32690 FQ	36480 MW	44970 TQ	USBLS	5/15
	Salt Lake City MSA, UT	Y	36690 FQ	46720 MW	61480 TQ	USBLS	5/15
	Vermont	Y	39470 FQ	50770 MW	61910 TQ	USBLS	5/15
	Burlington-South Burlington MSA, VT	Y	43880 FQ	54940 MW	74780 TQ	USBLS	5/15
	Virginia	Y	46400 FQ	57400 MW	72730 TQ	USBLS	5/15
	Richmond MSA, VA	Y	45460 FQ	59180 MW	75250 TQ	USBLS	5/15
	Virginia Beach-Norfolk-Newport News MSA, VA-NC	Y	48710 FQ	57910 MW	71150 TQ	USBLS	5/15
	Washington	H	19.82 FQ	24.22 MW	31.01 TQ	WABLS	3/16
	Seattle-Bellevue-Everett PMSA, WA	H	21.96 FQ	27.10 MW	33.29 TQ	WABLS	3/16
	Tacoma-Lakewood PMSA, WA	H	18.69 FQ	22.02 MW	27.37 TQ	WABLS	3/16
	West Virginia	Y	35320 FQ	44780 MW	55440 TQ	USBLS	5/15
	Huntington-Ashland MSA, WV-KY-OH	Y	33910 FQ	42530 MW	50150 TQ	USBLS	5/15
	Wisconsin	Y	34010 FQ	43820 MW	55170 TQ	USBLS	5/15
	Madison MSA, WI	Y	40560 FQ	45860 MW	52180 TQ	USBLS	5/15
	Milwaukee-Waukesha-West Allis MSA, WI	Y	37710 FQ	46540 MW	60010 TQ	USBLS	5/15
	Wyoming	Y	37310 FQ	48170 MW	63030 TQ	USBLS	5/15
	Cheyenne MSA, WY	Y	40390 FQ	52610 MW	64060 TQ	USBLS	5/15
	Puerto Rico	Y	25180 FQ	28580 MW	33340 TQ	USBLS	5/15
	San Juan-Carolina-Caguas MSA, PR	Y	25780 FQ	29110 MW	34630 TQ	USBLS	5/15
	Virgin Islands	Y	33350 FQ	38320 MW	49280 TQ	USBLS	5/15
	Guam	Y	24390 FQ	29550 MW	37820 TQ	USBLS	5/15
Football Technology Manager							
Michigan State University	East Lansing, MI	Y			72828 HI	MSUSAL	10/1/14-9/30/15
Foreign Language and Literature Teacher							
Postsecondary	Alabama	Y	43097 AE	68142 AW	80669 AEX	ALBLS	6/16
Postsecondary	Birmingham-Hoover MSA, AL	Y	42159 AE	60589 AW	69803 AEX	ALBLS	6/16
Postsecondary	Arizona	Y	41520 FQ	60790 MW	81470 TQ	USBLS	5/15
Postsecondary	Phoenix-Mesa-Scottsdale MSA, AZ	Y	50840 FQ	68010 MW	96310 TQ	USBLS	5/15
Postsecondary	Arkansas	Y	44590 FQ	53870 MW	65010 TQ	USBLS	5/15
Postsecondary	Little Rock-North Little Rock-Conway MSA, AR	Y	41870 FQ	53100 MW	62480 TQ	USBLS	5/15
Postsecondary	California	Y		86607 AW		CABLS	1/16-3/16
Postsecondary	Anaheim-Santa Ana-Irvine PMSA, CA	Y		120968 AW		CABLS	1/16-3/16
Postsecondary	Los Angeles-Long Beach-Glendale PMSA, CA	Y		85562 AW		CABLS	1/16-3/16
Postsecondary	Riverside-San Bernardino-Ontario MSA, CA	Y		96549 AW		CABLS	1/16-3/16

AE	Average entry wage	AWR	Average wage range	H	Hourly	LR	Low end range	MTC	Median total compensation	TCC	Total cash compensation
AEX	Average experienced wage	B	Biweekly	HI	Highest wage paid	M	Monthly	MW	Median wage paid	TQ	Third quartile wage
ATC	Average total compensation	D	Daily	HR	High end range	MCC	Median cash compensation	MWR	Median wage range	W	Weekly
AW	Average wage paid	FQ	First quartile wage	LO	Lowest wage paid	ME	Median entry wage	S	See annotated source	Y	Yearly

Occupation/Type/Industry	Location	Per	Low	Mid	High	Source	Date
Foreign Language and Literature Teacher							
Postsecondary	Sacramento–Roseville–Arden-Arcade MSA, CA	Y		82052 AW		CABLS	1/16-3/16
Postsecondary	San Diego-Carlsbad MSA, CA	Y		75265 AW		CABLS	1/16-3/16
Postsecondary	San Francisco-Redwood City-South San Francisco PMSA, CA	Y		110772 AW		CABLS	1/16-3/16
Postsecondary	Colorado	Y	34710 FQ	47570 MW	68950 TQ	USBLS	5/15
Postsecondary	Denver-Aurora-Lakewood MSA, CO	Y	33080 FQ	37890 MW	58790 TQ	USBLS	5/15
Postsecondary	Connecticut	Y		68904 MW		CTBLS	1/16-3/16
Postsecondary	Bridgeport-Stamford-Norwalk MSA, CT	Y	60590 FQ	76430 MW	116290 TQ	USBLS	5/15
Postsecondary	Hartford-West Hartford-East Hartford MSA, CT	Y	58980 FQ	72470 MW	94370 TQ	USBLS	5/15
Postsecondary	District of Columbia	Y	49490 FQ	58600 MW	73440 TQ	USBLS	5/15
Postsecondary	Washington-Arlington-Alexandria PMSA, DC-VA-MD-WV	Y	44960 FQ	55170 MW	68680 TQ	USBLS	5/15
Postsecondary	Florida	Y	47809 AE	76808 MW	91192 AEX	FLBLS	7/16-9/16
Postsecondary	Fort Lauderdale-Pompano Beach-Deerfield Beach PMSA, FL	Y	50452 AE	68125 MW	73496 AEX	FLBLS	7/16-9/16
Postsecondary	Miami-Miami Beach-Kendall PMSA, FL	Y	54992 AE	84580 MW	90989 AEX	FLBLS	7/16-9/16
Postsecondary	Tampa-St. Petersburg-Clearwater MSA, FL	Y	46197 AE	77675 MW	99917 AEX	FLBLS	7/16-9/16
Postsecondary	Georgia	Y	45070 FQ	57240 MW	71530 TQ	USBLS	5/15
Postsecondary	Atlanta-Sandy Springs-Roswell MSA, GA	Y	45600 FQ	59890 MW	72440 TQ	USBLS	5/15
Postsecondary	Hawaii	Y	33580 FQ	60510 MW	76290 TQ	USBLS	5/15
Postsecondary	Urban Honolulu MSA, HI	Y	32430 FQ	60040 MW	76470 TQ	USBLS	5/15
Postsecondary	Idaho	Y	35130 FQ	46820 MW	58910 TQ	USBLS	5/15
Postsecondary	Boise City MSA, ID	Y	19110 FQ	44510 MW	53800 TQ	USBLS	5/15
Postsecondary	Illinois	Y	51200 FQ	60900 MW	83040 TQ	USBLS	5/15
Postsecondary	Chicago-Naperville-Arlington Heights PMSA, IL	Y	52320 FQ	60140 MW	78100 TQ	USBLS	5/15
Postsecondary	Indiana	Y	45990 FQ	58720 MW	76480 TQ	USBLS	5/15
Postsecondary	Indianapolis-Carmel-Anderson MSA, IN	Y	46720 FQ	66400 MW	76810 TQ	USBLS	5/15
Postsecondary	Iowa	Y	52400 FQ	62240 MW	77750 TQ	USBLS	5/15
Postsecondary	Kansas	Y	34380 FQ	50770 MW	66590 TQ	USBLS	5/15
Postsecondary	Kentucky	Y	44880 FQ	59090 MW	79690 TQ	USBLS	5/15
Postsecondary	Louisville-Jefferson County MSA, KY-IN	Y	44080 FQ	53590 MW	65170 TQ	USBLS	5/15
Postsecondary	Louisiana	Y	36660 FQ	53360 MW	75720 TQ	USBLS	5/15
Postsecondary	Maine	Y	59320 FQ	76260 MW	95550 TQ	USBLS	5/15
Postsecondary	Maryland	Y	43346 AE	67803 MW	80032 AEX	MDBLS	4/16
Postsecondary	Baltimore-Columbia-Towson MSA, MD	Y	55820 FQ	65180 MW	80540 TQ	USBLS	5/15
Postsecondary	Salisbury MSA, MD-DE	Y	40140 FQ	55870 MW	70390 TQ	USBLS	5/15
Postsecondary	Massachusetts	Y	57030 FQ	70620 MW	97810 TQ	USBLS	5/15
Postsecondary	Boston-Cambridge-Newton NECTA, MA	Y	55770 FQ	66700 MW	96260 TQ	USBLS	5/15
Postsecondary	Worcester MSA, MA-CT	Y	58370 FQ	71290 MW	89830 TQ	USBLS	5/15
Postsecondary	Michigan	Y	42590 FQ	62150 MW	84770 TQ	USBLS	5/15
Postsecondary	Detroit-Dearborn-Livonia PMSA, MI	Y	60490 FQ	85000 MW	100890 TQ	USBLS	5/15
Postsecondary	Grand Rapids-Wyoming MSA, MI	Y	37840 FQ	59010 MW	80370 TQ	USBLS	5/15
Postsecondary	Minnesota	Y	50685 FQ	67529 MW	89938 TQ	MNBLS	1/16-3/16
Postsecondary	Minneapolis-St. Paul-Bloomington MSA, MN-WI	Y	46098 FQ	63054 MW	88094 TQ	MNBLS	1/16-3/16
Postsecondary	Mississippi	Y	40230 FQ	53250 MW	64910 TQ	USBLS	5/15
Postsecondary	Missouri	Y	39850 FQ	55710 MW	76560 TQ	USBLS	5/15
Postsecondary	Kansas City MSA, MO-KS	Y	35940 FQ	53260 MW	76610 TQ	USBLS	5/15
Postsecondary	St. Louis MSA, MO-IL	Y	41100 FQ	54340 MW	73790 TQ	USBLS	5/15
Postsecondary	Montana	Y	36810 FQ	47540 MW	60620 TQ	USBLS	5/15
Postsecondary	Nebraska	Y	49405 FQ	59875 MW	73520 TQ	NEBLS	7/16-9/16

AE Average entry wage	**AWR** Average wage range	**H** Hourly	**LR** Low end range	**MTC** Median total compensation	**TCC** Total cash compensation
AEX Average experienced wage	**B** Biweekly	**HI** Highest wage paid	**M** Monthly	**MW** Median wage paid	**TQ** Third quartile wage
ATC Average total compensation	**D** Daily	**HR** High end range	**MCC** Median cash compensation	**MWR** Median wage range	**W** Weekly
AW Average wage paid	**FQ** First quartile wage	**LO** Lowest wage paid	**ME** Median entry wage	**S** See annotated source	**Y** Yearly

Foreign Language and Literature Teacher

Occupation/Type/Industry	Location	Per	Low	Mid	High	Source	Date
Postsecondary	Omaha-Council Bluffs MSA, NE-IA	Y	35855 FQ	54975 MW	65155 TQ	NEBLS	7/16-9/16
Postsecondary	New Jersey	Y	51020 FQ	70680 MW	99270 TQ	USBLS	5/15
Postsecondary	Newark PMSA, NJ-PA	Y	64440 FQ	84880 MW	127320 TQ	USBLS	5/15
Postsecondary	Trenton MSA, NJ	Y	29810 FQ	44510 MW	65540 TQ	USBLS	5/15
Postsecondary	New Mexico	Y	49670 FQ	69600 MW	87380 TQ	USBLS	5/15
Postsecondary	New York	Y	42940 AE	68750 MW	106690 AEX	NYBLS	1/16-3/16
Postsecondary	Buffalo-Cheektowaga-Niagara Falls MSA, NY	Y	41250 FQ	66310 MW	88270 TQ	USBLS	5/15
Postsecondary	Nassau County-Suffolk County PMSA, NY	Y	44820 FQ	56510 MW	78780 TQ	USBLS	5/15
Postsecondary	New York-Jersey City-White Plains PMSA, NY-NJ	Y	51730 FQ	75660 MW	129890 TQ	USBLS	5/15
Postsecondary	Rochester MSA, NY	Y	46860 FQ	62040 MW	85000 TQ	USBLS	5/15
Postsecondary	North Carolina	Y	43950 FQ	54750 MW	69020 TQ	USBLS	5/15
Postsecondary	Charlotte-Concord-Gastonia MSA, NC-SC	Y	45100 FQ	56700 MW	75350 TQ	USBLS	5/15
Postsecondary	Raleigh MSA, NC	Y	41110 FQ	51390 MW	62180 TQ	USBLS	5/15
Postsecondary	North Dakota	Y	43870 FQ	60450 MW	86500 TQ	USBLS	5/15
Postsecondary	Fargo MSA, ND-MN	Y	51450 FQ	67670 MW	86340 TQ	USBLS	5/15
Postsecondary	Ohio	Y	44370 FQ	61090 MW	85370 TQ	USBLS	5/15
Postsecondary	Columbus MSA, OH	Y	52370 FQ	67870 MW	96870 TQ	USBLS	5/15
Postsecondary	Oklahoma	Y	39300 FQ	50780 MW	70230 TQ	USBLS	5/15
Postsecondary	Oklahoma City MSA, OK	Y	33760 FQ	40080 MW	51590 TQ	USBLS	5/15
Postsecondary	Oregon	Y	31865 FQ	53815 MW	73738 TQ	ORBLS	2016
Postsecondary	Portland-Vancouver-Hillsboro MSA, OR-WA	Y	28940 FQ	45240 MW	70460 TQ	USBLS	5/15
Postsecondary	Pennsylvania	Y	45400 FQ	62240 MW	86790 TQ	USBLS	5/15
Postsecondary	Allentown-Bethlehem-Easton MSA, PA-NJ	Y	22870 FQ	37270 MW	73080 TQ	USBLS	5/15
Postsecondary	Harrisburg-Carlisle MSA, PA	Y	57480 FQ	75620 MW	95910 TQ	USBLS	5/15
Postsecondary	Montgomery County-Bucks County-Chester County PMSA, PA	Y	23000 FQ	45230 MW	74070 TQ	USBLS	5/15
Postsecondary	Philadelphia PMSA, PA	Y	45440 FQ	58780 MW	84040 TQ	USBLS	5/15
Postsecondary	Pittsburgh MSA, PA	Y	52780 FQ	70660 MW	94820 TQ	USBLS	5/15
Postsecondary	Rhode Island	Y	50640 FQ	69110 MW	94520 TQ	USBLS	5/15
Postsecondary	Providence-Warwick MSA, RI-MA	Y	51690 FQ	68670 MW	92820 TQ	USBLS	5/15
Postsecondary	South Carolina	Y	42170 FQ	51600 MW	65820 TQ	USBLS	5/15
Postsecondary	Columbia MSA, SC	Y	43380 FQ	49890 MW	70070 TQ	USBLS	5/15
Postsecondary	South Dakota	Y	45600 FQ	54050 MW	62500 TQ	USBLS	5/15
Postsecondary	Tennessee	Y	34980 FQ	50560 MW	67850 TQ	USBLS	5/15
Postsecondary	Knoxville MSA, TN	Y	34970 FQ	42260 MW	63240 TQ	USBLS	5/15
Postsecondary	Memphis MSA, TN-MS-AR	Y	35160 FQ	50450 MW	62890 TQ	USBLS	5/15
Postsecondary	Nashville-Davidson–Murfreesboro–Franklin MSA, TN	Y	32450 FQ	52720 MW	76760 TQ	USBLS	5/15
Postsecondary	Texas	Y	36190 FQ	55130 MW	73130 TQ	USBLS	5/15
Postsecondary	Austin-Round Rock MSA, TX	Y	39040 FQ	58270 MW	75050 TQ	USBLS	5/15
Postsecondary	Dallas-Plano-Irving PMSA, TX	Y	34390 FQ	55460 MW	73400 TQ	NEBLS	5/15
Postsecondary	Fort Worth-Arlington PMSA, TX	Y	18900 FQ	40870 MW	62580 TQ	USBLS	5/15
Postsecondary	Houston-The Woodlands-Sugar Land MSA, TX	Y	42770 FQ	57390 MW	74540 TQ	USBLS	5/15
Postsecondary	San Antonio-New Braunfels MSA, TX	Y	24520 FQ	54360 MW	75210 TQ	USBLS	5/15
Postsecondary	Utah	Y	55630 FQ	75570 MW	95550 TQ	USBLS	5/15
Postsecondary	Provo-Orem MSA, UT	Y	60820 FQ	83560 MW	98140 TQ	USBLS	5/15
Postsecondary	Salt Lake City MSA, UT	Y	26980 FQ	47470 MW	62460 TQ	USBLS	5/15
Postsecondary	Vermont	Y	48170 FQ	68160 MW	77920 TQ	USBLS	5/15
Postsecondary	Burlington-South Burlington MSA, VT	Y	45960 FQ	58330 MW	73850 TQ	USBLS	5/15
Postsecondary	Virginia	Y	40700 FQ	49890 MW	62770 TQ	USBLS	5/15
Postsecondary	Richmond MSA, VA	Y	35450 FQ	46400 MW	72800 TQ	USBLS	5/15
Postsecondary	Virginia Beach-Norfolk-Newport News MSA, VA-NC	Y	44040 FQ	53140 MW	66250 TQ	USBLS	5/15
Postsecondary	Washington	Y		57958 AW		WABLS	3/16

AE	Average entry wage	AWR	Average wage range	H	Hourly	LR	Low end range	MTC Median total compensation TCC Total cash compensation
AEX	Average experienced wage	B	Biweekly	HI	Highest wage paid	M	Monthly	MW Median wage paid TQ Third quartile wage
ATC	Average total compensation	D	Daily	HR	High end range	MCC	Median cash compensation	MWR Median wage range W Weekly
AW	Average wage paid	FQ	First quartile wage	LO	Lowest wage paid	ME	Median entry wage	S See annotated source Y Yearly

Occupation/Type/Industry	Location	Per	Low	Mid	High	Source	Date
Foreign Language and Literature Teacher							
Postsecondary	Seattle-Bellevue-Everett PMSA, WA	Y		60525 AW		WABLS	3/16
Postsecondary	Tacoma-Lakewood PMSA, WA	Y		63172 AW		WABLS	3/16
Postsecondary	West Virginia	Y	37810 FQ	52290 MW	59570 TQ	USBLS	5/15
Postsecondary	Wisconsin	Y	42640 FQ	56130 MW	71740 TQ	USBLS	5/15
Postsecondary	Madison MSA, WI	Y	42380 FQ	63080 MW	86730 TQ	USBLS	5/15
Postsecondary	Milwaukee-Waukesha-West Allis MSA, WI	Y	38510 FQ	51440 MW	71400 TQ	USBLS	5/15
Postsecondary	Puerto Rico	Y	20260 FQ	56090 MW	81710 TQ	USBLS	5/15
Postsecondary	San Juan-Carolina-Caguas MSA, PR	Y	19390 FQ	50530 MW	84920 TQ	USBLS	5/15
Forensic Biologist							
County Government	Oakland County, MI	B	2233 LO		2929 HI	MIOAK2	10/1/16
Municipal Government	Detroit, MI	M	3467 LO		4858 HI	DETGOV	2016
Forensic Case Specialist							
State Government	North Carolina	Y	31904 LO		48800 HI	NCGOV	7/1/16
Forensic Chemist							
Municipal Government	Colorado Springs, CO	Y	56982 LO		78350 HI	COSPRS	2017
Forensic Coordinator							
Municipal Government	Santa Clara, CA	Y			93462 HI	CACIT	6/28/16
Forensic ID Specialist							
Municipal Government	Torrance, CA	Y		60414 AW		CACIT	6/28/16
Forensic Investigator							
Municipal Government	Elk Grove, CA	Y			75098 HI	CACIT	6/28/16
Forensic Laboratory Technician							
Sheriff's Department, Forensic Services Division	Ventura County, CA	M	3491 LO		4884 HI	CAC	12/15
Forensic Psychologist							
First-Year	United States	Y		50000 MW		APAC01	2016
Mental Health Department, State Government	Saline, MI	H	27.69 LO		39.48 HI	MIGOV	2016
Forensic Science Technician	Alabama	Y	39733 AE	56725 AW	65216 AEX	ALBLS	6/16
	Birmingham-Hoover MSA, AL	Y	45289 AE	68111 AW	79517 AEX	ALBLS	6/16
	Arizona	Y	42120 FQ	52830 MW	68950 TQ	USBLS	5/15
	Phoenix-Mesa-Scottsdale MSA, AZ	Y	44680 FQ	56050 MW	68970 TQ	USBLS	5/15
	Tucson MSA, AZ	Y	37760 FQ	47090 MW	60760 TQ	USBLS	5/15
	Arkansas	Y	32590 FQ	38910 MW	44050 TQ	USBLS	5/15
	Little Rock-North Little Rock-Conway MSA, AR	Y	32520 FQ	38910 MW	43860 TQ	USBLS	5/15
	California	H	29.71 FQ	37.65 MW	48.98 TQ	CABLS	1/16-3/16
	Anaheim-Santa Ana-Irvine PMSA, CA	H	32.24 FQ	39.70 MW	50.11 TQ	CABLS	1/16-3/16
	Los Angeles-Long Beach-Glendale PMSA, CA	H	33.41 FQ	44.67 MW	55.52 TQ	CABLS	1/16-3/16
	Oakland-Hayward-Berkeley PMSA, CA	H	30.44 FQ	39.34 MW	45.03 TQ	CABLS	1/16-3/16
	Riverside-San Bernardino-Ontario MSA, CA	H	24.45 FQ	30.91 MW	37.19 TQ	CABLS	1/16-3/16
	Sacramento-Roseville-Arden-Arcade MSA, CA	H	34.84 FQ	43.24 MW	52.29 TQ	CABLS	1/16-3/16
	San Diego-Carlsbad MSA, CA	H	29.73 FQ	37.42 MW	45.05 TQ	CABLS	1/16-3/16
	San Francisco-Redwood City-South San Francisco PMSA, CA	H	32.15 FQ	37.33 MW	52.65 TQ	CABLS	1/16-3/16
	Colorado	Y	48200 FQ	58810 MW	72160 TQ	USBLS	5/15
	Denver-Aurora-Lakewood MSA, CO	Y	50340 FQ	60590 MW	74220 TQ	USBLS	5/15
	Connecticut	Y		74342 MW		CTBLS	1/16-3/16

AE	Average entry wage	AWR	Average wage range	H	Hourly
AEX	Average experienced wage	B	Biweekly	HI	Highest wage paid
ATC	Average total compensation	D	Daily	HR	High end range
AW	Average wage paid	FQ	First quartile wage	LO	Lowest wage paid

LR	Low end range	MTC	Median total compensation
M	Monthly	MW	Median wage paid
MCC	Median cash compensation	MWR	Median wage range
ME	Median entry wage	S	See annotated source

TCC	Total cash compensation		
TQ	Third quartile wage		
W	Weekly		
Y	Yearly		

Forensic Science Technician

Occupation/Type/Industry	Location	Per	Low	Mid	High	Source	Date
Forensic Science Technician	Washington-Arlington-Alexandria PMSA, DC-VA-MD-WV	Y	51310 FQ	74810 MW	100350 TQ	USBLS	5/15
	Florida	H	16.27 AE	22.06 MW	26.95 AEX	FLBLS	7/16-9/16
	Fort Lauderdale-Pompano Beach-Deerfield Beach PMSA, FL	H	17.75 AE	23.90 MW	29.23 AEX	FLBLS	7/16-9/16
	Miami-Miami Beach-Kendall PMSA, FL	H	20.73 AE	28.71 MW	35.72 AEX	FLBLS	7/16-9/16
	Orlando-Kissimmee-Sanford MSA, FL	H	15.99 AE	22.03 MW	25.40 AEX	FLBLS	7/16-9/16
	Tampa-St. Petersburg-Clearwater MSA, FL	H	17.70 AE	22.50 MW	26.59 AEX	FLBLS	7/16-9/16
	Georgia	Y	32260 FQ	40820 MW	55590 TQ	USBLS	5/15
	Atlanta-Sandy Springs-Roswell MSA, GA	Y	37060 FQ	46330 MW	60500 TQ	USBLS	5/15
	Hawaii	Y	44800 FQ	50170 MW	61350 TQ	USBLS	5/15
	Idaho	Y	38750 FQ	46490 MW	57910 TQ	USBLS	5/15
	Boise City MSA, ID	Y	40940 FQ	48020 MW	58830 TQ	USBLS	5/15
	Illinois	Y	51960 FQ	65950 MW	97090 TQ	USBLS	5/15
	Chicago-Naperville-Arlington Heights PMSA, IL	Y	50090 FQ	63130 MW	82290 TQ	USBLS	5/15
	Lake County-Kenosha County PMSA, IL-WI	Y	51980 FQ	74310 MW	90820 TQ	USBLS	5/15
	Indiana	Y	46380 FQ	60350 MW	67190 TQ	USBLS	5/15
	Indianapolis-Carmel-Anderson MSA, IN	Y	47870 FQ	62140 MW	70950 TQ	USBLS	5/15
	Iowa	Y	48760 FQ	59360 MW	84450 TQ	USBLS	5/15
	Kansas	Y	35400 FQ	44380 MW	57940 TQ	USBLS	5/15
	Wichita MSA, KS	Y	40110 FQ	46700 MW	57480 TQ	USBLS	5/15
	Kentucky	Y	34760 FQ	42460 MW	48170 TQ	USBLS	5/15
	Louisiana	Y	36950 FQ	46440 MW	64150 TQ	USBLS	5/15
	Baton Rouge MSA, LA	Y	38720 FQ	47710 MW	63970 TQ	USBLS	5/15
	Maine	Y	35170 FQ	40230 MW	53180 TQ	USBLS	5/15
	Maryland	Y	36118 AE	64758 MW	79077 AEX	MDBLS	4/16
	Baltimore-Columbia-Towson MSA, MD	Y	43540 FQ	57860 MW	73010 TQ	USBLS	5/15
	Massachusetts	Y	52430 FQ	70480 MW	88850 TQ	USBLS	5/15
	Michigan	Y	45920 FQ	64150 MW	72560 TQ	USBLS	5/15
	Grand Rapids-Wyoming MSA, MI	Y	19570 FQ	57230 MW	72560 TQ	USBLS	5/15
	Minnesota	Y	50725 FQ	56975 MW	64808 TQ	MNBLS	1/16-3/16
	Minneapolis-St. Paul-Bloomington MSA, MN-WI	Y	49768 FQ	56733 MW	65090 TQ	MNBLS	1/16-3/16
	Mississippi	Y	42340 FQ	51630 MW	63660 TQ	USBLS	5/15
	Jackson MSA, MS	Y	44240 FQ	52190 MW	64570 TQ	USBLS	5/15
	Missouri	Y	38530 FQ	50770 MW	59490 TQ	USBLS	5/15
	Kansas City MSA, MO-KS	Y	34600 FQ	42540 MW	54550 TQ	USBLS	5/15
	St. Louis MSA, MO-IL	Y	46810 FQ	92690 MW	104130 TQ	USBLS	5/15
	Montana	Y	54520 FQ	58950 MW	64470 TQ	USBLS	5/15
	Nebraska	Y	44500 FQ	50595 MW	60090 TQ	NEBLS	7/16-9/16
	Omaha-Council Bluffs MSA, NE-IA	Y	44320 FQ	50255 MW	58745 TQ	NEBLS	7/16-9/16
	Nevada	Y	64030 FQ	73240 MW	85540 TQ	USBLS	5/15
	Las Vegas-Henderson-Paradise MSA, NV	Y	63750 FQ	72700 MW	84300 TQ	USBLS	5/15
	New Hampshire	H	27.48 AE	33.55 MW	36.56 AEX	NHBLS	6/16
	New Jersey	Y	42770 FQ	54240 MW	61710 TQ	USBLS	5/15
	Newark PMSA, NJ-PA	Y	37150 FQ	52690 MW	61720 TQ	USBLS	5/15
	New Mexico	Y	34540 FQ	51110 MW	65490 TQ	USBLS	5/15
	New York	Y	48290 AE	67100 MW	75620 AEX	NYBLS	1/16-3/16
	New York-Jersey City-White Plains PMSA, NY-NJ	Y	51830 FQ	65810 MW	78950 TQ	USBLS	5/15
	North Carolina	Y	36230 FQ	42170 MW	50450 TQ	USBLS	5/15
	Charlotte-Concord-Gastonia MSA, NC-SC	Y	40620 FQ	47170 MW	55610 TQ	USBLS	5/15
	Raleigh MSA, NC	Y	37000 FQ	42970 MW	54090 TQ	USBLS	5/15
	Ohio	Y	50600 FQ	57850 MW	72460 TQ	USBLS	5/15
	Columbus MSA, OH	Y	51090 FQ	57390 MW	69480 TQ	USBLS	5/15
	Oklahoma	Y	40270 FQ	61370 MW	73500 TQ	USBLS	5/15
	Oklahoma City MSA, OK	Y	44360 FQ	65040 MW	74610 TQ	USBLS	5/15
	Oregon	H	27.10 AE	31.91 MW	36.33 TQ	ORBLS	2016

AE	Average entry wage	AWR	Average wage range	H	Hourly	
AEX	Average experienced wage	B	Biweekly	HI	Highest wage paid	
ATC	Average total compensation	D	Daily	HR	High end range	
AW	Average wage paid	FQ	First quartile wage	LO	Lowest wage paid	
LR	Low end range	MTC	Median total compensation	TCC	Total cash compensation
M	Monthly	MW	Median wage paid	TQ	Third quartile wage
MCC	Median cash compensation	MWR	Median wage range	W	Weekly
ME	Median entry wage	S	See annotated source	Y	Yearly

Occupation/Type/Industry	Location	Per	Low	Mid	High	Source	Date
Forensic Science Technician	Portland-Vancouver-Hillsboro MSA, OR-WA	Y	57360 FQ	66900 MW	75510 TQ	USBLS	5/15
	Pennsylvania	Y	37090 FQ	44440 MW	57690 TQ	USBLS	5/15
	Montgomery County-Bucks County-Chester County PMSA, PA	Y	28150 FQ	33340 MW	43090 TQ	USBLS	5/15
	Philadelphia PMSA, PA	Y	43530 FQ	49540 MW	68460 TQ	USBLS	5/15
	South Carolina	Y	34760 FQ	43370 MW	49270 TQ	USBLS	5/15
	South Dakota	Y	41490 FQ	50610 MW	57790 TQ	USBLS	5/15
	Tennessee	Y	34080 FQ	42360 MW	57290 TQ	USBLS	5/15
	Knoxville MSA, TN	Y	36320 FQ	46090 MW	63050 TQ	USBLS	5/15
	Nashville-Davidson– Murfreesboro–Franklin MSA, TN	Y	32150 FQ	39030 MW	55940 TQ	USBLS	5/15
	Texas	Y	36890 FQ	45330 MW	58750 TQ	USBLS	5/15
	Austin-Round Rock MSA, TX	Y	38060 FQ	44750 MW	55970 TQ	USBLS	5/15
	Dallas-Plano-Irving PMSA, TX	Y	38850 FQ	46720 MW	58510 TQ	USBLS	5/15
	Fort Worth-Arlington PMSA, TX	Y	41890 FQ	51190 MW	61570 TQ	USBLS	5/15
	Houston-The Woodlands- Sugar Land MSA, TX	Y	45730 FQ	60530 MW	74350 TQ	USBLS	5/15
	San Antonio-New Braunfels MSA, TX	Y	32960 FQ	41800 MW	53480 TQ	USBLS	5/15
	Utah	Y	41690 FQ	49380 MW	58480 TQ	USBLS	5/15
	Salt Lake City MSA, UT	Y	43930 FQ	50570 MW	59370 TQ	USBLS	5/15
	Virginia	Y	41120 FQ	65330 MW	87110 TQ	USBLS	5/15
	Richmond MSA, VA	Y	43070 FQ	65230 MW	79100 TQ	USBLS	5/15
	Virginia Beach-Norfolk- Newport News MSA, VA-NC	Y	39930 FQ	48880 MW	69790 TQ	USBLS	5/15
	Washington	H	24.65 FQ	30.48 MW	36.04 TQ	WABLS	3/16
	Seattle-Bellevue-Everett PMSA, WA	H	27.96 FQ	32.96 MW	37.17 TQ	WABLS	3/16
	Tacoma-Lakewood PMSA, WA	H	27.24 FQ	31.59 MW	36.62 TQ	WABLS	3/16
	Wisconsin	Y	37390 FQ	43780 MW	55630 TQ	USBLS	5/15
	Madison MSA, WI	Y	36300 FQ	42280 MW	56480 TQ	USBLS	5/15
	Wyoming	Y	44600 FQ	66440 MW	75140 TQ	USBLS	5/15
	Puerto Rico	Y	24590 FQ	28770 MW	34660 TQ	USBLS	5/15
	San Juan-Carolina-Caguas MSA, PR	Y	24590 FQ	28770 MW	34660 TQ	USBLS	5/15
Forensic Scientist							
Department of Justice, State Government	Billings, MT	H	27.71 LO		29.50 HI	MTGOV	2016
State Police	Michigan	Y	37700 LO		64900 HI	MSP02	2017
Forensic Scientist Trainee							
Sheriff's Department, Forensic Services Division	Ventura County, CA	M	3491 LO		4884 HI	CAC	12/15
Forensic Specialist							
Police Department, Municipal Government	Beverly Hills, CA	Y		94895 AW		CACIT	6/28/16
Police Department, Municipal Government	Culver City, CA	Y		55881 AW		CACIT	6/28/16
Police Department, Municipal Government	Redlands, CA	Y		51243 AW		CACIT	6/27/16
Police Department, Municipal Government	Upland, CA	Y			62357 HI	CACIT	6/28/16
Forensic Toxicologist							
Health Department, State Government	Ohio	H			36.36 HI	OHGOV	2015
Medical Examiner	San Francisco, CA	B	6321 LO		7682 HI	SFGOV	2016-2018
Forensic Toxicologist Supervisor							
Municipal Government	San Francisco, CA	Y			112701 HI	CACIT	6/28/16
Forensic Toxicology Chemist							
County Government	Oakland County, MI	B	2233 LO		2929 HI	MIOAK2	10/1/16
Forest and Conservation Technician							
	Alabama	Y	34514 AE	45289 AW	50681 AEX	ALBLS	6/16
	Birmingham-Hoover MSA, AL	Y	36961 AE	47256 AW	52414 AEX	ALBLS	6/16
	Alaska	Y	34900 FQ	41680 MW	51860 TQ	USBLS	5/15
	Anchorage MSA, AK	Y	35870 FQ	40450 MW	48190 TQ	USBLS	5/15
	Arizona	Y	28550 FQ	31950 MW	43530 TQ	USBLS	5/15
	Phoenix-Mesa-Scottsdale MSA, AZ	Y	29200 FQ	34070 MW	47210 TQ	USBLS	5/15

AE	Average entry wage	**AWR**	Average wage range	**H**	Hourly
AEX	Average experienced wage	**B**	Biweekly	**HI**	Highest wage paid
ATC	Average total compensation	**D**	Daily	**HR**	High end range
AW	Average wage paid	**FQ**	First quartile wage	**LO**	Lowest wage paid

LR	Low end range	**MTC**	Median total compensation	**TCC**	Total cash compensation
M	Monthly	**MW**	Median wage paid	**TQ**	Third quartile wage
MCC	Median cash compensation	**MWR**	Median wage range	**W**	Weekly
ME	Median entry wage	**S**	See annotated source	**Y**	Yearly

Forest and Conservation Technician

Occupation/Type/Industry	Location	Per	Low	Mid	High	Source	Date
	Arkansas	Y	33650 FQ	42740 MW	50120 TQ	USBLS	5/15
	California	H	13.93 FQ	16.68 MW	22.57 TQ	CABLS	1/16-3/16
	Anaheim-Santa Ana-Irvine PMSA, CA	H	12.12 FQ	12.53 MW	16.33 TQ	CABLS	1/16-3/16
	Los Angeles-Long Beach-Glendale PMSA, CA	H	15.87 FQ	19.11 MW	24.51 TQ	CABLS	1/16-3/16
	Oakland-Hayward-Berkeley PMSA, CA	H	12.12 FQ	13.01 MW	35.23 TQ	CABLS	1/16-3/16
	Riverside-San Bernardino-Ontario MSA, CA	H	15.87 FQ	19.77 MW	25.09 TQ	CABLS	1/16-3/16
	Sacramento–Roseville–Arden-Arcade MSA, CA	H	12.54 FQ	14.91 MW	21.36 TQ	CABLS	1/16-3/16
	San Diego-Carlsbad MSA, CA	H	15.87 FQ	19.11 MW	24.24 TQ	CABLS	1/16-3/16
	San Francisco-Redwood City-South San Francisco PMSA, CA	H	13.27 FQ	15.88 MW	19.07 TQ	CABLS	1/16-3/16
	Colorado	Y	28550 FQ	31940 MW	43320 TQ	USBLS	5/15
	Denver-Aurora-Lakewood MSA, CO	Y	30650 FQ	34290 MW	48560 TQ	USBLS	5/15
	Connecticut	Y		76138 MW		CTBLS	1/16-3/16
	Washington-Arlington-Alexandria PMSA, DC-VA-MD-WV	Y	36610 FQ	49010 MW	63220 TQ	USBLS	5/15
	Florida	H	12.87 AE	20.78 MW	23.63 AEX	FLBLS	7/16-9/16
	Georgia	Y	37420 FQ	45970 MW	51890 TQ	USBLS	5/15
	Hawaii	Y	34780 FQ	39820 MW	47360 TQ	USBLS	5/15
	Urban Honolulu MSA, HI	Y	34760 FQ	38490 MW	48920 TQ	USBLS	5/15
	Idaho	Y	28550 FQ	31940 MW	42740 TQ	USBLS	5/15
	Boise City MSA, ID	Y	28560 FQ	35650 MW	48200 TQ	USBLS	5/15
	Illinois	Y	31290 FQ	39030 MW	50280 TQ	USBLS	5/15
	Chicago-Naperville-Arlington Heights PMSA, IL	Y	31300 FQ	35000 MW	45360 TQ	USBLS	5/15
	Indiana	Y	31300 FQ	38840 MW	45520 TQ	USBLS	5/15
	Iowa	Y	34790 FQ	44830 MW	51130 TQ	USBLS	5/15
	Kansas	Y	42210 FQ	47480 MW	51430 TQ	USBLS	5/15
	Kentucky	Y	28270 FQ	35610 MW	44840 TQ	USBLS	5/15
	Maine	Y	33700 FQ	39070 MW	43530 TQ	USBLS	5/15
	Maryland	Y	30859 AE	40980 MW	46041 AEX	MDBLS	4/16
	Baltimore-Columbia-Towson MSA, MD	Y	32420 FQ	38920 MW	46670 TQ	USBLS	5/15
	Massachusetts	Y	41430 FQ	49550 MW	61230 TQ	USBLS	5/15
	Boston-Cambridge-Newton NECTA, MA	Y	43970 FQ	54400 MW	69320 TQ	USBLS	5/15
	Michigan	Y	31940 FQ	40360 MW	50110 TQ	USBLS	5/15
	Minnesota	Y	32197 FQ	42782 MW	51834 TQ	MNBLS	1/16-3/16
	Minneapolis-St. Paul-Bloomington MSA, MN-WI	Y	30675 FQ	46491 MW	55332 TQ	MNBLS	1/16-3/16
	Mississippi	Y	33080 FQ	43520 MW	51430 TQ	USBLS	5/15
	Jackson MSA, MS	Y	28540 FQ	34650 MW	44830 TQ	USBLS	5/15
	Montana	Y	28550 FQ	31940 MW	41540 TQ	USBLS	5/15
	Billings MSA, MT	Y	28550 FQ	31940 MW	44830 TQ	USBLS	5/15
	Nebraska	Y	27590 FQ	36575 MW	47135 TQ	NEBLS	7/16-9/16
	Omaha-Council Bluffs MSA, NE-IA	Y	39705 FQ	43770 MW	48300 TQ	NEBLS	7/16-9/16
	Nevada	Y	28550 FQ	34200 MW	44840 TQ	USBLS	5/15
	Las Vegas-Henderson-Paradise MSA, NV	Y	28550 FQ	31950 MW	43530 TQ	USBLS	5/15
	New Hampshire	H	14.42 AE	15.66 MW	20.83 AEX	NHBLS	6/16
	New Jersey	Y	24210 FQ	38530 MW	49090 TQ	USBLS	5/15
	New Mexico	Y	28540 FQ	31940 MW	43530 TQ	USBLS	5/15
	Albuquerque MSA, NM	Y	28550 FQ	31940 MW	44020 TQ	USBLS	5/15
	New York	Y	38160 AE	47670 MW	54950 AEX	NYBLS	1/16-3/16
	North Carolina	Y	31940 FQ	38010 MW	44830 TQ	USBLS	5/15
	Charlotte-Concord-Gastonia MSA, NC-SC	Y	32790 FQ	36500 MW	39500 TQ	USBLS	5/15
	North Dakota	Y	33970 FQ	44650 MW	51420 TQ	USBLS	5/15
	Ohio	Y	32820 FQ	40650 MW	46010 TQ	USBLS	5/15
	Oklahoma	Y	36810 FQ	43920 MW	48210 TQ	USBLS	5/15
	Oregon	H	13.92 FQ	16.09 MW	22.52 TQ	ORBLS	2016
	Portland-Vancouver-Hillsboro MSA, OR-WA	Y	33690 FQ	44360 MW	56120 TQ	USBLS	5/15

AE	Average entry wage	AWR	Average wage range	H Hourly
AEX	Average experienced wage	B	Biweekly	HI Highest wage paid
ATC	Average total compensation	D	Daily	HR High end range
AW	Average wage paid	FQ	First quartile wage	LO Lowest wage paid

LR Low end range
M Monthly
MCC Median cash compensation
ME Median entry wage

MTC Median total compensation
MW Median wage paid
MWR Median wage range
S See annotated source

TCC Total cash compensation
TQ Third quartile wage
W Weekly
Y Yearly

Occupation/Type/Industry	Location	Per	Low	Mid	High	Source	Date
Forest and Conservation Technician	Pennsylvania	Y	32310 FQ	44000 MW	51360 TQ	USBLS	5/15
	Harrisburg-Carlisle MSA, PA	Y	19820 FQ	24230 MW	44010 TQ	USBLS	5/15
	Pittsburgh MSA, PA	Y	34340 FQ	38540 MW	51380 TQ	USBLS	5/15
	South Carolina	Y	29740 FQ	38130 MW	47480 TQ	USBLS	5/15
	Charleston-North Charleston MSA, SC	Y	31660 FQ	42730 MW	50120 TQ	USBLS	5/15
	Tennessee	Y	29630 FQ	36620 MW	44640 TQ	USBLS	5/15
	Knoxville MSA, TN	Y	31240 FQ	36880 MW	42870 TQ	USBLS	5/15
	Memphis MSA, TN-MS-AR	Y	32470 FQ	37330 MW	46160 TQ	USBLS	5/15
	Nashville-Davidson– Murfreesboro–Franklin MSA, TN	Y	34770 FQ	43870 MW	59340 TQ	USBLS	5/15
	Texas	Y	37120 FQ	38830 MW	43700 TQ	USBLS	5/15
	Austin-Round Rock MSA, TX	Y	34620 FQ	38430 MW	38830 TQ	USBLS	5/15
	Houston-The Woodlands- Sugar Land MSA, TX	Y	38810 FQ	38830 MW	43690 TQ	USBLS	5/15
	Utah	Y	25420 FQ	28550 MW	38870 TQ	USBLS	5/15
	Ogden-Clearfield MSA, UT	Y	19510 FQ	28550 MW	40880 TQ	USBLS	5/15
	Provo-Orem MSA, UT	Y	22760 FQ	27520 MW	35600 TQ	USBLS	5/15
	Salt Lake City MSA, UT	Y	25430 FQ	28560 MW	39410 TQ	USBLS	5/15
	Vermont	Y	31780 FQ	32460 MW	48790 TQ	USBLS	5/15
	Virginia	Y	28580 FQ	38210 MW	48200 TQ	USBLS	5/15
	Washington	H	13.93 FQ	16.62 MW	21.87 TQ	WABLS	3/16
	Seattle-Bellevue-Everett PMSA, WA	H	14.86 FQ	16.63 MW	21.83 TQ	WABLS	3/16
	Tacoma-Lakewood PMSA, WA	H	14.86 FQ	16.72 MW	25.47 TQ	WABLS	3/16
	Wisconsin	Y	28560 FQ	36680 MW	46290 TQ	USBLS	5/15
	Madison MSA, WI	Y	25520 FQ	32370 MW	38630 TQ	USBLS	5/15
	Milwaukee-Waukesha-West Allis MSA, WI	Y	26230 FQ	39400 MW	46780 TQ	USBLS	5/15
	Wyoming	Y	28540 FQ	31940 MW	40880 TQ	USBLS	5/15
	Puerto Rico	Y	21790 FQ	26120 MW	41530 TQ	USBLS	5/15
	San Juan-Carolina-Caguas MSA, PR	Y	20810 FQ	23730 MW	31940 TQ	USBLS	5/15
Forest and Conservation Worker	Alabama	Y	25254 AE	51794 AW	65065 AEX	ALBLS	6/16
	California	H	9.22 FQ	9.23 MW	10.51 TQ	CABLS	1/16-3/16
	Connecticut	Y		23530 MW		CTBLS	1/16-3/16
	Florida	H	10.84 AE	13.37 MW	17.14 AEX	FLBLS	7/16-9/16
	Georgia	Y	17060 FQ	18920 MW	26070 TQ	USBLS	5/15
	Illinois	Y	25600 FQ	32260 MW	38500 TQ	USBLS	5/15
	Iowa	Y	28940 FQ	29860 MW	39850 TQ	USBLS	5/15
	Kansas	Y	26880 FQ	28830 MW	30770 TQ	USBLS	5/15
	Louisiana	Y	29370 FQ	34590 MW	38900 TQ	USBLS	5/15
	Maryland	Y	20348 AE	40147 MW	50047 AEX	MDBLS	4/16
	Massachusetts	Y	31020 FQ	35670 MW	47000 TQ	USBLS	5/15
	Michigan	Y	18850 FQ	31810 MW	44730 TQ	USBLS	5/15
	Minnesota	Y	19181 FQ	27354 MW	42762 TQ	MNBLS	1/16-3/16
	Montana	Y	23230 FQ	26080 MW	29690 TQ	USBLS	5/15
	Nebraska	Y	31350 FQ	35255 MW	39960 TQ	NEBLS	7/16-9/16
	New Jersey	Y	30400 FQ	39360 MW	48200 TQ	USBLS	5/15
	New Mexico	Y	17560 FQ	25450 MW	30110 TQ	USBLS	5/15
	North Carolina	Y	21830 FQ	25030 MW	37010 TQ	USBLS	5/15
	North Dakota	Y	31860 FQ	34720 MW	37570 TQ	USBLS	5/15
	Oregon	H	13.69 FQ	16.51 MW	19.20 TQ	ORBLS	2016
	Pennsylvania	Y	35630 FQ	43050 MW	53750 TQ	USBLS	5/15
	South Carolina	Y	23600 FQ	25180 MW	28460 TQ	USBLS	5/15
	South Dakota	Y	21280 FQ	23340 MW	27990 TQ	USBLS	5/15
	Tennessee	Y	21220 FQ	23040 MW	25460 TQ	USBLS	5/15
	Texas	Y	30930 FQ	39730 MW	49180 TQ	USBLS	5/15
	Virginia	Y	31120 FQ	36540 MW	45530 TQ	USBLS	5/15
	Washington	H	9.58 FQ	9.73 MW	14.67 TQ	WABLS	3/16
	Wisconsin	Y	18600 FQ	23530 MW	30610 TQ	USBLS	5/15
	Wyoming	Y	25050 FQ	27650 MW	30220 TQ	USBLS	5/15
Forest Fire Inspector and Prevention Specialist	Alabama	Y	28397 AE	36026 AW	39846 AEX	ALBLS	6/16
	Arkansas	Y	32060 FQ	33240 MW	35710 TQ	USBLS	5/15
	California	H	23.68 FQ	35.03 MW	42.71 TQ	CABLS	1/16-3/16
	Georgia	Y	33140 FQ	36540 MW	41140 TQ	USBLS	5/15
	Massachusetts	Y	31080 FQ	36750 MW	45960 TQ	USBLS	5/15

AE	Average entry wage	AWR	Average wage range	H	Hourly	LR	Low end range	MTC	Median total compensation	TCC	Total cash compensation
AEX	Average experienced wage	B	Biweekly	HI	Highest wage paid	M	Monthly	MW	Median wage paid	TQ	Third quartile wage
ATC	Average total compensation	D	Daily	HR	High end range	MCC	Median cash compensation	MWR	Median wage range	W	Weekly
AW	Average wage paid	FQ	First quartile wage	LO	Lowest wage paid	ME	Median entry wage	S	See annotated source	Y	Yearly

Occupation/Type/Industry	Location	Per	Low	Mid	High	Source	Date
Forest Fire Inspector and Prevention Specialist	Minnesota	Y	51705 FQ	58451 MW	66146 TQ	MNBLS	1/16-3/16
	Mississippi	Y	20880 FQ	26420 MW	31730 TQ	USBLS	5/15
	New Jersey	Y	50470 FQ	59990 MW	70180 TQ	USBLS	5/15
	New York	Y	47660 AE	55890 MW	62040 AEX	NYBLS	1/16-3/16
	Oregon	H	24.56 FQ	25.78 MW	26.44 TQ	ORBLS	2016
	Texas	Y	36390 FQ	48240 MW	68400 TQ	USBLS	5/15
Forester	Alabama	Y	39703 AE	58754 AW	68274 AEX	ALBLS	6/16
	Birmingham-Hoover MSA, AL	Y	50507 AE	77183 AW	90526 AEX	ALBLS	6/16
	Alaska	Y	58580 FQ	68230 MW	78880 TQ	USBLS	5/15
	Arizona	Y	43500 FQ	53550 MW	66370 TQ	USBLS	5/15
	Phoenix-Mesa-Scottsdale MSA, AZ	Y	39600 FQ	48560 MW	81750 TQ	USBLS	5/15
	Arkansas	Y	42060 FQ	53240 MW	67080 TQ	USBLS	5/15
	Little Rock-North Little Rock-Conway MSA, AR	Y	38070 FQ	46870 MW	60250 TQ	USBLS	5/15
	California	H	29.32 FQ	35.84 MW	48.83 TQ	CABLS	1/16-3/16
	Los Angeles-Long Beach-Glendale PMSA, CA	H	27.00 FQ	32.06 MW	38.05 TQ	CABLS	1/16-3/16
	Riverside-San Bernardino-Ontario MSA, CA	H	29.57 FQ	33.79 MW	38.10 TQ	CABLS	1/16-3/16
	Sacramento–Roseville–Arden-Arcade MSA, CA	H	36.28 FQ	38.99 MW	46.37 TQ	CABLS	1/16-3/16
	San Diego-Carlsbad MSA, CA	H	30.85 FQ	33.92 MW	37.87 TQ	CABLS	1/16-3/16
	Colorado	Y	48400 FQ	59090 MW	70330 TQ	USBLS	5/15
	Connecticut	Y		80936 MW		CTBLS	1/16-3/16
	Hartford-West Hartford-East Hartford MSA, CT	Y	64660 FQ	78890 MW	83400 TQ	USBLS	5/15
	Florida	H	17.19 AE	21.77 MW	26.83 AEX	FLBLS	7/16-9/16
	Fort Lauderdale-Pompano Beach-Deerfield Beach PMSA, FL	H	21.89 AE	24.44 MW	28.42 AEX	FLBLS	7/16-9/16
	Orlando-Kissimmee-Sanford MSA, FL	H	18.77 AE	25.32 MW	30.59 AEX	FLBLS	7/16-9/16
	Tampa-St. Petersburg-Clearwater MSA, FL	H	17.65 AE	22.64 MW	26.32 AEX	FLBLS	7/16-9/16
	Georgia	Y	42970 FQ	55850 MW	75500 TQ	USBLS	5/15
	Atlanta-Sandy Springs-Roswell MSA, GA	Y	42920 FQ	50010 MW	85790 TQ	USBLS	5/15
	Idaho	Y	44780 FQ	52010 MW	60520 TQ	USBLS	5/15
	Illinois	Y	53970 FQ	61840 MW	75460 TQ	USBLS	5/15
	Chicago-Naperville-Arlington Heights PMSA, IL	Y	52570 FQ	59990 MW	76220 TQ	USBLS	5/15
	Indiana	Y	39000 FQ	49000 MW	60890 TQ	USBLS	5/15
	Iowa	Y	35690 FQ	43110 MW	68700 TQ	USBLS	5/15
	Kentucky	Y	39370 FQ	44690 MW	49700 TQ	USBLS	5/15
	Louisiana	Y	59460 FQ	70630 MW	97450 TQ	USBLS	5/15
	Maine	Y	46010 FQ	51340 MW	61490 TQ	USBLS	5/15
	Maryland	Y	43583 AE	60342 MW	68721 AEX	MDBLS	4/16
	Massachusetts	Y	51940 FQ	59960 MW	71010 TQ	USBLS	5/15
	Michigan	Y	53240 FQ	65380 MW	71100 TQ	USBLS	5/15
	Minnesota	Y	50685 FQ	59183 MW	69898 TQ	MNBLS	1/16-3/16
	Minneapolis-St. Paul-Bloomington MSA, MN-WI	Y	53044 FQ	60765 MW	73497 TQ	MNBLS	1/16-3/16
	Mississippi	Y	41790 FQ	53230 MW	66440 TQ	USBLS	5/15
	Missouri	Y	44770 FQ	51320 MW	62940 TQ	USBLS	5/15
	Montana	Y	44370 FQ	52620 MW	60510 TQ	USBLS	5/15
	Nebraska	Y	44950 FQ	57735 MW	77655 TQ	NEBLS	7/16-9/16
	New Hampshire	H	23.29 AE	30.04 MW	33.38 AEX	NHBLS	6/16
	New Jersey	Y	61510 FQ	72880 MW	85430 TQ	USBLS	5/15
	New Mexico	Y	36110 FQ	40200 MW	58730 TQ	USBLS	5/15
	New York	Y	53000 AE	62100 MW	69060 AEX	NYBLS	1/16-3/16
	New York-Jersey City-White Plains PMSA, NY-NJ	Y	54370 FQ	58000 MW	61540 TQ	USBLS	5/15
	North Carolina	Y	48560 FQ	58790 MW	72790 TQ	USBLS	5/15
	Charlotte-Concord-Gastonia MSA, NC-SC	Y	50580 FQ	57810 MW	69270 TQ	USBLS	5/15
	Raleigh MSA, NC	Y	49360 FQ	59920 MW	70850 TQ	USBLS	5/15
	North Dakota	Y	41770 FQ	49830 MW	61680 TQ	USBLS	5/15
	Ohio	Y	50490 FQ	54680 MW	62760 TQ	USBLS	5/15
	Oklahoma	Y	42790 FQ	49560 MW	58560 TQ	USBLS	5/15

AE	Average entry wage	**AWR**	Average wage range	**H**	Hourly
AEX	Average experienced wage	**B**	Biweekly	**HI**	Highest wage paid
ATC	Average total compensation	**D**	Daily	**HR**	High end range
AW	Average wage paid	**FQ**	First quartile wage	**LO**	Lowest wage paid

LR	Low end range	**MTC**	Median total compensation
M	Monthly	**MW**	Median wage paid
MCC	Median cash compensation	**MWR**	Median wage range
ME	Median entry wage	**S**	See annotated source

TCC	Total cash compensation		
TQ	Third quartile wage		
W	Weekly		
Y	Yearly		

Occupation/Type/Industry	Location	Per	Low	Mid	High	Source	Date
Forester	Oregon	H	26.19 FQ	29.87 MW	34.34 TQ	ORBLS	2016
	Portland-Vancouver-Hillsboro MSA, OR-WA	Y	53750 FQ	61020 MW	70430 TQ	USBLS	5/15
	Pennsylvania	Y	56540 FQ	64850 MW	75330 TQ	USBLS	5/15
	Philadelphia PMSA, PA	Y	65330 FQ	70300 MW	75260 TQ	USBLS	5/15
	South Carolina	Y	38380 FQ	52420 MW	66360 TQ	USBLS	5/15
	South Dakota	Y	40180 FQ	46560 MW	56810 TQ	USBLS	5/15
	Tennessee	Y	44630 FQ	53240 MW	65370 TQ	USBLS	5/15
	Texas	Y	43520 FQ	54860 MW	62930 TQ	USBLS	5/15
	Utah	Y	45890 FQ	55540 MW	64440 TQ	USBLS	5/15
	Vermont	Y	43950 FQ	56460 MW	65080 TQ	USBLS	5/15
	Virginia	Y	44010 FQ	54040 MW	64740 TQ	USBLS	5/15
	Richmond MSA, VA	Y	44830 FQ	53630 MW	67710 TQ	USBLS	5/15
	Washington	H	27.54 FQ	30.40 MW	37.03 TQ	WABLS	3/16
	Seattle-Bellevue-Everett PMSA, WA	H	24.02 FQ	28.23 MW	33.23 TQ	WABLS	3/16
	Tacoma-Lakewood PMSA, WA	H	30.48 FQ	32.51 MW	37.44 TQ	WABLS	3/16
	West Virginia	Y	33480 FQ	38380 MW	54730 TQ	USBLS	5/15
	Wisconsin	Y	47290 FQ	53380 MW	59210 TQ	USBLS	5/15
	Madison MSA, WI	Y	39720 FQ	51510 MW	61520 TQ	USBLS	5/15
	Wyoming	Y	50010 FQ	59690 MW	66020 TQ	USBLS	5/15
Forestry and Conservation Science Teacher							
Postsecondary	Arizona	Y	67280 FQ	90270 MW	114980 TQ	USBLS	5/15
Postsecondary	California	Y		124772 AW		CABLS	1/16-3/16
Postsecondary	Florida	Y	76552 FQ	108875 MW	131754 AEX	FLBLS	7/16-9/16
Postsecondary	Georgia	Y	83640 FQ	99960 MW	121030 TQ	USBLS	5/15
Postsecondary	Illinois	Y	44000 FQ	61330 MW	84420 TQ	USBLS	5/15
Postsecondary	Maine	Y	67080 FQ	78140 MW	110250 TQ	USBLS	5/15
Postsecondary	New York	Y	38780 AE	58830 MW	83440 AEX	NYBLS	1/16-3/16
Postsecondary	North Carolina	Y	68920 FQ	87580 MW	105000 TQ	USBLS	5/15
Postsecondary	Oregon	Y	74778 FQ	109061 MW	130355 TQ	ORBLS	2016
Postsecondary	Pennsylvania	Y	82370 FQ	109260 MW	136140 TQ	USBLS	5/15
Postsecondary	Tennessee	Y	78950 FQ	94410 MW	111680 TQ	USBLS	5/15
Postsecondary	Texas	Y	61050 FQ	85240 MW	104960 TQ	USBLS	5/15
Postsecondary	Washington	Y		101297 AW		WABLS	3/16
Postsecondary	West Virginia	Y	54740 FQ	71350 MW	82630 TQ	USBLS	5/15
Forestry Climber							
Municipal Government	Berkeley, CA	Y		64131 AW		CACIT	6/28/16
Forging Machine Setter, Operator, and Tender							
Metals and Plastics	Alabama	Y	28533 AE	50362 AW	61282 AEX	ALBLS	6/16
Metals and Plastics	Birmingham-Hoover MSA, AL	Y	27844 AE	40861 AW	47370 AEX	ALBLS	6/16
Metals and Plastics	Arkansas	Y	27660 FQ	33540 MW	37020 TQ	USBLS	5/15
Metals and Plastics	California	H	13.70 FQ	17.37 MW	22.01 TQ	CABLS	1/16-3/16
Metals and Plastics	Anaheim-Santa Ana-Irvine PMSA, CA	H	13.81 FQ	16.19 MW	21.23 TQ	CABLS	1/16-3/16
Metals and Plastics	Los Angeles-Long Beach-Glendale PMSA, CA	H	13.73 FQ	17.29 MW	21.54 TQ	CABLS	1/16-3/16
Metals and Plastics	Riverside-San Bernardino-Ontario MSA, CA	H	13.59 FQ	17.16 MW	21.64 TQ	CABLS	1/16-3/16
Metals and Plastics	San Diego-Carlsbad MSA, CA	H	25.40 FQ	28.91 MW	33.53 TQ	CABLS	1/16-3/16
Metals and Plastics	San Francisco-Redwood City-South San Francisco PMSA, CA	H	26.68 FQ	29.16 MW	31.38 TQ	CABLS	1/16-3/16
Metals and Plastics	Colorado	Y	34670 FQ	40410 MW	48520 TQ	USBLS	5/15
Metals and Plastics	Denver-Aurora-Lakewood MSA, CO	Y	40400 FQ	45300 MW	48790 TQ	USBLS	5/15
Metals and Plastics	Connecticut	Y		39840 MW		CTBLS	1/16-3/16
Metals and Plastics	Florida	H	10.97 AE	14.23 MW	16.05 AEX	FLBLS	7/16-9/16
Metals and Plastics	Georgia	Y	23590 FQ	29230 MW	38890 TQ	USBLS	5/15
Metals and Plastics	Illinois	Y	33030 FQ	40790 MW	53740 TQ	USBLS	5/15
Metals and Plastics	Chicago-Naperville-Arlington Heights PMSA, IL	Y	37430 FQ	48340 MW	56430 TQ	USBLS	5/15
Metals and Plastics	Indiana	Y	27620 FQ	31630 MW	38540 TQ	USBLS	5/15
Metals and Plastics	Indianapolis-Carmel-Anderson MSA, IN	Y	26620 FQ	29750 MW	35110 TQ	USBLS	5/15
Metals and Plastics	Iowa	Y	32360 FQ	35430 MW	38510 TQ	USBLS	5/15
Metals and Plastics	Kansas	Y	27940 FQ	33170 MW	37760 TQ	USBLS	5/15

Occupation/Type/Industry	Location	Per	Low	Mid	High	Source	Date
Forging Machine Setter, Operator, and Tender							
Metals and Plastics	Wichita MSA, KS	Y	29430 FQ	34990 MW	41010 TQ	USBLS	5/15
Metals and Plastics	Kentucky	Y	38770 FQ	51450 MW	57370 TQ	USBLS	5/15
Metals and Plastics	Louisville-Jefferson County MSA, KY-IN	Y	29550 FQ	38590 MW	47040 TQ	USBLS	5/15
Metals and Plastics	Maryland	Y	32615 AE	47219 MW	54521 AEX	MDBLS	4/16
Metals and Plastics	Baltimore-Columbia-Towson MSA, MD	Y	51440 FQ	55730 MW	59840 TQ	USBLS	5/15
Metals and Plastics	Massachusetts	Y	32090 FQ	36460 MW	43540 TQ	USBLS	5/15
Metals and Plastics	Boston-Cambridge-Newton NECTA, MA	Y	33870 FQ	36590 MW	39310 TQ	USBLS	5/15
Metals and Plastics	Worcester MSA, MA-CT	Y	35040 FQ	46000 MW	88830 TQ	USBLS	5/15
Metals and Plastics	Michigan	Y	21950 FQ	25770 MW	37290 TQ	USBLS	5/15
Metals and Plastics	Detroit-Dearborn-Livonia PMSA, MI	Y	19220 FQ	28330 MW	46020 TQ	USBLS	5/15
Metals and Plastics	Grand Rapids-Wyoming MSA, MI	Y	21220 FQ	34510 MW	44550 TQ	USBLS	5/15
Metals and Plastics	Minnesota	Y	25200 FQ	34251 MW	44244 TQ	MNBLS	1/16-3/16
Metals and Plastics	Mississippi	Y	23350 FQ	29090 MW	36290 TQ	USBLS	5/15
Metals and Plastics	Missouri	Y	22850 FQ	27780 MW	35530 TQ	USBLS	5/15
Metals and Plastics	Kansas City MSA, MO-KS	Y	21120 FQ	24040 MW	30070 TQ	USBLS	5/15
Metals and Plastics	St. Louis MSA, MO-IL	Y	22720 FQ	26210 MW	34690 TQ	USBLS	5/15
Metals and Plastics	New Hampshire	H	11.81 AE	17.41 MW	20.31 AEX	NHBLS	6/16
Metals and Plastics	Nashua NECTA, NH-MA	Y	32180 FQ	37860 MW	44810 TQ	USBLS	5/15
Metals and Plastics	New Jersey	Y	26490 FQ	33240 MW	40250 TQ	USBLS	5/15
Metals and Plastics	Newark PMSA, NJ-PA	Y	24180 FQ	29930 MW	37150 TQ	USBLS	5/15
Metals and Plastics	New York	Y	26270 AE	33540 MW	41670 AEX	NYBLS	1/16-3/16
Metals and Plastics	Nassau County-Suffolk County PMSA, NY	Y	32260 FQ	38330 MW	52500 TQ	USBLS	5/15
Metals and Plastics	New York-Jersey City-White Plains PMSA, NY-NJ	Y	31060 FQ	45370 MW	48850 TQ	USBLS	5/15
Metals and Plastics	Rochester MSA, NY	Y	27390 FQ	30360 MW	35050 TQ	USBLS	5/15
Metals and Plastics	North Carolina	Y	31820 FQ	36840 MW	43630 TQ	USBLS	5/15
Metals and Plastics	Charlotte-Concord-Gastonia MSA, NC-SC	Y	30970 FQ	37700 MW	46170 TQ	USBLS	5/15
Metals and Plastics	Ohio	Y	32360 FQ	37390 MW	45260 TQ	USBLS	5/15
Metals and Plastics	Cincinnati MSA, OH-KY-IN	Y	32650 FQ	38280 MW	46320 TQ	USBLS	5/15
Metals and Plastics	Cleveland-Elyria MSA, OH	Y	34990 FQ	43010 MW	54190 TQ	USBLS	5/15
Metals and Plastics	Columbus MSA, OH	Y	28310 FQ	33080 MW	38800 TQ	USBLS	5/15
Metals and Plastics	Oklahoma	Y	28760 FQ	42010 MW	53020 TQ	USBLS	5/15
Metals and Plastics	Tulsa MSA, OK	Y	36340 FQ	48310 MW	55530 TQ	USBLS	5/15
Metals and Plastics	Oregon	H	13.71 FQ	16.78 MW	20.96 TQ	ORBLS	2016
Metals and Plastics	Portland-Vancouver-Hillsboro MSA, OR-WA	Y	27720 FQ	33160 MW	40760 TQ	USBLS	5/15
Metals and Plastics	Pennsylvania	Y	34530 FQ	41240 MW	48730 TQ	USBLS	5/15
Metals and Plastics	Philadelphia PMSA, PA	Y	39250 FQ	48670 MW	52560 TQ	USBLS	5/15
Metals and Plastics	Pittsburgh MSA, PA	Y	34200 FQ	40840 MW	47570 TQ	USBLS	5/15
Metals and Plastics	Rhode Island	Y	28570 FQ	32300 MW	36640 TQ	USBLS	5/15
Metals and Plastics	Providence-Warwick MSA, RI-MA	Y	29090 FQ	33420 MW	38240 TQ	USBLS	5/15
Metals and Plastics	South Carolina	Y	25600 FQ	33300 MW	43170 TQ	USBLS	5/15
Metals and Plastics	South Dakota	Y	29000 FQ	33400 MW	39190 TQ	USBLS	5/15
Metals and Plastics	Tennessee	Y	25910 FQ	29720 MW	35540 TQ	USBLS	5/15.
Metals and Plastics	Knoxville MSA, TN	Y	29200 FQ	34950 MW	43800 TQ	USBLS	5/15
Metals and Plastics	Memphis MSA, TN-MS-AR	Y	22640 FQ	24980 MW	30670 TQ	USBLS	5/15
Metals and Plastics	Nashville-Davidson–Murfreesboro–Franklin MSA, TN	Y	27860 FQ	34140 MW	39590 TQ	USBLS	5/15
Metals and Plastics	Texas	Y	24350 FQ	32240 MW	43170 TQ	USBLS	5/15
Metals and Plastics	Dallas-Plano-Irving PMSA, TX	Y	25630 FQ	33570 MW	46080 TQ	USBLS	5/15
Metals and Plastics	Fort Worth-Arlington PMSA, TX	Y	23650 FQ	28330 MW	34320 TQ	USBLS	5/15
Metals and Plastics	Houston-The Woodlands-Sugar Land MSA, TX	Y	25610 FQ	37260 MW	48930 TQ	USBLS	5/15
Metals and Plastics	San Antonio-New Braunfels MSA, TX	Y	26390 FQ	30930 MW	36820 TQ	USBLS	5/15
Metals and Plastics	Utah	Y	27560 FQ	30710 MW	36180 TQ	USBLS	5/15
Metals and Plastics	Ogden-Clearfield MSA, UT	Y	27000 FQ	29620 MW	33190 TQ	USBLS	5/15
Metals and Plastics	Virginia	Y	35670 FQ	44830 MW	54010 TQ	USBLS	5/15
Metals and Plastics	Washington	H	11.51 FQ	14.50 MW	20.58 TQ	WABLS	3/16
Metals and Plastics	West Virginia	Y	26180 FQ	29150 MW	35370 TQ	USBLS	5/15

AE	Average entry wage	AWR	Average wage range	H	Hourly	LR	Low end range	MTC	Median total compensation	TCC	Total cash compensation
AEX	Average experienced wage	B	Biweekly	HI	Highest wage paid	M	Monthly	MW	Median wage paid	TQ	Third quartile wage
ATC	Average total compensation	D	Daily	HR	High end range	MCC	Median cash compensation	MWR	Median wage range	W	Weekly
AW	Average wage paid	FQ	First quartile wage	LO	Lowest wage paid	ME	Median entry wage	S	See annotated source	Y	Yearly

Occupation/Type/Industry	Location	Per	Low	Mid	High	Source	Date
Forging Machine Setter, Operator, and Tender							
Metals and Plastics	Wisconsin	Y	23240 FQ	30080 MW	37880 TQ	USBLS	5/15
Metals and Plastics	Milwaukee-Waukesha-West Allis MSA, WI	Y	24740 FQ	34490 MW	48040 TQ	USBLS	5/15
Metals and Plastics	Puerto Rico	Y	17060 FQ	18250 MW	19450 TQ	USBLS	5/15
Metals and Plastics	San Juan-Carolina-Caguas MSA, PR	Y	17060 FQ	18250 MW	19450 TQ	USBLS	5/15
Foster Coordinator							
Animal Services, Municipal Government	Louisville, KY	Y			33280 HI	LKY01	2017
Foundry Mold and Coremaker	Alabama	Y	27793 AE	39247 AW	44984 AEX	ALBLS	6/16
	Birmingham-Hoover MSA, AL	Y	28780 AE	35453 AW	38795 AEX	ALBLS	6/16
	Arizona	Y	25290 FQ	31920 MW	38250 TQ	USBLS	5/15
	Phoenix-Mesa-Scottsdale MSA, AZ	Y	24630 FQ	30930 MW	38440 TQ	USBLS	5/15
	Arkansas	Y	27810 FQ	32710 MW	36930 TQ	USBLS	5/15
	California	H	12.32 FQ	16.12 MW	19.18 TQ	CABLS	1/16-3/16
	Anaheim-Santa Ana-Irvine PMSA, CA	H	13.01 FQ	15.55 MW	18.50 TQ	CABLS	1/16-3/16
	Los Angeles-Long Beach-Glendale PMSA, CA	H	12.06 FQ	16.34 MW	19.01 TQ	CABLS	1/16-3/16
	Oakland-Hayward-Berkeley PMSA, CA	H	14.50 FQ	18.38 MW	21.47 TQ	CABLS	1/16-3/16
	Riverside-San Bernardino-Ontario MSA, CA	H	10.83 FQ	11.98 MW	14.53 TQ	CABLS	1/16-3/16
	Connecticut	Y		35042 MW		CTBLS	1/16-3/16
	Florida	H	10.48 AE	13.80 MW	16.34 AEX	FLBLS	7/16-9/16
	Georgia	Y	28930 FQ	34280 MW	39190 TQ	USBLS	5/15
	Atlanta-Sandy Springs-Roswell MSA, GA	Y	25390 FQ	29320 MW	35840 TQ	USBLS	5/15
	Illinois	Y	30320 FQ	36260 MW	46200 TQ	USBLS	5/15
	Indiana	Y	26580 FQ	31240 MW	36640 TQ	USBLS	5/15
	Indianapolis-Carmel-Anderson MSA, IN	Y	32330 FQ	35050 MW	37770 TQ	USBLS	5/15
	Iowa	Y	23710 FQ	30580 MW	41760 TQ	USBLS	5/15
	Kansas	Y	24460 FQ	32870 MW	37760 TQ	USBLS	5/15
	Kentucky	Y	28100 FQ	34070 MW	40240 TQ	USBLS	5/15
	Maryland	Y	22626 AE	28636 MW	31641 AEX	MDBLS	4/16
	Massachusetts	Y	32210 FQ	43020 MW	54520 TQ	USBLS	5/15
	Michigan	Y	27600 FQ	32610 MW	38820 TQ	USBLS	5/15
	Detroit-Dearborn-Livonia PMSA, MI	Y	25640 FQ	31680 MW	36720 TQ	USBLS	5/15
	Grand Rapids-Wyoming MSA, MI	Y	33630 FQ	35920 MW	38210 TQ	USBLS	5/15
	Minnesota	Y	34970 FQ	42584 MW	48618 TQ	MNBLS	1/16-3/16
	Minneapolis-St. Paul-Bloomington MSA, MN-WI	Y	36691 FQ	44234 MW	50714 TQ	MNBLS	1/16-3/16
	Missouri	Y	26970 FQ	31430 MW	36950 TQ	USBLS	5/15
	Kansas City MSA, MO-KS	Y	23960 FQ	32230 MW	36660 TQ	USBLS	5/15
	St. Louis MSA, MO-IL	Y	27320 FQ	32700 MW	37160 TQ	USBLS	5/15
	Nebraska	Y	22675 FQ	26355 MW	32155 TQ	NEBLS	7/16-9/16
	Omaha-Council Bluffs MSA, NE-IA	Y	29975 FQ	35760 MW	41715 TQ	NEBLS	7/16-9/16
	New Hampshire	H	12.30 AE	15.91 MW	17.70 AEX	NHBLS	6/16
	Nashua NECTA, NH-MA	Y	26880 FQ	31890 MW	36320 TQ	USBLS	5/15
	New Jersey	Y	26800 FQ	34340 MW	42460 TQ	USBLS	5/15
	New York	Y	25860 AE	36420 MW	42250 AEX	NYBLS	1/16-3/16
	North Carolina	Y	22850 FQ	28360 MW	38350 TQ	USBLS	5/15
	Ohio	Y	26580 FQ	32580 MW	37890 TQ	USBLS	5/15
	Cincinnati MSA, OH-KY-IN	Y	28870 FQ	33810 MW	37640 TQ	USBLS	5/15
	Cleveland-Elyria MSA, OH	Y	24150 FQ	31290 MW	36590 TQ	USBLS	5/15
	Columbus MSA, OH	Y	31460 FQ	35080 MW	38700 TQ	USBLS	5/15
	Oklahoma	Y	21950 FQ	25470 MW	32830 TQ	USBLS	5/15
	Tulsa MSA, OK	Y	22780 FQ	26440 MW	33400 TQ	USBLS	5/15
	Oregon	H	14.49 FQ	18.11 MW	22.07 TQ	ORBLS	2016
	Portland-Vancouver-Hillsboro MSA, OR-WA	Y	31600 FQ	39400 MW	46430 TQ	USBLS	5/15
	Pennsylvania	Y	28690 FQ	35230 MW	43800 TQ	USBLS	5/15
	Allentown-Bethlehem-Easton MSA, PA-NJ	Y	39510 FQ	43960 MW	48340 TQ	USBLS	5/15

AE Average entry wage	**AWR** Average wage range	**H** Hourly	**LR** Low end range	**MTC** Median total compensation	**TCC** Total cash compensation
AEX Average experienced wage	**B** Biweekly	**HI** Highest wage paid	**M** Monthly	**MW** Median wage paid	**TQ** Third quartile wage
ATC Average total compensation	**D** Daily	**HR** High end range	**MCC** Median cash compensation	**MWR** Median wage range	**W** Weekly
AW Average wage paid	**FQ** First quartile wage	**LO** Lowest wage paid	**ME** Median entry wage	**S** See annotated source	**Y** Yearly

Occupation/Type/Industry	Location	Per	Low	Mid	High	Source	Date
Foundry Mold and Coremaker	Montgomery County-Bucks County-Chester County PMSA, PA	Y	36620 FQ	44940 MW	54070 TQ	USBLS	5/15
	Philadelphia PMSA, PA	Y	26130 FQ	29960 MW	37860 TQ	USBLS	5/15
	Pittsburgh MSA, PA	Y	37370 FQ	42840 MW	47560 TQ	USBLS	5/15
	Providence-Warwick MSA, RI-MA	Y	25420 FQ	29800 MW	44950 TQ	USBLS	5/15
	South Carolina	Y	21880 FQ	23610 MW	26120 TQ	USBLS	5/15
	Greenville-Anderson-Mauldin MSA, SC	Y	27990 FQ	33340 MW	37530 TQ	USBLS	5/15
	Tennessee	Y	31180 FQ	36170 MW	42600 TQ	USBLS	5/15
	Texas	Y	23180 FQ	27880 MW	34060 TQ	USBLS	5/15
	Dallas-Plano-Irving PMSA, TX	Y	25300 FQ	32500 MW	39370 TQ	USBLS	5/15
	Fort Worth-Arlington PMSA, TX	Y	22620 FQ	26230 MW	29900 TQ	USBLS	5/15
	Houston-The Woodlands-Sugar Land MSA, TX	Y	24930 FQ	28260 MW	32580 TQ	USBLS	5/15
	Utah	Y	26710 FQ	32410 MW	39300 TQ	USBLS	5/15
	Provo-Orem MSA, UT	Y	26520 FQ	32450 MW	39290 TQ	USBLS	5/15
	Salt Lake City MSA, UT	Y	28140 FQ	34330 MW	42410 TQ	USBLS	5/15
	Washington	H	11.82 FQ	14.98 MW	18.91 TQ	WABLS	3/16
	Seattle-Bellevue-Everett PMSA, WA	H	11.66 FQ	14.25 MW	18.46 TQ	WABLS	3/16
	Tacoma-Lakewood PMSA, WA	H	11.19 FQ	12.54 MW	15.02 TQ	WABLS	3/16
	West Virginia	Y	24550 FQ	28040 MW	32510 TQ	USBLS	5/15
	Wisconsin	Y	28740 FQ	33680 MW	41300 TQ	USBLS	5/15
	Madison MSA, WI	Y	26560 FQ	28770 MW	30990 TQ	USBLS	5/15
	Milwaukee-Waukesha-West Allis MSA, WI	Y	28780 FQ	33420 MW	39920 TQ	USBLS	5/15
Fraud Investigator Board of Workers' Compensation, State Government	Ohio	H	24.47 LO		34.89 HI	OHGOV	2015
Fraud Prevention Technician Department of Public Health and Human Services, State Government	Helena, MT	H			14.00 HI	MTGOV	2016
FRIB Talent Manager Michigan State University	East Lansing, MI	Y			132796 HI	MSUSAL	10/1/14-9/30/15
Front-End Web Developer	United States	Y	83250-119500 LR			INFOW01	2017
Fueler Ramp Agent	United States	H		13.50 AW		AVJOB02	2016
Fundraiser	Alabama	Y	33977 AE	50172 AW	58269 AEX	ALBLS	6/16
	Birmingham-Hoover MSA, AL	Y	34633 AE	52252 AW	61057 AEX	ALBLS	6/16
	Alaska	Y	39800 FQ	48670 MW	60000 TQ	USBLS	5/15
	Anchorage MSA, AK	Y	50110 FQ	57850 MW	68790 TQ	USBLS	5/15
	Arizona	Y	38320 FQ	46580 MW	58870 TQ	USBLS	5/15
	Phoenix-Mesa-Scottsdale MSA, AZ	Y	38000 FQ	47430 MW	60340 TQ	USBLS	5/15
	Tucson MSA, AZ	Y	38640 FQ	45190 MW	53330 TQ	USBLS	5/15
	Arkansas	Y	21540 FQ	41200 MW	56260 TQ	USBLS	5/15
	Little Rock-North Little Rock-Conway MSA, AR	Y	25320 FQ	41840 MW	49730 TQ	USBLS	5/15
	California	H	20.42 FQ	28.95 MW	38.08 TQ	CABLS	1/16-3/16
	Anaheim-Santa Ana-Irvine PMSA, CA	H	19.26 FQ	27.37 MW	35.58 TQ	CABLS	1/16-3/16
	Los Angeles-Long Beach-Glendale PMSA, CA	H	25.33 FQ	33.69 MW	40.59 TQ	CABLS	1/16-3/16
	Oakland-Hayward-Berkeley PMSA, CA	H	21.01 FQ	29.85 MW	36.81 TQ	CABLS	1/16-3/16
	Riverside-San Bernardino-Ontario MSA, CA	H	19.59 FQ	26.76 MW	37.94 TQ	CABLS	1/16-3/16
	Sacramento–Roseville–Arden-Arcade MSA, CA	H	20.51 FQ	28.15 MW	39.91 TQ	CABLS	1/16-3/16
	San Diego-Carlsbad MSA, CA	H	17.51 FQ	22.61 MW	29.93 TQ	CABLS	1/16-3/16
	San Francisco-Redwood City-South San Francisco PMSA, CA	H	20.92 FQ	29.51 MW	38.87 TQ	CABLS	1/16-3/16
	Colorado	Y	40700 FQ	54990 MW	72860 TQ	USBLS	5/15

AE	Average entry wage	AWR	Average wage range	H	Hourly	LR	Low end range	MTC	Median total compensation	TCC	Total cash compensation
AEX	Average experienced wage	B	Biweekly	HI	Highest wage paid	M	Monthly	MW	Median wage paid	TQ	Third quartile wage
ATC	Average total compensation	D	Daily	HR	High end range	MCC	Median cash compensation	MWR	Median wage range	W	Weekly
AW	Average wage paid	FQ	First quartile wage	LO	Lowest wage paid	ME	Median entry wage	S	See annotated source	Y	Yearly

Occupation/Type/Industry	Location	Per	Low	Mid	High	Source	Date
Fundraiser	Denver-Aurora-Lakewood MSA, CO	Y	43980 FQ	57620 MW	75050 TQ	USBLS	5/15
	Connecticut	Y		55251 MW		CTBLS	1/16-3/16
	Bridgeport-Stamford-Norwalk MSA, CT	Y	41360 FQ	57950 MW	72830 TQ	USBLS	5/15
	Hartford-West Hartford-East Hartford MSA, CT	Y	41210 FQ	49740 MW	63330 TQ	USBLS	5/15
	Delaware	Y	39030 FQ	52390 MW	65020 TQ	USBLS	5/15
	Wilmington PMSA, DE-MD-NJ	Y	39980 FQ	54710 MW	67530 TQ	USBLS	5/15
	District of Columbia	Y	47800 FQ	68200 MW	91850 TQ	USBLS	5/15
	Washington-Arlington-Alexandria PMSA, DC-VA-MD-WV	Y	48720 FQ	69360 MW	91610 TQ	USBLS	5/15
	Florida	H	18.15 AE	25.91 MW	34.84 AEX	FLBLS	7/16-9/16
	Fort Lauderdale-Pompano Beach-Deerfield Beach PMSA, FL	H	16.20 AE	23.86 MW	29.97 AEX	FLBLS	7/16-9/16
	Miami-Miami Beach-Kendall PMSA, FL	H	21.61 AE	29.75 MW	42.22 AEX	FLBLS	7/16-9/16
	Orlando-Kissimmee-Sanford MSA, FL	H	17.39 AE	24.51 MW	29.64 AEX	FLBLS	7/16-9/16
	Tampa-St. Petersburg-Clearwater MSA, FL	H	18.71 AE	27.92 MW	34.81 AEX	FLBLS	7/16-9/16
	Georgia	Y	33270 FQ	43660 MW	56570 TQ	USBLS	5/15
	Atlanta-Sandy Springs-Roswell MSA, GA	Y	35340 FQ	45060 MW	57660 TQ	USBLS	5/15
	Augusta-Richmond County MSA, GA-SC	Y	32580 FQ	38720 MW	53940 TQ	USBLS	5/15
	Hawaii	Y	43760 FQ	59550 MW	78530 TQ	USBLS	5/15
	Urban Honolulu MSA, HI	Y	46020 FQ	63360 MW	83960 TQ	USBLS	5/15
	Idaho	Y	32310 FQ	45910 MW	58400 TQ	USBLS	5/15
	Boise City MSA, ID	Y	30030 FQ	45500 MW	59360 TQ	USBLS	5/15
	Illinois	Y	41100 FQ	51550 MW	66970 TQ	USBLS	5/15
	Chicago-Naperville-Arlington Heights PMSA, IL	Y	42360 FQ	54260 MW	68650 TQ	USBLS	5/15
	Lake County-Kenosha County PMSA, IL-WI	Y	44360 FQ	50410 MW	83270 TQ	USBLS	5/15
	Indiana	Y	37560 FQ	48110 MW	64750 TQ	USBLS	5/15
	Gary PMSA, IN	Y	34910 FQ	50910 MW	60990 TQ	USBLS	5/15
	Indianapolis-Carmel-Anderson MSA, IN	Y	40370 FQ	49400 MW	70740 TQ	USBLS	5/15
	Iowa	Y	35630 FQ	45610 MW	64370 TQ	USBLS	5/15
	Des Moines-West Des Moines MSA, IA	Y	37460 FQ	48570 MW	65440 TQ	USBLS	5/15
	Kansas	Y	38840 FQ	49510 MW	64640 TQ	USBLS	5/15
	Wichita MSA, KS	Y	38680 FQ	53090 MW	61970 TQ	USBLS	5/15
	Kentucky	Y	33190 FQ	44680 MW	57710 TQ	USBLS	5/15
	Louisville-Jefferson County MSA, KY-IN	Y	33990 FQ	45570 MW	62340 TQ	USBLS	5/15
	Louisiana	Y	38100 FQ	46160 MW	55810 TQ	USBLS	5/15
	Baton Rouge MSA, LA	Y	44290 FQ	50130 MW	58750 TQ	USBLS	5/15
	New Orleans-Metairie MSA, LA	Y	36530 FQ	44960 MW	54290 TQ	USBLS	5/15
	Maine	Y	39920 FQ	50720 MW	62460 TQ	USBLS	5/15
	Portland-South Portland MSA, ME	Y	39260 FQ	49820 MW	61020 TQ	USBLS	5/15
	Maryland	Y	30604 AE	57475 MW	70911 AEX	MDBLS	4/16
	Baltimore-Columbia-Towson MSA, MD	Y	36370 FQ	48450 MW	69430 TQ	USBLS	5/15
	Salisbury MSA, MD-DE	Y	25600 FQ	34630 MW	41630 TQ	USBLS	5/15
	Massachusetts	Y	43300 FQ	59850 MW	78310 TQ	USBLS	5/15
	Boston-Cambridge-Newton NECTA, MA	Y	46210 FQ	63850 MW	80270 TQ	USBLS	5/15
	Worcester MSA, MA-CT	Y	38390 FQ	49660 MW	69500 TQ	USBLS	5/15
	Michigan	Y	40680 FQ	55830 MW	72960 TQ	USBLS	5/15
	Detroit-Dearborn-Livonia PMSA, MI	Y	40430 FQ	59280 MW	75440 TQ	USBLS	5/15
	Grand Rapids-Wyoming MSA, MI	Y	36950 FQ	49710 MW	71930 TQ	USBLS	5/15
	Minnesota	Y	47818 FQ	62948 MW	77173 TQ	MNBLS	1/16-3/16

AE	Average entry wage	AWR	Average wage range	H	Hourly	LR	Low end range	MTC	Median total compensation	TCC	Total cash compensation
AEX	Average experienced wage	B	Biweekly	HI	Highest wage paid	M	Monthly	MW	Median wage paid	TQ	Third quartile wage
ATC	Average total compensation	D	Daily	HR	High end range	MCC	Median cash compensation	MWR	Median wage range	W	Weekly
AW	Average wage paid	FQ	First quartile wage	LO	Lowest wage paid	ME	Median entry wage	S	See annotated source	Y	Yearly

Occupation/Type/Industry	Location	Per	Low	Mid	High	Source	Date
Fundraiser	Minneapolis-St. Paul-Bloomington MSA, MN-WI	Y	50389 FQ	63903 MW	77864 TQ	MNBLS	1/16-3/16
	Mississippi	Y	33190 FQ	40960 MW	56060 TQ	USBLS	5/15
	Jackson MSA, MS	Y	24260 FQ	37420 MW	52890 TQ	USBLS	5/15
	Missouri	Y	39530 FQ	48660 MW	66790 TQ	USBLS	5/15
	Kansas City MSA, MO-KS	Y	37020 FQ	46560 MW	59260 TQ	USBLS	5/15
	St. Louis MSA, MO-IL	Y	41210 FQ	50270 MW	67390 TQ	USBLS	5/15
	Montana	Y	36340 FQ	45930 MW	58670 TQ	USBLS	5/15
	Billings MSA, MT	Y	34480 FQ	42970 MW	50220 TQ	USBLS	5/15
	Nebraska	Y	42385 FQ	52775 MW	72015 TQ	NEBLS	7/16-9/16
	Omaha-Council Bluffs MSA, NE-IA	Y	44690 FQ	57045 MW	73180 TQ	NEBLS	7/16-9/16
	Nevada	Y	40610 FQ	49540 MW	58240 TQ	USBLS	5/15
	Las Vegas-Henderson-Paradise MSA, NV	Y	40410 FQ	51610 MW	58640 TQ	USBLS	5/15
	New Hampshire	H	16.44 AE	25.92 MW	30.47 AEX	NHBLS	6/16
	Manchester NECTA, NH	H	16.45 AE	23.36 MW	27.63 AEX	NHBLS	6/16
	Nashua NECTA, NH-MA	Y	49140 FQ	56780 MW	63350 TQ	USBLS	5/15
	New Jersey	Y	47340 FQ	58650 MW	71750 TQ	USBLS	5/15
	Camden PMSA, NJ	Y	52030 FQ	59260 MW	69350 TQ	USBLS	5/15
	Newark PMSA, NJ-PA	Y	44600 FQ	56970 MW	71610 TQ	USBLS	5/15
	Trenton MSA, NJ	Y	42590 FQ	54300 MW	66760 TQ	USBLS	5/15
	New Mexico	Y	33870 FQ	48490 MW	64460 TQ	USBLS	5/15
	Albuquerque MSA, NM	Y	37760 FQ	51870 MW	62980 TQ	USBLS	5/15
	New York	Y	36780 AE	58280 MW	74170 AEX	NYBLS	1/16-3/16
	Buffalo-Cheektowaga-Niagara Falls MSA, NY	Y	35410 FQ	46020 MW	55620 TQ	USBLS	5/15
	Nassau County-Suffolk County PMSA, NY	Y	30310 FQ	54100 MW	68330 TQ	USBLS	5/15
	New York-Jersey City-White Plains PMSA, NY-NJ	Y	45380 FQ	60120 MW	79100 TQ	USBLS	5/15
	Rochester MSA, NY	Y	40840 FQ	49270 MW	60950 TQ	USBLS	5/15
	North Carolina	Y	40960 FQ	50020 MW	68080 TQ	USBLS	5/15
	Charlotte-Concord-Gastonia MSA, NC-SC	Y	41350 FQ	47660 MW	59060 TQ	USBLS	5/15
	Raleigh MSA, NC	Y	42140 FQ	51620 MW	68130 TQ	USBLS	5/15
	North Dakota	Y	39910 FQ	53840 MW	73440 TQ	USBLS	5/15
	Fargo MSA, ND-MN	Y	41820 FQ	56670 MW	84580 TQ	USBLS	5/15
	Ohio	Y	37720 FQ	48070 MW	61720 TQ	USBLS	5/15
	Cincinnati MSA, OH-KY-IN	Y	40670 FQ	49600 MW	63530 TQ	USBLS	5/15
	Cleveland-Elyria MSA, OH	Y	36820 FQ	48570 MW	62580 TQ	USBLS	5/15
	Columbus MSA, OH	Y	39660 FQ	50660 MW	65180 TQ	USBLS	5/15
	Oklahoma	Y	34740 FQ	41190 MW	56170 TQ	USBLS	5/15
	Oklahoma City MSA, OK	Y	34520 FQ	40770 MW	54260 TQ	USBLS	5/15
	Tulsa MSA, OK	Y	35970 FQ	45140 MW	59290 TQ	USBLS	5/15
	Oregon	H	17.65 FQ	22.80 MW	29.80 TQ	ORBLS	2016
	Portland-Vancouver-Hillsboro MSA, OR-WA	Y	37400 FQ	48080 MW	62270 TQ	USBLS	5/15
	Pennsylvania	Y	39100 FQ	50820 MW	65940 TQ	USBLS	5/15
	Allentown-Bethlehem-Easton MSA, PA-NJ	Y	33510 FQ	48520 MW	69510 TQ	USBLS	5/15
	Harrisburg-Carlisle MSA, PA	Y	35360 FQ	46520 MW	71420 TQ	USBLS	5/15
	Montgomery County-Bucks County-Chester County PMSA, PA	Y	38350 FQ	52480 MW	65430 TQ	USBLS	5/15
	Philadelphia PMSA, PA	Y	44200 FQ	60000 MW	75480 TQ	USBLS	5/15
	Pittsburgh MSA, PA	Y	39320 FQ	47330 MW	59740 TQ	USBLS	5/15
	Rhode Island	Y	39640 FQ	57970 MW	80580 TQ	USBLS	5/15
	Providence-Warwick MSA, RI-MA	Y	39820 FQ	58050 MW	80900 TQ	USBLS	5/15
	South Carolina	Y	36180 FQ	50740 MW	63730 TQ	USBLS	5/15
	Charleston-North Charleston MSA, SC	Y	40980 FQ	52330 MW	64620 TQ	USBLS	5/15
	Columbia MSA, SC	Y	35900 FQ	52630 MW	79020 TQ	USBLS	5/15
	Greenville-Anderson-Mauldin MSA, SC	Y	33830 FQ	46740 MW	62360 TQ	USBLS	5/15
	South Dakota	Y	36500 FQ	44060 MW	55650 TQ	USBLS	5/15
	Tennessee	Y	33750 FQ	44390 MW	60710 TQ	USBLS	5/15
	Knoxville MSA, TN	Y	25290 FQ	35880 MW	44610 TQ	USBLS	5/15
	Memphis MSA, TN-MS-AR	Y	36120 FQ	50360 MW	65140 TQ	USBLS	5/15

AE	Average entry wage	AWR	Average wage range	H	Hourly
AEX	Average experienced wage	B	Biweekly	HI	Highest wage paid
ATC	Average total compensation	D	Daily	HR	High end range
AW	Average wage paid	FQ	First quartile wage	LO	Lowest wage paid

LR Low end range   MTC Median total compensation TCC Total cash compensation
M Monthly   MW Median wage paid   TQ Third quartile wage
MCC Median cash compensation MWR Median wage range   W Weekly
ME Median entry wage   S See annotated source   Y Yearly

Occupation/Type/Industry	Location	Per	Low	Mid	High	Source	Date
Fundraiser	Nashville-Davidson– Murfreesboro–Franklin MSA, TN	Y	42100 FQ	55040 MW	77330 TQ	USBLS	5/15
	Texas	Y	42390 FQ	54040 MW	72140 TQ	USBLS	5/15
	Austin-Round Rock MSA, TX	Y	43040 FQ	56030 MW	69580 TQ	USBLS	5/15
	Dallas-Plano-Irving PMSA, TX	Y	44460 FQ	57230 MW	80640 TQ	USBLS	5/15
	Fort Worth-Arlington PMSA, TX	Y	39710 FQ	51770 MW	64620 TQ	USBLS	5/15
	Houston-The Woodlands- Sugar Land MSA, TX	Y	43710 FQ	56620 MW	73310 TQ	USBLS	5/15
	San Antonio-New Braunfels MSA, TX	Y	44130 FQ	52430 MW	68700 TQ	USBLS	5/15
	Utah	Y	37980 FQ	49660 MW	67050 TQ	USBLS	5/15
	Ogden-Clearfield MSA, UT	Y	36210 FQ	52810 MW	69010 TQ	USBLS	5/15
	Provo-Orem MSA, UT	Y	43830 FQ	58170 MW	70700 TQ	USBLS	5/15
	Salt Lake City MSA, UT	Y	38030 FQ	48050 MW	65890 TQ	USBLS	5/15
	Vermont	Y	37430 FQ	47230 MW	59380 TQ	USBLS	5/15
	Burlington-South Burlington MSA, VT	Y	42940 FQ	48540 MW	61540 TQ	USBLS	5/15
	Virginia	Y	42600 FQ	57760 MW	76900 TQ	USBLS	5/15
	Richmond MSA, VA	Y	40240 FQ	48080 MW	62950 TQ	USBLS	5/15
	Virginia Beach-Norfolk- Newport News MSA, VA-NC	Y	38970 FQ	53820 MW	69810 TQ	USBLS	5/15
	Washington	H	21.02 FQ	26.49 MW	34.07 TQ	WABLS	3/16
	Seattle-Bellevue-Everett PMSA, WA	H	21.93 FQ	27.90 MW	35.49 TQ	WABLS	3/16
	Tacoma-Lakewood PMSA, WA	H	18.86 FQ	25.77 MW	31.21 TQ	WABLS	3/16
	West Virginia	Y	30750 FQ	42730 MW	53930 TQ	USBLS	5/15
	Wisconsin	Y	41060 FQ	51010 MW	63160 TQ	USBLS	5/15
	Madison MSA, WI	Y	42650 FQ	52100 MW	61740 TQ	USBLS	5/15
	Milwaukee-Waukesha-West Allis MSA, WI	Y	42380 FQ	56930 MW	72750 TQ	USBLS	5/15
	Wyoming	Y	34800 FQ	51700 MW	61700 TQ	USBLS	5/15
Funeral Attendant	Alabama	Y	17359 AE	22754 AW	25452 AEX	ALBLS	6/16
	Birmingham-Hoover MSA, AL	Y	17225 AE	25133 AW	29086 AEX	ALBLS	6/16
	Arizona	Y	21690 FQ	25660 MW	29960 TQ	USBLS	5/15
	Phoenix-Mesa-Scottsdale MSA, AZ	Y	22430 FQ	26610 MW	30800 TQ	USBLS	5/15
	Arkansas	Y	17210 FQ	18800 MW	21980 TQ	USBLS	5/15
	Little Rock-North Little Rock- Conway MSA, AR	Y	20800 FQ	23420 MW	33830 TQ	USBLS	5/15
	California	H	10.95 FQ	14.11 MW	19.47 TQ	CABLS	1/16-3/16
	Los Angeles-Long Beach- Glendale PMSA, CA	H	11.05 FQ	14.49 MW	19.19 TQ	CABLS	1/16-3/16
	Oakland-Hayward-Berkeley PMSA, CA	H	18.55 FQ	20.83 MW	22.71 TQ	CABLS	1/16-3/16
	Riverside-San Bernardino- Ontario MSA, CA	H	10.91 FQ	12.94 MW	17.20 TQ	CABLS	1/16-3/16
	San Diego-Carlsbad MSA, CA	H	11.03 FQ	13.30 MW	17.16 TQ	CABLS	1/16-3/16
	San Francisco-Redwood City- South San Francisco PMSA, CA	H	13.73 FQ	16.86 MW	20.69 TQ	CABLS	1/16-3/16
	Colorado	Y	25670 FQ	27920 MW	30180 TQ	USBLS	5/15
	Denver-Aurora-Lakewood MSA, CO	Y	26210 FQ	27830 MW	29450 TQ	USBLS	5/15
	Connecticut	Y		38413 MW		CTBLS	1/16-3/16
	Hartford-West Hartford-East Hartford MSA, CT	Y	34420 FQ	41910 MW	46310 TQ	USBLS	5/15
	Delaware	Y	22390 FQ	32070 MW	37540 TQ	USBLS	5/15
	Wilmington PMSA, DE-MD- NJ	Y	30830 FQ	35330 MW	39520 TQ	USBLS	5/15
	Washington-Arlington- Alexandria PMSA, DC-VA- MD-WV	Y	23000 FQ	27600 MW	32390 TQ	USBLS	5/15
	Florida	H	9.48 AE	11.57 MW	13.85 AEX	FLBLS	7/16-9/16
	Fort Lauderdale-Pompano Beach-Deerfield Beach PMSA, FL	H	9.03 AE	11.24 MW	13.37 AEX	FLBLS	7/16-9/16
	Miami-Miami Beach-Kendall PMSA, FL	H	9.67 AE	11.45 MW	13.62 AEX	FLBLS	7/16-9/16

AE	Average entry wage	**AWR**	Average wage range	**H**	Hourly
AEX	Average experienced wage	**B**	Biweekly	**HI**	Highest wage paid
ATC	Average total compensation	**D**	Daily	**HR**	High end range
AW	Average wage paid	**FQ**	First quartile wage	**LO**	Lowest wage paid

LR	Low end range	**MTC**	Median total compensation	**TCC**	Total cash compensation
M	Monthly	**MW**	Median wage paid	**TQ**	Third quartile wage
MCC	Median cash compensation	**MWR**	Median wage range	**W**	Weekly
ME	Median entry wage	**S**	See annotated source	**Y**	Yearly

Funeral Attendant

Occupation/Type/Industry	Location	Per	Low	Mid	High	Source	Date
Funeral Attendant	Orlando-Kissimmee-Sanford MSA, FL	H	10.48 AE	16.34 MW	17.71 AEX	FLBLS	7/16-9/16
	Tampa-St. Petersburg-Clearwater MSA, FL	H	9.68 AE	11.47 MW	12.96 AEX	FLBLS	7/16-9/16
	Georgia	Y	19070 FQ	22530 MW	27830 TQ	USBLS	5/15
	Atlanta-Sandy Springs-Roswell MSA, GA	Y	20060 FQ	23040 MW	29430 TQ	USBLS	5/15
	Augusta-Richmond County MSA, GA-SC	Y	17420 FQ	20090 MW	24360 TQ	USBLS	5/15
	Idaho	Y	23570 FQ	27930 MW	31070 TQ	USBLS	5/15
	Illinois	Y	20310 FQ	23370 MW	29180 TQ	USBLS	5/15
	Chicago-Naperville-Arlington Heights PMSA, IL	Y	21070 FQ	24190 MW	40150 TQ	USBLS	5/15
	Lake County-Kenosha County PMSA, IL-WI	Y	21610 FQ	23740 MW	27440 TQ	USBLS	5/15
	Indiana	Y	20190 FQ	23240 MW	27280 TQ	USBLS	5/15
	Indianapolis-Carmel-Anderson MSA, IN	Y	18000 FQ	20380 MW	24000 TQ	USBLS	5/15
	Iowa	Y	19380 FQ	23540 MW	27840 TQ	USBLS	5/15
	Kansas	Y	18990 FQ	22790 MW	28580 TQ	USBLS	5/15
	Kentucky	Y	17350 FQ	19310 MW	22990 TQ	USBLS	5/15
	Louisville-Jefferson County MSA, KY-IN	Y	17910 FQ	20530 MW	24430 TQ	USBLS	5/15
	Louisiana	Y	18620 FQ	21940 MW	26080 TQ	USBLS	5/15
	Baton Rouge MSA, LA	Y	22360 FQ	25620 MW	31140 TQ	USBLS	5/15
	New Orleans-Metairie MSA, LA	Y	17950 FQ	20880 MW	25590 TQ	USBLS	5/15
	Maine	Y	19260 FQ	25570 MW	29170 TQ	USBLS	5/15
	Maryland	Y	19309 AE	28172 MW	32604 AEX	MDBLS	4/16
	Baltimore-Columbia-Towson MSA, MD	Y	19170 FQ	22790 MW	28120 TQ	USBLS	5/15
	Salisbury MSA, MD-DE	Y	23250 FQ	34860 MW	43730 TQ	USBLS	5/15
	Massachusetts	Y	31750 FQ	36180 MW	42800 TQ	USBLS	5/15
	Worcester MSA, MA-CT	Y	33560 FQ	36670 MW	51470 TQ	USBLS	5/15
	Michigan	Y	20650 FQ	23290 MW	29300 TQ	USBLS	5/15
	Detroit-Dearborn-Livonia PMSA, MI	Y	21620 FQ	23650 MW	27500 TQ	USBLS	5/15
	Grand Rapids-Wyoming MSA, MI	Y	22470 FQ	27190 MW	34150 TQ	USBLS	5/15
	Minnesota	Y	22874 FQ	27196 MW	32922 TQ	MNBLS	1/16-3/16
	Minneapolis-St. Paul-Bloomington MSA, MN-WI	Y	23994 FQ	27812 MW	31558 TQ	MNBLS	1/16-3/16
	Mississippi	Y	19940 FQ	22320 MW	24660 TQ	USBLS	5/15
	Jackson MSA, MS	Y	19970 FQ	22340 MW	24730 TQ	USBLS	5/15
	Missouri	Y	18490 FQ	22060 MW	27920 TQ	USBLS	5/15
	Kansas City MSA, MO-KS	Y	18920 FQ	22240 MW	27030 TQ	USBLS	5/15
	St. Louis MSA, MO-IL	Y	18300 FQ	21910 MW	28840 TQ	USBLS	5/15
	Montana	Y	25570 FQ	27750 MW	29940 TQ	USBLS	5/15
	Omaha-Council Bluffs MSA, NE-IA	Y	21915 FQ	27725 MW	31130 TQ	NEBLS	7/16-9/16
	Nevada	Y	21530 FQ	26220 MW	33420 TQ	USBLS	5/15
	New Hampshire	H	12.47 AE	18.05 MW	20.84 AEX	NHBLS	6/16
	New Jersey	Y	27270 FQ	34150 MW	41620 TQ	USBLS	5/15
	Camden PMSA, NJ	Y	22380 FQ	32180 MW	36360 TQ	USBLS	5/15
	Newark PMSA, NJ-PA	Y	27330 FQ	33430 MW	53930 TQ	USBLS	5/15
	New Mexico	Y	24960 FQ	29370 MW	39300 TQ	USBLS	5/15
	Albuquerque MSA, NM	Y	24480 FQ	40280 MW	44720 TQ	USBLS	5/15
	New York	Y	22000 AE	26120 MW	30460 AEX	NYBLS	1/16-3/16
	Nassau County-Suffolk County PMSA, NY	Y	25140 FQ	27330 MW	29530 TQ	USBLS	5/15
	New York-Jersey City-White Plains PMSA, NY-NJ	Y	23090 FQ	30100 MW	38790 TQ	USBLS	5/15
	Rochester MSA, NY	Y	25550 FQ	27750 MW	29950 TQ	USBLS	5/15
	North Carolina	Y	21450 FQ	24980 MW	29530 TQ	USBLS	5/15
	Charlotte-Concord-Gastonia MSA, NC-SC	Y	20210 FQ	22560 MW	25080 TQ	USBLS	5/15
	Raleigh MSA, NC	Y	19660 FQ	21800 MW	24060 TQ	USBLS	5/15
	North Dakota	Y	18550 FQ	23360 MW	28080 TQ	USBLS	5/15
	Fargo MSA, ND-MN	Y	19220 FQ	22280 MW	25270 TQ	USBLS	5/15
	Ohio	Y	18910 FQ	21830 MW	25850 TQ	USBLS	5/15
	Cincinnati MSA, OH-KY-IN	Y	21870 FQ	24320 MW	28060 TQ	USBLS	5/15
	Cleveland-Elyria MSA, OH	Y	18310 FQ	19850 MW	24670 TQ	USBLS	5/15

AE	Average entry wage	AWR	Average wage range	H	Hourly
AEX	Average experienced wage	B	Biweekly	HI	Highest wage paid
ATC	Average total compensation	D	Daily	HR	High end range
AW	Average wage paid	FQ	First quartile wage	LO	Lowest wage paid

LR	Low end range	MTC	Median total compensation	TCC	Total cash compensation
M	Monthly	MW	Median wage paid	TQ	Third quartile wage
MCC	Median cash compensation	MWR	Median wage range	W	Weekly
ME	Median entry wage	S	See annotated source	Y	Yearly

Occupation/Type/Industry	Location	Per	Low	Mid	High	Source	Date
Funeral Attendant	Columbus MSA, OH	Y	18790 FQ	21250 MW	24530 TQ	USBLS	5/15
	Oklahoma	Y	19300 FQ	22830 MW	28290 TQ	USBLS	5/15
	Oklahoma City MSA, OK	Y	20140 FQ	23110 MW	28360 TQ	USBLS	5/15
	Tulsa MSA, OK	Y	16710 FQ	18350 MW	21650 TQ	USBLS	5/15
	Oregon	H	10.41 FQ	11.71 MW	14.44 TQ	ORBLS	2016
	Portland-Vancouver-Hillsboro MSA, OR-WA	Y	20120 FQ	22270 MW	24420 TQ	USBLS	5/15
	Pennsylvania	Y	18240 FQ	22640 MW	28880 TQ	USBLS	5/15
	Allentown-Bethlehem-Easton MSA, PA-NJ	Y	19180 FQ	28400 MW	36960 TQ	USBLS	5/15
	Montgomery County-Bucks County-Chester County PMSA, PA	Y	18560 FQ	21760 MW	25410 TQ	USBLS	5/15
	Philadelphia PMSA, PA	Y	29630 FQ	33730 MW	38020 TQ	USBLS	5/15
	Pittsburgh MSA, PA	Y	16940 FQ	18640 MW	23610 TQ	USBLS	5/15
	Rhode Island	Y	27070 FQ	32470 MW	36000 TQ	USBLS	5/15
	Providence-Warwick MSA, RI-MA	Y	22510 FQ	28680 MW	34740 TQ	USBLS	5/15
	South Carolina	Y	17840 FQ	20820 MW	26510 TQ	USBLS	5/15
	Charleston-North Charleston MSA, SC	Y	18070 FQ	20870 MW	25520 TQ	USBLS	5/15
	Columbia MSA, SC	Y	17890 FQ	20630 MW	23400 TQ	USBLS	5/15
	Greenville-Anderson-Mauldin MSA, SC	Y	17810 FQ	20900 MW	26630 TQ	USBLS	5/15
	South Dakota	Y	19550 FQ	21810 MW	23950 TQ	USBLS	5/15
	Tennessee	Y	19610 FQ	23070 MW	28400 TQ	USBLS	5/15
	Knoxville MSA, TN	Y	21370 FQ	23180 MW	25820 TQ	USBLS	5/15
	Memphis MSA, TN-MS-AR	Y	17230 FQ	18960 MW	22010 TQ	USBLS	5/15
	Nashville-Davidson–Murfreesboro–Franklin MSA, TN	Y	20110 FQ	23480 MW	31840 TQ	USBLS	5/15
	Texas	Y	18690 FQ	22240 MW	26790 TQ	USBLS	5/15
	Austin-Round Rock MSA, TX	Y	21910 FQ	24080 MW	29450 TQ	USBLS	5/15
	Dallas-Plano-Irving PMSA, TX	Y	19210 FQ	23170 MW	27380 TQ	USBLS	5/15
	Fort Worth-Arlington PMSA, TX	Y	19690 FQ	22410 MW	25360 TQ	USBLS	5/15
	Houston-The Woodlands-Sugar Land MSA, TX	Y	19030 FQ	23400 MW	27700 TQ	USBLS	5/15
	Utah	Y	18190 FQ	24710 MW	32180 TQ	USBLS	5/15
	Vermont	Y	27260 FQ	33930 MW	40730 TQ	USBLS	5/15
	Virginia	Y	20470 FQ	23900 MW	30830 TQ	USBLS	5/15
	Richmond MSA, VA	Y	19450 FQ	22770 MW	32230 TQ	USBLS	5/15
	Virginia Beach-Norfolk-Newport News MSA, VA-NC	Y	24120 FQ	29840 MW	42140 TQ	USBLS	5/15
	Washington	H	10.60 FQ	11.83 MW	16.84 TQ	WABLS	3/16
	Seattle-Bellevue-Everett PMSA, WA	H	10.47 FQ	11.57 MW	15.93 TQ	WABLS	3/16
	Tacoma-Lakewood PMSA, WA	H	11.77 FQ	15.68 MW	18.97 TQ	WABLS	3/16
	West Virginia	Y	18770 FQ	22050 MW	27940 TQ	USBLS	5/15
	Huntington-Ashland MSA, WV-KY-OH	Y	20240 FQ	26980 MW	35820 TQ	USBLS	5/15
	Wisconsin	Y	21880 FQ	26380 MW	30670 TQ	USBLS	5/15
	Milwaukee-Waukesha-West Allis MSA, WI	Y	22750 FQ	26850 MW	30000 TQ	USBLS	5/15
	Wyoming	Y	21780 FQ	26150 MW	29760 TQ	USBLS	5/15
	Puerto Rico	Y	16660 FQ	17850 MW	19030 TQ	USBLS	5/15
	San Juan-Carolina-Caguas MSA, PR	Y	16710 FQ	17920 MW	19140 TQ	USBLS	5/15
Funeral Service Manager	Alabama	Y	48163 AE	68365 AW	78461 AEX	ALBLS	6/16
	Birmingham-Hoover MSA, AL	Y	67945 AE	73110 AW	75693 AEX	ALBLS	6/16
	Arizona	Y	58700 FQ	71000 MW	90450 TQ	USBLS	5/15
	Phoenix-Mesa-Scottsdale MSA, AZ	Y	63590 FQ	73160 MW	93640 TQ	USBLS	5/15
	Arkansas	Y	41040 FQ	52640 MW	77130 TQ	USBLS	5/15
	California	H	25.39 FQ	29.32 MW	35.48 TQ	CABLS	1/16-3/16
	Los Angeles-Long Beach-Glendale PMSA, CA	H	25.40 FQ	28.14 MW	31.00 TQ	CABLS	1/16-3/16
	Oakland-Hayward-Berkeley PMSA, CA	H	28.65 FQ	32.45 MW	36.08 TQ	CABLS	1/16-3/16
	Riverside-San Bernardino-Ontario MSA, CA	H	25.01 FQ	27.17 MW	29.32 TQ	CABLS	1/16-3/16

AE Average entry wage	AWR Average wage range	H Hourly	LR Low end range	MTC Median total compensation	TCC Total cash compensation
AEX Average experienced wage	B Biweekly	HI Highest wage paid	M Monthly	MW Median wage paid	TQ Third quartile wage
ATC Average total compensation	D Daily	HR High end range	MCC Median cash compensation	MWR Median wage range	W Weekly
AW Average wage paid	FQ First quartile wage	LO Lowest wage paid	ME Median entry wage	S See annotated source	Y Yearly

Occupation/Type/Industry	Location	Per	Low	Mid	High	Source	Date
Funeral Service Manager	Sacramento–Roseville–Arden-Arcade MSA, CA	H	18.97 FQ	29.53 MW	35.33 TQ	CABLS	1/16-3/16
	San Diego-Carlsbad MSA, CA	H	21.98 FQ	24.65 MW	30.49 TQ	CABLS	1/16-3/16
	San Francisco-Redwood City-South San Francisco PMSA, CA	H	26.06 FQ	33.03 MW	36.62 TQ	CABLS	1/16-3/16
	Colorado	Y	54860 FQ	65630 MW	74130 TQ	USBLS	5/15
	Denver-Aurora-Lakewood MSA, CO	Y	55690 FQ	64240 MW	73250 TQ	USBLS	5/15
	Connecticut	Y		92736 MW		CTBLS	1/16-3/16
	Delaware	Y	73460 FQ	89140 MW	117010 TQ	USBLS	5/15
	Washington-Arlington-Alexandria PMSA, DC-VA-MD-WV	Y	61130 FQ	72830 MW	109320 TQ	USBLS	5/15
	Florida	H	26.15 AE	39.43 MW	59.15 AEX	FLBLS	7/16-9/16
	Fort Lauderdale-Pompano Beach-Deerfield Beach PMSA, FL	H	22.65 AE	32.58 MW	36.46 AEX	FLBLS	7/16-9/16
	Orlando-Kissimmee-Sanford MSA, FL	H	28.82 AE	47.10 MW	51.59 AEX	FLBLS	7/16-9/16
	Tampa-St. Petersburg-Clearwater MSA, FL	H	35.83 AE	51.92 MW	65.37 AEX	FLBLS	7/16-9/16
	Georgia	Y	40320 FQ	56230 MW	101010 TQ	USBLS	5/15
	Illinois	Y	24050 FQ	65140 MW	87470 TQ	USBLS	5/15
	Chicago-Naperville-Arlington Heights PMSA, IL	Y	23200 FQ	70460 MW	108690 TQ	USBLS	5/15
	Lake County-Kenosha County PMSA, IL-WI	Y	57060 FQ	63650 MW	80380 TQ	USBLS	5/15
	Indiana	Y	53560 FQ	62940 MW	77160 TQ	USBLS	5/15
	Indianapolis-Carmel-Anderson MSA, IN	Y	57120 FQ	66120 MW	74500 TQ	USBLS	5/15
	Iowa	Y	53440 FQ	61920 MW	105640 TQ	USBLS	5/15
	Kansas	Y	55440 FQ	75280 MW	128080 TQ	USBLS	5/15
	Kentucky	Y	47090 FQ	63280 MW	79790 TQ	USBLS	5/15
	Louisville-Jefferson County MSA, KY-IN	Y	47570 FQ	62560 MW	76990 TQ	USBLS	5/15
	Louisiana	Y	38560 FQ	48130 MW	75370 TQ	USBLS	5/15
	New Orleans-Metairie MSA, LA	Y	42370 FQ	45740 MW	49110 TQ	USBLS	5/15
	Maine	Y	56670 FQ	69980 MW	94840 TQ	USBLS	5/15
	Maryland	Y	61084 AE	105827 MW	128198 AEX	MDBLS	4/16
	Baltimore-Columbia-Towson MSA, MD	Y	73770 FQ	98770 MW	126180 TQ	USBLS	5/15
	Massachusetts	Y	54910 FQ	66180 MW	123920 TQ	USBLS	5/15
	Michigan	Y	43430 FQ	63260 MW	87780 TQ	USBLS	5/15
	Minnesota	Y	75466 FQ	99202 MW	125773 TQ	MNBLS	1/16-3/16
	Minneapolis-St. Paul-Bloomington MSA, MN-WI	Y	58019 FQ	89813 MW	123070 TQ	MNBLS	1/16-3/16
	Mississippi	Y	22280 FQ	47640 MW	63280 TQ	USBLS	5/15
	Missouri	Y	53290 FQ	62030 MW	81990 TQ	USBLS	5/15
	Kansas City MSA, MO-KS	Y	53870 FQ	59440 MW	72500 TQ	USBLS	5/15
	St. Louis MSA, MO-IL	Y	46900 FQ	60240 MW	78220 TQ	USBLS	5/15
	Nevada	Y	62040 FQ	70080 MW	78390 TQ	USBLS	5/15
	Las Vegas-Henderson-Paradise MSA, NV	Y	63430 FQ	72040 MW	81340 TQ	USBLS	5/15
	New Hampshire	H	21.64 AE	24.51 MW	42.14 AEX	NHBLS	6/16
	New Jersey	Y	75890 FQ	109480 MW	155750 TQ	USBLS	5/15
	New Mexico	Y	51840 FQ	57710 MW	65470 TQ	USBLS	5/15
	Albuquerque MSA, NM	Y	52650 FQ	56290 MW	59930 TQ	USBLS	5/15
	New York	Y	68410 AE	115770 MW		NYBLS	1/16-3/16
	New York-Jersey City-White Plains PMSA, NY-NJ	Y	96080 FQ	126880 MW		USBLS	5/15
	North Carolina	Y	68920 FQ	84870 MW	136930 TQ	USBLS	5/15
	North Dakota	Y	55840 FQ	69200 MW	81590 TQ	USBLS	5/15
	Ohio	Y	60320 FQ	81600 MW	114660 TQ	USBLS	5/15
	Cincinnati MSA, OH-KY-IN	Y	52490 FQ	58800 MW	89110 TQ	USBLS	5/15
	Cleveland-Elyria MSA, OH	Y	63900 FQ	75220 MW	88210 TQ	USBLS	5/15
	Columbus MSA, OH	Y	52480 FQ	79470 MW	90170 TQ	USBLS	5/15
	Oklahoma	Y	45500 FQ	59720 MW	82430 TQ	USBLS	5/15
	Oklahoma City MSA, OK	Y	44730 FQ	49350 MW	79960 TQ	USBLS	5/15
	Oregon	H	24.71 FQ	30.15 MW	39.12 TQ	ORBLS	2016

AE	Average entry wage	AWR	Average wage range	H	Hourly	LR	Low end range	MTC	Median total compensation	TCC	Total cash compensation
AEX	Average experienced wage	B	Biweekly	HI	Highest wage paid	M	Monthly	MW	Median wage paid	TQ	Third quartile wage
ATC	Average total compensation	D	Daily	HR	High end range	MCC	Median cash compensation	MWR	Median wage range	W	Weekly
AW	Average wage paid	FQ	First quartile wage	LO	Lowest wage paid	ME	Median entry wage	S	See annotated source	Y	Yearly

Occupation/Type/Industry	Location	Per	Low	Mid	High	Source	Date
Funeral Service Manager	Portland-Vancouver-Hillsboro						
	MSA, OR-WA	Y	56530 FQ	68520 MW	96650 TQ	USBLS	5/15
	Pennsylvania	Y	74420 FQ	98640 MW	116240 TQ	USBLS	5/15
	Allentown-Bethlehem-Easton						
	MSA, PA-NJ	Y	69920 FQ	77340 MW	88330 TQ	USBLS	5/15
	Philadelphia PMSA, PA	Y	87400 FQ	94600 MW	101800 TQ	USBLS	5/15
	Pittsburgh MSA, PA	Y	78670 FQ	108200 MW	117560 TQ	USBLS	5/15
	Rhode Island	Y	59870 FQ	81670 MW	91280 TQ	USBLS	5/15
	Providence-Warwick MSA, RI-						
	MA	Y	59300 FQ	79100 MW	89970 TQ	USBLS	5/15
	South Carolina	Y	54290 FQ	80130 MW	102670 TQ	USBLS	5/15
	Tennessee	Y	53670 FQ	67890 MW	121820 TQ	USBLS	5/15
	Texas	Y	42770 FQ	67300 MW	81310 TQ	USBLS	5/15
	Dallas-Plano-Irving PMSA, TX	Y	48790 FQ	69430 MW	126170 TQ	USBLS	5/15
	Fort Worth-Arlington PMSA,						
	TX	Y	62890 FQ	69890 MW	77160 TQ	USBLS	5/15
	Houston-The Woodlands-						
	Sugar Land MSA, TX	Y	53810 FQ	72020 MW	80330 TQ	USBLS	5/15
	Utah	Y	40500 FQ	58440 MW	78510 TQ	USBLS	5/15
	Salt Lake City MSA, UT	Y	36780 FQ	54450 MW	82300 TQ	USBLS	5/15
	Virginia	Y	55550 FQ	89410 MW	108580 TQ	USBLS	5/15
	Washington	H	27.60 FQ	33.66 MW	45.47 TQ	WABLS	3/16
	Seattle-Bellevue-Everett						
	PMSA, WA	H	26.87 FQ	31.49 MW	40.63 TQ	WABLS	3/16
	West Virginia	Y	53100 FQ	67060 MW	90750 TQ	USBLS	5/15
	Wisconsin	Y	56760 FQ	81840 MW	112520 TQ	USBLS	5/15
	Puerto Rico	Y	26110 FQ	28650 MW	31290 TQ	USBLS	5/15
	San Juan-Carolina-Caguas						
	MSA, PR	Y	26700 FQ	28560 MW	30430 TQ	USBLS	5/15
Funeral Services Technician							
Cemetery, Municipal Government	Santa Monica, CA	Y			49000 HI	CACIT	6/28/16
Furnace, Kiln, Oven, Drier, and							
Kettle Operator and Tender	Alabama	Y	25243 AE	42424 AW	51020 AEX	ALBLS	6/16
	Birmingham-Hoover MSA, AL	Y	36533 AE	48511 AW	54506 AEX	ALBLS	6/16
	Arizona	Y	30700 FQ	36150 MW	42860 TQ	USBLS	5/15
	Phoenix-Mesa-Scottsdale						
	MSA, AZ	Y	29550 FQ	35940 MW	42730 TQ	USBLS	5/15
	Arkansas	Y	22450 FQ	29210 MW	40360 TQ	USBLS	5/15
	Little Rock-North Little Rock-						
	Conway MSA, AR	Y	16990 FQ	18380 MW	20700 TQ	USBLS	5/15
	California	H	11.92 FQ	15.19 MW	21.92 TQ	CABLS	1/16-3/16
	Los Angeles-Long Beach-						
	Glendale PMSA, CA	H	11.58 FQ	14.11 MW	19.50 TQ	CABLS	1/16-3/16
	Oakland-Hayward-Berkeley						
	PMSA, CA	H	11.18 FQ	13.66 MW	21.31 TQ	CABLS	1/16-3/16
	Sacramento–Roseville–						
	Arden-Arcade MSA, CA	H	13.05 FQ	13.94 MW	14.83 TQ	CABLS	1/16-3/16
	San Diego-Carlsbad MSA, CA	H	12.13 FQ	14.97 MW	19.33 TQ	CABLS	1/16-3/16
	Colorado	Y	29700 FQ	37470 MW	44420 TQ	USBLS	5/15
	Denver-Aurora-Lakewood						
	MSA, CO	Y	28600 FQ	33290 MW	38540 TQ	USBLS	5/15
	Connecticut	Y		34144 MW		CTBLS	1/16-3/16
	Florida	H	11.79 AE	14.22 MW	16.26 AEX	FLBLS	7/16-9/16
	Georgia	Y	27750 FQ	34060 MW	44120 TQ	USBLS	5/15
	Atlanta-Sandy Springs-						
	Roswell MSA, GA	Y	27720 FQ	34560 MW	44260 TQ	USBLS	5/15
	Augusta-Richmond County						
	MSA, GA-SC	Y	31180 FQ	36940 MW	43340 TQ	USBLS	5/15
	Idaho	Y	29230 FQ	36320 MW	44250 TQ	USBLS	5/15
	Illinois	Y	32330 FQ	36420 MW	42720 TQ	USBLS	5/15
	Chicago-Naperville-Arlington						
	Heights PMSA, IL	Y	32410 FQ	37010 MW	42680 TQ	USBLS	5/15
	Indiana	Y	32070 FQ	36650 MW	46630 TQ	USBLS	5/15
	Gary PMSA, IN	Y	34120 FQ	38420 MW	52520 TQ	USBLS	5/15
	Indianapolis-Carmel-Anderson						
	MSA, IN	Y	26090 FQ	31430 MW	36060 TQ	USBLS	5/15
	Iowa	Y	27590 FQ	31730 MW	38540 TQ	USBLS	5/15
	Kansas	Y	25410 FQ	31170 MW	44610 TQ	USBLS	5/15
	Kentucky	Y	27200 FQ	36910 MW	46060 TQ	USBLS	5/15
	Louisiana	Y	33090 FQ	39900 MW	49550 TQ	USBLS	5/15

AE	Average entry wage	AWR	Average wage range	H	Hourly
AEX	Average experienced wage	B	Biweekly	HI	Highest wage paid
ATC	Average total compensation	D	Daily	HR	High end range
AW	Average wage paid	FQ	First quartile wage	LO	Lowest wage paid

LR	Low end range	MTC	Median total compensation	TCC	Total cash compensation
M	Monthly	MW	Median wage paid	TQ	Third quartile wage
MCC	Median cash compensation	MWR	Median wage range	W	Weekly
ME	Median entry wage	S	See annotated source	Y	Yearly

Occupation/Type/Industry	Location	Per	Low	Mid	High	Source	Date
Furnace, Kiln, Oven, Drier, and Kettle Operator and Tender	New Orleans-Metairie MSA, LA	Y	39760 FQ	49410 MW	56490 TQ	USBLS	5/15
	Maine	Y	28650 FQ	35680 MW	50340 TQ	USBLS	5/15
	Maryland	Y	47610 AE	53887 MW	57025 AEX	MDBLS	4/16
	Baltimore-Columbia-Towson MSA, MD	Y	53450 FQ	57140 MW	60840 TQ	USBLS	5/15
	Massachusetts	Y	27090 FQ	33240 MW	37910 TQ	USBLS	5/15
	Worcester MSA, MA-CT	Y	32150 FQ	38380 MW	45760 TQ	USBLS	5/15
	Michigan	Y	29330 FQ	40920 MW	49180 TQ	USBLS	5/15
	Grand Rapids-Wyoming MSA, MI	Y	29530 FQ	36060 MW	46400 TQ	USBLS	5/15
	Minnesota	Y	32884 FQ	41328 MW	51888 TQ	MNBLS	1/16-3/16
	Minneapolis-St. Paul-Bloomington MSA, MN-WI	Y	35456 FQ	42695 MW	47818 TQ	MNBLS	1/16-3/16
	Mississippi	Y	27560 FQ	36410 MW	52230 TQ	USBLS	5/15
	Missouri	Y	30740 FQ	39040 MW	45440 TQ	USBLS	5/15
	Kansas City MSA, MO-KS	Y	21600 FQ	29110 MW	38860 TQ	USBLS	5/15
	St. Louis MSA, MO-IL	Y	33260 FQ	40140 MW	46970 TQ	USBLS	5/15
	Montana	Y	31100 FQ	41430 MW	49310 TQ	USBLS	5/15
	Nebraska	Y	28845 FQ	33980 MW	42350 TQ	NEBLS	7/16-9/16
	Nevada	Y	42730 FQ	45690 MW	48660 TQ	USBLS	5/15
	Las Vegas-Henderson-Paradise MSA, NV	Y	42730 FQ	45690 MW	48660 TQ	USBLS	5/15
	New Hampshire	H	14.32 AE	19.17 MW	22.45 AEX	NHBLS	6/16
	New Jersey	Y	25490 FQ	35160 MW	44800 TQ	USBLS	5/15
	Camden PMSA, NJ	Y	22620 FQ	25980 MW	30210 TQ	USBLS	5/15
	Newark PMSA, NJ-PA	Y	31350 FQ	35060 MW	38670 TQ	USBLS	5/15
	New York	Y	25410 AE	42730 MW	47470 AEX	NYBLS	1/16-3/16
	Buffalo-Cheektowaga-Niagara Falls MSA, NY	Y	27250 FQ	43060 MW	53380 TQ	USBLS	5/15
	New York-Jersey City-White Plains PMSA, NY-NJ	Y	29410 FQ	38130 MW	49020 TQ	USBLS	5/15
	Rochester MSA, NY	Y	30960 FQ	42130 MW	47030 TQ	USBLS	5/15
	North Carolina	Y	27300 FQ	34390 MW	40650 TQ	USBLS	5/15
	Charlotte-Concord-Gastonia MSA, NC-SC	Y	30860 FQ	34820 MW	38080 TQ	USBLS	5/15
	North Dakota	Y	28950 FQ	33450 MW	37240 TQ	USBLS	5/15
	Ohio	Y	27600 FQ	34610 MW	39260 TQ	USBLS	5/15
	Cincinnati MSA, OH-KY-IN	Y	31320 FQ	36760 MW	44740 TQ	USBLS	5/15
	Cleveland-Elyria MSA, OH	Y	26390 FQ	34850 MW	47100 TQ	USBLS	5/15
	Columbus MSA, OH	Y	24460 FQ	34030 MW	37260 TQ	USBLS	5/15
	Oklahoma	Y	28710 FQ	33720 MW	38280 TQ	USBLS	5/15
	Oklahoma City MSA, OK	Y	30060 FQ	34860 MW	39050 TQ	USBLS	5/15
	Tulsa MSA, OK	Y	28580 FQ	33390 MW	39330 TQ	USBLS	5/15
	Oregon	H	16.82 FQ	19.33 MW	22.15 TQ	ORBLS	2016
	Portland-Vancouver-Hillsboro MSA, OR-WA	Y	33270 FQ	39020 MW	45430 TQ	USBLS	5/15
	Pennsylvania	Y	31050 FQ	37550 MW	44640 TQ	USBLS	5/15
	Allentown-Bethlehem-Easton MSA, PA-NJ	Y	29600 FQ	38020 MW	46140 TQ	USBLS	5/15
	Pittsburgh MSA, PA	Y	34380 FQ	39600 MW	45330 TQ	USBLS	5/15
	Providence-Warwick MSA, RI-MA	Y	21460 FQ	23690 MW	34010 TQ	USBLS	5/15
	South Carolina	Y	30790 FQ	35110 MW	39990 TQ	USBLS	5/15
	Charleston-North Charleston MSA, SC	Y	32460 FQ	35410 MW	38370 TQ	USBLS	5/15
	Columbia MSA, SC	Y	33560 FQ	41020 MW	57810 TQ	USBLS	5/15
	South Dakota	Y	41090 FQ	47230 MW	55830 TQ	USBLS	5/15
	Tennessee	Y	26210 FQ	30780 MW	38180 TQ	USBLS	5/15
	Knoxville MSA, TN	Y	33530 FQ	41080 MW	48650 TQ	USBLS	5/15
	Memphis MSA, TN-MS-AR	Y	22300 FQ	26740 MW	32050 TQ	USBLS	5/15
	Nashville-Davidson–Murfreesboro–Franklin MSA, TN	Y	26670 FQ	30170 MW	35200 TQ	USBLS	5/15
	Texas	Y	26340 FQ	31840 MW	43050 TQ	USBLS	5/15
	Austin-Round Rock MSA, TX	Y	23760 FQ	30820 MW	36490 TQ	USBLS	5/15
	Dallas-Plano-Irving PMSA, TX	Y	25730 FQ	29340 MW	36640 TQ	USBLS	5/15
	Fort Worth-Arlington PMSA, TX	Y	22470 FQ	25150 MW	36550 TQ	USBLS	5/15
	Houston-The Woodlands-Sugar Land MSA, TX	Y	26150 FQ	30420 MW	38670 TQ	USBLS	5/15

AE Average entry wage	**AWR** Average wage range	**H** Hourly	**LR** Low end range	**MTC** Median total compensation	**TCC** Total cash compensation
AEX Average experienced wage	**B** Biweekly	**HI** Highest wage paid	**M** Monthly	**MW** Median wage paid	**TQ** Third quartile wage
ATC Average total compensation	**D** Daily	**HR** High end range	**MCC** Median cash compensation	**MWR** Median wage range	**W** Weekly
AW Average wage paid	**FQ** First quartile wage	**LO** Lowest wage paid	**ME** Median entry wage	**S** See annotated source	**Y** Yearly

Occupation/Type/Industry	Location	Per	Low	Mid	High	Source	Date
Furnace, Kiln, Oven, Drier, and Kettle Operator and Tender	San Antonio-New Braunfels MSA, TX	Y	25920 FQ	30090 MW	40680 TQ	USBLS	5/15
	Utah	Y	23080 FQ	29650 MW	43600 TQ	USBLS	5/15
	Salt Lake City MSA, UT	Y	22480 FQ	26300 MW	38300 TQ	USBLS	5/15
	Vermont	Y	19550 FQ	20070 MW	24900 TQ	USBLS	5/15
	Virginia	Y	34390 FQ	47190 MW	69670 TQ	USBLS	5/15
	Virginia Beach-Norfolk-Newport News MSA, VA-NC	Y	41490 FQ	47110 MW	54010 TQ	USBLS	5/15
	Washington	H	14.44 FQ	18.10 MW	22.59 TQ	WABLS	3/16
	Seattle-Bellevue-Everett PMSA, WA	H	14.18 FQ	17.14 MW	20.75 TQ	WABLS	3/16
	Tacoma-Lakewood PMSA, WA	H	15.60 FQ	23.36 MW	40.97 TQ	WABLS	3/16
	West Virginia	Y	27300 FQ	31460 MW	37660 TQ	USBLS	5/15
	Wisconsin	Y	27550 FQ	35820 MW	43960 TQ	USBLS	5/15
	Milwaukee-Waukesha-West Allis MSA, WI	Y	40500 FQ	44640 MW	48770 TQ	USBLS	5/15
	Wyoming	Y	39600 FQ	46260 MW	56100 TQ	USBLS	5/15
	Puerto Rico	Y	27040 FQ	28820 MW	30610 TQ	USBLS	5/15
Furniture Finisher	Alabama	Y	19875 AE	27525 AW	31350 AEX	ALBLS	6/16
	Arizona	Y	18910 FQ	24180 MW	29780 TQ	USBLS	5/15
	Phoenix-Mesa-Scottsdale MSA, AZ	Y	18370 FQ	20880 MW	29930 TQ	USBLS	5/15
	Tucson MSA, AZ	Y	24230 FQ	27110 MW	29460 TQ	USBLS	5/15
	California	H	10.42 FQ	12.94 MW	17.37 TQ	CABLS	1/16-3/16
	Anaheim-Santa Ana-Irvine PMSA, CA	H	12.11 FQ	14.77 MW	21.35 TQ	CABLS	1/16-3/16
	Los Angeles-Long Beach-Glendale PMSA, CA	H	9.95 FQ	11.66 MW	14.79 TQ	CABLS	1/16-3/16
	Oakland-Hayward-Berkeley PMSA, CA	H	15.42 FQ	19.81 MW	27.49 TQ	CABLS	1/16-3/16
	Riverside-San Bernardino-Ontario MSA, CA	H	10.00 FQ	11.59 MW	14.13 TQ	CABLS	1/16-3/16
	Sacramento-Roseville-Arden-Arcade MSA, CA	H	13.96 FQ	15.56 MW	20.25 TQ	CABLS	1/16-3/16
	Colorado	Y	30270 FQ	35360 MW	41130 TQ	USBLS	5/15
	Denver-Aurora-Lakewood MSA, CO	Y	29580 FQ	35040 MW	40520 TQ	USBLS	5/15
	Connecticut	Y		46077 MW		CTBLS	1/16-3/16
	Hartford-West Hartford-East Hartford MSA, CT	Y	41090 FQ	44630 MW	48180 TQ	USBLS	5/15
	Washington-Arlington-Alexandria PMSA, DC-VA-MD-WV	Y	30070 FQ	36650 MW	45570 TQ	USBLS	5/15
	Florida	H	10.78 AE	14.91 MW	17.88 AEX	FLBLS	7/16-9/16
	Fort Lauderdale-Pompano Beach-Deerfield Beach PMSA, FL	H	12.95 AE	16.71 MW	19.57 AEX	FLBLS	7/16-9/16
	Orlando-Kissimmee-Sanford MSA, FL	H	10.16 AE	15.73 MW	16.58 AEX	FLBLS	7/16-9/16
	Tampa-St. Petersburg-Clearwater MSA, FL	H	10.40 AE	12.03 MW	14.48 AEX	FLBLS	7/16-9/16
	Georgia	Y	21790 FQ	26460 MW	36020 TQ	USBLS	5/15
	Atlanta-Sandy Springs-Roswell MSA, GA	Y	22380 FQ	27130 MW	35580 TQ	USBLS	5/15
	Idaho	Y	23840 FQ	27760 MW	30910 TQ	USBLS	5/15
	Boise City MSA, ID	Y	22650 FQ	26530 MW	29570 TQ	USBLS	5/15
	Illinois	Y	23070 FQ	28630 MW	36140 TQ	USBLS	5/15
	Chicago-Naperville-Arlington Heights PMSA, IL	Y	23430 FQ	30980 MW	36920 TQ	USBLS	5/15
	Indiana	Y	25500 FQ	28530 MW	31640 TQ	USBLS	5/15
	Iowa	Y	23890 FQ	28010 MW	31810 TQ	USBLS	5/15
	Kansas	Y	24550 FQ	29370 MW	36060 TQ	USBLS	5/15
	Kentucky	Y	21820 FQ	25010 MW	32470 TQ	USBLS	5/15
	Louisville-Jefferson County MSA, KY-IN	Y	22760 FQ	26130 MW	29840 TQ	USBLS	5/15
	Maine	Y	27340 FQ	30600 MW	36850 TQ	USBLS	5/15
	Maryland	Y	20623 AE	35021 MW	42220 AEX	MDBLS	4/16
	Baltimore-Columbia-Towson MSA, MD	Y	22440 FQ	34020 MW	44110 TQ	USBLS	5/15
	Massachusetts	Y	35650 FQ	42520 MW	54840 TQ	USBLS	5/15

Occupation/Type/Industry	Location	Per	Low	Mid	High	Source	Date
Furniture Finisher	Boston-Cambridge-Newton NECTA, MA	Y	44430 FQ	53670 MW	59000 TQ	USBLS	5/15
	Michigan	Y	27160 FQ	32860 MW	37930 TQ	USBLS	5/15
	Grand Rapids-Wyoming MSA, MI	Y	28860 FQ	33060 MW	36570 TQ	USBLS	5/15
	Minnesota	Y	27366 FQ	33016 MW	39334 TQ	MNBLS	1/16-3/16
	Minneapolis-St. Paul-Bloomington MSA, MN-WI	Y	29341 FQ	35567 MW	41733 TQ	MNBLS	1/16-3/16
	Mississippi	Y	26910 FQ	33250 MW	39120 TQ	USBLS	5/15
	Missouri	Y	18660 FQ	26650 MW	32860 TQ	USBLS	5/15
	Kansas City MSA, MO-KS	Y	18410 FQ	23690 MW	31850 TQ	USBLS	5/15
	St. Louis MSA, MO-IL	Y	23150 FQ	27170 MW	30750 TQ	USBLS	5/15
	Nebraska	Y	33725 FQ	40920 MW	53775 TQ	NEBLS	7/16-9/16
	Nevada	Y	25780 FQ	31960 MW	39600 TQ	USBLS	5/15
	Las Vegas-Henderson-Paradise MSA, NV	Y	25570 FQ	32140 MW	38300 TQ	USBLS	5/15
	New Jersey	Y	30960 FQ	38110 MW	47710 TQ	USBLS	5/15
	Newark PMSA, NJ-PA	Y	34400 FQ	40290 MW	46700 TQ	USBLS	5/15
	New York	Y	25450 AE	30370 MW	37710 AEX	NYBLS	1/16-3/16
	Nassau County-Suffolk County PMSA, NY	Y	25950 FQ	30850 MW	44840 TQ	USBLS	5/15
	New York-Jersey City-White Plains PMSA, NY-NJ	Y	28230 FQ	34380 MW	45360 TQ	USBLS	5/15
	Rochester MSA, NY	Y	26180 FQ	29420 MW	35930 TQ	USBLS	5/15
	North Carolina	Y	22120 FQ	26820 MW	31650 TQ	USBLS	5/15
	Charlotte-Concord-Gastonia MSA, NC-SC	Y	22050 FQ	27770 MW	35040 TQ	USBLS	5/15
	North Dakota	Y	22710 FQ	25160 MW	36700 TQ	USBLS	5/15
	Ohio	Y	21250 FQ	26280 MW	33240 TQ	USBLS	5/15
	Cleveland-Elyria MSA, OH	Y	23250 FQ	30150 MW	35920 TQ	USBLS	5/15
	Columbus MSA, OH	Y	26440 FQ	32210 MW	37010 TQ	USBLS	5/15
	Oklahoma	Y	25190 FQ	30580 MW	38930 TQ	USBLS	5/15
	Oklahoma City MSA, OK	Y	24590 FQ	29670 MW	36960 TQ	USBLS	5/15
	Tulsa MSA, OK	Y	25460 FQ	31290 MW	41270 TQ	USBLS	5/15
	Oregon	H	9.71 FQ	9.88 MW	13.45 TQ	ORBLS	2016
	Portland-Vancouver-Hillsboro MSA, OR-WA	Y	26800 FQ	30980 MW	38340 TQ	USBLS	5/15
	Pennsylvania	Y	27120 FQ	32400 MW	40060 TQ	USBLS	5/15
	Allentown-Bethlehem-Easton MSA, PA-NJ	Y	26650 FQ	30960 MW	43500 TQ	USBLS	5/15
	Montgomery County-Bucks County-Chester County PMSA, PA	Y	35240 FQ	48920 MW	56130 TQ	USBLS	5/15
	Pittsburgh MSA, PA	Y	21990 FQ	30210 MW	37690 TQ	USBLS	5/15
	South Carolina	Y	25660 FQ	32120 MW	36950 TQ	USBLS	5/15
	Greenville-Anderson-Mauldin MSA, SC	Y	23550 FQ	27420 MW	32470 TQ	USBLS	5/15
	Tennessee	Y	21920 FQ	24900 MW	30430 TQ	USBLS	5/15
	Memphis MSA, TN-MS-AR	Y	25000 FQ	27650 MW	30300 TQ	USBLS	5/15
	Nashville-Davidson–Murfreesboro–Franklin MSA, TN	Y	22750 FQ	25580 MW	37930 TQ	USBLS	5/15
	Texas	Y	23070 FQ	27600 MW	31670 TQ	USBLS	5/15
	Austin-Round Rock MSA, TX	Y	24390 FQ	28870 MW	35100 TQ	USBLS	5/15
	Dallas-Plano-Irving PMSA, TX	Y	23550 FQ	27850 MW	32420 TQ	USBLS	5/15
	Fort Worth-Arlington PMSA, TX	Y	22660 FQ	29850 MW	37470 TQ	USBLS	5/15
	Houston-The Woodlands-Sugar Land MSA, TX	Y	25190 FQ	27950 MW	30690 TQ	USBLS	5/15
	San Antonio-New Braunfels MSA, TX	Y	25350 FQ	31430 MW	35340 TQ	USBLS	5/15
	Utah	Y	28050 FQ	34620 MW	41150 TQ	USBLS	5/15
	Provo-Orem MSA, UT	Y	26820 FQ	30520 MW	35980 TQ	USBLS	5/15
	Salt Lake City MSA, UT	Y	31900 FQ	38310 MW	44360 TQ	USBLS	5/15
	Vermont	Y	23140 FQ	26490 MW	30150 TQ	USBLS	5/15
	Virginia	Y	21970 FQ	28010 MW	36190 TQ	USBLS	5/15
	Richmond MSA, VA	Y	26910 FQ	33400 MW	37770 TQ	USBLS	5/15
	Washington	H	13.24 FQ	15.60 MW	18.76 TQ	WABLS	3/16
	Seattle-Bellevue-Everett PMSA, WA	H	13.38 FQ	15.63 MW	19.01 TQ	WABLS	3/16
	Tacoma-Lakewood PMSA, WA	H	16.80 FQ	18.24 MW	25.62 TQ	WABLS	3/16
	West Virginia	Y	25750 FQ	28640 MW	31470 TQ	USBLS	5/15

AE	Average entry wage	AWR	Average wage range	H	Hourly	LR	Low end range	MTC	Median total compensation	TCC	Total cash compensation
AEX	Average experienced wage	B	Biweekly	HI	Highest wage paid	M	Monthly	MCC	Median cash compensation	TQ	Third quartile wage
ATC	Average total compensation	D	Daily	HR	High end range	MCC	Median cash compensation	MW	Median wage paid	W	Weekly
AW	Average wage paid	FQ	First quartile wage	LO	Lowest wage paid	ME	Median entry wage	MWR	Median wage range	Y	Yearly
						S	See annotated source		

Occupation/Type/Industry	Location	Per	Low	Mid	High	Source	Date
Furniture Finisher	Wisconsin	Y	27440 FQ	32710 MW	39120 TQ	USBLS	5/15
	Madison MSA, WI	Y	27710 FQ	32790 MW	36800 TQ	USBLS	5/15
	Milwaukee-Waukesha-West Allis MSA, WI	Y	29930 FQ	36340 MW	43690 TQ	USBLS	5/15
	Puerto Rico	Y	16940 FQ	18100 MW	19260 TQ	USBLS	5/15
	San Juan-Carolina-Caguas MSA, PR	Y	17030 FQ	18200 MW	19370 TQ	USBLS	5/15
Fusion Welder							
Port, Municipal Government	San Francisco, CA	Y		92860 AW		CACIT	6/28/16
Gaming and Sports Book Writer and Runner	Alabama	Y	21364 AE	27264 AW	30219 AEX	ALBLS	6/16
	Alaska	Y	21150 FQ	23880 MW	34470 TQ	USBLS	5/15
	Arizona	Y	18790 FQ	21950 MW	29190 TQ	USBLS	5/15
	California	H	10.39 FQ	19.59 MW	22.24 TQ	CABLS	1/16-3/16
	Delaware	Y	27100 FQ	42110 MW	47870 TQ	USBLS	5/15
	Florida	H	9.50 AE	12.97 MW	16.49 AEX	FLBLS	7/16-9/16
	Kentucky	Y	27810 FQ	34130 MW	44780 TQ	USBLS	5/15
	Louisiana	Y	18670 FQ	21050 MW	23180 TQ	USBLS	5/15
	Michigan	Y	21340 FQ	23500 MW	29450 TQ	USBLS	5/15
	Minnesota	Y	17996 FQ	19097 MW	21672 TQ	MNBLS	1/16-3/16
	Mississippi	Y	16900 FQ	18390 MW	21470 TQ	USBLS	5/15
	Montana	Y	17950 FQ	19130 MW	21830 TQ	USBLS	5/15
	Nevada	Y	18370 FQ	21990 MW	27020 TQ	USBLS	5/15
	New Jersey	Y	22620 FQ	31530 MW	43130 TQ	USBLS	5/15
	New Mexico	Y	17170 FQ	18360 MW	19650 TQ	USBLS	5/15
	New York	Y	21320 AE	28030 MW	33490 AEX	NYBLS	1/16-3/16
	North Dakota	Y	16920 FQ	18330 MW	19850 TQ	USBLS	5/15
	Ohio	Y	26260 FQ	28750 MW	33260 TQ	USBLS	5/15
	Oklahoma	Y	16670 FQ	18160 MW	20160 TQ	USBLS	5/15
	Oregon	H	9.93 FQ	10.82 MW	11.72 TQ	ORBLS	2016
	Pennsylvania	Y	18530 FQ	22970 MW	28790 TQ	USBLS	5/15
	South Carolina	Y	16980 FQ	18540 MW	21150 TQ	USBLS	5/15
	South Dakota	Y	21580 FQ	24560 MW	29630 TQ	USBLS	5/15
	Texas	Y	17560 FQ	19570 MW	32380 TQ	USBLS	5/15
	Washington	H	10.41 FQ	11.39 MW	13.28 TQ	WABLS	3/16
Gaming Cage Worker	Arizona	Y	19740 FQ	23170 MW	28580 TQ	USBLS	5/15
	California	H	10.77 FQ	13.03 MW	17.23 TQ	CABLS	1/16-3/16
	Colorado	Y	27330 FQ	29780 MW	34190 TQ	USBLS	5/15
	Delaware	Y	20680 FQ	23830 MW	29220 TQ	USBLS	5/15
	Florida	H	9.12 AE	11.46 MW	13.84 AEX	FLBLS	7/16-9/16
	Idaho	Y	22280 FQ	25830 MW	31990 TQ	USBLS	5/15
	Illinois	Y	21780 FQ	26990 MW	35480 TQ	USBLS	5/15
	Indiana	Y	20280 FQ	24100 MW	29300 TQ	USBLS	5/15
	Iowa	Y	21910 FQ	25930 MW	32310 TQ	USBLS	5/15
	Kansas	Y	22730 FQ	26740 MW	29960 TQ	USBLS	5/15
	Louisiana	Y	18890 FQ	22430 MW	26220 TQ	USBLS	5/15
	Maryland	Y	22951 AE	27013 MW	29044 AEX	MDBLS	4/16
	Michigan	Y	22360 FQ	28230 MW	37130 TQ	USBLS	5/15
	Minnesota	Y	20903 FQ	25423 MW	31542 TQ	MNBLS	1/16-3/16
	Mississippi	Y	20890 FQ	24890 MW	29870 TQ	USBLS	5/15
	Missouri	Y	20940 FQ	24740 MW	29550 TQ	USBLS	5/15
	Montana	Y	18010 FQ	19220 MW	22910 TQ	USBLS	5/15
	Nevada	Y	24060 FQ	31050 MW	38020 TQ	USBLS	5/15
	New Jersey	Y	28450 FQ	33920 MW	38950 TQ	USBLS	5/15
	New Mexico	Y	21340 FQ	23710 MW	28240 TQ	USBLS	5/15
	New York	Y	22130 AE	27960 MW	31670 AEX	NYBLS	1/16-3/16
	North Dakota	Y	17750 FQ	19850 MW	34770 TQ	USBLS	5/15
	Ohio	Y	22540 FQ	27480 MW	33310 TQ	USBLS	5/15
	Oklahoma	Y	19150 FQ	22260 MW	26270 TQ	USBLS	5/15
	Oregon	H	10.78 FQ	12.08 MW	14.26 TQ	ORBLS	2016
	Pennsylvania	Y	24470 FQ	27980 MW	31510 TQ	USBLS	5/15
	South Dakota	Y	21500 FQ	23790 MW	27400 TQ	USBLS	5/15
	Texas	Y	19340 FQ	22470 MW	26070 TQ	USBLS	5/15
	Washington	H	9.98 FQ	11.48 MW	14.52 TQ	WABLS	3/16
	Wisconsin	Y	19960 FQ	22960 MW	27920 TQ	USBLS	5/15
	Puerto Rico	Y	16720 FQ	18100 MW	19720 TQ	USBLS	5/15
Gaming Change Person and Booth Cashier	Alaska	Y	18770 FQ	20390 MW	24160 TQ	USBLS	5/15

AE Average entry wage	**AWR** Average wage range	**H** Hourly	**LR** Low end range	**MTC** Median total compensation	**TCC** Total cash compensation
AEX Average experienced wage	**B** Biweekly	**HI** Highest wage paid	**M** Monthly	**MCC** Median cash compensation	**TQ** Third quartile wage
ATC Average total compensation	**D** Daily	**HR** High end range	**MCC** Median cash compensation	**MWR** Median wage range	**W** Weekly
AW Average wage paid	**FQ** First quartile wage	**LO** Lowest wage paid	**ME** Median entry wage	**S** See annotated source	**Y** Yearly

Occupation/Type/Industry	Location	Per	Low	Mid	High	Source	Date
Gaming Change Person and Booth Cashier	Arizona	Y	19590 FQ	23740 MW	30080 TQ	USBLS	5/15
	California	H	9.64 FQ	11.15 MW	13.31 TQ	CABLS	1/16-3/16
	Colorado	Y	23900 FQ	27750 MW	31680 TQ	USBLS	5/15
	Delaware	Y	20820 FQ	23150 MW	27650 TQ	USBLS	5/15
	Florida	H	9.05 AE	11.04 MW	13.49 AEX	FLBLS	7/16-9/16
	Idaho	Y	22260 FQ	28320 MW	34170 TQ	USBLS	5/15
	Illinois	Y	21830 FQ	26840 MW	30620 TQ	USBLS	5/15
	Indiana	Y	21820 FQ	24550 MW	28690 TQ	USBLS	5/15
	Iowa	Y	19230 FQ	23000 MW	27860 TQ	USBLS	5/15
	Kansas	Y	19890 FQ	26920 MW	40960 TQ	USBLS	5/15
	Kentucky	Y	21340 FQ	26630 MW	38440 TQ	USBLS	5/15
	Louisiana	Y	18440 FQ	21910 MW	26050 TQ	USBLS	5/15
	Maryland	Y	21120 AE	26787 MW	29621 AEX	MDBLS	4/16
	Michigan	Y	22120 FQ	26510 MW	31870 TQ	USBLS	5/15
	Minnesota	Y	21105 FQ	23323 MW	26580 TQ	MNBLS	1/16-3/16
	Mississippi	Y	20880 FQ	24870 MW	29540 TQ	USBLS	5/15
	Missouri	Y	22090 FQ	25680 MW	29390 TQ	USBLS	5/15
	Nevada	Y	18380 FQ	22280 MW	29050 TQ	USBLS	5/15
	New Jersey	Y	24420 FQ	29410 MW	35080 TQ	USBLS	5/15
	New Mexico	Y	19990 FQ	22940 MW	27140 TQ	USBLS	5/15
	New York	Y	21130 AE	24860 MW	31260 AEX	NYBLS	1/16-3/16
	North Dakota	Y	17790 FQ	25280 MW	30660 TQ	USBLS	5/15
	Ohio	Y	20090 FQ	22560 MW	25710 TQ	USBLS	5/15
	Oklahoma	Y	18390 FQ	21640 MW	25390 TQ	USBLS	5/15
	Oregon	H	10.78 FQ	12.20 MW	14.00 TQ	ORBLS	2016
	Pennsylvania	Y	22770 FQ	28230 MW	34590 TQ	USBLS	5/15
	South Dakota	Y	20690 FQ	22730 MW	24910 TQ	USBLS	5/15
	Tennessee	Y	17150 FQ	18610 MW	20200 TQ	USBLS	5/15
	Texas	Y	16830 FQ	18210 MW	19750 TQ	USBLS	5/15
	Washington	H	10.15 FQ	11.83 MW	14.40 TQ	WABLS	3/16
	West Virginia	Y	17530 FQ	18410 MW	19310 TQ	USBLS	5/15
	Wisconsin	Y	19440 FQ	22660 MW	27740 TQ	USBLS	5/15
	Puerto Rico	Y	16930 FQ	18550 MW	21420 TQ	USBLS	5/15
Gaming Dealer	Alaska	Y	20450 FQ	24090 MW	31360 TQ	USBLS	5/15
	Arizona	Y	17800 FQ	18820 MW	21280 TQ	USBLS	5/15
	California	H	9.50 FQ	10.39 MW	14.94 TQ	CABLS	1/16-3/16
	Colorado	Y	17880 FQ	18630 MW	19420 TQ	USBLS	5/15
	Florida	H	8.96 AE	9.42 MW	14.93 AEX	FLBLS	7/16-9/16
	Illinois	Y	18360 FQ	19190 MW	23740 TQ	USBLS	5/15
	Indiana	Y	16790 FQ	18100 MW	19450 TQ	USBLS	5/15
	Iowa	Y	16580 FQ	17700 MW	18830 TQ	USBLS	5/15
	Kansas	Y	18170 FQ	37210 MW	44160 TQ	USBLS	5/15
	Louisiana	Y	16630 FQ	17810 MW	18990 TQ	USBLS	5/15
	Maryland	Y	17674 AE	18868 MW	19465 AEX	MDBLS	4/16
	Michigan	Y	18960 FQ	22730 MW	28570 TQ	USBLS	5/15
	Minnesota	Y	17774 FQ	18662 MW	19591 TQ	MNBLS	1/16-3/16
	Mississippi	Y	16770 FQ	18100 MW	19500 TQ	USBLS	5/15
	Missouri	Y	16890 FQ	17860 MW	18830 TQ	USBLS	5/15
	Montana	Y	17480 FQ	18210 MW	18930 TQ	USBLS	5/15
	Nevada	Y	16550 FQ	17660 MW	18770 TQ	USBLS	5/15
	New Mexico	Y	16880 FQ	17860 MW	18840 TQ	CABLS	5/15
	New York	Y	19360 AE	20120 MW	32260 AEX	NYBLS	1/16-3/16
	North Carolina	Y	16350 FQ	17500 MW	18650 TQ	USBLS	5/15
	North Dakota	Y	17200 FQ	18840 MW	23770 TQ	USBLS	5/15
	Oklahoma	Y	17050 FQ	18690 MW	23880 TQ	USBLS	5/15
	Oregon	H	9.60 FQ	9.74 MW	10.94 TQ	ORBLS	2016
	Pennsylvania	Y	16780 FQ	18160 MW	19690 TQ	USBLS	5/15
	South Carolina	Y	16700 FQ	18090 MW	19690 TQ	USBLS	5/15
	South Dakota	Y	22700 FQ	26460 MW	30970 TQ	USBLS	5/15
	Texas	Y	19570 FQ	24720 MW	43560 TQ	USBLS	5/15
	Washington	H	9.72 FQ	10.02 MW	13.04 TQ	WABLS	3/16
	West Virginia	Y	17530 FQ	18420 MW	19300 TQ	USBLS	5/15
	Wisconsin	Y	21180 FQ	28510 MW	33480 TQ	USBLS	5/15
	Puerto Rico	Y	16790 FQ	18280 MW	20580 TQ	USBLS	5/15
Gaming Manager	Arizona	Y	46570 FQ	58190 MW	78510 TQ	USBLS	5/15
	California	H	29.39 FQ	38.23 MW	53.20 TQ	CABLS	1/16-3/16
	Colorado	Y	45910 FQ	52630 MW	65920 TQ	USBLS	5/15
	Florida	H	18.91 AE	30.93 MW	45.16 AEX	FLBLS	7/16-9/16
	Indiana	Y	48100 FQ	57830 MW	74870 TQ	USBLS	5/15

AE	Average entry wage	AWR	Average wage range	H	Hourly	LR	Low end range	MTC	Median total compensation	TCC	Total cash compensation
AEX	Average experienced wage	B	Biweekly	HI	Highest wage paid	M	Monthly	MW	Median wage paid	TQ	Third quartile wage
ATC	Average total compensation	D	Daily	HR	High end range	MCC	Median cash compensation	MWR	Median wage range	W	Weekly
AW	Average wage paid	FQ	First quartile wage	LO	Lowest wage paid	ME	Median entry wage	S	See annotated source	Y	Yearly

Occupation/Type/Industry	Location	Per	Low	Mid	High	Source	Date
Gaming Manager	Iowa	Y	46990 FQ	57930 MW	81350 TQ	USBLS	5/15
	Kansas	Y	60500 FQ	68890 MW	76260 TQ	USBLS	5/15
	Louisiana	Y	58640 FQ	70080 MW	85490 TQ	USBLS	5/15
	Michigan	Y	54960 FQ	79080 MW	102830 TQ	USBLS	5/15
	Minnesota	Y	54890 FQ	73678 MW	103165 TQ	MNBLS	1/16-3/16
	Mississippi	Y	56180 FQ	66530 MW	80920 TQ	USBLS	5/15
	Missouri	Y	45100 FQ	57450 MW	73860 TQ	USBLS	5/15
	Nebraska	Y	61850 FQ	81530 MW	95990 TQ	NEBLS	7/16-9/16
	Nevada	Y	65180 FQ	80240 MW	108880 TQ	USBLS	5/15
	New Jersey	Y	67950 FQ	75970 MW	91830 TQ	USBLS	5/15
	New Mexico	Y	48760 FQ	60820 MW	86880 TQ	USBLS	5/15
	New York	Y	53230 AE	66300 MW	79910 AEX	NYBLS	1/16-3/16
	North Dakota	Y	55590 FQ	81820 MW		USBLS	5/15
	Ohio	Y	55100 FQ	63170 MW	77500 TQ	USBLS	5/15
	Oklahoma	Y	43770 FQ	52580 MW	61280 TQ	USBLS	5/15
	Oregon	H	22.42 FQ	27.61 MW	45.20 TQ	ORBLS	2016
	Pennsylvania	Y	58840 FQ	72110 MW	93190 TQ	USBLS	5/15
	Washington	H	25.75 FQ	32.23 MW	44.76 TQ	WABLS	3/16
	Wisconsin	Y	48040 FQ	61030 MW	75160 TQ	USBLS	5/15
	Puerto Rico	Y	46140 FQ	58720 MW	78640 TQ	USBLS	5/15
Gaming Supervisor	Alabama	Y	33442 AE	43532 AW	48577 AEX	ALBLS	6/16
	Alaska	Y	24290 FQ	41730 MW	50540 TQ	USBLS	5/15
	Arizona	Y	36190 FQ	45070 MW	56210 TQ	USBLS	5/15
	Arkansas	Y	27450 FQ	30790 MW	39660 TQ	USBLS	5/15
	California	H	18.45 FQ	23.44 MW	28.30 TQ	CABLS	1/16-3/16
	Colorado	Y	42840 FQ	46920 MW	53310 TQ	USBLS	5/15
	Connecticut	Y		58176 MW		CTBLS	1/16-3/16
	Delaware	Y	47870 FQ	54650 MW	60330 TQ	USBLS	5/15
	Florida	H	16.09 AE	22.23 MW	29.72 AEX	FLBLS	7/16-9/16
	Illinois	Y	39710 FQ	50180 MW	58550 TQ	USBLS	5/15
	Indiana	Y	44690 FQ	51840 MW	58570 TQ	USBLS	5/15
	Iowa	Y	36280 FQ	43140 MW	51590 TQ	USBLS	5/15
	Kansas	Y	42960 FQ	52140 MW	57850 TQ	USBLS	5/15
	Louisiana	Y	40950 FQ	46260 MW	53400 TQ	USBLS	5/15
	Maryland	Y	49151 AE	59553 MW	64754 AEX	MDBLS	4/16
	Michigan	Y	33250 FQ	42580 MW	59140 TQ	USBLS	5/15
	Minnesota	Y	21288 FQ	30468 MW	42263 TQ	MNBLS	1/16-3/16
	Mississippi	Y	39330 FQ	48180 MW	56690 TQ	USBLS	5/15
	Missouri	Y	41430 FQ	49750 MW	57790 TQ	USBLS	5/15
	Montana	Y	18370 FQ	22440 MW	28600 TQ	USBLS	5/15
	Nevada	Y	42830 FQ	56090 MW	69560 TQ	USBLS	5/15
	New Jersey	Y	52190 FQ	58330 MW	66730 TQ	USBLS	5/15
	New Mexico	Y	35700 FQ	43060 MW	49700 TQ	USBLS	5/15
	New York	Y	28170 AE	46140 MW	56590 AEX	NYBLS	1/16-3/16
	North Carolina	Y	42330 FQ	48330 MW	55930 TQ	USBLS	5/15
	North Dakota	Y	23680 FQ	35210 MW	48610 TQ	USBLS	5/15
	Ohio	Y	38100 FQ	47180 MW	56610 TQ	USBLS	5/15
	Oklahoma	Y	26930 FQ	33640 MW	39590 TQ	USBLS	5/15
	Oregon	H	17.96 FQ	21.15 MW	24.79 TQ	ORBLS	2016
	Pennsylvania	Y	42430 FQ	51010 MW	58890 TQ	USBLS	5/15
	South Carolina	Y	23310 FQ	31180 MW	46300 TQ	USBLS	5/15
	South Dakota	Y	34250 FQ	38330 MW	44120 TQ	USBLS	5/15
	Tennessee	Y	23330 FQ	29160 MW	52660 TQ	USBLS	5/15
	Texas	Y	19450 FQ	29030 MW	36100 TQ	USBLS	5/15
	Washington	H	18.95 FQ	23.45 MW	28.08 TQ	WABLS	3/16
	Wisconsin	Y	31310 FQ	40990 MW	54440 TQ	USBLS	5/15
	Puerto Rico	Y	24560 FQ	29830 MW	38930 TQ	USBLS	5/15
Gaming Surveillance Officer and Gaming Investigator	Arizona	Y	23150 FQ	30590 MW	41490 TQ	USBLS	5/15
	California	H	13.49 FQ	16.35 MW	19.11 TQ	CABLS	1/16-3/16
	Colorado	Y	29340 FQ	33720 MW	37600 TQ	USBLS	5/15
	Delaware	Y	24570 FQ	31100 MW	36250 TQ	USBLS	5/15
	Florida	H	11.62 AE	15.22 MW	17.75 AEX	FLBLS	7/16-9/16
	Idaho	Y	26650 FQ	30110 MW	34780 TQ	USBLS	5/15
	Illinois	Y	26210 FQ	30940 MW	44010 TQ	USBLS	5/15
	Indiana	Y	25240 FQ	38250 MW	55170 TQ	USBLS	5/15
	Iowa	Y	23660 FQ	29020 MW	37250 TQ	USBLS	5/15
	Kansas	Y	26650 FQ	29100 MW	36610 TQ	USBLS	5/15
	Louisiana	Y	25970 FQ	30790 MW	37080 TQ	USBLS	5/15
	Maryland	Y	27307 AE	29373 MW	30407 AEX	MDBLS	4/16

AE	Average entry wage	AWR	Average wage range	H	Hourly	LR	Low end range	MTC	Median total compensation	TCC	Total cash compensation
AEX	Average experienced wage	B	Biweekly	HI	Highest wage paid	M	Monthly	MW	Median wage paid	TQ	Third quartile wage
ATC	Average total compensation	D	Daily	HR	High end range	MCC	Median cash compensation	MWR	Median wage range	W	Weekly
AW	Average wage paid	FQ	First quartile wage	LO	Lowest wage paid	ME	Median entry wage	S	See annotated source	Y	Yearly

Occupation/Type/Industry	Location	Per	Low	Mid	High	Source	Date
Gaming Surveillance Officer and Gaming Investigator	Michigan	Y	31280 FQ	36780 MW	51440 TQ	USBLS	5/15
	Minnesota	Y	25863 FQ	31286 MW	36153 TQ	MNBLS	1/16-3/16
	Mississippi	Y	27820 FQ	32510 MW	39340 TQ	USBLS	5/15
	Missouri	Y	27420 FQ	31320 MW	37850 TQ	USBLS	5/15
	Montana	Y	22020 FQ	27180 MW	42080 TQ	USBLS	5/15
	Nevada	Y	31160 FQ	37240 MW	45380 TQ	USBLS	5/15
	New Jersey	Y	28900 FQ	34420 MW	40800 TQ	USBLS	5/15
	New Mexico	Y	23340 FQ	27680 MW	34220 TQ	USBLS	5/15
	New York	Y	22370 AE	27530 MW	35300 AEX	NYBLS	1/16-3/16
	North Dakota	Y	31520 FQ	35520 MW	39700 TQ	USBLS	5/15
	Ohio	Y	36480 FQ	44060 MW	47740 TQ	USBLS	5/15
	Oklahoma	Y	21980 FQ	26250 MW	31190 TQ	USBLS	5/15
	Oregon	H	12.32 FQ	13.90 MW	15.84 TQ	ORBLS	2016
	Pennsylvania	Y	25940 FQ	29590 MW	39890 TQ	USBLS	5/15
	South Dakota	Y	24210 FQ	27830 MW	31290 TQ	USBLS	5/15
	Washington	H	12.39 FQ	14.88 MW	19.77 TQ	WABLS	3/16
	West Virginia	Y	18620 FQ	21870 MW	27370 TQ	USBLS	5/15
	Wisconsin	Y	26840 FQ	32590 MW	38070 TQ	USBLS	5/15
	Puerto Rico	Y	17020 FQ	18790 MW	23240 TQ	USBLS	5/15
Gang Analyst							
Police Department, Municipal Government	Hawthorne, CA	Y			71233 HI	CACIT	6/28/16
Garage Attendant							
Airports, Municipal Government	Los Angeles, CA	Y		52768 AW		CACIT	6/23/16
Garbage Truck Driver Apprentice	Oakland, CA	H			20.00 HI	CBS03	2016
Gardening Specialist							
California State University	California	Y	29904 LO		58188 HI	CALST	2016-2017
Gas Compressor and Gas Pumping Station Operator	Alabama	Y	40842 AE	57030 AW	65114 AEX	ALBLS	6/16
	Arizona	Y	18920 FQ	52690 MW	67850 TQ	USBLS	5/15
	California	H	24.24 FQ	28.37 MW	36.36 TQ	CABLS	1/16-3/16
	Colorado	Y	48190 FQ	58100 MW	69150 TQ	USBLS	5/15
	Connecticut	Y		47819 MW		CTBLS	1/16-3/16
	Florida	H	26.20 AE	34.23 MW	36.05 AEX	FLBLS	7/16-9/16
	Illinois	Y	44650 FQ	57310 MW	66660 TQ	USBLS	5/15
	Indiana	Y	49970 FQ	55940 MW	61630 TQ	USBLS	5/15
	Kansas	Y	35630 FQ	46130 MW	56550 TQ	USBLS	5/15
	Kentucky	Y	32800 FQ	39460 MW	57130 TQ	USBLS	5/15
	Massachusetts	Y	50500 FQ	59900 MW	69990 TQ	USBLS	5/15
	Mississippi	Y	55170 FQ	64500 MW	73170 TQ	USBLS	5/15
	Montana	Y	53400 FQ	59460 MW	68990 TQ	USBLS	5/15
	Nebraska	Y	54600 FQ	59080 MW	63590 TQ	NEBLS	7/16-9/16
	New Jersey	Y	44800 FQ	49920 MW	59940 TQ	USBLS	5/15
	New Mexico	Y	52650 FQ	60500 MW	69060 TQ	USBLS	5/15
	New York	Y	48820 AE	58030 MW	60250 AEX	NYBLS	1/16-3/16
	North Dakota	Y	53260 FQ	61150 MW	72810 TQ	USBLS	5/15
	Ohio	Y	60320 FQ	67360 MW	74250 TQ	USBLS	5/15
	Oklahoma	Y	50750 FQ	61350 MW	71350 TQ	USBLS	5/15
	Pennsylvania	Y	46420 FQ	56450 MW	63920 TQ	USBLS	5/15
	Texas	Y	45830 FQ	56130 MW	63320 TQ	USBLS	5/15
	Utah	Y	40990 FQ	54630 MW	66590 TQ	USBLS	5/15
	Virginia	Y	51830 FQ	57130 MW	62430 TQ	USBLS	5/15
	West Virginia	Y	53730 FQ	59310 MW	65830 TQ	USBLS	5/15
	Wyoming	Y	54980 FQ	63070 MW	72870 TQ	USBLS	5/15
Gas Construction Worker							
Department of Public Works, Municipal Government	LaFayette, GA	H	12.37 LO		20.69 HI	GACTY02	2016
Department of Public Works, Municipal Government	Trion, GA	H	13.86 LO		15.00 HI	GACTY02	2016
Gas Distribution Technician							
Department of Public Works, Municipal Government	Americus, GA	Y	27085 LO		37919 HI	GACTY02	2016
Department of Public Works, Municipal Government	Hartwell, GA	Y	25000 LO		45552 HI	GACTY02	2016

AE	Average entry wage	**AWR**	Average wage range	**H**	Hourly	**LR**	Low end range	**MTC**	Median total compensation	**TCC**	Total cash compensation
AEX	Average experienced wage	**B**	Biweekly	**HI**	Highest wage paid	**M**	Monthly	**MCC**	Median cash compensation	**TQ**	Third quartile wage
ATC	Average total compensation	**D**	Daily	**HR**	High end range	**MCC**	Median cash compensation	**MWR**	Median wage range	**W**	Weekly
AW	Average wage paid	**FQ**	First quartile wage	**LO**	Lowest wage paid	**ME**	Median entry wage	**S**	See annotated source	**Y**	Yearly

Occupation/Type/Industry	Location	Per	Low	Mid	High	Source	Date
Gas Plant Operator	Alabama	Y	51719 AE	67852 AW	75923 AEX	ALBLS	6/16
	Alaska	Y	53970 FQ	62110 MW	83890 TQ	USBLS	5/15
	Arkansas	Y	51800 FQ	60670 MW	70740 TQ	USBLS	5/15
	California	H	34.37 FQ	38.11 MW	45.79 TQ	CABLS	1/16-3/16
	Colorado	Y	60270 FQ	73810 MW	86680 TQ	USBLS	5/15
	Connecticut	Y		75933 MW		CTBLS	1/16-3/16
	Delaware	Y	52190 FQ	60740 MW	85430 TQ	USBLS	5/15
	Florida	H	19.89 AE	28.78 MW	33.84 AEX	FLBLS	7/16-9/16
	Georgia	Y	37910 FQ	52650 MW	61430 TQ	USBLS	5/15
	Illinois	Y	54730 FQ	66980 MW	79600 TQ	USBLS	5/15
	Indiana	Y	55790 FQ	65140 MW	76080 TQ	USBLS	5/15
	Iowa	Y	47620 FQ	58770 MW	68940 TQ	USBLS	5/15
	Kansas	Y	47060 FQ	56520 MW	64640 TQ	USBLS	5/15
	Kentucky	Y	56380 FQ	67420 MW	77180 TQ	USBLS	5/15
	Louisiana	Y	51060 FQ	60980 MW	72820 TQ	USBLS	5/15
	Maryland	Y	55354 AE	66711 MW	72389 AEX	MDBLS	4/16
	Massachusetts	Y	67040 FQ	72650 MW	78270 TQ	USBLS	5/15
	Michigan	Y	63790 FQ	70180 MW	76420 TQ	USBLS	5/15
	Minnesota	Y	51837 FQ	59552 MW	70234 TQ	MNBLS	1/16-3/16
	Mississippi	Y	53470 FQ	57800 MW	62130 TQ	USBLS	5/15
	Missouri	Y	53050 FQ	63210 MW	73710 TQ	USBLS	5/15
	Montana	Y	58390 FQ	69160 MW	80860 TQ	USBLS	5/15
	Nebraska	Y	52940 FQ	60210 MW	70380 TQ	NEBLS	7/16-9/16
	New Hampshire	H	27.12 AE	35.21 MW	36.72 AEX	NHBLS	6/16
	New Jersey	Y	59770 FQ	70810 MW	81410 TQ	USBLS	5/15
	New Mexico	Y	62930 FQ	70960 MW	77980 TQ	USBLS	5/15
	New York	Y	55930 AE	74200 MW	85810 AEX	NYBLS	1/16-3/16
	North Carolina	Y	50230 FQ	57200 MW	64680 TQ	USBLS	5/15
	Ohio	Y	54530 FQ	67870 MW	76580 TQ	USBLS	5/15
	Oklahoma	Y	44720 FQ	56190 MW	65540 TQ	USBLS	5/15
	Oregon	H	32.49 FQ	36.27 MW	41.34 TQ	ORBLS	2016
	Pennsylvania	Y	44680 FQ	54290 MW	62000 TQ	USBLS	5/15
	South Carolina	Y	51710 FQ	56510 MW	61310 TQ	USBLS	5/15
	Tennessee	Y	41520 FQ	55420 MW	66880 TQ	USBLS	5/15
	Texas	Y	52110 FQ	62060 MW	73250 TQ	USBLS	5/15
	Utah	Y	55640 FQ	69360 MW	85230 TQ	USBLS	5/15
	Virginia	Y	48070 FQ	62140 MW	76250 TQ	USBLS	5/15
	Washington	H	32.45 FQ	34.93 MW	37.42 TQ	WABLS	3/16
	West Virginia	Y	54990 FQ	65720 MW	74780 TQ	USBLS	5/15
	Wisconsin	Y	81390 FQ	89700 MW	97910 TQ	USBLS	5/15
	Wyoming	Y	55060 FQ	65070 MW	74520 TQ	USBLS	5/15
Gastroenterologist	Great Lakes	Y		407000 AW		BGIE	2016
	North Central	Y		339000 AW		BGIE	2016
	Northeast	Y		378000 AW		BGIE	2016
	Northwest	Y		475000 AW		BGIE	2016
	South Central	Y		318000 AW		BGIE	2016
	Southeast	Y		378000 AW		BGIE	2016
	Southwest	Y		406000 AW		BGIE	2016
	West	Y		410000 AW		BGIE	2016
Gem Worker	United States	Y		42000 AW		SKU01	2016
General and Operations Manager	Alabama	Y	66038 AE	125465 AW	155179 AEX	ALBLS	6/16
	Birmingham-Hoover MSA, AL	Y	71860 AE	135797 AW	167755 AEX	ALBLS	6/16
	Alaska	Y	64780 FQ	89690 MW	128390 TQ	USBLS	5/15
	Anchorage MSA, AK	Y	69890 FQ	99220 MW	140240 TQ	USBLS	5/15
	Arizona	Y	54660 FQ	80350 MW	121560 TQ	USBLS	5/15
	Phoenix-Mesa-Scottsdale MSA, AZ	Y	58020 FQ	86570 MW	130660 TQ	USBLS	5/15
	Tucson MSA, AZ	Y	50090 FQ	69910 MW	96910 TQ	USBLS	5/15
	Arkansas	Y	42040 FQ	66260 MW	106200 TQ	USBLS	5/15
	Little Rock-North Little Rock-Conway MSA, AR	Y	49960 FQ	73500 MW	114970 TQ	USBLS	5/15
	California	H	34.28 FQ	51.47 MW	81.41 TQ	CABLS	1/16-3/16
	Anaheim-Santa Ana-Irvine PMSA, CA	H	36.40 FQ	56.51 MW	89.14 TQ	CABLS	1/16-3/16
	Los Angeles-Long Beach-Glendale PMSA, CA	H	33.75 FQ	51.92 MW	83.07 TQ	CABLS	1/16-3/16
	Oakland-Hayward-Berkeley PMSA, CA	H	38.83 FQ	55.90 MW	87.47 TQ	CABLS	1/16-3/16

Occupation/Type/Industry	Location	Per	Low	Mid	High	Source	Date
General and Operations Manager	Riverside-San Bernardino-Ontario MSA, CA	H	31.64 FQ	43.51 MW	63.51 TQ	CABLS	1/16-3/16
	Sacramento–Roseville–Arden-Arcade MSA, CA	H	32.45 FQ	46.29 MW	68.02 TQ	CABLS	1/16-3/16
	San Diego-Carlsbad MSA, CA	H	34.12 FQ	51.44 MW	81.00 TQ	CABLS	1/16-3/16
	San Francisco-Redwood City-South San Francisco PMSA, CA	H	41.08 FQ	65.95 MW		CABLS	1/16-3/16
	Colorado	Y	68130 FQ	104560 MW	162160 TQ	USBLS	5/15
	Denver-Aurora-Lakewood MSA, CO	Y	76070 FQ	115360 MW	179800 TQ	USBLS	5/15
	Connecticut	Y		119005 MW		CTBLS	1/16-3/16
	Bridgeport-Stamford-Norwalk MSA, CT	Y	92630 FQ	150250 MW		USBLS	5/15
	Hartford-West Hartford-East Hartford MSA, CT	Y	68110 FQ	105560 MW	164830 TQ	USBLS	5/15
	Delaware	Y	91770 FQ	120370 MW	178500 TQ	USBLS	5/15
	Wilmington PMSA, DE-MD-NJ	Y	93030 FQ	123560 MW	179980 TQ	USBLS	5/15
	District of Columbia	Y	106660 FQ	134670 MW	164550 TQ	USBLS	5/15
	Washington-Arlington-Alexandria PMSA, DC-VA-MD-WV	Y	95960 FQ	134540 MW	178660 TQ	USBLS	5/15
	Florida	H	32.35 AE	53.61 MW	79.38 AEX	FLBLS	7/16-9/16
	Fort Lauderdale-Pompano Beach-Deerfield Beach PMSA, FL	H	33.61 AE	55.62 MW	86.42 AEX	FLBLS	7/16-9/16
	Miami-Miami Beach-Kendall PMSA, FL	H	35.14 AE	59.73 MW	87.72 AEX	FLBLS	7/16-9/16
	Orlando-Kissimmee-Sanford MSA, FL	H	31.98 AE	51.34 MW	74.04 AEX	FLBLS	7/16-9/16
	Tampa-St. Petersburg-Clearwater MSA, FL	H	32.92 AE	55.39 MW	79.61 AEX	FLBLS	7/16-9/16
	Georgia	Y	59950 FQ	93510 MW	145490 TQ	USBLS	5/15
	Atlanta-Sandy Springs-Roswell MSA, GA	Y	68270 FQ	104990 MW	161390 TQ	USBLS	5/15
	Augusta-Richmond County MSA, GA-SC	Y	51130 FQ	73440 MW	111700 TQ	USBLS	5/15
	Hawaii	Y	59820 FQ	85500 MW	122630 TQ	USBLS	5/15
	Urban Honolulu MSA, HI	Y	61100 FQ	88840 MW	126730 TQ	USBLS	5/15
	Idaho	Y	45840 FQ	65920 MW	98680 TQ	USBLS	5/15
	Boise City MSA, ID	Y	45690 FQ	64670 MW	96240 TQ	USBLS	5/15
	Illinois	Y	58390 FQ	93660 MW	145820 TQ	USBLS	5/15
	Chicago-Naperville-Arlington Heights PMSA, IL	Y	64970 FQ	101810 MW	157880 TQ	USBLS	5/15
	Lake County-Kenosha County PMSA, IL-WI	Y	63140 FQ	113530 MW	167430 TQ	USBLS	5/15
	Indiana	Y	52990 FQ	81460 MW	126730 TQ	USBLS	5/15
	Gary PMSA, IN	Y	52910 FQ	77870 MW	122360 TQ	USBLS	5/15
	Indianapolis-Carmel-Anderson MSA, IN	Y	58870 FQ	95700 MW	148120 TQ	USBLS	5/15
	Iowa	Y	49650 FQ	72610 MW	109900 TQ	USBLS	5/15
	Des Moines-West Des Moines MSA, IA	Y	59340 FQ	89550 MW	130260 TQ	USBLS	5/15
	Kansas	Y	60840 FQ	84730 MW	123410 TQ	USBLS	5/15
	Wichita MSA, KS	Y	64410 FQ	85720 MW	120040 TQ	USBLS	5/15
	Kentucky	Y	49220 FQ	74190 MW	109830 TQ	USBLS	5/15
	Louisville-Jefferson County MSA, KY-IN	Y	52560 FQ	78790 MW	117290 TQ	USBLS	5/15
	Louisiana	Y	61180 FQ	86260 MW	130390 TQ	USBLS	5/15
	Baton Rouge MSA, LA	Y	67130 FQ	93820 MW	138120 TQ	USBLS	5/15
	New Orleans-Metairie MSA, LA	Y	63200 FQ	90110 MW	139350 TQ	USBLS	5/15
	Maine	Y	52180 FQ	75310 MW	112480 TQ	USBLS	5/15
	Portland-South Portland MSA, ME	Y	55730 FQ	83330 MW	126630 TQ	USBLS	5/15
	Maryland	Y	62225 AE	131069 MW	165490 AEX	MDBLS	4/16
	Baltimore-Columbia-Towson MSA, MD	Y	79770 FQ	116270 MW	165050 TQ	USBLS	5/15
	Salisbury MSA, MD-DE	Y	64880 FQ	83470 MW	116740 TQ	USBLS	5/15
	Massachusetts	Y	72960 FQ	108200 MW	171800 TQ	USBLS	5/15

Occupation/Type/Industry	Location	Per	Low	Mid	High	Source	Date
General and Operations Manager	Boston-Cambridge-Newton NECTA, MA	Y	81760 FQ	126850 MW		USBLS	5/15
	Worcester MSA, MA-CT	Y	68200 FQ	98910 MW	154280 TQ	USBLS	5/15
	Michigan	Y	62650 FQ	93150 MW	139690 TQ	USBLS	5/15
	Detroit-Dearborn-Livonia PMSA, MI	Y	69540 FQ	100180 MW	150520 TQ	USBLS	5/15
	Grand Rapids-Wyoming MSA, MI	Y	67200 FQ	94610 MW	139170 TQ	USBLS	5/15
	Minnesota	Y	61210 FQ	86877 MW	129848 TQ	MNBLS	1/16-3/16
	Minneapolis-St. Paul-Bloomington MSA, MN-WI	Y	68018 FQ	97780 MW	146095 TQ	MNBLS	1/16-3/16
	Mississippi	Y	47740 FQ	69990 MW	108500 TQ	USBLS	5/15
	Jackson MSA, MS	Y	50830 FQ	72300 MW	111620 TQ	USBLS	5/15
	Missouri	Y	54920 FQ	81900 MW	125290 TQ	USBLS	5/15
	Kansas City MSA, MO-KS	Y	61630 FQ	92340 MW	137100 TQ	USBLS	5/15
	St. Louis MSA, MO-IL	Y	61840 FQ	92190 MW	139930 TQ	USBLS	5/15
	Montana	Y	52760 FQ	78960 MW	109750 TQ	USBLS	5/15
	Billings MSA, MT	Y	62550 FQ	85810 MW	130930 TQ	USBLS	5/15
	Nebraska	Y	61995 FQ	90490 MW	133690 TQ	NEBLS	7/16-9/16
	Omaha-Council Bluffs MSA, NE-IA	Y	64955 FQ	93910 MW	139550 TQ	NEBLS	7/16-9/16
	Nevada	Y	59820 FQ	84490 MW	125870 TQ	USBLS	5/15
	Las Vegas-Henderson-Paradise MSA, NV	Y	60140 FQ	83080 MW	127050 TQ	USBLS	5/15
	New Hampshire	H	29.17 AE	50.53 MW	77.60 AEX	NHBLS	6/16
	Manchester NECTA, NH	H	31.42 AE	51.46 MW	77.25 AEX	NHBLS	6/16
	Nashua NECTA, NH-MA	Y	75280 FQ	110640 MW	178510 TQ	USBLS	5/15
	New Jersey	Y	95670 FQ	140770 MW		USBLS	5/15
	Camden PMSA, NJ	Y	86160 FQ	123010 MW		USBLS	5/15
	Newark PMSA, NJ-PA	Y	98370 FQ	148210 MW		USBLS	5/15
	Trenton MSA, NJ	Y	97620 FQ	139440 MW		USBLS	5/15
	New Mexico	Y	54100 FQ	79500 MW	121510 TQ	USBLS	5/15
	Albuquerque MSA, NM	Y	56230 FQ	83070 MW	124640 TQ	USBLS	5/15
	New York	Y	62660 AE	123440 MW		NYBLS	1/16-3/16
	Buffalo-Cheektowaga-Niagara Falls MSA, NY	Y	58790 FQ	87540 MW	130010 TQ	USBLS	5/15
	Nassau County-Suffolk County PMSA, NY	Y	77690 FQ	119280 MW	183430 TQ	USBLS	5/15
	New York-Jersey City-White Plains PMSA, NY-NJ	Y	90560 FQ	145620 MW		USBLS	5/15
	Rochester MSA, NY	Y	67690 FQ	97960 MW	153920 TQ	USBLS	5/15
	North Carolina	Y	75560 FQ	107320 MW	159550 TQ	USBLS	5/15
	Charlotte-Concord-Gastonia MSA, NC-SC	Y	77620 FQ	113220 MW	169510 TQ	USBLS	5/15
	Raleigh MSA, NC	Y	80180 FQ	117990 MW	167440 TQ	USBLS	5/15
	North Dakota	Y	69480 FQ	91360 MW	123530 TQ	USBLS	5/15
	Fargo MSA, ND-MN	Y	65990 FQ	86730 MW	119040 TQ	USBLS	5/15
	Ohio	Y	60390 FQ	89950 MW	135200 TQ	USBLS	5/15
	Cincinnati MSA, OH-KY-IN	Y	61460 FQ	93460 MW	146730 TQ	USBLS	5/15
	Cleveland-Elyria MSA, OH	Y	62460 FQ	93020 MW	142200 TQ	USBLS	5/15
	Columbus MSA, OH	Y	65270 FQ	95260 MW	144640 TQ	USBLS	5/15
	Oklahoma	Y	55090 FQ	78940 MW	119710 TQ	USBLS	5/15
	Oklahoma City MSA, OK	Y	56580 FQ	82850 MW	124360 TQ	USBLS	5/15
	Tulsa MSA, OK	Y	59730 FQ	85770 MW	128470 TQ	USBLS	5/15
	Oregon	H	27.06 FQ	39.52 MW	60.41 TQ	ORBLS	2016
	Portland-Vancouver-Hillsboro MSA, OR-WA	Y	61280 FQ	90310 MW	140510 TQ	USBLS	5/15
	Pennsylvania	Y	70430 FQ	104210 MW	154880 TQ	USBLS	5/15
	Allentown-Bethlehem-Easton MSA, PA-NJ	Y	73350 FQ	104450 MW	144690 TQ	USBLS	5/15
	Harrisburg-Carlisle MSA, PA	Y	67740 FQ	97760 MW	148900 TQ	USBLS	5/15
	Montgomery County-Bucks County-Chester County PMSA, PA	Y	80860 FQ	122010 MW	177500 TQ	USBLS	5/15
	Philadelphia PMSA, PA	Y	82370 FQ	121380 MW	178440 TQ	USBLS	5/15
	Pittsburgh MSA, PA	Y	71200 FQ	103930 MW	158950 TQ	USBLS	5/15
	Rhode Island	Y	86520 FQ	117940 MW	165030 TQ	USBLS	5/15
	Providence-Warwick MSA, RI-MA	Y	81750 FQ	111500 MW	159280 TQ	USBLS	5/15
	South Carolina	Y	52840 FQ	78950 MW	119370 TQ	USBLS	5/15
	Charleston-North Charleston MSA, SC	Y	62090 FQ	84370 MW	121570 TQ	USBLS	5/15

AE Average entry wage	**AWR** Average wage range	**H** Hourly	**LR** Low end range	**MTC** Median total compensation	**TCC** Total cash compensation
AEX Average experienced wage	**B** Biweekly	**HI** Highest wage paid	**M** Monthly	**MW** Median wage paid	**TQ** Third quartile wage
ATC Average total compensation	**D** Daily	**HR** High end range	**MCC** Median cash compensation	**MWR** Median wage range	**W** Weekly
AW Average wage paid	**FQ** First quartile wage	**LO** Lowest wage paid	**ME** Median entry wage	**S** See annotated source	**Y** Yearly

Occupation/Type/Industry	Location	Per	Low	Mid	High	Source	Date
General and Operations Manager	Columbia MSA, SC	Y	64460 FQ	92230 MW	127420 TQ	USBLS	5/15
	Greenville-Anderson-Mauldin MSA, SC	Y	50690 FQ	77630 MW	123400 TQ	USBLS	5/15
	South Dakota	Y	80440 FQ	106610 MW	136500 TQ	USBLS	5/15
	Sioux Falls MSA, SD	Y	85600 FQ	113640 MW	150060 TQ	USBLS	5/15
	Tennessee	Y	56090 FQ	82730 MW	130020 TQ	USBLS	5/15
	Knoxville MSA, TN	Y	56110 FQ	88410 MW	139640 TQ	USBLS	5/15
	Memphis MSA, TN-MS-AR	Y	58120 FQ	86540 MW	137630 TQ	USBLS	5/15
	Nashville-Davidson– Murfreesboro–Franklin MSA, TN	Y	61870 FQ	89350 MW	139670 TQ	USBLS	5/15
	Texas	Y	69870 FQ	104960 MW	167570 TQ	USBLS	5/15
	Austin-Round Rock MSA, TX	Y	65650 FQ	97350 MW	161640 TQ	USBLS	5/15
	Dallas-Plano-Irving PMSA, TX	Y	78490 FQ	120600 MW		USBLS	5/15
	Fort Worth-Arlington PMSA, TX	Y	69700 FQ	105470 MW	158490 TQ	USBLS	5/15
	Houston-The Woodlands- Sugar Land MSA, TX	Y	80490 FQ	122180 MW		USBLS	5/15
	San Antonio-New Braunfels MSA, TX	Y	67370 FQ	98830 MW	146050 TQ	USBLS	5/15
	Utah	Y	44980 FQ	70150 MW	106060 TQ	USBLS	5/15
	Ogden-Clearfield MSA, UT	Y	36040 FQ	63990 MW	95650 TQ	USBLS	5/15
	Provo-Orem MSA, UT	Y	42420 FQ	70980 MW	103260 TQ	USBLS	5/15
	Salt Lake City MSA, UT	Y	53980 FQ	77430 MW	121080 TQ	USBLS	5/15
	Vermont	Y	66200 FQ	94580 MW	135720 TQ	USBLS	5/15
	Burlington-South Burlington MSA, VT	Y	74720 FQ	111660 MW	149440 TQ	USBLS	5/15
	Virginia	Y	74340 FQ	117520 MW	169830 TQ	USBLS	5/15
	Richmond MSA, VA	Y	71260 FQ	105370 MW	153800 TQ	USBLS	5/15
	Virginia Beach-Norfolk- Newport News MSA, VA-NC	Y	71920 FQ	105460 MW	149920 TQ	USBLS	5/15
	Washington	H	36.48 FQ	49.21 MW	70.91 TQ	WABLS	3/16
	Seattle-Bellevue-Everett PMSA, WA	H	40.58 FQ	57.05 MW	81.82 TQ	WABLS	3/16
	Tacoma-Lakewood PMSA, WA	H	34.27 FQ	44.98 MW	64.59 TQ	WABLS	3/16
	West Virginia	Y	51160 FQ	72400 MW	104920 TQ	USBLS	5/15
	Huntington-Ashland MSA, WV-KY-OH	Y	46130 FQ	73280 MW	106910 TQ	USBLS	5/15
	Wisconsin	Y	56830 FQ	88290 MW	139500 TQ	USBLS	5/15
	Madison MSA, WI	Y	67480 FQ	97940 MW	145620 TQ	USBLS	5/15
	Milwaukee-Waukesha-West Allis MSA, WI	Y	66950 FQ	106190 MW	170860 TQ	USBLS	5/15
	Wyoming	Y	64370 FQ	88810 MW	127830 TQ	USBLS	5/15
	Cheyenne MSA, WY	Y	61480 FQ	84720 MW	119210 TQ	USBLS	5/15
	Puerto Rico	Y	42540 FQ	60770 MW	93010 TQ	USBLS	5/15
	Arecibo MSA, PR	Y	29820 FQ	44620 MW	76340 TQ	USBLS	5/15
	San Juan-Carolina-Caguas MSA, PR	Y	43740 FQ	62070 MW	94780 TQ	USBLS	5/15
	Virgin Islands	Y	28260 FQ	45220 MW	71110 TQ	USBLS	5/15
	Guam	Y	35180 FQ	50310 MW	75610 TQ	USBLS	5/15
Genetic Counselor	United States	Y		67500 MW		FORB01	2015
	California	H	31.12 FQ	41.94 MW	52.72 TQ	CABLS	1/16-3/16
	Anaheim-Santa Ana-Irvine PMSA, CA	H	35.61 FQ	44.57 MW	54.28 TQ	CABLS	1/16-3/16
	Los Angeles-Long Beach- Glendale PMSA, CA	H	35.75 FQ	42.70 MW	50.33 TQ	CABLS	1/16-3/16
	Oakland-Hayward-Berkeley PMSA, CA	H	30.78 FQ	40.09 MW	56.44 TQ	CABLS	1/16-3/16
	Sacramento–Roseville– Arden-Arcade MSA, CA	H	32.42 FQ	42.60 MW	46.62 TQ	CABLS	1/16-3/16
	San Diego-Carlsbad MSA, CA	H	48.62 FQ	54.43 MW	58.94 TQ	CABLS	1/16-3/16
	San Francisco-Redwood City- South San Francisco PMSA, CA	H	27.88 FQ	35.60 MW	49.10 TQ	CABLS	1/16-3/16
	Colorado	Y	64920 FQ	72460 MW	80290 TQ	USBLS	5/15
	Denver-Aurora-Lakewood MSA, CO	Y	68140 FQ	74110 MW	80500 TQ	USBLS	5/15
	Florida	H	24.52 AE	36.57 MW	42.54 AEX	FLBLS	7/16-9/16
	Miami-Miami Beach-Kendall PMSA, FL	H	27.52 AE	29.83 MW	33.23 AEX	FLBLS	7/16-9/16

AE	Average entry wage	AWR	Average wage range	H	Hourly	LR	Low end range	MTC	Median total compensation	TCC	Total cash compensation
AEX	Average experienced wage	B	Biweekly	HI	Highest wage paid	M	Monthly	MW	Median wage paid	TQ	Third quartile wage
ATC	Average total compensation	D	Daily	HR	High end range	MCC	Median cash compensation	MWR	Median wage range	W	Weekly
AW	Average wage paid	FQ	First quartile wage	LO	Lowest wage paid	ME	Median entry wage	S	See annotated source	Y	Yearly

700

Occupation/Type/Industry	Location	Per	Low	Mid	High	Source	Date
Genetic Counselor	Orlando-Kissimmee-Sanford MSA, FL	H	25.80 AE	35.19 MW	38.75 AEX	FLBLS	7/16-9/16
	Tampa-St. Petersburg-Clearwater MSA, FL	H	31.81 AE	39.71 MW	46.18 AEX	FLBLS	7/16-9/16
	Georgia	Y	44700 FQ	52500 MW	62980 TQ	USBLS	5/15
	Illinois	Y	64770 FQ	74630 MW	92790 TQ	USBLS	5/15
	Chicago-Naperville-Arlington Heights PMSA, IL	Y	64930 FQ	74700 MW	93440 TQ	USBLS	5/15
	Indiana	Y	56490 FQ	64860 MW	75320 TQ	USBLS	5/15
	Indianapolis-Carmel-Anderson MSA, IN	Y	57020 FQ	64610 MW	74190 TQ	USBLS	5/15
	Baltimore-Columbia-Towson MSA, MD	Y	86670 FQ	96470 MW	108190 TQ	USBLS	5/15
	Massachusetts	Y	61040 FQ	70350 MW	78720 TQ	USBLS	5/15
	Boston-Cambridge-Newton NECTA, MA	Y	60840 FQ	70100 MW	78620 TQ	USBLS	5/15
	Michigan	Y	36090 FQ	45520 MW	60710 TQ	USBLS	5/15
	Minnesota	Y	68759 FQ	74515 MW	80352 TQ	MNBLS	1/16-3/16
	Minneapolis-St. Paul-Bloomington MSA, MN-WI	Y	68668 FQ	73678 MW	78699 TQ	MNBLS	1/16-3/16
	New Jersey	Y	71570 FQ	85510 MW	99940 TQ	USBLS	5/15
	New York	Y	51130 AE	74770 MW	84730 AEX	NYBLS	1/16-3/16
	New York-Jersey City-White Plains PMSA, NY-NJ	Y	69940 FQ	78230 MW	93590 TQ	USBLS	5/15
	North Carolina	Y	51820 FQ	58100 MW	64930 TQ	USBLS	5/15
	Ohio	Y	55760 FQ	62490 MW	73780 TQ	USBLS	5/15
	Cincinnati MSA, OH-KY-IN	Y	55540 FQ	62640 MW	76280 TQ	USBLS	5/15
	Cleveland-Elyria MSA, OH	Y	54750 FQ	60280 MW	71630 TQ	USBLS	5/15
	Oregon	H	32.46 FQ	41.78 MW	45.94 TQ	ORBLS	2016
	Pennsylvania	Y	55400 FQ	61000 MW	70350 TQ	USBLS	5/15
	South Carolina	Y	60410 FQ	105570 MW	117270 TQ	USBLS	5/15
	Texas	Y	64590 FQ	71620 MW	78650 TQ	USBLS	5/15
	Utah	Y	51020 FQ	60860 MW	74800 TQ	USBLS	5/15
	Salt Lake City MSA, UT	Y	50580 FQ	60690 MW	74980 TQ	USBLS	5/15
	Virginia	Y	55700 FQ	68020 MW	79950 TQ	USBLS	5/15
	Washington	H	32.37 FQ	36.26 MW	41.94 TQ	WABLS	3/16
	Seattle-Bellevue-Everett PMSA, WA	H	32.77 FQ	36.47 MW	42.12 TQ	WABLS	3/16
	Wisconsin	Y	54840 FQ	62300 MW	71360 TQ	USBLS	5/15
Genetic Laboratory Technologist Michigan State University	East Lansing, MI	Y			41371 HI	MSUSAL	10/1/14-9/30/15
Geneticist	United States	Y		113043 AW		TSCI	2016
Geographer	Alabama	Y	56919 AE	71210 AW	78355 AEX	ALBLS	6/16
	California	H	34.28 FQ	41.54 MW	47.04 TQ	CABLS	1/16-3/16
	Colorado	Y	62850 FQ	77840 MW	97930 TQ	USBLS	5/15
	Florida	H	31.21 AE	38.03 MW	42.17 AEX	FLBLS	7/16-9/16
	Georgia	Y	35580 FQ	39540 MW	83130 TQ	USBLS	5/15
	Illinois	Y	68600 FQ	74860 MW	105740 TQ	USBLS	5/15
	Maryland	Y	76780 AE	88888 MW	94943 AEX	MDBLS	4/16
	Minnesota	Y	57116 FQ	68598 MW	77146 TQ	MNBLS	1/16-3/16
	Missouri	Y	62930 FQ	73690 MW	83460 TQ	USBLS	5/15
	Nebraska	Y	60520 FQ	77210 MW	81890 TQ	NEBLS	7/16-9/16
	Oklahoma	Y	43970 FQ	48720 MW	69570 TQ	USBLS	5/15
	Oregon	H	33.32 FQ	36.14 MW	44.52 TQ	ORBLS	2016
	South Dakota	Y	57210 FQ	68320 MW	77370 TQ	USBLS	5/15
	Texas	Y	52610 FQ	59660 MW	70150 TQ	USBLS	5/15
	Virginia	Y	78920 FQ	94420 MW	108990 TQ	USBLS	5/15
	Washington	H	33.53 FQ	40.90 MW	47.50 TQ	WABLS	3/16
Geography Teacher Postsecondary	Alabama	Y	53708 AE	86714 AW	103217 AEX	ALBLS	6/16
Postsecondary	Arizona	Y	58010 FQ	74980 MW	96420 TQ	USBLS	5/15
Postsecondary	Arkansas	Y	59840 FQ	75460 MW	98370 TQ	USBLS	5/15
Postsecondary	California	Y		102312 AW		CABLS	1/16-3/16
Postsecondary	Colorado	Y	38550 FQ	63320 MW	82850 TQ	USBLS	5/15
Postsecondary	Florida	Y	77186 AE	103610 MW	125069 AEX	FLBLS	7/16-9/16
Postsecondary	Georgia	Y	65900 FQ	74850 MW	87410 TQ	USBLS	5/15
Postsecondary	Hawaii	Y	55190 FQ	74850 MW	97910 TQ	USBLS	5/15
Postsecondary	Illinois	Y	61490 FQ	82460 MW	106670 TQ	USBLS	5/15

AE	Average entry wage	AWR	Average wage range	H	Hourly	LR	Low end range	MTC	Median total compensation	TCC Total cash compensation
AEX	Average experienced wage	B	Biweekly	HI	Highest wage paid	M	Monthly	MW	Median wage paid	TQ Third quartile wage
ATC	Average total compensation	D	Daily	HR	High end range	MCC	Median cash compensation	MWR	Median wage range	W Weekly
AW	Average wage paid	FQ	First quartile wage	LO	Lowest wage paid	ME	Median entry wage	S	See annotated source	Y Yearly

Occupation/Type/Industry	Location	Per	Low	Mid	High	Source	Date
Geography Teacher							
Postsecondary	Indiana	Y	51670 FQ	69640 MW	89920 TQ	USBLS	5/15
Postsecondary	Kentucky	Y	53430 FQ	69310 MW	101860 TQ	USBLS	5/15
Postsecondary	Louisiana	Y	65840 FQ	72390 MW	79470 TQ	USBLS	5/15
Postsecondary	Maryland	Y	47912 AE	82131 MW	99240 AEX	MDBLS	4/16
Postsecondary	Massachusetts	Y	59460 FQ	73590 MW	93650 TQ	USBLS	5/15
Postsecondary	Michigan	Y	65210 FQ	87370 MW	110850 TQ	USBLS	5/15
Postsecondary	Minnesota	Y	64687 FQ	80977 MW	101259 TQ	MNBLS	1/16-3/16
Postsecondary	Missouri	Y	53210 FQ	67330 MW	79590 TQ	USBLS	5/15
Postsecondary	Nebraska	Y	48265 FQ	58705 MW	81470 TQ	NEBLS	7/16-9/16
Postsecondary	New Jersey	Y	68260 FQ	88280 MW	111470 TQ	USBLS	5/15
Postsecondary	New Mexico	Y	83330 FQ	91710 MW	100080 TQ	USBLS	5/15
Postsecondary	New York	Y	48520 AE	79090 MW	103580 AEX	NYBLS	1/16-3/16
Postsecondary	North Carolina	Y	56700 FQ	68470 MW	81600 TQ	USBLS	5/15
Postsecondary	Ohio	Y	62010 FQ	78710 MW	104800 TQ	USBLS	5/15
Postsecondary	Oklahoma	Y	58900 FQ	79770 MW	94220 TQ	USBLS	5/15
Postsecondary	Oregon	Y	63016 FQ	75842 MW	98800 TQ	ORBLS	2016
Postsecondary	Pennsylvania	Y	51240 FQ	80040 MW	102080 TQ	USBLS	5/15
Postsecondary	Tennessee	Y	35960 FQ	57760 MW	75740 TQ	USBLS	5/15
Postsecondary	Texas	Y	53080 FQ	73940 MW	98590 TQ	USBLS	5/15
Postsecondary	Utah	Y	56700 FQ	73000 MW	89450 TQ	USBLS	5/15
Postsecondary	Vermont	Y	46810 FQ	85370 MW	99500 TQ	USBLS	5/15
Postsecondary	Virginia	Y	39960 FQ	60950 MW	90680 TQ	USBLS	5/15
Postsecondary	Washington	Y		61184 AW		WABLS	3/16
Postsecondary	West Virginia	Y	48600 FQ	61870 MW	78110 TQ	USBLS	5/15
Postsecondary	Wisconsin	Y	52190 FQ	68560 MW	88650 TQ	USBLS	5/15
Geological and Petroleum Technician							
	Alabama	Y	33312 AE	54697 AW	65379 AEX	ALBLS	6/16
	Alaska	Y	54000 FQ	68510 MW	88780 TQ	USBLS	5/15
	Arizona	Y	31870 FQ	38980 MW	53080 TQ	USBLS	5/15
	California	H	22.59 FQ	31.04 MW	39.76 TQ	CABLS	1/16-3/16
	Colorado	Y	46320 FQ	59820 MW	87640 TQ	USBLS	5/15
	Florida	H	12.04 AE	16.48 MW	21.64 AEX	FLBLS	7/16-9/16
	Georgia	Y	40700 FQ	54030 MW	68740 TQ	USBLS	5/15
	Hawaii	Y	35190 FQ	39640 MW	53890 TQ	USBLS	5/15
	Idaho	Y	35550 FQ	48690 MW	72250 TQ	USBLS	5/15
	Illinois	Y	51160 FQ	58950 MW	69350 TQ	USBLS	5/15
	Indiana	Y	39290 FQ	58350 MW	74420 TQ	USBLS	5/15
	Kansas	Y	41920 FQ	51940 MW	59470 TQ	USBLS	5/15
	Kentucky	Y	36210 FQ	45660 MW	68350 TQ	USBLS	5/15
	Louisiana	Y	37410 FQ	48530 MW	73480 TQ	USBLS	5/15
	Maryland	Y	38923 AE	57679 MW	67057 AEX	MDBLS	4/16
	Michigan	Y	30360 FQ	39410 MW	56320 TQ	USBLS	5/15
	Minnesota	Y	40241 FQ	54153 MW	65150 TQ	MNBLS	1/16-3/16
	Mississippi	Y	31220 FQ	46060 MW	65040 TQ	USBLS	5/15
	Missouri	Y	35430 FQ	43540 MW	58400 TQ	USBLS	5/15
	Montana	Y	49920 FQ	55630 MW	61240 TQ	USBLS	5/15
	Nevada	Y	29280 FQ	43570 MW	57530 TQ	USBLS	5/15
	New Hampshire	H	11.72 AE	17.50 MW	24.17 AEX	NHBLS	6/16
	New Jersey	Y	41700 FQ	53850 MW	59860 TQ	USBLS	5/15
	New York	Y	37850 AE	46030 MW	59580 AEX	NYBLS	1/16-3/16
	North Dakota	Y	52370 FQ	65070 MW	85520 TQ	USBLS	5/15
	Ohio	Y	29970 FQ	50240 MW	64540 TQ	USBLS	5/15
	Oklahoma	Y	43400 FQ	60310 MW	78490 TQ	USBLS	5/15
	Oregon	H	22.29 FQ	26.64 MW	31.42 TQ	ORBLS	2016
	Pennsylvania	Y	38860 FQ	55960 MW	73290 TQ	USBLS	5/15
	South Carolina	Y	34020 FQ	39310 MW	48980 TQ	USBLS	5/15
	Tennessee	Y	41060 FQ	51610 MW	60680 TQ	USBLS	5/15
	Texas	Y	34130 FQ	56670 MW	79880 TQ	USBLS	5/15
	Utah	Y	38690 FQ	58950 MW	81410 TQ	USBLS	5/15
	Washington	H	14.14 FQ	19.40 MW	27.48 TQ	WABLS	3/16
	West Virginia	Y	39790 FQ	58070 MW	75920 TQ	USBLS	5/15
	Wyoming	Y	38070 FQ	48150 MW	71850 TQ	USBLS	5/15
Geophysicist	United States	Y		119380 MW		CNBC05	2016
Geoscientist							
Except Hydrologists and Geographers	Alabama	Y	50018 AE	83258 AW	99884 AEX	ALBLS	6/16
Except Hydrologists and Geographers	Birmingham-Hoover MSA, AL	Y	61047 AE	105153 AW	127212 AEX	ALBLS	6/16
Except Hydrologists and Geographers	Alaska	Y	78320 FQ	101130 MW	135510 TQ	USBLS	5/15
Except Hydrologists and Geographers	Anchorage MSA, AK	Y	88820 FQ	117330 MW	151980 TQ	USBLS	5/15

Occupation/Type/Industry	Location	Per	Low	Mid	High	Source	Date
Geoscientist							
Except Hydrologists and Geographers	Arizona	Y	55570 FQ	70190 MW	91820 TQ	USBLS	5/15
Except Hydrologists and Geographers	Phoenix-Mesa-Scottsdale MSA, AZ	Y	57280 FQ	70430 MW	91750 TQ	USBLS	5/15
Except Hydrologists and Geographers	Tucson MSA, AZ	Y	60360 FQ	74190 MW	101980 TQ	USBLS	5/15
Except Hydrologists and Geographers	Arkansas	Y	41680 FQ	55920 MW	77920 TQ	USBLS	5/15
Except Hydrologists and Geographers	Little Rock-North Little Rock-Conway MSA, AR	Y	40870 FQ	54350 MW	70180 TQ	USBLS	5/15
Except Hydrologists and Geographers	California	H	30.48 FQ	45.53 MW	57.01 TQ	CABLS	1/16-3/16
Except Hydrologists and Geographers	Anaheim-Santa Ana-Irvine PMSA, CA	H	30.90 FQ	38.35 MW	46.63 TQ	CABLS	1/16-3/16
Except Hydrologists and Geographers	Los Angeles-Long Beach-Glendale PMSA, CA	H	28.10 FQ	42.39 MW	53.79 TQ	CABLS	1/16-3/16
Except Hydrologists and Geographers	Riverside-San Bernardino-Ontario MSA, CA	H	29.25 FQ	38.18 MW	55.78 TQ	CABLS	1/16-3/16
Except Hydrologists and Geographers	Sacramento–Roseville–Arden-Arcade MSA, CA	H	37.20 FQ	48.14 MW	51.35 TQ	CABLS	1/16-3/16
Except Hydrologists and Geographers	San Diego-Carlsbad MSA, CA	H	27.37 FQ	40.14 MW	55.28 TQ	CABLS	1/16-3/16
Except Hydrologists and Geographers	San Francisco-Redwood City-South San Francisco PMSA, CA	H	43.24 FQ	54.18 MW	70.18 TQ	CABLS	1/16-3/16
Except Hydrologists and Geographers	Colorado	Y	70190 FQ	106470 MW	147170 TQ	USBLS	5/15
Except Hydrologists and Geographers	Denver-Aurora-Lakewood MSA, CO	Y	81460 FQ	116460 MW	157230 TQ	USBLS	5/15
Except Hydrologists and Geographers	Connecticut	Y		80226 MW		CTBLS	1/16-3/16
Except Hydrologists and Geographers	Hartford-West Hartford-East Hartford MSA, CT	Y	58690 FQ	76060 MW	113890 TQ	USBLS	5/15
Except Hydrologists and Geographers	Delaware	Y	66360 FQ	89230 MW	117540 TQ	USBLS	5/15
Except Hydrologists and Geographers	Wilmington PMSA, DE-MD-NJ	Y	64490 FQ	89830 MW	119930 TQ	USBLS	5/15
Except Hydrologists and Geographers	District of Columbia	Y	102930 FQ	118070 MW	158690 TQ	USBLS	5/15
Except Hydrologists and Geographers	Washington-Arlington-Alexandria PMSA, DC-VA-MD-WV	Y	93870 FQ	118070 MW	157730 TQ	USBLS	5/15
Except Hydrologists and Geographers	Florida	H	26.69 AE	41.47 MW	50.20 AEX	FLBLS	7/16-9/16
Except Hydrologists and Geographers	Miami-Miami Beach-Kendall PMSA, FL	H	43.30 AE	52.28 MW	58.41 AEX	FLBLS	7/16-9/16
Except Hydrologists and Geographers	Orlando-Kissimmee-Sanford MSA, FL	H	24.23 AE	33.42 MW	46.75 AEX	FLBLS	7/16-9/16
Except Hydrologists and Geographers	Tampa-St. Petersburg-Clearwater MSA, FL	H	28.26 AE	45.06 MW	52.90 AEX	FLBLS	7/16-9/16
Except Hydrologists and Geographers	Georgia	Y	51300 FQ	66210 MW	79180 TQ	USBLS	5/15
Except Hydrologists and Geographers	Atlanta-Sandy Springs-Roswell MSA, GA	Y	48260 FQ	60760 MW	76700 TQ	USBLS	5/15
Except Hydrologists and Geographers	Hawaii	Y	68620 FQ	93130 MW	127790 TQ	USBLS	5/15
Except Hydrologists and Geographers	Urban Honolulu MSA, HI	Y	65890 FQ	93140 MW	134000 TQ	USBLS	5/15
Except Hydrologists and Geographers	Idaho	Y	62470 FQ	70150 MW	77210 TQ	USBLS	5/15
Except Hydrologists and Geographers	Boise City MSA, ID	Y	53230 FQ	70230 MW	78170 TQ	USBLS	5/15
Except Hydrologists and Geographers	Illinois	Y	68710 FQ	91250 MW	108130 TQ	USBLS	5/15
Except Hydrologists and Geographers	Chicago-Naperville-Arlington Heights PMSA, IL	Y	64840 FQ	95480 MW	112590 TQ	USBLS	5/15
Except Hydrologists and Geographers	Indiana	Y	44950 FQ	55710 MW	70190 TQ	USBLS	5/15
Except Hydrologists and Geographers	Indianapolis-Carmel-Anderson MSA, IN	Y	44050 FQ	54480 MW	68920 TQ	USBLS	5/15
Except Hydrologists and Geographers	Iowa	Y	57800 FQ	80580 MW	91270 TQ	USBLS	5/15
Except Hydrologists and Geographers	Des Moines-West Des Moines MSA, IA	Y	60850 FQ	78350 MW	80600 TQ	USBLS	5/15
Except Hydrologists and Geographers	Kansas	Y	47870 FQ	69920 MW	91480 TQ	USBLS	5/15
Except Hydrologists and Geographers	Wichita MSA, KS	Y	60310 FQ	85440 MW	95000 TQ	USBLS	5/15
Except Hydrologists and Geographers	Kentucky	Y	44630 FQ	61700 MW	77360 TQ	USBLS	5/15
Except Hydrologists and Geographers	Louisville-Jefferson County MSA, KY-IN	Y	62670 FQ	78500 MW	94600 TQ	USBLS	5/15
Except Hydrologists and Geographers	Louisiana	Y	57580 FQ	79730 MW	121440 TQ	USBLS	5/15
Except Hydrologists and Geographers	Baton Rouge MSA, LA	Y	52020 FQ	63360 MW	81600 TQ	USBLS	5/15
Except Hydrologists and Geographers	New Orleans-Metairie MSA, LA	Y	76530 FQ	108500 MW	145580 TQ	USBLS	5/15
Except Hydrologists and Geographers	Maine	Y	54430 FQ	61050 MW	71210 TQ	USBLS	5/15
Except Hydrologists and Geographers	Portland-South Portland MSA, ME	Y	53560 FQ	60450 MW	71000 TQ	USBLS	5/15
Except Hydrologists and Geographers	Maryland	Y	54609 AE	95079 MW	115314 AEX	MDBLS	4/16
Except Hydrologists and Geographers	Baltimore-Columbia-Towson MSA, MD	Y	53850 FQ	70450 MW	85350 TQ	USBLS	5/15

AE	Average entry wage	AWR	Average wage range	H	Hourly	LR	Low end range	MTC	Median total compensation	TCC	Total cash compensation
AEX	Average experienced wage	B	Biweekly	HI	Highest wage paid	M	Monthly	MW	Median wage paid	TQ	Third quartile wage
ATC	Average total compensation	D	Daily	HR	High end range	MCC	Median cash compensation	MWR	Median wage range	W	Weekly
AW	Average wage paid	FQ	First quartile wage	LO	Lowest wage paid	ME	Median entry wage	S	See annotated source	Y	Yearly

Occupation/Type/Industry	Location	Per	Low	Mid	High	Source	Date
Geoscientist							
Except Hydrologists and Geographers	Massachusetts	Y	55820 FQ	70420 MW	99200 TQ	USBLS	5/15
Except Hydrologists and Geographers	Boston-Cambridge-Newton NECTA, MA	Y	53080 FQ	62010 MW	94660 TQ	USBLS	5/15
Except Hydrologists and Geographers	Michigan	Y	55520 FQ	71100 MW	80310 TQ	USBLS	5/15
Except Hydrologists and Geographers	Minnesota	Y	57429 FQ	72217 MW	94979 TQ	MNBLS	1/16-3/16
Except Hydrologists and Geographers	Minneapolis-St. Paul-Bloomington MSA, MN-WI	Y	57116 FQ	73285 MW	96884 TQ	MNBLS	1/16-3/16
Except Hydrologists and Geographers	Mississippi	Y	66350 FQ	89030 MW	108500 TQ	USBLS	5/15
Except Hydrologists and Geographers	Jackson MSA, MS	Y	47920 FQ	58480 MW	69930 TQ	USBLS	5/15
Except Hydrologists and Geographers	Missouri	Y	47000 FQ	64740 MW	82300 TQ	USBLS	5/15
Except Hydrologists and Geographers	Kansas City MSA, MO-KS	Y	70190 FQ	86570 MW	97110 TQ	USBLS	5/15
Except Hydrologists and Geographers	St. Louis MSA, MO-IL	Y	50430 FQ	66050 MW	79850 TQ	USBLS	5/15
Except Hydrologists and Geographers	Montana	Y	63350 FQ	83300 MW	110840 TQ	USBLS	5/15
Except Hydrologists and Geographers	Billings MSA, MT	Y	48520 FQ	75200 MW	155890 TQ	USBLS	5/15
Except Hydrologists and Geographers	Nebraska	Y	45445 FQ	70185 MW	97695 TQ	NEBLS	7/16-9/16
Except Hydrologists and Geographers	Omaha-Council Bluffs MSA, NE-IA	Y	42855 FQ	72290 MW	98925 TQ	NEBLS	7/16-9/16
Except Hydrologists and Geographers	Nevada	Y	71550 FQ	99200 MW	116750 TQ	USBLS	5/15
Except Hydrologists and Geographers	Las Vegas-Henderson-Paradise MSA, NV	Y	54200 FQ	66480 MW	100210 TQ	USBLS	5/15
Except Hydrologists and Geographers	New Hampshire	H	26.18 AE	37.84 MW	50.31 AEX	NHBLS	6/16
Except Hydrologists and Geographers	Manchester NECTA, NH	H	24.19 AE	36.71 MW	52.07 AEX	NHBLS	6/16
Except Hydrologists and Geographers	New Jersey	Y	66140 FQ	80030 MW	94560 TQ	USBLS	5/15
Except Hydrologists and Geographers	Camden PMSA, NJ	Y	58100 FQ	69100 MW	79350 TQ	USBLS	5/15
Except Hydrologists and Geographers	Newark PMSA, NJ-PA	Y	68850 FQ	85680 MW	101370 TQ	USBLS	5/15
Except Hydrologists and Geographers	Trenton MSA, NJ	Y	74250 FQ	87360 MW	95630 TQ	USBLS	5/15
Except Hydrologists and Geographers	New Mexico	Y	64000 FQ	82670 MW	129540 TQ	USBLS	5/15
Except Hydrologists and Geographers	Albuquerque MSA, NM	Y	54430 FQ	80410 MW	108490 TQ	USBLS	5/15
Except Hydrologists and Geographers	New York	Y	50670 AE	80490 MW	93840 AEX	NYBLS	1/16-3/16
Except Hydrologists and Geographers	Buffalo-Cheektowaga-Niagara Falls MSA, NY	Y	56840 FQ	73000 MW	100150 TQ	USBLS	5/15
Except Hydrologists and Geographers	Nassau County-Suffolk County PMSA, NY	Y	51120 FQ	61310 MW	78470 TQ	USBLS	5/15
Except Hydrologists and Geographers	New York-Jersey City-White Plains PMSA, NY-NJ	Y	66300 FQ	85040 MW	97260 TQ	USBLS	5/15
Except Hydrologists and Geographers	Rochester MSA, NY	Y	68940 FQ	84170 MW	97240 TQ	USBLS	5/15
Except Hydrologists and Geographers	North Carolina	Y	56580 FQ	71360 MW	90060 TQ	USBLS	5/15
Except Hydrologists and Geographers	Charlotte-Concord-Gastonia MSA, NC-SC	Y	62110 FQ	71940 MW	83260 TQ	USBLS	5/15
Except Hydrologists and Geographers	Raleigh MSA, NC	Y	56840 FQ	73410 MW	99140 TQ	USBLS	5/15
Except Hydrologists and Geographers	North Dakota	Y	54630 FQ	64230 MW	77880 TQ	USBLS	5/15
Except Hydrologists and Geographers	Ohio	Y	49790 FQ	65640 MW	78050 TQ	USBLS	5/15
Except Hydrologists and Geographers	Cincinnati MSA, OH-KY-IN	Y	45980 FQ	56950 MW	76020 TQ	USBLS	5/15
Except Hydrologists and Geographers	Cleveland-Elyria MSA, OH	Y	49060 FQ	73340 MW	107520 TQ	USBLS	5/15
Except Hydrologists and Geographers	Columbus MSA, OH	Y	50230 FQ	69100 MW	78710 TQ	USBLS	5/15
Except Hydrologists and Geographers	Oklahoma	Y	69910 FQ	108080 MW	137600 TQ	USBLS	5/15
Except Hydrologists and Geographers	Oklahoma City MSA, OK	Y	65930 FQ	101630 MW	123410 TQ	USBLS	5/15
Except Hydrologists and Geographers	Tulsa MSA, OK	Y	100580 FQ	131210 MW		USBLS	5/15
Except Hydrologists and Geographers	Oregon	H	26.88 FQ	31.66 MW	40.51 TQ	ORBLS	2016
Except Hydrologists and Geographers	Portland-Vancouver-Hillsboro MSA, OR-WA	Y	54260 FQ	61470 MW	86330 TQ	USBLS	5/15
Except Hydrologists and Geographers	Pennsylvania	Y	53180 FQ	68650 MW	88250 TQ	USBLS	5/15
Except Hydrologists and Geographers	Harrisburg-Carlisle MSA, PA	Y	57310 FQ	70010 MW	85240 TQ	USBLS	5/15
Except Hydrologists and Geographers	Montgomery County-Bucks County-Chester County PMSA, PA	Y	58100 FQ	72350 MW	93360 TQ	USBLS	5/15
Except Hydrologists and Geographers	Pittsburgh MSA, PA	Y	54920 FQ	76890 MW	109040 TQ	USBLS	5/15
Except Hydrologists and Geographers	Rhode Island	Y	49920 FQ	62450 MW	82630 TQ	USBLS	5/15
Except Hydrologists and Geographers	Providence-Warwick MSA, RI-MA	Y	49920 FQ	62450 MW	82630 TQ	USBLS	5/15
Except Hydrologists and Geographers	South Carolina	Y	69220 FQ	104570 MW	125970 TQ	USBLS	5/15
Except Hydrologists and Geographers	Charleston-North Charleston MSA, SC	Y	77460 FQ	105970 MW	126970 TQ	USBLS	5/15
Except Hydrologists and Geographers	Greenville-Anderson-Mauldin MSA, SC	Y	73940 FQ	110080 MW	125700 TQ	USBLS	5/15
Except Hydrologists and Geographers	South Dakota	Y	49230 FQ	61640 MW	77500 TQ	USBLS	5/15
Except Hydrologists and Geographers	Tennessee	Y	47420 FQ	63510 MW	84230 TQ	USBLS	5/15
Except Hydrologists and Geographers	Knoxville MSA, TN	Y	50500 FQ	81160 MW	98780 TQ	USBLS	5/15
Except Hydrologists and Geographers	Nashville-Davidson–Murfreesboro–Franklin MSA, TN	Y	50480 FQ	65880 MW	79550 TQ	USBLS	5/15

AE	Average entry wage	AWR	Average wage range	H	Hourly
AEX	Average experienced wage	B	Biweekly	HI	Highest wage paid
ATC	Average total compensation	D	Daily	HR	High end range
AW	Average wage paid	FQ	First quartile wage	LO	Lowest wage paid

LR	Low end range	MTC	Median total compensation	TCC	Total cash compensation
M	Monthly	MW	Median wage paid	TQ	Third quartile wage
MCC	Median cash compensation	MWR	Median wage range	W	Weekly
ME	Median entry wage	S	See annotated source	Y	Yearly

Occupation/Type/Industry	Location	Per	Low	Mid	High	Source	Date
Geoscientist							
Except Hydrologists and Geographers	Texas	Y	76960 FQ	122610 MW		USBLS	5/15
Except Hydrologists and Geographers	Austin-Round Rock MSA, TX	Y	59640 FQ	74130 MW	99430 TQ	USBLS	5/15
Except Hydrologists and Geographers	Dallas-Plano-Irving PMSA, TX	Y	60520 FQ	115490 MW		USBLS	5/15
Except Hydrologists and Geographers	Fort Worth-Arlington PMSA, TX	Y	29400 FQ	57870 MW	122350 TQ	USBLS	5/15
Except Hydrologists and Geographers	Houston-The Woodlands-Sugar Land MSA, TX	Y	89230 FQ	138650 MW		USBLS	5/15
Except Hydrologists and Geographers	San Antonio-New Braunfels MSA, TX	Y	51160 FQ	82640 MW	104310 TQ	USBLS	5/15
Except Hydrologists and Geographers	Utah	Y	49320 FQ	68560 MW	90280 TQ	USBLS	5/15
Except Hydrologists and Geographers	Salt Lake City MSA, UT	Y	61080 FQ	74320 MW	94720 TQ	USBLS	5/15
Except Hydrologists and Geographers	Vermont	Y	56710 FQ	77500 MW	100560 TQ	USBLS	5/15
Except Hydrologists and Geographers	Virginia	Y	56770 FQ	81910 MW	117320 TQ	USBLS	5/15
Except Hydrologists and Geographers	Richmond MSA, VA	Y	51140 FQ	57000 MW	62630 TQ	USBLS	5/15
Except Hydrologists and Geographers	Washington	H	29.97 FQ	39.77 MW	52.44 TQ	WABLS	3/16
Except Hydrologists and Geographers	Seattle-Bellevue-Everett PMSA, WA	H	29.17 FQ	38.96 MW	51.75 TQ	WABLS	3/16
Except Hydrologists and Geographers	Tacoma-Lakewood PMSA, WA	H	30.33 FQ	36.83 MW	45.14 TQ	WABLS	3/16
Except Hydrologists and Geographers	West Virginia	Y	44980 FQ	62950 MW	91430 TQ	USBLS	5/15
Except Hydrologists and Geographers	Huntington-Ashland MSA, WV-KY-OH	Y	33390 FQ	54540 MW	88160 TQ	USBLS	5/15
Except Hydrologists and Geographers	Wisconsin	Y	56180 FQ	71060 MW	89940 TQ	USBLS	5/15
Except Hydrologists and Geographers	Madison MSA, WI	Y	54870 FQ	64330 MW	84710 TQ	USBLS	5/15
Except Hydrologists and Geographers	Milwaukee-Waukesha-West Allis MSA, WI	Y	54930 FQ	75850 MW	92960 TQ	USBLS	5/15
Except Hydrologists and Geographers	Wyoming	Y	62230 FQ	71280 MW	84950 TQ	USBLS	5/15
Except Hydrologists and Geographers	Cheyenne MSA, WY	Y	38750 FQ	65210 MW	75520 TQ	USBLS	5/15
Except Hydrologists and Geographers	Puerto Rico	Y	52360 FQ	60620 MW	108690 TQ	USBLS	5/15
Except Hydrologists and Geographers	San Juan-Carolina-Caguas MSA, PR	Y	53220 FQ	61190 MW	110500 TQ	USBLS	5/15
Geospacial Database Administrator							
County Government	Douglas County, CO	Y			88117 HI	DCOGOV	2016
Geotechnical Specialist							
Department of Transportation, State Government	Helena, MT	H			25.12 HI	MTGOV	2016
Gerontological Nurse Practitioner	United States	Y		75000 AW		SCR01	2016
Gerontology Nurse	United States	Y		96460 MW		FTIME	2016
Gerontology Specialist							
Parks, Recreation and Neighborhood Services, Municipal Government	San Jose, CA	Y		60650 AW		CACIT	6/28/16
GIS Analyst							
Municipal Government	Bakersfield, CA	Y			63530 HI	CACIT	6/28/16
Municipal Government	Cerritos, CA	Y			74320 HI	CACIT	6/28/16
Municipal Government	Chico, CA	Y			67840 HI	CACIT	6/28/16
Municipal Government	Lompoc, CA	Y			59331 HI	CACIT	6/28/16
GIS Coordinator							
Environmental Services Department, Municipal Government	Arcata, CA	Y			58783 HI	CACIT	6/28/16
GIS Manager							
Information Technology Services, Municipal Government	Fremont, CA	Y			141220 HI	CACIT	6/28/16
GIS Specialist							
Public Works Department, Municipal Government	Buena Park, CA	Y			65095 HI	CACIT	6/28/16
Public Works Department, Municipal Government	Thousand Oaks, CA	Y			79880 HI	CACIT	6/28/16
GIS Technician							
Municipal Government	Carlsbad, CA	H	26.69 LO	30.80 MW	34.91 HI	CCCA01	6/28/16
Glass Blower	United States	Y		32000 AW		SKU01	2016

AE Average entry wage	**AWR** Average wage range	**H** Hourly	**LR** Low end range	**MTC** Median total compensation	**TCC** Total cash compensation
AEX Average experienced wage	**B** Biweekly	**HI** Highest wage paid	**M** Monthly	**MW** Median wage paid	**TQ** Third quartile wage
ATC Average total compensation	**D** Daily	**HR** High end range	**MCC** Median cash compensation	**MWR** Median wage range	**W** Weekly
AW Average wage paid	**FQ** First quartile wage	**LO** Lowest wage paid	**ME** Median entry wage	**S** See annotated source	**Y** Yearly

Glazier

Occupation/Type/Industry	Location	Per	Low	Mid	High	Source	Date
	Alabama	Y	25378 AE	36436 AW	41960 AEX	ALBLS	6/16
	Birmingham-Hoover MSA, AL	Y	31169 AE	42382 AW	47978 AEX	ALBLS	6/16
	Alaska	Y	51990 FQ	63690 MW	72410 TQ	USBLS	5/15
	Anchorage MSA, AK	Y	47930 FQ	60350 MW	72600 TQ	USBLS	5/15
	Arizona	Y	28770 FQ	34380 MW	45380 TQ	USBLS	5/15
	Phoenix-Mesa-Scottsdale MSA, AZ	Y	28990 FQ	34770 MW	49020 TQ	USBLS	5/15
	Tucson MSA, AZ	Y	24820 FQ	32200 MW	37730 TQ	USBLS	5/15
	Arkansas	Y	29520 FQ	35210 MW	40940 TQ	USBLS	5/15
	Little Rock-North Little Rock-Conway MSA, AR	Y	32110 FQ	35750 MW	39460 TQ	USBLS	5/15
	California	H	18.25 FQ	26.19 MW	38.87 TQ	CABLS	1/16-3/16
	Anaheim-Santa Ana-Irvine PMSA, CA	H	18.15 FQ	26.32 MW	39.27 TQ	CABLS	1/16-3/16
	Los Angeles-Long Beach-Glendale PMSA, CA	H	25.14 FQ	28.80 MW	39.93 TQ	CABLS	1/16-3/16
	Oakland-Hayward-Berkeley PMSA, CA	H	17.61 FQ	22.83 MW	29.39 TQ	CABLS	1/16-3/16
	Riverside-San Bernardino-Ontario MSA, CA	H	14.06 FQ	19.26 MW	28.13 TQ	CABLS	1/16-3/16
	Sacramento–Roseville–Arden-Arcade MSA, CA	H	17.44 FQ	21.42 MW	24.08 TQ	CABLS	1/16-3/16
	San Diego-Carlsbad MSA, CA	H	21.62 FQ	34.90 MW	43.53 TQ	CABLS	1/16-3/16
	San Francisco-Redwood City-South San Francisco PMSA, CA	H	39.91 FQ	43.54 MW	47.17 TQ	CABLS	1/16-3/16
	Colorado	Y	33470 FQ	42200 MW	54390 TQ	USBLS	5/15
	Denver-Aurora-Lakewood MSA, CO	Y	33140 FQ	43430 MW	55950 TQ	USBLS	5/15
	Connecticut	Y		48492 MW		CTBLS	1/16-3/16
	Bridgeport-Stamford-Norwalk MSA, CT	Y	38600 FQ	60950 MW	71980 TQ	USBLS	5/15
	Hartford-West Hartford-East Hartford MSA, CT	Y	41150 FQ	51010 MW	59020 TQ	USBLS	5/15
	District of Columbia	Y	33590 FQ	52470 MW	64080 TQ	USBLS	5/15
	Washington-Arlington-Alexandria PMSA, DC-VA-MD-WV	Y	40280 FQ	46670 MW	56110 TQ	USBLS	5/15
	Florida	H	11.94 AE	16.76 MW	19.07 AEX	FLBLS	7/16-9/16
	Fort Lauderdale-Pompano Beach-Deerfield Beach PMSA, FL	H	9.15 AE	16.25 MW	18.03 AEX	FLBLS	7/16-9/16
	Miami-Miami Beach-Kendall PMSA, FL	H	12.01 AE	16.05 MW	17.78 AEX	FLBLS	7/16-9/16
	Orlando-Kissimmee-Sanford MSA, FL	H	12.62 AE	16.91 MW	19.91 AEX	FLBLS	7/16-9/16
	Tampa-St. Petersburg-Clearwater MSA, FL	H	14.79 AE	17.49 MW	19.44 AEX	FLBLS	7/16-9/16
	Georgia	Y	26350 FQ	34670 MW	44730 TQ	USBLS	5/15
	Atlanta-Sandy Springs-Roswell MSA, GA	Y	27800 FQ	38550 MW	46030 TQ	USBLS	5/15
	Hawaii	Y	45090 FQ	64820 MW	73570 TQ	USBLS	5/15
	Urban Honolulu MSA, HI	Y	56040 FQ	68100 MW	75220 TQ	USBLS	5/15
	Idaho	Y	31120 FQ	38760 MW	45350 TQ	USBLS	5/15
	Boise City MSA, ID	Y	40190 FQ	43560 MW	46930 TQ	USBLS	5/15
	Illinois	Y	33740 FQ	40640 MW	75210 TQ	USBLS	5/15
	Chicago-Naperville-Arlington Heights PMSA, IL	Y	32940 FQ	38510 MW	72020 TQ	USBLS	5/15
	Lake County-Kenosha County PMSA, IL-WI	Y	31950 FQ	35900 MW	47270 TQ	USBLS	5/15
	Indiana	Y	33560 FQ	39830 MW	59570 TQ	USBLS	5/15
	Gary PMSA, IN	Y	32180 FQ	64830 MW	71600 TQ	USBLS	5/15
	Indianapolis-Carmel-Anderson MSA, IN	Y	40520 FQ	55380 MW	73400 TQ	USBLS	5/15
	Iowa	Y	32210 FQ	42500 MW	52830 TQ	USBLS	5/15
	Des Moines-West Des Moines MSA, IA	Y	40900 FQ	46860 MW	55530 TQ	USBLS	5/15
	Kansas	Y	30140 FQ	40610 MW	60980 TQ	USBLS	5/15
	Kentucky	Y	28610 FQ	35290 MW	43590 TQ	USBLS	5/15
	Louisville-Jefferson County MSA, KY-IN	Y	31100 FQ	36880 MW	44590 TQ	USBLS	5/15
	Louisiana	Y	28090 FQ	33110 MW	38640 TQ	USBLS	5/15

AE	Average entry wage	**AWR**	Average wage range	**H**	Hourly	**LR** Low end range	**MTC** Median total compensation	**TCC** Total cash compensation
AEX	Average experienced wage	**B**	Biweekly	**HI**	Highest wage paid	**M** Monthly	**MW** Median wage paid	**TQ** Third quartile wage
ATC	Average total compensation	**D**	Daily	**HR**	High end range	**MCC** Median cash compensation	**MWR** Median wage range	**W** Weekly
AW	Average wage paid	**FQ**	First quartile wage	**LO**	Lowest wage paid	**ME** Median entry wage	**S** See annotated source	**Y** Yearly

Glazier

Occupation/Type/Industry	Location	Per	Low	Mid	High	Source	Date
Glazier	Baton Rouge MSA, LA	Y	28030 FQ	33660 MW	41210 TQ	USBLS	5/15
	New Orleans-Metairie MSA, LA	Y	30650 FQ	35010 MW	39230 TQ	USBLS	5/15
	Maine	Y	32140 FQ	36410 MW	41440 TQ	USBLS	5/15
	Portland-South Portland MSA, ME	Y	34090 FQ	36650 MW	39220 TQ	USBLS	5/15
	Maryland	Y	34866 AE	47898 MW	54415 AEX	MDBLS	4/16
	Baltimore-Columbia-Towson MSA, MD	Y	33530 FQ	43620 MW	58330 TQ	USBLS	5/15
	Salisbury MSA, MD-DE	Y	31870 FQ	41010 MW	50430 TQ	USBLS	5/15
	Massachusetts	Y	36890 FQ	48590 MW	78770 TQ	USBLS	5/15
	Boston-Cambridge-Newton NECTA, MA	Y	40470 FQ	73580 MW	89320 TQ	USBLS	5/15
	Worcester MSA, MA-CT	Y	34300 FQ	38590 MW	45970 TQ	USBLS	5/15
	Michigan	Y	35930 FQ	45290 MW	56070 TQ	USBLS	5/15
	Detroit-Dearborn-Livonia PMSA, MI	Y	41600 FQ	53880 MW	61500 TQ	USBLS	5/15
	Grand Rapids-Wyoming MSA, MI	Y	37420 FQ	44210 MW	49810 TQ	USBLS	5/15
	Minnesota	Y	36163 FQ	57474 MW	74597 TQ	MNBLS	1/16-3/16
	Minneapolis-St. Paul-Bloomington MSA, MN-WI	Y	36103 FQ	65515 MW	76675 TQ	MNBLS	1/16-3/16
	Mississippi	Y	26930 FQ	30380 MW	35650 TQ	USBLS	5/15
	Missouri	Y	34700 FQ	46250 MW	68630 TQ	USBLS	5/15
	Kansas City MSA, MO-KS	Y	37190 FQ	45870 MW	65530 TQ	USBLS	5/15
	St. Louis MSA, MO-IL	Y	38740 FQ	63710 MW	72420 TQ	USBLS	5/15
	Montana	Y	33510 FQ	35830 MW	38150 TQ	USBLS	5/15
	Nebraska	Y	27890 FQ	34735 MW	43205 TQ	NEBLS	7/16-9/16
	Omaha-Council Bluffs MSA, NE-IA	Y	31490 FQ	38830 MW	46965 TQ	NEBLS	7/16-9/16
	Nevada	Y	34130 FQ	39110 MW	48580 TQ	USBLS	5/15
	Las Vegas-Henderson-Paradise MSA, NV	Y	33510 FQ	38040 MW	47590 TQ	USBLS	5/15
	New Hampshire	H	13.01 AE	15.02 MW	18.20 AEX	NHBLS	6/16
	New Jersey	Y	41480 FQ	60750 MW	89760 TQ	USBLS	5/15
	Camden PMSA, NJ	Y	55200 FQ	84720 MW	93830 TQ	USBLS	5/15
	Newark PMSA, NJ-PA	Y	39840 FQ	48250 MW	84580 TQ	USBLS	5/15
	Trenton MSA, NJ	Y	33900 FQ	38940 MW	46130 TQ	USBLS	5/15
	New Mexico	Y	22950 FQ	30130 MW	40370 TQ	USBLS	5/15
	Albuquerque MSA, NM	Y	30050 FQ	36960 MW	44360 TQ	USBLS	5/15
	New York	Y	29120 AE	54010 MW	72350 AEX	NYBLS	1/16-3/16
	Buffalo-Cheektowaga-Niagara Falls MSA, NY	Y	51760 FQ	55750 MW	59750 TQ	USBLS	5/15
	Nassau County-Suffolk County PMSA, NY	Y	38820 FQ	55670 MW	84360 TQ	USBLS	5/15
	New York-Jersey City-White Plains PMSA, NY-NJ	Y	35240 FQ	60830 MW	89910 TQ	USBLS	5/15
	Rochester MSA, NY	Y	27780 FQ	40190 MW	46960 TQ	USBLS	5/15
	North Carolina	Y	29460 FQ	34800 MW	39270 TQ	USBLS	5/15
	Charlotte-Concord-Gastonia MSA, NC-SC	Y	31900 FQ	36660 MW	42600 TQ	USBLS	5/15
	Raleigh MSA, NC	Y	35210 FQ	40630 MW	48580 TQ	USBLS	5/15
	North Dakota	Y	37150 FQ	45050 MW	58290 TQ	USBLS	5/15
	Fargo MSA, ND-MN	Y	43500 FQ	58020 MW	69220 TQ	USBLS	5/15
	Ohio	Y	32710 FQ	43280 MW	54610 TQ	USBLS	5/15
	Cincinnati MSA, OH-KY-IN	Y	31710 FQ	40090 MW	47910 TQ	USBLS	5/15
	Cleveland-Elyria MSA, OH	Y	38180 FQ	46330 MW	59520 TQ	USBLS	5/15
	Columbus MSA, OH	Y	42620 FQ	51190 MW	59340 TQ	USBLS	5/15
	Oklahoma	Y	27530 FQ	32880 MW	39080 TQ	USBLS	5/15
	Oklahoma City MSA, OK	Y	27360 FQ	30290 MW	36460 TQ	USBLS	5/15
	Tulsa MSA, OK	Y	29390 FQ	35320 MW	42430 TQ	USBLS	5/15
	Oregon	H	14.48 FQ	18.57 MW	33.33 TQ	ORBLS	2016
	Portland-Vancouver-Hillsboro MSA, OR-WA	Y	33070 FQ	42910 MW	67840 TQ	USBLS	5/15
	Pennsylvania	Y	31870 FQ	43180 MW	67490 TQ	USBLS	5/15
	Allentown-Bethlehem-Easton MSA, PA-NJ	Y	27970 FQ	32470 MW	59920 TQ	USBLS	5/15
	Harrisburg-Carlisle MSA, PA	Y	33710 FQ	40240 MW	45170 TQ	USBLS	5/15
	Montgomery County-Bucks County-Chester County PMSA, PA	Y	42210 FQ	60130 MW	86700 TQ	USBLS	5/15
	Philadelphia PMSA, PA	Y	49340 FQ	78100 MW	92360 TQ	USBLS	5/15

AE	Average entry wage	AWR	Average wage range	H	Hourly	LR	Low end range	MTC	Median total compensation	TCC	Total cash compensation
AEX	Average experienced wage	B	Biweekly	HI	Highest wage paid	M	Monthly	MW	Median wage paid	TQ	Third quartile wage
ATC	Average total compensation	D	Daily	HR	High end range	MCC	Median cash compensation	MWR	Median wage range	W	Weekly
AW	Average wage paid	FQ	First quartile wage	LO	Lowest wage paid	ME	Median entry wage	S	See annotated source	Y	Yearly

Occupation/Type/Industry	Location	Per	Low	Mid	High	Source	Date
Glazier	Pittsburgh MSA, PA	Y	29050 FQ	34780 MW	63710 TQ	USBLS	5/15
	Rhode Island	Y	30820 FQ	40840 MW	66330 TQ	USBLS	5/15
	Providence-Warwick MSA, RI-MA	Y	31590 FQ	40600 MW	64460 TQ	USBLS	5/15
	South Carolina	Y	31710 FQ	36570 MW	43300 TQ	USBLS	5/15
	Greenville-Anderson-Mauldin MSA, SC	Y	24580 FQ	32410 MW	35880 TQ	USBLS	5/15
	Myrtle Beach-Conway-North Myrtle Beach MSA, SC-NC	Y	25130 FQ	32470 MW	38520 TQ	USBLS	5/15
	South Dakota	Y	33060 FQ	36010 MW	38950 TQ	USBLS	5/15
	Tennessee	Y	26830 FQ	32450 MW	38500 TQ	USBLS	5/15
	Knoxville MSA, TN	Y	31680 FQ	34670 MW	37670 TQ	USBLS	5/15
	Memphis MSA, TN-MS-AR	Y	32010 FQ	35530 MW	39060 TQ	USBLS	5/15
	Nashville-Davidson–Murfreesboro–Franklin MSA, TN	Y	20820 FQ	27240 MW	32330 TQ	USBLS	5/15
	Texas	Y	29810 FQ	35560 MW	41620 TQ	USBLS	5/15
	Austin-Round Rock MSA, TX	Y	29510 FQ	35300 MW	40920 TQ	USBLS	5/15
	Dallas-Plano-Irving PMSA, TX	Y	29070 FQ	36270 MW	43130 TQ	USBLS	5/15
	Fort Worth-Arlington PMSA, TX	Y	31640 FQ	36980 MW	42930 TQ	USBLS	5/15
	Houston-The Woodlands-Sugar Land MSA, TX	Y	33250 FQ	38240 MW	46540 TQ	USBLS	5/15
	San Antonio-New Braunfels MSA, TX	Y	28980 FQ	35410 MW	40920 TQ	USBLS	5/15
	Utah	Y	32030 FQ	37090 MW	44110 TQ	USBLS	5/15
	Salt Lake City MSA, UT	Y	33940 FQ	40380 MW	46740 TQ	USBLS	5/15
	Vermont	Y	33570 FQ	36180 MW	38790 TQ	USBLS	5/15
	Virginia	Y	33510 FQ	40560 MW	46900 TQ	USBLS	5/15
	Richmond MSA, VA	Y	42160 FQ	46120 MW	50130 TQ	USBLS	5/15
	Virginia Beach-Norfolk-Newport News MSA, VA-NC	Y	35190 FQ	41240 MW	46080 TQ	USBLS	5/15
	Washington	H	19.46 FQ	24.72 MW	39.92 TQ	WABLS	3/16
	Seattle-Bellevue-Everett PMSA, WA	H	21.75 FQ	29.20 MW	41.66 TQ	WABLS	3/16
	Tacoma-Lakewood PMSA, WA	H	22.22 FQ	28.22 MW	42.22 TQ	WABLS	3/16
	West Virginia	Y	21290 FQ	28640 MW	37540 TQ	USBLS	5/15
	Wisconsin	Y	34990 FQ	47060 MW	64210 TQ	USBLS	5/15
	Madison MSA, WI	Y	45840 FQ	65650 MW	74720 TQ	USBLS	5/15
	Milwaukee-Waukesha-West Allis MSA, WI	Y	22950 FQ	35720 MW	67840 TQ	USBLS	5/15
	Wyoming	Y	30980 FQ	39300 MW	46980 TQ	USBLS	5/15
	Cheyenne MSA, WY	Y	29280 FQ	38180 MW	46700 TQ	USBLS	5/15
	Puerto Rico	Y	16850 FQ	18160 MW	19470 TQ	USBLS	5/15
	San Juan-Carolina-Caguas MSA, PR	Y	16850 FQ	18160 MW	19470 TQ	USBLS	5/15
Global Marketing Director	United States	Y		155000 MW		LI01	2017
Golf Course Manager							
Municipal Golf Course	San Clemente, CA	Y			111823 HI	CACIT	6/28/16
Municipal Golf Course	San Diego, CA	Y			71760 HI	CACIT	6/28/16
Municipal Golf Course	Detroit, MI	M	3300 LO		3408 HI	DETGOV	2016
Golf Course Mechanic							
Municipal Golf Course	San Clemente, CA	Y			57382 HI	CACIT	6/28/16
Golf Course Superintendent							
Municipal Golf Course	Colorado Springs, CO	Y	71715 LO		98608 HI	COSPRS	2017
Golf Course Technician							
Municipal Golf Course	Seattle, WA	H	21.61 LO		25.80 HI	CSSS	3/9/16
Golf Pro	United States	Y		72000 AW		SKU01	2016
Government Account Manager							
Copier Industry	United States	Y		125976 ATC		COPIER1	2016
Government Contracts Attorney	United States	H		50.00 AW		FORB03	2016
Government Fleet Manager	United States	Y		73481-118676 AWR		GOVFL	2015

Occupation/Type/Industry	Location	Per	Low	Mid	High	Source	Date
Government Meeting Professional	United States	Y		75833 AW		CVENE	2016
Governmental Efficiency Director							
State Government	Maryland	Y			150000 HI	MDGOV	2016
Governor	United States	Y		137415 AW		CSG	2016
	Alaska	Y			145000 HI	CSG	2016
	Colorado	Y			90000 HI	CSG	2016
	Delaware	Y			171000 HI	CSG	2016
	Georgia	Y			139339 HI	CSG	2016
	Idaho	Y			122597 HI	CSG	2016
	Kansas	Y			99636 HI	CSG	2016
	Louisiana	Y			130000 HI	CSG	2016
	Maine	Y			70000 HI	CSG	2016
	Michigan	Y			159300 HI	CSG	2016
	New Mexico	Y			110000 HI	CSG	2016
	North Carolina	Y			142265 HI	CSG	2016
	Pennsylvania	Y			190823 HI	CSG	2016
	Virginia	Y			175000 HI	CSG	2016
	Wisconsin	Y			147328 HI	CSG	2016
Grader and Sorter							
Agricultural Products	Alabama	Y	19833 AE	23773 AW	25748 AEX	ALBLS	6/16
Agricultural Products	Arizona	Y	18220 FQ	19810 MW	26910 TQ	USBLS	5/15
Agricultural Products	Phoenix-Mesa-Scottsdale MSA, AZ	Y	20880 FQ	27720 MW	36570 TQ	USBLS	5/15
Agricultural Products	Arkansas	Y	21050 FQ	22670 MW	24180 TQ	USBLS	5/15
Agricultural Products	California	H	9.38 FQ	9.58 MW	10.77 TQ	CABLS	1/16-3/16
Agricultural Products	Los Angeles-Long Beach-Glendale PMSA, CA	H	9.81 FQ	10.64 MW	11.48 TQ	CABLS	1/16-3/16
Agricultural Products	Riverside-San Bernardino-Ontario MSA, CA	H	9.29 FQ	9.36 MW	9.44 TQ	CABLS	1/16-3/16
Agricultural Products	Sacramento–Roseville–Arden-Arcade MSA, CA	H	12.88 FQ	14.22 MW	16.08 TQ	CABLS	1/16-3/16
Agricultural Products	Colorado	Y	18000 FQ	18890 MW	19780 TQ	USBLS	5/15
Agricultural Products	Denver-Aurora-Lakewood MSA, CO	Y	20090 FQ	21840 MW	23590 TQ	USBLS	5/15
Agricultural Products	Florida	H	8.96 AE	9.19 MW	9.75 AEX	FLBLS	7/16-9/16
Agricultural Products	Miami-Miami Beach-Kendall PMSA, FL	H	8.93 AE	8.99 MW	9.39 AEX	FLBLS	7/16-9/16
Agricultural Products	Orlando-Kissimmee-Sanford MSA, FL	H	8.89 AE	9.34 MW	10.51 AEX	FLBLS	7/16-9/16
Agricultural Products	Tampa-St. Petersburg-Clearwater MSA, FL	H	9.06 AE	9.15 MW	9.06 AEX	FLBLS	7/16-9/16
Agricultural Products	Georgia	Y	19280 FQ	21580 MW	23520 TQ	USBLS	5/15
Agricultural Products	Idaho	Y	16910 FQ	18340 MW	20130 TQ	USBLS	5/15
Agricultural Products	Boise City MSA, ID	Y	18290 FQ	27470 MW	34770 TQ	USBLS	5/15
Agricultural Products	Illinois	Y	19360 FQ	21660 MW	24780 TQ	USBLS	5/15
Agricultural Products	Chicago-Naperville-Arlington Heights PMSA, IL	Y	19140 FQ	21060 MW	24100 TQ	USBLS	5/15
Agricultural Products	Indiana	Y	17220 FQ	19350 MW	23430 TQ	USBLS	5/15
Agricultural Products	Indianapolis-Carmel-Anderson MSA, IN	Y	16860 FQ	18600 MW	21500 TQ	USBLS	5/15
Agricultural Products	Iowa	Y	24970 FQ	27940 MW	30970 TQ	USBLS	5/15
Agricultural Products	Kansas	Y	27580 FQ	30650 MW	35070 TQ	USBLS	5/15
Agricultural Products	Kentucky	Y	21390 FQ	23200 MW	25120 TQ	USBLS	5/15
Agricultural Products	Louisville-Jefferson County MSA, KY-IN	Y	22940 FQ	26180 MW	29560 TQ	USBLS	5/15
Agricultural Products	Louisiana	Y	23690 FQ	30520 MW	36190 TQ	USBLS	5/15
Agricultural Products	New Orleans-Metairie MSA, LA	Y	31940 FQ	35730 MW	39180 TQ	USBLS	5/15
Agricultural Products	Maine	Y	18950 FQ	22720 MW	29050 TQ	USBLS	5/15
Agricultural Products	Maryland	Y	25607 AE	37329 MW	43190 AEX	MDBLS	4/16
Agricultural Products	Baltimore-Columbia-Towson MSA, MD	Y	31290 FQ	41360 MW	45950 TQ	USBLS	5/15
Agricultural Products	Massachusetts	Y	19030 FQ	19340 MW	24430 TQ	USBLS	5/15
Agricultural Products	Boston-Cambridge-Newton NECTA, MA	Y	19000 FQ	19280 MW	24760 TQ	USBLS	5/15
Agricultural Products	Michigan	Y	19110 FQ	21800 MW	25390 TQ	USBLS	5/15
Agricultural Products	Detroit-Dearborn-Livonia PMSA, MI	Y	19320 FQ	21230 MW	23260 TQ	USBLS	5/15
Agricultural Products	Minnesota	Y	25084 FQ	29362 MW	36980 TQ	MNBLS	1/16-3/16

Occupation/Type/Industry	Location	Per	Low	Mid	High	Source	Date
Grader and Sorter							
Agricultural Products	Minneapolis-St. Paul-Bloomington MSA, MN-WI	Y	25609 FQ	34296 MW	40926 TQ	MNBLS	1/16-3/16
Agricultural Products	Mississippi	Y	18670 FQ	21390 MW	24160 TQ	USBLS	5/15
Agricultural Products	Missouri	Y	21090 FQ	22930 MW	24770 TQ	USBLS	5/15
Agricultural Products	Kansas City MSA, MO-KS	Y	27780 FQ	31870 MW	35900 TQ	USBLS	5/15
Agricultural Products	Montana	Y	19620 FQ	23170 MW	31740 TQ	USBLS	5/15
Agricultural Products	Nebraska	Y	26570 FQ	29160 MW	33135 TQ	NEBLS	7/16-9/16
Agricultural Products	Omaha-Council Bluffs MSA, NE-IA	Y	25240 FQ	27385 MW	29530 TQ	NEBLS	7/16-9/16
Agricultural Products	Nevada	Y	20140 FQ	22460 MW	24830 TQ	USBLS	5/15
Agricultural Products	Las Vegas-Henderson-Paradise MSA, NV	Y	20140 FQ	22460 MW	24830 TQ	USBLS	5/15
Agricultural Products	New Jersey	Y	18600 FQ	19980 MW	25650 TQ	USBLS	5/15
Agricultural Products	Camden PMSA, NJ	Y	18810 FQ	22830 MW	31880 TQ	USBLS	5/15
Agricultural Products	New Mexico	Y	17560 FQ	19350 MW	32650 TQ	USBLS	5/15
Agricultural Products	Las Cruces MSA, NM	Y	16700 FQ	17670 MW	18640 TQ	USBLS	5/15
Agricultural Products	New York	Y	19360 AE	19810 MW	24370 AEX	NYBLS	1/16-3/16
Agricultural Products	Rochester MSA, NY	Y	18600 FQ	18990 MW	19390 TQ	USBLS	5/15
Agricultural Products	North Carolina	Y	18580 FQ	21230 MW	23890 TQ	USBLS	5/15
Agricultural Products	Charlotte-Concord-Gastonia MSA, NC-SC	Y	19810 FQ	21620 MW	23420 TQ	USBLS	5/15
Agricultural Products	North Dakota	Y	25430 FQ	30510 MW	35470 TQ	USBLS	5/15
Agricultural Products	Ohio	Y	23870 FQ	29730 MW	35650 TQ	USBLS	5/15
Agricultural Products	Oklahoma	Y	20150 FQ	22870 MW	26450 TQ	USBLS	5/15
Agricultural Products	Tulsa MSA, OK	Y	17590 FQ	20930 MW	26690 TQ	USBLS	5/15
Agricultural Products	Oregon	H	9.54 FQ	9.72 MW	11.21 TQ	ORBLS	2016
Agricultural Products	Portland-Vancouver-Hillsboro MSA, OR-WA	Y	19330 FQ	19670 MW	22610 TQ	USBLS	5/15
Agricultural Products	Pennsylvania	Y	20690 FQ	24600 MW	28870 TQ	USBLS	5/15
Agricultural Products	South Carolina	Y	21610 FQ	23310 MW	25430 TQ	USBLS	5/15
Agricultural Products	South Dakota	Y	23370 FQ	26440 MW	29170 TQ	USBLS	5/15
Agricultural Products	Sioux Falls MSA, SD	Y	25630 FQ	27900 MW	30160 TQ	USBLS	5/15
Agricultural Products	Tennessee	Y	23300 FQ	24610 MW	25440 TQ	USBLS	5/15
Agricultural Products	Memphis MSA, TN-MS-AR	Y	23310 FQ	25430 MW	25440 TQ	USBLS	5/15
Agricultural Products	Texas	Y	18460 FQ	23200 MW	25660 TQ	USBLS	5/15
Agricultural Products	Dallas-Plano-Irving PMSA, TX	Y	18190 FQ	22250 MW	27360 TQ	USBLS	5/15
Agricultural Products	Fort Worth-Arlington PMSA, TX	Y	20400 FQ	22300 MW	24200 TQ	USBLS	5/15
Agricultural Products	Houston-The Woodlands-Sugar Land MSA, TX	Y	17020 FQ	18720 MW	22760 TQ	USBLS	5/15
Agricultural Products	San Antonio-New Braunfels MSA, TX	Y	17770 FQ	19880 MW	23330 TQ	USBLS	5/15
Agricultural Products	Vermont	Y	19770 FQ	22630 MW	26560 TQ	USBLS	5/15
Agricultural Products	Burlington-South Burlington MSA, VT	Y	19830 FQ	22420 MW	25430 TQ	USBLS	5/15
Agricultural Products	Virginia	Y	20790 FQ	30120 MW	36050 TQ	USBLS	5/15
Agricultural Products	Virginia Beach-Norfolk-Newport News MSA, VA-NC	Y	32270 FQ	35540 MW	38820 TQ	USBLS	5/15
Agricultural Products	Washington	H	10.71 FQ	12.42 MW	16.51 TQ	WABLS	3/16
Agricultural Products	Wisconsin	Y	25580 FQ	27860 MW	30300 TQ	USBLS	5/15
Agricultural Products	Milwaukee-Waukesha-West Allis MSA, WI	Y	25320 FQ	27360 MW	29420 TQ	USBLS	5/15
Graduate Teaching Assistant	Alabama	Y	17461 AE	18817 AW	19489 AEX	ALBLS	6/16
	Arizona	Y	34210 FQ	41440 MW	46370 TQ	USBLS	5/15
	Phoenix-Mesa-Scottsdale MSA, AZ	Y	18850 FQ	27120 MW	42260 TQ	USBLS	5/15
	Arkansas	Y	18210 FQ	21090 MW	26880 TQ	USBLS	5/15
	Little Rock-North Little Rock-Conway MSA, AR	Y	17770 FQ	19630 MW	23030 TQ	USBLS	5/15
	California	Y		31743 AW		CABLS	1/16-3/16
	Anaheim-Santa Ana-Irvine PMSA, CA	Y		30607 AW		CABLS	1/16-3/16
	Los Angeles-Long Beach-Glendale PMSA, CA	Y		32393 AW		CABLS	1/16-3/16
	Sacramento–Roseville–Arden-Arcade MSA, CA	Y		35548 AW		CABLS	1/16-3/16
	San Diego-Carlsbad MSA, CA	Y		32799 AW		CABLS	1/16-3/16
	San Francisco-Redwood City-South San Francisco PMSA, CA	Y		28386 AW		CABLS	1/16-3/16

AE	Average entry wage	AWR	Average wage range	H	Hourly
AEX	Average experienced wage	B	Biweekly	HI	Highest wage paid
ATC	Average total compensation	D	Daily	HR	High end range
AW	Average wage paid	FQ	First quartile wage	LO	Lowest wage paid

LR	Low end range	MTC	Median total compensation
M	Monthly	MW	Median wage paid
MCC	Median cash compensation	MWR	Median wage range
ME	Median entry wage	S	See annotated source

TCC	Total cash compensation
TQ	Third quartile wage
W	Weekly
Y	Yearly

Occupation/Type/Industry	Location	Per	Low	Mid	High	Source	Date
Graduate Teaching Assistant	Colorado	Y	28890 FQ	35790 MW	46340 TQ	USBLS	5/15
	Denver-Aurora-Lakewood MSA, CO	Y	31440 FQ	44680 MW	57530 TQ	USBLS	5/15
	Connecticut	Y		20310 MW		CTBLS	1/16-3/16
	Bridgeport-Stamford-Norwalk MSA, CT	Y	39010 FQ	47770 MW	58880 TQ	USBLS	5/15
	Hartford-West Hartford-East Hartford MSA, CT	Y	19390 FQ	19740 MW	20090 TQ	USBLS	5/15
	Washington-Arlington-Alexandria PMSA, DC-VA-MD-WV	Y	37280 FQ	43540 MW	48850 TQ	USBLS	5/15
	Florida	Y	18487 AE	18669 MW	20792 AEX	FLBLS	7/16-9/16
	Georgia	Y	17250 FQ	19040 MW	27550 TQ	USBLS	5/15
	Hawaii	Y	36680 FQ	41930 MW	47370 TQ	USBLS	5/15
	Urban Honolulu MSA, HI	Y	36710 FQ	41970 MW	47390 TQ	USBLS	5/15
	Idaho	Y	16970 FQ	18100 MW	19220 TQ	USBLS	5/15
	Illinois	Y	26280 FQ	32400 MW	48250 TQ	USBLS	5/15
	Chicago-Naperville-Arlington Heights PMSA, IL	Y	22760 FQ	28410 MW	35060 TQ	USBLS	5/15
	Indiana	Y	32140 FQ	39030 MW	45590 TQ	USBLS	5/15
	Iowa	Y	21890 FQ	24030 MW	37900 TQ	USBLS	5/15
	Kansas	Y	31640 FQ	43950 MW	51060 TQ	USBLS	5/15
	Kentucky	Y	17830 FQ	20650 MW	44260 TQ	USBLS	5/15
	Louisiana	Y	19500 FQ	31930 MW	38820 TQ	USBLS	5/15
	New Orleans-Metairie MSA, LA	Y	19300 FQ	30900 MW	37970 TQ	USBLS	5/15
	Maryland	Y	30118 AE	40974 MW	46402 AEX	MDBLS	4/16
	Baltimore-Columbia-Towson MSA, MD	Y	28260 FQ	34230 MW	40610 TQ	USBLS	5/15
	Massachusetts	Y	19840 FQ	27470 MW	37750 TQ	USBLS	5/15
	Boston-Cambridge-Newton NECTA, MA	Y	25850 FQ	29530 MW	37840 TQ	USBLS	5/15
	Worcester MSA, MA-CT	Y	19180 FQ	19640 MW	20100 TQ	USBLS	5/15
	Michigan	Y	21960 FQ	41210 MW	46390 TQ	USBLS	5/15
	Detroit-Dearborn-Livonia PMSA, MI	Y	40860 FQ	44570 MW	48280 TQ	USBLS	5/15
	Grand Rapids-Wyoming MSA, MI	Y	17700 FQ	18440 MW	19180 TQ	USBLS	5/15
	Minnesota	Y	19516 FQ	34596 MW	45030 TQ	MNBLS	1/16-3/16
	Minneapolis-St. Paul-Bloomington MSA, MN-WI	Y	19506 FQ	34818 MW	45130 TQ	MNBLS	1/16-3/16
	Mississippi	Y	17530 FQ	19370 MW	44180 TQ	USBLS	5/15
	Jackson MSA, MS	Y	52860 FQ	56860 MW	60860 TQ	USBLS	5/15
	Missouri	Y	21260 FQ	31100 MW	38510 TQ	USBLS	5/15
	Kansas City MSA, MO-KS	Y	17130 FQ	18340 MW	20060 TQ	USBLS	5/15
	St. Louis MSA, MO-IL	Y	26390 FQ	32740 MW	38320 TQ	USBLS	5/15
	Nebraska	Y	31395 FQ	44435 MW	50240 TQ	NEBLS	7/16-9/16
	Omaha-Council Bluffs MSA, NE-IA	Y	35190 FQ	44965 MW	50495 TQ	NEBLS	7/16-9/16
	Nevada	Y	37650 FQ	43090 MW	46920 TQ	USBLS	5/15
	Las Vegas-Henderson-Paradise MSA, NV	Y	33560 FQ	40180 MW	44990 TQ	USBLS	5/15
	New Jersey	Y	30820 FQ	41600 MW	53440 TQ	USBLS	5/15
	Camden PMSA, NJ	Y	19220 FQ	37890 MW	48790 TQ	USBLS	5/15
	New Mexico	Y	17390 FQ	18670 MW	20910 TQ	USBLS	5/15
	New York	Y	25030 AE	42470 MW	49760 AEX	NYBLS	1/16-3/16
	Buffalo-Cheektowaga-Niagara Falls MSA, NY	Y	18920 FQ	20460 MW	24480 TQ	USBLS	5/15
	New York-Jersey City-White Plains PMSA, NY-NJ	Y	32650 FQ	44260 MW	54870 TQ	USBLS	5/15
	Rochester MSA, NY	Y	53170 FQ	59060 MW	67400 TQ	USBLS	5/15
	Ohio	Y	25710 FQ	39570 MW	47250 TQ	USBLS	5/15
	Cleveland-Elyria MSA, OH	Y	18670 FQ	25090 MW	30990 TQ	USBLS	5/15
	Columbus MSA, OH	Y	38580 FQ	43690 MW	48430 TQ	USBLS	5/15
	Oklahoma	Y	33260 FQ	36260 MW	39250 TQ	USBLS	5/15
	Oregon	Y	33791 FQ	41809 MW	52096 TQ	ORBLS	2016
	Portland-Vancouver-Hillsboro MSA, OR-WA	Y	29240 FQ	36330 MW	54430 TQ	USBLS	5/15
	Pennsylvania	Y	18760 FQ	28530 MW	48040 TQ	USBLS	5/15
	Pittsburgh MSA, PA	Y	30440 FQ	38240 MW	50250 TQ	USBLS	5/15
	South Carolina	Y	20180 FQ	28620 MW	45860 TQ	USBLS	5/15

AE	Average entry wage	AWR	Average wage range	H	Hourly	LR	Low end range	MTC	Median total compensation	TCC	Total cash compensation
AEX	Average experienced wage	B	Biweekly	HI	Highest wage paid	M	Monthly	MW	Median wage paid	TQ	Third quartile wage
ATC	Average total compensation	D	Daily	HR	High end range	MCC	Median cash compensation	MWR	Median wage range	W	Weekly
AW	Average wage paid	FQ	First quartile wage	LO	Lowest wage paid	ME	Median entry wage	S	See annotated source	Y	Yearly

Occupation/Type/Industry	Location	Per	Low	Mid	High	Source	Date
Graduate Teaching Assistant	Greenville-Anderson-Mauldin MSA, SC	Y	29470 FQ	43220 MW	69440 TQ	USBLS	5/15
	Tennessee	Y	17790 FQ	19740 MW	28920 TQ	USBLS	5/15
	Nashville-Davidson–Murfreesboro–Franklin MSA, TN	Y	18710 FQ	26920 MW	33570 TQ	USBLS	5/15
	Texas	Y	19370 FQ	30700 MW	41810 TQ	USBLS	5/15
	Austin-Round Rock MSA, TX	Y	26640 FQ	33980 MW	43400 TQ	USBLS	5/15
	Dallas-Plano-Irving PMSA, TX	Y	16750 FQ	18210 MW	23280 TQ	USBLS	5/15
	Fort Worth-Arlington PMSA, TX	Y	27370 FQ	34390 MW	42290 TQ	USBLS	5/15
	Houston-The Woodlands-Sugar Land MSA, TX	Y	16930 FQ	18580 MW	27080 TQ	USBLS	5/15
	San Antonio-New Braunfels MSA, TX	Y	29770 FQ	41540 MW	47650 TQ	USBLS	5/15
	Utah	Y	38570 FQ	44330 MW	49360 TQ	USBLS	5/15
	Virginia	Y	27590 FQ	35270 MW	43970 TQ	USBLS	5/15
	Richmond MSA, VA	Y	31060 FQ	37020 MW	43800 TQ	USBLS	5/15
	Virginia Beach-Norfolk-Newport News MSA, VA-NC	Y	24180 FQ	36170 MW	48110 TQ	USBLS	5/15
	West Virginia	Y	22400 FQ	44400 MW	56690 TQ	USBLS	5/15
	Wisconsin	Y	27040 FQ	29400 MW	32180 TQ	USBLS	5/15
	Puerto Rico	Y	18220 FQ	29080 MW	45260 TQ	USBLS	5/15
	San Juan-Carolina-Caguas MSA, PR	Y	19400 FQ	33910 MW	47520 TQ	USBLS	5/15
Graffiti Abatement Coordinator							
Municipal Government	Chula Vista, CA	Y			75480 HI	CACIT	6/28/16
Municipal Government	El Monte, CA	Y			46250 HI	CACIT	6/24/16
Graffiti Abatement Specialist							
Police Department, Municipal Government	Santa Paula, CA	Y			38578 HI	CACIT	6/28/16
Graffiti Removal Technician							
Community Development - Neighborhood Services, Municipal Government	National City, CA	Y			45621 HI	CACIT	6/28/16
Grant Coordinator							
Municipal Government	Detroit, MI	M	3683 LO		5150 HI	DETGOV	2016
Grant Writer							
County Government	Oakland County, MI	B	1913 LO		2490 HI	MIOAK2	10/1/16
Finance Department, Municipal Government	Wasco, CA	Y			64852 HI	CACIT	6/28/16
Public Works Department, Municipal Government	Fresno, CA	Y			33754 HI	CACIT	6/28/16
Grants Manager							
Development Services, Municipal Government	Perris, CA	Y			77736 HI	CACIT	6/28/16
Graphic Aide							
Municipal Government	Seattle, WA	H	19.44 LO		22.61 HI	CSSS	1/13/16
Graphic Artist							
Police Department	San Francisco, CA	B	2079 LO		2527 HI	SFGOV	2016-2018
Graphic Delineator							
Municipal Government	Oakland, CA	Y			55104 HI	CACIT	6/28/16
Graphic Designer	Alabama	Y	27175 AE	41293 AW	48357 AEX	ALBLS	6/16
	Birmingham-Hoover MSA, AL	Y	29968 AE	41945 AW	47929 AEX	ALBLS	6/16
	Alaska	Y	38400 FQ	50610 MW	60670 TQ	USBLS	5/15
	Anchorage MSA, AK	Y	40140 FQ	52240 MW	61600 TQ	USBLS	5/15
	Arizona	Y	36060 FQ	44360 MW	53850 TQ	USBLS	5/15
	Phoenix-Mesa-Scottsdale MSA, AZ	Y	36930 FQ	44820 MW	54620 TQ	USBLS	5/15
	Tucson MSA, AZ	Y	36600 FQ	44100 MW	51370 TQ	USBLS	5/15
	Arkansas	Y	28440 FQ	35290 MW	45910 TQ	USBLS	5/15
	Little Rock-North Little Rock-Conway MSA, AR	Y	32450 FQ	37810 MW	49360 TQ	USBLS	5/15
	California	H	19.22 FQ	26.38 MW	35.95 TQ	CABLS	1/16-3/16

AE Average entry wage	**AWR** Average wage range	**H** Hourly	**LR** Low end range	**MTC** Median total compensation	**TCC** Total cash compensation
AEX Average experienced wage	**B** Biweekly	**HI** Highest wage paid	**M** Monthly	**MW** Median wage paid	**TQ** Third quartile wage
ATC Average total compensation	**D** Daily	**HR** High end range	**MCC** Median cash compensation	**MWR** Median wage range	**W** Weekly
AW Average wage paid	**FQ** First quartile wage	**LO** Lowest wage paid	**ME** Median entry wage	**S** See annotated source	**Y** Yearly

Occupation/Type/Industry	Location	Per	Low	Mid	High	Source	Date
Graphic Designer	Anaheim-Santa Ana-Irvine PMSA, CA	H	19.12 FQ	25.07 MW	32.62 TQ	CABLS	1/16-3/16
	Los Angeles-Long Beach-Glendale PMSA, CA	H	18.74 FQ	25.43 MW	34.95 TQ	CABLS	1/16-3/16
	Oakland-Hayward-Berkeley PMSA, CA	H	22.37 FQ	31.44 MW	38.50 TQ	CABLS	1/16-3/16
	Riverside-San Bernardino-Ontario MSA, CA	H	17.20 FQ	21.13 MW	25.54 TQ	CABLS	1/16-3/16
	Sacramento–Roseville–Arden-Arcade MSA, CA	H	17.59 FQ	23.06 MW	30.34 TQ	CABLS	1/16-3/16
	San Diego-Carlsbad MSA, CA	H	16.16 FQ	22.35 MW	30.52 TQ	CABLS	1/16-3/16
	San Francisco-Redwood City-South San Francisco PMSA, CA	H	27.68 FQ	35.97 MW	45.63 TQ	CABLS	1/16-3/16
	Colorado	Y	36980 FQ	49550 MW	65240 TQ	USBLS	5/15
	Denver-Aurora-Lakewood MSA, CO	Y	37390 FQ	50860 MW	66060 TQ	USBLS	5/15
	Connecticut	Y		52287 MW		CTBLS	1/16-3/16
	Bridgeport-Stamford-Norwalk MSA, CT	Y	46180 FQ	58670 MW	73870 TQ	USBLS	5/15
	Hartford-West Hartford-East Hartford MSA, CT	Y	35430 FQ	44760 MW	62940 TQ	USBLS	5/15
	Delaware	Y	40530 FQ	50590 MW	65870 TQ	USBLS	5/15
	Wilmington PMSA, DE-MD-NJ	Y	41800 FQ	53230 MW	67740 TQ	USBLS	5/15
	District of Columbia	Y	57200 FQ	73650 MW	90830 TQ	USBLS	5/15
	Washington-Arlington-Alexandria PMSA, DC-VA-MD-WV	Y	48180 FQ	64040 MW	83320 TQ	USBLS	5/15
	Florida	H	14.75 AE	21.03 MW	26.42 AEX	FLBLS	7/16-9/16
	Fort Lauderdale-Pompano Beach-Deerfield Beach PMSA, FL	H	15.80 AE	21.61 MW	26.01 AEX	FLBLS	7/16-9/16
	Miami-Miami Beach-Kendall PMSA, FL	H	13.66 AE	20.78 MW	28.10 AEX	FLBLS	7/16-9/16
	Orlando-Kissimmee-Sanford MSA, FL	H	15.01 AE	20.28 MW	25.59 AEX	FLBLS	7/16-9/16
	Tampa-St. Petersburg-Clearwater MSA, FL	H	14.72 AE	21.24 MW	26.32 AEX	FLBLS	7/16-9/16
	Georgia	Y	35180 FQ	48780 MW	63230 TQ	USBLS	5/15
	Atlanta-Sandy Springs-Roswell MSA, GA	Y	37270 FQ	51290 MW	65200 TQ	USBLS	5/15
	Augusta-Richmond County MSA, GA-SC	Y	29930 FQ	37660 MW	51610 TQ	USBLS	5/15
	Hawaii	Y	27380 FQ	40560 MW	52510 TQ	USBLS	5/15
	Urban Honolulu MSA, HI	Y	31470 FQ	42090 MW	54990 TQ	USBLS	5/15
	Idaho	Y	27560 FQ	35260 MW	48480 TQ	USBLS	5/15
	Boise City MSA, ID	Y	29120 FQ	36930 MW	52970 TQ	USBLS	5/15
	Illinois	Y	36240 FQ	47950 MW	62610 TQ	USBLS	5/15
	Chicago-Naperville-Arlington Heights PMSA, IL	Y	37550 FQ	49230 MW	64430 TQ	USBLS	5/15
	Lake County-Kenosha County PMSA, IL-WI	Y	40860 FQ	51940 MW	63510 TQ	USBLS	5/15
	Indiana	Y	30390 FQ	38360 MW	49200 TQ	USBLS	5/15
	Gary PMSA, IN	Y	33400 FQ	44640 MW	57920 TQ	USBLS	5/15
	Indianapolis-Carmel-Anderson MSA, IN	Y	31120 FQ	39610 MW	49750 TQ	USBLS	5/15
	Iowa	Y	31010 FQ	38320 MW	48460 TQ	USBLS	5/15
	Des Moines-West Des Moines MSA, IA	Y	35130 FQ	43130 MW	51770 TQ	USBLS	5/15
	Kansas	Y	33500 FQ	42260 MW	55490 TQ	USBLS	5/15
	Wichita MSA, KS	Y	32410 FQ	38540 MW	48480 TQ	USBLS	5/15
	Kentucky	Y	28370 FQ	37480 MW	48970 TQ	USBLS	5/15
	Louisville-Jefferson County MSA, KY-IN	Y	32370 FQ	40350 MW	51230 TQ	USBLS	5/15
	Louisiana	Y	30560 FQ	38310 MW	47200 TQ	USBLS	5/15
	Baton Rouge MSA, LA	Y	32190 FQ	39540 MW	47230 TQ	USBLS	5/15
	New Orleans-Metairie MSA, LA	Y	33260 FQ	42250 MW	49430 TQ	USBLS	5/15
	Maine	Y	29830 FQ	37520 MW	52920 TQ	USBLS	5/15
	Portland-South Portland MSA, ME	Y	35390 FQ	48710 MW	68570 TQ	USBLS	5/15

AE	Average entry wage	AWR	Average wage range	H Hourly	LR Low end range	MTC Median total compensation	TCC Total cash compensation
AEX	Average experienced wage	B	Biweekly	HI Highest wage paid	M Monthly	MW Median wage paid	TQ Third quartile wage
ATC	Average total compensation	D	Daily	HR High end range	MCC Median cash compensation	MWR Median wage range	W Weekly
AW	Average wage paid	FQ	First quartile wage	LO Lowest wage paid	ME Median entry wage	S See annotated source	Y Yearly

713

Occupation/Type/Industry	Location	Per	Low	Mid	High	Source	Date
Graphic Designer	Maryland	Y	36649 AE	58919 MW	70053 AEX	MDBLS	4/16
	Baltimore-Columbia-Towson MSA, MD	Y	40140 FQ	51480 MW	68160 TQ	USBLS	5/15
	Cumberland MSA, MD-WV	Y	22790 FQ	38680 MW	54960 TQ	USBLS	5/15
	Salisbury MSA, MD-DE	Y	33500 FQ	41220 MW	55860 TQ	USBLS	5/15
	Massachusetts	Y	41800 FQ	53990 MW	68240 TQ	USBLS	5/15
	Boston-Cambridge-Newton NECTA, MA	Y	45030 FQ	56730 MW	69990 TQ	USBLS	5/15
	Worcester MSA, MA-CT	Y	35080 FQ	45030 MW	59680 TQ	USBLS	5/15
	Michigan	Y	34160 FQ	44850 MW	58130 TQ	USBLS	5/15
	Detroit-Dearborn-Livonia PMSA, MI	Y	39530 FQ	47820 MW	61720 TQ	USBLS	5/15
	Grand Rapids-Wyoming MSA, MI	Y	32060 FQ	41060 MW	50530 TQ	USBLS	5/15
	Minnesota	Y	36542 FQ	48467 MW	61340 TQ	MNBLS	1/16-3/16
	Minneapolis-St. Paul-Bloomington MSA, MN-WI	Y	40937 FQ	52096 MW	63608 TQ	MNBLS	1/16-3/16
	Mississippi	Y	26370 FQ	31260 MW	42910 TQ	USBLS	5/15
	Jackson MSA, MS	Y	26540 FQ	33460 MW	51110 TQ	USBLS	5/15
	Missouri	Y	33070 FQ	43760 MW	59620 TQ	USBLS	5/15
	Kansas City MSA, MO-KS	Y	37840 FQ	48670 MW	63060 TQ	USBLS	5/15
	St. Louis MSA, MO-IL	Y	36960 FQ	49380 MW	63470 TQ	USBLS	5/15
	Montana	Y	28680 FQ	36420 MW	45650 TQ	USBLS	5/15
	Billings MSA, MT	Y	31600 FQ	36960 MW	46420 TQ	USBLS	5/15
	Nebraska	Y	31955 FQ	41345 MW	51990 TQ	NEBLS	7/16-9/16
	Omaha-Council Bluffs MSA, NE-IA	Y	34885 FQ	44410 MW	55815 TQ	NEBLS	7/16-9/16
	Nevada	Y	35770 FQ	44990 MW	57260 TQ	USBLS	5/15
	Las Vegas-Henderson-Paradise MSA, NV	Y	36800 FQ	45080 MW	55050 TQ	USBLS	5/15
	New Hampshire	H	14.89 AE	20.16 MW	25.97 AEX	NHBLS	6/16
	Manchester NECTA, NH	H	13.01 AE	19.34 MW	23.78 AEX	NHBLS	6/16
	Nashua NECTA, NH-MA	Y	33870 FQ	43890 MW	63400 TQ	USBLS	5/15
	New Jersey	Y	40060 FQ	52040 MW	69300 TQ	USBLS	5/15
	Camden PMSA, NJ	Y	39980 FQ	46980 MW	57210 TQ	USBLS	5/15
	Newark PMSA, NJ-PA	Y	41160 FQ	55530 MW	72870 TQ	USBLS	5/15
	Trenton MSA, NJ	Y	44850 FQ	60140 MW	76460 TQ	USBLS	5/15
	New Mexico	Y	26100 FQ	35540 MW	46500 TQ	USBLS	5/15
	Albuquerque MSA, NM	Y	26000 FQ	35890 MW	46690 TQ	USBLS	5/15
	New York	Y	36410 AE	58570 MW	77030 AEX	NYBLS	1/16-3/16
	Buffalo-Cheektowaga-Niagara Falls MSA, NY	Y	31810 FQ	41550 MW	51880 TQ	USBLS	5/15
	Nassau County-Suffolk County PMSA, NY	Y	33460 FQ	42780 MW	59680 TQ	USBLS	5/15
	New York-Jersey City-White Plains PMSA, NY-NJ	Y	45810 FQ	61930 MW	82190 TQ	USBLS	5/15
	Rochester MSA, NY	Y	34460 FQ	43740 MW	56890 TQ	USBLS	5/15
	North Carolina	Y	32550 FQ	42950 MW	58340 TQ	USBLS	5/15
	Charlotte-Concord-Gastonia MSA, NC-SC	Y	32920 FQ	43790 MW	59080 TQ	USBLS	5/15
	Raleigh MSA, NC	Y	35750 FQ	46320 MW	61770 TQ	USBLS	5/15
	North Dakota	Y	29440 FQ	35400 MW	43840 TQ	USBLS	5/15
	Fargo MSA, ND-MN	Y	29870 FQ	36470 MW	46710 TQ	USBLS	5/15
	Ohio	Y	33190 FQ	43100 MW	56380 TQ	USBLS	5/15
	Cincinnati MSA, OH-KY-IN	Y	36800 FQ	47240 MW	58650 TQ	USBLS	5/15
	Cleveland-Elyria MSA, OH	Y	31590 FQ	40440 MW	52710 TQ	USBLS	5/15
	Columbus MSA, OH	Y	40480 FQ	50410 MW	65490 TQ	USBLS	5/15
	Oklahoma	Y	31760 FQ	40790 MW	53850 TQ	USBLS	5/15
	Oklahoma City MSA, OK	Y	31280 FQ	39350 MW	52190 TQ	USBLS	5/15
	Tulsa MSA, OK	Y	36450 FQ	46010 MW	61940 TQ	USBLS	5/15
	Oregon	H	17.24 FQ	22.25 MW	29.64 TQ	ORBLS	2016
	Portland-Vancouver-Hillsboro MSA, OR-WA	Y	37090 FQ	48070 MW	64310 TQ	USBLS	5/15
	Pennsylvania	Y	33610 FQ	43960 MW	58390 TQ	USBLS	5/15
	Allentown-Bethlehem-Easton MSA, PA-NJ	Y	30600 FQ	43010 MW	55000 TQ	USBLS	5/15
	Bloomsburg-Berwick MSA, PA	Y	32740 FQ	36420 MW	41030 TQ	USBLS	5/15
	Harrisburg-Carlisle MSA, PA	Y	33770 FQ	41180 MW	51830 TQ	USBLS	5/15
	Montgomery County-Bucks County-Chester County PMSA, PA	Y	37760 FQ	48980 MW	64040 TQ	USBLS	5/15
	Philadelphia PMSA, PA	Y	44420 FQ	57460 MW	80280 TQ	USBLS	5/15

AE	Average entry wage	AWR	Average wage range	H	Hourly
AEX	Average experienced wage	B	Biweekly	HI	Highest wage paid
ATC	Average total compensation	D	Daily	HR	High end range
AW	Average wage paid	FQ	First quartile wage	LO	Lowest wage paid

LR	Low end range	MTC	Median total compensation	TCC	Total cash compensation
M	Monthly	MW	Median wage paid	TQ	Third quartile wage
MCC	Median cash compensation	MWR	Median wage range	W	Weekly
ME	Median entry wage	S	See annotated source	Y	Yearly

Occupation/Type/Industry	Location	Per	Low	Mid	High	Source	Date
Graphic Designer	Pittsburgh MSA, PA	Y	32160 FQ	39820 MW	50330 TQ	USBLS	5/15
	Rhode Island	Y	40180 FQ	52850 MW	62590 TQ	USBLS	5/15
	Providence-Warwick MSA, RI-MA	Y	39910 FQ	52950 MW	64430 TQ	USBLS	5/15
	South Carolina	Y	28990 FQ	36450 MW	46520 TQ	USBLS	5/15
	Charleston-North Charleston MSA, SC	Y	31770 FQ	38650 MW	47290 TQ	USBLS	5/15
	Columbia MSA, SC	Y	30840 FQ	39630 MW	52860 TQ	USBLS	5/15
	Greenville-Anderson-Mauldin MSA, SC	Y	28760 FQ	36680 MW	46230 TQ	USBLS	5/15
	South Dakota	Y	28380 FQ	33930 MW	39720 TQ	USBLS	5/15
	Sioux Falls MSA, SD	Y	32440 FQ	36650 MW	42820 TQ	USBLS	5/15
	Tennessee	Y	32330 FQ	40440 MW	55570 TQ	USBLS	5/15
	Knoxville MSA, TN	Y	33570 FQ	39490 MW	56110 TQ	USBLS	5/15
	Memphis MSA, TN-MS-AR	Y	34660 FQ	45660 MW	60100 TQ	USBLS	5/15
	Nashville-Davidson–Murfreesboro–Franklin MSA, TN	Y	34290 FQ	44530 MW	58050 TQ	USBLS	5/15
	Texas	Y	33870 FQ	43640 MW	57410 TQ	USBLS	5/15
	Austin-Round Rock MSA, TX	Y	35790 FQ	45060 MW	57280 TQ	USBLS	5/15
	Dallas-Plano-Irving PMSA, TX	Y	41510 FQ	52020 MW	66650 TQ	USBLS	5/15
	Fort Worth-Arlington PMSA, TX	Y	33720 FQ	43170 MW	59670 TQ	USBLS	5/15
	Houston-The Woodlands-Sugar Land MSA, TX	Y	35500 FQ	42800 MW	54950 TQ	USBLS	5/15
	San Antonio-New Braunfels MSA, TX	Y	32190 FQ	40950 MW	54570 TQ	USBLS	5/15
	Utah	Y	32960 FQ	44220 MW	58610 TQ	USBLS	5/15
	Ogden-Clearfield MSA, UT	Y	33990 FQ	42850 MW	55800 TQ	USBLS	5/15
	Provo-Orem MSA, UT	Y	29690 FQ	42170 MW	54720 TQ	USBLS	5/15
	Salt Lake City MSA, UT	Y	36110 FQ	46740 MW	63040 TQ	USBLS	5/15
	Vermont	Y	33060 FQ	40570 MW	52920 TQ	USBLS	5/15
	Burlington-South Burlington MSA, VT	Y	34280 FQ	43500 MW	54580 TQ	USBLS	5/15
	Virginia	Y	37270 FQ	51650 MW	70050 TQ	USBLS	5/15
	Richmond MSA, VA	Y	36750 FQ	48290 MW	64430 TQ	USBLS	5/15
	Virginia Beach-Norfolk-Newport News MSA, VA-NC	Y	34640 FQ	42390 MW	59920 TQ	USBLS	5/15
	Washington	H	19.17 FQ	25.93 MW	33.44 TQ	WABLS	3/16
	Seattle-Bellevue-Everett PMSA, WA	H	22.30 FQ	28.82 MW	35.87 TQ	WABLS	3/16
	Tacoma-Lakewood PMSA, WA	H	17.61 FQ	23.26 MW	30.84 TQ	WABLS	3/16
	West Virginia	Y	28500 FQ	36790 MW	49380 TQ	USBLS	5/15
	Huntington-Ashland MSA, WV-KY-OH	Y	34860 FQ	43520 MW	56020 TQ	USBLS	5/15
	Wisconsin	Y	34960 FQ	44630 MW	56430 TQ	USBLS	5/15
	Madison MSA, WI	Y	36890 FQ	46750 MW	57810 TQ	USBLS	5/15
	Milwaukee-Waukesha-West Allis MSA, WI	Y	40000 FQ	48250 MW	60090 TQ	USBLS	5/15
	Wyoming	Y	30190 FQ	38320 MW	48400 TQ	USBLS	5/15
	Puerto Rico	Y	20530 FQ	25450 MW	35060 TQ	USBLS	5/15
	San Juan-Carolina-Caguas MSA, PR	Y	20920 FQ	25920 MW	35260 TQ	USBLS	5/15
	Guam	Y	21510 FQ	24420 MW	29060 TQ	USBLS	5/15
Graphics Technician							
Main Library, Municipal Government	Santa Maria, CA	Y			30955 HI	CACIT	6/28/16
Green Waste Clerk							
Public Works Department, Municipal Government	Orland, CA	Y			13740 HI	CACIT	6/28/16
Grinding, Lapping, Polishing, and Buffing Machine Tool Setter, Operator, and Tender							
Metals and Plastics	Alabama	Y	21377 AE	29901 AW	34157 AEX	ALBLS	6/16
Metals and Plastics	Birmingham-Hoover MSA, AL	Y	21860 AE	30579 AW	34939 AEX	ALBLS	6/16
Metals and Plastics	Arizona	Y	26170 FQ	32820 MW	39610 TQ	USBLS	5/15
Metals and Plastics	Phoenix-Mesa-Scottsdale MSA, AZ	Y	27180 FQ	33820 MW	40510 TQ	USBLS	5/15
Metals and Plastics	Tucson MSA, AZ	Y	22010 FQ	26050 MW	29850 TQ	USBLS	5/15
Metals and Plastics	Arkansas	Y	22760 FQ	28160 MW	35180 TQ	USBLS	5/15

AE Average entry wage	**AWR** Average wage range	**H** Hourly	**LR** Low end range	**MTC** Median total compensation	**TCC** Total cash compensation
AEX Average experienced wage	**B** Biweekly	**HI** Highest wage paid	**M** Monthly	**MW** Median wage paid	**TQ** Third quartile wage
ATC Average total compensation	**D** Daily	**HR** High end range	**MCC** Median cash compensation	**MWR** Median wage range	**W** Weekly
AW Average wage paid	**FQ** First quartile wage	**LO** Lowest wage paid	**ME** Median entry wage	**S** See annotated source	**Y** Yearly

Occupation/Type/Industry	Location	Per	Low	Mid	High	Source	Date
Grinding, Lapping, Polishing, and Buffing Machine Tool Setter, Operator, and Tender							
Metals and Plastics	Little Rock-North Little Rock-Conway MSA, AR	Y	28120 FQ	34440 MW	41670 TQ	USBLS	5/15
Metals and Plastics	California	H	11.75 FQ	14.57 MW	18.41 TQ	CABLS	1/16-3/16
Metals and Plastics	Anaheim-Santa Ana-Irvine PMSA, CA	H	11.78 FQ	14.12 MW	17.95 TQ	CABLS	1/16-3/16
Metals and Plastics	Los Angeles-Long Beach-Glendale PMSA, CA	H	11.43 FQ	14.33 MW	18.40 TQ	CABLS	1/16-3/16
Metals and Plastics	Oakland-Hayward-Berkeley PMSA, CA	H	13.38 FQ	16.68 MW	19.65 TQ	CABLS	1/16-3/16
Metals and Plastics	Riverside-San Bernardino-Ontario MSA, CA	H	10.74 FQ	13.39 MW	17.34 TQ	CABLS	1/16-3/16
Metals and Plastics	Sacramento–Roseville–Arden-Arcade MSA, CA	H	12.97 FQ	16.17 MW	18.75 TQ	CABLS	1/16-3/16
Metals and Plastics	San Diego-Carlsbad MSA, CA	H	11.58 FQ	13.76 MW	16.62 TQ	CABLS	1/16-3/16
Metals and Plastics	San Francisco-Redwood City-South San Francisco PMSA, CA	H	11.06 FQ	13.00 MW	14.77 TQ	CABLS	1/16-3/16
Metals and Plastics	Colorado	Y	26800 FQ	31730 MW	42140 TQ	USBLS	5/15
Metals and Plastics	Denver-Aurora-Lakewood MSA, CO	Y	26560 FQ	32310 MW	43070 TQ	USBLS	5/15
Metals and Plastics	Connecticut	Y		39442 MW		CTBLS	1/16-3/16
Metals and Plastics	Bridgeport-Stamford-Norwalk MSA, CT	Y	28990 FQ	38680 MW	48060 TQ	USBLS	5/15
Metals and Plastics	Hartford-West Hartford-East Hartford MSA, CT	Y	32940 FQ	41670 MW	49510 TQ	USBLS	5/15
Metals and Plastics	Delaware	Y	23990 FQ	33970 MW	40660 TQ	USBLS	5/15
Metals and Plastics	Wilmington PMSA, DE-MD-NJ	Y	33030 FQ	37500 MW	44200 TQ	USBLS	5/15
Metals and Plastics	Florida	H	10.36 AE	13.91 MW	17.24 AEX	FLBLS	7/16-9/16
Metals and Plastics	Fort Lauderdale-Pompano Beach-Deerfield Beach PMSA, FL	H	10.04 AE	13.02 MW	16.70 AEX	FLBLS	7/16-9/16
Metals and Plastics	Miami-Miami Beach-Kendall PMSA, FL	H	9.96 AE	12.95 MW	18.55 AEX	FLBLS	7/16-9/16
Metals and Plastics	Orlando-Kissimmee-Sanford MSA, FL	H	11.76 AE	14.38 MW	18.32 AEX	FLBLS	7/16-9/16
Metals and Plastics	Tampa-St. Petersburg-Clearwater MSA, FL	H	9.96 AE	11.90 MW	15.10 AEX	FLBLS	7/16-9/16
Metals and Plastics	Georgia	Y	24980 FQ	31900 MW	38120 TQ	USBLS	5/15
Metals and Plastics	Atlanta-Sandy Springs-Roswell MSA, GA	Y	27460 FQ	33270 MW	38220 TQ	USBLS	5/15
Metals and Plastics	Augusta-Richmond County MSA, GA-SC	Y	23890 FQ	33160 MW	36730 TQ	USBLS	5/15
Metals and Plastics	Idaho	Y	20500 FQ	24430 MW	29580 TQ	USBLS	5/15
Metals and Plastics	Illinois	Y	27920 FQ	33460 MW	40450 TQ	USBLS	5/15
Metals and Plastics	Chicago-Naperville-Arlington Heights PMSA, IL	Y	27920 FQ	32950 MW	43930 TQ	USBLS	5/15
Metals and Plastics	Lake County-Kenosha County PMSA, IL-WI	Y	26720 FQ	32360 MW	38870 TQ	USBLS	5/15
Metals and Plastics	Indiana	Y	27200 FQ	34270 MW	44550 TQ	USBLS	5/15
Metals and Plastics	Gary PMSA, IN	Y	29820 FQ	35040 MW	39590 TQ	USBLS	5/15
Metals and Plastics	Indianapolis-Carmel-Anderson MSA, IN	Y	37460 FQ	46590 MW	56740 TQ	USBLS	5/15
Metals and Plastics	Iowa	Y	26410 FQ	33200 MW	39190 TQ	USBLS	5/15
Metals and Plastics	Kansas	Y	24300 FQ	30470 MW	37060 TQ	USBLS	5/15
Metals and Plastics	Wichita MSA, KS	Y	21650 FQ	25820 MW	31490 TQ	USBLS	5/15
Metals and Plastics	Kentucky	Y	19300 FQ	23390 MW	29620 TQ	USBLS	5/15
Metals and Plastics	Louisville-Jefferson County MSA, KY-IN	Y	23170 FQ	28450 MW	38650 TQ	USBLS	5/15
Metals and Plastics	Louisiana	Y	26130 FQ	33060 MW	42950 TQ	USBLS	5/15
Metals and Plastics	New Orleans-Metairie MSA, LA	Y	29310 FQ	45560 MW	56100 TQ	USBLS	5/15
Metals and Plastics	Maine	Y	20080 FQ	28760 MW	47740 TQ	USBLS	5/15
Metals and Plastics	Portland-South Portland MSA, ME	Y	31500 FQ	51340 MW	58350 TQ	USBLS	5/15
Metals and Plastics	Maryland	Y	25465 AE	33444 MW	37433 AEX	MDBLS	4/16
Metals and Plastics	Baltimore-Columbia-Towson MSA, MD	Y	26830 FQ	30520 MW	37410 TQ	USBLS	5/15

AE	Average entry wage	AWR	Average wage range	H	Hourly
AEX	Average experienced wage	B	Biweekly	HI	Highest wage paid
ATC	Average total compensation	D	Daily	HR	High end range
AW	Average wage paid	FQ	First quartile wage	LO	Lowest wage paid

LR	Low end range	MTC	Median total compensation
M	Monthly	MW	Median wage paid
MCC	Median cash compensation	MWR	Median wage range
ME	Median entry wage	S	See annotated source

TCC	Total cash compensation
TQ	Third quartile wage
W	Weekly
Y	Yearly

Grinding, Lapping, Polishing, and Buffing Machine Tool Setter, Operator, and Tender

Occupation/Type/Industry	Location	Per	Low	Mid	High	Source	Date
Metals and Plastics	Massachusetts	Y	30750 FQ	41150 MW	52300 TQ	USBLS	5/15
Metals and Plastics	Boston-Cambridge-Newton NECTA, MA	Y	37530 FQ	49440 MW	67000 TQ	USBLS	5/15
Metals and Plastics	Worcester MSA, MA-CT	Y	28390 FQ	34360 MW	44530 TQ	USBLS	5/15
Metals and Plastics	Michigan	Y	24260 FQ	32180 MW	39980 TQ	USBLS	5/15
Metals and Plastics	Detroit-Dearborn-Livonia PMSA, MI	Y	28290 FQ	35330 MW	42350 TQ	USBLS	5/15
Metals and Plastics	Grand Rapids-Wyoming MSA, MI	Y	23620 FQ	33270 MW	42840 TQ	USBLS	5/15
Metals and Plastics	Minnesota	Y	29148 FQ	35669 MW	43242 TQ	MNBLS	1/16-3/16
Metals and Plastics	Minneapolis-St. Paul-Bloomington MSA, MN-WI	Y	29705 FQ	36458 MW	43991 TQ	MNBLS	1/16-3/16
Metals and Plastics	Mississippi	Y	19950 FQ	34700 MW	53810 TQ	USBLS	5/15
Metals and Plastics	Missouri	Y	25180 FQ	32540 MW	43120 TQ	USBLS	5/15
Metals and Plastics	Kansas City MSA, MO-KS	Y	27480 FQ	37500 MW	51140 TQ	USBLS	5/15
Metals and Plastics	St. Louis MSA, MO-IL	Y	22240 FQ	27740 MW	33410 TQ	USBLS	5/15
Metals and Plastics	Montana	Y	21750 FQ	25400 MW	29570 TQ	USBLS	5/15
Metals and Plastics	Nebraska	Y	26815 FQ	30515 MW	35840 TQ	NEBLS	7/16-9/16
Metals and Plastics	Omaha-Council Bluffs MSA, NE-IA	Y	30555 FQ	36590 MW	47250 TQ	NEBLS	7/16-9/16
Metals and Plastics	Nevada	Y	23310 FQ	27780 MW	35190 TQ	USBLS	5/15
Metals and Plastics	Las Vegas-Henderson-Paradise MSA, NV	Y	22160 FQ	25460 MW	30130 TQ	USBLS	5/15
Metals and Plastics	New Hampshire	H	12.13 AE	19.36 MW	21.81 AEX	NHBLS	6/16
Metals and Plastics	Nashua NECTA, NH-MA	Y	30490 FQ	42860 MW	48580 TQ	USBLS	5/15
Metals and Plastics	New Jersey	Y	23340 FQ	28850 MW	35960 TQ	USBLS	5/15
Metals and Plastics	Camden PMSA, NJ	Y	30480 FQ	34880 MW	38200 TQ	USBLS	5/15
Metals and Plastics	Newark PMSA, NJ-PA	Y	21680 FQ	25130 MW	30930 TQ	USBLS	5/15
Metals and Plastics	New Mexico	Y	26480 FQ	30160 MW	40090 TQ	USBLS	5/15
Metals and Plastics	Albuquerque MSA, NM	Y	27510 FQ	32940 MW	47080 TQ	USBLS	5/15
Metals and Plastics	New York	Y	24660 AE	34990 MW	42020 AEX	NYBLS	1/16-3/16
Metals and Plastics	Buffalo-Cheektowaga-Niagara Falls MSA, NY	Y	32970 FQ	39400 MW	53590 TQ	USBLS	5/15
Metals and Plastics	Nassau County-Suffolk County PMSA, NY	Y	28320 FQ	36260 MW	45560 TQ	USBLS	5/15
Metals and Plastics	New York-Jersey City-White Plains PMSA, NY-NJ	Y	25320 FQ	31040 MW	38340 TQ	USBLS	5/15
Metals and Plastics	Rochester MSA, NY	Y	25140 FQ	30730 MW	37560 TQ	USBLS	5/15
Metals and Plastics	North Carolina	Y	26090 FQ	36010 MW	44440 TQ	USBLS	5/15
Metals and Plastics	Charlotte-Concord-Gastonia MSA, NC-SC	Y	34260 FQ	43280 MW	47820 TQ	USBLS	5/15
Metals and Plastics	Raleigh MSA, NC	Y	20260 FQ	23710 MW	36280 TQ	USBLS	5/15
Metals and Plastics	North Dakota	Y	24490 FQ	30960 MW	36410 TQ	USBLS	5/15
Metals and Plastics	Ohio	Y	25980 FQ	32290 MW	39340 TQ	USBLS	5/15
Metals and Plastics	Cincinnati MSA, OH-KY-IN	Y	26720 FQ	31190 MW	38060 TQ	USBLS	5/15
Metals and Plastics	Cleveland-Elyria MSA, OH	Y	28520 FQ	33920 MW	38770 TQ	USBLS	5/15
Metals and Plastics	Columbus MSA, OH	Y	18800 FQ	26380 MW	35190 TQ	USBLS	5/15
Metals and Plastics	Oklahoma	Y	23180 FQ	29400 MW	36250 TQ	USBLS	5/15
Metals and Plastics	Oklahoma City MSA, OK	Y	23140 FQ	29900 MW	36120 TQ	USBLS	5/15
Metals and Plastics	Tulsa MSA, OK	Y	26290 FQ	30880 MW	37150 TQ	USBLS	5/15
Metals and Plastics	Oregon	H	15.74 FQ	20.86 MW	26.00 TQ	ORBLS	2016
Metals and Plastics	Portland-Vancouver-Hillsboro MSA, OR-WA	Y	34000 FQ	44390 MW	59900 TQ	USBLS	5/15
Metals and Plastics	Pennsylvania	Y	29910 FQ	36130 MW	43900 TQ	USBLS	5/15
Metals and Plastics	Allentown-Bethlehem-Easton MSA, PA-NJ	Y	28770 FQ	34200 MW	40280 TQ	USBLS	5/15
Metals and Plastics	Harrisburg-Carlisle MSA, PA	Y	34670 FQ	42590 MW	51100 TQ	USBLS	5/15
Metals and Plastics	Montgomery County-Bucks County-Chester County PMSA, PA	Y	30610 FQ	40980 MW	49210 TQ	USBLS	5/15
Metals and Plastics	Philadelphia PMSA, PA	Y	36020 FQ	43950 MW	52990 TQ	USBLS	5/15
Metals and Plastics	Pittsburgh MSA, PA	Y	32300 FQ	36870 MW	43760 TQ	USBLS	5/15
Metals and Plastics	Rhode Island	Y	26040 FQ	32490 MW	38650 TQ	USBLS	5/15
Metals and Plastics	Providence-Warwick MSA, RI-MA	Y	26150 FQ	32580 MW	38730 TQ	USBLS	5/15
Metals and Plastics	South Carolina	Y	34270 FQ	41770 MW	46920 TQ	USBLS	5/15
Metals and Plastics	Charleston-North Charleston MSA, SC	Y	32880 FQ	38120 MW	62210 TQ	USBLS	5/15

AE	Average entry wage	AWR	Average wage range	H	Hourly	LR	Low end range	MTC	Median total compensation	TCC	Total cash compensation
AEX	Average experienced wage	B	Biweekly	HI	Highest wage paid	M	Monthly	MW	Median wage paid	TQ	Third quartile wage
ATC	Average total compensation	D	Daily	HR	High end range	MCC	Median cash compensation	MWR	Median wage range	W	Weekly
AW	Average wage paid	FQ	First quartile wage	LO	Lowest wage paid	ME	Median entry wage	S	See annotated source	Y	Yearly

Occupation/Type/Industry	Location	Per	Low	Mid	High	Source	Date
Grinding, Lapping, Polishing, and Buffing Machine Tool Setter, Operator, and Tender							
Metals and Plastics	Columbia MSA, SC	Y	32350 FQ	36750 MW	42250 TQ	USBLS	5/15
Metals and Plastics	Greenville-Anderson-Mauldin MSA, SC	Y	32580 FQ	38330 MW	44080 TQ	USBLS	5/15
Metals and Plastics	South Dakota	Y	23340 FQ	28770 MW	35740 TQ	USBLS	5/15
Metals and Plastics	Tennessee	Y	25910 FQ	34210 MW	44950 TQ	USBLS	5/15
Metals and Plastics	Knoxville MSA, TN	Y	23400 FQ	32730 MW	43020 TQ	USBLS	5/15
Metals and Plastics	Memphis MSA, TN-MS-AR	Y	29500 FQ	36800 MW	46530 TQ	USBLS	5/15
Metals and Plastics	Nashville-Davidson– Murfreesboro–Franklin MSA, TN	Y	27690 FQ	33530 MW	45570 TQ	USBLS	5/15
Metals and Plastics	Texas	Y	24430 FQ	30670 MW	38250 TQ	USBLS	5/15
Metals and Plastics	Austin-Round Rock MSA, TX	Y	21960 FQ	24660 MW	32760 TQ	USBLS	5/15
Metals and Plastics	Dallas-Plano-Irving PMSA, TX	Y	21480 FQ	26190 MW	33920 TQ	USBLS	5/15
Metals and Plastics	Fort Worth-Arlington PMSA, TX	Y	23940 FQ	33200 MW	65090 TQ	USBLS	5/15
Metals and Plastics	Houston-The Woodlands- Sugar Land MSA, TX	Y	27060 FQ	33020 MW	39120 TQ	USBLS	5/15
Metals and Plastics	San Antonio-New Braunfels MSA, TX	Y	25380 FQ	30790 MW	41600 TQ	USBLS	5/15
Metals and Plastics	Utah	Y	21620 FQ	27440 MW	33280 TQ	USBLS	5/15
Metals and Plastics	Ogden-Clearfield MSA, UT	Y	25450 FQ	30520 MW	35920 TQ	USBLS	5/15
Metals and Plastics	Provo-Orem MSA, UT	Y	25720 FQ	32110 MW	36110 TQ	USBLS	5/15
Metals and Plastics	Salt Lake City MSA, UT	Y	19260 FQ	24950 MW	30160 TQ	USBLS	5/15
Metals and Plastics	Vermont	Y	26490 FQ	32380 MW	37420 TQ	USBLS	5/15
Metals and Plastics	Virginia	Y	25510 FQ	33760 MW	42690 TQ	USBLS	5/15
Metals and Plastics	Virginia Beach-Norfolk- Newport News MSA, VA-NC	Y	29280 FQ	38250 MW	44600 TQ	USBLS	5/15
Metals and Plastics	Washington	H	13.00 FQ	15.89 MW	18.77 TQ	WABLS	3/16
Metals and Plastics	Seattle-Bellevue-Everett PMSA, WA	H	13.69 FQ	16.78 MW	20.17 TQ	WABLS	3/16
Metals and Plastics	Tacoma-Lakewood PMSA, WA	H	11.53 FQ	17.25 MW	32.39 TQ	WABLS	3/16
Metals and Plastics	West Virginia	Y	24040 FQ	31280 MW	45100 TQ	USBLS	5/15
Metals and Plastics	Huntington-Ashland MSA, WV-KY-OH	Y	26470 FQ	44050 MW	54350 TQ	USBLS	5/15
Metals and Plastics	Wisconsin	Y	27520 FQ	33630 MW	39720 TQ	USBLS	5/15
Metals and Plastics	Madison MSA, WI	Y	25360 FQ	28440 MW	31700 TQ	USBLS	5/15
Metals and Plastics	Milwaukee-Waukesha-West Allis MSA, WI	Y	28740 FQ	34140 MW	39280 TQ	USBLS	5/15
Metals and Plastics	Puerto Rico	Y	18380 FQ	20980 MW	23330 TQ	USBLS	5/15
Metals and Plastics	San Juan-Carolina-Caguas MSA, PR	Y	18380 FQ	20960 MW	23290 TQ	USBLS	5/15
Grinding and Polishing Worker							
Hand	Alabama	Y	20256 AE	26209 AW	29181 AEX	ALBLS	6/16
Hand	Birmingham-Hoover MSA, AL	Y	21819 AE	25839 AW	27844 AEX	ALBLS	6/16
Hand	Arizona	Y	30150 FQ	34500 MW	37940 TQ	USBLS	5/15
Hand	Phoenix-Mesa-Scottsdale MSA, AZ	Y	30830 FQ	34770 MW	38110 TQ	USBLS	5/15
Hand	Arkansas	Y	18040 FQ	21650 MW	30180 TQ	USBLS	5/15
Hand	California	H	10.14 FQ	12.50 MW	16.16 TQ	CABLS	1/16-3/16
Hand	Anaheim-Santa Ana-Irvine PMSA, CA	H	10.30 FQ	12.38 MW	14.55 TQ	CABLS	1/16-3/16
Hand	Los Angeles-Long Beach- Glendale PMSA, CA	H	9.74 FQ	11.81 MW	16.05 TQ	CABLS	1/16-3/16
Hand	Oakland-Hayward-Berkeley PMSA, CA	H	10.93 FQ	14.49 MW	20.47 TQ	CABLS	1/16-3/16
Hand	Riverside-San Bernardino- Ontario MSA, CA	H	10.77 FQ	13.06 MW	16.60 TQ	CABLS	1/16-3/16
Hand	Sacramento–Roseville– Arden-Arcade MSA, CA	H	10.74 FQ	12.20 MW	15.45 TQ	CABLS	1/16-3/16
Hand	San Diego-Carlsbad MSA, CA	H	11.38 FQ	14.96 MW	19.75 TQ	CABLS	1/16-3/16
Hand	San Francisco-Redwood City- South San Francisco PMSA, CA	H	14.21 FQ	19.29 MW	29.09 TQ	CABLS	1/16-3/16
Hand	Colorado	Y	24610 FQ	28520 MW	34010 TQ	USBLS	5/15
Hand	Denver-Aurora-Lakewood MSA, CO	Y	25020 FQ	28620 MW	34140 TQ	USBLS	5/15
Hand	Connecticut	Y		36839 MW		CTBLS	1/16-3/16

AE	Average entry wage	AWR	Average wage range	H	Hourly
AEX	Average experienced wage	B	Biweekly	HI	Highest wage paid
ATC	Average total compensation	D	Daily	HR	High end range
AW	Average wage paid	FQ	First quartile wage	LO	Lowest wage paid

LR	Low end range	MTC	Median total compensation
M	Monthly	MW	Median wage paid
MCC	Median cash compensation	MWR	Median wage range
ME	Median entry wage	S	See annotated source

TCC	Total cash compensation		
TQ	Third quartile wage		
W	Weekly		
Y	Yearly		

Occupation/Type/Industry	Location	Per	Low	Mid	High	Source	Date
Grinding and Polishing Worker							
Hand	Bridgeport-Stamford-Norwalk MSA, CT	Y	30640 FQ	38560 MW	45540 TQ	USBLS	5/15
Hand	Hartford-West Hartford-East Hartford MSA, CT	Y	31630 FQ	37920 MW	44520 TQ	USBLS	5/15
Hand	Washington-Arlington-Alexandria PMSA, DC-VA-MD-WV	Y	27390 FQ	30650 MW	48590 TQ	USBLS	5/15
Hand	Florida	H	11.28 AE	14.84 MW	17.55 AEX	FLBLS	7/16-9/16
Hand	Orlando-Kissimmee-Sanford MSA, FL	H	13.32 AE	18.44 MW	20.38 AEX	FLBLS	7/16-9/16
Hand	Tampa-St. Petersburg-Clearwater MSA, FL	H	11.67 AE	14.40 MW	15.89 AEX	FLBLS	7/16-9/16
Hand	Georgia	Y	21550 FQ	24550 MW	29960 TQ	USBLS	5/15
Hand	Atlanta-Sandy Springs-Roswell MSA, GA	Y	22450 FQ	25820 MW	29870 TQ	USBLS	5/15
Hand	Hawaii	Y	18740 FQ	26230 MW	34750 TQ	USBLS	5/15
Hand	Urban Honolulu MSA, HI	Y	18540 FQ	24940 MW	34270 TQ	USBLS	5/15
Hand	Idaho	Y	23240 FQ	27420 MW	31670 TQ	USBLS	5/15
Hand	Boise City MSA, ID	Y	23910 FQ	28280 MW	33100 TQ	USBLS	5/15
Hand	Illinois	Y	24220 FQ	30070 MW	37370 TQ	USBLS	5/15
Hand	Chicago-Naperville-Arlington Heights PMSA, IL	Y	24960 FQ	32150 MW	38120 TQ	USBLS	5/15
Hand	Lake County-Kenosha County PMSA, IL-WI	Y	25500 FQ	31260 MW	42620 TQ	USBLS	5/15
Hand	Indiana	Y	23600 FQ	27740 MW	31410 TQ	USBLS	5/15
Hand	Indianapolis-Carmel-Anderson MSA, IN	Y	18840 FQ	24990 MW	29540 TQ	USBLS	5/15
Hand	Iowa	Y	24580 FQ	34020 MW	38730 TQ	USBLS	5/15
Hand	Kansas	Y	25180 FQ	29830 MW	35480 TQ	USBLS	5/15
Hand	Wichita MSA, KS	Y	25830 FQ	29450 MW	34960 TQ	USBLS	5/15
Hand	Kentucky	Y	25300 FQ	28470 MW	32310 TQ	USBLS	5/15
Hand	Louisville-Jefferson County MSA, KY-IN	Y	25510 FQ	28260 MW	31270 TQ	USBLS	5/15
Hand	Louisiana	Y	25160 FQ	28920 MW	34520 TQ	USBLS	5/15
Hand	Maine	Y	29880 FQ	34220 MW	38240 TQ	USBLS	5/15
Hand	Maryland	Y	25683 AE	34206 MW	38467 AEX	MDBLS	4/16
Hand	Baltimore-Columbia-Towson MSA, MD	Y	27840 FQ	31720 MW	37610 TQ	USBLS	5/15
Hand	Massachusetts	Y	27020 FQ	34080 MW	40910 TQ	USBLS	5/15
Hand	Boston-Cambridge-Newton NECTA, MA	Y	25200 FQ	31360 MW	38290 TQ	USBLS	5/15
Hand	Worcester MSA, MA-CT	Y	28510 FQ	33000 MW	39560 TQ	USBLS	5/15
Hand	Michigan	Y	27060 FQ	32500 MW	40510 TQ	USBLS	5/15
Hand	Grand Rapids-Wyoming MSA, MI	Y	23980 FQ	30310 MW	35760 TQ	USBLS	5/15
Hand	Minnesota	Y	29017 FQ	34150 MW	39739 TQ	MNBLS	1/16-3/16
Hand	Minneapolis-St. Paul-Bloomington MSA, MN-WI	Y	29644 FQ	35334 MW	42199 TQ	MNBLS	1/16-3/16
Hand	Mississippi	Y	22440 FQ	28310 MW	38010 TQ	USBLS	5/15
Hand	Missouri	Y	23590 FQ	29030 MW	37890 TQ	USBLS	5/15
Hand	Kansas City MSA, MO-KS	Y	24940 FQ	31750 MW	36610 TQ	USBLS	5/15
Hand	St. Louis MSA, MO-IL	Y	23090 FQ	30650 MW	40680 TQ	USBLS	5/15
Hand	Montana	Y	28360 FQ	33900 MW	38730 TQ	USBLS	5/15
Hand	Nebraska	Y	26590 FQ	29725 MW	34390 TQ	NEBLS	7/16-9/16
Hand	Omaha-Council Bluffs MSA, NE-IA	Y	22405 FQ	26550 MW	33590 TQ	NEBLS	7/16-9/16
Hand	Nevada	Y	25310 FQ	29940 MW	35860 TQ	USBLS	5/15
Hand	Las Vegas-Henderson-Paradise MSA, NV	Y	23460 FQ	28460 MW	34400 TQ	USBLS	5/15
Hand	New Hampshire	H	11.90 AE	16.75 MW	19.34 AEX	NHBLS	6/16
Hand	Nashua NECTA, NH-MA	Y	26140 FQ	31950 MW	40450 TQ	USBLS	5/15
Hand	New Jersey	Y	25660 FQ	32090 MW	38430 TQ	USBLS	5/15
Hand	Camden PMSA, NJ	Y	23420 FQ	29550 MW	37020 TQ	USBLS	5/15
Hand	Newark PMSA, NJ-PA	Y	27180 FQ	32990 MW	38200 TQ	USBLS	5/15
Hand	New Mexico	Y	19660 FQ	24020 MW	30910 TQ	USBLS	5/15
Hand	Albuquerque MSA, NM	Y	21860 FQ	24790 MW	28730 TQ	USBLS	5/15
Hand	New York	Y	21130 AE	29160 MW	37220 AEX	NYBLS	1/16-3/16
Hand	Buffalo-Cheektowaga-Niagara Falls MSA, NY	Y	27180 FQ	31540 MW	36530 TQ	USBLS	5/15
Hand	Nassau County-Suffolk County PMSA, NY	Y	24210 FQ	31960 MW	38500 TQ	USBLS	5/15

Occupation/Type/Industry	Location	Per	Low	Mid	High	Source	Date
Grinding and Polishing Worker							
Hand	New York-Jersey City-White Plains PMSA, NY-NJ	Y	20840 FQ	26540 MW	35850 TQ	USBLS	5/15
Hand	Rochester MSA, NY	Y	20840 FQ	25880 MW	29950 TQ	USBLS	5/15
Hand	North Carolina	Y	21450 FQ	25810 MW	33790 TQ	USBLS	5/15
Hand	Charlotte-Concord-Gastonia MSA, NC-SC	Y	20490 FQ	24610 MW	36040 TQ	USBLS	5/15
Hand	Raleigh MSA, NC	Y	19400 FQ	25360 MW	34540 TQ	USBLS	5/15
Hand	Ohio	Y	25810 FQ	31060 MW	37280 TQ	USBLS	5/15
Hand	Cincinnati MSA, OH-KY-IN	Y	27420 FQ	31400 MW	37220 TQ	USBLS	5/15
Hand	Cleveland-Elyria MSA, OH	Y	26000 FQ	31740 MW	37490 TQ	USBLS	5/15
Hand	Columbus MSA, OH	Y	27860 FQ	32150 MW	36700 TQ	USBLS	5/15
Hand	Oklahoma	Y	23020 FQ	27810 MW	33850 TQ	USBLS	5/15
Hand	Oklahoma City MSA, OK	Y	22620 FQ	29310 MW	37200 TQ	USBLS	5/15
Hand	Tulsa MSA, OK	Y	23360 FQ	28020 MW	33800 TQ	USBLS	5/15
Hand	Oregon	H	10.71 FQ	13.15 MW	15.73 TQ	ORBLS	2016
Hand	Portland-Vancouver-Hillsboro MSA, OR-WA	Y	21410 FQ	27100 MW	33060 TQ	USBLS	5/15
Hand	Pennsylvania	Y	24910 FQ	29080 MW	35280 TQ	USBLS	5/15
Hand	Allentown-Bethlehem-Easton MSA, PA-NJ	Y	31090 FQ	35930 MW	41800 TQ	USBLS	5/15
Hand	Montgomery County-Bucks County-Chester County PMSA, PA	Y	25490 FQ	29240 MW	34640 TQ	USBLS	5/15
Hand	Philadelphia PMSA, PA	Y	27700 FQ	32420 MW	38690 TQ	USBLS	5/15
Hand	Pittsburgh MSA, PA	Y	27190 FQ	30150 MW	37500 TQ	USBLS	5/15
Hand	Rhode Island	Y	27110 FQ	32520 MW	38400 TQ	USBLS	5/15
Hand	Providence-Warwick MSA, RI-MA	Y	27480 FQ	33250 MW	37990 TQ	USBLS	5/15
Hand	South Carolina	Y	20900 FQ	27090 MW	32890 TQ	USBLS	5/15
Hand	Charleston-North Charleston MSA, SC	Y	21920 FQ	25120 MW	30140 TQ	USBLS	5/15
Hand	South Dakota	Y	25890 FQ	28830 MW	32440 TQ	USBLS	5/15
Hand	Tennessee	Y	22090 FQ	26760 MW	32780 TQ	USBLS	5/15
Hand	Knoxville MSA, TN	Y	21600 FQ	26470 MW	29900 TQ	USBLS	5/15
Hand	Nashville-Davidson–Murfreesboro–Franklin MSA, TN	Y	24860 FQ	31540 MW	39950 TQ	USBLS	5/15
Hand	Texas	Y	23580 FQ	28490 MW	36400 TQ	USBLS	5/15
Hand	Austin-Round Rock MSA, TX	Y	24910 FQ	30000 MW	42870 TQ	USBLS	5/15
Hand	Dallas-Plano-Irving PMSA, TX	Y	24920 FQ	29550 MW	41190 TQ	USBLS	5/15
Hand	Fort Worth-Arlington PMSA, TX	Y	22240 FQ	27560 MW	36450 TQ	USBLS	5/15
Hand	Houston-The Woodlands-Sugar Land MSA, TX	Y	23460 FQ	27500 MW	31370 TQ	USBLS	5/15
Hand	San Antonio-New Braunfels MSA, TX	Y	22630 FQ	26520 MW	30330 TQ	USBLS	5/15
Hand	Utah	Y	23460 FQ	27880 MW	34010 TQ	USBLS	5/15
Hand	Ogden-Clearfield MSA, UT	Y	23600 FQ	29070 MW	36620 TQ	USBLS	5/15
Hand	Provo-Orem MSA, UT	Y	23720 FQ	29140 MW	36750 TQ	USBLS	5/15
Hand	Vermont	Y	25520 FQ	41330 MW	47340 TQ	USBLS	5/15
Hand	Virginia	Y	23180 FQ	29010 MW	46240 TQ	USBLS	5/15
Hand	Virginia Beach-Norfolk-Newport News MSA, VA-NC	Y	23460 FQ	41970 MW	51590 TQ	USBLS	5/15
Hand	Washington	H	11.89 FQ	14.89 MW	18.58 TQ	WABLS	3/16
Hand	Seattle-Bellevue-Everett PMSA, WA	H	11.79 FQ	14.72 MW	18.68 TQ	WABLS	3/16
Hand	Tacoma-Lakewood PMSA, WA	H	12.51 FQ	14.97 MW	19.16 TQ	WABLS	3/16
Hand	Wisconsin	Y	26450 FQ	31240 MW	37920 TQ	USBLS	5/15
Hand	Milwaukee-Waukesha-West Allis MSA, WI	Y	27590 FQ	32130 MW	37210 TQ	USBLS	5/15
Grocery Director							
Supermarket, Large Company	United States	Y		175000 AW		SN01	2015
Supermarket, Medium Company	United States	Y		160000 AW		SN01	2015
Supermarket, Small Company	United States	Y		145000 AW		SN01	2015
Guidance Counselor							
Overseas School, United States Department of Defense	United States	Y	48950 LO		89215 HI	CPMS	2015-2016

Occupation/Type/Industry	Location	Per	Low	Mid	High	Source	Date
Gunnery Sergeant							
U.S. Marines, Active Duty, Pay Grade E-7	United States	M	2875 LO		5168 HI	DOD1	2017
Gymnastics Instructor							
Parks, Recreation and Community Services, Municipal Government	Novato, CA	Y		42126 AW		CACIT	6/28/16
Gypsy Moth Traptender							
Agriculture Department, State Government	Ohio	H			13.00 HI	OHGOV	2015
Hairdresser, Hairstylist, and Cosmetologist	Alabama	Y	17514 AE	25647 AW	29714 AEX	ALBLS	6/16
	Birmingham-Hoover MSA, AL	Y	17483 AE	24597 AW	28149 AEX	ALBLS	6/16
	Alaska	Y	25140 FQ	31700 MW	44420 TQ	USBLS	5/15
	Anchorage MSA, AK	Y	25080 FQ	30130 MW	42120 TQ	USBLS	5/15
	Arizona	Y	18300 FQ	20010 MW	27010 TQ	USBLS	5/15
	Phoenix-Mesa-Scottsdale MSA, AZ	Y	18220 FQ	19740 MW	26540 TQ	USBLS	5/15
	Tucson MSA, AZ	Y	18860 FQ	22540 MW	28000 TQ	USBLS	5/15
	Arkansas	Y	18390 FQ	21690 MW	26790 TQ	USBLS	5/15
	Little Rock-North Little Rock-Conway MSA, AR	Y	18350 FQ	21680 MW	27900 TQ	USBLS	5/15
	California	H	9.68 FQ	11.43 MW	15.11 TQ	CABLS	1/16-3/16
	Anaheim-Santa Ana-Irvine PMSA, CA	H	9.48 FQ	10.37 MW	14.33 TQ	CABLS	1/16-3/16
	Los Angeles-Long Beach-Glendale PMSA, CA	H	9.66 FQ	11.34 MW	14.31 TQ	CABLS	1/16-3/16
	Oakland-Hayward-Berkeley PMSA, CA	H	10.14 FQ	12.76 MW	16.10 TQ	CABLS	1/16-3/16
	Riverside-San Bernardino-Ontario MSA, CA	H	9.88 FQ	11.21 MW	15.44 TQ	CABLS	1/16-3/16
	Sacramento–Roseville–Arden-Arcade MSA, CA	H	10.20 FQ	11.82 MW	14.89 TQ	CABLS	1/16-3/16
	San Diego-Carlsbad MSA, CA	H	9.69 FQ	11.23 MW	14.49 TQ	CABLS	1/16-3/16
	San Francisco-Redwood City-South San Francisco PMSA, CA	H	10.79 FQ	14.99 MW	18.35 TQ	CABLS	1/16-3/16
	Colorado	Y	18560 FQ	21860 MW	31510 TQ	USBLS	5/15
	Denver-Aurora-Lakewood MSA, CO	Y	18430 FQ	21060 MW	30510 TQ	USBLS	5/15
	Connecticut	Y		25942 MW		CTBLS	1/16-3/16
	Bridgeport-Stamford-Norwalk MSA, CT	Y	19610 FQ	23780 MW	40670 TQ	USBLS	5/15
	Hartford-West Hartford-East Hartford MSA, CT	Y	21180 FQ	25250 MW	39430 TQ	USBLS	5/15
	Delaware	Y	21490 FQ	30350 MW	41270 TQ	USBLS	5/15
	Wilmington PMSA, DE-MD-NJ	Y	21920 FQ	30510 MW	39430 TQ	USBLS	5/15
	District of Columbia	Y	19920 FQ	26660 MW	48350 TQ	USBLS	5/15
	Washington-Arlington-Alexandria PMSA, DC-VA-MD-WV	Y	19780 FQ	27790 MW	44040 TQ	USBLS	5/15
	Florida	H	9.15 AE	11.65 MW	16.51 AEX	FLBLS	7/16-9/16
	Fort Lauderdale-Pompano Beach-Deerfield Beach PMSA, FL	H	9.04 AE	10.01 MW	14.17 AEX	FLBLS	7/16-9/16
	Miami-Miami Beach-Kendall PMSA, FL	H	9.04 AE	11.42 MW	15.37 AEX	FLBLS	7/16-9/16
	Orlando-Kissimmee-Sanford MSA, FL	H	9.00 AE	10.91 MW	14.85 AEX	FLBLS	7/16-9/16
	Tampa-St. Petersburg-Clearwater MSA, FL	H	9.44 AE	11.85 MW	15.62 AEX	FLBLS	7/16-9/16
	Georgia	Y	18690 FQ	23220 MW	31570 TQ	USBLS	5/15
	Atlanta-Sandy Springs-Roswell MSA, GA	Y	19130 FQ	23650 MW	32930 TQ	USBLS	5/15
	Augusta-Richmond County MSA, GA-SC	Y	17770 FQ	20520 MW	32540 TQ	USBLS	5/15
	Hawaii	Y	21560 FQ	31630 MW	47800 TQ	USBLS	5/15
	Urban Honolulu MSA, HI	Y	25180 FQ	33840 MW	48660 TQ	USBLS	5/15
	Idaho	Y	17570 FQ	20200 MW	30880 TQ	USBLS	5/15
	Boise City MSA, ID	Y	17880 FQ	22460 MW	35290 TQ	USBLS	5/15
	Illinois	Y	18880 FQ	22640 MW	31870 TQ	USBLS	5/15

AE Average entry wage	**AWR** Average wage range	**H** Hourly	**LR** Low end range	**MTC** Median total compensation	**TCC** Total cash compensation
AEX Average experienced wage	**B** Biweekly	**HI** Highest wage paid	**M** Monthly	**MW** Median wage paid	**TQ** Third quartile wage
ATC Average total compensation	**D** Daily	**HR** High end range	**MCC** Median cash compensation	**MWR** Median wage range	**W** Weekly
AW Average wage paid	**FQ** First quartile wage	**LO** Lowest wage paid	**ME** Median entry wage	**S** See annotated source	**Y** Yearly

Occupation/Type/Industry	Location	Per	Low	Mid	High	Source	Date
Hairdresser, Hairstylist, and Cosmetologist	Chicago-Naperville-Arlington Heights PMSA, IL	Y	18960 FQ	22970 MW	31830 TQ	USBLS	5/15
	Lake County-Kenosha County PMSA, IL-WI	Y	18900 FQ	23740 MW	34180 TQ	USBLS	5/15
	Indiana	Y	18290 FQ	22360 MW	29820 TQ	USBLS	5/15
	Gary PMSA, IN	Y	17500 FQ	19690 MW	29170 TQ	USBLS	5/15
	Indianapolis-Carmel-Anderson MSA, IN	Y	19700 FQ	25690 MW	33850 TQ	USBLS	5/15
	Iowa	Y	17900 FQ	21280 MW	29110 TQ	USBLS	5/15
	Des Moines-West Des Moines MSA, IA	Y	20310 FQ	28180 MW	38460 TQ	USBLS	5/15
	Kansas	Y	17790 FQ	21110 MW	30500 TQ	USBLS	5/15
	Wichita MSA, KS	Y	17830 FQ	23290 MW	29580 TQ	USBLS	5/15
	Kentucky	Y	18090 FQ	21580 MW	28350 TQ	USBLS	5/15
	Louisville-Jefferson County MSA, KY-IN	Y	18350 FQ	22810 MW	30650 TQ	USBLS	5/15
	Louisiana	Y	18660 FQ	22150 MW	27120 TQ	USBLS	5/15
	Baton Rouge MSA, LA	Y	17680 FQ	20120 MW	24560 TQ	USBLS	5/15
	New Orleans-Metairie MSA, LA	Y	19870 FQ	23350 MW	29520 TQ	USBLS	5/15
	Maine	Y	18840 FQ	23320 MW	33770 TQ	USBLS	5/15
	Portland-South Portland MSA, ME	Y	19420 FQ	27260 MW	35170 TQ	USBLS	5/15
	Maryland	Y	18534 AE	30907 MW	37093 AEX	MDBLS	4/16
	Baltimore-Columbia-Towson MSA, MD	Y	19500 FQ	24770 MW	38150 TQ	USBLS	5/15
	Salisbury MSA, MD-DE	Y	19010 FQ	26390 MW	38020 TQ	USBLS	5/15
	Massachusetts	Y	21370 FQ	31420 MW	45880 TQ	USBLS	5/15
	Boston-Cambridge-Newton NECTA, MA	Y	22790 FQ	34510 MW	48150 TQ	USBLS	5/15
	Worcester MSA, MA-CT	Y	20960 FQ	29520 MW	43640 TQ	USBLS	5/15
	Michigan	Y	18800 FQ	22950 MW	31660 TQ	USBLS	5/15
	Detroit-Dearborn-Livonia PMSA, MI	Y	19250 FQ	26520 MW	35120 TQ	USBLS	5/15
	Grand Rapids-Wyoming MSA, MI	Y	19010 FQ	24500 MW	35660 TQ	USBLS	5/15
	Minnesota	Y	19339 FQ	23853 MW	33073 TQ	MNBLS	1/16-3/16
	Minneapolis-St. Paul-Bloomington MSA, MN-WI	Y	19662 FQ	24560 MW	34123 TQ	MNBLS	1/16-3/16
	Mississippi	Y	17260 FQ	19110 MW	27570 TQ	USBLS	5/15
	Jackson MSA, MS	Y	16740 FQ	18120 MW	19570 TQ	USBLS	5/15
	Missouri	Y	18540 FQ	23150 MW	31970 TQ	USBLS	5/15
	Kansas City MSA, MO-KS	Y	18030 FQ	21730 MW	35050 TQ	USBLS	5/15
	St. Louis MSA, MO-IL	Y	18940 FQ	23520 MW	30500 TQ	USBLS	5/15
	Montana	Y	19350 FQ	24990 MW	35710 TQ	USBLS	5/15
	Billings MSA, MT	Y	21920 FQ	26390 MW	36110 TQ	USBLS	5/15
	Omaha-Council Bluffs MSA, NE-IA	Y	19385 FQ	24310 MW	37495 TQ	NEBLS	7/16-9/16
	Nevada	Y	18460 FQ	22600 MW	27940 TQ	USBLS	5/15
	Las Vegas-Henderson-Paradise MSA, NV	Y	18300 FQ	22780 MW	28390 TQ	USBLS	5/15
	New Hampshire	H	8.59 AE	12.29 MW	16.97 AEX	NHBLS	6/16
	Manchester NECTA, NH	H	10.33 AE	14.87 MW	18.42 AEX	NHBLS	6/16
	Nashua NECTA, NH-MA	Y	19960 FQ	27500 MW	37470 TQ	USBLS	5/15
	New Jersey	Y	24450 FQ	31700 MW	42750 TQ	USBLS	5/15
	Camden PMSA, NJ	Y	23090 FQ	29960 MW	38730 TQ	USBLS	5/15
	Newark PMSA, NJ-PA	Y	23550 FQ	30920 MW	45940 TQ	USBLS	5/15
	Trenton MSA, NJ	Y	22230 FQ	28210 MW	40890 TQ	USBLS	5/15
	New Mexico	Y	20530 FQ	23760 MW	30740 TQ	USBLS	5/15
	Albuquerque MSA, NM	Y	20500 FQ	23700 MW	31190 TQ	USBLS	5/15
	New York	Y	19300 AE	23170 MW	39360 AEX	NYBLS	1/16-3/16
	Buffalo-Cheektowaga-Niagara Falls MSA, NY	Y	18980 FQ	20360 MW	24180 TQ	USBLS	5/15
	Nassau County-Suffolk County PMSA, NY	Y	18890 FQ	19960 MW	31610 TQ	USBLS	5/15
	New York-Jersey City-White Plains PMSA, NY-NJ	Y	19850 FQ	29070 MW	43000 TQ	USBLS	5/15
	Rochester MSA, NY	Y	19290 FQ	22130 MW	27370 TQ	USBLS	5/15
	North Carolina	Y	18460 FQ	22910 MW	33640 TQ	USBLS	5/15
	Charlotte-Concord-Gastonia MSA, NC-SC	Y	18270 FQ	24180 MW	37100 TQ	USBLS	5/15

AE	Average entry wage	AWR	Average wage range	H	Hourly	LR	Low end range	MTC	Median total compensation	TCC	Total cash compensation
AEX	Average experienced wage	B	Biweekly	HI	Highest wage paid	M	Monthly	MW	Median wage paid	TQ	Third quartile wage
ATC	Average total compensation	D	Daily	HR	High end range	MCC	Median cash compensation	MWR	Median wage range	W	Weekly
AW	Average wage paid	FQ	First quartile wage	LO	Lowest wage paid	ME	Median entry wage	S	See annotateu source	Y	Yearly

Occupation/Type/Industry	Location	Per	Low	Mid	High	Source	Date
Hairdresser, Hairstylist, and Cosmetologist	Raleigh MSA, NC	Y	19620 FQ	22400 MW	28660 TQ	USBLS	5/15
	North Dakota	Y	21030 FQ	26960 MW	34590 TQ	USBLS	5/15
	Fargo MSA, ND-MN	Y	21640 FQ	26910 MW	31750 TQ	USBLS	5/15
	Ohio	Y	18490 FQ	20990 MW	28560 TQ	USBLS	5/15
	Cincinnati MSA, OH-KY-IN	Y	18540 FQ	21080 MW	27340 TQ	USBLS	5/15
	Cleveland-Elyria MSA, OH	Y	19930 FQ	25620 MW	34770 TQ	USBLS	5/15
	Columbus MSA, OH	Y	18420 FQ	20530 MW	25670 TQ	USBLS	5/15
	Oklahoma	Y	17910 FQ	20940 MW	25260 TQ	USBLS	5/15
	Oklahoma City MSA, OK	Y	18300 FQ	21210 MW	24100 TQ	USBLS	5/15
	Tulsa MSA, OK	Y	17650 FQ	21070 MW	28000 TQ	USBLS	5/15
	Oregon	H	9.93 FQ	11.98 MW	17.12 TQ	ORBLS	2016
	Portland-Vancouver-Hillsboro MSA, OR-WA	Y	21370 FQ	25530 MW	35470 TQ	USBLS	5/15
	Pennsylvania	Y	18800 FQ	23990 MW	30880 TQ	USBLS	5/15
	Allentown-Bethlehem-Easton MSA, PA-NJ	Y	18640 FQ	22370 MW	32110 TQ	USBLS	5/15
	Harrisburg-Carlisle MSA, PA	Y	19960 FQ	27210 MW	34450 TQ	USBLS	5/15
	Montgomery County-Bucks County-Chester County PMSA, PA	Y	19920 FQ	26700 MW	36040 TQ	USBLS	5/15
	Philadelphia PMSA, PA	Y	21350 FQ	26470 MW	33190 TQ	USBLS	5/15
	Pittsburgh MSA, PA	Y	18420 FQ	22960 MW	28560 TQ	USBLS	5/15
	Rhode Island	Y	19650 FQ	25360 MW	32940 TQ	USBLS	5/15
	Providence-Warwick MSA, RI-MA	Y	19810 FQ	26190 MW	35210 TQ	USBLS	5/15
	South Carolina	Y	17420 FQ	19490 MW	27340 TQ	USBLS	5/15
	Charleston-North Charleston MSA, SC	Y	18760 FQ	24280 MW	41580 TQ	USBLS	5/15
	Columbia MSA, SC	Y	17090 FQ	18870 MW	26640 TQ	USBLS	5/15
	Greenville-Anderson-Mauldin MSA, SC	Y	17690 FQ	19850 MW	24050 TQ	USBLS	5/15
	South Dakota	Y	23500 FQ	28200 MW	34160 TQ	USBLS	5/15
	Sioux Falls MSA, SD	Y	24460 FQ	30130 MW	36660 TQ	USBLS	5/15
	Tennessee	Y	18340 FQ	23250 MW	33600 TQ	USBLS	5/15
	Kingsport-Bristol-Bristol MSA, TN-VA	Y	17670 FQ	22400 MW	29320 TQ	USBLS	5/15
	Knoxville MSA, TN	Y	17280 FQ	19070 MW	25100 TQ	USBLS	5/15
	Memphis MSA, TN-MS-AR	Y	20380 FQ	26850 MW	37570 TQ	USBLS	5/15
	Nashville-Davidson–Murfreesboro–Franklin MSA, TN	Y	18590 FQ	24680 MW	35550 TQ	USBLS	5/15
	Texas	Y	18230 FQ	22330 MW	30920 TQ	USBLS	5/15
	Austin-Round Rock MSA, TX	Y	19660 FQ	29910 MW	40900 TQ	USBLS	5/15
	Dallas-Plano-Irving PMSA, TX	Y	18400 FQ	22500 MW	29300 TQ	USBLS	5/15
	Fort Worth-Arlington PMSA, TX	Y	18190 FQ	21930 MW	31380 TQ	USBLS	5/15
	Houston-The Woodlands-Sugar Land MSA, TX	Y	18080 FQ	21820 MW	31160 TQ	USBLS	5/15
	San Antonio-New Braunfels MSA, TX	Y	18370 FQ	21880 MW	27030 TQ	USBLS	5/15
	Utah	Y	19170 FQ	23980 MW	28770 TQ	USBLS	5/15
	Ogden-Clearfield MSA, UT	Y	20390 FQ	23490 MW	28390 TQ	USBLS	5/15
	Provo-Orem MSA, UT	Y	18530 FQ	25270 MW	28580 TQ	USBLS	5/15
	Salt Lake City MSA, UT	Y	19300 FQ	23420 MW	28630 TQ	USBLS	5/15
	Vermont	Y	19930 FQ	25980 MW	34530 TQ	USBLS	5/15
	Burlington-South Burlington MSA, VT	Y	19980 FQ	33660 MW	41490 TQ	USBLS	5/15
	Virginia	Y	19710 FQ	28540 MW	43830 TQ	USBLS	5/15
	Richmond MSA, VA	Y	21590 FQ	28230 MW	40040 TQ	USBLS	5/15
	Virginia Beach-Norfolk-Newport News MSA, VA-NC	Y	19430 FQ	31440 MW	47890 TQ	USBLS	5/15
	Washington	H	11.84 FQ	14.57 MW	22.00 TQ	WABLS	3/16
	Seattle-Bellevue-Everett PMSA, WA	H	11.87 FQ	16.30 MW	24.67 TQ	WABLS	3/16
	Tacoma-Lakewood PMSA, WA	H	12.40 FQ	14.58 MW	22.78 TQ	WABLS	3/16
	West Virginia	Y	18150 FQ	19770 MW	26430 TQ	USBLS	5/15
	Huntington-Ashland MSA, WV-KY-OH	Y	17310 FQ	18690 MW	25500 TQ	USBLS	5/15
	Wisconsin	Y	18950 FQ	23980 MW	31770 TQ	USBLS	5/15
	Madison MSA, WI	Y	18680 FQ	24930 MW	36560 TQ	USBLS	5/15

AE	Average entry wage	AWR	Average wage range	H	Hourly	LR	Low end range	MTC	Median total compensation	TCC	Total cash compensation
AEX	Average experienced wage	B	Biweekly	HI	Highest wage paid	M	Monthly	MW	Median wage paid	TQ	Third quartile wage
ATC	Average total compensation	D	Daily	HR	High end range	MCC	Median cash compensation	MWR	Median wage range	W	Weekly
AW	Average wage paid	FQ	First quartile wage	LO	Lowest wage paid	ME	Median entry wage	S	See annotated source	Y	Yearly

Occupation/Type/Industry	Location	Per	Low	Mid	High	Source	Date
Hairdresser, Hairstylist, and Cosmetologist	Milwaukee-Waukesha-West Allis MSA, WI	Y	19370 FQ	25070 MW	34640 TQ	USBLS	5/15
	Wyoming	Y	21890 FQ	27400 MW	34790 TQ	USBLS	5/15
	Cheyenne MSA, WY	Y	23720 FQ	29630 MW	44140 TQ	USBLS	5/15
	Puerto Rico	Y	16840 FQ	18250 MW	19840 TQ	USBLS	5/15
	San Juan-Carolina-Caguas MSA, PR	Y	16740 FQ	18070 MW	19420 TQ	USBLS	5/15
	Guam	Y	18200 FQ	19250 MW	25760 TQ	USBLS	5/15
Hairstylist							
Made for Television Motion Picture	United States	W	1182 LO			MPEG01	7/31/16-7/29/17
Harbor Master							
Municipal Government	Avalon, CA	Y			137427 HI	CACIT	6/28/16
Municipal Government	Pittsburg, CA	Y			102276 HI	CACIT	6/28/16
Harbor Pilot	United States	H		192.31 AW		HCHRON4	2017
Hazardous Materials Coordinator							
Public Works Department, Municipal Government	Folsom, CA	Y			68439 HI	CACIT	6/28/16
Hazardous Materials Removal Worker	Alabama	Y	27466 AE	36457 AW	40952 AEX	ALBLS	6/16
	Birmingham-Hoover MSA, AL	Y	28978 AE	35315 AW	38483 AEX	ALBLS	6/16
	Alaska	Y	46630 FQ	52560 MW	58390 TQ	USBLS	5/15
	Anchorage MSA, AK	Y	47340 FQ	52950 MW	58590 TQ	USBLS	5/15
	Arizona	Y	26960 FQ	30720 MW	37320 TQ	USBLS	5/15
	Phoenix-Mesa-Scottsdale MSA, AZ	Y	26650 FQ	30210 MW	36280 TQ	USBLS	5/15
	Tucson MSA, AZ	Y	28540 FQ	32690 MW	38130 TQ	USBLS	5/15
	Arkansas	Y	23090 FQ	27730 MW	33030 TQ	USBLS	5/15
	Little Rock-North Little Rock-Conway MSA, AR	Y	21860 FQ	26950 MW	33450 TQ	USBLS	5/15
	California	H	15.74 FQ	18.95 MW	23.96 TQ	CABLS	1/16-3/16
	Anaheim-Santa Ana-Irvine PMSA, CA	H	15.64 FQ	18.00 MW	22.78 TQ	CABLS	1/16-3/16
	Los Angeles-Long Beach-Glendale PMSA, CA	H	15.97 FQ	20.14 MW	26.50 TQ	CABLS	1/16-3/16
	Oakland-Hayward-Berkeley PMSA, CA	H	15.64 FQ	18.80 MW	22.46 TQ	CABLS	1/16-3/16
	Riverside-San Bernardino-Ontario MSA, CA	H	14.55 FQ	17.02 MW	20.25 TQ	CABLS	1/16-3/16
	Sacramento–Roseville–Arden-Arcade MSA, CA	H	17.95 FQ	21.83 MW	27.69 TQ	CABLS	1/16-3/16
	San Diego-Carlsbad MSA, CA	H	15.80 FQ	19.11 MW	23.84 TQ	CABLS	1/16-3/16
	San Francisco-Redwood City-South San Francisco PMSA, CA	H	16.03 FQ	19.33 MW	23.42 TQ	CABLS	1/16-3/16
	Colorado	Y	35940 FQ	40920 MW	46450 TQ	USBLS	5/15
	Denver-Aurora-Lakewood MSA, CO	Y	35670 FQ	40280 MW	45930 TQ	USBLS	5/15
	Connecticut	Y		42495 MW		CTBLS	1/16-3/16
	Bridgeport-Stamford-Norwalk MSA, CT	Y	34170 FQ	51680 MW	57900 TQ	USBLS	5/15
	Hartford-West Hartford-East Hartford MSA, CT	Y	34660 FQ	39260 MW	46060 TQ	USBLS	5/15
	Wilmington PMSA, DE-MD-NJ	Y	34900 FQ	38300 MW	43580 TQ	USBLS	5/15
	District of Columbia	Y	33570 FQ	42480 MW	48970 TQ	USBLS	5/15
	Washington-Arlington-Alexandria PMSA, DC-VA-MD-WV	Y	28850 FQ	34520 MW	45480 TQ	USBLS	5/15
	Florida	H	12.89 AE	15.41 MW	18.26 AEX	FLBLS	7/16-9/16
	Fort Lauderdale-Pompano Beach-Deerfield Beach PMSA, FL	H	13.33 AE	16.68 MW	18.48 AEX	FLBLS	7/16-9/16
	Miami-Miami Beach-Kendall PMSA, FL	H	13.63 AE	17.00 MW	18.44 AEX	FLBLS	7/16-9/16
	Orlando-Kissimmee-Sanford MSA, FL	H	13.21 AE	14.22 MW	15.22 AEX	FLBLS	7/16-9/16

AE	Average entry wage	AWR	Average wage range	H	Hourly
AEX	Average experienced wage	B	Biweekly	HI	Highest wage paid
ATC	Average total compensation	D	Daily	HR	High end range
AW	Average wage paid	FQ	First quartile wage	LO	Lowest wage paid

LR	Low end range	MTC	Median total compensation	TCC	Total cash compensation
M	Monthly	MW	Median wage paid	TQ	Third quartile wage
MCC	Median cash compensation	MWR	Median wage range	W	Weekly
ME	Median entry wage	S	See annotated source	Y	Yearly

Occupation/Type/Industry	Location	Per	Low	Mid	High	Source	Date
Hazardous Materials Removal Worker							
	Tampa-St. Petersburg-Clearwater MSA, FL	H	11.46 AE	13.51 MW	14.59 AEX	FLBLS	7/16-9/16
	Georgia	Y	29240 FQ	37320 MW	45660 TQ	USBLS	5/15
	Atlanta-Sandy Springs-Roswell MSA, GA	Y	32570 FQ	39940 MW	46190 TQ	USBLS	5/15
	Augusta-Richmond County MSA, GA-SC	Y	49700 FQ	54140 MW	58590 TQ	USBLS	5/15
	Hawaii	Y	18850 FQ	28030 MW	40230 TQ	USBLS	5/15
	Urban Honolulu MSA, HI	Y	18780 FQ	27140 MW	38870 TQ	USBLS	5/15
	Idaho	Y	65120 FQ	69990 MW	74860 TQ	USBLS	5/15
	Boise City MSA, ID	Y	29030 FQ	33480 MW	37700 TQ	USBLS	5/15
	Illinois	Y	31870 FQ	40650 MW	63140 TQ	USBLS	5/15
	Chicago-Naperville-Arlington Heights PMSA, IL	Y	30470 FQ	38960 MW	56820 TQ	USBLS	5/15
	Lake County-Kenosha County PMSA, IL-WI	Y	35880 FQ	50930 MW	67350 TQ	USBLS	5/15
	Indiana	Y	29220 FQ	36860 MW	47070 TQ	USBLS	5/15
	Gary PMSA, IN	Y	32220 FQ	65030 MW	72740 TQ	USBLS	5/15
	Indianapolis-Carmel-Anderson MSA, IN	Y	29950 FQ	40180 MW	47160 TQ	USBLS	5/15
	Iowa	Y	30830 FQ	37300 MW	50890 TQ	USBLS	5/15
	Des Moines-West Des Moines MSA, IA	Y	30390 FQ	36060 MW	45830 TQ	USBLS	5/15
	Kansas	Y	30970 FQ	37300 MW	53570 TQ	USBLS	5/15
	Wichita MSA, KS	Y	25180 FQ	28320 MW	31600 TQ	USBLS	5/15
	Kentucky	Y	25510 FQ	30790 MW	43650 TQ	USBLS	5/15
	Louisville-Jefferson County MSA, KY-IN	Y	25570 FQ	30820 MW	43920 TQ	USBLS	5/15
	Louisiana	Y	28450 FQ	35470 MW	44470 TQ	USBLS	5/15
	Baton Rouge MSA, LA	Y	30780 FQ	37520 MW	46310 TQ	USBLS	5/15
	New Orleans-Metairie MSA, LA	Y	32380 FQ	38550 MW	48400 TQ	USBLS	5/15
	Maine	Y	31720 FQ	39700 MW	45440 TQ	USBLS	5/15
	Maryland	Y	25882 AE	37329 MW	43053 AEX	MDBLS	4/16
	Baltimore-Columbia-Towson MSA, MD	Y	28820 FQ	34780 MW	40760 TQ	USBLS	5/15
	Massachusetts	Y	33750 FQ	38930 MW	49150 TQ	USBLS	5/15
	Boston-Cambridge-Newton NECTA, MA	Y	33550 FQ	38630 MW	46390 TQ	USBLS	5/15
	Worcester MSA, MA-CT	Y	34550 FQ	40780 MW	46770 TQ	USBLS	5/15
	Michigan	Y	36480 FQ	45930 MW	54850 TQ	USBLS	5/15
	Detroit-Dearborn-Livonia PMSA, MI	Y	37130 FQ	46760 MW	54670 TQ	USBLS	5/15
	Minnesota	Y	39089 FQ	53781 MW	61368 TQ	MNBLS	1/16-3/16
	Minneapolis-St. Paul-Bloomington MSA, MN-WI	Y	38343 FQ	53781 MW	61227 TQ	MNBLS	1/16-3/16
	Mississippi	Y	27140 FQ	32940 MW	38380 TQ	USBLS	5/15
	Missouri	Y	27370 FQ	35130 MW	46630 TQ	USBLS	5/15
	Kansas City MSA, MO-KS	Y	32910 FQ	42020 MW	56530 TQ	USBLS	5/15
	St. Louis MSA, MO-IL	Y	23900 FQ	36640 MW	52750 TQ	USBLS	5/15
	Montana	Y	35240 FQ	40040 MW	48250 TQ	USBLS	5/15
	Nebraska	Y	32065 FQ	34975 MW	37890 TQ	NEBLS	7/16-9/16
	Nevada	Y	31710 FQ	37300 MW	47290 TQ	USBLS	5/15
	Las Vegas-Henderson-Paradise MSA, NV	Y	31130 FQ	37450 MW	47670 TQ	USBLS	5/15
	New Hampshire	H	17.47 AE	19.40 MW	22.39 AEX	NHBLS	6/16
	Nashua NECTA, NH-MA	Y	43890 FQ	49020 MW	55940 TQ	USBLS	5/15
	New Jersey	Y	44290 FQ	51690 MW	61680 TQ	USBLS	5/15
	Camden PMSA, NJ	Y	41490 FQ	52050 MW	65170 TQ	USBLS	5/15
	Newark PMSA, NJ-PA	Y	44530 FQ	50540 MW	60680 TQ	USBLS	5/15
	New Mexico	Y	36380 FQ	63070 MW	74100 TQ	USBLS	5/15
	Albuquerque MSA, NM	Y	34820 FQ	58570 MW	73580 TQ	USBLS	5/15
	New York	Y	36820 AE	63870 MW	72530 AEX	NYBLS	1/16-3/16
	Buffalo-Cheektowaga-Niagara Falls MSA, NY	Y	32800 FQ	50990 MW	76890 TQ	USBLS	5/15
	Nassau County-Suffolk County PMSA, NY	Y	50310 FQ	63800 MW	72100 TQ	USBLS	5/15
	New York-Jersey City-White Plains PMSA, NY-NJ	Y	50610 FQ	65580 MW	74130 TQ	USBLS	5/15
	Rochester MSA, NY	Y	30300 FQ	37780 MW	51930 TQ	USBLS	5/15
	North Carolina	Y	27280 FQ	31650 MW	38030 TQ	USBLS	5/15

AE	Average entry wage	AWR	Average wage range	H	Hourly
AEX	Average experienced wage	B	Biweekly	HI	Highest wage paid
ATC	Average total compensation	D	Daily	HR	High end range
AW	Average wage paid	FQ	First quartile wage	LO	Lowest wage paid

LR	Low end range	MTC	Median total compensation	TCC	Total cash compensation
M	Monthly	MW	Median wage paid	TQ	Third quartile wage
MCC	Median cash compensation	MWR	Median wage range	W	Weekly
ME	Median entry wage	S	See annotated source	Y	Yearly

Occupation/Type/Industry	Location	Per	Low	Mid	High	Source	Date
Hazardous Materials Removal Worker							
	Charlotte-Concord-Gastonia MSA, NC-SC	Y	27040 FQ	30820 MW	35430 TQ	USBLS	5/15
	Raleigh MSA, NC	Y	28890 FQ	34260 MW	40080 TQ	USBLS	5/15
	North Dakota	Y	37610 FQ	51880 MW	58640 TQ	USBLS	5/15
	Ohio	Y	30350 FQ	38120 MW	64360 TQ	USBLS	5/15
	Cincinnati MSA, OH-KY-IN	Y	27620 FQ	34810 MW	41520 TQ	USBLS	5/15
	Cleveland-Elyria MSA, OH	Y	28380 FQ	34350 MW	51740 TQ	USBLS	5/15
	Columbus MSA, OH	Y	27620 FQ	32730 MW	39140 TQ	USBLS	5/15
	Oklahoma	Y	31810 FQ	34970 MW	38120 TQ	USBLS	5/15
	Oklahoma City MSA, OK	Y	32010 FQ	35970 MW	40390 TQ	USBLS	5/15
	Tulsa MSA, OK	Y	32730 FQ	35270 MW	37810 TQ	USBLS	5/15
	Oregon	H	14.51 FQ	17.25 MW	23.08 TQ	ORBLS	2016
	Portland-Vancouver-Hillsboro MSA, OR-WA	Y	29290 FQ	34450 MW	41270 TQ	USBLS	5/15
	Pennsylvania	Y	32510 FQ	43040 MW	54800 TQ	USBLS	5/15
	Allentown-Bethlehem-Easton MSA, PA-NJ	Y	35580 FQ	50970 MW	58540 TQ	USBLS	5/15
	Montgomery County-Bucks County-Chester County PMSA, PA	Y	25760 FQ	39650 MW	50140 TQ	USBLS	5/15
	Philadelphia PMSA, PA	Y	36580 FQ	52690 MW	58040 TQ	USBLS	5/15
	Pittsburgh MSA, PA	Y	33740 FQ	43230 MW	54620 TQ	USBLS	5/15
	Rhode Island	Y	35540 FQ	51120 MW	57210 TQ	USBLS	5/15
	Providence-Warwick MSA, RI-MA	Y	35750 FQ	45830 MW	54950 TQ	USBLS	5/15
	South Carolina	Y	39680 FQ	52780 MW	57950 TQ	USBLS	5/15
	Charleston-North Charleston MSA, SC	Y	27020 FQ	29960 MW	34470 TQ	USBLS	5/15
	Greenville-Anderson-Mauldin MSA, SC	Y	22990 FQ	30160 MW	45820 TQ	USBLS	5/15
	South Dakota	Y	29430 FQ	35040 MW	43340 TQ	USBLS	5/15
	Tennessee	Y	36750 FQ	49130 MW	69100 TQ	USBLS	5/15
	Knoxville MSA, TN	Y	56270 FQ	67850 MW	76140 TQ	USBLS	5/15
	Memphis MSA, TN-MS-AR	Y	31110 FQ	38240 MW	49940 TQ	USBLS	5/15
	Nashville-Davidson–Murfreesboro–Franklin MSA, TN	Y	18250 FQ	39990 MW	46050 TQ	USBLS	5/15
	Texas	Y	26840 FQ	30510 MW	38370 TQ	USBLS	5/15
	Austin-Round Rock MSA, TX	Y	31660 FQ	34890 MW	38130 TQ	USBLS	5/15
	Dallas-Plano-Irving PMSA, TX	Y	26610 FQ	30050 MW	36540 TQ	USBLS	5/15
	Fort Worth-Arlington PMSA, TX	Y	27120 FQ	29630 MW	35390 TQ	USBLS	5/15
	Houston-The Woodlands-Sugar Land MSA, TX	Y	26800 FQ	30030 MW	38120 TQ	USBLS	5/15
	San Antonio-New Braunfels MSA, TX	Y	25870 FQ	29110 MW	34590 TQ	USBLS	5/15
	Utah	Y	31080 FQ	37350 MW	48050 TQ	USBLS	5/15
	Ogden-Clearfield MSA, UT	Y	28840 FQ	32870 MW	36800 TQ	USBLS	5/15
	Salt Lake City MSA, UT	Y	34430 FQ	43240 MW	51330 TQ	USBLS	5/15
	Vermont	Y	34450 FQ	37610 MW	42810 TQ	USBLS	5/15
	Burlington-South Burlington MSA, VT	Y	34340 FQ	37500 MW	42550 TQ	USBLS	5/15
	Virginia	Y	28670 FQ	33960 MW	41960 TQ	USBLS	5/15
	Richmond MSA, VA	Y	29630 FQ	37530 MW	51010 TQ	USBLS	5/15
	Virginia Beach-Norfolk-Newport News MSA, VA-NC	Y	29080 FQ	33740 MW	37570 TQ	USBLS	5/15
	Washington	H	21.00 FQ	28.12 MW	34.91 TQ	WABLS	3/16
	Seattle-Bellevue-Everett PMSA, WA	H	27.06 FQ	31.17 MW	35.66 TQ	WABLS	3/16
	Tacoma-Lakewood PMSA, WA	H	16.55 FQ	18.98 MW	23.53 TQ	WABLS	3/16
	West Virginia	Y	29270 FQ	34550 MW	44270 TQ	USBLS	5/15
	Wisconsin	Y	32720 FQ	41540 MW	50630 TQ	USBLS	5/15
	Madison MSA, WI	Y	33930 FQ	39340 MW	48410 TQ	USBLS	5/15
	Milwaukee-Waukesha-West Allis MSA, WI	Y	24170 FQ	42460 MW	47360 TQ	USBLS	5/15
	Guam	Y	18780 FQ	25890 MW	29890 TQ	USBLS	5/15
Hazardous Materials Specialist							
Fire Department, Municipal Government	Bakersfield, CA	Y			76195 HI	CACIT	6/28/16
Fire Department, Municipal Government	Orange, CA	Y		91036 AW		CACIT	6/28/16
Fire Department, Municipal Government	Pasadena, CA	Y			92546 HI	CACIT	6/28/16

AE	Average entry wage	AWR	Average wage range	H	Hourly
AEX	Average experienced wage	B	Biweekly	HI	Highest wage paid
ATC	Average total compensation	D	Daily	HR	High end range
AW	Average wage paid	FQ	First quartile wage	LO	Lowest wage paid

LR	Low end range	MTC	Median total compensation	TCC	Total cash compensation
M	Monthly	MW	Median wage paid	TQ	Third quartile wage
MCC	Median cash compensation	MWR	Median wage range	W	Weekly
ME	Median entry wage	S	See annotated source	Y	Yearly

Occupation/Type/Industry	Location	Per	Low	Mid	High	Source	Date
Hazardous Materials Technician							
Fire Department, Municipal Government	Fremont, CA	Y		92789 ᴀᴡ		CACIT	6/28/16
Hazardous Waste Technician							
Municipal Government	Redding, CA	Y		54072 ᴀᴡ		CACIT	6/28/16
Head Athletic Trainer							
Michigan State University	East Lansing, MI	Y			97381 ʜɪ	MSUSAL	10/1/14-9/30/15
Head Boxing Coach							
Recreation Community Services Department, Municipal Government	Baldwin Park, CA	Y			16491 ʜɪ	CACIT	6/28/16
Head Coach							
Football, Big Ten Conference	United States	Y		3510000 ᴀᴡ		FORB02	2016
Football, Big Twelve Conference	United States	Y		3190000 ᴀᴡ		FORB02	2016
Football, Bowling Green State University	Bowling Green, OH	Y			410000 ʜɪ	USAT04	2016
Football, California State University, Fresno	Fresno, CA	Y			1518480 ʜɪ	USAT04	2016
Football, Kansas State University	Manhattan, KS	Y			3100000 ʜɪ	USAT04	2016
Football, Michigan State University	East Lansing, MI	Y			4300000 ʜɪ	USAT04	2016
Football, Ohio State University	Columbus, OH	Y			6003000 ʜɪ	USAT04	2016
Football, Old Dominion University	Norfolk, VA	Y			554590 ʜɪ	USAT04	2016
Football, Southeastern Conference	United States	Y		4100000 ᴀᴡ		FORB02	2016
Football, Stanford University	Stanford, CA	Y			4067219 ʜɪ	USAT04	2016
Football, United States Naval Academy	Annapolis, MD	Y			2000000 ʜɪ	USAT04	2016
Football, University of Alabama	Tuscaloosa, AL	Y			6939395 ʜɪ	USAT04	2016
Football, University of California, Los Angeles	Los Angeles, CA	Y			3450000 ʜɪ	USAT04	2016
Football, University of Michigan	Ann Arbor, MI	Y			9004000 ʜɪ	USAT04	2016
Football, Western Kentucky University	Bowling Green, KY	Y			805600 ʜɪ	USAT04	2016
Men's Basketball, Duke University	Durham, NC	Y			7300000 ʜɪ	FREEP04	2016
Men's Basketball, Michigan State University	East Lansing, MI	Y			4150359 ʜɪ	FREEP04	2016
Men's Basketball, University of Arizona	Tucson, AZ	Y			4945000 ʜɪ	FREEP04	2016
Men's Basketball, University of Michigan	Ann Arbor, MI	Y			3370000 ʜɪ	FREEP03	2017
Men's Cross Country/Track and Field, Eastern Michigan University	Ypsilanti, MI	Y			92990 ʜɪ	MLV02	2015
Men's Golf, Eastern Michigan University	Ypsilanti, MI	Y			58738 ʜɪ	MLV02	2015
Men's Soccer, Baccalaureate Institution	United States	Y		48535 ᴍᴡ		CHE02	2015-2016
Men's Soccer, Master's Institution	United States	Y		53000 ᴍᴡ		CHE02	2015-2016
Men's Soccer, Research University	United States	Y		83325 ᴍᴡ		CHE02	2015-2016
Strength and Conditioning, Baccalaureate Institution	United States	Y		42060 ᴍᴡ		CHE02	2015-2016
Strength and Conditioning, Master's Institution	United States	Y		47174 ᴍᴡ		CHE02	2015-2016
Strength and Conditioning, Research University	United States	Y		73814 ᴍᴡ		CHE02	2015-2016
Women's Cross Country/Track and Field, Eastern Michigan University	Ypsilanti, MI	Y			73062 ʜɪ	MLV02	2015
Women's Golf, Eastern Michigan University	Ypsilanti, MI	Y			67000 ʜɪ	MLV02	2015
Women's Soccer, Baccalaureate Institution	United States	Y		45990 ᴍᴡ		CHE02	2015-2016
Women's Soccer, Master's Institution	United States	Y		52152 ᴍᴡ		CHE02	2015-2016
Women's Soccer, Research University	United States	Y		76658 ᴍᴡ		CHE02	2015-2016
Head of Athletic Compliance							
Baccalaureate Institution	United States	Y		52671 ᴍᴡ		CHE02	2015-2016
Master's Institution	United States	Y		55052 ᴍᴡ		CHE02	2015-2016
Research University	United States	Y		77026 ᴍᴡ		CHE02	2015-2016
Head of Campus Mail Services							
College and University	United States	Y		47614 ᴀᴡ		HED01	2015-2016
Head of Campus Power Plants							
Baccalaureate Institution	United States	Y		75750 ᴍᴡ		CHE02	2015-2016
Master's Institution	United States	Y		67563 ᴍᴡ		CHE02	2015-2016
Research University	United States	Y		80613 ᴍᴡ		CHE02	2015-2016
Head of Catalog Sales							
Music Industry	United States	Y		275000 ᴀᴡ		BBRD01	2014

AE	Average entry wage	**AWR**	Average wage range	**H**	Hourly	**LR** Low end range	**MTC** Median total compensation	**TCC** Total cash compensation
AEX	Average experienced wage	**B**	Biweekly	**HI**	Highest wage paid	**M** Monthly	**MW** Median wage paid	**TQ** Third quartile wage
ATC	Average total compensation	**D**	Daily	**HR**	High end range	**MCC** Median cash compensation	**MWR** Median wage range	**W** Weekly
AW	Average wage paid	**FQ**	First quartile wage	**LO**	Lowest wage paid	**ME** Median entry wage	**S** See annotated source	**Y** Yearly

Occupation/Type/Industry	Location	Per	Low	Mid	High	Source	Date
Head of Licensing							
Independent Music Publishing Firm	United States	Y		150000-175000 AWR		BBRD01	2014
Large Music Publishing Firm	United States	Y		200000-350000 AWR		BBRD01	2014
Head of Minority and Multicultural Student Affairs							
Baccalaureate Institution	United States	Y		58773 MW		CHE02	2015-2016
Master's Institution	United States	Y		61746 MW		CHE02	2015-2016
Research University	United States	Y		80000 MW		CHE02	2015-2016
Head of Women's Athletics Programs							
Baccalaureate Institution	United States	Y		66307 MW		CHE02	2015-2016
Master's Institution	United States	Y		63142 MW		CHE02	2015-2016
Research University	United States	Y		105368 MW		CHE02	2015-2016
Health and Safety Engineer							
Except Mining Safety Engineers and Inspectors	Alabama	Y	65543 AE	95246 AW	110107 AEX	ALBLS	6/16
Except Mining Safety Engineers and Inspectors	Birmingham-Hoover MSA, AL	Y	67938 AE	88742 AW	99150 AEX	ALBLS	6/16
Except Mining Safety Engineers and Inspectors	Alaska	Y	102580 FQ	130250 MW	151830 TQ	USBLS	5/15
Except Mining Safety Engineers and Inspectors	Anchorage MSA, AK	Y	101800 FQ	134150 MW	154030 TQ	USBLS	5/15
Except Mining Safety Engineers and Inspectors	Arizona	Y	49690 FQ	74140 MW	97170 TQ	USBLS	5/15
Except Mining Safety Engineers and Inspectors	Phoenix-Mesa-Scottsdale MSA, AZ	Y	60660 FQ	80940 MW	102220 TQ	USBLS	5/15
Except Mining Safety Engineers and Inspectors	Tucson MSA, AZ	Y	41050 FQ	68180 MW	96620 TQ	USBLS	5/15
Except Mining Safety Engineers and Inspectors	Arkansas	Y	54430 FQ	65270 MW	79360 TQ	USBLS	5/15
Except Mining Safety Engineers and Inspectors	California	H	37.85 FQ	50.46 MW	57.59 TQ	CABLS	1/16-3/16
Except Mining Safety Engineers and Inspectors	Anaheim-Santa Ana-Irvine PMSA, CA	H	43.04 FQ	51.08 MW	56.87 TQ	CABLS	1/16-3/16
Except Mining Safety Engineers and Inspectors	Los Angeles-Long Beach-Glendale PMSA, CA	H	39.09 FQ	51.08 MW	58.17 TQ	CABLS	1/16-3/16
Except Mining Safety Engineers and Inspectors	Oakland-Hayward-Berkeley PMSA, CA	H	46.34 FQ	51.09 MW	58.38 TQ	CABLS	1/16-3/16
Except Mining Safety Engineers and Inspectors	Riverside-San Bernardino-Ontario MSA, CA	H	26.63 FQ	43.18 MW	51.21 TQ	CABLS	1/16-3/16
Except Mining Safety Engineers and Inspectors	Sacramento–Roseville–Arden-Arcade MSA, CA	H	41.92 FQ	51.08 MW	55.71 TQ	CABLS	1/16-3/16
Except Mining Safety Engineers and Inspectors	San Diego-Carlsbad MSA, CA	H	40.24 FQ	49.22 MW	56.28 TQ	CABLS	1/16-3/16
Except Mining Safety Engineers and Inspectors	San Francisco-Redwood City-South San Francisco PMSA, CA	H	31.88 FQ	51.08 MW	61.65 TQ	CABLS	1/16-3/16
Except Mining Safety Engineers and Inspectors	Colorado	Y	78120 FQ	95570 MW	116040 TQ	USBLS	5/15
Except Mining Safety Engineers and Inspectors	Denver-Aurora-Lakewood MSA, CO	Y	83720 FQ	98000 MW	117280 TQ	USBLS	5/15
Except Mining Safety Engineers and Inspectors	Connecticut	Y		97584 MW		CTBLS	1/16-3/16
Except Mining Safety Engineers and Inspectors	Hartford-West Hartford-East Hartford MSA, CT	Y	82420 FQ	97690 MW	113000 TQ	USBLS	5/15

Occupation/Type/Industry	Location	Per	Low	Mid	High	Source	Date
Health and Safety Engineer							
Except Mining Safety Engineers and Inspectors	Delaware	Y	69230 FQ	83840 MW	116890 TQ	USBLS	5/15
Except Mining Safety Engineers and Inspectors	Wilmington PMSA, DE-MD-NJ	Y	67770 FQ	80220 MW	111000 TQ	USBLS	5/15
Except Mining Safety Engineers and Inspectors	District of Columbia	Y	84140 FQ	99510 MW	115890 TQ	USBLS	5/15
Except Mining Safety Engineers and Inspectors	Washington-Arlington-Alexandria PMSA, DC-VA-MD-WV	Y	80640 FQ	100680 MW	126340 TQ	USBLS	5/15
Except Mining Safety Engineers and Inspectors	Florida	H	25.54 AE	34.59 MW	41.40 AEX	FLBLS	7/16-9/16
Except Mining Safety Engineers and Inspectors	Fort Lauderdale-Pompano Beach-Deerfield Beach PMSA, FL	H	22.77 AE	30.12 MW	35.56 AEX	FLBLS	7/16-9/16
Except Mining Safety Engineers and Inspectors	Miami-Miami Beach-Kendall PMSA, FL	H	26.28 AE	32.30 MW	38.66 AEX	FLBLS	7/16-9/16
Except Mining Safety Engineers and Inspectors	Orlando-Kissimmee-Sanford MSA, FL	H	24.04 AE	36.18 MW	43.14 AEX	FLBLS	7/16-9/16
Except Mining Safety Engineers and Inspectors	Tampa-St. Petersburg-Clearwater MSA, FL	H	29.58 AE	37.97 MW	43.41 AEX	FLBLS	7/16-9/16
Except Mining Safety Engineers and Inspectors	Georgia	Y	53260 FQ	70810 MW	91140 TQ	USBLS	5/15
Except Mining Safety Engineers and Inspectors	Atlanta-Sandy Springs-Roswell MSA, GA	Y	53070 FQ	72310 MW	94610 TQ	USBLS	5/15
Except Mining Safety Engineers and Inspectors	Augusta-Richmond County MSA, GA-SC	Y	65800 FQ	82930 MW	111960 TQ	USBLS	5/15
Except Mining Safety Engineers and Inspectors	Hawaii	Y	55270 FQ	69470 MW	85440 TQ	USBLS	5/15
Except Mining Safety Engineers and Inspectors	Urban Honolulu MSA, HI	Y	54220 FQ	68830 MW	84090 TQ	USBLS	5/15
Except Mining Safety Engineers and Inspectors	Idaho	Y	83130 FQ	100190 MW	116830 TQ	USBLS	5/15
Except Mining Safety Engineers and Inspectors	Illinois	Y	60280 FQ	83610 MW	100000 TQ	USBLS	5/15
Except Mining Safety Engineers and Inspectors	Chicago-Naperville-Arlington Heights PMSA, IL	Y	59690 FQ	85150 MW	97280 TQ	USBLS	5/15
Except Mining Safety Engineers and Inspectors	Lake County-Kenosha County PMSA, IL-WI	Y	59930 FQ	84420 MW	112810 TQ	USBLS	5/15
Except Mining Safety Engineers and Inspectors	Indiana	Y	60750 FQ	73200 MW	88620 TQ	USBLS	5/15
Except Mining Safety Engineers and Inspectors	Gary PMSA, IN	Y	68780 FQ	76240 MW	89550 TQ	USBLS	5/15
Except Mining Safety Engineers and Inspectors	Indianapolis-Carmel-Anderson MSA, IN	Y	66900 FQ	77920 MW	92940 TQ	USBLS	5/15
Except Mining Safety Engineers and Inspectors	Iowa	Y	67250 FQ	77860 MW	93410 TQ	USBLS	5/15
Except Mining Safety Engineers and Inspectors	Kansas	Y	57790 FQ	72850 MW	98180 TQ	USBLS	5/15
Except Mining Safety Engineers and Inspectors	Wichita MSA, KS	Y	64820 FQ	78220 MW	95720 TQ	USBLS	5/15
Except Mining Safety Engineers and Inspectors	Kentucky	Y	50760 FQ	72430 MW	90820 TQ	USBLS	5/15
Except Mining Safety Engineers and Inspectors	Louisville-Jefferson County MSA, KY-IN	Y	56060 FQ	70170 MW	80040 TQ	USBLS	5/15
Except Mining Safety Engineers and Inspectors	Louisiana	Y	58640 FQ	78290 MW	104520 TQ	USBLS	5/15
Except Mining Safety Engineers and Inspectors	Baton Rouge MSA, LA	Y	68190 FQ	83030 MW	98760 TQ	USBLS	5/15

AE	Average entry wage	AWR	Average wage range	H	Hourly	LR	Low end range	MTC	Median total compensation	TCC	Total cash compensation
AEX	Average experienced wage	B	Biweekly	HI	Highest wage paid	M	Monthly	MW	Median wage paid	TQ	Third quartile wage
ATC	Average total compensation	D	Daily	HR	High end range	MCC	Median cash compensation	MWR	Median wage range	W	Weekly
AW	Average wage paid	FQ	First quartile wage	LO	Lowest wage paid	ME	Median entry wage	S	See annotated source	Y	Yearly

Occupation/Type/Industry	Location	Per	Low	Mid	High	Source	Date
Health and Safety Engineer							
Except Mining Safety Engineers and Inspectors	New Orleans-Metairie MSA, LA	Y	59980 FQ	97680 MW	131560 TQ	USBLS	5/15
Except Mining Safety Engineers and Inspectors	Maine	Y	50510 FQ	70970 MW	87210 TQ	USBLS	5/15
Except Mining Safety Engineers and Inspectors	Maryland	Y	64242 AE	95569 MW	111232 AEX	MDBLS	4/16
Except Mining Safety Engineers and Inspectors	Baltimore-Columbia-Towson MSA, MD	Y	74150 FQ	93280 MW	117110 TQ	USBLS	5/15
Except Mining Safety Engineers and Inspectors	Massachusetts	Y	70460 FQ	91590 MW	115710 TQ	USBLS	5/15
Except Mining Safety Engineers and Inspectors	Boston-Cambridge-Newton NECTA, MA	Y	74010 FQ	99370 MW	120450 TQ	USBLS	5/15
Except Mining Safety Engineers and Inspectors	Worcester MSA, MA-CT	Y	38270 FQ	71930 MW	87660 TQ	USBLS	5/15
Except Mining Safety Engineers and Inspectors	Michigan	Y	73690 FQ	93410 MW	115760 TQ	USBLS	5/15
Except Mining Safety Engineers and Inspectors	Detroit-Dearborn-Livonia PMSA, MI	Y	86110 FQ	105910 MW	125880 TQ	USBLS	5/15
Except Mining Safety Engineers and Inspectors	Minnesota	Y	59828 FQ	79162 MW	102489 TQ	MNBLS	1/16-3/16
Except Mining Safety Engineers and Inspectors	Minneapolis-St. Paul-Bloomington MSA, MN-WI	Y	59596 FQ	77176 MW	100533 TQ	MNBLS	1/16-3/16
Except Mining Safety Engineers and Inspectors	Mississippi	Y	41210 FQ	58870 MW	77220 TQ	USBLS	5/15
Except Mining Safety Engineers and Inspectors	Missouri	Y	58710 FQ	81970 MW	111630 TQ	USBLS	5/15
Except Mining Safety Engineers and Inspectors	Kansas City MSA, MO-KS	Y	59380 FQ	76590 MW	105710 TQ	USBLS	5/15
Except Mining Safety Engineers and Inspectors	St. Louis MSA, MO-IL	Y	64960 FQ	82110 MW	108510 TQ	USBLS	5/15
Except Mining Safety Engineers and Inspectors	Montana	Y	35660 FQ	39690 MW	64390 TQ	USBLS	5/15
Except Mining Safety Engineers and Inspectors	Billings MSA, MT	Y	33900 FQ	36190 MW	38470 TQ	USBLS	5/15
Except Mining Safety Engineers and Inspectors	Nebraska	Y	65060 FQ	75930 MW	92510 TQ	NEBLS	7/16-9/16
Except Mining Safety Engineers and Inspectors	Omaha-Council Bluffs MSA, NE-IA	Y	65720 FQ	76560 MW	99135 TQ	NEBLS	7/16-9/16
Except Mining Safety Engineers and Inspectors	Nevada	Y	61730 FQ	79180 MW	113010 TQ	USBLS	5/15
Except Mining Safety Engineers and Inspectors	Las Vegas-Henderson-Paradise MSA, NV	Y	60460 FQ	79020 MW	113860 TQ	USBLS	5/15
Except Mining Safety Engineers and Inspectors	New Hampshire	H	29.77 AE	43.35 MW	54.22 AEX	NHBLS	6/16
Except Mining Safety Engineers and Inspectors	New Jersey	Y	80150 FQ	96050 MW	116100 TQ	USBLS	5/15
Except Mining Safety Engineers and Inspectors	Camden PMSA, NJ	Y	76140 FQ	93040 MW	111570 TQ	USBLS	5/15
Except Mining Safety Engineers and Inspectors	Newark PMSA, NJ-PA	Y	89690 FQ	105060 MW	121330 TQ	USBLS	5/15
Except Mining Safety Engineers and Inspectors	New Mexico	Y	54130 FQ	69190 MW	88550 TQ	USBLS	5/15
Except Mining Safety Engineers and Inspectors	Albuquerque MSA, NM	Y	55500 FQ	82150 MW	97970 TQ	USBLS	5/15
Except Mining Safety Engineers and Inspectors	New York	Y	62180 AE	89690 MW	104530 AEX	NYBLS	1/16-3/16
Except Mining Safety Engineers and Inspectors	Buffalo-Cheektowaga-Niagara Falls MSA, NY	Y	61920 FQ	81930 MW	92860 TQ	USBLS	5/15
Except Mining Safety Engineers and Inspectors	Nassau County-Suffolk County PMSA, NY	Y	84320 FQ	105930 MW	122260 TQ	USBLS	5/15

Occupation/Type/Industry	Location	Per	Low	Mid	High	Source	Date
Health and Safety Engineer							
Except Mining Safety Engineers and Inspectors	New York-Jersey City-White Plains PMSA, NY-NJ	Y	71830 FQ	90680 MW	110810 TQ	USBLS	5/15
Except Mining Safety Engineers and Inspectors	Rochester MSA, NY	Y	81840 FQ	105890 MW	121890 TQ	USBLS	5/15
Except Mining Safety Engineers and Inspectors	North Carolina	Y	59050 FQ	74980 MW	91590 TQ	USBLS	5/15
Except Mining Safety Engineers and Inspectors	Charlotte-Concord-Gastonia MSA, NC-SC	Y	57530 FQ	74600 MW	90230 TQ	USBLS	5/15
Except Mining Safety Engineers and Inspectors	Raleigh MSA, NC	Y	61160 FQ	76250 MW	90990 TQ	USBLS	5/15
Except Mining Safety Engineers and Inspectors	North Dakota	Y	65090 FQ	78450 MW	90240 TQ	USBLS	5/15
Except Mining Safety Engineers and Inspectors	Ohio	Y	65870 FQ	82320 MW	102140 TQ	USBLS	5/15
Except Mining Safety Engineers and Inspectors	Cincinnati MSA, OH-KY-IN	Y	69890 FQ	90160 MW	108600 TQ	USBLS	5/15
Except Mining Safety Engineers and Inspectors	Cleveland-Elyria MSA, OH	Y	63150 FQ	80260 MW	97090 TQ	USBLS	5/15
Except Mining Safety Engineers and Inspectors	Columbus MSA, OH	Y	67400 FQ	81210 MW	101640 TQ	USBLS	5/15
Except Mining Safety Engineers and Inspectors	Oklahoma	Y	61810 FQ	83010 MW	104860 TQ	USBLS	5/15
Except Mining Safety Engineers and Inspectors	Oklahoma City MSA, OK	Y	65280 FQ	89730 MW	108140 TQ	USBLS	5/15
Except Mining Safety Engineers and Inspectors	Tulsa MSA, OK	Y	64870 FQ	84600 MW	113070 TQ	USBLS	5/15
Except Mining Safety Engineers and Inspectors	Oregon	H	33.42 FQ	41.25 MW	47.81 TQ	ORBLS	2016
Except Mining Safety Engineers and Inspectors	Portland-Vancouver-Hillsboro MSA, OR-WA	Y	58800 FQ	78450 MW	95980 TQ	USBLS	5/15
Except Mining Safety Engineers and Inspectors	Pennsylvania	Y	60450 FQ	77400 MW	103880 TQ	USBLS	5/15
Except Mining Safety Engineers and Inspectors	Allentown-Bethlehem-Easton MSA, PA-NJ	Y	61900 FQ	85900 MW	117810 TQ	USBLS	5/15
Except Mining Safety Engineers and Inspectors	Harrisburg-Carlisle MSA, PA	Y	50200 FQ	62040 MW	80290 TQ	USBLS	5/15
Except Mining Safety Engineers and Inspectors	Montgomery County-Bucks County-Chester County PMSA, PA	Y	77600 FQ	95510 MW	118350 TQ	USBLS	5/15
Except Mining Safety Engineers and Inspectors	Philadelphia PMSA, PA	Y	63940 FQ	84870 MW	119420 TQ	USBLS	5/15
Except Mining Safety Engineers and Inspectors	Pittsburgh MSA, PA	Y	57050 FQ	69490 MW	107790 TQ	USBLS	5/15
Except Mining Safety Engineers and Inspectors	Providence-Warwick MSA, RI-MA	Y	61740 FQ	77570 MW	93780 TQ	USBLS	5/15
Except Mining Safety Engineers and Inspectors	South Carolina	Y	37150 FQ	62240 MW	86560 TQ	USBLS	5/15
Except Mining Safety Engineers and Inspectors	Charleston-North Charleston MSA, SC	Y	31120 FQ	36120 MW	45850 TQ	USBLS	5/15
Except Mining Safety Engineers and Inspectors	Greenville-Anderson-Mauldin MSA, SC	Y	36790 FQ	50660 MW	75570 TQ	USBLS	5/15
Except Mining Safety Engineers and Inspectors	South Dakota	Y	56220 FQ	68830 MW	83070 TQ	USBLS	5/15
Except Mining Safety Engineers and Inspectors	Tennessee	Y	63690 FQ	80450 MW	100670 TQ	USBLS	5/15
Except Mining Safety Engineers and Inspectors	Knoxville MSA, TN	Y	72220 FQ	87970 MW	106980 TQ	USBLS	5/15
Except Mining Safety Engineers and Inspectors	Memphis MSA, TN-MS-AR	Y	66020 FQ	79970 MW	106040 TQ	USBLS	5/15
Except Mining Safety Engineers and Inspectors	Nashville-Davidson–Murfreesboro–Franklin MSA, TN	Y	55570 FQ	70360 MW	85900 TQ	USBLS	5/15

AE	Average entry wage	AWR	Average wage range	H	Hourly	LR	Low end range	MTC	Median total compensation	TCC	Total cash compensation
AEX	Average experienced wage	B	Biweekly	HI	Highest wage paid	M	Monthly	MW	Median wage paid	TQ	Third quartile wage
ATC	Average total compensation	D	Daily	HR	High end range	MCC	Median cash compensation	MWR	Median wage range	W	Weekly
AW	Average wage paid	FQ	First quartile wage	LO	Lowest wage paid	ME	Median entry wage	S	See annotated source	Y	Yearly

Occupation/Type/Industry	Location	Per	Low	Mid	High	Source	Date
Health and Safety Engineer							
Except Mining Safety Engineers and Inspectors	Texas	Y	72900 FQ	94900 MW	126290 TQ	USBLS	5/15
Except Mining Safety Engineers and Inspectors	Austin-Round Rock MSA, TX	Y	75620 FQ	93940 MW	130650 TQ	USBLS	5/15
Except Mining Safety Engineers and Inspectors	Dallas-Plano-Irving PMSA, TX	Y	67820 FQ	84620 MW	101680 TQ	USBLS	5/15
Except Mining Safety Engineers and Inspectors	Fort Worth-Arlington PMSA, TX	Y	71850 FQ	88680 MW	114700 TQ	USBLS	5/15
Except Mining Safety Engineers and Inspectors	Houston-The Woodlands-Sugar Land MSA, TX	Y	81830 FQ	103310 MW	138500 TQ	USBLS	5/15
Except Mining Safety Engineers and Inspectors	San Antonio-New Braunfels MSA, TX	Y	60440 FQ	91260 MW	118670 TQ	USBLS	5/15
Except Mining Safety Engineers and Inspectors	Utah	Y	56870 FQ	73470 MW	96680 TQ	USBLS	5/15
Except Mining Safety Engineers and Inspectors	Ogden-Clearfield MSA, UT	Y	57890 FQ	70140 MW	84800 TQ	USBLS	5/15
Except Mining Safety Engineers and Inspectors	Provo-Orem MSA, UT	Y	54950 FQ	72220 MW	85210 TQ	USBLS	5/15
Except Mining Safety Engineers and Inspectors	Salt Lake City MSA, UT	Y	61010 FQ	84180 MW	106240 TQ	USBLS	5/15
Except Mining Safety Engineers and Inspectors	Vermont	Y	57880 FQ	79830 MW	99760 TQ	USBLS	5/15
Except Mining Safety Engineers and Inspectors	Burlington-South Burlington MSA, VT	Y	66530 FQ	84520 MW	100250 TQ	USBLS	5/15
Except Mining Safety Engineers and Inspectors	Virginia	Y	64760 FQ	87860 MW	112720 TQ	USBLS	5/15
Except Mining Safety Engineers and Inspectors	Richmond MSA, VA	Y	65870 FQ	86930 MW	105010 TQ	USBLS	5/15
Except Mining Safety Engineers and Inspectors	Virginia Beach-Norfolk-Newport News MSA, VA-NC	Y	55260 FQ	77120 MW	96720 TQ	USBLS	5/15
Except Mining Safety Engineers and Inspectors	Washington	H	37.95 FQ	45.75 MW	54.53 TQ	WABLS	3/16
Except Mining Safety Engineers and Inspectors	Seattle-Bellevue-Everett PMSA, WA	H	37.86 FQ	45.18 MW	53.24 TQ	WABLS	3/16
Except Mining Safety Engineers and Inspectors	Tacoma-Lakewood PMSA, WA	H	39.50 FQ	43.19 MW	46.68 TQ	WABLS	3/16
Except Mining Safety Engineers and Inspectors	West Virginia	Y	44720 FQ	67070 MW	102610 TQ	USBLS	5/15
Except Mining Safety Engineers and Inspectors	Huntington-Ashland MSA, WV-KY-OH	Y	54540 FQ	64660 MW	93950 TQ	USBLS	5/15
Except Mining Safety Engineers and Inspectors	Wisconsin	Y	48420 FQ	63970 MW	76870 TQ	USBLS	5/15
Except Mining Safety Engineers and Inspectors	Madison MSA, WI	Y	56160 FQ	70480 MW	83150 TQ	USBLS	5/15
Except Mining Safety Engineers and Inspectors	Milwaukee-Waukesha-West Allis MSA, WI	Y	47870 FQ	65140 MW	75840 TQ	USBLS	5/15
Except Mining Safety Engineers and Inspectors	Wyoming	Y	61460 FQ	73530 MW	90880 TQ	USBLS	5/15
Except Mining Safety Engineers and Inspectors	Puerto Rico	Y	30090 FQ	51280 MW	73940 TQ	USBLS	5/15
Except Mining Safety Engineers and Inspectors	San Juan-Carolina-Caguas MSA, PR	Y	29140 FQ	38820 MW	71900 TQ	USBLS	5/15
Health Coach							
Full-Time	United States	Y		83000 AW		HCARE1	2016
Health Educator	Alabama	Y	29652 AE	43831 AW	50915 AEX	ALBLS	6/16
	Birmingham-Hoover MSA, AL	Y	28725 AE	44351 AW	52159 AEX	ALBLS	6/16
	Alaska	Y	45180 FQ	59220 MW	72380 TQ	USBLS	5/15
	Anchorage MSA, AK	Y	46920 FQ	59700 MW	72120 TQ	USBLS	5/15
	Arizona	Y	33330 FQ	43040 MW	59520 TQ	USBLS	5/15

AE	Average entry wage	AWR	Average wage range	H	Hourly
AEX	Average experienced wage	B	Biweekly	HI	Highest wage paid
ATC	Average total compensation	D	Daily	HR	High end range
AW	Average wage paid	FQ	First quartile wage	LO	Lowest wage paid

LR	Low end range	MTC	Median total compensation	TCC	Total cash compensation
M	Monthly	MW	Median wage paid	TQ	Third quartile wage
MCC	Median cash compensation	MWR	Median wage range	W	Weekly
ME	Median entry wage	S	See annotated source	Y	Yearly

Health Educator

Occupation/Type/Industry	Location	Per	Low	Mid	High	Source	Date
Health Educator	Phoenix-Mesa-Scottsdale MSA, AZ	Y	35270 FQ	47130 MW	62680 TQ	USBLS	5/15
	Tucson MSA, AZ	Y	27640 FQ	32790 MW	41790 TQ	USBLS	5/15
	Arkansas	Y	30670 FQ	39470 MW	49770 TQ	USBLS	5/15
	Little Rock-North Little Rock-Conway MSA, AR	Y	31460 FQ	40210 MW	49110 TQ	USBLS	5/15
	California	H	19.87 FQ	26.42 MW	37.05 TQ	CABLS	1/16-3/16
	Anaheim-Santa Ana-Irvine PMSA, CA	H	20.68 FQ	24.65 MW	33.66 TQ	CABLS	1/16-3/16
	Los Angeles-Long Beach-Glendale PMSA, CA	H	18.47 FQ	25.05 MW	34.87 TQ	CABLS	1/16-3/16
	Oakland-Hayward-Berkeley PMSA, CA	H	21.90 FQ	30.43 MW	37.64 TQ	CABLS	1/16-3/16
	Riverside-San Bernardino-Ontario MSA, CA	H	20.27 FQ	27.56 MW	37.88 TQ	CABLS	1/16-3/16
	Sacramento–Roseville–Arden-Arcade MSA, CA	H	19.00 FQ	27.27 MW	38.88 TQ	CABLS	1/16-3/16
	San Diego-Carlsbad MSA, CA	H	19.36 FQ	24.36 MW	29.94 TQ	CABLS	1/16-3/16
	San Francisco-Redwood City-South San Francisco PMSA, CA	H	24.61 FQ	39.25 MW	50.38 TQ	CABLS	1/16-3/16
	Colorado	Y	38540 FQ	51490 MW	70790 TQ	USBLS	5/15
	Denver-Aurora-Lakewood MSA, CO	Y	40300 FQ	58980 MW	78550 TQ	USBLS	5/15
	Connecticut	Y		51800 MW		CTBLS	1/16-3/16
	Bridgeport-Stamford-Norwalk MSA, CT	Y	46470 FQ	60510 MW	83090 TQ	USBLS	5/15
	Hartford-West Hartford-East Hartford MSA, CT	Y	37420 FQ	50040 MW	67050 TQ	USBLS	5/15
	Delaware	Y	45280 FQ	61120 MW	77830 TQ	USBLS	5/15
	Wilmington PMSA, DE-MD-NJ	Y	48870 FQ	63310 MW	78150 TQ	USBLS	5/15
	District of Columbia	Y	55940 FQ	83570 MW	102300 TQ	USBLS	5/15
	Washington-Arlington-Alexandria PMSA, DC-VA-MD-WV	Y	55380 FQ	76040 MW	96980 TQ	USBLS	5/15
	Florida	H	15.21 AE	22.09 MW	29.09 AEX	FLBLS	7/16-9/16
	Fort Lauderdale-Pompano Beach-Deerfield Beach PMSA, FL	H	14.33 AE	20.28 MW	27.64 AEX	FLBLS	7/16-9/16
	Miami-Miami Beach-Kendall PMSA, FL	H	16.43 AE	26.85 MW	34.48 AEX	FLBLS	7/16-9/16
	Orlando-Kissimmee-Sanford MSA, FL	H	13.88 AE	21.80 MW	28.95 AEX	FLBLS	7/16-9/16
	Tampa-St. Petersburg-Clearwater MSA, FL	H	16.63 AE	22.70 MW	29.24 AEX	FLBLS	7/16-9/16
	Georgia	Y	50250 FQ	74060 MW	103070 TQ	USBLS	5/15
	Atlanta-Sandy Springs-Roswell MSA, GA	Y	58180 FQ	87230 MW	109550 TQ	USBLS	5/15
	Augusta-Richmond County MSA, GA-SC	Y	31770 FQ	52260 MW	70250 TQ	USBLS	5/15
	Hawaii	Y	40820 FQ	48970 MW	61000 TQ	USBLS	5/15
	Urban Honolulu MSA, HI	Y	43200 FQ	53940 MW	70380 TQ	USBLS	5/15
	Idaho	Y	41680 FQ	54530 MW	70610 TQ	USBLS	5/15
	Boise City MSA, ID	Y	46310 FQ	58080 MW	71830 TQ	USBLS	5/15
	Illinois	Y	41400 FQ	51020 MW	71430 TQ	USBLS	5/15
	Chicago-Naperville-Arlington Heights PMSA, IL	Y	42010 FQ	49250 MW	69370 TQ	USBLS	5/15
	Lake County-Kenosha County PMSA, IL-WI	Y	43990 FQ	56260 MW	73270 TQ	USBLS	5/15
	Indiana	Y	36950 FQ	56040 MW	74760 TQ	USBLS	5/15
	Gary PMSA, IN	Y	46790 FQ	57790 MW	72600 TQ	USBLS	5/15
	Indianapolis-Carmel-Anderson MSA, IN	Y	39990 FQ	59020 MW	80000 TQ	USBLS	5/15
	Iowa	Y	43480 FQ	54050 MW	67170 TQ	USBLS	5/15
	Des Moines-West Des Moines MSA, IA	Y	46910 FQ	56730 MW	74330 TQ	USBLS	5/15
	Kansas	Y	42750 FQ	51620 MW	66280 TQ	USBLS	5/15
	Wichita MSA, KS	Y	39110 FQ	47870 MW	60720 TQ	USBLS	5/15
	Kentucky	Y	34590 FQ	45880 MW	59840 TQ	USBLS	5/15
	Louisville-Jefferson County MSA, KY-IN	Y	44120 FQ	56650 MW	70330 TQ	USBLS	5/15

AE	Average entry wage	AWR	Average wage range	H	Hourly	LR	Low end range
AEX	Average experienced wage	B	Biweekly	HI	Highest wage paid	M	Monthly
ATC	Average total compensation	D	Daily	HR	High end range	MCC	Median cash compensation
AW	Average wage paid	FQ	First quartile wage	LO	Lowest wage paid	ME	Median entry wage

MTC	Median total compensation	TCC	Total cash compensation
MW	Median wage paid	TQ	Third quartile wage
MWR	Median wage range	W	Weekly
S	See annotated source	Y	Yearly

Health Educator

Occupation/Type/Industry	Location	Per	Low	Mid	High	Source	Date
	Louisiana	Y	35440 FQ	48410 MW	61900 TQ	USBLS	5/15
	Baton Rouge MSA, LA	Y	51890 FQ	60350 MW	74040 TQ	USBLS	5/15
	New Orleans-Metairie MSA, LA	Y	36110 FQ	48580 MW	63620 TQ	USBLS	5/15
	Maine	Y	38310 FQ	47280 MW	58830 TQ	USBLS	5/15
	Portland-South Portland MSA, ME	Y	40670 FQ	51230 MW	64270 TQ	USBLS	5/15
	Maryland	Y	47178 AE	86171 MW	105668 AEX	MDBLS	4/16
	Baltimore-Columbia-Towson MSA, MD	Y	40660 FQ	57440 MW	97750 TQ	USBLS	5/15
	Salisbury MSA, MD-DE	Y	36320 FQ	51320 MW	75110 TQ	USBLS	5/15
	Massachusetts	Y	37740 FQ	51860 MW	64650 TQ	USBLS	5/15
	Boston-Cambridge-Newton NECTA, MA	Y	41270 FQ	52910 MW	68370 TQ	USBLS	5/15
	Worcester MSA, MA-CT	Y	34950 FQ	44520 MW	57710 TQ	USBLS	5/15
	Michigan	Y	38710 FQ	50220 MW	67380 TQ	USBLS	5/15
	Detroit-Dearborn-Livonia PMSA, MI	Y	33840 FQ	55310 MW	70070 TQ	USBLS	5/15
	Grand Rapids-Wyoming MSA, MI	Y	35620 FQ	46440 MW	61660 TQ	USBLS	5/15
	Minnesota	Y	39082 FQ	48447 MW	62469 TQ	MNBLS	1/16-3/16
	Minneapolis-St. Paul-Bloomington MSA, MN-WI	Y	38901 FQ	48145 MW	63709 TQ	MNBLS	1/16-3/16
	Mississippi	Y	29010 FQ	33650 MW	47280 TQ	USBLS	5/15
	Jackson MSA, MS	Y	29020 FQ	35700 MW	48810 TQ	USBLS	5/15
	Missouri	Y	37190 FQ	45290 MW	59350 TQ	USBLS	5/15
	Kansas City MSA, MO-KS	Y	42820 FQ	51830 MW	68200 TQ	USBLS	5/15
	St. Louis MSA, MO-IL	Y	38160 FQ	48870 MW	64170 TQ	USBLS	5/15
	Montana	Y	32190 FQ	42360 MW	52160 TQ	USBLS	5/15
	Omaha-Council Bluffs MSA, NE-IA	Y	34350 FQ	43615 MW	57920 TQ	NEBLS	7/16-9/16
	Nevada	Y	49510 FQ	66950 MW	88110 TQ	USBLS	5/15
	Las Vegas-Henderson-Paradise MSA, NV	Y	52160 FQ	73060 MW	92220 TQ	USBLS	5/15
	New Hampshire	H	15.91 AE	23.88 MW	27.91 AEX	NHBLS	6/16
	Manchester NECTA, NH	H	20.22 AE	26.21 MW	29.52 AEX	NHBLS	6/16
	Nashua NECTA, NH-MA	Y	28370 FQ	40470 MW	47030 TQ	USBLS	5/15
	New Jersey	Y	45450 FQ	56540 MW	69530 TQ	USBLS	5/15
	Camden PMSA, NJ	Y	43990 FQ	55990 MW	67580 TQ	USBLS	5/15
	Newark PMSA, NJ-PA	Y	51960 FQ	61200 MW	76580 TQ	USBLS	5/15
	Trenton MSA, NJ	Y	44640 FQ	58250 MW	81440 TQ	USBLS	5/15
	New Mexico	Y	30990 FQ	45680 MW	66700 TQ	USBLS	5/15
	Albuquerque MSA, NM	Y	38510 FQ	59590 MW	71810 TQ	USBLS	5/15
	New York	Y	34180 AE	51480 MW	65540 AEX	NYBLS	1/16-3/16
	Buffalo-Cheektowaga-Niagara Falls MSA, NY	Y	22980 FQ	40570 MW	59190 TQ	USBLS	5/15
	Nassau County-Suffolk County PMSA, NY	Y	28750 FQ	46050 MW	66550 TQ	USBLS	5/15
	New York-Jersey City-White Plains PMSA, NY-NJ	Y	41800 FQ	52870 MW	65460 TQ	USBLS	5/15
	Rochester MSA, NY	Y	38820 FQ	50150 MW	58520 TQ	USBLS	5/15
	North Carolina	Y	39660 FQ	49260 MW	64120 TQ	USBLS	5/15
	Charlotte-Concord-Gastonia MSA, NC-SC	Y	40280 FQ	51740 MW	62460 TQ	USBLS	5/15
	Raleigh MSA, NC	Y	41270 FQ	48420 MW	60670 TQ	USBLS	5/15
	North Dakota	Y	45580 FQ	51390 MW	57360 TQ	USBLS	5/15
	Fargo MSA, ND-MN	Y	41390 FQ	54550 MW	66240 TQ	USBLS	5/15
	Ohio	Y	40060 FQ	54570 MW	69950 TQ	USBLS	5/15
	Cincinnati MSA, OH-KY-IN	Y	50330 FQ	61160 MW	79460 TQ	USBLS	5/15
	Cleveland-Elyria MSA, OH	Y	42890 FQ	55290 MW	72740 TQ	USBLS	5/15
	Columbus MSA, OH	Y	38020 FQ	52180 MW	67230 TQ	USBLS	5/15
	Oklahoma	Y	41310 FQ	49450 MW	64870 TQ	USBLS	5/15
	Oklahoma City MSA, OK	Y	41440 FQ	48310 MW	63910 TQ	USBLS	5/15
	Tulsa MSA, OK	Y	46400 FQ	61330 MW	72540 TQ	USBLS	5/15
	Oregon	H	21.49 FQ	29.29 MW	37.80 TQ	ORBLS	2016
	Portland-Vancouver-Hillsboro MSA, OR-WA	Y	45760 FQ	62830 MW	77500 TQ	USBLS	5/15
	Pennsylvania	Y	43690 FQ	56550 MW	74140 TQ	USBLS	5/15
	Allentown-Bethlehem-Easton MSA, PA-NJ	Y	45260 FQ	70420 MW	135600 TQ	USBLS	5/15
	Harrisburg-Carlisle MSA, PA	Y	55330 FQ	60440 MW	72800 TQ	USBLS	5/15

Occupation/Type/Industry	Location	Per	Low	Mid	High	Source	Date
Health Educator	Montgomery County-Bucks County-Chester County						
	PMSA, PA	Y	46470 FQ	65910 MW	80020 TQ	USBLS	5/15
	Philadelphia PMSA, PA	Y	45720 FQ	60020 MW	79670 TQ	USBLS	5/15
	Pittsburgh MSA, PA	Y	42390 FQ	54310 MW	65670 TQ	USBLS	5/15
	Rhode Island	Y	62910 FQ	76140 MW	87990 TQ	USBLS	5/15
	Providence-Warwick MSA, RI-MA	Y	47250 FQ	71860 MW	85650 TQ	USBLS	5/15
	South Carolina	Y	32770 FQ	45780 MW	64400 TQ	USBLS	5/15
	Charleston-North Charleston MSA, SC	Y	25290 FQ	32540 MW	53040 TQ	USBLS	5/15
	Columbia MSA, SC	Y	33920 FQ	39840 MW	62370 TQ	USBLS	5/15
	Greenville-Anderson-Mauldin MSA, SC	Y	34860 FQ	46850 MW	62390 TQ	USBLS	5/15
	South Dakota	Y	36180 FQ	46710 MW	57970 TQ	USBLS	5/15
	Sioux Falls MSA, SD	Y	35900 FQ	45260 MW	58380 TQ	USBLS	5/15
	Tennessee	Y	29000 FQ	36640 MW	48420 TQ	USBLS	5/15
	Knoxville MSA, TN	Y	37420 FQ	43630 MW	49040 TQ	USBLS	5/15
	Memphis MSA, TN-MS-AR	Y	31000 FQ	37440 MW	53640 TQ	USBLS*	5/15
	Nashville-Davidson–Murfreesboro–Franklin MSA, TN	Y	26380 FQ	32020 MW	46770 TQ	USBLS	5/15
	Texas	Y	36160 FQ	50150 MW	72230 TQ	USBLS	5/15
	Austin-Round Rock MSA, TX	Y	34600 FQ	42750 MW	56170 TQ	USBLS	5/15
	Dallas-Plano-Irving PMSA, TX	Y	35990 FQ	62070 MW	85830 TQ	USBLS	5/15
	Fort Worth-Arlington PMSA, TX	Y	34860 FQ	48460 MW	73380 TQ	USBLS	5/15
	Houston-The Woodlands-Sugar Land MSA, TX	Y	39900 FQ	50170 MW	70760 TQ	USBLS	5/15
	San Antonio-New Braunfels MSA, TX	Y	37380 FQ	49550 MW	66570 TQ	USBLS	5/15
	Utah	Y	33280 FQ	42950 MW	62070 TQ	USBLS	5/15
	Ogden-Clearfield MSA, UT	Y	31800 FQ	37380 MW	46230 TQ	USBLS	5/15
	Provo-Orem MSA, UT	Y	41600 FQ	48340 MW	60600 TQ	USBLS	5/15
	Salt Lake City MSA, UT	Y	32130 FQ	41150 MW	64370 TQ	USBLS	5/15
	Vermont	Y	42250 FQ	51310 MW	61060 TQ	USBLS	5/15
	Burlington-South Burlington MSA, VT	Y	43960 FQ	52670 MW	61060 TQ	USBLS	5/15
	Virginia	Y	40400 FQ	52180 MW	66970 TQ	USBLS	5/15
	Richmond MSA, VA	Y	40080 FQ	49950 MW	65530 TQ	USBLS	5/15
	Virginia Beach-Norfolk-Newport News MSA, VA-NC	Y	37180 FQ	45290 MW	57750 TQ	USBLS	5/15
	Washington	H	19.98 FQ	26.02 MW	33.55 TQ	WABLS	3/16
	Seattle-Bellevue-Everett PMSA, WA	H	19.19 FQ	24.70 MW	34.38 TQ	WABLS	3/16
	Tacoma-Lakewood PMSA, WA	H	15.31 FQ	20.06 MW	29.19 TQ	WABLS	3/16
	West Virginia	Y	24230 FQ	36130 MW	55690 TQ	USBLS	5/15
	Huntington-Ashland MSA, WV-KY-OH	Y	32820 FQ	37380 MW	47560 TQ	USBLS	5/15
	Wisconsin	Y	29940 FQ	51540 MW	64110 TQ	USBLS	5/15
	Madison MSA, WI	Y	30530 FQ	52380 MW	67880 TQ	USBLS	5/15
	Milwaukee-Waukesha-West Allis MSA, WI	Y	29420 FQ	52800 MW	65290 TQ	USBLS	5/15
	Wyoming	Y	35960 FQ	47450 MW	52840 TQ	USBLS	5/15
	Cheyenne MSA, WY	Y	46430 FQ	50570 MW	64900 TQ	USBLS	5/15
	Puerto Rico	Y	22600 FQ	29140 MW	36380 TQ	USBLS	5/15
	San Juan-Carolina-Caguas MSA, PR	Y	23000 FQ	29900 MW	37300 TQ	USBLS	5/15
Health Reference Librarian							
Municipal Government	Detroit, MI	M	3267 LO		3700 HI	DETGOV	2016
Health Services Administrator	United States	Y		92810 MW		AAHS	2016
Health Specialties Teacher							
Postsecondary	Alaska	Y	57830 FQ	76500 MW	91680 TQ	USBLS	5/15
Postsecondary	Arizona	Y	70930 FQ	98050 MW	166770 TQ	USBLS	5/15
Postsecondary	Phoenix-Mesa-Scottsdale MSA, AZ	Y	68700 FQ	92340 MW	131690 TQ	USBLS	5/15
Postsecondary	Tucson MSA, AZ	Y	85960 FQ	157490 MW		USBLS	5/15
Postsecondary	Arkansas	Y	48180 FQ	78470 MW	161550 TQ	USBLS	5/15

AE	Average entry wage	AWR	Average wage range	H	Hourly	LR	Low end range	MTC	Median total compensation	TCC	Total cash compensation
AEX	Average experienced wage	B	Biweekly	HI	Highest wage paid	M	Monthly	MW	Median wage paid	TQ	Third quartile teage
ATC	Average total compensation	D	Daily	HR	High end range	MCC	Median cash compensation	MWR	Median wage range	W	Weekly
AW	Average wage paid	FQ	First quartile wage	LO	Lowest wage paid	ME	Median entry wage	S	See annotated source	Y	Yearly

Health Specialties Teacher

Occupation/Type/Industry	Location	Per	Low	Mid	High	Source	Date
Health Specialties Teacher							
Postsecondary	Little Rock-North Little Rock-Conway MSA, AR	Y	63810 FQ	105720 MW		USBLS	5/15
Postsecondary	California	Y		119132 AW		CABLS	1/16-3/16
Postsecondary	Anaheim-Santa Ana-Irvine PMSA, CA	Y		130859 AW		CABLS	1/16-3/16
Postsecondary	Los Angeles-Long Beach-Glendale PMSA, CA	Y		116636 AW		CABLS	1/16-3/16
Postsecondary	Riverside-San Bernardino-Ontario MSA, CA	Y		116028 AW		CABLS	1/16-3/16
Postsecondary	Sacramento–Roseville–Arden-Arcade MSA, CA	Y		91964 AW		CABLS	1/16-3/16
Postsecondary	San Diego-Carlsbad MSA, CA	Y		117803 AW		CABLS	1/16-3/16
Postsecondary	San Francisco-Redwood City-South San Francisco PMSA, CA	Y		107516 AW		CABLS	1/16-3/16
Postsecondary	Colorado	Y	67470 FQ	110900 MW	178420 TQ	USBLS	5/15
Postsecondary	Denver-Aurora-Lakewood MSA, CO	Y	80500 FQ	125810 MW		USBLS	5/15
Postsecondary	Connecticut	Y		131001 MW		CTBLS	1/16-3/16
Postsecondary	Hartford-West Hartford-East Hartford MSA, CT	Y	71780 FQ	117220 MW		USBLS	5/15
Postsecondary	Delaware	Y	65870 FQ	73770 MW	91720 TQ	USBLS	5/15
Postsecondary	Wilmington PMSA, DE-MD-NJ	Y	64440 FQ	74380 MW	98360 TQ	USBLS	5/15
Postsecondary	Washington-Arlington-Alexandria PMSA, DC-VA-MD-WV	Y	58020 FQ	87600 MW	152280 TQ	USBLS	5/15
Postsecondary	Florida	Y	40488 AE	67394 MW	95261 AEX	FLBLS	7/16-9/16
Postsecondary	Fort Lauderdale-Pompano Beach-Deerfield Beach PMSA, FL	Y	59791 AE	91336 MW	116064 AEX	FLBLS	7/16-9/16
Postsecondary	Miami-Miami Beach-Kendall PMSA, FL	Y	48894 AE	86374 MW	113617 AEX	FLBLS	7/16-9/16
Postsecondary	Orlando-Kissimmee-Sanford MSA, FL	Y	37737 AE	60491 MW	92613 AEX	FLBLS	7/16-9/16
Postsecondary	Tampa-St. Petersburg-Clearwater MSA, FL	Y	49303 AE	65768 MW	83046 AEX	FLBLS	7/16-9/16
Postsecondary	Augusta-Richmond County MSA, GA-SC	Y	47120 FQ	54720 MW	60570 TQ	USBLS	5/15
Postsecondary	Idaho	Y	55120 FQ	81820 MW	119060 TQ	USBLS	5/15
Postsecondary	Boise City MSA, ID	Y	19780 FQ	45920 MW	56180 TQ	USBLS	5/15
Postsecondary	Indiana	Y	62720 FQ	94600 MW	157210 TQ	USBLS	5/15
Postsecondary	Iowa	Y	81470 FQ	122070 MW		USBLS	5/15
Postsecondary	Des Moines-West Des Moines MSA, IA	Y	54800 FQ	87060 MW	118320 TQ	USBLS	5/15
Postsecondary	Kansas	Y	62950 FQ	87950 MW	113470 TQ	USBLS	5/15
Postsecondary	Kentucky	Y	48620 FQ	66610 MW	85900 TQ	USBLS	5/15
Postsecondary	Louisville-Jefferson County MSA, KY-IN	Y	51100 FQ	67980 MW	87670 TQ	USBLS	5/15
Postsecondary	Salisbury MSA, MD-DE	Y	59460 FQ	70800 MW	84090 TQ	USBLS	5/15
Postsecondary	Massachusetts	Y	69930 FQ	102950 MW	155880 TQ	USBLS	5/15
Postsecondary	Boston-Cambridge-Newton NECTA, MA	Y	70570 FQ	108370 MW	169250 TQ	USBLS	5/15
Postsecondary	Worcester MSA, MA-CT	Y	76290 FQ	102830 MW	139800 TQ	USBLS	5/15
Postsecondary	Michigan	Y	73190 FQ	116410 MW		USBLS	5/15
Postsecondary	Detroit-Dearborn-Livonia PMSA, MI	Y	49120 FQ	78340 MW	94140 TQ	USBLS	5/15
Postsecondary	Grand Rapids-Wyoming MSA, MI	Y	51830 FQ	75280 MW	95680 TQ	USBLS	5/15
Postsecondary	Minnesota	Y	54848 FQ	76662 MW	124968 TQ	MNBLS	1/16-3/16
Postsecondary	Minneapolis-St. Paul-Bloomington MSA, MN-WI	Y	56058 FQ	81269 MW	131994 TQ	MNBLS	1/16-3/16
Postsecondary	Mississippi	Y	79520 FQ	122810 MW		USBLS	5/15
Postsecondary	Jackson MSA, MS	Y	87680 FQ	154500 MW		USBLS	5/15
Postsecondary	Missouri	Y	62060 FQ	91130 MW	154210 TQ	USBLS	5/15
Postsecondary	Kansas City MSA, MO-KS	Y	65030 FQ	91990 MW	123410 TQ	USBLS	5/15
Postsecondary	St. Louis MSA, MO-IL	Y	59710 FQ	81120 MW	115500 TQ	USBLS	5/15
Postsecondary	Montana	Y	34600 FQ	56790 MW	74000 TQ	USBLS	5/15
Postsecondary	Billings MSA, MT	Y	18030 FQ	19290 MW	45520 TQ	USBLS	5/15
Postsecondary	Nebraska	Y	57505 FQ	85735 MW	117230 TQ	NEBLS	7/16-9/16
Postsecondary	Nevada	Y	43360 FQ	85690 MW	171620 TQ	USBLS	5/15

AE Average entry wage	**AWR** Average wage range	**H** Hourly	**LR** Low end range	**MTC** Median total compensation	**TCC** Total cash compensation
AEX Average experienced wage	**B** Biweekly	**HI** Highest wage paid	**M** Monthly	**MW** Median wage paid	**TQ** Third quartile wage
ATC Average total compensation	**D** Daily	**HR** High end range	**MCC** Median cash compensation	**MWR** Median wage range	**W** Weekly
AW Average wage paid	**FQ** First quartile wage	**LO** Lowest wage paid	**ME** Median entry wage	**S** See annotated source	**Y** Yearly

Occupation/Type/Industry	Location	Per	Low	Mid	High	Source	Date
Health Specialties Teacher							
Postsecondary	Las Vegas-Henderson-Paradise MSA, NV	Y	42390 FQ	52360 MW	115260 TQ	USBLS	5/15
Postsecondary	New Hampshire	Y	64359 AE	98502 MW	153187 AEX	NHBLS	6/16
Postsecondary	Manchester NECTA, NH	Y	66234 AE	77062 MW	82054 AEX	NHBLS	6/16
Postsecondary	New Jersey	Y	66100 FQ	90960 MW	133860 TQ	USBLS	5/15
Postsecondary	Newark PMSA, NJ-PA	Y	69410 FQ	89780 MW	124370 TQ	USBLS	5/15
Postsecondary	New Mexico	Y	71950 FQ	112680 MW	180680 TQ	USBLS	5/15
Postsecondary	Albuquerque MSA, NM	Y	77900 FQ	128620 MW		USBLS	5/15
Postsecondary	New York	Y	55970 AE	102140 MW	154850 AEX	NYBLS	1/16-3/16
Postsecondary	Buffalo-Cheektowaga-Niagara Falls MSA, NY	Y	50340 FQ	72920 MW	104770 TQ	USBLS	5/15
Postsecondary	New York-Jersey City-White Plains PMSA, NY-NJ	Y	77860 FQ	110590 MW	163530 TQ	USBLS	5/15
Postsecondary	Rochester MSA, NY	Y	76890 FQ	117650 MW	175980 TQ	USBLS	5/15
Postsecondary	North Carolina	Y	57730 FQ	103990 MW	174000 TQ	USBLS	5/15
Postsecondary	Charlotte-Concord-Gastonia MSA, NC-SC	Y	57940 FQ	72530 MW	104230 TQ	USBLS	5/15
Postsecondary	Raleigh MSA, NC	Y	55010 FQ	91220 MW	127930 TQ	USBLS	5/15
Postsecondary	North Dakota	Y	74870 FQ	101360 MW	120570 TQ	USBLS	5/15
Postsecondary	Fargo MSA, ND-MN	Y	51120 FQ	65230 MW	106910 TQ	USBLS	5/15
Postsecondary	Ohio	Y	51340 FQ	80850 MW	139380 TQ	USBLS	5/15
Postsecondary	Cincinnati MSA, OH-KY-IN	Y	80820 FQ	139040 MW		USBLS	5/15
Postsecondary	Cleveland-Elyria MSA, OH	Y	38900 FQ	54770 MW	99700 TQ	USBLS	5/15
Postsecondary	Columbus MSA, OH	Y	50690 FQ	63490 MW	110140 TQ	USBLS	5/15
Postsecondary	Oklahoma	Y	57570 FQ	74470 MW	97670 TQ	USBLS	5/15
Postsecondary	Oklahoma City MSA, OK	Y	64460 FQ	78050 MW	102720 TQ	USBLS	5/15
Postsecondary	Tulsa MSA, OK	Y	41300 FQ	50650 MW	62700 TQ	USBLS	5/15
Postsecondary	Oregon	Y	76232 FQ	119264 MW		ORBLS	2016
Postsecondary	Portland-Vancouver-Hillsboro MSA, OR-WA	Y	82790 FQ	135670 MW		USBLS	5/15
Postsecondary	Pennsylvania	Y	52060 FQ	75210 MW	114550 TQ	USBLS	5/15
Postsecondary	Allentown-Bethlehem-Easton MSA, PA-NJ	Y	50820 FQ	63700 MW	91590 TQ	USBLS	5/15
Postsecondary	Montgomery County-Bucks County-Chester County PMSA, PA	Y	42190 FQ	61460 MW	89480 TQ	USBLS	5/15
Postsecondary	Philadelphia PMSA, PA	Y	59190 FQ	93990 MW	138990 TQ	USBLS	5/15
Postsecondary	Pittsburgh MSA, PA	Y	49430 FQ	71060 MW	105280 TQ	USBLS	5/15
Postsecondary	Rhode Island	Y	70360 FQ	86730 MW	100920 TQ	USBLS	5/15
Postsecondary	Providence-Warwick MSA, RI-MA	Y	67540 FQ	82670 MW	98540 TQ	USBLS	5/15
Postsecondary	South Carolina	Y	34180 FQ	63240 MW	92660 TQ	USBLS	5/15
Postsecondary	Columbia MSA, SC	Y	65840 FQ	82220 MW	105800 TQ	USBLS	5/15
Postsecondary	Greenville-Anderson-Mauldin MSA, SC	Y	18680 FQ	48390 MW	65720 TQ	USBLS	5/15
Postsecondary	South Dakota	Y	57790 FQ	73510 MW	96590 TQ	USBLS	5/15
Postsecondary	Tennessee	Y	39570 FQ	73990 MW	113070 TQ	USBLS	5/15
Postsecondary	Knoxville MSA, TN	Y	31020 FQ	55190 MW	95470 TQ	USBLS	5/15
Postsecondary	Memphis MSA, TN-MS-AR	Y	49690 FQ	86520 MW	120160 TQ	USBLS	5/15
Postsecondary	Nashville-Davidson–Murfreesboro–Franklin MSA, TN	Y	31590 FQ	68840 MW	100630 TQ	USBLS	5/15
Postsecondary	Texas	Y	56090 FQ	83460 MW	143230 TQ	USBLS	5/15
Postsecondary	Austin-Round Rock MSA, TX	Y	50390 FQ	66180 MW	83870 TQ	USBLS	5/15
Postsecondary	Houston-The Woodlands-Sugar Land MSA, TX	Y	57740 FQ	82360 MW	138220 TQ	USBLS	5/15
Postsecondary	Utah	Y	69650 FQ	125970 MW		USBLS	5/15
Postsecondary	Ogden-Clearfield MSA, UT	Y	40570 FQ	48760 MW	68920 TQ	USBLS	5/15
Postsecondary	Provo-Orem MSA, UT	Y	59350 FQ	85390 MW	109180 TQ	USBLS	5/15
Postsecondary	Salt Lake City MSA, UT	Y	79420 FQ	143550 MW		USBLS	5/15
Postsecondary	Vermont	Y	35550 FQ	43790 MW	65540 TQ	USBLS	5/15
Postsecondary	Virginia	Y	39430 FQ	63690 MW	114380 TQ	USBLS	5/15
Postsecondary	Virginia Beach-Norfolk-Newport News MSA, VA-NC	Y	53110 FQ	68400 MW	104220 TQ	USBLS	5/15
Postsecondary	Washington	Y		140639 AW		WABLS	3/16
Postsecondary	Seattle-Bellevue-Everett PMSA, WA	Y		142435 AW		WABLS	3/16
Postsecondary	West Virginia	Y	38760 FQ	54860 MW	63640 TQ	USBLS	5/15
Postsecondary	Wisconsin	Y	55640 FQ	79670 MW	145290 TQ	USBLS	5/15
Postsecondary	Madison MSA, WI	Y	51290 FQ	69230 MW	105950 TQ	USBLS	5/15

AE	Average entry wage	AWR	Average wage range	H	Hourly
AEX	Average experienced wage	B	Biweekly	HI	Highest wage paid
ATC	Average total compensation	D	Daily	HR	High end range
AW	Average wage paid	FQ	First quartile wage	LO	Lowest wage paid

LR	Low end range	MTC	Median total compensation	TCC	Total cash compensation
M	Monthly	MW	Median wage paid	TQ	Third quartile weage
MCC	Median cash compensation	MWR	Median wage range	W	Weekly
ME	Median entry wage	S	See annotated source	Y	Yearly

Occupation/Type/Industry	Location	Per	Low	Mid	High	Source	Date
Health Specialties Teacher							
Postsecondary	Milwaukee-Waukesha-West Allis MSA, WI	Y	70370 FQ	112450 MW		USBLS	5/15
Postsecondary	Wyoming	Y	43520 FQ	62380 MW	85990 TQ	USBLS	5/15
Postsecondary	Cheyenne MSA, WY	Y	38270 FQ	45000 MW	59440 TQ	USBLS	5/15
Postsecondary	Puerto Rico	Y	30690 FQ	53260 MW	85290 TQ	USBLS	5/15
Postsecondary	San Juan-Carolina-Caguas MSA, PR	Y	34900 FQ	58190 MW	87660 TQ	USBLS	5/15
Healthcare Analyst							
Public Health Department, Municipal Government	San Francisco, CA	Y		61560 AW		CACIT	6/28/16
Healthcare Coding Analyst							
Michigan State University	East Lansing, MI	Y			39250 HI	MSUSAL	10/1/14-9/30/15
Healthcare Marketer	United States	Y		139200 AW		MMM01	7/16
Healthcare Social Worker	Alabama	Y	33199 AE	47806 AW	55105 AEX	ALBLS	6/16
	Birmingham-Hoover MSA, AL	Y	33668 AE	48530 AW	55961 AEX	ALBLS	6/16
	Alaska	Y	42430 FQ	55990 MW	71420 TQ	USBLS	5/15
	Anchorage MSA, AK	Y	41480 FQ	58100 MW	73540 TQ	USBLS	5/15
	Arizona	Y	30350 FQ	39900 MW	56790 TQ	USBLS	5/15
	Phoenix-Mesa-Scottsdale MSA, AZ	Y	29420 FQ	37770 MW	54540 TQ	USBLS	5/15
	Tucson MSA, AZ	Y	33480 FQ	42700 MW	55150 TQ	USBLS	5/15
	Arkansas	Y	31380 FQ	41720 MW	56320 TQ	USBLS	5/15
	Little Rock-North Little Rock-Conway MSA, AR	Y	36970 FQ	51340 MW	60810 TQ	USBLS	5/15
	California	H	25.12 FQ	33.00 MW	42.41 TQ	CABLS	1/16-3/16
	Anaheim-Santa Ana-Irvine PMSA, CA	H	28.15 FQ	34.59 MW	42.45 TQ	CABLS	1/16-3/16
	Los Angeles-Long Beach-Glendale PMSA, CA	H	24.74 FQ	32.02 MW	40.93 TQ	CABLS	1/16-3/16
	Oakland-Hayward-Berkeley PMSA, CA	H	27.68 FQ	37.68 MW	46.26 TQ	CABLS	1/16-3/16
	Riverside-San Bernardino-Ontario MSA, CA	H	21.42 FQ	30.17 MW	37.78 TQ	CABLS	1/16-3/16
	Sacramento–Roseville–Arden-Arcade MSA, CA	H	22.66 FQ	33.03 MW	46.17 TQ	CABLS	1/16-3/16
	San Diego-Carlsbad MSA, CA	H	28.85 FQ	35.25 MW	43.69 TQ	CABLS	1/16-3/16
	San Francisco-Redwood City-South San Francisco PMSA, CA	H	24.01 FQ	35.04 MW	46.30 TQ	CABLS	1/16-3/16
	Colorado	Y	40900 FQ	52160 MW	63960 TQ	USBLS	5/15
	Denver-Aurora-Lakewood MSA, CO	Y	45130 FQ	54810 MW	67400 TQ	USBLS	5/15
	Connecticut	Per		63010 MW		CTBLS	1/16-3/16
	Bridgeport-Stamford-Norwalk MSA, CT	Y	56430 FQ	70880 MW	89240 TQ	USBLS	5/15
	Hartford-West Hartford-East Hartford MSA, CT	Y	52010 FQ	62220 MW	75550 TQ	USBLS	5/15
	Delaware	Y	41840 FQ	51310 MW	59620 TQ	USBLS	5/15
	Wilmington PMSA, DE-MD-NJ	Y	40070 FQ	49080 MW	57840 TQ	USBLS	5/15
	District of Columbia	Y	53230 FQ	64020 MW	77670 TQ	USBLS	5/15
	Washington-Arlington-Alexandria PMSA, DC-VA-MD-WV	Y	48120 FQ	60310 MW	72690 TQ	USBLS	5/15
	Florida	H	16.24 AE	23.45 MW	29.82 AEX	FLBLS	7/16-9/16
	Fort Lauderdale-Pompano Beach-Deerfield Beach PMSA, FL	H	20.16 AE	28.94 MW	36.69 AEX	FLBLS	7/16-9/16
	Miami-Miami Beach-Kendall PMSA, FL	H	14.97 AE	22.08 MW	26.77 AEX	FLBLS	7/16-9/16
	Orlando-Kissimmee-Sanford MSA, FL	H	19.68 AE	24.34 MW	32.47 AEX	FLBLS	7/16-9/16
	Tampa-St. Petersburg-Clearwater MSA, FL	H	14.86 AE	21.39 MW	29.35 AEX	FLBLS	7/16-9/16
	Georgia	Y	36180 FQ	45580 MW	57970 TQ	USBLS	5/15
	Atlanta-Sandy Springs-Roswell MSA, GA	Y	37530 FQ	46840 MW	59420 TQ	USBLS	5/15

AE	Average entry wage	AWR	Average wage range	H	Hourly	LR	Low end range	MTC	Median total compensation	TCC	Total cash compensation
AEX	Average experienced wage	B	Biweekly	HI	Highest wage paid	M	Monthly	MW	Median wage paid	TQ	Third quartile wage
ATC	Average total compensation	D	Daily	HR	High end range	MCC	Median cash compensation	MWR	Median wage range	W	Weekly
AW	Average wage paid	FQ	First quartile wage	LO	Lowest wage paid	ME	Median entry wage	S	See annotated source	Y	Yearly

Occupation/Type/Industry	Location	Per	Low	Mid	High	Source	Date
Healthcare Social Worker	Augusta-Richmond County						
	MSA, GA-SC	Y	39170 FQ	51340 MW	64610 TQ	USBLS	5/15
	Hawaii	Y	46380 FQ	60490 MW	73360 TQ	USBLS	5/15
	Urban Honolulu MSA, HI	Y	48680 FQ	62040 MW	74440 TQ	USBLS	5/15
	Idaho	Y	42080 FQ	50460 MW	60070 TQ	USBLS	5/15
	Boise City MSA, ID	Y	43120 FQ	50110 MW	60260 TQ	USBLS	5/15
	Illinois	Y	41570 FQ	55020 MW	69490 TQ	USBLS	5/15
	Chicago-Naperville-Arlington						
	Heights PMSA, IL	Y	44310 FQ	58700 MW	72240 TQ	USBLS	5/15
	Lake County-Kenosha County						
	PMSA, IL-WI	Y	37000 FQ	47100 MW	57820 TQ	USBLS	5/15
	Indiana	Y	34500 FQ	43930 MW	57760 TQ	USBLS	5/15
	Gary PMSA, IN	Y	41340 FQ	48390 MW	61890 TQ	USBLS	5/15
	Indianapolis-Carmel-Anderson						
	MSA, IN	Y	35580 FQ	47370 MW	61820 TQ	USBLS	5/15
	Iowa	Y	36130 FQ	45110 MW	54660 TQ	USBLS	5/15
	Des Moines-West Des Moines						
	MSA, IA	Y	43300 FQ	50540 MW	58350 TQ	USBLS	5/15
	Kansas	Y	39900 FQ	47560 MW	58090 TQ	USBLS	5/15
	Wichita MSA, KS	Y	40920 FQ	48760 MW	59910 TQ	USBLS	5/15
	Kentucky	Y	36210 FQ	45870 MW	55650 TQ	USBLS	5/15
	Louisville-Jefferson County						
	MSA, KY-IN	Y	38990 FQ	47910 MW	56880 TQ	USBLS	5/15
	Louisiana	Y	38990 FQ	47520 MW	58050 TQ	USBLS	5/15
	Baton Rouge MSA, LA	Y	36690 FQ	45910 MW	56740 TQ	USBLS	5/15
	New Orleans-Metairie MSA,						
	LA	Y	41700 FQ	47360 MW	56490 TQ	USBLS	5/15
	Maine	Y	42550 FQ	48280 MW	56770 TQ	USBLS	5/15
	Portland-South Portland MSA,						
	ME	Y	41400 FQ	49380 MW	58930 TQ	USBLS	5/15
	Maryland	Y	34431 AE	54313 MW	64255 AEX	MDBLS	4/16
	Baltimore-Columbia-Towson						
	MSA, MD	Y	43100 FQ	56550 MW	68810 TQ	USBLS	5/15
	Salisbury MSA, MD-DE	Y	42530 FQ	52260 MW	59180 TQ	USBLS	5/15
	Massachusetts	Y	38670 FQ	52940 MW	64880 TQ	USBLS	5/15
	Boston-Cambridge-Newton						
	NECTA, MA	Y	39810 FQ	52200 MW	63480 TQ	USBLS	5/15
	Worcester MSA, MA-CT	Y	41860 FQ	55190 MW	63580 TQ	USBLS	5/15
	Michigan	Y	42530 FQ	52360 MW	63800 TQ	USBLS	5/15
	Detroit-Dearborn-Livonia						
	PMSA, MI	Y	41120 FQ	48700 MW	61140 TQ	USBLS	5/15
	Grand Rapids-Wyoming MSA,						
	MI	Y	43980 FQ	54160 MW	63610 TQ	USBLS	5/15
	Minnesota	Y	44999 FQ	55463 MW	67005 TQ	MNBLS	1/16-3/16
	Minneapolis-St. Paul-						
	Bloomington MSA, MN-WI	Y	45372 FQ	56511 MW	68497 TQ	MNBLS	1/16-3/16
	Mississippi	Y	34590 FQ	43950 MW	56060 TQ	USBLS	5/15
	Jackson MSA, MS	Y	34540 FQ	44090 MW	55960 TQ	USBLS	5/15
	Missouri	Y	34470 FQ	45070 MW	57450 TQ	USBLS	5/15
	Kansas City MSA, MO-KS	Y	43070 FQ	52150 MW	61070 TQ	USBLS	5/15
	St. Louis MSA, MO-IL	Y	35080 FQ	45040 MW	58430 TQ	USBLS	5/15
	Montana	Y	35720 FQ	44570 MW	55010 TQ	USBLS	5/15
	Billings MSA, MT	Y	43540 FQ	49640 MW	57490 TQ	USBLS	5/15
	Omaha-Council Bluffs MSA,						
	NE-IA	Y	35980 FQ	43950 MW	54145 TQ	NEBLS	7/16-9/16
	Nevada	Y	52420 FQ	59720 MW	71620 TQ	USBLS	5/15
	Las Vegas-Henderson-Paradise						
	MSA, NV	Y	52980 FQ	60040 MW	72310 TQ	USBLS	5/15
	New Hampshire	H	20.18 AE	27.94 MW	31.16 AEX	NHBLS	6/16
	Manchester NECTA, NH	H	19.40 AE	27.74 MW	30.44 AEX	NHBLS	6/16
	Nashua NECTA, NH-MA	Y	45370 FQ	55800 MW	63470 TQ	USBLS	5/15
	New Jersey	Y	51340 FQ	58980 MW	69100 TQ	USBLS	5/15
	Camden PMSA, NJ	Y	52860 FQ	59780 MW	69040 TQ	USBLS	5/15
	Newark PMSA, NJ-PA	Y	52040 FQ	61200 MW	72360 TQ	USBLS	5/15
	Ocean City MSA, NJ	Y	51280 FQ	56960 MW	62880 TQ	USBLS	5/15
	Trenton MSA, NJ	Y	50650 FQ	57320 MW	65300 TQ	USBLS	5/15
	New Mexico	Y	39880 FQ	48700 MW	58250 TQ	USBLS	5/15
	Albuquerque MSA, NM	Y	42940 FQ	51730 MW	60340 TQ	USBLS	5/15
	New York	Y	39890 AE	57350 MW	68570 AEX	NYBLS	1/16-3/16
	Buffalo-Cheektowaga-Niagara						
	Falls MSA, NY	Y	35600 FQ	42140 MW	54040 TQ	USBLS	5/15

AE Average entry wage	**AWR** Average wage range	**H** Hourly	**LR** Low end range	**MTC** Median total compensation	**TCC** Total cash compensation
AEX Average experienced wage	**B** Biweekly	**HI** Highest wage paid	**M** Monthly	**MW** Median wage paid	**TQ** Third quartile wage
ATC Average total compensation	**D** Daily	**HR** High end range	**MCC** Median cash compensation	**MWR** Median wage range	**W** Weekly
AW Average wage paid	**FQ** First quartile wage	**LO** Lowest wage paid	**ME** Median entry wage	**S** See annotated source	**Y** Yearly

Healthcare Social Worker

Occupation/Type/Industry	Location	Per	Low	Mid	High	Source	Date
Healthcare Social Worker	Nassau County-Suffolk County PMSA, NY	Y	48880 FQ	61590 MW	73060 TQ	USBLS	5/15
	New York-Jersey City-White Plains PMSA, NY-NJ	Y	48440 FQ	59980 MW	73100 TQ	USBLS	5/15
	Rochester MSA, NY	Y	38690 FQ	48460 MW	57070 TQ	USBLS	5/15
	North Carolina	Y	41460 FQ	49410 MW	58490 TQ	USBLS	5/15
	Charlotte-Concord-Gastonia MSA, NC-SC	Y	43850 FQ	51480 MW	60270 TQ	USBLS	5/15
	Raleigh MSA, NC	Y	46410 FQ	54790 MW	60180 TQ	USBLS	5/15
	North Dakota	Y	41860 FQ	47600 MW	53730 TQ	USBLS	5/15
	Fargo MSA, ND-MN	Y	38590 FQ	45130 MW	49110 TQ	USBLS	5/15
	Ohio	Y	45870 FQ	54100 MW	60580 TQ	USBLS	5/15
	Cincinnati MSA, OH-KY-IN	Y	44510 FQ	54550 MW	62070 TQ	USBLS	5/15
	Cleveland-Elyria MSA, OH	Y	51900 FQ	56780 MW	61670 TQ	USBLS	5/15
	Columbus MSA, OH	Y	43820 FQ	50540 MW	60510 TQ	USBLS	5/15
	Oklahoma	Y	26940 FQ	38420 MW	54810 TQ	USBLS	5/15
	Oklahoma City MSA, OK	Y	28060 FQ	41230 MW	56540 TQ	USBLS	5/15
	Tulsa MSA, OK	Y	31240 FQ	39100 MW	58820 TQ	USBLS	5/15
	Oregon	H	25.86 FQ	30.98 MW	36.68 TQ	ORBLS	2016
	Portland-Vancouver-Hillsboro MSA, OR-WA	Y	54470 FQ	66660 MW	78900 TQ	USBLS	5/15
	Pennsylvania	Y	39370 FQ	48210 MW	58520 TQ	USBLS	5/15
	Allentown-Bethlehem-Easton MSA, PA-NJ	Y	41610 FQ	48930 MW	59010 TQ	USBLS	5/15
	Harrisburg-Carlisle MSA, PA	Y	32090 FQ	44140 MW	54470 TQ	USBLS	5/15
	Montgomery County-Bucks County-Chester County PMSA, PA	Y	42930 FQ	51600 MW	62120 TQ	USBLS	5/15
	Philadelphia PMSA, PA	Y	40280 FQ	50480 MW	60620 TQ	USBLS	5/15
	Pittsburgh MSA, PA	Y	40370 FQ	49070 MW	57770 TQ	USBLS	5/15
	South Carolina	Y	35890 FQ	47950 MW	60410 TQ	USBLS	5/15
	Charleston-North Charleston MSA, SC	Y	49800 FQ	60530 MW	73590 TQ	USBLS	5/15
	Columbia MSA, SC	Y	28820 FQ	39400 MW	51210 TQ	USBLS	5/15
	Greenville-Anderson-Mauldin MSA, SC	Y	40500 FQ	49040 MW	61480 TQ	USBLS	5/15
	South Dakota	Y	32970 FQ	38090 MW	46430 TQ	USBLS	5/15
	Sioux Falls MSA, SD	Y	38380 FQ	45070 MW	53800 TQ	USBLS	5/15
	Tennessee	Y	37930 FQ	50740 MW	64730 TQ	USBLS	5/15
	Knoxville MSA, TN	Y	34860 FQ	44800 MW	55000 TQ	USBLS	5/15
	Memphis MSA, TN-MS-AR	Y	39220 FQ	53360 MW	67570 TQ	USBLS	5/15
	Nashville-Davidson–Murfreesboro–Franklin MSA, TN	Y	43460 FQ	57590 MW	70910 TQ	USBLS	5/15
	Texas	Y	43070 FQ	54290 MW	64260 TQ	USBLS	5/15
	Austin-Round Rock MSA, TX	Y	45830 FQ	54240 MW	61340 TQ	USBLS	5/15
	Dallas-Plano-Irving PMSA, TX	Y	44880 FQ	56240 MW	69750 TQ	USBLS	5/15
	Fort Worth-Arlington PMSA, TX	Y	46960 FQ	56340 MW	66450 TQ	USBLS	5/15
	Houston-The Woodlands-Sugar Land MSA, TX	Y	44340 FQ	57440 MW	68990 TQ	USBLS	5/15
	San Antonio-New Braunfels MSA, TX	Y	50110 FQ	56890 MW	63960 TQ	USBLS	5/15
	Utah	Y	44480 FQ	54740 MW	64540 TQ	USBLS	5/15
	Ogden-Clearfield MSA, UT	Y	45400 FQ	54190 MW	64010 TQ	USBLS	5/15
	Provo-Orem MSA, UT	Y	35990 FQ	49470 MW	61020 TQ	USBLS	5/15
	Salt Lake City MSA, UT	Y	47740 FQ	57060 MW	67390 TQ	USBLS	5/15
	Vermont	Y	36960 FQ	46090 MW	57900 TQ	USBLS	5/15
	Burlington-South Burlington MSA, VT	Y	35310 FQ	39440 MW	53090 TQ	USBLS	5/15
	Virginia	Y	43470 FQ	53830 MW	65730 TQ	USBLS	5/15
	Richmond MSA, VA	Y	42940 FQ	50820 MW	63190 TQ	USBLS	5/15
	Virginia Beach-Norfolk-Newport News MSA, VA-NC	Y	45430 FQ	57580 MW	69140 TQ	USBLS	5/15
	Washington	H	22.72 FQ	28.53 MW	35.28 TQ	WABLS	3/16
	Seattle-Bellevue-Everett PMSA, WA	H	22.27 FQ	29.30 MW	36.26 TQ	WABLS	3/16
	Tacoma-Lakewood PMSA, WA	H	25.75 FQ	29.20 MW	34.38 TQ	WABLS	3/16
	West Virginia	Y	33770 FQ	44570 MW	56470 TQ	USBLS	5/15
	Huntington-Ashland MSA, WV-KY-OH	Y	36960 FQ	47110 MW	56560 TQ	USBLS	5/15
	Wisconsin	Y	41710 FQ	49720 MW	59150 TQ	USBLS	5/15

AE	Average entry wage	AWR	Average wage range	H	Hourly	LR	Low end range	MTC	Median total compensation	TCC	Total cash compensation
AEX	Average experienced wage	B	Biweekly	HI	Highest wage paid	M	Monthly	MW	Median wage paid	TQ	Third quartile wage
ATC	Average total compensation	D	Daily	HR	High end range	MCC	Median cash compensation	MWR	Median wage range	W	Weekly
AW	Average wage paid	FQ	First quartile wage	LO	Lowest wage paid	ME	Median entry wage	S	See annotated source	Y	Yearly

Occupation/Type/Industry	Location	Per	Low	Mid	High	Source	Date
Healthcare Social Worker	Madison MSA, WI	Y	43560 FQ	50660 MW	60360 TQ	USBLS	5/15
	Milwaukee-Waukesha-West Allis MSA, WI	Y	40630 FQ	48150 MW	58760 TQ	USBLS	5/15
	Wyoming	Y	36890 FQ	48710 MW	60770 TQ	USBLS	5/15
	Puerto Rico	Y	20720 FQ	27700 MW	35660 TQ	USBLS	5/15
	San Juan-Carolina-Caguas MSA, PR	Y	22270 FQ	30240 MW	37160 TQ	USBLS	5/15
Hearing Aid Specialist	United States	Y		43010 MW		FORB01	2015
	Alabama	Y	21987 AE	44657 AW	55991 AEX	ALBLS	6/16
	Arizona	Y	29950 FQ	47850 MW	68670 TQ	USBLS	5/15
	Phoenix-Mesa-Scottsdale MSA, AZ	Y	48340 FQ	67510 MW	74650 TQ	USBLS	5/15
	Tucson MSA, AZ	Y	18170 FQ	25400 MW	33360 TQ	USBLS	5/15
	Arkansas	Y	17900 FQ	32000 MW	41680 TQ	USBLS	5/15
	California	H	20.64 FQ	26.76 MW	33.81 TQ	CABLS	1/16-3/16
	Anaheim-Santa Ana-Irvine PMSA, CA	H	22.35 FQ	33.54 MW	43.37 TQ	CABLS	1/16-3/16
	Los Angeles-Long Beach-Glendale PMSA, CA	H	21.74 FQ	26.85 MW	34.12 TQ	CABLS	1/16-3/16
	Riverside-San Bernardino-Ontario MSA, CA	H	19.78 FQ	25.51 MW	34.39 TQ	CABLS	1/16-3/16
	Sacramento–Roseville–Arden-Arcade MSA, CA	H	20.04 FQ	25.61 MW	33.47 TQ	CABLS	1/16-3/16
	San Diego-Carlsbad MSA, CA	H	21.82 FQ	27.49 MW	31.38 TQ	CABLS	1/16-3/16
	Connecticut	Y		44567 MW		CTBLS	1/16-3/16
	Washington-Arlington-Alexandria PMSA, DC-VA-MD-WV	Y	34880 FQ	38170 MW	50760 TQ	USBLS	5/15
	Florida	H	17.21 AE	27.94 MW	33.98 AEX	FLBLS	7/16-9/16
	Fort Lauderdale-Pompano Beach-Deerfield Beach PMSA, FL	H	21.89 AE	23.89 MW	26.11 AEX	FLBLS	7/16-9/16
	Tampa-St. Petersburg-Clearwater MSA, FL	H	17.11 AE	27.05 MW	35.74 AEX	FLBLS	7/16-9/16
	Georgia	Y	29480 FQ	54360 MW	69670 TQ	USBLS	5/15
	Atlanta-Sandy Springs-Roswell MSA, GA	Y	29360 FQ	53590 MW	68140 TQ	USBLS	5/15
	Idaho	Y	39200 FQ	49590 MW	59720 TQ	USBLS	5/15
	Illinois	Y	23260 FQ	38580 MW	50760 TQ	USBLS	5/15
	Chicago-Naperville-Arlington Heights PMSA, IL	Y	22950 FQ	38340 MW	48570 TQ	USBLS	5/15
	Indiana	Y	28020 FQ	37420 MW	55980 TQ	USBLS	5/15
	Indianapolis-Carmel-Anderson MSA, IN	Y	25380 FQ	34540 MW	41360 TQ	USBLS	5/15
	Iowa	Y	41020 FQ	55520 MW	71340 TQ	USBLS	5/15
	Des Moines-West Des Moines MSA, IA	Y	44470 FQ	65130 MW	73430 TQ	USBLS	5/15
	Kansas	Y	31590 FQ	44200 MW	66620 TQ	USBLS	5/15
	Kentucky	Y	33110 FQ	49070 MW	65170 TQ	USBLS	5/15
	Maine	Y	85380 FQ	95910 MW	108310 TQ	USBLS	5/15
	Maryland	Y	28286 AE	48709 MW	58921 AEX	MDBLS	4/16
	Massachusetts	Y	27090 FQ	45860 MW	60770 TQ	USBLS	5/15
	Detroit-Dearborn-Livonia PMSA, MI	Y	31120 FQ	48370 MW	64020 TQ	USBLS	5/15
	Grand Rapids-Wyoming MSA, MI	Y	28970 FQ	40400 MW	47890 TQ	USBLS	5/15
	Minnesota	Y	51330 FQ	72761 MW	93789 TQ	MNBLS	1/16-3/16
	Minneapolis-St. Paul-Bloomington MSA, MN-WI	Y	54606 FQ	80362 MW	94384 TQ	MNBLS	1/16-3/16
	Missouri	Y	38620 FQ	43490 MW	47760 TQ	USBLS	5/15
	Kansas City MSA, MO-KS	Y	41660 FQ	44860 MW	48060 TQ	USBLS	5/15
	St. Louis MSA, MO-IL	Y	28460 FQ	36240 MW	48160 TQ	USBLS	5/15
	Montana	Y	21880 FQ	24590 MW	58710 TQ	USBLS	5/15
	Nebraska	Y	27280 FQ	29695 MW	36580 TQ	NEBLS	7/16-9/16
	New Jersey	Y	36780 FQ	44440 MW	61230 TQ	USBLS	5/15
	Camden PMSA, NJ	Y	29090 FQ	33120 MW	37420 TQ	USBLS	5/15
	Newark PMSA, NJ-PA	Y	42680 FQ	46510 MW	55310 TQ	USBLS	5/15
	New York	Y	27470 AE	41300 MW	59540 AEX	NYBLS	1/16-3/16
	Nassau County-Suffolk County PMSA, NY	Y	65170 FQ	72970 MW	102940 TQ	USBLS	5/15

AE	Average entry wage	AWR	Average wage range	H	Hourly
AEX	Average experienced wage	B	Biweekly	HI	Highest wage paid
ATC	Average total compensation	D	Daily	HR	High end range
AW	Average wage paid	FQ	First quartile wage	LO	Lowest wage paid

LR	Low end range	MTC	Median total compensation	TCC	Total cash compensation
M	Monthly	MW	Median wage paid	TQ	Third quartile wage
MCC	Median cash compensation	MWR	Median wage range	W	Weekly
ME	Median entry wage	S	See annotated source	Y	Yearly

Occupation/Type/Industry	Location	Per	Low	Mid	High	Source	Date
Hearing Aid Specialist	New York-Jersey City-White Plains PMSA, NY-NJ	Y	28140 FQ	38910 MW	56190 TQ	USBLS	5/15
	North Carolina	Y	34900 FQ	41370 MW	62860 TQ	USBLS	5/15
	Charlotte-Concord-Gastonia MSA, NC-SC	Y	33460 FQ	37070 MW	53290 TQ	USBLS	5/15
	Ohio	Y	32900 FQ	46370 MW	59630 TQ	USBLS	5/15
	Cincinnati MSA, OH-KY-IN	Y	34630 FQ	38160 MW	54500 TQ	USBLS	5/15
	Cleveland-Elyria MSA, OH	Y	38140 FQ	55000 MW	61370 TQ	USBLS	5/15
	Columbus MSA, OH	Y	29130 FQ	48530 MW	59750 TQ	USBLS	5/15
	Oregon	H	17.20 FQ	23.31 MW	28.02 TQ	ORBLS	2016
	Portland-Vancouver-Hillsboro MSA, OR-WA	Y	50360 FQ	55940 MW	61450 TQ	USBLS	5/15
	Pennsylvania	Y	45440 FQ	59750 MW	79670 TQ	USBLS	5/15
	Tennessee	Y	31160 FQ	37520 MW	47810 TQ	USBLS	5/15
	Texas	Y	33790 FQ	56010 MW	70750 TQ	USBLS	5/15
	Austin-Round Rock MSA, TX	Y	40260 FQ	54670 MW	69930 TQ	USBLS	5/15
	Dallas-Plano-Irving PMSA, TX	Y	62110 FQ	67580 MW	73030 TQ	USBLS	5/15
	Utah	Y	46450 FQ	54870 MW	60600 TQ	USBLS	5/15
	Provo-Orem MSA, UT	Y	52090 FQ	56340 MW	60590 TQ	USBLS	5/15
	Vermont	Y	31440 FQ	44710 MW	57650 TQ	USBLS	5/15
	Virginia	Y	34620 FQ	40760 MW	63750 TQ	USBLS	5/15
	Richmond MSA, VA	Y	51090 FQ	65300 MW	73150 TQ	USBLS	5/15
	Washington	H	19.33 FQ	25.13 MW	31.36 TQ	WABLS	3/16
	Seattle-Bellevue-Everett PMSA, WA	H	17.32 FQ	20.45 MW	25.77 TQ	WABLS	3/16
	West Virginia	Y	46820 FQ	54120 MW	59280 TQ	USBLS	5/15
	Wisconsin	Y	31870 FQ	50390 MW	62380 TQ	USBLS	5/15
	Puerto Rico	Y	20870 FQ	29200 MW	43750 TQ	USBLS	5/15
	San Juan-Carolina-Caguas MSA, PR	Y	22730 FQ	30220 MW	50280 TQ	USBLS	5/15
Hearing Consultant							
Municipal Government	Detroit, MI	M	3667 LO		3842 HI	DETGOV	2016
Hearing Examiner							
Municipal Government	Seattle, WA	H	46.59 LO		107.07 HI	CSSS	1/27/16
Heat Treating Equipment Setter, Operator, and Tender							
Metals and Plastics	Alabama	Y	31361 AE	51226 AW	61169 AEX	ALBLS	6/16
Metals and Plastics	Birmingham-Hoover MSA, AL	Y	38897 AE	47103 AW	51205 AEX	ALBLS	6/16
Metals and Plastics	Arizona	Y	33670 FQ	41750 MW	52090 TQ	USBLS	5/15
Metals and Plastics	Phoenix-Mesa-Scottsdale MSA, AZ	Y	32770 FQ	40660 MW	53540 TQ	USBLS	5/15
Metals and Plastics	Arkansas	Y	27590 FQ	34240 MW	39850 TQ	USBLS	5/15
Metals and Plastics	California	H	12.86 FQ	17.48 MW	22.92 TQ	CABLS	1/16-3/16
Metals and Plastics	Anaheim-Santa Ana-Irvine PMSA, CA	H	11.18 FQ	14.53 MW	20.05 TQ	CABLS	1/16-3/16
Metals and Plastics	Los Angeles-Long Beach-Glendale PMSA, CA	H	11.16 FQ	15.65 MW	21.48 TQ	CABLS	1/16-3/16
Metals and Plastics	Oakland-Hayward-Berkeley PMSA, CA	H	16.79 FQ	20.93 MW	23.64 TQ	CABLS	1/16-3/16
Metals and Plastics	Riverside-San Bernardino-Ontario MSA, CA	H	12.71 FQ	16.64 MW	31.57 TQ	CABLS	1/16-3/16
Metals and Plastics	San Diego-Carlsbad MSA, CA	H	15.94 FQ	19.48 MW	23.26 TQ	CABLS	1/16-3/16
Metals and Plastics	Colorado	Y	31360 FQ	41620 MW	51620 TQ	USBLS	5/15
Metals and Plastics	Denver-Aurora-Lakewood MSA, CO	Y	30350 FQ	45190 MW	52350 TQ	USBLS	5/15
Metals and Plastics	Connecticut	Y		37635 MW		CTBLS	1/16-3/16
Metals and Plastics	Hartford-West Hartford-East Hartford MSA, CT	Y	30160 FQ	36850 MW	45610 TQ	USBLS	5/15
Metals and Plastics	Florida	H	12.79 AE	16.49 MW	18.82 AEX	FLBLS	7/16-9/16
Metals and Plastics	Tampa-St. Petersburg-Clearwater MSA, FL	H	12.01 AE	14.23 MW	16.20 AEX	FLBLS	7/16-9/16
Metals and Plastics	Georgia	Y	27310 FQ	33210 MW	39520 TQ	USBLS	5/15
Metals and Plastics	Atlanta-Sandy Springs-Roswell MSA, GA	Y	26890 FQ	30910 MW	38060 TQ	USBLS	5/15
Metals and Plastics	Illinois	Y	26510 FQ	33120 MW	38950 TQ	USBLS	5/15
Metals and Plastics	Chicago-Naperville-Arlington Heights PMSA, IL	Y	25200 FQ	33610 MW	39600 TQ	USBLS	5/15
Metals and Plastics	Lake County-Kenosha County PMSA, IL-WI	Y	29770 FQ	36620 MW	45670 TQ	USBLS	5/15

AE	Average entry wage	AWR	Average wage range	H	Hourly
AEX	Average experienced wage	B	Biweekly	HI	Highest wage paid
ATC	Average total compensation	D	Daily	HR	High end range
AW	Average wage paid	FQ	First quartile wage	LO	Lowest wage paid

LR	Low end range	MTC	Median total compensation
M	Monthly	MW	Median wage paid
MCC	Median cash compensation	MWR	Median wage range
ME	Median entry wage	S	See annotated source

TCC	Total cash compensation
TQ	Third quartile wage
W	Weekly
Y	Yearly

Occupation/Type/Industry	Location	Per	Low	Mid	High	Source	Date
Heat Treating Equipment Setter, Operator, and Tender							
Metals and Plastics	Indiana	Y	34020 FQ	46310 MW	57520 TQ	USBLS	5/15
Metals and Plastics	Gary PMSA, IN	Y	42410 FQ	55710 MW	63250 TQ	USBLS	5/15
Metals and Plastics	Indianapolis-Carmel-Anderson MSA, IN	Y	37460 FQ	54010 MW	61560 TQ	USBLS	5/15
Metals and Plastics	Iowa	Y	28180 FQ	32130 MW	37510 TQ	USBLS	5/15
Metals and Plastics	Kansas	Y	24190 FQ	30180 MW	41840 TQ	USBLS	5/15
Metals and Plastics	Wichita MSA, KS	Y	24620 FQ	29200 MW	42620 TQ	USBLS	5/15
Metals and Plastics	Kentucky	Y	30190 FQ	35740 MW	41870 TQ	USBLS	5/15
Metals and Plastics	Louisville-Jefferson County MSA, KY-IN	Y	33040 FQ	35300 MW	37560 TQ	USBLS	5/15
Metals and Plastics	Louisiana	Y	38010 FQ	44800 MW	52530 TQ	USBLS	5/15
Metals and Plastics	New Orleans-Metairie MSA, LA	Y	37830 FQ	44510 MW	52780 TQ	USBLS	5/15
Metals and Plastics	Baltimore-Columbia-Towson MSA, MD	Y	18390 FQ	20710 MW	23960 TQ	USBLS	5/15
Metals and Plastics	Massachusetts	Y	28590 FQ	33890 MW	38670 TQ	USBLS	5/15
Metals and Plastics	Boston-Cambridge-Newton NECTA, MA	Y	29280 FQ	33910 MW	37720 TQ	USBLS	5/15
Metals and Plastics	Michigan	Y	31930 FQ	36800 MW	43320 TQ	USBLS	5/15
Metals and Plastics	Detroit-Dearborn-Livonia PMSA, MI	Y	30620 FQ	35360 MW	39720 TQ	USBLS	5/15
Metals and Plastics	Grand Rapids-Wyoming MSA, MI	Y	33190 FQ	37630 MW	43520 TQ	USBLS	5/15
Metals and Plastics	Minnesota	Y	32267 FQ	37764 MW	46633 TQ	MNBLS	1/16-3/16
Metals and Plastics	Minneapolis-St. Paul-Bloomington MSA, MN-WI	Y	31983 FQ	37521 MW	46573 TQ	MNBLS	1/16-3/16
Metals and Plastics	Mississippi	Y	35100 FQ	41840 MW	47070 TQ	USBLS	5/15
Metals and Plastics	Missouri	Y	22990 FQ	29650 MW	38700 TQ	USBLS	5/15
Metals and Plastics	Kansas City MSA, MO-KS	Y	20070 FQ	27800 MW	37860 TQ	USBLS	5/15
Metals and Plastics	St. Louis MSA, MO-IL	Y	23730 FQ	33180 MW	38610 TQ	USBLS	5/15
Metals and Plastics	Nebraska	Y	28420 FQ	34730 MW	42360 TQ	NEBLS	7/16-9/16
Metals and Plastics	Nevada	Y	27890 FQ	35690 MW	44300 TQ	USBLS	5/15
Metals and Plastics	New Hampshire	H	13.48 AE	18.51 MW	21.60 AEX	NHBLS	6/16
Metals and Plastics	Manchester NECTA, NH	H	20.37 AE	28.28 MW	35.27 AEX	NHBLS	6/16
Metals and Plastics	New Jersey	Y	26240 FQ	36060 MW	45470 TQ	USBLS	5/15
Metals and Plastics	Camden PMSA, NJ	Y	42280 FQ	46100 MW	49910 TQ	USBLS	5/15
Metals and Plastics	Newark PMSA, NJ-PA	Y	23310 FQ	28140 MW	34430 TQ	USBLS	5/15
Metals and Plastics	New York	Y	26700 AE	37300 MW	43650 AEX	NYBLS	1/16-3/16
Metals and Plastics	Buffalo-Cheektowaga-Niagara Falls MSA, NY	Y	33790 FQ	38440 MW	44720 TQ	USBLS	5/15
Metals and Plastics	New York-Jersey City-White Plains PMSA, NY-NJ	Y	25360 FQ	34360 MW	48650 TQ	USBLS	5/15
Metals and Plastics	North Carolina	Y	27090 FQ	37580 MW	45450 TQ	USBLS	5/15
Metals and Plastics	Charlotte-Concord-Gastonia MSA, NC-SC	Y	31390 FQ	42510 MW	47720 TQ	USBLS	5/15
Metals and Plastics	North Dakota	Y	33370 FQ	35980 MW	38590 TQ	USBLS	5/15
Metals and Plastics	Ohio	Y	28970 FQ	36910 MW	45560 TQ	USBLS	5/15
Metals and Plastics	Cincinnati MSA, OH-KY-IN	Y	36370 FQ	44120 MW	52860 TQ	USBLS	5/15
Metals and Plastics	Cleveland-Elyria MSA, OH	Y	27370 FQ	35370 MW	43880 TQ	USBLS	5/15
Metals and Plastics	Columbus MSA, OH	Y	27080 FQ	35160 MW	44190 TQ	USBLS	5/15
Metals and Plastics	Oklahoma	Y	28030 FQ	35010 MW	44560 TQ	USBLS	5/15
Metals and Plastics	Oklahoma City MSA, OK	Y	26540 FQ	30360 MW	50190 TQ	USBLS	5/15
Metals and Plastics	Tulsa MSA, OK	Y	30590 FQ	37240 MW	45080 TQ	USBLS	5/15
Metals and Plastics	Oregon	H	14.83 FQ	17.58 MW	21.04 TQ	ORBLS	2016
Metals and Plastics	Portland-Vancouver-Hillsboro MSA, OR-WA	Y	28740 FQ	34650 MW	41760 TQ	USBLS	5/15
Metals and Plastics	Pennsylvania	Y	32430 FQ	39800 MW	47960 TQ	USBLS	5/15
Metals and Plastics	Allentown-Bethlehem-Easton MSA, PA-NJ	Y	26760 FQ	33220 MW	38240 TQ	USBLS	5/15
Metals and Plastics	Harrisburg-Carlisle MSA, PA	Y	40170 FQ	43780 MW	47380 TQ	USBLS	5/15
Metals and Plastics	Montgomery County-Bucks County-Chester County PMSA, PA	Y	33700 FQ	39230 MW	46240 TQ	USBLS	5/15
Metals and Plastics	Philadelphia PMSA, PA	Y	52740 FQ	55010 MW	60060 TQ	USBLS	5/15
Metals and Plastics	Pittsburgh MSA, PA	Y	35540 FQ	41500 MW	47030 TQ	USBLS	5/15
Metals and Plastics	Rhode Island	Y	30830 FQ	36500 MW	45910 TQ	USBLS	5/15
Metals and Plastics	Providence-Warwick MSA, RI-MA	Y	29820 FQ	35590 MW	44110 TQ	USBLS	5/15
Metals and Plastics	South Carolina	Y	30510 FQ	36300 MW	44220 TQ	USBLS	5/15

AE	Average entry wage	AWR	Average wage range	H	Hourly
AEX	Average experienced wage	B	Biweekly	HI	Highest wage paid
ATC	Average total compensation	D	Daily	HR	High end range
AW	Average wage paid	FQ	First quartile wage	LO	Lowest wage paid

LR	Low end range	MTC	Median total compensation	TCC	Total cash compensation
M	Monthly	MW	Median wage paid	TQ	Third quartile wage
MCC	Median cash compensation	MWR	Median wage range	W	Weekly
ME	Median entry wage	S	See annotated source	Y	Yearly

Occupation/Type/Industry	Location	Per	Low	Mid	High	Source	Date
Heat Treating Equipment Setter, Operator, and Tender							
Metals and Plastics	Charleston-North Charleston MSA, SC	Y	39110 FQ	72350 MW	90140 TQ	USBLS	5/15
Metals and Plastics	Columbia MSA, SC	Y	31040 FQ	36110 MW	41880 TQ	USBLS	5/15
Metals and Plastics	Greenville-Anderson-Mauldin MSA, SC	Y	27790 FQ	33210 MW	38140 TQ	USBLS	5/15
Metals and Plastics	Tennessee	Y	26950 FQ	33360 MW	40670 TQ	USBLS	5/15
Metals and Plastics	Knoxville MSA, TN	Y	30680 FQ	38050 MW	44850 TQ	USBLS	5/15
Metals and Plastics	Nashville-Davidson–Murfreesboro–Franklin MSA, TN	Y	26960 FQ	30500 MW	41800 TQ	USBLS	5/15
Metals and Plastics	Texas	Y	29530 FQ	36070 MW	45750 TQ	USBLS	5/15
Metals and Plastics	Dallas-Plano-Irving PMSA, TX	Y	29170 FQ	36140 MW	47050 TQ	USBLS	5/15
Metals and Plastics	Fort Worth-Arlington PMSA, TX	Y	27490 FQ	35010 MW	45430 TQ	USBLS	5/15
Metals and Plastics	Houston-The Woodlands-Sugar Land MSA, TX	Y	29350 FQ	35430 MW	43890 TQ	USBLS	5/15
Metals and Plastics	Utah	Y	27230 FQ	30400 MW	36050 TQ	USBLS	5/15
Metals and Plastics	Ogden-Clearfield MSA, UT	Y	27370 FQ	30030 MW	35550 TQ	USBLS	5/15
Metals and Plastics	Salt Lake City MSA, UT	Y	27500 FQ	31480 MW	36760 TQ	USBLS	5/15
Metals and Plastics	Virginia	Y	39220 FQ	46580 MW	56890 TQ	USBLS	5/15
Metals and Plastics	Washington	H	14.95 FQ	18.93 MW	34.48 TQ	WABLS	3/16
Metals and Plastics	Seattle-Bellevue-Everett PMSA, WA	H	17.04 FQ	29.61 MW	38.89 TQ	WABLS	3/16
Metals and Plastics	Tacoma-Lakewood PMSA, WA	H	25.09 FQ	30.59 MW	38.15 TQ	WABLS	3/16
Metals and Plastics	West Virginia	Y	39390 FQ	43710 MW	47850 TQ	USBLS	5/15
Metals and Plastics	Wisconsin	Y	30430 FQ	38270 MW	47850 TQ	USBLS	5/15
Metals and Plastics	Milwaukee-Waukesha-West Allis MSA, WI	Y	31960 FQ	40290 MW	53120 TQ	USBLS	5/15
Metals and Plastics	Puerto Rico	Y	18850 FQ	21460 MW	24000 TQ	USBLS	5/15
Metals and Plastics	San Juan-Carolina-Caguas MSA, PR	Y	21530 FQ	23180 MW	24870 TQ	USBLS	5/15
Heating, Air Conditioning, and Refrigeration Mechanic and Installer							
	Alabama	Y	29249 AE	39725 AW	44962 AEX	ALBLS	6/16
	Birmingham-Hoover MSA, AL	Y	31578 AE	42440 AW	47871 AEX	ALBLS	6/16
	Alaska	Y	54060 FQ	64280 MW	75500 TQ	USBLS	5/15
	Anchorage MSA, AK	Y	54170 FQ	63240 MW	75340 TQ	USBLS	5/15
	Arizona	Y	34720 FQ	41680 MW	54550 TQ	USBLS	5/15
	Phoenix-Mesa-Scottsdale MSA, AZ	Y	34860 FQ	41190 MW	54070 TQ	USBLS	5/15
	Tucson MSA, AZ	Y	38270 FQ	49060 MW	61340 TQ	USBLS	5/15
	Arkansas	Y	27050 FQ	35380 MW	45260 TQ	USBLS	5/15
	Little Rock-North Little Rock-Conway MSA, AR	Y	28470 FQ	36770 MW	46660 TQ	USBLS	5/15
	California	H	18.43 FQ	24.86 MW	31.33 TQ	CABLS	1/16-3/16
	Anaheim-Santa Ana-Irvine PMSA, CA	H	19.22 FQ	23.70 MW	30.67 TQ	CABLS	1/16-3/16
	Los Angeles-Long Beach-Glendale PMSA, CA	H	18.15 FQ	25.37 MW	33.59 TQ	CABLS	1/16-3/16
	Oakland-Hayward-Berkeley PMSA, CA	H	22.53 FQ	27.95 MW	35.46 TQ	CABLS	1/16-3/16
	Riverside-San Bernardino-Ontario MSA, CA	H	17.96 FQ	22.95 MW	28.05 TQ	CABLS	1/16-3/16
	Sacramento–Roseville–Arden-Arcade MSA, CA	H	17.64 FQ	23.45 MW	29.81 TQ	CABLS	1/16-3/16
	San Diego-Carlsbad MSA, CA	H	20.91 FQ	26.56 MW	30.54 TQ	CABLS	1/16-3/16
	San Francisco-Redwood City-South San Francisco PMSA, CA	H	19.57 FQ	25.84 MW	36.74 TQ	CABLS	1/16-3/16
	Colorado	Y	43940 FQ	54250 MW	63590 TQ	USBLS	5/15
	Denver-Aurora-Lakewood MSA, CO	Y	44360 FQ	55090 MW	63940 TQ	USBLS	5/15
	Connecticut	Y		55280 MW		CTBLS	1/16-3/16
	Bridgeport-Stamford-Norwalk MSA, CT	Y	46460 FQ	57770 MW	70200 TQ	USBLS	5/15
	Hartford-West Hartford-East Hartford MSA, CT	Y	46030 FQ	54670 MW	62040 TQ	USBLS	5/15
	Delaware	Y	43070 FQ	49910 MW	59750 TQ	USBLS	5/15

AE	Average entry wage	AWR	Average wage range	H	Hourly
AEX	Average experienced wage	B	Biweekly	HI	Highest wage paid
ATC	Average total compensation	D	Daily	HR	High end range
AW	Average wage paid	FQ	First quartile wage	LO	Lowest wage paid

LR	Low end range	MTC	Median total compensation	TCC	Total cash compensation
M	Monthly	MW	Median wage paid	TQ	Third quartile wage
MCC	Median cash compensation	MWR	Median wage range	W	Weekly
ME	Median entry wage	S	See annotated source	Y	Yearly

Occupation/Type/Industry	Location	Per	Low	Mid	High	Source	Date
Heating, Air Conditioning, and Refrigeration Mechanic and Installer							
	Wilmington PMSA, DE-MD-NJ	Y	43580 FQ	52470 MW	61330 TQ	USBLS	5/15
	District of Columbia	Y	58660 FQ	66120 MW	74180 TQ	USBLS	5/15
	Washington-Arlington-Alexandria PMSA, DC-VA-MD-WV	Y	49840 FQ	58250 MW	67520 TQ	USBLS	5/15
	Florida	H	13.34 AE	18.54 MW	23.00 AEX	FLBLS	7/16-9/16
	Fort Lauderdale-Pompano Beach-Deerfield Beach PMSA, FL	H	14.59 AE	19.96 MW	26.05 AEX	FLBLS	7/16-9/16
	Miami-Miami Beach-Kendall PMSA, FL	H	12.00 AE	17.77 MW	23.01 AEX	FLBLS	7/16-9/16
	Orlando-Kissimmee-Sanford MSA, FL	H	13.18 AE	19.14 MW	24.29 AEX	FLBLS	7/16-9/16
	Tampa-St. Petersburg-Clearwater MSA, FL	H	13.53 AE	17.70 MW	21.69 AEX	FLBLS	7/16-9/16
	Georgia	Y	33670 FQ	42270 MW	50970 TQ	USBLS	5/15
	Atlanta-Sandy Springs-Roswell MSA, GA	Y	36160 FQ	44560 MW	54420 TQ	USBLS	5/15
	Augusta-Richmond County MSA, GA-SC	Y	36790 FQ	48380 MW	57350 TQ	USBLS	5/15
	Hawaii	Y	44410 FQ	61330 MW	75450 TQ	USBLS	5/15
	Urban Honolulu MSA, HI	Y	47330 FQ	62450 MW	76100 TQ	USBLS	5/15
	Idaho	Y	29210 FQ	37220 MW	47030 TQ	USBLS	5/15
	Boise City MSA, ID	Y	30920 FQ	38970 MW	49080 TQ	USBLS	5/15
	Illinois	Y	38550 FQ	52100 MW	61430 TQ	USBLS	5/15
	Chicago-Naperville-Arlington Heights PMSA, IL	Y	40580 FQ	53120 MW	62620 TQ	USBLS	5/15
	Lake County-Kenosha County PMSA, IL-WI	Y	51330 FQ	56740 MW	62310 TQ	USBLS	5/15
	Indiana	Y	33120 FQ	42050 MW	55370 TQ	USBLS	5/15
	Gary PMSA, IN	Y	24490 FQ	30710 MW	47480 TQ	USBLS	5/15
	Indianapolis-Carmel-Anderson MSA, IN	Y	36430 FQ	48680 MW	66160 TQ	USBLS	5/15
	Iowa	Y	37240 FQ	47820 MW	60780 TQ	USBLS	5/15
	Des Moines-West Des Moines MSA, IA	Y	36950 FQ	50460 MW	67500 TQ	USBLS	5/15
	Kansas	Y	36830 FQ	44910 MW	56260 TQ	USBLS	5/15
	Wichita MSA, KS	Y	38090 FQ	44570 MW	51010 TQ	USBLS	5/15
	Kentucky	Y	30520 FQ	38130 MW	48640 TQ	USBLS	5/15
	Louisville-Jefferson County MSA, KY-IN	Y	32540 FQ	38410 MW	46990 TQ	USBLS	5/15
	Louisiana	Y	33650 FQ	39900 MW	48950 TQ	USBLS	5/15
	Baton Rouge MSA, LA	Y	34280 FQ	43290 MW	53960 TQ	USBLS	5/15
	New Orleans-Metairie MSA, LA	Y	34190 FQ	39150 MW	46160 TQ	USBLS	5/15
	Maine	Y	36170 FQ	45700 MW	56740 TQ	USBLS	5/15
	Portland-South Portland MSA, ME	Y	39360 FQ	51910 MW	61000 TQ	USBLS	5/15
	Maryland	Y	36750 AE	54053 MW	62704 AEX	MDBLS	4/16
	Baltimore-Columbia-Towson MSA, MD	Y	44210 FQ	53470 MW	62400 TQ	USBLS	5/15
	Salisbury MSA, MD-DE	Y	37770 FQ	45000 MW	53320 TQ	USBLS	5/15
	Massachusetts	Y	44790 FQ	56520 MW	69640 TQ	USBLS	5/15
	Boston-Cambridge-Newton NECTA, MA	Y	45640 FQ	59380 MW	73680 TQ	USBLS	5/15
	Worcester MSA, MA-CT	Y	47550 FQ	56080 MW	64290 TQ	USBLS	5/15
	Michigan	Y	35830 FQ	45510 MW	57070 TQ	USBLS	5/15
	Detroit-Dearborn-Livonia PMSA, MI	Y	36310 FQ	46700 MW	57700 TQ	USBLS	5/15
	Grand Rapids-Wyoming MSA, MI	Y	35210 FQ	45370 MW	56510 TQ	USBLS	5/15
	Minnesota	Y	41293 FQ	52255 MW	63981 TQ	MNBLS	1/16-3/16
	Minneapolis-St. Paul-Bloomington MSA, MN-WI	Y	44129 FQ	56247 MW	71725 TQ	MNBLS	1/16-3/16
	Mississippi	Y	24860 FQ	33420 MW	43590 TQ	USBLS	5/15
	Jackson MSA, MS	Y	29010 FQ	38010 MW	46630 TQ	USBLS	5/15
	Missouri	Y	33950 FQ	46100 MW	60610 TQ	USBLS	5/15
	Kansas City MSA, MO-KS	Y	43520 FQ	56200 MW	68860 TQ	USBLS	5/15

AE	Average entry wage	AWR	Average wage range	H	Hourly
AEX	Average experienced wage	B	Biweekly	HI	Highest wage paid
ATC	Average total compensation	D	Daily	HR	High end range
AW	Average wage paid	FQ	First quartile wage	LO	Lowest wage paid

LR	Low end range	MTC	Median total compensation	TCC	Total cash compensation
M	Monthly	MW	Median wage paid	TQ	Third quartile wage
MCC	Median cash compensation	MWR	Median wage range	W	Weekly
ME	Median entry wage	S	See annotated source	Y	Yearly

Occupation/Type/Industry	Location	Per	Low	Mid	High	Source	Date
Heating, Air Conditioning, and Refrigeration Mechanic and Installer							
	St. Louis MSA, MO-IL	Y	31360 FQ	49090 MW	61130 TQ	USBLS	5/15
	Montana	Y	32290 FQ	40530 MW	57120 TQ	USBLS	5/15
	Billings MSA, MT	Y	29420 FQ	44100 MW	56740 TQ	USBLS	5/15
	Nebraska	Y	34730 FQ	44045 MW	59385 TQ	NEBLS	7/16-9/16
	Omaha-Council Bluffs MSA, NE-IA	Y	36090 FQ	49750 MW	65740 TQ	NEBLS	7/16-9/16
	Nevada	Y	41750 FQ	54550 MW	65730 TQ	USBLS	5/15
	Las Vegas-Henderson-Paradise MSA, NV	Y	41490 FQ	55850 MW	68590 TQ	USBLS	5/15
	New Hampshire	H	18.61 AE	24.70 MW	28.82 AEX	NHBLS	6/16
	Nashua NECTA, NH-MA	Y	42800 FQ	52480 MW	58780 TQ	USBLS	5/15
	New Jersey	Y	43290 FQ	55960 MW	71090 TQ	USBLS	5/15
	Camden PMSA, NJ	Y	43610 FQ	55270 MW	68590 TQ	USBLS	5/15
	Newark PMSA, NJ-PA	Y	40350 FQ	57650 MW	75250 TQ	USBLS	5/15
	Trenton MSA, NJ	Y	46290 FQ	55070 MW	61330 TQ	USBLS	5/15
	New Mexico	Y	33030 FQ	40590 MW	50100 TQ	USBLS	5/15
	Albuquerque MSA, NM	Y	34600 FQ	43940 MW	54690 TQ	USBLS	5/15
	New York	Y	35440 AE	50600 MW	64820 AEX	NYBLS	1/16-3/16
	Buffalo-Cheektowaga-Niagara Falls MSA, NY	Y	30450 FQ	40440 MW	57640 TQ	USBLS	5/15
	Nassau County-Suffolk County PMSA, NY	Y	45240 FQ	58520 MW	73810 TQ	USBLS	5/15
	New York-Jersey City-White Plains PMSA, NY-NJ	Y	42760 FQ	57500 MW	73440 TQ	USBLS	5/15
	Rochester MSA, NY	Y	34780 FQ	44490 MW	56030 TQ	USBLS	5/15
	North Carolina	Y	32100 FQ	39090 MW	49220 TQ	USBLS	5/15
	Charlotte-Concord-Gastonia MSA, NC-SC	Y	32210 FQ	38330 MW	49420 TQ	USBLS	5/15
	Raleigh MSA, NC	Y	32790 FQ	42810 MW	51350 TQ	USBLS	5/15
	North Dakota	Y	40380 FQ	51350 MW	60440 TQ	USBLS	5/15
	Fargo MSA, ND-MN	Y	44030 FQ	55310 MW	69610 TQ	USBLS	5/15
	Ohio	Y	35020 FQ	44150 MW	54560 TQ	USBLS	5/15
	Cincinnati MSA, OH-KY-IN	Y	39510 FQ	50470 MW	59680 TQ	USBLS	5/15
	Cleveland-Elyria MSA, OH	Y	36940 FQ	46070 MW	57890 TQ	USBLS	5/15
	Columbus MSA, OH	Y	36000 FQ	45220 MW	56330 TQ	USBLS	5/15
	Oklahoma	Y	32880 FQ	42300 MW	53360 TQ	USBLS	5/15
	Oklahoma City MSA, OK	Y	34980 FQ	44790 MW	56210 TQ	USBLS	5/15
	Tulsa MSA, OK	Y	34290 FQ	44230 MW	55460 TQ	USBLS	5/15
	Oregon	H	17.68 FQ	22.42 MW	27.78 TQ	ORBLS	2016
	Portland-Vancouver-Hillsboro MSA, OR-WA	Y	38360 FQ	50030 MW	61210 TQ	USBLS	5/15
	Pennsylvania	Y	36400 FQ	46000 MW	56770 TQ	USBLS	5/15
	Allentown-Bethlehem-Easton MSA, PA-NJ	Y	39470 FQ	45960 MW	54630 TQ	USBLS	5/15
	Harrisburg-Carlisle MSA, PA	Y	36480 FQ	44040 MW	52890 TQ	USBLS	5/15
	Montgomery County-Bucks County-Chester County PMSA, PA	Y	41130 FQ	52450 MW	61140 TQ	USBLS	5/15
	Philadelphia PMSA, PA	Y	43240 FQ	54580 MW	66660 TQ	USBLS	5/15
	Pittsburgh MSA, PA	Y	34750 FQ	43770 MW	52930 TQ	USBLS	5/15
	Rhode Island	Y	48260 FQ	55890 MW	62000 TQ	USBLS	5/15
	Providence-Warwick MSA, RI-MA	Y	47760 FQ	55640 MW	62140 TQ	USBLS	5/15
	South Carolina	Y	32280 FQ	39220 MW	48110 TQ	USBLS	5/15
	Charleston-North Charleston MSA, SC	Y	40220 FQ	48520 MW	63570 TQ	USBLS	5/15
	Columbia MSA, SC	Y	32340 FQ	39000 MW	50270 TQ	USBLS	5/15
	Greenville-Anderson-Mauldin MSA, SC	Y	35720 FQ	42940 MW	48880 TQ	USBLS	5/15
	South Dakota	Y	35770 FQ	45460 MW	55810 TQ	USBLS	5/15
	Sioux Falls MSA, SD	Y	40720 FQ	49900 MW	61720 TQ	USBLS	5/15
	Tennessee	Y	32090 FQ	39710 MW	52340 TQ	USBLS	5/15
	Knoxville MSA, TN	Y	31170 FQ	38890 MW	53410 TQ	USBLS	5/15
	Memphis MSA, TN-MS-AR	Y	33990 FQ	43450 MW	57190 TQ	USBLS	5/15
	Nashville-Davidson–Murfreesboro–Franklin MSA, TN	Y	33660 FQ	43840 MW	54120 TQ	USBLS	5/15
	Texas	Y	33110 FQ	40610 MW	51080 TQ	USBLS	5/15
	Austin-Round Rock MSA, TX	Y	33260 FQ	38780 MW	47190 TQ	USBLS	5/15

AE	Average entry wage	AWR	Average wage range	H	Hourly	LR	Low end range	MTC	Median total compensation	TCC	Total cash compensation
AEX	Average experienced wage	B	Biweekly	HI	Highest wage paid	M	Monthly	MW	Median wage paid	TQ	Third quartile wage
ATC	Average total compensation	D	Daily	HR	High end range	MCC	Median cash compensation	MWR	Median wage range	W	Weekly
AW	Average wage paid	FQ	First quartile wage	LO	Lowest wage paid	ME	Median entry wage	S	See annotated source	Y	Yearly

Occupation/Type/Industry	Location	Per	Low	Mid	High	Source	Date
Heating, Air Conditioning, and Refrigeration Mechanic and Installer	Dallas-Plano-Irving PMSA, TX	Y	35740 FQ	43560 MW	56010 TQ	USBLS	5/15
	Fort Worth-Arlington PMSA, TX	Y	34000 FQ	41810 MW	50810 TQ	USBLS	5/15
	Houston-The Woodlands-Sugar Land MSA, TX	Y	34680 FQ	44910 MW	56870 TQ	USBLS	5/15
	San Antonio-New Braunfels MSA, TX	Y	31080 FQ	40250 MW	49400 TQ	USBLS	5/15
	Utah	Y	36750 FQ	47010 MW	58550 TQ	USBLS	5/15
	Ogden-Clearfield MSA, UT	Y	31180 FQ	43760 MW	55550 TQ	USBLS	5/15
	Provo-Orem MSA, UT	Y	39040 FQ	46500 MW	54960 TQ	USBLS	5/15
	Salt Lake City MSA, UT	Y	42890 FQ	53480 MW	65540 TQ	USBLS	5/15
	Vermont	Y	41690 FQ	47480 MW	56410 TQ	USBLS	5/15
	Burlington-South Burlington MSA, VT	Y	43980 FQ	52960 MW	61320 TQ	USBLS	5/15
	Virginia	Y	36770 FQ	47370 MW	57990 TQ	USBLS	5/15
	Richmond MSA, VA	Y	36420 FQ	45980 MW	56290 TQ	USBLS	5/15
	Virginia Beach-Norfolk-Newport News MSA, VA-NC	Y	33990 FQ	43230 MW	51070 TQ	USBLS	5/15
	Washington	H	20.20 FQ	26.39 MW	32.41 TQ	WABLS	3/16
	Seattle-Bellevue-Everett PMSA, WA	H	24.48 FQ	29.23 MW	37.65 TQ	WABLS	3/16
	West Virginia	Y	27160 FQ	35370 MW	46110 TQ	USBLS	5/15
	Huntington-Ashland MSA, WV-KY-OH	Y	25920 FQ	31880 MW	41710 TQ	USBLS	5/15
	Wisconsin	Y	38520 FQ	46750 MW	58230 TQ	USBLS	5/15
	Madison MSA, WI	Y	40710 FQ	47850 MW	59230 TQ	USBLS	5/15
	Milwaukee-Waukesha-West Allis MSA, WI	Y	39320 FQ	49070 MW	61680 TQ	USBLS	5/15
	Wyoming	Y	36510 FQ	44860 MW	56730 TQ	USBLS	5/15
	Cheyenne MSA, WY	Y	39950 FQ	49270 MW	57290 TQ	USBLS	5/15
	Puerto Rico	Y	18450 FQ	21980 MW	27660 TQ	USBLS	5/15
	San Juan-Carolina-Caguas MSA, PR	Y	18830 FQ	22340 MW	27530 TQ	USBLS	5/15
	Virgin Islands	Y	33520 FQ	40180 MW	53830 TQ	USBLS	5/15
	Guam	Y	27540 FQ	33030 MW	38740 TQ	USBLS	5/15
Heavy and Tractor-Trailer Truck Driver	Alabama	Y	26659 AE	41253 AW	48545 AEX	ALBLS	6/16
	Birmingham-Hoover MSA, AL	Y	30084 AE	47023 AW	55488 AEX	ALBLS	6/16
	Dothan MSA, AL	Y	21743 AE	38281 AW	46550 AEX	ALBLS	6/16
	Alaska	Y	42600 FQ	51280 MW	61350 TQ	USBLS	5/15
	Anchorage MSA, AK	Y	41480 FQ	52580 MW	63800 TQ	USBLS	5/15
	Arizona	Y	32980 FQ	38680 MW	47650 TQ	USBLS	5/15
	Phoenix-Mesa-Scottsdale MSA, AZ	Y	33890 FQ	39380 MW	48850 TQ	USBLS	5/15
	Tucson MSA, AZ	Y	30120 FQ	37820 MW	46060 TQ	USBLS	5/15
	Arkansas	Y	29510 FQ	36310 MW	46150 TQ	USBLS	5/15
	Little Rock-North Little Rock-Conway MSA, AR	Y	28910 FQ	37120 MW	47690 TQ	USBLS	5/15
	California	H	16.57 FQ	20.58 MW	25.71 TQ	CABLS	1/16-3/16
	Anaheim-Santa Ana-Irvine PMSA, CA	H	16.63 FQ	19.26 MW	23.67 TQ	CABLS	1/16-3/16
	Los Angeles-Long Beach-Glendale PMSA, CA	H	15.47 FQ	19.57 MW	25.65 TQ	CABLS	1/16-3/16
	Oakland-Hayward-Berkeley PMSA, CA	H	18.37 FQ	22.12 MW	27.75 TQ	CABLS	1/16-3/16
	Riverside-San Bernardino-Ontario MSA, CA	H	18.26 FQ	22.75 MW	28.41 TQ	CABLS	1/16-3/16
	Sacramento–Roseville–Arden-Arcade MSA, CA	H	16.58 FQ	20.31 MW	24.11 TQ	CABLS	1/16-3/16
	San Diego-Carlsbad MSA, CA	H	15.24 FQ	19.14 MW	23.97 TQ	CABLS	1/16-3/16
	San Francisco-Redwood City-South San Francisco PMSA, CA	H	18.39 FQ	23.32 MW	29.02 TQ	CABLS	1/16-3/16
	Colorado	Y	36330 FQ	44370 MW	53180 TQ	USBLS	5/15
	Denver-Aurora-Lakewood MSA, CO	Y	37880 FQ	46300 MW	56990 TQ	USBLS	5/15
	Connecticut	Y		46536 MW		CTBLS	1/16-3/16

AE	Average entry wage	AWR	Average wage range	H	Hourly	LR	Low end range	MTC	Median total compensation	TCC	Total cash compensation
AEX	Average experienced wage	B	Biweekly	HI	Highest wage paid	M	Monthly	MW	Median wage paid	TQ	Third quartile wage
ATC	Average total compensation	D	Daily	HR	High range	MCC	Median cash compensation	MWR	Median wage range	W	Weekly
AW	Average wage paid	FQ	First quartile wage	LO	Lowest wage paid	ME	Median entry wage	S	See annotated source	Y	Yearly

Occupation/Type/Industry	Location	Per	Low	Mid	High	Source	Date
Heavy and Tractor-Trailer Truck Driver							
	Bridgeport-Stamford-Norwalk MSA, CT	Y	40400 FQ	49000 MW	58710 TQ	USBLS	5/15
	Hartford-West Hartford-East Hartford MSA, CT	Y	40750 FQ	45780 MW	52110 TQ	USBLS	5/15
	Delaware	Y	33920 FQ	40890 MW	50190 TQ	USBLS	5/15
	Wilmington PMSA, DE-MD-NJ	Y	36480 FQ	44540 MW	55930 TQ	USBLS	5/15
	District of Columbia	Y	42060 FQ	48250 MW	57630 TQ	USBLS	5/15
	Washington-Arlington-Alexandria PMSA, DC-VA-MD-WV	Y	34020 FQ	41350 MW	49740 TQ	USBLS	5/15
	Florida	H	12.74 AE	17.96 MW	21.89 AEX	FLBLS	7/16-9/16
	Fort Lauderdale-Pompano Beach-Deerfield Beach PMSA, FL	H	14.46 AE	19.40 MW	22.67 AEX	FLBLS	7/16-9/16
	Miami-Miami Beach-Kendall PMSA, FL	H	13.01 AE	17.68 MW	21.71 AEX	FLBLS	7/16-9/16
	Orlando-Kissimmee-Sanford MSA, FL	H	12.81 AE	19.09 MW	23.74 AEX	FLBLS	7/16-9/16
	Tampa-St. Petersburg-Clearwater MSA, FL	H	12.39 AE	17.92 MW	20.98 AEX	FLBLS	7/16-9/16
	Georgia	Y	29110 FQ	39630 MW	49660 TQ	USBLS	5/15
	Atlanta-Sandy Springs-Roswell MSA, GA	Y	30590 FQ	41420 MW	50790 TQ	USBLS	5/15
	Augusta-Richmond County MSA, GA-SC	Y	29980 FQ	40110 MW	53300 TQ	USBLS	5/15
	Hawaii	Y	36480 FQ	43930 MW	50410 TQ	USBLS	5/15
	Urban Honolulu MSA, HI	Y	36050 FQ	43610 MW	49710 TQ	USBLS	5/15
	Idaho	Y	29900 FQ	36810 MW	47340 TQ	USBLS	5/15
	Boise City MSA, ID	Y	29460 FQ	36670 MW	45390 TQ	USBLS	5/15
	Illinois	Y	34700 FQ	43750 MW	57670 TQ	USBLS	5/15
	Chicago-Naperville-Arlington Heights PMSA, IL	Y	36460 FQ	46780 MW	61370 TQ	USBLS	5/15
	Lake County-Kenosha County PMSA, IL-WI	Y	33300 FQ	39360 MW	52410 TQ	USBLS	5/15
	Indiana	Y	33400 FQ	40190 MW	50870 TQ	USBLS	5/15
	Gary PMSA, IN	Y	37650 FQ	45830 MW	56750 TQ	USBLS	5/15
	Indianapolis-Carmel-Anderson MSA, IN	Y	34950 FQ	41100 MW	53070 TQ	USBLS	5/15
	Iowa	Y	31900 FQ	39790 MW	48220 TQ	USBLS	5/15
	Des Moines-West Des Moines MSA, IA	Y	37630 FQ	44490 MW	51330 TQ	USBLS	5/15
	Kansas	Y	32100 FQ	38870 MW	48950 TQ	USBLS	5/15
	Wichita MSA, KS	Y	31990 FQ	38050 MW	45740 TQ	USBLS	5/15
	Kentucky	Y	30090 FQ	38210 MW	48330 TQ	USBLS	5/15
	Louisville-Jefferson County MSA, KY-IN	Y	35310 FQ	42920 MW	53000 TQ	USBLS	5/15
	Louisiana	Y	30960 FQ	37710 MW	48100 TQ	USBLS	5/15
	Baton Rouge MSA, LA	Y	33600 FQ	39710 MW	53320 TQ	USBLS	5/15
	New Orleans-Metairie MSA, LA	Y	30980 FQ	38550 MW	48850 TQ	USBLS	5/15
	Maine	Y	29550 FQ	36300 MW	45860 TQ	USBLS	5/15
	Portland-South Portland MSA, ME	Y	31840 FQ	36950 MW	44120 TQ	USBLS	5/15
	Maryland	Y	31427 AE	43737 MW	49893 AEX	MDBLS	4/16
	Baltimore-Columbia-Towson MSA, MD	Y	36690 FQ	43980 MW	50850 TQ	USBLS	5/15
	Salisbury MSA, MD-DE	Y	31330 FQ	37150 MW	45140 TQ	USBLS	5/15
	Massachusetts	Y	39490 FQ	46510 MW	57160 TQ	USBLS	5/15
	Boston-Cambridge-Newton NECTA, MA	Y	41950 FQ	48380 MW	59390 TQ	USBLS	5/15
	Worcester MSA, MA-CT	Y	39550 FQ	47610 MW	60940 TQ	USBLS	5/15
	Michigan	Y	32230 FQ	38570 MW	48280 TQ	USBLS	5/15
	Detroit-Dearborn-Livonia PMSA, MI	Y	32670 FQ	44060 MW	55700 TQ	USBLS	5/15
	Grand Rapids-Wyoming MSA, MI	Y	32750 FQ	39230 MW	48030 TQ	USBLS	5/15
	Minnesota	Y	34972 FQ	41878 MW	49117 TQ	MNBLS	1/16-3/16
	Minneapolis-St. Paul-Bloomington MSA, MN-WI	Y	37362 FQ	43874 MW	49833 TQ	MNBLS	1/16-3/16
	Mississippi	Y	29630 FQ	38080 MW	48850 TQ	USBLS	5/15

AE	Average entry wage	AWR	Average wage range	H	Hourly	LR	Low end range	MTC	Median total compensation	TCC	Total cash compensation
AEX	Average experienced wage	B	Biweekly	HI	Highest wage paid	M	Monthly	MW	Median wage paid	TQ	Third quartile wage
ATC	Average total compensation	D	Daily	HR	High end range	MCC	Median cash compensation	MWR	Median wage range	W	Weekly
AW	Average wage paid	FQ	First quartile wage	LO	Lowest wage paid	ME	Median entry wage	S	See annotated source	Y	Yearly

Occupation/Type/Industry	Location	Per	Low	Mid	High	Source	Date
Heavy and Tractor-Trailer Truck Driver	Jackson MSA, MS	Y	30680 FQ	43690 MW	58580 TQ	USBLS	5/15
	Missouri	Y	30880 FQ	39910 MW	48980 TQ	USBLS	5/15
	Kansas City MSA, MO-KS	Y	34540 FQ	42370 MW	51880 TQ	USBLS	5/15
	St. Louis MSA, MO-IL	Y	34430 FQ	41670 MW	49520 TQ	USBLS	5/15
	Montana	Y	34090 FQ	41360 MW	52010 TQ	USBLS	5/15
	Billings MSA, MT	Y	36820 FQ	44460 MW	55310 TQ	USBLS	5/15
	Nebraska	Y	33370 FQ	39665 MW	52635 TQ	NEBLS	7/16-9/16
	Omaha-Council Bluffs MSA, NE-IA	Y	33610 FQ	37665 MW	48070 TQ	NEBLS	7/16-9/16
	Nevada	Y	39740 FQ	47050 MW	56690 TQ	USBLS	5/15
	Las Vegas-Henderson-Paradise MSA, NV	Y	38870 FQ	45980 MW	55000 TQ	USBLS	5/15
	New Hampshire	H	15.72 AE	19.64 MW	23.05 AEX	NHBLS	6/16
	Manchester NECTA, NH	H	15.83 AE	19.45 MW	22.59 AEX	NHBLS	6/16
	Nashua NECTA, NH-MA	Y	34380 FQ	40940 MW	47590 TQ	USBLS	5/15
	New Jersey	Y	37310 FQ	45690 MW	56660 TQ	USBLS	5/15
	Camden PMSA, NJ	Y	36490 FQ	43310 MW	50090 TQ	USBLS	5/15
	Newark PMSA, NJ-PA	Y	39110 FQ	45830 MW	56050 TQ	USBLS	5/15
	Trenton MSA, NJ	Y	25970 FQ	39510 MW	52060 TQ	USBLS	5/15
	New Mexico	Y	33160 FQ	39870 MW	50960 TQ	USBLS	5/15
	Albuquerque MSA, NM	Y	33330 FQ	39740 MW	49200 TQ	USBLS	5/15
	New York	Y	31050 AE	45080 MW	57050 AEX	NYBLS	1/16-3/16
	Buffalo-Cheektowaga-Niagara Falls MSA, NY	Y	35560 FQ	42840 MW	50040 TQ	USBLS	5/15
	Nassau County-Suffolk County PMSA, NY	Y	43730 FQ	56370 MW	68920 TQ	USBLS	5/15
	New York-Jersey City-White Plains PMSA, NY-NJ	Y	36130 FQ	46770 MW	59680 TQ	USBLS	5/15
	Rochester MSA, NY	Y	32230 FQ	38510 MW	51190 TQ	USBLS	5/15
	North Carolina	Y	30510 FQ	38390 MW	47730 TQ	USBLS	5/15
	Charlotte-Concord-Gastonia MSA, NC-SC	Y	32940 FQ	40560 MW	48790 TQ	USBLS	5/15
	Raleigh MSA, NC	Y	33460 FQ	39300 MW	51010 TQ	USBLS	5/15
	North Dakota	Y	42560 FQ	49570 MW	60210 TQ	USBLS	5/15
	Fargo MSA, ND-MN	Y	36230 FQ	43710 MW	51030 TQ	USBLS	5/15
	Ohio	Y	33840 FQ	40860 MW	50090 TQ	USBLS	5/15
	Cincinnati MSA, OH-KY-IN	Y	35180 FQ	42180 MW	49750 TQ	USBLS	5/15
	Cleveland-Elyria MSA, OH	Y	35430 FQ	43460 MW	52190 TQ	USBLS	5/15
	Columbus MSA, OH	Y	35530 FQ	43310 MW	54650 TQ	USBLS	5/15
	Oklahoma	Y	32120 FQ	39940 MW	49180 TQ	USBLS	5/15
	Oklahoma City MSA, OK	Y	30760 FQ	38000 MW	48280 TQ	USBLS	5/15
	Tulsa MSA, OK	Y	32570 FQ	42280 MW	54100 TQ	USBLS	5/15
	Oregon	H	17.02 FQ	19.96 MW	23.34 TQ	ORBLS	2016
	Portland-Vancouver-Hillsboro MSA, OR-WA	Y	35910 FQ	42030 MW	47800 TQ	USBLS	5/15
	Pennsylvania	Y	34200 FQ	42100 MW	51960 TQ	USBLS	5/15
	Allentown-Bethlehem-Easton MSA, PA-NJ	Y	35700 FQ	43180 MW	50720 TQ	USBLS	5/15
	Harrisburg-Carlisle MSA, PA	Y	36460 FQ	45620 MW	56090 TQ	USBLS	5/15
	Montgomery County-Bucks County-Chester County PMSA, PA	Y	38810 FQ	45090 MW	53670 TQ	USBLS	5/15
	Philadelphia PMSA, PA	Y	33230 FQ	39210 MW	51860 TQ	USBLS	5/15
	Pittsburgh MSA, PA	Y	33690 FQ	41350 MW	50940 TQ	USBLS	5/15
	Rhode Island	Y	35220 FQ	41400 MW	49170 TQ	USBLS	5/15
	Providence-Warwick MSA, RI-MA	Y	35410 FQ	42140 MW	49410 TQ	USBLS	5/15
	South Carolina	Y	31200 FQ	38480 MW	47920 TQ	USBLS	5/15
	Charleston-North Charleston MSA, SC	Y	33790 FQ	40430 MW	48290 TQ	USBLS	5/15
	Columbia MSA, SC	Y	30070 FQ	39590 MW	51440 TQ	USBLS	5/15
	Greenville-Anderson-Mauldin MSA, SC	Y	31790 FQ	36470 MW	45000 TQ	USBLS	5/15
	South Dakota	Y	31150 FQ	37130 MW	46340 TQ	USBLS	5/15
	Sioux Falls MSA, SD	Y	31970 FQ	38490 MW	50890 TQ	USBLS	5/15
	Tennessee	Y	30570 FQ	38660 MW	50620 TQ	USBLS	5/15
	Knoxville MSA, TN	Y	33920 FQ	43550 MW	55880 TQ	USBLS	5/15
	Memphis MSA, TN-MS-AR	Y	32050 FQ	42070 MW	53090 TQ	USBLS	5/15

AE Average entry wage	**AWR** Average wage range	**H** Hourly	**LR** Low end range	**MTC** Median total compensation	**TCC** Total cash compensation
AEX Average experienced wage	**B** Biweekly	**HI** Highest wage paid	**M** Monthly	**MW** Median wage paid	**TQ** Third quartile wage
ATC Average total compensation	**D** Daily	**HR** High end range	**MCC** Median cash compensation	**MWR** Median wage range	**W** Weekly
AW Average wage paid	**FQ** First quartile wage	**LO** Lowest wage paid	**ME** Median entry wage	**S** See annotated source	**Y** Yearly

Occupation/Type/Industry	Location	Per	Low	Mid	High	Source	Date
Heavy and Tractor-Trailer Truck Driver							
	Nashville-Davidson–Murfreesboro–Franklin MSA, TN	Y	31140 FQ	37910 MW	50160 TQ	USBLS	5/15
	Texas	Y	31170 FQ	38280 MW	48580 TQ	USBLS	5/15
	Austin-Round Rock MSA, TX	Y	30840 FQ	36360 MW	45130 TQ	USBLS	5/15
	Dallas-Plano-Irving PMSA, TX	Y	30290 FQ	38740 MW	52210 TQ	USBLS	5/15
	Fort Worth-Arlington PMSA, TX	Y	31430 FQ	37660 MW	48330 TQ	USBLS	5/15
	Houston-The Woodlands-Sugar Land MSA, TX	Y	31970 FQ	38430 MW	48390 TQ	USBLS	5/15
	San Antonio-New Braunfels MSA, TX	Y	32310 FQ	40760 MW	49300 TQ	USBLS	5/15
	Utah	Y	34480 FQ	42380 MW	50950 TQ	USBLS	5/15
	Ogden-Clearfield MSA, UT	Y	36320 FQ	43120 MW	51090 TQ	USBLS	5/15
	Provo-Orem MSA, UT	Y	36120 FQ	42860 MW	51200 TQ	USBLS	5/15
	Salt Lake City MSA, UT	Y	32350 FQ	40550 MW	49560 TQ	USBLS	5/15
	Vermont	Y	34280 FQ	40040 MW	49040 TQ	USBLS	5/15
	Burlington-South Burlington MSA, VT	Y	34620 FQ	41520 MW	48710 TQ	USBLS	5/15
	Virginia	Y	31290 FQ	38270 MW	47870 TQ	USBLS	5/15
	Richmond MSA, VA	Y	32550 FQ	40960 MW	51150 TQ	USBLS	5/15
	Virginia Beach-Norfolk-Newport News MSA, VA-NC	Y	29990 FQ	36690 MW	46280 TQ	USBLS	5/15
	Washington	H	17.41 FQ	21.24 MW	26.02 TQ	WABLS	3/16
	Seattle-Bellevue-Everett PMSA, WA	H	17.29 FQ	21.64 MW	27.94 TQ	WABLS	3/16
	Tacoma-Lakewood PMSA, WA	H	18.99 FQ	22.16 MW	25.88 TQ	WABLS	3/16
	West Virginia	Y	29390 FQ	35690 MW	44760 TQ	USBLS	5/15
	Huntington-Ashland MSA, WV-KY-OH	Y	29570 FQ	36690 MW	49080 TQ	USBLS	5/15
	Wisconsin	Y	32830 FQ	39210 MW	49750 TQ	USBLS	5/15
	Madison MSA, WI	Y	36720 FQ	46300 MW	56020 TQ	USBLS	5/15
	Milwaukee-Waukesha-West Allis MSA, WI	Y	33440 FQ	39080 MW	49310 TQ	USBLS	5/15
	Wyoming	Y	39930 FQ	46580 MW	57160 TQ	USBLS	5/15
	Cheyenne MSA, WY	Y	35390 FQ	42640 MW	48790 TQ	USBLS	5/15
	Puerto Rico	Y	16940 FQ	18320 MW	19860 TQ	USBLS	5/15
	San Juan-Carolina-Caguas MSA, PR	Y	16990 FQ	18430 MW	20150 TQ	USBLS	5/15
	Virgin Islands	Y	27190 FQ	31150 MW	38240 TQ	USBLS	5/15
	Guam	Y	25600 FQ	29220 MW	34340 TQ	USBLS	5/15
Heavy Equipment Mechanic							
Municipal Government	Garden City, GA	Y	37351 LO		59762 HI	GACTY02	2016
Municipal Government	LaGrange, GA	Y	34944 LO		50482 HI	GACTY02	2016
Municipal Government	Rockmart, GA	Y	25781 LO		34547 HI	GACTY02	2016
Helicopter A&P Technician	United States	Y		57000 AW		AVJOB03	2016
Helicopter Mechanic							
Municipal Government	Anaheim, CA	Y			78913 HI	CACIT	6/28/16
Municipal Government	Long Beach, CA	Y			89037 HI	CACIT	6/28/16
Municipal Government	Los Angeles, CA	Y		84710 AW		CACIT	6/23/16
Municipal Government	Riverside, CA	Y			79095 HI	CACIT	7/6/16
Helicopter Pilot							
Municipal Government	El Monte, CA	Y			81493 HI	CACIT	6/24/16
Helper							
Carpenter	Alabama	Y	20173 AE	25234 AW	27764 AEX	ALBLS	6/16
Carpenter	Birmingham-Hoover MSA, AL	Y	22415 AE	26972 AW	29246 AEX	ALBLS	6/16
Carpenter	Alaska	Y	30670 FQ	36300 MW	44940 TQ	USBLS	5/15
Carpenter	Anchorage MSA, AK	Y	29930 FQ	36230 MW	49000 TQ	USBLS	5/15
Carpenter	Arizona	Y	23310 FQ	28350 MW	35740 TQ	USBLS	5/15
Carpenter	Phoenix-Mesa-Scottsdale MSA, AZ	Y	25520 FQ	30470 MW	38560 TQ	USBLS	5/15
Carpenter	Tucson MSA, AZ	Y	24110 FQ	28900 MW	35260 TQ	USBLS	5/15
Carpenter	Arkansas	Y	19060 FQ	23510 MW	28660 TQ	USBLS	5/15
Carpenter	Little Rock-North Little Rock-Conway MSA, AR	Y	20560 FQ	27180 MW	31270 TQ	USBLS	5/15
Carpenter	California	H	11.31 FQ	15.83 MW	18.74 TQ	CABLS	1/16-3/16

AE Average entry wage	**AWR** Average wage range	**H** Hourly	**LR** Low end range	**MTC** Median total compensation	**TCC** Total cash compensation
AEX Average experienced wage	**B** Biweekly	**HI** Highest wage paid	**M** Monthly	**MW** Median wage paid	**TQ** Third quartile wage
ATC Average total compensation	**D** Daily	**HR** High end range	**MCC** Median cash compensation	**MWR** Median wage range	**W** Weekly
AW Average wage paid	**FQ** First quartile wage	**LO** Lowest wage paid	**ME** Median entry wage	**S** See annotated source	**Y** Yearly

Helper

Occupation/Type/Industry	Location	Per	Low	Mid	High	Source	Date
Carpenter	Anaheim-Santa Ana-Irvine PMSA, CA	H	9.39 FQ	9.59 MW	15.64 TQ	CABLS	1/16-3/16
Carpenter	Los Angeles-Long Beach-Glendale PMSA, CA	H	12.03 FQ	16.59 MW	18.73 TQ	CABLS	1/16-3/16
Carpenter	Oakland-Hayward-Berkeley PMSA, CA	H	12.34 FQ	15.89 MW	18.45 TQ	CABLS	1/16-3/16
Carpenter	Riverside-San Bernardino-Ontario MSA, CA	H	12.91 FQ	15.01 MW	19.21 TQ	CABLS	1/16-3/16
Carpenter	Sacramento–Roseville–Arden-Arcade MSA, CA	H	12.77 FQ	16.41 MW	18.08 TQ	CABLS	1/16-3/16
Carpenter	San Diego-Carlsbad MSA, CA	H	10.95 FQ	13.53 MW	20.46 TQ	CABLS	1/16-3/16
Carpenter	San Francisco-Redwood City-South San Francisco PMSA, CA	H	16.15 FQ	17.60 MW	19.06 TQ	CABLS	1/16-3/16
Carpenter	Colorado	Y	20100 FQ	27290 MW	29910 TQ	USBLS	5/15
Carpenter	Connecticut	Y		29790 MW		CTBLS	1/16-3/16
Carpenter	Bridgeport-Stamford-Norwalk MSA, CT	Y	21750 FQ	26890 MW	30450 TQ	USBLS	5/15
Carpenter	Hartford-West Hartford-East Hartford MSA, CT	Y	27150 FQ	32180 MW	36320 TQ	USBLS	5/15
Carpenter	Delaware	Y	22700 FQ	25800 MW	29440 TQ	USBLS	5/15
Carpenter	Wilmington PMSA, DE-MD-NJ	Y	21190 FQ	23690 MW	27390 TQ	USBLS	5/15
Carpenter	District of Columbia	Y	32490 FQ	34850 MW	37200 TQ	USBLS	5/15
Carpenter	Washington-Arlington-Alexandria PMSA, DC-VA-MD-WV	Y	21730 FQ	28300 MW	34220 TQ	USBLS	5/15
Carpenter	Florida	H	10.21 AE	13.41 MW	15.65 AEX	FLBLS	7/16-9/16
Carpenter	Fort Lauderdale-Pompano Beach-Deerfield Beach PMSA, FL	H	9.37 AE	12.49 MW	15.25 AEX	FLBLS	7/16-9/16
Carpenter	Miami-Miami Beach-Kendall PMSA, FL	H	9.37 AE	14.21 MW	16.13 AEX	FLBLS	7/16-9/16
Carpenter	Orlando-Kissimmee-Sanford MSA, FL	H	11.01 AE	13.72 MW	15.24 AEX	FLBLS	7/16-9/16
Carpenter	Tampa-St. Petersburg-Clearwater MSA, FL	H	10.74 AE	12.49 MW	13.95 AEX	FLBLS	7/16-9/16
Carpenter	Georgia	Y	23780 FQ	28260 MW	33570 TQ	USBLS	5/15
Carpenter	Atlanta-Sandy Springs-Roswell MSA, GA	Y	25340 FQ	29010 MW	34040 TQ	USBLS	5/15
Carpenter	Augusta-Richmond County MSA, GA-SC	Y	29150 FQ	33970 MW	37740 TQ	USBLS	5/15
Carpenter	Hawaii	Y	32520 FQ	36620 MW	46100 TQ	USBLS	5/15
Carpenter	Urban Honolulu MSA, HI	Y	31200 FQ	36370 MW	52140 TQ	USBLS	5/15
Carpenter	Idaho	Y	26400 FQ	30010 MW	34670 TQ	USBLS	5/15
Carpenter	Illinois	Y	26330 FQ	29100 MW	32460 TQ	USBLS	5/15
Carpenter	Chicago-Naperville-Arlington Heights PMSA, IL	Y	26640 FQ	28400 MW	30160 TQ	USBLS	5/15
Carpenter	Lake County-Kenosha County PMSA, IL-WI	Y	25120 FQ	27500 MW	29860 TQ	USBLS	5/15
Carpenter	Indiana	Y	19040 FQ	24980 MW	32310 TQ	USBLS	5/15
Carpenter	Gary PMSA, IN	Y	17190 FQ	18910 MW	22460 TQ	USBLS	5/15
Carpenter	Indianapolis-Carmel-Anderson MSA, IN	Y	24000 FQ	30460 MW	35620 TQ	USBLS	5/15
Carpenter	Iowa	Y	23510 FQ	31070 MW	37640 TQ	USBLS	5/15
Carpenter	Kansas	Y	19400 FQ	24660 MW	29470 TQ	USBLS	5/15
Carpenter	Wichita MSA, KS	Y	21370 FQ	24280 MW	28650 TQ	USBLS	5/15
Carpenter	Kentucky	Y	27000 FQ	31980 MW	36200 TQ	USBLS	5/15
Carpenter	Louisville-Jefferson County MSA, KY-IN	Y	31570 FQ	34250 MW	36920 TQ	USBLS	5/15
Carpenter	Louisiana	Y	22560 FQ	27770 MW	34050 TQ	USBLS	5/15
Carpenter	Baton Rouge MSA, LA	Y	24120 FQ	28440 MW	33350 TQ	USBLS	5/15
Carpenter	New Orleans-Metairie MSA, LA	Y	25360 FQ	29710 MW	35550 TQ	USBLS	5/15
Carpenter	Maine	Y	25010 FQ	28000 MW	30980 TQ	USBLS	5/15
Carpenter	Portland-South Portland MSA, ME	Y	23360 FQ	27010 MW	30560 TQ	USBLS	5/15
Carpenter	Maryland	Y	18373 AE	27872 MW	32622 AEX	MDBLS	4/16
Carpenter	Baltimore-Columbia-Towson MSA, MD	Y	21340 FQ	27390 MW	34710 TQ	USBLS	5/15
Carpenter	Salisbury MSA, MD-DE	Y	19100 FQ	24180 MW	29170 TQ	USBLS	5/15

AE	Average entry wage	AWR	Average wage range	H	Hourly	LR	Low end range	MTC	Median total compensation	TCC	Total cash compensation
AEX	Average experienced wage	B	Biweekly	HI	Highest wage paid	M	Monthly	MW	Median wage paid	TQ	Third quartile wage
ATC	Average total compensation	D	Daily	HR	High end range	MCC	Median cash compensation	MWR	Median wage range	W	Weekly
AW	Average wage paid	FQ	First quartile wage	LO	Lowest wage paid	ME	Median entry wage	S	See annotated source	Y	Yearly

Helper

Occupation/Type/Industry	Location	Per	Low	Mid	High	Source	Date
Carpenter	Massachusetts	Y	27440 FQ	36020 MW	45120 TQ	USBLS	5/15
Carpenter	Boston-Cambridge-Newton NECTA, MA	Y	32470 FQ	42980 MW	48530 TQ	USBLS	5/15
Carpenter	Michigan	Y	19550 FQ	22790 MW	27450 TQ	USBLS	5/15
Carpenter	Detroit-Dearborn-Livonia PMSA, MI	Y	18590 FQ	19990 MW	24470 TQ	USBLS	5/15
Carpenter	Grand Rapids-Wyoming MSA, MI	Y	19580 FQ	23310 MW	28810 TQ	USBLS	5/15
Carpenter	Minnesota	Y	27284 FQ	35285 MW	52711 TQ	MNBLS	1/16-3/16
Carpenter	Minneapolis-St. Paul-Bloomington MSA, MN-WI	Y	29887 FQ	45557 MW	57181 TQ	MNBLS	1/16-3/16
Carpenter	Mississippi	Y	20600 FQ	24370 MW	32280 TQ	USBLS	5/15
Carpenter	Jackson MSA, MS	Y	17580 FQ	19470 MW	27420 TQ	USBLS	5/15
Carpenter	Missouri	Y	26050 FQ	31900 MW	39270 TQ	USBLS	5/15
Carpenter	Kansas City MSA, MO-KS	Y	18290 FQ	25830 MW	31060 TQ	USBLS	5/15
Carpenter	St. Louis MSA, MO-IL	Y	29300 FQ	34770 MW	41650 TQ	USBLS	5/15
Carpenter	Montana	Y	22620 FQ	26030 MW	31110 TQ	USBLS	5/15
Carpenter	Nebraska	Y	20565 FQ	22890 MW	26790 TQ	NEBLS	7/16-9/16
Carpenter	Omaha-Council Bluffs MSA, NE-IA	Y	19430 FQ	26010 MW	30645 TQ	NEBLS	7/16-9/16
Carpenter	Nevada	Y	25150 FQ	29180 MW	34680 TQ	USBLS	5/15
Carpenter	Las Vegas-Henderson-Paradise MSA, NV	Y	27310 FQ	31140 MW	36390 TQ	USBLS	5/15
Carpenter	New Hampshire	H	10.32 AE	14.38 MW	16.07 AEX	NHBLS	6/16
Carpenter	New Jersey	Y	22530 FQ	26200 MW	30940 TQ	USBLS	5/15
Carpenter	Camden PMSA, NJ	Y	25620 FQ	28070 MW	30530 TQ	USBLS	5/15
Carpenter	Newark PMSA, NJ-PA	Y	22310 FQ	24630 MW	28190 TQ	USBLS	5/15
Carpenter	New Mexico	Y	21520 FQ	26320 MW	29390 TQ	USBLS	5/15
Carpenter	Albuquerque MSA, NM	Y	26600 FQ	28230 MW	29850 TQ	USBLS	5/15
Carpenter	New York	Y	20640 AE	27850 MW	32600 AEX	NYBLS	1/16-3/16
Carpenter	Buffalo-Cheektowaga-Niagara Falls MSA, NY	Y	23180 FQ	32000 MW	36260 TQ	USBLS	5/15
Carpenter	Nassau County-Suffolk County PMSA, NY	Y	22830 FQ	27400 MW	30590 TQ	USBLS	5/15
Carpenter	New York-Jersey City-White Plains PMSA, NY-NJ	Y	22920 FQ	28130 MW	35420 TQ	USBLS	5/15
Carpenter	Rochester MSA, NY	Y	19700 FQ	24140 MW	29050 TQ	USBLS	5/15
Carpenter	North Carolina	Y	21630 FQ	24850 MW	28900 TQ	USBLS	5/15
Carpenter	Charlotte-Concord-Gastonia MSA, NC-SC	Y	25490 FQ	28120 MW	30770 TQ	USBLS	5/15
Carpenter	Raleigh MSA, NC	Y	23220 FQ	27080 MW	31450 TQ	USBLS	5/15
Carpenter	North Dakota	Y	24470 FQ	30070 MW	36180 TQ	USBLS	5/15
Carpenter	Fargo MSA, ND-MN	Y	25760 FQ	37450 MW	44270 TQ	USBLS	5/15
Carpenter	Ohio	Y	22170 FQ	27450 MW	31530 TQ	USBLS	5/15
Carpenter	Cincinnati MSA, OH-KY-IN	Y	21840 FQ	26730 MW	31440 TQ	USBLS	5/15
Carpenter	Cleveland-Elyria MSA, OH	Y	27010 FQ	29960 MW	55660 TQ	USBLS	5/15
Carpenter	Columbus MSA, OH	Y	25230 FQ	30420 MW	42980 TQ	USBLS	5/15
Carpenter	Oklahoma	Y	22430 FQ	27080 MW	31980 TQ	USBLS	5/15
Carpenter	Oklahoma City MSA, OK	Y	22300 FQ	27610 MW	34460 TQ	USBLS	5/15
Carpenter	Tulsa MSA, OK	Y	22220 FQ	26000 MW	30800 TQ	USBLS	5/15
Carpenter	Oregon	H	10.45 FQ	15.18 MW	17.29 TQ	ORBLS	2016
Carpenter	Portland-Vancouver-Hillsboro MSA, OR-WA	Y	21560 FQ	31950 MW	35790 TQ	USBLS	5/15
Carpenter	Pennsylvania	Y	23310 FQ	27870 MW	34710 TQ	USBLS	5/15
Carpenter	Allentown-Bethlehem-Easton MSA, PA-NJ	Y	25060 FQ	27100 MW	29130 TQ	USBLS	5/15
Carpenter	Montgomery County-Bucks County-Chester County PMSA, PA	Y	24240 FQ	29800 MW	35670 TQ	USBLS	5/15
Carpenter	Philadelphia PMSA, PA	Y	26520 FQ	29490 MW	36430 TQ	USBLS	5/15
Carpenter	Pittsburgh MSA, PA	Y	22500 FQ	29310 MW	41010 TQ	USBLS	5/15
Carpenter	Rhode Island	Y	23310 FQ	28530 MW	40990 TQ	USBLS	5/15
Carpenter	Providence-Warwick MSA, RI-MA	Y	23690 FQ	28310 MW	39780 TQ	USBLS	5/15
Carpenter	South Carolina	Y	22480 FQ	27860 MW	34360 TQ	USBLS	5/15
Carpenter	Charleston-North Charleston MSA, SC	Y	26590 FQ	28940 MW	31420 TQ	USBLS	5/15
Carpenter	Columbia MSA, SC	Y	25220 FQ	29480 MW	37960 TQ	USBLS	5/15
Carpenter	Greenville-Anderson-Mauldin MSA, SC	Y	19600 FQ	22290 MW	25000 TQ	USBLS	5/15
Carpenter	South Dakota	Y	20170 FQ	22090 MW	24010 TQ	USBLS	5/15

AE	Average entry wage	AWR	Average wage range	H	Hourly
AEX	Average experienced wage	B	Biweekly	HI	Highest wage paid
ATC	Average total compensation	D	Daily	HR	High end range
AW	Average wage paid	FQ	First quartile wage	LO	Lowest wage paid

LR	Low end range	MTC	Median total compensation	TCC	Total cash compensation
M	Monthly	MW	Median wage paid	TQ	Third quartile wage
MCC	Median cash compensation	MWR	Median wage range	W	Weekly
ME	Median entry wage	S	See annotated source	Y	Yearly

Helper

Occupation/Type/Industry	Location	Per	Low	Mid	High	Source	Date
Helper							
Carpenter	Sioux Falls MSA, SD	Y	20540 FQ	22330 MW	24110 TQ	USBLS	5/15
Carpenter	Tennessee	Y	21390 FQ	24760 MW	30480 TQ	USBLS	5/15
Carpenter	Knoxville MSA, TN	Y	21970 FQ	25900 MW	29720 TQ	USBLS	5/15
Carpenter	Memphis MSA, TN-MS-AR	Y	29670 FQ	34510 MW	38070 TQ	USBLS	5/15
Carpenter	Nashville-Davidson–Murfreesboro–Franklin MSA, TN	Y	22130 FQ	25010 MW	32910 TQ	USBLS	5/15
Carpenter	Texas	Y	22870 FQ	27910 MW	34010 TQ	USBLS	5/15
Carpenter	Austin-Round Rock MSA, TX	Y	27130 FQ	32140 MW	36280 TQ	USBLS	5/15
Carpenter	Dallas-Plano-Irving PMSA, TX	Y	24930 FQ	28380 MW	33420 TQ	USBLS	5/15
Carpenter	Fort Worth-Arlington PMSA, TX	Y	25350 FQ	27690 MW	30030 TQ	USBLS	5/15
Carpenter	Houston-The Woodlands-Sugar Land MSA, TX	Y	24650 FQ	30240 MW	37860 TQ	USBLS	5/15
Carpenter	San Antonio-New Braunfels MSA, TX	Y	19940 FQ	23460 MW	27930 TQ	USBLS	5/15
Carpenter	Utah	Y	20710 FQ	26960 MW	35460 TQ	USBLS	5/15
Carpenter	Salt Lake City MSA, UT	Y	23930 FQ	31610 MW	37260 TQ	USBLS	5/15
Carpenter	Vermont	Y	26940 FQ	30930 MW	35820 TQ	USBLS	5/15
Carpenter	Burlington-South Burlington MSA, VT	Y	29450 FQ	33720 MW	36880 TQ	USBLS	5/15
Carpenter	Virginia	Y	24490 FQ	27890 MW	31140 TQ	USBLS	5/15
Carpenter	Richmond MSA, VA	Y	26160 FQ	29000 MW	32890 TQ	USBLS	5/15
Carpenter	Virginia Beach-Norfolk-Newport News MSA, VA-NC	Y	26020 FQ	28060 MW	30130 TQ	USBLS	5/15
Carpenter	Washington	H	12.28 FQ	15.27 MW	18.38 TQ	WABLS	3/16
Carpenter	Seattle-Bellevue-Everett PMSA, WA	H	11.39 FQ	14.98 MW	18.23 TQ	WABLS	3/16
Carpenter	West Virginia	Y	18760 FQ	26910 MW	33630 TQ	USBLS	5/15
Carpenter	Huntington-Ashland MSA, WV-KY-OH	Y	19070 FQ	27230 MW	35170 TQ	USBLS	5/15
Carpenter	Wisconsin	Y	24300 FQ	29310 MW	36130 TQ	USBLS	5/15
Carpenter	Madison MSA, WI	Y	26750 FQ	33610 MW	38190 TQ	USBLS	5/15
Carpenter	Milwaukee-Waukesha-West Allis MSA, WI	Y	26250 FQ	30530 MW	36110 TQ	USBLS	5/15
Carpenter	Wyoming	Y	26270 FQ	29440 MW	34320 TQ	USBLS	5/15
Carpenter	Cheyenne MSA, WY	Y	25830 FQ	28590 MW	31310 TQ	USBLS	5/15
Carpenter	Puerto Rico	Y	16570 FQ	17680 MW	18780 TQ	USBLS	5/15
Carpenter	San Juan-Carolina-Caguas MSA, PR	Y	16660 FQ	17770 MW	18890 TQ	USBLS	5/15
Carpenter	Guam	Y	20620 FQ	22310 MW	24000 TQ	USBLS	5/15
Electrician	Alabama	Y	20759 AE	27980 AW	31601 AEX	ALBLS	6/16
Electrician	Birmingham-Hoover MSA, AL	Y	20944 AE	29554 AW	33854 AEX	ALBLS	6/16
Electrician	Alaska	Y	31410 FQ	38680 MW	47830 TQ	USBLS	5/15
Electrician	Anchorage MSA, AK	Y	31660 FQ	37880 MW	48460 TQ	USBLS	5/15
Electrician	Arizona	Y	18650 FQ	24450 MW	36160 TQ	USBLS	5/15
Electrician	Phoenix-Mesa-Scottsdale MSA, AZ	Y	18300 FQ	24970 MW	36950 TQ	USBLS	5/15
Electrician	Tucson MSA, AZ	Y	21400 FQ	23410 MW	26820 TQ	USBLS	5/15
Electrician	Arkansas	Y	18650 FQ	22720 MW	28800 TQ	USBLS	5/15
Electrician	Little Rock-North Little Rock-Conway MSA, AR	Y	18810 FQ	31440 MW	35430 TQ	USBLS	5/15
Electrician	California	H	13.34 FQ	16.19 MW	20.90 TQ	CABLS	1/16-3/16
Electrician	Anaheim-Santa Ana-Irvine PMSA, CA	H	13.22 FQ	16.16 MW	18.56 TQ	CABLS	1/16-3/16
Electrician	Los Angeles-Long Beach-Glendale PMSA, CA	H	13.02 FQ	16.06 MW	26.39 TQ	CABLS	1/16-3/16
Electrician	Oakland-Hayward-Berkeley PMSA, CA	H	14.03 FQ	17.90 MW	22.31 TQ	CABLS	1/16-3/16
Electrician	Riverside-San Bernardino-Ontario MSA, CA	H	12.88 FQ	14.74 MW	17.91 TQ	CABLS	1/16-3/16
Electrician	Sacramento–Roseville–Arden-Arcade MSA, CA	H	13.45 FQ	15.66 MW	20.41 TQ	CABLS	1/16-3/16
Electrician	San Diego-Carlsbad MSA, CA	H	15.73 FQ	18.85 MW	22.66 TQ	CABLS	1/16-3/16
Electrician	San Francisco-Redwood City-South San Francisco PMSA, CA	H	12.81 FQ	16.10 MW	20.70 TQ	CABLS	1/16-3/16
Electrician	Colorado	Y	27250 FQ	30670 MW	46160 TQ	USBLS	5/15
Electrician	Denver-Aurora-Lakewood MSA, CO	Y	27390 FQ	30690 MW	51330 TQ	USBLS	5/15
Electrician	Connecticut	Y		28937 MW		CTBLS	1/16-3/16

AE	Average entry wage	AWR	Average wage range	H	Hourly	LR	Low end range	MTC	Median total compensation	TCC	Total cash compensation
AEX	Average experienced wage	B	Biweekly	HI	Highest wage paid	M	Monthly	MW	Median wage paid	TQ	Third quartile wage
ATC	Average total compensation	D	Daily	HR	High end range	MCC	Median cash compensation	MWR	Median wage range	W	Weekly
AW	Average wage paid	FQ	First quartile wage	LO	Lowest wage paid	ME	Median entry wage	S	See annotated source	Y	Yearly

Occupation/Type/Industry	Location	Per	Low	Mid	High	Source	Date
Helper							
Electrician	Bridgeport-Stamford-Norwalk MSA, CT	Y	19320 FQ	19620 MW	23930 TQ	USBLS	5/15
Electrician	Hartford-West Hartford-East Hartford MSA, CT	Y	26440 FQ	32400 MW	36250 TQ	USBLS	5/15
Electrician	Delaware	Y	23460 FQ	28020 MW	32810 TQ	USBLS	5/15
Electrician	Wilmington PMSA, DE-MD-NJ	Y	25330 FQ	27970 MW	30610 TQ	USBLS	5/15
Electrician	District of Columbia	Y	27470 FQ	33670 MW	39730 TQ	USBLS	5/15
Electrician	Washington-Arlington-Alexandria PMSA, DC-VA-MD-WV	Y	23100 FQ	28540 MW	34960 TQ	USBLS	5/15
Electrician	Florida	H	9.80 AE	12.25 MW	14.03 AEX	FLBLS	7/16-9/16
Electrician	Fort Lauderdale-Pompano Beach-Deerfield Beach PMSA, FL	H	10.02 AE	12.69 MW	14.33 AEX	FLBLS	7/16-9/16
Electrician	Miami-Miami Beach-Kendall PMSA, FL	H	9.49 AE	12.28 MW	13.48 AEX	FLBLS	7/16-9/16
Electrician	Orlando-Kissimmee-Sanford MSA, FL	H	9.15 AE	11.85 MW	13.48 AEX	FLBLS	7/16-9/16
Electrician	Tampa-St. Petersburg-Clearwater MSA, FL	H	9.74 AE	11.55 MW	13.28 AEX	FLBLS	7/16-9/16
Electrician	Georgia	Y	22100 FQ	26860 MW	32610 TQ	USBLS	5/15
Electrician	Atlanta-Sandy Springs-Roswell MSA, GA	Y	22220 FQ	27780 MW	33980 TQ	USBLS	5/15
Electrician	Augusta-Richmond County MSA, GA-SC	Y	20950 FQ	24550 MW	28390 TQ	USBLS	5/15
Electrician	Hawaii	Y	29910 FQ	38340 MW	47210 TQ	USBLS	5/15
Electrician	Urban Honolulu MSA, HI	Y	40900 FQ	45950 MW	52050 TQ	USBLS	5/15
Electrician	Idaho	Y	21770 FQ	30220 MW	36420 TQ	USBLS	5/15
Electrician	Boise City MSA, ID	Y	19630 FQ	27350 MW	35100 TQ	USBLS	5/15
Electrician	Illinois	Y	27120 FQ	32080 MW	36970 TQ	USBLS	5/15
Electrician	Chicago-Naperville-Arlington Heights PMSA, IL	Y	28980 FQ	33650 MW	37110 TQ	USBLS	5/15
Electrician	Lake County-Kenosha County PMSA, IL-WI	Y	33500 FQ	37070 MW	44670 TQ	USBLS	5/15
Electrician	Indiana	Y	22850 FQ	26030 MW	28940 TQ	USBLS	5/15
Electrician	Indianapolis-Carmel-Anderson MSA, IN	Y	25330 FQ	27290 MW	29240 TQ	USBLS	5/15
Electrician	Iowa	Y	26750 FQ	31650 MW	37340 TQ	USBLS	5/15
Electrician	Des Moines-West Des Moines MSA, IA	Y	29430 FQ	33770 MW	37070 TQ	USBLS	5/15
Electrician	Kansas	Y	21090 FQ	25440 MW	33020 TQ	USBLS	5/15
Electrician	Wichita MSA, KS	Y	22800 FQ	27600 MW	35180 TQ	USBLS	5/15
Electrician	Kentucky	Y	25450 FQ	30170 MW	35940 TQ	USBLS	5/15
Electrician	Louisville-Jefferson County MSA, KY-IN	Y	24710 FQ	27360 MW	29990 TQ	USBLS	5/15
Electrician	Louisiana	Y	23260 FQ	28600 MW	35190 TQ	USBLS	5/15
Electrician	Baton Rouge MSA, LA	Y	24830 FQ	31200 MW	36670 TQ	USBLS	5/15
Electrician	New Orleans-Metairie MSA, LA	Y	23100 FQ	28350 MW	35540 TQ	USBLS	5/15
Electrician	Maine	Y	27380 FQ	31840 MW	36900 TQ	USBLS	5/15
Electrician	Portland-South Portland MSA, ME	Y	25860 FQ	28580 MW	31300 TQ	USBLS	5/15
Electrician	Maryland	Y	19420 AE	27966 MW	32238 AEX	MDBLS	4/16
Electrician	Baltimore-Columbia-Towson MSA, MD	Y	22030 FQ	29830 MW	36370 TQ	USBLS	5/15
Electrician	Salisbury MSA, MD-DE	Y	21170 FQ	28500 MW	33770 TQ	USBLS	5/15
Electrician	Massachusetts	Y	26880 FQ	31030 MW	40020 TQ	USBLS	5/15
Electrician	Boston-Cambridge-Newton NECTA, MA	Y	27210 FQ	30800 MW	39840 TQ	USBLS	5/15
Electrician	Worcester MSA, MA-CT	Y	34590 FQ	41010 MW	45770 TQ	USBLS	5/15
Electrician	Michigan	Y	20870 FQ	23340 MW	28460 TQ	USBLS	5/15
Electrician	Detroit-Dearborn-Livonia PMSA, MI	Y	21090 FQ	24880 MW	36370 TQ	USBLS	5/15
Electrician	Grand Rapids-Wyoming MSA, MI	Y	20360 FQ	22460 MW	24580 TQ	USBLS	5/15
Electrician	Minnesota	Y	21341 FQ	26910 MW	33045 TQ	MNBLS	1/16-3/16
Electrician	Minneapolis-St. Paul-Bloomington MSA, MN-WI	Y	24327 FQ	28757 MW	34529 TQ	MNBLS	1/16-3/16
Electrician	Mississippi	Y	21300 FQ	25140 MW	29670 TQ	USBLS	5/15
Electrician	Jackson MSA, MS	Y	21040 FQ	24290 MW	29790 TQ	USBLS	5/15

AE	Average entry wage	**AWR**	Average wage range	**H**	Hourly	**LR**	Low end range
AEX	Average experienced wage	**B**	Biweekly	**HI**	Highest wage paid	**M**	Monthly
ATC	Average total compensation	**D**	Daily	**HR**	High end range	**MCC**	Median cash compensation
AW	Average wage paid	**FQ**	First quartile wage	**LO**	Lowest wage paid	**ME**	Median entry wage

MTC	Median total compensation	**TCC**	Total cash compensation
MW	Median wage paid	**TQ**	Third quartile wage
MWR	Median wage range	**W**	Weekly
S	See annotated source	**Y**	Yearly

Helper

Occupation/Type/Industry	Location	Per	Low	Mid	High	Source	Date
Electrician	Missouri	Y	22900 FQ	27980 MW	35870 TQ	USBLS	5/15
Electrician	Kansas City MSA, MO-KS	Y	19090 FQ	25800 MW	36270 TQ	USBLS	5/15
Electrician	St. Louis MSA, MO-IL	Y	25060 FQ	28600 MW	38140 TQ	USBLS	5/15
Electrician	Montana	Y	24220 FQ	29450 MW	40670 TQ	USBLS	5/15
Electrician	Nebraska	Y	22475 FQ	27140 MW	33705 TQ	NEBLS	7/16-9/16
Electrician	Omaha-Council Bluffs MSA, NE-IA	Y	23685 FQ	29665 MW	40275 TQ	NEBLS	7/16-9/16
Electrician	Nevada	Y	27560 FQ	32540 MW	41700 TQ	USBLS	5/15
Electrician	Las Vegas-Henderson-Paradise MSA, NV	Y	27450 FQ	32160 MW	42100 TQ	USBLS	5/15
Electrician	New Hampshire	H	10.45 AE	12.66 MW	14.92 AEX	NHBLS	6/16
Electrician	New Jersey	Y	25700 FQ	29270 MW	34420 TQ	USBLS	5/15
Electrician	Camden PMSA, NJ	Y	19510 FQ	26800 MW	30020 TQ	USBLS	5/15
Electrician	Newark PMSA, NJ-PA	Y	25370 FQ	30650 MW	35530 TQ	USBLS	5/15
Electrician	New Mexico	Y	23830 FQ	29060 MW	34880 TQ	USBLS	5/15
Electrician	Albuquerque MSA, NM	Y	25730 FQ	31950 MW	36450 TQ	USBLS	5/15
Electrician	New York	Y	22610 AE	31210 MW	37880 AEX	NYBLS	1/16-3/16
Electrician	Buffalo-Cheektowaga-Niagara Falls MSA, NY	Y	19660 FQ	26870 MW	36350 TQ	USBLS	5/15
Electrician	Nassau County-Suffolk County PMSA, NY	Y	26350 FQ	29650 MW	35900 TQ	USBLS	5/15
Electrician	New York-Jersey City-White Plains PMSA, NY-NJ	Y	25180 FQ	31080 MW	37670 TQ	USBLS	5/15
Electrician	Rochester MSA, NY	Y	26050 FQ	31100 MW	40100 TQ	USBLS	5/15
Electrician	North Carolina	Y	23070 FQ	27280 MW	30860 TQ	USBLS	5/15
Electrician	Charlotte-Concord-Gastonia MSA, NC-SC	Y	24210 FQ	27980 MW	31540 TQ	USBLS	5/15
Electrician	Raleigh MSA, NC	Y	22870 FQ	26860 MW	30750 TQ	USBLS	5/15
Electrician	North Dakota	Y	26710 FQ	30400 MW	36060 TQ	USBLS	5/15
Electrician	Ohio	Y	23100 FQ	28180 MW	36660 TQ	USBLS	5/15
Electrician	Cincinnati MSA, OH-KY-IN	Y	23770 FQ	30000 MW	35810 TQ	USBLS	5/15
Electrician	Columbus MSA, OH	Y	22050 FQ	24450 MW	29970 TQ	USBLS	5/15
Electrician	Oklahoma	Y	25770 FQ	30580 MW	36360 TQ	USBLS	5/15
Electrician	Oklahoma City MSA, OK	Y	25980 FQ	31050 MW	36830 TQ	USBLS	5/15
Electrician	Tulsa MSA, OK	Y	26060 FQ	30990 MW	36760 TQ	USBLS	5/15
Electrician	Oregon	H	13.49 FQ	15.90 MW	19.68 TQ	ORBLS	2016
Electrician	Portland-Vancouver-Hillsboro MSA, OR-WA	Y	27690 FQ	33390 MW	41890 TQ	USBLS	5/15
Electrician	Pennsylvania	Y	25030 FQ	28650 MW	33670 TQ	USBLS	5/15
Electrician	Allentown-Bethlehem-Easton MSA, PA-NJ	Y	17220 FQ	19250 MW	40310 TQ	USBLS	5/15
Electrician	Harrisburg-Carlisle MSA, PA	Y	26080 FQ	29740 MW	34270 TQ	USBLS	5/15
Electrician	Montgomery County-Bucks County-Chester County PMSA, PA	Y	26220 FQ	29670 MW	34700 TQ	USBLS	5/15
Electrician	Philadelphia PMSA, PA	Y	27300 FQ	29900 MW	36200 TQ	USBLS	5/15
Electrician	Pittsburgh MSA, PA	Y	22280 FQ	26750 MW	29690 TQ	USBLS	5/15
Electrician	Providence-Warwick MSA, RI-MA	Y	21640 FQ	26910 MW	30540 TQ	USBLS	5/15
Electrician	South Carolina	Y	21570 FQ	26720 MW	31140 TQ	USBLS	5/15
Electrician	Charleston-North Charleston MSA, SC	Y	23630 FQ	28560 MW	33730 TQ	USBLS	5/15
Electrician	Columbia MSA, SC	Y	18700 FQ	24080 MW	30240 TQ	USBLS	5/15
Electrician	Greenville-Anderson-Mauldin MSA, SC	Y	23010 FQ	27480 MW	31670 TQ	USBLS	5/15
Electrician	South Dakota	Y	21930 FQ	24460 MW	29850 TQ	USBLS	5/15
Electrician	Sioux Falls MSA, SD	Y	22480 FQ	25270 MW	30190 TQ	USBLS	5/15
Electrician	Tennessee	Y	23960 FQ	28430 MW	33980 TQ	USBLS	5/15
Electrician	Knoxville MSA, TN	Y	22380 FQ	25630 MW	29300 TQ	USBLS	5/15
Electrician	Memphis MSA, TN-MS-AR	Y	24220 FQ	28830 MW	35120 TQ	USBLS	5/15
Electrician	Nashville-Davidson–Murfreesboro–Franklin MSA, TN	Y	27020 FQ	30880 MW	35560 TQ	USBLS	5/15
Electrician	Texas	Y	24680 FQ	30830 MW	36950 TQ	USBLS	5/15
Electrician	Austin-Round Rock MSA, TX	Y	25810 FQ	32570 MW	38560 TQ	USBLS	5/15
Electrician	Dallas-Plano-Irving PMSA, TX	Y	25370 FQ	30370 MW	35790 TQ	USBLS	5/15
Electrician	Fort Worth-Arlington PMSA, TX	Y	24680 FQ	30230 MW	35770 TQ	USBLS	5/15
Electrician	Houston-The Woodlands-Sugar Land MSA, TX	Y	26810 FQ	33880 MW	40810 TQ	USBLS	5/15

AE	Average entry wage	AWR	Average wage range	H	Hourly	LR	Low end range	MTC	Median total compensation	TCC	Total cash compensation
AEX	Average experienced wage	B	Biweekly	HI	Highest wage paid	M	Monthly	MW	Median wage paid	TQ	Third quartile wage
ATC	Average total compensation	D	Daily	HR	High end range	MCC	Median cash compensation	MWR	Median wage range	W	Weekly
AW	Average wage paid	FQ	First quartile wage	LO	Lowest wage paid	ME	Median entry wage	S	See annotated source	Y	Yearly

Occupation/Type/Industry	Location	Per	Low	Mid	High	Source	Date
Helper							
Electrician	San Antonio-New Braunfels MSA, TX	Y	27390 FQ	33060 MW	38110 TQ	USBLS	5/15
Electrician	Utah	Y	19570 FQ	24660 MW	28560 TQ	USBLS	5/15
Electrician	Provo-Orem MSA, UT	Y	23370 FQ	26340 MW	29000 TQ	USBLS	5/15
Electrician	Salt Lake City MSA, UT	Y	16750 FQ	18090 MW	19430 TQ	USBLS	5/15
Electrician	Vermont	Y	24090 FQ	28950 MW	34970 TQ	USBLS	5/15
Electrician	Virginia	Y	21910 FQ	27790 MW	34260 TQ	USBLS	5/15
Electrician	Richmond MSA, VA	Y	26360 FQ	32010 MW	37360 TQ	USBLS	5/15
Electrician	Virginia Beach-Norfolk-Newport News MSA, VA-NC	Y	18160 FQ	26240 MW	33990 TQ	USBLS	5/15
Electrician	Washington	H	14.35 FQ	18.23 MW	24.29 TQ	WABLS	3/16
Electrician	Seattle-Bellevue-Everett PMSA, WA	H	16.99 FQ	22.05 MW	27.27 TQ	WABLS	3/16
Electrician	West Virginia	Y	24620 FQ	30290 MW	39200 TQ	USBLS	5/15
Electrician	Huntington-Ashland MSA, WV-KY-OH	Y	27640 FQ	30410 MW	43270 TQ	USBLS	5/15
Electrician	Wisconsin	Y	25760 FQ	32780 MW	38790 TQ	USBLS	5/15
Electrician	Madison MSA, WI	Y	24900 FQ	33060 MW	41840 TQ	USBLS	5/15
Electrician	Milwaukee-Waukesha-West Allis MSA, WI	Y	23580 FQ	33130 MW	40760 TQ	USBLS	5/15
Electrician	Wyoming	Y	31750 FQ	36700 MW	44170 TQ	USBLS	5/15
Electrician	Puerto Rico	Y	17050 FQ	18480 MW	20040 TQ	USBLS	5/15
Electrician	San Juan-Carolina-Caguas MSA, PR	Y	17110 FQ	18610 MW	21670 TQ	USBLS	5/15
Electrician	Virgin Islands	Y	17440 FQ	19360 MW	30270 TQ	USBLS	5/15
Electrician	Guam	Y	19000 FQ	22660 MW	27240 TQ	USBLS	5/15
Extraction Worker	Alabama	Y	35068 AE	49696 AW	57000 AEX	ALBLS	6/16
Extraction Worker	Alaska	Y	39660 FQ	55450 MW	65740 TQ	USBLS	5/15
Extraction Worker	Arizona	Y	30210 FQ	35550 MW	41550 TQ	USBLS	5/15
Extraction Worker	Phoenix-Mesa-Scottsdale MSA, AZ	Y	30480 FQ	35060 MW	39180 TQ	USBLS	5/15
Extraction Worker	Tucson MSA, AZ	Y	28300 FQ	34740 MW	41740 TQ	USBLS	5/15
Extraction Worker	Arkansas	Y	27460 FQ	31130 MW	35780 TQ	USBLS	5/15
Extraction Worker	Little Rock-North Little Rock-Conway MSA, AR	Y	27470 FQ	30050 MW	34300 TQ	USBLS	5/15
Extraction Worker	California	H	14.61 FQ	17.73 MW	25.10 TQ	CABLS	1/16-3/16
Extraction Worker	Los Angeles-Long Beach-Glendale PMSA, CA	H	16.50 FQ	21.53 MW	26.76 TQ	CABLS	1/16-3/16
Extraction Worker	Sacramento–Roseville–Arden-Arcade MSA, CA	H	15.16 FQ	18.03 MW	23.29 TQ	CABLS	1/16-3/16
Extraction Worker	Colorado	Y	31700 FQ	37670 MW	45220 TQ	USBLS	5/15
Extraction Worker	Denver-Aurora-Lakewood MSA, CO	Y	33170 FQ	35860 MW	38550 TQ	USBLS	5/15
Extraction Worker	Greeley MSA, CO	Y	40510 FQ	44190 MW	47880 TQ	USBLS	5/15
Extraction Worker	Connecticut	Y		35869 MW		CTBLS	1/16-3/16
Extraction Worker	Washington-Arlington-Alexandria PMSA, DC-VA-MD-WV	Y	26890 FQ	29910 MW	34530 TQ	USBLS	5/15
Extraction Worker	Florida	H	11.08 AE	14.99 MW	16.49 AEX	FLBLS	7/16-9/16
Extraction Worker	Georgia	Y	21540 FQ	31060 MW	36840 TQ	USBLS	5/15
Extraction Worker	Atlanta-Sandy Springs-Roswell MSA, GA	Y	23860 FQ	33400 MW	37120 TQ	USBLS	5/15
Extraction Worker	Idaho	Y	32350 FQ	48560 MW	72670 TQ	USBLS	5/15
Extraction Worker	Illinois	Y	23380 FQ	30020 MW	39440 TQ	USBLS	5/15
Extraction Worker	Indiana	Y	31190 FQ	43610 MW	50280 TQ	USBLS	5/15
Extraction Worker	Kansas	Y	32260 FQ	42190 MW	46600 TQ	USBLS	5/15
Extraction Worker	Kentucky	Y	30220 FQ	41350 MW	46570 TQ	USBLS	5/15
Extraction Worker	Louisiana	Y	28470 FQ	33950 MW	39350 TQ	USBLS	5/15
Extraction Worker	Baton Rouge MSA, LA	Y	30000 FQ	35450 MW	41620 TQ	USBLS	5/15
Extraction Worker	Maryland	Y	18071 AE	22954 MW	25395 AEX	MDBLS	4/16
Extraction Worker	Michigan	Y	23760 FQ	27780 MW	32140 TQ	USBLS	5/15
Extraction Worker	Minnesota	Y	32783 FQ	36335 MW	40684 TQ	MNBLS	1/16-3/16
Extraction Worker	Mississippi	Y	22060 FQ	30250 MW	42120 TQ	USBLS	5/15
Extraction Worker	Jackson MSA, MS	Y	25940 FQ	28200 MW	30460 TQ	USBLS	5/15
Extraction Worker	Missouri	Y	23870 FQ	35520 MW	43090 TQ	USBLS	5/15
Extraction Worker	St. Louis MSA, MO-IL	Y	27380 FQ	29980 MW	38430 TQ	USBLS	5/15
Extraction Worker	Montana	Y	33190 FQ	39680 MW	53880 TQ	USBLS	5/15
Extraction Worker	Nevada	Y	32940 FQ	37130 MW	45600 TQ	USBLS	5/15
Extraction Worker	New Hampshire	H	15.79 AE	18.30 MW	19.81 AEX	NHBLS	6/16
Extraction Worker	New Jersey	Y	32160 FQ	38420 MW	47350 TQ	USBLS	5/15
Extraction Worker	New Mexico	Y	26990 FQ	31110 MW	40530 TQ	USBLS	5/15

AE	Average entry wage	**AWR**	Average wage range	**H**	Hourly	**LR**	Low end range	**MTC**	Median total compensation	**TCC**	Total cash compensation
AEX	Average experienced wage	**B**	Biweekly	**HI**	Highest wage paid	**M**	Monthly	**MW**	Median wage paid	**TQ**	Third quartile wage
ATC	Average total compensation	**D**	Daily	**HR**	High end range	**MCC**	Median cash compensation	**MWR**	Median wage range	**W**	Weekly
AW	Average wage paid	**FQ**	First quartile wage	**LO**	Lowest wage paid	**ME**	Median entry wage	**S**	See annotated source	**Y**	Yearly

Helper

Occupation/Type/Industry	Location	Per	Low	Mid	High	Source	Date
Extraction Worker	New York	Y	22240 AE	30000 MW	39200 AEX	NYBLS	1/16-3/16
Extraction Worker	North Carolina	Y	20710 FQ	27350 MW	34230 TQ	USBLS	5/15
Extraction Worker	North Dakota	Y	32970 FQ	39010 MW	46020 TQ	USBLS	5/15
Extraction Worker	Ohio	Y	28840 FQ	40610 MW	45780 TQ	USBLS	5/15
Extraction Worker	Cincinnati MSA, OH-KY-IN	Y	25870 FQ	27980 MW	30090 TQ	USBLS	5/15
Extraction Worker	Oklahoma	Y	30270 FQ	36040 MW	43590 TQ	USBLS	5/15
Extraction Worker	Oklahoma City MSA, OK	Y	24330 FQ	34300 MW	45650 TQ	USBLS	5/15
Extraction Worker	Tulsa MSA, OK	Y	33780 FQ	39750 MW	46160 TQ	USBLS	5/15
Extraction Worker	Oregon	H	14.65 FQ	18.07 MW	33.18 TQ	ORBLS	2016
Extraction Worker	Pennsylvania	Y	28360 FQ	38920 MW	46030 TQ	USBLS	5/15
Extraction Worker	Harrisburg-Carlisle MSA, PA	Y	33410 FQ	35740 MW	38070 TQ	USBLS	5/15
Extraction Worker	Pittsburgh MSA, PA	Y	24620 FQ	32840 MW	42420 TQ	USBLS	5/15
Extraction Worker	South Dakota	Y	21890 FQ	26490 MW	30640 TQ	USBLS	5/15
Extraction Worker	Tennessee	Y	31440 FQ	34380 MW	37280 TQ	USBLS	5/15
Extraction Worker	Memphis MSA, TN-MS-AR	Y	16940 FQ	18360 MW	19780 TQ	USBLS	5/15
Extraction Worker	Texas	Y	28380 FQ	33970 MW	41680 TQ	USBLS	5/15
Extraction Worker	Dallas-Plano-Irving PMSA, TX	Y	26640 FQ	30270 MW	40700 TQ	USBLS	5/15
Extraction Worker	Fort Worth-Arlington PMSA, TX	Y	32550 FQ	35810 MW	39070 TQ	USBLS	5/15
Extraction Worker	Houston-The Woodlands-Sugar Land MSA, TX	Y	28630 FQ	33730 MW	40830 TQ	USBLS	5/15
Extraction Worker	San Antonio-New Braunfels MSA, TX	Y	27640 FQ	33470 MW	40720 TQ	USBLS	5/15
Extraction Worker	Utah	Y	31900 FQ	36320 MW	42030 TQ	USBLS	5/15
Extraction Worker	Vermont	Y	26340 FQ	28550 MW	30770 TQ	USBLS	5/15
Extraction Worker	Virginia	Y	24400 FQ	28380 MW	32880 TQ	USBLS	5/15
Extraction Worker	Washington	H	15.67 FQ	20.34 MW	23.62 TQ	WABLS	3/16
Extraction Worker	West Virginia	Y	31900 FQ	41170 MW	49270 TQ	USBLS	5/15
Extraction Worker	Wisconsin	Y	28940 FQ	33800 MW	37280 TQ	USBLS	5/15
Extraction Worker	Wyoming	Y	34700 FQ	41990 MW	49730 TQ	USBLS	5/15
Installation and Repair Worker	Alabama	Y	17513 AE	25049 AW	28822 AEX	ALBLS	6/16
Installation and Repair Worker	Birmingham-Hoover MSA, AL	Y	17533 AE	26371 AW	30785 AEX	ALBLS	6/16
Installation and Repair Worker	Alaska	Y	25050 FQ	31560 MW	39620 TQ	USBLS	5/15
Installation and Repair Worker	Anchorage MSA, AK	Y	25180 FQ	30660 MW	41370 TQ	USBLS	5/15
Installation and Repair Worker	Arizona	Y	20670 FQ	25580 MW	31750 TQ	USBLS	5/15
Installation and Repair Worker	Phoenix-Mesa-Scottsdale MSA, AZ	Y	20130 FQ	25440 MW	30530 TQ	USBLS	5/15
Installation and Repair Worker	Tucson MSA, AZ	Y	22390 FQ	28010 MW	36290 TQ	USBLS	5/15
Installation and Repair Worker	Arkansas	Y	19210 FQ	23880 MW	31710 TQ	USBLS	5/15
Installation and Repair Worker	Little Rock-North Little Rock-Conway MSA, AR	Y	21000 FQ	25780 MW	33880 TQ	USBLS	5/15
Installation and Repair Worker	California	H	10.89 FQ	13.93 MW	17.83 TQ	CABLS	1/16-3/16
Installation and Repair Worker	Anaheim-Santa Ana-Irvine PMSA, CA	H	12.00 FQ	14.46 MW	17.53 TQ	CABLS	1/16-3/16
Installation and Repair Worker	Los Angeles-Long Beach-Glendale PMSA, CA	H	10.16 FQ	14.01 MW	18.26 TQ	CABLS	1/16-3/16
Installation and Repair Worker	Oakland-Hayward-Berkeley PMSA, CA	H	12.30 FQ	15.17 MW	18.93 TQ	CABLS	1/16-3/16
Installation and Repair Worker	Riverside-San Bernardino-Ontario MSA, CA	H	11.12 FQ	14.01 MW	17.99 TQ	CABLS	1/16-3/16
Installation and Repair Worker	Sacramento–Roseville–Arden-Arcade MSA, CA	H	10.09 FQ	11.77 MW	16.15 TQ	CABLS	1/16-3/16
Installation and Repair Worker	San Diego-Carlsbad MSA, CA	H	11.46 FQ	13.98 MW	17.27 TQ	CABLS	1/16-3/16
Installation and Repair Worker	San Francisco-Redwood City-South San Francisco PMSA, CA	H	12.78 FQ	15.06 MW	26.77 TQ	CABLS	1/16-3/16
Installation and Repair Worker	Colorado	Y	25340 FQ	31660 MW	38830 TQ	USBLS	5/15
Installation and Repair Worker	Denver-Aurora-Lakewood MSA, CO	Y	29760 FQ	35870 MW	45340 TQ	USBLS	5/15
Installation and Repair Worker	Connecticut	Y		29400 MW		CTBLS	1/16-3/16
Installation and Repair Worker	Bridgeport-Stamford-Norwalk MSA, CT	Y	25790 FQ	29200 MW	34960 TQ	USBLS	5/15
Installation and Repair Worker	Hartford-West Hartford-East Hartford MSA, CT	Y	20400 FQ	25800 MW	48080 TQ	USBLS	5/15
Installation and Repair Worker	Delaware	Y	21730 FQ	24710 MW	29320 TQ	USBLS	5/15
Installation and Repair Worker	Wilmington PMSA, DE-MD-NJ	Y	21500 FQ	24070 MW	29030 TQ	USBLS	5/15
Installation and Repair Worker	District of Columbia	Y	31960 FQ	38700 MW	46180 TQ	USBLS	5/15
Installation and Repair Worker	Washington-Arlington-Alexandria PMSA, DC-VA-MD-WV	Y	23800 FQ	30050 MW	41640 TQ	USBLS	5/15

AE	Average entry wage	**AWR**	Average wage range	**H**	Hourly	**LR**	Low end range	**MTC**	Median total compensation	**TCC**	Total cash compensation
AEX	Average experienced wage	**B**	Biweekly	**HI**	Highest wage paid	**M**	Monthly	**MW**	Median wage paid	**TQ**	Third quartile wage
ATC	Average total compensation	**D**	Daily	**HR**	High end range	**MCC**	Median cash compensation	**MWR**	Median wage range	**W**	Weekly
AW	Average wage paid	**FQ**	First quartile wage	**LO**	Lowest wage paid	**ME**	Median entry wage	**S**	See annotated source	**Y**	Yearly

Helper

Occupation/Type/Industry	Location	Per	Low	Mid	High	Source	Date
Helper							
Installation and Repair Worker	Florida	H	9.31 AE	11.65 MW	14.49 AEX	FLBLS	7/16-9/16
Installation and Repair Worker	Fort Lauderdale-Pompano Beach-Deerfield Beach PMSA, FL	H	9.77 AE	13.62 MW	17.46 AEX	FLBLS	7/16-9/16
Installation and Repair Worker	Miami-Miami Beach-Kendall PMSA, FL	H	8.97 AE	9.72 MW	12.72 AEX	FLBLS	7/16-9/16
Installation and Repair Worker	Orlando-Kissimmee-Sanford MSA, FL	H	9.78 AE	12.25 MW	15.69 AEX	FLBLS	7/16-9/16
Installation and Repair Worker	Tampa-St. Petersburg-Clearwater MSA, FL	H	9.50 AE	11.31 MW	12.97 AEX	FLBLS	7/16-9/16
Installation and Repair Worker	Georgia	Y	19250 FQ	24040 MW	29600 TQ	USBLS	5/15
Installation and Repair Worker	Atlanta-Sandy Springs-Roswell MSA, GA	Y	20200 FQ	25050 MW	30300 TQ	USBLS	5/15
Installation and Repair Worker	Augusta-Richmond County MSA, GA-SC	Y	18080 FQ	20210 MW	23760 TQ	USBLS	5/15
Installation and Repair Worker	Hawaii	Y	29690 FQ	38530 MW	47210 TQ	USBLS	5/15
Installation and Repair Worker	Urban Honolulu MSA, HI	Y	29380 FQ	38950 MW	48700 TQ	USBLS	5/15
Installation and Repair Worker	Idaho	Y	18830 FQ	22560 MW	28330 TQ	USBLS	5/15
Installation and Repair Worker	Boise City MSA, ID	Y	18960 FQ	23100 MW	29930 TQ	USBLS	5/15
Installation and Repair Worker	Illinois	Y	19920 FQ	25320 MW	33790 TQ	USBLS	5/15
Installation and Repair Worker	Chicago-Naperville-Arlington Heights PMSA, IL	Y	19990 FQ	26830 MW	35300 TQ	USBLS	5/15
Installation and Repair Worker	Lake County-Kenosha County PMSA, IL-WI	Y	21640 FQ	26310 MW	35390 TQ	USBLS	5/15
Installation and Repair Worker	Indiana	Y	20210 FQ	26600 MW	35250 TQ	USBLS	5/15
Installation and Repair Worker	Gary PMSA, IN	Y	20130 FQ	24530 MW	30090 TQ	USBLS	5/15
Installation and Repair Worker	Indianapolis-Carmel-Anderson MSA, IN	Y	25380 FQ	32050 MW	39600 TQ	USBLS	5/15
Installation and Repair Worker	Iowa	Y	21540 FQ	27550 MW	35000 TQ	USBLS	5/15
Installation and Repair Worker	Des Moines-West Des Moines MSA, IA	Y	22800 FQ	30710 MW	39460 TQ	USBLS	5/15
Installation and Repair Worker	Kansas	Y	19920 FQ	24010 MW	33640 TQ	USBLS	5/15
Installation and Repair Worker	Wichita MSA, KS	Y	21850 FQ	27890 MW	45110 TQ	USBLS	5/15
Installation and Repair Worker	Kentucky	Y	20490 FQ	26070 MW	33320 TQ	USBLS	5/15
Installation and Repair Worker	Louisville-Jefferson County MSA, KY-IN	Y	22170 FQ	26990 MW	34590 TQ	USBLS	5/15
Installation and Repair Worker	Louisiana	Y	21100 FQ	25220 MW	30670 TQ	USBLS	5/15
Installation and Repair Worker	Baton Rouge MSA, LA	Y	19920 FQ	24350 MW	29940 TQ	USBLS	5/15
Installation and Repair Worker	New Orleans-Metairie MSA, LA	Y	21730 FQ	25190 MW	30100 TQ	USBLS	5/15
Installation and Repair Worker	Maine	Y	19250 FQ	22980 MW	28610 TQ	USBLS	5/15
Installation and Repair Worker	Portland-South Portland MSA, ME	Y	21950 FQ	24460 MW	28620 TQ	USBLS	5/15
Installation and Repair Worker	Maryland	Y	19143 AE	29248 MW	34300 AEX	MDBLS	4/16
Installation and Repair Worker	Baltimore-Columbia-Towson MSA, MD	Y	18890 FQ	23610 MW	31590 TQ	USBLS	5/15
Installation and Repair Worker	Salisbury MSA, MD-DE	Y	19570 FQ	23660 MW	30020 TQ	USBLS	5/15
Installation and Repair Worker	Massachusetts	Y	25670 FQ	32450 MW	39960 TQ	USBLS	5/15
Installation and Repair Worker	Boston-Cambridge-Newton NECTA, MA	Y	26760 FQ	36370 MW	57480 TQ	USBLS	5/15
Installation and Repair Worker	Worcester MSA, MA-CT	Y	26840 FQ	30920 MW	36830 TQ	USBLS	5/15
Installation and Repair Worker	Michigan	Y	20350 FQ	24840 MW	31950 TQ	USBLS	5/15
Installation and Repair Worker	Detroit-Dearborn-Livonia PMSA, MI	Y	22970 FQ	29110 MW	37600 TQ	USBLS	5/15
Installation and Repair Worker	Grand Rapids-Wyoming MSA, MI	Y	19170 FQ	24020 MW	31830 TQ	USBLS	5/15
Installation and Repair Worker	Minnesota	Y	20838 FQ	26248 MW	34485 TQ	MNBLS	1/16-3/16
Installation and Repair Worker	Minneapolis-St. Paul-Bloomington MSA, MN-WI	Y	21773 FQ	27435 MW	36013 TQ	MNBLS	1/16-3/16
Installation and Repair Worker	Mississippi	Y	19410 FQ	25240 MW	33320 TQ	USBLS	5/15
Installation and Repair Worker	Jackson MSA, MS	Y	19420 FQ	25090 MW	36170 TQ	USBLS	5/15
Installation and Repair Worker	Missouri	Y	18360 FQ	22940 MW	29440 TQ	USBLS	5/15
Installation and Repair Worker	Kansas City MSA, MO-KS	Y	19180 FQ	23140 MW	31410 TQ	USBLS	5/15
Installation and Repair Worker	St. Louis MSA, MO-IL	Y	18500 FQ	22140 MW	28910 TQ	USBLS	5/15
Installation and Repair Worker	Montana	Y	21910 FQ	28020 MW	36780 TQ	USBLS	5/15
Installation and Repair Worker	Nebraska	Y	18665 FQ	23995 MW	29820 TQ	NEBLS	7/16-9/16
Installation and Repair Worker	Omaha-Council Bluffs MSA, NE-IA	Y	23165 FQ	29645 MW	41665 TQ	NEBLS	7/16-9/16
Installation and Repair Worker	Nevada	Y	23260 FQ	30100 MW	37930 TQ	USBLS	5/15
Installation and Repair Worker	Las Vegas-Henderson-Paradise MSA, NV	Y	23850 FQ	30360 MW	37410 TQ	USBLS	5/15

AE	Average entry wage	AWR	Average wage range	H	Hourly	LR	Low end range	MTC	Median total compensation	TCC	Total cash compensation
AEX	Average experienced wage	B	Biweekly	HI	Highest wage paid	M	Monthly	MW	Median wage paid	TQ	Third quartile wage
ATC	Average total compensation	D	Daily	HR	High end range	MCC	Median cash compensation	MWR	Median wage range	W	Weekly
AW	Average wage paid	FQ	First quartile wage	LO	Lowest wage paid	ME	Median entry wage	S	See annotated source	Y	Yearly

Helper

Occupation/Type/Industry	Location	Per	Low	Mid	High	Source	Date
Helper							
Installation and Repair Worker	New Hampshire	H	9.46 AE	12.22 MW	14.61 AEX	NHBLS	6/16
Installation and Repair Worker	Manchester NECTA, NH	H	9.83 AE	12.34 MW	14.31 AEX	NHBLS	6/16
Installation and Repair Worker	Nashua NECTA, NH-MA	Y	22160 FQ	26390 MW	30470 TQ	USBLS	5/15
Installation and Repair Worker	New Jersey	Y	22540 FQ	27790 MW	35700 TQ	USBLS	5/15
Installation and Repair Worker	Camden PMSA, NJ	Y	22680 FQ	27660 MW	32340 TQ	USBLS	5/15
Installation and Repair Worker	Newark PMSA, NJ-PA	Y	23120 FQ	29060 MW	38780 TQ	USBLS	5/15
Installation and Repair Worker	Trenton MSA, NJ	Y	19450 FQ	28460 MW	38030 TQ	USBLS	5/15
Installation and Repair Worker	New Mexico	Y	19840 FQ	26840 MW	34200 TQ	USBLS	5/15
Installation and Repair Worker	Albuquerque MSA, NM	Y	17800 FQ	19820 MW	27990 TQ	USBLS	5/15
Installation and Repair Worker	New York	Y	20590 AE	29960 MW	39980 AEX	NYBLS	1/16-3/16
Installation and Repair Worker	Buffalo-Cheektowaga-Niagara Falls MSA, NY	Y	21370 FQ	24520 MW	30260 TQ	USBLS	5/15
Installation and Repair Worker	Nassau County-Suffolk County PMSA, NY	Y	19420 FQ	23770 MW	35420 TQ	USBLS	5/15
Installation and Repair Worker	New York-Jersey City-White Plains PMSA, NY-NJ	Y	23210 FQ	29860 MW	45400 TQ	USBLS	5/15
Installation and Repair Worker	Rochester MSA, NY	Y	21240 FQ	28600 MW	35100 TQ	USBLS	5/15
Installation and Repair Worker	North Carolina	Y	19990 FQ	23820 MW	30470 TQ	USBLS	5/15
Installation and Repair Worker	Charlotte-Concord-Gastonia MSA, NC-SC	Y	22530 FQ	29230 MW	36780 TQ	USBLS	5/15
Installation and Repair Worker	Raleigh MSA, NC	Y	18700 FQ	22340 MW	27870 TQ	USBLS	5/15
Installation and Repair Worker	North Dakota	Y	24150 FQ	32480 MW	37010 TQ	USBLS	5/15
Installation and Repair Worker	Fargo MSA, ND-MN	Y	26750 FQ	31690 MW	36020 TQ	USBLS	5/15
Installation and Repair Worker	Ohio	Y	20920 FQ	27520 MW	35310 TQ	USBLS	5/15
Installation and Repair Worker	Cincinnati MSA, OH-KY-IN	Y	19060 FQ	24920 MW	35390 TQ	USBLS	5/15
Installation and Repair Worker	Cleveland-Elyria MSA, OH	Y	23120 FQ	28980 MW	38200 TQ	USBLS	5/15
Installation and Repair Worker	Columbus MSA, OH	Y	20860 FQ	26460 MW	34660 TQ	USBLS	5/15
Installation and Repair Worker	Oklahoma	Y	21230 FQ	26280 MW	31120 TQ	USBLS	5/15
Installation and Repair Worker	Oklahoma City MSA, OK	Y	20000 FQ	25910 MW	30170 TQ	USBLS	5/15
Installation and Repair Worker	Tulsa MSA, OK	Y	22340 FQ	27330 MW	33410 TQ	USBLS	5/15
Installation and Repair Worker	Portland-Vancouver-Hillsboro MSA, OR-WA	Y	22640 FQ	27650 MW	35310 TQ	USBLS	5/15
Installation and Repair Worker	Pennsylvania	Y	20950 FQ	26090 MW	32150 TQ	USBLS	5/15
Installation and Repair Worker	Allentown-Bethlehem-Easton MSA, PA-NJ	Y	19700 FQ	25250 MW	33030 TQ	USBLS	5/15
Installation and Repair Worker	Harrisburg-Carlisle MSA, PA	Y	19010 FQ	24590 MW	35270 TQ	USBLS	5/15
Installation and Repair Worker	Montgomery County-Bucks County-Chester County PMSA, PA	Y	22500 FQ	26360 MW	30870 TQ	USBLS	5/15
Installation and Repair Worker	Philadelphia PMSA, PA	Y	23890 FQ	30280 MW	35260 TQ	USBLS	5/15
Installation and Repair Worker	Pittsburgh MSA, PA	Y	18730 FQ	25610 MW	32470 TQ	USBLS	5/15
Installation and Repair Worker	Rhode Island	Y	20610 FQ	24930 MW	30970 TQ	USBLS	5/15
Installation and Repair Worker	Providence-Warwick MSA, RI-MA	Y	21130 FQ	25810 MW	32340 TQ	USBLS	5/15
Installation and Repair Worker	South Carolina	Y	20290 FQ	25000 MW	31290 TQ	USBLS	5/15
Installation and Repair Worker	Charleston-North Charleston MSA, SC	Y	18800 FQ	26790 MW	34110 TQ	USBLS	5/15
Installation and Repair Worker	Columbia MSA, SC	Y	21290 FQ	27660 MW	32550 TQ	USBLS	5/15
Installation and Repair Worker	Greenville-Anderson-Mauldin MSA, SC	Y	21810 FQ	24720 MW	33640 TQ	USBLS	5/15
Installation and Repair Worker	South Dakota	Y	18380 FQ	19080 MW	19860 TQ	USBLS	5/15
Installation and Repair Worker	Tennessee	Y	20230 FQ	24970 MW	32430 TQ	USBLS	5/15
Installation and Repair Worker	Knoxville MSA, TN	Y	18550 FQ	21910 MW	26110 TQ	USBLS	5/15
Installation and Repair Worker	Memphis MSA, TN-MS-AR	Y	19320 FQ	25460 MW	29690 TQ	USBLS	5/15
Installation and Repair Worker	Nashville-Davidson–Murfreesboro–Franklin MSA, TN	Y	21860 FQ	26650 MW	41100 TQ	USBLS	5/15
Installation and Repair Worker	Texas	Y	21410 FQ	26570 MW	32220 TQ	USBLS	5/15
Installation and Repair Worker	Austin-Round Rock MSA, TX	Y	18830 FQ	25190 MW	30840 TQ	USBLS	5/15
Installation and Repair Worker	Dallas-Plano-Irving PMSA, TX	Y	24980 FQ	29140 MW	34840 TQ	USBLS	5/15
Installation and Repair Worker	Fort Worth-Arlington PMSA, TX	Y	22940 FQ	27850 MW	33300 TQ	USBLS	5/15
Installation and Repair Worker	Houston-The Woodlands-Sugar Land MSA, TX	Y	21510 FQ	26480 MW	32610 TQ	USBLS	5/15
Installation and Repair Worker	San Antonio-New Braunfels MSA, TX	Y	20300 FQ	26820 MW	33890 TQ	USBLS	5/15
Installation and Repair Worker	Utah	Y	20850 FQ	26260 MW	33780 TQ	USBLS	5/15
Installation and Repair Worker	Ogden-Clearfield MSA, UT	Y	20490 FQ	23600 MW	31320 TQ	USBLS	5/15
Installation and Repair Worker	Provo-Orem MSA, UT	Y	18010 FQ	20310 MW	24240 TQ	USBLS	5/15
Installation and Repair Worker	Salt Lake City MSA, UT	Y	25180 FQ	28960 MW	34090 TQ	USBLS	5/15
Installation and Repair Worker	Vermont	Y	22410 FQ	27580 MW	32570 TQ	USBLS	5/15

AE	Average entry wage	AWR	Average wage range	H	Hourly
AEX	Average experienced wage	B	Biweekly	HI	Highest wage paid
ATC	Average total compensation	D	Daily	HR	High end range
AW	Average wage paid	FQ	First quartile wage	LO	Lowest wage paid

LR	Low end range	MTC	Median total compensation
M	Monthly	MW	Median wage paid
MCC	Median cash compensation	MWR	Median wage range
ME	Median entry wage	S	See annotated source

TCC	Total cash compensation
TQ	Third quartile wage
W	Weekly
Y	Yearly

Helper

Occupation/Type/Industry	Location	Per	Low	Mid	High	Source	Date
Helper							
Installation and Repair Worker	Burlington-South Burlington MSA, VT	Y	23720 FQ	27880 MW	31160 TQ	USBLS	5/15
Installation and Repair Worker	Virginia	Y	20670 FQ	26020 MW	31460 TQ	USBLS	5/15
Installation and Repair Worker	Richmond MSA, VA	Y	21330 FQ	25750 MW	31820 TQ	USBLS	5/15
Installation and Repair Worker	Virginia Beach-Norfolk-Newport News MSA, VA-NC	Y	21750 FQ	26400 MW	30430 TQ	USBLS	5/15
Installation and Repair Worker	Washington	H	12.38 FQ	15.15 MW	21.51 TQ	WABLS	3/16
Installation and Repair Worker	Seattle-Bellevue-Everett PMSA, WA	H	13.31 FQ	16.52 MW	21.77 TQ	WABLS	3/16
Installation and Repair Worker	Tacoma-Lakewood PMSA, WA	H	11.71 FQ	15.31 MW	22.66 TQ	WABLS	3/16
Installation and Repair Worker	West Virginia	Y	20530 FQ	27890 MW	34580 TQ	USBLS	5/15
Installation and Repair Worker	Huntington-Ashland MSA, WV-KY-OH	Y	19000 FQ	23700 MW	29460 TQ	USBLS	5/15
Installation and Repair Worker	Wisconsin	Y	20300 FQ	24620 MW	33690 TQ	USBLS	5/15
Installation and Repair Worker	Madison MSA, WI	Y	22860 FQ	29600 MW	35570 TQ	USBLS	5/15
Installation and Repair Worker	Milwaukee-Waukesha-West Allis MSA, WI	Y	20910 FQ	25200 MW	36130 TQ	USBLS	5/15
Installation and Repair Worker	Wyoming	Y	22690 FQ	29190 MW	41580 TQ	USBLS	5/15
Installation and Repair Worker	Puerto Rico	Y	17330 FQ	19090 MW	26220 TQ	USBLS	5/15
Installation and Repair Worker	San Juan-Carolina-Caguas MSA, PR	Y	17370 FQ	19190 MW	27500 TQ	USBLS	5/15
Installation and Repair Worker	Guam	Y	18390 FQ	19660 MW	22810 TQ	USBLS	5/15
Mason, Tile, and Marble Setter	Alabama	Y	20183 AE	27641 AW	31365 AEX	ALBLS	6/16
Mason, Tile, and Marble Setter	Birmingham-Hoover MSA, AL	Y	22631 AE	34266 AW	40088 AEX	ALBLS	6/16
Mason, Tile, and Marble Setter	Arizona	Y	19370 FQ	25630 MW	30030 TQ	USBLS	5/15
Mason, Tile, and Marble Setter	Phoenix-Mesa-Scottsdale MSA, AZ	Y	19420 FQ	25490 MW	29800 TQ	USBLS	5/15
Mason, Tile, and Marble Setter	Arkansas	Y	18150 FQ	20970 MW	24200 TQ	USBLS	5/15
Mason, Tile, and Marble Setter	Little Rock-North Little Rock-Conway MSA, AR	Y	20160 FQ	22440 MW	24720 TQ	USBLS	5/15
Mason, Tile, and Marble Setter	California	H	12.66 FQ	15.55 MW	18.85 TQ	CABLS	1/16-3/16
Mason, Tile, and Marble Setter	Anaheim-Santa Ana-Irvine PMSA, CA	H	12.83 FQ	15.37 MW	18.21 TQ	CABLS	1/16-3/16
Mason, Tile, and Marble Setter	Los Angeles-Long Beach-Glendale PMSA, CA	H	11.08 FQ	12.83 MW	16.56 TQ	CABLS	1/16-3/16
Mason, Tile, and Marble Setter	Riverside-San Bernardino-Ontario MSA, CA	H	13.37 FQ	16.22 MW	20.24 TQ	CABLS	1/16-3/16
Mason, Tile, and Marble Setter	Sacramento–Roseville–Arden-Arcade MSA, CA	H	14.68 FQ	17.47 MW	20.71 TQ	CABLS	1/16-3/16
Mason, Tile, and Marble Setter	San Diego-Carlsbad MSA, CA	H	13.46 FQ	16.37 MW	19.88 TQ	CABLS	1/16-3/16
Mason, Tile, and Marble Setter	San Francisco-Redwood City-South San Francisco PMSA, CA	H	12.73 FQ	15.64 MW	21.57 TQ	CABLS	1/16-3/16
Mason, Tile, and Marble Setter	Colorado	Y	26070 FQ	31640 MW	43210 TQ	USBLS	5/15
Mason, Tile, and Marble Setter	Connecticut	Y		51430 MW		CTBLS	1/16-3/16
Mason, Tile, and Marble Setter	Hartford-West Hartford-East Hartford MSA, CT	Y	38410 FQ	52130 MW	57870 TQ	USBLS	5/15
Mason, Tile, and Marble Setter	Delaware	Y	24620 FQ	30690 MW	36900 TQ	USBLS	5/15
Mason, Tile, and Marble Setter	Washington-Arlington-Alexandria PMSA, DC-VA-MD-WV	Y	23540 FQ	31360 MW	37240 TQ	USBLS	5/15
Mason, Tile, and Marble Setter	Florida	H	10.25 AE	11.93 MW	13.70 AEX	FLBLS	7/16-9/16
Mason, Tile, and Marble Setter	Orlando-Kissimmee-Sanford MSA, FL	H	11.04 AE	12.01 MW	13.35 AEX	FLBLS	7/16-9/16
Mason, Tile, and Marble Setter	Georgia	Y	22890 FQ	26540 MW	29150 TQ	USBLS	5/15
Mason, Tile, and Marble Setter	Atlanta-Sandy Springs-Roswell MSA, GA	Y	25300 FQ	27480 MW	29650 TQ	USBLS	5/15
Mason, Tile, and Marble Setter	Hawaii	Y	24480 FQ	43080 MW	59080 TQ	USBLS	5/15
Mason, Tile, and Marble Setter	Idaho	Y	23110 FQ	30910 MW	38740 TQ	USBLS	5/15
Mason, Tile, and Marble Setter	Boise City MSA, ID	Y	23480 FQ	32700 MW	39700 TQ	USBLS	5/15
Mason, Tile, and Marble Setter	Illinois	Y	25760 FQ	34760 MW	65360 TQ	USBLS	5/15
Mason, Tile, and Marble Setter	Lake County-Kenosha County PMSA, IL-WI	Y	37140 FQ	67590 MW	74140 TQ	USBLS	5/15
Mason, Tile, and Marble Setter	Indiana	Y	24840 FQ	28570 MW	34560 TQ	USBLS	5/15
Mason, Tile, and Marble Setter	Gary PMSA, IN	Y	26630 FQ	28230 MW	29820 TQ	USBLS	5/15
Mason, Tile, and Marble Setter	Indianapolis-Carmel-Anderson MSA, IN	Y	23490 FQ	28360 MW	36830 TQ	USBLS	5/15
Mason, Tile, and Marble Setter	Iowa	Y	23380 FQ	29100 MW	39910 TQ	USBLS	5/15
Mason, Tile, and Marble Setter	Kansas	Y	27120 FQ	31330 MW	38080 TQ	USBLS	5/15
Mason, Tile, and Marble Setter	Wichita MSA, KS	Y	25250 FQ	27570 MW	29890 TQ	USBLS	5/15
Mason, Tile, and Marble Setter	Kentucky	Y	23490 FQ	28120 MW	34940 TQ	USBLS	5/15

AE	Average entry wage	AWR	Average wage range	H	Hourly	LR	Low end range	MTC	Median total compensation	TCC	Total cash compensation
AEX	Average experienced wage	B	Biweekly	HI	Highest wage paid	M	Monthly	MW	Median wage paid	TQ	Third quartile wage
ATC	Average total compensation	D	Daily	HR	High end range	MCC	Median cash compensation	MWR	Median wage range	W	Weekly
AW	Average wage paid	FQ	First quartile wage	LO	Lowest wage paid	ME	Median entry wage	S	See annotated source	Y	Yearly

Occupation/Type/Industry	Location	Per	Low	Mid	High	Source	Date
Helper							
Mason, Tile, and Marble Setter	Louisville-Jefferson County MSA, KY-IN	Y	24250 FQ	28350 MW	32790 TQ	USBLS	5/15
Mason, Tile, and Marble Setter	Louisiana	Y	23190 FQ	27420 MW	31400 TQ	USBLS	5/15
Mason, Tile, and Marble Setter	Baton Rouge MSA, LA	Y	24150 FQ	28040 MW	32560 TQ	USBLS	5/15
Mason, Tile, and Marble Setter	New Orleans-Metairie MSA, LA	Y	26740 FQ	30020 MW	34520 TQ	USBLS	5/15
Mason, Tile, and Marble Setter	Maine	Y	27340 FQ	31810 MW	36270 TQ	USBLS	5/15
Mason, Tile, and Marble Setter	Portland-South Portland MSA, ME	Y	28480 FQ	32710 MW	36870 TQ	USBLS	5/15
Mason, Tile, and Marble Setter	Maryland	Y	20407 AE	28463 MW	32491 AEX	MDBLS	4/16
Mason, Tile, and Marble Setter	Baltimore-Columbia-Towson MSA, MD	Y	27370 FQ	31320 MW	36080 TQ	USBLS	5/15
Mason, Tile, and Marble Setter	Salisbury MSA, MD-DE	Y	21520 FQ	24170 MW	29450 TQ	USBLS	5/15
Mason, Tile, and Marble Setter	Massachusetts	Y	33850 FQ	40370 MW	58320 TQ	USBLS	5/15
Mason, Tile, and Marble Setter	Boston-Cambridge-Newton NECTA, MA	Y	33280 FQ	40840 MW	67180 TQ	USBLS	5/15
Mason, Tile, and Marble Setter	Worcester MSA, MA-CT	Y	28830 FQ	34450 MW	44680 TQ	USBLS	5/15
Mason, Tile, and Marble Setter	Michigan	Y	30260 FQ	38890 MW	45010 TQ	USBLS	5/15
Mason, Tile, and Marble Setter	Detroit-Dearborn-Livonia PMSA, MI	Y	32630 FQ	40050 MW	45690 TQ	USBLS	5/15
Mason, Tile, and Marble Setter	Grand Rapids-Wyoming MSA, MI	Y	33390 FQ	40170 MW	45780 TQ	USBLS	5/15
Mason, Tile, and Marble Setter	Minnesota	Y	28596 FQ	34095 MW	46939 TQ	MNBLS	1/16-3/16
Mason, Tile, and Marble Setter	Mississippi	Y	21580 FQ	25120 MW	29090 TQ	USBLS	5/15
Mason, Tile, and Marble Setter	Jackson MSA, MS	Y	21670 FQ	26040 MW	29820 TQ	USBLS	5/15
Mason, Tile, and Marble Setter	Missouri	Y	27000 FQ	34030 MW	52890 TQ	USBLS	5/15
Mason, Tile, and Marble Setter	Kansas City MSA, MO-KS	Y	26340 FQ	30690 MW	53510 TQ	USBLS	5/15
Mason, Tile, and Marble Setter	St. Louis MSA, MO-IL	Y	30020 FQ	36000 MW	55270 TQ	USBLS	5/15
Mason, Tile, and Marble Setter	Montana	Y	28510 FQ	34240 MW	42250 TQ	USBLS	5/15
Mason, Tile, and Marble Setter	Nebraska	Y	23270 FQ	30610 MW	35870 TQ	NEBLS	7/16-9/16
Mason, Tile, and Marble Setter	Nevada	Y	21480 FQ	26010 MW	30080 TQ	USBLS	5/15
Mason, Tile, and Marble Setter	Las Vegas-Henderson-Paradise MSA, NV	Y	21370 FQ	27360 MW	32310 TQ	USBLS	5/15
Mason, Tile, and Marble Setter	New Hampshire	H	13.25 AE	17.60 MW	19.75 AEX	NHBLS	6/16
Mason, Tile, and Marble Setter	New Jersey	Y	24070 FQ	27660 MW	30990 TQ	USBLS	5/15
Mason, Tile, and Marble Setter	Camden PMSA, NJ	Y	27430 FQ	30380 MW	64240 TQ	USBLS	5/15
Mason, Tile, and Marble Setter	Newark PMSA, NJ-PA	Y	22200 FQ	24390 MW	27930 TQ	USBLS	5/15
Mason, Tile, and Marble Setter	New Mexico	Y	24850 FQ	30980 MW	37430 TQ	USBLS	5/15
Mason, Tile, and Marble Setter	Albuquerque MSA, NM	Y	27190 FQ	30300 MW	34630 TQ	USBLS	5/15
Mason, Tile, and Marble Setter	New York	Y	21970 AE	25910 MW	41290 AEX	NYBLS	1/16-3/16
Mason, Tile, and Marble Setter	Nassau County-Suffolk County PMSA, NY	Y	24000 FQ	63450 MW	79250 TQ	USBLS	5/15
Mason, Tile, and Marble Setter	New York-Jersey City-White Plains PMSA, NY-NJ	Y	21390 FQ	23530 MW	35670 TQ	USBLS	5/15
Mason, Tile, and Marble Setter	North Carolina	Y	22730 FQ	26680 MW	30520 TQ	USBLS	5/15
Mason, Tile, and Marble Setter	Charlotte-Concord-Gastonia MSA, NC-SC	Y	23660 FQ	27730 MW	32250 TQ	USBLS	5/15
Mason, Tile, and Marble Setter	North Dakota	Y	26420 FQ	34590 MW	45690 TQ	USBLS	5/15
Mason, Tile, and Marble Setter	Ohio	Y	29550 FQ	35360 MW	42430 TQ	USBLS	5/15
Mason, Tile, and Marble Setter	Cincinnati MSA, OH-KY-IN	Y	20760 FQ	34270 MW	45840 TQ	USBLS	5/15
Mason, Tile, and Marble Setter	Cleveland-Elyria MSA, OH	Y	33570 FQ	36230 MW	38900 TQ	USBLS	5/15
Mason, Tile, and Marble Setter	Columbus MSA, OH	Y	31790 FQ	35740 MW	40090 TQ	USBLS	5/15
Mason, Tile, and Marble Setter	Oklahoma	Y	23110 FQ	25920 MW	28770 TQ	USBLS	5/15
Mason, Tile, and Marble Setter	Oklahoma City MSA, OK	Y	24550 FQ	27200 MW	29820 TQ	USBLS	5/15
Mason, Tile, and Marble Setter	Tulsa MSA, OK	Y	22880 FQ	25460 MW	28330 TQ	USBLS	5/15
Mason, Tile, and Marble Setter	Oregon	H	13.21 FQ	15.15 MW	18.14 TQ	ORBLS	2016
Mason, Tile, and Marble Setter	Portland-Vancouver-Hillsboro MSA, OR-WA	Y	26250 FQ	31480 MW	38620 TQ	USBLS	5/15
Mason, Tile, and Marble Setter	Pennsylvania	Y	27540 FQ	33710 MW	39520 TQ	USBLS	5/15
Mason, Tile, and Marble Setter	Harrisburg-Carlisle MSA, PA	Y	21940 FQ	27020 MW	30820 TQ	USBLS	5/15
Mason, Tile, and Marble Setter	Montgomery County-Bucks County-Chester County PMSA, PA	Y	30800 FQ	36030 MW	42520 TQ	USBLS	5/15
Mason, Tile, and Marble Setter	Pittsburgh MSA, PA	Y	25880 FQ	30360 MW	36450 TQ	USBLS	5/15
Mason, Tile, and Marble Setter	Rhode Island	Y	24870 FQ	53710 MW	60470 TQ	USBLS	5/15
Mason, Tile, and Marble Setter	Providence-Warwick MSA, RI-MA	Y	33410 FQ	52750 MW	60390 TQ	USBLS	5/15
Mason, Tile, and Marble Setter	South Carolina	Y	22430 FQ	25990 MW	31570 TQ	USBLS	5/15
Mason, Tile, and Marble Setter	Charleston-North Charleston MSA, SC	Y	21190 FQ	25140 MW	31300 TQ	USBLS	5/15
Mason, Tile, and Marble Setter	Columbia MSA, SC	Y	23120 FQ	26670 MW	30920 TQ	USBLS	5/15

AE	Average entry wage	AWR	Average wage range	H	Hourly
AEX	Average experienced wage	B	Biweekly	HI	Highest wage paid
ATC	Average total compensation	D	Daily	HR	High end range
AW	Average wage paid	FQ	First quartile wage	LO	Lowest wage paid

LR	Low end range	MTC	Median total compensation	TCC	Total cash compensation
M	Monthly	MW	Median wage paid	TQ	Third quartile wage
MCC	Median cash compensation	MWR	Median wage range	W	Weekly
ME	Median entry wage	S	See annotated source	Y	Yearly

Occupation/Type/Industry	Location	Per	Low	Mid	High	Source	Date
Helper							
Mason, Tile, and Marble Setter	Greenville-Anderson-Mauldin MSA, SC	Y	22400 FQ	25160 MW	31270 TQ	USBLS	5/15
Mason, Tile, and Marble Setter	South Dakota	Y	23790 FQ	27880 MW	34570 TQ	USBLS	5/15
Mason, Tile, and Marble Setter	Sioux Falls MSA, SD	Y	27660 FQ	31160 MW	37210 TQ	USBLS	5/15
Mason, Tile, and Marble Setter	Tennessee	Y	23390 FQ	27280 MW	30770 TQ	USBLS	5/15
Mason, Tile, and Marble Setter	Knoxville MSA, TN	Y	22220 FQ	25010 MW	28910 TQ	USBLS	5/15
Mason, Tile, and Marble Setter	Memphis MSA, TN-MS-AR	Y	26370 FQ	29700 MW	35730 TQ	USBLS	5/15
Mason, Tile, and Marble Setter	Nashville-Davidson–Murfreesboro–Franklin MSA, TN	Y	26250 FQ	28580 MW	30920 TQ	USBLS	5/15
Mason, Tile, and Marble Setter	Texas	Y	24490 FQ	27420 MW	30160 TQ	USBLS	5/15
Mason, Tile, and Marble Setter	Austin-Round Rock MSA, TX	Y	23590 FQ	26220 MW	28670 TQ	USBLS	5/15
Mason, Tile, and Marble Setter	Dallas-Plano-Irving PMSA, TX	Y	25890 FQ	28630 MW	31420 TQ	USBLS	5/15
Mason, Tile, and Marble Setter	Fort Worth-Arlington PMSA, TX	Y	24370 FQ	27560 MW	30560 TQ	USBLS	5/15
Mason, Tile, and Marble Setter	Houston-The Woodlands-Sugar Land MSA, TX	Y	25520 FQ	27910 MW	30300 TQ	USBLS	5/15
Mason, Tile, and Marble Setter	San Antonio-New Braunfels MSA, TX	Y	26000 FQ	27930 MW	29870 TQ	USBLS	5/15
Mason, Tile, and Marble Setter	Utah	Y	25590 FQ	31660 MW	36920 TQ	USBLS	5/15
Mason, Tile, and Marble Setter	Provo-Orem MSA, UT	Y	29150 FQ	34170 MW	38580 TQ	USBLS	5/15
Mason, Tile, and Marble Setter	Salt Lake City MSA, UT	Y	26500 FQ	32870 MW	37300 TQ	USBLS	5/15
Mason, Tile, and Marble Setter	Vermont	Y	30560 FQ	35910 MW	41730 TQ	USBLS	5/15
Mason, Tile, and Marble Setter	Burlington-South Burlington MSA, VT	Y	34580 FQ	38380 MW	43250 TQ	USBLS	5/15
Mason, Tile, and Marble Setter	Virginia	Y	25310 FQ	30040 MW	36990 TQ	USBLS	5/15
Mason, Tile, and Marble Setter	Richmond MSA, VA	Y	26270 FQ	30770 MW	40530 TQ	USBLS	5/15
Mason, Tile, and Marble Setter	Virginia Beach-Norfolk-Newport News MSA, VA-NC	Y	25730 FQ	28560 MW	32030 TQ	USBLS	5/15
Mason, Tile, and Marble Setter	Washington	H	18.67 FQ	26.10 MW	31.47 TQ	WABLS	3/16
Mason, Tile, and Marble Setter	Seattle-Bellevue-Everett PMSA, WA	H	18.67 FQ	28.54 MW	33.85 TQ	WABLS	3/16
Mason, Tile, and Marble Setter	Tacoma-Lakewood PMSA, WA	H	23.31 FQ	33.45 MW	36.55 TQ	WABLS	3/16
Mason, Tile, and Marble Setter	West Virginia	Y	20330 FQ	23500 MW	27650 TQ	USBLS	5/15
Mason, Tile, and Marble Setter	Huntington-Ashland MSA, WV-KY-OH	Y	19670 FQ	22080 MW	24280 TQ	USBLS	5/15
Mason, Tile, and Marble Setter	Wisconsin	Y	32180 FQ	37510 MW	44060 TQ	USBLS	5/15
Mason, Tile, and Marble Setter	Milwaukee-Waukesha-West Allis MSA, WI	Y	32440 FQ	40120 MW	45420 TQ	USBLS	5/15
Mason, Tile, and Marble Setter	Wyoming	Y	31730 FQ	38010 MW	43990 TQ	USBLS	5/15
Mason, Tile, and Marble Setter	Puerto Rico	Y	17330 FQ	19090 MW	23890 TQ	USBLS	5/15
Painter, Paperhanger, Plasterer	Alabama	Y	18784 AE	23207 AW	25419 AEX	ALBLS	6/16
Painter, Paperhanger, Plasterer	Birmingham-Hoover MSA, AL	Y	22909 AE	23392 AW	23639 AEX	ALBLS	6/16
Painter, Paperhanger, Plasterer	Arizona	Y	24700 FQ	32070 MW	35860 TQ	USBLS	5/15
Painter, Paperhanger, Plasterer	Phoenix-Mesa-Scottsdale MSA, AZ	Y	25640 FQ	33060 MW	36340 TQ	USBLS	5/15
Painter, Paperhanger, Plasterer	Arkansas	Y	18510 FQ	22710 MW	27280 TQ	USBLS	5/15
Painter, Paperhanger, Plasterer	California	H	10.98 FQ	13.94 MW	17.37 TQ	CABLS	1/16-3/16
Painter, Paperhanger, Plasterer	Anaheim-Santa Ana-Irvine PMSA, CA	H	13.14 FQ	14.06 MW	14.97 TQ	CABLS	1/16-3/16
Painter, Paperhanger, Plasterer	Los Angeles-Long Beach-Glendale PMSA, CA	H	9.34 FQ	9.47 MW	14.73 TQ	CABLS	1/16-3/16
Painter, Paperhanger, Plasterer	Oakland-Hayward-Berkeley PMSA, CA	H	13.07 FQ	14.39 MW	16.86 TQ	CABLS	1/16-3/16
Painter, Paperhanger, Plasterer	Riverside-San Bernardino-Ontario MSA, CA	H	12.36 FQ	13.71 MW	15.07 TQ	CABLS	1/16-3/16
Painter, Paperhanger, Plasterer	Sacramento–Roseville–Arden-Arcade MSA, CA	H	14.92 FQ	16.59 MW	18.01 TQ	CABLS	1/16-3/16
Painter, Paperhanger, Plasterer	San Diego-Carlsbad MSA, CA	H	13.62 FQ	16.76 MW	21.07 TQ	CABLS	1/16-3/16
Painter, Paperhanger, Plasterer	Colorado	Y	21290 FQ	23360 MW	32320 TQ	USBLS	5/15
Painter, Paperhanger, Plasterer	Delaware	Y	24360 FQ	28530 MW	34980 TQ	USBLS	5/15
Painter, Paperhanger, Plasterer	Wilmington PMSA, DE-MD-NJ	Y	25050 FQ	28960 MW	36120 TQ	USBLS	5/15
Painter, Paperhanger, Plasterer	Florida	H	9.43 AE	11.43 MW	13.80 AEX	FLBLS	7/16-9/16
Painter, Paperhanger, Plasterer	Orlando-Kissimmee-Sanford MSA, FL	H	8.97 AE	10.04 MW	11.53 AEX	FLBLS	7/16-9/16
Painter, Paperhanger, Plasterer	Tampa-St. Petersburg-Clearwater MSA, FL	H	9.02 AE	9.40 MW	10.41 AEX	FLBLS	7/16-9/16
Painter, Paperhanger, Plasterer	Georgia	Y	21590 FQ	25320 MW	28550 TQ	USBLS	5/15
Painter, Paperhanger, Plasterer	Atlanta-Sandy Springs-Roswell MSA, GA	Y	22670 FQ	26360 MW	29100 TQ	USBLS	5/15

AE	Average entry wage	AWR	Average wage range	H	Hourly	LR	Low end range	MTC	Median total compensation	TCC	Total cash compensation
AEX	Average experienced wage	B	Biweekly	HI	Highest wage paid	M	Monthly	MW	Median wage paid	TQ	Third quartile wage
ATC	Average total compensation	D	Daily	HR	High end range	MCC	Median cash compensation	MWR	Median wage range	W	Weekly
AW	Average wage paid	FQ	First quartile wage	LO	Lowest wage paid	ME	Median entry wage	S	See annotated source	Y	Yearly

762

Helper

Occupation/Type/Industry	Location	Per	Low	Mid	High	Source	Date
Painter, Paperhanger, Plasterer	Hawaii	Y	19840 FQ	26130 MW	33070 TQ	USBLS	5/15
Painter, Paperhanger, Plasterer	Urban Honolulu MSA, HI	Y	19140 FQ	23990 MW	33250 TQ	USBLS	5/15
Painter, Paperhanger, Plasterer	Idaho	Y	17790 FQ	19850 MW	24420 TQ	USBLS	5/15
Painter, Paperhanger, Plasterer	Illinois	Y	24660 FQ	34570 MW	53050 TQ	USBLS	5/15
Painter, Paperhanger, Plasterer	Chicago-Naperville-Arlington Heights PMSA, IL	Y	52060 FQ	59100 MW	85070 TQ	USBLS	5/15
Painter, Paperhanger, Plasterer	Indiana	Y	17800 FQ	21870 MW	27770 TQ	USBLS	5/15
Painter, Paperhanger, Plasterer	Iowa	Y	24420 FQ	27690 MW	31770 TQ	USBLS	5/15
Painter, Paperhanger, Plasterer	Kansas	Y	20380 FQ	24980 MW	43520 TQ	USBLS	5/15
Painter, Paperhanger, Plasterer	Louisiana	Y	22480 FQ	26270 MW	29830 TQ	USBLS	5/15
Painter, Paperhanger, Plasterer	Baton Rouge MSA, LA	Y	22990 FQ	26680 MW	30540 TQ	USBLS	5/15
Painter, Paperhanger, Plasterer	New Orleans-Metairie MSA, LA	Y	18660 FQ	22370 MW	27260 TQ	USBLS	5/15
Painter, Paperhanger, Plasterer	Maryland	Y	22841 AE	31419 MW	35708 AEX	MDBLS	4/16
Painter, Paperhanger, Plasterer	Massachusetts	Y	22300 FQ	29420 MW	38290 TQ	USBLS	5/15
Painter, Paperhanger, Plasterer	Michigan	Y	21260 FQ	24130 MW	27940 TQ	USBLS	5/15
Painter, Paperhanger, Plasterer	Detroit-Dearborn-Livonia PMSA, MI	Y	22310 FQ	24960 MW	29520 TQ	USBLS	5/15
Painter, Paperhanger, Plasterer	Minnesota	Y	27435 FQ	31320 MW	35679 TQ	MNBLS	1/16-3/16
Painter, Paperhanger, Plasterer	Mississippi	Y	19860 FQ	24690 MW	34560 TQ	USBLS	5/15
Painter, Paperhanger, Plasterer	Nebraska	Y	24175 FQ	28520 MW	33115 TQ	NEBLS	7/16-9/16
Painter, Paperhanger, Plasterer	Nevada	Y	23660 FQ	28960 MW	34180 TQ	USBLS	5/15
Painter, Paperhanger, Plasterer	Las Vegas-Henderson-Paradise MSA, NV	Y	26550 FQ	30760 MW	34910 TQ	USBLS	5/15
Painter, Paperhanger, Plasterer	New Jersey	Y	25400 FQ	27510 MW	29630 TQ	USBLS	5/15
Painter, Paperhanger, Plasterer	New Mexico	Y	21610 FQ	23700 MW	28540 TQ	USBLS	5/15
Painter, Paperhanger, Plasterer	Albuquerque MSA, NM	Y	21310 FQ	22930 MW	24560 TQ	USBLS	5/15
Painter, Paperhanger, Plasterer	New York	Y	22900 AE	29210 MW	37740 AEX	NYBLS	1/16-3/16
Painter, Paperhanger, Plasterer	New York-Jersey City-White Plains PMSA, NY-NJ	Y	24530 FQ	29990 MW	40750 TQ	USBLS	5/15
Painter, Paperhanger, Plasterer	North Carolina	Y	21290 FQ	24440 MW	28420 TQ	USBLS	5/15
Painter, Paperhanger, Plasterer	Charlotte-Concord-Gastonia MSA, NC-SC	Y	24500 FQ	26980 MW	29650 TQ	USBLS	5/15
Painter, Paperhanger, Plasterer	Ohio	Y	20850 FQ	23810 MW	27550 TQ	USBLS	5/15
Painter, Paperhanger, Plasterer	Oklahoma	Y	17320 FQ	19250 MW	27900 TQ	USBLS	5/15
Painter, Paperhanger, Plasterer	Oregon	H	10.29 FQ	11.78 MW	13.90 TQ	ORBLS	2016
Painter, Paperhanger, Plasterer	Portland-Vancouver-Hillsboro MSA, OR-WA	Y	21070 FQ	24070 MW	29810 TQ	USBLS	5/15
Painter, Paperhanger, Plasterer	Pennsylvania	Y	20850 FQ	22850 MW	25170 TQ	USBLS	5/15
Painter, Paperhanger, Plasterer	Montgomery County-Bucks County-Chester County PMSA, PA	Y	20810 FQ	24210 MW	27720 TQ	USBLS	5/15
Painter, Paperhanger, Plasterer	Pittsburgh MSA, PA	Y	20890 FQ	22390 MW	23900 TQ	USBLS	5/15
Painter, Paperhanger, Plasterer	South Carolina	Y	19440 FQ	21920 MW	24390 TQ	USBLS	5/15
Painter, Paperhanger, Plasterer	Tennessee	Y	21800 FQ	26350 MW	31530 TQ	USBLS	5/15
Painter, Paperhanger, Plasterer	Knoxville MSA, TN	Y	21050 FQ	27890 MW	34990 TQ	USBLS	5/15
Painter, Paperhanger, Plasterer	Nashville-Davidson–Murfreesboro–Franklin MSA, TN	Y	23360 FQ	26600 MW	29850 TQ	USBLS	5/15
Painter, Paperhanger, Plasterer	Texas	Y	22780 FQ	26760 MW	30100 TQ	USBLS	5/15
Painter, Paperhanger, Plasterer	Austin-Round Rock MSA, TX	Y	23790 FQ	26950 MW	29840 TQ	USBLS	5/15
Painter, Paperhanger, Plasterer	Dallas-Plano-Irving PMSA, TX	Y	20180 FQ	23200 MW	27630 TQ	USBLS	5/15
Painter, Paperhanger, Plasterer	Houston-The Woodlands-Sugar Land MSA, TX	Y	25420 FQ	28100 MW	30800 TQ	USBLS	5/15
Painter, Paperhanger, Plasterer	San Antonio-New Braunfels MSA, TX	Y	19690 FQ	25330 MW	28780 TQ	USBLS	5/15
Painter, Paperhanger, Plasterer	Utah	Y	21460 FQ	26750 MW	30650 TQ	USBLS	5/15
Painter, Paperhanger, Plasterer	Provo-Orem MSA, UT	Y	21360 FQ	26200 MW	29670 TQ	USBLS	5/15
Painter, Paperhanger, Plasterer	Salt Lake City MSA, UT	Y	24070 FQ	31560 MW	35960 TQ	USBLS	5/15
Painter, Paperhanger, Plasterer	Virginia	Y	22020 FQ	25800 MW	30000 TQ	USBLS	5/15
Painter, Paperhanger, Plasterer	Richmond MSA, VA	Y	27010 FQ	29030 MW	31060 TQ	USBLS	5/15
Painter, Paperhanger, Plasterer	Virginia Beach-Norfolk-Newport News MSA, VA-NC	Y	21330 FQ	23900 MW	30330 TQ	USBLS	5/15
Painter, Paperhanger, Plasterer	Washington	H	12.90 FQ	14.98 MW	17.15 TQ	WABLS	3/16
Painter, Paperhanger, Plasterer	Wisconsin	Y	21830 FQ	25650 MW	30310 TQ	USBLS	5/15
Painter, Paperhanger, Plasterer	Wyoming	Y	20770 FQ	24550 MW	29550 TQ	USBLS	5/15
Pipelayer, Plumber, Pipefitter, and Steamfitter	Alabama	Y	20193 AE	26684 AW	29925 AEX	ALBLS	6/16
Pipelayer, Plumber, Pipefitter, and Steamfitter	Birmingham-Hoover MSA, AL	Y	22364 AE	29986 AW	33803 AEX	ALBLS	6/16

AE	Average entry wage	AWR	Average wage range	H	Hourly	LR	Low end range	MTC	Median total compensation	TCC	Total cash compensation
AEX	Average experienced wage	B	Biweekly	HI	Highest wage paid	M	Monthly	MW	Median wage paid	TQ	Third quartile wage
ATC	Average total compensation	D	Daily	HR	High end range	MCC	Median cash compensation	MWR	Median wage range	W	Weekly
AW	Average wage paid	FQ	First quartile wage	LO	Lowest wage paid	ME	Median entry wage	S	See annotated source	Y	Yearly

Occupation/Type/Industry	Location	Per	Low	Mid	High	Source	Date
Helper							
Pipelayer, Plumber, Pipefitter, and Steamfitter	Arizona	Y	22370 FQ	26340 MW	31270 TQ	USBLS	5/15
Pipelayer, Plumber, Pipefitter, and Steamfitter	Phoenix-Mesa-Scottsdale MSA, AZ	Y	22280 FQ	26180 MW	31840 TQ	USBLS	5/15
Pipelayer, Plumber, Pipefitter, and Steamfitter	Tucson MSA, AZ	Y	24090 FQ	27680 MW	31310 TQ	USBLS	5/15
Pipelayer, Plumber, Pipefitter, and Steamfitter	Arkansas	Y	18410 FQ	21490 MW	24730 TQ	USBLS	5/15
Pipelayer, Plumber, Pipefitter, and Steamfitter	Little Rock-North Little Rock-Conway MSA, AR	Y	21060 FQ	23520 MW	27390 TQ	USBLS	5/15
Pipelayer, Plumber, Pipefitter, and Steamfitter	California	H	13.04 FQ	14.75 MW	17.73 TQ	CABLS	1/16-3/16
Pipelayer, Plumber, Pipefitter, and Steamfitter	Anaheim-Santa Ana-Irvine PMSA, CA	H	13.13 FQ	14.66 MW	17.44 TQ	CABLS	1/16-3/16
Pipelayer, Plumber, Pipefitter, and Steamfitter	Los Angeles-Long Beach-Glendale PMSA, CA	H	13.14 FQ	14.83 MW	17.32 TQ	CABLS	1/16-3/16
Pipelayer, Plumber, Pipefitter, and Steamfitter	Oakland-Hayward-Berkeley PMSA, CA	H	13.55 FQ	15.12 MW	17.83 TQ	CABLS	1/16-3/16
Pipelayer, Plumber, Pipefitter, and Steamfitter	Riverside-San Bernardino-Ontario MSA, CA	H	13.14 FQ	14.77 MW	17.89 TQ	CABLS	1/16-3/16
Pipelayer, Plumber, Pipefitter, and Steamfitter	Sacramento–Roseville–Arden-Arcade MSA, CA	H	14.18 FQ	17.32 MW	21.27 TQ	CABLS	1/16-3/16
Pipelayer, Plumber, Pipefitter, and Steamfitter	San Diego-Carlsbad MSA, CA	H	11.81 FQ	13.90 MW	18.15 TQ	CABLS	1/16-3/16
Pipelayer, Plumber, Pipefitter, and Steamfitter	Colorado	Y	19710 FQ	26900 MW	34770 TQ	USBLS	5/15
Pipelayer, Plumber, Pipefitter, and Steamfitter	Denver-Aurora-Lakewood MSA, CO	Y	18670 FQ	25520 MW	30010 TQ	USBLS	5/15
Pipelayer, Plumber, Pipefitter, and Steamfitter	Connecticut	Y		28703 MW		CTBLS	1/16-3/16
Pipelayer, Plumber, Pipefitter, and Steamfitter	Bridgeport-Stamford-Norwalk MSA, CT	Y	23150 FQ	27830 MW	34480 TQ	USBLS	5/15
Pipelayer, Plumber, Pipefitter, and Steamfitter	Delaware	Y	24780 FQ	27230 MW	29560 TQ	USBLS	5/15
Pipelayer, Plumber, Pipefitter, and Steamfitter	Wilmington PMSA, DE-MD-NJ	Y	22720 FQ	26940 MW	29770 TQ	USBLS	5/15
Pipelayer, Plumber, Pipefitter, and Steamfitter	District of Columbia	Y	27500 FQ	33600 MW	42310 TQ	USBLS	5/15
Pipelayer, Plumber, Pipefitter, and Steamfitter	Washington-Arlington-Alexandria PMSA, DC-VA-MD-WV	Y	25340 FQ	30800 MW	36670 TQ	USBLS	5/15
Pipelayer, Plumber, Pipefitter, and Steamfitter	Florida	H	9.92 AE	12.77 MW	14.55 AEX	FLBLS	7/16-9/16
Pipelayer, Plumber, Pipefitter, and Steamfitter	Fort Lauderdale-Pompano Beach-Deerfield Beach PMSA, FL	H	12.70 AE	14.29 MW	15.24 AEX	FLBLS	7/16-9/16
Pipelayer, Plumber, Pipefitter, and Steamfitter	Miami-Miami Beach-Kendall PMSA, FL	H	12.42 AE	15.47 MW	17.33 AEX	FLBLS	7/16-9/16
Pipelayer, Plumber, Pipefitter, and Steamfitter	Orlando-Kissimmee-Sanford MSA, FL	H	9.45 AE	11.65 MW	13.02 AEX	FLBLS	7/16-9/16
Pipelayer, Plumber, Pipefitter, and Steamfitter	Tampa-St. Petersburg-Clearwater MSA, FL	H	9.28 AE	11.54 MW	13.35 AEX	FLBLS	7/16-9/16
Pipelayer, Plumber, Pipefitter, and Steamfitter	Georgia	Y	22230 FQ	27250 MW	34160 TQ	USBLS	5/15

AE	Average entry wage	AWR	Average wage range	H	Hourly	LR	Low end range	MTC	Median total compensation	TCC	Total cash compensation
AEX	Average experienced wage	B	Biweekly	HI	Highest wage paid	M	Monthly	MW	Median wage paid	TQ	Third quartile wage
ATC	Average total compensation	D	Daily	HR	High end range	MCC	Median cash compensation	MWR	Median wage range	W	Weekly
AW	Average wage paid	FQ	First quartile wage	LO	Lowest wage paid	ME	Median entry wage	S	See annotated source	Y	Yearly

Helper

Occupation/Type/Industry	Location	Per	Low	Mid	High	Source	Date
Pipelayer, Plumber, Pipefitter, and Steamfitter	Atlanta-Sandy Springs-Roswell MSA, GA	Y	24660 FQ	29270 MW	36930 TQ	USBLS	5/15
Pipelayer, Plumber, Pipefitter, and Steamfitter	Augusta-Richmond County MSA, GA-SC	Y	20880 FQ	23130 MW	27020 TQ	USBLS	5/15
Pipelayer, Plumber, Pipefitter, and Steamfitter	Hawaii	Y	40800 FQ	45350 MW	49890 TQ	USBLS	5/15
Pipelayer, Plumber, Pipefitter, and Steamfitter	Urban Honolulu MSA, HI	Y	41390 FQ	45870 MW	50490 TQ	USBLS	5/15
Pipelayer, Plumber, Pipefitter, and Steamfitter	Idaho	Y	24880 FQ	31030 MW	44080 TQ	USBLS	5/15
Pipelayer, Plumber, Pipefitter, and Steamfitter	Boise City MSA, ID	Y	27480 FQ	34200 MW	49270 TQ	USBLS	5/15
Pipelayer, Plumber, Pipefitter, and Steamfitter	Illinois	Y	22930 FQ	27790 MW	34150 TQ	USBLS	5/15
Pipelayer, Plumber, Pipefitter, and Steamfitter	Chicago-Naperville-Arlington Heights PMSA, IL	Y	25950 FQ	30410 MW	38130 TQ	USBLS	5/15
Pipelayer, Plumber, Pipefitter, and Steamfitter	Lake County-Kenosha County PMSA, IL-WI	Y	19330 FQ	23180 MW	29750 TQ	USBLS	5/15
Pipelayer, Plumber, Pipefitter, and Steamfitter	Indiana	Y	25710 FQ	29060 MW	35470 TQ	USBLS	5/15
Pipelayer, Plumber, Pipefitter, and Steamfitter	Gary PMSA, IN	Y	20010 FQ	32650 MW	53570 TQ	USBLS	5/15
Pipelayer, Plumber, Pipefitter, and Steamfitter	Iowa	Y	25620 FQ	28150 MW	30680 TQ	USBLS	5/15
Pipelayer, Plumber, Pipefitter, and Steamfitter	Kansas	Y	24480 FQ	27800 MW	31880 TQ	USBLS	5/15
Pipelayer, Plumber, Pipefitter, and Steamfitter	Wichita MSA, KS	Y	26740 FQ	29300 MW	33410 TQ	USBLS	5/15
Pipelayer, Plumber, Pipefitter, and Steamfitter	Kentucky	Y	20010 FQ	24450 MW	29740 TQ	USBLS	5/15
Pipelayer, Plumber, Pipefitter, and Steamfitter	Louisville-Jefferson County MSA, KY-IN	Y	22470 FQ	26130 MW	31280 TQ	USBLS	5/15
Pipelayer, Plumber, Pipefitter, and Steamfitter	Louisiana	Y	24990 FQ	29060 MW	35230 TQ	USBLS	5/15
Pipelayer, Plumber, Pipefitter, and Steamfitter	Baton Rouge MSA, LA	Y	25040 FQ	30540 MW	37160 TQ	USBLS	5/15
Pipelayer, Plumber, Pipefitter, and Steamfitter	New Orleans-Metairie MSA, LA	Y	26220 FQ	28910 MW	32580 TQ	USBLS	5/15
Pipelayer, Plumber, Pipefitter, and Steamfitter	Maine	Y	25710 FQ	32980 MW	36420 TQ	USBLS	5/15
Pipelayer, Plumber, Pipefitter, and Steamfitter	Portland-South Portland MSA, ME	Y	21230 FQ	23170 MW	26920 TQ	USBLS	5/15
Pipelayer, Plumber, Pipefitter, and Steamfitter	Maryland	Y	23163 AE	30072 MW	33527 AEX	MDBLS	4/16
Pipelayer, Plumber, Pipefitter, and Steamfitter	Baltimore-Columbia-Towson MSA, MD	Y	24380 FQ	27860 MW	30960 TQ	USBLS	5/15
Pipelayer, Plumber, Pipefitter, and Steamfitter	Salisbury MSA, MD-DE	Y	19050 FQ	26170 MW	28720 TQ	USBLS	5/15
Pipelayer, Plumber, Pipefitter, and Steamfitter	Massachusetts	Y	26110 FQ	32090 MW	39900 TQ	USBLS	5/15
Pipelayer, Plumber, Pipefitter, and Steamfitter	Boston-Cambridge-Newton NECTA, MA	Y	26570 FQ	35270 MW	42650 TQ	USBLS	5/15
Pipelayer, Plumber, Pipefitter, and Steamfitter	Michigan	Y	20680 FQ	24990 MW	29680 TQ	USBLS	5/15
Pipelayer, Plumber, Pipefitter, and Steamfitter	Detroit-Dearborn-Livonia PMSA, MI	Y	24240 FQ	28630 MW	33580 TQ	USBLS	5/15
Pipelayer, Plumber, Pipefitter, and Steamfitter	Grand Rapids-Wyoming MSA, MI	Y	21820 FQ	24440 MW	28880 TQ	USBLS	5/15

Helper

Occupation/Type/Industry	Location	Per	Low	Mid	High	Source	Date
Pipelayer, Plumber, Pipefitter, and Steamfitter	Minnesota	Y	29080 FQ	35305 MW	42106 TQ	MNBLS	1/16-3/16
Pipelayer, Plumber, Pipefitter, and Steamfitter	Minneapolis-St. Paul-Bloomington MSA, MN-WI	Y	29009 FQ	35457 MW	41481 TQ	MNBLS	1/16-3/16
Pipelayer, Plumber, Pipefitter, and Steamfitter	Mississippi	Y	18670 FQ	23850 MW	29840 TQ	USBLS	5/15
Pipelayer, Plumber, Pipefitter, and Steamfitter	Jackson MSA, MS	Y	22110 FQ	26620 MW	30460 TQ	USBLS	5/15
Pipelayer, Plumber, Pipefitter, and Steamfitter	Missouri	Y	22680 FQ	28970 MW	37270 TQ	USBLS	5/15
Pipelayer, Plumber, Pipefitter, and Steamfitter	Kansas City MSA, MO-KS	Y	26910 FQ	29550 MW	34510 TQ	USBLS	5/15
Pipelayer, Plumber, Pipefitter, and Steamfitter	St. Louis MSA, MO-IL	Y	23790 FQ	30670 MW	37970 TQ	USBLS	5/15
Pipelayer, Plumber, Pipefitter, and Steamfitter	Montana	Y	28020 FQ	33120 MW	36390 TQ	USBLS	5/15
Pipelayer, Plumber, Pipefitter, and Steamfitter	Nebraska	Y	22695 FQ	28770 MW	36540 TQ	NEBLS	7/16-9/16
Pipelayer, Plumber, Pipefitter, and Steamfitter	Omaha-Council Bluffs MSA, NE-IA	Y	24875 FQ	32145 MW	38660 TQ	NEBLS	7/16-9/16
Pipelayer, Plumber, Pipefitter, and Steamfitter	Nevada	Y	20660 FQ	25820 MW	30060 TQ	USBLS	5/15
Pipelayer, Plumber, Pipefitter, and Steamfitter	Las Vegas-Henderson-Paradise MSA, NV	Y	20250 FQ	25460 MW	29790 TQ	USBLS	5/15
Pipelayer, Plumber, Pipefitter, and Steamfitter	New Hampshire	H	10.84 AE	15.26 MW	17.91 AEX	NHBLS	6/16
Pipelayer, Plumber, Pipefitter, and Steamfitter	New Jersey	Y	26230 FQ	32290 MW	37900 TQ	USBLS	5/15
Pipelayer, Plumber, Pipefitter, and Steamfitter	Camden PMSA, NJ	Y	26650 FQ	29240 MW	36270 TQ	USBLS	5/15
Pipelayer, Plumber, Pipefitter, and Steamfitter	Newark PMSA, NJ-PA	Y	22880 FQ	35490 MW	42990 TQ	USBLS	5/15
Pipelayer, Plumber, Pipefitter, and Steamfitter	New Mexico	Y	23220 FQ	28460 MW	34480 TQ	USBLS	5/15
Pipelayer, Plumber, Pipefitter, and Steamfitter	Albuquerque MSA, NM	Y	25730 FQ	31710 MW	36000 TQ	USBLS	5/15
Pipelayer, Plumber, Pipefitter, and Steamfitter	New York	Y	22310 AE	31220 MW	40790 AEX	NYBLS	1/16-3/16
Pipelayer, Plumber, Pipefitter, and Steamfitter	Buffalo-Cheektowaga-Niagara Falls MSA, NY	Y	26700 FQ	29530 MW	41230 TQ	USBLS	5/15
Pipelayer, Plumber, Pipefitter, and Steamfitter	Nassau County-Suffolk County PMSA, NY	Y	22190 FQ	24410 MW	36360 TQ	USBLS	5/15
Pipelayer, Plumber, Pipefitter, and Steamfitter	New York-Jersey City-White Plains PMSA, NY-NJ	Y	24740 FQ	32440 MW	39600 TQ	USBLS	5/15
Pipelayer, Plumber, Pipefitter, and Steamfitter	Rochester MSA, NY	Y	23880 FQ	36180 MW	45830 TQ	USBLS	5/15
Pipelayer, Plumber, Pipefitter, and Steamfitter	North Carolina	Y	22600 FQ	27400 MW	32940 TQ	USBLS	5/15
Pipelayer, Plumber, Pipefitter, and Steamfitter	Charlotte-Concord-Gastonia MSA, NC-SC	Y	22050 FQ	25410 MW	30070 TQ	USBLS	5/15
Pipelayer, Plumber, Pipefitter, and Steamfitter	Raleigh MSA, NC	Y	23860 FQ	30920 MW	36560 TQ	USBLS	5/15
Pipelayer, Plumber, Pipefitter, and Steamfitter	North Dakota	Y	25380 FQ	32790 MW	36690 TQ	USBLS	5/15
Pipelayer, Plumber, Pipefitter, and Steamfitter	Ohio	Y	19110 FQ	23820 MW	30130 TQ	USBLS	5/15
Pipelayer, Plumber, Pipefitter, and Steamfitter	Cincinnati MSA, OH-KY-IN	Y	19160 FQ	25670 MW	30980 TQ	USBLS	5/15
Pipelayer, Plumber, Pipefitter, and Steamfitter	Cleveland-Elyria MSA, OH	Y	18860 FQ	28790 MW	39750 TQ	USBLS	5/15
Pipelayer, Plumber, Pipefitter, and Steamfitter	Columbus MSA, OH	Y	19160 FQ	22310 MW	26540 TQ	USBLS	5/15

AE	Average entry wage	AWR	Average wage range	H	Hourly	LR	Low end range	MTC Median total compensation
AEX	Average experienced wage	B	Biweekly	HI	Highest wage paid	M	Monthly	MW Median wage paid
ATC	Average total compensation	D	Daily	HR	High end range	MCC	Median cash compensation	MWR Median wage range
AW	Average wage paid	FQ	First quartile wage	LO	Lowest wage paid	ME	Median entry wage	S See annotated source

TCC	Total cash compensation
TQ	Third quartile wage
W	Weekly
Y	Yearly

Helper

Occupation/Type/Industry	Location	Per	Low	Mid	High	Source	Date
Pipelayer, Plumber, Pipefitter, and Steamfitter	Oklahoma	Y	23020 FQ	27610 MW	33860 TQ	USBLS	5/15
Pipelayer, Plumber, Pipefitter, and Steamfitter	Oklahoma City MSA, OK	Y	23230 FQ	27240 MW	32540 TQ	USBLS	5/15
Pipelayer, Plumber, Pipefitter, and Steamfitter	Tulsa MSA, OK	Y	22560 FQ	27820 MW	35080 TQ	USBLS	5/15
Pipelayer, Plumber, Pipefitter, and Steamfitter	Oregon	H	13.40 FQ	15.95 MW	20.35 TQ	ORBLS	2016
Pipelayer, Plumber, Pipefitter, and Steamfitter	Portland-Vancouver-Hillsboro MSA, OR-WA	Y	29980 FQ	41360 MW	47890 TQ	USBLS	5/15
Pipelayer, Plumber, Pipefitter, and Steamfitter	Pennsylvania	Y	25410 FQ	30250 MW	37200 TQ	USBLS	5/15
Pipelayer, Plumber, Pipefitter, and Steamfitter	Harrisburg-Carlisle MSA, PA	Y	22860 FQ	29600 MW	35290 TQ	USBLS	5/15
Pipelayer, Plumber, Pipefitter, and Steamfitter	Montgomery County-Bucks County-Chester County PMSA, PA	Y	26410 FQ	29780 MW	37160 TQ	USBLS	5/15
Pipelayer, Plumber, Pipefitter, and Steamfitter	Philadelphia PMSA, PA	Y	23800 FQ	27940 MW	33570 TQ	USBLS	5/15
Pipelayer, Plumber, Pipefitter, and Steamfitter	Pittsburgh MSA, PA	Y	26960 FQ	30380 MW	39520 TQ	USBLS	5/15
Pipelayer, Plumber, Pipefitter, and Steamfitter	Rhode Island	Y	26330 FQ	28200 MW	30070 TQ	USBLS	5/15
Pipelayer, Plumber, Pipefitter, and Steamfitter	Providence-Warwick MSA, RI-MA	Y	26430 FQ	28350 MW	30270 TQ	USBLS	5/15
Pipelayer, Plumber, Pipefitter, and Steamfitter	South Carolina	Y	24120 FQ	27790 MW	31200 TQ	USBLS	5/15
Pipelayer, Plumber, Pipefitter, and Steamfitter	Charleston-North Charleston MSA, SC	Y	23310 FQ	26610 MW	29420 TQ	USBLS	5/15
Pipelayer, Plumber, Pipefitter, and Steamfitter	Columbia MSA, SC	Y	27590 FQ	32230 MW	39120 TQ	USBLS	5/15
Pipelayer, Plumber, Pipefitter, and Steamfitter	Greenville-Anderson-Mauldin MSA, SC	Y	23250 FQ	26680 MW	29380 TQ	USBLS	5/15
Pipelayer, Plumber, Pipefitter, and Steamfitter	South Dakota	Y	24590 FQ	27670 MW	30710 TQ	USBLS	5/15
Pipelayer, Plumber, Pipefitter, and Steamfitter	Sioux Falls MSA, SD	Y	25800 FQ	28510 MW	31230 TQ	USBLS	5/15
Pipelayer, Plumber, Pipefitter, and Steamfitter	Tennessee	Y	23850 FQ	29090 MW	35430 TQ	USBLS	5/15
Pipelayer, Plumber, Pipefitter, and Steamfitter	Knoxville MSA, TN	Y	22990 FQ	27960 MW	33940 TQ	USBLS	5/15
Pipelayer, Plumber, Pipefitter, and Steamfitter	Memphis MSA, TN-MS-AR	Y	23930 FQ	29330 MW	35390 TQ	USBLS	5/15
Pipelayer, Plumber, Pipefitter, and Steamfitter	Nashville-Davidson–Murfreesboro–Franklin MSA, TN	Y	23290 FQ	30660 MW	37160 TQ	USBLS	5/15
Pipelayer, Plumber, Pipefitter, and Steamfitter	Texas	Y	24960 FQ	29380 MW	35430 TQ	USBLS	5/15
Pipelayer, Plumber, Pipefitter, and Steamfitter	Austin-Round Rock MSA, TX	Y	23540 FQ	27440 MW	31270 TQ	USBLS	5/15
Pipelayer, Plumber, Pipefitter, and Steamfitter	Dallas-Plano-Irving PMSA, TX	Y	25100 FQ	28760 MW	33730 TQ	USBLS	5/15
Pipelayer, Plumber, Pipefitter, and Steamfitter	Fort Worth-Arlington PMSA, TX	Y	25800 FQ	30520 MW	35660 TQ	USBLS	5/15
Pipelayer, Plumber, Pipefitter, and Steamfitter	Houston-The Woodlands-Sugar Land MSA, TX	Y	26710 FQ	31700 MW	37750 TQ	USBLS	5/15
Pipelayer, Plumber, Pipefitter, and Steamfitter	San Antonio-New Braunfels MSA, TX	Y	24600 FQ	28890 MW	34530 TQ	USBLS	5/15
Pipelayer, Plumber, Pipefitter, and Steamfitter	Utah	Y	19510 FQ	23410 MW	27970 TQ	USBLS	5/15

AE Average entry wage	**AWR** Average wage range	**H** Hourly	**LR** Low end range	**MTC** Median total compensation	**TCC** Total cash compensation
AEX Average experienced wage	**B** Biweekly	**HI** Highest wage paid	**M** Monthly	**MW** Median wage paid	**TQ** Third quartile wage
ATC Average total compensation	**D** Daily	**HR** High end range	**MCC** Median cash compensation	**MWR** Median wage range	**W** Weekly
AW Average wage paid	**FQ** First quartile wage	**LO** Lowest wage paid	**ME** Median entry wage	**S** See annotated source	**Y** Yearly

Helper

Occupation/Type/Industry	Location	Per	Low	Mid	High	Source	Date
Pipelayer, Plumber, Pipefitter, and Steamfitter	Ogden-Clearfield MSA, UT	Y	20600 FQ	22310 MW	24010 TQ	USBLS	5/15
Pipelayer, Plumber, Pipefitter, and Steamfitter	Provo-Orem MSA, UT	Y	17620 FQ	24450 MW	28420 TQ	USBLS	5/15
Pipelayer, Plumber, Pipefitter, and Steamfitter	Salt Lake City MSA, UT	Y	19550 FQ	22430 MW	25550 TQ	USBLS	5/15
Pipelayer, Plumber, Pipefitter, and Steamfitter	Vermont	Y	26570 FQ	29150 MW	32870 TQ	USBLS	5/15
Pipelayer, Plumber, Pipefitter, and Steamfitter	Burlington-South Burlington MSA, VT	Y	26330 FQ	28880 MW	32730 TQ	USBLS	5/15
Pipelayer, Plumber, Pipefitter, and Steamfitter	Virginia	Y	23390 FQ	28740 MW	34530 TQ	USBLS	5/15
Pipelayer, Plumber, Pipefitter, and Steamfitter	Richmond MSA, VA	Y	26890 FQ	32360 MW	36550 TQ	USBLS	5/15
Pipelayer, Plumber, Pipefitter, and Steamfitter	Virginia Beach-Norfolk-Newport News MSA, VA-NC	Y	21290 FQ	24270 MW	28600 TQ	USBLS	5/15
Pipelayer, Plumber, Pipefitter, and Steamfitter	Washington	H	17.16 FQ	25.20 MW	28.24 TQ	WABLS	3/16
Pipelayer, Plumber, Pipefitter, and Steamfitter	Seattle-Bellevue-Everett PMSA, WA	H	24.39 FQ	26.67 MW	28.97 TQ	WABLS	3/16
Pipelayer, Plumber, Pipefitter, and Steamfitter	Tacoma-Lakewood PMSA, WA	H	16.64 FQ	18.30 MW	22.09 TQ	WABLS	3/16
Pipelayer, Plumber, Pipefitter, and Steamfitter	West Virginia	Y	21450 FQ	24420 MW	29860 TQ	USBLS	5/15
Pipelayer, Plumber, Pipefitter, and Steamfitter	Huntington-Ashland MSA, WV-KY-OH	Y	22120 FQ	25690 MW	30690 TQ	USBLS	5/15
Pipelayer, Plumber, Pipefitter, and Steamfitter	Wisconsin	Y	26640 FQ	33080 MW	39080 TQ	USBLS	5/15
Pipelayer, Plumber, Pipefitter, and Steamfitter	Madison MSA, WI	Y	32230 FQ	37290 MW	43840 TQ	USBLS	5/15
Pipelayer, Plumber, Pipefitter, and Steamfitter	Milwaukee-Waukesha-West Allis MSA, WI	Y	33180 FQ	36670 MW	41730 TQ	USBLS	5/15
Pipelayer, Plumber, Pipefitter, and Steamfitter	Wyoming	Y	24780 FQ	32250 MW	37060 TQ	USBLS	5/15
Pipelayer, Plumber, Pipefitter, and Steamfitter	Puerto Rico	Y	17360 FQ	19140 MW	26770 TQ	USBLS	5/15
Pipelayer, Plumber, Pipefitter, and Steamfitter	San Juan-Carolina-Caguas MSA, PR	Y	17480 FQ	19370 MW	27750 TQ	USBLS	5/15
Pipelayer, Plumber, Pipefitter, and Steamfitter	Guam	Y	18830 FQ	21300 MW	23740 TQ	USBLS	5/15
Production Worker	Alabama	Y	17603 AE	24379 AW	27772 AEX	ALBLS	6/16
Production Worker	Birmingham-Hoover MSA, AL	Y	21315 AE	27515 AW	30610 AEX	ALBLS	6/16
Production Worker	Alaska	Y	26480 FQ	32530 MW	37540 TQ	USBLS	5/15
Production Worker	Anchorage MSA, AK	Y	26780 FQ	32450 MW	44870 TQ	USBLS	5/15
Production Worker	Arizona	Y	19900 FQ	24500 MW	29820 TQ	USBLS	5/15
Production Worker	Phoenix-Mesa-Scottsdale MSA, AZ	Y	19490 FQ	23420 MW	28710 TQ	USBLS	5/15
Production Worker	Tucson MSA, AZ	Y	26150 FQ	29890 MW	38280 TQ	USBLS	5/15
Production Worker	Arkansas	Y	19010 FQ	22640 MW	29250 TQ	USBLS	5/15
Production Worker	Little Rock-North Little Rock-Conway MSA, AR	Y	18650 FQ	23410 MW	34650 TQ	USBLS	5/15
Production Worker	California	H	9.72 FQ	11.28 MW	14.08 TQ	CABLS	1/16-3/16
Production Worker	Anaheim-Santa Ana-Irvine PMSA, CA	H	9.95 FQ	11.25 MW	13.07 TQ	CABLS	1/16-3/16
Production Worker	Los Angeles-Long Beach-Glendale PMSA, CA	H	9.54 FQ	10.62 MW	12.76 TQ	CABLS	1/16-3/16
Production Worker	Oakland-Hayward-Berkeley PMSA, CA	H	9.80 FQ	12.58 MW	15.06 TQ	CABLS	1/16-3/16
Production Worker	Riverside-San Bernardino-Ontario MSA, CA	H	9.69 FQ	10.85 MW	13.08 TQ	CABLS	1/16-3/16
Production Worker	Sacramento–Roseville–Arden-Arcade MSA, CA	H	9.71 FQ	11.22 MW	13.54 TQ	CABLS	1/16-3/16
Production Worker	San Diego-Carlsbad MSA, CA	H	10.25 FQ	12.48 MW	15.58 TQ	CABLS	1/16-3/16

AE	Average entry wage	AWR	Average wage range	H	Hourly
AEX	Average experienced wage	B	Biweekly	HI	Highest wage paid
ATC	Average total compensation	D	Daily	HR	High end range
AW	Average wage paid	FQ	First quartile wage	LO	Lowest wage paid

LR	Low end range	MTC	Median total compensation	TCC	Total cash compensation
M	Monthly	MW	Median wage paid	TQ	Third quartile wage
MCC	Median cash compensation	MWR	Median wage range	W	Weekly
ME	Median entry wage	S	See annotated source	Y	Yearly

Occupation/Type/Industry	Location	Per	Low	Mid	High	Source	Date
Helper							
Production Worker	San Francisco-Redwood City-South San Francisco PMSA, CA	H	11.22 FQ	13.66 MW	17.50 TQ	CABLS	1/16-3/16
Production Worker	Colorado	Y	20970 FQ	26490 MW	32360 TQ	USBLS	5/15
Production Worker	Denver-Aurora-Lakewood MSA, CO	Y	21950 FQ	26540 MW	31230 TQ	USBLS	5/15
Production Worker	Connecticut	Y		27325 MW		CTBLS	1/16-3/16
Production Worker	Bridgeport-Stamford-Norwalk MSA, CT	Y	22140 FQ	32400 MW	41960 TQ	USBLS	5/15
Production Worker	Hartford-West Hartford-East Hartford MSA, CT	Y	22090 FQ	26250 MW	31880 TQ	USBLS	5/15
Production Worker	Delaware	Y	21580 FQ	25160 MW	30580 TQ	USBLS	5/15
Production Worker	Wilmington PMSA, DE-MD-NJ	Y	23910 FQ	29630 MW	35620 TQ	USBLS	5/15
Production Worker	District of Columbia	Y	21120 FQ	22740 MW	24350 TQ	USBLS	5/15
Production Worker	Washington-Arlington-Alexandria PMSA, DC-VA-MD-WV	Y	20020 FQ	25480 MW	33890 TQ	USBLS	5/15
Production Worker	Florida	H	9.25 AE	11.35 MW	13.41 AEX	FLBLS	7/16-9/16
Production Worker	Fort Lauderdale-Pompano Beach-Deerfield Beach PMSA, FL	H	9.88 AE	12.39 MW	14.51 AEX	FLBLS	7/16-9/16
Production Worker	Miami-Miami Beach-Kendall PMSA, FL	H	8.94 AE	9.67 MW	11.92 AEX	FLBLS	7/16-9/16
Production Worker	Orlando-Kissimmee-Sanford MSA, FL	H	10.16 AE	11.55 MW	13.26 AEX	FLBLS	7/16-9/16
Production Worker	Tampa-St. Petersburg-Clearwater MSA, FL	H	9.06 AE	10.20 MW	11.98 AEX	FLBLS	7/16-9/16
Production Worker	Georgia	Y	18450 FQ	22120 MW	27200 TQ	USBLS	5/15
Production Worker	Atlanta-Sandy Springs-Roswell MSA, GA	Y	17870 FQ	21050 MW	27820 TQ	USBLS	5/15
Production Worker	Augusta-Richmond County MSA, GA-SC	Y	18060 FQ	20160 MW	28000 TQ	USBLS	5/15
Production Worker	Hawaii	Y	17840 FQ	19600 MW	27180 TQ	USBLS	5/15
Production Worker	Urban Honolulu MSA, HI	Y	17640 FQ	19160 MW	25180 TQ	USBLS	5/15
Production Worker	Idaho	Y	21280 FQ	26080 MW	31830 TQ	USBLS	5/15
Production Worker	Boise City MSA, ID	Y	18990 FQ	22460 MW	27050 TQ	USBLS	5/15
Production Worker	Illinois	Y	21080 FQ	26140 MW	32560 TQ	USBLS	5/15
Production Worker	Chicago-Naperville-Arlington Heights PMSA, IL	Y	21510 FQ	26570 MW	31830 TQ	USBLS	5/15
Production Worker	Lake County-Kenosha County PMSA, IL-WI	Y	22630 FQ	26880 MW	31420 TQ	USBLS	5/15
Production Worker	Indiana	Y	20620 FQ	24500 MW	29730 TQ	USBLS	5/15
Production Worker	Gary PMSA, IN	Y	20200 FQ	23930 MW	29550 TQ	USBLS	5/15
Production Worker	Indianapolis-Carmel-Anderson MSA, IN	Y	19200 FQ	23430 MW	29730 TQ	USBLS	5/15
Production Worker	Iowa	Y	22210 FQ	26730 MW	32870 TQ	USBLS	5/15
Production Worker	Des Moines-West Des Moines MSA, IA	Y	21950 FQ	25050 MW	32200 TQ	USBLS	5/15
Production Worker	Kansas	Y	21930 FQ	26540 MW	30690 TQ	USBLS	5/15
Production Worker	Wichita MSA, KS	Y	17920 FQ	21180 MW	27840 TQ	USBLS	5/15
Production Worker	Kentucky	Y	19620 FQ	23770 MW	29610 TQ	USBLS	5/15
Production Worker	Louisville-Jefferson County MSA, KY-IN	Y	21880 FQ	24310 MW	29150 TQ	USBLS	5/15
Production Worker	Louisiana	Y	23370 FQ	28380 MW	34820 TQ	USBLS	5/15
Production Worker	Baton Rouge MSA, LA	Y	23570 FQ	29120 MW	36970 TQ	USBLS	5/15
Production Worker	New Orleans-Metairie MSA, LA	Y	22280 FQ	27500 MW	33540 TQ	USBLS	5/15
Production Worker	Maine	Y	20810 FQ	25740 MW	34410 TQ	USBLS	5/15
Production Worker	Portland-South Portland MSA, ME	Y	20350 FQ	23370 MW	28600 TQ	USBLS	5/15
Production Worker	Maryland	Y	21596 AE	30710 MW	35266 AEX	MDBLS	4/16
Production Worker	Baltimore-Columbia-Towson MSA, MD	Y	24800 FQ	29890 MW	36390 TQ	USBLS	5/15
Production Worker	Salisbury MSA, MD-DE	Y	19920 FQ	25530 MW	31780 TQ	USBLS	5/15
Production Worker	Massachusetts	Y	20090 FQ	23980 MW	30110 TQ	USBLS	5/15
Production Worker	Boston-Cambridge-Newton NECTA, MA	Y	20180 FQ	23720 MW	30330 TQ	USBLS	5/15
Production Worker	Worcester MSA, MA-CT	Y	20010 FQ	23850 MW	28740 TQ	USBLS	5/15
Production Worker	Michigan	Y	20430 FQ	24080 MW	30710 TQ	USBLS	5/15

AE	Average entry wage	AWR	Average wage range	H	Hourly
AEX	Average experienced wage	B	Biweekly	HI	Highest wage paid
ATC	Average total compensation	D	Daily	HR	High end range
AW	Average wage paid	FQ	First quartile wage	LO	Lowest wage paid

LR	Low end range	MTC	Median total compensation	TCC	Total cash compensation
M	Monthly	MW	Median wage paid	TQ	Third quartile wage
MCC	Median cash compensation	MWR	Median wage range	W	Weekly
ME	Median entry wage	S	See annotated source	Y	Yearly

Helper

Occupation/Type/Industry	Location	Per	Low	Mid	High	Source	Date
Production Worker	Detroit-Dearborn-Livonia PMSA, MI	Y	20060 FQ	22880 MW	27720 TQ	USBLS	5/15
Production Worker	Grand Rapids-Wyoming MSA, MI	Y	19510 FQ	23090 MW	30340 TQ	USBLS	5/15
Production Worker	Minnesota	Y	19905 FQ	23023 MW	28369 TQ	MNBLS	1/16-3/16
Production Worker	Minneapolis-St. Paul-Bloomington MSA, MN-WI	Y	19581 FQ	22436 MW	26830 TQ	MNBLS	1/16-3/16
Production Worker	Mississippi	Y	19850 FQ	23930 MW	30040 TQ	USBLS	5/15
Production Worker	Jackson MSA, MS	Y	18890 FQ	23560 MW	28160 TQ	USBLS	5/15
Production Worker	Missouri	Y	18960 FQ	23230 MW	29410 TQ	USBLS	5/15
Production Worker	Kansas City MSA, MO-KS	Y	23000 FQ	27920 MW	33450 TQ	USBLS	5/15
Production Worker	St. Louis MSA, MO-IL	Y	19380 FQ	23560 MW	30890 TQ	USBLS	5/15
Production Worker	Montana	Y	19800 FQ	23700 MW	29390 TQ	USBLS	5/15
Production Worker	Billings MSA, MT	Y	21360 FQ	24360 MW	28940 TQ	USBLS	5/15
Production Worker	Nebraska	Y	20125 FQ	23315 MW	28270 TQ	NEBLS	7/16-9/16
Production Worker	Omaha-Council Bluffs MSA, NE-IA	Y	18880 FQ	21920 MW	26940 TQ	NEBLS	7/16-9/16
Production Worker	Nevada	Y	20890 FQ	24140 MW	31790 TQ	USBLS	5/15
Production Worker	Las Vegas-Henderson-Paradise MSA, NV	Y	20450 FQ	23580 MW	32190 TQ	USBLS	5/15
Production Worker	New Hampshire	H	9.40 AE	11.70 MW	13.84 AEX	NHBLS	6/16
Production Worker	Manchester NECTA, NH	H	9.00 AE	10.59 MW	11.34 AEX	NHBLS	6/16
Production Worker	Nashua NECTA, NH-MA	Y	21300 FQ	23380 MW	26350 TQ	USBLS	5/15
Production Worker	New Jersey	Y	19630 FQ	23980 MW	30620 TQ	USBLS	5/15
Production Worker	Camden PMSA, NJ	Y	18850 FQ	20470 MW	27420 TQ	USBLS	5/15
Production Worker	Newark PMSA, NJ-PA	Y	21830 FQ	26430 MW	33870 TQ	USBLS	5/15
Production Worker	Trenton MSA, NJ	Y	19780 FQ	28460 MW	34170 TQ	USBLS	5/15
Production Worker	New Mexico	Y	18750 FQ	22220 MW	27090 TQ	USBLS	5/15
Production Worker	Albuquerque MSA, NM	Y	18410 FQ	21790 MW	28520 TQ	USBLS	5/15
Production Worker	New York	Y	19820 AE	24740 MW	31440 AEX	NYBLS	1/16-3/16
Production Worker	Buffalo-Cheektowaga-Niagara Falls MSA, NY	Y	22090 FQ	26730 MW	34610 TQ	USBLS	5/15
Production Worker	Nassau County-Suffolk County PMSA, NY	Y	19120 FQ	21470 MW	29650 TQ	USBLS	5/15
Production Worker	New York-Jersey City-White Plains PMSA, NY-NJ	Y	19470 FQ	23430 MW	29950 TQ	USBLS	5/15
Production Worker	Rochester MSA, NY	Y	20420 FQ	24560 MW	30620 TQ	USBLS	5/15
Production Worker	North Carolina	Y	18150 FQ	21520 MW	26680 TQ	USBLS	5/15
Production Worker	Charlotte-Concord-Gastonia MSA, NC-SC	Y	18180 FQ	21290 MW	26110 TQ	USBLS	5/15
Production Worker	Raleigh MSA, NC	Y	17920 FQ	20550 MW	24220 TQ	USBLS	5/15
Production Worker	North Dakota	Y	23910 FQ	31280 MW	41810 TQ	USBLS	5/15
Production Worker	Fargo MSA, ND-MN	Y	21490 FQ	25080 MW	31910 TQ	USBLS	5/15
Production Worker	Ohio	Y	21400 FQ	26260 MW	34380 TQ	USBLS	5/15
Production Worker	Cincinnati MSA, OH-KY-IN	Y	19190 FQ	23240 MW	33380 TQ	USBLS	5/15
Production Worker	Cleveland-Elyria MSA, OH	Y	20610 FQ	23840 MW	30620 TQ	USBLS	5/15
Production Worker	Columbus MSA, OH	Y	22270 FQ	29810 MW	35940 TQ	USBLS	5/15
Production Worker	Oklahoma	Y	20710 FQ	26370 MW	33090 TQ	USBLS	5/15
Production Worker	Oklahoma City MSA, OK	Y	18930 FQ	24380 MW	30140 TQ	USBLS	5/15
Production Worker	Tulsa MSA, OK	Y	22830 FQ	28100 MW	35400 TQ	USBLS	5/15
Production Worker	Oregon	H	12.06 FQ	15.06 MW	18.59 TQ	ORBLS	2016
Production Worker	Portland-Vancouver-Hillsboro MSA, OR-WA	Y	25660 FQ	30820 MW	38360 TQ	USBLS	5/15
Production Worker	Pennsylvania	Y	22210 FQ	27770 MW	34700 TQ	USBLS	5/15
Production Worker	Allentown-Bethlehem-Easton MSA, PA-NJ	Y	22410 FQ	27290 MW	32410 TQ	USBLS	5/15
Production Worker	Harrisburg-Carlisle MSA, PA	Y	19170 FQ	23050 MW	29510 TQ	USBLS	5/15
Production Worker	Montgomery County-Bucks County-Chester County PMSA, PA	Y	22650 FQ	26840 MW	31130 TQ	USBLS	5/15
Production Worker	Philadelphia PMSA, PA	Y	23200 FQ	27810 MW	32890 TQ	USBLS	5/15
Production Worker	Pittsburgh MSA, PA	Y	20580 FQ	27720 MW	34150 TQ	USBLS	5/15
Production Worker	Rhode Island	Y	19150 FQ	20530 MW	27310 TQ	USBLS	5/15
Production Worker	Providence-Warwick MSA, RI-MA	Y	19170 FQ	20750 MW	27700 TQ	USBLS	5/15
Production Worker	South Carolina	Y	18320 FQ	21340 MW	27970 TQ	USBLS	5/15
Production Worker	Charleston-North Charleston MSA, SC	Y	18050 FQ	20660 MW	24320 TQ	USBLS	5/15
Production Worker	Columbia MSA, SC	Y	17810 FQ	19830 MW	23850 TQ	USBLS	5/15
Production Worker	Greenville-Anderson-Mauldin MSA, SC	Y	17870 FQ	19990 MW	24640 TQ	USBLS	5/15

AE	Average entry wage	AWR	Average wage range	H	Hourly
AEX	Average experienced wage	B	Biweekly	HI	Highest wage paid
ATC	Average total compensation	D	Daily	HR	High end range
AW	Average wage paid	FQ	First quartile wage	LO	Lowest wage paid

LR	Low end range	MTC	Median total compensation	TCC	Total cash compensation
M	Monthly	MW	Median wage paid	TQ	Third quartile wage
MCC	Median cash compensation	MWR	Median wage range	W	Weekly
ME	Median entry wage	S	See annotated source	Y	Yearly

Helper

Occupation/Type/Industry	Location	Per	Low	Mid	High	Source	Date
Production Worker	Tennessee	Y	19010 FQ	22370 MW	28160 TQ	USBLS	5/15
Production Worker	Knoxville MSA, TN	Y	18770 FQ	22530 MW	27700 TQ	USBLS	5/15
Production Worker	Memphis MSA, TN-MS-AR	Y	20670 FQ	23080 MW	26890 TQ	USBLS	5/15
Production Worker	Nashville-Davidson–Murfreesboro–Franklin MSA, TN	Y	18490 FQ	21670 MW	27470 TQ	USBLS	5/15
Production Worker	Texas	Y	19330 FQ	23450 MW	28910 TQ	USBLS	5/15
Production Worker	Amarillo MSA, TX	Y	22310 FQ	25260 MW	28470 TQ	USBLS	5/15
Production Worker	Austin-Round Rock MSA, TX	Y	20260 FQ	22440 MW	24700 TQ	USBLS	5/15
Production Worker	Dallas-Plano-Irving PMSA, TX	Y	19250 FQ	22220 MW	25800 TQ	USBLS	5/15
Production Worker	Fort Worth-Arlington PMSA, TX	Y	17810 FQ	20800 MW	24400 TQ	USBLS	5/15
Production Worker	Houston-The Woodlands-Sugar Land MSA, TX	Y	20900 FQ	26140 MW	30360 TQ	USBLS	5/15
Production Worker	San Antonio-New Braunfels MSA, TX	Y	17180 FQ	19140 MW	23640 TQ	USBLS	5/15
Production Worker	Utah	Y	20180 FQ	23850 MW	29710 TQ	USBLS	5/15
Production Worker	Ogden-Clearfield MSA, UT	Y	18350 FQ	21560 MW	28240 TQ	USBLS	5/15
Production Worker	Provo-Orem MSA, UT	Y	20630 FQ	22770 MW	25130 TQ	USBLS	5/15
Production Worker	Salt Lake City MSA, UT	Y	20940 FQ	25370 MW	30070 TQ	USBLS	5/15
Production Worker	Vermont	Y	23600 FQ	27770 MW	32170 TQ	USBLS	5/15
Production Worker	Burlington-South Burlington MSA, VT	Y	24180 FQ	28540 MW	33590 TQ	USBLS	5/15
Production Worker	Virginia	Y	20560 FQ	24920 MW	30220 TQ	USBLS	5/15
Production Worker	Richmond MSA, VA	Y	20480 FQ	23990 MW	33420 TQ	USBLS	5/15
Production Worker	Virginia Beach-Norfolk-Newport News MSA, VA-NC	Y	22100 FQ	26510 MW	30150 TQ	USBLS	5/15
Production Worker	Washington	H	11.32 FQ	13.58 MW	16.60 TQ	WABLS	3/16
Production Worker	Seattle-Bellevue-Everett PMSA, WA	H	10.94 FQ	13.84 MW	17.56 TQ	WABLS	3/16
Production Worker	Tacoma-Lakewood PMSA, WA	H	12.00 FQ	14.15 MW	18.08 TQ	WABLS	3/16
Production Worker	West Virginia	Y	18810 FQ	22720 MW	31530 TQ	USBLS	5/15
Production Worker	Huntington-Ashland MSA, WV-KY-OH	Y	19810 FQ	26220 MW	35220 TQ	USBLS	5/15
Production Worker	Wisconsin	Y	20850 FQ	25970 MW	32820 TQ	USBLS	5/15
Production Worker	Madison MSA, WI	Y	21250 FQ	27140 MW	33590 TQ	USBLS	5/15
Production Worker	Milwaukee-Waukesha-West Allis MSA, WI	Y	18860 FQ	24360 MW	30580 TQ	USBLS	5/15
Production Worker	Wyoming	Y	25500 FQ	32720 MW	40900 TQ	USBLS	5/15
Production Worker	Puerto Rico	Y	17200 FQ	18890 MW	22580 TQ	USBLS	5/15
Production Worker	San Juan-Carolina-Caguas MSA, PR	Y	17270 FQ	19030 MW	22960 TQ	USBLS	5/15
Production Worker	Guam	Y	18040 FQ	18930 MW	20360 TQ	USBLS	5/15
Roofer	Alabama	Y	18979 AE	23557 AW	25851 AEX	ALBLS	6/16
Roofer	Birmingham-Hoover MSA, AL	Y	21705 AE	22549 AW	22971 AEX	ALBLS	6/16
Roofer	Arkansas	Y	18300 FQ	21380 MW	24950 TQ	USBLS	5/15
Roofer	Little Rock-North Little Rock-Conway MSA, AR	Y	18090 FQ	21690 MW	27190 TQ	USBLS	5/15
Roofer	California	H	12.37 FQ	15.08 MW	18.03 TQ	CABLS	1/16-3/16
Roofer	Colorado	Y	23200 FQ	27450 MW	32310 TQ	USBLS	5/15
Roofer	Denver-Aurora-Lakewood MSA, CO	Y	26270 FQ	29870 MW	35370 TQ	USBLS	5/15
Roofer	Connecticut	Y		33378 MW		CTBLS	1/16-3/16
Roofer	Washington-Arlington-Alexandria PMSA, DC-VA-MD-WV	Y	26740 FQ	31750 MW	36030 TQ	USBLS	5/15
Roofer	Florida	H	10.58 AE	13.33 MW	15.16 AEX	FLBLS	7/16-9/16
Roofer	Tampa-St. Petersburg-Clearwater MSA, FL	H	11.96 AE	14.53 MW	16.08 AEX	FLBLS	7/16-9/16
Roofer	Georgia	Y	23420 FQ	27850 MW	32610 TQ	USBLS	5/15
Roofer	Atlanta-Sandy Springs-Roswell MSA, GA	Y	26570 FQ	29920 MW	34500 TQ	USBLS	5/15
Roofer	Hawaii	Y	20430 FQ	22280 MW	24120 TQ	USBLS	5/15
Roofer	Urban Honolulu MSA, HI	Y	19270 FQ	21930 MW	24600 TQ	USBLS	5/15
Roofer	Idaho	Y	25040 FQ	28390 MW	32550 TQ	USBLS	5/15
Roofer	Boise City MSA, ID	Y	26600 FQ	29050 MW	31850 TQ	USBLS	5/15
Roofer	Illinois	Y	19410 FQ	27040 MW	34070 TQ	USBLS	5/15
Roofer	Indiana	Y	22400 FQ	25720 MW	28530 TQ	USBLS	5/15
Roofer	Indianapolis-Carmel-Anderson MSA, IN	Y	25250 FQ	27260 MW	29270 TQ	USBLS	5/15
Roofer	Iowa	Y	26600 FQ	31610 MW	35530 TQ	USBLS	5/15

AE	Average entry wage	AWR	Average wage range	H	Hourly
AEX	Average experienced wage	B	Biweekly	HI	Highest wage paid
ATC	Average total compensation	D	Daily	HR	High end range
AW	Average wage paid	FQ	First quartile wage	LO	Lowest wage paid

LR	Low end range	MTC	Median total compensation	TCC	Total cash compensation
M	Monthly	MW	Median wage paid	TQ	Third quartile wage
MCC	Median cash compensation	MWR	Median wage range	W	Weekly
ME	Median entry wage	S	See annotated source	Y	Yearly

Occupation/Type/Industry	Location	Per	Low	Mid	High	Source	Date
Helper							
Roofer	Kansas	Y	22490 FQ	26320 MW	31570 TQ	USBLS	5/15
Roofer	Kentucky	Y	22800 FQ	27220 MW	32070 TQ	USBLS	5/15
Roofer	Louisville-Jefferson County MSA, KY-IN	Y	23230 FQ	28030 MW	33810 TQ	USBLS	5/15
Roofer	Louisiana	Y	20740 FQ	24180 MW	28330 TQ	USBLS	5/15
Roofer	Maine	Y	21870 FQ	24280 MW	29550 TQ	USBLS	5/15
Roofer	Maryland	Y	25307 AE	31264 MW	34243 AEX	MDBLS	4/16
Roofer	Baltimore-Columbia-Towson MSA, MD	Y	25320 FQ	28610 MW	32830 TQ	USBLS	5/15
Roofer	Massachusetts	Y	22960 FQ	28620 MW	35830 TQ	USBLS	5/15
Roofer	Boston-Cambridge-Newton NECTA, MA	Y	23270 FQ	32200 MW	37920 TQ	USBLS	5/15
Roofer	Michigan	Y	20180 FQ	26580 MW	30680 TQ	USBLS	5/15
Roofer	Minnesota	Y	25599 FQ	30573 MW	36143 TQ	MNBLS	1/16-3/16
Roofer	Mississippi	Y	20280 FQ	22620 MW	25040 TQ	USBLS	5/15
Roofer	Missouri	Y	22890 FQ	28610 MW	35190 TQ	USBLS	5/15
Roofer	St. Louis MSA, MO-IL	Y	31360 FQ	36340 MW	42260 TQ	USBLS	5/15
Roofer	Nebraska	Y	22155 FQ	25490 MW	29100 TQ	NEBLS	7/16-9/16
Roofer	Nevada	Y	21510 FQ	22950 MW	24390 TQ	USBLS	5/15
Roofer	Las Vegas-Henderson-Paradise MSA, NV	Y	21510 FQ	22950 MW	24390 TQ	USBLS	5/15
Roofer	New Mexico	Y	20500 FQ	22480 MW	24460 TQ	USBLS	5/15
Roofer	New York	Y	21680 AE	24910 MW	29070 AEX	NYBLS	1/16-3/16
Roofer	New York-Jersey City-White Plains PMSA, NY-NJ	Y	22170 FQ	25680 MW	31960 TQ	USBLS	5/15
Roofer	North Carolina	Y	19810 FQ	25080 MW	28530 TQ	USBLS	5/15
Roofer	Charlotte-Concord-Gastonia MSA, NC-SC	Y	26120 FQ	27760 MW	29390 TQ	USBLS	5/15
Roofer	North Dakota	Y	29970 FQ	34230 MW	37890 TQ	USBLS	5/15
Roofer	Fargo MSA, ND-MN	Y	31590 FQ	35060 MW	38530 TQ	USBLS	5/15
Roofer	Ohio	Y	25610 FQ	29130 MW	33980 TQ	USBLS	5/15
Roofer	Cincinnati MSA, OH-KY-IN	Y	19780 FQ	27210 MW	29850 TQ	USBLS	5/15
Roofer	Oklahoma	Y	22110 FQ	25230 MW	29820 TQ	USBLS	5/15
Roofer	Oklahoma City MSA, OK	Y	26700 FQ	29690 MW	34640 TQ	USBLS	5/15
Roofer	Oregon	H	10.86 FQ	16.01 MW	25.12 TQ	ORBLS	2016
Roofer	Portland-Vancouver-Hillsboro MSA, OR-WA	Y	37040 FQ	49860 MW	56030 TQ	USBLS	5/15
Roofer	Pennsylvania	Y	26530 FQ	29970 MW	35760 TQ	USBLS	5/15
Roofer	Montgomery County-Bucks County-Chester County PMSA, PA	Y	31540 FQ	35390 MW	39250 TQ	USBLS	5/15
Roofer	Pittsburgh MSA, PA	Y	24920 FQ	26950 MW	29000 TQ	USBLS	5/15
Roofer	Rhode Island	Y	25830 FQ	30100 MW	36910 TQ	USBLS	5/15
Roofer	Providence-Warwick MSA, RI-MA	Y	25830 FQ	30100 MW	36910 TQ	USBLS	5/15
Roofer	South Carolina	Y	18400 FQ	21360 MW	24350 TQ	USBLS	5/15
Roofer	Greenville-Anderson-Mauldin MSA, SC	Y	20610 FQ	24990 MW	35860 TQ	USBLS	5/15
Roofer	South Dakota	Y	21090 FQ	22900 MW	25160 TQ	USBLS	5/15
Roofer	Tennessee	Y	24470 FQ	28290 MW	33780 TQ	USBLS	5/15
Roofer	Knoxville MSA, TN	Y	23260 FQ	27660 MW	31820 TQ	USBLS	5/15
Roofer	Memphis MSA, TN-MS-AR	Y	23270 FQ	28100 MW	38220 TQ	USBLS	5/15
Roofer	Nashville-Davidson–Murfreesboro–Franklin MSA, TN	Y	25860 FQ	28640 MW	32310 TQ	USBLS	5/15
Roofer	Texas	Y	23750 FQ	27520 MW	31290 TQ	USBLS	5/15
Roofer	Dallas-Plano-Irving PMSA, TX	Y	22740 FQ	26940 MW	32580 TQ	USBLS	5/15
Roofer	Houston-The Woodlands-Sugar Land MSA, TX	Y	25840 FQ	28180 MW	30530 TQ	USBLS	5/15
Roofer	San Antonio-New Braunfels MSA, TX	Y	26510 FQ	31720 MW	35370 TQ	USBLS	5/15
Roofer	Utah	Y	21800 FQ	24200 MW	27760 TQ	USBLS	5/15
Roofer	Vermont	Y	22130 FQ	24360 MW	27180 TQ	USBLS	5/15
Roofer	Virginia	Y	23760 FQ	28310 MW	34560 TQ	USBLS	5/15
Roofer	Richmond MSA, VA	Y	26100 FQ	35460 MW	42680 TQ	USBLS	5/15
Roofer	Virginia Beach-Norfolk-Newport News MSA, VA-NC	Y	22190 FQ	28030 MW	37370 TQ	USBLS	5/15
Roofer	Washington	H	11.53 FQ	13.96 MW	16.65 TQ	WABLS	3/16
Roofer	West Virginia	Y	20340 FQ	23670 MW	28330 TQ	USBLS	5/15
Roofer	Wisconsin	Y	23690 FQ	28420 MW	35000 TQ	USBLS	5/15

AE	Average entry wage	AWR	Average wage range	H	Hourly	LR	Low end range	MTC	Median total compensation	TCC	Total cash compensation
AEX	Average experienced wage	B	Biweekly	HI	Highest wage paid	M	Monthly	MW	Median wage paid	TQ	Third quartile wage
ATC	Average total compensation	D	Daily	HR	High end range	MCC	Median cash compensation	MWR	Median wage range	W	Weekly
AW	Average wage paid	FQ	First quartile wage	LO	Lowest wage paid	ME	Median entry wage	S	See annotated source	Y	Yearly

Occupation/Type/Industry	Location	Per	Low	Mid	High	Source	Date
Helper							
Roofer	Milwaukee-Waukesha-West Allis MSA, WI	Y	23960 FQ	28960 MW	34960 TQ	USBLS	5/15
Roofer	Puerto Rico	Y	16430 FQ	17490 MW	18550 TQ	USBLS	5/15
Roofer	San Juan-Carolina-Caguas MSA, PR	Y	16430 FQ	17490 MW	18550 TQ	USBLS	5/15
Herder							
Department of Fish, Wildlife, and Parks, State Government	Great Falls, MT	H	9.00 LO		9.35 HI	MTGOV	2016
High School Teacher	United States	Y		56882 MW		NHC01	2016
Highway Engineer							
State Government	Michigan	H	25.82 LO		36.56 HI	LSJ15	2016
Highway Maintenance Worker	Alabama	Y	22148 AE	29667 AW	33422 AEX	ALBLS	6/16
	Birmingham-Hoover MSA, AL	Y	24884 AE	31190 AW	34338 AEX	ALBLS	6/16
	Alaska	Y	50550 FQ	55260 MW	60060 TQ	USBLS	5/15
	Arizona	Y	33000 FQ	37710 MW	40830 TQ	USBLS	5/15
	Phoenix-Mesa-Scottsdale MSA, AZ	Y	34180 FQ	38370 MW	42970 TQ	USBLS	5/15
	Tucson MSA, AZ	Y	35830 FQ	39200 MW	42920 TQ	USBLS	5/15
	Arkansas	Y	22840 FQ	27980 MW	34040 TQ	USBLS	5/15
	Little Rock-North Little Rock-Conway MSA, AR	Y	24070 FQ	29970 MW	36840 TQ	USBLS	5/15
	California	H	19.35 FQ	23.65 MW	27.90 TQ	CABLS	1/16-3/16
	Anaheim-Santa Ana-Irvine PMSA, CA	H	17.82 FQ	21.27 MW	26.64 TQ	CABLS	1/16-3/16
	Los Angeles-Long Beach-Glendale PMSA, CA	H	19.35 FQ	24.57 MW	29.37 TQ	CABLS	1/16-3/16
	Oakland-Hayward-Berkeley PMSA, CA	H	21.20 FQ	27.23 MW	35.81 TQ	CABLS	1/16-3/16
	Riverside-San Bernardino-Ontario MSA, CA	H	17.83 FQ	21.12 MW	26.63 TQ	CABLS	1/16-3/16
	Sacramento–Roseville–Arden-Arcade MSA, CA	H	19.35 FQ	25.04 MW	27.75 TQ	CABLS	1/16-3/16
	San Diego-Carlsbad MSA, CA	H	19.36 FQ	23.41 MW	26.64 TQ	CABLS	1/16-3/16
	San Francisco-Redwood City-South San Francisco PMSA, CA	H	19.36 FQ	26.64 MW	42.73 TQ	CABLS	1/16-3/16
	Colorado	Y	35610 FQ	42810 MW	47100 TQ	USBLS	5/15
	Denver-Aurora-Lakewood MSA, CO	Y	37660 FQ	45190 MW	47830 TQ	USBLS	5/15
	Connecticut	Y		53127 MW		CTBLS	1/16-3/16
	Bridgeport-Stamford-Norwalk MSA, CT	Y	44220 FQ	52070 MW	60810 TQ	USBLS	5/15
	Hartford-West Hartford-East Hartford MSA, CT	Y	46130 FQ	53380 MW	60020 TQ	USBLS	5/15
	Delaware	Y	24120 FQ	34230 MW	41930 TQ	USBLS	5/15
	Wilmington PMSA, DE-MD-NJ	Y	28420 FQ	36990 MW	44130 TQ	USBLS	5/15
	Washington-Arlington-Alexandria PMSA, DC-VA-MD-WV	Y	32890 FQ	40570 MW	47050 TQ	USBLS	5/15
	Florida	H	11.91 AE	14.62 MW	18.16 AEX	FLBLS	7/16-9/16
	Fort Lauderdale-Pompano Beach-Deerfield Beach PMSA, FL	H	12.26 AE	16.52 MW	19.66 AEX	FLBLS	7/16-9/16
	Miami-Miami Beach-Kendall PMSA, FL	H	11.54 AE	15.19 MW	19.77 AEX	FLBLS	7/16-9/16
	Orlando-Kissimmee-Sanford MSA, FL	H	13.09 AE	14.78 MW	18.98 AEX	FLBLS	7/16-9/16
	Tampa-St. Petersburg-Clearwater MSA, FL	H	11.99 AE	15.97 MW	19.41 AEX	FLBLS	7/16-9/16
	Georgia	Y	22280 FQ	26920 MW	32210 TQ	USBLS	5/15
	Atlanta-Sandy Springs-Roswell MSA, GA	Y	24270 FQ	29740 MW	36630 TQ	USBLS	5/15
	Augusta-Richmond County MSA, GA-SC	Y	21030 FQ	24090 MW	29590 TQ	USBLS	5/15
	Idaho	Y	31960 FQ	35560 MW	40220 TQ	USBLS	5/15
	Boise City MSA, ID	Y	31740 FQ	35160 MW	39150 TQ	USBLS	5/15

AE	Average entry wage	AWR	Average wage range	H	Hourly
AEX	Average experienced wage	B	Biweekly	HI	Highest wage paid
ATC	Average total compensation	D	Daily	HR	High end range
AW	Average wage paid	FQ	First quartile wage	LO	Lowest wage paid

LR	Low end range	MTC	Median total compensation	TCC	Total cash compensation
M	Monthly	MW	Median wage paid	TQ	Third quartile wage
MCC	Median cash compensation	MWR	Median wage range	W	Weekly
ME	Median entry wage	S	See annotated source	Y	Yearly

Occupation/Type/Industry	Location	Per	Low	Mid	High	Source	Date
Highway Maintenance Worker	Illinois	Y	29440 FQ	46180 MW	56590 TQ	USBLS	5/15
	Chicago-Naperville-Arlington Heights PMSA, IL	Y	32290 FQ	51130 MW	65600 TQ	USBLS	5/15
	Lake County-Kenosha County PMSA, IL-WI	Y	43010 FQ	52030 MW	59050 TQ	USBLS	5/15
	Indiana	Y	28680 FQ	33930 MW	37830 TQ	USBLS	5/15
	Gary PMSA, IN	Y	28320 FQ	33630 MW	37750 TQ	USBLS	5/15
	Indianapolis-Carmel-Anderson MSA, IN	Y	31320 FQ	35530 MW	42560 TQ	USBLS	5/15
	Iowa	Y	38400 FQ	44430 MW	48560 TQ	USBLS	5/15
	Des Moines-West Des Moines MSA, IA	Y	41060 FQ	45960 MW	49070 TQ	USBLS	5/15
	Kansas	Y	24560 FQ	29750 MW	36180 TQ	USBLS	5/15
	Wichita MSA, KS	Y	24920 FQ	30060 MW	36200 TQ	USBLS	5/15
	Kentucky	Y	22680 FQ	27670 MW	37730 TQ	USBLS	5/15
	Louisville-Jefferson County MSA, KY-IN	Y	25610 FQ	29510 MW	35290 TQ	USBLS	5/15
	Louisiana	Y	22760 FQ	27390 MW	33060 TQ	USBLS	5/15
	Baton Rouge MSA, LA	Y	27080 FQ	30600 MW	35530 TQ	USBLS	5/15
	New Orleans-Metairie MSA, LA	Y	22050 FQ	24600 MW	29710 TQ	USBLS	5/15
	Maine	Y	27730 FQ	33700 MW	37020 TQ	USBLS	5/15
	Portland-South Portland MSA, ME	Y	28380 FQ	33980 MW	37020 TQ	USBLS	5/15
	Maryland	Y	27523 AE	37942 MW	43151 AEX	MDBLS	4/16
	Baltimore-Columbia-Towson MSA, MD	Y	29180 FQ	35360 MW	47630 TQ	USBLS	5/15
	Salisbury MSA, MD-DE	Y	28040 FQ	33640 MW	41770 TQ	USBLS	5/15
	Massachusetts	Y	41790 FQ	47380 MW	54850 TQ	USBLS	5/15
	Boston-Cambridge-Newton NECTA, MA	Y	43160 FQ	48450 MW	55610 TQ	USBLS	5/15
	Worcester MSA, MA-CT	Y	40100 FQ	46140 MW	53110 TQ	USBLS	5/15
	Michigan	Y	35680 FQ	42310 MW	46440 TQ	USBLS	5/15
	Detroit-Dearborn-Livonia PMSA, MI	Y	36740 FQ	43100 MW	47600 TQ	USBLS	5/15
	Grand Rapids-Wyoming MSA, MI	Y	32680 FQ	43100 MW	48790 TQ	USBLS	5/15
	Minnesota	Y	40512 FQ	47989 MW	52136 TQ	MNBLS	1/16-3/16
	Duluth MSA, MN-WI	Y	41470 FQ	47460 MW	50720 TQ	USBLS	5/15
	Minneapolis-St. Paul-Bloomington MSA, MN-WI	Y	42086 FQ	48261 MW	54517 TQ	MNBLS	1/16-3/16
	Mississippi	Y	22410 FQ	27030 MW	31720 TQ	USBLS	5/15
	Jackson MSA, MS	Y	21250 FQ	24510 MW	29910 TQ	USBLS	5/15
	Missouri	Y	28290 FQ	33310 MW	36760 TQ	USBLS	5/15
	Kansas City MSA, MO-KS	Y	27030 FQ	33310 MW	38100 TQ	USBLS	5/15
	St. Louis MSA, MO-IL	Y	33300 FQ	41740 MW	50300 TQ	USBLS	5/15
	Montana	Y	40380 FQ	42310 MW	45660 TQ	USBLS	5/15
	Billings MSA, MT	Y	40490 FQ	43930 MW	46180 TQ	USBLS	5/15
	Nebraska	Y	28855 FQ	33685 MW	38310 TQ	NEBLS	7/16-9/16
	Omaha-Council Bluffs MSA, NE-IA	Y	31885 FQ	37455 MW	43655 TQ	NEBLS	7/16-9/16
	Nevada	Y	34500 FQ	40690 MW	52560 TQ	USBLS	5/15
	Las Vegas-Henderson-Paradise MSA, NV	Y	34320 FQ	39140 MW	52250 TQ	USBLS	5/15
	New Hampshire	H	12.75 FQ	17.05 MW	20.05 AEX	NHBLS	6/16
	Manchester NECTA, NH	H	15.18 AE	21.13 MW	23.92 AEX	NHBLS	6/16
	Nashua NECTA, NH-MA	Y	32730 FQ	39460 MW	46580 TQ	USBLS	5/15
	New Jersey	Y	39960 FQ	50330 MW	68870 TQ	USBLS	5/15
	Camden PMSA, NJ	Y	46360 FQ	61190 MW	72630 TQ	USBLS	5/15
	Newark PMSA, NJ-PA	Y	37840 FQ	49640 MW	67920 TQ	USBLS	5/15
	Trenton MSA, NJ	Y	36370 FQ	44540 MW	55420 TQ	USBLS	5/15
	New Mexico	Y	29950 FQ	32460 MW	36220 TQ	USBLS	5/15
	Albuquerque MSA, NM	Y	29990 FQ	32950 MW	37270 TQ	USBLS	5/15
	New York	Y	32060 AE	42000 MW	48970 AEX	NYBLS	1/16-3/16
	Buffalo-Cheektowaga-Niagara Falls MSA, NY	Y	35910 FQ	43560 MW	50740 TQ	USBLS	5/15
	Nassau County-Suffolk County PMSA, NY	Y	34170 FQ	44970 MW	55510 TQ	USBLS	5/15
	New York-Jersey City-White Plains PMSA, NY-NJ	Y	43560 FQ	56870 MW	68490 TQ	USBLS	5/15
	Rochester MSA, NY	Y	36330 FQ	44040 MW	52090 TQ	USBLS	5/15
	North Carolina	Y	28250 FQ	30910 MW	34520 TQ	USBLS	5/15

AE	Average entry wage	AWR	Average wage range	H	Hourly	LR	Low end range
AEX	Average experienced wage	B	Biweekly	HI	Highest wage paid	M	Monthly
ATC	Average total compensation	D	Daily	HR	High end range	MCC	Median cash compensation
AW	Average wage paid	FQ	First quartile wage	LO	Lowest wage paid	ME	Median entry wage

MTC	Median total compensation	TCC	Total cash compensation
MW	Median wage paid	TQ	Third quartile wage
MWR	Median wage range	W	Weekly
S	See annotated source	Y	Yearly

Occupation/Type/Industry	Location	Per	Low	Mid	High	Source	Date
Highway Maintenance Worker	Charlotte-Concord-Gastonia MSA, NC-SC	Y	27040 FQ	30410 MW	34200 TQ	USBLS	5/15
	Raleigh MSA, NC	Y	28200 FQ	30190 MW	34560 TQ	USBLS	5/15
	North Dakota	Y	37200 FQ	44510 MW	50430 TQ	USBLS	5/15
	Fargo MSA, ND-MN	Y	37010 FQ	43880 MW	49060 TQ	USBLS	5/15
	Ohio	Y	30780 FQ	37120 MW	46010 TQ	USBLS	5/15
	Cincinnati MSA, OH-KY-IN	Y	30520 FQ	38920 MW	48850 TQ	USBLS	5/15
	Cleveland-Elyria MSA, OH	Y	34810 FQ	43040 MW	50580 TQ	USBLS	5/15
	Columbus MSA, OH	Y	32300 FQ	39320 MW	47770 TQ	USBLS	5/15
	Oklahoma	Y	25520 FQ	30440 MW	36320 TQ	USBLS	5/15
	Oklahoma City MSA, OK	Y	27700 FQ	33410 MW	38750 TQ	USBLS	5/15
	Tulsa MSA, OK	Y	23130 FQ	28860 MW	34440 TQ	USBLS	5/15
	Oregon	H	19.43 FQ	22.05 MW	23.48 TQ	ORBLS	2016
	Portland-Vancouver-Hillsboro MSA, OR-WA	Y	40990 FQ	46160 MW	51560 TQ	USBLS	5/15
	Pennsylvania	Y	30480 FQ	38760 MW	47430 TQ	USBLS	5/15
	Allentown-Bethlehem-Easton MSA, PA-NJ	Y	35250 FQ	42890 MW	48560 TQ	USBLS	5/15
	Harrisburg-Carlisle MSA, PA	Y	32670 FQ	41130 MW	48640 TQ	USBLS	5/15
	Montgomery County-Bucks County-Chester County PMSA, PA	Y	41060 FQ	47850 MW	56630 TQ	USBLS	5/15
	Philadelphia PMSA, PA	Y	40390 FQ	45940 MW	52910 TQ	USBLS	5/15
	Pittsburgh MSA, PA	Y	30360 FQ	40730 MW	49130 TQ	USBLS	5/15
	Rhode Island	Y	38020 FQ	42780 MW	47400 TQ	USBLS	5/15
	Providence-Warwick MSA, RI-MA	Y	38080 FQ	43300 MW	48200 TQ	USBLS	5/15
	South Carolina	Y	22890 FQ	27190 MW	31470 TQ	USBLS	5/15
	Columbia MSA, SC	Y	21520 FQ	25140 MW	30540 TQ	USBLS	5/15
	Greenville-Anderson-Mauldin MSA, SC	Y	22740 FQ	26860 MW	31020 TQ	USBLS	5/15
	South Dakota	Y	27090 FQ	30480 MW	35530 TQ	USBLS	5/15
	Sioux Falls MSA, SD	Y	27230 FQ	30400 MW	35970 TQ	USBLS	5/15
	Tennessee	Y	24130 FQ	27760 MW	31160 TQ	USBLS	5/15
	Knoxville MSA, TN	Y	25120 FQ	28370 MW	32580 TQ	USBLS	5/15
	Memphis MSA, TN-MS-AR	Y	23290 FQ	27400 MW	31830 TQ	USBLS	5/15
	Nashville-Davidson–Murfreesboro–Franklin MSA, TN	Y	25980 FQ	31030 MW	35890 TQ	USBLS	5/15
	Texas	Y	25950 FQ	32000 MW	39430 TQ	USBLS	5/15
	Austin-Round Rock MSA, TX	Y	28880 FQ	34530 MW	41450 TQ	USBLS	5/15
	Dallas-Plano-Irving PMSA, TX	Y	27030 FQ	31690 MW	38690 TQ	USBLS	5/15
	Fort Worth-Arlington PMSA, TX	Y	29070 FQ	37180 MW	45820 TQ	USBLS	5/15
	Houston-The Woodlands-Sugar Land MSA, TX	Y	26950 FQ	35460 MW	44580 TQ	USBLS	5/15
	San Antonio-New Braunfels MSA, TX	Y	22210 FQ	25570 MW	32640 TQ	USBLS	5/15
	Utah	Y	32060 FQ	37030 MW	43440 TQ	USBLS	5/15
	Ogden-Clearfield MSA, UT	Y	34100 FQ	40520 MW	44540 TQ	USBLS	5/15
	Provo-Orem MSA, UT	Y	32740 FQ	38250 MW	45450 TQ	USBLS	5/15
	Salt Lake City MSA, UT	Y	29700 FQ	35980 MW	42600 TQ	USBLS	5/15
	Vermont	Y	34500 FQ	39310 MW	45670 TQ	USBLS	5/15
	Burlington-South Burlington MSA, VT	Y	33340 FQ	38690 MW	46230 TQ	USBLS	5/15
	Virginia	Y	30850 FQ	35920 MW	41780 TQ	USBLS	5/15
	Richmond MSA, VA	Y	31850 FQ	35970 MW	37890 TQ	USBLS	5/15
	Virginia Beach-Norfolk-Newport News MSA, VA-NC	Y	26720 FQ	32280 MW	38200 TQ	USBLS	5/15
	Washington	H	20.43 FQ	22.56 MW	26.68 TQ	WABLS	3/16
	Seattle-Bellevue-Everett PMSA, WA	H	20.44 FQ	25.46 MW	28.75 TQ	WABLS	3/16
	Tacoma-Lakewood PMSA, WA	H	20.44 FQ	26.00 MW	29.23 TQ	WABLS	3/16
	West Virginia	Y	22110 FQ	25160 MW	29110 TQ	USBLS	5/15
	Huntington-Ashland MSA, WV-KY-OH	Y	21400 FQ	23820 MW	28370 TQ	USBLS	5/15
	Wisconsin	Y	33240 FQ	41950 MW	48720 TQ	USBLS	5/15
	Madison MSA, WI	Y	40100 FQ	45100 MW	50200 TQ	USBLS	5/15
	Milwaukee-Waukesha-West Allis MSA, WI	Y	38040 FQ	50820 MW	57000 TQ	USBLS	5/15
	Wyoming	Y	36280 FQ	38290 MW	44440 TQ	USBLS	5/15
	Puerto Rico	Y	16430 FQ	17510 MW	18600 TQ	USBLS	5/15

AE Average entry wage	**AWR** Average wage range	**H** Hourly	**LR** Low end range	**MTC** Median total compensation	**TCC** Total cash compensation
AEX Average experienced wage	**B** Biweekly	**HI** Highest wage paid	**M** Monthly	**MW** Median wage paid	**TQ** Third quartile wage
ATC Average total compensation	**D** Daily	**HR** High end range	**MCC** Median cash compensation	**MWR** Median wage range	**W** Weekly
AW Average wage paid	**FQ** First quartile wage	**LO** Lowest wage paid	**ME** Median entry wage	**S** See annotated source	**Y** Yearly

Occupation/Type/Industry	Location	Per	Low	Mid	High	Source	Date
Highway Maintenance Worker	San Juan-Carolina-Caguas MSA, PR	Y	16350 FQ	17430 MW	18500 TQ	USBLS	5/15
Highway Patrol Cadet Public Safety Department, State Government	Ohio	H			18.66 HI	OHGOV	2015
Highway Patrol Communication Technician Public Safety Department, State Government	Ohio	H			21.87 HI	OHGOV	2015
Highway Patrol Trooper Public Safety Department, State Government	Ohio	H	21.52 LO		31.67 HI	OHGOV	2015
HIPAA Business Coordinator State Government	North Carolina	Y	54887 LO		90780 HI	NCGOV	7/1/16
HIPAA Compliance Specialist Department of Public Health and Human Services, State Government	Helena, MT	H			21.05 HI	MTGOV	2016
Histology Technician County Government	Oakland County, MI	B	1439 LO		1874 HI	MIOAK2	10/1/16
Historian	Alabama	Y	38571 AE	65522 AW	78998 AEX	ALBLS	6/16
	California	H	24.47 FQ	33.60 MW	43.68 TQ	CABLS	1/16-3/16
	Colorado	Y	51940 FQ	69120 MW	86200 TQ	USBLS	5/15
	Connecticut	Y		76452 MW		CTBLS	1/16-3/16
	District of Columbia	Y	84030 FQ	99910 MW	115460 TQ	USBLS	5/15
	Georgia	Y	38980 FQ	47980 MW	74180 TQ	USBLS	5/15
	Hawaii	Y	67770 FQ	90860 MW	96540 TQ	USBLS	5/15
	Idaho	Y	47690 FQ	56670 MW	65970 TQ	USBLS	5/15
	Illinois	Y	41230 FQ	69030 MW	91760 TQ	USBLS	5/15
	Indiana	Y	25850 FQ	33810 MW	48620 TQ	USBLS	5/15
	Kentucky	Y	32450 FQ	36980 MW	45020 TQ	USBLS	5/15
	Maryland	Y	41464 AE	83330 MW	104263 AEX	MDBLS	4/16
	Massachusetts	Y	30770 FQ	57760 MW	86090 TQ	USBLS	5/15
	Michigan	Y	53860 FQ	59460 MW	66080 TQ	USBLS	5/15
	Minnesota	Y	36038 FQ	48417 MW	69767 TQ	MNBLS	1/16-3/16
	Mississippi	Y	32780 FQ	38380 MW	46010 TQ	USBLS	5/15
	Missouri	Y	34990 FQ	38980 MW	45470 TQ	USBLS	5/15
	Nebraska	Y	48480 FQ	62480 MW	91255 TQ	NEBLS	7/16-9/16
	New Jersey	Y	64190 FQ	73050 MW	79330 TQ	USBLS	5/15
	New York	Y	27430 AE	29670 MW	38580 AEX	NYBLS	1/16-3/16
	North Carolina	Y	44160 FQ	54860 MW	77230 TQ	USBLS	5/15
	Ohio	Y	41110 FQ	47010 MW	62680 TQ	USBLS	5/15
	Oklahoma	Y	35030 FQ	39760 MW	60520 TQ	USBLS	5/15
	Oregon	H	20.26 FQ	31.94 MW	38.56 TQ	ORBLS	2016
	Pennsylvania	Y	43740 FQ	57330 MW	71780 TQ	USBLS	5/15
	Tennessee	Y	42410 FQ	46170 MW	50020 TQ	USBLS	5/15
	Texas	Y	48400 FQ	70260 MW	86520 TQ	USBLS	5/15
	Virginia	Y	42790 FQ	72220 MW	99280 TQ	USBLS	5/15
	Washington	H	30.48 FQ	34.54 MW	40.27 TQ	WABLS	3/16
	Wisconsin	Y	48100 FQ	57470 MW	65580 TQ	USBLS	5/15
State Government	New Mexico	H	17.01 LO		29.60 HI	NMGOV	7/30/16
Historic Preservation Specialist Municipal Government	Louisville, KY	Y		43285 AW		LKY01	2017
Historic Publications Editor State Government	North Carolina	Y	33001 LO		69177 HI	NCGOV	7/1/16
Historical Conservator Municipal Government	Detroit, MI	M	3050 LO		3300 HI	DETGOV	2016
Historical Museum Curator Municipal Government	Arcadia, CA	Y			69952 HI	CACIT	6/28/16

Occupation/Type/Industry	Location	Per	Low	Mid	High	Source	Date
Historical Museum Graphic Designer							
Municipal Government	Detroit, MI	M	2983 LO		3267 HI	DETGOV	2016
History Teacher							
Postsecondary	Alabama	Y	41782 AE	68223 AW	81454 AEX	ALBLS	6/16
Postsecondary	Birmingham-Hoover MSA, AL	Y	53117 AE	73361 AW	83472 AEX	ALBLS	6/16
Postsecondary	Arizona	Y	42070 FQ	59090 MW	81580 TQ	USBLS	5/15
Postsecondary	Arkansas	Y	42830 FQ	50980 MW	64910 TQ	USBLS	5/15
Postsecondary	Little Rock-North Little Rock-Conway MSA, AR	Y	42600 FQ	53630 MW	66950 TQ	USBLS	5/15
Postsecondary	California	Y		97229 AW		CABLS	1/16-3/16
Postsecondary	Anaheim-Santa Ana-Irvine PMSA, CA	Y		126112 AW		CABLS	1/16-3/16
Postsecondary	Los Angeles-Long Beach-Glendale PMSA, CA	Y		103225 AW		CABLS	1/16-3/16
Postsecondary	Riverside-San Bernardino-Ontario MSA, CA	Y		103499 AW		CABLS	1/16-3/16
Postsecondary	Sacramento–Roseville–Arden-Arcade MSA, CA	Y		78014 AW		CABLS	1/16-3/16
Postsecondary	San Diego-Carlsbad MSA, CA	Y		97290 AW		CABLS	1/16-3/16
Postsecondary	San Francisco-Redwood City-South San Francisco PMSA, CA	Y		87277 AW		CABLS	1/16-3/16
Postsecondary	Colorado	Y	36000 FQ	56160 MW	75310 TQ	USBLS	5/15
Postsecondary	Denver-Aurora-Lakewood MSA, CO	Y	34700 FQ	48450 MW	64030 TQ	USBLS	5/15
Postsecondary	Connecticut	Y		78917 MW		CTBLS	1/16-3/16
Postsecondary	Bridgeport-Stamford-Norwalk MSA, CT	Y	69990 FQ	83680 MW	116950 TQ	USBLS	5/15
Postsecondary	Hartford-West Hartford-East Hartford MSA, CT	Y	60210 FQ	76590 MW	108990 TQ	USBLS	5/15
Postsecondary	Delaware	Y	54610 FQ	70900 MW	92740 TQ	USBLS	5/15
Postsecondary	Wilmington PMSA, DE-MD-NJ	Y	54540 FQ	70060 MW	90600 TQ	USBLS	5/15
Postsecondary	District of Columbia	Y	66780 FQ	83930 MW	101260 TQ	USBLS	5/15
Postsecondary	Washington-Arlington-Alexandria PMSA, DC-VA-MD-WV	Y	54190 FQ	69630 MW	90760 TQ	USBLS	5/15
Postsecondary	Florida	Y	49596 AE	77370 MW	95719 AEX	FLBLS	7/16-9/16
Postsecondary	Fort Lauderdale-Pompano Beach-Deerfield Beach PMSA, FL	Y	55789 AE	70883 MW	80916 AEX	FLBLS	7/16-9/16
Postsecondary	Miami-Miami Beach-Kendall PMSA, FL	Y	59307 AE	85773 MW	98299 AEX	FLBLS	7/16-9/16
Postsecondary	Orlando-Kissimmee-Sanford MSA, FL	Y	52855 AE	83574 MW	93935 AEX	FLBLS	7/16-9/16
Postsecondary	Tampa-St. Petersburg-Clearwater MSA, FL	Y	55953 AE	80522 MW	101226 AEX	FLBLS	7/16-9/16
Postsecondary	Georgia	Y	51030 FQ	63820 MW	77120 TQ	USBLS	5/15
Postsecondary	Atlanta-Sandy Springs-Roswell MSA, GA	Y	53740 FQ	65630 MW	78260 TQ	USBLS	5/15
Postsecondary	Hawaii	Y	52210 FQ	69850 MW	81510 TQ	USBLS	5/15
Postsecondary	Urban Honolulu MSA, HI	Y	54020 FQ	71950 MW	83040 TQ	USBLS	5/15
Postsecondary	Idaho	Y	42570 FQ	55310 MW	71830 TQ	USBLS	5/15
Postsecondary	Boise City MSA, ID	Y	43000 FQ	50660 MW	67110 TQ	USBLS	5/15
Postsecondary	Illinois	Y	67520 FQ	81110 MW	100730 TQ	USBLS	5/15
Postsecondary	Chicago-Naperville-Arlington Heights PMSA, IL	Y	70030 FQ	83270 MW	102400 TQ	USBLS	5/15
Postsecondary	Indiana	Y	52270 FQ	66610 MW	85010 TQ	USBLS	5/15
Postsecondary	Indianapolis-Carmel-Anderson MSA, IN	Y	53050 FQ	63320 MW	76210 TQ	USBLS	5/15
Postsecondary	Iowa	Y	54400 FQ	65210 MW	75810 TQ	USBLS	5/15
Postsecondary	Des Moines-West Des Moines MSA, IA	Y	50210 FQ	56290 MW	62200 TQ	USBLS	5/15
Postsecondary	Kansas	Y	41990 FQ	47410 MW	57830 TQ	USBLS	5/15
Postsecondary	Kentucky	Y	51950 FQ	65610 MW	86140 TQ	USBLS	5/15
Postsecondary	Louisville-Jefferson County MSA, KY-IN	Y	56920 FQ	68030 MW	88380 TQ	USBLS	5/15
Postsecondary	Louisiana	Y	42840 FQ	55440 MW	72720 TQ	USBLS	5/15
Postsecondary	Maine	Y	58500 FQ	75390 MW	97100 TQ	USBLS	5/15
Postsecondary	Maryland	Y	48965 AE	77697 MW	92064 AEX	MDBLS	4/16

AE	Average entry wage	AWR	Average wage range	H	Hourly	LR	Low end range	MTC	Median total compensation	TCC	Total cash compensation
AEX	Average experienced wage	B	Biweekly	HI	Highest wage paid	M	Monthly	MW	Median wage paid	TQ	Third quartile wage
ATC	Average total compensation	D	Daily	HR	High end range	MCC	Median cash compensation	MWR	Median wage range	W	Weekly
AW	Average wage paid	FQ	First quartile wage	LO	Lowest wage paid	ME	Median entry wage	S	See annotated source	Y	Yearly

Occupation/Type/Industry	Location	Per	Low	Mid	High	Source	Date
History Teacher							
Postsecondary	Baltimore-Columbia-Towson MSA, MD	Y	61860 FQ	74650 MW	100140 TQ	USBLS	5/15
Postsecondary	Massachusetts	Y	63460 FQ	83380 MW	105240 TQ	USBLS	5/15
Postsecondary	Boston-Cambridge-Newton NECTA, MA	Y	70630 FQ	91950 MW	122270 TQ	USBLS	5/15
Postsecondary	Worcester MSA, MA-CT	Y	53700 FQ	66250 MW	88570 TQ	USBLS	5/15
Postsecondary	Michigan	Y	62080 FQ	84890 MW	114760 TQ	USBLS	5/15
Postsecondary	Grand Rapids-Wyoming MSA, MI	Y	51680 FQ	64890 MW	77910 TQ	USBLS	5/15
Postsecondary	Minnesota	Y	64112 FQ	75785 MW	94001 TQ	MNBLS	1/16-3/16
Postsecondary	Minneapolis-St. Paul-Bloomington MSA, MN-WI	Y	64193 FQ	76602 MW	97065 TQ	MNBLS	1/16-3/16
Postsecondary	Mississippi	Y	47180 FQ	57200 MW	71990 TQ	USBLS	5/15
Postsecondary	Jackson MSA, MS	Y	43700 FQ	52140 MW	68320 TQ	USBLS	5/15
Postsecondary	Missouri	Y	52020 FQ	67090 MW	87640 TQ	USBLS	5/15
Postsecondary	Kansas City MSA, MO-KS	Y	58460 FQ	74500 MW	94640 TQ	USBLS	5/15
Postsecondary	St. Louis MSA, MO-IL	Y	50300 FQ	64270 MW	80970 TQ	USBLS	5/15
Postsecondary	Montana	Y	43730 FQ	55320 MW	72270 TQ	USBLS	5/15
Postsecondary	Nebraska	Y	53245 FQ	66625 MW	84855 TQ	NEBLS	7/16-9/16
Postsecondary	New Hampshire	Y	66304 AE	83251 MW	97305 AEX	NHBLS	6/16
Postsecondary	New Jersey	Y	57930 FQ	75880 MW	105160 TQ	USBLS	5/15
Postsecondary	Camden PMSA, NJ	Y	51670 FQ	71040 MW	95690 TQ	USBLS	5/15
Postsecondary	Newark PMSA, NJ-PA	Y	59650 FQ	76660 MW	105120 TQ	USBLS	5/15
Postsecondary	New Mexico	Y	56350 FQ	76290 MW	93840 TQ	USBLS	5/15
Postsecondary	New York	Y	45650 AE	78680 MW	114670 AEX	NYBLS	1/16-3/16
Postsecondary	Buffalo-Cheektowaga-Niagara Falls MSA, NY	Y	44710 FQ	66900 MW	83270 TQ	USBLS	5/15
Postsecondary	Nassau County-Suffolk County PMSA, NY	Y	48470 FQ	68830 MW	95190 TQ	USBLS	5/15
Postsecondary	New York-Jersey City-White Plains PMSA, NY-NJ	Y	60840 FQ	85500 MW	130070 TQ	USBLS	5/15
Postsecondary	Rochester MSA, NY	Y	62550 FQ	94630 MW	170720 TQ	USBLS	5/15
Postsecondary	North Carolina	Y	49990 FQ	63150 MW	78750 TQ	USBLS	5/15
Postsecondary	Charlotte-Concord-Gastonia MSA, NC-SC	Y	48160 FQ	60750 MW	78790 TQ	USBLS	5/15
Postsecondary	Raleigh MSA, NC	Y	39990 FQ	53490 MW	70930 TQ	USBLS	5/15
Postsecondary	North Dakota	Y	54980 FQ	76400 MW	94790 TQ	USBLS	5/15
Postsecondary	Fargo MSA, ND-MN	Y	69750 FQ	79780 MW	96950 TQ	USBLS	5/15
Postsecondary	Ohio	Y	50100 FQ	67230 MW	89620 TQ	USBLS	5/15
Postsecondary	Cleveland-Elyria MSA, OH	Y	57400 FQ	78580 MW	109560 TQ	USBLS	5/15
Postsecondary	Columbus MSA, OH	Y	52100 FQ	66040 MW	87100 TQ	USBLS	5/15
Postsecondary	Oklahoma	Y	41200 FQ	52590 MW	77650 TQ	USBLS	5/15
Postsecondary	Oklahoma City MSA, OK	Y	35130 FQ	44980 MW	54540 TQ	USBLS	5/15
Postsecondary	Oregon	Y	64728 FQ	75898 MW	94073 TQ	ORBLS	2016
Postsecondary	Portland-Vancouver-Hillsboro MSA, OR-WA	Y	58370 FQ	72250 MW	88120 TQ	USBLS	5/15
Postsecondary	Pennsylvania	Y	52650 FQ	72130 MW	93140 TQ	USBLS	5/15
Postsecondary	Allentown-Bethlehem-Easton MSA, PA-NJ	Y	55660 FQ	74000 MW	107640 TQ	USBLS	5/15
Postsecondary	Harrisburg-Carlisle MSA, PA	Y	59320 FQ	81410 MW	98710 TQ	USBLS	5/15
Postsecondary	Montgomery County-Bucks County-Chester County PMSA, PA	Y	24680 FQ	59160 MW	85450 TQ	USBLS	5/15
Postsecondary	Philadelphia PMSA, PA	Y	50660 FQ	72240 MW	93480 TQ	USBLS	5/15
Postsecondary	Pittsburgh MSA, PA	Y	52170 FQ	68890 MW	88950 TQ	USBLS	5/15
Postsecondary	Rhode Island	Y	61300 FQ	75480 MW	96900 TQ	USBLS	5/15
Postsecondary	Providence-Warwick MSA, RI-MA	Y	61120 FQ	75460 MW	95800 TQ	USBLS	5/15
Postsecondary	South Carolina	Y	52190 FQ	66450 MW	80470 TQ	USBLS	5/15
Postsecondary	Columbia MSA, SC	Y	63820 FQ	75050 MW	90600 TQ	USBLS	5/15
Postsecondary	Greenville-Anderson-Mauldin MSA, SC	Y	60370 FQ	73200 MW	92870 TQ	USBLS	5/15
Postsecondary	South Dakota	Y	54010 FQ	60960 MW	75490 TQ	USBLS	5/15
Postsecondary	Tennessee	Y	34050 FQ	52410 MW	72680 TQ	USBLS	5/15
Postsecondary	Knoxville MSA, TN	Y	36880 FQ	47270 MW	63330 TQ	USBLS	5/15
Postsecondary	Memphis MSA, TN-MS-AR	Y	34730 FQ	52860 MW	68370 TQ	USBLS	5/15
Postsecondary	Nashville-Davidson–Murfreesboro–Franklin MSA, TN	Y	42470 FQ	63920 MW	88670 TQ	USBLS	5/15
Postsecondary	Texas	Y	41240 FQ	59070 MW	82840 TQ	USBLS	5/15
Postsecondary	Austin-Round Rock MSA, TX	Y	50830 FQ	62310 MW	89750 TQ	USBLS	5/15

AE Average entry wage	**AWR** Average wage range	**H** Hourly	**LR** Low end range	**MTC** Median total compensation	**TCC** Total cash compensation
AEX Average experienced wage	**B** Biweekly	**HI** Highest wage paid	**M** Monthly	**MW** Median wage paid	**TQ** Third quartile wage
ATC Average total compensation	**D** Daily	**HR** High end range	**MCC** Median cash compensation	**MWR** Median wage range	**W** Weekly
AW Average wage paid	**FQ** First quartile wage	**LO** Lowest wage paid	**ME** Median entry wage	**S** See annotated source	**Y** Yearly

Occupation/Type/Industry	Location	Per	Low	Mid	High	Source	Date
History Teacher							
Postsecondary	Dallas-Plano-Irving PMSA, TX	Y	46080 FQ	61170 MW	80500 TQ	USBLS	5/15
Postsecondary	Fort Worth-Arlington PMSA, TX	Y	25980 FQ	48300 MW	67560 TQ	USBLS	5/15
Postsecondary	Houston-The Woodlands-Sugar Land MSA, TX	Y	47970 FQ	71530 MW	98960 TQ	USBLS	5/15
Postsecondary	San Antonio-New Braunfels MSA, TX	Y	22270 FQ	24600 MW	73230 TQ	USBLS	5/15
Postsecondary	Utah	Y	60730 FQ	78740 MW	97590 TQ	USBLS	5/15
Postsecondary	Provo-Orem MSA, UT	Y	72640 FQ	87440 MW	100210 TQ	USBLS	5/15
Postsecondary	Salt Lake City MSA, UT	Y	51010 FQ	70640 MW	96550 TQ	USBLS	5/15
Postsecondary	Vermont	Y	55390 FQ	72260 MW	92220 TQ	USBLS	5/15
Postsecondary	Virginia	Y	44080 FQ	59920 MW	79190 TQ	USBLS	5/15
Postsecondary	Richmond MSA, VA	Y	35500 FQ	56160 MW	81340 TQ	USBLS	5/15
Postsecondary	Virginia Beach-Norfolk-Newport News MSA, VA-NC	Y	41770 FQ	55730 MW	73070 TQ	USBLS	5/15
Postsecondary	Washington	Y		66946 AW		WABLS	3/16
Postsecondary	Seattle-Bellevue-Everett PMSA, WA	Y		74596 AW		WABLS	3/16
Postsecondary	Tacoma-Lakewood PMSA, WA	Y		70994 AW		WABLS	3/16
Postsecondary	West Virginia	Y	36850 FQ	55760 MW	68540 TQ	USBLS	5/15
Postsecondary	Wisconsin	Y	54150 FQ	69350 MW	92200 TQ	USBLS	5/15
Postsecondary	Milwaukee-Waukesha-West Allis MSA, WI	Y	55230 FQ	70770 MW	90430 TQ	USBLS	5/15
Postsecondary	Puerto Rico	Y	49100 FQ	66320 MW	78300 TQ	USBLS	5/15
Hockey Player							
National Hockey League	United States	Y		1175000 MW		USAT02	2014-2015
Hodcarrier							
Department of Public Works, Municipal Government	San Francisco, CA	Y		69628 AW		CACIT	6/28/16
Hoist and Winch Operator	Alabama	Y	24859 AE	44966 AW	55015 AEX	ALBLS	6/16
	Florida	H	12.06 AE	17.67 MW	22.22 AEX	FLBLS	7/16-9/16
	Illinois	Y	86530 FQ	92470 MW	98420 TQ	USBLS	5/15
	Indiana	Y	26880 FQ	34220 MW	39680 TQ	USBLS	5/15
	Iowa	Y	29730 FQ	39230 MW	60940 TQ	USBLS	5/15
	Kentucky	Y	24720 FQ	38020 MW	47160 TQ	USBLS	5/15
	Maryland	Y	35263 AE	50831 MW	58615 AEX	MDBLS	4/16
	Massachusetts	Y	36400 FQ	42250 MW	48200 TQ	USBLS	5/15
	Michigan	Y	33070 FQ	36310 MW	39550 TQ	USBLS	5/15
	Minnesota	Y	67011 FQ	74774 MW	82819 TQ	MNBLS	1/16-3/16
	Mississippi	Y	37310 FQ	45200 MW	60980 TQ	USBLS	5/15
	Missouri	Y	41140 FQ	48960 MW	65440 TQ	USBLS	5/15
	Nebraska	Y	26405 FQ	28630 MW	30850 TQ	NEBLS	7/16-9/16
	New Mexico	Y	26800 FQ	35670 MW	46500 TQ	USBLS	5/15
	New York	Y	31460 AE	67740 MW	90200 AEX	NYBLS	1/16-3/16
	Ohio	Y	31780 FQ	38010 MW	48400 TQ	USBLS	5/15
	Oregon	H	17.64 FQ	21.19 MW	26.85 TQ	ORBLS	2016
	Pennsylvania	Y	34750 FQ	43550 MW	57500 TQ	USBLS	5/15
	Tennessee	Y	24480 FQ	34060 MW	37830 TQ	USBLS	5/15
	Texas	Y	34170 FQ	38180 MW	54940 TQ	USBLS	5/15
	Virginia	Y	31940 FQ	36030 MW	42360 TQ	USBLS	5/15
	Washington	H	20.29 FQ	26.50 MW	30.76 TQ	WABLS	3/16
	West Virginia	Y	45630 FQ	53960 MW	61290 TQ	USBLS	5/15
	Wyoming	Y	51110 FQ	57350 MW	66680 TQ	USBLS	5/15
Home Appliance Repairer	Alabama	Y	24164 AE	36521 AW	42694 AEX	ALBLS	6/16
	Birmingham-Hoover MSA, AL	Y	26992 AE	33165 AW	36247 AEX	ALBLS	6/16
	Alaska	Y	35610 FQ	46640 MW	62980 TQ	USBLS	5/15
	Anchorage MSA, AK	Y	26760 FQ	41640 MW	46800 TQ	USBLS	5/15
	Arizona	Y	28180 FQ	41210 MW	53550 TQ	USBLS	5/15
	Phoenix-Mesa-Scottsdale MSA, AZ	Y	30400 FQ	41300 MW	49140 TQ	USBLS	5/15
	Tucson MSA, AZ	Y	24250 FQ	39080 MW	49790 TQ	USBLS	5/15
	Arkansas	Y	26240 FQ	33740 MW	42310 TQ	USBLS	5/15
	Little Rock-North Little Rock-Conway MSA, AR	Y	29040 FQ	35580 MW	42380 TQ	USBLS	5/15
	California	H	16.07 FQ	19.37 MW	25.07 TQ	CABLS	1/16-3/16
	Anaheim-Santa Ana-Irvine PMSA, CA	H	16.11 FQ	17.78 MW	19.50 TQ	CABLS	1/16-3/16

Occupation/Type/Industry	Location	Per	Low	Mid	High	Source	Date
Home Appliance Repairer	Los Angeles-Long Beach-Glendale PMSA, CA	H	13.48 FQ	18.90 MW	28.50 TQ	CABLS	1/16-3/16
	Oakland-Hayward-Berkeley PMSA, CA	H	16.39 FQ	18.77 MW	22.65 TQ	CABLS	1/16-3/16
	Riverside-San Bernardino-Ontario MSA, CA	H	18.04 FQ	22.23 MW	26.95 TQ	CABLS	1/16-3/16
	Sacramento–Roseville–Arden-Arcade MSA, CA	H	17.74 FQ	20.87 MW	23.55 TQ	CABLS	1/16-3/16
	San Diego-Carlsbad MSA, CA	H	15.55 FQ	19.02 MW	23.45 TQ	CABLS	1/16-3/16
	San Francisco-Redwood City-South San Francisco PMSA, CA	H	15.70 FQ	18.23 MW	24.24 TQ	CABLS	1/16-3/16
	Colorado	Y	28770 FQ	42580 MW	61770 TQ	USBLS	5/15
	Denver-Aurora-Lakewood MSA, CO	Y	30860 FQ	48210 MW	67030 TQ	USBLS	5/15
	Connecticut	Y		39392 MW		CTBLS	1/16-3/16
	Bridgeport-Stamford-Norwalk MSA, CT	Y	30910 FQ	37190 MW	45690 TQ	USBLS	5/15
	Hartford-West Hartford-East Hartford MSA, CT	Y	40210 FQ	45610 MW	52410 TQ	USBLS	5/15
	Delaware	Y	29560 FQ	35520 MW	45440 TQ	USBLS	5/15
	Wilmington PMSA, DE-MD-NJ	Y	32120 FQ	37470 MW	46590 TQ	USBLS	5/15
	Washington-Arlington-Alexandria PMSA, DC-VA-MD-WV	Y	33620 FQ	40190 MW	47720 TQ	USBLS	5/15
	Florida	H	11.37 AE	14.99 MW	19.07 AEX	FLBLS	7/16-9/16
	Fort Lauderdale-Pompano Beach-Deerfield Beach PMSA, FL	H	12.15 AE	14.30 MW	16.78 AEX	FLBLS	7/16-9/16
	Miami-Miami Beach-Kendall PMSA, FL	H	11.11 AE	15.19 MW	21.85 AEX	FLBLS	7/16-9/16
	Orlando-Kissimmee-Sanford MSA, FL	H	10.79 AE	16.00 MW	21.47 AEX	FLBLS	7/16-9/16
	Tampa-St. Petersburg-Clearwater MSA, FL	H	12.90 AE	18.56 MW	22.08 AEX	FLBLS	7/16-9/16
	Georgia	Y	26680 FQ	34730 MW	42450 TQ	USBLS	5/15
	Atlanta-Sandy Springs-Roswell MSA, GA	Y	27800 FQ	35970 MW	43480 TQ	USBLS	5/15
	Augusta-Richmond County MSA, GA-SC	Y	19790 FQ	31120 MW	35310 TQ	USBLS	5/15
	Hawaii	Y	47260 FQ	55910 MW	62340 TQ	USBLS	5/15
	Urban Honolulu MSA, HI	Y	43430 FQ	55000 MW	61040 TQ	USBLS	5/15
	Idaho	Y	24020 FQ	33970 MW	42990 TQ	USBLS	5/15
	Boise City MSA, ID	Y	23970 FQ	31270 MW	36870 TQ	USBLS	5/15
	Illinois	Y	35210 FQ	53080 MW	72630 TQ	USBLS	5/15
	Chicago-Naperville-Arlington Heights PMSA, IL	Y	36380 FQ	53090 MW	72040 TQ	USBLS	5/15
	Indiana	Y	24400 FQ	36110 MW	46800 TQ	USBLS	5/15
	Indianapolis-Carmel-Anderson MSA, IN	Y	34990 FQ	43450 MW	49710 TQ	USBLS	5/15
	Iowa	Y	25430 FQ	31170 MW	38550 TQ	USBLS	5/15
	Kansas	Y	27010 FQ	31190 MW	37480 TQ	USBLS	5/15
	Wichita MSA, KS	Y	30520 FQ	35230 MW	38970 TQ	USBLS	5/15
	Kentucky	Y	23630 FQ	30010 MW	38490 TQ	USBLS	5/15
	Louisville-Jefferson County MSA, KY-IN	Y	24130 FQ	32690 MW	37280 TQ	USBLS	5/15
	Louisiana	Y	22400 FQ	29240 MW	35020 TQ	USBLS	5/15
	Maine	Y	34460 FQ	40680 MW	49460 TQ	USBLS	5/15
	Portland-South Portland MSA, ME	Y	34910 FQ	43140 MW	54480 TQ	USBLS	5/15
	Maryland	Y	24365 AE	38499 MW	45565 AEX	MDBLS	4/16
	Baltimore-Columbia-Towson MSA, MD	Y	25000 FQ	33850 MW	56580 TQ	USBLS	5/15
	Salisbury MSA, MD-DE	Y	27740 FQ	30210 MW	39750 TQ	USBLS	5/15
	Massachusetts	Y	34180 FQ	41840 MW	48430 TQ	USBLS	5/15
	Boston-Cambridge-Newton NECTA, MA	Y	37540 FQ	43590 MW	47980 TQ	USBLS	5/15
	Worcester MSA, MA-CT	Y	26780 FQ	30500 MW	43170 TQ	USBLS	5/15
	Michigan	Y	29090 FQ	35100 MW	45870 TQ	USBLS	5/15
	Detroit-Dearborn-Livonia PMSA, MI	Y	33120 FQ	36150 MW	40530 TQ	USBLS	5/15

AE	Average entry wage	AWR	Average wage range	H	Hourly
AEX	Average experienced wage	B	Biweekly	HI	Highest wage paid
ATC	Average total compensation	D	Daily	HR	High end range
AW	Average wage paid	FQ	First quartile wage	LO	Lowest wage paid

LR	Low end range	MTC	Median total compensation
M	Monthly	MW	Median wage paid
MCC	Median cash compensation	MWR	Median wage range
ME	Median entry wage	S	See annotated source

TCC	Total cash compensation
TQ	Third quartile wage
W	Weekly
Y	Yearly

Occupation/Type/Industry	Location	Per	Low	Mid	High	Source	Date
Home Appliance Repairer	Grand Rapids-Wyoming MSA, MI	Y	25100 FQ	32320 MW	38590 TQ	USBLS	5/15
	Minnesota	Y	36084 FQ	45617 MW	57756 TQ	MNBLS	1/16-3/16
	Minneapolis-St. Paul-Bloomington MSA, MN-WI	Y	38909 FQ	50384 MW	64363 TQ	MNBLS	1/16-3/16
	Mississippi	Y	30440 FQ	35700 MW	40380 TQ	USBLS	5/15
	Jackson MSA, MS	Y	30050 FQ	36770 MW	44220 TQ	USBLS	5/15
	Missouri	Y	24220 FQ	41010 MW	54690 TQ	USBLS	5/15
	St. Louis MSA, MO-IL	Y	39280 FQ	53320 MW	59010 TQ	USBLS	5/15
	Montana	Y	23490 FQ	28960 MW	35300 TQ	USBLS	5/15
	Nebraska	Y	26195 FQ	32265 MW	46765 TQ	NEBLS	7/16-9/16
	Omaha-Council Bluffs MSA, NE-IA	Y	23115 FQ	29560 MW	44365 TQ	NEBLS	7/16-9/16
	Nevada	Y	29600 FQ	37010 MW	48140 TQ	USBLS	5/15
	Las Vegas-Henderson-Paradise MSA, NV	Y	32910 FQ	37600 MW	45670 TQ	USBLS	5/15
	New Hampshire	H	15.74 AE	20.09 MW	21.65 AEX	NHBLS	6/16
	New Jersey	Y	38680 FQ	51540 MW	68100 TQ	USBLS	5/15
	Newark PMSA, NJ-PA	Y	46300 FQ	59520 MW	71750 TQ	USBLS	5/15
	New Mexico	Y	23670 FQ	28120 MW	36490 TQ	USBLS	5/15
	Albuquerque MSA, NM	Y	21430 FQ	30730 MW	43710 TQ	USBLS	5/15
	New York	Y	23020 AE	38790 MW	47500 AEX	NYBLS	1/16-3/16
	Buffalo-Cheektowaga-Niagara Falls MSA, NY	Y	30480 FQ	42240 MW	47530 TQ	USBLS	5/15
	Nassau County-Suffolk County PMSA, NY	Y	22310 FQ	25000 MW	44520 TQ	USBLS	5/15
	New York-Jersey City-White Plains PMSA, NY-NJ	Y	29080 FQ	42760 MW	58740 TQ	USBLS	5/15
	Rochester MSA, NY	Y	35230 FQ	42850 MW	48270 TQ	USBLS	5/15
	North Carolina	Y	29210 FQ	36690 MW	44750 TQ	USBLS	5/15
	Charlotte-Concord-Gastonia MSA, NC-SC	Y	44370 FQ	53100 MW	58910 TQ	USBLS	5/15
	North Dakota	Y	34630 FQ	41190 MW	46550 TQ	USBLS	5/15
	Fargo MSA, ND-MN	Y	36780 FQ	43630 MW	48580 TQ	USBLS	5/15
	Ohio	Y	24080 FQ	31630 MW	38270 TQ	USBLS	5/15
	Cincinnati MSA, OH-KY-IN	Y	24850 FQ	33170 MW	50440 TQ	USBLS	5/15
	Cleveland-Elyria MSA, OH	Y	25600 FQ	32870 MW	36740 TQ	USBLS	5/15
	Columbus MSA, OH	Y	21760 FQ	29170 MW	41990 TQ	USBLS	5/15
	Oklahoma	Y	28040 FQ	34510 MW	39600 TQ	USBLS	5/15
	Oklahoma City MSA, OK	Y	31830 FQ	34680 MW	37540 TQ	USBLS	5/15
	Tulsa MSA, OK	Y	28520 FQ	34360 MW	43020 TQ	USBLS	5/15
	Oregon	H	11.11 FQ	14.66 MW	18.99 TQ	ORBLS	2016
	Portland-Vancouver-Hillsboro MSA, OR-WA	Y	24600 FQ	33750 MW	44070 TQ	USBLS	5/15
	Pennsylvania	Y	27220 FQ	36230 MW	44490 TQ	USBLS	5/15
	Allentown-Bethlehem-Easton MSA, PA-NJ	Y	26340 FQ	34940 MW	41630 TQ	USBLS	5/15
	Harrisburg-Carlisle MSA, PA	Y	39250 FQ	47670 MW	56440 TQ	USBLS	5/15
	Montgomery County-Bucks County-Chester County PMSA, PA	Y	33520 FQ	40630 MW	48520 TQ	USBLS	5/15
	Philadelphia PMSA, PA	Y	36150 FQ	41750 MW	47260 TQ	USBLS	5/15
	Pittsburgh MSA, PA	Y	19030 FQ	30150 MW	39150 TQ	USBLS	5/15
	Rhode Island	Y	42310 FQ	50560 MW	56410 TQ	USBLS	5/15
	Providence-Warwick MSA, RI-MA	Y	33360 FQ	39320 MW	50510 TQ	USBLS	5/15
	South Carolina	Y	25290 FQ	29220 MW	35470 TQ	USBLS	5/15
	Charleston-North Charleston MSA, SC	Y	26060 FQ	34750 MW	50340 TQ	USBLS	5/15
	Greenville-Anderson-Mauldin MSA, SC	Y	26300 FQ	30350 MW	35370 TQ	USBLS	5/15
	South Dakota	Y	24850 FQ	29970 MW	38740 TQ	USBLS	5/15
	Sioux Falls MSA, SD	Y	27940 FQ	50550 MW	61780 TQ	USBLS	5/15
	Tennessee	Y	25540 FQ	29620 MW	38160 TQ	USBLS	5/15
	Knoxville MSA, TN	Y	25850 FQ	35420 MW	42180 TQ	USBLS	5/15
	Memphis MSA, TN-MS-AR	Y	26150 FQ	31910 MW	36350 TQ	USBLS	5/15
	Nashville-Davidson–Murfreesboro–Franklin MSA, TN	Y	24310 FQ	28790 MW	35900 TQ	USBLS	5/15
	Texas	Y	28830 FQ	35660 MW	43620 TQ	USBLS	5/15
	Austin-Round Rock MSA, TX	Y	29980 FQ	36630 MW	47480 TQ	USBLS	5/15
	Dallas-Plano-Irving PMSA, TX	Y	25490 FQ	31920 MW	37900 TQ	USBLS	5/15

AE	Average entry wage	AWR	Average wage range	H	Hourly	LR	Low end range	MTC	Median total compensation	TCC	Total cash compensation
AEX	Average experienced wage	B	Biweekly	HI	Highest wage paid	M	Monthly	MW	Median wage paid	TQ	Third quartile wage
ATC	Average total compensation	D	Daily	HR	High end range	MCC	Median cash compensation	MWR	Median wage range	W	Weekly
AW	Average wage paid	FQ	First quartile wage	LO	Lowest wage paid	ME	Median entry wage	S	See annotated source	Y	Yearly

Occupation/Type/Industry	Location	Per	Low	Mid	High	Source	Date
Home Appliance Repairer	Fort Worth-Arlington PMSA, TX	Y	28930 FQ	36760 MW	44450 TQ	USBLS	5/15
	Houston-The Woodlands-Sugar Land MSA, TX	Y	33420 FQ	38920 MW	46230 TQ	USBLS	5/15
	San Antonio-New Braunfels MSA, TX	Y	29000 FQ	34170 MW	39990 TQ	USBLS	5/15
	Utah	Y	22010 FQ	35500 MW	49040 TQ	USBLS	5/15
	Ogden-Clearfield MSA, UT	Y	21020 FQ	27930 MW	41540 TQ	USBLS	5/15
	Provo-Orem MSA, UT	Y	17960 FQ	22690 MW	35040 TQ	USBLS	5/15
	Salt Lake City MSA, UT	Y	33320 FQ	42800 MW	65490 TQ	USBLS	5/15
	Vermont	Y	30920 FQ	35290 MW	39260 TQ	USBLS	5/15
	Virginia	Y	28100 FQ	36770 MW	49760 TQ	USBLS	5/15
	Richmond MSA, VA	Y	31430 FQ	39330 MW	53590 TQ	USBLS	5/15
	Virginia Beach-Norfolk-Newport News MSA, VA-NC	Y	20070 FQ	27250 MW	50950 TQ	USBLS	5/15
	Washington	H	14.55 FQ	17.93 MW	22.58 TQ	WABLS	3/16
	Seattle-Bellevue-Everett PMSA, WA	H	14.06 FQ	17.12 MW	21.13 TQ	WABLS	3/16
	Tacoma-Lakewood PMSA, WA	H	19.81 FQ	21.90 MW	23.97 TQ	WABLS	3/16
	West Virginia	Y	19720 FQ	24930 MW	34230 TQ	USBLS	5/15
	Huntington-Ashland MSA, WV-KY-OH	Y	20710 FQ	28230 MW	37080 TQ	USBLS	5/15
	Wisconsin	Y	29060 FQ	34650 MW	39950 TQ	USBLS	5/15
	Madison MSA, WI	Y	36710 FQ	44400 MW	50860 TQ	USBLS	5/15
	Milwaukee-Waukesha-West Allis MSA, WI	Y	27470 FQ	31610 MW	42540 TQ	USBLS	5/15
	Wyoming	Y	32510 FQ	41160 MW	45840 TQ	USBLS	5/15
Home Economics Teacher							
Postsecondary	Alabama	Y	42343 AE	85338 AW	106825 AEX	ALBLS	6/16
Postsecondary	Arkansas	Y	29670 FQ	43800 MW	67610 TQ	USBLS	5/15
Postsecondary	California	Y		84933 AW		CABLS	1/16-3/16
Postsecondary	Connecticut	Y		61428 MW		CTBLS	1/16-3/16
Postsecondary	Florida	Y	51862 AE	83118 MW	98330 AEX	FLBLS	7/16-9/16
Postsecondary	Georgia	Y	61230 FQ	78710 MW	100310 TQ	USBLS	5/15
Postsecondary	Illinois	Y	36100 FQ	64440 MW	97270 TQ	USBLS	5/15
Postsecondary	Indiana	Y	48110 FQ	67340 MW	86750 TQ	USBLS	5/15
Postsecondary	Kentucky	Y	55060 FQ	69650 MW	92040 TQ	USBLS	5/15
Postsecondary	Louisiana	Y	51950 FQ	58110 MW	67460 TQ	USBLS	5/15
Postsecondary	Mississippi	Y	51360 FQ	64930 MW	82070 TQ	USBLS	5/15
Postsecondary	Missouri	Y	50650 FQ	67870 MW	94710 TQ	USBLS	5/15
Postsecondary	Nebraska	Y	53655 FQ	64665 MW	80415 TQ	NEBLS	7/16-9/16
Postsecondary	North Carolina	Y	53370 FQ	61880 MW	74790 TQ	USBLS	5/15
Postsecondary	Oklahoma	Y	36510 FQ	47860 MW	75020 TQ	USBLS	5/15
Postsecondary	Oregon	Y	44922 FQ	55410 MW	75297 TQ	ORBLS	2016
Postsecondary	Pennsylvania	Y	53250 FQ	77460 MW	98060 TQ	USBLS	5/15
Postsecondary	Tennessee	Y	52040 FQ	71310 MW	93580 TQ	USBLS	5/15
Postsecondary	Texas	Y	35250 FQ	61470 MW	79650 TQ	USBLS	5/15
Postsecondary	Utah	Y	43760 FQ	58420 MW	76070 TQ	USBLS	5/15
Postsecondary	Washington	Y		55077 AW		WABLS	3/16
Postsecondary	Wisconsin	Y	33510 FQ	39530 MW	62640 TQ	USBLS	5/15
Home Health Aide	Alabama	Y	17462 AE	20304 AW	21725 AEX	ALBLS	6/16
	Birmingham-Hoover MSA, AL	Y	17483 AE	18934 AW	19655 AEX	ALBLS	6/16
	Alaska	Y	25510 FQ	30780 MW	35210 TQ	USBLS	5/15
	Anchorage MSA, AK	Y	24360 FQ	29290 MW	34210 TQ	USBLS	5/15
	Arizona	Y	19010 FQ	22260 MW	26490 TQ	USBLS	5/15
	Phoenix-Mesa-Scottsdale MSA, AZ	Y	19000 FQ	22170 MW	26270 TQ	USBLS	5/15
	Tucson MSA, AZ	Y	19350 FQ	22890 MW	27090 TQ	USBLS	5/15
	Arkansas	Y	16090 FQ	17960 MW	21120 TQ	USBLS	5/15
	Little Rock-North Little Rock-Conway MSA, AR	Y	18260 FQ	21020 MW	22710 TQ	USBLS	5/15
	California	H	10.00 FQ	11.65 MW	15.01 TQ	CABLS	1/16-3/16
	Anaheim-Santa Ana-Irvine PMSA, CA	H	9.76 FQ	11.03 MW	12.96 TQ	CABLS	1/16-3/16
	Los Angeles-Long Beach-Glendale PMSA, CA	H	9.60 FQ	11.54 MW	14.96 TQ	CABLS	1/16-3/16
	Oakland-Hayward-Berkeley PMSA, CA	H	10.52 FQ	12.22 MW	15.83 TQ	CABLS	1/16-3/16
	Riverside-San Bernardino-Ontario MSA, CA	H	10.14 FQ	11.60 MW	17.04 TQ	CABLS	1/16-3/16

Home Health Aide

Occupation/Type/Industry	Location	Per	Low	Mid	High	Source	Date
Home Health Aide	Sacramento–Roseville–Arden-Arcade MSA, CA	H	9.75 FQ	12.06 MW	16.24 TQ	CABLS	1/16-3/16
	San Diego-Carlsbad MSA, CA	H	10.89 FQ	12.75 MW	15.62 TQ	CABLS	1/16-3/16
	San Francisco-Redwood City-South San Francisco PMSA, CA	H	10.20 FQ	12.34 MW	16.62 TQ	CABLS	1/16-3/16
	Colorado	Y	20730 FQ	24000 MW	29720 TQ	USBLS	5/15
	Denver-Aurora-Lakewood MSA, CO	Y	21410 FQ	24850 MW	30970 TQ	USBLS	5/15
	Connecticut	Y		27360 MW		CTBLS	1/16-3/16
	Bridgeport-Stamford-Norwalk MSA, CT	Y	22610 FQ	25990 MW	28950 TQ	USBLS	5/15
	Hartford-West Hartford-East Hartford MSA, CT	Y	23560 FQ	27020 MW	29810 TQ	USBLS	5/15
	Delaware	Y	23820 FQ	27170 MW	30340 TQ	USBLS	5/15
	Wilmington PMSA, DE-MD-NJ	Y	24180 FQ	27710 MW	31140 TQ	USBLS	5/15
	District of Columbia	Y	23250 FQ	26230 MW	28760 TQ	USBLS	5/15
	Washington-Arlington-Alexandria PMSA, DC-VA-MD-WV	Y	22510 FQ	25780 MW	28700 TQ	USBLS	5/15
	Florida	H	9.50 AE	11.03 MW	12.41 AEX	FLBLS	7/16-9/16
	Fort Lauderdale-Pompano Beach-Deerfield Beach PMSA, FL	H	9.03 AE	9.87 MW	11.34 AEX	FLBLS	7/16-9/16
	Jacksonville MSA, FL	H	9.40 AE	10.91 MW	12.61 AEX	FLBLS	7/16-9/16
	Miami-Miami Beach-Kendall PMSA, FL	H	9.80 AE	11.73 MW	13.60 AEX	FLBLS	7/16-9/16
	Orlando-Kissimmee-Sanford MSA, FL	H	9.48 AE	10.99 MW	12.05 AEX	FLBLS	7/16-9/16
	Tampa-St. Petersburg-Clearwater MSA, FL	H	9.48 AE	10.91 MW	11.83 AEX	FLBLS	7/16-9/16
	Georgia	Y	17650 FQ	19800 MW	23510 TQ	USBLS	5/15
	Atlanta-Sandy Springs-Roswell MSA, GA	Y	18150 FQ	20630 MW	23870 TQ	USBLS	5/15
	Augusta-Richmond County MSA, GA-SC	Y	17140 FQ	18920 MW	22000 TQ	USBLS	5/15
	Hawaii	Y	20450 FQ	26460 MW	30570 TQ	USBLS	5/15
	Urban Honolulu MSA, HI	Y	21120 FQ	26910 MW	31030 TQ	USBLS	5/15
	Idaho	Y	17610 FQ	19770 MW	24860 TQ	USBLS	5/15
	Boise City MSA, ID	Y	18410 FQ	22140 MW	27180 TQ	USBLS	5/15
	Illinois	Y	19950 FQ	22270 MW	24630 TQ	USBLS	5/15
	Chicago-Naperville-Arlington Heights PMSA, IL	Y	19950 FQ	22230 MW	24530 TQ	USBLS	5/15
	Lake County-Kenosha County PMSA, IL-WI	Y	21030 FQ	23100 MW	25820 TQ	USBLS	5/15
	Indiana	Y	19430 FQ	21850 MW	24220 TQ	USBLS	5/15
	Gary PMSA, IN	Y	18790 FQ	23230 MW	30900 TQ	USBLS	5/15
	Indianapolis-Carmel-Anderson MSA, IN	Y	20000 FQ	22490 MW	25050 TQ	USBLS	5/15
	Iowa	Y	20850 FQ	23220 MW	26780 TQ	USBLS	5/15
	Des Moines-West Des Moines MSA, IA	Y	21760 FQ	24130 MW	28090 TQ	USBLS	5/15
	Kansas	Y	20850 FQ	22680 MW	24500 TQ	USBLS	5/15
	Wichita MSA, KS	Y	20190 FQ	22130 MW	24070 TQ	USBLS	5/15
	Kentucky	Y	18670 FQ	21910 MW	26810 TQ	USBLS	5/15
	Louisville-Jefferson County MSA, KY-IN	Y	18900 FQ	21210 MW	23690 TQ	USBLS	5/15
	Louisiana	Y	17110 FQ	18750 MW	22220 TQ	USBLS	5/15
	Baton Rouge MSA, LA	Y	16910 FQ	18290 MW	19730 TQ	USBLS	5/15
	New Orleans-Metairie MSA, LA	Y	18030 FQ	21220 MW	27020 TQ	USBLS	5/15
	Maine	Y	20590 FQ	22860 MW	26150 TQ	USBLS	5/15
	Portland-South Portland MSA, ME	Y	21330 FQ	23160 MW	25870 TQ	USBLS	5/15
	Maryland	Y	20858 AE	24271 MW	25978 AEX	MDBLS	4/16
	Baltimore-Columbia-Towson MSA, MD	Y	21250 FQ	23190 MW	25980 TQ	USBLS	5/15
	Salisbury MSA, MD-DE	Y	20820 FQ	22510 MW	24200 TQ	USBLS	5/15
	Massachusetts	Y	25310 FQ	28010 MW	30730 TQ	USBLS	5/15
	Boston-Cambridge-Newton NECTA, MA	Y	25980 FQ	28720 MW	32140 TQ	USBLS	5/15

AE	Average entry wage	AWR	Average wage range	H	Hourly
AEX	Average experienced wage	B	Biweekly	HI	Highest wage paid
ATC	Average total compensation	D	Daily	HR	High end range
AW	Average wage paid	FQ	First quartile wage	LO	Lowest wage paid

LR	Low end range	MTC	Median total compensation
M	Monthly	MW	Median wage paid
MCC	Median cash compensation	MWR	Median wage range
ME	Median entry wage	S	See annotated source

TCC	Total cash compensation		
TQ	Third quartile wage		
W	Weekly		
Y	Yearly		

Home Health Aide

Occupation/Type/Industry	Location	Per	Low	Mid	High	Source	Date
Home Health Aide	Worcester MSA, MA-CT	Y	25400 FQ	27890 MW	30390 TQ	USBLS	5/15
	Michigan	Y	18690 FQ	20880 MW	23850 TQ	USBLS	5/15
	Detroit-Dearborn-Livonia PMSA, MI	Y	18310 FQ	19620 MW	24040 TQ	USBLS	5/15
	Grand Rapids-Wyoming MSA, MI	Y	18520 FQ	20480 MW	23340 TQ	USBLS	5/15
	Minnesota	Y	22207 FQ	24944 MW	28751 TQ	MNBLS	1/16-3/16
	Minneapolis-St. Paul-Bloomington MSA, MN-WI	Y	22954 FQ	26125 MW	29357 TQ	MNBLS	1/16-3/16
	Mississippi	Y	20030 FQ	21720 MW	23410 TQ	USBLS	5/15
	Jackson MSA, MS	Y	20930 FQ	22280 MW	23630 TQ	USBLS	5/15
	Missouri	Y	19960 FQ	22500 MW	23950 TQ	USBLS	5/15
	Kansas City MSA, MO-KS	Y	21910 FQ	23370 MW	26610 TQ	USBLS	5/15
	St. Louis MSA, MO-IL	Y	20280 FQ	22350 MW	23760 TQ	USBLS	5/15
	Montana	Y	20730 FQ	22310 MW	23890 TQ	USBLS	5/15
	Billings MSA, MT	Y	23070 FQ	26130 MW	28640 TQ	USBLS	5/15
	Nebraska	Y	21065 FQ	23425 MW	27280 TQ	NEBLS	7/16-9/16
	Omaha-Council Bluffs MSA, NE-IA	Y	20255 FQ	22225 MW	24190 TQ	NEBLS	7/16-9/16
	Nevada	Y	20360 FQ	22850 MW	27160 TQ	USBLS	5/15
	Las Vegas-Henderson-Paradise MSA, NV	Y	20680 FQ	22950 MW	27240 TQ	USBLS	5/15
	New Hampshire	H	10.85 AE	12.98 MW	14.37 AEX	NHBLS	6/16
	Manchester NECTA, NH	H	11.19 AE	13.21 MW	13.98 AEX	NHBLS	6/16
	Nashua NECTA, NH-MA	Y	23680 FQ	26540 MW	29100 TQ	USBLS	5/15
	New Jersey	Y	20060 FQ	22270 MW	24500 TQ	USBLS	5/15
	Camden PMSA, NJ	Y	19380 FQ	21510 MW	23610 TQ	USBLS	5/15
	Newark PMSA, NJ-PA	Y	20350 FQ	22750 MW	26100 TQ	USBLS	5/15
	Trenton MSA, NJ	Y	21740 FQ	24060 MW	27770 TQ	USBLS	5/15
	New Mexico	Y	18030 FQ	20730 MW	29800 TQ	USBLS	5/15
	Albuquerque MSA, NM	Y	19500 FQ	23800 MW	32900 TQ	USBLS	5/15
	New York	Y	21080 AE	23010 MW	25200 AEX	NYBLS	1/16-3/16
	Buffalo-Cheektowaga-Niagara Falls MSA, NY	Y	21180 FQ	23380 MW	27150 TQ	USBLS	5/15
	Nassau County-Suffolk County PMSA, NY	Y	20600 FQ	22770 MW	25080 TQ	USBLS	5/15
	New York-Jersey City-White Plains PMSA, NY-NJ	Y	20300 FQ	22310 MW	24310 TQ	USBLS	5/15
	Rochester MSA, NY	Y	20800 FQ	23200 MW	27310 TQ	USBLS	5/15
	North Carolina	Y	17200 FQ	18970 MW	22180 TQ	USBLS	5/15
	Charlotte-Concord-Gastonia MSA, NC-SC	Y	17070 FQ	18740 MW	21690 TQ	USBLS	5/15
	Raleigh MSA, NC	Y	18340 FQ	21000 MW	23540 TQ	USBLS	5/15
	North Dakota	Y	25130 FQ	29380 MW	34970 TQ	USBLS	5/15
	Fargo MSA, ND-MN	Y	24580 FQ	28130 MW	31950 TQ	USBLS	5/15
	Ohio	Y	18510 FQ	20450 MW	23080 TQ	USBLS	5/15
	Cincinnati MSA, OH-KY-IN	Y	20140 FQ	22070 MW	23990 TQ	USBLS	5/15
	Cleveland-Elyria MSA, OH	Y	18550 FQ	20640 MW	23340 TQ	USBLS	5/15
	Columbus MSA, OH	Y	19780 FQ	21630 MW	23430 TQ	USBLS	5/15
	Oklahoma	Y	18780 FQ	22080 MW	26490 TQ	USBLS	5/15
	Oklahoma City MSA, OK	Y	20140 FQ	22720 MW	26820 TQ	USBLS	5/15
	Tulsa MSA, OK	Y	20380 FQ	24240 MW	28980 TQ	USBLS	5/15
	Oregon	H	10.25 FQ	11.09 MW	11.94 TQ	ORBLS	2016
	Portland-Vancouver-Hillsboro MSA, OR-WA	Y	20870 FQ	22900 MW	25630 TQ	USBLS	5/15
	Pennsylvania	Y	18410 FQ	21350 MW	24520 TQ	USBLS	5/15
	Allentown-Bethlehem-Easton MSA, PA-NJ	Y	18870 FQ	21830 MW	24630 TQ	USBLS	5/15
	Harrisburg-Carlisle MSA, PA	Y	19630 FQ	22210 MW	24900 TQ	USBLS	5/15
	Montgomery County-Bucks County-Chester County PMSA, PA	Y	19690 FQ	22540 MW	26100 TQ	USBLS	5/15
	Philadelphia PMSA, PA	Y	18100 FQ	20870 MW	23990 TQ	USBLS	5/15
	Pittsburgh MSA, PA	Y	18630 FQ	21700 MW	24790 TQ	USBLS	5/15
	Rhode Island	Y	21580 FQ	24030 MW	30190 TQ	USBLS	5/15
	Providence-Warwick MSA, RI-MA	Y	21650 FQ	24220 MW	30070 TQ	USBLS	5/15
	South Carolina	Y	17660 FQ	19940 MW	22860 TQ	USBLS	5/15
	Charleston-North Charleston MSA, SC	Y	18620 FQ	20870 MW	23250 TQ	USBLS	5/15
	Columbia MSA, SC	Y	17940 FQ	20570 MW	23010 TQ	USBLS	5/15

Occupation/Type/Industry	Location	Per	Low	Mid	High	Source	Date
Home Health Aide	Greenville-Anderson-Mauldin						
	MSA, SC	Y	17200 FQ	18980 MW	22070 TQ	USBLS	5/15
	South Dakota	Y	22910 FQ	26200 MW	29420 TQ	USBLS	5/15
	Sioux Falls MSA, SD	Y	22330 FQ	25390 MW	29450 TQ	USBLS	5/15
	Tennessee	Y	17280 FQ	19040 MW	21900 TQ	USBLS	5/15
	Knoxville MSA, TN	Y	17040 FQ	18490 MW	20080 TQ	USBLS	5/15
	Memphis MSA, TN-MS-AR	Y	17200 FQ	18880 MW	21450 TQ	USBLS	5/15
	Nashville-Davidson–						
	Murfreesboro–Franklin						
	MSA, TN	Y	17430 FQ	19330 MW	22140 TQ	USBLS	5/15
	Texas	Y	16900 FQ	18420 MW	21260 TQ	USBLS	5/15
	Austin-Round Rock MSA, TX	Y	17810 FQ	20830 MW	25820 TQ	USBLS	5/15
	Dallas-Plano-Irving PMSA, TX	Y	17720 FQ	20750 MW	27090 TQ	USBLS	5/15
	Fort Worth-Arlington PMSA,						
	TX	Y	17430 FQ	19380 MW	24230 TQ	USBLS	5/15
	Houston-The Woodlands-						
	Sugar Land MSA, TX	Y	16780 FQ	18200 MW	19830 TQ	USBLS	5/15
	San Antonio-New Braunfels						
	MSA, TX	Y	17810 FQ	20800 MW	24090 TQ	USBLS	5/15
	Utah	Y	19400 FQ	22660 MW	27390 TQ	USBLS	5/15
	Ogden-Clearfield MSA, UT	Y	19440 FQ	22730 MW	27390 TQ	USBLS	5/15
	Provo-Orem MSA, UT	Y	18460 FQ	20910 MW	23350 TQ	USBLS	5/15
	Salt Lake City MSA, UT	Y	20560 FQ	24990 MW	29250 TQ	USBLS	5/15
	Vermont	Y	23230 FQ	26480 MW	29350 TQ	USBLS	5/15
	Burlington-South Burlington						
	MSA, VT	Y	22290 FQ	25420 MW	28460 TQ	USBLS	5/15
	Virginia	Y	18390 FQ	21830 MW	26030 TQ	USBLS	5/15
	Richmond MSA, VA	Y	17070 FQ	18630 MW	21910 TQ	USBLS	5/15
	Virginia Beach-Norfolk-						
	Newport News MSA, VA-NC	Y	19490 FQ	21910 MW	24270 TQ	USBLS	5/15
	Washington	H	10.68 FQ	11.74 MW	13.74 TQ	WABLS	3/16
	Seattle-Bellevue-Everett						
	PMSA, WA	H	10.89 FQ	12.05 MW	14.04 TQ	WABLS	3/16
	Tacoma-Lakewood PMSA, WA	H	10.36 FQ	11.65 MW	13.56 TQ	WABLS	3/16
	West Virginia	Y	17580 FQ	18530 MW	19530 TQ	USBLS	5/15
	Huntington-Ashland MSA,						
	WV-KY-OH	Y	17990 FQ	19360 MW	22450 TQ	USBLS	5/15
	Wisconsin	Y	20830 FQ	23110 MW	27460 TQ	USBLS	5/15
	Madison MSA, WI	Y	21710 FQ	24510 MW	29860 TQ	USBLS	5/15
	Milwaukee-Waukesha-West						
	Allis MSA, WI	Y	20410 FQ	22500 MW	24610 TQ	USBLS	5/15
	Wyoming	Y	25120 FQ	27420 MW	29720 TQ	USBLS	5/15
	Cheyenne MSA, WY	Y	26210 FQ	29420 MW	34230 TQ	USBLS	5/15
	Puerto Rico	Y	16520 FQ	17620 MW	18720 TQ	USBLS	5/15
	San Juan-Carolina-Caguas						
	MSA, PR	Y	16550 FQ	17650 MW	18750 TQ	USBLS	5/15
	Virgin Islands	Y	21410 FQ	23540 MW	26610 TQ	USBLS	5/15
Home Rehabilitation Coordinator							
Environmental Services, Municipal							
Government	Simi Valley, CA	Y			78094 HI	CACIT	6/28/16
Homeland Security Specialist							
County Government	Oakland County, MI	B	2121 LO		2774 HI	MIOAK2	10/1/16
State Government	New Mexico	H	17.01 LO		29.60 HI	NMGOV	7/30/16
Homeless Programs Coordinator							
Municipal Government	Glendale, CA	Y			47760 HI	CACIT	6/28/16
Homeless Services Officer							
Municipal Government	Long Beach, CA	Y			63857 HI	CACIT	6/28/16
Homicide Detective							
Municipal Government	Seattle, WA	H	35.76 LO		46.03 HI	CSSS	1/1/14
Horse Trainer	United States	Y		31000 AW		SKU01	2016
Horticulturist							
Municipal Government	San Diego, CA	Y		60553 AW		CACIT	6/28/16
Municipal Government	Colorado Springs, CO	Y	55377 LO		76143 HI	COSPRS	2017
Hospitalist	United States	Y		222000 MW		HCHRON1	2017

AE Average entry wage	**AWR** Average wage range	**H** Hourly	**LR** Low end range	**MTC** Median total compensation	**TCC** Total cash compensation
AEX Average experienced wage	**B** Biweekly	**HI** Highest wage paid	**M** Monthly	**MW** Median wage paid	**TQ** Third quartile wage
ATC Average total compensation	**D** Daily	**HR** High end range	**MCC** Median cash compensation	**MWR** Median wage range	**W** Weekly
AW Average wage paid	**FQ** First quartile wage	**LO** Lowest wage paid	**ME** Median entry wage	**S** See annotated source	**Y** Yearly

Host and Hostess

Occupation/Type/Industry	Location	Per	Low	Mid	High	Source	Date
Restaurant, Lounge, and Coffee Shop	Alabama	Y	17472 AE	18378 AW	18831 AEX	ALBLS	6/16
Restaurant, Lounge, and Coffee Shop	Birmingham-Hoover MSA, AL	Y	17503 AE	18481 AW	18976 AEX	ALBLS	6/16
Restaurant, Lounge, and Coffee Shop	Alaska	Y	18790 FQ	19380 MW	22240 TQ	USBLS	5/15
Restaurant, Lounge, and Coffee Shop	Anchorage MSA, AK	Y	18760 FQ	19320 MW	21770 TQ	USBLS	5/15
Restaurant, Lounge, and Coffee Shop	Arizona	Y	17830 FQ	18880 MW	21250 TQ	USBLS	5/15
Restaurant, Lounge, and Coffee Shop	Phoenix-Mesa-Scottsdale MSA, AZ	Y	17860 FQ	18950 MW	21610 TQ	USBLS	5/15
Restaurant, Lounge, and Coffee Shop	Tucson MSA, AZ	Y	17750 FQ	18740 MW	20420 TQ	USBLS	5/15
Restaurant, Lounge, and Coffee Shop	Arkansas	Y	16850 FQ	18090 MW	19340 TQ	USBLS	5/15
Restaurant, Lounge, and Coffee Shop	Little Rock-North Little Rock-Conway MSA, AR	Y	16930 FQ	18230 MW	19610 TQ	USBLS	5/15
Restaurant, Lounge, and Coffee Shop	California	H	9.42 FQ	9.67 MW	11.61 TQ	CABLS	1/16-3/16
Restaurant, Lounge, and Coffee Shop	Anaheim-Santa Ana-Irvine PMSA, CA	H	9.42 FQ	9.66 MW	11.84 TQ	CABLS	1/16-3/16
Restaurant, Lounge, and Coffee Shop	Los Angeles-Long Beach-Glendale PMSA, CA	H	9.44 FQ	9.73 MW	12.26 TQ	CABLS	1/16-3/16
Restaurant, Lounge, and Coffee Shop	Oakland-Hayward-Berkeley PMSA, CA	H	9.40 FQ	9.64 MW	11.13 TQ	CABLS	1/16-3/16
Restaurant, Lounge, and Coffee Shop	Riverside-San Bernardino-Ontario MSA, CA	H	9.42 FQ	9.67 MW	11.06 TQ	CABLS	1/16-3/16
Restaurant, Lounge, and Coffee Shop	Sacramento–Roseville–Arden-Arcade MSA, CA	H	9.41 FQ	9.66 MW	11.24 TQ	CABLS	1/16-3/16
Restaurant, Lounge, and Coffee Shop	San Diego-Carlsbad MSA, CA	H	9.39 FQ	9.62 MW	11.03 TQ	CABLS	1/16-3/16
Restaurant, Lounge, and Coffee Shop	San Francisco-Redwood City-South San Francisco PMSA, CA	H	9.55 FQ	11.31 MW	14.12 TQ	CABLS	1/16-3/16
Restaurant, Lounge, and Coffee Shop	Colorado	Y	18260 FQ	19430 MW	23090 TQ	USBLS	5/15
Restaurant, Lounge, and Coffee Shop	Denver-Aurora-Lakewood MSA, CO	Y	18200 FQ	19310 MW	22810 TQ	USBLS	5/15
Restaurant, Lounge, and Coffee Shop	Connecticut	Y		20007 MW		CTBLS	1/16-3/16
Restaurant, Lounge, and Coffee Shop	Bridgeport-Stamford-Norwalk MSA, CT	Y	19290 FQ	19620 MW	22630 TQ	USBLS	5/15
Restaurant, Lounge, and Coffee Shop	Hartford-West Hartford-East Hartford MSA, CT	Y	19200 FQ	19560 MW	22190 TQ	USBLS	5/15
Restaurant, Lounge, and Coffee Shop	Delaware	Y	17480 FQ	18570 MW	19750 TQ	USBLS	5/15
Restaurant, Lounge, and Coffee Shop	Wilmington PMSA, DE-MD-NJ	Y	17570 FQ	18660 MW	20000 TQ	USBLS	5/15
Restaurant, Lounge, and Coffee Shop	District of Columbia	Y	19920 FQ	22680 MW	27370 TQ	USBLS	5/15
Restaurant, Lounge, and Coffee Shop	Washington-Arlington-Alexandria PMSA, DC-VA-MD-WV	Y	18840 FQ	20970 MW	24370 TQ	USBLS	5/15
Restaurant, Lounge, and Coffee Shop	Florida	H	8.99 AE	9.67 MW	11.40 AEX	FLBLS	7/16-9/16
Restaurant, Lounge, and Coffee Shop	Fort Lauderdale-Pompano Beach-Deerfield Beach PMSA, FL	H	8.96 AE	9.74 MW	11.01 AEX	FLBLS	7/16-9/16
Restaurant, Lounge, and Coffee Shop	Miami-Miami Beach-Kendall PMSA, FL	H	9.31 AE	11.58 MW	13.23 AEX	FLBLS	7/16-9/16
Restaurant, Lounge, and Coffee Shop	Orlando-Kissimmee-Sanford MSA, FL	H	9.00 AE	9.95 MW	12.24 AEX	FLBLS	7/16-9/16
Restaurant, Lounge, and Coffee Shop	Tampa-St. Petersburg-Clearwater MSA, FL	H	9.00 AE	9.47 MW	10.75 AEX	FLBLS	7/16-9/16
Restaurant, Lounge, and Coffee Shop	Georgia	Y	16690 FQ	17940 MW	19190 TQ	USBLS	5/15
Restaurant, Lounge, and Coffee Shop	Atlanta-Sandy Springs-Roswell MSA, GA	Y	16730 FQ	18000 MW	19280 TQ	USBLS	5/15
Restaurant, Lounge, and Coffee Shop	Augusta-Richmond County MSA, GA-SC	Y	16750 FQ	18090 MW	19470 TQ	USBLS	5/15
Restaurant, Lounge, and Coffee Shop	Hawaii	Y	18300 FQ	21470 MW	29450 TQ	USBLS	5/15
Restaurant, Lounge, and Coffee Shop	Urban Honolulu MSA, HI	Y	18060 FQ	20700 MW	28600 TQ	USBLS	5/15
Restaurant, Lounge, and Coffee Shop	Idaho	Y	16630 FQ	17880 MW	19130 TQ	USBLS	5/15
Restaurant, Lounge, and Coffee Shop	Boise City MSA, ID	Y	16530 FQ	17700 MW	18870 TQ	USBLS	5/15
Restaurant, Lounge, and Coffee Shop	Illinois	Y	18370 FQ	19220 MW	22090 TQ	USBLS	5/15
Restaurant, Lounge, and Coffee Shop	Chicago-Naperville-Arlington Heights PMSA, IL	Y	18490 FQ	19500 MW	22990 TQ	USBLS	5/15
Restaurant, Lounge, and Coffee Shop	Lake County-Kenosha County PMSA, IL-WI	Y	17970 FQ	18740 MW	19780 TQ	USBLS	5/15
Restaurant, Lounge, and Coffee Shop	Indiana	Y	16640 FQ	17880 MW	19120 TQ	USBLS	5/15
Restaurant, Lounge, and Coffee Shop	Gary PMSA, IN	Y	16750 FQ	18040 MW	19360 TQ	USBLS	5/15
Restaurant, Lounge, and Coffee Shop	Indianapolis-Carmel-Anderson MSA, IN	Y	16690 FQ	18010 MW	19350 TQ	USBLS	5/15
Restaurant, Lounge, and Coffee Shop	Iowa	Y	16670 FQ	17960 MW	19250 TQ	USBLS	5/15

AE	Average entry wage	AWR	Average wage range	H	Hourly	LR	Low end range	MTC	Median total compensation	TCC	Total cash compensation
AEX	Average experienced wage	B	Biweekly	HI	Highest wage paid	M	Monthly	MW	Median wage paid	TQ	Third quartile wage
ATC	Average total compensation	D	Daily	HR	High end range	MCC	Median cash compensation	MWR	Median wage range	W	Weekly
AW	Average wage paid	FQ	First quartile wage	LO	Lowest wage paid	ME	Median entry wage	S	See annotated source	Y	Yearly

Occupation/Type/Industry	Location	Per	Low	Mid	High	Source	Date
Host and Hostess							
Restaurant, Lounge, and Coffee Shop	Des Moines-West Des Moines MSA, IA	Y	16650 FQ	17930 MW	19220 TQ	USBLS	5/15
Restaurant, Lounge, and Coffee Shop	Kansas	Y	17080 FQ	18770 MW	22120 TQ	USBLS	5/15
Restaurant, Lounge, and Coffee Shop	Wichita MSA, KS	Y	16950 FQ	18440 MW	20720 TQ	USBLS	5/15
Restaurant, Lounge, and Coffee Shop	Kentucky	Y	16680 FQ	17940 MW	19200 TQ	USBLS	5/15
Restaurant, Lounge, and Coffee Shop	Louisville-Jefferson County MSA, KY-IN	Y	16720 FQ	18030 MW	19360 TQ	USBLS	5/15
Restaurant, Lounge, and Coffee Shop	Louisiana	Y	16710 FQ	18010 MW	19310 TQ	USBLS	5/15
Restaurant, Lounge, and Coffee Shop	Baton Rouge MSA, LA	Y	16620 FQ	17800 MW	18980 TQ	USBLS	5/15
Restaurant, Lounge, and Coffee Shop	New Orleans-Metairie MSA, LA	Y	16780 FQ	18190 MW	19770 TQ	USBLS	5/15
Restaurant, Lounge, and Coffee Shop	Maine	Y	17310 FQ	18630 MW	20510 TQ	USBLS	5/15
Restaurant, Lounge, and Coffee Shop	Portland-South Portland MSA, ME	Y	17570 FQ	19140 MW	21850 TQ	USBLS	5/15
Restaurant, Lounge, and Coffee Shop	Maryland	Y	18065 AE	20466 MW	21666 AEX	MDBLS	4/16
Restaurant, Lounge, and Coffee Shop	Baltimore-Columbia-Towson MSA, MD	Y	17980 FQ	19310 MW	22340 TQ	USBLS	5/15
Restaurant, Lounge, and Coffee Shop	Salisbury MSA, MD-DE	Y	17560 FQ	18600 MW	19710 TQ	USBLS	5/15
Restaurant, Lounge, and Coffee Shop	Massachusetts	Y	19920 FQ	22720 MW	26430 TQ	USBLS	5/15
Restaurant, Lounge, and Coffee Shop	Boston-Cambridge-Newton NECTA, MA	Y	20560 FQ	23350 MW	27330 TQ	USBLS	5/15
Restaurant, Lounge, and Coffee Shop	Worcester MSA, MA-CT	Y	19510 FQ	21410 MW	23770 TQ	USBLS	5/15
Restaurant, Lounge, and Coffee Shop	Michigan	Y	17880 FQ	18710 MW	19660 TQ	USBLS	5/15
Restaurant, Lounge, and Coffee Shop	Detroit-Dearborn-Livonia PMSA, MI	Y	17790 FQ	18560 MW	19450 TQ	USBLS	5/15
Restaurant, Lounge, and Coffee Shop	Grand Rapids-Wyoming MSA, MI	Y	17850 FQ	18640 MW	19470 TQ	USBLS	5/15
Restaurant, Lounge, and Coffee Shop	Minnesota	Y	18006 FQ	19117 MW	22530 TQ	MNBLS	1/16-3/16
Restaurant, Lounge, and Coffee Shop	Minneapolis-St. Paul-Bloomington MSA, MN-WI	Y	18087 FQ	19299 MW	24065 TQ	MNBLS	1/16-3/16
Restaurant, Lounge, and Coffee Shop	Mississippi	Y	16910 FQ	18370 MW	20160 TQ	USBLS	5/15
Restaurant, Lounge, and Coffee Shop	Jackson MSA, MS	Y	17090 FQ	18670 MW	21100 TQ	USBLS	5/15
Restaurant, Lounge, and Coffee Shop	Missouri	Y	17170 FQ	18400 MW	19710 TQ	USBLS	5/15
Restaurant, Lounge, and Coffee Shop	Kansas City MSA, MO-KS	Y	17460 FQ	19190 MW	22450 TQ	USBLS	5/15
Restaurant, Lounge, and Coffee Shop	St. Louis MSA, MO-IL	Y	17490 FQ	18660 MW	19900 TQ	USBLS	5/15
Restaurant, Lounge, and Coffee Shop	Montana	Y	17710 FQ	18640 MW	19690 TQ	USBLS	5/15
Restaurant, Lounge, and Coffee Shop	Billings MSA, MT	Y	17790 FQ	18820 MW	20980 TQ	USBLS	5/15
Restaurant, Lounge, and Coffee Shop	Nebraska	Y	17605 FQ	18565 MW	19635 TQ	NEBLS	7/16-9/16
Restaurant, Lounge, and Coffee Shop	Omaha-Council Bluffs MSA, NE-IA	Y	17435 FQ	18375 MW	19330 TQ	NEBLS	7/16-9/16
Restaurant, Lounge, and Coffee Shop	Nevada	Y	17780 FQ	21390 MW	31940 TQ	USBLS	5/15
Restaurant, Lounge, and Coffee Shop	Las Vegas-Henderson-Paradise MSA, NV	Y	18010 FQ	22990 MW	33070 TQ	USBLS	5/15
Restaurant, Lounge, and Coffee Shop	New Hampshire	H	8.43 AE	9.49 MW	10.73 AEX	NHBLS	6/16
Restaurant, Lounge, and Coffee Shop	Manchester NECTA, NH	H	8.41 AE	10.60 MW	11.99 AEX	NHBLS	6/16
Restaurant, Lounge, and Coffee Shop	Nashua NECTA, NH-MA	Y	17590 FQ	19720 MW	23910 TQ	USBLS	5/15
Restaurant, Lounge, and Coffee Shop	New Jersey	Y	18920 FQ	20960 MW	23990 TQ	USBLS	5/15
Restaurant, Lounge, and Coffee Shop	Camden PMSA, NJ	Y	18380 FQ	19250 MW	22630 TQ	USBLS	5/15
Restaurant, Lounge, and Coffee Shop	Newark PMSA, NJ-PA	Y	19790 FQ	21760 MW	23730 TQ	USBLS	5/15
Restaurant, Lounge, and Coffee Shop	Trenton MSA, NJ	Y	18680 FQ	20100 MW	23150 TQ	USBLS	5/15
Restaurant, Lounge, and Coffee Shop	New Mexico	Y	17340 FQ	18710 MW	21200 TQ	USBLS	5/15
Restaurant, Lounge, and Coffee Shop	Albuquerque MSA, NM	Y	17200 FQ	18420 MW	19700 TQ	USBLS	5/15
Restaurant, Lounge, and Coffee Shop	New York	Y	19260 AE	21430 MW	26200 AEX	NYBLS	1/16-3/16
Restaurant, Lounge, and Coffee Shop	Buffalo-Cheektowaga-Niagara Falls MSA, NY	Y	18770 FQ	19350 MW	21670 TQ	USBLS	5/15
Restaurant, Lounge, and Coffee Shop	Nassau County-Suffolk County PMSA, NY	Y	18970 FQ	20760 MW	24120 TQ	USBLS	5/15
Restaurant, Lounge, and Coffee Shop	New York-Jersey City-White Plains PMSA, NY-NJ	Y	19240 FQ	22210 MW	26990 TQ	USBLS	5/15
Restaurant, Lounge, and Coffee Shop	Rochester MSA, NY	Y	18700 FQ	19210 MW	20410 TQ	USBLS	5/15
Restaurant, Lounge, and Coffee Shop	North Carolina	Y	16780 FQ	18130 MW	19520 TQ	USBLS	5/15
Restaurant, Lounge, and Coffee Shop	Charlotte-Concord-Gastonia MSA, NC-SC	Y	16970 FQ	18500 MW	21100 TQ	USBLS	5/15
Restaurant, Lounge, and Coffee Shop	Raleigh MSA, NC	Y	16700 FQ	17950 MW	19190 TQ	USBLS	5/15
Restaurant, Lounge, and Coffee Shop	North Dakota	Y	16910 FQ	18430 MW	20820 TQ	USBLS	5/15
Restaurant, Lounge, and Coffee Shop	Fargo MSA, ND-MN	Y	16690 FQ	17980 MW	19260 TQ	USBLS	5/15
Restaurant, Lounge, and Coffee Shop	Ohio	Y	17750 FQ	18620 MW	19620 TQ	USBLS	5/15
Restaurant, Lounge, and Coffee Shop	Cincinnati MSA, OH-KY-IN	Y	17610 FQ	18550 MW	19630 TQ	USBLS	5/15
Restaurant, Lounge, and Coffee Shop	Cleveland-Elyria MSA, OH	Y	17710 FQ	18560 MW	19500 TQ	USBLS	5/15
Restaurant, Lounge, and Coffee Shop	Columbus MSA, OH	Y	17900 FQ	18930 MW	21780 TQ	USBLS	5/15
Restaurant, Lounge, and Coffee Shop	Oklahoma	Y	16750 FQ	18120 MW	19630 TQ	USBLS	5/15

AE	Average entry wage	AWR	Average wage range	H	Hourly	LR	Low end range	MTC	Median total compensation	TCC	Total cash compensation
AEX	Average experienced wage	B	Biweekly	HI	Highest wage paid	M	Monthly	MW	Median wage paid	TQ	Third quartile wage
ATC	Average total compensation	D	Daily	HR	High end range	MCC	Median cash compensation	MWR	Median wage range	W	Weekly
AW	Average wage paid	FQ	First quartile wage	LO	Lowest wage paid	ME	Median entry wage	S	See annotated source	Y	Yearly

Occupation/Type/Industry	Location	Per	Low	Mid	High	Source	Date
Host and Hostess							
Restaurant, Lounge, and Coffee Shop	Oklahoma City MSA, OK	Y	17010 FQ	18620 MW	22470 TQ	USBLS	5/15
Restaurant, Lounge, and Coffee Shop	Tulsa MSA, OK	Y	16460 FQ	17630 MW	18800 TQ	USBLS	5/15
Restaurant, Lounge, and Coffee Shop	Oregon	H	9.57 FQ	9.70 MW	10.97 TQ	ORBLS	2016
Restaurant, Lounge, and Coffee Shop	Portland-Vancouver-Hillsboro MSA, OR-WA	Y	19540 FQ	19880 MW	22760 TQ	USBLS	5/15
Restaurant, Lounge, and Coffee Shop	Pennsylvania	Y	17130 FQ	18860 MW	22860 TQ	USBLS	5/15
Restaurant, Lounge, and Coffee Shop	Allentown-Bethlehem-Easton MSA, PA-NJ	Y	17250 FQ	18820 MW	22930 TQ	USBLS	5/15
Restaurant, Lounge, and Coffee Shop	Harrisburg-Carlisle MSA, PA	Y	17010 FQ	18570 MW	21360 TQ	USBLS	5/15
Restaurant, Lounge, and Coffee Shop	Montgomery County-Bucks County-Chester County PMSA, PA	Y	17440 FQ	19410 MW	24800 TQ	USBLS	5/15
Restaurant, Lounge, and Coffee Shop	Philadelphia PMSA, PA	Y	18020 FQ	20960 MW	26390 TQ	USBLS	5/15
Restaurant, Lounge, and Coffee Shop	Pittsburgh MSA, PA	Y	17140 FQ	18920 MW	22880 TQ	USBLS	5/15
Restaurant, Lounge, and Coffee Shop	Rhode Island	Y	19070 FQ	19620 MW	22770 TQ	USBLS	5/15
Restaurant, Lounge, and Coffee Shop	Providence-Warwick MSA, RI-MA	Y	19110 FQ	19750 MW	23300 TQ	USBLS	5/15
Restaurant, Lounge, and Coffee Shop	South Carolina	Y	16910 FQ	18380 MW	20280 TQ	USBLS	5/15
Restaurant, Lounge, and Coffee Shop	Charleston-North Charleston MSA, SC	Y	17210 FQ	19000 MW	22070 TQ	USBLS	5/15
Restaurant, Lounge, and Coffee Shop	Columbia MSA, SC	Y	16650 FQ	17830 MW	19010 TQ	USBLS	5/15
Restaurant, Lounge, and Coffee Shop	Greenville-Anderson-Mauldin MSA, SC	Y	16890 FQ	18230 MW	19580 TQ	USBLS	5/15
Restaurant, Lounge, and Coffee Shop	South Dakota	Y	18570 FQ	19480 MW	22150 TQ	USBLS	5/15
Restaurant, Lounge, and Coffee Shop	Sioux Falls MSA, SD	Y	18670 FQ	19780 MW	22740 TQ	USBLS	5/15
Restaurant, Lounge, and Coffee Shop	Tennessee	Y	16760 FQ	18090 MW	19470 TQ	USBLS	5/15
Restaurant, Lounge, and Coffee Shop	Knoxville MSA, TN	Y	16700 FQ	17940 MW	19180 TQ	USBLS	5/15
Restaurant, Lounge, and Coffee Shop	Memphis MSA, TN-MS-AR	Y	16760 FQ	18060 MW	19380 TQ	USBLS	5/15
Restaurant, Lounge, and Coffee Shop	Nashville-Davidson–Murfreesboro–Franklin MSA, TN	Y	16890 FQ	18370 MW	20390 TQ	USBLS	5/15
Restaurant, Lounge, and Coffee Shop	Texas	Y	16900 FQ	18370 MW	20340 TQ	USBLS	5/15
Restaurant, Lounge, and Coffee Shop	Austin-Round Rock MSA, TX	Y	17230 FQ	19020 MW	22280 TQ	USBLS	5/15
Restaurant, Lounge, and Coffee Shop	Dallas-Plano-Irving PMSA, TX	Y	17160 FQ	18900 MW	22890 TQ	USBLS	5/15
Restaurant, Lounge, and Coffee Shop	Fort Worth-Arlington PMSA, TX	Y	17090 FQ	18740 MW	21760 TQ	USBLS	5/15
Restaurant, Lounge, and Coffee Shop	Houston-The Woodlands-Sugar Land MSA, TX	Y	16850 FQ	18260 MW	19770 TQ	USBLS	5/15
Restaurant, Lounge, and Coffee Shop	San Antonio-New Braunfels MSA, TX	Y	16810 FQ	18220 MW	19710 TQ	USBLS	5/15
Restaurant, Lounge, and Coffee Shop	Utah	Y	17140 FQ	18830 MW	21770 TQ	USBLS	5/15
Restaurant, Lounge, and Coffee Shop	Ogden-Clearfield MSA, UT	Y	17110 FQ	18750 MW	21040 TQ	USBLS	5/15
Restaurant, Lounge, and Coffee Shop	Provo-Orem MSA, UT	Y	16700 FQ	17950 MW	19200 TQ	USBLS	5/15
Restaurant, Lounge, and Coffee Shop	Salt Lake City MSA, UT	Y	17490 FQ	19500 MW	22720 TQ	USBLS	5/15
Restaurant, Lounge, and Coffee Shop	Vermont	Y	20040 FQ	22450 MW	25080 TQ	USBLS	5/15
Restaurant, Lounge, and Coffee Shop	Burlington-South Burlington MSA, VT	Y	20340 FQ	22060 MW	23780 TQ	USBLS	5/15
Restaurant, Lounge, and Coffee Shop	Virginia	Y	17190 FQ	18930 MW	22330 TQ	USBLS	5/15
Restaurant, Lounge, and Coffee Shop	Richmond MSA, VA	Y	16850 FQ	18200 MW	19580 TQ	USBLS	5/15
Restaurant, Lounge, and Coffee Shop	Virginia Beach-Norfolk-Newport News MSA, VA-NC	Y	16850 FQ	18230 MW	19660 TQ	USBLS	5/15
Restaurant, Lounge, and Coffee Shop	Washington	H	10.09 FQ	11.12 MW	12.21 TQ	WABLS	3/16
Restaurant, Lounge, and Coffee Shop	Seattle-Bellevue-Everett PMSA, WA	H	10.22 FQ	11.36 MW	13.23 TQ	WABLS	3/16
Restaurant, Lounge, and Coffee Shop	Tacoma-Lakewood PMSA, WA	H	10.30 FQ	11.19 MW	12.08 TQ	WABLS	3/16
Restaurant, Lounge, and Coffee Shop	West Virginia	Y	17480 FQ	18320 MW	19160 TQ	USBLS	5/15
Restaurant, Lounge, and Coffee Shop	Huntington-Ashland MSA, WV-KY-OH	Y	17160 FQ	18070 MW	18980 TQ	USBLS	5/15
Restaurant, Lounge, and Coffee Shop	Wisconsin	Y	16830 FQ	18230 MW	19740 TQ	USBLS	5/15
Restaurant, Lounge, and Coffee Shop	Madison MSA, WI	Y	17210 FQ	19010 MW	22110 TQ	USBLS	5/15
Restaurant, Lounge, and Coffee Shop	Milwaukee-Waukesha-West Allis MSA, WI	Y	16760 FQ	18090 MW	19430 TQ	USBLS	5/15
Restaurant, Lounge, and Coffee Shop	Wyoming	Y	17140 FQ	18950 MW	22970 TQ	USBLS	5/15
Restaurant, Lounge, and Coffee Shop	Cheyenne MSA, WY	Y	16580 FQ	17800 MW	19020 TQ	USBLS	5/15
Restaurant, Lounge, and Coffee Shop	Puerto Rico	Y	16490 FQ	17570 MW	18650 TQ	USBLS	5/15
Restaurant, Lounge, and Coffee Shop	San Juan-Carolina-Caguas MSA, PR	Y	16500 FQ	17580 MW	18660 TQ	USBLS	5/15
Restaurant, Lounge, and Coffee Shop	Virgin Islands	Y	16880 FQ	18230 MW	19650 TQ	USBLS	5/15
Restaurant, Lounge, and Coffee Shop	Guam	Y	17770 FQ	18390 MW	19000 TQ	USBLS	5/15

AE	Average entry wage	AWR	Average wage range	H	Hourly
AEX	Average experienced wage	B	Biweekly	HI	Highest wage paid
ATC	Average total compensation	D	Daily	HR	High end range
AW	Average wage paid	FQ	First quartile wage	LO	Lowest wage paid

LR	Low end range	MTC	Median total compensation	TCC	Total cash compensation
M	Monthly	MW	Median wage paid	TQ	Third quartile wage
MCC	Median cash compensation	MWR	Median wage range	W	Weekly
ME	Median entry wage	S	See annotated source	Y	Yearly

Occupation/Type/Industry	Location	Per	Low	Mid	High	Source	Date
Hotel, Motel, and Resort Desk Clerk							
	Alabama	Y	17592 AE	19890 AW	21034 AEX	ALBLS	6/16
	Birmingham-Hoover MSA, AL	Y	17633 AE	20272 AW	21581 AEX	ALBLS	6/16
	Alaska	Y	21930 FQ	25400 MW	29380 TQ	USBLS	5/15
	Anchorage MSA, AK	Y	21340 FQ	24790 MW	28800 TQ	USBLS	5/15
	Arizona	Y	18610 FQ	20700 MW	24290 TQ	USBLS	5/15
	Phoenix-Mesa-Scottsdale MSA, AZ	Y	19050 FQ	21740 MW	25560 TQ	USBLS	5/15
	Tucson MSA, AZ	Y	17980 FQ	19140 MW	21910 TQ	USBLS	5/15
	Arkansas	Y	16830 FQ	18000 MW	19170 TQ	USBLS	5/15
	Little Rock-North Little Rock-Conway MSA, AR	Y	16810 FQ	17940 MW	19070 TQ	USBLS	5/15
	California	H	10.48 FQ	12.17 MW	14.73 TQ	CABLS	1/16-3/16
	Anaheim-Santa Ana-Irvine PMSA, CA	H	11.27 FQ	13.16 MW	14.84 TQ	CABLS	1/16-3/16
	Los Angeles-Long Beach-Glendale PMSA, CA	H	10.24 FQ	11.70 MW	14.58 TQ	CABLS	1/16-3/16
	Oakland-Hayward-Berkeley PMSA, CA	H	11.97 FQ	13.99 MW	16.67 TQ	CABLS	1/16-3/16
	Riverside-San Bernardino-Ontario MSA, CA	H	9.81 FQ	11.63 MW	13.86 TQ	CABLS	1/16-3/16
	Sacramento–Roseville–Arden-Arcade MSA, CA	H	10.05 FQ	11.01 MW	11.97 TQ	CABLS	1/16-3/16
	San Diego-Carlsbad MSA, CA	H	11.11 FQ	12.78 MW	14.54 TQ	CABLS	1/16-3/16
	San Francisco-Redwood City-South San Francisco PMSA, CA	H	13.26 FQ	16.96 MW	22.24 TQ	CABLS	1/16-3/16
	Colorado	Y	19680 FQ	22620 MW	26960 TQ	USBLS	5/15
	Denver-Aurora-Lakewood MSA, CO	Y	20790 FQ	22900 MW	25320 TQ	USBLS	5/15
	Connecticut	Y		22667 MW		CTBLS	1/16-3/16
	Bridgeport-Stamford-Norwalk MSA, CT	Y	20790 FQ	22660 MW	24530 TQ	USBLS	5/15
	Hartford-West Hartford-East Hartford MSA, CT	Y	19600 FQ	22290 MW	26200 TQ	USBLS	5/15
	Delaware	Y	18670 FQ	21600 MW	26790 TQ	USBLS	5/15
	Wilmington PMSA, DE-MD-NJ	Y	18870 FQ	21650 MW	25550 TQ	USBLS	5/15
	District of Columbia	Y	28290 FQ	34290 MW	38570 TQ	USBLS	5/15
	Washington-Arlington-Alexandria PMSA, DC-VA-MD-WV	Y	21630 FQ	25130 MW	30650 TQ	USBLS	5/15
	Florida	H	9.05 AE	10.63 MW	12.10 AEX	FLBLS	7/16-9/16
	Fort Lauderdale-Pompano Beach-Deerfield Beach PMSA, FL	H	9.03 AE	10.01 MW	11.42 AEX	FLBLS	7/16-9/16
	Miami-Miami Beach-Kendall PMSA, FL	H	9.20 AE	11.80 MW	13.51 AEX	FLBLS	7/16-9/16
	Orlando-Kissimmee-Sanford MSA, FL	H	9.67 AE	10.95 MW	11.88 AEX	FLBLS	7/16-9/16
	Tampa-St. Petersburg-Clearwater MSA, FL	H	9.18 AE	10.65 MW	11.69 AEX	FLBLS	7/16-9/16
	Georgia	Y	17260 FQ	18970 MW	22040 TQ	USBLS	5/15
	Atlanta-Sandy Springs-Roswell MSA, GA	Y	17800 FQ	20000 MW	23640 TQ	USBLS	5/15
	Augusta-Richmond County MSA, GA-SC	Y	17010 FQ	18530 MW	20770 TQ	USBLS	5/15
	Hawaii	Y	32170 FQ	40340 MW	45320 TQ	USBLS	5/15
	Urban Honolulu MSA, HI	Y	33300 FQ	40800 MW	45500 TQ	USBLS	5/15
	Idaho	Y	18390 FQ	21150 MW	23930 TQ	USBLS	5/15
	Boise City MSA, ID	Y	18230 FQ	20900 MW	23690 TQ	USBLS	5/15
	Illinois	Y	18990 FQ	21150 MW	24380 TQ	USBLS	5/15
	Chicago-Naperville-Arlington Heights PMSA, IL	Y	19620 FQ	22540 MW	26840 TQ	USBLS	5/15
	Lake County-Kenosha County PMSA, IL-WI	Y	18560 FQ	21310 MW	27030 TQ	USBLS	5/15
	Indiana	Y	17120 FQ	18660 MW	20900 TQ	USBLS	5/15
	Gary PMSA, IN	Y	17200 FQ	18930 MW	21950 TQ	USBLS	5/15
	Indianapolis-Carmel-Anderson MSA, IN	Y	17620 FQ	19530 MW	22830 TQ	USBLS	5/15
	Iowa	Y	17780 FQ	20130 MW	22760 TQ	USBLS	5/15

AE	Average entry wage	AWR	Average wage range	H	Hourly
AEX	Average experienced wage	B	Biweekly	HI	Highest wage paid
ATC	Average total compensation	D	Daily	HR	High end range
AW	Average wage paid	FQ	First quartile wage	LO	Lowest wage paid

LR	Low end range	MTC	Median total compensation
M	Monthly	MW	Median wage paid
MCC	Median cash compensation	MWR	Median wage range
ME	Median entry wage	S	See annotated source

TCC	Total cash compensation		
TQ	Third quartile wage		
W	Weekly		
Y	Yearly		

Occupation/Type/Industry	Location	Per	Low	Mid	High	Source	Date
Hotel, Motel, and Resort Desk Clerk							
	Des Moines-West Des Moines MSA, IA	Y	19340 FQ	21660 MW	23660 TQ	USBLS	5/15
	Kansas	Y	17280 FQ	18960 MW	21490 TQ	USBLS	5/15
	Wichita MSA, KS	Y	17660 FQ	19740 MW	22750 TQ	USBLS	5/15
	Kentucky	Y	16980 FQ	18470 MW	20540 TQ	USBLS	5/15
	Louisville-Jefferson County MSA, KY-IN	Y	17400 FQ	19300 MW	22230 TQ	USBLS	5/15
	Louisiana	Y	17640 FQ	19900 MW	23520 TQ	USBLS	5/15
	Baton Rouge MSA, LA	Y	17120 FQ	18670 MW	21110 TQ	USBLS	5/15
	New Orleans-Metairie MSA, LA	Y	18890 FQ	22130 MW	25510 TQ	USBLS	5/15
	Maine	Y	20850 FQ	24990 MW	29240 TQ	USBLS	5/15
	Portland-South Portland MSA, ME	Y	21870 FQ	24600 MW	28090 TQ	USBLS	5/15
	Maryland	Y	20170 AE	25428 MW	28057 AEX	MDBLS	4/16
	Baltimore-Columbia-Towson MSA, MD	Y	21430 FQ	24750 MW	29530 TQ	USBLS	5/15
	Salisbury MSA, MD-DE	Y	19270 FQ	22200 MW	26290 TQ	USBLS	5/15
	Massachusetts	Y	22330 FQ	25730 MW	33040 TQ	USBLS	5/15
	Boston-Cambridge-Newton NECTA, MA	Y	22700 FQ	27300 MW	35570 TQ	USBLS	5/15
	Worcester MSA, MA-CT	Y	20170 FQ	23240 MW	28340 TQ	USBLS	5/15
	Michigan	Y	18390 FQ	19690 MW	23040 TQ	USBLS	5/15
	Detroit-Dearborn-Livonia PMSA, MI	Y	18770 FQ	21100 MW	26730 TQ	USBLS	5/15
	Grand Rapids-Wyoming MSA, MI	Y	18190 FQ	19250 MW	21810 TQ	USBLS	5/15
	Minnesota	Y	19113 FQ	21338 MW	23947 TQ	MNBLS	1/16-3/16
	Minneapolis-St. Paul-Bloomington MSA, MN-WI	Y	21166 FQ	23128 MW	25211 TQ	MNBLS	1/16-3/16
	Mississippi	Y	17030 FQ	18560 MW	20800 TQ	USBLS	5/15
	Jackson MSA, MS	Y	17110 FQ	18680 MW	21060 TQ	USBLS	5/15
	Missouri	Y	17750 FQ	19570 MW	22720 TQ	USBLS	5/15
	Kansas City MSA, MO-KS	Y	17770 FQ	19640 MW	22580 TQ	USBLS	5/15
	St. Louis MSA, MO-IL	Y	18800 FQ	21220 MW	23570 TQ	USBLS	5/15
	Montana	Y	18610 FQ	20550 MW	23690 TQ	USBLS	5/15
	Billings MSA, MT	Y	18790 FQ	20700 MW	23380 TQ	USBLS	5/15
	Nebraska	Y	18530 FQ	20395 MW	23590 TQ	NEBLS	7/16-9/16
	Omaha-Council Bluffs MSA, NE-IA	Y	18910 FQ	21575 MW	24420 TQ	NEBLS	7/16-9/16
	Nevada	Y	21000 FQ	30250 MW	36360 TQ	USBLS	5/15
	Las Vegas-Henderson-Paradise MSA, NV	Y	24280 FQ	33580 MW	37630 TQ	USBLS	5/15
	New Hampshire	H	9.50 AE	11.18 MW	12.52 AEX	NHBLS	6/16
	Manchester NECTA, NH	H	8.90 AE	11.12 MW	12.37 AEX	NHBLS	6/16
	Nashua NECTA, NH-MA	Y	17790 FQ	20350 MW	22900 TQ	USBLS	5/15
	New Jersey	Y	19850 FQ	22830 MW	26680 TQ	USBLS	5/15
	Camden PMSA, NJ	Y	19380 FQ	21520 MW	23920 TQ	USBLS	5/15
	Newark PMSA, NJ-PA	Y	18840 FQ	22690 MW	27190 TQ	USBLS	5/15
	Trenton MSA, NJ	Y	19990 FQ	21960 MW	24020 TQ	USBLS	5/15
	New Mexico	Y	17640 FQ	19200 MW	22420 TQ	USBLS	5/15
	Albuquerque MSA, NM	Y	17860 FQ	19700 MW	23470 TQ	USBLS	5/15
	New York	Y	20450 AE	25260 MW	34980 AEX	NYBLS	1/16-3/16
	Buffalo-Cheektowaga-Niagara Falls MSA, NY	Y	18840 FQ	19480 MW	22350 TQ	USBLS	5/15
	Nassau County-Suffolk County PMSA, NY	Y	21190 FQ	24070 MW	28920 TQ	USBLS	5/15
	New York-Jersey City-White Plains PMSA, NY-NJ	Y	23870 FQ	30530 MW	42050 TQ	USBLS	5/15
	Rochester MSA, NY	Y	18900 FQ	19680 MW	21910 TQ	USBLS	5/15
	North Carolina	Y	17460 FQ	19390 MW	23030 TQ	USBLS	5/15
	Charlotte-Concord-Gastonia MSA, NC-SC	Y	17490 FQ	19360 MW	22320 TQ	USBLS	5/15
	Raleigh MSA, NC	Y	20130 FQ	22980 MW	26490 TQ	USBLS	5/15
	North Dakota	Y	20680 FQ	24290 MW	29830 TQ	USBLS	5/15
	Fargo MSA, ND-MN	Y	19180 FQ	22610 MW	26860 TQ	USBLS	5/15
	Ohio	Y	18010 FQ	19100 MW	21460 TQ	USBLS	5/15
	Cincinnati MSA, OH-KY-IN	Y	17920 FQ	19290 MW	22390 TQ	USBLS	5/15
	Cleveland-Elyria MSA, OH	Y	18260 FQ	19680 MW	22570 TQ	USBLS	5/15
	Columbus MSA, OH	Y	18090 FQ	19280 MW	22200 TQ	USBLS	5/15
	Oklahoma	Y	16990 FQ	18530 MW	20840 TQ	USBLS	5/15

AE	Average entry wage	AWR	Average wage range	H	Hourly
AEX	Average experienced wage	B	Biweekly	HI	Highest wage paid
ATC	Average total compensation	D	Daily	HR	High end range
AW	Average wage paid	FQ	First quartile wage	LO	Lowest wage paid

LR	Low end range	MTC	Median total compensation
M	Monthly	MW	Median wage paid
MCC	Median cash compensation	MWR	Median wage range
ME	Median entry wage	S	See annotated source

TCC	Total cash compensation	
TQ	Third quartile wage	
W	Weekly	
Y	Yearly	

Occupation/Type/Industry	Location	Per	Low	Mid	High	Source	Date
Hotel, Motel, and Resort Desk Clerk	Oklahoma City MSA, OK	Y	17140 FQ	18860 MW	21930 TQ	USBLS	5/15
	Tulsa MSA, OK	Y	16860 FQ	18300 MW	20110 TQ	USBLS	5/15
	Oregon	H	9.71 FQ	10.61 MW	11.81 TQ	ORBLS	2016
	Portland-Vancouver-Hillsboro MSA, OR-WA	Y	20100 FQ	21880 MW	23690 TQ	USBLS	5/15
	Pennsylvania	Y	18170 FQ	21160 MW	24770 TQ	USBLS	5/15
	Allentown-Bethlehem-Easton MSA, PA-NJ	Y	18010 FQ	20950 MW	25200 TQ	USBLS	5/15
	Harrisburg-Carlisle MSA, PA	Y	17150 FQ	18800 MW	21570 TQ	USBLS	5/15
	Montgomery County-Bucks County-Chester County PMSA, PA	Y	20900 FQ	24430 MW	29200 TQ	USBLS	5/15
	Philadelphia PMSA, PA	Y	23480 FQ	27090 MW	30120 TQ	USBLS	5/15
	Pittsburgh MSA, PA	Y	17880 FQ	20280 MW	23470 TQ	USBLS	5/15
	Rhode Island	Y	19790 FQ	23220 MW	28180 TQ	USBLS	5/15
	Providence-Warwick MSA, RI-MA	Y	19670 FQ	22680 MW	27560 TQ	USBLS	5/15
	South Carolina	Y	17560 FQ	19620 MW	22770 TQ	USBLS	5/15
	Charleston-North Charleston MSA, SC	Y	17450 FQ	19440 MW	22690 TQ	USBLS	5/15
	Columbia MSA, SC	Y	17590 FQ	19470 MW	22300 TQ	USBLS	5/15
	Greenville-Anderson-Mauldin MSA, SC	Y	17080 FQ	18660 MW	21290 TQ	USBLS	5/15
	South Dakota	Y	19000 FQ	20850 MW	23440 TQ	USBLS	5/15
	Sioux Falls MSA, SD	Y	19570 FQ	21310 MW	23140 TQ	USBLS	5/15
	Tennessee	Y	17360 FQ	19190 MW	22280 TQ	USBLS	5/15
	Knoxville MSA, TN	Y	16950 FQ	18420 MW	20410 TQ	USBLS	5/15
	Memphis MSA, TN-MS-AR	Y	17760 FQ	19780 MW	22620 TQ	USBLS	5/15
	Nashville-Davidson–Murfreesboro–Franklin MSA, TN	Y	18270 FQ	20810 MW	23300 TQ	USBLS	5/15
	Texas	Y	17370 FQ	19190 MW	22550 TQ	USBLS	5/15
	Austin-Round Rock MSA, TX	Y	17900 FQ	20410 MW	23840 TQ	USBLS	5/15
	Dallas-Plano-Irving PMSA, TX	Y	17640 FQ	19760 MW	23140 TQ	USBLS	5/15
	Fort Worth-Arlington PMSA, TX	Y	17910 FQ	20170 MW	23920 TQ	USBLS	5/15
	Houston-The Woodlands-Sugar Land MSA, TX	Y	17370 FQ	19200 MW	22400 TQ	USBLS	5/15
	San Antonio-New Braunfels MSA, TX	Y	18710 FQ	21350 MW	24080 TQ	USBLS	5/15
	Utah	Y	17480 FQ	19660 MW	22910 TQ	USBLS	5/15
	Ogden-Clearfield MSA, UT	Y	16980 FQ	18380 MW	19890 TQ	USBLS	5/15
	Provo-Orem MSA, UT	Y	17210 FQ	19140 MW	22510 TQ	USBLS	5/15
	Salt Lake City MSA, UT	Y	18400 FQ	21160 MW	23420 TQ	USBLS	5/15
	Vermont	Y	20870 FQ	23760 MW	27890 TQ	USBLS	5/15
	Burlington-South Burlington MSA, VT	Y	19990 FQ	22270 MW	24600 TQ	USBLS	5/15
	Virginia	Y	17850 FQ	20430 MW	24400 TQ	USBLS	5/15
	Richmond MSA, VA	Y	17500 FQ	19420 MW	22920 TQ	USBLS	5/15
	Virginia Beach-Norfolk-Newport News MSA, VA-NC	Y	17600 FQ	19720 MW	23890 TQ	USBLS	5/15
	Washington	H	10.49 FQ	11.50 MW	13.12 TQ	WABLS	3/16
	Seattle-Bellevue-Everett PMSA, WA	H	10.73 FQ	11.93 MW	13.97 TQ	WABLS	3/16
	Tacoma-Lakewood PMSA, WA	H	11.36 FQ	13.23 MW	14.89 TQ	WABLS	3/16
	West Virginia	Y	17630 FQ	18620 MW	19690 TQ	USBLS	5/15
	Huntington-Ashland MSA, WV-KY-OH	Y	17480 FQ	18550 MW	19710 TQ	USBLS	5/15
	Wisconsin	Y	17880 FQ	20370 MW	23450 TQ	USBLS	5/15
	Madison MSA, WI	Y	18430 FQ	21210 MW	23570 TQ	USBLS	5/15
	Milwaukee-Waukesha-West Allis MSA, WI	Y	19400 FQ	21790 MW	24190 TQ	USBLS	5/15
	Racine MSA, WI	Y	18110 FQ	20470 MW	23740 TQ	USBLS	5/15
	Wyoming	Y	19080 FQ	22560 MW	26730 TQ	USBLS	5/15
	Cheyenne MSA, WY	Y	17190 FQ	19100 MW	25870 TQ	USBLS	5/15
	Puerto Rico	Y	16820 FQ	18110 MW	19400 TQ	USBLS	5/15
	San Juan-Carolina-Caguas MSA, PR	Y	16820 FQ	18100 MW	19390 TQ	USBLS	5/15
	Virgin Islands	Y	19820 FQ	24090 MW	31660 TQ	USBLS	5/15
	Guam	Y	17960 FQ	18760 MW	19630 TQ	USBLS	5/15

AE	Average entry wage	AWR	Average wage range	H	Hourly
AEX	Average experienced wage	B	Biweekly	HI	Highest wage paid
ATC	Average total compensation	D	Daily	HR	High end range
AW	Average wage paid	FQ	First quartile wage	LO	Lowest wage paid

LR	Low end range	MTC	Median total compensation
M	Monthly	MW	Median wage paid
MCC	Median cash compensation	MWR	Median wage range
ME	Median entry wage	S	See annotated source

TCC	Total cash compensation
TQ	Third quartile wage
W	Weekly
Y	Yearly

Occupation/Type/Industry	Location	Per	Low	Mid	High	Source	Date
Household Hazardous Waste Technician							
Municipal Government	Lompoc, CA	Y			46758 ʜɪ	CACIT	6/28/16
Housing Analyst							
Municipal Government	Brentwood, CA	Y			87811 ʜɪ	CACIT	6/28/16
Municipal Government	Fountain Valley, CA	Y			77996 ʜɪ	CACIT	6/28/16
Housing Assistance Officer							
Municipal Government	Long Beach, CA	Y			103816 ʜɪ	CACIT	6/28/16
Housing Inspector							
Municipal Government	Baldwin Park, CA	Y			51136 ʜɪ	CACIT	6/28/16
Housing Ordinance Specialist							
Municipal Government	Seattle, WA	H	28.38 ʟᴏ		33.00 ʜɪ	CSSS	1/13/16
Housing Rehabilitation Specialist							
Municipal Government	Brea, CA	Y			12425 ʜɪ	CACIT	6/28/16
Housing Systems Analyst							
Municipal Government	Glendale, CA	Y			92322 ʜɪ	CACIT	6/28/16
Human Resources Assistant							
Except Payroll and Timekeeping	Alabama	Y	26455 ᴀᴇ	36648 ᴀᴡ	41739 ᴀᴇx	ALBLS	6/16
Except Payroll and Timekeeping	Birmingham-Hoover MSA, AL	Y	28723 ᴀᴇ	37081 ᴀᴡ	41265 ᴀᴇx	ALBLS	6/16
Except Payroll and Timekeeping	Alaska	Y	38920 ꜰQ	46260 ᴍᴡ	52540 ᴛQ	USBLS	5/15
Except Payroll and Timekeeping	Anchorage MSA, AK	Y	36780 ꜰQ	44520 ᴍᴡ	53150 ᴛQ	USBLS	5/15
Except Payroll and Timekeeping	Arizona	Y	28960 ꜰQ	34870 ᴍᴡ	41760 ᴛQ	USBLS	5/15
Except Payroll and Timekeeping	Phoenix-Mesa-Scottsdale MSA, AZ	Y	29280 ꜰQ	35030 ᴍᴡ	42110 ᴛQ	USBLS	5/15
Except Payroll and Timekeeping	Tucson MSA, AZ	Y	28320 ꜰQ	33470 ᴍᴡ	38820 ᴛQ	USBLS	5/15
Except Payroll and Timekeeping	Arkansas	Y	27690 ꜰQ	34560 ᴍᴡ	40960 ᴛQ	USBLS	5/15
Except Payroll and Timekeeping	Little Rock-North Little Rock-Conway MSA, AR	Y	27990 ꜰQ	35610 ᴍᴡ	44830 ᴛQ	USBLS	5/15
Except Payroll and Timekeeping	California	H	16.83 ꜰQ	21.13 ᴍᴡ	25.76 ᴛQ	CABLS	1/16-3/16
Except Payroll and Timekeeping	Anaheim-Santa Ana-Irvine PMSA, CA	H	15.88 ꜰQ	19.45 ᴍᴡ	26.24 ᴛQ	CABLS	1/16-3/16
Except Payroll and Timekeeping	Los Angeles-Long Beach-Glendale PMSA, CA	H	16.70 ꜰQ	21.15 ᴍᴡ	26.11 ᴛQ	CABLS	1/16-3/16
Except Payroll and Timekeeping	Oakland-Hayward-Berkeley PMSA, CA	H	17.50 ꜰQ	22.37 ᴍᴡ	27.82 ᴛQ	CABLS	1/16-3/16
Except Payroll and Timekeeping	Riverside-San Bernardino-Ontario MSA, CA	H	13.55 ꜰQ	18.76 ᴍᴡ	22.67 ᴛQ	CABLS	1/16-3/16
Except Payroll and Timekeeping	Sacramento–Roseville–Arden-Arcade MSA, CA	H	18.76 ꜰQ	21.55 ᴍᴡ	24.79 ᴛQ	CABLS	1/16-3/16
Except Payroll and Timekeeping	San Diego-Carlsbad MSA, CA	H	17.10 ꜰQ	20.52 ᴍᴡ	23.65 ᴛQ	CABLS	1/16-3/16
Except Payroll and Timekeeping	San Francisco-Redwood City-South San Francisco PMSA, CA	H	20.93 ꜰQ	25.68 ᴍᴡ	29.79 ᴛQ	CABLS	1/16-3/16
Except Payroll and Timekeeping	Colorado	Y	34170 ꜰQ	40460 ᴍᴡ	47230 ᴛQ	USBLS	5/15
Except Payroll and Timekeeping	Denver-Aurora-Lakewood MSA, CO	Y	35350 ꜰQ	42280 ᴍᴡ	48460 ᴛQ	USBLS	5/15
Except Payroll and Timekeeping	Connecticut	Y		42837 ᴍᴡ		CTBLS	1/16-3/16
Except Payroll and Timekeeping	Bridgeport-Stamford-Norwalk MSA, CT	Y	28990 ꜰQ	37840 ᴍᴡ	47010 ᴛQ	USBLS	5/15
Except Payroll and Timekeeping	Hartford-West Hartford-East Hartford MSA, CT	Y	34450 ꜰQ	42990 ᴍᴡ	55500 ᴛQ	USBLS	5/15
Except Payroll and Timekeeping	Delaware	Y	32130 ꜰQ	35770 ᴍᴡ	39400 ᴛQ	USBLS	5/15
Except Payroll and Timekeeping	Wilmington PMSA, DE-MD-NJ	Y	32520 ꜰQ	36340 ᴍᴡ	41200 ᴛQ	USBLS	5/15
Except Payroll and Timekeeping	District of Columbia	Y	44200 ꜰQ	51790 ᴍᴡ	59000 ᴛQ	USBLS	5/15
Except Payroll and Timekeeping	Washington-Arlington-Alexandria PMSA, DC-VA-MD-WV	Y	38210 ꜰQ	45630 ᴍᴡ	54050 ᴛQ	USBLS	5/15
Except Payroll and Timekeeping	Florida	H	13.10 ᴀᴇ	17.28 ᴍᴡ	19.91 ᴀᴇx	FLBLS	7/16-9/16
Except Payroll and Timekeeping	Fort Lauderdale-Pompano Beach-Deerfield Beach PMSA, FL	H	13.25 ᴀᴇ	17.10 ᴍᴡ	20.69 ᴀᴇx	FLBLS	7/16-9/16
Except Payroll and Timekeeping	Miami-Miami Beach-Kendall PMSA, FL	H	13.66 ᴀᴇ	18.17 ᴍᴡ	20.72 ᴀᴇx	FLBLS	7/16-9/16

AE	Average entry wage	AWR	Average wage range	H	Hourly	LR Low end range	MTC Median total compensation	TCC Total cash compensation
AEX	Average experienced wage	B	Biweekly	HI	Highest wage paid	M Monthly	MW Median wage paid	TQ Third quartile wage
ATC	Average total compensation	D	Daily	HR	High end range	MCC Median cash compensation	MWR Median wage range	W Weekly
AW	Average wage paid	FQ	First quartile wage	LO	Lowest wage paid	ME Median entry wage	S See annotated source	Y Yearly

792

Occupation/Type/Industry	Location	Per	Low	Mid	High	Source	Date
Human Resources Assistant							
Except Payroll and Timekeeping	Orlando-Kissimmee-Sanford MSA, FL	H	13.26 AE	16.09 MW	18.39 AEX	FLBLS	7/16-9/16
Except Payroll and Timekeeping	Tampa-St. Petersburg-Clearwater MSA, FL	H	13.47 AE	17.50 MW	19.91 AEX	FLBLS	7/16-9/16
Except Payroll and Timekeeping	Georgia	Y	28290 FQ	36210 MW	44940 TQ	USBLS	5/15
Except Payroll and Timekeeping	Atlanta-Sandy Springs-Roswell MSA, GA	Y	28450 FQ	37710 MW	48250 TQ	USBLS	5/15
Except Payroll and Timekeeping	Augusta-Richmond County MSA, GA-SC	Y	29900 FQ	33320 MW	40470 TQ	USBLS	5/15
Except Payroll and Timekeeping	Hawaii	Y	34560 FQ	40560 MW	46340 TQ	USBLS	5/15
Except Payroll and Timekeeping	Urban Honolulu MSA, HI	Y	34630 FQ	40780 MW	46300 TQ	USBLS	5/15
Except Payroll and Timekeeping	Idaho	Y	29230 FQ	35470 MW	42110 TQ	USBLS	5/15
Except Payroll and Timekeeping	Boise City MSA, ID	Y	30370 FQ	35810 MW	41570 TQ	USBLS	5/15
Except Payroll and Timekeeping	Illinois	Y	34360 FQ	41600 MW	48190 TQ	USBLS	5/15
Except Payroll and Timekeeping	Champaign-Urbana MSA, IL	Y	29220 FQ	39310 MW	46160 TQ	USBLS	5/15
Except Payroll and Timekeeping	Chicago-Naperville-Arlington Heights PMSA, IL	Y	35370 FQ	42680 MW	48890 TQ	USBLS	5/15
Except Payroll and Timekeeping	Lake County-Kenosha County PMSA, IL-WI	Y	36480 FQ	42900 MW	48390 TQ	USBLS	5/15
Except Payroll and Timekeeping	Indiana	Y	29910 FQ	36490 MW	43840 TQ	USBLS	5/15
Except Payroll and Timekeeping	Gary PMSA, IN	Y	28770 FQ	35530 MW	43150 TQ	USBLS	5/15
Except Payroll and Timekeeping	Indianapolis-Carmel-Anderson MSA, IN	Y	32990 FQ	40240 MW	46410 TQ	USBLS	5/15
Except Payroll and Timekeeping	Iowa	Y	30160 FQ	37270 MW	45500 TQ	USBLS	5/15
Except Payroll and Timekeeping	Des Moines-West Des Moines MSA, IA	Y	36200 FQ	42820 MW	48250 TQ	USBLS	5/15
Except Payroll and Timekeeping	Kansas	Y	31940 FQ	37510 MW	43530 TQ	USBLS	5/15
Except Payroll and Timekeeping	Wichita MSA, KS	Y	30590 FQ	36930 MW	44200 TQ	USBLS	5/15
Except Payroll and Timekeeping	Kentucky	Y	31940 FQ	39570 MW	45940 TQ	USBLS	5/15
Except Payroll and Timekeeping	Louisville-Jefferson County MSA, KY-IN	Y	30360 FQ	37240 MW	43800 TQ	USBLS	5/15
Except Payroll and Timekeeping	Louisiana	Y	29300 FQ	36400 MW	43910 TQ	USBLS	5/15
Except Payroll and Timekeeping	Baton Rouge MSA, LA	Y	29390 FQ	35510 MW	42250 TQ	USBLS	5/15
Except Payroll and Timekeeping	New Orleans-Metairie MSA, LA	Y	31930 FQ	38760 MW	45120 TQ	USBLS	5/15
Except Payroll and Timekeeping	Maine	Y	30540 FQ	36350 MW	42740 TQ	USBLS	5/15
Except Payroll and Timekeeping	Portland-South Portland MSA, ME	Y	30340 FQ	36160 MW	41920 TQ	USBLS	5/15
Except Payroll and Timekeeping	Maryland	Y	30050 AE	42255 MW	48358 AEX	MDBLS	4/16
Except Payroll and Timekeeping	Baltimore-Columbia-Towson MSA, MD	Y	33730 FQ	41810 MW	49130 TQ	USBLS	5/15
Except Payroll and Timekeeping	Salisbury MSA, MD-DE	Y	30330 FQ	35990 MW	39960 TQ	USBLS	5/15
Except Payroll and Timekeeping	Massachusetts	Y	34260 FQ	43610 MW	54280 TQ	USBLS	5/15
Except Payroll and Timekeeping	Boston-Cambridge-Newton NECTA, MA	Y	35360 FQ	45390 MW	56090 TQ	USBLS	5/15
Except Payroll and Timekeeping	Worcester MSA, MA-CT	Y	31790 FQ	40380 MW	49960 TQ	USBLS	5/15
Except Payroll and Timekeeping	Michigan	Y	31350 FQ	38160 MW	47020 TQ	USBLS	5/15
Except Payroll and Timekeeping	Detroit-Dearborn-Livonia PMSA, MI	Y	31590 FQ	39960 MW	49830 TQ	USBLS	5/15
Except Payroll and Timekeeping	Grand Rapids-Wyoming MSA, MI	Y	32960 FQ	38060 MW	46420 TQ	USBLS	5/15
Except Payroll and Timekeeping	Minnesota	Y	33058 FQ	39237 MW	47783 TQ	MNBLS	1/16-3/16
Except Payroll and Timekeeping	Minneapolis-St. Paul-Bloomington MSA, MN-WI	Y	34232 FQ	40886 MW	49451 TQ	MNBLS	1/16-3/16
Except Payroll and Timekeeping	Mississippi	Y	29750 FQ	36540 MW	44470 TQ	USBLS	5/15
Except Payroll and Timekeeping	Jackson MSA, MS	Y	34360 FQ	39560 MW	46000 TQ	USBLS	5/15
Except Payroll and Timekeeping	Missouri	Y	30500 FQ	37910 MW	45610 TQ	USBLS	5/15
Except Payroll and Timekeeping	Kansas City MSA, MO-KS	Y	33710 FQ	40100 MW	46520 TQ	USBLS	5/15
Except Payroll and Timekeeping	St. Louis MSA, MO-IL	Y	31930 FQ	40210 MW	48330 TQ	USBLS	5/15
Except Payroll and Timekeeping	Montana	Y	28480 FQ	34500 MW	40920 TQ	USBLS	5/15
Except Payroll and Timekeeping	Billings MSA, MT	Y	32530 FQ	36900 MW	43530 TQ	USBLS	5/15
Except Payroll and Timekeeping	Nebraska	Y	29760 FQ	35730 MW	42805 TQ	NEBLS	7/16-9/16
Except Payroll and Timekeeping	Omaha-Council Bluffs MSA, NE-IA	Y	30705 FQ	36485 MW	43915 TQ	NEBLS	7/16-9/16
Except Payroll and Timekeeping	Nevada	Y	29500 FQ	35880 MW	43510 TQ	USBLS	5/15
Except Payroll and Timekeeping	Las Vegas-Henderson-Paradise MSA, NV	Y	29280 FQ	35480 MW	42580 TQ	USBLS	5/15
Except Payroll and Timekeeping	New Hampshire	H	13.60 AE	18.49 MW	20.95 AEX	NHBLS	6/16
Except Payroll and Timekeeping	Manchester NECTA, NH	H	14.71 AE	18.03 MW	20.10 AEX	NHBLS	6/16
Except Payroll and Timekeeping	Nashua NECTA, NH-MA	Y	26700 FQ	33400 MW	39710 TQ	USBLS	5/15
Except Payroll and Timekeeping	New Jersey	Y	33500 FQ	40740 MW	48250 TQ	USBLS	5/15

AE	Average entry wage	AWR	Average wage range	H	Hourly
AEX	Average experienced wage	B	Biweekly	HI	Highest wage paid
ATC	Average total compensation	D	Daily	HR	High end range
AW	Average wage paid	FQ	First quartile wage	LO	Lowest wage paid

LR	Low end range	MTC	Median total compensation
M	Monthly	MW	Median wage paid
MCC	Median cash compensation	MWR	Median wage range
ME	Median entry wage	S	See annotated source

TCC	Total cash compensation		
TQ	Third quartile wage		
W	Weekly		
Y	Yearly		

Human Resources Assistant

Occupation/Type/Industry	Location	Per	Low	Mid	High	Source	Date
Except Payroll and Timekeeping	Camden PMSA, NJ	Y	33070 FQ	38730 MW	46660 TQ	USBLS	5/15
Except Payroll and Timekeeping	Newark PMSA, NJ-PA	Y	33930 FQ	41750 MW	48710 TQ	USBLS	5/15
Except Payroll and Timekeeping	Trenton MSA, NJ	Y	34780 FQ	43950 MW	51670 TQ	USBLS	5/15
Except Payroll and Timekeeping	New Mexico	Y	28640 FQ	35610 MW	43530 TQ	USBLS	5/15
Except Payroll and Timekeeping	Albuquerque MSA, NM	Y	31410 FQ	37270 MW	44400 TQ	USBLS	5/15
Except Payroll and Timekeeping	New York	Y	29830 AE	40440 MW	47880 AEX	NYBLS	1/16-3/16
Except Payroll and Timekeeping	Buffalo-Cheektowaga-Niagara Falls MSA, NY	Y	29430 FQ	38190 MW	46020 TQ	USBLS	5/15
Except Payroll and Timekeeping	Nassau County-Suffolk County PMSA, NY	Y	32990 FQ	42840 MW	55380 TQ	USBLS	5/15
Except Payroll and Timekeeping	New York-Jersey City-White Plains PMSA, NY-NJ	Y	33260 FQ	40740 MW	48790 TQ	USBLS	5/15
Except Payroll and Timekeeping	Rochester MSA, NY	Y	29990 FQ	35480 MW	42210 TQ	USBLS	5/15
Except Payroll and Timekeeping	North Carolina	Y	28410 FQ	35340 MW	42700 TQ	USBLS	5/15
Except Payroll and Timekeeping	Charlotte-Concord-Gastonia MSA, NC-SC	Y	29440 FQ	35200 MW	42640 TQ	USBLS	5/15
Except Payroll and Timekeeping	Raleigh MSA, NC	Y	27750 FQ	36110 MW	43880 TQ	USBLS	5/15
Except Payroll and Timekeeping	North Dakota	Y	32090 FQ	38450 MW	45160 TQ	USBLS	5/15
Except Payroll and Timekeeping	Fargo MSA, ND-MN	Y	32070 FQ	37360 MW	44480 TQ	USBLS	5/15
Except Payroll and Timekeeping	Ohio	Y	31210 FQ	36950 MW	44070 TQ	USBLS	5/15
Except Payroll and Timekeeping	Cincinnati MSA, OH-KY-IN	Y	31720 FQ	37360 MW	45680 TQ	USBLS	5/15
Except Payroll and Timekeeping	Cleveland-Elyria MSA, OH	Y	32430 FQ	38020 MW	44630 TQ	USBLS	5/15
Except Payroll and Timekeeping	Columbus MSA, OH	Y	33250 FQ	39020 MW	45660 TQ	USBLS	5/15
Except Payroll and Timekeeping	Oklahoma	Y	27570 FQ	34780 MW	42180 TQ	USBLS	5/15
Except Payroll and Timekeeping	Oklahoma City MSA, OK	Y	29250 FQ	35750 MW	42300 TQ	USBLS	5/15
Except Payroll and Timekeeping	Tulsa MSA, OK	Y	27860 FQ	35980 MW	45390 TQ	USBLS	5/15
Except Payroll and Timekeeping	Oregon	H	16.14 FQ	19.14 MW	22.71 TQ	ORBLS	2016
Except Payroll and Timekeeping	Portland-Vancouver-Hillsboro MSA, OR-WA	Y	33960 FQ	40400 MW	47600 TQ	USBLS	5/15
Except Payroll and Timekeeping	Pennsylvania	Y	30540 FQ	36600 MW	44380 TQ	USBLS	5/15
Except Payroll and Timekeeping	Allentown-Bethlehem-Easton MSA, PA-NJ	Y	30770 FQ	36170 MW	43880 TQ	USBLS	5/15
Except Payroll and Timekeeping	Harrisburg-Carlisle MSA, PA	Y	30470 FQ	37290 MW	42460 TQ	USBLS	5/15
Except Payroll and Timekeeping	Montgomery County-Bucks County-Chester County PMSA, PA	Y	28270 FQ	35510 MW	45070 TQ	USBLS	5/15
Except Payroll and Timekeeping	Philadelphia PMSA, PA	Y	33320 FQ	38590 MW	47840 TQ	USBLS	5/15
Except Payroll and Timekeeping	Pittsburgh MSA, PA	Y	29730 FQ	35490 MW	41490 TQ	USBLS	5/15
Except Payroll and Timekeeping	Rhode Island	Y	32920 FQ	40530 MW	46690 TQ	USBLS	5/15
Except Payroll and Timekeeping	Providence-Warwick MSA, RI-MA	Y	32290 FQ	39750 MW	46480 TQ	USBLS	5/15
Except Payroll and Timekeeping	South Carolina	Y	30330 FQ	31070 MW	35670 TQ	USBLS	5/15
Except Payroll and Timekeeping	Charleston-North Charleston MSA, SC	Y	29450 FQ	31930 MW	37900 TQ	USBLS	5/15
Except Payroll and Timekeeping	Columbia MSA, SC	Y	30000 FQ	31940 MW	36820 TQ	USBLS	5/15
Except Payroll and Timekeeping	Greenville-Anderson-Mauldin MSA, SC	Y	30990 FQ	31010 MW	35210 TQ	USBLS	5/15
Except Payroll and Timekeeping	South Dakota	Y	27430 FQ	32300 MW	37830 TQ	USBLS	5/15
Except Payroll and Timekeeping	Sioux Falls MSA, SD	Y	27540 FQ	32080 MW	37250 TQ	USBLS	5/15
Except Payroll and Timekeeping	Tennessee	Y	28900 FQ	36610 MW	44520 TQ	USBLS	5/15
Except Payroll and Timekeeping	Knoxville MSA, TN	Y	18620 FQ	31480 MW	41540 TQ	USBLS	5/15
Except Payroll and Timekeeping	Memphis MSA, TN-MS-AR	Y	33250 FQ	39170 MW	45230 TQ	USBLS	5/15
Except Payroll and Timekeeping	Nashville-Davidson–Murfreesboro–Franklin MSA, TN	Y	29580 FQ	37200 MW	45310 TQ	USBLS	5/15
Except Payroll and Timekeeping	Texas	Y	30750 FQ	37370 MW	45130 TQ	USBLS	5/15
Except Payroll and Timekeeping	Austin-Round Rock MSA, TX	Y	32140 FQ	37280 MW	44330 TQ	USBLS	5/15
Except Payroll and Timekeeping	Dallas-Plano-Irving PMSA, TX	Y	33010 FQ	39850 MW	47620 TQ	USBLS	5/15
Except Payroll and Timekeeping	Fort Worth-Arlington PMSA, TX	Y	32290 FQ	39610 MW	46690 TQ	USBLS	5/15
Except Payroll and Timekeeping	Houston-The Woodlands-Sugar Land MSA, TX	Y	32890 FQ	39190 MW	47670 TQ	USBLS	5/15
Except Payroll and Timekeeping	San Antonio-New Braunfels MSA, TX	Y	31830 FQ	38220 MW	44640 TQ	USBLS	5/15
Except Payroll and Timekeeping	Utah	Y	28780 FQ	36770 MW	44940 TQ	USBLS	5/15
Except Payroll and Timekeeping	Ogden-Clearfield MSA, UT	Y	35140 FQ	43520 MW	48820 TQ	USBLS	5/15
Except Payroll and Timekeeping	Provo-Orem MSA, UT	Y	24920 FQ	31840 MW	41760 TQ	USBLS	5/15
Except Payroll and Timekeeping	Salt Lake City MSA, UT	Y	28950 FQ	36110 MW	43530 TQ	USBLS	5/15
Except Payroll and Timekeeping	Vermont	Y	32430 FQ	38270 MW	45020 TQ	USBLS	5/15
Except Payroll and Timekeeping	Burlington-South Burlington MSA, VT	Y	33680 FQ	39190 MW	44840 TQ	USBLS	5/15

AE Average entry wage	AWR Average wage range	H Hourly	LR Low end range	MTC Median total compensation	TCC Total cash compensation
AEX Average experienced wage	B Biweekly	HI Highest wage paid	M Monthly	MW Median wage paid	TQ Third quartile wage
ATC Average total compensation	D Daily	HR High end range	MCC Median cash compensation	MWR Median wage range	W Weekly
AW Average wage paid	FQ First quartile wage	LO Lowest wage paid	ME Median entry wage	S See annotated source	Y Yearly

Occupation/Type/Industry	Location	Per	Low	Mid	High	Source	Date
Human Resources Assistant							
Except Payroll and Timekeeping	Virginia	Y	33000 FQ	38980 MW	46500 TQ	USBLS	5/15
Except Payroll and Timekeeping	Richmond MSA, VA	Y	31770 FQ	37050 MW	43390 TQ	USBLS	5/15
Except Payroll and Timekeeping	Virginia Beach-Norfolk-						
	Newport News MSA, VA-NC	Y	31950 FQ	36210 MW	42270 TQ	USBLS	5/15
Except Payroll and Timekeeping	Washington	H	17.06 FQ	20.29 MW	23.28 TQ	WABLS	3/16
Except Payroll and Timekeeping	Seattle-Bellevue-Everett						
	PMSA, WA	H	17.89 FQ	21.23 MW	24.18 TQ	WABLS	3/16
Except Payroll and Timekeeping	Tacoma-Lakewood PMSA, WA	H	17.89 FQ	20.75 MW	23.36 TQ	WABLS	3/16
Except Payroll and Timekeeping	West Virginia	Y	29450 FQ	35970 MW	44830 TQ	USBLS	5/15
Except Payroll and Timekeeping	Huntington-Ashland MSA,						
	WV-KY-OH	Y	26070 FQ	33110 MW	40340 TQ	USBLS	5/15
Except Payroll and Timekeeping	Wisconsin	Y	31020 FQ	37430 MW	45030 TQ	USBLS	5/15
Except Payroll and Timekeeping	Madison MSA, WI	Y	35720 FQ	42040 MW	48730 TQ	USBLS	5/15
Except Payroll and Timekeeping	Milwaukee-Waukesha-West						
	Allis MSA, WI	Y	32350 FQ	37830 MW	45330 TQ	USBLS	5/15
Except Payroll and Timekeeping	Wyoming	Y	33590 FQ	39180 MW	47140 TQ	USBLS	5/15
Except Payroll and Timekeeping	Cheyenne MSA, WY	Y	35770 FQ	40880 MW	47090 TQ	USBLS	5/15
Except Payroll and Timekeeping	Puerto Rico	Y	17320 FQ	19220 MW	25860 TQ	USBLS	5/15
Except Payroll and Timekeeping	San Juan-Carolina-Caguas						
	MSA, PR	Y	17300 FQ	19190 MW	26200 TQ	USBLS	5/15
Except Payroll and Timekeeping	Virgin Islands	Y	29430 FQ	35270 MW	41270 TQ	USBLS	5/15
Except Payroll and Timekeeping	Guam	Y	21350 FQ	29130 MW	36030 TQ	USBLS	5/15
Human Resources Consultant							
Municipal Government	Detroit, MI	H			175.00 HI	FREEP02	2016
Human Resources Manager	Alabama	Y	64408 AE	102158 AW	121038 AEX	ALBLS	6/16
	Birmingham-Hoover MSA, AL	Y	69267 AE	113330 AW	135356 AEX	ALBLS	6/16
	Alaska	Y	88040 FQ	106770 MW	130790 TQ	USBLS	5/15
	Anchorage MSA, AK	Y	87030 FQ	106350 MW	139380 TQ	USBLS	5/15
	Arizona	Y	68340 FQ	89660 MW	120370 TQ	USBLS	5/15
	Phoenix-Mesa-Scottsdale						
	MSA, AZ	Y	69140 FQ	92470 MW	124450 TQ	USBLS	5/15
	Tucson MSA, AZ	Y	64580 FQ	80900 MW	99680 TQ	USBLS	5/15
	Arkansas	Y	57110 FQ	81280 MW	111460 TQ	USBLS	5/15
	Little Rock-North Little Rock-						
	Conway MSA, AR	Y	44440 FQ	66230 MW	92800 TQ	USBLS	5/15
	California	H	43.32 FQ	58.98 MW	78.14 TQ	CABLS	1/16-3/16
	Anaheim-Santa Ana-Irvine						
	PMSA, CA	H	45.02 FQ	58.33 MW	84.56 TQ	CABLS	1/16-3/16
	Los Angeles-Long Beach-						
	Glendale PMSA, CA	H	41.88 FQ	57.72 MW	75.31 TQ	CABLS	1/16-3/16
	Oakland-Hayward-Berkeley						
	PMSA, CA	H	47.93 FQ	62.46 MW	79.23 TQ	CABLS	1/16-3/16
	Riverside-San Bernardino-						
	Ontario MSA, CA	H	37.58 FQ	49.23 MW	61.13 TQ	CABLS	1/16-3/16
	Sacramento–Roseville–						
	Arden-Arcade MSA, CA	H	32.81 FQ	47.02 MW	63.55 TQ	CABLS	1/16-3/16
	San Diego-Carlsbad MSA, CA	H	43.28 FQ	57.76 MW	72.87 TQ	CABLS	1/16-3/16
	San Francisco-Redwood City-						
	South San Francisco PMSA,						
	CA	H	54.12 FQ	70.97 MW		CABLS	1/16-3/16
	Colorado	Y	98950 FQ	125210 MW	162010 TQ	USBLS	5/15
	Denver-Aurora-Lakewood						
	MSA, CO	Y	104650 FQ	132820 MW	172590 TQ	USBLS	5/15
	Connecticut	Y		118033 MW		CTBLS	1/16-3/16
	Bridgeport-Stamford-Norwalk						
	MSA, CT	Y	90830 FQ	122940 MW	177070 TQ	USBLS	5/15
	Hartford-West Hartford-East						
	Hartford MSA, CT	Y	93200 FQ	116800 MW	146100 TQ	USBLS	5/15
	Delaware	Y	103510 FQ	126090 MW	156370 TQ	USBLS	5/15
	Wilmington PMSA, DE-MD-						
	NJ	Y	107990 FQ	129370 MW	158960 TQ	USBLS	5/15
	District of Columbia	Y	122290 FQ	144080 MW	158700 TQ	USBLS	5/15
	Washington-Arlington-						
	Alexandria PMSA, DC-VA-						
	MD-WV	Y	115610 FQ	142850 MW	160140 TQ	USBLS	5/15
	Florida	H	35.61 AE	51.06 MW	66.60 AEX	FLBLS	7/16-9/16
	Fort Lauderdale-Pompano						
	Beach-Deerfield Beach						
	PMSA, FL	H	32.37 AE	47.49 MW	63.33 AEX	FLBLS	7/16-9/16

AE	Average entry wage	AWR	Average wage range	H	Hourly	LR	Low end range	MTC	Median total compensation	TCC	Total cash compensation
AEX	Average experienced wage	B	Biweekly	HI	Highest wage paid	M	Monthly	MW	Median wage paid	TQ	Third quartile wage
ATC	Average total compensation	D	Daily	HR	High end range	MCC	Median cash compensation	MWR	Median wage range	W	Weekly
AW	Average wage paid	FQ	First quartile wage	LO	Lowest wage paid	ME	Median entry wage	S	See annotated source	Y	Yearly

Occupation/Type/Industry	Location	Per	Low	Mid	High	Source	Date
Human Resources Manager	Miami-Miami Beach-Kendall PMSA, FL	H	37.27 AE	54.71 MW	70.90 AEX	FLBLS	7/16-9/16
	Orlando-Kissimmee-Sanford MSA, FL	H	36.16 AE	52.34 MW	67.79 AEX	FLBLS	7/16-9/16
	Tampa-St. Petersburg-Clearwater MSA, FL	H	35.38 AE	49.74 MW	65.84 AEX	FLBLS	7/16-9/16
	Georgia	Y	78670 FQ	99440 MW	133920 TQ	USBLS	5/15
	Atlanta-Sandy Springs-Roswell MSA, GA	Y	80800 FQ	101850 MW	139270 TQ	USBLS	5/15
	Augusta-Richmond County MSA, GA-SC	Y	63790 FQ	80640 MW	107010 TQ	USBLS	5/15
	Hawaii	Y	66000 FQ	81840 MW	101110 TQ	USBLS	5/15
	Urban Honolulu MSA, HI	Y	69610 FQ	85120 MW	101580 TQ	USBLS	5/15
	Idaho	Y	61200 FQ	78130 MW	101980 TQ	USBLS	5/15
	Boise City MSA, ID	Y	64810 FQ	81660 MW	109500 TQ	USBLS	5/15
	Illinois	Y	69670 FQ	93780 MW	122190 TQ	USBLS	5/15
	Chicago-Naperville-Arlington Heights PMSA, IL	Y	73930 FQ	96800 MW	124310 TQ	USBLS	5/15
	Lake County-Kenosha County PMSA, IL-WI	Y	71400 FQ	105340 MW	151980 TQ	USBLS	5/15
	Indiana	Y	74850 FQ	94010 MW	121450 TQ	USBLS	5/15
	Gary PMSA, IN	Y	65320 FQ	80580 MW	99760 TQ	USBLS	5/15
	Indianapolis-Carmel-Anderson MSA, IN	Y	78640 FQ	96180 MW	125480 TQ	USBLS	5/15
	Iowa	Y	68640 FQ	85980 MW	106370 TQ	USBLS	5/15
	Des Moines-West Des Moines MSA, IA	Y	74070 FQ	91560 MW	117850 TQ	USBLS	5/15
	Kansas	Y	70920 FQ	90660 MW	120230 TQ	USBLS	5/15
	Wichita MSA, KS	Y	70850 FQ	81540 MW	104240 TQ	USBLS	5/15
	Kentucky	Y	65340 FQ	85370 MW	109710 TQ	USBLS	5/15
	Louisville-Jefferson County MSA, KY-IN	Y	72930 FQ	92480 MW	116420 TQ	USBLS	5/15
	Louisiana	Y	55760 FQ	71710 MW	93720 TQ	USBLS	5/15
	Baton Rouge MSA, LA	Y	64720 FQ	80760 MW	95800 TQ	USBLS	5/15
	New Orleans-Metairie MSA, LA	Y	55040 FQ	70940 MW	104730 TQ	USBLS	5/15
	Maine	Y	73420 FQ	92510 MW	115500 TQ	USBLS	5/15
	Portland-South Portland MSA, ME	Y	76660 FQ	95540 MW	123110 TQ	USBLS	5/15
	Maryland	Y	90071 AE	133074 MW	154576 AEX	MDBLS	4/16
	Baltimore-Columbia-Towson MSA, MD	Y	98560 FQ	121160 MW	147300 TQ	USBLS	5/15
	Salisbury MSA, MD-DE	Y	103790 FQ	121890 MW	157730 TQ	USBLS	5/15
	Massachusetts	Y	82040 FQ	109210 MW	146740 TQ	USBLS	5/15
	Boston-Cambridge-Newton NECTA, MA	Y	87480 FQ	116500 MW	153880 TQ	USBLS	5/15
	Worcester MSA, MA-CT	Y	63590 FQ	87030 MW	117890 TQ	USBLS	5/15
	Michigan	Y	71370 FQ	91590 MW	122510 TQ	USBLS	5/15
	Detroit-Dearborn-Livonia PMSA, MI	Y	80310 FQ	103950 MW	138010 TQ	USBLS	5/15
	Grand Rapids-Wyoming MSA, MI	Y	62040 FQ	79600 MW	101380 TQ	USBLS	5/15
	Minnesota	Y	81857 FQ	106396 MW	138647 TQ	MNBLS	1/16-3/16
	Minneapolis-St. Paul-Bloomington MSA, MN-WI	Y	85647 FQ	112239 MW	147701 TQ	MNBLS	1/16-3/16
	Mississippi	Y	52590 FQ	71520 MW	98790 TQ	USBLS	5/15
	Jackson MSA, MS	Y	57700 FQ	73060 MW	100300 TQ	USBLS	5/15
	Missouri	Y	81660 FQ	105400 MW	137870 TQ	USBLS	5/15
	Kansas City MSA, MO-KS	Y	81390 FQ	105210 MW	130910 TQ	USBLS	5/15
	St. Louis MSA, MO-IL	Y	80950 FQ	110020 MW	148070 TQ	USBLS	5/15
	Montana	Y	73310 FQ	86900 MW	108090 TQ	USBLS	5/15
	Billings MSA, MT	Y	69640 FQ	86620 MW	106170 TQ	USBLS	5/15
	Nebraska	Y	83520 FQ	102515 MW	132290 TQ	NEBLS	7/16-9/16
	Omaha-Council Bluffs MSA, NE-IA	Y	84160 FQ	104460 MW	134000 TQ	NEBLS	7/16-9/16
	Nevada	Y	71890 FQ	92410 MW	115180 TQ	USBLS	5/15
	Las Vegas-Henderson-Paradise MSA, NV	Y	70270 FQ	92500 MW	116360 TQ	USBLS	5/15
	New Hampshire	H	34.27 AE	51.99 MW	64.33 AEX	NHBLS	6/16
	Manchester NECTA, NH	H	31.01 AE	44.46 MW	59.83 AEX	NHBLS	6/16
	Nashua NECTA, NH-MA	Y	95190 FQ	114120 MW	131040 TQ	USBLS	5/15
	New Jersey	Y	106790 FQ	134370 MW	178990 TQ	USBLS	5/15

Occupation/Type/Industry	Location	Per	Low	Mid	High	Source	Date
Human Resources Manager	Camden PMSA, NJ	Y	85140 FQ	103980 MW	128410 TQ	USBLS	5/15
	Newark PMSA, NJ-PA	Y	115280 FQ	148530 MW		USBLS	5/15
	Trenton MSA, NJ	Y	100090 FQ	116620 MW	144410 TQ	USBLS	5/15
	New Mexico	Y	66390 FQ	83390 MW	109110 TQ	USBLS	5/15
	Albuquerque MSA, NM	Y	68220 FQ	87420 MW	114640 TQ	USBLS	5/15
	New York	Y	79190 AE	122390 MW	171740 AEX	NYBLS	1/16-3/16
	Buffalo-Cheektowaga-Niagara Falls MSA, NY	Y	81000 FQ	97450 MW	130750 TQ	USBLS	5/15
	Nassau County-Suffolk County PMSA, NY	Y	103820 FQ	133010 MW	174080 TQ	USBLS	5/15
	New York-Jersey City-White Plains PMSA, NY-NJ	Y	91800 FQ	127590 MW	179640 TQ	USBLS	5/15
	Rochester MSA, NY	Y	82280 FQ	100230 MW	130740 TQ	USBLS	5/15
	North Carolina	Y	81360 FQ	103510 MW	144370 TQ	USBLS	5/15
	Charlotte-Concord-Gastonia MSA, NC-SC	Y	85550 FQ	112210 MW	156540 TQ	USBLS	5/15
	Raleigh MSA, NC	Y	80480 FQ	101120 MW	134670 TQ	USBLS	5/15
	North Dakota	Y	73290 FQ	88540 MW	108860 TQ	USBLS	5/15
	Fargo MSA, ND-MN	Y	70880 FQ	86790 MW	113410 TQ	USBLS	5/15
	Ohio	Y	80680 FQ	100130 MW	128840 TQ	USBLS	5/15
	Cincinnati MSA, OH-KY-IN	Y	85550 FQ	107520 MW	129800 TQ	USBLS	5/15
	Cleveland-Elyria MSA, OH	Y	83690 FQ	99930 MW	134460 TQ	USBLS	5/15
	Columbus MSA, OH	Y	83010 FQ	100750 MW	138540 TQ	USBLS	5/15
	Oklahoma	Y	63260 FQ	81740 MW	103950 TQ	USBLS	5/15
	Oklahoma City MSA, OK	Y	65440 FQ	83980 MW	107610 TQ	USBLS	5/15
	Tulsa MSA, OK	Y	68280 FQ	86510 MW	111270 TQ	USBLS	5/15
	Oregon	H	30.71 FQ	43.54 MW	59.97 TQ	ORBLS	2016
	Portland-Vancouver-Hillsboro MSA, OR-WA	Y	64850 FQ	94250 MW	132230 TQ	USBLS	5/15
	Pennsylvania	Y	89770 FQ	116100 MW	157720 TQ	USBLS	5/15
	Allentown-Bethlehem-Easton MSA, PA-NJ	Y	94200 FQ	125930 MW	176990 TQ	USBLS	5/15
	Harrisburg-Carlisle MSA, PA	Y	80160 FQ	97770 MW	119970 TQ	USBLS	5/15
	Montgomery County-Bucks County-Chester County PMSA, PA	Y	101860 FQ	138000 MW		USBLS	5/15
	Philadelphia PMSA, PA	Y	94080 FQ	127370 MW	170630 TQ	USBLS	5/15
	Pittsburgh MSA, PA	Y	90070 FQ	114160 MW	150800 TQ	USBLS	5/15
	Rhode Island	Y	96760 FQ	125060 MW	163950 TQ	USBLS	5/15
	Providence-Warwick MSA, RI-MA	Y	90070 FQ	114740 MW	153690 TQ	USBLS	5/15
	South Carolina	Y	67830 FQ	87910 MW	114180 TQ	USBLS	5/15
	Charleston-North Charleston MSA, SC	Y	74770 FQ	90750 MW	110830 TQ	USBLS	5/15
	Columbia MSA, SC	Y	69060 FQ	86810 MW	108010 TQ	USBLS	5/15
	Greenville-Anderson-Mauldin MSA, SC	Y	65830 FQ	86220 MW	112710 TQ	USBLS	5/15
	South Dakota	Y	75240 FQ	89880 MW	105360 TQ	USBLS	5/15
	Sioux Falls MSA, SD	Y	83440 FQ	94320 MW	109360 TQ	USBLS	5/15
	Tennessee	Y	58550 FQ	77990 MW	100730 TQ	USBLS	5/15
	Knoxville MSA, TN	Y	55860 FQ	73740 MW	99560 TQ	USBLS	5/15
	Memphis MSA, TN-MS-AR	Y	70130 FQ	90980 MW	116740 TQ	USBLS	5/15
	Nashville-Davidson–Murfreesboro–Franklin MSA, TN	Y	61890 FQ	80480 MW	99350 TQ	USBLS	5/15
	Texas	Y	91460 FQ	117990 MW	154080 TQ	USBLS	5/15
	Austin-Round Rock MSA, TX	Y	87950 FQ	115030 MW	150620 TQ	USBLS	5/15
	Dallas-Plano-Irving PMSA, TX	Y	98400 FQ	122070 MW	156310 TQ	USBLS	5/15
	Fort Worth-Arlington PMSA, TX	Y	82910 FQ	104520 MW	131250 TQ	USBLS	5/15
	Houston-The Woodlands-Sugar Land MSA, TX	Y	103500 FQ	129020 MW	169780 TQ	USBLS	5/15
	San Antonio-New Braunfels MSA, TX	Y	85930 FQ	109070 MW	159390 TQ	USBLS	5/15
	Utah	Y	74830 FQ	92760 MW	118680 TQ	USBLS	5/15
	Ogden-Clearfield MSA, UT	Y	74350 FQ	90940 MW	105160 TQ	USBLS	5/15
	Provo-Orem MSA, UT	Y	74540 FQ	90550 MW	121770 TQ	USBLS	5/15
	Salt Lake City MSA, UT	Y	75700 FQ	94490 MW	121300 TQ	USBLS	5/15
	Vermont	Y	75200 FQ	102400 MW	143470 TQ	USBLS	5/15
	Burlington-South Burlington MSA, VT	Y	66960 FQ	105940 MW	135570 TQ	USBLS	5/15
	Virginia	Y	92720 FQ	122650 MW	153280 TQ	USBLS	5/15

AE	Average entry wage	AWR	Average wage range	H	Hourly
AEX	Average experienced wage	B	Biweekly	HI	Highest wage paid
ATC	Average total compensation	D	Daily	HR	High end range
AW	Average wage paid	FQ	First quartile wage	LO	Lowest wage paid

LR	Low end range	MTC	Median total compensation
M	Monthly	MW	Median wage paid
MCC	Median cash compensation	MWR	Median wage range
ME	Median entry wage	S	See annotated source

TCC	Total cash compensation	
TQ	Third quartile wage	
W	Weekly	
Y	Yearly	

Occupation/Type/Industry	Location	Per	Low	Mid	High	Source	Date
Human Resources Manager	Richmond MSA, VA	Y	87360 FQ	103250 MW	134460 TQ	USBLS	5/15
	Virginia Beach-Norfolk-						
	Newport News MSA, VA-NC	Y	75190 FQ	98630 MW	125280 TQ	USBLS	5/15
	Washington	H	41.61 FQ	53.86 MW	68.36 TQ	WABLS	3/16
	Seattle-Bellevue-Everett						
	PMSA, WA	H	44.38 FQ	57.61 MW	72.63 TQ	WABLS	3/16
	Tacoma-Lakewood PMSA, WA	H	33.60 FQ	42.78 MW	53.97 TQ	WABLS	3/16
	West Virginia	Y	57910 FQ	78130 MW	98100 TQ	USBLS	5/15
	Huntington-Ashland MSA,						
	WV-KY-OH	Y	60710 FQ	82520 MW	98410 TQ	USBLS	5/15
	Wisconsin	Y	72920 FQ	92660 MW	117680 TQ	USBLS	5/15
	Madison MSA, WI	Y	76720 FQ	96960 MW	118720 TQ	USBLS	5/15
	Milwaukee-Waukesha-West						
	Allis MSA, WI	Y	76410 FQ	97990 MW	126940 TQ	USBLS	5/15
	Wyoming	Y	74200 FQ	89010 MW	115940 TQ	USBLS	5/15
	Cheyenne MSA, WY	Y	73480 FQ	74890 MW	88090 TQ	USBLS	5/15
	Puerto Rico	Y	43040 FQ	59240 MW	86650 TQ	USBLS	5/15
	San Juan-Carolina-Caguas						
	MSA, PR	Y	45500 FQ	61440 MW	89310 TQ	USBLS	5/15
	Virgin Islands	Y	60970 FQ	82650 MW	102440 TQ	USBLS	5/15
	Guam	Y	43050 FQ	64360 MW	77520 TQ	USBLS	5/15
Human Resources Specialist	Alabama	Y	38108 AE	59622 AW	70384 AEX	ALBLS	6/16
	Birmingham-Hoover MSA, AL	Y	38364 AE	57172 AW	66581 AEX	ALBLS	6/16
	Alaska	Y	52280 FQ	61650 MW	77010 TQ	USBLS	5/15
	Anchorage MSA, AK	Y	50610 FQ	61100 MW	78880 TQ	USBLS	5/15
	Arizona	Y	41930 FQ	53080 MW	70800 TQ	USBLS	5/15
	Phoenix-Mesa-Scottsdale						
	MSA, AZ	Y	42480 FQ	53790 MW	71370 TQ	USBLS	5/15
	Tucson MSA, AZ	Y	40030 FQ	49710 MW	65480 TQ	USBLS	5/15
	Arkansas	Y	36110 FQ	46830 MW	61720 TQ	USBLS	5/15
	Little Rock-North Little Rock-						
	Conway MSA, AR	Y	36290 FQ	47240 MW	63240 TQ	USBLS	5/15
	California	H	24.91 FQ	33.20 MW	44.45 TQ	CABLS	1/16-3/16
	Anaheim-Santa Ana-Irvine						
	PMSA, CA	H	23.43 FQ	31.40 MW	43.35 TQ	CABLS	1/16-3/16
	Hanford-Corcoran MSA, CA	H	21.75 FQ	30.49 MW	42.60 TQ	CABLS	1/16-3/16
	Los Angeles-Long Beach-						
	Glendale PMSA, CA	H	23.84 FQ	31.87 MW	43.03 TQ	CABLS	1/16-3/16
	Oakland-Hayward-Berkeley						
	PMSA, CA	H	27.63 FQ	36.10 MW	49.08 TQ	CABLS	1/16-3/16
	Riverside-San Bernardino-						
	Ontario MSA, CA	H	23.09 FQ	29.08 MW	36.24 TQ	CABLS	1/16-3/16
	Sacramento–Roseville–						
	Arden-Arcade MSA, CA	H	25.16 FQ	31.45 MW	41.99 TQ	CABLS	1/16-3/16
	San Diego-Carlsbad MSA, CA	H	23.36 FQ	31.69 MW	41.20 TQ	CABLS	1/16-3/16
	San Francisco-Redwood City-						
	South San Francisco PMSA,						
	CA	H	31.31 FQ	40.67 MW	52.25 TQ	CABLS	1/16-3/16
	Colorado	Y	46720 FQ	62240 MW	80700 TQ	USBLS	5/15
	Denver-Aurora-Lakewood						
	MSA, CO	Y	48760 FQ	64880 MW	83980 TQ	USBLS	5/15
	Connecticut	Y		65136 MW		CTBLS	1/16-3/16
	Bridgeport-Stamford-Norwalk						
	MSA, CT	Y	51210 FQ	65210 MW	84870 TQ	USBLS	5/15
	Hartford-West Hartford-East						
	Hartford MSA, CT	Y	50500 FQ	65080 MW	81240 TQ	USBLS	5/15
	Delaware	Y	44940 FQ	57020 MW	74740 TQ	USBLS	5/15
	Wilmington PMSA, DE-MD-						
	NJ	Y	47390 FQ	60890 MW	79140 TQ	USBLS	5/15
	District of Columbia	Y	66530 FQ	90820 MW	111840 TQ	USBLS	5/15
	Washington-Arlington-						
	Alexandria PMSA, DC-VA-						
	MD-WV	Y	59990 FQ	81460 MW	105900 TQ	USBLS	5/15
	Florida	H	17.24 AE	24.75 MW	32.51 AEX	FLBLS	7/16-9/16
	Fort Lauderdale-Pompano						
	Beach-Deerfield Beach						
	PMSA, FL	H	18.29 AE	26.49 MW	34.00 AEX	FLBLS	7/16-9/16
	Miami-Miami Beach-Kendall						
	PMSA, FL	H	18.38 AE	27.61 MW	34.81 AEX	FLBLS	7/16-9/16
	Orlando-Kissimmee-Sanford						
	MSA, FL	H	16.89 AE	24.68 MW	33.82 AEX	FLBLS	7/16-9/16

AE	Average entry wage	**AWR** Average wage range	**H** Hourly	**LR** Low end range	**MTC** Median total compensation	**TCC** Total cash compensation
AEX	Average experienced wage	**B** Biweekly	**HI** Highest wage paid	**M** Monthly	**MW** Median wage paid	**TQ** Third quartile wage
ATC	Average total compensation	**D** Daily	**HR** High end range	**MCC** Median cash compensation	**MWR** Median wage range	**W** Weekly
AW	Average wage paid	**FQ** First quartile wage	**LO** Lowest wage paid	**ME** Median entry wage	**S** See annotated source	**Y** Yearly

Human Resources Specialist

Occupation/Type/Industry	Location	Per	Low	Mid	High	Source	Date
Human Resources Specialist	Tampa-St. Petersburg-Clearwater MSA, FL	H	17.43 AE	24.20 MW	31.19 AEX	FLBLS	7/16-9/16
	Georgia	Y	39170 FQ	54070 MW	73620 TQ	USBLS	5/15
	Atlanta-Sandy Springs-Roswell MSA, GA	Y	41460 FQ	56740 MW	76460 TQ	USBLS	5/15
	Augusta-Richmond County MSA, GA-SC	Y	37080 FQ	51190 MW	67280 TQ	USBLS	5/15
	Hawaii	Y	44260 FQ	57300 MW	73940 TQ	USBLS	5/15
	Urban Honolulu MSA, HI	Y	44980 FQ	59090 MW	76260 TQ	USBLS	5/15
	Idaho	Y	37310 FQ	50310 MW	68900 TQ	USBLS	5/15
	Boise City MSA, ID	Y	39580 FQ	53980 MW	71670 TQ	USBLS	5/15
	Illinois	Y	42870 FQ	55300 MW	72890 TQ	USBLS	5/15
	Chicago-Naperville-Arlington Heights PMSA, IL	Y	43280 FQ	55440 MW	74270 TQ	USBLS	5/15
	Lake County-Kenosha County PMSA, IL-WI	Y	41560 FQ	52720 MW	72160 TQ	USBLS	5/15
	Indiana	Y	35870 FQ	48470 MW	64250 TQ	USBLS	5/15
	Gary PMSA, IN	Y	34360 FQ	44550 MW	58980 TQ	USBLS	5/15
	Indianapolis-Carmel-Anderson MSA, IN	Y	37220 FQ	50820 MW	68040 TQ	USBLS	5/15
	Iowa	Y	38270 FQ	49820 MW	61440 TQ	USBLS	5/15
	Des Moines-West Des Moines MSA, IA	Y	42460 FQ	54490 MW	67370 TQ	USBLS	5/15
	Kansas	Y	40630 FQ	54460 MW	70180 TQ	USBLS	5/15
	Wichita MSA, KS	Y	41830 FQ	54510 MW	68570 TQ	USBLS	5/15
	Kentucky	Y	37400 FQ	50580 MW	66360 TQ	USBLS	5/15
	Louisville-Jefferson County MSA, KY-IN	Y	37110 FQ	48770 MW	66220 TQ	USBLS	5/15
	Louisiana	Y	38710 FQ	49120 MW	62350 TQ	USBLS	5/15
	Baton Rouge MSA, LA	Y	40150 FQ	49060 MW	59550 TQ	USBLS	5/15
	New Orleans-Metairie MSA, LA	Y	41430 FQ	51180 MW	67660 TQ	USBLS	5/15
	Maine	Y	42250 FQ	52120 MW	67010 TQ	USBLS	5/15
	Portland-South Portland MSA, ME	Y	42980 FQ	54830 MW	70330 TQ	USBLS	5/15
	Maryland	Y	43850 AE	71298 MW	85022 AEX	MDBLS	4/16
	Baltimore-Columbia-Towson MSA, MD	Y	49950 FQ	65220 MW	84020 TQ	USBLS	5/15
	Salisbury MSA, MD-DE	Y	38530 FQ	52120 MW	68350 TQ	USBLS	5/15
	Massachusetts	Y	49860 FQ	64790 MW	87020 TQ	USBLS	5/15
	Boston-Cambridge-Newton NECTA, MA	Y	53120 FQ	70060 MW	93480 TQ	USBLS	5/15
	Worcester MSA, MA-CT	Y	47680 FQ	60320 MW	77050 TQ	USBLS	5/15
	Michigan	Y	42390 FQ	55410 MW	71660 TQ	USBLS	5/15
	Detroit-Dearborn-Livonia PMSA, MI	Y	44960 FQ	59570 MW	77380 TQ	USBLS	5/15
	Grand Rapids-Wyoming MSA, MI	Y	39290 FQ	48870 MW	63460 TQ	USBLS	5/15
	Minnesota	Y	46019 FQ	58599 MW	75019 TQ	MNBLS	1/16-3/16
	Minneapolis-St. Paul-Bloomington MSA, MN-WI	Y	48316 FQ	61007 MW	77529 TQ	MNBLS	1/16-3/16
	Mississippi	Y	31270 FQ	43480 MW	63090 TQ	USBLS	5/15
	Jackson MSA, MS	Y	32860 FQ	46170 MW	61950 TQ	USBLS	5/15
	Missouri	Y	41880 FQ	54200 MW	72540 TQ	USBLS	5/15
	Kansas City MSA, MO-KS	Y	43830 FQ	57810 MW	75250 TQ	USBLS	5/15
	St. Louis MSA, MO-IL	Y	42770 FQ	56110 MW	75260 TQ	USBLS	5/15
	Montana	Y	37600 FQ	47930 MW	62470 TQ	USBLS	5/15
	Billings MSA, MT	Y	43790 FQ	57530 MW	79430 TQ	USBLS	5/15
	Nebraska	Y	39890 FQ	50360 MW	64715 TQ	NEBLS	7/16-9/16
	Omaha-Council Bluffs MSA, NE-IA	Y	41065 FQ	52635 MW	68255 TQ	NEBLS	7/16-9/16
	Nevada	Y	40610 FQ	50950 MW	65660 TQ	USBLS	5/15
	Las Vegas-Henderson-Paradise MSA, NV	Y	40440 FQ	50210 MW	63930 TQ	USBLS	5/15
	New Hampshire	H	19.13 AE	27.71 MW	34.68 AEX	NHBLS	6/16
	Manchester NECTA, NH	H	20.04 AE	29.66 MW	35.77 AEX	NHBLS	6/16
	Nashua NECTA, NH-MA	Y	46130 FQ	57180 MW	70970 TQ	USBLS	5/15
	New Jersey	Y	54750 FQ	68240 MW	83800 TQ	USBLS	5/15
	Camden PMSA, NJ	Y	50460 FQ	63880 MW	80210 TQ	USBLS	5/15
	Newark PMSA, NJ-PA	Y	57920 FQ	71570 MW	89970 TQ	USBLS	5/15
	Trenton MSA, NJ	Y	54550 FQ	68570 MW	81510 TQ	USBLS	5/15
	New Mexico	Y	39070 FQ	54000 MW	72230 TQ	USBLS	5/15

AE	Average entry wage	AWR	Average wage range	H	Hourly	LR	Low end range	MTC	Median total compensation
AEX	Average experienced wage	B	Biweekly	HI	Highest wage paid	M	Monthly	MW	Median wage paid
ATC	Average total compensation	D	Daily	HR	High end range	MCC	Median cash compensation	MWR	Median wage range
AW	Average wage paid	FQ	First quartile wage	LO	Lowest wage paid	ME	Median entry wage	S	See annotated source

TCC	Total cash compensation	
TQ	Third quartile wage	
W	Weekly	
Y	Yearly	

Occupation/Type/Industry	Location	Per	Low	Mid	High	Source	Date
Human Resources Specialist	Albuquerque MSA, NM	Y	43790 FQ	57870 MW	74860 TQ	USBLS	5/15
	New York	Y	46080 AE	67960 MW	88060 AEX	NYBLS	1/16-3/16
	Buffalo-Cheektowaga-Niagara Falls MSA, NY	Y	46990 FQ	57630 MW	72000 TQ	USBLS	5/15
	Nassau County-Suffolk County PMSA, NY	Y	48830 FQ	64380 MW	85610 TQ	USBLS	5/15
	New York-Jersey City-White Plains PMSA, NY-NJ	Y	53530 FQ	70080 MW	91580 TQ	USBLS	5/15
	Rochester MSA, NY	Y	47120 FQ	60540 MW	78180 TQ	USBLS	5/15
	North Carolina	Y	41440 FQ	54390 MW	73010 TQ	USBLS	5/15
	Charlotte-Concord-Gastonia MSA, NC-SC	Y	43900 FQ	60130 MW	79880 TQ	USBLS	5/15
	Raleigh MSA, NC	Y	41740 FQ	51620 MW	69630 TQ	USBLS	5/15
	North Dakota	Y	44750 FQ	54000 MW	64420 TQ	USBLS	5/15
	Fargo MSA, ND-MN	Y	44610 FQ	54120 MW	62800 TQ	USBLS	5/15
	Ohio	Y	41390 FQ	54670 MW	71310 TQ	USBLS	5/15
	Cincinnati MSA, OH-KY-IN	Y	43060 FQ	57350 MW	73390 TQ	USBLS	5/15
	Cleveland-Elyria MSA, OH	Y	42000 FQ	56080 MW	73280 TQ	USBLS	5/15
	Columbus MSA, OH	Y	43620 FQ	56690 MW	72790 TQ	USBLS	5/15
	Oklahoma	Y	37210 FQ	48110 MW	63060 TQ	USBLS	5/15
	Oklahoma City MSA, OK	Y	39100 FQ	48540 MW	64420 TQ	USBLS	5/15
	Tulsa MSA, OK	Y	36770 FQ	48040 MW	62200 TQ	USBLS	5/15
	Oregon	H	20.62 FQ	26.77 MW	34.87 TQ	ORBLS	2016
	Portland-Vancouver-Hillsboro MSA, OR-WA	Y	44970 FQ	57760 MW	76470 TQ	USBLS	5/15
	Pennsylvania	Y	46520 FQ	61000 MW	77270 TQ	USBLS	5/15
	Allentown-Bethlehem-Easton MSA, PA-NJ	Y	40990 FQ	57400 MW	74750 TQ	USBLS	5/15
	Harrisburg-Carlisle MSA, PA	Y	44790 FQ	55060 MW	67550 TQ	USBLS	5/15
	Montgomery County-Bucks County-Chester County PMSA, PA	Y	51840 FQ	68240 MW	85350 TQ	USBLS	5/15
	Philadelphia PMSA, PA	Y	52950 FQ	69040 MW	85380 TQ	USBLS	5/15
	Pittsburgh MSA, PA	Y	44720 FQ	58250 MW	73860 TQ	USBLS	5/15
	Rhode Island	Y	50500 FQ	60800 MW	77250 TQ	USBLS	5/15
	Providence-Warwick MSA, RI-MA	Y	46220 FQ	57800 MW	74870 TQ	USBLS	5/15
	South Carolina	Y	39330 FQ	49940 MW	64360 TQ	USBLS	5/15
	Charleston-North Charleston MSA, SC	Y	41540 FQ	53790 MW	71500 TQ	USBLS	5/15
	Columbia MSA, SC	Y	40950 FQ	52900 MW	66320 TQ	USBLS	5/15
	Greenville-Anderson-Mauldin MSA, SC	Y	34860 FQ	45690 MW	58470 TQ	USBLS	5/15
	South Dakota	Y	40050 FQ	48660 MW	60520 TQ	USBLS	5/15
	Sioux Falls MSA, SD	Y	42720 FQ	52410 MW	62450 TQ	USBLS	5/15
	Tennessee	Y	37000 FQ	49670 MW	65430 TQ	USBLS	5/15
	Knoxville MSA, TN	Y	34080 FQ	43850 MW	58800 TQ	USBLS	5/15
	Memphis MSA, TN-MS-AR	Y	38730 FQ	53230 MW	69840 TQ	USBLS	5/15
	Nashville-Davidson–Murfreesboro–Franklin MSA, TN	Y	40270 FQ	54140 MW	69300 TQ	USBLS	5/15
	Texas	Y	43310 FQ	58520 MW	78110 TQ	USBLS	5/15
	Austin-Round Rock MSA, TX	Y	44040 FQ	57150 MW	75680 TQ	USBLS	5/15
	Dallas-Plano-Irving PMSA, TX	Y	44950 FQ	62200 MW	84090 TQ	USBLS	5/15
	Fort Worth-Arlington PMSA, TX	Y	45010 FQ	58100 MW	75860 TQ	USBLS	5/15
	Houston-The Woodlands-Sugar Land MSA, TX	Y	47190 FQ	61090 MW	81420 TQ	USBLS	5/15
	San Antonio-New Braunfels MSA, TX	Y	44260 FQ	61280 MW	79550 TQ	USBLS	5/15
	Utah	Y	39370 FQ	52440 MW	70750 TQ	USBLS	5/15
	Ogden-Clearfield MSA, UT	Y	41810 FQ	58560 MW	75120 TQ	USBLS	5/15
	Provo-Orem MSA, UT	Y	32690 FQ	41570 MW	55740 TQ	USBLS	5/15
	Salt Lake City MSA, UT	Y	42360 FQ	55540 MW	74020 TQ	USBLS	5/15
	Vermont	Y	43460 FQ	55870 MW	73590 TQ	USBLS	5/15
	Burlington-South Burlington MSA, VT	Y	43300 FQ	58070 MW	75640 TQ	USBLS	5/15
	Virginia	Y	48750 FQ	65710 MW	89160 TQ	USBLS	5/15
	Richmond MSA, VA	Y	45430 FQ	59690 MW	75910 TQ	USBLS	5/15
	Virginia Beach-Norfolk-Newport News MSA, VA-NC	Y	45500 FQ	60020 MW	77820 TQ	USBLS	5/15
	Washington	H	23.70 FQ	30.20 MW	39.83 TQ	WABLS	3/16

AE	Average entry wage	AWR Average wage range	H Hourly	LR Low end range	MTC Median total compensation	TCC Total cash compensation
AEX	Average experienced wage	B Biweekly	HI Highest wage paid	M Monthly	MW Median wage paid	TQ Third quartile wage
ATC	Average total compensation	D Daily	HR High end range	MCC Median cash compensation	MWR Median wage range	W Weekly
AW	Average wage paid	FQ First quartile wage	LO Lowest wage paid	ME Median entry wage	S See annotated source	Y Yearly

Occupation/Type/Industry	Location	Per	Low	Mid	High	Source	Date
Human Resources Specialist	Seattle-Bellevue-Everett						
	PMSA, WA	H	25.73 FQ	33.45 MW	45.05 TQ	WABLS	3/16
	Tacoma-Lakewood PMSA, WA	H	22.46 FQ	28.41 MW	36.09 TQ	WABLS	3/16
	West Virginia	Y	39580 FQ	54850 MW	74580 TQ	USBLS	5/15
	Huntington-Ashland MSA,						
	WV-KY-OH	Y	38780 FQ	55170 MW	72770 TQ	USBLS	5/15
	Wisconsin	Y	40720 FQ	52230 MW	66370 TQ	USBLS	5/15
	Madison MSA, WI	Y	42980 FQ	56410 MW	71010 TQ	USBLS	5/15
	Milwaukee-Waukesha-West						
	Allis MSA, WI	Y	42770 FQ	56170 MW	72210 TQ	USBLS	5/15
	Wyoming	Y	43100 FQ	49120 MW	64250 TQ	USBLS	5/15
	Cheyenne MSA, WY	Y	44650 FQ	51470 MW	63040 TQ	USBLS	5/15
	Puerto Rico	Y	24610 FQ	31850 MW	42980 TQ	USBLS	5/15
	San Juan-Carolina-Caguas						
	MSA, PR	Y	25380 FQ	32870 MW	43950 TQ	USBLS	5/15
	Virgin Islands	Y	36620 FQ	44880 MW	60600 TQ	USBLS	5/15
	Guam	Y	34760 FQ	44150 MW	55160 TQ	USBLS	5/15
Human Rights Specialist							
Municipal Government	Detroit, MI	M	4133 LO		5775 HI	DETGOV	2016
Hydrant Worker							
Municipal Utilities	Stockton, CA	Y			38579 HI	CACIT	6/28/16
Hydrocrane Operator							
Municipal Government	Seattle, WA	H			38.14 HI	CSSS	1/27/16
Hydrogeologist							
State Government	Helena, MT	H			24.40 HI	MTGOV	2016
Hydrographer							
Municipal Government	Los Angeles, CA	Y		79748 AW		CACIT	6/23/16
Hydrography Aide							
Water Department, Municipal Government	San Diego, CA	Y			50887 HI	CACIT	6/28/16
Hydrologist	Alabama	Y	76531 AE	89741 AW	96357 AEX	ALBLS	6/16
	Alaska	Y	76650 FQ	81790 MW	99670 TQ	USBLS	5/15
	Anchorage MSA, AK	Y	77050 FQ	86890 MW	106370 TQ	USBLS	5/15
	Arizona	Y	57420 FQ	69650 MW	84490 TQ	USBLS	5/15
	Phoenix-Mesa-Scottsdale						
	MSA, AZ	Y	56400 FQ	67370 MW	87790 TQ	USBLS	5/15
	Tucson MSA, AZ	Y	57660 FQ	70190 MW	79900 TQ	USBLS	5/15
	California	H	39.45 FQ	51.23 MW	60.27 TQ	CABLS	1/16-3/16
	Anaheim-Santa Ana-Irvine						
	PMSA, CA	H	64.88 FQ	73.24 MW	81.60 TQ	CABLS	1/16-3/16
	Oakland-Hayward-Berkeley						
	PMSA, CA	H	46.87 FQ	56.61 MW	71.18 TQ	CABLS	1/16-3/16
	Sacramento–Roseville–						
	Arden-Arcade MSA, CA	H	33.64 FQ	40.32 MW	50.85 TQ	CABLS	1/16-3/16
	San Francisco-Redwood City-						
	South San Francisco PMSA,						
	CA	H	43.47 FQ	51.34 MW	61.90 TQ	CABLS	1/16-3/16
	Colorado	Y	79360 FQ	94320 MW	116460 TQ	USBLS	5/15
	Denver-Aurora-Lakewood						
	MSA, CO	Y	83630 FQ	97180 MW	127330 TQ	USBLS	5/15
	Connecticut	Y		76848 MW		CTBLS	1/16-3/16
	Hartford-West Hartford-East						
	Hartford MSA, CT	Y	75490 FQ	92840 MW	110400 TQ	USBLS	5/15
	Washington-Arlington-						
	Alexandria PMSA, DC-VA-						
	MD-WV	Y	73330 FQ	93370 MW	115030 TQ	USBLS	5/15
	Florida	H	29.14 AE	39.95 MW	46.09 AEX	FLBLS	7/16-9/16
	Tampa-St. Petersburg-						
	Clearwater MSA, FL	H	31.60 AE	40.00 MW	48.71 AEX	FLBLS	7/16-9/16
	Georgia	Y	88020 FQ	95360 MW	107560 TQ	USBLS	5/15
	Atlanta-Sandy Springs-						
	Roswell MSA, GA	Y	88020 FQ	95360 MW	107560 TQ	USBLS	5/15
	Idaho	Y	53710 FQ	68670 MW	84230 TQ	USBLS	5/15
	Boise City MSA, ID	Y	54040 FQ	68310 MW	85870 TQ	USBLS	5/15
	Illinois	Y	54910 FQ	72400 MW	90170 TQ	USBLS	5/15
	Chicago-Naperville-Arlington						
	Heights PMSA, IL	Y	46100 FQ	65730 MW	75990 TQ	USBLS	5/15

AE	Average entry wage	AWR	Average wage range	H	Hourly	LR	Low end range	
AEX	Average experienced wage	B	Biweekly	HI	Highest wage paid	M	Monthly	
ATC	Average total compensation	D	Daily	HR	High end range	MCC	Median cash compensation	
AW	Average wage paid	FQ	First quartile wage	LO	Lowest wage paid	ME	Median entry wage	

MTC	Median total compensation	TCC	Total cash compensation
MW	Median wage paid	TQ	Third quartile wage
MWR	Median wage range	W	Weekly
S	See annotated source	Y	Yearly

Occupation/Type/Industry	Location	Per	Low	Mid	High	Source	Date
Hydrologist	Indiana	Y	66670 FQ	78630 MW	91670 TQ	USBLS	5/15
	Maine	Y	57250 FQ	68950 MW	81910 TQ	USBLS	5/15
	Maryland	Y	68543 AE	92702 MW	104781 AEX	MDBLS	4/16
	Massachusetts	Y	77750 FQ	97050 MW	106450 TQ	USBLS	5/15
	Michigan	Y	64200 FQ	80120 MW	92890 TQ	USBLS	5/15
	Minnesota	Y	62751 FQ	75019 MW	82489 TQ	MNBLS	1/16-3/16
	Minneapolis-St. Paul-Bloomington MSA, MN-WI	Y	65070 FQ	80029 MW	86350 TQ	MNBLS	1/16-3/16
	Missouri	Y	50020 FQ	81900 MW	94370 TQ	USBLS	5/15
	Kansas City MSA, MO-KS	Y	51880 FQ	87120 MW	97370 TQ	USBLS	5/15
	Montana	Y	55880 FQ	68310 MW	77210 TQ	USBLS	5/15
	Nebraska	Y	41200 FQ	50425 MW	65830 TQ	NEBLS	7/16-9/16
	Nevada	Y	60520 FQ	88860 MW	120990 TQ	USBLS	5/15
	Las Vegas-Henderson-Paradise MSA, NV	Y	73100 FQ	97370 MW	128840 TQ	USBLS	5/15
	New Hampshire	H	29.65 AE	39.41 MW	45.05 AEX	NHBLS	6/16
	New Jersey	Y	54570 FQ	78790 MW	102880 TQ	USBLS	5/15
	Camden PMSA, NJ	Y	63000 FQ	98810 MW	114790 TQ	USBLS	5/15
	Newark PMSA, NJ-PA	Y	38390 FQ	68480 MW	80480 TQ	USBLS	5/15
	Trenton MSA, NJ	Y	81770 FQ	100250 MW	108400 TQ	USBLS	5/15
	New Mexico	Y	60520 FQ	76970 MW	95500 TQ	USBLS	5/15
	Albuquerque MSA, NM	Y	61190 FQ	79550 MW	96710 TQ	USBLS	5/15
	New York	Y	55210 AE	79120 MW	104840 AEX	NYBLS	1/16-3/16
	Nassau County-Suffolk County PMSA, NY	Y	67430 FQ	91390 MW	123200 TQ	USBLS	5/15
	New York-Jersey City-White Plains PMSA, NY-NJ	Y	55020 FQ	68720 MW	80380 TQ	USBLS	5/15
	North Carolina	Y	53610 FQ	59040 MW	67320 TQ	USBLS	5/15
	Raleigh MSA, NC	Y	53380 FQ	58620 MW	66240 TQ	USBLS	5/15
	Ohio	Y	59490 FQ	75110 MW	86690 TQ	USBLS	5/15
	Columbus MSA, OH	Y	60140 FQ	75120 MW	86680 TQ	USBLS	5/15
	Oklahoma	Y	66360 FQ	88920 MW	102960 TQ	USBLS	5/15
	Oregon	H	33.12 FQ	39.70 MW	46.93 TQ	ORBLS	2016
	Portland-Vancouver-Hillsboro MSA, OR-WA	Y	76480 FQ	91260 MW	105590 TQ	USBLS	5/15
	Pennsylvania	Y	67280 FQ	78720 MW	99280 TQ	USBLS	5/15
	South Carolina	Y	48720 FQ	59410 MW	72220 TQ	USBLS	5/15
	Columbia MSA, SC	Y	47650 FQ	56330 MW	65430 TQ	USBLS	5/15
	Tennessee	Y	69760 FQ	82770 MW	105720 TQ	USBLS	5/15
	Nashville-Davidson–Murfreesboro–Franklin MSA, TN	Y	68400 FQ	77700 MW	97240 TQ	USBLS	5/15
	Texas	Y	57230 FQ	69060 MW	90440 TQ	USBLS	5/15
	Austin-Round Rock MSA, TX	Y	54090 FQ	63710 MW	76120 TQ	USBLS	5/15
	Fort Worth-Arlington PMSA, TX	Y	69000 FQ	88220 MW	105880 TQ	USBLS	5/15
	Houston-The Woodlands-Sugar Land MSA, TX	Y	64770 FQ	87740 MW	133340 TQ	USBLS	5/15
	Salt Lake City MSA, UT	Y	61550 FQ	79540 MW	91410 TQ	USBLS	5/15
	Vermont	Y	59270 FQ	76130 MW	93290 TQ	USBLS	5/15
	Burlington-South Burlington MSA, VT	Y	58210 FQ	83220 MW	95690 TQ	USBLS	5/15
	Virginia	Y	73420 FQ	93710 MW	115030 TQ	USBLS	5/15
	Washington	H	36.14 FQ	42.20 MW	55.03 TQ	WABLS	3/16
	Seattle-Bellevue-Everett PMSA, WA	H	39.27 FQ	52.28 MW	59.35 TQ	WABLS	3/16
	Tacoma-Lakewood PMSA, WA	H	36.85 FQ	43.84 MW	49.62 TQ	WABLS	3/16
	Wisconsin	Y	55360 FQ	61290 MW	71700 TQ	USBLS	5/15
	Madison MSA, WI	Y	56050 FQ	63160 MW	72550 TQ	USBLS	5/15
	Milwaukee-Waukesha-West Allis MSA, WI	Y	55350 FQ	61180 MW	77540 TQ	USBLS	5/15
	Wyoming	Y	63600 FQ	70270 MW	76620 TQ	USBLS	5/15
Hypnotherapist	United States	Y		59000 AW		SKU01	2016
IBM Certified Solution Architect	United States	Y		137000 AW		CERTM02	2015
Ice Rink Specialist Municipal Government	Seattle, WA	H	26.04 LO		27.05 HI	CSSS	3/9/16
Ice Trucker	United States	Y		34000 AW		HCHRON2	2013

AE	Average entry wage	AWR	Average wage range	H	Hourly	LR	Low end range	MTC	Median total compensation	TCC	Total cash compensation
AEX	Average experienced wage	B	Biweekly	HI	Highest wage paid	M	Monthly	MW	Median wage paid	TQ	Third quartile wage
ATC	Average total compensation	D	Daily	HR	High end range	MCC	Median cash compensation	MWR	Median wage range	W	Weekly
AW	Average wage paid	FQ	First quartile wage	LO	Lowest wage paid	ME	Median entry wage	S	See annotated source	Y	Yearly

Occupation/Type/Industry	Location	Per	Low	Mid	High	Source	Date
Identification Technician							
Police Department, Municipal Government	Fountain Valley, CA	Y			57232 HI	CACIT	6/28/16
Police Department, Municipal Government	Detroit, MI	M	2433 LO		2800 HI	DETGOV	2016
Image Consultant	United States	S		39000 AW		JM02	2017
Implementation Consultant	United States	Y		75000 MW		MCCS	2016
Incident Support Specialist							
Fire Department, Municipal Government	San Francisco, CA	Y		114469 AW		CACIT	6/28/16
Income Tax Investigator							
Municipal Government	Detroit, MI	M	2122 LO		2750 HI	DETGOV	2016
Industrial Engineer	Alabama	Y	62138 AE	90353 AW	104460 AEX	ALBLS	6/16
	Birmingham-Hoover MSA, AL	Y	57643 AE	81984 AW	94155 AEX	ALBLS	6/16
	Alaska	Y	88480 FQ	113850 MW	146920 TQ	USBLS	5/15
	Anchorage MSA, AK	Y	79760 FQ	94140 MW	125270 TQ	USBLS	5/15
	Arizona	Y	74450 FQ	92120 MW	112400 TQ	USBLS	5/15
	Phoenix-Mesa-Scottsdale MSA, AZ	Y	75630 FQ	93930 MW	113760 TQ	USBLS	5/15
	Tucson MSA, AZ	Y	67030 FQ	80940 MW	94350 TQ	USBLS	5/15
	Arkansas	Y	59850 FQ	72170 MW	86440 TQ	USBLS	5/15
	Little Rock-North Little Rock-Conway MSA, AR	Y	64520 FQ	74010 MW	88080 TQ	USBLS	5/15
	California	H	37.99 FQ	48.06 MW	60.35 TQ	CABLS	1/16-3/16
	Anaheim-Santa Ana-Irvine PMSA, CA	H	34.32 FQ	45.35 MW	58.46 TQ	CABLS	1/16-3/16
	Los Angeles-Long Beach-Glendale PMSA, CA	H	38.67 FQ	48.14 MW	60.50 TQ	CABLS	1/16-3/16
	Oakland-Hayward-Berkeley PMSA, CA	H	36.84 FQ	47.02 MW	58.83 TQ	CABLS	1/16-3/16
	Riverside-San Bernardino-Ontario MSA, CA	H	29.25 FQ	35.76 MW	46.11 TQ	CABLS	1/16-3/16
	Sacramento–Roseville–Arden-Arcade MSA, CA	H	34.62 FQ	44.90 MW	55.37 TQ	CABLS	1/16-3/16
	San Diego-Carlsbad MSA, CA	H	37.35 FQ	45.44 MW	57.17 TQ	CABLS	1/16-3/16
	San Francisco-Redwood City-South San Francisco PMSA, CA	H	41.59 FQ	52.03 MW	61.73 TQ	CABLS	1/16-3/16
	Colorado	Y	71920 FQ	91960 MW	115820 TQ	USBLS	5/15
	Denver-Aurora-Lakewood MSA, CO	Y	72790 FQ	91440 MW	112770 TQ	USBLS	5/15
	Connecticut	Y		87175 MW		CTBLS	1/16-3/16
	Bridgeport-Stamford-Norwalk MSA, CT	Y	73940 FQ	91320 MW	111640 TQ	USBLS	5/15
	Hartford-West Hartford-East Hartford MSA, CT	Y	69390 FQ	83510 MW	98440 TQ	USBLS	5/15
	Delaware	Y	72060 FQ	88580 MW	109800 TQ	USBLS	5/15
	Wilmington PMSA, DE-MD-NJ	Y	72020 FQ	89690 MW	111010 TQ	USBLS	5/15
	District of Columbia	Y	68500 FQ	82160 MW	107940 TQ	USBLS	5/15
	Washington-Arlington-Alexandria PMSA, DC-VA-MD-WV	Y	75820 FQ	92600 MW	118370 TQ	USBLS	5/15
	Florida	H	21.90 AE	34.29 MW	43.12 AEX	FLBLS	7/16-9/16
	Fort Lauderdale-Pompano Beach-Deerfield Beach PMSA, FL	H	21.72 AE	29.93 MW	40.91 AEX	FLBLS	7/16-9/16
	Miami-Miami Beach-Kendall PMSA, FL	H	19.54 AE	31.80 MW	38.54 AEX	FLBLS	7/16-9/16
	Orlando-Kissimmee-Sanford MSA, FL	H	23.95 AE	37.21 MW	45.15 AEX	FLBLS	7/16-9/16
	Tampa-St. Petersburg-Clearwater MSA, FL	H	22.13 AE	33.00 MW	40.56 AEX	FLBLS	7/16-9/16
	Georgia	Y	63230 FQ	78880 MW	95810 TQ	USBLS	5/15
	Atlanta-Sandy Springs-Roswell MSA, GA	Y	66690 FQ	82020 MW	97700 TQ	USBLS	5/15
	Augusta-Richmond County MSA, GA-SC	Y	63430 FQ	74310 MW	93750 TQ	USBLS	5/15
	Hawaii	Y	59080 FQ	78000 MW	110270 TQ	USBLS	5/15
	Urban Honolulu MSA, HI	Y	59100 FQ	77830 MW	110750 TQ	USBLS	5/15
	Idaho	Y	74350 FQ	90670 MW	108830 TQ	USBLS	5/15

AE	Average entry wage	AWR	Average wage range	H	Hourly
AEX	Average experienced wage	B	Biweekly	HI	Highest wage paid
ATC	Average total compensation	D	Daily	HR	High end range
AW	Average wage paid	FQ	First quartile wage	LO	Lowest wage paid

LR	Low end range	MTC	Median total compensation	TCC	Total cash compensation
M	Monthly	MW	Median wage paid	TQ	Third quartile wage
MCC	Median cash compensation	MWR	Median wage range	W	Weekly
ME	Median entry wage	S	See annotated source	Y	Yearly

Industrial Engineer

Occupation/Type/Industry	Location	Per	Low	Mid	High	Source	Date
Industrial Engineer	Boise City MSA, ID	Y	74410 FQ	91020 MW	110240 TQ	USBLS	5/15
	Illinois	Y	61170 FQ	78150 MW	96190 TQ	USBLS	5/15
	Chicago-Naperville-Arlington Heights PMSA, IL	Y	60610 FQ	78700 MW	96850 TQ	USBLS	5/15
	Lake County-Kenosha County PMSA, IL-WI	Y	63470 FQ	83340 MW	101230 TQ	USBLS	5/15
	Indiana	Y	57990 FQ	71810 MW	88470 TQ	USBLS	5/15
	Gary PMSA, IN	Y	56750 FQ	69910 MW	85000 TQ	USBLS	5/15
	Indianapolis-Carmel-Anderson MSA, IN	Y	61860 FQ	73920 MW	89730 TQ	USBLS	5/15
	Iowa	Y	61410 FQ	72950 MW	87460 TQ	USBLS	5/15
	Des Moines-West Des Moines MSA, IA	Y	64880 FQ	75380 MW	89550 TQ	USBLS	5/15
	Kansas	Y	63050 FQ	79440 MW	97200 TQ	USBLS	5/15
	Wichita MSA, KS	Y	65150 FQ	80030 MW	97900 TQ	USBLS	5/15
	Kentucky	Y	64770 FQ	77430 MW	93910 TQ	USBLS	5/15
	Louisville-Jefferson County MSA, KY-IN	Y	60970 FQ	73520 MW	89200 TQ	USBLS	5/15
	Louisiana	Y	65380 FQ	93520 MW	123460 TQ	USBLS	5/15
	Baton Rouge MSA, LA	Y	56610 FQ	96350 MW	126420 TQ	USBLS	5/15
	New Orleans-Metairie MSA, LA	Y	81660 FQ	102610 MW	129980 TQ	USBLS	5/15
	Maine	Y	69360 FQ	82400 MW	96610 TQ	USBLS	5/15
	Portland-South Portland MSA, ME	Y	68750 FQ	83490 MW	100010 TQ	USBLS	5/15
	Maryland	Y	45035 AE	83234 MW	102333 AEX	MDBLS	4/16
	Baltimore-Columbia-Towson MSA, MD	Y	71080 FQ	88920 MW	113300 TQ	USBLS	5/15
	Salisbury MSA, MD-DE	Y	72840 FQ	86180 MW	97800 TQ	USBLS	5/15
	Massachusetts	Y	74330 FQ	92480 MW	115530 TQ	USBLS	5/15
	Boston-Cambridge-Newton NECTA, MA	Y	77850 FQ	97000 MW	121440 TQ	USBLS	5/15
	Worcester MSA, MA-CT	Y	65260 FQ	77790 MW	94970 TQ	USBLS	5/15
	Michigan	Y	69450 FQ	86390 MW	103980 TQ	USBLS	5/15
	Detroit-Dearborn-Livonia PMSA, MI	Y	76650 FQ	91540 MW	108570 TQ	USBLS	5/15
	Grand Rapids-Wyoming MSA, MI	Y	63420 FQ	74770 MW	91750 TQ	USBLS	5/15
	Minnesota	Y	68971 FQ	84747 MW	102347 TQ	MNBLS	1/16-3/16
	Minneapolis-St. Paul-Bloomington MSA, MN-WI	Y	71975 FQ	88154 MW	105956 TQ	MNBLS	1/16-3/16
	Mississippi	Y	64880 FQ	78340 MW	95950 TQ	USBLS	5/15
	Jackson MSA, MS	Y	65600 FQ	76120 MW	91250 TQ	USBLS	5/15
	Missouri	Y	64870 FQ	81010 MW	105670 TQ	USBLS	5/15
	Kansas City MSA, MO-KS	Y	64980 FQ	79160 MW	98680 TQ	USBLS	5/15
	St. Louis MSA, MO-IL	Y	68020 FQ	87280 MW	111520 TQ	USBLS	5/15
	Montana	Y	65870 FQ	82190 MW	99500 TQ	USBLS	5/15
	Billings MSA, MT	Y	69710 FQ	85630 MW	99140 TQ	USBLS	5/15
	Nebraska	Y	63275 FQ	76375 MW	95940 TQ	NEBLS	7/16-9/16
	Omaha-Council Bluffs MSA, NE-IA	Y	65775 FQ	85855 MW	111550 TQ	NEBLS	7/16-9/16
	Nevada	Y	67830 FQ	81740 MW	97040 TQ	USBLS	5/15
	Las Vegas-Henderson-Paradise MSA, NV	Y	65810 FQ	80110 MW	95400 TQ	USBLS	5/15
	New Hampshire	H	30.24 AE	38.93 MW	44.53 AEX	NHBLS	6/16
	Manchester NECTA, NH	H	31.96 AE	39.22 MW	44.24 AEX	NHBLS	6/16
	Nashua NECTA, NH-MA	Y	71260 FQ	85540 MW	101210 TQ	USBLS	5/15
	New Jersey	Y	71260 FQ	87590 MW	108620 TQ	USBLS	5/15
	Camden PMSA, NJ	Y	72800 FQ	89240 MW	108550 TQ	USBLS	5/15
	Newark PMSA, NJ-PA	Y	72190 FQ	91000 MW	113680 TQ	USBLS	5/15
	Trenton MSA, NJ	Y	65160 FQ	76890 MW	92160 TQ	USBLS	5/15
	New Mexico	Y	81930 FQ	91080 MW	100110 TQ	USBLS	5/15
	Albuquerque MSA, NM	Y	81460 FQ	89830 MW	98170 TQ	USBLS	5/15
	New York	Y	60520 AE	83660 MW	99800 AEX	NYBLS	1/16-3/16
	Buffalo-Cheektowaga-Niagara Falls MSA, NY	Y	64300 FQ	76850 MW	92760 TQ	USBLS	5/15
	Nassau County-Suffolk County PMSA, NY	Y	69760 FQ	87730 MW	108460 TQ	USBLS	5/15
	New York-Jersey City-White Plains PMSA, NY-NJ	Y	67950 FQ	85410 MW	105980 TQ	USBLS	5/15
	Rochester MSA, NY	Y	67090 FQ	79510 MW	94210 TQ	USBLS	5/15
	North Carolina	Y	65650 FQ	79880 MW	97230 TQ	USBLS	5/15

AE	Average entry wage	AWR	Average wage range	H	Hourly
AEX	Average experienced wage	B	Biweekly	HI	Highest wage paid
ATC	Average total compensation	D	Daily	HR	High end range
AW	Average wage paid	FQ	First quartile wage	LO	Lowest wage paid

LR	Low end range	MTC	Median total compensation
M	Monthly	MW	Median wage paid
MCC	Median cash compensation	MWR	Median wage range
ME	Median entry wage	S	See annotated source

TCC	Total cash compensation
TQ	Third quartile wage
W	Weekly
Y	Yearly

Occupation/Type/Industry	Location	Per	Low	Mid	High	Source	Date
Industrial Engineer	Charlotte-Concord-Gastonia						
	MSA, NC-SC	Y	65850 FQ	79490 MW	95130 TQ	USBLS	5/15
	Raleigh MSA, NC	Y	65470 FQ	82640 MW	97950 TQ	USBLS	5/15
	North Dakota	Y	55730 FQ	74620 MW	93920 TQ	USBLS	5/15
	Fargo MSA, ND-MN	Y	51540 FQ	70390 MW	94350 TQ	USBLS	5/15
	Ohio	Y	62570 FQ	76680 MW	94730 TQ	USBLS	5/15
	Cincinnati MSA, OH-KY-IN	Y	70460 FQ	86410 MW	105560 TQ	USBLS	5/15
	Cleveland-Elyria MSA, OH	Y	63370 FQ	76440 MW	93100 TQ	USBLS	5/15
	Columbus MSA, OH	Y	62010 FQ	75980 MW	93740 TQ	USBLS	5/15
	Oklahoma	Y	63620 FQ	79590 MW	101180 TQ	USBLS	5/15
	Oklahoma City MSA, OK	Y	68160 FQ	84440 MW	107730 TQ	USBLS	5/15
	Tulsa MSA, OK	Y	65120 FQ	79840 MW	99900 TQ	USBLS	5/15
	Oregon	H	38.22 FQ	47.16 MW	58.79 TQ	ORBLS	2016
	Portland-Vancouver-Hillsboro						
	MSA, OR-WA	Y	80200 FQ	97940 MW	121060 TQ	USBLS	5/15
	Pennsylvania	Y	65840 FQ	80770 MW	100410 TQ	USBLS	5/15
	Allentown-Bethlehem-Easton						
	MSA, PA-NJ	Y	61160 FQ	78530 MW	100610 TQ	USBLS	5/15
	Harrisburg-Carlisle MSA, PA	Y	66950 FQ	74610 MW	88310 TQ	USBLS	5/15
	Montgomery County-Bucks						
	County-Chester County						
	PMSA, PA	Y	71590 FQ	89470 MW	111010 TQ	USBLS	5/15
	Philadelphia PMSA, PA	Y	77190 FQ	92590 MW	111560 TQ	USBLS	5/15
	Pittsburgh MSA, PA	Y	67900 FQ	82440 MW	100920 TQ	USBLS	5/15
	Rhode Island	Y	66490 FQ	85030 MW	101350 TQ	USBLS	5/15
	Providence-Warwick MSA, RI-						
	MA	Y	66330 FQ	84800 MW	100850 TQ	USBLS	5/15
	South Carolina	Y	64820 FQ	78450 MW	95500 TQ	USBLS	5/15
	Charleston-North Charleston						
	MSA, SC	Y	66360 FQ	80980 MW	96590 TQ	USBLS	5/15
	Columbia MSA, SC	Y	67900 FQ	84120 MW	105910 TQ	USBLS	5/15
	Greenville-Anderson-Mauldin						
	MSA, SC	Y	61570 FQ	75300 MW	92420 TQ	USBLS	5/15
	South Dakota	Y	61790 FQ	72640 MW	87780 TQ	USBLS	5/15
	Sioux Falls MSA, SD	Y	58620 FQ	68770 MW	80710 TQ	USBLS	5/15
	Tennessee	Y	62440 FQ	77850 MW	98010 TQ	USBLS	5/15
	Knoxville MSA, TN	Y	68900 FQ	88990 MW	114290 TQ	USBLS	5/15
	Memphis MSA, TN-MS-AR	Y	64830 FQ	77020 MW	96500 TQ	USBLS	5/15
	Nashville-Davidson–						
	Murfreesboro–Franklin						
	MSA, TN	Y	64460 FQ	79520 MW	96590 TQ	USBLS	5/15
	Texas	Y	71550 FQ	92280 MW	118670 TQ	USBLS	5/15
	Austin-Round Rock MSA, TX	Y	73750 FQ	91040 MW	111200 TQ	USBLS	5/15
	Dallas-Plano-Irving PMSA, TX	Y	71800 FQ	94250 MW	117610 TQ	USBLS	5/15
	Fort Worth-Arlington PMSA,						
	TX	Y	66220 FQ	84980 MW	109690 TQ	USBLS	5/15
	Houston-The Woodlands-						
	Sugar Land MSA, TX	Y	78070 FQ	98870 MW	130220 TQ	USBLS	5/15
	San Antonio-New Braunfels						
	MSA, TX	Y	65530 FQ	77960 MW	95170 TQ	USBLS	5/15
	Utah	Y	63980 FQ	77310 MW	96470 TQ	USBLS	5/15
	Ogden-Clearfield MSA, UT	Y	61830 FQ	75820 MW	94400 TQ	USBLS	5/15
	Provo-Orem MSA, UT	Y	67730 FQ	78920 MW	94540 TQ	USBLS	5/15
	Salt Lake City MSA, UT	Y	64770 FQ	78930 MW	98360 TQ	USBLS	5/15
	Vermont	Y	66170 FQ	77010 MW	89380 TQ	USBLS	5/15
	Burlington-South Burlington						
	MSA, VT	Y	66500 FQ	76400 MW	87940 TQ	USBLS	5/15
	Virginia	Y	66840 FQ	83460 MW	102360 TQ	USBLS	5/15
	Richmond MSA, VA	Y	74650 FQ	93680 MW	116770 TQ	USBLS	5/15
	Virginia Beach-Norfolk-						
	Newport News MSA, VA-NC	Y	67560 FQ	84780 MW	98920 TQ	USBLS	5/15
	Washington	H	38.97 FQ	48.49 MW	59.02 TQ	WABLS	3/16
	Seattle-Bellevue-Everett						
	PMSA, WA	H	41.18 FQ	50.31 MW	60.45 TQ	WABLS	3/16
	Tacoma-Lakewood PMSA, WA	H	32.79 FQ	39.06 MW	50.74 TQ	WABLS	3/16
	West Virginia	Y	65520 FQ	78340 MW	95440 TQ	USBLS	5/15
	Huntington-Ashland MSA,						
	WV-KY-OH	Y	65710 FQ	76360 MW	97700 TQ	USBLS	5/15
	Wisconsin	Y	59860 FQ	73290 MW	90040 TQ	USBLS	5/15
	Madison MSA, WI	Y	59110 FQ	71790 MW	86740 TQ	USBLS	5/15
	Milwaukee-Waukesha-West						
	Allis MSA, WI	Y	62680 FQ	75560 MW	92510 TQ	USBLS	5/15

AE	Average entry wage	AWR	Average wage range	H	Hourly
AEX	Average experienced wage	B	Biweekly	HI	Highest wage paid
ATC	Average total compensation	D	Daily	HR	High end range
AW	Average wage paid	FQ	First quartile wage	LO	Lowest wage paid

LR	Low end range	MTC	Median total compensation
M	Monthly	MW	Median wage paid
MCC	Median cash compensation	MWR	Median wage range
ME	Median entry wage	S	See annotated source

TCC	Total cash compensation
TQ	Third quartile wage
W	Weekly
Y	Yearly

Occupation/Type/Industry	Location	Per	Low	Mid	High	Source	Date
Industrial Engineer	Wyoming	Y	77630 FQ	100110 MW	121590 TQ	USBLS	5/15
	Puerto Rico	Y	53450 FQ	69720 MW	87910 TQ	USBLS	5/15
	San Juan-Carolina-Caguas MSA, PR	Y	52410 FQ	69730 MW	89360 TQ	USBLS	5/15
Industrial Engineering Technician	Alabama	Y	40192 AE	59824 AW	69640 AEX	ALBLS	6/16
	Birmingham-Hoover MSA, AL	Y	38092 AE	50803 AW	57153 AEX	ALBLS	6/16
	Alaska	Y	73290 FQ	85380 MW	99960 TQ	USBLS	5/15
	Arizona	Y	50380 FQ	57140 MW	66170 TQ	USBLS	5/15
	Tucson MSA, AZ	Y	35540 FQ	43150 MW	56430 TQ	USBLS	5/15
	Arkansas	Y	36790 FQ	45090 MW	56680 TQ	USBLS	5/15
	Little Rock-North Little Rock-Conway MSA, AR	Y	37800 FQ	48370 MW	57960 TQ	USBLS	5/15
	California	H	22.34 FQ	28.36 MW	37.06 TQ	CABLS	1/16-3/16
	Anaheim-Santa Ana-Irvine PMSA, CA	H	21.82 FQ	27.55 MW	36.17 TQ	CABLS	1/16-3/16
	Los Angeles-Long Beach-Glendale PMSA, CA	H	22.21 FQ	28.94 MW	39.39 TQ	CABLS	1/16-3/16
	Oakland-Hayward-Berkeley PMSA, CA	H	21.48 FQ	27.84 MW	37.85 TQ	CABLS	1/16-3/16
	Riverside-San Bernardino-Ontario MSA, CA	H	19.75 FQ	23.72 MW	30.97 TQ	CABLS	1/16-3/16
	Sacramento–Roseville–Arden-Arcade MSA, CA	H	24.96 FQ	32.27 MW	40.24 TQ	CABLS	1/16-3/16
	San Diego-Carlsbad MSA, CA	H	22.59 FQ	27.30 MW	32.93 TQ	CABLS	1/16-3/16
	San Francisco-Redwood City-South San Francisco PMSA, CA	H	24.88 FQ	30.86 MW	37.99 TQ	CABLS	1/16-3/16
	Colorado	Y	44140 FQ	59290 MW	72520 TQ	USBLS	5/15
	Denver-Aurora-Lakewood MSA, CO	Y	40960 FQ	62390 MW	73550 TQ	USBLS	5/15
	Connecticut	Y		64096 MW		CTBLS	1/16-3/16
	Bridgeport-Stamford-Norwalk MSA, CT	Y	50140 FQ	57290 MW	63490 TQ	USBLS	5/15
	Hartford-West Hartford-East Hartford MSA, CT	Y	58960 FQ	69010 MW	77620 TQ	USBLS	5/15
	Delaware	Y	51020 FQ	59290 MW	69750 TQ	USBLS	5/15
	Wilmington PMSA, DE-MD-NJ	Y	51820 FQ	62170 MW	73740 TQ	USBLS	5/15
	Washington-Arlington-Alexandria PMSA, DC-VA-MD-WV	Y	47770 FQ	57130 MW	66940 TQ	USBLS	5/15
	Florida	H	16.06 AE	23.05 MW	28.18 AEX	FLBLS	7/16-9/16
	Fort Lauderdale-Pompano Beach-Deerfield Beach PMSA, FL	H	15.45 AE	22.06 MW	28.78 AEX	FLBLS	7/16-9/16
	Miami-Miami Beach-Kendall PMSA, FL	H	16.68 AE	23.01 MW	26.95 AEX	FLBLS	7/16-9/16
	Orlando-Kissimmee-Sanford MSA, FL	H	12.77 AE	17.58 MW	21.05 AEX	FLBLS	7/16-9/16
	Tampa-St. Petersburg-Clearwater MSA, FL	H	15.32 AE	23.19 MW	27.02 AEX	FLBLS	7/16-9/16
	Georgia	Y	42620 FQ	54560 MW	70080 TQ	USBLS	5/15
	Atlanta-Sandy Springs-Roswell MSA, GA	Y	41030 FQ	48870 MW	70110 TQ	USBLS	5/15
	Augusta-Richmond County MSA, GA-SC	Y	40680 FQ	48510 MW	60310 TQ	USBLS	5/15
	Idaho	Y	38160 FQ	46310 MW	56470 TQ	USBLS	5/15
	Boise City MSA, ID	Y	34890 FQ	42310 MW	50440 TQ	USBLS	5/15
	Illinois	Y	41910 FQ	52580 MW	68310 TQ	USBLS	5/15
	Chicago-Naperville-Arlington Heights PMSA, IL	Y	41650 FQ	52440 MW	65680 TQ	USBLS	5/15
	Lake County-Kenosha County PMSA, IL-WI	Y	41030 FQ	52700 MW	71190 TQ	USBLS	5/15
	Indiana	Y	38210 FQ	47080 MW	58070 TQ	USBLS	5/15
	Gary PMSA, IN	Y	40410 FQ	47800 MW	58670 TQ	USBLS	5/15
	Indianapolis-Carmel-Anderson MSA, IN	Y	41880 FQ	51880 MW	61500 TQ	USBLS	5/15
	Iowa	Y	42120 FQ	51200 MW	59870 TQ	USBLS	5/15
	Des Moines-West Des Moines MSA, IA	Y	41370 FQ	51040 MW	58160 TQ	USBLS	5/15
	Kansas	Y	45640 FQ	59030 MW	80920 TQ	USBLS	5/15

AE	Average entry wage	AWR	Average wage range	H	Hourly
AEX	Average experienced wage	B	Biweekly	HI	Highest wage paid
ATC	Average total compensation	D	Daily	HR	High end range
AW	Average wage paid	FQ	First quartile wage	LO	Lowest wage paid

LR	Low end range	MTC	Median total compensation	TCC	Total cash compensation
M	Monthly	MW	Median wage paid	TQ	Third quartile wage
MCC	Median cash compensation	MWR	Median wage range	W	Weekly
ME	Median entry wage	S	See annotated source	Y	Yearly

Occupation/Type/Industry	Location	Per	Low	Mid	High	Source	Date
Industrial Engineering Technician	Wichita MSA, KS	Y	57270 FQ	76420 MW	95690 TQ	USBLS	5/15
	Kentucky	Y	42430 FQ	55810 MW	75320 TQ	USBLS	5/15
	Louisville-Jefferson County MSA, KY-IN	Y	40160 FQ	49620 MW	66750 TQ	USBLS	5/15
	Louisiana	Y	33480 FQ	61570 MW	86330 TQ	USBLS	5/15
	Baton Rouge MSA, LA	Y	55430 FQ	90650 MW	118600 TQ	USBLS	5/15
	New Orleans-Metairie MSA, LA	Y	61040 FQ	74420 MW	93800 TQ	USBLS	5/15
	Maine	Y	47780 FQ	57340 MW	75990 TQ	USBLS	5/15
	Portland-South Portland MSA, ME	Y	48700 FQ	56510 MW	67510 TQ	USBLS	5/15
	Maryland	Y	43072 AE	61602 MW	70867 AEX	MDBLS	4/16
	Baltimore-Columbia-Towson MSA, MD	Y	45860 FQ	56500 MW	70790 TQ	USBLS	5/15
	Massachusetts	Y	45340 FQ	55930 MW	68340 TQ	USBLS	5/15
	Boston-Cambridge-Newton NECTA, MA	Y	48490 FQ	58670 MW	73140 TQ	USBLS	5/15
	Worcester MSA, MA-CT	Y	44250 FQ	53320 MW	62170 TQ	USBLS	5/15
	Michigan	Y	39510 FQ	50060 MW	66330 TQ	USBLS	5/15
	Detroit-Dearborn-Livonia PMSA, MI	Y	56210 FQ	68220 MW	77300 TQ	USBLS	5/15
	Grand Rapids-Wyoming MSA, MI	Y	37440 FQ	44870 MW	54050 TQ	USBLS	5/15
	Minnesota	Y	41995 FQ	50967 MW	60836 TQ	MNBLS	1/16-3/16
	Minneapolis-St. Paul-Bloomington MSA, MN-WI	Y	45030 FQ	54223 MW	62852 TQ	MNBLS	1/16-3/16
	Mississippi	Y	38780 FQ	52040 MW	60250 TQ	USBLS	5/15
	Missouri	Y	45390 FQ	60900 MW	81900 TQ	USBLS	5/15
	Kansas City MSA, MO-KS	Y	42330 FQ	50710 MW	62030 TQ	USBLS	5/15
	St. Louis MSA, MO-IL	Y	51820 FQ	72050 MW	89720 TQ	USBLS	5/15
	Montana	Y	39630 FQ	45450 MW	59170 TQ	USBLS	5/15
	Nebraska	Y	41150 FQ	48055 MW	59350 TQ	NEBLS	7/16-9/16
	Omaha-Council Bluffs MSA, NE-IA	Y	37925 FQ	44835 MW	51655 TQ	NEBLS	7/16-9/16
	Nevada	Y	37830 FQ	47080 MW	61770 TQ	USBLS	5/15
	Las Vegas-Henderson-Paradise MSA, NV	Y	36800 FQ	43400 MW	51950 TQ	USBLS	5/15
	New Hampshire	H	20.16 AE	24.86 MW	28.56 AEX	NHBLS	6/16
	Nashua NECTA, NH-MA	Y	46810 FQ	54110 MW	61940 TQ	USBLS	5/15
	New Jersey	Y	44070 FQ	53980 MW	67820 TQ	USBLS	5/15
	Camden PMSA, NJ	Y	43970 FQ	49780 MW	58520 TQ	USBLS	5/15
	Newark PMSA, NJ-PA	Y	45950 FQ	57500 MW	76960 TQ	USBLS	5/15
	Trenton MSA, NJ	Y	38220 FQ	43440 MW	48300 TQ	USBLS	5/15
	New Mexico	Y	43120 FQ	56240 MW	70830 TQ	USBLS	5/15
	Albuquerque MSA, NM	Y	42750 FQ	55860 MW	70370 TQ	USBLS	5/15
	New York	Y	38180 AE	54920 MW	64740 AEX	NYBLS	1/16-3/16
	Buffalo-Cheektowaga-Niagara Falls MSA, NY	Y	44000 FQ	54140 MW	65770 TQ	USBLS	5/15
	Nassau County-Suffolk County PMSA, NY	Y	49830 FQ	55280 MW	60600 TQ	USBLS	5/15
	New York-Jersey City-White Plains PMSA, NY-NJ	Y	30590 FQ	51800 MW	62420 TQ	USBLS	5/15
	Rochester MSA, NY	Y	40900 FQ	54510 MW	78480 TQ	USBLS	5/15
	North Carolina	Y	40260 FQ	50750 MW	60360 TQ	USBLS	5/15
	Charlotte-Concord-Gastonia MSA, NC-SC	Y	42450 FQ	48750 MW	58390 TQ	USBLS	5/15
	Raleigh MSA, NC	Y	40400 FQ	58770 MW	73000 TQ	USBLS	5/15
	North Dakota	Y	39370 FQ	44370 MW	48830 TQ	USBLS	5/15
	Fargo MSA, ND-MN	Y	32440 FQ	38880 MW	48680 TQ	USBLS	5/15
	Ohio	Y	40280 FQ	49130 MW	61350 TQ	USBLS	5/15
	Cincinnati MSA, OH-KY-IN	Y	45890 FQ	57720 MW	77620 TQ	USBLS	5/15
	Cleveland-Elyria MSA, OH	Y	38410 FQ	46830 MW	57840 TQ	USBLS	5/15
	Columbus MSA, OH	Y	41010 FQ	55010 MW	69110 TQ	USBLS	5/15
	Oklahoma	Y	43100 FQ	59690 MW	70280 TQ	USBLS	5/15
	Oklahoma City MSA, OK	Y	58860 FQ	66370 MW	74170 TQ	USBLS	5/15
	Tulsa MSA, OK	Y	37380 FQ	46970 MW	60520 TQ	USBLS	5/15
	Oregon	H	21.82 FQ	26.47 MW	33.69 TQ	ORBLS	2016
	Portland-Vancouver-Hillsboro MSA, OR-WA	Y	45000 FQ	54990 MW	70900 TQ	USBLS	5/15
	Pennsylvania	Y	40690 FQ	50620 MW	64310 TQ	USBLS	5/15
	Allentown-Bethlehem-Easton MSA, PA-NJ	Y	36350 FQ	47280 MW	62220 TQ	USBLS	5/15

AE	Average entry wage	AWR	Average wage range	H	Hourly
AEX	Average experienced wage	B	Biweekly	HI	Highest wage paid
ATC	Average total compensation	D	Daily	HR	High end range
AW	Average wage paid	FQ	First quartile wage	LO	Lowest wage paid

LR	Low end range	MTC	Median total compensation	TCC	Total cash compensation
M	Monthly	MW	Median wage paid	TQ	Third quartile wage
MCC	Median cash compensation	MWR	Median wage range	W	Weekly
ME	Median entry wage	S	See annotated source	Y	Yearly

Occupation/Type/Industry	Location	Per	Low	Mid	High	Source	Date
Industrial Engineering Technician	Harrisburg-Carlisle MSA, PA	Y	26410 FQ	34770 MW	54930 TQ	USBLS	5/15
	Montgomery County-Bucks County-Chester County PMSA, PA	Y	46630 FQ	59350 MW	79180 TQ	USBLS	5/15
	Philadelphia PMSA, PA	Y	46900 FQ	63740 MW	82270 TQ	USBLS	5/15
	Pittsburgh MSA, PA	Y	42570 FQ	51220 MW	61580 TQ	USBLS	5/15
	Rhode Island	Y	43360 FQ	50080 MW	59750 TQ	USBLS	5/15
	Providence-Warwick MSA, RI-MA	Y	43040 FQ	51000 MW	61600 TQ	USBLS	5/15
	South Carolina	Y	38690 FQ	46790 MW	57710 TQ	USBLS	5/15
	Charleston-North Charleston MSA, SC	Y	47200 FQ	55300 MW	62840 TQ	USBLS	5/15
	Columbia MSA, SC	Y	39910 FQ	50060 MW	60800 TQ	USBLS	5/15
	Greenville-Anderson-Mauldin MSA, SC	Y	37860 FQ	47570 MW	57650 TQ	USBLS	5/15
	South Dakota	Y	35140 FQ	41090 MW	48190 TQ	USBLS	5/15
	Sioux Falls MSA, SD	Y	35790 FQ	40260 MW	46140 TQ	USBLS	5/15
	Tennessee	Y	35240 FQ	43300 MW	57920 TQ	USBLS	5/15
	Knoxville MSA, TN	Y	38890 FQ	56600 MW	77980 TQ	USBLS	5/15
	Memphis MSA, TN-MS-AR	Y	37190 FQ	45040 MW	55580 TQ	USBLS	5/15
	Nashville-Davidson–Murfreesboro–Franklin MSA, TN	Y	33670 FQ	38940 MW	48080 TQ	USBLS	5/15
	Texas	Y	49050 FQ	62730 MW	79150 TQ	USBLS	5/15
	Austin-Round Rock MSA, TX	Y	53360 FQ	58590 MW	67100 TQ	USBLS	5/15
	Dallas-Plano-Irving PMSA, TX	Y	51850 FQ	66100 MW	79080 TQ	USBLS	5/15
	Fort Worth-Arlington PMSA, TX	Y	56200 FQ	75030 MW	95350 TQ	USBLS	5/15
	Houston-The Woodlands-Sugar Land MSA, TX	Y	45060 FQ	60470 MW	79660 TQ	USBLS	5/15
	San Antonio-New Braunfels MSA, TX	Y	43750 FQ	59360 MW	73280 TQ	USBLS	5/15
	Utah	Y	40870 FQ	53560 MW	67590 TQ	USBLS	5/15
	Ogden-Clearfield MSA, UT	Y	58560 FQ	66370 MW	72540 TQ	USBLS	5/15
	Provo-Orem MSA, UT	Y	43910 FQ	54520 MW	63160 TQ	USBLS	5/15
	Salt Lake City MSA, UT	Y	36790 FQ	44010 MW	50780 TQ	USBLS	5/15
	Vermont	Y	51240 FQ	55440 MW	59640 TQ	USBLS	5/15
	Burlington-South Burlington MSA, VT	Y	51590 FQ	55660 MW	59720 TQ	USBLS	5/15
	Virginia	Y	44610 FQ	55020 MW	67910 TQ	USBLS	5/15
	Richmond MSA, VA	Y	42610 FQ	60700 MW	79580 TQ	USBLS	5/15
	Virginia Beach-Norfolk-Newport News MSA, VA-NC	Y	44060 FQ	55120 MW	71480 TQ	USBLS	5/15
	Washington	H	32.32 FQ	38.72 MW	46.16 TQ	WABLS	3/16
	West Virginia	Y	40730 FQ	52150 MW	67620 TQ	USBLS	5/15
	Wisconsin	Y	39150 FQ	47540 MW	57780 TQ	USBLS	5/15
	Madison MSA, WI	Y	44060 FQ	51300 MW	57890 TQ	USBLS	5/15
	Milwaukee-Waukesha-West Allis MSA, WI	Y	37560 FQ	47650 MW	59190 TQ	USBLS	5/15
	Puerto Rico	Y	28870 FQ	36630 MW	48650 TQ	USBLS	5/15
	San Juan-Carolina-Caguas MSA, PR	Y	28730 FQ	37650 MW	51530 TQ	USBLS	5/15
Industrial Hygienist							
Airports, Municipal Government	Los Angeles, CA	Y			110032 HI	CACIT	6/23/16
Fire Department, Municipal Government	Los Angeles, CA	Y			94215 HI	CACIT	6/23/16
Industrial Machinery Mechanic	Alabama	Y	35128 AE	52244 AW	60808 AEX	ALBLS	6/16
	Birmingham-Hoover MSA, AL	Y	34162 AE	49091 AW	56556 AEX	ALBLS	6/16
	Alaska	Y	52150 FQ	70150 MW	83720 TQ	USBLS	5/15
	Anchorage MSA, AK	Y	46360 FQ	68690 MW	84220 TQ	USBLS	5/15
	Arizona	Y	40650 FQ	48880 MW	58770 TQ	USBLS	5/15
	Phoenix-Mesa-Scottsdale MSA, AZ	Y	40600 FQ	49960 MW	59470 TQ	USBLS	5/15
	Tucson MSA, AZ	Y	41130 FQ	45720 MW	51300 TQ	USBLS	5/15
	Arkansas	Y	34780 FQ	43360 MW	56180 TQ	USBLS	5/15
	Little Rock-North Little Rock-Conway MSA, AR	Y	35860 FQ	46140 MW	55990 TQ	USBLS	5/15
	California	H	21.34 FQ	27.52 MW	35.08 TQ	CABLS	1/16-3/16
	Anaheim-Santa Ana-Irvine PMSA, CA	H	21.44 FQ	27.06 MW	32.29 TQ	CABLS	1/16-3/16

AE	Average entry wage	AWR	Average wage range	H	Hourly	LR	Low end range	MTC	Median total compensation	TCC	Total cash compensation
AEX	Average experienced wage	B	Biweekly	HI	Highest wage paid	M	Monthly	MW	Median wage paid	TQ	Third quartile wage
ATC	Average total compensation	D	Daily	HR	High end range	MCC	Median cash compensation	MWR	Median wage range	W	Weekly
AW	Average wage paid	FQ	First quartile wage	LO	Lowest wage paid	ME	Median entry wage	S	See annotated source	Y	Yearly

Occupation/Type/Industry	Location	Per	Low	Mid	High	Source	Date
Industrial Machinery Mechanic	Los Angeles-Long Beach-Glendale PMSA, CA	H	22.12 FQ	29.12 MW	38.85 TQ	CABLS	1/16-3/16
	Oakland-Hayward-Berkeley PMSA, CA	H	25.14 FQ	30.49 MW	42.21 TQ	CABLS	1/16-3/16
	Riverside-San Bernardino-Ontario MSA, CA	H	20.01 FQ	24.25 MW	30.34 TQ	CABLS	1/16-3/16
	Sacramento–Roseville–Arden-Arcade MSA, CA	H	22.62 FQ	30.23 MW	36.22 TQ	CABLS	1/16-3/16
	San Diego-Carlsbad MSA, CA	H	20.98 FQ	25.85 MW	29.99 TQ	CABLS	1/16-3/16
	San Francisco-Redwood City-South San Francisco PMSA, CA	H	28.18 FQ	37.41 MW	45.63 TQ	CABLS	1/16-3/16
	Colorado	Y	40340 FQ	53950 MW	67320 TQ	USBLS	5/15
	Denver-Aurora-Lakewood MSA, CO	Y	39500 FQ	55130 MW	68680 TQ	USBLS	5/15
	Connecticut	Y		53753 MW		CTBLS	1/16-3/16
	Bridgeport-Stamford-Norwalk MSA, CT	Y	40790 FQ	50930 MW	62190 TQ	USBLS	5/15
	Hartford-West Hartford-East Hartford MSA, CT	Y	41980 FQ	55550 MW	68780 TQ	USBLS	5/15
	Delaware	Y	42480 FQ	53590 MW	64300 TQ	USBLS	5/15
	Wilmington PMSA, DE-MD-NJ	Y	52460 FQ	61910 MW	72800 TQ	USBLS	5/15
	District of Columbia	Y	54620 FQ	62930 MW	66270 TQ	USBLS	5/15
	Washington-Arlington-Alexandria PMSA, DC-VA-MD-WV	Y	45290 FQ	57000 MW	68140 TQ	USBLS	5/15
	Florida	H	15.87 AE	22.79 MW	26.88 AEX	FLBLS	7/16-9/16
	Fort Lauderdale-Pompano Beach-Deerfield Beach PMSA, FL	H	15.66 AE	20.83 MW	25.51 AEX	FLBLS	7/16-9/16
	Miami-Miami Beach-Kendall PMSA, FL	H	15.40 AE	22.26 MW	27.47 AEX	FLBLS	7/16-9/16
	Orlando-Kissimmee-Sanford MSA, FL	H	16.53 AE	23.99 MW	27.58 AEX	FLBLS	7/16-9/16
	Tampa-St. Petersburg-Clearwater MSA, FL	H	16.25 AE	22.66 MW	25.68 AEX	FLBLS	7/16-9/16
	Georgia	Y	34810 FQ	43970 MW	55830 TQ	USBLS	5/15
	Atlanta-Sandy Springs-Roswell MSA, GA	Y	35850 FQ	45020 MW	56480 TQ	USBLS	5/15
	Augusta-Richmond County MSA, GA-SC	Y	41680 FQ	52600 MW	59040 TQ	USBLS	5/15
	Hawaii	Y	46750 FQ	56860 MW	67790 TQ	USBLS	5/15
	Urban Honolulu MSA, HI	Y	52810 FQ	61050 MW	70330 TQ	USBLS	5/15
	Idaho	Y	41140 FQ	48470 MW	58420 TQ	USBLS	5/15
	Boise City MSA, ID	Y	37980 FQ	45880 MW	55440 TQ	USBLS	5/15
	Illinois	Y	43280 FQ	54490 MW	64630 TQ	USBLS	5/15
	Chicago-Naperville-Arlington Heights PMSA, IL	Y	42570 FQ	55630 MW	69770 TQ	USBLS	5/15
	Lake County-Kenosha County PMSA, IL-WI	Y	43530 FQ	53980 MW	61820 TQ	USBLS	5/15
	Indiana	Y	40140 FQ	48970 MW	61630 TQ	USBLS	5/15
	Gary PMSA, IN	Y	45230 FQ	52840 MW	66670 TQ	USBLS	5/15
	Indianapolis-Carmel-Anderson MSA, IN	Y	40120 FQ	48700 MW	60840 TQ	USBLS	5/15
	Iowa	Y	39360 FQ	46980 MW	57190 TQ	USBLS	5/15
	Des Moines-West Des Moines MSA, IA	Y	40020 FQ	47100 MW	56600 TQ	USBLS	5/15
	Kansas	Y	39760 FQ	48640 MW	60070 TQ	USBLS	5/15
	Wichita MSA, KS	Y	42860 FQ	55980 MW	68780 TQ	USBLS	5/15
	Kentucky	Y	38360 FQ	48050 MW	60090 TQ	USBLS	5/15
	Louisville-Jefferson County MSA, KY-IN	Y	40280 FQ	47410 MW	56780 TQ	USBLS	5/15
	Louisiana	Y	37560 FQ	48970 MW	62090 TQ	USBLS	5/15
	Baton Rouge MSA, LA	Y	39500 FQ	51890 MW	67500 TQ	USBLS	5/15
	New Orleans-Metairie MSA, LA	Y	36990 FQ	49170 MW	72350 TQ	USBLS	5/15
	Maine	Y	43240 FQ	52760 MW	59320 TQ	USBLS	5/15
	Portland-South Portland MSA, ME	Y	47600 FQ	55750 MW	62760 TQ	USBLS	5/15
	Maryland	Y	38583 AE	52878 MW	60025 AEX	MDBLS	4/16

Occupation/Type/Industry	Location	Per	Low	Mid	High	Source	Date
Industrial Machinery Mechanic	Baltimore-Columbia-Towson MSA, MD	Y	44160 FQ	52680 MW	59760 TQ	USBLS	5/15
	Salisbury MSA, MD-DE	Y	35230 FQ	42300 MW	49540 TQ	USBLS	5/15
	Massachusetts	Y	44730 FQ	55220 MW	68030 TQ	USBLS	5/15
	Boston-Cambridge-Newton NECTA, MA	Y	46020 FQ	57920 MW	72530 TQ	USBLS	5/15
	Worcester MSA, MA-CT	Y	43780 FQ	50970 MW	60220 TQ	USBLS	5/15
	Michigan	Y	38910 FQ	50760 MW	62670 TQ	USBLS	5/15
	Detroit-Dearborn-Livonia PMSA, MI	Y	48330 FQ	58540 MW	67920 TQ	USBLS	5/15
	Grand Rapids-Wyoming MSA, MI	Y	35890 FQ	44700 MW	54460 TQ	USBLS	5/15
	Minnesota	Y	42811 FQ	52446 MW	62462 TQ	MNBLS	1/16-3/16
	Minneapolis-St. Paul-Bloomington MSA, MN-WI	Y	44421 FQ	53773 MW	62875 TQ	MNBLS	1/16-3/16
	Mississippi	Y	37990 FQ	48690 MW	58840 TQ	USBLS	5/15
	Jackson MSA, MS	Y	50420 FQ	55730 MW	61310 TQ	USBLS	5/15
	Missouri	Y	40250 FQ	49370 MW	60020 TQ	USBLS	5/15
	Kansas City MSA, MO-KS	Y	40840 FQ	49940 MW	60660 TQ	USBLS	5/15
	St. Louis MSA, MO-IL	Y	45180 FQ	53510 MW	60010 TQ	USBLS	5/15
	Montana	Y	39950 FQ	54900 MW	68510 TQ	USBLS	5/15
	Billings MSA, MT	Y	32600 FQ	45190 MW	60010 TQ	USBLS	5/15
	Nebraska	Y	36275 FQ	44510 MW	54195 TQ	NEBLS	7/16-9/16
	Omaha-Council Bluffs MSA, NE-IA	Y	37725 FQ	45540 MW	55515 TQ	NEBLS	7/16-9/16
	Nevada	Y	45910 FQ	61030 MW	72060 TQ	USBLS	5/15
	Las Vegas-Henderson-Paradise MSA, NV	Y	39490 FQ	52020 MW	64340 TQ	USBLS	5/15
	New Hampshire	H	19.88 AE	26.09 MW	30.01 AEX	NHBLS	6/16
	Manchester NECTA, NH	H	19.03 AE	23.43 MW	26.89 AEX	NHBLS	6/16
	Nashua NECTA, NH-MA	Y	47860 FQ	57010 MW	65670 TQ	USBLS	5/15
	New Jersey	Y	43150 FQ	54250 MW	65560 TQ	USBLS	5/15
	Camden PMSA, NJ	Y	42010 FQ	51650 MW	61400 TQ	USBLS	5/15
	Newark PMSA, NJ-PA	Y	43860 FQ	53970 MW	66980 TQ	USBLS	5/15
	Trenton MSA, NJ	Y	54510 FQ	61280 MW	71760 TQ	USBLS	5/15
	New Mexico	Y	35910 FQ	45130 MW	59490 TQ	USBLS	5/15
	Albuquerque MSA, NM	Y	33850 FQ	38520 MW	48580 TQ	USBLS	5/15
	New York	Y	38420 AE	52000 MW	61700 AEX	NYBLS	1/16-3/16
	Buffalo-Cheektowaga-Niagara Falls MSA, NY	Y	44160 FQ	52600 MW	60940 TQ	USBLS	5/15
	Nassau County-Suffolk County PMSA, NY	Y	42670 FQ	54470 MW	70660 TQ	USBLS	5/15
	New York-Jersey City-White Plains PMSA, NY-NJ	Y	42930 FQ	54810 MW	67690 TQ	USBLS	5/15
	Rochester MSA, NY	Y	38720 FQ	44910 MW	51980 TQ	USBLS	5/15
	North Carolina	Y	35660 FQ	45790 MW	57920 TQ	USBLS	5/15
	Charlotte-Concord-Gastonia MSA, NC-SC	Y	33420 FQ	45940 MW	60500 TQ	USBLS	5/15
	Hickory-Lenoir-Morganton MSA, NC	Y	35000 FQ	42780 MW	52970 TQ	USBLS	5/15
	Raleigh MSA, NC	Y	40120 FQ	48070 MW	58830 TQ	USBLS	5/15
	North Dakota	Y	44980 FQ	57160 MW	71820 TQ	USBLS	5/15
	Fargo MSA, ND-MN	Y	37620 FQ	47650 MW	59810 TQ	USBLS	5/15
	Ohio	Y	37630 FQ	47040 MW	59090 TQ	USBLS	5/15
	Cincinnati MSA, OH-KY-IN	Y	40520 FQ	50280 MW	61450 TQ	USBLS	5/15
	Cleveland-Elyria MSA, OH	Y	36360 FQ	44000 MW	53490 TQ	USBLS	5/15
	Columbus MSA, OH	Y	39080 FQ	49350 MW	59890 TQ	USBLS	5/15
	Oklahoma	Y	37230 FQ	47890 MW	59300 TQ	USBLS	5/15
	Oklahoma City MSA, OK	Y	39210 FQ	48650 MW	57540 TQ	USBLS	5/15
	Tulsa MSA, OK	Y	36810 FQ	47250 MW	60320 TQ	USBLS	5/15
	Oregon	H	21.25 FQ	26.00 MW	30.67 TQ	ORBLS	2016
	Portland-Vancouver-Hillsboro MSA, OR-WA	Y	47450 FQ	57580 MW	70410 TQ	USBLS	5/15
	Pennsylvania	Y	40050 FQ	47620 MW	57570 TQ	USBLS	5/15
	Allentown-Bethlehem-Easton MSA, PA-NJ	Y	40450 FQ	48540 MW	58090 TQ	USBLS	5/15
	Harrisburg-Carlisle MSA, PA	Y	39370 FQ	47590 MW	56200 TQ	USBLS	5/15
	Montgomery County-Bucks County-Chester County PMSA, PA	Y	41540 FQ	48520 MW	59360 TQ	USBLS	5/15
	Philadelphia PMSA, PA	Y	42050 FQ	50010 MW	61920 TQ	USBLS	5/15
	Pittsburgh MSA, PA	Y	39810 FQ	47050 MW	57200 TQ	USBLS	5/15

AE	Average entry wage	**AWR**	Average wage range	**H**	Hourly
AEX	Average experienced wage	**B**	Biweekly	**HI**	Highest wage paid
ATC	Average total compensation	**D**	Daily	**HR**	High end range
AW	Average wage paid	**FQ**	First quartile wage	**LO**	Lowest wage paid

LR	Low end range	**MTC**	Median total compensation
M	Monthly	**MW**	Median wage paid
MCC	Median cash compensation	**MWR**	Median wage range
ME	Median entry wage	**S**	See annotated source

TCC	Total cash compensation
TQ	Third quartile wage
W	Weekly
Y	Yearly

Occupation/Type/Industry	Location	Per	Low	Mid	High	Source	Date
Industrial Machinery Mechanic	Rhode Island	Y	38090 FQ	49620 MW	60070 TQ	USBLS	5/15
	Providence-Warwick MSA, RI-MA	Y	37990 FQ	48230 MW	59540 TQ	USBLS	5/15
	South Carolina	Y	39470 FQ	49190 MW	61130 TQ	USBLS	5/15
	Charleston-North Charleston MSA, SC	Y	43110 FQ	52490 MW	73790 TQ	USBLS	5/15
	Columbia MSA, SC	Y	46140 FQ	55680 MW	65060 TQ	USBLS	5/15
	Greenville-Anderson-Mauldin MSA, SC	Y	36070 FQ	44420 MW	54630 TQ	USBLS	5/15
	South Dakota	Y	36780 FQ	42970 MW	49620 TQ	USBLS	5/15
	Sioux Falls MSA, SD	Y	35620 FQ	40220 MW	46950 TQ	USBLS	5/15
	Tennessee	Y	36300 FQ	48810 MW	64830 TQ	USBLS	5/15
	Knoxville MSA, TN	Y	37190 FQ	47950 MW	58810 TQ	USBLS	5/15
	Memphis MSA, TN-MS-AR	Y	36240 FQ	48750 MW	61830 TQ	USBLS	5/15
	Nashville-Davidson–Murfreesboro–Franklin MSA, TN	Y	41710 FQ	55960 MW	69630 TQ	USBLS	5/15
	Texas	Y	37190 FQ	48840 MW	63750 TQ	USBLS	5/15
	Austin-Round Rock MSA, TX	Y	42120 FQ	54480 MW	67510 TQ	USBLS	5/15
	Dallas-Plano-Irving PMSA, TX	Y	38080 FQ	49170 MW	61760 TQ	USBLS	5/15
	Fort Worth-Arlington PMSA, TX	Y	38670 FQ	48150 MW	58050 TQ	USBLS	5/15
	Houston-The Woodlands-Sugar Land MSA, TX	Y	37040 FQ	51700 MW	70030 TQ	USBLS	5/15
	San Antonio-New Braunfels MSA, TX	Y	41130 FQ	48430 MW	60000 TQ	USBLS	5/15
	Utah	Y	43470 FQ	52550 MW	61420 TQ	USBLS	5/15
	Ogden-Clearfield MSA, UT	Y	46700 FQ	55470 MW	61080 TQ	USBLS	5/15
	Provo-Orem MSA, UT	Y	35200 FQ	43260 MW	48230 TQ	USBLS	5/15
	Salt Lake City MSA, UT	Y	43820 FQ	52400 MW	59870 TQ	USBLS	5/15
	Vermont	Y	42570 FQ	50130 MW	59690 TQ	USBLS	5/15
	Burlington-South Burlington MSA, VT	Y	43760 FQ	49810 MW	57380 TQ	USBLS	5/15
	Virginia	Y	37170 FQ	47860 MW	58690 TQ	USBLS	5/15
	Richmond MSA, VA	Y	40170 FQ	53600 MW	64240 TQ	USBLS	5/15
	Virginia Beach-Norfolk-Newport News MSA, VA-NC	Y	41350 FQ	50390 MW	60330 TQ	USBLS	5/15
	Washington	H	21.52 FQ	26.92 MW	33.62 TQ	WABLS	3/16
	Seattle-Bellevue-Everett PMSA, WA	H	24.16 FQ	29.24 MW	38.18 TQ	WABLS	3/16
	Tacoma-Lakewood PMSA, WA	H	22.03 FQ	27.82 MW	38.59 TQ	WABLS	3/16
	West Virginia	Y	34270 FQ	42450 MW	50880 TQ	USBLS	5/15
	Huntington-Ashland MSA, WV-KY-OH	Y	37370 FQ	46220 MW	58800 TQ	USBLS	5/15
	Wisconsin	Y	41310 FQ	48880 MW	58270 TQ	USBLS	5/15
	Madison MSA, WI	Y	42280 FQ	48100 MW	56500 TQ	USBLS	5/15
	Milwaukee-Waukesha-West Allis MSA, WI	Y	44420 FQ	53690 MW	63260 TQ	USBLS	5/15
	Wyoming	Y	44890 FQ	58180 MW	73450 TQ	USBLS	5/15
	Casper MSA, WY	Y	40690 FQ	51390 MW	63560 TQ	USBLS	5/15
	Cheyenne MSA, WY	Y	44050 FQ	55580 MW	60440 TQ	USBLS	5/15
	Puerto Rico	Y	24250 FQ	29410 MW	37350 TQ	USBLS	5/15
	San Juan-Carolina-Caguas MSA, PR	Y	24890 FQ	29880 MW	37840 TQ	USBLS	5/15
	Guam	Y	40650 FQ	45670 MW	51820 TQ	USBLS	5/15
Industrial-Organizational Psychologist	California	H	33.92 FQ	39.78 MW	85.35 TQ	CABLS	1/16-3/16
	Florida	H	24.76 AE	34.91 MW	44.80 AEX	FLBLS	7/16-9/16
	Massachusetts	Y	65930 FQ	82790 MW	101270 TQ	USBLS	5/15
	Minnesota	Y	63719 FQ	102841 MW	121541 TQ	MNBLS	1/16-3/16
	North Carolina	Y	67730 FQ	73360 MW	79200 TQ	USBLS	5/15
	Ohio	Y	57350 FQ	68950 MW	90710 TQ	USBLS	5/15
	Pennsylvania	Y	65540 FQ	101520 MW	148590 TQ	USBLS	5/15
	West Virginia	Y	66270 FQ	71720 MW	77180 TQ	USBLS	5/15
Industrial Production Manager	Alabama	Y	66653 AE	99411 AW	115800 AEX	ALBLS	6/16
	Birmingham-Hoover MSA, AL	Y	65987 AE	92841 AW	106278 AEX	ALBLS	6/16
	Alaska	Y	70080 FQ	92600 MW	121470 TQ	USBLS	5/15
	Anchorage MSA, AK	Y	65690 FQ	93740 MW	134230 TQ	USBLS	5/15
	Arizona	Y	70800 FQ	92310 MW	125150 TQ	USBLS	5/15

AE Average entry wage	**AWR** Average wage range	**H** Hourly	**LR** Low end range	**MTC** Median total compensation	**TCC** Total cash compensation
AEX Average experienced wage	**B** Biweekly	**HI** Highest wage paid	**M** Monthly	**MW** Median wage paid	**TQ** Third quartile wage
ATC Average total compensation	**D** Daily	**HR** High end range	**MCC** Median cash compensation	**MWR** Median wage range	**W** Weekly
AW Average wage paid	**FQ** First quartile wage	**LO** Lowest wage paid	**ME** Median entry wage	**S** See annotated source	**Y** Yearly

Occupation/Type/Industry	Location	Per	Low	Mid	High	Source	Date
Industrial Production Manager	Phoenix-Mesa-Scottsdale MSA, AZ	Y	72650 FQ	93470 MW	125530 TQ	USBLS	5/15
	Tucson MSA, AZ	Y	65700 FQ	89330 MW	127000 TQ	USBLS	5/15
	Arkansas	Y	63150 FQ	78340 MW	101500 TQ	USBLS	5/15
	Little Rock-North Little Rock-Conway MSA, AR	Y	67340 FQ	82530 MW	103810 TQ	USBLS	5/15
	California	H	35.50 FQ	47.68 MW	67.23 TQ	CABLS	1/16-3/16
	Anaheim-Santa Ana-Irvine PMSA, CA	H	35.42 FQ	46.49 MW	63.03 TQ	CABLS	1/16-3/16
	Los Angeles-Long Beach-Glendale PMSA, CA	H	33.64 FQ	46.10 MW	64.45 TQ	CABLS	1/16-3/16
	Oakland-Hayward-Berkeley PMSA, CA	H	35.59 FQ	49.23 MW	70.24 TQ	CABLS	1/16-3/16
	Riverside-San Bernardino-Ontario MSA, CA	H	33.96 FQ	45.52 MW	58.37 TQ	CABLS	1/16-3/16
	Sacramento–Roseville–Arden-Arcade MSA, CA	H	34.74 FQ	44.08 MW	62.43 TQ	CABLS	1/16-3/16
	San Diego-Carlsbad MSA, CA	H	36.31 FQ	45.18 MW	60.64 TQ	CABLS	1/16-3/16
	San Francisco-Redwood City-South San Francisco PMSA, CA	H	47.31 FQ	62.50 MW	80.23 TQ	CABLS	1/16-3/16
	Colorado	Y	79470 FQ	102230 MW	130690 TQ	USBLS	5/15
	Denver-Aurora-Lakewood MSA, CO	Y	78120 FQ	101640 MW	133070 TQ	USBLS	5/15
	Connecticut	Y		108107 MW		CTBLS	1/16-3/16
	Bridgeport-Stamford-Norwalk MSA, CT	Y	83470 FQ	112300 MW	142300 TQ	USBLS	5/15
	Hartford-West Hartford-East Hartford MSA, CT	Y	82120 FQ	99790 MW	126590 TQ	USBLS	5/15
	Delaware	Y	95300 FQ	117530 MW	159780 TQ	USBLS	5/15
	Wilmington PMSA, DE-MD-NJ	Y	100230 FQ	123940 MW	167810 TQ	USBLS	5/15
	District of Columbia	Y	79100 FQ	116320 MW	147290 TQ	USBLS	5/15
	Washington-Arlington-Alexandria PMSA, DC-VA-MD-WV	Y	96930 FQ	125910 MW	153680 TQ	USBLS	5/15
	Florida	H	37.20 AE	48.73 MW	67.64 AEX	FLBLS	7/16-9/16
	Fort Lauderdale-Pompano Beach-Deerfield Beach PMSA, FL	H	37.75 AE	48.00 MW	63.12 AEX	FLBLS	7/16-9/16
	Miami-Miami Beach-Kendall PMSA, FL	H	37.93 AE	51.80 MW	73.85 AEX	FLBLS	7/16-9/16
	Orlando-Kissimmee-Sanford MSA, FL	H	38.24 AE	47.61 MW	63.16 AEX	FLBLS	7/16-9/16
	Tampa-St. Petersburg-Clearwater MSA, FL	H	34.19 AE	46.50 MW	59.02 AEX	FLBLS	7/16-9/16
	Georgia	Y	68760 FQ	87530 MW	112230 TQ	USBLS	5/15
	Atlanta-Sandy Springs-Roswell MSA, GA	Y	70750 FQ	90810 MW	115600 TQ	USBLS	5/15
	Augusta-Richmond County MSA, GA-SC	Y	80220 FQ	107280 MW	151090 TQ	USBLS	5/15
	Hawaii	Y	54830 FQ	73550 MW	93930 TQ	USBLS	5/15
	Urban Honolulu MSA, HI	Y	55670 FQ	73290 MW	94300 TQ	USBLS	5/15
	Idaho	Y	57550 FQ	74890 MW	102270 TQ	USBLS	5/15
	Boise City MSA, ID	Y	56010 FQ	73340 MW	97130 TQ	USBLS	5/15
	Illinois	Y	69420 FQ	89330 MW	115470 TQ	USBLS	5/15
	Chicago-Naperville-Arlington Heights PMSA, IL	Y	72210 FQ	92420 MW	119320 TQ	USBLS	5/15
	Lake County-Kenosha County PMSA, IL-WI	Y	66990 FQ	86840 MW	118370 TQ	USBLS	5/15
	Indiana	Y	67280 FQ	84650 MW	105440 TQ	USBLS	5/15
	Gary PMSA, IN	Y	75980 FQ	96940 MW	115460 TQ	USBLS	5/15
	Indianapolis-Carmel-Anderson MSA, IN	Y	72040 FQ	89060 MW	115860 TQ	USBLS	5/15
	Iowa	Y	66730 FQ	82660 MW	104760 TQ	USBLS	5/15
	Des Moines-West Des Moines MSA, IA	Y	74430 FQ	90460 MW	109650 TQ	USBLS	5/15
	Kansas	Y	64090 FQ	78620 MW	101070 TQ	USBLS	5/15
	Wichita MSA, KS	Y	64620 FQ	85000 MW	107570 TQ	USBLS	5/15
	Kentucky	Y	65910 FQ	81640 MW	103030 TQ	USBLS	5/15
	Louisville-Jefferson County MSA, KY-IN	Y	62870 FQ	78480 MW	98350 TQ	USBLS	5/15

AE	Average entry wage	AWR	Average wage range	H	Hourly
AEX	Average experienced wage	B	Biweekly	HI	Highest wage paid
ATC	Average total compensation	D	Daily	HR	High end range
AW	Average wage paid	FQ	First quartile wage	LO	Lowest wage paid

LR	Low end range	MTC	Median total compensation	TCC	Total cash compensation
M	Monthly	MW	Median wage paid	TQ	Third quartile wage
MCC	Median cash compensation	MWR	Median wage range	W	Weekly
ME	Median entry wage	S	See annotated source	Y	Yearly

Occupation/Type/Industry	Location	Per	Low	Mid	High	Source	Date
Industrial Production Manager	Louisiana	Y	73150 FQ	98570 MW	140900 TQ	USBLS	5/15
	Baton Rouge MSA, LA	Y	88960 FQ	121190 MW	160630 TQ	USBLS	5/15
	New Orleans-Metairie MSA, LA	Y	74470 FQ	112870 MW	163350 TQ	USBLS	5/15
	Maine	Y	65760 FQ	84960 MW	109660 TQ	USBLS	5/15
	Portland-South Portland MSA, ME	Y	71980 FQ	85620 MW	115950 TQ	USBLS	5/15
	Maryland	Y	74397 AE	118507 MW	140562 AEX	MDBLS	4/16
	Baltimore-Columbia-Towson MSA, MD	Y	85920 FQ	110000 MW	145070 TQ	USBLS	5/15
	Salisbury MSA, MD-DE	Y	84710 FQ	99550 MW	122940 TQ	USBLS	5/15
	Massachusetts	Y	82900 FQ	102300 MW	131920 TQ	USBLS	5/15
	Boston-Cambridge-Newton NECTA, MA	Y	87600 FQ	108370 MW	140460 TQ	USBLS	5/15
	Worcester MSA, MA-CT	Y	74100 FQ	93880 MW	116840 TQ	USBLS	5/15
	Michigan	Y	80710 FQ	102950 MW	129620 TQ	USBLS	5/15
	Detroit-Dearborn-Livonia PMSA, MI	Y	96410 FQ	120210 MW	149400 TQ	USBLS	5/15
	Grand Rapids-Wyoming MSA, MI	Y	70840 FQ	90350 MW	114460 TQ	USBLS	5/15
	Minnesota	Y	74541 FQ	93675 MW	122024 TQ	MNBLS	1/16-3/16
	Minneapolis-St. Paul-Bloomington MSA, MN-WI	Y	78138 FQ	98684 MW	128192 TQ	MNBLS	1/16-3/16
	Mississippi	Y	63760 FQ	83530 MW	103830 TQ	USBLS	5/15
	Jackson MSA, MS	Y	59560 FQ	84150 MW	97790 TQ	USBLS	5/15
	Missouri	Y	67610 FQ	89810 MW	119820 TQ	USBLS	5/15
	Kansas City MSA, MO-KS	Y	70540 FQ	90290 MW	112990 TQ	USBLS	5/15
	St. Louis MSA, MO-IL	Y	70070 FQ	93100 MW	125830 TQ	USBLS	5/15
	Montana	Y	68130 FQ	83820 MW	125210 TQ	USBLS	5/15
	Nebraska	Y	65220 FQ	82410 MW	102425 TQ	NEBLS	7/16-9/16
	Omaha-Council Bluffs MSA, NE-IA	Y	68835 FQ	86600 MW	109290 TQ	NEBLS	7/16-9/16
	Nevada	Y	66120 FQ	86020 MW	112960 TQ	USBLS	5/15
	Las Vegas-Henderson-Paradise MSA, NV	Y	63820 FQ	81580 MW	114070 TQ	USBLS	5/15
	New Hampshire	H	38.03 AE	52.83 MW	65.94 AEX	NHBLS	6/16
	Manchester NECTA, NH	H	33.79 AE	53.09 MW	65.85 AEX	NHBLS	6/16
	Nashua NECTA, NH-MA	Y	93920 FQ	119220 MW	154300 TQ	USBLS	5/15
	New Jersey	Y	90350 FQ	112850 MW	145850 TQ	USBLS	5/15
	Camden PMSA, NJ	Y	84040 FQ	100580 MW	130380 TQ	USBLS	5/15
	Newark PMSA, NJ-PA	Y	91810 FQ	114070 MW	149870 TQ	USBLS	5/15
	Trenton MSA, NJ	Y	85470 FQ	105320 MW	137270 TQ	USBLS	5/15
	New Mexico	Y	68830 FQ	96480 MW	133730 TQ	USBLS	5/15
	Albuquerque MSA, NM	Y	62490 FQ	83100 MW	122250 TQ	USBLS	5/15
	New York	Y	73760 AE	111150 MW	147930 AEX	NYBLS	1/16-3/16
	Buffalo-Cheektowaga-Niagara Falls MSA, NY	Y	79700 FQ	106960 MW	129430 TQ	USBLS	5/15
	Nassau County-Suffolk County PMSA, NY	Y	87190 FQ	114180 MW	146110 TQ	USBLS	5/15
	New York-Jersey City-White Plains PMSA, NY-NJ	Y	92470 FQ	117960 MW	158290 TQ	USBLS	5/15
	Rochester MSA, NY	Y	73240 FQ	90050 MW	116110 TQ	USBLS	5/15
	North Carolina	Y	77060 FQ	96190 MW	123470 TQ	USBLS	5/15
	Charlotte-Concord-Gastonia MSA, NC-SC	Y	76660 FQ	94280 MW	123960 TQ	USBLS	5/15
	Raleigh MSA, NC	Y	81330 FQ	105260 MW	140710 TQ	USBLS	5/15
	North Dakota	Y	68800 FQ	90900 MW	122690 TQ	USBLS	5/15
	Fargo MSA, ND-MN	Y	68270 FQ	86280 MW	115350 TQ	USBLS	5/15
	Ohio	Y	66360 FQ	85260 MW	113300 TQ	USBLS	5/15
	Cincinnati MSA, OH-KY-IN	Y	73060 FQ	94910 MW	125830 TQ	USBLS	5/15
	Cleveland-Elyria MSA, OH	Y	67070 FQ	82890 MW	109810 TQ	USBLS	5/15
	Columbus MSA, OH	Y	67080 FQ	87530 MW	107680 TQ	USBLS	5/15
	Oklahoma	Y	66030 FQ	87180 MW	120500 TQ	USBLS	5/15
	Oklahoma City MSA, OK	Y	59860 FQ	78080 MW	107400 TQ	USBLS	5/15
	Tulsa MSA, OK	Y	73970 FQ	99650 MW	135920 TQ	USBLS	5/15
	Oregon	H	32.26 FQ	40.49 MW	50.90 TQ	ORBLS	2016
	Portland-Vancouver-Hillsboro MSA, OR-WA	Y	68820 FQ	85770 MW	108140 TQ	USBLS	5/15
	Pennsylvania	Y	77610 FQ	97370 MW	125070 TQ	USBLS	5/15
	Allentown-Bethlehem-Easton MSA, PA-NJ	Y	81610 FQ	104270 MW	128610 TQ	USBLS	5/15
	Harrisburg-Carlisle MSA, PA	Y	74420 FQ	92130 MW	112100 TQ	USBLS	5/15

AE Average entry wage	**AWR** Average wage range	**H** Hourly	**LR** Low end range	**MTC** Median total compensation	**TCC** Total cash compensation
AEX Average experienced wage	**B** Biweekly	**HI** Highest wage paid	**M** Monthly	**MW** Median wage paid	**TQ** Third quartile wage
ATC Average total compensation	**D** Daily	**HR** High end range	**MCC** Median cash compensation	**MWR** Median wage range	**W** Weekly
AW Average wage paid	**FQ** First quartile wage	**LO** Lowest wage paid	**ME** Median entry wage	**S** See annotated source	**Y** Yearly

Occupation/Type/Industry	Location	Per	Low	Mid	High	Source	Date
Industrial Production Manager	Montgomery County-Bucks County-Chester County						
	PMSA, PA	Y	84210 FQ	104710 MW	136600 TQ	USBLS	5/15
	Philadelphia PMSA, PA	Y	92690 FQ	115660 MW	146320 TQ	USBLS	5/15
	Pittsburgh MSA, PA	Y	78260 FQ	97970 MW	128330 TQ	USBLS	5/15
	Rhode Island	Y	83250 FQ	97550 MW	123240 TQ	USBLS	5/15
	Providence-Warwick MSA, RI-MA	Y	79200 FQ	95210 MW	118960 TQ	USBLS	5/15
	South Carolina	Y	82210 FQ	104780 MW	137550 TQ	USBLS	5/15
	Charleston-North Charleston MSA, SC	Y	73930 FQ	107150 MW	139380 TQ	USBLS	5/15
	Columbia MSA, SC	Y	83060 FQ	101070 MW	127120 TQ	USBLS	5/15
	Greenville-Anderson-Mauldin MSA, SC	Y	78380 FQ	99780 MW	125310 TQ	USBLS	5/15
	South Dakota	Y	76170 FQ	90270 MW	104820 TQ	USBLS	5/15
	Sioux Falls MSA, SD	Y	79490 FQ	91400 MW	104140 TQ	USBLS	5/15
	Tennessee	Y	55680 FQ	74890 MW	102140 TQ	USBLS	5/15
	Knoxville MSA, TN	Y	57860 FQ	78570 MW	117110 TQ	USBLS	5/15
	Memphis MSA, TN-MS-AR	Y	49240 FQ	76570 MW	100810 TQ	USBLS	5/15
	Nashville-Davidson–Murfreesboro–Franklin MSA, TN	Y	58360 FQ	74080 MW	103120 TQ	USBLS	5/15
	Texas	Y	75050 FQ	99660 MW	134500 TQ	USBLS	5/15
	Austin-Round Rock MSA, TX	Y	63150 FQ	96490 MW	138150 TQ	USBLS	5/15
	Dallas-Plano-Irving PMSA, TX	Y	76130 FQ	101020 MW	128080 TQ	USBLS	5/15
	Fort Worth-Arlington PMSA, TX	Y	73580 FQ	93500 MW	122490 TQ	USBLS	5/15
	Houston-The Woodlands-Sugar Land MSA, TX	Y	83440 FQ	109300 MW	151500 TQ	USBLS	5/15
	San Antonio-New Braunfels MSA, TX	Y	73160 FQ	91850 MW	118860 TQ	USBLS	5/15
	Utah	Y	63560 FQ	89840 MW	119710 TQ	USBLS	5/15
	Ogden-Clearfield MSA, UT	Y	65210 FQ	96950 MW	127480 TQ	USBLS	5/15
	Provo-Orem MSA, UT	Y	68150 FQ	93140 MW	116910 TQ	USBLS	5/15
	Salt Lake City MSA, UT	Y	68140 FQ	91830 MW	120000 TQ	USBLS	5/15
	Vermont	Y	68780 FQ	90310 MW	119120 TQ	USBLS	5/15
	Burlington-South Burlington MSA, VT	Y	82160 FQ	106970 MW	130360 TQ	USBLS	5/15
	Virginia	Y	81960 FQ	107460 MW	142530 TQ	USBLS	5/15
	Richmond MSA, VA	Y	88270 FQ	123340 MW	154610 TQ	USBLS	5/15
	Virginia Beach-Norfolk-Newport News MSA, VA-NC	Y	83570 FQ	107230 MW	137790 TQ	USBLS	5/15
	Washington	H	36.51 FQ	49.75 MW	65.53 TQ	WABLS	3/16
	Seattle-Bellevue-Everett PMSA, WA	H	43.05 FQ	55.73 MW	70.23 TQ	WABLS	3/16
	Tacoma-Lakewood PMSA, WA	H	30.87 FQ	39.64 MW	56.14 TQ	WABLS	3/16
	West Virginia	Y	70180 FQ	92690 MW	117740 TQ	USBLS	5/15
	Huntington-Ashland MSA, WV-KY-OH	Y	74680 FQ	95890 MW	128840 TQ	USBLS	5/15
	Wisconsin	Y	74990 FQ	94670 MW	123770 TQ	USBLS	5/15
	Madison MSA, WI	Y	77520 FQ	99700 MW	126130 TQ	USBLS	5/15
	Milwaukee-Waukesha-West Allis MSA, WI	Y	79700 FQ	98120 MW	128470 TQ	USBLS	5/15
	Wyoming	Y	93090 FQ	117530 MW	146120 TQ	USBLS	5/15
	Puerto Rico	Y	67040 FQ	97460 MW	126390 TQ	USBLS	5/15
	San Juan-Carolina-Caguas MSA, PR	Y	63670 FQ	98930 MW	129970 TQ	USBLS	5/15
Industrial Rehabilitation Nurse							
Workers' Compensation, State Government	Ohio	H	22.60 LO		34.73 HI	OHGOV	2015
Industrial Truck and Tractor Operator							
	Alabama	Y	21969 AE	32172 AW	37273 AEX	ALBLS	6/16
	Birmingham-Hoover MSA, AL	Y	23038 AE	32460 AW	37170 AEX	ALBLS	6/16
	Alaska	Y	39010 FQ	47650 MW	63420 TQ	USBLS	5/15
	Anchorage MSA, AK	Y	39340 FQ	47630 MW	73530 TQ	USBLS	5/15
	Arizona	Y	26270 FQ	30870 MW	39850 TQ	USBLS	5/15
	Phoenix-Mesa-Scottsdale MSA, AZ	Y	26560 FQ	30860 MW	41080 TQ	USBLS	5/15
	Tucson MSA, AZ	Y	28620 FQ	33760 MW	37780 TQ	USBLS	5/15
	Arkansas	Y	22980 FQ	27810 MW	34140 TQ	USBLS	5/15

Industrial Truck and Tractor Operator

Occupation/Type/Industry	Location	Per	Low	Mid	High	Source	Date
Industrial Truck and Tractor Operator	Little Rock-North Little Rock-Conway MSA, AR	Y	22980 FQ	27430 MW	34960 TQ	USBLS	5/15
	California	H	12.98 FQ	17.08 MW	22.37 TQ	CABLS	1/16-3/16
	Anaheim-Santa Ana-Irvine PMSA, CA	H	12.30 FQ	15.51 MW	20.17 TQ	CABLS	1/16-3/16
	Los Angeles-Long Beach-Glendale PMSA, CA	H	13.55 FQ	19.57 MW	29.69 TQ	CABLS	1/16-3/16
	Oakland-Hayward-Berkeley PMSA, CA	H	16.13 FQ	20.88 MW	26.08 TQ	CABLS	1/16-3/16
	Riverside-San Bernardino-Ontario MSA, CA	H	12.82 FQ	15.48 MW	19.35 TQ	CABLS	1/16-3/16
	Sacramento–Roseville–Arden-Arcade MSA, CA	H	12.13 FQ	14.40 MW	19.05 TQ	CABLS	1/16-3/16
	San Diego-Carlsbad MSA, CA	H	14.48 FQ	18.65 MW	22.51 TQ	CABLS	1/16-3/16
	San Francisco-Redwood City-South San Francisco PMSA, CA	H	14.21 FQ	18.15 MW	23.77 TQ	CABLS	1/16-3/16
	Colorado	Y	26780 FQ	33220 MW	39470 TQ	USBLS	5/15
	Denver-Aurora-Lakewood MSA, CO	Y	27010 FQ	33530 MW	40130 TQ	USBLS	5/15
	Connecticut	Y		34545 MW		CTBLS	1/16-3/16
	Bridgeport-Stamford-Norwalk MSA, CT	Y	30030 FQ	37370 MW	46970 TQ	USBLS	5/15
	Hartford-West Hartford-East Hartford MSA, CT	Y	30380 FQ	35910 MW	45850 TQ	USBLS	5/15
	Delaware	Y	26560 FQ	31200 MW	39740 TQ	USBLS	5/15
	Wilmington PMSA, DE-MD-NJ	Y	29990 FQ	37040 MW	49300 TQ	USBLS	5/15
	District of Columbia	Y	49880 FQ	51860 MW	55030 TQ	USBLS	5/15
	Washington-Arlington-Alexandria PMSA, DC-VA-MD-WV	Y	30950 FQ	36500 MW	43770 TQ	USBLS	5/15
	Florida	H	11.46 AE	15.37 MW	18.17 AEX	FLBLS	7/16-9/16
	Fort Lauderdale-Pompano Beach-Deerfield Beach PMSA, FL	H	12.74 AE	16.15 MW	19.08 AEX	FLBLS	7/16-9/16
	Miami-Miami Beach-Kendall PMSA, FL	H	10.72 AE	14.22 MW	17.10 AEX	FLBLS	7/16-9/16
	Orlando-Kissimmee-Sanford MSA, FL	H	11.97 AE	16.46 MW	19.39 AEX	FLBLS	7/16-9/16
	Tampa-St. Petersburg-Clearwater MSA, FL	H	11.17 AE	14.80 MW	18.14 AEX	FLBLS	7/16-9/16
	Georgia	Y	24140 FQ	29250 MW	36110 TQ	USBLS	5/15
	Atlanta-Sandy Springs-Roswell MSA, GA	Y	24910 FQ	30060 MW	37400 TQ	USBLS	5/15
	Augusta-Richmond County MSA, GA-SC	Y	20470 FQ	25530 MW	30450 TQ	USBLS	5/15
	Hawaii	Y	36370 FQ	44560 MW	56520 TQ	USBLS	5/15
	Urban Honolulu MSA, HI	Y	35620 FQ	44620 MW	59630 TQ	USBLS	5/15
	Idaho	Y	26730 FQ	33020 MW	37740 TQ	USBLS	5/15
	Boise City MSA, ID	Y	23140 FQ	32240 MW	37260 TQ	USBLS	5/15
	Illinois	Y	26510 FQ	32780 MW	40130 TQ	USBLS	5/15
	Chicago-Naperville-Arlington Heights PMSA, IL	Y	26920 FQ	33230 MW	42450 TQ	USBLS	5/15
	Lake County-Kenosha County PMSA, IL-WI	Y	26280 FQ	31240 MW	38190 TQ	USBLS	5/15
	Indiana	Y	27230 FQ	32280 MW	38640 TQ	USBLS	5/15
	Gary PMSA, IN	Y	26050 FQ	29900 MW	38520 TQ	USBLS	5/15
	Indianapolis-Carmel-Anderson MSA, IN	Y	26650 FQ	30540 MW	37280 TQ	USBLS	5/15
	Iowa	Y	26670 FQ	31660 MW	37610 TQ	USBLS	5/15
	Des Moines-West Des Moines MSA, IA	Y	27850 FQ	32550 MW	37940 TQ	USBLS	5/15
	Kansas	Y	27420 FQ	32920 MW	41470 TQ	USBLS	5/15
	Wichita MSA, KS	Y	26320 FQ	30990 MW	36330 TQ	USBLS	5/15
	Kentucky	Y	25370 FQ	29960 MW	36570 TQ	USBLS	5/15
	Louisville-Jefferson County MSA, KY-IN	Y	25820 FQ	29740 MW	35550 TQ	USBLS	5/15
	Louisiana	Y	27170 FQ	33370 MW	39140 TQ	USBLS	5/15
	Baton Rouge MSA, LA	Y	27750 FQ	34780 MW	42580 TQ	USBLS	5/15

AE	Average entry wage	AWR	Average wage range	H	Hourly	LR	Low end range	MTC	Median total compensation	TCC	Total cash compensation
AEX	Average experienced wage	B	Biweekly	HI	Highest wage paid	M	Monthly	MW	Median wage paid	TQ	Third quartile wage
ATC	Average total compensation	D	Daily	HR	High end range	MCC	Median cash compensation	MWR	Median wage range	W	Weekly
AW	Average wage paid	FQ	First quartile wage	LO	Lowest wage paid	ME	Median entry wage	S	See annotated source	Y	Yearly

Occupation/Type/Industry	Location	Per	Low	Mid	High	Source	Date
Industrial Truck and Tractor Operator							
	New Orleans-Metairie MSA, LA	Y	28010 FQ	33290 MW	39180 TQ	USBLS	5/15
	Maine	Y	27420 FQ	32220 MW	38620 TQ	USBLS	5/15
	Portland-South Portland MSA, ME	Y	30260 FQ	34810 MW	38680 TQ	USBLS	5/15
	Maryland	Y	26632 AE	39705 MW	46241 AEX	MDBLS	4/16
	Baltimore-Columbia-Towson MSA, MD	Y	29280 FQ	37470 MW	49670 TQ	USBLS	5/15
	Salisbury MSA, MD-DE	Y	26450 FQ	29520 MW	34480 TQ	USBLS	5/15
	Massachusetts	Y	29180 FQ	37820 MW	46520 TQ	USBLS	5/15
	Boston-Cambridge-Newton NECTA, MA	Y	29460 FQ	37920 MW	45680 TQ	USBLS	5/15
	Worcester MSA, MA-CT	Y	29110 FQ	35800 MW	46600 TQ	USBLS	5/15
	Michigan	Y	24760 FQ	30870 MW	40530 TQ	USBLS	5/15
	Detroit-Dearborn-Livonia PMSA, MI	Y	25740 FQ	32220 MW	46330 TQ	USBLS	5/15
	Grand Rapids-Wyoming MSA, MI	Y	23930 FQ	28470 MW	35130 TQ	USBLS	5/15
	Minnesota	Y	30617 FQ	36565 MW	43461 TQ	MNBLS	1/16-3/16
	Minneapolis-St. Paul-Bloomington MSA, MN-WI	Y	31545 FQ	36928 MW	43582 TQ	MNBLS	1/16-3/16
	Mississippi	Y	22350 FQ	26840 MW	35050 TQ	USBLS	5/15
	Jackson MSA, MS	Y	22910 FQ	27150 MW	32110 TQ	USBLS	5/15
	Missouri	Y	24620 FQ	31280 MW	39900 TQ	USBLS	5/15
	Kansas City MSA, MO-KS	Y	27850 FQ	35350 MW	43090 TQ	USBLS	5/15
	St. Louis MSA, MO-IL	Y	23600 FQ	29630 MW	38220 TQ	USBLS	5/15
	Montana	Y	25890 FQ	31940 MW	40470 TQ	USBLS	5/15
	Billings MSA, MT	Y	25490 FQ	31530 MW	39090 TQ	USBLS	5/15
	Nebraska	Y	27340 FQ	31640 MW	37505 TQ	NEBLS	7/16-9/16
	Omaha-Council Bluffs MSA, NE-IA	Y	28245 FQ	34230 MW	39380 TQ	NEBLS	7/16-9/16
	Nevada	Y	27840 FQ	35890 MW	45000 TQ	USBLS	5/15
	Las Vegas-Henderson-Paradise MSA, NV	Y	28890 FQ	37000 MW	45160 TQ	USBLS	5/15
	New Hampshire	H	12.51 AE	17.92 MW	20.87 AEX	NHBLS	6/16
	Manchester NECTA, NH	H	12.95 AE	16.64 MW	19.25 AEX	NHBLS	6/16
	Nashua NECTA, NH-MA	Y	28910 FQ	36160 MW	44120 TQ	USBLS	5/15
	New Jersey	Y	26490 FQ	33850 MW	42460 TQ	USBLS	5/15
	Camden PMSA, NJ	Y	29030 FQ	35810 MW	45260 TQ	USBLS	5/15
	Newark PMSA, NJ-PA	Y	28680 FQ	35460 MW	44540 TQ	USBLS	5/15
	Trenton MSA, NJ	Y	33350 FQ	39600 MW	45400 TQ	USBLS	5/15
	New Mexico	Y	22510 FQ	29810 MW	40070 TQ	USBLS	5/15
	Albuquerque MSA, NM	Y	22660 FQ	31180 MW	40920 TQ	USBLS	5/15
	New York	Y	25890 AE	36070 MW	43410 AEX	NYBLS	1/16-3/16
	Buffalo-Cheektowaga-Niagara Falls MSA, NY	Y	28490 FQ	34490 MW	43700 TQ	USBLS	5/15
	Nassau County-Suffolk County PMSA, NY	Y	31510 FQ	41580 MW	49130 TQ	USBLS	5/15
	New York-Jersey City-White Plains PMSA, NY-NJ	Y	25270 FQ	32060 MW	41180 TQ	USBLS	5/15
	Rochester MSA, NY	Y	28160 FQ	33900 MW	39000 TQ	USBLS	5/15
	North Carolina	Y	24580 FQ	29690 MW	36170 TQ	USBLS	5/15
	Charlotte-Concord-Gastonia MSA, NC-SC	Y	25670 FQ	30980 MW	37000 TQ	USBLS	5/15
	Raleigh MSA, NC	Y	22780 FQ	30680 MW	37520 TQ	USBLS	5/15
	North Dakota	Y	32320 FQ	38310 MW	49700 TQ	USBLS	5/15
	Fargo MSA, ND-MN	Y	29220 FQ	33820 MW	39570 TQ	USBLS	5/15
	Ohio	Y	26260 FQ	31500 MW	38380 TQ	USBLS	5/15
	Cincinnati MSA, OH-KY-IN	Y	25400 FQ	31000 MW	37850 TQ	USBLS	5/15
	Cleveland-Elyria MSA, OH	Y	26850 FQ	32730 MW	40790 TQ	USBLS	5/15
	Columbus MSA, OH	Y	26380 FQ	30050 MW	35740 TQ	USBLS	5/15
	Oklahoma	Y	25990 FQ	31280 MW	38360 TQ	USBLS	5/15
	Oklahoma City MSA, OK	Y	27110 FQ	33530 MW	40210 TQ	USBLS	5/15
	Tulsa MSA, OK	Y	25210 FQ	30750 MW	38600 TQ	USBLS	5/15
	Oregon	H	14.23 FQ	17.41 MW	21.01 TQ	ORBLS	2016
	Medford MSA, OR	Y	27450 FQ	33640 MW	43050 TQ	USBLS	5/15
	Portland-Vancouver-Hillsboro MSA, OR-WA	Y	30240 FQ	37490 MW	45360 TQ	USBLS	5/15
	Pennsylvania	Y	30070 FQ	35930 MW	43150 TQ	USBLS	5/15
	Allentown-Bethlehem-Easton MSA, PA-NJ	Y	29620 FQ	34440 MW	39870 TQ	USBLS	5/15

AE	Average entry wage	AWR	Average wage range	H	Hourly	LR	Low end range	MTC	Median total compensation	TCC	Total cash compensation
AEX	Average experienced wage	B	Biweekly	HI	Highest wage paid	M	Monthly	MW	Median wage paid	TQ	Third quartile wage
ATC	Average total compensation	D	Daily	HR	High end range	MCC	Median cash compensation	MWR	Median wage range	W	Weekly
AW	Average wage paid	FQ	First quartile wage	LO	Lowest wage paid	ME	Median entry wage	S	See annotated source	Y	Yearly

Occupation/Type/Industry	Location	Per	Low	Mid	High	Source	Date
Industrial Truck and Tractor Operator	Harrisburg-Carlisle MSA, PA	Y	27980 FQ	32080 MW	41210 TQ	USBLS	5/15
	Montgomery County-Bucks County-Chester County PMSA, PA	Y	31620 FQ	37090 MW	44860 TQ	USBLS	5/15
	Philadelphia PMSA, PA	Y	34730 FQ	41280 MW	47420 TQ	USBLS	5/15
	Pittsburgh MSA, PA	Y	32470 FQ	40040 MW	46760 TQ	USBLS	5/15
	Rhode Island	Y	29760 FQ	35910 MW	43220 TQ	USBLS	5/15
	Providence-Warwick MSA, RI-MA	Y	29190 FQ	35800 MW	43610 TQ	USBLS	5/15
	South Carolina	Y	24450 FQ	29040 MW	35360 TQ	USBLS	5/15
	Charleston-North Charleston MSA, SC	Y	25200 FQ	31220 MW	40650 TQ	USBLS	5/15
	Columbia MSA, SC	Y	25100 FQ	29780 MW	37630 TQ	USBLS	5/15
	Greenville-Anderson-Mauldin MSA, SC	Y	23280 FQ	28120 MW	34510 TQ	USBLS	5/15
	South Dakota	Y	27570 FQ	31320 MW	36520 TQ	USBLS	5/15
	Sioux Falls MSA, SD	Y	26350 FQ	29310 MW	33370 TQ	USBLS	5/15
	Tennessee	Y	23940 FQ	28400 MW	34410 TQ	USBLS	5/15
	Knoxville MSA, TN	Y	23790 FQ	28870 MW	36750 TQ	USBLS	5/15
	Memphis MSA, TN-MS-AR	Y	23570 FQ	27180 MW	30750 TQ	USBLS	5/15
	Nashville-Davidson–Murfreesboro–Franklin MSA, TN	Y	25090 FQ	30020 MW	36830 TQ	USBLS	5/15
	Texas	Y	23440 FQ	28840 MW	35640 TQ	USBLS	5/15
	Austin-Round Rock MSA, TX	Y	25200 FQ	30060 MW	37750 TQ	USBLS	5/15
	Dallas-Plano-Irving PMSA, TX	Y	23070 FQ	27570 MW	33100 TQ	USBLS	5/15
	Fort Worth-Arlington PMSA, TX	Y	24720 FQ	29530 MW	36320 TQ	USBLS	5/15
	Houston-The Woodlands-Sugar Land MSA, TX	Y	26740 FQ	31530 MW	37770 TQ	USBLS	5/15
	San Antonio-New Braunfels MSA, TX	Y	21950 FQ	27180 MW	32910 TQ	USBLS	5/15
	Utah	Y	27140 FQ	33520 MW	41690 TQ	USBLS	5/15
	Ogden-Clearfield MSA, UT	Y	25110 FQ	31330 MW	38630 TQ	USBLS	5/15
	Provo-Orem MSA, UT	Y	28980 FQ	34120 MW	39050 TQ	USBLS	5/15
	Salt Lake City MSA, UT	Y	27160 FQ	33400 MW	42130 TQ	USBLS	5/15
	Vermont	Y	29690 FQ	34700 MW	39080 TQ	USBLS	5/15
	Burlington-South Burlington MSA, VT	Y	33200 FQ	37480 MW	43670 TQ	USBLS	5/15
	Virginia	Y	26250 FQ	33540 MW	39700 TQ	USBLS	5/15
	Richmond MSA, VA	Y	28110 FQ	34540 MW	39130 TQ	USBLS	5/15
	Virginia Beach-Norfolk-Newport News MSA, VA-NC	Y	25860 FQ	34590 MW	47330 TQ	USBLS	5/15
	Winchester MSA, VA-WV	Y	29220 FQ	34030 MW	38040 TQ	USBLS	5/15
	Washington	H	14.98 FQ	18.84 MW	23.48 TQ	WABLS	3/16
	Seattle-Bellevue-Everett PMSA, WA	H	15.86 FQ	20.53 MW	26.11 TQ	WABLS	3/16
	Tacoma-Lakewood PMSA, WA	H	15.77 FQ	20.15 MW	24.07 TQ	WABLS	3/16
	West Virginia	Y	23920 FQ	30350 MW	40740 TQ	USBLS	5/15
	Huntington-Ashland MSA, WV-KY-OH	Y	27600 FQ	37730 MW	45050 TQ	USBLS	5/15
	Parkersburg-Vienna MSA, WV	Y	27180 FQ	29460 MW	31720 TQ	USBLS	5/15
	Wisconsin	Y	27430 FQ	33320 MW	40060 TQ	USBLS	5/15
	Madison MSA, WI	Y	27480 FQ	32670 MW	38210 TQ	USBLS	5/15
	Milwaukee-Waukesha-West Allis MSA, WI	Y	28700 FQ	34000 MW	39030 TQ	USBLS	5/15
	Wyoming	Y	30130 FQ	35260 MW	39610 TQ	USBLS	5/15
	Cheyenne MSA, WY	Y	30740 FQ	34570 MW	37920 TQ	USBLS	5/15
	Puerto Rico	Y	17320 FQ	19020 MW	23540 TQ	USBLS	5/15
	San Juan-Carolina-Caguas MSA, PR	Y	17340 FQ	19060 MW	23810 TQ	USBLS	5/15
	Virgin Islands	Y	19580 FQ	24040 MW	32270 TQ	USBLS	5/15
	Guam	Y	27560 FQ	32710 MW	39910 TQ	USBLS	5/15
Industrial Waste Inspector							
Municipal Government	Bakersfield, CA	Y		59530 AW		CACIT	6/28/16
Municipal Government	Chico, CA	Y			16680 HI	CACIT	6/28/16
Infection Preventionist	United States	Y		74687 AW		HPN01	2016
Information Architect	United States	Y		98800 MW		GLKN	2016

Occupation/Type/Industry	Location	Per	Low	Mid	High	Source	Date
Information Architect	Mid-Atlantic	Y		109706 AW		IAI	4/11/16-5/9/16
	Midwest	Y		94815 AW		IAI	4/11/16-5/9/16
	Northeast	Y		117143 AW		IAI	4/11/16-5/9/16
	Southeast	Y		115000 AW		IAI	4/11/16-5/9/16
	Southwest	Y		108077 AW		IAI	4/11/16-5/9/16
Information Security Analyst	United States	Y		90120 MW		BHICR	2016
	Alabama	Y	61363 AE	87264 AW	100220 AEX	ALBLS	6/16
	Birmingham-Hoover MSA, AL	Y	64360 AE	88702 AW	100872 AEX	ALBLS	6/16
	Alaska	Y	70340 MW	87740 MW	101110 TQ	USBLS	5/15
	Anchorage MSA, AK	Y	66460 FQ	84110 MW	96030 MW	USBLS	5/15
	Arizona	Y	62210 FQ	76010 MW	97180 TQ	USBLS	5/15
	Phoenix-Mesa-Scottsdale MSA, AZ	Y	63250 FQ	76300 MW	97320 TQ	USBLS	5/15
	Tucson MSA, AZ	Y	48120 FQ	68260 MW	88650 TQ	USBLS	5/15
	Arkansas	Y	52330 FQ	73610 MW	88190 TQ	USBLS	5/15
	Little Rock-North Little Rock-Conway MSA, AR	Y	53530 FQ	74550 MW	88970 TQ	USBLS	5/15
	California	H	40.72 FQ	52.30 MW	63.10 TQ	CABLS	1/16-3/16
	Anaheim-Santa Ana-Irvine PMSA, CA	H	35.98 FQ	45.34 MW	57.79 TQ	CABLS	1/16-3/16
	Los Angeles-Long Beach-Glendale PMSA, CA	H	41.56 FQ	50.45 MW	59.28 TQ	CABLS	1/16-3/16
	Oakland-Hayward-Berkeley PMSA, CA	H	50.83 FQ	56.89 MW	63.18 TQ	CABLS	1/16-3/16
	Riverside-San Bernardino-Ontario MSA, CA	H	34.47 FQ	43.91 MW	53.48 TQ	CABLS	1/16-3/16
	San Diego-Carlsbad MSA, CA	H	35.66 FQ	46.99 MW	63.59 TQ	CABLS	1/16-3/16
	San Francisco-Redwood City-South San Francisco PMSA, CA	H	39.70 FQ	53.98 MW	66.07 TQ	CABLS	1/16-3/16
	Colorado	Y	80320 FQ	98140 MW	119760 TQ	USBLS	5/15
	Denver-Aurora-Lakewood MSA, CO	Y	78280 FQ	95450 MW	118870 TQ	USBLS	5/15
	Connecticut	Y		94399 MW		CTBLS	1/16-3/16
	Bridgeport-Stamford-Norwalk MSA, CT	Y	73810 FQ	93450 MW	120530 TQ	USBLS	5/15
	Hartford-West Hartford-East Hartford MSA, CT	Y	77870 FQ	94110 MW	111960 TQ	USBLS	5/15
	Delaware	Y	76450 FQ	95750 MW	117630 TQ	USBLS	5/15
	Wilmington PMSA, DE-MD-NJ	Y	78390 FQ	97440 MW	119450 TQ	USBLS	5/15
	District of Columbia	Y	84870 FQ	111490 MW	143250 TQ	USBLS	5/15
	Washington-Arlington-Alexandria PMSA, DC-VA-MD-WV	Y	84270 FQ	107610 MW	137140 TQ	USBLS	5/15
	Florida	H	25.81 AE	40.00 MW	48.92 AEX	FLBLS	7/16-9/16
	Fort Lauderdale-Pompano Beach-Deerfield Beach PMSA, FL	H	23.49 AE	32.63 MW	41.32 AEX	FLBLS	7/16-9/16
	Miami-Miami Beach-Kendall PMSA, FL	H	21.42 AE	32.45 MW	42.69 AEX	FLBLS	7/16-9/16
	Orlando-Kissimmee-Sanford MSA, FL	H	30.43 AE	42.99 MW	51.27 AEX	FLBLS	7/16-9/16
	Tampa-St. Petersburg-Clearwater MSA, FL	H	27.74 AE	42.74 MW	50.39 AEX	FLBLS	7/16-9/16
	Georgia	Y	66850 FQ	86580 MW	105280 TQ	USBLS	5/15
	Atlanta-Sandy Springs-Roswell MSA, GA	Y	69810 FQ	89010 MW	107890 TQ	USBLS	5/15
	Augusta-Richmond County MSA, GA-SC	Y	64060 FQ	83310 MW	101240 TQ	USBLS	5/15
	Hawaii	Y	69510 FQ	84300 MW	97100 TQ	USBLS	5/15
	Urban Honolulu MSA, HI	Y	69130 FQ	83700 MW	96620 TQ	USBLS	5/15
	Idaho	Y	57780 FQ	83840 MW	128900 TQ	USBLS	5/15
	Boise City MSA, ID	Y	62620 FQ	77570 MW	93700 TQ	USBLS	5/15
	Illinois	Y	68650 FQ	87690 MW	112610 TQ	USBLS	5/15
	Chicago-Naperville-Arlington Heights PMSA, IL	Y	72470 FQ	92450 MW	117400 TQ	USBLS	5/15
	Lake County-Kenosha County PMSA, IL-WI	Y	75770 FQ	100400 MW	125090 TQ	USBLS	5/15
	Indiana	Y	58390 FQ	76400 MW	94280 TQ	USBLS	5/15

Occupation/Type/Industry	Location	Per	Low	Mid	High	Source	Date
Information Security Analyst	Indianapolis-Carmel-Anderson MSA, IN	Y	62570 FQ	83530 MW	95890 TQ	USBLS	5/15
	Iowa	Y	55900 FQ	72010 MW	89700 TQ	USBLS	5/15
	Des Moines-West Des Moines MSA, IA	Y	56570 FQ	71250 MW	88350 TQ	USBLS	5/15
	Kansas	Y	49330 FQ	63640 MW	86890 TQ	USBLS	5/15
	Wichita MSA, KS	Y	53550 FQ	60390 MW	79660 TQ	USBLS	5/15
	Kentucky	Y	47600 FQ	69270 MW	96420 TQ	USBLS	5/15
	Louisville-Jefferson County MSA, KY-IN	Y	55540 FQ	75820 MW	105770 TQ	USBLS	5/15
	Louisiana	Y	43430 FQ	62300 MW	92950 TQ	USBLS	5/15
	Baton Rouge MSA, LA	Y	59020 FQ	73310 MW	110290 TQ	USBLS	5/15
	New Orleans-Metairie MSA, LA	Y	58890 FQ	84060 MW	112690 TQ	USBLS	5/15
	Maryland	Y	62929 AE	102952 MW	122963 AEX	MDBLS	4/16
	Baltimore-Columbia-Towson MSA, MD	Y	73870 FQ	101450 MW	134650 TQ	USBLS	5/15
	Salisbury MSA, MD-DE	Y	62020 FQ	82480 MW	125010 TQ	USBLS	5/15
	Massachusetts	Y	62950 FQ	89100 MW	117900 TQ	USBLS	5/15
	Boston-Cambridge-Newton NECTA, MA	Y	58790 FQ	87520 MW	118310 TQ	USBLS	5/15
	Springfield MSA, MA-CT	Y	70200 FQ	86160 MW	96830 TQ	USBLS	5/15
	Worcester MSA, MA-CT	Y	72820 FQ	91800 MW	112610 TQ	USBLS	5/15
	Michigan	Y	61440 FQ	85930 MW	104050 TQ	USBLS	5/15
	Detroit-Dearborn-Livonia PMSA, MI	Y	61740 FQ	84180 MW	105280 TQ	USBLS	5/15
	Grand Rapids-Wyoming MSA, MI	Y	55380 FQ	79280 MW	97420 TQ	USBLS	5/15
	Minnesota	Y	70836 FQ	89414 MW	108829 TQ	MNBLS	1/16-3/16
	Minneapolis-St. Paul-Bloomington MSA, MN-WI	Y	71370 FQ	89323 MW	107347 TQ	MNBLS	1/16-3/16
	Mississippi	Y	45280 FQ	61320 MW	80410 TQ	USBLS	5/15
	Jackson MSA, MS	Y	47480 FQ	61360 MW	86000 TQ	USBLS	5/15
	Missouri	Y	56130 FQ	78350 MW	98420 TQ	USBLS	5/15
	Kansas City MSA, MO-KS	Y	61290 FQ	81990 MW	100410 TQ	USBLS	5/15
	St. Louis MSA, MO-IL	Y	51900 FQ	74830 MW	95870 TQ	USBLS	5/15
	Montana	Y	45370 FQ	57810 MW	73730 TQ	USBLS	5/15
	Billings MSA, MT	Y	42390 FQ	54400 MW	77420 TQ	USBLS	5/15
	Nebraska	Y	53445 FQ	74460 MW	92600 TQ	NEBLS	7/16-9/16
	Omaha-Council Bluffs MSA, NE-IA	Y	54290 FQ	74735 MW	92450 TQ	NEBLS	7/16-9/16
	Nevada	Y	55340 FQ	69710 MW	87240 TQ	USBLS	5/15
	Las Vegas-Henderson-Paradise MSA, NV	Y	56860 FQ	70790 MW	87580 TQ	USBLS	5/15
	New Hampshire	H	32.11 AE	46.50 MW	55.63 AEX	NHBLS	6/16
	Nashua NECTA, NH-MA	Y	73620 FQ	100290 MW	119080 TQ	USBLS	5/15
	New Jersey	Y	86650 FQ	110210 MW	133020 TQ	USBLS	5/15
	Camden PMSA, NJ	Y	73410 FQ	85360 MW	102480 TQ	USBLS	5/15
	Newark PMSA, NJ-PA	Y	88310 FQ	108220 MW	129440 TQ	USBLS	5/15
	Trenton MSA, NJ	Y	93920 FQ	118760 MW	139870 TQ	USBLS	5/15
	New Mexico	Y	79630 FQ	102950 MW	118240 TQ	USBLS	5/15
	Albuquerque MSA, NM	Y	85640 FQ	106760 MW	120710 TQ	USBLS	5/15
	New York	Y	68320 AE	109240 MW	135020 AEX	NYBLS	1/16-3/16
	Buffalo-Cheektowaga-Niagara Falls MSA, NY	Y	51330 FQ	79010 MW	93260 TQ	USBLS	5/15
	Nassau County-Suffolk County PMSA, NY	Y	61020 FQ	89400 MW	119890 TQ	USBLS	5/15
	New York-Jersey City-White Plains PMSA, NY-NJ	Y	89220 FQ	117370 MW	146850 TQ	USBLS	5/15
	Rochester MSA, NY	Y	55490 FQ	76340 MW	101400 TQ	USBLS	5/15
	North Carolina	Y	67040 FQ	87580 MW	110920 TQ	USBLS	5/15
	Charlotte-Concord-Gastonia MSA, NC-SC	Y	73020 FQ	95590 MW	118990 TQ	USBLS	5/15
	Raleigh MSA, NC	Y	71500 FQ	90510 MW	108560 TQ	USBLS	5/15
	North Dakota	Y	56960 FQ	68270 MW	80860 TQ	USBLS	5/15
	Fargo MSA, ND-MN	Y	58870 FQ	69670 MW	80680 TQ	USBLS	5/15
	Ohio	Y	64980 FQ	80780 MW	103400 TQ	USBLS	5/15
	Cincinnati MSA, OH-KY-IN	Y	61390 FQ	77380 MW	98590 TQ	USBLS	5/15
	Cleveland-Elyria MSA, OH	Y	69780 FQ	93610 MW	114510 TQ	USBLS	5/15
	Columbus MSA, OH	Y	66090 FQ	78320 MW	101040 TQ	USBLS	5/15
	Oklahoma	Y	42810 FQ	60220 MW	82480 TQ	USBLS	5/15
	Oklahoma City MSA, OK	Y	37920 FQ	59010 MW	80950 TQ	USBLS	5/15

AE	Average entry wage	AWR	Average wage range	H	Hourly	LR	Low end range	MTC	Median total compensation	TCC	Total cash compensation
AEX	Average experienced wage	B	Biweekly	HI	Highest wage paid	M	Monthly	MW	Median wage paid	TQ	Third quartile wage
ATC	Average total compensation	D	Daily	HR	High end range	MCC	Median cash compensation	MWR	Median wage range	W	Weekly
AW	Average wage paid	FQ	First quartile wage	LO	Lowest wage paid	ME	Median entry wage	S	See annotated source	Y	Yearly

Occupation/Type/Industry	Location	Per	Low	Mid	High	Source	Date
Information Security Analyst	Tulsa MSA, OK	Y	50050 FQ	62530 MW	88280 TQ	USBLS	5/15
	Oregon	H	39.65 FQ	45.33 MW	54.69 TQ	ORBLS	2016
	Portland-Vancouver-Hillsboro MSA, OR-WA	Y	82010 FQ	93250 MW	111690 TQ	USBLS	5/15
	Pennsylvania	Y	63260 FQ	84360 MW	106360 TQ	USBLS	5/15
	Allentown-Bethlehem-Easton MSA, PA-NJ	Y	73920 FQ	100570 MW	124890 TQ	USBLS	5/15
	Harrisburg-Carlisle MSA, PA	Y	60220 FQ	75340 MW	98990 TQ	USBLS	5/15
	Montgomery County-Bucks County-Chester County PMSA, PA	Y	68510 FQ	88930 MW	109140 TQ	USBLS	5/15
	Philadelphia PMSA, PA	Y	67150 FQ	88080 MW	109720 TQ	USBLS	5/15
	Pittsburgh MSA, PA	Y	49070 FQ	70630 MW	94260 TQ	USBLS	5/15
	Rhode Island	Y	71190 FQ	88830 MW	109730 TQ	USBLS	5/15
	Providence-Warwick MSA, RI-MA	Y	71230 FQ	88760 MW	109470 TQ	USBLS	5/15
	South Carolina	Y	53660 FQ	68580 MW	87100 TQ	USBLS	5/15
	Charleston-North Charleston MSA, SC	Y	54610 FQ	70350 MW	93940 TQ	USBLS	5/15
	Columbia MSA, SC	Y	59470 FQ	71590 MW	86350 TQ	USBLS	5/15
	Greenville-Anderson-Mauldin MSA, SC	Y	37960 FQ	59400 MW	84620 TQ	USBLS	5/15
	South Dakota	Y	70420 FQ	85690 MW	101170 TQ	USBLS	5/15
	Sioux Falls MSA, SD	Y	72310 FQ	88790 MW	102380 TQ	USBLS	5/15
	Tennessee	Y	50580 FQ	71920 MW	96380 TQ	USBLS	5/15
	Knoxville MSA, TN	Y	43370 FQ	79160 MW	95820 TQ	USBLS	5/15
	Memphis MSA, TN-MS-AR	Y	44730 FQ	59550 MW	81560 TQ	USBLS	5/15
	Nashville-Davidson–Murfreesboro–Franklin MSA, TN	Y	54730 FQ	72330 MW	95290 TQ	USBLS	5/15
	Texas	Y	68960 FQ	89790 MW	111170 TQ	USBLS	5/15
	Austin-Round Rock MSA, TX	Y	81220 FQ	96920 MW	130960 TQ	USBLS	5/15
	Dallas-Plano-Irving PMSA, TX	Y	65920 FQ	90040 MW	108870 TQ	USBLS	5/15
	Fort Worth-Arlington PMSA, TX	Y	71600 FQ	90890 MW	116470 TQ	USBLS	5/15
	Houston-The Woodlands-Sugar Land MSA, TX	Y	74190 FQ	94770 MW	116740 TQ	USBLS	5/15
	San Antonio-New Braunfels MSA, TX	Y	65690 FQ	83310 MW	101530 TQ	USBLS	5/15
	Utah	Y	57620 FQ	74660 MW	96000 TQ	USBLS	5/15
	Ogden-Clearfield MSA, UT	Y	58590 FQ	71240 MW	86910 TQ	USBLS	5/15
	Provo-Orem MSA, UT	Y	58030 FQ	83010 MW	97750 TQ	USBLS	5/15
	Salt Lake City MSA, UT	Y	57750 FQ	74440 MW	98530 TQ	USBLS	5/15
	Vermont	Y	62850 FQ	74060 MW	103620 TQ	USBLS	5/15
	Burlington-South Burlington MSA, VT	Y	57900 FQ	77450 MW	112100 TQ	USBLS	5/15
	Virginia	Y	80960 FQ	102710 MW	133480 TQ	USBLS	5/15
	Richmond MSA, VA	Y	75820 FQ	97490 MW	135020 TQ	USBLS	5/15
	Virginia Beach-Norfolk-Newport News MSA, VA-NC	Y	59410 FQ	80120 MW	104290 TQ	USBLS	5/15
	Washington	H	35.59 FQ	46.89 MW	57.16 TQ	WABLS	3/16
	Seattle-Bellevue-Everett PMSA, WA	H	38.77 FQ	49.98 MW	58.13 TQ	WABLS	3/16
	Tacoma-Lakewood PMSA, WA	H	31.56 FQ	42.18 MW	55.15 TQ	WABLS	3/16
	West Virginia	Y	60360 FQ	85640 MW	106710 TQ	USBLS	5/15
	Wisconsin	Y	54340 FQ	74390 MW	94160 TQ	USBLS	5/15
	Madison MSA, WI	Y	62090 FQ	77610 MW	94880 TQ	USBLS	5/15
	Milwaukee-Waukesha-West Allis MSA, WI	Y	64660 FQ	81010 MW	99640 TQ	USBLS	5/15
	Puerto Rico	Y	33010 FQ	40780 MW	53040 TQ	USBLS	5/15
	San Juan-Carolina-Caguas MSA, PR	Y	33140 FQ	41320 MW	53390 TQ	USBLS	5/15
Information Systems Specialist							
Public Library	Arcadia, CA	Y			52464 HI	CACIT	6/28/16
Information Systems/Technology Specialist							
County Government	Douglas County, GA	Y	36933 LO		75580 HI	GACTY04	2016
County Government	Peach County, GA	Y	34806 LO		52183 HI	GACTY04	2016

AE	Average entry wage	AWR	Average wage range	H	Hourly	LR	Low end range	MTC	Median total compensation	TCC	Total cash compensation
AEX	Average experienced wage	B	Biweekly	HI	Highest wage paid	M	Monthly	MW	Median wage paid	TQ	Third quartile wage
ATC	Average total compensation	D	Daily	HR	High end range	MCC	Median cash compensation	MWR	Median wage range	W	Weekly
AW	Average wage paid	FQ	First quartile wage	LO	Lowest wage paid	ME	Median entry wage	S	See annotated source	Y	Yearly

Occupation/Type/Industry	Location	Per	Low	Mid	High	Source	Date
Information Technology Analyst							
Municipal Government	Los Altos, CA	Y			88324 HI	CACIT	6/28/16
Information Technology Manager							
Municipal Government	Alameda, CA	Y			136513 HI	CACIT	6/28/16
Information Technology Training Manager							
	Central	Y		70067 AW		TRAIN	2015-2016
	Great Lakes	Y		72167 AW		TRAIN	2015-2016
	Mountain	Y		45000 AW		TRAIN	2015-2016
	Northeast	Y		92250 AW		TRAIN	2015-2016
	Pacific	Y		99808 AW		TRAIN	2015-2016
	Southeast	Y		84326 AW		TRAIN	2015-2016
Infusion Therapy Nurse	United States	Y		79139 AW		SCR02	2015
Inmate Caseworker							
County Government	Oakland County, MI	B	2014 LO		2628 HI	MIOAK2	10/1/16
Inorganic Chemist							
Municipal Government	Fresno, CA	Y		49512 AW		CACIT	6/28/16
Inspector, Tester, Sorter, Sampler, and Weigher	Alabama	Y	20040 AE	32965 AW	39432 AEX	ALBLS	6/16
	Birmingham-Hoover MSA, AL	Y	19536 AE	32265 AW	38630 AEX	ALBLS	6/16
	Alaska	Y	51650 FQ	64570 MW	80450 TQ	USBLS	5/15
	Anchorage MSA, AK	Y	52140 FQ	60250 MW	73720 TQ	USBLS	5/15
	Arizona	Y	29260 FQ	37540 MW	50060 TQ	USBLS	5/15
	Phoenix-Mesa-Scottsdale MSA, AZ	Y	29930 FQ	37810 MW	50380 TQ	USBLS	5/15
	Tucson MSA, AZ	Y	33040 FQ	43000 MW	54640 TQ	USBLS	5/15
	Arkansas	Y	24780 FQ	30440 MW	40220 TQ	USBLS	5/15
	Little Rock-North Little Rock-Conway MSA, AR	Y	25670 FQ	39520 MW	48230 TQ	USBLS	5/15
	California	H	13.29 FQ	18.17 MW	24.70 TQ	CABLS	1/16-3/16
	Anaheim-Santa Ana-Irvine PMSA, CA	H	13.90 FQ	18.23 MW	23.60 TQ	CABLS	1/16-3/16
	Los Angeles-Long Beach-Glendale PMSA, CA	H	12.43 FQ	17.41 MW	24.09 TQ	CABLS	1/16-3/16
	Oakland-Hayward-Berkeley PMSA, CA	H	15.59 FQ	20.97 MW	28.15 TQ	CABLS	1/16-3/16
	Riverside-San Bernardino-Ontario MSA, CA	H	12.48 FQ	16.43 MW	21.37 TQ	CABLS	1/16-3/16
	Sacramento–Roseville–Arden-Arcade MSA, CA	H	12.37 FQ	16.43 MW	25.01 TQ	CABLS	1/16-3/16
	San Diego-Carlsbad MSA, CA	H	14.98 FQ	19.97 MW	25.75 TQ	CABLS	1/16-3/16
	San Francisco-Redwood City-South San Francisco PMSA, CA	H	13.44 FQ	20.16 MW	29.99 TQ	CABLS	1/16-3/16
	Colorado	Y	28870 FQ	38140 MW	49630 TQ	USBLS	5/15
	Denver-Aurora-Lakewood MSA, CO	Y	29160 FQ	38750 MW	53440 TQ	USBLS	5/15
	Connecticut	Y		43984 MW		CTBLS	1/16-3/16
	Bridgeport-Stamford-Norwalk MSA, CT	Y	34720 FQ	43650 MW	55370 TQ	USBLS	5/15
	Hartford-West Hartford-East Hartford MSA, CT	Y	35760 FQ	46190 MW	60370 TQ	USBLS	5/15
	Delaware	Y	27040 FQ	34500 MW	50250 TQ	USBLS	5/15
	Wilmington PMSA, DE-MD-NJ	Y	32960 FQ	44310 MW	57020 TQ	USBLS	5/15
	District of Columbia	Y	49140 FQ	53880 MW	53890 TQ	USBLS	5/15
	Washington-Arlington-Alexandria PMSA, DC-VA-MD-WV	Y	24150 FQ	38120 MW	55100 TQ	USBLS	5/15
	Florida	H	11.32 AE	16.60 MW	21.97 AEX	FLBLS	7/16-9/16
	Fort Lauderdale-Pompano Beach-Deerfield Beach PMSA, FL	H	10.61 AE	16.17 MW	23.16 AEX	FLBLS	7/16-9/16
	Miami-Miami Beach-Kendall PMSA, FL	H	11.54 AE	16.68 MW	22.44 AEX	FLBLS	7/16-9/16
	Orlando-Kissimmee-Sanford MSA, FL	H	11.30 AE	17.03 MW	22.63 AEX	FLBLS	7/16-9/16

AE	Average entry wage	AWR	Average wage range	H	Hourly
AEX	Average experienced wage	B	Biweekly	HI	Highest wage paid
ATC	Average total compensation	D	Daily	HR	High end range
AW	Average wage paid	FQ	First quartile wage	LO	Lowest wage paid

LR	Low end range	MTC	Median total compensation
M	Monthly	MW	Median wage paid
MCC	Median cash compensation	MWR	Median wage range
ME	Median entry wage	S	See annotated source

TCC	Total cash compensation
TQ	Third quartile wage
W	Weekly
Y	Yearly

Occupation/Type/Industry	Location	Per	Low	Mid	High	Source	Date
Inspector, Tester, Sorter, Sampler, and Weigher							
	Tampa-St. Petersburg-Clearwater MSA, FL	H	11.08 AE	15.84 MW	20.77 AEX	FLBLS	7/16-9/16
	Georgia	Y	24490 FQ	31990 MW	41370 TQ	USBLS	5/15
	Atlanta-Sandy Springs-Roswell MSA, GA	Y	24770 FQ	32230 MW	43720 TQ	USBLS	5/15
	Augusta-Richmond County MSA, GA-SC	Y	22150 FQ	33390 MW	42440 TQ	USBLS	5/15
	Hawaii	Y	26610 FQ	42960 MW	60260 TQ	USBLS	5/15
	Urban Honolulu MSA, HI	Y	24950 FQ	46170 MW	62660 TQ	USBLS	5/15
	Idaho	Y	25420 FQ	33240 MW	43010 TQ	USBLS	5/15
	Boise City MSA, ID	Y	26700 FQ	34610 MW	43690 TQ	USBLS	5/15
	Illinois	Y	24500 FQ	34320 MW	46920 TQ	USBLS	5/15
	Chicago-Naperville-Arlington Heights PMSA, IL	Y	23410 FQ	33470 MW	47650 TQ	USBLS	5/15
	Lake County-Kenosha County PMSA, IL-WI	Y	25760 FQ	34260 MW	45270 TQ	USBLS	5/15
	Indiana	Y	26610 FQ	34360 MW	44330 TQ	USBLS	5/15
	Gary PMSA, IN	Y	25960 FQ	35680 MW	46700 TQ	USBLS	5/15
	Indianapolis-Carmel-Anderson MSA, IN	Y	26610 FQ	35580 MW	47430 TQ	USBLS	5/15
	Iowa	Y	27610 FQ	34670 MW	44810 TQ	USBLS	5/15
	Des Moines-West Des Moines MSA, IA	Y	25740 FQ	31550 MW	41090 TQ	USBLS	5/15
	Kansas	Y	32630 FQ	42250 MW	55590 TQ	USBLS	5/15
	Wichita MSA, KS	Y	39200 FQ	53000 MW	62270 TQ	USBLS	5/15
	Kentucky	Y	25710 FQ	33180 MW	47160 TQ	USBLS	5/15
	Louisville-Jefferson County MSA, KY-IN	Y	25970 FQ	33300 MW	52800 TQ	USBLS	5/15
	Louisiana	Y	32680 FQ	43000 MW	56970 TQ	USBLS	5/15
	Baton Rouge MSA, LA	Y	32880 FQ	45990 MW	60040 TQ	USBLS	5/15
	New Orleans-Metairie MSA, LA	Y	34380 FQ	44540 MW	56700 TQ	USBLS	5/15
	Maine	Y	32240 FQ	42530 MW	55350 TQ	USBLS	5/15
	Portland-South Portland MSA, ME	Y	33340 FQ	41350 MW	52370 TQ	USBLS	5/15
	Maryland	Y	26901 AE	47097 MW	57195 AEX	MDBLS	4/16
	Baltimore-Columbia-Towson MSA, MD	Y	30330 FQ	43230 MW	56060 TQ	USBLS	5/15
	Salisbury MSA, MD-DE	Y	23760 FQ	29110 MW	38690 TQ	USBLS	5/15
	Massachusetts	Y	33540 FQ	42890 MW	54740 TQ	USBLS	5/15
	Boston-Cambridge-Newton NECTA, MA	Y	35030 FQ	44930 MW	56770 TQ	USBLS	5/15
	Worcester MSA, MA-CT	Y	32600 FQ	39470 MW	49870 TQ	USBLS	5/15
	Michigan	Y	23660 FQ	31510 MW	42370 TQ	USBLS	5/15
	Battle Creek MSA, MI	Y	23440 FQ	29560 MW	39970 TQ	USBLS	5/15
	Detroit-Dearborn-Livonia PMSA, MI	Y	24080 FQ	34620 MW	48130 TQ	USBLS	5/15
	Grand Rapids-Wyoming MSA, MI	Y	23240 FQ	29840 MW	38460 TQ	USBLS	5/15
	Minnesota	Y	30404 FQ	37987 MW	47302 TQ	MNBLS	1/16-3/16
	Minneapolis-St. Paul-Bloomington MSA, MN-WI	Y	31518 FQ	39577 MW	49053 TQ	MNBLS	1/16-3/16
	Mississippi	Y	22720 FQ	29580 MW	38230 TQ	USBLS	5/15
	Jackson MSA, MS	Y	22630 FQ	29080 MW	44450 TQ	USBLS	5/15
	Missouri	Y	28150 FQ	36520 MW	51070 TQ	USBLS	5/15
	Kansas City MSA, MO-KS	Y	30230 FQ	42180 MW	55390 TQ	USBLS	5/15
	St. Louis MSA, MO-IL	Y	29550 FQ	38990 MW	56040 TQ	USBLS	5/15
	Montana	Y	31600 FQ	39380 MW	53160 TQ	USBLS	5/15
	Billings MSA, MT	Y	39490 FQ	50480 MW	62680 TQ	USBLS	5/15
	Nebraska	Y	29145 FQ	35865 MW	44545 TQ	NEBLS	7/16-9/16
	Omaha-Council Bluffs MSA, NE-IA	Y	25945 FQ	33025 MW	42170 TQ	NEBLS	7/16-9/16
	Nevada	Y	22060 FQ	32510 MW	45970 TQ	USBLS	5/15
	Las Vegas-Henderson-Paradise MSA, NV	Y	19830 FQ	25660 MW	43540 TQ	USBLS	5/15
	New Hampshire	H	14.55 AE	18.95 MW	23.31 AEX	NHBLS	6/16
	Manchester NECTA, NH	H	12.74 AE	18.47 MW	24.86 AEX	NHBLS	6/16
	Nashua NECTA, NH-MA	Y	32600 FQ	37780 MW	48520 TQ	USBLS	5/15
	New Jersey	Y	27010 FQ	35970 MW	46440 TQ	USBLS	5/15
	Camden PMSA, NJ	Y	28820 FQ	38310 MW	47680 TQ	USBLS	5/15
	Newark PMSA, NJ-PA	Y	28730 FQ	37540 MW	47790 TQ	USBLS	5/15

AE Average entry wage	**AWR** Average wage range	**H** Hourly	**LR** Low end range	**MTC** Median total compensation	**TCC** Total cash compensation
AEX Average experienced wage	**B** Biweekly	**HI** Highest wage paid	**M** Monthly	**MW** Median wage paid	**TQ** Third quartile wage
ATC Average total compensation	**D** Daily	**HR** High end range	**MCC** Median cash compensation	**MWR** Median wage range	**W** Weekly
AW Average wage paid	**FQ** First quartile wage	**LO** Lowest wage paid	**ME** Median entry wage	**S** See annotated source	**Y** Yearly

Occupation/Type/Industry	Location	Per	Low	Mid	High	Source	Date
Inspector, Tester, Sorter, Sampler, and Weigher	Trenton MSA, NJ	Y	30890 FQ	38490 MW	45470 TQ	USBLS	5/15
	New Mexico	Y	31800 FQ	42150 MW	62160 TQ	USBLS	5/15
	Albuquerque MSA, NM	Y	33540 FQ	43260 MW	58620 TQ	USBLS	5/15
	New York	Y	24670 AE	38500 MW	50140 AEX	NYBLS	1/16-3/16
	Buffalo-Cheektowaga-Niagara Falls MSA, NY	Y	26680 FQ	35020 MW	46880 TQ	USBLS	5/15
	Nassau County-Suffolk County PMSA, NY	Y	33290 FQ	43010 MW	56640 TQ	USBLS	5/15
	New York-Jersey City-White Plains PMSA, NY-NJ	Y	25730 FQ	35900 MW	49290 TQ	USBLS	5/15
	Rochester MSA, NY	Y	26750 FQ	35520 MW	46130 TQ	USBLS	5/15
	North Carolina	Y	23560 FQ	30740 MW	43500 TQ	USBLS	5/15
	Charlotte-Concord-Gastonia MSA, NC-SC	Y	24800 FQ	34700 MW	47960 TQ	USBLS	5/15
	Raleigh MSA, NC	Y	25890 FQ	32430 MW	52890 TQ	USBLS	5/15
	North Dakota	Y	34350 FQ	46280 MW	62970 TQ	USBLS	5/15
	Fargo MSA, ND-MN	Y	34720 FQ	44720 MW	60640 TQ	USBLS	5/15
	Ohio	Y	28220 FQ	36170 MW	46200 TQ	USBLS	5/15
	Cincinnati MSA, OH-KY-IN	Y	29800 FQ	38520 MW	49630 TQ	USBLS	5/15
	Cleveland-Elyria MSA, OH	Y	29400 FQ	37060 MW	48330 TQ	USBLS	5/15
	Columbus MSA, OH	Y	29050 FQ	37260 MW	49140 TQ	USBLS	5/15
	Oklahoma	Y	26200 FQ	36690 MW	48880 TQ	USBLS	5/15
	Oklahoma City MSA, OK	Y	27100 FQ	38440 MW	51310 TQ	USBLS	5/15
	Tulsa MSA, OK	Y	27100 FQ	39340 MW	50830 TQ	USBLS	5/15
	Oregon	H	13.77 FQ	17.68 MW	22.57 TQ	ORBLS	2016
	Portland-Vancouver-Hillsboro MSA, OR-WA	Y	29710 FQ	38270 MW	48250 TQ	USBLS	5/15
	Pennsylvania	Y	29330 FQ	37140 MW	47130 TQ	USBLS	5/15
	Allentown-Bethlehem-Easton MSA, PA-NJ	Y	30170 FQ	37500 MW	47860 TQ	USBLS	5/15
	Harrisburg-Carlisle MSA, PA	Y	31730 FQ	37600 MW	45000 TQ	USBLS	5/15
	Montgomery County-Bucks County-Chester County PMSA, PA	Y	32900 FQ	41470 MW	50360 TQ	USBLS	5/15
	Philadelphia PMSA, PA	Y	29240 FQ	41660 MW	59350 TQ	USBLS	5/15
	Pittsburgh MSA, PA	Y	32290 FQ	38900 MW	48350 TQ	USBLS	5/15
	Rhode Island	Y	26950 FQ	34350 MW	44400 TQ	USBLS	5/15
	Providence-Warwick MSA, RI-MA	Y	26910 FQ	34050 MW	44380 TQ	USBLS	5/15
	South Carolina	Y	26350 FQ	34030 MW	43800 TQ	USBLS	5/15
	Charleston-North Charleston MSA, SC	Y	30540 FQ	41180 MW	48950 TQ	USBLS	5/15
	Columbia MSA, SC	Y	29290 FQ	40070 MW	52280 TQ	USBLS	5/15
	Greenville-Anderson-Mauldin MSA, SC	Y	27840 FQ	34400 MW	44880 TQ	USBLS	5/15
	South Dakota	Y	28550 FQ	33500 MW	39010 TQ	USBLS	5/15
	Sioux Falls MSA, SD	Y	27550 FQ	31200 MW	35970 TQ	USBLS	5/15
	Tennessee	Y	25140 FQ	31660 MW	39630 TQ	USBLS	5/15
	Knoxville MSA, TN	Y	23820 FQ	34430 MW	50860 TQ	USBLS	5/15
	Memphis MSA, TN-MS-AR	Y	25770 FQ	33590 MW	43350 TQ	USBLS	5/15
	Nashville-Davidson–Murfreesboro–Franklin MSA, TN	Y	25110 FQ	31850 MW	39880 TQ	USBLS	5/15
	Texas	Y	27730 FQ	37910 MW	52750 TQ	USBLS	5/15
	Austin-Round Rock MSA, TX	Y	25380 FQ	32680 MW	48430 TQ	USBLS	5/15
	Dallas-Plano-Irving PMSA, TX	Y	27300 FQ	35400 MW	47150 TQ	USBLS	5/15
	Fort Worth-Arlington PMSA, TX	Y	28940 FQ	39140 MW	53730 TQ	USBLS	5/15
	Houston-The Woodlands-Sugar Land MSA, TX	Y	32980 FQ	42920 MW	59220 TQ	USBLS	5/15
	San Antonio-New Braunfels MSA, TX	Y	25170 FQ	35500 MW	48250 TQ	USBLS	5/15
	Utah	Y	27390 FQ	35730 MW	47420 TQ	USBLS	5/15
	Ogden-Clearfield MSA, UT	Y	29130 FQ	37710 MW	49770 TQ	USBLS	5/15
	Provo-Orem MSA, UT	Y	24130 FQ	30610 MW	39290 TQ	USBLS	5/15
	Salt Lake City MSA, UT	Y	28330 FQ	37700 MW	49230 TQ	USBLS	5/15
	Vermont	Y	28110 FQ	35000 MW	43350 TQ	USBLS	5/15
	Burlington-South Burlington MSA, VT	Y	26890 FQ	34690 MW	44240 TQ	USBLS	5/15
	Virginia	Y	26160 FQ	36160 MW	47880 TQ	USBLS	5/15
	Richmond MSA, VA	Y	28380 FQ	40560 MW	48530 TQ	USBLS	5/15

AE	Average entry wage	AWR	Average wage range	H	Hourly
AEX	Average experienced wage	B	Biweekly	HI	Highest wage paid
ATC	Average total compensation	D	Daily	HR	High end range
AW	Average wage paid	FQ	First quartile wage	LO	Lowest wage paid

LR	Low end range	MTC	Median total compensation	TCC	Total cash compensation
M	Monthly	MW	Median wage paid	TQ	Third quartile wage
MCC	Median cash compensation	MWR	Median wage range	W	Weekly
ME	Median entry wage	S	See annotated source	Y	Yearly

Occupation/Type/Industry	Location	Per	Low	Mid	High	Source	Date
Inspector, Tester, Sorter, Sampler, and Weigher							
	Virginia Beach-Norfolk- Newport News MSA, VA-NC	Y	31970 FQ	44530 MW	54650 TQ	USBLS	5/15
	Washington	H	17.93 FQ	23.82 MW	35.08 TQ	WABLS	3/16
	Seattle-Bellevue-Everett PMSA, WA	H	20.06 FQ	27.04 MW	39.40 TQ	WABLS	3/16
	Tacoma-Lakewood PMSA, WA	H	19.18 FQ	25.78 MW	34.74 TQ	WABLS	3/16
	West Virginia	Y	29270 FQ	38640 MW	53590 TQ	USBLS	5/15
	Huntington-Ashland MSA, WV-KY-OH	Y	26560 FQ	41900 MW	54890 TQ	USBLS	5/15
	Wisconsin	Y	28390 FQ	35550 MW	44350 TQ	USBLS	5/15
	Madison MSA, WI	Y	27560 FQ	35470 MW	45690 TQ	USBLS	5/15
	Milwaukee-Waukesha-West Allis MSA, WI	Y	29460 FQ	36950 MW	47000 TQ	USBLS	5/15
	Wyoming	Y	36210 FQ	47480 MW	59860 TQ	USBLS	5/15
	Puerto Rico	Y	18740 FQ	23050 MW	33060 TQ	USBLS	5/15
	San Juan-Carolina-Caguas MSA, PR	Y	19090 FQ	23980 MW	38200 TQ	USBLS	5/15
	Guam	Y	26020 FQ	29270 MW	34770 TQ	USBLS	5/15
Installer and Repairer							
Radio, Cellular, and Tower Equipment	Alabama	Y	33155 AE	48400 AW	56028 AEX	ALBLS	6/16
Radio, Cellular, and Tower Equipment	Birmingham-Hoover MSA, AL	Y	35199 AE	49244 AW	56272 AEX	ALBLS	6/16
Radio, Cellular, and Tower Equipment	Alaska	Y	54620 FQ	71000 MW	82350 TQ	USBLS	5/15
Radio, Cellular, and Tower Equipment	Anchorage MSA, AK	Y	49380 FQ	69640 MW	81230 TQ	USBLS	5/15
Radio, Cellular, and Tower Equipment	Arizona	Y	42600 FQ	56750 MW	70510 TQ	USBLS	5/15
Radio, Cellular, and Tower Equipment	Phoenix-Mesa-Scottsdale MSA, AZ	Y	43540 FQ	57870 MW	71090 TQ	USBLS	5/15
Radio, Cellular, and Tower Equipment	Arkansas	Y	29050 FQ	47360 MW	68370 TQ	USBLS	5/15
Radio, Cellular, and Tower Equipment	California	H	19.52 FQ	27.54 MW	33.90 TQ	CABLS	1/16-3/16
Radio, Cellular, and Tower Equipment	Anaheim-Santa Ana-Irvine PMSA, CA	H	17.44 FQ	24.41 MW	29.84 TQ	CABLS	1/16-3/16
Radio, Cellular, and Tower Equipment	Los Angeles-Long Beach- Glendale PMSA, CA	H	18.49 FQ	27.23 MW	34.56 TQ	CABLS	1/16-3/16
Radio, Cellular, and Tower Equipment	Oakland-Hayward-Berkeley PMSA, CA	H	16.22 FQ	27.41 MW	32.27 TQ	CABLS	1/16-3/16
Radio, Cellular, and Tower Equipment	Riverside-San Bernardino- Ontario MSA, CA	H	14.58 FQ	25.61 MW	29.44 TQ	CABLS	1/16-3/16
Radio, Cellular, and Tower Equipment	Sacramento–Roseville– Arden-Arcade MSA, CA	H	26.36 FQ	29.36 MW	32.29 TQ	CABLS	1/16-3/16
Radio, Cellular, and Tower Equipment	San Diego-Carlsbad MSA, CA	H	17.63 FQ	25.48 MW	30.29 TQ	CABLS	1/16-3/16
Radio, Cellular, and Tower Equipment	Colorado	Y	37430 FQ	48830 MW	59650 TQ	USBLS	5/15
Radio, Cellular, and Tower Equipment	Denver-Aurora-Lakewood MSA, CO	Y	44200 FQ	52920 MW	60350 TQ	USBLS	5/15
Radio, Cellular, and Tower Equipment	Connecticut	Y		48484 MW		CTBLS	1/16-3/16
Radio, Cellular, and Tower Equipment	Delaware	Y	38800 FQ	44270 MW	56200 TQ	USBLS	5/15
Radio, Cellular, and Tower Equipment	Washington-Arlington- Alexandria PMSA, DC-VA- MD-WV	Y	44940 FQ	57140 MW	73240 TQ	USBLS	5/15
Radio, Cellular, and Tower Equipment	Florida	H	15.95 AE	27.95 MW	33.40 AEX	FLBLS	7/16-9/16
Radio, Cellular, and Tower Equipment	Miami-Miami Beach-Kendall PMSA, FL	H	31.00 AE	35.17 MW	36.95 AEX	FLBLS	7/16-9/16
Radio, Cellular, and Tower Equipment	Orlando-Kissimmee-Sanford MSA, FL	H	20.34 AE	27.40 MW	30.92 AEX	FLBLS	7/16-9/16
Radio, Cellular, and Tower Equipment	Tampa-St. Petersburg- Clearwater MSA, FL	H	21.01 AE	33.18 MW	39.19 AEX	FLBLS	7/16-9/16
Radio, Cellular, and Tower Equipment	Georgia	Y	39350 FQ	47980 MW	69440 TQ	USBLS	5/15
Radio, Cellular, and Tower Equipment	Atlanta-Sandy Springs- Roswell MSA, GA	Y	39880 FQ	46350 MW	65470 TQ	USBLS	5/15
Radio, Cellular, and Tower Equipment	Hawaii	Y	38240 FQ	48830 MW	57500 TQ	USBLS	5/15
Radio, Cellular, and Tower Equipment	Urban Honolulu MSA, HI	Y	37690 FQ	51540 MW	58210 TQ	USBLS	5/15
Radio, Cellular, and Tower Equipment	Idaho	Y	25270 FQ	36050 MW	51770 TQ	USBLS	5/15
Radio, Cellular, and Tower Equipment	Illinois	Y	34490 FQ	40540 MW	56090 TQ	USBLS	5/15
Radio, Cellular, and Tower Equipment	Chicago-Naperville-Arlington Heights PMSA, IL	Y	35200 FQ	40890 MW	55830 TQ	USBLS	5/15
Radio, Cellular, and Tower Equipment	Lake County-Kenosha County PMSA, IL-WI	Y	45150 FQ	58990 MW	70710 TQ	USBLS	5/15
Radio, Cellular, and Tower Equipment	Indiana	Y	37040 FQ	47740 MW	66090 TQ	USBLS	5/15
Radio, Cellular, and Tower Equipment	Indianapolis-Carmel-Anderson MSA, IN	Y	53940 FQ	67400 MW	74290 TQ	USBLS	5/15
Radio, Cellular, and Tower Equipment	Iowa	Y	41470 FQ	45050 MW	48640 TQ	USBLS	5/15
Radio, Cellular, and Tower Equipment	Kansas	Y	36780 FQ	47980 MW	61740 TQ	USBLS	5/15

AE	Average entry wage	AWR	Average wage range	H	Hourly	LR	Low end range	MTC	Median total compensation	TCC	Total cash compensation
AEX	Average experienced wage	B	Biweekly	HI	Highest wage paid	M	Monthly	MW	Median wage paid	TQ	Third quartile wage
ATC	Average total compensation	D	Daily	HR	High end range	MCC	Median cash compensation	MWR	Median wage range	W	Weekly
AW	Average wage paid	FQ	First quartile wage	LO	Lowest wage paid	ME	Median entry wage	S	See annotated source	Y	Yearly

Occupation/Type/Industry	Location	Per	Low	Mid	High	Source	Date
Installer and Repairer							
Radio, Cellular, and Tower Equipment	Wichita MSA, KS	Y	37810 FQ	45150 MW	56560 TQ	USBLS	5/15
Radio, Cellular, and Tower Equipment	Kentucky	Y	41320 FQ	61850 MW	73710 TQ	USBLS	5/15
Radio, Cellular, and Tower Equipment	Louisville-Jefferson County MSA, KY-IN	Y	38820 FQ	68240 MW	75830 TQ	USBLS	5/15
Radio, Cellular, and Tower Equipment	Louisiana	Y	36870 FQ	51710 MW	60230 TQ	USBLS	5/15
Radio, Cellular, and Tower Equipment	Baton Rouge MSA, LA	Y	46320 FQ	55240 MW	61380 TQ	USBLS	5/15
Radio, Cellular, and Tower Equipment	Maine	Y	33760 FQ	36530 MW	39300 TQ	USBLS	5/15
Radio, Cellular, and Tower Equipment	Portland-South Portland MSA, ME	Y	33690 FQ	36770 MW	40140 TQ	USBLS	5/15
Radio, Cellular, and Tower Equipment	Maryland	Y	42562 AE	64488 MW	75451 AEX	MDBLS	4/16
Radio, Cellular, and Tower Equipment	Baltimore-Columbia-Towson MSA, MD	Y	47130 FQ	65890 MW	75620 TQ	USBLS	5/15
Radio, Cellular, and Tower Equipment	Massachusetts	Y	45340 FQ	56980 MW	70210 TQ	USBLS	5/15
Radio, Cellular, and Tower Equipment	Boston-Cambridge-Newton NECTA, MA	Y	53490 FQ	60570 MW	73100 TQ	USBLS	5/15
Radio, Cellular, and Tower Equipment	Worcester MSA, MA-CT	Y	35200 FQ	38640 MW	54090 TQ	USBLS	5/15
Radio, Cellular, and Tower Equipment	Michigan	Y	48740 FQ	65250 MW	74580 TQ	USBLS	5/15
Radio, Cellular, and Tower Equipment	Minnesota	Y	55010 FQ	59023 MW	64655 TQ	MNBLS	1/16-3/16
Radio, Cellular, and Tower Equipment	Minneapolis-St. Paul-Bloomington MSA, MN-WI	Y	55232 FQ	59968 MW	64926 TQ	MNBLS	1/16-3/16
Radio, Cellular, and Tower Equipment	Mississippi	Y	61930 FQ	69690 MW	75980 TQ	USBLS	5/15
Radio, Cellular, and Tower Equipment	Missouri	Y	34300 FQ	44620 MW	69530 TQ	USBLS	5/15
Radio, Cellular, and Tower Equipment	Kansas City MSA, MO-KS	Y	41690 FQ	60720 MW	71530 TQ	USBLS	5/15
Radio, Cellular, and Tower Equipment	St. Louis MSA, MO-IL	Y	35390 FQ	42920 MW	65550 TQ	USBLS	5/15
Radio, Cellular, and Tower Equipment	Nebraska	Y	40390 FQ	51145 MW	70930 TQ	NEBLS	7/16-9/16
Radio, Cellular, and Tower Equipment	Nevada	Y	40870 FQ	49040 MW	62260 TQ	USBLS	5/15
Radio, Cellular, and Tower Equipment	Las Vegas-Henderson-Paradise MSA, NV	Y	40030 FQ	46770 MW	59530 TQ	USBLS	5/15
Radio, Cellular, and Tower Equipment	New Hampshire	H	16.27 AE	21.69 MW	27.78 AEX	NHBLS	6/16
Radio, Cellular, and Tower Equipment	New Jersey	Y	55350 FQ	67970 MW	74020 TQ	USBLS	5/15
Radio, Cellular, and Tower Equipment	New Mexico	Y	47070 FQ	68150 MW	86430 TQ	USBLS	5/15
Radio, Cellular, and Tower Equipment	New York	Y	31950 AE	73810 MW	82810 AEX	NYBLS	1/16-3/16
Radio, Cellular, and Tower Equipment	Nassau County-Suffolk County PMSA, NY	Y	24510 FQ	56780 MW	71680 TQ	USBLS	5/15
Radio, Cellular, and Tower Equipment	New York-Jersey City-White Plains PMSA, NY-NJ	Y	66570 FQ	73360 MW	85720 TQ	USBLS	5/15
Radio, Cellular, and Tower Equipment	North Carolina	Y	34940 FQ	44760 MW	60250 TQ	USBLS	5/15
Radio, Cellular, and Tower Equipment	Charlotte-Concord-Gastonia MSA, NC-SC	Y	33260 FQ	39040 MW	53620 TQ	USBLS	5/15
Radio, Cellular, and Tower Equipment	Raleigh MSA, NC	Y	34590 FQ	44280 MW	57690 TQ	USBLS	5/15
Radio, Cellular, and Tower Equipment	North Dakota	Y	44740 FQ	54810 MW	60570 TQ	USBLS	5/15
Radio, Cellular, and Tower Equipment	Ohio	Y	42630 FQ	57380 MW	71280 TQ	USBLS	5/15
Radio, Cellular, and Tower Equipment	Cincinnati MSA, OH-KY-IN	Y	47270 FQ	57950 MW	68240 TQ	USBLS	5/15
Radio, Cellular, and Tower Equipment	Cleveland-Elyria MSA, OH	Y	34600 FQ	55790 MW	88430 TQ	USBLS	5/15
Radio, Cellular, and Tower Equipment	Columbus MSA, OH	Y	47170 FQ	66020 MW	73990 TQ	USBLS	5/15
Radio, Cellular, and Tower Equipment	Oklahoma	Y	34490 FQ	41540 MW	49320 TQ	USBLS	5/15
Radio, Cellular, and Tower Equipment	Oklahoma City MSA, OK	Y	31800 FQ	35650 MW	39860 TQ	USBLS	5/15
Radio, Cellular, and Tower Equipment	Oregon	H	19.14 FQ	22.76 MW	29.13 TQ	ORBLS	2016
Radio, Cellular, and Tower Equipment	Portland-Vancouver-Hillsboro MSA, OR-WA	Y	34240 FQ	44070 MW	68820 TQ	USBLS	5/15
Radio, Cellular, and Tower Equipment	Pennsylvania	Y	59560 FQ	69300 MW	75830 TQ	USBLS	5/15
Radio, Cellular, and Tower Equipment	Montgomery County-Bucks County-Chester County PMSA, PA	Y	65470 FQ	70570 MW	75660 TQ	USBLS	5/15
Radio, Cellular, and Tower Equipment	Philadelphia PMSA, PA	Y	51720 FQ	62870 MW	72160 TQ	USBLS	5/15
Radio, Cellular, and Tower Equipment	Pittsburgh MSA, PA	Y	64200 FQ	72960 MW	81300 TQ	USBLS	5/15
Radio, Cellular, and Tower Equipment	South Carolina	Y	38270 FQ	44950 MW	53710 TQ	USBLS	5/15
Radio, Cellular, and Tower Equipment	Charleston-North Charleston MSA, SC	Y	38570 FQ	44240 MW	49620 TQ	USBLS	5/15
Radio, Cellular, and Tower Equipment	Columbia MSA, SC	Y	34430 FQ	45810 MW	67330 TQ	USBLS	5/15
Radio, Cellular, and Tower Equipment	Tennessee	Y	30980 FQ	45960 MW	59520 TQ	USBLS	5/15
Radio, Cellular, and Tower Equipment	Knoxville MSA, TN	Y	48700 FQ	59070 MW	70320 TQ	USBLS	5/15
Radio, Cellular, and Tower Equipment	Memphis MSA, TN-MS-AR	Y	43400 FQ	51640 MW	64720 TQ	USBLS	5/15
Radio, Cellular, and Tower Equipment	Nashville-Davidson–Murfreesboro–Franklin MSA, TN	Y	26210 FQ	30510 MW	51390 TQ	USBLS	5/15
Radio, Cellular, and Tower Equipment	Texas	Y	33780 FQ	41750 MW	59140 TQ	USBLS	5/15
Radio, Cellular, and Tower Equipment	Austin-Round Rock MSA, TX	Y	27340 FQ	33440 MW	38900 TQ	USBLS	5/15
Radio, Cellular, and Tower Equipment	Dallas-Plano-Irving PMSA, TX	Y	33990 FQ	39530 MW	55800 TQ	USBLS	5/15
Radio, Cellular, and Tower Equipment	Houston-The Woodlands-Sugar Land MSA, TX	Y	46210 FQ	60900 MW	72740 TQ	USBLS	5/15

AE Average entry wage	**AWR** Average wage range	**H** Hourly	**LR** Low end range	**MTC** Median total compensation	**TCC** Total cash compensation
AEX Average experienced wage	**B** Biweekly	**HI** Highest wage paid	**M** Monthly	**MW** Median wage paid	**TQ** Third quartile wage
ATC Average total compensation	**D** Daily	**HR** High end range	**MCC** Median cash compensation	**MWR** Median wage range	**W** Weekly
AW Average wage paid	**FQ** First quartile wage	**LO** Lowest wage paid	**ME** Median entry wage	**S** See annotated source	**Y** Yearly

Occupation/Type/Industry	Location	Per	Low	Mid	High	Source	Date
Installer and Repairer							
Radio, Cellular, and Tower Equipment	San Antonio-New Braunfels MSA, TX	Y	41130 FQ	50140 MW	63020 TQ	USBLS	5/15
Radio, Cellular, and Tower Equipment	Utah	Y	41320 FQ	47190 MW	56910 TQ	USBLS	5/15
Radio, Cellular, and Tower Equipment	Vermont	Y	36070 FQ	47630 MW	63590 TQ	USBLS	5/15
Radio, Cellular, and Tower Equipment	Virginia	Y	45720 FQ	52900 MW	59660 TQ	USBLS	5/15
Radio, Cellular, and Tower Equipment	Virginia Beach-Norfolk-Newport News MSA, VA-NC	Y	52110 FQ	58830 MW	59660 TQ	USBLS	5/15
Radio, Cellular, and Tower Equipment	Washington	H	24.25 FQ	29.87 MW	36.02 TQ	WABLS	3/16
Radio, Cellular, and Tower Equipment	Seattle-Bellevue-Everett PMSA, WA	H	24.57 FQ	29.70 MW	35.56 TQ	WABLS	3/16
Radio, Cellular, and Tower Equipment	West Virginia	Y	29380 FQ	45420 MW	65850 TQ	USBLS	5/15
Radio, Cellular, and Tower Equipment	Huntington-Ashland MSA, WV-KY-OH	Y	39510 FQ	46500 MW	61800 TQ	USBLS	5/15
Radio, Cellular, and Tower Equipment	Wisconsin	Y	34130 FQ	42580 MW	51910 TQ	USBLS	5/15
Radio, Cellular, and Tower Equipment	Milwaukee-Waukesha-West Allis MSA, WI	Y	36090 FQ	42860 MW	50210 TQ	USBLS	5/15
Radio, Cellular, and Tower Equipment	Wyoming	Y	39750 FQ	51490 MW	61260 TQ	USBLS	5/15
Radio, Cellular, and Tower Equipment	Puerto Rico	Y	27260 FQ	34580 MW	43050 TQ	USBLS	5/15
Radio, Cellular, and Tower Equipment	San Juan-Carolina-Caguas MSA, PR	Y	26430 FQ	31790 MW	39750 TQ	USBLS	5/15
Instructional Coordinator	Alabama	Y	48092 AE	69141 AW	79670 AEX	ALBLS	6/16
	Birmingham-Hoover MSA, AL	Y	50324 AE	69763 AW	79477 AEX	ALBLS	6/16
	Alaska	Y	57840 FQ	75710 MW	91650 TQ	USBLS	5/15
	Anchorage MSA, AK	Y	56450 FQ	75410 MW	93270 TQ	USBLS	5/15
	Arizona	Y	40500 FQ	50430 MW	62550 TQ	USBLS	5/15
	Phoenix-Mesa-Scottsdale MSA, AZ	Y	41030 FQ	51100 MW	63250 TQ	USBLS	5/15
	Tucson MSA, AZ	Y	37500 FQ	46400 MW	58090 TQ	USBLS	5/15
	Arkansas	Y	44990 FQ	56480 MW	67280 TQ	USBLS	5/15
	Little Rock-North Little Rock-Conway MSA, AR	Y	50750 FQ	58370 MW	66950 TQ	USBLS	5/15
	California	H	26.80 FQ	36.14 MW	45.68 TQ	CABLS	1/16-3/16
	Anaheim-Santa Ana-Irvine PMSA, CA	H	29.46 FQ	41.23 MW	50.09 TQ	CABLS	1/16-3/16
	Los Angeles-Long Beach-Glendale PMSA, CA	H	25.47 FQ	34.26 MW	42.98 TQ	CABLS	1/16-3/16
	Oakland-Hayward-Berkeley PMSA, CA	H	25.03 FQ	33.45 MW	44.11 TQ	CABLS	1/16-3/16
	Riverside-San Bernardino-Ontario MSA, CA	H	35.79 FQ	44.59 MW	51.46 TQ	CABLS	1/16-3/16
	Sacramento–Roseville–Arden-Arcade MSA, CA	H	30.48 FQ	40.67 MW	46.28 TQ	CABLS	1/16-3/16
	San Diego-Carlsbad MSA, CA	H	25.74 FQ	36.03 MW	47.70 TQ	CABLS	1/16-3/16
	San Francisco-Redwood City-South San Francisco PMSA, CA	H	27.84 FQ	34.86 MW	41.84 TQ	CABLS	1/16-3/16
	Colorado	Y	54570 FQ	67290 MW	80770 TQ	USBLS	5/15
	Denver-Aurora-Lakewood MSA, CO	Y	56000 FQ	67280 MW	79950 TQ	USBLS	5/15
	Connecticut	Y		80875 MW		CTBLS	1/16-3/16
	Bridgeport-Stamford-Norwalk MSA, CT	Y	42440 FQ	68360 MW	96450 TQ	USBLS	5/15
	Hartford-West Hartford-East Hartford MSA, CT	Y	69190 FQ	89960 MW	109780 TQ	USBLS	5/15
	Delaware	Y	52150 FQ	68280 MW	82700 TQ	USBLS	5/15
	Wilmington PMSA, DE-MD-NJ	Y	53010 FQ	69440 MW	88870 TQ	USBLS	5/15
	District of Columbia	Y	65500 FQ	84210 MW	109530 TQ	USBLS	5/15
	Washington-Arlington-Alexandria PMSA, DC-VA-MD-WV	Y	56250 FQ	74520 MW	96070 TQ	USBLS	5/15
	Florida	H	18.65 AE	27.40 MW	33.79 AEX	FLBLS	7/16-9/16
	Fort Lauderdale-Pompano Beach-Deerfield Beach PMSA, FL	H	15.96 AE	25.02 MW	34.21 AEX	FLBLS	7/16-9/16
	Miami-Miami Beach-Kendall PMSA, FL	H	21.26 AE	28.84 MW	34.32 AEX	FLBLS	7/16-9/16
	Orlando-Kissimmee-Sanford MSA, FL	H	19.76 AE	29.70 MW	36.40 AEX	FLBLS	7/16-9/16

AE	Average entry wage	AWR	Average wage range	H	Hourly	LR	Low end range	MTC	Median total compensation	TCC	Total cash compensation
AEX	Average experienced wage	B	Biweekly	HI	Highest wage paid	M	Monthly	MW	Median wage paid	TQ	Third quartile wage
ATC	Average total compensation	D	Daily	HR	High end range	MCC	Median cash compensation	MWR	Median wage range	W	Weekly
AW	Average wage paid	FQ	First quartile wage	LO	Lowest wage paid	ME	Median entry wage	S	See annotated source	Y	Yearly

Instructional Coordinator

Occupation/Type/Industry	Location	Per	Low	Mid	High	Source	Date
Instructional Coordinator	Tampa-St. Petersburg-Clearwater MSA, FL	H	18.30 AE	26.51 MW	35.89 AEX	FLBLS	7/16-9/16
	Georgia	Y	42400 FQ	60640 MW	74880 TQ	USBLS	5/15
	Atlanta-Sandy Springs-Roswell MSA, GA	Y	41370 FQ	57190 MW	73860 TQ	USBLS	5/15
	Augusta-Richmond County MSA, GA-SC	Y	38000 FQ	50640 MW	68320 TQ	USBLS	5/15
	Hawaii	Y	50290 FQ	63180 MW	77480 TQ	USBLS	5/15
	Urban Honolulu MSA, HI	Y	52140 FQ	64850 MW	78400 TQ	USBLS	5/15
	Idaho	Y	38970 FQ	49790 MW	60810 TQ	USBLS	5/15
	Boise City MSA, ID	Y	43130 FQ	51230 MW	61740 TQ	USBLS	5/15
	Illinois	Y	42960 FQ	57850 MW	73730 TQ	USBLS	5/15
	Chicago-Naperville-Arlington Heights PMSA, IL	Y	44430 FQ	59590 MW	74520 TQ	USBLS	5/15
	Lake County-Kenosha County PMSA, IL-WI	Y	51320 FQ	66320 MW	86680 TQ	USBLS	5/15
	Indiana	Y	37600 FQ	54590 MW	70360 TQ	USBLS	5/15
	Gary PMSA, IN	Y	41480 FQ	57680 MW	72470 TQ	USBLS	5/15
	Indianapolis-Carmel-Anderson MSA, IN	Y	37550 FQ	55410 MW	70840 TQ	USBLS	5/15
	Iowa	Y	47190 FQ	66590 MW	78610 TQ	USBLS	5/15
	Des Moines-West Des Moines MSA, IA	Y	67160 FQ	77470 MW	83610 TQ	USBLS	5/15
	Kansas	Y	37180 FQ	52430 MW	68400 TQ	USBLS	5/15
	Wichita MSA, KS	Y	46100 FQ	56500 MW	65980 TQ	USBLS	5/15
	Kentucky	Y	46470 FQ	58840 MW	74380 TQ	USBLS	5/15
	Louisville-Jefferson County MSA, KY-IN	Y	42100 FQ	53070 MW	74970 TQ	USBLS	5/15
	Louisiana	Y	39950 FQ	51320 MW	61830 TQ	USBLS	5/15
	Baton Rouge MSA, LA	Y	42280 FQ	53510 MW	62710 TQ	USBLS	5/15
	New Orleans-Metairie MSA, LA	Y	35950 FQ	44750 MW	58910 TQ	USBLS	5/15
	Maine	Y	43170 FQ	55310 MW	68590 TQ	USBLS	5/15
	Portland-South Portland MSA, ME	Y	43770 FQ	57870 MW	73610 TQ	USBLS	5/15
	Maryland	Y	46764 AE	68487 MW	79349 AEX	MDBLS	4/16
	Baltimore-Columbia-Towson MSA, MD	Y	53960 FQ	66630 MW	82190 TQ	USBLS	5/15
	Salisbury MSA, MD-DE	Y	37280 FQ	63310 MW	76230 TQ	USBLS	5/15
	Massachusetts	Y	46290 FQ	64230 MW	85190 TQ	USBLS	5/15
	Boston-Cambridge-Newton NECTA, MA	Y	45180 FQ	62300 MW	85440 TQ	USBLS	5/15
	Worcester MSA, MA-CT	Y	49320 FQ	71890 MW	87780 TQ	USBLS	5/15
	Michigan	Y	49870 FQ	68940 MW	81830 TQ	USBLS	5/15
	Detroit-Dearborn-Livonia PMSA, MI	Y	62140 FQ	72520 MW	84580 TQ	USBLS	5/15
	Grand Rapids-Wyoming MSA, MI	Y	47140 FQ	68470 MW	80860 TQ	USBLS	5/15
	Minnesota	Y	43185 FQ	58759 MW	78719 TQ	MNBLS	1/16-3/16
	Minneapolis-St. Paul-Bloomington MSA, MN-WI	Y	43467 FQ	60463 MW	81955 TQ	MNBLS	1/16-3/16
	Mississippi	Y	40500 FQ	53150 MW	68230 TQ	USBLS	5/15
	Jackson MSA, MS	Y	39140 FQ	45950 MW	59590 TQ	USBLS	5/15
	Missouri	Y	45080 FQ	56830 MW	70890 TQ	USBLS	5/15
	Kansas City MSA, MO-KS	Y	51270 FQ	63280 MW	77890 TQ	USBLS	5/15
	St. Louis MSA, MO-IL	Y	37420 FQ	50420 MW	62890 TQ	USBLS	5/15
	Montana	Y	36800 FQ	47310 MW	57500 TQ	USBLS	5/15
	Nebraska	Y	43630 FQ	57075 MW	71970 TQ	NEBLS	7/16-9/16
	Omaha-Council Bluffs MSA, NE-IA	Y	45515 FQ	60195 MW	75305 TQ	NEBLS	7/16-9/16
	Nevada	Y	42700 FQ	52740 MW	63520 TQ	USBLS	5/15
	Las Vegas-Henderson-Paradise MSA, NV	Y	43060 FQ	51510 MW	63730 TQ	USBLS	5/15
	New Hampshire	H	23.27 AE	30.81 MW	38.32 AEX	NHBLS	6/16
	Manchester NECTA, NH	H	24.30 AE	31.42 MW	36.30 AEX	NHBLS	6/16
	Nashua NECTA, NH-MA	Y	53020 FQ	61610 MW	71820 TQ	USBLS	5/15
	New Jersey	Y	61290 FQ	80580 MW	95760 TQ	USBLS	5/15
	Camden PMSA, NJ	Y	40130 FQ	78070 MW	92000 TQ	USBLS	5/15
	Newark PMSA, NJ-PA	Y	60980 FQ	78070 MW	93750 TQ	USBLS	5/15
	Trenton MSA, NJ	Y	79960 FQ	94070 MW	110800 TQ	USBLS	5/15
	New Mexico	Y	47770 FQ	63910 MW	81080 TQ	USBLS	5/15
	Albuquerque MSA, NM	Y	51840 FQ	68890 MW	84220 TQ	USBLS	5/15

AE	Average entry wage	AWR	Average wage range	H	Hourly
AEX	Average experienced wage	B	Biweekly	HI	Highest wage paid
ATC	Average total compensation	D	Daily	HR	High end range
AW	Average wage paid	FQ	First quartile wage	LO	Lowest wage paid

LR	Low end range	MTC	Median total compensation
M	Monthly	MW	Median wage paid
MCC	Median cash compensation	MWR	Median wage range
ME	Median entry wage	S	See annotated source

TCC	Total cash compensation
TQ	Third quartile wage
W	Weekly
Y	Yearly

Occupation/Type/Industry	Location	Per	Low	Mid	High	Source	Date
Instructional Coordinator	New York	Y	45020 AE	63330 MW	81100 AEX	NYBLS	1/16-3/16
	Buffalo-Cheektowaga-Niagara Falls MSA, NY	Y	41480 FQ	55640 MW	67780 TQ	USBLS	5/15
	Nassau County-Suffolk County PMSA, NY	Y	53530 FQ	78030 MW	112520 TQ	USBLS	5/15
	New York-Jersey City-White Plains PMSA, NY-NJ	Y	51230 FQ	65840 MW	82860 TQ	USBLS	5/15
	Rochester MSA, NY	Y	53890 FQ	62040 MW	77390 TQ	USBLS	5/15
	North Carolina	Y	46050 FQ	56950 MW	70550 TQ	USBLS	5/15
	Charlotte-Concord-Gastonia MSA, NC-SC	Y	49880 FQ	60540 MW	74120 TQ	USBLS	5/15
	Raleigh MSA, NC	Y	51750 FQ	62160 MW	74960 TQ	USBLS	5/15
	North Dakota	Y	44350 FQ	57520 MW	77780 TQ	USBLS	5/15
	Fargo MSA, ND-MN	Y	39600 FQ	50110 MW	67820 TQ	USBLS	5/15
	Ohio	Y	41470 FQ	59600 MW	77410 TQ	USBLS	5/15
	Cincinnati MSA, OH-KY-IN	Y	43760 FQ	62960 MW	79010 TQ	USBLS	5/15
	Cleveland-Elyria MSA, OH	Y	54730 FQ	74390 MW	92100 TQ	USBLS	5/15
	Columbus MSA, OH	Y	50430 FQ	63370 MW	78200 TQ	USBLS	5/15
	Oklahoma	Y	38040 FQ	50370 MW	67680 TQ	USBLS	5/15
	Oklahoma City MSA, OK	Y	37350 FQ	51510 MW	66570 TQ	USBLS	5/15
	Tulsa MSA, OK	Y	40760 FQ	50220 MW	72920 TQ	USBLS	5/15
	Oregon	H	21.92 FQ	30.71 MW	39.43 TQ	ORBLS	2016
	Portland-Vancouver-Hillsboro MSA, OR-WA	Y	53610 FQ	68760 MW	86430 TQ	USBLS	5/15
	Pennsylvania	Y	43140 FQ	57220 MW	75590 TQ	USBLS	5/15
	Allentown-Bethlehem-Easton MSA, PA-NJ	Y	48590 FQ	67400 MW	79070 TQ	USBLS	5/15
	Harrisburg-Carlisle MSA, PA	Y	51460 FQ	66660 MW	78590 TQ	USBLS	5/15
	Montgomery County-Bucks County-Chester County PMSA, PA	Y	37140 FQ	58430 MW	87230 TQ	USBLS	5/15
	Philadelphia PMSA, PA	Y	45070 FQ	57240 MW	72660 TQ	USBLS	5/15
	Pittsburgh MSA, PA	Y	44410 FQ	56740 MW	72820 TQ	USBLS	5/15
	Rhode Island	Y	44400 FQ	54250 MW	66490 TQ	USBLS	5/15
	Providence-Warwick MSA, RI-MA	Y	44450 FQ	54540 MW	68110 TQ	USBLS	5/15
	South Carolina	Y	42370 FQ	53730 MW	68850 TQ	USBLS	5/15
	Charleston-North Charleston MSA, SC	Y	29130 FQ	49000 MW	68430 TQ	USBLS	5/15
	Columbia MSA, SC	Y	42080 FQ	56750 MW	71830 TQ	USBLS	5/15
	Greenville-Anderson-Mauldin MSA, SC	Y	43630 FQ	50420 MW	63100 TQ	USBLS	5/15
	South Dakota	Y	47680 FQ	57060 MW	67730 TQ	USBLS	5/15
	Sioux Falls MSA, SD	Y	45630 FQ	54580 MW	67820 TQ	USBLS	5/15
	Tennessee	Y	43590 FQ	57430 MW	71990 TQ	USBLS	5/15
	Knoxville MSA, TN	Y	43470 FQ	58070 MW	71880 TQ	USBLS	5/15
	Memphis MSA, TN-MS-AR	Y	52090 FQ	61290 MW	74440 TQ	USBLS	5/15
	Nashville-Davidson–Murfreesboro–Franklin MSA, TN	Y	45930 FQ	59550 MW	75360 TQ	USBLS	5/15
	Texas	Y	54540 FQ	66230 MW	78610 TQ	USBLS	5/15
	Austin-Round Rock MSA, TX	Y	54340 FQ	66550 MW	76940 TQ	USBLS	5/15
	Dallas-Plano-Irving PMSA, TX	Y	55710 FQ	67560 MW	79260 TQ	USBLS	5/15
	Fort Worth-Arlington PMSA, TX	Y	54130 FQ	64270 MW	81040 TQ	USBLS	5/15
	Houston-The Woodlands-Sugar Land MSA, TX	Y	57300 FQ	68040 MW	80810 TQ	USBLS	5/15
	San Antonio-New Braunfels MSA, TX	Y	52370 FQ	64330 MW	77040 TQ	USBLS	5/15
	Utah	Y	35980 FQ	49930 MW	71530 TQ	USBLS	5/15
	Ogden-Clearfield MSA, UT	Y	41400 FQ	57120 MW	75140 TQ	USBLS	5/15
	Provo-Orem MSA, UT	Y	33190 FQ	37170 MW	51510 TQ	USBLS	5/15
	Salt Lake City MSA, UT	Y	53590 FQ	69950 MW	83870 TQ	USBLS	5/15
	Vermont	Y	37500 FQ	52270 MW	68210 TQ	USBLS	5/15
	Burlington-South Burlington MSA, VT	Y	43840 FQ	56250 MW	82050 TQ	USBLS	5/15
	Virginia	Y	52530 FQ	69510 MW	87530 TQ	USBLS	5/15
	Richmond MSA, VA	Y	51120 FQ	69000 MW	81740 TQ	USBLS	5/15
	Virginia Beach-Norfolk-Newport News MSA, VA-NC	Y	46580 FQ	64350 MW	77240 TQ	USBLS	5/15
	Washington	H	23.55 FQ	29.06 MW	35.12 TQ	WABLS	3/16

Occupation/Type/Industry	Location	Per	Low	Mid	High	Source	Date
Instructional Coordinator	Seattle-Bellevue-Everett PMSA, WA	H	24.96 FQ	30.51 MW	36.00 TQ	WABLS	3/16
	Tacoma-Lakewood PMSA, WA	H	23.11 FQ	27.97 MW	33.31 TQ	WABLS	3/16
	West Virginia	Y	43430 FQ	56030 MW	70190 TQ	USBLS	5/15
	Huntington-Ashland MSA, WV-KY-OH	Y	28270 FQ	44410 MW	70030 TQ	USBLS	5/15
	Wisconsin	Y	49930 FQ	59610 MW	75920 TQ	USBLS	5/15
	Madison MSA, WI	Y	52550 FQ	63110 MW	76460 TQ	USBLS	5/15
	Milwaukee-Waukesha-West Allis MSA, WI	Y	52900 FQ	60060 MW	83050 TQ	USBLS	5/15
	Wyoming	Y	57120 FQ	66470 MW	76410 TQ	USBLS	5/15
	Cheyenne MSA, WY	Y	59370 FQ	64920 MW	76370 TQ	USBLS	5/15
	Puerto Rico	Y	25950 FQ	30240 MW	38750 TQ	USBLS	5/15
	San Juan-Carolina-Caguas MSA, PR	Y	26000 FQ	30370 MW	39070 TQ	USBLS	5/15
Instructional Designer	Central	Y		65374 AW		TRAIN	2015-2016
	Great Lakes	Y		67526 AW		TRAIN	2015-2016
	Mountain	Y		66682 AW		TRAIN	2015-2016
	Northeast	Y		70459 AW		TRAIN	2015-2016
	Pacific	Y		80511 AW		TRAIN	2015-2016
	Southeast	Y		78101 AW		TRAIN	2015-2016
Instructional System Specialist							
Overseas School, United States Department of Defense	United States	Y	59340 LO		104615 HI	CPMS	2015-2016
Instructor							
Accounting	United States	Y		77500 AW		AACSB	2014-2015
Entrepreneurship	United States	Y		83900 AW		AACSB	2014-2015
Female, 2-Year For-Profit Institution	United States	Y		40125 AW		CHE03	2014-2015
Female, 2-Year Private Institution	United States	Y		42279 AW		CHE03	2014-2015
Female, 2-Year Public Institution	United States	Y		60011 AW		CHE03	2014-2015
Female, 4-Year For-Profit Institution	United States	Y		44076 AW		CHE03	2014-2015
Female, 4-Year Private Institution	United States	Y		48477 AW		CHE03	2014-2015
Female, 4-Year Public Institution	United States	Y		48210 AW		CHE03	2014-2015
Male, 2-Year For-Profit Institution	United States	Y		38116 AW		CHE03	2014-2015
Male, 2-Year Private Institution	United States	Y		22268 AW		CHE03	2014-2015
Male, 2-Year Public Institution	United States	Y		61951 AW		CHE03	2014-2015
Male, 4-Year For-Profit Institution	United States	Y		43368 AW		CHE03	2014-2015
Male, 4-Year Private Institution	United States	Y		46902 AW		CHE03	2014-2015
Male, 4-Year Public Institution	United States	Y		50445 AW		CHE03	2014-2015
Instrument Calibration Technician							
Department of Transportation, State Government	Helena, MT	H			23.57 HI	MTGOV	2016
Insulation Worker							
Floor, Ceiling, and Wall	Alabama	Y	19370 AE	31714 AW	37887 AEX	ALBLS	6/16
Floor, Ceiling, and Wall	Alaska	Y	39710 FQ	57370 MW	73280 TQ	USBLS	5/15
Floor, Ceiling, and Wall	Anchorage MSA, AK	Y	36550 FQ	65190 MW	81430 TQ	USBLS	5/15
Floor, Ceiling, and Wall	Arizona	Y	24990 FQ	29780 MW	37540 TQ	USBLS	5/15
Floor, Ceiling, and Wall	Phoenix-Mesa-Scottsdale MSA, AZ	Y	22610 FQ	27530 MW	37100 TQ	USBLS	5/15
Floor, Ceiling, and Wall	Tucson MSA, AZ	Y	27760 FQ	30830 MW	37950 TQ	USBLS	5/15
Floor, Ceiling, and Wall	Arkansas	Y	22760 FQ	28820 MW	35800 TQ	USBLS	5/15
Floor, Ceiling, and Wall	Little Rock-North Little Rock-Conway MSA, AR	Y	25910 FQ	29880 MW	35490 TQ	USBLS	5/15
Floor, Ceiling, and Wall	California	H	16.56 FQ	21.17 MW	36.08 TQ	CABLS	1/16-3/16
Floor, Ceiling, and Wall	Los Angeles-Long Beach-Glendale PMSA, CA	H	14.60 FQ	19.28 MW	43.29 TQ	CABLS	1/16-3/16
Floor, Ceiling, and Wall	Oakland-Hayward-Berkeley PMSA, CA	H	35.51 FQ	42.77 MW	46.74 TQ	CABLS	1/16-3/16
Floor, Ceiling, and Wall	Riverside-San Bernardino-Ontario MSA, CA	H	23.71 FQ	34.00 MW	37.90 TQ	CABLS	1/16-3/16
Floor, Ceiling, and Wall	Colorado	Y	26860 FQ	34620 MW	47570 TQ	USBLS	5/15
Floor, Ceiling, and Wall	Denver-Aurora-Lakewood MSA, CO	Y	32970 FQ	44990 MW	60510 TQ	USBLS	5/15
Floor, Ceiling, and Wall	Connecticut	Y		36560 MW		CTBLS	1/16-3/16
Floor, Ceiling, and Wall	Bridgeport-Stamford-Norwalk MSA, CT	Y	33530 FQ	35950 MW	38380 TQ	USBLS	5/15

Occupation/Type/Industry	Location	Per	Low	Mid	High	Source	Date
Insulation Worker							
Floor, Ceiling, and Wall	Washington-Arlington-Alexandria PMSA, DC-VA-MD-WV	Y	29070 FQ	35110 MW	42980 TQ	USBLS	5/15
Floor, Ceiling, and Wall	Florida	H	12.11 AE	15.50 MW	18.48 AEX	FLBLS	7/16-9/16
Floor, Ceiling, and Wall	Miami-Miami Beach-Kendall PMSA, FL	H	12.07 AE	15.08 MW	18.43 AEX	FLBLS	7/16-9/16
Floor, Ceiling, and Wall	Orlando-Kissimmee-Sanford MSA, FL	H	13.25 AE	15.42 MW	18.05 AEX	FLBLS	7/16-9/16
Floor, Ceiling, and Wall	Tampa-St. Petersburg-Clearwater MSA, FL	H	12.42 AE	15.30 MW	18.66 AEX	FLBLS	7/16-9/16
Floor, Ceiling, and Wall	Georgia	Y	26490 FQ	30770 MW	40180 TQ	USBLS	5/15
Floor, Ceiling, and Wall	Atlanta-Sandy Springs-Roswell MSA, GA	Y	27420 FQ	31570 MW	41330 TQ	USBLS	5/15
Floor, Ceiling, and Wall	Augusta-Richmond County MSA, GA-SC	Y	21780 FQ	37360 MW	48480 TQ	USBLS	5/15
Floor, Ceiling, and Wall	Idaho	Y	27190 FQ	35600 MW	47940 TQ	USBLS	5/15
Floor, Ceiling, and Wall	Boise City MSA, ID	Y	34360 FQ	42600 MW	52690 TQ	USBLS	5/15
Floor, Ceiling, and Wall	Illinois	Y	28700 FQ	38360 MW	56500 TQ	USBLS	5/15
Floor, Ceiling, and Wall	Chicago-Naperville-Arlington Heights PMSA, IL	Y	34930 FQ	51120 MW	74730 TQ	USBLS	5/15
Floor, Ceiling, and Wall	Indiana	Y	27470 FQ	33610 MW	39460 TQ	USBLS	5/15
Floor, Ceiling, and Wall	Iowa	Y	26660 FQ	34530 MW	52880 TQ	USBLS	5/15
Floor, Ceiling, and Wall	Des Moines-West Des Moines MSA, IA	Y	27930 FQ	50520 MW	58170 TQ	USBLS	5/15
Floor, Ceiling, and Wall	Kansas	Y	27710 FQ	32240 MW	37150 TQ	USBLS	5/15
Floor, Ceiling, and Wall	Wichita MSA, KS	Y	27680 FQ	31050 MW	37220 TQ	USBLS	5/15
Floor, Ceiling, and Wall	Kentucky	Y	26600 FQ	33240 MW	38730 TQ	USBLS	5/15
Floor, Ceiling, and Wall	Louisville-Jefferson County MSA, KY-IN	Y	27090 FQ	33240 MW	39900 TQ	USBLS	5/15
Floor, Ceiling, and Wall	Louisiana	Y	30260 FQ	36950 MW	45760 TQ	USBLS	5/15
Floor, Ceiling, and Wall	Maine	Y	33140 FQ	39860 MW	45440 TQ	USBLS	5/15
Floor, Ceiling, and Wall	Portland-South Portland MSA, ME	Y	28060 FQ	33950 MW	39200 TQ	USBLS	5/15
Floor, Ceiling, and Wall	Maryland	Y	22772 AE	39208 MW	47426 AEX	MDBLS	4/16
Floor, Ceiling, and Wall	Massachusetts	Y	31400 FQ	36150 MW	42520 TQ	USBLS	5/15
Floor, Ceiling, and Wall	Boston-Cambridge-Newton NECTA, MA	Y	29690 FQ	34010 MW	38030 TQ	USBLS	5/15
Floor, Ceiling, and Wall	Michigan	Y	27280 FQ	34120 MW	50710 TQ	USBLS	5/15
Floor, Ceiling, and Wall	Detroit-Dearborn-Livonia PMSA, MI	Y	29730 FQ	35160 MW	42260 TQ	USBLS	5/15
Floor, Ceiling, and Wall	Grand Rapids-Wyoming MSA, MI	Y	20810 FQ	26430 MW	33670 TQ	USBLS	5/15
Floor, Ceiling, and Wall	Minnesota	Y	28353 FQ	39251 MW	80187 TQ	MNBLS	1/16-3/16
Floor, Ceiling, and Wall	Mississippi	Y	22850 FQ	27060 MW	33280 TQ	USBLS	5/15
Floor, Ceiling, and Wall	Jackson MSA, MS	Y	27960 FQ	32240 MW	39090 TQ	USBLS	5/15
Floor, Ceiling, and Wall	Missouri	Y	23280 FQ	35400 MW	54310 TQ	USBLS	5/15
Floor, Ceiling, and Wall	Kansas City MSA, MO-KS	Y	31140 FQ	36110 MW	45500 TQ	USBLS	5/15
Floor, Ceiling, and Wall	Montana	Y	18910 FQ	26340 MW	42930 TQ	USBLS	5/15
Floor, Ceiling, and Wall	Nebraska	Y	31005 FQ	34950 MW	38740 TQ	NEBLS	7/16-9/16
Floor, Ceiling, and Wall	Nevada	Y	34050 FQ	36600 MW	39150 TQ	USBLS	5/15
Floor, Ceiling, and Wall	Las Vegas-Henderson-Paradise MSA, NV	Y	34000 FQ	36410 MW	38810 TQ	USBLS	5/15
Floor, Ceiling, and Wall	New Hampshire	H	12.96 AE	16.82 MW	20.78 AEX	NHBLS	6/16
Floor, Ceiling, and Wall	New Jersey	Y	30400 FQ	36520 MW	45680 TQ	USBLS	5/15
Floor, Ceiling, and Wall	Camden PMSA, NJ	Y	35830 FQ	41440 MW	51230 TQ	USBLS	5/15
Floor, Ceiling, and Wall	Newark PMSA, NJ-PA	Y	27570 FQ	33970 MW	38920 TQ	USBLS	5/15
Floor, Ceiling, and Wall	New Mexico	Y	27070 FQ	29220 MW	31510 TQ	USBLS	5/15
Floor, Ceiling, and Wall	New York	Y	29840 AE	45260 MW	63930 AEX	NYBLS	1/16-3/16
Floor, Ceiling, and Wall	Buffalo-Cheektowaga-Niagara Falls MSA, NY	Y	25620 FQ	31010 MW	40950 TQ	USBLS	5/15
Floor, Ceiling, and Wall	Nassau County-Suffolk County PMSA, NY	Y	54790 FQ	62910 MW	90670 TQ	USBLS	5/15
Floor, Ceiling, and Wall	New York-Jersey City-White Plains PMSA, NY-NJ	Y	29690 FQ	37770 MW	50110 TQ	USBLS	5/15
Floor, Ceiling, and Wall	Rochester MSA, NY	Y	27410 FQ	32390 MW	40940 TQ	USBLS	5/15
Floor, Ceiling, and Wall	North Carolina	Y	26750 FQ	30180 MW	37340 TQ	USBLS	5/15
Floor, Ceiling, and Wall	Charlotte-Concord-Gastonia MSA, NC-SC	Y	26920 FQ	30490 MW	36240 TQ	USBLS	5/15
Floor, Ceiling, and Wall	Raleigh MSA, NC	Y	29050 FQ	36000 MW	46910 TQ	USBLS	5/15
Floor, Ceiling, and Wall	North Dakota	Y	31170 FQ	39690 MW	54400 TQ	USBLS	5/15
Floor, Ceiling, and Wall	Fargo MSA, ND-MN	Y	29670 FQ	35670 MW	47730 TQ	USBLS	5/15

AE	Average entry wage	AWR	Average wage range	H	Hourly	LR	Low end range	MTC	Median total compensation	TCC	Total cash compensation
AEX	Average experienced wage	B	Biweekly	HI	Highest wage paid	M	Monthly	MW	Median wage paid	TQ	Third quartile wage
ATC	Average total compensation	D	Daily	HR	High end range	MCC	Median cash compensation	MWR	Median wage range	W	Weekly
AW	Average wage paid	FQ	First quartile wage	LO	Lowest wage paid	ME	Median entry wage	S	See annotated source	Y	Yearly

Occupation/Type/Industry	Location	Per	Low	Mid	High	Source	Date
Insulation Worker							
Floor, Ceiling, and Wall	Ohio	Y	26570 FQ	33290 MW	39340 TQ	USBLS	5/15
Floor, Ceiling, and Wall	Cincinnati MSA, OH-KY-IN	Y	24580 FQ	28170 MW	31810 TQ	USBLS	5/15
Floor, Ceiling, and Wall	Oklahoma	Y	24920 FQ	33760 MW	42530 TQ	USBLS	5/15
Floor, Ceiling, and Wall	Oklahoma City MSA, OK	Y	28770 FQ	36090 MW	43640 TQ	USBLS	5/15
Floor, Ceiling, and Wall	Oregon	H	13.70 FQ	17.17 MW	23.11 TQ	ORBLS	2016
Floor, Ceiling, and Wall	Portland-Vancouver-Hillsboro MSA, OR-WA	Y	33910 FQ	40100 MW	50880 TQ	USBLS	5/15
Floor, Ceiling, and Wall	Pennsylvania	Y	30200 FQ	36220 MW	48000 TQ	USBLS	5/15
Floor, Ceiling, and Wall	Allentown-Bethlehem-Easton MSA, PA-NJ	Y	31150 FQ	34220 MW	37290 TQ	USBLS	5/15
Floor, Ceiling, and Wall	South Carolina	Y	24840 FQ	31700 MW	39220 TQ	USBLS	5/15
Floor, Ceiling, and Wall	South Dakota	Y	25330 FQ	28890 MW	35720 TQ	USBLS	5/15
Floor, Ceiling, and Wall	Tennessee	Y	25940 FQ	32840 MW	42590 TQ	USBLS	5/15
Floor, Ceiling, and Wall	Knoxville MSA, TN	Y	27360 FQ	33490 MW	42980 TQ	USBLS	5/15
Floor, Ceiling, and Wall	Nashville-Davidson– Murfreesboro–Franklin MSA, TN	Y	23660 FQ	30930 MW	41280 TQ	USBLS	5/15
Floor, Ceiling, and Wall	Texas	Y	27690 FQ	33830 MW	41000 TQ	USBLS	5/15
Floor, Ceiling, and Wall	Austin-Round Rock MSA, TX	Y	29050 FQ	37350 MW	45580 TQ	USBLS	5/15
Floor, Ceiling, and Wall	Dallas-Plano-Irving PMSA, TX	Y	24410 AE	31730 MW	38140 TQ	USBLS	5/15
Floor, Ceiling, and Wall	Houston-The Woodlands- Sugar Land MSA, TX	Y	30820 FQ	37000 MW	45170 TQ	USBLS	5/15
Floor, Ceiling, and Wall	Utah	Y	31600 FQ	38030 MW	47500 TQ	USBLS	5/15
Floor, Ceiling, and Wall	Ogden-Clearfield MSA, UT	Y	31420 FQ	35210 MW	38910 TQ	USBLS	5/15
Floor, Ceiling, and Wall	Provo-Orem MSA, UT	Y	32160 FQ	37350 MW	44230 TQ	USBLS	5/15
Floor, Ceiling, and Wall	Vermont	Y	28380 FQ	32800 MW	38850 TQ	USBLS	5/15
Floor, Ceiling, and Wall	Virginia	Y	30820 FQ	36380 MW	43940 TQ	USBLS	5/15
Floor, Ceiling, and Wall	Richmond MSA, VA	Y	35220 FQ	42770 MW	52320 TQ	USBLS	5/15
Floor, Ceiling, and Wall	Virginia Beach-Norfolk- Newport News MSA, VA-NC	Y	31790 FQ	35340 MW	38900 TQ	USBLS	5/15
Floor, Ceiling, and Wall	Washington	H	16.57 FQ	20.52 MW	27.29 TQ	WABLS	3/16
Floor, Ceiling, and Wall	Seattle-Bellevue-Everett PMSA, WA	H	14.66 FQ	18.35 MW	23.68 TQ	WABLS	3/16
Floor, Ceiling, and Wall	Tacoma-Lakewood PMSA, WA	H	24.81 FQ	30.93 MW	36.39 TQ	WABLS	3/16
Floor, Ceiling, and Wall	West Virginia	Y	29300 FQ	39850 MW	71390 TQ	USBLS	5/15
Floor, Ceiling, and Wall	Wisconsin	Y	31800 FQ	36510 MW	46260 TQ	USBLS	5/15
Floor, Ceiling, and Wall	Madison MSA, WI	Y	31320 FQ	38070 MW	47740 TQ	USBLS	5/15
Floor, Ceiling, and Wall	Milwaukee-Waukesha-West Allis MSA, WI	Y	33640 FQ	37870 MW	65340 TQ	USBLS	5/15
Floor, Ceiling, and Wall	Wyoming	Y	30270 FQ	35140 MW	39420 TQ	USBLS	5/15
Floor, Ceiling, and Wall	Cheyenne MSA, WY	Y	26320 FQ	29950 MW	36040 TQ	USBLS	5/15
Floor, Ceiling, and Wall	Puerto Rico	Y	16860 FQ	18230 MW	19690 TQ	USBLS	5/15
Floor, Ceiling, and Wall	San Juan-Carolina-Caguas MSA, PR	Y	16720 FQ	17920 MW	19130 TQ	USBLS	5/15
Mechanical	Alabama	Y	26499 AE	38884 AW	45077 AEX	ALBLS	6/16
Mechanical	Birmingham-Hoover MSA, AL	Y	24977 AE	31169 AW	34266 AEX	ALBLS	6/16
Mechanical	Alaska	Y	56440 FQ	63250 MW	73120 TQ	USBLS	5/15
Mechanical	Anchorage MSA, AK	Y	67950 FQ	73830 MW	83140 TQ	USBLS	5/15
Mechanical	Arizona	Y	47120 FQ	55280 MW	60290 TQ	USBLS	5/15
Mechanical	Phoenix-Mesa-Scottsdale MSA, AZ	Y	47180 FQ	55310 MW	60300 TQ	USBLS	5/15
Mechanical	Arkansas	Y	24210 FQ	31320 MW	40600 TQ	USBLS	5/15
Mechanical	California	H	16.95 FQ	23.27 MW	31.50 TQ	CABLS	1/16-3/16
Mechanical	Anaheim-Santa Ana-Irvine PMSA, CA	H	18.58 FQ	26.42 MW	33.88 TQ	CABLS	1/16-3/16
Mechanical	Oakland-Hayward-Berkeley PMSA, CA	H	18.81 FQ	24.67 MW	35.32 TQ	CABLS	1/16-3/16
Mechanical	San Diego-Carlsbad MSA, CA	H	15.12 FQ	24.42 MW	32.34 TQ	CABLS	1/16-3/16
Mechanical	Colorado	Y	31030 FQ	36450 MW	44980 TQ	USBLS	5/15
Mechanical	Denver-Aurora-Lakewood MSA, CO	Y	30410 FQ	35480 MW	41890 TQ	USBLS	5/15
Mechanical	Connecticut	Y		56501 MW		CTBLS	1/16-3/16
Mechanical	Delaware	Y	34620 FQ	43720 MW	50750 TQ	USBLS	5/15
Mechanical	Wilmington PMSA, DE-MD-NJ	Y	38600 FQ	45310 MW	51560 TQ	USBLS	5/15
Mechanical	District of Columbia	Y	43150 FQ	64040 MW	72300 TQ	USBLS	5/15
Mechanical	Washington-Arlington-Alexandria PMSA, DC-VA-MD-WV	Y	31670 FQ	45740 MW	64530 TQ	USBLS	5/15
Mechanical	Florida	H	13.16 AE	17.75 MW	22.11 AEX	FLBLS	7/16-9/16

Occupation/Type/Industry	Location	Per	Low	Mid	High	Source	Date
Insulation Worker							
Mechanical	Orlando-Kissimmee-Sanford MSA, FL	H	11.25 AE	16.58 MW	21.25 AEX	FLBLS	7/16-9/16
Mechanical	Tampa-St. Petersburg-Clearwater MSA, FL	H	15.21 AE	17.37 MW	18.23 AEX	FLBLS	7/16-9/16
Mechanical	Georgia	Y	30890 FQ	35500 MW	40980 TQ	USBLS	5/15
Mechanical	Atlanta-Sandy Springs-Roswell MSA, GA	Y	33150 FQ	37530 MW	43840 TQ	USBLS	5/15
Mechanical	Augusta-Richmond County MSA, GA-SC	Y	25480 FQ	30950 MW	35810 TQ	USBLS	5/15
Mechanical	Hawaii	Y	37290 FQ	51830 MW	70340 TQ	USBLS	5/15
Mechanical	Urban Honolulu MSA, HI	Y	37290 FQ	51830 MW	70340 TQ	USBLS	5/15
Mechanical	Illinois	Y	68160 FQ	81240 MW	90940 TQ	USBLS	5/15
Mechanical	Chicago-Naperville-Arlington Heights PMSA, IL	Y	69830 FQ	83820 MW	92030 TQ	USBLS	5/15
Mechanical	Indiana	Y	66650 FQ	102000 MW	112620 TQ	USBLS	5/15
Mechanical	Gary PMSA, IN	Y	99960 FQ	107710 MW	115550 TQ	USBLS	5/15
Mechanical	Indianapolis-Carmel-Anderson MSA, IN	Y	35320 FQ	53560 MW	87810 TQ	USBLS	5/15
Mechanical	Iowa	Y	31040 FQ	37830 MW	47920 TQ	USBLS	5/15
Mechanical	Des Moines-West Des Moines MSA, IA	Y	36270 FQ	42410 MW	47970 TQ	USBLS	5/15
Mechanical	Kansas	Y	27590 FQ	35890 MW	44160 TQ	USBLS	5/15
Mechanical	Wichita MSA, KS	Y	33340 FQ	37410 MW	42930 TQ	USBLS	5/15
Mechanical	Kentucky	Y	43400 FQ	52490 MW	58040 TQ	USBLS	5/15
Mechanical	Louisiana	Y	34930 FQ	43150 MW	52050 TQ	USBLS	5/15
Mechanical	Baton Rouge MSA, LA	Y	34500 FQ	42490 MW	50480 TQ	USBLS	5/15
Mechanical	New Orleans-Metairie MSA, LA	Y	35480 FQ	39790 MW	45600 TQ	USBLS	5/15
Mechanical	Maine	Y	30590 FQ	39520 MW	46420 TQ	USBLS	5/15
Mechanical	Maryland	Y	26005 AE	43303 MW	51952 AEX	MDBLS	4/16
Mechanical	Baltimore-Columbia-Towson MSA, MD	Y	27670 FQ	38320 MW	49860 TQ	USBLS	5/15
Mechanical	Salisbury MSA, MD-DE	Y	21920 FQ	24160 MW	29910 TQ	USBLS	5/15
Mechanical	Massachusetts	Y	36530 FQ	51750 MW	81000 TQ	USBLS	5/15
Mechanical	Boston-Cambridge-Newton NECTA, MA	Y	37670 FQ	48920 MW	85150 TQ	USBLS	5/15
Mechanical	Worcester MSA, MA-CT	Y	36350 FQ	50880 MW	80730 TQ	USBLS	5/15
Mechanical	Michigan	Y	39440 FQ	54340 MW	65580 TQ	USBLS	5/15
Mechanical	Minnesota	Y	44447 FQ	62731 MW	88037 TQ	MNBLS	1/16-3/16
Mechanical	Minneapolis-St. Paul-Bloomington MSA, MN-WI	Y	49079 FQ	69693 MW	91992 TQ	MNBLS	1/16-3/16
Mechanical	Mississippi	Y	33430 FQ	46550 MW	56440 TQ	USBLS	5/15
Mechanical	Jackson MSA, MS	Y	30200 FQ	41300 MW	49320 TQ	USBLS	5/15
Mechanical	Missouri	Y	53890 FQ	58220 MW	62550 TQ	USBLS	5/15
Mechanical	St. Louis MSA, MO-IL	Y	54750 FQ	59940 MW	68240 TQ	USBLS	5/15
Mechanical	Montana	Y	34880 FQ	43940 MW	67220 TQ	USBLS	5/15
Mechanical	Nebraska	Y	37310 FQ	47865 MW	69730 TQ	NEBLS	7/16-9/16
Mechanical	Nevada	Y	34770 FQ	45760 MW	76920 TQ	USBLS	5/15
Mechanical	Las Vegas-Henderson-Paradise MSA, NV	Y	37450 FQ	48280 MW	86840 TQ	USBLS	5/15
Mechanical	New Jersey	Y	42020 FQ	70180 MW	91230 TQ	USBLS	5/15
Mechanical	Camden PMSA, NJ	Y	47480 FQ	87890 MW	95710 TQ	USBLS	5/15
Mechanical	New Mexico	Y	38540 FQ	48790 MW	69930 TQ	USBLS	5/15
Mechanical	Albuquerque MSA, NM	Y	41840 FQ	61610 MW	71590 TQ	USBLS	5/15
Mechanical	New York	Y	31320 AE	57400 MW	93950 AEX	NYBLS	1/16-3/16
Mechanical	Buffalo-Cheektowaga-Niagara Falls MSA, NY	Y	33870 FQ	51520 MW	67260 TQ	USBLS	5/15
Mechanical	Nassau County-Suffolk County PMSA, NY	Y	72810 FQ	109700 MW	120920 TQ	USBLS	5/15
Mechanical	Rochester MSA, NY	Y	31520 FQ	38200 MW	52150 TQ	USBLS	5/15
Mechanical	North Carolina	Y	28390 FQ	33880 MW	38660 TQ	USBLS	5/15
Mechanical	Charlotte-Concord-Gastonia MSA, NC-SC	Y	26970 FQ	32060 MW	36160 TQ	USBLS	5/15
Mechanical	Raleigh MSA, NC	Y	25730 FQ	32940 MW	38130 TQ	USBLS	5/15
Mechanical	North Dakota	Y	35500 FQ	41830 MW	47240 TQ	USBLS	5/15
Mechanical	Fargo MSA, ND-MN	Y	31550 FQ	36360 MW	46590 TQ	USBLS	5/15
Mechanical	Ohio	Y	34430 FQ	48690 MW	62080 TQ	USBLS	5/15
Mechanical	Columbus MSA, OH	Y	27460 FQ	40400 MW	58080 TQ	USBLS	5/15
Mechanical	Oklahoma	Y	29740 FQ	38720 MW	55560 TQ	USBLS	5/15
Mechanical	Oklahoma City MSA, OK	Y	29350 FQ	51370 MW	62970 TQ	USBLS	5/15
Mechanical	Tulsa MSA, OK	Y	30880 FQ	38020 MW	46910 TQ	USBLS	5/15

AE	Average entry wage	AWR	Average wage range	H	Hourly	LR	Low end range	MTC	Median total compensation	TCC	Total cash compensation
AEX	Average experienced wage	B	Biweekly	HI	Highest wage paid	M	Monthly	MW	Median wage paid	TQ	Third quartile wage
ATC	Average total compensation	D	Daily	HR	High end range	MCC	Median cash compensation	MWR	Median wage range	W	Weekly
AW	Average wage paid	FQ	First quartile wage	LO	Lowest wage paid	ME	Median entry wage	S	See annotated source	Y	Yearly

Insulation Worker

Occupation/Type/Industry	Location	Per	Low	Mid	High	Source	Date
Insulation Worker							
Mechanical	Oregon	H	34.37 ꜰQ	40.86 ᴍᴡ	46.53 ᴛQ	ORBLS	2016
Mechanical	Pennsylvania	Y	46170 ꜰQ	61770 ᴍᴡ	74870 ᴛQ	USBLS	5/15
Mechanical	Pittsburgh MSA, PA	Y	58950 ꜰQ	68360 ᴍᴡ	75290 ᴛQ	USBLS	5/15
Mechanical	Rhode Island	Y	65420 ꜰQ	74960 ᴍᴡ	86000 ᴛQ	USBLS	5/15
Mechanical	Providence-Warwick MSA, RI-MA	Y	58010 ꜰQ	72240 ᴍᴡ	84290 ᴛQ	USBLS	5/15
Mechanical	South Carolina	Y	30130 ꜰQ	35540 ᴍᴡ	41360 ᴛQ	USBLS	5/15
Mechanical	Columbia MSA, SC	Y	26970 ꜰQ	33150 ᴍᴡ	39560 ᴛQ	USBLS	5/15
Mechanical	Greenville-Anderson-Mauldin MSA, SC	Y	33120 ꜰQ	39880 ᴍᴡ	45750 ᴛQ	USBLS	5/15
Mechanical	South Dakota	Y	27490 ꜰQ	30580 ᴍᴡ	35770 ᴛQ	USBLS	5/15
Mechanical	Tennessee	Y	31440 ꜰQ	37770 ᴍᴡ	46720 ᴛQ	USBLS	5/15
Mechanical	Knoxville MSA, TN	Y	30770 ꜰQ	36100 ᴍᴡ	46170 ᴛQ	USBLS	5/15
Mechanical	Memphis MSA, TN-MS-AR	Y	37100 ꜰQ	44560 ᴍᴡ	51490 ᴛQ	USBLS	5/15
Mechanical	Texas	Y	33350 ꜰQ	39540 ᴍᴡ	47000 ᴛQ	USBLS	5/15
Mechanical	Austin-Round Rock MSA, TX	Y	31230 ꜰQ	35130 ᴍᴡ	38990 ᴛQ	USBLS	5/15
Mechanical	Dallas-Plano-Irving PMSA, TX	Y	32160 ꜰQ	36700 ᴍᴡ	45600 ᴛQ	USBLS	5/15
Mechanical	Fort Worth-Arlington PMSA, TX	Y	29970 ꜰQ	34520 ᴍᴡ	38620 ᴛQ	USBLS	5/15
Mechanical	Houston-The Woodlands-Sugar Land MSA, TX	Y	39670 ꜰQ	44290 ᴍᴡ	48920 ᴛQ	USBLS	5/15
Mechanical	San Antonio-New Braunfels MSA, TX	Y	31500 ꜰQ	38010 ᴍᴡ	45760 ᴛQ	USBLS	5/15
Mechanical	Utah	Y	29410 ꜰQ	34440 ᴍᴡ	38300 ᴛQ	USBLS	5/15
Mechanical	Ogden-Clearfield MSA, UT	Y	29140 ꜰQ	34090 ᴍᴡ	38580 ᴛQ	USBLS	5/15
Mechanical	Virginia	Y	33970 ꜰQ	43060 ᴍᴡ	50020 ᴛQ	USBLS	5/15
Mechanical	Washington	H	21.05 ꜰQ	27.69 ᴍᴡ	35.01 ᴛQ	WABLS	3/16
Mechanical	Seattle-Bellevue-Everett PMSA, WA	H	19.82 ꜰQ	24.99 ᴍᴡ	35.21 ᴛQ	WABLS	3/16
Mechanical	West Virginia	Y	50690 ꜰQ	67600 ᴍᴡ	73790 ᴛQ	USBLS	5/15
Mechanical	Wisconsin	Y	49830 ꜰQ	67310 ᴍᴡ	74090 ᴛQ	USBLS	5/15
Mechanical	Madison MSA, WI	Y	65850 ꜰQ	71320 ᴍᴡ	76800 ᴛQ	USBLS	5/15
Mechanical	Milwaukee-Waukesha-West Allis MSA, WI	Y	63480 ꜰQ	69250 ᴍᴡ	75060 ᴛQ	USBLS	5/15
Mechanical	Wyoming	Y	34650 ꜰQ	39100 ᴍᴡ	46440 ᴛQ	USBLS	5/15
Mechanical	Cheyenne MSA, WY	Y	36320 ꜰQ	41440 ᴍᴡ	46850 ᴛQ	USBLS	5/15
Mechanical	Puerto Rico	Y	16460 ꜰQ	17620 ᴍᴡ	18780 ᴛQ	USBLS	5/15
Mechanical	San Juan-Carolina-Caguas MSA, PR	Y	16460 ꜰQ	17620 ᴍᴡ	18780 ᴛQ	USBLS	5/15
Insurance Appraiser							
Auto Damage	Alabama	Y	53267 ᴀᴇ	70917 ᴀᴡ	79742 ᴀᴇx	ALBLS	6/16
Auto Damage	Birmingham-Hoover MSA, AL	Y	51104 ᴀᴇ	65269 ᴀᴡ	72342 ᴀᴇx	ALBLS	6/16
Auto Damage	Arizona	Y	51940 ꜰQ	66880 ᴍᴡ	76300 ᴛQ	USBLS	5/15
Auto Damage	Phoenix-Mesa-Scottsdale MSA, AZ	Y	56840 ꜰQ	68730 ᴍᴡ	77240 ᴛQ	USBLS	5/15
Auto Damage	California	H	25.30 ꜰQ	32.06 ᴍᴡ	39.07 ᴛQ	CABLS	1/16-3/16
Auto Damage	Anaheim-Santa Ana-Irvine PMSA, CA	H	25.50 ꜰQ	31.85 ᴍᴡ	37.86 ᴛQ	CABLS	1/16-3/16
Auto Damage	Los Angeles-Long Beach-Glendale PMSA, CA	H	24.22 ꜰQ	30.96 ᴍᴡ	43.08 ᴛQ	CABLS	1/16-3/16
Auto Damage	Oakland-Hayward-Berkeley PMSA, CA	H	32.51 ꜰQ	36.41 ᴍᴡ	41.40 ᴛQ	CABLS	1/16-3/16
Auto Damage	Sacramento–Roseville–Arden-Arcade MSA, CA	H	25.77 ꜰQ	33.49 ᴍᴡ	42.07 ᴛQ	CABLS	1/16-3/16
Auto Damage	San Diego-Carlsbad MSA, CA	H	27.54 ꜰQ	31.94 ᴍᴡ	37.13 ᴛQ	CABLS	1/16-3/16
Auto Damage	San Francisco-Redwood City-South San Francisco PMSA, CA	H	27.27 ꜰQ	33.23 ᴍᴡ	37.15 ᴛQ	CABLS	1/16-3/16
Auto Damage	Colorado	Y	37180 ꜰQ	61260 ᴍᴡ	78060 ᴛQ	USBLS	5/15
Auto Damage	Denver-Aurora-Lakewood MSA, CO	Y	58730 ꜰQ	71430 ᴍᴡ	83590 ᴛQ	USBLS	5/15
Auto Damage	Connecticut	Y		68851 ᴍᴡ		CTBLS	1/16-3/16
Auto Damage	Hartford-West Hartford-East Hartford MSA, CT	Y	60040 ꜰQ	70470 ᴍᴡ	78770 ᴛQ	USBLS	5/15
Auto Damage	Washington-Arlington-Alexandria PMSA, DC-VA-MD-WV	Y	53130 ꜰQ	60210 ᴍᴡ	74470 ᴛQ	USBLS	5/15
Auto Damage	Florida	H	23.56 ᴀᴇ	31.46 ᴍᴡ	36.20 ᴀᴇx	FLBLS	7/16-9/16

AE Average entry wage	**AWR** Average wage range	**H** Hourly	**LR** Low end range	**MTC** Median total compensation	**TCC** Total cash compensation
AEX Average experienced wage	**B** Biweekly	**HI** Highest wage paid	**M** Monthly	**MW** Median wage paid	**TQ** Third quartile wage
ATC Average total compensation	**D** Daily	**HR** High end range	**MCC** Median cash compensation	**MWR** Median wage range	**W** Weekly
AW Average wage paid	**FQ** First quartile wage	**LO** Lowest wage paid	**ME** Median entry wage	**S** See annotated source	**Y** Yearly

Insurance Appraiser

Occupation/Type/Industry	Location	Per	Low	Mid	High	Source	Date
Insurance Appraiser							
Auto Damage	Fort Lauderdale-Pompano Beach-Deerfield Beach PMSA, FL	H	26.90 AE	30.37 MW	34.58 AEX	FLBLS	7/16-9/16
Auto Damage	Miami-Miami Beach-Kendall PMSA, FL	H	21.96 AE	30.09 MW	34.48 AEX	FLBLS	7/16-9/16
Auto Damage	Orlando-Kissimmee-Sanford MSA, FL	H	21.21 AE	26.82 MW	31.65 AEX	FLBLS	7/16-9/16
Auto Damage	Tampa-St. Petersburg-Clearwater MSA, FL	H	24.66 AE	32.97 MW	37.02 AEX	FLBLS	7/16-9/16
Auto Damage	Georgia	Y	52540 FQ	66480 MW	77830 TQ	USBLS	5/15
Auto Damage	Atlanta-Sandy Springs-Roswell MSA, GA	Y	56600 FQ	69270 MW	80380 TQ	USBLS	5/15
Auto Damage	Hawaii	Y	59840 FQ	70600 MW	80910 TQ	USBLS	5/15
Auto Damage	Urban Honolulu MSA, HI	Y	59840 FQ	70600 MW	80910 TQ	USBLS	5/15
Auto Damage	Illinois	Y	57730 FQ	69010 MW	80670 TQ	USBLS	5/15
Auto Damage	Chicago-Naperville-Arlington Heights PMSA, IL	Y	57730 FQ	68830 MW	79490 TQ	USBLS	5/15
Auto Damage	Indiana	Y	52910 FQ	68910 MW	91820 TQ	USBLS	5/15
Auto Damage	Indianapolis-Carmel-Anderson MSA, IN	Y	63380 FQ	79360 MW	100640 TQ	USBLS	5/15
Auto Damage	Kansas	Y	58270 FQ	68310 MW	77000 TQ	USBLS	5/15
Auto Damage	Wichita MSA, KS	Y	61070 FQ	71740 MW	81320 TQ	USBLS	5/15
Auto Damage	Kentucky	Y	43220 FQ	52830 MW	58540 TQ	USBLS	5/15
Auto Damage	Louisville-Jefferson County MSA, KY-IN	Y	43590 FQ	53100 MW	58700 TQ	USBLS	5/15
Auto Damage	Louisiana	Y	49780 FQ	63190 MW	83390 TQ	USBLS	5/15
Auto Damage	New Orleans-Metairie MSA, LA	Y	49050 FQ	63240 MW	85320 TQ	USBLS	5/15
Auto Damage	Maine	Y	56120 FQ	63080 MW	75710 TQ	USBLS	5/15
Auto Damage	Maryland	Y	49423 AE	67102 MW	75942 AEX	MDBLS	4/16
Auto Damage	Baltimore-Columbia-Towson MSA, MD	Y	51050 FQ	62450 MW	79570 TQ	USBLS	5/15
Auto Damage	Massachusetts	Y	55480 FQ	65770 MW	76940 TQ	USBLS	5/15
Auto Damage	Boston-Cambridge-Newton NECTA, MA	Y	61230 FQ	70850 MW	80930 TQ	USBLS	5/15
Auto Damage	Worcester MSA, MA-CT	Y	47030 FQ	55420 MW	63530 TQ	USBLS	5/15
Auto Damage	Grand Rapids-Wyoming MSA, MI	Y	54320 FQ	59550 MW	66000 TQ	USBLS	5/15
Auto Damage	Mississippi	Y	53950 FQ	58730 MW	64350 TQ	USBLS	5/15
Auto Damage	Missouri	Y	59340 FQ	69170 MW	78420 TQ	USBLS	5/15
Auto Damage	Kansas City MSA, MO-KS	Y	59070 FQ	68320 MW	76540 TQ	USBLS	5/15
Auto Damage	St. Louis MSA, MO-IL	Y	59190 FQ	69360 MW	79140 TQ	USBLS	5/15
Auto Damage	Nevada	Y	44610 FQ	49740 MW	58920 TQ	USBLS	5/15
Auto Damage	Las Vegas-Henderson-Paradise MSA, NV	Y	44580 FQ	49690 MW	58870 TQ	USBLS	5/15
Auto Damage	New Hampshire	H	22.33 AE	30.06 MW	34.75 AEX	NHBLS	6/16
Auto Damage	New Jersey	Y	60340 FQ	71960 MW	82220 TQ	USBLS	5/15
Auto Damage	Newark PMSA, NJ-PA	Y	67410 FQ	75700 MW	86830 TQ	USBLS	5/15
Auto Damage	New Mexico	Y	37680 FQ	46930 MW	59850 TQ	USBLS	5/15
Auto Damage	Albuquerque MSA, NM	Y	37630 FQ	46790 MW	59530 TQ	USBLS	5/15
Auto Damage	New York	Y	50480 AE	63380 MW	74800 AEX	NYBLS	1/16-3/16
Auto Damage	Buffalo-Cheektowaga-Niagara Falls MSA, NY	Y	43210 FQ	52890 MW	62400 TQ	USBLS	5/15
Auto Damage	Nassau County-Suffolk County PMSA, NY	Y	53830 FQ	61630 MW	74910 TQ	USBLS	5/15
Auto Damage	New York-Jersey City-White Plains PMSA, NY-NJ	Y	64150 FQ	75240 MW	89720 TQ	USBLS	5/15
Auto Damage	Rochester MSA, NY	Y	83330 FQ	89190 MW	95060 TQ	USBLS	5/15
Auto Damage	North Carolina	Y	54040 FQ	62910 MW	73380 TQ	USBLS	5/15
Auto Damage	Charlotte-Concord-Gastonia MSA, NC-SC	Y	50370 FQ	58540 MW	68570 TQ	USBLS	5/15
Auto Damage	Raleigh MSA, NC	Y	53600 FQ	65330 MW	75230 TQ	USBLS	5/15
Auto Damage	Ohio	Y	53040 FQ	61440 MW	72480 TQ	USBLS	5/15
Auto Damage	Cincinnati MSA, OH-KY-IN	Y	56990 FQ	66040 MW	86010 TQ	USBLS	5/15
Auto Damage	Columbus MSA, OH	Y	46850 FQ	55190 MW	63760 TQ	USBLS	5/15
Auto Damage	Oklahoma	Y	54260 FQ	62390 MW	72400 TQ	USBLS	5/15
Auto Damage	Oklahoma City MSA, OK	Y	55650 FQ	63200 MW	72770 TQ	USBLS	5/15
Auto Damage	Oregon	H	29.10 FQ	33.74 MW	37.83 TQ	ORBLS	2016
Auto Damage	Portland-Vancouver-Hillsboro MSA, OR-WA	Y	60550 FQ	69320 MW	77260 TQ	USBLS	5/15
Auto Damage	Pennsylvania	Y	51100 FQ	62990 MW	73870 TQ	USBLS	5/15

AE	Average entry wage	AWR	Average wage range	H	Hourly
AEX	Average experienced wage	B	Biweekly	HI	Highest wage paid
ATC	Average total compensation	D	Daily	HR	High end range
AW	Average wage paid	FQ	First quartile wage	LO	Lowest wage paid

LR	Low end range	MTC	Median total compensation
M	Monthly	MW	Median wage paid
MCC	Median cash compensation	MWR	Median wage range
ME	Median entry wage	S	See annotated source

TCC	Total cash compensation	
TQ	Third quartile wage	
W	Weekly	
Y	Yearly	

Occupation/Type/Industry	Location	Per	Low	Mid	High	Source	Date
Insurance Appraiser							
Auto Damage	Montgomery County-Bucks County-Chester County PMSA, PA	Y	50460 FQ	62950 MW	74090 TQ	USBLS	5/15
Auto Damage	Pittsburgh MSA, PA	Y	56760 FQ	66210 MW	74530 TQ	USBLS	5/15
Auto Damage	South Carolina	Y	64490 FQ	71030 MW	77570 TQ	USBLS	5/15
Auto Damage	Tennessee	Y	55370 FQ	66010 MW	79020 TQ	USBLS	5/15
Auto Damage	Nashville-Davidson– Murfreesboro–Franklin MSA, TN	Y	54390 FQ	63340 MW	75010 TQ	USBLS	5/15
Auto Damage	Texas	Y	46810 FQ	57550 MW	72560 TQ	USBLS	5/15
Auto Damage	Austin-Round Rock MSA, TX	Y	56830 FQ	71930 MW	93780 TQ	USBLS	5/15
Auto Damage	Dallas-Plano-Irving PMSA, TX	Y	50410 FQ	59020 MW	71840 TQ	USBLS	5/15
Auto Damage	Fort Worth-Arlington PMSA, TX	Y	54600 FQ	66460 MW	76120 TQ	USBLS	5/15
Auto Damage	Houston-The Woodlands- Sugar Land MSA, TX	Y	49710 FQ	58720 MW	72800 TQ	USBLS	5/15
Auto Damage	Utah	Y	55250 FQ	67380 MW	76540 TQ	USBLS	5/15
Auto Damage	Salt Lake City MSA, UT	Y	55390 FQ	67830 MW	76770 TQ	USBLS	5/15
Auto Damage	Virginia	Y	53020 FQ	61860 MW	79700 TQ	USBLS	5/15
Auto Damage	Richmond MSA, VA	Y	48590 FQ	61260 MW	75210 TQ	USBLS	5/15
Auto Damage	Washington	H	27.09 FQ	33.89 MW	39.28 TQ	WABLS	3/16
Auto Damage	Seattle-Bellevue-Everett PMSA, WA	H	29.56 FQ	34.69 MW	38.90 TQ	WABLS	3/16
Auto Damage	Wisconsin	Y	60670 FQ	68470 MW	74980 TQ	USBLS	5/15
Auto Damage	Madison MSA, WI	Y	66630 FQ	71150 MW	75680 TQ	USBLS	5/15
Auto Damage	Puerto Rico	Y	27370 FQ	33430 MW	38220 TQ	USBLS	5/15
Auto Damage	San Juan-Carolina-Caguas MSA, PR	Y	26580 FQ	32680 MW	38600 TQ	USBLS	5/15
Insurance Claims and Policy Processing Clerk	Alabama	Y	25631 AE	34041 AW	38245 AEX	ALBLS	6/16
	Birmingham-Hoover MSA, AL	Y	28558 AE	35988 AW	39709 AEX	ALBLS	6/16
	Alaska	Y	33250 FQ	41220 MW	51600 TQ	USBLS	5/15
	Anchorage MSA, AK	Y	35880 FQ	43710 MW	56790 TQ	USBLS	5/15
	Arizona	Y	30460 FQ	35480 MW	41600 TQ	USBLS	5/15
	Phoenix-Mesa-Scottsdale MSA, AZ	Y	31220 FQ	36030 MW	42500 TQ	USBLS	5/15
	Tucson MSA, AZ	Y	31260 FQ	35440 MW	39560 TQ	USBLS	5/15
	Arkansas	Y	25920 FQ	33070 MW	40960 TQ	USBLS	5/15
	Fayetteville-Springdale-Rogers MSA, AR-MO	Y	21330 FQ	23340 MW	32390 TQ	USBLS	5/15
	Little Rock-North Little Rock- Conway MSA, AR	Y	32700 FQ	38140 MW	45300 TQ	USBLS	5/15
	California	H	16.13 FQ	19.81 MW	23.85 TQ	CABLS	1/16-3/16
	Anaheim-Santa Ana-Irvine PMSA, CA	H	16.23 FQ	20.08 MW	23.96 TQ	CABLS	1/16-3/16
	Los Angeles-Long Beach- Glendale PMSA, CA	H	15.90 FQ	19.76 MW	23.53 TQ	CABLS	1/16-3/16
	Oakland-Hayward-Berkeley PMSA, CA	H	17.24 FQ	22.19 MW	27.81 TQ	CABLS	1/16-3/16
	Riverside-San Bernardino- Ontario MSA, CA	H	14.36 FQ	18.15 MW	22.00 TQ	CABLS	1/16-3/16
	Sacramento–Roseville– Arden-Arcade MSA, CA	H	17.50 FQ	20.80 MW	23.83 TQ	CABLS	1/16-3/16
	San Diego-Carlsbad MSA, CA	H	15.74 FQ	18.72 MW	23.09 TQ	CABLS	1/16-3/16
	San Francisco-Redwood City- South San Francisco PMSA, CA	H	18.81 FQ	22.44 MW	26.93 TQ	CABLS	1/16-3/16
	Colorado	Y	37100 FQ	44620 MW	52880 TQ	USBLS	5/15
	Denver-Aurora-Lakewood MSA, CO	Y	38700 FQ	45820 MW	54810 TQ	USBLS	5/15
	Connecticut	Y		47535 MW		CTBLS	1/16-3/16
	Bridgeport-Stamford-Norwalk MSA, CT	Y	38240 FQ	48820 MW	59310 TQ	USBLS	5/15
	Hartford-West Hartford-East Hartford MSA, CT	Y	40840 FQ	46540 MW	56710 TQ	USBLS	5/15
	Delaware	Y	32180 FQ	38950 MW	50090 TQ	USBLS	5/15
	Wilmington PMSA, DE-MD- NJ	Y	34060 FQ	41940 MW	51040 TQ	USBLS	5/15
	District of Columbia	Y	42470 FQ	48080 MW	60770 TQ	USBLS	5/15

AE	Average entry wage	AWR	Average wage range	H	Hourly	LR	Low end range	MTC Median total compensation	TCC Total cash compensation
AEX	Average experienced wage	B	Biweekly	HI	Highest wage paid	M	Monthly	MW Median wage paid	TQ Third quartile wage
ATC	Average total compensation	D	Daily	HR	High end range	MCC Median cash compensation		MWR Median wage range	W Weekly
AW	Average wage paid	FQ	First quartile wage	LO	Lowest wage paid	ME Median entry wage		S See annotated source	Y Yearly

Occupation/Type/Industry	Location	Per	Low	Mid	High	Source	Date
Insurance Claims and Policy Processing Clerk	Washington-Arlington-Alexandria PMSA, DC-VA-MD-WV	Y	27610 FQ	34430 MW	43660 TQ	USBLS	5/15
	Florida	H	12.97 AE	17.36 MW	20.27 AEX	FLBLS	7/16-9/16
	Fort Lauderdale-Pompano Beach-Deerfield Beach PMSA, FL	H	12.80 AE	16.31 MW	18.68 AEX	FLBLS	7/16-9/16
	Miami-Miami Beach-Kendall PMSA, FL	H	12.64 AE	17.97 MW	21.30 AEX	FLBLS	7/16-9/16
	Orlando-Kissimmee-Sanford MSA, FL	H	13.85 AE	17.64 MW	20.32 AEX	FLBLS	7/16-9/16
	Tampa-St. Petersburg-Clearwater MSA, FL	H	12.85 AE	18.07 MW	21.18 AEX	FLBLS	7/16-9/16
	Georgia	Y	28300 FQ	33330 MW	41690 TQ	USBLS	5/15
	Atlanta-Sandy Springs-Roswell MSA, GA	Y	28330 FQ	33830 MW	45460 TQ	USBLS	5/15
	Augusta-Richmond County MSA, GA-SC	Y	28530 FQ	33440 MW	37800 TQ	USBLS	5/15
	Hawaii	Y	29790 FQ	37120 MW	45050 TQ	USBLS	5/15
	Urban Honolulu MSA, HI	Y	29900 FQ	37120 MW	45160 TQ	USBLS	5/15
	Idaho	Y	29270 FQ	34550 MW	40060 TQ	USBLS	5/15
	Boise City MSA, ID	Y	32120 FQ	36890 MW	44590 TQ	USBLS	5/15
	Illinois	Y	29440 FQ	36640 MW	46060 TQ	USBLS	5/15
	Chicago-Naperville-Arlington Heights PMSA, IL	Y	29350 FQ	38240 MW	47800 TQ	USBLS	5/15
	Lake County-Kenosha County PMSA, IL-WI	Y	32560 FQ	36040 MW	39550 TQ	USBLS	5/15
	Indiana	Y	29270 FQ	35280 MW	42410 TQ	USBLS	5/15
	Gary PMSA, IN	Y	32360 FQ	36210 MW	41260 TQ	USBLS	5/15
	Indianapolis-Carmel-Anderson MSA, IN	Y	32140 FQ	37820 MW	46420 TQ	USBLS	5/15
	Iowa	Y	31890 FQ	36260 MW	42370 TQ	USBLS	5/15
	Des Moines-West Des Moines MSA, IA	Y	33490 FQ	37350 MW	43860 TQ	USBLS	5/15
	Kansas	Y	28880 FQ	34950 MW	41220 TQ	USBLS	5/15
	Wichita MSA, KS	Y	27390 FQ	36910 MW	45300 TQ	USBLS	5/15
	Kentucky	Y	27690 FQ	33270 MW	38300 TQ	USBLS	5/15
	Louisville-Jefferson County MSA, KY-IN	Y	28220 FQ	33630 MW	38200 TQ	USBLS	5/15
	Louisiana	Y	29700 FQ	36820 MW	45600 TQ	USBLS	5/15
	Baton Rouge MSA, LA	Y	31640 FQ	37580 MW	45230 TQ	USBLS	5/15
	New Orleans-Metairie MSA, LA	Y	30350 FQ	38120 MW	47670 TQ	USBLS	5/15
	Maine	Y	29810 FQ	36200 MW	43840 TQ	USBLS	5/15
	Portland-South Portland MSA, ME	Y	30060 FQ	37080 MW	45960 TQ	USBLS	5/15
	Maryland	Y	32652 AE	42996 MW	48167 AEX	MDBLS	4/16
	Baltimore-Columbia-Towson MSA, MD	Y	35430 FQ	41190 MW	47860 TQ	USBLS	5/15
	Salisbury MSA, MD-DE	Y	27850 FQ	33010 MW	38900 TQ	USBLS	5/15
	Massachusetts	Y	36160 FQ	43620 MW	50540 TQ	USBLS	5/15
	Boston-Cambridge-Newton NECTA, MA	Y	40090 FQ	45960 MW	54740 TQ	USBLS	5/15
	Worcester MSA, MA-CT	Y	31220 FQ	37890 MW	46740 TQ	USBLS	5/15
	Michigan	Y	29470 FQ	38570 MW	55470 TQ	USBLS	5/15
	Detroit-Dearborn-Livonia PMSA, MI	Y	28790 FQ	37880 MW	59550 TQ	USBLS	5/15
	Grand Rapids-Wyoming MSA, MI	Y	34130 FQ	39770 MW	47100 TQ	USBLS	5/15
	Minnesota	Y	35678 FQ	41968 MW	48774 TQ	MNBLS	1/16-3/16
	Minneapolis-St. Paul-Bloomington MSA, MN-WI	Y	36547 FQ	42473 MW	48602 TQ	MNBLS	1/16-3/16
	Mississippi	Y	25050 FQ	30940 MW	40420 TQ	USBLS	5/15
	Jackson MSA, MS	Y	28330 FQ	35970 MW	47170 TQ	USBLS	5/15
	Missouri	Y	33010 FQ	40530 MW	49900 TQ	USBLS	5/15
	Kansas City MSA, MO-KS	Y	31200 FQ	37640 MW	47410 TQ	USBLS	5/15
	St. Louis MSA, MO-IL	Y	33630 FQ	41800 MW	51600 TQ	USBLS	5/15
	Montana	Y	31280 FQ	36390 MW	44280 TQ	USBLS	5/15
	Billings MSA, MT	Y	32540 FQ	38290 MW	47440 TQ	USBLS	5/15
	Nebraska	Y	32285 FQ	36535 MW	42710 TQ	NEBLS	7/16-9/16

AE	Average entry wage	AWR	Average wage range	H	Hourly	LR	Low end range	MTC	Median total compensation	TCC	Total cash compensation
AEX	Average experienced wage	B	Biweekly	HI	Highest wage paid	M	Monthly	MW	Median wage paid	TQ	Third quartile wage
ATC	Average total compensation	D	Daily	HR	High end range	MCC	Median cash compensation	MWR	Median wage range	W	Weekly
AW	Average wage paid	FQ	First quartile wage	LO	Lowest wage paid	ME	Median entry wage	S	See annotated source	Y	Yearly

Occupation/Type/Industry	Location	Per	Low	Mid	High	Source	Date
Insurance Claims and Policy Processing Clerk	Omaha-Council Bluffs MSA, NE-IA	Y	32705 FQ	36630 MW	42325 TQ	NEBLS	7/16-9/16
	Nevada	Y	26830 FQ	36120 MW	47960 TQ	USBLS	5/15
	Las Vegas-Henderson-Paradise MSA, NV	Y	26120 FQ	38790 MW	49750 TQ	USBLS	5/15
	New Hampshire	H	15.37 AE	18.82 MW	22.82 AEX	NHBLS	6/16
	Manchester NECTA, NH	H	15.75 AE	19.73 MW	24.91 AEX	NHBLS	6/16
	Nashua NECTA, NH-MA	Y	28870 FQ	33500 MW	38450 TQ	USBLS	5/15
	New Jersey	Y	35040 FQ	42760 MW	49880 TQ	USBLS	5/15
	Camden PMSA, NJ	Y	36820 FQ	43060 MW	48350 TQ	USBLS	5/15
	Newark PMSA, NJ-PA	Y	35730 FQ	43560 MW	50280 TQ	USBLS	5/15
	Trenton MSA, NJ	Y	37420 FQ	46340 MW	55650 TQ	USBLS	5/15
	New Mexico	Y	26940 FQ	29900 MW	37680 TQ	USBLS	5/15
	Albuquerque MSA, NM	Y	27910 FQ	31330 MW	41000 TQ	USBLS	5/15
	New York	Y	32400 AE	43770 MW	54540 AEX	NYBLS	1/16-3/16
	Buffalo-Cheektowaga-Niagara Falls MSA, NY	Y	31960 FQ	36860 MW	44930 TQ	USBLS	5/15
	Nassau County-Suffolk County PMSA, NY	Y	35130 FQ	41400 MW	50130 TQ	USBLS	5/15
	New York-Jersey City-White Plains PMSA, NY-NJ	Y	36390 FQ	45810 MW	60560 TQ	USBLS	5/15
	Rochester MSA, NY	Y	33660 FQ	40490 MW	49050 TQ	USBLS	5/15
	North Carolina	Y	32530 FQ	38130 MW	46150 TQ	USBLS	5/15
	Charlotte-Concord-Gastonia MSA, NC-SC	Y	34950 FQ	40810 MW	48340 TQ	USBLS	5/15
	Raleigh MSA, NC	Y	32800 FQ	38200 MW	46030 TQ	USBLS	5/15
	North Dakota	Y	32350 FQ	36920 MW	44230 TQ	USBLS	5/15
	Fargo MSA, ND-MN	Y	30780 FQ	35830 MW	42680 TQ	USBLS	5/15
	Ohio	Y	29710 FQ	36190 MW	44400 TQ	USBLS	5/15
	Cincinnati MSA, OH-KY-IN	Y	31520 FQ	38270 MW	47230 TQ	USBLS	5/15
	Cleveland-Elyria MSA, OH	Y	29560 FQ	35920 MW	44450 TQ	USBLS	5/15
	Columbus MSA, OH	Y	33450 FQ	39010 MW	46380 TQ	USBLS	5/15
	Oklahoma	Y	25990 FQ	31200 MW	39780 TQ	USBLS	5/15
	Oklahoma City MSA, OK	Y	27240 FQ	33830 MW	40670 TQ	USBLS	5/15
	Tulsa MSA, OK	Y	25770 FQ	31070 MW	44480 TQ	USBLS	5/15
	Oregon	H	16.07 FQ	18.65 MW	22.74 TQ	ORBLS	2016
	Portland-Vancouver-Hillsboro MSA, OR-WA	Y	34050 FQ	39190 MW	47890 TQ	USBLS	5/15
	Pennsylvania	Y	31810 FQ	38510 MW	46690 TQ	USBLS	5/15
	Allentown-Bethlehem-Easton MSA, PA-NJ	Y	35850 FQ	42900 MW	48050 TQ	USBLS	5/15
	Harrisburg-Carlisle MSA, PA	Y	30790 FQ	37170 MW	44780 TQ	USBLS	5/15
	Montgomery County-Bucks County-Chester County PMSA, PA	Y	35930 FQ	43030 MW	49770 TQ	USBLS	5/15
	Philadelphia PMSA, PA	Y	34090 FQ	40110 MW	48290 TQ	USBLS	5/15
	Pittsburgh MSA, PA	Y	28510 FQ	33910 MW	40730 TQ	USBLS	5/15
	Rhode Island	Y	35260 FQ	41460 MW	47880 TQ	USBLS	5/15
	Providence-Warwick MSA, RI-MA	Y	34290 FQ	40430 MW	47330 TQ	USBLS	5/15
	South Carolina	Y	27200 FQ	32830 MW	39680 TQ	USBLS	5/15
	Charleston-North Charleston MSA, SC	Y	28900 FQ	34210 MW	39560 TQ	USBLS	5/15
	Columbia MSA, SC	Y	26650 FQ	31840 MW	38450 TQ	USBLS	5/15
	Greenville-Anderson-Mauldin MSA, SC	Y	30120 FQ	40310 MW	48910 TQ	USBLS	5/15
	South Dakota	Y	25600 FQ	29210 MW	34200 TQ	USBLS	5/15
	Sioux Falls MSA, SD	Y	25760 FQ	29550 MW	35050 TQ	USBLS	5/15
	Tennessee	Y	28570 FQ	34350 MW	43650 TQ	USBLS	5/15
	Knoxville MSA, TN	Y	27760 FQ	32140 MW	37950 TQ	USBLS	5/15
	Memphis MSA, TN-MS-AR	Y	28030 FQ	31970 MW	39230 TQ	USBLS	5/15
	Nashville-Davidson–Murfreesboro–Franklin MSA, TN	Y	29210 FQ	35680 MW	45180 TQ	USBLS	5/15
	Texas	Y	28960 FQ	36410 MW	46540 TQ	USBLS	5/15
	Austin-Round Rock MSA, TX	Y	33620 FQ	41470 MW	50900 TQ	USBLS	5/15
	Dallas-Plano-Irving PMSA, TX	Y	27650 FQ	35810 MW	46630 TQ	USBLS	5/15
	Fort Worth-Arlington PMSA, TX	Y	27900 FQ	34480 MW	44130 TQ	USBLS	5/15
	Houston-The Woodlands-Sugar Land MSA, TX	Y	32460 FQ	38610 MW	48130 TQ	USBLS	5/15

AE	Average entry wage	AWR	Average wage range	H	Hourly
AEX	Average experienced wage	B	Biweekly	HI	Highest wage paid
ATC	Average total compensation	D	Daily	HR	High end range
AW	Average wage paid	FQ	First quartile wage	LO	Lowest wage paid

LR	Low end range	MTC	Median total compensation
M	Monthly	MW	Median wage paid
MCC	Median cash compensation	MWR	Median wage range
ME	Median entry wage	S`	See annotated source

TCC	Total cash compensation
TQ	Third quartile wage
W	Weekly
Y	Yearly

Occupation/Type/Industry	Location	Per	Low	Mid	High	Source	Date
Insurance Claims and Policy Processing Clerk	San Antonio-New Braunfels MSA, TX	Y	28670 FQ	34370 MW	42610 TQ	USBLS	5/15
	Utah	Y	31240 FQ	38330 MW	47540 TQ	USBLS	5/15
	Ogden-Clearfield MSA, UT	Y	28010 FQ	34010 MW	40760 TQ	USBLS	5/15
	Provo-Orem MSA, UT	Y	32120 FQ	37270 MW	45200 TQ	USBLS	5/15
	Salt Lake City MSA, UT	Y	31610 FQ	38760 MW	48170 TQ	USBLS	5/15
	Vermont	Y	29830 FQ	36690 MW	44560 TQ	USBLS	5/15
	Burlington-South Burlington MSA, VT	Y	27490 FQ	30920 MW	42070 TQ	USBLS	5/15
	Virginia	Y	27520 FQ	33340 MW	39630 TQ	USBLS	5/15
	Richmond MSA, VA	Y	27910 FQ	33310 MW	39480 TQ	USBLS	5/15
	Virginia Beach-Norfolk-Newport News MSA, VA-NC	Y	27570 FQ	33260 MW	39070 TQ	USBLS	5/15
	Washington	H	17.13 FQ	20.27 MW	23.87 TQ	WABLS	3/16
	Seattle-Bellevue-Everett PMSA, WA	H	17.33 FQ	20.90 MW	24.62 TQ	WABLS	3/16
	Tacoma-Lakewood PMSA, WA	H	16.32 FQ	18.71 MW	22.20 TQ	WABLS	3/16
	West Virginia	Y	27030 FQ	32270 MW	41640 TQ	USBLS	5/15
	Wisconsin	Y	30000 FQ	35950 MW	44120 TQ	USBLS	5/15
	Madison MSA, WI	Y	31400 FQ	37000 MW	44300 TQ	USBLS	5/15
	Milwaukee-Waukesha-West Allis MSA, WI	Y	33660 FQ	40040 MW	53550 TQ	USBLS	5/15
	Wyoming	Y	28940 FQ	34690 MW	41150 TQ	USBLS	5/15
	Cheyenne MSA, WY	Y	31010 FQ	35650 MW	40820 TQ	USBLS	5/15
	Puerto Rico	Y	18730 FQ	22700 MW	29580 TQ	USBLS	5/15
	San Juan-Carolina-Caguas MSA, PR	Y	18810 FQ	22870 MW	29960 TQ	USBLS	5/15
	Guam	Y	20810 FQ	23380 MW	27500 TQ	USBLS	5/15
Insurance Examination Data Specialist State Government	Ohio	H	25.67 LO		39.38 HI	OHGOV	2015
Insurance Industry Professional Without a College Degree	United States	Y		66448 AW		TC02	2016
Insurance Sales Agent	Alabama	Y	28680 AE	60214 AW	75976 AEX	ALBLS	6/16
	Birmingham-Hoover MSA, AL	Y	30417 AE	61652 AW	77269 AEX	ALBLS	6/16
	Alaska	Y	37850 FQ	47330 MW	58550 TQ	USBLS	5/15
	Anchorage MSA, AK	Y	35260 FQ	42910 MW	54340 TQ	USBLS	5/15
	Arizona	Y	35010 FQ	46850 MW	60720 TQ	USBLS	5/15
	Phoenix-Mesa-Scottsdale MSA, AZ	Y	35540 FQ	47400 MW	60320 TQ	USBLS	5/15
	Tucson MSA, AZ	Y	30920 FQ	41400 MW	72260 TQ	USBLS	5/15
	Arkansas	Y	27940 FQ	37450 MW	59630 TQ	USBLS	5/15
	Little Rock-North Little Rock-Conway MSA, AR	Y	28570 FQ	45380 MW	83300 TQ	USBLS	5/15
	California	H	18.25 FQ	26.55 MW	41.97 TQ	CABLS	1/16-3/16
	Anaheim-Santa Ana-Irvine PMSA, CA	H	18.57 FQ	27.50 MW	44.69 TQ	CABLS	1/16-3/16
	Los Angeles-Long Beach-Glendale PMSA, CA	H	16.66 FQ	23.69 MW	35.14 TQ	CABLS	1/16-3/16
	Oakland-Hayward-Berkeley PMSA, CA	H	23.25 FQ	32.76 MW	64.40 TQ	CABLS	1/16-3/16
	Riverside-San Bernardino-Ontario MSA, CA	H	14.65 FQ	25.38 MW	35.72 TQ	CABLS	1/16-3/16
	Sacramento–Roseville–Arden-Arcade MSA, CA	H	18.65 FQ	27.03 MW	46.05 TQ	CABLS	1/16-3/16
	San Diego-Carlsbad MSA, CA	H	19.48 FQ	23.49 MW	37.92 TQ	CABLS	1/16-3/16
	San Francisco-Redwood City-South San Francisco PMSA, CA	H	20.48 FQ	32.41 MW	56.00 TQ	CABLS	1/16-3/16
	Colorado	Y	32350 FQ	43800 MW	59290 TQ	USBLS	5/15
	Denver-Aurora-Lakewood MSA, CO	Y	27510 FQ	40230 MW	61810 TQ	USBLS	5/15
	Connecticut	Y		57649 MW		CTBLS	1/16-3/16
	Bridgeport-Stamford-Norwalk MSA, CT	Y	35950 FQ	51250 MW	92500 TQ	USBLS	5/15
	Hartford-West Hartford-East Hartford MSA, CT	Y	46500 FQ	59040 MW	78210 TQ	USBLS	5/15
	Delaware	Y	31650 FQ	45660 MW	70130 TQ	USBLS	5/15

AE	Average entry wage	AWR	Average wage range	H	Hourly	LR	Low end range	MTC	Median total compensation	TCC	Total cash compensation
AEX	Average experienced wage	B	Biweekly	HI	Highest wage paid	M	Monthly	MW	Median wage paid	TQ	Third quartile wage
ATC	Average total compensation	D	Daily	HR	High end range	MCC	Median cash compensation	MWR	Median wage range	W	Weekly
AW	Average wage paid	FQ	First quartile wage	LO	Lowest wage paid	ME	Median entry wage	S	See annotated source	Y	Yearly

Occupation/Type/Industry	Location	Per	Low	Mid	High	Source	Date
Insurance Sales Agent	Wilmington PMSA, DE-MD-NJ	Y	30070 FQ	44420 MW	65510 TQ	USBLS	5/15
	District of Columbia	Y	36130 FQ	47700 MW	79710 TQ	USBLS	5/15
	Washington-Arlington-Alexandria PMSA, DC-VA-MD-WV	Y	37170 FQ	50530 MW	87050 TQ	USBLS	5/15
	Florida	H	17.45 AE	25.21 MW	41.66 AEX	FLBLS	7/16-9/16
	Fort Lauderdale-Pompano Beach-Deerfield Beach PMSA, FL	H	17.83 AE	24.80 MW	38.05 AEX	FLBLS	7/16-9/16
	Miami-Miami Beach-Kendall PMSA, FL	H	18.66 AE	32.08 MW	49.87 AEX	FLBLS	7/16-9/16
	Orlando-Kissimmee-Sanford MSA, FL	H	15.91 AE	24.28 MW	40.63 AEX	FLBLS	7/16-9/16
	Tampa-St. Petersburg-Clearwater MSA, FL	H	17.77 AE	24.52 MW	49.23 AEX	FLBLS	7/16-9/16
	Georgia	Y	30870 FQ	43660 MW	69120 TQ	USBLS	5/15
	Atlanta-Sandy Springs-Roswell MSA, GA	Y	35640 FQ	47910 MW	83370 TQ	USBLS	5/15
	Augusta-Richmond County MSA, GA-SC	Y	27990 FQ	33780 MW	50360 TQ	USBLS	5/15
	Hawaii	Y	39040 FQ	54000 MW	80180 TQ	USBLS	5/15
	Urban Honolulu MSA, HI	Y	40650 FQ	55430 MW	92610 TQ	USBLS	5/15
	Idaho	Y	30630 FQ	44650 MW	70250 TQ	USBLS	5/15
	Boise City MSA, ID	Y	44680 FQ	61140 MW	82500 TQ	USBLS	5/15
	Illinois	Y	28090 FQ	39110 MW	64020 TQ	USBLS	5/15
	Chicago-Naperville-Arlington Heights PMSA, IL	Y	27510 FQ	37550 MW	62690 TQ	USBLS	5/15
	Lake County-Kenosha County PMSA, IL-WI	Y	41030 FQ	59770 MW	143380 TQ	USBLS	5/15
	Indiana	Y	30040 FQ	44640 MW	68400 TQ	USBLS	5/15
	Gary PMSA, IN	Y	29660 FQ	38990 MW	61160 TQ	USBLS	5/15
	Indianapolis-Carmel-Anderson MSA, IN	Y	30540 FQ	48790 MW	69960 TQ	USBLS	5/15
	Iowa	Y	30390 FQ	42150 MW	60900 TQ	USBLS	5/15
	Des Moines-West Des Moines MSA, IA	Y	33340 FQ	44680 MW	61250 TQ	USBLS	5/15
	Kansas	Y	36470 FQ	52880 MW	69700 TQ	USBLS	5/15
	Wichita MSA, KS	Y	34930 FQ	46070 MW	63800 TQ	USBLS	5/15
	Kentucky	Y	27980 FQ	39350 MW	59820 TQ	USBLS	5/15
	Louisville-Jefferson County MSA, KY-IN	Y	29790 FQ	43150 MW	62290 TQ	USBLS	5/15
	Owensboro MSA, KY	Y	26660 FQ	29720 MW	33820 TQ	USBLS	5/15
	Louisiana	Y	31510 FQ	43120 MW	60190 TQ	USBLS	5/15
	Baton Rouge MSA, LA	Y	36770 FQ	47150 MW	62530 TQ	USBLS	5/15
	New Orleans-Metairie MSA, LA	Y	32170 FQ	44710 MW	61070 TQ	USBLS	5/15
	Maine	Y	33980 FQ	48420 MW	66250 TQ	USBLS	5/15
	Portland-South Portland MSA, ME	Y	31470 FQ	48220 MW	69070 TQ	USBLS	5/15
	Maryland	Y	30686 AE	61860 MW	77447 AEX	MDBLS	4/16
	Baltimore-Columbia-Towson MSA, MD	Y	41910 FQ	53840 MW	73650 TQ	USBLS	5/15
	Salisbury MSA, MD-DE	Y	37490 FQ	50000 MW	72500 TQ	USBLS	5/15
	Massachusetts	Y	47800 FQ	62910 MW	92830 TQ	USBLS	5/15
	Boston-Cambridge-Newton NECTA, MA	Y	49840 FQ	66170 MW	94230 TQ	USBLS	5/15
	Worcester MSA, MA-CT	Y	45970 FQ	59050 MW	84490 TQ	USBLS	5/15
	Michigan	Y	34690 FQ	47090 MW	76100 TQ	USBLS	5/15
	Detroit-Dearborn-Livonia PMSA, MI	Y	39500 FQ	53270 MW	78960 TQ	USBLS	5/15
	Grand Rapids-Wyoming MSA, MI	Y	40910 FQ	49060 MW	78850 TQ	USBLS	5/15
	Minnesota	Y	46152 FQ	61056 MW	119944 TQ	MNBLS	1/16-3/16
	Minneapolis-St. Paul-Bloomington MSA, MN-WI	Y	49540 FQ	67187 MW	139102 TQ	MNBLS	1/16-3/16
	Mississippi	Y	24470 FQ	37050 MW	62260 TQ	USBLS	5/15
	Jackson MSA, MS	Y	34040 FQ	44950 MW	62970 TQ	USBLS	5/15
	Missouri	Y	31880 FQ	47270 MW	85660 TQ	USBLS	5/15
	Kansas City MSA, MO-KS	Y	36000 FQ	54300 MW	72950 TQ	USBLS	5/15
	St. Louis MSA, MO-IL	Y	32490 FQ	54360 MW	96470 TQ	USBLS	5/15
	Montana	Y	28960 FQ	45660 MW	73160 TQ	USBLS	5/15

AE	Average entry wage	AWR	Average wage range	H	Hourly
AEX	Average experienced wage	B	Biweekly	HI	Highest wage paid
ATC	Average total compensation	D	Daily	HR	High end range
AW	Average wage paid	FQ	First quartile wage	LO	Lowest wage paid

LR	Low end range	MTC	Median total compensation
M	Monthly	MW	Median wage paid
MCC	Median cash compensation	MWR	Median wage range
ME	Median entry wage	S	See annotated source

TCC	Total cash compensation		
TQ	Third quartile wage		
W	Weekly		
Y	Yearly		

Insurance Sales Agent

Occupation/Type/Industry	Location	Per	Low	Mid	High	Source	Date
Insurance Sales Agent	Billings MSA, MT	Y	26690 FQ	44000 MW	75690 TQ	USBLS	5/15
	Nebraska	Y	32000 FQ	42665 MW	61330 TQ	NEBLS	7/16-9/16
	Omaha-Council Bluffs MSA, NE-IA	Y	33010 FQ	41090 MW	58485 TQ	NEBLS	7/16-9/16
	Nevada	Y	33380 FQ	41200 MW	61190 TQ	USBLS	5/15
	Las Vegas-Henderson-Paradise MSA, NV	Y	33950 FQ	40640 MW	58070 TQ	USBLS	5/15
	New Hampshire	H	17.89 AE	26.87 MW	37.47 AEX	NHBLS	6/16
	Manchester NECTA, NH	H	16.91 AE	28.33 MW	36.87 AEX	NHBLS	6/16
	Nashua NECTA, NH-MA	Y	36200 FQ	48770 MW	64510 TQ	USBLS	5/15
	New Jersey	Y	39750 FQ	59520 MW	85510 TQ	USBLS	5/15
	Camden PMSA, NJ	Y	43780 FQ	59490 MW	90370 TQ	USBLS	5/15
	Newark PMSA, NJ-PA	Y	42140 FQ	63080 MW	94550 TQ	USBLS	5/15
	Trenton MSA, NJ	Y	56970 FQ	76810 MW	98730 TQ	USBLS	5/15
	New Mexico	Y	31120 FQ	39080 MW	56620 TQ	USBLS	5/15
	Albuquerque MSA, NM	Y	34260 FQ	41830 MW	63560 TQ	USBLS	5/15
	New York	Y	36370 AE	64910 MW	106970 AEX	NYBLS	1/16-3/16
	Buffalo-Cheektowaga-Niagara Falls MSA, NY	Y	38320 FQ	46360 MW	60410 TQ	USBLS	5/15
	Nassau County-Suffolk County PMSA, NY	Y	46470 FQ	69530 MW	105500 TQ	USBLS	5/15
	New York-Jersey City-White Plains PMSA, NY-NJ	Y	42820 FQ	64720 MW	97060 TQ	USBLS	5/15
	Rochester MSA, NY	Y	44110 FQ	57810 MW	76030 TQ	USBLS	5/15
	North Carolina	Y	31620 FQ	44420 MW	67370 TQ	USBLS	5/15
	Charlotte-Concord-Gastonia MSA, NC-SC	Y	38470 FQ	53870 MW	78310 TQ	USBLS	5/15
	Raleigh MSA, NC	Y	28910 FQ	43800 MW	68880 TQ	USBLS	5/15
	North Dakota	Y	33570 FQ	54740 MW	76150 TQ	USBLS	5/15
	Bismarck MSA, ND	Y	31910 FQ	40570 MW	63160 TQ	USBLS	5/15
	Fargo MSA, ND-MN	Y	50540 FQ	70980 MW	87610 TQ	USBLS	5/15
	Ohio	Y	34680 FQ	48460 MW	74960 TQ	USBLS	5/15
	Cincinnati MSA, OH-KY-IN	Y	31120 FQ	48570 MW	76440 TQ	USBLS	5/15
	Cleveland-Elyria MSA, OH	Y	34830 FQ	46550 MW	74280 TQ	USBLS	5/15
	Columbus MSA, OH	Y	37910 FQ	52640 MW	73960 TQ	USBLS	5/15
	Oklahoma	Y	29200 FQ	38900 MW	53940 TQ	USBLS	5/15
	Oklahoma City MSA, OK	Y	31920 FQ	38720 MW	57410 TQ	USBLS	5/15
	Tulsa MSA, OK	Y	28230 FQ	40540 MW	49400 TQ	USBLS	5/15
	Oregon	H	16.91 FQ	23.37 MW	36.39 TQ	ORBLS	2016
	Corvallis MSA, OR	Y	43390 FQ	53320 MW	62070 TQ	USBLS	5/15
	Portland-Vancouver-Hillsboro MSA, OR-WA	Y	36220 FQ	55280 MW	77560 TQ	USBLS	5/15
	Pennsylvania	Y	36480 FQ	55000 MW	84640 TQ	USBLS	5/15
	Allentown-Bethlehem-Easton MSA, PA-NJ	Y	32540 FQ	55110 MW	101970 TQ	USBLS	5/15
	Harrisburg-Carlisle MSA, PA	Y	28860 FQ	42900 MW	71810 TQ	USBLS	5/15
	Montgomery County-Bucks County-Chester County PMSA, PA	Y	41330 FQ	63590 MW	104410 TQ	USBLS	5/15
	Philadelphia PMSA, PA	Y	38290 FQ	59380 MW	95690 TQ	USBLS	5/15
	Pittsburgh MSA, PA	Y	36800 FQ	56990 MW	79410 TQ	USBLS	5/15
	Rhode Island	Y	45430 FQ	60690 MW	91370 TQ	USBLS	5/15
	Providence-Warwick MSA, RI-MA	Y	45050 FQ	60070 MW	90780 TQ	USBLS	5/15
	South Carolina	Y	28170 FQ	36700 MW	54700 TQ	USBLS	5/15
	Charleston-North Charleston MSA, SC	Y	32660 FQ	39030 MW	55060 TQ	USBLS	5/15
	Columbia MSA, SC	Y	31050 FQ	46530 MW	60530 TQ	USBLS	5/15
	Greenville-Anderson-Mauldin MSA, SC	Y	27260 FQ	33820 MW	46610 TQ	USBLS	5/15
	South Dakota	Y	38700 FQ	50920 MW	76100 TQ	USBLS	5/15
	Sioux Falls MSA, SD	Y	37480 FQ	52880 MW	66460 TQ	USBLS	5/15
	Tennessee	Y	31350 FQ	43090 MW	63070 TQ	USBLS	5/15
	Knoxville MSA, TN	Y	26690 FQ	35070 MW	59900 TQ	USBLS	5/15
	Memphis MSA, TN-MS-AR	Y	31510 FQ	46430 MW	72730 TQ	USBLS	5/15
	Nashville-Davidson–Murfreesboro–Franklin MSA, TN	Y	33370 FQ	44120 MW	63990 TQ	USBLS	5/15
	Texas	Y	32390 FQ	44130 MW	67790 TQ	USBLS	5/15
	Austin-Round Rock MSA, TX	Y	34990 FQ	46130 MW	84950 TQ	USBLS	5/15
	Dallas-Plano-Irving PMSA, TX	Y	34280 FQ	50630 MW	77350 TQ	USBLS	5/15

AE	Average entry wage	AWR	Average wage range	H	Hourly	LR	Low end range	MTC	Median total compensation	TCC	Total cash compensation
AEX	Average experienced wage	B	Biweekly	HI	Highest wage paid	M	Monthly	MW	Median wage paid	TQ	Third quartile wage
ATC	Average total compensation	D	Daily	HR	High end range	MCC	Median cash compensation	MWR	Median wage range	W	Weekly
AW	Average wage paid	FQ	First quartile wage	LO	Lowest wage paid	ME	Median entry wage	S	See annotated source	Y	Yearly

Occupation/Type/Industry	Location	Per	Low	Mid	High	Source	Date
Insurance Sales Agent	Fort Worth-Arlington PMSA, TX	Y	31780 FQ	41600 MW	56970 TQ	USBLS	5/15
	Houston-The Woodlands-Sugar Land MSA, TX	Y	32140 FQ	45560 MW	86030 TQ	USBLS	5/15
	San Antonio-New Braunfels MSA, TX	Y	34610 FQ	43890 MW	57120 TQ	USBLS	5/15
	Utah	Y	26690 FQ	39950 MW	57930 TQ	USBLS	5/15
	Ogden-Clearfield MSA, UT	Y	24600 FQ	32170 MW	51230 TQ	USBLS	5/15
	Provo-Orem MSA, UT	Y	25650 FQ	36270 MW	45230 TQ	USBLS	5/15
	Salt Lake City MSA, UT	Y	27910 FQ	44230 MW	70960 TQ	USBLS	5/15
	Vermont	Y	37970 FQ	46650 MW	63830 TQ	USBLS	5/15
	Burlington-South Burlington MSA, VT	Y	38090 FQ	48750 MW	62800 TQ	USBLS	5/15
	Virginia	Y	32700 FQ	44710 MW	68980 TQ	USBLS	5/15
	Richmond MSA, VA	Y	31090 FQ	43430 MW	66340 TQ	USBLS	5/15
	Virginia Beach-Norfolk-Newport News MSA, VA-NC	Y	31840 FQ	39340 MW	56510 TQ	USBLS	5/15
	Washington	H	15.06 FQ	20.85 MW	29.67 TQ	WABLS	3/16
	Seattle-Bellevue-Everett PMSA, WA	H	17.73 FQ	23.64 MW	36.90 TQ	WABLS	3/16
	Tacoma-Lakewood PMSA, WA	H	13.91 FQ	20.09 MW	28.68 TQ	WABLS	3/16
	West Virginia	Y	26610 FQ	33950 MW	55630 TQ	USBLS	5/15
	Huntington-Ashland MSA, WV-KY-OH	Y	26310 FQ	31420 MW	46330 TQ	USBLS	5/15
	Wisconsin	Y	37050 FQ	55070 MW	84600 TQ	USBLS	5/15
	Madison MSA, WI	Y	37540 FQ	49800 MW	73410 TQ	USBLS	5/15
	Milwaukee-Waukesha-West Allis MSA, WI	Y	47040 FQ	70440 MW	128070 TQ	USBLS	5/15
	Wyoming	Y	29030 FQ	38270 MW	53510 TQ	USBLS	5/15
	Cheyenne MSA, WY	Y	22230 FQ	31210 MW	60690 TQ	USBLS	5/15
	Puerto Rico	Y	24650 FQ	29940 MW	37050 TQ	USBLS	5/15
	San Juan-Carolina-Caguas MSA, PR	Y	26510 FQ	31010 MW	37950 TQ	USBLS	5/15
Insurance Services Technician City Attorney's Office	Glendale, CA	Y			60496 HI	CACIT	6/28/16
Insurance Underwriter	Alabama	Y	37380 AE	57213 AW	67135 AEX	ALBLS	6/16
	Birmingham-Hoover MSA, AL	Y	41900 AE	62769 AW	73203 AEX	ALBLS	6/16
	Anchorage MSA, AK	Y	34210 FQ	50670 MW	69910 TQ	USBLS	5/15
	Arizona	Y	47000 FQ	62600 MW	85570 TQ	USBLS	5/15
	Phoenix-Mesa-Scottsdale MSA, AZ	Y	48190 FQ	64430 MW	87930 TQ	USBLS	5/15
	Arkansas	Y	40250 FQ	58400 MW	86010 TQ	USBLS	5/15
	Little Rock-North Little Rock-Conway MSA, AR	Y	39110 FQ	57160 MW	83800 TQ	USBLS	5/15
	California	H	25.59 FQ	32.27 MW	44.31 TQ	CABLS	1/16-3/16
	Anaheim-Santa Ana-Irvine PMSA, CA	H	24.12 FQ	32.50 MW	45.66 TQ	CABLS	1/16-3/16
	Los Angeles-Long Beach-Glendale PMSA, CA	H	25.47 FQ	31.35 MW	44.01 TQ	CABLS	1/16-3/16
	Oakland-Hayward-Berkeley PMSA, CA	H	25.21 FQ	31.19 MW	44.62 TQ	CABLS	1/16-3/16
	Riverside-San Bernardino-Ontario MSA, CA	H	20.12 FQ	27.44 MW	34.82 TQ	CABLS	1/16-3/16
	Sacramento–Roseville–Arden-Arcade MSA, CA	H	26.96 FQ	33.22 MW	42.75 TQ	CABLS	1/16-3/16
	San Diego-Carlsbad MSA, CA	H	25.15 FQ	32.36 MW	46.82 TQ	CABLS	1/16-3/16
	San Francisco-Redwood City-South San Francisco PMSA, CA	H	27.10 FQ	35.05 MW	46.54 TQ	CABLS	1/16-3/16
	Colorado	Y	54440 FQ	70050 MW	91470 TQ	USBLS	5/15
	Denver-Aurora-Lakewood MSA, CO	Y	56830 FQ	72040 MW	93720 TQ	USBLS	5/15
	Connecticut	Y		74009 MW		CTBLS	1/16-3/16
	Bridgeport-Stamford-Norwalk MSA, CT	Y	50580 FQ	74140 MW	121560 TQ	USBLS	5/15
	Hartford-West Hartford-East Hartford MSA, CT	Y	53550 FQ	73010 MW	99250 TQ	USBLS	5/15
	Delaware	Y	45920 FQ	60490 MW	79890 TQ	USBLS	5/15
	Wilmington PMSA, DE-MD-NJ	Y	46390 FQ	60890 MW	79280 TQ	USBLS	5/15

AE	Average entry wage	**AWR**	Average wage range	**H**	Hourly	**LR**	Low end range	**MTC**	Median total compensation	**TCC** Total cash compensation
AEX	Average experienced wage	**B**	Biweekly	**HI**	Highest wage paid	**M**	Monthly	**MW**	Median wage paid	**TQ** Third quartile wage
ATC	Average total compensation	**D**	Daily	**HR**	High end range	**MCC**	Median cash compensation	**MWR**	Median wage range	**W** Weekly
AW	Average wage paid	**FQ**	First quartile wage	**LO**	Lowest wage paid	**ME**	Median entry wage	**S**	See annotated source	**Y** Yearly

Occupation/Type/Industry	Location	Per	Low	Mid	High	Source	Date
Insurance Underwriter	District of Columbia	Y	59190 FQ	75110 MW	100000 TQ	USBLS	5/15
	Washington-Arlington-Alexandria PMSA, DC-VA-MD-WV	Y	53420 FQ	62760 MW	76810 TQ	USBLS	5/15
	Florida	H	19.75 AE	28.21 MW	36.64 AEX	FLBLS	7/16-9/16
	Fort Lauderdale-Pompano Beach-Deerfield Beach PMSA, FL	H	19.89 AE	26.36 MW	32.62 AEX	FLBLS	7/16-9/16
	Miami-Miami Beach-Kendall PMSA, FL	H	20.32 AE	29.24 MW	36.26 AEX	FLBLS	7/16-9/16
	Orlando-Kissimmee-Sanford MSA, FL	H	22.25 AE	30.10 MW	36.70 AEX	FLBLS	7/16-9/16
	Tampa-St. Petersburg-Clearwater MSA, FL	H	19.30 AE	27.69 MW	33.29 AEX	FLBLS	7/16-9/16
	Georgia	Y	44160 FQ	61330 MW	93380 TQ	USBLS	5/15
	Atlanta-Sandy Springs-Roswell MSA, GA	Y	45360 FQ	62590 MW	95740 TQ	USBLS	5/15
	Hawaii	Y	44180 FQ	58030 MW	77830 TQ	USBLS	5/15
	Urban Honolulu MSA, HI	Y	43580 FQ	57050 MW	78420 TQ	USBLS	5/15
	Idaho	Y	40370 FQ	51050 MW	69820 TQ	USBLS	5/15
	Boise City MSA, ID	Y	42340 FQ	52540 MW	74040 TQ	USBLS	5/15
	Illinois	Y	44740 FQ	59980 MW	82290 TQ	USBLS	5/15
	Chicago-Naperville-Arlington Heights PMSA, IL	Y	46260 FQ	63060 MW	88240 TQ	USBLS	5/15
	Lake County-Kenosha County PMSA, IL-WI	Y	43680 FQ	54670 MW	73120 TQ	USBLS	5/15
	Indiana	Y	48230 FQ	61020 MW	77400 TQ	USBLS	5/15
	Indianapolis-Carmel-Anderson MSA, IN	Y	52190 FQ	66210 MW	82420 TQ	USBLS	5/15
	Iowa	Y	44140 FQ	57200 MW	73610 TQ	USBLS	5/15
	Des Moines-West Des Moines MSA, IA	Y	47460 FQ	60250 MW	77430 TQ	USBLS	5/15
	Kansas	Y	50830 FQ	62200 MW	82100 TQ	USBLS	5/15
	Wichita MSA, KS	Y	41570 FQ	61150 MW	81730 TQ	USBLS	5/15
	Kentucky	Y	43620 FQ	56440 MW	74230 TQ	USBLS	5/15
	Louisville-Jefferson County MSA, KY-IN	Y	43350 FQ	55900 MW	71610 TQ	USBLS	5/15
	Louisiana	Y	44970 FQ	60010 MW	76740 TQ	USBLS	5/15
	Baton Rouge MSA, LA	Y	50090 FQ	63390 MW	77480 TQ	USBLS	5/15
	New Orleans-Metairie MSA, LA	Y	43960 FQ	59420 MW	76790 TQ	USBLS	5/15
	Maine	Y	45870 FQ	63800 MW	85610 TQ	USBLS	5/15
	Portland-South Portland MSA, ME	Y	47220 FQ	68940 MW	87540 TQ	USBLS	5/15
	Maryland	Y	43728 AE	76284 MW	92562 AEX	MDBLS	4/16
	Baltimore-Columbia-Towson MSA, MD	Y	58030 FQ	74710 MW	105590 TQ	USBLS	5/15
	Salisbury MSA, MD-DE	Y	52100 FQ	57120 MW	62140 TQ	USBLS	5/15
	Massachusetts	Y	58130 FQ	74840 MW	96510 TQ	USBLS	5/15
	Boston-Cambridge-Newton NECTA, MA	Y	59880 FQ	76210 MW	98180 TQ	USBLS	5/15
	Worcester MSA, MA-CT	Y	56360 FQ	67870 MW	79140 TQ	USBLS	5/15
	Michigan	Y	47490 FQ	59770 MW	73780 TQ	USBLS	5/15
	Detroit-Dearborn-Livonia PMSA, MI	Y	48030 FQ	62450 MW	74920 TQ	USBLS	5/15
	Minnesota	Y	46883 FQ	62409 MW	79002 TQ	MNBLS	1/16-3/16
	Minneapolis-St. Paul-Bloomington MSA, MN-WI	Y	48742 FQ	64533 MW	79886 TQ	MNBLS	1/16-3/16
	Mississippi	Y	40170 FQ	49510 MW	69290 TQ	USBLS	5/15
	Jackson MSA, MS	Y	38920 FQ	48450 MW	68460 TQ	USBLS	5/15
	Missouri	Y	46630 FQ	60860 MW	79960 TQ	USBLS	5/15
	Kansas City MSA, MO-KS	Y	48550 FQ	61640 MW	83870 TQ	USBLS	5/15
	St. Louis MSA, MO-IL	Y	52410 FQ	69210 MW	93030 TQ	USBLS	5/15
	Montana	Y	39440 FQ	59660 MW	90140 TQ	USBLS	5/15
	Nebraska	Y	40120 FQ	52235 MW	71090 TQ	NEBLS	7/16-9/16
	Omaha-Council Bluffs MSA, NE-IA	Y	39375 FQ	51795 MW	69160 TQ	NEBLS	7/16-9/16
	Nevada	Y	52030 FQ	69750 MW	91110 TQ	USBLS	5/15
	Las Vegas-Henderson-Paradise MSA, NV	Y	56570 FQ	77230 MW	93240 TQ	USBLS	5/15
	New Hampshire	H	25.71 AE	37.73 MW	47.06 AEX	NHBLS	6/16
	Manchester NECTA, NH	H	24.36 AE	35.17 MW	42.73 AEX	NHBLS	6/16

AE	Average entry wage	AWR	Average wage range	H	Hourly
AEX	Average experienced wage	B	Biweekly	HI	Highest wage paid
ATC	Average total compensation	D	Daily	HR	High end range
AW	Average wage paid	FQ	First quartile wage	LO	Lowest wage paid

LR	Low end range	MTC	Median total compensation	TCC	Total cash compensation
M	Monthly	MW	Median wage paid	TQ	Third quartile wage
MCC	Median cash compensation	MWR	Median wage range	W	Weekly
ME	Median entry wage	S	See annotated source	Y	Yearly

Occupation/Type/Industry	Location	Per	Low	Mid	High	Source	Date
Insurance Underwriter	New Jersey	Y	64640 FQ	82340 MW	102680 TQ	USBLS	5/15
	Camden PMSA, NJ	Y	61860 FQ	79550 MW	99890 TQ	USBLS	5/15
	Newark PMSA, NJ-PA	Y	68610 FQ	84590 MW	99870 TQ	USBLS	5/15
	New Mexico	Y	50790 FQ	61080 MW	81530 TQ	USBLS	5/15
	Albuquerque MSA, NM	Y	48200 FQ	59010 MW	81390 TQ	USBLS	5/15
	New York	Y	53050 AE	81380 MW	115280 AEX	NYBLS	1/16-3/16
	Buffalo-Cheektowaga-Niagara Falls MSA, NY	Y	44860 FQ	56730 MW	86020 TQ	USBLS	5/15
	Nassau County-Suffolk County PMSA, NY	Y	53060 FQ	63730 MW	81850 TQ	USBLS	5/15
	New York-Jersey City-White Plains PMSA, NY-NJ	Y	67260 FQ	89320 MW	124250 TQ	USBLS	5/15
	Rochester MSA, NY	Y	56740 FQ	71600 MW	99760 TQ	USBLS	5/15
	North Carolina	Y	52550 FQ	74280 MW	101030 TQ	USBLS	5/15
	Charlotte-Concord-Gastonia MSA, NC-SC	Y	65860 FQ	89850 MW	119330 TQ	USBLS	5/15
	Raleigh MSA, NC	Y	41910 FQ	55560 MW	78330 TQ	USBLS	5/15
	North Dakota	Y	41990 FQ	53020 MW	75760 TQ	USBLS	5/15
	Fargo MSA, ND-MN	Y	37170 FQ	46700 MW	83740 TQ	USBLS	5/15
	Ohio	Y	48290 FQ	61340 MW	77920 TQ	USBLS	5/15
	Cincinnati MSA, OH-KY-IN	Y	47910 FQ	60360 MW	74880 TQ	USBLS	5/15
	Cleveland-Elyria MSA, OH	Y	50650 FQ	64560 MW	80520 TQ	USBLS	5/15
	Columbus MSA, OH	Y	51620 FQ	63020 MW	82590 TQ	USBLS	5/15
	Oklahoma	Y	42230 FQ	55890 MW	73550 TQ	USBLS	5/15
	Oklahoma City MSA, OK	Y	46010 FQ	57970 MW	74280 TQ	USBLS	5/15
	Tulsa MSA, OK	Y	41310 FQ	57070 MW	74380 TQ	USBLS	5/15
	Oregon	H	26.36 FQ	32.84 MW	42.03 TQ	ORBLS	2016
	Portland-Vancouver-Hillsboro MSA, OR-WA	Y	53680 FQ	67420 MW	86710 TQ	USBLS	5/15
	Pennsylvania	Y	53470 FQ	68130 MW	91720 TQ	USBLS	5/15
	Harrisburg-Carlisle MSA, PA	Y	50890 FQ	63940 MW	79320 TQ	USBLS	5/15
	Montgomery County-Bucks County-Chester County PMSA, PA	Y	54150 FQ	67900 MW	90070 TQ	USBLS	5/15
	Philadelphia PMSA, PA	Y	57410 FQ	75140 MW	104360 TQ	USBLS	5/15
	Pittsburgh MSA, PA	Y	57100 FQ	74820 MW	97220 TQ	USBLS	5/15
	Rhode Island	Y	54040 FQ	65350 MW	81820 TQ	USBLS	5/15
	Providence-Warwick MSA, RI-MA	Y	54150 FQ	65820 MW	82320 TQ	USBLS	5/15
	South Carolina	Y	40530 FQ	47790 MW	58680 TQ	USBLS	5/15
	Charleston-North Charleston MSA, SC	Y	38600 FQ	46380 MW	57590 TQ	USBLS	5/15
	Columbia MSA, SC	Y	38410 FQ	44800 MW	52140 TQ	USBLS	5/15
	Greenville-Anderson-Mauldin MSA, SC	Y	51590 FQ	57400 MW	65300 TQ	USBLS	5/15
	South Dakota	Y	65140 FQ	72540 MW	81270 TQ	USBLS	5/15
	Sioux Falls MSA, SD	Y	61660 FQ	76540 MW	97300 TQ	USBLS	5/15
	Tennessee	Y	46060 FQ	65340 MW	84050 TQ	USBLS	5/15
	Knoxville MSA, TN	Y	48780 FQ	73090 MW	93500 TQ	USBLS	5/15
	Memphis MSA, TN-MS-AR	Y	48650 FQ	71140 MW	79020 TQ	USBLS	5/15
	Nashville-Davidson–Murfreesboro–Franklin MSA, TN	Y	44870 FQ	62420 MW	82620 TQ	USBLS	5/15
	Texas	Y	47570 FQ	63810 MW	82280 TQ	USBLS	5/15
	Austin-Round Rock MSA, TX	Y	53190 FQ	69340 MW	79870 TQ	USBLS	5/15
	Dallas-Plano-Irving PMSA, TX	Y	45120 FQ	59360 MW	82950 AEX	USBLS	5/15
	Fort Worth-Arlington PMSA, TX	Y	49350 FQ	65640 MW	85280 TQ	USBLS	5/15
	Houston-The Woodlands-Sugar Land MSA, TX	Y	49620 FQ	64530 MW	86820 TQ	USBLS	5/15
	San Antonio-New Braunfels MSA, TX	Y	58020 FQ	71600 MW	86250 TQ	USBLS	5/15
	Utah	Y	40420 FQ	54230 MW	86770 TQ	USBLS	5/15
	Salt Lake City MSA, UT	Y	40200 FQ	54050 MW	90040 TQ	USBLS	5/15
	Vermont	Y	44710 FQ	53780 MW	73570 TQ	USBLS	5/15
	Burlington-South Burlington MSA, VT	Y	45990 FQ	56260 MW	73350 TQ	USBLS	5/15
	Virginia	Y	50930 FQ	61890 MW	76670 TQ	USBLS	5/15
	Richmond MSA, VA	Y	51710 FQ	64130 MW	80150 TQ	USBLS	5/15
	Virginia Beach-Norfolk-Newport News MSA, VA-NC	Y	44470 FQ	54950 MW	66520 TQ	USBLS	5/15
	Washington	H	27.80 FQ	35.25 MW	44.71 TQ	WABLS	3/16

AE	Average entry wage	AWR	Average wage range	H	Hourly
AEX	Average experienced wage	B	Biweekly	HI	Highest wage paid
ATC	Average total compensation	D	Daily	HR	High end range
AW	Average wage paid	FQ	First quartile wage	LO	Lowest wage paid

LR	Low end range	MTC	Median total compensation	TCC	Total cash compensation
M	Monthly	MW	Median wage paid	TQ	Third quartile wage
MCC	Median cash compensation	MWR	Median wage range	W	Weekly
ME	Median entry wage	S	See annotated source	Y	Yearly

Occupation/Type/Industry	Location	Per	Low	Mid	High	Source	Date
Insurance Underwriter	Seattle-Bellevue-Everett						
	PMSA, WA	H	30.14 FQ	36.54 MW	46.39 TQ	WABLS	3/16
	West Virginia	Y	38400 FQ	60040 MW	81540 TQ	USBLS	5/15
	Wisconsin	Y	46410 FQ	60130 MW	76900 TQ	USBLS	5/15
	Madison MSA, WI	Y	50860 FQ	61430 MW	76760 TQ	USBLS	5/15
	Milwaukee-Waukesha-West						
	Allis MSA, WI	Y	48980 FQ	66470 MW	83690 TQ	USBLS	5/15
	Wyoming	Y	42020 FQ	60610 MW	75050 TQ	USBLS	5/15
	Cheyenne MSA, WY	Y	45120 FQ	65700 MW	73460 TQ	USBLS	5/15
	Puerto Rico	Y	29540 FQ	42630 MW	59070 TQ	USBLS	5/15
	San Juan-Carolina-Caguas						
	MSA, PR	Y	29460 FQ	43150 MW	59860 TQ	USBLS	5/15
	Guam	Y	29720 FQ	42800 MW	53740 TQ	USBLS	5/15
Integrated Circuit Design							
Engineer	United States	Y		127500 MW		CNBC02	2016
Intellectual Property Officer							
Michigan State University	East Lansing, MI	Y	66720 LO		111430 HI	MSUSAL	10/1/14-9/30/15
Intelligence Analyst	United States	Y		62400 MW		TSTR	2017
Intensivist	United States	Y		214321-399692 MWR		MHLTH03	2015
Interactive Designer							
Central Intelligence Agency	District of Columbia	Y	51603 LO		69480 HI	CIA08	2016
Interactive/Web Copywriter							
1 to 5 Years Experience	United States	Y	50250 LO		74500 HI	RH02	2017
Interior Designer	Alabama	Y	23353 AE	64228 AW	84655 AEX	ALBLS	6/16
	Alaska	Y	35330 FQ	50680 MW	58940 TQ	USBLS	5/15
	Anchorage MSA, AK	Y	34380 FQ	47340 MW	57600 TQ	USBLS	5/15
	Arizona	Y	33120 FQ	46150 MW	70190 TQ	USBLS	5/15
	Phoenix-Mesa-Scottsdale						
	MSA, AZ	Y	36550 FQ	48240 MW	73600 TQ	USBLS	5/15
	Tucson MSA, AZ	Y	18760 FQ	29290 MW	43690 TQ	USBLS	5/15
	Arkansas	Y	27180 FQ	32960 MW	43120 TQ	USBLS	5/15
	Little Rock-North Little Rock-						
	Conway MSA, AR	Y	28040 FQ	36370 MW	47620 TQ	USBLS	5/15
	California	H	19.78 FQ	27.12 MW	36.53 TQ	CABLS	1/16-3/16
	Anaheim-Santa Ana-Irvine						
	PMSA, CA	H	20.16 FQ	25.18 MW	33.84 TQ	CABLS	1/16-3/16
	Los Angeles-Long Beach-						
	Glendale PMSA, CA	H	20.44 FQ	28.88 MW	41.29 TQ	CABLS	1/16-3/16
	Oakland-Hayward-Berkeley						
	PMSA, CA	H	21.58 FQ	26.75 MW	33.77 TQ	CABLS	1/16-3/16
	Riverside-San Bernardino-						
	Ontario MSA, CA	H	17.58 FQ	22.67 MW	31.40 TQ	CABLS	1/16-3/16
	Sacramento–Roseville–						
	Arden-Arcade MSA, CA	H	18.11 FQ	25.62 MW	33.28 TQ	CABLS	1/16-3/16
	San Diego-Carlsbad MSA, CA	H	15.33 FQ	21.83 MW	29.88 TQ	CABLS	1/16-3/16
	San Francisco-Redwood City-						
	South San Francisco PMSA,						
	CA	H	26.02 FQ	31.41 MW	42.26 TQ	CABLS	1/16-3/16
	Colorado	Y	35980 FQ	46220 MW	59730 TQ	USBLS	5/15
	Colorado Springs MSA, CO	Y	19090 FQ	36160 MW	47950 TQ	USBLS	5/15
	Denver-Aurora-Lakewood						
	MSA, CO	Y	36620 FQ	47000 MW	60970 TQ	USBLS	5/15
	Connecticut	Y		49223 MW		CTBLS	1/16-3/16
	Hartford-West Hartford-East						
	Hartford MSA, CT	Y	44120 FQ	52640 MW	61310 TQ	USBLS	5/15
	Delaware	Y	30820 FQ	42420 MW	62580 TQ	USBLS	5/15
	Wilmington PMSA, DE-MD-						
	NJ	Y	35950 FQ	45680 MW	78080 TQ	USBLS	5/15
	District of Columbia	Y	53580 FQ	67970 MW	91860 TQ	USBLS	5/15
	Washington-Arlington-						
	Alexandria PMSA, DC-VA-						
	MD-WV	Y	45500 FQ	60740 MW	82130 TQ	USBLS	5/15
	Florida	H	13.11 AE	20.45 MW	28.70 AEX	FLBLS	7/16-9/16

AE	Average entry wage	AWR	Average wage range	H	Hourly	LR	Low end range
AEX	Average experienced wage	B	Biweekly	HI	Highest wage paid	M	Monthly
ATC	Average total compensation	D	Daily	HR	High end range	MCC	Median cash compensation
AW	Average wage paid	FQ	First quartile wage	LO	Lowest wage paid	ME	Median entry wage

MTC	Median total compensation	TCC	Total cash compensation
MW	Median wage paid	TQ	Third quartile wage
MWR	Median wage range	W	Weekly
S	See annotated source	Y	Yearly

844

Occupation/Type/Industry	Location	Per	Low	Mid	High	Source	Date
Interior Designer	Fort Lauderdale-Pompano Beach-Deerfield Beach PMSA, FL	H	12.96 AE	21.21 MW	27.27 AEX	FLBLS	7/16-9/16
	Miami-Miami Beach-Kendall PMSA, FL	H	13.11 AE	23.20 MW	29.77 AEX	FLBLS	7/16-9/16
	Orlando-Kissimmee-Sanford MSA, FL	H	12.61 AE	18.72 MW	25.66 AEX	FLBLS	7/16-9/16
	Tampa-St. Petersburg-Clearwater MSA, FL	H	15.61 AE	20.61 MW	27.92 AEX	FLBLS	7/16-9/16
	Georgia	Y	34880 FQ	48090 MW	60580 TQ	USBLS	5/15
	Atlanta-Sandy Springs-Roswell MSA, GA	Y	36270 FQ	50310 MW	61650 TQ	USBLS	5/15
	Hawaii	Y	34910 FQ	46530 MW	60110 TQ	USBLS	5/15
	Urban Honolulu MSA, HI	Y	35770 FQ	47870 MW	60240 TQ	USBLS	5/15
	Idaho	Y	27960 FQ	35980 MW	48480 TQ	USBLS	5/15
	Boise City MSA, ID	Y	29150 FQ	36520 MW	48530 TQ	USBLS	5/15
	Illinois	Y	33480 FQ	47840 MW	69130 TQ	USBLS	5/15
	Chicago-Naperville-Arlington Heights PMSA, IL	Y	33320 FQ	47670 MW	66060 TQ	USBLS	5/15
	Lake County-Kenosha County PMSA, IL-WI	Y	34700 FQ	54930 MW	96980 TQ	USBLS	5/15
	Indiana	Y	31520 FQ	41070 MW	61560 TQ	USBLS	5/15
	Gary PMSA, IN	Y	31560 FQ	37160 MW	49590 TQ	USBLS	5/15
	Indianapolis-Carmel-Anderson MSA, IN	Y	34540 FQ	44660 MW	69190 TQ	USBLS	5/15
	Iowa	Y	29250 FQ	38070 MW	49310 TQ	USBLS	5/15
	Des Moines-West Des Moines MSA, IA	Y	33130 FQ	39060 MW	57230 TQ	USBLS	5/15
	Kansas	Y	30120 FQ	39250 MW	49960 TQ	USBLS	5/15
	Wichita MSA, KS	Y	32540 FQ	38470 MW	46880 TQ	USBLS	5/15
	Kentucky	Y	29140 FQ	48900 MW	64710 TQ	USBLS	5/15
	Louisville-Jefferson County MSA, KY-IN	Y	43510 FQ	60520 MW	73830 TQ	USBLS	5/15
	Louisiana	Y	34810 FQ	42990 MW	49260 TQ	USBLS	5/15
	Baton Rouge MSA, LA	Y	29490 FQ	39770 MW	52110 TQ	USBLS	5/15
	New Orleans-Metairie MSA, LA	Y	40510 FQ	44350 MW	48200 TQ	USBLS	5/15
	Maine	Y	32100 FQ	43410 MW	60920 TQ	USBLS	5/15
	Portland-South Portland MSA, ME	Y	30640 FQ	43160 MW	59740 TQ	USBLS	5/15
	Maryland	Y	35831 AE	55649 MW	65558 AEX	MDBLS	4/16
	Baltimore-Columbia-Towson MSA, MD	Y	43470 FQ	51840 MW	66520 TQ	USBLS	5/15
	Salisbury MSA, MD-DE	Y	28460 FQ	37260 MW	60100 TQ	USBLS	5/15
	Massachusetts	Y	45680 FQ	58230 MW	78930 TQ	USBLS	5/15
	Boston-Cambridge-Newton NECTA, MA	Y	48870 FQ	60030 MW	82390 TQ	USBLS	5/15
	Worcester MSA, MA-CT	Y	47160 FQ	55730 MW	61740 TQ	USBLS	5/15
	Michigan	Y	29120 FQ	38830 MW	57920 TQ	USBLS	5/15
	Detroit-Dearborn-Livonia PMSA, MI	Y	42090 FQ	58010 MW	74390 TQ	USBLS	5/15
	Grand Rapids-Wyoming MSA, MI	Y	25520 FQ	36320 MW	48950 TQ	USBLS	5/15
	Minnesota	Y	35352 FQ	45221 MW	60927 TQ	MNBLS	1/16-3/16
	Minneapolis-St. Paul-Bloomington MSA, MN-WI	Y	37066 FQ	46804 MW	64294 TQ	MNBLS	1/16-3/16
	Mississippi	Y	22780 FQ	28840 MW	38000 TQ	USBLS	5/15
	Jackson MSA, MS	Y	22880 FQ	27210 MW	34940 TQ	USBLS	5/15
	Missouri	Y	37790 FQ	47570 MW	66410 TQ	USBLS	5/15
	Kansas City MSA, MO-KS	Y	35550 FQ	49350 MW	68690 TQ	USBLS	5/15
	St. Louis MSA, MO-IL	Y	39880 FQ	48130 MW	70200 TQ	USBLS	5/15
	Montana	Y	25270 FQ	32320 MW	44600 TQ	USBLS	5/15
	Nebraska	Y	30840 FQ	43935 MW	56930 TQ	NEBLS	7/16-9/16
	Omaha-Council Bluffs MSA, NE-IA	Y	35750 FQ	46170 MW	57820 TQ	NEBLS	7/16-9/16
	Nevada	Y	34360 FQ	48400 MW	64300 TQ	USBLS	5/15
	Las Vegas-Henderson-Paradise MSA, NV	Y	32620 FQ	48220 MW	63200 TQ	USBLS	5/15
	New Hampshire	H	15.32 AE	20.69 MW	28.02 AEX	NHBLS	6/16
	New Jersey	Y	42500 FQ	53280 MW	72470 TQ	USBLS	5/15
	Camden PMSA, NJ	Y	25320 FQ	64630 MW	109880 TQ	USBLS	5/15
	Newark PMSA, NJ-PA	Y	43720 FQ	52560 MW	74180 TQ	USBLS	5/15

AE Average entry wage	**AWR** Average wage range	**H** Hourly	**LR** Low end range	**MTC** Median total compensation	**TCC** Total cash compensation
AEX Average experienced wage	**B** Biweekly	**HI** Highest wage paid	**M** Monthly	**MW** Median wage paid	**TQ** Third quartile wage
ATC Average total compensation	**D** Daily	**HR** High end range	**MCC** Median cash compensation	**MWR** Median wage range	**W** Weekly
AW Average wage paid	**FQ** First quartile wage	**LO** Lowest wage paid	**ME** Median entry wage	**S** See annotated source	**Y** Yearly

Occupation/Type/Industry	Location	Per	Low	Mid	High	Source	Date
Interior Designer	Trenton MSA, NJ	Y	39200 FQ	51200 MW	59800 TQ	USBLS	5/15
	New Mexico	Y	24680 FQ	43370 MW	79230 TQ	USBLS	5/15
	Albuquerque MSA, NM	Y	37040 FQ	50350 MW	89190 TQ	USBLS	5/15
	New York	Y	36900 AE	64690 MW	82450 AEX	NYBLS	1/16-3/16
	Buffalo-Cheektowaga-Niagara Falls MSA, NY	Y	28550 FQ	36990 MW	50540 TQ	USBLS	5/15
	Nassau County-Suffolk County PMSA, NY	Y	40550 FQ	45850 MW	54700 TQ	USBLS	5/15
	New York-Jersey City-White Plains PMSA, NY-NJ	Y	47590 FQ	66660 MW	84490 TQ	USBLS	5/15
	Rochester MSA, NY	Y	32110 FQ	40040 MW	51310 TQ	USBLS	5/15
	North Carolina	Y	29350 FQ	45130 MW	65010 TQ	USBLS	5/15
	Charlotte-Concord-Gastonia MSA, NC-SC	Y	29520 FQ	52190 MW	70800 TQ	USBLS	5/15
	Raleigh MSA, NC	Y	38030 FQ	45720 MW	58060 TQ	USBLS	5/15
	North Dakota	Y	35580 FQ	43540 MW	53020 TQ	USBLS	5/15
	Fargo MSA, ND-MN	Y	35990 FQ	46640 MW	56180 TQ	USBLS	5/15
	Ohio	Y	31780 FQ	44400 MW	59030 TQ	USBLS	5/15
	Cincinnati MSA, OH-KY-IN	Y	35550 FQ	47260 MW	62680 TQ	USBLS	5/15
	Cleveland-Elyria MSA, OH	Y	33360 FQ	43130 MW	54580 TQ	USBLS	5/15
	Columbus MSA, OH	Y	25860 FQ	41100 MW	58240 TQ	USBLS	5/15
	Oklahoma	Y	24920 FQ	37620 MW	54930 TQ	USBLS	5/15
	Oklahoma City MSA, OK	Y	29380 FQ	37640 MW	53260 TQ	USBLS	5/15
	Tulsa MSA, OK	Y	20560 FQ	39660 MW	58830 TQ	USBLS	5/15
	Oregon	H	17.35 FQ	21.72 MW	28.73 TQ	ORBLS	2016
	Portland-Vancouver-Hillsboro MSA, OR-WA	Y	37650 FQ	46350 MW	60160 TQ	USBLS	5/15
	Pennsylvania	Y	33660 FQ	44980 MW	60470 TQ	USBLS	5/15
	Allentown-Bethlehem-Easton MSA, PA-NJ	Y	36250 FQ	43540 MW	49640 TQ	USBLS	5/15
	Harrisburg-Carlisle MSA, PA	Y	35820 FQ	46170 MW	56690 TQ	USBLS	5/15
	Montgomery County-Bucks County-Chester County PMSA, PA	Y	42460 FQ	56190 MW	66410 TQ	USBLS	5/15
	Philadelphia PMSA, PA	Y	37030 FQ	49540 MW	70970 TQ	USBLS	5/15
	Pittsburgh MSA, PA	Y	25160 FQ	33590 MW	48570 TQ	USBLS	5/15
	Rhode Island	Y	65160 FQ	72450 MW	80570 TQ	USBLS	5/15
	Providence-Warwick MSA, RI-MA	Y	64230 FQ	72240 MW	81020 TQ	USBLS	5/15
	South Carolina	Y	26400 FQ	37020 MW	51380 TQ	USBLS	5/15
	Charleston-North Charleston MSA, SC	Y	23510 FQ	35640 MW	58140 TQ	USBLS	5/15
	Columbia MSA, SC	Y	22980 FQ	36640 MW	55460 TQ	USBLS	5/15
	Greenville-Anderson-Mauldin MSA, SC	Y	35140 FQ	39240 MW	47960 TQ	USBLS	5/15
	South Dakota	Y	40900 FQ	48240 MW	61690 TQ	USBLS	5/15
	Sioux Falls MSA, SD	Y	42880 FQ	49590 MW	67450 TQ	USBLS	5/15
	Tennessee	Y	28990 FQ	39580 MW	50400 TQ	USBLS	5/15
	Knoxville MSA, TN	Y	25370 FQ	34370 MW	43090 TQ	USBLS	5/15
	Memphis MSA, TN-MS-AR	Y	39710 FQ	46280 MW	61300 TQ	USBLS	5/15
	Nashville-Davidson–Murfreesboro–Franklin MSA, TN	Y	29920 FQ	40710 MW	50980 TQ	USBLS	5/15
	Texas	Y	41580 FQ	56670 MW	80770 TQ	USBLS	5/15
	Austin-Round Rock MSA, TX	Y	37920 FQ	48620 MW	61800 TQ	USBLS	5/15
	Dallas-Plano-Irving PMSA, TX	Y	42760 FQ	57380 MW	83840 TQ	USBLS	5/15
	Fort Worth-Arlington PMSA, TX	Y	32530 FQ	47260 MW	61900 TQ	USBLS	5/15
	Houston-The Woodlands-Sugar Land MSA, TX	Y	47770 FQ	66120 MW	85170 TQ	USBLS	5/15
	San Antonio-New Braunfels MSA, TX	Y	44350 FQ	63070 MW	84630 TQ	USBLS	5/15
	Utah	Y	37260 FQ	56950 MW	70820 TQ	USBLS	5/15
	Ogden-Clearfield MSA, UT	Y	31510 FQ	49840 MW	57560 TQ	USBLS	5/15
	Provo-Orem MSA, UT	Y	41800 FQ	54530 MW	64130 TQ	USBLS	5/15
	Vermont	Y	38100 FQ	43720 MW	48720 TQ	USBLS	5/15
	Virginia	Y	36580 FQ	48470 MW	67950 TQ	USBLS	5/15
	Richmond MSA, VA	Y	36240 FQ	45900 MW	57580 TQ	USBLS	5/15
	Virginia Beach-Norfolk-Newport News MSA, VA-NC	Y	22240 FQ	30620 MW	69690 TQ	USBLS	5/15
	Washington	H	20.45 FQ	25.75 MW	30.34 TQ	WABLS	3/16

AE	Average entry wage	AWR	Average wage range	H	Hourly
AEX	Average experienced wage	B	Biweekly	HI	Highest wage paid
ATC	Average total compensation	D	Daily	HR	High end range
AW	Average wage paid	FQ	First quartile wage	LO	Lowest wage paid

LR	Low end range	MTC	Median total compensation	TCC	Total cash compensation
M	Monthly	MW	Median wage paid	TQ	Third quartile wage
MCC	Median cash compensation	MWR	Median wage range	W	Weekly
ME	Median entry wage	S	See annotated source	Y	Yearly

Occupation/Type/Industry	Location	Per	Low	Mid	High	Source	Date
Interior Designer	Seattle-Bellevue-Everett						
	PMSA, WA	H	21.14 FQ	26.33 MW	30.51 TQ	WABLS	3/16
	Tacoma-Lakewood PMSA, WA	H	20.95 FQ	23.95 MW	30.86 TQ	WABLS	3/16
	West Virginia	Y	28620 FQ	41380 MW	47060 TQ	USBLS	5/15
	Wisconsin	Y	27940 FQ	36840 MW	49880 TQ	USBLS	5/15
	Madison MSA, WI	Y	27280 FQ	39550 MW	50970 TQ	USBLS	5/15
	Milwaukee-Waukesha-West						
	Allis MSA, WI	Y	36630 FQ	45980 MW	57510 TQ	USBLS	5/15
	Wyoming	Y	28680 FQ	43150 MW	67960 TQ	USBLS	5/15
	Puerto Rico	Y	18180 FQ	26820 MW	54640 TQ	USBLS	5/15
	San Juan-Carolina-Caguas						
	MSA, PR	Y	18310 FQ	30150 MW	56810 TQ	USBLS	5/15
Intern							
Amazon	United States	S		6000 AW		DTREND01	2016
Box	United States	S		6700 AW		DTREND01	2016
Dropbox	United States	S		6300 AW		DTREND01	2016
Goldman Sachs	United States	S		7100 AW		DTREND01	2016
Pinterest	United States	S		9000 AW		DTREND01	2016
Snapchat	United States	S		10000 AW		DTREND01	2016
Internal Auditor	United States	Y		52900 MW		INVPED	2015
Public Schools	Baldwin County, AL	Y	51538 LO		58883 HI	BCPSSS	2016-2017
Internist	Alabama	Y		255177 AW		ALBLS	6/16
	Birmingham-Hoover MSA, AL	Y		255402 AW		ALBLS	6/16
	Alaska	Y	148180 FQ	215070 AW		USBLS	5/15
	Anchorage MSA, AK	Y	134310 FQ	196120 AW		USBLS	5/15
	Arizona	Y	164310 FQ	192040 AW		USBLS	5/15
	Phoenix-Mesa-Scottsdale						
	MSA, AZ	Y	154870 FQ	182970 MW		USBLS	5/15
	Arkansas	Y		265360 AW		USBLS	5/15
	Little Rock-North Little Rock-						
	Conway MSA, AR	Y		254730 AW		USBLS	5/15
	California	H	53.85 FQ	97.16 AW		CABLS	1/16-3/16
	Anaheim-Santa Ana-Irvine						
	PMSA, CA	H		131.05 AW		CABLS	1/16-3/16
	Los Angeles-Long Beach-						
	Glendale PMSA, CA	H	46.45 FQ	85.69 MW		CABLS	1/16-3/16
	Oakland-Hayward-Berkeley						
	PMSA, CA	H	57.17 FQ	103.78 AW		CABLS	1/16-3/16
	Riverside-San Bernardino-						
	Ontario MSA, CA	H	28.31 FQ	43.63 MW	87.21 TQ	CABLS	1/16-3/16
	Sacramento–Roseville–						
	Arden-Arcade MSA, CA	H	86.65 FQ	101.78 AW		CABLS	1/16-3/16
	San Diego-Carlsbad MSA, CA	H	70.73 FQ	100.05 AW		CABLS	1/16-3/16
	San Francisco-Redwood City-						
	South San Francisco PMSA,						
	CA	H	46.20 FQ	82.96 MW		CABLS	1/16-3/16
	Colorado	Y	153160 FQ	193140 AW		USBLS	5/15
	Denver-Aurora-Lakewood						
	MSA, CO	Y	131150 FQ	157330 MW		USBLS	5/15
	Connecticut	Y		196172 AW		CTBLS	1/16-3/16
	Bridgeport-Stamford-Norwalk						
	MSA, CT	Y	128850 FQ	209080 AW		USBLS	5/15
	Hartford-West Hartford-East						
	Hartford MSA, CT	Y	59490 FQ	173990 MW		USBLS	5/15
	Delaware	Y	134380 FQ	196570 AW		USBLS	5/15
	Wilmington PMSA, DE-MD-						
	NJ	Y	158570 FQ	210160 AW		USBLS	5/15
	District of Columbia	Y	55800 FQ	62920 MW	173760 TQ	USBLS	5/15
	Washington-Arlington-						
	Alexandria PMSA, DC-VA-						
	MD-WV	Y	59110 FQ	123240 MW		USBLS	5/15
	Florida	H	54.43 AE	101.17 AW	124.53 AEX	FLBLS	7/16-9/16
	Fort Lauderdale-Pompano						
	Beach-Deerfield Beach						
	PMSA, FL	H	47.72 AE	59.18 MW	78.40 AEX	FLBLS	7/16-9/16
	Miami-Miami Beach-Kendall						
	PMSA, FL	H	59.97 AE	104.91 AW	127.38 AEX	FLBLS	7/16-9/16
	Orlando-Kissimmee-Sanford						
	MSA, FL	H	41.06 AE	99.72 AW	129.05 AEX	FLBLS	7/16-9/16

AE	Average entry wage	AWR	Average wage range	H	Hourly	LR	Low end range	MTC	Median total compensation	TCC	Total cash compensation
AEX	Average experienced wage	B	Biweekly	HI	Highest wage paid	M	Monthly	MW	Median wage paid	TQ	Third quartile wage
ATC	Average total compensation	D	Daily	HR	High end range	MCC	Median cash compensation	MWR	Median wage range	W	Weekly
AW	Average wage paid	FQ	First quartile wage	LO	Lowest wage paid	ME	Median entry wage	S	See annotated source	Y	Yearly

Occupation/Type/Industry	Location	Per	Low	Mid	High	Source	Date
Internist	Tampa-St. Petersburg-Clearwater MSA, FL	H	67.01 AE	92.20 MW	121.69 AEX	FLBLS	7/16-9/16
	Georgia	Y		260370 AW		USBLS	5/15
	Atlanta-Sandy Springs-Roswell MSA, GA	Y		268350 AW		USBLS	5/15
	Augusta-Richmond County MSA, GA-SC	Y	96660 FQ	185460 MW		USBLS	5/15
	Hawaii	Y	142850 FQ	209180 AW		USBLS	5/15
	Urban Honolulu MSA, HI	Y	135770 FQ	179190 MW		USBLS	5/15
	Illinois	Y	107180 FQ	176120 MW		USBLS	5/15
	Chicago-Naperville-Arlington Heights PMSA, IL	Y	72140 FQ	159300 MW		USBLS	5/15
	Lake County-Kenosha County PMSA, IL-WI	Y	180130 FQ	238070 AW		USBLS	5/15
	Indiana	Y		252310 AW		USBLS	5/15
	Indianapolis-Carmel-Anderson MSA, IN	Y		260070 AW		USBLS	5/15
	Iowa	Y	159060 FQ	218990 AW		USBLS	5/15
	Des Moines-West Des Moines MSA, IA	Y	158270 FQ	202910 AW		USBLS	5/15
	Kansas	Y	143820 FQ	203840 AW		USBLS	5/15
	Wichita MSA, KS	Y		270810 AW		USBLS	5/15
	Kentucky	Y	166910 FQ	222770 AW		USBLS	5/15
	Louisville-Jefferson County MSA, KY-IN	Y	170730 FQ	230820 AW		USBLS	5/15
	Louisiana	Y	185810 FQ	237820 AW		USBLS	5/15
	Baton Rouge MSA, LA	Y	180940 FQ	222940 AW		USBLS	5/15
	New Orleans-Metairie MSA, LA	Y		250690 AW		USBLS	5/15
	Maine	Y	160430 FQ	204820 AW		USBLS	5/15
	Portland-South Portland MSA, ME	Y	148090 FQ	208970 AW		USBLS	5/15
	Maryland	Y	119412 AE	210963 MW	256739 AEX	MDBLS	4/16
	Baltimore-Columbia-Towson MSA, MD	Y	120120 FQ	163470 MW		USBLS	5/15
	Salisbury MSA, MD-DE	Y	158140 FQ	178550 MW		USBLS	5/15
	Massachusetts	Y	174880 FQ	230440 AW		USBLS	5/15
	Boston-Cambridge-Newton NECTA, MA	Y	177490 FQ	234080 AW		USBLS	5/15
	Michigan	Y	59780 FQ	97560 MW		USBLS	5/15
	Detroit-Dearborn-Livonia PMSA, MI	Y	56750 FQ	157960 MW		USBLS	5/15
	Grand Rapids-Wyoming MSA, MI	Y	138840 FQ	163760 MW		USBLS	5/15
	Minnesota	Y	174907 FQ	234392 AW		MNBLS	1/16-3/16
	Minneapolis-St. Paul-Bloomington MSA, MN-WI	Y		250289 AW		MNBLS	1/16-3/16
	Mississippi	Y		240780 AW		USBLS	5/15
	Missouri	Y	172180 FQ	223600 AW		USBLS	5/15
	Kansas City MSA, MO-KS	Y	137890 FQ	183470 MW		USBLS	5/15
	St. Louis MSA, MO-IL	Y		264480 AW		USBLS	5/15
	Montana	Y	159660 FQ	222950 AW		USBLS	5/15
	Omaha-Council Bluffs MSA, NE-IA	Y	124545 FQ	179455 MW		NEBLS	7/16-9/16
	Nevada	Y	152350 FQ	227340 AW		USBLS	5/15
	Las Vegas-Henderson-Paradise MSA, NV	Y	159960 FQ	229040 AW		USBLS	5/15
	New Hampshire	H	72.17 AE	109.54 AW	128.22 AEX	NHBLS	6/16
	Nashua NECTA, NH-MA	Y		249360 AW		USBLS	5/15
	New Jersey	Y	146160 FQ	210840 AW		USBLS	5/15
	Camden PMSA, NJ	Y	158010 FQ	210930 AW		USBLS	5/15
	Trenton MSA, NJ	Y	152570 FQ	230850 AW		USBLS	5/15
	New Mexico	Y	160250 FQ	233710 AW		USBLS	5/15
	Albuquerque MSA, NM	Y	111270 FQ	216090 AW		USBLS	5/15
	New York	Y	73600 AE	189890 AW		NYBLS	1/16-3/16
	Nassau County-Suffolk County PMSA, NY	Y	158790 FQ	229650 AW		USBLS	5/15
	New York-Jersey City-White Plains PMSA, NY-NJ	Y	135630 FQ	203040 AW		USBLS	5/15
	North Carolina	Y		249070 AW		USBLS	5/15
	Charlotte-Concord-Gastonia MSA, NC-SC	Y		248430 AW		USBLS	5/15

AE	Average entry wage	**AWR**	Average wage range	**H**	Hourly	**LR**	Low end range	**MTC**	Median total compensation	**TCC**	Total cash compensation
AEX	Average experienced wage	**B**	Biweekly	**HI**	Highest wage paid	**M**	Monthly	**MW**	Median wage paid	**TQ**	Third quartile wage
ATC	Average total compensation	**D**	Daily	**HR**	High end range	**MCC**	Median cash compensation	**MWR**	Median wage range	**W**	Weekly
AW	Average wage paid	**FQ**	First quartile wage	**LO**	Lowest wage paid	**ME**	Median entry wage	**S**	See annotated source	**Y**	Yearly

Occupation/Type/Industry	Location	Per	Low	Mid	High	Source	Date
Internist	Raleigh MSA, NC	Y		252130 AW		USBLS	5/15
	Ohio	Y	108850 FQ	199250 AW		USBLS	5/15
	Cincinnati MSA, OH-KY-IN	Y	57450 FQ	130450 MW		USBLS	5/15
	Cleveland-Elyria MSA, OH	Y	61960 FQ	152830 MW		USBLS	5/15
	Columbus MSA, OH	Y		258470 AW		USBLS	5/15
	Oklahoma	Y	78780 FQ	197830 AW		USBLS	5/15
	Oklahoma City MSA, OK	Y	74500 FQ	158760 MW		USBLS	5/15
	Tulsa MSA, OK	Y		260700 AW		USBLS	5/15
	Oregon	H	83.98 FQ	104.78 AW		ORBLS	2016
	Portland-Vancouver-Hillsboro MSA, OR-WA	Y	168840 FQ	210640 AW		USBLS	5/15
	Pennsylvania	Y	82060 FQ	168080 MW		USBLS	5/15
	Allentown-Bethlehem-Easton MSA, PA-NJ	Y	141710 FQ	191990 AW		USBLS	5/15
	Montgomery County-Bucks County-Chester County PMSA, PA	Y	115620 FQ	157220 MW		USBLS	5/15
	Pittsburgh MSA, PA	Y	173140 FQ	216600 AW		USBLS	5/15
	Rhode Island	Y	130600 FQ	194090 AW		USBLS	5/15
	Providence-Warwick MSA, RI-MA	Y	133170 FQ	197070 AW		USBLS	5/15
	South Carolina	Y	164470 FQ	214970 AW		USBLS	5/15
	Charleston-North Charleston MSA, SC	Y	157600 FQ	176200 MW		USBLS	5/15
	Columbia MSA, SC	Y	181180 FQ	232020 AW		USBLS	5/15
	Greenville-Anderson-Mauldin MSA, SC	Y	136220 FQ	195180 AW		USBLS	5/15
	South Dakota	Y		257260 AW		USBLS	5/15
	Sioux Falls MSA, SD	Y		260260 AW		USBLS	5/15
	Tennessee	Y	43390 FQ	175000 AW		USBLS	5/15
	Memphis MSA, TN-MS-AR	Y		274720 AW		USBLS	5/15
	Nashville-Davidson–Murfreesboro–Franklin MSA, TN	Y	25080 FQ	174060 MW		USBLS	5/15
	Texas	Y	98590 FQ	149500 MW		USBLS	5/15
	Austin-Round Rock MSA, TX	Y		245980 AW		USBLS	5/15
	Dallas-Plano-Irving PMSA, TX	Y	94540 FQ	116740 MW		USBLS	5/15
	Fort Worth-Arlington PMSA, TX	Y	97400 FQ	160770 MW		USBLS	5/15
	Houston-The Woodlands-Sugar Land MSA, TX	Y	85190 FQ	148960 MW		USBLS	5/15
	San Antonio-New Braunfels MSA, TX	Y	79370 FQ	212510 AW		USBLS	5/15
	Utah	Y	152970 FQ	217580 AW		USBLS	5/15
	Salt Lake City MSA, UT	Y	139670 FQ	212610 AW		USBLS	5/15
	Vermont	Y	119000 FQ	164580 MW		USBLS	5/15
	Virginia	Y	132060 FQ	180320 MW		USBLS	5/15
	Richmond MSA, VA	Y	161130 FQ	184390 MW		USBLS	5/15
	Virginia Beach-Norfolk-Newport News MSA, VA-NC	Y	145830 FQ	160830 MW		USBLS	5/15
	Washington	H	78.94 FQ	105.23 AW		WABLS	3/16
	Seattle-Bellevue-Everett PMSA, WA	H	77.03 FQ	101.77 AW		WABLS	3/16
	Tacoma-Lakewood PMSA, WA	H	86.36 FQ	117.97 AW		WABLS	3/16
	Wisconsin	Y	175520 FQ	227440 AW		USBLS	5/15
	Madison MSA, WI	Y		249480 AW		USBLS	5/15
	Milwaukee-Waukesha-West Allis MSA, WI	Y	155820 FQ	212570 AW		USBLS	5/15
	Wyoming	Y	179380 FQ	231040 AW		USBLS	5/15
	Puerto Rico	Y	56920 FQ	69300 MW	77820 TQ	USBLS	5/15
	Mayaguez MSA, PR	Y	18630 FQ	73350 MW	91670 TQ	USBLS	5/15
	San Juan-Carolina-Caguas MSA, PR	Y	64110 FQ	69750 MW	75410 TQ	USBLS	5/15
Interpreter							
Deaf and Hard of Hearing, Genesee Area Skill Center	Flint, MI	H	16.91 LO		22.33 HI	MIGOV	2016
Interpreter and Translator	Alabama	Y	33271 AE	47378 AW	54432 AEX	ALBLS	6/16
	Birmingham-Hoover MSA, AL	Y	39947 AE	46165 AW	49274 AEX	ALBLS	6/16
	Alaska	Y	40720 FQ	51660 MW	62430 TQ	USBLS	5/15
	Anchorage MSA, AK	Y	32550 FQ	41980 MW	53410 TQ	USBLS	5/15

AE	Average entry wage	AWR	Average wage range	H	Hourly
AEX	Average experienced wage	B	Biweekly	HI	Highest wage paid
ATC	Average total compensation	D	Daily	HR	High end range
AW	Average wage paid	FQ	First quartile wage	LO	Lowest wage paid

LR	Low end range	MTC	Median total compensation
M	Monthly	MW	Median wage paid
MCC	Median cash compensation	MWR	Median wage range
ME	Median entry wage	S	See annotated source

TCC	Total cash compensation		
TQ	Third quartile wage		
W	Weekly		
Y	Yearly		

Occupation/Type/Industry	Location	Per	Low	Mid	High	Source	Date
Interpreter and Translator	Arizona	Y	33370 FQ	43910 MW	61150 TQ	USBLS	5/15
	Phoenix-Mesa-Scottsdale MSA, AZ	Y	29630 FQ	43630 MW	61250 TQ	USBLS	5/15
	Tucson MSA, AZ	Y	35520 FQ	43650 MW	59600 TQ	USBLS	5/15
	Arkansas	Y	22450 FQ	31120 MW	41560 TQ	USBLS	5/15
	Little Rock-North Little Rock-Conway MSA, AR	Y	24330 FQ	33310 MW	42120 TQ	USBLS	5/15
	California	H	15.43 FQ	21.84 MW	29.20 TQ	CABLS	1/16-3/16
	Anaheim-Santa Ana-Irvine PMSA, CA	H	17.78 FQ	21.96 MW	26.57 TQ	CABLS	1/16-3/16
	Los Angeles-Long Beach-Glendale PMSA, CA	H	18.68 FQ	25.16 MW	29.51 TQ	CABLS	1/16-3/16
	Oakland-Hayward-Berkeley PMSA, CA	H	24.23 FQ	30.24 MW	35.28 TQ	CABLS	1/16-3/16
	Riverside-San Bernardino-Ontario MSA, CA	H	13.01 FQ	17.70 MW	23.66 TQ	CABLS	1/16-3/16
	Sacramento–Roseville–Arden-Arcade MSA, CA	H	18.92 FQ	25.53 MW	29.33 TQ	CABLS	1/16-3/16
	San Diego-Carlsbad MSA, CA	H	18.36 FQ	23.87 MW	32.51 TQ	CABLS	1/16-3/16
	San Francisco-Redwood City-South San Francisco PMSA, CA	H	13.86 FQ	26.58 MW	34.98 TQ	CABLS	1/16-3/16
	Colorado	Y	41670 FQ	52610 MW	71860 TQ	USBLS	5/15
	Denver-Aurora-Lakewood MSA, CO	Y	47260 FQ	63390 MW	84840 TQ	USBLS	5/15
	Connecticut	Y		52013 MW		CTBLS	1/16-3/16
	Hartford-West Hartford-East Hartford MSA, CT	Y	45690 FQ	56390 MW	68440 TQ	USBLS	5/15
	District of Columbia	Y	62560 FQ	85120 MW	101310 TQ	USBLS	5/15
	Washington-Arlington-Alexandria PMSA, DC-VA-MD-WV	Y	46780 FQ	68600 MW	101450 TQ	USBLS	5/15
	Florida	H	10.10 AE	16.53 MW	23.91 AEX	FLBLS	7/16-9/16
	Miami-Miami Beach-Kendall PMSA, FL	H	8.90 AE	18.35 MW	29.72 AEX	FLBLS	7/16-9/16
	Orlando-Kissimmee-Sanford MSA, FL	H	13.30 AE	18.56 MW	23.41 AEX	FLBLS	7/16-9/16
	Tampa-St. Petersburg-Clearwater MSA, FL	H	16.90 AE	25.88 MW	30.83 AEX	FLBLS	7/16-9/16
	Georgia	Y	28880 FQ	46120 MW	65070 TQ	USBLS	5/15
	Atlanta-Sandy Springs-Roswell MSA, GA	Y	31970 FQ	44160 MW	65010 TQ	USBLS	5/15
	Hawaii	Y	36700 FQ	44630 MW	56460 TQ	USBLS	5/15
	Urban Honolulu MSA, HI	Y	36710 FQ	44050 MW	50080 TQ	USBLS	5/15
	Idaho	Y	28570 FQ	35330 MW	42280 TQ	USBLS	5/15
	Boise City MSA, ID	Y	28130 FQ	34810 MW	41440 TQ	USBLS	5/15
	Illinois	Y	33850 FQ	40840 MW	50820 TQ	USBLS	5/15
	Chicago-Naperville-Arlington Heights PMSA, IL	Y	34380 FQ	40120 MW	49500 TQ	USBLS	5/15
	Lake County-Kenosha County PMSA, IL-WI	Y	37250 FQ	50170 MW	60140 TQ	USBLS	5/15
	Indiana	Y	32230 FQ	39940 MW	50160 TQ	USBLS	5/15
	Gary PMSA, IN	Y	18410 FQ	25920 MW	34390 TQ	USBLS	5/15
	Indianapolis-Carmel-Anderson MSA, IN	Y	35940 FQ	43130 MW	50240 TQ	USBLS	5/15
	Iowa	Y	30190 FQ	35730 MW	42440 TQ	USBLS	5/15
	Des Moines-West Des Moines MSA, IA	Y	32460 FQ	38000 MW	44680 TQ	USBLS	5/15
	Kansas	Y	23970 FQ	30700 MW	46210 TQ	USBLS	5/15
	Wichita MSA, KS	Y	30820 FQ	39620 MW	53750 TQ	USBLS	5/15
	Kentucky	Y	40470 FQ	47610 MW	62460 TQ	USBLS	5/15
	Louisville-Jefferson County MSA, KY-IN	Y	34190 FQ	41290 MW	55960 TQ	USBLS	5/15
	Louisiana	Y	34710 FQ	39300 MW	57880 TQ	USBLS	5/15
	Maine	Y	41430 FQ	45410 MW	49410 TQ	USBLS	5/15
	Portland-South Portland MSA, ME	Y	42620 FQ	46190 MW	51270 TQ	USBLS	5/15
	Maryland	Y	35527 AE	62917 MW	76611 AEX	MDBLS	4/16
	Baltimore-Columbia-Towson MSA, MD	Y	40120 FQ	52690 MW	77160 TQ	USBLS	5/15
	Massachusetts	Y	43880 FQ	55720 MW	73200 TQ	USBLS	5/15

AE	Average entry wage	AWR	Average wage range	H	Hourly	LR	Low end range	MTC	Median total compensation	TCC	Total cash compensation
AEX	Average experienced wage	B	Biweekly	HI	Highest wage paid	M	Monthly	MW	Median wage paid	TQ	Third quartile wage
ATC	Average total compensation	D	Daily	HR	High end range	MCC	Median cash compensation	MWR	Median wage range	W	Weekly
AW	Average wage paid	FQ	First quartile wage	LO	Lowest wage paid	ME	Median entry wage	S	See annotated source	Y	Yearly

Occupation/Type/Industry	Location	Per	Low	Mid	High	Source	Date
Interpreter and Translator	Boston-Cambridge-Newton NECTA, MA	Y	51580 FQ	61510 MW	82060 TQ	USBLS	5/15
	Worcester MSA, MA-CT	Y	39860 FQ	46290 MW	58280 TQ	USBLS	5/15
	Michigan	Y	33660 FQ	41230 MW	54350 TQ	USBLS	5/15
	Detroit-Dearborn-Livonia PMSA, MI	Y	33520 FQ	42820 MW	59030 TQ	USBLS	5/15
	Grand Rapids-Wyoming MSA, MI	Y	37280 FQ	46800 MW	59940 TQ	USBLS	5/15
	Minnesota	Y	36965 FQ	46774 MW	56350 TQ	MNBLS	1/16-3/16
	Minneapolis-St. Paul-Bloomington MSA, MN-WI	Y	39062 FQ	48417 MW	57620 TQ	MNBLS	1/16-3/16
	Mississippi	Y	23740 FQ	30220 MW	38980 TQ	USBLS	5/15
	Missouri	Y	34250 FQ	45930 MW	58980 TQ	USBLS	5/15
	Kansas City MSA, MO-KS	Y	28020 FQ	39140 MW	57110 TQ	USBLS	5/15
	St. Louis MSA, MO-IL	Y	33460 FQ	44050 MW	58410 TQ	USBLS	5/15
	Montana	Y	25100 FQ	32220 MW	37550 TQ	USBLS	5/15
	Nebraska	Y	29475 FQ	38435 MW	45910 TQ	NEBLS	7/16-9/16
	Omaha-Council Bluffs MSA, NE-IA	Y	32315 FQ	37745 MW	47720 TQ	NEBLS	7/16-9/16
	Nevada	Y	32010 FQ	45870 MW	58950 TQ	USBLS	5/15
	Las Vegas-Henderson-Paradise MSA, NV	Y	27290 FQ	43680 MW	57550 TQ	USBLS	5/15
	New Hampshire	H	17.98 AE	21.95 MW	25.12 AEX	NHBLS	6/16
	Manchester NECTA, NH	H	15.29 AE	22.37 MW	28.30 AEX	NHBLS	6/16
	Nashua NECTA, NH-MA	Y	40760 FQ	54010 MW	61620 TQ	USBLS	5/15
	New Jersey	Y	46370 FQ	64570 MW	81450 TQ	USBLS	5/15
	Trenton MSA, NJ	Y	43610 FQ	48990 MW	80700 TQ	USBLS	5/15
	New Mexico	Y	35030 FQ	41550 MW	56280 TQ	USBLS	5/15
	Albuquerque MSA, NM	Y	34060 FQ	38100 MW	46180 TQ	USBLS	5/15
	New York	Y	26140 AE	49440 MW	64510 AEX	NYBLS	1/16-3/16
	Buffalo-Cheektowaga-Niagara Falls MSA, NY	Y	26540 FQ	29010 MW	35710 TQ	USBLS	5/15
	Nassau County-Suffolk County PMSA, NY	Y	37870 FQ	55320 MW	86460 TQ	USBLS	5/15
	New York-Jersey City-White Plains PMSA, NY-NJ	Y	31670 FQ	55790 MW	70940 TQ	USBLS	5/15
	Rochester MSA, NY	Y	34380 FQ	40800 MW	53660 TQ	USBLS	5/15
	North Carolina	Y	28420 FQ	36450 MW	63420 TQ	USBLS	5/15
	Charlotte-Concord-Gastonia MSA, NC-SC	Y	33080 FQ	39400 MW	52010 TQ	USBLS	5/15
	Raleigh MSA, NC	Y	33370 FQ	50130 MW	69890 TQ	USBLS	5/15
	North Dakota	Y	26160 FQ	33070 MW	38890 TQ	USBLS	5/15
	Fargo MSA, ND-MN	Y	32460 FQ	35780 MW	39100 TQ	USBLS	5/15
	Ohio	Y	31230 FQ	41370 MW	52480 TQ	USBLS	5/15
	Cincinnati MSA, OH-KY-IN	Y	40560 FQ	45490 MW	50650 TQ	USBLS	5/15
	Cleveland-Elyria MSA, OH	Y	33930 FQ	39060 MW	46800 TQ	USBLS	5/15
	Columbus MSA, OH	Y	29070 FQ	45730 MW	61770 TQ	USBLS	5/15
	Oklahoma	Y	25830 FQ	31230 MW	38920 TQ	USBLS	5/15
	Oklahoma City MSA, OK	Y	26730 FQ	31120 MW	37750 TQ	USBLS	5/15
	Tulsa MSA, OK	Y	23060 FQ	32150 MW	38610 TQ	USBLS	5/15
	Oregon	H	16.79 FQ	19.63 MW	23.23 TQ	ORBLS	2016
	Portland-Vancouver-Hillsboro MSA, OR-WA	Y	35330 FQ	40620 MW	47220 TQ	USBLS	5/15
	Pennsylvania	Y	31550 FQ	45630 MW	61050 TQ	USBLS	5/15
	Allentown-Bethlehem-Easton MSA, PA-NJ	Y	27440 FQ	30660 MW	41360 TQ	USBLS	5/15
	Philadelphia PMSA, PA	Y	41600 FQ	48110 MW	58420 TQ	USBLS	5/15
	Pittsburgh MSA, PA	Y	31150 FQ	45560 MW	65750 TQ	USBLS	5/15
	Rhode Island	Y	40380 FQ	45020 MW	50640 TQ	USBLS	5/15
	Providence-Warwick MSA, RI-MA	Y	38850 FQ	44310 MW	50640 TQ	USBLS	5/15
	South Carolina	Y	28780 FQ	36110 MW	44060 TQ	USBLS	5/15
	Charleston-North Charleston MSA, SC	Y	35730 FQ	41520 MW	46660 TQ	USBLS	5/15
	Columbia MSA, SC	Y	28270 FQ	35950 MW	48380 TQ	USBLS	5/15
	Greenville-Anderson-Mauldin MSA, SC	Y	32990 FQ	37400 MW	43530 TQ	USBLS	5/15
	South Dakota	Y	31900 FQ	36610 MW	44770 TQ	USBLS	5/15
	Sioux Falls MSA, SD	Y	31250 FQ	36510 MW	46210 TQ	USBLS	5/15
	Tennessee	Y	25810 FQ	34790 MW	45580 TQ	USBLS	5/15
	Knoxville MSA, TN	Y	33250 FQ	43980 MW	57430 TQ	USBLS	5/15
	Memphis MSA, TN-MS-AR	Y	35500 FQ	44530 MW	49970 TQ	USBLS	5/15

AE	Average entry wage	AWR	Average wage range	H	Hourly
AEX	Average experienced wage	B	Biweekly	HI	Highest wage paid
ATC	Average total compensation	D	Daily	HR	High end range
AW	Average wage paid	FQ	First quartile wage	LO	Lowest wage paid

LR	Low end range	MTC	Median total compensation	TCC	Total cash compensation
M	Monthly	MW	Median wage paid	TQ	Third quartile wage
HR	High end range	MCC	Median cash compensation	MWR	Median wage range	W	Weekly
ME	Median entry wage	S	See annotated source	Y	Yearly

Occupation/Type/Industry	Location	Per	Low	Mid	High	Source	Date
Interpreter and Translator	Nashville-Davidson–Murfreesboro–Franklin						
	MSA, TN	Y	25980 FQ	33630 MW	41100 TQ	USBLS	5/15
	Texas	Y	34760 FQ	49350 MW	62710 TQ	USBLS	5/15
	Austin-Round Rock MSA, TX	Y	39140 FQ	58100 MW	79570 TQ	USBLS	5/15
	Dallas-Plano-Irving PMSA, TX	Y	29920 FQ	37180 MW	46730 TQ	USBLS	5/15
	Fort Worth-Arlington PMSA, TX	Y	30240 FQ	40120 MW	53970 TQ	USBLS	5/15
	Houston-The Woodlands-Sugar Land MSA, TX	Y	45160 FQ	56270 MW	68370 TQ	USBLS	5/15
	San Antonio-New Braunfels MSA, TX	Y	36280 FQ	52610 MW	67750 TQ	USBLS	5/15
	Utah	Y	29400 FQ	39580 MW	52620 TQ	USBLS	5/15
	Ogden-Clearfield MSA, UT	Y	38670 FQ	45040 MW	59030 TQ	USBLS	5/15
	Provo-Orem MSA, UT	Y	31950 FQ	44010 MW	58770 TQ	USBLS	5/15
	Salt Lake City MSA, UT	Y	28410 FQ	37830 MW	52610 TQ	USBLS	5/15
	Vermont	Y	34570 FQ	38180 MW	44920 TQ	USBLS	5/15
	Virginia	Y	42600 FQ	62410 MW	88270 TQ	USBLS	5/15
	Richmond MSA, VA	Y	34250 FQ	54730 MW	77660 TQ	USBLS	5/15
	Virginia Beach-Norfolk-Newport News MSA, VA-NC	Y	47160 FQ	65730 MW	90210 TQ	USBLS	5/15
	Washington	H	9.62 FQ	19.86 MW	23.74 TQ	WABLS	3/16
	Seattle-Bellevue-Everett PMSA, WA	H	9.62 FQ	19.49 MW	23.18 TQ	WABLS	3/16
	Tacoma-Lakewood PMSA, WA	H	14.34 FQ	18.51 MW	26.07 TQ	WABLS	3/16
	West Virginia	Y	22990 FQ	26430 MW	30900 TQ	USBLS	5/15
	Wisconsin	Y	34820 FQ	45750 MW	56870 TQ	USBLS	5/15
	Madison MSA, WI	Y	40850 FQ	45660 MW	50750 TQ	USBLS	5/15
	Milwaukee-Waukesha-West Allis MSA, WI	Y	41410 FQ	50300 MW	61100 TQ	USBLS	5/15
	Wyoming	Y	34790 FQ	41260 MW	49440 TQ	USBLS	5/15
	Puerto Rico	Y	35200 FQ	50880 MW	62930 TQ	USBLS	5/15
	San Juan-Carolina-Caguas MSA, PR	Y	35200 FQ	50880 MW	62930 TQ	USBLS	5/15
Interpretive Naturalist							
Environmental Services Department, Municipal Government	Arcata, CA	Y			16475 HI	CACIT	6/28/16
Interviewer							
Except Eligibility and Loan	Alabama	Y	21096 AE	29331 AW	33453 AEX	ALBLS	6/16
Except Eligibility and Loan	Birmingham-Hoover MSA, AL	Y	21962 AE	30083 AW	34154 AEX	ALBLS	6/16
Except Eligibility and Loan	Alaska	Y	32500 FQ	37200 MW	43580 TQ	USBLS	5/15
Except Eligibility and Loan	Anchorage MSA, AK	Y	33130 FQ	38270 MW	45160 TQ	USBLS	5/15
Except Eligibility and Loan	Arizona	Y	19680 FQ	28300 MW	36830 TQ	USBLS	5/15
Except Eligibility and Loan	Phoenix-Mesa-Scottsdale MSA, AZ	Y	20810 FQ	30350 MW	37870 TQ	USBLS	5/15
Except Eligibility and Loan	Tucson MSA, AZ	Y	17810 FQ	18880 MW	26630 TQ	USBLS	5/15
Except Eligibility and Loan	Arkansas	Y	20220 FQ	24630 MW	34900 TQ	USBLS	5/15
Except Eligibility and Loan	Little Rock-North Little Rock-Conway MSA, AR	Y	24970 FQ	34670 MW	43260 TQ	USBLS	5/15
Except Eligibility and Loan	California	H	13.79 FQ	18.11 MW	24.05 TQ	CABLS	1/16-3/16
Except Eligibility and Loan	Anaheim-Santa Ana-Irvine PMSA, CA	H	12.99 FQ	17.74 MW	22.25 TQ	CABLS	1/16-3/16
Except Eligibility and Loan	Los Angeles-Long Beach-Glendale PMSA, CA	H	14.19 FQ	17.56 MW	22.15 TQ	CABLS	1/16-3/16
Except Eligibility and Loan	Oakland-Hayward-Berkeley PMSA, CA	H	16.78 FQ	25.36 MW	28.49 TQ	CABLS	1/16-3/16
Except Eligibility and Loan	Riverside-San Bernardino-Ontario MSA, CA	H	15.65 FQ	18.44 MW	22.03 TQ	CABLS	1/16-3/16
Except Eligibility and Loan	Sacramento–Roseville–Arden-Arcade MSA, CA	H	15.91 FQ	20.94 MW	24.16 TQ	CABLS	1/16-3/16
Except Eligibility and Loan	San Diego-Carlsbad MSA, CA	H	15.25 FQ	18.01 MW	22.21 TQ	CABLS	1/16-3/16
Except Eligibility and Loan	San Francisco-Redwood City-South San Francisco PMSA, CA	H	17.22 FQ	25.60 MW	29.49 TQ	CABLS	1/16-3/16
Except Eligibility and Loan	Colorado	Y	27230 FQ	33580 MW	39560 TQ	USBLS	5/15
Except Eligibility and Loan	Denver-Aurora-Lakewood MSA, CO	Y	31200 FQ	35950 MW	42090 TQ	USBLS	5/15
Except Eligibility and Loan	Connecticut	Y		38631 MW		CTBLS	1/16-3/16
Except Eligibility and Loan	Bridgeport-Stamford-Norwalk MSA, CT	Y	33710 FQ	41460 MW	48290 TQ	USBLS	5/15

AE	Average entry wage	AWR	Average wage range	H	Hourly	LR	Low end range	MTC	Median total compensation	TCC	Total cash compensation
AEX	Average experienced wage	B	Biweekly	HI	Highest wage paid	M	Monthly	MCC	Median cash compensation	TQ	Third quartile wage
ATC	Average total compensation	D	Daily	HR	High end range	MCC	Median cash compensation	MWR	Median wage range	W	Weekly
AW	Average wage paid	FQ	First quartile wage	LO	Lowest wage paid	ME	Median entry wage	S	See annotated source	Y	Yearly

Occupation/Type/Industry	Location	Per	Low	Mid	High	Source	Date
Interviewer							
Except Eligibility and Loan	Hartford-West Hartford-East Hartford MSA, CT	Y	32840 FQ	39740 MW	47930 TQ	USBLS	5/15
Except Eligibility and Loan	Delaware	Y	30450 FQ	35710 MW	41600 TQ	USBLS	5/15
Except Eligibility and Loan	Wilmington PMSA, DE-MD-NJ	Y	32340 FQ	36540 MW	42110 TQ	USBLS	5/15
Except Eligibility and Loan	District of Columbia	Y	32710 FQ	38520 MW	49030 TQ	USBLS	5/15
Except Eligibility and Loan	Washington-Arlington-Alexandria PMSA, DC-VA-MD-WV	Y	28460 FQ	34350 MW	39410 TQ	USBLS	5/15
Except Eligibility and Loan	Florida	H	11.78 AE	15.08 MW	17.33 AEX	FLBLS	7/16-9/16
Except Eligibility and Loan	Fort Lauderdale-Pompano Beach-Deerfield Beach PMSA, FL	H	12.81 AE	17.42 MW	21.08 AEX	FLBLS	7/16-9/16
Except Eligibility and Loan	Miami-Miami Beach-Kendall PMSA, FL	H	12.53 AE	16.18 MW	17.85 AEX	FLBLS	7/16-9/16
Except Eligibility and Loan	Orlando-Kissimmee-Sanford MSA, FL	H	11.94 AE	14.56 MW	16.31 AEX	FLBLS	7/16-9/16
Except Eligibility and Loan	Tampa-St. Petersburg-Clearwater MSA, FL	H	12.29 AE	16.38 MW	18.58 AEX	FLBLS	7/16-9/16
Except Eligibility and Loan	Georgia	Y	23430 FQ	28830 MW	36200 TQ	USBLS	5/15
Except Eligibility and Loan	Atlanta-Sandy Springs-Roswell MSA, GA	Y	23420 FQ	29190 MW	37580 TQ	USBLS	5/15
Except Eligibility and Loan	Augusta-Richmond County MSA, GA-SC	Y	26310 FQ	29410 MW	33880 TQ	USBLS	5/15
Except Eligibility and Loan	Hawaii	Y	29740 FQ	35610 MW	42660 TQ	USBLS	5/15
Except Eligibility and Loan	Urban Honolulu MSA, HI	Y	29180 FQ	35950 MW	43930 TQ	USBLS	5/15
Except Eligibility and Loan	Idaho	Y	22380 FQ	29000 MW	35530 TQ	USBLS	5/15
Except Eligibility and Loan	Boise City MSA, ID	Y	26860 FQ	29960 MW	35740 TQ	USBLS	5/15
Except Eligibility and Loan	Illinois	Y	20470 FQ	28930 MW	37520 TQ	USBLS	5/15
Except Eligibility and Loan	Chicago-Naperville-Arlington Heights PMSA, IL	Y	19890 FQ	28150 MW	37410 TQ	USBLS	5/15
Except Eligibility and Loan	Lake County-Kenosha County PMSA, IL-WI	Y	20730 FQ	27850 MW	36480 TQ	USBLS	5/15
Except Eligibility and Loan	Indiana	Y	25640 FQ	29400 MW	34600 TQ	USBLS	5/15
Except Eligibility and Loan	Gary PMSA, IN	Y	26840 FQ	30150 MW	34850 TQ	USBLS	5/15
Except Eligibility and Loan	Indianapolis-Carmel-Anderson MSA, IN	Y	26440 FQ	30380 MW	36070 TQ	USBLS	5/15
Except Eligibility and Loan	Iowa	Y	23730 FQ	27670 MW	31300 TQ	USBLS	5/15
Except Eligibility and Loan	Des Moines-West Des Moines MSA, IA	Y	26720 FQ	29510 MW	34040 TQ	USBLS	5/15
Except Eligibility and Loan	Kansas	Y	24290 FQ	28630 MW	33900 TQ	USBLS	5/15
Except Eligibility and Loan	Wichita MSA, KS	Y	19260 FQ	24390 MW	29230 TQ	USBLS	5/15
Except Eligibility and Loan	Kentucky	Y	23770 FQ	29480 MW	35420 TQ	USBLS	5/15
Except Eligibility and Loan	Louisville-Jefferson County MSA, KY-IN	Y	27520 FQ	31630 MW	36380 TQ	USBLS	5/15
Except Eligibility and Loan	Louisiana	Y	20590 FQ	24780 MW	29660 TQ	USBLS	5/15
Except Eligibility and Loan	Baton Rouge MSA, LA	Y	22080 FQ	25670 MW	29510 TQ	USBLS	5/15
Except Eligibility and Loan	New Orleans-Metairie MSA, LA	Y	17700 FQ	21050 MW	26770 TQ	USBLS	5/15
Except Eligibility and Loan	Maine	Y	25010 FQ	28360 MW	31750 TQ	USBLS	5/15
Except Eligibility and Loan	Portland-South Portland MSA, ME	Y	26990 FQ	30260 MW	35020 TQ	USBLS	5/15
Except Eligibility and Loan	Baltimore-Columbia-Towson MSA, MD	Y	28350 FQ	34050 MW	38900 TQ	USBLS	5/15
Except Eligibility and Loan	Salisbury MSA, MD-DE	Y	27420 FQ	31350 MW	37700 TQ	USBLS	5/15
Except Eligibility and Loan	Massachusetts	Y	29760 FQ	36220 MW	44660 TQ	USBLS	5/15
Except Eligibility and Loan	Boston-Cambridge-Newton NECTA, MA	Y	29830 FQ	37080 MW	46840 TQ	USBLS	5/15
Except Eligibility and Loan	Worcester MSA, MA-CT	Y	32940 FQ	37730 MW	45040 TQ	USBLS	5/15
Except Eligibility and Loan	Michigan	Y	26510 FQ	31450 MW	38180 TQ	USBLS	5/15
Except Eligibility and Loan	Detroit-Dearborn-Livonia PMSA, MI	Y	27260 FQ	31330 MW	38790 TQ	USBLS	5/15
Except Eligibility and Loan	Grand Rapids-Wyoming MSA, MI	Y	19810 FQ	28290 MW	36420 TQ	USBLS	5/15
Except Eligibility and Loan	Minnesota	Y	29509 FQ	34788 MW	39662 TQ	MNBLS	1/16-3/16
Except Eligibility and Loan	Minneapolis-St. Paul-Bloomington MSA, MN-WI	Y	31087 FQ	36173 MW	41988 TQ	MNBLS	1/16-3/16
Except Eligibility and Loan	Mississippi	Y	21160 FQ	25360 MW	33430 TQ	USBLS	5/15
Except Eligibility and Loan	Jackson MSA, MS	Y	22090 FQ	27900 MW	39110 TQ	USBLS	5/15
Except Eligibility and Loan	Missouri	Y	24950 FQ	30270 MW	37830 TQ	USBLS	5/15
Except Eligibility and Loan	Kansas City MSA, MO-KS	Y	25840 FQ	30240 MW	35990 TQ	USBLS	5/15

AE Average entry wage	**AWR** Average wage range	**H** Hourly	**LR** Low end range	**MTC** Median total compensation	**TCC** Total cash compensation
AEX Average experienced wage	**B** Biweekly	**HI** Highest wage paid	**M** Monthly	**MW** Median wage paid	**TQ** Third quartile wage
ATC Average total compensation	**D** Daily	**HR** High end range	**MCC** Median cash compensation	**MWR** Median wage range	**W** Weekly
AW Average wage paid	**FQ** First quartile wage	**LO** Lowest wage paid	**ME** Median entry wage	**S** See annotated source	**Y** Yearly

Occupation/Type/Industry	Location	Per	Low	Mid	High	Source	Date
Interviewer							
Except Eligibility and Loan	St. Louis MSA, MO-IL	Y	26250 FQ	31100 MW	38520 TQ	USBLS	5/15
Except Eligibility and Loan	Montana	Y	26500 FQ	30180 MW	36080 TQ	USBLS	5/15
Except Eligibility and Loan	Billings MSA, MT	Y	28110 FQ	31780 MW	36830 TQ	USBLS	5/15
Except Eligibility and Loan	Nebraska	Y	20380 FQ	26230 MW	33710 TQ	NEBLS	7/16-9/16
Except Eligibility and Loan	Omaha-Council Bluffs MSA, NE-IA	Y	21485 FQ	27095 MW	34470 TQ	NEBLS	7/16-9/16
Except Eligibility and Loan	Nevada	Y	21930 FQ	34300 MW	45930 TQ	USBLS	5/15
Except Eligibility and Loan	Las Vegas-Henderson-Paradise MSA, NV	Y	18620 FQ	33390 MW	44800 TQ	USBLS	5/15
Except Eligibility and Loan	New Hampshire	H	12.23 AE	16.01 MW	18.46 AEX	NHBLS	6/16
Except Eligibility and Loan	Manchester NECTA, NH	H	14.63 AE	18.35 MW	20.66 AEX	NHBLS	6/16
Except Eligibility and Loan	Nashua NECTA, NH-MA	Y	25890 MW	30700 MW	36330 MW	USBLS	5/15
Except Eligibility and Loan	New Jersey	Y	29170 FQ	34670 MW	40120 TQ	USBLS	5/15
Except Eligibility and Loan	Camden PMSA, NJ	Y	30010 FQ	34400 MW	38650 TQ	USBLS	5/15
Except Eligibility and Loan	Newark PMSA, NJ-PA	Y	29810 FQ	35660 MW	42550 TQ	USBLS	5/15
Except Eligibility and Loan	Trenton MSA, NJ	Y	27140 FQ	31470 MW	36660 TQ	USBLS	5/15
Except Eligibility and Loan	New Mexico	Y	26820 FQ	31240 MW	37190 TQ	USBLS	5/15
Except Eligibility and Loan	Albuquerque MSA, NM	Y	28440 FQ	32580 MW	37130 TQ	USBLS	5/15
Except Eligibility and Loan	New York	Y	25960 AE	38320 MW	44130 AEX	NYBLS	1/16-3/16
Except Eligibility and Loan	Buffalo-Cheektowaga-Niagara Falls MSA, NY	Y	32440 FQ	37250 MW	43700 TQ	USBLS	5/15
Except Eligibility and Loan	Nassau County-Suffolk County PMSA, NY	Y	37520 FQ	43030 MW	47810 TQ	USBLS	5/15
Except Eligibility and Loan	New York-Jersey City-White Plains PMSA, NY-NJ	Y	30380 FQ	38000 MW	45480 TQ	USBLS	5/15
Except Eligibility and Loan	Rochester MSA, NY	Y	25890 FQ	29100 MW	33780 TQ	USBLS	5/15
Except Eligibility and Loan	North Carolina	Y	25550 FQ	29010 MW	33840 TQ	USBLS	5/15
Except Eligibility and Loan	Charlotte-Concord-Gastonia MSA, NC-SC	Y	26540 FQ	29680 MW	34480 TQ	USBLS	5/15
Except Eligibility and Loan	Raleigh MSA, NC	Y	23840 FQ	28570 MW	34800 TQ	USBLS	5/15
Except Eligibility and Loan	North Dakota	Y	23720 FQ	27930 MW	32640 TQ	USBLS	5/15
Except Eligibility and Loan	Ohio	Y	25520 FQ	29530 MW	35210 TQ	USBLS	5/15
Except Eligibility and Loan	Cincinnati MSA, OH-KY-IN	Y	25600 FQ	30210 MW	36080 TQ	USBLS	5/15
Except Eligibility and Loan	Cleveland-Elyria MSA, OH	Y	27260 FQ	31220 MW	37260 TQ	USBLS	5/15
Except Eligibility and Loan	Columbus MSA, OH	Y	26890 FQ	30950 MW	36770 TQ	USBLS	5/15
Except Eligibility and Loan	Oklahoma	Y	26720 FQ	31320 MW	36330 TQ	USBLS	5/15
Except Eligibility and Loan	Oklahoma City MSA, OK	Y	27320 FQ	32360 MW	36810 TQ	USBLS	5/15
Except Eligibility and Loan	Tulsa MSA, OK	Y	27090 FQ	30990 MW	36380 TQ	USBLS	5/15
Except Eligibility and Loan	Oregon	H	12.46 FQ	16.22 MW	19.04 TQ	ORBLS	2016
Except Eligibility and Loan	Portland-Vancouver-Hillsboro MSA, OR-WA	Y	32000 FQ	36790 MW	43000 TQ	USBLS	5/15
Except Eligibility and Loan	Pennsylvania	Y	26730 FQ	32630 MW	39890 TQ	USBLS	5/15
Except Eligibility and Loan	Allentown-Bethlehem-Easton MSA, PA-NJ	Y	25270 FQ	30440 MW	36310 TQ	USBLS	5/15
Except Eligibility and Loan	Harrisburg-Carlisle MSA, PA	Y	28520 FQ	33300 MW	39300 TQ	USBLS	5/15
Except Eligibility and Loan	Montgomery County-Bucks County-Chester County PMSA, PA	Y	26750 FQ	33760 MW	43040 TQ	USBLS	5/15
Except Eligibility and Loan	Philadelphia PMSA, PA	Y	30200 FQ	37100 MW	45240 TQ	USBLS	5/15
Except Eligibility and Loan	Pittsburgh MSA, PA	Y	27020 FQ	31380 MW	38050 TQ	USBLS	5/15
Except Eligibility and Loan	Rhode Island	Y	33860 FQ	41440 MW	49410 TQ	USBLS	5/15
Except Eligibility and Loan	Providence-Warwick MSA, RI-MA	Y	33230 FQ	39270 MW	47970 TQ	USBLS	5/15
Except Eligibility and Loan	South Carolina	Y	23230 FQ	27730 MW	32590 TQ	USBLS	5/15
Except Eligibility and Loan	Charleston-North Charleston MSA, SC	Y	26210 FQ	29310 MW	33550 TQ	USBLS	5/15
Except Eligibility and Loan	Columbia MSA, SC	Y	23670 FQ	28700 MW	34560 TQ	USBLS	5/15
Except Eligibility and Loan	Greenville-Anderson-Mauldin MSA, SC	Y	23110 FQ	26930 MW	30870 TQ	USBLS	5/15
Except Eligibility and Loan	South Dakota	Y	24200 FQ	27970 MW	31820 TQ	USBLS	5/15
Except Eligibility and Loan	Tennessee	Y	23240 FQ	27990 MW	33700 TQ	USBLS	5/15
Except Eligibility and Loan	Knoxville MSA, TN	Y	22250 FQ	26130 MW	30070 TQ	USBLS	5/15
Except Eligibility and Loan	Memphis MSA, TN-MS-AR	Y	26720 FQ	30410 MW	36320 TQ	USBLS	5/15
Except Eligibility and Loan	Nashville-Davidson–Murfreesboro–Franklin MSA, TN	Y	25180 FQ	30140 MW	35620 TQ	USBLS	5/15
Except Eligibility and Loan	Texas	Y	25150 FQ	31280 MW	37950 TQ	USBLS	5/15
Except Eligibility and Loan	Austin-Round Rock MSA, TX	Y	23030 FQ	28390 MW	35240 TQ	USBLS	5/15
Except Eligibility and Loan	Dallas-Plano-Irving PMSA, TX	Y	27100 FQ	33130 MW	37980 TQ	USBLS	5/15
Except Eligibility and Loan	Fort Worth-Arlington PMSA, TX	Y	27440 FQ	34840 MW	47160 TQ	USBLS	5/15

AE	Average entry wage	AWR	Average wage range	
AEX	Average experienced wage	B	Biweekly	
ATC	Average total compensation	D	Daily	
AW	Average wage paid	FQ	First quartile wage	

H	Hourly	LR	Low end range
HI	Highest wage paid	M	Monthly
HR	High end range	MCC	Median cash compensation
LO	Lowest wage paid	ME	Median entry wage

MTC	Median total compensation	TCC	Total cash compensation
MW	Median wage paid	TQ	Third quartile wage
MWR	Median wage range	W	Weekly
S	See annotated source	Y	Yearly

Occupation/Type/Industry	Location	Per	Low	Mid	High	Source	Date
Interviewer							
Except Eligibility and Loan	Houston-The Woodlands-Sugar Land MSA, TX	Y	24920 FQ	33570 MW	39600 TQ	USBLS	5/15
Except Eligibility and Loan	San Antonio-New Braunfels MSA, TX	Y	26670 FQ	31850 MW	37710 TQ	USBLS	5/15
Except Eligibility and Loan	Utah	Y	22230 FQ	27460 MW	32360 TQ	USBLS	5/15
Except Eligibility and Loan	Ogden-Clearfield MSA, UT	Y	26590 FQ	29790 MW	34980 TQ	USBLS	5/15
Except Eligibility and Loan	Provo-Orem MSA, UT	Y	20840 FQ	23900 MW	29290 TQ	USBLS	5/15
Except Eligibility and Loan	Salt Lake City MSA, UT	Y	26930 FQ	30850 MW	37460 TQ	USBLS	5/15
Except Eligibility and Loan	Vermont	Y	28120 FQ	32880 MW	38210 TQ	USBLS	5/15
Except Eligibility and Loan	Burlington-South Burlington MSA, VT	Y	28200 FQ	33610 MW	38830 TQ	USBLS	5/15
Except Eligibility and Loan	Virginia	Y	25790 FQ	29860 MW	35930 TQ	USBLS	5/15
Except Eligibility and Loan	Richmond MSA, VA	Y	25750 FQ	29510 MW	35480 TQ	USBLS	5/15
Except Eligibility and Loan	Virginia Beach-Norfolk-Newport News MSA, VA-NC	Y	25400 FQ	28550 MW	32560 TQ	USBLS	5/15
Except Eligibility and Loan	Washington	H	15.65 FQ	18.36 MW	21.93 TQ	WABLS	3/16
Except Eligibility and Loan	Seattle-Bellevue-Everett PMSA, WA	H	15.76 FQ	18.81 MW	22.37 TQ	WABLS	3/16
Except Eligibility and Loan	Tacoma-Lakewood PMSA, WA	H	16.93 FQ	19.96 MW	23.35 TQ	WABLS	3/16
Except Eligibility and Loan	West Virginia	Y	23960 FQ	28120 MW	32960 TQ	USBLS	5/15
Except Eligibility and Loan	Huntington-Ashland MSA, WV-KY-OH	Y	25560 FQ	30500 MW	36810 TQ	USBLS	5/15
Except Eligibility and Loan	Wisconsin	Y	27440 FQ	32840 MW	39870 TQ	USBLS	5/15
Except Eligibility and Loan	Madison MSA, WI	Y	29620 FQ	34940 MW	40580 TQ	USBLS	5/15
Except Eligibility and Loan	Milwaukee-Waukesha-West Allis MSA, WI	Y	27960 FQ	33060 MW	39250 TQ	USBLS	5/15
Except Eligibility and Loan	Wyoming	Y	25800 FQ	30720 MW	37750 TQ	USBLS	5/15
Except Eligibility and Loan	Cheyenne MSA, WY	Y	30590 FQ	34890 MW	39100 TQ	USBLS	5/15
Except Eligibility and Loan	Puerto Rico	Y	17550 FQ	19440 MW	29220 TQ	USBLS	5/15
Except Eligibility and Loan	San Juan-Carolina-Caguas MSA, PR	Y	17640 FQ	19620 MW	30020 TQ	USBLS	5/15
Except Eligibility and Loan	Guam	Y	19450 FQ	24830 MW	29680 TQ	USBLS	5/15
Intramural Sports Coordinator							
Michigan State University	East Lansing, MI	Y	47376 LO		52253 HI	MSUSAL	10/1/14-9/30/15
Investigative Specialist							
Municipal Government	Colorado Springs, CO	Y	52277 LO		71881 HI	COSPRS	2017
Investigator							
District Attorney's Office	San Francisco, CA	B	3387 LO		4323 HI	SFGOV	2016-2018
Investigator/Detective							
Municipal Public Safety Department	Barnesville, GA	Y	41788 LO		57605 HI	GACTY01	2016
Municipal Public Safety Department	Brunswick, GA	Y	30077 LO		49061 HI	GACTY01	2016
Municipal Public Safety Department	Valdosta, GA	Y	28730 LO		50837 HI	GACTY01	2016
Investment Analyst							
Municipal Government	Detroit, MI	M	4492 LO		6300 HI	DETGOV	2016
Iron Worker							
Open Shop	Central	H		27.42 AW		ENR01	2016
Open Shop	Central Mountain	H		28.07 AW		ENR01	2016
Open Shop	Great Lakes	H		28.34 AW		ENR01	2016
Open Shop	Mid-Atlantic	H		28.19 AW		ENR01	2016
Open Shop	New England	H		28.84 AW		ENR01	2016
Open Shop	New York and New Jersey Region	H		29.02 AW		ENR01	2016
Open Shop	Northwest	H		28.21 AW		ENR01	2016
Open Shop	South Central	H		28.35 AW		ENR01	2016
Open Shop	Southeast	H		28.21 AW		ENR01	2016
Open Shop	West	H		28.55 AW		ENR01	2016
Irrigation Repair Specialist							
Parks Department, Municipal Government	Burlingame, CA	Y			71836 HI	CACIT	6/28/16
Irrigation Technician							
Cemetery, Municipal Government	Santa Monica, CA	Y			60956 HI	CACIT	6/28/16
Public Works Department, Municipal Government	Redondo Beach, CA	Y			60564 HI	CACIT	6/28/16

Occupation/Type/Industry	Location	Per	Low	Mid	High	Source	Date
Jail Administrator							
Municipal Government	Long Beach, CA	Y			87481 HI	CACIT	6/28/16
Jail Inspector							
State Government	Ohio	H	33.12 LO		34.89 HI	OHGOV	2015
Jail Library Technician							
County Government	Oakland County, MI	B	1243 LO		1619 HI	MIOAK2	10/1/16
Jail Supervisor							
Municipal Government	Beverly Hills, CA	Y			83313 HI	CACIT	6/28/16
Janitor and Cleaner							
Except Maids and Housekeeping Cleaners	Alabama	Y	17503 AE	22116 AW	24422 AEX	ALBLS	6/16
Except Maids and Housekeeping Cleaners	Birmingham-Hoover MSA, AL	Y	17534 AE	22301 AW	24680 AEX	ALBLS	6/16
Except Maids and Housekeeping Cleaners	Alaska	Y	24950 FQ	30540 MW	37460 TQ	USBLS	5/15
Except Maids and Housekeeping Cleaners	Anchorage MSA, AK	Y	23660 FQ	30060 MW	36870 TQ	USBLS	5/15
Except Maids and Housekeeping Cleaners	Arizona	Y	18910 FQ	21740 MW	25650 TQ	USBLS	5/15
Except Maids and Housekeeping Cleaners	Phoenix-Mesa-Scottsdale MSA, AZ	Y	19050 FQ	21810 MW	25240 TQ	USBLS	5/15
Except Maids and Housekeeping Cleaners	Tucson MSA, AZ	Y	18570 FQ	21510 MW	26710 TQ	USBLS	5/15
Except Maids and Housekeeping Cleaners	Arkansas	Y	17490 FQ	19380 MW	23930 TQ	USBLS	5/15
Except Maids and Housekeeping Cleaners	Little Rock-North Little Rock-Conway MSA, AR	Y	17420 FQ	19250 MW	23760 TQ	USBLS	5/15
Except Maids and Housekeeping Cleaners	California	H	10.24 FQ	12.64 MW	16.83 TQ	CABLS	1/16-3/16
Except Maids and Housekeeping Cleaners	Anaheim-Santa Ana-Irvine PMSA, CA	H	9.65 FQ	11.13 MW	14.06 TQ	CABLS	1/16-3/16
Except Maids and Housekeeping Cleaners	Los Angeles-Long Beach-Glendale PMSA, CA	H	10.37 FQ	13.02 MW	16.85 TQ	CABLS	1/16-3/16
Except Maids and Housekeeping Cleaners	Oakland-Hayward-Berkeley PMSA, CA	H	11.59 FQ	15.04 MW	18.79 TQ	CABLS	1/16-3/16
Except Maids and Housekeeping Cleaners	Riverside-San Bernardino-Ontario MSA, CA	H	9.75 FQ	13.03 MW	17.14 TQ	CABLS	1/16-3/16
Except Maids and Housekeeping Cleaners	Sacramento–Roseville–Arden-Arcade MSA, CA	H	9.69 FQ	12.75 MW	16.43 TQ	CABLS	1/16-3/16
Except Maids and Housekeeping Cleaners	San Diego-Carlsbad MSA, CA	H	10.41 FQ	12.80 MW	16.90 TQ	CABLS	1/16-3/16
Except Maids and Housekeeping Cleaners	San Francisco-Redwood City-South San Francisco PMSA, CA	H	11.08 FQ	13.03 MW	16.34 TQ	CABLS	1/16-3/16
Except Maids and Housekeeping Cleaners	Colorado	Y	19830 FQ	23880 MW	29380 TQ	USBLS	5/15
Except Maids and Housekeeping Cleaners	Denver-Aurora-Lakewood MSA, CO	Y	19720 FQ	23360 MW	28560 TQ	USBLS	5/15
Except Maids and Housekeeping Cleaners	Connecticut	Y		28420 MW		CTBLS	1/16-3/16
Except Maids and Housekeeping Cleaners	Bridgeport-Stamford-Norwalk MSA, CT	Y	21120 FQ	27580 MW	39180 TQ	USBLS	5/15
Except Maids and Housekeeping Cleaners	Hartford-West Hartford-East Hartford MSA, CT	Y	20820 FQ	28910 MW	41250 TQ	USBLS	5/15
Except Maids and Housekeeping Cleaners	Delaware	Y	18820 FQ	22810 MW	29980 TQ	USBLS	5/15
Except Maids and Housekeeping Cleaners	Wilmington PMSA, DE-MD-NJ	Y	18710 FQ	22920 MW	30150 TQ	USBLS	5/15
Except Maids and Housekeeping Cleaners	District of Columbia	Y	24100 FQ	28390 MW	34230 TQ	USBLS	5/15
Except Maids and Housekeeping Cleaners	Washington-Arlington-Alexandria PMSA, DC-VA-MD-WV	Y	20130 FQ	25630 MW	31700 TQ	USBLS	5/15
Except Maids and Housekeeping Cleaners	Florida	H	8.99 AE	10.38 MW	12.48 AEX	FLBLS	7/16-9/16
Except Maids and Housekeeping Cleaners	Fort Lauderdale-Pompano Beach-Deerfield Beach PMSA, FL	H	8.98 AE	9.54 MW	11.63 AEX	FLBLS	7/16-9/16
Except Maids and Housekeeping Cleaners	Miami-Miami Beach-Kendall PMSA, FL	H	8.99 AE	9.85 MW	11.84 AEX	FLBLS	7/16-9/16
Except Maids and Housekeeping Cleaners	Orlando-Kissimmee-Sanford MSA, FL	H	9.10 AE	10.75 MW	12.31 AEX	FLBLS	7/16-9/16
Except Maids and Housekeeping Cleaners	Tampa-St. Petersburg-Clearwater MSA, FL	H	8.98 AE	10.68 MW	12.73 AEX	FLBLS	7/16-9/16
Except Maids and Housekeeping Cleaners	Georgia	Y	17890 FQ	20930 MW	25940 TQ	USBLS	5/15
Except Maids and Housekeeping Cleaners	Atlanta-Sandy Springs-Roswell MSA, GA	Y	18600 FQ	22280 MW	27570 TQ	USBLS	5/15
Except Maids and Housekeeping Cleaners	Augusta-Richmond County MSA, GA-SC	Y	17610 FQ	19960 MW	26300 TQ	USBLS	5/15
Except Maids and Housekeeping Cleaners	Rome MSA, GA	Y	19790 FQ	23490 MW	30300 TQ	USBLS	5/15
Except Maids and Housekeeping Cleaners	Hawaii	Y	18770 FQ	24990 MW	34490 TQ	USBLS	5/15
Except Maids and Housekeeping Cleaners	Urban Honolulu MSA, HI	Y	18550 FQ	24030 MW	33610 TQ	USBLS	5/15

AE	Average entry wage	**AWR**	Average wage range	**H**	Hourly	**LR**	Low end range	**MTC**	Median total compensation	**TCC** Total cash compensation
AEX	Average experienced wage	**B**	Biweekly	**HI**	Highest wage paid	**M**	Monthly	**MW**	Median wage paid	**TQ** Third quartile wage
ATC	Average total compensation	**D**	Daily	**HR**	High end range	**MCC**	Median cash compensation	**MWR**	Median wage range	**W** Weekly
AW	Average wage paid	**FQ**	First quartile wage	**LO**	Lowest wage paid	**ME**	Median entry wage	**S**	See annotated source	**Y** Yearly

Occupation/Type/Industry	Location	Per	Low	Mid	High	Source	Date
Janitor and Cleaner							
Except Maids and Housekeeping Cleaners	Idaho	Y	18730 FQ	22220 MW	26780 TQ	USBLS	5/15
Except Maids and Housekeeping Cleaners	Boise City MSA, ID	Y	19180 FQ	22480 MW	26730 TQ	USBLS	5/15
Except Maids and Housekeeping Cleaners	Illinois	Y	20420 FQ	25460 MW	34010 TQ	USBLS	5/15
Except Maids and Housekeeping Cleaners	Chicago-Naperville-Arlington Heights PMSA, IL	Y	21270 FQ	26970 MW	35220 TQ	USBLS	5/15
Except Maids and Housekeeping Cleaners	Lake County-Kenosha County PMSA, IL-WI	Y	21250 FQ	24790 MW	33420 TQ	USBLS	5/15
Except Maids and Housekeeping Cleaners	Indiana	Y	19240 FQ	23210 MW	29420 TQ	USBLS	5/15
Except Maids and Housekeeping Cleaners	Gary PMSA, IN	Y	19910 FQ	25560 MW	32610 TQ	USBLS	5/15
Except Maids and Housekeeping Cleaners	Indianapolis-Carmel-Anderson MSA, IN	Y	19500 FQ	23050 MW	28700 TQ	USBLS	5/15
Except Maids and Housekeeping Cleaners	Iowa	Y	19290 FQ	23810 MW	31560 TQ	USBLS	5/15
Except Maids and Housekeeping Cleaners	Des Moines-West Des Moines MSA, IA	Y	18390 FQ	22460 MW	29840 TQ	USBLS	5/15
Except Maids and Housekeeping Cleaners	Kansas	Y	19050 FQ	23100 MW	28720 TQ	USBLS	5/15
Except Maids and Housekeeping Cleaners	Wichita MSA, KS	Y	18850 FQ	23470 MW	30050 TQ	USBLS	5/15
Except Maids and Housekeeping Cleaners	Kentucky	Y	18080 FQ	21310 MW	26560 TQ	USBLS	5/15
Except Maids and Housekeeping Cleaners	Louisville-Jefferson County MSA, KY-IN	Y	17760 FQ	20650 MW	27760 TQ	USBLS	5/15
Except Maids and Housekeeping Cleaners	Louisiana	Y	17540 FQ	19690 MW	23950 TQ	USBLS	5/15
Except Maids and Housekeeping Cleaners	Baton Rouge MSA, LA	Y	17210 FQ	18940 MW	23060 TQ	USBLS	5/15
Except Maids and Housekeeping Cleaners	New Orleans-Metairie MSA, LA	Y	18260 FQ	21600 MW	25950 TQ	USBLS	5/15
Except Maids and Housekeeping Cleaners	Maine	Y	21230 FQ	25810 MW	32400 TQ	USBLS	5/15
Except Maids and Housekeeping Cleaners	Portland-South Portland MSA, ME	Y	21860 FQ	26830 MW	34820 TQ	USBLS	5/15
Except Maids and Housekeeping Cleaners	Maryland	Y	18188 AE	26264 MW	30302 AEX	MDBLS	4/16
Except Maids and Housekeeping Cleaners	Baltimore-Columbia-Towson MSA, MD	Y	18980 FQ	23470 MW	31010 TQ	USBLS	5/15
Except Maids and Housekeeping Cleaners	Salisbury MSA, MD-DE	Y	19210 FQ	22850 MW	30640 TQ	USBLS	5/15
Except Maids and Housekeeping Cleaners	Massachusetts	Y	24070 FQ	32070 MW	40560 TQ	USBLS	5/15
Except Maids and Housekeeping Cleaners	Boston-Cambridge-Newton NECTA, MA	Y	26370 FQ	34360 MW	42720 TQ	USBLS	5/15
Except Maids and Housekeeping Cleaners	Worcester MSA, MA-CT	Y	22710 FQ	30400 MW	40730 TQ	USBLS	5/15
Except Maids and Housekeeping Cleaners	Michigan	Y	19080 FQ	23320 MW	30850 TQ	USBLS	5/15
Except Maids and Housekeeping Cleaners	Detroit-Dearborn-Livonia PMSA, MI	Y	18870 FQ	23220 MW	31280 TQ	USBLS	5/15
Except Maids and Housekeeping Cleaners	Grand Rapids-Wyoming MSA, MI	Y	19060 FQ	21890 MW	25740 TQ	USBLS	5/15
Except Maids and Housekeeping Cleaners	Minnesota	Y	21399 FQ	26014 MW	33154 TQ	MNBLS	1/16-3/16
Except Maids and Housekeeping Cleaners	Minneapolis-St. Paul-Bloomington MSA, MN-WI	Y	21581 FQ	26004 MW	33750 TQ	MNBLS	1/16-3/16
Except Maids and Housekeeping Cleaners	Mississippi	Y	17270 FQ	19140 MW	23440 TQ	USBLS	5/15
Except Maids and Housekeeping Cleaners	Jackson MSA, MS	Y	17230 FQ	19220 MW	23350 TQ	USBLS	5/15
Except Maids and Housekeeping Cleaners	Missouri	Y	18650 FQ	22000 MW	26940 TQ	USBLS	5/15
Except Maids and Housekeeping Cleaners	Kansas City MSA, MO-KS	Y	18960 FQ	23930 MW	30520 TQ	USBLS	5/15
Except Maids and Housekeeping Cleaners	St. Louis MSA, MO-IL	Y	18710 FQ	22050 MW	27150 TQ	USBLS	5/15
Except Maids and Housekeeping Cleaners	Montana	Y	19570 FQ	23810 MW	30440 TQ	USBLS	5/15
Except Maids and Housekeeping Cleaners	Billings MSA, MT	Y	20290 FQ	25250 MW	30780 TQ	USBLS	5/15
Except Maids and Housekeeping Cleaners	Nebraska	Y	19240 FQ	22860 MW	28465 TQ	NEBLS	7/16-9/16
Except Maids and Housekeeping Cleaners	Omaha-Council Bluffs MSA, NE-IA	Y	19570 FQ	23085 MW	29165 TQ	NEBLS	7/16-9/16
Except Maids and Housekeeping Cleaners	Nevada	Y	19460 FQ	29570 MW	35450 TQ	USBLS	5/15
Except Maids and Housekeeping Cleaners	Las Vegas-Henderson-Paradise MSA, NV	Y	21370 FQ	31840 MW	36020 TQ	USBLS	5/15
Except Maids and Housekeeping Cleaners	New Hampshire	H	9.54 AE	12.61 MW	15.72 AEX	NHBLS	6/16
Except Maids and Housekeeping Cleaners	Manchester NECTA, NH	H	9.64 AE	11.26 MW	13.54 AEX	NHBLS	6/16
Except Maids and Housekeeping Cleaners	Nashua NECTA, NH-MA	Y	21150 FQ	29660 MW	42140 TQ	USBLS	5/15
Except Maids and Housekeeping Cleaners	New Jersey	Y	21570 FQ	27380 MW	35680 TQ	USBLS	5/15
Except Maids and Housekeeping Cleaners	Camden PMSA, NJ	Y	21740 FQ	27560 MW	36240 TQ	USBLS	5/15
Except Maids and Housekeeping Cleaners	Newark PMSA, NJ-PA	Y	22710 FQ	27830 MW	35380 TQ	USBLS	5/15
Except Maids and Housekeeping Cleaners	Trenton MSA, NJ	Y	19820 FQ	26180 MW	36870 TQ	USBLS	5/15
Except Maids and Housekeeping Cleaners	New Mexico	Y	18420 FQ	21380 MW	25290 TQ	USBLS	5/15
Except Maids and Housekeeping Cleaners	Albuquerque MSA, NM	Y	18400 FQ	21330 MW	24850 TQ	USBLS	5/15
Except Maids and Housekeeping Cleaners	New York	Y	20530 AE	28700 MW	37580 AEX	NYBLS	1/16-3/16
Except Maids and Housekeeping Cleaners	Buffalo-Cheektowaga-Niagara Falls MSA, NY	Y	19540 FQ	24430 MW	31210 TQ	USBLS	5/15
Except Maids and Housekeeping Cleaners	Nassau County-Suffolk County PMSA, NY	Y	19880 FQ	26110 MW	40010 TQ	USBLS	5/15
Except Maids and Housekeeping Cleaners	New York-Jersey City-White Plains PMSA, NY-NJ	Y	22350 FQ	30510 MW	42620 TQ	USBLS	5/15

AE Average entry wage	**AWR** Average wage range	**H** Hourly	**LR** Low end range	**MTC** Median total compensation	**TCC** Total cash compensation
AEX Average experienced wage	**B** Biweekly	**HI** Highest wage paid	**M** Monthly	**MW** Median wage paid	**TQ** Third quartile wage
ATC Average total compensation	**D** Daily	**HR** High end range	**MCC** Median cash compensation	**MWR** Median wage range	**W** Weekly
AW Average wage paid	**FQ** First quartile wage	**LO** Lowest wage paid	**ME** Median entry wage	**S** See annotated source	**Y** Yearly

Janitor and Cleaner

Occupation/Type/Industry	Location	Per	Low	Mid	High	Source	Date
Except Maids and Housekeeping Cleaners	Rochester MSA, NY	Y	19490 FQ	22840 MW	28210 TQ	USBLS	5/15
Except Maids and Housekeeping Cleaners	North Carolina	Y	17840 FQ	20690 MW	24970 TQ	USBLS	5/15
Except Maids and Housekeeping Cleaners	Charlotte-Concord-Gastonia MSA, NC-SC	Y	17890 FQ	21130 MW	26100 TQ	USBLS	5/15
Except Maids and Housekeeping Cleaners	Raleigh MSA, NC	Y	17660 FQ	19860 MW	24390 TQ	USBLS	5/15
Except Maids and Housekeeping Cleaners	North Dakota	Y	22390 FQ	27330 MW	33600 TQ	USBLS	5/15
Except Maids and Housekeeping Cleaners	Fargo MSA, ND-MN	Y	21710 FQ	25630 MW	30390 TQ	USBLS	5/15
Except Maids and Housekeeping Cleaners	Ohio	Y	18700 FQ	22310 MW	30260 TQ	USBLS	5/15
Except Maids and Housekeeping Cleaners	Cincinnati MSA, OH-KY-IN	Y	18950 FQ	22680 MW	28730 TQ	USBLS	5/15
Except Maids and Housekeeping Cleaners	Cleveland-Elyria MSA, OH	Y	18590 FQ	22120 MW	30850 TQ	USBLS	5/15
Except Maids and Housekeeping Cleaners	Columbus MSA, OH	Y	18960 FQ	22870 MW	31970 TQ	USBLS	5/15
Except Maids and Housekeeping Cleaners	Youngstown-Warren-Boardman MSA, OH-PA	Y	18350 FQ	21410 MW	31160 TQ	USBLS	5/15
Except Maids and Housekeeping Cleaners	Oklahoma	Y	17900 FQ	20790 MW	24650 TQ	USBLS	5/15
Except Maids and Housekeeping Cleaners	Oklahoma City MSA, OK	Y	18080 FQ	21380 MW	25980 TQ	USBLS	5/15
Except Maids and Housekeeping Cleaners	Tulsa MSA, OK	Y	18380 FQ	21280 MW	24540 TQ	USBLS	5/15
Except Maids and Housekeeping Cleaners	Oregon	H	10.44 FQ	12.40 MW	15.09 TQ	ORBLS	2016
Except Maids and Housekeeping Cleaners	Portland-Vancouver-Hillsboro MSA, OR-WA	Y	21470 FQ	25990 MW	31150 TQ	USBLS	5/15
Except Maids and Housekeeping Cleaners	Pennsylvania	Y	19830 FQ	24910 MW	32230 TQ	USBLS	5/15
Except Maids and Housekeeping Cleaners	Allentown-Bethlehem-Easton MSA, PA-NJ	Y	19530 FQ	27190 MW	38980 TQ	USBLS	5/15
Except Maids and Housekeeping Cleaners	Harrisburg-Carlisle MSA, PA	Y	19050 FQ	23290 MW	28900 TQ	USBLS	5/15
Except Maids and Housekeeping Cleaners	Montgomery County-Bucks County-Chester County PMSA, PA	Y	23310 FQ	29770 MW	36610 TQ	USBLS	5/15
Except Maids and Housekeeping Cleaners	Philadelphia PMSA, PA	Y	21100 FQ	26150 MW	32260 TQ	USBLS	5/15
Except Maids and Housekeeping Cleaners	Pittsburgh MSA, PA	Y	19680 FQ	24400 MW	32120 TQ	USBLS	5/15
Except Maids and Housekeeping Cleaners	Rhode Island	Y	20020 FQ	23970 MW	34340 TQ	USBLS	5/15
Except Maids and Housekeeping Cleaners	Providence-Warwick MSA, RI-MA	Y	20000 FQ	24320 MW	34960 TQ	USBLS	5/15
Except Maids and Housekeeping Cleaners	South Carolina	Y	17500 FQ	19770 MW	23940 TQ	USBLS	5/15
Except Maids and Housekeeping Cleaners	Charleston-North Charleston MSA, SC	Y	17260 FQ	19460 MW	24010 TQ	USBLS	5/15
Except Maids and Housekeeping Cleaners	Columbia MSA, SC	Y	17590 FQ	20230 MW	24100 TQ	USBLS	5/15
Except Maids and Housekeeping Cleaners	Greenville-Anderson-Mauldin MSA, SC	Y	17290 FQ	19140 MW	22830 TQ	USBLS	5/15
Except Maids and Housekeeping Cleaners	South Dakota	Y	19870 FQ	22830 MW	26910 TQ	USBLS	5/15
Except Maids and Housekeeping Cleaners	Sioux Falls MSA, SD	Y	19510 FQ	22860 MW	27660 TQ	USBLS	5/15
Except Maids and Housekeeping Cleaners	Tennessee	Y	17780 FQ	20480 MW	25060 TQ	USBLS	5/15
Except Maids and Housekeeping Cleaners	Knoxville MSA, TN	Y	17980 FQ	21140 MW	26280 TQ	USBLS	5/15
Except Maids and Housekeeping Cleaners	Memphis MSA, TN-MS-AR	Y	17550 FQ	19620 MW	24520 TQ	USBLS	5/15
Except Maids and Housekeeping Cleaners	Nashville-Davidson–Murfreesboro–Franklin MSA, TN	Y	18320 FQ	22000 MW	27400 TQ	USBLS	5/15
Except Maids and Housekeeping Cleaners	Texas	Y	17760 FQ	20300 MW	24370 TQ	USBLS	5/15
Except Maids and Housekeeping Cleaners	Austin-Round Rock MSA, TX	Y	18560 FQ	22180 MW	26790 TQ	USBLS	5/15
Except Maids and Housekeeping Cleaners	Dallas-Plano-Irving PMSA, TX	Y	17320 FQ	19200 MW	23310 TQ	USBLS	5/15
Except Maids and Housekeeping Cleaners	Fort Worth-Arlington PMSA, TX	Y	17720 FQ	20270 MW	24680 TQ	USBLS	5/15
Except Maids and Housekeeping Cleaners	Houston-The Woodlands-Sugar Land MSA, TX	Y	17770 FQ	20270 MW	24480 TQ	USBLS	5/15
Except Maids and Housekeeping Cleaners	San Antonio-New Braunfels MSA, TX	Y	18110 FQ	20960 MW	24370 TQ	USBLS	5/15
Except Maids and Housekeeping Cleaners	Utah	Y	17330 FQ	19250 MW	24950 TQ	USBLS	5/15
Except Maids and Housekeeping Cleaners	Ogden-Clearfield MSA, UT	Y	17510 FQ	19670 MW	28020 TQ	USBLS	5/15
Except Maids and Housekeeping Cleaners	Provo-Orem MSA, UT	Y	16930 FQ	18470 MW	21750 TQ	USBLS	5/15
Except Maids and Housekeeping Cleaners	Salt Lake City MSA, UT	Y	17150 FQ	18900 MW	23160 TQ	USBLS	5/15
Except Maids and Housekeeping Cleaners	Vermont	Y	22640 FQ	27390 MW	33510 TQ	USBLS	5/15
Except Maids and Housekeeping Cleaners	Burlington-South Burlington MSA, VT	Y	23870 FQ	28310 MW	33800 TQ	USBLS	5/15
Except Maids and Housekeeping Cleaners	Virginia	Y	18460 FQ	22150 MW	27840 TQ	USBLS	5/15
Except Maids and Housekeeping Cleaners	Richmond MSA, VA	Y	18310 FQ	21860 MW	26960 TQ	USBLS	5/15
Except Maids and Housekeeping Cleaners	Virginia Beach-Norfolk-Newport News MSA, VA-NC	Y	18460 FQ	21990 MW	27050 TQ	USBLS	5/15
Except Maids and Housekeeping Cleaners	Washington	H	11.56 FQ	14.34 MW	17.66 TQ	WABLS	3/16
Except Maids and Housekeeping Cleaners	Seattle-Bellevue-Everett PMSA, WA	H	11.74 FQ	14.74 MW	18.35 TQ	WABLS	3/16
Except Maids and Housekeeping Cleaners	Tacoma-Lakewood PMSA, WA	H	12.44 FQ	15.61 MW	18.26 TQ	WABLS	3/16
Except Maids and Housekeeping Cleaners	West Virginia	Y	18470 FQ	21200 MW	26790 TQ	USBLS	5/15

AE	Average entry wage	AWR	Average wage range	H	Hourly
AEX	Average experienced wage	B	Biweekly	HI	Highest wage paid
ATC	Average total compensation	D	Daily	HR	High end range
AW	Average wage paid	FQ	First quartile wage	LO	Lowest wage paid

LR	Low end range	MTC	Median total compensation
M	Monthly	MW	Median wage paid
MCC	Median cash compensation	MWR	Median wage range
ME	Median entry wage	S	See annotated source

TCC	Total cash compensation		
TQ	Third quartile wage		
W	Weekly		
Y	Yearly		

Occupation/Type/Industry	Location	Per	Low	Mid	High	Source	Date
Janitor and Cleaner							
Except Maids and Housekeeping Cleaners	Huntington-Ashland MSA, WV-KY-OH	Y	18600 FQ	21450 MW	25560 TQ	USBLS	5/15
Except Maids and Housekeeping Cleaners	Wisconsin	Y	18930 FQ	23070 MW	29800 TQ	USBLS	5/15
Except Maids and Housekeeping Cleaners	Madison MSA, WI	Y	18130 FQ	22060 MW	28210 TQ	USBLS	5/15
Except Maids and Housekeeping Cleaners	Milwaukee-Waukesha-West Allis MSA, WI	Y	18320 FQ	21650 MW	27650 TQ	USBLS	5/15
Except Maids and Housekeeping Cleaners	Wyoming	Y	21850 FQ	27170 MW	34190 TQ	USBLS	5/15
Except Maids and Housekeeping Cleaners	Cheyenne MSA, WY	Y	20350 FQ	24820 MW	32390 TQ	USBLS	5/15
Except Maids and Housekeeping Cleaners	Puerto Rico	Y	16720 FQ	18030 MW	19360 TQ	USBLS	5/15
Except Maids and Housekeeping Cleaners	San Juan-Carolina-Caguas MSA, PR	Y	16700 FQ	18010 MW	19340 TQ	USBLS	5/15
Except Maids and Housekeeping Cleaners	Virgin Islands	Y	17830 FQ	20490 MW	23930 TQ	USBLS	5/15
Except Maids and Housekeeping Cleaners	Guam	Y	17900 FQ	18630 MW	19420 TQ	USBLS	5/15
Jazz Music Instructor	United States	H		51.05-78.75 AWR		FORB03	2016
Jeweler and Precious Stone and Metal Worker							
	Alabama	Y	27690 AE	40635 AW	47113 AEX	ALBLS	6/16
	Birmingham-Hoover MSA, AL	Y	28502 AE	43267 AW	50650 AEX	ALBLS	6/16
	Arizona	Y	27020 FQ	32410 MW	45570 TQ	USBLS	5/15
	Phoenix-Mesa-Scottsdale MSA, AZ	Y	28410 FQ	37030 MW	46690 TQ	USBLS	5/15
	Tucson MSA, AZ	Y	24930 FQ	29790 MW	41090 TQ	USBLS	5/15
	Arkansas	Y	30520 FQ	53050 MW	62390 TQ	USBLS	5/15
	Little Rock-North Little Rock-Conway MSA, AR	Y	53830 FQ	58670 MW	63510 TQ	USBLS	5/15
	California	H	13.38 FQ	16.73 MW	22.87 TQ	CABLS	1/16-3/16
	Anaheim-Santa Ana-Irvine PMSA, CA	H	13.20 FQ	14.58 MW	21.91 TQ	CABLS	1/16-3/16
	Los Angeles-Long Beach-Glendale PMSA, CA	H	13.18 FQ	16.57 MW	20.35 TQ	CABLS	1/16-3/16
	Oakland-Hayward-Berkeley PMSA, CA	H	12.53 FQ	16.88 MW	24.70 TQ	CABLS	1/16-3/16
	Riverside-San Bernardino-Ontario MSA, CA	H	9.63 FQ	13.99 MW	21.77 TQ	CABLS	1/16-3/16
	Sacramento–Roseville–Arden-Arcade MSA, CA	H	14.93 FQ	20.53 MW	30.57 TQ	CABLS	1/16-3/16
	San Diego-Carlsbad MSA, CA	H	14.49 FQ	16.78 MW	18.86 TQ	CABLS	1/16-3/16
	San Francisco-Redwood City-South San Francisco PMSA, CA	H	19.03 FQ	24.11 MW	33.42 TQ	CABLS	1/16-3/16
	Colorado	Y	25470 FQ	29140 MW	44500 TQ	USBLS	5/15
	Denver-Aurora-Lakewood MSA, CO	Y	25920 FQ	28340 MW	31650 TQ	USBLS	5/15
	Connecticut	Y		47352 MW		CTBLS	1/16-3/16
	Washington-Arlington-Alexandria PMSA, DC-VA-MD-WV	Y	26670 FQ	28310 MW	29950 TQ	USBLS	5/15
	Florida	H	12.62 AE	17.86 MW	20.68 AEX	FLBLS	7/16-9/16
	Fort Lauderdale-Pompano Beach-Deerfield Beach PMSA, FL	H	14.82 AE	18.62 MW	20.54 AEX	FLBLS	7/16-9/16
	Miami-Miami Beach-Kendall PMSA, FL	H	12.94 AE	18.10 MW	20.61 AEX	FLBLS	7/16-9/16
	Orlando-Kissimmee-Sanford MSA, FL	H	9.06 AE	9.90 MW	18.45 AEX	FLBLS	7/16-9/16
	Tampa-St. Petersburg-Clearwater MSA, FL	H	16.35 AE	19.40 MW	21.28 AEX	FLBLS	7/16-9/16
	Georgia	Y	28360 FQ	38340 MW	54010 TQ	USBLS	5/15
	Atlanta-Sandy Springs-Roswell MSA, GA	Y	34470 FQ	50040 MW	58460 TQ	USBLS	5/15
	Augusta-Richmond County MSA, GA-SC	Y	28700 FQ	32760 MW	36390 TQ	USBLS	5/15
	Hawaii	Y	27150 FQ	34010 MW	40980 TQ	USBLS	5/15
	Urban Honolulu MSA, HI	Y	25720 FQ	33510 MW	44170 TQ	USBLS	5/15
	Idaho	Y	34660 FQ	43480 MW	54240 TQ	USBLS	5/15
	Illinois	Y	24200 FQ	33140 MW	41330 TQ	USBLS	5/15
	Chicago-Naperville-Arlington Heights PMSA, IL	Y	24100 FQ	32150 MW	39220 TQ	USBLS	5/15
	Indiana	Y	32870 FQ	41940 MW	49480 TQ	USBLS	5/15

AE	Average entry wage	**AWR**	Average wage range	**H**	Hourly
AEX	Average experienced wage	**B**	Biweekly	**HI**	Highest wage paid
ATC	Average total compensation	**D**	Daily	**HR**	High end range
AW	Average wage paid	**FQ**	First quartile wage	**LO**	Lowest wage paid

LR	Low end range	**MTC**	Median total compensation	**TCC**	Total cash compensation
M	Monthly	**MW**	Median wage paid	**TQ**	Third quartile wage
MCC	Median cash compensation	**MWR**	Median wage range	**W**	Weekly
ME	Median entry wage	**S**	See annotated source	**Y**	Yearly

Occupation/Type/Industry	Location	Per	Low	Mid	High	Source	Date
Jeweler and Precious Stone and Metal Worker							
	Gary PMSA, IN	Y	27170 FQ	31450 MW	47780 TQ	USBLS	5/15
	Indianapolis-Carmel-Anderson MSA, IN	Y	39650 FQ	46520 MW	54140 TQ	USBLS	5/15
	Iowa	Y	32640 FQ	37400 MW	47550 TQ	USBLS	5/15
	Kansas	Y	26860 FQ	36880 MW	48040 TQ	USBLS	5/15
	Wichita MSA, KS	Y	41280 FQ	47380 MW	55510 TQ	USBLS	5/15
	Kentucky	Y	21640 FQ	32800 MW	42320 TQ	USBLS	5/15
	Louisiana	Y	23850 FQ	28990 MW	38480 TQ	USBLS	5/15
	Baton Rouge MSA, LA	Y	31620 FQ	34250 MW	36880 TQ	USBLS	5/15
	New Orleans-Metairie MSA, LA	Y	21970 FQ	24160 MW	41560 TQ	USBLS	5/15
	Maine	Y	24440 FQ	29890 MW	40680 TQ	USBLS	5/15
	Portland-South Portland MSA, ME	Y	25340 FQ	28860 MW	33510 TQ	USBLS	5/15
	Maryland	Y	19835 AE	40272 MW	50490 AEX	MDBLS	4/16
	Baltimore-Columbia-Towson MSA, MD	Y	22450 FQ	33010 MW	36800 TQ	USBLS	5/15
	Massachusetts	Y	33610 FQ	42930 MW	57830 TQ	USBLS	5/15
	Boston-Cambridge-Newton NECTA, MA	Y	36900 FQ	50390 MW	63560 TQ	USBLS	5/15
	Michigan	Y	24350 FQ	33960 MW	39080 TQ	USBLS	5/15
	Detroit-Dearborn-Livonia PMSA, MI	Y	19760 FQ	29010 MW	38560 TQ	USBLS	5/15
	Minnesota	Y	32591 FQ	40407 MW	48557 TQ	MNBLS	1/16-3/16
	Minneapolis-St. Paul-Bloomington MSA, MN-WI	Y	38838 FQ	54804 MW	64078 TQ	MNBLS	1/16-3/16
	Missouri	Y	19680 FQ	31600 MW	43870 TQ	USBLS	5/15
	Kansas City MSA, MO-KS	Y	30070 FQ	36350 MW	45720 TQ	USBLS	5/15
	Montana	Y	19040 FQ	28530 MW	35990 TQ	USBLS	5/15
	Nebraska	Y	30560 FQ	37615 MW	46875 TQ	NEBLS	7/16-9/16
	Omaha-Council Bluffs MSA, NE-IA	Y	31370 FQ	36785 MW	44095 TQ	NEBLS	7/16-9/16
	Nevada	Y	27860 FQ	34530 MW	46550 TQ	USBLS	5/15
	Las Vegas-Henderson-Paradise MSA, NV	Y	28470 FQ	35620 MW	46290 TQ	USBLS	5/15
	New Hampshire	H	11.17 AE	15.74 MW	22.21 AEX	NHBLS	6/16
	New Jersey	Y	35360 FQ	50020 MW	58060 TQ	USBLS	5/15
	Newark PMSA, NJ-PA	Y	41690 FQ	48730 MW	60180 TQ	USBLS	5/15
	New Mexico	Y	20010 FQ	26470 MW	31400 TQ	USBLS	5/15
	Albuquerque MSA, NM	Y	22670 FQ	26830 MW	30320 TQ	USBLS	5/15
	New York	Y	25300 AE	42090 MW	63340 AEX	NYBLS	1/16-3/16
	Buffalo-Cheektowaga-Niagara Falls MSA, NY	Y	28490 FQ	40120 MW	51070 TQ	USBLS	5/15
	New York-Jersey City-White Plains PMSA, NY-NJ	Y	28490 FQ	41650 MW	57470 TQ	USBLS	5/15
	Rochester MSA, NY	Y	35840 FQ	42940 MW	47270 TQ	USBLS	5/15
	North Carolina	Y	27180 FQ	34880 MW	43100 TQ	USBLS	5/15
	Charlotte-Concord-Gastonia MSA, NC-SC	Y	24060 FQ	32290 MW	40320 TQ	USBLS	5/15
	Raleigh MSA, NC	Y	23600 FQ	29530 MW	37310 TQ	USBLS	5/15
	North Dakota	Y	29220 FQ	35600 MW	45950 TQ	USBLS	5/15
	Ohio	Y	27980 FQ	37420 MW	54580 TQ	USBLS	5/15
	Cincinnati MSA, OH-KY-IN	Y	22530 FQ	29620 MW	40660 TQ	USBLS	5/15
	Columbus MSA, OH	Y	32790 FQ	39280 MW	56380 TQ	USBLS	5/15
	Oklahoma	Y	30730 FQ	39230 MW	49210 TQ	USBLS	5/15
	Oklahoma City MSA, OK	Y	33310 FQ	38470 MW	54030 TQ	USBLS	5/15
	Oregon	H	15.15 FQ	18.99 MW	24.82 TQ	ORBLS	2016
	Portland-Vancouver-Hillsboro MSA, OR-WA	Y	32000 FQ	37820 MW	55050 TQ	USBLS	5/15
	Montgomery County-Bucks County-Chester County PMSA, PA	Y	35600 FQ	39480 MW	46050 TQ	USBLS	5/15
	Pittsburgh MSA, PA	Y	36990 FQ	53240 MW	61390 TQ	USBLS	5/15
	Rhode Island	Y	24690 FQ	36460 MW	64860 TQ	USBLS	5/15
	Providence-Warwick MSA, RI-MA	Y	25020 FQ	36470 MW	60840 TQ	USBLS	5/15
	South Carolina	Y	26860 FQ	34210 MW	51850 TQ	USBLS	5/15
	Charleston-North Charleston MSA, SC	Y	37370 FQ	55790 MW	68110 TQ	USBLS	5/15
	Columbia MSA, SC	Y	26410 FQ	32660 MW	36090 TQ	USBLS	5/15

Occupation/Type/Industry	Location	Per	Low	Mid	High	Source	Date
Jeweler and Precious Stone and Metal Worker	Greenville-Anderson-Mauldin						
	MSA, SC	Y	36640 FQ	51280 MW	59250 TQ	USBLS	5/15
	South Dakota	Y	27540 FQ	31720 MW	41820 TQ	USBLS	5/15
	Tennessee	Y	24040 FQ	36560 MW	49130 TQ	USBLS	5/15
	Knoxville MSA, TN	Y	37230 FQ	43220 MW	47420 TQ	USBLS	5/15
	Nashville-Davidson– Murfreesboro–Franklin						
	MSA, TN	Y	33650 FQ	37170 MW	58050 TQ	USBLS	5/15
	Texas	Y	26480 FQ	40000 MW	51490 TQ	USBLS	5/15
	Austin-Round Rock MSA, TX	Y	24040 FQ	30910 MW	46280 TQ	USBLS	5/15
	Dallas-Plano-Irving PMSA, TX	Y	30920 FQ	43720 MW	58020 TQ	USBLS	5/15
	Houston-The Woodlands- Sugar Land MSA, TX	Y	22040 FQ	26680 MW	45670 TQ	USBLS	5/15
	San Antonio-New Braunfels MSA, TX	Y	28060 FQ	39500 MW	69830 TQ	USBLS	5/15
	Utah	Y	22460 FQ	26500 MW	41600 TQ	USBLS	5/15
	Provo-Orem MSA, UT	Y	28480 FQ	41500 MW	47460 TQ	USBLS	5/15
	Salt Lake City MSA, UT	Y	22050 FQ	24110 MW	30070 TQ	USBLS	5/15
	Vermont	Y	33320 FQ	39310 MW	46840 TQ	USBLS	5/15
	Burlington-South Burlington MSA, VT	Y	29760 FQ	43690 MW	56200 TQ	USBLS	5/15
	Virginia	Y	27340 FQ	30620 MW	39170 TQ	USBLS	5/15
	Richmond MSA, VA	Y	27000 FQ	33560 MW	38010 TQ	USBLS	5/15
	Washington	H	17.42 FQ	22.24 MW	29.90 TQ	WABLS	3/16
	Seattle-Bellevue-Everett PMSA, WA	H	19.91 FQ	27.45 MW	34.81 TQ	WABLS	3/16
	West Virginia	Y	26630 FQ	30380 MW	41090 TQ	USBLS	5/15
	Wisconsin	Y	32470 FQ	38580 MW	48530 TQ	USBLS	5/15
	Madison MSA, WI	Y	30420 FQ	35320 MW	43710 TQ	USBLS	5/15
	Milwaukee-Waukesha-West Allis MSA, WI	Y	34970 FQ	40930 MW	57550 TQ	USBLS	5/15
	Puerto Rico	Y	17070 FQ	18370 MW	19720 TQ	USBLS	5/15
	San Juan-Carolina-Caguas MSA, PR	Y	16870 FQ	17960 MW	19050 TQ	USBLS	5/15
Jingle Writer	United States	Y		55000 AW		SKU01	2016
JROTC Instructor							
Bachelor's Degree, Public Schools	Baldwin County, AL	Y	23021 LO		32512 HI	BCPSSS	2016-2017
Judge							
Court of International Trade	United States	Y			205100 HI	OPM01	2017
General Jurisdiction Trial Courts	United States	Y		149605 MW		NCSC	1/1/17
Juvenile Court	Charlton County, GA	Y			31875 HI	GACTY04	2016
Juvenile Court	Cherokee County, GA	Y			131403 HI	GACTY04	2016
Probate Court	Coweta County, GA	Y			105713 HI	GACTY03	2016
Probate Court	Jones County, GA	Y			83662 HI	GACTY03	2016
State Court	Decatur County, GA	Y			60516 HI	GACTY03	2016
State Court	Miller County, GA	Y			16000 HI	GACTY03	2016
Superior Court	Bryan County, GA	Y			135000 HI	GACTY03	2016
Superior Court	Charlton County, GA	Y			16800 HI	GACTY03	2016
Judge, Magistrate Judge, and Magistrate	Alabama	Y	32017 AE	63453 AW	79171 AEX	ALBLS	6/16
	Birmingham-Hoover MSA, AL	Y	32272 AE	50579 AW	59732 AEX	ALBLS	6/16
	Alaska	Y	140260 FQ	163790 MW		USBLS	5/15
	Arizona	Y	73330 FQ	95650 MW	144490 TQ	USBLS	5/15
	Phoenix-Mesa-Scottsdale MSA, AZ	Y	73330 FQ	129270 MW	149810 TQ	USBLS	5/15
	Tucson MSA, AZ	Y	73320 FQ	73340 MW	114680 TQ	USBLS	5/15
	Arkansas	Y	38750 FQ	126930 MW	141970 TQ	USBLS	5/15
	Little Rock-North Little Rock- Conway MSA, AR	Y	93530 FQ	141960 MW	141980 TQ	USBLS	5/15
	California	H	86.37 FQ	86.38 MW		CABLS	1/16-3/16
	Oakland-Hayward-Berkeley PMSA, CA	H	86.37 FQ	86.38 MW		CABLS	1/16-3/16
	Sacramento–Roseville– Arden-Arcade MSA, CA	H	86.37 FQ	86.38 MW		CABLS	1/16-3/16
	Colorado	Y	125690 FQ	140570 MW	146880 TQ	USBLS	5/15
	Denver-Aurora-Lakewood MSA, CO	Y	132590 FQ	146870 MW	146890 TQ	USBLS	5/15

AE	Average entry wage	AWR	Average wage range	H	Hourly
AEX	Average experienced wage	B	Biweekly	HI	Highest wage paid
ATC	Average total compensation	D	Daily	HR	High end range
AW	Average wage paid	FQ	First quartile wage	LO	Lowest wage paid

LR	Low end range	MTC	Median total compensation	TCC	Total cash compensation
M	Monthly	MW	Median wage paid	TQ	Third quartile wage
MCC	Median cash compensation	MWR	Median wage range	W	Weekly
ME	Median entry wage	S	See annotated source	Y	Yearly

Occupation/Type/Industry	Location	Per	Low	Mid	High	Source	Date
Judge, Magistrate Judge, and Magistrate							
	Connecticut	Y		184242 MW		CTBLS	1/16-3/16
	Bridgeport-Stamford-Norwalk MSA, CT	Y	99760 FQ	178720 MW		USBLS	5/15
	Delaware	Y	83950 FQ	83970 MW		USBLS	5/15
	Wilmington PMSA, DE-MD-NJ	Y	83960 FQ	166860 MW		USBLS	5/15
	Washington-Arlington-Alexandria PMSA, DC-VA-MD-WV	Y	142930 FQ	156200 MW		USBLS	5/15
	Florida	H	55.00 AE	69.11 MW	71.32 AEX	FLBLS	7/16-9/16
	Georgia	Y	56140 FQ	87420 MW	121450 TQ	USBLS	5/15
	Atlanta-Sandy Springs-Roswell MSA, GA	Y	69750 FQ	109190 MW	133100 TQ	USBLS	5/15
	Augusta-Richmond County MSA, GA-SC	Y	63840 FQ	76520 MW	116290 TQ	USBLS	5/15
	Hawaii	Y	177310 FQ	189300 AW		USBLS	5/15
	Idaho	Y	113290 FQ	113290 MW	125430 TQ	USBLS	5/15
	Indiana	Y	78040 FQ	135270 MW	135280 TQ	USBLS	5/15
	Gary PMSA, IN	Y	66470 FQ	118090 MW	135280 TQ	USBLS	5/15
	Indianapolis-Carmel-Anderson MSA, IN	Y	74360 FQ	135260 MW	135270 TQ	USBLS	5/15
	Iowa	Y	39900 FQ	39910 MW	129360 TQ	USBLS	5/15
	Kansas	Y	70120 FQ	115350 MW	152100 TQ	USBLS	5/15
	Kentucky	Y	115580 FQ	133750 MW	149710 TQ	USBLS	5/15
	Louisville-Jefferson County MSA, KY-IN	Y	39640 FQ	128450 MW	135280 TQ	USBLS	5/15
	Louisiana	Y	50500 FQ	74560 MW	96670 TQ	USBLS	5/15
	New Orleans-Metairie MSA, LA	Y	53630 FQ	59790 MW	130850 TQ	USBLS	5/15
	Maine	Y	89430 FQ	122500 MW	122510 TQ	USBLS	5/15
	Maryland	Y	121643 AE	143674 MW	154690 AEX	MDBLS	4/16
	Baltimore-Columbia-Towson MSA, MD	Y	142930 FQ	156190 MW	156200 MW	USBLS	5/15
	Salisbury MSA, MD-DE	Y	81430 FQ	111220 MW		USBLS	5/15
	Michigan	Y	44360 FQ	49770 MW	87120 TQ	USBLS	5/15
	Detroit-Dearborn-Livonia PMSA, MI	Y	44320 FQ	48890 MW	71350 TQ	USBLS	5/15
	Grand Rapids-Wyoming MSA, MI	Y	43770 FQ	48820 MW	84240 TQ	USBLS	5/15
	Mississippi	Y	24620 FQ	39260 MW	54920 TQ	USBLS	5/15
	Jackson MSA, MS	Y	33420 FQ	47930 MW	126350 TQ	USBLS	5/15
	Missouri	Y	129600 FQ	135240 MW	147000 TQ	USBLS	5/15
	Kansas City MSA, MO-KS	Y	60600 FQ	135230 MW	147010 TQ	USBLS	5/15
	St. Louis MSA, MO-IL	Y	135220 FQ	147000 MW	164770 TQ	USBLS	5/15
	Montana	Y	31800 FQ	44550 MW	60090 TQ	USBLS	5/15
	Nevada	Y	136000 FQ	166140 MW		USBLS	5/15
	Las Vegas-Henderson-Paradise MSA, NV	Y	143850 FQ	167810 MW		USBLS	5/15
	New Jersey	Y	141840 FQ	166870 MW	179140 TQ	USBLS	5/15
	Camden PMSA, NJ	Y	143540 FQ	166870 MW	182710 TQ	USBLS	5/15
	Newark PMSA, NJ-PA	Y	141290 FQ	166870 MW	177550 TQ	USBLS	5/15
	Trenton MSA, NJ	Y	94560 FQ	170170 MW		USBLS	5/15
	New Mexico	Y	17990 FQ	22940 MW	50150 TQ	USBLS	5/15
	New York	Y	132650 AE	154490 MW	166060 AEX	NYBLS	1/16-3/16
	Buffalo-Cheektowaga-Niagara Falls MSA, NY	Y	134910 FQ	147280 MW	161130 TQ	USBLS	5/15
	Nassau County-Suffolk County PMSA, NY	Y	138620 FQ	158430 MW	182840 TQ	USBLS	5/15
	New York-Jersey City-White Plains PMSA, NY-NJ	Y	142770 FQ	166860 MW	183120 TQ	USBLS	5/15
	Rochester MSA, NY	Y	134550 FQ	145740 MW	157480 TQ	USBLS	5/15
	Charlotte-Concord-Gastonia MSA, NC-SC	Y	41300 FQ	57550 MW	112950 TQ	USBLS	5/15
	North Dakota	Y	137160 FQ	137170 MW	141130 TQ	USBLS	5/15
	Ohio	Y	42950 FQ	67960 MW	103290 TQ	USBLS	5/15
	Cincinnati MSA, OH-KY-IN	Y	68250 FQ	96680 MW	134800 TQ	USBLS	5/15
	Cleveland-Elyria MSA, OH	Y	34240 FQ	45310 MW	80040 TQ	USBLS	5/15
	Columbus MSA, OH	Y	61280 FQ	66350 MW	83340 TQ	USBLS	5/15
	Oklahoma	Y	37510 FQ	54560 MW	125500 TQ	USBLS	5/15
	Oklahoma City MSA, OK	Y	37760 FQ	55020 MW	127750 TQ	USBLS	5/15
	Tulsa MSA, OK	Y	41370 FQ	75030 MW	126920 TQ	USBLS	5/15

AE	Average entry wage	AWR	Average wage range	H	Hourly	LR	Low end range	MTC	Median total compensation	TCC	Total cash compensation
AEX	Average experienced wage	B	Biweekly	HI	Highest wage paid	M	Monthly	MCC	Median cash compensation	TQ	Third quartile wage
ATC	Average total compensation	D	Daily	HR	High end range	MCC	Median cash compensation	MWR	Median wage range	W	Weekly
AW	Average wage paid	FQ	First quartile wage	LO	Lowest wage paid	ME	Median entry wage	S	See annotated source	Y	Yearly

Occupation/Type/Industry	Location	Per	Low	Mid	High	Source	Date
Judge, Magistrate Judge, and Magistrate	Oregon	H	61.40 FQ	61.41 MW	61.41 TQ	ORBLS	2016
	Portland-Vancouver-Hillsboro MSA, OR-WA	Y	125880 FQ	125890 MW	125900 TQ	USBLS	5/15
	Pennsylvania	Y	51000 FQ	58310 MW	69100 TQ	USBLS	5/15
	Rhode Island	Y	115620 FQ	158290 AW		USBLS	5/15
	Providence-Warwick MSA, RI-MA	Y	123810 FQ	159170 AW		USBLS	5/15
	South Carolina	Y	30360 FQ	61190 MW	97940 TQ	USBLS	5/15
	Charleston-North Charleston MSA, SC	Y	21510 FQ	33350 MW	86290 TQ	USBLS	5/15
	Columbia MSA, SC	Y	45300 FQ	89020 MW	138450 TQ	USBLS	5/15
	Greenville-Anderson-Mauldin MSA, SC	Y	46480 FQ	69490 MW	119480 TQ	USBLS	5/15
	South Dakota	Y	81210 FQ	92480 MW	111600 TQ	USBLS	5/15
	Tennessee	Y	36890 FQ	114290 MW	181440 TQ	USBLS	5/15
	Knoxville MSA, TN	Y	56100 FQ	99430 MW	160640 TQ	USBLS	5/15
	Memphis MSA, TN-MS-AR	Y	34370 FQ	84660 MW	142270 TQ	USBLS	5/15
	Nashville-Davidson–Murfreesboro–Franklin MSA, TN	Y	39240 FQ	167180 MW		USBLS	5/15
	Texas	Y	35490 FQ	80220 MW	141590 TQ	USBLS	5/15
	Austin-Round Rock MSA, TX	Y	39260 FQ	110950 MW	141590 TQ	USBLS	5/15
	Dallas-Plano-Irving PMSA, TX	Y	48790 FQ	122810 MW	142870 TQ	USBLS	5/15
	Fort Worth-Arlington PMSA, TX	Y	63030 FQ	100060 MW	141590 TQ	USBLS	5/15
	Houston-The Woodlands-Sugar Land MSA, TX	Y	55130 FQ	118670 MW	141600 TQ	USBLS	5/15
	San Antonio-New Braunfels MSA, TX	Y	40400 FQ	86250 MW	141590 TQ	USBLS	5/15
	Utah	Y	52380 FQ	81530 MW	112290 TQ	USBLS	5/15
	Vermont	Y	66850 FQ	136910 MW	136920 TQ	USBLS	5/15
	Washington	H	38.56 FQ	53.03 MW	71.02 TQ	WABLS	3/16
	Seattle-Bellevue-Everett PMSA, WA	H	31.40 FQ	53.39 MW	67.58 TQ	WABLS	3/16
	Tacoma-Lakewood PMSA, WA	H	38.57 FQ	50.00 MW	60.49 TQ	WABLS	3/16
	West Virginia	Y	55200 FQ	60780 MW	111390 TQ	USBLS	5/15
	Huntington-Ashland MSA, WV-KY-OH	Y	51770 FQ	60360 MW	119760 TQ	USBLS	5/15
	Wisconsin	Y	28640 FQ	67430 MW	119050 TQ	USBLS	5/15
	Wyoming	Y	71560 FQ	111320 MW	136330 TQ	USBLS	5/15
Judicial Law Clerk	Alabama	Y	26278 AE	41476 AW	49070 AEX	ALBLS	6/16
	Arizona	Y	34710 FQ	38810 MW	48630 TQ	USBLS	5/15
	Phoenix-Mesa-Scottsdale MSA, AZ	Y	35560 FQ	41100 MW	52710 TQ	USBLS	5/15
	Tucson MSA, AZ	Y	34370 FQ	37700 MW	44850 TQ	USBLS	5/15
	Arkansas	Y	22700 FQ	51090 MW	57780 TQ	USBLS	5/15
	Little Rock-North Little Rock-Conway MSA, AR	Y	51090 FQ	52490 MW	59650 TQ	USBLS	5/15
	California	H	21.15 FQ	24.29 MW	30.07 TQ	CABLS	1/16-3/16
	Los Angeles-Long Beach-Glendale PMSA, CA	H	23.06 FQ	29.13 MW	34.19 TQ	CABLS	1/16-3/16
	Oakland-Hayward-Berkeley PMSA, CA	H	22.60 FQ	28.34 MW	38.39 TQ	CABLS	1/16-3/16
	Sacramento–Roseville–Arden-Arcade MSA, CA	H	26.66 FQ	28.48 MW	30.23 TQ	CABLS	1/16-3/16
	Colorado	Y	40330 FQ	44510 MW	52940 TQ	USBLS	5/15
	Denver-Aurora-Lakewood MSA, CO	Y	40330 FQ	50190 MW	52940 TQ	USBLS	5/15
	Connecticut	Y		77020 MW		CTBLS	1/16-3/16
	Wilmington PMSA, DE-MD-NJ	Y	38580 FQ	53870 MW	54220 TQ	USBLS	5/15
	Washington-Arlington-Alexandria PMSA, DC-VA-MD-WV	Y	47860 FQ	54090 MW	67410 TQ	USBLS	5/15
	Florida	H	16.64 AE	22.28 MW	24.93 AEX	FLBLS	7/16-9/16
	Georgia	Y	41090 FQ	48690 MW	59250 TQ	USBLS	5/15
	Atlanta-Sandy Springs-Roswell MSA, GA	Y	44510 FQ	53030 MW	61740 TQ	USBLS	5/15
	Augusta-Richmond County MSA, GA-SC	Y	30770 FQ	35520 MW	40140 TQ	USBLS	5/15

AE	Average entry wage	**AWR**	Average wage range	**H**	Hourly	**LR**	Low end range	**MTC**	Median total compensation	**TCC**	Total cash compensation
AEX	Average experienced wage	**B**	Biweekly	**HI**	Highest wage paid	**M**	Monthly	**MW**	Median wage paid	**TQ**	Third quartile wage
ATC	Average total compensation	**D**	Daily	**HR**	High end range	**MCC**	Median cash compensation	**MWR**	Median wage range	**W**	Weekly
AW	Average wage paid	**FQ**	First quartile wage	**LO**	Lowest wage paid	**ME**	Median entry wage	**S**	See annotated source	**Y**	Yearly

Occupation/Type/Industry	Location	Per	Low	Mid	High	Source	Date
Judicial Law Clerk	Idaho	Y	41090 FQ	51520 MW	56320 TQ	USBLS	5/15
	Illinois	Y	43290 FQ	81010 MW	92480 TQ	USBLS	5/15
	Indiana	Y	24530 FQ	29950 MW	43890 TQ	USBLS	5/15
	Kansas	Y	27640 FQ	33260 MW	40420 TQ	USBLS	5/15
	Louisiana	Y	35050 FQ	42580 MW	51440 TQ	USBLS	5/15
	Baton Rouge MSA, LA	Y	41460 FQ	45860 MW	51320 TQ	USBLS	5/15
	Maine	Y	45740 FQ	45750 MW	47520 TQ	USBLS	5/15
	Maryland	Y	44580 AE	65199 MW	75509 AEX	MDBLS	4/16
	Baltimore-Columbia-Towson MSA, MD	Y	48850 FQ	61920 MW	78280 TQ	USBLS	5/15
	Salisbury MSA, MD-DE	Y	47880 FQ	54210 MW	67990 TQ	USBLS	5/15
	Michigan	Y	34870 FQ	41920 MW	48490 TQ	USBLS	5/15
	Detroit-Dearborn-Livonia PMSA, MI	Y	32240 FQ	37990 MW	44380 TQ	USBLS	5/15
	Minnesota	Y	47459 FQ	48669 MW	48679 TQ	MNBLS	1/16-3/16
	Mississippi	Y	19810 FQ	30120 MW	42660 TQ	USBLS	5/15
	Missouri	Y	46120 FQ	50110 MW	52150 TQ	USBLS	5/15
	Kansas City MSA, MO-KS	Y	48230 FQ	52150 MW	52160 TQ	USBLS	5/15
	Montana	Y	32410 FQ	37680 MW	45560 TQ	USBLS	5/15
	Nevada	Y	53290 FQ	60100 MW	70530 TQ	USBLS	5/15
	New Jersey	Y	46620 FQ	46630 MW	51280 TQ	USBLS	5/15
	Camden PMSA, NJ	Y	46620 FQ	46630 MW	46630 TQ	USBLS	5/15
	Newark PMSA, NJ-PA	Y	46620 FQ	46630 MW	55930 TQ	USBLS	5/15
	New York	Y	82540 AE	131370 MW	138930 AEX	NYBLS	1/16-3/16
	New York-Jersey City-White Plains PMSA, NY-NJ	Y	46620 FQ	46630 MW	68040 TQ	USBLS	5/15
	North Dakota	Y	63740 FQ	66150 MW	75540 TQ	USBLS	5/15
	Ohio	Y	31900 FQ	43050 MW	58750 TQ	USBLS	5/15
	Cleveland-Elyria MSA, OH	Y	39400 FQ	47570 MW	66200 TQ	USBLS	5/15
	Columbus MSA, OH	Y	28530 FQ	43020 MW	90740 TQ	USBLS	5/15
	Oklahoma	Y	28820 FQ	41830 MW	53100 TQ	USBLS	5/15
	Oregon	H	23.29 FQ	23.30 MW	24.46 TQ	ORBLS	2016
	Pennsylvania	Y	31060 FQ	40240 MW	50400 TQ	USBLS	5/15
	Allentown-Bethlehem-Easton MSA, PA-NJ	Y	45300 FQ	53290 MW	60680 TQ	USBLS	5/15
	Montgomery County-Bucks County-Chester County PMSA, PA	Y	32140 FQ	42820 MW	50790 TQ	USBLS	5/15
	Philadelphia PMSA, PA	Y	38620 FQ	45020 MW	52900 TQ	USBLS	5/15
	Pittsburgh MSA, PA	Y	34210 FQ	41050 MW	56420 TQ	USBLS	5/15
	South Carolina	Y	26320 FQ	32370 MW	39660 TQ	USBLS	5/15
	Tennessee	Y	32350 FQ	52740 MW	64180 TQ	USBLS	5/15
	Nashville-Davidson– Murfreesboro–Franklin MSA, TN	Y	45120 FQ	57210 MW	72620 TQ	USBLS	5/15
	Texas	Y	31790 FQ	43010 MW	54370 TQ	USBLS	5/15
	Austin-Round Rock MSA, TX	Y	36540 FQ	43010 MW	52200 TQ	USBLS	5/15
	Dallas-Plano-Irving PMSA, TX	Y	31620 FQ	46200 MW	57710 TQ	USBLS	5/15
	Fort Worth-Arlington PMSA, TX	Y	43440 FQ	53470 MW	61200 TQ	USBLS	5/15
	Houston-The Woodlands- Sugar Land MSA, TX	Y	47010 FQ	53010 MW	60980 TQ	USBLS	5/15
	Utah	Y	32350 FQ	33390 MW	37710 TQ	USBLS	5/15
	Ogden-Clearfield MSA, UT	Y	32660 FQ	34490 MW	40340 TQ	USBLS	5/15
	Provo-Orem MSA, UT	Y	29540 FQ	33760 MW	37010 TQ	USBLS	5/15
	Salt Lake City MSA, UT	Y	32360 FQ	33200 MW	39240 TQ	USBLS	5/15
	Virginia	Y	42380 FQ	50160 MW	58380 TQ	USBLS	5/15
	Washington	H	22.65 FQ	25.59 MW	36.92 TQ	WABLS	3/16
	Seattle-Bellevue-Everett PMSA, WA	H	21.85 FQ	24.49 MW	32.75 TQ	WABLS	3/16
	Tacoma-Lakewood PMSA, WA	H	23.76 FQ	32.38 MW	40.90 TQ	WABLS	3/16
	West Virginia	Y	44890 FQ	51810 MW	57760 TQ	USBLS	5/15
	Wisconsin	Y	35100 FQ	40100 MW	47780 TQ	USBLS	5/15
	Milwaukee-Waukesha-West Allis MSA, WI	Y	34520 FQ	38220 MW	43450 TQ	USBLS	5/15
Juvenile Court Counselor							
State Government	North Carolina	Y	38125 LO		60604 HI	NCGOV	7/1/16
Juvenile Justice Program Coordinator							
Municipal Government	Carlsbad, CA	H	26.16 LO	30.20 MW	34.23 HI	CCCA01	6/28/16

AE	Average entry wage	AWR	Average wage range	H	Hourly
AEX	Average experienced wage	B	Biweekly	HI	Highest wage paid
ATC	Average total compensation	D	Daily	HR	High end range
AW	Average wage paid	FQ	First quartile wage	LO	Lowest wage paid

LR	Low end range	MTC	Median total compensation	TCC	Total cash compensation
M	Monthly	MW	Median wage paid	TQ	Third quartile wage
MCC	Median cash compensation	MWR	Median wage range	W	Weekly
ME	Median entry wage	S	See annotated source	Y	Yearly

Occupation/Type/Industry	Location	Per	Low	Mid	High	Source	Date
K9 Police Officer							
Municipal Government	Eureka, CA	Y		61908 ᴬᵂ		CACIT	6/28/16
Municipal Government	Seattle, WA	H	34.46 ʟᴏ		44.73 ʜɪ	CSSS	1/1/14
Kennel Attendant							
Police Department, Municipal Government	Burbank, CA	Y		39275 ᴬᵂ		CACIT	6/28/16
KGB Executive Director							
County Government	Forsyth County, GA	Y	44932 ʟᴏ		66077 ʜɪ	GACTY04	2016
County Government	Walton County, GA	Y	48140 ʟᴏ		72210 ʜɪ	GACTY04	2016
Kindergarten Teacher							
Except Special Education	Alabama	Y	37052 ᴬᴱ	47602 ᴬᵂ	52872 ᴬᴱˣ	ALBLS	6/16
Except Special Education	Birmingham-Hoover MSA, AL	Y	37603 ᴬᴱ	47776 ᴬᵂ	52862 ᴬᴱˣ	ALBLS	6/16
Except Special Education	Alaska	Y	55970 ꜰǫ	66820 ᴹᵂ	86060 ᵀǫ	USBLS	5/15
Except Special Education	Arizona	Y	34570 ꜰǫ	40230 ᴹᵂ	47410 ᵀǫ	USBLS	5/15
Except Special Education	Phoenix-Mesa-Scottsdale MSA, AZ	Y	35240 ꜰǫ	41300 ᴹᵂ	47980 ᵀǫ	USBLS	5/15
Except Special Education	Tucson MSA, AZ	Y	32240 ꜰǫ	36510 ᴹᵂ	42640 ᵀǫ	USBLS	5/15
Except Special Education	Arkansas	Y	39660 ꜰǫ	45390 ᴹᵂ	51960 ᵀǫ	USBLS	5/15
Except Special Education	Little Rock-North Little Rock-Conway MSA, AR	Y	36730 ꜰǫ	44540 ᴹᵂ	52320 ᵀǫ	USBLS	5/15
Except Special Education	California	Y		64968 ᴬᵂ		CABLS	1/16-3/16
Except Special Education	Anaheim-Santa Ana-Irvine PMSA, CA	Y		67301 ᴬᵂ		CABLS	1/16-3/16
Except Special Education	Los Angeles-Long Beach-Glendale PMSA, CA	Y		63162 ᴬᵂ		CABLS	1/16-3/16
Except Special Education	Oakland-Hayward-Berkeley PMSA, CA	Y		61194 ᴬᵂ		CABLS	1/16-3/16
Except Special Education	Riverside-San Bernardino-Ontario MSA, CA	Y		67859 ᴬᵂ		CABLS	1/16-3/16
Except Special Education	Sacramento–Roseville–Arden-Arcade MSA, CA	Y		61955 ᴬᵂ		CABLS	1/16-3/16
Except Special Education	San Diego-Carlsbad MSA, CA	Y		61468 ᴬᵂ		CABLS	1/16-3/16
Except Special Education	San Francisco-Redwood City-South San Francisco PMSA, CA	Y		71420 ᴬᵂ		CABLS	1/16-3/16
Except Special Education	Colorado	Y	37970 ꜰǫ	46190 ᴹᵂ	58050 ᵀǫ	USBLS	5/15
Except Special Education	Denver-Aurora-Lakewood MSA, CO	Y	39340 ꜰǫ	48770 ᴹᵂ	62340 ᵀǫ	USBLS	5/15
Except Special Education	Connecticut	Y		72080 ᴹᵂ		CTBLS	1/16-3/16
Except Special Education	Bridgeport-Stamford-Norwalk MSA, CT	Y	60060 ꜰǫ	76680 ᴹᵂ	92660 ᵀǫ	USBLS	5/15
Except Special Education	Hartford-West Hartford-East Hartford MSA, CT	Y	52160 ꜰǫ	68850 ᴹᵂ	87290 ᵀǫ	USBLS	5/15
Except Special Education	Delaware	Y	50520 ꜰǫ	58540 ᴹᵂ	70180 ᵀǫ	USBLS	5/15
Except Special Education	Wilmington PMSA, DE-MD-NJ	Y	49330 ꜰǫ	60070 ᴹᵂ	73950 ᵀǫ	USBLS	5/15
Except Special Education	District of Columbia	Y	34590 ꜰǫ	52010 ᴹᵂ	61130 ᵀǫ	USBLS	5/15
Except Special Education	Washington-Arlington-Alexandria PMSA, DC-VA-MD-WV	Y	49480 ꜰǫ	66470 ᴹᵂ	83450 ᵀǫ	USBLS	5/15
Except Special Education	Florida	Y	36432 ᴬᴱ	46762 ᴹᵂ	53760 ᴬᴱˣ	FLBLS	7/16-9/16
Except Special Education	Fort Lauderdale-Pompano Beach-Deerfield Beach PMSA, FL	Y	29471 ᴬᴱ	46011 ᴹᵂ	54995 ᴬᴱˣ	FLBLS	7/16-9/16
Except Special Education	Miami-Miami Beach-Kendall PMSA, FL	Y	35935 ᴬᴱ	46843 ᴹᵂ	53922 ᴬᴱˣ	FLBLS	7/16-9/16
Except Special Education	Orlando-Kissimmee-Sanford MSA, FL	Y	37241 ᴬᴱ	46674 ᴹᵂ	52823 ᴬᴱˣ	FLBLS	7/16-9/16
Except Special Education	Tampa-St. Petersburg-Clearwater MSA, FL	Y	34402 ᴬᴱ	44429 ᴹᵂ	50969 ᴬᴱˣ	FLBLS	7/16-9/16
Except Special Education	Georgia	Y	44470 ꜰǫ	53840 ᴹᵂ	61650 ᵀǫ	USBLS	5/15
Except Special Education	Atlanta-Sandy Springs-Roswell MSA, GA	Y	44820 ꜰǫ	53750 ᴹᵂ	61430 ᵀǫ	USBLS	5/15
Except Special Education	Augusta-Richmond County MSA, GA-SC	Y	41830 ꜰǫ	53950 ᴹᵂ	62830 ᵀǫ	USBLS	5/15
Except Special Education	Hawaii	Y	37920 ꜰǫ	44350 ᴹᵂ	50880 ᵀǫ	USBLS	5/15
Except Special Education	Urban Honolulu MSA, HI	Y	38200 ꜰǫ	44900 ᴹᵂ	52900 ᵀǫ	USBLS	5/15
Except Special Education	Idaho	Y	36540 ꜰǫ	44070 ᴹᵂ	54120 ᵀǫ	USBLS	5/15
Except Special Education	Boise City MSA, ID	Y	40170 ꜰǫ	48230 ᴹᵂ	57700 ᵀǫ	USBLS	5/15
Except Special Education	Illinois	Y	40400 ꜰǫ	48710 ᴹᵂ	62550 ᵀǫ	USBLS	5/15

AE Average entry wage	**AWR** Average wage range	**H** Hourly	**LR** Low end range	**MTC** Median total compensation	**TCC** Total cash compensation
AEX Average experienced wage	**B** Biweekly	**HI** Highest wage paid	**M** Monthly	**MW** Median wage paid	**TQ** Third quartile wage
ATC Average total compensation	**D** Daily	**HR** High end range	**MCC** Median cash compensation	**MWR** Median wage range	**W** Weekly
AW Average wage paid	**FQ** First quartile wage	**LO** Lowest wage paid	**ME** Median entry wage	**S** See annotated source	**Y** Yearly

Kindergarten Teacher

Occupation/Type/Industry	Location	Per	Low	Mid	High	Source	Date
Except Special Education	Chicago-Naperville-Arlington Heights PMSA, IL	Y	41600 FQ	50200 MW	68360 TQ	USBLS	5/15
Except Special Education	Lake County-Kenosha County PMSA, IL-WI	Y	42810 FQ	54110 MW	71470 TQ	USBLS	5/15
Except Special Education	Indiana	Y	36620 FQ	44970 MW	56220 TQ	USBLS	5/15
Except Special Education	Gary PMSA, IN	Y	36080 FQ	44270 MW	57380 TQ	USBLS	5/15
Except Special Education	Indianapolis-Carmel-Anderson MSA, IN	Y	36890 FQ	44680 MW	56760 TQ	USBLS	5/15
Except Special Education	Iowa	Y	40020 FQ	50030 MW	57570 TQ	USBLS	5/15
Except Special Education	Des Moines-West Des Moines MSA, IA	Y	44370 FQ	53070 MW	58270 TQ	USBLS	5/15
Except Special Education	Kansas	Y	39900 FQ	44880 MW	49910 TQ	USBLS	5/15
Except Special Education	Wichita MSA, KS	Y	41010 FQ	45770 MW	50570 TQ	USBLS	5/15
Except Special Education	Kentucky	Y	44180 FQ	52370 MW	59700 TQ	USBLS	5/15
Except Special Education	Louisville-Jefferson County MSA, KY-IN	Y	49760 FQ	58910 MW	70010 TQ	USBLS	5/15
Except Special Education	Louisiana	Y	42900 FQ	47340 MW	53230 TQ	USBLS	5/15
Except Special Education	Baton Rouge MSA, LA	Y	43720 FQ	48540 MW	55610 TQ	USBLS	5/15
Except Special Education	New Orleans-Metairie MSA, LA	Y	43240 FQ	48170 MW	54880 TQ	USBLS	5/15
Except Special Education	Maine	Y	38580 FQ	49960 MW	59870 TQ	USBLS	5/15
Except Special Education	Portland-South Portland MSA, ME	Y	46390 FQ	56920 MW	67320 TQ	USBLS	5/15
Except Special Education	Maryland	Y	40110 AE	58822 MW	68178 AEX	MDBLS	4/16
Except Special Education	Baltimore-Columbia-Towson MSA, MD	Y	45740 FQ	55320 MW	69320 TQ	USBLS	5/15
Except Special Education	Salisbury MSA, MD-DE	Y	49920 FQ	56510 MW	64360 TQ	USBLS	5/15
Except Special Education	Massachusetts	Y	53780 FQ	67170 MW	80750 TQ	USBLS	5/15
Except Special Education	Boston-Cambridge-Newton NECTA, MA	Y	53210 FQ	67880 MW	84860 TQ	USBLS	5/15
Except Special Education	Worcester MSA, MA-CT	Y	51090 FQ	60470 MW	72520 TQ	USBLS	5/15
Except Special Education	Michigan	Y	37510 FQ	52460 MW	67690 TQ	USBLS	5/15
Except Special Education	Detroit-Dearborn-Livonia PMSA, MI	Y	34180 FQ	44880 MW	61100 TQ	USBLS	5/15
Except Special Education	Grand Rapids-Wyoming MSA, MI	Y	37420 FQ	60940 MW	72950 TQ	USBLS	5/15
Except Special Education	Minnesota	Y	39828 FQ	53538 MW	68729 TQ	MNBLS	1/16-3/16
Except Special Education	Minneapolis-St. Paul-Bloomington MSA, MN-WI	Y	41794 FQ	56441 MW	72358 TQ	MNBLS	1/16-3/16
Except Special Education	Mississippi	Y	34410 FQ	39800 MW	47240 TQ	USBLS	5/15
Except Special Education	Jackson MSA, MS	Y	33230 FQ	38280 MW	45460 TQ	USBLS	5/15
Except Special Education	Missouri	Y	36420 FQ	45070 MW	56770 TQ	USBLS	5/15
Except Special Education	Kansas City MSA, MO-KS	Y	36350 FQ	44170 MW	55540 TQ	USBLS	5/15
Except Special Education	St. Louis MSA, MO-IL	Y	40760 FQ	49540 MW	59720 TQ	USBLS	5/15
Except Special Education	Montana	Y	34680 FQ	44230 MW	55290 TQ	USBLS	5/15
Except Special Education	Nebraska	Y	41430 FQ	47910 MW	56980 TQ	NEBLS	7/16-9/16
Except Special Education	Omaha-Council Bluffs MSA, NE-IA	Y	41955 FQ	47590 MW	55230 TQ	NEBLS	7/16-9/16
Except Special Education	Nevada	Y	41090 FQ	48700 MW	59070 TQ	USBLS	5/15
Except Special Education	Las Vegas-Henderson-Paradise MSA, NV	Y	41260 FQ	48490 MW	59120 TQ	USBLS	5/15
Except Special Education	New Hampshire	Y	32709 AE	52271 MW	59371 AEX	NHBLS	6/16
Except Special Education	Manchester NECTA, NH	Y	28082 AE	51066 MW	59599 AEX	NHBLS	6/16
Except Special Education	Nashua NECTA, NH-MA	Y	38740 FQ	52570 MW	58560 TQ	USBLS	5/15
Except Special Education	New Jersey	Y	53440 FQ	61350 MW	77150 TQ	USBLS	5/15
Except Special Education	Camden PMSA, NJ	Y	52540 FQ	60110 MW	73910 TQ	USBLS	5/15
Except Special Education	Newark PMSA, NJ-PA	Y	55060 FQ	63750 MW	79260 TQ	USBLS	5/15
Except Special Education	Trenton MSA, NJ	Y	44970 FQ	57840 MW	73700 TQ	USBLS	5/15
Except Special Education	New Mexico	Y	43550 FQ	52870 MW	69540 TQ	USBLS	5/15
Except Special Education	Albuquerque MSA, NM	Y	45970 FQ	60560 MW	80920 TQ	USBLS	5/15
Except Special Education	New York	Y	42330 AE	60990 MW	82610 AEX	NYBLS	1/16-3/16
Except Special Education	Buffalo-Cheektowaga-Niagara Falls MSA, NY	Y	46840 FQ	59800 MW	73720 TQ	USBLS	5/15
Except Special Education	Nassau County-Suffolk County PMSA, NY	Y	88320 FQ	108190 MW	121360 TQ	USBLS	5/15
Except Special Education	New York-Jersey City-White Plains PMSA, NY-NJ	Y	48760 FQ	57850 MW	77140 TQ	USBLS	5/15
Except Special Education	Rochester MSA, NY	Y	48510 FQ	56800 MW	66800 TQ	USBLS	5/15
Except Special Education	North Carolina	Y	35150 FQ	39930 MW	47680 TQ	USBLS	5/15
Except Special Education	Burlington MSA, NC	Y	34280 FQ	37300 MW	41560 TQ	USBLS	5/15

AE   Average entry wage   AWR Average wage range   H   Hourly   LR   Low end range   MTC Median total compensation   TCC Total cash compensation
AEX Average experienced wage   B   Biweekly   HI   Highest wage paid   M   Monthly   MW   Median wage paid   TQ   Third quartile wage
ATC Average total compensation   D   Daily   HR   High end range   MCC Median cash compensation   MWR Median wage range   W   Weekly
AW   Average wage paid   FQ   First quartile wage   LO   Lowest wage paid   ME   Median entry wage   S   See annotated source   Y   Yearly

Occupation/Type/Industry	Location	Per	Low	Mid	High	Source	Date

Kindergarten Teacher

Occupation/Type/Industry	Location	Per	Low	Mid	High	Source	Date
Except Special Education	Charlotte-Concord-Gastonia MSA, NC-SC	Y	35580 FQ	41660 MW	49700 TQ	USBLS	5/15
Except Special Education	Raleigh MSA, NC	Y	36920 FQ	43960 MW	53740 TQ	USBLS	5/15
Except Special Education	North Dakota	Y	37700 FQ	44360 MW	51840 TQ	USBLS	5/15
Except Special Education	Fargo MSA, ND-MN	Y	37330 FQ	43500 MW	50410 TQ	USBLS	5/15
Except Special Education	Ohio	Y	40920 FQ	52470 MW	67770 TQ	USBLS	5/15
Except Special Education	Cincinnati MSA, OH-KY-IN	Y	43600 FQ	54930 MW	67500 TQ	USBLS	5/15
Except Special Education	Cleveland-Elyria MSA, OH	Y	35000 FQ	47560 MW	69370 TQ	USBLS	5/15
Except Special Education	Columbus MSA, OH	Y	41570 FQ	50810 MW	69070 TQ	USBLS	5/15
Except Special Education	Oklahoma	Y	34470 FQ	38750 MW	47400 TQ	USBLS	5/15
Except Special Education	Oklahoma City MSA, OK	Y	34200 FQ	38100 MW	44670 TQ	USBLS	5/15
Except Special Education	Tulsa MSA, OK	Y	36300 FQ	49040 MW	58930 TQ	USBLS	5/15
Except Special Education	Oregon	Y	45403 FQ	57721 MW	69791 TQ	ORBLS	2016
Except Special Education	Portland-Vancouver-Hillsboro MSA, OR-WA	Y	43700 FQ	56280 MW	69510 TQ	USBLS	5/15
Except Special Education	Pennsylvania	Y	41150 FQ	51050 MW	62530 TQ	USBLS	5/15
Except Special Education	Allentown-Bethlehem-Easton MSA, PA-NJ	Y	39950 FQ	54430 MW	64080 TQ	USBLS	5/15
Except Special Education	Harrisburg-Carlisle MSA, PA	Y	40740 FQ	48400 MW	58690 TQ	USBLS	5/15
Except Special Education	Montgomery County-Bucks County-Chester County PMSA, PA	Y	28700 FQ	53020 MW	78820 TQ	USBLS	5/15
Except Special Education	Philadelphia PMSA, PA	Y	43460 FQ	53260 MW	67310 TQ	USBLS	5/15
Except Special Education	Pittsburgh MSA, PA	Y	41750 FQ	51010 MW	59030 TQ	USBLS	5/15
Except Special Education	Rhode Island	Y	54680 FQ	69870 MW	78930 TQ	USBLS	5/15
Except Special Education	Providence-Warwick MSA, RI-MA	Y	54900 FQ	69850 MW	79070 TQ	USBLS	5/15
Except Special Education	South Carolina	Y	40050 FQ	51150 MW	60140 TQ	USBLS	5/15
Except Special Education	Charleston-North Charleston MSA, SC	Y	37890 FQ	49820 MW	60660 TQ	USBLS	5/15
Except Special Education	Columbia MSA, SC	Y	40310 FQ	49900 MW	59100 TQ	USBLS	5/15
Except Special Education	Greenville-Anderson-Mauldin MSA, SC	Y	45190 FQ	53770 MW	60210 TQ	USBLS	5/15
Except Special Education	South Dakota	Y	34230 FQ	38560 MW	46230 TQ	USBLS	5/15
Except Special Education	Sioux Falls MSA, SD	Y	34950 FQ	40690 MW	49850 TQ	USBLS	5/15
Except Special Education	Tennessee	Y	40490 FQ	47950 MW	58180 TQ	USBLS	5/15
Except Special Education	Knoxville MSA, TN	Y	40050 FQ	46330 MW	54020 TQ	USBLS	5/15
Except Special Education	Memphis MSA, TN-MS-AR	Y	30740 FQ	42250 MW	49820 TQ	USBLS	5/15
Except Special Education	Nashville-Davidson–Murfreesboro–Franklin MSA, TN	Y	43230 FQ	55650 MW	66340 TQ	USBLS	5/15
Except Special Education	Texas	Y	43100 FQ	50910 MW	59370 TQ	USBLS	5/15
Except Special Education	Austin-Round Rock MSA, TX	Y	43020 FQ	47060 MW	53020 TQ	USBLS	5/15
Except Special Education	Dallas-Plano-Irving PMSA, TX	Y	44590 FQ	53890 MW	61990 TQ	USBLS	5/15
Except Special Education	Fort Worth-Arlington PMSA, TX	Y	45290 FQ	52830 MW	58500 TQ	USBLS	5/15
Except Special Education	Houston-The Woodlands-Sugar Land MSA, TX	Y	43050 FQ	53780 MW	62510 TQ	USBLS	5/15
Except Special Education	San Antonio-New Braunfels MSA, TX	Y	47130 FQ	53580 MW	58570 TQ	USBLS	5/15
Except Special Education	Utah	Y	33390 FQ	43320 MW	58260 TQ	USBLS	5/15
Except Special Education	Provo-Orem MSA, UT	Y	33800 FQ	43110 MW	49610 TQ	USBLS	5/15
Except Special Education	Salt Lake City MSA, UT	Y	30110 FQ	39270 MW	65820 TQ	USBLS	5/15
Except Special Education	Vermont	Y	43850 FQ	53080 MW	62750 TQ	USBLS	5/15
Except Special Education	Burlington-South Burlington MSA, VT	Y	51470 FQ	59380 MW	74440 TQ	USBLS	5/15
Except Special Education	Virginia	Y	45630 FQ	57100 MW	72850 TQ	USBLS	5/15
Except Special Education	Richmond MSA, VA	Y	46640 FQ	55920 MW	62800 TQ	USBLS	5/15
Except Special Education	Virginia Beach-Norfolk-Newport News MSA, VA-NC	Y	47880 FQ	58680 MW	73360 TQ	USBLS	5/15
Except Special Education	Washington	Y		55746 AW		WABLS	3/16
Except Special Education	Seattle-Bellevue-Everett PMSA, WA	Y		56355 AW		WABLS	3/16
Except Special Education	Tacoma-Lakewood PMSA, WA	Y		59683 AW		WABLS	3/16
Except Special Education	West Virginia	Y	40400 FQ	47880 MW	55550 TQ	USBLS	5/15
Except Special Education	Huntington-Ashland MSA, WV-KY-OH	Y	40140 FQ	47700 MW	55900 TQ	USBLS	5/15
Except Special Education	Wisconsin	Y	39610 FQ	48700 MW	61130 TQ	USBLS	5/15
Except Special Education	Madison MSA, WI	Y	38320 FQ	48630 MW	61800 TQ	USBLS	5/15
Except Special Education	Milwaukee-Waukesha-West Allis MSA, WI	Y	36310 FQ	54440 MW	70760 TQ	USBLS	5/15

AE	Average entry wage	AWR	Average wage range	H	Hourly	LR	Low end range	MTC	Median total compensation	TCC	Total cash compensation
AEX	Average experienced wage	B	Biweekly	HI	Highest wage paid	M	Monthly	MW	Median wage paid	TQ	Third quartile wage
ATC	Average total compensation	D	Daily	HR	High end range	MCC	Median cash compensation	MWR	Median wage range	W	Weekly
AW	Average wage paid	FQ	First quartile wage	LO	Lowest wage paid	ME	Median entry wage	S	See annotated source	Y	Yearly

Occupation/Type/Industry	Location	Per	Low	Mid	High	Source	Date
Kindergarten Teacher							
Except Special Education	Wyoming	Y	49260 FQ	56190 MW	63070 TQ	USBLS	5/15
Except Special Education	Puerto Rico	Y	16900 FQ	18420 MW	20640 TQ	USBLS	5/15
Except Special Education	San Juan-Carolina-Caguas MSA, PR	Y	16810 FQ	18260 MW	20230 TQ	USBLS	5/15
Except Special Education	Virgin Islands	Y	18830 FQ	22600 MW	29230 TQ	USBLS	5/15
Except Special Education	Guam	Y	29540 FQ	48020 MW	57380 TQ	USBLS	5/15
Labor Market Analyst							
State Government	North Carolina	Y	34190 LO		53063 HI	NCGOV	7/1/16
Labor Relations Mediator							
Employee Relations Board, State Government	Ohio	H	31.45 LO		48.09 HI	OHGOV	2015
Labor Relations Specialist	Alabama	Y	17496 AE	53780 AW	71921 AEX	ALBLS	6/16
	Birmingham-Hoover MSA, AL	Y	47425 AE	80562 AW	97135 AEX	ALBLS	6/16
	Montgomery MSA, AL	Y	17588 AE	30882 AW	37534 AEX	ALBLS	6/16
	Alaska	Y	77780 FQ	99800 MW	115870 TQ	USBLS	5/15
	Anchorage MSA, AK	Y	66210 FQ	100120 MW	119940 TQ	USBLS	5/15
	Arizona	Y	40310 FQ	47280 MW	72090 TQ	USBLS	5/15
	Phoenix-Mesa-Scottsdale MSA, AZ	Y	41660 FQ	47860 MW	73240 TQ	USBLS	5/15
	Tucson MSA, AZ	Y	19210 FQ	23770 MW	56560 TQ	USBLS	5/15
	Arkansas	Y	21180 FQ	43080 MW	75990 TQ	USBLS	5/15
	Little Rock-North Little Rock-Conway MSA, AR	Y	36750 FQ	51430 MW	83050 TQ	USBLS	5/15
	California	H	29.96 FQ	39.84 MW	49.95 TQ	CABLS	1/16-3/16
	Anaheim-Santa Ana-Irvine PMSA, CA	H	19.68 FQ	33.89 MW	44.41 TQ	CABLS	1/16-3/16
	Los Angeles-Long Beach-Glendale PMSA, CA	H	31.87 FQ	44.44 MW	52.67 TQ	CABLS	1/16-3/16
	Oakland-Hayward-Berkeley PMSA, CA	H	30.59 FQ	37.14 MW	48.23 TQ	CABLS	1/16-3/16
	Riverside-San Bernardino-Ontario MSA, CA	H	27.98 FQ	33.89 MW	43.56 TQ	CABLS	1/16-3/16
	Sacramento–Roseville–Arden-Arcade MSA, CA	H	29.30 FQ	36.51 MW	45.49 TQ	CABLS	1/16-3/16
	San Diego-Carlsbad MSA, CA	H	30.01 FQ	39.04 MW	56.21 TQ	CABLS	1/16-3/16
	San Francisco-Redwood City-South San Francisco PMSA, CA	H	31.21 FQ	38.53 MW	49.20 TQ	CABLS	1/16-3/16
	Connecticut	Y		54637 MW		CTBLS	1/16-3/16
	Bridgeport-Stamford-Norwalk MSA, CT	Y	19910 FQ	56470 MW	82900 TQ	USBLS	5/15
	Hartford-West Hartford-East Hartford MSA, CT	Y	39920 FQ	70780 MW	97920 TQ	USBLS	5/15
	Delaware	Y	45790 FQ	63280 MW	74400 TQ	USBLS	5/15
	Wilmington PMSA, DE-MD-NJ	Y	53930 FQ	68100 MW	82320 TQ	USBLS	5/15
	District of Columbia	Y	64040 FQ	83120 MW	97020 TQ	USBLS	5/15
	Washington-Arlington-Alexandria PMSA, DC-VA-MD-WV	Y	52270 FQ	68080 MW	89720 TQ	USBLS	5/15
	Florida	H	14.26 AE	28.79 MW	37.29 AEX	FLBLS	7/16-9/16
	Fort Lauderdale-Pompano Beach-Deerfield Beach PMSA, FL	H	10.42 AE	29.17 MW	36.68 AEX	FLBLS	7/16-9/16
	Miami-Miami Beach-Kendall PMSA, FL	H	18.78 AE	28.47 MW	33.03 AEX	FLBLS	7/16-9/16
	Orlando-Kissimmee-Sanford MSA, FL	H	25.79 AE	37.10 MW	46.97 AEX	FLBLS	7/16-9/16
	Tampa-St. Petersburg-Clearwater MSA, FL	H	13.36 AE	27.03 MW	33.80 AEX	FLBLS	7/16-9/16
	Georgia	Y	43240 FQ	52070 MW	69490 TQ	USBLS	5/15
	Atlanta-Sandy Springs-Roswell MSA, GA	Y	45860 FQ	55430 MW	72680 TQ	USBLS	5/15
	Augusta-Richmond County MSA, GA-SC	Y	49910 FQ	83720 MW	93610 TQ	USBLS	5/15
	Hawaii	Y	51170 FQ	67740 MW	82410 TQ	USBLS	5/15
	Urban Honolulu MSA, HI	Y	50060 FQ	67550 MW	84510 TQ	USBLS	5/15
	Idaho	Y	19330 FQ	59650 MW	76400 TQ	USBLS	5/15

Occupation/Type/Industry	Location	Per	Low	Mid	High	Source	Date
Labor Relations Specialist	Boise City MSA, ID	Y	48940 FQ	63660 MW	72370 TQ	USBLS	5/15
	Illinois	Y	19200 FQ	55100 MW	80210 TQ	USBLS	5/15
	Chicago-Naperville-Arlington Heights PMSA, IL	Y	19810 FQ	59670 MW	88510 TQ	USBLS	5/15
	Lake County-Kenosha County PMSA, IL-WI	Y	18200 FQ	19920 MW	79850 TQ	USBLS	5/15
	Indiana	Y	19910 FQ	47880 MW	71050 TQ	USBLS	5/15
	Gary PMSA, IN	Y	18230 FQ	25920 MW	47410 TQ	USBLS	5/15
	Indianapolis-Carmel-Anderson MSA, IN	Y	42230 FQ	57660 MW	78150 TQ	USBLS	5/15
	Terre Haute MSA, IN	Y	18700 FQ	76790 MW	101950 TQ	USBLS	5/15
	Iowa	Y	19800 FQ	48650 MW	78700 TQ	USBLS	5/15
	Des Moines-West Des Moines MSA, IA	Y	19440 FQ	64080 MW	81970 TQ	USBLS	5/15
	Kansas	Y	19860 FQ	53870 MW	62640 TQ	USBLS	5/15
	Wichita MSA, KS	Y	54240 FQ	58780 MW	82040 TQ	USBLS	5/15
	Kentucky	Y	17880 FQ	44180 MW	61060 TQ	USBLS	5/15
	Louisville-Jefferson County MSA, KY-IN	Y	18800 FQ	53870 MW	62020 TQ	USBLS	5/15
	Louisiana	Y	37040 FQ	48220 MW	70170 TQ	USBLS	5/15
	Baton Rouge MSA, LA	Y	45620 FQ	54250 MW	62850 TQ	USBLS	5/15
	New Orleans-Metairie MSA, LA	Y	45090 FQ	56170 MW	85830 TQ	USBLS	5/15
	Maine	Y	60760 FQ	75330 MW	88680 TQ	USBLS	5/15
	Portland-South Portland MSA, ME	Y	68060 FQ	80490 MW	88410 TQ	USBLS	5/15
	Maryland	Y	18095 AE	48730 MW	64048 AEX	MDBLS	4/16
	Baltimore-Columbia-Towson MSA, MD	Y	18710 FQ	42830 MW	71710 TQ	USBLS	5/15
	Massachusetts	Y	39820 FQ	63760 MW	86430 TQ	USBLS	5/15
	Boston-Cambridge-Newton NECTA, MA	Y	36710 FQ	60450 MW	78970 TQ	USBLS	5/15
	Worcester MSA, MA-CT	Y	47610 FQ	80250 MW	92650 TQ	USBLS	5/15
	Michigan	Y	39200 FQ	61020 MW	77670 TQ	USBLS	5/15
	Detroit-Dearborn-Livonia PMSA, MI	Y	40050 FQ	59720 MW	78170 TQ	USBLS	5/15
	Grand Rapids-Wyoming MSA, MI	Y	55690 FQ	70690 MW	79660 TQ	USBLS	5/15
	Minnesota	Y	35025 FQ	69654 MW	92394 TQ	MNBLS	1/16-3/16
	Minneapolis-St. Paul-Bloomington MSA, MN-WI	Y	35340 FQ	69695 MW	97139 TQ	MNBLS	1/16-3/16
	Mississippi	Y	38900 FQ	53290 MW	66390 TQ	USBLS	5/15
	Jackson MSA, MS	Y	48520 FQ	58100 MW	82910 TQ	USBLS	5/15
	Missouri	Y	52160 FQ	65660 MW	82190 TQ	USBLS	5/15
	Kansas City MSA, MO-KS	Y	53690 FQ	62200 MW	86020 TQ	USBLS	5/15
	St. Louis MSA, MO-IL	Y	19920 FQ	65770 MW	82810 TQ	USBLS	5/15
	Montana	Y	43540 FQ	61790 MW	76090 TQ	USBLS	5/15
	Nebraska	Y	41785 FQ	55170 MW	72235 TQ	NEBLS	7/16-9/16
	Omaha-Council Bluffs MSA, NE-IA	Y	43270 FQ	51590 MW	73150 TQ	NEBLS	7/16-9/16
	Nevada	Y	46000 FQ	61300 MW	79880 TQ	USBLS	5/15
	Las Vegas-Henderson-Paradise MSA, NV	Y	45910 FQ	59360 MW	81830 TQ	USBLS	5/15
	New Hampshire	H	14.63 AE	36.44 MW	44.33 AEX	NHBLS	6/16
	New Jersey	Y	51810 FQ	75970 MW	100760 TQ	USBLS	5/15
	Camden PMSA, NJ	Y	60000 FQ	84880 MW	102350 TQ	USBLS	5/15
	Newark PMSA, NJ-PA	Y	39150 FQ	61950 MW	94760 TQ	USBLS	5/15
	Trenton MSA, NJ	Y	66370 FQ	81150 MW	102470 TQ	USBLS	5/15
	New Mexico	Y	18280 FQ	47600 MW	67480 TQ	USBLS	5/15
	Albuquerque MSA, NM	Y	17840 FQ	27040 MW	57530 TQ	USBLS	5/15
	New York	Y	47490 AE	68190 MW	93140 AEX	NYBLS	1/16-3/16
	Buffalo-Cheektowaga-Niagara Falls MSA, NY	Y	45920 FQ	73960 MW	92860 TQ	USBLS	5/15
	Nassau County-Suffolk County PMSA, NY	Y	58240 FQ	79230 MW	155810 TQ	USBLS	5/15
	New York-Jersey City-White Plains PMSA, NY-NJ	Y	55700 FQ	67010 MW	95820 TQ	USBLS	5/15
	Rochester MSA, NY	Y	48180 FQ	59560 MW	87210 TQ	USBLS	5/15
	North Carolina	Y	19020 FQ	51970 MW	68410 TQ	USBLS	5/15
	Charlotte-Concord-Gastonia MSA, NC-SC	Y	19350 FQ	63890 MW	78840 TQ	USBLS	5/15
	Raleigh MSA, NC	Y	37690 FQ	47010 MW	58810 TQ	USBLS	5/15

AE	Average entry wage	AWR	Average wage range	H	Hourly
AEX	Average experienced wage	B	Biweekly	HI	Highest wage paid
ATC	Average total compensation	D	Daily	HR	High end range
AW	Average wage paid	FQ	First quartile wage	LO	Lowest wage paid

LR	Low end range	MTC	Median total compensation	TCC	Total cash compensation
M	Monthly	MW	Median wage paid	TQ	Third quartile wage
MCC	Median cash compensation	MWR	Median wage range	W	Weekly
ME	Median entry wage	S	See annotated source	Y	Yearly

Occupation/Type/Industry	Location	Per	Low	Mid	High	Source	Date
Labor Relations Specialist	North Dakota	Y	47780 FQ	57040 MW	72980 TQ	USBLS	5/15
	Ohio	Y	18140 FQ	19390 MW	53830 TQ	USBLS	5/15
	Cincinnati MSA, OH-KY-IN	Y	18610 FQ	21280 MW	55760 TQ	USBLS	5/15
	Cleveland-Elyria MSA, OH	Y	17920 FQ	18960 MW	22900 TQ	USBLS	5/15
	Columbus MSA, OH	Y	19500 FQ	56240 MW	72880 TQ	USBLS	5/15
	Oklahoma	Y	19240 FQ	42770 MW	76520 TQ	USBLS	5/15
	Oklahoma City MSA, OK	Y	42440 FQ	57700 MW	79440 TQ	USBLS	5/15
	Tulsa MSA, OK	Y	18550 FQ	23180 MW	74620 TQ	USBLS	5/15
	Oregon	H	23.09 FQ	30.22 MW	45.44 TQ	ORBLS	2016
	Portland-Vancouver-Hillsboro MSA, OR-WA	Y	45850 FQ	62880 MW	98950 TQ	USBLS	5/15
	Pennsylvania	Y	18020 FQ	34480 MW	62580 TQ	USBLS	5/15
	Allentown-Bethlehem-Easton MSA, PA-NJ	Y	20250 FQ	47740 MW	60960 TQ	USBLS	5/15
	Harrisburg-Carlisle MSA, PA	Y	54180 FQ	63200 MW	82710 TQ	USBLS	5/15
	Philadelphia PMSA, PA	Y	18520 FQ	34470 MW	84400 TQ	USBLS	5/15
	Pittsburgh MSA, PA	Y	17400 FQ	19020 MW	43880 TQ	USBLS	5/15
	Rhode Island	Y	28170 FQ	62780 MW	103260 TQ	USBLS	5/15
	Providence-Warwick MSA, RI-MA	Y	25960 FQ	60210 MW	100130 TQ	USBLS	5/15
	South Carolina	Y	35230 FQ	53490 MW	77810 TQ	USBLS	5/15
	Columbia MSA, SC	Y	36420 FQ	47560 MW	62410 TQ	USBLS	5/15
	Greenville-Anderson-Mauldin MSA, SC	Y	47490 FQ	61430 MW	118640 TQ	USBLS	5/15
	Tennessee	Y	19810 FQ	59670 MW	77140 TQ	USBLS	5/15
	Knoxville MSA, TN	Y	17980 FQ	46900 MW	81340 TQ	USBLS	5/15
	Memphis MSA, TN-MS-AR	Y	49820 FQ	63770 MW	76310 TQ	USBLS	5/15
	Nashville-Davidson–Murfreesboro–Franklin MSA, TN	Y	58040 FQ	70250 MW	79080 TQ	USBLS	5/15
	Texas	Y	39410 FQ	67780 MW	92830 TQ	USBLS	5/15
	Austin-Round Rock MSA, TX	Y	46510 FQ	68990 MW	85050 TQ	USBLS	5/15
	Dallas-Plano-Irving PMSA, TX	Y	18990 FQ	65820 MW	91200 TQ	USBLS	5/15
	Houston-The Woodlands-Sugar Land MSA, TX	Y	44570 FQ	67240 MW	95760 TQ	USBLS	5/15
	San Antonio-New Braunfels MSA, TX	Y	17790 FQ	52470 MW	72530 TQ	USBLS	5/15
	Utah	Y	19330 FQ	54310 MW	60460 TQ	USBLS	5/15
	Salt Lake City MSA, UT	Y	18910 FQ	53940 MW	59770 TQ	USBLS	5/15
	Vermont	Y	47110 FQ	62190 MW	93380 TQ	USBLS	5/15
	Burlington-South Burlington MSA, VT	Y	56160 FQ	76040 MW	104730 TQ	USBLS	5/15
	Virginia	Y	46240 FQ	59090 MW	76500 TQ	USBLS	5/15
	Richmond MSA, VA	Y	51360 FQ	58940 MW	71830 TQ	USBLS	5/15
	Virginia Beach-Norfolk-Newport News MSA, VA-NC	Y	43820 FQ	56440 MW	78270 TQ	USBLS	5/15
	Washington	H	25.00 FQ	35.50 MW	47.23 TQ	WABLS	3/16
	Seattle-Bellevue-Everett PMSA, WA	H	24.13 FQ	35.18 MW	48.58 TQ	WABLS	3/16
	Tacoma-Lakewood PMSA, WA	H	26.72 FQ	41.68 MW	49.43 TQ	WABLS	3/16
	West Virginia	Y	18380 FQ	36040 MW	66660 TQ	USBLS	5/15
	Huntington-Ashland MSA, WV-KY-OH	Y	17530 FQ	19420 MW	43660 TQ	USBLS	5/15
	Wisconsin	Y	17360 FQ	19160 MW	44210 TQ	USBLS	5/15
	Madison MSA, WI	Y	17570 FQ	19560 MW	77570 TQ	USBLS	5/15
	Milwaukee-Waukesha-West Allis MSA, WI	Y	17800 FQ	22860 MW	61810 TQ	USBLS	5/15
	Wyoming	Y	18400 FQ	58220 MW	81940 TQ	USBLS	5/15
	Puerto Rico	Y	28790 FQ	42960 MW	56660 TQ	USBLS	5/15
	San Juan-Carolina-Caguas MSA, PR	Y	29300 FQ	43510 MW	56770 TQ	USBLS	5/15
Laboratory Chemist Public Works Department, Municipal Government	Thousand Oaks, CA	Y			88794 HI	CACIT	6/28/16
Laboratory Worker Cannabis Testing Facility, ACT Laboratories	Lansing, MI	Y			35000 HI	LSJ13	2018

AE	Average entry wage	AWR	Average wage range	H	Hourly	LR	Low end range	MTC	Median total compensation	TCC	Total cash compensation
AEX	Average experienced wage	B	Biweekly	HI	Highest wage paid	M	Monthly	MW	Median wage paid	TQ	Third quartile wage
ATC	Average total compensation	D	Daily	HR	High end range	MCC	Median cash compensation	MWR	Median wage range	W	Weekly
AW	Average wage paid	FQ	First quartile wage	LO	Lowest wage paid	ME	Median entry wage	S	See annotated source	Y	Yearly

Occupation/Type/Industry	Location	Per	Low	Mid	High	Source	Date
Laborer and Freight, Stock, and Material Mover							
Hand	Alabama	Y	17742 AE	25157 AW	28860 AEX	ALBLS	6/16
Hand	Birmingham-Hoover MSA, AL	Y	19151 AE	26103 AW	29580 AEX	ALBLS	6/16
Hand	Alaska	Y	25520 FQ	33640 MW	43720 TQ	USBLS	5/15
Hand	Anchorage MSA, AK	Y	24490 FQ	31720 MW	39080 TQ	USBLS	5/15
Hand	Arizona	Y	19910 FQ	25380 MW	31140 TQ	USBLS	5/15
Hand	Phoenix-Mesa-Scottsdale MSA, AZ	Y	19970 FQ	25910 MW	31390 TQ	USBLS	5/15
Hand	Tucson MSA, AZ	Y	20130 FQ	23610 MW	31290 TQ	USBLS	5/15
Hand	Arkansas	Y	18850 FQ	22070 MW	26760 TQ	USBLS	5/15
Hand	Little Rock-North Little Rock-Conway MSA, AR	Y	18800 FQ	23050 MW	28950 TQ	USBLS	5/15
Hand	California	H	10.02 FQ	12.30 MW	16.08 TQ	CABLS	1/16-3/16
Hand	Anaheim-Santa Ana-Irvine PMSA, CA	H	9.62 FQ	11.24 MW	14.56 TQ	CABLS	1/16-3/16
Hand	Los Angeles-Long Beach-Glendale PMSA, CA	H	9.92 FQ	11.92 MW	15.20 TQ	CABLS	1/16-3/16
Hand	Oakland-Hayward-Berkeley PMSA, CA	H	11.16 FQ	14.56 MW	19.45 TQ	CABLS	1/16-3/16
Hand	Riverside-San Bernardino-Ontario MSA, CA	H	9.89 FQ	12.33 MW	15.80 TQ	CABLS	1/16-3/16
Hand	Sacramento–Roseville–Arden-Arcade MSA, CA	H	10.10 FQ	12.68 MW	17.40 TQ	CABLS	1/16-3/16
Hand	San Diego-Carlsbad MSA, CA	H	9.91 FQ	11.87 MW	15.04 TQ	CABLS	1/16-3/16
Hand	San Francisco-Redwood City-South San Francisco PMSA, CA	H	11.84 FQ	14.09 MW	17.36 TQ	CABLS	1/16-3/16
Hand	Colorado	Y	21180 FQ	26320 MW	33280 TQ	USBLS	5/15
Hand	Denver-Aurora-Lakewood MSA, CO	Y	21270 FQ	26220 MW	33190 TQ	USBLS	5/15
Hand	Connecticut	Y		28922 MW		CTBLS	1/16-3/16
Hand	Bridgeport-Stamford-Norwalk MSA, CT	Y	23080 FQ	28770 MW	37730 TQ	USBLS	5/15
Hand	Hartford-West Hartford-East Hartford MSA, CT	Y	22260 FQ	28280 MW	36490 TQ	USBLS	5/15
Hand	Delaware	Y	21580 FQ	25210 MW	35390 TQ	USBLS	5/15
Hand	Wilmington PMSA, DE-MD-NJ	Y	22070 FQ	27340 MW	36050 TQ	USBLS	5/15
Hand	District of Columbia	Y	28490 FQ	35100 MW	44990 TQ	USBLS	5/15
Hand	Washington-Arlington-Alexandria PMSA, DC-VA-MD-WV	Y	21810 FQ	25260 MW	32570 TQ	USBLS	5/15
Hand	Florida	H	9.07 AE	11.43 MW	14.64 AEX	FLBLS	7/16-9/16
Hand	Fort Lauderdale-Pompano Beach-Deerfield Beach PMSA, FL	H	9.04 AE	11.25 MW	14.96 AEX	FLBLS	7/16-9/16
Hand	Miami-Miami Beach-Kendall PMSA, FL	H	9.46 AE	11.94 MW	15.12 AEX	FLBLS	7/16-9/16
Hand	Orlando-Kissimmee-Sanford MSA, FL	H-	9.04 AE	10.99 MW	14.15 AEX	FLBLS	7/16-9/16
Hand	Tampa-St. Petersburg-Clearwater MSA, FL	H	9.14 AE	11.48 MW	14.72 AEX	FLBLS	7/16-9/16
Hand	Georgia	Y	19670 FQ	23840 MW	31210 TQ	USBLS	5/15
Hand	Atlanta-Sandy Springs-Roswell MSA, GA	Y	19870 FQ	23950 MW	30880 TQ	USBLS	5/15
Hand	Augusta-Richmond County MSA, GA-SC	Y	18270 FQ	21590 MW	27210 TQ	USBLS	5/15
Hand	Hawaii	Y	22840 FQ	28820 MW	36810 TQ	USBLS	5/15
Hand	Urban Honolulu MSA, HI	Y	22960 FQ	28600 MW	36610 TQ	USBLS	5/15
Hand	Idaho	Y	19840 FQ	25500 MW	31160 TQ	USBLS	5/15
Hand	Boise City MSA, ID	Y	19830 FQ	24860 MW	31170 TQ	USBLS	5/15
Hand	Illinois	Y	19890 FQ	24310 MW	33020 TQ	USBLS	5/15
Hand	Chicago-Naperville-Arlington Heights PMSA, IL	Y	19640 FQ	23790 MW	32380 TQ	USBLS	5/15
Hand	Lake County-Kenosha County PMSA, IL-WI	Y	22920 FQ	29410 MW	37760 TQ	USBLS	5/15
Hand	Indiana	Y	21010 FQ	25180 MW	30990 TQ	USBLS	5/15
Hand	Gary PMSA, IN	Y	21190 FQ	25310 MW	34560 TQ	USBLS	5/15
Hand	Indianapolis-Carmel-Anderson MSA, IN	Y	21210 FQ	24920 MW	30490 TQ	USBLS	5/15
Hand	Iowa	Y	22060 FQ	27150 MW	33780 TQ	USBLS	5/15

AE	Average entry wage	AWR	Average wage range	H	Hourly	LR	Low end range
AEX	Average experienced wage	B	Biweekly	HI	Highest wage paid	M	Monthly
ATC	Average total compensation	D	Daily	HR	High end range	MCC	Median cash compensation
AW	Average wage paid	FQ	First quartile wage	LO	Lowest wage paid	ME	Median entry wage

MTC	Median total compensation	TCC	Total cash compensation
MW	Median wage paid	TQ	Third quartile wage
MWR	Median wage range	W	Weekly
S	See annotated source	Y	Yearly

871

Occupation/Type/Industry	Location	Per	Low	Mid	High	Source	Date
Laborer and Freight, Stock, and Material Mover							
Hand	Des Moines-West Des Moines MSA, IA	Y	21310 FQ	25470 MW	32860 TQ	USBLS	5/15
Hand	Kansas	Y	20950 FQ	26320 MW	32960 TQ	USBLS	5/15
Hand	Wichita MSA, KS	Y	19190 FQ	23660 MW	29080 TQ	USBLS	5/15
Hand	Kentucky	Y	20450 FQ	24600 MW	31050 TQ	USBLS	5/15
Hand	Louisville-Jefferson County MSA, KY-IN	Y	21340 FQ	25200 MW	33200 TQ	USBLS	5/15
Hand	Louisiana	Y	19410 FQ	24030 MW	30410 TQ	USBLS	5/15
Hand	Baton Rouge MSA, LA	Y	19020 FQ	24950 MW	32610 TQ	USBLS	5/15
Hand	New Orleans-Metairie MSA, LA	Y	19550 FQ	23960 MW	29620 TQ	USBLS	5/15
Hand	Maine	Y	22090 FQ	26310 MW	33170 TQ	USBLS	5/15
Hand	Portland-South Portland MSA, ME	Y	22580 FQ	27500 MW	35280 TQ	USBLS	5/15
Hand	Maryland	Y	20140 AE	28450 MW	32605 AEX	MDBLS	4/16
Hand	Baltimore-Columbia-Towson MSA, MD	Y	20740 FQ	25540 MW	34070 TQ	USBLS	5/15
Hand	Salisbury MSA, MD-DE	Y	21110 FQ	24090 MW	29660 TQ	USBLS	5/15
Hand	Massachusetts	Y	22430 FQ	28080 MW	36960 TQ	USBLS	5/15
Hand	Boston-Cambridge-Newton NECTA, MA	Y	23540 FQ	29610 MW	38370 TQ	USBLS	5/15
Hand	Worcester MSA, MA-CT	Y	22040 FQ	28610 MW	37590 TQ	USBLS	5/15
Hand	Michigan	Y	20680 FQ	25950 MW	33050 TQ	USBLS	5/15
Hand	Detroit-Dearborn-Livonia PMSA, MI	Y	23140 FQ	28510 MW	36270 TQ	USBLS	5/15
Hand	Grand Rapids-Wyoming MSA, MI	Y	19060 FQ	22610 MW	28640 TQ	USBLS	5/15
Hand	Minnesota	Y	23349 FQ	29014 MW	36152 TQ	MNBLS	1/16-3/16
Hand	Minneapolis-St. Paul-Bloomington MSA, MN-WI	Y	23580 FQ	29135 MW	36676 TQ	MNBLS	1/16-3/16
Hand	Mississippi	Y	18410 FQ	21940 MW	27840 TQ	USBLS	5/15
Hand	Jackson MSA, MS	Y	19460 FQ	23720 MW	30540 TQ	USBLS	5/15
Hand	Missouri	Y	20820 FQ	25940 MW	33740 TQ	USBLS	5/15
Hand	Kansas City MSA, MO-KS	Y	21050 FQ	26330 MW	34080 TQ	USBLS	5/15
Hand	St. Louis MSA, MO-IL	Y	22090 FQ	28660 MW	37820 TQ	USBLS	5/15
Hand	Montana	Y	21900 FQ	26650 MW	32930 TQ	USBLS	5/15
Hand	Billings MSA, MT	Y	22230 FQ	26400 MW	31740 TQ	USBLS	5/15
Hand	Nebraska	Y	21245 FQ	26735 MW	32880 TQ	NEBLS	7/16-9/16
Hand	Omaha-Council Bluffs MSA, NE-IA	Y	20595 FQ	26350 MW	33280 TQ	NEBLS	7/16-9/16
Hand	Nevada	Y	21110 FQ	27110 MW	36340 TQ	USBLS	5/15
Hand	Las Vegas-Henderson-Paradise MSA, NV	Y	20860 FQ	27370 MW	36930 TQ	USBLS	5/15
Hand	New Hampshire	H	9.49 AE	12.21 MW	15.09 AEX	NHBLS	6/16
Hand	Manchester NECTA, NH	H	9.40 AE	12.21 MW	15.74 AEX	NHBLS	6/16
Hand	Nashua NECTA, NH-MA	Y	20680 FQ	25050 MW	30160 TQ	USBLS	5/15
Hand	New Jersey	Y	19690 FQ	24530 MW	33010 TQ	USBLS	5/15
Hand	Camden PMSA, NJ	Y	22680 FQ	29100 MW	37120 TQ	USBLS	5/15
Hand	Newark PMSA, NJ-PA	Y	19280 FQ	24500 MW	34720 TQ	USBLS	5/15
Hand	Trenton MSA, NJ	Y	22300 FQ	27880 MW	35980 TQ	USBLS	5/15
Hand	New Mexico	Y	19700 FQ	24110 MW	30500 TQ	USBLS	5/15
Hand	Albuquerque MSA, NM	Y	19960 FQ	24490 MW	32650 TQ	USBLS	5/15
Hand	New York	Y	20200 AE	26180 MW	35800 AEX	NYBLS	1/16-3/16
Hand	Buffalo-Cheektowaga-Niagara Falls MSA, NY	Y	20630 FQ	25000 MW	32450 TQ	USBLS	5/15
Hand	Nassau County-Suffolk County PMSA, NY	Y	21080 FQ	26260 MW	34610 TQ	USBLS	5/15
Hand	New York-Jersey City-White Plains PMSA, NY-NJ	Y	19550 FQ	24160 MW	33580 TQ	USBLS	5/15
Hand	Rochester MSA, NY	Y	19970 FQ	24750 MW	32100 TQ	USBLS	5/15
Hand	North Carolina	Y	19750 FQ	24040 MW	30680 TQ	USBLS	5/15
Hand	Charlotte-Concord-Gastonia MSA, NC-SC	Y	20920 FQ	25310 MW	34330 TQ	USBLS	5/15
Hand	Raleigh MSA, NC	Y	20150 FQ	24650 MW	30960 TQ	USBLS	5/15
Hand	North Dakota	Y	24300 FQ	30520 MW	37590 TQ	USBLS	5/15
Hand	Fargo MSA, ND-MN	Y	22190 FQ	27770 MW	35250 TQ	USBLS	5/15
Hand	Ohio	Y	19650 FQ	24370 MW	31630 TQ	USBLS	5/15
Hand	Cincinnati MSA, OH-KY-IN	Y	21070 FQ	26190 MW	33540 TQ	USBLS	5/15
Hand	Cleveland-Elyria MSA, OH	Y	19780 FQ	24310 MW	32620 TQ	USBLS	5/15
Hand	Columbus MSA, OH	Y	19630 FQ	23700 MW	29910 TQ	USBLS	5/15

AE	Average entry wage	AWR	Average wage range	H	Hourly
AEX	Average experienced wage	B	Biweekly	HI	Highest wage paid
ATC	Average total compensation	D	Daily	HR	High end range
AW	Average wage paid	FQ	First quartile wage	LO	Lowest wage paid

LR	Low end range	MTC	Median total compensation
M	Monthly	MW	Median wage paid
MCC	Median cash compensation	MWR	Median wage range
ME	Median entry wage	S	See annotated source

TCC	Total cash compensation	
TQ	Third quartile wage	
W	Weekly	
Y	Yearly	

Occupation/Type/Industry	Location	Per	Low	Mid	High	Source	Date
Laborer and Freight, Stock, and Material Mover							
Hand	Oklahoma	Y	20450 FQ	25430 MW	32440 TQ	USBLS	5/15
Hand	Oklahoma City MSA, OK	Y	20760 FQ	25700 MW	32720 TQ	USBLS	5/15
Hand	Tulsa MSA, OK	Y	20490 FQ	25700 MW	31230 TQ	USBLS	5/15
Hand	Oregon	H	10.73 FQ	13.05 MW	16.77 TQ	ORBLS	2016
Hand	Portland-Vancouver-Hillsboro MSA, OR-WA	Y	22040 FQ	26370 MW	33890 TQ	USBLS	5/15
Hand	Pennsylvania	Y	22100 FQ	28220 MW	36260 TQ	USBLS	5/15
Hand	Allentown-Bethlehem-Easton MSA, PA-NJ	Y	24520 FQ	28740 MW	34890 TQ	USBLS	5/15
Hand	Harrisburg-Carlisle MSA, PA	Y	23420 FQ	29190 MW	40090 TQ	USBLS	5/15
Hand	Montgomery County-Bucks County-Chester County PMSA, PA	Y	22600 FQ	28720 MW	36760 TQ	USBLS	5/15
Hand	Philadelphia PMSA, PA	Y	20890 FQ	28710 MW	37970 TQ	USBLS	5/15
Hand	Pittsburgh MSA, PA	Y	20970 FQ	27020 MW	36220 TQ	USBLS	5/15
Hand	Rhode Island	Y	20140 FQ	25670 MW	34220 TQ	USBLS	5/15
Hand	Providence-Warwick MSA, RI-MA	Y	20110 FQ	25590 MW	33690 TQ	USBLS	5/15
Hand	South Carolina	Y	19940 FQ	24410 MW	31300 TQ	USBLS	5/15
Hand	Charleston-North Charleston MSA, SC	Y	20860 FQ	24630 MW	30310 TQ	USBLS	5/15
Hand	Columbia MSA, SC	Y	21210 FQ	26700 MW	33220 TQ	USBLS	5/15
Hand	Greenville-Anderson-Mauldin MSA, SC	Y	19710 FQ	24770 MW	33270 TQ	USBLS	5/15
Hand	South Dakota	Y	21390 FQ	24390 MW	28900 TQ	USBLS	5/15
Hand	Sioux Falls MSA, SD	Y	22460 FQ	25910 MW	29850 TQ	USBLS	5/15
Hand	Tennessee	Y	20220 FQ	25040 MW	31980 TQ	USBLS	5/15
Hand	Knoxville MSA, TN	Y	20300 FQ	24220 MW	30060 TQ	USBLS	5/15
Hand	Memphis MSA, TN-MS-AR	Y	21420 FQ	26410 MW	33640 TQ	USBLS	5/15
Hand	Nashville-Davidson–Murfreesboro–Franklin MSA, TN	Y	19690 FQ	24280 MW	30540 TQ	USBLS	5/15
Hand	Texas	Y	19570 FQ	23780 MW	30360 TQ	USBLS	5/15
Hand	Austin-Round Rock MSA, TX	Y	19460 FQ	23260 MW	29560 TQ	USBLS	5/15
Hand	Dallas-Plano-Irving PMSA, TX	Y	19810 FQ	24120 MW	30410 TQ	USBLS	5/15
Hand	Fort Worth-Arlington PMSA, TX	Y	20040 FQ	23690 MW	29150 TQ	USBLS	5/15
Hand	Houston-The Woodlands-Sugar Land MSA, TX	Y	20410 FQ	24580 MW	32290 TQ	USBLS	5/15
Hand	San Antonio-New Braunfels MSA, TX	Y	18920 FQ	22970 MW	29960 TQ	USBLS	5/15
Hand	Utah	Y	21080 FQ	25840 MW	31720 TQ	USBLS	5/15
Hand	Ogden-Clearfield MSA, UT	Y	21380 FQ	26720 MW	33870 TQ	USBLS	5/15
Hand	Provo-Orem MSA, UT	Y	19820 FQ	23700 MW	29340 TQ	USBLS	5/15
Hand	Salt Lake City MSA, UT	Y	21680 FQ	26550 MW	31990 TQ	USBLS	5/15
Hand	Vermont	Y	22340 FQ	26620 MW	31830 TQ	USBLS	5/15
Hand	Burlington-South Burlington MSA, VT	Y	24220 FQ	29660 MW	36790 TQ	USBLS	5/15
Hand	Virginia	Y	20680 FQ	24430 MW	30910 TQ	USBLS	5/15
Hand	Richmond MSA, VA	Y	21120 FQ	25210 MW	32140 TQ	USBLS	5/15
Hand	Virginia Beach-Norfolk-Newport News MSA, VA-NC	Y	19860 FQ	23930 MW	30670 TQ	USBLS	5/15
Hand	Washington	H	11.40 FQ	14.01 MW	18.15 TQ	WABLS	3/16
Hand	Seattle-Bellevue-Everett PMSA, WA	H	11.72 FQ	14.17 MW	18.12 TQ	WABLS	3/16
Hand	Tacoma-Lakewood PMSA, WA	H	12.85 FQ	16.60 MW	22.72 TQ	WABLS	3/16
Hand	West Virginia	Y	19240 FQ	23060 MW	29590 TQ	USBLS	5/15
Hand	Huntington-Ashland MSA, WV-KY-OH	Y	19630 FQ	23890 MW	31140 TQ	USBLS	5/15
Hand	Wisconsin	Y	21920 FQ	27980 MW	35950 TQ	USBLS	5/15
Hand	Madison MSA, WI	Y	23150 FQ	28590 MW	34710 TQ	USBLS	5/15
Hand	Milwaukee-Waukesha-West Allis MSA, WI	Y	21510 FQ	27350 MW	36330 TQ	USBLS	5/15
Hand	Wyoming	Y	24450 FQ	30940 MW	37790 TQ	USBLS	5/15
Hand	Cheyenne MSA, WY	Y	25060 FQ	32130 MW	37790 TQ	USBLS	5/15
Hand	Puerto Rico	Y	17130 FQ	18690 MW	22360 TQ	USBLS	5/15
Hand	San Juan-Carolina-Caguas MSA, PR	Y	17170 FQ	18740 MW	22670 TQ	USBLS	5/15
Hand	Virgin Islands	Y	18910 FQ	22350 MW	27140 TQ	USBLS	5/15
Hand	Guam	Y	18620 FQ	23660 MW	34680 TQ	USBLS	5/15

AE	Average entry wage	**AWR**	Average wage range	**H**	Hourly
AEX	Average experienced wage	**B**	Biweekly	**HI**	Highest wage paid
ATC	Average total compensation	**D**	Daily	**HR**	High end range
AW	Average wage paid	**FQ**	First quartile wage	**LO**	Lowest wage paid

LR	Low end range	**MTC**	Median total compensation	**TCC**	Total cash compensation
M	Monthly	**MW**	Median wage paid	**TQ**	Third quartile wage
MCC	Median cash compensation	**MWR**	Median wage range	**W**	Weekly
ME	Median entry wage	**S**	See annotated source	**Y**	Yearly

Occupation/Type/Industry	Location	Per	Low	Mid	High	Source	Date
Lactation Specialist							
County Government	Oakland County, MI	B			1093 HI	MIOAK2	10/1/16
Lake Level Technician							
County Government	Oakland County, MI	H	17.99 LO		23.43 HI	MIOAK2	10/1/16
Lance Corporal							
U.S. Marines, Active Duty, Pay Grade E-3	United States	M	1886 LO		2126 HI	DOD1	2017
Landfill Manager							
Certified, Municipal Government	Fitzgerald, GA	Y			39790 HI	GACTY02	2016
Certified, Municipal Government	Savannah, GA	Y	58732 LO		88232 HI	GACTY02	2016
Landscape Architect	Alabama	Y	52057 AE	69120 AW	77662 AEX	ALBLS	6/16
	Arizona	Y	46560 FQ	55410 MW	70000 TQ	USBLS	5/15
	Phoenix-Mesa-Scottsdale MSA, AZ	Y	44490 FQ	49980 MW	69880 TQ	USBLS	5/15
	Tucson MSA, AZ	Y	53710 FQ	59270 MW	68480 TQ	USBLS	5/15
	Arkansas	Y	34800 FQ	45050 MW	55740 TQ	USBLS	5/15
	California	H	28.03 FQ	35.18 MW	47.12 TQ	CABLS	1/16-3/16
	Anaheim-Santa Ana-Irvine PMSA, CA	H	27.78 FQ	32.90 MW	41.54 TQ	CABLS	1/16-3/16
	Los Angeles-Long Beach-Glendale PMSA, CA	H	28.92 FQ	40.77 MW	48.44 TQ	CABLS	1/16-3/16
	Oakland-Hayward-Berkeley PMSA, CA	H	29.66 FQ	41.62 MW	51.93 TQ	CABLS	1/16-3/16
	Riverside-San Bernardino-Ontario MSA, CA	H	27.78 FQ	30.71 MW	45.20 TQ	CABLS	1/16-3/16
	Sacramento-Roseville-Arden-Arcade MSA, CA	H	40.01 FQ	49.44 MW	55.24 TQ	CABLS	1/16-3/16
	San Diego-Carlsbad MSA, CA	H	29.33 FQ	39.94 MW	51.08 TQ	CABLS	1/16-3/16
	Colorado	Y	64460 FQ	74020 MW	89100 TQ	USBLS	5/15
	Denver-Aurora-Lakewood MSA, CO	Y	68000 FQ	77400 MW	95670 TQ	USBLS	5/15
	Connecticut	Y		74758 MW		CTBLS	1/16-3/16
	Bridgeport-Stamford-Norwalk MSA, CT	Y	56420 FQ	71660 MW	91860 TQ	USBLS	5/15
	Hartford-West Hartford-East Hartford MSA, CT	Y	47780 FQ	70380 MW	112090 TQ	USBLS	5/15
	Delaware	Y	44110 FQ	48670 MW	82540 TQ	USBLS	5/15
	District of Columbia	Y	76390 FQ	89300 MW	105970 TQ	USBLS	5/15
	Washington-Arlington-Alexandria PMSA, DC-VA-MD-WV	Y	47510 FQ	66190 MW	91650 TQ	USBLS	5/15
	Florida	H	24.14 AE	31.67 MW	39.80 AEX	FLBLS	7/16-9/16
	Fort Lauderdale-Pompano Beach-Deerfield Beach PMSA, FL	H	22.29 AE	28.12 MW	43.03 AEX	FLBLS	7/16-9/16
	Miami-Miami Beach-Kendall PMSA, FL	H	27.73 AE	34.12 MW	40.64 AEX	FLBLS	7/16-9/16
	Orlando-Kissimmee-Sanford MSA, FL	H	26.77 AE	35.37 MW	40.62 AEX	FLBLS	7/16-9/16
	Tampa-St. Petersburg-Clearwater MSA, FL	H	28.95 AE	33.94 MW	35.66 AEX	FLBLS	7/16-9/16
	Georgia	Y	51220 FQ	70830 MW	84520 TQ	USBLS	5/15
	Atlanta-Sandy Springs-Roswell MSA, GA	Y	49380 FQ	70090 MW	83060 TQ	USBLS	5/15
	Idaho	Y	47850 FQ	64720 MW	72840 TQ	USBLS	5/15
	Illinois	Y	44090 FQ	50400 MW	70980 TQ	USBLS	5/15
	Chicago-Naperville-Arlington Heights PMSA, IL	Y	43300 FQ	47340 MW	63250 TQ	USBLS	5/15
	Lake County-Kenosha County PMSA, IL-WI	Y	49590 FQ	65980 MW	82880 TQ	USBLS	5/15
	Gary PMSA, IN	Y	40710 FQ	45950 MW	52380 TQ	USBLS	5/15
	Indianapolis-Carmel-Anderson MSA, IN	Y	24570 FQ	40420 MW	50020 TQ	USBLS	5/15
	Iowa	Y	34590 FQ	46550 MW	61020 TQ	USBLS	5/15
	Des Moines-West Des Moines MSA, IA	Y	40080 FQ	49420 MW	62760 TQ	USBLS	5/15
	Kansas	Y	43250 FQ	48340 MW	63220 TQ	USBLS	5/15
	Wichita MSA, KS	Y	41870 FQ	46350 MW	54550 TQ	USBLS	5/15
	Kentucky	Y	45240 FQ	57190 MW	71590 TQ	USBLS	5/15

AE Average entry wage | AWR Average wage range | H Hourly | LR Low end range | MTC Median total compensation | TCC Total cash compensation
AEX Average experienced wage | B Biweekly | HI Highest wage paid | M Monthly | MW Median wage paid | TQ Third quartile wage
ATC Average total compensation | D Daily | HR High end range | MCC Median cash compensation | MWR Median wage range | W Weekly
AW Average wage paid | FQ First quartile wage | LO Lowest wage paid | ME Median entry wage | S See annotated source | Y Yearly

Occupation/Type/Industry	Location	Per	Low	Mid	High	Source	Date
Landscape Architect	Lexington-Fayette MSA, KY	Y	53600 FQ	59470 MW	71010 TQ	USBLS	5/15
	Louisiana	Y	33190 FQ	38020 MW	53320 TQ	USBLS	5/15
	Baton Rouge MSA, LA	Y	31730 FQ	35450 MW	39260 TQ	USBLS	5/15
	Maine	Y	48230 FQ	56840 MW	67480 TQ	USBLS	5/15
	Portland-South Portland MSA, ME	Y	47200 FQ	54950 MW	63800 TQ	USBLS	5/15
	Maryland	Y	52504 AE	64251 MW	70125 AEX	MDBLS	4/16
	Baltimore-Columbia-Towson MSA, MD	Y	54650 FQ	59820 MW	75020 TQ	USBLS	5/15
	Massachusetts	Y	60880 FQ	77870 MW	97220 TQ	USBLS	5/15
	Boston-Cambridge-Newton NECTA, MA	Y	59650 FQ	75130 MW	97260 TQ	USBLS	5/15
	Worcester MSA, MA-CT	Y	60350 FQ	70590 MW	89920 TQ	USBLS	5/15
	Michigan	Y	44510 FQ	57800 MW	73210 TQ	USBLS	5/15
	Detroit-Dearborn-Livonia PMSA, MI	Y	48550 FQ	63070 MW	77330 TQ	USBLS	5/15
	Grand Rapids-Wyoming MSA, MI	Y	47960 FQ	65490 MW	75510 TQ	USBLS	5/15
	Minnesota	Y	47469 FQ	56612 MW	68628 TQ	MNBLS	1/16-3/16
	Minneapolis-St. Paul-Bloomington MSA, MN-WI	Y	47096 FQ	55846 MW	66743 TQ	MNBLS	1/16-3/16
	Mississippi	Y	41860 FQ	45230 MW	48610 TQ	USBLS	5/15
	Jackson MSA, MS	Y	42210 FQ	44950 MW	47700 TQ	USBLS	5/15
	Missouri	Y	49910 FQ	60290 MW	77020 TQ	USBLS	5/15
	Kansas City MSA, MO-KS	Y	49330 FQ	64250 MW	80730 TQ	USBLS	5/15
	St. Louis MSA, MO-IL	Y	49550 FQ	59030 MW	73400 TQ	USBLS	5/15
	Montana	Y	55220 FQ	67750 MW	74260 TQ	USBLS	5/15
	Nebraska	Y	38375 FQ	48230 MW	81865 TQ	NEBLS	7/16-9/16
	Omaha-Council Bluffs MSA, NE-IA	Y	36790 FQ	47460 MW	82405 TQ	NEBLS	7/16-9/16
	New Jersey	Y	29350 FQ	50330 MW	77510 TQ	USBLS	5/15
	Camden PMSA, NJ	Y	63400 FQ	69570 MW	75740 TQ	USBLS	5/15
	Newark PMSA, NJ-PA	Y	42620 FQ	50490 MW	64990 TQ	USBLS	5/15
	Trenton MSA, NJ	Y	65180 FQ	71450 MW	77730 TQ	USBLS	5/15
	Albuquerque MSA, NM	Y	26980 FQ	29260 MW	52270 TQ	USBLS	5/15
	New York	Y	48690 AE	69220 MW	84450 AEX	NYBLS	1/16-3/16
	Nassau County-Suffolk County PMSA, NY	Y	72500 FQ	90810 MW	112770 TQ	USBLS	5/15
	New York-Jersey City-White Plains PMSA, NY-NJ	Y	45080 FQ	61200 MW	84040 TQ	USBLS	5/15
	Rochester MSA, NY	Y	53610 FQ	68390 MW	86360 TQ	USBLS	5/15
	North Carolina	Y	54130 FQ	69020 MW	93330 TQ	USBLS	5/15
	Raleigh MSA, NC	Y	55340 FQ	70350 MW	81290 TQ	USBLS	5/15
	North Dakota	Y	44700 FQ	50030 MW	62800 TQ	USBLS	5/15
	Ohio	Y	46850 FQ	57280 MW	72080 TQ	USBLS	5/15
	Cincinnati MSA, OH-KY-IN	Y	43500 FQ	50590 MW	76080 TQ	USBLS	5/15
	Cleveland-Elyria MSA, OH	Y	51230 FQ	57760 MW	65900 TQ	USBLS	5/15
	Columbus MSA, OH	Y	42980 FQ	56970 MW	74270 TQ	USBLS	5/15
	Oklahoma	Y	54380 FQ	65120 MW	79260 TQ	USBLS	5/15
	Oklahoma City MSA, OK	Y	53790 FQ	62910 MW	78210 TQ	USBLS	5/15
	Tulsa MSA, OK	Y	50820 FQ	65230 MW	76990 TQ	USBLS	5/15
	Oregon	H	22.81 FQ	28.04 MW	35.68 TQ	ORBLS	2016
	Portland-Vancouver-Hillsboro MSA, OR-WA	Y	47140 FQ	59110 MW	76090 TQ	USBLS	5/15
	Pennsylvania	Y	52320 FQ	62140 MW	82480 TQ	USBLS	5/15
	Harrisburg-Carlisle MSA, PA	Y	59160 FQ	76200 MW	107060 TQ	USBLS	5/15
	Montgomery County-Bucks County-Chester County PMSA, PA	Y	45660 FQ	55440 MW	62760 TQ	USBLS	5/15
	Philadelphia PMSA, PA	Y	61340 FQ	74090 MW	91470 TQ	USBLS	5/15
	Pittsburgh MSA, PA	Y	45640 FQ	51370 MW	61830 TQ	USBLS	5/15
	South Carolina	Y	44070 FQ	57090 MW	67660 TQ	USBLS	5/15
	Charleston-North Charleston MSA, SC	Y	53900 FQ	58740 MW	63590 TQ	USBLS	5/15
	Greenville-Anderson-Mauldin MSA, SC	Y	38710 FQ	57120 MW	70290 TQ	USBLS	5/15
	South Dakota	Y	39480 FQ	60930 MW	71730 TQ	USBLS	5/15
	Sioux Falls MSA, SD	Y	38280 FQ	57410 MW	67500 TQ	USBLS	5/15
	Tennessee	Y	64150 FQ	80620 MW	104760 TQ	USBLS	5/15
	Knoxville MSA, TN	Y	77020 FQ	88520 MW	99520 TQ	USBLS	5/15
	Memphis MSA, TN-MS-AR	Y	63300 FQ	74990 MW	91480 TQ	USBLS	5/15

AE Average entry wage	AWR Average wage range	H Hourly	LR Low end range	MTC Median total compensation	TCC Total cash compensation
AEX Average experienced wage	B Biweekly	HI Highest wage paid	M Monthly	MW Median wage paid	TQ Third quartile wage
ATC Average total compensation	D Daily	HR High end range	MCC Median cash compensation	MWR Median wage range	W Weekly
AW Average wage paid	FQ First quartile wage	LO Lowest wage paid	ME Median entry wage	S See annotated source	Y Yearly

Occupation/Type/Industry	Location	Per	Low	Mid	High	Source	Date
Landscape Architect	Nashville-Davidson–Murfreesboro–Franklin MSA, TN	Y	63970 FQ	71920 MW	79400 TQ	USBLS	5/15
	Texas	Y	47190 FQ	59270 MW	78510 TQ	USBLS	5/15
	Austin-Round Rock MSA, TX	Y	44430 FQ	57900 MW	72970 TQ	USBLS	5/15
	Dallas-Plano-Irving PMSA, TX	Y	55480 FQ	65060 MW	89250 TQ	USBLS	5/15
	Fort Worth-Arlington PMSA, TX	Y	43450 FQ	47770 MW	58130 TQ	USBLS	5/15
	Houston-The Woodlands-Sugar Land MSA, TX	Y	55770 FQ	63000 MW	97970 TQ	USBLS	5/15
	San Antonio-New Braunfels MSA, TX	Y	28980 FQ	35410 MW	53510 TQ	USBLS	5/15
	Utah	Y	43100 FQ	48290 MW	71950 TQ	USBLS	5/15
	Provo-Orem MSA, UT	Y	42110 FQ	45640 MW	49160 TQ	USBLS	5/15
	Salt Lake City MSA, UT	Y	42840 FQ	46510 MW	63730 TQ	USBLS	5/15
	Vermont	Y	51720 FQ	62570 MW	77640 TQ	USBLS	5/15
	Burlington-South Burlington MSA, VT	Y	50750 FQ	62130 MW	80080 TQ	USBLS	5/15
	Virginia	Y	48010 FQ	61440 MW	86940 TQ	USBLS	5/15
	Richmond MSA, VA	Y	45400 FQ	64530 MW	94040 TQ	USBLS	5/15
	Virginia Beach-Norfolk-Newport News MSA, VA-NC	Y	49050 FQ	57160 MW	89190 TQ	USBLS	5/15
	Washington	H	24.40 FQ	34.51 MW	42.59 TQ	WABLS	3/16
	Seattle-Bellevue-Everett PMSA, WA	H	24.35 FQ	34.63 MW	42.69 TQ	WABLS	3/16
	Tacoma-Lakewood PMSA, WA	H	30.69 FQ	33.56 MW	38.08 TQ	WABLS	3/16
	West Virginia	Y	59200 FQ	71200 MW	78270 TQ	USBLS	5/15
	Wisconsin	Y	38060 FQ	47880 MW	66410 TQ	USBLS	5/15
	Madison MSA, WI	Y	44980 FQ	50400 MW	68260 TQ	USBLS	5/15
	Milwaukee-Waukesha-West Allis MSA, WI	Y	36460 FQ	55540 MW	74510 TQ	USBLS	5/15
	Wyoming	Y	41200 FQ	63590 MW	74600 TQ	USBLS	5/15
Landscape Architectural Aide Public Works Department, Municipal Government	Pasadena, CA	Y			57525 HI	CACIT	6/28/16
Landscape Inspector Public Works Department, Municipal Government	Yorba Linda, CA	Y			75827 HI	CACIT	6/28/16
Landscaping and Groundskeeping Worker	Alabama	Y	17699 AE	25771 AW	29807 AEX	ALBLS	6/16
	Birmingham-Hoover MSA, AL	Y	19161 AE	26955 AW	30857 AEX	ALBLS	6/16
	Alaska	Y	25400 FQ	31300 MW	37910 TQ	USBLS	5/15
	Anchorage MSA, AK	Y	26310 FQ	31840 MW	37620 TQ	USBLS	5/15
	Arizona	Y	19720 FQ	22930 MW	28110 TQ	USBLS	5/15
	Phoenix-Mesa-Scottsdale MSA, AZ	Y	19610 FQ	22610 MW	27410 TQ	USBLS	5/15
	Tucson MSA, AZ	Y	19950 FQ	23810 MW	28830 TQ	USBLS	5/15
	Arkansas	Y	19490 FQ	22310 MW	25930 TQ	USBLS	5/15
	Little Rock-North Little Rock-Conway MSA, AR	Y	20150 FQ	22420 MW	25020 TQ	USBLS	5/15
	California	H	10.63 FQ	12.99 MW	17.09 TQ	CABLS	1/16-3/16
	Anaheim-Santa Ana-Irvine PMSA, CA	H	9.96 FQ	11.66 MW	14.60 TQ	CABLS	1/16-3/16
	Los Angeles-Long Beach-Glendale PMSA, CA	H	10.68 FQ	12.58 MW	17.19 TQ	CABLS	1/16-3/16
	Oakland-Hayward-Berkeley PMSA, CA	H	11.81 FQ	14.09 MW	18.41 TQ	CABLS	1/16-3/16
	Riverside-San Bernardino-Ontario MSA, CA	H	9.79 FQ	11.40 MW	14.41 TQ	CABLS	1/16-3/16
	Sacramento–Roseville–Arden-Arcade MSA, CA	H	10.91 FQ	13.10 MW	16.62 TQ	CABLS	1/16-3/16
	San Diego-Carlsbad MSA, CA	H	10.27 FQ	12.70 MW	17.41 TQ	CABLS	1/16-3/16
	San Francisco-Redwood City-South San Francisco PMSA, CA	H	12.95 FQ	18.13 MW	26.34 TQ	CABLS	1/16-3/16
	Colorado	Y	22190 FQ	27350 MW	34000 TQ	USBLS	5/15
	Denver-Aurora-Lakewood MSA, CO	Y	22620 FQ	27320 MW	33460 TQ	USBLS	5/15
	Connecticut	Y		31112 MW		CTBLS	1/16-3/16

AE	Average entry wage	AWR	Average wage range	H	Hourly
AEX	Average experienced wage	B	Biweekly	HI	Highest wage paid
ATC	Average total compensation	D	Daily	HR	High end range
AW	Average wage paid	FQ	First quartile wage	LO	Lowest wage paid

LR	Low end range	MTC	Median total compensation	TCC	Total cash compensation
M	Monthly	MW	Median wage paid	TQ	Third quartile wage
MCC	Median cash compensation	MWR	Median wage range	W	Weekly
ME	Median entry wage	S	See annotated source	Y	Yearly

Occupation/Type/Industry	Location	Per	Low	Mid	High	Source	Date
Landscaping and Groundskeeping Worker							
	Bridgeport-Stamford-Norwalk MSA, CT	Y	26680 FQ	31870 MW	37350 TQ	USBLS	5/15
	Hartford-West Hartford-East Hartford MSA, CT	Y	22460 FQ	27260 MW	35220 TQ	USBLS	5/15
	Delaware	Y	22150 FQ	26230 MW	32310 TQ	USBLS	5/15
	Wilmington PMSA, DE-MD-NJ	Y	22010 FQ	25740 MW	32160 TQ	USBLS	5/15
	District of Columbia	Y	28790 FQ	35060 MW	45870 TQ	USBLS	5/15
	Washington-Arlington-Alexandria PMSA, DC-VA-MD-WV	Y	22830 FQ	27300 MW	32580 TQ	USBLS	5/15
	Florida	H	9.42 AE	11.34 MW	13.50 AEX	FLBLS	7/16-9/16
	Fort Lauderdale-Pompano Beach-Deerfield Beach PMSA, FL	H	10.06 AE	11.95 MW	14.76 AEX	FLBLS	7/16-9/16
	Miami-Miami Beach-Kendall PMSA, FL	H	9.00 AE	11.04 MW	13.53 AEX	FLBLS	7/16-9/16
	Orlando-Kissimmee-Sanford MSA, FL	H	9.51 AE	11.43 MW	13.57 AEX	FLBLS	7/16-9/16
	Tampa-St. Petersburg-Clearwater MSA, FL	H	9.80 AE	11.35 MW	12.91 AEX	FLBLS	7/16-9/16
	Georgia	Y	20400 FQ	24820 MW	29800 TQ	USBLS	5/15
	Atlanta-Sandy Springs-Roswell MSA, GA	Y	21290 FQ	26100 MW	30560 TQ	USBLS	5/15
	Augusta-Richmond County MSA, GA-SC	Y	20100 FQ	22810 MW	26260 TQ	USBLS	5/15
	Hawaii	Y	23750 FQ	31050 MW	36980 TQ	USBLS	5/15
	Urban Honolulu MSA, HI	Y	22290 FQ	28180 MW	36660 TQ	USBLS	5/15
	Idaho	Y	21310 FQ	27020 MW	34120 TQ	USBLS	5/15
	Boise City MSA, ID	Y	22260 FQ	26660 MW	30870 TQ	USBLS	5/15
	Illinois	Y	21400 FQ	26100 MW	33140 TQ	USBLS	5/15
	Chicago-Naperville-Arlington Heights PMSA, IL	Y	22010 FQ	26590 MW	34510 TQ	USBLS	5/15
	Lake County-Kenosha County PMSA, IL-WI	Y	20780 FQ	26980 MW	33490 TQ	USBLS	5/15
	Indiana	Y	19820 FQ	23850 MW	29980 TQ	USBLS	5/15
	Gary PMSA, IN	Y	19440 FQ	25060 MW	29620 TQ	USBLS	5/15
	Indianapolis-Carmel-Anderson MSA, IN	Y	20990 FQ	24330 MW	29450 TQ	USBLS	5/15
	Iowa	Y	20310 FQ	24710 MW	30710 TQ	USBLS	5/15
	Des Moines-West Des Moines MSA, IA	Y	23980 FQ	28260 MW	33970 TQ	USBLS	5/15
	Kansas	Y	20220 FQ	24450 MW	29620 TQ	USBLS	5/15
	Wichita MSA, KS	Y	19480 FQ	23710 MW	30430 TQ	USBLS	5/15
	Kentucky	Y	19580 FQ	23340 MW	28280 TQ	USBLS	5/15
	Louisville-Jefferson County MSA, KY-IN	Y	21060 FQ	24650 MW	29490 TQ	USBLS	5/15
	Louisiana	Y	18730 FQ	22640 MW	28770 TQ	USBLS	5/15
	Baton Rouge MSA, LA	Y	19060 FQ	24760 MW	31820 TQ	USBLS	5/15
	New Orleans-Metairie MSA, LA	Y	18820 FQ	22510 MW	27720 TQ	USBLS	5/15
	Maine	Y	24850 FQ	29060 MW	35160 TQ	USBLS	5/15
	Portland-South Portland MSA, ME	Y	25090 FQ	28930 MW	35110 TQ	USBLS	5/15
	Maryland	Y	20204 AE	28324 MW	32385 AEX	MDBLS	4/16
	Baltimore-Columbia-Towson MSA, MD	Y	22530 FQ	28550 MW	36070 TQ	USBLS	5/15
	Salisbury MSA, MD-DE	Y	21370 FQ	24950 MW	30230 TQ	USBLS	5/15
	Massachusetts	Y	26570 FQ	32820 MW	39600 TQ	USBLS	5/15
	Boston-Cambridge-Newton NECTA, MA	Y	26750 FQ	33650 MW	41050 TQ	USBLS	5/15
	Worcester MSA, MA-CT	Y	24720 FQ	29610 MW	38230 TQ	USBLS	5/15
	Michigan	Y	20530 FQ	24060 MW	30420 TQ	USBLS	5/15
	Detroit-Dearborn-Livonia PMSA, MI	Y	20090 FQ	23890 MW	30920 TQ	USBLS	5/15
	Grand Rapids-Wyoming MSA, MI	Y	21320 FQ	24360 MW	29760 TQ	USBLS	5/15
	Minnesota	Y	21177 FQ	26065 MW	34709 TQ	MNBLS	1/16-3/16
	Minneapolis-St. Paul-Bloomington MSA, MN-WI	Y	21975 FQ	27337 MW	36012 TQ	MNBLS	1/16-3/16
	Mississippi	Y	18430 FQ	21910 MW	26360 TQ	USBLS	5/15

AE Average entry wage	**AWR** Average wage range	**H** Hourly	**LR** Low end range	**MTC** Median total compensation	**TCC** Total cash compensation
AEX Average experienced wage	**B** Biweekly	**HI** Highest wage paid	**M** Monthly	**MW** Median wage paid	**TQ** Third quartile wage
ATC Average total compensation	**D** Daily	**HR** High end range	**MCC** Median cash compensation	**MWR** Median wage range	**W** Weekly
AW Average wage paid	**FQ** First quartile wage	**LO** Lowest wage paid	**ME** Median entry wage	**S** See annotated source	**Y** Yearly

Occupation/Type/Industry	Location	Per	Low	Mid	High	Source	Date
Landscaping and Groundskeeping Worker							
	Jackson MSA, MS	Y	19750 FQ	22980 MW	27350 TQ	USBLS	5/15
	Missouri	Y	20550 FQ	24750 MW	30180 TQ	USBLS	5/15
	Kansas City MSA, MO-KS	Y	21960 FQ	26010 MW	30130 TQ	USBLS	5/15
	St. Louis MSA, MO-IL	Y	21830 FQ	25600 MW	31250 TQ	USBLS	5/15
	Montana	Y	20300 FQ	24370 MW	29890 TQ	USBLS	5/15
	Billings MSA, MT	Y	19920 FQ	22970 MW	31410 TQ	USBLS	5/15
	Nebraska	Y	20955 FQ	24730 MW	30070 TQ	NEBLS	7/16-9/16
	Omaha-Council Bluffs MSA, NE-IA	Y	22335 FQ	26755 MW	31005 TQ	NEBLS	7/16-9/16
	Nevada	Y	20020 FQ	23820 MW	29990 TQ	USBLS	5/15
	Las Vegas-Henderson-Paradise MSA, NV	Y	19570 FQ	23180 MW	29250 TQ	USBLS	5/15
	New Hampshire	H	10.84 AE	14.19 MW	16.69 AEX	NHBLS	6/16
	Manchester NECTA, NH	H	10.94 AE	14.54 MW	17.68 AEX	NHBLS	6/16
	Nashua NECTA, NH-MA	Y	22120 FQ	25290 MW	29670 TQ	USBLS	5/15
	New Jersey	Y	21670 FQ	25650 MW	32280 TQ	USBLS	5/15
	Camden PMSA, NJ	Y	19260 FQ	22210 MW	27360 TQ	USBLS	5/15
	Newark PMSA, NJ-PA	Y	21790 FQ	25190 MW	31840 TQ	USBLS	5/15
	Trenton MSA, NJ	Y	22170 FQ	26950 MW	33920 TQ	USBLS	5/15
	New Mexico	Y	19120 FQ	23310 MW	28370 TQ	USBLS	5/15
	Albuquerque MSA, NM	Y	19530 FQ	23900 MW	28120 TQ	USBLS	5/15
	New York	Y	21370 AE	29830 MW	37410 AEX	NYBLS	1/16-3/16
	Buffalo-Cheektowaga-Niagara Falls MSA, NY	Y	21210 FQ	25760 MW	31340 TQ	USBLS	5/15
	Nassau County-Suffolk County PMSA, NY	Y	23590 FQ	31320 MW	38350 TQ	USBLS	5/15
	New York-Jersey City-White Plains PMSA, NY-NJ	Y	23870 FQ	29820 MW	38030 TQ	USBLS	5/15
	Rochester MSA, NY	Y	21910 FQ	27330 MW	33370 TQ	USBLS	5/15
	North Carolina	Y	20470 FQ	23990 MW	29010 TQ	USBLS	5/15
	Charlotte-Concord-Gastonia MSA, NC-SC	Y	20770 FQ	24130 MW	28930 TQ	USBLS	5/15
	Raleigh MSA, NC	Y	20770 FQ	24060 MW	29020 TQ	USBLS	5/15
	North Dakota	Y	21700 FQ	25570 MW	32300 TQ	USBLS	5/15
	Fargo MSA, ND-MN	Y	21680 FQ	23960 MW	31680 TQ	USBLS	5/15
	Ohio	Y	19190 FQ	23410 MW	29990 TQ	USBLS	5/15
	Cincinnati MSA, OH-KY-IN	Y	19270 FQ	23390 MW	29310 TQ	USBLS	5/15
	Cleveland-Elyria MSA, OH	Y	18900 FQ	24470 MW	31200 TQ	USBLS	5/15
	Columbus MSA, OH	Y	20490 FQ	24070 MW	29980 TQ	USBLS	5/15
	Oklahoma	Y	19360 FQ	22680 MW	27490 TQ	USBLS	5/15
	Oklahoma City MSA, OK	Y	18860 FQ	22520 MW	27700 TQ	USBLS	5/15
	Tulsa MSA, OK	Y	20600 FQ	23450 MW	28290 TQ	USBLS	5/15
	Oregon	H	11.15 FQ	13.59 MW	17.04 TQ	ORBLS	2016
	Portland-Vancouver-Hillsboro MSA, OR-WA	Y	23790 FQ	29150 MW	37120 TQ	USBLS	5/15
	Pennsylvania	Y	21330 FQ	26100 MW	32830 TQ	USBLS	5/15
	Allentown-Bethlehem-Easton MSA, PA-NJ	Y	20310 FQ	24950 MW	30610 TQ	USBLS	5/15
	Harrisburg-Carlisle MSA, PA	Y	22370 FQ	27420 MW	32590 TQ	USBLS	5/15
	Montgomery County-Bucks County-Chester County PMSA, PA	Y	23680 FQ	28260 MW	34840 TQ	USBLS	5/15
	Philadelphia PMSA, PA	Y	22610 FQ	27590 MW	34440 TQ	USBLS	5/15
	Pittsburgh MSA, PA	Y	20830 FQ	25130 MW	31720 TQ	USBLS	5/15
	Rhode Island	Y	23870 FQ	28540 MW	35570 TQ	USBLS	5/15
	Providence-Warwick MSA, RI-MA	Y	23860 FQ	28530 MW	35000 TQ	USBLS	5/15
	South Carolina	Y	18710 FQ	22310 MW	27110 TQ	USBLS	5/15
	Charleston-North Charleston MSA, SC	Y	20850 FQ	23810 MW	28160 TQ	USBLS	5/15
	Columbia MSA, SC	Y	18260 FQ	21610 MW	25750 TQ	USBLS	5/15
	Greenville-Anderson-Mauldin MSA, SC	Y	17870 FQ	21790 MW	28420 TQ	USBLS	5/15
	South Dakota	Y	20680 FQ	23690 MW	28420 TQ	USBLS	5/15
	Sioux Falls MSA, SD	Y	21540 FQ	24690 MW	30170 TQ	USBLS	5/15
	Tennessee	Y	21080 FQ	24840 MW	29500 TQ	USBLS	5/15
	Knoxville MSA, TN	Y	21490 FQ	26600 MW	36240 TQ	USBLS	5/15
	Memphis MSA, TN-MS-AR	Y	21070 FQ	24240 MW	28310 TQ	USBLS	5/15

AE	Average entry wage	AWR	Average wage range	H	Hourly	LR	Low end range	MTC	Median total compensation	TCC	Total cash compensation
AEX	Average experienced wage	B	Biweekly	HI	Highest wage paid	M	Monthly	MW	Median wage paid	TQ	Third quartile wage
ATC	Average total compensation	D	Daily	HR	High end range	MCC	Median cash compensation	MWR	Median wage range	W	Weekly
AW	Average wage paid	FQ	First quartile wage	LO	Lowest wage paid	ME	Median entry wage	S	See annotated source	Y	Yearly

Occupation/Type/Industry	Location	Per	Low	Mid	High	Source	Date
Landscaping and Groundskeeping Worker	Nashville-Davidson–Murfreesboro–Franklin MSA, TN	Y	22170 FQ	26210 MW	29450 TQ	USBLS	5/15
	Texas	Y	20150 FQ	23450 MW	28810 TQ	USBLS	5/15
	Austin-Round Rock MSA, TX	Y	21690 FQ	24980 MW	30230 TQ	USBLS	5/15
	Dallas-Plano-Irving PMSA, TX	Y	20400 FQ	23660 MW	29630 TQ	USBLS	5/15
	Fort Worth-Arlington PMSA, TX	Y	21170 FQ	25210 MW	30080 TQ	USBLS	5/15
	Houston-The Woodlands-Sugar Land MSA, TX	Y	19690 FQ	22940 MW	28170 TQ	USBLS	5/15
	San Antonio-New Braunfels MSA, TX	Y	20160 FQ	22930 MW	27080 TQ	USBLS	5/15
	Utah	Y	19840 FQ	24700 MW	29460 TQ	USBLS	5/15
	Ogden-Clearfield MSA, UT	Y	18590 FQ	22530 MW	28580 TQ	USBLS	5/15
	Provo-Orem MSA, UT	Y	19610 FQ	24550 MW	28620 TQ	USBLS	5/15
	Salt Lake City MSA, UT	Y	21150 FQ	26210 MW	30080 TQ	USBLS	5/15
	Vermont	Y	23490 FQ	29020 MW	35810 TQ	USBLS	5/15
	Burlington-South Burlington MSA, VT	Y	23990 FQ	28500 MW	34100 TQ	USBLS	5/15
	Virginia	Y	21580 FQ	25500 MW	30410 TQ	USBLS	5/15
	Richmond MSA, VA	Y	21850 FQ	26240 MW	32520 TQ	USBLS	5/15
	Virginia Beach-Norfolk-Newport News MSA, VA-NC	Y	20150 FQ	22930 MW	27260 TQ	USBLS	5/15
	Washington	H	12.03 FQ	14.28 MW	18.35 TQ	WABLS	3/16
	Seattle-Bellevue-Everett PMSA, WA	H	13.11 FQ	14.90 MW	19.46 TQ	WABLS	3/16
	Tacoma-Lakewood PMSA, WA	H	11.70 FQ	14.44 MW	18.96 TQ	WABLS	3/16
	West Virginia	Y	18740 FQ	22220 MW	27420 TQ	USBLS	5/15
	Huntington-Ashland MSA, WV-KY-OH	Y	18630 FQ	21290 MW	24380 TQ	USBLS	5/15
	Wisconsin	Y	20590 FQ	25240 MW	30940 TQ	USBLS	5/15
	Madison MSA, WI	Y	21900 FQ	26730 MW	32260 TQ	USBLS	5/15
	Milwaukee-Waukesha-West Allis MSA, WI	Y	20450 FQ	25530 MW	30910 TQ	USBLS	5/15
	Wyoming	Y	22590 FQ	28810 MW	36100 TQ	USBLS	5/15
	Cheyenne MSA, WY	Y	21700 FQ	24780 MW	30460 TQ	USBLS	5/15
	Puerto Rico	Y	16710 FQ	17990 MW	19280 TQ	USBLS	5/15
	San Juan-Carolina-Caguas MSA, PR	Y	16780 FQ	18130 MW	19560 TQ	USBLS	5/15
	Virgin Islands	Y	19970 FQ	24060 MW	29400 TQ	USBLS	5/15
	Guam	Y	17980 FQ	18800 MW	19760 TQ	USBLS	5/15
Latent Fingerprint Examiner							
Police Department, Municipal Government	Bakersfield, CA	Y			51609 HI	CACIT	6/28/16
Police Department, Municipal Government	Huntington Beach, CA	Y		64401 AW		CACIT	6/28/16
Police Department, Municipal Government	Oakland, CA	M	6391 LO		9082 HI	CAC	7/15
Police Department, Municipal Government	Seattle, WA	H	33.00 LO		38.44 HI	CSSS	1/13/16
State Department of Public Safety	Arizona	M	3705 LO		5304 HI	CAC	1/14
Latent Fingerprint Technician							
Police Department, Municipal Government	Salinas, CA	Y			64780 HI	CACIT	6/28/16
Police Department, Municipal Government	Detroit, MI	M	2742 LO		3233 HI	DETGOV	2016
Lathe and Turning Machine Tool Setter, Operator, and Tender							
Metals and Plastics	Alabama	Y	26178 AE	37221 AW	42743 AEX	ALBLS	6/16
Metals and Plastics	Birmingham-Hoover MSA, AL	Y	24986 AE	28245 AW	29880 AEX	ALBLS	6/16
Metals and Plastics	Arizona	Y	27510 FQ	34030 MW	40890 TQ	USBLS	5/15
Metals and Plastics	Phoenix-Mesa-Scottsdale MSA, AZ	Y	27810 FQ	34220 MW	41940 TQ	USBLS	5/15
Metals and Plastics	Arkansas	Y	23530 FQ	31890 MW	40720 TQ	USBLS	5/15
Metals and Plastics	Little Rock-North Little Rock-Conway MSA, AR	Y	33920 FQ	39670 MW	44820 TQ	USBLS	5/15
Metals and Plastics	California	H	13.33 FQ	17.21 MW	22.20 TQ	CABLS	1/16-3/16
Metals and Plastics	Anaheim-Santa Ana-Irvine PMSA, CA	H	11.49 FQ	14.54 MW	21.36 TQ	CABLS	1/16-3/16
Metals and Plastics	Los Angeles-Long Beach-Glendale PMSA, CA	H	14.97 FQ	17.94 MW	22.14 TQ	CABLS	1/16-3/16
Metals and Plastics	Oakland-Hayward-Berkeley PMSA, CA	H	13.20 FQ	18.78 MW	25.57 TQ	CABLS	1/16-3/16

AE	Average entry wage	AWR	Average wage range	H	Hourly	LR	Low end range	MTC	Median total compensation	TCC	Total cash compensation
AEX	Average experienced wage	B	Biweekly	HI	Highest wage paid	M	Monthly	MW	Median wage paid	TQ	Third quartile wage
ATC	Average total compensation	D	Daily	HR	High end range	MCC	Median cash compensation	MWR	Median wage range	W	Weekly
AW	Average wage paid	FQ	First quartile wage	LO	Lowest wage paid	ME	Median entry wage	S	See annotated source	Y	Yearly

Occupation/Type/Industry	Location	Per	Low	Mid	High	Source	Date
Lathe and Turning Machine Tool Setter, Operator, and Tender							
Metals and Plastics	Riverside-San Bernardino-Ontario MSA, CA	H	12.87 FQ	16.90 MW	21.37 TQ	CABLS	1/16-3/16
Metals and Plastics	Sacramento–Roseville–Arden-Arcade MSA, CA	H	16.83 FQ	20.03 MW	25.66 TQ	CABLS	1/16-3/16
Metals and Plastics	San Diego-Carlsbad MSA, CA	H	13.67 FQ	17.30 MW	21.79 TQ	CABLS	1/16-3/16
Metals and Plastics	San Francisco-Redwood City-South San Francisco PMSA, CA	H	12.34 FQ	16.87 MW	22.16 TQ	CABLS	1/16-3/16
Metals and Plastics	Colorado	Y	29440 FQ	35460 MW	42030 TQ	USBLS	5/15
Metals and Plastics	Denver-Aurora-Lakewood MSA, CO	Y	34430 FQ	39880 MW	46040 TQ	USBLS	5/15
Metals and Plastics	Connecticut	Y		36737 MW		CTBLS	1/16-3/16
Metals and Plastics	Bridgeport-Stamford-Norwalk MSA, CT	Y	40250 FQ	47290 MW	56370 TQ	USBLS	5/15
Metals and Plastics	Hartford-West Hartford-East Hartford MSA, CT	Y	32130 FQ	39520 MW	48420 TQ	USBLS	5/15
Metals and Plastics	Florida	H	11.23 AE	15.92 MW	18.37 AEX	FLBLS	7/16-9/16
Metals and Plastics	Fort Lauderdale-Pompano Beach-Deerfield Beach PMSA, FL	H	15.15 AE	18.73 MW	21.75 AEX	FLBLS	7/16-9/16
Metals and Plastics	Miami-Miami Beach-Kendall PMSA, FL	H	11.27 AE	15.12 MW	17.89 AEX	FLBLS	7/16-9/16
Metals and Plastics	Orlando-Kissimmee-Sanford MSA, FL	H	13.18 AE	16.59 MW	18.73 AEX	FLBLS	7/16-9/16
Metals and Plastics	Tampa-St. Petersburg-Clearwater MSA, FL	H	10.94 AE	13.66 MW	16.14 AEX	FLBLS	7/16-9/16
Metals and Plastics	Georgia	Y	34580 FQ	40090 MW	45320 TQ	USBLS	5/15
Metals and Plastics	Atlanta-Sandy Springs-Roswell MSA, GA	Y	34850 FQ	40270 MW	45240 TQ	USBLS	5/15
Metals and Plastics	Idaho	Y	32830 FQ	37960 MW	45600 TQ	USBLS	5/15
Metals and Plastics	Illinois	Y	31560 FQ	39010 MW	47970 TQ	USBLS	5/15
Metals and Plastics	Chicago-Naperville-Arlington Heights PMSA, IL	Y	32630 FQ	39220 MW	47680 TQ	USBLS	5/15
Metals and Plastics	Lake County-Kenosha County PMSA, IL-WI	Y	28950 FQ	35900 MW	44170 TQ	USBLS	5/15
Metals and Plastics	Indiana	Y	30070 FQ	36190 MW	44850 TQ	USBLS	5/15
Metals and Plastics	Gary PMSA, IN	Y	41010 FQ	45600 MW	50160 TQ	USBLS	5/15
Metals and Plastics	Indianapolis-Carmel-Anderson MSA, IN	Y	30550 FQ	38870 MW	53480 TQ	USBLS	5/15
Metals and Plastics	Iowa	Y	31970 FQ	37050 MW	43350 TQ	USBLS	5/15
Metals and Plastics	Kansas	Y	32370 FQ	38170 MW	46310 TQ	USBLS	5/15
Metals and Plastics	Wichita MSA, KS	Y	34070 FQ	39950 MW	48570 TQ	USBLS	5/15
Metals and Plastics	Kentucky	Y	32720 FQ	37120 MW	43330 TQ	USBLS	5/15
Metals and Plastics	Louisville-Jefferson County MSA, KY-IN	Y	31030 FQ	43390 MW	48640 TQ	USBLS	5/15
Metals and Plastics	Louisiana	Y	31850 FQ	39610 MW	47680 TQ	USBLS	5/15
Metals and Plastics	Maine	Y	38770 FQ	44470 MW	49330 TQ	USBLS	5/15
Metals and Plastics	Maryland	Y	27563 AE	41530 MW	48514 AEX	MDBLS	4/16
Metals and Plastics	Baltimore-Columbia-Towson MSA, MD	Y	36380 FQ	47010 MW	64140 TQ	USBLS	5/15
Metals and Plastics	Massachusetts	Y	37090 FQ	46790 MW	60690 TQ	USBLS	5/15
Metals and Plastics	Boston-Cambridge-Newton NECTA, MA	Y	36660 FQ	46430 MW	62930 TQ	USBLS	5/15
Metals and Plastics	Worcester MSA, MA-CT	Y	33420 FQ	43060 MW	55410 TQ	USBLS	5/15
Metals and Plastics	Michigan	Y	26070 FQ	33160 MW	40410 TQ	USBLS	5/15
Metals and Plastics	Detroit-Dearborn-Livonia PMSA, MI	Y	28880 FQ	37660 MW	45530 TQ	USBLS	5/15
Metals and Plastics	Grand Rapids-Wyoming MSA, MI	Y	32110 FQ	35650 MW	39190 TQ	USBLS	5/15
Metals and Plastics	Minnesota	Y	33350 FQ	40123 MW	48628 TQ	MNBLS	1/16-3/16
Metals and Plastics	Minneapolis-St. Paul-Bloomington MSA, MN-WI	Y	36114 FQ	42341 MW	49701 TQ	MNBLS	1/16-3/16
Metals and Plastics	Mississippi	Y	26600 FQ	35530 MW	43510 TQ	USBLS	5/15
Metals and Plastics	Missouri	Y	28940 FQ	37170 MW	46270 TQ	USBLS	5/15
Metals and Plastics	Kansas City MSA, MO-KS	Y	31700 FQ	37330 MW	43980 TQ	USBLS	5/15
Metals and Plastics	St. Louis MSA, MO-IL	Y	28620 FQ	38040 MW	47790 TQ	USBLS	5/15
Metals and Plastics	Nebraska	Y	31350 FQ	40440 MW	45920 TQ	NEBLS	7/16-9/16
Metals and Plastics	Omaha-Council Bluffs MSA, NE-IA	Y	42360 FQ	45345 MW	48325 TQ	NEBLS	7/16-9/16
Metals and Plastics	Nevada	Y	27180 FQ	30690 MW	39000 TQ	USBLS	5/15

AE	Average entry wage	AWR	Average wage range	H	Hourly	LR	Low end range	MTC	Median total compensation	TCC	Total cash compensation
AEX	Average experienced wage	B	Biweekly	HI	Highest wage paid	M	Monthly	MW	Median wage paid	TQ	Third quartile wage
ATC	Average total compensation	D	Daily	HR	High end range	MCC	Median cash compensation	MWR	Median wage range	W	Weekly
AW	Average wage paid	FQ	First quartile wage	LO	Lowest wage paid	ME	Median entry wage	S	See annotated source	Y	Yearly

Occupation/Type/Industry	Location	Per	Low	Mid	High	Source	Date
Lathe and Turning Machine Tool Setter, Operator, and Tender							
Metals and Plastics	New Hampshire	H	13.82 AE	19.65 MW	22.91 AEX	NHBLS	6/16
Metals and Plastics	Nashua NECTA, NH-MA	Y	27190 FQ	32470 MW	40470 TQ	USBLS	5/15
Metals and Plastics	New Jersey	Y	26900 FQ	33160 MW	45460 TQ	USBLS	5/15
Metals and Plastics	Camden PMSA, NJ	Y	33820 FQ	37550 MW	45420 TQ	USBLS	5/15
Metals and Plastics	Newark PMSA, NJ-PA	Y	25940 FQ	30220 MW	40750 TQ	USBLS	5/15
Metals and Plastics	New York	Y	27250 AE	37690 MW	46130 AEX	NYBLS	1/16-3/16
Metals and Plastics	Buffalo-Cheektowaga-Niagara Falls MSA, NY	Y	27980 FQ	34800 MW	43450 TQ	USBLS	5/15
Metals and Plastics	Nassau County-Suffolk County PMSA, NY	Y	32130 FQ	38450 MW	55390 TQ	USBLS	5/15
Metals and Plastics	New York-Jersey City-White Plains PMSA, NY-NJ	Y	32900 FQ	43230 MW	57510 TQ	USBLS	5/15
Metals and Plastics	Rochester MSA, NY	Y	27520 FQ	34680 MW	42750 TQ	USBLS	5/15
Metals and Plastics	North Carolina	Y	32090 FQ	39020 MW	46180 TQ	USBLS	5/15
Metals and Plastics	Charlotte-Concord-Gastonia MSA, NC-SC	Y	37230 FQ	45460 MW	52730 TQ	USBLS	5/15
Metals and Plastics	Raleigh MSA, NC	Y	33980 FQ	37100 MW	41230 TQ	USBLS	5/15
Metals and Plastics	Ohio	Y	29870 FQ	37920 MW	46180 TQ	USBLS	5/15
Metals and Plastics	Cincinnati MSA, OH-KY-IN	Y	33540 FQ	39560 MW	46210 TQ	USBLS	5/15
Metals and Plastics	Cleveland-Elyria MSA, OH	Y	28730 FQ	35180 MW	42560 TQ	USBLS	5/15
Metals and Plastics	Columbus MSA, OH	Y	24230 FQ	29470 MW	40160 TQ	USBLS	5/15
Metals and Plastics	Oklahoma	Y	33120 FQ	39020 MW	45910 TQ	USBLS	5/15
Metals and Plastics	Oklahoma City MSA, OK	Y	32540 FQ	35890 MW	39240 TQ	USBLS	5/15
Metals and Plastics	Tulsa MSA, OK	Y	37240 FQ	43580 MW	48370 TQ	USBLS	5/15
Metals and Plastics	Oregon	H	18.55 FQ	25.02 MW	28.98 TQ	ORBLS	2016
Metals and Plastics	Portland-Vancouver-Hillsboro MSA, OR-WA	Y	37720 FQ	51920 MW	59640 TQ	USBLS	5/15
Metals and Plastics	Pennsylvania	Y	30150 FQ	36050 MW	43010 TQ	USBLS	5/15
Metals and Plastics	Allentown-Bethlehem-Easton MSA, PA-NJ	Y	30390 FQ	38020 MW	45840 TQ	USBLS	5/15
Metals and Plastics	Montgomery County-Bucks County-Chester County PMSA, PA	Y	34110 FQ	41470 MW	47920 TQ	USBLS	5/15
Metals and Plastics	Philadelphia PMSA, PA	Y	27930 FQ	32800 MW	44720 TQ	USBLS	5/15
Metals and Plastics	Pittsburgh MSA, PA	Y	27410 FQ	34470 MW	40150 TQ	USBLS	5/15
Metals and Plastics	Rhode Island	Y	30700 FQ	36500 MW	43830 TQ	USBLS	5/15
Metals and Plastics	Providence-Warwick MSA, RI-MA	Y	32110 FQ	37800 MW	46720 TQ	USBLS	5/15
Metals and Plastics	South Carolina	Y	28460 FQ	34830 MW	39840 TQ	USBLS	5/15
Metals and Plastics	Charleston-North Charleston MSA, SC	Y	28500 FQ	31670 MW	38790 TQ	USBLS	5/15
Metals and Plastics	Greenville-Anderson-Mauldin MSA, SC	Y	30280 FQ	35640 MW	41290 TQ	USBLS	5/15
Metals and Plastics	South Dakota	Y	27570 FQ	30430 MW	35940 TQ	USBLS	5/15
Metals and Plastics	Tennessee	Y	28970 FQ	36640 MW	45620 TQ	USBLS	5/15
Metals and Plastics	Knoxville MSA, TN	Y	26200 FQ	31350 MW	42920 TQ	USBLS	5/15
Metals and Plastics	Memphis MSA, TN-MS-AR	Y	23690 FQ	29320 MW	35140 TQ	USBLS	5/15
Metals and Plastics	Nashville-Davidson–Murfreesboro–Franklin MSA, TN	Y	27620 FQ	34850 MW	41990 TQ	USBLS	5/15
Metals and Plastics	Texas	Y	27920 FQ	36410 MW	46920 TQ	USBLS	5/15
Metals and Plastics	Austin-Round Rock MSA, TX	Y	32600 FQ	38850 MW	46440 TQ	USBLS	5/15
Metals and Plastics	Dallas-Plano-Irving PMSA, TX	Y	27970 FQ	36670 MW	44900 TQ	USBLS	5/15
Metals and Plastics	Fort Worth-Arlington PMSA, TX	Y	33250 FQ	39950 MW	51430 TQ	USBLS	5/15
Metals and Plastics	Houston-The Woodlands-Sugar Land MSA, TX	Y	26170 FQ	33040 MW	45600 TQ	USBLS	5/15
Metals and Plastics	San Antonio-New Braunfels MSA, TX	Y	30980 FQ	34750 MW	38460 TQ	USBLS	5/15
Metals and Plastics	Utah	Y	27240 FQ	32150 MW	40680 TQ	USBLS	5/15
Metals and Plastics	Ogden-Clearfield MSA, UT	Y	27000 FQ	29610 MW	35080 TQ	USBLS	5/15
Metals and Plastics	Salt Lake City MSA, UT	Y	27780 FQ	36460 MW	45300 TQ	USBLS	5/15
Metals and Plastics	Vermont	Y	25670 FQ	32500 MW	38510 TQ	USBLS	5/15
Metals and Plastics	Burlington-South Burlington MSA, VT	Y	24550 FQ	33840 MW	41070 TQ	USBLS	5/15
Metals and Plastics	Virginia	Y	36440 FQ	44590 MW	63250 TQ	USBLS	5/15
Metals and Plastics	Washington	H	14.55 FQ	18.71 MW	24.05 TQ	WABLS	3/16
Metals and Plastics	Seattle-Bellevue-Everett PMSA, WA	H	14.19 FQ	18.01 MW	23.92 TQ	WABLS	3/16
Metals and Plastics	West Virginia	Y	30480 FQ	41980 MW	49760 TQ	USBLS	5/15

AE Average entry wage	**AWR** Average wage range	**H** Hourly	**LR** Low end range	**MTC** Median total compensation	**TCC** Total cash compensation
AEX Average experienced wage	**B** Biweekly	**HI** Highest wage paid	**M** Monthly	**MW** Median wage paid	**TQ** Third quartile wage
ATC Average total compensation	**D** Daily	**HR** High end range	**MCC** Median cash compensation	**MWR** Median wage range	**W** Weekly
AW Average wage paid	**FQ** First quartile wage	**LO** Lowest wage paid	**ME** Median entry wage	**S** See annotated source	**Y** Yearly

Occupation/Type/Industry	Location	Per	Low	Mid	High	Source	Date
Lathe and Turning Machine Tool Setter, Operator, and Tender							
Metals and Plastics	Huntington-Ashland MSA, WV-KY-OH	Y	29310 FQ	38270 MW	45800 TQ	USBLS	5/15
Metals and Plastics	Wisconsin	Y	32190 FQ	38230 MW	46230 TQ	USBLS	5/15
Metals and Plastics	Milwaukee-Waukesha-West Allis MSA, WI	Y	31180 FQ	37170 MW	45870 TQ	USBLS	5/15
Laundry and Dry-Cleaning Worker							
	Alabama	Y	17521 AE	19999 AW	21243 AEX	ALBLS	6/16
	Birmingham-Hoover MSA, AL	Y	17541 AE	19166 AW	19989 AEX	ALBLS	6/16
	Alaska	Y	20300 FQ	25270 MW	33600 TQ	USBLS	5/15
	Anchorage MSA, AK	Y	20420 FQ	26040 MW	35010 TQ	USBLS	5/15
	Arizona	Y	18730 FQ	20960 MW	23870 TQ	USBLS	5/15
	Phoenix-Mesa-Scottsdale MSA, AZ	Y	19140 FQ	21500 MW	24200 TQ	USBLS	5/15
	Tucson MSA, AZ	Y	17840 FQ	18890 MW	21320 TQ	USBLS	5/15
	Arkansas	Y	16990 FQ	18300 MW	19740 TQ	USBLS	5/15
	Little Rock-North Little Rock-Conway MSA, AR	Y	17070 FQ	18500 MW	21030 TQ	USBLS	5/15
	California	H	9.85 FQ	11.60 MW	14.08 TQ	CABLS	1/16-3/16
	Anaheim-Santa Ana-Irvine PMSA, CA	H	9.62 FQ	11.73 MW	14.15 TQ	CABLS	1/16-3/16
	Los Angeles-Long Beach-Glendale PMSA, CA	H	9.63 FQ	10.88 MW	13.13 TQ	CABLS	1/16-3/16
	Oakland-Hayward-Berkeley PMSA, CA	H	9.84 FQ	11.46 MW	13.72 TQ'	CABLS	1/16-3/16
	Riverside-San Bernardino-Ontario MSA, CA	H	9.79 FQ	11.39 MW	14.48 TQ	CABLS	1/16-3/16
	Sacramento–Roseville–Arden-Arcade MSA, CA	H	10.50 FQ	12.35 MW	14.15 TQ	CABLS	1/16-3/16
	San Diego-Carlsbad MSA, CA	H	10.70 FQ	12.15 MW	14.18 TQ	CABLS	1/16-3/16
	San Francisco-Redwood City-South San Francisco PMSA, CA	H	12.19 FQ	15.45 MW	20.51 TQ	CABLS	1/16-3/16
	Colorado	Y	18730 FQ	21080 MW	24740 TQ	USBLS	5/15
	Denver-Aurora-Lakewood MSA, CO	Y	19020 FQ	21760 MW	25860 TQ	USBLS	5/15
	Connecticut	Y		24324 MW		CTBLS	1/16-3/16
	Bridgeport-Stamford-Norwalk MSA, CT	Y	19950 FQ	24360 MW	31120 TQ	USBLS	5/15
	Hartford-West Hartford-East Hartford MSA, CT	Y	21460 FQ	23770 MW	28520 TQ	USBLS	5/15
	Delaware	Y	18240 FQ	21010 MW	25250 TQ	USBLS	5/15
	Wilmington PMSA, DE-MD-NJ	Y	18220 FQ	21260 MW	25970 TQ	USBLS	5/15
	District of Columbia	Y	22460 FQ	32620 MW	37940 TQ	USBLS	5/15
	Washington-Arlington-Alexandria PMSA, DC-VA-MD-WV	Y	18790 FQ	21800 MW	26710 TQ	USBLS	5/15
	Florida	H	8.99 AE	9.64 MW	11.22 AEX	FLBLS	7/16-9/16
	Fort Lauderdale-Pompano Beach-Deerfield Beach PMSA, FL	H	8.95 AE	9.52 MW	10.48 AEX	FLBLS	7/16-9/16
	Miami-Miami Beach-Kendall PMSA, FL	H	9.00 AE	9.55 MW	11.02 AEX	FLBLS	7/16-9/16
	Orlando-Kissimmee-Sanford MSA, FL	H	9.02 AE	9.89 MW	11.37 AEX	FLBLS	7/16-9/16
	Tampa-St. Petersburg-Clearwater MSA, FL	H	8.96 AE	9.65 MW	11.24 AEX	FLBLS	7/16-9/16
	Georgia	Y	17840 FQ	20250 MW	23130 TQ	USBLS	5/15
	Atlanta-Sandy Springs-Roswell MSA, GA	Y	18850 FQ	21440 MW	23780 TQ	USBLS	5/15
	Augusta-Richmond County MSA, GA-SC	Y	17180 FQ	18860 MW	21530 TQ	USBLS	5/15
	Hawaii	Y	25980 FQ	32500 MW	39610 TQ	USBLS	5/15
	Urban Honolulu MSA, HI	Y	24940 FQ	28980 MW	36640 TQ	USBLS	5/15
	Idaho	Y	17250 FQ	18980 MW	23150 TQ	USBLS	5/15
	Boise City MSA, ID	Y	17120 FQ	18590 MW	20240 TQ	USBLS	5/15
	Illinois	Y	18850 FQ	20610 MW	24530 TQ	USBLS	5/15

AE	Average entry wage	AWR	Average wage range	H	Hourly	LR	Low end range	MTC	Median total compensation	TCC	Total cash compensation
AEX	Average experienced wage	B	Biweekly	HI	Highest wage paid	M	Monthly	MW	Median wage paid	TQ	Third quartile wage
ATC	Average total compensation	D	Daily	HR	High end range	MCC	Median cash compensation	MWR	Median wage range	W	Weekly
AW	Average wage paid	FQ	First quartile wage	LO	Lowest wage paid	ME	Median entry wage	S	See annotated source	Y	Yearly

Occupation/Type/Industry	Location	Per	Low	Mid	High	Source	Date
Laundry and Dry-Cleaning Worker							
	Chicago-Naperville-Arlington Heights PMSA, IL	Y	18950 FQ	21090 MW	25460 TQ	USBLS	5/15
	Lake County-Kenosha County PMSA, IL-WI	Y	18920 FQ	20950 MW	24090 TQ	USBLS	5/15
	Indiana	Y	17730 FQ	20070 MW	23880 TQ	USBLS	5/15
	Gary PMSA, IN	Y	17100 FQ	18700 MW	21980 TQ	USBLS	5/15
	Indianapolis-Carmel-Anderson MSA, IN	Y	19800 FQ	22570 MW	25060 TQ	USBLS	5/15
	Iowa	Y	18900 FQ	21650 MW	24320 TQ	USBLS	5/15
	Des Moines-West Des Moines MSA, IA	Y	18950 FQ	21610 MW	24180 TQ	USBLS	5/15
	Kansas	Y	17790 FQ	20220 MW	23990 TQ	USBLS	5/15
	Wichita MSA, KS	Y	17270 FQ	18990 MW	22440 TQ	USBLS	5/15
	Kentucky	Y	17740 FQ	20040 MW	23590 TQ	USBLS	5/15
	Louisville-Jefferson County MSA, KY-IN	Y	17660 FQ	19790 MW	23260 TQ	USBLS	5/15
	Louisiana	Y	17080 FQ	18660 MW	21380 TQ	USBLS	5/15
	Baton Rouge MSA, LA	Y	16890 FQ	18430 MW	20990 TQ	USBLS	5/15
	New Orleans-Metairie MSA, LA	Y	17400 FQ	19340 MW	23200 TQ	USBLS	5/15
	Maine	Y	19210 FQ	21810 MW	24180 TQ	USBLS	5/15
	Portland-South Portland MSA, ME	Y	20760 FQ	22790 MW	24840 TQ	USBLS	5/15
	Maryland	Y	18065 AE	23152 MW	25696 AEX	MDBLS	4/16
	Baltimore-Columbia-Towson MSA, MD	Y	19520 FQ	23050 MW	29390 TQ	USBLS	5/15
	Salisbury MSA, MD-DE	Y	18330 FQ	20470 MW	23720 TQ	USBLS	5/15
	Massachusetts	Y	19420 FQ	21980 MW	26050 TQ	USBLS	5/15
	Boston-Cambridge-Newton NECTA, MA	Y	19410 FQ	22340 MW	26870 TQ	USBLS	5/15
	Worcester MSA, MA-CT	Y	20450 FQ	23130 MW	27460 TQ	USBLS	5/15
	Michigan	Y	18940 FQ	21930 MW	26430 TQ	USBLS	5/15
	Detroit-Dearborn-Livonia PMSA, MI	Y	19120 FQ	22220 MW	26320 TQ	USBLS	5/15
	Grand Rapids-Wyoming MSA, MI	Y	19640 FQ	23680 MW	27950 TQ	USBLS	5/15
	Minnesota	Y	21191 FQ	25220 MW	30191 TQ	MNBLS	1/16-3/16
	Minneapolis-St. Paul-Bloomington MSA, MN-WI	Y	22193 FQ	26374 MW	30981 TQ	MNBLS	1/16-3/16
	Mississippi	Y	17010 FQ	18510 MW	20460 TQ	USBLS	5/15
	Jackson MSA, MS	Y	17170 FQ	18700 MW	20970 TQ	USBLS	5/15
	Missouri	Y	17630 FQ	19350 MW	23200 TQ	USBLS	5/15
	Kansas City MSA, MO-KS	Y	17840 FQ	19910 MW	24150 TQ	USBLS	5/15
	St. Louis MSA, MO-IL	Y	18100 FQ	19950 MW	24000 TQ	USBLS	5/15
	Montana	Y	19760 FQ	22050 MW	24410 TQ	USBLS	5/15
	Billings MSA, MT	Y	20440 FQ	22430 MW	24420 TQ	USBLS	5/15
	Nebraska	Y	18695 FQ	21165 MW	24650 TQ	NEBLS	7/16-9/16
	Omaha-Council Bluffs MSA, NE-IA	Y	18705 FQ	21080 MW	24650 TQ	NEBLS	7/16-9/16
	Nevada	Y	20720 FQ	22610 MW	24510 TQ	USBLS	5/15
	Las Vegas-Henderson-Paradise MSA, NV	Y	21110 FQ	22850 MW	24640 TQ	USBLS	5/15
	New Hampshire	H	8.51 AE	10.82 MW	12.72 AEX	NHBLS	6/16
	Manchester NECTA, NH	H	8.51 AE	9.44 MW	11.31 AEX	NHBLS	6/16
	Nashua NECTA, NH-MA	Y	17680 FQ	19690 MW	24340 TQ	USBLS	5/15
	New Jersey	Y	19050 FQ	22250 MW	28570 TQ	USBLS	5/15
	Camden PMSA, NJ	Y	19040 FQ	21440 MW	24510 TQ	USBLS	5/15
	Newark PMSA, NJ-PA	Y	19060 FQ	22750 MW	29110 TQ	USBLS	5/15
	Trenton MSA, NJ	Y	18830 FQ	20670 MW	28240 TQ	USBLS	5/15
	New Mexico	Y	17740 FQ	19420 MW	22640 TQ	USBLS	5/15
	Albuquerque MSA, NM	Y	17660 FQ	19200 MW	22200 TQ	USBLS	5/15
	New York	Y	19350 AE	20350 MW	27020 AEX	NYBLS	1/16-3/16
	Buffalo-Cheektowaga-Niagara Falls MSA, NY	Y	18940 FQ	19670 MW	23920 TQ	USBLS	5/15
	Nassau County-Suffolk County PMSA, NY	Y	19070 FQ	21140 MW	28380 TQ	USBLS	5/15
	New York-Jersey City-White Plains PMSA, NY-NJ	Y	18900 FQ	19820 MW	25840 TQ	USBLS	5/15
	Rochester MSA, NY	Y	20690 FQ	24730 MW	29520 TQ	USBLS	5/15
	North Carolina	Y	17510 FQ	19460 MW	22800 TQ	USBLS	5/15

AE	Average entry wage	AWR	Average wage range	H	Hourly	LR	Low end range	MTC	Median total compensation	TCC	Total cash compensation
AEX	Average experienced wage	B	Biweekly	HI	Highest wage paid	M	Monthly	MW	Median wage paid	TQ	Third quartile wage
ATC	Average total compensation	D	Daily	HR	High end range	MCC	Median cash compensation	MWR	Median wage range	W	Weekly
AW	Average wage paid	FQ	First quartile wage	LO	Lowest wage paid	ME	Median entry wage	S	See annotated source	Y	Yearly

Occupation/Type/Industry	Location	Per	Low	Mid	High	Source	Date
Laundry and Dry-Cleaning Worker	Charlotte-Concord-Gastonia MSA, NC-SC	Y	17270 FQ	18880 MW	21620 TQ	USBLS	5/15
	Raleigh MSA, NC	Y	17850 FQ	20500 MW	23400 TQ	USBLS	5/15
	North Dakota	Y	19790 FQ	24940 MW	29260 TQ	USBLS	5/15
	Fargo MSA, ND-MN	Y	20690 FQ	25310 MW	28860 TQ	USBLS	5/15
	Ohio	Y	18400 FQ	20070 MW	23460 TQ	USBLS	5/15
	Cincinnati MSA, OH-KY-IN	Y	18210 FQ	20310 MW	24160 TQ	USBLS	5/15
	Cleveland-Elyria MSA, OH	Y	18700 FQ	21020 MW	23990 TQ	USBLS	5/15
	Columbus MSA, OH	Y	18740 FQ	20890 MW	23880 TQ	USBLS	5/15
	Oklahoma	Y	18000 FQ	20610 MW	24330 TQ	USBLS	5/15
	Oklahoma City MSA, OK	Y	18010 FQ	20430 MW	24380 TQ	USBLS	5/15
	Tulsa MSA, OK	Y	18400 FQ	21640 MW	25210 TQ	USBLS	5/15
	Oregon	H	9.97 FQ	11.20 MW	12.94 TQ	ORBLS	2016
	Portland-Vancouver-Hillsboro MSA, OR-WA	Y	20700 FQ	23340 MW	29530 TQ	USBLS	5/15
	Pennsylvania	Y	19000 FQ	22840 MW	28280 TQ	USBLS	5/15
	Allentown-Bethlehem-Easton MSA, PA-NJ	Y	22480 FQ	27750 MW	33610 TQ	USBLS	5/15
	Harrisburg-Carlisle MSA, PA	Y	18630 FQ	21950 MW	26270 TQ	USBLS	5/15
	Montgomery County-Bucks County-Chester County PMSA, PA	Y	19470 FQ	23310 MW	28550 TQ	USBLS	5/15
	Philadelphia PMSA, PA	Y	19370 FQ	24460 MW	30000 TQ	USBLS	5/15
	Pittsburgh MSA, PA	Y	18500 FQ	22020 MW	27600 TQ	USBLS	5/15
	Rhode Island	Y	19150 FQ	20880 MW	25770 TQ	USBLS	5/15
	Providence-Warwick MSA, RI-MA	Y	19170 FQ	20960 MW	25750 TQ	USBLS	5/15
	South Carolina	Y	17590 FQ	19800 MW	23350 TQ	USBLS	5/15
	Charleston-North Charleston MSA, SC	Y	18150 FQ	20670 MW	23130 TQ	USBLS	5/15
	Columbia MSA, SC	Y	18420 FQ	22350 MW	29950 TQ	USBLS	5/15
	Greenville-Anderson-Mauldin MSA, SC	Y	17560 FQ	19600 MW	22600 TQ	USBLS	5/15
	South Dakota	Y	18730 FQ	20000 MW	23110 TQ	USBLS	5/15
	Sioux Falls MSA, SD	Y	19240 FQ	21670 MW	24250 TQ	USBLS	5/15
	Tennessee	Y	17110 FQ	18720 MW	21520 TQ	USBLS	5/15
	Knoxville MSA, TN	Y	17650 FQ	19910 MW	22620 TQ	USBLS	5/15
	Memphis MSA, TN-MS-AR	Y	17040 FQ	18490 MW	20130 TQ	USBLS	5/15
	Nashville-Davidson–Murfreesboro–Franklin MSA, TN	Y	17210 FQ	18930 MW	22240 TQ	USBLS	5/15
	Texas	Y	17440 FQ	19340 MW	23320 TQ	USBLS	5/15
	Austin-Round Rock MSA, TX	Y	17120 FQ	18620 MW	20820 TQ	USBLS	5/15
	Dallas-Plano-Irving PMSA, TX	Y	17890 FQ	19960 MW	22930 TQ	USBLS	5/15
	Fort Worth-Arlington PMSA, TX	Y	17740 FQ	20290 MW	23630 TQ	USBLS	5/15
	Houston-The Woodlands-Sugar Land MSA, TX	Y	17200 FQ	18880 MW	22650 TQ	USBLS	5/15
	San Antonio-New Braunfels MSA, TX	Y	18580 FQ	21270 MW	24060 TQ	USBLS	5/15
	Utah	Y	18080 FQ	20860 MW	23710 TQ	USBLS	5/15
	Ogden-Clearfield MSA, UT	Y	18310 FQ	21310 MW	24160 TQ	USBLS	5/15
	Provo-Orem MSA, UT	Y	17660 FQ	19960 MW	23660 TQ	USBLS	5/15
	Salt Lake City MSA, UT	Y	17890 FQ	20620 MW	23580 TQ	USBLS	5/15
	Vermont	Y	20110 FQ	22650 MW	25570 TQ	USBLS	5/15
	Burlington-South Burlington MSA, VT	Y	20830 FQ	23160 MW	26790 TQ	USBLS	5/15
	Virginia	Y	18060 FQ	20870 MW	24250 TQ	USBLS	5/15
	Richmond MSA, VA	Y	19470 FQ	21670 MW	23950 TQ	USBLS	5/15
	Virginia Beach-Norfolk-Newport News MSA, VA-NC	Y	17230 FQ	19100 MW	23170 TQ	USBLS	5/15
	Washington	H	10.81 FQ	12.12 MW	15.08 TQ	WABLS	3/16
	Seattle-Bellevue-Everett PMSA, WA	H	11.26 FQ	13.44 MW	16.47 TQ	WABLS	3/16
	Tacoma-Lakewood PMSA, WA	H	10.48 FQ	11.35 MW	12.25 TQ	WABLS	3/16
	West Virginia	Y	18260 FQ	20370 MW	24800 TQ	USBLS	5/15
	Huntington-Ashland MSA, WV-KY-OH	Y	18560 FQ	22230 MW	29860 TQ	USBLS	5/15
	Wisconsin	Y	17780 FQ	20200 MW	25700 TQ	USBLS	5/15
	Madison MSA, WI	Y	18290 FQ	23290 MW	30320 TQ	USBLS	5/15

AE	Average entry wage	AWR	Average wage range	H	Hourly	LR	Low end range	MTC	Median total compensation	TCC	Total cash compensation
AEX	Average experienced wage	B	Biweekly	HI	Highest wage paid	M	Monthly	MW	Median wage paid	TQ	Third quartile wage
ATC	Average total compensation	D	Daily	HR	High end range	MCC	Median cash compensation	MWR	Median wage range	W	Weekly
AW	Average wage paid	FQ	First quartile wage	LO	Lowest wage paid	ME	Median entry wage	S	See annotated source	Y	Yearly

Occupation/Type/Industry	Location	Per	Low	Mid	High	Source	Date
Laundry and Dry-Cleaning Worker							
	Milwaukee-Waukesha-West Allis MSA, WI	Y	17560 FQ	19570 MW	25110 TQ	USBLS	5/15
	Wyoming	Y	19960 FQ	22820 MW	26340 TQ	USBLS	5/15
	Cheyenne MSA, WY	Y	19440 FQ	23150 MW	26830 TQ	USBLS	5/15
	Puerto Rico	Y	16820 FQ	18110 MW	19340 TQ	USBLS	5/15
	San Juan-Carolina-Caguas MSA, PR	Y	16840 FQ	18130 MW	19360 TQ	USBLS	5/15
	Virgin Islands	Y	18990 FQ	23170 MW	27190 TQ	USBLS	5/15
	Guam	Y	17790 FQ	18410 MW	19040 TQ	USBLS	5/15
Law Librarian							
City Attorney's Office	Los Angeles, CA	Y			88240 HI	CACIT	6/23/16
Law Revision Counsel							
United States House of Representatives	United States	Y			172500 HI	CRS01	2016
Law Teacher							
Postsecondary	Alabama	Y	35615 AE	87957 AW	114134 AEX	ALBLS	6/16
Postsecondary	Arizona	Y	65620 FQ	117940 MW	166370 TQ	USBLS	5/15
Postsecondary	Arkansas	Y	69570 FQ	118690 MW	164970 TQ	USBLS	5/15
Postsecondary	California	Y		122926 AW		CABLS	1/16-3/16
Postsecondary	Los Angeles-Long Beach-Glendale PMSA, CA	Y		144362 AW		CABLS	1/16-3/16
Postsecondary	Sacramento–Roseville–Arden-Arcade MSA, CA	Y		120441 AW		CABLS	1/16-3/16
Postsecondary	San Diego-Carlsbad MSA, CA	Y		85319 AW		CABLS	1/16-3/16
Postsecondary	Colorado	Y	52330 FQ	94000 MW	146680 TQ	USBLS	5/15
Postsecondary	Denver-Aurora-Lakewood MSA, CO	Y	64160 FQ	102340 MW	142500 TQ	USBLS	5/15
Postsecondary	Connecticut	Y		76939 MW		CTBLS	1/16-3/16
Postsecondary	Delaware	Y	42390 FQ	98080 MW	186940 TQ	USBLS	5/15
Postsecondary	District of Columbia	Y	72360 FQ	95910 MW	155440 TQ	USBLS	5/15
Postsecondary	Washington-Arlington-Alexandria PMSA, DC-VA-MD-WV	Y	69430 FQ	94180 MW	154760 TQ	USBLS	5/15
Postsecondary	Florida	Y	61309 AE	100634 MW	159358 AEX	FLBLS	7/16-9/16
Postsecondary	Miami-Miami Beach-Kendall PMSA, FL	Y	63518 AE	95466 MW	143752 AEX	FLBLS	7/16-9/16
Postsecondary	Orlando-Kissimmee-Sanford MSA, FL	Y	83233 AE	135851 MW	170647 AEX	FLBLS	7/16-9/16
Postsecondary	Tampa-St. Petersburg-Clearwater MSA, FL	Y	56919 AE	62745 MW	105515 AEX	FLBLS	7/16-9/16
Postsecondary	Georgia	Y	60420 FQ	96430 MW	158850 TQ	USBLS	5/15
Postsecondary	Atlanta-Sandy Springs-Roswell MSA, GA	Y	54400 FQ	83690 MW	102230 TQ	USBLS	5/15
Postsecondary	Chicago-Naperville-Arlington Heights PMSA, IL	Y	77950 FQ	124050 MW		USBLS	5/15
Postsecondary	Iowa	Y	106510 FQ	144110 MW	183980 TQ	USBLS	5/15
Postsecondary	Kentucky	Y	81330 FQ	132200 MW	173900 TQ	USBLS	5/15
Postsecondary	Maine	Y	89830 FQ	111270 MW	128730 TQ	USBLS	5/15
Postsecondary	Maryland	Y	63406 AE	142732 MW	182395 AEX	MDBLS	4/16
Postsecondary	Massachusetts	Y	82120 FQ	135290 MW	184620 TQ	USBLS	5/15
Postsecondary	Boston-Cambridge-Newton NECTA, MA	Y	83550 FQ	138340 MW		USBLS	5/15
Postsecondary	Michigan	Y	59770 FQ	112130 MW		USBLS	5/15
Postsecondary	Minnesota	Y	54939 FQ	76955 MW	125432 TQ	MNBLS	1/16-3/16
Postsecondary	Mississippi	Y	59360 FQ	76410 MW	117440 TQ	USBLS	5/15
Postsecondary	Jackson MSA, MS	Y	55870 FQ	72060 MW	113720 TQ	USBLS	5/15
Postsecondary	Missouri	Y	52380 FQ	99920 MW	157270 TQ	USBLS	5/15
Postsecondary	New Mexico	Y	63280 FQ	136360 MW	160420 TQ	USBLS	5/15
Postsecondary	New York	Y	46910 AE	88250 MW	179240 AEX	NYBLS	1/16-3/16
Postsecondary	Buffalo-Cheektowaga-Niagara Falls MSA, NY	Y	38020 FQ	86380 MW	143830 TQ	USBLS	5/15
Postsecondary	New York-Jersey City-White Plains PMSA, NY-NJ	Y	54430 FQ	72330 MW	186360 TQ	USBLS	5/15
Postsecondary	North Carolina	Y	63630 FQ	102440 MW	178850 TQ	USBLS	5/15
Postsecondary	Ohio	Y	45820 FQ	96260 MW	153400 TQ	ALBLS	5/15
Postsecondary	Columbus MSA, OH	Y	45290 FQ	102960 MW	154780 TQ	USBLS	5/15
Postsecondary	Oklahoma	Y	46000 FQ	87150 MW	123660 TQ	USBLS	5/15
Postsecondary	Portland-Vancouver-Hillsboro MSA, OR-WA	Y	52150 FQ	89980 MW	147430 TQ	USBLS	5/15

Occupation/Type/Industry	Location	Per	Low	Mid	High	Source	Date
Law Teacher							
Postsecondary	Pennsylvania	Y	67610 FQ	103560 MW	148290 TQ	USBLS	5/15
Postsecondary	Philadelphia PMSA, PA	Y	72460 FQ	102550 MW	148700 TQ	USBLS	5/15
Postsecondary	Tennessee	Y	86640 FQ	131410 MW	186660 TQ	USBLS	5/15
Postsecondary	Texas	Y	50600 FQ	100430 MW	162070 TQ	USBLS	5/15
Postsecondary	Houston-The Woodlands-Sugar Land MSA, TX	Y	19010 FQ	66100 MW	126010 TQ	USBLS	5/15
Postsecondary	Utah	Y	73300 FQ	143850 MW		USBLS	5/15
Postsecondary	Salt Lake City MSA, UT	Y	56660 FQ	164010 MW		USBLS	5/15
Postsecondary	Virginia	Y	56560 FQ	104740 MW	178440 TQ	USBLS	5/15
Postsecondary	Washington	Y		112162 AW		WABLS	3/16
Postsecondary	Seattle-Bellevue-Everett PMSA, WA	Y		109971 AW		WABLS	3/16
Postsecondary	West Virginia	Y	70460 FQ	104550 MW	126900 TQ	USBLS	5/15
Postsecondary	Wisconsin	Y	64460 FQ	96010 MW	133910 TQ	USBLS	5/15
Postsecondary	Madison MSA, WI	Y	70750 FQ	103040 MW	146660 TQ	USBLS	5/15
Postsecondary	Puerto Rico	Y	19680 FQ	69810 MW	107830 TQ	USBLS	5/15
Lawyer	Alabama	Y	58458 AE	117039 AW	146324 AEX	ALBLS	6/16
	Birmingham-Hoover MSA, AL	Y	63188 AE	123980 AW	154366 AEX	ALBLS	6/16
	Alaska	Y	92990 FQ	112500 MW	136250 TQ	USBLS	5/15
	Anchorage MSA, AK	Y	94480 FQ	113080 MW	140680 TQ	USBLS	5/15
	Arizona	Y	79320 FQ	102390 MW	156100 TQ	USBLS*	5/15
	Phoenix-Mesa-Scottsdale MSA, AZ	Y	82900 FQ	107710 MW	165570 TQ	USBLS	5/15
	Tucson MSA, AZ	Y	67840 FQ	94060 MW	129000 TQ	USBLS	5/15
	Arkansas	Y	58580 FQ	86510 MW	122770 TQ	USBLS	5/15
	Little Rock-North Little Rock-Conway MSA, AR	Y	68790 FQ	91150 MW	116140 TQ	USBLS	5/15
	California	H	49.25 FQ	71.24 MW		CABLS	1/16-3/16
	Anaheim-Santa Ana-Irvine PMSA, CA	H	46.13 FQ	70.37 MW		CABLS	1/16-3/16
	Los Angeles-Long Beach-Glendale PMSA, CA	H	53.25 FQ	77.37 MW		CABLS	1/16-3/16
	Oakland-Hayward-Berkeley PMSA, CA	H	46.57 FQ	66.96 MW		CABLS	1/16-3/16
	Riverside-San Bernardino-Ontario MSA, CA	H	43.50 FQ	63.68 MW	75.31 TQ	CABLS	1/16-3/16
	Sacramento–Roseville–Arden-Arcade MSA, CA	H	44.50 FQ	58.35 MW	76.62 TQ	CABLS	1/16-3/16
	San Diego-Carlsbad MSA, CA	H	38.90 FQ	60.58 MW	83.86 TQ	CABLS	1/16-3/16
	San Francisco-Redwood City-South San Francisco PMSA, CA	H	56.94 FQ	77.49 MW		CABLS	1/16-3/16
	Colorado	Y	72340 FQ	111140 MW	173130 TQ	USBLS	5/15
	Denver-Aurora-Lakewood MSA, CO	Y	76770 FQ	120480 MW	186020 TQ	USBLS	5/15
	Connecticut	Y		129926 MW		CTBLS	1/16-3/16
	Bridgeport-Stamford-Norwalk MSA, CT	Y	98140 FQ	158590 MW		USBLS	5/15
	Hartford-West Hartford-East Hartford MSA, CT	Y	96280 FQ	126190 MW	158210 TQ	USBLS	5/15
	Delaware	Y	102610 FQ	134320 MW		USBLS	5/15
	Wilmington PMSA, DE-MD-NJ	Y	101810 FQ	136640 MW		USBLS	5/15
	District of Columbia	Y	128790 FQ	158690 MW		USBLS	5/15
	Washington-Arlington-Alexandria PMSA, DC-VA-MD-WV	Y	119330 FQ	155700 MW		USBLS	5/15
	Florida	H	28.12 AE	47.81 MW	80.51 AEX	FLBLS	7/16-9/16
	Miami-Miami Beach-Kendall PMSA, FL	H	33.65 AE	60.49 MW	87.63 AEX	FLBLS	7/16-9/16
	Orlando-Kissimmee-Sanford MSA, FL	H	34.38 AE	66.28 MW	103.35 AEX	FLBLS	7/16-9/16
	Tampa-St. Petersburg-Clearwater MSA, FL	H	25.53 AE	44.39 MW	77.48 AEX	FLBLS	7/16-9/16
	Georgia	Y	71360 FQ	110290 MW	164650 TQ	USBLS	5/15
	Atlanta-Sandy Springs-Roswell MSA, GA	Y	76760 FQ	117620 MW	173750 TQ	USBLS	5/15
	Augusta-Richmond County MSA, GA-SC	Y	58190 FQ	72260 MW	108240 TQ	USBLS	5/15
	Hawaii	Y	75950 FQ	92760 MW	118060 TQ	USBLS	5/15

AE	Average entry wage	AWR	Average wage range	H	Hourly
AEX	Average experienced wage	B	Biweekly	HI	Highest wage paid
ATC	Average total compensation	D	Daily	HR	High end range
AW	Average wage paid	FQ	First quartile wage	LO	Lowest wage paid

LR	Low end range	MTC	Median total compensation	TCC	Total cash compensation
M	Monthly	MW	Median wage paid	TQ	Third quartile wage
MCC	Median cash compensation	MWR	Median wage range	W	Weekly
ME	Median entry wage	S	See annotated source	Y	Yearly

Lawyer

Occupation/Type/Industry	Location	Per	Low	Mid	High	Source	Date
Lawyer	Urban Honolulu MSA, HI	Y	75400 FQ	91730 MW	116160 TQ	USBLS	5/15
	Idaho	Y	57520 FQ	76920 MW	120550 TQ	USBLS	5/15
	Boise City MSA, ID	Y	60470 FQ	81950 MW	126480 TQ	USBLS	5/15
	Illinois	Y	68130 FQ	100130 MW	160980 TQ	USBLS	5/15
	Chicago-Naperville-Arlington Heights PMSA, IL	Y	70310 FQ	102750 MW	165570 TQ	USBLS	5/15
	Lake County-Kenosha County PMSA, IL-WI	Y	79280 FQ	141630 MW		USBLS	5/15
	Indiana	Y	60750 FQ	93370 MW	135060 TQ	USBLS	5/15
	Gary PMSA, IN	Y	44630 FQ	58170 MW	99790 TQ	USBLS	5/15
	Indianapolis-Carmel-Anderson MSA, IN	Y	78870 FQ	106930 MW	144800 TQ	USBLS	5/15
	Iowa	Y	61450 FQ	88260 MW	126840 TQ	USBLS	5/15
	Des Moines-West Des Moines MSA, IA	Y	71330 FQ	107580 MW	155160 TQ	USBLS	5/15
	Kansas	Y	60610 FQ	79350 MW	127230 TQ	USBLS	5/15
	Wichita MSA, KS	Y	64580 FQ	80280 MW	119900 TQ	USBLS	5/15
	Kentucky	Y	52920 FQ	74880 MW	113550 TQ	USBLS	5/15
	Louisville-Jefferson County MSA, KY-IN	Y	59390 FQ	90180 MW	129250 TQ	USBLS	5/15
	Louisiana	Y	63220 FQ	89210 MW	130250 TQ	USBLS	5/15
	Baton Rouge MSA, LA	Y	70070 FQ	95350 MW	121540 TQ	USBLS	5/15
	New Orleans-Metairie MSA, LA	Y	73070 FQ	100720 MW	154430 TQ	USBLS	5/15
	Maine	Y	60710 FQ	83750 MW	114900 TQ	USBLS	5/15
	Portland-South Portland MSA, ME	Y	64290 FQ	97460 MW	129090 TQ	USBLS	5/15
	Maryland	Y	61921 AE	121530 MW	151335 AEX	MDBLS	4/16
	Baltimore-Columbia-Towson MSA, MD	Y	67500 FQ	95550 MW	135910 TQ	USBLS	5/15
	Salisbury MSA, MD-DE	Y	65790 FQ	94090 MW	118930 TQ	USBLS	5/15
	Massachusetts	Y	83030 FQ	132890 MW		USBLS	5/15
	Boston-Cambridge-Newton NECTA, MA	Y	91240 FQ	147990 MW		USBLS	5/15
	Worcester MSA, MA-CT	Y	69430 FQ	88330 MW	124570 TQ	USBLS	5/15
	Michigan	Y	67680 FQ	93750 MW	131310 TQ	USBLS	5/15
	Detroit-Dearborn-Livonia PMSA, MI	Y	77590 FQ	99440 MW	129900 TQ	USBLS	5/15
	Grand Rapids-Wyoming MSA, MI	Y	65940 FQ	84020 MW	125870 TQ	USBLS	5/15
	Minnesota	Y	82197 FQ	111279 MW	157014 TQ	MNBLS	1/16-3/16
	Minneapolis-St. Paul-Bloomington MSA, MN-WI	Y	87731 FQ	117660 MW	162941 TQ	MNBLS	1/16-3/16
	Mississippi	Y	43750 FQ	87120 MW	143350 TQ	USBLS	5/15
	Jackson MSA, MS	Y	63830 FQ	102050 MW	151380 TQ	USBLS	5/15
	Missouri	Y	60430 FQ	93230 MW	144770 TQ	USBLS	5/15
	Kansas City MSA, MO-KS	Y	66340 FQ	101930 MW	147620 TQ	USBLS	5/15
	St. Louis MSA, MO-IL	Y	59500 FQ	94010 MW	148280 TQ	USBLS	5/15
	Montana	Y	53580 FQ	71670 MW	93650 TQ	USBLS	5/15
	Billings MSA, MT	Y	57180 FQ	68570 MW	97020 TQ	USBLS	5/15
	Nebraska	Y	58330 FQ	78095 MW	124365 TQ	NEBLS	7/16-9/16
	Omaha-Council Bluffs MSA, NE-IA	Y	62230 FQ	90150 MW	130855 TQ	NEBLS	7/16-9/16
	Nevada	Y	80280 FQ	106720 MW	139810 TQ	USBLS	5/15
	Las Vegas-Henderson-Paradise MSA, NV	Y	78190 FQ	105680 MW	142780 TQ	USBLS	5/15
	New Hampshire	H	31.82 AE	48.40 MW	68.23 AEX	NHBLS	6/16
	Manchester NECTA, NH	H	38.48 AE	57.33 MW	82.16 AEX	NHBLS	6/16
	Nashua NECTA, NH-MA	Y	77580 FQ	98610 MW	114720 TQ	USBLS	5/15
	New Jersey	Y	87280 FQ	128710 MW	186630 TQ	USBLS	5/15
	Camden PMSA, NJ	Y	74610 FQ	104160 MW	164580 TQ	USBLS	5/15
	Newark PMSA, NJ-PA	Y	104860 FQ	153600 MW		USBLS	5/15
	Trenton MSA, NJ	Y	76080 FQ	105390 MW	158850 TQ	USBLS	5/15
	New Mexico	Y	62960 FQ	78140 MW	113320 TQ	USBLS	5/15
	Albuquerque MSA, NM	Y	61990 FQ	77050 MW	120160 TQ	USBLS	5/15
	New York	Y	73020 AE	136560 MW		NYBLS	1/16-3/16
	Buffalo-Cheektowaga-Niagara Falls MSA, NY	Y	63060 FQ	84440 MW	113930 TQ	USBLS	5/15
	Nassau County-Suffolk County PMSA, NY	Y	80970 FQ	108480 MW	163780 TQ	USBLS	5/15
	New York-Jersey City-White Plains PMSA, NY-NJ	Y	94280 FQ	153120 MW		USBLS	5/15

AE	Average entry wage	AWR	Average wage range	H	Hourly	LR	Low end range	MTC	Median total compensation	TCC	Total cash compensation
AEX	Average experienced wage	B	Biweekly	HI	Highest wage paid	M	Monthly	MW	Median wage paid	TQ	Third quartile wage
ATC	Average total compensation	D	Daily	HR	High end range	MCC	Median cash compensation	MWR	Median wage range	W	Weekly
AW	Average wage paid	FQ	First quartile wage	LO	Lowest wage paid	ME	Median entry wage	S	See annotated source	Y	Yearly

Occupation/Type/Industry	Location	Per	Low	Mid	High	Source	Date
Lawyer	Rochester MSA, NY	Y	67090 FQ	91390 MW	124320 TQ	USBLS	5/15
	North Carolina	Y	60120 FQ	96060 MW	164200 TQ	USBLS	5/15
	Charlotte-Concord-Gastonia MSA, NC-SC	Y	58630 FQ	121010 MW		USBLS	5/15
	Raleigh MSA, NC	Y	63560 FQ	98110 MW	159650 TQ	USBLS	5/15
	North Dakota	Y	65510 FQ	83800 MW	112120 TQ	USBLS	5/15
	Fargo MSA, ND-MN	Y	73640 FQ	94580 MW	119990 TQ	USBLS	5/15
	Ohio	Y	68220 FQ	96190 MW	141580 TQ	USBLS	5/15
	Cincinnati MSA, OH-KY-IN	Y	69590 FQ	101030 MW	148970 TQ	USBLS	5/15
	Cleveland-Elyria MSA, OH	Y	70520 FQ	97790 MW	139780 TQ	USBLS	5/15
	Columbus MSA, OH	Y	72450 FQ	100480 MW	142640 TQ	USBLS	5/15
	Oklahoma	Y	61980 FQ	91510 MW	145250 TQ	USBLS	5/15
	Oklahoma City MSA, OK	Y	62420 FQ	87240 MW	130040 TQ	USBLS	5/15
	Tulsa MSA, OK	Y	74140 FQ	118370 MW		USBLS	5/15
	Oregon	H	36.14 FQ	51.14 MW	67.48 TQ	ORBLS	2016
	Portland-Vancouver-Hillsboro MSA, OR-WA	Y	80460 FQ	111030 MW	144970 TQ	USBLS	5/15
	Pennsylvania	Y	74590 FQ	112960 MW	165380 TQ	USBLS	5/15
	Allentown-Bethlehem-Easton MSA, PA-NJ	Y	72090 FQ	110860 MW	175540 TQ	USBLS	5/15
	Harrisburg-Carlisle MSA, PA	Y	83100 FQ	115300 MW	150540 TQ	USBLS	5/15
	Montgomery County-Bucks County-Chester County PMSA, PA	Y	81130 FQ	111150 MW	158700 TQ	USBLS	5/15
	Philadelphia PMSA, PA	Y	79930 FQ	126260 MW	176180 TQ	USBLS	5/15
	Pittsburgh MSA, PA	Y	78180 FQ	120400 MW	182270 TQ	USBLS	5/15
	Rhode Island	Y	82810 FQ	112650 MW	159700 TQ	USBLS	5/15
	Providence-Warwick MSA, RI-MA	Y	81200 FQ	109940 MW	158690 TQ	USBLS	5/15
	South Carolina	Y	58430 FQ	82290 MW	135370 TQ	USBLS	5/15
	Charleston-North Charleston MSA, SC	Y	46170 FQ	66700 MW	106960 TQ	USBLS	5/15
	Columbia MSA, SC	Y	61350 FQ	77210 MW	122360 TQ	USBLS	5/15
	Greenville-Anderson-Mauldin MSA, SC	Y	85430 FQ	128660 MW		USBLS	5/15
	South Dakota	Y	66320 FQ	79720 MW	119120 TQ	USBLS	5/15
	Sioux Falls MSA, SD	Y	65020 FQ	83070 MW	121420 TQ	USBLS	5/15
	Tennessee	Y	70360 FQ	105890 MW	153180 TQ	USBLS	5/15
	Knoxville MSA, TN	Y	76000 FQ	110060 MW	158680 TQ	USBLS	5/15
	Memphis MSA, TN-MS-AR	Y	67090 FQ	107210 MW	160770 TQ	USBLS	5/15
	Nashville-Davidson–Murfreesboro–Franklin MSA, TN	Y	71600 FQ	108870 MW	152680 TQ	USBLS	5/15
	Texas	Y	83020 FQ	121180 MW	186720 TQ	USBLS	5/15
	Austin-Round Rock MSA, TX	Y	75800 FQ	101860 MW		USBLS	5/15
	Dallas-Plano-Irving PMSA, TX	Y	94110 FQ	132310 MW		USBLS	5/15
	Fort Worth-Arlington PMSA, TX	Y	72000 FQ	100000 MW	140660 TQ	USBLS	5/15
	Houston-The Woodlands-Sugar Land MSA, TX	Y	91680 FQ	146500 MW		USBLS	5/15
	San Antonio-New Braunfels MSA, TX	Y	72470 FQ	110310 MW	155210 TQ	USBLS	5/15
	Utah	Y	68900 FQ	100590 MW	132080 TQ	USBLS	5/15
	Ogden-Clearfield MSA, UT	Y	58900 FQ	82870 MW	113710 TQ	USBLS	5/15
	Provo-Orem MSA, UT	Y	82260 FQ	102540 MW	119090 TQ	USBLS	5/15
	Salt Lake City MSA, UT	Y	74460 FQ	104880 MW	144800 TQ	USBLS	5/15
	Vermont	Y	62380 FQ	91580 MW	128620 TQ	USBLS	5/15
	Burlington-South Burlington MSA, VT	Y	70180 FQ	99150 MW	143100 TQ	USBLS	5/15
	Virginia	Y	80200 FQ	123230 MW	164880 TQ	USBLS	5/15
	Richmond MSA, VA	Y	80490 FQ	120700 MW	170040 TQ	USBLS	5/15
	Virginia Beach-Norfolk-Newport News MSA, VA-NC	Y	70740 FQ	105390 MW	146410 TQ	USBLS	5/15
	Washington	H	38.03 FQ	52.90 MW	74.04 TQ	WABLS	3/16
	Seattle-Bellevue-Everett PMSA, WA	H	40.69 FQ	58.71 MW	81.03 TQ	WABLS	3/16
	Tacoma-Lakewood PMSA, WA	H	37.87 FQ	46.75 MW	59.06 TQ	WABLS	3/16
	West Virginia	Y	65370 FQ	86030 MW	115460 TQ	USBLS	5/15
	Huntington-Ashland MSA, WV-KY-OH	Y	65490 FQ	88810 MW	109320 TQ	USBLS	5/15
	Wisconsin	Y	56070 FQ	82980 MW	130370 TQ	USBLS	5/15
	Madison MSA, WI	Y	71150 FQ	93270 MW	126470 TQ	USBLS	5/15

AE	Average entry wage	AWR	Average wage range	H	Hourly	LR	Low end range	MTC	Median total compensation	TCC	Total cash compensation
AEX	Average experienced wage	B	Biweekly	HI	Highest wage paid	M	Monthly	MW	Median wage paid	TQ	Third quartile wage
ATC	Average total compensation	D	Daily	HR	High end range	MCC	Median cash compensation	MWR	Median wage range	W	Weekly
AW	Average wage paid	FQ	First quartile wage	LO	Lowest wage paid	ME	Median entry wage	S	See annotated source	Y	Yearly

Occupation/Type/Industry	Location	Per	Low	Mid	High	Source	Date
Lawyer	Milwaukee-Waukesha-West						
	Allis MSA, WI	Y	50620 FQ	82790 MW	147890 TQ	USBLS	5/15
	Wyoming	Y	62850 FQ	83380 MW	111250 TQ	USBLS	5/15
	Cheyenne MSA, WY	Y	65040 FQ	77550 MW	101160 TQ	USBLS	5/15
	Puerto Rico	Y	43040 FQ	60340 MW	88140 TQ	USBLS	5/15
	San Juan-Carolina-Caguas						
	MSA, PR	Y	43270 FQ	61020 MW	89450 TQ	USBLS	5/15
	Virgin Islands	Y	80340 FQ	107390 MW	128870 TQ	USBLS	5/15
	Guam	Y	66990 FQ	86910 MW	103520 TQ	USBLS	5/15
Layout Worker							
Metals and Plastics	Alabama	Y	28862 AE	40265 AW	45691 AEX	ALBLS	6/16
Metals and Plastics	Birmingham-Hoover MSA, AL	Y	28338 AE	35381 AW	38908 AEX	ALBLS	6/16
Metals and Plastics	Arizona	Y	30600 FQ	37020 MW	44050 TQ	USBLS	5/15
Metals and Plastics	Phoenix-Mesa-Scottsdale						
	MSA, AZ	Y	31260 FQ	37520 MW	44350 TQ	USBLS	5/15
Metals and Plastics	Arkansas	Y	30870 FQ	38860 MW	47630 TQ	USBLS	5/15
Metals and Plastics	California	H	13.02 FQ	19.03 MW	25.77 TQ	CABLS	1/16-3/16
Metals and Plastics	Anaheim-Santa Ana-Irvine						
	PMSA, CA	H	11.85 FQ	13.96 MW	19.82 TQ	CABLS	1/16-3/16
Metals and Plastics	Los Angeles-Long Beach-						
	Glendale PMSA, CA	H	13.41 FQ	15.60 MW	24.81 TQ	CABLS	1/16-3/16
Metals and Plastics	Riverside-San Bernardino-						
	Ontario MSA, CA	H	15.27 FQ	17.95 MW	22.36 TQ	CABLS	1/16-3/16
Metals and Plastics	San Diego-Carlsbad MSA, CA	H	9.49 FQ	21.44 MW	26.20 TQ	CABLS	1/16-3/16
Metals and Plastics	Colorado	Y	31920 FQ	34730 MW	37540 TQ	USBLS	5/15
Metals and Plastics	Connecticut	Y		47740 MW		CTBLS	1/16-3/16
Metals and Plastics	Florida	H	15.06 AE	20.95 MW	23.19 AEX	FLBLS	7/16-9/16
Metals and Plastics	Tampa-St. Petersburg-						
	Clearwater MSA, FL	H	15.48 AE	22.16 MW	23.88 AEX	FLBLS	7/16-9/16
Metals and Plastics	Georgia	Y	32800 FQ	43100 MW	50370 TQ	USBLS	5/15
Metals and Plastics	Hawaii	Y	57310 FQ	70330 MW	70340 TQ	USBLS	5/15
Metals and Plastics	Urban Honolulu MSA, HI	Y	57310 FQ	70330 MW	70340 TQ	USBLS	5/15
Metals and Plastics	Illinois	Y	39230 FQ	54790 MW	62000 TQ	USBLS	5/15
Metals and Plastics	Chicago-Naperville-Arlington						
	Heights PMSA, IL	Y	52140 FQ	55590 MW	59040 TQ	USBLS	5/15
Metals and Plastics	Indiana	Y	35340 FQ	40770 MW	46830 TQ	USBLS	5/15
Metals and Plastics	Indianapolis-Carmel-Anderson						
	MSA, IN	Y	40800 FQ	44460 MW	48130 TQ	USBLS	5/15
Metals and Plastics	Iowa	Y	39730 FQ	44330 MW	49020 TQ	USBLS	5/15
Metals and Plastics	Kansas	Y	52820 FQ	61420 MW	87200 TQ	USBLS	5/15
Metals and Plastics	Wichita MSA, KS	Y	53620 FQ	61950 MW	87760 TQ	USBLS	5/15
Metals and Plastics	Kentucky	Y	30330 FQ	35570 MW	44180 TQ	USBLS	5/15
Metals and Plastics	Louisiana	Y	42860 FQ	51230 MW	58780 TQ	USBLS	5/15
Metals and Plastics	Maine	Y	36520 FQ	50220 MW	55180 TQ	USBLS	5/15
Metals and Plastics	Baltimore-Columbia-Towson						
	MSA, MD	Y	31890 FQ	39060 MW	54880 TQ	USBLS	5/15
Metals and Plastics	Massachusetts	Y	35040 FQ	42140 MW	54280 TQ	USBLS	5/15
Metals and Plastics	Michigan	Y	41730 FQ	49740 MW	64490 TQ	USBLS	5/15
Metals and Plastics	Minnesota	Y	36509 FQ	45742 MW	61294 TQ	MNBLS	1/16-3/16
Metals and Plastics	Minneapolis-St. Paul-						
	Bloomington MSA, MN-WI	Y	41166 FQ	47474 MW	62134 TQ	MNBLS	1/16-3/16
Metals and Plastics	Mississippi	Y	37060 FQ	46450 MW	55470 TQ	USBLS	5/15
Metals and Plastics	Missouri	Y	34000 FQ	38410 MW	47720 TQ	USBLS	5/15
Metals and Plastics	Kansas City MSA, MO-KS	Y	35540 FQ	40070 MW	45870 TQ	USBLS	5/15
Metals and Plastics	St. Louis MSA, MO-IL	Y	34060 FQ	45980 MW	70410 TQ	USBLS	5/15
Metals and Plastics	New York	Y	22110 AE	28770 MW	37960 AEX	NYBLS	1/16-3/16
Metals and Plastics	Nassau County-Suffolk County						
	PMSA, NY	Y	20200 FQ	24040 MW	36520 TQ	USBLS	5/15
Metals and Plastics	North Carolina	Y	29070 FQ	36220 MW	43220 TQ	USBLS	5/15
Metals and Plastics	Ohio	Y	33130 FQ	37350 MW	46290 TQ	USBLS	5/15
Metals and Plastics	Cincinnati MSA, OH-KY-IN	Y	31060 FQ	37900 MW	48200 TQ	USBLS	5/15
Metals and Plastics	Columbus MSA, OH	Y	34380 FQ	36940 MW	39500 TQ	USBLS	5/15
Metals and Plastics	Oklahoma	Y	30590 FQ	43010 MW	47960 TQ	USBLS	5/15
Metals and Plastics	Oregon	H	15.47 FQ	19.56 MW	27.24 TQ	ORBLS	2016
Metals and Plastics	Pennsylvania	Y	31000 FQ	40400 MW	45700 TQ	USBLS	5/15
Metals and Plastics	Montgomery County-Bucks						
	County-Chester County						
	PMSA, PA	Y	31700 FQ	35410 MW	39140 TQ	USBLS	5/15
Metals and Plastics	Pittsburgh MSA, PA	Y	29140 FQ	40910 MW	45710 TQ	USBLS	5/15
Metals and Plastics	Providence-Warwick MSA, RI-						
	MA	Y	35920 FQ	40630 MW	51110 TQ	USBLS	5/15

AE	Average entry wage	AWR	Average wage range	H	Hourly
AEX	Average experienced wage	B	Biweekly	HI	Highest wage paid
ATC	Average total compensation	D	Daily	HR	High end range
AW	Average wage paid	FQ	First quartile wage	LO	Lowest wage paid

LR	Low end range	MTC	Median total compensation
M	Monthly	MW	Median wage paid
MCC	Median cash compensation	MWR	Median wage range
ME	Median entry wage	S	See annotated source

TCC	Total cash compensation		
TQ	Third quartile wage		
W	Weekly		
Y	Yearly		

Occupation/Type/Industry	Location	Per	Low	Mid	High	Source	Date
Layout Worker							
Metals and Plastics	South Carolina	Y	18370 FQ	38890 MW	55480 TQ	USBLS	5/15
Metals and Plastics	Tennessee	Y	31600 FQ	38440 MW	45380 TQ	USBLS	5/15
Metals and Plastics	Nashville-Davidson–Murfreesboro–Franklin MSA, TN	Y	32080 FQ	35840 MW	39600 TQ	USBLS	5/15
Metals and Plastics	Texas	Y	33280 FQ	41090 MW	47990 TQ	USBLS	5/15
Metals and Plastics	Dallas-Plano-Irving PMSA, TX	Y	33870 FQ	40560 MW	46640 TQ	USBLS	5/15
Metals and Plastics	Houston-The Woodlands-Sugar Land MSA, TX	Y	31590 FQ	41960 MW	47260 TQ	USBLS	5/15
Metals and Plastics	Utah	Y	36020 FQ	50540 MW	69980 TQ	USBLS	5/15
Metals and Plastics	Ogden-Clearfield MSA, UT	Y	44050 FQ	66850 MW	73500 TQ	USBLS	5/15
Metals and Plastics	Virginia	Y	41720 FQ	47070 MW	51710 TQ	USBLS	5/15
Metals and Plastics	Virginia Beach-Norfolk-Newport News MSA, VA-NC	Y	41720 FQ	47310 MW	51710 TQ	USBLS	5/15
Metals and Plastics	Washington	H	21.17 FQ	28.55 MW	31.96 TQ	WABLS	3/16
Metals and Plastics	Seattle-Bellevue-Everett PMSA, WA	H	31.23 FQ	36.24 MW	43.68 TQ	WABLS	3/16
Metals and Plastics	Wisconsin	Y	35210 FQ	45400 MW	56050 TQ	USBLS	5/15
LBGT Resource Center Manager							
Michigan State University	East Lansing, MI	Y			75123 HI	MSUSAL	10/1/14-9/30/15
Lecturer							
Female, 2-Year For-Profit Institution	United States	Y		46876 AW		CHE03	2014-2015
Female, 2-Year Public Institution	United States	Y		49762 AW		CHE03	2014-2015
Female, 4-Year For-Profit Institution	United States	Y		49673 AW		CHE03	2014-2015
Female, 4-Year Private Institution	United States	Y		59420 AW		CHE03	2014-2015
Female, 4-Year Public Institution	United States	Y		53275 AW		CHE03	2014-2015
Male, 2-Year For-Profit Institution	United States	Y		41994 AW		CHE03	2014-2015
Male, 2-Year Public Institution	United States	Y		50423 AW		CHE03	2014-2015
Male, 4-Year For-Profit Institution	United States	Y		44424 AW		CHE03	2014-2015
Male, 4-Year Private Institution	United States	Y		66107 AW		CHE03	2014-2015
Male, 4-Year Public Institution	United States	Y		59546 AW		CHE03	2014-2015
Legal Advisor							
Police Department, Municipal Government	Detroit, MI	M			5617 HI	DETGOV	2016
Legal Counsel							
United States Senate	United States	Y			172500 HI	CRS01	2016
Legal Intern							
Municipal Government	Seattle, WA	H			22.61 HI	CSSS	1/13/16
Legal Investigator							
Municipal Government	Detroit, MI	M	2617 LO		2933 HI	DETGOV	2016
Legal Research Analyst							
Judiciary, State Government	Ohio	H	27.07 LO		30.08 HI	OHGOV	2015
Legal Secretary	Alabama	Y	27177 AE	39678 AW	45934 AEX	ALBLS	6/16
	Birmingham-Hoover MSA, AL	Y	32794 AE	46902 AW	53962 AEX	ALBLS	6/16
	Alaska	Y	38450 FQ	44730 MW	56570 TQ	USBLS	5/15
	Anchorage MSA, AK	Y	40790 FQ	45850 MW	58590 TQ	USBLS	5/15
	Arizona	Y	32950 FQ	41230 MW	53680 TQ	USBLS	5/15
	Phoenix-Mesa-Scottsdale MSA, AZ	Y	34760 FQ	45800 MW	56110 TQ	USBLS	5/15
	Tucson MSA, AZ	Y	28730 FQ	35010 MW	40570 TQ	USBLS	5/15
	Arkansas	Y	26550 FQ	31000 MW	40090 TQ	USBLS	5/15
	Little Rock-North Little Rock-Conway MSA, AR	Y	26350 FQ	32840 MW	42320 TQ	USBLS	5/15
	California	H	18.86 FQ	24.86 MW	33.13 TQ	CABLS	1/16-3/16
	Anaheim-Santa Ana-Irvine PMSA, CA	H	17.02 FQ	22.76 MW	29.74 TQ	CABLS	1/16-3/16
	Los Angeles-Long Beach-Glendale PMSA, CA	H	18.28 FQ	25.29 MW	34.19 TQ	CABLS	1/16-3/16
	Oakland-Hayward-Berkeley PMSA, CA	H	23.48 FQ	28.84 MW	35.48 TQ	CABLS	1/16-3/16
	Riverside-San Bernardino-Ontario MSA, CA	H	14.86 FQ	18.20 MW	22.96 TQ	CABLS	1/16-3/16
	Sacramento–Roseville–Arden-Arcade MSA, CA	H	20.31 FQ	23.22 MW	30.51 TQ	CABLS	1/16-3/16
	San Diego-Carlsbad MSA, CA	H	19.90 FQ	23.17 MW	28.50 TQ	CABLS	1/16-3/16

AE	Average entry wage	AWR	Average wage range	
AEX	Average experienced wage	B	Biweekly	
ATC	Average total compensation	D	Daily	
AW	Average wage paid	FQ	First quartile wage	

H	Hourly
HI	Highest wage paid
HR	High end range
LO	Lowest wage paid

LR	Low end range
M	Monthly
MCC	Median cash compensation
ME	Median entry wage

MTC	Median total compensation
MW	Median wage paid
MWR	Median wage range
S	See annotated source

TCC	Total cash compensation
TQ	Third quartile wage
W	Weekly
Y	Yearly

Occupation/Type/Industry	Location	Per	Low	Mid	High	Source	Date
Legal Secretary	San Francisco-Redwood City-South San Francisco PMSA, CA	H	25.44 FQ	32.57 MW	42.36 TQ	CABLS	1/16-3/16
	Colorado	Y	31710 FQ	45270 MW	57170 TQ	USBLS	5/15
	Denver-Aurora-Lakewood MSA, CO	Y	40570 FQ	50020 MW	62230 TQ	USBLS	5/15
	Connecticut	Y		42193 MW		CTBLS	1/16-3/16
	Bridgeport-Stamford-Norwalk MSA, CT	Y	35450 FQ	39470 MW	55840 TQ	USBLS	5/15
	Hartford-West Hartford-East Hartford MSA, CT	Y	32980 FQ	47430 MW	58870 TQ	USBLS	5/15
	Delaware	Y	41160 FQ	53310 MW	64950 TQ	USBLS	5/15
	Wilmington PMSA, DE-MD-NJ	Y	44030 FQ	53550 MW	66040 TQ	USBLS	5/15
	District of Columbia	Y	63140 FQ	77370 MW	90680 TQ	USBLS	5/15
	Washington-Arlington-Alexandria PMSA, DC-VA-MD-WV	Y	47090 FQ	69610 MW	86610 TQ	USBLS	5/15
	Florida	H	14.27 AE	19.13 MW	24.03 AEX	FLBLS	7/16-9/16
	Fort Lauderdale-Pompano Beach-Deerfield Beach PMSA, FL	H	15.19 AE	18.41 MW	22.90 AEX	FLBLS	7/16-9/16
	Miami-Miami Beach-Kendall PMSA, FL	H	14.17 AE	20.91 MW	26.55 AEX	FLBLS	7/16-9/16
	Orlando-Kissimmee-Sanford MSA, FL	H	13.98 AE	20.70 MW	24.58 AEX	FLBLS	7/16-9/16
	Tampa-St. Petersburg-Clearwater MSA, FL	H	15.88 AE	20.63 MW	24.92 AEX	FLBLS	7/16-9/16
	Georgia	Y	30460 FQ	38130 MW	49680 TQ	USBLS	5/15
	Atlanta-Sandy Springs-Roswell MSA, GA	Y	31740 FQ	41030 MW	56380 TQ	USBLS	5/15
	Augusta-Richmond County MSA, GA-SC	Y	30990 FQ	34940 MW	38610 TQ	USBLS	5/15
	Hawaii	Y	40680 FQ	47540 MW	55650 TQ	USBLS	5/15
	Urban Honolulu MSA, HI	Y	42270 FQ	50170 MW	57430 TQ	USBLS	5/15
	Idaho	Y	28560 FQ	35670 MW	42340 TQ	USBLS	5/15
	Boise City MSA, ID	Y	34510 FQ	40440 MW	48840 TQ	USBLS	5/15
	Illinois	Y	32420 FQ	45260 MW	60140 TQ	USBLS	5/15
	Chicago-Naperville-Arlington Heights PMSA, IL	Y	35620 FQ	50010 MW	64970 TQ	USBLS	5/15
	Lake County-Kenosha County PMSA, IL-WI	Y	35060 FQ	46330 MW	55920 TQ	USBLS	5/15
	Indiana	Y	28930 FQ	35080 MW	45470 TQ	USBLS	5/15
	Gary PMSA, IN	Y	28390 FQ	32500 MW	37510 TQ	USBLS	5/15
	Indianapolis-Carmel-Anderson MSA, IN	Y	29930 FQ	37960 MW	52650 TQ	USBLS	5/15
	Iowa	Y	26890 FQ	34270 MW	45570 TQ	USBLS	5/15
	Des Moines-West Des Moines MSA, IA	Y	41420 FQ	50370 MW	57650 TQ	USBLS	5/15
	Kansas	Y	27000 FQ	32960 MW	42250 TQ	USBLS	5/15
	Wichita MSA, KS	Y	30700 FQ	36400 MW	43210 TQ	USBLS	5/15
	Kentucky	Y	25850 FQ	32410 MW	37850 TQ	USBLS	5/15
	Louisville-Jefferson County MSA, KY-IN	Y	30790 FQ	36790 MW	46760 TQ	USBLS	5/15
	Louisiana	Y	26780 FQ	34560 MW	40460 TQ	USBLS	5/15
	Baton Rouge MSA, LA	Y	28350 FQ	34760 MW	45870 TQ	USBLS	5/15
	New Orleans-Metairie MSA, LA	Y	30290 FQ	35920 MW	42500 TQ	USBLS	5/15
	Maine	Y	32970 FQ	37310 MW	43290 TQ	USBLS	5/15
	Portland-South Portland MSA, ME	Y	34870 FQ	38510 MW	46580 TQ	USBLS	5/15
	Maryland	Y	29595 AE	42262 MW	48595 AEX	MDBLS	4/16
	Baltimore-Columbia-Towson MSA, MD	Y	30350 FQ	37590 MW	49020 TQ	USBLS	5/15
	Salisbury MSA, MD-DE	Y	29930 FQ	39340 MW	48230 TQ	USBLS	5/15
	Massachusetts	Y	36490 FQ	46940 MW	65080 TQ	USBLS	5/15
	Boston-Cambridge-Newton NECTA, MA	Y	39210 FQ	54640 MW	71450 TQ	USBLS	5/15
	Worcester MSA, MA-CT	Y	35780 FQ	42190 MW	54970 TQ	USBLS	5/15
	Michigan	Y	35150 FQ	46710 MW	57010 TQ	USBLS	5/15
	Detroit-Dearborn-Livonia PMSA, MI	Y	40210 FQ	49960 MW	57800 TQ	USBLS	5/15

AE	Average entry wage	AWR	Average wage range	H	Hourly	LR	Low end range	MTC	Median total compensation	TCC	Total cash compensation
AEX	Average experienced wage	B	Biweekly	HI	Highest wage paid	M	Monthly	MW	Median wage paid	TQ	Third quartile wage
ATC	Average total compensation	D	Daily	HR	High end range	MCC	Median cash compensation	MWR	Median wage range	W	Weekly
AW	Average wage paid	FQ	First quartile wage	LO	Lowest wage paid	ME	Median entry wage	S	See annotated source	Y	Yearly

891

Occupation/Type/Industry	Location	Per	Low	Mid	High	Source	Date
Legal Secretary	Grand Rapids-Wyoming MSA, MI	Y	38960 FQ	48750 MW	57030 TQ	USBLS	5/15
	Minnesota	Y	37043 FQ	49451 MW	61152 TQ	MNBLS	1/16-3/16
	Minneapolis-St. Paul-Bloomington MSA, MN-WI	Y	39480 FQ	53284 MW	63427 TQ	MNBLS	1/16-3/16
	Mississippi	Y	30710 FQ	38240 MW	47920 TQ	USBLS	5/15
	Jackson MSA, MS	Y	38600 FQ	45360 MW	52800 TQ	USBLS	5/15
	Missouri	Y	31760 FQ	43740 MW	54990 TQ	USBLS	5/15
	Kansas City MSA, MO-KS	Y	32350 FQ	42620 MW	52880 TQ	USBLS	5/15
	St. Louis MSA, MO-IL	Y	30640 FQ	44880 MW	55340 TQ	USBLS	5/15
	Montana	Y	26590 FQ	33550 MW	38590 TQ	USBLS	5/15
	Billings MSA, MT	Y	28520 FQ	36410 MW	44570 TQ	USBLS	5/15
	Nebraska	Y	27615 FQ	34800 MW	44920 TQ	NEBLS	7/16-9/16
	Omaha-Council Bluffs MSA, NE-IA	Y	28405 FQ	39680 MW	50390 TQ	NEBLS	7/16-9/16
	Nevada	Y	38430 FQ	47200 MW	56380 TQ	USBLS	5/15
	Las Vegas-Henderson-Paradise MSA, NV	Y	38100 FQ	46510 MW	55580 TQ	USBLS	5/15
	New Hampshire	H	14.69 AE	20.92 MW	23.88 AEX	NHBLS	6/16
	Manchester NECTA, NH	H	20.92 AE	26.26 MW	28.24 AEX	NHBLS	6/16
	New Jersey	Y	34680 FQ	44400 MW	57010 TQ	USBLS	5/15
	Camden PMSA, NJ	Y	43600 FQ	52760 MW	60200 TQ	USBLS	5/15
	Newark PMSA, NJ-PA	Y	34220 FQ	46360 MW	60830 TQ	USBLS	5/15
	Trenton MSA, NJ	Y	43540 FQ	51810 MW	59790 TQ	USBLS	5/15
	New Mexico	Y	28840 FQ	33380 MW	41090 TQ	USBLS	5/15
	Albuquerque MSA, NM	Y	28450 FQ	33240 MW	42470 TQ	USBLS	5/15
	New York	Y	37050 AE	60130 MW	73940 AEX	NYBLS	1/16-3/16
	Buffalo-Cheektowaga-Niagara Falls MSA, NY	Y	34210 FQ	41340 MW	50550 TQ	USBLS	5/15
	Nassau County-Suffolk County PMSA, NY	Y	48500 FQ	60030 MW	69900 TQ	USBLS	5/15
	New York-Jersey City-White Plains PMSA, NY-NJ	Y	39990 FQ	58510 MW	78180 TQ	USBLS	5/15
	Rochester MSA, NY	Y	32000 FQ	38600 MW	51700 TQ	USBLS	5/15
	North Carolina	Y	34610 FQ	47020 MW	61050 TQ	USBLS	5/15
	Charlotte-Concord-Gastonia MSA, NC-SC	Y	45160 FQ	57640 MW	68530 TQ	USBLS	5/15
	Raleigh MSA, NC	Y	51680 FQ	59060 MW	69080 TQ	USBLS	5/15
	North Dakota	Y	32750 FQ	37200 MW	43150 TQ	USBLS	5/15
	Fargo MSA, ND-MN	Y	33610 FQ	40060 MW	45880 TQ	USBLS	5/15
	Ohio	Y	28580 FQ	37070 MW	48870 TQ	USBLS	5/15
	Cincinnati MSA, OH-KY-IN	Y	29760 FQ	38040 MW	51670 TQ	USBLS	5/15
	Cleveland-Elyria MSA, OH	Y	32860 FQ	41960 MW	53370 TQ	USBLS	5/15
	Columbus MSA, OH	Y	31710 FQ	42200 MW	51420 TQ	USBLS	5/15
	Oklahoma	Y	31310 FQ	37680 MW	45670 TQ	USBLS	5/15
	Oklahoma City MSA, OK	Y	31060 FQ	40040 MW	47310 TQ	USBLS	5/15
	Tulsa MSA, OK	Y	33130 FQ	38890 MW	46380 TQ	USBLS	5/15
	Oregon	H	16.93 FQ	22.20 MW	29.02 TQ	ORBLS	2016
	Portland-Vancouver-Hillsboro MSA, OR-WA	Y	40720 FQ	54650 MW	64830 TQ	USBLS	5/15
	Pennsylvania	Y	34200 FQ	42100 MW	52490 TQ	USBLS	5/15
	Allentown-Bethlehem-Easton MSA, PA-NJ	Y	34610 FQ	40040 MW	49970 TQ	USBLS	5/15
	Harrisburg-Carlisle MSA, PA	Y	39720 FQ	45020 MW	50920 TQ	USBLS	5/15
	Montgomery County-Bucks County-Chester County PMSA, PA	Y	40880 FQ	46600 MW	55280 TQ	USBLS	5/15
	Philadelphia PMSA, PA	Y	36920 FQ	45190 MW	56750 TQ	USBLS	5/15
	Pittsburgh MSA, PA	Y	34670 FQ	42690 MW	53890 TQ	USBLS	5/15
	Rhode Island	Y	38610 FQ	46880 MW	59160 TQ	USBLS	5/15
	Providence-Warwick MSA, RI-MA	Y	34120 FQ	44400 MW	57040 TQ	USBLS	5/15
	South Carolina	Y	31010 FQ	37790 MW	47310 TQ	USBLS	5/15
	Charleston-North Charleston MSA, SC	Y	32170 FQ	39280 MW	51680 TQ	USBLS	5/15
	Columbia MSA, SC	Y	35700 FQ	43390 MW	49460 TQ	USBLS	5/15
	Greenville-Anderson-Mauldin MSA, SC	Y	32880 FQ	38170 MW	46930 TQ	USBLS	5/15
	South Dakota	Y	28660 FQ	33740 MW	40830 TQ	USBLS	5/15
	Sioux Falls MSA, SD	Y	33120 FQ	37830 MW	44050 TQ	USBLS	5/15
	Tennessee	Y	28500 FQ	36270 MW	46890 TQ	USBLS	5/15
	Knoxville MSA, TN	Y	32060 FQ	38710 MW	46250 TQ	USBLS	5/15

AE	Average entry wage	AWR	Average wage range	H	Hourly	LR	Low end range	MTC	Median total compensation	TCC	Total cash compensation
AEX	Average experienced wage	B	Biweekly	HI	Highest wage paid	M	Monthly	MW	Median wage paid	TQ	Third quartile wage
ATC	Average total compensation	D	Daily	HR	High end range	MCC	Median cash compensation	MWR	Median wage range	W	Weekly
AW	Average wage paid	FQ	First quartile wage	LO	Lowest wage paid	ME	Median entry wage	S	See annotated source	Y	Yearly

Occupation/Type/Industry	Location	Per	Low	Mid	High	Source	Date
Legal Secretary	Memphis MSA, TN-MS-AR	Y	30250 FQ	39960 MW	54520 TQ	USBLS	5/15
	Nashville-Davidson–Murfreesboro–Franklin MSA, TN	Y	31400 FQ	38420 MW	52720 TQ	USBLS	5/15
	Texas	Y	32410 FQ	40230 MW	54310 TQ	USBLS	5/15
	Austin-Round Rock MSA, TX	Y	37110 FQ	43360 MW	50370 TQ	USBLS	5/15
	Dallas-Plano-Irving PMSA, TX	Y	33040 FQ	41070 MW	63570 TQ	USBLS	5/15
	Fort Worth-Arlington PMSA, TX	Y	32810 FQ	39960 MW	56400 TQ	USBLS	5/15
	Houston-The Woodlands-Sugar Land MSA, TX	Y	39800 FQ	50020 MW	64830 TQ	USBLS	5/15
	San Antonio-New Braunfels MSA, TX	Y	29550 FQ	37170 MW	47540 TQ	USBLS	5/15
	Utah	Y	29450 FQ	36070 MW	49350 TQ	USBLS	5/15
	Ogden-Clearfield MSA, UT	Y	31150 FQ	43500 MW	49320 TQ	USBLS	5/15
	Provo-Orem MSA, UT	Y	27510 FQ	30030 MW	34190 TQ	USBLS	5/15
	Salt Lake City MSA, UT	Y	31320 FQ	39710 MW	54740 TQ	USBLS	5/15
	Vermont	Y	42130 FQ	47130 MW	54740 TQ	USBLS	5/15
	Burlington-South Burlington MSA, VT	Y	46330 FQ	53520 MW	59100 TQ	USBLS	5/15
	Virginia	Y	33150 FQ	39350 MW	53630 TQ	USBLS	5/15
	Richmond MSA, VA	Y	36330 FQ	43360 MW	53810 TQ	USBLS	5/15
	Virginia Beach-Norfolk-Newport News MSA, VA-NC	Y	32250 FQ	36760 MW	45040 TQ	USBLS	5/15
	Washington	H	17.36 FQ	21.74 MW	28.46 TQ	WABLS	3/16
	Seattle-Bellevue-Everett PMSA, WA	H	19.03 FQ	25.70 MW	33.39 TQ	WABLS	3/16
	Tacoma-Lakewood PMSA, WA	H	21.74 FQ	25.13 MW	28.11 TQ	WABLS	3/16
	West Virginia	Y	26820 FQ	35060 MW	44100 TQ	USBLS	5/15
	Huntington-Ashland MSA, WV-KY-OH	Y	29470 FQ	34190 MW	38520 TQ	USBLS	5/15
	Wisconsin	Y	33330 FQ	40630 MW	49080 TQ	USBLS	5/15
	Madison MSA, WI	Y	35160 FQ	39370 MW	48990 TQ	USBLS	5/15
	Milwaukee-Waukesha-West Allis MSA, WI	Y	34940 FQ	45050 MW	53460 TQ	USBLS	5/15
	Wyoming	Y	28790 FQ	35290 MW	42670 TQ	USBLS	5/15
	Cheyenne MSA, WY	Y	25610 FQ	30850 MW	39030 TQ	USBLS	5/15
	Puerto Rico	Y	19890 FQ	24090 MW	31660 TQ	USBLS	5/15
	San Juan-Carolina-Caguas MSA, PR	Y	20880 FQ	24810 MW	32470 TQ	USBLS	5/15
	Virgin Islands	Y	35170 FQ	43120 MW	50400 TQ	USBLS	5/15
	Guam	Y	30520 FQ	35250 MW	41010 TQ	USBLS	5/15
Legal Technician							
City Attorney's Office	Benicia, CA	Y			51428 HI	CACIT	6/28/16
City Attorney's Office	Carlsbad, CA	Y			81393 HI	CACIT	6/28/16
Legislation Clerk							
Board of Supervisors	San Francisco, CA	B	2660 LO		3234 HI	SFGOV	2016-2018
Legislative Analyst							
Department of Water and Power, Municipal Government	Burbank, CA	Y			96823 HI	CACIT	6/28/16
Municipal Government	Seattle, WA	H	39.18 LO		45.66 HI	CSSS	1/13/16
Legislative Assistant							
Municipal Government	Berkeley, CA	Y			12159 HI	CACIT	6/28/16
Legislative Counsel							
United States House of Representatives	United States	Y			172500 HI	CRS01	2016
United States Senate	United States	Y			172500 HI	CRS01	2016
Legislative/Executive Fellow							
California State University	California	M	1972 LO		3121 HI	CALST	2016-2017
Legislator	Alabama	Y	17517 AE	23256 AW	26126 AEX	ALBLS	6/16
	Birmingham-Hoover MSA, AL	Y	17578 AE	20448 AW	21883 AEX	ALBLS	6/16
	Arizona	Y	19860 FQ	26240 MW	48920 TQ	USBLS	5/15
	Phoenix-Mesa-Scottsdale MSA, AZ	Y	24280 FQ	31400 MW	52540 TQ	USBLS	5/15
	Tucson MSA, AZ	Y	18920 FQ	23160 MW	24290 TQ	USBLS	5/15
	Arkansas	Y	16320 FQ	17530 MW	18740 TQ	USBLS	5/15

AE	Average entry wage	AWR	Average wage range	H	Hourly	LR	Low end range	MTC Median total compensation TCC Total cash compensation
AEX	Average experienced wage	B	Biweekly	HI	Highest wage paid	M	Monthly	MW Median wage paid TQ Third quartile wage
ATC	Average total compensation	D	Daily	HR	High end range	MCC	Median cash compensation	MWR Median wage range W Weekly
AW	Average wage paid	FQ	First quartile wage	LO	Lowest wage paid	ME	Median entry wage	S See annotated source Y Yearly

Legislator

Occupation/Type/Industry	Location	Per	Low	Mid	High	Source	Date
Legislator	Little Rock-North Little Rock-Conway MSA, AR	Y	16060 FQ	17390 MW	18730 TQ	USBLS	5/15
	California	Y		60705 AW		CABLS	1/16-3/16
	Anaheim-Santa Ana-Irvine PMSA, CA	Y		75994 AW		CABLS	1/16-3/16
	Los Angeles-Long Beach-Glendale PMSA, CA	Y		65720 AW		CABLS	1/16-3/16
	Oakland-Hayward-Berkeley PMSA, CA	Y		61882 AW		CABLS	1/16-3/16
	Riverside-San Bernardino-Ontario MSA, CA	Y		50564 AW		CABLS	1/16-3/16
	Sacramento–Roseville–Arden-Arcade MSA, CA	Y		79504 AW		CABLS	1/16-3/16
	San Diego-Carlsbad MSA, CA	Y		62875 AW		CABLS	1/16-3/16
	San Francisco-Redwood City-South San Francisco PMSA, CA	Y		67234 AW		CABLS	1/16-3/16
	Colorado	Y	19050 FQ	55570 MW	86940 TQ	USBLS	5/15
	Denver-Aurora-Lakewood MSA, CO	Y	21040 FQ	80330 MW	101230 TQ	USBLS	5/15
	Connecticut	Y		35459 MW		CTBLS	1/16-3/16
	Bridgeport-Stamford-Norwalk MSA, CT	Y	19660 FQ	72460 MW	95630 TQ	USBLS	5/15
	Hartford-West Hartford-East Hartford MSA, CT	Y	31720 FQ	34890 MW	38070 TQ	USBLS	5/15
	Washington-Arlington-Alexandria PMSA, DC-VA-MD-WV	Y	17890 FQ	19510 MW	69310 TQ	USBLS	5/15
	Florida	Y	25029 AE	34116 MW	50911 AEX	FLBLS	7/16-9/16
	Fort Lauderdale-Pompano Beach-Deerfield Beach PMSA, FL	Y	26976 AE	32753 MW	51163 AEX	FLBLS	7/16-9/16
	Miami-Miami Beach-Kendall PMSA, FL	Y	25708 AE	35007 MW	44809 AEX	FLBLS	7/16-9/16
	Orlando-Kissimmee-Sanford MSA, FL	Y	26230 AE	41112 MW	60951 AEX	FLBLS	7/16-9/16
	Tampa-St. Petersburg-Clearwater MSA, FL	Y	26963 AE	39216 MW	64233 AEX	FLBLS	7/16-9/16
	Georgia	Y	16850 FQ	18220 MW	19730 TQ	USBLS	5/15
	Atlanta-Sandy Springs-Roswell MSA, GA	Y	16950 FQ	18470 MW	22350 TQ	USBLS	5/15
	Augusta-Richmond County MSA, GA-SC	Y	16770 FQ	17940 MW	19120 TQ	USBLS	5/15
	Hawaii	Y	54190 FQ	57970 MW	61750 TQ	USBLS	5/15
	Idaho	Y	16650 FQ	17900 MW	19340 TQ	USBLS	5/15
	Boise City MSA, ID	Y	16650 FQ	16900 MW	19430 TQ	USBLS	5/15
	Illinois	Y	18740 FQ	20800 MW	68020 TQ	USBLS	5/15
	Chicago-Naperville-Arlington Heights PMSA, IL	Y	18960 FQ	40180 MW	78280 TQ	USBLS	5/15
	Lake County-Kenosha County PMSA, IL-WI	Y	18440 FQ	19480 MW	66440 TQ	USBLS	5/15
	Indiana	Y	17600 FQ	19700 MW	31060 TQ	USBLS	5/15
	Gary PMSA, IN	Y	17830 FQ	21490 MW	29540 TQ	USBLS	5/15
	Indianapolis-Carmel-Anderson MSA, IN	Y	17530 FQ	19430 MW	26800 TQ	USBLS	5/15
	Iowa	Y	17020 FQ	18670 MW	25480 TQ	USBLS	5/15
	Des Moines-West Des Moines MSA, IA	Y	16550 FQ	17810 MW	19070 TQ	USBLS	5/15
	Kansas	Y	17290 FQ	19090 MW	34250 TQ	USBLS	5/15
	Wichita MSA, KS	Y	17050 FQ	18480 MW	20000 TQ	USBLS	5/15
	Louisiana	Y	16820 FQ	18200 MW	19780 TQ	USBLS	5/15
	Baton Rouge MSA, LA	Y	16710 FQ	17820 MW	18920 TQ	USBLS	5/15
	New Orleans-Metairie MSA, LA	Y	17320 FQ	19210 MW	32340 TQ	USBLS	5/15
	Maryland	Y	18052 AE	40175 MW	51236 AEX	MDBLS	4/16
	Baltimore-Columbia-Towson MSA, MD	Y	18250 FQ	33640 MW	62650 TQ	USBLS	5/15
	Salisbury MSA, MD-DE	Y	19480 FQ	22150 MW	24550 TQ	USBLS	5/15
	Michigan	Y	18070 FQ	19030 MW	27750 TQ	USBLS	5/15
	Detroit-Dearborn-Livonia PMSA, MI	Y	18420 FQ	28220 MW	102950 TQ	USBLS	5/15

AE	Average entry wage	AWR	Average wage range	H	Hourly	LR	Low end range	MTC	Median total compensation	TCC	Total cash compensation
AEX	Average experienced wage	B	Biweekly	HI	Highest wage paid	M	Monthly	MW	Median wage paid	TQ	Third quartile wage
ATC	Average total compensation	D	Daily	HR	High end range	MCC	Median cash compensation	MWR	Median wage range	W	Weekly
AW	Average wage paid	FQ	First quartile wage	LO	Lowest wage paid	ME	Median entry wage	S	See annotated source	Y	Yearly

Occupation/Type/Industry	Location	Per	Low	Mid	High	Source	Date
Legislator	Grand Rapids-Wyoming MSA, MI	Y	18120 FQ	19200 MW	28620 TQ	USBLS	5/15
	Lansing-East Lansing MSA, MI	Y	19010 FQ	24570 MW	108380 TQ	USBLS	5/15
	Minnesota	Y	18026 FQ	18971 MW	20200 TQ	MNBLS	1/16-3/16
	Minneapolis-St. Paul-Bloomington MSA, MN-WI	Y	17853 FQ	18747 MW	19702 TQ	MNBLS	1/16-3/16
	Mississippi	Y	16990 FQ	18470 MW	22970 TQ	USBLS	5/15
	Jackson MSA, MS	Y	17160 FQ	18660 MW	24530 TQ	USBLS	5/15
	Missouri	Y	17060 FQ	18190 MW	19360 TQ	USBLS	5/15
	Kansas City MSA, MO-KS	Y	17720 FQ	19780 MW	38960 TQ	USBLS	5/15
	St. Louis MSA, MO-IL	Y	17730 FQ	18970 MW	22490 TQ	USBLS	5/15
	Montana	Y	18370 FQ	25340 MW	50460 TQ	USBLS	5/15
	Billings MSA, MT	Y	25540 FQ	30600 MW	81470 TQ	USBLS	5/15
	Nebraska	Y	17735 FQ	18830 MW	20130 TQ	NEBLS	7/16-9/16
	Omaha-Council Bluffs MSA, NE-IA	Y	19450 FQ	25805 MW	53660 TQ	NEBLS	7/16-9/16
	Nevada	Y	28610 FQ	35940 MW	57820 TQ	USBLS	5/15
	Las Vegas-Henderson-Paradise MSA, NV	Y	42350 FQ	57690 MW	74420 TQ	USBLS	5/15
	New Hampshire	Y	17449 AE	18273 MW	22700 AEX	NHBLS	6/16
	Manchester NECTA, NH	Y	17451 AE	18217 MW	20197 AEX	NHBLS	6/16
	Nashua NECTA, NH-MA	Y	16540 FQ	17610 MW	18680 TQ	USBLS	5/15
	New Mexico	Y	17360 FQ	18680 MW	21550 TQ	USBLS	5/15
	Albuquerque MSA, NM	Y	17170 FQ	18340 MW	19670 TQ	USBLS	5/15
	New York	Y	74700 AE	89470 MW	94620 AEX	NYBLS	1/16-3/16
	Buffalo-Cheektowaga-Niagara Falls MSA, NY	Y	75630 FQ	86330 MW	94230 TQ	USBLS	5/15
	Nassau County-Suffolk County PMSA, NY	Y	76480 FQ	87860 MW	97190 TQ	USBLS	5/15
	New York-Jersey City-White Plains PMSA, NY-NJ	Y	19370 FQ	66760 MW	90730 TQ	USBLS	5/15
	Rochester MSA, NY	Y	79470 FQ	87440 MW	94870 TQ	USBLS	5/15
	Charlotte-Concord-Gastonia MSA, NC-SC	Y	16690 FQ	17770 MW	18840 TQ	USBLS	5/15
	Ohio	Y	17780 FQ	18680 MW	20380 TQ	USBLS	5/15
	Cincinnati MSA, OH-KY-IN	Y	17860 FQ	18910 MW	26780 TQ	USBLS	5/15
	Cleveland-Elyria MSA, OH	Y	17860 FQ	18840 MW	35420 TQ	USBLS	5/15
	Columbus MSA, OH	Y	17760 FQ	18640 MW	19910 TQ	USBLS	5/15
	Oklahoma	Y	19400 FQ	40860 MW	48020 TQ	USBLS	5/15
	Oklahoma City MSA, OK	Y	24150 FQ	42460 MW	47910 TQ	USBLS	5/15
	Tulsa MSA, OK	Y	22000 FQ	42990 MW	49040 TQ	USBLS	5/15
	Oregon	Y	23884 FQ	23893 MW	23901 TQ	ORBLS	2016
	Portland-Vancouver-Hillsboro MSA, OR-WA	Y	19710 FQ	53000 MW	88900 TQ	USBLS	5/15
	Pennsylvania	Y	17390 FQ	19210 MW	54500 TQ	USBLS	5/15
	Allentown-Bethlehem-Easton MSA, PA-NJ	Y	17940 FQ	19220 MW	46080 TQ	USBLS	5/15
	Harrisburg-Carlisle MSA, PA	Y	17320 FQ	19140 MW	66620 TQ	USBLS	5/15
	Montgomery County-Bucks County-Chester County PMSA, PA	Y	17200 FQ	18930 MW	45840 TQ	USBLS	5/15
	Philadelphia PMSA, PA	Y	17560 FQ	20120 MW	75630 TQ	USBLS	5/15
	Pittsburgh MSA, PA	Y	17900 FQ	29090 MW	62920 TQ	USBLS	5/15
	Rhode Island	Y	19070 FQ	19470 MW	24830 TQ	USBLS	5/15
	Providence-Warwick MSA, RI-MA	Y	19010 FQ	19370 MW	25850 TQ	USBLS	5/15
	South Carolina	Y	16710 FQ	17840 MW	18980 TQ	USBLS	5/15
	Charleston-North Charleston MSA, SC	Y	16840 FQ	18090 MW	19340 TQ	USBLS	5/15
	Columbia MSA, SC	Y	16630 FQ	17770 MW	18920 TQ	USBLS	5/15
	Greenville-Anderson-Mauldin MSA, SC	Y	16680 FQ	17820 MW	18960 TQ	USBLS	5/15
	South Dakota	Y	40560 FQ	43940 MW	47320 TQ	USBLS	5/15
	Tennessee	Y	17210 FQ	18870 MW	23160 TQ	USBLS	5/15
	Memphis MSA, TN-MS-AR	Y	17210 FQ	18890 MW	28610 TQ	USBLS	5/15
	Nashville-Davidson–Murfreesboro–Franklin MSA, TN	Y	18110 FQ	20520 MW	24050 TQ	USBLS	5/15
	Texas	Y	17710 FQ	27780 MW	51710 TQ	USBLS	5/15
	Austin-Round Rock MSA, TX	Y	17120 FQ	18850 MW	65550 TQ	USBLS	5/15
	Dallas-Plano-Irving PMSA, TX	Y	17290 FQ	19280 MW	63310 TQ	USBLS	5/15

AE	Average entry wage	AWR	Average wage range	H	Hourly
AEX	Average experienced wage	B	Biweekly	HI	Highest wage paid
ATC	Average total compensation	D	Daily	HR	High end range
AW	Average wage paid	FQ	First quartile wage	LO	Lowest wage paid

LR	Low end range	MTC	Median total compensation	TCC	Total cash compensation
M	Monthly	MW	Median wage paid	TQ	Third quartile wage
MCC	Median cash compensation	MWR	Median wage range	W	Weekly
ME	Median entry wage	S	See annotated source	Y	Yearly

Occupation/Type/Industry	Location	Per	Low	Mid	High	Source	Date
Legislator	Fort Worth-Arlington PMSA, TX	Y	17600 FQ	26830 MW	69530 TQ	USBLS	5/15
	Houston-The Woodlands-Sugar Land MSA, TX	Y	17130 FQ	18900 MW	51640 TQ	USBLS	5/15
	San Antonio-New Braunfels MSA, TX	Y	19200 FQ	28390 MW	60120 TQ	USBLS	5/15
	Utah	Y	17320 FQ	19210 MW	34230 TQ	USBLS	5/15
	Ogden-Clearfield MSA, UT	Y	16770 FQ	18200 MW	44910 TQ	USBLS	5/15
	Provo-Orem MSA, UT	Y	17130 FQ	18800 MW	24320 TQ	USBLS	5/15
	Salt Lake City MSA, UT	Y	27210 FQ	34220 MW	34230 TQ	USBLS	5/15
	Virginia	Y	16890 FQ	18270 MW	19790 TQ	USBLS	5/15
	Richmond MSA, VA	Y	17110 FQ	18650 MW	26720 TQ	USBLS	5/15
	Virginia Beach-Norfolk-Newport News MSA, VA-NC	Y	17550 FQ	19850 MW	23310 TQ	USBLS	5/15
	Washington	Y		86882 AW		WABLS	3/16
	Seattle-Bellevue-Everett PMSA, WA	Y		71471 AW		WABLS	3/16
	Tacoma-Lakewood PMSA, WA	Y		112169 AW		WABLS	3/16
	West Virginia	Y	17830 FQ	19020 MW	32360 TQ	USBLS	5/15
	Huntington-Ashland MSA, WV-KY-OH	Y	17680 FQ	18620 MW	20120 TQ	USBLS	5/15
	Wisconsin	Y	16940 FQ	18260 MW	19590 TQ	USBLS	5/15
	Milwaukee-Waukesha-West Allis MSA, WI	Y	17410 FQ	19230 MW	64060 TQ	USBLS	5/15
	Wyoming	Y	26850 FQ	32730 MW	52640 TQ	USBLS	5/15
State Government	Alaska	Y			50400 HI	NCSL	2016
State Government	Arizona	Y			24000 HI	NCSL	2016
State Government	Arkansas	Y			39400 HI	NCSL	2016
State Government	California	Y			100113 HI	NCSL	2016
State Government	Colorado	Y			30000 HI	NCSL	2016
State Government	Connecticut	Y			28000 HI	NCSL	2016
State Government	Delaware	Y			44541 HI	NCSL	2016
State Government	Florida	Y			29697 HI	NCSL	2016
State Government	Georgia	Y			17342 HI	NCSL	2016
State Government	Hawaii	Y			60180 HI	NCSL	2016
State Government	Idaho	Y			16684 HI	NCSL	2016
State Government	Illinois	Y			67836 HI	NCSL	2016
State Government	Indiana	Y			24671 HI	NCSL	2016
State Government	Iowa	Y			25000 HI	NCSL	2016
State Government	Louisiana	Y			16800 HI	NCSL	2016
State Government	Maine	Y			14074 HI	NCSL	2016
State Government	Maryland	Y			46061 HI	NCSL	2016
State Government	Massachusetts	Y			60032 HI	NCSL	2016
State Government	Michigan	Y			71685 HI	NCSL	2016
State Government	Minnesota	Y			31141 HI	NCSL	2016
State Government	Mississippi	Y			10000 HI	NCSL	2016
State Government	Missouri	Y			35915 HI	NCSL	2016
State Government	Nebraska	Y			12000 HI	NCSL	2016
State Government	New Jersey	Y			49000 HI	NCSL	2016
State Government	New York	Y			79500 HI	NCSL	2016
State Government	North Carolina	Y			13951 HI	NCSL	2016
State Government	Ohio	Y			60584 HI	NCSL	2016
State Government	Oklahoma	Y			38400 HI	NCSL	2016
State Government	Oregon	Y			23568 HI	NCSL	2016
State Government	Pennsylvania	Y			85339 HI	NCSL	2016
State Government	Rhode Island	Y			15414 HI	NCSL	2016
State Government	South Carolina	Y			10400 HI	NCSL	2016
State Government	South Dakota	Y			6000 HI	NCSL	2016
State Government	Tennessee	Y			20884 HI	NCSL	2016
State Government	Texas	Y			7200 HI	NCSL	2016
State Government	Washington	Y			45474 HI	NCSL	2016
State Government	West Virginia	Y			20000 HI	NCSL	2016
State Government	Wisconsin	Y			50950 HI	NCSL	2016
State House of Representatives	Virginia	Y			17640 HI	NCSL	2016
State Senate	Virginia	Y			18000 HI	NCSL	2016
Librarian	Midwest	Y	46000 ME			LJ01	2015
	Mountain	Y	45000 ME			LJ01	2015
	Northeast	Y	47650 ME			LJ01	2015
	Pacific	Y	55000 ME			LJ01	2015
	South Central	Y	40175 ME			LJ01	2015
	Southeast	Y	44500 ME			LJ01	2015

AE	Average entry wage	AWR	Average wage range	H	Hourly	LR	Low end range	MTC	Median total compensation
AEX	Average experienced wage	B	Biweekly	HI	Highest wage paid	M	Monthly	MCC	Median cash compensation
ATC	Average total compensation	D	Daily	HR	High end range	MCC	Median cash compensation	MWR	Median wage range
AW	Average wage paid	FQ	First quartile wage	LO	Lowest wage paid	ME	Median entry wage	S	See annotated source

TCC Total cash compensation
TQ Third quartile wage
W Weekly
Y Yearly
MW Median wage paid

Occupation/Type/Industry	Location	Per	Low	Mid	High	Source	Date
Librarian	Alabama	Y	39754 AE	53637 AW	60589 AEX	ALBLS	6/16
	Birmingham-Hoover MSA, AL	Y	43637 AE	56776 AW	63351 AEX	ALBLS	6/16
	Alaska	Y	53360 FQ	67110 MW	83930 TQ	USBLS	5/15
	Anchorage MSA, AK	Y	64960 FQ	78030 MW	95410 TQ	USBLS	5/15
	Arizona	Y	32670 FQ	46090 MW	58450 TQ	USBLS	5/15
	Phoenix-Mesa-Scottsdale MSA, AZ	Y	30590 FQ	46990 MW	59280 TQ	USBLS	5/15
	Tucson MSA, AZ	Y	40080 FQ	49070 MW	61840 TQ	USBLS	5/15
	Arkansas	Y	42520 FQ	50560 MW	59400 TQ	USBLS	5/15
	Little Rock-North Little Rock-Conway MSA, AR	Y	44340 FQ	53340 MW	60460 TQ	USBLS	5/15
	California	H	26.84 FQ	34.61 MW	42.69 TQ	CABLS	1/16-3/16
	Anaheim-Santa Ana-Irvine PMSA, CA	H	29.30 FQ	37.48 MW	45.74 TQ	CABLS	1/16-3/16
	Los Angeles-Long Beach-Glendale PMSA, CA	H	29.35 FQ	36.16 MW	44.01 TQ	CABLS	1/16-3/16
	Oakland-Hayward-Berkeley PMSA, CA	H	27.81 FQ	33.53 MW	38.58 TQ	CABLS	1/16-3/16
	Riverside-San Bernardino-Ontario MSA, CA	H	21.59 FQ	26.34 MW	36.58 TQ	CABLS	1/16-3/16
	Sacramento–Roseville–Arden-Arcade MSA, CA	H	29.30 FQ	34.46 MW	39.79 TQ	CABLS	1/16-3/16
	San Diego-Carlsbad MSA, CA	H	27.23 FQ	32.77 MW	38.49 TQ	CABLS	1/16-3/16
	San Francisco-Redwood City-South San Francisco PMSA, CA	H	33.15 FQ	40.53 MW	45.92 TQ	CABLS	1/16-3/16
	Colorado	Y	48790 FQ	61510 MW	81210 TQ	USBLS	5/15
	Denver-Aurora-Lakewood MSA, CO	Y	48350 FQ	60690 MW	81530 TQ	USBLS	5/15
	Connecticut	Y		66429 MW		CTBLS	1/16-3/16
	Bridgeport-Stamford-Norwalk MSA, CT	Y	59410 FQ	75780 MW	96890 TQ	USBLS	5/15
	Hartford-West Hartford-East Hartford MSA, CT	Y	51000 FQ	67830 MW	87040 TQ	USBLS	5/15
	Delaware	Y	54090 FQ	70120 MW	83040 TQ	USBLS	5/15
	Wilmington PMSA, DE-MD-NJ	Y	61030 FQ	77340 MW	89010 TQ	USBLS	5/15
	District of Columbia	Y	65470 FQ	79990 MW	95600 TQ	USBLS	5/15
	Washington-Arlington-Alexandria PMSA, DC-VA-MD-WV	Y	58700 FQ	76300 MW	94590 TQ	USBLS	5/15
	Florida	H	19.64 AE	27.27 MW	33.01 AEX	FLBLS	7/16-9/16
	Fort Lauderdale-Pompano Beach-Deerfield Beach PMSA, FL	H	21.50 AE	27.75 MW	35.17 AEX	FLBLS	7/16-9/16
	Miami-Miami Beach-Kendall PMSA, FL	H	23.50 AE	32.61 MW	37.48 AEX	FLBLS	7/16-9/16
	Orlando-Kissimmee-Sanford MSA, FL	H	19.36 AE	25.93 MW	31.53 AEX	FLBLS	7/16-9/16
	Tampa-St. Petersburg-Clearwater MSA, FL	H	19.28 AE	27.07 MW	32.95 AEX	FLBLS	7/16-9/16
	Georgia	Y	50220 FQ	59200 MW	69620 TQ	USBLS	5/15
	Atlanta-Sandy Springs-Roswell MSA, GA	Y	48250 FQ	58570 MW	69420 TQ	USBLS	5/15
	Augusta-Richmond County MSA, GA-SC	Y	53320 FQ	61850 MW	71750 TQ	USBLS	5/15
	Hawaii	Y	53730 FQ	63690 MW	75470 TQ	USBLS	5/15
	Urban Honolulu MSA, HI	Y	55450 FQ	66000 MW	76580 TQ	USBLS	5/15
	Idaho	Y	25990 FQ	38970 MW	51850 TQ	USBLS	5/15
	Boise City MSA, ID	Y	30600 FQ	38630 MW	52710 TQ	USBLS	5/15
	Illinois	Y	40990 FQ	52870 MW	68230 TQ	USBLS	5/15
	Chicago-Naperville-Arlington Heights PMSA, IL	Y	46200 FQ	57470 MW	73190 TQ	USBLS	5/15
	Lake County-Kenosha County PMSA, IL-WI	Y	43860 FQ	52820 MW	63530 TQ	USBLS	5/15
	Indiana	Y	34970 FQ	46600 MW	61240 TQ	USBLS	5/15
	Gary PMSA, IN	Y	29350 FQ	46050 MW	60970 TQ	USBLS	5/15
	Indianapolis-Carmel-Anderson MSA, IN	Y	35240 FQ	45110 MW	60420 TQ	USBLS	5/15
	Iowa	Y	31810 FQ	46070 MW	60970 TQ	USBLS	5/15
	Des Moines-West Des Moines MSA, IA	Y	37000 FQ	58740 MW	72270 TQ	USBLS	5/15

AE	Average entry wage	AWR	Average wage range	H	Hourly
AEX	Average experienced wage	B	Biweekly	HI	Highest wage paid
ATC	Average total compensation	D	Daily	HR	High end range
AW	Average wage paid	FQ	First quartile wage	LO	Lowest wage paid

LR	Low end range	MTC	Median total compensation	TCC	Total cash compensation
M	Monthly	MW	Median wage paid	TQ	Third quartile wage
MCC	Median cash compensation	MWR	Median wage range	W	Weekly
ME	Median entry wage	S	See annotated source	Y	Yearly

Occupation/Type/Industry	Location	Per	Low	Mid	High	Source	Date
Librarian	Kansas	Y	39710 FQ	49850 MW	59270 TQ	USBLS	5/15
	Wichita MSA, KS	Y	39650 FQ	50690 MW	59490 TQ	USBLS	5/15
	Kentucky	Y	45470 FQ	55490 MW	63720 TQ	USBLS	5/15
	Louisville-Jefferson County MSA, KY-IN	Y	45720 FQ	59520 MW	73180 TQ	USBLS	5/15
	Louisiana	Y	44840 FQ	52660 MW	59750 TQ	USBLS	5/15
	Baton Rouge MSA, LA	Y	47120 FQ	55250 MW	62390 TQ	USBLS	5/15
	New Orleans-Metairie MSA, LA	Y	43100 FQ	52970 MW	60520 TQ	USBLS	5/15
	Maine	Y	35190 FQ	47330 MW	60120 TQ	USBLS	5/15
	Portland-South Portland MSA, ME	Y	43000 FQ	53470 MW	65900 TQ	USBLS	5/15
	Maryland	Y	43306 AE	67994 MW	80338 AEX	MDBLS	4/16
	Baltimore-Columbia-Towson MSA, MD	Y	51650 FQ	60830 MW	75060 TQ	USBLS	5/15
	Salisbury MSA, MD-DE	Y	40230 FQ	52860 MW	69770 TQ	USBLS	5/15
	Massachusetts	Y	52650 FQ	66390 MW	81100 TQ	USBLS	5/15
	Boston-Cambridge-Newton NECTA, MA	Y	57950 FQ	71880 MW	87850 TQ	USBLS	5/15
	Worcester MSA, MA-CT	Y	45210 FQ	58130 MW	71770 TQ	USBLS	5/15
	Michigan	Y	38130 FQ	50180 MW	62100 TQ	USBLS	5/15
	Detroit-Dearborn-Livonia PMSA, MI	Y	42520 FQ	51170 MW	60160 TQ	USBLS	5/15
	Grand Rapids-Wyoming MSA, MI	Y	39060 FQ	55290 MW	67200 TQ	USBLS	5/15
	Minnesota	Y	44042 FQ	54536 MW	67439 TQ	MNBLS	1/16-3/16
	Minneapolis-St. Paul-Bloomington MSA, MN-WI	Y	46078 FQ	56894 MW	69918 TQ	MNBLS	1/16-3/16
	Mississippi	Y	35720 FQ	44830 MW	54300 TQ	USBLS	5/15
	Gulfport-Biloxi-Pascagoula MSA, MS	Y	41140 FQ	48940 MW	60590 TQ	USBLS	5/15
	Jackson MSA, MS	Y	32790 FQ	43240 MW	50420 TQ	USBLS	5/15
	Missouri	Y	39110 FQ	51280 MW	61610 TQ	USBLS	5/15
	Kansas City MSA, MO-KS	Y	44220 FQ	55080 MW	66140 TQ	USBLS	5/15
	St. Louis MSA, MO-IL	Y	45160 FQ	55900 MW	67300 TQ	USBLS	5/15
	Montana	Y	34140 FQ	45650 MW	57290 TQ	USBLS	5/15
	Billings MSA, MT	Y	41960 FQ	50090 MW	61080 TQ	USBLS	5/15
	Nebraska	Y	31620 FQ	48260 MW	59950 TQ	NEBLS	7/16-9/16
	Omaha-Council Bluffs MSA, NE-IA	Y	43215 FQ	52835 MW	61565 TQ	NEBLS	7/16-9/16
	Nevada	Y	54660 FQ	65470 MW	74500 TQ	USBLS	5/15
	Las Vegas-Henderson-Paradise MSA, NV	Y	56930 FQ	67080 MW	75230 TQ	USBLS	5/15
	New Hampshire	H	18.58 AE	26.44 MW	31.18 AEX	NHBLS	6/16
	Manchester NECTA, NH	H	21.55 AE	28.35 MW	32.16 AEX	NHBLS	6/16
	Nashua NECTA, NH-MA	Y	44800 FQ	56440 MW	69250 TQ	USBLS	5/15
	New Jersey	Y	53630 FQ	64590 MW	80170 TQ	USBLS	5/15
	Camden PMSA, NJ	Y	46670 FQ	59850 MW	77810 TQ	USBLS	5/15
	Newark PMSA, NJ-PA	Y	54670 FQ	65890 MW	79240 TQ	USBLS	5/15
	Trenton MSA, NJ	Y	60150 FQ	75430 MW	89140 TQ	USBLS	5/15
	New Mexico	Y	36220 FQ	46780 MW	63490 TQ	USBLS	5/15
	Albuquerque MSA, NM	Y	38710 FQ	46120 MW	60170 TQ	USBLS	5/15
	New York	Y	46100 AE	64410 MW	79550 AEX	NYBLS	1/16-3/16
	Buffalo-Cheektowaga-Niagara Falls MSA, NY	Y	39870 FQ	51640 MW	63560 TQ	USBLS	5/15
	Nassau County-Suffolk County PMSA, NY	Y	59090 FQ	73630 MW	96620 TQ	USBLS	5/15
	New York-Jersey City-White Plains PMSA, NY-NJ	Y	54950 FQ	66160 MW	81640 TQ	USBLS	5/15
	Rochester MSA, NY	Y	45090 FQ	54810 MW	64970 TQ	USBLS	5/15
	North Carolina	Y	42360 FQ	50340 MW	60310 TQ	USBLS	5/15
	Charlotte-Concord-Gastonia MSA, NC-SC	Y	44450 FQ	53690 MW	61620 TQ	USBLS	5/15
	Raleigh MSA, NC	Y	45550 FQ	55400 MW	67080 TQ	USBLS	5/15
	North Dakota	Y	35430 FQ	47180 MW	57750 TQ	USBLS	5/15
	Fargo MSA, ND-MN	Y	43700 FQ	51400 MW	65290 TQ	USBLS	5/15
	Ohio	Y	37810 FQ	50260 MW	65350 TQ	USBLS	5/15
	Cincinnati MSA, OH-KY-IN	Y	45860 FQ	55780 MW	67140 TQ	USBLS	5/15
	Cleveland-Elyria MSA, OH	Y	40930 FQ	54090 MW	71450 TQ	USBLS	5/15
	Columbus MSA, OH	Y	45240 FQ	57770 MW	74560 TQ	USBLS	5/15
	Oklahoma	Y	35860 FQ	43910 MW	52260 TQ	USBLS	5/15
	Oklahoma City MSA, OK	Y	35290 FQ	42310 MW	49540 TQ	USBLS	5/15

AE	Average entry wage	AWR	Average wage range	H	Hourly
AEX	Average experienced wage	B	Biweekly	HI	Highest wage paid
ATC	Average total compensation	D	Daily	HR	High end range
AW	Average wage paid	FQ	First quartile wage	LO	Lowest wage paid

LR	Low end range	MTC	Median total compensation	TCC	Total cash compensation
M	Monthly	MW	Median wage paid	TQ	Third quartile wage
MCC	Median cash compensation	MWR	Median wage range	W	Weekly
ME	Median entry wage	S	See annotated source	Y	Yearly

Occupation/Type/Industry	Location	Per	Low	Mid	High	Source	Date
Librarian	Tulsa MSA, OK	Y	43210 FQ	52000 MW	65800 TQ	USBLS	5/15
	Oregon	H	22.74 FQ	28.53 MW	34.89 TQ	ORBLS	2016
	Portland-Vancouver-Hillsboro MSA, OR-WA	Y	51460 FQ	62030 MW	74070 TQ	USBLS	5/15
	Pennsylvania	Y	40110 FQ	54330 MW	70030 TQ	USBLS	5/15
	Allentown-Bethlehem-Easton MSA, PA-NJ	Y	44550 FQ	58800 MW	71500 TQ	USBLS	5/15
	Harrisburg-Carlisle MSA, PA	Y	47400 FQ	58510 MW	68430 TQ	USBLS	5/15
	Montgomery County-Bucks County-Chester County PMSA, PA	Y	44110 FQ	56730 MW	74850 TQ	USBLS	5/15
	Philadelphia PMSA, PA	Y	46340 FQ	60120 MW	77090 TQ	USBLS	5/15
	Pittsburgh MSA, PA	Y	37810 FQ	51940 MW	67260 TQ	USBLS	5/15
	Rhode Island	Y	50790 FQ	62380 MW	76030 TQ	USBLS	5/15
	Providence-Warwick MSA, RI-MA	Y	50690 FQ	61960 MW	75250 TQ	USBLS	5/15
	South Carolina	Y	43650 FQ	53430 MW	63140 TQ	USBLS	5/15
	Charleston-North Charleston MSA, SC	Y	42720 FQ	51410 MW	63310 TQ	USBLS	5/15
	Columbia MSA, SC	Y	44770 FQ	54000 MW	63400 TQ	USBLS	5/15
	Greenville-Anderson-Mauldin MSA, SC	Y	43090 FQ	51700 MW	60630 TQ	USBLS	5/15
	Spartanburg MSA, SC	Y	51400 FQ	60480 MW	70660 TQ	USBLS	5/15
	South Dakota	Y	31490 FQ	37900 MW	49170 TQ	USBLS	5/15
	Sioux Falls MSA, SD	Y	37020 FQ	49160 MW	59080 TQ	USBLS	5/15
	Tennessee	Y	42030 FQ	50910 MW	61630 TQ	USBLS	5/15
	Knoxville MSA, TN	Y	41580 FQ	49880 MW	58990 TQ	USBLS	5/15
	Memphis MSA, TN-MS-AR	Y	43520 FQ	57510 MW	69920 TQ	USBLS	5/15
	Nashville-Davidson–Murfreesboro–Franklin MSA, TN	Y	45130 FQ	54860 MW	65630 TQ	USBLS	5/15
	Texas	Y	49070 FQ	56530 MW	63850 TQ	USBLS	5/15
	Austin-Round Rock MSA, TX	Y	51680 FQ	59900 MW	71760 TQ	USBLS	5/15
	Dallas-Plano-Irving PMSA, TX	Y	52320 FQ	58660 MW	67050 TQ	USBLS	5/15
	Fort Worth-Arlington PMSA, TX	Y	50070 FQ	56280 MW	62480 TQ	USBLS	5/15
	Houston-The Woodlands-Sugar Land MSA, TX	Y	51730 FQ	58230 MW	67010 TQ	USBLS	5/15
	San Antonio-New Braunfels MSA, TX	Y	49460 FQ	55650 MW	61650 TQ	USBLS	5/15
	Utah	Y	37220 FQ	48350 MW	65340 TQ	USBLS	5/15
	Ogden-Clearfield MSA, UT	Y	32920 FQ	39500 MW	46350 TQ	USBLS	5/15
	Provo-Orem MSA, UT	Y	33810 FQ	42670 MW	59250 TQ	USBLS	5/15
	Salt Lake City MSA, UT	Y	43580 FQ	57670 MW	77780 TQ	USBLS	5/15
	Vermont	Y	35160 FQ	45250 MW	59100 TQ	USBLS	5/15
	Burlington-South Burlington MSA, VT	Y	39990 FQ	51160 MW	72880 TQ	USBLS	5/15
	Virginia	Y	47640 FQ	60200 MW	77480 TQ	USBLS	5/15
	Richmond MSA, VA	Y	48790 FQ	58890 MW	70850 TQ	USBLS	5/15
	Virginia Beach-Norfolk-Newport News MSA, VA-NC	Y	46970 FQ	58170 MW	72790 TQ	USBLS	5/15
	Washington	H	27.63 FQ	32.87 MW	36.80 TQ	WABLS	3/16
	Seattle-Bellevue-Everett PMSA, WA	H	30.72 FQ	34.31 MW	37.77 TQ	WABLS	3/16
	Tacoma-Lakewood PMSA, WA	H	29.14 FQ	33.21 MW	36.53 TQ	WABLS	3/16
	West Virginia	Y	34670 FQ	44090 MW	55280 TQ	USBLS	5/15
	Huntington-Ashland MSA, WV-KY-OH	Y	40430 FQ	49100 MW	61170 TQ	USBLS	5/15
	Wisconsin	Y	41210 FQ	52270 MW	64550 TQ	USBLS	5/15
	Madison MSA, WI	Y	45830 FQ	57300 MW	68190 TQ	USBLS	5/15
	Milwaukee-Waukesha-West Allis MSA, WI	Y	44690 FQ	55850 MW	71340 TQ	USBLS	5/15
	Wyoming	Y	37980 FQ	49690 MW	63480 TQ	USBLS	5/15
	Puerto Rico	Y	26850 FQ	35840 MW	44980 TQ	USBLS	5/15
	San Juan-Carolina-Caguas MSA, PR	Y	25090 FQ	33200 MW	44070 TQ	USBLS	5/15
	Virgin Islands	Y	35900 FQ	43980 MW	50950 TQ	USBLS	5/15
	Guam	Y	35760 FQ	46970 MW	57590 TQ	USBLS	5/15
Adult Services	United States	Y	45000 ME			LJ01	2015
Archival and Preservation	United States	Y	42450 ME			LJ01	2015

Occupation/Type/Industry	Location	Per	Low	Mid	High	Source	Date
Librarian							
Emerging Technology, College and University	United States	Y		55371 AW		HED01	2015-2016
Government Documents/Publications, College and University	United States	Y		59392 AW		HED01	2015-2016
Head of Cataloging, Baccalaureate Institution	United States	Y		61171 MW		CHE02	2015-2016
Head of Cataloging, Master's Institution	United States	Y		58583 MW		CHE02	2015-2016
Head of Cataloging, Research University	United States	Y		73547 MW		CHE02	2015-2016
Head of Technical Services, Baccalaureate Institution	United States	Y		59720 MW		CHE02	2015-2016
Head of Technical Services, Master's Institution	United States	Y		64422 MW		CHE02	2015-2016
Head of Technical Services, Research University	United States	Y		92642 MW		CHE02	2015-2016
Patron Programming	United States	Y	40500 ME			LJ01	2015
Website Design	United States	Y	43000 ME			LJ01	2015
Young Adult/Teen Services	United States	Y	46300 ME			LJ01	2015
Librarian Specialist							
Public Library	Glendale, CA	Y		66328 AW		CACIT	6/28/16
Library Aide							
Public Library	Bernardston, MA	H			12.82 HI	FRCOG	2016
Library Assistant							
Clerical	Alabama	Y	17613 AE	22982 AW	25672 AEX	ALBLS	6/16
Clerical	Birmingham-Hoover MSA, AL	Y	17551 AE	27105 AW	31876 AEX	ALBLS	6/16
Clerical	Alaska	Y	33260 FQ	38610 MW	45960 TQ	USBLS	5/15
Clerical	Anchorage MSA, AK	Y	33330 FQ	37630 MW	43380 TQ	USBLS	5/15
Clerical	Arizona	Y	20590 FQ	23560 MW	27890 TQ	USBLS	5/15
Clerical	Phoenix-Mesa-Scottsdale MSA, AZ	Y	19900 FQ	24290 MW	29040 TQ	USBLS	5/15
Clerical	Tucson MSA, AZ	Y	20990 FQ	22400 MW	23820 TQ	USBLS	5/15
Clerical	Arkansas	Y	17630 FQ	19550 MW	23580 TQ	USBLS	5/15
Clerical	Little Rock-North Little Rock-Conway MSA, AR	Y	17990 FQ	20210 MW	27230 TQ	USBLS	5/15
Clerical	California	H	11.07 FQ	14.18 MW	18.49 TQ	CABLS	1/16-3/16
Clerical	Anaheim-Santa Ana-Irvine PMSA, CA	H	9.84 FQ	15.78 MW	19.00 TQ	CABLS	1/16-3/16
Clerical	Los Angeles-Long Beach-Glendale PMSA, CA	H	11.21 FQ	13.42 MW	16.58 TQ	CABLS	1/16-3/16
Clerical	Oakland-Hayward-Berkeley PMSA, CA	H	11.85 FQ	17.05 MW	19.93 TQ	CABLS	1/16-3/16
Clerical	Riverside-San Bernardino-Ontario MSA, CA	H	9.72 FQ	11.30 MW	14.35 TQ	CABLS	1/16-3/16
Clerical	Sacramento–Roseville–Arden-Arcade MSA, CA	H	9.61 FQ	13.96 MW	17.94 TQ	CABLS	1/16-3/16
Clerical	San Diego-Carlsbad MSA, CA	H	10.88 FQ	12.86 MW	17.25 TQ	CABLS	1/16-3/16
Clerical	San Francisco-Redwood City-South San Francisco PMSA, CA	H	12.35 FQ	19.31 MW	23.74 TQ	CABLS	1/16-3/16
Clerical	Colorado	Y	20570 FQ	25660 MW	30630 TQ	USBLS	5/15
Clerical	Denver-Aurora-Lakewood MSA, CO	Y	23730 FQ	27560 MW	31150 TQ	USBLS	5/15
Clerical	Connecticut	Y		28285 MW		CTBLS	1/16-3/16
Clerical	Bridgeport-Stamford-Norwalk MSA, CT	Y	19740 FQ	24250 MW	31900 TQ	USBLS	5/15
Clerical	Hartford-West Hartford-East Hartford MSA, CT	Y	20250 FQ	32270 MW	41890 TQ	USBLS	5/15
Clerical	Delaware	Y	20020 FQ	22040 MW	24100 TQ	USBLS	5/15
Clerical	Wilmington PMSA, DE-MD-NJ	Y	20510 FQ	22410 MW	24300 TQ	USBLS	5/15
Clerical	District of Columbia	Y	22970 FQ	34930 MW	45450 TQ	USBLS	5/15
Clerical	Washington-Arlington-Alexandria PMSA, DC-VA-MD-WV	Y	23130 FQ	33400 MW	43350 TQ	USBLS	5/15
Clerical	Florida	H	9.93 AE	12.67 MW	14.56 AEX	FLBLS	7/16-9/16
Clerical	Fort Lauderdale-Pompano Beach-Deerfield Beach PMSA, FL	H	10.73 AE	13.42 MW	15.04 AEX	FLBLS	7/16-9/16

AE	Average entry wage	**AWR**	Average wage range	**H**	Hourly
AEX	Average experienced wage	**B**	Biweekly	**HI**	Highest wage paid
ATC	Average total compensation	**D**	Daily	**HR**	High end range
AW	Average wage paid	**FQ**	First quartile wage	**LO**	Lowest wage paid

LR	Low end range	**MTC**	Median total compensation	**TCC**	Total cash compensation
M	Monthly	**MW**	Median wage paid	**TQ**	Third quartile wage
MCC	Median cash compensation	**MWR**	Median wage range	**W**	Weekly
ME	Median entry wage	**S**	See annotated source	**Y**	Yearly

Occupation/Type/Industry	Location	Per	Low	Mid	High	Source	Date
Library Assistant							
Clerical	Miami-Miami Beach-Kendall PMSA, FL	H	9.18 AE	12.74 MW	15.25 AEX	FLBLS	7/16-9/16
Clerical	Orlando-Kissimmee-Sanford MSA, FL	H	10.57 AE	12.65 MW	14.14 AEX	FLBLS	7/16-9/16
Clerical	Tampa-St. Petersburg-Clearwater MSA, FL	H	10.13 AE	12.83 MW	14.85 AEX	FLBLS	7/16-9/16
Clerical	Georgia	Y	18360 FQ	21870 MW	26750 TQ	USBLS	5/15
Clerical	Atlanta-Sandy Springs-Roswell MSA, GA	Y	18660 FQ	22140 MW	26810 TQ	USBLS	5/15
Clerical	Augusta-Richmond County MSA, GA-SC	Y	17060 FQ	18610 MW	21410 TQ	USBLS	5/15
Clerical	Hawaii	Y	26980 FQ	30370 MW	35570 TQ	USBLS	5/15
Clerical	Urban Honolulu MSA, HI	Y	27100 FQ	30980 MW	36160 TQ	USBLS	5/15
Clerical	Idaho	Y	17790 FQ	20250 MW	25810 TQ	USBLS	5/15
Clerical	Boise City MSA, ID	Y	17810 FQ	20670 MW	24370 TQ	USBLS	5/15
Clerical	Illinois	Y	20300 FQ	24340 MW	30580 TQ	USBLS	5/15
Clerical	Chicago-Naperville-Arlington Heights PMSA, IL	Y	21870 FQ	26300 MW	32370 TQ	USBLS	5/15
Clerical	Lake County-Kenosha County PMSA, IL-WI	Y	20660 FQ	25170 MW	33280 TQ	USBLS	5/15
Clerical	Indiana	Y	18710 FQ	23190 MW	28580 TQ	USBLS	5/15
Clerical	Gary PMSA, IN	Y	18580 FQ	24080 MW	29010 TQ	USBLS	5/15
Clerical	Indianapolis-Carmel-Anderson MSA, IN	Y	20220 FQ	23980 MW	28080 TQ	USBLS	5/15
Clerical	Iowa	Y	18170 FQ	21360 MW	27460 TQ	USBLS	5/15
Clerical	Des Moines-West Des Moines MSA, IA	Y	20480 FQ	23950 MW	29530 TQ	USBLS	5/15
Clerical	Kansas	Y	18380 FQ	21670 MW	26020 TQ	USBLS	5/15
Clerical	Wichita MSA, KS	Y	18140 FQ	20810 MW	25080 TQ	USBLS	5/15
Clerical	Kentucky	Y	18120 FQ	21860 MW	27790 TQ	USBLS	5/15
Clerical	Louisville-Jefferson County MSA, KY-IN	Y	23810 FQ	28200 MW	32630 TQ	USBLS	5/15
Clerical	Baton Rouge MSA, LA	Y	18430 FQ	21540 MW	27590 TQ	USBLS	5/15
Clerical	New Orleans-Metairie MSA, LA	Y	18060 FQ	21080 MW	30250 TQ	USBLS	5/15
Clerical	Maine	Y	18660 FQ	23040 MW	28350 TQ	USBLS	5/15
Clerical	Portland-South Portland MSA, ME	Y	18660 FQ	25780 MW	29660 TQ	USBLS	5/15
Clerical	Maryland	Y	18029 AE	26410 MW	30601 AEX	MDBLS	4/16
Clerical	Baltimore-Columbia-Towson MSA, MD	Y	18720 FQ	22650 MW	31460 TQ	USBLS	5/15
Clerical	Salisbury MSA, MD-DE	Y	19160 FQ	22130 MW	26490 TQ	USBLS	5/15
Clerical	Massachusetts	Y	21460 FQ	29550 MW	38530 TQ	USBLS	5/15
Clerical	Boston-Cambridge-Newton NECTA, MA	Y	22020 FQ	32770 MW	42450 TQ	USBLS	5/15
Clerical	Worcester MSA, MA-CT	Y	20510 FQ	25560 MW	32030 TQ	USBLS	5/15
Clerical	Michigan	Y	18550 FQ	20410 MW	26530 TQ	USBLS	5/15
Clerical	Detroit-Dearborn-Livonia PMSA, MI	Y	18470 FQ	19900 MW	26090 TQ	USBLS	5/15
Clerical	Grand Rapids-Wyoming MSA, MI	Y	18620 FQ	21390 MW	29040 TQ	USBLS	5/15
Clerical	Minnesota	Y	20498 FQ	27881 MW	34434 TQ	MNBLS	1/16-3/16
Clerical	Minneapolis-St. Paul-Bloomington MSA, MN-WI	Y	25474 FQ	30652 MW	36325 TQ	MNBLS	1/16-3/16
Clerical	Mississippi	Y	17170 FQ	18780 MW	23010 TQ	USBLS	5/15
Clerical	Jackson MSA, MS	Y	16810 FQ	18060 MW	19340 TQ	USBLS	5/15
Clerical	Missouri	Y	18970 FQ	22340 MW	27450 TQ	USBLS	5/15
Clerical	Kansas City MSA, MO-KS	Y	20030 FQ	23190 MW	27880 TQ	USBLS	5/15
Clerical	St. Louis MSA, MO-IL	Y	20790 FQ	23540 MW	28190 TQ	USBLS	5/15
Clerical	Montana	Y	19730 FQ	25340 MW	29990 TQ	USBLS	5/15
Clerical	Nebraska	Y	18305 FQ	20180 MW	24985 TQ	NEBLS	7/16-9/16
Clerical	Omaha-Council Bluffs MSA, NE-IA	Y	18465 FQ	21500 MW	27280 TQ	NEBLS	7/16-9/16
Clerical	Las Vegas-Henderson-Paradise MSA, NV	Y	30310 FQ	36970 MW	44590 TQ	USBLS	5/15
Clerical	New Hampshire	H	9.19 AE	12.75 MW	14.76 AEX	NHBLS	6/16
Clerical	Manchester NECTA, NH	H	11.20 AE	13.93 MW	15.46 AEX	NHBLS	6/16
Clerical	Nashua NECTA, NH-MA	Y	20210 FQ	26880 MW	33760 TQ	USBLS	5/15
Clerical	New Jersey	Y	20340 FQ	27650 MW	34630 TQ	USBLS	5/15
Clerical	Camden PMSA, NJ	Y	18980 FQ	27140 MW	34100 TQ	USBLS	5/15
Clerical	Newark PMSA, NJ-PA	Y	20900 FQ	27440 MW	34590 TQ	USBLS	5/15

AE	Average entry wage	AWR	Average wage range	H	Hourly
AEX	Average experienced wage	B	Biweekly	HI	Highest wage paid
ATC	Average total compensation	D	Daily	HR	High end range
AW	Average wage paid	FQ	First quartile wage	LO	Lowest wage paid

LR	Low end range	MTC	Median total compensation	TCC	Total cash compensation
M	Monthly	MW	Median wage paid	TQ	Third quartile wage
MCC	Median cash compensation	MWR	Median wage range	W	Weekly
ME	Median entry wage	S	See annotated source	Y	Yearly

Occupation/Type/Industry	Location	Per	Low	Mid	High	Source	Date
Library Assistant							
Clerical	Trenton MSA, NJ	Y	21370 FQ	29440 MW	40660 TQ	USBLS	5/15
Clerical	New Mexico	Y	18270 FQ	21940 MW	27860 TQ	USBLS	5/15
Clerical	Albuquerque MSA, NM	Y	19090 FQ	24050 MW	28480 TQ	USBLS	5/15
Clerical	New York	Y	20360 AE	28720 MW	35670 AEX	NYBLS	1/16-3/16
Clerical	Buffalo-Cheektowaga-Niagara Falls MSA, NY	Y	26770 FQ	31870 MW	38780 TQ	USBLS	5/15
Clerical	Nassau County-Suffolk County PMSA, NY	Y	27580 FQ	35050 MW	42380 TQ	USBLS	5/15
Clerical	New York-Jersey City-White Plains PMSA, NY-NJ	Y	19820 FQ	27610 MW	35770 TQ	USBLS	5/15
Clerical	Rochester MSA, NY	Y	20450 FQ	24570 MW	31020 TQ	USBLS	5/15
Clerical	North Carolina	Y	19190 FQ	24480 MW	30870 TQ	USBLS	5/15
Clerical	Charlotte-Concord-Gastonia MSA, NC-SC	Y	22160 FQ	27150 MW	33270 TQ	USBLS	5/15
Clerical	Raleigh MSA, NC	Y	17010 FQ	18620 MW	22080 TQ	USBLS	5/15
Clerical	North Dakota	Y	19120 FQ	23720 MW	29520 TQ	USBLS	5/15
Clerical	Ohio	Y	18990 FQ	23720 MW	30970 TQ	USBLS	5/15
Clerical	Cincinnati MSA, OH-KY-IN	Y	20080 FQ	24530 MW	30790 TQ	USBLS	5/15
Clerical	Cleveland-Elyria MSA, OH	Y	18850 FQ	24780 MW	36020 TQ	USBLS	5/15
Clerical	Columbus MSA, OH	Y	20520 FQ	25920 MW	30140 TQ	USBLS	5/15
Clerical	Oklahoma	Y	17430 FQ	19300 MW	23600 TQ	USBLS	5/15
Clerical	Oklahoma City MSA, OK	Y	17480 FQ	19400 MW	25340 TQ	USBLS	5/15
Clerical	Tulsa MSA, OK	Y	17710 FQ	19730 MW	23950 TQ	USBLS	5/15
Clerical	Oregon	H	11.98 FQ	14.83 MW	17.89 TQ	ORBLS	2016
Clerical	Portland-Vancouver-Hillsboro MSA, OR-WA	Y	27610 FQ	32600 MW	37510 TQ	USBLS	5/15
Clerical	Pennsylvania	Y	18220 FQ	22300 MW	28340 TQ	USBLS	5/15
Clerical	Allentown-Bethlehem-Easton MSA, PA-NJ	Y	19160 FQ	24930 MW	31660 TQ	USBLS	5/15
Clerical	Harrisburg-Carlisle MSA, PA	Y	18430 FQ	22630 MW	27850 TQ	USBLS	5/15
Clerical	Montgomery County-Bucks County-Chester County PMSA, PA	Y	20080 FQ	24290 MW	29790 TQ	USBLS	5/15
Clerical	Philadelphia PMSA, PA	Y	19960 FQ	26460 MW	30790 TQ	USBLS	5/15
Clerical	Pittsburgh MSA, PA	Y	17290 FQ	19050 MW	23080 TQ	USBLS	5/15
Clerical	Rhode Island	Y	19260 FQ	21550 MW	32390 TQ	USBLS	5/15
Clerical	Providence-Warwick MSA, RI-MA	Y	19310 FQ	22120 MW	33160 TQ	USBLS	5/15
Clerical	South Carolina	Y	18150 FQ	21750 MW	27370 TQ	USBLS	5/15
Clerical	Charleston-North Charleston MSA, SC	Y	17440 FQ	19620 MW	23800 TQ	USBLS	5/15
Clerical	Columbia MSA, SC	Y	19660 FQ	23250 MW	27960 TQ	USBLS	5/15
Clerical	Greenville-Anderson-Mauldin MSA, SC	Y	17820 FQ	20890 MW	30450 TQ	USBLS	5/15
Clerical	Tennessee	Y	19780 FQ	24510 MW	30300 TQ	USBLS	5/15
Clerical	Knoxville MSA, TN	Y	20760 FQ	24960 MW	33970 TQ	USBLS	5/15
Clerical	Memphis MSA, TN-MS-AR	Y	23050 FQ	27050 MW	29960 TQ	USBLS	5/15
Clerical	Nashville-Davidson–Murfreesboro–Franklin MSA, TN	Y	21320 FQ	25460 MW	30650 TQ	USBLS	5/15
Clerical	Texas	Y	18940 FQ	23230 MW	28430 TQ	USBLS	5/15
Clerical	Austin-Round Rock MSA, TX	Y	23020 FQ	27110 MW	30740 TQ	USBLS	5/15
Clerical	Dallas-Plano-Irving PMSA, TX	Y	18930 FQ	24310 MW	29170 TQ	USBLS	5/15
Clerical	Fort Worth-Arlington PMSA, TX	Y	18820 FQ	23910 MW	28910 TQ	USBLS	5/15
Clerical	Houston-The Woodlands-Sugar Land MSA, TX	Y	19000 FQ	24910 MW	29300 TQ	USBLS	5/15
Clerical	San Antonio-New Braunfels MSA, TX	Y	19710 FQ	22670 MW	27740 TQ	USBLS	5/15
Clerical	Utah	Y	20650 FQ	24560 MW	29160 TQ	USBLS	5/15
Clerical	Ogden-Clearfield MSA, UT	Y	17860 FQ	21270 MW	26890 TQ	USBLS	5/15
Clerical	Provo-Orem MSA, UT	Y	17710 FQ	20620 MW	24140 TQ	USBLS	5/15
Clerical	Salt Lake City MSA, UT	Y	23500 FQ	26900 MW	30270 TQ	USBLS	5/15
Clerical	Vermont	Y	20200 FQ	26480 MW	32170 TQ	USBLS	5/15
Clerical	Burlington-South Burlington MSA, VT	Y	21570 FQ	27970 MW	33150 TQ	USBLS	5/15
Clerical	Virginia	Y	20150 FQ	26880 MW	34720 TQ	USBLS	5/15
Clerical	Richmond MSA, VA	Y	20090 FQ	26000 MW	33130 TQ	USBLS	5/15
Clerical	Virginia Beach-Norfolk-Newport News MSA, VA-NC	Y	19540 FQ	25580 MW	31850 TQ	USBLS	5/15
Clerical	Washington	H	11.93 FQ	13.89 MW	16.38 TQ	WABLS	3/16

AE	Average entry wage	AWR	Average wage range	H	Hourly
AEX	Average experienced wage	B	Biweekly	HI	Highest wage paid
ATC	Average total compensation	D	Daily	HR	High end range
AW	Average wage paid	FQ	First quartile wage	LO	Lowest wage paid

LR	Low end range	MTC	Median total compensation	TCC	Total cash compensation
M	Monthly	MW	Median wage paid	TQ	Third quartile wage
MCC	Median cash compensation	MWR	Median wage range	W	Weekly
ME	Median entry wage	S	See annotated source	Y	Yearly

Occupation/Type/Industry	Location	Per	Low	Mid	High	Source	Date
Library Assistant							
Clerical	Seattle-Bellevue-Everett PMSA, WA	H	12.40 FQ	13.71 MW	15.02 TQ	WABLS	3/16
Clerical	Tacoma-Lakewood PMSA, WA	H	13.86 FQ	15.52 MW	17.73 TQ	WABLS	3/16
Clerical	West Virginia	Y	17830 FQ	19020 MW	23110 TQ	USBLS	5/15
Clerical	Huntington-Ashland MSA, WV-KY-OH	Y	17880 FQ	19550 MW	26060 TQ	USBLS	5/15
Clerical	Wisconsin	Y	18930 FQ	24380 MW	30840 TQ	USBLS	5/15
Clerical	Madison MSA, WI	Y	18670 FQ	24610 MW	34430 TQ	USBLS	5/15
Clerical	Milwaukee-Waukesha-West Allis MSA, WI	Y	17660 FQ	19800 MW	29540 TQ	USBLS	5/15
Clerical	Wyoming	Y	20320 FQ	23510 MW	30710 TQ	USBLS	5/15
Clerical	Puerto Rico	Y	16580 FQ	17750 MW	18920 TQ	USBLS	5/15
Clerical	San Juan-Carolina-Caguas MSA, PR	Y	16680 FQ	17940 MW	19190 TQ	USBLS	5/15
Library Copy Catalog Clerk							
Public Library	Detroit, MI	M	1720 LO		2338 HI	DETGOV	2016
Library Director							
Public Library	Larkspur, CA	Y			102336 HI	CACIT	6/28/16
Public Library	Gill, MA	H			18.12 HI	FRCOG	2016
Library Intern							
Public Library	Benicia, CA	Y			1429 HI	CACIT	6/28/16
Library Literacy Clerk							
Public Library	Commerce, CA	Y			21129 HI	CACIT	6/28/16
Library Media Supervisor							
Public Library	Whittier, CA	Y			73438 HI	CACIT	6/27/16
Library Science Teacher							
Postsecondary	Alabama	Y	48938 AE	66215 AW	74859 AEX	ALBLS	6/16
Postsecondary	California	Y		99755 AW		CABLS	1/16-3/16
Postsecondary	Colorado	Y	54050 FQ	64170 MW	77680 TQ	USBLS	5/15
Postsecondary	District of Columbia	Y	55240 FQ	66360 MW	89380 TQ	USBLS	5/15
Postsecondary	Florida	Y	64119 AE	96443 MW	131812 AEX	FLBLS	7/16-9/16
Postsecondary	Georgia	Y	47980 FQ	56850 MW	70550 TQ	USBLS	5/15
Postsecondary	Hawaii	Y	62930 FQ	75770 MW	89490 TQ	USBLS	5/15
Postsecondary	Illinois	Y	59820 FQ	78810 MW	101210 TQ	USBLS	5/15
Postsecondary	Indiana	Y	53100 FQ	64580 MW	80030 TQ	USBLS	5/15
Postsecondary	Kentucky	Y	49280 FQ	59310 MW	74660 TQ	USBLS	5/15
Postsecondary	Louisiana	Y	49320 FQ	59590 MW	72510 TQ	USBLS	5/15
Postsecondary	Massachusetts	Y	36600 FQ	55310 MW	71570 TQ	USBLS	5/15
Postsecondary	Michigan	Y	64620 FQ	76090 MW	93440 TQ	USBLS	5/15
Postsecondary	Minnesota	Y	54586 FQ	63336 MW	76844 TQ	MNBLS	1/16-3/16
Postsecondary	Mississippi	Y	45200 FQ	53860 MW	69740 TQ	USBLS	5/15
Postsecondary	Missouri	Y	48150 FQ	58490 MW	74070 TQ	USBLS	5/15
Postsecondary	New Jersey	Y	67200 FQ	82960 MW	97180 TQ	USBLS	5/15
Postsecondary	New Mexico	Y	56090 FQ	63610 MW	82470 TQ	USBLS	5/15
Postsecondary	New York	Y	48850 AE	73470 MW	95810 AEX	NYBLS	1/16-3/16
Postsecondary	North Carolina	Y	48850 FQ	64920 MW	83490 TQ	USBLS	5/15
Postsecondary	Ohio	Y	46810 FQ	64600 MW	82360 TQ	USBLS	5/15
Postsecondary	Oklahoma	Y	44510 FQ	53680 MW	69880 TQ	USBLS	5/15
Postsecondary	Oregon	Y	63892 FQ	73899 MW	88065 TQ	ORBLS	2016
Postsecondary	Pennsylvania	Y	57920 FQ	72520 MW	91120 TQ	USBLS	5/15
Postsecondary	South Carolina	Y	47750 FQ	56450 MW	64530 TQ	USBLS	5/15
Postsecondary	Tennessee	Y	51940 FQ	64650 MW	76310 TQ	USBLS	5/15
Postsecondary	Texas	Y	51090 FQ	62520 MW	81610 TQ	USBLS	5/15
Postsecondary	Utah	Y	33510 FQ	56510 MW	71430 TQ	USBLS	5/15
Postsecondary	Virginia	Y	45250 FQ	60690 MW	74920 TQ	USBLS	5/15
Postsecondary	Washington	Y		73997 AW		WABLS	3/16
Postsecondary	Wisconsin	Y	44180 FQ	50510 MW	61180 TQ	USBLS	5/15
Library Technician	Alabama	Y	20764 AE	29193 AW	33413 AEX	ALBLS	6/16
	Birmingham-Hoover MSA, AL	Y	19377 AE	31049 AW	36879 AEX	ALBLS	6/16
	Alaska	Y	32170 FQ	39450 MW	49900 TQ	USBLS	5/15
	Anchorage MSA, AK	Y	31710 FQ	37900 MW	46940 TQ	USBLS	5/15
	Arizona	Y	25890 FQ	31830 MW	38490 TQ	USBLS	5/15
	Phoenix-Mesa-Scottsdale MSA, AZ	Y	25960 FQ	30190 MW	36760 TQ	USBLS	5/15
	Tucson MSA, AZ	Y	31670 FQ	36750 MW	43200 TQ	USBLS	5/15

AE	Average entry wage	AWR	Average wage range	H	Hourly	LR	Low end range
AEX	Average experienced wage	B	Biweekly	HI	Highest wage paid	M	Monthly
ATC	Average total compensation	D	Daily	HR	High end range	MCC	Median cash compensation
AW	Average wage paid	FQ	First quartile wage	LO	Lowest wage paid	ME	Median entry wage

MTC	Median total compensation	TCC	Total cash compensation
MW	Median wage paid	TQ	Third quartile wage
MWR	Median wage range	W	Weekly
S	See annotated source	Y	Yearly

Occupation/Type/Industry	Location	Per	Low	Mid	High	Source	Date
Library Technician	Arkansas	Y	20920 FQ	25530 MW	31540 TQ	USBLS	5/15
	Little Rock-North Little Rock-Conway MSA, AR	Y	23080 FQ	27780 MW	32670 TQ	USBLS	5/15
	California	H	16.73 FQ	20.42 MW	24.01 TQ	CABLS	1/16-3/16
	Anaheim-Santa Ana-Irvine PMSA, CA	H	19.65 FQ	21.92 MW	24.19 TQ	CABLS	1/16-3/16
	Los Angeles-Long Beach-Glendale PMSA, CA	H	16.30 FQ	20.08 MW	24.27 TQ	CABLS	1/16-3/16
	Oakland-Hayward-Berkeley PMSA, CA	H	17.59 FQ	21.28 MW	24.12 TQ	CABLS	1/16-3/16
	Riverside-San Bernardino-Ontario MSA, CA	H	15.58 FQ	18.27 MW	21.92 TQ	CABLS	1/16-3/16
	Sacramento–Roseville–Arden-Arcade MSA, CA	H	16.07 FQ	18.78 MW	22.26 TQ	CABLS	1/16-3/16
	San Diego-Carlsbad MSA, CA	H	19.91 FQ	22.04 MW	24.23 TQ	CABLS	1/16-3/16
	San Francisco-Redwood City-South San Francisco PMSA, CA	H	21.53 FQ	25.50 MW	31.33 TQ	CABLS	1/16-3/16
	Colorado	Y	26750 FQ	33330 MW	39410 TQ	USBLS	5/15
	Denver-Aurora-Lakewood MSA, CO	Y	27110 FQ	34790 MW	42550 TQ	USBLS	5/15
	Connecticut	Y		40113 MW		CTBLS	1/16-3/16
	Bridgeport-Stamford-Norwalk MSA, CT	Y	31950 FQ	39590 MW	54210 TQ	USBLS	5/15
	Hartford-West Hartford-East Hartford MSA, CT	Y	29680 FQ	40010 MW	53050 TQ	USBLS	5/15
	Delaware	Y	30080 FQ	38740 MW	47920 TQ	USBLS	5/15
	Wilmington PMSA, DE-MD-NJ	Y	34560 FQ	40950 MW	49220 TQ	USBLS	5/15
	District of Columbia	Y	40800 FQ	47230 MW	55390 TQ	USBLS	5/15
	Washington-Arlington-Alexandria PMSA, DC-VA-MD-WV	Y	33530 FQ	42380 MW	52450 TQ	USBLS	5/15
	Florida	H	12.23 AE	16.70 MW	20.41 AEX	FLBLS	7/16-9/16
	Fort Lauderdale-Pompano Beach-Deerfield Beach PMSA, FL	H	16.20 AE	18.86 MW	21.09 AEX	FLBLS	7/16-9/16
	Miami-Miami Beach-Kendall PMSA, FL	H	12.94 AE	16.64 MW	18.80 AEX	FLBLS	7/16-9/16
	Orlando-Kissimmee-Sanford MSA, FL	H	11.76 AE	15.33 MW	17.16 AEX	FLBLS	7/16-9/16
	Tampa-St. Petersburg-Clearwater MSA, FL	H	11.69 AE	16.97 MW	24.29 AEX	FLBLS	7/16-9/16
	Georgia	Y	18960 FQ	25100 MW	31980 TQ	USBLS	5/15
	Atlanta-Sandy Springs-Roswell MSA, GA	Y	21480 FQ	27620 MW	34700 TQ	USBLS	5/15
	Augusta-Richmond County MSA, GA-SC	Y	17570 FQ	19600 MW	30400 TQ	USBLS	5/15
	Hawaii	Y	35720 FQ	42390 MW	48080 TQ	USBLS	5/15
	Urban Honolulu MSA, HI	Y	36950 FQ	43020 MW	47720 TQ	USBLS	5/15
	Idaho	Y	20600 FQ	25670 MW	29590 TQ	USBLS	5/15
	Boise City MSA, ID	Y	22210 FQ	26040 MW	30480 TQ	USBLS	5/15
	Illinois	Y	24390 FQ	32010 MW	41540 TQ	USBLS	5/15
	Chicago-Naperville-Arlington Heights PMSA, IL	Y	26510 FQ	33730 MW	42880 TQ	USBLS	5/15
	Lake County-Kenosha County PMSA, IL-WI	Y	23040 FQ	30560 MW	37710 TQ	USBLS	5/15
	Indiana	Y	20190 FQ	25370 MW	30920 TQ	USBLS	5/15
	Fort Wayne MSA, IN	Y	22880 FQ	26290 MW	30460 TQ	USBLS	5/15
	Gary PMSA, IN	Y	18370 FQ	24550 MW	30080 TQ	USBLS	5/15
	Indianapolis-Carmel-Anderson MSA, IN	Y	21140 FQ	26790 MW	31350 TQ	USBLS	5/15
	Iowa	Y	20110 FQ	26790 MW	38760 TQ	USBLS	5/15
	Des Moines-West Des Moines MSA, IA	Y	21820 FQ	30410 MW	42440 TQ	USBLS	5/15
	Kansas	Y	22960 FQ	27750 MW	33240 TQ	USBLS	5/15
	Wichita MSA, KS	Y	25660 FQ	28510 MW	31600 TQ	USBLS	5/15
	Kentucky	Y	24030 FQ	28790 MW	34590 TQ	USBLS	5/15
	Louisville-Jefferson County MSA, KY-IN	Y	24460 FQ	32000 MW	36300 TQ	USBLS	5/15
	Louisiana	Y	25350 FQ	32880 MW	41010 TQ	USBLS	5/15
	Baton Rouge MSA, LA	Y	33370 FQ	38380 MW	47980 TQ	USBLS	5/15

AE	Average entry wage	AWR	Average wage range	H	Hourly	LR	Low end range	MTC	Median total compensation	TCC	Total cash compensation
AEX	Average experienced wage	B	Biweekly	HI	Highest wage paid	M	Monthly	MW	Median wage paid	TQ	Third quartile wage
ATC	Average total compensation	D	Daily	HR	High end range	MCC	Median cash compensation	MWR	Median wage range	W	Weekly
AW	Average wage paid	FQ	First quartile wage	LO	Lowest wage paid	ME	Median entry wage	S	See annotated source	Y	Yearly

Occupation/Type/Industry	Location	Per	Low	Mid	High	Source	Date
Library Technician	New Orleans-Metairie MSA, LA	Y	25850 FQ	30120 MW	36880 TQ	USBLS	5/15
	Maine	Y	26410 FQ	31830 MW	37970 TQ	USBLS	5/15
	Portland-South Portland MSA, ME	Y	25160 FQ	33430 MW	40780 TQ	USBLS	5/15
	Maryland	Y	29576 AE	41683 MW	47736 AEX	MDBLS	4/16
	Baltimore-Columbia-Towson MSA, MD	Y	31870 FQ	38170 MW	46040 TQ	USBLS	5/15
	Salisbury MSA, MD-DE	Y	24990 FQ	28390 MW	32580 TQ	USBLS	5/15
	Massachusetts	Y	32390 FQ	41640 MW	51470 TQ	USBLS	5/15
	Boston-Cambridge-Newton NECTA, MA	Y	36560 FQ	46100 MW	56580 TQ	USBLS	5/15
	Worcester MSA, MA-CT	Y	29770 FQ	36470 MW	44760 TQ	USBLS	5/15
	Michigan	Y	23590 FQ	29470 MW	37000 TQ	USBLS	5/15
	Detroit-Dearborn-Livonia PMSA, MI	Y	24930 FQ	32270 MW	37680 TQ	USBLS	5/15
	Grand Rapids-Wyoming MSA, MI	Y	31580 FQ	38120 MW	44820 TQ	USBLS	5/15
	Minnesota	Y	28417 FQ	38377 MW	46259 TQ	MNBLS	1/16-3/16
	Minneapolis-St. Paul-Bloomington MSA, MN-WI	Y	25504 FQ	37510 MW	45776 TQ	MNBLS	1/16-3/16
	Mississippi	Y	18440 FQ	22320 MW	30180 TQ	USBLS	5/15
	Jackson MSA, MS	Y	18750 FQ	24700 MW	31880 TQ	USBLS	5/15
	Missouri	Y	26460 FQ	33720 MW	41850 TQ	USBLS	5/15
	Kansas City MSA, MO-KS	Y	27220 FQ	31060 MW	38470 TQ	USBLS	5/15
	St. Louis MSA, MO-IL	Y	31360 FQ	37070 MW	46640 TQ	USBLS	5/15
	Montana	Y	20880 FQ	25870 MW	30370 TQ	USBLS	5/15
	Billings MSA, MT	Y	25450 FQ	29840 MW	35570 TQ	USBLS	5/15
	Nebraska	Y	21985 FQ	27905 MW	35005 TQ	NEBLS	7/16-9/16
	Omaha-Council Bluffs MSA, NE-IA	Y	23830 FQ	29175 MW	36390 TQ	NEBLS	7/16-9/16
	Nevada	Y	21740 FQ	24410 MW	38530 TQ	USBLS	5/15
	Las Vegas-Henderson-Paradise MSA, NV	Y	21300 FQ	23350 MW	30680 TQ	USBLS	5/15
	New Hampshire	H	12.72 AE	16.99 MW	19.49 AEX	NHBLS	6/16
	Nashua NECTA, NH-MA	Y	26660 FQ	31280 MW	37120 TQ	USBLS	5/15
	New Jersey	Y	30920 FQ	40020 MW	52690 TQ	USBLS	5/15
	Camden PMSA, NJ	Y	22550 FQ	32380 MW	44880 TQ	USBLS	5/15
	Newark PMSA, NJ-PA	Y	38040 FQ	47840 MW	57590 TQ	USBLS	5/15
	Trenton MSA, NJ	Y	38450 FQ	48480 MW	57000 TQ	USBLS	5/15
	New Mexico	Y	24300 FQ	31310 MW	38650 TQ	USBLS	5/15
	Albuquerque MSA, NM	Y	27910 FQ	33690 MW	37950 TQ	USBLS	5/15
	New York	Y	19690 AE	28440 MW	38910 AEX	NYBLS	1/16-3/16
	Buffalo-Cheektowaga-Niagara Falls MSA, NY	Y	18610 FQ	19010 MW	19410 TQ	USBLS	5/15
	Nassau County-Suffolk County PMSA, NY	Y	19600 FQ	28290 MW	40960 TQ	USBLS	5/15
	New York-Jersey City-White Plains PMSA, NY-NJ	Y	23800 FQ	34680 MW	45740 TQ	USBLS	5/15
	Rochester MSA, NY	Y	18960 FQ	20130 MW	27460 TQ	USBLS	5/15
	North Carolina	Y	25010 FQ	30010 MW	36710 TQ	USBLS	5/15
	Charlotte-Concord-Gastonia MSA, NC-SC	Y	28000 FQ	31790 MW	37240 TQ	USBLS	5/15
	Fayetteville MSA, NC	Y	30440 FQ	34320 MW	37730 TQ	USBLS	5/15
	Raleigh MSA, NC	Y	26850 FQ	32460 MW	37690 TQ	USBLS	5/15
	North Dakota	Y	26190 FQ	29770 MW	36580 AEX	USBLS	5/15
	Fargo MSA, ND-MN	Y	28060 FQ	32250 MW	40890 TQ	USBLS	5/15
	Ohio	Y	24970 FQ	30550 MW	38080 TQ	USBLS	5/15
	Cincinnati MSA, OH-KY-IN	Y	24310 FQ	31220 MW	37750 TQ	USBLS	5/15
	Cleveland-Elyria MSA, OH	Y	28820 FQ	37040 MW	46750 TQ	USBLS	5/15
	Columbus MSA, OH	Y	27600 FQ	32740 MW	38760 TQ	USBLS	5/15
	Oklahoma	Y	18850 FQ	24610 MW	30690 TQ	USBLS	5/15
	Oklahoma City MSA, OK	Y	19410 FQ	23840 MW	30960 TQ	USBLS	5/15
	Tulsa MSA, OK	Y	23260 FQ	28690 MW	36130 TQ	USBLS	5/15
	Oregon	H	15.16 FQ	17.91 MW	21.46 TQ	ORBLS	2016
	Portland-Vancouver-Hillsboro MSA, OR-WA	Y	32410 FQ	37420 MW	44770 TQ	USBLS	5/15
	Pennsylvania	Y	21810 FQ	29530 MW	38330 TQ	USBLS	5/15
	Allentown-Bethlehem-Easton MSA, PA-NJ	Y	19490 FQ	28840 MW	46600 TQ	USBLS	5/15
	Chambersburg-Waynesboro MSA, PA	Y	18590 FQ	22590 MW	28640 TQ	USBLS	5/15

AE Average entry wage	**AWR** Average wage range	**H** Hourly	**LR** Low end range	**MTC** Median total compensation	**TCC** Total cash compensation
AEX Average experienced wage	**B** Biweekly	**HI** Highest wage paid	**M** Monthly	**MW** Median wage paid	**TQ** Third quartile wage
ATC Average total compensation	**D** Daily	**HR** High end range	**MCC** Median cash compensation	**MWR** Median wage range	**W** Weekly
AW Average wage paid	**FQ** First quartile wage	**LO** Lowest wage paid	**ME** Median entry wage	**S** See annotated source	**Y** Yearly

Occupation/Type/Industry	Location	Per	Low	Mid	High	Source	Date
Library Technician	Harrisburg-Carlisle MSA, PA	Y	24160 FQ	30260 MW	39390 TQ	USBLS	5/15
	Johnstown MSA, PA	Y	18250 FQ	23810 MW	30740 MW	USBLS	5/15
	Montgomery County-Bucks County-Chester County PMSA, PA	Y	23850 FQ	33560 MW	39440 TQ	USBLS	5/15
	Philadelphia PMSA, PA	Y	27370 FQ	36040 MW	49510 TQ	USBLS	5/15
	Pittsburgh MSA, PA	Y	21410 FQ	26480 MW	33150 TQ	USBLS	5/15
	Rhode Island	Y	29460 FQ	36990 MW	49510 TQ	USBLS	5/15
	Providence-Warwick MSA, RI-MA	Y	29370 FQ	37060 MW	49300 TQ	USBLS	5/15
	South Carolina	Y	22650 FQ	27930 MW	34210 TQ	USBLS	5/15
	Charleston-North Charleston MSA, SC	Y	23710 FQ	28630 MW	35260 TQ	USBLS	5/15
	Columbia MSA, SC	Y	25620 FQ	29830 MW	36200 TQ	USBLS	5/15
	Greenville-Anderson-Mauldin MSA, SC	Y	22180 FQ	28050 MW	34180 TQ	USBLS	5/15
	South Dakota	Y	20660 FQ	23200 MW	27430 TQ	USBLS	5/15
	Sioux Falls MSA, SD	Y	21560 FQ	24780 MW	39660 TQ	USBLS	5/15
	Tennessee	Y	22140 FQ	28280 MW	37070 TQ	USBLS	5/15
	Knoxville MSA, TN	Y	23570 FQ	29300 MW	38520 TQ	USBLS	5/15
	Memphis MSA, TN-MS-AR	Y	23870 FQ	28150 MW	32120 TQ	USBLS	5/15
	Nashville-Davidson–Murfreesboro–Franklin MSA, TN	Y	22820 FQ	29130 MW	37060 TQ	USBLS	5/15
	Texas	Y	21390 FQ	27150 MW	34760 TQ	USBLS	5/15
	Austin-Round Rock MSA, TX	Y	25480 FQ	32580 MW	39190 TQ	USBLS	5/15
	Dallas-Plano-Irving PMSA, TX	Y	21150 FQ	27480 MW	35320 TQ	USBLS	5/15
	Fort Worth-Arlington PMSA, TX	Y	21890 FQ	30050 MW	36940 TQ	USBLS	5/15
	Houston-The Woodlands-Sugar Land MSA, TX	Y	26430 FQ	32870 MW	38340 TQ	USBLS	5/15
	San Antonio-New Braunfels MSA, TX	Y	24300 FQ	31850 MW	38200 TQ	USBLS	5/15
	Utah	Y	22060 FQ	28790 MW	37940 TQ	USBLS	5/15
	Ogden-Clearfield MSA, UT	Y	27580 FQ	32260 MW	39860 TQ	USBLS	5/15
	Provo-Orem MSA, UT	Y	18170 FQ	22350 MW	33420 TQ	USBLS	5/15
	Salt Lake City MSA, UT	Y	25480 FQ	29990 MW	40640 TQ	USBLS	5/15
	Vermont	Y	25480 FQ	29250 MW	35250 TQ	USBLS	5/15
	Burlington-South Burlington MSA, VT	Y	25760 FQ	28780 MW	32260 TQ	USBLS	5/15
	Virginia	Y	24050 FQ	30800 MW	39330 TQ	USBLS	5/15
	Richmond MSA, VA	Y	23040 FQ	27190 MW	33310 TQ	USBLS	5/15
	Virginia Beach-Norfolk-Newport News MSA, VA-NC	Y	27060 FQ	32740 MW	37970 TQ	USBLS	5/15
	Washington	H	14.93 FQ	19.61 MW	23.22 TQ	WABLS	3/16
	Seattle-Bellevue-Everett PMSA, WA	H	19.21 FQ	21.85 MW	24.56 TQ	WABLS	3/16
	Tacoma-Lakewood PMSA, WA	H	16.85 FQ	21.77 MW	25.97 TQ	WABLS	3/16
	West Virginia	Y	20240 FQ	26160 MW	30820 TQ	USBLS	5/15
	Huntington-Ashland MSA, WV-KY-OH	Y	23000 FQ	28690 MW	34750 TQ	USBLS	5/15
	Wisconsin	Y	21250 FQ	27590 MW	35390 TQ	USBLS	5/15
	Madison MSA, WI	Y	23210 FQ	28700 MW	35830 TQ	USBLS	5/15
	Milwaukee-Waukesha-West Allis MSA, WI	Y	21290 FQ	26670 MW	33540 TQ	USBLS	5/15
	Wyoming	Y	26760 FQ	31730 MW	37240 TQ	USBLS	5/15
	Cheyenne MSA, WY	Y	24460 FQ	29440 MW	34580 TQ	USBLS	5/15
	Puerto Rico	Y	17970 FQ	22050 MW	29110 TQ	USBLS	5/15
	San Juan-Carolina-Caguas MSA, PR	Y	17930 FQ	21360 MW	28590 TQ	USBLS	5/15
	Guam	Y	26800 FQ	30280 MW	35270 TQ	USBLS	5/15
Librettist	United States	Y		69000 AW		SKU01	2016
License Examiner Specialist Department of Agriculture, State Government	Helena, MT	H			24.80 HI	MTGOV	2016
Licensed Pesticide Applicator Municipal Government	Lakewood, CA	Y			53150 HI	CACIT	6/28/16

AE	Average entry wage	AWR	Average wage range	H	Hourly	LR	Low end range	MTC	Median total compensation	TCC	Total cash compensation
AEX	Average experienced wage	B	Biweekly	HI	Highest wage paid	M	Monthly	MW	Median wage paid	TQ	Third quartile wage
ATC	Average total compensation	D	Daily	HR	High end range	MCC	Median cash compensation	MWR	Median wage range	W	Weekly
AW	Average wage paid	FQ	First quartile wage	LO	Lowest wage paid	ME	Median entry wage	S	See annotated source	Y	Yearly

Occupation/Type/Industry	Location	Per	Low	Mid	High	Source	Date
Licensed Practical and Licensed Vocational Nurse							
	Alabama	Y	29448 AE	36798 AW	40467 AEX	ALBLS	6/16
	Birmingham-Hoover MSA, AL	Y	33261 AE	39030 AW	33261 AEX	ALBLS	6/16
	Alaska	Y	48030 FQ	54960 MW	61160 TQ	USBLS	5/15
	Anchorage MSA, AK	Y	46250 FQ	54390 MW	61420 TQ	USBLS	5/15
	Arizona	Y	43700 FQ	49760 MW	56950 TQ	USBLS	5/15
	Phoenix-Mesa-Scottsdale MSA, AZ	Y	44740 FQ	51070 MW	58060 TQ	USBLS	5/15
	Tucson MSA, AZ	Y	42710 FQ	48380 MW	54810 TQ	USBLS	5/15
	Arkansas	Y	31990 FQ	36170 MW	40890 TQ	USBLS	5/15
	Little Rock-North Little Rock-Conway MSA, AR	Y	33750 FQ	38020 MW	43710 TQ	USBLS	5/15
	California	H	20.97 FQ	25.36 MW	29.34 TQ	CABLS	1/16-3/16
	Anaheim-Santa Ana-Irvine PMSA, CA	H	20.51 FQ	24.14 MW	29.17 TQ	CABLS	1/16-3/16
	Los Angeles-Long Beach-Glendale PMSA, CA	H	19.83 FQ	24.07 MW	28.82 TQ	CABLS	1/16-3/16
	Oakland-Hayward-Berkeley PMSA, CA	H	25.10 FQ	28.73 MW	33.80 TQ	CABLS	1/16-3/16
	Riverside-San Bernardino-Ontario MSA, CA	H	18.51 FQ	22.66 MW	26.84 TQ	CABLS	1/16-3/16
	Sacramento–Roseville–Arden-Arcade MSA, CA	H	25.97 FQ	28.15 MW	30.66 TQ	CABLS	1/16-3/16
	San Diego-Carlsbad MSA, CA	H	22.71 FQ	26.30 MW	29.61 TQ	CABLS	1/16-3/16
	San Francisco-Redwood City-South San Francisco PMSA, CA	H	25.86 FQ	28.96 MW	35.00 TQ	CABLS	1/16-3/16
	Colorado	Y	41300 FQ	46540 MW	53630 TQ	USBLS	5/15
	Denver-Aurora-Lakewood MSA, CO	Y	43250 FQ	48780 MW	56130 TQ	USBLS	5/15
	Connecticut	Y		56548 MW		CTBLS	1/16-3/16
	Bridgeport-Stamford-Norwalk MSA, CT	Y	50310 FQ	56370 MW	61970 TQ	USBLS	5/15
	Hartford-West Hartford-East Hartford MSA, CT	Y	50030 FQ	56250 MW	61960 TQ	USBLS	5/15
	Delaware	Y	42450 FQ	49440 MW	57180 TQ	USBLS	5/15
	Wilmington PMSA, DE-MD-NJ	Y	46680 FQ	53750 MW	59200 TQ	USBLS	5/15
	District of Columbia	Y	45480 FQ	52140 MW	59110 TQ	USBLS	5/15
	Washington-Arlington-Alexandria PMSA, DC-VA-MD-WV	Y	42790 FQ	48390 MW	56050 TQ	USBLS	5/15
	Florida	H	16.68 AE	20.64 MW	22.92 AEX	FLBLS	7/16-9/16
	Fort Lauderdale-Pompano Beach-Deerfield Beach PMSA, FL	H	17.23 AE	21.45 MW	23.75 AEX	FLBLS	7/16-9/16
	Miami-Miami Beach-Kendall PMSA, FL	H	17.21 AE	21.51 MW	23.80 AEX	FLBLS	7/16-9/16
	Orlando-Kissimmee-Sanford MSA, FL	H	16.12 AE	19.27 MW	21.66 AEX	FLBLS	7/16-9/16
	Tampa-St. Petersburg-Clearwater MSA, FL	H	17.06 AE	21.50 MW	23.97 AEX	FLBLS	7/16-9/16
	Georgia	Y	33210 FQ	38210 MW	44780 TQ	USBLS	5/15
	Atlanta-Sandy Springs-Roswell MSA, GA	Y	34310 FQ	40970 MW	46960 TQ	USBLS	5/15
	Augusta-Richmond County MSA, GA-SC	Y	34140 FQ	39150 MW	45350 TQ	USBLS	5/15
	Hawaii	Y	41720 FQ	46390 MW	52340 TQ	USBLS	5/15
	Urban Honolulu MSA, HI	Y	42910 FQ	47800 MW	54900 TQ	USBLS	5/15
	Idaho	Y	34710 FQ	39500 MW	45320 TQ	USBLS	5/15
	Boise City MSA, ID	Y	35170 FQ	40030 MW	45630 TQ	USBLS	5/15
	Illinois	Y	39370 FQ	45870 MW	54290 TQ	USBLS	5/15
	Chicago-Naperville-Arlington Heights PMSA, IL	Y	42160 FQ	49280 MW	58320 TQ	USBLS	5/15
	Lake County-Kenosha County PMSA, IL-WI	Y	44180 FQ	50960 MW	57190 TQ	USBLS	5/15
	Indiana	Y	35540 FQ	40660 MW	46160 TQ	USBLS	5/15
	Gary PMSA, IN	Y	35820 FQ	42280 MW	47500 TQ	USBLS	5/15
	Indianapolis-Carmel-Anderson MSA, IN	Y	36440 FQ	41820 MW	46830 TQ	USBLS	5/15
	Iowa	Y	34560 FQ	39140 MW	45170 TQ	USBLS	5/15

AE	Average entry wage	AWR	Average wage range	H	Hourly	LR	Low end range	MTC	Median total compensation	TCC	Total cash compensation
AEX	Average experienced wage	B	Biweekly	HI	Highest wage paid	M	Monthly	MW	Median wage paid	TQ	Third quartile wage
ATC	Average total compensation	D	Daily	HR	High end range	MCC	Median cash compensation	MWR	Median wage range	W	Weekly
AW	Average wage paid	FQ	First quartile wage	LO	Lowest wage paid	ME	Median entry wage	S	See annotated source	Y	Yearly

Occupation/Type/Industry	Location	Per	Low	Mid	High	Source	Date
Licensed Practical and Licensed Vocational Nurse							
	Des Moines-West Des Moines MSA, IA	Y	36960 FQ	42570 MW	47010 TQ	USBLS	5/15
	Kansas	Y	34990 FQ	39370 MW	45410 TQ	USBLS	5/15
	Wichita MSA, KS	Y	36170 FQ	40950 MW	45930 TQ	USBLS	5/15
	Kentucky	Y	33850 FQ	38720 MW	45050 TQ	USBLS	5/15
	Louisville-Jefferson County MSA, KY-IN	Y	35680 FQ	40630 MW	46210 TQ	USBLS	5/15
	Louisiana	Y	32860 FQ	37340 MW	43630 TQ	USBLS	5/15
	Baton Rouge MSA, LA	Y	34480 FQ	38400 MW	44420 TQ	USBLS	5/15
	New Orleans-Metairie MSA, LA	Y	34840 FQ	40910 MW	46150 TQ	USBLS	5/15
	Maine	Y	37550 FQ	42720 MW	47230 TQ	USBLS	5/15
	Portland-South Portland MSA, ME	Y	40480 FQ	44820 MW	49060 TQ	USBLS	5/15
	Maryland	Y	42010 AE	51147 MW	55715 AEX	MDBLS	4/16
	Baltimore-Columbia-Towson MSA, MD	Y	44560 FQ	50950 MW	58890 TQ	USBLS	5/15
	Salisbury MSA, MD-DE	Y	37540 FQ	44050 MW	50630 TQ	USBLS	5/15
	Massachusetts	Y	47270 FQ	54330 MW	60520 TQ	USBLS	5/15
	Boston-Cambridge-Newton NECTA, MA	Y	49290 FQ	55320 MW	60940 TQ	USBLS	5/15
	Worcester MSA, MA-CT	Y	47480 FQ	54120 MW	60540 TQ	USBLS	5/15
	Michigan	Y	40280 FQ	45650 MW	50950 TQ	USBLS	5/15
	Detroit-Dearborn-Livonia PMSA, MI	Y	43400 FQ	49040 MW	55500 TQ	USBLS	5/15
	Grand Rapids-Wyoming MSA, MI	Y	40490 FQ	44570 MW	48550 TQ	USBLS	5/15
	Minnesota	Y	37409 FQ	43014 MW	48024 TQ	MNBLS	1/16-3/16
	Minneapolis-St. Paul-Bloomington MSA, MN-WI	Y	41118 FQ	45040 MW	48961 TQ	MNBLS	1/16-3/16
	Mississippi	Y	31950 FQ	36230 MW	41460 TQ	USBLS	5/15
	Jackson MSA, MS	Y	33480 FQ	37900 MW	43970 TQ	USBLS	5/15
	Missouri	Y	33190 FQ	37750 MW	43930 TQ	USBLS	5/15
	Kansas City MSA, MO-KS	Y	35420 FQ	40810 MW	46370 TQ	USBLS	5/15
	St. Louis MSA, MO-IL	Y	36940 FQ	42380 MW	47360 TQ	USBLS	5/15
	Montana	Y	34270 FQ	39420 MW	45380 TQ	USBLS	5/15
	Billings MSA, MT	Y	34060 FQ	40250 MW	45380 TQ	USBLS	5/15
	Nebraska	Y	34555 FQ	39040 MW	45125 TQ	NEBLS	7/16-9/16
	Omaha-Council Bluffs MSA, NE-IA	Y	35980 FQ	41050 MW	46775 TQ	NEBLS	7/16-9/16
	Nevada	Y	45870 FQ	52210 MW	58980 TQ	USBLS	5/15
	Las Vegas-Henderson-Paradise MSA, NV	Y	46020 FQ	52390 MW	59560 TQ	USBLS	5/15
	New Hampshire	H	19.22 AE	23.19 MW	25.52 AEX	NHBLS	6/16
	Manchester NECTA, NH	H	21.40 AE	24.55 MW	27.34 AEX	NHBLS	6/16
	Nashua NECTA, NH-MA	Y	42750 FQ	49450 MW	56120 TQ	USBLS	5/15
	New Jersey	Y	47240 FQ	54290 MW	59730 TQ	USBLS	5/15
	Camden PMSA, NJ	Y	44710 FQ	51670 MW	58000 TQ	USBLS	5/15
	Newark PMSA, NJ-PA	Y	49720 FQ	55490 MW	60550 TQ	USBLS	5/15
	Trenton MSA, NJ	Y	47800 FQ	54630 MW	60030 TQ	USBLS	5/15
	New Mexico	Y	40200 FQ	46620 MW	54870 TQ	USBLS	5/15
	Albuquerque MSA, NM	Y	42420 FQ	47720 MW	55530 TQ	USBLS	5/15
	New York	Y	35500 AE	46720 MW	53010 AEX	NYBLS	1/16-3/16
	Buffalo-Cheektowaga-Niagara Falls MSA, NY	Y	35100 FQ	39800 MW	46680 TQ	USBLS	5/15
	Nassau County-Suffolk County PMSA, NY	Y	46480 FQ	53350 MW	59190 TQ	USBLS	5/15
	New York-Jersey City-White Plains PMSA, NY-NJ	Y	46030 FQ	53690 MW	59830 TQ	USBLS	5/15
	Rochester MSA, NY	Y	35050 FQ	39780 MW	45570 TQ	USBLS	5/15
	North Carolina	Y	36680 FQ	42160 MW	47220 TQ	USBLS	5/15
	Charlotte-Concord-Gastonia MSA, NC-SC	Y	35810 FQ	41900 MW	47630 TQ	USBLS	5/15
	Raleigh MSA, NC	Y	39260 FQ	43490 MW	47620 TQ	USBLS	5/15
	North Dakota	Y	36020 FQ	41520 MW	46590 TQ	USBLS	5/15
	Fargo MSA, ND-MN	Y	34220 FQ	38960 MW	45020 TQ	USBLS	5/15
	Ohio	Y	35430 FQ	40750 MW	46690 TQ	USBLS	5/15
	Cincinnati MSA, OH-KY-IN	Y	37910 FQ	43410 MW	48210 TQ	USBLS	5/15
	Cleveland-Elyria MSA, OH	Y	39740 FQ	44080 MW	48320 TQ	USBLS	5/15
	Columbus MSA, OH	Y	36110 FQ	41350 MW	46760 TQ	USBLS	5/15
	Oklahoma	Y	33410 FQ	38000 MW	44400 TQ	USBLS	5/15

AE	Average entry wage	AWR	Average wage range	H	Hourly
AEX	Average experienced wage	B	Biweekly	HI	Highest wage paid
ATC	Average total compensation	D	Daily	HR	High end range
AW	Average wage paid	FQ	First quartile wage	LO	Lowest wage paid

LR	Low end range	MTC	Median total compensation
M	Monthly	MW	Median wage paid
MCC	Median cash compensation	MWR	Median wage range
ME	Median entry wage	S	See annotated source

TCC	Total cash compensation
TQ	Third quartile wage
W	Weekly
Y	Yearly

Occupation/Type/Industry	Location	Per	Low	Mid	High	Source	Date
Licensed Practical and Licensed Vocational Nurse	Oklahoma City MSA, OK	Y	34080 FQ	39200 MW	45870 TQ	USBLS	5/15
	Tulsa MSA, OK	Y	34420 FQ	39100 MW	45310 TQ	USBLS	5/15
	Oregon	H	21.25 FQ	23.72 MW	27.01 TQ	ORBLS	2016
	Portland-Vancouver-Hillsboro MSA, OR-WA	Y	45320 FQ	50990 MW	57090 TQ	USBLS	5/15
	Pennsylvania	Y	37330 FQ	44020 MW	50430 TQ	USBLS	5/15
	Allentown-Bethlehem-Easton MSA, PA-NJ	Y	41300 FQ	45690 MW	50390 TQ	USBLS	5/15
	Harrisburg-Carlisle MSA, PA	Y	40290 FQ	45450 MW	51500 TQ	USBLS	5/15
	Montgomery County-Bucks County-Chester County PMSA, PA	Y	43560 FQ	51550 MW	58840 TQ	USBLS	5/15
	Philadelphia PMSA, PA	Y	42620 FQ	50700 MW	59110 TQ	USBLS	5/15
	Pittsburgh MSA, PA	Y	37190 FQ	42870 MW	47550 TQ	USBLS	5/15
	Rhode Island	Y	50000 FQ	55730 MW	61270 TQ	USBLS	5/15
	Providence-Warwick MSA, RI-MA	Y	46610 FQ	53780 MW	59970 TQ	USBLS	5/15
	South Carolina	Y	33970 FQ	39250 MW	45470 TQ	USBLS	5/15
	Charleston-North Charleston MSA, SC	Y	37060 FQ	42320 MW	46780 TQ	USBLS	5/15
	Columbia MSA, SC	Y	35640 FQ	41850 MW	46740 TQ	USBLS	5/15
	Greenville-Anderson-Mauldin MSA, SC	Y	31870 FQ	36580 MW	42440 TQ	USBLS	5/15
	South Dakota	Y	32040 FQ	36080 MW	40400 TQ	USBLS	5/15
	Sioux Falls MSA, SD	Y	31790 FQ	35750 MW	40110 TQ	USBLS	5/15
	Tennessee	Y	32540 FQ	36670 MW	42170 TQ	USBLS	5/15
	Knoxville MSA, TN	Y	32960 FQ	36580 MW	41050 TQ	USBLS	5/15
	Memphis MSA, TN-MS-AR	Y	36350 FQ	42050 MW	46920 TQ	USBLS	5/15
	Nashville-Davidson–Murfreesboro–Franklin MSA, TN	Y	34350 FQ	38710 MW	45340 TQ	USBLS	5/15
	Texas	Y	38170 FQ	44200 MW	50030 TQ	USBLS	5/15
	Austin-Round Rock MSA, TX	Y	40770 FQ	45430 MW	50610 TQ	USBLS	5/15
	Dallas-Plano-Irving PMSA, TX	Y	39070 FQ	45700 MW	54680 TQ	USBLS	5/15
	Fort Worth-Arlington PMSA, TX	Y	42040 FQ	46880 MW	53580 TQ	USBLS	5/15
	Houston-The Woodlands-Sugar Land MSA, TX	Y	41620 FQ	47220 MW	57480 TQ	USBLS	5/15
	San Antonio-New Braunfels MSA, TX	Y	38000 FQ	43330 MW	48300 TQ	USBLS	5/15
	Utah	Y	36590 FQ	42820 MW	48370 TQ	USBLS	5/15
	Ogden-Clearfield MSA, UT	Y	35770 FQ	41640 MW	48660 TQ	USBLS	5/15
	Provo-Orem MSA, UT	Y	34080 FQ	40310 MW	45830 TQ	USBLS	5/15
	Salt Lake City MSA, UT	Y	41840 FQ	46370 MW	51770 TQ	USBLS	5/15
	Vermont	Y	40290 FQ	45500 MW	51490 TQ	USBLS	5/15
	Burlington-South Burlington MSA, VT	Y	42540 FQ	48410 MW	55990 TQ	USBLS	5/15
	Virginia	Y	34720 FQ	40240 MW	47060 TQ	USBLS	5/15
	Richmond MSA, VA	Y	34500 FQ	38750 MW	45770 TQ	USBLS	5/15
	Virginia Beach-Norfolk-Newport News MSA, VA-NC	Y	34930 FQ	39250 MW	45750 TQ	USBLS	5/15
	Washington	H	21.01 FQ	23.82 MW	27.73 TQ	WABLS	3/16
	Seattle-Bellevue-Everett PMSA, WA	H	22.29 FQ	25.97 MW	29.56 TQ	WABLS	3/16
	Tacoma-Lakewood PMSA, WA	H	21.50 FQ	23.99 MW	27.27 TQ	WABLS	3/16
	West Virginia	Y	29980 FQ	34940 MW	39530 TQ	USBLS	5/15
	Huntington-Ashland MSA, WV-KY-OH	Y	29820 FQ	34490 MW	38900 TQ	USBLS	5/15
	Wisconsin	Y	37520 FQ	43400 MW	48150 TQ	USBLS	5/15
	Madison MSA, WI	Y	40600 FQ	45720 MW	51230 TQ	USBLS	5/15
	Milwaukee-Waukesha-West Allis MSA, WI	Y	41110 FQ	45840 MW	51030 TQ	USBLS	5/15
	Wyoming	Y	39700 FQ	44380 MW	48860 TQ	USBLS	5/15
	Cheyenne MSA, WY	Y	37850 FQ	42640 MW	46780 TQ	USBLS	5/15
	Puerto Rico	Y	18080 FQ	20910 MW	24590 TQ	USBLS	5/15
	Guayama MSA, PR	Y	18130 FQ	21100 MW	24200 TQ	USBLS	5/15
	San Juan-Carolina-Caguas MSA, PR	Y	18460 FQ	21520 MW	25430 TQ	USBLS	5/15
	Virgin Islands	Y	34930 FQ	41950 MW	50360 TQ	USBLS	5/15
	Guam	Y	29570 FQ	35810 MW	43050 TQ	USBLS	5/15

AE	Average entry wage	AWR	Average wage range	H	Hourly	LR	Low end range	MTC	Median total compensation	TCC	Total cash compensation
AEX	Average experienced wage	B	Biweekly	HI	Highest wage paid	M	Monthly	MW	Median wage paid	TQ	Third quartile wage
ATC	Average total compensation	D	Daily	HR	High end range	MCC	Median cash compensation	MWR	Median wage range	W	Weekly
AW	Average wage paid	FQ	First quartile wage	LO	Lowest wage paid	ME	Median entry wage	S	See annotated source	Y	Yearly

Occupation/Type/Industry	Location	Per	Low	Mid	High	Source	Date
Lifeguard, Ski Patrol, and Other Recreational Protective Service Worker							
	Alabama	Y	17462 AE	18770 AW	19418 AEX	ALBLS	6/16
	Birmingham-Hoover MSA, AL	Y	17483 AE	18275 AW	18677 AEX	ALBLS	6/16
	Alaska	Y	23860 FQ	33030 MW	38200 TQ	USBLS	5/15
	Anchorage MSA, AK	Y	20870 FQ	30640 MW	36160 TQ	USBLS	5/15
	Arizona	Y	18580 FQ	20560 MW	23080 TQ	USBLS	5/15
	Phoenix-Mesa-Scottsdale MSA, AZ	Y	18540 FQ	20510 MW	23130 TQ	USBLS	5/15
	Tucson MSA, AZ	Y	20400 FQ	21970 MW	23540 TQ	USBLS	5/15
	Arkansas	Y	16700 FQ	17800 MW	18900 TQ	USBLS	5/15
	Little Rock-North Little Rock-Conway MSA, AR	Y	16660 FQ	17720 MW	18780 TQ	USBLS	5/15
	California	H	10.60 FQ	13.50 MW	17.51 TQ	CABLS	1/16-3/16
	Anaheim-Santa Ana-Irvine PMSA, CA	H	10.81 FQ	12.58 MW	17.52 TQ	CABLS	1/16-3/16
	Los Angeles-Long Beach-Glendale PMSA, CA	H	11.73 FQ	16.47 MW	22.54 TQ	CABLS	1/16-3/16
	Oakland-Hayward-Berkeley PMSA, CA	H	9.96 FQ	11.03 MW	12.15 TQ	CABLS	1/16-3/16
	Riverside-San Bernardino-Ontario MSA, CA	H	9.55 FQ	10.86 MW	15.60 TQ	CABLS	1/16-3/16
	Sacramento–Roseville–Arden-Arcade MSA, CA	H	9.40 FQ	10.29 MW	12.70 TQ	CABLS	1/16-3/16
	San Diego-Carlsbad MSA, CA	H	11.89 FQ	15.39 MW	17.85 TQ	CABLS	1/16-3/16
	San Francisco-Redwood City-South San Francisco PMSA, CA	H	11.47 FQ	13.89 MW	16.46 TQ	CABLS	1/16-3/16
	Colorado	Y	18240 FQ	19400 MW	22720 TQ	USBLS	5/15
	Denver-Aurora-Lakewood MSA, CO	Y	18100 FQ	19080 MW	21610 TQ	USBLS	5/15
	Connecticut	Y		22557 MW		CTBLS	1/16-3/16
	Bridgeport-Stamford-Norwalk MSA, CT	Y	20260 FQ	22670 MW	25290 TQ	USBLS	5/15
	Hartford-West Hartford-East Hartford MSA, CT	Y	19600 FQ	21690 MW	24020 TQ	USBLS	5/15
	Delaware	Y	18220 FQ	21330 MW	27110 TQ	USBLS	5/15
	District of Columbia	Y	22880 FQ	31720 MW	34980 TQ	USBLS	5/15
	Washington-Arlington-Alexandria PMSA, DC-VA-MD-WV	Y	18450 FQ	21940 MW	26940 TQ	USBLS	5/15
	Florida	H	9.04 AE	10.71 MW	12.72 AEX	FLBLS	7/16-9/16
	Fort Lauderdale-Pompano Beach-Deerfield Beach PMSA, FL	H	10.72 AE	13.43 MW	15.90 AEX	FLBLS	7/16-9/16
	Miami-Miami Beach-Kendall PMSA, FL	H	9.64 AE	11.63 MW	13.78 AEX	FLBLS	7/16-9/16
	Orlando-Kissimmee-Sanford MSA, FL	H	9.26 AE	10.59 MW	11.45 AEX	FLBLS	7/16-9/16
	Tampa-St. Petersburg-Clearwater MSA, FL	H	9.00 AE	9.79 MW	10.86 AEX	FLBLS	7/16-9/16
	Georgia	Y	16920 FQ	18420 MW	20520 TQ	USBLS	5/15
	Atlanta-Sandy Springs-Roswell MSA, GA	Y	16940 FQ	18460 MW	20680 TQ	USBLS	5/15
	Augusta-Richmond County MSA, GA-SC	Y	16770 FQ	18120 MW	19520 TQ	USBLS	5/15
	Hawaii	Y	26010 FQ	36540 MW	44560 TQ	USBLS	5/15
	Urban Honolulu MSA, HI	Y	19830 FQ	34920 MW	43310 TQ	USBLS	5/15
	Idaho	Y	16720 FQ	17960 MW	19210 TQ	USBLS	5/15
	Boise City MSA, ID	Y	16730 FQ	17870 MW	19010 TQ	USBLS	5/15
	Illinois	Y	18390 FQ	19240 MW	22430 TQ	USBLS	5/15
	Chicago-Naperville-Arlington Heights PMSA, IL	Y	18550 FQ	19610 MW	24040 TQ	USBLS	5/15
	Lake County-Kenosha County PMSA, IL-WI	Y	18210 FQ	19020 MW	19920 TQ	USBLS	5/15
	Indiana	Y	17010 FQ	18620 MW	21130 TQ	USBLS	5/15
	Gary PMSA, IN	Y	16560 FQ	17750 MW	18940 TQ	USBLS	5/15
	Indianapolis-Carmel-Anderson MSA, IN	Y	18050 FQ	20450 MW	22750 TQ	USBLS	5/15
	Iowa	Y	16680 FQ	17930 MW	19180 TQ	USBLS	5/15

AE	Average entry wage	AWR	Average wage range	H	Hourly	LR	Low end range	MTC	Median total compensation	TCC	Total cash compensation
AEX	Average experienced wage	B	Biweekly	HI	Highest wage paid	M	Monthly	MW	Median wage paid	TQ	Third quartile wage
ATC	Average total compensation	D	Daily	HR	High end range	MCC	Median cash compensation	MWR	Median wage range	W	Weekly
AW	Average wage paid	FQ	First quartile wage	LO	Lowest wage paid	ME	Median entry wage	S	See annotated source	Y	Yearly

Occupation/Type/Industry	Location	Per	Low	Mid	High	Source	Date
Lifeguard, Ski Patrol, and Other Recreational Protective Service Worker	Des Moines-West Des Moines MSA, IA	Y	16690 FQ	18030 MW	19390 TQ	USBLS	5/15
	Kansas	Y	16600 FQ	17800 MW	19000 TQ	USBLS	5/15
	Wichita MSA, KS	Y	16390 FQ	17560 MW	18740 TQ	USBLS	5/15
	Kentucky	Y	16610 FQ	17830 MW	19050 TQ	USBLS	5/15
	Louisville-Jefferson County MSA, KY-IN	Y	16600 FQ	17900 MW	19200 TQ	USBLS	5/15
	Louisiana	Y	16940 FQ	18440 MW	20990 TQ	USBLS	5/15
	Baton Rouge MSA, LA	Y	17120 FQ	18780 MW	24680 TQ	USBLS	5/15
	New Orleans-Metairie MSA, LA	Y	16880 FQ	18240 MW	19640 TQ	USBLS	5/15
	Maine	Y	17460 FQ	18980 MW	21900 TQ	USBLS	5/15
	Portland-South Portland MSA, ME	Y	17280 FQ	18600 MW	20680 TQ	USBLS	5/15
	Maryland	Y	18071 AE	19645 MW	20432 AEX	MDBLS	4/16
	Baltimore-Columbia-Towson MSA, MD	Y	17770 FQ	18910 MW	20810 TQ	USBLS	5/15
	Salisbury MSA, MD-DE	Y	18590 FQ	25550 MW	28710 TQ	USBLS	5/15
	Massachusetts	Y	19400 FQ	21420 MW	24510 TQ	USBLS	5/15
	Boston-Cambridge-Newton NECTA, MA	Y	19570 FQ	22000 MW	25130 TQ	USBLS	5/15
	Worcester MSA, MA-CT	Y	19180 FQ	20830 MW	23080 TQ	USBLS	5/15
	Michigan	Y	18080 FQ	19110 MW	21800 TQ	USBLS	5/15
	Detroit-Dearborn-Livonia PMSA, MI	Y	18150 FQ	19250 MW	22240 TQ	USBLS	5/15
	Grand Rapids-Wyoming MSA, MI	Y	18080 FQ	19090 MW	21780 TQ	USBLS	5/15
	Minnesota	Y	18582 FQ	20591 MW	23833 TQ	MNBLS	1/16-3/16
	Minneapolis-St. Paul-Bloomington MSA, MN-WI	Y	18743 FQ	21137 MW	24308 TQ	MNBLS	1/16-3/16
	Mississippi	Y	16680 FQ	18010 MW	19400 TQ	USBLS	5/15
	Missouri	Y	16960 FQ	18000 MW	19040 TQ	USBLS	5/15
	Kansas City MSA, MO-KS	Y	16850 FQ	17980 MW	19110 TQ	USBLS	5/15
	St. Louis MSA, MO-IL	Y	17190 FQ	18240 MW	19180 TQ	USBLS	5/15
	Montana	Y	17640 FQ	18510 MW	19430 TQ	USBLS	5/15
	Nebraska	Y	17500 FQ	18365 MW	19225 TQ	NEBLS	7/16-9/16
	Omaha-Council Bluffs MSA, NE-IA	Y	17450 FQ	18300 MW	19150 TQ	NEBLS	7/16-9/16
	Nevada	Y	19690 FQ	21880 MW	24010 TQ	USBLS	5/15
	Las Vegas-Henderson-Paradise MSA, NV	Y	20280 FQ	22150 MW	24020 TQ	USBLS	5/15
	New Hampshire	H	8.46 AE	11.08 MW	12.31 AEX	NHBLS	6/16
	Manchester NECTA, NH	H	8.33 AE	9.77 MW	11.59 AEX	NHBLS	6/16
	New Jersey	Y	18550 FQ	19760 MW	23610 TQ	USBLS	5/15
	Camden PMSA, NJ	Y	18260 FQ	19040 MW	21420 TQ	USBLS	5/15
	Newark PMSA, NJ-PA	Y	18780 FQ	20670 MW	24390 TQ	USBLS	5/15
	Trenton MSA, NJ	Y	18810 FQ	20910 MW	23310 TQ	USBLS	5/15
	New Mexico	Y	17120 FQ	18520 MW	21370 TQ	USBLS	5/15
	Albuquerque MSA, NM	Y	16830 FQ	17980 MW	19130 TQ	USBLS	5/15
	New York	Y	20000 AE	23470 MW	27830 AEX	NYBLS	1/16-3/16
	Buffalo-Cheektowaga-Niagara Falls MSA, NY	Y	19010 FQ	19820 MW	22580 TQ	USBLS	5/15
	Nassau County-Suffolk County PMSA, NY	Y	20430 FQ	23950 MW	28430 TQ	USBLS	5/15
	New York-Jersey City-White Plains PMSA, NY-NJ	Y	19520 FQ	23080 MW	28760 TQ	USBLS	5/15
	Rochester MSA, NY	Y	18960 FQ	19930 MW	23350 TQ	USBLS	5/15
	North Carolina	Y	16780 FQ	18180 MW	19660 TQ	USBLS	5/15
	Charlotte-Concord-Gastonia MSA, NC-SC	Y	16790 FQ	18140 MW	19510 TQ	USBLS	5/15
	Raleigh MSA, NC	Y	16790 FQ	18220 MW	19820 TQ	USBLS	5/15
	North Dakota	Y	17150 FQ	18790 MW	23200 TQ	USBLS	5/15
	Fargo MSA, ND-MN	Y	16980 FQ	18320 MW	19670 TQ	USBLS	5/15
	Ohio	Y	17690 FQ	18510 MW	19350 TQ	USBLS	5/15
	Cincinnati MSA, OH-KY-IN	Y	17620 FQ	18460 MW	19330 TQ	USBLS	5/15
	Cleveland-Elyria MSA, OH	Y	17680 FQ	18490 MW	19340 TQ	USBLS	5/15
	Columbus MSA, OH	Y	17780 FQ	18680 MW	19610 TQ	USBLS	5/15
	Oklahoma	Y	16710 FQ	18060 MW	19460 TQ	USBLS	5/15
	Oklahoma City MSA, OK	Y	16750 FQ	18180 MW	20080 TQ	USBLS	5/15

AE	Average entry wage	AWR	Average wage range	H	Hourly
AEX	Average experienced wage	B	Biweekly	HI	Highest wage paid
ATC	Average total compensation	D	Daily	HR	High end range
AW	Average wage paid	FQ	First quartile wage	LO	Lowest wage paid

LR	Low end range	MTC	Median total compensation
M	Monthly	MW	Median wage paid
MCC	Median cash compensation	MWR	Median wage range
ME	Median entry wage	S	See annotated source

TCC	Total cash compensation
TQ	Third quartile wage
W	Weekly
Y	Yearly

Occupation/Type/Industry	Location	Per	Low	Mid	High	Source	Date
Lifeguard, Ski Patrol, and Other Recreational Protective Service Worker							
	Tulsa MSA, OK	Y	16680 FQ	18000 MW	19350 TQ	USBLS	5/15
	Oregon	H	9.71 FQ	10.57 MW	11.50 TQ	ORBLS	2016
	Portland-Vancouver-Hillsboro MSA, OR-WA	Y	20440 FQ	22080 MW	23720 TQ	USBLS	5/15
	Pennsylvania	Y	16870 FQ	18320 MW	20170 TQ	USBLS	5/15
	Allentown-Bethlehem-Easton MSA, PA-NJ	Y	17330 FQ	19150 MW	24100 TQ	USBLS	5/15
	Harrisburg-Carlisle MSA, PA	Y	17280 FQ	19150 MW	22920 TQ	USBLS	5/15
	Montgomery County-Bucks County-Chester County PMSA, PA	Y	16930 FQ	18480 MW	21560 TQ	USBLS	5/15
	Philadelphia PMSA, PA	Y	16690 FQ	18070 MW	19530 TQ	USBLS	5/15
	Pittsburgh MSA, PA	Y	16800 FQ	18160 MW	19590 TQ	USBLS	5/15
	Rhode Island	Y	19280 FQ	22010 MW	28450 TQ	USBLS	5/15
	Providence-Warwick MSA, RI-MA	Y	19350 FQ	21750 MW	25660 TQ	USBLS	5/15
	South Carolina	Y	17110 FQ	18710 MW	21990 TQ	USBLS	5/15
	Charleston-North Charleston MSA, SC	Y	18110 FQ	21300 MW	26070 TQ	USBLS	5/15
	South Dakota	Y	18450 FQ	19220 MW	21540 TQ	USBLS	5/15
	Sioux Falls MSA, SD	Y	18410 FQ	19140 MW	21420 TQ	USBLS	5/15
	Tennessee	Y	16570 FQ	17760 MW	18960 TQ	USBLS	5/15
	Knoxville MSA, TN	Y	16460 FQ	17650 MW	18840 TQ	USBLS	5/15
	Memphis MSA, TN-MS-AR	Y	16750 FQ	17970 MW	19180 TQ	USBLS	5/15
	Nashville-Davidson–Murfreesboro–Franklin MSA, TN	Y	16570 FQ	17810 MW	19050 TQ	USBLS	5/15
	Texas	Y	16770 FQ	18230 MW	20180 TQ	USBLS	5/15
	Austin-Round Rock MSA, TX	Y	17290 FQ	19230 MW	23190 TQ	USBLS	5/15
	Dallas-Plano-Irving PMSA, TX	Y	16700 FQ	18180 MW	20110 TQ	USBLS	5/15
	Fort Worth-Arlington PMSA, TX	Y	16850 FQ	18430 MW	20820 TQ	USBLS	5/15
	Houston-The Woodlands-Sugar Land MSA, TX	Y	16650 FQ	17950 MW	19250 TQ	USBLS	5/15
	San Antonio-New Braunfels MSA, TX	Y	16930 FQ	18530 MW	21540 TQ	USBLS	5/15
	Utah	Y	16930 FQ	18560 MW	21580 TQ	USBLS	5/15
	Ogden-Clearfield MSA, UT	Y	17350 FQ	19410 MW	22720 TQ	USBLS	5/15
	Provo-Orem MSA, UT	Y	16930 FQ	18750 MW	22080 TQ	USBLS	5/15
	Vermont	Y	19350 FQ	21180 MW	24020 TQ	USBLS	5/15
	Burlington-South Burlington MSA, VT	Y	19360 FQ	19930 MW	22520 TQ	USBLS	5/15
	Virginia	Y	18030 FQ	20930 MW	24890 TQ	USBLS	5/15
	Richmond MSA, VA	Y	17430 FQ	19440 MW	23470 TQ	USBLS	5/15
	Virginia Beach-Norfolk-Newport News MSA, VA-NC	Y	18220 FQ	21020 MW	24060 TQ	USBLS	5/15
	Washington	H	10.37 FQ	11.31 MW	12.61 TQ	WABLS	3/16
	Seattle-Bellevue-Everett PMSA, WA	H	10.40 FQ	11.48 MW	13.91 TQ	WABLS	3/16
	Tacoma-Lakewood PMSA, WA	H	10.54 FQ	11.38 MW	12.69 TQ	WABLS	3/16
	West Virginia	Y	17450 FQ	18260 MW	19080 TQ	USBLS	5/15
	Huntington-Ashland MSA, WV-KY-OH	Y	17450 FQ	18250 MW	19060 TQ	USBLS	5/15
	Wisconsin	Y	16860 FQ	18260 MW	19790 TQ	USBLS	5/15
	Madison MSA, WI	Y	16790 FQ	18320 MW	21510 TQ	USBLS	5/15
	Milwaukee-Waukesha-West Allis MSA, WI	Y	17300 FQ	19060 MW	21850 TQ	USBLS	5/15
	Wyoming	Y	18480 FQ	21290 MW	24870 TQ	USBLS	5/15
	Puerto Rico	Y	16770 FQ	18200 MW	19950 TQ	USBLS	5/15
	San Juan-Carolina-Caguas MSA, PR	Y	16970 FQ	18640 MW	23180 TQ	USBLS	5/15
	Virgin Islands	Y	21220 FQ	24900 MW	28280 TQ	USBLS	5/15
	Guam	Y	18210 FQ	19250 MW	22320 TQ	USBLS	5/15
Light Truck or Delivery Services Driver							
	Alabama	Y	19079 AE	30567 AW	36316 AEX	ALBLS	6/16
	Birmingham-Hoover MSA, AL	Y	19367 AE	31297 AW	37263 AEX	ALBLS	6/16
	Alaska	Y	31100 FQ	38670 MW	53320 TQ	USBLS	5/15
	Anchorage MSA, AK	Y	29720 FQ	37090 MW	48830 TQ	USBLS	5/15

AE	Average entry wage	AWR	Average wage range	H	Hourly
AEX	Average experienced wage	B	Biweekly	HI	Highest wage paid
ATC	Average total compensation	D	Daily	HR	High end range
AW	Average wage paid	FQ	First quartile wage	LO	Lowest wage paid

LR	Low end range	MTC	Median total compensation
M	Monthly	MW	Median wage paid
MCC	Median cash compensation	MWR	Median wage range
ME	Median entry wage	S	See annotated source

TCC	Total cash compensation
TQ	Third quartile wage
W	Weekly
Y	Yearly

Light Truck or Delivery Services Driver

Occupation/Type/Industry	Location	Per	Low	Mid	High	Source	Date
Light Truck or Delivery Services Driver	Arizona	Y	22730 FQ	29400 MW	39710 TQ	USBLS	5/15
	Phoenix-Mesa-Scottsdale MSA, AZ	Y	23110 FQ	29170 MW	39340 TQ	USBLS	5/15
	Tucson MSA, AZ	Y	19860 FQ	28460 MW	39560 TQ	USBLS	5/15
	Arkansas	Y	19060 FQ	25000 MW	33670 TQ	USBLS	5/15
	Little Rock-North Little Rock-Conway MSA, AR	Y	19340 FQ	24650 MW	31110 TQ	USBLS	5/15
	California	H	11.54 FQ	15.54 MW	23.13 TQ	CABLS	1/16-3/16
	Anaheim-Santa Ana-Irvine PMSA, CA	H	12.20 FQ	16.07 MW	23.24 TQ	CABLS	1/16-3/16
	Los Angeles-Long Beach-Glendale PMSA, CA	H	10.99 FQ	14.48 MW	21.62 TQ	CABLS	1/16-3/16
	Oakland-Hayward-Berkeley PMSA, CA	H	12.89 FQ	17.16 MW	23.83 TQ	CABLS	1/16-3/16
	Riverside-San Bernardino-Ontario MSA, CA	H	12.39 FQ	17.29 MW	26.61 TQ	CABLS	1/16-3/16
	Sacramento–Roseville–Arden-Arcade MSA, CA	H	11.50 FQ	16.22 MW	24.07 TQ	CABLS	1/16-3/16
	San Diego-Carlsbad MSA, CA	H	10.75 FQ	14.77 MW	21.98 TQ	CABLS	1/16-3/16
	San Francisco-Redwood City-South San Francisco PMSA, CA	H	13.10 FQ	17.19 MW	26.57 TQ	CABLS	1/16-3/16
	Colorado	Y	24480 FQ	32110 MW	40740 TQ	USBLS	5/15
	Denver-Aurora-Lakewood MSA, CO	Y	26170 FQ	33230 MW	42890 TQ	USBLS	5/15
	Connecticut	Y		33547 MW		CTBLS	1/16-3/16
	Bridgeport-Stamford-Norwalk MSA, CT	Y	23000 FQ	33360 MW	43550 TQ	USBLS	5/15
	Hartford-West Hartford-East Hartford MSA, CT	Y	25220 FQ	32510 MW	43360 TQ	USBLS	5/15
	Delaware	Y	22340 FQ	29390 MW	40360 TQ	USBLS	5/15
	Wilmington PMSA, DE-MD-NJ	Y	22930 FQ	30810 MW	43920 TQ	USBLS	5/15
	District of Columbia	Y	23080 FQ	30190 MW	37530 TQ	USBLS	5/15
	Washington-Arlington-Alexandria PMSA, DC-VA-MD-WV	Y	24890 FQ	34640 MW	48910 TQ	USBLS	5/15
	Florida	H	10.24 AE	14.32 MW	19.29 AEX	FLBLS	7/16-9/16
	Fort Lauderdale-Pompano Beach-Deerfield Beach PMSA, FL	H	11.17 AE	15.91 MW	21.32 AEX	FLBLS	7/16-9/16
	Miami-Miami Beach-Kendall PMSA, FL	H	10.16 AE	13.68 MW	17.58 AEX	FLBLS	7/16-9/16
	Orlando-Kissimmee-Sanford MSA, FL	H	10.17 AE	14.49 MW	19.18 AEX	FLBLS	7/16-9/16
	Tampa-St. Petersburg-Clearwater MSA, FL	H	10.08 AE	14.42 MW	20.43 AEX	FLBLS	7/16-9/16
	Georgia	Y	21930 FQ	29610 MW	40910 TQ	USBLS	5/15
	Atlanta-Sandy Springs-Roswell MSA, GA	Y	24980 FQ	31480 MW	44480 TQ	USBLS	5/15
	Augusta-Richmond County MSA, GA-SC	Y	19200 FQ	25540 MW	36060 TQ	USBLS	5/15
	Hawaii	Y	24290 FQ	30170 MW	38460 TQ	USBLS	5/15
	Urban Honolulu MSA, HI	Y	24190 FQ	30140 MW	38330 TQ	USBLS	5/15
	Idaho	Y	19890 FQ	27690 MW	39540 TQ	USBLS	5/15
	Boise City MSA, ID	Y	20810 FQ	26310 MW	35030 TQ	USBLS	5/15
	Illinois	Y	22240 FQ	30950 MW	44100 TQ	USBLS	5/15
	Chicago-Naperville-Arlington Heights PMSA, IL	Y	23260 FQ	32000 MW	47390 TQ	USBLS	5/15
	Lake County-Kenosha County PMSA, IL-WI	Y	20440 FQ	31180 MW	42120 TQ	USBLS	5/15
	Indiana	Y	21380 FQ	28960 MW	38930 TQ	USBLS	5/15
	Gary PMSA, IN	Y	19420 FQ	29210 MW	39500 TQ	USBLS	5/15
	Indianapolis-Carmel-Anderson MSA, IN	Y	23030 FQ	30990 MW	43730 TQ	USBLS	5/15
	Iowa	Y	21220 FQ	28430 MW	37680 TQ	USBLS	5/15
	Des Moines-West Des Moines MSA, IA	Y	23990 FQ	31890 MW	39150 TQ	USBLS	5/15
	Kansas	Y	20970 FQ	29050 MW	39630 TQ	USBLS	5/15
	Wichita MSA, KS	Y	18580 FQ	23040 MW	32910 TQ	USBLS	5/15
	Kentucky	Y	21830 FQ	28500 MW	38330 TQ	USBLS	5/15

AE	Average entry wage	AWR	Average wage range	H	Hourly	LR	Low end range	MTC	Median total compensation	TCC	Total cash compensation
AEX	Average experienced wage	B	Biweekly	HI	Highest wage paid	M	Monthly	MW	Median wage paid	TQ	Third quartile wage
ATC	Average total compensation	D	Daily	HR	High end range	MCC	Median cash compensation	MWR	Median wage range	W	Weekly
AW	Average wage paid	FQ	First quartile wage	LO	Lowest wage paid	ME	Median entry wage	S	See annotated source	Y	Yearly

Occupation/Type/Industry	Location	Per	Low	Mid	High	Source	Date
Light Truck or Delivery Services Driver	Louisville-Jefferson County MSA, KY-IN	Y	24580 FQ	33060 MW	45760 TQ	USBLS	5/15
	Louisiana	Y	20730 FQ	27630 MW	37700 TQ	USBLS	5/15
	Baton Rouge MSA, LA	Y	19560 FQ	24380 MW	35110 TQ	USBLS	5/15
	New Orleans-Metairie MSA, LA	Y	23850 FQ	30220 MW	41240 TQ	USBLS	5/15
	Maine	Y	21530 FQ	26640 MW	34590 TQ	USBLS	5/15
	Portland-South Portland MSA, ME	Y	23280 FQ	29050 MW	37880 TQ	USBLS	5/15
	Maryland	Y	22798 AE	37464 MW	44796 AEX	MDBLS	4/16
	Baltimore-Columbia-Towson MSA, MD	Y	26600 FQ	35140 MW	45850 TQ	USBLS	5/15
	Salisbury MSA, MD-DE	Y	22070 FQ	29230 MW	36870 TQ	USBLS	5/15
	Massachusetts	Y	24010 FQ	33680 MW	44700 TQ	USBLS	5/15
	Boston-Cambridge-Newton NECTA, MA	Y	25180 FQ	34890 MW	45350 TQ	USBLS	5/15
	Worcester MSA, MA-CT	Y	24510 FQ	35500 MW	45560 TQ	USBLS	5/15
	Michigan	Y	22080 FQ	29620 MW	40400 TQ	USBLS	5/15
	Detroit-Dearborn-Livonia PMSA, MI	Y	24670 FQ	34130 MW	47710 TQ	USBLS	5/15
	Grand Rapids-Wyoming MSA, MI	Y	22750 FQ	30620 MW	38900 TQ	USBLS	5/15
	Minnesota	Y	24508 FQ	33370 MW	44288 TQ	MNBLS	1/16-3/16
	Minneapolis-St. Paul-Bloomington MSA, MN-WI	Y	25466 FQ	34882 MW	47090 TQ	MNBLS	1/16-3/16
	Mississippi	Y	19280 FQ	25810 MW	35450 TQ	USBLS	5/15
	Jackson MSA, MS	Y	21130 FQ	27710 MW	40220 TQ	USBLS	5/15
	Missouri	Y	22400 FQ	30420 MW	39420 TQ	USBLS	5/15
	Kansas City MSA, MO-KS	Y	23820 FQ	32420 MW	43620 TQ	USBLS	5/15
	St. Louis MSA, MO-IL	Y	22920 FQ	33340 MW	45110 TQ	USBLS	5/15
	Montana	Y	21730 FQ	29980 MW	38620 TQ	USBLS	5/15
	Billings MSA, MT	Y	23010 FQ	30070 MW	43070 TQ	USBLS	5/15
	Nebraska	Y	22250 FQ	29075 MW	38435 TQ	NEBLS	7/16-9/16
	Omaha-Council Bluffs MSA, NE-IA	Y	23825 FQ	30120 MW	38820 TQ	NEBLS	7/16-9/16
	Nevada	Y	23800 FQ	30980 MW	40740 TQ	USBLS	5/15
	Las Vegas-Henderson-Paradise MSA, NV	Y	23540 FQ	30520 MW	39740 TQ	USBLS	5/15
	New Hampshire	H	9.27 AE	13.37 MW	17.56 AEX	NHBLS	6/16
	Manchester NECTA, NH	H	9.94 AE	14.50 MW	18.68 AEX	NHBLS	6/16
	Nashua NECTA, NH-MA	Y	21280 FQ	30230 MW	41880 TQ	USBLS	5/15
	New Jersey	Y	22760 FQ	31820 MW	45700 TQ	USBLS	5/15
	Camden PMSA, NJ	Y	20760 FQ	29460 MW	39460 TQ	USBLS	5/15
	Newark PMSA, NJ-PA	Y	21880 FQ	30070 MW	41480 TQ	USBLS	5/15
	Trenton MSA, NJ	Y	22840 FQ	30650 MW	44210 TQ	USBLS	5/15
	New Mexico	Y	20700 FQ	28820 MW	37290 TQ	USBLS	5/15
	Albuquerque MSA, NM	Y	22580 FQ	29860 MW	37180 TQ	USBLS	5/15
	New York	Y	21010 AE	31600 MW	43990 AEX	NYBLS	1/16-3/16
	Buffalo-Cheektowaga-Niagara Falls MSA, NY	Y	22730 FQ	31390 MW	38960 TQ	USBLS	5/15
	Nassau County-Suffolk County PMSA, NY	Y	27110 FQ	36710 MW	52870 TQ	USBLS	5/15
	New York-Jersey City-White Plains PMSA, NY-NJ	Y	22470 FQ	31860 MW	48080 TQ	USBLS	5/15
	Rochester MSA, NY	Y	21070 FQ	27590 MW	37280 TQ	USBLS	5/15
	North Carolina	Y	21490 FQ	28520 MW	37400 TQ	USBLS	5/15
	Charlotte-Concord-Gastonia MSA, NC-SC	Y	21470 FQ	28860 MW	38130 TQ	USBLS	5/15
	Raleigh MSA, NC	Y	23550 FQ	30390 MW	37510 TQ	USBLS	5/15
	North Dakota	Y	26050 FQ	33420 MW	43220 TQ	USBLS	5/15
	Fargo MSA, ND-MN	Y	22940 FQ	29530 MW	40900 TQ	USBLS	5/15
	Ohio	Y	20690 FQ	28230 MW	38770 TQ	USBLS	5/15
	Cincinnati MSA, OH-KY-IN	Y	22910 FQ	30150 MW	39570 TQ	USBLS	5/15
	Cleveland-Elyria MSA, OH	Y	20110 FQ	27960 MW	39090 TQ	USBLS	5/15
	Columbus MSA, OH	Y	24200 FQ	31230 MW	41420 TQ	USBLS	5/15
	Oklahoma	Y	22480 FQ	29840 MW	39080 TQ	USBLS	5/15
	Oklahoma City MSA, OK	Y	25680 FQ	33260 MW	46700 TQ	USBLS	5/15
	Tulsa MSA, OK	Y	22430 FQ	30580 MW	38920 TQ	USBLS	5/15
	Oregon	H	11.60 FQ	14.71 MW	19.73 TQ	ORBLS	2016
	Portland-Vancouver-Hillsboro MSA, OR-WA	Y	24480 FQ	30470 MW	41070 TQ	USBLS	5/15

AE	Average entry wage	AWR	Average wage range	H	Hourly	LR	Low end range	MTC	Median total compensation	TCC	Total cash compensation
AEX	Average experienced wage	B	Biweekly	HI	Highest wage paid	M	Monthly	MW	Median wage paid	TQ	Third quartile wage
ATC	Average total compensation	D	Daily	HR	High end range	MCC	Median cash compensation	MWR	Median wage range	W	Weekly
AW	Average wage paid	FQ	First quartile wage	LO	Lowest wage paid	ME	Median entry wage	S	See annotated source	Y	Yearly

Occupation/Type/Industry	Location	Per	Low	Mid	High	Source	Date
Light Truck or Delivery Services Driver	Pennsylvania	Y	21380 FQ	29110 MW	39520 TQ	USBLS	5/15
	Allentown-Bethlehem-Easton MSA, PA-NJ	Y	22540 FQ	30630 MW	46990 TQ	USBLS	5/15
	Harrisburg-Carlisle MSA, PA	Y	24290 FQ	31100 MW	45480 TQ	USBLS	5/15
	Montgomery County-Bucks County-Chester County PMSA, PA	Y	21140 FQ	28840 MW	39360 TQ	USBLS	5/15
	Philadelphia PMSA, PA	Y	24820 FQ	34890 MW	52970 TQ	USBLS	5/15
	Pittsburgh MSA, PA	Y	21930 FQ	29400 MW	38480 TQ	USBLS	5/15
	Rhode Island	Y	24930 FQ	34100 MW	44680 TQ	USBLS	5/15
	Providence-Warwick MSA, RI-MA	Y	23160 FQ	33030 MW	43000 TQ	USBLS	5/15
	South Carolina	Y	20650 FQ	27720 MW	37260 TQ	USBLS	5/15
	Charleston-North Charleston MSA, SC	Y	23020 FQ	27520 MW	32200 TQ	USBLS	5/15
	Columbia MSA, SC	Y	21550 FQ	30190 MW	41700 TQ	USBLS	5/15
	Greenville-Anderson-Mauldin MSA, SC	Y	21340 FQ	28910 MW	37760 TQ	USBLS	5/15
	South Dakota	Y	22330 FQ	28040 MW	36640 TQ	USBLS	5/15
	Sioux Falls MSA, SD	Y	24110 FQ	28210 MW	34210 TQ	USBLS	5/15
	Tennessee	Y	24970 FQ	29180 MW	36340 TQ	USBLS	5/15
	Knoxville MSA, TN	Y	21390 FQ	27060 MW	36730 TQ	USBLS	5/15
	Memphis MSA, TN-MS-AR	Y	26060 FQ	32650 MW	39110 TQ	USBLS	5/15
	Nashville-Davidson–Murfreesboro–Franklin MSA, TN	Y	26130 FQ	32690 MW	40890 TQ	USBLS	5/15
	Texas	Y	21400 FQ	28220 MW	36840 TQ	USBLS	5/15
	Austin-Round Rock MSA, TX	Y	22540 FQ	29450 MW	38810 TQ	USBLS	5/15
	Dallas-Plano-Irving PMSA, TX	Y	22970 FQ	30170 MW	39740 TQ	USBLS	5/15
	Fort Worth-Arlington PMSA, TX	Y	23400 FQ	31780 MW	38280 TQ	USBLS	5/15
	Houston-The Woodlands-Sugar Land MSA, TX	Y	23310 FQ	29780 MW	37270 TQ	USBLS	5/15
	San Antonio-New Braunfels MSA, TX	Y	19510 FQ	24040 MW	34240 TQ	USBLS	5/15
	Utah	Y	21540 FQ	28100 MW	37200 TQ	USBLS	5/15
	Ogden-Clearfield MSA, UT	Y	20890 FQ	24810 MW	33200 TQ	USBLS	5/15
	Provo-Orem MSA, UT	Y	19150 FQ	26230 MW	33370 TQ	USBLS	5/15
	Salt Lake City MSA, UT	Y	22320 FQ	28900 MW	38360 TQ	USBLS	5/15
	Vermont	Y	24450 FQ	31790 MW	41240 TQ	USBLS	5/15
	Burlington-South Burlington MSA, VT	Y	26780 FQ	34350 MW	43430 TQ	USBLS	5/15
	Virginia	Y	21710 FQ	29530 MW	40780 TQ	USBLS	5/15
	Richmond MSA, VA	Y	22300 FQ	31480 MW	39950 TQ	USBLS	5/15
	Virginia Beach-Norfolk-Newport News MSA, VA-NC	Y	22020 FQ	28870 MW	39960 TQ	USBLS	5/15
	Washington	H	12.88 FQ	16.57 MW	22.63 TQ	WABLS	3/16
	Seattle-Bellevue-Everett PMSA, WA	H	13.44 FQ	16.84 MW	22.78 TQ	WABLS	3/16
	Tacoma-Lakewood PMSA, WA	H	13.78 FQ	18.16 MW	24.65 TQ	WABLS	3/16
	West Virginia	Y	19360 FQ	25650 MW	34830 TQ	USBLS	5/15
	Huntington-Ashland MSA, WV-KY-OH	Y	18900 FQ	23550 MW	30950 TQ	USBLS	5/15
	Wisconsin	Y	21090 FQ	27940 MW	37530 TQ	USBLS	5/15
	Madison MSA, WI	Y	22850 FQ	29810 MW	38990 TQ	USBLS	5/15
	Milwaukee-Waukesha-West Allis MSA, WI	Y	22620 FQ	29880 MW	41220 TQ	USBLS	5/15
	Wyoming	Y	26200 FQ	33700 MW	42080 TQ	USBLS	5/15
	Cheyenne MSA, WY	Y	23040 FQ	35090 MW	44430 TQ	USBLS	5/15
	Puerto Rico	Y	16990 FQ	18380 MW	19950 TQ	USBLS	5/15
	San Juan-Carolina-Caguas MSA, PR	Y	17030 FQ	18470 MW	20180 TQ	USBLS	5/15
	Virgin Islands	Y	18760 FQ	22640 MW	28670 TQ	USBLS	5/15
	Guam	Y	18100 FQ	19030 MW	21510 TQ	USBLS	5/15
Lighting Engineer Theater Administration, Municipal Government	La Mirada, CA	Y			67227 HI	CACIT	6/28/16
Literacy Outreach Coordinator Public Library	Watsonville, CA	Y			67759 HI	CACIT	6/28/16

AE Average entry wage	**AWR** Average wage range	**H** Hourly	**LR** Low end range	**MTC** Median total compensation	**TCC** Total cash compensation
AEX Average experienced wage	**B** Biweekly	**HI** Highest wage paid	**M** Monthly	**MW** Median wage paid	**TQ** Third quartile wage
ATC Average total compensation	**D** Daily	**HR** High end range	**MCC** Median cash compensation	**MWR** Median wage range	**W** Weekly
AW Average wage paid	**FQ** First quartile wage	**LO** Lowest wage paid	**ME** Median entry wage	**S** See annotated source	**Y** Yearly

Occupation/Type/Industry	Location	Per	Low	Mid	High	Source	Date
Literacy Program Assistant							
Public Library	Colton, CA	Y		16028 AW		CACIT	6/28/16
Literacy Program Specialist							
Public Library	San Jose, CA	Y		49103 AW		CACIT	6/28/16
Lithographic Press Operator							
Department of Administration, State Government	Helena, MT	H	14.00 LO		16.00 HI	MTGOV	2016
Livestock Crime Investigator							
State Government	Chinook, MT	H			19.88 HI	MTGOV	2016
Livestock Inspector							
State Government	Glasgow, MT	H			13.34 HI	MTGOV	2016
Loading Machine Operator							
Underground Mining	Alabama	Y	42559 AE	54253 AW	60095 AEX	ALBLS	6/16
Underground Mining	Arizona	Y	35580 FQ	39750 MW	52040 TQ	USBLS	5/15
Underground Mining	Idaho	Y	40230 FQ	49290 MW	61760 TQ	USBLS	5/15
Underground Mining	Illinois	Y	34420 FQ	51990 MW	60170 TQ	USBLS	5/15
Underground Mining	Indiana	Y	48750 FQ	55890 MW	60710 TQ	USBLS	5/15
Underground Mining	Kentucky	Y	39360 FQ	48820 MW	62070 TQ	USBLS	5/15
Underground Mining	Mississippi	Y	29580 FQ	44080 MW	65110 TQ	USBLS	5/15
Underground Mining	Missouri	Y	28700 FQ	38100 MW	45220 TQ	USBLS	5/15
Underground Mining	New York	Y	33350 AE	44820 MW	46350 AEX	NYBLS	1/16-3/16
Underground Mining	Pennsylvania	Y	37150 FQ	52390 MW	60310 TQ	USBLS	5/15
Underground Mining	Texas	Y	29600 FQ	43160 MW	48280 TQ	USBLS	5/15
Underground Mining	West Virginia	Y	32840 FQ	49060 MW	58640 TQ	USBLS	5/15
Loan Interviewer and Clerk	Alabama	Y	25198 AE	33525 AW	37689 AEX	ALBLS	6/16
	Birmingham-Hoover MSA, AL	Y	27094 AE	34700 AW	38503 AEX	ALBLS	6/16
	Alaska	Y	32720 FQ	38430 MW	45760 TQ	USBLS	5/15
	Anchorage MSA, AK	Y	32790 FQ	38470 MW	45350 TQ	USBLS	5/15
	Arizona	Y	32650 FQ	42270 MW	50320 TQ	USBLS	5/15
	Phoenix-Mesa-Scottsdale MSA, AZ	Y	33120 FQ	42660 MW	50270 TQ	USBLS	5/15
	Tucson MSA, AZ	Y	29960 FQ	39620 MW	52340 TQ	USBLS	5/15
	Arkansas	Y	28450 FQ	33950 MW	39540 TQ	USBLS	5/15
	Little Rock-North Little Rock-Conway MSA, AR	Y	29000 FQ	35580 MW	44580 TQ	USBLS	5/15
	California	H	16.83 FQ	21.33 MW	25.81 TQ	CABLS	1/16-3/16
	Anaheim-Santa Ana-Irvine PMSA, CA	H	15.53 FQ	21.60 MW	26.46 TQ	CABLS	1/16-3/16
	Los Angeles-Long Beach-Glendale PMSA, CA	H	18.26 FQ	22.03 MW	26.14 TQ	CABLS	1/16-3/16
	Oakland-Hayward-Berkeley PMSA, CA	H	16.01 FQ	22.17 MW	27.17 TQ	CABLS	1/16-3/16
	Riverside-San Bernardino-Ontario MSA, CA	H	14.43 FQ	18.86 MW	23.34 TQ	CABLS	1/16-3/16
	Sacramento–Roseville–Arden-Arcade MSA, CA	H	15.59 FQ	18.71 MW	23.21 TQ	CABLS	1/16-3/16
	San Diego-Carlsbad MSA, CA	H	17.41 FQ	21.30 MW	25.75 TQ	CABLS	1/16-3/16
	San Francisco-Redwood City-South San Francisco PMSA, CA	H	17.67 FQ	23.27 MW	28.04 TQ	CABLS	1/16-3/16
	Colorado	Y	35640 FQ	43890 MW	51470 TQ	USBLS	5/15
	Denver-Aurora-Lakewood MSA, CO	Y	36620 FQ	44310 MW	51170 TQ	USBLS	5/15
	Connecticut	Y		42111 MW		CTBLS	1/16-3/16
	Bridgeport-Stamford-Norwalk MSA, CT	Y	25920 FQ	38050 MW	46430 TQ	USBLS	5/15
	Hartford-West Hartford-East Hartford MSA, CT	Y	36070 FQ	42950 MW	48800 TQ	USBLS	5/15
	Delaware	Y	28670 FQ	34700 MW	44020 TQ	USBLS	5/15
	Wilmington PMSA, DE-MD-NJ	Y	28790 FQ	34490 MW	43670 TQ	USBLS	5/15
	District of Columbia	Y	33080 FQ	45040 MW	57340 TQ	USBLS	5/15
	Washington-Arlington-Alexandria PMSA, DC-VA-MD-WV	Y	31230 FQ	40530 MW	52590 TQ	USBLS	5/15
	Florida	H	14.35 AE	19.23 MW	22.02 AEX	FLBLS	7/16-9/16

Occupation/Type/Industry	Location	Per	Low	Mid	High	Source	Date
Loan Interviewer and Clerk	Fort Lauderdale-Pompano Beach-Deerfield Beach PMSA, FL	H	13.78 AE	18.35 MW	21.23 AEX	FLBLS	7/16-9/16
	Miami-Miami Beach-Kendall PMSA, FL	H	12.75 AE	17.90 MW	22.23 AEX	FLBLS	7/16-9/16
	Orlando-Kissimmee-Sanford MSA, FL	H	13.75 AE	18.80 MW	21.68 AEX	FLBLS	7/16-9/16
	Tampa-St. Petersburg-Clearwater MSA, FL	H	15.08 AE	20.26 MW	22.80 AEX	FLBLS	7/16-9/16
	Georgia	Y	24520 FQ	33690 MW	40760 TQ	USBLS	5/15
	Atlanta-Sandy Springs-Roswell MSA, GA	Y	24180 FQ	35010 MW	41810 TQ	USBLS	5/15
	Augusta-Richmond County MSA, GA-SC	Y	27030 FQ	32380 MW	38820 TQ	USBLS	5/15
	Hawaii	Y	29050 FQ	35680 MW	44450 TQ	USBLS	5/15
	Urban Honolulu MSA, HI	Y	28130 FQ	34530 MW	42750 TQ	USBLS	5/15
	Idaho	Y	29620 FQ	36010 MW	44050 TQ	USBLS	5/15
	Boise City MSA, ID	Y	30650 FQ	37080 MW	44920 TQ	USBLS	5/15
	Illinois	Y	31960 FQ	39760 MW	48160 TQ	USBLS	5/15
	Chicago-Naperville-Arlington Heights PMSA, IL	Y	33300 FQ	42190 MW	49580 TQ	USBLS	5/15
	Lake County-Kenosha County PMSA, IL-WI	Y	34180 FQ	41810 MW	49820 TQ	USBLS	5/15
	Indiana	Y	25730 FQ	32220 MW	40330 TQ	USBLS	5/15
	Gary PMSA, IN	Y	27620 FQ	33390 MW	41720 TQ	USBLS	5/15
	Indianapolis-Carmel-Anderson MSA, IN	Y	26370 FQ	33760 MW	42580 TQ	USBLS	5/15
	Iowa	Y	31290 FQ	35490 MW	39600 TQ	USBLS	5/15
	Kansas	Y	29920 FQ	35840 MW	43810 TQ	USBLS	5/15
	Wichita MSA, KS	Y	29400 FQ	34040 MW	37830 TQ	USBLS	5/15
	Kentucky	Y	26040 FQ	30790 MW	38140 TQ	USBLS	5/15
	Louisville-Jefferson County MSA, KY-IN	Y	26080 FQ	34640 MW	42580 TQ	USBLS	5/15
	Louisiana	Y	25450 FQ	31000 MW	39060 TQ	USBLS	5/15
	Baton Rouge MSA, LA	Y	32680 FQ	42000 MW	48830 TQ	USBLS	5/15
	New Orleans-Metairie MSA, LA	Y	24880 FQ	31330 MW	40070 TQ	USBLS	5/15
	Maine	Y	28460 FQ	33120 MW	38450 TQ	USBLS	5/15
	Portland-South Portland MSA, ME	Y	31930 FQ	37210 MW	43390 TQ	USBLS	5/15
	Maryland	Y	29894 AE	43429 MW	50197 AEX	MDBLS	4/16
	Baltimore-Columbia-Towson MSA, MD	Y	31080 FQ	42590 MW	52120 TQ	USBLS	5/15
	Salisbury MSA, MD-DE	Y	26660 FQ	33830 MW	44220 TQ	USBLS	5/15
	Massachusetts	Y	36960 FQ	44510 MW	51860 TQ	USBLS	5/15
	Boston-Cambridge-Newton NECTA, MA	Y	40280 FQ	46050 MW	53560 TQ	USBLS	5/15
	Worcester MSA, MA-CT	Y	30790 FQ	40310 MW	52350 TQ	USBLS	5/15
	Michigan	Y	28650 FQ	34390 MW	40370 TQ	USBLS	5/15
	Detroit-Dearborn-Livonia PMSA, MI	Y	29420 FQ	34790 MW	41220 TQ	USBLS	5/15
	Grand Rapids-Wyoming MSA, MI	Y	27650 FQ	33370 MW	40740 TQ	USBLS	5/15
	Minnesota	Y	33776 FQ	40087 MW	47338 TQ	MNBLS	1/16-3/16
	Minneapolis-St. Paul-Bloomington MSA, MN-WI	Y	34545 FQ	41240 MW	47874 TQ	MNBLS	1/16-3/16
	Mississippi	Y	26980 FQ	33580 MW	39670 TQ	USBLS	5/15
	Jackson MSA, MS	Y	25540 FQ	34290 MW	44960 TQ	USBLS	5/15
	Missouri	Y	26960 FQ	33880 MW	40790 TQ	USBLS	5/15
	Kansas City MSA, MO-KS	Y	29770 FQ	37420 MW	47200 TQ	USBLS	5/15
	St. Louis MSA, MO-IL	Y	31860 FQ	37530 MW	44610 TQ	USBLS	5/15
	Montana	Y	28900 FQ	34000 MW	39470 TQ	USBLS	5/15
	Nebraska	Y	30185 FQ	36140 MW	43645 TQ	NEBLS	7/16-9/16
	Omaha-Council Bluffs MSA, NE-IA	Y	32200 FQ	37435 MW	44460 TQ	NEBLS	7/16-9/16
	Las Vegas-Henderson-Paradise MSA, NV	Y	34070 FQ	42360 MW	53400 TQ	USBLS	5/15
	New Hampshire	H	12.59 AE	17.41 MW	20.69 AEX	NHBLS	6/16
	Manchester NECTA, NH	H	13.74 AE	18.70 MW	22.31 AEX	NHBLS	6/16
	Nashua NECTA, NH-MA	Y	24360 FQ	34290 MW	39170 TQ	USBLS	5/15
	New Jersey	Y	31080 FQ	39000 MW	49710 TQ	USBLS	5/15
	Camden PMSA, NJ	Y	34750 FQ	40930 MW	54700 TQ	USBLS	5/15

AE	Average entry wage	AWR	Average wage range	H	Hourly	LR	Low end range	MTC	Median total compensation	TCC	Total cash compensation
AEX	Average experienced wage	B	Biweekly	HI	Highest wage paid	M	Monthly	MW	Median wage paid	TQ	Third quartile wage
ATC	Average total compensation	D	Daily	HR	High end range	MCC	Median cash compensation	MWR	Median wage range	W	Weekly
AW	Average wage paid	FQ	First quartile wage	LO	Lowest wage paid	ME	Median entry wage	S	See annotated source	Y	Yearly

Occupation/Type/Industry	Location	Per	Low	Mid	High	Source	Date
Loan Interviewer and Clerk	Newark PMSA, NJ-PA	Y	24750 FQ	38220 MW	48450 TQ	USBLS	5/15
	Trenton MSA, NJ	Y	32600 FQ	37900 MW	45280 TQ	USBLS	5/15
	New Mexico	Y	19660 FQ	28480 MW	36490 TQ	USBLS	5/15
	Albuquerque MSA, NM	Y	29220 FQ	35950 MW	43850 TQ	USBLS	5/15
	New York	Y	29230 AE	39640 MW	50360 AEX	NYBLS	1/16-3/16
	Buffalo-Cheektowaga-Niagara Falls MSA, NY	Y	31700 FQ	35250 MW	38790 TQ	USBLS	5/15
	Nassau County-Suffolk County PMSA, NY	Y	31860 FQ	39960 MW	52950 TQ	USBLS	5/15
	New York-Jersey City-White Plains PMSA, NY-NJ	Y	32060 FQ	39670 MW	51950 TQ	USBLS	5/15
	Rochester MSA, NY	Y	34580 FQ	41040 MW	47140 TQ	USBLS	5/15
	North Carolina	Y	31340 FQ	37500 MW	45530 TQ	USBLS	5/15
	Charlotte-Concord-Gastonia MSA, NC-SC	Y	33650 FQ	40250 MW	46890 TQ	USBLS	5/15
	Raleigh MSA, NC	Y	32610 FQ	38030 MW	45870 TQ	USBLS	5/15
	North Dakota	Y	32010 FQ	36880 MW	44080 TQ	USBLS	5/15
	Fargo MSA, ND-MN	Y	33330 FQ	37650 MW	43700 TQ	USBLS	5/15
	Ohio	Y	29320 FQ	35990 MW	44040 TQ	USBLS	5/15
	Cincinnati MSA, OH-KY-IN	Y	30970 FQ	38330 MW	46160 TQ	USBLS	5/15
	Cleveland-Elyria MSA, OH	Y	28650 FQ	36910 MW	44940 TQ	USBLS	5/15
	Columbus MSA, OH	Y	32860 FQ	37640 MW	46390 TQ	USBLS	5/15
	Oklahoma	Y	23880 FQ	29830 MW	39430 TQ	USBLS	5/15
	Oklahoma City MSA, OK	Y	24180 FQ	31520 MW	43320 TQ	USBLS	5/15
	Tulsa MSA, OK	Y	24540 FQ	30810 MW	41640 TQ	USBLS	5/15
	Oregon	H	16.72 FQ	19.43 MW	23.22 TQ	ORBLS	2016
	Portland-Vancouver-Hillsboro MSA, OR-WA	Y	34990 FQ	41270 MW	48190 TQ	USBLS	5/15
	Pennsylvania	Y	31110 FQ	36790 MW	44400 TQ	USBLS	5/15
	Allentown-Bethlehem-Easton MSA, PA-NJ	Y	28300 FQ	33210 MW	39370 TQ	USBLS	5/15
	Harrisburg-Carlisle MSA, PA	Y	32760 FQ	37580 MW	43620 TQ	USBLS	5/15
	Montgomery County-Bucks County-Chester County PMSA, PA	Y	34410 FQ	41080 MW	47990 TQ	USBLS	5/15
	Philadelphia PMSA, PA	Y	34420 FQ	40360 MW	48210 TQ	USBLS	5/15
	Pittsburgh MSA, PA	Y	30710 FQ	36200 MW	43170 TQ	USBLS	5/15
	Rhode Island	Y	33250 FQ	38310 MW	45710 TQ	USBLS	5/15
	Providence-Warwick MSA, RI-MA	Y	33190 FQ	38230 MW	45620 TQ	USBLS	5/15
	South Carolina	Y	26790 FQ	33430 MW	39340 TQ	USBLS	5/15
	Charleston-North Charleston MSA, SC	Y	24580 FQ	31320 MW	41050 TQ	USBLS	5/15
	Columbia MSA, SC	Y	32630 FQ	36340 MW	40180 TQ	USBLS	5/15
	Greenville-Anderson-Mauldin MSA, SC	Y	24820 FQ	30660 MW	36640 TQ	USBLS	5/15
	South Dakota	Y	28020 FQ	32740 MW	37920 TQ	USBLS	5/15
	Sioux Falls MSA, SD	Y	28490 FQ	33360 MW	38360 TQ	USBLS	5/15
	Tennessee	Y	28180 FQ	35050 MW	43690 TQ	USBLS	5/15
	Knoxville MSA, TN	Y	26920 FQ	32010 MW	37950 TQ	USBLS	5/15
	Memphis MSA, TN-MS-AR	Y	32150 FQ	37150 MW	45470 TQ	USBLS	5/15
	Nashville-Davidson–Murfreesboro–Franklin MSA, TN	Y	32730 FQ	39800 MW	48120 TQ	USBLS	5/15
	Texas	Y	34280 FQ	41530 MW	50100 TQ	USBLS	5/15
	Austin-Round Rock MSA, TX	Y	35220 FQ	44080 MW	54060 TQ	USBLS	5/15
	Dallas-Plano-Irving PMSA, TX	Y	36290 FQ	43050 MW	51330 TQ	USBLS	5/15
	Fort Worth-Arlington PMSA, TX	Y	32450 FQ	39690 MW	49080 TQ	USBLS	5/15
	Houston-The Woodlands-Sugar Land MSA, TX	Y	33040 FQ	42890 MW	51740 TQ	USBLS	5/15
	San Antonio-New Braunfels MSA, TX	Y	34060 FQ	39630 MW	48010 TQ	USBLS	5/15
	Utah	Y	26210 FQ	32140 MW	38810 TQ	USBLS	5/15
	Ogden-Clearfield MSA, UT	Y	25730 FQ	33150 MW	38730 TQ	USBLS	5/15
	Provo-Orem MSA, UT	Y	25930 FQ	30520 MW	39320 TQ	USBLS	5/15
	Salt Lake City MSA, UT	Y	26820 FQ	32410 MW	38940 TQ	USBLS	5/15
	Vermont	Y	31140 FQ	36270 MW	43750 TQ	USBLS	5/15
	Burlington-South Burlington MSA, VT	Y	31210 FQ	36220 MW	43260 TQ	USBLS	5/15
	Virginia	Y	29240 FQ	37200 MW	47150 TQ	USBLS	5/15
	Richmond MSA, VA	Y	29260 FQ	38980 MW	45950 TQ	USBLS	5/15

AE	Average entry wage	AWR	Average wage range	
AEX	Average experienced wage	B	Biweekly	
ATC	Average total compensation	D	Daily	
AW	Average wage paid	FQ	First quartile wage	

H	Hourly	LR	Low end range	
HI	Highest wage paid	M	Monthly	
HR	High end range	MCC	Median cash compensation	
LO	Lowest wage paid	ME	Median entry wage	

MTC	Median total compensation	TCC	Total cash compensation
MW	Median wage paid	TQ	Third quartile wage
MWR	Median wage range	W	Weekly
S	See annotated source	Y	Yearly

Occupation/Type/Industry	Location	Per	Low	Mid	High	Source	Date
Loan Interviewer and Clerk	Virginia Beach-Norfolk-Newport News MSA, VA-NC	Y	29160 FQ	36520 MW	45130 TQ	USBLS	5/15
	Washington	H	14.51 FQ	18.10 MW	22.68 TQ	WABLS	3/16
	Seattle-Bellevue-Everett PMSA, WA	H	13.30 FQ	17.60 MW	23.05 TQ	WABLS	3/16
	Tacoma-Lakewood PMSA, WA	H	15.06 FQ	17.70 MW	21.00 TQ	WABLS	3/16
	West Virginia	Y	24400 FQ	28400 MW	33300 TQ	USBLS	5/15
	Huntington-Ashland MSA, WV-KY-OH	Y	24070 FQ	28950 MW	35450 TQ	USBLS	5/15
	Wisconsin	Y	29450 FQ	35570 MW	42830 TQ	USBLS	5/15
	Madison MSA, WI	Y	29740 FQ	35630 MW	42800 TQ	USBLS	5/15
	Milwaukee-Waukesha-West Allis MSA, WI	Y	31450 FQ	38510 MW	46050 TQ	USBLS	5/15
	Wyoming	Y	27380 FQ	34470 MW	40330 TQ	USBLS	5/15
	Cheyenne MSA, WY	Y	26200 FQ	34540 MW	38910 TQ	USBLS	5/15
	Puerto Rico	Y	17970 FQ	21180 MW	26710 TQ	USBLS	5/15
	San Juan-Carolina-Caguas MSA, PR	Y	18190 FQ	21950 MW	27730 TQ	USBLS	5/15
	Guam	Y	20460 FQ	24250 MW	29900 TQ	USBLS	5/15
Loan Officer	Alabama	Y	39092 AE	69749 AW	85082 AEX	ALBLS	6/16
	Birmingham-Hoover MSA, AL	Y	38395 AE	68816 AW	84026 AEX	ALBLS	6/16
	Alaska	Y	50890 FQ	62630 MW	90290 TQ	USBLS	5/15
	Anchorage MSA, AK	Y	50330 FQ	62220 MW	91100 TQ	USBLS	5/15
	Arizona	Y	44790 FQ	63190 MW	83210 TQ	USBLS	5/15
	Phoenix-Mesa-Scottsdale MSA, AZ	Y	46270 FQ	64370 MW	83870 TQ	USBLS	5/15
	Tucson MSA, AZ	Y	35920 FQ	48250 MW	73010 TQ	USBLS	5/15
	Arkansas	Y	40820 FQ	58570 MW	78740 TQ	USBLS	5/15
	Little Rock-North Little Rock-Conway MSA, AR	Y	37430 FQ	54050 MW	77220 TQ	USBLS	5/15
	California	H	25.06 FQ	36.18 MW	51.48 TQ	CABLS	1/16-3/16
	Anaheim-Santa Ana-Irvine PMSA, CA	H	27.52 FQ	38.63 MW	55.05 TQ	CABLS	1/16-3/16
	Los Angeles-Long Beach-Glendale PMSA, CA	H	24.14 FQ	37.02 MW	52.02 TQ	CABLS	1/16-3/16
	Oakland-Hayward-Berkeley PMSA, CA	H	27.44 FQ	37.02 MW	55.84 TQ	CABLS	1/16-3/16
	Riverside-San Bernardino-Ontario MSA, CA	H	27.14 FQ	40.23 MW	48.11 TQ	CABLS	1/16-3/16
	Sacramento–Roseville–Arden-Arcade MSA, CA	H	21.06 FQ	31.80 MW	46.40 TQ	CABLS	1/16-3/16
	San Diego-Carlsbad MSA, CA	H	29.87 FQ	38.71 MW	49.45 TQ	CABLS	1/16-3/16
	San Francisco-Redwood City-South San Francisco PMSA, CA	H	25.99 FQ	36.28 MW	55.76 TQ	CABLS	1/16-3/16
	Colorado	Y	44230 FQ	62100 MW	88150 TQ	USBLS	5/15
	Denver-Aurora-Lakewood MSA, CO	Y	42290 FQ	59740 MW	85870 TQ	USBLS	5/15
	Connecticut	Y		71634 MW		CTBLS	1/16-3/16
	Bridgeport-Stamford-Norwalk MSA, CT	Y	46570 FQ	71340 MW	110770 TQ	USBLS	5/15
	Hartford-West Hartford-East Hartford MSA, CT	Y	47400 FQ	64850 MW	87690 TQ	USBLS	5/15
	Delaware	Y	55610 FQ	69130 MW	87230 TQ	USBLS	5/15
	Wilmington PMSA, DE-MD-NJ	Y	54930 FQ	67710 MW	89260 TQ	USBLS	5/15
	District of Columbia	Y	54610 FQ	86830 MW	123040 TQ	USBLS	5/15
	Washington-Arlington-Alexandria PMSA, DC-VA-MD-WV	Y	49580 FQ	73630 MW	110820 TQ	USBLS	5/15
	Florida	H	22.41 AE	34.86 MW	49.75 AEX	FLBLS	7/16-9/16
	Fort Lauderdale-Pompano Beach-Deerfield Beach PMSA, FL	H	22.54 AE	34.59 MW	51.63 AEX	FLBLS	7/16-9/16
	Miami-Miami Beach-Kendall PMSA, FL	H	21.72 AE	39.18 MW	63.40 AEX	FLBLS	7/16-9/16
	Orlando-Kissimmee-Sanford MSA, FL	H	22.73 AE	32.23 MW	44.88 AEX	FLBLS	7/16-9/16
	Sebastian-Vero Beach MSA, FL	Y	58980 FQ	107740 MW	140970 TQ	USBLS	5/15

Occupation/Type/Industry	Location	Per	Low	Mid	High	Source	Date
Loan Officer							
	Tampa-St. Petersburg-Clearwater MSA, FL	H	23.12 AE	35.90 MW	47.07 AEX	FLBLS	7/16-9/16
	Georgia	Y	39570 FQ	58590 MW	88930 TQ	USBLS	5/15
	Atlanta-Sandy Springs-Roswell MSA, GA	Y	40180 FQ	61200 MW	94090 TQ	USBLS	5/15
	Augusta-Richmond County MSA, GA-SC	Y	37200 FQ	47620 MW	70510 TQ	USBLS	5/15
	Hawaii	Y	42730 FQ	54720 MW	75330 TQ	USBLS	5/15
	Urban Honolulu MSA, HI	Y	42410 FQ	55050 MW	74510 TQ	USBLS	5/15
	Idaho	Y	35550 FQ	52260 MW	76760 TQ	USBLS	5/15
	Boise City MSA, ID	Y	34410 FQ	54690 MW	78470 TQ	USBLS	5/15
	Illinois	Y	45940 FQ	65860 MW	94220 TQ	USBLS	5/15
	Chicago-Naperville-Arlington Heights PMSA, IL	Y	51580 FQ	70560 MW	100140 TQ	USBLS	5/15
	Lake County-Kenosha County PMSA, IL-WI	Y	32670 FQ	53870 MW	83930 TQ	USBLS	5/15
	Indiana	Y	40670 FQ	56920 MW	84700 TQ	USBLS	5/15
	Gary PMSA, IN	Y	40500 FQ	58280 MW	86190 TQ	USBLS	5/15
	Indianapolis-Carmel-Anderson MSA, IN	Y	41550 FQ	59470 MW	90300 TQ	USBLS	5/15
	Iowa	Y	45080 FQ	62110 MW	83350 TQ	USBLS	5/15
	Des Moines-West Des Moines MSA, IA	Y	44440 FQ	58590 MW	78670 TQ	USBLS	5/15
	Kansas	Y	48720 FQ	65780 MW	91320 TQ	USBLS	5/15
	Wichita MSA, KS	Y	46990 FQ	70130 MW	95730 TQ	USBLS	5/15
	Kentucky	Y	44270 FQ	61000 MW	87860 TQ	USBLS	5/15
	Louisville-Jefferson County MSA, KY-IN	Y	46020 FQ	68480 MW	103420 TQ	USBLS	5/15
	Louisiana	Y	35830 FQ	47270 MW	66530 TQ	USBLS	5/15
	Baton Rouge MSA, LA	Y	46110 FQ	64000 MW	80850 TQ	USBLS	5/15
	New Orleans-Metairie MSA, LA	Y	36170 FQ	48190 MW	66920 TQ	USBLS	5/15
	Maine	Y	43150 FQ	54650 MW	79190 TQ	USBLS	5/15
	Portland-South Portland MSA, ME	Y	47360 FQ	58710 MW	84660 TQ	USBLS	5/15
	Maryland	Y	35109 AE	75659 MW	95934 AEX	MDBLS	4/16
	Baltimore-Columbia-Towson MSA, MD	Y	35560 FQ	54890 MW	81610 TQ	USBLS	5/15
	Salisbury MSA, MD-DE	Y	48820 FQ	66270 MW	80650 TQ	USBLS	5/15
	Massachusetts	Y	55770 FQ	76580 MW	121530 TQ	USBLS	5/15
	Boston-Cambridge-Newton NECTA, MA	Y	60930 FQ	84390 MW	130570 TQ	USBLS	5/15
	Worcester MSA, MA-CT	Y	46240 FQ	71110 MW	104800 TQ	USBLS	5/15
	Michigan	Y	37230 FQ	49520 MW	67850 TQ	USBLS	5/15
	Grand Rapids-Wyoming MSA, MI	Y	37960 FQ	49080 MW	66190 TQ	USBLS	5/15
	Minnesota	Y	51273 FQ	71381 MW	98847 TQ	MNBLS	1/16-3/16
	Minneapolis-St. Paul-Bloomington MSA, MN-WI	Y	56363 FQ	77051 MW	104222 TQ	MNBLS	1/16-3/16
	Mississippi	Y	36680 FQ	49970 MW	74910 TQ	USBLS	5/15
	Jackson MSA, MS	Y	38660 FQ	54210 MW	86440 TQ	USBLS	5/15
	Missouri	Y	38840 FQ	58090 MW	81340 TQ	USBLS	5/15
	Kansas City MSA, MO-KS	Y	46190 FQ	68750 MW	98640 TQ	USBLS	5/15
	St. Louis MSA, MO-IL	Y	38060 FQ	59530 MW	81790 TQ	USBLS	5/15
	Montana	Y	44870 FQ	59640 MW	78700 TQ	USBLS	5/15
	Billings MSA, MT	Y	39680 FQ	57870 MW	79460 TQ	USBLS	5/15
	Nebraska	Y	49060 FQ	69535 MW	96655 TQ	NEBLS	7/16-9/16
	Omaha-Council Bluffs MSA, NE-IA	Y	45495 FQ	65975 MW	107185 TQ	NEBLS	7/16-9/16
	Nevada	Y	37930 FQ	55060 MW	90870 TQ	USBLS	5/15
	Las Vegas-Henderson-Paradise MSA, NV	Y	38790 FQ	56690 MW	87190 TQ	USBLS	5/15
	New Hampshire	H	21.65 AE	35.61 MW	55.60 AEX	NHBLS	6/16
	Manchester NECTA, NH	H	23.04 AE	36.92 MW	52.64 AEX	NHBLS	6/16
	Nashua NECTA, NH-MA	Y	45320 FQ	61150 MW	97460 TQ	USBLS	5/15
	New Jersey	Y	53340 FQ	74260 MW	103000 TQ	USBLS	5/15
	Camden PMSA, NJ	Y	46150 FQ	67920 MW	101470 TQ	USBLS	5/15
	Newark PMSA, NJ-PA	Y	55960 FQ	74370 MW	99490 TQ	USBLS	5/15
	Trenton MSA, NJ	Y	57000 FQ	75430 MW	103210 TQ	USBLS	5/15
	New Mexico	Y	35550 FQ	46480 MW	69270 TQ	USBLS	5/15
	Albuquerque MSA, NM	Y	36240 FQ	45380 MW	65300 TQ	USBLS	5/15
	New York	Y	40730 AE	75810 MW	125060 AEX	NYBLS	1/16-3/16

AE Average entry wage	AWR Average wage range	H Hourly	LR Low end range	MTC Median total compensation	TCC Total cash compensation
AEX Average experienced wage	B Biweekly	HI Highest wage paid	M Monthly	MW Median wage paid	TQ Third quartile wage
ATC Average total compensation	D Daily	HR High end range	MCC Median cash compensation	MWR Median wage range	W Weekly
AW Average wage paid	FQ First quartile wage	LO Lowest wage paid	ME Median entry wage	S See annotated source	Y Yearly

Occupation/Type/Industry	Location	Per	Low	Mid	High	Source	Date
Loan Officer	Buffalo-Cheektowaga-Niagara Falls MSA, NY	Y	36590 FQ	46820 MW	66920 TQ	USBLS	5/15
	Nassau County-Suffolk County PMSA, NY	Y	48790 FQ	72340 MW	108860 TQ	USBLS	5/15
	New York-Jersey City-White Plains PMSA, NY-NJ	Y	60350 FQ	88960 MW	144650 TQ	USBLS	5/15
	Rochester MSA, NY	Y	47510 FQ	67540 MW	95000 TQ	USBLS	5/15
	North Carolina	Y	45360 FQ	64840 MW	90770 TQ	USBLS	5/15
	Charlotte-Concord-Gastonia MSA, NC-SC	Y	49910 FQ	68540 MW	89890 TQ	USBLS	5/15
	Raleigh MSA, NC	Y	42860 FQ	58910 MW	93320 TQ	USBLS	5/15
	North Dakota	Y	50130 FQ	66820 MW	85710 TQ	USBLS	5/15
	Fargo MSA, ND-MN	Y	47880 FQ	67720 MW	82110 TQ	USBLS	5/15
	Ohio	Y	41070 FQ	57530 MW	82140 TQ	USBLS	5/15
	Cincinnati MSA, OH-KY-IN	Y	45320 FQ	68080 MW	95830 TQ	USBLS	5/15
	Cleveland-Elyria MSA, OH	Y	38660 FQ	65020 MW	86450 TQ	USBLS	5/15
	Columbus MSA, OH	Y	43080 FQ	56480 MW	76700 TQ	USBLS	5/15
	Oklahoma	Y	38100 FQ	56130 MW	80190 TQ	USBLS	5/15
	Oklahoma City MSA, OK	Y	37650 FQ	57680 MW	84630 TQ	USBLS	5/15
	Tulsa MSA, OK	Y	36500 FQ	56710 MW	83830 TQ	USBLS	5/15
	Oregon	H	25.06 FQ	35.48 MW	48.24 TQ	ORBLS	2016
	Portland-Vancouver-Hillsboro MSA, OR-WA	Y	54050 FQ	74430 MW	101100 TQ	USBLS	5/15
	Pennsylvania	Y	45360 FQ	60110 MW	82630 TQ	USBLS	5/15
	Allentown-Bethlehem-Easton MSA, PA-NJ	Y	48710 FQ	65170 MW	82350 TQ	USBLS	5/15
	Harrisburg-Carlisle MSA, PA	Y	40950 FQ	52680 MW	74180 TQ	USBLS	5/15
	Montgomery County-Bucks County-Chester County PMSA, PA	Y	47120 FQ	62010 MW	86770 TQ	USBLS	5/15
	Philadelphia PMSA, PA	Y	50720 FQ	71890 MW	105030 TQ	USBLS	5/15
	Pittsburgh MSA, PA	Y	40530 FQ	56100 MW	72530 TQ	USBLS	5/15
	Rhode Island	Y	46210 FQ	65820 MW	111140 TQ	USBLS	5/15
	Providence-Warwick MSA, RI-MA	Y	45460 FQ	65170 MW	107860 TQ	USBLS	5/15
	South Carolina	Y	39310 FQ	54600 MW	80240 TQ	USBLS	5/15
	Charleston-North Charleston MSA, SC	Y	47810 FQ	63480 MW	108900 TQ	USBLS	5/15
	Columbia MSA, SC	Y	43490 FQ	57300 MW	82870 TQ	USBLS	5/15
	Greenville-Anderson-Mauldin MSA, SC	Y	34510 FQ	49590 MW	86780 TQ	USBLS	5/15
	South Dakota	Y	50580 FQ	60550 MW	74180 TQ	USBLS	5/15
	Sioux Falls MSA, SD	Y	49960 FQ	60890 MW	76410 TQ	USBLS	5/15
	Tennessee	Y	37050 FQ	55290 MW	77490 TQ	USBLS	5/15
	Knoxville MSA, TN	Y	35500 FQ	50330 MW	64460 TQ	USBLS	5/15
	Memphis MSA, TN-MS-AR	Y	43620 FQ	57260 MW	76350 TQ	USBLS	5/15
	Nashville-Davidson–Murfreesboro–Franklin MSA, TN	Y	52800 FQ	68270 MW	98300 TQ	USBLS	5/15
	Texas	Y	46660 FQ	64680 MW	97450 TQ	USBLS	5/15
	Austin-Round Rock MSA, TX	Y	48890 FQ	75520 MW	131610 TQ	USBLS	5/15
	Dallas-Plano-Irving PMSA, TX	Y	51660 FQ	69370 MW	97860 TQ	USBLS	5/15
	Fort Worth-Arlington PMSA, TX	Y	37910 FQ	55110 MW	77330 TQ	USBLS	5/15
	Houston-The Woodlands-Sugar Land MSA, TX	Y	44230 FQ	66040 MW	115330 TQ	USBLS	5/15
	San Antonio-New Braunfels MSA, TX	Y	48500 FQ	61760 MW	84600 TQ	USBLS	5/15
	Utah	Y	33360 FQ	50460 MW	78270 TQ	USBLS	5/15
	Ogden-Clearfield MSA, UT	Y	31600 FQ	48420 MW	70090 TQ	USBLS	5/15
	Provo-Orem MSA, UT	Y	44440 FQ	71690 MW	100940 TQ	USBLS	5/15
	Salt Lake City MSA, UT	Y	32670 FQ	48790 MW	75050 TQ	USBLS	5/15
	Vermont	Y	45780 FQ	60410 MW	91270 TQ	USBLS	5/15
	Burlington-South Burlington MSA, VT	Y	44390 FQ	58120 MW	100130 TQ	USBLS	5/15
	Virginia	Y	46210 FQ	64860 MW	95370 TQ	USBLS	5/15
	Richmond MSA, VA	Y	45390 FQ	60480 MW	82450 TQ	USBLS	5/15
	Virginia Beach-Norfolk-Newport News MSA, VA-NC	Y	41140 FQ	56530 MW	78460 TQ	USBLS	5/15
	Washington	H	19.85 FQ	29.73 MW	43.24 TQ	WABLS	3/16
	Seattle-Bellevue-Everett PMSA, WA	H	18.14 FQ	31.07 MW	44.16 TQ	WABLS	3/16

AE Average entry wage	**AWR** Average wage range	**H** Hourly	**LR** Low end range	**MTC** Median total compensation	**TCC** Total cash compensation
AEX Average experienced wage	**B** Biweekly	**HI** Highest wage paid	**M** Monthly	**MW** Median wage paid	**TQ** Third quartile wage
ATC Average total compensation	**D** Daily	**HR** High end range	**MCC** Median cash compensation	**MWR** Median wage range	**W** Weekly
AW Average wage paid	**FQ** First quartile wage	**LO** Lowest wage paid	**ME** Median entry wage	**S** See annotated source	**Y** Yearly

Occupation/Type/Industry	Location	Per	Low	Mid	High	Source	Date
Loan Officer	Tacoma-Lakewood PMSA, WA	H	20.73 FQ	29.01 MW	47.64 TQ	WABLS	3/16
	West Virginia	Y	30740 FQ	44150 MW	70400 TQ	USBLS	5/15
	Huntington-Ashland MSA, WV-KY-OH	Y	30970 FQ	42180 MW	71900 TQ	USBLS	5/15
	Wisconsin	Y	44220 FQ	61150 MW	83530 TQ	USBLS	5/15
	Madison MSA, WI	Y	51130 FQ	63200 MW	100750 TQ	USBLS	5/15
	Milwaukee-Waukesha-West Allis MSA, WI	Y	46210 FQ	66300 MW	96930 TQ	USBLS	5/15
	Wyoming	Y	40590 FQ	63020 MW	81000 TQ	USBLS	5/15
	Cheyenne MSA, WY	Y	36540 FQ	51740 MW	72160 TQ	USBLS	5/15
	Puerto Rico	Y	23080 FQ	28560 MW	40600 TQ	USBLS	5/15
	San Juan-Carolina-Caguas MSA, PR	Y	23080 FQ	28720 MW	41580 TQ	USBLS	5/15
	Guam	Y	31450 FQ	41140 MW	54390 TQ	USBLS	5/15
Loan Specialist Community Development Department, Municipal Government	Santa Ana, CA	Y			73756 HI	CACIT	6/28/16
Local History Archivist Public Library	Fullerton, CA	Y			53794 HI	CACIT	6/28/16
Locker Room, Coatroom, and Dressing Room Attendant	Alabama	Y	17359 AE	23949 AW	27243 AEX	ALBLS	6/16
	Birmingham-Hoover MSA, AL	Y	17328 AE	20592 AW	22229 AEX	ALBLS	6/16
	Alaska	Y	24970 FQ	28140 MW	31430 TQ	USBLS	5/15
	Anchorage MSA, AK	Y	24970 FQ	28140 MW	31430 TQ	USBLS	5/15
	Arizona	Y	18910 FQ	21450 MW	24450 TQ	USBLS	5/15
	Phoenix-Mesa-Scottsdale MSA, AZ	Y	19040 FQ	21580 MW	24430 TQ	USBLS	5/15
	Tucson MSA, AZ	Y	18430 FQ	20480 MW	24120 TQ	USBLS	5/15
	California	H	9.78 FQ	13.28 MW	16.91 TQ	CABLS	1/16-3/16
	Anaheim-Santa Ana-Irvine PMSA, CA	H	10.02 FQ	11.60 MW	14.80 TQ	CABLS	1/16-3/16
	Los Angeles-Long Beach-Glendale PMSA, CA	H	9.53 FQ	15.31 MW	17.76 TQ	CABLS	1/16-3/16
	Oakland-Hayward-Berkeley PMSA, CA	H	12.10 FQ	14.67 MW	17.17 TQ	CABLS	1/16-3/16
	Riverside-San Bernardino-Ontario MSA, CA	H	9.82 FQ	11.76 MW	15.36 TQ	CABLS	1/16-3/16
	Sacramento–Roseville–Arden-Arcade MSA, CA	H	9.48 FQ	9.97 MW	13.60 TQ	CABLS	1/16-3/16
	San Diego-Carlsbad MSA, CA	H	10.29 FQ	12.39 MW	14.56 TQ	CABLS	1/16-3/16
	San Francisco-Redwood City-South San Francisco PMSA, CA	H	10.04 FQ	13.10 MW	18.78 TQ	CABLS	1/16-3/16
	Colorado	Y	19670 FQ	24160 MW	28020 TQ	USBLS	5/15
	Denver-Aurora-Lakewood MSA, CO	Y	19610 FQ	23610 MW	27660 TQ	USBLS	5/15
	Connecticut	Y		23801 MW		CTBLS	1/16-3/16
	Delaware	Y	17360 FQ	18470 MW	20410 TQ	USBLS	5/15
	Wilmington PMSA, DE-MD-NJ	Y	17330 FQ	18410 MW	20110 TQ	USBLS	5/15
	Washington-Arlington-Alexandria PMSA, DC-VA-MD-WV	Y	18760 FQ	22380 MW	27500 TQ	USBLS	5/15
	Florida	H	9.08 AE	11.10 MW	13.94 AEX	FLBLS	7/16-9/16
	Fort Lauderdale-Pompano Beach-Deerfield Beach PMSA, FL	H	9.23 AE	11.53 MW	14.15 AEX	FLBLS	7/16-9/16
	Miami-Miami Beach-Kendall PMSA, FL	H	10.19 AE	12.09 MW	13.90 AEX	FLBLS	7/16-9/16
	Orlando-Kissimmee-Sanford MSA, FL	H	8.98 AE	10.34 MW	12.04 AEX	FLBLS	7/16-9/16
	Tampa-St. Petersburg-Clearwater MSA, FL	H	9.05 AE	9.50 MW	11.21 AEX	FLBLS	7/16-9/16
	Georgia	Y	17900 FQ	20650 MW	23910 TQ	USBLS	5/15
	Atlanta-Sandy Springs-Roswell MSA, GA	Y	19380 FQ	22060 MW	24940 TQ	USBLS	5/15
	Hawaii	Y	19460 FQ	28150 MW	39930 TQ	USBLS	5/15
	Urban Honolulu MSA, HI	Y	18190 FQ	21860 MW	29830 TQ	USBLS	5/15
	Illinois	Y	18710 FQ	20380 MW	24970 TQ	USBLS	5/15

AE	Average entry wage	AWR	Average wage range	H	Hourly	LR	Low end range	MTC	Median total compensation	TCC	Total cash compensation
AEX	Average experienced wage	B	Biweekly	HI	Highest wage paid	M	Monthly	MW	Median wage paid	TQ	Third quartile wage
ATC	Average total compensation	D	Daily	HR	High end range	MCC	Median cash compensation	MWR	Median wage range	W	Weekly
AW	Average wage paid	FQ	First quartile wage	LO	Lowest wage paid	ME	Median entry wage	S	See annotated source	Y	Yearly

922

Occupation/Type/Industry	Location	Per	Low	Mid	High	Source	Date
Locker Room, Coatroom, and Dressing Room Attendant	Chicago-Naperville-Arlington Heights PMSA, IL	Y	18910 FQ	21280 MW	26680 TQ	USBLS	5/15
	Lake County-Kenosha County PMSA, IL-WI	Y	17880 FQ	18610 MW	20060 TQ	USBLS	5/15
	Indiana	Y	17050 FQ	18430 MW	19810 TQ	USBLS	5/15
	Iowa	Y	16450 FQ	17620 MW	18790 TQ	USBLS	5/15
	Kansas	Y	16750 FQ	17970 MW	19180 TQ	USBLS	5/15
	Louisiana	Y	22250 FQ	26830 MW	30470 TQ	USBLS	5/15
	Maine	Y	16850 FQ	17890 MW	18940 TQ	USBLS	5/15
	Portland-South Portland MSA, ME	Y	16910 FQ	17860 MW	18810 TQ	USBLS	5/15
	Maryland	Y	18845 AE	23093 MW	25217 AEX	MDBLS	4/16
	Baltimore-Columbia-Towson MSA, MD	Y	19120 FQ	21830 MW	24670 TQ	USBLS	5/15
	Massachusetts	Y	22510 FQ	27970 MW	34290 TQ	USBLS	5/15
	Boston-Cambridge-Newton NECTA, MA	Y	25240 FQ	30450 MW	36730 TQ	USBLS	5/15
	Michigan	Y	17980 FQ	18900 MW	21010 TQ	USBLS	5/15
	Detroit-Dearborn-Livonia PMSA, MI	Y	18810 FQ	21210 MW	23900 TQ	USBLS	5/15
	Grand Rapids-Wyoming MSA, MI	Y	17860 FQ	18630 MW	19440 TQ	USBLS	5/15
	Minnesota	Y	18238 FQ	19632 MW	26731 TQ	MNBLS	1/16-3/16
	Minneapolis-St. Paul-Bloomington MSA, MN-WI	Y	18743 FQ	23288 MW	28801 TQ	MNBLS	1/16-3/16
	Mississippi	Y	16530 FQ	17870 MW	19200 TQ	USBLS	5/15
	Missouri	Y	17070 FQ	18210 MW	19410 TQ	USBLS	5/15
	Kansas City MSA, MO-KS	Y	16990 FQ	18250 MW	19740 TQ	USBLS	5/15
	St. Louis MSA, MO-IL	Y	17050 FQ	18150 MW	19210 TQ	USBLS	5/15
	Montana	Y	17460 FQ	18180 MW	18890 TQ	USBLS	5/15
	Omaha-Council Bluffs MSA, NE-IA	Y	17685 FQ	19565 MW	24610 TQ	NEBLS	7/16-9/16
	Nevada	Y	20190 FQ	22710 MW	25870 TQ	USBLS	5/15
	Las Vegas-Henderson-Paradise MSA, NV	Y	20880 FQ	23170 MW	26450 TQ	USBLS	5/15
	New Hampshire	H	8.40 AE	9.19 MW	10.77 AEX	NHBLS	6/16
	New Jersey	Y	18600 FQ	19750 MW	24800 TQ	USBLS	5/15
	Camden PMSA, NJ	Y	18310 FQ	19120 MW	23170 TQ	USBLS	5/15
	Newark PMSA, NJ-PA	Y	18580 FQ	20060 MW	27700 TQ	USBLS	5/15
	New York	Y	20820 AE	27010 MW	35920 AEX	NYBLS	1/16-3/16
	Buffalo-Cheektowaga-Niagara Falls MSA, NY	Y	19000 FQ	19880 MW	27270 TQ	USBLS	5/15
	Nassau County-Suffolk County PMSA, NY	Y	20620 FQ	24580 MW	33430 TQ	USBLS	5/15
	New York-Jersey City-White Plains PMSA, NY-NJ	Y	20220 FQ	25080 MW	40150 TQ	USBLS	5/15
	Rochester MSA, NY	Y	18720 FQ	19240 MW	23290 TQ	USBLS	5/15
	North Carolina	Y	17290 FQ	19330 MW	23430 TQ	USBLS	5/15
	North Dakota	Y	18400 FQ	26970 MW	34640 TQ	USBLS	5/15
	Ohio	Y	18260 FQ	19790 MW	26760 TQ	USBLS	5/15
	Cincinnati MSA, OH-KY-IN	Y	18010 FQ	19200 MW	32720 TQ	USBLS	5/15
	Cleveland-Elyria MSA, OH	Y	18260 FQ	19760 MW	25960 TQ	USBLS	5/15
	Columbus MSA, OH	Y	18230 FQ	19720 MW	25570 TQ	USBLS	5/15
	Oklahoma	Y	17640 FQ	20070 MW	23410 TQ	USBLS	5/15
	Oregon	H	9.65 FQ	10.55 MW	11.86 TQ	ORBLS	2016
	Portland-Vancouver-Hillsboro MSA, OR-WA	Y	19720 FQ	21450 MW	23910 TQ	USBLS	5/15
	Pennsylvania	Y	18270 FQ	22170 MW	27540 TQ	USBLS	5/15
	Allentown-Bethlehem-Easton MSA, PA-NJ	Y	18450 FQ	25040 MW	33200 TQ	USBLS	5/15
	Harrisburg-Carlisle MSA, PA	Y	20670 FQ	22790 MW	25930 TQ	USBLS	5/15
	Montgomery County-Bucks County-Chester County PMSA, PA	Y	19890 FQ	23390 MW	28030 TQ	USBLS	5/15
	Philadelphia PMSA, PA	Y	17810 FQ	21220 MW	26220 TQ	USBLS	5/15
	Pittsburgh MSA, PA	Y	18010 FQ	22270 MW	27660 TQ	USBLS	5/15
	Rhode Island	Y	19310 FQ	23280 MW	30920 TQ	USBLS	5/15
	Providence-Warwick MSA, RI-MA	Y	19290 FQ	22630 MW	29600 TQ	USBLS	5/15
	South Carolina	Y	17890 FQ	20540 MW	23450 TQ	USBLS	5/15
	South Dakota	Y	18240 FQ	18800 MW	19360 TQ	USBLS	5/15

AE	Average entry wage	AWR	Average wage range	H	Hourly	LR	Low end range	MTC	Median total compensation	TCC	Total cash compensation
AEX	Average experienced wage	B	Biweekly	HI	Highest wage paid	M	Monthly	MW	Median wage paid	TQ	Third quartile wage
ATC	Average total compensation	D	Daily	HR	High end range	MCC	Median cash compensation	MWR	Median wage range	W	Weekly
AW	Average wage paid	FQ	First quartile wage	LO	Lowest wage paid	ME	Median entry wage	S	See annotated source	Y	Yearly

Occupation/Type/Industry	Location	Per	Low	Mid	High	Source	Date
Locker Room, Coatroom, and Dressing Room Attendant	Texas	Y	17320 FQ	19250 MW	23440 TQ	USBLS	5/15
	Austin-Round Rock MSA, TX	Y	17790 FQ	19930 MW	24000 TQ	USBLS	5/15
	Dallas-Plano-Irving PMSA, TX	Y	17970 FQ	20730 MW	26450 TQ	USBLS	5/15
	Fort Worth-Arlington PMSA, TX	Y	17570 FQ	19610 MW	24210 TQ	USBLS	5/15
	Houston-The Woodlands-Sugar Land MSA, TX	Y	17090 FQ	18890 MW	22680 TQ	USBLS	5/15
	San Antonio-New Braunfels MSA, TX	Y	17180 FQ	18910 MW	21930 TQ	USBLS	5/15
	Utah	Y	18010 FQ	20920 MW	24610 TQ	USBLS	5/15
	Virginia	Y	17640 FQ	20360 MW	24300 TQ	USBLS	5/15
	Richmond MSA, VA	Y	18160 FQ	21250 MW	25030 TQ	USBLS	5/15
	Washington	H	10.40 FQ	11.80 MW	14.07 TQ	WABLS	3/16
	Seattle-Bellevue-Everett PMSA, WA	H	10.34 FQ	11.90 MW	14.31 TQ	WABLS	3/16
	West Virginia	Y	17920 FQ	19200 MW	23940 TQ	USBLS	5/15
	Wisconsin	Y	16910 FQ	18290 MW	19740 TQ	USBLS	5/15
	Milwaukee-Waukesha-West Allis MSA, WI	Y	17250 FQ	18940 MW	21850 TQ	USBLS	5/15
	Puerto Rico	Y	17490 FQ	20070 MW	22630 TQ	USBLS	5/15
	San Juan-Carolina-Caguas MSA, PR	Y	17760 FQ	20460 MW	22820 TQ	USBLS	5/15
Locksmith and Safe Repairer	Alabama	Y	20778 AE	33114 AW	39287 AEX	ALBLS	6/16
	Birmingham-Hoover MSA, AL	Y	22537 AE	30073 AW	33836 AEX	ALBLS	6/16
	Arizona	Y	34750 FQ	40430 MW	47230 TQ	USBLS	5/15
	Phoenix-Mesa-Scottsdale MSA, AZ	Y	35080 FQ	41030 MW	47580 TQ	USBLS	5/15
	Tucson MSA, AZ	Y	35830 FQ	40160 MW	45970 TQ	USBLS	5/15
	Arkansas	Y	26370 FQ	29770 MW	35740 TQ	USBLS	5/15
	Little Rock-North Little Rock-Conway MSA, AR	Y	26570 FQ	29310 MW	32230 TQ	USBLS	5/15
	California	H	19.74 FQ	23.99 MW	28.87 TQ	CABLS	1/16-3/16
	Anaheim-Santa Ana-Irvine PMSA, CA	H	21.85 FQ	25.06 MW	31.74 TQ	CABLS	1/16-3/16
	Los Angeles-Long Beach-Glendale PMSA, CA	H	20.34 FQ	23.86 MW	28.52 TQ	CABLS	1/16-3/16
	Oakland-Hayward-Berkeley PMSA, CA	H	20.02 FQ	23.88 MW	28.45 TQ	CABLS	1/16-3/16
	Riverside-San Bernardino-Ontario MSA, CA	H	23.16 FQ	26.21 MW	28.28 TQ	CABLS	1/16-3/16
	Sacramento–Roseville–Arden-Arcade MSA, CA	H	19.55 FQ	22.21 MW	24.98 TQ	CABLS	1/16-3/16
	San Diego-Carlsbad MSA, CA	H	19.18 FQ	22.86 MW	26.89 TQ	CABLS	1/16-3/16
	San Francisco-Redwood City-South San Francisco PMSA, CA	H	22.45 FQ	31.59 MW	36.47 TQ	CABLS	1/16-3/16
	Colorado	Y	27070 FQ	31290 MW	43970 TQ	USBLS	5/15
	Denver-Aurora-Lakewood MSA, CO	Y	34760 FQ	43560 MW	53910 TQ	USBLS	5/15
	Connecticut	Y		48625 MW		CTBLS	1/16-3/16
	Bridgeport-Stamford-Norwalk MSA, CT	Y	34500 FQ	37770 MW	43160 TQ	USBLS	5/15
	Hartford-West Hartford-East Hartford MSA, CT	Y	51280 FQ	55520 MW	60140 TQ	USBLS	5/15
	Delaware	Y	30410 FQ	34760 MW	38760 TQ	USBLS	5/15
	Wilmington PMSA, DE-MD-NJ	Y	31810 FQ	35120 MW	38430 TQ	USBLS	5/15
	District of Columbia	Y	52590 FQ	59680 MW	62970 TQ	USBLS	5/15
	Washington-Arlington-Alexandria PMSA, DC-VA-MD-WV	Y	37810 FQ	50530 MW	59680 TQ	USBLS	5/15
	Florida	H	11.32 AE	16.56 MW	19.69 AEX	FLBLS	7/16-9/16
	Fort Lauderdale-Pompano Beach-Deerfield Beach PMSA, FL	H	17.27 AE	22.86 MW	25.45 AEX	FLBLS	7/16-9/16
	Miami-Miami Beach-Kendall PMSA, FL	H	10.14 AE	14.91 MW	18.19 AEX	FLBLS	7/16-9/16
	Orlando-Kissimmee-Sanford MSA, FL	H	12.94 AE	17.58 MW	20.21 AEX	FLBLS	7/16-9/16

AE	Average entry wage	AWR	Average wage range	H	Hourly	LR Low end range	MTC Median total compensation	TCC Total cash compensation
AEX	Average experienced wage	B	Biweekly	HI	Highest wage paid	M Monthly	MW Median wage paid	TQ Third quartile wage
ATC	Average total compensation	D	Daily	HR	High end range	MCC Median cash compensation	MWR Median wage range	W Weekly
AW	Average wage paid	FQ	First quartile wage	LO	Lowest wage paid	ME Median entry wage	S See annotated source	Y Yearly

Occupation/Type/Industry	Location	Per	Low	Mid	High	Source	Date
Locksmith and Safe Repairer	Tampa-St. Petersburg-Clearwater MSA, FL	H	11.16 AE	15.03 MW	17.36 AEX	FLBLS	7/16-9/16
	Georgia	Y	30270 FQ	35720 MW	43040 TQ	USBLS	5/15
	Atlanta-Sandy Springs-Roswell MSA, GA	Y	31380 FQ	35570 MW	39700 TQ	USBLS	5/15
	Augusta-Richmond County MSA, GA-SC	Y	22130 FQ	24140 MW	33740 TQ	USBLS	5/15
	Hawaii	Y	37380 FQ	52440 MW	62400 TQ	USBLS	5/15
	Idaho	Y	23950 FQ	29220 MW	38580 TQ	USBLS	5/15
	Illinois	Y	29450 FQ	39310 MW	54500 TQ	USBLS	5/15
	Chicago-Naperville-Arlington Heights PMSA, IL	Y	22730 FQ	38920 MW	54340 TQ	USBLS	5/15
	Lake County-Kenosha County PMSA, IL-WI	Y	19720 FQ	43750 MW	54610 TQ	USBLS	5/15
	Indiana	Y	30190 FQ	36570 MW	47380 TQ	USBLS	5/15
	Gary PMSA, IN	Y	32380 FQ	37260 MW	49280 TQ	USBLS	5/15
	Indianapolis-Carmel-Anderson MSA, IN	Y	34160 FQ	37450 MW	42010 TQ	USBLS	5/15
	Iowa	Y	31050 FQ	41010 MW	51230 TQ	USBLS	5/15
	Des Moines-West Des Moines MSA, IA	Y	38110 FQ	45400 MW	55050 TQ	USBLS	5/15
	Kansas	Y	26060 FQ	35740 MW	48420 TQ	USBLS	5/15
	Kentucky	Y	27770 FQ	33290 MW	39750 TQ	USBLS	5/15
	Louisiana	Y	29310 FQ	35510 MW	49800 TQ	USBLS	5/15
	New Orleans-Metairie MSA, LA	Y	37670 FQ	51190 MW	59800 TQ	USBLS	5/15
	Maine	Y	32440 FQ	43830 MW	51240 TQ	USBLS	5/15
	Maryland	Y	30487 AE	46092 MW	53894 AEX	MDBLS	4/16
	Baltimore-Columbia-Towson MSA, MD	Y	36840 FQ	49340 MW	58250 TQ	USBLS	5/15
	Massachusetts	Y	39080 FQ	50000 MW	59890 TQ	USBLS	5/15
	Boston-Cambridge-Newton NECTA, MA	Y	45120 FQ	53310 MW	62390 TQ	USBLS	5/15
	Worcester MSA, MA-CT	Y	36470 FQ	51660 MW	58930 TQ	USBLS	5/15
	Michigan	Y	33270 FQ	42210 MW	52220 TQ	USBLS	5/15
	Grand Rapids-Wyoming MSA, MI	Y	31820 FQ	40060 MW	46430 TQ	USBLS	5/15
	Minnesota	Y	34947 FQ	38668 MW	46573 TQ	MNBLS	1/16-3/16
	Minneapolis-St. Paul-Bloomington MSA, MN-WI	Y	35299 FQ	38658 MW	45245 TQ	MNBLS	1/16-3/16
	Mississippi	Y	17440 FQ	19390 MW	27550 TQ	USBLS	5/15
	Jackson MSA, MS	Y	17300 FQ	19100 MW	26240 TQ	USBLS	5/15
	Missouri	Y	31630 FQ	40820 MW	53760 TQ	USBLS	5/15
	Kansas City MSA, MO-KS	Y	31430 FQ	41430 MW	54240 TQ	USBLS	5/15
	St. Louis MSA, MO-IL	Y	32710 FQ	37790 MW	53570 TQ	USBLS	5/15
	Montana	Y	22110 FQ	33430 MW	39010 TQ	USBLS	5/15
	Nebraska	Y	23980 FQ	31130 MW	37985 TQ	NEBLS	7/16-9/16
	Omaha-Council Bluffs MSA, NE-IA	Y	27695 FQ	31725 MW	42485 TQ	NEBLS	7/16-9/16
	Nevada	Y	26840 FQ	44590 MW	60840 TQ	USBLS	5/15
	Las Vegas-Henderson-Paradise MSA, NV	Y	25470 FQ	43570 MW	61770 TQ	USBLS	5/15
	New Hampshire	H	17.72 AE	25.71 MW	28.46 AEX	NHBLS	6/16
	Nashua NECTA, NH-MA	Y	42900 FQ	52580 MW	59220 TQ	USBLS	5/15
	New Jersey	Y	36210 FQ	46320 MW	57600 TQ	USBLS	5/15
	Camden PMSA, NJ	Y	37970 FQ	50720 MW	57860 TQ	USBLS	5/15
	Newark PMSA, NJ-PA	Y	38890 FQ	51490 MW	62460 TQ	USBLS	5/15
	New Mexico	Y	32460 FQ	38610 MW	45230 TQ	USBLS	5/15
	Albuquerque MSA, NM	Y	35270 FQ	41740 MW	46130 TQ	USBLS	5/15
	New York	Y	29000 AE	41310 MW	52420 AEX	NYBLS	1/16-3/16
	Buffalo-Cheektowaga-Niagara Falls MSA, NY	Y	28280 FQ	32600 MW	37720 TQ	USBLS	5/15
	New York-Jersey City-White Plains PMSA, NY-NJ	Y	32750 FQ	38910 MW	51990 TQ	USBLS	5/15
	North Carolina	Y	22390 FQ	30130 MW	39360 TQ	USBLS	5/15
	Charlotte-Concord-Gastonia MSA, NC-SC	Y	18960 FQ	24090 MW	30770 TQ	USBLS	5/15
	North Dakota	Y	26650 FQ	31330 MW	38840 TQ	USBLS	5/15
	Fargo MSA, ND-MN	Y	27140 FQ	33820 MW	39250 TQ	USBLS	5/15
	Ohio	Y	29770 FQ	38450 MW	47730 TQ	USBLS	5/15
	Cincinnati MSA, OH-KY-IN	Y	31860 FQ	44530 MW	49620 TQ	USBLS	5/15
	Cleveland-Elyria MSA, OH	Y	29200 FQ	36830 MW	49410 TQ	USBLS	5/15

AE	Average entry wage	AWR	Average wage range	H	Hourly
AEX	Average experienced wage	B	Biweekly	HI	Highest wage paid
ATC	Average total compensation	D	Daily	HR	High end range
AW	Average wage paid	FQ	First quartile wage	LO	Lowest wage paid

LR	Low end range	MTC	Median total compensation	TCC	Total cash compensation
M	Monthly	MW	Median wage paid	TQ	Third quartile wage
MCC	Median cash compensation	MWR	Median wage range	W	Weekly
ME	Median entry wage	S	See annotated source	Y	Yearly

Occupation/Type/Industry	Location	Per	Low	Mid	High	Source	Date
Locksmith and Safe Repairer	Columbus MSA, OH	Y	30090 FQ	44100 MW	51150 TQ	USBLS	5/15
	Oklahoma	Y	25530 FQ	37450 MW	47060 TQ	USBLS	5/15
	Oklahoma City MSA, OK	Y	24340 FQ	33590 MW	47460 TQ	USBLS	5/15
	Tulsa MSA, OK	Y	32770 FQ	41320 MW	46310 TQ	USBLS	5/15
	Oregon	H	12.69 FQ	16.57 MW	20.58 TQ	ORBLS	2016
	Portland-Vancouver-Hillsboro MSA, OR-WA	Y	28120 FQ	36250 MW	47530 TQ	USBLS	5/15
	Pennsylvania	Y	32180 FQ	38310 MW	50630 TQ	USBLS	5/15
	Philadelphia PMSA, PA	Y	43940 FQ	51470 MW	58380 TQ	USBLS	5/15
	Pittsburgh MSA, PA	Y	32920 FQ	35900 MW	38880 TQ	USBLS	5/15
	Rhode Island	Y	37270 FQ	47770 MW	56010 TQ	USBLS	5/15
	Providence-Warwick MSA, RI-MA	Y	37270 FQ	47770 MW	56010 TQ	USBLS	5/15
	South Carolina	Y	25430 FQ	31550 MW	39450 TQ	USBLS	5/15
	Columbia MSA, SC	Y	23820 FQ	28140 MW	36020 TQ	USBLS	5/15
	Tennessee	Y	25990 FQ	33020 MW	43350 TQ	USBLS	5/15
	Memphis MSA, TN-MS-AR	Y	29500 FQ	37880 MW	46340 TQ	USBLS	5/15
	Nashville-Davidson–Murfreesboro–Franklin MSA, TN	Y	30920 FQ	38380 MW	44420 TQ	USBLS	5/15
	Texas	Y	28770 FQ	37660 MW	47220 TQ	USBLS	5/15
	Dallas-Plano-Irving PMSA, TX	Y	29360 FQ	37900 MW	59080 TQ	USBLS	5/15
	Fort Worth-Arlington PMSA, TX	Y	24800 FQ	42190 MW	46550 TQ	USBLS	5/15
	Houston-The Woodlands-Sugar Land MSA, TX	Y	29750 FQ	42290 MW	50680 TQ	USBLS	5/15
	San Antonio-New Braunfels MSA, TX	Y	31830 FQ	39100 MW	46400 TQ	USBLS	5/15
	Utah	Y	32230 FQ	40420 MW	51520 TQ	USBLS	5/15
	Provo-Orem MSA, UT	Y	29650 FQ	37360 MW	52260 TQ	USBLS	5/15
	Salt Lake City MSA, UT	Y	39320 FQ	47020 MW	57570 TQ	USBLS	5/15
	Virginia	Y	28280 FQ	41690 MW	50600 TQ	USBLS	5/15
	Richmond MSA, VA	Y	26700 FQ	36840 MW	48280 TQ	USBLS	5/15
	Virginia Beach-Norfolk-Newport News MSA, VA-NC	Y	34400 FQ	43950 MW	52230 TQ	USBLS	5/15
	Washington	H	14.03 FQ	21.77 MW	27.28 TQ	WABLS	3/16
	Tacoma-Lakewood PMSA, WA	H	10.50 FQ	11.41 MW	25.89 TQ	WABLS	3/16
	West Virginia	Y	24070 FQ	33800 MW	39590 TQ	USBLS	5/15
	Wisconsin	Y	31910 FQ	38140 MW	45450 TQ	USBLS	5/15
	Madison MSA, WI	Y	33510 FQ	36810 MW	40490 TQ	USBLS	5/15
	Milwaukee-Waukesha-West Allis MSA, WI	Y	33240 FQ	43120 MW	48490 TQ	USBLS	5/15
Locomotive Engineer	Alabama	Y	46478 AE	57576 AW	63129 AEX	ALBLS	6/16
	Arizona	Y	49420 FQ	58870 MW	73660 TQ	USBLS	5/15
	Arkansas	Y	46450 FQ	55700 MW	63520 TQ	USBLS	5/15
	California	H	20.91 FQ	24.23 MW	30.97 TQ	CABLS	1/16-3/16
	Colorado	Y	29200 FQ	43650 MW	51820 TQ	USBLS	5/15
	Delaware	Y	51590 FQ	60480 MW	72700 TQ	USBLS	5/15
	Florida	H	25.97 AE	28.56 MW	31.88 AEX	FLBLS	7/16-9/16
	Georgia	Y	50930 FQ	62970 MW	72770 TQ	USBLS	5/15
	Idaho	Y	45510 FQ	54140 MW	63150 TQ	USBLS	5/15
	Illinois	Y	51470 FQ	60350 MW	73120 TQ	USBLS	5/15
	Indiana	Y	46750 FQ	54810 MW	65340 TQ	USBLS	5/15
	Iowa	Y	50850 FQ	60660 MW	72340 TQ	USBLS	5/15
	Kansas	Y	43250 FQ	50370 MW	57530 TQ	USBLS	5/15
	Kentucky	Y	53010 FQ	61030 MW	74960 TQ	USBLS	5/15
	Louisiana	Y	49420 FQ	57990 MW	68940 TQ	USBLS	5/15
	Maine	Y	49140 FQ	61260 MW	72390 TQ	USBLS	5/15
	Maryland	Y	44205 AE	53424 MW	58034 AEX	MDBLS	4/16
	Massachusetts	Y	42630 FQ	50570 MW	58260 TQ	USBLS	5/15
	Michigan	Y	51120 FQ	63160 MW	74610 TQ	USBLS	5/15
	Minnesota	Y	51798 FQ	57021 MW	62253 TQ	MNBLS	1/16-3/16
	Mississippi	Y	52530 FQ	62600 MW	75700 TQ	USBLS	5/15
	Missouri	Y	47620 FQ	54930 MW	61080 TQ	USBLS	5/15
	Montana	Y	46950 FQ	53850 MW	59910 TQ	USBLS	5/15
	Nebraska	Y	50230 FQ	54535 MW	58840 TQ	NEBLS	7/16-9/16
	Nevada	Y	48610 FQ	57170 MW	64150 TQ	USBLS	5/15
	New Jersey	Y	60250 FQ	68760 MW	75210 TQ	USBLS	5/15
	New York	Y	49810 AE	65950 MW	70210 AEX	NYBLS	1/16-3/16
	North Carolina	Y	45080 FQ	52730 MW	60050 TQ	USBLS	5/15
	Ohio	Y	42130 FQ	45880 MW	49640 TQ	USBLS	5/15

Occupation/Type/Industry	Location	Per	Low	Mid	High	Source	Date
Locomotive Engineer	Oklahoma	Y	34830 FQ	38000 MW	50150 TQ	USBLS	5/15
	Pennsylvania	Y	46100 FQ	54850 MW	64200 TQ	USBLS	5/15
	South Carolina	Y	43770 FQ	48120 MW	54070 TQ	USBLS	5/15
	South Dakota	Y	46160 FQ	52820 MW	59380 TQ	USBLS	5/15
	Tennessee	Y	47570 FQ	54800 MW	60680 TQ	USBLS	5/15
	Texas	Y	42270 FQ	54270 MW	63110 TQ	USBLS	5/15
	Utah	Y	45570 FQ	53900 MW	64450 TQ	USBLS	5/15
	Virginia	Y	47360 FQ	54840 MW	61030 TQ	USBLS	5/15
	Washington	H	27.16 FQ	40.31 MW	45.69 TQ	WABLS	3/16
	West Virginia	Y	44340 FQ	50520 MW	58020 TQ	USBLS	5/15
	Wisconsin	Y	54070 FQ	63130 MW	74790 TQ	USBLS	5/15
	Wyoming	Y	50490 FQ	58750 MW	70180 TQ	USBLS	5/15
Locomotive Firer	Arkansas	Y	43480 FQ	46560 MW	49650 TQ	USBLS	5/15
	Pennsylvania	Y	45520 FQ	50970 MW	84460 TQ	USBLS	5/15
Lodging Manager	Alabama	Y	36376 AE	49577 AW	56178 AEX	ALBLS	6/16
	Birmingham-Hoover MSA, AL	Y	41675 AE	52375 AW	57726 AEX	ALBLS	6/16
	Alaska	Y	41930 FQ	56200 MW	75000 TQ	USBLS	5/15
	Anchorage MSA, AK	Y	48260 FQ	68830 MW	84780 TQ	USBLS	5/15
	Arizona	Y	61590 FQ	73130 MW	92150 TQ	USBLS	5/15
	Phoenix-Mesa-Scottsdale MSA, AZ	Y	67550 FQ	76420 MW	97520 TQ	USBLS	5/15
	Tucson MSA, AZ	Y	37170 FQ	50490 MW	71780 TQ	USBLS	5/15
	Arkansas	Y	29770 FQ	43570 MW	56860 TQ	USBLS	5/15
	Little Rock-North Little Rock-Conway MSA, AR	Y	31650 FQ	44070 MW	52060 TQ	USBLS	5/15
	California	H	20.11 FQ	26.48 MW	32.98 TQ	CABLS	1/16-3/16
	Anaheim-Santa Ana-Irvine PMSA, CA	H	23.38 FQ	28.74 MW	34.54 TQ	CABLS	1/16-3/16
	Los Angeles-Long Beach-Glendale PMSA, CA	H	20.24 FQ	25.16 MW	33.89 TQ	CABLS	1/16-3/16
	Oakland-Hayward-Berkeley PMSA, CA	H	27.64 FQ	33.43 MW	38.65 TQ	CABLS	1/16-3/16
	Riverside-San Bernardino-Ontario MSA, CA	H	16.37 FQ	19.88 MW	28.69 TQ	CABLS	1/16-3/16
	Sacramento–Roseville–Arden-Arcade MSA, CA	H	14.93 FQ	21.39 MW	28.94 TQ	CABLS	1/16-3/16
	San Diego-Carlsbad MSA, CA	H	25.37 FQ	27.92 MW	30.45 TQ	CABLS	1/16-3/16
	San Francisco-Redwood City-South San Francisco PMSA, CA	H	28.55 FQ	34.36 MW	39.52 TQ	CABLS	1/16-3/16
	Colorado	Y	44210 FQ	57880 MW	74190 TQ	USBLS	5/15
	Denver-Aurora-Lakewood MSA, CO	Y	44310 FQ	52230 MW	71180 TQ	USBLS	5/15
	Connecticut	Y		51372 MW		CTBLS	1/16-3/16
	Hartford-West Hartford-East Hartford MSA, CT	Y	37880 FQ	44180 MW	50240 TQ	USBLS	5/15
	Delaware	Y	52340 FQ	60140 MW	82240 TQ	USBLS	5/15
	Wilmington PMSA, DE-MD-NJ	Y	51260 FQ	60000 MW	83260 TQ	USBLS	5/15
	District of Columbia	Y	49770 FQ	64540 MW	110820 TQ	USBLS	5/15
	Washington-Arlington-Alexandria PMSA, DC-VA-MD-WV	Y	55860 FQ	82940 MW	99600 TQ	USBLS	5/15
	Florida	H	19.29 AE	27.33 MW	38.80 AEX	FLBLS	7/16-9/16
	Fort Lauderdale-Pompano Beach-Deerfield Beach PMSA, FL	H	18.82 AE	24.53 MW	31.48 AEX	FLBLS	7/16-9/16
	Miami-Miami Beach-Kendall PMSA, FL	H	23.46 AE	41.19 MW	63.34 AEX	FLBLS	7/16-9/16
	Orlando-Kissimmee-Sanford MSA, FL	H	21.90 AE	35.34 MW	45.75 AEX	FLBLS	7/16-9/16
	Tampa-St. Petersburg-Clearwater MSA, FL	H	21.42 AE	27.13 MW	30.05 AEX	FLBLS	7/16-9/16
	Georgia	Y	32100 FQ	43230 MW	62840 TQ	USBLS	5/15
	Atlanta-Sandy Springs-Roswell MSA, GA	Y	36710 FQ	48430 MW	71200 TQ	USBLS	5/15
	Augusta-Richmond County MSA, GA-SC	Y	33570 FQ	39720 MW	46420 TQ	USBLS	5/15
	Hawaii	Y	45670 FQ	56220 MW	75250 TQ	USBLS	5/15
	Urban Honolulu MSA, HI	Y	44530 FQ	54150 MW	66450 TQ	USBLS	5/15

AE	Average entry wage	AWR	Average wage range	H	Hourly	LR	Low end range	MTC	Median total compensation	TCC	Total cash compensation
AEX	Average experienced wage	B	Biweekly	HI	Highest wage paid	M	Monthly	MW	Median wage paid	TQ	Third quartile wage
ATC	Average total compensation	D	Daily	HR	High end range	MCC	Median cash compensation	MWR	Median wage range	W	Weekly
AW	Average wage paid	FQ	First quartile wage	LO	Lowest wage paid	ME	Median entry wage	S	See annotated source	Y	Yearly

927

Occupation/Type/Industry	Location	Per	Low	Mid	High	Source	Date
Lodging Manager	Idaho	Y	42840 FQ	52850 MW	65710 TQ	USBLS	5/15
	Boise City MSA, ID	Y	40060 FQ	52430 MW	60130 TQ	USBLS	5/15
	Illinois	Y	29970 FQ	39830 MW	53630 TQ	USBLS	5/15
	Chicago-Naperville-Arlington Heights PMSA, IL	Y	37650 FQ	45690 MW	56720 TQ	USBLS	5/15
	Lake County-Kenosha County PMSA, IL-WI	Y	50690 FQ	58050 MW	72270 TQ	USBLS	5/15
	Indiana	Y	26640 FQ	36930 MW	49000 TQ	USBLS	5/15
	Gary PMSA, IN	Y	31310 FQ	37370 MW	47050 TQ	USBLS	5/15
	Indianapolis-Carmel-Anderson MSA, IN	Y	23840 FQ	40400 MW	49670 TQ	USBLS	5/15
	Iowa	Y	26060 FQ	40820 MW	47510 TQ	USBLS	5/15
	Des Moines-West Des Moines MSA, IA	Y	39690 FQ	47170 MW	85240 TQ	USBLS	5/15
	Kansas	Y	30260 FQ	40230 MW	72210 TQ	USBLS	5/15
	Kentucky	Y	33980 FQ	44800 MW	61520 TQ	USBLS	5/15
	Louisville-Jefferson County MSA, KY-IN	Y	34190 FQ	38280 MW	53770 TQ	USBLS	5/15
	Louisiana	Y	38020 FQ	47100 MW	60210 TQ	USBLS	5/15
	Baton Rouge MSA, LA	Y	41220 FQ	44560 MW	47890 TQ	USBLS	5/15
	New Orleans-Metairie MSA, LA	Y	38520 FQ	52810 MW	64730 TQ	USBLS	5/15
	Maine	Y	37670 FQ	47770 MW	58970 TQ	USBLS	5/15
	Portland-South Portland MSA, ME	Y	35360 FQ	39430 MW	59980 TQ	USBLS	5/15
	Maryland	Y	41834 AE	73517 MW	89358 AEX	MDBLS	4/16
	Baltimore-Columbia-Towson MSA, MD	Y	53180 FQ	68920 MW	81050 TQ	USBLS	5/15
	Salisbury MSA, MD-DE	Y	33080 FQ	55380 MW	72410 TQ	USBLS	5/15
	Massachusetts	Y	51870 FQ	64560 MW	91480 TQ	USBLS	5/15
	Boston-Cambridge-Newton NECTA, MA	Y	57760 FQ	74220 MW	102610 TQ	USBLS	5/15
	Worcester MSA, MA-CT	Y	33980 FQ	58410 MW	74470 TQ	USBLS	5/15
	Michigan	Y	28560 FQ	34520 MW	53210 TQ	USBLS	5/15
	Detroit-Dearborn-Livonia PMSA, MI	Y	37810 FQ	51220 MW	73490 TQ	USBLS	5/15
	Grand Rapids-Wyoming MSA, MI	Y	27970 FQ	30890 MW	39460 TQ	USBLS	5/15
	Minnesota	Y	32810 FQ	40502 MW	55124 TQ	MNBLS	1/16-3/16
	Minneapolis-St. Paul-Bloomington MSA, MN-WI	Y	37484 FQ	49748 MW	69014 TQ	MNBLS	1/16-3/16
	Mississippi	Y	28340 FQ	40540 MW	54770 TQ	USBLS	5/15
	Jackson MSA, MS	Y	29670 FQ	43700 MW	50800 TQ	USBLS	5/15
	Missouri	Y	28610 FQ	40150 MW	59140 TQ	USBLS	5/15
	Kansas City MSA, MO-KS	Y	19730 FQ	33560 MW	67570 TQ	USBLS	5/15
	St. Louis MSA, MO-IL	Y	31880 FQ	46890 MW	64690 TQ	USBLS	5/15
	Montana	Y	28510 FQ	31870 MW	58130 TQ	USBLS	5/15
	Nebraska	Y	50580 FQ	58955 MW	105900 TQ	NEBLS	7/16-9/16
	Omaha-Council Bluffs MSA, NE-IA	Y	25315 FQ	45010 MW	55495 TQ	NEBLS	7/16-9/16
	Nevada	Y	50490 FQ	64070 MW	96850 TQ	USBLS	5/15
	Las Vegas-Henderson-Paradise MSA, NV	Y	55650 FQ	72410 MW	121160 TQ	USBLS	5/15
	New Hampshire	H	19.65 AE	27.98 MW	36.42 AEX	NHBLS	6/16
	New Jersey	Y	57210 FQ	68430 MW	81920 TQ	USBLS	5/15
	Camden PMSA, NJ	Y	54820 FQ	59110 MW	63400 TQ	USBLS	5/15
	New Mexico	Y	27780 FQ	43770 MW	53390 TQ	USBLS	5/15
	New York	Y	44370 AE	63160 MW	89670 AEX	NYBLS	1/16-3/16
	Buffalo-Cheektowaga-Niagara Falls MSA, NY	Y	29190 FQ	34440 MW	41820 TQ	USBLS	5/15
	Nassau County-Suffolk County PMSA, NY	Y	44790 FQ	49980 MW	60610 TQ	USBLS	5/15
	New York-Jersey City-White Plains PMSA, NY-NJ	Y	61730 FQ	72870 MW	91810 TQ	USBLS	5/15
	North Carolina	Y	37830 FQ	48570 MW	61050 TQ	USBLS	5/15
	Charlotte-Concord-Gastonia MSA, NC-SC	Y	35830 FQ	45710 MW	57620 TQ	USBLS	5/15
	Raleigh MSA, NC	Y	43370 FQ	54310 MW	83780 TQ	USBLS	5/15
	North Dakota	Y	48030 FQ	57730 MW	75730 TQ	USBLS	5/15
	Fargo MSA, ND-MN	Y	50210 FQ	55810 MW	61780 TQ	USBLS	5/15
	Ohio	Y	29930 FQ	40980 MW	57590 TQ	USBLS	5/15
	Cincinnati MSA, OH-KY-IN	Y	28700 FQ	36460 MW	57120 TQ	USBLS	5/15

AE	Average entry wage	AWR Average wage range	H Hourly	LR Low end range	MTC Median total compensation	TCC Total cash compensation
AEX	Average experienced wage	B Biweekly	HI Highest wage paid	M Monthly	MW Median wage paid	TQ Third quartile wage
ATC	Average total compensation	D Daily	HR High end range	MCC Median cash compensation	MWR Median wage range	W Weekly
AW	Average wage paid	FQ First quartile wage	LO Lowest wage paid	ME Median entry wage	S See annotated source	Y Yearly

Occupation/Type/Industry	Location	Per	Low	Mid	High	Source	Date
Lodging Manager	Cleveland-Elyria MSA, OH	Y	35620 FQ	46940 MW	60390 TQ	USBLS	5/15
	Columbus MSA, OH	Y	45150 FQ	66500 MW	100160 TQ	USBLS	5/15
	Oklahoma	Y	21750 FQ	38000 MW	47210 TQ	USBLS	5/15
	Oklahoma City MSA, OK	Y	22020 FQ	24560 MW	44870 TQ	USBLS	5/15
	Tulsa MSA, OK	Y	41650 FQ	45580 MW	49520 TQ	USBLS	5/15
	Oregon	H	20.80 FQ	26.22 MW	33.82 TQ	ORBLS	2016
	Portland-Vancouver-Hillsboro MSA, OR-WA	Y	34540 FQ	48210 MW	72160 TQ	USBLS	5/15
	Pennsylvania	Y	33800 FQ	40600 MW	56570 TQ	USBLS	5/15
	Harrisburg-Carlisle MSA, PA	Y	35940 FQ	43390 MW	50010 TQ	USBLS	5/15
	Montgomery County-Bucks County-Chester County PMSA, PA	Y	34830 FQ	51790 MW	79680 TQ	USBLS	5/15
	Philadelphia PMSA, PA	Y	39010 FQ	52500 MW	63660 TQ	USBLS	5/15
	Pittsburgh MSA, PA	Y	35410 FQ	39860 MW	49820 TQ	USBLS	5/15
	Rhode Island	Y	37670 FQ	80220 MW	90760 TQ	USBLS	5/15
	Providence-Warwick MSA, RI-MA	Y	37280 FQ	79840 MW	90530 TQ	USBLS	5/15
	South Carolina	Y	34880 FQ	44190 MW	55220 TQ	USBLS	5/15
	Charleston-North Charleston MSA, SC	Y	36870 FQ	51150 MW	59280 TQ	USBLS	5/15
	Greenville-Anderson-Mauldin MSA, SC	Y	29920 FQ	40080 MW	45830 TQ	USBLS	5/15
	South Dakota	Y	44310 FQ	49770 MW	57380 TQ	USBLS	5/15
	Tennessee	Y	32730 FQ	47460 MW	74340 TQ	USBLS	5/15
	Knoxville MSA, TN	Y	34420 FQ	53190 MW	66310 TQ	USBLS	5/15
	Memphis MSA, TN-MS-AR	Y	47690 FQ	62000 MW	86340 TQ	USBLS	5/15
	Nashville-Davidson–Murfreesboro–Franklin MSA, TN	Y	36750 FQ	57290 MW	79000 TQ	USBLS	5/15
	Texas	Y	36910 FQ	46400 MW	63520 TQ	USBLS	5/15
	Austin-Round Rock MSA, TX	Y	33150 FQ	59520 MW	83420 TQ	USBLS	5/15
	Dallas-Plano-Irving PMSA, TX	Y	30540 FQ	45190 MW	74220 TQ	USBLS	5/15
	Fort Worth-Arlington PMSA, TX	Y	43340 FQ	47230 MW	58140 TQ	USBLS	5/15
	Houston-The Woodlands-Sugar Land MSA, TX	Y	39110 FQ	47160 MW	67570 TQ	USBLS	5/15
	San Antonio-New Braunfels MSA, TX	Y	43420 FQ	48560 MW	60110 TQ	USBLS	5/15
	Utah	Y	29250 FQ	44240 MW	64450 TQ	USBLS	5/15
	Salt Lake City MSA, UT	Y	28450 FQ	39400 MW	67440 TQ	USBLS	5/15
	Vermont	Y	31010 FQ	55770 MW	72190 TQ	USBLS	5/15
	Burlington-South Burlington MSA, VT	Y	38150 FQ	54830 MW	72340 TQ	USBLS	5/15
	Virginia	Y	49990 FQ	74700 MW	96220 TQ	USBLS	5/15
	Richmond MSA, VA	Y	40220 FQ	48920 MW	61600 TQ	USBLS	5/15
	Virginia Beach-Norfolk-Newport News MSA, VA-NC	Y	41710 FQ	56500 MW	66650 TQ	USBLS	5/15
	Washington	H	19.26 FQ	23.62 MW	28.63 TQ	WABLS	3/16
	Seattle-Bellevue-Everett PMSA, WA	H	21.54 FQ	26.49 MW	29.88 TQ	WABLS	3/16
	Tacoma-Lakewood PMSA, WA	H	20.40 FQ	26.66 MW	30.18 TQ	WABLS	3/16
	West Virginia	Y	31220 FQ	42530 MW	56400 TQ	USBLS	5/15
	Huntington-Ashland MSA, WV-KY-OH	Y	28190 FQ	34900 MW	50960 TQ	USBLS	5/15
	Wisconsin	Y	36530 FQ	49510 MW	64090 TQ	USBLS	5/15
	Madison MSA, WI	Y	29280 FQ	48040 MW	62710 TQ	USBLS	5/15
	Milwaukee-Waukesha-West Allis MSA, WI	Y	37240 FQ	59790 MW	81570 TQ	USBLS	5/15
	Wyoming	Y	34820 FQ	45500 MW	56800 TQ	USBLS	5/15
	Puerto Rico	Y	36520 FQ	47920 MW	76090 TQ	USBLS	5/15
	San Juan-Carolina-Caguas MSA, PR	Y	47160 FQ	64150 MW	87760 TQ	USBLS	5/15
	Virgin Islands	Y	43650 FQ	64940 MW	96460 TQ	USBLS	5/15
	Guam	Y	20880 FQ	29310 MW	37200 TQ	USBLS	5/15
Log Grader and Scaler	Alabama	Y	28844 AE	38216 AW	42896 AEX	ALBLS	6/16
	Arkansas	Y	27450 FQ	35480 MW	43680 TQ	USBLS	5/15
	California	H	14.71 FQ	19.43 MW	22.29 TQ	CABLS	1/16-3/16
	Georgia	Y	28870 FQ	33460 MW	38460 TQ	USBLS	5/15
	Idaho	Y	36090 FQ	41270 MW	45850 TQ	USBLS	5/15
	Indiana	Y	30940 FQ	34640 MW	38180 TQ	USBLS	5/15

AE	Average entry wage	AWR	Average wage range	H	Hourly	LR	Low end range	MTC	Median total compensation	TCC Total cash compensation
AEX	Average experienced wage	B	Biweekly	HI	Highest wage paid	M	Monthly	MW	Median wage paid	TQ Third quartile wage
ATC	Average total compensation	D	Daily	HR	High end range	MCC	Median cash compensation	MWR	Median wage range	W Weekly
AW	Average wage paid	FQ	First quartile wage	LO	Lowest wage paid	ME	Median entry wage	S	See annotated source	Y Yearly

Occupation/Type/Industry	Location	Per	Low	Mid	High	Source	Date
Log Grader and Scaler	Kentucky	Y	22820 FQ	27270 MW	30220 TQ	USBLS	5/15
	Louisiana	Y	25750 FQ	29980 MW	37290 TQ	USBLS	5/15
	Maine	Y	32270 FQ	35230 MW	38180 TQ	USBLS	5/15
	Michigan	Y	32980 FQ	35640 MW	38310 TQ	USBLS	5/15
	Minnesota	Y	30220 FQ	37142 MW	44316 TQ	MNBLS	1/16-3/16
	Mississippi	Y	28750 FQ	35730 MW	44120 TQ	USBLS	5/15
	Missouri	Y	22480 FQ	29260 MW	42080 TQ	USBLS	5/15
	New Hampshire	H	13.69 AE	15.61 MW	17.93 AEX	NHBLS	6/16
	New York	Y	28840 AE	37750 MW	47030 AEX	NYBLS	1/16-3/16
	North Carolina	Y	26730 FQ	33880 MW	38410 TQ	USBLS	5/15
	Oklahoma	Y	34770 FQ	39620 MW	45340 TQ	USBLS	5/15
	Oregon	H	20.05 FQ	22.42 MW	25.01 TQ	ORBLS	2016
	Pennsylvania	Y	26520 FQ	30050 MW	37660 TQ	USBLS	5/15
	South Carolina	Y	25290 FQ	33100 MW	37530 TQ	USBLS	5/15
	Tennessee	Y	31210 FQ	36260 MW	44190 TQ	USBLS	5/15
	Texas	Y	25270 FQ	29240 MW	35480 TQ	USBLS	5/15
	Virginia	Y	21010 FQ	31590 MW	50630 TQ	USBLS	5/15
	Washington	H	19.70 FQ	22.09 MW	24.61 TQ	WABLS	3/16
	West Virginia	Y	27140 FQ	31560 MW	42270 TQ	USBLS	5/15
	Wisconsin	Y	27570 FQ	31990 MW	40420 TQ	USBLS	5/15
Logger	United States	Y		35160 MW		CBS02	2016
Logging Equipment Operator	Alabama	Y	24966 AE	34379 AW	39090 AEX	ALBLS	6/16
	Arkansas	Y	25180 FQ	34210 MW	46260 TQ	USBLS	5/15
	California	H	17.54 AE	20.19 MW	22.68 TQ	CABLS	1/16-3/16
	Colorado	Y	31080 FQ	37130 MW	45050 TQ	USBLS	5/15
	Florida	H	11.66 AE	17.32 MW	20.99 AEX	FLBLS	7/16-9/16
	Georgia	Y	30120 FQ	36160 MW	43380 TQ	USBLS	5/15
	Idaho	Y	35250 FQ	45570 MW	67870 TQ	USBLS	5/15
	Indiana	Y	25160 FQ	28260 MW	32240 TQ	USBLS	5/15
	Kentucky	Y	25750 FQ	29800 MW	36010 TQ	USBLS	5/15
	Louisiana	Y	29210 FQ	36980 MW	45260 TQ	USBLS	5/15
	Maine	Y	30710 FQ	36140 MW	42700 TQ	USBLS	5/15
	Maryland	Y	22914 AE	31722 MW	36126 AEX	MDBLS	4/16
	Michigan	Y	24910 FQ	28800 MW	35000 TQ	USBLS	5/15
	Minnesota	Y	31693 FQ	36082 MW	41703 TQ	MNBLS	1/16-3/16
	Mississippi	Y	29630 FQ	34590 MW	38690 TQ	USBLS	5/15
	Missouri	Y	19190 FQ	23590 MW	30840 TQ	USBLS	5/15
	Montana	Y	35350 FQ	40110 MW	46310 TQ	USBLS	5/15
	New Hampshire	H	14.59 AE	17.54 MW	18.98 AEX	NHBLS	6/16
	New York	Y	24190 AE	29320 MW	33400 AEX	NYBLS	1/16-3/16
	North Carolina	Y	27530 FQ	33890 MW	43380 TQ	USBLS	5/15
	Ohio	Y	22570 FQ	28180 MW	40930 TQ	USBLS	5/15
	Oklahoma	Y	29370 FQ	38320 MW	45990 TQ	USBLS	5/15
	Oregon	H	19.30 FQ	21.26 MW	23.22 TQ	ORBLS	2016
	Pennsylvania	Y	22960 FQ	28780 MW	36610 TQ	USBLS	5/15
	South Carolina	Y	30570 FQ	35740 MW	42230 TQ	USBLS	5/15
	South Dakota	Y	32010 FQ	36440 MW	42620 TQ	USBLS	5/15
	Tennessee	Y	23760 FQ	29090 MW	35540 TQ	USBLS	5/15
	Texas	Y	27420 FQ	40050 MW	47160 TQ	USBLS	5/15
	Vermont	Y	33540 FQ	43790 MW	51110 TQ	USBLS	5/15
	Virginia	Y	24830 FQ	31790 MW	40610 TQ	USBLS	5/15
	Washington	H	20.95 FQ	23.64 MW	27.32 TQ	WABLS	3/16
	West Virginia	Y	18500 FQ	21770 MW	29640 TQ	USBLS	5/15
	Wisconsin	Y	29740 FQ	35090 MW	40940 TQ	USBLS	5/15
	Wyoming	Y	29240 FQ	35900 MW	54440 TQ	USBLS	5/15
Logistical Services Officer							
Police Department, Municipal Government	Arcadia, CA	Y			50468 HI	CACIT	6/28/16
Logistician	Alabama	Y	59776 AE	86845 AW	100385 AEX	ALBLS	6/16
	Birmingham-Hoover MSA, AL	Y	47128 AE	69113 AW	80101 AEX	ALBLS	6/16
	Alaska	Y	68740 FQ	83150 MW	104590 TQ	USBLS	5/15
	Anchorage MSA, AK	Y	70350 FQ	84330 MW	105810 TQ	USBLS	5/15
	Arizona	Y	52790 FQ	67760 MW	87420 TQ	USBLS	5/15
	Phoenix-Mesa-Scottsdale MSA, AZ	Y	52160 FQ	67260 MW	89600 TQ	USBLS	5/15
	Tucson MSA, AZ	Y	56580 FQ	70210 MW	84660 TQ	USBLS	5/15
	Arkansas	Y	52130 FQ	61020 MW	75600 TQ	USBLS	5/15
	Little Rock-North Little Rock-Conway MSA, AR	Y	54890 FQ	66360 MW	83460 TQ	USBLS	5/15
	California	H	31.78 FQ	41.09 MW	51.18 TQ	CABLS	1/16-3/16

AE	Average entry wage	AWR	Average wage range	H	Hourly	LR	Low end range	MTC	Median total compensation	TCC	Total cash compensation
AEX	Average experienced wage	B	Biweekly	HI	Highest wage paid	M	Monthly	MW	Median wage paid	TQ	Third quartile wage
ATC	Average total compensation	D	Daily	HR	High end range	MCC	Median cash compensation	MWR	Median wage range	W	Weekly
AW	Average wage paid	FQ	First quartile wage	LO	Lowest wage paid	ME	Median entry wage	S	See annotated source	Y	Yearly

Logistician

Occupation/Type/Industry	Location	Per	Low	Mid	High	Source	Date
Logistician	Anaheim-Santa Ana-Irvine PMSA, CA	H	30.66 FQ	39.16 MW	49.96 TQ	CABLS	1/16-3/16
	Los Angeles-Long Beach-Glendale PMSA, CA	H	31.84 FQ	42.08 MW	51.11 TQ	CABLS	1/16-3/16
	Oakland-Hayward-Berkeley PMSA, CA	H	27.92 FQ	35.93 MW	48.48 TQ	CABLS	1/16-3/16
	Riverside-San Bernardino-Ontario MSA, CA	H	27.24 FQ	34.95 MW	46.16 TQ	CABLS	1/16-3/16
	Sacramento–Roseville–Arden-Arcade MSA, CA	H	30.69 FQ	38.47 MW	47.59 TQ	CABLS	1/16-3/16
	San Diego-Carlsbad MSA, CA	H	33.40 FQ	40.97 MW	48.33 TQ	CABLS	1/16-3/16
	San Francisco-Redwood City-South San Francisco PMSA, CA	H	32.52 FQ	39.69 MW	50.48 TQ	CABLS	1/16-3/16
	Colorado	Y	57630 FQ	74220 MW	94720 TQ	USBLS	5/15
	Denver-Aurora-Lakewood MSA, CO	Y	59240 FQ	74100 MW	95290 TQ	USBLS	5/15
	Connecticut	Y		74469 MW		CTBLS	1/16-3/16
	Bridgeport-Stamford-Norwalk MSA, CT	Y	67370 FQ	75290 MW	86300 TQ	USBLS	5/15
	Hartford-West Hartford-East Hartford MSA, CT	Y	64010 FQ	81230 MW	95360 TQ	USBLS	5/15
	District of Columbia	Y	76480 FQ	101140 MW	125200 TQ	USBLS	5/15
	Washington-Arlington-Alexandria PMSA, DC-VA-MD-WV	Y	75060 FQ	98960 MW	119440 TQ	USBLS	5/15
	Florida	H	23.03 AE	32.82 MW	40.62 AEX	FLBLS	7/16-9/16
	Fort Lauderdale-Pompano Beach-Deerfield Beach PMSA, FL	H	18.60 AE	28.10 MW	34.77 AEX	FLBLS	7/16-9/16
	Miami-Miami Beach-Kendall PMSA, FL	H	21.32 AE	28.85 MW	35.81 AEX	FLBLS	7/16-9/16
	Orlando-Kissimmee-Sanford MSA, FL	H	25.63 AE	36.57 MW	43.08 AEX	FLBLS	7/16-9/16
	Tampa-St. Petersburg-Clearwater MSA, FL	H	25.19 AE	34.35 MW	42.68 AEX	FLBLS	7/16-9/16
	Georgia	Y	53620 FQ	68440 MW	83820 TQ	USBLS	5/15
	Atlanta-Sandy Springs-Roswell MSA, GA	Y	48700 FQ	61860 MW	79480 TQ	USBLS	5/15
	Augusta-Richmond County MSA, GA-SC	Y	53230 FQ	65730 MW	82320 TQ	USBLS	5/15
	Hawaii	Y	65790 FQ	83150 MW	99380 TQ	USBLS	5/15
	Urban Honolulu MSA, HI	Y	65750 FQ	83360 MW	99390 TQ	USBLS	5/15
	Idaho	Y	50620 FQ	62190 MW	78190 TQ	USBLS	5/15
	Boise City MSA, ID	Y	54220 FQ	66790 MW	84040 TQ	USBLS	5/15
	Illinois	Y	53460 FQ	66600 MW	83610 TQ	USBLS	5/15
	Chicago-Naperville-Arlington Heights PMSA, IL	Y	51470 FQ	62200 MW	78290 TQ	USBLS	5/15
	Lake County-Kenosha County PMSA, IL-WI	Y	54290 FQ	68870 MW	82430 TQ	USBLS	5/15
	Indiana	Y	51750 FQ	68850 MW	86570 TQ	USBLS	5/15
	Gary PMSA, IN	Y	51020 FQ	67590 MW	81340 TQ	USBLS	5/15
	Indianapolis-Carmel-Anderson MSA, IN	Y	47910 FQ	67100 MW	85270 TQ	USBLS	5/15
	Iowa	Y	48070 FQ	58080 MW	71090 TQ	USBLS	5/15
	Des Moines-West Des Moines MSA, IA	Y	42160 FQ	52040 MW	64300 TQ	USBLS	5/15
	Kansas	Y	54920 FQ	66360 MW	81120 TQ	USBLS	5/15
	Wichita MSA, KS	Y	56660 FQ	66670 MW	80930 TQ	USBLS	5/15
	Kentucky	Y	57010 FQ	70270 MW	87920 TQ	USBLS	5/15
	Louisville-Jefferson County MSA, KY-IN	Y	59430 FQ	76860 MW	115120 TQ	USBLS	5/15
	Louisiana	Y	50960 FQ	68330 MW	88940 TQ	USBLS	5/15
	Baton Rouge MSA, LA	Y	53240 FQ	68440 MW	89790 TQ	USBLS	5/15
	New Orleans-Metairie MSA, LA	Y	50020 FQ	70460 MW	87690 TQ	USBLS	5/15
	Maine	Y	53130 FQ	64020 MW	75080 TQ	USBLS	5/15
	Portland-South Portland MSA, ME	Y	51440 FQ	62760 MW	73850 TQ	USBLS	5/15
	Maryland	Y	62841 AE	89256 MW	102463 AEX	MDBLS	4/16
	Baltimore-Columbia-Towson MSA, MD	Y	70080 FQ	84020 MW	99920 TQ	USBLS	5/15

AE	Average entry wage	**AWR**	Average wage range	**H**	Hourly
AEX	Average experienced wage	**B**	Biweekly	**HI**	Highest wage paid
ATC	Average total compensation	**D**	Daily	**HR**	High end range
AW	Average wage paid	**FQ**	First quartile wage	**LO**	Lowest wage paid

LR	Low end range	**MTC**	Median total compensation
M	Monthly	**MW**	Median wage paid
MCC	Median cash compensation	**MWR**	Median wage range
ME	Median entry wage	**S**	See annotated source

TCC	Total cash compensation
TQ	Third quartile wage
W	Weekly
Y	Yearly

Occupation/Type/Industry	Location	Per	Low	Mid	High	Source	Date
Logistician	Salisbury MSA, MD-DE	Y	64130 FQ	89080 MW	100940 TQ	USBLS	5/15
	Massachusetts	Y	59960 FQ	75860 MW	98160 TQ	USBLS	5/15
	Boston-Cambridge-Newton NECTA, MA	Y	60100 FQ	79090 MW	103400 TQ	USBLS	5/15
	Worcester MSA, MA-CT	Y	54650 FQ	66400 MW	79270 TQ	USBLS	5/15
	Michigan	Y	60400 FQ	81000 MW	99810 TQ	USBLS	5/15
	Detroit-Dearborn-Livonia PMSA, MI	Y	66090 FQ	88290 MW	103340 TQ	USBLS	5/15
	Grand Rapids-Wyoming MSA, MI	Y	49040 FQ	63310 MW	73670 TQ	USBLS	5/15
	Minnesota	Y	57024 FQ	71290 MW	88604 TQ	MNBLS	1/16-3/16
	Minneapolis-St. Paul-Bloomington MSA, MN-WI	Y	58314 FQ	72072 MW	89976 TQ	MNBLS	1/16-3/16
	Mississippi	Y	56460 FQ	69880 MW	87450 TQ	USBLS	5/15
	Jackson MSA, MS	Y	50360 FQ	59740 MW	72540 TQ	USBLS	5/15
	Missouri	Y	53050 FQ	67620 MW	88430 TQ	USBLS	5/15
	Kansas City MSA, MO-KS	Y	53010 FQ	65610 MW	81370 TQ	USBLS	5/15
	St. Louis MSA, MO-IL	Y	55390 FQ	72960 MW	92170 TQ	USBLS	5/15
	Montana	Y	53450 FQ	59090 MW	64790 TQ	USBLS	5/15
	Nebraska	Y	51645 FQ	61640 MW	78790 TQ	NEBLS	7/16-9/16
	Omaha-Council Bluffs MSA, NE-IA	Y	50370 FQ	59500 MW	77225 TQ	NEBLS	7/16-9/16
	Nevada	Y	54860 FQ	63160 MW	73560 TQ	USBLS	5/15
	Las Vegas-Henderson-Paradise MSA, NV	Y	54500 FQ	61320 MW	73980 TQ	USBLS	5/15
	New Hampshire	H	23.21 AE	34.88 MW	41.16 AEX	NHBLS	6/16
	Manchester NECTA, NH	H	29.34 AE	35.05 MW	38.30 AEX	NHBLS	6/16
	Nashua NECTA, NH-MA	Y	50200 FQ	73960 MW	91350 TQ	USBLS	5/15
	New Jersey	Y	60840 FQ	77020 MW	96400 TQ	USBLS	5/15
	Camden PMSA, NJ	Y	60030 FQ	72640 MW	89710 TQ	USBLS	5/15
	Newark PMSA, NJ-PA	Y	61450 FQ	79980 MW	100440 TQ	USBLS	5/15
	Trenton MSA, NJ	Y	61080 FQ	76530 MW	95980 TQ	USBLS	5/15
	New Mexico	Y	56460 FQ	69230 MW	86190 TQ	USBLS	5/15
	Albuquerque MSA, NM	Y	54190 FQ	65430 MW	80000 TQ	USBLS	5/15
	New York	Y	50520 AE	72160 MW	88230 AEX	NYBLS	1/16-3/16
	Buffalo-Cheektowaga-Niagara Falls MSA, NY	Y	50960 FQ	61020 MW	78470 TQ	USBLS	5/15
	Nassau County-Suffolk County PMSA, NY	Y	60970 FQ	76800 MW	97470 TQ	USBLS	5/15
	New York-Jersey City-White Plains PMSA, NY-NJ	Y	59880 FQ	75340 MW	94330 TQ	USBLS	5/15
	Rochester MSA, NY	Y	53940 FQ	66390 MW	84530 TQ	USBLS	5/15
	North Carolina	Y	54380 FQ	70270 MW	87890 TQ	USBLS	5/15
	Charlotte-Concord-Gastonia MSA, NC-SC	Y	52280 FQ	67370 MW	93640 TQ	USBLS	5/15
	Raleigh MSA, NC	Y	55260 FQ	71960 MW	89220 TQ	USBLS	5/15
	North Dakota	Y	51600 FQ	58560 MW	67460 TQ	USBLS	5/15
	Fargo MSA, ND-MN	Y	42970 FQ	54000 MW	63900 TQ	USBLS	5/15
	Ohio	Y	55070 FQ	69590 MW	85770 TQ	USBLS	5/15
	Cincinnati MSA, OH-KY-IN	Y	56180 FQ	70550 MW	86380 TQ	USBLS	5/15
	Cleveland-Elyria MSA, OH	Y	53500 FQ	67000 MW	80590 TQ	USBLS	5/15
	Columbus MSA, OH	Y	55920 FQ	66900 MW	77950 TQ	USBLS	5/15
	Oklahoma	Y	58560 FQ	72530 MW	84230 TQ	USBLS	5/15
	Oklahoma City MSA, OK	Y	60370 FQ	73070 MW	84230 TQ	USBLS	5/15
	Tulsa MSA, OK	Y	53200 FQ	66300 MW	81650 TQ	USBLS	5/15
	Oregon	H	24.63 FQ	33.29 MW	40.14 TQ	ORBLS	2016
	Portland-Vancouver-Hillsboro MSA, OR-WA	Y	51070 FQ	68740 MW	83630 TQ	USBLS	5/15
	Pennsylvania	Y	58350 FQ	74250 MW	89870 TQ	USBLS	5/15
	Allentown-Bethlehem-Easton MSA, PA-NJ	Y	51230 FQ	66890 MW	88140 TQ	USBLS	5/15
	Harrisburg-Carlisle MSA, PA	Y	58560 FQ	74880 MW	88900 TQ	USBLS	5/15
	Montgomery County-Bucks County-Chester County PMSA, PA	Y	60530 FQ	76700 MW	94040 TQ	USBLS	5/15
	Philadelphia PMSA, PA	Y	66630 FQ	81210 MW	94980 TQ	USBLS	5/15
	Pittsburgh MSA, PA	Y	55650 FQ	66510 MW	80690 TQ	USBLS	5/15
	Rhode Island	Y	56600 FQ	72800 MW	91800 TQ	USBLS	5/15
	Providence-Warwick MSA, RI-MA	Y	56960 FQ	72630 MW	90790 TQ	USBLS	5/15
	South Carolina	Y	50880 FQ	62680 MW	82630 TQ	USBLS	5/15

AE	Average entry wage	AWR	Average wage range	H	Hourly
AEX	Average experienced wage	B	Biweekly	HI	Highest wage paid
ATC	Average total compensation	D	Daily	HR	High end range
AW	Average wage paid	FQ	First quartile wage	LO	Lowest wage paid

LR	Low end range	MTC	Median total compensation	TCC	Total cash compensation
M	Monthly	MW	Median wage paid	TQ	Third quartile wage
MCC	Median cash compensation	MWR	Median wage range	W	Weekly
ME	Median entry wage	S	See annotated source	Y	Yearly

Occupation/Type/Industry	Location	Per	Low	Mid	High	Source	Date
Logistician	Charleston-North Charleston						
	MSA, SC	Y	50910 FQ	64960 MW	82540 TQ	USBLS	5/15
	Columbia MSA, SC	Y	51040 FQ	62470 MW	77220 TQ	USBLS	5/15
	Greenville-Anderson-Mauldin						
	MSA, SC	Y	52150 FQ	61290 MW	74960 TQ	USBLS	5/15
	South Dakota	Y	53240 FQ	61300 MW	75900 TQ	USBLS	5/15
	Tennessee	Y	47480 FQ	61760 MW	79550 TQ	USBLS	5/15
	Knoxville MSA, TN	Y	39110 FQ	51390 MW	79610 TQ	USBLS	5/15
	Memphis MSA, TN-MS-AR	Y	48810 FQ	61140 MW	77220 TQ	USBLS	5/15
	Nashville-Davidson–						
	Murfreesboro–Franklin						
	MSA, TN	Y	50300 FQ	61810 MW	76370 TQ	USBLS	5/15
	Texas	Y	58690 FQ	76190 MW	97950 TQ	USBLS	5/15
	Austin-Round Rock MSA, TX	Y	61970 FQ	80590 MW	102400 TQ	USBLS	5/15
	Dallas-Plano-Irving PMSA, TX	Y	56130 FQ	71410 MW	90910 TQ	USBLS	5/15
	Fort Worth-Arlington PMSA,						
	TX	Y	56280 FQ	75360 MW	95220 TQ	USBLS	5/15
	Houston-The Woodlands-						
	Sugar Land MSA, TX	Y	64290 FQ	82790 MW	112250 TQ	USBLS	5/15
	San Antonio-New Braunfels						
	MSA, TX	Y	58080 FQ	73330 MW	88920 TQ	USBLS	5/15
	Utah	Y	57450 FQ	71890 MW	84930 TQ	USBLS	5/15
	Ogden-Clearfield MSA, UT	Y	62470 FQ	74880 MW	86240 TQ	USBLS	5/15
	Provo-Orem MSA, UT	Y	48900 FQ	59150 MW	73180 TQ	USBLS	5/15
	Salt Lake City MSA, UT	Y	53240 FQ	65730 MW	86580 TQ	USBLS	5/15
	Vermont	Y	50010 FQ	60510 MW	74850 TQ	USBLS	5/15
	Burlington-South Burlington						
	MSA, VT	Y	50260 FQ	62280 MW	77770 TQ	USBLS	5/15
	Virginia	Y	64950 FQ	84240 MW	108510 TQ	USBLS	5/15
	Richmond MSA, VA	Y	59700 FQ	73990 MW	88330 TQ	USBLS	5/15
	Virginia Beach-Norfolk-						
	Newport News MSA, VA-NC	Y	59690 FQ	74190 MW	91260 TQ	USBLS	5/15
	Tacoma-Lakewood PMSA, WA	H	31.33 FQ	40.08 MW	49.56 TQ	WABLS	3/16
	West Virginia	Y	44090 FQ	58090 MW	75310 TQ	USBLS	5/15
	Huntington-Ashland MSA,						
	WV-KY-OH	Y	49740 FQ	67080 MW	97470 TQ	USBLS	5/15
	Wisconsin	Y	48780 FQ	60870 MW	76130 TQ	USBLS	5/15
	Madison MSA, WI	Y	47610 FQ	56430 MW	67130 TQ	USBLS	5/15
	Milwaukee-Waukesha-West						
	Allis MSA, WI	Y	53940 FQ	67610 MW	83420 TQ	USBLS	5/15
	Wyoming	Y	59300 FQ	72850 MW	86580 TQ	USBLS	5/15
	Cheyenne MSA, WY	Y	56450 FQ	68320 MW	77220 AEX	USBLS	5/15
	Puerto Rico	Y	34620 FQ	48130 MW	65150 TQ	USBLS	5/15
	San Juan-Carolina-Caguas						
	MSA, PR	Y	33870 FQ	46400 MW	62470 TQ	USBLS	5/15
Logistics Management							
Professional							
Lean Black Belt	United States	Y		96900 ATC		LOGMGT	2015
Lean Black Belt - Master	United States	Y		130200 ATC		LOGMGT	2015
Lean Champion	United States	Y		79200 ATC		LOGMGT	2015
Logistics Professional							
Fleet Operations	United States	Y		75000 MW		SCHAIN	2016
Import/Export Operations	United States	Y		80000 MW		SCHAIN	2016
Long-Haul Truck Driver	United States	Y		57000 AW		CNBC03	2015
Lottery Delivery Worker							
Lottery Commission, State Government	Ohio	H	20.98 LO		21.33 HI	OHGOV	2015
Lottery Security Specialist							
State Government	Maryland	Y	34390 LO		54186 HI	MDGOV	2016
Lounge Performer							
Cruise Ship	United States	M	2500 LO		4800 HI	CRU02	2016
Low Vision Specialist							
State Government	North Carolina	Y	41125 LO		66204 HI	NCGOV	7/1/16
Machine Design Engineer	United States	Y		99933 AW		MDES	2016
Machine Feeder and Offbearer	Alabama	Y	20303 AE	30464 AW	35535 AEX	ALBLS	6/16

AE Average entry wage	**AWR** Average wage range	**H** Hourly	**LR** Low end range	**MTC** Median total compensation	**TCC** Total cash compensation
AEX Average experienced wage	**B** Biweekly	**HI** Highest wage paid	**M** Monthly	**MW** Median wage paid	**TQ** Third quartile wage
ATC Average total compensation	**D** Daily	**HR** High end range	**MCC** Median cash compensation	**MWR** Median wage range	**W** Weekly
AW Average wage paid	**FQ** First quartile wage	**LO** Lowest wage paid	**ME** Median entry wage	**S** See annotated source	**Y** Yearly

Occupation/Type/Industry	Location	Per	Low	Mid	High	Source	Date
Machine Feeder and Offbearer	Birmingham-Hoover MSA, AL	Y	21578 AE	34589 AW	41099 AEX	ALBLS	6/16
	Alaska	Y	18600 FQ	19000 MW	19530 TQ	USBLS	5/15
	Arizona	Y	29480 FQ	40580 MW	45930 TQ	USBLS	5/15
	Phoenix-Mesa-Scottsdale MSA, AZ	Y	29890 FQ	40700 MW	45900 TQ	USBLS	5/15
	Arkansas	Y	20720 FQ	23290 MW	28600 TQ	USBLS	5/15
	California	H	10.55 FQ	13.50 MW	18.05 TQ	CABLS	1/16-3/16
	Anaheim-Santa Ana-Irvine PMSA, CA	H	9.68 FQ	11.22 MW	14.43 TQ	CABLS	1/16-3/16
	Los Angeles-Long Beach-Glendale PMSA, CA	H	9.98 FQ	12.09 MW	15.65 TQ	CABLS	1/16-3/16
	Oakland-Hayward-Berkeley PMSA, CA	H	10.96 FQ	15.21 MW	18.10 TQ	CABLS	1/16-3/16
	Riverside-San Bernardino-Ontario MSA, CA	H	10.53 FQ	11.81 MW	17.39 TQ	CABLS	1/16-3/16
	Sacramento–Roseville–Arden-Arcade MSA, CA	H	9.92 FQ	12.91 MW	15.24 TQ	CABLS	1/16-3/16
	San Diego-Carlsbad MSA, CA	H	9.92 FQ	13.11 MW	16.78 TQ	CABLS	1/16-3/16
	San Francisco-Redwood City-South San Francisco PMSA, CA	H	10.33 FQ	13.80 MW	18.37 TQ	CABLS	1/16-3/16
	Colorado	Y	22530 FQ	35550 MW	43630 TQ	USBLS	5/15
	Denver-Aurora-Lakewood MSA, CO	Y	19030 FQ	22410 MW	29570 TQ	USBLS	5/15
	Connecticut	Y		27628 MW		CTBLS	1/16-3/16
	Bridgeport-Stamford-Norwalk MSA, CT	Y	21830 FQ	27500 MW	33710 TQ	USBLS	5/15
	Hartford-West Hartford-East Hartford MSA, CT	Y	23490 FQ	27230 MW	31240 TQ	USBLS	5/15
	Delaware	Y	36980 FQ	43300 MW	47210 TQ	USBLS	5/15
	Wilmington PMSA, DE-MD-NJ	Y	25480 FQ	28850 MW	33010 TQ	USBLS	5/15
	Washington-Arlington-Alexandria PMSA, DC-VA-MD-WV	Y	25100 FQ	32970 MW	40730 TQ	USBLS	5/15
	Florida	H	10.64 AE	17.68 MW	20.05 AEX	FLBLS	7/16-9/16
	Fort Lauderdale-Pompano Beach-Deerfield Beach PMSA, FL	H	9.21 AE	13.36 MW	16.26 AEX	FLBLS	7/16-9/16
	Miami-Miami Beach-Kendall PMSA, FL	H	9.03 AE	11.59 MW	13.24 AEX	FLBLS	7/16-9/16
	Orlando-Kissimmee-Sanford MSA, FL	H	10.38 AE	14.46 MW	17.21 AEX	FLBLS	7/16-9/16
	Tampa-St. Petersburg-Clearwater MSA, FL	H	10.94 AE	17.69 MW	19.65 AEX	FLBLS	7/16-9/16
	Georgia	Y	22470 FQ	27220 MW	33730 TQ	USBLS	5/15
	Atlanta-Sandy Springs-Roswell MSA, GA	Y	21450 FQ	24900 MW	29570 TQ	USBLS	5/15
	Augusta-Richmond County MSA, GA-SC	Y	21300 FQ	24710 MW	30690 TQ	USBLS	5/15
	Hawaii	Y	22590 FQ	26960 MW	31880 TQ	USBLS	5/15
	Urban Honolulu MSA, HI	Y	22270 FQ	26410 MW	32540 TQ	USBLS	5/15
	Idaho	Y	27400 FQ	33480 MW	41540 TQ	USBLS	5/15
	Boise City MSA, ID	Y	25530 FQ	28920 MW	33980 TQ	USBLS	5/15
	Illinois	Y	21830 FQ	29350 MW	38390 TQ	USBLS	5/15
	Chicago-Naperville-Arlington Heights PMSA, IL	Y	20370 FQ	24010 MW	34030 TQ	USBLS	5/15
	Lake County-Kenosha County PMSA, IL-WI	Y	23130 FQ	28880 MW	36440 TQ	USBLS	5/15
	Indiana	Y	23060 FQ	29040 MW	37330 TQ	USBLS	5/15
	Gary PMSA, IN	Y	24090 FQ	28790 MW	35070 TQ	USBLS	5/15
	Indianapolis-Carmel-Anderson MSA, IN	Y	22530 FQ	28110 MW	35920 TQ	USBLS	5/15
	Iowa	Y	23580 FQ	28880 MW	36190 TQ	USBLS	5/15
	Des Moines-West Des Moines MSA, IA	Y	25660 FQ	28360 MW	31070 TQ	USBLS	5/15
	Kansas	Y	25320 FQ	31260 MW	42210 TQ	USBLS	5/15
	Wichita MSA, KS	Y	26180 FQ	28410 MW	30640 TQ	USBLS	5/15
	Kentucky	Y	23230 FQ	28730 MW	36580 TQ	USBLS	5/15
	Louisville-Jefferson County MSA, KY-IN	Y	27020 FQ	33420 MW	38800 TQ	USBLS	5/15
	Louisiana	Y	32980 FQ	38500 MW	44540 TQ	USBLS	5/15

AE	Average entry wage	AWR	Average wage range	H	Hourly
AEX	Average experienced wage	B	Biweekly	HI	Highest wage paid
ATC	Average total compensation	D	Daily	HR	High end range
AW	Average wage paid	FQ	First quartile wage	LO	Lowest wage paid

LR	Low end range	MTC	Median total compensation
M	Monthly	MW	Median wage paid
MCC	Median cash compensation	MWR	Median wage range
ME	Median entry wage	S	See annotated source

TCC	Total cash compensation		
TQ	Third quartile wage		
W	Weekly		
Y	Yearly		

Occupation/Type/Industry	Location	Per	Low	Mid	High	Source	Date
Machine Feeder and Offbearer	Baton Rouge MSA, LA	Y	21230 FQ	23400 MW	27040 TQ	USBLS	5/15
	New Orleans-Metairie MSA, LA	Y	22350 FQ	24870 MW	30080 TQ	USBLS	5/15
	Maine	Y	23380 FQ	30490 MW	42800 TQ	USBLS	5/15
	Portland-South Portland MSA, ME	Y	21830 FQ	26880 MW	33450 TQ	USBLS	5/15
	Maryland	Y	20326 AE	27885 MW	31664 AEX	MDBLS	4/16
	Baltimore-Columbia-Towson MSA, MD	Y	20960 FQ	24400 MW	32730 TQ	USBLS	5/15
	Massachusetts	Y	23850 FQ	30180 MW	37030 TQ	USBLS	5/15
	Boston-Cambridge-Newton NECTA, MA	Y	22210 FQ	28430 MW	35230 TQ	USBLS	5/15
	Worcester MSA, MA-CT	Y	25980 FQ	31340 MW	40460 TQ	USBLS	5/15
	Michigan	Y	21780 FQ	29180 MW	42360 TQ	USBLS	5/15
	Grand Rapids-Wyoming MSA, MI	Y	19580 FQ	25000 MW	31870 TQ	USBLS	5/15
	Minnesota	Y	27532 FQ	34468 MW	42271 TQ	MNBLS	1/16-3/16
	Minneapolis-St. Paul-Bloomington MSA, MN-WI	Y	30244 FQ	36777 MW	44489 TQ	MNBLS	1/16-3/16
	Mississippi	Y	19560 FQ	24150 MW	35500 TQ	USBLS	5/15
	Jackson MSA, MS	Y	17620 FQ	20290 MW	26710 TQ	USBLS	5/15
	Missouri	Y	28020 FQ	37550 MW	47630 TQ	USBLS	5/15
	Kansas City MSA, MO-KS	Y	33220 FQ	47080 MW	55680 TQ	USBLS	5/15
	St. Louis MSA, MO-IL	Y	27850 FQ	34640 MW	42750 TQ	USBLS	5/15
	Montana	Y	23090 FQ	27720 MW	33930 TQ	USBLS	5/15
	Nebraska	Y	28515 FQ	33895 MW	38530 TQ	NEBLS	7/16-9/16
	Omaha-Council Bluffs MSA, NE-IA	Y	27420 FQ	33335 MW	37930 TQ	NEBLS	7/16-9/16
	Nevada	Y	35660 FQ	42810 MW	46520 TQ	USBLS	5/15
	Las Vegas-Henderson-Paradise MSA, NV	Y	32000 FQ	38520 MW	44890 TQ	USBLS	5/15
	New Hampshire	H	14.06 AE	19.10 MW	20.86 AEX	NHBLS	6/16
	Nashua NECTA, NH-MA	Y	25370 FQ	30380 MW	37490 TQ	USBLS	5/15
	New Jersey	Y	18840 FQ	21270 MW	29290 TQ	USBLS	5/15
	Camden PMSA, NJ	Y	23360 FQ	28720 MW	36870 TQ	USBLS	5/15
	Newark PMSA, NJ-PA	Y	18630 FQ	20110 MW	25090 TQ	USBLS	5/15
	Trenton MSA, NJ	Y	26860 FQ	29200 MW	31550 TQ	USBLS	5/15
	New Mexico	Y	37260 FQ	42860 MW	46990 TQ	USBLS	5/15
	Albuquerque MSA, NM	Y	39310 FQ	43480 MW	47300 TQ	USBLS	5/15
	New York	Y	21000 AE	29040 MW	36070 AEX	NYBLS	1/16-3/16
	Buffalo-Cheektowaga-Niagara Falls MSA, NY	Y	20590 FQ	23030 MW	27710 TQ	USBLS	5/15
	Nassau County-Suffolk County PMSA, NY	Y	20780 FQ	26500 MW	31780 TQ	USBLS	5/15
	New York-Jersey City-White Plains PMSA, NY-NJ	Y	19020 FQ	21040 MW	32150 TQ	USBLS	5/15
	Rochester MSA, NY	Y	21650 FQ	25040 MW	33040 TQ	USBLS	5/15
	North Carolina	Y	21480 FQ	27100 MW	35990 TQ	USBLS	5/15
	Charlotte-Concord-Gastonia MSA, NC-SC	Y	20030 FQ	24170 MW	29590 TQ	USBLS	5/15
	Raleigh MSA, NC	Y	20900 FQ	23650 MW	28170 TQ	USBLS	5/15
	North Dakota	Y	18920 FQ	23540 MW	34030 TQ	USBLS	5/15
	Ohio	Y	21540 FQ	29860 MW	42970 TQ	USBLS	5/15
	Cincinnati MSA, OH-KY-IN	Y	24800 FQ	32190 MW	43240 TQ	USBLS	5/15
	Cleveland-Elyria MSA, OH	Y	27520 FQ	35930 MW	53260 TQ	USBLS	5/15
	Columbus MSA, OH	Y	19660 FQ	21920 MW	24240 TQ	USBLS	5/15
	Oklahoma	Y	30530 FQ	38120 MW	44510 TQ	USBLS	5/15
	Oklahoma City MSA, OK	Y	17950 FQ	27600 MW	36580 TQ	USBLS	5/15
	Tulsa MSA, OK	Y	25560 FQ	31940 MW	38640 TQ	USBLS	5/15
	Oregon	H	10.97 FQ	14.72 MW	17.82 TQ	ORBLS	2016
	Portland-Vancouver-Hillsboro MSA, OR-WA	Y	21010 FQ	24970 MW	33390 TQ	USBLS	5/15
	Pennsylvania	Y	26260 FQ	33890 MW	41710 TQ	USBLS	5/15
	Allentown-Bethlehem-Easton MSA, PA-NJ	Y	24920 FQ	30170 MW	37220 TQ	USBLS	5/15
	Harrisburg-Carlisle MSA, PA	Y	28940 FQ	33820 MW	38010 TQ	USBLS	5/15
	Montgomery County-Bucks County-Chester County PMSA, PA	Y	24500 FQ	30920 MW	38740 TQ	USBLS	5/15
	Philadelphia PMSA, PA	Y	25400 FQ	29810 MW	39030 TQ	USBLS	5/15
	Pittsburgh MSA, PA	Y	25060 FQ	28950 MW	35680 TQ	USBLS	5/15
	Rhode Island	Y	20630 FQ	26020 MW	35110 TQ	USBLS	5/15

Occupation/Type/Industry	Location	Per	Low	Mid	High	Source	Date
Machine Feeder and Offbearer	Providence-Warwick MSA, RI-MA	Y	20750 FQ	25130 MW	33950 TQ	USBLS	5/15
	South Carolina	Y	22630 FQ	31750 MW	38220 TQ	USBLS	5/15
	Charleston-North Charleston MSA, SC	Y	33750 FQ	36230 MW	38710 TQ	USBLS	5/15
	Columbia MSA, SC	Y	26100 FQ	32740 MW	38910 TQ	USBLS	5/15
	Greenville-Anderson-Mauldin MSA, SC	Y	24160 FQ	32740 MW	36360 TQ	USBLS	5/15
	South Dakota	Y	22030 FQ	25620 MW	30270 TQ	USBLS	5/15
	Sioux Falls MSA, SD	Y	23300 FQ	26920 MW	31020 TQ	USBLS	5/15
	Tennessee	Y	21140 FQ	25060 MW	31030 TQ	USBLS	5/15
	Knoxville MSA, TN	Y	21080 FQ	23340 MW	26730 TQ	USBLS	5/15
	Memphis MSA, TN-MS-AR	Y	24700 FQ	30630 MW	35720 TQ	USBLS	5/15
	Nashville-Davidson–Murfreesboro–Franklin MSA, TN	Y	20980 FQ	24320 MW	28050 TQ	USBLS	5/15
	Texas	Y	21910 FQ	29160 MW	36950 TQ	USBLS	5/15
	Austin-Round Rock MSA, TX	Y	20720 FQ	25340 MW	28240 TQ	USBLS	5/15
	Dallas-Plano-Irving PMSA, TX	Y	23030 FQ	33930 MW	41170 TQ	USBLS	5/15
	Fort Worth-Arlington PMSA, TX	Y	21300 FQ	27010 MW	34970 TQ	USBLS	5/15
	Houston-The Woodlands-Sugar Land MSA, TX	Y	19660 FQ	24790 MW	34450 TQ	USBLS	5/15
	San Antonio-New Braunfels MSA, TX	Y	23180 FQ	30720 MW	35940 TQ	USBLS	5/15
	Utah	Y	32260 FQ	38000 MW	44120 TQ	USBLS	5/15
	Ogden-Clearfield MSA, UT	Y	30900 FQ	37260 MW	43930 TQ	USBLS	5/15
	Salt Lake City MSA, UT	Y	27070 FQ	34460 MW	39120 TQ	USBLS	5/15
	Vermont	Y	22060 FQ	28810 MW	35140 TQ	USBLS	5/15
	Virginia	Y	23420 FQ	29180 MW	38300 TQ	USBLS	5/15
	Richmond MSA, VA	Y	23730 FQ	29050 MW	35570 TQ	USBLS	5/15
	Virginia Beach-Norfolk-Newport News MSA, VA-NC	Y	24740 FQ	32110 MW	40910 TQ	USBLS	5/15
	Washington	H	12.57 FQ	14.97 MW	19.01 TQ	WABLS	3/16
	Seattle-Bellevue-Everett PMSA, WA	H	12.00 FQ	14.28 MW	16.99 TQ	WABLS	3/16
	Tacoma-Lakewood PMSA, WA	H	12.48 FQ	14.67 MW	18.25 TQ	WABLS	3/16
	West Virginia	Y	24840 FQ	30180 MW	36050 TQ	USBLS	5/15
	Wisconsin	Y	22100 FQ	26910 MW	35520 TQ	USBLS	5/15
	Madison MSA, WI	Y	24240 FQ	27320 MW	30250 TQ	USBLS	5/15
	Milwaukee-Waukesha-West Allis MSA, WI	Y	21240 FQ	24340 MW	31120 TQ	USBLS	5/15
	Wyoming	Y	32190 FQ	36350 MW	40850 TQ	USBLS	5/15
	Puerto Rico	Y	19260 FQ	21710 MW	23740 TQ	USBLS	5/15
	San Juan-Carolina-Caguas MSA, PR	Y	20180 FQ	21980 MW	23780 TQ	USBLS	5/15
Machinist	Alabama	Y	27217 AE	41036 AW	47935 AEX	ALBLS	6/16
	Birmingham-Hoover MSA, AL	Y	28420 AE	41982 AW	48768 AEX	ALBLS	6/16
	Alaska	Y	39610 FQ	48080 MW	64290 TQ	USBLS	5/15
	Anchorage MSA, AK	Y	45450 FQ	53550 MW	63250 TQ	USBLS	5/15
	Arizona	Y	28790 FQ	39220 MW	50320 TQ	USBLS	5/15
	Phoenix-Mesa-Scottsdale MSA, AZ	Y	28910 FQ	40160 MW	51180 TQ	USBLS	5/15
	Tucson MSA, AZ	Y	30830 FQ	38180 MW	47180 TQ	USBLS	5/15
	Arkansas	Y	29700 FQ	37110 MW	46610 TQ	USBLS	5/15
	Little Rock-North Little Rock-Conway MSA, AR	Y	33250 FQ	38450 MW	47790 TQ	USBLS	5/15
	California	H	14.29 FQ	19.55 MW	26.77 TQ	CABLS	1/16-3/16
	Anaheim-Santa Ana-Irvine PMSA, CA	H	14.34 FQ	18.37 MW	24.32 TQ	CABLS	1/16-3/16
	Los Angeles-Long Beach-Glendale PMSA, CA	H	12.18 FQ	16.96 MW	23.45 TQ	CABLS	1/16-3/16
	Oakland-Hayward-Berkeley PMSA, CA	H	18.90 FQ	26.78 MW	33.47 TQ	CABLS	1/16-3/16
	Riverside-San Bernardino-Ontario MSA, CA	H	12.43 FQ	16.52 MW	22.27 TQ	CABLS	1/16-3/16
	Sacramento–Roseville–Arden-Arcade MSA, CA	H	18.82 FQ	24.48 MW	31.74 TQ	CABLS	1/16-3/16
	San Diego-Carlsbad MSA, CA	H	17.49 FQ	24.62 MW	28.62 TQ	CABLS	1/16-3/16

AE	Average entry wage	AWR	Average wage range	H	Hourly	LR	Low end range	MTC	Median total compensation	TCC	Total cash compensation
AEX	Average experienced wage	B	Biweekly	HI	Highest wage paid	M	Monthly	MW	Median wage paid	TQ	Third quartile wage
ATC	Average total compensation	D	Daily	HR	High end range	MCC	Median cash compensation	MWR	Median wage range	W	Weekly
AW	Average wage paid	FQ	First quartile wage	LO	Lowest wage paid	ME	Median entry wage	S	See annotated source	Y	Yearly

Occupation/Type/Industry	Location	Per	Low	Mid	High	Source	Date
Machinist	San Francisco-Redwood City-South San Francisco PMSA, CA	H	16.92 FQ	25.23 MW	39.24 TQ	CABLS	1/16-3/16
	Colorado	Y	33020 FQ	43530 MW	54820 TQ	USBLS	5/15
	Denver-Aurora-Lakewood MSA, CO	Y	32170 FQ	44010 MW	55330 TQ	USBLS	5/15
	Connecticut	Y		46628 MW		CTBLS	1/16-3/16
	Bridgeport-Stamford-Norwalk MSA, CT	Y	40020 FQ	52460 MW	60470 TQ	USBLS	5/15
	Hartford-West Hartford-East Hartford MSA, CT	Y	36340 FQ	46590 MW	57550 TQ	USBLS	5/15
	Delaware	Y	42300 FQ	53440 MW	60930 TQ	USBLS	5/15
	Wilmington PMSA, DE-MD-NJ	Y	43750 FQ	55210 MW	64770 TQ	USBLS	5/15
	District of Columbia	Y	54450 FQ	58850 MW	62980 TQ	USBLS	5/15
	Washington-Arlington-Alexandria PMSA, DC-VA-MD-WV	Y	41790 FQ	52130 MW	60220 TQ	USBLS	5/15
	Florida	H	12.68 AE	18.73 MW	22.13 AEX	FLBLS	7/16-9/16
	Fort Lauderdale-Pompano Beach-Deerfield Beach PMSA, FL	H	12.49 AE	18.71 MW	22.06 AEX	FLBLS	7/16-9/16
	Miami-Miami Beach-Kendall PMSA, FL	H	10.22 AE	16.42 MW	20.93 AEX	FLBLS	7/16-9/16
	Orlando-Kissimmee-Sanford MSA, FL	H	13.10 AE	19.31 MW	22.57 AEX	FLBLS	7/16-9/16
	Tampa-St. Petersburg-Clearwater MSA, FL	H	13.91 AE	19.40 MW	22.39 AEX	FLBLS	7/16-9/16
	Georgia	Y	29460 FQ	37120 MW	48870 TQ	USBLS	5/15
	Atlanta-Sandy Springs-Roswell MSA, GA	Y	28420 FQ	36290 MW	49040 TQ	USBLS	5/15
	Augusta-Richmond County MSA, GA-SC	Y	33450 FQ	42300 MW	49330 TQ	USBLS	5/15
	Hawaii	Y	43800 FQ	59540 MW	70330 TQ	USBLS	5/15
	Urban Honolulu MSA, HI	Y	49820 FQ	62800 MW	70330 TQ	USBLS	5/15
	Idaho	Y	33420 FQ	41470 MW	49180 TQ	USBLS	5/15
	Boise City MSA, ID	Y	33290 FQ	41290 MW	48470 TQ	USBLS	5/15
	Illinois	Y	28350 FQ	36620 MW	48030 TQ	USBLS	5/15
	Chicago-Naperville-Arlington Heights PMSA, IL	Y	28890 FQ	36620 MW	48230 TQ	USBLS	5/15
	Lake County-Kenosha County PMSA, IL-WI	Y	23720 FQ	33410 MW	47440 TQ	USBLS	5/15
	Indiana	Y	31770 FQ	39410 MW	48390 TQ	USBLS	5/15
	Gary PMSA, IN	Y	34160 FQ	40240 MW	47390 TQ	USBLS	5/15
	Indianapolis-Carmel-Anderson MSA, IN	Y	33850 FQ	40970 MW	49410 TQ	USBLS	5/15
	Iowa	Y	29900 FQ	36610 MW	44310 TQ	USBLS	5/15
	Des Moines-West Des Moines MSA, IA	Y	31730 FQ	39490 MW	47930 TQ	USBLS	5/15
	Kansas	Y	33050 FQ	38630 MW	47280 TQ	USBLS	5/15
	Wichita MSA, KS	Y	33790 FQ	38020 MW	45680 TQ	USBLS	5/15
	Kentucky	Y	32790 FQ	41890 MW	51390 TQ	USBLS	5/15
	Louisville-Jefferson County MSA, KY-IN	Y	35180 FQ	45500 MW	54820 TQ	USBLS	5/15
	Louisiana	Y	36540 FQ	44730 MW	54950 TQ	USBLS	5/15
	Baton Rouge MSA, LA	Y	39670 FQ	51530 MW	60460 TQ	USBLS	5/15
	New Orleans-Metairie MSA, LA	Y	37660 FQ	47490 MW	60260 TQ	USBLS	5/15
	Maine	Y	37240 FQ	44730 MW	52230 TQ	USBLS	5/15
	Portland-South Portland MSA, ME	Y	34200 FQ	39020 MW	46380 TQ	USBLS	5/15
	Maryland	Y	32330 AE	47075 MW	54448 AEX	MDBLS	4/16
	Baltimore-Columbia-Towson MSA, MD	Y	38720 FQ	49000 MW	58180 TQ	USBLS	5/15
	Salisbury MSA, MD-DE	Y	34470 FQ	41000 MW	48930 TQ	USBLS	5/15
	Massachusetts	Y	38950 FQ	47710 MW	59200 TQ	USBLS	5/15
	Boston-Cambridge-Newton NECTA, MA	Y	39190 FQ	48790 MW	60960 TQ	USBLS	5/15
	Worcester MSA, MA-CT	Y	38290 FQ	46160 MW	55350 TQ	USBLS	5/15
	Michigan	Y	31530 FQ	39610 MW	50190 TQ	USBLS	5/15
	Detroit-Dearborn-Livonia PMSA, MI	Y	33670 FQ	40550 MW	50150 TQ	USBLS	5/15

Occupation/Type/Industry	Location	Per	Low	Mid	High	Source	Date
Machinist	Grand Rapids-Wyoming MSA, MI	Y	29770 FQ	38630 MW	48220 TQ	USBLS	5/15
	Minnesota	Y	37481 FQ	46107 MW	55472 TQ	MNBLS	1/16-3/16
	Minneapolis-St. Paul-Bloomington MSA, MN-WI	Y	40640 FQ	48577 MW	57679 TQ	MNBLS	1/16-3/16
	Mississippi	Y	32720 FQ	41330 MW	49110 TQ	USBLS	5/15
	Jackson MSA, MS	Y	30190 FQ	42850 MW	53720 TQ	USBLS	5/15
	Missouri	Y	30880 FQ	39850 MW	52730 TQ	USBLS	5/15
	Kansas City MSA, MO-KS	Y	34110 FQ	42790 MW	49810 TQ	USBLS	5/15
	St. Louis MSA, MO-IL	Y	34240 FQ	45850 MW	58380 TQ	USBLS	5/15
	Montana	Y	24440 FQ	38120 MW	47000 TQ	USBLS	5/15
	Billings MSA, MT	Y	36370 FQ	48090 MW	57760 TQ	USBLS	5/15
	Nebraska	Y	29175 FQ	38055 MW	46380 TQ	NEBLS	7/16-9/16
	Omaha-Council Bluffs MSA, NE-IA	Y	24130 FQ	32565 MW	42560 TQ	NEBLS	7/16-9/16
	Nevada	Y	28410 FQ	36280 MW	50330 TQ	USBLS	5/15
	Las Vegas-Henderson-Paradise MSA, NV	Y	26800 FQ	31920 MW	46410 TQ	USBLS	5/15
	New Hampshire	H	15.41 AE	21.15 MW	25.30 AEX	NHBLS	6/16
	Manchester NECTA, NH	H	19.16 AE	24.37 MW	30.23 AEX	NHBLS	6/16
	Nashua NECTA, NH-MA	Y	41440 FQ	49060 MW	58530 TQ	USBLS	5/15
	New Jersey	Y	38740 FQ	48170 MW	60330 TQ	USBLS	5/15
	Camden PMSA, NJ	Y	41000 FQ	48620 MW	57400 TQ	USBLS	5/15
	Newark PMSA, NJ-PA	Y	37220 FQ	48210 MW	62180 TQ	USBLS	5/15
	Trenton MSA, NJ	Y	36470 FQ	50220 MW	60600 TQ	USBLS	5/15
	New Mexico	Y	38190 FQ	47200 MW	62380 TQ	USBLS	5/15
	Albuquerque MSA, NM	Y	35200 FQ	43840 MW	50050 TQ	USBLS	5/15
	New York	Y	29630 AE	43080 MW	51880 AEX	NYBLS	1/16-3/16
	Buffalo-Cheektowaga-Niagara Falls MSA, NY	Y	35790 FQ	43730 MW	53700 TQ	USBLS	5/15
	Nassau County-Suffolk County PMSA, NY	Y	37290 FQ	50950 MW	65990 TQ	USBLS	5/15
	New York-Jersey City-White Plains PMSA, NY-NJ	Y	36180 FQ	46640 MW	59650 TQ	USBLS	5/15
	Rochester MSA, NY	Y	31990 FQ	39870 MW	48260 TQ	USBLS	5/15
	North Carolina	Y	31650 FQ	38930 MW	47560 TQ	USBLS	5/15
	Charlotte-Concord-Gastonia MSA, NC-SC	Y	34210 FQ	40900 MW	48970 TQ	USBLS	5/15
	Raleigh MSA, NC	Y	28050 FQ	34170 MW	43850 TQ	USBLS	5/15
	North Dakota	Y	35090 FQ	41950 MW	48550 TQ	USBLS	5/15
	Fargo MSA, ND-MN	Y	33710 FQ	38970 MW	46840 TQ	USBLS	5/15
	Ohio	Y	32050 FQ	39670 MW	50250 TQ	USBLS	5/15
	Cincinnati MSA, OH-KY-IN	Y	33160 FQ	43080 MW	54570 TQ	USBLS	5/15
	Cleveland-Elyria MSA, OH	Y	30490 FQ	38470 MW	48320 TQ	USBLS	5/15
	Columbus MSA, OH	Y	32040 FQ	37610 MW	46220 TQ	USBLS	5/15
	Oklahoma	Y	31080 FQ	38900 MW	47900 TQ	USBLS	5/15
	Oklahoma City MSA, OK	Y	29730 FQ	38140 MW	53630 TQ	USBLS	5/15
	Tulsa MSA, OK	Y	32260 FQ	39570 MW	47110 TQ	USBLS	5/15
	Oregon	H	18.25 FQ	22.85 MW	28.08 TQ	ORBLS	2016
	Portland-Vancouver-Hillsboro MSA, OR-WA	Y	37940 FQ	47290 MW	57760 TQ	USBLS	5/15
	Pennsylvania	Y	32030 FQ	40450 MW	48640 TQ	USBLS	5/15
	Allentown-Bethlehem-Easton MSA, PA-NJ	Y	30870 FQ	40760 MW	50740 TQ	USBLS	5/15
	Harrisburg-Carlisle MSA, PA	Y	38550 FQ	45040 MW	50930 TQ	USBLS	5/15
	Montgomery County-Bucks County-Chester County PMSA, PA	Y	36980 FQ	45340 MW	54350 TQ	USBLS	5/15
	Philadelphia PMSA, PA	Y	33250 FQ	44490 MW	55340 TQ	USBLS	5/15
	Pittsburgh MSA, PA	Y	31580 FQ	38750 MW	46600 TQ	USBLS	5/15
	Rhode Island	Y	35040 FQ	42500 MW	50860 TQ	USBLS	5/15
	Providence-Warwick MSA, RI-MA	Y	35720 FQ	43010 MW	50220 TQ	USBLS	5/15
	South Carolina	Y	31540 FQ	38580 MW	48150 TQ	USBLS	5/15
	Charleston-North Charleston MSA, SC	Y	34170 FQ	41310 MW	49130 TQ	USBLS	5/15
	Columbia MSA, SC	Y	33630 FQ	43090 MW	49560 TQ	USBLS	5/15
	Greenville-Anderson-Mauldin MSA, SC	Y	32020 FQ	40760 MW	54880 TQ	USBLS	5/15
	South Dakota	Y	32470 FQ	36670 MW	42370 TQ	USBLS	5/15
	Sioux Falls MSA, SD	Y	32800 FQ	37040 MW	43110 TQ	USBLS	5/15
	Tennessee	Y	31390 FQ	38130 MW	49390 TQ	USBLS	5/15

AE	Average entry wage	AWR	Average wage range	H	Hourly	LR	Low end range	MTC	Median total compensation	TCC	Total cash compensation
AEX	Average experienced wage	B	Biweekly	HI	Highest wage paid	M	Monthly	MW	Median wage paid	TQ	Third quartile wage
ATC	Average total compensation	D	Daily	HR	High end range	MCC	Median cash compensation	MWR	Median wage range	W	Weekly
AW	Average wage paid	FQ	First quartile wage	LO	Lowest wage paid	ME	Median entry wage	S	See annotated source	Y	Yearly

Occupation/Type/Industry	Location	Per	Low	Mid	High	Source	Date
Machinist	Knoxville MSA, TN	Y	27250 FQ	38100 MW	65630 TQ	USBLS	5/15
	Memphis MSA, TN-MS-AR	Y	36610 FQ	46950 MW	56640 TQ	USBLS	5/15
	Nashville-Davidson–Murfreesboro–Franklin MSA, TN	Y	32900 FQ	38360 MW	51140 TQ	USBLS	5/15
	Texas	Y	31610 FQ	39520 MW	49790 TQ	USBLS	5/15
	Austin-Round Rock MSA, TX	Y	32520 FQ	38490 MW	46370 TQ	USBLS	5/15
	Dallas-Plano-Irving PMSA, TX	Y	27500 FQ	35560 MW	44710 TQ	USBLS	5/15
	Fort Worth-Arlington PMSA, TX	Y	29090 FQ	38130 MW	50760 TQ	USBLS	5/15
	Houston-The Woodlands-Sugar Land MSA, TX	Y	32810 FQ	41200 MW	50700 TQ	USBLS	5/15
	San Antonio-New Braunfels MSA, TX	Y	32220 FQ	38040 MW	46730 TQ	USBLS	5/15
	Utah	Y	36330 FQ	46150 MW	56550 TQ	USBLS	5/15
	Ogden-Clearfield MSA, UT	Y	40300 FQ	52030 MW	59910 TQ	USBLS	5/15
	Provo-Orem MSA, UT	Y	33040 FQ	39520 MW	52110 TQ	USBLS	5/15
	Salt Lake City MSA, UT	Y	37920 FQ	46280 MW	55530 TQ	USBLS	5/15
	Vermont	Y	33300 FQ	39620 MW	48080 TQ	USBLS	5/15
	Burlington-South Burlington MSA, VT	Y	33540 FQ	39620 MW	49060 TQ	USBLS	5/15
	Virginia	Y	34350 FQ	43600 MW	51730 TQ	USBLS	5/15
	Richmond MSA, VA	Y	33030 FQ	42980 MW	54800 TQ	USBLS	5/15
	Virginia Beach-Norfolk-Newport News MSA, VA-NC	Y	41600 FQ	48430 MW	55560 TQ	USBLS	5/15
	Washington	H	17.98 FQ	22.85 MW	28.76 TQ	WABLS	3/16
	Seattle-Bellevue-Everett PMSA, WA	H	18.66 FQ	23.59 MW	29.47 TQ	WABLS	3/16
	Tacoma-Lakewood PMSA, WA	H	23.50 FQ	27.52 MW	31.09 TQ	WABLS	3/16
	West Virginia	Y	32210 FQ	40000 MW	47490 TQ	USBLS	5/15
	Huntington-Ashland MSA, WV-KY-OH	Y	29020 FQ	35320 MW	43440 TQ	USBLS	5/15
	Wisconsin	Y	33650 FQ	41250 MW	48670 TQ	USBLS	5/15
	Madison MSA, WI	Y	38050 FQ	44260 MW	49430 TQ	USBLS	5/15
	Milwaukee-Waukesha-West Allis MSA, WI	Y	34330 FQ	41640 MW	48860 TQ	USBLS	5/15
	Wyoming	Y	36500 FQ	48500 MW	59040 TQ	USBLS	5/15
	Puerto Rico	Y	18000 FQ	20930 MW	26630 TQ	USBLS	5/15
	San Juan-Carolina-Caguas MSA, PR	Y	18430 FQ	22270 MW	28210 TQ	USBLS	5/15
Magnetic Resonance Imaging Technologist	United States	Y		57370 MW		FTIME	2016
	Alabama	Y	51486 AE	61007 AW	65767 AEX	ALBLS	6/16
	Birmingham-Hoover MSA, AL	Y	55380 AE	63269 AW	55380 AEX	ALBLS	6/16
	Alaska	Y	64310 FQ	77390 MW	88920 TQ	USBLS	5/15
	Anchorage MSA, AK	Y	62140 FQ	74010 MW	86420 TQ	USBLS	5/15
	Arizona	Y	63520 FQ	73760 MW	85680 TQ	USBLS	5/15
	Phoenix-Mesa-Scottsdale MSA, AZ	Y	61630 FQ	73320 MW	85100 TQ	USBLS	5/15
	Tucson MSA, AZ	Y	59300 FQ	69970 MW	79830 TQ	USBLS	5/15
	Arkansas	Y	43370 FQ	50700 MW	61270 TQ	USBLS	5/15
	Little Rock-North Little Rock-Conway MSA, AR	Y	44160 FQ	50800 MW	64330 TQ	USBLS	5/15
	California	H	32.92 FQ	42.77 MW	54.61 TQ	CABLS	1/16-3/16
	Anaheim-Santa Ana-Irvine PMSA, CA	H	27.95 FQ	35.56 MW	44.07 TQ	CABLS	1/16-3/16
	Los Angeles-Long Beach-Glendale PMSA, CA	H	34.33 FQ	43.14 MW	52.80 TQ	CABLS	1/16-3/16
	Oakland-Hayward-Berkeley PMSA, CA	H	37.24 FQ	54.59 MW	61.19 TQ	CABLS	1/16-3/16
	Riverside-San Bernardino-Ontario MSA, CA	H	33.68 FQ	38.12 MW	48.88 TQ	CABLS	1/16-3/16
	Sacramento–Roseville–Arden-Arcade MSA, CA	H	42.42 FQ	52.43 MW	59.47 TQ	CABLS	1/16-3/16
	San Diego-Carlsbad MSA, CA	H	35.42 FQ	44.32 MW	54.55 TQ	CABLS	1/16-3/16
	San Francisco-Redwood City-South San Francisco PMSA, CA	H	29.06 FQ	45.56 MW	57.22 TQ	CABLS	1/16-3/16
	Colorado	Y	68280 FQ	76720 MW	87540 TQ	USBLS	5/15
	Denver-Aurora-Lakewood MSA, CO	Y	70570 FQ	78590 MW	88850 TQ	USBLS	5/15

AE	Average entry wage	AWR	Average wage range	H	Hourly	LR	Low end range	MTC Median total compensation	TCC Total cash compensation
AEX	Average experienced wage	B	Biweekly	HI	Highest wage paid	M	Monthly	MW Median wage paid	TQ Third quartile wage
ATC	Average total compensation	D	Daily	HR	High end range	MCC Median cash compensation	MWR Median wage range	W Weekly
AW	Average wage paid	FQ	First quartile wage	LO	Lowest wage paid	ME Median entry wage	S See annotated source	Y Yearly

Occupation/Type/Industry	Location	Per	Low	Mid	High	Source	Date
Magnetic Resonance Imaging Technologist	Connecticut	Y		77000 MW		CTBLS	1/16-3/16
	Bridgeport-Stamford-Norwalk MSA, CT	Y	72170 FQ	82540 MW	92670 TQ	USBLS	5/15
	Hartford-West Hartford-East Hartford MSA, CT	Y	70760 FQ	79420 MW	90620 TQ	USBLS	5/15
	Delaware	Y	64810 FQ	71380 MW	78020 TQ	USBLS	5/15
	Wilmington PMSA, DE-MD-NJ	Y	66020 FQ	72340 MW	79460 TQ	USBLS	5/15
	District of Columbia	Y	74200 FQ	86650 MW	97490 TQ	USBLS	5/15
	Washington-Arlington-Alexandria PMSA, DC-VA-MD-WV	Y	63480 FQ	77980 MW	94500 TQ	USBLS	5/15
	Florida	H	25.46 AE	32.16 MW	35.12 AEX	FLBLS	7/16-9/16
	Fort Lauderdale-Pompano Beach-Deerfield Beach PMSA, FL	H	28.21 AE	34.64 MW	37.94 AEX	FLBLS	7/16-9/16
	Miami-Miami Beach-Kendall PMSA, FL	H	25.09 AE	32.90 MW	35.95 AEX	FLBLS	7/16-9/16
	Orlando-Kissimmee-Sanford MSA, FL	H	25.07 AE	32.02 MW	34.04 AEX	FLBLS	7/16-9/16
	Tampa-St. Petersburg-Clearwater MSA, FL	H	26.68 AE	33.53 MW	36.64 AEX	FLBLS	7/16-9/16
	Georgia	Y	51450 FQ	62270 MW	72680 TQ	USBLS	5/15
	Atlanta-Sandy Springs-Roswell MSA, GA	Y	53540 FQ	64100 MW	73470 TQ	USBLS	5/15
	Augusta-Richmond County MSA, GA-SC	Y	49330 FQ	57270 MW	65430 TQ	USBLS	5/15
	Hawaii	Y	78010 FQ	86960 MW	94660 TQ	USBLS	5/15
	Urban Honolulu MSA, HI	Y	81870 FQ	88690 MW	95520 TQ	USBLS	5/15
	Idaho	Y	55720 FQ	65600 MW	75080 TQ	USBLS	5/15
	Boise City MSA, ID	Y	48260 FQ	57220 MW	69150 TQ	USBLS	5/15
	Illinois	Y	55980 FQ	69050 MW	83280 TQ	USBLS	5/15
	Chicago-Naperville-Arlington Heights PMSA; IL	Y	61350 FQ	73730 MW	87950 TQ	USBLS	5/15
	Lake County-Kenosha County PMSA, IL-WI	Y	64720 FQ	72660 MW	84040 TQ	USBLS	5/15
	Indiana	Y	53030 FQ	63090 MW	72580 TQ	USBLS	5/15
	Gary PMSA, IN	Y	59520 FQ	68920 MW	75830 TQ	USBLS	5/15
	Indianapolis-Carmel-Anderson MSA, IN	Y	57010 FQ	66160 MW	74300 TQ	USBLS	5/15
	Iowa	Y	52640 FQ	58660 MW	66730 TQ	USBLS	5/15
	Des Moines-West Des Moines MSA, IA	Y	55110 FQ	60330 MW	69190 TQ	USBLS	5/15
	Kansas	Y	53210 FQ	59260 MW	67600 TQ	USBLS	5/15
	Wichita MSA, KS	Y	53040 FQ	59550 MW	68100 TQ	USBLS	5/15
	Kentucky	Y	54300 FQ	61780 MW	71470 TQ	USBLS	5/15
	Louisville-Jefferson County MSA, KY-IN	Y	52350 FQ	60250 MW	69970 TQ	USBLS	5/15
	Louisiana	Y	46760 FQ	55280 MW	62660 TQ	USBLS	5/15
	Baton Rouge MSA, LA	Y	44200 FQ	55090 MW	64440 TQ	USBLS	5/15
	New Orleans-Metairie MSA, LA	Y	49540 FQ	56150 MW	62880 TQ	USBLS	5/15
	Maine	Y	64770 FQ	73950 MW	84130 TQ	USBLS	5/15
	Portland-South Portland MSA, ME	Y	63620 FQ	72860 MW	82300 TQ	USBLS	5/15
	Maryland	Y	62062 AE	75544 MW	82286 AEX	MDBLS	4/16
	Baltimore-Columbia-Towson MSA, MD	Y	67660 FQ	74140 MW	81320 TQ	USBLS	5/15
	Salisbury MSA, MD-DE	Y	58250 FQ	69050 MW	79220 TQ	USBLS	5/15
	Massachusetts	Y	71200 FQ	84830 MW	96380 TQ	USBLS	5/15
	Boston-Cambridge-Newton NECTA, MA	Y	70430 FQ	86480 MW	97920 TQ	USBLS	5/15
	Worcester MSA, MA-CT	Y	76620 FQ	87930 MW	98710 TQ	USBLS	5/15
	Michigan	Y	50650 FQ	60320 MW	70880 TQ	USBLS	5/15
	Detroit-Dearborn-Livonia PMSA, MI	Y	55370 FQ	64520 MW	74810 TQ	USBLS	5/15
	Grand Rapids-Wyoming MSA, MI	Y	53630 FQ	62000 MW	72320 TQ	USBLS	5/15
	Minnesota	Y	63558 FQ	71400 MW	79061 TQ	MNBLS	1/16-3/16
	Minneapolis-St. Paul-Bloomington MSA, MN-WI	Y	66431 FQ	73225 MW	80271 TQ	MNBLS	1/16-3/16

Occupation/Type/Industry	Location	Per	Low	Mid	High	Source	Date
Magnetic Resonance Imaging Technologist							
	Mississippi	Y	48200 FQ	57060 MW	66390 TQ	USBLS	5/15
	Jackson MSA, MS	Y	46690 FQ	56090 MW	66500 TQ	USBLS	5/15
	Missouri	Y	48650 FQ	58320 MW	68960 TQ	USBLS	5/15
	Kansas City MSA, MO-KS	Y	55650 FQ	62320 MW	71190 TQ	USBLS	5/15
	St. Louis MSA, MO-IL	Y	47110 FQ	57520 MW	68930 TQ	USBLS	5/15
	Montana	Y	48290 FQ	60590 MW	72230 TQ	USBLS	5/15
	Nebraska	Y	54775 FQ	62015 MW	72520 TQ	NEBLS	7/16-9/16
	Omaha-Council Bluffs MSA, NE-IA	Y	54150 FQ	61645 MW	72720 TQ	NEBLS	7/16-9/16
	Nevada	Y	71270 FQ	84050 MW	95610 TQ	USBLS	5/15
	Las Vegas-Henderson-Paradise MSA, NV	Y	71920 FQ	85080 MW	96760 TQ	USBLS	5/15
	New Hampshire	H	28.40 AE	34.56 MW	37.62 AEX	NHBLS	6/16
	New Jersey	Y	70870 FQ	80740 MW	91580 TQ	USBLS	5/15
	Camden PMSA, NJ	Y	67850 FQ	75140 MW	83540 TQ	USBLS	5/15
	Newark PMSA, NJ-PA	Y	73530 FQ	84650 MW	93870 TQ	USBLS	5/15
	Trenton MSA, NJ	Y	69610 FQ	76980 MW	87060 TQ	USBLS	5/15
	New Mexico	Y	58660 FQ	68070 MW	77320 TQ	USBLS	5/15
	Albuquerque MSA, NM	Y	63650 FQ	71440 MW	79840 TQ	USBLS	5/15
	New York	Y	54820 AE	75130 MW	83080 AEX	NYBLS	1/16-3/16
	Buffalo-Cheektowaga-Niagara Falls MSA, NY	Y	51850 FQ	57890 MW	65220 TQ	USBLS	5/15
	Nassau County-Suffolk County PMSA, NY	Y	69590 FQ	78820 MW	90030 TQ	USBLS	5/15
	New York-Jersey City-White Plains PMSA, NY-NJ	Y	69830 FQ	81120 MW	91690 TQ	USBLS	5/15
	Rochester MSA, NY	Y	56310 FQ	63600 MW	72040 TQ	USBLS	5/15
	North Carolina	Y	57270 FQ	66160 MW	74510 TQ	USBLS	5/15
	Charlotte-Concord-Gastonia MSA, NC-SC	Y	60610 FQ	68100 MW	74670 TQ	USBLS	5/15
	Raleigh MSA, NC	Y	59710 FQ	67830 MW	74810 TQ	USBLS	5/15
	North Dakota	Y	47410 FQ	57520 MW	69450 TQ	USBLS	5/15
	Fargo MSA, ND-MN	Y	43950 FQ	51010 MW	62270 TQ	USBLS	5/15
	Ohio	Y	54750 FQ	61170 MW	70350 TQ	USBLS	5/15
	Cincinnati MSA, OH-KY-IN	Y	58020 FQ	67240 MW	74540 TQ	USBLS	5/15
	Cleveland-Elyria MSA, OH	Y	56390 FQ	62920 MW	72020 TQ	USBLS	5/15
	Columbus MSA, OH	Y	55080 FQ	62660 MW	71700 TQ	USBLS	5/15
	Oklahoma	Y	46730 FQ	58840 MW	70510 TQ	USBLS	5/15
	Oklahoma City MSA, OK	Y	42110 FQ	59700 MW	71080 TQ	USBLS	5/15
	Tulsa MSA, OK	Y	48810 FQ	58530 MW	70640 TQ	USBLS	5/15
	Oregon	H	33.30 FQ	40.04 MW	45.05 TQ	ORBLS	2016
	Portland-Vancouver-Hillsboro MSA, OR-WA	Y	73530 FQ	85850 MW	94370 TQ	USBLS	5/15
	Pennsylvania	Y	53890 FQ	62060 MW	74170 TQ	USBLS	5/15
	Allentown-Bethlehem-Easton MSA, PA-NJ	Y	54720 FQ	67010 MW	78030 TQ	USBLS	5/15
	Harrisburg-Carlisle MSA, PA	Y	49910 FQ	58020 MW	68850 TQ	USBLS	5/15
	Montgomery County-Bucks County-Chester County PMSA, PA	Y	56850 FQ	65130 MW	74490 TQ	USBLS	5/15
	Philadelphia PMSA, PA	Y	60670 FQ	71820 MW	82360 TQ	USBLS	5/15
	Pittsburgh MSA, PA	Y	50930 FQ	58600 MW	69720 TQ	USBLS	5/15
	Rhode Island	Y	68280 FQ	76890 MW	87500 TQ	USBLS	5/15
	Providence-Warwick MSA, RI-MA	Y	68480 FQ	77080 MW	87890 TQ	USBLS	5/15
	South Carolina	Y	51870 FQ	59420 MW	70220 TQ	USBLS	5/15
	Charleston-North Charleston MSA, SC	Y	39380 FQ	58490 MW	69010 TQ	USBLS	5/15
	South Dakota	Y	51860 FQ	56730 MW	61600 TQ	USBLS	5/15
	Tennessee	Y	48140 FQ	57370 MW	67060 TQ	USBLS	5/15
	Knoxville MSA, TN	Y	44110 FQ	53340 MW	60770 TQ	USBLS	5/15
	Memphis MSA, TN-MS-AR	Y	53260 FQ	60510 MW	69700 TQ	USBLS	5/15
	Nashville-Davidson–Murfreesboro–Franklin MSA, TN	Y	51680 FQ	60930 MW	71310 TQ	USBLS	5/15
	Texas	Y	60110 FQ	69160 MW	77000 TQ	USBLS	5/15
	Austin-Round Rock MSA, TX	Y	58340 FQ	67160 MW	76220 TQ	USBLS	5/15
	Dallas-Plano-Irving PMSA, TX	Y	66040 FQ	73980 MW	83460 TQ	USBLS	5/15
	Fort Worth-Arlington PMSA, TX	Y	65700 FQ	73090 MW	81250 TQ	USBLS	5/15

AE	Average entry wage	AWR	Average wage range	H	Hourly
AEX	Average experienced wage	B	Biweekly	HI	Highest wage paid
ATC	Average total compensation	D	Daily	HR	High end range
AW	Average wage paid	FQ	First quartile wage	LO	Lowest wage paid

LR	Low end range	MTC	Median total compensation
M	Monthly	MW	Median wage paid
MCC	Median cash compensation	MWR	Median wage range
ME	Median entry wage	S	See annotated source

TCC	Total cash compensation
TQ	Third quartile wage
W	Weekly
Y	Yearly

Occupation/Type/Industry	Location	Per	Low	Mid	High	Source	Date
Magnetic Resonance Imaging Technologist	Houston-The Woodlands-Sugar Land MSA, TX	Y	59490 FQ	67730 MW	74830 TQ	USBLS	5/15
	San Antonio-New Braunfels MSA, TX	Y	58600 FQ	68370 MW	75410 TQ	USBLS	5/15
	Utah	Y	52480 FQ	62260 MW	73060 TQ	USBLS	5/15
	Ogden-Clearfield MSA, UT	Y	49160 FQ	57970 MW	68340 TQ	USBLS	5/15
	Salt Lake City MSA, UT	Y	50730 FQ	60890 MW	72720 TQ	USBLS	5/15
	Vermont	Y	62130 FQ	72100 MW	84250 TQ	USBLS	5/15
	Virginia	Y	57290 FQ	68670 MW	78820 TQ	USBLS	5/15
	Richmond MSA, VA	Y	54310 FQ	63670 MW	73240 TQ	USBLS	5/15
	Virginia Beach-Norfolk-Newport News MSA, VA-NC	Y	64410 FQ	70940 MW	77470 TQ	USBLS	5/15
	Washington	H	31.22 FQ	38.95 MW	45.54 TQ	WABLS	3/16
	Seattle-Bellevue-Everett PMSA, WA	H	34.74 FQ	41.49 MW	46.71 TQ	WABLS	3/16
	Tacoma-Lakewood PMSA, WA	H	24.67 FQ	38.46 MW	46.17 TQ	WABLS	3/16
	West Virginia	Y	52590 FQ	60730 MW	71230 TQ	USBLS	5/15
	Huntington-Ashland MSA, WV-KY-OH	Y	49200 FQ	58040 MW	71920 TQ	USBLS	5/15
	Wisconsin	Y	60860 FQ	68880 MW	75890 TQ	USBLS	5/15
	Milwaukee-Waukesha-West Allis MSA, WI	Y	64570 FQ	70890 MW	77180 TQ	USBLS	5/15
	Wyoming	Y	53630 FQ	63900 MW	81090 TQ	USBLS	5/15
	Puerto Rico	Y	24260 FQ	32480 MW	39400 TQ	USBLS	5/15
	San Juan-Carolina-Caguas MSA, PR	Y	23640 FQ	33720 MW	41660 TQ	USBLS	5/15
Maid and Housekeeping Cleaner	Alabama	Y	17472 AE	19346 AW	20283 AEX	ALBLS	6/16
	Birmingham-Hoover MSA, AL	Y	17442 AE	18811 AW	19501 AEX	ALBLS	6/16
	Alaska	Y	21520 FQ	25390 MW	30100 TQ	USBLS	5/15
	Anchorage MSA, AK	Y	22080 FQ	24870 MW	29570 TQ	USBLS	5/15
	Arizona	Y	18260 FQ	19780 MW	23150 TQ	USBLS	5/15
	Phoenix-Mesa-Scottsdale MSA, AZ	Y	18630 FQ	20750 MW	23730 TQ	USBLS	5/15
	Tucson MSA, AZ	Y	17830 FQ	18880 MW	21130 TQ	USBLS	5/15
	Arkansas	Y	16870 FQ	18120 MW	19390 TQ	USBLS	5/15
	Little Rock-North Little Rock-Conway MSA, AR	Y	17020 FQ	18420 MW	20320 TQ	USBLS	5/15
	California	H	9.71 FQ	11.43 MW	15.10 TQ	CABLS	1/16-3/16
	Anaheim-Santa Ana-Irvine PMSA, CA	H	9.64 FQ	10.98 MW	12.87 TQ	CABLS	1/16-3/16
	Los Angeles-Long Beach-Glendale PMSA, CA	H	9.66 FQ	11.48 MW	15.77 TQ	CABLS	1/16-3/16
	Oakland-Hayward-Berkeley PMSA, CA	H	11.04 FQ	14.47 MW	19.78 TQ	CABLS	1/16-3/16
	Riverside-San Bernardino-Ontario MSA, CA	H	9.62 FQ	10.76 MW	12.29 TQ	CABLS	1/16-3/16
	Sacramento–Roseville–Arden-Arcade MSA, CA	H	9.48 FQ	10.35 MW	14.69 TQ	CABLS	1/16-3/16
	San Diego-Carlsbad MSA, CA	H	9.61 FQ	10.93 MW	13.19 TQ	CABLS	1/16-3/16
	San Francisco-Redwood City-South San Francisco PMSA, CA	H	12.87 FQ	19.08 MW	22.31 TQ	CABLS	1/16-3/16
	Colorado	Y	18800 FQ	21060 MW	24180 TQ	USBLS	5/15
	Denver-Aurora-Lakewood MSA, CO	Y	18660 FQ	20490 MW	23570 TQ	USBLS	5/15
	Connecticut	Y		24025 MW		CTBLS	1/16-3/16
	Bridgeport-Stamford-Norwalk MSA, CT	Y	20660 FQ	24110 MW	28940 TQ	USBLS	5/15
	Hartford-West Hartford-East Hartford MSA, CT	Y	21810 FQ	24730 MW	29590 TQ	USBLS	5/15
	Delaware	Y	18220 FQ	20330 MW	25470 TQ	USBLS	5/15
	Wilmington PMSA, DE-MD-NJ	Y	18470 FQ	21060 MW	25500 TQ	USBLS	5/15
	District of Columbia	Y	27110 FQ	34030 MW	38880 TQ	USBLS	5/15
	Washington-Arlington-Alexandria PMSA, DC-VA-MD-WV	Y	19930 FQ	24130 MW	31200 TQ	USBLS	5/15
	Florida	H	9.00 AE	9.83 MW	11.21 AEX	FLBLS	7/16-9/16

AE	Average entry wage	AWR	Average wage range	H	Hourly
AEX	Average experienced wage	B	Biweekly	HI	Highest wage paid
ATC	Average total compensation	D	Daily	HR	High end range
AW	Average wage paid	FQ	First quartile wage	LO	Lowest wage paid

LR	Low end range	MTC	Median total compensation	TCC	Total cash compensation
M	Monthly	MW	Median wage paid	TQ	Third quartile wage
MCC	Median cash compensation	MWR	Median wage range	W	Weekly
ME	Median entry wage	S	See annotated source	Y	Yearly

Occupation/Type/Industry	Location	Per	Low	Mid	High	Source	Date
Maid and Housekeeping Cleaner	Fort Lauderdale-Pompano Beach-Deerfield Beach PMSA, FL	H	8.99 AE	10.02 MW	11.53 AEX	FLBLS	7/16-9/16
	Miami-Miami Beach-Kendall PMSA, FL	H	9.01 AE	10.32 MW	11.53 AEX	FLBLS	7/16-9/16
	Orlando-Kissimmee-Sanford MSA, FL	H	9.01 AE	10.12 MW	11.49 AEX	FLBLS	7/16-9/16
	Tampa-St. Petersburg-Clearwater MSA, FL	H	8.99 AE	9.53 MW	10.56 AEX	FLBLS	7/16-9/16
	Georgia	Y	16960 FQ	18470 MW	20790 TQ	USBLS	5/15
	Atlanta-Sandy Springs-Roswell MSA, GA	Y	17070 FQ	18700 MW	21610 TQ	USBLS	5/15
	Augusta-Richmond County MSA, GA-SC	Y	16860 FQ	18220 MW	19620 TQ	USBLS	5/15
	Hawaii	Y	31490 FQ	35510 MW	39580 TQ	USBLS	5/15
	Urban Honolulu MSA, HI	Y	31620 FQ	36170 MW	41360 TQ	USBLS	5/15
	Idaho	Y	17870 FQ	20530 MW	23970 TQ	USBLS	5/15
	Boise City MSA, ID	Y	18620 FQ	21590 MW	24630 TQ	USBLS	5/15
	Illinois	Y	19040 FQ	22010 MW	28750 TQ	USBLS	5/15
	Chicago-Naperville-Arlington Heights PMSA, IL	Y	19610 FQ	23850 MW	32010 TQ	USBLS	5/15
	Lake County-Kenosha County PMSA, IL-WI	Y	18810 FQ	21190 MW	24350 TQ	USBLS	5/15
	Indiana	Y	17330 FQ	19200 MW	22600 TQ	USBLS	5/15
	Gary PMSA, IN	Y	18280 FQ	21310 MW	24570 TQ	USBLS	5/15
	Indianapolis-Carmel-Anderson MSA, IN	Y	17360 FQ	19250 MW	22630 TQ	USBLS	5/15
	Iowa	Y	17750 FQ	20380 MW	24410 TQ	USBLS	5/15
	Des Moines-West Des Moines MSA, IA	Y	17680 FQ	20140 MW	24610 TQ	USBLS	5/15
	Kansas	Y	17220 FQ	18990 MW	22000 TQ	USBLS	5/15
	Wichita MSA, KS	Y	17290 FQ	19170 MW	22180 TQ	USBLS	5/15
	Kentucky	Y	17120 FQ	18790 MW	22270 TQ	USBLS	5/15
	Louisville-Jefferson County MSA, KY-IN	Y	17700 FQ	20200 MW	24490 TQ	USBLS	5/15
	Louisiana	Y	16920 FQ	18430 MW	20730 TQ	USBLS	5/15
	Baton Rouge MSA, LA	Y	16900 FQ	18380 MW	20460 TQ	USBLS	5/15
	New Orleans-Metairie MSA, LA	Y	17490 FQ	19570 MW	22820 TQ	USBLS	5/15
	Maine	Y	18260 FQ	20760 MW	23430 TQ	USBLS	5/15
	Portland-South Portland MSA, ME	Y	18230 FQ	20550 MW	23390 TQ	USBLS	5/15
	Maryland	Y	18136 AE	23431 MW	26079 AEX	MDBLS	4/16
	Baltimore-Columbia-Towson MSA, MD	Y	19320 FQ	22660 MW	26630 TQ	USBLS	5/15
	Salisbury MSA, MD-DE	Y	18090 FQ	19700 MW	24090 TQ	USBLS	5/15
	Massachusetts	Y	20660 FQ	25460 MW	34390 TQ	USBLS	5/15
	Boston-Cambridge-Newton NECTA, MA	Y	21890 FQ	30800 MW	36980 TQ	USBLS	5/15
	Worcester MSA, MA-CT	Y	19460 FQ	22670 MW	28650 TQ	USBLS	5/15
	Michigan	Y	18790 FQ	21600 MW	26010 TQ	USBLS	5/15
	Detroit-Dearborn-Livonia PMSA, MI	Y	19630 FQ	23010 MW	28880 TQ	USBLS	5/15
	Grand Rapids-Wyoming MSA, MI	Y	18490 FQ	20220 MW	23630 TQ	USBLS	5/15
	Minnesota	Y	19238 FQ	22146 MW	25964 TQ	MNBLS	1/16-3/16
	Minneapolis-St. Paul-Bloomington MSA, MN-WI	Y	19753 FQ	22631 MW	26782 TQ	MNBLS	1/16-3/16
	Mississippi	Y	16690 FQ	18020 MW	19380 TQ	USBLS	5/15
	Jackson MSA, MS	Y	16720 FQ	18080 MW	19520 TQ	USBLS	5/15
	Missouri	Y	17570 FQ	19220 MW	22680 TQ	USBLS	5/15
	Kansas City MSA, MO-KS	Y	17660 FQ	19480 MW	23220 TQ	USBLS	5/15
	St. Louis MSA, MO-IL	Y	18290 FQ	20410 MW	23630 TQ	USBLS	5/15
	Montana	Y	18360 FQ	20340 MW	23870 TQ	USBLS	5/15
	Billings MSA, MT	Y	19060 FQ	21540 MW	24350 TQ	USBLS	5/15
	Nebraska	Y	18030 FQ	19435 MW	22910 TQ	NEBLS	7/16-9/16
	Omaha-Council Bluffs MSA, NE-IA	Y	17915 FQ	19455 MW	23455 TQ	NEBLS	7/16-9/16
	Nevada	Y	22990 FQ	32280 MW	36040 TQ	USBLS	5/15
	Las Vegas-Henderson-Paradise MSA, NV	Y	27590 FQ	33390 MW	36590 TQ	USBLS	5/15
	New Hampshire	H	8.42 AE	10.54 MW	12.05 AEX	NHBLS	6/16

AE	Average entry wage	AWR	Average wage range	H	Hourly
AEX	Average experienced wage	B	Biweekly	HI	Highest wage paid
ATC	Average total compensation	D	Daily	HR	High end range
AW	Average wage paid	FQ	First quartile wage	LO	Lowest wage paid

LR	Low end range	MTC	Median total compensation	TCC	Total cash compensation
M	Monthly	MW	Median wage paid	TQ	Third quartile wage
MCC	Median cash compensation	MWR	Median wage range	W	Weekly
ME	Median entry wage	S	See annotated source	Y	Yearly

Occupation/Type/Industry	Location	Per	Low	Mid	High	Source	Date
Maid and Housekeeping Cleaner	Manchester NECTA, NH	H	8.42 AE	9.85 MW	11.60 AEX	NHBLS	6/16
	Nashua NECTA, NH-MA	Y	17770 FQ	20430 MW	23200 TQ	USBLS	5/15
	New Jersey	Y	19850 FQ	23020 MW	27560 TQ	USBLS	5/15
	Camden PMSA, NJ	Y	19140 FQ	21890 MW	25770 TQ	USBLS	5/15
	Newark PMSA, NJ-PA	Y	19930 FQ	23190 MW	28070 TQ	USBLS	5/15
	Trenton MSA, NJ	Y	21470 FQ	25340 MW	30210 TQ	USBLS	5/15
	New Mexico	Y	17390 FQ	18800 MW	21210 TQ	USBLS	5/15
	Albuquerque MSA, NM	Y	17370 FQ	18720 MW	20770 TQ	USBLS	5/15
	New York	Y	20130 AE	27120 MW	38260 AEX	NYBLS	1/16-3/16
	Buffalo-Cheektowaga-Niagara Falls MSA, NY	Y	19140 FQ	21290 MW	27050 TQ	USBLS	5/15
	Nassau County-Suffolk County PMSA, NY	Y	20700 FQ	24190 MW	32030 TQ	USBLS	5/15
	New York-Jersey City-White Plains PMSA, NY-NJ	Y	22530 FQ	32090 MW	47580 TQ	USBLS	5/15
	Rochester MSA, NY	Y	19130 FQ	20990 MW	25360 TQ	USBLS	5/15
	North Carolina	Y	17180 FQ	18920 MW	22040 TQ	USBLS	5/15
	Charlotte-Concord-Gastonia MSA, NC-SC	Y	17060 FQ	18670 MW	21210 TQ	USBLS	5/15
	Raleigh MSA, NC	Y	17250 FQ	19090 MW	22450 TQ	USBLS	5/15
	North Dakota	Y	19210 FQ	23100 MW	27790 TQ	USBLS	5/15
	Fargo MSA, ND-MN	Y	17560 FQ	19420 MW	23980 TQ	USBLS	5/15
	Ohio	Y	18240 FQ	19660 MW	23370 TQ	USBLS	5/15
	Cincinnati MSA, OH-KY-IN	Y	18290 FQ	20590 MW	24690 TQ	USBLS	5/15
	Cleveland-Elyria MSA, OH	Y	18640 FQ	21090 MW	24590 TQ	USBLS	5/15
	Columbus MSA, OH	Y	18310 FQ	19790 MW	23450 TQ	USBLS	5/15
	Oklahoma	Y	16990 FQ	18560 MW	21110 TQ	USBLS	5/15
	Oklahoma City MSA, OK	Y	16970 FQ	18530 MW	21230 TQ	USBLS	5/15
	Tulsa MSA, OK	Y	17440 FQ	19440 MW	22500 TQ	USBLS	5/15
	Oregon	H	9.69 FQ	10.95 MW	12.92 TQ	ORBLS	2016
	Portland-Vancouver-Hillsboro MSA, OR-WA	Y	20010 FQ	23500 MW	29870 TQ	USBLS	5/15
	Pennsylvania	Y	18150 FQ	21270 MW	25190 TQ	USBLS	5/15
	Allentown-Bethlehem-Easton MSA, PA-NJ	Y	18250 FQ	21420 MW	25520 TQ	USBLS	5/15
	Harrisburg-Carlisle MSA, PA	Y	17400 FQ	19320 MW	22390 TQ	USBLS	5/15
	Montgomery County-Bucks County-Chester County PMSA, PA	Y	19790 FQ	23070 MW	28280 TQ	USBLS	5/15
	Philadelphia PMSA, PA	Y	22000 FQ	26230 MW	30670 TQ	USBLS	5/15
	Pittsburgh MSA, PA	Y	18360 FQ	21370 MW	24600 TQ	USBLS	5/15
	Rhode Island	Y	20570 FQ	25450 MW	30520 TQ	USBLS	5/15
	Providence-Warwick MSA, RI-MA	Y	20080 FQ	24880 MW	30090 TQ	USBLS	5/15
	South Carolina	Y	16880 FQ	18350 MW	20420 TQ	USBLS	5/15
	Charleston-North Charleston MSA, SC	Y	17120 FQ	18850 MW	22350 TQ	USBLS	5/15
	Columbia MSA, SC	Y	17010 FQ	18540 MW	21120 TQ	USBLS	5/15
	Greenville-Anderson-Mauldin MSA, SC	Y	16830 FQ	18240 MW	19740 TQ	USBLS	5/15
	South Dakota	Y	18530 FQ	19420 MW	22320 TQ	USBLS	5/15
	Sioux Falls MSA, SD	Y	18560 FQ	19460 MW	22610 TQ	USBLS	5/15
	Tennessee	Y	17210 FQ	19010 MW	22290 TQ	USBLS	5/15
	Knoxville MSA, TN	Y	16870 FQ	18360 MW	20730 TQ	USBLS	5/15
	Memphis MSA, TN-MS-AR	Y	17230 FQ	19090 MW	22260 TQ	USBLS	5/15
	Morristown MSA, TN	Y	16950 FQ	18430 MW	20450 TQ	USBLS	5/15
	Nashville-Davidson–Murfreesboro–Franklin MSA, TN	Y	17670 FQ	20200 MW	23680 TQ	USBLS	5/15
	Texas	Y	17120 FQ	18810 MW	21900 TQ	USBLS	5/15
	Abilene MSA, TX	Y	16680 FQ	17920 MW	19150 TQ	USBLS	5/15
	Austin-Round Rock MSA, TX	Y	17420 FQ	19440 MW	23070 TQ	USBLS	5/15
	Dallas-Plano-Irving PMSA, TX	Y	17170 FQ	18890 MW	22400 TQ	USBLS	5/15
	Fort Worth-Arlington PMSA, TX	Y	17440 FQ	19480 MW	23570 TQ	USBLS	5/15
	Houston-The Woodlands-Sugar Land MSA, TX	Y	17230 FQ	19010 MW	22090 TQ	USBLS	5/15
	San Antonio-New Braunfels MSA, TX	Y	17620 FQ	19860 MW	22860 TQ	USBLS	5/15
	Utah	Y	17620 FQ	19870 MW	23580 TQ	USBLS	5/15
	Ogden-Clearfield MSA, UT	Y	17320 FQ	19220 MW	22980 TQ	USBLS	5/15
	Provo-Orem MSA, UT	Y	17210 FQ	19030 MW	22080 TQ	USBLS	5/15

AE Average entry wage	**AWR** Average wage range	**H** Hourly	**LR** Low end range	**MTC** Median total compensation	**TCC** Total cash compensation
AEX Average experienced wage	**B** Biweekly	**HI** Highest wage paid	**M** Monthly	**MW** Median wage paid	**TQ** Third quartile wage
ATC Average total compensation	**D** Daily	**HR** High end range	**MCC** Median cash compensation	**MWR** Median wage range	**W** Weekly
AW Average wage paid	**FQ** First quartile wage	**LO** Lowest wage paid	**ME** Median entry wage	**S** See annotated source	**Y** Yearly

Occupation/Type/Industry	Location	Per	Low	Mid	High	Source	Date
Maid and Housekeeping Cleaner	Salt Lake City MSA, UT	Y	18400 FQ	21480 MW	24670 TQ	USBLS	5/15
	Vermont	Y	20450 FQ	23350 MW	28380 TQ	USBLS	5/15
	Burlington-South Burlington MSA, VT	Y	19940 FQ	22270 MW	24720 TQ	USBLS	5/15
	Virginia	Y	17860 FQ	20390 MW	23900 TQ	USBLS	5/15
	Harrisonburg MSA, VA	Y	17010 FQ	18610 MW	21780 TQ	USBLS	5/15
	Richmond MSA, VA	Y	18350 FQ	21010 MW	23530 TQ	USBLS	5/15
	Virginia Beach-Norfolk-Newport News MSA, VA-NC	Y	17540 FQ	19610 MW	22950 TQ	USBLS	5/15
	Washington	H	10.31 FQ	11.36 MW	13.03 TQ	WABLS	3/16
	Seattle-Bellevue-Everett PMSA, WA	H	10.63 FQ	11.80 MW	14.10 TQ	WABLS	3/16
	Tacoma-Lakewood PMSA, WA	H	10.32 FQ	11.33 MW	12.72 TQ	WABLS	3/16
	West Virginia	Y	17790 FQ	18950 MW	21600 TQ	USBLS	5/15
	Huntington-Ashland MSA, WV-KY-OH	Y	17750 FQ	19090 MW	23660 TQ	USBLS	5/15
	Wisconsin	Y	17690 FQ	20170 MW	24090 TQ	USBLS	5/15
	Madison MSA, WI	Y	17750 FQ	20250 MW	24150 TQ	USBLS	5/15
	Milwaukee-Waukesha-West Allis MSA, WI	Y	18580 FQ	21670 MW	24720 TQ	USBLS	5/15
	Wyoming	Y	18210 FQ	21000 MW	23920 TQ	USBLS	5/15
	Cheyenne MSA, WY	Y	17030 FQ	18720 MW	21540 TQ	USBLS	5/15
	Puerto Rico	Y	16730 FQ	18070 MW	19440 TQ	USBLS	5/15
	San Juan-Carolina-Caguas MSA, PR	Y	16850 FQ	18290 MW	19960 TQ	USBLS	5/15
	Virgin Islands	Y	18370 FQ	22400 MW	27260 TQ	USBLS	5/15
	Guam	Y	17820 FQ	18470 MW	19130 TQ	USBLS	5/15
Mail Clerk and Mail Machine Operator							
Except Postal Service	Alabama	Y	20179 AE	29722 AW	34484 AEX	ALBLS	6/16
Except Postal Service	Birmingham-Hoover MSA, AL	Y	22591 AE	31382 AW	35772 AEX	ALBLS	6/16
Except Postal Service	Alaska	Y	31800 FQ	35810 MW	40210 TQ	USBLS	5/15
Except Postal Service	Anchorage MSA, AK	Y	31380 FQ	36120 MW	41680 TQ	USBLS	5/15
Except Postal Service	Arizona	Y	19440 FQ	23020 MW	29700 TQ	USBLS	5/15
Except Postal Service	Phoenix-Mesa-Scottsdale MSA, AZ	Y	19420 FQ	22910 MW	29760 TQ	USBLS	5/15
Except Postal Service	Tucson MSA, AZ	Y	21020 FQ	26730 MW	30200 TQ	USBLS	5/15
Except Postal Service	Arkansas	Y	22630 FQ	28220 MW	30880 TQ	USBLS	5/15
Except Postal Service	Little Rock-North Little Rock-Conway MSA, AR	Y	22440 FQ	27580 MW	30790 TQ	USBLS	5/15
Except Postal Service	California	H	12.52 FQ	15.92 MW	19.61 TQ	CABLS	1/16-3/16
Except Postal Service	Anaheim-Santa Ana-Irvine PMSA, CA	H	11.57 FQ	14.45 MW	17.74 TQ	CABLS	1/16-3/16
Except Postal Service	Los Angeles-Long Beach-Glendale PMSA, CA	H	12.12 FQ	16.09 MW	20.79 TQ	CABLS	1/16-3/16
Except Postal Service	Oakland-Hayward-Berkeley PMSA, CA	H	11.27 FQ	18.30 MW	22.40 TQ	CABLS	1/16-3/16
Except Postal Service	Riverside-San Bernardino-Ontario MSA, CA	H	11.12 FQ	14.10 MW	17.36 TQ	CABLS	1/16-3/16
Except Postal Service	Sacramento–Roseville–Arden-Arcade MSA, CA	H	13.89 FQ	18.01 MW	20.22 TQ	CABLS	1/16-3/16
Except Postal Service	San Diego-Carlsbad MSA, CA	H	15.23 FQ	17.43 MW	19.43 TQ	CABLS	1/16-3/16
Except Postal Service	San Francisco-Redwood City-South San Francisco PMSA, CA	H	14.96 FQ	18.48 MW	22.10 TQ	CABLS	1/16-3/16
Except Postal Service	Colorado	Y	26230 FQ	34010 MW	40640 TQ	USBLS	5/15
Except Postal Service	Denver-Aurora-Lakewood MSA, CO	Y	29430 FQ	35860 MW	43650 TQ	USBLS	5/15
Except Postal Service	Connecticut	Y		34651 MW		CTBLS	1/16-3/16
Except Postal Service	Bridgeport-Stamford-Norwalk MSA, CT	Y	21430 FQ	28730 MW	37160 TQ	USBLS	5/15
Except Postal Service	Hartford-West Hartford-East Hartford MSA, CT	Y	29470 FQ	36460 MW	44170 TQ	USBLS	5/15
Except Postal Service	Delaware	Y	20990 FQ	26880 MW	34020 TQ	USBLS	5/15
Except Postal Service	Wilmington PMSA, DE-MD-NJ	Y	20050 FQ	27660 MW	35350 TQ	USBLS	5/15
Except Postal Service	District of Columbia	Y	36070 FQ	43510 MW	48870 TQ	USBLS	5/15
Except Postal Service	Washington-Arlington-Alexandria PMSA, DC-VA-MD-WV	Y	22140 FQ	33460 MW	44590 TQ	USBLS	5/15
Except Postal Service	Florida	H	9.68 AE	12.42 MW	14.94 AEX	FLBLS	7/16-9/16

AE	Average entry wage	AWR	Average wage range	H	Hourly	LR Low end range
AEX	Average experienced wage	B	Biweekly	HI	Highest wage paid	M Monthly
ATC	Average total compensation	D	Daily	HR	High end range	MCC Median cash compensation
AW	Average wage paid	FQ	First quartile wage	LO	Lowest wage paid	ME Median entry wage

MTC Median total compensation   TCC Total cash compensation
MW Median wage paid   TQ Third quartile wage
MWR Median wage range   W Weekly
S See annotated source   Y Yearly

Occupation/Type/Industry	Location	Per	Low	Mid	High	Source	Date
Mail Clerk and Mail Machine Operator							
Except Postal Service	Fort Lauderdale-Pompano Beach-Deerfield Beach PMSA, FL	H	10.42 AE	12.10 MW	14.45 AEX	FLBLS	7/16-9/16
Except Postal Service	Miami-Miami Beach-Kendall PMSA, FL	H	9.66 AE	13.45 MW	15.88 AEX	FLBLS	7/16-9/16
Except Postal Service	Orlando-Kissimmee-Sanford MSA, FL	H	8.97 AE	11.25 MW	13.93 AEX	FLBLS	7/16-9/16
Except Postal Service	Tampa-St. Petersburg-Clearwater MSA, FL	H	9.65 AE	13.64 MW	15.89 AEX	FLBLS	7/16-9/16
Except Postal Service	Georgia	Y	21450 FQ	27670 MW	34820 TQ	USBLS	5/15
Except Postal Service	Atlanta-Sandy Springs-Roswell MSA, GA	Y	22100 FQ	28820 MW	35810 TQ	USBLS	5/15
Except Postal Service	Augusta-Richmond County MSA, GA-SC	Y	19540 FQ	23870 MW	34270 TQ	USBLS	5/15
Except Postal Service	Hawaii	Y	23310 FQ	29840 MW	36950 TQ	USBLS	5/15
Except Postal Service	Urban Honolulu MSA, HI	Y	25170 FQ	31280 MW	38940 TQ	USBLS	5/15
Except Postal Service	Idaho	Y	22220 FQ	25720 MW	29900 TQ	USBLS	5/15
Except Postal Service	Boise City MSA, ID	Y	22410 FQ	26240 MW	29960 TQ	USBLS	5/15
Except Postal Service	Illinois	Y	20580 FQ	28220 MW	37220 TQ	USBLS	5/15
Except Postal Service	Chicago-Naperville-Arlington Heights PMSA, IL	Y	21460 FQ	29050 MW	38020 TQ	USBLS	5/15
Except Postal Service	Lake County-Kenosha County PMSA, IL-WI	Y	19440 FQ	32380 MW	40630 TQ	USBLS	5/15
Except Postal Service	Indiana	Y	19490 FQ	25790 MW	32020 TQ	USBLS	5/15
Except Postal Service	Gary PMSA, IN	Y	21830 FQ	27190 MW	30770 TQ	USBLS	5/15
Except Postal Service	Indianapolis-Carmel-Anderson MSA, IN	Y	20580 FQ	25760 MW	31080 TQ	USBLS	5/15
Except Postal Service	Iowa	Y	20440 FQ	26920 MW	32470 TQ	USBLS	5/15
Except Postal Service	Des Moines-West Des Moines MSA, IA	Y	21830 FQ	28810 MW	35010 TQ	USBLS	5/15
Except Postal Service	Kansas	Y	21680 FQ	28540 MW	36440 TQ	USBLS	5/15
Except Postal Service	Kentucky	Y	22880 FQ	29050 MW	34210 TQ	USBLS	5/15
Except Postal Service	Louisville-Jefferson County MSA, KY-IN	Y	22520 FQ	26500 MW	32070 TQ	USBLS	5/15
Except Postal Service	Louisiana	Y	20450 FQ	25930 MW	33340 TQ	USBLS	5/15
Except Postal Service	Baton Rouge MSA, LA	Y	18740 FQ	26320 MW	31730 TQ	USBLS	5/15
Except Postal Service	New Orleans-Metairie MSA, LA	Y	23150 FQ	28730 MW	36110 TQ	USBLS	5/15
Except Postal Service	Maine	Y	21750 FQ	26990 MW	32010 TQ	USBLS	5/15
Except Postal Service	Portland-South Portland MSA, ME	Y	20330 FQ	24840 MW	31010 TQ	USBLS	5/15
Except Postal Service	Maryland	Y	20483 AE	32675 MW	38771 AEX	MDBLS	4/16
Except Postal Service	Baltimore-Columbia-Towson MSA, MD	Y	23550 FQ	31430 MW	39900 TQ	USBLS	5/15
Except Postal Service	Salisbury MSA, MD-DE	Y	22620 FQ	26640 MW	34190 TQ	USBLS	5/15
Except Postal Service	Massachusetts	Y	27890 FQ	34290 MW	40600 TQ	USBLS	5/15
Except Postal Service	Boston-Cambridge-Newton NECTA, MA	Y	28500 FQ	35100 MW	41110 TQ	USBLS	5/15
Except Postal Service	Worcester MSA, MA-CT	Y	26050 FQ	30720 MW	36960 TQ	USBLS	5/15
Except Postal Service	Michigan	Y	21820 FQ	27380 MW	34760 TQ	USBLS	5/15
Except Postal Service	Detroit-Dearborn-Livonia PMSA, MI	Y	23830 FQ	31040 MW	37230 TQ	USBLS	5/15
Except Postal Service	Grand Rapids-Wyoming MSA, MI	Y	25150 FQ	29180 MW	34120 TQ	USBLS	5/15
Except Postal Service	Minnesota	Y	23067 FQ	29266 MW	37528 TQ	MNBLS	1/16-3/16
Except Postal Service	Minneapolis-St. Paul-Bloomington MSA, MN-WI	Y	24614 FQ	31339 MW	39076 TQ	MNBLS	1/16-3/16
Except Postal Service	Mississippi	Y	19150 FQ	23650 MW	30600 TQ	USBLS	5/15
Except Postal Service	Jackson MSA, MS	Y	18800 FQ	23420 MW	30470 TQ	USBLS	5/15
Except Postal Service	Missouri	Y	23840 FQ	28560 MW	33480 TQ	USBLS	5/15
Except Postal Service	Kansas City MSA, MO-KS	Y	21720 FQ	28000 MW	33730 TQ	USBLS	5/15
Except Postal Service	St. Louis MSA, MO-IL	Y	26670 FQ	30440 MW	35250 TQ	USBLS	5/15
Except Postal Service	Montana	Y	19020 FQ	22820 MW	28180 TQ	USBLS	5/15
Except Postal Service	Billings MSA, MT	Y	20880 FQ	24400 MW	32660 TQ	USBLS	5/15
Except Postal Service	Nebraska	Y	21130 FQ	26270 MW	31205 TQ	NEBLS	7/16-9/16
Except Postal Service	Omaha-Council Bluffs MSA, NE-IA	Y	24370 FQ	28485 MW	33325 TQ	NEBLS	7/16-9/16
Except Postal Service	Nevada	Y	26060 FQ	30380 MW	36140 TQ	USBLS	5/15

AE	Average entry wage	AWR	Average wage range	H	Hourly	LR	Low end range	MTC	Median total compensation	TCC	Total cash compensation
AEX	Average experienced wage	B	Biweekly	HI	Highest wage paid	M	Monthly	MW	Median wage paid	TQ	Third quartile wage
ATC	Average total compensation	D	Daily	HR	High end range	MCC	Median cash compensation	MWR	Median wage range	W	Weekly
AW	Average wage paid	FQ	First quartile wage	LO	Lowest wage paid	ME	Median entry wage	S	See annotated source	Y	Yearly

Mail Clerk and Mail Machine Operator

Occupation/Type/Industry	Location	Per	Low	Mid	High	Source	Date
Except Postal Service	Las Vegas-Henderson-Paradise MSA, NV	Y	25770 FQ	32440 MW	37320 TQ	USBLS	5/15
Except Postal Service	New Hampshire	H	10.44 AE	13.90 MW	16.14 AEX	NHBLS	6/16
Except Postal Service	Manchester NECTA, NH	H	10.24 AE	12.73 MW	14.88 AEX	NHBLS	6/16
Except Postal Service	Nashua NECTA, NH-MA	Y	22610 FQ	28150 MW	38370 TQ	USBLS	5/15
Except Postal Service	New Jersey	Y	22380 FQ	29400 MW	38130 TQ	USBLS	5/15
Except Postal Service	Camden PMSA, NJ	Y	23410 FQ	27660 MW	33510 TQ	USBLS	5/15
Except Postal Service	Newark PMSA, NJ-PA	Y	22260 FQ	30540 MW	38220 TQ	USBLS	5/15
Except Postal Service	Trenton MSA, NJ	Y	28510 FQ	37390 MW	46530 TQ	USBLS	5/15
Except Postal Service	New Mexico	Y	23160 FQ	28520 MW	34260 TQ	USBLS	5/15
Except Postal Service	Albuquerque MSA, NM	Y	26530 FQ	30460 MW	37470 TQ	USBLS	5/15
Except Postal Service	New York	Y	22360 AE	32090 MW	39420 AEX	NYBLS	1/16-3/16
Except Postal Service	Buffalo-Cheektowaga-Niagara Falls MSA, NY	Y	27810 FQ	33680 MW	40200 TQ	USBLS	5/15
Except Postal Service	Nassau County-Suffolk County PMSA, NY	Y	21410 FQ	29110 MW	39760 TQ	USBLS	5/15
Except Postal Service	New York-Jersey City-White Plains PMSA, NY-NJ	Y	23230 FQ	30820 MW	39710 TQ	USBLS	5/15
Except Postal Service	Rochester MSA, NY	Y	24550 FQ	29200 MW	35820 TQ	USBLS	5/15
Except Postal Service	North Carolina	Y	20810 FQ	26840 MW	33160 TQ	USBLS	5/15
Except Postal Service	Charlotte-Concord-Gastonia MSA, NC-SC	Y	19920 FQ	25110 MW	30550 TQ	USBLS	5/15
Except Postal Service	Raleigh MSA, NC	Y	22330 FQ	26870 MW	30810 TQ	USBLS	5/15
Except Postal Service	North Dakota	Y	22690 FQ	26810 MW	32260 TQ	USBLS	5/15
Except Postal Service	Fargo MSA, ND-MN	Y	24920 FQ	29010 MW	34050 TQ	USBLS	5/15
Except Postal Service	Ohio	Y	21930 FQ	27600 MW	35440 TQ	USBLS	5/15
Except Postal Service	Cincinnati MSA, OH-KY-IN	Y	20730 FQ	27110 MW	33450 TQ	USBLS	5/15
Except Postal Service	Cleveland-Elyria MSA, OH	Y	26220 FQ	30610 MW	39310 TQ	USBLS	5/15
Except Postal Service	Columbus MSA, OH	Y	23070 FQ	28560 MW	36330 TQ	USBLS	5/15
Except Postal Service	Oklahoma	Y	20580 FQ	26640 MW	34080 TQ	USBLS	5/15
Except Postal Service	Oklahoma City MSA, OK	Y	22420 FQ	29700 MW	36690 TQ	USBLS	5/15
Except Postal Service	Tulsa MSA, OK	Y	19580 FQ	25580 MW	30990 TQ	USBLS	5/15
Except Postal Service	Oregon	H	12.74 FQ	14.93 MW	18.27 TQ	ORBLS	2016
Except Postal Service	Portland-Vancouver-Hillsboro MSA, OR-WA	Y	27220 FQ	31130 MW	38270 TQ	USBLS	5/15
Except Postal Service	Pennsylvania	Y	21890 FQ	27890 MW	35530 TQ	USBLS	5/15
Except Postal Service	Allentown-Bethlehem-Easton MSA, PA-NJ	Y	21530 FQ	26030 MW	33700 TQ	USBLS	5/15
Except Postal Service	Harrisburg-Carlisle MSA, PA	Y	25840 FQ	30000 MW	35980 TQ	USBLS	5/15
Except Postal Service	Montgomery County-Bucks County-Chester County PMSA, PA	Y	22520 FQ	27900 MW	38430 TQ	USBLS	5/15
Except Postal Service	Philadelphia PMSA, PA	Y	27350 FQ	32270 MW	39390 TQ	USBLS	5/15
Except Postal Service	Pittsburgh MSA, PA	Y	19540 FQ	22960 MW	29780 TQ	USBLS	5/15
Except Postal Service	Rhode Island	Y	27650 FQ	33190 MW	39520 TQ	USBLS	5/15
Except Postal Service	Providence-Warwick MSA, RI-MA	Y	27790 FQ	33300 MW	39540 TQ	USBLS	5/15
Except Postal Service	South Carolina	Y	21390 FQ	25210 MW	31480 TQ	USBLS	5/15
Except Postal Service	Charleston-North Charleston MSA, SC	Y	25180 FQ	29790 MW	36300 TQ	USBLS	5/15
Except Postal Service	Columbia MSA, SC	Y	23540 FQ	28110 MW	33110 TQ	USBLS	5/15
Except Postal Service	Greenville-Anderson-Mauldin MSA, SC	Y	19490 FQ	22480 MW	25810 TQ	USBLS	5/15
Except Postal Service	South Dakota	Y	20400 FQ	23500 MW	27710 TQ	USBLS	5/15
Except Postal Service	Sioux Falls MSA, SD	Y	21340 FQ	24200 MW	27870 TQ	USBLS	5/15
Except Postal Service	Tennessee	Y	20950 FQ	27600 MW	34540 TQ	USBLS	5/15
Except Postal Service	Knoxville MSA, TN	Y	18430 FQ	26020 MW	32180 TQ	USBLS	5/15
Except Postal Service	Memphis MSA, TN-MS-AR	Y	20590 FQ	29500 MW	37110 TQ	USBLS	5/15
Except Postal Service	Nashville-Davidson–Murfreesboro–Franklin MSA, TN	Y	22980 FQ	28950 MW	35220 TQ	USBLS	5/15
Except Postal Service	Texas	Y	22550 FQ	28060 MW	34090 TQ	USBLS	5/15
Except Postal Service	Austin-Round Rock MSA, TX	Y	24720 FQ	28670 MW	33060 TQ	USBLS	5/15
Except Postal Service	Dallas-Plano-Irving PMSA, TX	Y	23660 FQ	28570 MW	34590 TQ	USBLS	5/15
Except Postal Service	Fort Worth-Arlington PMSA, TX	Y	25630 FQ	29090 MW	33970 TQ	USBLS	5/15
Except Postal Service	Houston-The Woodlands-Sugar Land MSA, TX	Y	21680 FQ	28790 MW	37480 TQ	USBLS	5/15

AE	Average entry wage	AWR	Average wage range	H	Hourly	LR	Low end range	MTC	Median total compensation	TCC	Total cash compensation
AEX	Average experienced wage	B	Biweekly	HI	Highest wage paid	M	Monthly	MW	Median wage paid	TQ	Third quartile wage
ATC	Average total compensation	D	Daily	HR	High end range	MCC	Median cash compensation	MWR	Median wage range	W	Weekly
AW	Average wage paid	FQ	First quartile wage	LO	Lowest wage paid	ME	Median entry wage	S	See annotated source	Y	Yearly

Occupation/Type/Industry	Location	Per	Low	Mid	High	Source	Date
Mail Clerk and Mail Machine Operator							
Except Postal Service	San Antonio-New Braunfels MSA, TX	Y	19220 FQ	25070 MW	33220 TQ	USBLS	5/15
Except Postal Service	Utah	Y	24880 FQ	29140 MW	34010 TQ	USBLS	5/15
Except Postal Service	Ogden-Clearfield MSA, UT	Y	25430 FQ	29680 MW	33300 TQ	USBLS	5/15
Except Postal Service	Salt Lake City MSA, UT	Y	25350 FQ	29180 MW	34830 TQ	USBLS	5/15
Except Postal Service	Vermont	Y	25420 FQ	32310 MW	36660 TQ	USBLS	5/15
Except Postal Service	Burlington-South Burlington MSA, VT	Y	28140 FQ	33860 MW	37430 TQ	USBLS	5/15
Except Postal Service	Virginia	Y	19650 FQ	25920 MW	33910 TQ	USBLS	5/15
Except Postal Service	Richmond MSA, VA	Y	26020 FQ	29830 MW	35910 TQ	USBLS	5/15
Except Postal Service	Virginia Beach-Norfolk-Newport News MSA, VA-NC	Y	22510 FQ	28550 MW	36200 TQ	USBLS	5/15
Except Postal Service	Washington	H	12.62 FQ	16.41 MW	20.46 TQ	WABLS	3/16
Except Postal Service	Seattle-Bellevue-Everett PMSA, WA	H	13.83 FQ	17.58 MW	21.54 TQ	WABLS	3/16
Except Postal Service	Tacoma-Lakewood PMSA, WA	H	15.25 FQ	18.94 MW	22.09 TQ	WABLS	3/16
Except Postal Service	West Virginia	Y	18810 FQ	24320 MW	33770 TQ	USBLS	5/15
Except Postal Service	Huntington-Ashland MSA, WV-KY-OH	Y	20740 FQ	31390 MW	36240 TQ	USBLS	5/15
Except Postal Service	Wisconsin	Y	21360 FQ	28210 MW	34520 TQ	USBLS	5/15
Except Postal Service	Madison MSA, WI	Y	21310 FQ	28340 MW	35070 TQ	USBLS	5/15
Except Postal Service	Milwaukee-Waukesha-West Allis MSA, WI	Y	21440 FQ	27690 MW	33040 TQ	USBLS	5/15
Except Postal Service	Wyoming	Y	17990 FQ	22450 MW	30360 TQ	USBLS	5/15
Except Postal Service	Cheyenne MSA, WY	Y	22500 FQ	26010 MW	30850 TQ	USBLS	5/15
Except Postal Service	Puerto Rico	Y	17420 FQ	19450 MW	34700 TQ	USBLS	5/15
Except Postal Service	San Juan-Carolina-Caguas MSA, PR	Y	17230 FQ	19040 MW	33740 TQ	USBLS	5/15
Except Postal Service	Virgin Islands	Y	21770 FQ	24040 MW	32490 TQ	USBLS	5/15
Mail Courier							
Municipal Government	Seattle, WA	H	16.17 LO		18.04 HI	CSSS	1/13/16
Mailing Coordinator							
College and University	United States	Y		31173 AW		HED03	2015-2016
Mailroom Supervisor							
Municipal Government	Detroit, MI	M	2575 LO		3342 HI	DETGOV	2016
Maintenance and Repair Worker							
General	Alabama	Y	24825 AE	38138 AW	44789 AEX	ALBLS	6/16
General	Birmingham-Hoover MSA, AL	Y	27215 AE	39674 AW	45908 AEX	ALBLS	6/16
General	Tuscaloosa MSA, AL	Y	24825 AE	36236 AW	41932 AEX	ALBLS	6/16
General	Alaska	Y	37240 FQ	48040 MW	61170 TQ	USBLS	5/15
General	Anchorage MSA, AK	Y	35680 FQ	46100 MW	59770 TQ	USBLS	5/15
General	Arizona	Y	26110 FQ	33910 MW	44280 TQ	USBLS	5/15
General	Phoenix-Mesa-Scottsdale MSA, AZ	Y	26590 FQ	34630 MW	45140 TQ	USBLS	5/15
General	Tucson MSA, AZ	Y	25600 FQ	32260 MW	41130 TQ	USBLS	5/15
General	Arkansas	Y	22780 FQ	30610 MW	38360 TQ	USBLS	5/15
General	Little Rock-North Little Rock-Conway MSA, AR	Y	22250 FQ	31070 MW	38970 TQ	USBLS	5/15
General	California	H	14.80 FQ	19.47 MW	26.19 TQ	CABLS	1/16-3/16
General	Anaheim-Santa Ana-Irvine PMSA, CA	H	14.33 FQ	18.80 MW	24.73 TQ	CABLS	1/16-3/16
General	Los Angeles-Long Beach-Glendale PMSA, CA	H	15.03 FQ	20.04 MW	26.61 TQ	CABLS	1/16-3/16
General	Oakland-Hayward-Berkeley PMSA, CA	H	15.42 FQ	19.60 MW	27.61 TQ	CABLS	1/16-3/16
General	Riverside-San Bernardino-Ontario MSA, CA	H	13.77 FQ	18.16 MW	24.34 TQ	CABLS	1/16-3/16
General	Sacramento–Roseville–Arden-Arcade MSA, CA	H	14.61 FQ	18.97 MW	25.76 TQ	CABLS	1/16-3/16
General	San Diego-Carlsbad MSA, CA	H	14.32 FQ	18.72 MW	24.65 TQ	CABLS	1/16-3/16
General	San Francisco-Redwood City-South San Francisco PMSA, CA	H	18.95 FQ	27.16 MW	35.71 TQ	CABLS	1/16-3/16
General	Colorado	Y	28360 FQ	36600 MW	47410 TQ	USBLS	5/15
General	Denver-Aurora-Lakewood MSA, CO	Y	29180 FQ	36730 MW	47890 TQ	USBLS	5/15

AE	Average entry wage	AWR	Average wage range	H	Hourly	LR	Low end range	MTC	Median total compensation	TCC	Total cash compensation
AEX	Average experienced wage	B	Biweekly	HI	Highest wage paid	M	Monthly	MW	Median wage paid	TQ	Third quartile wage
ATC	Average total compensation	D	Daily	HR	High end range	MCC	Median cash compensation	MWR	Median wage range	W	Weekly
AW	Average wage paid	FQ	First quartile wage	LO	Lowest wage paid	ME	Median entry wage	S	See annotated source	Y	Yearly

Occupation/Type/Industry	Location	Per	Low	Mid	High	Source	Date
Maintenance and Repair Worker							
General	Connecticut	Y		44206 MW		CTBLS	1/16-3/16
General	Bridgeport-Stamford-Norwalk MSA, CT	Y	36840 FQ	47370 MW	60810 TQ	USBLS	5/15
General	Hartford-West Hartford-East Hartford MSA, CT	Y	32340 FQ	42130 MW	52420 TQ	USBLS	5/15
General	Delaware	Y	31750 FQ	38670 MW	48930 TQ	USBLS	5/15
General	Wilmington PMSA, DE-MD-NJ	Y	31310 FQ	40070 MW	52220 TQ	USBLS	5/15
General	District of Columbia	Y	33730 FQ	44360 MW	56780 TQ	USBLS	5/15
General	Washington-Arlington-Alexandria PMSA, DC-VA-MD-WV	Y	33550 FQ	42950 MW	55740 TQ	USBLS	5/15
General	Florida	H	11.50 AE	15.66 MW	19.36 AEX	FLBLS	7/16-9/16
General	Fort Lauderdale-Pompano Beach-Deerfield Beach PMSA, FL	H	12.12 AE	15.63 MW	19.33 AEX	FLBLS	7/16-9/16
General	Miami-Miami Beach-Kendall PMSA, FL	H	11.19 AE	15.11 MW	18.77 AEX	FLBLS	7/16-9/16
General	Orlando-Kissimmee-Sanford MSA, FL	H	11.49 AE	15.56 MW	19.19 AEX	FLBLS	7/16-9/16
General	Tampa-St. Petersburg-Clearwater MSA, FL	H	11.00 AE	15.19 MW	18.61 AEX	FLBLS	7/16-9/16
General	Georgia	Y	26120 FQ	34340 MW	44190 TQ	USBLS	5/15
General	Atlanta-Sandy Springs-Roswell MSA, GA	Y	27960 FQ	36490 MW	46400 TQ	USBLS	5/15
General	Augusta-Richmond County MSA, GA-SC	Y	25640 FQ	32430 MW	47940 TQ	USBLS	5/15
General	Hawaii	Y	33940 FQ	43740 MW	55400 TQ	USBLS	5/15
General	Urban Honolulu MSA, HI	Y	32420 FQ	42320 MW	54820 TQ	USBLS	5/15
General	Idaho	Y	24060 FQ	31980 MW	42130 TQ	USBLS	5/15
General	Boise City MSA, ID	Y	23350 FQ	29710 MW	37870 TQ	USBLS	5/15
General	Illinois	Y	29570 FQ	40700 MW	54630 TQ	USBLS	5/15
General	Chicago-Naperville-Arlington Heights PMSA, IL	Y	30730 FQ	42430 MW	56820 TQ	USBLS	5/15
General	Lake County-Kenosha County PMSA, IL-WI	Y	30820 FQ	42030 MW	56570 TQ	USBLS	5/15
General	Indiana	Y	28380 FQ	36800 MW	46440 TQ	USBLS	5/15
General	Gary PMSA, IN	Y	27540 FQ	36610 MW	47200 TQ	USBLS	5/15
General	Indianapolis-Carmel-Anderson MSA, IN	Y	29920 FQ	37330 MW	46270 TQ	USBLS	5/15
General	Iowa	Y	28310 FQ	36570 MW	46200 TQ	USBLS	5/15
General	Des Moines-West Des Moines MSA, IA	Y	29200 FQ	37720 MW	46940 TQ	USBLS	5/15
General	Kansas	Y	26890 FQ	34720 MW	45670 TQ	USBLS	5/15
General	Wichita MSA, KS	Y	25540 FQ	33850 MW	45450 TQ	USBLS	5/15
General	Kentucky	Y	26260 FQ	35110 MW	46090 TQ	USBLS	5/15
General	Louisville-Jefferson County MSA, KY-IN	Y	29750 FQ	37980 MW	48980 TQ	USBLS	5/15
General	Louisiana	Y	25780 FQ	33710 MW	43930 TQ	USBLS	5/15
General	Baton Rouge MSA, LA	Y	24240 FQ	33950 MW	45770 TQ	USBLS	5/15
General	New Orleans-Metairie MSA, LA	Y	27760 FQ	35310 MW	45270 TQ	USBLS	5/15
General	Maine	Y	30380 FQ	36880 MW	46520 TQ	USBLS	5/15
General	Portland-South Portland MSA, ME	Y	32840 FQ	38430 MW	48850 TQ	USBLS	5/15
General	Maryland	Y	26597 AE	40905 MW	48059 AEX	MDBLS	4/16
General	Baltimore-Columbia-Towson MSA, MD	Y	31040 FQ	40100 MW	49560 TQ	USBLS	5/15
General	Salisbury MSA, MD-DE	Y	24960 FQ	32290 MW	39830 TQ	USBLS	5/15
General	Massachusetts	Y	33620 FQ	42890 MW	54440 TQ	USBLS	5/15
General	Boston-Cambridge-Newton NECTA, MA	Y	35630 FQ	45230 MW	56690 TQ	USBLS	5/15
General	Worcester MSA, MA-CT	Y	32280 FQ	42320 MW	53400 TQ	USBLS	5/15
General	Michigan	Y	25970 FQ	34760 MW	45820 TQ	USBLS	5/15
General	Detroit-Dearborn-Livonia PMSA, MI	Y	27430 FQ	37970 MW	48880 TQ	USBLS	5/15
General	Grand Rapids-Wyoming MSA, MI	Y	26640 FQ	36180 MW	46150 TQ	USBLS	5/15
General	Minnesota	Y	33026 FQ	41745 MW	51078 TQ	MNBLS	1/16-3/16
General	Minneapolis-St. Paul-Bloomington MSA, MN-WI	Y	35370 FQ	44431 MW	54457 TQ	MNBLS	1/16-3/16

AE	Average entry wage	AWR	Average wage range	H	Hourly	LR	Low end range	MTC	Median total compensation	TCC	Total cash compensation
AEX	Average experienced wage	B	Biweekly	HI	Highest wage paid	M	Monthly	MW	Median wage paid	TQ	Third quartile wage
ATC	Average total compensation	D	Daily	HR	High end range	MCC	Median cash compensation	MWR	Median wage range	W	Weekly
AW	Average wage paid	FQ	First quartile wage	LO	Lowest wage paid	ME	Median entry wage	S	See annotated source	Y	Yearly

Maintenance and Repair Worker

Occupation/Type/Industry	Location	Per	Low	Mid	High	Source	Date
General	Mississippi	Y	23120 FQ	29590 MW	38130 TQ	USBLS	5/15
General	Jackson MSA, MS	Y	22390 FQ	29100 MW	38190 TQ	USBLS	5/15
General	Missouri	Y	25890 FQ	33350 MW	42870 TQ	USBLS	5/15
General	Kansas City MSA, MO-KS	Y	27090 FQ	34740 MW	45420 TQ	USBLS	5/15
General	St. Louis MSA, MO-IL	Y	28570 FQ	36990 MW	49710 TQ	USBLS	5/15
General	Montana	Y	24870 FQ	31800 MW	42590 TQ	USBLS	5/15
General	Billings MSA, MT	Y	25420 FQ	29730 MW	36970 TQ	USBLS	5/15
General	Nebraska	Y	28490 FQ	36225 MW	45040 TQ	NEBLS	7/16-9/16
General	Omaha-Council Bluffs MSA, NE-IA	Y	29235 FQ	37300 MW	46405 TQ	NEBLS	7/16-9/16
General	Nevada	Y	30840 FQ	43130 MW	58010 TQ	USBLS	5/15
General	Las Vegas-Henderson-Paradise MSA, NV	Y	32840 FQ	47320 MW	60460 TQ	USBLS	5/15
General	New Hampshire	H	14.13 AE	18.97 MW	22.70 AEX	NHBLS	6/16
General	Manchester NECTA, NH	H	15.12 AE	19.94 MW	24.24 AEX	NHBLS	6/16
General	Nashua NECTA, NH-MA	Y	31240 FQ	40220 MW	50480 TQ	USBLS	5/15
General	New Jersey	Y	31600 FQ	41230 MW	55070 TQ	USBLS	5/15
General	Camden PMSA, NJ	Y	32630 FQ	42080 MW	53110 TQ	USBLS	5/15
General	Newark PMSA, NJ-PA	Y	31030 FQ	40160 MW	54920 TQ	USBLS	5/15
General	Trenton MSA, NJ	Y	33970 FQ	45000 MW	58630 TQ	USBLS	5/15
General	New Mexico	Y	25100 FQ	32130 MW	42020 TQ	USBLS	5/15
General	Albuquerque MSA, NM	Y	24060 FQ	32750 MW	42220 TQ	USBLS	5/15
General	Farmington MSA, NM	Y	27790 FQ	35590 MW	47660 TQ	USBLS	5/15
General	New York	Y	27380 AE	42200 MW	51790 AEX	NYBLS	1/16-3/16
General	Buffalo-Cheektowaga-Niagara Falls MSA, NY	Y	29080 FQ	37560 MW	47560 TQ	USBLS	5/15
General	Nassau County-Suffolk County PMSA, NY	Y	33480 FQ	46060 MW	59890 TQ	USBLS	5/15
General	New York-Jersey City-White Plains PMSA, NY-NJ	Y	31470 FQ	42940 MW	56050 TQ	USBLS	5/15
General	Rochester MSA, NY	Y	30530 FQ	38230 MW	48220 TQ	USBLS	5/15
General	North Carolina	Y	28940 FQ	36710 MW	46220 TQ	USBLS	5/15
General	Charlotte-Concord-Gastonia MSA, NC-SC	Y	31210 FQ	39060 MW	48410 TQ	USBLS	5/15
General	Raleigh MSA, NC	Y	30930 FQ	37550 MW	47110 TQ	USBLS	5/15
General	North Dakota	Y	32330 FQ	38950 MW	49380 TQ	USBLS	5/15
General	Fargo MSA, ND-MN	Y	32040 FQ	37220 MW	46620 TQ	USBLS	5/15
General	Ohio	Y	29100 FQ	37520 MW	47270 TQ	USBLS	5/15
General	Cincinnati MSA, OH-KY-IN	Y	29720 FQ	38810 MW	49860 TQ	USBLS	5/15
General	Cleveland-Elyria MSA, OH	Y	29250 FQ	38440 MW	48470 TQ	USBLS	5/15
General	Columbus MSA, OH	Y	30420 FQ	38750 MW	48450 TQ	USBLS	5/15
General	Oklahoma	Y	24650 FQ	32060 MW	40700 TQ	USBLS	5/15
General	Oklahoma City MSA, OK	Y	26020 FQ	33310 MW	40070 TQ	USBLS	5/15
General	Tulsa MSA, OK	Y	26240 FQ	33500 MW	43570 TQ	USBLS	5/15
General	Oregon	H	14.34 FQ	18.41 MW	24.00 TQ	ORBLS	2016
General	Portland-Vancouver-Hillsboro MSA, OR-WA	Y	31200 FQ	40540 MW	54090 TQ	USBLS	5/15
General	Pennsylvania	Y	28350 FQ	36980 MW	47340 TQ	USBLS	5/15
General	Allentown-Bethlehem-Easton MSA, PA-NJ	Y	27520 FQ	36310 MW	47680 TQ	USBLS	5/15
General	Harrisburg-Carlisle MSA, PA	Y	30090 FQ	37780 MW	46320 TQ	USBLS	5/15
General	Montgomery County-Bucks County-Chester County PMSA, PA	Y	29950 FQ	39770 MW	50630 TQ	USBLS	5/15
General	Philadelphia PMSA, PA	Y	31780 FQ	39780 MW	52190 TQ	USBLS	5/15
General	Pittsburgh MSA, PA	Y	28950 FQ	37370 MW	48120 TQ	USBLS	5/15
General	Rhode Island	Y	32310 FQ	40580 MW	49850 TQ	USBLS	5/15
General	Providence-Warwick MSA, RI-MA	Y	32320 FQ	40680 MW	49760 TQ	USBLS	5/15
General	South Carolina	Y	25830 FQ	33300 MW	44090 TQ	USBLS	5/15
General	Charleston-North Charleston MSA, SC	Y	27040 FQ	35880 MW	47160 TQ	USBLS	5/15
General	Columbia MSA, SC	Y	26580 FQ	33640 MW	43250 TQ	USBLS	5/15
General	Greenville-Anderson-Mauldin MSA, SC	Y	27620 FQ	35270 MW	46100 TQ	USBLS	5/15
General	South Dakota	Y	28900 FQ	33760 MW	38730 TQ	USBLS	5/15
General	Sioux Falls MSA, SD	Y	27960 FQ	32310 MW	37660 TQ	USBLS	5/15
General	Tennessee	Y	28450 FQ	36290 MW	46210 TQ	USBLS	5/15
General	Knoxville MSA, TN	Y	28310 FQ	36260 MW	46570 TQ	USBLS	5/15
General	Memphis MSA, TN-MS-AR	Y	28400 FQ	36120 MW	46180 TQ	USBLS	5/15

AE	Average entry wage	AWR	Average wage range	H	Hourly	LR	Low end range	MTC	Median total compensation	TCC	Total cash compensation
AEX	Average experienced wage	B	Biweekly	HI	Highest wage paid	M	Monthly	MW	Median wage paid	TQ	Third quartile wage
ATC	Average total compensation	D	Daily	HR	High end range	MCC	Median cash compensation	MWR	Median wage range	W	Weekly
AW	Average wage paid	FQ	First quartile wage	LO	Lowest wage paid	ME	Median entry wage	S	See annotated source	Y	Yearly

Occupation/Type/Industry	Location	Per	Low	Mid	High	Source	Date
Maintenance and Repair Worker							
General	Nashville-Davidson– Murfreesboro–Franklin MSA, TN	Y	30060 FQ	37070 MW	46480 TQ	USBLS	5/15
General	Texas	Y	25150 FQ	32870 MW	42660 TQ	USBLS	5/15
General	Austin-Round Rock MSA, TX	Y	27310 FQ	34380 MW	42060 TQ	USBLS	5/15
General	Dallas-Plano-Irving PMSA, TX	Y	27520 FQ	35740 MW	45210 TQ	USBLS	5/15
General	Fort Worth-Arlington PMSA, TX	Y	26080 FQ	34150 MW	44470 TQ	USBLS	5/15
General	Houston-The Woodlands-Sugar Land MSA, TX	Y	26950 FQ	35350 MW	46960 TQ	USBLS	5/15
General	San Antonio-New Braunfels MSA, TX	Y	24880 FQ	30220 MW	38580 TQ	USBLS	5/15
General	Utah	Y	26440 FQ	34910 MW	46540 TQ	USBLS	5/15
General	Ogden-Clearfield MSA, UT	Y	26320 FQ	35500 MW	47790 TQ	USBLS	5/15
General	Provo-Orem MSA, UT	Y	25990 FQ	32600 MW	43990 TQ	USBLS	5/15
General	Salt Lake City MSA, UT	Y	27740 FQ	36500 MW	49130 TQ	USBLS	5/15
General	Vermont	Y	29630 FQ	36640 MW	45510 TQ	USBLS	5/15
General	Burlington-South Burlington MSA, VT	Y	29320 FQ	36380 MW	46730 TQ	USBLS	5/15
General	Virginia	Y	28880 FQ	37230 MW	48030 TQ	USBLS	5/15
General	Richmond MSA, VA	Y	29850 FQ	37580 MW	47970 TQ	USBLS	5/15
General	Virginia Beach-Norfolk-Newport News MSA, VA-NC	Y	26630 FQ	34630 MW	43650 TQ	USBLS	5/15
General	Washington	H	15.45 FQ	20.13 MW	26.21 TQ	WABLS	3/16
General	Seattle-Bellevue-Everett PMSA, WA	H	16.33 FQ	20.70 MW	26.98 TQ	WABLS	3/16
General	Tacoma-Lakewood PMSA, WA	H	15.17 FQ	21.35 MW	26.92 TQ	WABLS	3/16
General	West Virginia	Y	21330 FQ	27770 MW	36850 TQ	USBLS	5/15
General	Huntington-Ashland MSA, WV-KY-OH	Y	22720 FQ	30510 MW	39490 TQ	USBLS	5/15
General	Wisconsin	Y	29190 FQ	37920 MW	47470 TQ *	USBLS	5/15
General	Madison MSA, WI	Y	31740 FQ	39320 MW	48280 TQ	USBLS	5/15
General	Milwaukee-Waukesha-West Allis MSA, WI	Y	28420 FQ	37980 MW	48660 TQ	USBLS	5/15
General	Wyoming	Y	29770 FQ	38800 MW	56030 TQ	USBLS	5/15
General	Cheyenne MSA, WY	Y	25850 FQ	36810 MW	46170 TQ	USBLS	5/15
General	Puerto Rico	Y	17320 FQ	19140 MW	25370 TQ	USBLS	5/15
General	San Juan-Carolina-Caguas MSA, PR	Y	17330 FQ	19150 MW	25270 TQ	USBLS	5/15
General	Virgin Islands	Y	22770 FQ	30660 MW	38380 TQ	USBLS	5/15
General	Guam	Y	19790 FQ	24830 MW	33200 TQ	USBLS	5/15
Maintenance Superintendent							
Department of Public Works, Municipal Government	Auburn, GA	Y	36275 LO		53602 HI	GACTY02	2016
Department of Public Works, Municipal Government	Hiram, GA	Y	30000 LO		40000 HI	GACTY02	2016
Department of Public Works, Municipal Government	Smyrna, GA	Y	49676 LO		74514 HI	GACTY02	2016
Maintenance Worker							
Machinery	Alabama	Y	26442 AE	39643 AW	46254 AEX	ALBLS	6/16
Machinery	Birmingham-Hoover MSA, AL	Y	29453 AE	38637 AW	43233 AEX	ALBLS	6/16
Machinery	Alaska	Y	46280 FQ	55760 MW	65780 TQ	USBLS	5/15
Machinery	Arizona	Y	33670 FQ	40820 MW	48860 TQ	USBLS	5/15
Machinery	Phoenix-Mesa-Scottsdale MSA, AZ	Y	33010 FQ	41420 MW	49870 TQ	USBLS	5/15
Machinery	Tucson MSA, AZ	Y	37520 FQ	43780 MW	49520 TQ	USBLS	5/15
Machinery	Arkansas	Y	28740 FQ	40110 MW	48730 TQ	USBLS	5/15
Machinery	Little Rock-North Little Rock-Conway MSA, AR	Y	38130 FQ	46180 MW	54060 TQ	USBLS	5/15
Machinery	California	H	15.46 FQ	19.44 MW	26.63 TQ	CABLS	1/16-3/16
Machinery	Anaheim-Santa Ana-Irvine PMSA, CA	H	15.67 FQ	18.59 MW	23.20 TQ	CABLS	1/16-3/16
Machinery	Los Angeles-Long Beach-Glendale PMSA, CA	H	14.52 FQ	18.60 MW	27.51 TQ	CABLS	1/16-3/16
Machinery	Oakland-Hayward-Berkeley PMSA, CA	H	20.72 FQ	31.41 MW	37.11 TQ	CABLS	1/16-3/16
Machinery	Riverside-San Bernardino-Ontario MSA, CA	H	15.77 FQ	19.72 MW	23.91 TQ	CABLS	1/16-3/16

AE	Average entry wage	AWR	Average wage range	H	Hourly
AEX	Average experienced wage	B	Biweekly	HI	Highest wage paid
ATC	Average total compensation	D	Daily	HR	High end range
AW	Average wage paid	FQ	First quartile wage	LO	Lowest wage paid

LR	Low end range	MTC	Median total compensation	TCC	Total cash compensation
M	Monthly	MW	Median wage paid	TQ	Third quartile wage
MCC	Median cash compensation	MWR	Median wage range	W	Weekly
ME	Median entry wage	S	See annotated source	Y	Yearly

Occupation/Type/Industry	Location	Per	Low	Mid	High	Source	Date
Maintenance Worker							
Machinery	Sacramento–Roseville–Arden-Arcade MSA, CA	H	17.64 FQ	21.73 MW	26.85 TQ	CABLS	1/16-3/16
Machinery	San Diego-Carlsbad MSA, CA	H	17.34 FQ	22.11 MW	26.92 TQ	CABLS	1/16-3/16
Machinery	San Francisco-Redwood City-South San Francisco PMSA, CA	H	14.65 FQ	17.99 MW	25.70 TQ	CABLS	1/16-3/16
Machinery	Colorado	Y	36460 FQ	48750 MW	58790 TQ	USBLS	5/15
Machinery	Denver-Aurora-Lakewood MSA, CO	Y	36030 FQ	48980 MW	59590 TQ	USBLS	5/15
Machinery	Connecticut	Y		48464 MW		CTBLS	1/16-3/16
Machinery	Bridgeport-Stamford-Norwalk MSA, CT	Y	32990 FQ	43690 MW	52250 TQ	USBLS	5/15
Machinery	Hartford-West Hartford-East Hartford MSA, CT	Y	36170 FQ	47970 MW	58180 TQ	USBLS	5/15
Machinery	Delaware	Y	40190 FQ	45740 MW	53600 TQ	USBLS	5/15
Machinery	Wilmington PMSA, DE-MD-NJ	Y	37600 FQ	44960 MW	55790 TQ	USBLS	5/15
Machinery	District of Columbia	Y	37430 FQ	48510 MW	59290 TQ	USBLS	5/15
Machinery	Washington-Arlington-Alexandria PMSA, DC-VA-MD-WV	Y	35710 FQ	45560 MW	56500 TQ	USBLS	5/15
Machinery	Florida	H	13.16 AE	18.80 MW	23.54 AEX	FLBLS	7/16-9/16
Machinery	Fort Lauderdale-Pompano Beach-Deerfield Beach PMSA, FL	H	14.45 AE	21.03 MW	25.03 AEX	FLBLS	7/16-9/16
Machinery	Miami-Miami Beach-Kendall PMSA, FL	H	10.03 AE	15.06 MW	19.37 AEX	FLBLS	7/16-9/16
Machinery	Orlando-Kissimmee-Sanford MSA, FL	H	14.94 AE	24.18 MW	26.61 AEX	FLBLS	7/16-9/16
Machinery	Tampa-St. Petersburg-Clearwater MSA, FL	H	13.60 AE	19.34 MW	23.52 AEX	FLBLS	7/16-9/16
Machinery	Georgia	Y	30970 FQ	39370 MW	49420 TQ	USBLS	5/15
Machinery	Atlanta-Sandy Springs-Roswell MSA, GA	Y.	24340 FQ	38350 MW	49840 TQ	USBLS	5/15
Machinery	Augusta-Richmond County MSA, GA-SC	Y	32010 FQ	50530 MW	68380 TQ	USBLS	5/15
Machinery	Hawaii	Y	34450 FQ	38060 MW	61240 TQ	USBLS	5/15
Machinery	Urban Honolulu MSA, HI	Y	34790 FQ	38600 MW	66230 TQ	USBLS	5/15
Machinery	Idaho	Y	35030 FQ	42130 MW	49450 TQ	USBLS	5/15
Machinery	Boise City MSA, ID	Y	36590 FQ	42990 MW	48960 TQ	USBLS	5/15
Machinery	Illinois	Y	32190 FQ	43580 MW	55270 TQ	USBLS	5/15
Machinery	Chicago-Naperville-Arlington Heights PMSA, IL	Y	28780 FQ	41690 MW	53390 TQ	USBLS	5/15
Machinery	Lake County-Kenosha County PMSA, IL-WI	Y	38290 FQ	48670 MW	62420 TQ	USBLS	5/15
Machinery	Indiana	Y	36620 FQ	45160 MW	54860 TQ	USBLS	5/15
Machinery	Gary PMSA, IN	Y	41060 FQ	46390 MW	52670 TQ	USBLS	5/15
Machinery	Indianapolis-Carmel-Anderson MSA, IN	Y	37640 FQ	45760 MW	54820 TQ	USBLS	5/15
Machinery	Iowa	Y	33730 FQ	41870 MW	50930 TQ	USBLS	5/15
Machinery	Des Moines-West Des Moines MSA, IA	Y	36350 FQ	48440 MW	58690 TQ	USBLS	5/15
Machinery	Kansas	Y	36120 FQ	42950 MW	48610 TQ	USBLS	5/15
Machinery	Wichita MSA, KS	Y	36260 FQ	41860 MW	48170 TQ	USBLS	5/15
Machinery	Kentucky	Y	36420 FQ	44940 MW	53210 TQ	USBLS	5/15
Machinery	Louisville-Jefferson County MSA, KY-IN	Y	35750 FQ	45090 MW	54160 TQ	USBLS	5/15
Machinery	Louisiana	Y	32730 FQ	39240 MW	52170 TQ	USBLS	5/15
Machinery	Baton Rouge MSA, LA	Y	34690 FQ	41880 MW	53550 TQ	USBLS	5/15
Machinery	New Orleans-Metairie MSA, LA	Y	30610 FQ	38910 MW	52410 TQ	USBLS	5/15
Machinery	Maine	Y	35210 FQ	47630 MW	55960 TQ	USBLS	5/15
Machinery	Maryland	Y	30324 AE	44488 MW	51570 AEX	MDBLS	4/16
Machinery	Baltimore-Columbia-Towson MSA, MD	Y	32410 FQ	39920 MW	51560 TQ	USBLS	5/15
Machinery	Massachusetts	Y	37220 FQ	45940 MW	57150 TQ	USBLS	5/15
Machinery	Boston-Cambridge-Newton NECTA, MA	Y	38550 FQ	49390 MW	62110 TQ	USBLS	5/15
Machinery	Worcester MSA, MA-CT	Y	37530 FQ	45020 MW	53120 TQ	USBLS	5/15
Machinery	Michigan	Y	34300 FQ	42870 MW	51460 TQ	USBLS	5/15

AE	Average entry wage	AWR	Average wage range	H	Hourly
AEX	Average experienced wage	B	Biweekly	HI	Highest wage paid
ATC	Average total compensation	D	Daily	HR	High end range
AW	Average wage paid	FQ	First quartile wage	LO	Lowest wage paid

LR	Low end range	MTC	Median total compensation	TCC	Total cash compensation
M	Monthly	MW	Median wage paid	TQ	Third quartile wage
MCC	Median cash compensation	MWR	Median wage range	W	Weekly
ME	Median entry wage	S	See annotated source	Y	Yearly

Occupation/Type/Industry	Location	Per	Low	Mid	High	Source	Date
Maintenance Worker							
Machinery	Detroit-Dearborn-Livonia PMSA, MI	Y	36330 FQ	45460 MW	54760 TQ	USBLS	5/15
Machinery	Grand Rapids-Wyoming MSA, MI	Y	34340 FQ	42260 MW	53000 TQ	USBLS	5/15
Machinery	Minnesota	Y	32131 FQ	41052 MW	48453 TQ	MNBLS	1/16-3/16
Machinery	Minneapolis-St. Paul-Bloomington MSA, MN-WI	Y	33901 FQ	43515 MW	52194 TQ	MNBLS	1/16-3/16
Machinery	Mississippi	Y	30980 FQ	39420 MW	50060 TQ	USBLS	5/15
Machinery	Jackson MSA, MS	Y	32230 FQ	40600 MW	47920 TQ	USBLS	5/15
Machinery	Missouri	Y	36990 FQ	44740 MW	53400 TQ	USBLS	5/15
Machinery	Kansas City MSA, MO-KS	Y	39510 FQ	46530 MW	55290 TQ	USBLS	5/15
Machinery	St. Louis MSA, MO-IL	Y	37820 FQ	45580 MW	54850 TQ	USBLS	5/15
Machinery	Montana	Y	33620 FQ	39790 MW	65360 TQ	USBLS	5/15
Machinery	Nebraska	Y	33315 FQ	39525 MW	48005 TQ	NEBLS	7/16-9/16
Machinery	Omaha-Council Bluffs MSA, NE-IA	Y	36550 FQ	44905 MW	53225 TQ	NEBLS	7/16-9/16
Machinery	Nevada	Y	38210 FQ	47890 MW	58650 TQ	USBLS	5/15
Machinery	Las Vegas-Henderson-Paradise MSA, NV	Y	37080 FQ	51800 MW	63270 TQ	USBLS	5/15
Machinery	New Hampshire	H	13.62 AE	18.44 MW	22.71 AEX	NHBLS	6/16
Machinery	Nashua NECTA, NH-MA	Y	31600 FQ	39550 MW	51350 TQ	USBLS	5/15
Machinery	New Jersey	Y	33860 FQ	42170 MW	53410 TQ	USBLS	5/15
Machinery	Camden PMSA, NJ	Y	41240 FQ	52180 MW	60810 TQ	USBLS	5/15
Machinery	Newark PMSA, NJ-PA	Y	33110 FQ	44120 MW	59260 TQ	USBLS	5/15
Machinery	Trenton MSA, NJ	Y	27090 FQ	37320 MW	51170 TQ	USBLS	5/15
Machinery	New Mexico	Y	26130 FQ	31670 MW	39930 TQ	USBLS	5/15
Machinery	Albuquerque MSA, NM	Y	28720 FQ	36240 MW	44610 AEX	USBLS	5/15
Machinery	New York	Y	31970 AE	47780 MW	62340 AEX	NYBLS	1/16-3/16
Machinery	Buffalo-Cheektowaga-Niagara Falls MSA, NY	Y	36420 FQ	46730 MW	57380 TQ	USBLS	5/15
Machinery	Nassau County-Suffolk County PMSA, NY	Y	32600 FQ	44790 MW	63390 TQ	USBLS	5/15
Machinery	New York-Jersey City-White Plains PMSA, NY-NJ	Y	35810 FQ	47580 MW	71050 TQ	USBLS	5/15
Machinery	Rochester MSA, NY	Y	38030 FQ	44820 MW	51300 TQ	USBLS	5/15
Machinery	North Carolina	Y	30550 FQ	38160 MW	48980 TQ	USBLS	5/15
Machinery	Charlotte-Concord-Gastonia MSA, NC-SC	Y	31450 FQ	38070 MW	48340 TQ	USBLS	5/15
Machinery	Raleigh MSA, NC	Y	26050 FQ	31370 MW	37600 TQ	USBLS	5/15
Machinery	North Dakota	Y	39250 FQ	48240 MW	58490 TQ	USBLS	5/15
Machinery	Fargo MSA, ND-MN	Y	36710 FQ	42250 MW	48760 TQ	USBLS	5/15
Machinery	Ohio	Y	36040 FQ	44440 MW	53800 TQ	USBLS	5/15
Machinery	Cincinnati MSA, OH-KY-IN	Y	37460 FQ	46140 MW	55290 TQ	USBLS	5/15
Machinery	Cleveland-Elyria MSA, OH	Y	32610 FQ	39500 MW	50310 TQ	USBLS	5/15
Machinery	Columbus MSA, OH	Y	41520 FQ	49030 MW	57630 TQ	USBLS	5/15
Machinery	Oklahoma	Y	30990 FQ	39290 MW	49340 TQ	USBLS	5/15
Machinery	Oklahoma City MSA, OK	Y	31230 FQ	38080 MW	47410 TQ	USBLS	5/15
Machinery	Tulsa MSA, OK	Y	29370 FQ	39510 MW	48190 TQ	USBLS	5/15
Machinery	Oregon	H	17.51 FQ	21.47 MW	25.68 TQ	ORBLS	2016
Machinery	Portland-Vancouver-Hillsboro MSA, OR-WA	Y	39110 FQ	46650 MW	56180 TQ	USBLS	5/15
Machinery	Pennsylvania	Y	39940 FQ	46840 MW	55670 TQ	USBLS	5/15
Machinery	Allentown-Bethlehem-Easton MSA, PA-NJ	Y	39900 FQ	52380 MW	59700 TQ	USBLS	5/15
Machinery	Harrisburg-Carlisle MSA, PA	Y	40780 FQ	48010 MW	55960 TQ	USBLS	5/15
Machinery	Montgomery County-Bucks County-Chester County PMSA, PA	Y	41850 FQ	49610 MW	58690 TQ	USBLS	5/15
Machinery	Philadelphia PMSA, PA	Y	45790 FQ	57190 MW	67560 TQ	USBLS	5/15
Machinery	Pittsburgh MSA, PA	Y	41010 FQ	48500 MW	57220 TQ	USBLS	5/15
Machinery	Rhode Island	Y	33930 FQ	39470 MW	50050 TQ	USBLS	5/15
Machinery	Providence-Warwick MSA, RI-MA	Y	35350 FQ	43460 MW	54450 TQ	USBLS	5/15
Machinery	South Carolina	Y	36380 FQ	45380 MW	55910 TQ	USBLS	5/15
Machinery	Charleston-North Charleston MSA, SC	Y	37400 FQ	50440 MW	58240 TQ	USBLS	5/15
Machinery	Columbia MSA, SC	Y	34070 FQ	42760 MW	51890 TQ	USBLS	5/15
Machinery	Greenville-Anderson-Mauldin MSA, SC	Y	32310 FQ	40200 MW	48400 TQ	USBLS	5/15
Machinery	South Dakota	Y	26010 FQ	29150 MW	33290 TQ	USBLS	5/15
Machinery	Tennessee	Y	30660 FQ	44490 MW	54260 TQ	USBLS	5/15

AE	Average entry wage	AWR	Average wage range	H	Hourly
AEX	Average experienced wage	B	Biweekly	HI	Highest wage paid
ATC	Average total compensation	D	Daily	HR	High end range
AW	Average wage paid	FQ	First quartile wage	LO	Lowest wage paid

LR	Low end range	
M	Monthly	
MCC	Median cash compensation	
ME	Median entry wage	

MTC	Median total compensation	
MW	Median wage paid	
MWR	Median wage range	
S	See annotated source	

TCC	Total cash compensation	
TQ	Third quartile wage	
W	Weekly	
Y	Yearly	

Occupation/Type/Industry	Location	Per	Low	Mid	High	Source	Date
Maintenance Worker							
Machinery	Knoxville MSA, TN	Y	34580 FQ	48280 MW	57470 TQ	USBLS	5/15
Machinery	Memphis MSA, TN-MS-AR	Y	32360 FQ	44320 MW	53950 TQ	USBLS	5/15
Machinery	Nashville-Davidson–Murfreesboro–Franklin MSA, TN	Y	29260 FQ	42240 MW	51700 TQ	USBLS	5/15
Machinery	Texas	Y	32780 FQ	40990 MW	53270 TQ	USBLS	5/15
Machinery	Austin-Round Rock MSA, TX	Y	34300 FQ	47180 MW	61970 TQ	USBLS	5/15
Machinery	Dallas-Plano-Irving PMSA, TX	Y	34130 FQ	42920 MW	52200 TQ	USBLS	5/15
Machinery	Fort Worth-Arlington PMSA, TX	Y	31760 FQ	39150 MW	49750 TQ	USBLS	5/15
Machinery	Houston-The Woodlands-Sugar Land MSA, TX	Y	34870 FQ	44360 MW	55650 TQ	USBLS	5/15
Machinery	San Antonio-New Braunfels MSA, TX	Y	31640 FQ	37340 MW	47030 TQ	USBLS	5/15
Machinery	Utah	Y	38580 FQ	46190 MW	55240 TQ	USBLS	5/15
Machinery	Ogden-Clearfield MSA, UT	Y	42670 FQ	51760 MW	62510 TQ	USBLS	5/15
Machinery	Provo-Orem MSA, UT	Y	41600 FQ	50200 MW	57180 TQ	USBLS	5/15
Machinery	Salt Lake City MSA, UT	Y	36750 FQ	44330 MW	50890 TQ	USBLS	5/15
Machinery	Vermont	Y	35920 FQ	42240 MW	47730 TQ	USBLS	5/15
Machinery	Burlington-South Burlington MSA, VT	Y	35580 FQ	40920 MW	48980 TQ	USBLS	5/15
Machinery	Virginia	Y	32540 FQ	42860 MW	51650 TQ	USBLS	5/15
Machinery	Richmond MSA, VA	Y	26830 FQ	42750 MW	60720 TQ	USBLS	5/15
Machinery	Virginia Beach-Norfolk-Newport News MSA, VA-NC	Y	37070 FQ	46200 MW	56110 TQ	USBLS	5/15
Machinery	Washington	H	18.85 FQ	23.88 MW	30.51 TQ	WABLS	3/16
Machinery	Seattle-Bellevue-Everett PMSA, WA	H	18.75 FQ	23.41 MW	30.95 TQ	WABLS	3/16
Machinery	Tacoma-Lakewood PMSA, WA	H	25.42 FQ	28.69 MW	33.50 TQ	WABLS	3/16
Machinery	West Virginia	Y	23720 FQ	31970 MW	40890 TQ	USBLS	5/15
Machinery	Huntington-Ashland MSA, WV-KY-OH	Y	29780 FQ	37480 MW	50030 TQ	USBLS	5/15
Machinery	Wisconsin	Y	40860 FQ	47560 MW	56510 TQ	USBLS	5/15
Machinery	Madison MSA, WI	Y	40290 FQ	44940 MW	49630 TQ	USBLS	5/15
Machinery	Milwaukee-Waukesha-West Allis MSA, WI	Y	43190 FQ	52460 MW	60380 TQ	USBLS	5/15
Machinery	Wyoming	Y	50940 FQ	58770 MW	68920 TQ	USBLS	5/15
Machinery	Puerto Rico	Y	17460 FQ	19410 MW	24540 TQ	USBLS	5/15
Machinery	San Juan-Carolina-Caguas MSA, PR	Y	17670 FQ	19810 MW	25900 TQ	USBLS	5/15
Machinery	Guam	Y	19070 FQ	23690 MW	36850 TQ	USBLS	5/15
Majority Leader							
United States House of Representatives	United States	Y			193400 HI	OPM01	2017
United States Senate	United States	Y			193400 HI	OPM01	2017
MakerSpace Facilitator							
Public Library, County Government	Johnson County, KS	H	23.20 FQ	25.08 MW	26.96 TQ	JCOKS	2017
Makeup Artist							
Theatrical and Performance	California	H	18.39 FQ	37.55 MW	53.51 TQ	CABLS	1/16-3/16
Theatrical and Performance	District of Columbia	Y	27720 FQ	104350 MW	139070 TQ	USBLS	5/15
Theatrical and Performance	Florida	H	9.67 AE	14.90 MW	23.95 AEX	FLBLS	7/16-9/16
Theatrical and Performance	Georgia	Y	25120 FQ	40010 MW	84100 TQ	USBLS	5/15
Theatrical and Performance	Hawaii	Y	35840 FQ	40890 MW	46460 TQ	USBLS	5/15
Theatrical and Performance	Indiana	Y	16810 FQ	17930 MW	19060 TQ	USBLS	5/15
Theatrical and Performance	New Jersey	Y	21270 FQ	22890 MW	24510 TQ	USBLS	5/15
Theatrical and Performance	New York	Y	42680 AE	87520 MW	109670 AEX	NYBLS	1/16-3/16
Theatrical and Performance	Oregon	H	25.87 FQ	27.54 MW	29.22 TQ	ORBLS	2016
Theatrical and Performance	Pennsylvania	Y	19780 FQ	24460 MW	47140 TQ	USBLS	5/15
Theatrical and Performance	Tennessee	Y	53070 FQ	91210 MW	119170 TQ	USBLS	5/15
Theatrical and Performance	Texas	Y	26580 FQ	35530 MW	51850 TQ	USBLS	5/15
Theatrical and Performance	Washington	H	20.23 FQ	22.41 MW	25.26 TQ	WABLS	3/16
Mammologist	United States	Y		63000 AW		SKU01	2016
Management Analyst	Alabama	Y	52201 AE	93292 AW	113842 AEX	ALBLS	6/16
	Birmingham-Hoover MSA, AL	Y	46318 AE	89469 AW	111044 AEX	ALBLS	6/16
	Alaska	Y	63970 FQ	80950 MW	100630 TQ	USBLS	5/15
	Anchorage MSA, AK	Y	64020 FQ	83140 MW	104920 TQ	USBLS	5/15
	Arizona	Y	51970 FQ	68090 MW	92910 TQ	USBLS	5/15

AE	Average entry wage	AWR	Average wage range	H	Hourly	LR	Low end range	MTC	Median total compensation
AEX	Average experienced wage	B	Biweekly	HI	Highest wage paid	M	Monthly	MW	Median wage paid
ATC	Average total compensation	D	Daily	HR	High end range	MCC	Median cash compensation	MWR	Median wage range
AW	Average wage paid	FQ	First quartile wage	LO	Lowest wage paid	ME	Median entry wage	S	See annotated source

TCC	Total cash compensation		
TQ	Third quartile wage		
W	Weekly		
Y	Yearly		

Management Analyst

Occupation/Type/Industry	Location	Per	Low	Mid	High	Source	Date
Management Analyst	Phoenix-Mesa-Scottsdale MSA, AZ	Y	51200 FQ	68760 MW	93430 TQ	USBLS	5/15
	Tucson MSA, AZ	Y	53240 FQ	72890 MW	102950 TQ	USBLS	5/15
	Arkansas	Y	32070 FQ	50920 MW	72070 TQ	USBLS	5/15
	Little Rock-North Little Rock-Conway MSA, AR	Y	30510 FQ	47590 MW	63290 TQ	USBLS	5/15
	California	H	31.08 FQ	41.18 MW	57.37 TQ	CABLS	1/16-3/16
	Anaheim-Santa Ana-Irvine PMSA, CA	H	32.46 FQ	44.69 MW	57.70 TQ	CABLS	1/16-3/16
	Los Angeles-Long Beach-Glendale PMSA, CA	H	32.92 FQ	43.05 MW	57.39 TQ	CABLS	1/16-3/16
	Oakland-Hayward-Berkeley PMSA, CA	H	32.08 FQ	43.71 MW	58.03 TQ	CABLS	1/16-3/16
	Riverside-San Bernardino-Ontario MSA, CA	H	29.34 FQ	36.08 MW	44.83 TQ	CABLS	1/16-3/16
	Sacramento–Roseville–Arden-Arcade MSA, CA	H	27.11 FQ	32.59 MW	34.17 TQ	CABLS	1/16-3/16
	San Diego-Carlsbad MSA, CA	H	30.73 FQ	40.52 MW	54.89 TQ	CABLS	1/16-3/16
	San Francisco-Redwood City-South San Francisco PMSA, CA	H	37.01 FQ	52.38 MW	73.51 TQ	CABLS	1/16-3/16
	Colorado	Y	62440 FQ	81060 MW	107690 TQ	USBLS	5/15
	Denver-Aurora-Lakewood MSA, CO	Y	63150 FQ	81140 MW	106720 TQ	USBLS	5/15
	Connecticut	Y		91109 MW		CTBLS	1/16-3/16
	Bridgeport-Stamford-Norwalk MSA, CT	Y	71030 FQ	93080 MW	128030 TQ	USBLS	5/15
	Hartford-West Hartford-East Hartford MSA, CT	Y	72570 FQ	90280 MW	111180 TQ	USBLS	5/15
	Delaware	Y	57240 FQ	75450 MW	101500 TQ	USBLS	5/15
	Wilmington PMSA, DE-MD-NJ	Y	60080 FQ	79050 MW	104210 TQ	USBLS	5/15
	District of Columbia	Y	76390 FQ	94700 MW	112400 TQ	USBLS	5/15
	Washington-Arlington-Alexandria PMSA, DC-VA-MD-WV	Y	77510 FQ	99130 MW	122010 TQ	USBLS	5/15
	Florida	H	21.45 AE	33.54 MW	50.74 AEX	FLBLS	7/16-9/16
	Fort Lauderdale-Pompano Beach-Deerfield Beach PMSA, FL	H	20.09 AE	30.19 MW	43.14 AEX	FLBLS	7/16-9/16
	Miami-Miami Beach-Kendall PMSA, FL	H	22.74 AE	34.50 MW	59.90 AEX	FLBLS	7/16-9/16
	Orlando-Kissimmee-Sanford MSA, FL	H	23.20 AE	35.66 MW	51.47 AEX	FLBLS	7/16-9/16
	Tampa-St. Petersburg-Clearwater MSA, FL	H	21.71 AE	35.60 MW	48.65 AEX	FLBLS	7/16-9/16
	Georgia	Y	58760 FQ	80670 MW	111150 TQ	USBLS	5/15
	Atlanta-Sandy Springs-Roswell MSA, GA	Y	59710 FQ	83150 MW	113480 TQ	USBLS	5/15
	Augusta-Richmond County MSA, GA-SC	Y	58080 FQ	75540 MW	96830 TQ	USBLS	5/15
	Hawaii	Y	57260 FQ	73630 MW	90860 TQ	USBLS	5/15
	Urban Honolulu MSA, HI	Y	57450 FQ	73710 MW	90860 TQ	USBLS	5/15
	Idaho	Y	46870 FQ	60810 MW	104970 TQ	USBLS	5/15
	Boise City MSA, ID	Y	47880 FQ	60710 MW	108120 TQ	USBLS	5/15
	Illinois	Y	61530 FQ	81210 MW	106450 TQ	USBLS	5/15
	Chicago-Naperville-Arlington Heights PMSA, IL	Y	63420 FQ	84280 MW	111740 TQ	USBLS	5/15
	Lake County-Kenosha County PMSA, IL-WI	Y	64010 FQ	78760 MW	99590 TQ	USBLS	5/15
	Indiana	Y	51380 FQ	68930 MW	93200 TQ	USBLS	5/15
	Gary PMSA, IN	Y	44780 FQ	67450 MW	118100 TQ	USBLS	5/15
	Indianapolis-Carmel-Anderson MSA, IN	Y	51180 FQ	68500 MW	92800 TQ	USBLS	5/15
	Iowa	Y	55240 FQ	71230 MW	92640 TQ	USBLS	5/15
	Des Moines-West Des Moines MSA, IA	Y	59240 FQ	74500 MW	94410 TQ	USBLS	5/15
	Kansas	Y	55130 FQ	73080 MW	97370 TQ	USBLS	5/15
	Wichita MSA, KS	Y	54750 FQ	72250 MW	90690 TQ	USBLS	5/15
	Kentucky	Y	52410 FQ	70470 MW	92930 TQ	USBLS	5/15
	Louisville-Jefferson County MSA, KY-IN	Y	51950 FQ	70560 MW	94000 TQ	USBLS	5/15

AE	Average entry wage	AWR	Average wage range	
AEX	Average experienced wage	B	Biweekly	
ATC	Average total compensation	D	Daily	
AW	Average wage paid	FQ	First quartile wage	
H	Hourly			
HI	Highest wage paid			
HR	High end range			
LO	Lowest wage paid			
LR	Low end range			
M	Monthly			
MCC	Median cash compensation			
ME	Median entry wage			
MTC	Median total compensation			
MW	Median wage paid			
MWR	Median wage range			
S	See annotated source			
TCC	Total cash compensation			
TQ	Third quartile wage			
W	Weekly			
Y	Yearly			

Occupation/Type/Industry	Location	Per	Low	Mid	High	Source	Date
Management Analyst	Louisiana	Y	51030 FQ	66850 MW	86580 TQ	USBLS	5/15
	Baton Rouge MSA, LA	Y	41110 FQ	56570 MW	80490 TQ	USBLS	5/15
	New Orleans-Metairie MSA, LA	Y	57840 FQ	70270 MW	86580 TQ	USBLS	5/15
	Maine	Y	48190 FQ	59800 MW	76740 TQ	USBLS	5/15
	Portland-South Portland MSA, ME	Y	49510 FQ	64760 MW	77770 TQ	USBLS	5/15
	Maryland	Y	61483 AE	96489 MW	113991 AEX	MDBLS	4/16
	Baltimore-Columbia-Towson MSA, MD	Y	76380 FQ	92150 MW	108990 TQ	USBLS	5/15
	Salisbury MSA, MD-DE	Y	48470 FQ	68300 MW	104550 TQ	USBLS	5/15
	Massachusetts	Y	68690 FQ	91480 MW	121470 TQ	USBLS	5/15
	Boston-Cambridge-Newton NECTA, MA	Y	69410 FQ	93710 MW	123830 TQ	USBLS	5/15
	Worcester MSA, MA-CT	Y	63110 FQ	76270 MW	96410 TQ	USBLS	5/15
	Michigan	Y	60690 FQ	79480 MW	102950 TQ	USBLS	5/15
	Detroit-Dearborn-Livonia PMSA, MI	Y	66280 FQ	84570 MW	111960 TQ	USBLS	5/15
	Grand Rapids-Wyoming MSA, MI	Y	55770 FQ	69490 MW	89240 TQ	USBLS	5/15
	Minnesota	Y	60113 FQ	76380 MW	100757 TQ	MNBLS	1/16-3/16
	Minneapolis-St. Paul-Bloomington MSA, MN-WI	Y	60672 FQ	77183 MW	102565 TQ	MNBLS	1/16-3/16
	Mississippi	Y	48230 FQ	63290 MW	82930 TQ	USBLS	5/15
	Jackson MSA, MS	Y	42820 FQ	55190 MW	77060 TQ	USBLS	5/15
	Missouri	Y	56260 FQ	73930 MW	92150 TQ	USBLS	5/15
	Kansas City MSA, MO-KS	Y	62680 FQ	80000 MW	100310 TQ	USBLS	5/15
	St. Louis MSA, MO-IL	Y	56330 FQ	74680 MW	92700 TQ	USBLS	5/15
	Montana	Y	56470 FQ	76140 MW	109660 TQ	USBLS	5/15
	Billings MSA, MT	Y	70740 FQ	99500 MW	137550 TQ	USBLS	5/15
	Nebraska	Y	59820 FQ	76035 MW	93860 TQ	NEBLS	7/16-9/16
	Omaha-Council Bluffs MSA, NE-IA	Y	63015 FQ	78890 MW	95645 TQ	NEBLS	7/16-9/16
	Nevada	Y	52600 FQ	67330 MW	89350 TQ	USBLS	5/15
	Las Vegas-Henderson-Paradise MSA, NV	Y	53640 FQ	70000 MW	91330 TQ	USBLS	5/15
	New Hampshire	H	25.65 AE	41.48 MW	58.76 AEX	NHBLS	6/16
	Manchester NECTA, NH	H	27.01 AE	40.82 MW	50.85 AEX	NHBLS	6/16
	Nashua NECTA, NH-MA	Y	63280 FQ	92250 MW	118130 TQ	USBLS	5/15
	New Jersey	Y	68950 FQ	90390 MW	118040 TQ	USBLS	5/15
	Camden PMSA, NJ	Y	60430 FQ	78290 MW	99610 TQ	USBLS	5/15
	Newark PMSA, NJ-PA	Y	73900 FQ	96190 MW	128090 TQ	USBLS	5/15
	Trenton MSA, NJ	Y	80870 FQ	97050 MW	115540 TQ	USBLS	5/15
	New Mexico	Y	47870 FQ	63220 MW	87770 TQ	USBLS	5/15
	Albuquerque MSA, NM	Y	50600 FQ	70380 MW	92170 TQ	USBLS	5/15
	New York	Y	57080 AE	93440 MW	135350 AEX	NYBLS	1/16-3/16
	Buffalo-Cheektowaga-Niagara Falls MSA, NY	Y	56140 FQ	72010 MW	92990 TQ	USBLS	5/15
	Nassau County-Suffolk County PMSA, NY	Y	62500 FQ	94280 MW	175170 TQ	USBLS	5/15
	New York-Jersey City-White Plains PMSA, NY-NJ	Y	70050 FQ	96980 MW	138800 TQ	USBLS	5/15
	Rochester MSA, NY	Y	60110 FQ	77230 MW	103360 TQ	USBLS	5/15
	North Carolina	Y	58090 FQ	79310 MW	110510 TQ	USBLS	5/15
	Charlotte-Concord-Gastonia MSA, NC-SC	Y	60730 FQ	81330 MW	115220 TQ	USBLS	5/15
	Raleigh MSA, NC	Y	51300 FQ	79210 MW	118920 TQ	USBLS	5/15
	North Dakota	Y	49870 FQ	60530 MW	83470 TQ	USBLS	5/15
	Fargo MSA, ND-MN	Y	43780 FQ	56250 MW	71880 TQ	USBLS	5/15
	Ohio	Y	55770 FQ	74290 MW	96620 TQ	USBLS	5/15
	Cincinnati MSA, OH-KY-IN	Y	53610 FQ	71740 MW	95330 TQ	USBLS	5/15
	Cleveland-Elyria MSA, OH	Y	55360 FQ	75410 MW	99430 TQ	USBLS	5/15
	Columbus MSA, OH	Y	57000 FQ	75400 MW	97090 TQ	USBLS	5/15
	Oklahoma	Y	49910 FQ	64890 MW	82790 TQ	USBLS	5/15
	Oklahoma City MSA, OK	Y	50320 FQ	66140 MW	80700 TQ	USBLS	5/15
	Tulsa MSA, OK	Y	52520 FQ	69970 MW	96820 TQ	USBLS	5/15
	Oregon	H	31.19 FQ	37.71 MW	47.39 TQ	ORBLS	2016
	Portland-Vancouver-Hillsboro MSA, OR-WA	Y	65610 FQ	81520 MW	108100 TQ	USBLS	5/15
	Pennsylvania	Y	55610 FQ	76150 MW	101740 TQ	USBLS	5/15
	Allentown-Bethlehem-Easton MSA, PA-NJ	Y	55760 FQ	75620 MW	99860 TQ	USBLS	5/15

Occupation/Type/Industry	Location	Per	Low	Mid	High	Source	Date
Management Analyst	Harrisburg-Carlisle MSA, PA	Y	51810 FQ	62960 MW	82390 TQ	USBLS	5/15
	Montgomery County-Bucks County-Chester County PMSA, PA	Y	55570 FQ	81620 MW	111450 TQ	USBLS	5/15
	Philadelphia PMSA, PA	Y	64230 FQ	84870 MW	111770 TQ	USBLS	5/15
	Pittsburgh MSA, PA	Y	54280 FQ	71530 MW	93830 TQ	USBLS	5/15
	Rhode Island	Y	65310 FQ	82230 MW	105840 TQ	USBLS	5/15
	Providence-Warwick MSA, RI-MA	Y	65270 FQ	82230 MW	105490 TQ	USBLS	5/15
	South Carolina	Y	50050 FQ	66860 MW	85650 TQ	USBLS	5/15
	Charleston-North Charleston MSA, SC	Y	56080 FQ	70530 MW	89070 TQ	USBLS	5/15
	Columbia MSA, SC	Y	49130 FQ	65250 MW	82430 TQ	USBLS	5/15
	Greenville-Anderson-Mauldin MSA, SC	Y	49210 FQ	63970 MW	84690 TQ	USBLS	5/15
	South Dakota	Y	51580 FQ	63490 MW	84210 TQ	USBLS	5/15
	Sioux Falls MSA, SD	Y	52950 FQ	65100 MW	88190 TQ	USBLS	5/15
	Tennessee	Y	54860 FQ	72950 MW	95790 TQ	USBLS	5/15
	Knoxville MSA, TN	Y	55850 FQ	77620 MW	102780 TQ	USBLS	5/15
	Memphis MSA, TN-MS-AR	Y	56200 FQ	72610 MW	89030 TQ	USBLS	5/15
	Nashville-Davidson–Murfreesboro–Franklin MSA, TN	Y	55600 FQ	74060 MW	99260 TQ	USBLS	5/15
	Texas	Y	64570 FQ	86240 MW	115130 TQ	USBLS	5/15
	Austin-Round Rock MSA, TX	Y	67080 FQ	87920 MW	126370 TQ	USBLS	5/15
	Dallas-Plano-Irving PMSA, TX	Y	65210 FQ	86100 MW	108970 TQ	USBLS	5/15
	Fort Worth-Arlington PMSA, TX	Y	59700 FQ	81810 MW	107750 TQ	USBLS	5/15
	Houston-The Woodlands-Sugar Land MSA, TX	Y	70950 FQ	95970 MW	132910 TQ	USBLS	5/15
	San Antonio-New Braunfels MSA, TX	Y	62830 FQ	79550 MW	96090 TQ	USBLS	5/15
	Utah	Y	50400 FQ	70850 MW	92910 TQ	USBLS	5/15
	Ogden-Clearfield MSA, UT	Y	48420 FQ	68880 MW	86580 TQ	USBLS	5/15
	Provo-Orem MSA, UT	Y	46680 FQ	62670 MW	97900 TQ	USBLS	5/15
	Salt Lake City MSA, UT	Y	54890 FQ	74580 MW	95540 TQ	USBLS	5/15
	Vermont	Y	58560 FQ	78540 MW	114050 TQ	USBLS	5/15
	Burlington-South Burlington MSA, VT	Y	60510 FQ	83590 MW	115370 TQ	USBLS	5/15
	Virginia	Y	72550 FQ	94930 MW	122530 TQ	USBLS	5/15
	Richmond MSA, VA	Y	61860 FQ	78780 MW	100290 TQ	USBLS	5/15
	Virginia Beach-Norfolk-Newport News MSA, VA-NC	Y	66360 FQ	86530 MW	100170 TQ	USBLS	5/15
	Washington	H	34.07 FQ	46.88 MW	62.41 TQ	WABLS	3/16
	Seattle-Bellevue-Everett PMSA, WA	H	38.29 FQ	51.08 MW	66.30 TQ	WABLS	3/16
	Tacoma-Lakewood PMSA, WA	H	28.51 FQ	35.41 MW	44.39 TQ	WABLS	3/16
	West Virginia	Y	50170 FQ	69540 MW	86840 TQ	USBLS	5/15
	Huntington-Ashland MSA, WV-KY-OH	Y	53060 FQ	66360 MW	76150 TQ	USBLS	5/15
	Wisconsin	Y	56390 FQ	71230 MW	91180 TQ	USBLS	5/15
	Madison MSA, WI	Y	59200 FQ	73020 MW	90390 TQ	USBLS	5/15
	Milwaukee-Waukesha-West Allis MSA, WI	Y	56800 FQ	74490 MW	96360 TQ	USBLS	5/15
	Wyoming	Y	58310 FQ	77220 MW	150770 TQ	USBLS	5/15
	Cheyenne MSA, WY	Y	60520 FQ	74880 MW	97380 TQ	USBLS	5/15
	Puerto Rico	Y	33110 FQ	46380 MW	66070 TQ	USBLS	5/15
	San Juan-Carolina-Caguas MSA, PR	Y	32910 FQ	47350 MW	67610 TQ	USBLS	5/15
	Guam	Y	44260 FQ	58940 MW	74860 TQ	USBLS	5/15
Emergency Preparedness, Municipal Government	Laguna Niguel, CA	Y			78722 HI	CACIT	6/28/16
Management Consultant	United States	Y		81329 MW		CCAST01	2016
Managing Editor							
Association Magazine	United States	Y		65300 AW		FOLIO01	4/22/15-5/22/15
B2B Magazine	United States	Y		59900 AW		FOLIO01	4/22/15-5/22/15
Consumer Magazine	United States	Y		69900 AW		FOLIO01	4/22/15-5/22/15
Female	United States	Y		60100 AW		FOLIO01	4/22/15-5/22/15
Male	United States	Y		72600 AW		FOLIO01	4/22/15-5/22/15

AE Average entry wage	**AWR** Average wage range	**H** Hourly	**LR** Low end range	**MTC** Median total compensation	**TCC** Total cash compensation
AEX Average experienced wage	**B** Biweekly	**HI** Highest wage paid	**M** Monthly	**MW** Median wage paid	**TQ** Third quartile wage
ATC Average total compensation	**D** Daily	**HR** High end range	**MCC** Median cash compensation	**MWR** Median wage range	**W** Weekly
AW Average wage paid	**FQ** First quartile wage	**LO** Lowest wage paid	**ME** Median entry wage	**S** See annotated source	**Y** Yearly

Occupation/Type/Industry	Location	Per	Low	Mid	High	Source	Date
Manicurist and Pedicurist	Alabama	Y	17452 AE	22868 AW	25575 AEX	ALBLS	6/16
	Birmingham-Hoover MSA, AL	Y	17617 AE	23568 AW	26543 AEX	ALBLS	6/16
	Alaska	Y	26250 FQ	28040 MW	29820 TQ	USBLS	5/15
	Anchorage MSA, AK	Y	26100 FQ	27730 MW	29360 TQ	USBLS	5/15
	Arizona	Y	18690 FQ	22220 MW	31500 TQ	USBLS	5/15
	Phoenix-Mesa-Scottsdale MSA, AZ	Y	18950 FQ	22730 MW	30350 TQ	USBLS	5/15
	Tucson MSA, AZ	Y	18380 FQ	21160 MW	35890 TQ	USBLS	5/15
	Arkansas	Y	17410 FQ	19230 MW	23740 TQ	USBLS	5/15
	California	H	9.42 FQ	9.72 MW	11.70 TQ	CABLS	1/16-3/16
	Anaheim-Santa Ana-Irvine PMSA, CA	H	9.41 FQ	9.78 MW	11.71 TQ	CABLS	1/16-3/16
	Los Angeles-Long Beach-Glendale PMSA, CA	H	9.38 FQ	9.54 MW	10.25 TQ	CABLS	1/16-3/16
	Oakland-Hayward-Berkeley PMSA, CA	H	9.66 FQ	11.58 MW	13.71 TQ	CABLS	1/16-3/16
	Riverside-San Bernardino-Ontario MSA, CA	H	9.33 FQ	9.47 MW	10.13 TQ	CABLS	1/16-3/16
	Sacramento–Roseville–Arden-Arcade MSA, CA	H	9.71 FQ	10.81 MW	12.02 TQ	CABLS	1/16-3/16
	San Diego-Carlsbad MSA, CA	H	9.35 FQ	9.48 MW	9.81 TQ	CABLS	1/16-3/16
	San Francisco-Redwood City-South San Francisco PMSA, CA	H	9.88 FQ	12.06 MW	13.65 TQ	CABLS	1/16-3/16
	Colorado	Y	18300 FQ	19710 MW	32460 TQ	USBLS	5/15
	Denver-Aurora-Lakewood MSA, CO	Y	18280 FQ	19950 MW	31690 TQ	USBLS	5/15
	Connecticut	Y		20150 MW		CTBLS	1/16-3/16
	Bridgeport-Stamford-Norwalk MSA, CT	Y	19240 FQ	19740 MW	22530 TQ	USBLS	5/15
	Delaware	Y	18190 FQ	20940 MW	23330 TQ	USBLS	5/15
	Wilmington PMSA, DE-MD-NJ	Y	18170 FQ	20790 MW	22990 TQ	USBLS	5/15
	District of Columbia	Y	26230 FQ	31970 MW	36720 TQ	USBLS	5/15
	Washington-Arlington-Alexandria PMSA, DC-VA-MD-WV	Y	18600 FQ	21520 MW	24830 TQ	USBLS	5/15
	Florida	H	9.42 AE	12.30 MW	17.15 AEX	FLBLS	7/16-9/16
	Fort Lauderdale-Pompano Beach-Deerfield Beach PMSA, FL	H	9.04 AE	10.34 MW	13.32 AEX	FLBLS	7/16-9/16
	Miami-Miami Beach-Kendall PMSA, FL	H	9.08 AE	9.48 MW	13.23 AEX	FLBLS	7/16-9/16
	Orlando-Kissimmee-Sanford MSA, FL	H	9.01 AE	12.96 MW	19.17 AEX	FLBLS	7/16-9/16
	Tampa-St. Petersburg-Clearwater MSA, FL	H	9.40 AE	13.53 MW	16.76 AEX	FLBLS	7/16-9/16
	Georgia	Y	18860 FQ	22200 MW	26510 TQ	USBLS	5/15
	Atlanta-Sandy Springs-Roswell MSA, GA	Y	19730 FQ	22570 MW	26420 TQ	USBLS	5/15
	Hawaii	Y	18130 FQ	20230 MW	24520 TQ	USBLS	5/15
	Urban Honolulu MSA, HI	Y	17960 FQ	19810 MW	22980 TQ	USBLS	5/15
	Idaho	Y	17730 FQ	20600 MW	27790 TQ	USBLS	5/15
	Illinois	Y	19130 FQ	21470 MW	24080 TQ	USBLS	5/15
	Chicago-Naperville-Arlington Heights PMSA, IL	Y	18990 FQ	21120 MW	23580 TQ	USBLS	5/15
	Lake County-Kenosha County PMSA, IL-WI	Y	19880 FQ	22190 MW	24560 TQ	USBLS	5/15
	Indiana	Y	16950 FQ	18480 MW	21140 TQ	USBLS	5/15
	Gary PMSA, IN	Y	17040 FQ	18690 MW	22380 TQ	USBLS	5/15
	Indianapolis-Carmel-Anderson MSA, IN	Y	17300 FQ	18970 MW	22100 TQ	USBLS	5/15
	Iowa	Y	18490 FQ	30400 MW	37190 TQ	USBLS	5/15
	Des Moines-West Des Moines MSA, IA	Y	31970 FQ	40300 MW	44790 TQ	USBLS	5/15
	Kansas	Y	17880 FQ	22760 MW	33440 TQ	USBLS	5/15
	Wichita MSA, KS	Y	18620 FQ	22790 MW	28890 TQ	USBLS	5/15
	Kentucky	Y	18130 FQ	22330 MW	29030 TQ	USBLS	5/15
	Louisville-Jefferson County MSA, KY-IN	Y	19360 FQ	23480 MW	33780 TQ	USBLS	5/15
	Louisiana	Y	17720 FQ	20170 MW	24330 TQ	USBLS	5/15
	Baton Rouge MSA, LA	Y	16950 FQ	18420 MW	20640 TQ	USBLS	5/15

AE	Average entry wage	AWR	Average wage range	H	Hourly	LR	Low end range	MTC	Median total compensation	TCC	Total cash compensation
AEX	Average experienced wage	B	Biweekly	HI	Highest wage paid	M	Monthly	MW	Median wage paid	TQ	Third quartile wage
ATC	Average total compensation	D	Daily	HR	High end range	MCC	Median cash compensation	MWR	Median wage range	W	Weekly
AW	Average wage paid	FQ	First quartile wage	LO	Lowest wage paid	ME	Median entry wage	S	See annotated source	Y	Yearly

Occupation/Type/Industry	Location	Per	Low	Mid	High	Source	Date
Manicurist and Pedicurist	New Orleans-Metairie MSA, LA	Y	18900 FQ	21820 MW	24750 TQ	USBLS	5/15
	Maine	Y	17150 FQ	18540 MW	22330 TQ	USBLS	5/15
	Portland-South Portland MSA, ME	Y	16960 FQ	18220 MW	20860 TQ	USBLS	5/15
	Maryland	Y	18046 AE	25031 MW	28524 AEX	MDBLS	4/16
	Baltimore-Columbia-Towson MSA, MD	Y	18330 FQ	20740 MW	24760 TQ	USBLS	5/15
	Salisbury MSA, MD-DE	Y	18870 FQ	21760 MW	24790 TQ	USBLS	5/15
	Massachusetts	Y	20350 FQ	22990 MW	26640 TQ	USBLS	5/15
	Boston-Cambridge-Newton NECTA, MA	Y	20960 FQ	23440 MW	26850 TQ	USBLS	5/15
	Worcester MSA, MA-CT	Y	20350 FQ	22050 MW	23750 TQ	USBLS	5/15
	Michigan	Y	19180 FQ	27300 MW	35130 TQ	USBLS	5/15
	Detroit-Dearborn-Livonia PMSA, MI	Y	18080 FQ	19150 MW	28110 TQ	USBLS	5/15
	Grand Rapids-Wyoming MSA, MI	Y	24750 FQ	29780 MW	35950 TQ	USBLS	5/15
	Minnesota	Y	20086 FQ	23227 MW	28377 TQ	MNBLS	1/16-3/16
	Minneapolis-St. Paul-Bloomington MSA, MN-WI	Y	20440 FQ	23217 MW	27852 TQ	MNBLS	1/16-3/16
	Mississippi	Y	18000 FQ	20620 MW	24170 TQ	USBLS	5/15
	Jackson MSA, MS	Y	17930 FQ	20750 MW	26970 TQ	USBLS	5/15
	Missouri	Y	17710 FQ	19510 MW	25860 TQ	USBLS	5/15
	Kansas City MSA, MO-KS	Y	17620 FQ	19550 MW	25080 TQ	USBLS	5/15
	St. Louis MSA, MO-IL	Y	18250 FQ	19990 MW	32750 TQ	USBLS	5/15
	Montana	Y	25070 FQ	27490 MW	29910 TQ	USBLS	5/15
	Omaha-Council Bluffs MSA, NE-IA	Y	19790 FQ	24985 MW	36520 TQ	NEBLS	7/16-9/16
	Nevada	Y	16830 FQ	18190 MW	19600 TQ	USBLS	5/15
	Las Vegas-Henderson-Paradise MSA, NV	Y	16860 FQ	18240 MW	19700 TQ	USBLS	5/15
	New Hampshire	H	8.54 AE	12.38 MW	14.87 AEX	NHBLS	6/16
	Manchester NECTA, NH	H	8.38 AE	9.05 MW	10.60 AEX	NHBLS	6/16
	Nashua NECTA, NH-MA	Y	25170 FQ	32050 MW	36990 TQ	USBLS	5/15
	New Jersey	Y	21640 FQ	26330 MW	30830 TQ	USBLS	5/15
	Camden PMSA, NJ	Y	18680 FQ	24020 MW	28410 TQ	USBLS	5/15
	Newark PMSA, NJ-PA	Y	22500 FQ	26310 MW	30470 TQ	USBLS	5/15
	Trenton MSA, NJ	Y	27050 FQ	30970 MW	34800 TQ	USBLS	5/15
	New York	Y	19310 AE	19570 MW	21400 AEX	NYBLS	1/16-3/16
	Buffalo-Cheektowaga-Niagara Falls MSA, NY	Y	19110 FQ	20980 MW	23550 TQ	USBLS	5/15
	Nassau County-Suffolk County PMSA, NY	Y	18730 FQ	19270 MW	21030 TQ	USBLS	5/15
	New York-Jersey City-White Plains PMSA, NY-NJ	Y	18760 FQ	19350 MW	22240 TQ	USBLS	5/15
	Rochester MSA, NY	Y	18810 FQ	19420 MW	25590 TQ	USBLS	5/15
	North Carolina	Y	21600 FQ	29390 MW	34970 TQ	USBLS	5/15
	Charlotte-Concord-Gastonia MSA, NC-SC	Y	24440 FQ	29760 MW	34650 TQ	USBLS	5/15
	Raleigh MSA, NC	Y	25900 FQ	33550 MW	36490 TQ	USBLS	5/15
	North Dakota	Y	17080 FQ	18580 MW	21220 TQ	USBLS	5/15
	Ohio	Y	18010 FQ	19140 MW	23850 TQ	USBLS	5/15
	Cincinnati MSA, OH-KY-IN	Y	18010 FQ	19200 MW	25730 TQ	USBLS	5/15
	Cleveland-Elyria MSA, OH	Y	17860 FQ	18820 MW	19840 TQ	USBLS	5/15
	Columbus MSA, OH	Y	18640 FQ	21720 MW	28070 TQ	USBLS	5/15
	Oklahoma	Y	17350 FQ	19140 MW	22780 TQ	USBLS	5/15
	Oklahoma City MSA, OK	Y	18450 FQ	22110 MW	27300 TQ	USBLS	5/15
	Tulsa MSA, OK	Y	17110 FQ	18650 MW	21070 TQ	USBLS	5/15
	Oregon	H	9.57 FQ	9.77 MW	12.93 TQ	ORBLS	2016
	Portland-Vancouver-Hillsboro MSA, OR-WA	Y	19560 FQ	21510 MW	27760 TQ	USBLS	5/15
	Pennsylvania	Y	17980 FQ	21020 MW	24910 TQ	USBLS	5/15
	Allentown-Bethlehem-Easton MSA, PA-NJ	Y	18800 FQ	21970 MW	26880 TQ	USBLS	5/15
	Harrisburg-Carlisle MSA, PA	Y	20630 FQ	32950 MW	36640 TQ	USBLS	5/15
	Montgomery County-Bucks County-Chester County PMSA, PA	Y	17300 FQ	19260 MW	22940 TQ	USBLS	5/15
	Philadelphia PMSA, PA	Y	20370 FQ	24530 MW	32720 TQ	USBLS	5/15
	Pittsburgh MSA, PA	Y	17350 FQ	19840 MW	23410 TQ	USBLS	5/15
	Reading MSA, PA	Y	22140 FQ	24670 MW	28230 TQ	USBLS	5/15

Occupation/Type/Industry	Location	Per	Low	Mid	High	Source	Date
Manicurist and Pedicurist	Rhode Island	Y	21260 FQ	22840 MW	24420 TQ	USBLS	5/15
	Providence-Warwick MSA, RI-MA	Y	21030 FQ	22720 MW	24420 TQ	USBLS	5/15
	South Carolina	Y	18430 FQ	22430 MW	30620 TQ	USBLS	5/15
	Charleston-North Charleston MSA, SC	Y	16910 FQ	18550 MW	23420 TQ	USBLS	5/15
	Columbia MSA, SC	Y	18980 FQ	33540 MW	44980 TQ	USBLS	5/15
	Greenville-Anderson-Mauldin MSA, SC	Y	21790 FQ	23850 MW	28490 TQ	USBLS	5/15
	South Dakota	Y	25800 FQ	29110 MW	33660 TQ	USBLS	5/15
	Tennessee	Y	18630 FQ	22780 MW	30770 TQ	USBLS	5/15
	Knoxville MSA, TN	Y	20060 FQ	22590 MW	27170 TQ	USBLS	5/15
	Memphis MSA, TN-MS-AR	Y	17460 FQ	19520 MW	34650 TQ	USBLS	5/15
	Nashville-Davidson–Murfreesboro–Franklin MSA, TN	Y	18950 FQ	27460 MW	34830 TQ	USBLS	5/15
	Texas	Y	17540 FQ	19850 MW	27690 TQ	USBLS	5/15
	Austin-Round Rock MSA, TX	Y	16710 FQ	18270 MW	24600 TQ	USBLS	5/15
	Dallas-Plano-Irving PMSA, TX	Y	20910 FQ	29180 MW	37790 TQ	USBLS	5/15
	Fort Worth-Arlington PMSA, TX	Y	17940 FQ	22550 MW	35230 TQ	USBLS	5/15
	Houston-The Woodlands-Sugar Land MSA, TX	Y	17420 FQ	19200 MW	27590 TQ	USBLS	5/15
	San Antonio-New Braunfels MSA, TX	Y	18340 FQ	21260 MW	24410 TQ	USBLS	5/15
	Utah	Y	19690 FQ	22390 MW	31390 TQ	USBLS	5/15
	Ogden-Clearfield MSA, UT	Y	20880 FQ	28800 MW	34620 TQ	USBLS	5/15
	Provo-Orem MSA, UT	Y	18830 FQ	21190 MW	23060 TQ	USBLS	5/15
	Salt Lake City MSA, UT	Y	20600 FQ	24320 MW	35230 TQ	USBLS	5/15
	Vermont	Y	25920 FQ	34340 MW	56000 TQ	USBLS	5/15
	Burlington-South Burlington MSA, VT	Y	27210 FQ	37940 MW	58950 TQ	USBLS	5/15
	Virginia	Y	17670 FQ	20030 MW	23720 TQ	USBLS	5/15
	Richmond MSA, VA	Y	17090 FQ	18870 MW	23080 TQ	USBLS	5/15
	Virginia Beach-Norfolk-Newport News MSA, VA-NC	Y	17050 FQ	18750 MW	27310 TQ	USBLS	5/15
	Washington	H	11.12 FQ	13.07 MW	17.22 TQ	WABLS	3/16
	Seattle-Bellevue-Everett PMSA, WA	H	11.27 FQ	13.94 MW	18.02 TQ	WABLS	3/16
	Tacoma-Lakewood PMSA, WA	H	10.53 FQ	11.36 MW	12.22 TQ	WABLS	3/16
	West Virginia	Y	17670 FQ	18710 MW	21360 TQ	USBLS	5/15
	Wisconsin	Y	18870 FQ	24260 MW	34090 TQ	USBLS	5/15
	Madison MSA, WI	Y	17600 FQ	19580 MW	32290 TQ	USBLS	5/15
	Milwaukee-Waukesha-West Allis MSA, WI	Y	20510 FQ	25300 MW	33540 TQ	USBLS	5/15
	Wyoming	Y	26790 FQ	29910 MW	44550 TQ	USBLS	5/15
	Puerto Rico	Y	16710 FQ	17870 MW	19030 TQ	USBLS	5/15
	San Juan-Carolina-Caguas MSA, PR	Y	16730 FQ	17900 MW	19070 TQ	USBLS	5/15
Manufactured Building and Mobile Home Installer	Alabama	Y	25141 AE	31283 AW	34355 AEX	ALBLS	6/16
	California	H	10.37 FQ	11.28 MW	12.20 TQ	CABLS	1/16-3/16
	Florida	H	9.49 AE	11.85 MW	15.18 AEX	FLBLS	7/16-9/16
	Georgia	Y	21150 FQ	28250 MW	35950 TQ	USBLS	5/15
	Illinois	Y	24330 FQ	32140 MW	37060 TQ	USBLS	5/15
	Indiana	Y	23770 FQ	31790 MW	39140 TQ	USBLS	5/15
	Iowa	Y	26860 FQ	30320 MW	35340 TQ	USBLS	5/15
	Maine	Y	24860 FQ	28020 MW	31140 TQ	USBLS	5/15
	Michigan	Y	19520 FQ	28460 MW	33840 TQ	USBLS	5/15
	Minnesota	Y	33056 FQ	35349 MW	37642 TQ	MNBLS	1/16-3/16
	Mississippi	Y	20500 FQ	26650 MW	31220 TQ	USBLS	5/15
	Missouri	Y	26270 FQ	28810 MW	31380 TQ	USBLS	5/15
	Montana	Y	28260 FQ	33980 MW	39140 TQ	USBLS	5/15
	New Hampshire	H	14.23 AE	18.27 MW	22.45 AEX	NHBLS	6/16
	New Mexico	Y	34880 FQ	42760 MW	47830 TQ	USBLS	5/15
	New York	Y	27380 AE	29530 MW	31760 AEX	NYBLS	1/16-3/16
	North Carolina	Y	20790 FQ	25340 MW	29750 TQ	USBLS	5/15
	North Dakota	Y	28130 FQ	34220 MW	38680 TQ	USBLS	5/15
	Ohio	Y	21500 FQ	24280 MW	29930 TQ	USBLS	5/15
	Oklahoma	Y	20850 FQ	28920 MW	34560 TQ	USBLS	5/15
	Pennsylvania	Y	24280 FQ	31390 MW	36400 TQ	USBLS	5/15

AE	Average entry wage	AWR	Average wage range	H	Hourly
AEX	Average experienced wage	B	Biweekly	HI	Highest wage paid
ATC	Average total compensation	D	Daily	HR	High end range
AW	Average wage paid	FQ	First quartile wage	LO	Lowest wage paid

LR	Low end range	MTC	Median total compensation	TCC	Total cash compensation
M	Monthly	MW	Median wage paid	TQ	Third quartile wage
MCC	Median cash compensation	MWR	Median wage range	W	Weekly
ME	Median entry wage	S	See annotated source	Y	Yearly

Occupation/Type/Industry	Location	Per	Low	Mid	High	Source	Date
Manufactured Building and Mobile Home Installer	South Dakota	Y	29670 FQ	36970 MW	44050 TQ	USBLS	5/15
	Tennessee	Y	18740 FQ	25510 MW	30200 TQ	USBLS	5/15
	Virginia	Y	25850 FQ	29960 MW	34860 TQ	USBLS	5/15
	Washington	H	11.10 FQ	14.53 MW	19.04 TQ	WABLS	3/16
	West Virginia	Y	21540 FQ	25780 MW	30090 TQ	USBLS	5/15
	Wyoming	Y	27540 FQ	30240 MW	37190 TQ	USBLS	5/15
Manufacturing Manager							
Apparel and Textile Industries	United States	Y		105424 AW		INDWK	2015
Chemical Industry	United States	Y		135411 AW		INDWK	2015
Female	United States	Y		90482 AW		INDWK	2015
Male	United States	Y		117662 AW		INDWK	2015
Petroleum and Coal Industries	United States	Y		113731 AW		INDWK	2015
Manufacturing Worker	United States	Y		81289 ATC		LSJ09	2016
Mapping Supervisor							
Municipal Government	Roseville, CA	Y			103715 HI	CACIT	6/28/16
Municipal Government	Seattle, WA	H	41.18 LO		47.92 HI	CSSS	1/13/16
Marine Deputy							
County Government	Oakland County, MI	H	16.88 LO		19.31 HI	MIOAK2	10/1/16
Marine Engineer and Naval Architect	California	H	37.25 FQ	47.51 MW	64.43 TQ	CABLS	1/16-3/16
	San Diego-Carlsbad MSA, CA	H	35.39 FQ	42.72 MW	59.07 TQ	CABLS	1/16-3/16
	District of Columbia	Y	105960 FQ	127820 MW	147300 TQ	USBLS	5/15
	Washington-Arlington-Alexandria PMSA, DC-VA-MD-WV	Y	87690 FQ	113100 MW	137330 TQ	USBLS	5/15
	Florida	H	32.87 AE	45.74 MW	52.03 AEX	FLBLS	7/16-9/16
	Fort Lauderdale-Pompano Beach-Deerfield Beach PMSA, FL	H	32.58 AE	41.49 MW	46.33 AEX	FLBLS	7/16-9/16
	Tampa-St. Petersburg-Clearwater MSA, FL	H	32.83 AE	45.18 MW	49.81 AEX	FLBLS	7/16-9/16
	Hawaii	Y	70010 FQ	80860 MW	95190 TQ	USBLS	5/15
	Urban Honolulu MSA, HI	Y	68700 FQ	80580 MW	93710 TQ	USBLS	5/15
	Idaho	Y	67910 FQ	73000 MW	78090 TQ	USBLS	5/15
	Louisiana	Y	61160 FQ	72740 MW	84170 TQ	USBLS	5/15
	Baton Rouge MSA, LA	Y	61140 FQ	72920 MW	86550 TQ	USBLS	5/15
	New Orleans-Metairie MSA, LA	Y	69170 FQ	91260 MW	111660 TQ	USBLS	5/15
	Maryland	Y	63684 AE	118462 MW	145852 AEX	MDBLS	4/16
	Baltimore-Columbia-Towson MSA, MD	Y	57940 FQ	64520 MW	124410 TQ	USBLS	5/15
	Massachusetts	Y	60500 FQ	81350 MW	96310 TQ	USBLS	5/15
	Mississippi	Y	69950 FQ	80750 MW	102260 TQ	USBLS	5/15
	New Jersey	Y	72570 FQ	87000 MW	113580 TQ	USBLS	5/15
	Newark PMSA, NJ-PA	Y	75340 FQ	98950 MW	118270 TQ	USBLS	5/15
	New York	Y	76760 AE	95560 MW	101110 AEX	NYBLS	1/16-3/16
	New York-Jersey City-White Plains PMSA, NY-NJ	Y	84840 FQ	96560 MW	107430 TQ	USBLS	5/15
	Oregon	H	30.04 FQ	36.68 MW	52.57 TQ	ORBLS	2016
	Portland-Vancouver-Hillsboro MSA, OR-WA	Y	61340 FQ	77370 MW	96780 TQ	USBLS	5/15
	Texas	Y	82580 FQ	107090 MW	137600 TQ	USBLS	5/15
	Houston-The Woodlands-Sugar Land MSA, TX	Y	86520 FQ	110110 MW	140170 TQ	USBLS	5/15
	Virginia	Y	71530 FQ	88990 MW	108510 TQ	USBLS	5/15
	Virginia Beach-Norfolk-Newport News MSA, VA-NC	Y	67570 FQ	83470 MW	99350 TQ	USBLS	5/15
	Washington	H	35.19 FQ	42.20 MW	48.94 TQ	WABLS	3/16
	Seattle-Bellevue-Everett PMSA, WA	H	36.34 FQ	43.85 MW	50.71 TQ	WABLS	3/16
	Wisconsin	Y	59980 FQ	70010 MW	79060 TQ	USBLS	5/15
Marine Equipment Servicer							
Municipal Government	Seattle, WA	H	35.05 LO		36.35 HI	CSSS	1/13/16

AE	Average entry wage	AWR	Average wage range	H	Hourly	LR	Low end range	MTC	Median total compensation	TCC	Total cash compensation
AEX	Average experienced wage	B	Biweekly	HI	Highest wage paid	M	Monthly	MW	Median wage paid	TQ	Third quartile wage
ATC	Average total compensation	D	Daily	HR	High end range	MCC	Median cash compensation	MWR	Median wage range	W	Weekly
AW	Average wage paid	FQ	First quartile wage	LO	Lowest wage paid	ME	Median entry wage	S	See annotated source	Y	Yearly

Occupation/Type/Industry	Location	Per	Low	Mid	High	Source	Date
Marine Mechanic							
County Government	Oakland County, MI	H			19.90 HI	MIOAK2	10/1/16
Fire-Rescue, Municipal Government	San Diego, CA	Y		48410 AW		CACIT	6/28/16
Marine Museum Exhibitor							
Municipal Government	Detroit, MI	M	3500 LO		3675 HI	DETGOV	2016
Marine Protection Officer							
Municipal Government	Laguna Beach, CA	Y			72631 HI	CACIT	6/28/16
Marine Safety Captain							
Fire Department, Municipal Government	Long Beach, CA	Y		111106 AW		CACIT	6/28/16
Marine Safety Sergeant							
Municipal Government	Encinitas, CA	Y		68548 AW		CACIT	6/28/16
Market Master							
County Government	Oakland County, MI	B	1740 LO		2265 HI	MIOAK2	10/1/16
Municipal Government	Detroit, MI	M	2700 LO		3233 HI	DETGOV	2016
Market Research Analyst and Marketing Specialist							
	Alabama	Y	35597 AE	61457 AW	74381 AEX	ALBLS	6/16
	Birmingham-Hoover MSA, AL	Y	36970 AE	65198 AW	79322 AEX	ALBLS	6/16
	Alaska	Y	50100 FQ	64680 MW	78920 TQ	USBLS	5/15
	Anchorage MSA, AK	Y	52740 FQ	66300 MW	80600 TQ	USBLS	5/15
	Arizona	Y	39360 FQ	56490 MW	77980 TQ	USBLS	5/15
	Phoenix-Mesa-Scottsdale MSA, AZ	Y	39810 FQ	57690 MW	78920 TQ	USBLS	5/15
	Tucson MSA, AZ	Y	38240 FQ	52100 MW	74300 TQ	USBLS	5/15
	Arkansas	Y	41750 FQ	58740 MW	77810 TQ	USBLS	5/15
	Little Rock-North Little Rock-Conway MSA, AR	Y	43050 FQ	56360 MW	73280 TQ	USBLS	5/15
	California	H	24.54 FQ	35.32 MW	51.32 TQ	CABLS	1/16-3/16
	Anaheim-Santa Ana-Irvine PMSA, CA	H	21.91 FQ	32.49 MW	44.39 TQ	CABLS	1/16-3/16
	Los Angeles-Long Beach-Glendale PMSA, CA	H	22.38 FQ	31.47 MW	44.75 TQ	CABLS	1/16-3/16
	Oakland-Hayward-Berkeley PMSA, CA	H	27.76 FQ	39.43 MW	58.96 TQ	CABLS	1/16-3/16
	Riverside-San Bernardino-Ontario MSA, CA	H	19.22 FQ	25.33 MW	34.76 TQ	CABLS	1/16-3/16
	Sacramento–Roseville–Arden-Arcade MSA, CA	H	22.02 FQ	32.90 MW	43.97 TQ	CABLS	1/16-3/16
	San Diego-Carlsbad MSA, CA	H	22.10 FQ	31.98 MW	46.79 TQ	CABLS	1/16-3/16
	San Francisco-Redwood City-South San Francisco PMSA, CA	H	29.81 FQ	41.15 MW	59.65 TQ	CABLS	1/16-3/16
	Colorado	Y	47610 FQ	68380 MW	95450 TQ	USBLS	5/15
	Denver-Aurora-Lakewood MSA, CO	Y	52280 FQ	73590 MW	99250 TQ	USBLS	5/15
	Connecticut	Y		63069 MW		CTBLS	1/16-3/16
	Bridgeport-Stamford-Norwalk MSA, CT	Y	46700 FQ	63510 MW	86340 TQ	USBLS	5/15
	Hartford-West Hartford-East Hartford MSA, CT	Y	52050 FQ	63880 MW	83650 TQ	USBLS	5/15
	Delaware	Y	57490 FQ	73040 MW	95390 TQ	USBLS	5/15
	Wilmington PMSA, DE-MD-NJ	Y	59140 FQ	74250 MW	96410 TQ	USBLS	5/15
	District of Columbia	Y	49890 FQ	68120 MW	90010 TQ	USBLS	5/15
	Washington-Arlington-Alexandria PMSA, DC-VA-MD-WV	Y	50000 FQ	69780 MW	95760 TQ	USBLS	5/15
	Florida	H	17.56 AE	28.04 MW	37.16 AEX	FLBLS	7/16-9/16
	Fort Lauderdale-Pompano Beach-Deerfield Beach PMSA, FL	H	18.07 AE	26.94 MW	35.60 AEX	FLBLS	7/16-9/16
	Miami-Miami Beach-Kendall PMSA, FL	H	18.06 AE	29.30 MW	39.83 AEX	FLBLS	7/16-9/16
	Orlando-Kissimmee-Sanford MSA, FL	H	16.82 AE	26.95 MW	35.68 AEX	FLBLS	7/16-9/16
	Tampa-St. Petersburg-Clearwater MSA, FL	H	18.40 AE	28.92 MW	38.42 AEX	FLBLS	7/16-9/16

AE	Average entry wage	AWR	Average wage range	H	Hourly
AEX	Average experienced wage	B	Biweekly	HI	Highest wage paid
ATC	Average total compensation	D	Daily	HR	High end range
AW	Average wage paid	FQ	First quartile wage	LO	Lowest wage paid

LR	Low end range	MTC	Median total compensation	TCC	Total cash compensation
M	Monthly	MW	Median wage paid	TQ	Third quartile wage
MCC	Median cash compensation	MWR	Median wage range	W	Weekly
ME	Median entry wage	S	See annotated source	Y	Yearly

Occupation/Type/Industry	Location	Per	Low	Mid	High	Source	Date
Market Research Analyst and Marketing Specialist							
	Georgia	Y	41070 FQ	56910 MW	79320 TQ	USBLS	5/15
	Atlanta-Sandy Springs-Roswell MSA, GA	Y	42150 FQ	57950 MW	81490 TQ	USBLS	5/15
	Augusta-Richmond County MSA, GA-SC	Y	36860 FQ	51650 MW	66560 TQ	USBLS	5/15
	Hawaii	Y	42120 FQ	51700 MW	67270 TQ	USBLS	5/15
	Urban Honolulu MSA, HI	Y	42550 FQ	51810 MW	68240 TQ	USBLS	5/15
	Idaho	Y	37320 FQ	51330 MW	72000 TQ	USBLS	5/15
	Boise City MSA, ID	Y	39600 FQ	54000 MW	74340 TQ	USBLS	5/15
	Illinois	Y	41870 FQ	57180 MW	77560 TQ	USBLS	5/15
	Chicago-Naperville-Arlington Heights PMSA, IL	Y	43020 FQ	57990 MW	77820 TQ	USBLS	5/15
	Lake County-Kenosha County PMSA, IL-WI	Y	44170 FQ	63080 MW	83480 TQ	USBLS	5/15
	Indiana	Y	39210 FQ	50380 MW	68210 TQ	USBLS	5/15
	Gary PMSA, IN	Y	37390 FQ	50540 MW	69080 TQ	USBLS	5/15
	Indianapolis-Carmel-Anderson MSA, IN	Y	41910 FQ	52440 MW	71940 TQ	USBLS	5/15
	Iowa	Y	40570 FQ	53800 MW	71470 TQ	USBLS	5/15
	Des Moines-West Des Moines MSA, IA	Y	50980 FQ	66210 MW	80460 TQ	USBLS	5/15
	Kansas	Y	43930 FQ	57370 MW	76060 TQ	USBLS	5/15
	Wichita MSA, KS	Y	41690 FQ	53480 MW	77310 TQ	USBLS	5/15
	Kentucky	Y	36770 FQ	48660 MW	66900 TQ	USBLS	5/15
	Louisville-Jefferson County MSA, KY-IN	Y	39170 FQ	49110 MW	72190 TQ	USBLS	5/15
	Louisiana	Y	36190 FQ	47300 MW	60090 TQ	USBLS	5/15
	Baton Rouge MSA, LA	Y	39460 FQ	48110 MW	58210 TQ	USBLS	5/15
	New Orleans-Metairie MSA, LA	Y	37500 FQ	48090 MW	60690 TQ	USBLS	5/15
	Maine	Y	51390 FQ	67880 MW	86000 TQ	USBLS	5/15
	Portland-South Portland MSA, ME	Y	49230 FQ	65530 MW	84980 TQ	USBLS	5/15
	Maryland	Y	36069 AE	65679 MW	80485 AEX	MDBLS	4/16
	Baltimore-Columbia-Towson MSA, MD	Y	43370 FQ	57260 MW	76430 TQ	USBLS	5/15
	Salisbury MSA, MD-DE	Y	39280 FQ	53940 MW	67650 TQ	USBLS	5/15
	Massachusetts	Y	49120 FQ	68330 MW	96400 TQ	USBLS	5/15
	Boston-Cambridge-Newton NECTA, MA	Y	48730 FQ	68630 MW	97840 TQ	USBLS	5/15
	Worcester MSA, MA-CT	Y	50050 FQ	68460 MW	86370 TQ	USBLS	5/15
	Michigan	Y	44050 FQ	60140 MW	86330 TQ	USBLS	5/15
	Detroit-Dearborn-Livonia PMSA, MI	Y	61660 FQ	87580 MW	112730 TQ	USBLS	5/15
	Grand Rapids-Wyoming MSA, MI	Y	41170 FQ	52140 MW	69680 TQ	USBLS	5/15
	Minnesota	Y	48306 FQ	63283 MW	83219 TQ	MNBLS	1/16-3/16
	Minneapolis-St. Paul-Bloomington MSA, MN-WI	Y	50013 FQ	65122 MW	85840 TQ	MNBLS	1/16-3/16
	Mississippi	Y	34440 FQ	47850 MW	69740 TQ	USBLS	5/15
	Jackson MSA, MS	Y	34120 FQ	46900 MW	63010 TQ	USBLS	5/15
	Missouri	Y	42370 FQ	60260 MW	83770 TQ	USBLS	5/15
	Kansas City MSA, MO-KS	Y	46050 FQ	61750 MW	84030 TQ	USBLS	5/15
	St. Louis MSA, MO-IL	Y	45990 FQ	64210 MW	87050 TQ	USBLS	5/15
	Montana	Y	38590 FQ	50270 MW	68470 TQ	USBLS	5/15
	Billings MSA, MT	Y	46340 FQ	54790 MW	67220 TQ	USBLS	5/15
	Nebraska	Y	41655 FQ	54435 MW	72820 TQ	NEBLS	7/16-9/16
	Omaha-Council Bluffs MSA, NE-IA	Y	44435 FQ	56835 MW	74645 TQ	NEBLS	7/16-9/16
	Nevada	Y	36620 FQ	51920 MW	67950 TQ	USBLS	5/15
	Las Vegas-Henderson-Paradise MSA, NV	Y	37140 FQ	52030 MW	63730 TQ	USBLS	5/15
	New Hampshire	H	20.18 AE	30.49 MW	40.71 AEX	NHBLS	6/16
	Dover-Durham MSA, NH-ME	Y	53580 FQ	61260 MW	71520 TQ	USBLS	5/15
	Manchester NECTA, NH	H	19.08 AE	29.62 MW	36.16 AEX	NHBLS	6/16
	Nashua NECTA, NH-MA	Y	55220 FQ	68500 MW	98240 TQ	USBLS	5/15
	New Jersey	Y	51930 FQ	70110 MW	93940 TQ	USBLS	5/15
	Camden PMSA, NJ	Y	43090 FQ	55610 MW	76080 TQ	USBLS	5/15
	Newark PMSA, NJ-PA	Y	55700 FQ	76000 MW	101170 TQ	USBLS	5/15
	Trenton MSA, NJ	Y	51850 FQ	68040 MW	85930 TQ	USBLS	5/15
	New Mexico	Y	36910 FQ	46910 MW	60430 TQ	USBLS	5/15

AE	Average entry wage	AWR	Average wage range	H	Hourly
AEX	Average experienced wage	B	Biweekly	HI	Highest wage paid
ATC	Average total compensation	D	Daily	HR	High end range
AW	Average wage paid	FQ	First quartile wage	LO	Lowest wage paid

LR	Low end range	MTC	Median total compensation	TCC	Total cash compensation
M	Monthly	MW	Median wage paid	TQ	Third quartile wage
MCC	Median cash compensation	MWR	Median wage range	W	Weekly
ME	Median entry wage	S	See annotated source	Y	Yearly

Market Research Analyst and Marketing Specialist

Occupation/Type/Industry	Location	Per	Low	Mid	High	Source	Date
Market Research Analyst and Marketing Specialist	Albuquerque MSA, NM	Y	36970 FQ	47180 MW	59680 TQ	USBLS	5/15
	New York	Y	45520 AE	73160 MW	95870 AEX	NYBLS	1/16-3/16
	Buffalo-Cheektowaga-Niagara Falls MSA, NY	Y	40820 FQ	57560 MW	76820 TQ	USBLS	5/15
	Nassau County-Suffolk County PMSA, NY	Y	45910 FQ	67020 MW	95780 TQ	USBLS	5/15
	New York-Jersey City-White Plains PMSA, NY-NJ	Y	54860 FQ	73270 MW	97340 TQ	USBLS	5/15
	Rochester MSA, NY	Y	46240 FQ	65650 MW	92710 TQ	USBLS	5/15
	North Carolina	Y	45300 FQ	61930 MW	85830 TQ	USBLS	5/15
	Raleigh MSA, NC	Y	43150 FQ	59030 MW	85320 TQ	USBLS	5/15
	North Dakota	Y	40910 FQ	52110 MW	64280 TQ	USBLS	5/15
	Fargo MSA, ND-MN	Y	40380 FQ	52330 MW	62470 TQ	USBLS	5/15
	Ohio	Y	44280 FQ	59510 MW	79420 TQ	USBLS	5/15
	Cincinnati MSA, OH-KY-IN	Y	43330 FQ	58480 MW	77210 TQ	USBLS	5/15
	Cleveland-Elyria MSA, OH	Y	44680 FQ	60870 MW	83690 TQ	USBLS	5/15
	Columbus MSA, OH	Y	49570 FQ	63800 MW	86590 TQ	USBLS	5/15
	Oklahoma	Y	36980 FQ	51260 MW	72480 TQ	USBLS	5/15
	Oklahoma City MSA, OK	Y	36840 FQ	48590 MW	68750 TQ	USBLS	5/15
	Tulsa MSA, OK	Y	43300 FQ	61830 MW	82850 TQ	USBLS	5/15
	Oregon	H	20.61 FQ	27.69 MW	38.77 TQ	ORBLS	2016
	Portland-Vancouver-Hillsboro MSA, OR-WA	Y	44200 FQ	58700 MW	81720 TQ	USBLS	5/15
	Pennsylvania	Y	44320 FQ	59640 MW	82450 TQ	USBLS	5/15
	Allentown-Bethlehem-Easton MSA, PA-NJ	Y	37670 FQ	53710 MW	73700 TQ	USBLS	5/15
	Harrisburg-Carlisle MSA, PA	Y	43580 FQ	56200 MW	72110 TQ	USBLS	5/15
	Montgomery County-Bucks County-Chester County PMSA, PA	Y	49250 FQ	64580 MW	95540 TQ	USBLS	5/15
	Philadelphia PMSA, PA	Y	48860 FQ	63420 MW	90510 TQ	USBLS	5/15
	Pittsburgh MSA, PA	Y	44240 FQ	60110 MW	79080 TQ	USBLS	5/15
	Rhode Island	Y	46110 FQ	59400 MW	79910 TQ	USBLS	5/15
	Providence-Warwick MSA, RI-MA	Y	45850 FQ	59600 MW	80440 TQ	USBLS	5/15
	Charleston-North Charleston MSA, SC	Y	31280 FQ	43190 MW	64230 TQ	USBLS	5/15
	Columbia MSA, SC	Y	37060 FQ	51830 MW	76070 TQ	USBLS	5/15
	Greenville-Anderson-Mauldin MSA, SC	Y	42320 FQ	60610 MW	81720 TQ	USBLS	5/15
	South Dakota	Y	41460 FQ	49050 MW	60290 TQ	USBLS	5/15
	Sioux Falls MSA, SD	Y	42830 FQ	49620 MW	60680 TQ	USBLS	5/15
	Tennessee	Y	36370 FQ	49990 MW	71270 TQ	USBLS	5/15
	Knoxville MSA, TN	Y	32970 FQ	43950 MW	62440 TQ	USBLS	5/15
	Memphis MSA, TN-MS-AR	Y	40580 FQ	54260 MW	70020 TQ	USBLS	5/15
	Nashville-Davidson–Murfreesboro–Franklin MSA, TN	Y	36620 FQ	50400 MW	76240 TQ	USBLS	5/15
	Texas	Y	48530 FQ	66740 MW	96000 TQ	USBLS	5/15
	Austin-Round Rock MSA, TX	Y	53360 FQ	76220 MW	104970 TQ	USBLS	5/15
	Dallas-Plano-Irving PMSA, TX	Y	52460 FQ	71310 MW	100310 TQ	USBLS	5/15
	Fort Worth-Arlington PMSA, TX	Y	45650 FQ	62590 MW	93330 TQ	USBLS	5/15
	Houston-The Woodlands-Sugar Land MSA, TX	Y	46820 FQ	61560 MW	90840 TQ	USBLS	5/15
	San Antonio-New Braunfels MSA, TX	Y	42140 FQ	66900 MW	96200 TQ	USBLS	5/15
	Utah	Y	39470 FQ	53120 MW	73990 TQ	USBLS	5/15
	Ogden-Clearfield MSA, UT	Y	36610 FQ	50700 MW	63760 TQ	USBLS	5/15
	Provo-Orem MSA, UT	Y	40540 FQ	52390 MW	74640 TQ	USBLS	5/15
	Salt Lake City MSA, UT	Y	40930 FQ	55380 MW	77780 TQ	USBLS	5/15
	Vermont	Y	39700 FQ	49430 MW	66570 TQ	USBLS	5/15
	Burlington-South Burlington MSA, VT	Y	39820 FQ	49560 MW	68910 TQ	USBLS	5/15
	Virginia	Y	45000 FQ	63250 MW	90780 TQ	USBLS	5/15
	Richmond MSA, VA	Y	45670 FQ	65110 MW	92160 TQ	USBLS	5/15
	Virginia Beach-Norfolk-Newport News MSA, VA-NC	Y	38860 FQ	51670 MW	68610 TQ	USBLS	5/15
	Washington	H	23.90 FQ	34.00 MW	50.13 TQ	WABLS	3/16
	Seattle-Bellevue-Everett PMSA, WA	H	26.28 FQ	37.11 MW	55.40 TQ	WABLS	3/16

AE	Average entry wage	AWR	Average wage range	H	Hourly	LR	Low end range	MTC	Median total compensation	TCC	Total cash compensation
AEX	Average experienced wage	B	Biweekly	HI	Highest wage paid	M	Monthly	MW	Median wage paid	TQ	Third quartile wage
ATC	Average total compensation	D	Daily	HR	High end range	MCC	Median cash compensation	MWR	Median wage range	W	Weekly
AW	Average wage paid	FQ	First quartile wage	LO	Lowest wage paid	ME	Median entry wage	S	See annotated source	Y	Yearly

Occupation/Type/Industry	Location	Per	Low	Mid	High	Source	Date
Market Research Analyst and Marketing Specialist	Tacoma-Lakewood PMSA, WA	H	17.74 FQ	23.05 MW	30.96 TQ	WABLS	3/16
	West Virginia	Y	32610 FQ	42250 MW	55890 TQ	USBLS	5/15
	Huntington-Ashland MSA, WV-KY-OH	Y	31630 FQ	43530 MW	52580 TQ	USBLS	5/15
	Wisconsin	Y	40140 FQ	51260 MW	68960 TQ	USBLS	5/15
	Madison MSA, WI	Y	43290 FQ	55350 MW	72800 TQ	USBLS	5/15
	Milwaukee-Waukesha-West Allis MSA, WI	Y	41230 FQ	55940 MW	74980 TQ	USBLS	5/15
	Wyoming	Y	38350 FQ	51570 MW	62900 TQ	USBLS	5/15
	Cheyenne MSA, WY	Y	40790 FQ	50900 MW	61760 TQ	USBLS	5/15
	Puerto Rico	Y	22140 FQ	28820 MW	40800 TQ	USBLS	5/15
	San Juan-Carolina-Caguas MSA, PR	Y	22510 FQ	29420 MW	41680 TQ	USBLS	5/15
	Guam	Y	26890 FQ	36110 MW	49220 TQ	USBLS	5/15
Marketing Associate Management Services Department, Municipal Government	Indian Wells, CA	Y			88664 HI	CACIT	6/28/16
Marketing Director Pharmaceutical, Medical Device, and Healthcare Industries	United States	Y		147900 AW		MMM01	7/16
Marketing Executive	United States	H		57.42 MW		ADAGE01	2015
Credit Union	United States	Y		131084 MW		CUMGT	2016
Marketing Manager	Alabama	Y	75693 AE	142387 AW	175740 AEX	ALBLS	6/16
	Birmingham-Hoover MSA, AL	Y	77241 AE	151540 AW	188695 AEX	ALBLS	6/16
	Alaska	Y	72840 FQ	91070 MW	123140 TQ	USBLS	5/15
	Anchorage MSA, AK	Y	72880 FQ	91730 MW	125540 TQ	USBLS	5/15
	Arizona	Y	68170 FQ	98700 MW	147060 TQ	USBLS	5/15
	Phoenix-Mesa-Scottsdale MSA, AZ	Y	70810 FQ	102210 MW	150280 TQ	USBLS	5/15
	Tucson MSA, AZ	Y	60970 FQ	87410 MW	133450 TQ	USBLS	5/15
	Arkansas	Y	76540 FQ	108730 MW	160460 TQ	USBLS	5/15
	Little Rock-North Little Rock-Conway MSA, AR	Y	64380 FQ	93250 MW	144060 TQ	USBLS	5/15
	California	H	54.29 FQ	75.28 MW		CABLS	1/16-3/16
	Anaheim-Santa Ana-Irvine PMSA, CA	H	44.96 FQ	61.64 MW	83.91 TQ	CABLS	1/16-3/16
	Los Angeles-Long Beach-Glendale PMSA, CA	H	47.21 FQ	68.43 MW	89.29 TQ	CABLS	1/16-3/16
	Oakland-Hayward-Berkeley PMSA, CA	H	60.34 FQ	77.92 MW		CABLS	1/16-3/16
	Riverside-San Bernardino-Ontario MSA, CA	H	36.21 FQ	49.62 MW	69.37 TQ	CABLS	1/16-3/16
	Sacramento–Roseville–Arden-Arcade MSA, CA	H	33.03 FQ	57.22 MW	76.21 TQ	CABLS	1/16-3/16
	San Diego-Carlsbad MSA, CA	H	49.26 FQ	69.45 MW		CABLS	1/16-3/16
	San Francisco-Redwood City-South San Francisco PMSA, CA	H	66.76 FQ	86.22 MW		CABLS	1/16-3/16
	Colorado	Y	99190 FQ	135990 MW	182200 TQ	USBLS	5/15
	Denver-Aurora-Lakewood MSA, CO	Y	99870 FQ	132880 MW	181850 TQ	USBLS	5/15
	Connecticut	Y		130283 MW		CTBLS	1/16-3/16
	Bridgeport-Stamford-Norwalk MSA, CT	Y	108980 FQ	147750 MW		USBLS	5/15
	Hartford-West Hartford-East Hartford MSA, CT	Y	102950 FQ	121930 MW	152780 TQ	USBLS	5/15
	Delaware	Y	116730 FQ	150870 MW	187100 TQ	USBLS	5/15
	Wilmington PMSA, DE-MD-NJ	Y	116380 FQ	150460 MW	186660 TQ	USBLS	5/15
	District of Columbia	Y	106000 FQ	145910 MW		USBLS	5/15
	Washington-Arlington-Alexandria PMSA, DC-VA-MD-WV	Y	109400 FQ	146910 MW		USBLS	5/15
	Florida	H	31.96 AE	54.36 MW	73.38 AEX	FLBLS	7/16-9/16
	Fort Lauderdale-Pompano Beach-Deerfield Beach PMSA, FL	H	35.83 AE	58.45 MW	73.40 AEX	FLBLS	7/16-9/16

965

Occupation/Type/Industry	Location	Per	Low	Mid	High	Source	Date
Marketing Manager	Miami-Miami Beach-Kendall PMSA, FL	H	30.21 AE	58.52 MW	72.92 AEX	FLBLS	7/16-9/16
	Orlando-Kissimmee-Sanford MSA, FL	H	30.53 AE	49.44 MW	67.82 AEX	FLBLS	7/16-9/16
	Tampa-St. Petersburg-Clearwater MSA, FL	H	33.00 AE	54.74 MW	72.96 AEX	FLBLS	7/16-9/16
	Georgia	Y	93060 FQ	122980 MW	159830 TQ	USBLS	5/15
	Atlanta-Sandy Springs-Roswell MSA, GA	Y	95320 FQ	125130 MW	162050 TQ	USBLS	5/15
	Augusta-Richmond County MSA, GA-SC	Y	83830 FQ	109140 MW	163340 TQ	USBLS	5/15
	Hawaii	Y	66070 FQ	87110 MW	127590 TQ	USBLS	5/15
	Urban Honolulu MSA, HI	Y	66820 FQ	86100 MW	120800 TQ	USBLS	5/15
	Idaho	Y	68680 FQ	100220 MW	142570 TQ	USBLS	5/15
	Boise City MSA, ID	Y	82880 FQ	114750 MW	155270 TQ	USBLS	5/15
	Illinois	Y	77900 FQ	110090 MW	150310 TQ	USBLS	5/15
	Chicago-Naperville-Arlington Heights PMSA, IL	Y	80350 FQ	111740 MW	151590 TQ	USBLS	5/15
	Lake County-Kenosha County PMSA, IL-WI	Y	99680 FQ	127950 MW	162120 TQ	USBLS	5/15
	Indiana	Y	73630 FQ	98410 MW	131270 TQ	USBLS	5/15
	Bloomington MSA, IN	Y	83130 FQ	103130 MW	137240 TQ	USBLS	5/15
	Gary PMSA, IN	Y	54540 FQ	77930 MW	108570 TQ	USBLS	5/15
	Indianapolis-Carmel-Anderson MSA, IN	Y	74450 FQ	103080 MW	139560 TQ	USBLS	5/15
	Iowa	Y	74150 FQ	99810 MW	134080 TQ	USBLS	5/15
	Des Moines-West Des Moines MSA, IA	Y	81420 FQ	112750 MW	145280 TQ	USBLS	5/15
	Kansas	Y	84830 FQ	114210 MW	153140 TQ	USBLS	5/15
	Wichita MSA, KS	Y	88420 FQ	114310 MW	145780 TQ	USBLS	5/15
	Kentucky	Y	65990 FQ	91770 MW	123170 TQ	USBLS	5/15
	Louisville-Jefferson County MSA, KY-IN	Y	74630 FQ	98160 MW	129550 TQ	USBLS	5/15
	Louisiana	Y	60190 FQ	79910 MW	116410 TQ	USBLS	5/15
	Baton Rouge MSA, LA	Y	62270 FQ	85900 MW	102980 TQ	USBLS	5/15
	New Orleans-Metairie MSA, LA	Y	60040 FQ	82660 MW	127180 TQ	USBLS	5/15
	Maine	Y	66220 FQ	91960 MW	120700 TQ	USBLS	5/15
	Portland-South Portland MSA, ME	Y	70190 FQ	94950 MW	121980 TQ	USBLS	5/15
	Maryland	Y	74827 AE	140322 MW	173069 AEX	MDBLS	4/16
	Baltimore-Columbia-Towson MSA, MD	Y	88360 FQ	117710 MW	164250 TQ	USBLS	5/15
	Salisbury MSA, MD-DE	Y	86800 FQ	117620 MW	155850 TQ	USBLS	5/15
	Massachusetts	Y	96160 FQ	129100 MW	170200 TQ	USBLS	5/15
	Boston-Cambridge-Newton NECTA, MA	Y	100090 FQ	132780 MW	173820 TQ	USBLS	5/15
	Worcester MSA, MA-CT	Y	85020 FQ	111660 MW	156970 TQ	USBLS	5/15
	Michigan	Y	76010 FQ	110140 MW	150040 TQ	USBLS	5/15
	Detroit-Dearborn-Livonia PMSA, MI	Y	107340 FQ	143530 MW	178770 TQ	USBLS	5/15
	Grand Rapids-Wyoming MSA, MI	Y	69250 FQ	91090 MW	116440 TQ	USBLS	5/15
	Minnesota	Y	95879 FQ	123436 MW	160727 TQ	MNBLS	1/16-3/16
	Minneapolis-St. Paul-Bloomington MSA, MN-WI	Y	99233 FQ	126606 MW	165147 TQ	MNBLS	1/16-3/16
	Mississippi	Y	55450 FQ	74730 MW	104970 TQ	USBLS	5/15
	Jackson MSA, MS	Y	57280 FQ	75100 MW	97630 TQ	USBLS	5/15
	Missouri	Y	92680 FQ	120840 MW	155340 TQ	USBLS	5/15
	Kansas City MSA, MO-KS	Y	88720 FQ	115350 MW	153140 TQ	USBLS	5/15
	St. Louis MSA, MO-IL	Y	96850 FQ	127870 MW	160430 TQ	USBLS	5/15
	Montana	Y	70630 FQ	94400 MW	122850 TQ	USBLS	5/15
	Nebraska	Y	64605 FQ	93425 MW	136680 TQ	NEBLS	7/16-9/16
	Omaha-Council Bluffs MSA, NE-IA	Y	67920 FQ	97895 MW	142700 TQ	NEBLS	7/16-9/16
	Nevada	Y	71940 FQ	94080 MW	128020 TQ	USBLS	5/15
	Las Vegas-Henderson-Paradise MSA, NV	Y	73420 FQ	97350 MW	137350 TQ	USBLS	5/15
	New Hampshire	H	37.71 AE	59.42 MW	74.54 AEX	NHBLS	6/16
	Manchester NECTA, NH	H	34.86 AE	56.66 MW	68.27 AEX	NHBLS	6/16
	Nashua NECTA, NH-MA	Y	105500 FQ	136100 MW	155960 TQ	USBLS	5/15
	New Jersey	Y	112690 FQ	149060 MW		USBLS	5/15

AE	Average entry wage	AWR	Average wage range	H	Hourly
AEX	Average experienced wage	B	Biweekly	HI	Highest wage paid
ATC	Average total compensation	D	Daily	HR	High end range
AW	Average wage paid	FQ	First quartile wage	LO	Lowest wage paid

LR	Low end range	MTC	Median total compensation	TCC	Total cash compensation
M	Monthly	MW	Median wage paid	TQ	Third quartile wage
MCC	Median cash compensation	MWR	Median wage range	W	Weekly
ME	Median entry wage	S	See annotated source	Y	Yearly

Occupation/Type/Industry	Location	Per	Low	Mid	High	Source	Date
Marketing Manager	Camden PMSA, NJ	Y	93880 FQ	123460 MW	153800 TQ	USBLS	5/15
	Newark PMSA, NJ-PA	Y	121350 FQ	158920 MW		USBLS	5/15
	Trenton MSA, NJ	Y	109160 FQ	139890 MW	183720 TQ	USBLS	5/15
	New Mexico	Y	54480 FQ	75100 MW	99320 TQ	USBLS	5/15
	Albuquerque MSA, NM	Y	49440 FQ	73730 MW	99140 TQ	USBLS	5/15
	New York	Y	110470 AE	178890 MW		NYBLS	1/16-3/16
	Binghamton MSA, NY	Y	107790 FQ	138400 MW		USBLS	5/15
	Buffalo-Cheektowaga-Niagara Falls MSA, NY	Y	92300 FQ	130600 MW	179140 TQ	USBLS	5/15
	Nassau County-Suffolk County PMSA, NY	Y	123280 FQ	157180 MW		USBLS	5/15
	New York-Jersey City-White Plains PMSA, NY-NJ	Y	127680 FQ	171900 MW		USBLS	5/15
	Rochester MSA, NY	Y	82090 FQ	109930 MW	147320 TQ	USBLS	5/15
	North Carolina	Y	94110 FQ	125000 MW	167750 TQ	USBLS	5/15
	Charlotte-Concord-Gastonia MSA, NC-SC	Y	91430 FQ	123900 MW	164880 TQ	USBLS	5/15
	Raleigh MSA, NC	Y	100540 FQ	129420 MW	166150 TQ	USBLS	5/15
	North Dakota	Y	67600 FQ	90110 MW	129310 TQ	USBLS	5/15
	Fargo MSA, ND-MN	Y	68510 FQ	88780 MW	128940 TQ	USBLS	5/15
	Ohio	Y	89130 FQ	118730 MW	154720 TQ	USBLS	5/15
	Cincinnati MSA, OH-KY-IN	Y	89620 FQ	117300 MW	156980 TQ	USBLS	5/15
	Cleveland-Elyria MSA, OH	Y	87610 FQ	119100 MW	153420 TQ	USBLS	5/15
	Columbus MSA, OH	Y	97260 FQ	128170 MW	162660 TQ	USBLS	5/15
	Oklahoma	Y	58580 FQ	79230 MW	119360 TQ	USBLS	5/15
	Oklahoma City MSA, OK	Y	59950 FQ	77890 MW	112980 TQ	USBLS	5/15
	Tulsa MSA, OK	Y	60120 FQ	87820 MW	132680 TQ	USBLS	5/15
	Oregon	H	34.65 FQ	50.27 MW	68.14 TQ	ORBLS	2016
	Portland-Vancouver-Hillsboro MSA, OR-WA	Y	77910 FQ	110520 MW	145450 TQ	USBLS	5/15
	Pennsylvania	Y	104260 FQ	141700 MW	185600 TQ	USBLS	5/15
	Allentown-Bethlehem-Easton MSA, PA-NJ	Y	95570 FQ	145340 MW	183210 TQ	USBLS	5/15
	Harrisburg-Carlisle MSA, PA	Y	89910 FQ	115310 MW	157050 TQ	USBLS	5/15
	Montgomery County-Bucks County-Chester County PMSA, PA	Y	113530 FQ	150550 MW		USBLS	5/15
	Philadelphia PMSA, PA	Y	117550 FQ	153060 MW		USBLS	5/15
	Pittsburgh MSA, PA	Y	105660 FQ	133770 MW	179090 TQ	USBLS	5/15
	Rhode Island	Y	96960 FQ	126360 MW	158070 TQ	USBLS	5/15
	Providence-Warwick MSA, RI-MA	Y	94280 FQ	122470 MW	157850 TQ	USBLS	5/15
	South Carolina	Y	73390 FQ	97730 MW	134870 TQ	USBLS	5/15
	Charleston-North Charleston MSA, SC	Y	57630 FQ	88400 MW	128300 TQ	USBLS	5/15
	Columbia MSA, SC	Y	81660 FQ	100530 MW	136340 TQ	USBLS	5/15
	Greenville-Anderson-Mauldin MSA, SC	Y	79640 FQ	107110 MW	133170 TQ	USBLS	5/15
	South Dakota	Y	87280 FQ	106200 MW	123060 TQ	USBLS	5/15
	Sioux Falls MSA, SD	Y	91000 FQ	107270 MW	125630 TQ	USBLS	5/15
	Tennessee	Y	56390 FQ	80660 MW	126110 TQ	USBLS	5/15
	Knoxville MSA, TN	Y	57220 FQ	86590 MW	121530 TQ	USBLS	5/15
	Memphis MSA, TN-MS-AR	Y	54880 FQ	78460 MW	118520 TQ	USBLS	5/15
	Nashville-Davidson–Murfreesboro–Franklin MSA, TN	Y	57240 FQ	81360 MW	135540 TQ	USBLS	5/15
	Texas	Y	107670 FQ	141040 MW	179790 TQ	USBLS	5/15
	Austin-Round Rock MSA, TX	Y	112460 FQ	147130 MW	184450 TQ	USBLS	5/15
	Dallas-Plano-Irving PMSA, TX	Y	111060 FQ	139050 MW	167990 TQ	USBLS	5/15
	Fort Worth-Arlington PMSA, TX	Y	83980 FQ	112210 MW	163730 TQ	USBLS	5/15
	Houston-The Woodlands-Sugar Land MSA, TX	Y	111070 FQ	149820 MW		USBLS	5/15
	San Antonio-New Braunfels MSA, TX	Y	100000 FQ	133020 MW	169750 TQ	USBLS	5/15
	Utah	Y	75280 FQ	109570 MW	150330 TQ	USBLS	5/15
	Ogden-Clearfield MSA, UT	Y	58260 FQ	79530 MW	120660 TQ	USBLS	5/15
	Provo-Orem MSA, UT	Y	69070 FQ	99530 MW	144900 TQ	USBLS	5/15
	Salt Lake City MSA, UT	Y	84900 FQ	118050 MW	156260 TQ	USBLS	5/15
	Vermont	Y	80100 FQ	107330 MW	156270 TQ	USBLS	5/15
	Burlington-South Burlington MSA, VT	Y	87740 FQ	113060 MW	154470 TQ	USBLS	5/15

Occupation/Type/Industry	Location	Per	Low	Mid	High	Source	Date
Marketing Manager	Virginia	Y	107440 FQ	144270 MW	184420 TQ	USBLS	5/15
	Richmond MSA, VA	Y	101550 FQ	141450 MW	183120 TQ	USBLS	5/15
	Virginia Beach-Norfolk-Newport News MSA, VA-NC	Y	85900 FQ	112610 MW	159070 TQ	USBLS	5/15
	Washington	H	48.65 FQ	64.39 MW	82.67 TQ	WABLS	3/16
	Seattle-Bellevue-Everett PMSA, WA	H	51.69 FQ	67.11 MW	85.47 TQ	WABLS	3/16
	Tacoma-Lakewood PMSA, WA	H	36.48 FQ	43.84 MW	55.89 TQ	WABLS	3/16
	West Virginia	Y	58310 FQ	77820 MW	115240 TQ	USBLS	5/15
	Huntington-Ashland MSA, WV-KY-OH	Y	56310 FQ	70340 MW	121410 TQ	USBLS	5/15
	Wisconsin	Y	81580 FQ	103200 MW	131500 TQ	USBLS	5/15
	Madison MSA, WI	Y	84100 FQ	104610 MW	128090 TQ	USBLS	5/15
	Milwaukee-Waukesha-West Allis MSA, WI	Y	82320 FQ	107430 MW	137070 TQ	USBLS	5/15
	Puerto Rico	Y	49670 FQ	68850 MW	101800 TQ	USBLS	5/15
	San Juan-Carolina-Caguas MSA, PR	Y	50640 FQ	70100 MW	102560 TQ	USBLS	5/15
	Guam	Y	36130 FQ	54880 MW	70270 TQ	USBLS	5/15
Marketing Specialist							
County Government	Rockdale County, GA	Y	29973 LO		48769 HI	GACTY04	2016
Municipal Government	Bellflower, CA	Y			71229 HI	CACIT	6/28/16
Marriage and Family Therapist	Alabama	Y	29020 AE	40528 AW	46287 AEX	ALBLS	6/16
	Birmingham-Hoover MSA, AL	Y	37552 AE	45819 AW	49957 AEX	ALBLS	6/16
	Alaska	Y	53790 FQ	59390 MW	66420 TQ	USBLS	5/15
	Tucson MSA, AZ	Y	35260 FQ	42710 MW	48930 TQ	USBLS	5/15
	Arkansas	Y	42830 FQ	50530 MW	64440 TQ	USBLS	5/15
	California	H	19.53 FQ	24.13 MW	30.62 TQ	CABLS	1/16-3/16
	Anaheim-Santa Ana-Irvine PMSA, CA	H	18.73 FQ	27.67 MW	35.11 TQ	CABLS	1/16-3/16
	Los Angeles-Long Beach-Glendale PMSA, CA	H	17.02 FQ	22.07 MW	26.93 TQ	CABLS	1/16-3/16
	Oakland-Hayward-Berkeley PMSA, CA	H	23.68 FQ	29.10 MW	37.58 TQ	CABLS	1/16-3/16
	Riverside-San Bernardino-Ontario MSA, CA	H	23.24 FQ	27.78 MW	31.62 TQ	CABLS	1/16-3/16
	Sacramento–Roseville–Arden-Arcade MSA, CA	H	20.07 FQ	23.70 MW	29.93 TQ	CABLS	1/16-3/16
	San Diego-Carlsbad MSA, CA	H	17.62 FQ	22.53 MW	35.29 TQ	CABLS	1/16-3/16
	San Francisco-Redwood City-South San Francisco PMSA, CA	H	20.08 FQ	23.08 MW	28.22 TQ	CABLS	1/16-3/16
	Colorado	Y	34660 FQ	51270 MW	71200 TQ	USBLS	5/15
	Denver-Aurora-Lakewood MSA, CO	Y	33340 FQ	49380 MW	74680 TQ	USBLS	5/15
	Connecticut	Y		47823 MW		CTBLS	1/16-3/16
	Bridgeport-Stamford-Norwalk MSA, CT	Y	35310 FQ	39250 MW	48140 TQ	USBLS	5/15
	Hartford-West Hartford-East Hartford MSA, CT	Y	40990 FQ	49550 MW	60380 TQ	USBLS	5/15
	Delaware	Y	47580 FQ	50940 MW	53820 TQ	USBLS	5/15
	Wilmington PMSA, DE-MD-NJ	Y	47590 FQ	51810 MW	59590 TQ	USBLS	5/15
	Washington-Arlington-Alexandria PMSA, DC-VA-MD-WV	Y	40790 FQ	51070 MW	62430 TQ	USBLS	5/15
	Florida	H	15.16 AE	19.56 MW	24.76 AEX	FLBLS	7/16-9/16
	Fort Lauderdale-Pompano Beach-Deerfield Beach PMSA, FL	H	15.52 AE	19.34 MW	25.19 AEX	FLBLS	7/16-9/16
	Miami-Miami Beach-Kendall PMSA, FL	H	14.90 AE	21.34 MW	24.48 AEX	FLBLS	7/16-9/16
	Tampa-St. Petersburg-Clearwater MSA, FL	H	13.26 AE	16.59 MW	19.90 AEX	FLBLS	7/16-9/16
	Georgia	Y	40460 FQ	52520 MW	58200 TQ	USBLS	5/15
	Atlanta-Sandy Springs-Roswell MSA, GA	Y	49500 FQ	54440 MW	59040 TQ	USBLS	5/15
	Hawaii	Y	43670 FQ	57470 MW	72550 TQ	USBLS	5/15
	Urban Honolulu MSA, HI	Y	40600 FQ	46990 MW	61430 TQ	USBLS	5/15
	Illinois	Y	34920 FQ	43870 MW	66540 TQ	USBLS	5/15

AE	Average entry wage	AWR	Average wage range	H	Hourly
AEX	Average experienced wage	B	Biweekly	HI	Highest wage paid
ATC	Average total compensation	D	Daily	HR	High end range
AW	Average wage paid	FQ	First quartile wage	LO	Lowest wage paid

LR	Low end range	MTC	Median total compensation	TCC	Total cash compensation
M	Monthly	MW	Median wage paid	TQ	Third quartile wage
MCC	Median cash compensation	MWR	Median wage range	W	Weekly
ME	Median entry wage	S	See annotated source	Y	Yearly

Occupation/Type/Industry	Location	Per	Low	Mid	High	Source	Date
Marriage and Family Therapist	Lake County-Kenosha County						
	PMSA, IL-WI	Y	34360 FQ	47440 MW	64770 TQ	USBLS	5/15
	Indiana	Y	37980 FQ	48180 MW	74060 TQ	USBLS	5/15
	Gary PMSA, IN	Y	37700 FQ	50960 MW	59830 TQ	USBLS	5/15
	Indianapolis-Carmel-Anderson						
	MSA, IN	Y	47860 FQ	76730 MW	89470 TQ	USBLS	5/15
	Iowa	Y	38690 FQ	45250 MW	53890 TQ	USBLS	5/15
	Des Moines-West Des Moines						
	MSA, IA	Y	39300 FQ	46920 MW	58410 TQ	USBLS	5/15
	Kansas	Y	38270 FQ	45270 MW	66970 TQ	USBLS	5/15
	Kentucky	Y	27700 FQ	36050 MW	44440 TQ	USBLS	5/15
	Louisville-Jefferson County						
	MSA, KY-IN	Y	19830 FQ	35080 MW	44150 TQ	USBLS	5/15
	Louisiana	Y	32360 FQ	38870 MW	51260 TQ	USBLS	5/15
	Maine	Y	53530 FQ	59510 MW	65310 TQ	USBLS	5/15
	Maryland	Y	33614 AE	51796 MW	60886 AEX	MDBLS	4/16
	Baltimore-Columbia-Towson						
	MSA, MD	Y	38990 FQ	52000 MW	59360 TQ	USBLS	5/15
	Salisbury MSA, MD-DE	Y	36620 FQ	47580 MW	53770 TQ	USBLS	5/15
	Massachusetts	Y	35600 FQ	42300 MW	52130 TQ	USBLS	5/15
	Boston-Cambridge-Newton						
	NECTA, MA	Y	36300 FQ	42660 MW	49120 TQ	USBLS	5/15
	Worcester MSA, MA-CT	Y	39030 FQ	46820 MW	70160 TQ	USBLS	5/15
	Michigan	Y	35430 FQ	40140 MW	46680 TQ	USBLS	5/15
	Detroit-Dearborn-Livonia						
	PMSA, MI	Y	35540 FQ	39940 MW	45950 TQ	USBLS	5/15
	Minnesota	Y	40302 FQ	49082 MW	59435 TQ	MNBLS	1/16-3/16
	Minneapolis-St. Paul-						
	Bloomington MSA, MN-WI	Y	44526 FQ	51229 MW	62489 TQ	MNBLS	1/16-3/16
	Mississippi	Y	35190 FQ	39290 MW	49600 TQ	USBLS	5/15
	Missouri	Y	35770 FQ	42400 MW	57470 TQ	USBLS	5/15
	Kansas City MSA, MO-KS	Y	36010 FQ	43110 MW	83270 TQ	USBLS	5/15
	St. Louis MSA, MO-IL	Y	35360 FQ	43460 MW	64720 TQ	USBLS	5/15
	Omaha-Council Bluffs MSA,						
	NE-IA	Y	37205 FQ	43955 MW	50275 TQ	NEBLS	7/16-9/16
	Nevada	Y	44850 FQ	53580 MW	68240 TQ	USBLS	5/15
	Las Vegas-Henderson-Paradise						
	MSA, NV	Y	43480 FQ	49820 MW	59090 TQ	USBLS	5/15
	New Hampshire	H	17.60 AE	29.62 MW	33.52 AEX	NHBLS	6/16
	New Jersey	Y	65230 FQ	74720 MW	84770 TQ	USBLS	5/15
	Camden PMSA, NJ	Y	64640 FQ	74720 MW	84770 TQ	USBLS	5/15
	Newark PMSA, NJ-PA	Y	67150 FQ	74720 MW	84760 TQ	USBLS	5/15
	Trenton MSA, NJ	Y	67060 FQ	75740 MW	87250 TQ	USBLS	5/15
	New Mexico	Y	41140 FQ	47250 MW	60790 TQ	USBLS	5/15
	New York	Y	34600 AE	41050 MW	50640 AEX	NYBLS	1/16-3/16
	Buffalo-Cheektowaga-Niagara						
	Falls MSA, NY	Y	33270 FQ	35940 MW	38610 TQ	USBLS	5/15
	Nassau County-Suffolk County						
	PMSA, NY	Y	37990 FQ	49860 MW	56050 TQ	USBLS	5/15
	New York-Jersey City-White						
	Plains PMSA, NY-NJ	Y	57050 FQ	72200 MW	81960 TQ	USBLS	5/15
	North Carolina	Y	44140 FQ	50800 MW	57280 TQ	USBLS	5/15
	Charlotte-Concord-Gastonia						
	MSA, NC-SC	Y	47600 FQ	52580 MW	57490 TQ	USBLS	5/15
	North Dakota	Y	37020 FQ	44710 MW	54830 TQ	USBLS	5/15
	Fargo MSA, ND-MN	Y	35310 FQ	44630 MW	56590 TQ	USBLS	5/15
	Ohio	Y	40190 FQ	48140 MW	64180 TQ	USBLS	5/15
	Cincinnati MSA, OH-KY-IN	Y	32800 FQ	36130 MW	39440 TQ	USBLS	5/15
	Cleveland-Elyria MSA, OH	Y	35640 FQ	42620 MW	48870 TQ	USBLS	5/15
	Oklahoma	Y	29400 FQ	38730 MW	46040 TQ	USBLS	5/15
	Oklahoma City MSA, OK	Y	19100 FQ	36710 MW	43240 TQ	USBLS	5/15
	Tulsa MSA, OK	Y	38150 FQ	43690 MW	49020 TQ	USBLS	5/15
	Oregon	H	15.62 FQ	19.09 MW	25.19 TQ	ORBLS	2016
	Portland-Vancouver-Hillsboro						
	MSA, OR-WA	Y	23650 FQ	40880 MW	54090 TQ	USBLS	5/15
	Pennsylvania	Y	36450 FQ	45150 MW	59980 TQ	USBLS	5/15
	Allentown-Bethlehem-Easton						
	MSA, PA-NJ	Y	49430 FQ	64730 MW	77270 TQ	USBLS	5/15
	Montgomery County-Bucks						
	County-Chester County						
	PMSA, PA	Y	38050 FQ	63220 MW	72150 TQ	USBLS	5/15
	Philadelphia PMSA, PA	Y	40610 FQ	48290 MW	61900 TQ	USBLS	5/15

AE	Average entry wage	AWR	Average wage range	H	Hourly
AEX	Average experienced wage	B	Biweekly	HI	Highest wage paid
ATC	Average total compensation	D	Daily	HR	High end range
AW	Average wage paid	FQ	First quartile wage	LO	Lowest wage paid

LR	Low end range	MTC	Median total compensation
M	Monthly	MW	Median wage paid
MCC	Median cash compensation	MWR	Median wage range
ME	Median entry wage	S	See annotated source

TCC	Total cash compensation		
TQ	Third quartile wage		
W	Weekly		
Y	Yearly		

Occupation/Type/Industry	Location	Per	Low	Mid	High	Source	Date
Marriage and Family Therapist	Pittsburgh MSA, PA	Y	34120 FQ	39590 MW	48760 TQ	USBLS	5/15
	South Carolina	Y	27540 FQ	30310 MW	43200 TQ	USBLS	5/15
	South Dakota	Y	34830 FQ	41210 MW	47940 TQ	USBLS	5/15
	Tennessee	Y	27630 FQ	33170 MW	39360 TQ	USBLS	5/15
	Knoxville MSA, TN	Y	28540 FQ	32540 MW	37410 TQ	USBLS	5/15
	Memphis MSA, TN-MS-AR	Y	19210 FQ	28150 MW	33390 TQ	USBLS	5/15
	Nashville-Davidson–Murfreesboro–Franklin MSA, TN	Y	29540 FQ	34270 MW	38140 TQ	USBLS	5/15
	Texas	Y	33620 FQ	42980 MW	53840 TQ	USBLS	5/15
	Dallas-Plano-Irving PMSA, TX	Y	33650 FQ	40310 MW	48020 TQ	USBLS	5/15
	Fort Worth-Arlington PMSA, TX	Y	35690 FQ	45130 MW	56830 TQ	USBLS	5/15
	Houston-The Woodlands-Sugar Land MSA, TX	Y	37250 FQ	48820 MW	58630 TQ	USBLS	5/15
	San Antonio-New Braunfels MSA, TX	Y	29570 FQ	39900 MW	50490 TQ	USBLS	5/15
	Utah	Y	39970 FQ	49430 MW	61030 TQ	USBLS	5/15
	Ogden-Clearfield MSA, UT	Y	30200 FQ	45990 MW	60450 TQ	USBLS	5/15
	Provo-Orem MSA, UT	Y	43850 FQ	52930 MW	59230 TQ	USBLS	5/15
	Salt Lake City MSA, UT	Y	39390 FQ	45390 MW	52930 TQ	USBLS	5/15
	Virginia	Y	38930 FQ	47570 MW	57550 TQ	USBLS	5/15
	Richmond MSA, VA	Y	36550 FQ	44390 MW	51070 TQ	USBLS	5/15
	Virginia Beach-Norfolk-Newport News MSA, VA-NC	Y	43430 FQ	53140 MW	58520 TQ	USBLS	5/15
	Washington	H.	19.41 FQ	23.71 MW	33.79 TQ	WABLS	3/16
	Seattle-Bellevue-Everett PMSA, WA	H	17.11 FQ	20.50 MW	24.17 TQ	WABLS	3/16
	Tacoma-Lakewood PMSA, WA	H	22.03 FQ	26.93 MW	38.52 TQ	WABLS	3/16
	West Virginia	Y	28930 FQ	34870 MW	40870 TQ	USBLS	5/15
	Huntington-Ashland MSA, WV-KY-OH	Y	27150 FQ	31580 MW	36750 TQ	USBLS	5/15
	Wisconsin	Y	29270 FQ	38310 MW	51010 TQ	USBLS	5/15
	Madison MSA, WI	Y	38940 FQ	45240 MW	54050 TQ	USBLS	5/15
	Milwaukee-Waukesha-West Allis MSA, WI	Y	27280 FQ	32790 MW	42000 TQ	USBLS	5/15
Massage Therapist	Alabama	Y	17544 AE	34512 AW	42996 AEX	ALBLS	6/16
	Birmingham-Hoover MSA, AL	Y	52005 AE	84283 AW	100428 AEX	ALBLS	6/16
	Alaska	Y	67930 FQ'	80430 MW	108220 TQ	USBLS	5/15
	Anchorage MSA, AK	Y	68790 FQ	80870 MW	108810 TQ	USBLS	5/15
	Arizona	Y	30180 FQ	37750 MW	64660 TQ	USBLS	5/15
	Phoenix-Mesa-Scottsdale MSA, AZ	Y	27970 FQ	37310 MW	64800 TQ	USBLS	5/15
	Tucson MSA, AZ	Y	34580 FQ	45030 MW	67180 TQ	USBLS	5/15
	Arkansas	Y	27800 FQ	40210 MW	46250 TQ	USBLS	5/15
	Little Rock-North Little Rock-Conway MSA, AR	Y	32670 FQ	41180 MW	45580 TQ	USBLS	5/15
	California	H	12.53 FQ	19.09 MW	27.32 TQ	CABLS	1/16-3/16
	Anaheim-Santa Ana-Irvine PMSA, CA	H	13.45 FQ	19.25 MW	28.96 TQ	CABLS	1/16-3/16
	Los Angeles-Long Beach-Glendale PMSA, CA	H	12.34 FQ	19.97 MW	26.22 TQ	CABLS	1/16-3/16
	Oakland-Hayward-Berkeley PMSA, CA	H	21.77 FQ	30.77 MW	35.56 TQ	CABLS	1/16-3/16
	Riverside-San Bernardino-Ontario MSA, CA	H	14.39 FQ	17.42 MW	26.33 TQ	CABLS	1/16-3/16
	Sacramento–Roseville–Arden-Arcade MSA, CA	H	15.22 FQ	17.24 MW	19.25 TQ	CABLS	1/16-3/16
	Salinas MSA, CA	H	11.85 FQ	21.24 MW	28.12 TQ	CABLS	1/16-3/16
	San Diego-Carlsbad MSA, CA	H	9.63 FQ	18.07 MW	26.01 TQ	CABLS	1/16-3/16
	San Francisco-Redwood City-South San Francisco PMSA, CA	H	10.85 FQ	12.22 MW	23.68 TQ	CABLS	1/16-3/16
	Colorado	Y	24140 FQ	40980 MW	58440 TQ	USBLS	5/15
	Denver-Aurora-Lakewood MSA, CO	Y	24060 FQ	40540 MW	57620 TQ	USBLS	5/15
	Connecticut	Y		45970 MW		CTBLS	1/16-3/16
	Bridgeport-Stamford-Norwalk MSA, CT	Y	40020 FQ	47330 MW	63400 TQ	USBLS	5/15
	Hartford-West Hartford-East Hartford MSA, CT	Y	34250 FQ	44640 MW	57910 TQ	USBLS	5/15

AE	Average entry wage	**AWR**	Average wage range	**H**	Hourly	**LR** Low end range	**MTC** Median total compensation	**TCC** Total cash compensation
AEX	Average experienced wage	**B**	Biweekly	**HI**	Highest wage paid	**M** Monthly	**MCC** Median cash compensation	**TQ** Third quartile wage
ATC	Average total compensation	**D**	Daily	**HR**	High end range	**MCC** Median cash compensation	**MWR** Median wage range	**W** Weekly
AW	Average wage paid	**FQ**	First quartile wage	**LO**	Lowest wage paid	**ME** Median entry wage	**S** See annotated source	**Y** Yearly

970

Massage Therapist

Occupation/Type/Industry	Location	Per	Low	Mid	High	Source	Date
Massage Therapist	Delaware	Y	31950 FQ	40890 MW	69370 TQ	USBLS	5/15
	Wilmington PMSA, DE-MD-NJ	Y	36750 FQ	47650 MW	83660 TQ	USBLS	5/15
	District of Columbia	Y	19920 FQ	23390 MW	44020 TQ	USBLS	5/15
	Washington-Arlington-Alexandria PMSA, DC-VA-MD-WV	Y	26930 FQ	40030 MW	57900 TQ	USBLS	5/15
	Florida	H	11.97 AE	18.54 MW	25.67 AEX	FLBLS	7/16-9/16
	Fort Lauderdale-Pompano Beach-Deerfield Beach PMSA, FL	H	14.93 AE	20.44 MW	25.74 AEX	FLBLS	7/16-9/16
	Miami-Miami Beach-Kendall PMSA, FL	H	11.48 AE	17.01 MW	24.29 AEX	FLBLS	7/16-9/16
	Orlando-Kissimmee-Sanford MSA, FL	H	10.68 AE	18.37 MW	26.15 AEX	FLBLS	7/16-9/16
	Tampa-St. Petersburg-Clearwater MSA, FL	H	11.09 AE	19.20 MW	25.92 AEX	FLBLS	7/16-9/16
	Georgia	Y	18130 FQ	27290 MW	39780 TQ	USBLS	5/15
	Atlanta-Sandy Springs-Roswell MSA, GA	Y	17890 FQ	25860 MW	39080 TQ	USBLS	5/15
	Augusta-Richmond County MSA, GA-SC	Y	17260 FQ	19070 MW	33690 TQ	USBLS	5/15
	Hawaii	Y	18490 FQ	36590 MW	67360 TQ	USBLS	5/15
	Urban Honolulu MSA, HI	Y	18520 FQ	33180 MW	56120 TQ	USBLS	5/15
	Idaho	Y	25240 FQ	33630 MW	43500 TQ	USBLS	5/15
	Boise City MSA, ID	Y	18830 FQ	34210 MW	44210 TQ	USBLS	5/15
	Illinois	Y	20650 FQ	32720 MW	50630 TQ	USBLS	5/15
	Chicago-Naperville-Arlington Heights PMSA, IL	Y	20460 FQ	31950 MW	49670 TQ	USBLS	5/15
	Lake County-Kenosha County PMSA, IL-WI	Y	26940 FQ	39170 MW	58730 TQ	USBLS	5/15
	Indiana	Y	23380 FQ	30560 MW	44450 TQ	USBLS	5/15
	Gary PMSA, IN	Y	21610 FQ	25900 MW	28860 TQ	USBLS	5/15
	Indianapolis-Carmel-Anderson MSA, IN	Y	19840 FQ	32090 MW	52970 TQ	USBLS	5/15
	Iowa	Y	25180 FQ	36040 MW	48220 TQ	USBLS	5/15
	Des Moines-West Des Moines MSA, IA	Y	26130 FQ	36350 MW	43010 TQ	USBLS	5/15
	Kansas	Y	18400 FQ	22540 MW	34280 TQ	USBLS	5/15
	Wichita MSA, KS	Y	18940 FQ	23480 MW	32600 TQ	USBLS	5/15
	Kentucky	Y	27970 FQ	35830 MW	49020 TQ	USBLS	5/15
	Louisville-Jefferson County MSA, KY-IN	Y	28830 FQ	40820 MW	52100 TQ	USBLS	5/15
	Louisiana	Y	22850 FQ	29930 MW	42570 TQ	USBLS	5/15
	Baton Rouge MSA, LA	Y	26220 FQ	35550 MW	83660 TQ	USBLS	5/15
	New Orleans-Metairie MSA, LA	Y	25790 FQ	29210 MW	41460 TQ	USBLS	5/15
	Maine	Y	23580 FQ	35460 MW	45510 TQ	USBLS	5/15
	Portland-South Portland MSA, ME	Y	32200 FQ	35740 MW	39280 TQ	USBLS	5/15
	Maryland	Y	24789 AE	49228 MW	61447 AEX	MDBLS	4/16
	Baltimore-Columbia-Towson MSA, MD	Y	29730 FQ	43900 MW	57010 TQ	USBLS	5/15
	Salisbury MSA, MD-DE	Y	31050 FQ	35530 MW	41000 TQ	USBLS	5/15
	Massachusetts	Y	36370 FQ	47550 MW	60130 TQ	USBLS	5/15
	Boston-Cambridge-Newton NECTA, MA	Y	34030 FQ	44120 MW	55630 TQ	USBLS	5/15
	Worcester MSA, MA-CT	Y	33610 FQ	52050 MW	59790 TQ	USBLS	5/15
	Michigan	Y	29450 FQ	46730 MW	60830 TQ	USBLS	5/15
	Detroit-Dearborn-Livonia PMSA, MI	Y	19290 FQ	39290 MW	55960 TQ	USBLS	5/15
	Grand Rapids-Wyoming MSA, MI	Y	40900 FQ	55530 MW	62940 TQ	USBLS	5/15
	Minnesota	Y	33356 FQ	41374 MW	57462 TQ	MNBLS	1/16-3/16
	Minneapolis-St. Paul-Bloomington MSA, MN-WI	Y	33376 FQ	41182 MW	57886 TQ	MNBLS	1/16-3/16
	Mississippi	Y	17180 FQ	18930 MW	27930 TQ	USBLS	5/15
	Jackson MSA, MS	Y	16710 FQ	18080 MW	19660 TQ	USBLS	5/15
	Missouri	Y	18920 FQ	24220 MW	37660 TQ	USBLS	5/15
	Kansas City MSA, MO-KS	Y	18230 FQ	23350 MW	43730 TQ	USBLS	5/15
	St. Louis MSA, MO-IL	Y	18810 FQ	24320 MW	37910 TQ	USBLS	5/15
	Montana	Y	19700 FQ	30510 MW	46110 TQ	USBLS	5/15

AE	Average entry wage	AWR	Average wage range	H	Hourly	LR	Low end range	MTC	Median total compensation	TCC	Total cash compensation
AEX	Average experienced wage	B	Biweekly	HI	Highest wage paid	M	Monthly	MW	Median wage paid	TQ	Third quartile wage
ATC	Average total compensation	D	Daily	HR	High end range	MCC	Median cash compensation	MWR	Median wage range	W	Weekly
AW	Average wage paid	FQ	First quartile wage	LO	Lowest wage paid	ME	Median entry wage	S	See annotated source	Y	Yearly

Occupation/Type/Industry	Location	Per	Low	Mid	High	Source	Date
Massage Therapist	Nebraska	Y	25175 FQ	28990 MW	35380 TQ	NEBLS	7/16-9/16
	Omaha-Council Bluffs MSA, NE-IA	Y	26305 FQ	29510 MW	35685 TQ	NEBLS	7/16-9/16
	Nevada	Y	17580 FQ	19690 MW	34990 TQ	USBLS	5/15
	Las Vegas-Henderson-Paradise MSA, NV	Y	17650 FQ	19870 MW	35840 TQ	USBLS	5/15
	New Hampshire	H	11.52 AE	20.36 MW	24.60 AEX	NHBLS	6/16
	Manchester NECTA, NH	H	11.21 AE	25.59 MW	26.39 AEX	NHBLS	6/16
	Nashua NECTA, NH-MA	Y	32950 FQ	35790 MW	38630 TQ	USBLS	
	New Jersey	Y	32300 FQ	39250 MW	55590 TQ	USBLS	5/15
	Camden PMSA, NJ	Y	33050 FQ	36680 MW	41830 TQ	USBLS	5/15
	Newark PMSA, NJ-PA	Y	31700 FQ	37480 MW	57230 TQ	USBLS	5/15
	Trenton MSA, NJ	Y	40440 FQ	45620 MW	56600 TQ	USBLS	5/15
	New Mexico	Y	18170 FQ	23410 MW	33890 TQ	USBLS	5/15
	Albuquerque MSA, NM	Y	17820 FQ	19500 MW	29990 TQ	USBLS	5/15
	Buffalo-Cheektowaga-Niagara Falls MSA, NY	Y	31240 FQ	40870 MW	48750 TQ	USBLS	5/15
	Nassau County-Suffolk County PMSA, NY	Y	31110 FQ	55480 MW	74690 TQ	USBLS	5/15
	New York-Jersey City-White Plains PMSA, NY-NJ	Y	39780 FQ	61970 MW	84020 TQ	USBLS	5/15
	Rochester MSA, NY	Y	32920 FQ	49090 MW	75340 TQ	USBLS	5/15
	North Carolina	Y	29320 FQ	38110 MW	54540 TQ	USBLS	5/15
	Charlotte-Concord-Gastonia MSA, NC-SC	Y	32480 FQ	37720 MW	45790 TQ	USBLS	5/15
	Raleigh MSA, NC	Y	24120 FQ	36350 MW	65560 TQ	USBLS	5/15
	North Dakota	Y	34420 FQ	46420 MW	56740 TQ	USBLS	5/15
	Fargo MSA, ND-MN	Y	32270 FQ	51100 MW	58490 TQ	USBLS	5/15
	Ohio	Y	24340 FQ	33160 MW	46020 TQ	USBLS	5/15
	Cincinnati MSA, OH-KY-IN	Y	24050 FQ	35300 MW	54730 TQ	USBLS	5/15
	Cleveland-Elyria MSA, OH	Y	24970 FQ	33770 MW	49040 TQ	USBLS	5/15
	Columbus MSA, OH	Y	25090 FQ	32190 MW	38550 TQ	USBLS	5/15
	Oklahoma	Y	27470 FQ	34040 MW	42530 TQ	USBLS	5/15
	Oklahoma City MSA, OK	Y	26810 FQ	33350 MW	37800 TQ	USBLS	5/15
	Tulsa MSA, OK	Y	25510 FQ	28650 MW	59470 TQ	USBLS	5/15
	Oregon	H	15.56 FQ	27.50 MW	32.63 TQ	ORBLS	2016
	Portland-Vancouver-Hillsboro MSA, OR-WA	Y	37130 FQ	55130 MW	63740 TQ	USBLS	5/15
	Pennsylvania	Y	18980 FQ	31560 MW	46820 TQ	USBLS	5/15
	Allentown-Bethlehem-Easton MSA, PA-NJ	Y	18800 FQ	32380 MW	45600 TQ	USBLS	5/15
	Harrisburg-Carlisle MSA, PA	Y	29350 FQ	34980 MW	39120 TQ	USBLS	5/15
	Montgomery County-Bucks County-Chester County PMSA, PA	Y	18040 FQ	23190 MW	47290 TQ	USBLS	5/15
	Philadelphia PMSA, PA	Y	18910 FQ	34390 MW	57440 TQ	USBLS	5/15
	Pittsburgh MSA, PA	Y	26020 FQ	32950 MW	66970 TQ	USBLS	5/15
	Rhode Island	Yr	19660 FQ	35110 MW	47820 TQ	USBLS	5/15
	Providence-Warwick MSA, RI-MA	Y	19690 FQ	34670 MW	48450 TQ	USBLS	5/15
	South Carolina	Y	21310 FQ	32640 MW	46370 TQ	USBLS	5/15
	Charleston-North Charleston MSA, SC	Y	18910 FQ	23140 MW	40140 TQ	USBLS	5/15
	Columbia MSA, SC	Y	23560 FQ	34580 MW	46250 TQ	USBLS	5/15
	Greenville-Anderson-Mauldin MSA, SC	Y	19860 FQ	30870 MW	48020 TQ	USBLS	5/15
	South Dakota	Y	30220 FQ	34640 MW	38800 TQ	USBLS	5/15
	Tennessee	Y	25250 FQ	34020 MW	43310 TQ	NHBLS	5/15
	Knoxville MSA, TN	Y	32600 FQ	36100 MW	39640 TQ	USBLS	5/15
	Memphis MSA, TN-MS-AR	Y	16990 FQ	18590 MW	23780 TQ	USBLS	5/15
	Nashville-Davidson–Murfreesboro–Franklin MSA, TN	Y	27620 FQ	34980 MW	43110 TQ	USBLS	5/15
	Texas	Y	21100 FQ	35540 MW	46590 TQ	USBLS	5/15
	Austin-Round Rock MSA, TX	Y	27780 FQ	38080 MW	57820 TQ	USBLS	5/15
	Dallas-Plano-Irving PMSA, TX	Y	18450 FQ	33220 MW	46890 TQ	USBLS	5/15
	Fort Worth-Arlington PMSA, TX	Y	18090 FQ	41940 MW	63290 TQ	USBLS	5/15
	Houston-The Woodlands-Sugar Land MSA, TX	Y	19400 FQ	35200 MW	40410 TQ	USBLS	5/15
	San Antonio-New Braunfels MSA, TX	Y	26390 FQ	40680 MW	46070 TQ	USBLS	5/15

AE	Average entry wage	AWR	Average wage range	H	Hourly	LR	Low end range	MTC	Median total compensation	TCC	Total cash compensation
AEX	Average experienced wage	B	Biweekly	HI	Highest wage paid	M	Monthly	MW	Median wage paid	TQ	Third quartile wage
ATC	Average total compensation	D	Daily	HR	High end range	MCC	Median cash compensation	MWR	Median wage range	W	Weekly
AW	Average wage paid	FQ	First quartile wage	LO	Lowest wage paid	ME	Median entry wage	S	See annotated source	Y	Yearly

Occupation/Type/Industry	Location	Per	Low	Mid	High	Source	Date
Massage Therapist	Utah	Y	23860 FQ	33330 MW	39080 TQ	USBLS	5/15
	Ogden-Clearfield MSA, UT	Y	29970 FQ	34800 MW	38780 TQ	USBLS	5/15
	Provo-Orem MSA, UT	Y	32320 FQ	36980 MW	44200 TQ	USBLS	5/15
	Salt Lake City MSA, UT	Y	21660 FQ	30870 MW	37940 TQ	USBLS	5/15
	Vermont	Y	36230 FQ	54740 MW	68720 TQ	USBLS	5/15
	Burlington-South Burlington MSA, VT	Y	39750 FQ	60980 MW	72650 TQ	USBLS	5/15
	Virginia	Y	22410 FQ	33570 MW	50090 TQ	USBLS	5/15
	Richmond MSA, VA	Y	20700 FQ	25210 MW	40030 TQ	USBLS	5/15
	Virginia Beach-Norfolk-Newport News MSA, VA-NC	Y	23540 FQ	31970 MW	37850 TQ	USBLS	5/15
	Washington	H	18.20 FQ	26.75 MW	33.17 TQ	WABLS	3/16
	Seattle-Bellevue-Everett PMSA, WA	H	17.46 FQ	26.67 MW	34.32 TQ	WABLS	3/16
	Tacoma-Lakewood PMSA, WA	H	18.80 FQ	26.03 MW	29.25 TQ	WABLS	3/16
	West Virginia	Y	21740 FQ	27610 MW	43870 TQ	USBLS	5/15
	Huntington-Ashland MSA, WV-KY-OH	Y	18950 FQ	26600 MW	44050 TQ	USBLS	5/15
	Wisconsin	Y	25330 FQ	35400 MW	45290 TQ	USBLS	5/15
	Madison MSA, WI	Y	27950 FQ	47330 MW	56890 TQ	USBLS	5/15
	Milwaukee-Waukesha-West Allis MSA, WI	Y	31030 FQ	35220 MW	39360 TQ	USBLS	5/15
	Wyoming	Y	19130 FQ	37060 MW	66570 TQ	USBLS	5/15
	Puerto Rico	Y	17030 FQ	18680 MW	21720 TQ	USBLS	5/15
	San Juan-Carolina-Caguas MSA, PR	Y	17100 FQ	18860 MW	22200 TQ	USBLS	5/15
	Guam	Y	18020 FQ	18870 MW	19690 TQ	USBLS	5/15
Master Chief Petty Officer U.S. Navy, Active Duty, Pay Grade E-9	United States	M	5053 LO		7845 HI	DOD1	2017
Master Gunnery Sergeant U.S. Marines, Active Duty, Pay Grade E-9	United States	M	5053 LO		7845 HI	DOD1	2017
Master Sergeant U.S. Air Force, Active Duty, Pay Grade E-7	United States	M	2875 LO		5168 HI	DOD1	2017
U.S. Army, Active Duty, Pay Grade E-8	United States	M	4136 LO		5899 HI	DOD1	2017
U.S. Marines, Active Duty, Pay Grade E-8	United States	M	4136 LO		5899 HI	DOD1	2017
Materials Engineer	Alabama	Y	69059 AE	103940 AW	121371 AEX	ALBLS	6/16
	Birmingham-Hoover MSA, AL	Y	71006 AE	103247 AW	119373 AEX	ALBLS	6/16
	Arizona	Y	72160 FQ	94350 MW	125370 TQ	USBLS	5/15
	Tucson MSA, AZ	Y	71390 FQ	95960 MW	118790 TQ	USBLS	5/15
	Arkansas	Y	66490 FQ	94960 MW	104650 TQ	USBLS	5/15
	California	H	42.04 FQ	53.83 MW	63.21 TQ	CABLS	1/16-3/16
	Anaheim-Santa Ana-Irvine PMSA, CA	H	37.99 FQ	53.06 MW	69.28 TQ	CABLS	1/16-3/16
	Los Angeles-Long Beach-Glendale PMSA, CA	H	36.76 FQ	48.59 MW	61.39 TQ	CABLS	1/16-3/16
	Riverside-San Bernardino-Ontario MSA, CA	H	33.97 FQ	37.51 MW	49.40 TQ	CABLS	1/16-3/16
	Sacramento–Roseville–Arden-Arcade MSA, CA	H	37.50 FQ	51.09 MW	60.19 TQ	CABLS	1/16-3/16
	San Diego-Carlsbad MSA, CA	H	37.41 FQ	45.50 MW	57.56 TQ	CABLS	1/16-3/16
	Colorado	Y	82030 FQ	108100 MW	129980 TQ	USBLS	5/15
	Denver-Aurora-Lakewood MSA, CO	Y	78710 FQ	104400 MW	121360 TQ	USBLS	5/15
	Connecticut	Y		100546 MW		CTBLS	1/16-3/16
	Bridgeport-Stamford-Norwalk MSA, CT	Y	82910 FQ	91480 MW	99990 TQ	USBLS	5/15
	Delaware	Y	72130 FQ	89460 MW	113060 TQ	USBLS	5/15
	District of Columbia	Y	91670 FQ	112930 MW	132100 TQ	USBLS	5/15
	Washington-Arlington-Alexandria PMSA, DC-VA-MD-WV	Y	88750 FQ	111600 MW	132000 TQ	USBLS	5/15
	Florida	H	31.28 AE	41.95 MW	48.28 AEX	FLBLS	7/16-9/16
	Fort Lauderdale-Pompano Beach-Deerfield Beach PMSA, FL	H	33.75 AE	45.09 MW	52.80 AEX	FLBLS	7/16-9/16
	Miami-Miami Beach-Kendall PMSA, FL	H	34.10 AE	44.07 MW	48.57 AEX	FLBLS	7/16-9/16

AE	Average entry wage	AWR	Average wage range	H	Hourly	LR	Low end range	MTC	Median total compensation	TCC	Total cash compensation
AEX	Average experienced wage	B	Biweekly	HI	Highest wage paid	M	Monthly	MW	Median wage paid	TQ	Third quartile wage
ATC	Average total compensation	D	Daily	HR	High end range	MCC	Median cash compensation	MWR	Median wage range	W	Weekly
AW	Average wage paid	FQ	First quartile wage	LO	Lowest wage paid	ME	Median entry wage	S	See annotated source	Y	Yearly

Occupation/Type/Industry	Location	Per	Low	Mid	High	Source	Date
Materials Engineer	Orlando-Kissimmee-Sanford MSA, FL	H	29.45 AE	40.45 MW	44.53 AEX	FLBLS	7/16-9/16
	Tampa-St. Petersburg-Clearwater MSA, FL	H	31.62 AE	41.44 MW	45.90 AEX	FLBLS	7/16-9/16
	Georgia	Y	54120 FQ	64870 MW	97120 TQ	USBLS	5/15
	Atlanta-Sandy Springs-Roswell MSA, GA	Y	53020 FQ	68110 MW	109970 TQ	USBLS	5/15
	Idaho	Y	71900 FQ	92490 MW	119220 TQ	USBLS	5/15
	Illinois	Y	77080 FQ	96290 MW	115950 TQ	USBLS	5/15
	Chicago-Naperville-Arlington Heights PMSA, IL	Y	86300 FQ	103970 MW	121040 TQ	USBLS	5/15
	Lake County-Kenosha County PMSA, IL-WI	Y	69320 FQ	84330 MW	101980 TQ	USBLS	5/15
	Indiana	Y	50610 FQ	68070 MW	87710 TQ	USBLS	5/15
	Gary PMSA, IN	Y	46780 FQ	62350 MW	92410 TQ	USBLS	5/15
	Indianapolis-Carmel-Anderson MSA, IN	Y	65730 FQ	78220 MW	92070 TQ	USBLS	5/15
	Iowa	Y	58600 FQ	72830 MW	93190 TQ	USBLS	5/15
	Kansas	Y	80620 FQ	102960 MW	119090 TQ	USBLS	5/15
	Wichita MSA, KS	Y	87580 FQ	108070 MW	121640 TQ	USBLS	5/15
	Kentucky	Y	65550 FQ	78040 MW	91520 TQ	USBLS	5/15
	Louisiana	Y	77530 FQ	94410 MW	132100 TQ	USBLS	5/15
	New Orleans-Metairie MSA, LA	Y	80020 FQ	92470 MW	110530 TQ	USBLS	5/15
	Maine	Y	59090 FQ	72520 MW	97920 TQ	USBLS	5/15
	Maryland	Y	71791 AE	107003 MW	124609 AEX	MDBLS	4/16
	Baltimore-Columbia-Towson MSA, MD	Y	73040 FQ	93570 MW	118070 TQ	USBLS	5/15
	Massachusetts	Y	68180 FQ	90990 MW	119060 TQ	USBLS	5/15
	Boston-Cambridge-Newton NECTA, MA	Y	65450 FQ	90000 MW	121900 TQ	USBLS	5/15
	Worcester MSA, MA-CT	Y	73150 FQ	97900 MW	117170 TQ	USBLS	5/15
	Michigan	Y	60390 FQ	74370 MW	92260 TQ	USBLS	5/15
	Detroit-Dearborn-Livonia PMSA, MI	Y	59380 FQ	74030 MW	95480 TQ	USBLS	5/15
	Grand Rapids-Wyoming MSA, MI	Y	57620 FQ	67750 MW	83020 TQ	USBLS	5/15
	Minnesota	Y	75745 FQ	94303 MW	118960 TQ	MNBLS	1/16-3/16
	Minneapolis-St. Paul-Bloomington MSA, MN-WI	Y	80382 FQ	97509 MW	121480 TQ	MNBLS	1/16-3/16
	Mississippi	Y	66690 FQ	76960 MW	95250 TQ	USBLS	5/15
	Missouri	Y	62520 FQ	86640 MW	118600 TQ	USBLS	5/15
	Kansas City MSA, MO-KS	Y	48490 FQ	64560 MW	80370 TQ	USBLS	5/15
	Montana	Y	50360 FQ	53140 MW	69390 TQ	USBLS	5/15
	Nebraska	Y	55820 FQ	67340 MW	87250 TQ	NEBLS	7/16-9/16
	Omaha-Council Bluffs MSA, NE-IA	Y	54645 FQ	62920 MW	92000 TQ	NEBLS	7/16-9/16
	Nevada	Y	71340 FQ	88160 MW	105150 TQ	USBLS	5/15
	New Hampshire	H	32.93 AE	44.46 MW	50.26 AEX	NHBLS	6/16
	New Jersey	Y	76560 FQ	96280 MW	115350 TQ	USBLS	5/15
	Camden PMSA, NJ	Y	84590 FQ	97710 MW	112470 TQ	USBLS	5/15
	Newark PMSA, NJ-PA	Y	90230 FQ	106660 MW	122370 TQ	USBLS	5/15
	Trenton MSA, NJ	Y	68670 FQ	82110 MW	100420 TQ	USBLS	5/15
	New Mexico	Y	84030 FQ	107000 MW	127970 TQ	USBLS	5/15
	Albuquerque MSA, NM	Y	100380 FQ	115070 MW	136870 TQ	USBLS	5/15
	New York	Y	62520 AE	87410 MW	102540 AEX	NYBLS	1/16-3/16
	Buffalo-Cheektowaga-Niagara Falls MSA, NY	Y	67190 FQ	83100 MW	100230 TQ	USBLS	5/15
	Nassau County-Suffolk County PMSA, NY	Y	77240 FQ	105960 MW	135450 TQ	USBLS	5/15
	New York-Jersey City-White Plains PMSA, NY-NJ	Y	78930 FQ	89160 MW	99460 TQ	USBLS	5/15
	Rochester MSA, NY	Y	61260 FQ	74400 MW	95590 TQ	USBLS	5/15
	North Carolina	Y	70460 FQ	86110 MW	104580 TQ	USBLS	5/15
	Charlotte-Concord-Gastonia MSA, NC-SC	Y	67060 FQ	86870 MW	109590 TQ	USBLS	5/15
	Raleigh MSA, NC	Y	61190 FQ	77500 MW	91530 TQ	USBLS	5/15
	Ohio	Y	69580 FQ	89680 MW	118250 TQ	USBLS	5/15
	Cincinnati MSA, OH-KY-IN	Y	67150 FQ	85290 MW	117990 TQ	USBLS	5/15
	Cleveland-Elyria MSA, OH	Y	70140 FQ	89400 MW	120950 TQ	USBLS	5/15
	Columbus MSA, OH	Y	65210 FQ	83620 MW	102580 TQ	USBLS	5/15
	Oklahoma	Y	59990 FQ	74640 MW	93690 TQ	USBLS	5/15

AE	Average entry wage	AWR	Average wage range	H	Hourly	LR	Low end range	MTC	Median total compensation	TCC	Total cash compensation
AEX	Average experienced wage	B	Biweekly	HI	Highest wage paid	M	Monthly	MW	Median wage paid	TQ	Third quartile wage
ATC	Average total compensation	D	Daily	HR	High end range	MCC	Median cash compensation	MWR	Median wage range	W	Weekly
AW	Average wage paid	FQ	First quartile wage	LO	Lowest wage paid	ME	Median entry wage	S	See annotated source	Y	Yearly

Occupation/Type/Industry	Location	Per	Low	Mid	High	Source	Date
Materials Engineer	Oklahoma City MSA, OK	Y	58640 FQ	77220 MW	94800 TQ	USBLS	5/15
	Tulsa MSA, OK	Y	61670 FQ	75640 MW	99360 TQ	USBLS	5/15
	Pennsylvania	Y	65910 FQ	81560 MW	102390 TQ	USBLS	5/15
	Harrisburg-Carlisle MSA, PA	Y	62920 FQ	76080 MW	92130 TQ	USBLS	5/15
	Montgomery County-Bucks County-Chester County PMSA, PA	Y	73190 FQ	89950 MW	110690 TQ	USBLS	5/15
	Pittsburgh MSA, PA	Y	62230 FQ	76500 MW	95460 TQ	USBLS	5/15
	Rhode Island	Y	70190 FQ	88890 MW	110480 TQ	USBLS	5/15
	Providence-Warwick MSA, RI-MA	Y	69950 FQ	87580 MW	109080 TQ	USBLS	5/15
	South Carolina	Y	57870 FQ	74760 MW	93160 TQ	USBLS	5/15
	Charleston-North Charleston MSA, SC	Y	63820 FQ	78990 MW	94300 TQ	USBLS	5/15
	Columbia MSA, SC	Y	52370 FQ	69750 MW	85580 TQ	USBLS	5/15
	Greenville-Anderson-Mauldin MSA, SC	Y	57770 FQ	79380 MW	93870 TQ	USBLS	5/15
	Tennessee	Y	42890 FQ	58900 MW	86820 TQ	USBLS	5/15
	Knoxville MSA, TN	Y	55910 FQ	63290 MW	89840 TQ	USBLS	5/15
	Memphis MSA, TN-MS-AR	Y	101400 FQ	109530 MW	117650 TQ	USBLS	5/15
	Nashville-Davidson–Murfreesboro–Franklin MSA, TN	Y	63940 FQ	77950 MW	95760 TQ	USBLS	5/15
	Texas	Y	69790 FQ	93390 MW	120020 TQ	USBLS	5/15
	Austin-Round Rock MSA, TX	Y	65520 FQ	80020 MW	108980 TQ	USBLS	5/15
	Dallas-Plano-Irving PMSA, TX	Y	72120 FQ	93500 MW	119150 TQ	USBLS	5/15
	Fort Worth-Arlington PMSA, TX	Y	80830 FQ	107680 MW	125080 TQ	USBLS	5/15
	Houston-The Woodlands-Sugar Land MSA, TX	Y	80820 FQ	105640 MW	127390 TQ	USBLS	5/15
	San Antonio-New Braunfels MSA, TX	Y	18970 FQ	61570 MW	88960 TQ	USBLS	5/15
	Utah	Y	62390 FQ	75070 MW	92150 TQ	USBLS	5/15
	Ogden-Clearfield MSA, UT	Y	60990 FQ	72890 MW	86900 TQ	USBLS	5/15
	Provo-Orem MSA, UT	Y	67160 FQ	88370 MW	122750 TQ	USBLS	5/15
	Salt Lake City MSA, UT	Y	63400 FQ	75140 MW	93360 TQ	USBLS	5/15
	Vermont	Y	74730 FQ	89000 MW	104170 TQ	USBLS	5/15
	Virginia	Y	68490 FQ	87590 MW	116380 TQ	USBLS	5/15
	Virginia Beach-Norfolk-Newport News MSA, VA-NC	Y	80360 FQ	105220 MW	128210 TQ	USBLS	5/15
	West Virginia	Y	57790 FQ	79090 MW	99480 TQ	USBLS	5/15
	Wisconsin	Y	59550 FQ	74330 MW	92460 TQ	USBLS	5/15
	Madison MSA, WI	Y	68660 FQ	84990 MW	98910 TQ	USBLS	5/15
	Milwaukee-Waukesha-West Allis MSA, WI	Y	52000 FQ	74830 MW	93760 TQ	USBLS	5/15
Materials Handling Professional	United States	Y		91625 AW		MMH01	9/16
	Mid-Atlantic	Y		94915 AW		MMH01	9/16
	Midwest	Y		89560 AW		MMH01	9/16
	Mountain	Y		79550 AW		MMH01	9/16
	New England	Y		92140 AW		MMH01	9/16
	South	Y		97450 AW		MMH01	9/16
	Southeast	Y		95930 AW		MMH01	9/16
	West	Y		95510 AW		MMH01	9/16
Materials Scientist	Alabama	Y	51782 AE	91474 AW	111320 AEX	ALBLS	6/16
	Arizona	Y	55670 FQ	80050 MW	134510 TQ	USBLS	5/15
	Phoenix-Mesa-Scottsdale MSA, AZ	Y	62950 FQ	92630 MW	154020 TQ	USBLS	5/15
	California	H	36.00 FQ	47.77 MW	63.90 TQ	CABLS	1/16-3/16
	Anaheim-Santa Ana-Irvine PMSA, CA	H	36.89 FQ	48.78 MW	60.81 TQ	CABLS	1/16-3/16
	Los Angeles-Long Beach-Glendale PMSA, CA	H	28.94 FQ	42.69 MW	55.06 TQ	CABLS	1/16-3/16
	Oakland-Hayward-Berkeley PMSA, CA	H	45.71 FQ	58.66 MW	74.60 TQ	CABLS	1/16-3/16
	Riverside-San Bernardino-Ontario MSA, CA	H	39.28 FQ	44.12 MW	49.07 TQ	CABLS	1/16-3/16
	San Diego-Carlsbad MSA, CA	H	22.70 FQ	31.26 MW	48.74 TQ	CABLS	1/16-3/16
	San Francisco-Redwood City-South San Francisco PMSA, CA	H	38.99 FQ	47.54 MW	67.01 TQ	CABLS	1/16-3/16

AE	Average entry wage	AWR	Average wage range	H	Hourly	LR	Low end range	MTC Median total compensation TCC Total cash compensation
AEX	Average experienced wage	B	Biweekly	HI	Highest wage paid	M	Monthly	MW Median wage paid TQ Third quartile wage
ATC	Average total compensation	D	Daily	HR	High end range	MCC	Median cash compensation	MWR Median wage range W Weekly
AW	Average wage paid	FQ	First quartile wage	LO	Lowest wage paid	ME	Median entry wage	S See annotated source Y Yearly

Occupation/Type/Industry	Location	Per	Low	Mid	High	Source	Date
Materials Scientist	Colorado	Y	75610 FQ	101580 MW	135330 TQ	USBLS	5/15
	Denver-Aurora-Lakewood MSA, CO	Y	71390 FQ	92190 MW	113480 TQ	USBLS	5/15
	Connecticut	Y		98568 MW		CTBLS	1/16-3/16
	Hartford-West Hartford-East Hartford MSA, CT	Y	86090 FQ	104780 MW	125930 TQ	USBLS	5/15
	Delaware	Y	43570 FQ	67070 MW	105750 TQ	USBLS	5/15
	Wilmington PMSA, DE-MD-NJ	Y	43530 FQ	66500 MW	105310 TQ	USBLS	5/15
	Washington-Arlington-Alexandria PMSA, DC-VA-MD-WV	Y	82690 FQ	100230 MW	159340 TQ	USBLS	5/15
	Florida	H	28.00 AE	38.34 MW	50.85 AEX	FLBLS	7/16-9/16
	Orlando-Kissimmee-Sanford MSA, FL	H	23.20 AE	38.09 MW	52.75 AEX	FLBLS	7/16-9/16
	Tampa-St. Petersburg-Clearwater MSA, FL	H	26.00 AE	36.86 MW	42.49 AEX	FLBLS	7/16-9/16
	Georgia	Y	70950 FQ	86250 MW	99060 TQ	USBLS	5/15
	Illinois	Y	81470 FQ	99380 MW	121940 TQ	USBLS	5/15
	Chicago-Naperville-Arlington Heights PMSA, IL	Y	80240 FQ	98230 MW	121380 TQ	USBLS	5/15
	Indiana	Y	59540 FQ	87140 MW	108500 TQ	USBLS	5/15
	Louisiana	Y	94710 FQ	112070 MW	124040 TQ	USBLS	5/15
	New Orleans-Metairie MSA, LA	Y	105860 FQ	115180 MW	124490 TQ	USBLS	5/15
	Maryland	Y	48422 AE	96102 MW	119942 AEX	MDBLS	4/16
	Baltimore-Columbia-Towson MSA, MD	Y	49870 FQ	67970 MW	133330 TQ	USBLS	5/15
	Massachusetts	Y	58780 FQ	78260 MW	98080 TQ	USBLS	5/15
	Boston-Cambridge-Newton NECTA, MA	Y	55790 FQ	76060 MW	95350 TQ	USBLS	5/15
	Michigan	Y	61620 FQ	84510 MW	112660 TQ	USBLS	5/15
	Grand Rapids-Wyoming MSA, MI	Y	58980 FQ	93250 MW	117970 TQ	USBLS	5/15
	Minnesota	Y	89263 FQ	113547 MW	138708 TQ	MNBLS	1/16-3/16
	Minneapolis-St. Paul-Bloomington MSA, MN-WI	Y	89041 FQ	113678 MW	139141 TQ	MNBLS	1/16-3/16
	Missouri	Y	56950 FQ	77980 MW	103700 TQ	USBLS	5/15
	St. Louis MSA, MO-IL	Y	60300 FQ	73250 MW	86070 TQ	USBLS	5/15
	New Hampshire	H	29.74 AE	42.70 MW	54.99 AEX	NHBLS	6/16
	New Jersey	Y	71620 FQ	86930 MW	114580 TQ	USBLS	5/15
	New York	Y	49780 AE	92470 MW	125390 AEX	NYBLS	1/16-3/16
	Nassau County-Suffolk County PMSA, NY	Y	75380 FQ	106340 MW	127520 TQ	USBLS	5/15
	New York-Jersey City-White Plains PMSA, NY-NJ	Y	67760 FQ	93200 MW	121860 TQ	USBLS	5/15
	North Carolina	Y	72840 FQ	91900 MW	111700 TQ	USBLS	5/15
	Charlotte-Concord-Gastonia MSA, NC-SC	Y	53550 FQ	79910 MW	101360 TQ	USBLS	5/15
	Raleigh MSA, NC	Y	55240 FQ	89250 MW	115410 TQ	USBLS	5/15
	Ohio	Y	62620 FQ	91640 MW	124570 TQ	USBLS	5/15
	Cincinnati MSA, OH-KY-IN	Y	55190 FQ	88490 MW	134810 TQ	USBLS	5/15
	Cleveland-Elyria MSA, OH	Y	85320 FQ	104160 MW	135030 TQ	USBLS	5/15
	Oklahoma	Y	42240 FQ	57970 MW	77360 TQ	USBLS	5/15
	Oregon	H	33.19 AE	43.91 MW	52.92 TQ	ORBLS	2016
	Pennsylvania	Y	73250 FQ	90200 MW	112420 TQ	USBLS	5/15
	Montgomery County-Bucks County-Chester County PMSA, PA	Y	76760 FQ	91320 MW	107320 TQ	USBLS	5/15
	Philadelphia PMSA, PA	Y	73570 FQ	86700 MW	97530 TQ	USBLS	5/15
	South Carolina	Y	57310 FQ	72950 MW	88820 TQ	USBLS	5/15
	Tennessee	Y	56120 FQ	70930 MW	91950 TQ	USBLS	5/15
	Knoxville MSA, TN	Y	55150 FQ	82340 MW	93980 TQ	USBLS	5/15
	Texas	Y	64560 FQ	89350 MW	117760 TQ	USBLS	5/15
	Austin-Round Rock MSA, TX	Y	60590 FQ	73630 MW	115530 TQ	USBLS	5/15
	Dallas-Plano-Irving PMSA, TX	Y	67690 FQ	90830 MW	121880 TQ	USBLS	5/15
	Houston-The Woodlands-Sugar Land MSA, TX	Y	68460 FQ	93650 MW	115550 TQ	USBLS	5/15
	Utah	Y	65040 FQ	75360 MW	101030 TQ	USBLS	5/15
	Virginia	Y	76090 FQ	97300 MW	124210 TQ	USBLS	5/15
	West Virginia	Y	64710 FQ	98250 MW	117470 TQ	USBLS	5/15
	Wisconsin	Y	67490 FQ	79360 MW	105460 TQ	USBLS	5/15

AE	Average entry wage	AWR	Average wage range	H	Hourly
AEX	Average experienced wage	B	Biweekly	HI	Highest wage paid
ATC	Average total compensation	D	Daily	HR	High end range
AW	Average wage paid	FQ	First quartile wage	LO	Lowest wage paid

LR	Low end range	MTC	Median total compensation	TCC	Total cash compensation
M	Monthly	MW	Median wage paid	TQ	Third quartile wage
MCC	Median cash compensation	MWR	Median wage range	W	Weekly
ME	Median entry wage	S	See annotated source	Y	Yearly

Occupation/Type/Industry	Location	Per	Low	Mid	High	Source	Date
Mathematical Modeler	United States	Y	80000 LO			NYFA	2015
Mathematical Science Teacher							
Postsecondary	Alabama	Y	46165 AE	72494 AW	85654 AEX	ALBLS	6/16
Postsecondary	Birmingham-Hoover MSA, AL	Y	53474 AE	89303 AW	107212 AEX	ALBLS	6/16
Postsecondary	Alaska	Y	68860 FQ	85350 MW	101420 TQ	USBLS	5/15
Postsecondary	Arizona	Y	45510 FQ	66410 MW	93080 TQ	USBLS	5/15
Postsecondary	Phoenix-Mesa-Scottsdale MSA, AZ	Y	50110 FQ	70900 MW	94830 TQ	USBLS	5/15
Postsecondary	Arkansas	Y	42980 FQ	52010 MW	62240 TQ	USBLS	5/15
Postsecondary	Little Rock-North Little Rock-Conway MSA, AR	Y	45970 FQ	57170 MW	69590 TQ	USBLS	5/15
Postsecondary	California	Y		96701 AW		CABLS	1/16-3/16
Postsecondary	Anaheim-Santa Ana-Irvine PMSA, CA	Y		112203 AW		CABLS	1/16-3/16
Postsecondary	Los Angeles-Long Beach-Glendale PMSA, CA	Y		97107 AW		CABLS	1/16-3/16
Postsecondary	Riverside-San Bernardino-Ontario MSA, CA	Y		99441 AW		CABLS	1/16-3/16
Postsecondary	Sacramento–Roseville–Arden-Arcade MSA, CA	Y		89072 AW		CABLS	1/16-3/16
Postsecondary	San Diego-Carlsbad MSA, CA	Y		96468 AW		CABLS	1/16-3/16
Postsecondary	San Francisco-Redwood City-South San Francisco PMSA, CA	Y		90097 AW		CABLS	1/16-3/16
Postsecondary	Colorado	Y	34030 FQ	45100 MW	67940 TQ	USBLS	5/15
Postsecondary	Denver-Aurora-Lakewood MSA, CO	Y	33920 FQ	38870 MW	60280 TQ	USBLS	5/15
Postsecondary	Connecticut	Y		71359 MW		CTBLS	1/16-3/16
Postsecondary	Bridgeport-Stamford-Norwalk MSA, CT	Y	57820 FQ	72950 MW	109360 TQ	USBLS	5/15
Postsecondary	Hartford-West Hartford-East Hartford MSA, CT	Y	58380 FQ	76370 MW	103300 TQ	USBLS	5/15
Postsecondary	Delaware	Y	64580 FQ	71460 MW	78280 TQ	USBLS	5/15
Postsecondary	Wilmington PMSA, DE-MD-NJ	Y	57890 FQ	70050 MW	80150 TQ	USBLS	5/15
Postsecondary	District of Columbia	Y	61380 FQ	76120 MW	94090 TQ	USBLS	5/15
Postsecondary	Washington-Arlington-Alexandria PMSA, DC-VA-MD-WV	Y	49640 FQ	69570 MW	93040 TQ	USBLS	5/15
Postsecondary	Florida	Y	45096 AE	69805 MW	87366 AEX	FLBLS	7/16-9/16
Postsecondary	Fort Lauderdale-Pompano Beach-Deerfield Beach PMSA, FL	Y	49621 AE	65016 MW	71934 AEX	FLBLS	7/16-9/16
Postsecondary	Miami-Miami Beach-Kendall PMSA, FL	Y	60219 AE	86804 MW	94238 AEX	FLBLS	7/16-9/16
Postsecondary	Tampa-St. Petersburg-Clearwater MSA, FL	Y	39986 AE	68868 MW	86957 AEX	FLBLS	7/16-9/16
Postsecondary	Georgia	Y	47950 FQ	60680 MW	78210 TQ	USBLS	5/15
Postsecondary	Atlanta-Sandy Springs-Roswell MSA, GA	Y	50190 FQ	64110 MW	81310 TQ	USBLS	5/15
Postsecondary	Hawaii	Y	41680 FQ	61920 MW	81940 TQ	USBLS	5/15
Postsecondary	Urban Honolulu MSA, HI	Y	46680 FQ	65890 MW	89930 TQ	USBLS	5/15
Postsecondary	Idaho	Y	40310 FQ	48570 MW	65840 TQ	USBLS	5/15
Postsecondary	Boise City MSA, ID	Y	40200 FQ	45360 MW	50520 TQ	USBLS	5/15
Postsecondary	Illinois	Y	51860 FQ	71330 MW	99590 TQ	USBLS	5/15
Postsecondary	Chicago-Naperville-Arlington Heights PMSA, IL	Y	51200 FQ	69340 MW	93640 TQ	USBLS	5/15
Postsecondary	Indiana	Y	48860 FQ	62990 MW	86160 TQ	USBLS	5/15
Postsecondary	Indianapolis-Carmel-Anderson MSA, IN	Y	50600 FQ	61520 MW	83360 TQ	USBLS	5/15
Postsecondary	Iowa	Y	52500 FQ	68360 MW	92770 TQ	USBLS	5/15
Postsecondary	Des Moines-West Des Moines MSA, IA	Y	42910 FQ	57830 MW	71820 TQ	USBLS	5/15
Postsecondary	Kansas	Y	40260 FQ	49790 MW	65380 TQ	USBLS	5/15
Postsecondary	Kentucky	Y	45230 FQ	58730 MW	81710 TQ	USBLS	5/15
Postsecondary	Louisville-Jefferson County MSA, KY-IN	Y	43700 FQ	55540 MW	75450 TQ	USBLS	5/15
Postsecondary	Louisiana	Y	38110 FQ	54560 MW	79460 TQ	USBLS	5/15
Postsecondary	Maine	Y	40210 FQ	61390 MW	76300 TQ	USBLS	5/15
Postsecondary	Portland-South Portland MSA, ME	Y	29770 FQ	37690 MW	57710 TQ	USBLS	5/15

AE	Average entry wage	AWR	Average wage range	H	Hourly	LR	Low end range	MTC	Median total compensation	TCC	Total cash compensation
AEX	Average experienced wage	B	Biweekly	HI	Highest wage paid	M	Monthly	MW	Median wage paid	TQ	Third quartile wage
ATC	Average total compensation	D	Daily	HR	High end range	MCC	Median cash compensation	MWR	Median wage range	W	Weekly
AW	Average wage paid	FQ	First quartile wage	LO	Lowest wage paid	ME	Median entry wage	S	See annotated source	Y	Yearly

Occupation/Type/Industry	Location	Per	Low	Mid	High	Source	Date
Mathematical Science Teacher							
Postsecondary	Maryland	Y	45192 AE	82653 MW	101384 AEX	MDBLS	4/16
Postsecondary	Baltimore-Columbia-Towson MSA, MD	Y	58970 FQ	75380 MW	97640 TQ	USBLS	5/15
Postsecondary	Salisbury MSA, MD-DE	Y	45870 FQ	66060 MW	76090 TQ	USBLS	5/15
Postsecondary	Massachusetts	Y	57760 FQ	75370 MW	104850 TQ	USBLS	5/15
Postsecondary	Boston-Cambridge-Newton NECTA, MA	Y	61670 FQ	84800 MW	121010 TQ	USBLS	5/15
Postsecondary	Worcester MSA, MA-CT	Y	48920 FQ	58260 MW	73320 TQ	USBLS	5/15
Postsecondary	Michigan	Y	45780 FQ	73750 MW	98850 TQ	USBLS	5/15
Postsecondary	Detroit-Dearborn-Livonia PMSA, MI	Y	54680 FQ	79450 MW	96240 TQ	USBLS	5/15
Postsecondary	Grand Rapids-Wyoming MSA, MI	Y	37300 FQ	49730 MW	76370 TQ	USBLS	5/15
Postsecondary	Minnesota	Y	50282 FQ	64122 MW	82106 TQ	MNBLS	1/16-3/16
Postsecondary	Minneapolis-St. Paul-Bloomington MSA, MN-WI	Y	47731 FQ	62247 MW	84283 TQ	MNBLS	1/16-3/16
Postsecondary	Mississippi	Y	41310 FQ	54110 MW	69050 TQ	USBLS	5/15
Postsecondary	Jackson MSA, MS	Y	41900 FQ	51040 MW	61460 TQ	USBLS	5/15
Postsecondary	Missouri	Y	49680 FQ	70330 MW	93870 TQ	USBLS	5/15
Postsecondary	Kansas City MSA, MO-KS	Y	57340 FQ	70730 MW	90510 TQ	USBLS	5/15
Postsecondary	St. Louis MSA, MO-IL	Y	51400 FQ	72620 MW	98390 TQ	USBLS	5/15
Postsecondary	Montana	Y	39800 FQ	52250 MW	70860 TQ	USBLS	5/15
Postsecondary	Nebraska	Y	51820 FQ	64420 MW	81665 TQ	NEBLS	7/16-9/16
Postsecondary	Omaha-Council Bluffs MSA, NE-IA	Y	48330 FQ	57905 MW	71460 TQ	NEBLS	7/16-9/16
Postsecondary	Nevada	Y	38100 FQ	58100 MW	79020 TQ	USBLS	5/15
Postsecondary	Las Vegas-Henderson-Paradise MSA, NV	Y	37720 FQ	56580 MW	75790 TQ	USBLS	5/15
Postsecondary	New Hampshire	Y	61277 AE	82721 MW	105367 AEX	NHBLS	6/16
Postsecondary	New Jersey	Y	57060 FQ	76150 MW	111370 TQ	USBLS	5/15
Postsecondary	Newark PMSA, NJ-PA	Y	58790 FQ	78790 MW	110980 TQ	USBLS	5/15
Postsecondary	New Mexico	Y	51200 FQ	65970 MW	87030 TQ	USBLS	5/15
Postsecondary	Albuquerque MSA, NM	Y	66790 FQ	87540 MW	97760 TQ	USBLS	5/15
Postsecondary	New York	Y	45170 AE	77610 MW	116160 AEX	NYBLS	1/16-3/16
Postsecondary	Buffalo-Cheektowaga-Niagara Falls MSA, NY	Y	42710 FQ	66330 MW	88240 TQ	USBLS	5/15
Postsecondary	Nassau County-Suffolk County PMSA, NY	Y	49880 FQ	69080 MW	93970 TQ	USBLS	5/15
Postsecondary	New York-Jersey City-White Plains PMSA, NY-NJ	Y	59840 FQ	89730 MW	143060 TQ	USBLS	5/15
Postsecondary	Rochester MSA, NY	Y	56560 FQ	77910 MW	98640 TQ	USBLS	5/15
Postsecondary	North Carolina	Y	50100 FQ	60930 MW	81120 TQ	USBLS	5/15
Postsecondary	Charlotte-Concord-Gastonia MSA, NC-SC	Y	48780 FQ	58810 MW	76000 TQ	USBLS	5/15
Postsecondary	Raleigh MSA, NC	Y	54530 FQ	85010 MW	106710 TQ	USBLS	5/15
Postsecondary	North Dakota	Y	42560 FQ	66750 MW	91960 TQ	USBLS	5/15
Postsecondary	Fargo MSA, ND-MN	Y	64730 FQ	79380 MW	97190 TQ	USBLS	5/15
Postsecondary	Ohio	Y	48570 FQ	68630 MW	100680 TQ	USBLS	5/15
Postsecondary	Cincinnati MSA, OH-KY-IN	Y	49380 FQ	70300 MW	102220 TQ	USBLS	5/15
Postsecondary	Cleveland-Elyria MSA, OH	Y	47720 FQ	67990 MW	97500 TQ	USBLS	5/15
Postsecondary	Columbus MSA, OH	Y	63540 FQ	96820 MW	112270 TQ	USBLS	5/15
Postsecondary	Oklahoma	Y	36770 FQ	49940 MW	65120 TQ	USBLS	5/15
Postsecondary	Oklahoma City MSA, OK	Y	32060 FQ	43740 MW	62990 TQ	USBLS	5/15
Postsecondary	Oregon	Y	55935 FQ	72306 MW	94363 TQ	ORBLS	2016
Postsecondary	Portland-Vancouver-Hillsboro MSA, OR-WA	Y	50840 FQ	68030 MW	90440 TQ	USBLS	5/15
Postsecondary	Pennsylvania	Y	55120 FQ	73740 MW	99710 TQ	USBLS	5/15
Postsecondary	Allentown-Bethlehem-Easton MSA, PA-NJ	Y	58860 FQ	78550 MW	110520 TQ	USBLS	5/15
Postsecondary	Harrisburg-Carlisle MSA, PA	Y	56600 FQ	74280 MW	96470 TQ	USBLS	5/15
Postsecondary	Montgomery County-Bucks County-Chester County PMSA, PA	Y	34830 FQ	59540 MW	79200 TQ	USBLS	5/15
Postsecondary	Philadelphia PMSA, PA	Y	56340 FQ	76130 MW	107520 TQ	USBLS	5/15
Postsecondary	Pittsburgh MSA, PA	Y	55450 FQ	72550 MW	98560 TQ	USBLS	5/15
Postsecondary	Rhode Island	Y	58560 FQ	74830 MW	104910 TQ	USBLS	5/15
Postsecondary	Providence-Warwick MSA, RI-MA	Y	57450 FQ	72690 MW	100130 TQ	USBLS	5/15
Postsecondary	South Carolina	Y	51860 FQ	64180 MW	78970 TQ	USBLS	5/15
Postsecondary	Charleston-North Charleston MSA, SC	Y	22660 FQ	66240 MW	78830 TQ	USBLS	5/15

AE	Average entry wage	AWR	Average wage range	H	Hourly	LR	Low end range	MTC	Median total compensation	TCC	Total cash compensation
AEX	Average experienced wage	B	Biweekly	HI	Highest wage paid	M	Monthly	MW	Median wage paid	TQ	Third quartile wage
ATC	Average total compensation	D	Daily	HR	High end range	MCC	Median cash compensation	MWR	Median wage range	W	Weekly
AW	Average wage paid	FQ	First quartile wage	LO	Lowest wage paid	ME	Median entry wage	S	See annotated source	Y	Yearly

Occupation/Type/Industry	Location	Per	Low	Mid	High	Source	Date
Mathematical Science Teacher							
Postsecondary	Columbia MSA, SC	Y	55210 FQ	70470 MW	85910 TQ	USBLS	5/15
Postsecondary	Greenville-Anderson-Mauldin MSA, SC	Y	48980 FQ	64230 MW	83560 TQ	USBLS	5/15
Postsecondary	South Dakota	Y	48210 FQ	59210 MW	72620 TQ	USBLS	5/15
Postsecondary	Tennessee	Y	35920 FQ	52320 MW	74460 TQ	USBLS	5/15
Postsecondary	Knoxville MSA, TN	Y	32140 FQ	40630 MW	59880 TQ	USBLS	5/15
Postsecondary	Memphis MSA, TN-MS-AR	Y	38960 FQ	54890 MW	76340 TQ	USBLS	5/15
Postsecondary	Nashville-Davidson–Murfreesboro–Franklin MSA, TN	Y	40750 FQ	58510 MW	83160 TQ	USBLS	5/15
Postsecondary	Texas	Y	43870 FQ	61400 MW	82870 TQ	USBLS	5/15
Postsecondary	Austin-Round Rock MSA, TX	Y	48090 FQ	58940 MW	76440 TQ	USBLS	5/15
Postsecondary	Beaumont-Port Arthur MSA, TX	Y	39850 FQ	53260 MW	71200 TQ	USBLS	5/15
Postsecondary	Dallas-Plano-Irving PMSA, TX	Y	42680 FQ	61560 MW	86390 TQ	USBLS	5/15
Postsecondary	Fort Worth-Arlington PMSA, TX	Y	27530 FQ	49370 MW	63920 TQ	USBLS	5/15
Postsecondary	Houston-The Woodlands-Sugar Land MSA, TX	Y	45760 FQ	66460 MW	90450 TQ	USBLS	5/15
Postsecondary	San Antonio-New Braunfels MSA, TX	Y	37110 FQ	72770 MW	94500 TQ	USBLS	5/15
Postsecondary	Utah	Y	50550 FQ	68830 MW	94980 TQ	USBLS	5/15
Postsecondary	Ogden-Clearfield MSA, UT	Y	41270 FQ	48420 MW	62530 TQ	USBLS	5/15
Postsecondary	Provo-Orem MSA, UT	Y	57320 FQ	76390 MW	100180 TQ	USBLS	5/15
Postsecondary	Salt Lake City MSA, UT	Y	48070 FQ	67060 MW	92920 TQ	USBLS	5/15
Postsecondary	Vermont	Y	39620 FQ	49150 MW	87890 TQ	USBLS	5/15
Postsecondary	Burlington-South Burlington MSA, VT	Y	38750 FQ	48170 MW	95070 TQ	USBLS	5/15
Postsecondary	Virginia	Y	38080 FQ	50550 MW	72230 TQ	USBLS	5/15
Postsecondary	Richmond MSA, VA	Y	33220 FQ	40440 MW	57720 TQ	USBLS	5/15
Postsecondary	Virginia Beach-Norfolk-Newport News MSA, VA-NC	Y	38660 FQ	49540 MW	67300 TQ	USBLS	5/15
Postsecondary	Washington	Y		69543 AW		WABLS	3/16
Postsecondary	Seattle-Bellevue-Everett PMSA, WA	Y		85288 AW		WABLS	3/16
Postsecondary	Tacoma-Lakewood PMSA, WA	Y		59358 AW		WABLS	3/16
Postsecondary	West Virginia	Y	35750 FQ	48450 MW	66410 TQ	USBLS	5/15
Postsecondary	Huntington-Ashland MSA, WV-KY-OH	Y	33620 FQ	44010 MW	60640 TQ	USBLS	5/15
Postsecondary	Wisconsin	Y	48460 FQ	63540 MW	90770 TQ	USBLS	5/15
Postsecondary	Milwaukee-Waukesha-West Allis MSA, WI	Y	45890 FQ	68220 MW	94640 TQ	USBLS	5/15
Postsecondary	Wyoming	Y	52470 FQ	64720 MW	76640 TQ	USBLS	5/15
Postsecondary	Puerto Rico	Y	44510 FQ	63910 MW	78640 TQ	USBLS	5/15
Postsecondary	San Juan-Carolina-Caguas MSA, PR	Y	36430 FQ	60770 MW	78460 TQ	USBLS	5/15
Mathematical Technician	Florida	H	16.50 AE	18.45 MW	22.15 AEX	FLBLS	7/16-9/16
	Georgia	Y	29840 FQ	34150 MW	37750 TQ	USBLS	5/15
	New York	Y	33840 AE	51190 MW	83490 AEX	NYBLS	1/16-3/16
	Texas	Y	41360 FQ	51740 MW	69850 TQ	USBLS	5/15
Mathematician	California	H	40.12 FQ	57.57 MW	68.69 TQ	CABLS	1/16-3/16
	District of Columbia	Y	90630 FQ	118130 MW	151510 TQ	USBLS	5/15
	Florida	H	30.11 AE	46.31 MW	51.36 AEX	FLBLS	7/16-9/16
	Maryland	Y	92572 AE	134047 MW	154785 AEX	MDBLS	4/16
	Massachusetts	Y	61450 FQ	111030 MW	134890 TQ	USBLS	5/15
	Michigan	Y	59810 FQ	84900 MW	97850 TQ	USBLS	5/15
	Minnesota	Y	85090 FQ	91642 MW	98184 TQ	MNBLS	1/16-3/16
	New Jersey	Y	110640 FQ	145360 MW		USBLS	5/15
	New Mexico	Y	96400 FQ	108510 MW	136810 TQ	USBLS	5/15
	New York	Y	71880 AE	84050 MW	97160 AEX	NYBLS	1/16-3/16
	Ohio	Y	76230 FQ	93650 MW	109070 TQ	USBLS	5/15
	Rhode Island	Y	74730 FQ	101820 MW	118610 TQ	USBLS	5/15
	Texas	Y	42460 FQ	53900 MW	84820 TQ	USBLS	5/15
	Virginia	Y	93890 FQ	112610 MW	126780 TQ	USBLS	5/15
Mayor	Burbank, CA	Y			9217 HI	CACIT	6/28/16
	San Francisco, CA	B			11270 HI	SFGOV	2016-2018
	Sand City, CA	Y			3600 HI	CACIT	6/28/16
	Greenfield, MA	Y			76115 HI	FRCOG	2016

AE Average entry wage	AWR Average wage range	H Hourly	LR Low end range	MTC Median total compensation	TCC Total cash compensation
AEX Average experienced wage	B Biweekly	HI Highest wage paid	M Monthly	MW Median wage paid	TQ Third quartile wage
ATC Average total compensation	D Daily	HR High end range	MCC Median cash compensation	MWR Median wage range	W Weekly
AW Average wage paid	FQ First quartile wage	LO Lowest wage paid	ME Median entry wage	S See annotated source	Y Yearly

Occupation/Type/Industry	Location	Per	Low	Mid	High	Source	Date
Mayor	Detroit, MI	Y			166487 HI	FREEP02	2016
	Lansing, MI	Y			128400 HI	LSJ16	2017
	Seattle, WA	H			91.20 HI	CSSS	1/13/16
Meat, Poultry, and Fish Cutter and Trimmer	Alabama	Y	20307 AE	23392 AW	24945 AEX	ALBLS	6/16
	Birmingham-Hoover MSA, AL	Y	20780 AE	24790 AW	26785 AEX	ALBLS	6/16
	Alaska	Y	18840 FQ	19560 MW	23250 TQ	USBLS	5/15
	Arizona	Y	22390 FQ	26200 MW	28690 TQ	USBLS	5/15
	Tucson MSA, AZ	Y	18020 FQ	19120 MW	20260 TQ	USBLS	5/15
	Arkansas	Y	20750 FQ	22790 MW	25000 TQ	USBLS	5/15
	California	H	9.67 FQ	10.90 MW	13.12 TQ	CABLS	1/16-3/16
	Anaheim-Santa Ana-Irvine PMSA, CA	H	9.60 FQ	10.47 MW	12.35 TQ	CABLS	1/16-3/16
	Los Angeles-Long Beach-Glendale PMSA, CA	H	9.61 FQ	10.53 MW	12.98 TQ	CABLS	1/16-3/16
	Oakland-Hayward-Berkeley PMSA, CA	H	9.70 FQ	11.00 MW	12.99 TQ	CABLS	1/16-3/16
	Riverside-San Bernardino-Ontario MSA, CA	H	9.60 FQ	11.14 MW	13.93 TQ	CABLS	1/16-3/16
	Sacramento–Roseville–Arden-Arcade MSA, CA	H	9.51 FQ	10.31 MW	12.27 TQ	CABLS	1/16-3/16
	San Diego-Carlsbad MSA, CA	H	9.60 FQ	10.77 MW	14.15 TQ	CABLS	1/16-3/16
	San Francisco-Redwood City-South San Francisco PMSA, CA	H	10.20 FQ	11.16 MW	12.11 TQ	CABLS	1/16-3/16
	Colorado	Y	23460 FQ	30980 MW	35870 TQ	USBLS	5/15
	Denver-Aurora-Lakewood MSA, CO	Y	20860 FQ	25480 MW	32810 TQ	USBLS	5/15
	Connecticut	Y		24406 MW		CTBLS	1/16-3/16
	Hartford-West Hartford-East Hartford MSA, CT	Y	21760 FQ	24150 MW	27540 TQ	USBLS	5/15
	Delaware	Y	20560 FQ	23500 MW	27210 TQ	USBLS	5/15
	Wilmington PMSA, DE-MD-NJ	Y	22260 FQ	26880 MW	29190 TQ	USBLS	5/15
	Washington-Arlington-Alexandria PMSA, DC-VA-MD-WV	Y	21680 FQ	28480 MW	38930 TQ	USBLS	5/15
	Florida	H	9.51 AE	11.33 MW	13.26 AEX	FLBLS	7/16-9/16
	Fort Lauderdale-Pompano Beach-Deerfield Beach PMSA, FL	H	9.90 AE	12.41 MW	14.54 AEX	FLBLS	7/16-9/16
	Miami-Miami Beach-Kendall PMSA, FL	H	8.99 AE	10.03 MW	12.32 AEX	FLBLS	7/16-9/16
	Orlando-Kissimmee-Sanford MSA, FL	H	9.07 AE	11.23 MW	13.78 AEX	FLBLS	7/16-9/16
	Tampa-St. Petersburg-Clearwater MSA, FL	H	10.08 AE	11.94 MW	13.82 AEX	FLBLS	7/16-9/16
	Georgia	Y	18900 FQ	21550 MW	23930 TQ	USBLS	5/15
	Atlanta-Sandy Springs-Roswell MSA, GA	Y	17870 FQ	19970 MW	24030 TQ	USBLS	5/15
	Augusta-Richmond County MSA, GA-SC	Y	18190 FQ	20500 MW	24160 TQ	USBLS	5/15
	Hawaii	Y	19050 FQ	27260 MW	33780 TQ	USBLS	5/15
	Urban Honolulu MSA, HI	Y	18540 FQ	25240 MW	31110 TQ	USBLS	5/15
	Idaho	Y	19470 FQ	22770 MW	27110 TQ	USBLS	5/15
	Boise City MSA, ID	Y	18540 FQ	25120 MW	31070 TQ	USBLS	5/15
	Illinois	Y	19730 FQ	24380 MW	29080 TQ	USBLS	5/15
	Chicago-Naperville-Arlington Heights PMSA, IL	Y	19650 FQ	23870 MW	29140 TQ	USBLS	5/15
	Lake County-Kenosha County PMSA, IL-WI	Y	19980 FQ	26260 MW	31770 TQ	USBLS	5/15
	Indiana	Y	25340 FQ	27340 MW	29340 TQ	USBLS	5/15
	Indianapolis-Carmel-Anderson MSA, IN	Y	20160 FQ	24420 MW	28390 TQ	USBLS	5/15
	Iowa	Y	25900 FQ	28300 MW	30700 TQ	USBLS	5/15
	Des Moines-West Des Moines MSA, IA	Y	26030 FQ	28330 MW	30620 TQ	USBLS	5/15
	Kansas	Y	26630 FQ	28780 MW	30940 TQ	USBLS	5/15
	Wichita MSA, KS	Y	20500 FQ	32080 MW	35940 TQ	USBLS	5/15
	Kentucky	Y	20400 FQ	23330 MW	27180 TQ	USBLS	5/15

AE	Average entry wage	AWR	Average wage range	H	Hourly
AEX	Average experienced wage	B	Biweekly	HI	Highest wage paid
ATC	Average total compensation	D	Daily	HR	High end range
AW	Average wage paid	FQ	First quartile wage	LO	Lowest wage paid

LR	Low end range	MTC	Median total compensation	TCC	Total cash compensation
M	Monthly	MW	Median wage paid	TQ	Third quartile wage
MCC	Median cash compensation	MWR	Median wage range	W	Weekly
ME	Median entry wage	S	See annotated source	Y	Yearly

Occupation/Type/Industry	Location	Per	Low	Mid	High	Source	Date
Meat, Poultry, and Fish Cutter and Trimmer							
	Louisville-Jefferson County MSA, KY-IN	Y	24140 FQ	26950 MW	29260 TQ	USBLS	5/15
	Louisiana	Y	17770 FQ	20020 MW	23400 TQ	USBLS	5/15
	Baton Rouge MSA, LA	Y	17930 FQ	21760 MW	28040 TQ	USBLS	5/15
	New Orleans-Metairie MSA, LA	Y	19380 FQ	22970 MW	27560 TQ	USBLS	5/15
	Maine	Y	18230 FQ	21020 MW	26040 TQ	USBLS	5/15
	Portland-South Portland MSA, ME	Y	18340 FQ	21150 MW	24790 TQ	USBLS	5/15
	Maryland	Y	20625 AE	36776 MW	44852 AEX	MDBLS	4/16
	Baltimore-Columbia-Towson MSA, MD	Y	18320 FQ	22320 MW	38540 TQ	USBLS	5/15
	Salisbury MSA, MD-DE	Y	19990 FQ	23880 MW	28010 TQ	USBLS	5/15
	Massachusetts	Y	21970 FQ	28010 MW	36480 TQ	USBLS	5/15
	Boston-Cambridge-Newton NECTA, MA	Y	24210 FQ	29810 MW	40300 TQ	USBLS	5/15
	Michigan	Y	20450 FQ	23290 MW	27130 TQ	USBLS	5/15
	Detroit-Dearborn-Livonia PMSA, MI	Y	24040 FQ	26600 MW	28790 TQ	USBLS	5/15
	Grand Rapids-Wyoming MSA, MI	Y	20950 FQ	23460 MW	27110 TQ	USBLS	5/15
	Minnesota	Y	25868 FQ	27903 MW	29938 TQ	MNBLS	1/16-3/16
	Minneapolis-St. Paul-Bloomington MSA, MN-WI	Y	23428 FQ	27123 MW	29513 TQ	MNBLS	1/16-3/16
	Mississippi	Y	20250 FQ	23540 MW	27530 TQ	USBLS	5/15
	Jackson MSA, MS	Y	20780 FQ	22360 MW	23940 TQ	USBLS	5/15
	Missouri	Y	21910 FQ	25810 MW	28780 TQ	USBLS	5/15
	Kansas City MSA, MO-KS	Y	19520 FQ	22360 MW	25690 TQ	USBLS	5/15
	Montana	Y	20740 FQ	28150 MW	34910 TQ	USBLS	5/15
	Nebraska	Y	25850 FQ	28685 MW	31480 TQ	NEBLS	7/16-9/16
	Omaha-Council Bluffs MSA, NE-IA	Y	21555 FQ	25645 MW	29075 TQ	NEBLS	7/16-9/16
	Nevada	Y	17980 FQ	21250 MW	26540 TQ	USBLS	5/15
	Las Vegas-Henderson-Paradise MSA, NV	Y	17870 FQ	20800 MW	24890 TQ	USBLS	5/15
	New Hampshire	H	8.42 AE	11.65 MW	13.73 AEX	NHBLS	6/16
	New Jersey	Y	19920 FQ	23270 MW	29370 TQ	USBLS	5/15
	Camden PMSA, NJ	Y	19460 FQ	24030 MW	29620 TQ	USBLS	5/15
	Newark PMSA, NJ-PA	Y	19240 FQ	21720 MW	24860 TQ	USBLS	5/15
	Trenton MSA, NJ	Y	21930 FQ	26620 MW	29610 TQ	USBLS	5/15
	New Mexico	Y	18580 FQ	22800 MW	28910 TQ	USBLS	5/15
	Albuquerque MSA, NM	Y	21290 FQ	26020 MW	33210 TQ	USBLS	5/15
	New York	Y	19490 AE	25160 MW	37860 AEX	NYBLS	1/16-3/16
	Buffalo-Cheektowaga-Niagara Falls MSA, NY	Y	21630 FQ	25470 MW	37380 TQ	USBLS	5/15
	Nassau County-Suffolk County PMSA, NY	Y	19000 FQ	19860 MW	36340 TQ	USBLS	5/15
	New York-Jersey City-White Plains PMSA, NY-NJ	Y	19730 FQ	24350 MW	35990 TQ	USBLS	5/15
	Rochester MSA, NY	Y	22980 FQ	28280 MW	41140 TQ	USBLS	5/15
	North Carolina	Y	19720 FQ	22670 MW	26320 TQ	USBLS	5/15
	Charlotte-Concord-Gastonia MSA, NC-SC	Y	20910 FQ	22540 MW	24170 TQ	USBLS	5/15
	North Dakota	Y	18290 FQ	21550 MW	25680 TQ	USBLS	5/15
	Ohio	Y	19540 FQ	23850 MW	29130 TQ	USBLS	5/15
	Cincinnati MSA, OH-KY-IN	Y	18960 FQ	22360 MW	27630 TQ	USBLS	5/15
	Cleveland-Elyria MSA, OH	Y	27510 FQ	32460 MW	36070 TQ	USBLS	5/15
	Columbus MSA, OH	Y	19290 FQ	22520 MW	27460 TQ	USBLS	5/15
	Oklahoma	Y	20670 FQ	22540 MW	24400 TQ	USBLS	5/15
	Oklahoma City MSA, OK	Y	20090 FQ	23740 MW	29290 TQ	USBLS	5/15
	Tulsa MSA, OK	Y	24900 FQ	27760 MW	30420 TQ	USBLS	5/15
	Oregon	H	9.60 FQ	10.60 MW	13.46 TQ	ORBLS	2016
	Portland-Vancouver-Hillsboro MSA, OR-WA	Y	19830 FQ	22470 MW	28330 TQ	USBLS	5/15
	Pennsylvania	Y	25060 FQ	28290 MW	31980 TQ	USBLS	5/15
	Allentown-Bethlehem-Easton MSA, PA-NJ	Y	21340 FQ	24460 MW	32800 TQ	USBLS	5/15
	Montgomery County-Bucks County-Chester County PMSA, PA	Y	25590 FQ	28280 MW	31110 TQ	USBLS	5/15
	Philadelphia PMSA, PA	Y	22840 FQ	28010 MW	34190 TQ	USBLS	5/15

AE	Average entry wage	AWR	Average wage range	H	Hourly
AEX	Average experienced wage	B	Biweekly	HI	Highest wage paid
ATC	Average total compensation	D	Daily	HR	High end range
AW	Average wage paid	FQ	First quartile wage	LO	Lowest wage paid

LR	Low end range	MTC	Median total compensation	TCC	Total cash compensation
M	Monthly	MW	Median wage paid	TQ	Third quartile wage
MCC	Median cash compensation	MWR	Median wage range	W	Weekly
ME	Median entry wage	S	See annotated source	Y	Yearly

Occupation/Type/Industry	Location	Per	Low	Mid	High	Source	Date
Meat, Poultry, and Fish Cutter and Trimmer	Pittsburgh MSA, PA	Y	20160 FQ	24170 MW	29500 TQ	USBLS	5/15
	Rhode Island	Y	24990 FQ	27890 MW	30970 TQ	USBLS	5/15
	Providence-Warwick MSA, RI-MA	Y	25240 FQ	28840 MW	34100 TQ	USBLS	5/15
	South Carolina	Y	19250 FQ	22040 MW	25370 TQ	USBLS	5/15
	Charleston-North Charleston MSA, SC	Y	18100 FQ	20790 MW	26810 TQ	USBLS	5/15
	Tennessee	Y	17860 FQ	20590 MW	23300 TQ	USBLS	5/15
	Knoxville MSA, TN	Y	19140 FQ	21970 MW	24190 TQ	USBLS	5/15
	Memphis MSA, TN-MS-AR	Y	17340 FQ	19280 MW	23410 TQ	USBLS	5/15
	Nashville-Davidson–Murfreesboro–Franklin MSA, TN	Y	22950 FQ	26620 MW	29280 TQ	USBLS	5/15
	Texas	Y	19000 FQ	22020 MW	25430 TQ	USBLS	5/15
	Dallas-Plano-Irving PMSA, TX	Y	17450 FQ	19220 MW	26190 TQ	USBLS	5/15
	Fort Worth-Arlington PMSA, TX	Y	18080 FQ	20170 MW	22970 TQ	USBLS	5/15
	Houston-The Woodlands-Sugar Land MSA, TX	Y	17300 FQ	18990 MW	22010 TQ	USBLS	5/15
	San Antonio-New Braunfels MSA, TX	Y	20140 FQ	22380 MW	24770 TQ	USBLS	5/15
	Utah	Y	22080 FQ	26400 MW	29590 TQ	USBLS	5/15
	Ogden-Clearfield MSA, UT	Y	24220 FQ	27090 MW	29800 TQ	USBLS	5/15
	Provo-Orem MSA, UT	Y	21160 FQ	27470 MW	31420 TQ	USBLS	5/15
	Salt Lake City MSA, UT	Y	21830 FQ	25070 MW	28340 TQ	USBLS	5/15
	Vermont	Y	22130 FQ	26030 MW	36150 TQ	USBLS	5/15
	Burlington-South Burlington MSA, VT	Y	22560 FQ	27570 MW	40140 TQ	USBLS	5/15
	Virginia	Y	20790 FQ	23010 MW	25660 TQ	USBLS	5/15
	Virginia Beach-Norfolk-Newport News MSA, VA-NC	Y	19360 FQ	21570 MW	23600 TQ	USBLS	5/15
	Washington	H	10.75 FQ	12.01 MW	14.82 TQ	WABLS	3/16
	Seattle-Bellevue-Everett PMSA, WA	H	10.61 FQ	11.96 MW	15.47 TQ	WABLS	3/16
	Tacoma-Lakewood PMSA, WA	H	11.36 FQ	13.98 MW	17.28 TQ	WABLS	3/16
	West Virginia	Y	20290 FQ	23360 MW	27650 TQ	USBLS	5/15
	Wisconsin	Y	23610 FQ	27480 MW	30620 TQ	USBLS	5/15
	Madison MSA, WI	Y	26520 FQ	28760 MW	30990 TQ	USBLS	5/15
	Milwaukee-Waukesha-West Allis MSA, WI	Y	20450 FQ	22680 MW	26320 TQ	USBLS	5/15
	Wyoming	Y	25550 FQ	31220 MW	35860 TQ	USBLS	5/15
	Puerto Rico	Y	17610 FQ	19580 MW	25200 TQ	USBLS	5/15
	San Juan-Carolina-Caguas MSA, PR	Y	17560 FQ	19730 MW	24670 TQ	USBLS	5/15
Meat Inspector							
Agriculture Department, State Government	Ohio	H	18.82 LO		26.35 HI	OHGOV	2015
Meat Laboratory Manager							
Michigan State University	East Lansing, MI	Y			60947 HI	MSUSAL	10/1/14-9/30/15
Mechanical Door Repairer	Alabama	Y	28110 AE	35962 AW	39877 AEX	ALBLS	6/16
	Arizona	Y	39190 FQ	45680 MW	53320 TQ	USBLS	5/15
	Arkansas	Y	23310 FQ	27370 MW	31220 TQ	USBLS	5/15
	California	H	17.03 FQ	19.85 MW	23.65 TQ	CABLS	1/16-3/16
	Colorado	Y	33960 FQ	39340 MW	50800 TQ	USBLS	5/15
	Connecticut	Y		43781 MW		CTBLS	1/16-3/16
	Florida	H	11.48 AE	17.27 MW	20.88 AEX	FLBLS	7/16-9/16
	Georgia	Y	32270 FQ	40170 MW	47730 TQ	USBLS	5/15
	Idaho	Y	35620 FQ	40150 MW	46210 TQ	USBLS	5/15
	Illinois	Y	35000 FQ	48670 MW	70980 TQ	USBLS	5/15
	Indiana	Y	28340 FQ	34820 MW	40680 TQ	USBLS	5/15
	Iowa	Y	29100 FQ	34880 MW	41460 TQ	USBLS	5/15
	Kansas	Y	28490 FQ	35300 MW	43080 TQ	USBLS	5/15
	Kentucky	Y	30880 FQ	40720 MW	46250 TQ	USBLS	5/15
	Louisiana	Y	32750 FQ	36870 MW	42450 TQ	USBLS	5/15
	Maryland	Y	33141 AE	49399 MW	57527 AEX	MDBLS	4/16
	Massachusetts	Y	24560 FQ	36120 MW	46370 TQ	USBLS	5/15
	Michigan	Y	30110 FQ	39570 MW	47680 TQ	USBLS	5/15
	Minnesota	Y	39714 FQ	44732 MW	49338 TQ	MNBLS	1/16-3/16
	Mississippi	Y	25840 FQ	33040 MW	39390 TQ	USBLS	5/15

AE	Average entry wage	**AWR**	Average wage range	**H**	Hourly	**LR** Low end range	**MTC** Median total compensation	**TCC** Total cash compensation
AEX	Average experienced wage	**B**	Biweekly	**HI**	Highest wage paid	**M** Monthly	**MW** Median wage paid	**TQ** Third quartile wage
ATC	Average total compensation	**D**	Daily	**HR**	High end range	**MCC** Median cash compensation	**MWR** Median wage range	**W** Weekly
AW	Average wage paid	**FQ**	First quartile wage	**LO**	Lowest wage paid	**ME** Median entry wage	**S** See annotated source	**Y** Yearly

Occupation/Type/Industry	Location	Per	Low	Mid	High	Source	Date
Mechanical Door Repairer	Missouri	Y	29930 FQ	35210 MW	39690 TQ	USBLS	5/15
	Montana	Y	32670 FQ	36650 MW	41540 TQ	USBLS	5/15
	Nebraska	Y	31025 FQ	36175 MW	43355 TQ	NEBLS	7/16-9/16
	Nevada	Y	35420 FQ	42400 MW	51280 TQ	USBLS	5/15
	New Hampshire	H	16.22 AE	18.99 MW	23.59 AEX	NHBLS	6/16
	New Jersey	Y	40930 FQ	45760 MW	51620 TQ	USBLS	5/15
	New Mexico	Y	30360 FQ	35020 MW	39260 TQ	USBLS	5/15
	New York	Y	24480 AE	40150 MW	49860 AEX	NYBLS	1/16-3/16
	North Carolina	Y	30440 FQ	38210 MW	48100 TQ	USBLS	5/15
	North Dakota	Y	33370 FQ	40300 MW	45680 TQ	USBLS	5/15
	Ohio	Y	28000 FQ	33720 MW	39420 TQ	USBLS	5/15
	Oklahoma	Y	23700 FQ	28130 MW	34550 TQ	USBLS	5/15
	Oregon	H	14.67 FQ	17.36 MW	20.50 TQ	ORBLS	2016
	Pennsylvania	Y	32240 FQ	36080 MW	40270 TQ	USBLS	5/15
	South Carolina	Y	26880 FQ	31990 MW	38200 TQ	USBLS	5/15
	Tennessee	Y	28190 FQ	33980 MW	39700 TQ	USBLS	5/15
	Texas	Y	28680 FQ	35380 MW	44410 TQ	USBLS	5/15
	Utah	Y	31540 FQ	40260 MW	48800 TQ	USBLS	5/15
	Virginia	Y	31740 FQ	40660 MW	49840 TQ	USBLS	5/15
	Washington	H	19.62 FQ	22.25 MW	25.73 TQ	WABLS	3/16
	West Virginia	Y	27160 FQ	38760 MW	47680 TQ	USBLS	5/15
	Wisconsin	Y	29420 FQ	35000 MW	40950 TQ	USBLS	5/15
Mechanical Drafter	Alabama	Y	38031 AE	59916 AW	70853 AEX	ALBLS	6/16
	Birmingham-Hoover MSA, AL	Y	35330 AE	54187 AW	63616 AEX	ALBLS	6/16
	Arizona	Y	43620 FQ	58370 MW	75420 TQ	USBLS	5/15
	Phoenix-Mesa-Scottsdale MSA, AZ	Y	44370 FQ	59060 MW	76570 TQ	USBLS	5/15
	Tucson MSA, AZ	Y	38480 FQ	53200 MW	67320 TQ	USBLS	5/15
	Arkansas	Y	40890 FQ	49410 MW	57960 TQ	USBLS	5/15
	Little Rock-North Little Rock-Conway MSA, AR	Y	46200 FQ	53260 MW	58790 TQ	USBLS	5/15
	California	H	21.27 FQ	27.54 MW	35.79 TQ	CABLS	1/16-3/16
	Anaheim-Santa Ana-Irvine PMSA, CA	H	22.48 FQ	28.61 MW	36.08 TQ	CABLS	1/16-3/16
	Los Angeles-Long Beach-Glendale PMSA, CA	H	20.90 FQ	25.07 MW	32.30 TQ	CABLS	1/16-3/16
	Oakland-Hayward-Berkeley PMSA, CA	H	21.44 FQ	30.09 MW	39.89 TQ	CABLS	1/16-3/16
	Riverside-San Bernardino-Ontario MSA, CA	H	18.45 FQ	24.09 MW	29.58 TQ	CABLS	1/16-3/16
	Sacramento–Roseville–Arden-Arcade MSA, CA	H	21.21 FQ	28.43 MW	34.40 TQ	CABLS	1/16-3/16
	San Diego-Carlsbad MSA, CA	H	22.12 FQ	29.37 MW	38.82 TQ	CABLS	1/16-3/16
	San Francisco-Redwood City-South San Francisco PMSA, CA	H	26.42 FQ	32.74 MW	42.60 TQ	CABLS	1/16-3/16
	Colorado	Y	40040 FQ	53110 MW	67120 TQ	USBLS	5/15
	Denver-Aurora-Lakewood MSA, CO	Y	40260 FQ	51230 MW	67410 TQ	USBLS	5/15
	Connecticut	Y		59246 MW		CTBLS	1/16-3/16
	Bridgeport-Stamford-Norwalk MSA, CT	Y	53830 FQ	60350 MW	73580 TQ	USBLS	5/15
	Hartford-West Hartford-East Hartford MSA, CT	Y	51750 FQ	61320 MW	73550 TQ	USBLS	5/15
	Delaware	Y	43540 FQ	54290 MW	72090 TQ	USBLS	5/15
	Wilmington PMSA, DE-MD-NJ	Y	44180 FQ	58140 MW	79590 TQ	USBLS	5/15
	Washington-Arlington-Alexandria PMSA, DC-VA-MD-WV	Y	46970 FQ	57670 MW	73190 TQ	USBLS	5/15
	Florida	H	17.29 AE	24.15 MW	30.20 AEX	FLBLS	7/16-9/16
	Fort Lauderdale-Pompano Beach-Deerfield Beach PMSA, FL	H	20.25 AE	23.98 MW	30.35 AEX	FLBLS	7/16-9/16
	Miami-Miami Beach-Kendall PMSA, FL	H	17.72 AE	23.65 MW	30.97 AEX	FLBLS	7/16-9/16
	Orlando-Kissimmee-Sanford MSA, FL	H	17.13 AE	22.93 MW	27.92 AEX	FLBLS	7/16-9/16
	Tampa-St. Petersburg-Clearwater MSA, FL	H	15.97 AE	24.45 MW	28.66 AEX	FLBLS	7/16-9/16
	Georgia	Y	40440 FQ	54580 MW	70930 TQ	USBLS	5/15

AE Average entry wage	**AWR** Average wage range	**H** Hourly	**LR** Low end range	**MTC** Median total compensation	**TCC** Total cash compensation
AEX Average experienced wage	**B** Biweekly	**HI** Highest wage paid	**M** Monthly	**MW** Median wage paid	**TQ** Third quartile wage
ATC Average total compensation	**D** Daily	**HR** High end range	**MCC** Median cash compensation	**MWR** Median wage range	**W** Weekly
AW Average wage paid	**FQ** First quartile wage	**LO** Lowest wage paid	**ME** Median entry wage	**S** See annotated source	**Y** Yearly

Occupation/Type/Industry	Location	Per	Low	Mid	High	Source	Date
Mechanical Drafter	Atlanta-Sandy Springs-Roswell MSA, GA	Y	40730 FQ	53760 MW	62890 TQ	USBLS	5/15
	Augusta-Richmond County MSA, GA-SC	Y	44740 FQ	56080 MW	65520 TQ	USBLS	5/15
	Hawaii	Y	40840 FQ	51060 MW	62800 TQ	USBLS	5/15
	Urban Honolulu MSA, HI	Y	40170 FQ	52940 MW	63430 TQ	USBLS	5/15
	Idaho	Y	35260 FQ	43120 MW	53430 TQ	USBLS	5/15
	Boise City MSA, ID	Y	35070 FQ	42770 MW	54970 TQ	USBLS	5/15
	Illinois	Y	42670 FQ	52190 MW	66600 TQ	USBLS	5/15
	Chicago-Naperville-Arlington Heights PMSA, IL	Y	45280 FQ	56490 MW	72060 TQ	USBLS	5/15
	Lake County-Kenosha County PMSA, IL-WI	Y	43070 FQ	48210 MW	57610 TQ	USBLS	5/15
	Indiana	Y	39360 FQ	48720 MW	60400 TQ	USBLS	5/15
	Gary PMSA, IN	Y	38920 FQ	47280 MW	57050 TQ	USBLS	5/15
	Indianapolis-Carmel-Anderson MSA, IN	Y	44180 FQ	58700 MW	71700 TQ	USBLS	5/15
	Iowa	Y	36610 FQ	46250 MW	57880 TQ	USBLS	5/15
	Des Moines-West Des Moines MSA, IA	Y	39090 FQ	48310 MW	68110 TQ	USBLS	5/15
	Kansas	Y	37120 FQ	46280 MW	58400 TQ	USBLS	5/15
	Wichita MSA, KS	Y	41710 FQ	49740 MW	64260 TQ	USBLS	5/15
	Kentucky	Y	37440 FQ	46480 MW	57440 TQ	USBLS	5/15
	Louisville-Jefferson County MSA, KY-IN	Y	40050 FQ	46620 MW	54410 TQ	USBLS	5/15
	Louisiana	Y	45190 FQ	58520 MW	83160 TQ	USBLS	5/15
	Baton Rouge MSA, LA	Y	47600 FQ	63110 MW	87640 TQ	USBLS	5/15
	New Orleans-Metairie MSA, LA	Y	46660 FQ	59290 MW	85050 TQ	USBLS	5/15
	Maine	Y	51270 FQ	55440 MW	59620 TQ	USBLS	5/15
	Portland-South Portland MSA, ME	Y	47970 FQ	55180 MW	61910 TQ	USBLS	5/15
	Maryland	Y	38930 AE	60095 MW	70677 AEX	MDBLS	4/16
	Baltimore-Columbia-Towson MSA, MD	Y	42700 FQ	54560 MW	75030 TQ	USBLS	5/15
	Salisbury MSA, MD-DE	Y	40930 FQ	45480 MW	50380 TQ	USBLS	5/15
	Massachusetts	Y	47990 FQ	61260 MW	79710 TQ	USBLS	5/15
	Boston-Cambridge-Newton NECTA, MA	Y	49240 FQ	61270 MW	84920 TQ	USBLS	5/15
	Worcester MSA, MA-CT	Y	40190 FQ	51230 MW	62710 TQ	USBLS	5/15
	Michigan	Y	41010 FQ	53780 MW	66930 TQ	USBLS	5/15
	Detroit-Dearborn-Livonia PMSA, MI	Y	47860 FQ	63120 MW	80140 TQ	USBLS	5/15
	Grand Rapids-Wyoming MSA, MI	Y	41290 FQ	50890 MW	59850 TQ	USBLS	5/15
	Minnesota	Y	46441 FQ	56632 MW	68507 TQ	MNBLS	1/16-3/16
	Minneapolis-St. Paul-Bloomington MSA, MN-WI	Y	50907 FQ	60090 MW	72287 TQ	MNBLS	1/16-3/16
	Mississippi	Y	37520 FQ	45990 MW	57450 TQ	USBLS	5/15
	Jackson MSA, MS	Y	41160 FQ	49370 MW	62350 TQ	USBLS	5/15
	Missouri	Y	37600 FQ	47000 MW	58100 TQ	USBLS	5/15
	Kansas City MSA, MO-KS	Y	40190 FQ	47490 MW	57950 TQ	USBLS	5/15
	St. Louis MSA, MO-IL	Y	39260 FQ	47940 MW	59050 TQ	USBLS	5/15
	Montana	Y	42090 FQ	52840 MW	60540 TQ	USBLS	5/15
	Billings MSA, MT	Y	41150 FQ	51920 MW	61460 TQ	USBLS	5/15
	Nebraska	Y	36705 FQ	43855 MW	52885 TQ	NEBLS	7/16-9/16
	Omaha-Council Bluffs MSA, NE-IA	Y	39230 FQ	46085 MW	55620 TQ	NEBLS	7/16-9/16
	Nevada	Y	34880 FQ	40330 MW	53550 TQ	USBLS	5/15
	Las Vegas-Henderson-Paradise MSA, NV	Y	33800 FQ	40880 MW	61910 TQ	USBLS	5/15
	New Hampshire	H	20.42 AE	30.18 MW	34.08 AEX	NHBLS	6/16
	Manchester NECTA, NH	H	20.96 AE	29.46 MW	33.34 AEX	NHBLS	6/16
	Nashua NECTA, NH-MA	Y	38640 FQ	53430 MW	69930 TQ	USBLS	5/15
	New Jersey	Y	42210 FQ	57440 MW	75580 TQ	USBLS	5/15
	Camden PMSA, NJ	Y	45910 FQ	57800 MW	76030 TQ	USBLS	5/15
	Newark PMSA, NJ-PA	Y	45330 FQ	57700 MW	73780 TQ	USBLS	5/15
	Trenton MSA, NJ	Y	36640 FQ	53460 MW	62590 TQ	USBLS	5/15
	New Mexico	Y	45840 FQ	59860 MW	74080 TQ	USBLS	5/15
	Albuquerque MSA, NM	Y	50020 FQ	62370 MW	75450 TQ	USBLS	5/15
	New York	Y	37930 AE	53230 MW	65790 AEX	NYBLS	1/16-3/16

984

Occupation/Type/Industry	Location	Per	Low	Mid	High	Source	Date
Mechanical Drafter	Buffalo-Cheektowaga-Niagara Falls MSA, NY	Y	43440 FQ	51720 MW	60890 TQ	USBLS	5/15
	Nassau County-Suffolk County PMSA, NY	Y	50950 FQ	62090 MW	76760 TQ	USBLS	5/15
	New York-Jersey City-White Plains PMSA, NY-NJ	Y	39480 FQ	50360 MW	71160 TQ	USBLS	5/15
	Rochester MSA, NY	Y	40590 FQ	49540 MW	59310 TQ	USBLS	5/15
	North Carolina	Y	40850 FQ	52230 MW	62240 TQ	USBLS	5/15
	Charlotte-Concord-Gastonia MSA, NC-SC	Y	39410 FQ	51350 MW	62100 TQ	USBLS	5/15
	Raleigh MSA, NC	Y	49650 FQ	57430 MW	66570 TQ	USBLS	5/15
	North Dakota	Y	37990 FQ	46400 MW	55550 TQ	USBLS	5/15
	Fargo MSA, ND-MN	Y	37290 FQ	44350 MW	52010 TQ	USBLS	5/15
	Ohio	Y	40990 FQ	49230 MW	59760 TQ	USBLS	5/15
	Cincinnati MSA, OH-KY-IN	Y	42380 FQ	52490 MW	62020 TQ	USBLS	5/15
	Cleveland-Elyria MSA, OH	Y	39380 FQ	50490 MW	60070 TQ	USBLS	5/15
	Columbus MSA, OH	Y	40990 FQ	47510 MW	58540 TQ	USBLS	5/15
	Oklahoma	Y	39450 FQ	50160 MW	62100 TQ	USBLS	5/15
	Oklahoma City MSA, OK	Y	35760 FQ	44340 MW	55780 TQ	USBLS	5/15
	Tulsa MSA, OK	Y	44350 FQ	55040 MW	70190 TQ	USBLS	5/15
	Oregon	H	20.73 FQ	24.93 MW	34.88 TQ	ORBLS	2016
	Portland-Vancouver-Hillsboro MSA, OR-WA	Y	44970 FQ	58940 MW	86480 TQ	USBLS	5/15
	Pennsylvania	Y	40140 FQ	51320 MW	62600 TQ	USBLS	5/15
	Allentown-Bethlehem-Easton MSA, PA-NJ	Y	40680 FQ	50600 MW	59470 TQ	USBLS	5/15
	Harrisburg-Carlisle MSA, PA	Y	42860 FQ	49940 MW	57940 TQ	USBLS	5/15
	Montgomery County-Bucks County-Chester County PMSA, PA	Y	51810 FQ	60760 MW	75040 TQ	USBLS	5/15
	Philadelphia PMSA, PA	Y	43930 FQ	58260 MW	75860 TQ	USBLS	5/15
	Pittsburgh MSA, PA	Y	38560 FQ	50340 MW	61170 TQ	USBLS	5/15
	Rhode Island	Y	42380 FQ	50410 MW	60360 TQ	USBLS	5/15
	Providence-Warwick MSA, RI-MA	Y	41830 FQ	48430 MW	58840 TQ	USBLS	5/15
	South Carolina	Y	45770 FQ	58380 MW	73920 TQ	USBLS	5/15
	Charleston-North Charleston MSA, SC	Y	49520 FQ	64050 MW	88670 TQ	USBLS	5/15
	Columbia MSA, SC	Y	39100 FQ	54130 MW	70670 TQ	USBLS	5/15
	Greenville-Anderson-Mauldin MSA, SC	Y	47840 FQ	65490 MW	108790 TQ	USBLS	5/15
	South Dakota	Y	35560 FQ	40840 MW	46850 TQ	USBLS	5/15
	Sioux Falls MSA, SD	Y	37300 FQ	43510 MW	51640 TQ	USBLS	5/15
	Tennessee	Y	40750 FQ	50130 MW	68800 TQ	USBLS	5/15
	Knoxville MSA, TN	Y	40580 FQ	57470 MW	92460 TQ	USBLS	5/15
	Memphis MSA, TN-MS-AR	Y	37760 FQ	45860 MW	56330 TQ	USBLS	5/15
	Nashville-Davidson–Murfreesboro–Franklin MSA, TN	Y	46290 FQ	57070 MW	73550 TQ	USBLS	5/15
	Texas	Y	45210 FQ	58070 MW	77440 TQ	USBLS	5/15
	Austin-Round Rock MSA, TX	Y	43000 FQ	50240 MW	61460 TQ	USBLS	5/15
	Dallas-Plano-Irving PMSA, TX	Y	48890 FQ	64400 MW	82590 TQ	USBLS	5/15
	Fort Worth-Arlington PMSA, TX	Y	43070 FQ	49650 MW	59160 TQ	USBLS	5/15
	Houston-The Woodlands-Sugar Land MSA, TX	Y	48370 FQ	65420 MW	85350 TQ	USBLS	5/15
	San Antonio-New Braunfels MSA, TX	Y	43180 FQ	52580 MW	64260 TQ	USBLS	5/15
	Utah	Y	40340 FQ	49750 MW	62670 TQ	USBLS	5/15
	Ogden-Clearfield MSA, UT	Y	39720 FQ	48640 MW	61280 TQ	USBLS	5/15
	Provo-Orem MSA, UT	Y	39210 FQ	45430 MW	53960 TQ	USBLS	5/15
	Salt Lake City MSA, UT	Y	43240 FQ	55160 MW	68040 TQ	USBLS	5/15
	Vermont	Y	44750 FQ	59370 MW	75430 TQ	USBLS	5/15
	Burlington-South Burlington MSA, VT	Y	44820 FQ	56340 MW	76570 TQ	USBLS	5/15
	Virginia	Y	44710 FQ	55000 MW	68270 TQ	USBLS	5/15
	Richmond MSA, VA	Y	43010 FQ	55920 MW	73570 TQ	USBLS	5/15
	Washington	H	27.29 FQ	35.83 MW	44.78 TQ	WABLS	3/16
	Seattle-Bellevue-Everett PMSA, WA	H	31.77 FQ	38.96 MW	46.67 TQ	WABLS	3/16
	Tacoma-Lakewood PMSA, WA	H	21.90 FQ	27.00 MW	30.97 TQ	WABLS	3/16
	West Virginia	Y	41480 FQ	51980 MW	66150 TQ	USBLS	5/15

AE	Average entry wage	AWR	Average wage range	H	Hourly	LR	Low end range	MTC	Median total compensation	TCC	Total cash compensation
AEX	Average experienced wage	B	Biweekly	HI	Highest wage paid	M	Monthly	MW	Median wage paid	TQ	Third quartile wage
ATC	Average total compensation	D	Daily	HR	High end range	MCC	Median cash compensation	MWR	Median wage range	W	Weekly
AW	Average wage paid	FQ	First quartile wage	LO	Lowest wage paid	ME	Median entry wage	S	See annotated source	Y	Yearly

Occupation/Type/Industry	Location	Per	Low	Mid	High	Source	Date
Mechanical Drafter	Wisconsin	Y	40920 FQ	48880 MW	60130 TQ	USBLS	5/15
	Madison MSA, WI	Y	38430 FQ	47510 MW	57710 TQ	USBLS	5/15
	Milwaukee-Waukesha-West Allis MSA, WI	Y	43430 FQ	51710 MW	62530 TQ	USBLS	5/15
	Wyoming	Y	34910 FQ	52470 MW	62610 TQ	USBLS	5/15
	Puerto Rico	Y	24550 FQ	29500 MW	37150 TQ	USBLS	5/15
	San Juan-Carolina-Caguas MSA, PR	Y	19740 FQ	26410 MW	31860 TQ	USBLS	5/15
Mechanical Engineer	Alabama	Y	62831 AE	89690 AW	103115 AEX	ALBLS	6/16
	Birmingham-Hoover MSA, AL	Y	57235 AE	80914 AW	92758 AEX	ALBLS	6/16
	Alaska	Y	95720 FQ	123610 MW	152400 TQ	USBLS	5/15
	Anchorage MSA, AK	Y	98390 FQ	128460 MW	154120 TQ	USBLS	5/15
	Arizona	Y	69610 FQ	85350 MW	103690 TQ	USBLS	5/15
	Phoenix-Mesa-Scottsdale MSA, AZ	Y	70780 FQ	88610 MW	110470 TQ	USBLS	5/15
	Tucson MSA, AZ	Y	68220 FQ	80380 MW	94410 TQ	USBLS	5/15
	Arkansas	Y	53080 FQ	68480 MW	91020 TQ	USBLS	5/15
	Little Rock-North Little Rock-Conway MSA, AR	Y	53180 FQ	69620 MW	91250 TQ	USBLS	5/15
	California	H	35.91 FQ	46.56 MW	59.48 TQ	CABLS	1/16-3/16
	Anaheim-Santa Ana-Irvine PMSA, CA	H	34.81 FQ	45.22 MW	58.03 TQ	CABLS	1/16-3/16
	Los Angeles-Long Beach-Glendale PMSA, CA	H	35.11 FQ	46.49 MW	60.83 TQ	CABLS	1/16-3/16
	Oakland-Hayward-Berkeley PMSA, CA	H	39.84 FQ	48.11 MW	59.62 TQ	CABLS	1/16-3/16
	Riverside-San Bernardino-Ontario MSA, CA	H	30.95 FQ	38.14 MW	52.64 TQ	CABLS	1/16-3/16
	Sacramento–Roseville–Arden-Arcade MSA, CA	H	35.13 FQ	44.90 MW	55.78 TQ	CABLS	1/16-3/16
	San Diego-Carlsbad MSA, CA	H	33.47 FQ	42.84 MW	52.36 TQ	CABLS	1/16-3/16
	San Francisco-Redwood City-South San Francisco PMSA, CA	H	37.17 FQ	49.25 MW	63.57 TQ	CABLS	1/16-3/16
	Colorado	Y	67030 FQ	82770 MW	107990 TQ	USBLS	5/15
	Denver-Aurora-Lakewood MSA, CO	Y	69650 FQ	85480 MW	111520 TQ	USBLS	5/15
	Connecticut	Y		83259 MW		CTBLS	1/16-3/16
	Bridgeport-Stamford-Norwalk MSA, CT	Y	66600 FQ	82230 MW	109790 TQ	USBLS	5/15
	Hartford-West Hartford-East Hartford MSA, CT	Y	67690 FQ	81320 MW	96820 TQ	USBLS	5/15
	Delaware	Y	77060 FQ	97330 MW	126620 TQ	USBLS	5/15
	Wilmington PMSA, DE-MD-NJ	Y	76720 FQ	95500 MW	121440 TQ	USBLS	5/15
	District of Columbia	Y	76390 FQ	96880 MW	118070 TQ	USBLS	5/15
	Washington-Arlington-Alexandria PMSA, DC-VA-MD-WV	Y	80460 FQ	102990 MW	131120 TQ	USBLS	5/15
	Florida	H	27.33 AE	40.97 MW	48.69 AEX	FLBLS	7/16-9/16
	Fort Lauderdale-Pompano Beach-Deerfield Beach PMSA, FL	H	24.28 AE	36.12 MW	45.60 AEX	FLBLS	7/16-9/16
	Miami-Miami Beach-Kendall PMSA, FL	H	23.42 AE	32.30 MW	40.63 AEX	FLBLS	7/16-9/16
	Orlando-Kissimmee-Sanford MSA, FL	H	29.57 AE	43.95 MW	53.35 AEX	FLBLS	7/16-9/16
	Tampa-St. Petersburg-Clearwater MSA, FL	H	24.62 AE	34.68 MW	41.36 AEX	FLBLS	7/16-9/16
	Georgia	Y	60870 FQ	75660 MW	96400 TQ	USBLS	5/15
	Atlanta-Sandy Springs-Roswell MSA, GA	Y	63380 FQ	77540 MW	100890 TQ	USBLS	5/15
	Augusta-Richmond County MSA, GA-SC	Y	82670 FQ	99230 MW	114920 TQ	USBLS	5/15
	Hawaii	Y	62110 FQ	80540 MW	96540 TQ	USBLS	5/15
	Urban Honolulu MSA, HI	Y	60800 FQ	78470 MW	96540 TQ	USBLS	5/15
	Idaho	Y	61610 FQ	76850 MW	100210 TQ	USBLS	5/15
	Boise City MSA, ID	Y	59690 FQ	72820 MW	91190 TQ	USBLS	5/15
	Illinois	Y	68140 FQ	84540 MW	105100 TQ	USBLS	5/15
	Chicago-Naperville-Arlington Heights PMSA, IL	Y	68440 FQ	82150 MW	100340 TQ	USBLS	5/15

AE	Average entry wage	AWR	Average wage range	H	Hourly
AEX	Average experienced wage	B	Biweekly	HI	Highest wage paid
ATC	Average total compensation	D	Daily	HR	High end range
AW	Average wage paid	FQ	First quartile wage	LO	Lowest wage paid

LR	Low end range	MTC	Median total compensation	TCC	Total cash compensation
M	Monthly	MW	Median wage paid	TQ	Third quartile wage
MCC	Median cash compensation	MWR	Median wage range	W	Weekly
ME	Median entry wage	S	See annotated source	Y	Yearly

Mechanical Engineer

Occupation/Type/Industry	Location	Per	Low	Mid	High	Source	Date
Mechanical Engineer	Lake County-Kenosha County PMSA, IL-WI	Y	64080 FQ	76990 MW	106610 TQ	USBLS	5/15
	Indiana	Y	61280 FQ	74190 MW	90880 TQ	USBLS	5/15
	Gary PMSA, IN	Y	58710 FQ	70880 MW	89090 TQ	USBLS	5/15
	Indianapolis-Carmel-Anderson MSA, IN	Y	63750 FQ	77280 MW	92400 TQ	USBLS	5/15
	Iowa	Y	57530 FQ	71570 MW	89970 TQ	USBLS	5/15
	Des Moines-West Des Moines MSA, IA	Y	59950 FQ	76100 MW	94690 TQ	USBLS	5/15
	Kansas	Y	57940 FQ	70680 MW	86220 TQ	USBLS	5/15
	Wichita MSA, KS	Y	60840 FQ	72360 MW	88990 TQ	USBLS	5/15
	Kentucky	Y	62050 FQ	76920 MW	95270 TQ	USBLS	5/15
	Louisville-Jefferson County MSA, KY-IN	Y	61050 FQ	77590 MW	97370 TQ	USBLS	5/15
	Louisiana	Y	68040 FQ	88290 MW	120600 TQ	USBLS	5/15
	Baton Rouge MSA, LA	Y	73430 FQ	98850 MW	131620 TQ	USBLS	5/15
	New Orleans-Metairie MSA, LA	Y	70010 FQ	90980 MW	128880 TQ	USBLS	5/15
	Maine	Y	64440 FQ	79300 MW	94840 TQ	USBLS	5/15
	Portland-South Portland MSA, ME	Y	68220 FQ	81460 MW	96630 TQ	USBLS	5/15
	Maryland	Y	61066 AE	98370 MW	117023 AEX	MDBLS	4/16
	Baltimore-Columbia-Towson MSA, MD	Y	63730 FQ	85670 MW	118000 TQ	USBLS	5/15
	Salisbury MSA, MD-DE	Y	74330 FQ	108990 MW	138710 TQ	USBLS	5/15
	Massachusetts	Y	71170 FQ	87790 MW	108630 TQ	USBLS	5/15
	Boston-Cambridge-Newton NECTA, MA	Y	71310 FQ	87730 MW	106380 TQ	USBLS	5/15
	Worcester MSA, MA-CT	Y	66980 FQ	78920 MW	93810 TQ	USBLS	5/15
	Michigan	Y	70980 FQ	89120 MW	108320 TQ	USBLS	5/15
	Detroit-Dearborn-Livonia PMSA, MI	Y	78680 FQ	94850 MW	112650 TQ	USBLS	5/15
	Grand Rapids-Wyoming MSA, MI	Y	56950 FQ	69790 MW	86160 TQ	USBLS	5/15
	Minnesota	Y	64374 FQ	78043 MW	97247 TQ	MNBLS	1/16-3/16
	Minneapolis-St. Paul-Bloomington MSA, MN-WI	Y	66289 FQ	80049 MW	99051 TQ	MNBLS	1/16-3/16
	Mississippi	Y	63180 FQ	83750 MW	102950 TQ	USBLS	5/15
	Jackson MSA, MS	Y	52550 FQ	68510 MW	94740 TQ	USBLS	5/15
	Missouri	Y	62710 FQ	77210 MW	98390 TQ	USBLS	5/15
	Kansas City MSA, MO-KS	Y	60250 FQ	73540 MW	92930 TQ	USBLS	5/15
	St. Louis MSA, MO-IL	Y	66880 FQ	80090 MW	101500 TQ	USBLS	5/15
	Montana	Y	65500 FQ	74900 MW	91250 TQ	USBLS	5/15
	Billings MSA, MT	Y	65700 FQ	73520 MW	85840 TQ	USBLS	5/15
	Nebraska	Y	61880 FQ	73315 MW	89715 TQ	NEBLS	7/16-9/16
	Omaha-Council Bluffs MSA, NE-IA	Y	59485 FQ	72455 MW	90690 TQ	NEBLS	7/16-9/16
	Nevada	Y	64230 FQ	77690 MW	99650 TQ	USBLS	5/15
	Las Vegas-Henderson-Paradise MSA, NV	Y	66360 FQ	80120 MW	104130 TQ	USBLS	5/15
	New Hampshire	H	30.62 AE	39.82 MW	49.19 AEX	NHBLS	6/16
	Manchester NECTA, NH	H	32.70 AE	38.05 MW	43.73 AEX	NHBLS	6/16
	Nashua NECTA, NH-MA	Y	72250 FQ	89580 MW	114000 TQ	USBLS	5/15
	New Jersey	Y	70150 FQ	88210 MW	108610 TQ	USBLS	5/15
	Camden PMSA, NJ	Y	64980 FQ	82340 MW	107170 TQ	USBLS	5/15
	Newark PMSA, NJ-PA	Y	73250 FQ	89410 MW	106840 TQ	USBLS	5/15
	Trenton MSA, NJ	Y	77120 FQ	107890 MW	136930 TQ	USBLS	5/15
	New Mexico	Y	85870 FQ	102020 MW	121630 TQ	USBLS	5/15
	Albuquerque MSA, NM	Y	89480 FQ	105670 MW	123700 TQ	USBLS	5/15
	New York	Y	60290 AE	82930 MW	100480 AEX	NYBLS	1/16-3/16
	Buffalo-Cheektowaga-Niagara Falls MSA, NY	Y	60980 FQ	72970 MW	88710 TQ	USBLS	5/15
	Nassau County-Suffolk County PMSA, NY	Y	73500 FQ	91230 MW	114120 TQ	USBLS	5/15
	New York-Jersey City-White Plains PMSA, NY-NJ	Y	68410 FQ	87490 MW	107740 TQ	USBLS	5/15
	Rochester MSA, NY	Y	64310 FQ	78690 MW	98480 TQ	USBLS	5/15
	North Carolina	Y	65200 FQ	79260 MW	96830 TQ	USBLS	5/15
	Charlotte-Concord-Gastonia MSA, NC-SC	Y	63270 FQ	78730 MW	97570 TQ	USBLS	5/15
	Raleigh MSA, NC	Y	68550 FQ	86460 MW	105840 TQ	USBLS	5/15
	North Dakota	Y	51760 FQ	72270 MW	91040 TQ	USBLS	5/15

AE	Average entry wage	AWR	Average wage range	H	Hourly	LR	Low end range	MTC	Median total compensation	TCC	Total cash compensation
AEX	Average experienced wage	B	Biweekly	HI	Highest wage paid	M	Monthly	MCC	Median cash compensation	MWR	Median wage range	TQ	Third quartile wage
ATC	Average total compensation	D	Daily	HR	High end range	MCC	Median cash compensation	MWR	Median wage range	W	Weekly
AW	Average wage paid	FQ	First quartile wage	LO	Lowest wage paid	ME	Median entry wage	S	See annotated source	Y	Yearly

Occupation/Type/Industry	Location	Per	Low	Mid	High	Source	Date
Mechanical Engineer	Fargo MSA, ND-MN	Y	67700 FQ	81850 MW	101240 TQ	USBLS	5/15
	Ohio	Y	59530 FQ	73010 MW	89950 TQ	USBLS	5/15
	Cincinnati MSA, OH-KY-IN	Y	61670 FQ	75030 MW	94130 TQ	USBLS	5/15
	Cleveland-Elyria MSA, OH	Y	59900 FQ	73360 MW	90110 TQ	USBLS	5/15
	Columbus MSA, OH	Y	64500 FQ	76270 MW	94800 TQ	USBLS	5/15
	Oklahoma	Y	65410 FQ	80520 MW	99690 TQ	USBLS	5/15
	Oklahoma City MSA, OK	Y	67540 FQ	81900 MW	97730 TQ	USBLS	5/15
	Tulsa MSA, OK	Y	64660 FQ	80620 MW	99640 TQ	USBLS	5/15
	Oregon	H	33.46 FQ	41.70 MW	50.20 TQ	ORBLS	2016
	Portland-Vancouver-Hillsboro MSA, OR-WA	Y	69890 FQ	86690 MW	103060 TQ	USBLS	5/15
	Pennsylvania	Y	62510 FQ	79250 MW	101860 TQ	USBLS	5/15
	Allentown-Bethlehem-Easton MSA, PA-NJ	Y	62310 FQ	77130 MW	98780 TQ	USBLS	5/15
	Harrisburg-Carlisle MSA, PA	Y	65870 FQ	78080 MW	96720 TQ	USBLS	5/15
	Montgomery County-Bucks County-Chester County PMSA, PA	Y	64370 FQ	84260 MW	105620 TQ	USBLS	5/15
	Philadelphia PMSA, PA	Y	71540 FQ	94990 MW	112800 TQ	USBLS	5/15
	Pittsburgh MSA, PA	Y	68040 FQ	84810 MW	107950 TQ	USBLS	5/15
	Rhode Island	Y	68640 FQ	90100 MW	114310 TQ	USBLS	5/15
	Providence-Warwick MSA, RI-MA	Y	70000 FQ	89680 MW	113780 TQ	USBLS	5/15
	South Carolina	Y	66180 FQ	86330 MW	106950 TQ	USBLS	5/15
	Charleston-North Charleston MSA, SC	Y	68230 FQ	89670 MW	108500 TQ	USBLS	5/15
	Columbia MSA, SC	Y	50530 FQ	63370 MW	79340 TQ	USBLS	5/15
	Greenville-Anderson-Mauldin MSA, SC	Y	69650 FQ	89000 MW	117220 TQ	USBLS	5/15
	South Dakota	Y	57870 FQ	69000 MW	80880 TQ	USBLS	5/15
	Sioux Falls MSA, SD	Y	57880 FQ	69330 MW	84600 TQ	USBLS	5/15
	Tennessee	Y	63950 FQ	82230 MW	101610 TQ	USBLS	5/15
	Knoxville MSA, TN	Y	62600 FQ	87090 MW	107890 TQ	USBLS	5/15
	Memphis MSA, TN-MS-AR	Y	68250 FQ	85870 MW	104830 TQ	USBLS	5/15
	Nashville-Davidson–Murfreesboro–Franklin MSA, TN	Y	60530 FQ	74640 MW	93270 TQ	USBLS	5/15
	Texas	Y	71780 FQ	92330 MW	120690 TQ	USBLS	5/15
	Austin-Round Rock MSA, TX	Y	72970 FQ	91290 MW	112930 TQ	USBLS	5/15
	Dallas-Plano-Irving PMSA, TX	Y	73930 FQ	96650 MW	122280 TQ	USBLS	5/15
	Fort Worth-Arlington PMSA, TX	Y	63440 FQ	82850 MW	103950 TQ	USBLS	5/15
	Houston-The Woodlands-Sugar Land MSA, TX	Y	75150 FQ	97140 MW	129110 TQ	USBLS	5/15
	San Antonio-New Braunfels MSA, TX	Y	58580 FQ	75990 MW	94980 TQ	USBLS	5/15
	Utah	Y	63070 FQ	76740 MW	94380 TQ	USBLS	5/15
	Ogden-Clearfield MSA, UT	Y	67190 FQ	81010 MW	95710 TQ	USBLS	5/15
	Provo-Orem MSA, UT	Y	63800 FQ	74690 MW	91350 TQ	USBLS	5/15
	Salt Lake City MSA, UT	Y	61380 FQ	74410 MW	93700 TQ	USBLS	5/15
	Vermont	Y	61300 FQ	74840 MW	96750 TQ	USBLS	5/15
	Burlington-South Burlington MSA, VT	Y	63170 FQ	78910 MW	103210 TQ	USBLS	5/15
	Virginia	Y	71550 FQ	91260 MW	115880 TQ	USBLS	5/15
	Richmond MSA, VA	Y	63300 FQ	75670 MW	96270 TQ	USBLS	5/15
	Virginia Beach-Norfolk-Newport News MSA, VA-NC	Y	70190 FQ	85630 MW	100920 TQ	USBLS	5/15
	Washington	H	33.57 FQ	42.77 MW	53.25 TQ	WABLS	3/16
	Seattle-Bellevue-Everett PMSA, WA	H	35.04 FQ	45.02 MW	56.49 TQ	WABLS	3/16
	Tacoma-Lakewood PMSA, WA	H	32.87 FQ	40.44 MW	49.48 TQ	WABLS	3/16
	West Virginia	Y	64820 FQ	79580 MW	100170 TQ	USBLS	5/15
	Huntington-Ashland MSA, WV-KY-OH	Y	70860 FQ	83100 MW	96390 TQ	USBLS	5/15
	Wisconsin	Y	58380 FQ	71190 MW	85900 TQ	USBLS	5/15
	Madison MSA, WI	Y	63040 FQ	74840 MW	90590 TQ	USBLS	5/15
	Milwaukee-Waukesha-West Allis MSA, WI	Y	59830 FQ	71900 MW	85880 TQ	USBLS	5/15
	Wyoming	Y	64000 FQ	81340 MW	108940 TQ	USBLS	5/15
	Cheyenne MSA, WY	Y	56720 FQ	80030 MW	139140 TQ	USBLS	5/15
	Puerto Rico	Y	36150 FQ	45870 MW	59080 TQ	USBLS	5/15

Occupation/Type/Industry	Location	Per	Low	Mid	High	Source	Date
Mechanical Engineer	San Juan-Carolina-Caguas						
	MSA, PR	Y	26240 FQ	45460 MW	69940 TQ	USBLS	5/15
	Guam	Y	44780 FQ	57820 MW	79270 TQ	USBLS	5/15
Mechanical Engineering							
Technician	Alabama	Y	36716 AE	54513 AW	63412 AEX	ALBLS	6/16
	Birmingham-Hoover MSA, AL	Y	36655 AE	54422 AW	63300 AEX	ALBLS	6/16
	Alaska	Y	51790 FQ	63010 MW	76290 TQ	USBLS	5/15
	Anchorage MSA, AK	Y	51100 FQ	67860 MW	84350 TQ	USBLS	5/15
	Arizona	Y	40220 FQ	49120 MW	61420 TQ	USBLS	5/15
	Phoenix-Mesa-Scottsdale						
	MSA, AZ	Y	40440 FQ	48980 MW	61020 TQ	USBLS	5/15
	Arkansas	Y	37150 FQ	44900 MW	53770 TQ	USBLS	5/15
	Little Rock-North Little Rock-						
	Conway MSA, AR	Y	35750 FQ	42490 MW	53040 TQ	USBLS	5/15
	California	H	23.18 FQ	29.85 MW	36.40 TQ	CABLS	1/16-3/16
	Anaheim-Santa Ana-Irvine						
	PMSA, CA	H	22.12 FQ	27.63 MW	35.41 TQ	CABLS	1/16-3/16
	Los Angeles-Long Beach-						
	Glendale PMSA, CA	H	25.75 FQ	32.32 MW	37.65 TQ	CABLS	1/16-3/16
	Oakland-Hayward-Berkeley						
	PMSA, CA	H	25.35 FQ	32.26 MW	38.17 TQ	CABLS	1/16-3/16
	Riverside-San Bernardino-						
	Ontario MSA, CA	H	14.98 FQ	22.29 MW	30.22 TQ	CABLS	1/16-3/16
	Sacramento–Roseville–						
	Arden-Arcade MSA, CA	H	18.68 FQ	27.47 MW	35.19 TQ	CABLS	1/16-3/16
	San Diego-Carlsbad MSA, CA	H	26.89 FQ	32.32 MW	36.87 TQ	CABLS	1/16-3/16
	San Francisco-Redwood City-						
	South San Francisco PMSA,						
	CA	H	28.22 FQ	33.67 MW	37.16 TQ	CABLS	1/16-3/16
	Colorado	Y	50730 FQ	63700 MW	80860 TQ	USBLS	5/15
	Denver-Aurora-Lakewood						
	MSA, CO	Y	48470 FQ	63770 MW	79750 TQ	USBLS	5/15
	Connecticut	Y		63558 MW		CTBLS	1/16-3/16
	Bridgeport-Stamford-Norwalk						
	MSA, CT	Y	44740 FQ	54740 MW	65730 TQ	USBLS	5/15
	Hartford-West Hartford-East						
	Hartford MSA, CT	Y	60090 FQ	73950 MW	88630 TQ	USBLS	5/15
	Delaware	Y	58610 FQ	68540 MW	80070 TQ	USBLS	5/15
	Wilmington PMSA, DE-MD-						
	NJ	Y	59590 FQ	69430 MW	78620 TQ	USBLS	5/15
	Washington-Arlington-						
	Alexandria PMSA, DC-VA-						
	MD-WV	Y	50520 FQ	57030 MW	66260 TQ	USBLS	5/15
	Florida	H	16.74 AE	23.61 MW	27.97 AEX	FLBLS	7/16-9/16
	Fort Lauderdale-Pompano						
	Beach-Deerfield Beach						
	PMSA, FL	H	18.52 AE	23.63 MW	26.18 AEX	FLBLS	7/16-9/16
	Miami-Miami Beach-Kendall						
	PMSA, FL	H	19.66 AE	23.61 MW	28.70 AEX	FLBLS	7/16-9/16
	Orlando-Kissimmee-Sanford						
	MSA, FL	H	13.70 AE	23.02 MW	26.80 AEX	FLBLS	7/16-9/16
	Tampa-St. Petersburg-						
	Clearwater MSA, FL	H	16.14 AE	23.29 MW	28.33 AEX	FLBLS	7/16-9/16
	Georgia	Y	41880 FQ	53110 MW	64980 TQ	USBLS	5/15
	Atlanta-Sandy Springs-						
	Roswell MSA, GA	Y	42980 FQ	53980 MW	62750 TQ	USBLS	5/15
	Augusta-Richmond County						
	MSA, GA-SC	Y	43770 FQ	52250 MW	60560 TQ	USBLS	5/15
	Hawaii	Y	46810 FQ	58460 MW	74120 TQ	USBLS	5/15
	Urban Honolulu MSA, HI	Y	45910 FQ	56010 MW	72080 TQ	USBLS	5/15
	Idaho	Y	43080 FQ	49240 MW	64800 TQ	USBLS	5/15
	Boise City MSA, ID	Y	42770 FQ	47390 MW	59880 TQ	USBLS	5/15
	Illinois	Y	44180 FQ	52800 MW	63580 TQ	USBLS	5/15
	Chicago-Naperville-Arlington						
	Heights PMSA, IL	Y	46040 FQ	55250 MW	66190 TQ	USBLS	5/15
	Lake County-Kenosha County						
	PMSA, IL-WI	Y	43670 FQ	52180 MW	63030 TQ	USBLS	5/15
	Indiana	Y	39160 FQ	50300 MW	61200 TQ	USBLS	5/15
	Gary PMSA, IN	Y	35600 FQ	64830 MW	72910 TQ	USBLS	5/15
	Indianapolis-Carmel-Anderson						
	MSA, IN	Y	45480 FQ	60470 MW	82700 TQ	USBLS	5/15

AE	Average entry wage	AWR	Average wage range	H	Hourly
AEX	Average experienced wage	B	Biweekly	HI	Highest wage paid
ATC	Average total compensation	D	Daily	HR	High end range
AW	Average wage paid	FQ	First quartile wage	LO	Lowest wage paid

LR	Low end range	MTC	Median total compensation
M	Monthly	MW	Median wage paid
MCC	Median cash compensation	MWR	Median wage range
ME	Median entry wage	S	See annotated source

TCC	Total cash compensation	
TQ	Third quartile wage	
W	Weekly	
Y	Yearly	

**Mechanical Engineering
Technician**

Occupation/Type/Industry	Location	Per	Low	Mid	High	Source	Date
	Iowa	Y	37140 FQ	47380 MW	58240 TQ	USBLS	5/15
	Kansas	Y	41360 FQ	48890 MW	58660 TQ	USBLS	5/15
	Wichita MSA, KS	Y	42410 FQ	52210 MW	59340 TQ	USBLS	5/15
	Kentucky	Y	38960 FQ	47610 MW	58140 TQ	USBLS	5/15
	Louisville-Jefferson County MSA, KY-IN	Y	35190 FQ	41590 MW	51340 TQ	USBLS	5/15
	Louisiana	Y	44510 FQ	56990 MW	74810 TQ	USBLS	5/15
	New Orleans-Metairie MSA, LA	Y	48470 FQ	61720 MW	87160 TQ	USBLS	5/15
	Maine	Y	51340 FQ	62390 MW	76790 TQ	USBLS	5/15
	Portland-South Portland MSA, ME	Y	60830 FQ	84190 MW	103700 TQ	USBLS	5/15
	Maryland	Y	40418 AE	57553 MW	66120 AEX	MDBLS	4/16
	Baltimore-Columbia-Towson MSA, MD	Y	46700 FQ	55740 MW	65630 TQ	USBLS	5/15
	Massachusetts	Y	45090 FQ	56020 MW	68270 TQ	USBLS	5/15
	Boston-Cambridge-Newton NECTA, MA	Y	44170 FQ	56000 MW	69860 TQ	USBLS	5/15
	Worcester MSA, MA-CT	Y	44040 FQ	55230 MW	64160 TQ	USBLS	5/15
	Michigan	Y	44940 FQ	58030 MW	72310 TQ	USBLS	5/15
	Detroit-Dearborn-Livonia PMSA, MI	Y	45020 FQ	59730 MW	75370 TQ	USBLS	5/15
	Grand Rapids-Wyoming MSA, MI	Y	37830 FQ	46760 MW	60700 TQ	USBLS	5/15
	Minnesota	Y	43850 FQ	54546 MW	70342 TQ	MNBLS	1/16-3/16
	Minneapolis-St. Paul-Bloomington MSA, MN-WI	Y	44415 FQ	55977 MW	72358 TQ	MNBLS	1/16-3/16
	Mississippi	Y	34290 FQ	37990 MW	54390 TQ	USBLS	5/15
	Missouri	Y	37340 FQ	48080 MW	65030 TQ	USBLS	5/15
	Kansas City MSA, MO-KS	Y	38480 FQ	46640 MW	57830 TQ	USBLS	5/15
	St. Louis MSA, MO-IL	Y	39240 FQ	57610 MW	72930 TQ	USBLS	5/15
	Nebraska	Y	47020 FQ	56230 MW	64340 TQ	NEBLS	7/16-9/16
	Omaha-Council Bluffs MSA, NE-IA	Y	48560 FQ	56385 MW	63080 TQ	NEBLS	7/16-9/16
	Nevada	Y	29750 FQ	43370 MW	65310 TQ	USBLS	5/15
	Las Vegas-Henderson-Paradise MSA, NV	Y	32870 FQ	45500 MW	62350 TQ	USBLS	5/15
	New Hampshire	H	18.54 AE	25.74 MW	29.30 AEX	NHBLS	6/16
	Manchester NECTA, NH	H	14.69 AE	20.11 MW	26.02 AEX	NHBLS	6/16
	Nashua NECTA, NH-MA	Y	43970 FQ	55190 MW	66340 TQ	USBLS	5/15
	New Jersey	Y	42340 FQ	64020 MW	76610 TQ	USBLS	5/15
	Camden PMSA, NJ	Y	49380 FQ	64350 MW	75960 TQ	USBLS	5/15
	Newark PMSA, NJ-PA	Y	29330 FQ	39630 MW	75560 TQ	USBLS	5/15
	New Mexico	Y	60670 FQ	68430 MW	74840 TQ	USBLS	5/15
	Albuquerque MSA, NM	Y	62370 FQ	69790 MW	77210 TQ	USBLS	5/15
	New York	Y	39350 AE	53460 MW	67080 AEX	NYBLS	1/16-3/16
	Buffalo-Cheektowaga-Niagara Falls MSA, NY	Y	41270 FQ	50110 MW	57970 TQ	USBLS	5/15
	Nassau County-Suffolk County PMSA, NY	Y	51790 FQ	68460 MW	82320 TQ	USBLS	5/15
	New York-Jersey City-White Plains PMSA, NY-NJ	Y	45730 FQ	64980 MW	77790 TQ	USBLS	5/15
	Rochester MSA, NY	Y	43690 FQ	52130 MW	64510 TQ	USBLS	5/15
	North Carolina	Y	42150 FQ	51020 MW	60510 TQ	USBLS	5/15
	Charlotte-Concord-Gastonia MSA, NC-SC	Y	42700 FQ	49540 MW	59050 TQ	USBLS	5/15
	Raleigh MSA, NC	Y	45890 FQ	56700 MW	73380 TQ	USBLS	5/15
	North Dakota	Y	45270 FQ	55780 MW	67410 TQ	USBLS	5/15
	Fargo MSA, ND-MN	Y	50220 FQ	57150 MW	63480 TQ	USBLS	5/15
	Ohio	Y	39530 FQ	48280 MW	59320 TQ	USBLS	5/15
	Cincinnati MSA, OH-KY-IN	Y	36760 FQ	45340 MW	60550 TQ	USBLS	5/15
	Cleveland-Elyria MSA, OH	Y	42130 FQ	50490 MW	61330 TQ	USBLS	5/15
	Columbus MSA, OH	Y	45140 FQ	54350 MW	64550 TQ	USBLS	5/15
	Oklahoma	Y	42100 FQ	51400 MW	62800 TQ	USBLS	5/15
	Oklahoma City MSA, OK	Y	43880 FQ	53380 MW	67260 TQ	USBLS	5/15
	Tulsa MSA, OK	Y	42150 FQ	51880 MW	60780 TQ	USBLS	5/15
	Oregon	H	20.32 FQ	24.10 MW	28.64 TQ	ORBLS	2016
	Portland-Vancouver-Hillsboro MSA, OR-WA	Y	41820 FQ	50290 MW	59660 TQ	USBLS	5/15
	Pennsylvania	Y	38250 FQ	47830 MW	59120 TQ	USBLS	5/15

Occupation/Type/Industry	Location	Per	Low	Mid	High	Source	Date
Mechanical Engineering Technician	Allentown-Bethlehem-Easton MSA, PA-NJ	Y	44480 FQ	51010 MW	62250 TQ	USBLS	5/15
	Harrisburg-Carlisle MSA, PA	Y	39500 FQ	54270 MW	60010 TQ	USBLS	5/15
	Montgomery County-Bucks County-Chester County PMSA, PA	Y	38000 FQ	47200 MW	61940 TQ	USBLS	5/15
	Philadelphia PMSA, PA	Y	29150 FQ	37730 MW	52620 TQ	USBLS	5/15
	Pittsburgh MSA, PA	Y	41080 FQ	49000 MW	58700 TQ	USBLS	5/15
	Rhode Island	Y	42600 FQ	47970 MW	69800 TQ	USBLS	5/15
	Providence-Warwick MSA, RI-MA	Y	47200 FQ	57550 MW	69440 TQ	USBLS	5/15
	South Carolina	Y	43300 FQ	51070 MW	60000 TQ	USBLS	5/15
	Charleston-North Charleston MSA, SC	Y	47770 FQ	55310 MW	61070 TQ	USBLS	5/15
	Columbia MSA, SC	Y	44190 FQ	49660 MW	57480 TQ	USBLS	5/15
	Greenville-Anderson-Mauldin MSA, SC	Y	42940 FQ	52490 MW	61190 TQ	USBLS	5/15
	South Dakota	Y	34540 FQ	38510 MW	44640 TQ	USBLS	5/15
	Sioux Falls MSA, SD	Y	36140 FQ	41700 MW	46550 TQ	USBLS	5/15
	Tennessee	Y	42060 FQ	52030 MW	62090 TQ	USBLS	5/15
	Knoxville MSA, TN	Y	43020 FQ	52060 MW	63300 TQ	USBLS	5/15
	Memphis MSA, TN-MS-AR	Y	38740 FQ	48820 MW	61420 TQ	USBLS	5/15
	Nashville-Davidson–Murfreesboro–Franklin MSA, TN	Y	46350 FQ	56360 MW	64420 TQ	USBLS	5/15
	Texas	Y	41330 FQ	54910 MW	71430 TQ	USBLS	5/15
	Austin-Round Rock MSA, TX	Y	36120 FQ	44680 MW	57990 TQ	USBLS	5/15
	Dallas-Plano-Irving PMSA, TX	Y	42330 FQ	54010 MW	62620 TQ	USBLS	5/15
	Fort Worth-Arlington PMSA, TX	Y	27640 FQ	42050 MW	56950 TQ	USBLS	5/15
	Houston-The Woodlands-Sugar Land MSA, TX	Y	46130 FQ	59240 MW	82350 TQ	USBLS	5/15
	San Antonio-New Braunfels MSA, TX	Y	42180 FQ	54160 MW	62400 TQ	USBLS	5/15
	Utah	Y	38000 FQ	48710 MW	62320 TQ	USBLS	5/15
	Ogden-Clearfield MSA, UT	Y	37350 FQ	44190 MW	51030 TQ	USBLS	5/15
	Provo-Orem MSA, UT	Y	34590 FQ	38600 MW	54720 TQ	USBLS	5/15
	Salt Lake City MSA, UT	Y	43270 FQ	55720 MW	69330 TQ	USBLS	5/15
	Vermont	Y	43290 FQ	50680 MW	62400 TQ	USBLS	5/15
	Virginia	Y	46670 FQ	55310 MW	65160 TQ	USBLS	5/15
	Virginia Beach-Norfolk-Newport News MSA, VA-NC	Y	43120 FQ	50350 MW	60570 TQ	USBLS	5/15
	Washington	H	22.93 FQ	29.45 MW	37.21 TQ	WABLS	3/16
	Seattle-Bellevue-Everett PMSA, WA	H	22.44 FQ	29.50 MW	36.47 TQ	WABLS	3/16
	Tacoma-Lakewood PMSA, WA	H	32.93 FQ	39.53 MW	45.21 TQ	WABLS	3/16
	West Virginia	Y	28890 FQ	37550 MW	58150 TQ	USBLS	5/15
	Wisconsin	Y	40390 FQ	50560 MW	61330 TQ	USBLS	5/15
	Madison MSA, WI	Y	40460 FQ	51080 MW	63340 TQ	USBLS	5/15
	Milwaukee-Waukesha-West Allis MSA, WI	Y	42080 FQ	52430 MW	62100 TQ	USBLS	5/15
	Wyoming	Y	34720 FQ	38990 MW	71260 TQ	USBLS	5/15
	Puerto Rico	Y	18740 FQ	27330 MW	38460 TQ	USBLS	5/15
	San Juan-Carolina-Caguas MSA, PR	Y	18190 FQ	24460 MW	34630 TQ	USBLS	5/15
Mechatronics/Robotics Technician	South Carolina	Y		50000 AW		UBJ01	2015
Medi-Spa Physician Cruise Ship	United States	M	3000 LO		5200 HI	CRU01	2016
Media Director Pharmaceutical, Medical Device, and Healthcare Industries	United States	Y		108600 AW		MMM01	7/16
Media Planner	United States	Y		45000 MW		MCCS	2016
Media Production Specialist City Manager's Office	Arcata, CA	Y			14713 HI	CACIT	6/28/16
Public Library	San Francisco, CA	B	2371 LO		2882 HI	SFGOV	2016-2018

AE	Average entry wage	**AWR**	Average wage range	**H**	Hourly	**LR** Low end range	**MTC** Median total compensation	**TCC** Total cash compensation
AEX	Average experienced wage	**B**	Biweekly	**HI**	Highest wage paid	**M** Monthly	**MW** Median wage paid	**TQ** Third quartile wage
ATC	Average total compensation	**D**	Daily	**HR**	High end range	**MCC** Median cash compensation	**MWR** Median wage range	**W** Weekly
AW	Average wage paid	**FQ**	First quartile wage	**LO**	Lowest wage paid	**ME** Median entry wage	**S** See annotated source	**Y** Yearly

Occupation/Type/Industry	Location	Per	Low	Mid	High	Source	Date
Media Relations Specialist							
Public Library	Detroit, MI	M	3538 LO		3890 HI	DETGOV	2016
Media Training Specialist							
Public Library	San Francisco, CA	Y			93884 HI	CACIT	6/28/16
Medicaid Fraud Deputy							
State Government	North Carolina	Y	75006 LO		125529 HI	NCGOV	7/1/16
Medicaid Fraud Intake Officer							
Attorney General's Office, State Government	Ohio	H	17.97 LO		18.58 HI	OHGOV	2015
Medical and Clinical Laboratory Technician							
	Alabama	Y	24678 AE	36237 AW	42027 AEX	ALBLS	6/16
	Birmingham-Hoover MSA, AL	Y	28755 AE	39529 AW	28755 AEX	ALBLS	6/16
	Alaska	Y	38160 FQ	45070 MW	54860 TQ	USBLS	5/15
	Anchorage MSA, AK	Y	38160 FQ	44660 MW	54020 TQ	USBLS	5/15
	Arizona	Y	30820 FQ	37270 MW	48770 TQ	USBLS	5/15
	Phoenix-Mesa-Scottsdale MSA, AZ	Y	30570 FQ	37290 MW	48060 TQ	USBLS	5/15
	Tucson MSA, AZ	Y	32190 FQ	37490 MW	54660 TQ	USBLS	5/15
	Arkansas	Y	28070 FQ	35470 MW	43980 TQ	USBLS	5/15
	Little Rock-North Little Rock-Conway MSA, AR	Y	26870 FQ	34350 MW	42320 TQ	USBLS	5/15
	California	H	17.35 FQ	22.33 MW	28.07 TQ	CABLS	1/16-3/16
	Anaheim-Santa Ana-Irvine PMSA, CA	H	16.34 FQ	20.37 MW	25.94 TQ	CABLS	1/16-3/16
	Los Angeles-Long Beach-Glendale PMSA, CA	H	16.14 FQ	20.19 MW	25.26 TQ	CABLS	1/16-3/16
	Oakland-Hayward-Berkeley PMSA, CA	H	20.64 FQ	25.50 MW	29.73 TQ	CABLS	1/16-3/16
	Riverside-San Bernardino-Ontario MSA, CA	H	16.98 FQ	20.44 MW	23.91 TQ	CABLS	1/16-3/16
	Sacramento–Roseville–Arden-Arcade MSA, CA	H	18.92 FQ	24.80 MW	28.79 TQ	CABLS	1/16-3/16
	San Diego-Carlsbad MSA, CA	H	17.14 FQ	22.85 MW	28.24 TQ	CABLS	1/16-3/16
	San Francisco-Redwood City-South San Francisco PMSA, CA	H	25.93 FQ	28.55 MW	31.37 TQ	CABLS	1/16-3/16
	Colorado	Y	31410 FQ	38250 MW	48220 TQ	USBLS	5/15
	Denver-Aurora-Lakewood MSA, CO	Y	32010 FQ	38490 MW	48370 TQ	USBLS	5/15
	Connecticut	Y		47559 MW		CTBLS	1/16-3/16
	Bridgeport-Stamford-Norwalk MSA, CT	Y	34150 FQ	45000 MW	63170 TQ	USBLS	5/15
	Hartford-West Hartford-East Hartford MSA, CT	Y	42320 FQ	53710 MW	66400 TQ	USBLS	5/15
	Delaware	Y	34860 FQ	42680 MW	52480 TQ	USBLS	5/15
	Wilmington PMSA, DE-MD-NJ	Y	36060 FQ	44310 MW	54500 TQ	USBLS	5/15
	District of Columbia	Y	35330 FQ	40540 MW	55500 TQ	USBLS	5/15
	Washington-Arlington-Alexandria PMSA, DC-VA-MD-WV	Y	32740 FQ	39050 MW	51540 TQ	USBLS	5/15
	Florida	H	12.81 AE	17.49 MW	21.25 AEX	FLBLS	7/16-9/16
	Fort Lauderdale-Pompano Beach-Deerfield Beach PMSA, FL	H	12.96 AE	16.76 MW	18.92 AEX	FLBLS	7/16-9/16
	Miami-Miami Beach-Kendall PMSA, FL	H	13.35 AE	17.20 MW	20.27 AEX	FLBLS	7/16-9/16
	Orlando-Kissimmee-Sanford MSA, FL	H	13.15 AE	17.00 MW	20.79 AEX	FLBLS	7/16-9/16
	Tampa-St. Petersburg-Clearwater MSA, FL	H	12.67 AE	17.70 MW	21.59 AEX	FLBLS	7/16-9/16
	Georgia	Y	28030 FQ	34830 MW	45060 TQ	USBLS	5/15
	Albany MSA, GA	Y	23560 FQ	28090 MW	34600 TQ	USBLS	5/15
	Atlanta-Sandy Springs-Roswell MSA, GA	Y	29520 FQ	36090 MW	48030 TQ	USBLS	5/15
	Augusta-Richmond County MSA, GA-SC	Y	24200 FQ	35710 MW	47530 TQ	USBLS	5/15
	Hawaii	Y	41240 FQ,	45770 MW	50430 TQ	USBLS	5/15

AE	Average entry wage	AWR	Average wage range	H	Hourly	LR	Low end range	MTC	Median total compensation	TCC	Total cash compensation
AEX	Average experienced wage	B	Biweekly	HI	Highest wage paid	M	Monthly	MW	Median wage paid	TQ	Third quartile wage
ATC	Average total compensation	D	Daily	HR	High end range	MCC	Median cash compensation	MWR	Median wage range	W	Weekly
AW	Average wage paid	FQ	First quartile wage	LO	Lowest wage paid	ME	Median entry wage	S	See annotated source	Y	Yearly

Occupation/Type/Industry	Location	Per	Low	Mid	High	Source	Date
Medical and Clinical Laboratory Technician	Urban Honolulu MSA, HI	Y	41230 FQ	45870 MW	51160 TQ	USBLS	5/15
	Idaho	Y	26460 FQ	30620 MW	37750 TQ	USBLS	5/15
	Boise City MSA, ID	Y	25110 FQ	29860 MW	37510 TQ	USBLS	5/15
	Illinois	Y	34400 FQ	44270 MW	56910 TQ	USBLS	5/15
	Chicago-Naperville-Arlington Heights PMSA, IL	Y	35030 FQ	45230 MW	58880 TQ	USBLS	5/15
	Lake County-Kenosha County PMSA, IL-WI	Y	38060 FQ	47310 MW	56910 TQ	USBLS	5/15
	Indiana	Y	28600 FQ	34900 MW	43900 TQ	USBLS	5/15
	Gary PMSA, IN	Y	28360 FQ	34270 MW	42860 TQ	USBLS	5/15
	Indianapolis-Carmel-Anderson MSA, IN	Y	28970 FQ	34620 MW	41740 TQ	USBLS	5/15
	Iowa	Y	33820 FQ	41620 MW	49570 TQ	USBLS	5/15
	Des Moines-West Des Moines MSA, IA	Y	31660 FQ	39330 MW	47350 TQ	USBLS	5/15
	Kansas	Y	29860 FQ	36300 MW	44200 TQ	USBLS	5/15
	Wichita MSA, KS	Y	32110 FQ	38220 MW	45200 TQ	USBLS	5/15
	Kentucky	Y	32240 FQ	39350 MW	47230 TQ	USBLS	5/15
	Louisville-Jefferson County MSA, KY-IN	Y	30870 FQ	39430 MW	48180 TQ	USBLS	5/15
	Louisiana	Y	24990 FQ	31950 MW	39330 TQ	USBLS	5/15
	Baton Rouge MSA, LA	Y	29660 FQ	38330 MW	48170 TQ	USBLS	5/15
	New Orleans-Metairie MSA, LA	Y	24900 FQ	31080 MW	36720 TQ	USBLS	5/15
	Maine	Y	30260 FQ	37660 MW	50120 TQ	USBLS	5/15
	Portland-South Portland MSA, ME	Y	27850 FQ	34630 MW	41770 TQ	USBLS	5/15
	Maryland	Y	29315 AE	41563 MW	47687 AEX	MDBLS	4/16
	Baltimore-Columbia-Towson MSA, MD	Y	29840 FQ	35490 MW	42750 TQ	USBLS	5/15
	Salisbury MSA, MD-DE	Y	37850 FQ	46290 MW	54460 TQ	USBLS	5/15
	Massachusetts	Y	33940 FQ	40260 MW	49130 TQ	USBLS	5/15
	Boston-Cambridge-Newton NECTA, MA	Y	33920 FQ	39000 MW	48230 TQ	USBLS	5/15
	Worcester MSA, MA-CT	Y	35820 FQ	43380 MW	50370 TQ	USBLS	5/15
	Michigan	Y	27140 FQ	32290 MW	39780 TQ	USBLS	5/15
	Detroit-Dearborn-Livonia PMSA, MI	Y	27160 FQ	31900 MW	38290 TQ	USBLS	5/15
	Grand Rapids-Wyoming MSA, MI	Y	27200 FQ	29910 MW	35470 TQ	USBLS	5/15
	Minnesota	Y	38175 FQ	44747 MW	51350 TQ	MNBLS	1/16-3/16
	Minneapolis-St. Paul-Bloomington MSA, MN-WI	Y	37671 FQ	44606 MW	51774 TQ	MNBLS	1/16-3/16
	Mississippi	Y	27680 FQ	34800 MW	41150 TQ	USBLS	5/15
	Jackson MSA, MS	Y	27110 FQ	35330 MW	42520 TQ	USBLS	5/15
	Missouri	Y	26590 FQ	32940 MW	45650 TQ	USBLS	5/15
	Kansas City MSA, MO-KS	Y	29500 FQ	36150 MW	48510 TQ	USBLS	5/15
	St. Louis MSA, MO-IL	Y	27840 FQ	34050 MW	45220 TQ	USBLS	5/15
	Montana	Y	29420 FQ	39350 MW	55280 TQ	USBLS	5/15
	Billings MSA, MT	Y	31430 FQ	36600 MW	45870 TQ	USBLS	5/15
	Nebraska	Y	29980 FQ	38125 MW	46590 TQ	NEBLS	7/16-9/16
	Omaha-Council Bluffs MSA, NE-IA	Y	30490 FQ	41100 MW	48095 TQ	NEBLS	7/16-9/16
	Nevada	Y	32960 FQ	38020 MW	48840 TQ	USBLS	5/15
	Las Vegas-Henderson-Paradise MSA, NV	Y	32300 FQ	37130 MW	47530 TQ	USBLS	5/15
	New Hampshire	H	15.09 AE	19.27 MW	22.64 AEX	NHBLS	6/16
	Manchester NECTA, NH	H	15.94 AE	21.34 MW	24.16 AEX	NHBLS	6/16
	New Jersey	Y	38600 FQ	48190 MW	57830 TQ	USBLS	5/15
	Camden PMSA, NJ	Y	46440 FQ	54410 MW	61150 TQ	USBLS	5/15
	Newark PMSA, NJ-PA	Y	42150 FQ	49840 MW	58020 TQ	USBLS	5/15
	Trenton MSA, NJ	Y	40830 FQ	47860 MW	57130 TQ	USBLS	5/15
	New Mexico	Y	31660 FQ	38520 MW	47480 TQ	USBLS	5/15
	Albuquerque MSA, NM	Y	31540 FQ	37270 MW	45360 TQ	USBLS	5/15
	New York	Y	32330 AE	46620 MW	55350 AEX	NYBLS	1/16-3/16
	Buffalo-Cheektowaga-Niagara Falls MSA, NY	Y	39000 FQ	46450 MW	54820 TQ	USBLS	5/15
	Nassau County-Suffolk County PMSA, NY	Y	35300 FQ	48170 MW	62330 TQ	USBLS	5/15
	New York-Jersey City-White Plains PMSA, NY-NJ	Y	38590 FQ	47450 MW	58590 TQ	USBLS	5/15

Medical and Clinical Laboratory Technician

Occupation/Type/Industry	Location	Per	Low	Mid	High	Source	Date
Medical and Clinical Laboratory Technician							
	Rochester MSA, NY	Y	28100 FQ	34600 MW	42330 TQ	USBLS	5/15
	North Carolina	Y	33580 FQ	38890 MW	46330 TQ	USBLS	5/15
	Charlotte-Concord-Gastonia MSA, NC-SC	Y	32390 FQ	39590 MW	48760 TQ	USBLS	5/15
	Raleigh MSA, NC	Y	33120 FQ	40350 MW	47790 TQ	USBLS	5/15
	North Dakota	Y	34980 FQ	40300 MW	46920 TQ	USBLS	5/15
	Fargo MSA, ND-MN	Y	33180 FQ	37260 MW	44570 TQ	USBLS	5/15
	Ohio	Y	34300 FQ	41850 MW	49790 TQ	USBLS	5/15
	Cincinnati MSA, OH-KY-IN	Y	33010 FQ	38670 MW	47830 TQ	USBLS	5/15
	Cleveland-Elyria MSA, OH	Y	36910 FQ	44170 MW	51190 TQ	USBLS	5/15
	Columbus MSA, OH	Y	32560 FQ	40190 MW	48410 TQ	USBLS	5/15
	Oklahoma	Y	24590 FQ	30870 MW	40070 TQ	USBLS	5/15
	Oklahoma City MSA, OK	Y	23690 FQ	30810 MW	40500 TQ	USBLS	5/15
	Tulsa MSA, OK	Y	26960 FQ	30750 MW	37950 TQ	USBLS	5/15
	Oregon	H	16.16 FQ	19.69 MW	24.14 TQ	ORBLS	2016
	Portland-Vancouver-Hillsboro MSA, OR-WA	Y	33050 FQ	41700 MW	50750 TQ	USBLS	5/15
	Pennsylvania	Y	31550 FQ	38510 MW	49250 TQ	USBLS	5/15
	Allentown-Bethlehem-Easton MSA, PA-NJ	Y	34500 FQ	41370 MW	51230 TQ	USBLS	5/15
	Harrisburg-Carlisle MSA, PA	Y	32020 FQ	39220 MW	48070 TQ	USBLS	5/15
	Montgomery County-Bucks County-Chester County PMSA, PA	Y	34750 FQ	43170 MW	57970 TQ	USBLS	5/15
	Philadelphia PMSA, PA	Y	33100 FQ	40360 MW	53000 TQ	USBLS	5/15
	Pittsburgh MSA, PA	Y	28730 FQ	35340 MW	44370 TQ	USBLS	5/15
	Rhode Island	Y	49410 FQ	58330 MW	69050 TQ	USBLS	5/15
	Providence-Warwick MSA, RI-MA	Y	43010 FQ	54420 MW	66360 TQ	USBLS	5/15
	South Carolina	Y	27540 FQ	35880 MW	45950 TQ	USBLS	5/15
	Charleston-North Charleston MSA, SC	Y	30730 FQ	39420 MW	47530 TQ	USBLS	5/15
	Columbia MSA, SC	Y	24240 FQ	36680 MW	50380 TQ	USBLS	5/15
	Greenville-Anderson-Mauldin MSA, SC	Y	25880 FQ	31400 MW	38790 TQ	USBLS	5/15
	South Dakota	Y	29420 FQ	35260 MW	41710 TQ	USBLS	5/15
	Sioux Falls MSA, SD	Y	27700 FQ	34310 MW	41060 TQ	USBLS	5/15
	Tennessee	Y	28260 FQ	35770 MW	44790 TQ	USBLS	5/15
	Knoxville MSA, TN	Y	24580 FQ	29990 MW	40290 TQ	USBLS	5/15
	Memphis MSA, TN-MS-AR	Y	30410 FQ	39150 MW	47590 TQ	USBLS	5/15
	Nashville-Davidson–Murfreesboro–Franklin MSA, TN	Y	29350 FQ	36140 MW	44780 TQ	USBLS	5/15
	Texas	Y	29630 FQ	36980 MW	46650 TQ	USBLS	5/15
	Austin-Round Rock MSA, TX	Y	31510 FQ	40530 MW	48850 TQ	USBLS	5/15
	Dallas-Plano-Irving PMSA, TX	Y	31300 FQ	37300 MW	47710 TQ	USBLS	5/15
	Fort Worth-Arlington PMSA, TX	Y	28470 FQ	35510 MW	44350 TQ	USBLS	5/15
	Houston-The Woodlands-Sugar Land MSA, TX	Y	30910 FQ	38410 MW	47790 TQ	USBLS	5/15
	San Antonio-New Braunfels MSA, TX	Y	28290 FQ	35570 MW	45340 TQ	USBLS	5/15
	Utah	Y	26430 FQ	31000 MW	37900 TQ	USBLS	5/15
	Ogden-Clearfield MSA, UT	Y	26290 FQ	32510 MW	50330 TQ	USBLS	5/15
	Provo-Orem MSA, UT	Y	28510 FQ	34470 MW	39630 TQ	USBLS	5/15
	Salt Lake City MSA, UT	Y	26390 FQ	30720 MW	37400 TQ	USBLS	5/15
	Vermont	Y	45490 FQ	55430 MW	65740 TQ	USBLS	5/15
	Burlington-South Burlington MSA, VT	Y	44070 FQ	55520 MW	67400 TQ	USBLS	5/15
	Virginia	Y	29610 FQ	37000 MW	46980 TQ	USBLS	5/15
	Richmond MSA, VA	Y	28040 FQ	35670 MW	45080 TQ	USBLS	5/15
	Virginia Beach-Norfolk-Newport News MSA, VA-NC	Y	28600 FQ	37110 MW	46170 TQ	USBLS	5/15
	Washington	H	17.54 FQ	21.49 MW	26.23 TQ	WABLS	3/16
	Seattle-Bellevue-Everett PMSA, WA	H	17.84 FQ	21.19 MW	24.51 TQ	WABLS	3/16
	Tacoma-Lakewood PMSA, WA	H	14.85 FQ	18.85 MW	23.47 TQ	WABLS	3/16
	West Virginia	Y	28410 FQ	36630 MW	46340 TQ	USBLS	5/15
	Huntington-Ashland MSA, WV-KY-OH	Y	31150 FQ	37120 MW	47790 TQ	USBLS	5/15
	Wisconsin	Y	36140 FQ	43940 MW	54240 TQ	USBLS	5/15

AE Average entry wage	**AWR** Average wage range	**H** Hourly	**LR** Low end range	**MTC** Median total compensation	**TCC** Total cash compensation
AEX Average experienced wage	**B** Biweekly	**HI** Highest wage paid	**M** Monthly	**MW** Median wage paid	**TQ** Third quartile wage
ATC Average total compensation	**D** Daily	**HR** High end range	**MCC** Median cash compensation	**MWR** Median wage range	**W** Weekly
AW Average wage paid	**FQ** First quartile wage	**LO** Lowest wage paid	**ME** Median entry wage	**S** See annotated source	**Y** Yearly

Occupation/Type/Industry	Location	Per	Low	Mid	High	Source	Date
Medical and Clinical Laboratory Technician	Madison MSA, WI	Y	37630 FQ	45890 MW	56820 TQ	USBLS	5/15
	Milwaukee-Waukesha-West Allis MSA, WI	Y	36000 FQ	44290 MW	57940 TQ	USBLS	5/15
	Wyoming	Y	33370 FQ	40720 MW	48340 TQ	USBLS	5/15
	Cheyenne MSA, WY	Y	30960 FQ	34980 MW	39420 TQ	USBLS	5/15
	Puerto Rico	Y	17810 FQ	21040 MW	27990 TQ	USBLS	5/15
	San Juan-Carolina-Caguas MSA, PR	Y	17360 FQ	19420 MW	29750 TQ	USBLS	5/15
	Guam	Y	23780 FQ	27970 MW	33440 TQ	USBLS	5/15
Medical and Clinical Laboratory Technologist	Alabama	Y	40355 AE	54259 AW	61221 AEX	ALBLS	6/16
	Birmingham-Hoover MSA, AL	Y	44106 AE	58591 AW	44106 AEX	ALBLS	6/16
	Alaska	Y	58780 FQ	70440 MW	81030 TQ	USBLS	5/15
	Anchorage MSA, AK	Y	59560 FQ	71370 MW	82580 TQ	USBLS	5/15
	Arizona	Y	51690 FQ	59510 MW	69870 TQ	USBLS	5/15
	Phoenix-Mesa-Scottsdale MSA, AZ	Y	49590 FQ	61860 MW	73620 TQ	USBLS	5/15
	Tucson MSA, AZ	Y	52380 FQ	57000 MW	61590 TQ	USBLS	5/15
	Arkansas	Y	39430 FQ	51050 MW	61310 TQ	USBLS	5/15
	Little Rock-North Little Rock-Conway MSA, AR	Y	40920 FQ	54910 MW	64430 TQ	USBLS	5/15
	California	H	33.27 FQ	40.55 MW	47.84 TQ	CABLS	1/16-3/16
	Anaheim-Santa Ana-Irvine PMSA, CA	H	30.92 FQ	36.39 MW	43.64 TQ	CABLS	1/16-3/16
	Los Angeles-Long Beach-Glendale PMSA, CA	H	34.44 FQ	41.13 MW	47.33 TQ	CABLS	1/16-3/16
	Oakland-Hayward-Berkeley PMSA, CA	H	30.08 FQ	40.10 MW	49.61 TQ	CABLS	1/16-3/16
	Riverside-San Bernardino-Ontario MSA, CA	H	33.44 FQ	40.26 MW	45.95 TQ	CABLS	1/16-3/16
	Sacramento–Roseville–Arden-Arcade MSA, CA	H	40.48 FQ	47.27 MW	55.92 TQ	CABLS	1/16-3/16
	San Diego-Carlsbad MSA, CA	H	31.74 FQ	37.64 MW	44.88 TQ	CABLS	1/16-3/16
	San Francisco-Redwood City-South San Francisco PMSA, CA	H	29.69 FQ	40.03 MW	51.23 TQ	CABLS	1/16-3/16
	Colorado	Y	53240 FQ	63740 MW	74610 TQ	USBLS	5/15
	Denver-Aurora-Lakewood MSA, CO	Y	52680 FQ	63860 MW	75000 TQ	USBLS	5/15
	Connecticut	Y		72039 MW		CTBLS	1/16-3/16
	Bridgeport-Stamford-Norwalk MSA, CT	Y	61280 FQ	71140 MW	81870 TQ	USBLS	5/15
	Hartford-West Hartford-East Hartford MSA, CT	Y	61540 FQ	73610 MW	87410 TQ	USBLS	5/15
	Delaware	Y	56420 FQ	65900 MW	73580 TQ	USBLS	5/15
	Wilmington PMSA, DE-MD-NJ	Y	59030 FQ	67200 MW	73930 TQ	USBLS	5/15
	District of Columbia	Y	57590 FQ	69480 MW	80710 TQ	USBLS	5/15
	Washington-Arlington-Alexandria PMSA, DC-VA-MD-WV	Y	54510 FQ	64930 MW	76470 TQ	USBLS	5/15
	Florida	H	24.63 AE	29.12 MW	32.24 AEX	FLBLS	7/16-9/16
	Fort Lauderdale-Pompano Beach-Deerfield Beach PMSA, FL	H	26.02 AE	30.06 MW	33.17 AEX	FLBLS	7/16-9/16
	Miami-Miami Beach-Kendall PMSA, FL	H	24.98 AE	30.27 MW	33.57 AEX	FLBLS	7/16-9/16
	Orlando-Kissimmee-Sanford MSA, FL	H	23.28 AE	28.51 MW	32.40 AEX	FLBLS	7/16-9/16
	Tampa-St. Petersburg-Clearwater MSA, FL	H	25.44 AE	29.42 MW	32.30 AEX	FLBLS	7/16-9/16
	Georgia	Y	48980 FQ	58190 MW	68470 TQ	USBLS	5/15
	Atlanta-Sandy Springs-Roswell MSA, GA	Y	51260 FQ	60340 MW	70700 TQ	USBLS	5/15
	Augusta-Richmond County MSA, GA-SC	Y	49150 FQ	55980 MW	62930 TQ	USBLS	5/15
	Hawaii	Y	57360 FQ	67570 MW	76570 TQ	USBLS	5/15
	Urban Honolulu MSA, HI	Y	58880 FQ	68290 MW	76980 TQ	USBLS	5/15
	Idaho	Y	53020 FQ	60450 MW	70030 TQ	USBLS	5/15

AE	Average entry wage	**AWR**	Average wage range	**H**	Hourly	**LR**	Low end range	**MTC**	Median total compensation	**TCC**	Total cash compensation
AEX	Average experienced wage	**B**	Biweekly	**HI**	Highest wage paid	**M**	Monthly	**MWR**	Median wage range	**TQ**	Third quartile wage
ATC	Average total compensation	**D**	Daily	**HR**	High end range	**MCC**	Median cash compensation	**MWR**	Median wage range	**W**	Weekly
AW	Average wage paid	**FQ**	First quartile wage	**LO**	Lowest wage paid	**ME**	Median entry wage	**S**	See annotated source	**Y**	Yearly

995

Medical and Clinical Laboratory Technologist

Occupation/Type/Industry	Location	Per	Low	Mid	High	Source	Date
	Boise City MSA, ID	Y	53240 FQ	60110 MW	69550 TQ	USBLS	5/15
	Illinois	Y	50530 FQ	60080 MW	73230 TQ	USBLS	5/15
	Chicago-Naperville-Arlington Heights PMSA, IL	Y	51450 FQ	60710 MW	73160 TQ	USBLS	5/15
	Lake County-Kenosha County PMSA, IL-WI	Y	57710 FQ	70200 MW	88000 TQ	USBLS	5/15
	Indiana	Y	47820 FQ	58260 MW	70140 TQ	USBLS	5/15
	Gary PMSA, IN	Y	50230 FQ	58670 MW	68610 TQ	USBLS	5/15
	Indianapolis-Carmel-Anderson MSA, IN	Y	49910 FQ	62210 MW	74710 TQ	USBLS	5/15
	Iowa	Y	46410 FQ	54770 MW	61980 TQ	USBLS	5/15
	Des Moines-West Des Moines MSA, IA	Y	49640 FQ	57160 MW	64420 TQ	USBLS	5/15
	Kansas	Y	44760 FQ	55140 MW	65400 TQ	USBLS	5/15
	Wichita MSA, KS	Y	45250 FQ	54000 MW	64320 TQ	USBLS	5/15
	Kentucky	Y	48490 FQ	56760 MW	65300 TQ	USBLS	5/15
	Louisville-Jefferson County MSA, KY-IN	Y	50340 FQ	60430 MW	70280 TQ	USBLS	5/15
	Louisiana	Y	41070 FQ	50270 MW	59130 TQ	USBLS	5/15
	Baton Rouge MSA, LA	Y	39550 FQ	47820 MW	59590 TQ	USBLS	5/15
	New Orleans-Metairie MSA, LA	Y	43720 FQ	52210 MW	59390 TQ	USBLS	5/15
	Maine	Y	49480 FQ	56140 MW	62420 TQ	USBLS	5/15
	Portland-South Portland MSA, ME	Y	48370 FQ	55510 MW	61890 TQ	USBLS	5/15
	Maryland	Y	40025 AE	59471 MW	69195 AEX	MDBLS	4/16
	Baltimore-Columbia-Towson MSA, MD	Y	44530 FQ	55380 MW	70930 TQ	USBLS	5/15
	Salisbury MSA, MD-DE	Y	46880 FQ	57760 MW	70260 TQ	USBLS	5/15
	Massachusetts	Y	60170 FQ	71830 MW	84370 TQ	USBLS	5/15
	Boston-Cambridge-Newton NECTA, MA	Y	61210 FQ	73080 MW	87100 TQ	USBLS	5/15
	Worcester MSA, MA-CT	Y	57950 FQ	70710 MW	83480 TQ	USBLS	5/15
	Michigan	Y	49710 FQ	57450 MW	65910 TQ	USBLS	5/15
	Detroit-Dearborn-Livonia PMSA, MI	Y	51160 FQ	58370 MW	66820 TQ	USBLS	5/15
	Grand Rapids-Wyoming MSA, MI	Y	50700 FQ	57550 MW	65450 TQ	USBLS	5/15
	Minnesota	Y	55634 FQ	65160 MW	74838 TQ	MNBLS	1/16-3/16
	Minneapolis-St. Paul-Bloomington MSA, MN-WI	Y	54062 FQ	64435 MW	73991 TQ	MNBLS	1/16-3/16
	Mississippi	Y	44580 FQ	55970 MW	68150 TQ	USBLS	5/15
	Jackson MSA, MS	Y	46590 FQ	58080 MW	69770 TQ	USBLS	5/15
	Missouri	Y	48300 FQ	57570 MW	67340 TQ	USBLS	5/15
	Kansas City MSA, MO-KS	Y	48680 FQ	58830 MW	69330 TQ	USBLS	5/15
	St. Louis MSA, MO-IL	Y	50360 FQ	58470 MW	68030 TQ	USBLS	5/15
	Montana	Y	51300 FQ	59930 MW	69500 TQ	USBLS	5/15
	Billings MSA, MT	Y	56310 FQ	63780 MW	73290 TQ	USBLS	5/15
	Nebraska	Y	46135 FQ	55030 MW	63910 TQ	NEBLS	7/16-9/16
	Omaha-Council Bluffs MSA, NE-IA	Y	44555 FQ	53435 MW	62940 TQ	NEBLS	7/16-9/16
	Nevada	Y	55000 FQ	68890 MW	80280 TQ	USBLS	5/15
	Las Vegas-Henderson-Paradise MSA, NV	Y	54770 FQ	68150 MW	79040 TQ	USBLS	5/15
	New Hampshire	H	25.34 AE	32.22 MW	35.25 AEX	NHBLS	6/16
	New Jersey	Y	58730 FQ	68610 MW	77030 TQ	USBLS	5/15
	Camden PMSA, NJ	Y	57560 FQ	66580 MW	75420 TQ	USBLS	5/15
	Newark PMSA, NJ-PA	Y	56080 FQ	67050 MW	76030 TQ	USBLS	5/15
	Trenton MSA, NJ	Y	59780 FQ	70120 MW	79190 TQ	USBLS	5/15
	New Mexico	Y	36560 FQ	47020 MW	58860 TQ	USBLS	5/15
	Albuquerque MSA, NM	Y	37220 FQ	46860 MW	58330 TQ	USBLS	5/15
	New York	Y	53040 AE	67310 MW	74840 AEX	NYBLS	1/16-3/16
	Buffalo-Cheektowaga-Niagara Falls MSA, NY	Y	51870 FQ	57630 MW	64470 TQ	USBLS	5/15
	Nassau County-Suffolk County PMSA, NY	Y	66200 FQ	72470 MW	79000 TQ	USBLS	5/15
	New York-Jersey City-White Plains PMSA, NY-NJ	Y	59770 FQ	69370 MW	77910 TQ	USBLS	5/15
	Rochester MSA, NY	Y	51460 FQ	57540 MW	64590 TQ	USBLS	5/15
	North Carolina	Y	50660 FQ	57310 MW	64410 TQ	USBLS	5/15

AE Average entry wage	**AWR** Average wage range	**H** Hourly	**LR** Low end range	**MTC** Median total compensation	**TCC** Total cash compensation
AEX Average experienced wage	**B** Biweekly	**HI** Highest wage paid	**M** Monthly	**MW** Median wage paid	**TQ** Third quartile wage
ATC Average total compensation	**D** Daily	**HR** High end range	**MCC** Median cash compensation	**MWR** Median wage range	**W** Weekly
AW Average wage paid	**FQ** First quartile wage	**LO** Lowest wage paid	**ME** Median entry wage	**S** See annotated source	**Y** Yearly

Occupation/Type/Industry	Location	Per	Low	Mid	High	Source	Date
Medical and Clinical Laboratory Technologist	Charlotte-Concord-Gastonia MSA, NC-SC	Y	50840 FQ	56960 MW	63250 TQ	USBLS	5/15
	Raleigh MSA, NC	Y	45410 FQ	54720 MW	62860 TQ	USBLS	5/15
	North Dakota	Y	44880 FQ	53200 MW	61270 TQ	USBLS	5/15
	Fargo MSA, ND-MN	Y	43190 FQ	51440 MW	58860 TQ	USBLS	5/15
	Ohio	Y	52080 FQ	58060 MW	64820 TQ	USBLS	5/15
	Cincinnati MSA, OH-KY-IN	Y	50040 FQ	58920 MW	69810 TQ	USBLS	5/15
	Cleveland-Elyria MSA, OH	Y	53160 FQ	58320 MW	63530 TQ	USBLS	5/15
	Columbus MSA, OH	Y	50170 FQ	57110 MW	64280 TQ	USBLS	5/15
	Oklahoma	Y	45450 FQ	55380 MW	64740 TQ	USBLS	5/15
	Oklahoma City MSA, OK	Y	47660 FQ	58280 MW	69710 TQ	USBLS	5/15
	Tulsa MSA, OK	Y	45270 FQ	53160 MW	61270 TQ	USBLS	5/15
	Oregon	H	28.45 FQ	33.75 MW	37.86 TQ	ORBLS	2016
	Portland-Vancouver-Hillsboro MSA, OR-WA	Y	56640 FQ	69090 MW	77670 TQ	USBLS	5/15
	Pennsylvania	Y	49350 FQ	58240 MW	69200 TQ	USBLS	5/15
	Allentown-Bethlehem-Easton MSA, PA-NJ	Y	51490 FQ	58680 MW	68520 TQ	USBLS	5/15
	Harrisburg-Carlisle MSA, PA	Y	53470 FQ	61740 MW	72030 TQ	USBLS	5/15
	Montgomery County-Bucks County-Chester County PMSA, PA	Y	54830 FQ	66590 MW	77320 TQ	USBLS	5/15
	Philadelphia PMSA, PA	Y	47440 FQ	59660 MW	71810 TQ	USBLS	5/15
	Pittsburgh MSA, PA	Y	47620 FQ	55120 MW	61470 TQ	USBLS	5/15
	Rhode Island	Y	58730 FQ	69490 MW	78380 TQ	USBLS	5/15
	Providence-Warwick MSA, RI-MA	Y	58270 FQ	69560 MW	78930 TQ	USBLS	5/15
	South Carolina	Y	35920 FQ	48870 MW	61540 TQ	USBLS	5/15
	Charleston-North Charleston MSA, SC	Y	42930 FQ	54730 MW	64350 TQ	USBLS	5/15
	Columbia MSA, SC	Y	34190 FQ	45600 MW	58090 TQ	USBLS	5/15
	Greenville-Anderson-Mauldin MSA, SC	Y	40800 FQ	54640 MW	67280 TQ	USBLS	5/15
	South Dakota	Y	43340 FQ	51120 MW	62930 TQ	USBLS	5/15
	Tennessee	Y	50440 FQ	59140 MW	70100 TQ	USBLS	5/15
	Knoxville MSA, TN	Y	45520 FQ	54520 MW	62380 TQ	USBLS	5/15
	Memphis MSA, TN-MS-AR	Y	55390 FQ	63800 MW	75750 TQ	USBLS	5/15
	Nashville-Davidson–Murfreesboro–Franklin MSA, TN	Y	51680 FQ	59690 MW	70300 TQ	USBLS	5/15
	Texas	Y	49270 FQ	58170 MW	69340 TQ	USBLS	5/15
	Austin-Round Rock MSA, TX	Y	44310 FQ	52640 MW	61400 TQ	USBLS	5/15
	Dallas-Plano-Irving PMSA, TX	Y	53220 FQ	61690 MW	74410 TQ	USBLS	5/15
	Fort Worth-Arlington PMSA, TX	Y	48130 FQ	59090 MW	70260 TQ	USBLS	5/15
	Houston-The Woodlands-Sugar Land MSA, TX	Y	52510 FQ	61120 MW	72140 TQ	USBLS	5/15
	San Antonio-New Braunfels MSA, TX	Y	44810 FQ	54850 MW	63060 TQ	USBLS	5/15
	Utah	Y	41730 FQ	51040 MW	62920 TQ	USBLS	5/15
	Ogden-Clearfield MSA, UT	Y	32280 FQ	45060 MW	65670 TQ	USBLS	5/15
	Provo-Orem MSA, UT	Y	45230 FQ	54450 MW	66520 TQ	USBLS	5/15
	Salt Lake City MSA, UT	Y	41640 FQ	50450 MW	61390 TQ	USBLS	5/15
	Vermont	Y	56580 FQ	67510 MW	79050 TQ	USBLS	5/15
	Virginia	Y	48960 FQ	58020 MW	68850 TQ	USBLS	5/15
	Richmond MSA, VA	Y	52380 FQ	59380 MW	68270 TQ	USBLS	5/15
	Virginia Beach-Norfolk-Newport News MSA, VA-NC	Y	44820 FQ	53580 MW	61310 TQ	USBLS	5/15
	Washington	H	28.05 FQ	33.19 MW	38.08 TQ	WABLS	3/16
	Seattle-Bellevue-Everett PMSA, WA	H	28.18 FQ	33.36 MW	38.22 TQ	WABLS	3/16
	Tacoma-Lakewood PMSA, WA	H	28.55 FQ	33.04 MW	37.97 TQ	WABLS	3/16
	West Virginia	Y	43940 FQ	52900 MW	60680 TQ	USBLS	5/15
	Huntington-Ashland MSA, WV-KY-OH	Y	51230 FQ	60230 MW	70320 TQ	USBLS	5/15
	Wisconsin	Y	48640 FQ	57480 MW	67450 TQ	USBLS	5/15
	Madison MSA, WI	Y	52540 FQ	60770 MW	72830 TQ	USBLS	5/15
	Milwaukee-Waukesha-West Allis MSA, WI	Y	46270 FQ	56770 MW	67890 TQ	USBLS	5/15
	Wyoming	Y	53110 FQ	61020 MW	70270 TQ	USBLS	5/15
	Cheyenne MSA, WY	Y	52030 FQ	63890 MW	70270 TQ	USBLS	5/15

AE Average entry wage	**AWR** Average wage range	**H** Hourly	**LR** Low end range	**MTC** Median total compensation	**TCC** Total cash compensation
AEX Average experienced wage	**B** Biweekly	**HI** Highest wage paid	**M** Monthly	**MW** Median wage paid	**TQ** Third quartile wage
ATC Average total compensation	**D** Daily	**HR** High end range	**MCC** Median cash compensation	**MWR** Median wage range	**W** Weekly
AW Average wage paid	**FQ** First quartile wage	**LO** Lowest wage paid	**ME** Median entry wage	**S** See annotated source	**Y** Yearly

Occupation/Type/Industry	Location	Per	Low	Mid	High	Source	Date
Medical and Clinical Laboratory Technologist	Puerto Rico	Y	24520 FQ	30510 MW	37610 TQ	USBLS	5/15
	San Juan-Carolina-Caguas MSA, PR	Y	26200 FQ	32640 MW	38840 TQ	USBLS	5/15
Medical and Health Services Manager	Alabama	Y	64347 AE	101512 AW	120095 AEX	ALBLS	6/16
	Birmingham-Hoover MSA, AL	Y	68570 AE	111270 AW	132609 AEX	ALBLS	6/16
	Alaska	Y	84350 FQ	107530 MW	133290 TQ	USBLS	5/15
	Anchorage MSA, AK	Y	81020 FQ	107560 MW	157330 TQ	USBLS	5/15
	Arizona	Y	72400 FQ	92780 MW	122750 TQ	USBLS	5/15
	Phoenix-Mesa-Scottsdale MSA, AZ	Y	72650 FQ	92480 MW	123950 TQ	USBLS	5/15
	Tucson MSA, AZ	Y	65690 FQ	91590 MW	125150 TQ	USBLS	5/15
	Arkansas	Y	57720 FQ	74100 MW	97380 TQ	USBLS	5/15
	Little Rock-North Little Rock-Conway MSA, AR	Y	66470 FQ	84810 MW	113870 TQ	USBLS	5/15
	California	H	40.88 FQ	57.89 MW	75.24 TQ	CABLS	1/16-3/16
	Anaheim-Santa Ana-Irvine PMSA, CA	H	30.38 FQ	43.85 MW	62.98 TQ	CABLS	1/16-3/16
	Los Angeles-Long Beach-Glendale PMSA, CA	H	40.79 FQ	56.73 MW	71.94 TQ	CABLS	1/16-3/16
	Oakland-Hayward-Berkeley PMSA, CA	H	48.28 FQ	67.79 MW	82.12 TQ	CABLS	1/16-3/16
	Riverside-San Bernardino-Ontario MSA, CA	H	35.48 FQ	51.57 MW	64.76 TQ	CABLS	1/16-3/16
	Sacramento–Roseville–Arden-Arcade MSA, CA	H	46.75 FQ	67.18 MW	80.49 TQ	CABLS	1/16-3/16
	San Diego-Carlsbad MSA, CA	H	38.58 FQ	54.76 MW	68.63 TQ	CABLS	1/16-3/16
	San Francisco-Redwood City-South San Francisco PMSA, CA	H	56.69 FQ	72.68 MW	87.23 TQ	CABLS	1/16-3/16
	Colorado	Y	79070 FQ	102380 MW	132210 TQ	USBLS	5/15
	Denver-Aurora-Lakewood MSA, CO	Y	84090 FQ	110820 MW	140700 TQ	USBLS	5/15
	Connecticut	Y		109580 MW		CTBLS	1/16-3/16
	Bridgeport-Stamford-Norwalk MSA, CT	Y	87370 FQ	108310 MW	148620 TQ	USBLS	5/15
	Hartford-West Hartford-East Hartford MSA, CT	Y	85510 FQ	104330 MW	149010 TQ	USBLS	5/15
	Delaware	Y	86210 FQ	102560 MW	126720 TQ	USBLS	5/15
	Wilmington PMSA, DE-MD-NJ	Y	87370 FQ	103820 MW	129220 TQ	USBLS	5/15
	District of Columbia	Y	95090 FQ	121620 MW	158680 TQ	USBLS	5/15
	Washington-Arlington-Alexandria PMSA, DC-VA-MD-WV	Y	88310 FQ	109510 MW	139510 TQ	USBLS	5/15
	Florida	H	34.96 AE	49.43 MW	66.33 AEX	FLBLS	7/16-9/16
	Fort Lauderdale-Pompano Beach-Deerfield Beach PMSA, FL	H	40.46 AE	54.32 MW	78.57 AEX	FLBLS	7/16-9/16
	Miami-Miami Beach-Kendall PMSA, FL	H	34.46 AE	52.72 MW	68.68 AEX	FLBLS	7/16-9/16
	Orlando-Kissimmee-Sanford MSA, FL	H	36.68 AE	55.26 MW	72.05 AEX	FLBLS	7/16-9/16
	Tampa-St. Petersburg-Clearwater MSA, FL	H	36.07 AE	49.79 MW	65.42 AEX	FLBLS	7/16-9/16
	Georgia	Y	69700 FQ	91330 MW	119220 TQ	USBLS	5/15
	Atlanta-Sandy Springs-Roswell MSA, GA	Y	72060 FQ	97600 MW	124770 TQ	USBLS	5/15
	Augusta-Richmond County MSA, GA-SC	Y	70570 FQ	86580 MW	115490 TQ	USBLS	5/15
	Hawaii	Y	81760 FQ	104250 MW	133050 TQ	USBLS	5/15
	Urban Honolulu MSA, HI	Y	89270 FQ	110100 MW	138520 TQ	USBLS	5/15
	Idaho	Y	58200 FQ	76860 MW	97600 TQ	USBLS	5/15
	Boise City MSA, ID	Y	59470 FQ	78880 MW	97650 TQ	USBLS	5/15
	Illinois	Y	72220 FQ	94820 MW	119500 TQ	USBLS	5/15
	Chicago-Naperville-Arlington Heights PMSA, IL	Y	79340 FQ	100220 MW	123500 TQ	USBLS	5/15
	Lake County-Kenosha County PMSA, IL-WI	Y	65050 FQ	93700 MW	121860 TQ	USBLS	5/15

AE	Average entry wage	AWR	Average wage range	H	Hourly
AEX	Average experienced wage	B	Biweekly	HI	Highest wage paid
ATC	Average total compensation	D	Daily	HR	High end range
AW	Average wage paid	FQ	First quartile wage	LO	Lowest wage paid

LR	Low end range	MTC	Median total compensation	TCC	Total cash compensation
M	Monthly	MW	Median wage paid	TQ	Third quartile wage
MCC	Median cash compensation	MWR	Median wage range	W	Weekly
ME	Median entry wage	S	See annotated source	Y	Yearly

Occupation/Type/Industry	Location	Per	Low	Mid	High	Source	Date
Medical and Health Services Manager	Indiana	Y	62390 FQ	80580 MW	100470 TQ	USBLS	5/15
	Gary PMSA, IN	Y	58790 FQ	83230 MW	100180 TQ	USBLS	5/15
	Indianapolis-Carmel-Anderson MSA, IN	Y	66850 FQ	86960 MW	113520 TQ	USBLS	5/15
	Iowa	Y	58580 FQ	73940 MW	94140 TQ	USBLS	5/15
	Des Moines-West Des Moines MSA, IA	Y	62170 FQ	78060 MW	96950 TQ	USBLS	5/15
	Kansas	Y	61810 FQ	75470 MW	95190 TQ	USBLS	5/15
	Wichita MSA, KS	Y	59410 FQ	73040 MW	91040 TQ	USBLS	5/15
	Kentucky	Y	64150 FQ	81170 MW	107350 TQ	USBLS	5/15
	Louisville-Jefferson County MSA, KY-IN	Y	67910 FQ	84720 MW	112820 TQ	USBLS	5/15
	Louisiana	Y	67690 FQ	81470 MW	99700 TQ	USBLS	5/15
	Baton Rouge MSA, LA	Y	67750 FQ	83760 MW	107160 TQ	USBLS	5/15
	New Orleans-Metairie MSA, LA	Y	71050 FQ	84640 MW	101930 TQ	USBLS	5/15
	Maine	Y	67250 FQ	82390 MW	104210 TQ	USBLS	5/15
	Portland-South Portland MSA, ME	Y	73240 FQ	87890 MW	111590 TQ	USBLS	5/15
	Maryland	Y	72875 AE	111420 MW	130693 AEX	MDBLS	4/16
	Baltimore-Columbia-Towson MSA, MD	Y	78290 FQ	96660 MW	124660 TQ	USBLS	5/15
	Salisbury MSA, MD-DE	Y	68770 FQ	88470 MW	112760 TQ	USBLS	5/15
	Massachusetts	Y	79720 FQ	100130 MW	131530 TQ	USBLS	5/15
	Boston-Cambridge-Newton NECTA, MA	Y	85250 FQ	107470 MW	143550 TQ	USBLS	5/15
	Worcester MSA, MA-CT	Y	70310 FQ	91410 MW	119390 TQ	USBLS	5/15
	Michigan	Y	68770 FQ	88050 MW	114430 TQ	USBLS	5/15
	Detroit-Dearborn-Livonia PMSA, MI	Y	75190 FQ	95720 MW	126810 TQ	USBLS	5/15
	Grand Rapids-Wyoming MSA, MI	Y	71070 FQ	86670 MW	116950 TQ	USBLS	5/15
	Minnesota	Y	74684 FQ	95219 MW	120276 TQ	MNBLS	1/16-3/16
	Minneapolis-St. Paul-Bloomington MSA, MN-WI	Y	78270 FQ	98257 MW	123406 TQ	MNBLS	1/16-3/16
	Mississippi	Y	57390 FQ	75130 MW	96370 TQ	USBLS	5/15
	Jackson MSA, MS	Y	67990 FQ	84500 MW	105720 TQ	USBLS	5/15
	Missouri	Y	70370 FQ	91280 MW	117640 TQ	USBLS	5/15
	Kansas City MSA, MO-KS	Y	73110 FQ	90600 MW	114450 TQ	USBLS	5/15
	St. Louis MSA, MO-IL	Y	75120 FQ	94850 MW	122740 TQ	USBLS	5/15
	Montana	Y	62680 FQ	80350 MW	101170 TQ	USBLS	5/15
	Billings MSA, MT	Y	72170 FQ	88700 MW	106940 TQ	USBLS	5/15
	Nebraska	Y	68100 FQ	85855 MW	108825 TQ	NEBLS	7/16-9/16
	Omaha-Council Bluffs MSA, NE-IA	Y	71335 FQ	89755 MW	114320 TQ	NEBLS	7/16-9/16
	Nevada	Y	70580 FQ	98720 MW	125870 TQ	USBLS	5/15
	Las Vegas-Henderson-Paradise MSA, NV	Y	66210 FQ	97220 MW	124350 TQ	USBLS	5/15
	New Hampshire	H	33.22 AE	46.18 MW	61.48 AEX	NHBLS	6/16
	Manchester NECTA, NH	H	36.48 AE	48.87 MW	65.16 AEX	NHBLS	6/16
	Nashua NECTA, NH-MA	Y	70560 FQ	83980 MW	99830 TQ	USBLS	5/15
	New Jersey	Y	93150 FQ	110930 MW	129760 TQ	USBLS	5/15
	Camden PMSA, NJ	Y	92890 FQ	111730 MW	128580 TQ	USBLS	5/15
	Newark PMSA, NJ-PA	Y	93900 FQ	111810 MW	131800 TQ	USBLS	5/15
	Trenton MSA, NJ	Y	89680 FQ	106140 MW	129330 TQ	USBLS	5/15
	New Mexico	Y	66520 FQ	87810 MW	112880 TQ	USBLS	5/15
	Albuquerque MSA, NM	Y	63840 FQ	88940 MW	115870 TQ	USBLS	5/15
	New York	Y	78990 AE	116290 MW	157710 AEX	NYBLS	1/16-3/16
	Buffalo-Cheektowaga-Niagara Falls MSA, NY	Y	78230 FQ	95080 MW	121720 TQ	USBLS	5/15
	Nassau County-Suffolk County PMSA, NY	Y	103250 FQ	123010 MW	163100 TQ	USBLS	5/15
	New York-Jersey City-White Plains PMSA, NY-NJ	Y	94230 FQ	118190 MW	150840 TQ	USBLS	5/15
	Rochester MSA, NY	Y	72890 FQ	90400 MW	120300 TQ	USBLS	5/15
	North Carolina	Y	77450 FQ	94580 MW	121120 TQ	USBLS	5/15
	Charlotte-Concord-Gastonia MSA, NC-SC	Y	77540 FQ	95090 MW	128620 TQ	USBLS	5/15
	Raleigh MSA, NC	Y	75600 FQ	93370 MW	117910 TQ	USBLS	5/15
	North Dakota	Y	65110 FQ	78660 MW	100210 TQ	USBLS	5/15
	Fargo MSA, ND-MN	Y	69960 FQ	92130 MW	124290 TQ	USBLS	5/15

AE	Average entry wage	AWR	Average wage range	H	Hourly
AEX	Average experienced wage	B	Biweekly	HI	Highest wage paid
ATC	Average total compensation	D	Daily	HR	High end range
AW	Average wage paid	FQ	First quartile wage	LO	Lowest wage paid

LR	Low end range	MTC	Median total compensation	TCC	Total cash compensation
M	Monthly	MW	Median wage paid	TQ	Third quartile wage
MCC	Median cash compensation	MWR	Median wage range	W	Weekly
ME	Median entry wage	S	See annotated source	Y	Yearly

Occupation/Type/Industry	Location	Per	Low	Mid	High	Source	Date
Medical and Health Services Manager	Ohio	Y	71370 FQ	87430 MW	109500 TQ	USBLS	5/15
	Cincinnati MSA, OH-KY-IN	Y	76230 FQ	93780 MW	117610 TQ	USBLS	5/15
	Cleveland-Elyria MSA, OH	Y	73680 FQ	89180 MW	109930 TQ	USBLS	5/15
	Columbus MSA, OH	Y	71890 FQ	90490 MW	116360 TQ	USBLS	5/15
	Oklahoma	Y	59490 FQ	75800 MW	96990 TQ	USBLS	5/15
	Oklahoma City MSA, OK	Y	58390 FQ	76180 MW	101310 TQ	USBLS	5/15
	Tulsa MSA, OK	Y	63980 FQ	76730 MW	94140 TQ	USBLS	5/15
	Oregon	H	35.74 FQ	48.09 MW	63.21 TQ	ORBLS	2016
	Portland-Vancouver-Hillsboro MSA, OR-WA	Y	74460 FQ	102180 MW	144500 TQ	USBLS	5/15
	Pennsylvania	Y	65530 FQ	85930 MW	112510 TQ	USBLS	5/15
	Allentown-Bethlehem-Easton MSA, PA-NJ	Y	66550 FQ	84620 MW	101460 TQ	USBLS	5/15
	Harrisburg-Carlisle MSA, PA	Y	66970 FQ	87660 MW	126070 TQ	USBLS	5/15
	Montgomery County-Bucks County-Chester County PMSA, PA	Y	73760 FQ	93710 MW	115580 TQ	USBLS	5/15
	Philadelphia PMSA, PA	Y	79260 FQ	100850 MW	129510 TQ	USBLS	5/15
	Pittsburgh MSA, PA	Y	63230 FQ	78860 MW	106030 TQ	USBLS	5/15
	Rhode Island	Y	80520 FQ	99920 MW	128110 TQ	USBLS	5/15
	Providence-Warwick MSA, RI-MA	Y	77280 FQ	97240 MW	124530 TQ	USBLS	5/15
	South Carolina	Y	62790 FQ	81320 MW	107690 TQ	USBLS	5/15
	Charleston-North Charleston MSA, SC	Y	70960 FQ	89710 MW	116990 TQ	USBLS	5/15
	Columbia MSA, SC	Y	59210 FQ	78840 MW	109290 TQ	USBLS	5/15
	Greenville-Anderson-Mauldin MSA, SC	Y	53180 FQ	69440 MW	94720 TQ	USBLS	5/15
	South Dakota	Y	77460 FQ	96580 MW	116980 TQ	USBLS	5/15
	Sioux Falls MSA, SD	Y	83280 FQ	104800 MW	124810 TQ	USBLS	5/15
	Tennessee	Y	61990 FQ	80090 MW	104340 TQ	USBLS	5/15
	Knoxville MSA, TN	Y	58900 FQ	73590 MW	92950 TQ	USBLS	5/15
	Memphis MSA, TN-MS-AR	Y	68240 FQ	89480 MW	113770 TQ	USBLS	5/15
	Nashville-Davidson–Murfreesboro–Franklin MSA, TN	Y	64140 FQ	84460 MW	115870 TQ	USBLS	5/15
	Texas	Y	70980 FQ	91310 MW	117240 TQ	USBLS	5/15
	Austin-Round Rock MSA, TX	Y	73040 FQ	89470 MW	103590 TQ	USBLS	5/15
	Dallas-Plano-Irving PMSA, TX	Y	71860 FQ	94080 MW	125880 TQ	USBLS	5/15
	Fort Worth-Arlington PMSA, TX	Y	70620 FQ	90280 MW	124430 TQ	USBLS	5/15
	Houston-The Woodlands-Sugar Land MSA, TX	Y	77870 FQ	101080 MW	125180 TQ	USBLS	5/15
	San Antonio-New Braunfels MSA, TX	Y	73620 FQ	92590 MW	113110 TQ	USBLS	5/15
	Utah	Y	68400 FQ	90120 MW	120090 TQ	USBLS	5/15
	Ogden-Clearfield MSA, UT	Y	68140 FQ	84820 MW	107100 TQ	USBLS	5/15
	Provo-Orem MSA, UT	Y	57240 FQ	84180 MW	107820 TQ	USBLS	5/15
	Salt Lake City MSA, UT	Y	72540 FQ	94590 MW	127560 TQ	USBLS	5/15
	Vermont	Y	65560 FQ	84310 MW	110950 TQ	USBLS	5/15
	Burlington-South Burlington MSA, VT	Y	61220 FQ	82420 MW	110800 TQ	USBLS	5/15
	Virginia	Y	76610 FQ	95580 MW	121720 TQ	USBLS	5/15
	Richmond MSA, VA	Y	77940 FQ	98970 MW	125710 TQ	USBLS	5/15
	Virginia Beach-Norfolk-Newport News MSA, VA-NC	Y	74620 FQ	91250 MW	113870 TQ	USBLS	5/15
	Washington	H	38.48 FQ	50.20 MW	66.10 TQ	WABLS	3/16
	Seattle-Bellevue-Everett PMSA, WA	H	43.11 FQ	56.17 MW	74.33 TQ	WABLS	3/16
	Tacoma-Lakewood PMSA, WA	H	36.84 FQ	46.41 MW	58.29 TQ	WABLS	3/16
	West Virginia	Y	69600 FQ	90700 MW	118010 TQ	USBLS	5/15
	Huntington-Ashland MSA, WV-KY-OH	Y	71330 FQ	92310 MW	116230 TQ	USBLS	5/15
	Wisconsin	Y	65210 FQ	83760 MW	103480 TQ	USBLS	5/15
	Madison MSA, WI	Y	76080 FQ	92390 MW	115420 TQ	USBLS	5/15
	Milwaukee-Waukesha-West Allis MSA, WI	Y	66780 FQ	86400 MW	109610 TQ	USBLS	5/15
	Wyoming	Y	66950 FQ	85040 MW	108510 TQ	USBLS	5/15
	Cheyenne MSA, WY	Y	67740 FQ	86980 MW	115560 TQ	USBLS	5/15
	Puerto Rico	Y	45610 FQ	59660 MW	91630 TQ	USBLS	5/15

AE	Average entry wage	AWR	Average wage range	H	Hourly
AEX	Average experienced wage	B	Biweekly	HI	Highest wage paid
ATC	Average total compensation	D	Daily	HR	High end range
AW	Average wage paid	FQ	First quartile wage	LO	Lowest wage paid

LR	Low end range	MTC	Median total compensation	TCC	Total cash compensation
M	Monthly	MW	Median wage paid	TQ	Third quartile wage
MCC	Median cash compensation	MWR	Median wage range	W	Weekly
ME	Median entry wage	S	See annotated source	Y	Yearly

Occupation/Type/Industry	Location	Per	Low	Mid	High	Source	Date
Medical and Health Services Manager	San Juan-Carolina-Caguas MSA, PR	Y	47980 FQ	63120 MW	97760 TQ	USBLS	5/15
	Virgin Islands	Y	44640 FQ	65540 MW	75680 TQ	USBLS	5/15
Medical Appliance Technician	Alabama	Y	24934 AE	34815 AW	39761 AEX	ALBLS	6/16
	Birmingham-Hoover MSA, AL	Y	23022 AE	31093 AW	35124 AEX	ALBLS	6/16
	Arizona	Y	28780 FQ	34280 MW	39850 TQ	USBLS	5/15
	Phoenix-Mesa-Scottsdale MSA, AZ	Y	29260 FQ	34880 MW	42630 TQ	USBLS	5/15
	Arkansas	Y	29910 FQ	35160 MW	39890 TQ	USBLS	5/15
	Little Rock-North Little Rock-Conway MSA, AR	Y	32620 FQ	37050 MW	43300 TQ	USBLS	5/15
	California	H	14.93 FQ	20.40 MW	30.72 TQ	CABLS	1/16-3/16
	Anaheim-Santa Ana-Irvine PMSA, CA	H	13.33 FQ	18.35 MW	23.45 TQ	CABLS	1/16-3/16
	Los Angeles-Long Beach-Glendale PMSA, CA	H	14.07 FQ	18.64 MW	24.46 TQ	CABLS	1/16-3/16
	Oakland-Hayward-Berkeley PMSA, CA	H	14.74 FQ	20.04 MW	30.94 TQ	CABLS	1/16-3/16
	Riverside-San Bernardino-Ontario MSA, CA	H	12.74 FQ	16.00 MW	42.37 TQ	CABLS	1/16-3/16
	Sacramento–Roseville–Arden-Arcade MSA, CA	H	19.27 FQ	33.58 MW	41.28 TQ	CABLS	1/16-3/16
	San Diego-Carlsbad MSA, CA	H	17.05 FQ	23.23 MW	38.16 TQ	CABLS	1/16-3/16
	San Francisco-Redwood City-South San Francisco PMSA, CA	H	25.72 FQ	35.68 MW	51.47 TQ	CABLS	1/16-3/16
	Colorado	Y	27670 FQ	33940 MW	45820 TQ	USBLS	5/15
	Denver-Aurora-Lakewood MSA, CO	Y	28870 FQ	37150 MW	45970 TQ	USBLS	5/15
	Connecticut	Y		34409 MW		CTBLS	1/16-3/16
	Bridgeport-Stamford-Norwalk MSA, CT	Y	25210 FQ	32510 MW	73220 TQ	USBLS	5/15
	Hartford-West Hartford-East Hartford MSA, CT	Y	30780 FQ	36290 MW	49530 TQ	USBLS	5/15
	Delaware	Y	27510 FQ	35740 MW	47740 TQ	USBLS	5/15
	Wilmington PMSA, DE-MD-NJ	Y	32950 FQ	41650 MW	58790 TQ	USBLS	5/15
	Washington-Arlington-Alexandria PMSA, DC-VA-MD-WV	Y	30070 FQ	34300 MW	38470 TQ	USBLS	5/15
	Florida	H	12.45 AE	17.37 MW	21.39 AEX	FLBLS	7/16-9/16
	Fort Lauderdale-Pompano Beach-Deerfield Beach PMSA, FL	H	19.12 AE	23.54 MW	25.47 AEX	FLBLS	7/16-9/16
	Miami-Miami Beach-Kendall PMSA, FL	H	13.31 AE	14.92 MW	18.52 AEX	FLBLS	7/16-9/16
	Orlando-Kissimmee-Sanford MSA, FL	H	12.35 AE	19.36 MW	22.67 AEX	FLBLS	7/16-9/16
	Tampa-St. Petersburg-Clearwater MSA, FL	H	10.81 AE	13.54 MW	19.17 AEX	FLBLS	7/16-9/16
	Georgia	Y	29510 FQ	37620 MW	53830 TQ	USBLS	5/15
	Atlanta-Sandy Springs-Roswell MSA, GA	Y	27020 FQ	36920 MW	50820 TQ	USBLS	5/15
	Illinois	Y	26380 FQ	35130 MW	46720 TQ	USBLS	5/15
	Chicago-Naperville-Arlington Heights PMSA, IL	Y	26960 FQ	36900 MW	48960 TQ	USBLS	5/15
	Lake County-Kenosha County PMSA, IL-WI	Y	27370 FQ	33510 MW	42450 TQ	USBLS	5/15
	Gary PMSA, IN	Y	18740 FQ	22340 MW	30400 TQ	USBLS	5/15
	Indianapolis-Carmel-Anderson MSA, IN	Y	26270 FQ	32480 MW	36470 TQ	USBLS	5/15
	Iowa	Y	31790 FQ	37750 MW	44500 TQ	USBLS	5/15
	Des Moines-West Des Moines MSA, IA	Y	33800 FQ	40750 MW	46280 TQ	USBLS	5/15
	Kansas	Y	24510 FQ	34800 MW	44470 TQ	USBLS	5/15
	Louisiana	Y	25100 FQ	33860 MW	45480 TQ	USBLS	5/15
	New Orleans-Metairie MSA, LA	Y	22850 FQ	26030 MW	41830 TQ	USBLS	5/15
	Maine	Y	24470 FQ	37420 MW	54110 TQ	USBLS	5/15
	Maryland	Y	20990 AE	33820 MW	40235 AEX	MDBLS	4/16

AE	Average entry wage	AWR	Average wage range	H	Hourly	LR	Low end range	MTC	Median total compensation	TCC	Total cash compensation
AEX	Average experienced wage	B	Biweekly	HI	Highest wage paid	M	Monthly	MW	Median wage paid	TQ	Third quartile wage
ATC	Average total compensation	D	Daily	HR	High end range	MCC	Median cash compensation	MWR	Median wage range	W	Weekly
AW	Average wage paid	FQ	First quartile wage	LO	Lowest wage paid	ME	Median entry wage	S	See annotated source	Y	Yearly

Occupation/Type/Industry	Location	Per	Low	Mid	High	Source	Date
Medical Appliance Technician	Baltimore-Columbia-Towson MSA, MD	Y	21210 FQ	24030 MW	32210 TQ	USBLS	5/15
	Salisbury MSA, MD-DE	Y	20480 FQ	23680 MW	29310 TQ	USBLS	5/15
	Massachusetts	Y	32690 FQ	40150 MW	54400 TQ	USBLS	5/15
	Boston-Cambridge-Newton NECTA, MA	Y	33360 FQ	47450 MW	58600 TQ	USBLS	5/15
	Michigan	Y	27280 FQ	29580 MW	32780 TQ	USBLS	5/15
	Minnesota	Y	30748 FQ	36246 MW	43454 TQ	MNBLS	1/16-3/16
	Minneapolis-St. Paul-Bloomington MSA, MN-WI	Y	30637 FQ	35993 MW	42422 TQ	MNBLS	1/16-3/16
	Mississippi	Y	32850 FQ	37100 MW	43530 TQ	USBLS	5/15
	Missouri	Y	32260 FQ	42630 MW	56400 TQ	USBLS	5/15
	Kansas City MSA, MO-KS	Y	25460 FQ	34250 MW	43990 TQ	USBLS	5/15
	St. Louis MSA, MO-IL	Y	49840 FQ	55570 MW	60520 TQ	USBLS	5/15
	Nebraska	Y	42995 FQ	51950 MW	58510 TQ	NEBLS	7/16-9/16
	Omaha-Council Bluffs MSA, NE-IA	Y	40335 FQ	45425 MW	55300 TQ	NEBLS	7/16-9/16
	Nevada	Y	34770 FQ	45440 MW	67600 TQ	USBLS	5/15
	Las Vegas-Henderson-Paradise MSA, NV	Y	29970 FQ	54680 MW	73220 TQ	USBLS	5/15
	New Hampshire	H	14.24 AE	22.26 MW	24.89 AEX	NHBLS	6/16
	New Jersey	Y	32330 FQ	37890 MW	50890 TQ	USBLS	5/15
	Newark PMSA, NJ-PA	Y	28780 FQ	33730 MW	38000 TQ	USBLS	5/15
	New Mexico	Y	25590 FQ	29490 MW	34650 TQ	USBLS	5/15
	New York	Y	22090 AE	32730 MW	43180 AEX	NYBLS	1/16-3/16
	Buffalo-Cheektowaga-Niagara Falls MSA, NY	Y	22440 FQ	27460 MW	36430 TQ	USBLS	5/15
	Nassau County-Suffolk County PMSA, NY	Y	35650 FQ	44390 MW	54740 TQ	USBLS	5/15
	New York-Jersey City-White Plains PMSA, NY-NJ	Y	31380 FQ	39530 MW	58480 TQ	USBLS	5/15
	North Carolina	Y	26800 FQ	34070 MW	45250 TQ	USBLS	5/15
	Charlotte-Concord-Gastonia MSA, NC-SC	Y	26670 FQ	36030 MW	53240 TQ	USBLS	5/15
	Raleigh MSA, NC	Y	22180 FQ	28020 MW	37990 TQ	USBLS	5/15
	Ohio	Y	23230 FQ	30820 MW	39250 TQ	USBLS	5/15
	Cleveland-Elyria MSA, OH	Y	20680 FQ	26710 MW	36590 TQ	USBLS	5/15
	Columbus MSA, OH	Y	23990 FQ	29340 MW	41110 TQ	USBLS	5/15
	Oklahoma	Y	20760 FQ	29370 MW	38170 TQ	USBLS	5/15
	Oklahoma City MSA, OK	Y	18230 FQ	24780 MW	38800 TQ	USBLS	5/15
	Oregon	H	19.79 FQ	25.86 MW	35.27 TQ	ORBLS	2016
	Portland-Vancouver-Hillsboro MSA, OR-WA	Y	40750 FQ	50310 MW	68560 TQ	USBLS	5/15
	Pennsylvania	Y	26620 FQ	33040 MW	42680 TQ	USBLS	5/15
	Montgomery County-Bucks County-Chester County PMSA, PA	Y	25280 FQ	31580 MW	39750 TQ	USBLS	5/15
	Philadelphia PMSA, PA	Y	32440 FQ	39120 MW	49230 TQ	USBLS	5/15
	Pittsburgh MSA, PA	Y	29310 FQ	36680 MW	46230 TQ	USBLS	5/15
	Rhode Island	Y	28060 FQ	33640 MW	40070 TQ	USBLS	5/15
	Providence-Warwick MSA, RI-MA	Y	28840 FQ	35540 MW	43160 TQ	USBLS	5/15
	South Carolina	Y	31190 FQ	36830 MW	46950 TQ	USBLS	5/15
	Greenville-Anderson-Mauldin MSA, SC	Y	28170 FQ	33700 MW	39450 TQ	USBLS	5/15
	South Dakota	Y	27320 FQ	31620 MW	38150 TQ	USBLS	5/15
	Tennessee	Y	27310 FQ	31550 MW	38010 TQ	USBLS	5/15
	Knoxville MSA, TN	Y	27990 FQ	33130 MW	42690 TQ	USBLS	5/15
	Memphis MSA, TN-MS-AR	Y	24730 FQ	31380 MW	39420 TQ	USBLS	5/15
	Nashville-Davidson–Murfreesboro–Franklin MSA, TN	Y	27390 FQ	31380 MW	37460 TQ	USBLS	5/15
	Texas	Y	27780 FQ	36120 MW	48450 TQ	USBLS	5/15
	Austin-Round Rock MSA, TX	Y	27920 FQ	31150 MW	36040 TQ	USBLS	5/15
	Dallas-Plano-Irving PMSA, TX	Y	32910 FQ	38930 MW	55390 TQ	USBLS	5/15
	Houston-The Woodlands-Sugar Land MSA, TX	Y	26630 FQ	35940 MW	46330 TQ	USBLS	5/15
	San Antonio-New Braunfels MSA, TX	Y	34060 FQ	44770 MW	72190 TQ	USBLS	5/15
	Utah	Y	18180 FQ	22820 MW	36200 TQ	USBLS	5/15
	Salt Lake City MSA, UT	Y	17650 FQ	19550 MW	30120 TQ	USBLS	5/15
	Virginia	Y	30920 FQ	35760 MW	43060 TQ	USBLS	5/15

AE	Average entry wage	AWR	Average wage range	H	Hourly	LR	Low end range	MTC	Median total compensation	TCC	Total cash compensation
AEX	Average experienced wage	B	Biweekly	HI	Highest wage paid	M	Monthly	MW	Median wage paid	TQ	Third quartile wage
ATC	Average total compensation	D	Daily	HR	High end range	MCC	Median cash compensation	MWR	Median wage range	W	Weekly
AW	Average wage paid	FQ	First quartile wage	LO	Lowest wage paid	ME	Median entry wage	S	See annotated source	Y	Yearly

Occupation/Type/Industry	Location	Per	Low	Mid	High	Source	Date
Medical Appliance Technician	Richmond MSA, VA	Y	36080 FQ	43790 MW	47920 TQ	USBLS	5/15
	Washington	H	17.90 FQ	22.16 MW	28.20 TQ	WABLS	3/16
	Seattle-Bellevue-Everett PMSA, WA	H	24.31 FQ	28.20 MW	31.57 TQ	WABLS	3/16
	West Virginia	Y	29580 FQ	35270 MW	45370 TQ	USBLS	5/15
	Wisconsin	Y	26500 FQ	31320 MW	38420 TQ	USBLS	5/15
	Milwaukee-Waukesha-West Allis MSA, WI	Y	25540 FQ	30370 MW	36700 TQ	USBLS	5/15
	Puerto Rico	Y	17270 FQ	18990 MW	26330 TQ	USBLS	5/15
	San Juan-Carolina-Caguas MSA, PR	Y	17680 FQ	19710 MW	27690 TQ	USBLS	5/15
Medical Assistant	Alabama	Y	21128 AE	27532 AW	30734 AEX	ALBLS	6/16
	Birmingham-Hoover MSA, AL	Y	23835 AE	30456 AW	33761 AEX	ALBLS	6/16
	Alaska	Y	33050 FQ	38320 MW	45380 TQ	USBLS	5/15
	Anchorage MSA, AK	Y	32100 FQ	36720 MW	43180 TQ	USBLS	5/15
	Arizona	Y	26590 FQ	30440 MW	36630 TQ	USBLS	5/15
	Phoenix-Mesa-Scottsdale MSA, AZ	Y	26980 FQ	31570 MW	37390 TQ	USBLS	5/15
	Tucson MSA, AZ	Y	26000 FQ	28710 MW	32000 TQ	USBLS	5/15
	Arkansas	Y	23500 FQ	27710 MW	31550 TQ	USBLS	5/15
	Jonesboro MSA, AR	Y	21150 FQ	25440 MW	29530 TQ	USBLS	5/15
	Little Rock-North Little Rock-Conway MSA, AR	Y	25440 FQ	28770 MW	33580 TQ	USBLS	5/15
	California	H	13.48 FQ	16.60 MW	20.46 TQ	CABLS	1/16-3/16
	Anaheim-Santa Ana-Irvine PMSA, CA	H	13.27 FQ	16.44 MW	20.58 TQ	CABLS	1/16-3/16
	Los Angeles-Long Beach-Glendale PMSA, CA	H	12.95 FQ	16.02 MW	19.13 TQ	CABLS	1/16-3/16
	Oakland-Hayward-Berkeley PMSA, CA	H	17.90 FQ	21.41 MW	24.51 TQ	CABLS	1/16-3/16
	Riverside-San Bernardino-Ontario MSA, CA	H	11.90 FQ	13.84 MW	16.54 TQ	CABLS	1/16-3/16
	Sacramento–Roseville–Arden-Arcade MSA, CA	H	13.73 FQ	16.37 MW	19.35 TQ	CABLS	1/16-3/16
	San Diego-Carlsbad MSA, CA	H	15.15 FQ	17.28 MW	19.75 TQ	CABLS	1/16-3/16
	San Francisco-Redwood City-South San Francisco PMSA, CA	H	17.46 FQ	21.09 MW	24.75 TQ	CABLS	1/16-3/16
	Colorado	Y	28210 FQ	32780 MW	37560 TQ	USBLS	5/15
	Denver-Aurora-Lakewood MSA, CO	Y	29520 FQ	34230 MW	38720 TQ	USBLS	5/15
	Connecticut	Y		34865 MW		CTBLS	1/16-3/16
	Bridgeport-Stamford-Norwalk MSA, CT	Y	28750 FQ	34380 MW	42980 TQ	USBLS	5/15
	Hartford-West Hartford-East Hartford MSA, CT	Y	29430 FQ	35100 MW	41880 TQ	USBLS	5/15
	Delaware	Y	26590 FQ	30650 MW	35600 TQ	USBLS	5/15
	Wilmington PMSA, DE-MD-NJ	Y	27720 FQ	32210 MW	36690 TQ	USBLS	5/15
	District of Columbia	Y	33950 FQ	38670 MW	45930 TQ	USBLS	5/15
	Washington-Arlington-Alexandria PMSA, DC-VA-MD-WV	Y	28990 FQ	35030 MW	41960 TQ	USBLS	5/15
	Florida	H	12.19 AE	14.76 MW	16.52 AEX	FLBLS	7/16-9/16
	Fort Lauderdale-Pompano Beach-Deerfield Beach PMSA, FL	H	12.59 AE	15.20 MW	16.92 AEX	FLBLS	7/16-9/16
	Miami-Miami Beach-Kendall PMSA, FL	H	11.79 AE	15.30 MW	17.64 AEX	FLBLS	7/16-9/16
	Orlando-Kissimmee-Sanford MSA, FL	H	12.15 AE	14.38 MW	15.79 AEX	FLBLS	7/16-9/16
	Tampa-St. Petersburg-Clearwater MSA, FL	H	12.35 AE	14.73 MW	16.43 AEX	FLBLS	7/16-9/16
	Georgia	Y	25160 FQ	29220 MW	34760 TQ	USBLS	5/15
	Atlanta-Sandy Springs-Roswell MSA, GA	Y	26100 FQ	30520 MW	36110 TQ	USBLS	5/15
	Augusta-Richmond County MSA, GA-SC	Y	25000 FQ	28730 MW	34040 TQ	USBLS	5/15
	Hawaii	Y	27340 FQ	33620 MW	40310 TQ	USBLS	5/15
	Urban Honolulu MSA, HI	Y	27830 FQ	33990 MW	41390 TQ	USBLS	5/15
	Idaho	Y	26180 FQ	29470 MW	34560 TQ	USBLS	5/15

AE	Average entry wage	AWR	Average wage range	H	Hourly
AEX	Average experienced wage	B	Biweekly	HI	Highest wage paid
ATC	Average total compensation	D	Daily	HR	High end range
AW	Average wage paid	FQ	First quartile wage	LO	Lowest wage paid

LR	Low end range	MTC	Median total compensation	TCC	Total cash compensation
M	Monthly	MW	Median wage paid	TQ	Third quartile wage
MCC	Median cash compensation	MWR	Median wage range	W	Weekly
ME	Median entry wage	S	See annotated source	Y	Yearly

Occupation/Type/Industry	Location	Per	Low	Mid	High	Source	Date
Medical Assistant	Boise City MSA, ID	Y	26180 FQ	29500 MW	34220 TQ	USBLS	5/15
	Illinois	Y	25740 FQ	30800 MW	37230 TQ	USBLS	5/15
	Chicago-Naperville-Arlington Heights PMSA, IL	Y	26070 FQ	32270 MW	38500 TQ	USBLS	5/15
	Lake County-Kenosha County PMSA, IL-WI	Y	28170 FQ	33200 MW	37820 TQ	USBLS	5/15
	Indiana	Y	25730 FQ	28990 MW	33730 TQ	USBLS	5/15
	Gary PMSA, IN	Y	25740 FQ	28920 MW	34450 TQ	USBLS	5/15
	Indianapolis-Carmel-Anderson MSA, IN	Y	27050 FQ	30480 MW	35930 TQ	USBLS	5/15
	Iowa	Y	25870 FQ	30180 MW	36280 TQ	USBLS	5/15
	Des Moines-West Des Moines MSA, IA	Y	29750 FQ	35070 MW	41450 TQ	USBLS	5/15
	Kansas	Y	24530 FQ	28550 MW	34010 TQ	USBLS	5/15
	Manhattan MSA, KS	Y	20480 FQ	22430 MW	24380 TQ	USBLS	5/15
	Wichita MSA, KS	Y	23560 FQ	27460 MW	31310 TQ	USBLS	5/15
	Kentucky	Y	24270 FQ	28350 MW	33450 TQ	USBLS	5/15
	Louisville-Jefferson County MSA, KY-IN	Y	25840 FQ	29680 MW	34910 TQ	USBLS	5/15
	Louisiana	Y	22060 FQ	26630 MW	30740 TQ	USBLS	5/15
	Baton Rouge MSA, LA	Y	23430 FQ	27400 MW	31130 TQ	USBLS	5/15
	New Orleans-Metairie MSA, LA	Y	24990 FQ	28220 MW	31910 TQ	USBLS	5/15
	Maine	Y	27380 FQ	31230 MW	36240 TQ	USBLS	5/15
	Portland-South Portland MSA, ME	Y	29500 FQ	34340 MW	38790 TQ	USBLS	5/15
	Maryland	Y	25938 AE	34121 MW	38213 AEX	MDBLS	4/16
	Baltimore-Columbia-Towson MSA, MD	Y	28520 FQ	33420 MW	38070 TQ	USBLS	5/15
	Salisbury MSA, MD-DE	Y	25580 FQ	29760 MW	35590 TQ	USBLS	5/15
	Massachusetts	Y	31980 FQ	36560 MW	43310 TQ	USBLS	5/15
	Boston-Cambridge-Newton NECTA, MA	Y	32640 FQ	37420 MW	45350 TQ	USBLS	5/15
	Worcester MSA, MA-CT	Y	30870 FQ	35480 MW	40340 TQ	USBLS	5/15
	Michigan	Y	25590 FQ	29080 MW	34040 TQ	USBLS	5/15
	Detroit-Dearborn-Livonia PMSA, MI	Y	24660 FQ	28280 MW	32540 TQ	USBLS	5/15
	Grand Rapids-Wyoming MSA, MI	Y	27010 FQ	31270 MW	36950 TQ	USBLS	5/15
	Minnesota	Y	32255 FQ	36274 MW	40960 TQ	MNBLS	1/16-3/16
	Minneapolis-St. Paul-Bloomington MSA, MN-WI	Y	32548 FQ	36487 MW	41243 TQ	MNBLS	1/16-3/16
	Mississippi	Y	23080 FQ	27570 MW	32660 TQ	USBLS	5/15
	Jackson MSA, MS	Y	25890 FQ	29750 MW	34810 TQ	USBLS	5/15
	Missouri	Y	24410 FQ	28470 MW	33700 TQ	USBLS	5/15
	Kansas City MSA, MO-KS	Y	27430 FQ	32210 MW	37990 TQ	USBLS	5/15
	St. Louis MSA, MO-IL	Y	25010 FQ	28570 MW	33160 TQ	USBLS	5/15
	Montana	Y	26470 FQ	30580 MW	35960 TQ	USBLS	5/15
	Billings MSA, MT	Y	26940 FQ	30890 MW	36200 TQ	USBLS	5/15
	Nebraska	Y	25600 FQ	29620 MW	35705 TQ	NEBLS	7/16-9/16
	Omaha-Council Bluffs MSA, NE-IA	Y	26945 FQ	30605 MW	36710 TQ	NEBLS	7/16-9/16
	Nevada	Y	26540 FQ	30730 MW	36070 TQ	USBLS	5/15
	Las Vegas-Henderson-Paradise MSA, NV	Y	26010 FQ	30190 MW	35580 TQ	USBLS	5/15
	New Hampshire	H	13.46 AE	16.47 MW	18.20 AEX	NHBLS	6/16
	Manchester NECTA, NH	H	13.44 AE	16.18 MW	18.02 AEX	NHBLS	6/16
	Nashua NECTA, NH-MA	Y	28760 FQ	32940 MW	37210 TQ	USBLS	5/15
	New Jersey	Y	28650 FQ	33690 MW	38420 TQ	USBLS	5/15
	Camden PMSA, NJ	Y	29010 FQ	34240 MW	39000 TQ	USBLS	5/15
	Newark PMSA, NJ-PA	Y	29410 FQ	34500 MW	39230 TQ	USBLS	5/15
	Trenton MSA, NJ	Y	27960 FQ	33080 MW	39180 TQ	USBLS	5/15
	New Mexico	Y	24850 FQ	28230 MW	32220 TQ	USBLS	5/15
	Albuquerque MSA, NM	Y	25700 FQ	28610 MW	32250 TQ	USBLS	5/15
	New York	Y	26310 AE	34360 MW	39270 AEX	NYBLS	1/16-3/16
	Buffalo-Cheektowaga-Niagara Falls MSA, NY	Y	28550 FQ	33500 MW	37990 TQ	USBLS	5/15
	Nassau County-Suffolk County PMSA, NY	Y	30910 FQ	35980 MW	42130 TQ	USBLS	5/15
	New York-Jersey City-White Plains PMSA, NY-NJ	Y	28180 FQ	33850 MW	38920 TQ	USBLS	5/15
	Rochester MSA, NY	Y	26110 FQ	29050 MW	34050 TQ	USBLS	5/15

AE	Average entry wage	AWR	Average wage range	H	Hourly
AEX	Average experienced wage	B	Biweekly	HI	Highest wage paid
ATC	Average total compensation	D	Daily	HR	High end range
AW	Average wage paid	FQ	First quartile wage	LO	Lowest wage paid

LR	Low end range	MTC	Median total compensation	TCC	Total cash compensation
M	Monthly	MW	Median wage paid	TQ	Third quartile wage
MCC	Median cash compensation	MWR	Median wage range	W	Weekly
ME	Median entry wage	S	See annotated source	Y	Yearly

Occupation/Type/Industry	Location	Per	Low	Mid	High	Source	Date
Medical Assistant	North Carolina	Y	26160 FQ	29830 MW	35080 TQ	USBLS	5/15
	Charlotte-Concord-Gastonia MSA, NC-SC	Y	26810 FQ	30700 MW	36800 TQ	USBLS	5/15
	Raleigh MSA, NC	Y	27330 FQ	32080 MW	36060 TQ	USBLS	5/15
	North Dakota	Y	28010 FQ	32530 MW	37430 TQ	USBLS	5/15
	Fargo MSA, ND-MN	Y	26770 FQ	30440 MW	36110 TQ	USBLS	5/15
	Ohio	Y	25220 FQ	28600 MW	33060 TQ	USBLS	5/15
	Cincinnati MSA, OH-KY-IN	Y	26350 FQ	29930 MW	35240 TQ	USBLS	5/15
	Cleveland-Elyria MSA, OH	Y	26350 FQ	29160 MW	33310 TQ	USBLS	5/15
	Columbus MSA, OH	Y	26580 FQ	30070 MW	35950 TQ	USBLS	5/15
	Oklahoma	Y	24200 FQ	28160 MW	32540 TQ	USBLS	5/15
	Oklahoma City MSA, OK	Y	23970 FQ	27860 MW	31480 TQ	USBLS	5/15
	Tulsa MSA, OK	Y	26230 FQ	30000 MW	35060 TQ	USBLS	5/15
	Oregon	H	14.66 FQ	17.08 MW	19.21 TQ	ORBLS	2016
	Portland-Vancouver-Hillsboro MSA, OR-WA	Y	31510 FQ	35920 MW	41130 TQ	USBLS	5/15
	Pennsylvania	Y	25520 FQ	29490 MW	35340 TQ	USBLS	5/15
	Allentown-Bethlehem-Easton MSA, PA-NJ	Y	26320 FQ	30330 MW	35730 TQ	USBLS	5/15
	Harrisburg-Carlisle MSA, PA	Y	26290 FQ	30030 MW	35680 TQ	USBLS	5/15
	Montgomery County-Bucks County-Chester County PMSA, PA	Y	26810 FQ	33000 MW	38750 TQ	USBLS	5/15
	Philadelphia PMSA, PA	Y	28000 FQ	33220 MW	37690 TQ	USBLS	5/15
	Pittsburgh MSA, PA	Y	25320 FQ	28640 MW	33250 TQ	USBLS	5/15
	Rhode Island	Y	28930 FQ	33240 MW	37390 TQ	USBLS	5/15
	Providence-Warwick MSA, RI-MA	Y	28680 FQ	32930 MW	37330 TQ	USBLS	5/15
	South Carolina	Y	24640 FQ	28310 MW	33170 TQ	USBLS	5/15
	Charleston-North Charleston MSA, SC	Y	25620 FQ	28900 MW	34110 TQ	USBLS	5/15
	Columbia MSA, SC	Y	23540 FQ	27600 MW	31440 TQ	USBLS	5/15
	Greenville-Anderson-Mauldin MSA, SC	Y	23450 FQ	27530 MW	31550 TQ	USBLS	5/15
	South Dakota	Y	25380 FQ	28230 MW	31240 TQ	USBLS	5/15
	Sioux Falls MSA, SD	Y	26430 FQ	29220 MW	33220 TQ	USBLS	5/15
	Tennessee	Y	24850 FQ	28840 MW	34360 TQ	USBLS	5/15
	Knoxville MSA, TN	Y	24830 FQ	28450 MW	33140 TQ	USBLS	5/15
	Memphis MSA, TN-MS-AR	Y	24500 FQ	28380 MW	33290 TQ	USBLS	5/15
	Nashville-Davidson–Murfreesboro–Franklin MSA, TN	Y	27510 FQ	32320 MW	37370 TQ	USBLS	5/15
	Texas	Y	23620 FQ	28350 MW	34140 TQ	USBLS	5/15
	Austin-Round Rock MSA, TX	Y	27170 FQ	31800 MW	36510 TQ	USBLS	5/15
	Dallas-Plano-Irving PMSA, TX	Y	26380 FQ	31130 MW	37010 TQ	USBLS	5/15
	Fort Worth-Arlington PMSA, TX	Y	25980 FQ	30170 MW	35260 TQ	USBLS	5/15
	Houston-The Woodlands-Sugar Land MSA, TX	Y	23680 FQ	28430 MW	34410 TQ	USBLS	5/15
	San Antonio-New Braunfels MSA, TX	Y	24210 FQ	27930 MW	31750 TQ	USBLS	5/15
	Utah	Y	25860 FQ	29080 MW	33840 TQ	USBLS	5/15
	Ogden-Clearfield MSA, UT	Y	25830 FQ	29400 MW	34660 TQ	USBLS	5/15
	Provo-Orem MSA, UT	Y	23560 FQ	26970 MW	30190 TQ	USBLS	5/15
	Salt Lake City MSA, UT	Y	26660 FQ	29610 MW	34520 TQ	USBLS	5/15
	Vermont	Y	29150 FQ	33990 MW	38520 TQ	USBLS	5/15
	Burlington-South Burlington MSA, VT	Y	29220 FQ	33860 MW	38440 TQ	USBLS	5/15
	Virginia	Y	25860 FQ	30400 MW	36530 TQ	USBLS	5/15
	Richmond MSA, VA	Y	24890 FQ	30360 MW	35710 TQ	USBLS	5/15
	Virginia Beach-Norfolk-Newport News MSA, VA-NC	Y	25810 FQ	29260 MW	34280 TQ	USBLS	5/15
	Washington	H	15.50 FQ	17.61 MW	20.21 TQ	WABLS	3/16
	Seattle-Bellevue-Everett PMSA, WA	H	16.33 FQ	18.35 MW	21.32 TQ	WABLS	3/16
	Tacoma-Lakewood PMSA, WA	H	15.38 FQ	17.47 MW	19.79 TQ	WABLS	3/16
	West Virginia	Y	21400 FQ	25080 MW	29030 TQ	USBLS	5/15
	Huntington-Ashland MSA, WV-KY-OH	Y	21940 FQ	25200 MW	29240 TQ	USBLS	5/15
	Wisconsin	Y	27500 FQ	32170 MW	37090 TQ	USBLS	5/15
	Madison MSA, WI	Y	28680 FQ	33770 MW	38460 TQ	USBLS	5/15

Occupation/Type/Industry	Location	Per	Low	Mid	High	Source	Date
Medical Assistant	Milwaukee-Waukesha-West						
	Allis MSA, WI	Y	26920 FQ	31750 MW	36670 TQ	USBLS	5/15
	Wyoming	Y	25640 FQ	30130 MW	35810 TQ	USBLS	5/15
	Cheyenne MSA, WY	Y	26430 FQ	30220 MW	35900 TQ	USBLS	5/15
	Puerto Rico	Y	16730 FQ	18210 MW	21140 TQ	USBLS	5/15
	San Juan-Carolina-Caguas						
	MSA, PR	Y	16590 FQ	17950 MW	19310 TQ	USBLS	5/15
	Virgin Islands	Y	21730 FQ	26550 MW	31020 TQ	USBLS	5/15
	Guam	Y	19130 FQ	22820 MW	27490 TQ	USBLS	5/15
Department of Corrections, State							
Government	Billings, MT	H			16.36 HI	MTGOV	2016
Medical Director	United States	Y		230000 MW		LI01	2017
Medical Equipment Preparer	Alabama	Y	20757 AE	26564 AW	29467 AEX	ALBLS	6/16
	Birmingham-Hoover MSA, AL	Y	21632 AE	27943 AW	31104 AEX	ALBLS	6/16
	Alaska	Y	35790 FQ	40930 MW	47670 TQ	USBLS	5/15
	Anchorage MSA, AK	Y	35740 FQ	40820 MW	47460 TQ	USBLS	5/15
	Arizona	Y	28680 FQ	34000 MW	39450 TQ	USBLS	5/15
	Phoenix-Mesa-Scottsdale						
	MSA, AZ	Y	29660 FQ	34940 MW	41110 TQ	USBLS	5/15
	Tucson MSA, AZ	Y	27220 FQ	30800 MW	36890 TQ	USBLS	5/15
	Arkansas	Y	22080 FQ	26400 MW	34570 TQ	USBLS	5/15
	Little Rock-North Little Rock-						
	Conway MSA, AR	Y	22530 FQ	28440 MW	40270 TQ	USBLS	5/15
	California	H	16.64 FQ	21.82 MW	27.16 TQ	CABLS	1/16-3/16
	Anaheim-Santa Ana-Irvine						
	PMSA, CA	H	14.52 FQ	19.94 MW	26.70 TQ	CABLS	1/16-3/16
	Los Angeles-Long Beach-						
	Glendale PMSA, CA	H	16.64 FQ	19.95 MW	24.20 TQ	CABLS	1/16-3/16
	Oakland-Hayward-Berkeley						
	PMSA, CA	H	21.28 FQ	26.98 MW	29.98 TQ	CABLS	1/16-3/16
	Riverside-San Bernardino-						
	Ontario MSA, CA	H	16.72 FQ	21.90 MW	26.69 TQ	CABLS	1/16-3/16
	Sacramento–Roseville–						
	Arden-Arcade MSA, CA	H	19.46 FQ	24.18 MW	29.37 TQ	CABLS	1/16-3/16
	San Diego-Carlsbad MSA, CA	H	15.10 FQ	19.33 MW	24.39 TQ	CABLS	1/16-3/16
	San Francisco-Redwood City-						
	South San Francisco PMSA,						
	CA	H	24.86 FQ	27.43 MW	29.92 TQ	CABLS	1/16-3/16
	Colorado	Y	31030 FQ	36210 MW	43250 TQ	USBLS	5/15
	Denver-Aurora-Lakewood						
	MSA, CO	Y	33270 FQ	38090 MW	45400 TQ	USBLS	5/15
	Connecticut	Y		38220 MW		CTBLS	1/16-3/16
	Bridgeport-Stamford-Norwalk						
	MSA, CT	Y	32130 FQ	35920 MW	40190 TQ	USBLS	5/15
	Hartford-West Hartford-East						
	Hartford MSA, CT	Y	32840 FQ	36700 MW	42850 TQ	USBLS	5/15
	Delaware	Y	31470 FQ	36070 MW	41780 TQ	USBLS	5/15
	Wilmington PMSA, DE-MD-						
	NJ	Y	31580 FQ	36090 MW	41650 TQ	USBLS	5/15
	District of Columbia	Y	34070 FQ	38760 MW	46820 TQ	USBLS	5/15
	Washington-Arlington-						
	Alexandria PMSA, DC-VA-						
	MD-WV	Y	32020 FQ	36790 MW	44330 TQ	USBLS	5/15
	Florida	H	11.37 AE	14.19 MW	16.22 AEX	FLBLS	7/16-9/16
	Fort Lauderdale-Pompano						
	Beach-Deerfield Beach						
	PMSA, FL	H	12.16 AE	16.10 MW	18.31 AEX	FLBLS	7/16-9/16
	Miami-Miami Beach-Kendall						
	PMSA, FL	H	10.76 AE	13.81 MW	16.22 AEX	FLBLS	7/16-9/16
	Orlando-Kissimmee-Sanford						
	MSA, FL	H	11.75 AE	14.47 MW	16.58 AEX	FLBLS	7/16-9/16
	Tampa-St. Petersburg-						
	Clearwater MSA, FL	H	11.50 AE	14.11 MW	15.83 AEX	FLBLS	7/16-9/16
	Georgia	Y	24970 FQ	29790 MW	36200 TQ	USBLS	5/15
	Atlanta-Sandy Springs-						
	Roswell MSA, GA	Y	27290 FQ	32610 MW	38010 TQ	USBLS	5/15
	Augusta-Richmond County						
	MSA, GA-SC	Y	22530 FQ	26460 MW	35120 TQ	USBLS	5/15
	Hawaii	Y	32370 FQ	39640 MW	47400 TQ	USBLS	5/15
	Urban Honolulu MSA, HI	Y	34250 FQ	41340 MW	47430 TQ	USBLS	5/15

AE	Average entry wage	AWR	Average wage range	H	Hourly	LR	Low end range	MTC	Median total compensation	TCC	Total cash compensation
AEX	Average experienced wage	B	Biweekly	HI	Highest wage paid	M	Monthly	MW	Median wage paid	TQ	Third quartile wage
ATC	Average total compensation	D	Daily	HR	High end range	MCC	Median cash compensation	MWR	Median wage range	W	Weekly
AW	Average wage paid	FQ	First quartile wage	LO	Lowest wage paid	ME	Median entry wage	S	See annotated source	Y	Yearly

Medical Equipment Preparer

Occupation/Type/Industry	Location	Per	Low	Mid	High	Source	Date
Medical Equipment Preparer	Idaho	Y	25490 FQ	28800 MW	33700 TQ	USBLS	5/15
	Boise City MSA, ID	Y	25530 FQ	28440 MW	32140 TQ	USBLS	5/15
	Illinois	Y	27950 FQ	34200 MW	41110 TQ	USBLS	5/15
	Chicago-Naperville-Arlington Heights PMSA, IL	Y	30900 FQ	36700 MW	43480 TQ	USBLS	5/15
	Lake County-Kenosha County PMSA, IL-WI	Y	28010 FQ	33480 MW	38890 TQ	USBLS	5/15
	Indiana	Y	26710 FQ	30750 MW	36580 TQ	USBLS	5/15
	Gary PMSA, IN	Y	25530 FQ	28960 MW	33480 TQ	USBLS	5/15
	Indianapolis-Carmel-Anderson MSA, IN	Y	27850 FQ	31700 MW	37510 TQ	USBLS	5/15
	Iowa	Y	27270 FQ	30950 MW	38330 TQ	USBLS	5/15
	Des Moines-West Des Moines MSA, IA	Y	27730 FQ	31930 MW	39750 TQ	USBLS	5/15
	Kansas	Y	25330 FQ	29190 MW	34250 TQ	USBLS	5/15
	Kentucky	Y	27000 FQ	31680 MW	36130 TQ	USBLS	5/15
	Louisville-Jefferson County MSA, KY-IN	Y	28190 FQ	32540 MW	36090 TQ	USBLS	5/15
	Louisiana	Y	23510 FQ	27570 MW	31580 TQ	USBLS	5/15
	Baton Rouge MSA, LA	Y	25630 FQ	29140 MW	33510 TQ	USBLS	5/15
	New Orleans-Metairie MSA, LA	Y	23390 FQ	27840 MW	33430 TQ	USBLS	5/15
	Maine	Y	26640 FQ	31740 MW	37020 TQ	USBLS	5/15
	Portland-South Portland MSA, ME	Y	26680 FQ	31310 MW	37830 TQ	USBLS	5/15
	Maryland	Y	24252 AE	35362 MW	40918 AEX	MDBLS	4/16
	Baltimore-Columbia-Towson MSA, MD	Y	27420 FQ	35390 MW	43420 TQ	USBLS	5/15
	Salisbury MSA, MD-DE	Y	27450 FQ	32330 MW	37960 TQ	USBLS	5/15
	Massachusetts	Y	33910 FQ	40760 MW	48430 TQ	USBLS	5/15
	Boston-Cambridge-Newton NECTA, MA	Y	37070 FQ	43410 MW	49260 TQ	USBLS	5/15
	Worcester MSA, MA-CT	Y	29380 FQ	34650 MW	42310 TQ	USBLS	5/15
	Michigan	Y	29270 FQ	33970 MW	38110 TQ	USBLS	5/15
	Detroit-Dearborn-Livonia PMSA, MI	Y	29910 FQ	33790 MW	37180 TQ	USBLS	5/15
	Grand Rapids-Wyoming MSA, MI	Y	26800 FQ	30810 MW	35780 TQ	USBLS	5/15
	Minnesota	Y	33901 FQ	38415 MW	44555 TQ	MNBLS	1/16-3/16
	Minneapolis-St. Paul-Bloomington MSA, MN-WI	Y	36598 FQ	41778 MW	46757 TQ	MNBLS	1/16-3/16
	Mississippi	Y	21900 FQ	26370 MW	30550 TQ	USBLS	5/15
	Jackson MSA, MS	Y	23640 FQ	27540 MW	31870 TQ	USBLS	5/15
	Missouri	Y	24710 FQ	29170 MW	34930 TQ	USBLS	5/15
	Kansas City MSA, MO-KS	Y	24240 FQ	29590 MW	35510 TQ	USBLS	5/15
	St. Louis MSA, MO-IL	Y	25530 FQ	29820 MW	35340 TQ	USBLS	5/15
	Montana	Y	24900 FQ	29430 MW	35390 TQ	USBLS	5/15
	Billings MSA, MT	Y	25120 FQ	30810 MW	37710 TQ	USBLS	5/15
	Nebraska	Y	27875 FQ	33240 MW	38370 TQ	NEBLS	7/16-9/16
	Omaha-Council Bluffs MSA, NE-IA	Y	29035 FQ	34080 MW	38945 TQ	NEBLS	7/16-9/16
	Nevada	Y	32550 FQ	41820 MW	48430 TQ	USBLS	5/15
	Las Vegas-Henderson-Paradise MSA, NV	Y	40610 FQ	45330 MW	50420 TQ	USBLS	5/15
	New Hampshire	H	13.09 AE	16.31 MW	18.49 AEX	NHBLS	6/16
	Manchester NECTA, NH	H	13.10 AE	16.04 MW	18.73 AEX	NHBLS	6/16
	New Jersey	Y	30510 FQ	35230 MW	39930 TQ	USBLS	5/15
	Camden PMSA, NJ	Y	31290 FQ	35420 MW	39670 TQ	USBLS	5/15
	Newark PMSA, NJ-PA	Y	30740 FQ	35150 MW	39280 TQ	USBLS	5/15
	Trenton MSA, NJ	Y	31950 FQ	35010 MW	38060 TQ	USBLS	5/15
	New Mexico	Y	26550 FQ	32460 MW	38110 TQ	USBLS	5/15
	Albuquerque MSA, NM	Y	30320 FQ	35380 MW	39820 TQ	USBLS	5/15
	New York	Y	29420 AE	38970 MW	44090 AEX	NYBLS	1/16-3/16
	Buffalo-Cheektowaga-Niagara Falls MSA, NY	Y	30640 FQ	34820 MW	38810 TQ	USBLS	5/15
	Nassau County-Suffolk County PMSA, NY	Y	37060 FQ	42970 MW	48410 TQ	USBLS	5/15
	New York-Jersey City-White Plains PMSA, NY-NJ	Y	32490 FQ	37790 MW	44710 TQ	USBLS	5/15
	Rochester MSA, NY	Y	25360 FQ	29100 MW	34410 TQ	USBLS	5/15
	North Carolina	Y	24130 FQ	28260 MW	33540 TQ	USBLS	5/15

AE	Average entry wage	AWR	Average wage range	H	Hourly
AEX	Average experienced wage	B	Biweekly	HI	Highest wage paid
ATC	Average total compensation	D	Daily	HR	High end range
AW	Average wage paid	FQ	First quartile wage	LO	Lowest wage paid

LR	Low end range	MTC	Median total compensation
M	Monthly	MW	Median wage paid
MCC	Median cash compensation	MWR	Median wage range
ME	Median entry wage	S	See annotated source

TCC	Total cash compensation		
TQ	Third quartile wage		
W	Weekly		
Y	Yearly		

Medical Equipment Preparer

Occupation/Type/Industry	Location	Per	Low	Mid	High	Source	Date
Medical Equipment Preparer	Charlotte-Concord-Gastonia						
	MSA, NC-SC	Y	20910 FQ	26480 MW	31140 TQ	USBLS	5/15
	Raleigh MSA, NC	Y	28580 FQ	34740 MW	39700 TQ	USBLS	5/15
	Ohio	Y	27380 FQ	31570 MW	36220 TQ	USBLS	5/15
	Cincinnati MSA, OH-KY-IN	Y	28220 FQ	32390 MW	37450 TQ	USBLS	5/15
	Cleveland-Elyria MSA, OH	Y	28150 FQ	32780 MW	36530 TQ	USBLS	5/15
	Columbus MSA, OH	Y	28390 FQ	32970 MW	37570 TQ	USBLS	5/15
	Oklahoma	Y	24590 FQ	29830 MW	36770 TQ	USBLS	5/15
	Oklahoma City MSA, OK	Y	25110 FQ	30470 MW	37640 TQ	USBLS	5/15
	Tulsa MSA, OK	Y	27050 FQ	30550 MW	36620 TQ	USBLS	5/15
	Oregon	H	15.56 FQ	18.07 MW	21.71 TQ	ORBLS	2016
	Portland-Vancouver-Hillsboro						
	MSA, OR-WA	Y	34650 FQ	40620 MW	47730 TQ	USBLS	5/15
	Pennsylvania	Y	27750 FQ	33000 MW	39480 TQ	USBLS	5/15
	Allentown-Bethlehem-Easton						
	MSA, PA-NJ	Y	26180 FQ	30500 MW	37900 TQ	USBLS	5/15
	Montgomery County-Bucks						
	County-Chester County						
	PMSA, PA	Y	30160 FQ	35830 MW	42840 TQ	USBLS	5/15
	Philadelphia PMSA, PA	Y	32630 FQ	38390 MW	44640 TQ	USBLS	5/15
	Pittsburgh MSA, PA	Y	26020 FQ	29590 MW	34860 TQ	USBLS	5/15
	Rhode Island	Y	30130 FQ	35800 MW	43070 TQ	USBLS	5/15
	Providence-Warwick MSA, RI-						
	MA	Y	30950 FQ	37280 MW	45890 TQ	USBLS	5/15
	South Carolina	Y	24490 FQ	29390 MW	35600 TQ	USBLS	5/15
	Charleston-North Charleston						
	MSA, SC	Y	24850 FQ	28750 MW	34180 TQ	USBLS	5/15
	Columbia MSA, SC	Y	24250 FQ	29600 MW	35690 TQ	USBLS	5/15
	Greenville-Anderson-Mauldin						
	MSA, SC	Y	24680 FQ	29070 MW	35480 TQ	USBLS	5/15
	Tennessee	Y	24450 FQ	29570 MW	35880 TQ	USBLS	5/15
	Knoxville MSA, TN	Y	22090 FQ	24990 MW	29670 TQ	USBLS	5/15
	Memphis MSA, TN-MS-AR	Y	25630 FQ	31880 MW	37250 TQ	USBLS	5/15
	Nashville-Davidson–						
	Murfreesboro–Franklin						
	MSA, TN	Y	27280 FQ	31990 MW	37890 TQ	USBLS	5/15
	Texas	Y	24310 FQ	29400 MW	36630 TQ	USBLS	5/15
	Austin-Round Rock MSA, TX	Y	22430 FQ	25120 MW	30270 TQ	USBLS	5/15
	Dallas-Plano-Irving PMSA, TX	Y	26190 FQ	31330 MW	38540 TQ	USBLS	5/15
	Fort Worth-Arlington PMSA,						
	TX	Y	27160 FQ	32070 MW	37260 TQ	USBLS	5/15
	Houston-The Woodlands-						
	Sugar Land MSA, TX	Y	26680 FQ	32470 MW	38770 TQ	USBLS	5/15
	San Antonio-New Braunfels						
	MSA, TX	Y	22900 FQ	26930 MW	32510 TQ	USBLS	5/15
	Utah	Y	26700 FQ	30790 MW	36440 TQ	USBLS	5/15
	Salt Lake City MSA, UT	Y	27940 FQ	31820 MW	37120 TQ	USBLS	5/15
	Vermont	Y	27740 FQ	32470 MW	39310 TQ	USBLS	5/15
	Virginia	Y	26410 FQ	30630 MW	37050 TQ	USBLS	5/15
	Richmond MSA, VA	Y	25700 FQ	30470 MW	38710 TQ	USBLS	5/15
	Virginia Beach-Norfolk-						
	Newport News MSA, VA-NC	Y	25360 FQ	28540 MW	32810 TQ	USBLS	5/15
	Washington	H	14.52 FQ	17.91 MW	21.90 TQ	WABLS	3/16
	Seattle-Bellevue-Everett						
	PMSA, WA	H	15.07 FQ	18.66 MW	22.66 TQ	WABLS	3/16
	Tacoma-Lakewood PMSA, WA	H	14.89 FQ	17.53 MW	21.18 TQ	WABLS	3/16
	West Virginia	Y	22800 FQ	26700 MW	31400 TQ	USBLS	5/15
	Huntington-Ashland MSA,						
	WV-KY-OH	Y	23700 FQ	28660 MW	34850 TQ	USBLS	5/15
	Wisconsin	Y	29360 FQ	34740 MW	41090 TQ	USBLS	5/15
	Madison MSA, WI	Y	30800 FQ	35520 MW	41290 TQ	USBLS	5/15
	Milwaukee-Waukesha-West						
	Allis MSA, WI	Y	29440 FQ	35640 MW	42980 TQ	USBLS	5/15
	Wyoming	Y	27340 FQ	33850 MW	39770 TQ	USBLS	5/15
	Puerto Rico	Y	17160 FQ	19140 MW	26460 TQ	USBLS	5/15
	San Juan-Carolina-Caguas						
	MSA, PR	Y	17140 FQ	19100 MW	24000 TQ	USBLS	5/15
Medical Equipment Repairer	Alabama	Y	30683 AE	47688 AW	56190 AEX	ALBLS	6/16
	Birmingham-Hoover MSA, AL	Y	33734 AE	51878 AW	60950 AEX	ALBLS	6/16
	Alaska	Y	55460 FQ	64340 MW	77490 TQ	USBLS	5/15
	Anchorage MSA, AK	Y	55280 FQ	64040 MW	77140 TQ	USBLS	5/15

AE	Average entry wage	AWR	Average wage range	H	Hourly
AEX	Average experienced wage	B	Biweekly	HI	Highest wage paid
ATC	Average total compensation	D	Daily	HR	High end range
AW	Average wage paid	FQ	First quartile wage	LO	Lowest wage paid

LR	Low end range	MTC	Median total compensation	TCC	Total cash compensation
M	Monthly	MW	Median wage paid	TQ	Third quartile wage
MCC	Median cash compensation	MWR	Median wage range	W	Weekly
ME	Median entry wage	S	See annotated source	Y	Yearly

Medical Equipment Repairer

Occupation/Type/Industry	Location	Per	Low	Mid	High	Source	Date
Medical Equipment Repairer	Arizona	Y	30720 FQ	35840 MW	42870 TQ	USBLS	5/15
	Phoenix-Mesa-Scottsdale MSA, AZ	Y	30590 FQ	35340 MW	39640 TQ	USBLS	5/15
	Tucson MSA, AZ	Y	33060 FQ	43120 MW	54450 TQ	USBLS	5/15
	Arkansas	Y	27710 FQ	33700 MW	41420 TQ	USBLS	5/15
	Little Rock-North Little Rock-Conway MSA, AR	Y	33790 FQ	37210 MW	42300 TQ	USBLS	5/15
	California	H	18.09 FQ	24.14 MW	31.17 TQ	CABLS	1/16-3/16
	Anaheim-Santa Ana-Irvine PMSA, CA	H	17.91 FQ	22.50 MW	30.85 TQ	CABLS	1/16-3/16
	Los Angeles-Long Beach-Glendale PMSA, CA	H	20.47 FQ	27.45 MW	34.51 TQ	CABLS	1/16-3/16
	Oakland-Hayward-Berkeley PMSA, CA	H	18.17 FQ	22.82 MW	28.28 TQ	CABLS	1/16-3/16
	Riverside-San Bernardino-Ontario MSA, CA	H	15.84 FQ	21.03 MW	30.64 TQ	CABLS	1/16-3/16
	Sacramento–Roseville–Arden-Arcade MSA, CA	H	21.22 FQ	27.68 MW	37.03 TQ	CABLS	1/16-3/16
	San Diego-Carlsbad MSA, CA	H	20.23 FQ	27.80 MW	38.50 TQ	CABLS	1/16-3/16
	San Francisco-Redwood City-South San Francisco PMSA, CA	H	22.98 FQ	27.50 MW	31.64 TQ	CABLS	1/16-3/16
	Colorado	Y	37500 FQ	49570 MW	60010 TQ	USBLS	5/15
	Denver-Aurora-Lakewood MSA, CO	Y	41000 FQ	51290 MW	60830 TQ	USBLS	5/15
	Connecticut	Y		49394 MW		CTBLS	1/16-3/16
	Bridgeport-Stamford-Norwalk MSA, CT	Y	40440 FQ	52530 MW	64920 TQ	USBLS	5/15
	Hartford-West Hartford-East Hartford MSA, CT	Y	41750 FQ	47470 MW	61400 TQ	USBLS	5/15
	Delaware	Y	45740 FQ	55510 MW	64240 TQ	USBLS	5/15
	Wilmington PMSA, DE-MD-NJ	Y	48480 FQ	56670 MW	66430 TQ	USBLS	5/15
	District of Columbia	Y	41410 FQ	47600 MW	54570 TQ	USBLS	5/15
	Washington-Arlington-Alexandria PMSA, DC-VA-MD-WV	Y	37960 FQ	55710 MW	70630 TQ	USBLS	5/15
	Florida	H	14.78 AE	19.74 MW	25.15 AEX	FLBLS	7/16-9/16
	Fort Lauderdale-Pompano Beach-Deerfield Beach PMSA, FL	H	17.71 AE	27.45 MW	33.81 AEX	FLBLS	7/16-9/16
	Miami-Miami Beach-Kendall PMSA, FL	H	13.57 AE	16.10 MW	21.41 AEX	FLBLS	7/16-9/16
	Orlando-Kissimmee-Sanford MSA, FL	H	15.62 AE	23.04 MW	28.24 AEX	FLBLS	7/16-9/16
	Tampa-St. Petersburg-Clearwater MSA, FL	H	15.72 AE	19.97 MW	24.06 AEX	FLBLS	7/16-9/16
	Georgia	Y	30860 FQ	38020 MW	53380 TQ	USBLS	5/15
	Atlanta-Sandy Springs-Roswell MSA, GA	Y	31360 FQ	38920 MW	56380 TQ	USBLS	5/15
	Augusta-Richmond County MSA, GA-SC	Y	28730 FQ	34590 MW	48580 TQ	USBLS	5/15
	Hawaii	Y	38840 FQ	47650 MW	80720 TQ	USBLS	5/15
	Urban Honolulu MSA, HI	Y	38540 FQ	48290 MW	82960 TQ	USBLS	5/15
	Idaho	Y	39330 FQ	48440 MW	64060 TQ	USBLS	5/15
	Boise City MSA, ID	Y	39420 FQ	49790 MW	63130 TQ	USBLS	5/15
	Illinois	Y	35900 FQ	47600 MW	61740 TQ	USBLS	5/15
	Chicago-Naperville-Arlington Heights PMSA, IL	Y	38940 FQ	52130 MW	67690 TQ	USBLS	5/15
	Lake County-Kenosha County PMSA, IL-WI	Y	31740 FQ	43530 MW	57640 TQ	USBLS	5/15
	Indiana	Y	35900 FQ	47240 MW	62220 TQ	USBLS	5/15
	Indianapolis-Carmel-Anderson MSA, IN	Y	41170 FQ	54360 MW	70680 TQ	USBLS	5/15
	Iowa	Y	32290 FQ	39450 MW	53280 TQ	USBLS	5/15
	Des Moines-West Des Moines MSA, IA	Y	31700 FQ	37350 MW	48890 TQ	USBLS	5/15
	Kansas	Y	35510 FQ	49260 MW	58140 TQ	USBLS	5/15
	Wichita MSA, KS	Y	31780 FQ	38610 MW	53200 TQ	USBLS	5/15
	Kentucky	Y	28680 FQ	38040 MW	57080 TQ	USBLS	5/15
	Louisville-Jefferson County MSA, KY-IN	Y	28420 FQ	35550 MW	48080 TQ	USBLS	5/15

AE	Average entry wage	AWR	Average wage range	H	Hourly	LR	Low end range	MTC	Median total compensation	TCC	Total cash compensation
AEX	Average experienced wage	B	Biweekly	HI	Highest wage paid	M	Monthly	MW	Median wage paid	TQ	Third quartile wage
ATC	Average total compensation	D	Daily	HR	High end range	MCC	Median cash compensation	MWR	Median wage range	W	Weekly
AW	Average wage paid	FQ	First quartile wage	LO	Lowest wage paid	ME	Median entry wage	S	See annotated source	Y	Yearly

Occupation/Type/Industry	Location	Per	Low	Mid	High	Source	Date
Medical Equipment Repairer	Louisiana	Y	28250 FQ	36060 MW	46990 TQ	USBLS	5/15
	Baton Rouge MSA, LA	Y	33170 FQ	37790 MW	54100 TQ	USBLS	5/15
	New Orleans-Metairie MSA, LA	Y	26850 FQ	33710 MW	40230 TQ	USBLS	5/15
	Maine	Y	47970 FQ	56640 MW	65190 TQ	USBLS	5/15
	Portland-South Portland MSA, ME	Y	50060 FQ	57590 MW	66560 TQ	USBLS	5/15
	Maryland	Y	33263 AE	49696 MW	57913 AEX	MDBLS	4/16
	Baltimore-Columbia-Towson MSA, MD	Y	39310 FQ	52680 MW	67990 TQ	USBLS	5/15
	Salisbury MSA, MD-DE	Y	43260 FQ	47630 MW	54990 TQ	USBLS	5/15
	Massachusetts	Y	37990 FQ	53660 MW	71630 TQ	USBLS	5/15
	Boston-Cambridge-Newton NECTA, MA	Y	50940 FQ	66870 MW	78220 TQ	USBLS	5/15
	Worcester MSA, MA-CT	Y	35410 FQ	47890 MW	59780 TQ	USBLS	5/15
	Michigan	Y	29960 FQ	40140 MW	52550 TQ	USBLS	5/15
	Detroit-Dearborn-Livonia PMSA, MI	Y	24640 FQ	38870 MW	49980 TQ	USBLS	5/15
	Grand Rapids-Wyoming MSA, MI	Y	30990 FQ	41240 MW	58970 TQ	USBLS	5/15
	Minnesota	Y	43696 FQ	56780 MW	70146 TQ	MNBLS	1/16-3/16
	Minneapolis-St. Paul-Bloomington MSA, MN-WI	Y	42600 FQ	54739 MW	65962 TQ	MNBLS	1/16-3/16
	Mississippi	Y	34730 FQ	45630 MW	54790 TQ	USBLS	5/15
	Jackson MSA, MS	Y	27150 FQ	42640 MW	55220 TQ	USBLS	5/15
	Missouri	Y	34230 FQ	42700 MW	56440 TQ	USBLS	5/15
	Kansas City MSA, MO-KS	Y	38190 FQ	50980 MW	58640 TQ	USBLS	5/15
	St. Louis MSA, MO-IL	Y	35640 FQ	44400 MW	58210 TQ	USBLS	5/15
	Montana	Y	37140 FQ	55080 MW	69380 TQ	USBLS	5/15
	Nebraska	Y	38435 FQ	46750 MW	65230 TQ	NEBLS	7/16-9/16
	Omaha-Council Bluffs MSA, NE-IA	Y	37795 FQ	47205 MW	63285 TQ	NEBLS	7/16-9/16
	Nevada	Y	38460 FQ	51050 MW	70820 TQ	USBLS	5/15
	Las Vegas-Henderson-Paradise MSA, NV	Y	46630 FQ	56540 MW	71510 TQ	USBLS	5/15
	New Hampshire	H	18.02 AE	27.00 MW	31.00 AEX	NHBLS	6/16
	Manchester NECTA, NH	H	17.92 AE	24.85 MW	28.33 AEX	NHBLS	6/16
	New Jersey	Y	44240 FQ	58390 MW	72090 TQ	USBLS	5/15
	Camden PMSA, NJ	Y	40610 FQ	49430 MW	59210 TQ	USBLS	5/15
	Newark PMSA, NJ-PA	Y	52890 FQ	65460 MW	77590 TQ	USBLS	5/15
	New Mexico	Y	37100 FQ	47530 MW	61020 TQ	USBLS	5/15
	Albuquerque MSA, NM	Y	37570 FQ	47130 MW	61310 TQ	USBLS	5/15
	New York	Y	37570 AE	56130 MW	68740 AEX	NYBLS	1/16-3/16
	Buffalo-Cheektowaga-Niagara Falls MSA, NY	Y	33140 FQ	37700 MW	46520 TQ	USBLS	5/15
	Nassau County-Suffolk County PMSA, NY	Y	39530 FQ	48480 MW	68440 TQ	USBLS	5/15
	New York-Jersey City-White Plains PMSA, NY-NJ	Y	50880 FQ	64930 MW	76630 TQ	USBLS	5/15
	Rochester MSA, NY	Y	42380 FQ	53000 MW	61060 TQ	USBLS	5/15
	North Carolina	Y	33300 FQ	43460 MW	55490 TQ	USBLS	5/15
	Charlotte-Concord-Gastonia MSA, NC-SC	Y	33830 FQ	42220 MW	54220 TQ	USBLS	5/15
	Raleigh MSA, NC	Y	29770 FQ	40330 MW	47380 TQ	USBLS	5/15
	North Dakota	Y	42140 FQ	55050 MW	62500 TQ	USBLS	5/15
	Fargo MSA, ND-MN	Y	39960 FQ	57830 MW	71780 TQ	USBLS	5/15
	Ohio	Y	37930 FQ	50500 MW	63960 TQ	USBLS	5/15
	Cincinnati MSA, OH-KY-IN	Y	45590 FQ	57580 MW	69690 TQ	USBLS	5/15
	Cleveland-Elyria MSA, OH	Y	41460 FQ	56070 MW	70740 TQ	USBLS	5/15
	Columbus MSA, OH	Y	40450 FQ	48720 MW	59690 TQ	USBLS	5/15
	Oklahoma	Y	32260 FQ	38870 MW	48970 TQ	USBLS	5/15
	Oklahoma City MSA, OK	Y	31990 FQ	37870 MW	45690 TQ	USBLS	5/15
	Tulsa MSA, OK	Y	33640 FQ	40900 MW	53610 TQ	USBLS	5/15
	Oregon	H	17.89 FQ	27.57 MW	35.69 TQ	ORBLS	2016
	Portland-Vancouver-Hillsboro MSA, OR-WA	Y	41230 FQ	64840 MW	76590 TQ	USBLS	5/15
	Pennsylvania	Y	37360 FQ	48570 MW	64000 TQ	USBLS	5/15
	Allentown-Bethlehem-Easton MSA, PA-NJ	Y	40700 FQ	53970 MW	62780 TQ	USBLS	5/15
	Harrisburg-Carlisle MSA, PA	Y	32280 FQ	41500 MW	59660 TQ	USBLS	5/15

AE	Average entry wage	AWR	Average wage range	H	Hourly	LR	Low end range	MTC	Median total compensation	TCC	Total cash compensation
AEX	Average experienced wage	B	Biweekly	HI	Highest wage paid	M	Monthly	MW	Median wage paid	TQ	Third quartile wage
ATC	Average total compensation	D	Daily	HR	High end range	MCC	Median cash compensation	MWR	Median wage range	W	Weekly
AW	Average wage paid	FQ	First quartile wage	LO	Lowest wage paid	ME	Median entry wage	S	See annotated source	Y	Yearly

Occupation/Type/Industry	Location	Per	Low	Mid	High	Source	Date
Medical Equipment Repairer	Montgomery County-Bucks County-Chester County						
	PMSA, PA	Y	43480 FQ	52390 MW	69050 TQ	USBLS	5/15
	Philadelphia PMSA, PA	Y	45520 FQ	62550 MW	73420 TQ	USBLS	5/15
	Pittsburgh MSA, PA	Y	35380 FQ	44510 MW	55090 TQ	USBLS	5/15
	Rhode Island	Y	41270 FQ	57360 MW	72430 TQ	USBLS	5/15
	Providence-Warwick MSA, RI-MA	Y	34080 FQ	52320 MW	70260 TQ	USBLS	5/15
	South Carolina	Y	29920 FQ	39420 MW	55350 TQ	USBLS	5/15
	Charleston-North Charleston MSA, SC	Y	37010 FQ	49240 MW	58780 TQ	USBLS	5/15
	Columbia MSA, SC	Y	28090 FQ	33600 MW	53850 TQ	USBLS	5/15
	Greenville-Anderson-Mauldin MSA, SC	Y	25400 FQ	34680 MW	48530 TQ	USBLS	5/15
	South Dakota	Y	41260 FQ	46160 MW	52140 TQ	USBLS	5/15
	Sioux Falls MSA, SD	Y	42590 FQ	47530 MW	55240 TQ	USBLS	5/15
	Tennessee	Y	32820 FQ	41960 MW	54840 TQ	USBLS	5/15
	Knoxville MSA, TN	Y	28700 FQ	38550 MW	51360 TQ	USBLS	5/15
	Memphis MSA, TN-MS-AR	Y	35630 FQ	47240 MW	63610 TQ	USBLS	5/15
	Nashville-Davidson–Murfreesboro–Franklin MSA, TN	Y	34800 FQ	42330 MW	54910 TQ	USBLS	5/15
	Texas	Y	33070 FQ	44560 MW	57110 TQ	USBLS	5/15
	Austin-Round Rock MSA, TX	Y	40940 FQ	47080 MW	59190 TQ	USBLS	5/15
	Dallas-Plano-Irving PMSA, TX	Y	43040 FQ	53880 MW	65610 TQ	USBLS	5/15
	Fort Worth-Arlington PMSA, TX	Y	34450 FQ	42330 MW	49790 TQ	USBLS	5/15
	Houston-The Woodlands-Sugar Land MSA, TX	Y	35730 FQ	47340 MW	62990 TQ	USBLS	5/15
	San Antonio-New Braunfels MSA, TX	Y	28970 FQ	36130 MW	44950 TQ	USBLS	5/15
	Utah	Y	35950 FQ	53430 MW	61350 TQ	USBLS	5/15
	Ogden-Clearfield MSA, UT	Y	28920 FQ	42790 MW	57710 TQ	USBLS	5/15
	Salt Lake City MSA, UT	Y	39630 FQ	55360 MW	62270 TQ	USBLS	5/15
	Vermont	Y	42830 FQ	51410 MW	60700 TQ	USBLS	5/15
	Burlington-South Burlington MSA, VT	Y	42630 FQ	50280 MW	59730 TQ	USBLS	5/15
	Virginia	Y	35070 FQ	52170 MW	67520 TQ	USBLS	5/15
	Richmond MSA, VA	Y	33800 FQ	49890 MW	74300 TQ	USBLS	5/15
	Virginia Beach-Norfolk-Newport News MSA, VA-NC	Y	30160 FQ	37560 MW	55240 TQ	USBLS	5/15
	Washington	H	18.94 FQ	25.38 MW	32.80 TQ	WABLS	3/16
	Seattle-Bellevue-Everett PMSA, WA	H	20.53 FQ	26.61 MW	33.06 TQ	WABLS	3/16
	Tacoma-Lakewood PMSA, WA	H	17.62 FQ	21.42 MW	30.19 TQ	WABLS	3/16
	West Virginia	Y	28570 FQ	39000 MW	49330 TQ	USBLS	5/15
	Huntington-Ashland MSA, WV-KY-OH	Y	32330 FQ	45000 MW	55000 TQ	USBLS	5/15
	Wisconsin	Y	36400 FQ	45750 MW	57680 TQ	USBLS	5/15
	Madison MSA, WI	Y	34900 FQ	40240 MW	59880 TQ	USBLS	5/15
	Milwaukee-Waukesha-West Allis MSA, WI	Y	39460 FQ	47000 MW	57060 TQ	USBLS	5/15
	Wyoming	Y	23800 FQ	37970 MW	56270 TQ	USBLS	5/15
	Puerto Rico	Y	21100 FQ	31070 MW	41580 TQ	USBLS	5/15
	San Juan-Carolina-Caguas MSA, PR	Y	22530 FQ	32580 MW	42570 TQ	USBLS	5/15
Medical Examiner							
County Government	Augusta/Richmond County, GA	Y	49994 LO		75393 HI	GACTY04	2016
State Government	Missoula, MT	H	97.13 LO		113.96 HI	MTGOV	2016
Medical Illustrator	United States	Y	69250 LO		94500 HI	RH02	2017
Medical Informatics Executive							
Healthcare System	United States	Y		338700 MCC		MHLTH01	2015
Medical Meeting Professional	United States	Y		71750 AW		CVENE	2016
Medical Perfusionist	United States	Y		93500 MW		FTIME	2016
Medical Record Librarian							
Municipal Government	Detroit, MI	M	3092 LO		3308 HI	DETGOV	2016

AE	Average entry wage	AWR	Average wage range	H	Hourly	LR	Low end range	MTC Median total compensation TCC Total cash compensation
AEX	Average experienced wage	B	Biweekly	HI	Highest wage paid	M	Monthly	MW Median wage paid TQ Third quartile wage
ATC	Average total compensation	D	Daily	HR	High end range	MCC	Median cash compensation	MWR Median wage range W Weekly
AW	Average wage paid	FQ	First quartile wage	LO	Lowest wage paid	ME	Median entry wage	S See annotated source Y Yearly

Occupation/Type/Industry	Location	Per	Low	Mid	High	Source	Date
Medical Records and Health Information Technician	Alabama	Y	22242 AE	33821 AW	39611 AEX	ALBLS	6/16
	Birmingham-Hoover MSA, AL	Y	23924 AE	36268 AW	23924 AEX	ALBLS	6/16
	Alaska	Y	36940 FQ	43750 MW	50690 TQ	USBLS	5/15
	Anchorage MSA, AK	Y	35610 FQ	41540 MW	49430 TQ	USBLS	5/15
	Arizona	Y	29720 FQ	36890 MW	48910 TQ	USBLS	5/15
	Phoenix-Mesa-Scottsdale MSA, AZ	Y	30080 FQ	36970 MW	50400 TQ	USBLS	5/15
	Tucson MSA, AZ	Y	27360 FQ	35610 MW	44640 TQ	USBLS	5/15
	Arkansas	Y	25120 FQ	31180 MW	39610 TQ	USBLS	5/15
	Little Rock-North Little Rock-Conway MSA, AR	Y	29560 FQ	36490 MW	44560 TQ	USBLS	5/15
	California	H	16.05 FQ	21.38 MW	28.76 TQ	CABLS	1/16-3/16
	Anaheim-Santa Ana-Irvine PMSA, CA	H	15.90 FQ	22.13 MW	32.36 TQ	CABLS	1/16-3/16
	Los Angeles-Long Beach-Glendale PMSA, CA	H	16.09 FQ	20.77 MW	27.93 TQ	CABLS	1/16-3/16
	Oakland-Hayward-Berkeley PMSA, CA	H	20.29 FQ	26.38 MW	33.81 TQ	CABLS	1/16-3/16
	Riverside-San Bernardino-Ontario MSA, CA	H	14.61 FQ	20.54 MW	27.78 TQ	CABLS	1/16-3/16
	Sacramento–Roseville–Arden-Arcade MSA, CA	H	17.20 FQ	22.92 MW	29.73 TQ	CABLS	1/16-3/16
	San Diego-Carlsbad MSA, CA	H	14.93 FQ	19.36 MW	26.83 TQ	CABLS	1/16-3/16
	San Francisco-Redwood City-South San Francisco PMSA, CA	H	20.91 FQ	26.40 MW	30.75 TQ	CABLS	1/16-3/16
	Colorado	Y	35700 FQ	45610 MW	58080 TQ	USBLS	5/15
	Denver-Aurora-Lakewood MSA, CO	Y	39060 FQ	51630 MW	62590 TQ	USBLS	5/15
	Connecticut	Y		43806 MW		CTBLS	1/16-3/16
	Bridgeport-Stamford-Norwalk MSA, CT	Y	32640 FQ	39910 MW	46830 TQ	USBLS	5/15
	Hartford-West Hartford-East Hartford MSA, CT	Y	32900 FQ	40060 MW	54600 TQ	USBLS	5/15
	Delaware	Y	31630 FQ	38150 MW	45790 TQ	USBLS	5/15
	Wilmington PMSA, DE-MD-NJ	Y	33980 FQ	40410 MW	47650 TQ	USBLS	5/15
	District of Columbia	Y	40180 FQ	48740 MW	62100 TQ	USBLS	5/15
	Washington-Arlington-Alexandria PMSA, DC-VA-MD-WV	Y	35280 FQ	44530 MW	58150 TQ	USBLS	5/15
	Florida	H	12.79 AE	18.11 MW	23.02 AEX	FLBLS	7/16-9/16
	Deltona-Daytona Beach-Ormond Beach MSA, FL	H	12.18 AE	16.63 MW	19.54 AEX	FLBLS	7/16-9/16
	Fort Lauderdale-Pompano Beach-Deerfield Beach PMSA, FL	H	12.46 AE	18.69 MW	24.54 AEX	FLBLS	7/16-9/16
	Miami-Miami Beach-Kendall PMSA, FL	H	13.07 AE	18.28 MW	24.60 AEX	FLBLS	7/16-9/16
	Orlando-Kissimmee-Sanford MSA, FL	H	14.73 AE	19.63 MW	22.61 AEX	FLBLS	7/16-9/16
	Tampa-St. Petersburg-Clearwater MSA, FL	H	13.75 AE	18.40 MW	23.64 AEX	FLBLS	7/16-9/16
	Georgia	Y	27280 FQ	34760 MW	45580 TQ	USBLS	5/15
	Atlanta-Sandy Springs-Roswell MSA, GA	Y	28670 FQ	36270 MW	47470 TQ	USBLS	5/15
	Augusta-Richmond County MSA, GA-SC	Y	31430 FQ	39550 MW	48210 TQ	USBLS	5/15
	Hawaii	Y	34240 FQ	44230 MW	58960 TQ	USBLS	5/15
	Urban Honolulu MSA, HI	Y	37580 FQ	48710 MW	63620 TQ	USBLS	5/15
	Idaho	Y	28000 FQ	34130 MW	40850 TQ	USBLS	5/15
	Boise City MSA, ID	Y	29900 FQ	35600 MW	42840 TQ	USBLS	5/15
	Illinois	Y	28370 FQ	36830 MW	48340 TQ	USBLS	5/15
	Chicago-Naperville-Arlington Heights PMSA, IL	Y	30720 FQ	39750 MW	51330 TQ	USBLS	5/15
	Lake County-Kenosha County PMSA, IL-WI	Y	33630 FQ	44480 MW	59220 TQ	USBLS	5/15
	Indiana	Y	27180 FQ	33690 MW	43260 TQ	USBLS	5/15
	Gary PMSA, IN	Y	24900 FQ	30100 MW	37990 TQ	USBLS	5/15
	Indianapolis-Carmel-Anderson MSA, IN	Y	28880 FQ	35760 MW	45980 TQ	USBLS	5/15

AE	Average entry wage	AWR	Average wage range	H	Hourly
AEX	Average experienced wage	B	Biweekly	HI	Highest wage paid
ATC	Average total compensation	D	Daily	HR	High end range
AW	Average wage paid	FQ	First quartile wage	LO	Lowest wage paid

LR	Low end range	MTC	Median total compensation	TCC	Total cash compensation
M	Monthly	MW	Median wage paid	TQ	Third quartile wage
MCC	Median cash compensation	MWR	Median wage range	W	Weekly
ME	Median entry wage	S	See annotated source	Y	Yearly

Occupation/Type/Industry	Location	Per	Low	Mid	High	Source	Date
Medical Records and Health Information Technician	Iowa	Y	30810 FQ	37030 MW	46350 TQ	USBLS	5/15
	Des Moines-West Des Moines MSA, IA	Y	31630 FQ	37730 MW	47360 TQ	USBLS	5/15
	Kansas	Y	26840 FQ	33390 MW	42280 TQ	USBLS	5/15
	Wichita MSA, KS	Y	26290 FQ	31810 MW	38430 TQ	USBLS	5/15
	Kentucky	Y	26890 FQ	34020 MW	43620 TQ	USBLS	5/15
	Louisville-Jefferson County MSA, KY-IN	Y	27900 FQ	34900 MW	42940 TQ	USBLS	5/15
	Louisiana	Y	24550 FQ	30500 MW	38520 TQ	USBLS	5/15
	Baton Rouge MSA, LA	Y	24360 FQ	29710 MW	41770 TQ	USBLS	5/15
	New Orleans-Metairie MSA, LA	Y	24830 FQ	31190 MW	38090 TQ	USBLS	5/15
	Maine	Y	28970 FQ	35100 MW	42600 TQ	USBLS	5/15
	Portland-South Portland MSA, ME	Y	31250 FQ	36730 MW	45270 TQ	USBLS	5/15
	Maryland	Y	30333 AE	47928 MW	56726 AEX	MDBLS	4/16
	Baltimore-Columbia-Towson MSA, MD	Y	33660 FQ	46040 MW	59820 TQ	USBLS	5/15
	Salisbury MSA, MD-DE	Y	28170 FQ	34670 MW	44530 TQ	USBLS	5/15
	Massachusetts	Y	34270 FQ	42830 MW	55500 TQ	USBLS	5/15
	Boston-Cambridge-Newton NECTA, MA	Y	36700 FQ	46700 MW	58680 TQ	USBLS	5/15
	Worcester MSA, MA-CT	Y	33140 FQ	41280 MW	51600 TQ	USBLS	5/15
	Michigan	Y	28840 FQ	36200 MW	46620 TQ	USBLS	5/15
	Detroit-Dearborn-Livonia PMSA, MI	Y	28250 FQ	34860 MW	45590 TQ	USBLS	5/15
	Grand Rapids-Wyoming MSA, MI	Y	30700 FQ	34950 MW	38940 TQ	USBLS	5/15
	Minnesota	Y	37469 FQ	44546 MW	51985 TQ	MNBLS	1/16-3/16
	Minneapolis-St. Paul-Bloomington MSA, MN-WI	Y	37711 FQ	44768 MW	51915 TQ	MNBLS	1/16-3/16
	Mississippi	Y	22370 FQ	28120 MW	36490 TQ	USBLS	5/15
	Jackson MSA, MS	Y	26340 FQ	31130 MW	41520 TQ	USBLS	5/15
	Missouri	Y	29470 FQ	36910 MW	46800 TQ	USBLS	5/15
	Kansas City MSA, MO-KS	Y	30460 FQ	36320 MW	45280 TQ	USBLS	5/15
	St. Louis MSA, MO-IL	Y	31180 FQ	40760 MW	49440 TQ	USBLS	5/15
	Montana	Y	26440 FQ	31370 MW	41440 TQ	USBLS	5/15
	Billings MSA, MT	Y	26440 FQ	36670 MW	55320 TQ	USBLS	5/15
	Nebraska	Y	31320 FQ	37175 MW	46045 TQ	NEBLS	7/16-9/16
	Omaha-Council Bluffs MSA, NE-IA	Y	33280 FQ	38670 MW	48005 TQ	NEBLS	7/16-9/16
	Nevada	Y	30660 FQ	40630 MW	54220 TQ	USBLS	5/15
	Las Vegas-Henderson-Paradise MSA, NV	Y	31000 FQ	42170 MW	54870 TQ	USBLS	5/15
	New Hampshire	H	13.56 AE	17.84 MW	21.91 AEX	NHBLS	6/16
	Manchester NECTA, NH	H	13.96 AE	18.30 MW	21.12 AEX	NHBLS	6/16
	Nashua NECTA, NH-MA	Y	28910 FQ	34830 MW	44660 TQ	USBLS	5/15
	New Jersey	Y	46780 FQ	58420 MW	71210 TQ	USBLS	5/15
	Camden PMSA, NJ	Y	35660 FQ	48230 MW	59690 TQ	USBLS	5/15
	Newark PMSA, NJ-PA	Y	50920 FQ	60980 MW	74150 TQ	USBLS	5/15
	Trenton MSA, NJ	Y	39750 FQ	51060 MW	61270 TQ	USBLS	5/15
	New Mexico	Y	24170 FQ	30610 MW	41530 TQ	USBLS	5/15
	Albuquerque MSA, NM	Y	24600 FQ	31450 MW	43780 TQ	USBLS	5/15
	New York	Y	30370 AE	42200 MW	51280 AEX	NYBLS	1/16-3/16
	Buffalo-Cheektowaga-Niagara Falls MSA, NY	Y	33970 FQ	41600 MW	52250 TQ	USBLS	5/15
	Nassau County-Suffolk County PMSA, NY	Y	40070 FQ	46800 MW	57380 TQ	USBLS	5/15
	New York-Jersey City-White Plains PMSA, NY-NJ	Y	36830 FQ	46540 MW	59260 TQ	USBLS	5/15
	Rochester MSA, NY	Y	29260 FQ	36960 MW	46050 TQ	USBLS	5/15
	North Carolina	Y	27200 FQ	32980 MW	41830 TQ	USBLS	5/15
	Charlotte-Concord-Gastonia MSA, NC-SC	Y	27420 FQ	33380 MW	41550 TQ	USBLS	5/15
	Raleigh MSA, NC	Y	27420 FQ	33250 MW	40870 TQ	USBLS	5/15
	North Dakota	Y	30810 FQ	38300 MW	45910 TQ	USBLS	5/15
	Fargo MSA, ND-MN	Y	35180 FQ	42110 MW	48780 TQ	USBLS	5/15
	Ohio	Y	29720 FQ	36070 MW	45330 TQ	USBLS	5/15
	Cincinnati MSA, OH-KY-IN	Y	32780 FQ	39380 MW	51800 TQ	USBLS	5/15
	Cleveland-Elyria MSA, OH	Y	29300 FQ	36050 MW	45000 TQ	USBLS	5/15
	Columbus MSA, OH	Y	30070 FQ	35490 MW	41860 TQ	USBLS	5/15

AE Average entry wage	**AWR** Average wage range	**H** Hourly	**LR** Low end range	**MTC** Median total compensation	**TCC** Total cash compensation
AEX Average experienced wage	**B** Biweekly	**HI** Highest wage paid	**M** Monthly	**MW** Median wage paid	**TQ** Third quartile wage
ATC Average total compensation	**D** Daily	**HR** High end range	**MCC** Median cash compensation	**MWR** Median wage range	**W** Weekly
AW Average wage paid	**FQ** First quartile wage	**LO** Lowest wage paid	**ME** Median entry wage	**S** See annotated source	**Y** Yearly

Occupation/Type/Industry	Location	Per	Low	Mid	High	Source	Date
Medical Records and Health Information Technician							
	Oklahoma	Y	25570 FQ	31000 MW	40370 TQ	USBLS	5/15
	Oklahoma City MSA, OK	Y	24840 FQ	31890 MW	39650 TQ	USBLS	5/15
	Tulsa MSA, OK	Y	26740 FQ	30860 MW	40840 TQ	USBLS	5/15
	Oregon	H	15.82 FQ	19.99 MW	24.70 TQ	ORBLS	2016
	Portland-Vancouver-Hillsboro MSA, OR-WA	Y	34490 FQ	43270 MW	52540 TQ	USBLS	5/15
	Pennsylvania	Y	29590 FQ	35970 MW	44760 TQ	USBLS	5/15
	Allentown-Bethlehem-Easton MSA, PA-NJ	Y	27320 FQ	32370 MW	39030 TQ	USBLS	5/15
	Harrisburg-Carlisle MSA, PA	Y	30910 FQ	38940 MW	48590 TQ	USBLS	5/15
	Montgomery County-Bucks County-Chester County PMSA, PA	Y	29900 FQ	35170 MW	42280 TQ	USBLS	5/15
	Philadelphia PMSA, PA	Y	31820 FQ	38510 MW	48870 TQ	USBLS	5/15
	Pittsburgh MSA, PA	Y	29320 FQ	36090 MW	44680 TQ	USBLS	5/15
	Rhode Island	Y	29890 FQ	39220 MW	49130 TQ	USBLS	5/15
	Providence-Warwick MSA, RI-MA	Y	30150 FQ	38430 MW	48310 TQ	USBLS	5/15
	South Carolina	Y	26580 FQ	32700 MW	43030 TQ	USBLS	5/15
	Charleston-North Charleston MSA, SC	Y	28740 FQ	35690 MW	44240 TQ	USBLS	5/15
	Columbia MSA, SC	Y	26960 FQ	35330 MW	47480 TQ	USBLS	5/15
	Greenville-Anderson-Mauldin MSA, SC	Y	25540 FQ	31140 MW	41870 TQ	USBLS	5/15
	South Dakota	Y	28610 FQ	35140 MW	44990 TQ	USBLS	5/15
	Tennessee	Y	26100 FQ	31940 MW	39860 TQ	USBLS	5/15
	Knoxville MSA, TN	Y	24830 FQ	29960 MW	37190 TQ	USBLS	5/15
	Memphis MSA, TN-MS-AR	Y	24140 FQ	32560 MW	42670 TQ	USBLS	5/15
	Nashville-Davidson–Murfreesboro–Franklin MSA, TN	Y	27770 FQ	33290 MW	43600 TQ	USBLS	5/15
	Texas	Y	26600 FQ	34990 MW	48590 TQ	USBLS	5/15
	Austin-Round Rock MSA, TX	Y	25970 FQ	32770 MW	41920 TQ	USBLS	5/15
	Dallas-Plano-Irving PMSA, TX	Y	31700 FQ	41370 MW	55910 TQ	USBLS	5/15
	Fort Worth-Arlington PMSA, TX	Y	29270 FQ	37540 MW	54440 TQ	USBLS	5/15
	Houston-The Woodlands-Sugar Land MSA, TX	Y	29090 FQ	38500 MW	53850 TQ	USBLS	5/15
	San Antonio-New Braunfels MSA, TX	Y	27530 FQ	34220 MW	42460 TQ	USBLS	5/15
	Utah	Y	28640 FQ	35130 MW	45010 TQ	USBLS	5/15
	Ogden-Clearfield MSA, UT	Y	24770 FQ	29900 MW	37440 TQ	USBLS	5/15
	Provo-Orem MSA, UT	Y	28890 FQ	35420 MW	44290 TQ	USBLS	5/15
	Salt Lake City MSA, UT	Y	30000 FQ	36800 MW	47550 TQ	USBLS	5/15
	Vermont	Y	29790 FQ	36340 MW	48030 TQ	USBLS	5/15
	Burlington-South Burlington MSA, VT	Y	29820 FQ	35030 MW	42890 TQ	USBLS	5/15
	Virginia	Y	29110 FQ	35960 MW	45990 TQ	USBLS	5/15
	Richmond MSA, VA	Y	27450 FQ	32060 MW	40660 TQ	USBLS	5/15
	Virginia Beach-Norfolk-Newport News MSA, VA-NC	Y	28490 FQ	33850 MW	41530 TQ	USBLS	5/15
	Washington	H	16.31 FQ	19.77 MW	25.20 TQ	WABLS	3/16
	Seattle-Bellevue-Everett PMSA, WA	H	17.54 FQ	21.79 MW	27.79 TQ	WABLS	3/16
	Tacoma-Lakewood PMSA, WA	H	16.73 FQ	20.07 MW	24.60 TQ	WABLS	3/16
	West Virginia	Y	25970 FQ	32300 MW	42490 TQ	USBLS	5/15
	Huntington-Ashland MSA, WV-KY-OH	Y	26800 FQ	33910 MW	49480 TQ	USBLS	5/15
	Wisconsin	Y	30890 FQ	37770 MW	48480 TQ	USBLS	5/15
	Madison MSA, WI	Y	33260 FQ	39880 MW	48330 TQ	USBLS	5/15
	Milwaukee-Waukesha-West Allis MSA, WI	Y	31880 FQ	39430 MW	52910 TQ	USBLS	5/15
	Wyoming	Y	30070 FQ	36740 MW	46730 TQ	USBLS	5/15
	Cheyenne MSA, WY	Y	32970 FQ	41530 MW	49140 TQ	USBLS	5/15
	Puerto Rico	Y	17350 FQ	19330 MW	24700 TQ	USBLS	5/15
	San Juan-Carolina-Caguas MSA, PR	Y	17420 FQ	19550 MW	25680 TQ	USBLS	5/15
	Guam	Y	19150 FQ	26210 MW	33590 TQ	USBLS	5/15
Medical Resident	United States	Y		56500 AW		MED01	2016
Critical Care	United States	Y		62000 AW		MED01	2016

AE	Average entry wage	AWR	Average wage range	H	Hourly	LR	Low end range	MTC	Median total compensation	TCC	Total cash compensation
AEX	Average experienced wage	B	Biweekly	HI	Highest wage paid	M	Monthly	MW	Median wage paid	TQ	Third quartile wage
ATC	Average total compensation	D	Daily	HR	High end range	MCC	Median cash compensation	MWR	Median wage range	W	Weekly
AW	Average wage paid	FQ	First quartile wage	LO	Lowest wage paid	ME	Median entry wage	S	See annotated source	Y	Yearly

Occupation/Type/Industry	Location	Per	Low	Mid	High	Source	Date
Medical Resident							
Internal Medicine, Obstetrics and Gynecology, Ophthalmology	United States	Y		55000 AW		MED01	2016
Preventative Medicine	United States	Y		58000 AW		MED01	2016
Medical Review Nurse							
Health Department, State Government	Ohio	H	25.52 LO		40.80 HI	OHGOV	2015
Medical Scientist							
Except Epidemiologist	Alabama	Y	41537 AE	58081 AW	66358 AEX	ALBLS	6/16
Except Epidemiologist	Arizona	Y	48860 FQ	62970 MW	87980 TQ	USBLS	5/15
Except Epidemiologist	Phoenix-Mesa-Scottsdale MSA, AZ	Y	52920 FQ	63760 MW	78830 TQ	USBLS	5/15
Except Epidemiologist	Tucson MSA, AZ	Y	42540 FQ	57730 MW	90620 TQ	USBLS	5/15
Except Epidemiologist	Arkansas	Y	36630 FQ	51600 MW	105600 TQ	USBLS	5/15
Except Epidemiologist	Little Rock-North Little Rock-Conway MSA, AR	Y	31080 FQ	43280 MW	64600 TQ	USBLS	5/15
Except Epidemiologist	California	H	39.29 FQ	50.71 MW	61.66 TQ	CABLS	1/16-3/16
Except Epidemiologist	Anaheim-Santa Ana-Irvine PMSA, CA	H	34.69 FQ	47.99 MW	60.33 TQ	CABLS	1/16-3/16
Except Epidemiologist	Los Angeles-Long Beach-Glendale PMSA, CA	H	31.25 FQ	40.56 MW	53.25 TQ	CABLS	1/16-3/16
Except Epidemiologist	Oakland-Hayward-Berkeley PMSA, CA	H	43.10 FQ	54.73 MW	65.17 TQ	CABLS	1/16-3/16
Except Epidemiologist	Riverside-San Bernardino-Ontario MSA, CA	H	39.58 FQ	46.10 MW	54.05 TQ	CABLS	1/16-3/16
Except Epidemiologist	Sacramento–Roseville–Arden-Arcade MSA, CA	H	41.67 FQ	47.37 MW	55.74 TQ	CABLS	1/16-3/16
Except Epidemiologist	San Diego-Carlsbad MSA, CA	H	39.96 FQ	49.40 MW	69.31 TQ	CABLS	1/16-3/16
Except Epidemiologist	San Francisco-Redwood City-South San Francisco PMSA, CA	H	48.59 FQ	57.62 MW	71.67 TQ	CABLS	1/16-3/16
Except Epidemiologist	Colorado	Y	44560 FQ	56390 MW	86040 TQ	USBLS	5/15
Except Epidemiologist	Colorado Springs MSA, CO	Y	38910 FQ	56140 MW	71500 TQ	USBLS	5/15
Except Epidemiologist	Connecticut	Y		113836 MW		CTBLS	1/16-3/16
Except Epidemiologist	Bridgeport-Stamford-Norwalk MSA, CT	Y	65720 FQ	86790 MW	122890 TQ	USBLS	5/15
Except Epidemiologist	Hartford-West Hartford-East Hartford MSA, CT	Y	65830 FQ	78350 MW	101360 TQ	USBLS	5/15
Except Epidemiologist	District of Columbia	Y	59740 FQ	85360 MW	127540 TQ	USBLS	5/15
Except Epidemiologist	Washington-Arlington-Alexandria PMSA, DC-VA-MD-WV	Y	63250 FQ	96410 MW	135360 TQ	USBLS	5/15
Except Epidemiologist	Florida	H	21.31 AE	32.59 MW	48.08 AEX	FLBLS	7/16-9/16
Except Epidemiologist	Fort Lauderdale-Pompano Beach-Deerfield Beach PMSA, FL	H	21.61 AE	33.40 MW	60.14 AEX	FLBLS	7/16-9/16
Except Epidemiologist	Miami-Miami Beach-Kendall PMSA, FL	H	20.61 AE	28.74 MW	53.30 AEX	FLBLS	7/16-9/16
Except Epidemiologist	Orlando-Kissimmee-Sanford MSA, FL	H	26.42 AE	37.76 MW	50.66 AEX	FLBLS	7/16-9/16
Except Epidemiologist	Tampa-St. Petersburg-Clearwater MSA, FL	H	20.86 AE	23.90 MW	33.77 AEX	FLBLS	7/16-9/16
Except Epidemiologist	Georgia	Y	37360 FQ	54480 MW	80980 TQ	USBLS	5/15
Except Epidemiologist	Augusta-Richmond County MSA, GA-SC	Y	38740 FQ	53890 MW	85990 TQ	USBLS	5/15
Except Epidemiologist	Hawaii	Y	53820 FQ	66110 MW	95210 TQ	USBLS	5/15
Except Epidemiologist	Urban Honolulu MSA, HI	Y	53920 FQ	65820 MW	97800 TQ	USBLS	5/15
Except Epidemiologist	Idaho	Y	46290 FQ	67260 MW	88240 TQ	USBLS	5/15
Except Epidemiologist	Boise City MSA, ID	Y	46730 FQ	67270 MW	85000 TQ	USBLS	5/15
Except Epidemiologist	Lake County-Kenosha County PMSA, IL-WI	Y	81660 FQ	106020 MW	132830 TQ	USBLS	5/15
Except Epidemiologist	Indiana	Y	38310 FQ	80430 MW	117560 TQ	USBLS	5/15
Except Epidemiologist	Indianapolis-Carmel-Anderson MSA, IN	Y	37970 FQ	82840 MW	117700 TQ	USBLS	5/15
Except Epidemiologist	Iowa	Y	51300 FQ	59920 MW	71850 TQ	USBLS	5/15
Except Epidemiologist	Des Moines-West Des Moines MSA, IA	Y	42380 FQ	60860 MW	80600 TQ	USBLS	5/15
Except Epidemiologist	Kansas	Y	61290 FQ	85840 MW	127730 TQ	USBLS	5/15
Except Epidemiologist	Kentucky	Y	43030 FQ	50590 MW	61690 TQ	USBLS	5/15
Except Epidemiologist	Louisville-Jefferson County MSA, KY-IN	Y	42500 FQ	51480 MW	61000 TQ	USBLS	5/15

AE	Average entry wage	AWR	Average wage range	H	Hourly	LR	Low end range	MTC	Median total compensation	TCC	Total cash compensation
AEX	Average experienced wage	B	Biweekly	HI	Highest wage paid	M	Monthly	MW	Median wage paid	TQ	Third quartile wage
ATC	Average total compensation	D	Daily	HR	High end range	MCC	Median cash compensation	MWR	Median wage range	W	Weekly
AW	Average wage paid	FQ	First quartile wage	LO	Lowest wage paid	ME	Median entry wage	S	See annotated source	Y	Yearly

1015

Medical Scientist

Occupation/Type/Industry	Location	Per	Low	Mid	High	Source	Date
Except Epidemiologist	Louisiana	Y	58340 FQ	74890 MW	119270 TQ	USBLS	5/15
Except Epidemiologist	Maine	Y	53330 FQ	73820 MW	148320 TQ	USBLS	5/15
Except Epidemiologist	Portland-South Portland MSA, ME	Y	48750 FQ	62160 MW	96600 TQ	USBLS	5/15
Except Epidemiologist	Maryland	Y	55073 AE	103377 MW	127529 AEX	MDBLS	4/16
Except Epidemiologist	Baltimore-Columbia-Towson MSA, MD	Y	56970 FQ	78340 MW	113690 TQ	USBLS	5/15
Except Epidemiologist	Massachusetts	Y	59870 FQ	83790 MW	116050 TQ	USBLS	5/15
Except Epidemiologist	Boston-Cambridge-Newton NECTA, MA	Y	58490 FQ	82400 MW	114030 TQ	USBLS	5/15
Except Epidemiologist	Worcester MSA, MA-CT	Y	45080 FQ	57280 MW	77700 TQ	USBLS	5/15
Except Epidemiologist	Michigan	Y	46270 FQ	58180 MW	76320 TQ	USBLS	5/15
Except Epidemiologist	Detroit-Dearborn-Livonia PMSA, MI	Y	36260 FQ	45640 MW	70020 TQ	USBLS	5/15
Except Epidemiologist	Grand Rapids-Wyoming MSA, MI	Y	45440 FQ	53540 MW	77050 TQ	USBLS	5/15
Except Epidemiologist	Minnesota	Y	45876 FQ	59294 MW	81088 TQ	MNBLS	1/16-3/16
Except Epidemiologist	Minneapolis-St. Paul-Bloomington MSA, MN-WI	Y	45675 FQ	60927 MW	82670 TQ	MNBLS	1/16-3/16
Except Epidemiologist	Mississippi	Y	32080 FQ	44290 MW	60200 TQ	USBLS	5/15
Except Epidemiologist	Jackson MSA, MS	Y	30210 FQ	40870 MW	51360 TQ	USBLS	5/15
Except Epidemiologist	Missouri	Y	57670 FQ	72910 MW	99220 TQ	USBLS	5/15
Except Epidemiologist	Kansas City MSA, MO-KS	Y	60260 FQ	83510 MW	126050 TQ	USBLS	5/15
Except Epidemiologist	St. Louis MSA, MO-IL	Y	58030 FQ	72390 MW	96890 TQ	USBLS	5/15
Except Epidemiologist	Montana	Y	46340 FQ	59150 MW	117360 TQ	USBLS	5/15
Except Epidemiologist	New Hampshire	H	22.33 AE	29.29 MW	36.10 AEX	NHBLS	6/16
Except Epidemiologist	New Jersey	Y	88650 FQ	110860 MW	126110 TQ	USBLS	5/15
Except Epidemiologist	Camden PMSA, NJ	Y	67490 FQ	85120 MW	108520 TQ	USBLS	5/15
Except Epidemiologist	Newark PMSA, NJ-PA	Y	92120 FQ	113110 MW	127990 TQ	USBLS	5/15
Except Epidemiologist	Trenton MSA, NJ	Y	76130 FQ	100510 MW	114170 TQ	USBLS	5/15
Except Epidemiologist	New Mexico	Y	49500 FQ	66160 MW	91840 TQ	USBLS	5/15
Except Epidemiologist	Albuquerque MSA, NM	Y	49090 FQ	64040 MW	90640 TQ	USBLS	5/15
Except Epidemiologist	New York	Y	49120 AE	77020 MW	117720 AEX	NYBLS	1/16-3/16
Except Epidemiologist	Buffalo-Cheektowaga-Niagara Falls MSA, NY	Y	60620 FQ	73980 MW	103560 TQ	USBLS	5/15
Except Epidemiologist	Nassau County-Suffolk County PMSA, NY	Y	58460 FQ	77810 MW	110610 TQ	USBLS	5/15
Except Epidemiologist	New York-Jersey City-White Plains PMSA, NY-NJ	Y	52930 FQ	72840 MW	109530 TQ	USBLS	5/15
Except Epidemiologist	North Carolina	Y	65480 FQ	89410 MW	115230 TQ	USBLS	5/15
Except Epidemiologist	Ohio	Y	52430 FQ	70320 MW	104180 TQ	USBLS	5/15
Except Epidemiologist	Cincinnati MSA, OH-KY-IN	Y	46160 FQ	56930 MW	76510 TQ	USBLS	5/15
Except Epidemiologist	Cleveland-Elyria MSA, OH	Y	69400 FQ	91710 MW	183410 TQ	USBLS	5/15
Except Epidemiologist	Columbus MSA, OH	Y	45710 FQ	57530 MW	74340 TQ	USBLS	5/15
Except Epidemiologist	Oklahoma	Y	43980 FQ	53670 MW	71490 TQ	USBLS	5/15
Except Epidemiologist	Oklahoma City MSA, OK	Y	44050 FQ	53610 MW	70530 TQ	USBLS	5/15
Except Epidemiologist	Oregon	H	25.24 FQ	32.74 MW	46.78 TQ	ORBLS	2016
Except Epidemiologist	Portland-Vancouver-Hillsboro MSA, OR-WA	Y	51560 FQ	67130 MW	96550 TQ	USBLS	5/15
Except Epidemiologist	Pennsylvania	Y	62710 FQ	82490 MW	115750 TQ	USBLS	5/15
Except Epidemiologist	Allentown-Bethlehem-Easton MSA, PA-NJ	Y	71790 FQ	94310 MW	131760 TQ	USBLS	5/15
Except Epidemiologist	Harrisburg-Carlisle MSA, PA	Y	86920 FQ	119140 MW	150540 TQ	USBLS	5/15
Except Epidemiologist	Montgomery County-Bucks County-Chester County PMSA, PA	Y	69590 FQ	92950 MW	126220 TQ	USBLS	5/15
Except Epidemiologist	Pittsburgh MSA, PA	Y	59340 FQ	73320 MW	94740 TQ	USBLS	5/15
Except Epidemiologist	Rhode Island	Y	62650 FQ	83460 MW	117490 TQ	USBLS	5/15
Except Epidemiologist	Providence-Warwick MSA, RI-MA	Y	62300 FQ	82810 MW	116020 TQ	USBLS	5/15
Except Epidemiologist	South Carolina	Y	36940 FQ	50410 MW	75430 TQ	USBLS	5/15
Except Epidemiologist	Charleston-North Charleston MSA, SC	Y	38690 FQ	56240 MW	86420 TQ	USBLS	5/15
Except Epidemiologist	Greenville-Anderson-Mauldin MSA, SC	Y	37680 FQ	47140 MW	57920 TQ	USBLS	5/15
Except Epidemiologist	South Dakota	Y	45600 FQ	58660 MW	74310 TQ	USBLS	5/15
Except Epidemiologist	Tennessee	Y	47980 FQ	62110 MW	79480 TQ	USBLS	5/15
Except Epidemiologist	Knoxville MSA, TN	Y	35400 FQ	49060 MW	66730 TQ	USBLS	5/15
Except Epidemiologist	Memphis MSA, TN-MS-AR	Y	58000 FQ	72430 MW	91840 TQ	USBLS	5/15

AE	Average entry wage	AWR	Average wage range	H	Hourly
AEX	Average experienced wage	B	Biweekly	HI	Highest wage paid
ATC	Average total compensation	D	Daily	HR	High end range
AW	Average wage paid	FQ	First quartile wage	LO	Lowest wage paid

LR	Low end range	MTC	Median total compensation	TCC	Total cash compensation
M	Monthly	MW	Median wage paid	TQ	Third quartile wage
MCC	Median cash compensation	MWR	Median wage range	W	Weekly
ME	Median entry wage	S	See annotated source	Y	Yearly

Occupation/Type/Industry	Location	Per	Low	Mid	High	Source	Date
Medical Scientist							
Except Epidemiologist	Nashville-Davidson–Murfreesboro–Franklin MSA, TN	Y	46510 FQ	57410 MW	75190 TQ	USBLS	5/15
Except Epidemiologist	Texas	Y	46150 FQ	59580 MW	83760 TQ	USBLS	5/15
Except Epidemiologist	Austin-Round Rock MSA, TX	Y	55370 FQ	66940 MW	89100 TQ	USBLS	5/15
Except Epidemiologist	Dallas-Plano-Irving PMSA, TX	Y	43510 FQ	49420 MW	61160 TQ	USBLS	5/15
Except Epidemiologist	Fort Worth-Arlington PMSA, TX	Y	38030 FQ	51620 MW	75200 TQ	USBLS	5/15
Except Epidemiologist	Houston-The Woodlands-Sugar Land MSA, TX	Y	56680 FQ	74110 MW	96690 TQ	USBLS	5/15
Except Epidemiologist	San Antonio-New Braunfels MSA, TX	Y	49240 FQ	63030 MW	94600 TQ	USBLS	5/15
Except Epidemiologist	Utah	Y	63120 FQ	80400 MW	99940 TQ	USBLS	5/15
Except Epidemiologist	Ogden-Clearfield MSA, UT	Y	75140 FQ	97520 MW	157800 TQ	USBLS	5/15
Except Epidemiologist	Provo-Orem MSA, UT	Y	68680 FQ	89130 MW	104000 TQ	USBLS	5/15
Except Epidemiologist	Salt Lake City MSA, UT	Y	61420 FQ	77680 MW	97150 TQ	USBLS	5/15
Except Epidemiologist	Burlington-South Burlington MSA, VT	Y	59350 FQ	110950 MW	181580 TQ	USBLS	5/15
Except Epidemiologist	Virginia	Y	61970 FQ	85040 MW	115020 TQ	USBLS	5/15
Except Epidemiologist	Richmond MSA, VA	Y	46120 FQ	58810 MW	88530 TQ	USBLS	5/15
Except Epidemiologist	Virginia Beach-Norfolk-Newport News MSA, VA-NC	Y	88710 FQ	99190 MW	114190 TQ	USBLS	5/15
Except Epidemiologist	Washington	H	24.59 FQ	31.82 MW	44.78 TQ	WABLS	3/16
Except Epidemiologist	Seattle-Bellevue-Everett PMSA, WA	H	24.30 FQ	31.32 MW	43.86 TQ	WABLS	3/16
Except Epidemiologist	Tacoma-Lakewood PMSA, WA	H	33.10 FQ	39.16 MW	45.33 TQ	WABLS	3/16
Except Epidemiologist	Wisconsin	Y	50670 FQ	63460 MW	83860 TQ	USBLS	5/15
Except Epidemiologist	Madison MSA, WI	Y	39520 FQ	57580 MW	72720 TQ	USBLS	5/15
Except Epidemiologist	Milwaukee-Waukesha-West Allis MSA, WI	Y	50830 FQ	58740 MW	70370 TQ	USBLS	5/15
Except Epidemiologist	Puerto Rico	Y	23700 FQ	35890 MW	45590 TQ	USBLS	5/15
Except Epidemiologist	San Juan-Carolina-Caguas MSA, PR	Y	22220 FQ	34910 MW	43720 TQ	USBLS	5/15
Medical Secretary	Alabama	Y	23580 AE	32402 AW	36813 AEX	ALBLS	6/16
	Birmingham-Hoover MSA, AL	Y	26806 AE	35586 AW	39967 AEX	ALBLS	6/16
	Alaska	Y	29960 FQ	36590 MW	44630 TQ	USBLS	5/15
	Anchorage MSA, AK	Y	29450 FQ	35190 MW	42470 TQ	USBLS	5/15
	Arizona	Y	25810 FQ	30820 MW	37220 TQ	USBLS	5/15
	Phoenix-Mesa-Scottsdale MSA, AZ	Y	25930 FQ	30890 MW	37380 TQ	USBLS	5/15
	Tucson MSA, AZ	Y	27110 FQ	33710 MW	39970 TQ	USBLS	5/15
	Arkansas	Y	23830 FQ	28760 MW	34950 TQ	USBLS	5/15
	Little Rock-North Little Rock-Conway MSA, AR	Y	25610 FQ	30220 MW	37000 TQ	USBLS	5/15
	California	H	14.57 FQ	18.34 MW	23.25 TQ	CABLS	1/16-3/16
	Anaheim-Santa Ana-Irvine PMSA, CA	H	15.74 FQ	18.12 MW	22.31 TQ	CABLS	1/16-3/16
	Los Angeles-Long Beach-Glendale PMSA, CA	H	13.38 FQ	17.64 MW	22.76 TQ	CABLS	1/16-3/16
	Oakland-Hayward-Berkeley PMSA, CA	H	17.61 FQ	22.14 MW	27.01 TQ	CABLS	1/16-3/16
	Riverside-San Bernardino-Ontario MSA, CA	H	12.76 FQ	14.90 MW	18.66 TQ	CABLS	1/16-3/16
	Sacramento–Roseville–Arden-Arcade MSA, CA	H	15.84 FQ	19.82 MW	23.25 TQ	CABLS	1/16-3/16
	San Diego-Carlsbad MSA, CA	H	15.05 FQ	18.09 MW	22.12 TQ	CABLS	1/16-3/16
	San Francisco-Redwood City-South San Francisco PMSA, CA	H	17.24 FQ	21.55 MW	27.10 TQ	CABLS	1/16-3/16
	Colorado	Y	29580 FQ	35510 MW	42240 TQ	USBLS	5/15
	Denver-Aurora-Lakewood MSA, CO	Y	32080 FQ	37460 MW	44570 TQ	USBLS	5/15
	Connecticut	Y		39921 MW		CTBLS	1/16-3/16
	Bridgeport-Stamford-Norwalk MSA, CT	Y	34490 FQ	39810 MW	47810 TQ	USBLS	5/15
	Hartford-West Hartford-East Hartford MSA, CT	Y	32150 FQ	38630 MW	47520 TQ	USBLS	5/15
	Delaware	Y	28840 FQ	34470 MW	39500 TQ	USBLS	5/15
	Wilmington PMSA, DE-MD-NJ	Y	29800 FQ	35270 MW	41060 TQ	USBLS	5/15

Occupation/Type/Industry	Location	Per	Low	Mid	High	Source	Date
Medical Secretary	District of Columbia	Y	32690 ꜰQ	38070 ᴍw	45610 ᴛQ	USBLS	5/15
	Washington-Arlington-Alexandria PMSA, DC-VA-MD-WV	Y	31620 ꜰQ	36800 ᴍw	44820 ᴛQ	USBLS	5/15
	Florida	H	12.23 ᴀᴇ	14.93 ᴍw	17.23 ᴀᴇx	FLBLS	7/16-9/16
	Fort Lauderdale-Pompano Beach-Deerfield Beach PMSA, FL	H	13.10 ᴀᴇ	16.24 ᴍw	17.84 ᴀᴇx	FLBLS	7/16-9/16
	Miami-Miami Beach-Kendall PMSA, FL	H	12.52 ᴀᴇ	15.31 ᴍw	17.94 ᴀᴇx	FLBLS	7/16-9/16
	Orlando-Kissimmee-Sanford MSA, FL	H	12.51 ᴀᴇ	14.89 ᴍw	16.74 ᴀᴇx	FLBLS	7/16-9/16
	Tampa-St. Petersburg-Clearwater MSA, FL	H	12.34 ᴀᴇ	14.49 ᴍw	16.65 ᴀᴇx	FLBLS	7/16-9/16
	Georgia	Y	25840 ꜰQ	30390 ᴍw	36640 ᴛQ	USBLS	5/15
	Atlanta-Sandy Springs-Roswell MSA, GA	Y	27810 ꜰQ	32820 ᴍw	37880 ᴛQ	USBLS	5/15
	Augusta-Richmond County MSA, GA-SC	Y	25950 ꜰQ	29940 ᴍw	36140 ᴛQ	USBLS	5/15
	Hawaii	Y	31360 ꜰQ	36620 ᴍw	43860 ᴛQ	USBLS	5/15
	Urban Honolulu MSA, HI	Y	31200 ꜰQ	36760 ᴍw	43710 ᴛQ	USBLS	5/15
	Idaho	Y	27110 ꜰQ	30850 ᴍw	36390 ᴛQ	USBLS	5/15
	Boise City MSA, ID	Y	28470 ꜰQ	31760 ᴍw	38160 ᴛQ	USBLS	5/15
	Illinois	Y	27100 ꜰQ	33870 ᴍw	40010 ᴛQ	USBLS	5/15
	Chicago-Naperville-Arlington Heights PMSA, IL	Y	27500 ꜰQ	34430 ᴍw	40210 ᴛQ	USBLS	5/15
	Lake County-Kenosha County PMSA, IL-WI	Y	28770 ꜰQ	33720 ᴍw	38940 ᴛQ	USBLS	5/15
	Indiana	Y	25910 ꜰQ	31380 ᴍw	37830 ᴛQ	USBLS	5/15
	Gary PMSA, IN	Y	28290 ꜰQ	33230 ᴍw	38110 ᴛQ	USBLS	5/15
	Indianapolis-Carmel-Anderson MSA, IN	Y	25870 ꜰQ	32770 ᴍw	39080 ᴛQ	USBLS	5/15
	Iowa	Y	26310 ꜰQ	31340 ᴍw	37420 ᴛQ	USBLS	5/15
	Des Moines-West Des Moines MSA, IA	Y	27270 ꜰQ	33200 ᴍw	38130 ᴛQ	USBLS	5/15
	Kansas	Y	25720 ꜰQ	30720 ᴍw	36860 ᴛQ	USBLS	5/15
	Wichita MSA, KS	Y	25310 ꜰQ	29970 ᴍw	36400 ᴛQ	USBLS	5/15
	Kentucky	Y	23700 ꜰQ	28490 ᴍw	34090 ᴛQ	USBLS	5/15
	Louisville-Jefferson County MSA, KY-IN	Y	25420 ꜰQ	30330 ᴍw	35900 ᴛQ	USBLS	5/15
	Louisiana	Y	24740 ꜰQ	28560 ᴍw	33390 ᴛQ	USBLS	5/15
	Baton Rouge MSA, LA	Y	24420 ꜰQ	28150 ᴍw	32960 ᴛQ	USBLS	5/15
	New Orleans-Metairie MSA, LA	Y	26040 ꜰQ	30450 ᴍw	35470 ᴛQ	USBLS	5/15
	Maine	Y	26980 ꜰQ	31360 ᴍw	37310 ᴛQ	USBLS	5/15
	Portland-South Portland MSA, ME	Y	30430 ꜰQ	35200 ᴍw	39340 ᴛQ	USBLS	5/15
	Maryland	Y	25643 ᴀᴇ	35226 ᴍw	40018 ᴀᴇx	MDBLS	4/16
	Baltimore-Columbia-Towson MSA, MD	Y	30510 ꜰQ	35900 ᴍw	41910 ᴛQ	USBLS	5/15
	Salisbury MSA, MD-DE	Y	26320 ꜰQ	31520 ᴍw	37260 ᴛQ	USBLS	5/15
	Massachusetts	Y	33830 ꜰQ	39610 ᴍw	47820 ᴛQ	USBLS	5/15
	Boston-Cambridge-Newton NECTA, MA	Y	34970 ꜰQ	41330 ᴍw	49730 ᴛQ	USBLS	5/15
	Worcester MSA, MA-CT	Y	34320 ꜰQ	40150 ᴍw	46640 ᴛQ	USBLS	5/15
	Michigan	Y	26100 ꜰQ	31310 ᴍw	36830 ᴛQ	USBLS	5/15
	Detroit-Dearborn-Livonia PMSA, MI	Y	27740 ꜰQ	33840 ᴍw	38240 ᴛQ	USBLS	5/15
	Grand Rapids-Wyoming MSA, MI	Y	27450 ꜰQ	31820 ᴍw	36720 ᴛQ	USBLS	5/15
	Minnesota	Y	34211 ꜰQ	39510 ᴍw	45952 ᴛQ	MNBLS	1/16-3/16
	Minneapolis-St. Paul-Bloomington MSA, MN-WI	Y	35475 ꜰQ	41189 ᴍw	47065 ᴛQ	MNBLS	1/16-3/16
	Mississippi	Y	25040 ꜰQ	29320 ᴍw	35480 ᴛQ	USBLS	5/15
	Jackson MSA, MS	Y	26620 ꜰQ	31220 ᴍw	37680 ᴛQ	USBLS	5/15
	Missouri	Y	25730 ꜰQ	31450 ᴍw	37760 ᴛQ	USBLS	5/15
	Kansas City MSA, MO-KS	Y	29120 ꜰQ	34330 ᴍw	38500 ᴛQ	USBLS	5/15
	St. Louis MSA, MO-IL	Y	26730 ꜰQ	31870 ᴍw	38260 ᴛQ	USBLS	5/15
	Montana	Y	25640 ꜰQ	30380 ᴍw	36780 ᴛQ	USBLS	5/15
	Billings MSA, MT	Y	28080 ꜰQ	33810 ᴍw	38990 ᴛQ	USBLS	5/15
	Nebraska	Y	27490 ꜰQ	31525 ᴍw	37210 ᴛQ	NEBLS	7/16-9/16

AE	Average entry wage	AWR	Average wage range	H	Hourly	LR	Low end range	MTC	Median total compensation	TCC	Total cash compensation
AEX	Average experienced wage	B	Biweekly	HI	Highest wage paid	M	Monthly	MW	Median wage paid	TQ	Third quartile wage
ATC	Average total compensation	D	Daily	HR	High end range	MCC	Median cash compensation	MWR	Median wage range	W	Weekly
AW	Average wage paid	FQ	First quartile wage	LO	Lowest wage paid	ME	Median entry wage	S	See annotated source	Y	Yearly

1018

Occupation/Type/Industry	Location	Per	Low	Mid	High	Source	Date
Medical Secretary	Omaha-Council Bluffs MSA, NE-IA	Y	28715 FQ	33015 MW	38040 TQ	NEBLS	7/16-9/16
	Nevada	Y	27630 FQ	35240 MW	45250 TQ	USBLS	5/15
	Las Vegas-Henderson-Paradise MSA, NV	Y	27460 FQ	35120 MW	46310 TQ	USBLS	5/15
	New Hampshire	H	13.89 AE	17.46 MW	19.66 AEX	NHBLS	6/16
	Manchester NECTA, NH	H	16.02 AE	19.43 MW	21.77 AEX	NHBLS	6/16
	Nashua NECTA, NH-MA	Y	28230 FQ	34340 MW	43440 TQ	USBLS	5/15
	New Jersey	Y	33340 FQ	39260 MW	48720 TQ	USBLS	5/15
	Camden PMSA, NJ	Y	31810 FQ	36870 MW	43070 TQ	USBLS	5/15
	Newark PMSA, NJ-PA	Y	33960 FQ	38730 MW	48330 TQ	USBLS	5/15
	Trenton MSA, NJ	Y	31940 FQ	36620 MW	42410 TQ	USBLS	5/15
	New Mexico	Y	25750 FQ	30960 MW	36550 TQ	USBLS	5/15
	Albuquerque MSA, NM	Y	28070 FQ	32490 MW	37320 TQ	USBLS	5/15
	New York	Y	27870 AE	37530 MW	44620 AEX	NYBLS	1/16-3/16
	Buffalo-Cheektowaga-Niagara Falls MSA, NY	Y	27990 FQ	33180 MW	39320 TQ	USBLS	5/15
	Nassau County-Suffolk County PMSA, NY	Y	34030 FQ	40690 MW	48060 TQ	USBLS	5/15
	New York-Jersey City-White Plains PMSA, NY-NJ	Y	34380 FQ	42880 MW	51250 TQ	USBLS	5/15
	Rochester MSA, NY	Y	26970 FQ	30420 MW	35260 TQ	USBLS	5/15
	North Carolina	Y	26440 FQ	30450 MW	35770 TQ	USBLS	5/15
	Charlotte-Concord-Gastonia MSA, NC-SC	Y	28740 FQ	33410 MW	37760 TQ	USBLS	5/15
	Raleigh MSA, NC	Y	27700 FQ	31100 MW	36070 TQ	USBLS	5/15
	North Dakota	Y	26190 FQ	30030 MW	35870 TQ	USBLS	5/15
	Fargo MSA, ND-MN	Y	25380 FQ	28790 MW	34290 TQ	USBLS	5/15
	Ohio	Y	25730 FQ	30190 MW	36140 TQ	USBLS	5/15
	Cincinnati MSA, OH-KY-IN	Y	27170 FQ	31390 MW	37200 TQ	USBLS	5/15
	Cleveland-Elyria MSA, OH	Y	25760 FQ	31710 MW	36810 TQ	USBLS	5/15
	Columbus MSA, OH	Y	27450 FQ	32480 MW	38320 TQ	USBLS	5/15
	Oklahoma	Y	24850 FQ	29300 MW	35460 TQ	USBLS	5/15
	Oklahoma City MSA, OK	Y	26090 FQ	30660 MW	37040 TQ	USBLS	5/15
	Tulsa MSA, OK	Y	26700 FQ	30130 MW	35590 TQ	USBLS	5/15
	Oregon	H	14.65 FQ	17.49 MW	21.01 TQ	ORBLS	2016
	Portland-Vancouver-Hillsboro MSA, OR-WA	Y	31790 FQ	37740 MW	45520 TQ	USBLS	5/15
	Pennsylvania	Y	27330 FQ	32930 MW	39050 TQ	USBLS	5/15
	Allentown-Bethlehem-Easton MSA, PA-NJ	Y	24500 FQ	30660 MW	36110 TQ	USBLS	5/15
	Harrisburg-Carlisle MSA, PA	Y	28150 FQ	32570 MW	36720 TQ	USBLS	5/15
	Montgomery County-Bucks County-Chester County PMSA, PA	Y	30420 FQ	37050 MW	44450 TQ	USBLS	5/15
	Philadelphia PMSA, PA	Y	32580 FQ	37400 MW	44370 TQ	USBLS	5/15
	Pittsburgh MSA, PA	Y	27500 FQ	31860 MW	36890 TQ	USBLS	5/15
	Rhode Island	Y	32160 FQ	36710 MW	43070 TQ	USBLS	5/15
	Providence-Warwick MSA, RI-MA	Y	31940 FQ	36520 MW	42750 TQ	USBLS	5/15
	South Carolina	Y	25940 FQ	30480 MW	37060 TQ	USBLS	5/15
	Charleston-North Charleston MSA, SC	Y	26970 FQ	32080 MW	38580 TQ	USBLS	5/15
	Columbia MSA, SC	Y	25520 FQ	30730 MW	37120 TQ	USBLS	5/15
	Greenville-Anderson-Mauldin MSA, SC	Y	24990 FQ	29110 MW	34930 TQ	USBLS	5/15
	South Dakota	Y	29040 FQ	33970 MW	38610 TQ	USBLS	5/15
	Sioux Falls MSA, SD	Y	30820 FQ	35240 MW	39530 TQ	USBLS	5/15
	Tennessee	Y	24580 FQ	28850 MW	34710 TQ	USBLS	5/15
	Knoxville MSA, TN	Y	23270 FQ	27850 MW	34020 TQ	USBLS	5/15
	Memphis MSA, TN-MS-AR	Y	25570 FQ	29120 MW	34960 TQ	USBLS	5/15
	Nashville-Davidson–Murfreesboro–Franklin MSA, TN	Y	26960 FQ	31670 MW	37030 TQ	USBLS	5/15
	Texas	Y	25030 FQ	30120 MW	36730 TQ	USBLS	5/15
	Austin-Round Rock MSA, TX	Y	28440 FQ	33910 MW	41970 TQ	USBLS	5/15
	Dallas-Plano-Irving PMSA, TX	Y	26180 FQ	31840 MW	37430 TQ	USBLS	5/15
	Fort Worth-Arlington PMSA, TX	Y	26990 FQ	32290 MW	37950 TQ	USBLS	5/15
	Houston-The Woodlands-Sugar Land MSA, TX	Y	26410 FQ	31810 MW	38060 TQ	USBLS	5/15

Occupation/Type/Industry	Location	Per	Low	Mid	High	Source	Date
Medical Secretary	San Antonio-New Braunfels						
	MSA, TX	Y	25080 FQ	29030 MW	34560 TQ	USBLS	5/15
	Utah	Y	26560 FQ	30390 MW	36290 TQ	USBLS	5/15
	Ogden-Clearfield MSA, UT	Y	27690 FQ	31310 MW	37640 TQ	USBLS	5/15
	Provo-Orem MSA, UT	Y	25700 FQ	29610 MW	35070 TQ	USBLS	5/15
	Salt Lake City MSA, UT	Y	26920 FQ	30950 MW	37030 TQ	USBLS	5/15
	Vermont	Y	32000 FQ	36520 MW	43210 TQ	USBLS	5/15
	Burlington-South Burlington						
	MSA, VT	Y	33460 FQ	37320 MW	44260 TQ	USBLS	5/15
	Virginia	Y	27690 FQ	32970 MW	40060 TQ	USBLS	5/15
	Richmond MSA, VA	Y	27770 FQ	31560 MW	38130 TQ	USBLS	5/15
	Virginia Beach-Norfolk-						
	Newport News MSA, VA-NC	Y	26610 FQ	29320 MW	33510 TQ	USBLS	5/15
	Washington	H	16.92 FQ	20.07 MW	24.12 TQ	WABLS	3/16
	Seattle-Bellevue-Everett						
	PMSA, WA	H	18.32 FQ	21.94 MW	25.78 TQ	WABLS	3/16
	Tacoma-Lakewood PMSA, WA	H	17.16 FQ	19.44 MW	22.77 TQ	WABLS	3/16
	West Virginia	Y	22760 FQ	27110 MW	33210 TQ	USBLS	5/15
	Huntington-Ashland MSA,						
	WV-KY-OH	Y	24220 FQ	29110 MW	35040 TQ	USBLS	5/15
	Wisconsin	Y	29280 FQ	34100 MW	38730 TQ	USBLS	5/15
	Madison MSA, WI	Y	32200 FQ	36290 MW	40730 TQ	USBLS	5/15
	Milwaukee-Waukesha-West						
	Allis MSA, WI	Y	29920 FQ	34550 MW	38910 TQ	USBLS	5/15
	Wyoming	Y	26460 FQ	31120 MW	36990 TQ	USBLS	5/15
	Cheyenne MSA, WY	Y	24280 FQ	28700 MW	35280 TQ	USBLS	5/15
	Puerto Rico	Y	17180 FQ	18800 MW	22290 TQ	USBLS	5/15
	San Juan-Carolina-Caguas						
	MSA, PR	Y	17630 FQ	19670 MW	24650 TQ	USBLS	5/15
	Virgin Islands	Y	27660 FQ	31470 MW	37660 TQ	USBLS	5/15
	Guam	Y	18690 FQ	20480 MW	24870 TQ	USBLS	5/15
Medical Services Manager	United States	Y		94500 AW		CBS05	2017
Medical Social Worker							
Human Services Department, Municipal Government	San Francisco, CA	Y		71372 AW		CACIT	6/28/16
Medical Transcriptionist	Alabama	Y	23403 AE	35264 AW	41205 AEX	ALBLS	6/16
	Birmingham-Hoover MSA, AL	Y	33411 AE	43532 AW	48587 AEX	ALBLS	6/16
	Gadsden MSA, AL	Y	27030 FQ	29750 MW	35120 TQ	USBLS	5/15
	Alaska	Y	27710 FQ	31750 MW	44180 TQ	USBLS	5/15
	Anchorage MSA, AK	Y	27360 FQ	30690 MW	47010 TQ	USBLS	5/15
	Arizona	Y	30940 FQ	37790 MW	44700 TQ	USBLS	5/15
	Phoenix-Mesa-Scottsdale						
	MSA, AZ	Y	29540 FQ	38100 MW	45070 TQ	USBLS	5/15
	Tucson MSA, AZ	Y	34510 FQ	37990 MW	44270 TQ	USBLS	5/15
	Arkansas	Y	23470 FQ	29620 MW	35680 TQ	USBLS	5/15
	Little Rock-North Little Rock-						
	Conway MSA, AR	Y	22660 FQ	29880 MW	36550 TQ	USBLS	5/15
	California	H	15.95 FQ	22.24 MW	27.55 TQ	CABLS	1/16-3/16
	Anaheim-Santa Ana-Irvine						
	PMSA, CA	H	17.22 FQ	20.69 MW	26.93 TQ	CABLS	1/16-3/16
	Los Angeles-Long Beach-						
	Glendale PMSA, CA	H	22.97 FQ	26.27 MW	28.80 TQ	CABLS	1/16-3/16
	Oakland-Hayward-Berkeley						
	PMSA, CA	H	11.96 FQ	14.33 MW	19.05 TQ	CABLS	1/16-3/16
	Riverside-San Bernardino-						
	Ontario MSA, CA	H	21.71 FQ	25.80 MW	28.80 TQ	CABLS	1/16-3/16
	Sacramento–Roseville–						
	Arden-Arcade MSA, CA	H	17.35 FQ	21.85 MW	27.55 TQ	CABLS	1/16-3/16
	San Diego-Carlsbad MSA, CA	H	19.36 FQ	24.12 MW	28.47 TQ	CABLS	1/16-3/16
	San Francisco-Redwood City- South San Francisco PMSA,						
	CA	H	24.79 FQ	29.59 MW	34.39 TQ	CABLS	1/16-3/16
	Colorado	Y	32530 FQ	41950 MW	49950 TQ	USBLS	5/15
	Denver-Aurora-Lakewood						
	MSA, CO	Y	34540 FQ	43580 MW	51680 TQ	USBLS	5/15
	Connecticut	Y		43308 MW		CTBLS	1/16-3/16
	Bridgeport-Stamford-Norwalk						
	MSA, CT	Y	40200 FQ	44380 MW	48550 TQ	USBLS	5/15

AE	Average entry wage	AWR	Average wage range	H	Hourly	LR	Low end range	MTC	Median total compensation	TCC	Total cash compensation
AEX	Average experienced wage	B	Biweekly	HI	Highest wage paid	M	Monthly	MW	Median wage paid	TQ	Third quartile wage
ATC	Average total compensation	D	Daily	HR	High end range	MCC	Median cash compensation	MWR	Median wage range	W	Weekly
AW	Average wage paid	FQ	First quartile wage	LO	Lowest wage paid	ME	Median entry wage	S	See annotated source	Y	Yearly

Medical Transcriptionist

Occupation/Type/Industry	Location	Per	Low	Mid	High	Source	Date
Medical Transcriptionist	Hartford-West Hartford-East Hartford MSA, CT	Y	33360 FQ	41090 MW	47570 TQ	USBLS	5/15
	Delaware	Y	23550 FQ	31950 MW	39230 TQ	USBLS	5/15
	Wilmington PMSA, DE-MD-NJ	Y	29940 FQ	36200 MW	42520 TQ	USBLS	5/15
	District of Columbia	Y	43160 FQ	50630 MW	56960 TQ	USBLS	5/15
	Washington-Arlington-Alexandria PMSA, DC-VA-MD-WV	Y	37600 FQ	45680 MW	54890 TQ	USBLS	5/15
	Florida	H	11.50 AE	16.23 MW	18.87 AEX	FLBLS	7/16-9/16
	Fort Lauderdale-Pompano Beach-Deerfield Beach PMSA, FL	H	15.24 AE	18.27 MW	19.90 AEX	FLBLS	7/16-9/16
	Miami-Miami Beach-Kendall PMSA, FL	H	13.14 AE	16.58 MW	19.23 AEX	FLBLS	7/16-9/16
	Orlando-Kissimmee-Sanford MSA, FL	H	9.86 AE	12.05 MW	15.49 AEX	FLBLS	7/16-9/16
	Tampa-St. Petersburg-Clearwater MSA, FL	H	14.69 AE	20.52 MW	22.08 AEX	FLBLS	7/16-9/16
	Georgia	Y	22880 FQ	32460 MW	42540 TQ	USBLS	5/15
	Atlanta-Sandy Springs-Roswell MSA, GA	Y	21950 FQ	32140 MW	43780 TQ	USBLS	5/15
	Augusta-Richmond County MSA, GA-SC	Y	32950 FQ	38720 MW	43770 TQ	USBLS	5/15
	Hawaii	Y	22500 FQ	27590 MW	42350 TQ	USBLS	5/15
	Urban Honolulu MSA, HI	Y	21600 FQ	23530 MW	28940 TQ	USBLS	5/15
	Idaho	Y	29800 FQ	34500 MW	38490 TQ	USBLS	5/15
	Boise City MSA, ID	Y	29030 FQ	34260 MW	38580 TQ	USBLS	5/15
	Illinois	Y	28700 FQ	34300 MW	41540 TQ	USBLS	5/15
	Chicago-Naperville-Arlington Heights PMSA, IL	Y	28440 FQ	33620 MW	42100 TQ	USBLS	5/15
	Lake County-Kenosha County PMSA, IL-WI	Y	33430 FQ	38210 MW	44160 TQ	USBLS	5/15
	Indiana	Y	29990 FQ	34500 MW	38350 TQ	USBLS	5/15
	Gary PMSA, IN	Y	22440 FQ	32580 MW	36660 TQ	USBLS	5/15
	Indianapolis-Carmel-Anderson MSA, IN	Y	31860 FQ	35570 MW	39290 TQ	USBLS	5/15
	Iowa	Y	27220 FQ	32300 MW	37960 TQ	USBLS	5/15
	Des Moines-West Des Moines MSA, IA	Y	28180 FQ	32780 MW	40550 TQ	USBLS	5/15
	Kansas	Y	24110 FQ	31610 MW	37180 TQ	USBLS	5/15
	Wichita MSA, KS	Y	26890 FQ	34360 MW	40170 TQ	USBLS	5/15
	Kentucky	Y	26750 FQ	31770 MW	37790 TQ	USBLS	5/15
	Louisville-Jefferson County MSA, KY-IN	Y	32740 FQ	37290 MW	45860 TQ	USBLS	5/15
	Louisiana	Y	25070 FQ	30650 MW	36200 TQ	USBLS	5/15
	Baton Rouge MSA, LA	Y	20600 FQ	25690 MW	33630 TQ	USBLS	5/15
	New Orleans-Metairie MSA, LA	Y	26480 FQ	31710 MW	36620 TQ	USBLS	5/15
	Maine	Y	27040 FQ	32840 MW	37780 TQ	USBLS	5/15
	Portland-South Portland MSA, ME	Y	28150 FQ	32700 MW	37330 TQ	USBLS	5/15
	Maryland	Y	22088 AE	36333 MW	43456 AEX	MDBLS	4/16
	Baltimore-Columbia-Towson MSA, MD	Y	20640 FQ	28340 MW	44430 TQ	USBLS	5/15
	Salisbury MSA, MD-DE	Y	28170 FQ	33150 MW	37650 TQ	USBLS	5/15
	Massachusetts	Y	37830 FQ	44850 MW	52860 TQ	USBLS	5/15
	Boston-Cambridge-Newton NECTA, MA	Y	39930 FQ	47500 MW	57670 TQ	USBLS	5/15
	Worcester MSA, MA-CT	Y	33910 FQ	39680 MW	47170 TQ	USBLS	5/15
	Michigan	Y	25080 FQ	31530 MW	37400 TQ	USBLS	5/15
	Detroit-Dearborn-Livonia PMSA, MI	Y	31790 FQ	35460 MW	39230 TQ	USBLS	5/15
	Grand Rapids-Wyoming MSA, MI	Y	22460 FQ	27080 MW	31740 TQ	USBLS	5/15
	Minnesota	Y	29953 FQ	39082 MW	45050 TQ	MNBLS	1/16-3/16
	Minneapolis-St. Paul-Bloomington MSA, MN-WI	Y	23520 FQ	35578 MW	44091 TQ	MNBLS	1/16-3/16
	Mississippi	Y	23560 FQ	29070 MW	35550 TQ	USBLS	5/15
	Jackson MSA, MS	Y	26380 FQ	32290 MW	37480 TQ	USBLS	5/15
	Missouri	Y	28350 FQ	35330 MW	42720 TQ	USBLS	5/15
	Kansas City MSA, MO-KS	Y	23770 FQ	33380 MW	38760 TQ	USBLS	5/15

AE	Average entry wage	AWR	Average wage range	H	Hourly	LR	Low end range	MTC	Median total compensation	TCC	Total cash compensation
AEX	Average experienced wage	B	Biweekly	HI	Highest wage paid	M	Monthly	MW	Median wage paid	TQ	Third quartile wage
ATC	Average total compensation	D	Daily	HR	High end range	MCC	Median cash compensation	MWR	Median wage range	W	Weekly
AW	Average wage paid	FQ	First quartile wage	LO	Lowest wage paid	ME	Median entry wage	S	See annotated source	Y	Yearly

Occupation/Type/Industry	Location	Per	Low	Mid	High	Source	Date
Medical Transcriptionist	St. Louis MSA, MO-IL	Y	32810 FQ	38140 MW	45570 TQ	USBLS	5/15
	Montana	Y	27180 FQ	30400 MW	35750 TQ	USBLS	5/15
	Nebraska	Y	30275 FQ	34640 MW	38685 TQ	NEBLS	7/16-9/16
	Omaha-Council Bluffs MSA, NE-IA	Y	32735 FQ	36000 MW	39280 TQ	NEBLS	7/16-9/16
	Nevada	Y	27790 FQ	31170 MW	36370 TQ	USBLS	5/15
	Las Vegas-Henderson-Paradise MSA, NV	Y	27650 FQ	30800 MW	35930 TQ	USBLS	5/15
	New Hampshire	H	14.85 AE	18.97 MW	20.88 AEX	NHBLS	6/16
	Manchester NECTA, NH	H	20.39 AE	22.03 MW	22.80 AEX	NHBLS	6/16
	Nashua NECTA, NH-MA	Y	35800 FQ	41160 MW	46090 TQ	USBLS	5/15
	New Jersey	Y	32420 FQ	38790 MW	47880 TQ	USBLS	5/15
	Camden PMSA, NJ	Y	33370 FQ	40570 MW	45580 TQ	USBLS	5/15
	Newark PMSA, NJ-PA	Y	34930 FQ	42940 MW	51980 TQ	USBLS	5/15
	Trenton MSA, NJ	Y	33730 FQ	38190 MW	45840 TQ	USBLS	5/15
	New Mexico	Y	27260 FQ	35640 MW	46670 TQ	USBLS	5/15
	Albuquerque MSA, NM	Y	33150 FQ	38890 MW	52310 TQ	USBLS	5/15
	New York	Y	26180 AE	36630 MW	43430 AEX	NYBLS	1/16-3/16
	Buffalo-Cheektowaga-Niagara Falls MSA, NY	Y	32580 FQ	36410 MW	40630 TQ	USBLS	5/15
	Nassau County-Suffolk County PMSA, NY	Y	31840 FQ	37660 MW	44420 TQ	USBLS	5/15
	New York-Jersey City-White Plains PMSA, NY-NJ	Y	29570 FQ	38040 MW	48950 TQ	USBLS	5/15
	Rochester MSA, NY	Y	29430 FQ	33490 MW	37080 TQ	USBLS	5/15
	North Carolina	Y	28090 FQ	33950 MW	39990 TQ	USBLS	5/15
	Charlotte-Concord-Gastonia MSA, NC-SC	Y	28710 FQ	35070 MW	41730 TQ	USBLS	5/15
	Raleigh MSA, NC	Y	17870 FQ	25410 MW	48450 TQ	USBLS	5/15
	North Dakota	Y	29210 FQ	34100 MW	38830 TQ	USBLS	5/15
	Fargo MSA, ND-MN	Y	27550 FQ	31230 MW	36390 TQ	USBLS	5/15
	Ohio	Y	27800 FQ	33860 MW	38740 TQ	USBLS	5/15
	Cincinnati MSA, OH-KY-IN	Y	33420 FQ	40680 MW	45810 TQ	USBLS	5/15
	Cleveland-Elyria MSA, OH	Y	30100 FQ	34840 MW	38990 TQ	USBLS	5/15
	Columbus MSA, OH	Y	32290 FQ	36470 MW	41760 TQ	USBLS	5/15
	Oklahoma	Y	28970 FQ	33870 MW	38250 TQ	USBLS	5/15
	Oklahoma City MSA, OK	Y	32540 FQ	36070 MW	40280 TQ	USBLS	5/15
	Tulsa MSA, OK	Y	30060 FQ	34490 MW	38670 TQ	USBLS	5/15
	Oregon	H	15.58 FQ	18.68 MW	22.42 TQ	ORBLS	2016
	Portland-Vancouver-Hillsboro MSA, OR-WA	Y	32780 FQ	41570 MW	48480 TQ	USBLS	5/15
	Pennsylvania	Y	30020 FQ	34830 MW	39230 TQ	USBLS	5/15
	Allentown-Bethlehem-Easton MSA, PA-NJ	Y	31960 FQ	35480 MW	39010 TQ	USBLS	5/15
	Harrisburg-Carlisle MSA, PA	Y	32450 FQ	36290 MW	40880 TQ	USBLS	5/15
	Montgomery County-Bucks County-Chester County PMSA, PA	Y	32750 FQ	37150 MW	42970 TQ	USBLS	5/15
	Philadelphia PMSA, PA	Y	31640 FQ	37210 MW	44750 TQ	USBLS	5/15
	Pittsburgh MSA, PA	Y	31570 FQ	35220 MW	38870 TQ	USBLS	5/15
	Rhode Island	Y	33680 FQ	40490 MW	46520 TQ	USBLS	5/15
	Providence-Warwick MSA, RI-MA	Y	33620 FQ	40820 MW	46830 TQ	USBLS	5/15
	South Carolina	Y	28600 FQ	34310 MW	39600 TQ	USBLS	5/15
	Charleston-North Charleston MSA, SC	Y	32260 FQ	36040 MW	40490 TQ	USBLS	5/15
	Columbia MSA, SC	Y	27930 FQ	35200 MW	42560 TQ	USBLS	5/15
	Greenville-Anderson-Mauldin MSA, SC	Y	26460 FQ	30480 MW	35500 TQ	USBLS	5/15
	South Dakota	Y	27220 FQ	30330 MW	34900 TQ	USBLS	5/15
	Sioux Falls MSA, SD	Y	28330 FQ	31850 MW	36260 TQ	USBLS	5/15
	Tennessee	Y	26720 FQ	32020 MW	37540 TQ	USBLS	5/15
	Knoxville MSA, TN	Y	28380 FQ	34420 MW	41210 TQ	USBLS	5/15
	Memphis MSA, TN-MS-AR	Y	26780 FQ	32830 MW	37700 TQ	USBLS	5/15
	Nashville-Davidson–Murfreesboro–Franklin MSA, TN	Y	26020 FQ	31390 MW	37400 TQ	USBLS	5/15
	Texas	Y	22380 FQ	35000 MW	45220 TQ	USBLS	5/15
	Austin-Round Rock MSA, TX	Y	28850 FQ	39210 MW	45440 TQ	USBLS	5/15
	Dallas-Plano-Irving PMSA, TX	Y	34080 FQ	42280 MW	48480 TQ	USBLS	5/15
	Fort Worth-Arlington PMSA, TX	Y	28140 FQ	40780 MW	52850 TQ	USBLS	5/15

AE	Average entry wage	AWR	Average wage range	H	Hourly	LR	Low end range	MTC	Median total compensation	TCC	Total cash compensation
AEX	Average experienced wage	B	Biweekly	HI	Highest wage paid	M	Monthly	MW	Median wage paid	TQ	Third quartile wage
ATC	Average total compensation	D	Daily	HR	High end range	MCC	Median cash compensation	MWR	Median wage range	W	Weekly
AW	Average wage paid	FQ	First quartile wage	LO	Lowest wage paid	ME	Median entry wage	S	See annotated source	Y	Yearly

Occupation/Type/Industry	Location	Per	Low	Mid	High	Source	Date
Medical Transcriptionist	Houston-The Woodlands-Sugar Land MSA, TX	Y	34680 FQ	41640 MW	47840 TQ	USBLS	5/15
	San Antonio-New Braunfels MSA, TX	Y	16760 FQ	18410 MW	22480 TQ	USBLS	5/15
	Utah	Y	25850 FQ	30830 MW	37250 TQ	USBLS	5/15
	Ogden-Clearfield MSA, UT	Y	33250 FQ	36300 MW	39420 TQ	USBLS	5/15
	Provo-Orem MSA, UT	Y	17530 FQ	19540 MW	28540 TQ	USBLS	5/15
	Salt Lake City MSA, UT	Y	28670 FQ	33760 MW	39860 TQ	USBLS	5/15
	Vermont	Y	31900 FQ	37140 MW	44090 TQ	USBLS	5/15
	Burlington-South Burlington MSA, VT	Y	34490 FQ	41520 MW	47250 TQ	USBLS	5/15
	Virginia	Y	24020 FQ	31650 MW	37290 TQ	USBLS	5/15
	Richmond MSA, VA	Y	20270 FQ	24890 MW	36250 TQ	USBLS	5/15
	Virginia Beach-Norfolk-Newport News MSA, VA-NC	Y	22350 FQ	30020 MW	34880 TQ	USBLS	5/15
	Washington	H	15.71 FQ	19.18 MW	25.07 TQ	WABLS	3/16
	Seattle-Bellevue-Everett PMSA, WA	H	17.03 FQ	21.58 MW	27.14 TQ	WABLS	3/16
	Tacoma-Lakewood PMSA, WA	H	13.38 FQ	17.56 MW	23.53 TQ	WABLS	3/16
	West Virginia	Y	24950 FQ	29800 MW	36390 TQ	USBLS	5/15
	Huntington-Ashland MSA, WV-KY-OH	Y	26170 FQ	29620 MW	34610 TQ	USBLS	5/15
	Wisconsin	Y	33340 FQ	37520 MW	43570 TQ	USBLS	5/15
	Madison MSA, WI	Y	34270 FQ	38780 MW	45430 TQ	USBLS	5/15
	Milwaukee-Waukesha-West Allis MSA, WI	Y	33320 FQ	38350 MW	44400 TQ	USBLS	5/15
	Wyoming	Y	26430 FQ	32830 MW	38110 TQ	USBLS	5/15
	Cheyenne MSA, WY	Y	19030 FQ	32710 MW	37450 TQ	USBLS	5/15
	Puerto Rico	Y	21220 FQ	25050 MW	29120 TQ	USBLS	5/15
	San Juan-Carolina-Caguas MSA, PR	Y	22950 FQ	26750 MW	30230 TQ	USBLS	5/15
Medical Writer							
3 to 5 Years Experience	United States	Y	73500 LO		98500 HI	RH02	2017
Pharmaceutical, Medical Device, and Healthcare Industries	United States	Y		75300 AW		MMM01	7/16
Medication Aide							
Department of Public Health and Human Services, State Government	Lewistown, MT	H			16.00 HI	MTGOV	2016
Meeting, Convention, and Event Planner	Alabama	Y	32870 AE	50141 AW	58771 AEX	ALBLS	6/16
	Birmingham-Hoover MSA, AL	Y	35228 AE	50705 AW	58443 AEX	ALBLS	6/16
	Alaska	Y	43150 FQ	49400 MW	60580 TQ	USBLS	5/15
	Anchorage MSA, AK	Y	44020 FQ	49590 MW	71440 TQ	USBLS	5/15
	Arizona	Y	24050 FQ	40310 MW	56280 TQ	USBLS	5/15
	Phoenix-Mesa-Scottsdale MSA, AZ	Y	25820 FQ	42260 MW	58370 TQ	USBLS	5/15
	Tucson MSA, AZ	Y	22040 FQ	32180 MW	47350 TQ	USBLS	5/15
	Arkansas	Y	29320 FQ	37470 MW	48860 TQ	USBLS	5/15
	Little Rock-North Little Rock-Conway MSA, AR	Y	30110 FQ	40040 MW	48310 TQ	USBLS	5/15
	California	H	18.56 FQ	25.12 MW	34.47 TQ	CABLS	1/16-3/16
	Anaheim-Santa Ana-Irvine PMSA, CA	H	21.67 FQ	27.50 MW	35.64 TQ	CABLS	1/16-3/16
	Los Angeles-Long Beach-Glendale PMSA, CA	H	20.01 FQ	25.71 MW	34.90 TQ	CABLS	1/16-3/16
	Oakland-Hayward-Berkeley PMSA, CA	H	17.62 FQ	23.51 MW	30.58 TQ	CABLS	1/16-3/16
	Riverside-San Bernardino-Ontario MSA, CA	H	12.87 FQ	17.97 MW	26.82 TQ	CABLS	1/16-3/16
	Sacramento–Roseville–Arden-Arcade MSA, CA	H	16.98 FQ	23.76 MW	36.85 TQ	CABLS	1/16-3/16
	San Diego-Carlsbad MSA, CA	H	16.15 FQ	22.43 MW	30.94 TQ	CABLS	1/16-3/16
	San Francisco-Redwood City-South San Francisco PMSA, CA	H	22.08 FQ	29.17 MW	39.62 TQ	CABLS	1/16-3/16
	Colorado	Y	29450 FQ	39710 MW	53360 TQ	USBLS	5/15
	Denver-Aurora-Lakewood MSA, CO	Y	28340 FQ	39190 MW	53740 TQ	USBLS	5/15
	Connecticut	Y		61575 MW		CTBLS	1/16-3/16

AE	Average entry wage	**AWR**	Average wage range	**H**	Hourly	
AEX	Average experienced wage	**B**	Biweekly	**HI**	Highest wage paid	
ATC	Average total compensation	**D**	Daily	**HR**	High end range	
AW	Average wage paid	**FQ**	First quartile wage	**LO**	Lowest wage paid	
LR	Low end range	**MTC**	Median total compensation	**TCC**	Total cash compensation
M	Monthly	**MW**	Median wage paid	**TQ**	Third quartile wage
MCC	Median cash compensation	**MWR**	Median wage range	**W**	Weekly
ME	Median entry wage	**S**	See annotated source	**Y**	Yearly

Occupation/Type/Industry	Location	Per	Low	Mid	High	Source	Date
Meeting, Convention, and Event Planner							
	Bridgeport-Stamford-Norwalk MSA, CT	Y	48610 FQ	67440 MW	87030 TQ	USBLS	5/15
	Hartford-West Hartford-East Hartford MSA, CT	Y	50140 FQ	67040 MW	88090 TQ	USBLS	5/15
	Delaware	Y	36740 FQ	45980 MW	57540 TQ	USBLS	5/15
	Wilmington PMSA, DE-MD-NJ	Y	36450 FQ	46160 MW	58160 TQ	USBLS	5/15
	District of Columbia	Y	52330 FQ	62930 MW	78970 TQ	USBLS	5/15
	Washington-Arlington-Alexandria PMSA, DC-VA-MD-WV	Y	49510 FQ	61960 MW	78400 TQ	USBLS	5/15
	Florida	H	13.64 AE	21.09 MW	27.28 AEX	FLBLS	7/16-9/16
	Fort Lauderdale-Pompano Beach-Deerfield Beach PMSA, FL	H	17.09 AE	25.91 MW	29.48 AEX	FLBLS	7/16-9/16
	Miami-Miami Beach-Kendall PMSA, FL	H	10.91 AE	19.36 MW	25.74 AEX	FLBLS	7/16-9/16
	Orlando-Kissimmee-Sanford MSA, FL	H	14.02 AE	21.58 MW	28.78 AEX	FLBLS	7/16-9/16
	Tampa-St. Petersburg-Clearwater MSA, FL	H	11.54 AE	18.85 MW	27.14 AEX	FLBLS	7/16-9/16
	Georgia	Y	34160 FQ	45260 MW	59870 TQ	USBLS	5/15
	Atlanta-Sandy Springs-Roswell MSA, GA	Y	35560 FQ	47400 MW	62250 TQ	USBLS	5/15
	Augusta-Richmond County MSA, GA-SC	Y	27410 FQ	46240 MW	62790 TQ	USBLS	5/15
	Hawaii	Y	38710 FQ	47170 MW	59450 TQ	USBLS	5/15
	Urban Honolulu MSA, HI	Y	39510 FQ	46900 MW	57500 TQ	USBLS	5/15
	Idaho	Y	27790 FQ	34930 MW	48580 TQ	USBLS	5/15
	Boise City MSA, ID	Y	28940 FQ	35590 MW	47110 TQ	USBLS	5/15
	Illinois	Y	36580 FQ	48570 MW	61950 TQ	USBLS	5/15
	Chicago-Naperville-Arlington Heights PMSA, IL	Y	40820 FQ	51080 MW	63280 TQ	USBLS	5/15
	Lake County-Kenosha County PMSA, IL-WI	Y	38020 FQ	55030 MW	72050 TQ	USBLS	5/15
	Indiana	Y	33050 FQ	41990 MW	52870 TQ	USBLS	5/15
	Gary PMSA, IN	Y	31340 FQ	38140 MW	48770 TQ	USBLS	5/15
	Indianapolis-Carmel-Anderson MSA, IN	Y	39810 FQ	48050 MW	58330 TQ	USBLS	5/15
	Iowa	Y	30100 FQ	41350 MW	54030 TQ	USBLS	5/15
	Des Moines-West Des Moines MSA, IA	Y	37440 FQ	47480 MW	58270 TQ	USBLS	5/15
	Kansas	Y	32760 FQ	40880 MW	51880 TQ	USBLS	5/15
	Wichita MSA, KS	Y	32920 FQ	37730 MW	46060 TQ	USBLS	5/15
	Kentucky	Y	29830 FQ	37740 MW	48190 TQ	USBLS	5/15
	Louisville-Jefferson County MSA, KY-IN	Y	31580 FQ	39770 MW	51540 TQ	USBLS	5/15
	Louisiana	Y	32450 FQ	41100 MW	52390 TQ	USBLS	5/15
	Baton Rouge MSA, LA	Y	32750 FQ	40850 MW	50450 TQ	USBLS	5/15
	New Orleans-Metairie MSA, LA	Y	31880 FQ	41640 MW	52950 TQ	USBLS	5/15
	Maine	Y	28920 FQ	37940 MW	48820 TQ	USBLS	5/15
	Portland-South Portland MSA, ME	Y	24580 FQ	35630 MW	46630 TQ	USBLS	5/15
	Maryland	Y	34186 AE	57789 MW	69591 AEX	MDBLS	4/16
	Baltimore-Columbia-Towson MSA, MD	Y	40940 FQ	51600 MW	66910 TQ	USBLS	5/15
	Salisbury MSA, MD-DE	Y	28800 FQ	44330 MW	63240 TQ	USBLS	5/15
	Massachusetts	Y	44980 FQ	56760 MW	71640 TQ	USBLS	5/15
	Boston-Cambridge-Newton NECTA, MA	Y	48400 FQ	59110 MW	74810 TQ	USBLS	5/15
	Worcester MSA, MA-CT	Y	39600 FQ	49930 MW	61910 TQ	USBLS	5/15
	Michigan	Y	33150 FQ	43160 MW	56060 TQ	USBLS	5/15
	Detroit-Dearborn-Livonia PMSA, MI	Y	38200 FQ	48070 MW	62080 TQ	USBLS	5/15
	Grand Rapids-Wyoming MSA, MI	Y	34880 FQ	46760 MW	58580 TQ	USBLS	5/15
	Minnesota	Y	35574 FQ	49007 MW	61647 TQ	MNBLS	1/16-3/16
	Minneapolis-St. Paul-Bloomington MSA, MN-WI	Y	36590 FQ	50378 MW	62917 TQ	MNBLS	1/16-3/16
	Mississippi	Y	28370 FQ	35020 MW	42370 TQ	USBLS	5/15

AE	Average entry wage	AWR	Average wage range	H	Hourly	LR	Low end range	MTC	Median total compensation	TCC	Total cash compensation
AEX	Average experienced wage	B	Biweekly	HI	Highest wage paid	M	Monthly	MW	Median wage paid	TQ	Third quartile wage
ATC	Average total compensation	D	Daily	HR	High end range	MCC	Median cash compensation	MWR	Median wage range	W	Weekly
AW	Average wage paid	FQ	First quartile wage	LO	Lowest wage paid	ME	Median entry wage	S	See annotated source	Y	Yearly

Occupation/Type/Industry	Location	Per	Low	Mid	High	Source	Date
Meeting, Convention, and Event Planner	Jackson MSA, MS	Y	27140 FQ	33920 MW	41010 TQ	USBLS	5/15
	Missouri	Y	33900 FQ	44840 MW	60200 TQ	USBLS	5/15
	Kansas City MSA, MO-KS	Y	33930 FQ	45610 MW	58180 TQ	USBLS	5/15
	St. Louis MSA, MO-IL	Y	34860 FQ	46800 MW	65660 TQ	USBLS	5/15
	Montana	Y	27410 FQ	38430 MW	49770 TQ	USBLS	5/15
	Billings MSA, MT	Y	30800 FQ	44320 MW	95230 TQ	USBLS	5/15
	Nebraska	Y	31495 FQ	42415 MW	50650 TQ	NEBLS	7/16-9/16
	Omaha-Council Bluffs MSA, NE-IA	Y	29310 FQ	40355 MW	51055 TQ	NEBLS	7/16-9/16
	Nevada	Y	35510 FQ	45750 MW	58890 TQ	USBLS	5/15
	Las Vegas-Henderson-Paradise MSA, NV	Y	36930 FQ	46530 MW	60260 TQ	USBLS	5/15
	New Hampshire	H	17.58 AE	23.19 MW	28.07 AEX	NHBLS	6/16
	Manchester NECTA, NH	H	15.39 AE	20.94 MW	24.59 AEX	NHBLS	6/16
	New Jersey	Y	42740 FQ	54600 MW	72140 TQ	USBLS	5/15
	Camden PMSA, NJ	Y	37750 FQ	52000 MW	68640 TQ	USBLS	5/15
	Newark PMSA, NJ-PA	Y	44320 FQ	57630 MW	78650 TQ	USBLS	5/15
	Trenton MSA, NJ	Y	43680 FQ	50900 MW	63320 TQ	USBLS	5/15
	New Mexico	Y	39560 FQ	44370 MW	49140 TQ	USBLS	5/15
	Albuquerque MSA, NM	Y	41270 FQ	44990 MW	48710 TQ	USBLS	5/15
	New York	Y	33880 AE	56040 MW	75220 AEX	NYBLS	1/16-3/16
	Buffalo-Cheektowaga-Niagara Falls MSA, NY	Y	23840 FQ	30530 MW	47280 TQ	USBLS	5/15
	Nassau County-Suffolk County PMSA, NY	Y	32910 FQ	46530 MW	65980 TQ	USBLS	5/15
	New York-Jersey City-White Plains PMSA, NY-NJ	Y	44160 FQ	58770 MW	79930 TQ	USBLS	5/15
	Rochester MSA, NY	Y	37000 FQ	45390 MW	56130 TQ	USBLS	5/15
	North Carolina	Y	32200 FQ	43930 MW	57900 TQ	USBLS	5/15
	Charlotte-Concord-Gastonia MSA, NC-SC	Y	32600 FQ	46210 MW	60810 TQ	USBLS	5/15
	Raleigh MSA, NC	Y	36170 FQ	46340 MW	65860 TQ	USBLS	5/15
	North Dakota	Y	35520 FQ	44480 MW	54090 TQ	USBLS	5/15
	Fargo MSA, ND-MN	Y	35620 FQ	47310 MW	56680 TQ	USBLS	5/15
	Ohio	Y	30000 FQ	39030 MW	49390 TQ	USBLS	5/15
	Cincinnati MSA, OH-KY-IN	Y	29700 FQ	39120 MW	49570 TQ	USBLS	5/15
	Cleveland-Elyria MSA, OH	Y	31970 FQ	37530 MW	48430 TQ	USBLS	5/15
	Columbus MSA, OH	Y	29060 FQ	41110 MW	49630 TQ	USBLS	5/15
	Oklahoma	Y	23830 FQ	35100 MW	48670 TQ	USBLS	5/15
	Tulsa MSA, OK	Y	26960 FQ	37800 MW	49450 TQ	USBLS	5/15
	Oregon	H	17.37 FQ	22.62 MW	28.25 TQ	ORBLS	2016
	Portland-Vancouver-Hillsboro MSA, OR-WA	Y	38290 FQ	48360 MW	58910 TQ	USBLS	5/15
	Pennsylvania	Y	34460 FQ	45120 MW	57530 TQ	USBLS	5/15
	Allentown-Bethlehem-Easton MSA, PA-NJ	Y	28280 FQ	38570 MW	53040 TQ	USBLS	5/15
	Harrisburg-Carlisle MSA, PA	Y	33650 FQ	43290 MW	54920 TQ	USBLS	5/15
	Montgomery County-Bucks County-Chester County PMSA, PA	Y	33940 FQ	47050 MW	60570 TQ	USBLS	5/15
	Philadelphia PMSA, PA	Y	42140 FQ	50780 MW	67860 TQ	USBLS	5/15
	Pittsburgh MSA, PA	Y	32070 FQ	42940 MW	52340 TQ	USBLS	5/15
	Rhode Island	Y	36390 FQ	46980 MW	61680 TQ	USBLS	5/15
	Providence-Warwick MSA, RI-MA	Y	36480 FQ	47090 MW	61740 TQ	USBLS	5/15
	South Carolina	Y	28310 FQ	37310 MW	49260 TQ	USBLS	5/15
	Charleston-North Charleston MSA, SC	Y	31750 FQ	40860 MW	49520 TQ	USBLS	5/15
	Columbia MSA, SC	Y	34300 FQ	39620 MW	58420 TQ	USBLS	5/15
	Greenville-Anderson-Mauldin MSA, SC	Y	22170 FQ	30770 MW	42350 TQ	USBLS	5/15
	South Dakota	Y	27230 FQ	30630 MW	36840 TQ	USBLS	5/15
	Sioux Falls MSA, SD	Y	32110 FQ	35530 MW	38950 TQ	USBLS	5/15
	Tennessee	Y	28000 FQ	36970 MW	51170 TQ	USBLS	5/15
	Knoxville MSA, TN	Y	29050 FQ	36680 MW	47700 TQ	USBLS	5/15
	Memphis MSA, TN-MS-AR	Y	29450 FQ	39190 MW	53830 TQ	USBLS	5/15
	Nashville-Davidson–Murfreesboro–Franklin MSA, TN	Y	27790 FQ	36730 MW	51690 TQ	USBLS	5/15
	Texas	Y	34320 FQ	45500 MW	59850 TQ	USBLS	5/15
	Austin-Round Rock MSA, TX	Y	36180 FQ	45760 MW	57640 TQ	USBLS	5/15

AE	Average entry wage	AWR	Average wage range	H	Hourly	LR	Low end range	MTC	Median total compensation	TCC	Total cash compensation
AEX	Average experienced wage	B	Biweekly	HI	Highest wage paid	M	Monthly	MW	Median wage paid	TQ	Third quartile wage
ATC	Average total compensation	D	Daily	HR	High end range	MCC	Median cash compensation	MWR	Median wage range	W	Weekly
AW	Average wage paid	FQ	First quartile wage	LO	Lowest wage paid	ME	Median entry wage	S	See annotated source	Y	Yearly

Occupation/Type/Industry	Location	Per	Low	Mid	High	Source	Date
Meeting, Convention, and Event Planner							
	Corpus Christi MSA, TX	Y	26600 FQ	37770 MW	45240 TQ	USBLS	5/15
	Dallas-Plano-Irving PMSA, TX	Y	41690 FQ	54150 MW	70070 TQ	USBLS	5/15
	Fort Worth-Arlington PMSA, TX	Y	28440 FQ	38980 MW	53940 TQ	USBLS	5/15
	Houston-The Woodlands-Sugar Land MSA, TX	Y	35700 FQ	46830 MW	59920 TQ	USBLS	5/15
	San Antonio-New Braunfels MSA, TX	Y	28670 FQ	39070 MW	53180 TQ	USBLS	5/15
	Utah	Y	25790 FQ	36540 MW	55200 TQ	USBLS	5/15
	Ogden-Clearfield MSA, UT	Y	22700 FQ	27980 MW	44580 TQ	USBLS	5/15
	Provo-Orem MSA, UT	Y	24120 FQ	34410 MW	53820 TQ	USBLS	5/15
	Salt Lake City MSA, UT	Y	28140 FQ	38460 MW	58770 TQ	USBLS	5/15
	Vermont	Y	30750 FQ	40930 MW	50660 TQ	USBLS	5/15
	Burlington-South Burlington MSA, VT	Y	28570 FQ	41020 MW	50420 TQ	USBLS	5/15
	Virginia	Y	41740 FQ	53180 MW	72400 TQ	USBLS	5/15
	Richmond MSA, VA	Y	39240 FQ	46530 MW	61820 TQ	USBLS	5/15
	Virginia Beach-Norfolk-Newport News MSA, VA-NC	Y	31110 FQ	40040 MW	48160 TQ	USBLS	5/15
	Tacoma-Lakewood PMSA, WA	H	15.04 FQ	20.12 MW	26.46 TQ	WABLS	3/16
	West Virginia	Y	25750 FQ	36780 MW	47030 TQ	USBLS	5/15
	Huntington-Ashland MSA, WV-KY-OH	Y	23500 FQ	38650 MW	46320 TQ	USBLS	5/15
	Wisconsin	Y	30290 FQ	39400 MW	51080 TQ	USBLS	5/15
	Madison MSA, WI	Y	36590 FQ	46240 MW	57870 TQ	USBLS	5/15
	Milwaukee-Waukesha-West Allis MSA, WI	Y	30960 FQ	40480 MW	55810 TQ	USBLS	5/15
	Wyoming	Y	32540 FQ	40520 MW	47520 TQ	USBLS	5/15
	Puerto Rico	Y	18400 FQ	23100 MW	30820 TQ	USBLS	5/15
	San Juan-Carolina-Caguas MSA, PR	Y	19420 FQ	24650 MW	32600 TQ	USBLS	5/15
	Virgin Islands	Y	28560 FQ	35400 MW	53500 TQ	USBLS	5/15
	Guam	Y	19170 FQ	23680 MW	35230 TQ	USBLS	5/15
Mental Health and Substance Abuse Social Worker							
	Alabama	Y	26146 AE	37481 AW	43138 AEX	ALBLS	6/16
	Birmingham-Hoover MSA, AL	Y	28286 AE	38367 AW	43403 AEX	ALBLS	6/16
	Alaska	Y	36170 FQ	44610 MW	53430 TQ	USBLS	5/15
	Anchorage MSA, AK	Y	34470 FQ	43220 MW	51000 TQ	USBLS	5/15
	Arizona	Y	24690 FQ	31790 MW	36710 TQ	USBLS	5/15
	Phoenix-Mesa-Scottsdale MSA, AZ	Y	24680 FQ	32060 MW	36710 TQ	USBLS	5/15
	Tucson MSA, AZ	Y	23710 FQ	29700 MW	35960 TQ	USBLS	5/15
	Arkansas	Y	26920 FQ	33990 MW	46820 TQ	USBLS	5/15
	Little Rock-North Little Rock-Conway MSA, AR	Y	27670 FQ	33910 MW	39460 TQ	USBLS	5/15
	California	H	17.13 FQ	23.11 MW	34.10 TQ	CABLS	1/16-3/16
	Anaheim-Santa Ana-Irvine PMSA, CA	H	16.48 FQ	22.04 MW	30.18 TQ	CABLS	1/16-3/16
	Oakland-Hayward-Berkeley PMSA, CA	H	18.78 FQ	27.57 MW	41.73 TQ	CABLS	1/16-3/16
	Riverside-San Bernardino-Ontario MSA, CA	H	17.05 FQ	21.60 MW	40.86 TQ	CABLS	1/16-3/16
	Sacramento–Roseville–Arden-Arcade MSA, CA	H	12.10 FQ	16.02 MW	23.59 TQ	CABLS	1/16-3/16
	San Diego-Carlsbad MSA, CA	H	15.16 FQ	20.14 MW	27.33 TQ	CABLS	1/16-3/16
	San Francisco-Redwood City-South San Francisco PMSA, CA	H	21.85 FQ	27.67 MW	41.62 TQ	CABLS	1/16-3/16
	Colorado	Y	32210 FQ	39370 MW	50910 TQ	USBLS	5/15
	Denver-Aurora-Lakewood MSA, CO	Y	32350 FQ	37760 MW	48890 TQ	USBLS	5/15
	Connecticut	Y		60819 MW		CTBLS	1/16-3/16
	Bridgeport-Stamford-Norwalk MSA, CT	Y	48550 FQ	67010 MW	82020 TQ	USBLS	5/15
	Hartford-West Hartford-East Hartford MSA, CT	Y	41800 FQ	55450 MW	72270 TQ	USBLS	5/15
	Delaware	Y	40250 FQ	46620 MW	54100 TQ	USBLS	5/15
	Wilmington PMSA, DE-MD-NJ	Y	40900 FQ	47380 MW	55950 TQ	USBLS	5/15

Mental Health and Substance Abuse Social Worker

Occupation/Type/Industry	Location	Per	Low	Mid	High	Source	Date
Mental Health and Substance Abuse Social Worker	District of Columbia	Y	39860 FQ	47620 MW	60640 TQ	USBLS	5/15
	Washington-Arlington-Alexandria PMSA, DC-VA-MD-WV	Y	42480 FQ	56310 MW	72990 TQ	USBLS	5/15
	Florida	H	13.40 AE	18.32 MW	23.60 AEX	FLBLS	7/16-9/16
	Fort Lauderdale-Pompano Beach-Deerfield Beach PMSA, FL	H	13.45 AE	19.49 MW	23.37 AEX	FLBLS	7/16-9/16
	Miami-Miami Beach-Kendall PMSA, FL	H	11.52 AE	17.28 MW	21.97 AEX	FLBLS	7/16-9/16
	Orlando-Kissimmee-Sanford MSA, FL	H	13.60 AE	17.14 MW	20.82 AEX	FLBLS	7/16-9/16
	Tampa-St. Petersburg-Clearwater MSA, FL	H	13.47 AE	19.50 MW	28.83 AEX	FLBLS	7/16-9/16
	Georgia	Y	33980 FQ	42550 MW	66050 TQ	USBLS	5/15
	Atlanta-Sandy Springs-Roswell MSA, GA	Y	32420 FQ	38720 MW	47800 TQ	USBLS	5/15
	Augusta-Richmond County MSA, GA-SC	Y	31570 FQ	35760 MW	39750 TQ	USBLS	5/15
	Hawaii	Y	41820 FQ	48690 MW	63210 TQ	USBLS	5/15
	Urban Honolulu MSA, HI	Y	41260 FQ	50980 MW	68390 TQ	USBLS	5/15
	Idaho	Y	29900 FQ	39680 MW	49120 TQ	USBLS	5/15
	Boise City MSA, ID	Y	24530 FQ	40250 MW	48930 TQ	USBLS	5/15
	Illinois	Y	32040 FQ	38490 MW	54880 TQ	USBLS	5/15
	Indiana	Y	31580 FQ	37950 MW	48140 TQ	USBLS	5/15
	Gary PMSA, IN	Y	29230 FQ	35960 MW	56380 TQ	USBLS	5/15
	Indianapolis-Carmel-Anderson MSA, IN	Y	34120 FQ	39890 MW	50910 TQ	USBLS	5/15
	Iowa	Y	32260 FQ	37590 MW	46380 TQ	USBLS	5/15
	Des Moines-West Des Moines MSA, IA	Y	35240 FQ	40910 MW	46340 TQ	USBLS	5/15
	Kansas	Y	31190 FQ	39350 MW	47110 TQ	USBLS	5/15
	Wichita MSA, KS	Y	32680 FQ	42350 MW	51770 TQ	USBLS	5/15
	Kentucky	Y	29240 FQ	35350 MW	43910 TQ	USBLS	5/15
	Louisville-Jefferson County MSA, KY-IN	Y	33470 FQ	39790 MW	47910 TQ	USBLS	5/15
	Louisiana	Y	29130 FQ	38130 MW	50100 TQ	USBLS	5/15
	Baton Rouge MSA, LA	Y	24300 FQ	36700 MW	49740 TQ	USBLS	5/15
	New Orleans-Metairie MSA, LA	Y	29760 FQ	39200 MW	51800 TQ	USBLS	5/15
	Maine	Y	44690 FQ	53830 MW	70260 TQ	USBLS	5/15
	Portland-South Portland MSA, ME	Y	47300 FQ	55030 MW	64180 TQ	USBLS	5/15
	Maryland	Y	28229 AE	48131 MW	58082 AEX	MDBLS	4/16
	Baltimore-Columbia-Towson MSA, MD	Y	36050 FQ	49390 MW	59310 TQ	USBLS	5/15
	Salisbury MSA, MD-DE	Y	21710 FQ	24080 MW	38080 TQ	USBLS	5/15
	Massachusetts	Y	29980 FQ	41990 MW	62470 TQ	USBLS	5/15
	Boston-Cambridge-Newton NECTA, MA	Y	33950 FQ	50420 MW	73190 TQ	USBLS	5/15
	Worcester MSA, MA-CT	Y	30410 FQ	41700 MW	66320 TQ	USBLS	5/15
	Michigan	Y	38640 FQ	45930 MW	54820 TQ	USBLS	5/15
	Detroit-Dearborn-Livonia PMSA, MI	Y	36970 FQ	43840 MW	50370 TQ	USBLS	5/15
	Grand Rapids-Wyoming MSA, MI	Y	38650 FQ	48890 MW	58610 TQ	USBLS	5/15
	Minnesota	Y	38437 FQ	46794 MW	59566 TQ	MNBLS	1/16-3/16
	Minneapolis-St. Paul-Bloomington MSA, MN-WI	Y	38266 FQ	45907 MW	59536 TQ	MNBLS	1/16-3/16
	Mississippi	Y	24420 FQ	32590 MW	43140 TQ	USBLS	5/15
	Jackson MSA, MS	Y	27140 FQ	31230 MW	43550 TQ	USBLS	5/15
	Missouri	Y	25310 FQ	34990 MW	43440 TQ	USBLS	5/15
	Kansas City MSA, MO-KS	Y	34310 FQ	39030 MW	47680 TQ	USBLS	5/15
	St. Louis MSA, MO-IL	Y	33810 FQ	37600 MW	46580 TQ	USBLS	5/15
	Montana	Y	27100 FQ	33200 MW	43290 TQ	USBLS	5/15
	Billings MSA, MT	Y	28880 FQ	35410 MW	47770 TQ	USBLS	5/15
	Omaha-Council Bluffs MSA, NE-IA	Y	27570 FQ	31475 MW	37720 TQ	NEBLS	7/16-9/16
	Nevada	Y	43380 FQ	50090 MW	62930 TQ	USBLS	5/15
	Las Vegas-Henderson-Paradise MSA, NV	Y	44130 FQ	51360 MW	63650 TQ	USBLS	5/15

AE	Average entry wage	AWR	Average wage range	H	Hourly
AEX	Average experienced wage	B	Biweekly	HI	Highest wage paid
ATC	Average total compensation	D	Daily	HR	High end range
AW	Average wage paid	FQ	First quartile wage	LO	Lowest wage paid

LR	Low end range	MTC	Median total compensation	TCC	Total cash compensation
M	Monthly	MW	Median wage paid	TQ	Third quartile wage
MCC	Median cash compensation	MWR	Median wage range	W	Weekly
ME	Median entry wage	S	See annotated source	Y	Yearly

Mental Health and Substance Abuse Social Worker

Occupation/Type/Industry	Location	Per	Low	Mid	High	Source	Date
Mental Health and Substance Abuse Social Worker	New Hampshire	H	18.93 AE	25.48 MW	33.41 AEX	NHBLS	6/16
	Manchester NECTA, NH	H	17.94 AE	23.71 MW	29.55 AEX	NHBLS	6/16
	New Jersey	Y	50610 FQ	63050 MW	83870 TQ	USBLS	5/15
	Camden PMSA, NJ	Y	37510 FQ	46210 MW	60500 TQ	USBLS	5/15
	Newark PMSA, NJ-PA	Y	50080 FQ	58250 MW	70340 TQ	USBLS	5/15
	Trenton MSA, NJ	Y	56570 FQ	67720 MW	79600 TQ	USBLS	5/15
	New Mexico	Y	27170 FQ	37050 MW	46720 TQ	USBLS	5/15
	Albuquerque MSA, NM	Y	24730 FQ	29820 MW	41340 TQ	USBLS	5/15
	New York	Y	38580 AE	51750 MW	65220 AEX	NYBLS	1/16-3/16
	Buffalo-Cheektowaga-Niagara Falls MSA, NY	Y	36430 FQ	43230 MW	49770 TQ	USBLS	5/15
	Nassau County-Suffolk County PMSA, NY	Y	44400 FQ	55230 MW	69570 TQ	USBLS	5/15
	New York-Jersey City-White Plains PMSA, NY-NJ	Y	42600 FQ	53900 MW	70680 TQ	USBLS	5/15
	Rochester MSA, NY	Y	37240 FQ	45910 MW	57810 TQ	USBLS	5/15
	North Carolina	Y	37750 FQ	44530 MW	51730 TQ	USBLS	5/15
	Charlotte-Concord-Gastonia MSA, NC-SC	Y	41240 FQ	46840 MW	54490 TQ	USBLS	5/15
	Raleigh MSA, NC	Y	41020 FQ	46710 MW	55710 TQ	USBLS	5/15
	North Dakota	Y	41440 FQ	46890 MW	50410 TQ	USBLS	5/15
	Fargo MSA, ND-MN	Y	39560 FQ	45570 MW	48950 TQ	USBLS	5/15
	Ohio	Y	31600 FQ	37310 MW	48080 TQ	USBLS	5/15
	Cincinnati MSA, OH-KY-IN	Y	31090 FQ	35610 MW	41230 TQ	USBLS	5/15
	Cleveland-Elyria MSA, OH	Y	32400 FQ	37460 MW	48440 TQ	USBLS	5/15
	Columbus MSA, OH	Y	30050 FQ	39960 MW	53830 TQ	USBLS	5/15
	Oklahoma	Y	18770 FQ	25230 MW	37860 TQ	USBLS	5/15
	Oklahoma City MSA, OK	Y	25920 FQ	31110 MW	40140 TQ	USBLS	5/15
	Tulsa MSA, OK	Y	17850 FQ	19800 MW	31800 TQ	USBLS	5/15
	Oregon	H	16.13 FQ	21.31 MW	26.51 TQ	ORBLS	2016
	Portland-Vancouver-Hillsboro MSA, OR-WA	Y	30530 FQ	39270 MW	48070 TQ	USBLS	5/15
	Pennsylvania	Y	29060 FQ	36000 MW	45890 TQ	USBLS	5/15
	Allentown-Bethlehem-Easton MSA, PA-NJ	Y	29980 FQ	35600 MW	43050 TQ	USBLS	5/15
	Harrisburg-Carlisle MSA, PA	Y	28590 FQ	35010 MW	44000 TQ	USBLS	5/15
	Montgomery County-Bucks County-Chester County PMSA, PA	Y	31140 FQ	40230 MW	49590 TQ	USBLS	5/15
	Philadelphia PMSA, PA	Y	33080 FQ	38870 MW	48820 TQ	USBLS	5/15
	Pittsburgh MSA, PA	Y	28470 FQ	35250 MW	46160 TQ	USBLS	5/15
	South Carolina	Y	34580 FQ	39710 MW	47630 TQ	USBLS	5/15
	Columbia MSA, SC	Y	36200 FQ	41930 MW	49770 TQ	USBLS	5/15
	Greenville-Anderson-Mauldin MSA, SC	Y	31650 FQ	41120 MW	50150 TQ	USBLS	5/15
	South Dakota	Y	31620 FQ	36160 MW	41740 TQ	USBLS	5/15
	Sioux Falls MSA, SD	Y	31420 FQ	35430 MW	39410 TQ	USBLS	5/15
	Tennessee	Y	27410 FQ	30820 MW	38810 TQ	USBLS	5/15
	Knoxville MSA, TN	Y	27570 FQ	30970 MW	37500 TQ	USBLS	5/15
	Memphis MSA, TN-MS-AR	Y	29170 FQ	36340 MW	46950 TQ	USBLS	5/15
	Nashville-Davidson– Murfreesboro–Franklin MSA, TN	Y	27250 FQ	30190 MW	37630 TQ	USBLS	5/15
	Texas	Y	35310 FQ	41130 MW	49220 TQ	USBLS	5/15
	Austin-Round Rock MSA, TX	Y	35030 FQ	40770 MW	49150 TQ	USBLS	5/15
	Dallas-Plano-Irving PMSA, TX	Y	35970 FQ	42880 MW	50260 TQ	USBLS	5/15
	Fort Worth-Arlington PMSA, TX	Y	38880 FQ	46230 MW	57420 TQ	USBLS	5/15
	Houston-The Woodlands– Sugar Land MSA, TX	Y	39070 FQ	45950 MW	54850 TQ	USBLS	5/15
	San Antonio-New Braunfels MSA, TX	Y	39510 FQ	43800 MW	48440 TQ	USBLS	5/15
	Utah	Y	33100 FQ	45100 MW	57000 TQ	USBLS	5/15
	Ogden-Clearfield MSA, UT	Y	28730 FQ	39550 MW	54440 TQ	USBLS	5/15
	Provo-Orem MSA, UT	Y	41930 FQ	52670 MW	61050 TQ	USBLS	5/15
	Salt Lake City MSA, UT	Y	36430 FQ	44780 MW	54970 TQ	USBLS	5/15
	Vermont	Y	33220 FQ	38990 MW	48260 TQ	USBLS	5/15
	Burlington-South Burlington MSA, VT	Y	32190 FQ	37590 MW	47630 TQ	USBLS	5/15
	Virginia	Y	36030 FQ	44730 MW	56360 TQ	USBLS	5/15
	Richmond MSA, VA	Y	40710 FQ	46500 MW	55350 TQ	USBLS	5/15

AE	Average entry wage	AWR	Average wage range	H	Hourly	LR	Low end range	MTC	Median total compensation	TCC	Total cash compensation
AEX	Average experienced wage	B	Biweekly	HI	Highest wage paid	M	Monthly	MW	Median wage paid	TQ	Third quartile wage
ATC	Average total compensation	D	Daily	HR	High end range	MCC	Median cash compensation	MWR	Median wage range	W	Weekly
AW	Average wage paid	FQ	First quartile wage	LO	Lowest wage paid	ME	Median entry wage	S	See annotated source	Y	Yearly

Occupation/Type/Industry	Location	Per	Low	Mid	High	Source	Date
Mental Health and Substance Abuse Social Worker	Virginia Beach-Norfolk-Newport News MSA, VA-NC	Y	38130 FQ	46880 MW	59420 TQ	USBLS	5/15
	Washington	H	20.13 FQ	24.63 MW	28.78 TQ	WABLS	3/16
	Seattle-Bellevue-Everett PMSA, WA	H	21.45 FQ	26.89 MW	34.07 TQ	WABLS	3/16
	Tacoma-Lakewood PMSA, WA	H	18.32 FQ	22.80 MW	27.54 TQ	WABLS	3/16
	West Virginia	Y	20220 FQ	24160 MW	35480 TQ	USBLS	5/15
	Huntington-Ashland MSA, WV-KY-OH	Y	32790 FQ	37180 MW	42710 TQ	USBLS	5/15
	Wisconsin	Y	37430 FQ	47500 MW	56760 TQ	USBLS	5/15
	Madison MSA, WI	Y	35890 FQ	42090 MW	53670 TQ	USBLS	5/15
	Milwaukee-Waukesha-West Allis MSA, WI	Y	38630 FQ	47790 MW	56640 TQ	USBLS	5/15
	Wyoming	Y	42920 FQ	57520 MW	72870 TQ	USBLS	5/15
	Puerto Rico	Y	17070 FQ	18750 MW	22620 TQ	USBLS	5/15
	San Juan-Carolina-Caguas MSA, PR	Y	17230 FQ	19180 MW	23660 TQ	USBLS	5/15
	Guam	Y	27360 FQ	30010 MW	43920 TQ	USBLS	5/15
Mental Health Counselor	Alabama	Y	33413 AE	47847 AW	55054 AEX	ALBLS	6/16
	Birmingham-Hoover MSA, AL	Y	32578 AE	47256 AW	54605 AEX	ALBLS	6/16
	Alaska	Y	48990 FQ	60150 MW	72730 TQ	USBLS	5/15
	Anchorage MSA, AK	Y	53430 FQ	64730 MW	74720 TQ	USBLS	5/15
	Arizona	Y	39750 FQ	47000 MW	57010 TQ	USBLS	5/15
	Phoenix-Mesa-Scottsdale MSA, AZ	Y	41330 FQ	48490 MW	58480 TQ	USBLS	5/15
	Tucson MSA, AZ	Y	33800 FQ	44080 MW	51090 TQ	USBLS	5/15
	Arkansas	Y	41540 FQ	49100 MW	58490 TQ	USBLS	5/15
	Little Rock-North Little Rock-Conway MSA, AR	Y	41660 FQ	47720 MW	57340 TQ	USBLS	5/15
	California	H	16.17 FQ	20.35 MW	28.37 TQ	CABLS	1/16-3/16
	Anaheim-Santa Ana-Irvine PMSA, CA	H	16.07 FQ	19.06 MW	23.38 TQ	CABLS	1/16-3/16
	Los Angeles-Long Beach-Glendale PMSA, CA	H	17.20 FQ	23.00 MW	34.31 TQ	CABLS	1/16-3/16
	Oakland-Hayward-Berkeley PMSA, CA	H	17.72 FQ	23.18 MW	35.77 TQ	CABLS	1/16-3/16
	Riverside-San Bernardino-Ontario MSA, CA	H	15.90 FQ	18.57 MW	25.54 TQ	CABLS	1/16-3/16
	Sacramento–Roseville–Arden-Arcade MSA, CA	H	11.38 FQ	14.44 MW	22.27 TQ	CABLS	1/16-3/16
	San Diego-Carlsbad MSA, CA	H	15.59 FQ	19.20 MW	26.60 TQ	CABLS	1/16-3/16
	San Francisco-Redwood City-South San Francisco PMSA, CA	H	17.23 FQ	19.61 MW	22.93 TQ	CABLS	1/16-3/16
	Colorado	Y	34060 FQ	44950 MW	59860 TQ	USBLS	5/15
	Denver-Aurora-Lakewood MSA, CO	Y	31770 FQ	42410 MW	57510 TQ	USBLS	5/15
	Connecticut	Y		44983 MW		CTBLS	1/16-3/16
	Bridgeport-Stamford-Norwalk MSA, CT	Y	34980 FQ	41340 MW	54330 TQ	USBLS	5/15
	Hartford-West Hartford-East Hartford MSA, CT	Y	37210 FQ	45290 MW	54990 TQ	USBLS	5/15
	Delaware	Y	29030 FQ	36940 MW	46480 TQ	USBLS	5/15
	Wilmington PMSA, DE-MD-NJ	Y	29270 FQ	37010 MW	46460 TQ	USBLS	5/15
	District of Columbia	Y	28030 FQ	42150 MW	58440 TQ	USBLS	5/15
	Washington-Arlington-Alexandria PMSA, DC-VA-MD-WV	Y	35340 FQ	47390 MW	60710 TQ	USBLS	5/15
	Florida	H	13.64 AE	19.63 MW	24.92 AEX	FLBLS	7/16-9/16
	Fort Lauderdale-Pompano Beach-Deerfield Beach PMSA, FL	H	13.23 AE	18.29 MW	26.80 AEX	FLBLS	7/16-9/16
	Miami-Miami Beach-Kendall PMSA, FL	H	16.71 AE	25.40 MW	27.79 AEX	FLBLS	7/16-9/16
	Orlando-Kissimmee-Sanford MSA, FL	H	9.57 AE	14.58 MW	20.61 AEX	FLBLS	7/16-9/16
	Tampa-St. Petersburg-Clearwater MSA, FL	H	12.54 AE	17.49 MW	22.93 AEX	FLBLS	7/16-9/16
	Georgia	Y	36130 FQ	45320 MW	55490 TQ	USBLS	5/15

AE Average entry wage	**AWR** Average wage range	**H** Hourly	**LR** Low end range	**MTC** Median total compensation	**TCC** Total cash compensation
AEX Average experienced wage	**B** Biweekly	**HI** Highest wage paid	**M** Monthly	**MW** Median wage paid	**TQ** Third quartile wage
ATC Average total compensation	**D** Daily	**HR** High end range	**MCC** Median cash compensation	**MWR** Median wage range	**W** Weekly
AW Average wage paid	**FQ** First quartile wage	**LO** Lowest wage paid	**ME** Median entry wage	**S** See annotated source	**Y** Yearly

Occupation/Type/Industry	Location	Per	Low	Mid	High	Source	Date
Mental Health Counselor	Atlanta-Sandy Springs-Roswell MSA, GA	Y	40090 FQ	50090 MW	58730 TQ	USBLS	5/15
	Hawaii	Y	29500 FQ	38720 MW	59280 TQ	USBLS	5/15
	Urban Honolulu MSA, HI	Y	28780 FQ	37060 MW	58870 TQ	USBLS	5/15
	Idaho	Y	35750 FQ	51920 MW	59550 TQ	USBLS	5/15
	Boise City MSA, ID	Y	38530 FQ	53860 MW	59210 TQ	USBLS	5/15
	Illinois	Y	29010 FQ	37660 MW	52400 TQ	USBLS	5/15
	Chicago-Naperville-Arlington Heights PMSA, IL	Y	30440 FQ	40330 MW	57740 TQ	USBLS	5/15
	Lake County-Kenosha County PMSA, IL-WI	Y	30490 FQ	39450 MW	63870 TQ	USBLS	5/15
	Indiana	Y	33020 FQ	41370 MW	50040 TQ	USBLS	5/15
	Gary PMSA, IN	Y	33160 FQ	39790 MW	48470 TQ	USBLS	5/15
	Indianapolis-Carmel-Anderson MSA, IN	Y	31430 FQ	39600 MW	49020 TQ	USBLS	5/15
	Iowa	Y	27340 FQ	36270 MW	46790 TQ	USBLS	5/15
	Des Moines-West Des Moines MSA, IA	Y	32860 FQ	39430 MW	48240 TQ	USBLS	5/15
	Kansas	Y	30830 FQ	40290 MW	48020 TQ	USBLS	5/15
	Wichita MSA, KS	Y	35720 FQ	43170 MW	48160 TQ	USBLS	5/15
	Kentucky	Y	30450 FQ	36020 MW	44580 TQ	USBLS	5/15
	Louisville-Jefferson County MSA, KY-IN	Y	29760 FQ	37240 MW	46180 TQ	USBLS	5/15
	Louisiana	Y	25890 FQ	33190 MW	39490 TQ	USBLS	5/15
	Baton Rouge MSA, LA	Y	22290 FQ	29960 MW	38110 TQ	USBLS	5/15
	New Orleans-Metairie MSA, LA	Y	28500 FQ	34740 MW	42980 TQ	USBLS	5/15
	Maine	Y	39260 FQ	50450 MW	57720 TQ	USBLS	5/15
	Portland-South Portland MSA, ME	Y	44380 FQ	50810 MW	57520 TQ	USBLS	5/15
	Maryland	Y	25575 AE	41476 MW	49427 AEX	MDBLS	4/16
	Baltimore-Columbia-Towson MSA, MD	Y	33990 FQ	41160 MW	49900 TQ	USBLS	5/15
	Salisbury MSA, MD-DE	Y	21930 FQ	24350 MW	29100 TQ	USBLS	5/15
	Massachusetts	Y	30360 FQ	38540 MW	52610 TQ	USBLS	5/15
	Boston-Cambridge-Newton NECTA, MA	Y	29000 FQ	36510 MW	48960 TQ	USBLS	5/15
	Worcester MSA, MA-CT	Y	29340 FQ	40680 MW	52440 TQ	USBLS	5/15
	Michigan	Y	34970 FQ	45820 MW	56340 TQ	USBLS	5/15
	Detroit-Dearborn-Livonia PMSA, MI	Y	29510 FQ	39990 MW	46920 TQ	USBLS	5/15
	Grand Rapids-Wyoming MSA, MI	Y	36670 FQ	47250 MW	57190 TQ	USBLS	5/15
	Minnesota	Y	36431 FQ	45040 MW	55181 TQ	MNBLS	1/16-3/16
	Minneapolis-St. Paul-Bloomington MSA, MN-WI	Y	38014 FQ	45856 MW	55241 TQ	MNBLS	1/16-3/16
	Mississippi	Y	34000 FQ	43120 MW	50920 TQ	USBLS	5/15
	Jackson MSA, MS	Y	35330 FQ	44960 MW	52540 TQ	USBLS	5/15
	Missouri	Y	29210 FQ	38470 MW	50470 TQ	USBLS	5/15
	Kansas City MSA, MO-KS	Y	28950 FQ	39230 MW	53600 TQ	USBLS	5/15
	St. Louis MSA, MO-IL	Y	33510 FQ	41570 MW	49200 TQ	USBLS	5/15
	Montana	Y	24790 FQ	33270 MW	43130 TQ	USBLS	5/15
	Billings MSA, MT	Y	31630 FQ	39610 MW	48520 TQ	USBLS	5/15
	Omaha-Council Bluffs MSA, NE-IA	Y	37010 FQ	46095 MW	59380 TQ	NEBLS	7/16-9/16
	Nevada	Y	37430 FQ	46250 MW	58350 TQ	USBLS	5/15
	Las Vegas-Henderson-Paradise MSA, NV	Y	38560 FQ	45670 MW	55560 TQ	USBLS	5/15
	New Hampshire	H	15.44 AE	21.24 MW	27.89 AEX	NHBLS	6/16
	Manchester NECTA, NH	H	15.35 AE	22.06 MW	31.32 AEX	NHBLS	6/16
	Nashua NECTA, NH-MA	Y	37420 FQ	43520 MW	50280 TQ	USBLS	5/15
	New Jersey	Y	40370 FQ	48800 MW	60150 TQ	USBLS	5/15
	Camden PMSA, NJ	Y	42070 FQ	50130 MW	61250 TQ	USBLS	5/15
	Newark PMSA, NJ-PA	Y	39780 FQ	50980 MW	61780 TQ	USBLS	5/15
	New Mexico	Y	24310 FQ	33440 MW	49290 TQ	USBLS	5/15
	Albuquerque MSA, NM	Y	23200 FQ	29180 MW	47800 TQ	USBLS	5/15
	New York	Y	29740 AE	40360 MW	49990 AEX	NYBLS	1/16-3/16
	Buffalo-Cheektowaga-Niagara Falls MSA, NY	Y	29030 FQ	35110 MW	46040 TQ	USBLS	5/15
	Nassau County-Suffolk County PMSA, NY	Y	32430 FQ	37910 MW	49430 TQ	USBLS	5/15

AE	Average entry wage	AWR	Average wage range	H	Hourly
AEX	Average experienced wage	B	Biweekly	HI	Highest wage paid
ATC	Average total compensation	D	Daily	HR	High end range
AW	Average wage paid	FQ	First quartile wage	LO	Lowest wage paid

LR	Low end range	MTC	Median total compensation
M	Monthly	MW	Median wage paid
MCC	Median cash compensation	MWR	Median wage range
ME	Median entry wage	S	See annotated source

TCC	Total cash compensation		
TQ	Third quartile wage		
W	Weekly		
Y	Yearly		

Occupation/Type/Industry	Location	Per	Low	Mid	High	Source	Date
Mental Health Counselor	New York-Jersey City-White Plains PMSA, NY-NJ	Y	35660 FQ	43720 MW	53220 TQ	USBLS	5/15
	Rochester MSA, NY	Y	33340 FQ	41130 MW	48150 TQ	USBLS	5/15
	North Carolina	Y	37550 FQ	46110 MW	57000 TQ	USBLS	5/15
	Charlotte-Concord-Gastonia MSA, NC-SC	Y	38640 FQ	46260 MW	56620 TQ	USBLS	5/15
	Raleigh MSA, NC	Y	34060 FQ	50290 MW	61620 TQ	USBLS	5/15
	North Dakota	Y	33940 FQ	44150 MW	52080 TQ	USBLS	5/15
	Fargo MSA, ND-MN	Y	40680 FQ	48950 MW	60800 TQ	USBLS	5/15
	Ohio	Y	35540 FQ	43270 MW	53580 TQ	USBLS	5/15
	Cincinnati MSA, OH-KY-IN	Y	35940 FQ	41930 MW	47610 TQ	USBLS	5/15
	Cleveland-Elyria MSA, OH	Y	34090 FQ	40280 MW	56420 TQ	USBLS	5/15
	Columbus MSA, OH	Y	34740 FQ	42610 MW	57800 TQ	USBLS	5/15
	Oklahoma	Y	34050 FQ	43090 MW	53530 TQ	USBLS	5/15
	Oklahoma City MSA, OK	Y	32900 FQ	40670 MW	54820 TQ	USBLS	5/15
	Tulsa MSA, OK	Y	41370 FQ	47940 MW	56480 TQ	USBLS	5/15
	Oregon	H	17.89 FQ	23.30 MW	32.96 TQ	ORBLS	2016
	Portland-Vancouver-Hillsboro MSA, OR-WA	Y	36900 FQ	47690 MW	68730 TQ	USBLS	5/15
	Pennsylvania	Y	32970 FQ	41640 MW	52750 TQ	USBLS	5/15
	Allentown-Bethlehem-Easton MSA, PA-NJ	Y	40690 FQ	49120 MW	62240 TQ	USBLS	5/15
	Harrisburg-Carlisle MSA, PA	Y	28880 FQ	41310 MW	55830 TQ	USBLS	5/15
	Montgomery County-Bucks County-Chester County PMSA, PA	Y	35950 FQ	44320 MW	57430 TQ	USBLS	5/15
	Philadelphia PMSA, PA	Y	33050 FQ	40750 MW	49450 TQ	USBLS	5/15
	Pittsburgh MSA, PA	Y	33150 FQ	40360 MW	51280 TQ	USBLS	5/15
	Rhode Island	Y	27070 FQ	29660 MW	37090 TQ	USBLS	5/15
	Providence-Warwick MSA, RI-MA	Y	27700 FQ	30920 MW	41030 TQ	USBLS	5/15
	South Carolina	Y	27880 FQ	35820 MW	52820 TQ	USBLS	5/15
	Charleston-North Charleston MSA, SC	Y	35940 FQ	42440 MW	81220 TQ	USBLS	5/15
	Columbia MSA, SC	Y	23830 FQ	28840 MW	50740 TQ	USBLS	5/15
	Greenville-Anderson-Mauldin MSA, SC	Y	27500 FQ	30380 MW	37560 TQ	USBLS	5/15
	South Dakota	Y	35100 FQ	42680 MW	49820 TQ	USBLS	5/15
	Sioux Falls MSA, SD	Y	33900 FQ	41730 MW	53950 TQ	USBLS	5/15
	Tennessee	Y	25620 FQ	30450 MW	40140 TQ	USBLS	5/15
	Knoxville MSA, TN	Y	22790 FQ	26980 MW	41650 TQ	USBLS	5/15
	Memphis MSA, TN-MS-AR	Y	22460 FQ	27520 MW	33610 TQ	USBLS	5/15
	Nashville-Davidson–Murfreesboro–Franklin MSA, TN	Y	29190 FQ	36410 MW	47120 TQ	USBLS	5/15
	Texas	Y	33750 FQ	42450 MW	55170 TQ	USBLS	5/15
	Austin-Round Rock MSA, TX	Y	33860 FQ	38610 MW	47180 TQ	USBLS	5/15
	Dallas-Plano-Irving PMSA, TX	Y	36790 FQ	47310 MW	60180 TQ	USBLS	5/15
	Fort Worth-Arlington PMSA, TX	Y	39470 FQ	51250 MW	66120 TQ	USBLS	5/15
	Houston-The Woodlands-Sugar Land MSA, TX	Y	35900 FQ	46850 MW	58660 TQ	USBLS	5/15
	San Antonio-New Braunfels MSA, TX	Y	35490 FQ	48070 MW	57290 TQ	USBLS	5/15
	Utah	Y	38510 FQ	49410 MW	62700 TQ	USBLS	5/15
	Ogden-Clearfield MSA, UT	Y	28200 FQ	37320 MW	58180 TQ	USBLS	5/15
	Provo-Orem MSA, UT	Y	42260 FQ	53060 MW	66120 TQ	USBLS	5/15
	Salt Lake City MSA, UT	Y	42880 FQ	51990 MW	68770 TQ	USBLS	5/15
	Vermont	Y	32790 FQ	38520 MW	49060 TQ	USBLS	5/15
	Burlington-South Burlington MSA, VT	Y	35910 FQ	42720 MW	52930 TQ	USBLS	5/15
	Virginia	Y	35460 FQ	43460 MW	53510 TQ	USBLS	5/15
	Richmond MSA, VA	Y	34460 FQ	41150 MW	49070 TQ	USBLS	5/15
	Virginia Beach-Norfolk-Newport News MSA, VA-NC	Y	35420 FQ	42400 MW	49350 TQ	USBLS	5/15
	Washington	H	16.96 FQ	21.67 MW	26.73 TQ	WABLS	3/16
	Seattle-Bellevue-Everett PMSA, WA	H	15.53 FQ	19.69 MW	24.67 TQ	WABLS	3/16
	Tacoma-Lakewood PMSA, WA	H	18.95 FQ	23.05 MW	27.70 TQ	WABLS	3/16
	West Virginia	Y	24760 FQ	31300 MW	37810 TQ	USBLS	5/15
	Huntington-Ashland MSA, WV-KY-OH	Y	28150 FQ	35070 MW	43210 TQ	USBLS	5/15

Occupation/Type/Industry	Location	Per	Low	Mid	High	Source	Date
Mental Health Counselor	Wisconsin	Y	27610 FQ	42870 MW	58810 TQ	USBLS	5/15
	Madison MSA, WI	Y	42160 FQ	48230 MW	63910 TQ	USBLS	5/15
	Milwaukee-Waukesha-West Allis MSA, WI	Y	33530 FQ	45610 MW	59850 TQ	USBLS	5/15
	Wyoming	Y	42990 FQ	51430 MW	61030 TQ	USBLS	5/15
	Cheyenne MSA, WY	Y	36810 FQ	44770 MW	56530 TQ	USBLS	5/15
	Puerto Rico	Y	18630 FQ	22520 MW	31900 TQ	USBLS	5/15
	San Juan-Carolina-Caguas MSA, PR	Y	19320 FQ	23560 MW	33790 TQ	USBLS	5/15
Mental Health Treatment Specialist							
Public Health Department, Municipal Government	San Francisco, CA	Y		94118 AW		CACIT	6/28/16
Merchandise Displayer and Window Trimmer							
	Alabama	Y	17267 AE	26931 AW	31752 AEX	ALBLS	6/16
	Birmingham-Hoover MSA, AL	Y	20672 AE	31314 AW	36634 AEX	ALBLS	6/16
	Alaska	Y	28440 FQ	34050 MW	39310 TQ	USBLS	5/15
	Anchorage MSA, AK	Y	27720 FQ	32870 MW	38530 TQ	USBLS	5/15
	Arizona	Y	23280 FQ	28270 MW	38990 TQ	USBLS	5/15
	Phoenix-Mesa-Scottsdale MSA, AZ	Y	23050 FQ	27920 MW	40720 TQ	USBLS	5/15
	Tucson MSA, AZ	Y	24500 FQ	28230 MW	31610 TQ	USBLS	5/15
	Arkansas	Y	23440 FQ	30000 MW	43550 TQ	USBLS	5/15
	Little Rock-North Little Rock-Conway MSA, AR	Y	25240 FQ	29460 MW	40780 TQ	USBLS	5/15
	California	H	10.92 FQ	13.49 MW	17.51 TQ	CABLS	1/16-3/16
	Anaheim-Santa Ana-Irvine PMSA, CA	H	10.79 FQ	12.11 MW	15.62 TQ	CABLS	1/16-3/16
	Los Angeles-Long Beach-Glendale PMSA, CA	H	10.58 FQ	14.13 MW	18.01 TQ	CABLS	1/16-3/16
	Oakland-Hayward-Berkeley PMSA, CA	H	10.68 FQ	11.84 MW	14.98 TQ	CABLS	1/16-3/16
	Riverside-San Bernardino-Ontario MSA, CA	H	10.49 FQ	12.73 MW	17.24 TQ	CABLS	1/16-3/16
	Sacramento–Roseville–Arden-Arcade MSA, CA	H	11.33 FQ	15.33 MW	18.77 TQ	CABLS	1/16-3/16
	San Diego-Carlsbad MSA, CA	H	10.71 FQ	13.42 MW	17.49 TQ	CABLS	1/16-3/16
	San Francisco-Redwood City-South San Francisco PMSA, CA	H	14.75 FQ	17.52 MW	21.98 TQ	CABLS	1/16-3/16
	Colorado	Y	24340 FQ	29810 MW	38100 TQ	USBLS	5/15
	Denver-Aurora-Lakewood MSA, CO	Y	25450 FQ	30350 MW	38270 TQ	USBLS	5/15
	Connecticut	Y		25332 MW		CTBLS	1/16-3/16
	Bridgeport-Stamford-Norwalk MSA, CT	Y	25090 FQ	29310 MW	47910 TQ	USBLS	5/15
	Hartford-West Hartford-East Hartford MSA, CT	Y	21890 FQ	24240 MW	30120 TQ	USBLS	5/15
	Delaware	Y	21670 FQ	28070 MW	35430 TQ	USBLS	5/15
	Wilmington PMSA, DE-MD-NJ	Y	21520 FQ	27160 MW	34980 TQ	USBLS	5/15
	District of Columbia	Y	36170 FQ	49070 MW	59090 TQ	USBLS	5/15
	Washington-Arlington-Alexandria PMSA, DC-VA-MD-WV	Y	25230 FQ	31910 MW	43380 TQ	USBLS	5/15
	Florida	H	9.68 AE	13.11 MW	16.20 AEX	FLBLS	7/16-9/16
	Fort Lauderdale-Pompano Beach-Deerfield Beach PMSA, FL	H	9.31 AE	12.80 MW	15.62 AEX	FLBLS	7/16-9/16
	Miami-Miami Beach-Kendall PMSA, FL	H	8.95 AE	11.96 MW	17.38 AEX	FLBLS	7/16-9/16
	Orlando-Kissimmee-Sanford MSA, FL	H	9.45 AE	12.94 MW	16.52 AEX	FLBLS	7/16-9/16
	Tampa-St. Petersburg-Clearwater MSA, FL	H	10.25 AE	13.22 MW	15.84 AEX	FLBLS	7/16-9/16
	Georgia	Y	21970 FQ	26630 MW	39540 TQ	USBLS	5/15
	Atlanta-Sandy Springs-Roswell MSA, GA	Y	22060 FQ	26430 MW	40330 TQ	USBLS	5/15

AE	Average entry wage	AWR	Average wage range	H	Hourly	LR	Low end range	MTC Median total compensation · TCC Total cash compensation
AEX	Average experienced wage	B	Biweekly	HI	Highest wage paid	M	Monthly	MW Median wage paid · TQ Third quartile wage
ATC	Average total compensation	D	Daily	HR	High end range	MCC	Median cash compensation	MWR Median wage range · W Weekly
AW	Average wage paid	FQ	First quartile wage	LO	Lowest wage paid	ME	Median entry wage	S See annotated source · Y Yearly

Occupation/Type/Industry	Location	Per	Low	Mid	High	Source	Date
Merchandise Displayer and Window Trimmer							
	Augusta-Richmond County MSA, GA-SC	Y	24280 FQ	29510 MW	35080 TQ	USBLS	5/15
	Hawaii	Y	21860 FQ	25920 MW	33560 TQ	USBLS	5/15
	Urban Honolulu MSA, HI	Y	21810 FQ	25770 MW	33440 TQ	USBLS	5/15
	Idaho	Y	19970 FQ	24670 MW	31470 TQ	USBLS	5/15
	Boise City MSA, ID	Y	23490 FQ	27630 MW	31180 TQ	USBLS	5/15
	Illinois	Y	21020 FQ	25530 MW	33520 TQ	USBLS	5/15
	Chicago-Naperville-Arlington Heights PMSA, IL	Y	21090 FQ	24650 MW	33920 TQ	USBLS	5/15
	Lake County-Kenosha County PMSA, IL-WI	Y	19360 FQ	26240 MW	38620 TQ	USBLS	5/15
	Indiana	Y	21120 FQ	26280 MW	34220 TQ	USBLS	5/15
	Gary PMSA, IN	Y	20130 FQ	22830 MW	27990 TQ	USBLS	5/15
	Indianapolis-Carmel-Anderson MSA, IN	Y	20450 FQ	26660 MW	34020 TQ	USBLS	5/15
	Iowa	Y	21450 FQ	23910 MW	30000 TQ	USBLS	5/15
	Des Moines-West Des Moines MSA, IA	Y	21850 FQ	23900 MW	28580 TQ	USBLS	5/15
	Kansas	Y	21990 FQ	28090 MW	35510 TQ	USBLS	5/15
	Wichita MSA, KS	Y	24750 FQ	28390 MW	34400 TQ	USBLS	5/15
	Kentucky	Y	21150 FQ	26050 MW	33600 TQ	USBLS	5/15
	Louisville-Jefferson County MSA, KY-IN	Y	21860 FQ	26970 MW	37120 TQ	USBLS	5/15
	Louisiana	Y	21620 FQ	25630 MW	33000 TQ	USBLS	5/15
	Baton Rouge MSA, LA	Y	23490 FQ	28810 MW	33930 TQ	USBLS	5/15
	New Orleans-Metairie MSA, LA	Y	21550 FQ	24210 MW	32460 TQ	USBLS	5/15
	Maine	Y	21930 FQ	26700 MW	31740 TQ	USBLS	5/15
	Portland-South Portland MSA, ME	Y	24090 FQ	28280 MW	33760 TQ	USBLS	5/15
	Maryland	Y	20800 AE	29012 MW	33118 AEX	MDBLS	4/16
	Baltimore-Columbia-Towson MSA, MD	Y	22720 FQ	27930 MW	34180 TQ	USBLS	5/15
	Salisbury MSA, MD-DE	Y	22090 FQ	31520 MW	37140 TQ	USBLS	5/15
	Massachusetts	Y	21750 FQ	28510 MW	38040 TQ	USBLS	5/15
	Boston-Cambridge-Newton NECTA, MA	Y	24570 FQ	29650 MW	41610 TQ	USBLS	5/15
	Worcester MSA, MA-CT	Y	30280 FQ	34260 MW	37760 TQ	USBLS	5/15
	Michigan	Y	20660 FQ	23920 MW	30510 TQ	USBLS	5/15
	Detroit-Dearborn-Livonia PMSA, MI	Y	20820 FQ	22950 MW	25940 TQ	USBLS	5/15
	Grand Rapids-Wyoming MSA, MI	Y	21610 FQ	25000 MW	33300 TQ	USBLS	5/15
	Minnesota	Y	22681 FQ	27046 MW	33447 TQ	MNBLS	1/16-3/16
	Minneapolis-St. Paul-Bloomington MSA, MN-WI	Y	22510 FQ	26623 MW	33246 TQ	MNBLS	1/16-3/16
	Mississippi	Y	20740 FQ	24780 MW	29570 TQ	USBLS	5/15
	Jackson MSA, MS	Y	20010 FQ	23280 MW	27670 TQ	USBLS	5/15
	Missouri	Y	22910 FQ	26900 MW	30570 TQ	USBLS	5/15
	Kansas City MSA, MO-KS	Y	24830 FQ	27990 MW	31960 TQ	USBLS	5/15
	St. Louis MSA, MO-IL	Y	21510 FQ	26220 MW	31270 TQ	USBLS	5/15
	Montana	Y	22400 FQ	27370 MW	34040 TQ	USBLS	5/15
	Billings MSA, MT	Y	22480 FQ	26140 MW	30180 TQ	USBLS	5/15
	Nebraska	Y	25430 FQ	31020 MW	36185 TQ	NEBLS	7/16-9/16
	Omaha-Council Bluffs MSA, NE-IA	Y	26710 FQ	31475 MW	36090 TQ	NEBLS	7/16-9/16
	Nevada	Y	18540 FQ	22970 MW	30410 TQ	USBLS	5/15
	Las Vegas-Henderson-Paradise MSA, NV	Y	18040 FQ	22580 MW	30720 TQ	USBLS	5/15
	New Hampshire	H	8.63 AE	11.64 MW	15.99 AEX	NHBLS	6/16
	Manchester NECTA, NH	H	8.46 AE	11.10 MW	15.08 AEX	NHBLS	6/16
	Nashua NECTA, NH-MA	Y	18930 FQ	26750 MW	33990 TQ	USBLS	5/15
	New Jersey	Y	21370 FQ	24790 MW	32340 TQ	USBLS	5/15
	Camden PMSA, NJ	Y	26750 FQ	35560 MW	43920 TQ	USBLS	5/15
	Newark PMSA, NJ-PA	Y	20270 FQ	30340 MW	38590 TQ	USBLS	5/15
	Trenton MSA, NJ	Y	18360 FQ	19280 MW	30650 TQ	USBLS	5/15
	New Mexico	Y	21140 FQ	25000 MW	29600 TQ	USBLS	5/15
	Albuquerque MSA, NM	Y	21140 FQ	24790 MW	29110 TQ	USBLS	5/15
	New York	Y	20920 AE	30720 MW	43080 AEX	NYBLS	1/16-3/16
	Buffalo-Cheektowaga-Niagara Falls MSA, NY	Y	19310 FQ	25640 MW	34410 TQ	USBLS	5/15

AE	Average entry wage	AWR	Average wage range	H	Hourly
AEX	Average experienced wage	B	Biweekly	HI	Highest wage paid
ATC	Average total compensation	D	Daily	HR	High end range
AW	Average wage paid	FQ	First quartile wage	LO	Lowest wage paid

LR	Low end range	MTC	Median total compensation
M	Monthly	MW	Median wage paid
MCC	Median cash compensation	MWR	Median wage range
ME	Median entry wage	S	See annotated source

TCC	Total cash compensation	
TQ	Third quartile wage	
W	Weekly	
Y	Yearly	

Occupation/Type/Industry	Location	Per	Low	Mid	High	Source	Date
Merchandise Displayer and Window Trimmer	Nassau County-Suffolk County PMSA, NY	Y	19230 FQ	22650 MW	29230 TQ	USBLS	5/15
	New York-Jersey City-White Plains PMSA, NY-NJ	Y	23440 FQ	30240 MW	44400 TQ	USBLS	5/15
	Rochester MSA, NY	Y	20150 FQ	27550 MW	34700 TQ	USBLS	5/15
	North Carolina	Y	20820 FQ	25880 MW	33570 TQ	USBLS	5/15
	Charlotte-Concord-Gastonia MSA, NC-SC	Y	19270 FQ	23990 MW	31260 TQ	USBLS	5/15
	Raleigh MSA, NC	Y	22690 FQ	26180 MW	30760 TQ	USBLS	5/15
	North Dakota	Y	26600 FQ	31050 MW	36280 TQ	USBLS	5/15
	Fargo MSA, ND-MN	Y	25510 FQ	29230 MW	34540 TQ	USBLS	5/15
	Ohio	Y	22590 FQ	28650 MW	36140 TQ	USBLS	5/15
	Cincinnati MSA, OH-KY-IN	Y	23140 FQ	29660 MW	36480 TQ	USBLS	5/15
	Cleveland-Elyria MSA, OH	Y	20440 FQ	26790 MW	34890 TQ	USBLS	5/15
	Columbus MSA, OH	Y	25320 FQ	31150 MW	39130 TQ	USBLS	5/15
	Oklahoma	Y	21950 FQ	26480 MW	36620 TQ	USBLS	5/15
	Oklahoma City MSA, OK	Y	21030 FQ	24160 MW	29570 TQ	USBLS	5/15
	Tulsa MSA, OK	Y	24790 FQ	37540 MW	45820 TQ	USBLS	5/15
	Oregon	H	11.15 FQ	13.86 MW	18.11 TQ	ORBLS	2016
	Portland-Vancouver-Hillsboro MSA, OR-WA	Y	22850 FQ	29610 MW	38270 TQ	USBLS	5/15
	Pennsylvania	Y	21210 FQ	26830 MW	34860 TQ	USBLS	5/15
	Allentown-Bethlehem-Easton MSA, PA-NJ	Y	20720 FQ	25780 MW	31340 TQ	USBLS	5/15
	Harrisburg-Carlisle MSA, PA	Y	18470 FQ	25560 MW	34240 TQ	USBLS	5/15
	Montgomery County-Bucks County-Chester County PMSA, PA	Y	21240 FQ	25250 MW	34850 TQ	USBLS	5/15
	Philadelphia PMSA, PA	Y	20850 FQ	28090 MW	36260 TQ	USBLS	5/15
	Pittsburgh MSA, PA	Y	22140 FQ	28130 MW	34920 TQ	USBLS	5/15
	Rhode Island	Y	28390 FQ	36300 MW	48910 TQ	USBLS	5/15
	Providence-Warwick MSA, RI-MA	Y	24940 FQ	34100 MW	46140 TQ	USBLS	5/15
	South Carolina	Y	21470 FQ	26770 MW	34010 TQ	USBLS	5/15
	Charleston-North Charleston MSA, SC	Y	23140 FQ	27650 MW	30800 TQ	USBLS	5/15
	Columbia MSA, SC	Y	25040 FQ	32690 MW	38550 TQ	USBLS	5/15
	Greenville-Anderson-Mauldin MSA, SC	Y	21210 FQ	25690 MW	33450 TQ	USBLS	5/15
	South Dakota	Y	20700 FQ	23860 MW	30290 TQ	USBLS	5/15
	Sioux Falls MSA, SD	Y	20350 FQ	23600 MW	28220 TQ	USBLS	5/15
	Tennessee	Y	22790 FQ	28480 MW	36970 TQ	USBLS	5/15
	Knoxville MSA, TN	Y	21460 FQ	24720 MW	28730 TQ	USBLS	5/15
	Memphis MSA, TN-MS-AR	Y	20700 FQ	24580 MW	33870 TQ	USBLS	5/15
	Nashville-Davidson–Murfreesboro–Franklin MSA, TN	Y	25560 FQ	32780 MW	43110 TQ	USBLS	5/15
	Texas	Y	21420 FQ	25390 MW	30140 TQ	USBLS	5/15
	Austin-Round Rock MSA, TX	Y	21070 FQ	24280 MW	32760 TQ	USBLS	5/15
	Dallas-Plano-Irving PMSA, TX	Y	22740 FQ	27540 MW	31700 TQ	USBLS	5/15
	Fort Worth-Arlington PMSA, TX	Y	23420 FQ	27740 MW	32470 TQ	USBLS	5/15
	Houston-The Woodlands-Sugar Land MSA, TX	Y	21200 FQ	24310 MW	28970 TQ	USBLS	5/15
	San Antonio-New Braunfels MSA, TX	Y	20700 FQ	23800 MW	27880 TQ	USBLS	5/15
	Utah	Y	23780 FQ	28220 MW	34380 TQ	USBLS	5/15
	Ogden-Clearfield MSA, UT	Y	21290 FQ	26680 MW	34070 TQ	USBLS	5/15
	Provo-Orem MSA, UT	Y	29760 FQ	42300 MW	47190 TQ	USBLS	5/15
	Salt Lake City MSA, UT	Y	24570 FQ	28160 MW	32000 TQ	USBLS	5/15
	Vermont	Y	23410 FQ	27900 MW	31160 TQ	USBLS	5/15
	Burlington-South Burlington MSA, VT	Y	21770 FQ	27560 MW	30830 TQ	USBLS	5/15
	Virginia	Y	23310 FQ	30520 MW	38090 TQ	USBLS	5/15
	Richmond MSA, VA	Y	21190 FQ	32930 MW	36780 TQ	USBLS	5/15
	Virginia Beach-Norfolk-Newport News MSA, VA-NC	Y	23780 FQ	29170 MW	35890 TQ	USBLS	5/15
	Washington	H	11.97 FQ	15.20 MW	18.01 TQ	WABLS	3/16
	Seattle-Bellevue-Everett PMSA, WA	H	11.72 FQ	15.09 MW	17.86 TQ	WABLS	3/16
	Tacoma-Lakewood PMSA, WA	H	15.29 FQ	17.82 MW	21.30 TQ	WABLS	3/16

Occupation/Type/Industry	Location	Per	Low	Mid	High	Source	Date
Merchandise Displayer and Window Trimmer	West Virginia	Y	18930 FQ	22020 MW	26470 TQ	USBLS	5/15
	Huntington-Ashland MSA, WV-KY-OH	Y	18660 FQ	23760 MW	28650 TQ	USBLS	5/15
	Wisconsin	Y	19590 FQ	26300 MW	35710 TQ	USBLS	5/15
	Madison MSA, WI	Y	21350 FQ	30690 MW	43530 TQ	USBLS	5/15
	Milwaukee-Waukesha-West Allis MSA, WI	Y	18150 FQ	24990 MW	34030 TQ	USBLS	5/15
	Wyoming	Y	21940 FQ	24180 MW	28150 TQ	USBLS	5/15
	Puerto Rico	Y	17930 FQ	21190 MW	24310 TQ	USBLS	5/15
	San Juan-Carolina-Caguas MSA, PR	Y	17400 FQ	19830 MW	24040 TQ	USBLS	5/15
Metal-Refining Furnace Operator and Tender	Alabama	Y	40306 AE	55174 AW	62608 AEX	ALBLS	6/16
	Birmingham-Hoover MSA, AL	Y	32923 AE	43596 AW	48933 AEX	ALBLS	6/16
	Phoenix-Mesa-Scottsdale MSA, AZ	Y	31450 FQ	35560 MW	39670 TQ	USBLS	5/15
	Arkansas	Y	30820 FQ	43420 MW	55220 TQ	USBLS	5/15
	California	H	15.60 FQ	18.78 MW	23.33 TQ	CABLS	1/16-3/16
	Los Angeles-Long Beach-Glendale PMSA, CA	H	16.14 FQ	19.23 MW	25.45 TQ	CABLS	1/16-3/16
	Oakland-Hayward-Berkeley PMSA, CA	H	17.76 FQ	20.30 MW	23.43 TQ	CABLS	1/16-3/16
	Riverside-San Bernardino-Ontario MSA, CA	H	13.10 FQ	15.85 MW	18.46 TQ	CABLS	1/16-3/16
	Colorado	Y	36640 FQ	42530 MW	46460 TQ	USBLS	5/15
	Connecticut	Y		34501 MW		CTBLS	1/16-3/16
	Florida	H	12.68 AE	16.21 MW	18.60 AEX	FLBLS	7/16-9/16
	Fort Lauderdale-Pompano Beach-Deerfield Beach PMSA, FL	H	12.32 AE	16.05 MW	18.42 AEX	FLBLS	7/16-9/16
	Miami-Miami Beach-Kendall PMSA, FL	H	9.44 AE	13.68 MW	17.18 AEX	FLBLS	7/16-9/16
	Tampa-St. Petersburg-Clearwater MSA, FL	H	13.36 AE	16.85 MW	18.93 AEX	FLBLS	7/16-9/16
	Georgia	Y	28110 FQ	39520 MW	48080 TQ	USBLS	5/15
	Illinois	Y	37440 FQ	45880 MW	54220 TQ	USBLS	5/15
	Chicago-Naperville-Arlington Heights PMSA, IL	Y	31920 FQ	40030 MW	45440 TQ	USBLS	5/15
	Indiana	Y	34790 FQ	44180 MW	54590 TQ	USBLS	5/15
	Gary PMSA, IN	Y	37960 FQ	49660 MW	57240 TQ	USBLS	5/15
	Indianapolis-Carmel-Anderson MSA, IN	Y	32230 FQ	36820 MW	45030 TQ	USBLS	5/15
	Iowa	Y	31820 FQ	36590 MW	44890 TQ	USBLS	5/15
	Kansas	Y	27900 FQ	35400 MW	44860 TQ	USBLS	5/15
	Kentucky	Y	36260 FQ	42660 MW	47220 TQ	USBLS	5/15
	Massachusetts	Y	39680 FQ	44580 MW	49390 TQ	USBLS	5/15
	Michigan	Y	28990 FQ	34990 MW	41140 TQ	USBLS	5/15
	Detroit-Dearborn-Livonia PMSA, MI	Y	29050 FQ	37360 MW	44700 TQ	USBLS	5/15
	Grand Rapids-Wyoming MSA, MI	Y	27220 FQ	29960 MW	39780 TQ	USBLS	5/15
	Minnesota	Y	37531 FQ	42614 MW	46937 TQ	MNBLS	1/16-3/16
	Minneapolis-St. Paul-Bloomington MSA, MN-WI	Y	36701 FQ	41601 MW	46066 TQ	MNBLS	1/16-3/16
	Mississippi	Y	30910 FQ	40640 MW	50440 TQ	USBLS	5/15
	Missouri	Y	33240 FQ	42060 MW	46410 TQ	USBLS	5/15
	Nebraska	Y	25125 FQ	29305 MW	33900 TQ	NEBLS	7/16-9/16
	Nevada	Y	47210 FQ	55200 MW	62290 TQ	USBLS	5/15
	New Hampshire	H	13.15 AE	18.15 MW	21.42 AEX	NHBLS	6/16
	New Jersey	Y	39550 FQ	49610 MW	60850 TQ	USBLS	5/15
	Newark PMSA, NJ-PA	Y	50700 FQ	56090 MW	61480 TQ	USBLS	5/15
	New York	Y	35690 AE	44180 MW	47280 AEX	NYBLS	1/16-3/16
	New York-Jersey City-White Plains PMSA, NY-NJ	Y	34070 FQ	42200 MW	56390 TQ	USBLS	5/15
	North Carolina	Y	40970 FQ	51250 MW	57910 TQ	USBLS	5/15
	Charlotte-Concord-Gastonia MSA, NC-SC	Y	43120 FQ	49450 MW	57060 TQ	USBLS	5/15
	Ohio	Y	33100 FQ	38480 MW	44910 TQ	USBLS	5/15
	Cincinnati MSA, OH-KY-IN	Y	31990 FQ	35750 MW	39540 TQ	USBLS	5/15

AE	Average entry wage	AWR	Average wage range	H	Hourly
AEX	Average experienced wage	B	Biweekly	HI	Highest wage paid
ATC	Average total compensation	D	Daily	HR	High end range
AW	Average wage paid	FQ	First quartile wage	LO	Lowest wage paid

LR	Low end range	MTC	Median total compensation	TCC	Total cash compensation
M	Monthly	MW	Median wage paid	TQ	Third quartile wage
MCC	Median cash compensation	MWR	Median wage range	W	Weekly
ME	Median entry wage	S	See annotated source	Y	Yearly

Occupation/Type/Industry	Location	Per	Low	Mid	High	Source	Date
Metal-Refining Furnace Operator and Tender	Cleveland-Elyria MSA, OH	Y	32570 FQ	37010 MW	42990 TQ	USBLS	5/15
	Oklahoma	Y	25790 FQ	33420 MW	51130 TQ	USBLS	5/15
	Tulsa MSA, OK	Y	23340 FQ	27740 MW	33110 TQ	USBLS	5/15
	Oregon	H	18.30 FQ	22.64 MW	27.03 TQ	ORBLS	2016
	Portland-Vancouver-Hillsboro MSA, OR-WA	Y	31830 FQ	38130 MW	47780 TQ	USBLS	5/15
	Pennsylvania	Y	36130 FQ	45100 MW	54350 TQ	USBLS	5/15
	Allentown-Bethlehem-Easton MSA, PA-NJ	Y	34650 FQ	44350 MW	53220 TQ	USBLS	5/15
	Montgomery County-Bucks County-Chester County PMSA, PA	Y	40890 FQ	53400 MW	66340 TQ	USBLS	5/15
	Pittsburgh MSA, PA	Y	40450 FQ	48670 MW	56330 TQ	USBLS	5/15
	Rhode Island	Y	30820 FQ	35380 MW	40110 TQ	USBLS	5/15
	Providence-Warwick MSA, RI-MA	Y	30800 FQ	35300 MW	39910 TQ	USBLS	5/15
	South Carolina	Y	34430 FQ	44760 MW	58590 TQ	USBLS	5/15
	South Dakota	Y	28480 FQ	31940 MW	39120 TQ	USBLS	5/15
	Tennessee	Y	33890 FQ	41860 MW	48330 TQ	USBLS	5/15
	Knoxville MSA, TN	Y	42290 FQ	45850 MW	49410 TQ	USBLS	5/15
	Nashville-Davidson–Murfreesboro–Franklin MSA, TN	Y	35470 FQ	43700 MW	50590 TQ	USBLS	5/15
	Texas	Y	27710 FQ	34470 MW	40350 TQ	USBLS	5/15
	Dallas-Plano-Irving PMSA, TX	Y	31750 FQ	39250 MW	45880 TQ	USBLS	5/15
	Fort Worth-Arlington PMSA, TX	Y	29740 FQ	35850 MW	42890 TQ	USBLS	5/15
	Houston-The Woodlands-Sugar Land MSA, TX	Y	29120 FQ	33690 MW	38010 TQ	USBLS	5/15
	Utah	Y	40740 FQ	45200 MW	50280 TQ	USBLS	5/15
	Salt Lake City MSA, UT	Y	41120 FQ	45460 MW	50670 TQ	USBLS	5/15
	Virginia	Y	43870 FQ	49220 MW	56810 TQ	USBLS	5/15
	Richmond MSA, VA	Y	44470 FQ	49980 MW	58930 TQ	USBLS	5/15
	Washington	H	18.04 FQ	20.97 MW	23.28 TQ	WABLS	3/16
	Seattle-Bellevue-Everett PMSA, WA	H	14.27 FQ	17.84 MW	22.35 TQ	WABLS	3/16
	West Virginia	Y	35980 FQ	41410 MW	47130 TQ	USBLS	5/15
	Wisconsin	Y	30360 FQ	36520 MW	44470 TQ	USBLS	5/15
	Madison MSA, WI	Y	23210 FQ	32510 MW	38310 TQ	USBLS	5/15
	Milwaukee-Waukesha-West Allis MSA, WI	Y	27800 FQ	32640 MW	42040 TQ	USBLS	5/15
Meter Mechanic							
Water and Power Department, Municipal Government	Pasadena, CA	Y			56741 HI	CACIT	6/28/16
Meter Reader							
Utilities	Alabama	Y	23807 AE	36102 AW	42254 AEX	ALBLS	6/16
Utilities	Birmingham-Hoover MSA, AL	Y	27012 AE	38771 AW	44656 AEX	ALBLS	6/16
Utilities	Alaska	Y	52030 FQ	66660 MW	74590 TQ	USBLS	5/15
Utilities	Arizona	Y	34270 FQ	42030 MW	49920 TQ	USBLS	5/15
Utilities	Phoenix-Mesa-Scottsdale MSA, AZ	Y	39500 FQ	46760 MW	63280 TQ	USBLS	5/15
Utilities	Arkansas	Y	22630 FQ	28850 MW	36700 TQ	USBLS	5/15
Utilities	Little Rock-North Little Rock-Conway MSA, AR	Y	25010 FQ	37440 MW	45180 TQ	USBLS	5/15
Utilities	California	H	20.31 FQ	23.78 MW	32.57 TQ	CABLS	1/16-3/16
Utilities	Anaheim-Santa Ana-Irvine PMSA, CA	H	20.12 FQ	22.76 MW	27.86 TQ	CABLS	1/16-3/16
Utilities	Los Angeles-Long Beach-Glendale PMSA, CA	H	20.63 FQ	23.32 MW	33.39 TQ	CABLS	1/16-3/16
Utilities	Oakland-Hayward-Berkeley PMSA, CA	H	31.57 FQ	35.20 MW	38.82 TQ	CABLS	1/16-3/16
Utilities	Riverside-San Bernardino-Ontario MSA, CA	H	17.91 FQ	22.26 MW	26.68 TQ	CABLS	1/16-3/16
Utilities	San Diego-Carlsbad MSA, CA	H	23.53 FQ	29.55 MW	35.32 TQ	CABLS	1/16-3/16
Utilities	Colorado	Y	31710 FQ	45210 MW	56960 TQ	USBLS	5/15
Utilities	Denver-Aurora-Lakewood MSA, CO	Y	30720 FQ	50960 MW	58920 TQ	USBLS	5/15
Utilities	Connecticut	Y		63089 MW		CTBLS	1/16-3/16

AE	Average entry wage	AWR	Average wage range	H	Hourly
AEX	Average experienced wage	B	Biweekly	HI	Highest wage paid
ATC	Average total compensation	D	Daily	HR	High end range
AW	Average wage paid	FQ	First quartile wage	LO	Lowest wage paid

LR	Low end range	MTC	Median total compensation
M	Monthly	MW	Median wage paid
MCC	Median cash compensation	MWR	Median wage range
ME	Median entry wage	S	See annotated source

TCC	Total cash compensation
TQ	Third quartile wage
W	Weekly
Y	Yearly

Meter Reader

Occupation/Type/Industry	Location	Per	Low	Mid	High	Source	Date
Meter Reader							
Utilities	Bridgeport-Stamford-Norwalk MSA, CT	Y	52010 FQ	58510 MW	67380 TQ	USBLS	5/15
Utilities	Hartford-West Hartford-East Hartford MSA, CT	Y	56380 FQ	66600 MW	73920 TQ	USBLS	5/15
Utilities	Delaware	Y	33770 FQ	44210 MW	54520 TQ	USBLS	5/15
Utilities	Wilmington PMSA, DE-MD-NJ	Y	32440 FQ	44610 MW	54780 TQ	USBLS	5/15
Utilities	Washington-Arlington-Alexandria PMSA, DC-VA-MD-WV	Y	38470 FQ	45260 MW	53640 TQ	USBLS	5/15
Utilities	Florida	H	11.37 AE	14.72 MW	17.72 AEX	FLBLS	7/16-9/16
Utilities	Fort Lauderdale-Pompano Beach-Deerfield Beach PMSA, FL	H	9.78 AE	13.95 MW	17.98 AEX	FLBLS	7/16-9/16
Utilities	Miami-Miami Beach-Kendall PMSA, FL	H	11.54 AE	17.15 MW	19.64 AEX	FLBLS	7/16-9/16
Utilities	Orlando-Kissimmee-Sanford MSA, FL	H	12.45 AE	17.19 MW	19.28 AEX	FLBLS	7/16-9/16
Utilities	Tampa-St. Petersburg-Clearwater MSA, FL	H	11.38 AE	14.18 MW	16.29 AEX	FLBLS	7/16-9/16
Utilities	Georgia	Y	26540 FQ	31260 MW	39560 TQ	USBLS	5/15
Utilities	Atlanta-Sandy Springs-Roswell MSA, GA	Y	27810 FQ	33110 MW	43720 TQ	USBLS	5/15
Utilities	Augusta-Richmond County MSA, GA-SC	Y	26900 FQ	33860 MW	51080 TQ	USBLS	5/15
Utilities	Hawaii	Y	35720 FQ	49870 MW	57330 TQ	USBLS	5/15
Utilities	Urban Honolulu MSA, HI	Y	44490 FQ	53500 MW	58720 TQ	USBLS	5/15
Utilities	Idaho	Y	28690 FQ	37170 MW	49400 TQ	USBLS	5/15
Utilities	Illinois	Y	28150 FQ	37130 MW	53630 TQ	USBLS	5/15
Utilities	Chicago-Naperville-Arlington Heights PMSA, IL	Y	31350 FQ	45050 MW	65360 TQ	USBLS	5/15
Utilities	Indiana	Y	31570 FQ	37440 MW	44810 TQ	USBLS	5/15
Utilities	Gary PMSA, IN	Y	24540 FQ	34460 MW	55480 TQ	USBLS	5/15
Utilities	Indianapolis-Carmel-Anderson MSA, IN	Y	34220 FQ	38730 MW	44970 TQ	USBLS	5/15
Utilities	Iowa	Y	23970 FQ	31700 MW	45420 TQ	USBLS	5/15
Utilities	Des Moines-West Des Moines MSA, IA	Y	27940 FQ	30610 MW	46290 TQ	USBLS	5/15
Utilities	Kansas	Y	24670 FQ	32850 MW	41710 TQ	USBLS	5/15
Utilities	Wichita MSA, KS	Y	26410 FQ	30750 MW	40390 TQ	USBLS	5/15
Utilities	Kentucky	Y	20690 FQ	26980 MW	39190 TQ	USBLS	5/15
Utilities	Louisville-Jefferson County MSA, KY-IN	Y	21390 FQ	29250 MW	39200 TQ	USBLS	5/15
Utilities	Louisiana	Y	21730 FQ	25420 MW	33930 TQ	USBLS	5/15
Utilities	Baton Rouge MSA, LA	Y	22630 FQ	26020 MW	33970 TQ	USBLS	5/15
Utilities	New Orleans-Metairie MSA, LA	Y	21330 FQ	23570 MW	33820 TQ	USBLS	5/15
Utilities	Maine	Y	38550 FQ	43690 MW	48530 TQ	USBLS	5/15
Utilities	Maryland	Y	30405 AE	45862 MW	53590 AEX	MDBLS	4/16
Utilities	Baltimore-Columbia-Towson MSA, MD	Y	39180 FQ	50590 MW	60010 TQ	USBLS	5/15
Utilities	Salisbury MSA, MD-DE	Y	34760 FQ	48180 MW	58360 TQ	USBLS	5/15
Utilities	Massachusetts	Y	46110 FQ	58630 MW	73830 TQ	USBLS	5/15
Utilities	Boston-Cambridge-Newton NECTA, MA	Y	48710 FQ	55860 MW	62730 TQ	USBLS	5/15
Utilities	Michigan	Y	26960 FQ	43570 MW	51020 TQ	USBLS	5/15
Utilities	Detroit-Dearborn-Livonia PMSA, MI	Y	30320 FQ	43510 MW	52380 TQ	USBLS	5/15
Utilities	Grand Rapids-Wyoming MSA, MI	Y	35990 FQ	43090 MW	48080 TQ	USBLS	5/15
Utilities	Minnesota	Y	39692 FQ	50139 MW	59645 TQ	MNBLS	1/16-3/16
Utilities	Minneapolis-St. Paul-Bloomington MSA, MN-WI	Y	36911 FQ	48612 MW	59149 TQ	MNBLS	1/16-3/16
Utilities	Mississippi	Y	20760 FQ	27690 MW	36220 TQ	USBLS	5/15
Utilities	Jackson MSA, MS	Y	19660 FQ	27690 MW	37990 TQ	USBLS	5/15
Utilities	Missouri	Y	29450 FQ	38870 MW	53780 TQ	USBLS	5/15
Utilities	Kansas City MSA, MO-KS	Y	34600 FQ	42640 MW	51180 TQ	USBLS	5/15
Utilities	St. Louis MSA, MO-IL	Y	30930 FQ	47320 MW	62160 TQ	USBLS	5/15
Utilities	Montana	Y	34020 FQ	46580 MW	57480 TQ	USBLS	5/15
Utilities	Nebraska	Y	32135 FQ	40060 MW	48095 TQ	NEBLS	7/16-9/16
Utilities	Nevada	Y	49350 FQ	56180 MW	62560 TQ	USBLS	5/15

AE	Average entry wage	AWR	Average wage range	H	Hourly
AEX	Average experienced wage	B	Biweekly	HI	Highest wage paid
ATC	Average total compensation	D	Daily	HR	High end range
AW	Average wage paid	FQ	First quartile wage	LO	Lowest wage paid

LR	Low end range	MTC	Median total compensation
M	Monthly	MW	Median wage paid
MCC	Median cash compensation	MWR	Median wage range
ME	Median entry wage	S	See annotated source

TCC	Total cash compensation		
TQ	Third quartile wage		
W	Weekly		
Y	Yearly		

Occupation/Type/Industry	Location	Per	Low	Mid	High	Source	Date
Meter Reader							
Utilities	Las Vegas-Henderson-Paradise MSA, NV	Y	51350 FQ	57590 MW	64800 TQ	USBLS	5/15
Utilities	New Hampshire	H	19.81 AE	26.62 MW	28.55 AEX	NHBLS	6/16
Utilities	New Jersey	Y	34320 FQ	50120 MW	58570 TQ	USBLS	5/15
Utilities	Camden PMSA, NJ	Y	34940 FQ	42800 MW	56880 TQ	USBLS	5/15
Utilities	Newark PMSA, NJ-PA	Y	40050 FQ	52970 MW	59050 TQ	USBLS	5/15
Utilities	New Mexico	Y	28450 FQ	34460 MW	41600 TQ	USBLS	5/15
Utilities	Albuquerque MSA, NM	Y	34060 FQ	38870 MW	44770 TQ	USBLS	5/15
Utilities	New York	Y	39590 AE	53870 MW	64150 AEX	NYBLS	1/16-3/16
Utilities	Buffalo-Cheektowaga-Niagara Falls MSA, NY	Y	30330 FQ	46490 MW	56930 TQ	USBLS	5/15
Utilities	Nassau County-Suffolk County PMSA, NY	Y	45350 FQ	55470 MW	72810 TQ	USBLS	5/15
Utilities	New York-Jersey City-White Plains PMSA, NY-NJ	Y	43310 FQ	52870 MW	63220 TQ	USBLS	5/15
Utilities	Rochester MSA, NY	Y	44910 FQ	49650 MW	56880 TQ	USBLS	5/15
Utilities	North Carolina	Y	24860 FQ	30000 MW	37870 TQ	USBLS	5/15
Utilities	Charlotte-Concord-Gastonia MSA, NC-SC	Y	22400 FQ	27030 MW	35990 TQ	USBLS	5/15
Utilities	Raleigh MSA, NC	Y	27520 FQ	33680 MW	43280 TQ	USBLS	5/15
Utilities	North Dakota	Y	36620 FQ	48030 MW	60440 TQ	USBLS	5/15
Utilities	Ohio	Y	31020 FQ	41920 MW	52500 TQ	USBLS	5/15
Utilities	Cincinnati MSA, OH-KY-IN	Y	25000 FQ	29350 MW	40860 TQ	USBLS	5/15
Utilities	Cleveland-Elyria MSA, OH	Y	40630 FQ	45750 MW	52860 TQ	USBLS	5/15
Utilities	Columbus MSA, OH	Y	26760 FQ	36610 MW	52420 TQ	USBLS	5/15
Utilities	Oklahoma	Y	22850 FQ	28060 MW	35140 TQ	USBLS	5/15
Utilities	Tulsa MSA, OK	Y	25330 FQ	28380 MW	32520 TQ	USBLS	5/15
Utilities	Oregon	H	14.33 FQ	19.55 MW	23.88 TQ	ORBLS	2016
Utilities	Portland-Vancouver-Hillsboro MSA, OR-WA	Y	27310 FQ	29830 MW	43380 TQ	USBLS	5/15
Utilities	Pennsylvania	Y	37630 FQ	51440 MW	59100 TQ	USBLS	5/15
Utilities	Allentown-Bethlehem-Easton MSA, PA-NJ	Y	41220 FQ	46790 MW	54560 TQ	USBLS	5/15
Utilities	Harrisburg-Carlisle MSA, PA	Y	44360 FQ	51070 MW	57270 TQ	USBLS	5/15
Utilities	Montgomery County-Bucks County-Chester County PMSA, PA	Y	48290 FQ	55030 MW	59700 TQ	USBLS	5/15
Utilities	Philadelphia PMSA, PA	Y	38480 FQ	52700 MW	59020 TQ	USBLS	5/15
Utilities	Pittsburgh MSA, PA	Y	36250 FQ	53560 MW	60630 TQ	USBLS	5/15
Utilities	Providence-Warwick MSA, RI-MA	Y	43260 FQ	49980 MW	66220 TQ	USBLS	5/15
Utilities	South Carolina	Y	27540 FQ	34720 MW	44910 TQ	USBLS	5/15
Utilities	Columbia MSA, SC	Y	27930 FQ	32670 MW	42080 TQ	USBLS	5/15
Utilities	Greenville-Anderson-Mauldin MSA, SC	Y	29430 FQ	38900 MW	47700 TQ	USBLS	5/15
Utilities	South Dakota	Y	30240 FQ	35950 MW	43460 TQ	USBLS	5/15
Utilities	Tennessee	Y	27900 FQ	35360 MW	47970 TQ	USBLS	5/15
Utilities	Knoxville MSA, TN	Y	28710 FQ	38110 MW	54910 TQ	USBLS	5/15
Utilities	Memphis MSA, TN-MS-AR	Y	27970 FQ	33540 MW	44540 TQ	USBLS	5/15
Utilities	Nashville-Davidson–Murfreesboro–Franklin MSA, TN	Y	28360 FQ	37030 MW	49590 TQ	USBLS	5/15
Utilities	Texas	Y	24940 FQ	30080 MW	38740 TQ	USBLS	5/15
Utilities	Austin-Round Rock MSA, TX	Y	28250 FQ	34490 MW	43710 TQ	USBLS	5/15
Utilities	Dallas-Plano-Irving PMSA, TX	Y	27010 FQ	30100 MW	36810 TQ	USBLS	5/15
Utilities	Fort Worth-Arlington PMSA, TX	Y	25930 FQ	31120 MW	36690 TQ	USBLS	5/15
Utilities	Houston-The Woodlands-Sugar Land MSA, TX	Y	25740 FQ	30480 MW	40360 TQ	USBLS	5/15
Utilities	San Antonio-New Braunfels MSA, TX	Y	21300 FQ	31040 MW	57080 TQ	USBLS	5/15
Utilities	Utah	Y	28930 FQ	42990 MW	57250 TQ	USBLS	5/15
Utilities	Ogden-Clearfield MSA, UT	Y	28570 FQ	51310 MW	61930 TQ	USBLS	5/15
Utilities	Vermont	Y	28410 FQ	40040 MW	52640 TQ	USBLS	5/15
Utilities	Virginia	Y	28040 FQ	36330 MW	46840 TQ	USBLS	5/15
Utilities	Richmond MSA, VA	Y	25330 FQ	31430 MW	41320 TQ	USBLS	5/15
Utilities	Virginia Beach-Norfolk-Newport News MSA, VA-NC	Y	27920 FQ	33030 MW	43240 TQ	USBLS	5/15
Utilities	Washington	H	17.60 FQ	22.62 MW	27.17 TQ	WABLS	3/16
Utilities	Seattle-Bellevue-Everett PMSA, WA	H	20.69 FQ	23.55 MW	27.26 TQ	WABLS	3/16

AE	Average entry wage	AWR	Average wage range	H	Hourly
AEX	Average experienced wage	B	Biweekly	HI	Highest wage paid
ATC	Average total compensation	D	Daily	HR	High end range
AW	Average wage paid	FQ	First quartile wage	LO	Lowest wage paid

LR	Low end range	MTC	Median total compensation	TCC	Total cash compensation
M	Monthly	MW	Median wage paid	TQ	Third quartile wage
MCC	Median cash compensation	MWR	Median wage range	W	Weekly
ME	Median entry wage	S	See annotated source	Y	Yearly

Occupation/Type/Industry	Location	Per	Low	Mid	High	Source	Date
Meter Reader							
Utilities	Tacoma-Lakewood PMSA, WA	H	21.74 FQ	24.62 MW	29.82 TQ	WABLS	3/16
Utilities	West Virginia	Y	23190 FQ	34090 MW	45850 TQ	USBLS	5/15
Utilities	Huntington-Ashland MSA, WV-KY-OH	Y	30870 FQ	36680 MW	43960 TQ	USBLS	5/15
Utilities	Wisconsin	Y	35560 FQ	49460 MW	60420 TQ	USBLS	5/15
Utilities	Milwaukee-Waukesha-West Allis MSA, WI	Y	33730 FQ	46770 MW	59340 TQ	USBLS	5/15
Utilities	Wyoming	Y	36980 FQ	43900 MW	50740 TQ	USBLS	5/15
Utilities	Puerto Rico	Y	18570 FQ	42460 MW	46530 TQ	USBLS	5/15
Utilities	San Juan-Carolina-Caguas MSA, PR	Y	18730 FQ	42630 MW	46620 TQ	USBLS	5/15
Metrologist							
State Government	Helena, MT	H			25.80 HI	MTGOV	2016
State Government	North Carolina	Y	34190 LO		58006 HI	NCGOV	7/1/16
Microbiologist							
	Alabama	Y	39397 AE	72545 AW	89119 AEX	ALBLS	6/16
	Alaska	Y	56590 FQ	69990 MW	79480 TQ	USBLS	5/15
	Arizona	Y	57590 FQ	69580 MW	79750 TQ	USBLS	5/15
	Phoenix-Mesa-Scottsdale MSA, AZ	Y	56260 FQ	68090 MW	79160 TQ	USBLS	5/15
	Arkansas	Y	56870 FQ	72540 MW	94590 TQ	USBLS	5/15
	Little Rock-North Little Rock-Conway MSA, AR	Y	36330 FQ	56870 MW	62930 TQ	USBLS	5/15
	California	H	28.71 FQ	41.24 MW	54.66 TQ	CABLS	1/16-3/16
	Anaheim-Santa Ana-Irvine PMSA, CA	H	26.29 FQ	32.31 MW	48.30 TQ	CABLS	1/16-3/16
	Los Angeles-Long Beach-Glendale PMSA, CA	H	25.64 FQ	34.21 MW	44.54 TQ	CABLS	1/16-3/16
	Oakland-Hayward-Berkeley PMSA, CA	H	29.25 FQ	39.85 MW	48.64 TQ	CABLS	1/16-3/16
	Riverside-San Bernardino-Ontario MSA, CA	H	27.34 FQ	36.43 MW	46.63 TQ	CABLS	1/16-3/16
	Sacramento–Roseville–Arden-Arcade MSA, CA	H	24.47 FQ	30.05 MW	39.24 TQ	CABLS	1/16-3/16
	San Diego-Carlsbad MSA, CA	H	25.16 FQ	31.09 MW	52.48 TQ	CABLS	1/16-3/16
	San Francisco-Redwood City-South San Francisco PMSA, CA	H	42.65 FQ	52.08 MW	62.14 TQ	CABLS	1/16-3/16
	Colorado	Y	50510 FQ	60000 MW	79600 TQ	USBLS	5/15
	Denver-Aurora-Lakewood MSA, CO	Y	53140 FQ	61380 MW	81130 TQ	USBLS	5/15
	Connecticut	Y		82681 MW		CTBLS	1/16-3/16
	Hartford-West Hartford-East Hartford MSA, CT	Y	53780 FQ	60900 MW	83320 TQ	USBLS	5/15
	Wilmington PMSA, DE-MD-NJ	Y	45320 FQ	55860 MW	75100 TQ	USBLS	5/15
	District of Columbia	Y	98570 FQ	114470 MW	139520 TQ	USBLS	5/15
	Washington-Arlington-Alexandria PMSA, DC-VA-MD-WV	Y	66380 FQ	90830 MW	118080 TQ	USBLS	5/15
	Florida	H	17.44 AE	26.44 MW	36.05 AEX	FLBLS	7/16-9/16
	Fort Lauderdale-Pompano Beach-Deerfield Beach PMSA, FL	H	17.09 AE	18.67 MW	25.95 AEX	FLBLS	7/16-9/16
	Miami-Miami Beach-Kendall PMSA, FL	H	17.09 AE	26.22 MW	33.99 AEX	FLBLS	7/16-9/16
	Orlando-Kissimmee-Sanford MSA, FL	H	18.11 AE	26.75 MW	37.57 AEX	FLBLS	7/16-9/16
	Tampa-St. Petersburg-Clearwater MSA, FL	H	26.59 AE	44.00 MW	47.40 AEX	FLBLS	7/16-9/16
	Georgia	Y	66350 FQ	83130 MW	102370 TQ	USBLS	5/15
	Atlanta-Sandy Springs-Roswell MSA, GA	Y	69350 FQ	85580 MW	101770 TQ	USBLS	5/15
	Hawaii	Y	52940 FQ	60960 MW	77440 TQ	USBLS	5/15
	Urban Honolulu MSA, HI	Y	52940 FQ	60230 MW	73260 TQ	USBLS	5/15
	Idaho	Y	47710 FQ	57280 MW	77520 TQ	USBLS	5/15
	Boise City MSA, ID	Y	41830 FQ	51820 MW	57410 TQ	USBLS	5/15
	Illinois	Y	39790 FQ	56360 MW	84840 TQ	USBLS	5/15
	Chicago-Naperville-Arlington Heights PMSA, IL	Y	36860 FQ	50890 MW	77170 TQ	USBLS	5/15

AE	Average entry wage	AWR	Average wage range	H	Hourly	LR	Low end range	MTC	Median total compensation	TCC	Total cash compensation
AEX	Average experienced wage	B	Biweekly	HI	Highest wage paid	M	Monthly	MW	Median wage paid	TQ	Third quartile wage
ATC	Average total compensation	D	Daily	HR	High end range	MCC	Median cash compensation	MWR	Median wage range	W	Weekly
AW	Average wage paid	FQ	First quartile wage	LO	Lowest wage paid	ME	Median entry wage	S	See annotated source	Y	Yearly

Occupation/Type/Industry	Location	Per	Low	Mid	High	Source	Date
Microbiologist	Indiana	Y	34920 FQ	38540 MW	44810 TQ	USBLS	5/15
	Indianapolis-Carmel-Anderson MSA, IN	Y	34710 FQ	38080 MW	43230 TQ	USBLS	5/15
	Iowa	Y	56430 FQ	72350 MW	97370 TQ	USBLS	5/15
	Kansas	Y	42360 FQ	49060 MW	58230 TQ	USBLS	5/15
	Kentucky	Y	44730 FQ	51390 MW	64370 TQ	USBLS	5/15
	Maine	Y	44900 FQ	52840 MW	61810 TQ	USBLS	5/15
	Portland-South Portland MSA, ME	Y	50440 FQ	57840 MW	78070 TQ	USBLS	5/15
	Maryland	Y	49270 AE	93657 MW	115851 AEX	MDBLS	4/16
	Baltimore-Columbia-Towson MSA, MD	Y	63420 FQ	81670 MW	118070 TQ	USBLS	5/15
	Massachusetts	Y	49700 FQ	61610 MW	84550 TQ	USBLS	5/15
	Boston-Cambridge-Newton NECTA, MA	Y	55380 FQ	68750 MW	91620 TQ	USBLS	5/15
	Worcester MSA, MA-CT	Y	36990 FQ	45510 MW	62820 TQ	USBLS	5/15
	Michigan	Y	45740 FQ	55560 MW	71110 TQ	USBLS	5/15
	Minnesota	Y	51673 FQ	62882 MW	83557 TQ	MNBLS	1/16-3/16
	Minneapolis-St. Paul-Bloomington MSA, MN-WI	Y	52046 FQ	63013 MW	84737 TQ	MNBLS	1/16-3/16
	Mississippi	Y	42700 FQ	64480 MW	79020 TQ	USBLS	5/15
	Missouri	Y	43470 FQ	66430 MW	96450 TQ	USBLS	5/15
	Kansas City MSA, MO-KS	Y	46960 FQ	67580 MW	112780 TQ	USBLS	5/15
	St. Louis MSA, MO-IL	Y	36630 FQ	60030 MW	91260 TQ	USBLS	5/15
	Montana	Y	46870 FQ	69490 MW	90710 TQ	USBLS	5/15
	Nebraska	Y	48365 FQ	59885 MW	87250 TQ	NEBLS	7/16-9/16
	Omaha-Council Bluffs MSA, NE-IA	Y	47235 FQ	56805 MW	85035 TQ	NEBLS	7/16-9/16
	Nevada	Y	56490 FQ	69970 MW	105320 TQ	USBLS	5/15
	New Jersey	Y	55060 FQ	73150 MW	94570 TQ	USBLS	5/15
	Newark PMSA, NJ-PA	Y	53200 FQ	71990 MW	94540 TQ	USBLS	5/15
	Trenton MSA, NJ	Y	74630 FQ	89870 MW	101950 TQ	USBLS	5/15
	New Mexico	Y	40830 FQ	49740 MW	79460 TQ	USBLS	5/15
	Albuquerque MSA, NM	Y	40680 FQ	49730 MW	81930 TQ	USBLS	5/15
	New York	Y	47700 AE	72580 MW	95220 AEX	NYBLS	1/16-3/16
	Buffalo-Cheektowaga-Niagara Falls MSA, NY	Y	50560 FQ	62980 MW	79710 TQ	USBLS	5/15
	Nassau County-Suffolk County PMSA, NY	Y	66970 FQ	84430 MW	108920 TQ	USBLS	5/15
	New York-Jersey City-White Plains PMSA, NY-NJ	Y	51580 FQ	69070 MW	92410 TQ	USBLS	5/15
	Rochester MSA, NY	Y	53700 FQ	63630 MW	85840 TQ	USBLS	5/15
	North Carolina	Y	47160 FQ	64940 MW	82040 TQ	USBLS	5/15
	Charlotte-Concord-Gastonia MSA, NC-SC	Y	43950 FQ	48420 MW	59050 TQ	USBLS	5/15
	Raleigh MSA, NC	Y	39040 FQ	47470 MW	65740 TQ	USBLS	5/15
	Ohio	Y	44240 FQ	67690 MW	91900 TQ	USBLS	5/15
	Cincinnati MSA, OH-KY-IN	Y	40500 FQ	61470 MW	80200 TQ	USBLS	5/15
	Cleveland-Elyria MSA, OH	Y	59590 FQ	74610 MW	99400 TQ	USBLS	5/15
	Columbus MSA, OH	Y	38140 FQ	56180 MW	84890 TQ	USBLS	5/15
	Oklahoma	Y	44460 FQ	56000 MW	70450 TQ	USBLS	5/15
	Oklahoma City MSA, OK	Y	46020 FQ	59010 MW	71890 TQ	USBLS	5/15
	Oregon	H	22.58 FQ	29.76 MW	34.35 TQ	ORBLS	2016
	Portland-Vancouver-Hillsboro MSA, OR-WA	Y	53620 FQ	65870 MW	81400 TQ	USBLS	5/15
	Pennsylvania	Y	50150 FQ	63410 MW	96150 TQ	USBLS	5/15
	Harrisburg-Carlisle MSA, PA	Y	51990 FQ	60020 MW	70010 TQ	USBLS	5/15
	Montgomery County-Bucks County-Chester County PMSA, PA	Y	51360 FQ	68050 MW	106160 TQ	USBLS	5/15
	Pittsburgh MSA, PA	Y	46510 FQ	59630 MW	95530 TQ	USBLS	5/15
	South Carolina	Y	41210 FQ	49210 MW	75220 TQ	USBLS	5/15
	South Dakota	Y	41900 FQ	50060 MW	62620 TQ	USBLS	5/15
	Tennessee	Y	49880 FQ	58830 MW	86440 TQ	USBLS	5/15
	Knoxville MSA, TN	Y	49880 FQ	58690 MW	80890 TQ	USBLS	5/15
	Memphis MSA, TN-MS-AR	Y	59150 FQ	88140 MW	103470 TQ	USBLS	5/15
	Nashville-Davidson–Murfreesboro–Franklin MSA, TN	Y	44630 FQ	53360 MW	62260 TQ	USBLS	5/15
	Texas	Y	39760 FQ	47940 MW	61260 TQ	USBLS	5/15
	Austin-Round Rock MSA, TX	Y	37390 FQ	44220 MW	52120 TQ	USBLS	5/15
	Dallas-Plano-Irving PMSA, TX	Y	36970 FQ	47200 MW	98650 TQ	USBLS	5/15

AE	Average entry wage	AWR	Average wage range	H	Hourly
AEX	Average experienced wage	B	Biweekly	HI	Highest wage paid
ATC	Average total compensation	D	Daily	HR	High end range
AW	Average wage paid	FQ	First quartile wage	LO	Lowest wage paid

LR	Low end range	MTC	Median total compensation
M	Monthly	MW	Median wage paid
MCC	Median cash compensation	MWR	Median wage range
ME	Median entry wage	S	See annotated source

TCC	Total cash compensation
TQ	Third quartile wage
W	Weekly
Y	Yearly

Occupation/Type/Industry	Location	Per	Low	Mid	High	Source	Date
Microbiologist	Houston-The Woodlands-Sugar Land MSA, TX	Y	42290 FQ	51150 MW	63920 TQ	USBLS	5/15
	San Antonio-New Braunfels MSA, TX	Y	62930 FQ	74180 MW	88900 TQ	USBLS	5/15
	Utah	Y	45110 FQ	53660 MW	71790 TQ	USBLS	5/15
	Virginia	Y	48880 FQ	70430 MW	104750 TQ	USBLS	5/15
	Richmond MSA, VA	Y	43240 FQ	49790 MW	83050 TQ	USBLS	5/15
	Virginia Beach-Norfolk-Newport News MSA, VA-NC	Y	49660 FQ	72940 MW	92820 TQ	USBLS	5/15
	Washington	H	25.73 FQ	33.16 MW	41.40 TQ	WABLS	3/16
	Seattle-Bellevue-Everett PMSA, WA	H	24.03 FQ	30.87 MW	40.60 TQ	WABLS	3/16
	Tacoma-Lakewood PMSA, WA	H	26.58 FQ	33.52 MW	37.60 TQ	WABLS	3/16
	West Virginia	Y	28940 FQ	35400 MW	50440 TQ	USBLS	5/15
	Wisconsin	Y	45700 FQ	57840 MW	73450 TQ	USBLS	5/15
	Madison MSA, WI	Y	45200 FQ	56820 MW	72950 TQ	USBLS	5/15
	Puerto Rico	Y	39030 FQ	46450 MW	59950 TQ	USBLS	5/15
	San Juan-Carolina-Caguas MSA, PR	Y	39490 FQ	47310 MW	61800 TQ	USBLS	5/15
Environmental Services, Municipal Government	San Jose, CA	Y			77594 HI	CACIT	6/28/16
Municipal Government	Detroit, MI	M	3700 LO		4217 HI	DETGOV	2016
Public Health, Municipal Government	San Francisco, CA	Y		54699 AW		CACIT	6/28/16
Water Utilities, Municipal Government	Oceanside, CA	Y			58067 HI	CACIT	6/28/16
Microphoto/Imaging Technician							
Assessor's Office, Municipal Government	San Francisco, CA	Y			43632 HI	CACIT	6/28/16
Microsoft Certified Solutions Expert							
Desktop Infrastructure	United States	Y		115120 AW		CERTM02	2015
Middle School Teacher							
Except Special and Career/Technical Education	Alabama	Y	41242 AE	49835 AW	54126 AEX	ALBLS	6/16
Except Special and Career/Technical Education	Birmingham-Hoover MSA, AL	Y	41650 AE	50783 AW	55359 AEX	ALBLS	6/16
Except Special and Career/Technical Education	Alaska	Y	66470 FQ	81690 MW	94220 TQ	USBLS	5/15
Except Special and Career/Technical Education	Arizona	Y	35270 FQ	41200 MW	48310 TQ	USBLS	5/15
Except Special and Career/Technical Education	Phoenix-Mesa-Scottsdale MSA, AZ	Y	35800 FQ	42320 MW	48930 TQ	USBLS	5/15
Except Special and Career/Technical Education	Tucson MSA, AZ	Y	34110 FQ	37610 MW	43780 TQ	USBLS	5/15
Except Special and Career/Technical Education	Arkansas	Y	40720 FQ	46540 MW	54440 TQ	USBLS	5/15
Except Special and Career/Technical Education	Little Rock-North Little Rock-Conway MSA, AR	Y	39440 FQ	45390 MW	52810 TQ	USBLS	5/15
Except Special and Career/Technical Education	California	Y		70020 AW		CABLS	1/16-3/16
Except Special and Career/Technical Education	Anaheim-Santa Ana-Irvine PMSA, CA	Y		76067 AW		CABLS	1/16-3/16
Except Special and Career/Technical Education	Los Angeles-Long Beach-Glendale PMSA, CA	Y		69259 AW		CABLS	1/16-3/16
Except Special and Career/Technical Education	Oakland-Hayward-Berkeley PMSA, CA	Y		68448 AW		CABLS	1/16-3/16
Except Special and Career/Technical Education	Riverside-San Bernardino-Ontario MSA, CA	Y		76584 AW		CABLS	1/16-3/16
Except Special and Career/Technical Education	Sacramento–Roseville–Arden-Arcade MSA, CA	Y		67119 AW		CABLS	1/16-3/16
Except Special and Career/Technical Education	San Diego-Carlsbad MSA, CA	Y		66368 AW		CABLS	1/16-3/16

AE Average entry wage	**AWR** Average wage range	**H** Hourly	**LR** Low end range	**MTC** Median total compensation	**TCC** Total cash compensation
AEX Average experienced wage	**B** Biweekly	**HI** Highest wage paid	**M** Monthly	**MW** Median wage paid	**TQ** Third quartile wage
ATC Average total compensation	**D** Daily	**HR** High end range	**MCC** Median cash compensation	**MWR** Median wage range	**W** Weekly
AW Average wage paid	**FQ** First quartile wage	**LO** Lowest wage paid	**ME** Median entry wage	**S** See annotated source	**Y** Yearly

1041

Occupation/Type/Industry	Location	Per	Low	Mid	High	Source	Date
Middle School Teacher							
Except Special and Career/Technical Education	San Francisco-Redwood City-South San Francisco PMSA, CA	Y		72952 AW		CABLS	1/16-3/16
Except Special and Career/Technical Education	Colorado	Y	40250 FQ	48490 MW	60860 TQ	USBLS	5/15
Except Special and Career/Technical Education	Denver-Aurora-Lakewood MSA, CO	Y	42290 FQ	50850 MW	65470 TQ	USBLS	5/15
Except Special and Career/Technical Education	Connecticut	Y		78643 MW		CTBLS	1/16-3/16
Except Special and Career/Technical Education	Bridgeport-Stamford-Norwalk MSA, CT	Y	63830 FQ	81730 MW	95980 TQ	USBLS	5/15
Except Special and Career/Technical Education	Hartford-West Hartford-East Hartford MSA, CT	Y	61390 FQ	75880 MW	90540 TQ	USBLS	5/15
Except Special and Career/Technical Education	Delaware	Y	48600 FQ	58760 MW	70280 TQ	USBLS	5/15
Except Special and Career/Technical Education	Wilmington PMSA, DE-MD-NJ	Y	47680 FQ	58790 MW	71980 TQ	USBLS	5/15
Except Special and Career/Technical Education	District of Columbia	Y	56620 FQ	68320 MW	80200 TQ	USBLS	5/15
Except Special and Career/Technical Education	Washington-Arlington-Alexandria PMSA, DC-VA-MD-WV	Y	54500 FQ	69560 MW	87860 TQ	USBLS	5/15
Except Special and Career/Technical Education	Florida	Y	39025 AE	47468 MW	54535 AEX	FLBLS	7/16-9/16
Except Special and Career/Technical Education	Fort Lauderdale-Pompano Beach-Deerfield Beach PMSA, FL	Y	37053 AE	48585 MW	56951 AEX	FLBLS	7/16-9/16
Except Special and Career/Technical Education	Miami-Miami Beach-Kendall PMSA, FL	Y	40264 AE	49880 MW	59501 AEX	FLBLS	7/16-9/16
Except Special and Career/Technical Education	Orlando-Kissimmee-Sanford MSA, FL	Y	41021 AE	48115 MW	54069 AEX	FLBLS	7/16-9/16
Except Special and Career/Technical Education	Tampa-St. Petersburg-Clearwater MSA, FL	Y	36474 AE	45088 MW	50770 AEX	FLBLS	7/16-9/16
Except Special and Career/Technical Education	Georgia	Y	44710 FQ	54030 MW	63000 TQ	USBLS	5/15
Except Special and Career/Technical Education	Atlanta-Sandy Springs-Roswell MSA, GA	Y	44810 FQ	53780 MW	63120 TQ	USBLS	5/15
Except Special and Career/Technical Education	Augusta-Richmond County MSA, GA-SC	Y	44640 FQ	53660 MW	61430 TQ	USBLS	5/15
Except Special and Career/Technical Education	Hawaii	Y	48630 FQ	56820 MW	64580 TQ	USBLS	5/15
Except Special and Career/Technical Education	Urban Honolulu MSA, HI	Y	48110 FQ	56960 MW	65320 TQ	USBLS	5/15
Except Special and Career/Technical Education	Idaho	Y	36810 FQ	46630 MW	59180 TQ	USBLS	5/15
Except Special and Career/Technical Education	Boise City MSA, ID	Y	37860 FQ	48470 MW	60490 TQ	USBLS	5/15
Except Special and Career/Technical Education	Illinois	Y	49150 FQ	62870 MW	83890 TQ	USBLS	5/15
Except Special and Career/Technical Education	Chicago-Naperville-Arlington Heights PMSA, IL	Y	54200 FQ	68940 MW	88660 TQ	USBLS	5/15
Except Special and Career/Technical Education	Lake County-Kenosha County PMSA, IL-WI	Y	49940 FQ	62380 MW	81270 TQ	USBLS	5/15
Except Special and Career/Technical Education	Indiana	Y	39740 FQ	49660 MW	61200 TQ	USBLS	5/15

AE	Average entry wage	AWR	Average wage range	H	Hourly	LR	Low end range	MTC	Median total compensation	TCC	Total cash compensation
AEX	Average experienced wage	B	Biweekly	HI	Highest wage paid	M	Monthly	MW	Median wage paid	TQ	Third quartile wage
ATC	Average total compensation	D	Daily	HR	High end range	MCC	Median cash compensation	MWR	Median wage range	W	Weekly
AW	Average wage paid	FQ	First quartile wage	LO	Lowest wage paid	ME	Median entry wage	S	See annotated source	Y	Yearly

Middle School Teacher

Occupation/Type/Industry	Location	Per	Low	Mid	High	Source	Date
Middle School Teacher							
Except Special and Career/Technical Education							
Except Special and Career/Technical Education	Gary PMSA, IN	Y	39170 FQ	47740 MW	59970 TQ	USBLS	5/15
Except Special and Career/Technical Education	Indianapolis-Carmel-Anderson MSA, IN	Y	39580 FQ	49280 MW	62260 TQ	USBLS	5/15
Except Special and Career/Technical Education	Iowa	Y	44670 FQ	54720 MW	64740 TQ	USBLS	5/15
Except Special and Career/Technical Education	Des Moines-West Des Moines MSA, IA	Y	49250 FQ	59890 MW	72510 TQ	USBLS	5/15
Except Special and Career/Technical Education	Kansas	Y	41330 FQ	47150 MW	55290 TQ	USBLS	5/15
Except Special and Career/Technical Education	Wichita MSA, KS	Y	40640 FQ	45600 MW	50690 TQ	USBLS	5/15
Except Special and Career/Technical Education	Kentucky	Y	44070 FQ	52030 MW	60100 TQ	USBLS	5/15
Except Special and Career/Technical Education	Louisville-Jefferson County MSA, KY-IN	Y	46920 FQ	56620 MW	67990 TQ	USBLS	5/15
Except Special and Career/Technical Education	Louisiana	Y	42390 FQ	46840 MW	52430 TQ	USBLS	5/15
Except Special and Career/Technical Education	Baton Rouge MSA, LA	Y	43780 FQ	48580 MW	56190 TQ	USBLS	5/15
Except Special and Career/Technical Education	New Orleans-Metairie MSA, LA	Y	42000 FQ	46480 MW	51340 TQ	USBLS	5/15
Except Special and Career/Technical Education	Maine	Y	42300 FQ	52240 MW	61150 TQ	USBLS	5/15
Except Special and Career/Technical Education	Portland-South Portland MSA, ME	Y	46780 FQ	54950 MW	62090 TQ	USBLS	5/15
Except Special and Career/Technical Education	Maryland	Y	42962 AE	65941 MW	77430 AEX	MDBLS	4/16
Except Special and Career/Technical Education	Baltimore-Columbia-Towson MSA, MD	Y	46280 FQ	58620 MW	73230 TQ	USBLS	5/15
Except Special and Career/Technical Education	Salisbury MSA, MD-DE	Y	48780 FQ	58170 MW	68510 TQ	USBLS	5/15
Except Special and Career/Technical Education	Massachusetts	Y	57550 FQ	70990 MW	84630 TQ	USBLS	5/15
Except Special and Career/Technical Education	Boston-Cambridge-Newton NECTA, MA	Y	59300 FQ	74970 MW	89320 TQ	USBLS	5/15
Except Special and Career/Technical Education	Worcester MSA, MA-CT	Y	58680 FQ	69650 MW	78640 TQ	USBLS	5/15
Except Special and Career/Technical Education	Michigan	Y	48390 FQ	65050 MW	77290 TQ	USBLS	5/15
Except Special and Career/Technical Education	Detroit-Dearborn-Livonia PMSA, MI	Y	45830 FQ	65950 MW	81000 TQ	USBLS	5/15
Except Special and Career/Technical Education	Grand Rapids-Wyoming MSA, MI	Y	47620 FQ	64550 MW	77600 TQ	USBLS	5/15
Except Special and Career/Technical Education	Minnesota	Y	46189 FQ	58900 MW	74878 TQ	MNBLS	1/16-3/16
Except Special and Career/Technical Education	Minneapolis-St. Paul-Bloomington MSA, MN-WI	Y	47681 FQ	62086 MW	78537 TQ	MNBLS	1/16-3/16
Except Special and Career/Technical Education	Mississippi	Y	35370 FQ	40170 MW	46960 TQ	USBLS	5/15
Except Special and Career/Technical Education	Jackson MSA, MS	Y	34860 FQ	39460 MW	46380 TQ	USBLS	5/15
Except Special and Career/Technical Education	Missouri	Y	40070 FQ	49600 MW	64420 TQ	USBLS	5/15
Except Special and Career/Technical Education	Kansas City MSA, MO-KS	Y	41130 FQ	48630 MW	59770 TQ	USBLS	5/15
Except Special and Career/Technical Education	St. Louis MSA, MO-IL	Y	44780 FQ	56270 MW	72430 TQ	USBLS	5/15
Except Special and Career/Technical Education	Montana	Y	43620 FQ	55890 MW	71030 TQ	USBLS	5/15

AE	Average entry wage	AWR	Average wage range	H	Hourly	LR	Low end range	MTC	Median total compensation	TCC	Total cash compensation
AEX	Average experienced wage	B	Biweekly	HI	Highest wage paid	M	Monthly	MW	Median wage paid	TQ	Third quartile wage
ATC	Average total compensation	D	Daily	HR	High end range	MCC	Median cash compensation	MWR	Median wage range	W	Weekly
AW	Average wage paid	FQ	First quartile wage	LO	Lowest wage paid	ME	Median entry wage	S	See annotated source	Y	Yearly

Occupation/Type/Industry	Location	Per	Low	Mid	High	Source	Date
Middle School Teacher							
Except Special and Career/Technical Education	Billings MSA, MT	Y	39240 FQ	45770 MW	53210 TQ	USBLS	5/15
Except Special and Career/Technical Education	Nebraska	Y	43895 FQ	50820 MW	59970 TQ	NEBLS	7/16-9/16
Except Special and Career/Technical Education	Omaha-Council Bluffs MSA, NE-IA	Y	42295 FQ	48880 MW	57645 TQ	NEBLS	7/16-9/16
Except Special and Career/Technical Education	Nevada	Y	44680 FQ	54010 MW	64940 TQ	USBLS	5/15
Except Special and Career/Technical Education	Las Vegas-Henderson-Paradise MSA, NV	Y	44510 FQ	53680 MW	65270 TQ	USBLS	5/15
Except Special and Career/Technical Education	New Hampshire	Y	41689 AE	57538 MW	67427 AEX	NHBLS	6/16
Except Special and Career/Technical Education	Manchester NECTA, NH	Y	40690 AE	57392 MW	63969 AEX	NHBLS	6/16
Except Special and Career/Technical Education	Nashua NECTA, NH-MA	Y	47350 FQ	57930 MW	68430 TQ	USBLS	5/15
Except Special and Career/Technical Education	New Jersey	Y	56390 FQ	65530 MW	82640 TQ	USBLS	5/15
Except Special and Career/Technical Education	Camden PMSA, NJ	Y	56650 FQ	64960 MW	81030 TQ	USBLS	5/15
Except Special and Career/Technical Education	Newark PMSA, NJ-PA	Y	56130 FQ	64590 MW	79820 TQ	USBLS	5/15
Except Special and Career/Technical Education	Trenton MSA, NJ	Y	56240 FQ	67570 MW	84530 TQ	USBLS	5/15
Except Special and Career/Technical Education	New Mexico	Y	42290 FQ	50900 MW	62030 TQ	USBLS	5/15
Except Special and Career/Technical Education	Albuquerque MSA, NM	Y	38350 FQ	47580 MW	57800 TQ	USBLS	5/15
Except Special and Career/Technical Education	New York	Y	49470 AE	75130 MW	92630 AEX	NYBLS	1/16-3/16
Except Special and Career/Technical Education	Buffalo-Cheektowaga-Niagara Falls MSA, NY	Y	41950 FQ	57340 MW	72850 TQ	USBLS	5/15
Except Special and Career/Technical Education	Nassau County-Suffolk County PMSA, NY	Y	86560 FQ	104210 MW	119690 TQ	USBLS	5/15
Except Special and Career/Technical Education	New York-Jersey City-White Plains PMSA, NY-NJ	Y	57800 FQ	72820 MW	93060 TQ	USBLS	5/15
Except Special and Career/Technical Education	Rochester MSA, NY	Y	47710 FQ	57640 MW	70200 TQ	USBLS	5/15
Except Special and Career/Technical Education	North Carolina	Y	35810 FQ	41470 MW	48870 TQ	USBLS	5/15
Except Special and Career/Technical Education	Charlotte-Concord-Gastonia MSA, NC-SC	Y	36270 FQ	43130 MW	52010 TQ	USBLS	5/15
Except Special and Career/Technical Education	Raleigh MSA, NC	Y	36410 FQ	43600 MW	53610 TQ	USBLS	5/15
Except Special and Career/Technical Education	North Dakota	Y	44120 FQ	52680 MW	61160 TQ	USBLS	5/15
Except Special and Career/Technical Education	Fargo MSA, ND-MN	Y	42980 FQ	53750 MW	65650 TQ	USBLS	5/15
Except Special and Career/Technical Education	Ohio	Y	45550 FQ	58750 MW	71250 TQ	USBLS	5/15
Except Special and Career/Technical Education	Cincinnati MSA, OH-KY-IN	Y	45860 FQ	57290 MW	70190 TQ	USBLS	5/15
Except Special and Career/Technical Education	Cleveland-Elyria MSA, OH	Y	39350 FQ	57350 MW	72640 TQ	USBLS	5/15
Except Special and Career/Technical Education	Columbus MSA, OH	Y	48090 FQ	61930 MW	74200 TQ	USBLS	5/15
Except Special and Career/Technical Education	Oklahoma	Y	35360 FQ	40720 MW	48470 TQ	USBLS	5/15
Except Special and Career/Technical Education	Oklahoma City MSA, OK	Y	34520 FQ	38960 MW	46080 TQ	USBLS	5/15
Except Special and Career/Technical Education	Tulsa MSA, OK	Y	36470 FQ	44280 MW	55550 TQ	USBLS	5/15
Except Special and Career/Technical Education	Oregon	Y	48631 FQ	59953 MW	73770 TQ	ORBLS	2016

AE	Average entry wage	AWR	Average wage range	H	Hourly
AEX	Average experienced wage	B	Biweekly	HI	Highest wage paid
ATC	Average total compensation	D	Daily	HR	High end range
AW	Average wage paid	FQ	First quartile wage	LO	Lowest wage paid

LR	Low end range	MTC	Median total compensation	TCC	Total cash compensation
M	Monthly	MW	Median wage paid	TQ	Third quartile wage
MCC	Median cash compensation	MWR	Median wage range	W	Weekly
ME	Median entry wage	S	See annotated source	Y	Yearly

Occupation/Type/Industry	Location	Per	Low	Mid	High	Source	Date
Middle School Teacher							
Except Special and Career/Technical Education	Portland-Vancouver-Hillsboro MSA, OR-WA	Y	52940 FQ	66050 MW	77760 TQ	USBLS	5/15
Except Special and Career/Technical Education	Pennsylvania	Y	46870 FQ	57290 MW	70270 TQ	USBLS	5/15
Except Special and Career/Technical Education	Allentown-Bethlehem-Easton MSA, PA-NJ	Y	50650 FQ	58790 MW	71600 TQ	USBLS	5/15
Except Special and Career/Technical Education	Harrisburg-Carlisle MSA, PA	Y	48030 FQ	57480 MW	68380 TQ	USBLS	5/15
Except Special and Career/Technical Education	Montgomery County-Bucks County-Chester County PMSA, PA	Y	49170 FQ	59260 MW	74560 TQ	USBLS	5/15
Except Special and Career/Technical Education	Philadelphia PMSA, PA	Y	44260 FQ	54160 MW	68010 TQ	USBLS	5/15
Except Special and Career/Technical Education	Pittsburgh MSA, PA	Y	50500 FQ	59660 MW	73310 TQ	USBLS	5/15
Except Special and Career/Technical Education	Rhode Island	Y	56460 FQ	69880 MW	79730 TQ	USBLS	5/15
Except Special and Career/Technical Education	Providence-Warwick MSA, RI-MA	Y	56610 FQ	69840 MW	80010 TQ	USBLS	5/15
Except Special and Career/Technical Education	South Carolina	Y	40470 FQ	48860 MW	58650 TQ	USBLS	5/15
Except Special and Career/Technical Education	Charleston-North Charleston MSA, SC	Y	39550 FQ	49620 MW	60160 TQ	USBLS	5/15
Except Special and Career/Technical Education	Columbia MSA, SC	Y	39460 FQ	46100 MW	54730 TQ	USBLS	5/15
Except Special and Career/Technical Education	Greenville-Anderson-Mauldin MSA, SC	Y	45360 FQ	54290 MW	61830 TQ	USBLS	5/15
Except Special and Career/Technical Education	South Dakota	Y	35360 FQ	41670 MW	50130 TQ	USBLS	5/15
Except Special and Career/Technical Education	Sioux Falls MSA, SD	Y	35450 FQ	42710 MW	52730 TQ	USBLS	5/15
Except Special and Career/Technical Education	Tennessee	Y	40910 FQ	47460 MW	57200 TQ	USBLS	5/15
Except Special and Career/Technical Education	Knoxville MSA, TN	Y	40850 FQ	47100 MW	55530 TQ	USBLS	5/15
Except Special and Career/Technical Education	Memphis MSA, TN-MS-AR	Y	40280 FQ	46010 MW	54180 TQ	USBLS	5/15
Except Special and Career/Technical Education	Nashville-Davidson–Murfreesboro–Franklin MSA, TN	Y	41520 FQ	50010 MW	60730 TQ	USBLS	5/15
Except Special and Career/Technical Education	Texas	Y	45470 FQ	52710 MW	59850 TQ	USBLS	5/15
Except Special and Career/Technical Education	Austin-Round Rock MSA, TX	Y	44700 FQ	50690 MW	59830 TQ	USBLS	5/15
Except Special and Career/Technical Education	Dallas-Plano-Irving PMSA, TX	Y	46990 FQ	54120 MW	60820 TQ	USBLS	5/15
Except Special and Career/Technical Education	Fort Worth-Arlington PMSA, TX	Y	50800 FQ	55760 MW	60730 TQ	USBLS	5/15
Except Special and Career/Technical Education	Houston-The Woodlands-Sugar Land MSA, TX	Y	49960 FQ	56370 MW	62580 TQ	USBLS	5/15
Except Special and Career/Technical Education	Odessa MSA, TX	Y	45250 FQ	51440 MW	57710 TQ	USBLS	5/15
Except Special and Career/Technical Education	San Antonio-New Braunfels MSA, TX	Y	49320 FQ	54240 MW	59050 TQ	USBLS	5/15
Except Special and Career/Technical Education	Utah	Y	42810 FQ	53420 MW	63160 TQ	USBLS	5/15
Except Special and Career/Technical Education	Ogden-Clearfield MSA, UT	Y	47000 FQ	56730 MW	67720 TQ	USBLS	5/15
Except Special and Career/Technical Education	Provo-Orem MSA, UT	Y	37040 FQ	46120 MW	57460 TQ	USBLS	5/15

AE	Average entry wage	AWR	Average wage range	H	Hourly	LR	Low end range	MTC	Median total compensation	TCC	Total cash compensation
AEX	Average experienced wage	B	Biweekly	HI	Highest wage paid	M	Monthly	MW	Median wage paid	TQ	Third quartile wage
ATC	Average total compensation	D	Daily	HR	High end range	MCC	Median cash compensation	MWR	Median wage range	W	Weekly
AW	Average wage paid	FQ	First quartile wage	LO	Lowest wage paid	ME	Median entry wage	S	See annotated source	Y	Yearly

Occupation/Type/Industry	Location	Per	Low	Mid	High	Source	Date
Middle School Teacher							
Except Special and Career/Technical Education	Salt Lake City MSA, UT	Y	44080 FQ	55090 MW	64450 TQ	USBLS	5/15
Except Special and Career/Technical Education	Vermont	Y	45970 FQ	55960 MW	66080 TQ	USBLS	5/15
Except Special and Career/Technical Education	Burlington-South Burlington MSA, VT	Y	56970 FQ	69240 MW	81540 TQ	USBLS	5/15
Except Special and Career/Technical Education	Virginia	Y	46230 FQ	57790 MW	74020 TQ	USBLS	5/15
Except Special and Career/Technical Education	Richmond MSA, VA	Y	48090 FQ	56380 MW	63240 TQ	USBLS	5/15
Except Special and Career/Technical Education	Virginia Beach-Norfolk-Newport News MSA, VA-NC	Y	46900 FQ	57120 MW	71420 TQ	USBLS	5/15
Except Special and Career/Technical Education	Washington	Y		62148 AW		WABLS	3/16
Except Special and Career/Technical Education	Seattle-Bellevue-Everett PMSA, WA	Y		63477 AW		WABLS	3/16
Except Special and Career/Technical Education	Tacoma-Lakewood PMSA, WA	Y		62970 AW		WABLS	3/16
Except Special and Career/Technical Education	West Virginia	Y	38580 FQ	45310 MW	52960 TQ	USBLS	5/15
Except Special and Career/Technical Education	Huntington-Ashland MSA, WV-KY-OH	Y	40400 FQ	47940 MW	56630 TQ	USBLS	5/15
Except Special and Career/Technical Education	Wisconsin	Y	44740 FQ	55300 MW	66550 TQ	USBLS	5/15
Except Special and Career/Technical Education	Madison MSA, WI	Y	44220 FQ	53620 MW	62000 TQ	USBLS	5/15
Except Special and Career/Technical Education	Milwaukee-Waukesha-West Allis MSA, WI	Y	46090 FQ	59260 MW	71370 TQ	USBLS	5/15
Except Special and Career/Technical Education	Wyoming	Y	51470 FQ	59740 MW	69620 TQ	USBLS	5/15
Except Special and Career/Technical Education	Puerto Rico	Y	17110 FQ	18870 MW	24360 TQ	USBLS	5/15
Except Special and Career/Technical Education	San Juan-Carolina-Caguas MSA, PR	Y	17110 FQ	18900 MW	23840 TQ	USBLS	5/15
Except Special and Career/Technical Education	Virgin Islands	Y	26210 FQ	30860 MW	48680 TQ	USBLS	5/15
Except Special and Career/Technical Education	Guam	Y	33780 FQ	41460 MW	52740 TQ	USBLS	5/15
Military General	United States	Y		205114 MW		CNBC06	2016
Milling and Planing Machine Setter, Operator, and Tender							
Metals and Plastics	Alabama	Y	33016 AE	37026 AW	39031 AEX	ALBLS	6/16
Metals and Plastics	Birmingham-Hoover MSA, AL	Y	31577 AE	35710 AW	37777 AEX	ALBLS	6/16
Metals and Plastics	Arizona	Y	40250 FQ	46170 MW	53200 TQ	USBLS	5/15
Metals and Plastics	Phoenix-Mesa-Scottsdale MSA, AZ	Y	36920 FQ	45110 MW	53580 TQ	USBLS	5/15
Metals and Plastics	Tucson MSA, AZ	Y	40970 FQ	44510 MW	48060 TQ	USBLS	5/15
Metals and Plastics	Arkansas	Y	29200 FQ	40860 MW	48440 TQ	USBLS	5/15
Metals and Plastics	Little Rock-North Little Rock-Conway MSA, AR	Y	21020 FQ	32460 MW	42550 TQ	USBLS	5/15
Metals and Plastics	California	H	13.50 FQ	18.11 MW	22.82 TQ	CABLS	1/16-3/16
Metals and Plastics	Anaheim-Santa Ana-Irvine PMSA, CA	H	11.31 FQ	15.97 MW	21.11 TQ	CABLS	1/16-3/16
Metals and Plastics	Los Angeles-Long Beach-Glendale PMSA, CA	H	14.86 FQ	20.00 MW	23.58 TQ	CABLS	1/16-3/16
Metals and Plastics	Oakland-Hayward-Berkeley PMSA, CA	H	15.06 FQ	19.48 MW	27.19 TQ	CABLS	1/16-3/16
Metals and Plastics	Riverside-San Bernardino-Ontario MSA, CA	H	12.39 FQ	16.84 MW	20.64 TQ	CABLS	1/16-3/16
Metals and Plastics	Sacramento–Roseville–Arden-Arcade MSA, CA	H	18.36 FQ	23.32 MW	30.88 TQ	CABLS	1/16-3/16
Metals and Plastics	San Diego-Carlsbad MSA, CA	H	14.18 FQ	17.01 MW	20.08 TQ	CABLS	1/16-3/16

AE	Average entry wage	**AWR**	Average wage range	**H**	Hourly	**LR** Low end range
AEX	Average experienced wage	**B**	Biweekly	**HI**	Highest wage paid	**M** Monthly
ATC	Average total compensation	**D**	Daily	**HR**	High end range	**MCC** Median cash compensation
AW	Average wage paid	**FQ**	First quartile wage	**LO**	Lowest wage paid	**ME** Median entry wage

MTC Median total compensation	**TCC** Total cash compensation		
MW Median wage paid	**TQ** Third quartile wage		
MWR Median wage range	**W** Weekly		
S See annotated source	**Y** Yearly		

Milling and Planing Machine Setter, Operator, and Tender

Occupation/Type/Industry	Location	Per	Low	Mid	High	Source	Date
Metals and Plastics	San Francisco-Redwood City-South San Francisco PMSA, CA	H	18.08 FQ	21.64 MW	24.21 TQ	CABLS	1/16-3/16
Metals and Plastics	Colorado	Y	30290 FQ	35290 MW	39480 TQ	USBLS	5/15
Metals and Plastics	Connecticut	Y		43606 MW		CTBLS	1/16-3/16
Metals and Plastics	Bridgeport-Stamford-Norwalk MSA, CT	Y	38720 FQ	49860 MW	69810 TQ	USBLS	5/15
Metals and Plastics	Hartford-West Hartford-East Hartford MSA, CT	Y	32270 FQ	41800 MW	50580 TQ	USBLS	5/15
Metals and Plastics	Florida	H	14.99 AE	17.84 MW	19.89 AEX	FLBLS	7/16-9/16
Metals and Plastics	Tampa-St. Petersburg-Clearwater MSA, FL	H	15.92 AE	18.42 MW	21.52 AEX	FLBLS	7/16-9/16
Metals and Plastics	Georgia	Y	25520 FQ	29750 MW	37880 TQ	USBLS	5/15
Metals and Plastics	Atlanta-Sandy Springs-Roswell MSA, GA	Y	25160 FQ	29110 MW	37350 TQ	USBLS	5/15
Metals and Plastics	Idaho	Y	25290 FQ	33220 MW	41890 TQ	USBLS	5/15
Metals and Plastics	Boise City MSA, ID	Y	24880 FQ	32520 MW	40340 TQ	USBLS	5/15
Metals and Plastics	Illinois	Y	30040 FQ	37880 MW	47660 TQ	USBLS	5/15
Metals and Plastics	Chicago-Naperville-Arlington Heights PMSA, IL	Y	30580 FQ	39770 MW	49200 TQ	USBLS	5/15
Metals and Plastics	Lake County-Kenosha County PMSA, IL-WI	Y	28630 FQ	35080 MW	43520 TQ	USBLS	5/15
Metals and Plastics	Indiana	Y	28780 FQ	35090 MW	43510 TQ	USBLS	5/15
Metals and Plastics	Indianapolis-Carmel-Anderson MSA, IN	Y	34050 FQ	38330 MW	44390 TQ	USBLS	5/15
Metals and Plastics	Iowa	Y	30780 FQ	38700 MW	44980 TQ	USBLS	5/15
Metals and Plastics	Kansas	Y	34550 FQ	44790 MW	55630 TQ	USBLS	5/15
Metals and Plastics	Wichita MSA, KS	Y	44380 FQ	54720 MW	59670 TQ	USBLS	5/15
Metals and Plastics	Kentucky	Y	28020 FQ	33440 MW	38490 TQ	USBLS	5/15
Metals and Plastics	Louisville-Jefferson County MSA, KY-IN	Y	43520 FQ	62970 MW	71370 TQ	USBLS	5/15
Metals and Plastics	Louisiana	Y	32810 FQ	41440 MW	50210 TQ	USBLS	5/15
Metals and Plastics	Maine	Y	40880 FQ	47630 MW	54670 TQ	USBLS	5/15
Metals and Plastics	Maryland	Y	39928 AE	49646 MW	54505 AEX	MDBLS	4/16
Metals and Plastics	Baltimore-Columbia-Towson MSA, MD	Y	42650 FQ	50750 MW	58110 TQ	USBLS	5/15
Metals and Plastics	Massachusetts	Y	37190 FQ	46140 MW	57510 TQ	USBLS	5/15
Metals and Plastics	Boston-Cambridge-Newton NECTA, MA	Y	41330 FQ	47820 MW	59530 TQ	USBLS	5/15
Metals and Plastics	Worcester MSA, MA-CT	Y	32470 FQ	39090 MW	51840 TQ	USBLS	5/15
Metals and Plastics	Michigan	Y	26120 FQ	32810 MW	41260 TQ	USBLS	5/15
Metals and Plastics	Detroit-Dearborn-Livonia PMSA, MI	Y	25020 FQ	29120 MW	38320 TQ	USBLS	5/15
Metals and Plastics	Grand Rapids-Wyoming MSA, MI	Y	29400 FQ	36280 MW	45400 TQ	USBLS	5/15
Metals and Plastics	Minnesota	Y	30647 FQ	36560 MW	43404 TQ	MNBLS	1/16-3/16
Metals and Plastics	Minneapolis-St. Paul-Bloomington MSA, MN-WI	Y	29665 FQ	35638 MW	41865 TQ	MNBLS	1/16-3/16
Metals and Plastics	Mississippi	Y	20830 FQ	24910 MW	31210 TQ	USBLS	5/15
Metals and Plastics	Missouri	Y	28050 FQ	34900 MW	43940 TQ	USBLS	5/15
Metals and Plastics	Kansas City MSA, MO-KS	Y	23220 FQ	29670 MW	38160 TQ	USBLS	5/15
Metals and Plastics	St. Louis MSA, MO-IL	Y	29810 FQ	37210 MW	47820 TQ	USBLS	5/15
Metals and Plastics	Nebraska	Y	35930 FQ	43010 MW	48875 TQ	NEBLS	7/16-9/16
Metals and Plastics	Nevada	Y	29690 FQ	37370 MW	45740 TQ	USBLS	5/15
Metals and Plastics	New Hampshire	H	15.25 AE	20.98 MW	23.81 AEX	NHBLS	6/16
Metals and Plastics	New Jersey	Y	34610 FQ	42260 MW	49120 TQ	USBLS	5/15
Metals and Plastics	Newark PMSA, NJ-PA	Y	34930 FQ	41620 MW	50170 TQ	USBLS	5/15
Metals and Plastics	New York	Y	27120 AE	37990 MW	44210 AEX	NYBLS	1/16-3/16
Metals and Plastics	Buffalo-Cheektowaga-Niagara Falls MSA, NY	Y	32690 FQ	40360 MW	46230 TQ	USBLS	5/15
Metals and Plastics	Nassau County-Suffolk County PMSA, NY	Y	33230 FQ	42780 MW	49830 TQ	USBLS	5/15
Metals and Plastics	New York-Jersey City-White Plains PMSA, NY-NJ	Y	31810 FQ	41680 MW	46620 TQ	USBLS	5/15
Metals and Plastics	Rochester MSA, NY	Y	32810 FQ	37290 MW	46310 TQ	USBLS	5/15
Metals and Plastics	North Carolina	Y	26010 FQ	34160 MW	45270 TQ	USBLS	5/15
Metals and Plastics	Charlotte-Concord-Gastonia MSA, NC-SC	Y	30390 FQ	39410 MW	47570 TQ	USBLS	5/15
Metals and Plastics	Ohio	Y	31330 FQ	38820 MW	45680 TQ	USBLS	5/15
Metals and Plastics	Cincinnati MSA, OH-KY-IN	Y	32700 FQ	40420 MW	46360 TQ	USBLS	5/15

AE	Average entry wage	AWR	Average wage range	H	Hourly	LR	Low end range	MTC	Median total compensation	TCC	Total cash compensation
AEX	Average experienced wage	B	Biweekly	HI	Highest wage paid	M	Monthly	MW	Median wage	TQ	Third quartile wage
ATC	Average total compensation	D	Daily	HR	High end range	MCC	Median cash compensation	MWR	Median wage range	W	Weekly
AW	Average wage paid	FQ	First quartile wage	LO	Lowest wage paid	ME	Median entry wage	S	See annotated source	Y	Yearly

Occupation/Type/Industry	Location	Per	Low	Mid	High	Source	Date
Milling and Planing Machine Setter, Operator, and Tender							
Metals and Plastics	Cleveland-Elyria MSA, OH	Y	31800 FQ	38820 MW	46030 TQ	USBLS	5/15
Metals and Plastics	Columbus MSA, OH	Y	19110 FQ	28150 MW	39200 TQ	USBLS	5/15
Metals and Plastics	Oklahoma	Y	25720 FQ	32400 MW	40180 TQ	USBLS	5/15
Metals and Plastics	Oklahoma City MSA, OK	Y	26970 FQ	33940 MW	39520 TQ	USBLS	5/15
Metals and Plastics	Tulsa MSA, OK	Y	29510 FQ	35840 MW	43250 TQ	USBLS	5/15
Metals and Plastics	Oregon	H	15.93 FQ	17.89 MW	20.41 TQ	ORBLS	2016
Metals and Plastics	Portland-Vancouver-Hillsboro MSA, OR-WA	Y	32930 FQ	36160 MW	39390 TQ	USBLS	5/15
Metals and Plastics	Pennsylvania	Y	35460 FQ	43890 MW	54590 TQ	USBLS	5/15
Metals and Plastics	Allentown-Bethlehem-Easton MSA, PA-NJ	Y	37120 FQ	44840 MW	54300 TQ	USBLS	5/15
Metals and Plastics	Montgomery County-Bucks County-Chester County PMSA, PA	Y	35750 FQ	44860 MW	56220 TQ	USBLS	5/15
Metals and Plastics	Philadelphia PMSA, PA	Y	40620 FQ	46650 MW	56100 TQ	USBLS	5/15
Metals and Plastics	Pittsburgh MSA, PA	Y	39970 FQ	46470 MW	64890 TQ	USBLS	5/15
Metals and Plastics	Providence-Warwick MSA, RI-MA	Y	34560 FQ	44880 MW	55620 TQ	USBLS	5/15
Metals and Plastics	South Carolina	Y	26280 FQ	31110 MW	47420 TQ	USBLS	5/15
Metals and Plastics	South Dakota	Y	27970 FQ	32830 MW	38300 TQ	USBLS	5/15
Metals and Plastics	Tennessee	Y	26490 FQ	33860 MW	39980 TQ	USBLS	5/15
Metals and Plastics	Knoxville MSA, TN	Y	19370 FQ	23830 MW	41390 TQ	USBLS	5/15
Metals and Plastics	Memphis MSA, TN-MS-AR	Y	27280 FQ	31610 MW	35830 TQ	USBLS	5/15
Metals and Plastics	Nashville-Davidson–Murfreesboro–Franklin MSA, TN	Y	31560 FQ	36700 MW	43130 TQ	USBLS	5/15
Metals and Plastics	Texas	Y	33170 FQ	42120 MW	51930 TQ	USBLS	5/15
Metals and Plastics	Austin-Round Rock MSA, TX	Y	35630 FQ	43030 MW	53660 TQ	USBLS	5/15
Metals and Plastics	Dallas-Plano-Irving PMSA, TX	Y	34760 FQ	43990 MW	51950 TQ	USBLS	5/15
Metals and Plastics	Fort Worth-Arlington PMSA, TX	Y	32140 FQ	42620 MW	49330 TQ	USBLS	5/15
Metals and Plastics	Houston-The Woodlands-Sugar Land MSA, TX	Y	34960 FQ	43080 MW	53500 TQ	USBLS	5/15
Metals and Plastics	San Antonio-New Braunfels MSA, TX	Y	25100 FQ	28520 MW	34060 TQ	USBLS	5/15
Metals and Plastics	Utah	Y	30120 FQ	34370 MW	38190 TQ	USBLS	5/15
Metals and Plastics	Ogden-Clearfield MSA, UT	Y	33200 FQ	36000 MW	38790 TQ	USBLS	5/15
Metals and Plastics	Salt Lake City MSA, UT	Y	32060 FQ	35480 MW	38900 TQ	USBLS	5/15
Metals and Plastics	Vermont	Y	26900 FQ	30590 MW	36940 TQ	USBLS	5/15
Metals and Plastics	Virginia	Y	28320 FQ	34000 MW	43860 TQ	USBLS	5/15
Metals and Plastics	Washington	H	16.68 FQ	21.62 MW	31.92 TQ	WABLS	3/16
Metals and Plastics	Seattle-Bellevue-Everett PMSA, WA	H	17.72 FQ	22.18 MW	30.22 TQ	WABLS	3/16
Metals and Plastics	Tacoma-Lakewood PMSA, WA	H	16.43 FQ	24.74 MW	35.63 TQ	WABLS	3/16
Metals and Plastics	West Virginia	Y	41840 FQ	46710 MW	53010 TQ	USBLS	5/15
Metals and Plastics	Huntington-Ashland MSA, WV-KY-OH	Y	32160 FQ	36200 MW	41160 TQ	USBLS	5/15
Metals and Plastics	Wisconsin	Y	34930 FQ	42060 MW	48410 TQ	USBLS	5/15
Metals and Plastics	Milwaukee-Waukesha-West Allis MSA, WI	Y	35690 FQ	45200 MW	57970 TQ	USBLS	5/15
Millwright	Alabama	Y	30938 AE	43559 AW	49864 AEX	ALBLS	6/16
	Birmingham-Hoover MSA, AL	Y	33287 AE	43854 AW	49142 AEX	ALBLS	6/16
	Alaska	Y	47670 FQ	69230 MW	79680 TQ	USBLS	5/15
	Arizona	Y	35670 FQ	46330 MW	57280 TQ	USBLS	5/15
	Phoenix-Mesa-Scottsdale MSA, AZ	Y	37990 FQ	47250 MW	57990 TQ	USBLS	5/15
	Arkansas	Y	33150 FQ	39840 MW	49060 TQ	USBLS	5/15
	Little Rock-North Little Rock-Conway MSA, AR	Y	28410 FQ	33080 MW	38720 TQ	USBLS	5/15
	California	H	20.44 FQ	27.74 MW	34.68 TQ	CABLS	1/16-3/16
	Anaheim-Santa Ana-Irvine PMSA, CA	H	16.33 FQ	23.85 MW	32.56 TQ	CABLS	1/16-3/16
	Los Angeles-Long Beach-Glendale PMSA, CA	H	26.35 FQ	33.69 MW	37.59 TQ	CABLS	1/16-3/16
	Oakland-Hayward-Berkeley PMSA, CA	H	18.62 FQ	29.93 MW	38.74 TQ	CABLS	1/16-3/16
	Riverside-San Bernardino-Ontario MSA, CA	H	18.94 FQ	23.03 MW	26.99 TQ	CABLS	1/16-3/16

AE	Average entry wage	AWR	Average wage range	H	Hourly	LR	Low end range	MTC	Median total compensation	TCC	Total cash compensation
AEX	Average experienced wage	B	Biweekly	HI	Highest wage paid	M	Monthly	MW	Median wage paid	TQ	Third quartile wage
ATC	Average total compensation	D	Daily	HR	High end range	MCC	Median cash compensation	MWR	Median wage range	W	Weekly
AW	Average wage paid	FQ	First quartile wage	LO	Lowest wage paid	ME	Median entry wage	S	See annotated source	Y	Yearly

Occupation/Type/Industry	Location	Per	Low	Mid	High	Source	Date
Millwright	Sacramento–Roseville–Arden-Arcade MSA, CA	H	27.30 FQ	31.20 MW	34.90 TQ	CABLS	1/16-3/16
	San Diego-Carlsbad MSA, CA	H	21.23 FQ	27.54 MW	33.70 TQ	CABLS	1/16-3/16
	Colorado	Y	41080 FQ	50380 MW	60430 TQ	USBLS	5/15
	Denver-Aurora-Lakewood MSA, CO	Y	45920 FQ	53830 MW	62740 TQ	USBLS	5/15
	Connecticut	Y		53005 MW		CTBLS	1/16-3/16
	Bridgeport-Stamford-Norwalk MSA, CT	Y	44330 FQ	55760 MW	71440 TQ	USBLS	5/15
	Delaware	Y	38260 FQ	52160 MW	59850 TQ	USBLS	5/15
	Wilmington PMSA, DE-MD-NJ	Y	42250 FQ	53500 MW	59780 TQ	USBLS	5/15
	Washington-Arlington-Alexandria PMSA, DC-VA-MD-WV	Y	50410 FQ	55000 MW	59240 TQ	USBLS	5/15
	Florida	H	15.81 AE	21.92 MW	24.44 AEX	FLBLS	7/16-9/16
	Orlando-Kissimmee-Sanford MSA, FL	H	22.23 AE	27.20 MW	27.93 AEX	FLBLS	7/16-9/16
	Tampa-St. Petersburg-Clearwater MSA, FL	H	23.77 AE	27.21 MW	27.97 AEX	FLBLS	7/16-9/16
	Georgia	Y	36580 FQ	46960 MW	57100 TQ	USBLS	5/15
	Atlanta-Sandy Springs-Roswell MSA, GA	Y	39860 FQ	53100 MW	59390 TQ	USBLS	5/15
	Augusta-Richmond County MSA, GA-SC	Y	27640 FQ	31570 MW	36720 TQ	USBLS	5/15
	Idaho	Y	36520 FQ	43850 MW	52980 TQ	USBLS	5/15
	Illinois	Y	40120 FQ	49490 MW	65580 TQ	USBLS	5/15
	Chicago-Naperville-Arlington Heights PMSA, IL	Y	36870 FQ	53170 MW	69490 TQ	USBLS	5/15
	Indiana	Y	41110 FQ	57960 MW	70310 TQ	USBLS	5/15
	Gary PMSA, IN	Y	43750 FQ	55560 MW	71440 TQ	USBLS	5/15
	Indianapolis-Carmel-Anderson MSA, IN	Y	35680 FQ	61380 MW	72090 TQ	USBLS	5/15
	Iowa	Y	41960 FQ	48240 MW	58160 TQ	USBLS	5/15
	Des Moines-West Des Moines MSA, IA	Y	39760 FQ	45730 MW	52450 TQ	USBLS	5/15
	Kansas	Y	44160 FQ	65090 MW	80170 TQ	USBLS	5/15
	Kentucky	Y	41980 FQ	51920 MW	62770 TQ	USBLS	5/15
	Louisville-Jefferson County MSA, KY-IN	Y	38120 FQ	59280 MW	71970 TQ	USBLS	5/15
	Louisiana	Y	38980 FQ	49090 MW	57790 TQ	USBLS	5/15
	Baton Rouge MSA, LA	Y	36600 FQ	48330 MW	56560 TQ	USBLS	5/15
	New Orleans-Metairie MSA, LA	Y	42410 FQ	53310 MW	63380 TQ	USBLS	5/15
	Maine	Y	44790 FQ	52540 MW	58390 TQ	USBLS	5/15
	Portland-South Portland MSA, ME	Y	48010 FQ	53980 MW	58800 TQ	USBLS	5/15
	Maryland	Y	37456 AE	52105 MW	59430 AEX	MDBLS	4/16
	Baltimore-Columbia-Towson MSA, MD	Y	41940 FQ	53660 MW	62050 TQ	USBLS	5/15
	Massachusetts	Y	49510 FQ	57870 MW	68930 TQ	USBLS	5/15
	Boston-Cambridge-Newton NECTA, MA	Y	52590 FQ	58260 MW	66940 TQ	USBLS	5/15
	Worcester MSA, MA-CT	Y	49160 FQ	58910 MW	68780 TQ	USBLS	5/15
	Michigan	Y	51500 FQ	66200 MW	74210 TQ	USBLS	5/15
	Detroit-Dearborn-Livonia PMSA, MI	Y	29300 FQ	67510 MW	76980 TQ	USBLS	5/15
	Grand Rapids-Wyoming MSA, MI	Y	50750 FQ	65940 MW	73450 TQ	USBLS	5/15
	Minnesota	Y	39181 FQ	50575 MW	62925 TQ	MNBLS	1/16-3/16
	Minneapolis-St. Paul-Bloomington MSA, MN-WI	Y	45165 FQ	57162 MW	65640 TQ	MNBLS	1/16-3/16
	Mississippi	Y	41220 FQ	50160 MW	56780 TQ	USBLS	5/15
	Jackson MSA, MS	Y	23470 FQ	42760 MW	47210 TQ	USBLS	5/15
	Missouri	Y	36580 FQ	47140 MW	69000 TQ	USBLS	5/15
	Kansas City MSA, MO-KS	Y	63880 FQ	71210 MW	78370 TQ	USBLS	5/15
	St. Louis MSA, MO-IL	Y	42480 FQ	47720 MW	59370 TQ	USBLS	5/15
	Montana	Y	37100 FQ	46070 MW	54380 TQ	USBLS	5/15
	Nebraska	Y	34375 FQ	48505 MW	57350 TQ	NEBLS	7/16-9/16
	Omaha-Council Bluffs MSA, NE-IA	Y	46115 FQ	55615 MW	61010 TQ	NEBLS	7/16-9/16
	Nevada	Y	37970 FQ	51540 MW	69270 TQ	USBLS	5/15

AE	Average entry wage	AWR	Average wage range	H	Hourly	LR	Low end range	MTC	Median total compensation	TCC	Total cash compensation
AEX	Average experienced wage	B	Biweekly	HI	Highest wage paid	M	Monthly	MW	Median wage paid	TQ	Third quartile wage
ATC	Average total compensation	D	Daily	HR	High end range	MCC	Median cash compensation	MWR	Median wage range	W	Weekly
AW	Average wage paid	FQ	First quartile wage	LO	Lowest wage paid	ME	Median entry wage	S	See annotated source	Y	Yearly

1049

Occupation/Type/Industry	Location	Per	Low	Mid	High	Source	Date
Millwright	Las Vegas-Henderson-Paradise						
	MSA, NV	Y	38530 FQ	54180 MW	72530 TQ	USBLS	5/15
	New Hampshire	H	21.60 AE	26.79 MW	29.72 AEX	NHBLS	6/16
	New Jersey	Y	43390 FQ	55510 MW	73950 TQ	USBLS	5/15
	Camden PMSA, NJ	Y	37190 FQ	70180 MW	90890 TQ	USBLS	5/15
	Newark PMSA, NJ-PA	Y	46900 FQ	58310 MW	70060 TQ	USBLS	5/15
	Trenton MSA, NJ	Y	42360 FQ	51540 MW	61490 TQ	USBLS	5/15
	New Mexico	Y	52550 FQ	59980 MW	69310 TQ	USBLS	5/15
	Albuquerque MSA, NM	Y	51400 FQ	57600 MW	64760 TQ	USBLS	5/15
	New York	Y	40720 AE	59300 MW	69930 AEX	NYBLS	1/16-3/16
	Buffalo-Cheektowaga-Niagara						
	Falls MSA, NY	Y	60050 FQ	68670 MW	74920 TQ	USBLS	5/15
	Nassau County-Suffolk County						
	PMSA, NY	Y	29070 FQ	44380 MW	58180 TQ	USBLS	5/15
	New York-Jersey City-White						
	Plains PMSA, NY-NJ	Y	55000 FQ	84240 MW	96400 TQ	USBLS	5/15
	Rochester MSA, NY	Y	43250 FQ	55040 MW	63130 TQ	USBLS	5/15
	North Carolina	Y	36960 FQ	44930 MW	52510 TQ	USBLS	5/15
	Charlotte-Concord-Gastonia						
	MSA, NC-SC	Y	42390 FQ	49110 MW	57370 TQ	USBLS	5/15
	Raleigh MSA, NC	Y	37670 FQ	43770 MW	49470 TQ	USBLS	5/15
	North Dakota	Y	40050 FQ	47180 MW	62400 TQ	USBLS	5/15
	Ohio	Y	46990 FQ	62470 MW	72550 TQ	USBLS	5/15
	Cincinnati MSA, OH-KY-IN	Y	40110 FQ	55350 MW	70000 TQ	USBLS	5/15
	Cleveland-Elyria MSA, OH	Y	64620 FQ	69900 MW	75180 TQ	USBLS	5/15
	Columbus MSA, OH	Y	50710 FQ	60030 MW	70490 TQ	USBLS	5/15
	Oklahoma	Y	35930 FQ	42230 MW	50650 TQ	USBLS	5/15
	Tulsa MSA, OK	Y	35460 FQ	42730 MW	50570 TQ	USBLS	5/15
	Oregon	H	20.81 FQ	24.07 MW	29.04 TQ	ORBLS	2016
	Portland-Vancouver-Hillsboro						
	MSA, OR-WA	Y	44070 FQ	52050 MW	62310 TQ	USBLS	5/15
	Pennsylvania	Y	41820 FQ	50720 MW	65310 TQ	USBLS	5/15
	Allentown-Bethlehem-Easton						
	MSA, PA-NJ	Y	50910 FQ	56020 MW	61120 TQ	USBLS	5/15
	Harrisburg-Carlisle MSA, PA	Y	42200 FQ	50450 MW	69550 TQ	USBLS	5/15
	Montgomery County-Bucks						
	County-Chester County						
	PMSA, PA	Y	42470 FQ	64740 MW	75460 TQ	USBLS	5/15
	Pittsburgh MSA, PA	Y	37750 FQ	46440 MW	61780 TQ	USBLS	5/15
	Providence-Warwick MSA, RI-						
	MA	Y	46130 FQ	56620 MW	67290 TQ	USBLS	5/15
	South Carolina	Y	36260 FQ	43880 MW	53700 TQ	USBLS	5/15
	Charleston-North Charleston						
	MSA, SC	Y	39450 FQ	51300 MW	59180 TQ	USBLS	5/15
	Columbia MSA, SC	Y	40040 FQ	47100 MW	60380 TQ	USBLS	5/15
	Greenville-Anderson-Mauldin						
	MSA, SC	Y	37260 FQ	43750 MW	49060 TQ	USBLS	5/15
	South Dakota	Y	36890 FQ	41980 MW	46840 TQ	USBLS	5/15
	Sioux Falls MSA, SD	Y	39050 FQ	43480 MW	47500 TQ	USBLS	5/15
	Tennessee	Y	40790 FQ	47460 MW	55820 TQ	USBLS	5/15
	Knoxville MSA, TN	Y	37480 FQ	43660 MW	49160 TQ	USBLS	5/15
	Memphis MSA, TN-MS-AR	Y	42280 FQ	47710 MW	55750 TQ	USBLS	5/15
	Nashville-Davidson–						
	Murfreesboro–Franklin						
	MSA, TN	Y	44580 FQ	51900 MW	57530 TQ	USBLS	5/15
	Texas	Y	33420 FQ	44740 MW	55980 TQ	USBLS	5/15
	Austin-Round Rock MSA, TX	Y	30210 FQ	34290 MW	38080 TQ	USBLS	5/15
	Dallas-Plano-Irving PMSA, TX	Y	39710 FQ	45600 MW	53570 TQ	USBLS	5/15
	Fort Worth-Arlington PMSA,						
	TX	Y	35120 FQ	61080 MW	84920 TQ	USBLS	5/15
	Houston-The Woodlands-						
	Sugar Land MSA, TX	Y	36750 FQ	48550 MW	58960 TQ	USBLS	5/15
	San Antonio-New Braunfels						
	MSA, TX	Y	24900 FQ	42940 MW	51960 TQ	USBLS	5/15
	Salt Lake City MSA, UT	Y	64370 FQ	69670 MW	74960 TQ	USBLS	5/15
	Virginia	Y	43680 FQ	52530 MW	62270 TQ	USBLS	5/15
	Richmond MSA, VA	Y	45640 FQ	57140 MW	72490 TQ	USBLS	5/15
	Virginia Beach-Norfolk-						
	Newport News MSA, VA-NC	Y	50460 FQ	54660 MW	58870 TQ	USBLS	5/15
	Washington	H	21.67 FQ	29.88 MW	40.95 TQ	WABLS	3/16
	Seattle-Bellevue-Everett						
	PMSA, WA	H	32.38 FQ	41.71 MW	46.92 TQ	WABLS	3/16

AE	Average entry wage	AWR	Average wage range	H	Hourly
AEX	Average experienced wage	B	Biweekly	HI	Highest wage paid
ATC	Average total compensation	D	Daily	HR	High end range
AW	Average wage paid	FQ	First quartile wage	LO	Lowest wage paid

LR	Low end range	MTC	Median total compensation	TCC	Total cash compensation
M	Monthly	MW	Median wage paid	TQ	Third quartile wage
MCC	Median cash compensation	MWR	Median wage range	W	Weekly
ME	Median entry wage	S	See annotated source	Y	Yearly

Occupation/Type/Industry	Location	Per	Low	Mid	High	Source	Date
Millwright	Tacoma-Lakewood PMSA, WA	H	18.98 FQ	27.20 MW	35.26 TQ	WABLS	3/16
	West Virginia	Y	40360 FQ	44990 MW	49650 TQ	USBLS	5/15
	Wisconsin	Y	41340 FQ	53790 MW	61080 TQ	USBLS	5/15
	Milwaukee-Waukesha-West Allis MSA, WI	Y	52580 FQ	58280 MW	65410 TQ	USBLS	5/15
	Wyoming	Y	58810 FQ	66940 MW	73080 TQ	USBLS	5/15
Mine Cutting and Channeling Machine Operator	Alabama	Y	30099 AE	45571 AW	53317 AEX	ALBLS	6/16
	Alaska	Y	44550 FQ	49900 MW	62380 TQ	USBLS	5/15
	Arizona	Y	50990 FQ	57180 MW	63670 TQ	USBLS	5/15
	Arkansas	Y	32140 FQ	38840 MW	46020 TQ	USBLS	5/15
	California	H	23.98 FQ	27.88 MW	30.93 TQ	CABLS	1/16-3/16
	Colorado	Y	43750 FQ	53880 MW	60270 TQ	USBLS	5/15
	Florida	H	16.90 AE	21.53 MW	22.35 AEX	FLBLS	7/16-9/16
	Georgia	Y	34900 FQ	43590 MW	51530 TQ	USBLS	5/15
	Illinois	Y	35140 FQ	46650 MW	65330 TQ	USBLS	5/15
	Indiana	Y	39010 FQ	43100 MW	47190 TQ	USBLS	5/15
	Kansas	Y	29230 FQ	34490 MW	38410 TQ	USBLS	5/15
	Kentucky	Y	46840 FQ	53990 MW	60290 TQ	USBLS	5/15
	Missouri	Y	25250 FQ	30290 MW	44120 TQ	USBLS	5/15
	Montana	Y	57510 FQ	67420 MW	74130 TQ	USBLS	5/15
	Nevada	Y	55440 FQ	61950 MW	70320 TQ	USBLS	5/15
	New York	Y	32750 AE	38970 MW	43050 AEX	NYBLS	1/16-3/16
	Ohio	Y	35690 FQ	41960 MW	64710 TQ	USBLS	5/15
	Oklahoma	Y	24590 FQ	32280 MW	36750 TQ	USBLS	5/15
	Pennsylvania	Y	35620 FQ	50350 MW	57680 TQ	USBLS	5/15
	South Carolina	Y	35950 FQ	41240 MW	45890 TQ	USBLS	5/15
	Tennessee	Y	27960 FQ	39040 MW	47700 TQ	USBLS	5/15
	Texas	Y	22460 FQ	25780 MW	35000 TQ	USBLS	5/15
	Utah	Y	52270 FQ	57950 MW	64390 TQ	USBLS	5/15
	Virginia	Y	31510 FQ	38180 MW	47120 TQ	USBLS	5/15
	West Virginia	Y	41410 FQ	52560 MW	61620 TQ	USBLS	5/15
	Wyoming	Y	66770 FQ	72030 MW	77280 TQ	USBLS	5/15
Mine Rescue Operations Coordinator							
State Government	Ohio	H	26.38 LO		27.96 HI	OHGOV	2015
Mine Safety Manager							
State Government	Ohio	H			43.60 HI	OHGOV	2015
Mine Shuttle Car Operator	Alabama	Y	58553 AE	58655 AW	58707 AEX	ALBLS	6/16
	Colorado	Y	53190 FQ	57380 MW	61570 TQ	USBLS	5/15
	Kentucky	Y	43740 FQ	48100 MW	55950 TQ	USBLS	5/15
	Pennsylvania	Y	52740 FQ	57340 MW	61930 TQ	USBLS	5/15
	Utah	Y	52830 FQ	56520 MW	60210 TQ	USBLS	5/15
	West Virginia	Y	51340 FQ	56020 MW	60640 TQ	USBLS	5/15
	Wyoming	Y	71470 FQ	78840 MW	87120 TQ	USBLS	5/15
Mining and Geological Engineer							
Including Mining Safety Engineers	Alabama	Y	57255 AE	88946 AW	104786 AEX	ALBLS	6/16
Including Mining Safety Engineers	Alaska	Y	92170 FQ	112870 MW	137210 TQ	USBLS	5/15
Including Mining Safety Engineers	Arizona	Y	65960 FQ	80900 MW	102260 TQ	USBLS	5/15
Including Mining Safety Engineers	California	H	45.19 FQ	60.18 MW	62.14 TQ	CABLS	1/16-3/16
Including Mining Safety Engineers	Colorado	Y	83400 FQ	102090 MW	155900 TQ	USBLS	5/15
Including Mining Safety Engineers	Florida	H	24.04 AE	36.38 MW	46.73 AEX	FLBLS	7/16-9/16
Including Mining Safety Engineers	Georgia	Y	51590 FQ	68380 MW	94090 TQ	USBLS	5/15
Including Mining Safety Engineers	Idaho	Y	81660 FQ	96390 MW	125980 TQ	USBLS	5/15
Including Mining Safety Engineers	Indiana	Y	53990 FQ	72540 MW	93180 TQ	USBLS	5/15
Including Mining Safety Engineers	Maryland	Y	49748 AE	83578 MW	100493 AEX	MDBLS	4/16
Including Mining Safety Engineers	Michigan	Y	57800 FQ	73020 MW	94630 TQ	USBLS	5/15
Including Mining Safety Engineers	Minnesota	Y	70039 FQ	90523 MW	118628 TQ	MNBLS	1/16-3/16
Including Mining Safety Engineers	Missouri	Y	58370 FQ	75060 MW	93550 TQ	USBLS	5/15
Including Mining Safety Engineers	Montana	Y	69570 FQ	84240 MW	100360 TQ	USBLS	5/15
Including Mining Safety Engineers	Nevada	Y	73230 FQ	89010 MW	108310 TQ	USBLS	5/15
Including Mining Safety Engineers	New Mexico	Y	66100 FQ	73970 MW	91260 TQ	USBLS	5/15
Including Mining Safety Engineers	New York	Y	64910 AE	93160 MW	106590 AEX	NYBLS	1/16-3/16
Including Mining Safety Engineers	North Carolina	Y	66920 FQ	77190 MW	97590 TQ	USBLS	5/15
Including Mining Safety Engineers	North Dakota	Y	64490 FQ	87400 MW	111300 TQ	USBLS	5/15
Including Mining Safety Engineers	Ohio	Y	57010 FQ	65620 MW	89160 TQ	USBLS	5/15
Including Mining Safety Engineers	Oklahoma	Y	86150 FQ	105620 MW	131160 TQ	USBLS	5/15

AE	Average entry wage	AWR	Average wage range	H	Hourly	LR	Low end range	MTC	Median total compensation	TCC	Total cash compensation
AEX	Average experienced wage	B	Biweekly	HI	Highest wage paid	M	Monthly	MW	Median wage paid	TQ	Third quartile wage
ATC	Average total compensation	D	Daily	HR	High end range	MCC	Median cash compensation	MWR	Median wage range	W	Weekly
AW	Average wage paid	FQ	First quartile wage	LO	Lowest wage paid	ME	Median entry wage	S	See annotated source	Y	Yearly

1051

Occupation/Type/Industry	Location	Per	Low	Mid	High	Source	Date
Mining and Geological Engineer							
Including Mining Safety Engineers	Oregon	H	39.36 FQ	49.11 MW	51.44 TQ	ORBLS	2016
Including Mining Safety Engineers	Pennsylvania	Y	66510 FQ	81840 MW	96610 TQ	USBLS	5/15
Including Mining Safety Engineers	Tennessee	Y	64480 FQ	85930 MW	115320 TQ	USBLS	5/15
Including Mining Safety Engineers	Texas	Y	94850 FQ	156890 MW		USBLS	5/15
Including Mining Safety Engineers	Utah	Y	69550 FQ	87830 MW	106430 TQ	USBLS	5/15
Including Mining Safety Engineers	Virginia	Y	51860 FQ	61450 MW	108620 TQ	USBLS	5/15
Including Mining Safety Engineers	Washington	H	35.65 FQ	44.51 MW	59.86 TQ	WABLS	3/16
Including Mining Safety Engineers	West Virginia	Y	56670 FQ	68780 MW	114050 TQ	USBLS	5/15
Including Mining Safety Engineers	Wyoming	Y	71090 FQ	85270 MW	106360 TQ	USBLS	5/15
Minister							
Music/Worship, Southern Baptist Convention	United States	Y		68080 AW		LWAY02	2016
Minority Leader							
United States House of Representatives	United States	Y			193400 HI	OPM01	2017
United States Senate	United States	Y			193400 HI	OPM01	2017
MIS Manager	United States	Y		108218 AW		DICE01	10/6/15-11/25/15
Missing Persons Specialist							
Police Department, Municipal Government	Oxnard, CA	Y			35343 HI	CACIT	6/28/16
Missing Persons Supervisor							
State Government	North Carolina	Y	38125 LO		60604 HI	NCGOV	7/1/16
Mission Pastor							
Southern Baptist Convention	United States	Y		68159 AW		LWAY02	2016
Mixing and Blending Machine Setter, Operator, and Tender	Alabama	Y	25222 AE	40985 AW	48861 AEX	ALBLS	6/16
	Birmingham-Hoover MSA, AL	Y	21901 AE	34867 AW	41355 AEX	ALBLS	6/16
	Alaska	Y	40770 FQ	56160 MW	67630 TQ	USBLS	5/15
	Anchorage MSA, AK	Y	36240 FQ	53610 MW	58620 TQ	USBLS	5/15
	Arizona	Y	24760 FQ	29760 MW	36860 TQ	USBLS	5/15
	Phoenix-Mesa-Scottsdale MSA, AZ	Y	24660 FQ	29500 MW	36550 TQ	USBLS	5/15
	Tucson MSA, AZ	Y	25810 FQ	31450 MW	38620 TQ	USBLS	5/15
	Arkansas	Y	27650 FQ	36870 MW	44970 TQ	USBLS	5/15
	Little Rock-North Little Rock-Conway MSA, AR	Y	28170 FQ	35230 MW	40070 TQ	USBLS	5/15
	California	H	11.46 FQ	14.60 MW	19.13 TQ	CABLS	1/16-3/16
	Anaheim-Santa Ana-Irvine PMSA, CA	H	11.52 FQ	16.33 MW	20.50 TQ	CABLS	1/16-3/16
	Los Angeles-Long Beach-Glendale PMSA, CA	H	11.02 FQ	13.48 MW	16.10 TQ	CABLS	1/16-3/16
	Oakland-Hayward-Berkeley PMSA, CA	H	15.22 FQ	19.56 MW	26.70 TQ	CABLS	1/16-3/16
	Riverside-San Bernardino-Ontario MSA, CA	H	11.14 FQ	14.47 MW	18.59 TQ	CABLS	1/16-3/16
	Sacramento–Roseville–Arden-Arcade MSA, CA	H	12.40 FQ	14.96 MW	19.74 TQ	CABLS	1/16-3/16
	San Diego-Carlsbad MSA, CA	H	12.33 FQ	15.10 MW	19.97 TQ	CABLS	1/16-3/16
	San Francisco-Redwood City-South San Francisco PMSA, CA	H	14.55 FQ	21.56 MW	27.26 TQ	CABLS	1/16-3/16
	Colorado	Y	21650 FQ	28410 MW	41830 TQ	USBLS	5/15
	Denver-Aurora-Lakewood MSA, CO	Y	20610 FQ	25630 MW	36470 TQ	USBLS	5/15
	Connecticut	Y		36073 MW		CTBLS	1/16-3/16
	Bridgeport-Stamford-Norwalk MSA, CT	Y	31770 FQ	35380 MW	38980 TQ	USBLS	5/15
	Hartford-West Hartford-East Hartford MSA, CT	Y	29660 FQ	34260 MW	38580 TQ	USBLS	5/15
	Delaware	Y	34270 FQ	39620 MW	48910 TQ	USBLS	5/15
	Wilmington PMSA, DE-MD-NJ	Y	34410 FQ	39640 MW	50300 TQ	USBLS	5/15
	Washington-Arlington-Alexandria PMSA, DC-VA-MD-WV	Y	32540 FQ	40360 MW	56280 TQ	USBLS	5/15
	Florida	H	11.38 AE	15.06 MW	17.87 AEX	FLBLS	7/16-9/16

AE	Average entry wage	AWR	Average wage range	H	Hourly	LR	Low end range	MTC	Median total compensation	TCC	Total cash compensation
AEX	Average experienced wage	B	Biweekly	HI	Highest wage paid	M	Monthly	MW	Median wage paid	TQ	Third quartile wage
ATC	Average total compensation	D	Daily	HR	High end range	MCC	Median cash compensation	MWR	Median wage range	W	Weekly
AW	Average wage paid	FQ	First quartile wage	LO	Lowest wage paid	ME	Median entry wage	S	See annotated source	Y	Yearly

Occupation/Type/Industry	Location	Per	Low	Mid	High	Source	Date
Mixing and Blending Machine Setter, Operator, and Tender	Fort Lauderdale-Pompano Beach-Deerfield Beach PMSA, FL	H	11.74 AE	14.04 MW	16.13 AEX	FLBLS	7/16-9/16
	Miami-Miami Beach-Kendall PMSA, FL	H	9.98 AE	13.74 MW	16.52 AEX	FLBLS	7/16-9/16
	Orlando-Kissimmee-Sanford MSA, FL	H	12.32 AE	16.28 MW	18.62 AEX	FLBLS	7/16-9/16
	Tampa-St. Petersburg-Clearwater MSA, FL	H	11.25 AE	15.84 MW	18.20 AEX	FLBLS	7/16-9/16
	Georgia	Y	28480 FQ	35230 MW	42420 TQ	USBLS	5/15
	Atlanta-Sandy Springs-Roswell MSA, GA	Y	29480 FQ	35890 MW	44470 TQ	USBLS	5/15
	Augusta-Richmond County MSA, GA-SC	Y	32570 FQ	40300 MW	48920 TQ	USBLS	5/15
	Hawaii	Y	26240 FQ	32840 MW	45800 TQ	USBLS	5/15
	Urban Honolulu MSA, HI	Y	26330 FQ	31230 MW	46020 TQ	USBLS	5/15
	Idaho	Y	24710 FQ	29260 MW	38560 TQ	USBLS	5/15
	Boise City MSA, ID	Y	25180 FQ	27890 MW	30610 TQ	USBLS	5/15
	Illinois	Y	26810 FQ	34760 MW	44750 TQ	USBLS	5/15
	Chicago-Naperville-Arlington Heights PMSA, IL	Y	26010 FQ	33780 MW	43560 TQ	USBLS	5/15
	Lake County-Kenosha County PMSA, IL-WI	Y	32920 FQ	42690 MW	54120 TQ	USBLS	5/15
	Indiana	Y	27920 FQ	35830 MW	44880 TQ	USBLS	5/15
	Gary PMSA, IN	Y	31120 FQ	39400 MW	50570 TQ	USBLS	5/15
	Indianapolis-Carmel-Anderson MSA, IN	Y	32050 FQ	40890 MW	47250 TQ	USBLS	5/15
	Iowa	Y	27810 FQ	33430 MW	43090 TQ	USBLS	5/15
	Des Moines-West Des Moines MSA, IA	Y	27450 FQ	31300 MW	41410 TQ	USBLS	5/15
	Kansas	Y	29850 FQ	36520 MW	44680 TQ	USBLS	5/15
	Wichita MSA, KS	Y	24640 FQ	35000 MW	44830 TQ	USBLS	5/15
	Kentucky	Y	28210 FQ	33960 MW	38960 TQ	USBLS	5/15
	Louisville-Jefferson County MSA, KY-IN	Y	29500 FQ	35620 MW	45040 TQ	USBLS	5/15
	Louisiana	Y	34690 FQ	45030 MW	55830 TQ	USBLS	5/15
	Baton Rouge MSA, LA	Y	37720 FQ	46710 MW	56950 TQ	USBLS	5/15
	Maine	Y	34920 FQ	45160 MW	55350 TQ	USBLS	5/15
	Portland-South Portland MSA, ME	Y	31260 FQ	36170 MW	40770 TQ	USBLS	5/15
	Maryland	Y	28367 AE	49275 MW	59729 AEX	MDBLS	4/16
	Baltimore-Columbia-Towson MSA, MD	Y	31200 FQ	42620 MW	55610 TQ	USBLS	5/15
	Salisbury MSA, MD-DE	Y	28210 FQ	35750 MW	49250 TQ	USBLS	5/15
	Massachusetts	Y	32270 FQ	38090 MW	44980 TQ	USBLS	5/15
	Boston-Cambridge-Newton NECTA, MA	Y	33670 FQ	39400 MW	46140 TQ	USBLS	5/15
	Worcester MSA, MA-CT	Y	30600 FQ	38140 MW	45330 TQ	USBLS	5/15
	Michigan	Y	25770 FQ	34590 MW	44810 TQ	USBLS	5/15
	Detroit-Dearborn-Livonia PMSA, MI	Y	24900 FQ	33930 MW	46490 TQ	USBLS	5/15
	Grand Rapids-Wyoming MSA, MI	Y	25440 FQ	33200 MW	39890 TQ	USBLS	5/15
	Minnesota	Y	32489 FQ	38676 MW	47403 TQ	MNBLS	1/16-3/16
	Minneapolis-St. Paul-Bloomington MSA, MN-WI	Y	32763 FQ	39334 MW	49691 TQ	MNBLS	1/16-3/16
	Mississippi	Y	27850 FQ	34840 MW	42510 TQ	USBLS	5/15
	Jackson MSA, MS	Y	33780 FQ	42370 MW	48120 TQ	USBLS	5/15
	Missouri	Y	28510 FQ	39850 MW	50620 TQ	USBLS	5/15
	Kansas City MSA, MO-KS	Y	30900 FQ	37690 MW	45950 TQ	USBLS	5/15
	St. Louis MSA, MO-IL	Y	31180 FQ	42120 MW	49880 TQ	USBLS	5/15
	Montana	Y	27190 FQ	33330 MW	37520 TQ	USBLS	5/15
	Billings MSA, MT	Y	26410 FQ	31050 MW	52140 TQ	USBLS	5/15
	Nebraska	Y	26825 FQ	33465 MW	40480 TQ	NEBLS	7/16-9/16
	Omaha-Council Bluffs MSA, NE-IA	Y	30200 FQ	36375 MW	44010 TQ	NEBLS	7/16-9/16
	Nevada	Y	29200 FQ	37190 MW	45080 TQ	USBLS	5/15
	Las Vegas-Henderson-Paradise MSA, NV	Y	27360 FQ	32830 MW	44110 TQ	USBLS	5/15
	New Hampshire	H	14.46 AE	18.46 MW	21.62 AEX	NHBLS	6/16
	Nashua NECTA, NH-MA	Y	33120 FQ	36720 MW	42570 TQ	USBLS	5/15

AE	Average entry wage	AWR	Average wage range	H	Hourly
AEX	Average experienced wage	B	Biweekly	HI	Highest wage paid
ATC	Average total compensation	D	Daily	HR	High end range
AW	Average wage paid	FQ	First quartile wage	LO	Lowest wage paid

LR	Low end range	MTC	Median total compensation
M	Monthly	MW	Median wage paid
MCC	Median cash compensation	MWR	Median wage range
ME	Median entry wage	S	See annotated source

TCC	Total cash compensation
TQ	Third quartile wage
W	Weekly
Y	Yearly

Occupation/Type/Industry	Location	Per	Low	Mid	High	Source	Date
Mixing and Blending Machine Setter, Operator, and Tender							
	New Jersey	Y	28870 FQ	37560 MW	47980 TQ	USBLS	5/15
	Camden PMSA, NJ	Y	33520 FQ	38440 MW	45790 TQ	USBLS	5/15
	Newark PMSA, NJ-PA	Y	28740 FQ	37760 MW	51980 TQ	USBLS	5/15
	Trenton MSA, NJ	Y	31120 FQ	41830 MW	48640 TQ	USBLS	5/15
	New Mexico	Y	29600 FQ	35350 MW	42550 TQ	USBLS	5/15
	Albuquerque MSA, NM	Y	23010 FQ	30720 MW	40470 TQ	USBLS	5/15
	New York	Y	24090 AE	39090 MW	47260 AEX	NYBLS	1/16-3/16
	Buffalo-Cheektowaga-Niagara Falls MSA, NY	Y	30240 FQ	39540 MW	47460 TQ	USBLS	5/15
	Nassau County-Suffolk County PMSA, NY	Y	24310 FQ	31620 MW	43610 TQ	USBLS	5/15
	New York-Jersey City-White Plains PMSA, NY-NJ	Y	26530 FQ	36390 MW	49010 TQ	USBLS	5/15
	Rochester MSA, NY	Y	26650 FQ	41300 MW	46010 TQ	USBLS	5/15
	North Carolina	Y	26960 FQ	33010 MW	41090 TQ	USBLS	5/15
	Charlotte-Concord-Gastonia MSA, NC-SC	Y	27470 FQ	32800 MW	39050 TQ	USBLS	5/15
	Raleigh MSA, NC	Y	26840 FQ	33520 MW	45090 TQ	USBLS	5/15
	North Dakota	Y	33670 FQ	41240 MW	46870 TQ	USBLS	5/15
	Fargo MSA, ND-MN	Y	38390 FQ	42810 MW	46630 TQ	USBLS	5/15
	Ohio	Y	28260 FQ	35910 MW	45090 TQ	USBLS	5/15
	Cincinnati MSA, OH-KY-IN	Y	30400 FQ	39870 MW	50700 TQ	USBLS	5/15
	Cleveland-Elyria MSA, OH	Y	28740 FQ	34540 MW	39560 TQ	USBLS	5/15
	Columbus MSA, OH	Y	26220 FQ	34000 MW	42160 TQ	USBLS	5/15
	Oklahoma	Y	23770 FQ	29950 MW	37370 TQ	USBLS	5/15
	Oklahoma City MSA, OK	Y	23200 FQ	31770 MW	38780 TQ	USBLS	5/15
	Tulsa MSA, OK	Y	27280 FQ	34290 MW	47000 TQ	USBLS	5/15
	Oregon	H	13.52 FQ	16.46 MW	21.30 TQ	ORBLS	2016
	Portland-Vancouver-Hillsboro MSA, OR-WA	Y	26060 FQ	31530 MW	42740 TQ	USBLS	5/15
	Pennsylvania	Y	31070 FQ	36980 MW	45530 TQ	USBLS	5/15
	Allentown-Bethlehem-Easton MSA, PA-NJ	Y	34080 FQ	44040 MW	54040 TQ	USBLS	5/15
	Harrisburg-Carlisle MSA, PA	Y	30030 FQ	37270 MW	44740 TQ	USBLS	5/15
	Montgomery County-Bucks County-Chester County PMSA, PA	Y	34220 FQ	39260 MW	48030 TQ	USBLS	5/15
	Philadelphia PMSA, PA	Y	36190 FQ	43500 MW	54090 TQ	USBLS	5/15
	Pittsburgh MSA, PA	Y	29680 FQ	35080 MW	40890 TQ	USBLS	5/15
	Rhode Island	Y	30090 FQ	37430 MW	44820 TQ	USBLS	5/15
	Providence-Warwick MSA, RI-MA	Y	30320 FQ	36920 MW	44200 TQ	USBLS	5/15
	South Carolina	Y	28980 FQ	35760 MW	44230 TQ	USBLS	5/15
	Charleston-North Charleston MSA, SC	Y	28430 FQ	33850 MW	38020 TQ	USBLS	5/15
	Columbia MSA, SC	Y	32850 FQ	36750 MW	42180 TQ	USBLS	5/15
	Greenville-Anderson-Mauldin MSA, SC	Y	33150 FQ	38620 MW	46260 TQ	USBLS	5/15
	South Dakota	Y	27420 FQ	30530 MW	36230 TQ	USBLS	5/15
	Sioux Falls MSA, SD	Y	27970 FQ	31580 MW	38030 TQ	USBLS	5/15
	Tennessee	Y	29420 FQ	36980 MW	45150 TQ	USBLS	5/15
	Knoxville MSA, TN	Y	23550 FQ	28720 MW	38480 TQ	USBLS	5/15
	Memphis MSA, TN-MS-AR	Y	27110 FQ	35550 MW	44010 TQ	USBLS	5/15
	Nashville-Davidson–Murfreesboro–Franklin MSA, TN	Y	28830 FQ	36960 MW	44410 TQ	USBLS	5/15
	Texas	Y	25330 FQ	32180 MW	38760 TQ	USBLS	5/15
	Austin-Round Rock MSA, TX	Y	27370 FQ	33160 MW	36940 TQ	USBLS	5/15
	Dallas-Plano-Irving PMSA, TX	Y	25590 FQ	31630 MW	41750 TQ	USBLS	5/15
	Fort Worth-Arlington PMSA, TX	Y	23130 FQ	28370 MW	34870 TQ	USBLS	5/15
	Houston-The Woodlands-Sugar Land MSA, TX	Y	28060 FQ	34940 MW	40430 TQ	USBLS	5/15
	San Antonio-New Braunfels MSA, TX	Y	22830 FQ	27670 MW	33920 TQ	USBLS	5/15
	Utah	Y	22160 FQ	28010 MW	36810 TQ	USBLS	5/15
	Ogden-Clearfield MSA, UT	Y	22860 FQ	29450 MW	37050 TQ	USBLS	5/15
	Provo-Orem MSA, UT	Y	23660 FQ	29190 MW	37700 TQ	USBLS	5/15
	Salt Lake City MSA, UT	Y	21250 FQ	24370 MW	35290 TQ	USBLS	5/15
	Vermont	Y	27870 FQ	32560 MW	37440 TQ	USBLS	5/15

Occupation/Type/Industry	Location	Per	Low	Mid	High	Source	Date
Mixing and Blending Machine Setter, Operator, and Tender	Burlington-South Burlington MSA, VT	Y	26730 FQ	31070 MW	35950 TQ	USBLS	5/15
	Virginia	Y	26130 FQ	37060 MW	51810 TQ	USBLS	5/15
	Richmond MSA, VA	Y	24000 FQ	41460 MW	57750 TQ	USBLS	5/15
	Virginia Beach-Norfolk-Newport News MSA, VA-NC	Y	19540 FQ	28380 MW	39260 TQ	USBLS	5/15
	Washington	H	12.51 FQ	16.60 MW	20.53 TQ	WABLS	3/16
	Seattle-Bellevue-Everett PMSA, WA	H	12.14 FQ	16.68 MW	22.09 TQ	WABLS	3/16
	Tacoma-Lakewood PMSA, WA	H	13.72 FQ	16.30 MW	21.23 TQ	WABLS	3/16
	West Virginia	Y	23190 FQ	36420 MW	49120 TQ	USBLS	5/15
	Huntington-Ashland MSA, WV-KY-OH	Y	28000 FQ	32710 MW	39450 TQ	USBLS	5/15
	Wisconsin	Y	28970 FQ	35890 MW	44440 TQ	USBLS	5/15
	Madison MSA, WI	Y	29290 FQ	34740 MW	40320 TQ	USBLS	5/15
	Milwaukee-Waukesha-West Allis MSA, WI	Y	28330 FQ	34820 MW	44620 TQ	USBLS	5/15
	Wyoming	Y	31560 FQ	40130 MW	48740 TQ	USBLS	5/15
	Puerto Rico	Y	19070 FQ	25960 MW	35890 TQ	USBLS	5/15
	San Juan-Carolina-Caguas MSA, PR	Y	19690 FQ	27300 MW	36950 TQ	USBLS	5/15
Mobile Applications Designer	United States	Y	81000 LO		117000 HI	ADAGE02	2015
Mobile Applications Developer	United States	Y	118750 LO		182250 HI	DATAM2	2017
Mobile Heavy Equipment Mechanic							
Except Engines	Alabama	Y	32138 AE	45908 AW	52793 AEX	ALBLS	6/16
Except Engines	Birmingham-Hoover MSA, AL	Y	30989 AE	46081 AW	53627 AEX	ALBLS	6/16
Except Engines	Alaska	Y	54500 FQ	66370 MW	74720 TQ	USBLS	5/15
Except Engines	Anchorage MSA, AK	Y	38700 FQ	65180 MW	76860 TQ	USBLS	5/15
Except Engines	Arizona	Y	39370 FQ	48120 MW	57640 TQ	USBLS	5/15
Except Engines	Phoenix-Mesa-Scottsdale MSA, AZ	Y	39060 FQ	47890 MW	57520 TQ	USBLS	5/15
Except Engines	Tucson MSA, AZ	Y	41810 FQ	49610 MW	58530 TQ	USBLS	5/15
Except Engines	Arkansas	Y	29920 FQ	38320 MW	46550 TQ	USBLS	5/15
Except Engines	Little Rock-North Little Rock-Conway MSA, AR	Y	34510 FQ	41110 MW	47820 TQ	USBLS	5/15
Except Engines	California	H	22.71 FQ	27.74 MW	34.10 TQ	CABLS	1/16-3/16
Except Engines	Anaheim-Santa Ana-Irvine PMSA, CA	H	23.40 FQ	28.57 MW	35.17 TQ	CABLS	1/16-3/16
Except Engines	Los Angeles-Long Beach-Glendale PMSA, CA	H	23.39 FQ	29.42 MW	40.38 TQ	CABLS	1/16-3/16
Except Engines	Oakland-Hayward-Berkeley PMSA, CA	H	28.68 FQ	34.65 MW	40.40 TQ	CABLS	1/16-3/16
Except Engines	Riverside-San Bernardino-Ontario MSA, CA	H	19.94 FQ	26.60 MW	30.00 TQ	CABLS	1/16-3/16
Except Engines	Sacramento–Roseville–Arden-Arcade MSA, CA	H	22.13 FQ	25.62 MW	30.36 TQ	CABLS	1/16-3/16
Except Engines	San Diego-Carlsbad MSA, CA	H	22.92 FQ	26.31 MW	29.06 TQ	CABLS	1/16-3/16
Except Engines	San Francisco-Redwood City-South San Francisco PMSA, CA	H	26.55 FQ	34.86 MW	52.45 TQ	CABLS	1/16-3/16
Except Engines	Colorado	Y	38640 FQ	48430 MW	58400 TQ	USBLS	5/15
Except Engines	Denver-Aurora-Lakewood MSA, CO	Y	37990 FQ	48880 MW	58730 TQ	USBLS	5/15
Except Engines	Connecticut	Y		56615 MW		CTBLS	1/16-3/16
Except Engines	Bridgeport-Stamford-Norwalk MSA, CT	Y	44250 FQ	54340 MW	66270 TQ	USBLS	5/15
Except Engines	Hartford-West Hartford-East Hartford MSA, CT	Y	51160 FQ	57980 MW	66450 TQ	USBLS	5/15
Except Engines	Delaware	Y	37340 FQ	48970 MW	58450 TQ	USBLS	5/15
Except Engines	Wilmington PMSA, DE-MD-NJ	Y	38580 FQ	50190 MW	60060 TQ	USBLS	5/15
Except Engines	District of Columbia	Y	50890 FQ	67770 MW	82940 TQ	USBLS	5/15
Except Engines	Washington-Arlington-Alexandria PMSA, DC-VA-MD-WV	Y	41630 FQ	53760 MW	64920 TQ	USBLS	5/15
Except Engines	Florida	H	15.31 AE	20.67 MW	24.42 AEX	FLBLS	7/16-9/16

AE Average entry wage	**AWR** Average wage range	**H** Hourly	**LR** Low end range	**MTC** Median total compensation	**TCC** Total cash compensation
AEX Average experienced wage	**B** Biweekly	**HI** Highest wage paid	**M** Monthly	**MCC** Median cash compensation	**TQ** Third quartile wage
ATC Average total compensation	**D** Daily	**HR** High end range	**MCC** Median cash compensation	**MWR** Median wage range	**W** Weekly
AW Average wage paid	**FQ** First quartile wage	**LO** Lowest wage paid	**ME** Median entry wage	**S** See annotated source	**Y** Yearly

Occupation/Type/Industry	Location	Per	Low	Mid	High	Source	Date
Mobile Heavy Equipment							
Mechanic							
Except Engines	Fort Lauderdale-Pompano Beach-Deerfield Beach PMSA, FL	H	16.67 AE	21.62 MW	25.70 AEX	FLBLS	7/16-9/16
Except Engines	Miami-Miami Beach-Kendall PMSA, FL	H	15.71 AE	23.26 MW	27.45 AEX	FLBLS	7/16-9/16
Except Engines	Orlando-Kissimmee-Sanford MSA, FL	H	16.39 AE	20.58 MW	23.86 AEX	FLBLS	7/16-9/16
Except Engines	Tampa-St. Petersburg-Clearwater MSA, FL	H	13.56 AE	18.56 MW	21.88 AEX	FLBLS	7/16-9/16
Except Engines	Georgia	Y	35580 FQ	45330 MW	55860 TQ	USBLS	5/15
Except Engines	Atlanta-Sandy Springs-Roswell MSA, GA	Y	36000 FQ	45300 MW	57180 TQ	USBLS	5/15
Except Engines	Augusta-Richmond County MSA, GA-SC	Y	51550 FQ	64930 MW	72070 TQ	USBLS	5/15
Except Engines	Hawaii	Y	52810 FQ	63950 MW	71100 TQ	USBLS	5/15
Except Engines	Urban Honolulu MSA, HI	Y	60270 FQ	69200 MW	74790 TQ	USBLS	5/15
Except Engines	Idaho	Y	36520 FQ	46580 MW	57610 TQ	USBLS	5/15
Except Engines	Boise City MSA, ID	Y	39450 FQ	50980 MW	57120 TQ	USBLS	5/15
Except Engines	Illinois	Y	40580 FQ	55440 MW	72540 TQ	USBLS	5/15
Except Engines	Chicago-Naperville-Arlington Heights PMSA, IL	Y	46820 FQ	64730 MW	85470 TQ	USBLS	5/15
Except Engines	Lake County-Kenosha County PMSA, IL-WI	Y	53110 FQ	59510 MW	74010 TQ	USBLS	5/15
Except Engines	Indiana	Y	36450 FQ	45940 MW	57350 TQ	USBLS	5/15
Except Engines	Gary PMSA, IN	Y	40720 FQ	50950 MW	70090 TQ	USBLS	5/15
Except Engines	Indianapolis-Carmel-Anderson MSA, IN	Y	35840 FQ	45610 MW	58210 TQ	USBLS	5/15
Except Engines	Iowa	Y	38180 FQ	46110 MW	54980 TQ	USBLS	5/15
Except Engines	Des Moines-West Des Moines MSA, IA	Y	37130 FQ	47400 MW	56650 TQ	USBLS	5/15
Except Engines	Kansas	Y	36680 FQ	45700 MW	56810 TQ	USBLS	5/15
Except Engines	Wichita MSA, KS	Y	38620 FQ	52320 MW	62700 TQ	USBLS	5/15
Except Engines	Kentucky	Y	38140 FQ	45620 MW	54280 TQ	USBLS	5/15
Except Engines	Louisville-Jefferson County MSA, KY-IN	Y	39100 FQ	47500 MW	55730 TQ	USBLS	5/15
Except Engines	Louisiana	Y	32840 FQ	42430 MW	54780 TQ	USBLS	5/15
Except Engines	Baton Rouge MSA, LA	Y	33380 FQ	38410 MW	53460 TQ	USBLS	5/15
Except Engines	New Orleans-Metairie MSA, LA	Y	32170 FQ	44980 MW	55010 TQ	USBLS	5/15
Except Engines	Maine	Y	36510 FQ	42900 MW	51040 TQ	USBLS	5/15
Except Engines	Portland-South Portland MSA, ME	Y	42230 FQ	48950 MW	59170 TQ	USBLS	5/15
Except Engines	Maryland	Y	36426 AE	50293 MW	57227 AEX	MDBLS	4/16
Except Engines	Baltimore-Columbia-Towson MSA, MD	Y	42880 FQ	50830 MW	59550 TQ	USBLS	5/15
Except Engines	Salisbury MSA, MD-DE	Y	36990 FQ	48130 MW	57170 TQ	USBLS	5/15
Except Engines	Massachusetts	Y	48280 FQ	58400 MW	75810 TQ	USBLS	5/15
Except Engines	Worcester MSA, MA-CT	Y	49420 FQ	58400 MW	72660 TQ	USBLS	5/15
Except Engines	Michigan	Y	37870 FQ	46390 MW	56110 TQ	USBLS	5/15
Except Engines	Detroit-Dearborn-Livonia PMSA, MI	Y	44800 FQ	53740 MW	59780 TQ	USBLS	5/15
Except Engines	Grand Rapids-Wyoming MSA, MI	Y	41620 FQ	45970 MW	50320 TQ	USBLS	5/15
Except Engines	Minnesota	Y	45959 FQ	54950 MW	61678 TQ	MNBLS	1/16-3/16
Except Engines	Minneapolis-St. Paul-Bloomington MSA, MN-WI	Y	48976 FQ	56448 MW	64232 TQ	MNBLS	1/16-3/16
Except Engines	Mississippi	Y	35170 FQ	43490 MW	50530 TQ	USBLS	5/15
Except Engines	Jackson MSA, MS	Y	33670 FQ	43670 MW	51410 TQ	USBLS	5/15
Except Engines	Missouri	Y	41100 FQ	49410 MW	58140 TQ	USBLS	5/15
Except Engines	Kansas City MSA, MO-KS	Y	42330 FQ	48830 MW	60550 TQ	USBLS	5/15
Except Engines	St. Louis MSA, MO-IL	Y	44550 FQ	52740 MW	58450 TQ	USBLS	5/15
Except Engines	Montana	Y	40650 FQ	52560 MW	61520 TQ	USBLS	5/15
Except Engines	Billings MSA, MT	Y	43670 FQ	53120 MW	63530 TQ	USBLS	5/15
Except Engines	Nebraska	Y	38295 FQ	46390 MW	54485 TQ	NEBLS	7/16-9/16
Except Engines	Omaha-Council Bluffs MSA, NE-IA	Y	43040 FQ	49735 MW	57125 TQ	NEBLS	7/16-9/16
Except Engines	Nevada	Y	50580 FQ	64040 MW	72600 TQ	USBLS	5/15
Except Engines	Las Vegas-Henderson-Paradise MSA, NV	Y	44050 FQ	57020 MW	67430 TQ	USBLS	5/15
Except Engines	New Hampshire	H	17.91 AE	22.64 MW	25.98 AEX	NHBLS	6/16

AE	Average entry wage	AWR	Average wage range	H	Hourly	LR	Low end range	MTC	Median total compensation	TCC	Total cash compensation
AEX	Average experienced wage	B	Biweekly	HI	Highest wage paid	M	Monthly	MW	Median wage paid	TQ	Third quartile wage
ATC	Average total compensation	D	Daily	HR	High end range	MCC	Median cash compensation	MWR	Median wage range	W	Weekly
AW	Average wage paid	FQ	First quartile wage	LO	Lowest wage paid	ME	Median entry wage	S	See annotated source	Y	Yearly

Occupation/Type/Industry	Location	Per	Low	Mid	High	Source	Date
Mobile Heavy Equipment Mechanic							
Except Engines	Manchester NECTA, NH	H	18.14 AE	23.54 MW	27.57 AEX	NHBLS	6/16
Except Engines	Nashua NECTA, NH-MA	Y	38140 FQ	46980 MW	56200 TQ	USBLS	5/15
Except Engines	New Jersey	Y	44670 FQ	55220 MW	64310 TQ	USBLS	5/15
Except Engines	Camden PMSA, NJ	Y	48460 FQ	57170 MW	63130 TQ	USBLS	5/15
Except Engines	Newark PMSA, NJ-PA	Y	45780 FQ	56760 MW	67220 TQ	USBLS	5/15
Except Engines	Trenton MSA, NJ	Y	41660 FQ	48140 MW	58300 TQ	USBLS	5/15
Except Engines	New Mexico	Y	39710 FQ	47850 MW	58060 TQ	USBLS	5/15
Except Engines	Albuquerque MSA, NM	Y	41260 FQ	48670 MW	58200 TQ	USBLS	5/15
Except Engines	New York	Y	38190 AE	50680 MW	60430 AEX	NYBLS	1/16-3/16
Except Engines	Buffalo-Cheektowaga-Niagara Falls MSA, NY	Y	40140 FQ	47570 MW	57060 TQ	USBLS	5/15
Except Engines	Nassau County-Suffolk County PMSA, NY	Y	44920 FQ	55860 MW	71080 TQ	USBLS	5/15
Except Engines	New York-Jersey City-White Plains PMSA, NY-NJ	Y	46600 FQ	56860 MW	67280 TQ	USBLS	5/15
Except Engines	Rochester MSA, NY	Y	37940 FQ	44270 MW	50030 TQ	USBLS	5/15
Except Engines	North Carolina	Y	34750 FQ	42480 MW	50030 TQ	USBLS	5/15
Except Engines	Charlotte-Concord-Gastonia MSA, NC-SC	Y	34760 FQ	42760 MW	49380 TQ	USBLS	5/15
Except Engines	Raleigh MSA, NC	Y	36240 FQ	43540 MW	51310 TQ	USBLS	5/15
Except Engines	North Dakota	Y	46570 FQ	58410 MW	84490 TQ	USBLS	5/15
Except Engines	Fargo MSA, ND-MN	Y	37430 FQ	47020 MW	59290 TQ	USBLS	5/15
Except Engines	Ohio	Y	38400 FQ	47480 MW	58000 TQ	USBLS	5/15
Except Engines	Cincinnati MSA, OH-KY-IN	Y	36210 FQ	44790 MW	54330 TQ	USBLS	5/15
Except Engines	Cleveland-Elyria MSA, OH	Y	42810 FQ	54100 MW	65910 TQ	USBLS	5/15
Except Engines	Columbus MSA, OH	Y	39120 FQ	48330 MW	58010 TQ	USBLS	5/15
Except Engines	Toledo MSA, OH	Y	52850 FQ	61020 MW	68440 TQ	USBLS	5/15
Except Engines	Oklahoma	Y	34280 FQ	41920 MW	51890 TQ	USBLS	5/15
Except Engines	Oklahoma City MSA, OK	Y	34400 FQ	43750 MW	54430 TQ	USBLS	5/15
Except Engines	Tulsa MSA, OK	Y	35500 FQ	42350 MW	49860 TQ	USBLS	5/15
Except Engines	Oregon	H	20.28 FQ	24.23 MW	28.36 TQ	ORBLS	2016
Except Engines	Portland-Vancouver-Hillsboro MSA, OR-WA	Y	41590 FQ	50550 MW	58630 TQ	USBLS	5/15
Except Engines	Pennsylvania	Y	40450 FQ	49250 MW	57780 TQ	USBLS	5/15
Except Engines	Allentown-Bethlehem-Easton MSA, PA-NJ	Y	37700 FQ	44550 MW	50770 TQ	USBLS	5/15
Except Engines	Harrisburg-Carlisle MSA, PA	Y	45210 FQ	51330 MW	58470 TQ	USBLS	5/15
Except Engines	Montgomery County-Bucks County-Chester County PMSA, PA	Y	42550 FQ	52690 MW	63150 TQ	USBLS	5/15
Except Engines	Philadelphia PMSA, PA	Y	50740 FQ	56370 MW	61950 TQ	USBLS	5/15
Except Engines	Pittsburgh MSA, PA	Y	39560 FQ	49770 MW	58660 TQ	USBLS	5/15
Except Engines	Rhode Island	Y	46520 FQ	53230 MW	59350 TQ	USBLS	5/15
Except Engines	Providence-Warwick MSA, RI-MA	Y	45180 FQ	52840 MW	59290 TQ	USBLS	5/15
Except Engines	South Carolina	Y	38170 FQ	48380 MW	59330 TQ	USBLS	5/15
Except Engines	Charleston-North Charleston MSA, SC	Y	37360 FQ	45910 MW	54810 TQ	USBLS	5/15
Except Engines	Columbia MSA, SC	Y	38140 FQ	47500 MW	55460 TQ	USBLS	5/15
Except Engines	Greenville-Anderson-Mauldin MSA, SC	Y	35390 FQ	44740 MW	54090 TQ	USBLS	5/15
Except Engines	South Dakota	Y	40620 FQ	48390 MW	58330 TQ	USBLS	5/15
Except Engines	Sioux Falls MSA, SD	Y	38750 FQ	47190 MW	55230 TQ	USBLS	5/15
Except Engines	Tennessee	Y	34040 FQ	41460 MW	49930 TQ	USBLS	5/15
Except Engines	Knoxville MSA, TN	Y	35740 FQ	45480 MW	55450 TQ	USBLS	5/15
Except Engines	Memphis MSA, TN-MS-AR	Y	34590 FQ	43030 MW	51480 TQ	USBLS	5/15
Except Engines	Nashville-Davidson–Murfreesboro–Franklin MSA, TN	Y	34570 FQ	42000 MW	50080 TQ	USBLS	5/15
Except Engines	Texas	Y	38920 FQ	47640 MW	56610 TQ	USBLS	5/15
Except Engines	Austin-Round Rock MSA, TX	Y	34100 FQ	40480 MW	49210 TQ	USBLS	5/15
Except Engines	Dallas-Plano-Irving PMSA, TX	Y	37350 FQ	45890 MW	55770 TQ	USBLS	5/15
Except Engines	Fort Worth-Arlington PMSA, TX	Y	38600 FQ	47180 MW	56570 TQ	USBLS	5/15
Except Engines	Houston-The Woodlands-Sugar Land MSA, TX	Y	41290 FQ	50900 MW	59200 TQ	USBLS	5/15
Except Engines	San Antonio-New Braunfels MSA, TX	Y	37620 FQ	44530 MW	50290 TQ	USBLS	5/15
Except Engines	Utah	Y	42230 FQ	51860 MW	60070 TQ	USBLS	5/15
Except Engines	Ogden-Clearfield MSA, UT	Y	37610 FQ	47510 MW	56550 TQ	USBLS	5/15

AE	Average entry wage	AWR	Average wage range	H	Hourly
AEX	Average experienced wage	B	Biweekly	HI	Highest wage paid
ATC	Average total compensation	D	Daily	HR	High end range
AW	Average wage paid	FQ	First quartile wage	LO	Lowest wage paid

LR	Low end range	MTC	Median total compensation
M	Monthly	MW	Median wage paid
MCC	Median cash compensation	MWR	Median wage range
ME	Median entry wage	S	See annotated source

TCC	Total cash compensation		
TQ	Third quartile wage		
W	Weekly		
Y	Yearly		

Occupation/Type/Industry	Location	Per	Low	Mid	High	Source	Date
Mobile Heavy Equipment Mechanic							
Except Engines	Provo-Orem MSA, UT	Y	39070 FQ	46290 MW	58510 TQ	USBLS	5/15
Except Engines	Salt Lake City MSA, UT	Y	44650 FQ	53750 MW	61960 TQ	USBLS	5/15
Except Engines	Vermont	Y	34840 FQ	42620 MW	50430 TQ	USBLS	5/15
Except Engines	Burlington-South Burlington MSA, VT	Y	38850 FQ	47060 MW	57580 TQ	USBLS	5/15
Except Engines	Virginia	Y	38940 FQ	46800 MW	55970 TQ	USBLS	5/15
Except Engines	Richmond MSA, VA	Y	40520 FQ	48420 MW	57340 TQ	USBLS	5/15
Except Engines	Virginia Beach-Norfolk-Newport News MSA, VA-NC	Y	42440 FQ	48790 MW	57340 TQ	USBLS	5/15
Except Engines	Washington	H	19.33 FQ	25.49 MW	31.63 TQ	WABLS	3/16
Except Engines	Seattle-Bellevue-Everett PMSA, WA	H	18.30 FQ	24.29 MW	32.14 TQ	WABLS	3/16
Except Engines	Tacoma-Lakewood PMSA, WA	H	24.10 FQ	29.18 MW	32.69 TQ	WABLS	3/16
Except Engines	West Virginia	Y	35350 FQ	44710 MW	55620 TQ	USBLS	5/15
Except Engines	Huntington-Ashland MSA, WV-KY-OH	Y	25220 FQ	36980 MW	46780 TQ	USBLS	5/15
Except Engines	Wisconsin	Y	40640 FQ	47600 MW	56820 TQ	USBLS	5/15
Except Engines	Madison MSA, WI	Y	42760 FQ	48690 MW	56120 TQ	USBLS	5/15
Except Engines	Milwaukee-Waukesha-West Allis MSA, WI	Y	41430 FQ	50580 MW	60010 TQ	USBLS	5/15
Except Engines	Wyoming	Y	47610 FQ	60140 MW	72070 TQ	USBLS	5/15
Except Engines	Cheyenne MSA, WY	Y	48370 FQ	54920 MW	62600 TQ	USBLS	5/15
Except Engines	Puerto Rico	Y	19370 FQ	26090 MW	31440 TQ	USBLS	5/15
Except Engines	San Juan-Carolina-Caguas MSA, PR	Y	20640 FQ	26350 MW	30890 TQ	USBLS	5/15
Except Engines	Guam	Y	31360 FQ	40530 MW	46030 TQ	USBLS	5/15
Mobile Specialist/Technologist	United States	Y		83900 AW		CWRLD3	2016
Model	Arizona	Y	33570 FQ	37520 MW	44020 TQ	USBLS	5/15
	California	H	13.71 FQ	20.38 MW	24.61 TQ	CABLS	1/16-3/16
	Florida	H	8.90 AE	9.75 MW	42.44 AEX	FLBLS	7/16-9/16
	Idaho	Y	25150 FQ	28890 MW	33700 TQ	USBLS	5/15
	Illinois	Y	31540 FQ	42710 MW	49110 TQ	USBLS	5/15
	Iowa	Y	16920 FQ	18020 MW	19110 TQ	USBLS	5/15
	Kentucky	Y	32660 FQ	35800 MW	38950 TQ	USBLS	5/15
	Missouri	Y	26950 FQ	29210 MW	32000 TQ	USBLS	5/15
	New York	Y	19100 AE	37600 MW	67860 AEX	NYBLS	1/16-3/16
	Ohio	Y	32060 FQ	41850 MW	46430 TQ	USBLS	5/15
	Oregon	H	15.04 FQ	17.00 MW	18.84 TQ	ORBLS	2016
	Pennsylvania	Y	36020 FQ	42790 MW	47300 TQ	USBLS	5/15
	Texas	Y	16700 FQ	18140 MW	21060 TQ	USBLS	5/15
	Washington	H	12.95 FQ	16.44 MW	18.52 TQ	WABLS	3/16
	Wisconsin	Y	30240 FQ	39180 MW	57010 TQ	USBLS	5/15
Model Maker							
Metals and Plastics	Alabama	Y	28564 AE	40625 AW	46660 AEX	ALBLS	6/16
Metals and Plastics	California	H	18.19 FQ	22.77 MW	29.64 TQ	CABLS	1/16-3/16
Metals and Plastics	Anaheim-Santa Ana-Irvine PMSA, CA	H	19.03 FQ	22.42 MW	30.39 TQ	CABLS	1/16-3/16
Metals and Plastics	Los Angeles-Long Beach-Glendale PMSA, CA	H	18.00 FQ	23.32 MW	29.78 TQ	CABLS	1/16-3/16
Metals and Plastics	Oakland-Hayward-Berkeley PMSA, CA	H	16.12 FQ	19.20 MW	28.26 TQ	CABLS	1/16-3/16
Metals and Plastics	Sacramento–Roseville–Arden-Arcade MSA, CA	H	17.95 FQ	20.15 MW	23.83 TQ	CABLS	1/16-3/16
Metals and Plastics	San Diego-Carlsbad MSA, CA	H	18.10 FQ	27.23 MW	34.99 TQ	CABLS	1/16-3/16
Metals and Plastics	San Francisco-Redwood City-South San Francisco PMSA, CA	H	23.08 FQ	42.26 MW	47.50 TQ	CABLS	1/16-3/16
Metals and Plastics	Colorado	Y	44540 FQ	57720 MW	66830 TQ	USBLS	5/15
Metals and Plastics	Denver-Aurora-Lakewood MSA, CO	Y	53060 FQ	61550 MW	69860 TQ	USBLS	5/15
Metals and Plastics	Connecticut	Y		50476 MW		CTBLS	1/16-3/16
Metals and Plastics	Hartford-West Hartford-East Hartford MSA, CT	Y	47290 FQ	56790 MW	66610 TQ	USBLS	5/15
Metals and Plastics	Florida	H	15.96 AE	21.24 MW	26.73 AEX	FLBLS	7/16-9/16
Metals and Plastics	Fort Lauderdale-Pompano Beach-Deerfield Beach PMSA, FL	H	15.33 AE	18.74 MW	21.66 AEX	FLBLS	7/16-9/16

Model Maker

Occupation/Type/Industry	Location	Per	Low	Mid	High	Source	Date
Model Maker							
Metals and Plastics	Illinois	Y	34740 FQ	45320 MW	58420 TQ	USBLS	5/15
Metals and Plastics	Chicago-Naperville-Arlington Heights PMSA, IL	Y	32760 FQ	46330 MW	60960 TQ	USBLS	5/15
Metals and Plastics	Indiana	Y	31750 FQ	39250 MW	48970 TQ	USBLS	5/15
Metals and Plastics	Indianapolis-Carmel-Anderson MSA, IN	Y	31550 FQ	38770 MW	50220 TQ	USBLS	5/15
Metals and Plastics	Iowa	Y	36380 FQ	42750 MW	49640 TQ	USBLS	5/15
Metals and Plastics	Kansas	Y	22550 FQ	27360 MW	60020 TQ	USBLS	5/15
Metals and Plastics	Kentucky	Y	23340 FQ	30640 MW	48040 TQ	USBLS	5/15
Metals and Plastics	Baltimore-Columbia-Towson MSA, MD	Y	45330 FQ	50240 MW	61760 TQ	USBLS	5/15
Metals and Plastics	Massachusetts	Y	42190 FQ	55600 MW	69540 TQ	USBLS	5/15
Metals and Plastics	Boston-Cambridge-Newton NECTA, MA	Y	59620 FQ	70510 MW	80680 TQ	USBLS	5/15
Metals and Plastics	Michigan	Y	50930 FQ	66320 MW	74730 TQ	USBLS	5/15
Metals and Plastics	Detroit-Dearborn-Livonia PMSA, MI	Y	49500 FQ	71210 MW	82490 TQ	USBLS	5/15
Metals and Plastics	Minnesota	Y	30282 FQ	40164 MW	54935 TQ	MNBLS	1/16-3/16
Metals and Plastics	Minneapolis-St. Paul-Bloomington MSA, MN-WI	Y	39809 FQ	54024 MW	71367 TQ	MNBLS	1/16-3/16
Metals and Plastics	Mississippi	Y	28500 FQ	32720 MW	36510 TQ	USBLS	5/15
Metals and Plastics	Missouri	Y	33390 FQ	45590 MW	56140 TQ	USBLS	5/15
Metals and Plastics	St. Louis MSA, MO-IL	Y	42160 FQ	53210 MW	61780 TQ	USBLS	5/15
Metals and Plastics	New Jersey	Y	40960 FQ	49380 MW	64290 TQ	USBLS	5/15
Metals and Plastics	Camden PMSA, NJ	Y	46690 FQ	56210 MW	70260 TQ	USBLS	5/15
Metals and Plastics	Newark PMSA, NJ-PA	Y	37030 FQ	46680 MW	60780 TQ	USBLS	5/15
Metals and Plastics	New Mexico	Y	48430 FQ	53610 MW	58400 TQ	USBLS	5/15
Metals and Plastics	New York	Y	36220 AE	48250 MW	59740 AEX	NYBLS	1/16-3/16
Metals and Plastics	New York-Jersey City-White Plains PMSA, NY-NJ	Y	39700 FQ	47290 MW	61810 TQ	USBLS	5/15
Metals and Plastics	Rochester MSA, NY	Y	30960 FQ	48370 MW	58360 TQ	USBLS	5/15
Metals and Plastics	North Carolina	Y	30740 FQ	39330 MW	53020 TQ	USBLS	5/15
Metals and Plastics	Charlotte-Concord-Gastonia MSA, NC-SC	Y	32990 FQ	42820 MW	52660 TQ	USBLS	5/15
Metals and Plastics	Ohio	Y	35910 FQ	45400 MW	63070 TQ	USBLS	5/15
Metals and Plastics	Cincinnati MSA, OH-KY-IN	Y	36950 FQ	52460 MW	69490 TQ	USBLS	5/15
Metals and Plastics	Cleveland-Elyria MSA, OH	Y	47660 FQ	68870 MW	78390 TQ	USBLS	5/15
Metals and Plastics	Oregon	H	26.40 FQ	32.57 MW	36.42 TQ	ORBLS	2016
Metals and Plastics	Pennsylvania	Y	37270 FQ	51470 MW	60790 TQ	USBLS	5/15
Metals and Plastics	Montgomery County-Bucks County-Chester County PMSA, PA	Y	55810 FQ	66720 MW	74720 TQ	USBLS	5/15
Metals and Plastics	Pittsburgh MSA, PA	Y	41190 FQ	52960 MW	60000 TQ	USBLS	5/15
Metals and Plastics	Rhode Island	Y	27560 FQ	30180 MW	44940 TQ	USBLS	5/15
Metals and Plastics	Providence-Warwick MSA, RI-MA	Y	29190 FQ	40690 MW	49630 TQ	USBLS	5/15
Metals and Plastics	South Carolina	Y	22940 FQ	27550 MW	34570 TQ	USBLS	5/15
Metals and Plastics	Memphis MSA, TN-MS-AR	Y	33170 FQ	35380 MW	37600 TQ	USBLS	5/15
Metals and Plastics	Texas	Y	34800 FQ	43190 MW	56530 TQ	USBLS	5/15
Metals and Plastics	Houston-The Woodlands-Sugar Land MSA, TX	Y	36680 FQ	43610 MW	51800 TQ	USBLS	5/15
Metals and Plastics	Utah	Y	34160 FQ	41960 MW	49070 TQ	USBLS	5/15
Metals and Plastics	Vermont	Y	40770 FQ	44060 MW	47350 TQ	USBLS	5/15
Metals and Plastics	Virginia	Y	33670 FQ	48900 MW	64800 TQ	USBLS	5/15
Metals and Plastics	Washington	H	20.54 FQ	29.81 MW	44.06 TQ	WABLS	3/16
Metals and Plastics	Seattle-Bellevue-Everett PMSA, WA	H	23.36 FQ	40.91 MW	46.35 TQ	WABLS	3/16
Metals and Plastics	Tacoma-Lakewood PMSA, WA	H	22.21 FQ	24.92 MW	30.97 TQ	WABLS	3/16
Metals and Plastics	Wisconsin	Y	41350 FQ	52120 MW	60570 TQ	USBLS	5/15
Metals and Plastics	Milwaukee-Waukesha-West Allis MSA, WI	Y	50450 FQ	56890 MW	63970 TQ	USBLS	5/15
Wood	California	H	14.53 FQ	19.03 MW	27.38 TQ	CABLS	1/16-3/16
Wood	Los Angeles-Long Beach-Glendale PMSA, CA	H	11.91 FQ	16.29 MW	26.54 TQ	CABLS	1/16-3/16
Wood	Georgia	Y	23130 FQ	35490 MW	53010 TQ	USBLS	5/15
Wood	Illinois	Y	26640 FQ	28850 MW	31050 TQ	USBLS	5/15
Wood	Chicago-Naperville-Arlington Heights PMSA, IL	Y	26720 FQ	28670 MW	30620 TQ	USBLS	5/15
Wood	New York	Y	29820 AE	44440 MW	59130 AEX	NYBLS	1/16-3/16
Wood	North Carolina	Y	30340 FQ	35600 MW	41060 TQ	USBLS	5/15
Wood	Pennsylvania	Y	25020 FQ	31290 MW	36750 TQ	USBLS	5/15

Occupation/Type/Industry	Location	Per	Low	Mid	High	Source	Date
Model Maker							
Wood	South Carolina	Y	19230 FQ	22850 MW	29420 TQ	USBLS	5/15
Wood	Tennessee	Y	22440 FQ	26610 MW	36620 TQ	USBLS	5/15
Molder, Shaper, and Caster							
Except Metals and Plastics	Alabama	Y	18107 AE	26199 AW	30250 AEX	ALBLS	6/16
Except Metals and Plastics	Birmingham-Hoover MSA, AL	Y	24071 AE	31011 AW	34486 AEX	ALBLS	6/16
Except Metals and Plastics	Alaska	Y	34130 FQ	43030 MW	54840 TQ	USBLS	5/15
Except Metals and Plastics	Anchorage MSA, AK	Y	35030 FQ	46100 MW	55800 TQ	USBLS	5/15
Except Metals and Plastics	Arizona	Y	25900 FQ	29820 MW	35240 TQ	USBLS	5/15
Except Metals and Plastics	Phoenix-Mesa-Scottsdale MSA, AZ	Y	26580 FQ	29970 MW	34700 TQ	USBLS	5/15
Except Metals and Plastics	Arkansas	Y	21720 FQ	25640 MW	30270 TQ	USBLS	5/15
Except Metals and Plastics	California	H	11.14 FQ	14.01 MW	17.92 TQ	CABLS	1/16-3/16
Except Metals and Plastics	Anaheim-Santa Ana-Irvine PMSA, CA	H	11.62 FQ	16.05 MW	20.84 TQ	CABLS	1/16-3/16
Except Metals and Plastics	Los Angeles-Long Beach-Glendale PMSA, CA	H	9.97 FQ	11.94 MW	14.68 TQ	CABLS	1/16-3/16
Except Metals and Plastics	Oakland-Hayward-Berkeley PMSA, CA	H	9.50 FQ	14.48 MW	18.02 TQ	CABLS	1/16-3/16
Except Metals and Plastics	Riverside-San Bernardino-Ontario MSA, CA	H	11.01 FQ	14.40 MW	18.70 TQ	CABLS	1/16-3/16
Except Metals and Plastics	Sacramento–Roseville–Arden-Arcade MSA, CA	H	13.23 FQ	17.30 MW	21.61 TQ	CABLS	1/16-3/16
Except Metals and Plastics	San Diego-Carlsbad MSA, CA	H	12.78 FQ	14.59 MW	17.29 TQ	CABLS	1/16-3/16
Except Metals and Plastics	San Francisco-Redwood City-South San Francisco PMSA, CA	H	13.16 FQ	14.36 MW	19.87 TQ	CABLS	1/16-3/16
Except Metals and Plastics	Colorado	Y	26750 FQ	31060 MW	42620 TQ	USBLS	5/15
Except Metals and Plastics	Denver-Aurora-Lakewood MSA, CO	Y	27280 FQ	31070 MW	50960 TQ	USBLS	5/15
Except Metals and Plastics	Connecticut	Y		39932 MW		CTBLS	1/16-3/16
Except Metals and Plastics	Hartford-West Hartford-East Hartford MSA, CT	Y	23040 FQ	31110 MW	36200 TQ	USBLS	5/15
Except Metals and Plastics	Delaware	Y	32220 FQ	35040 MW	37850 TQ	USBLS	5/15
Except Metals and Plastics	Wilmington PMSA, DE-MD-NJ	Y	27480 FQ	31980 MW	37880 TQ	USBLS	5/15
Except Metals and Plastics	Washington-Arlington-Alexandria PMSA, DC-VA-MD-WV	Y	28310 FQ	34780 MW	42140 TQ	USBLS	5/15
Except Metals and Plastics	Florida	H	10.46 AE	13.69 MW	16.71 AEX	FLBLS	7/16-9/16
Except Metals and Plastics	Fort Lauderdale-Pompano Beach-Deerfield Beach PMSA, FL	H	9.35 AE	15.57 MW	18.66 AEX	FLBLS	7/16-9/16
Except Metals and Plastics	Miami-Miami Beach-Kendall PMSA, FL	H	9.69 AE	13.81 MW	15.63 AEX	FLBLS	7/16-9/16
Except Metals and Plastics	Orlando-Kissimmee-Sanford MSA, FL	H	11.27 AE	14.51 MW	17.06 AEX	FLBLS	7/16-9/16
Except Metals and Plastics	Tampa-St. Petersburg-Clearwater MSA, FL	H	10.55 AE	11.50 MW	12.48 AEX	FLBLS	7/16-9/16
Except Metals and Plastics	Georgia	Y	22660 FQ	28420 MW	37900 TQ	USBLS	5/15
Except Metals and Plastics	Atlanta-Sandy Springs-Roswell MSA, GA	Y	23500 FQ	29240 MW	37840 TQ	USBLS	5/15
Except Metals and Plastics	Hawaii	Y	29830 FQ	35250 MW	43640 TQ	USBLS	5/15
Except Metals and Plastics	Urban Honolulu MSA, HI	Y	29970 FQ	35750 MW	43780 TQ	USBLS	5/15
Except Metals and Plastics	Idaho	Y	20040 FQ	32580 MW	36710 TQ	USBLS	5/15
Except Metals and Plastics	Boise City MSA, ID	Y	32690 FQ	35160 MW	37640 TQ	USBLS	5/15
Except Metals and Plastics	Illinois	Y	22980 FQ	31780 MW	45560 TQ	USBLS	5/15
Except Metals and Plastics	Chicago-Naperville-Arlington Heights PMSA, IL	Y	26100 FQ	38590 MW	52640 TQ	USBLS	5/15
Except Metals and Plastics	Lake County-Kenosha County PMSA, IL-WI	Y	19550 FQ	30250 MW	38570 TQ	USBLS	5/15
Except Metals and Plastics	Indiana	Y	20520 FQ	25410 MW	35120 TQ	USBLS	5/15
Except Metals and Plastics	Gary PMSA, IN	Y	20350 FQ	25130 MW	44980 TQ	USBLS	5/15
Except Metals and Plastics	Indianapolis-Carmel-Anderson MSA, IN	Y	22750 FQ	27450 MW	36040 TQ	USBLS	5/15
Except Metals and Plastics	Iowa	Y	27180 FQ	33610 MW	38420 TQ	USBLS	5/15
Except Metals and Plastics	Des Moines-West Des Moines MSA, IA	Y	26730 FQ	29860 MW	36040 TQ	USBLS	5/15
Except Metals and Plastics	Kansas	Y	24000 FQ	28970 MW	34540 TQ	USBLS	5/15
Except Metals and Plastics	Wichita MSA, KS	Y	26210 FQ	30210 MW	35030 TQ	USBLS	5/15
Except Metals and Plastics	Kentucky	Y	21910 FQ	26710 MW	33000 TQ	USBLS	5/15

Occupation/Type/Industry	Location	Per	Low	Mid	High	Source	Date
Molder, Shaper, and Caster							
Except Metals and Plastics	Louisville-Jefferson County MSA, KY-IN	Y	18270 FQ	22600 MW	27750 TQ	USBLS	5/15
Except Metals and Plastics	Louisiana	Y	31780 FQ	38520 MW	44330 TQ	USBLS	5/15
Except Metals and Plastics	Maine	Y	25980 FQ	29810 MW	34950 TQ	USBLS	5/15
Except Metals and Plastics	Maryland	Y	20007 AE	31296 MW	36940 AEX	MDBLS	4/16
Except Metals and Plastics	Baltimore-Columbia-Towson MSA, MD	Y	20590 FQ	24970 MW	31420 TQ	USBLS	5/15
Except Metals and Plastics	Salisbury MSA, MD-DE	Y	31830 FQ	34570 MW	37310 TQ	USBLS	5/15
Except Metals and Plastics	Massachusetts	Y	23580 FQ	34960 MW	46750 TQ	USBLS	5/15
Except Metals and Plastics	Boston-Cambridge-Newton NECTA, MA	Y	32670 FQ	41980 MW	46920 TQ	USBLS	5/15
Except Metals and Plastics	Worcester MSA, MA-CT	Y	31620 FQ	38510 MW	48790 TQ	USBLS	5/15
Except Metals and Plastics	Michigan	Y	25110 FQ	30540 MW	35980 TQ	USBLS	5/15
Except Metals and Plastics	Detroit-Dearborn-Livonia PMSA, MI	Y	24170 FQ	29040 MW	34380 TQ	USBLS	5/15
Except Metals and Plastics	Grand Rapids-Wyoming MSA, MI	Y	21910 FQ	26100 MW	32640 TQ	USBLS	5/15
Except Metals and Plastics	Minnesota	Y	26192 FQ	33937 MW	40771 TQ	MNBLS	1/16-3/16
Except Metals and Plastics	Minneapolis-St. Paul-Bloomington MSA, MN-WI	Y	23155 FQ	29078 MW	38007 TQ	MNBLS	1/16-3/16
Except Metals and Plastics	Mississippi	Y	22070 FQ	26310 MW	30670 TQ	USBLS	5/15
Except Metals and Plastics	Jackson MSA, MS	Y	22320 FQ	25780 MW	30580 TQ	USBLS	5/15
Except Metals and Plastics	Missouri	Y	25780 FQ	31870 MW	37600 TQ	USBLS	5/15
Except Metals and Plastics	Kansas City MSA, MO-KS	Y	23650 FQ	29640 MW	35680 TQ	USBLS	5/15
Except Metals and Plastics	St. Louis MSA, MO-IL	Y	26510 FQ	33140 MW	39240 TQ	USBLS	5/15
Except Metals and Plastics	Montana	Y	27880 FQ	33150 MW	38140 TQ	USBLS	5/15
Except Metals and Plastics	Nebraska	Y	23820 FQ	31320 MW	37900 TQ	NEBLS	7/16-9/16
Except Metals and Plastics	Nevada	Y	28840 FQ	33430 MW	38360 TQ	USBLS	5/15
Except Metals and Plastics	Las Vegas-Henderson-Paradise MSA, NV	Y	28880 FQ	33360 MW	38110 TQ	USBLS	5/15
Except Metals and Plastics	New Hampshire	H	11.06 AE	14.17 MW	17.08 AEX	NHBLS	6/16
Except Metals and Plastics	New Jersey	Y	28420 FQ	34310 MW	40650 TQ	USBLS	5/15
Except Metals and Plastics	Camden PMSA, NJ	Y	19970 FQ	32240 MW	38230 TQ	USBLS	5/15
Except Metals and Plastics	Newark PMSA, NJ-PA	Y	29260 FQ	34160 MW	38700 TQ	USBLS	5/15
Except Metals and Plastics	New Mexico	Y	34120 FQ	38650 MW	46570 TQ	USBLS	5/15
Except Metals and Plastics	New York	Y	22480 AE	34490 MW	40780 AEX	NYBLS	1/16-3/16
Except Metals and Plastics	Buffalo-Cheektowaga-Niagara Falls MSA, NY	Y	32130 FQ	41810 MW	47180 TQ	USBLS	5/15
Except Metals and Plastics	Nassau County-Suffolk County PMSA, NY	Y	27320 FQ	33080 MW	40280 TQ	USBLS	5/15
Except Metals and Plastics	New York-Jersey City-White Plains PMSA, NY-NJ	Y	26200 FQ	33340 MW	41810 TQ	USBLS	5/15
Except Metals and Plastics	Rochester MSA, NY	Y	19860 FQ	24500 MW	34910 TQ	USBLS	5/15
Except Metals and Plastics	North Carolina	Y	26080 FQ	29580 MW	37180 TQ	USBLS	5/15
Except Metals and Plastics	Charlotte-Concord-Gastonia MSA, NC-SC	Y	27360 FQ	33120 MW	37810 TQ	USBLS	5/15
Except Metals and Plastics	Raleigh MSA, NC	Y	21130 FQ	23810 MW	38310 TQ	USBLS	5/15
Except Metals and Plastics	North Dakota	Y	32820 FQ	35060 MW	37300 TQ	USBLS	5/15
Except Metals and Plastics	Ohio	Y	24800 FQ	30910 MW	39110 TQ	USBLS	5/15
Except Metals and Plastics	Cincinnati MSA, OH-KY-IN	Y	22460 FQ	30250 MW	38280 TQ	USBLS	5/15
Except Metals and Plastics	Cleveland-Elyria MSA, OH	Y	27380 FQ	38920 MW	51480 TQ	USBLS	5/15
Except Metals and Plastics	Columbus MSA, OH	Y	28750 FQ	34480 MW	45040 TQ	USBLS	5/15
Except Metals and Plastics	Oklahoma	Y	22350 FQ	32080 MW	36930 TQ	USBLS	5/15
Except Metals and Plastics	Oklahoma City MSA, OK	Y	27000 FQ	34220 MW	37440 TQ	USBLS	5/15
Except Metals and Plastics	Tulsa MSA, OK	Y	26820 FQ	29900 MW	36690 AEX	USBLS	5/15
Except Metals and Plastics	Oregon	H	13.34 FQ	16.52 MW	23.60 TQ	ORBLS	2016
Except Metals and Plastics	Portland-Vancouver-Hillsboro MSA, OR-WA	Y	27590 FQ	35180 MW	52950 TQ	USBLS	5/15
Except Metals and Plastics	Pennsylvania	Y	25630 FQ	30290 MW	37850 TQ	USBLS	5/15
Except Metals and Plastics	Allentown-Bethlehem-Easton MSA, PA-NJ	Y	28070 FQ	33250 MW	37880 TQ	USBLS	5/15
Except Metals and Plastics	Harrisburg-Carlisle MSA, PA	Y	21950 FQ	29640 MW	45720 TQ	USBLS	5/15
Except Metals and Plastics	Montgomery County-Bucks County-Chester County PMSA, PA	Y	26750 FQ	30130 MW	37300 TQ	USBLS	5/15
Except Metals and Plastics	Philadelphia PMSA, PA	Y	35180 FQ	39410 MW	45350 TQ	USBLS	5/15
Except Metals and Plastics	Pittsburgh MSA, PA	Y	26230 FQ	29290 MW	35930 TQ	USBLS	5/15
Except Metals and Plastics	Rhode Island	Y	28100 FQ	33970 MW	39000 TQ	USBLS	5/15
Except Metals and Plastics	Providence-Warwick MSA, RI-MA	Y	27900 FQ	34460 MW	44730 TQ	USBLS	5/15
Except Metals and Plastics	South Carolina	Y	25470 FQ	30260 MW	36660 TQ	USBLS	5/15

Occupation/Type/Industry	Location	Per	Low	Mid	High	Source	Date
Molder, Shaper, and Caster							
Except Metals and Plastics	Charleston-North Charleston MSA, SC	Y	22870 FQ	26360 MW	34330 TQ	USBLS	5/15
Except Metals and Plastics	Greenville-Anderson-Mauldin MSA, SC	Y	22440 FQ	25670 MW	35400 TQ	USBLS	5/15
Except Metals and Plastics	Tennessee	Y	22170 FQ	27720 MW	33000 TQ	USBLS	5/15
Except Metals and Plastics	Knoxville MSA, TN	Y	23660 FQ	27830 MW	31350 TQ	USBLS	5/15
Except Metals and Plastics	Nashville-Davidson–Murfreesboro–Franklin MSA, TN	Y	23920 FQ	32300 MW	37180 TQ	USBLS	5/15
Except Metals and Plastics	Texas	Y	21190 FQ	24190 MW	29010 TQ	USBLS	5/15
Except Metals and Plastics	Austin-Round Rock MSA, TX	Y	22120 FQ	24780 MW	29440 TQ	USBLS	5/15
Except Metals and Plastics	Dallas-Plano-Irving PMSA, TX	Y	21610 FQ	23820 MW	27710 TQ	USBLS	5/15
Except Metals and Plastics	Fort Worth-Arlington PMSA, TX	Y	19710 FQ	22370 MW	25500 TQ	USBLS	5/15
Except Metals and Plastics	Houston-The Woodlands-Sugar Land MSA, TX	Y	21380 FQ	24240 MW	29620 TQ	USBLS	5/15
Except Metals and Plastics	San Antonio-New Braunfels MSA, TX	Y	22000 FQ	25530 MW	28740 TQ	USBLS	5/15
Except Metals and Plastics	Utah	Y	27110 FQ	32850 MW	39100 TQ	USBLS	5/15
Except Metals and Plastics	Ogden-Clearfield MSA, UT	Y	27760 FQ	40080 MW	58550 TQ	USBLS	5/15
Except Metals and Plastics	Salt Lake City MSA, UT	Y	28350 FQ	33230 MW	38460 TQ	USBLS	5/15
Except Metals and Plastics	Vermont	Y	36750 FQ	50370 MW	58500 TQ	USBLS	5/15
Except Metals and Plastics	Virginia	Y	25590 FQ	31230 MW	39420 TQ	USBLS	5/15
Except Metals and Plastics	Richmond MSA, VA	Y	25620 FQ	31270 MW	38270 TQ	USBLS	5/15
Except Metals and Plastics	Virginia Beach-Norfolk-Newport News MSA, VA-NC	Y	27220 FQ	31670 MW	42650 TQ	USBLS	5/15
Except Metals and Plastics	Washington	H	15.98 FQ	18.24 MW	22.59 TQ	WABLS	3/16
Except Metals and Plastics	Seattle-Bellevue-Everett PMSA, WA	H	16.53 FQ	21.21 MW	26.29 TQ	WABLS	3/16
Except Metals and Plastics	Tacoma-Lakewood PMSA, WA	H	16.70 FQ	18.36 MW	22.89 TQ	WABLS	3/16
Except Metals and Plastics	West Virginia	Y	26290 FQ	29390 MW	33970 TQ	USBLS	5/15
Except Metals and Plastics	Wisconsin	Y	26190 FQ	29550 MW	36000 TQ	USBLS	5/15
Except Metals and Plastics	Madison MSA, WI	Y	18770 FQ	27780 MW	36770 TQ	USBLS	5/15
Except Metals and Plastics	Milwaukee-Waukesha-West Allis MSA, WI	Y	24530 FQ	30650 MW	43780 TQ	USBLS	5/15
Except Metals and Plastics	Puerto Rico	Y	17130 FQ	18460 MW	19800 TQ	USBLS	5/15
Except Metals and Plastics	San Juan-Carolina-Caguas MSA, PR	Y	16990 FQ	18180 MW	19360 TQ	USBLS	5/15
Molding, Coremaking, and Casting Machine Setter, Operator, and Tender							
Metals and Plastics	Alabama	Y	22240 AE	35885 AW	42712 AEX	ALBLS	6/16
Metals and Plastics	Birmingham-Hoover MSA, AL	Y	24410 AE	38373 AW	45355 AEX	ALBLS	6/16
Metals and Plastics	Arizona	Y	21930 FQ	26690 MW	33490 TQ	USBLS	5/15
Metals and Plastics	Phoenix-Mesa-Scottsdale MSA, AZ	Y	21980 FQ	26960 MW	33160 TQ	USBLS	5/15
Metals and Plastics	Tucson MSA, AZ	Y	20970 FQ	22920 MW	25230 TQ	USBLS	5/15
Metals and Plastics	Arkansas	Y	23260 FQ	28230 MW	34860 TQ	USBLS	5/15
Metals and Plastics	Little Rock-North Little Rock-Conway MSA, AR	Y	28400 FQ	32590 MW	36870 TQ	USBLS	5/15
Metals and Plastics	California	H	10.60 FQ	13.51 MW	17.56 TQ	CABLS	1/16-3/16
Metals and Plastics	Anaheim-Santa Ana-Irvine PMSA, CA	H	10.15 FQ	12.62 MW	16.86 TQ	CABLS	1/16-3/16
Metals and Plastics	Los Angeles-Long Beach-Glendale PMSA, CA	H	9.81 FQ	11.45 MW	15.29 TQ	CABLS	1/16-3/16
Metals and Plastics	Oakland-Hayward-Berkeley PMSA, CA	H	12.23 FQ	19.67 MW	22.75 TQ	CABLS	1/16-3/16
Metals and Plastics	Riverside-San Bernardino-Ontario MSA, CA	H	11.74 FQ	14.34 MW	17.75 TQ	CABLS	1/16-3/16
Metals and Plastics	Sacramento–Roseville–Arden-Arcade MSA, CA	H	9.66 FQ	12.16 MW	15.92 TQ	CABLS	1/16-3/16
Metals and Plastics	San Diego-Carlsbad MSA, CA	H	14.43 FQ	16.80 MW	18.78 TQ	CABLS	1/16-3/16
Metals and Plastics	San Francisco-Redwood City-South San Francisco PMSA, CA	H	13.02 FQ	14.50 MW	18.20 TQ	CABLS	1/16-3/16
Metals and Plastics	Colorado	Y	20620 FQ	24570 MW	31980 TQ	USBLS	5/15
Metals and Plastics	Denver-Aurora-Lakewood MSA, CO	Y	19980 FQ	23860 MW	31250 TQ	USBLS	5/15
Metals and Plastics	Connecticut	Y		28397 MW		CTBLS	1/16-3/16

AE	Average entry wage	AWR	Average wage range	H	Hourly	LR	Low end range	MTC	Median total compensation	TCC	Total cash compensation
AEX	Average experienced wage	B	Biweekly	HI	Highest wage paid	M	Monthly	MW	Median wage paid	TQ	Third quartile wage
ATC	Average total compensation	D	Daily	HR	High end range	MCC	Median cash compensation	MWR	Median wage range	W	Weekly
AW	Average wage paid	FQ	First quartile wage	LO	Lowest wage paid	ME	Median entry wage	S	See annotated source	Y	Yearly

1062

Occupation/Type/Industry	Location	Per	Low	Mid	High	Source	Date
Molding, Coremaking, and Casting Machine Setter, Operator, and Tender							
Metals and Plastics	Bridgeport-Stamford-Norwalk MSA, CT	Y	25320 FQ	31870 MW	38700 TQ	USBLS	5/15
Metals and Plastics	Hartford-West Hartford-East Hartford MSA, CT	Y	19620 FQ	24310 MW	31630 TQ	USBLS	5/15
Metals and Plastics	Delaware	Y	22090 FQ	24460 MW	29420 TQ	USBLS	5/15
Metals and Plastics	Wilmington PMSA, DE-MD-NJ	Y	23840 FQ	28590 MW	36490 TQ	USBLS	5/15
Metals and Plastics	Washington-Arlington-Alexandria PMSA, DC-VA-MD-WV	Y	24690 FQ	34260 MW	38020 TQ	USBLS	5/15
Metals and Plastics	Florida	H	10.49 AE	14.83 MW	18.52 AEX	FLBLS	7/16-9/16
Metals and Plastics	Fort Lauderdale-Pompano Beach-Deerfield Beach PMSA, FL	H	9.93 AE	12.42 MW	16.01 AEX	FLBLS	7/16-9/16
Metals and Plastics	Miami-Miami Beach-Kendall PMSA, FL	H	9.05 AE	11.99 MW	13.52 AEX	FLBLS	7/16-9/16
Metals and Plastics	Orlando-Kissimmee-Sanford MSA, FL	H	13.35 AE	15.37 MW	17.53 AEX	FLBLS	7/16-9/16
Metals and Plastics	Tampa-St. Petersburg-Clearwater MSA, FL	H	9.81 AE	16.20 MW	20.69 AEX	FLBLS	7/16-9/16
Metals and Plastics	Georgia	Y	20860 FQ	24910 MW	31980 TQ	USBLS	5/15
Metals and Plastics	Atlanta-Sandy Springs-Roswell MSA, GA	Y	20630 FQ	25410 MW	32490 TQ	USBLS	5/15
Metals and Plastics	Augusta-Richmond County MSA, GA-SC	Y	21580 FQ	23540 MW	29590 TQ	USBLS	5/15
Metals and Plastics	Hawaii	Y	28310 FQ	43520 MW	66330 TQ	USBLS	5/15
Metals and Plastics	Urban Honolulu MSA, HI	Y	29860 FQ	48520 MW	68800 TQ	USBLS	5/15
Metals and Plastics	Idaho	Y	23050 FQ	28030 MW	34050 TQ	USBLS	5/15
Metals and Plastics	Illinois	Y	25520 FQ	32680 MW	42840 TQ	USBLS	5/15
Metals and Plastics	Chicago-Naperville-Arlington Heights PMSA, IL	Y	23390 FQ	30500 MW	42930 TQ	USBLS	5/15
Metals and Plastics	Lake County-Kenosha County PMSA, IL-WI	Y	25640 FQ	29510 MW	35940 TQ	USBLS	5/15
Metals and Plastics	Indiana	Y	24170 FQ	29660 MW	37520 TQ	USBLS	5/15
Metals and Plastics	Gary PMSA, IN	Y	28130 FQ	42420 MW	59130 TQ	USBLS	5/15
Metals and Plastics	Indianapolis-Carmel-Anderson MSA, IN	Y	22360 FQ	26310 MW	35790 TQ	USBLS	5/15
Metals and Plastics	Iowa	Y	23800 FQ	30580 MW	37390 TQ	USBLS	5/15
Metals and Plastics	Des Moines-West Des Moines MSA, IA	Y	20720 FQ	22960 MW	27820 TQ	USBLS	5/15
Metals and Plastics	Kansas	Y	22270 FQ	27990 MW	35480 TQ	USBLS	5/15
Metals and Plastics	Wichita MSA, KS	Y	23350 FQ	28050 MW	36590 TQ	USBLS	5/15
Metals and Plastics	Kentucky	Y	27600 FQ	33730 MW	38560 TQ	USBLS	5/15
Metals and Plastics	Louisville-Jefferson County MSA, KY-IN	Y	22340 FQ	30780 MW	40120 TQ	USBLS	5/15
Metals and Plastics	Louisiana	Y	23490 FQ	28180 MW	34390 TQ	USBLS	5/15
Metals and Plastics	Maine	Y	21540 FQ	32770 MW	50220 TQ	USBLS	5/15
Metals and Plastics	Maryland	Y	22572 AE	33438 MW	38871 AEX	MDBLS	4/16
Metals and Plastics	Baltimore-Columbia-Towson MSA, MD	Y	25180 FQ	32710 MW	38610 TQ	USBLS	5/15
Metals and Plastics	Salisbury MSA, MD-DE	Y	22000 FQ	24290 MW	29140 TQ	USBLS	5/15
Metals and Plastics	Massachusetts	Y	26360 FQ	34180 MW	44910 TQ	USBLS	5/15
Metals and Plastics	Boston-Cambridge-Newton NECTA, MA	Y	27440 FQ	40780 MW	55610 TQ	USBLS	5/15
Metals and Plastics	Worcester MSA, MA-CT	Y	26940 FQ	30290 MW	36890 TQ	USBLS	5/15
Metals and Plastics	Michigan	Y	22560 FQ	27530 MW	33580 TQ	USBLS	5/15
Metals and Plastics	Detroit-Dearborn-Livonia PMSA, MI	Y	25960 FQ	28730 MW	31500 TQ	USBLS	5/15
Metals and Plastics	Grand Rapids-Wyoming MSA, MI	Y	20590 FQ	25700 MW	30530 TQ	USBLS	5/15
Metals and Plastics	Minnesota	Y	29725 FQ	35537 MW	41419 TQ	MNBLS	1/16-3/16
Metals and Plastics	Minneapolis-St. Paul-Bloomington MSA, MN-WI	Y	30211 FQ	35658 MW	40832 TQ	MNBLS	1/16-3/16
Metals and Plastics	Mississippi	Y	19670 FQ	22510 MW	27360 TQ	USBLS	5/15
Metals and Plastics	Jackson MSA, MS	Y	20260 FQ	22230 MW	24200 TQ	USBLS	5/15
Metals and Plastics	Missouri	Y	20760 FQ	25810 MW	34890 TQ	USBLS	5/15
Metals and Plastics	Kansas City MSA, MO-KS	Y	23030 FQ	27890 MW	34600 TQ	USBLS	5/15
Metals and Plastics	St. Louis MSA, MO-IL	Y	21480 FQ	28450 MW	37670 TQ	USBLS	5/15

AE Average entry wage	**AWR** Average wage range	**H** Hourly	**LR** Low end range	**MTC** Median total compensation	**TCC** Total cash compensation
AEX Average experienced wage	**B** Biweekly	**HI** Highest wage paid	**M** Monthly	**MW** Median wage paid	**TQ** Third quartile wage
ATC Average total compensation	**D** Daily	**HR** High end range	**MCC** Median cash compensation	**MWR** Median wage range	**W** Weekly
AW Average wage paid	**FQ** First quartile wage	**LO** Lowest wage paid	**ME** Median entry wage	**S** See annotated source	**Y** Yearly

Occupation/Type/Industry	Location	Per	Low	Mid	High	Source	Date
Molding, Coremaking, and Casting Machine Setter, Operator, and Tender							
Metals and Plastics	Montana	Y	21240 FQ	27120 MW	34610 TQ	USBLS	5/15
Metals and Plastics	Nebraska	Y	23995 FQ	30545 MW	38025 TQ	NEBLS	7/16-9/16
Metals and Plastics	Omaha-Council Bluffs MSA, NE-IA	Y	24860 FQ	30730 MW	36305 TQ	NEBLS	7/16-9/16
Metals and Plastics	Nevada	Y	21060 FQ	26540 MW	33400 TQ	USBLS	5/15
Metals and Plastics	Las Vegas-Henderson-Paradise MSA, NV	Y	17970 FQ	20340 MW	28970 TQ	USBLS	5/15
Metals and Plastics	New Hampshire	H	10.72 AE	14.08 MW	17.15 AEX	NHBLS	6/16
Metals and Plastics	Manchester NECTA, NH	H	11.63 AE	14.42 MW	17.66 AEX	NHBLS	6/16
Metals and Plastics	Nashua NECTA, NH-MA	Y	22870 FQ	28050 MW	36150 TQ	USBLS	5/15
Metals and Plastics	New Jersey	Y	22360 FQ	27990 MW	38180 TQ	USBLS	5/15
Metals and Plastics	Camden PMSA, NJ	Y	27040 FQ	33550 MW	42420 TQ	USBLS	5/15
Metals and Plastics	Newark PMSA, NJ-PA	Y	21130 FQ	24250 MW	33500 TQ	USBLS	5/15
Metals and Plastics	New Mexico	Y	21050 FQ	24490 MW	32360 TQ	USBLS	5/15
Metals and Plastics	Albuquerque MSA, NM	Y	21100 FQ	24200 MW	32580 TQ	USBLS	5/15
Metals and Plastics	New York	Y	21860 AE	32510 MW	41210 AEX	NYBLS	1/16-3/16
Metals and Plastics	Buffalo-Cheektowaga-Niagara Falls MSA, NY	Y	20880 FQ	27010 MW	42320 TQ	USBLS	5/15
Metals and Plastics	Nassau County-Suffolk County PMSA, NY	Y	19800 FQ	23260 MW	32280 TQ	USBLS	5/15
Metals and Plastics	New York-Jersey City-White Plains PMSA, NY-NJ	Y	21560 FQ	30480 MW	42500 TQ	USBLS	5/15
Metals and Plastics	Rochester MSA, NY	Y	27680 FQ	40130 MW	49440 TQ	USBLS	5/15
Metals and Plastics	North Carolina	Y	23150 FQ	28350 MW	35930 TQ	USBLS	5/15
Metals and Plastics	Charlotte-Concord-Gastonia MSA, NC-SC	Y	24580 FQ	29570 MW	37910 TQ	USBLS	5/15
Metals and Plastics	Raleigh MSA, NC	Y	21250 FQ	24700 MW	34880 TQ	USBLS	5/15
Metals and Plastics	North Dakota	Y	30630 FQ	34980 MW	38580 TQ	USBLS	5/15
Metals and Plastics	Ohio	Y	23930 FQ	29980 MW	37630 TQ	USBLS	5/15
Metals and Plastics	Cincinnati MSA, OH-KY-IN	Y	25860 FQ	33320 MW	40910 TQ	USBLS	5/15
Metals and Plastics	Cleveland-Elyria MSA, OH	Y	23380 FQ	29100 MW	36890 TQ	USBLS	5/15
Metals and Plastics	Columbus MSA, OH	Y	21350 FQ	27550 MW	36480 TQ	USBLS	5/15
Metals and Plastics	Oklahoma	Y	22380 FQ	27040 MW	33670 TQ	USBLS	5/15
Metals and Plastics	Oklahoma City MSA, OK	Y	22070 FQ	27290 MW	38940 TQ	USBLS	5/15
Metals and Plastics	Tulsa MSA, OK	Y	21510 FQ	24450 MW	29000 TQ	USBLS	5/15
Metals and Plastics	Oregon	H	13.07 FQ	15.59 MW	18.69 TQ	ORBLS	2016
Metals and Plastics	Portland-Vancouver-Hillsboro MSA, OR-WA	Y	26100 FQ	30940 MW	38150 TQ	USBLS	5/15
Metals and Plastics	Pennsylvania	Y	26130 FQ	33270 MW	40600 TQ	USBLS	5/15
Metals and Plastics	Allentown-Bethlehem-Easton MSA, PA-NJ	Y	29310 FQ	36650 MW	49100 TQ	USBLS	5/15
Metals and Plastics	Montgomery County-Bucks County-Chester County PMSA, PA	Y	25560 FQ	33050 MW	42870 TQ	USBLS	5/15
Metals and Plastics	Philadelphia PMSA, PA	Y	30870 FQ	39010 MW	46660 TQ	USBLS	5/15
Metals and Plastics	Pittsburgh MSA, PA	Y	24190 FQ	33330 MW	44000 TQ	USBLS	5/15
Metals and Plastics	Rhode Island	Y	23130 FQ	28570 MW	36390 TQ	USBLS	5/15
Metals and Plastics	Providence-Warwick MSA, RI-MA	Y	22930 FQ	28300 MW	36340 TQ	USBLS	5/15
Metals and Plastics	South Carolina	Y	23360 FQ	28770 MW	37180 TQ	USBLS	5/15
Metals and Plastics	Columbia MSA, SC	Y	22430 FQ	25080 MW	30830 TQ	USBLS	5/15
Metals and Plastics	Greenville-Anderson-Mauldin MSA, SC	Y	24480 FQ	28860 MW	35920 TQ	USBLS	5/15
Metals and Plastics	South Dakota	Y	23800 FQ	28140 MW	34020 TQ	USBLS	5/15
Metals and Plastics	Sioux Falls MSA, SD	Y	30380 FQ	35290 MW	41180 TQ	USBLS	5/15
Metals and Plastics	Tennessee	Y	24210 FQ	30620 MW	36470 TQ	USBLS	5/15
Metals and Plastics	Knoxville MSA, TN	Y	19100 FQ	23330 MW	30110 TQ	USBLS	5/15
Metals and Plastics	Memphis MSA, TN-MS-AR	Y	24520 FQ	33960 MW	38460 TQ	USBLS	5/15
Metals and Plastics	Nashville-Davidson–Murfreesboro–Franklin MSA, TN	Y	25300 FQ	29810 MW	36170 TQ	USBLS	5/15
Metals and Plastics	Texas	Y	20690 FQ	26390 MW	32680 TQ	USBLS	5/15
Metals and Plastics	Austin-Round Rock MSA, TX	Y	21570 FQ	23860 MW	27830 TQ	USBLS	5/15
Metals and Plastics	Dallas-Plano-Irving PMSA, TX	Y	19310 FQ	23810 MW	29570 TQ	USBLS	5/15
Metals and Plastics	Fort Worth-Arlington PMSA, TX	Y	18630 FQ	23470 MW	32660 TQ	USBLS	5/15
Metals and Plastics	Houston-The Woodlands-Sugar Land MSA, TX	Y	24570 FQ	28230 MW	32910 TQ	USBLS	5/15

AE	Average entry wage	AWR	Average wage range	H	Hourly	LR	Low end range	MTC	Median total compensation	TCC	Total cash compensation
AEX	Average experienced wage	B	Biweekly	HI	Highest wage paid	M	Monthly	MW	Median wage paid	TQ	Third quartile wage
ATC	Average total compensation	D	Daily	HR	High end range	MCC	Median cash compensation	MWR	Median wage range	W	Weekly
AW	Average wage paid	FQ	First quartile wage	LO	Lowest wage paid	ME	Median entry wage	S	See annotated source	Y	Yearly

Occupation/Type/Industry	Location	Per	Low	Mid	High	Source	Date
Molding, Coremaking, and Casting Machine Setter, Operator, and Tender							
Metals and Plastics	San Antonio-New Braunfels MSA, TX	Y	25490 FQ	31130 MW	38330 TQ	USBLS	5/15
Metals and Plastics	Utah	Y	25340 FQ	28770 MW	34990 TQ	USBLS	5/15
Metals and Plastics	Ogden-Clearfield MSA, UT	Y	26720 FQ	32890 MW	39750 TQ	USBLS	5/15
Metals and Plastics	Provo-Orem MSA, UT	Y	25790 FQ	28790 MW	34030 TQ	USBLS	5/15
Metals and Plastics	Salt Lake City MSA, UT	Y	25450 FQ	27950 MW	30450 TQ	USBLS	5/15
Metals and Plastics	Vermont	Y	22410 FQ	24880 MW	31080 TQ	USBLS	5/15
Metals and Plastics	Virginia	Y	23600 FQ	32120 MW	37890 TQ	USBLS	5/15
Metals and Plastics	Virginia Beach-Norfolk-Newport News MSA, VA-NC	Y	32200 FQ	35410 MW	38630 TQ	USBLS	5/15
Metals and Plastics	Washington	H	13.34 FQ	16.25 MW	20.61 TQ	WABLS	3/16
Metals and Plastics	Seattle-Bellevue-Everett PMSA, WA	H	12.89 FQ	14.45 MW	17.00 TQ	WABLS	3/16
Metals and Plastics	Tacoma-Lakewood PMSA, WA	H	12.46 FQ	16.08 MW	21.33 TQ	WABLS	3/16
Metals and Plastics	West Virginia	Y	28200 FQ	41610 MW	54220 TQ	USBLS	5/15
Metals and Plastics	Wisconsin	Y	25500 FQ	30530 MW	40680 TQ	USBLS	5/15
Metals and Plastics	Madison MSA, WI	Y	24320 FQ	29520 MW	37620 TQ	USBLS	5/15
Metals and Plastics	Milwaukee-Waukesha-West Allis MSA, WI	Y	23480 FQ	30530 MW	43210 TQ	USBLS	5/15
Metals and Plastics	Wyoming	Y	22880 FQ	27300 MW	32890 TQ	USBLS	5/15
Metals and Plastics	Puerto Rico	Y	18110 FQ	21520 MW	26830 TQ	USBLS	5/15
Metals and Plastics	San Juan-Carolina-Caguas MSA, PR	Y	17630 FQ	19940 MW	25140 TQ	USBLS	5/15
Molecular Biologist	United States	Y		83673 AW		TSCI	2016
Morgue Attendant							
Department of Public Health, Acute Care, Hospital	San Francisco, CA	B	2407 LO		2926 HI	SFGOV	2016-2018
Mortician, Undertaker, and Funeral Director							
	Alabama	Y	34574 AE	44870 AW	50029 AEX	ALBLS	6/16
	Birmingham-Hoover MSA, AL	Y	41431 AE	45622 AW	47712 AEX	ALBLS	6/16
	Alaska	Y	37190 FQ	46810 MW	58990 TQ	USBLS	5/15
	Arizona	Y	34930 FQ	43290 MW	56580 TQ	USBLS	5/15
	Phoenix-Mesa-Scottsdale MSA, AZ	Y	35060 FQ	42480 MW	53700 TQ	USBLS	5/15
	Arkansas	Y	31300 FQ	39740 MW	50190 TQ	USBLS	5/15
	California	H	15.93 FQ	18.87 MW	26.60 TQ	CABLS	1/16-3/16
	Los Angeles-Long Beach-Glendale PMSA, CA	H	16.04 FQ	18.56 MW	26.20 TQ	CABLS	1/16-3/16
	Oakland-Hayward-Berkeley PMSA, CA	H	16.68 FQ	17.99 MW	19.28 TQ	CABLS	1/16-3/16
	Riverside-San Bernardino-Ontario MSA, CA	H	17.71 FQ	37.85 MW	43.51 TQ	CABLS	1/16-3/16
	Sacramento–Roseville–Arden-Arcade MSA, CA	H	10.70 FQ	11.86 MW	17.95 TQ	CABLS	1/16-3/16
	San Diego-Carlsbad MSA, CA	H	16.27 FQ	17.36 MW	18.44 TQ	CABLS	1/16-3/16
	San Francisco-Redwood City-South San Francisco PMSA, CA	H	20.21 FQ	26.45 MW	28.91 TQ	CABLS	1/16-3/16
	Colorado	Y	25650 FQ	38610 MW	47120 TQ	USBLS	5/15
	Denver-Aurora-Lakewood MSA, CO	Y	22570 FQ	40750 MW	46670 TQ	USBLS	5/15
	Connecticut	Y		58176 MW		CTBLS	1/16-3/16
	Hartford-West Hartford-East Hartford MSA, CT	Y	44230 FQ	48970 MW	67090 TQ	USBLS	5/15
	Delaware	Y	61750 FQ	78570 MW	92420 TQ	USBLS	5/15
	Wilmington PMSA, DE-MD-NJ	Y	55670 FQ	69070 MW	96090 TQ	USBLS	5/15
	Washington-Arlington-Alexandria PMSA, DC-VA-MD-WV	Y	43980 FQ	58800 MW	76520 TQ	USBLS	5/15
	Florida	H	17.99 AE	24.74 MW	31.76 AEX	FLBLS	7/16-9/16
	Fort Lauderdale-Pompano Beach-Deerfield Beach PMSA, FL	H	15.06 AE	21.87 MW	26.53 AEX	FLBLS	7/16-9/16

AE	Average entry wage	AWR	Average wage range	H	Hourly	LR	Low end range	MTC	Median total compensation	TCC	Total cash compensation
AEX	Average experienced wage	B	Biweekly	HI	Highest wage paid	M	Monthly	MCC	Median cash compensation	TQ	Third quartile wage
ATC	Average total compensation	D	Daily	HR	High end range	MCC	Median cash compensation	MWR	Median wage range	W	Weekly
AW	Average wage paid	FQ	First quartile wage	LO	Lowest wage paid	ME	Median entry wage	S	See annotated source	Y	Yearly

1065

Occupation/Type/Industry	Location	Per	Low	Mid	High	Source	Date
Mortician, Undertaker, and Funeral Director							
	Miami-Miami Beach-Kendall PMSA, FL	H	19.20 AE	24.39 MW	31.31 AEX	FLBLS	7/16-9/16
	Orlando-Kissimmee-Sanford MSA, FL	H	30.16 AE	36.02 MW	39.67 AEX	FLBLS	7/16-9/16
	Tampa-St. Petersburg-Clearwater MSA, FL	H	17.57 AE	23.44 MW	29.68 AEX	FLBLS	7/16-9/16
	Georgia	Y	27820 FQ	37710 MW	56270 TQ	USBLS	5/15
	Atlanta-Sandy Springs-Roswell MSA, GA	Y	27510 FQ	37540 MW	57170 TQ	USBLS	5/15
	Augusta-Richmond County MSA, GA-SC	Y	24160 FQ	33240 MW	70190 TQ	USBLS	5/15
	Hawaii	Y	27610 FQ	30770 MW	54980 TQ	USBLS	5/15
	Urban Honolulu MSA, HI	Y	27610 FQ	30770 MW	54980 TQ	USBLS	5/15
	Idaho	Y	28750 FQ	46170 MW	67100 TQ	USBLS	5/15
	Illinois	Y	38500 FQ	59050 MW	85470 TQ	USBLS	5/15
	Chicago-Naperville-Arlington Heights PMSA, IL	Y	38220 FQ	57410 MW	97920 TQ	USBLS	5/15
	Lake County-Kenosha County PMSA, IL-WI	Y	31580 FQ	50520 MW	76930 TQ	USBLS	5/15
	Indiana	Y	29900 FQ	43190 MW	53820 TQ	USBLS	5/15
	Gary PMSA, IN	Y	41880 FQ	53840 MW	85020 TQ	USBLS	5/15
	Indianapolis-Carmel-Anderson MSA, IN	Y	39070 FQ	47680 MW	54600 TQ	USBLS	5/15
	Iowa	Y	43510 FQ	60510 MW	74710 TQ	USBLS	5/15
	Des Moines-West Des Moines MSA, IA	Y	39470 FQ	44370 MW	49460 TQ	USBLS	5/15
	Kansas	Y	36650 FQ	48820 MW	62140 TQ	USBLS	5/15
	Wichita MSA, KS	Y	38820 FQ	49370 MW	58390 TQ	USBLS	5/15
	Kentucky	Y	26340 FQ	38090 MW	49930 TQ	USBLS	5/15
	Louisville-Jefferson County MSA, KY-IN	Y	38660 FQ	52690 MW	60970 TQ	USBLS	5/15
	Louisiana	Y	28250 FQ	38380 MW	51650 TQ	USBLS	5/15
	Baton Rouge MSA, LA	Y	37550 FQ	51820 MW	61640 TQ	USBLS	5/15
	New Orleans-Metairie MSA, LA	Y	27780 FQ	31070 MW	44560 TQ	USBLS	5/15
	Maine	Y	40740 FQ	52390 MW	68400 TQ	USBLS	5/15
	Maryland	Y	40137 AE	57313 MW	65900 AEX	MDBLS	4/16
	Baltimore-Columbia-Towson MSA, MD	Y	45900 FQ	57270 MW	70450 TQ	USBLS	5/15
	Salisbury MSA, MD-DE	Y	45280 FQ	58290 MW	73620 TQ	USBLS	5/15
	Massachusetts	Y	43790 FQ	58140 MW	79860 TQ	USBLS	5/15
	Boston-Cambridge-Newton NECTA, MA	Y	46120 FQ	66760 MW	95770 TQ	USBLS	5/15
	Worcester MSA, MA-CT	Y	24630 FQ	35570 MW	53500 TQ	USBLS	5/15
	Michigan	Y	32510 FQ	50520 MW	70190 TQ	USBLS	5/15
	Grand Rapids-Wyoming MSA, MI	Y	39870 FQ	65200 MW	73310 TQ	USBLS	5/15
	Minnesota	Y	48969 FQ	60400 MW	73730 TQ	MNBLS	1/16-3/16
	Minneapolis-St. Paul-Bloomington MSA, MN-WI	Y	52493 FQ	61269 MW	75013 TQ	MNBLS	1/16-3/16
	Mississippi	Y	28130 FQ	39170 MW	48800 TQ	USBLS	5/15
	Jackson MSA, MS	Y	32480 FQ	42710 MW	61300 TQ	USBLS	5/15
	Missouri	Y	34140 FQ	38620 MW	51210 TQ	USBLS	5/15
	Kansas City MSA, MO-KS	Y	33550 FQ	41050 MW	48600 TQ	USBLS	5/15
	St. Louis MSA, MO-IL	Y	37160 FQ	54410 MW	70190 TQ	USBLS	5/15
	Montana	Y	35200 FQ	41060 MW	61080 TQ	USBLS	5/15
	Omaha-Council Bluffs MSA, NE-IA	Y	30560 FQ	37695 MW	46420 TQ	NEBLS	7/16-9/16
	Nevada	Y	34000 FQ	38770 MW	46350 TQ	USBLS	5/15
	Las Vegas-Henderson-Paradise MSA, NV	Y	35200 FQ	40630 MW	46730 TQ	USBLS	5/15
	New Hampshire	H	11.20 AE	19.36 MW	26.81 AEX	NHBLS	6/16
	New Jersey	Y	59320 FQ	70920 MW	83630 TQ	USBLS	5/15
	Newark PMSA, NJ-PA	Y	65030 FQ	73780 MW	85310 TQ	USBLS	5/15
	New Mexico	Y	41610 FQ	47220 MW	56850 TQ	USBLS	5/15
	Albuquerque MSA, NM	Y	41160 FQ	48510 MW	55500 TQ	USBLS	5/15
	New York	Y	37890 AE	51700 MW	66260 AEX	NYBLS	1/16-3/16
	Nassau County-Suffolk County PMSA, NY	Y	64030 FQ	73630 MW	83230 TQ	USBLS	5/15
	New York-Jersey City-White Plains PMSA, NY-NJ	Y	42680 FQ	50820 MW	68680 TQ	USBLS	5/15

AE	Average entry wage	AWR	Average wage range	H	Hourly
AEX	Average experienced wage	B	Biweekly	HI	Highest wage paid
ATC	Average total compensation	D	Daily	HR	High end range
AW	Average wage paid	FQ	First quartile wage	LO	Lowest wage paid

LR	Low end range	MTC	Median total compensation	TCC	Total cash compensation
M	Monthly	MW	Median wage paid	TQ	Third quartile wage
MCC	Median cash compensation	MWR	Median wage range	W	Weekly
ME	Median entry wage	S	See annotated source	Y	Yearly

Occupation/Type/Industry	Location	Per	Low	Mid	High	Source	Date
Mortician, Undertaker, and Funeral Director	Rochester MSA, NY	Y	35850 FQ	69090 MW	74320 TQ	USBLS	5/15
	North Carolina	Y	44450 FQ	54520 MW	63760 TQ	USBLS	5/15
	Charlotte-Concord-Gastonia MSA, NC-SC	Y	40750 FQ	46060 MW	56110 TQ	USBLS	5/15
	Raleigh MSA, NC	Y	53440 FQ	58740 MW	65430 TQ	USBLS	5/15
	North Dakota	Y	30150 FQ	50660 MW	60670 TQ	USBLS	5/15
	Ohio	Y	39230 FQ	51400 MW	60800 TQ	USBLS	5/15
	Cincinnati MSA, OH-KY-IN	Y	40080 FQ	50340 MW	57600 TQ	USBLS	5/15
	Cleveland-Elyria MSA, OH	Y	41850 FQ	54430 MW	61250 TQ	USBLS	5/15
	Columbus MSA, OH	Y	49440 FQ	64680 MW	71610 TQ	USBLS	5/15
	Oklahoma	Y	24510 FQ	47010 MW	61200 TQ	USBLS	5/15
	Oregon	H	18.41 FQ	23.94 MW	31.37 TQ	ORBLS	2016
	Portland-Vancouver-Hillsboro MSA, OR-WA	Y	39680 FQ	53480 MW	70000 TQ	USBLS	5/15
	Pennsylvania	Y	32330 FQ	42950 MW	61190 TQ	USBLS	5/15
	Allentown-Bethlehem-Easton MSA, PA-NJ	Y	28390 FQ	36680 MW	68730 TQ	USBLS	5/15
	Harrisburg-Carlisle MSA, PA	Y	42200 FQ	44890 MW	47570 TQ	USBLS	5/15
	Montgomery County-Bucks County-Chester County PMSA, PA	Y	41220 FQ	53890 MW	71030 TQ	USBLS	5/15
	Philadelphia PMSA, PA	Y	50620 FQ	61370 MW	77220 TQ	USBLS	5/15
	Pittsburgh MSA, PA	Y	27370 FQ	30310 MW	43020 TQ	USBLS	5/15
	Rhode Island	Y	45760 FQ	65520 MW	73190 TQ	USBLS	5/15
	Providence-Warwick MSA, RI-MA	Y	44300 FQ	63940 MW	71770 TQ	USBLS	5/15
	South Carolina	Y	22890 FQ	40970 MW	56740 TQ	USBLS	5/15
	Columbia MSA, SC	Y	24620 FQ	40750 MW	52240 TQ	USBLS	5/15
	Greenville-Anderson-Mauldin MSA, SC	Y	32240 FQ	48510 MW	60190 TQ	USBLS	5/15
	South Dakota	Y	51460 FQ	58420 MW	70190 TQ	USBLS	5/15
	Sioux Falls MSA, SD	Y	54390 FQ	62580 MW	86070 TQ	USBLS	5/15
	Tennessee	Y	34240 FQ	43670 MW	58830 TQ	USBLS	5/15
	Knoxville MSA, TN	Y	40260 FQ	45710 MW	54740 TQ	USBLS	5/15
	Memphis MSA, TN-MS-AR	Y	22100 FQ	24700 MW	64390 TQ	USBLS	5/15
	Nashville-Davidson–Murfreesboro–Franklin MSA, TN	Y	41800 FQ	57880 MW	87900 TQ	USBLS	5/15
	Texas	Y	36660 FQ	47740 MW	62810 TQ	USBLS	5/15
	Austin-Round Rock MSA, TX	Y	35430 FQ	41260 MW	61600 TQ	USBLS	5/15
	Dallas-Plano-Irving PMSA, TX	Y	38460 FQ	45420 MW	55800 TQ	USBLS	5/15
	Fort Worth-Arlington PMSA, TX	Y	38520 FQ	48890 MW	56020 TQ	USBLS	5/15
	Houston-The Woodlands-Sugar Land MSA, TX	Y	39610 FQ	65960 MW	83680 TQ	USBLS	5/15
	San Antonio-New Braunfels MSA, TX	Y	47860 FQ	59240 MW	69780 TQ	USBLS	5/15
	Utah	Y	42120 FQ	47700 MW	58080 TQ	USBLS	5/15
	Salt Lake City MSA, UT	Y	40860 FQ	45450 MW	52740 TQ	USBLS	5/15
	Vermont	Y	42650 FQ	53660 MW	61140 TQ	USBLS	5/15
	Burlington-South Burlington MSA, VT	Y	44660 FQ	55000 MW	59970 TQ	USBLS	5/15
	Virginia	Y	42080 FQ	51190 MW	65650 TQ	USBLS	5/15
	Richmond MSA, VA	Y	42750 FQ	48200 MW	57990 TQ	USBLS	5/15
	Virginia Beach-Norfolk-Newport News MSA, VA-NC	Y	39340 FQ	48030 MW	68290 TQ	USBLS	5/15
	Washington	H	19.40 FQ	24.91 MW	28.99 TQ	WABLS	3/16
	Seattle-Bellevue-Everett PMSA, WA	H	25.09 FQ	27.93 MW	30.88 TQ	WABLS	3/16
	Tacoma-Lakewood PMSA, WA	H	20.49 FQ	24.37 MW	28.70 TQ	WABLS	3/16
	West Virginia	Y	32430 FQ	44400 MW	56030 TQ	USBLS	5/15
	Huntington-Ashland MSA, WV-KY-OH	Y	40630 FQ	48830 MW	58190 TQ	USBLS	5/15
	Wisconsin	Y	45320 FQ	58140 MW	74250 TQ	USBLS	5/15
	Madison MSA, WI	Y	37390 FQ	54080 MW	66240 TQ	USBLS	5/15
	Milwaukee-Waukesha-West Allis MSA, WI	Y	40670 FQ	56690 MW	75530 TQ	USBLS	5/15
	Wyoming	Y	35630 FQ	46570 MW	63260 TQ	USBLS	5/15
Motion Designer	United States	Y	70500 LO		103500 HI	RH02	2017

AE	Average entry wage	AWR	Average wage range	H	Hourly	LR	Low end range	MTC	Median total compensation	TCC	Total cash compensation
AEX	Average experienced wage	B	Biweekly	HI	Highest wage paid	M	Monthly	MW	Median wage paid	TQ	Third quartile wage
ATC	Average total compensation	D	Daily	HR	High end range	MCC	Median cash compensation	MWR	Median wage range	W	Weekly
AW	Average wage paid	FQ	First quartile wage	LO	Lowest wage paid	ME	Median entry wage	S	See annotated source	Y	Yearly

Occupation/Type/Industry	Location	Per	Low	Mid	High	Source	Date
Motion Picture Editor							
On Call, Subscription Video on Demand, High Budget	United States	H	49.08 LO			MPEG01	7/31/16-7/29/17
Motion Picture Projectionist	Alabama	Y	17472 AE	21158 AW	23001 AEX	ALBLS	6/16
	Arizona	Y	18530 FQ	21870 MW	28140 TQ	USBLS	5/15
	Phoenix-Mesa-Scottsdale MSA, AZ	Y	18600 FQ	21030 MW	26410 TQ	USBLS	5/15
	Arkansas	Y	16880 FQ	18090 MW	19310 TQ	USBLS	5/15
	California	H	9.72 FQ	11.22 MW	16.32 TQ	CABLS	1/16-3/16
	Los Angeles-Long Beach-Glendale PMSA, CA	H	9.74 FQ	11.78 MW	18.36 TQ	CABLS	1/16-3/16
	Colorado	Y	17800 FQ	18480 MW	19160 TQ	USBLS	5/15
	Denver-Aurora-Lakewood MSA, CO	Y	17750 FQ	18380 MW	19000 TQ	USBLS	5/15
	Connecticut	Y		19977 MW		CTBLS	1/16-3/16
	Washington-Arlington-Alexandria PMSA, DC-VA-MD-WV	Y	20600 FQ	23570 MW	27720 TQ	USBLS	5/15
	Florida	H	9.05 AE	10.48 MW	12.09 AEX	FLBLS	7/16-9/16
	Fort Lauderdale-Pompano Beach-Deerfield Beach PMSA, FL	H	9.13 AE	10.35 MW	10.96 AEX	FLBLS	7/16-9/16
	Miami-Miami Beach-Kendall PMSA, FL	H	9.04 AE	9.95 MW	11.13 AEX	FLBLS	7/16-9/16
	Orlando-Kissimmee-Sanford MSA, FL	H	9.10 AE	10.12 MW	11.42 AEX	FLBLS	7/16-9/16
	Tampa-St. Petersburg-Clearwater MSA, FL	H	8.96 AE	9.26 MW	9.55 AEX	FLBLS	7/16-9/16
	Georgia	Y	17500 FQ	19420 MW	27150 TQ	USBLS	5/15
	Idaho	Y	20400 FQ	22400 MW	24390 TQ	USBLS	5/15
	Illinois	Y	18330 FQ	19280 MW	26570 TQ	USBLS	5/15
	Indiana	Y	17200 FQ	18890 MW	22000 TQ	USBLS	5/15
	Iowa	Y	16410 FQ	17570 MW	18720 TQ	USBLS	5/15
	Kansas	Y	18680 FQ	22270 MW	27410 TQ	USBLS	5/15
	Louisiana	Y	18890 FQ	21860 MW	24510 TQ	USBLS	5/15
	Maine	Y	22280 FQ	24880 MW	37060 TQ	USBLS	5/15
	Massachusetts	Y	23180 FQ	26820 MW	30480 TQ	USBLS	5/15
	Boston-Cambridge-Newton NECTA, MA	Y	23690 FQ	27230 MW	30630 TQ	USBLS	5/15
	Michigan	Y	19430 FQ	23430 MW	32500 TQ	USBLS	5/15
	Minnesota	Y	18218 FQ	19501 MW	22187 TQ	MNBLS	1/16-3/16
	Minneapolis-St. Paul-Bloomington MSA, MN-WI	Y	17955 FQ	18986 MW	20005 TQ	MNBLS	1/16-3/16
	Mississippi	Y	19200 FQ	22130 MW	26060 TQ	USBLS	5/15
	Missouri	Y	24900 FQ	29600 MW	37790 TQ	USBLS	5/15
	New Jersey	Y	20370 FQ	31860 MW	35860 TQ	USBLS	5/15
	New York	Y	19910 AE	25280 MW	39410 AEX	NYBLS	1/16-3/16
	New York-Jersey City-White Plains PMSA, NY-NJ	Y	20910 FQ	24830 MW	38780 TQ	USBLS	5/15
	North Carolina	Y	17500 FQ	19720 MW	24770 TQ	USBLS	5/15
	Charlotte-Concord-Gastonia MSA, NC-SC	Y	16950 FQ	18580 MW	21100 TQ	USBLS	5/15
	Ohio	Y	20360 FQ	23010 MW	34940 TQ	USBLS	5/15
	Cleveland-Elyria MSA, OH	Y	33450 FQ	36790 MW	41020 TQ	USBLS	5/15
	Oklahoma	Y	17990 FQ	20990 MW	25950 TQ	USBLS	5/15
	Oregon	H	9.69 FQ	10.69 MW	13.48 TQ	ORBLS	2016
	Pennsylvania	Y	18530 FQ	21670 MW	24800 TQ	USBLS	5/15
	Montgomery County-Bucks County-Chester County PMSA, PA	Y	18160 FQ	21120 MW	24200 TQ	USBLS	5/15
	Pittsburgh MSA, PA	Y	19200 FQ	22080 MW	24750 TQ	USBLS	5/15
	South Carolina	Y	18250 FQ	21740 MW	26910 TQ	USBLS	5/15
	Tennessee	Y	17700 FQ	19950 MW	24600 TQ	USBLS	5/15
	Texas	Y	17560 FQ	20080 MW	28790 TQ	USBLS	5/15
	Dallas-Plano-Irving PMSA, TX	Y	19100 FQ	26790 MW	31790 TQ	USBLS	5/15
	Fort Worth-Arlington PMSA, TX	Y	16730 FQ	18180 MW	20680 TQ	USBLS	5/15
	Houston-The Woodlands-Sugar Land MSA, TX	Y	17620 FQ	19600 MW	29600 TQ	USBLS	5/15
	Utah	Y	18820 FQ	22650 MW	29830 TQ	USBLS	5/15
	Virginia	Y	18440 FQ	21580 MW	26070 TQ	USBLS	5/15

AE	Average entry wage	AWR	Average wage range	H	Hourly
AEX	Average experienced wage	B	Biweekly	HI	Highest wage paid
ATC	Average total compensation	D	Daily	HR	High end range
AW	Average wage paid	FQ	First quartile wage	LO	Lowest wage paid

LR	Low end range	MTC	Median total compensation	TCC	Total cash compensation
M	Monthly	MW	Median wage paid	TQ	Third quartile wage
MCC	Median cash compensation	MWR	Median wage range	W	Weekly
ME	Median entry wage	S	See annotated source	Y	Yearly

Occupation/Type/Industry	Location	Per	Low	Mid	High	Source	Date
Motion Picture Projectionist	Virginia Beach-Norfolk-Newport News MSA, VA-NC	Y	17020 FQ	18340 MW	19660 TQ	USBLS	5/15
	Washington	H	9.78 FQ	11.24 MW	13.82 TQ	WABLS	3/16
	Seattle-Bellevue-Everett PMSA, WA	H	9.80 FQ	12.47 MW	15.67 TQ	WABLS	3/16
	Wisconsin	Y	18040 FQ	21220 MW	25990 TQ	USBLS	5/15
	Milwaukee-Waukesha-West Allis MSA, WI	Y	19250 FQ	24630 MW	29630 TQ	USBLS	5/15
	Puerto Rico	Y	16560 FQ	17740 MW	18920 TQ	USBLS	5/15
	San Juan-Carolina-Caguas MSA, PR	Y	16540 FQ	17710 MW	18880 TQ	USBLS	5/15
Motivational Speaker	United States	Y		63000 AW		SKU01	2016
Motorboat Mechanic and Service Technician	Alabama	Y	29982 AE	38860 AW	43305 AEX	ALBLS	6/16
	Alaska	Y	38070 FQ	44150 MW	48940 TQ	USBLS	5/15
	Anchorage MSA, AK	Y	28050 FQ	36140 MW	50750 TQ	USBLS	5/15
	Arizona	Y	28140 FQ	40690 MW	49980 TQ	USBLS	5/15
	Phoenix-Mesa-Scottsdale MSA, AZ	Y	26570 FQ	32660 MW	45990 TQ	USBLS	5/15
	Arkansas	Y	27010 FQ	33420 MW	38200 TQ	USBLS	5/15
	California	H	14.21 FQ	18.50 MW	23.15 TQ	CABLS	1/16-3/16
	Anaheim-Santa Ana-Irvine PMSA, CA	H	16.58 FQ	19.82 MW	22.43 TQ	CABLS	1/16-3/16
	Los Angeles-Long Beach-Glendale PMSA, CA	H	14.89 FQ	19.75 MW	22.76 TQ	CABLS	1/16-3/16
	Oakland-Hayward-Berkeley PMSA, CA	H	13.50 FQ	18.03 MW	22.72 TQ	CABLS	1/16-3/16
	Riverside-San Bernardino-Ontario MSA, CA	H	14.96 FQ	17.36 MW	20.57 TQ	CABLS	1/16-3/16
	Sacramento–Roseville–Arden-Arcade MSA, CA	H	9.66 FQ	17.76 MW	25.75 TQ	CABLS	1/16-3/16
	San Diego-Carlsbad MSA, CA	H	9.54 FQ	9.83 MW	21.93 TQ	CABLS	1/16-3/16
	San Francisco-Redwood City-South San Francisco PMSA, CA	H	22.22 FQ	26.31 MW	29.83 TQ	CABLS	1/16-3/16
	Colorado	Y	18950 FQ	34200 MW	43830 TQ	USBLS	5/15
	Connecticut	Y		50021 MW		CTBLS	1/16-3/16
	Bridgeport-Stamford-Norwalk MSA, CT	Y	42080 FQ	52750 MW	61790 TQ	USBLS	5/15
	Delaware	Y	32490 FQ	42550 MW	48040 TQ	USBLS	5/15
	Wilmington PMSA, DE-MD-NJ	Y	41310 FQ	45130 MW	48950 TQ	USBLS	5/15
	Washington-Arlington-Alexandria PMSA, DC-VA-MD-WV	Y	32540 FQ	35300 MW	38050 TQ	USBLS	5/15
	Florida	H	12.80 AE	17.88 MW	21.99 AEX	FLBLS	7/16-9/16
	Fort Lauderdale-Pompano Beach-Deerfield Beach PMSA, FL	H	12.46 AE	18.04 MW	21.90 AEX	FLBLS	7/16-9/16
	Miami-Miami Beach-Kendall PMSA, FL	H	15.33 AE	19.05 MW	23.04 AEX	FLBLS	7/16-9/16
	Orlando-Kissimmee-Sanford MSA, FL	H	14.06 AE	19.48 MW	24.01 AEX	FLBLS	7/16-9/16
	Tampa-St. Petersburg-Clearwater MSA, FL	H	13.01 AE	16.58 MW	19.13 AEX	FLBLS	7/16-9/16
	Georgia	Y	27870 FQ	41580 MW	50490 TQ	USBLS	5/15
	Augusta-Richmond County MSA, GA-SC	Y	41530 FQ	44980 MW	48430 TQ	USBLS	5/15
	Idaho	Y	27580 FQ	35680 MW	48860 TQ	USBLS	5/15
	Illinois	Y	19640 FQ	28440 MW	37810 TQ	USBLS	5/15
	Chicago-Naperville-Arlington Heights PMSA, IL	Y	18900 FQ	19840 MW	28330 TQ	USBLS	5/15
	Lake County-Kenosha County PMSA, IL-WI	Y	34530 FQ	44890 MW	53970 TQ	USBLS	5/15
	Indiana	Y	25440 FQ	33220 MW	40780 TQ	USBLS	5/15
	Gary PMSA, IN	Y	28140 FQ	35010 MW	44000 TQ	USBLS	5/15
	Indianapolis-Carmel-Anderson MSA, IN	Y	23900 FQ	30010 MW	35190 TQ	USBLS	5/15
	Iowa	Y	26070 FQ	30260 MW	36750 TQ	USBLS	5/15
	Kansas	Y	27720 FQ	40530 MW	49530 TQ	USBLS	5/15

AE	Average entry wage	AWR	Average wage range	H	Hourly	LR	Low end range	MTC	Median total compensation	TCC	Total cash compensation
AEX	Average experienced wage	B	Biweekly	HI	Highest wage paid	M	Monthly	MW	Median wage paid	TQ	Third quartile wage
ATC	Average total compensation	D	Daily	HR	High end range	MCC	Median cash compensation	MWR	Median wage range	W	Weekly
AW	Average wage paid	FQ	First quartile wage	LO	Lowest wage paid	ME	Median entry wage	S	See annotated source	Y	Yearly

Motorboat Mechanic and Service Technician

Occupation/Type/Industry	Location	Per	Low	Mid	High	Source	Date
Motorboat Mechanic and Service Technician	Kentucky	Y	26160 FQ	31450 MW	40830 TQ	USBLS	5/15
	Louisiana	Y	25970 FQ	35380 MW	46890 TQ	USBLS	5/15
	Maine	Y	30710 FQ	36990 MW	44570 TQ	USBLS	5/15
	Portland-South Portland MSA, ME	Y	24150 FQ	36090 MW	44940 TQ	USBLS	5/15
	Maryland	Y	29415 AE	43955 MW	51224 AEX	MDBLS	4/16
	Baltimore-Columbia-Towson MSA, MD	Y	36170 FQ	44130 MW	55670 TQ	USBLS	5/15
	Salisbury MSA, MD-DE	Y	30300 FQ	37630 MW	47440 TQ	USBLS	5/15
	Massachusetts	Y	36820 FQ	43710 MW	50580 TQ	USBLS	5/15
	Boston-Cambridge-Newton NECTA, MA	Y	36440 FQ	42730 MW	49500 TQ	USBLS	5/15
	Michigan	Y	28330 FQ	38460 MW	53110 TQ	USBLS	5/15
	Grand Rapids-Wyoming MSA, MI	Y	30810 FQ	37990 MW	48670 TQ	USBLS	5/15
	Minnesota	Y	30422 FQ	38568 MW	49560 TQ	MNBLS	1/16-3/16
	Minneapolis-St. Paul-Bloomington MSA, MN-WI	Y	32272 FQ	43536 MW	53693 TQ	MNBLS	1/16-3/16
	Mississippi	Y	26940 FQ	30180 MW	38860 TQ	USBLS	5/15
	Jackson MSA, MS	Y	26100 FQ	28530 MW	30950 TQ	USBLS	5/15
	Missouri	Y	23550 FQ	30340 MW	37700 TQ	USBLS	5/15
	St. Louis MSA, MO-IL	Y	24240 FQ	31610 MW	40100 TQ	USBLS	5/15
	Montana	Y	26570 FQ	32260 MW	42680 TQ	USBLS	5/15
	Nebraska	Y	28700 FQ	37585 MW	52340 TQ	NEBLS	7/16-9/16
	Nevada	Y	32330 FQ	39110 MW	52770 TQ	USBLS	5/15
	New Hampshire	H	15.97 AE	21.19 MW	22.79 AEX	NHBLS	6/16
	New Jersey	Y	39370 FQ	46580 MW	55010 TQ	USBLS	5/15
	New York	Y	23940 AE	36850 MW	43540 AEX	NYBLS	1/16-3/16
	Buffalo-Cheektowaga-Niagara Falls MSA, NY	Y	35140 FQ	41450 MW	45860 TQ	USBLS	5/15
	Nassau County-Suffolk County PMSA, NY	Y	25310 FQ	40290 MW	49840 TQ	USBLS	5/15
	New York-Jersey City-White Plains PMSA, NY-NJ	Y	38560 FQ	45290 MW	52000 TQ	USBLS	5/15
	Rochester MSA, NY	Y	22950 FQ	27400 MW	35950 TQ	USBLS	5/15
	North Carolina	Y	28130 FQ	35530 MW	43520 TQ	USBLS	5/15
	Charlotte-Concord-Gastonia MSA, NC-SC	Y	29810 FQ	37240 MW	57740 TQ	USBLS	5/15
	North Dakota	Y	29070 FQ	40820 MW	48610 TQ	USBLS	5/15
	Fargo MSA, ND-MN	Y	36010 FQ	46830 MW	58220 TQ	USBLS	5/15
	Ohio	Y	29330 FQ	35860 MW	43920 TQ	USBLS	5/15
	Cincinnati MSA, OH-KY-IN	Y	27200 FQ	29350 MW	31950 TQ	USBLS	5/15
	Cleveland-Elyria MSA, OH	Y	25790 FQ	31230 MW	42780 TQ	USBLS	5/15
	Oklahoma	Y	28190 FQ	36540 MW	48820 TQ	USBLS	5/15
	Oregon	H	14.80 FQ	17.55 MW	21.17 TQ	ORBLS	2016
	Portland-Vancouver-Hillsboro MSA, OR-WA	Y	31290 FQ	39770 MW	45950 TQ	USBLS	5/15
	Pennsylvania	Y	27660 FQ	37400 MW	44800 TQ	USBLS	5/15
	Rhode Island	Y	36570 FQ	45810 MW	55330 TQ	USBLS	5/15
	Providence-Warwick MSA, RI-MA	Y	36080 FQ	44410 MW	54570 TQ	USBLS	5/15
	South Carolina	Y	24270 FQ	34410 MW	43310 TQ	USBLS	5/15
	Charleston-North Charleston MSA, SC	Y	27340 FQ	35810 MW	55570 TQ	USBLS	5/15
	Greenville-Anderson-Mauldin MSA, SC	Y	18630 FQ	34370 MW	38500 TQ	USBLS	5/15
	South Dakota	Y	28860 FQ	33870 MW	37710 TQ	USBLS	5/15
	Tennessee	Y	29360 FQ	40630 MW	47840 TQ	USBLS	5/15
	Knoxville MSA, TN	Y	26900 FQ	29240 MW	34380 TQ	USBLS	5/15
	Nashville-Davidson–Murfreesboro–Franklin MSA, TN	Y	41150 FQ	44630 MW	48110 TQ	USBLS	5/15
	Texas	Y	33040 FQ	44350 MW	54390 TQ	USBLS	5/15
	Dallas-Plano-Irving PMSA, TX	Y	40400 FQ	45550 MW	52730 TQ	USBLS	5/15
	Fort Worth-Arlington PMSA, TX	Y	30860 FQ	39820 MW	54220 TQ	USBLS	5/15
	Houston-The Woodlands-Sugar Land MSA, TX	Y	41990 FQ	47350 MW	55730 TQ	USBLS	5/15
	San Antonio-New Braunfels MSA, TX	Y	25760 FQ	40080 MW	46800 TQ	USBLS	5/15
	Utah	Y	32270 FQ	37690 MW	53780 TQ	USBLS	5/15

AE	Average entry wage	AWR	Average wage range	H	Hourly	LR	Low end range	MTC	Median total compensation	TCC	Total cash compensation
AEX	Average experienced wage	B	Biweekly	HI	Highest wage paid	M	Monthly	MW	Median wage paid	TQ	Third quartile wage
ATC	Average total compensation	D	Daily	HR	High end range	MCC	Median cash compensation	MWR	Median wage range	W	Weekly
AW	Average wage paid	FQ	First quartile wage	LO	Lowest wage paid	ME	Median entry wage	S	See annotated source	Y	Yearly

Occupation/Type/Industry	Location	Per	Low	Mid	High	Source	Date
Motorboat Mechanic and Service Technician	Salt Lake City MSA, UT	Y	28520 FQ	35970 MW	55690 TQ	USBLS	5/15
	Vermont	Y	34100 FQ	39350 MW	45280 TQ	USBLS	5/15
	Burlington-South Burlington MSA, VT	Y	33020 FQ	37200 MW	43040 TQ	USBLS	5/15
	Virginia	Y	34000 FQ	40310 MW	46510 TQ	USBLS	5/15
	Virginia Beach-Norfolk-Newport News MSA, VA-NC	Y	33830 FQ	41800 MW	47040 TQ	USBLS	5/15
	Washington	H	17.85 FQ	22.16 MW	27.41 TQ	WABLS	3/16
	Seattle-Bellevue-Everett PMSA, WA	H	20.85 FQ	26.00 MW	30.30 TQ	WABLS	3/16
	Tacoma-Lakewood PMSA, WA	H	17.82 FQ	21.63 MW	25.85 TQ	WABLS	3/16
	Huntington-Ashland MSA, WV-KY-OH	Y	27010 FQ	32450 MW	44990 TQ	USBLS	5/15
	Wisconsin	Y	30300 FQ	37270 MW	45430 TQ	USBLS	5/15
	Puerto Rico	Y	18430 FQ	24160 MW	32030 TQ	USBLS	5/15
	San Juan-Carolina-Caguas MSA, PR	Y	19720 FQ	25770 MW	33640 TQ	USBLS	5/15
	Virgin Islands	Y	25800 FQ	30870 MW	40620 TQ	USBLS	5/15
Motorboat Operator	Alaska	Y	62460 FQ	68440 MW	73600 TQ	USBLS	5/15
	Arizona	Y	35670 FQ	39960 MW	46650 TQ	USBLS	5/15
	California	H	11.75 FQ	23.00 MW	29.99 TQ	CABLS	1/16-3/16
	Florida	H	10.41 AE	14.42 MW	20.76 AEX	FLBLS	7/16-9/16
	Hawaii	Y	33790 FQ	38690 MW	44790 TQ	USBLS	5/15
	Louisiana	Y	30710 FQ	55790 MW	64170 TQ	USBLS	5/15
	Maryland	Y	47774 AE	62324 MW	69598 AEX	MDBLS	4/16
	Massachusetts	Y	23360 FQ	47020 MW	67090 TQ	USBLS	5/15
	New Jersey	Y	19640 FQ	27210 MW	33550 TQ	USBLS	5/15
	New York	Y	24460 AE	37110 MW	50330 AEX	NYBLS	1/16-3/16
	Oregon	H	17.82 FQ	22.19 MW	28.03 TQ	ORBLS	2016
	South Carolina	Y	32200 FQ	60480 MW	70750 TQ	USBLS	5/15
	Texas	Y	22500 FQ	31750 MW	56880 TQ	USBLS	5/15
	Washington	H	29.66 FQ	30.88 MW	31.90 TQ	WABLS	3/16
Motorcycle Mechanic	Alabama	Y	26381 AE	36399 AW	41403 AEX	ALBLS	6/16
	Alaska	Y	36510 FQ	45840 MW	58520 TQ	USBLS	5/15
	Anchorage MSA, AK	Y	38860 FQ	48510 MW	59370 TQ	USBLS	5/15
	Arizona	Y	24150 FQ	33420 MW	46330 TQ	USBLS	5/15
	Phoenix-Mesa-Scottsdale MSA, AZ	Y	23710 FQ	33240 MW	48960 TQ	USBLS	5/15
	Tucson MSA, AZ	Y	24600 FQ	40510 MW	53870 TQ	USBLS	5/15
	Arkansas	Y	22800 FQ	27360 MW	31190 TQ	USBLS	5/15
	California	H	15.33 FQ	20.40 MW	27.13 TQ	CABLS	1/16-3/16
	Anaheim-Santa Ana-Irvine PMSA, CA	H	10.81 FQ	16.52 MW	24.15 TQ	CABLS	1/16-3/16
	Los Angeles-Long Beach-Glendale PMSA, CA	H	14.50 FQ	19.16 MW	25.13 TQ	CABLS	1/16-3/16
	Oakland-Hayward-Berkeley PMSA, CA	H	15.87 FQ	20.12 MW	23.33 TQ	CABLS	1/16-3/16
	Riverside-San Bernardino-Ontario MSA, CA	H	14.77 FQ	23.16 MW	30.16 TQ	CABLS	1/16-3/16
	Sacramento–Roseville–Arden-Arcade MSA, CA	H	16.38 FQ	17.67 MW	18.95 TQ	CABLS	1/16-3/16
	San Diego-Carlsbad MSA, CA	H	18.87 FQ	26.35 MW	28.84 TQ	CABLS	1/16-3/16
	Colorado	Y	31720 FQ	40430 MW	50270 TQ	USBLS	5/15
	Denver-Aurora-Lakewood MSA, CO	Y	35740 FQ	47200 MW	61160 TQ	USBLS	5/15
	Connecticut	Y		36783 MW		CTBLS	1/16-3/16
	Hartford-West Hartford-East Hartford MSA, CT	Y	30990 FQ	37770 MW	46920 TQ	USBLS	5/15
	Washington-Arlington-Alexandria PMSA, DC-VA-MD-WV	Y	28830 FQ	37730 MW	48420 TQ	USBLS	5/15
	Florida	H	11.41 AE	15.81 MW	18.32 AEX	FLBLS	7/16-9/16
	Fort Lauderdale-Pompano Beach-Deerfield Beach PMSA, FL	H	11.04 AE	11.67 MW	14.95 AEX	FLBLS	7/16-9/16
	Miami-Miami Beach-Kendall PMSA, FL	H	11.19 AE	16.31 MW	21.09 AEX	FLBLS	7/16-9/16
	Orlando-Kissimmee-Sanford MSA, FL	H	10.89 AE	14.59 MW	17.13 AEX	FLBLS	7/16-9/16

AE	Average entry wage	**AWR**	Average wage range	**H**	Hourly	**LR** Low end range	**MTC** Median total compensation	**TCC** Total cash compensation
AEX	Average experienced wage	**B**	Biweekly	**HI**	Highest wage paid	**M** Monthly	**MW** Median wage paid	**TQ** Third quartile wage
ATC	Average total compensation	**D**	Daily	**HR**	High end range	**MCC** Median cash compensation	**MWR** Median wage range	**W** Weekly
AW	Average wage paid	**FQ**	First quartile wage	**LO**	Lowest wage paid	**ME** Median entry wage	**S** See annotated source	**Y** Yearly

Occupation/Type/Industry	Location	Per	Low	Mid	High	Source	Date
Motorcycle Mechanic	Tampa-St. Petersburg-Clearwater MSA, FL	H	12.86 AE	16.51 MW	17.85 AEX	FLBLS	7/16-9/16
	Georgia	Y	24290 FQ	29600 MW	38510 TQ	USBLS	5/15
	Atlanta-Sandy Springs-Roswell MSA, GA	Y	25390 FQ	36110 MW	52250 TQ	USBLS	5/15
	Hawaii	Y	36070 FQ	48760 MW	71210 TQ	USBLS	5/15
	Urban Honolulu MSA, HI	Y	42470 FQ	57320 MW	72700 TQ	USBLS	5/15
	Idaho	Y	25980 FQ	29790 MW	40890 TQ	USBLS	5/15
	Boise City MSA, ID	Y	26320 FQ	29550 MW	41730 TQ	USBLS	5/15
	Illinois	Y	27320 FQ	34930 MW	43170 TQ	USBLS	5/15
	Chicago-Naperville-Arlington Heights PMSA, IL	Y	30100 FQ	41480 MW	47330 TQ	USBLS	5/15
	Indiana	Y	29730 FQ	35400 MW	40940 TQ	USBLS	5/15
	Indianapolis-Carmel-Anderson MSA, IN	Y	32670 FQ	37010 MW	48030 TQ	USBLS	5/15
	Iowa	Y	27560 FQ	33060 MW	37820 TQ	USBLS	5/15
	Des Moines-West Des Moines MSA, IA	Y	26370 FQ	33520 MW	38230 TQ	USBLS	5/15
	Kansas	Y	31120 FQ	34680 MW	38170 TQ	USBLS	5/15
	Kentucky	Y	23310 FQ	33580 MW	41160 TQ	USBLS	5/15
	Louisiana	Y	27150 FQ	36260 MW	48370 TQ	USBLS	5/15
	New Orleans-Metairie MSA, LA	Y	36470 FQ	45950 MW	55770 TQ	USBLS	5/15
	Maine	Y	27250 FQ	32270 MW	38260 TQ	USBLS	5/15
	Maryland	Y	25862 AE	41019 MW	48597 AEX	MDBLS	4/16
	Baltimore-Columbia-Towson MSA, MD	Y	30570 FQ	44270 MW	53060 TQ	USBLS	5/15
	Massachusetts	Y	24350 FQ	35460 MW	42260 TQ	USBLS	5/15
	Boston-Cambridge-Newton NECTA, MA	Y	33850 FQ	38070 MW	44090 TQ	USBLS	5/15
	Michigan	Y	25390 FQ	32240 MW	45200 TQ	USBLS	5/15
	Minnesota	Y	28229 FQ	31618 MW	39121 TQ	MNBLS	1/16-3/16
	Minneapolis-St. Paul-Bloomington MSA, MN-WI	Y	28078 FQ	30814 MW	36556 TQ	MNBLS	1/16-3/16
	Mississippi	Y	27340 FQ	33120 MW	40110 TQ	USBLS	5/15
	Missouri	Y	23830 FQ	30410 MW	38730 TQ	USBLS	5/15
	Kansas City MSA, MO-KS	Y	29070 FQ	35600 MW	43950 TQ	USBLS	5/15
	St. Louis MSA, MO-IL	Y	26830 FQ	32610 MW	39220 TQ	USBLS	5/15
	Montana	Y	27330 FQ	32270 MW	38840 TQ	USBLS	5/15
	Nebraska	Y	27135 FQ	32240 MW	43585 TQ	NEBLS	7/16-9/16
	Nevada	Y	27850 FQ	35990 MW	55050 TQ	USBLS	5/15
	Las Vegas-Henderson-Paradise MSA, NV	Y	32820 FQ	46660 MW	69020 TQ	USBLS	5/15
	New Hampshire	H	14.43 AE	20.07 MW	23.74 AEX	NHBLS	6/16
	New Jersey	Y	32910 FQ	42710 MW	50030 TQ	USBLS	5/15
	Camden PMSA, NJ	Y	19120 FQ	39080 MW	45840 TQ	USBLS	5/15
	Newark PMSA, NJ-PA	Y	41990 FQ	50260 MW	56740 TQ	USBLS	5/15
	New Mexico	Y	22120 FQ	24920 MW	34570 TQ	USBLS	5/15
	Albuquerque MSA, NM	Y	21410 FQ	23800 MW	30400 TQ	USBLS	5/15
	New York	Y	26710 AE	38060 MW	44240 AEX	NYBLS	1/16-3/16
	Buffalo-Cheektowaga-Niagara Falls MSA, NY	Y	23560 FQ	33270 MW	38330 TQ	USBLS	5/15
	Nassau County-Suffolk County PMSA, NY	Y	28680 FQ	40170 MW	45640 TQ	USBLS	5/15
	New York-Jersey City-White Plains PMSA, NY-NJ	Y	33230 FQ	42130 MW	48690 TQ	USBLS	5/15
	North Carolina	Y	26240 FQ	31340 MW	43000 TQ	USBLS	5/15
	Charlotte-Concord-Gastonia MSA, NC-SC	Y	35630 FQ	44960 MW	50890 TQ	USBLS	5/15
	Raleigh MSA, NC	Y	27860 FQ	33750 MW	44630 TQ	USBLS	5/15
	North Dakota	Y	25100 FQ	35000 MW	45220 TQ	USBLS	5/15
	Ohio	Y	26410 FQ	31980 MW	37340 TQ	USBLS	5/15
	Cincinnati MSA, OH-KY-IN	Y	25780 FQ	29090 MW	34100 TQ	USBLS	5/15
	Cleveland-Elyria MSA, OH	Y	29550 FQ	35820 MW	51820 TQ	USBLS	5/15
	Columbus MSA, OH	Y	29320 FQ	33510 MW	37750 TQ	USBLS	5/15
	Oklahoma	Y	27650 FQ	34730 MW	39660 TQ	USBLS	5/15
	Oklahoma City MSA, OK	Y	24070 FQ	33840 MW	37670 TQ	USBLS	5/15
	Tulsa MSA, OK	Y	35260 FQ	42460 MW	47900 TQ	USBLS	5/15
	Oregon	H	14.19 FQ	19.59 MW	22.14 TQ	ORBLS	2016
	Portland-Vancouver-Hillsboro MSA, OR-WA	Y	31750 FQ	42060 MW	46580 TQ	USBLS	5/15
	Pennsylvania	Y	26200 FQ	32980 MW	40820 TQ	USBLS	5/15

AE	Average entry wage	AWR	Average wage range	H	Hourly
AEX	Average experienced wage	B	Biweekly	HI	Highest wage paid
ATC	Average total compensation	D	Daily	HR	High end range
AW	Average wage paid	FQ	First quartile wage	LO	Lowest wage paid

LR	Low end range	MTC	Median total compensation
M	Monthly	MW	Median wage paid
MCC	Median cash compensation	MWR	Median wage range
ME	Median entry wage	S	See annotated source

TCC	Total cash compensation		
TQ	Third quartile wage		
W	Weekly		
Y	Yearly		

Occupation/Type/Industry	Location	Per	Low	Mid	High	Source	Date
Motorcycle Mechanic	Montgomery County-Bucks County-Chester County						
	PMSA, PA	Y	31770 FQ	41060 MW	47960 TQ	USBLS	5/15
	Pittsburgh MSA, PA	Y	20120 FQ	31120 MW	38980 TQ	USBLS	5/15
	Rhode Island	Y	35580 FQ	41970 MW	46380 TQ	USBLS	5/15
	Providence-Warwick MSA, RI-MA	Y	32800 FQ	41110 MW	45970 TQ	USBLS	5/15
	South Carolina	Y	26560 FQ	35690 MW	45100 TQ	USBLS	5/15
	Columbia MSA, SC	Y	35000 FQ	40280 MW	50790 TQ	USBLS	5/15
	Greenville-Anderson-Mauldin MSA, SC	Y	29480 FQ	38610 MW	46220 TQ	USBLS	5/15
	South Dakota	Y	25450 FQ	29500 MW	36370 TQ	USBLS	5/15
	Tennessee	Y	31660 FQ	38230 MW	44440 TQ	USBLS	5/15
	Memphis MSA, TN-MS-AR	Y	24560 FQ	35740 MW	43430 TQ	USBLS	5/15
	Nashville-Davidson–Murfreesboro–Franklin MSA, TN	Y	40690 FQ	43920 MW	47150 TQ	USBLS	5/15
	Texas	Y	25230 FQ	33520 MW	46430 TQ	USBLS	5/15
	Austin-Round Rock MSA, TX	Y	24690 FQ	34020 MW	40510 TQ	USBLS	5/15
	Dallas-Plano-Irving PMSA, TX	Y	24880 FQ	40630 MW	46350 TQ	USBLS	5/15
	Fort Worth-Arlington PMSA, TX	Y	29370 FQ	42480 MW	52290 TQ	USBLS	5/15
	Houston-The Woodlands-Sugar Land MSA, TX	Y	23920 FQ	27810 MW	39540 TQ	USBLS	5/15
	San Antonio-New Braunfels MSA, TX	Y	27760 FQ	33190 MW	40350 TQ	USBLS	5/15
	Utah	Y	30140 FQ	40040 MW	48950 TQ	USBLS	5/15
	Provo-Orem MSA, UT	Y	27240 FQ	30070 MW	47710 TQ	USBLS	5/15
	Salt Lake City MSA, UT	Y	33540 FQ	42250 MW	49370 TQ	USBLS	5/15
	Vermont	Y	25130 FQ	27950 MW	30860 TQ	USBLS	5/15
	Virginia	Y	26620 FQ	34450 MW	45060 TQ	USBLS	5/15
	Richmond MSA, VA	Y	33980 FQ	41700 MW	54200 TQ	USBLS	5/15
	Washington	H	14.10 FQ	17.86 MW	24.73 TQ	WABLS	3/16
	Seattle-Bellevue-Everett PMSA, WA	H	17.66 FQ	25.20 MW	28.06 TQ	WABLS	3/16
	West Virginia	Y	19440 FQ	25220 MW	31500 TQ	USBLS	5/15
	Huntington-Ashland MSA, WV-KY-OH	Y	18440 FQ	39700 MW	45160 TQ	USBLS	5/15
	Wisconsin	Y	21310 FQ	29500 MW	36190 TQ	USBLS	5/15
	Milwaukee-Waukesha-West Allis MSA, WI	Y	21370 FQ	33630 MW	38860 TQ	USBLS	5/15
	Wyoming	Y	28830 FQ	41280 MW	47680 TQ	USBLS	5/15
Motorcycle Officer							
Police Department, Municipal Government	Menlo Park, CA	Y			114454 HI	CACIT	6/28/16
Mounted Deputy							
County Government	Oakland County, MI	H			16.88 HI	MIOAK2	10/1/16
Multimedia Artist and Animator	Alabama	Y	43015 AE	65298 AW	76429 AEX	ALBLS	6/16
	Birmingham-Hoover MSA, AL	Y	40273 AE	69365 AW	83911 AEX	ALBLS	6/16
	Arizona	Y	43310 FQ	56280 MW	69050 TQ	USBLS	5/15
	Phoenix-Mesa-Scottsdale MSA, AZ	Y	41770 FQ	53010 MW	65400 TQ	USBLS	5/15
	Tucson MSA, AZ	Y	60680 FQ	67540 MW	73010 TQ	USBLS	5/15
	Arkansas	Y	26730 FQ	34290 MW	51090 TQ	USBLS	5/15
	Little Rock-North Little Rock-Conway MSA, AR	Y	31440 FQ	36420 MW	50880 TQ	USBLS	5/15
	California	H	27.94 FQ	39.21 MW	49.09 TQ	CABLS	1/16-3/16
	Anaheim-Santa Ana-Irvine PMSA, CA	H	25.67 FQ	32.57 MW	42.48 TQ	CABLS	1/16-3/16
	Los Angeles-Long Beach-Glendale PMSA, CA	H	28.64 FQ	40.94 MW	49.87 TQ	CABLS	1/16-3/16
	Oakland-Hayward-Berkeley PMSA, CA	H	28.63 FQ	37.42 MW	48.18 TQ	CABLS	1/16-3/16
	Riverside-San Bernardino-Ontario MSA, CA	H	19.99 FQ	30.99 MW	43.49 TQ	CABLS	1/16-3/16
	Sacramento–Roseville–Arden-Arcade MSA, CA	H	24.09 FQ	30.89 MW	39.86 TQ	CABLS	1/16-3/16
	San Diego-Carlsbad MSA, CA	H	18.84 FQ	29.69 MW	45.71 TQ	CABLS	1/16-3/16

AE	Average entry wage	AWR	Average wage range	H	Hourly	LR	Low end range	
AEX	Average experienced wage	B	Biweekly	HI	Highest wage paid	M	Monthly	
ATC	Average total compensation	D	Daily	HR	High end range	MCC	Median cash compensation	
AW	Average wage paid	FQ	First quartile wage	LO	Lowest wage paid	ME	Median entry wage	

MTC	Median total compensation	TCC	Total cash compensation
MW	Median wage paid	TQ	Third quartile wage
MWR	Median wage range	W	Weekly
S	See annotated source	Y	Yearly

Multimedia Artist and Animator

Occupation/Type/Industry	Location	Per	Low	Mid	High	Source	Date
Multimedia Artist and Animator	San Francisco-Redwood City-South San Francisco PMSA, CA	H	33.87 FQ	42.15 MW	53.89 TQ	CABLS	1/16-3/16
	Colorado	Y	48630 FQ	58920 MW	72320 TQ	USBLS	5/15
	Denver-Aurora-Lakewood MSA, CO	Y	49400 FQ	59310 MW	72730 TQ	USBLS	5/15
	Connecticut	Y		74839 MW		CTBLS	1/16-3/16
	Bridgeport-Stamford-Norwalk MSA, CT	Y	46460 FQ	68530 MW	92510 TQ	USBLS	5/15
	Wilmington PMSA, DE-MD-NJ	Y	56740 FQ	68610 MW	79570 TQ	USBLS	5/15
	District of Columbia	Y	65030 FQ	74280 MW	85990 TQ	USBLS	5/15
	Washington-Arlington-Alexandria PMSA, DC-VA-MD-WV	Y	54470 FQ	69320 MW	87680 TQ	USBLS	5/15
	Florida	H	19.00 AE	26.96 MW	32.61 AEX	FLBLS	7/16-9/16
	Fort Lauderdale-Pompano Beach-Deerfield Beach PMSA, FL	H	23.84 AE	29.64 MW	36.04 AEX	FLBLS	7/16-9/16
	Miami-Miami Beach-Kendall PMSA, FL	H	17.57 AE	26.89 MW	34.83 AEX	FLBLS	7/16-9/16
	Orlando-Kissimmee-Sanford MSA, FL	H	18.72 AE	28.55 MW	35.27 AEX	FLBLS	7/16-9/16
	Tampa-St. Petersburg-Clearwater MSA, FL	H	18.58 AE	26.35 MW	30.17 AEX	FLBLS	7/16-9/16
	Georgia	Y	42280 FQ	50180 MW	61540 TQ	USBLS	5/15
	Atlanta-Sandy Springs-Roswell MSA, GA	Y	42650 FQ	50720 MW	62080 TQ	USBLS	5/15
	Hawaii	Y	36110 FQ	59770 MW	74110 TQ	USBLS	5/15
	Urban Honolulu MSA, HI	Y	36110 FQ	59770 MW	74110 TQ	USBLS	5/15
	Idaho	Y	54940 FQ	67810 MW	79470 TQ	USBLS	5/15
	Boise City MSA, ID	Y	56770 FQ	67620 MW	77800 TQ	USBLS	5/15
	Illinois	Y	48540 FQ	64120 MW	85200 TQ	USBLS	5/15
	Chicago-Naperville-Arlington Heights PMSA, IL	Y	50470 FQ	66140 MW	87010 TQ	USBLS	5/15
	Indiana	Y	37790 FQ	48210 MW	60660 TQ	USBLS	5/15
	Indianapolis-Carmel-Anderson MSA, IN	Y	38610 FQ	49090 MW	62090 TQ	USBLS	5/15
	Iowa	Y	31460 FQ	47270 MW	71440 TQ	USBLS	5/15
	Kansas	Y	35250 FQ	45840 MW	57300 TQ	USBLS	5/15
	Wichita MSA, KS	Y	31660 FQ	41730 MW	51310 TQ	USBLS	5/15
	Kentucky	Y	35690 FQ	44570 MW	68610 TQ	USBLS	5/15
	Louisville-Jefferson County MSA, KY-IN	Y	34970 FQ	42560 MW	56090 TQ	USBLS	5/15
	New Orleans-Metairie MSA, LA	Y	54100 FQ	67600 MW	85870 TQ	USBLS	5/15
	Maryland	Y	43095 AE	68756 MW	81587 AEX	MDBLS	4/16
	Baltimore-Columbia-Towson MSA, MD	Y	48170 FQ	66760 MW	90590 TQ	USBLS	5/15
	Massachusetts	Y	54570 FQ	67560 MW	85720 TQ	USBLS	5/15
	Boston-Cambridge-Newton NECTA, MA	Y	55650 FQ	68920 MW	89510 TQ	USBLS	5/15
	Worcester MSA, MA-CT	Y	49840 FQ	68500 MW	84550 TQ	USBLS	5/15
	Michigan	Y	37570 FQ	50340 MW	68020 TQ	USBLS	5/15
	Detroit-Dearborn-Livonia PMSA, MI	Y	46020 FQ	61360 MW	76520 TQ	USBLS	5/15
	Grand Rapids-Wyoming MSA, MI	Y	33690 FQ	37920 MW	46830 TQ	USBLS	5/15
	Minnesota	Y	44032 FQ	64112 MW	77136 TQ	MNBLS	1/16-3/16
	Minneapolis-St. Paul-Bloomington MSA, MN-WI	Y	43568 FQ	61904 MW	76189 TQ	MNBLS	1/16-3/16
	Missouri	Y	42850 FQ	57330 MW	75320 TQ	USBLS	5/15
	Kansas City MSA, MO-KS	Y	42410 FQ	54710 MW	70580 TQ	USBLS	5/15
	St. Louis MSA, MO-IL	Y	52300 FQ	66630 MW	87370 TQ	USBLS	5/15
	Nebraska	Y	40985 FQ	49970 MW	59475 TQ	NEBLS	7/16-9/16
	Omaha-Council Bluffs MSA, NE-IA	Y	42405 FQ	49225 MW	59250 TQ	NEBLS	7/16-9/16
	Nevada	Y	50210 FQ	63620 MW	77970 TQ	USBLS	5/15
	Las Vegas-Henderson-Paradise MSA, NV	Y	49730 FQ	62270 MW	76560 TQ	USBLS	5/15
	New Hampshire	H	19.92 AE	27.21 MW	34.03 AEX	NHBLS	6/16
	Manchester NECTA, NH	H	20.20 AE	27.70 MW	31.16 AEX	NHBLS	6/16

AE	Average entry wage	AWR	Average wage range	H	Hourly
AEX	Average experienced wage	B	Biweekly	HI	Highest wage paid
ATC	Average total compensation	D	Daily	HR	High end range
AW	Average wage paid	FQ	First quartile wage	LO	Lowest wage paid

LR	Low end range	MTC	Median total compensation
M	Monthly	MCC	Median cash compensation
MCC	Median cash compensation	MWR	Median wage range
ME	Median entry wage	S	See annotated source

MTC	Median total compensation	TCC	Total cash compensation
MW	Median wage paid	TQ	Third quartile wage
MWR	Median wage range	W	Weekly
S	See annotated source	Y	Yearly

Occupation/Type/Industry	Location	Per	Low	Mid	High	Source	Date
Multimedia Artist and Animator	New Jersey	Y	51560 FQ	61900 MW	81640 TQ	USBLS	5/15
	Camden PMSA, NJ	Y	47700 FQ	78830 MW	107790 TQ	USBLS	5/15
	Newark PMSA, NJ-PA	Y	61740 FQ	74720 MW	92840 TQ	USBLS	5/15
	Trenton MSA, NJ	Y	48430 FQ	58420 MW	73350 TQ	USBLS	5/15
	New Mexico	Y	36280 FQ	48820 MW	103540 TQ	USBLS	5/15
	New York	Y	45580 AE	65030 MW	83140 AEX	NYBLS	1/16-3/16
	Nassau County-Suffolk County PMSA, NY	Y	42450 FQ	54300 MW	69550 TQ	USBLS	5/15
	New York-Jersey City-White Plains PMSA, NY-NJ	Y	53480 FQ	64600 MW	84240 TQ	USBLS	5/15
	Rochester MSA, NY	Y	40990 FQ	48270 MW	66280 TQ	USBLS	5/15
	North Carolina	Y	39290 FQ	54760 MW	69610 TQ	USBLS	5/15
	Charlotte-Concord-Gastonia MSA, NC-SC	Y	42970 FQ	55440 MW	65770 TQ	USBLS	5/15
	Raleigh MSA, NC	Y	39150 FQ	54980 MW	68300 TQ	USBLS	5/15
	Ohio	Y	42380 FQ	50780 MW	62770 TQ	USBLS	5/15
	Cincinnati MSA, OH-KY-IN	Y	40240 FQ	49470 MW	62330 TQ	USBLS	5/15
	Cleveland-Elyria MSA, OH	Y	43940 FQ	50790 MW	61440 TQ	USBLS	5/15
	Columbus MSA, OH	Y	48980 FQ	56620 MW	63770 TQ	USBLS	5/15
	Oklahoma	Y	38300 FQ	45670 MW	59120 TQ	USBLS	5/15
	Oklahoma City MSA, OK	Y	40660 FQ	48200 MW	67430 TQ	USBLS	5/15
	Portland-Vancouver-Hillsboro MSA, OR-WA	Y	48530 FQ	61300 MW	97150 TQ	USBLS	5/15
	Pennsylvania	Y	38700 FQ	50200 MW	67430 TQ	USBLS	5/15
	Montgomery County-Bucks County-Chester County PMSA, PA	Y	44360 FQ	54300 MW	71760 TQ	USBLS	5/15
	Philadelphia PMSA, PA	Y	35880 FQ	40490 MW	57920 TQ	USBLS	5/15
	Pittsburgh MSA, PA	Y	40420 FQ	49040 MW	58780 TQ	USBLS	5/15
	Rhode Island	Y	51390 FQ	56730 MW	62070 TQ	USBLS	5/15
	Providence-Warwick MSA, RI-MA	Y	51390 FQ	56730 MW	62070 TQ	USBLS	5/15
	South Carolina	Y	35220 FQ	48440 MW	64330 TQ	USBLS	5/15
	Charleston-North Charleston MSA, SC	Y	45130 FQ	53820 MW	65100 TQ	USBLS	5/15
	South Dakota	Y	32330 FQ	38860 MW	45780 TQ	USBLS	5/15
	Sioux Falls MSA, SD	Y	35070 FQ	41200 MW	47400 TQ	USBLS	5/15
	Tennessee	Y	36780 FQ	45780 MW	58390 TQ	USBLS	5/15
	Nashville-Davidson–Murfreesboro–Franklin MSA, TN	Y	40100 FQ	46380 MW	57610 TQ	USBLS	5/15
	Texas	Y	41340 FQ	58540 MW	77500 TQ	USBLS	5/15
	Austin-Round Rock MSA, TX	Y	38250 FQ	52580 MW	73150 TQ	USBLS	5/15
	Dallas-Plano-Irving PMSA, TX	Y	45910 FQ	62400 MW	77810 TQ	USBLS	5/15
	Fort Worth-Arlington PMSA, TX	Y	38420 FQ	56040 MW	68740 TQ	USBLS	5/15
	Houston-The Woodlands-Sugar Land MSA, TX	Y	45200 FQ	66150 MW	80450 TQ	USBLS	5/15
	San Antonio-New Braunfels MSA, TX	Y	46550 FQ	76790 MW	101030 TQ	USBLS	5/15
	Utah	Y	45930 FQ	59380 MW	72390 TQ	USBLS	5/15
	Salt Lake City MSA, UT	Y	53490 FQ	62770 MW	75550 TQ	USBLS	5/15
	Virginia	Y	53630 FQ	65990 MW	81220 TQ	USBLS	5/15
	Richmond MSA, VA	Y	63840 FQ	70780 MW	77590 TQ	USBLS	5/15
	Virginia Beach-Norfolk-Newport News MSA, VA-NC	Y	51290 FQ	58400 MW	68680 TQ	USBLS	5/15
	Washington	H	25.82 FQ	37.68 MW	49.68 TQ	WABLS	3/16
	Seattle-Bellevue-Everett PMSA, WA	H	26.96 FQ	38.33 MW	50.31 TQ	WABLS	3/16
	Wisconsin	Y	41090 FQ	49280 MW	58850 TQ	USBLS	5/15
	Madison MSA, WI	Y	41390 FQ	49970 MW	59640 TQ	USBLS	5/15
	Milwaukee-Waukesha-West Allis MSA, WI	Y	44030 FQ	53080 MW	61850 TQ	USBLS	5/15
Multimedia Journalist							
Television	United States	Y		32000 MW		RTDNA	2016
Multiple Machine Tool Setter, Operator, and Tender							
Metals and Plastics	Alabama	Y	22991 AE	33098 AW	38157 AEX	ALBLS	6/16
Metals and Plastics	Birmingham-Hoover MSA, AL	Y	26456 AE	36615 AW	41694 AEX	ALBLS	6/16
Metals and Plastics	Alaska	Y	41810 FQ	47400 MW	54510 TQ	USBLS	5/15

AE Average entry wage	**AWR** Average wage range	**H** Hourly	**LR** Low end range	**MTC** Median total compensation	**TCC** Total cash compensation
AEX Average experienced wage	**B** Biweekly	**HI** Highest wage paid	**M** Monthly	**MW** Median wage paid	**TQ** Third quartile wage
ATC Average total compensation	**D** Daily	**HR** High end range	**MCC** Median cash compensation	**MWR** Median wage range	**W** Weekly
AW Average wage paid	**FQ** First quartile wage	**LO** Lowest wage paid	**ME** Median entry wage	**S** See annotated source	**Y** Yearly

Occupation/Type/Industry	Location	Per	Low	Mid	High	Source	Date
Multiple Machine Tool Setter, Operator, and Tender							
Metals and Plastics	Arizona	Y	28470 FQ	36670 MW	49360 TQ	USBLS	5/15
Metals and Plastics	Phoenix-Mesa-Scottsdale MSA, AZ	Y	28710 FQ	37650 MW	49900 TQ	USBLS	5/15
Metals and Plastics	Tucson MSA, AZ	Y	29970 FQ	36970 MW	49610 TQ	USBLS	5/15
Metals and Plastics	Arkansas	Y	29930 FQ	35520 MW	40960 TQ	USBLS	5/15
Metals and Plastics	Little Rock-North Little Rock-Conway MSA, AR	Y	28010 FQ	33830 MW	38240 TQ	USBLS	5/15
Metals and Plastics	California	H	12.45 FQ	17.10 MW	22.40 TQ	CABLS	1/16-3/16
Metals and Plastics	Anaheim-Santa Ana-Irvine PMSA, CA	H	12.24 FQ	16.51 MW	21.04 TQ	CABLS	1/16-3/16
Metals and Plastics	Los Angeles-Long Beach-Glendale PMSA, CA	H	11.93 FQ	17.64 MW	23.07 TQ	CABLS	1/16-3/16
Metals and Plastics	Oakland-Hayward-Berkeley PMSA, CA	H	16.14 FQ	20.62 MW	23.21 TQ	CABLS	1/16-3/16
Metals and Plastics	Riverside-San Bernardino-Ontario MSA, CA	H	11.29 FQ	14.24 MW	19.52 TQ	CABLS	1/16-3/16
Metals and Plastics	Sacramento–Roseville–Arden-Arcade MSA, CA	H	11.08 FQ	13.00 MW	15.87 TQ	CABLS	1/16-3/16
Metals and Plastics	San Diego-Carlsbad MSA, CA	H	14.06 FQ	16.94 MW	20.21 TQ	CABLS	1/16-3/16
Metals and Plastics	San Francisco-Redwood City-South San Francisco PMSA, CA	H	13.74 FQ	18.03 MW	22.79 TQ	CABLS	1/16-3/16
Metals and Plastics	Colorado	Y	25540 FQ	29380 MW	35860 TQ	USBLS	5/15
Metals and Plastics	Denver-Aurora-Lakewood MSA, CO	Y	25510 FQ	29100 MW	35460 TQ	USBLS	5/15
Metals and Plastics	Connecticut	Y		37492 MW		CTBLS	1/16-3/16
Metals and Plastics	Bridgeport-Stamford-Norwalk MSA, CT	Y	30100 FQ	39000 MW	56250 TQ	USBLS	5/15
Metals and Plastics	Hartford-West Hartford-East Hartford MSA, CT	Y	33480 FQ	42360 MW	53420 TQ	USBLS	5/15
Metals and Plastics	Waterbury MSA, CT	Y	21450 FQ	23610 MW	30190 TQ	USBLS	5/15
Metals and Plastics	Washington-Arlington-Alexandria PMSA, DC-VA-MD-WV	Y	31090 FQ	44040 MW	55380 TQ	USBLS	5/15
Metals and Plastics	Florida	H	11.56 AE	15.78 MW	19.17 AEX	FLBLS	7/16-9/16
Metals and Plastics	Fort Lauderdale-Pompano Beach-Deerfield Beach PMSA, FL	H	11.04 AE	15.11 MW	19.89 AEX	FLBLS	7/16-9/16
Metals and Plastics	Miami-Miami Beach-Kendall PMSA, FL	H	12.45 AE	15.58 MW	19.43 AEX	FLBLS	7/16-9/16
Metals and Plastics	Orlando-Kissimmee-Sanford MSA, FL	H	12.02 AE	15.99 MW	17.42 AEX	FLBLS	7/16-9/16
Metals and Plastics	Tampa-St. Petersburg-Clearwater MSA, FL	H	11.69 AE	17.43 MW	20.11 AEX	FLBLS	7/16-9/16
Metals and Plastics	Georgia	Y	23270 FQ	28250 MW	33780 TQ	USBLS	5/15
Metals and Plastics	Atlanta-Sandy Springs-Roswell MSA, GA	Y	25860 FQ	28690 MW	32560 TQ	USBLS	5/15
Metals and Plastics	Illinois	Y	27420 FQ	35500 MW	45050 TQ	USBLS	5/15
Metals and Plastics	Chicago-Naperville-Arlington Heights PMSA, IL	Y	27850 FQ	38740 MW	47500 TQ	USBLS	5/15
Metals and Plastics	Lake County-Kenosha County PMSA, IL-WI	Y	23350 FQ	29200 MW	35470 TQ	USBLS	5/15
Metals and Plastics	Indiana	Y	28800 FQ	35820 MW	43760 TQ	USBLS	5/15
Metals and Plastics	Gary PMSA, IN	Y	32060 FQ	36330 MW	42060 TQ	USBLS	5/15
Metals and Plastics	Indianapolis-Carmel-Anderson MSA, IN	Y	26620 FQ	33330 MW	41310 TQ	USBLS	5/15
Metals and Plastics	Iowa	Y	27090 FQ	32750 MW	38240 TQ	USBLS	5/15
Metals and Plastics	Des Moines-West Des Moines MSA, IA	Y	24470 FQ	29260 MW	36050 TQ	USBLS	5/15
Metals and Plastics	Kansas	Y	30820 FQ	37730 MW	47930 TQ	USBLS	5/15
Metals and Plastics	Wichita MSA, KS	Y	24520 FQ	28540 MW	34470 TQ	USBLS	5/15
Metals and Plastics	Kentucky	Y	29620 FQ	35430 MW	40600 TQ	USBLS	5/15
Metals and Plastics	Louisville-Jefferson County MSA, KY-IN	Y	26590 FQ	34330 MW	38840 TQ	USBLS	5/15
Metals and Plastics	Louisiana	Y	32190 FQ	37830 MW	48430 TQ	USBLS	5/15
Metals and Plastics	Maine	Y	28250 FQ	34380 MW	44370 TQ	USBLS	5/15
Metals and Plastics	Portland-South Portland MSA, ME	Y	28210 FQ	35240 MW	45970 TQ	USBLS	5/15
Metals and Plastics	Maryland	Y	24619 AE	35771 MW	41347 AEX	MDBLS	4/16

AE	Average entry wage	AWR	Average wage range	H	Hourly
AEX	Average experienced wage	B	Biweekly	HI	Highest wage paid
ATC	Average total compensation	D	Daily	HR	High end range
AW	Average wage paid	FQ	First quartile wage	LO	Lowest wage paid

LR	Low end range	MTC	Median total compensation	TCC	Total cash compensation
M	Monthly	MW	Median wage paid	TQ	Third quartile wage
MCC	Median cash compensation	MWR	Median wage range	W	Weekly
ME	Median entry wage	S	See annotated source	Y	Yearly

Occupation/Type/Industry	Location	Per	Low	Mid	High	Source	Date
Multiple Machine Tool Setter, Operator, and Tender							
Metals and Plastics	Baltimore-Columbia-Towson MSA, MD	Y	31250 FQ	38620 MW	45860 TQ	USBLS	5/15
Metals and Plastics	Massachusetts	Y	26880 FQ	35150 MW	45010 TQ	USBLS	5/15
Metals and Plastics	Boston-Cambridge-Newton NECTA, MA	Y	31770 FQ	38790 MW	49320 TQ	USBLS	5/15
Metals and Plastics	Worcester MSA, MA-CT	Y	23280 FQ	29560 MW	39820 TQ	USBLS	5/15
Metals and Plastics	Michigan	Y	23640 FQ	31580 MW	42920 TQ	USBLS	5/15
Metals and Plastics	Grand Rapids-Wyoming MSA, MI	Y	19050 FQ	24240 MW	30480 TQ	USBLS	5/15
Metals and Plastics	Minnesota	Y	31993 FQ	37349 MW	44851 TQ	MNBLS	1/16-3/16
Metals and Plastics	Minneapolis-St. Paul-Bloomington MSA, MN-WI	Y	34008 FQ	40650 MW	47889 TQ	MNBLS	1/16-3/16
Metals and Plastics	Mississippi	Y	23990 FQ	29440 MW	37610 TQ	USBLS	5/15
Metals and Plastics	Missouri	Y	26260 FQ	29780 MW	36660 TQ	USBLS	5/15
Metals and Plastics	Kansas City MSA, MO-KS	Y	24840 FQ	32200 MW	38800 TQ	USBLS	5/15
Metals and Plastics	St. Louis MSA, MO-IL	Y	31370 FQ	38060 MW	45500 TQ	USBLS	5/15
Metals and Plastics	Montana	Y	31790 FQ	37040 MW	44420 TQ	USBLS	5/15
Metals and Plastics	Nebraska	Y	31845 FQ	36070 MW	41935 TQ	NEBLS	7/16-9/16
Metals and Plastics	Omaha-Council Bluffs MSA, NE-IA	Y	27440 FQ	33430 MW	38385 TQ	NEBLS	7/16-9/16
Metals and Plastics	Nevada	Y	27070 FQ	30170 MW	35420 TQ	USBLS	5/15
Metals and Plastics	New Hampshire	H	14.26 AE	18.37 MW	22.48 AEX	NHBLS	6/16
Metals and Plastics	Manchester NECTA, NH	H	15.48 AE	22.88 MW	25.91 AEX	NHBLS	6/16
Metals and Plastics	Nashua NECTA, NH-MA	Y	41250 FQ	47310 MW	60440 TQ	USBLS	5/15
Metals and Plastics	New Jersey	Y	27270 FQ	33630 MW	41140 TQ	USBLS	5/15
Metals and Plastics	Camden PMSA, NJ	Y	30550 FQ	37380 MW	46960 TQ	USBLS	5/15
Metals and Plastics	Newark PMSA, NJ-PA	Y	26620 FQ	32030 MW	38250 TQ	USBLS	5/15
Metals and Plastics	New York	Y	24190 AE	34870 MW	42380 AEX	NYBLS	1/16-3/16
Metals and Plastics	Buffalo-Cheektowaga-Niagara Falls MSA, NY	Y	31490 FQ	36210 MW	48120 TQ	USBLS	5/15
Metals and Plastics	Nassau County-Suffolk County PMSA, NY	Y	20760 FQ	32970 MW	50350 TQ	USBLS	5/15
Metals and Plastics	New York-Jersey City-White Plains PMSA, NY-NJ	Y	24560 FQ	31850 MW	40420 TQ	USBLS	5/15
Metals and Plastics	Rochester MSA, NY	Y	22720 FQ	32660 MW	42270 TQ	USBLS	5/15
Metals and Plastics	North Carolina	Y	29220 FQ	36310 MW	49430 TQ	USBLS	5/15
Metals and Plastics	Charlotte-Concord-Gastonia MSA, NC-SC	Y	32490 FQ	41820 MW	53400 TQ	USBLS	5/15
Metals and Plastics	Raleigh MSA, NC	Y	30560 FQ	35240 MW	39540 TQ	USBLS	5/15
Metals and Plastics	North Dakota	Y	28800 FQ	34470 MW	41760 TQ	USBLS	5/15
Metals and Plastics	Ohio	Y	27020 FQ	33820 MW	40000 TQ	USBLS	5/15
Metals and Plastics	Cincinnati MSA, OH-KY-IN	Y	31090 FQ	39780 MW	64530 TQ	USBLS	5/15
Metals and Plastics	Cleveland-Elyria MSA, OH	Y	24350 FQ	31650 MW	39200 TQ	USBLS	5/15
Metals and Plastics	Columbus MSA, OH	Y	27880 FQ	34110 MW	42410 TQ	USBLS	5/15
Metals and Plastics	Oklahoma	Y	26540 FQ	31540 MW	38140 TQ	USBLS	5/15
Metals and Plastics	Oklahoma City MSA, OK	Y	23400 FQ	28300 MW	34030 TQ	USBLS	5/15
Metals and Plastics	Tulsa MSA, OK	Y	28180 FQ	32830 MW	39990 TQ	USBLS	5/15
Metals and Plastics	Oregon	H	14.73 FQ	17.48 MW	20.36 TQ	ORBLS	2016
Metals and Plastics	Portland-Vancouver-Hillsboro MSA, OR-WA	Y	31400 FQ	36090 MW	41900 TQ	USBLS	5/15
Metals and Plastics	Pennsylvania	Y	27800 FQ	34730 MW	42560 TQ	USBLS	5/15
Metals and Plastics	Allentown-Bethlehem-Easton MSA, PA-NJ	Y	31810 FQ	36640 MW	43360 TQ	USBLS	5/15
Metals and Plastics	Harrisburg-Carlisle MSA, PA	Y	26470 FQ	31090 MW	37230 TQ	USBLS	5/15
Metals and Plastics	Montgomery County-Bucks County-Chester County PMSA, PA	Y	29490 FQ	37360 MW	45870 TQ	USBLS	5/15
Metals and Plastics	Philadelphia PMSA, PA	Y	36110 FQ	46410 MW	61740 TQ	USBLS	5/15
Metals and Plastics	Pittsburgh MSA, PA	Y	28230 FQ	33050 MW	38480 TQ	USBLS	5/15
Metals and Plastics	Rhode Island	Y	37110 FQ	46010 MW	54850 TQ	USBLS	5/15
Metals and Plastics	Providence-Warwick MSA, RI-MA	Y	33620 FQ	41650 MW	53210 TQ	USBLS	5/15
Metals and Plastics	South Carolina	Y	34740 FQ	40900 MW	47350 TQ	USBLS	5/15
Metals and Plastics	Columbia MSA, SC	Y	31170 FQ	38980 MW	46230 TQ	USBLS	5/15
Metals and Plastics	Greenville-Anderson-Mauldin MSA, SC	Y	32750 FQ	49880 MW	56160 TQ	USBLS	5/15
Metals and Plastics	South Dakota	Y	23480 FQ	35790 MW	45640 TQ	USBLS	5/15
Metals and Plastics	Tennessee	Y	24930 FQ	29420 MW	36800 TQ	USBLS	5/15
Metals and Plastics	Knoxville MSA, TN	Y	22600 FQ	27560 MW	35330 TQ	USBLS	5/15
Metals and Plastics	Memphis MSA, TN-MS-AR	Y	27940 FQ	32870 MW	38690 TQ	USBLS	5/15

AE	Average entry wage	AWR	Average wage range	H	Hourly	LR	Low end range	MTC	Median total compensation	TCC	Total cash compensation
AEX	Average experienced wage	B	Biweekly	HI	Highest wage paid	M	Monthly	MW	Median wage paid	TQ	Third quartile wage
ATC	Average total compensation	D	Daily	HR	High end range	MCC	Median cash compensation	MWR	Median wage range	W	Weekly
AW	Average wage paid	FQ	First quartile wage	LO	Lowest wage paid	ME	Median entry wage	S	See annotated source	Y	Yearly

Occupation/Type/Industry	Location	Per	Low	Mid	High	Source	Date
Multiple Machine Tool Setter, Operator, and Tender							
Metals and Plastics	Nashville-Davidson–Murfreesboro–Franklin MSA, TN	Y	22570 FQ	26950 MW	34170 TQ	USBLS	5/15
Metals and Plastics	Texas	Y	25720 FQ	31930 MW	39340 TQ	USBLS	5/15
Metals and Plastics	Austin-Round Rock MSA, TX	Y	22660 FQ	29700 MW	39530 TQ	USBLS	5/15
Metals and Plastics	Dallas-Plano-Irving PMSA, TX	Y	25860 FQ	30470 MW	38590 TQ	USBLS	5/15
Metals and Plastics	Fort Worth-Arlington PMSA, TX	Y	24720 FQ	29030 MW	35970 TQ	USBLS	5/15
Metals and Plastics	Houston-The Woodlands-Sugar Land MSA, TX	Y	27420 FQ	34470 MW	40820 TQ	USBLS	5/15
Metals and Plastics	San Antonio-New Braunfels MSA, TX	Y	27410 FQ	32020 MW	37620 TQ	USBLS	5/15
Metals and Plastics	Utah	Y	25200 FQ	32780 MW	40370 TQ	USBLS	5/15
Metals and Plastics	Provo-Orem MSA, UT	Y	20840 FQ	22870 MW	24880 TQ	USBLS	5/15
Metals and Plastics	Vermont	Y	28090 FQ	33280 MW	38810 TQ	USBLS	5/15
Metals and Plastics	Burlington-South Burlington MSA, VT	Y	27500 FQ	31800 MW	37910 TQ	USBLS	5/15
Metals and Plastics	Virginia	Y	22940 FQ	32060 MW	43610 TQ	USBLS	5/15
Metals and Plastics	Richmond MSA, VA	Y	22140 FQ	29820 MW	39420 TQ	USBLS	5/15
Metals and Plastics	Washington	H	14.95 FQ	18.24 MW	23.32 TQ	WABLS	3/16
Metals and Plastics	Seattle-Bellevue-Everett PMSA, WA	H	15.74 FQ	18.63 MW	24.58 TQ	WABLS	3/16
Metals and Plastics	Tacoma-Lakewood PMSA, WA	H	12.42 FQ	13.49 MW	14.57 TQ	WABLS	3/16
Metals and Plastics	West Virginia	Y	23300 FQ	30580 MW	43690 TQ	USBLS	5/15
Metals and Plastics	Huntington-Ashland MSA, WV-KY-OH	Y	21620 FQ	23600 MW	29920 TQ	USBLS	5/15
Metals and Plastics	Wisconsin	Y	28460 FQ	34460 MW	41860 TQ	USBLS	5/15
Metals and Plastics	Madison MSA, WI	Y	31920 FQ	35520 MW	39110 TQ	USBLS	5/15
Metals and Plastics	Milwaukee-Waukesha-West Allis MSA, WI	Y	28580 FQ	35720 MW	45130 TQ	USBLS	5/15
Metals and Plastics	Puerto Rico	Y	16900 FQ	18210 MW	19530 TQ	USBLS	5/15
Multiple Picture Performer							
Film	United States	W	3239 LO			AFTRA2	7/1/16-6/30/17
Municipal Court Marshal	Seattle, WA	H	28.45 LO		34.52 HI	CSSS	1/13/16
Municipal Judge	Seattle, WA	H			70.72 HI	CSSS	9/1/15
Municipal/Town Clerk	Apple Valley, CA	Y			155331 HI	CACIT	6/28/16
	Moraga, CA	Y			109578 HI	CACIT	6/28/16
	Conway, MA	Y			26986 HI	FRCOG	2016
	Montague, MA	Y			67420 HI	FRCOG	2016
	Sunderland, MA	Y			40415 HI	FRCOG	2016
Museum Collections Specialist							
Municipal Government	Campbell, CA	Y			47181 HI	CACIT	6/28/16
Museum Curator							
Municipal Government	Capitola, CA	Y			27204 HI	CACIT	6/28/16
Municipal Government	Fortuna, CA	Y			15926 HI	CACIT	6/28/16
Municipal Government	Colorado Springs, CO	Y	56982 LO		78350 HI	COSPRS	2017
Museum Director							
Municipal Government	Angels, CA	Y			76763 HI	CACIT	6/28/16
Museum Educator							
Municipal Government	Fullerton, CA	Y			51123 HI	CACIT	6/28/16
Museum Exhibit Designer							
Municipal Government	Colorado Springs, CO	Y	50500 LO		65946 HI	COSPRS	2017
Museum Exhibit Specialist							
State Government	Helena, MT	H			20.27 HI	MTGOV	2016
Museum Exhibit Technician							
State Government	Virginia City, MT	H	14.41 LO		15.50 HI	MTGOV	2016
Museum Guard							
Municipal Government	Detroit, MI	M	2217 LO		2483 HI	DETGOV	2016

AE Average entry wage AWR Average wage range H Hourly LR Low end range MTC Median total compensation TCC Total cash compensation
AEX Average experienced wage B Biweekly HI Highest wage paid M Monthly MW Median wage paid TQ Third quartile wage
ATC Average total compensation D Daily HR High end range MCC Median cash compensation MWR Median wage range W Weekly
AW Average wage paid FQ First quartile wage LO Lowest wage paid ME Median entry wage S See annotated source Y Yearly

Occupation/Type/Industry	Location	Per	Low	Mid	High	Source	Date
Museum Publication Director							
State Government	New Mexico	H	21.53 LO		37.46 HI	NMGOV	7/30/16
Museum Registrar							
Michigan State University	East Lansing, MI	Y			56377 HI	MSUSAL	10/1/14-9/30/15
Museum Technician and Conservator							
	Alabama	Y	27471 AE	38459 AW	43953 AEX	ALBLS	6/16
	Alaska	Y	32710 FQ	43220 MW	55060 TQ	USBLS	5/15
	Arizona	Y	34090 FQ	40370 MW	47700 TQ	USBLS	5/15
	Phoenix-Mesa-Scottsdale MSA, AZ	Y	35540 FQ	41370 MW	46810 TQ	USBLS	5/15
	Arkansas	Y	21730 FQ	29060 MW	35280 TQ	USBLS	5/15
	California	H	16.89 FQ	21.81 MW	28.01 TQ	CABLS	1/16-3/16
	Anaheim-Santa Ana-Irvine PMSA, CA	H	15.62 FQ	18.65 MW	22.10 TQ	CABLS	1/16-3/16
	Los Angeles-Long Beach-Glendale PMSA, CA	H	17.87 FQ	24.17 MW	28.98 TQ	CABLS	1/16-3/16
	Oakland-Hayward-Berkeley PMSA, CA	H	13.13 FQ	20.33 MW	23.67 TQ	CABLS	1/16-3/16
	Riverside-San Bernardino-Ontario MSA, CA	H	13.88 FQ	18.51 MW	21.40 TQ	CABLS	1/16-3/16
	Sacramento–Roseville–Arden-Arcade MSA, CA	H	11.47 FQ	20.88 MW	22.49 TQ	CABLS	1/16-3/16
	San Diego-Carlsbad MSA, CA	H	17.39 FQ	20.57 MW	24.32 TQ	CABLS	1/16-3/16
	San Francisco-Redwood City-South San Francisco PMSA, CA	H	17.49 FQ	21.49 MW	33.83 TQ	CABLS	1/16-3/16
	Colorado	Y	26870 FQ	35380 MW	45110 TQ	USBLS	5/15
	Denver-Aurora-Lakewood MSA, CO	Y	33320 FQ	38210 MW	47800 TQ	USBLS	5/15
	Connecticut	Y		52916 MW		CTBLS	1/16-3/16
	Bridgeport-Stamford-Norwalk MSA, CT	Y	27940 FQ	31290 MW	46100 TQ	USBLS	5/15
	Delaware	Y	29630 FQ	34430 MW	49910 TQ	USBLS	5/15
	Wilmington PMSA, DE-MD-NJ	Y	31950 FQ	42770 MW	61640 TQ	USBLS	5/15
	District of Columbia	Y	51500 FQ	65850 MW	80720 TQ	USBLS	5/15
	Washington-Arlington-Alexandria PMSA, DC-VA-MD-WV	Y	47030 FQ	63720 MW	80730 TQ	USBLS	5/15
	Florida	H	12.84 AE	18.80 MW	23.94 AEX	FLBLS	7/16-9/16
	Fort Lauderdale-Pompano Beach-Deerfield Beach PMSA, FL	H	11.67 AE	16.29 MW	24.29 AEX	FLBLS	7/16-9/16
	Miami-Miami Beach-Kendall PMSA, FL	H	13.90 AE	20.05 MW	23.80 AEX	FLBLS	7/16-9/16
	Orlando-Kissimmee-Sanford MSA, FL	H	11.10 AE	16.39 MW	18.13 AEX	FLBLS	7/16-9/16
	Georgia	Y	31540 FQ	40040 MW	51640 TQ	USBLS	5/15
	Atlanta-Sandy Springs-Roswell MSA, GA	Y	31980 FQ	39720 MW	52360 TQ	USBLS	5/15
	Hawaii	Y	27780 FQ	35900 MW	55780 TQ	USBLS	5/15
	Urban Honolulu MSA, HI	Y	27680 FQ	38630 MW	57290 TQ	USBLS	5/15
	Illinois	Y	27020 FQ	41220 MW	54910 TQ	USBLS	5/15
	Chicago-Naperville-Arlington Heights PMSA, IL	Y	23460 FQ	40250 MW	52760 TQ	USBLS	5/15
	Indiana	Y	28050 FQ	34780 MW	41210 TQ	USBLS	5/15
	Indianapolis-Carmel-Anderson MSA, IN	Y	28690 FQ	35450 MW	41550 TQ	USBLS	5/15
	Iowa	Y	31090 FQ	47640 MW	71390 TQ	USBLS	5/15
	Kansas	Y	30470 FQ	35130 MW	40370 TQ	USBLS	5/15
	Louisiana	Y	23490 FQ	29500 MW	38260 TQ	USBLS	5/15
	Maine	Y	29820 FQ	34970 MW	38150 TQ	USBLS	5/15
	Portland-South Portland MSA, ME	Y	32110 FQ	34880 MW	37640 TQ	USBLS	5/15
	Maryland	Y	32288 AE	59825 MW	73593 AEX	MDBLS	4/16
	Baltimore-Columbia-Towson MSA, MD	Y	18990 FQ	40090 MW	54410 TQ	USBLS	5/15
	Massachusetts	Y	39920 FQ	52680 MW	62350 TQ	USBLS	5/15
	Boston-Cambridge-Newton NECTA, MA	Y	43840 FQ	55300 MW	65470 TQ	USBLS	5/15

AE	Average entry wage	AWR	Average wage range	H	Hourly	LR	Low end range	MTC	Median total compensation	TCC	Total cash compensation
AEX	Average experienced wage	B	Biweekly	HI	Highest wage paid	M	Monthly	MW	Median wage paid	TQ	Third quartile wage
ATC	Average total compensation	D	Daily	HR	High end range	MCC	Median cash compensation	MWR	Median wage range	W	Weekly
AW	Average wage paid	FQ	First quartile wage	LO	Lowest wage paid	ME	Median entry wage	S	See annotated source	Y	Yearly

Occupation/Type/Industry	Location	Per	Low	Mid	High	Source	Date
Museum Technician and Conservator	Michigan	Y	22460 FQ	30590 MW	41560 TQ	USBLS	5/15
	Minnesota	Y	22288 FQ	34042 MW	45100 TQ	MNBLS	1/16-3/16
	Minneapolis-St. Paul-Bloomington MSA, MN-WI	Y	33800 FQ	41552 MW	48830 TQ	MNBLS	1/16-3/16
	Missouri	Y	28540 FQ	35230 MW	41540 TQ	USBLS	5/15
	Kansas City MSA, MO-KS	Y	29510 FQ	35230 MW	42220 TQ	USBLS	5/15
	St. Louis MSA, MO-IL	Y	26290 FQ	35230 MW	41530 TQ	USBLS	5/15
	Montana	Y	20090 FQ	27880 MW	34260 TQ	USBLS	5/15
	Nebraska	Y	19515 FQ	31810 MW	38120 TQ	NEBLS	7/16-9/16
	Omaha-Council Bluffs MSA, NE-IA	Y	18580 FQ	33195 MW	37735 TQ	NEBLS	7/16-9/16
	Nevada	Y	22730 FQ	32410 MW	36130 TQ	USBLS	5/15
	Las Vegas-Henderson-Paradise MSA, NV	Y	22110 FQ	31760 MW	35720 TQ	USBLS	5/15
	New Jersey	Y	36390 FQ	51890 MW	72280 TQ	USBLS	5/15
	New Mexico	Y	33180 FQ	39570 MW	45930 TQ	USBLS	5/15
	New York	Y	36160 AE	56640 MW	72190 AEX	NYBLS	1/16-3/16
	Nassau County-Suffolk County PMSA, NY	Y	34310 FQ	37970 MW	48340 TQ	USBLS	5/15
	New York-Jersey City-White Plains PMSA, NY-NJ	Y	47470 FQ	60900 MW	75880 TQ	USBLS	5/15
	Rochester MSA, NY	Y	38330 FQ	44790 MW	55550 TQ	USBLS	5/15
	North Carolina	Y	33940 FQ	40190 MW	46250 TQ	USBLS	5/15
	Raleigh MSA, NC	Y	37190 FQ	42020 MW	46730 TQ	USBLS	5/15
	Ohio	Y	29080 FQ	35710 MW	46320 TQ	USBLS	5/15
	Cincinnati MSA, OH-KY-IN	Y	32960 FQ	38650 MW	46430 TQ	USBLS	5/15
	Cleveland-Elyria MSA, OH	Y	35920 FQ	48110 MW	63500 TQ	USBLS	5/15
	Columbus MSA, OH	Y	25120 FQ	31030 MW	41870 TQ	USBLS	5/15
	Oklahoma	Y	26990 FQ	34760 MW	43620 TQ	USBLS	5/15
	Oregon	H	11.87 FQ	16.93 MW	20.84 TQ	ORBLS	2016
	Portland-Vancouver-Hillsboro MSA, OR-WA	Y	33830 FQ	39030 MW	45520 TQ	USBLS	5/15
	Pennsylvania	Y	28160 FQ	37890 MW	49320 TQ	USBLS	5/15
	Harrisburg-Carlisle MSA, PA	Y	37250 FQ	45110 MW	57310 TQ	USBLS	5/15
	Montgomery County-Bucks County-Chester County PMSA, PA	Y	31510 FQ	45070 MW	54880 TQ	USBLS	5/15
	Philadelphia PMSA, PA	Y	27910 FQ	37580 MW	49120 TQ	USBLS	5/15
	Pittsburgh MSA, PA	Y	24350 FQ	36570 MW	47140 TQ	USBLS	5/15
	Rhode Island	Y	41060 FQ	45070 MW	49090 TQ	USBLS	5/15
	Providence-Warwick MSA, RI-MA	Y	41060 FQ	45070 MW	49090 TQ	USBLS	5/15
	South Carolina	Y	22080 FQ	30280 MW	42650 TQ	USBLS	5/15
	Charleston-North Charleston MSA, SC	Y	21490 FQ	28200 MW	47330 TQ	USBLS	5/15
	South Dakota	Y	26480 FQ	30380 MW	37020 TQ	USBLS	5/15
	Tennessee	Y	28040 FQ	35260 MW	45700 TQ	USBLS	5/15
	Nashville-Davidson–Murfreesboro–Franklin MSA, TN	Y	29140 FQ	40290 MW	47630 TQ	USBLS	5/15
	Texas	Y	30190 FQ	38020 MW	47690 TQ	USBLS	5/15
	Austin-Round Rock MSA, TX	Y	36760 FQ	45160 MW	49550 TQ	USBLS	5/15
	Dallas-Plano-Irving PMSA, TX	Y	33140 FQ	40150 MW	47210 TQ	USBLS	5/15
	Fort Worth-Arlington PMSA, TX	Y	32270 FQ	41650 MW	52140 TQ	USBLS	5/15
	Houston-The Woodlands-Sugar Land MSA, TX	Y	35360 FQ	42500 MW	55330 TQ	USBLS	5/15
	San Antonio-New Braunfels MSA, TX	Y	30080 FQ	38780 MW	48920 TQ	USBLS	5/15
	Utah	Y	25350 FQ	28960 MW	37630 TQ	USBLS	5/15
	Provo-Orem MSA, UT	Y	26060 FQ	28390 MW	30720 TQ	USBLS	5/15
	Vermont	Y	29760 FQ	34750 MW	38450 TQ	USBLS	5/15
	Burlington-South Burlington MSA, VT	Y	30910 FQ	34440 MW	37470 TQ	USBLS	5/15
	Virginia	Y	33090 FQ	40620 MW	59250 TQ	USBLS	5/15
	Richmond MSA, VA	Y	33850 FQ	42920 MW	55700 TQ	USBLS	5/15
	Virginia Beach-Norfolk-Newport News MSA, VA-NC	Y	30140 FQ	36240 MW	48420 TQ	USBLS	5/15
	Washington	H	13.36 FQ	18.70 MW	23.94 TQ	WABLS	3/16
	Seattle-Bellevue-Everett PMSA, WA	H	17.04 FQ	20.80 MW	24.53 TQ	WABLS	3/16

AE Average entry wage	AWR Average wage range	H Hourly	LR Low end range	MTC Median total compensation TCC Total cash compensation
AEX Average experienced wage	B Biweekly	HI Highest wage paid	M Monthly	MW Median wage paid TQ Third quartile wage
ATC Average total compensation	D Daily	HR High end range	MCC Median cash compensation	MWR Median wage range W Weekly
AW Average wage paid	FQ First quartile wage	LO Lowest wage paid	ME Median entry wage	S See annotated source Y Yearly

Occupation/Type/Industry	Location	Per	Low	Mid	High	Source	Date
Museum Technician and Conservator	Tacoma-Lakewood PMSA, WA	H	10.91 FQ	12.16 MW	19.07 TQ	WABLS	3/16
	West Virginia	Y	23420 FQ	31740 MW	40740 TQ	USBLS	5/15
	Wisconsin	Y	27290 FQ	32790 MW	39440 TQ	USBLS	5/15
	Milwaukee-Waukesha-West Allis MSA, WI	Y	28070 FQ	33460 MW	38490 TQ	USBLS	5/15
	Wyoming	Y	28720 FQ	35190 MW	46280 TQ	USBLS	5/15
Music Blogger	United States	Y		25000-75000 AWR		BBRD01	2014
Music Critic	United States	Y		44000 AW		SKU01	2016
Music Director and Composer	Alabama	Y	19031 AE	41680 AW	53005 AEX	ALBLS	6/16
	Birmingham-Hoover MSA, AL	Y	41864 AE	44228 AW	45401 AEX	ALBLS	6/16
	Arizona	Y	27190 FQ	36170 MW	47350 TQ	USBLS	5/15
	Phoenix-Mesa-Scottsdale MSA, AZ	Y	27830 FQ	36330 MW	45920 TQ	USBLS	5/15
	Arkansas	Y	42160 FQ	49000 MW	58700 TQ	USBLS	5/15
	California	H	20.98 FQ	27.15 MW	36.71 TQ	CABLS	1/16-3/16
	Anaheim-Santa Ana-Irvine PMSA, CA	H	21.88 FQ	27.74 MW	38.77 TQ	CABLS	1/16-3/16
	Los Angeles-Long Beach-Glendale PMSA, CA	H	20.33 FQ	24.93 MW	40.53 TQ	CABLS	1/16-3/16
	Oakland-Hayward-Berkeley PMSA, CA	H	23.31 FQ	27.90 MW	33.20 TQ	CABLS	1/16-3/16
	Riverside-San Bernardino-Ontario MSA, CA	H	14.97 FQ	23.70 MW	29.77 TQ	CABLS	1/16-3/16
	Sacramento–Roseville–Arden-Arcade MSA, CA	H	16.30 FQ	23.94 MW	33.79 TQ	CABLS	1/16-3/16
	San Diego-Carlsbad MSA, CA	H	21.30 FQ	26.02 MW	30.43 TQ	CABLS	1/16-3/16
	San Francisco-Redwood City-South San Francisco PMSA, CA	H	24.62 FQ	31.98 MW	39.34 TQ	CABLS	1/16-3/16
	Colorado	Y	30870 FQ	46960 MW	62180 TQ	USBLS	5/15
	Denver-Aurora-Lakewood MSA, CO	Y	28890 FQ	48370 MW	66830 TQ	USBLS	5/15
	Connecticut	Y		35152 MW		CTBLS	1/16-3/16
	Bridgeport-Stamford-Norwalk MSA, CT	Y	63660 FQ	70700 MW	77330 TQ	USBLS	5/15
	Hartford-West Hartford-East Hartford MSA, CT	Y	19380 FQ	19970 MW	39420 TQ	USBLS	5/15
	District of Columbia	Y	40110 FQ	52510 MW	71170 TQ	USBLS	5/15
	Washington-Arlington-Alexandria PMSA, DC-VA-MD-WV	Y	41930 FQ	56720 MW	76940 TQ	USBLS	5/15
	Florida	H	13.74 AE	22.95 MW	36.34 AEX	FLBLS	7/16-9/16
	Fort Lauderdale-Pompano Beach-Deerfield Beach PMSA, FL	H	12.90 AE	26.35 MW	30.51 AEX	FLBLS	7/16-9/16
	Miami-Miami Beach-Kendall PMSA, FL	H	13.35 AE	20.64 MW	26.47 AEX	FLBLS	7/16-9/16
	Orlando-Kissimmee-Sanford MSA, FL	H	13.87 AE	21.79 MW	31.29 AEX	FLBLS	7/16-9/16
	Tampa-St. Petersburg-Clearwater MSA, FL	H	11.22 AE	18.41 MW	24.85 AEX	FLBLS	7/16-9/16
	Georgia	Y	43010 FQ	54190 MW	63900 TQ	USBLS	5/15
	Atlanta-Sandy Springs-Roswell MSA, GA	Y	50200 FQ	57940 MW	67350 TQ	USBLS	5/15
	Hawaii	Y	20510 FQ	37410 MW	46730 TQ	USBLS	5/15
	Urban Honolulu MSA, HI	Y	19290 FQ	35730 MW	45230 TQ	USBLS	5/15
	Idaho	Y	18570 FQ	25070 MW	50380 TQ	USBLS	5/15
	Illinois	Y	36830 FQ	54200 MW	81790 TQ	USBLS	5/15
	Chicago-Naperville-Arlington Heights PMSA, IL	Y	36390 FQ	55390 MW	74340 TQ	USBLS	5/15
	Lake County-Kenosha County PMSA, IL-WI	Y	37320 FQ	47620 MW	62970 TQ	USBLS	5/15
	Indiana	Y	38620 FQ	52240 MW	68400 TQ	USBLS	5/15
	Gary PMSA, IN	Y	34320 FQ	40850 MW	49520 TQ	USBLS	5/15
	Indianapolis-Carmel-Anderson MSA, IN	Y	48260 FQ	66150 MW	76430 TQ	USBLS	5/15
	Iowa	Y	39150 FQ	47620 MW	59820 TQ	USBLS	5/15

Occupation/Type/Industry	Location	Per	Low	Mid	High	Source	Date
Music Director and Composer	Des Moines-West Des Moines MSA, IA	Y	43860 FQ	53610 MW	59420 TQ	USBLS	5/15
	Kansas	Y	40030 FQ	44190 MW	48350 TQ	USBLS	5/15
	Wichita MSA, KS	Y	40220 FQ	44110 MW	47990 TQ	USBLS	5/15
	Louisville-Jefferson County MSA, KY-IN	Y	17620 FQ	19870 MW	54040 TQ	USBLS	5/15
	Louisiana	Y	40070 FQ	49150 MW	59170 TQ	USBLS	5/15
	New Orleans-Metairie MSA, LA	Y	42150 FQ	49760 MW	57390 TQ	USBLS	5/15
	Baltimore-Columbia-Towson MSA, MD	Y	43940 FQ	51590 MW	60010 TQ	USBLS	5/15
	Massachusetts	Y	44340 FQ	60750 MW	92950 TQ	USBLS	5/15
	Boston-Cambridge-Newton NECTA, MA	Y	42570 FQ	60840 MW	93490 TQ	USBLS	5/15
	Worcester MSA, MA-CT	Y	39400 FQ	64530 MW	78510 TQ	USBLS	5/15
	Michigan	Y	27510 FQ	46420 MW	67550 TQ	USBLS	5/15
	Detroit-Dearborn-Livonia PMSA, MI	Y	24980 FQ	40090 MW	71850 TQ	USBLS	5/15
	Grand Rapids-Wyoming MSA, MI	Y	18570 FQ	25930 MW	61250 TQ	USBLS	5/15
	Minnesota	Y	38961 FQ	57368 MW	73437 TQ	MNBLS	1/16-3/16
	Minneapolis-St. Paul-Bloomington MSA, MN-WI	Y	51653 FQ	68114 MW	80563 TQ	MNBLS	1/16-3/16
	Mississippi	Y	35610 FQ	45500 MW	55810 TQ	USBLS	5/15
	Jackson MSA, MS	Y	38390 FQ	55140 MW	62100 TQ	USBLS	5/15
	Missouri	Y	41650 FQ	51400 MW	62550 TQ	USBLS	5/15
	Kansas City MSA, MO-KS	Y	39920 FQ	49310 MW	59470 TQ	USBLS	5/15
	St. Louis MSA, MO-IL	Y	34930 FQ	52330 MW	65230 TQ	USBLS	5/15
	Montana	Y	19060 FQ	33750 MW	49700 TQ	USBLS	5/15
	Billings MSA, MT	Y	18450 FQ	28300 MW	39070 TQ	USBLS	5/15
	Nebraska	Y	42130 FQ	49495 MW	58460 TQ	NEBLS	7/16-9/16
	Omaha-Council Bluffs MSA, NE-IA	Y	41355 FQ	49305 MW	57450 TQ	NEBLS	7/16-9/16
	New Hampshire	H	13.78 AE	27.12 MW	34.49 AEX	NHBLS	6/16
	New Jersey	Y	35390 FQ	50140 MW	63080 TQ	USBLS	5/15
	Newark PMSA, NJ-PA	Y	39320 FQ	46130 MW	53670 TQ	USBLS	5/15
	Trenton MSA, NJ	Y	55480 FQ	62720 MW	104290 TQ	USBLS	5/15
	New York	Y	27840 AE	54560 MW	103310 AEX	NYBLS	1/16-3/16
	Buffalo-Cheektowaga-Niagara Falls MSA, NY	Y	19150 FQ	23170 MW	41910 TQ	USBLS	5/15
	New York-Jersey City-White Plains PMSA, NY-NJ	Y	37220 FQ	59570 MW	109080 TQ	USBLS	5/15
	Rochester MSA, NY	Y	42860 FQ	50540 MW	103280 TQ	USBLS	5/15
	North Carolina	Y	36920 FQ	45770 MW	56210 TQ	USBLS	5/15
	Charlotte-Concord-Gastonia MSA, NC-SC	Y	34190 FQ	42250 MW	56130 TQ	USBLS	5/15
	Ohio	Y	41670 FQ	59660 MW	80470 TQ	USBLS	5/15
	Cincinnati MSA, OH-KY-IN	Y	46010 FQ	61920 MW	79320 TQ	USBLS	5/15
	Cleveland-Elyria MSA, OH	Y	47500 FQ	74450 MW	90330 TQ	USBLS	5/15
	Columbus MSA, OH	Y	19410 FQ	61090 MW	72040 TQ	USBLS	5/15
	Oklahoma	Y	32520 FQ	39520 MW	47080 TQ	USBLS	5/15
	Oklahoma City MSA, OK	Y	32870 FQ	41240 MW	47990 TQ	USBLS	5/15
	Oregon	H	12.09 FQ	18.86 MW	25.52 TQ	ORBLS	2016
	Portland-Vancouver-Hillsboro MSA, OR-WA	Y	23600 FQ	37800 MW	47050 TQ	USBLS	5/15
	Pennsylvania	Y	26920 FQ	38650 MW	58240 TQ	USBLS	5/15
	Allentown-Bethlehem-Easton MSA, PA-NJ	Y	24530 FQ	34430 MW	39770 TQ	USBLS	5/15
	Harrisburg-Carlisle MSA, PA	Y	27210 FQ	31020 MW	52340 TQ	USBLS	5/15
	Montgomery County-Bucks County-Chester County PMSA, PA	Y	28610 FQ	35780 MW	45920 TQ	USBLS	5/15
	Philadelphia PMSA, PA	Y	37610 FQ	47890 MW	106700 TQ	USBLS	5/15
	Pittsburgh MSA, PA	Y	26540 FQ	30030 MW	36420 TQ	USBLS	5/15
	Rhode Island	Y	33210 FQ	55640 MW	84450 TQ	USBLS	5/15
	Providence-Warwick MSA, RI-MA	Y	33460 FQ	57000 MW	85480 TQ	USBLS	5/15
	South Carolina	Y	30760 FQ	37150 MW	52010 TQ	USBLS	5/15
	Charleston-North Charleston MSA, SC	Y	18340 FQ	37010 MW	48630 TQ	USBLS	5/15
	Columbia MSA, SC	Y	34080 FQ	41610 MW	50800 TQ	USBLS	5/15

AE	Average entry wage	AWR	Average wage range	H	Hourly
AEX	Average experienced wage	B	Biweekly	HI	Highest wage paid
ATC	Average total compensation	D	Daily	HR	High end range
AW	Average wage paid	FQ	First quartile wage	LO	Lowest wage paid
LR	Low end range	MTC	Median total compensation	TCC	Total cash compensation
M	Monthly	MW	Median wage paid	TQ	Third quartile wage
MCC	Median cash compensation	MWR	Median wage range	W	Weekly
ME	Median entry wage	S	See annotated source	Y	Yearly

Occupation/Type/Industry	Location	Per	Low	Mid	High	Source	Date
Music Director and Composer	Greenville-Anderson-Mauldin						
	MSA, SC	Y	29450 FQ	33820 MW	38040 TQ	USBLS	5/15
	Tennessee	Y	22340 FQ	27420 MW	51580 TQ	USBLS	5/15
	Nashville-Davidson–						
	Murfreesboro–Franklin						
	MSA, TN	Y	22010 FQ	24020 MW	48250 TQ	USBLS	5/15
	Texas	Y	42020 FQ	51920 MW	60580 TQ	USBLS	5/15
	Austin-Round Rock MSA, TX	Y	42240 FQ	49090 MW	57660 TQ	USBLS	5/15
	Fort Worth-Arlington PMSA,						
	TX	Y	28370 FQ	51780 MW	58640 TQ	USBLS	5/15
	Houston-The Woodlands-						
	Sugar Land MSA, TX	Y	49720 FQ	56070 MW	62280 TQ	USBLS	5/15
	San Antonio-New Braunfels						
	MSA, TX	Y	47400 FQ	53980 MW	59030 TQ	USBLS	5/15
	Utah	Y	32930 FQ	39080 MW	62710 TQ	USBLS	5/15
	Salt Lake City MSA, UT	Y	32160 FQ	36740 MW	44060 TQ	USBLS	5/15
	Vermont	Y	31660 FQ	47780 MW	70370 TQ	USBLS	5/15
	Burlington-South Burlington						
	MSA, VT	Y	42030 FQ	55220 MW	89480 TQ	USBLS	5/15
	Virginia	Y	37180 FQ	51320 MW	75330 TQ	USBLS	5/15
	Richmond MSA, VA	Y	34670 FQ	42670 MW	57170 TQ	USBLS	5/15
	Virginia Beach-Norfolk-						
	Newport News MSA, VA-NC	Y	34260 FQ	60900 MW	83000 TQ	USBLS	5/15
	Washington	H	15.07 FQ	30.49 MW	47.80 TQ	WABLS	3/16
	Seattle-Bellevue-Everett						
	PMSA, WA	H	22.94 FQ	37.74 MW	61.11 TQ	WABLS	3/16
	Tacoma-Lakewood PMSA, WA	H	13.49 FQ	26.98 MW	39.37 TQ	WABLS	3/16
	Wisconsin	Y	41680 FQ	52780 MW	63220 TQ	USBLS	5/15
	Madison MSA, WI	Y	38810 FQ	49400 MW	57330 TQ	USBLS	5/15
	Milwaukee-Waukesha-West						
	Allis MSA, WI	Y	46420 FQ	57860 MW	82030 TQ	USBLS	5/15
	Wyoming	Y	48030 FQ	60620 MW	70570 TQ	USBLS	5/15
Music Education Teacher	United States	Y		56000 AW		MSC	2015
Music Film Editor							
Subscription Video on Demand, High							
Budget	United States	H	41.85 LO			MPEG01	7/31/16-7/29/17
Music Therapist							
State Government	Maryland	Y	34390 LO		57808 HI	MDGOV	2016
Musical Instrument Repairer and Tuner							
	Alabama	Y	21256 AE	33216 AW	39196 AEX	ALBLS	6/16
	Arizona	Y	27110 FQ	32770 MW	45420 TQ	USBLS	5/15
	Arkansas	Y	27450 FQ	35480 MW	52980 TQ	USBLS	5/15
	California	H	12.39 FQ	17.76 MW	27.66 TQ	CABLS	1/16-3/16
	Los Angeles-Long Beach-						
	Glendale PMSA, CA	H	17.72 FQ	27.57 MW	34.14 TQ	CABLS	1/16-3/16
	San Diego-Carlsbad MSA, CA	H	11.11 FQ	12.54 MW	14.27 TQ	CABLS	1/16-3/16
	Colorado	Y	23330 FQ	33520 MW	47110 TQ	USBLS	5/15
	Connecticut	Y		40808 MW		CTBLS	1/16-3/16
	Washington-Arlington-						
	Alexandria PMSA, DC-VA-						
	MD-WV	Y	32520 FQ	35360 MW	38200 TQ	USBLS	5/15
	Florida	H	10.43 AE	14.32 MW	17.86 AEX	FLBLS	7/16-9/16
	Georgia	Y	25020 FQ	33210 MW	42410 TQ	USBLS	5/15
	Illinois	Y	21010 FQ	36410 MW	48450 TQ	USBLS	5/15
	Chicago-Naperville-Arlington						
	Heights PMSA, IL	Y	26620 FQ	38200 MW	49400 TQ	USBLS	5/15
	Indiana	Y	27050 FQ	37000 MW	53020 TQ	USBLS	5/15
	Indianapolis-Carmel-Anderson						
	MSA, IN	Y	19380 FQ	28550 MW	62070 TQ	USBLS	5/15
	Iowa	Y	21760 FQ	25380 MW	38890 TQ	USBLS	5/15
	Kansas	Y	24840 FQ	32880 MW	39530 TQ	USBLS	5/15
	Kentucky	Y	31030 FQ	36580 MW	47720 TQ	USBLS	5/15
	Louisville-Jefferson County						
	MSA, KY-IN	Y	31730 FQ	47300 MW	56200 TQ	USBLS	5/15
	Louisiana	Y	33280 FQ	38380 MW	45130 TQ	USBLS	5/15
	Maryland	Y	21500 AE	37718 MW	45827 AEX	MDBLS	4/16
	Baltimore-Columbia-Towson						
	MSA, MD	Y	21200 FQ	32060 MW	40550 TQ	USBLS	5/15

AE	Average entry wage	AWR	Average wage range	H	Hourly	LR	Low end range	MTC	Median total compensation	TCC	Total cash compensation
AEX	Average experienced wage	B	Biweekly	HI	Highest wage paid	M	Monthly	MW	Median wage paid	TQ	Third quartile wage
ATC	Average total compensation	D	Daily	HR	High end range	MCC	Median cash compensation	MWR	Median wage range	W	Weekly
AW	Average wage paid	FQ	First quartile wage	LO	Lowest wage paid	ME	Median entry wage	S	See annotated source	Y	Yearly

Occupation/Type/Industry	Location	Per	Low	Mid	High	Source	Date
Musical Instrument Repairer and Tuner							
	Michigan	Y	30290 FQ	38540 MW	50680 TQ	USBLS	5/15
	Minnesota	Y	30170 FQ	37783 MW	45738 TQ	MNBLS	1/16-3/16
	Minneapolis-St. Paul-Bloomington MSA, MN-WI	Y	29426 FQ	37019 MW	44813 TQ	MNBLS	1/16-3/16
	Missouri	Y	23870 FQ	36740 MW	46440 TQ	USBLS	5/15
	Kansas City MSA, MO-KS	Y	24510 FQ	27370 MW	30060 TQ	USBLS	5/15
	St. Louis MSA, MO-IL	Y	23500 FQ	32170 MW	45910 TQ	USBLS	5/15
	Nebraska	Y	19940 FQ	34185 MW	39275 TQ	NEBLS	7/16-9/16
	Nevada	Y	28470 FQ	43240 MW	49250 TQ	USBLS	5/15
	Las Vegas-Henderson-Paradise MSA, NV	Y	28670 FQ	43590 MW	49480 TQ	USBLS	5/15
	New Hampshire	H	16.16 AE	19.74 MW	21.56 AEX	NHBLS	6/16
	New Jersey	Y	34270 FQ	38600 MW	60260 TQ	USBLS	5/15
	Newark PMSA, NJ-PA	Y	32440 FQ	42360 MW	54350 TQ	USBLS	5/15
	New York	Y	22160 AE	35810 MW	49710 AEX	NYBLS	1/16-3/16
	New York-Jersey City-White Plains PMSA, NY-NJ	Y	25990 FQ	33850 MW	46940 TQ	USBLS	5/15
	North Carolina	Y	23800 FQ	31710 MW	38540 TQ	USBLS	5/15
	Ohio	Y	20340 FQ	32200 MW	39450 TQ	USBLS	5/15
	Cincinnati MSA, OH-KY-IN	Y	33260 FQ	36720 MW	45300 TQ	USBLS	5/15
	Cleveland-Elyria MSA, OH	Y	23920 FQ	28580 MW	36100 TQ	USBLS	5/15
	Oklahoma	Y	29940 FQ	35650 MW	41340 TQ	USBLS	5/15
	Oklahoma City MSA, OK	Y	28630 FQ	32970 MW	38650 TQ	USBLS	5/15
	Oregon	H	13.30 FQ	18.34 MW	23.01 TQ	ORBLS	2016
	Portland-Vancouver-Hillsboro MSA, OR-WA	Y	29400 FQ	41080 MW	48340 TQ	USBLS	5/15
	Pennsylvania	Y	33610 FQ	43490 MW	51230 TQ	USBLS	5/15
	Allentown-Bethlehem-Easton MSA, PA-NJ	Y	38740 FQ	45330 MW	53270 TQ	USBLS	5/15
	Montgomery County-Bucks County-Chester County PMSA, PA	Y	30500 FQ	41730 MW	53030 TQ	USBLS	5/15
	Pittsburgh MSA, PA	Y	36570 FQ	44320 MW	50400 TQ	USBLS	5/15
	South Carolina	Y	23450 FQ	33420 MW	40410 TQ	USBLS	5/15
	Columbia MSA, SC	Y	22980 FQ	32430 MW	36820 TQ	USBLS	5/15
	Tennessee	Y	30000 FQ	35100 MW	39480 TQ	USBLS	5/15
	Nashville-Davidson–Murfreesboro–Franklin MSA, TN	Y	32220 FQ	37070 MW	45890 TQ	USBLS	5/15
	Texas	Y	29480 FQ	37110 MW	49890 TQ	USBLS	5/15
	Dallas-Plano-Irving PMSA, TX	Y	33320 FQ	39900 MW	54340 TQ	USBLS	5/15
	Houston-The Woodlands-Sugar Land MSA, TX	Y	25470 FQ	32120 MW	38750 TQ	USBLS	5/15
	San Antonio-New Braunfels MSA, TX	Y	20610 FQ	28210 MW	37470 TQ	USBLS	5/15
	Utah	Y	27460 FQ	33100 MW	38390 TQ	USBLS	5/15
	Provo-Orem MSA, UT	Y	27900 FQ	34320 MW	39000 TQ	USBLS	5/15
	Virginia	Y	26100 FQ	31130 MW	36650 TQ	USBLS	5/15
	Washington	H	14.52 FQ	20.26 MW	23.37 TQ	WABLS	3/16
	Seattle-Bellevue-Everett PMSA, WA	H	11.06 FQ	14.53 MW	19.15 TQ	WABLS	3/16
	Tacoma-Lakewood PMSA, WA	H	19.44 FQ	21.77 MW	24.07 TQ	WABLS	3/16
	West Virginia	Y	23100 FQ	27650 MW	32760 TQ	USBLS	5/15
	Wisconsin	Y	29610 FQ	35760 MW	40800 TQ	USBLS	5/15
	Milwaukee-Waukesha-West Allis MSA, WI	Y	32090 FQ	35320 MW	38550 TQ	USBLS	5/15
Musician and Singer	Arizona	H	20.63 FQ	25.36 MW	30.20 TQ	USBLS	5/15
	California	H	17.11 FQ	30.77 MW	53.67 TQ	CABLS	1/16-3/16
	Colorado	H	13.95 FQ	23.14 MW	29.11 TQ	USBLS	5/15
	Connecticut	H		26.27 MW		CTBLS	1/16-3/16
	District of Columbia	H	23.41 FQ	27.32 MW	30.38 TQ	USBLS	5/15
	Florida	H	10.41 AE	19.24 MW	48.45 AEX	FLBLS	7/16-9/16
	Hawaii	H	19.54 FQ	25.98 MW	53.79 TQ	USBLS	5/15
	Illinois	H	14.48 FQ	22.23 MW	36.34 TQ	USBLS	5/15
	Indiana	H	10.68 FQ	21.33 MW	36.19 TQ	USBLS	5/15
	Maryland	H	17.50 AE	33.50 MW	41.75 AEX	MDBLS	4/16
	Massachusetts	H	19.29 FQ	31.65 MW	45.19 TQ	USBLS	5/15
	Michigan	H	10.71 FQ	16.54 MW	23.33 TQ	USBLS	5/15
	Minnesota	H	11.98 FQ	23.94 MW	51.74 TQ	MNBLS	1/16-3/16
	Missouri	H	12.08 FQ	24.43 MW	35.16 TQ	USBLS	5/15

AE	Average entry wage	AWR	Average wage range	H	Hourly	LR	Low end range	MTC	Median total compensation	TCC	Total cash compensation
AEX	Average experienced wage	B	Biweekly	HI	Highest wage paid	M	Monthly	MW	Median wage paid	TQ	Third quartile wage
ATC	Average total compensation	D	Daily	HR	High end range	MCC	Median cash compensation	MWR	Median wage range	W	Weekly
AW	Average wage paid	FQ	First quartile wage	LO	Lowest wage paid	ME	Median entry wage	S	See annotated source	Y	Yearly

Occupation/Type/Industry	Location	Per	Low	Mid	High	Source	Date
Musician and Singer	Montana	H	9.49 FQ	14.17 MW	23.59 TQ	USBLS	5/15
	Nevada	H	17.68 FQ	35.17 MW	44.24 TQ	USBLS	5/15
	New Jersey	H	11.33 FQ	21.53 MW	35.49 TQ	USBLS	5/15
	North Carolina	H	15.74 FQ	19.31 MW	23.42 TQ	USBLS	5/15
	Ohio	H	9.18 FQ	16.57 MW	28.51 TQ	USBLS	5/15
	Oregon	H	12.01 FQ	23.61 MW	40.72 TQ	ORBLS	2016
	Pennsylvania	H	11.36 FQ	27.57 MW	53.81 TQ	USBLS	5/15
	Rhode Island	H	9.20 FQ	9.40 MW	13.65 TQ	USBLS	5/15
	South Carolina	H	9.16 FQ	12.92 MW	20.28 TQ	USBLS	5/15
	Tennessee	H	19.54 FQ	28.46 MW	50.42 TQ	USBLS	5/15
	Texas	H	13.88 FQ	22.23 MW	47.29 TQ	USBLS	5/15
	Vermont	H	24.56 FQ	26.90 MW	29.24 TQ	USBLS	5/15
	Virginia	H	15.12 FQ	19.86 MW	30.35 TQ	USBLS	5/15
	Washington	H	18.54 FQ	33.59 MW	41.51 TQ	WABLS	3/16
	Wisconsin	H	8.45 FQ	11.85 MW	26.73 TQ	USBLS	5/15
Nail Technician	United States	W		630 AW		NLSM01	2015-2016
Nanny	United States	H		18.66 AW		INA	2014
International Nanny Association Credential	United States	H		19.96 AW		INA	2014
Nanosystems Engineer	United States	Y		98000 AW		SKU01	2016
Narcotics Abatement Officer							
Police Department, Municipal Government	Menlo Park, CA	Y			114454 HI	CACIT	6/28/16
National Account Manager							
Copier Industry	United States	Y		121423 ATC		COPIER1	2016
Native Vegetation Specialist							
Municipal Parks	Coralville, IA	Y			43666 HI	ICPC	2014
Natural Sciences Manager	Alabama	Y	83032 AE	113135 AW	128192 AEX	ALBLS	6/16
	Birmingham-Hoover MSA, AL	Y	96684 AE	150218 AW	176980 AEX	ALBLS	6/16
	Alaska	Y	88630 FQ	100280 MW	112620 TQ	USBLS	5/15
	Anchorage MSA, AK	Y	86890 FQ	98990 MW	112430 TQ	USBLS	5/15
	Arizona	Y	81900 FQ	100610 MW	134400 TQ	USBLS	5/15
	Phoenix-Mesa-Scottsdale MSA, AZ	Y	82910 FQ	104070 MW	142460 TQ	USBLS	5/15
	Tucson MSA, AZ	Y	84240 FQ	109200 MW	150830 TQ	USBLS	5/15
	Arkansas	Y	57970 FQ	87940 MW	110220 TQ	USBLS	5/15
	Little Rock-North Little Rock-Conway MSA, AR	Y	65790 FQ	92420 MW	108860 TQ	USBLS	5/15
	California	H	54.22 FQ	70.86 MW		CABLS	1/16-3/16
	Anaheim-Santa Ana-Irvine PMSA, CA	H	56.85 FQ	73.55 MW		CABLS	1/16-3/16
	Los Angeles-Long Beach-Glendale PMSA, CA	H	46.49 FQ	63.22 MW		CABLS	1/16-3/16
	Oakland-Hayward-Berkeley PMSA, CA	H	55.49 FQ	71.36 MW		CABLS	1/16-3/16
	Riverside-San Bernardino-Ontario MSA, CA	H	42.61 FQ	51.46 MW	60.34 TQ	CABLS	1/16-3/16
	Sacramento–Roseville–Arden-Arcade MSA, CA	H	49.82 FQ	58.41 MW	67.53 TQ	CABLS	1/16-3/16
	San Diego-Carlsbad MSA, CA	H	58.08 FQ	74.68 MW		CABLS	1/16-3/16
	San Francisco-Redwood City-South San Francisco PMSA, CA	H	68.81 FQ	98.60 AW		CABLS	1/16-3/16
	Colorado	Y	101520 FQ	123490 MW	154340 TQ	USBLS	5/15
	Denver-Aurora-Lakewood MSA, CO	Y	104510 FQ	122710 MW	155130 TQ	USBLS	5/15
	Connecticut	Y		138940 MW		CTBLS	1/16-3/16
	Bridgeport-Stamford-Norwalk MSA, CT	Y	115510 FQ	152450 MW		USBLS	5/15
	Hartford-West Hartford-East Hartford MSA, CT	Y	114400 FQ	140220 MW	161260 TQ	USBLS	5/15
	Delaware	Y	143070 FQ	176030 MW		USBLS	5/15
	Wilmington PMSA, DE-MD-NJ	Y	148260 FQ	180520 MW		USBLS	5/15
	District of Columbia	Y	109600 FQ	130730 MW	151500 TQ	USBLS	5/15
	Washington-Arlington-Alexandria PMSA, DC-VA-MD-WV	Y	112010 FQ	133270 MW	155700 TQ	USBLS	5/15

AE	Average entry wage	AWR	Average wage range	H	Hourly
AEX	Average experienced wage	B	Biweekly	HI	Highest wage paid
ATC	Average total compensation	D	Daily	HR	High end range
AW	Average wage paid	FQ	First quartile wage	LO	Lowest wage paid

LR	Low end range	MTC	Median total compensation
M	Monthly	MW	Median wage paid
MCC	Median cash compensation	MWR	Median wage range
ME	Median entry wage	S	See annotated source

TCC	Total cash compensation		
TQ	Third quartile wage		
W	Weekly		
Y	Yearly		

Occupation/Type/Industry	Location	Per	Low	Mid	High	Source	Date
Natural Sciences Manager	Florida	H	33.31 AE	49.75 MW	64.54 AEX	FLBLS	7/16-9/16
	Fort Lauderdale-Pompano Beach-Deerfield Beach PMSA, FL	H	42.91 AE	56.25 MW	81.91 AEX	FLBLS	7/16-9/16
	Miami-Miami Beach-Kendall PMSA, FL	H	41.90 AE	55.16 MW	71.25 AEX	FLBLS	7/16-9/16
	Orlando-Kissimmee-Sanford MSA, FL	H	33.14 AE	50.44 MW	73.54 AEX	FLBLS	7/16-9/16
	Tampa-St. Petersburg-Clearwater MSA, FL	H	30.33 AE	40.49 MW	50.70 AEX	FLBLS	7/16-9/16
	Georgia	Y	72800 FQ	95940 MW	115040 TQ	USBLS	5/15
	Atlanta-Sandy Springs-Roswell MSA, GA	Y	73040 FQ	96400 MW	117900 TQ	USBLS	5/15
	Augusta-Richmond County MSA, GA-SC	Y	74690 FQ	93330 MW	110360 TQ	USBLS	5/15
	Hawaii	Y	87860 FQ	104010 MW	127210 TQ	USBLS	5/15
	Urban Honolulu MSA, HI	Y	85980 FQ	102230 MW	126660 TQ	USBLS	5/15
	Idaho	Y	78980 FQ	91250 MW	105720 TQ	USBLS	5/15
	Boise City MSA, ID	Y	79360 FQ	94580 MW	108630 TQ	USBLS	5/15
	Illinois	Y	89190 FQ	115010 MW	144440 TQ	USBLS	5/15
	Chicago-Naperville-Arlington Heights PMSA, IL	Y	79370 FQ	106080 MW	125130 TQ	USBLS	5/15
	Lake County-Kenosha County PMSA, IL-WI	Y	113060 FQ	150580 MW		USBLS	5/15
	Indiana	Y	46160 FQ	55360 MW	71910 TQ	USBLS	5/15
	Gary PMSA, IN	Y	43850 FQ	51750 MW	88550 TQ	USBLS	5/15
	Indianapolis-Carmel-Anderson MSA, IN	Y	45600 FQ	54050 MW	66370 TQ	USBLS	5/15
	Iowa	Y	86860 FQ	101990 MW	121320 TQ	USBLS	5/15
	Des Moines-West Des Moines MSA, IA	Y	105730 FQ	115050 MW	126750 TQ	USBLS	5/15
	Kansas	Y	83460 FQ	94580 MW	108510 TQ	USBLS	5/15
	Kentucky	Y	71320 FQ	96860 MW	127630 TQ	USBLS	5/15
	Louisville-Jefferson County MSA, KY-IN	Y	90810 FQ	117050 MW	138980 TQ	USBLS	5/15
	Louisiana	Y	72550 FQ	91830 MW	109570 TQ	USBLS	5/15
	Baton Rouge MSA, LA	Y	68090 FQ	80950 MW	101270 TQ	USBLS	5/15
	New Orleans-Metairie MSA, LA	Y	83450 FQ	102940 MW	122410 TQ	USBLS	5/15
	Maine	Y	73150 FQ	93590 MW	121110 TQ	USBLS	5/15
	Portland-South Portland MSA, ME	Y	71980 FQ	102790 MW	130770 TQ	USBLS	5/15
	Maryland	Y	93507 AE	133580 MW	153617 AEX	MDBLS	4/16
	Baltimore-Columbia-Towson MSA, MD	Y	90820 FQ	113320 MW	151500 TQ	USBLS	5/15
	Massachusetts	Y	110850 FQ	152970 MW		USBLS	5/15
	Boston-Cambridge-Newton NECTA, MA	Y	114300 FQ	163770 MW		USBLS	5/15
	Worcester MSA, MA-CT	Y	97470 FQ	125060 MW	149400 TQ	USBLS	5/15
	Michigan	Y	81580 FQ	100650 MW	137030 TQ	USBLS	5/15
	Detroit-Dearborn-Livonia PMSA, MI	Y	82840 FQ	99180 MW	141260 TQ	USBLS	5/15
	Grand Rapids-Wyoming MSA, MI	Y	46640 FQ	68630 MW	111680 TQ	USBLS	5/15
	Minnesota	Y	84662 FQ	104770 MW	127450 TQ	MNBLS	1/16-3/16
	Minneapolis-St. Paul-Bloomington MSA, MN-WI	Y	91947 FQ	111192 MW	133353 TQ	MNBLS	1/16-3/16
	Mississippi	Y	84230 FQ	97380 MW	118360 TQ	USBLS	5/15
	Jackson MSA, MS	Y	79540 FQ	91260 MW	100160 TQ	USBLS	5/15
	Missouri	Y	86760 FQ	104800 MW	134900 TQ	USBLS	5/15
	Kansas City MSA, MO-KS	Y	89740 FQ	102650 MW	126530 TQ	USBLS	5/15
	St. Louis MSA, MO-IL	Y	92850 FQ	111790 MW	145120 TQ	USBLS	5/15
	Montana	Y	76230 FQ	88910 MW	105720 TQ	USBLS	5/15
	Nebraska	Y	66075 FQ	97370 MW	118355 TQ	NEBLS	7/16-9/16
	Omaha-Council Bluffs MSA, NE-IA	Y	67620 FQ	91830 MW	111795 TQ	NEBLS	7/16-9/16
	Nevada	Y	84230 FQ	98280 MW	118370 TQ	USBLS	5/15
	Las Vegas-Henderson-Paradise MSA, NV	Y	91260 FQ	105220 MW	133120 TQ	USBLS	5/15
	New Hampshire	H	43.45 AE	60.46 MW	82.29 AEX	NHBLS	6/16
	New Jersey	Y	126490 FQ	173320 MW		USBLS	5/15
	Camden PMSA, NJ	Y	111160 FQ	143210 MW		USBLS	5/15

AE	Average entry wage	**AWR**	Average wage range	**H**	Hourly	**LR**	Low end range	**MTC**	Median total compensation	**TCC**	Total cash compensation
AEX	Average experienced wage	**B**	Biweekly	**HI**	Highest wage paid	**M**	Monthly	**MW**	Median wage paid	**TQ**	Third quartile wage
ATC	Average total compensation	**D**	Daily	**HR**	High end range	**MCC**	Median cash compensation	**MWR**	Median wage range	**W**	Weekly
AW	Average wage paid	**FQ**	First quartile wage	**LO**	Lowest wage paid	**ME**	Median entry wage	**S**	See annotated source	**Y**	Yearly

Occupation/Type/Industry	Location	Per	Low	Mid	High	Source	Date
Natural Sciences Manager	Newark PMSA, NJ-PA	Y	140310 FQ	185350 MW		USBLS	5/15
	Trenton MSA, NJ	Y	113460 FQ	127700 MW	181680 TQ	USBLS	5/15
	New Mexico	Y	79940 FQ	97550 MW	123290 TQ	USBLS	5/15
	Albuquerque MSA, NM	Y	86250 FQ	99680 MW	114460 TQ	USBLS	5/15
	New York	Y	82970 AE	125250 MW	177640 AEX	NYBLS	1/16-3/16
	Buffalo-Cheektowaga-Niagara Falls MSA, NY	Y	91230 FQ	102390 MW	128290 TQ	USBLS	5/15
	Nassau County-Suffolk County PMSA, NY	Y	116230 FQ	154030 MW		USBLS	5/15
	New York-Jersey City-White Plains PMSA, NY-NJ	Y	112290 FQ	147490 MW		USBLS	5/15
	Rochester MSA, NY	Y	67260 FQ	76980 MW	96910 TQ	USBLS	5/15
	North Carolina	Y	102160 FQ	127700 MW	166820 TQ	USBLS	5/15
	Charlotte-Concord-Gastonia MSA, NC-SC	Y	89940 FQ	107950 MW	140670 TQ	USBLS	5/15
	Raleigh MSA, NC	Y	96060 FQ	116870 MW	152050 TQ	USBLS	5/15
	North Dakota	Y	80580 FQ	91820 MW	106170 TQ	USBLS	5/15
	Ohio	Y	79560 FQ	111910 MW	144590 TQ	USBLS	5/15
	Cincinnati MSA, OH-KY-IN	Y	91580 FQ	118660 MW	146880 TQ	USBLS	5/15
	Cleveland-Elyria MSA, OH	Y	92480 FQ	127350 MW	163770 TQ	USBLS	5/15
	Columbus MSA, OH	Y	75780 FQ	105160 MW	135980 TQ	USBLS	5/15
	Oklahoma	Y	61390 FQ	88770 MW	113440 TQ	USBLS	5/15
	Oklahoma City MSA, OK	Y	55450 FQ	68530 MW	108500 TQ	USBLS	5/15
	Tulsa MSA, OK	Y	66560 FQ	84780 MW	115070 TQ	USBLS	5/15
	Oregon	H	41.82 FQ	49.06 MW	59.68 TQ	ORBLS	2016
	Portland-Vancouver-Hillsboro MSA, OR-WA	Y	93870 FQ	111450 MW	134540 TQ	USBLS	5/15
	Pennsylvania	Y	98170 FQ	134770 MW		USBLS	5/15
	Allentown-Bethlehem-Easton MSA, PA-NJ	Y	75900 FQ	119360 MW		USBLS	5/15
	Harrisburg-Carlisle MSA, PA	Y	84080 FQ	102950 MW	119460 TQ	USBLS	5/15
	Montgomery County-Bucks County-Chester County PMSA, PA	Y	113240 FQ	148540 MW		USBLS	5/15
	Philadelphia PMSA, PA	Y	89860 FQ	115760 MW	172050 TQ	USBLS	5/15
	Rhode Island	Y	105980 FQ	120960 MW	161350 TQ	USBLS	5/15
	Providence-Warwick MSA, RI-MA	Y	103990 FQ	120960 MW	161040 TQ	USBLS	5/15
	South Carolina	Y	70200 FQ	85230 MW	111780 TQ	USBLS	5/15
	Charleston-North Charleston MSA, SC	Y	72900 FQ	94090 MW	130350 TQ	USBLS	5/15
	Columbia MSA, SC	Y	66620 FQ	73830 MW	89040 TQ	USBLS	5/15
	Greenville-Anderson-Mauldin MSA, SC	Y	84970 FQ	97590 MW	171360 TQ	USBLS	5/15
	South Dakota	Y	84230 FQ	97380 MW	115080 TQ	USBLS	5/15
	Tennessee	Y	84460 FQ	102680 MW	136510 TQ	USBLS	5/15
	Knoxville MSA, TN	Y	90210 FQ	110730 MW	138910 TQ	USBLS	5/15
	Memphis MSA, TN-MS-AR	Y	84320 FQ	104750 MW	130060 TQ	USBLS	5/15
	Nashville-Davidson–Murfreesboro–Franklin MSA, TN	Y	87640 FQ	97190 MW	130570 TQ	USBLS	5/15
	Texas	Y	89180 FQ	110200 MW	144240 TQ	USBLS	5/15
	Austin-Round Rock MSA, TX	Y	101590 FQ	126770 MW	147160 TQ	USBLS	5/15
	Dallas-Plano-Irving PMSA, TX	Y	104730 AE	125790 MW	161900 TQ	USBLS	5/15
	Fort Worth-Arlington PMSA, TX	Y	108020 FQ	121620 MW	136550 TQ	USBLS	5/15
	Houston-The Woodlands-Sugar Land MSA, TX	Y	87040 FQ	118620 MW	179400 TQ	USBLS	5/15
	San Antonio-New Braunfels MSA, TX	Y	88050 FQ	108500 MW	145580 TQ	USBLS	5/15
	Utah	Y	74970 FQ	94590 MW	121870 TQ	USBLS	5/15
	Ogden-Clearfield MSA, UT	Y	86580 FQ	102940 MW	120010 TQ	USBLS	5/15
	Provo-Orem MSA, UT	Y	68800 FQ	100440 MW	123670 TQ	USBLS	5/15
	Salt Lake City MSA, UT	Y	76510 FQ	95110 MW	124930 TQ	USBLS	5/15
	Vermont	Y	78500 FQ	91260 MW	102960 TQ	USBLS	5/15
	Virginia	Y	101060 FQ	126220 MW	158690 TQ	USBLS	5/15
	Richmond MSA, VA	Y	82050 FQ	106910 MW	147380 TQ	USBLS	5/15
	Virginia Beach-Norfolk-Newport News MSA, VA-NC	Y	89030 FQ	102940 MW	117850 TQ	USBLS	5/15
	Washington	H	49.27 FQ	61.00 MW	84.82 TQ	WABLS	3/16
	Seattle-Bellevue-Everett PMSA, WA	H	53.21 FQ	67.45 MW		WABLS	3/16

AE	Average entry wage	AWR	Average wage range	H	Hourly	LR	Low end range	MTC	Median total compensation	TCC	Total cash compensation
AEX	Average experienced wage	B	Biweekly	HI	Highest wage paid	M	Monthly	MW	Median wage paid	TQ	Third quartile wage
ATC	Average total compensation	D	Daily	HR	High end range	MCC	Median cash compensation	MWR	Median wage range	W	Weekly
AW	Average wage paid	FQ	First quartile wage	LO	Lowest wage paid	ME	Median entry wage	S	See annotated source	Y	Yearly

Occupation/Type/Industry	Location	Per	Low	Mid	High	Source	Date
Natural Sciences Manager	Tacoma-Lakewood PMSA, WA	H	50.35 FQ	58.34 MW	66.90 TQ	WABLS	3/16
	West Virginia	Y	87210 FQ	100910 MW	123750 TQ	USBLS	5/15
	Wisconsin	Y	86420 FQ	98620 MW	117400 TQ	USBLS	5/15
	Madison MSA, WI	Y	89040 FQ	101040 MW	121650 TQ	USBLS	5/15
	Milwaukee-Waukesha-West Allis MSA, WI	Y	76560 FQ	96230 MW	110690 TQ	USBLS	5/15
	Wyoming	Y	81910 FQ	89030 MW	97370 TQ	USBLS	5/15
	Puerto Rico	Y	86580 FQ	97380 MW	108510 TQ	USBLS	5/15
Naturalist							
Municipal Government	Detroit, MI	M	2858 LO		3200 HI	DETGOV	2016
Naturopathic Physician	United States	Y		85000 AW		EXHC03	2016
Neighborhood Counselor							
Human Services Department, Municipal Government	Hawaiian Gardens, CA	Y			57745 HI	CACIT	6/28/16
Neighborhood Improvement Officer							
Municipal Government	Long Beach, CA	Y			115288 HI	CACIT	6/28/16
Neighborhood Services Manager							
Municipal Government	Escondido, CA	Y			58246 HI	CACIT	6/28/16
Municipal Government	Lodi, CA	Y			103355 HI	CACIT	6/28/16
Municipal Government	Colorado Springs, CO	Y	67751 LO		93157 HI	COSPRS	2017
Neighborhood Watch Coordinator							
Police Department, Municipal Government	Bell Gardens, CA	Y			58737 HI	CACIT	6/28/16
Nematologist							
State Government	North Carolina	Y	50238 LO		82872 HI	NCGOV	7/1/16
Nephrologist	United States	Y		273000 AW		MED02	2016
Network and Computer Systems Administrator	Alabama	Y	49498 AE	72392 AW	83839 AEX	ALBLS	6/16
	Birmingham-Hoover MSA, AL	Y	51323 AE	75848 AW	88110 AEX	ALBLS	6/16
	Alaska	Y	65600 FQ	78480 MW	95740 TQ	USBLS	5/15
	Anchorage MSA, AK	Y	64340 FQ	77650 MW	96630 TQ	USBLS	5/15
	Arizona	Y	56490 FQ	74240 MW	95160 TQ	USBLS	5/15
	Phoenix-Mesa-Scottsdale MSA, AZ	Y	58500 FQ	77810 MW	98140 TQ	USBLS	5/15
	Prescott MSA, AZ	Y	51750 FQ	60680 MW	73270 TQ	USBLS	5/15
	Tucson MSA, AZ	Y	51770 FQ	61790 MW	75310 TQ	USBLS	5/15
	Arkansas	Y	51270 FQ	64550 MW	77800 TQ	USBLS	5/15
	Little Rock-North Little Rock-Conway MSA, AR	Y	51560 FQ	64340 MW	75250 TQ	USBLS	5/15
	California	H	32.92 FQ	43.33 MW	55.79 TQ	CABLS	1/16-3/16
	Anaheim-Santa Ana-Irvine PMSA, CA	H	31.23 FQ	42.27 MW	54.74 TQ	CABLS	1/16-3/16
	Los Angeles-Long Beach-Glendale PMSA, CA	H	30.27 FQ	40.34 MW	51.34 TQ	CABLS	1/16-3/16
	Oakland-Hayward-Berkeley PMSA, CA	H	40.73 FQ	49.96 MW	61.60 TQ	CABLS	1/16-3/16
	Riverside-San Bernardino-Ontario MSA, CA	H	27.98 FQ	35.19 MW	43.00 TQ	CABLS	1/16-3/16
	Sacramento–Roseville–Arden-Arcade MSA, CA	H	30.61 FQ	40.88 MW	48.61 TQ	CABLS	1/16-3/16
	San Diego-Carlsbad MSA, CA	H	31.62 FQ	39.49 MW	51.15 TQ	CABLS	1/16-3/16
	San Francisco-Redwood City-South San Francisco PMSA, CA	H	39.08 FQ	52.05 MW	64.08 TQ	CABLS	1/16-3/16
	Colorado	Y	63770 FQ	80260 MW	100200 TQ	USBLS	5/15
	Denver-Aurora-Lakewood MSA, CO	Y	67050 FQ	85550 MW	104660 TQ	USBLS	5/15
	Connecticut	Y		83412 MW		CTBLS	1/16-3/16
	Bridgeport-Stamford-Norwalk MSA, CT	Y	72320 FQ	91740 MW	116100 TQ	USBLS	5/15
	Hartford-West Hartford-East Hartford MSA, CT	Y	66710 FQ	81110 MW	97980 TQ	USBLS	5/15
	Delaware	Y	56030 FQ	69810 MW	89710 TQ	USBLS	5/15

AE	Average entry wage	AWR	Average wage range	H	Hourly
AEX	Average experienced wage	B	Biweekly	HI	Highest wage paid
ATC	Average total compensation	D	Daily	HR	High end range
AW	Average wage paid	FQ	First quartile wage	LO	Lowest wage paid

LR	Low end range	MTC	Median total compensation	TCC	Total cash compensation
M	Monthly	MW	Median wage paid	TQ	Third quartile wage
MCC	Median cash compensation	MWR	Median wage range	W	Weekly
ME	Median entry wage	S	See annotated source	Y	Yearly

Occupation/Type/Industry	Location	Per	Low	Mid	High	Source	Date
Network and Computer Systems Administrator	Wilmington PMSA, DE-MD-NJ	Y	58840 FQ	73780 MW	94110 TQ	USBLS	5/15
	District of Columbia	Y	72610 FQ	90870 MW	111580 TQ	USBLS	5/15
	Washington-Arlington-Alexandria PMSA, DC-VA-MD-WV	Y	76240 FQ	97020 MW	120120 TQ	USBLS	5/15
	Florida	H	26.11 AE	37.90 MW	46.46 AEX	FLBLS	7/16-9/16
	Fort Lauderdale-Pompano Beach-Deerfield Beach PMSA, FL	H	27.16 AE	38.16 MW	46.86 AEX	FLBLS	7/16-9/16
	Miami-Miami Beach-Kendall PMSA, FL	H	27.86 AE	38.57 MW	46.16 AEX	FLBLS	7/16-9/16
	Orlando-Kissimmee-Sanford MSA, FL	H	28.38 AE	40.36 MW	48.89 AEX	FLBLS	7/16-9/16
	Tampa-St. Petersburg-Clearwater MSA, FL	H	25.61 AE	38.07 MW	45.32 AEX	FLBLS	7/16-9/16
	Georgia	Y	60540 FQ	78050 MW	101160 TQ	USBLS	5/15
	Atlanta-Sandy Springs-Roswell MSA, GA	Y	63150 FQ	81850 MW	105180 TQ	USBLS	5/15
	Augusta-Richmond County MSA, GA-SC	Y	53760 FQ	67910 MW	88760 TQ	USBLS	5/15
	Hawaii	Y	59280 FQ	71330 MW	85110 TQ	USBLS	5/15
	Urban Honolulu MSA, HI	Y	59400 FQ	71440 MW	85280 TQ	USBLS	5/15
	Idaho	Y	45960 FQ	60930 MW	78120 TQ	USBLS	5/15
	Boise City MSA, ID	Y	44080 FQ	62070 MW	83420 TQ	USBLS	5/15
	Illinois	Y	63570 FQ	80070 MW	97590 TQ	USBLS	5/15
	Chicago-Naperville-Arlington Heights PMSA, IL	Y	65740 FQ	82170 MW	101460 TQ	USBLS	5/15
	Lake County-Kenosha County PMSA, IL-WI	Y	63450 FQ	86510 MW	108840 TQ	USBLS	5/15
	Indiana	Y	51650 FQ	65120 MW	81890 TQ	USBLS	5/15
	Gary PMSA, IN	Y	50610 FQ	64530 MW	80890 TQ	USBLS	5/15
	Indianapolis-Carmel-Anderson MSA, IN	Y	56800 FQ	71780 MW	91120 TQ	USBLS	5/15
	Iowa	Y	53500 FQ	66870 MW	81480 TQ	USBLS	5/15
	Des Moines-West Des Moines MSA, IA	Y	54990 FQ	72210 MW	92350 TQ	USBLS	5/15
	Kansas	Y	52540 FQ	66830 MW	82370 TQ	USBLS	5/15
	Wichita MSA, KS	Y	47640 FQ	58580 MW	71680 TQ	USBLS	5/15
	Kentucky	Y	47080 FQ	60500 MW	78330 TQ	USBLS	5/15
	Louisville-Jefferson County MSA, KY-IN	Y	50850 FQ	65040 MW	84330 TQ	USBLS	5/15
	Louisiana	Y	45730 FQ	59780 MW	76400 TQ	USBLS	5/15
	Baton Rouge MSA, LA	Y	49790 FQ	63380 MW	77550 TQ	USBLS	5/15
	New Orleans-Metairie MSA, LA	Y	45000 FQ	57760 MW	75680 TQ	USBLS	5/15
	Maine	Y	52710 FQ	64530 MW	81320 TQ	USBLS	5/15
	Portland-South Portland MSA, ME	Y	55980 FQ	69470 MW	88700 TQ	USBLS	5/15
	Maryland	Y	64923 AE	100629 MW	118483 AEX	MDBLS	4/16
	Baltimore-Columbia-Towson MSA, MD	Y	74210 FQ	94660 MW	122490 TQ	USBLS	5/15
	Salisbury MSA, MD-DE	Y	56440 FQ	69500 MW	81060 TQ	USBLS	5/15
	Massachusetts	Y	67230 FQ	83140 MW	102610 TQ	USBLS	5/15
	Boston-Cambridge-Newton NECTA, MA	Y	70660 FQ	87740 MW	108220 TQ	USBLS	5/15
	Worcester MSA, MA-CT	Y	63560 FQ	80660 MW	95960 TQ	USBLS	5/15
	Michigan	Y	55020 FQ	71170 MW	89980 TQ	USBLS	5/15
	Detroit-Dearborn-Livonia PMSA, MI	Y	58580 FQ	79500 MW	95860 TQ	USBLS	5/15
	Grand Rapids-Wyoming MSA, MI	Y	54990 FQ	68420 MW	81890 TQ	USBLS	5/15
	Minnesota	Y	64445 FQ	80120 MW	98497 TQ	MNBLS	1/16-3/16
	Minneapolis-St. Paul-Bloomington MSA, MN-WI	Y	67469 FQ	83769 MW	101783 TQ	MNBLS	1/16-3/16
	Mississippi	Y	47060 FQ	63790 MW	79860 TQ	USBLS	5/15
	Jackson MSA, MS	Y	51080 FQ	69000 MW	83610 TQ	USBLS	5/15
	Missouri	Y	55510 FQ	71380 MW	90610 TQ	USBLS	5/15
	Kansas City MSA, MO-KS	Y	59900 FQ	74080 MW	91400 TQ	USBLS	5/15
	St. Louis MSA, MO-IL	Y	61520 FQ	78260 MW	96010 TQ	USBLS	5/15
	Montana	Y	48230 FQ	58650 MW	71520 TQ	USBLS	5/15

AE	Average entry wage	AWR	Average wage range	H	Hourly	LR	Low end range	MTC Median total compensation TCC Total cash compensation
AEX	Average experienced wage	B	Biweekly	HI	Highest wage paid	M	Monthly	MW Median wage paid TQ Third quartile wage
ATC	Average total compensation	D	Daily	HR	High end range	MCC	Median cash compensation	MWR Median wage range W Weekly
AW	Average wage paid	FQ	First quartile wage	LO	Lowest wage paid	ME	Median entry wage	S See annotated source Y Yearly

Occupation/Type/Industry	Location	Per	Low	Mid	High	Source	Date
Network and Computer Systems Administrator	Billings MSA, MT	Y	49030 FQ	59820 MW	73480 TQ	USBLS	5/15
	Nebraska	Y	53200 FQ	66845 MW	83560 TQ	NEBLS	7/16-9/16
	Omaha-Council Bluffs MSA, NE-IA	Y	57955 FQ	71740 MW	89470 TQ	NEBLS	7/16-9/16
	Nevada	Y	61770 FQ	82880 MW	102780 TQ	USBLS	5/15
	Las Vegas-Henderson-Paradise MSA, NV	Y	62680 FQ	87500 MW	113790 TQ	USBLS	5/15
	New Hampshire	H	25.93 AE	36.46 MW	42.92 AEX	NHBLS	6/16
	Manchester NECTA, NH	H	20.93 AE	34.32 MW	39.08 AEX	NHBLS	6/16
	Nashua NECTA, NH-MA	Y	54580 FQ	66240 MW	87150 TQ	USBLS	5/15
	New Jersey	Y	70480 FQ	88920 MW	116030 TQ	USBLS	5/15
	Camden PMSA, NJ	Y	60790 FQ	76900 MW	93170 TQ	USBLS	5/15
	Newark PMSA, NJ-PA	Y	71370 FQ	94980 MW	117640 TQ	USBLS	5/15
	Trenton MSA, NJ	Y	66710 FQ	78980 MW	102000 TQ	USBLS	5/15
	New Mexico	Y	56140 FQ	70820 MW	87480 TQ	USBLS	5/15
	Albuquerque MSA, NM	Y	56250 FQ	69070 MW	85800 TQ	USBLS	5/15
	New York	Y	56490 AE	85070 MW	107270 AEX	NYBLS	1/16-3/16
	Buffalo-Cheektowaga-Niagara Falls MSA, NY	Y	51810 FQ	65700 MW	82020 TQ	USBLS	5/15
	Nassau County-Suffolk County PMSA, NY	Y	67010 FQ	83390 MW	102460 TQ	USBLS	5/15
	New York-Jersey City-White Plains PMSA, NY-NJ	Y	71420 FQ	92250 MW	120090 TQ	USBLS	5/15
	Rochester MSA, NY	Y	56880 FQ	70580 MW	87130 TQ	USBLS	5/15
	North Carolina	Y	59290 FQ	77630 MW	97520 TQ	USBLS	5/15
	Charlotte-Concord-Gastonia MSA, NC-SC	Y	59230 FQ	77900 MW	97890 TQ	USBLS	5/15
	Raleigh MSA, NC	Y	67060 FQ	86110 MW	106580 TQ	USBLS	5/15
	North Dakota	Y	55110 FQ	64500 MW	79050 TQ	USBLS	5/15
	Fargo MSA, ND-MN	Y	56080 FQ	66830 MW	82330 TQ	USBLS	5/15
	Ohio	Y	56100 FQ	69550 MW	86550 TQ	USBLS	5/15
	Cincinnati MSA, OH-KY-IN	Y	60550 FQ	75350 MW	92530 TQ	USBLS	5/15
	Cleveland-Elyria MSA, OH	Y	57280 FQ	70310 MW	87880 TQ	USBLS	5/15
	Columbus MSA, OH	Y	55140 FQ	68740 MW	86570 TQ	USBLS	5/15
	Oklahoma	Y	49030 FQ	62710 MW	80780 TQ	USBLS	5/15
	Oklahoma City MSA, OK	Y	48350 FQ	61490 MW	79670 TQ	USBLS	5/15
	Tulsa MSA, OK	Y	55140 FQ	71900 MW	92370 TQ	USBLS	5/15
	Oregon	H	27.03 FQ	35.18 MW	43.85 TQ	ORBLS	2016
	Portland-Vancouver-Hillsboro MSA, OR-WA	Y	58430 FQ	74180 MW	92640 TQ	USBLS	5/15
	Pennsylvania	Y	57510 FQ	71760 MW	90120 TQ	USBLS	5/15
	Allentown-Bethlehem-Easton MSA, PA-NJ	Y	57370 FQ	72310 MW	93280 TQ	USBLS	5/15
	Harrisburg-Carlisle MSA, PA	Y	54040 FQ	68640 MW	81570 TQ	USBLS	5/15
	Montgomery County-Bucks County-Chester County PMSA, PA	Y	65280 FQ	78930 MW	100040 TQ	USBLS	5/15
	Philadelphia PMSA, PA	Y	63020 FQ	76490 MW	95610 TQ	USBLS	5/15
	Pittsburgh MSA, PA	Y	56330 FQ	68920 MW	85250 TQ	USBLS	5/15
	Rhode Island	Y	67200 FQ	83110 MW	96770 TQ	USBLS	5/15
	Providence-Warwick MSA, RI-MA	Y	65790 FQ	81750 MW	96090 TQ	USBLS	5/15
	South Carolina	Y	51360 FQ	65670 MW	87050 TQ	USBLS	5/15
	Charleston-North Charleston MSA, SC	Y	57450 FQ	77280 MW	98850 TQ	USBLS	5/15
	Columbia MSA, SC	Y	56160 FQ	72310 MW	93140 TQ	USBLS	5/15
	Greenville-Anderson-Mauldin MSA, SC	Y	47810 FQ	60350 MW	74730 TQ	USBLS	5/15
	South Dakota	Y	51060 FQ	59630 MW	71930 TQ	USBLS	5/15
	Sioux Falls MSA, SD	Y	51850 FQ	60810 MW	73260 TQ	USBLS	5/15
	Tennessee	Y	55350 FQ	71560 MW	92690 TQ	USBLS	5/15
	Knoxville MSA, TN	Y	54700 FQ	69570 MW	88310 TQ	USBLS	5/15
	Memphis MSA, TN-MS-AR	Y	64800 FQ	78190 MW	96740 TQ	USBLS	5/15
	Nashville-Davidson–Murfreesboro–Franklin MSA, TN	Y	61920 FQ	77950 MW	100740 TQ	USBLS	5/15
	Texas	Y	63020 FQ	80340 MW	103020 TQ	USBLS	5/15
	Austin-Round Rock MSA, TX	Y	60080 FQ	79830 MW	109480 TQ	USBLS	5/15
	Dallas-Plano-Irving PMSA, TX	Y	67600 FQ	83990 MW	103010 TQ	USBLS	5/15
	Fort Worth-Arlington PMSA, TX	Y	63190 FQ	79000 MW	96980 TQ	USBLS	5/15

Occupation/Type/Industry	Location	Per	Low	Mid	High	Source	Date
Network and Computer Systems Administrator	Houston-The Woodlands-Sugar Land MSA, TX	Y	69250 FQ	88640 MW	114020 TQ	USBLS	5/15
	San Antonio-New Braunfels MSA, TX	Y	59560 FQ	75560 MW	96290 TQ	USBLS	5/15
	Utah	Y	57580 FQ	73130 MW	91590 TQ	USBLS	5/15
	Ogden-Clearfield MSA, UT	Y	63730 FQ	79310 MW	95120 TQ	USBLS	5/15
	Provo-Orem MSA, UT	Y	54770 FQ	68910 MW	83520 TQ	USBLS	5/15
	Salt Lake City MSA, UT	Y	59520 FQ	75840 MW	95090 TQ	USBLS	5/15
	Vermont	Y	54830 FQ	72740 MW	95710 TQ	USBLS	5/15
	Burlington-South Burlington MSA, VT	Y	61280 FQ	80910 MW	103750 TQ	USBLS	5/15
	Virginia	Y	69410 FQ	90050 MW	114920 TQ	USBLS	5/15
	Richmond MSA, VA	Y	65360 FQ	86670 MW	108190 TQ	USBLS	5/15
	Virginia Beach-Norfolk-Newport News MSA, VA-NC	Y	62100 FQ	76030 MW	95550 TQ	USBLS	5/15
	Washington	H	32.24 FQ	41.01 MW	49.09 TQ	WABLS	3/16
	Seattle-Bellevue-Everett PMSA, WA	H	34.90 FQ	43.76 MW	51.87 TQ	WABLS	3/16
	Tacoma-Lakewood PMSA, WA	H	28.29 FQ	34.90 MW	42.20 TQ	WABLS	3/16
	West Virginia	Y	45290 FQ	57430 MW	74460 TQ	USBLS	5/15
	Huntington-Ashland MSA, WV-KY-OH	Y	44360 FQ	53230 MW	65140 TQ	USBLS	5/15
	Wisconsin	Y	52460 FQ	66220 MW	80800 TQ	USBLS	5/15
	Madison MSA, WI	Y	52690 FQ	67700 MW	82470 TQ	USBLS	5/15
	Milwaukee-Waukesha-West Allis MSA, WI	Y	55300 FQ	70940 MW	87980 TQ	USBLS	5/15
	Wyoming	Y	50660 FQ	62280 MW	76320 TQ	USBLS	5/15
	Cheyenne MSA, WY	Y	48150 FQ	55840 MW	67290 TQ	USBLS	5/15
	Puerto Rico	Y	31650 FQ	42290 MW	56090 TQ	USBLS	5/15
	San Juan-Carolina-Caguas MSA, PR	Y	32840 FQ	43600 MW	56880 TQ	USBLS	5/15
	Virgin Islands	Y	52070 FQ	61800 MW	74390 TQ	USBLS	5/15
	Guam	Y	41020 FQ	49500 MW	63930 TQ	USBLS	5/15
Network Technician	United States	Y		56000 MW		GLKN	2016
Neurologist	United States	Y	225000 ME			AAMC	2016
Neuroscientist	United States	Y		98013 AW		TSCI	2016
Neurosurgeon							
Multispecialty Practice	United States	Y		737849 MW		BSR	2014
Single-Specialty Practice	United States	Y		752141 MW		BSR	2014
New Accounts Clerk	Alabama	Y	28022 AE	34133 AW	37194 AEX	ALBLS	6/16
	Birmingham-Hoover MSA, AL	Y	28310 AE	33670 AW	36349 AEX	ALBLS	6/16
	Alaska	Y	31040 FQ	35990 MW	41690 TQ	USBLS	5/15
	Arizona	Y	33500 FQ	36840 MW	40650 TQ	USBLS	5/15
	Phoenix-Mesa-Scottsdale MSA, AZ	Y	33820 FQ	37090 MW	41230 TQ	USBLS	5/15
	Tucson MSA, AZ	Y	34810 FQ	38970 MW	46820 TQ	USBLS	5/15
	Arkansas	Y	25580 FQ	29680 MW	35370 TQ	USBLS	5/15
	Little Rock-North Little Rock-Conway MSA, AR	Y	27150 FQ	30820 MW	35730 TQ	USBLS	5/15
	California	H	17.01 FQ	20.26 MW	23.30 TQ	CABLS	1/16-3/16
	Anaheim-Santa Ana-Irvine PMSA, CA	H	17.85 FQ	21.14 MW	24.07 TQ	CABLS	1/16-3/16
	Los Angeles-Long Beach-Glendale PMSA, CA	H	17.26 FQ	19.34 MW	22.36 TQ	CABLS	1/16-3/16
	Oakland-Hayward-Berkeley PMSA, CA	H	19.72 FQ	21.54 MW	23.36 TQ	CABLS	1/16-3/16
	Riverside-San Bernardino-Ontario MSA, CA	H	13.87 FQ	15.50 MW	21.18 TQ	CABLS	1/16-3/16
	Sacramento–Roseville–Arden-Arcade MSA, CA	H	17.46 FQ	20.83 MW	24.50 TQ	CABLS	1/16-3/16
	San Diego-Carlsbad MSA, CA	H	19.44 FQ	21.74 MW	23.84 TQ	CABLS	1/16-3/16
	San Francisco-Redwood City-South San Francisco PMSA, CA	H	20.69 FQ	23.34 MW	27.94 TQ	CABLS	1/16-3/16
	Colorado	Y	33040 FQ	36960 MW	42750 TQ	USBLS	5/15

Occupation/Type/Industry	Location	Per	Low	Mid	High	Source	Date
New Accounts Clerk	Denver-Aurora-Lakewood MSA, CO	Y	34160 FQ	37200 MW	41050 TQ	USBLS	5/15
	Connecticut	Y		42193 MW		CTBLS	1/16-3/16
	Bridgeport-Stamford-Norwalk MSA, CT	Y	43650 FQ	49750 MW	65180 TQ	USBLS	5/15
	Delaware	Y	32560 FQ	38350 MW	48440 TQ	USBLS	5/15
	Wilmington PMSA, DE-MD-NJ	Y	33030 FQ	41570 MW	51490 TQ	USBLS	5/15
	District of Columbia	Y	40130 FQ	43980 MW	47820 TQ	USBLS	5/15
	Washington-Arlington-Alexandria PMSA, DC-VA-MD-WV	Y	32840 FQ	38150 MW	45760 TQ	USBLS	5/15
	Florida	H	15.12 AE	17.95 MW	19.89 AEX	FLBLS	7/16-9/16
	Fort Lauderdale-Pompano Beach-Deerfield Beach PMSA, FL	H	17.49 AE	19.20 MW	22.09 AEX	FLBLS	7/16-9/16
	Miami-Miami Beach-Kendall PMSA, FL	H	17.47 AE	18.90 MW	21.77 AEX	FLBLS	7/16-9/16
	Orlando-Kissimmee-Sanford MSA, FL	H	14.47 AE	17.61 MW	19.42 AEX	FLBLS	7/16-9/16
	Tampa-St. Petersburg-Clearwater MSA, FL	H	15.55 AE	17.64 MW	18.92 AEX	FLBLS	7/16-9/16
	Georgia	Y	29730 FQ	35460 MW	41630 TQ	USBLS	5/15
	Atlanta-Sandy Springs-Roswell MSA, GA	Y	37030 FQ	42560 MW	46710 TQ	USBLS	5/15
	Augusta-Richmond County MSA, GA-SC	Y	29480 FQ	34280 MW	38100 TQ	USBLS	5/15
	Hawaii	Y	26980 FQ	30030 MW	35820 TQ	USBLS	5/15
	Urban Honolulu MSA, HI	Y	26630 FQ	29690 MW	35720 TQ	USBLS	5/15
	Idaho	Y	31150 FQ	35170 MW	39030 TQ	USBLS	5/15
	Boise City MSA, ID	Y	34000 FQ	37720 MW	43110 TQ	USBLS	5/15
	Illinois	Y	29040 FQ	34540 MW	41620 TQ	USBLS	5/15
	Chicago-Naperville-Arlington Heights PMSA, IL	Y	30530 FQ	36290 MW	44200 TQ	USBLS	5/15
	Lake County-Kenosha County PMSA, IL-WI	Y	31150 FQ	35820 MW	42670 TQ	USBLS	5/15
	Indiana	Y	28020 FQ	32270 MW	37720 TQ	USBLS	5/15
	Gary PMSA, IN	Y	32740 FQ	36610 MW	41220 TQ	USBLS	5/15
	Indianapolis-Carmel-Anderson MSA, IN	Y	28850 FQ	33760 MW	38470 TQ	USBLS	5/15
	Iowa	Y	29340 FQ	33970 MW	38380 TQ	USBLS	5/15
	Des Moines-West Des Moines MSA, IA	Y	29870 FQ	34470 MW	38690 TQ	USBLS	5/15
	Kansas	Y	27280 FQ	30320 MW	35060 TQ	USBLS	5/15
	Wichita MSA, KS	Y	27260 FQ	29420 MW	31580 TQ	USBLS	5/15
	Kentucky	Y	28720 FQ	33430 MW	37990 TQ	USBLS	5/15
	Louisville-Jefferson County MSA, KY-IN	Y	30370 FQ	34880 MW	39250 TQ	USBLS	5/15
	Louisiana	Y	27040 FQ	31200 MW	36160 TQ	USBLS	5/15
	Baton Rouge MSA, LA	Y	29910 FQ	33850 MW	36780 TQ	USBLS	5/15
	New Orleans-Metairie MSA, LA	Y	27120 FQ	31040 MW	36690 TQ	USBLS	5/15
	Maine	Y	31260 FQ	34210 MW	37210 TQ	USBLS	5/15
	Portland-South Portland MSA, ME	Y	33080 FQ	35440 MW	37800 TQ	USBLS	5/15
	Maryland	Y	27115 AE	36895 MW	41785 AEX	MDBLS	4/16
	Baltimore-Columbia-Towson MSA, MD	Y	30450 FQ	37210 MW	45340 TQ	USBLS	5/15
	Salisbury MSA, MD-DE	Y	27190 FQ	33650 MW	37150 TQ	USBLS	5/15
	Massachusetts	Y	33710 FQ	38880 MW	46070 TQ	USBLS	5/15
	Boston-Cambridge-Newton NECTA, MA	Y	36790 FQ	42880 MW	49060 TQ	USBLS	5/15
	Worcester MSA, MA-CT	Y	34030 FQ	37700 MW	43510 TQ	USBLS	5/15
	Michigan	Y	26130 FQ	31500 MW	38380 TQ	USBLS	5/15
	Detroit-Dearborn-Livonia PMSA, MI	Y	28280 FQ	34860 MW	42010 TQ	USBLS	5/15
	Minnesota	Y	29873 FQ	34950 MW	40198 TQ	MNBLS	1/16-3/16
	Minneapolis-St. Paul-Bloomington MSA, MN-WI	Y	31299 FQ	36123 MW	42119 TQ	MNBLS	1/16-3/16
	Mississippi	Y	27270 FQ	31610 MW	36810 TQ	USBLS	5/15
	Jackson MSA, MS	Y	30040 FQ	34250 MW	38380 TQ	USBLS	5/15
	Missouri	Y	26570 FQ	30640 MW	36380 TQ	USBLS	5/15

AE Average entry wage; AEX Average experienced wage; ATC Average total compensation; AW Average wage paid; AWR Average wage range; B Biweekly; D Daily; FQ First quartile wage; H Hourly; HI Highest wage paid; HR High end range; LO Lowest wage paid; LR Low end range; M Monthly; MCC Median cash compensation; ME Median entry wage; MTC Median total compensation; MW Median wage paid; MWR Median wage range; S See annotated source; TCC Total cash compensation; TQ Third quartile wage; W Weekly; Y Yearly

1092

Occupation/Type/Industry	Location	Per	Low	Mid	High	Source	Date
New Accounts Clerk	Kansas City MSA, MO-KS	Y	27870 FQ	31440 MW	36270 TQ	USBLS	5/15
	St. Louis MSA, MO-IL	Y	27230 FQ	31310 MW	36500 TQ	USBLS	5/15
	Montana	Y	27230 FQ	31230 MW	36740 TQ	USBLS	5/15
	Billings MSA, MT	Y	32480 FQ	36810 MW	42730 TQ	USBLS	5/15
	Nebraska	Y	28055 FQ	31720 MW	36465 TQ	NEBLS	7/16-9/16
	Omaha-Council Bluffs MSA, NE-IA	Y	27690 FQ	30620 MW	35770 TQ	NEBLS	7/16-9/16
	Nevada	Y	32360 FQ	35270 MW	38180 TQ	USBLS	5/15
	Las Vegas-Henderson-Paradise MSA, NV	Y	33500 FQ	36100 MW	38690 TQ	USBLS	5/15
	New Hampshire	H	13.88 AE	16.40 MW	18.01 AEX	NHBLS	6/16
	Manchester NECTA, NH	H	15.12 AE	17.85 MW	19.32 AEX	NHBLS	6/16
	New Jersey	Y	39680 FQ	44330 MW	48800 TQ	USBLS	5/15
	Camden PMSA, NJ	Y	40370 FQ	46550 MW	53510 TQ	USBLS	5/15
	Newark PMSA, NJ-PA	Y	43010 FQ	46850 MW	51930 TQ	USBLS	5/15
	Trenton MSA, NJ	Y	42300 FQ	45640 MW	48980 TQ	USBLS	5/15
	New Mexico	Y	26540 FQ	29840 MW	35150 TQ	USBLS	5/15
	Albuquerque MSA, NM	Y	27770 FQ	30720 MW	35540 TQ	USBLS	5/15
	New York	Y	32050 AE	37650 MW	43160 AEX	NYBLS	1/16-3/16
	Nassau County-Suffolk County PMSA, NY	Y	34080 FQ	36820 MW	39580 TQ	USBLS	5/15
	New York-Jersey City-White Plains PMSA, NY-NJ	Y	36000 FQ	42470 MW	48060 TQ	USBLS	5/15
	Rochester MSA, NY	Y	29780 FQ	34010 MW	38170 TQ	USBLS	5/15
	North Carolina	Y	32460 FQ	37720 MW	44850 TQ	USBLS	5/15
	Charlotte-Concord-Gastonia MSA, NC-SC	Y	32480 FQ	39880 MW	45240 TQ	USBLS	5/15
	Raleigh MSA, NC	Y	33330 FQ	38080 MW	47120 TQ	USBLS	5/15
	North Dakota	Y	27280 FQ	32850 MW	36920 TQ	USBLS	5/15
	Fargo MSA, ND-MN	Y	24640 FQ	28270 MW	32640 TQ	USBLS	5/15
	Ohio	Y	27410 FQ	32090 MW	40560 TQ	USBLS	5/15
	Cincinnati MSA, OH-KY-IN	Y	28330 FQ	32810 MW	41500 TQ	USBLS	5/15
	Cleveland-Elyria MSA, OH	Y	25330 FQ	29280 MW	38350 TQ	USBLS	5/15
	Columbus MSA, OH	Y	31570 FQ	39650 MW	47200 TQ	USBLS	5/15
	Oklahoma	Y	26380 FQ	30210 MW	36410 TQ	USBLS	5/15
	Oklahoma City MSA, OK	Y	28230 FQ	32330 MW	38620 TQ	USBLS	5/15
	Tulsa MSA, OK	Y	26900 FQ	31280 MW	37030 TQ	USBLS	5/15
	Oregon	H	14.99 FQ	17.35 MW	19.41 TQ	ORBLS	2016
	Portland-Vancouver-Hillsboro MSA, OR-WA	Y	33060 FQ	36360 MW	39710 TQ	USBLS	5/15
	Pennsylvania	Y	27680 FQ	32270 MW	37530 TQ	USBLS	5/15
	Allentown-Bethlehem-Easton MSA, PA-NJ	Y	31570 FQ	37050 MW	43650 TQ	USBLS	5/15
	Harrisburg-Carlisle MSA, PA	Y	23800 FQ	28780 MW	37500 TQ	USBLS	5/15
	Montgomery County-Bucks County-Chester County PMSA, PA	Y	35630 FQ	42410 MW	46250 TQ	USBLS	5/15
	Philadelphia PMSA, PA	Y	32640 FQ	35520 MW	38410 TQ	USBLS	5/15
	Pittsburgh MSA, PA	Y	26220 FQ	28890 MW	33060 TQ	USBLS	5/15
	Rhode Island	Y	32210 FQ	34970 MW	37730 TQ	USBLS	5/15
	Providence-Warwick MSA, RI-MA	Y	32190 FQ	35260 MW	38330 TQ	USBLS	5/15
	South Carolina	Y	29730 FQ	34190 MW	38530 TQ	USBLS	5/15
	Charleston-North Charleston MSA, SC	Y	27870 FQ	31460 MW	39040 TQ	USBLS	5/15
	Columbia MSA, SC	Y	31280 FQ	34790 MW	37990 TQ	USBLS	5/15
	Greenville-Anderson-Mauldin MSA, SC	Y	30980 FQ	34750 MW	38500 TQ	USBLS	5/15
	South Dakota	Y	29340 FQ	33900 MW	38430 TQ	USBLS	5/15
	Tennessee	Y	27010 FQ	31250 MW	37490 TQ	USBLS	5/15
	Knoxville MSA, TN	Y	25560 FQ	27410 MW	29260 TQ	USBLS	5/15
	Memphis MSA, TN-MS-AR	Y	32350 FQ	35460 MW	38570 TQ	USBLS	5/15
	Nashville-Davidson–Murfreesboro–Franklin MSA, TN	Y	27100 FQ	32090 MW	41680 TQ	USBLS	5/15
	Texas	Y	28510 FQ	33650 MW	37750 TQ	USBLS	5/15
	Austin-Round Rock MSA, TX	Y	33070 FQ	35370 MW	37660 TQ	USBLS	5/15
	Dallas-Plano-Irving PMSA, TX	Y	29420 FQ	33950 MW	38180 TQ	USBLS	5/15
	Fort Worth-Arlington PMSA, TX	Y	32670 FQ	35680 MW	38690 TQ	USBLS	5/15
	Houston-The Woodlands-Sugar Land MSA, TX	Y	32750 FQ	35760 MW	38770 TQ	USBLS	5/15

AE	Average entry wage	AWR	Average wage range	H	Hourly	LR	Low end range	MTC	Median total compensation	TCC	Total cash compensation
AEX	Average experienced wage	B	Biweekly	HI	Highest wage paid	M	Monthly	MW	Median wage paid	TQ	Third quartile wage
ATC	Average total compensation	D	Daily	HR	High end range	MCC	Median cash compensation	MWR	Median wage range	W	Weekly
AW	Average wage paid	FQ	First quartile wage	LO	Lowest wage paid	ME	Median entry wage	S	See annotated source	Y	Yearly

Occupation/Type/Industry	Location	Per	Low	Mid	High	Source	Date
New Accounts Clerk	San Antonio-New Braunfels						
	MSA, TX	Y	27170 FQ	31050 MW	37420 TQ	USBLS	5/15
	Utah	Y	29980 FQ	34590 MW	38270 TQ	USBLS	5/15
	Ogden-Clearfield MSA, UT	Y	26810 FQ	33320 MW	36780 TQ	USBLS	5/15
	Provo-Orem MSA, UT	Y	28580 FQ	33110 MW	36510 TQ	USBLS	5/15
	Salt Lake City MSA, UT	Y	32610 FQ	36230 MW	39980 TQ	USBLS	5/15
	Vermont	Y	31220 FQ	34640 MW	37770 TQ	USBLS	5/15
	Virginia	Y	31110 FQ	35760 MW	40510 TQ	USBLS	5/15
	Richmond MSA, VA	Y	34080 FQ	36460 MW	38850 TQ	USBLS	5/15
	Virginia Beach-Norfolk-						
	Newport News MSA, VA-NC	Y	31310 FQ	35830 MW	40500 TQ	USBLS	5/15
	Washington	H	16.52 FQ	18.43 MW	21.22 TQ	WABLS	3/16
	Seattle-Bellevue-Everett						
	PMSA, WA	H	17.59 FQ	19.70 MW	22.75 TQ	WABLS	3/16
	Tacoma-Lakewood PMSA, WA	H	15.71 FQ	17.42 MW	19.13 TQ	WABLS	3/16
	West Virginia	Y	25940 FQ	29430 MW	33950 TQ	USBLS	5/15
	Huntington-Ashland MSA,						
	WV-KY-OH	Y	26130 FQ	28910 MW	31640 TQ	USBLS	5/15
	Wisconsin	Y	30690 FQ	34410 MW	38200 TQ	USBLS	5/15
	Madison MSA, WI	Y	28790 FQ	32170 MW	37310 TQ	USBLS	5/15
	Milwaukee-Waukesha-West						
	Allis MSA, WI	Y	32750 FQ	35540 MW	38320 TQ	USBLS	5/15
	Wyoming	Y	26530 FQ	30260 MW	36790 TQ	USBLS	5/15
	Cheyenne MSA, WY	Y	24450 FQ	27700 MW	30830 TQ	USBLS	5/15
	Puerto Rico	Y	18830 FQ	21670 MW	24530 TQ	USBLS	5/15
	San Juan-Carolina-Caguas						
	MSA, PR	Y	18510 FQ	21480 MW	24750 TQ	USBLS	5/15
News Anchor							
Radio	United States	Y		40000 MW		RTDNA	2016
Television	United States	Y		70000 MW		RTDNA	2016
News Reporter							
Radio	United States	Y		36000 MW		RTDNA	2016
Television	United States	Y		41000 MW		RTDNA	2016
News Secretary							
City Attorney's Office	Los Angeles, CA	Y			118811 HI	CACIT	6/23/16
News Writer							
Television	United States	Y		30500 MW		RTDNA	2016
Noise Abatement Officer							
Airport, Municipal Government	Long Beach, CA	Y			118662 HI	CACIT	6/28/16
Noise Control Program Specialist							
Municipal Government	Seattle, WA	H	36.35 LO		42.32 HI	CSSS	1/13/16
Nonfarm Animal Caretaker	Alabama	Y	17483 AE	20870 AW	22569 AEX	ALBLS	6/16
	Birmingham-Hoover MSA, AL	Y	17534 AE	21210 AW	23043 AEX	ALBLS	6/16
	Alaska	Y	19640 FQ	23130 MW	28080 TQ	USBLS	5/15
	Anchorage MSA, AK	Y	19330 FQ	21600 MW	24670 TQ	USBLS	5/15
	Arizona	Y	18400 FQ	20900 MW	26920 TQ	USBLS	5/15
	Phoenix-Mesa-Scottsdale						
	MSA, AZ	Y	18410 FQ	21120 MW	27310 TQ	USBLS	5/15
	Tucson MSA, AZ	Y	18360 FQ	20280 MW	28300 TQ	USBLS	5/15
	Arkansas	Y	17090 FQ	18560 MW	21720 TQ	USBLS	5/15
	Little Rock-North Little Rock-						
	Conway MSA, AR	Y	17180 FQ	18750 MW	23950 TQ	USBLS	5/15
	California	H	9.78 FQ	11.50 MW	15.62 TQ	CABLS	1/16-3/16
	Anaheim-Santa Ana-Irvine						
	PMSA, CA	H	9.62 FQ	10.89 MW	13.41 TQ	CABLS	1/16-3/16
	Los Angeles-Long Beach-						
	Glendale PMSA, CA	H	9.67 FQ	11.44 MW	17.40 TQ	CABLS	1/16-3/16
	Oakland-Hayward-Berkeley						
	PMSA, CA	H	10.09 FQ	11.46 MW	13.92 TQ	CABLS	1/16-3/16
	Riverside-San Bernardino-						
	Ontario MSA, CA	H	9.70 FQ	11.35 MW	14.25 TQ	CABLS	1/16-3/16
	Sacramento–Roseville–						
	Arden-Arcade MSA, CA	H	9.58 FQ	11.14 MW	14.62 TQ	CABLS	1/16-3/16
	San Diego-Carlsbad MSA, CA	H	10.45 FQ	12.09 MW	18.53 TQ	CABLS	1/16-3/16

AE	Average entry wage	AWR	Average wage range	H	Hourly	LR	Low end range	MTC	Median total compensation	TCC	Total cash compensation
AEX	Average experienced wage	B	Biweekly	HI	Highest wage paid	M	Monthly	MW	Median wage paid	TQ	Third quartile wage
ATC	Average total compensation	D	Daily	HR	High end range	MCC	Median cash compensation	MWR	Median wage range	W	Weekly
AW	Average wage paid	FQ	First quartile wage	LO	Lowest wage paid	ME	Median entry wage	S	See annotated source	Y	Yearly

Occupation/Type/Industry	Location	Per	Low	Mid	High	Source	Date
Nonfarm Animal Caretaker	San Francisco-Redwood City-South San Francisco PMSA, CA	H	9.99 FQ	14.65 MW	19.44 TQ	CABLS	1/16-3/16
	Colorado	Y	18500 FQ	20130 MW	23700 TQ	USBLS	5/15
	Denver-Aurora-Lakewood MSA, CO	Y	18480 FQ	20110 MW	23840 TQ	USBLS	5/15
	Connecticut	Y		23066 MW		CTBLS	1/16-3/16
	Bridgeport-Stamford-Norwalk MSA, CT	Y	20130 FQ	23960 MW	33150 TQ	USBLS	5/15
	Hartford-West Hartford-East Hartford MSA, CT	Y	19710 FQ	22230 MW	25880 TQ	USBLS	5/15
	Delaware	Y	17840 FQ	19250 MW	23110 TQ	USBLS	5/15
	Wilmington PMSA, DE-MD-NJ	Y	18370 FQ	21150 MW	27480 TQ	USBLS	5/15
	District of Columbia	Y	24280 FQ	27810 MW	33210 TQ	USBLS	5/15
	Washington-Arlington-Alexandria PMSA, DC-VA-MD-WV	Y	19480 FQ	22730 MW	28450 TQ	USBLS	5/15
	Florida	H	8.98 AE	10.38 MW	12.90 AEX	FLBLS	7/16-9/16
	Fort Lauderdale-Pompano Beach-Deerfield Beach PMSA, FL	H	9.11 AE	11.74 MW	14.32 AEX	FLBLS	7/16-9/16
	Miami-Miami Beach-Kendall PMSA, FL	H	9.04 AE	11.08 MW	13.37 AEX	FLBLS	7/16-9/16
	Orlando-Kissimmee-Sanford MSA, FL	H	8.99 AE	10.29 MW	13.26 AEX	FLBLS	7/16-9/16
	Tampa-St. Petersburg-Clearwater MSA, FL	H	9.06 AE	11.64 MW	14.12 AEX	FLBLS	7/16-9/16
	Georgia	Y	17840 FQ	20600 MW	26090 TQ	USBLS	5/15
	Atlanta-Sandy Springs-Roswell MSA, GA	Y	18110 FQ	21270 MW	27470 TQ	USBLS	5/15
	Augusta-Richmond County MSA, GA-SC	Y	17650 FQ	20390 MW	25790 TQ	USBLS	5/15
	Hawaii	Y	19130 FQ	30380 MW	43260 TQ	USBLS	5/15
	Urban Honolulu MSA, HI	Y	18660 FQ	32400 MW	44250 TQ	USBLS	5/15
	Idaho	Y	17340 FQ	19210 MW	23470 TQ	USBLS	5/15
	Boise City MSA, ID	Y	17360 FQ	19200 MW	23800 TQ	USBLS	5/15
	Illinois	Y	18700 FQ	20450 MW	24550 TQ	USBLS	5/15
	Chicago-Naperville-Arlington Heights PMSA, IL	Y	18730 FQ	20580 MW	24940 TQ	USBLS	5/15
	Lake County-Kenosha County PMSA, IL-WI	Y	18690 FQ	20400 MW	24240 TQ	USBLS	5/15
	Indiana	Y	17220 FQ	18990 MW	23300 TQ	USBLS	5/15
	Gary PMSA, IN	Y	16960 FQ	18460 MW	21380 TQ	USBLS	5/15
	Indianapolis-Carmel-Anderson MSA, IN	Y	17600 FQ	19680 MW	25070 TQ	USBLS	5/15
	Iowa	Y	17550 FQ	19750 MW	24380 TQ	USBLS	5/15
	Des Moines-West Des Moines MSA, IA	Y	18110 FQ	20970 MW	24490 TQ	USBLS	5/15
	Kansas	Y	17370 FQ	19360 MW	24550 TQ	USBLS	5/15
	Wichita MSA, KS	Y	17390 FQ	19530 MW	26020 TQ	USBLS	5/15
	Kentucky	Y	17700 FQ	20270 MW	25330 TQ	USABLS	5/15
	Louisville-Jefferson County MSA, KY-IN	Y	17450 FQ	19510 MW	24700 TQ	USBLS	5/15
	Louisiana	Y	17850 FQ	20620 MW	24260 TQ	USBLS	5/15
	Baton Rouge MSA, LA	Y	17720 FQ	20790 MW	25930 TQ	USBLS	5/15
	New Orleans-Metairie MSA, LA	Y	18980 FQ	21970 MW	25100 TQ	USBLS	5/15
	Maine	Y	18020 FQ	20690 MW	25480 TQ	USBLS	5/15
	Portland-South Portland MSA, ME	Y	21250 FQ	25100 MW	28200 TQ	USBLS	5/15
	Maryland	Y	18047 AE	24362 MW	27519 AEX	MDBLS	4/16
	Baltimore-Columbia-Towson MSA, MD	Y	18350 FQ	20770 MW	25530 TQ	USBLS	5/15
	Salisbury MSA, MD-DE	Y	17800 FQ	19090 MW	22230 TQ	USBLS	5/15
	Massachusetts	Y	19830 FQ	22920 MW	27930 TQ	USBLS	5/15
	Boston-Cambridge-Newton NECTA, MA	Y	19970 FQ	23040 MW	27730 TQ	USBLS	5/15
	Worcester MSA, MA-CT	Y	19210 FQ	21170 MW	25370 TQ	USBLS	5/15
	Michigan	Y	18300 FQ	19590 MW	23850 TQ	USBLS	5/15
	Detroit-Dearborn-Livonia PMSA, MI	Y	18330 FQ	19680 MW	24340 TQ	USBLS	5/15

AE Average entry wage	**AWR** Average wage range	**H** Hourly	**LR** Low end range	**MTC** Median total compensation	**TCC** Total cash compensation
AEX Average experienced wage	**B** Biweekly	**HI** Highest wage paid	**M** Monthly	**MW** Median wage paid	**TQ** Third quartile wage
ATC Average total compensation	**D** Daily	**HR** High end range	**MCC** Median cash compensation	**MWR** Median wage range	**W** Weekly
AW Average wage paid	**FQ** First quartile wage	**LO** Lowest wage paid	**ME** Median entry wage	**S** See annotated source	**Y** Yearly

Occupation/Type/Industry	Location	Per	Low	Mid	High	Source	Date
Nonfarm Animal Caretaker	Grand Rapids-Wyoming MSA, MI	Y	18440 FQ	19840 MW	24840 TQ	USBLS	5/15
	Minnesota	Y	18874 FQ	22066 MW	28458 TQ	MNBLS	1/16-3/16
	Minneapolis-St. Paul-Bloomington MSA, MN-WI	Y	19329 FQ	22631 MW	30508 TQ	MNBLS	1/16-3/16
	Mississippi	Y	17370 FQ	19350 MW	26440 TQ	USBLS	5/15
	Jackson MSA, MS	Y	17400 FQ	20100 MW	28550 TQ	USBLS	5/15
	Missouri	Y	17450 FQ	18960 MW	22940 TQ	USBLS	5/15
	Kansas City MSA, MO-KS	Y	17620 FQ	19790 MW	26210 TQ	USBLS	5/15
	St. Louis MSA, MO-IL	Y	17890 FQ	19260 MW	22990 TQ	USBLS	5/15
	Montana	Y	18400 FQ	20470 MW	24500 TQ	USBLS	5/15
	Billings MSA, MT	Y	19060 FQ	21650 MW	24780 TQ	USBLS	5/15
	Omaha-Council Bluffs MSA, NE-IA	Y	18925 FQ	23105 MW	29660 TQ	NEBLS	7/16-9/16
	Nevada	Y	18160 FQ	21140 MW	24430 TQ	USBLS	5/15
	Las Vegas-Henderson-Paradise MSA, NV	Y	18060 FQ	21050 MW	24450 TQ	USBLS	5/15
	New Hampshire	H	8.40 AE	10.44 MW	12.18 AEX	NHBLS	6/16
	Manchester NECTA, NH	H	8.41 AE	10.53 MW	11.50 AEX	NHBLS	6/16
	Nashua NECTA, NH-MA	Y	18140 FQ	21710 MW	26930 TQ	USBLS	5/15
	New Jersey	Y	19220 FQ	22570 MW	28260 TQ	USBLS	5/15
	Camden PMSA, NJ	Y	18650 FQ	20000 MW	23700 TQ	USBLS	5/15
	Newark PMSA, NJ-PA	Y	20620 FQ	23120 MW	27770 TQ	USBLS	5/15
	Trenton MSA, NJ	Y	19870 FQ	24360 MW	32960 TQ	USBLS	5/15
	New Mexico	Y	18820 FQ	23110 MW	29510 TQ	USBLS	5/15
	Albuquerque MSA, NM	Y	19170 FQ	24020 MW	31930 TQ	USBLS	5/15
	New York	Y	19440 AE	23410 MW	29350 AEX	NYBLS	1/16-3/16
	Buffalo-Cheektowaga-Niagara Falls MSA, NY	Y	19170 FQ	21120 MW	24220 TQ	USBLS	5/15
	Nassau County-Suffolk County PMSA, NY	Y	19560 FQ	22980 MW	29530 TQ	USBLS	5/15
	New York-Jersey City-White Plains PMSA, NY-NJ	Y	19260 FQ	24540 MW	30040 TQ	USBLS	5/15
	Rochester MSA, NY	Y	18950 FQ	20640 MW	25810 TQ	USBLS	5/15
	North Carolina	Y	17370 FQ	19350 MW	23720 TQ	USBLS	5/15
	Charlotte-Concord-Gastonia MSA, NC-SC	Y	17430 FQ	19510 MW	23690 TQ	USBLS	5/15
	Raleigh MSA, NC	Y	17660 FQ	19920 MW	25630 TQ	USBLS	5/15
	North Dakota	Y	17710 FQ	20270 MW	24100 TQ	USBLS	5/15
	Fargo MSA, ND-MN	Y	17170 FQ	18850 MW	26290 TQ	USBLS	5/15
	Ohio	Y	18100 FQ	19340 MW	23330 TQ	USBLS	5/15
	Cincinnati MSA, OH-KY-IN	Y	18000 FQ	19340 MW	24340 TQ	USBLS	5/15
	Cleveland-Elyria MSA, OH	Y	18100 FQ	19310 MW	22770 TQ	USBLS	5/15
	Columbus MSA, OH	Y	18640 FQ	21400 MW	26270 TQ	USBLS	5/15
	Oklahoma	Y	17140 FQ	18860 MW	23280 TQ	USBLS	5/15
	Oklahoma City MSA, OK	Y	17150 FQ	18830 MW	22090 TQ	USBLS	5/15
	Tulsa MSA, OK	Y	16980 FQ	18640 MW	25380 TQ	USBLS	5/15
	Oregon	H	10.10 FQ	11.33 MW	13.28 TQ	ORBLS	2016
	Portland-Vancouver-Hillsboro MSA, OR-WA	Y	21260 FQ	23700 MW	28330 TQ	USBLS	5/15
	Pennsylvania	Y	17510 FQ	19680 MW	23830 TQ	USBLS	5/15
	Allentown-Bethlehem-Easton MSA, PA-NJ	Y	17150 FQ	18770 MW	22720 TQ	USBLS	5/15
	Harrisburg-Carlisle MSA, PA	Y	17370 FQ	19290 MW	24240 TQ	USBLS	5/15
	Montgomery County-Bucks County-Chester County PMSA, PA	Y	17960 FQ	21010 MW	24690 TQ	USBLS	5/15
	Philadelphia PMSA, PA	Y	18750 FQ	22070 MW	27010 TQ	USBLS	5/15
	Pittsburgh MSA, PA	Y	17400 FQ	19280 MW	23160 TQ	USBLS	5/15
	Rhode Island	Y	19490 FQ	23140 MW	33390 TQ	USBLS	5/15
	Providence-Warwick MSA, RI-MA	Y	19530 FQ	22270 MW	29940 TQ	USBLS	5/15
	South Carolina	Y	17450 FQ	19490 MW	24290 TQ	USBLS	5/15
	Charleston-North Charleston MSA, SC	Y	17320 FQ	19220 MW	25520 TQ	USBLS	5/15
	Columbia MSA, SC	Y	17560 FQ	19590 MW	23780 TQ	USBLS	5/15
	Greenville-Anderson-Mauldin MSA, SC	Y	17290 FQ	19160 MW	22550 TQ	USBLS	5/15
	South Dakota	Y	18570 FQ	19480 MW	23400 TQ	USBLS	5/15
	Sioux Falls MSA, SD	Y	18720 FQ	20130 MW	24890 TQ	USBLS	5/15
	Tennessee	Y	17580 FQ	19880 MW	23500 TQ	USBLS	5/15
	Knoxville MSA, TN	Y	17380 FQ	19330 MW	22950 TQ	USBLS	5/15

AE	Average entry wage	AWR	Average wage range	H	Hourly
AEX	Average experienced wage	B	Biweekly	HI	Highest wage paid
ATC	Average total compensation	D	Daily	HR	High end range
AW	Average wage paid	FQ	First quartile wage	LO	Lowest wage paid

LR	Low end range	MTC	Median total compensation	TCC	Total cash compensation
M	Monthly	MW	Median wage paid	TQ	Third quartile wage
MCC	Median cash compensation	MWR	Median wage range	W	Weekly
ME	Median entry wage	S	See annotated source	Y	Yearly

Occupation/Type/Industry	Location	Per	Low	Mid	High	Source	Date
Nonfarm Animal Caretaker	Memphis MSA, TN-MS-AR	Y	18050 FQ	21420 MW	27080 TQ	USBLS	5/15
	Nashville-Davidson–Murfreesboro–Franklin MSA, TN	Y	17470 FQ	19610 MW	22980 TQ	USBLS	5/15
	Texas	Y	17550 FQ	19720 MW	24090 TQ	USBLS	5/15
	Austin-Round Rock MSA, TX	Y	18950 FQ	21410 MW	23860 TQ	USBLS	5/15
	Dallas-Plano-Irving PMSA, TX	Y	17600 FQ	19780 MW	24560 TQ	USBLS	5/15
	Fort Worth-Arlington PMSA, TX	Y	17800 FQ	20900 MW	27120 TQ	USBLS	5/15
	Houston-The Woodlands-Sugar Land MSA, TX	Y	17100 FQ	18810 MW	22600 TQ	USBLS	5/15
	San Antonio-New Braunfels MSA, TX	Y	19680 FQ	22470 MW	29300 TQ	USBLS	5/15
	Utah	Y	17320 FQ	19230 MW	25830 TQ	USBLS	5/15
	Ogden-Clearfield MSA, UT	Y	17050 FQ	18720 MW	22070 TQ	USBLS	5/15
	Provo-Orem MSA, UT	Y	17390 FQ	19650 MW	23590 TQ	USBLS	5/15
	Salt Lake City MSA, UT	Y	17010 FQ	18570 MW	21490 TQ	USBLS	5/15
	Vermont	Y	20100 FQ	23800 MW	28330 TQ	USBLS	5/15
	Burlington-South Burlington MSA, VT	Y	21350 FQ	24730 MW	28950 TQ	USBLS	5/15
	Virginia	Y	18060 FQ	20990 MW	24710 TQ	USBLS	5/15
	Richmond MSA, VA	Y	17650 FQ	20010 MW	23960 TQ	USBLS	5/15
	Virginia Beach-Norfolk-Newport News MSA, VA-NC	Y	17340 FQ	19310 MW	23790 TQ	USBLS	5/15
	Washington	H	10.57 FQ	11.58 MW	13.65 TQ	WABLS	3/16
	Seattle-Bellevue-Everett PMSA, WA	H	10.65 FQ	11.67 MW	13.72 TQ	WABLS	3/16
	Tacoma-Lakewood PMSA, WA	H	10.37 FQ	11.47 MW	13.85 TQ	WABLS	3/16
	West Virginia	Y	18020 FQ	19420 MW	23700 TQ	USBLS	5/15
	Huntington-Ashland MSA, WV-KY-OH	Y	17830 FQ	19150 MW	25280 TQ	USBLS	5/15
	Wisconsin	Y	17090 FQ	18770 MW	22760 TQ	USBLS	5/15
	Madison MSA, WI	Y	16750 FQ	18050 MW	19360 TQ	USBLS	5/15
	Milwaukee-Waukesha-West Allis MSA, WI	Y	17250 FQ	19100 MW	24480 TQ	USBLS	5/15
	Wyoming	Y	18970 FQ	22220 MW	25790 TQ	USBLS	5/15
	Cheyenne MSA, WY	Y	19570 FQ	22310 MW	25150 TQ	USBLS	5/15
	Puerto Rico	Y	16700 FQ	18030 MW	19450 TQ	USBLS	5/15
	San Juan-Carolina-Caguas MSA, PR	Y	16680 FQ	18000 MW	19350 TQ	USBLS	5/15
Noxious Weed Support Specialist							
County Government	Douglas County, CO	Y			50525 HI	DCOGOV	2016
Nuclear Boiler Inspector							
State Government	Ohio	H			34.56 HI	OHGOV	2015
Nuclear Engineer	Alabama	Y	85480 AE	126529 AW	147058 AEX	ALBLS	6/16
	California	H	58.51 FQ	70.61 MW	82.61 TQ	CABLS	1/16-3/16
	Connecticut	Y		116301 MW		CTBLS	1/16-3/16
	District of Columbia	Y	127490 FQ	156470 MW	168710 TQ	USBLS	5/15
	Florida	H	41.12 AE	47.49 MW	52.59 AEX	FLBLS	7/16-9/16
	Georgia	Y	80100 FQ	90510 MW	107560 TQ	USBLS	5/15
	Idaho	Y	94630 FQ	115130 MW	138690 TQ	USBLS	5/15
	Illinois	Y	103750 FQ	115690 MW	130730 TQ	USBLS	5/15
	Kansas	Y	80860 FQ	100760 MW	121450 TQ	USBLS	5/15
	Louisiana	Y	84010 FQ	104340 MW	119680 TQ	USBLS	5/15
	Maryland	Y	77939 AE*	108138 MW	123238 AEX	MDBLS	4/16
	Michigan	Y	91700 FQ	106390 MW	120640 TQ	USBLS	5/15
	Minnesota	Y	88477 FQ	95301 MW	102136 TQ	MNBLS	1/16-3/16
	Nebraska	Y	77550 FQ	101440 MW	116130 TQ	NEBLS	7/16-9/16
	New Hampshire	H	40.38 AE	54.05 MW	60.41 AEX	NHBLS	6/16
	New Jersey	Y	83320 FQ	98320 MW	116140 TQ	USBLS	5/15
	New Mexico	Y	126110 FQ	159380 MW		USBLS	5/15
	New York	Y	82450 AE	114490 MW	128110 AEX	NYBLS	1/16-3/16
	Pennsylvania	Y	70390 FQ	91610 MW	114680 TQ	USBLS	5/15
	South Carolina	Y	82770 FQ	96240 MW	114770 TQ	USBLS	5/15
	Tennessee	Y	99700 FQ	116750 MW	130390 TQ	USBLS	5/15
	Texas	Y	93480 FQ	111700 MW	125670 TQ	USBLS	5/15
	Virginia	Y	70200 FQ	87790 MW	106280 TQ	USBLS	5/15
	Washington	H	38.96 FQ	46.34 MW	54.26 TQ	WABLS	3/16
	Wisconsin	Y	83170 FQ	90920 MW	98350 TQ	USBLS	5/15

AE	Average entry wage	AWR	Average wage range	H	Hourly
AEX	Average experienced wage	B	Biweekly	HI	Highest wage paid
ATC	Average total compensation	D	Daily	HR	High end range
AW	Average wage paid	FQ	First quartile wage	LO	Lowest wage paid

LR	Low end range	MTC	Median total compensation	TCC	Total cash compensation
M	Monthly	MW	Median wage paid	TQ	Third quartile wage
MCC	Median cash compensation	MWR	Median wage range	W	Weekly
ME	Median entry wage	S	See annotated source	Y	Yearly

Occupation/Type/Industry	Location	Per	Low	Mid	High	Source	Date
Nuclear Medicine Technologist	Alabama	Y	48469 AE	62077 AW	68876 AEX	ALBLS	6/16
	Birmingham-Hoover MSA, AL	Y	54850 AE	66287 AW	54850 AEX	ALBLS	6/16
	Alaska	Y	70340 FQ	82890 MW	93370 TQ	USBLS	5/15
	Anchorage MSA, AK	Y	71000 FQ	84560 MW	94360 TQ	USBLS	5/15
	Arizona	Y	69280 FQ	78240 MW	89670 TQ	USBLS	5/15
	Phoenix-Mesa-Scottsdale MSA, AZ	Y	69580 FQ	78760 MW	90130 TQ	USBLS	5/15
	Arkansas	Y	60420 FQ	69380 MW	77390 TQ	USBLS	5/15
	Little Rock-North Little Rock-Conway MSA, AR	Y	60130 FQ	68710 MW	76290 TQ	USBLS	5/15
	California	H	43.46 FQ	51.34 MW	60.22 TQ	CABLS	1/16-3/16
	Anaheim-Santa Ana-Irvine PMSA, CA	H	45.38 FQ	53.50 MW	61.24 TQ	CABLS	1/16-3/16
	Los Angeles-Long Beach-Glendale PMSA, CA	H	42.43 FQ	48.52 MW	57.08 TQ	CABLS	1/16-3/16
	Oakland-Hayward-Berkeley PMSA, CA	H	50.43 FQ	56.75 MW	64.11 TQ	CABLS	1/16-3/16
	Riverside-San Bernardino-Ontario MSA, CA	H	42.61 FQ	46.77 MW	54.11 TQ	CABLS	1/16-3/16
	Sacramento–Roseville–Arden-Arcade MSA, CA	H	51.94 FQ	57.97 MW	64.14 TQ	CABLS	1/16-3/16
	San Diego-Carlsbad MSA, CA	H	32.34 FQ	45.28 MW	55.50 TQ	CABLS	1/16-3/16
	San Francisco-Redwood City-South San Francisco PMSA, CA	H	46.51 FQ	56.67 MW	68.07 TQ	CABLS	1/16-3/16
	Colorado	Y	66080 FQ	76780 MW	89170 TQ	USBLS	5/15
	Denver-Aurora-Lakewood MSA, CO	Y	66270 FQ	76390 MW	88460 TQ	USBLS	5/15
	Connecticut	Y		90757 MW		CTBLS	1/16-3/16
	Bridgeport-Stamford-Norwalk MSA, CT	Y	87270 FQ	99220 MW	110930 TQ	USBLS	5/15
	Hartford-West Hartford-East Hartford MSA, CT	Y	72020 FQ	81740 MW	92070 TQ	USBLS	5/15
	Delaware	Y	67910 FQ	75750 MW	87390 TQ	USBLS	5/15
	Wilmington PMSA, DE-MD-NJ	Y	69000 FQ	76370 MW	87820 TQ	USBLS	5/15
	District of Columbia	Y	69940 FQ	78140 MW	95050 TQ	USBLS	5/15
	Washington-Arlington-Alexandria PMSA, DC-VA-MD-WV	Y	69860 FQ	79470 MW	92760 TQ	USBLS	5/15
	Florida	H	28.40 AE	35.44 MW	39.70 AEX	FLBLS	7/16-9/16
	Fort Lauderdale-Pompano Beach-Deerfield Beach PMSA, FL	H	31.01 AE	36.76 MW	39.62 AEX	FLBLS	7/16-9/16
	Miami-Miami Beach-Kendall PMSA, FL	H	26.93 AE	36.31 MW	39.93 AEX	FLBLS	7/16-9/16
	Orlando-Kissimmee-Sanford MSA, FL	H	30.82 AE	35.96 MW	38.38 AEX	FLBLS	7/16-9/16
	Tampa-St. Petersburg-Clearwater MSA, FL	H	27.00 AE	34.36 MW	43.25 AEX	FLBLS	7/16-9/16
	Georgia	Y	61280 FQ	71130 MW	80410 TQ	USBLS	5/15
	Atlanta-Sandy Springs-Roswell MSA, GA	Y	66860 FQ	74930 MW	83880 TQ	USBLS	5/15
	Augusta-Richmond County MSA, GA-SC	Y	53240 FQ	57240 MW	63960 TQ	USBLS	5/15
	Hawaii	Y	81500 FQ	88720 MW	95870 TQ	USBLS	5/15
	Urban Honolulu MSA, HI	Y	84710 FQ	91040 MW	97380 TQ	USBLS	5/15
	Idaho	Y	64840 FQ	72250 MW	79920 TQ	USBLS	5/15
	Illinois	Y	64220 FQ	73050 MW	83400 TQ	USBLS	5/15
	Chicago-Naperville-Arlington Heights PMSA, IL	Y	63530 FQ	72620 MW	82970 TQ	USBLS	5/15
	Lake County-Kenosha County PMSA, IL-WI	Y	71010 FQ	83180 MW	92740 TQ	USBLS	5/15
	Indiana	Y	60230 FQ	69280 MW	77390 TQ	USBLS	5/15
	Gary PMSA, IN	Y	64840 FQ	81330 MW	92070 TQ	USBLS	5/15
	Indianapolis-Carmel-Anderson MSA, IN	Y	64280 FQ	71890 MW	80370 TQ	USBLS	5/15
	Iowa	Y	61870 FQ	71000 MW	79970 TQ	USBLS	5/15
	Des Moines-West Des Moines MSA, IA	Y	63520 FQ	71190 MW	78950 TQ	USBLS	5/15
	Kansas	Y	61180 FQ	70280 MW	79320 TQ	USBLS	5/15
	Kentucky	Y	51310 FQ	58660 MW	68690 TQ	USBLS	5/15

Occupation/Type/Industry	Location	Per	Low	Mid	High	Source	Date
Nuclear Medicine Technologist	Louisville-Jefferson County MSA, KY-IN	Y	52790 FQ	60200 MW	69810 TQ	USBLS	5/15
	Louisiana	Y	49200 FQ	63650 MW	73270 TQ	USBLS	5/15
	Baton Rouge MSA, LA	Y	37790 FQ	62520 MW	72990 TQ	USBLS	5/15
	New Orleans-Metairie MSA, LA	Y	59290 FQ	67770 MW	74530 TQ	USBLS	5/15
	Maine	Y	65570 FQ	76470 MW	88140 TQ	USBLS	5/15
	Maryland	Y	66515 AE	77981 MW	83714 AEX	MDBLS	4/16
	Baltimore-Columbia-Towson MSA, MD	Y	69520 FQ	78560 MW	90240 TQ	USBLS	5/15
	Massachusetts	Y	61990 FQ	76430 MW	91620 TQ	USBLS	5/15
	Boston-Cambridge-Newton NECTA, MA	Y	61390 FQ	78350 MW	93000 TQ	USBLS	5/15
	Michigan	Y	57880 FQ	67050 MW	74800 TQ	USBLS	5/15
	Detroit-Dearborn-Livonia PMSA, MI	Y	55270 FQ	65240 MW	73820 TQ	USBLS	5/15
	Grand Rapids-Wyoming MSA, MI	Y	57410 FQ	66300 MW	74040 TQ	USBLS	5/15
	Minnesota	Y	70221 FQ	78699 MW	90624 TQ	MNBLS	1/16-3/16
	Minneapolis-St. Paul-Bloomington MSA, MN-WI	Y	69677 FQ	77348 MW	89465 TQ	MNBLS	1/16-3/16
	Mississippi	Y	55970 FQ	67570 MW	77170 TQ	USBLS	5/15
	Jackson MSA, MS	Y	62470 FQ	70520 MW	77660 TQ	USBLS	5/15
	Missouri	Y	60340 FQ	69850 MW	78840 TQ	USBLS	5/15
	Kansas City MSA, MO-KS	Y	61100 FQ	69400 MW	76590 TQ	USBLS	5/15
	St. Louis MSA, MO-IL	Y	60720 FQ	70230 MW	79800 TQ	USBLS	5/15
	Montana	Y	64320 FQ	71060 MW	77780 TQ	USBLS	5/15
	Nebraska	Y	58140 FQ	66590 MW	75010 TQ	NEBLS	7/16-9/16
	Omaha-Council Bluffs MSA, NE-IA	Y	57185 FQ	64000 MW	74130 TQ	NEBLS	7/16-9/16
	Nevada	Y	71430 FQ	83630 MW	93350 TQ	USBLS	5/15
	Las Vegas-Henderson-Paradise MSA, NV	Y	69610 FQ	80370 MW	92400 TQ	USBLS	5/15
	New Hampshire	H	28.84 AE	36.40 MW	39.99 AEX	NHBLS	6/16
	New Jersey	Y	77080 FQ	87180 MW	97010 TQ	USBLS	5/15
	Camden PMSA, NJ	Y	73190 FQ	81550 MW	92280 TQ	USBLS	5/15
	Newark PMSA, NJ-PA	Y	82100 FQ	91230 MW	101250 TQ	USBLS	5/15
	Trenton MSA, NJ	Y	83010 FQ	92460 MW	103920 TQ	USBLS	5/15
	New Mexico	Y	65780 FQ	74260 MW	85740 TQ	USBLS	5/15
	Albuquerque MSA, NM	Y	65830 FQ	73840 MW	84370 TQ	USBLS	5/15
	New York	Y	66240 AE	79420 MW	88260 AEX	NYBLS	1/16-3/16
	Buffalo-Cheektowaga-Niagara Falls MSA, NY	Y	65640 FQ	71380 MW	77120 TQ	USBLS	5/15
	Nassau County-Suffolk County PMSA, NY	Y	70910 FQ	81690 MW	94830 TQ	USBLS	5/15
	New York-Jersey City-White Plains PMSA, NY-NJ	Y	73180 FQ	83920 MW	95710 TQ	USBLS	5/15
	Rochester MSA, NY	Y	61920 FQ	72540 MW	83570 TQ	USBLS	5/15
	North Carolina	Y	57240 FQ	65700 MW	75480 TQ	USBLS	5/15
	Charlotte-Concord-Gastonia MSA, NC-SC	Y	58870 FQ	67270 MW	76320 TQ	USBLS	5/15
	Raleigh MSA, NC	Y	60430 FQ	68060 MW	75580 TQ	USBLS	5/15
	Ohio	Y	59590 FQ	68060 MW	75130 TQ	USBLS	5/15
	Cincinnati MSA, OH-KY-IN	Y	62260 FQ	69610 MW	75800 TQ	USBLS	5/15
	Cleveland-Elyria MSA, OH	Y	63850 FQ	70690 MW	77340 TQ	USBLS	5/15
	Columbus MSA, OH	Y	60810 FQ	69280 MW	76600 TQ	USBLS	5/15
	Oklahoma	Y	52700 FQ	61750 MW	73540 TQ	USBLS	5/15
	Oklahoma City MSA, OK	Y	58770 FQ	69370 MW	79800 TQ	USBLS	5/15
	Tulsa MSA, OK	Y	49250 FQ	57890 MW	67680 TQ	USBLS	5/15
	Oregon	H	35.28 FQ	40.58 MW	45.45 TQ	ORBLS	2016
	Portland-Vancouver-Hillsboro MSA, OR-WA	Y	75630 FQ	86710 MW	95690 TQ	USBLS	5/15
	Pennsylvania	Y	56110 FQ	67810 MW	84280 TQ	USBLS	5/15
	Allentown-Bethlehem-Easton MSA, PA-NJ	Y	61170 FQ	72700 MW	86590 TQ	USBLS	5/15
	Harrisburg-Carlisle MSA, PA	Y	64090 FQ	72370 MW	82690 TQ	USBLS	5/15
	Montgomery County-Bucks County-Chester County PMSA, PA	Y	63800 FQ	74250 MW	87260 TQ	USBLS	5/15
	Philadelphia PMSA, PA	Y	64400 FQ	86190 MW	97580 TQ	USBLS	5/15
	Pittsburgh MSA, PA	Y	50520 FQ	58540 MW	68800 TQ	USBLS	5/15
	Rhode Island	Y	78410 FQ	85960 MW	93450 TQ	USBLS	5/15

AE	Average entry wage	AWR	Average wage range	H	Hourly
AEX	Average experienced wage	B	Biweekly	HI	Highest wage paid
ATC	Average total compensation	D	Daily	HR	High end range
AW	Average wage paid	FQ	First quartile wage	LO	Lowest wage paid

LR	Low end range	MTC	Median total compensation
M	Monthly	MW	Median wage paid
MCC	Median cash compensation	MWR	Median wage range
ME	Median entry wage	S	See annotated source

TCC	Total cash compensation		
TQ	Third quartile wage		
W	Weekly		
Y	Yearly		

Occupation/Type/Industry	Location	Per	Low	Mid	High	Source	Date
Nuclear Medicine Technologist	Providence-Warwick MSA, RI-MA	Y	80210 FQ	87960 MW	95190 TQ	USBLS	5/15
	South Carolina	Y	56590 FQ	66850 MW	75790 TQ	USBLS	5/15
	Charleston-North Charleston MSA, SC	Y	62960 FQ	70390 MW	77490 TQ	USBLS	5/15
	Columbia MSA, SC	Y	47950 FQ	60450 MW	72420 TQ	USBLS	5/15
	Greenville-Anderson-Mauldin MSA, SC	Y	56230 FQ	65740 MW	74230 TQ	USBLS	5/15
	South Dakota	Y	47900 FQ	57290 MW	68220 TQ	USBLS	5/15
	Tennessee	Y	56990 FQ	66530 MW	74640 TQ	USBLS	5/15
	Knoxville MSA, TN	Y	56430 FQ	63290 MW	72470 TQ	USBLS	5/15
	Memphis MSA, TN-MS-AR	Y	66950 FQ	72540 MW	78140 TQ	USBLS	5/15
	Nashville-Davidson–Murfreesboro–Franklin MSA, TN	Y	56500 FQ	66510 MW	74660 TQ	USBLS	5/15
	Texas	Y	64100 FQ	74080 MW	87940 TQ	USBLS	5/15
	Austin-Round Rock MSA, TX	Y	60360 FQ	73010 MW	85940 TQ	USBLS	5/15
	Dallas-Plano-Irving PMSA, TX	Y	68610 FQ	76860 MW	89730 TQ	USBLS	5/15
	Fort Worth-Arlington PMSA, TX	Y	47080 FQ	83240 MW	93990 TQ	USBLS	5/15
	Houston-The Woodlands-Sugar Land MSA, TX	Y	66640 FQ	73690 MW	82630 TQ	USBLS	5/15
	San Antonio-New Braunfels MSA, TX	Y	60850 FQ	68880 MW	77100 TQ	USBLS	5/15
	Utah	Y	61300 FQ	71580 MW	81320 TQ	USBLS	5/15
	Salt Lake City MSA, UT	Y	62970 FQ	72360 MW	81870 TQ	USBLS	5/15
	Virginia	Y	61010 FQ	69620 MW	77930 TQ	USBLS	5/15
	Richmond MSA, VA	Y	62610 FQ	69700 MW	76200 TQ	USBLS	5/15
	Virginia Beach-Norfolk-Newport News MSA, VA-NC	Y	57500 FQ	64190 MW	72310 TQ	USBLS	5/15
	Washington	H	37.26 FQ	42.92 MW	47.97 TQ	WABLS	3/16
	Seattle-Bellevue-Everett PMSA, WA	H	38.52 FQ	43.76 MW	49.01 TQ	WABLS	3/16
	Tacoma-Lakewood PMSA, WA	H	38.79 FQ	43.54 MW	48.14 TQ	WABLS	3/16
	West Virginia	Y	52590 FQ	58470 MW	65970 TQ	USBLS	5/15
	Wisconsin	Y	64650 FQ	73760 MW	85300 TQ	USBLS	5/15
	Milwaukee-Waukesha-West Allis MSA, WI	Y	64870 FQ	73760 MW	85070 TQ	USBLS	5/15
	Wyoming	Y	55790 FQ	62120 MW	72180 TQ	USBLS	5/15
	Puerto Rico	Y	33470 FQ	38810 MW	46270 TQ	USBLS	5/15
	San Juan-Carolina-Caguas MSA, PR	Y	34910 FQ	40130 MW	47190 TQ	USBLS	5/15
Nuclear Power Reactor Operator	California	H	39.75 FQ	47.06 MW	55.67 TQ	CABLS	1/16-3/16
	Louisiana	Y	69410 FQ	80860 MW	90440 TQ	USBLS	5/15
	Michigan	Y	83250 FQ	93840 MW	108160 TQ	USBLS	5/15
	Mississippi	Y	68200 FQ	78690 MW	94560 TQ	USBLS	5/15
	New Jersey	Y	81530 FQ	89890 MW	97910 TQ	USBLS	5/15
	New York	Y	87240 AE	105610 MW	116270 AEX	NYBLS	1/16-3/16
	North Carolina	Y	82470 FQ	90260 MW	98050 TQ	USBLS	5/15
	Tennessee	Y	82000 FQ	82010 MW	98620 TQ	USBLS	5/15
Nuclear Technician	Alabama	Y	49661 AE	68305 AW	77622 AEX	ALBLS	6/16
	California	H	36.21 FQ	42.44 MW	48.52 TQ	CABLS	1/16-3/16
	Connecticut	Y		85086 MW		CTBLS	1/16-3/16
	Idaho	Y	68060 FQ	73310 MW	78560 TQ	USBLS	5/15
	Illinois	Y	61030 FQ	71800 MW	86450 TQ	USBLS	5/15
	Louisiana	Y	43970 FQ	68140 MW	87500 TQ	USBLS	5/15
	Michigan	Y	63170 FQ	79020 MW	90930 TQ	USBLS	5/15
	Mississippi	Y	57230 FQ	73930 MW	89450 TQ	USBLS	5/15
	Missouri	Y	57280 FQ	70170 MW	80340 TQ	USBLS	5/15
	New Jersey	Y	58320 FQ	68300 MW	76240 TQ	USBLS	5/15
	New York	Y	61720 AE	93830 MW	105120 AEX	NYBLS	1/16-3/16
	North Carolina	Y	75290 FQ	87050 MW	95730 TQ	USBLS	5/15
	Pennsylvania	Y	65400 FQ	80380 MW	93070 TQ	USBLS	5/15
	South Carolina	Y	71940 FQ	84770 MW	93610 TQ	USBLS	5/15
	Texas	Y	68590 FQ	80620 MW	92300 TQ	USBLS	5/15
Nurse							
Home Healthcare	United States	H		24.00 AW		HCARE2	2015
Pediatric Endocrinology	United States	Y		81000 AW		SCR01	2016
Nurse Anesthetist	Alabama	Y	122951 AE	163122 AW	183203 AEX	ALBLS	6/16

AE	Average entry wage	AWR	Average wage range	H	Hourly	LR	Low end range	MTC	Median total compensation	TCC	Total cash compensation
AEX	Average experienced wage	B	Biweekly	HI	Highest wage paid	M	Monthly	MW	Median wage paid	TQ	Third quartile wage
ATC	Average total compensation	D	Daily	HR	High end range	MCC	Median cash compensation	MWR	Median wage range	W	Weekly
AW	Average wage paid	FQ	First quartile wage	LO	Lowest wage paid	ME	Median entry wage	S	See annotated source	Y	Yearly

Nurse Anesthetist

Occupation/Type/Industry	Location	Per	Low	Mid	High	Source	Date
Nurse Anesthetist	Birmingham-Hoover MSA, AL	Y	115958 AE	169320 AW	195996 AEX	ALBLS	6/16
	Alaska	Y	107260 FQ	116690 MW	186750 TQ	USBLS	5/15
	Arizona	Y	39570 FQ	137900 MW	177200 TQ	USBLS	5/15
	Phoenix-Mesa-Scottsdale MSA, AZ	Y	36270 FQ	72710 MW	103410 TQ	USBLS	5/15
	Tucson MSA, AZ	Y	139860 FQ	161730 MW	183070 TQ	USBLS	5/15
	Arkansas	Y	122000 FQ	143570 MW	184870 TQ	USBLS	5/15
	Little Rock-North Little Rock-Conway MSA, AR	Y	118560 FQ	134670 MW	161420 TQ	USBLS	5/15
	California	H	77.86 FQ	100.55 AW		CABLS	1/16-3/16
	Los Angeles-Long Beach-Glendale PMSA, CA	H	74.75 FQ	86.06 MW		CABLS	1/16-3/16
	Oakland-Hayward-Berkeley PMSA, CA	H	83.42 FQ	104.90 AW		CABLS	1/16-3/16
	Riverside-San Bernardino-Ontario MSA, CA	H	71.06 FQ	84.64 MW		CABLS	1/16-3/16
	San Diego-Carlsbad MSA, CA	H	85.43 FQ	117.99 AW		CABLS	1/16-3/16
	San Francisco-Redwood City-South San Francisco PMSA, CA	H	39.67 FQ	89.87 AW		CABLS	1/16-3/16
	Colorado	Y	93350 FQ	151240 MW	182410 TQ	USBLS	5/15
	Denver-Aurora-Lakewood MSA, CO	Y	85990 FQ	100930 MW	162040 TQ	USBLS	5/15
	Connecticut	Y		171186 MW		CTBLS	1/16-3/16
	Bridgeport-Stamford-Norwalk MSA, CT	Y	147370 FQ	175150 MW		USBLS	5/15
	District of Columbia	Y	143080 FQ	158610 MW	180980 TQ	USBLS	5/15
	Washington-Arlington-Alexandria PMSA, DC-VA-MD-WV	Y	135220 FQ	157710 MW		USBLS	5/15
	Florida	H	50.72 AE	70.74 MW	82.28 AEX	FLBLS	7/16-9/16
	Fort Lauderdale-Pompano Beach-Deerfield Beach PMSA, FL	H	39.38 AE	85.93 MW	89.24 AEX	FLBLS	7/16-9/16
	Miami-Miami Beach-Kendall PMSA, FL	H	59.27 AE	76.07 MW	109.12 AEX	FLBLS	7/16-9/16
	Orlando-Kissimmee-Sanford MSA, FL	H	54.61 AE	63.48 MW	69.09 AEX	FLBLS	7/16-9/16
	Tampa-St. Petersburg-Clearwater MSA, FL	H	53.29 AE	73.43 MW	79.89 AEX	FLBLS	7/16-9/16
	Georgia	Y	119510 FQ	144180 MW	162700 TQ	USBLS	5/15
	Atlanta-Sandy Springs-Roswell MSA, GA	Y	111020 FQ	123240 MW	157270 TQ	USBLS	5/15
	Augusta-Richmond County MSA, GA-SC	Y	158410 FQ	165910 MW		USBLS	5/15
	Hawaii	Y	168680 FQ	185550 MW		USBLS	5/15
	Urban Honolulu MSA, HI	Y	170170 FQ	186550 MW		USBLS	5/15
	Idaho	Y	143600 FQ	160170 MW		USBLS	5/15
	Illinois	Y	60530 FQ	135980 MW	172970 TQ	USBLS	5/15
	Chicago-Naperville-Arlington Heights PMSA, IL	Y	57020 FQ	73780 MW	145460 TQ	USBLS	5/15
	Lake County-Kenosha County PMSA, IL-WI	Y	59980 FQ	155030 MW	176550 TQ	USBLS	5/15
	Indiana	Y	110710 FQ	146770 MW		USBLS	5/15
	Gary PMSA, IN	Y	136330 FQ	154460 MW	179260 TQ	USBLS	5/15
	Indianapolis-Carmel-Anderson MSA, IN	Y	68570 FQ	114530 MW	141350 TQ	USBLS	5/15
	Iowa	Y	149000 FQ	174010 MW		USBLS	5/15
	Des Moines-West Des Moines MSA, IA	Y	113470 FQ	172440 MW		USBLS	5/15
	Kansas	Y	129770 FQ	145170 MW	174350 TQ	USBLS	5/15
	Wichita MSA, KS	Y	124230 FQ	154570 MW		USBLS	5/15
	Kentucky	Y	127840 FQ	154360 MW	184750 TQ	USBLS	5/15
	Louisville-Jefferson County MSA, KY-IN	Y	135150 FQ	166390 MW		USBLS	5/15
	Louisiana	Y	87270 FQ	134640 MW	161300 TQ	USBLS	5/15
	New Orleans-Metairie MSA, LA	Y	78200 FQ	124800 MW	168710 TQ	USBLS	5/15
	Maine	Y	131480 FQ	158170 MW		USBLS	5/15
	Portland-South Portland MSA, ME	Y	138410 FQ	154560 MW	174020 TQ	USBLS	5/15
	Maryland	Y	91509 AE	156109 MW	188409 AEX	MDBLS	4/16

AE	Average entry wage	AWR	Average wage range	H	Hourly	LR	Low end range	MTC	Median total compensation	TCC	Total cash compensation
AEX	Average experienced wage	B	Biweekly	HI	Highest wage paid	M	Monthly	MW	Median wage paid	TQ	Third quartile wage
ATC	Average total compensation	D	Daily	HR	High end range	MCC	Median cash compensation	MWR	Median wage range	W	Weekly
AW	Average wage paid	FQ	First quartile wage	LO	Lowest wage paid	ME	Median entry wage	S	See annotated source	Y	Yearly

Occupation/Type/Industry	Location	Per	Low	Mid	High	Source	Date
Nurse Anesthetist	Baltimore-Columbia-Towson MSA, MD	Y	116750 FQ	142120 MW	157900 TQ	USBLS	5/15
	Massachusetts	Y	137370 FQ	164410 MW		USBLS	5/15
	Boston-Cambridge-Newton NECTA, MA	Y	134230 FQ	155800 MW	178370 TQ	USBLS	5/15
	Worcester MSA, MA-CT	Y	132130 FQ	165760 MW	186770 TQ	USBLS	5/15
	Michigan	Y	165360 FQ	180230 MW		USBLS	5/15
	Detroit-Dearborn-Livonia PMSA, MI	Y	174220 FQ	186460 MW		USBLS	5/15
	Grand Rapids-Wyoming MSA, MI	Y	136050 FQ	150510 MW	164110 TQ	USBLS	5/15
	Minnesota	Y	157679 FQ	174978 MW		MNBLS	1/16-3/16
	Minneapolis-St. Paul-Bloomington MSA, MN-WI	Y	150260 FQ	165562 MW	188092 TQ	MNBLS	1/16-3/16
	Mississippi	Y	138290 FQ	161300 MW		USBLS	5/15
	Missouri	Y	134540 FQ	153990 MW	182010 TQ	USBLS	5/15
	Kansas City MSA, MO-KS	Y	124740 FQ	147350 MW	170690 TQ	USBLS	5/15
	St. Louis MSA, MO-IL	Y	135050 FQ	151530 MW	172430 TQ	USBLS	5/15
	Montana	Y	183210 FQ	243550 AW		USBLS	5/15
	Nebraska	Y	125140 FQ	158865 MW	187930 TQ	NEBLS	7/16-9/16
	Omaha-Council Bluffs MSA, NE-IA	Y	92975 FQ	151050 MW	184525 TQ	NEBLS	7/16-9/16
	New Hampshire	H	70.98 AE	106.62 AW	124.44 AEX	NHBLS	6/16
	New Jersey	Y	165990 FQ	182130 MW		USBLS	5/15
	Newark PMSA, NJ-PA	Y	157060 FQ	207550 AW		USBLS	5/15
	New Mexico	Y	40050 FQ	164020 MW		USBLS	5/15
	New York	Y	136540 AE	162020 MW	176170 AEX	NYBLS	1/16-3/16
	Buffalo-Cheektowaga-Niagara Falls MSA, NY	Y	139870 FQ	150830 MW	164760 TQ	USBLS	5/15
	Nassau County-Suffolk County PMSA, NY	Y	164490 FQ	174730 MW	184980 TQ	USBLS	5/15
	New York-Jersey City-White Plains PMSA, NY-NJ	Y	143270 FQ	165590 MW		USBLS	5/15
	Rochester MSA, NY	Y	144360 FQ	159170 MW		USBLS	5/15
	North Carolina	Y	134240 FQ	154540 MW	182740 TQ	USBLS	5/15
	Charlotte-Concord-Gastonia MSA, NC-SC	Y	133470 FQ	164010 MW		USBLS	5/15
	Raleigh MSA, NC	Y	119740 FQ	137780 MW	153140 TQ	USBLS	5/15
	North Dakota	Y	167090 FQ	181470 MW		USBLS	5/15
	Ohio	Y	130160 FQ	145610 MW	163710 TQ	USBLS	5/15
	Cincinnati MSA, OH-KY-IN	Y	127660 FQ	142220 MW	156340 TQ	USBLS	5/15
	Cleveland-Elyria MSA, OH	Y	128780 FQ	145710 MW	163510 TQ	USBLS	5/15
	Columbus MSA, OH	Y	131940 FQ	147830 MW	164950 TQ	USBLS	5/15
	Oklahoma	Y	145780 FQ	167900 MW		USBLS	5/15
	Oklahoma City MSA, OK	Y	145720 FQ	171400 MW		USBLS	5/15
	Tulsa MSA, OK	Y	141430 FQ	163060 MW		USBLS	5/15
	Oregon	H	76.81 FQ	89.06 MW		ORBLS	2016
	Portland-Vancouver-Hillsboro MSA, OR-WA	Y	162330 FQ	181780 MW		USBLS	5/15
	Pennsylvania	Y	136360 FQ	150520 MW	166120 TQ	USBLS	5/15
	Allentown-Bethlehem-Easton MSA, PA-NJ	Y	133140 FQ	143270 MW	153410 TQ	USBLS	5/15
	Harrisburg-Carlisle MSA, PA	Y	161210 FQ	175370 MW		USBLS	5/15
	Philadelphia PMSA, PA	Y	139760 FQ	160570 MW		USBLS	5/15
	Pittsburgh MSA, PA	Y	135820 FQ	147240 MW	158540 TQ	USBLS	5/15
	Providence-Warwick MSA, RI-MA	Y	158790 FQ	241660 AW		USBLS	5/15
	South Carolina	Y	135450 FQ	152100 MW	183500 TQ	USBLS	5/15
	Charleston-North Charleston MSA, SC	Y	133090 FQ	146140 MW	170600 TQ	USBLS	5/15
	Greenville-Anderson-Mauldin MSA, SC	Y	37510 FQ	160590 MW		USBLS	5/15
	South Dakota	Y	157930 FQ	173920 MW		USBLS	5/15
	Sioux Falls MSA, SD	Y	164770 FQ	179030 MW		USBLS	5/15
	Tennessee	Y	125880 FQ	143920 MW	166720 TQ	USBLS	5/15
	Knoxville MSA, TN	Y	125410 FQ	148380 MW		USBLS	5/15
	Memphis MSA, TN-MS-AR	Y	111450 FQ	121130 MW	140210 TQ	USBLS	5/15
	Nashville-Davidson–Murfreesboro–Franklin MSA, TN	Y	128980 FQ	143970 MW	158890 TQ	USBLS	5/15
	Texas	Y	126290 FQ	153800 MW	181390 TQ	USBLS	5/15
	Dallas-Plano-Irving PMSA, TX	Y	140430 FQ	154350 MW	175680 TQ	USBLS	5/15

AE	Average entry wage	AWR	Average wage range	H	Hourly	LR	Low end range	MTC	Median total compensation	TCC	Total cash compensation
AEX	Average experienced wage	B	Biweekly	HI	Highest wage paid	M	Monthly	MW	Median wage paid	TQ	Third quartile wage
ATC	Average total compensation	D	Daily	HR	High end range	MCC	Median cash compensation	MWR	Median wage range	W	Weekly
AW	Average wage paid	FQ	First quartile wage	LO	Lowest wage paid	ME	Median entry wage	S	See annotated source	Y	Yearly

1102

Occupation/Type/Industry	Location	Per	Low	Mid	High	Source	Date
Nurse Anesthetist	Houston-The Woodlands-Sugar Land MSA, TX	Y	137620 FQ	158980 MW	185660 TQ	USBLS	5/15
	San Antonio-New Braunfels MSA, TX	Y	166880 FQ	183220 MW		USBLS	5/15
	Utah	Y	137960 FQ	154980 MW	185790 TQ	USBLS	5/15
	Salt Lake City MSA, UT	Y	137790 FQ	159350 MW		USBLS	5/15
	Vermont	Y	138490 FQ	151220 MW	165400 TQ	USBLS	5/15
	Virginia	Y	135200 FQ	155010 MW		USBLS	5/15
	Richmond MSA, VA	Y	126410 FQ	146750 MW	184390 TQ	USBLS	5/15
	Virginia Beach-Norfolk-Newport News MSA, VA-NC	Y	140010 FQ	160490 MW		USBLS	5/15
	Washington	H	76.24 FQ	86.95 MW		WABLS	3/16
	Seattle-Bellevue-Everett PMSA, WA	H	79.98 FQ	86.91 MW		WABLS	3/16
	West Virginia	Y	147520 FQ	163710 MW		USBLS	5/15
	Huntington-Ashland MSA, WV-KY-OH	Y	143710 FQ	162660 MW	183910 TQ	USBLS	5/15
	Wisconsin	Y	171570 FQ	207220 AW		USBLS	5/15
	Milwaukee-Waukesha-West Allis MSA, WI	Y	142030 FQ	169760 MW	183910 TQ	USBLS	5/15
	Wyoming	Y	165490 FQ	210210 AW		USBLS	5/15
	Puerto Rico	Y	45080 FQ	55080 MW	60880 TQ	USBLS	5/15
	San Juan-Carolina-Caguas MSA, PR	Y	39110 FQ	54820 MW	61350 TQ	USBLS	5/15
Nurse Clinician Public Health Department, Municipal Government	Detroit, MI	M	4067 LO		4375 HI	DETGOV	2016
Nurse Manager	United States	Y		77000 MW		TSTR	2017
Nurse Midwife	Alaska	Y	85860 FQ	96840 MW	119210 TQ	USBLS	5/15
	Arizona	Y	64800 FQ	84520 MW	98160 TQ	USBLS	5/15
	California	H	53.91 FQ	66.98 MW	83.55 TQ	CABLS	1/16-3/16
	Anaheim-Santa Ana-Irvine PMSA, CA	H	51.44 FQ	67.05 MW	81.95 TQ	CABLS	1/16-3/16
	Los Angeles-Long Beach-Glendale PMSA, CA	H	51.95 FQ	68.70 MW	87.32 TQ	CABLS	1/16-3/16
	Oakland-Hayward-Berkeley PMSA, CA	H	67.11 FQ	73.55 MW	83.11 TQ	CABLS	1/16-3/16
	Riverside-San Bernardino-Ontario MSA, CA	H	54.05 FQ	63.24 MW	86.74 TQ	CABLS	1/16-3/16
	Sacramento–Roseville–Arden-Arcade MSA, CA	H	49.02 FQ	56.46 MW	63.33 TQ	CABLS	1/16-3/16
	San Diego-Carlsbad MSA, CA	H	44.97 FQ	55.94 MW	84.61 TQ	CABLS	1/16-3/16
	San Francisco-Redwood City-South San Francisco PMSA, CA	H	55.96 FQ	61.51 MW	70.36 TQ	CABLS	1/16-3/16
	Colorado	Y	86130 FQ	94140 MW	101850 TQ	USBLS	5/15
	Denver-Aurora-Lakewood MSA, CO	Y	85500 FQ	101540 MW	115180 TQ	USBLS	5/15
	Connecticut	Y		105457 MW		CTBLS	1/16-3/16
	Hartford-West Hartford-East Hartford MSA, CT	Y	91740 FQ	101470 MW	113190 TQ	USBLS	5/15
	Delaware	Y	79800 FQ	90420 MW	100180 TQ	USBLS	5/15
	Washington-Arlington-Alexandria PMSA, DC-VA-MD-WV	Y	87470 FQ	96380 MW	113670 TQ	USBLS	5/15
	Florida	H	33.73 AE	44.80 MW	48.38 AEX	FLBLS	7/16-9/16
	Miami-Miami Beach-Kendall PMSA, FL	H	34.70 AE	44.08 MW	45.10 AEX	FLBLS	7/16-9/16
	Orlando-Kissimmee-Sanford MSA, FL	H	35.51 AE	41.58 MW	45.26 AEX	FLBLS	7/16-9/16
	Tampa-St. Petersburg-Clearwater MSA, FL	H	42.74 AE	45.28 MW	53.07 AEX	FLBLS	7/16-9/16
	Georgia	Y	83040 FQ	93330 MW	105420 TQ	USBLS	5/15
	Atlanta-Sandy Springs-Roswell MSA, GA	Y	83060 FQ	93000 MW	104270 TQ	USBLS	5/15
	Illinois	Y	37810 FQ	84840 MW	107210 TQ	USBLS	5/15
	Chicago-Naperville-Arlington Heights PMSA, IL	Y	32520 FQ	76860 MW	99840 TQ	USBLS	5/15
	Indiana	Y	84650 FQ	95960 MW	113100 TQ	USBLS	5/15

AE	Average entry wage	AWR	Average wage range	H	Hourly
AEX	Average experienced wage	B	Biweekly	HI	Highest wage paid
ATC	Average total compensation	D	Daily	HR	High end range
AW	Average wage paid	FQ	First quartile wage	LO	Lowest wage paid

LR	Low end range	MTC	Median total compensation	TCC	Total cash compensation
M	Monthly	MW	Median wage paid	TQ	Third quartile wage
MCC	Median cash compensation	MWR	Median wage range	W	Weekly
ME	Median entry wage	S	See annotated source	Y	Yearly

Occupation/Type/Industry	Location	Per	Low	Mid	High	Source	Date
Nurse Midwife	Iowa	Y	86480 FQ	100900 MW	130290 TQ	USBLS	5/15
	Kentucky	Y	80970 FQ	92970 MW	108570 TQ	USBLS	5/15
	Louisville-Jefferson County MSA, KY-IN	Y	81740 FQ	93140 MW	106820 TQ	USBLS	5/15
	Maine	Y	86130 FQ	96280 MW	107610 TQ	USBLS	5/15
	Maryland	Y	51173 AE	88908 MW	107775 AEX	MDBLS	4/16
	Baltimore-Columbia-Towson MSA, MD	Y	82930 FQ	101580 MW	117000 TQ	USBLS	5/15
	Massachusetts	Y	88590 FQ	110590 MW	135790 TQ	USBLS	5/15
	Boston-Cambridge-Newton NECTA, MA	Y	92430 FQ	112630 MW	136810 TQ	USBLS	5/15
	Worcester MSA, MA-CT	Y	131820 FQ	142210 MW	152600 TQ	USBLS	5/15
	Michigan	Y	87120 FQ	97070 MW	108320 TQ	USBLS	5/15
	Warren-Troy-Farmington Hills PMSA, MI	Y	86160 FQ	93060 MW	99980 TQ	USBLS	5/15
	Minnesota	Y	96108 FQ	110815 MW	125573 TQ	MNBLS	1/16-3/16
	Minneapolis-St. Paul-Bloomington MSA, MN-WI	Y	96430 FQ	111198 MW	125754 TQ	MNBLS	1/16-3/16
	Mississippi	Y	78820 FQ	89580 MW	99570 TQ	USBLS	5/15
	Nebraska	Y	45525 FQ	72450 MW	90635 TQ	NEBLS	7/16-9/16
	Omaha-Council Bluffs MSA, NE-IA	Y	38895 FQ	49650 MW	88335 TQ	NEBLS	7/16-9/16
	New Hampshire	H	39.58 AE	48.10 MW	53.47 AEX	NHBLS	6/16
	New Jersey	Y	103030 FQ	112970 MW	122570 TQ	USBLS	5/15
	New Mexico	Y	86630 FQ	98670 MW	110770 TQ	USBLS	5/15
	Albuquerque MSA, NM	Y	86310 FQ	98770 MW	110590 TQ	USBLS	5/15
	New York	Y	79390 AE	98330 MW	108280 AEX	NYBLS	1/16-3/16
	New York-Jersey City-White Plains PMSA, NY-NJ	Y	88760 FQ	103530 MW	118570 TQ	USBLS	5/15
	North Carolina	Y	80400 FQ	92440 MW	106080 TQ	USBLS	5/15
	Ohio	Y	83330 FQ	94520 MW	109290 TQ	USBLS	5/15
	Cleveland-Elyria MSA, OH	Y	75590 FQ	93390 MW	111020 TQ	USBLS	5/15
	Columbus MSA, OH	Y	92750 FQ	103710 MW	117370 TQ	USBLS	5/15
	Oregon	H	50.67 FQ	59.54 MW	70.77 TQ	ORBLS	2016
	Portland-Vancouver-Hillsboro MSA, OR-WA	Y	110770 FQ	132210 MW	148660 TQ	USBLS	5/15
	Pennsylvania	Y	75540 FQ	93430 MW	112130 TQ	USBLS	5/15
	Pittsburgh MSA, PA	Y	68910 FQ	77010 MW	100500 TQ	USBLS	5/15
	South Carolina	Y	67580 FQ	85700 MW	103780 TQ	USBLS	5/15
	Tennessee	Y	61570 FQ	71750 MW	81790 TQ	USBLS	5/15
	Texas	Y	79870 FQ	97110 MW	116610 TQ	USBLS	5/15
	Dallas-Plano-Irving PMSA, TX	Y	87620 FQ	107540 MW	127730 TQ	USBLS	5/15
	Houston-The Woodlands-Sugar Land MSA, TX	Y	73960 FQ	94360 MW	111740 TQ	USBLS	5/15
	Utah	Y	79490 FQ	88750 MW	98630 TQ	USBLS	5/15
	Provo-Orem MSA, UT	Y	77450 FQ	85040 MW	92680 TQ	USBLS	5/15
	Vermont	Y	86150 FQ	95620 MW	106420 TQ	USBLS	5/15
	Washington	H	41.61 FQ	45.81 MW	51.81 TQ	WABLS	3/16
	Seattle-Bellevue-Everett PMSA, WA	H	41.90 FQ	45.95 MW	51.65 TQ	WABLS	3/16
	West Virginia	Y	84730 FQ	95070 MW	117380 TQ	USBLS	5/15
	Wisconsin	Y	47600 FQ	67450 MW	93500 TQ	USBLS	5/15
	Madison MSA, WI	Y	44710 FQ	51260 MW	65930 TQ	USBLS	5/15
	Milwaukee-Waukesha-West Allis MSA, WI	Y	87970 FQ	95220 MW	102590 TQ	USBLS	5/15
Nurse Practitioner	Alabama	Y	66389 AE	95633 AW	110260 AEX	ALBLS	6/16
	Birmingham-Hoover MSA, AL	Y	77764 AE	103777 AW	116784 AEX	ALBLS	6/16
	Alaska	Y	95040 FQ	115040 MW	138600 TQ	USBLS	5/15
	Anchorage MSA, AK	Y	90560 FQ	110080 MW	133400 TQ	USBLS	5/15
	Arizona	Y	85930 FQ	104120 MW	121250 TQ	USBLS	5/15
	Lake Havasu City-Kingman MSA, AZ	Y	77250 FQ	102840 MW	117630 TQ	USBLS	5/15
	Phoenix-Mesa-Scottsdale MSA, AZ	Y	87460 FQ	106690 MW	122740 TQ	USBLS	5/15
	Tucson MSA, AZ	Y	79020 FQ	94520 MW	116700 TQ	USBLS	5/15
	Arkansas	Y	76400 FQ	91510 MW	116730 TQ	USBLS	5/15
	Little Rock-North Little Rock-Conway MSA, AR	Y	82690 FQ	96080 MW	131130 TQ	USBLS	5/15
	California	H	48.39 FQ	57.55 MW	69.67 TQ	CABLS	1/16-3/16
	Anaheim-Santa Ana-Irvine PMSA, CA	H	47.64 FQ	55.10 MW	61.05 TQ	CABLS	1/16-3/16

AE Average entry wage	**AWR** Average wage range	**H** Hourly	**LR** Low end range	**MTC** Median total compensation	**TCC** Total cash compensation
AEX Average experienced wage	**B** Biweekly	**HI** Highest wage paid	**M** Monthly	**MW** Median wage paid	**TQ** Third quartile wage
ATC Average total compensation	**D** Daily	**HR** High end range	**MCC** Median cash compensation	**MWR** Median wage range	**W** Weekly
AW Average wage paid	**FQ** First quartile wage	**LO** Lowest wage paid	**ME** Median entry wage	**S** See annotated source	**Y** Yearly

Nurse Practitioner

Occupation/Type/Industry	Location	Per	Low	Mid	High	Source	Date
Nurse Practitioner	Los Angeles-Long Beach-Glendale PMSA, CA	H	51.13 FQ	58.87 MW	69.29 TQ	CABLS	1/16-3/16
	Oakland-Hayward-Berkeley PMSA, CA	H	53.89 FQ	61.97 MW	79.71 TQ	CABLS	1/16-3/16
	Riverside-San Bernardino-Ontario MSA, CA	H	43.57 FQ	52.60 MW	60.89 TQ	CABLS	1/16-3/16
	Sacramento–Roseville–Arden-Arcade MSA, CA	H	46.12 FQ	61.55 MW	72.52 TQ	CABLS	1/16-3/16
	San Diego-Carlsbad MSA, CA	H	46.32 FQ	55.60 MW	68.31 TQ	CABLS	1/16-3/16
	San Francisco-Redwood City-South San Francisco PMSA, CA	H	54.21 FQ	66.95 MW	86.19 TQ	CABLS	1/16-3/16
	Colorado	Y	86610 FQ	101080 MW	120110 TQ	USBLS	5/15
	Denver-Aurora-Lakewood MSA, CO	Y	90850 FQ	107600 MW	127860 TQ	USBLS	5/15
	Connecticut	Y		102971 MW		CTBLS	1/16-3/16
	Bridgeport-Stamford-Norwalk MSA, CT	Y	85030 FQ	98180 MW	120260 TQ	USBLS	5/15
	Hartford-West Hartford-East Hartford MSA, CT	Y	91910 FQ	105890 MW	119170 TQ	USBLS	5/15
	Delaware	Y	86080 FQ	97560 MW	116600 TQ	USBLS	5/15
	Wilmington PMSA, DE-MD-NJ	Y	84170 FQ	93680 MW	104130 TQ	USBLS	5/15
	District of Columbia	Y	89650 FQ	100910 MW	116260 TQ	USBLS	5/15
	Washington-Arlington-Alexandria PMSA, DC-VA-MD-WV	Y	88020 FQ	102130 MW	118400 TQ	USBLS	5/15
	Florida	H	35.54 AE	45.75 MW	52.97 AEX	FLBLS	7/16-9/16
	Fort Lauderdale-Pompano Beach-Deerfield Beach PMSA, FL	H	26.09 AE	41.91 MW	47.84 AEX	FLBLS	7/16-9/16
	Miami-Miami Beach-Kendall PMSA, FL	H	39.33 AE	47.44 MW	50.74 AEX	FLBLS	7/16-9/16
	Orlando-Kissimmee-Sanford MSA, FL	H	41.28 AE	47.83 MW	58.45 AEX	FLBLS	7/16-9/16
	Tampa-St. Petersburg-Clearwater MSA, FL	H	35.22 AE	45.02 MW	49.88 AEX	FLBLS	7/16-9/16
	Georgia	Y	80770 FQ	92660 MW	106690 TQ	USBLS	5/15
	Atlanta-Sandy Springs-Roswell MSA, GA	Y	80840 FQ	91490 MW	102460 TQ	USBLS	5/15
	Augusta-Richmond County MSA, GA-SC	Y	81670 FQ	93370 MW	104420 TQ	USBLS	5/15
	Hawaii	Y	95860 FQ	114240 MW	129910 TQ	USBLS	5/15
	Urban Honolulu MSA, HI	Y	105230 FQ	119450 MW	138870 TQ	USBLS	5/15
	Idaho	Y	81330 FQ	92490 MW	105090 TQ	USBLS	5/15
	Boise City MSA, ID	Y	83540 FQ	95280 MW	110210 TQ	USBLS	5/15
	Illinois	Y	78740 FQ	93270 MW	109680 TQ	USBLS	5/15
	Chicago-Naperville-Arlington Heights PMSA, IL	Y	80750 FQ	97780 MW	114270 TQ	USBLS	5/15
	Lake County-Kenosha County PMSA, IL-WI	Y	63270 FQ	84480 MW	98800 TQ	USBLS	5/15
	Indiana	Y	84430 FQ	93360 MW	103920 TQ	USBLS	5/15
	Gary PMSA, IN	Y	74680 FQ	90880 MW	102650 TQ	USBLS	5/15
	Indianapolis-Carmel-Anderson MSA, IN	Y	86130 FQ	94020 MW	103980 TQ	USBLS	5/15
	Iowa	Y	84500 FQ	92760 MW	102020 TQ	USBLS	5/15
	Des Moines-West Des Moines MSA, IA	Y	85410 FQ	93080 MW	102320 TQ	USBLS	5/15
	Kansas	Y	81460 FQ	92290 MW	104010 TQ	USBLS	5/15
	Wichita MSA, KS	Y	72430 FQ	85550 MW	96640 TQ	USBLS	5/15
	Kentucky	Y	80600 FQ	91340 MW	103000 TQ	USBLS	5/15
	Louisville-Jefferson County MSA, KY-IN	Y	81260 FQ	90830 MW	100820 TQ	USBLS	5/15
	Louisiana	Y	76740 FQ	93270 MW	112990 TQ	USBLS	5/15
	Baton Rouge MSA, LA	Y	73200 FQ	91610 MW	110950 TQ	USBLS	5/15
	New Orleans-Metairie MSA, LA	Y	83440 FQ	96740 MW	113280 TQ	USBLS	5/15
	Maine	Y	84730 FQ	93990 MW	106280 TQ	USBLS	5/15
	Portland-South Portland MSA, ME	Y	82330 FQ	93740 MW	109260 TQ	USBLS	5/15
	Maryland	Y	72020 AE	96205 MW	108297 AEX	MDBLS	4/16

Occupation/Type/Industry	Location	Per	Low	Mid	High	Source	Date
Nurse Practitioner	Baltimore-Columbia-Towson MSA, MD	Y	84760 FQ	99080 MW	114860 TQ	USBLS	5/15
	Salisbury MSA, MD-DE	Y	87910 FQ	105090 MW	130250 TQ	USBLS	5/15
	Massachusetts	Y	91430 FQ	109600 MW	130200 TQ	USBLS	5/15
	Boston-Cambridge-Newton NECTA, MA	Y	94810 FQ	113360 MW	139960 TQ	USBLS	5/15
	Worcester MSA, MA-CT	Y	94100 FQ	109280 MW	122220 TQ	USBLS	5/15
	Michigan	Y	83160 FQ	93580 MW	106900 TQ	USBLS	5/15
	Detroit-Dearborn-Livonia PMSA, MI	Y	81310 FQ	92760 MW	106760 TQ	USBLS	5/15
	Grand Rapids-Wyoming MSA, MI	Y	81980 FQ	90990 MW	100450 TQ	USBLS	5/15
	Minnesota	Y	91329 FQ	105644 MW	120402 TQ	MNBLS	1/16-3/16
	Minneapolis-St. Paul-Bloomington MSA, MN-WI	Y	92559 FQ	105543 MW	120563 TQ	MNBLS	1/16-3/16
	Mississippi	Y	83840 FQ	95240 MW	112100 TQ	USBLS	5/15
	Jackson MSA, MS	Y	85420 FQ	95270 MW	108500 TQ	USBLS	5/15
	Missouri	Y	80090 FQ	91020 MW	102480 TQ	USBLS	5/15
	Kansas City MSA, MO-KS	Y	82420 FQ	93640 MW	106850 TQ	USBLS	5/15
	St. Louis MSA, MO-IL	Y	78610 FQ	89770 MW	102020 TQ	USBLS	5/15
	Montana	Y	80760 FQ	92000 MW	105150 TQ	USBLS	5/15
	Billings MSA, MT	Y	87220 FQ	95850 MW	108080 TQ	USBLS	5/15
	Nebraska	Y	76180 FQ	90405 MW	103710 TQ	NEBLS	7/16-9/16
	Omaha-Council Bluffs MSA, NE-IA	Y	78775 FQ	91975 MW	106410 TQ	NEBLS	7/16-9/16
	Nevada	Y	87250 FQ	99050 MW	115410 TQ	USBLS	5/15
	Las Vegas-Henderson-Paradise MSA, NV	Y	85430 FQ	97480 MW	114460 TQ	USBLS	5/15
	New Hampshire	H	39.55 AE	49.54 MW	58.30 AEX	NHBLS	6/16
	Manchester NECTA, NH	H	41.46 AE	50.28 MW	56.83 AEX	NHBLS	6/16
	Nashua NECTA, NH-MA	Y	85130 FQ	103730 MW	129950 TQ	USBLS	5/15
	New Jersey	Y	99770 FQ	112550 MW	124440 TQ	USBLS	5/15
	Camden PMSA, NJ	Y	90900 FQ	108960 MW	121780 TQ	USBLS	5/15
	Newark PMSA, NJ-PA	Y	104830 FQ	114900 MW	125190 TQ	USBLS	5/15
	Trenton MSA, NJ	Y	94880 FQ	109520 MW	121490 TQ	USBLS	5/15
	New Mexico	Y	86470 FQ	101990 MW	124790 TQ	USBLS	5/15
	Albuquerque MSA, NM	Y	90500 FQ	105910 MW	131770 TQ	USBLS	5/15
	New York	Y	83730 AE	108710 MW	120710 AEX	NYBLS	1/16-3/16
	Buffalo-Cheektowaga-Niagara Falls MSA, NY	Y	84680 FQ	96910 MW	112450 TQ	USBLS	5/15
	Nassau County-Suffolk County PMSA, NY	Y	103850 FQ	114220 MW	124640 TQ	USBLS	5/15
	New York-Jersey City-White Plains PMSA, NY-NJ	Y	100430 FQ	113920 MW	127100 TQ	USBLS	5/15
	Rochester MSA, NY	Y	80900 FQ	90040 MW	99330 TQ	USBLS	5/15
	North Carolina	Y	85500 FQ	96740 MW	114240 TQ	USBLS	5/15
	Charlotte-Concord-Gastonia MSA, NC-SC	Y	83450 FQ	94020 MW	108170 TQ	USBLS	5/15
	Raleigh MSA, NC	Y	88510 FQ	99450 MW	112580 TQ	USBLS	5/15
	North Dakota	Y	81450 FQ	92570 MW	105410 TQ	USBLS	5/15
	Fargo MSA, ND-MN	Y	85290 FQ	94880 MW	107240 TQ	USBLS	5/15
	Ohio	Y	85210 FQ	94560 MW	107300 TQ	USBLS	5/15
	Cincinnati MSA, OH-KY-IN	Y	87510 FQ	98520 MW	114350 TQ	USBLS	5/15
	Cleveland-Elyria MSA, OH	Y	86440 FQ	95500 MW	107540 TQ	USBLS	5/15
	Columbus MSA, OH	Y	84210 FQ	95000 MW	108550 TQ	USBLS	5/15
	Oklahoma	Y	49310 FQ	87900 MW	105460 TQ	USBLS	5/15
	Oklahoma City MSA, OK	Y	38140 FQ	83200 MW	99880 TQ	USBLS	5/15
	Tulsa MSA, OK	Y	47450 FQ	86540 MW	103750 TQ	USBLS	5/15
	Oregon	H	45.33 FQ	53.56 MW	61.77 TQ	ORBLS	2016
	Portland-Vancouver-Hillsboro MSA, OR-WA	Y	96050 FQ	113260 MW	129250 TQ	USBLS	5/15
	Pennsylvania	Y	80570 FQ	92740 MW	107120 TQ	USBLS	5/15
	Allentown-Bethlehem-Easton MSA, PA-NJ	Y	85180 FQ	96530 MW	114960 TQ	USBLS	5/15
	Harrisburg-Carlisle MSA, PA	Y	83510 FQ	99540 MW	117080 TQ	USBLS	5/15
	Montgomery County-Bucks County-Chester County PMSA, PA	Y	83770 FQ	94220 MW	105670 TQ	USBLS	5/15
	Philadelphia PMSA, PA	Y	82980 FQ	96200 MW	111660 TQ	USBLS	5/15
	Pittsburgh MSA, PA	Y	77390 FQ	88530 MW	98140 TQ	USBLS	5/15
	Rhode Island	Y	89660 FQ	103720 MW	124540 TQ	USBLS	5/15

AE	Average entry wage	AWR	Average wage range	H	Hourly	LR	Low end range	MTC	Median total compensation	TCC	Total cash compensation
AEX	Average experienced wage	B	Biweekly	HI	Highest wage paid	M	Monthly	MW	Median wage paid	TQ	Third quartile wage
ATC	Average total compensation	D	Daily	HR	High end range	MCC	Median cash compensation	MWR	Median wage range	W	Weekly
AW	Average wage paid	FQ	First quartile wage	LO	Lowest wage paid	ME	Median entry wage	S	See annotated source	Y	Yearly

Occupation/Type/Industry	Location	Per	Low	Mid	High	Source	Date
Nurse Practitioner	Providence-Warwick MSA, RI-MA	Y	89830 FQ	104450 MW	123760 TQ	USBLS	5/15
	South Carolina	Y	81060 FQ	90600 MW	100360 TQ	USBLS	5/15
	Charleston-North Charleston MSA, SC	Y	82260 FQ	91590 MW	102340 TQ	USBLS	5/15
	Columbia MSA, SC	Y	81690 FQ	90300 MW	99240 TQ	USBLS	5/15
	Greenville-Anderson-Mauldin MSA, SC	Y	80290 FQ	89010 MW	97410 TQ	USBLS	5/15
	South Dakota	Y	81960 FQ	93760 MW	109430 TQ	USBLS	5/15
	Sioux Falls MSA, SD	Y	82180 FQ	93970 MW	109350 TQ	USBLS	5/15
	Tennessee	Y	80060 FQ	91990 MW	105210 TQ	USBLS	5/15
	Knoxville MSA, TN	Y	79630 FQ	90220 MW	100910 TQ	USBLS	5/15
	Memphis MSA, TN-MS-AR	Y	88140 FQ	99410 MW	114280 TQ	USBLS	5/15
	Nashville-Davidson–Murfreesboro–Franklin MSA, TN	Y	70940 FQ	85550 MW	97210 TQ	USBLS	5/15
	Texas	Y	87910 FQ	104370 MW	121540 TQ	USBLS	5/15
	Austin-Round Rock MSA, TX	Y	71130 FQ	94370 MW	114810 TQ	USBLS	5/15
	Dallas-Plano-Irving PMSA, TX	Y	88760 FQ	102470 MW	120460 TQ	USBLS	5/15
	Fort Worth-Arlington PMSA, TX	Y	85550 FQ	102650 MW	117130 TQ	USBLS	5/15
	Houston-The Woodlands-Sugar Land MSA, TX	Y	100010 FQ	113770 MW	128480 TQ	USBLS	5/15
	San Antonio-New Braunfels MSA, TX	Y	83990 FQ	96870 MW	114180 TQ	USBLS	5/15
	Utah	Y	80880 FQ	94360 MW	111540 TQ	USBLS	5/15
	Ogden-Clearfield MSA, UT	Y	65920 FQ	90760 MW	112190 TQ	USBLS	5/15
	Provo-Orem MSA, UT	Y	85850 FQ	96700 MW	111380 TQ	USBLS	5/15
	Salt Lake City MSA, UT	Y	80940 FQ	94230 MW	111750 TQ	USBLS	5/15
	Burlington-South Burlington MSA, VT	Y	82840 FQ	94890 MW	109520 TQ	USBLS	5/15
	Virginia	Y	82760 FQ	94340 MW	110900 TQ	USBLS	5/15
	Richmond MSA, VA	Y	80330 FQ	90410 MW	101580 TQ	USBLS	5/15
	Virginia Beach-Norfolk-Newport News MSA, VA-NC	Y	82820 FQ	94840 MW	113740 TQ	USBLS	5/15
	Washington	H	43.28 FQ	50.20 MW	58.11 TQ	WABLS	3/16
	Seattle-Bellevue-Everett PMSA, WA	H	44.46 FQ	51.97 MW	58.51 TQ	WABLS	3/16
	Tacoma-Lakewood PMSA, WA	H	44.09 FQ	50.47 MW	58.48 TQ	WABLS	3/16
	West Virginia	Y	77570 FQ	88880 MW	99130 TQ	USBLS	5/15
	Huntington-Ashland MSA, WV-KY-OH	Y	79760 FQ	89680 MW	99210 TQ	USBLS	5/15
	Wisconsin	Y	84990 FQ	94260 MW	105140 TQ	USBLS	5/15
	Madison MSA, WI	Y	85070 FQ	94050 MW	104690 TQ	USBLS	5/15
	Milwaukee-Waukesha-West Allis MSA, WI	Y	84480 FQ	93170 MW	102080 TQ	USBLS	5/15
	Wyoming	Y	82220 FQ	96540 MW	117750 TQ	USBLS	5/15
	Cheyenne MSA, WY	Y	80980 FQ	96460 MW	133120 TQ	USBLS	5/15
	Puerto Rico	Y	18050 FQ	20880 MW	24650 TQ	USBLS	5/15
	San Juan-Carolina-Caguas MSA, PR	Y	19070 FQ	22230 MW	26600 TQ	USBLS	5/15
Pain Management	United States	Y		97940 AW		MLEVU2	2016
Pediatrics, Municipal Government	Detroit, MI	M	4858 LO		5117 HI	DETGOV	2016
Urgent Care	United States	Y		152165 AW		MLEVU2	2016
Women's Health	United States	Y		99062 AW		MLEVU2	2016
Nursing Assistant	Alabama	Y	17668 AE	22806 AW	25369 AEX	ALBLS	6/16
	Birmingham-Hoover MSA, AL	Y	17895 AE	23012 AW	25565 AEX	ALBLS	6/16
	Alaska	Y	33150 FQ	36820 MW	41940 TQ	USBLS	5/15
	Anchorage MSA, AK	Y	32450 FQ	36570 MW	41940 TQ	USBLS	5/15
	Arizona	Y	25120 FQ	28420 MW	32300 TQ	USBLS	5/15
	Phoenix-Mesa-Scottsdale MSA, AZ	Y	25710 FQ	28940 MW	33440 TQ	USBLS	5/15
	Tucson MSA, AZ	Y	24240 FQ	27350 MW	29920 TQ	USBLS	5/15
	Arkansas	Y	18980 FQ	21660 MW	24120 TQ	USBLS	5/15
	Little Rock-North Little Rock-Conway MSA, AR	Y	21070 FQ	23240 MW	25940 TQ	USBLS	5/15
	California	H	12.09 FQ	14.29 MW	17.79 TQ	CABLS	1/16-3/16
	Anaheim-Santa Ana-Irvine PMSA, CA	H	11.72 FQ	13.64 MW	15.57 TQ	CABLS	1/16-3/16
	Los Angeles-Long Beach-Glendale PMSA, CA	H	12.04 FQ	14.15 MW	17.41 TQ	CABLS	1/16-3/16

AE Average entry wage	**AWR** Average wage range	**H** Hourly	**LR** Low end range	**MTC** Median total compensation	**TCC** Total cash compensation
AEX Average experienced wage	**B** Biweekly	**HI** Highest wage paid	**M** Monthly	**MW** Median wage paid	**TQ** Third quartile wage
ATC Average total compensation	**D** Daily	**HR** High end range	**MCC** Median cash compensation	**MWR** Median wage range	**W** Weekly
AW Average wage paid	**FQ** First quartile wage	**LO** Lowest wage paid	**ME** Median entry wage	**S** See annotated source	**Y** Yearly

Occupation/Type/Industry	Location	Per	Low	Mid	High	Source	Date
Nursing Assistant	Oakland-Hayward-Berkeley PMSA, CA	H	12.00 FQ	16.01 MW	19.14 TQ	CABLS	1/16-3/16
	Riverside-San Bernardino-Ontario MSA, CA	H	11.58 FQ	13.60 MW	16.08 TQ	CABLS	1/16-3/16
	Sacramento–Roseville–Arden-Arcade MSA, CA	H	14.20 FQ	18.49 MW	22.10 TQ	CABLS	1/16-3/16
	San Diego-Carlsbad MSA, CA	H	12.40 FQ	14.20 MW	17.52 TQ	CABLS	1/16-3/16
	San Francisco-Redwood City-South San Francisco PMSA, CA	H	16.33 FQ	18.74 MW	22.74 TQ	CABLS	1/16-3/16
	Colorado	Y	24810 FQ	28710 MW	33730 TQ	USBLS	5/15
	Denver-Aurora-Lakewood MSA, CO	Y	26790 FQ	30480 MW	35530 TQ	USBLS	5/15
	Connecticut	Y		31357 MW		CTBLS	1/16-3/16
	Bridgeport-Stamford-Norwalk MSA, CT	Y	28600 FQ	32710 MW	37170 TQ	USBLS	5/15
	Hartford-West Hartford-East Hartford MSA, CT	Y	26300 FQ	29680 MW	35130 TQ	USBLS	5/15
	Delaware	Y	25200 FQ	28030 MW	31270 TQ	USBLS	5/15
	Wilmington PMSA, DE-MD-NJ	Y	25500 FQ	28510 MW	32220 TQ	USBLS	5/15
	District of Columbia	Y	27290 FQ	31980 MW	37410 TQ	USBLS	5/15
	Washington-Arlington-Alexandria PMSA, DC-VA-MD-WV	Y	23910 FQ	28130 MW	33260 TQ	USBLS	5/15
	Florida	H	10.24 AE	11.88 MW	13.24 AEX	FLBLS	7/16-9/16
	Fort Lauderdale-Pompano Beach-Deerfield Beach PMSA, FL	H	9.85 AE	12.23 MW	13.80 AEX	FLBLS	7/16-9/16
	Miami-Miami Beach-Kendall PMSA, FL	H	9.98 AE	11.47 MW	12.71 AEX	FLBLS	7/16-9/16
	Orlando-Kissimmee-Sanford MSA, FL	H	10.25 AE	12.00 MW	13.35 AEX	FLBLS	7/16-9/16
	Tampa-St. Petersburg-Clearwater MSA, FL	H	10.42 AE	12.03 MW	13.38 AEX	FLBLS	7/16-9/16
	Georgia	Y	19120 FQ	22060 MW	25080 TQ	USBLS	5/15
	Atlanta-Sandy Springs-Roswell MSA, GA	Y	20180 FQ	22980 MW	27050 TQ	USBLS	5/15
	Augusta-Richmond County MSA, GA-SC	Y	19290 FQ	22540 MW	27200 TQ	USBLS	5/15
	Hawaii	Y	26380 FQ	30410 MW	35740 TQ	USBLS	5/15
	Urban Honolulu MSA, HI	Y	26070 FQ	29870 MW	35270 TQ	USBLS	5/15
	Idaho	Y	20530 FQ	23690 MW	27820 TQ	USBLS	5/15
	Boise City MSA, ID	Y	20680 FQ	23870 MW	28110 TQ	USBLS	5/15
	Illinois	Y	21540 FQ	24450 MW	29400 TQ	USBLS	5/15
	Chicago-Naperville-Arlington Heights PMSA, IL	Y	21910 FQ	25490 MW	30290 TQ	USBLS	5/15
	Lake County-Kenosha County PMSA, IL-WI	Y	23950 FQ	27310 MW	30450 TQ	USBLS	5/15
	Indiana	Y	21080 FQ	23530 MW	27510 TQ	USBLS	5/15
	Gary PMSA, IN	Y	20610 FQ	23510 MW	27840 TQ	USBLS	5/15
	Indianapolis-Carmel-Anderson MSA, IN	Y	22020 FQ	24600 MW	28780 TQ	USBLS	5/15
	Iowa	Y	22120 FQ	25100 MW	29430 TQ	USBLS	5/15
	Des Moines-West Des Moines MSA, IA	Y	23340 FQ	27550 MW	31340 TQ	USBLS	5/15
	Kansas	Y	21190 FQ	23320 MW	26490 TQ	USBLS	5/15
	Wichita MSA, KS	Y	21310 FQ	23310 MW	26330 TQ	USBLS	5/15
	Kentucky	Y	20770 FQ	23980 MW	28300 TQ	USBLS	5/15
	Louisville-Jefferson County MSA, KY-IN	Y	22590 FQ	26190 MW	29590 TQ	USBLS	5/15
	Louisiana	Y	17700 FQ	20140 MW	23480 TQ	USBLS	5/15
	Baton Rouge MSA, LA	Y	18320 FQ	21080 MW	23840 TQ	USBLS	5/15
	New Orleans-Metairie MSA, LA	Y	19380 FQ	22270 MW	25270 TQ	USBLS	5/15
	Maine	Y	21600 FQ	24460 MW	28680 TQ	USBLS	5/15
	Portland-South Portland MSA, ME	Y	23790 FQ	27480 MW	31100 TQ	USBLS	5/15
	Maryland	Y	22275 AE	28741 MW	31973 AEX	MDBLS	4/16
	Baltimore-Columbia-Towson MSA, MD	Y	24190 FQ	28200 MW	33020 TQ	USBLS	5/15
	Salisbury MSA, MD-DE	Y	22510 FQ	25750 MW	29850 TQ	USBLS	5/15

AE	Average entry wage	**AWR** Average wage range	**H** Hourly	**LR** Low end range	**MTC** Median total compensation **TCC** Total cash compensation
AEX	Average experienced wage	**B** Biweekly	**HI** Highest wage paid	**M** Monthly	**MW** Median wage paid **TQ** Third quartile wage
ATC	Average total compensation	**D** Daily	**HR** High end range	**MCC** Median cash compensation **MWR** Median wage range	**W** Weekly
AW	Average wage paid	**FQ** First quartile wage	**LO** Lowest wage paid	**ME** Median entry wage	**S** See annotated source **Y** Yearly

Occupation/Type/Industry	Location	Per	Low	Mid	High	Source	Date
Nursing Assistant	Massachusetts	Y	25770 FQ	29120 MW	34190 TQ	USBLS	5/15
	Boston-Cambridge-Newton NECTA, MA	Y	26290 FQ	29560 MW	34950 TQ	USBLS	5/15
	Worcester MSA, MA-CT	Y	26400 FQ	30010 MW	35340 TQ	USBLS	5/15
	Michigan	Y	24330 FQ	27820 MW	31180 TQ	USBLS	5/15
	Detroit-Dearborn-Livonia PMSA, MI	Y	24890 FQ	28000 MW	31090 TQ	USBLS	5/15
	Grand Rapids-Wyoming MSA, MI	Y	25070 FQ	27630 MW	30190 TQ	USBLS	5/15
	Minnesota	Y	23974 FQ	28125 MW	33154 TQ	MNBLS	1/16-3/16
	Minneapolis-St. Paul-Bloomington MSA, MN-WI	Y	26539 FQ	30326 MW	35881 TQ	MNBLS	1/16-3/16
	Mississippi	Y	17690 FQ	20050 MW	23470 TQ	USBLS	5/15
	Jackson MSA, MS	Y	18340 FQ	21130 MW	23800 TQ	USBLS	5/15
	Missouri	Y	20020 FQ	23000 MW	27020 TQ	USBLS	5/15
	Kansas City MSA, MO-KS	Y	21820 FQ	24680 MW	28840 TQ	USBLS	5/15
	St. Louis MSA, MO-IL	Y	21410 FQ	23670 MW	27570 TQ	USBLS	5/15
	Montana	Y	21780 FQ	24360 MW	28470 TQ	USBLS	5/15
	Billings MSA, MT	Y	21890 FQ	24490 MW	28750 TQ	USBLS	5/15
	Nebraska	Y	21760 FQ	24130 MW	28465 TQ	NEBLS	7/16-9/16
	Omaha-Council Bluffs MSA, NE-IA	Y	21965 FQ	24495 MW	28925 TQ	NEBLS	7/16-9/16
	Nevada	Y	27280 FQ	31020 MW	37160 TQ	USBLS	5/15
	Las Vegas-Henderson-Paradise MSA, NV	Y	28000 FQ	32430 MW	38600 TQ	USBLS	5/15
	New Hampshire	H	11.99 AE	14.37 MW	16.08 AEX	NHBLS	6/16
	Manchester NECTA, NH	H	13.06 AE	15.27 MW	16.84 AEX	NHBLS	6/16
	Nashua NECTA, NH-MA	Y	24790 FQ	27680 MW	30470 TQ	USBLS	5/15
	New Jersey	Y	23880 FQ	27660 MW	31400 TQ	USBLS	5/15
	Camden PMSA, NJ	Y	22650 FQ	26450 MW	30760 TQ	USBLS	5/15
	Newark PMSA, NJ-PA	Y	23810 FQ	27750 MW	32130 TQ	USBLS	5/15
	Trenton MSA, NJ	Y	23910 FQ	27270 MW	30370 TQ	USBLS	5/15
	New Mexico	Y	22050 FQ	25880 MW	30560 TQ	USBLS	5/15
	Albuquerque MSA, NM	Y	23730 FQ	27850 MW	31680 TQ	USBLS	5/15
	New York	Y	25730 AE	34360 MW	38220 AEX	NYBLS	1/16-3/16
	Buffalo-Cheektowaga-Niagara Falls MSA, NY	Y	24970 FQ	29160 MW	34150 TQ	USBLS	5/15
	Nassau County-Suffolk County PMSA, NY	Y	32800 FQ	36670 MW	41780 TQ	USBLS	5/15
	New York-Jersey City-White Plains PMSA, NY-NJ	Y	29050 FQ	34250 MW	38610 TQ	USBLS	5/15
	Rochester MSA, NY	Y	23560 FQ	27110 MW	30330 TQ	USBLS	5/15
	North Carolina	Y	19430 FQ	22550 MW	26460 TQ	USBLS	5/15
	Charlotte-Concord-Gastonia MSA, NC-SC	Y	20120 FQ	22830 MW	26520 TQ	USBLS	5/15
	Raleigh MSA, NC	Y	20400 FQ	23340 MW	27510 TQ	USBLS	5/15
	North Dakota	Y	25950 FQ	29070 MW	33340 TQ	USBLS	5/15
	Fargo MSA, ND-MN	Y	25150 FQ	28020 MW	30900 TQ	USBLS	5/15
	Ohio	Y	21350 FQ	24150 MW	28610 TQ	USBLS	5/15
	Cincinnati MSA, OH-KY-IN	Y	22110 FQ	24850 MW	29300 TQ	USBLS	5/15
	Cleveland-Elyria MSA, OH	Y	21710 FQ	25100 MW	29140 TQ	USBLS	5/15
	Columbus MSA, OH	Y	21590 FQ	24230 MW	28300 TQ	USBLS	5/15
	Oklahoma	Y	20030 FQ	22490 MW	25150 TQ	USBLS	5/15
	Oklahoma City MSA, OK	Y	21020 FQ	23340 MW	26670 TQ	USBLS	5/15
	Tulsa MSA, OK	Y	20140 FQ	22720 MW	25820 TQ	USBLS	5/15
	Oregon	H	12.83 FQ	14.40 MW	16.78 TQ	ORBLS	2016
	Portland-Vancouver-Hillsboro MSA, OR-WA	Y	25490 FQ	28990 MW	34270 TQ	USBLS	5/15
	Pennsylvania	Y	24430 FQ	28000 MW	31810 TQ	USBLS	5/15
	Allentown-Bethlehem-Easton MSA, PA-NJ	Y	24760 FQ	27950 MW	31110 TQ	USBLS	5/15
	Harrisburg-Carlisle MSA, PA	Y	25560 FQ	28570 MW	32090 TQ	USBLS	5/15
	Montgomery County-Bucks County-Chester County PMSA, PA	Y	25840 FQ	29060 MW	33610 TQ	USBLS	5/15
	Philadelphia PMSA, PA	Y	24790 FQ	29090 MW	35300 TQ	USBLS	5/15
	Pittsburgh MSA, PA	Y	24990 FQ	28260 MW	31940 TQ	USBLS	5/15
	Rhode Island	Y	25030 FQ	28290 MW	32350 TQ	USBLS	5/15
	Providence-Warwick MSA, RI-MA	Y	24920 FQ	28170 MW	31950 TQ	USBLS	5/15
	South Carolina	Y	19560 FQ	22670 MW	26640 TQ	USBLS	5/15

AE	Average entry wage	AWR	Average wage range	H	Hourly	LR	Low end range	MTC	Median total compensation	TCC	Total cash compensation
AEX	Average experienced wage	B	Biweekly	HI	Highest wage paid	M	Monthly	MW	Median wage paid	TQ	Third quartile wage
ATC	Average total compensation	D	Daily	HR	High end range	MCC	Median cash compensation	MWR	Median wage range	W	Weekly
AW	Average wage paid	FQ	First quartile wage	LO	Lowest wage paid	ME	Median entry wage	S	See annotated source	Y	Yearly

Occupation/Type/Industry	Location	Per	Low	Mid	High	Source	Date
Nursing Assistant	Charleston-North Charleston						
	MSA, SC	Y	22010 FQ	26010 MW	29770 TQ	USBLS	5/15
	Columbia MSA, SC	Y	20260 FQ	23120 MW	27430 TQ	USBLS	5/15
	Greenville-Anderson-Mauldin						
	MSA, SC	Y	20030 FQ	23050 MW	27090 TQ	USBLS	5/15
	South Dakota	Y	20800 FQ	23320 MW	27130 TQ	USBLS	5/15
	Sioux Falls MSA, SD	Y	21480 FQ	23930 MW	27850 TQ	USBLS	5/15
	Tennessee	Y	19630 FQ	22390 MW	25700 TQ	USBLS	5/15
	Knoxville MSA, TN	Y	20960 FQ	23270 MW	26730 TQ	USBLS	5/15
	Memphis MSA, TN-MS-AR	Y	20640 FQ	23880 MW	27950 TQ	USBLS	5/15
	Nashville-Davidson–						
	Murfreesboro–Franklin						
	MSA, TN	Y	18730 FQ	22050 MW	26400 TQ	USBLS	5/15
	Texas	Y	20460 FQ	23350 MW	27850 TQ	USBLS	5/15
	Austin-Round Rock MSA, TX	Y	21980 FQ	25730 MW	29310 TQ	USBLS	5/15
	Dallas-Plano-Irving PMSA, TX	Y	21180 FQ	24170 MW	29340 TQ	USBLS	5/15
	Fort Worth-Arlington PMSA,						
	TX	Y	20930 FQ	23830 MW	28450 TQ	USBLS	5/15
	Houston-The Woodlands-						
	Sugar Land MSA, TX	Y	21200 FQ	24520 MW	29220 TQ	USBLS	5/15
	San Antonio-New Braunfels						
	MSA, TX	Y	21380 FQ	23850 MW	28050 TQ	USBLS	5/15
	Utah	Y	21130 FQ	23350 MW	26800 TQ	USBLS	5/15
	Ogden-Clearfield MSA, UT	Y	20560 FQ	22530 MW	24510 TQ	USBLS	5/15
	Provo-Orem MSA, UT	Y	20960 FQ	22740 MW	24530 TQ	USBLS	5/15
	Salt Lake City MSA, UT	Y	22100 FQ	24970 MW	28550 TQ	USBLS	5/15
	Vermont	Y	23850 FQ	27310 MW	30470 TQ	USBLS	5/15
	Burlington-South Burlington						
	MSA, VT	Y	25340 FQ	28350 MW	31640 TQ	USBLS	5/15
	Virginia	Y	21020 FQ	24450 MW	28870 TQ	USBLS	5/15
	Richmond MSA, VA	Y	21620 FQ	24860 MW	28800 TQ	USBLS	5/15
	Virginia Beach-Norfolk-						
	Newport News MSA, VA-NC	Y	21080 FQ	24190 MW	28070 TQ	USBLS	5/15
	Washington	H	11.94 FQ	13.95 MW	16.63 TQ	WABLS	3/16
	Seattle-Bellevue-Everett						
	PMSA, WA	H	13.41 FQ	15.13 MW	17.79 TQ	WABLS	3/16
	Tacoma-Lakewood PMSA, WA	H	11.97 FQ	13.93 MW	16.52 TQ	WABLS	3/16
	West Virginia	Y	20300 FQ	23020 MW	27110 TQ	USBLS	5/15
	Huntington-Ashland MSA,						
	WV-KY-OH	Y	20870 FQ	23400 MW	27750 TQ	USBLS	5/15
	Wisconsin	Y	23180 FQ	26940 MW	30540 TQ	USBLS	5/15
	Madison MSA, WI	Y	25450 FQ	28920 MW	34070 TQ	USBLS	5/15
	Milwaukee-Waukesha-West						
	Allis MSA, WI	Y	22770 FQ	26530 MW	30340 TQ	USBLS	5/15
	Wyoming	Y	24100 FQ	27650 MW	30570 TQ	USBLS	5/15
	Cheyenne MSA, WY	Y	22630 FQ	26600 MW	31930 TQ	USBLS	5/15
	Puerto Rico	Y	16870 FQ	18280 MW	19790 TQ	USBLS	5/15
	San Juan-Carolina-Caguas						
	MSA, PR	Y	17220 FQ	19090 MW	23980 TQ	USBLS	5/15
	Virgin Islands	Y	21120 FQ	24390 MW	28220 TQ	USBLS	5/15
	Guam	Y	19250 FQ	23210 MW	29360 TQ	USBLS	5/15
Nursing Instructor and Teacher							
Postsecondary	Alabama	Y	32945 AE	60660 AW	74513 AEX	ALBLS	6/16
Postsecondary	Alaska	Y	65750 FQ	77540 MW	97900 TQ	USBLS	5/15
Postsecondary	Arizona	Y	57070 FQ	70990 MW	87660 TQ	USBLS	5/15
Postsecondary	Phoenix-Mesa-Scottsdale						
	MSA, AZ	Y	55790 FQ	70100 MW	89040 TQ	USBLS	5/15
Postsecondary	Arkansas	Y	44260 FQ	57670 MW	74480 TQ	USBLS	5/15
Postsecondary	Little Rock-North Little Rock-						
	Conway MSA, AR	Y	36820 FQ	58730 MW	75980 TQ	USBLS	5/15
Postsecondary	California	Y		100962 AW		CABLS	1/16-3/16
Postsecondary	Anaheim-Santa Ana-Irvine						
	PMSA, CA	Y		96042 AW		CABLS	1/16-3/16
Postsecondary	Los Angeles-Long Beach-						
	Glendale PMSA, CA	Y		105233 AW		CABLS	1/16-3/16
Postsecondary	Riverside-San Bernardino-						
	Ontario MSA, CA	Y		90929 AW		CABLS	1/16-3/16
Postsecondary	San Diego-Carlsbad MSA, CA	Y		89843 AW		CABLS	1/16-3/16
Postsecondary	San Francisco-Redwood City-						
	South San Francisco PMSA,						
	CA	Y		88271 AW		CABLS	1/16-3/16

AE	Average entry wage	**AWR** Average wage range	**H** Hourly	**LR** Low end range	**MTC** Median total compensation	**TCC** Total cash compensation
AEX	Average experienced wage	**B** Biweekly	**HI** Highest wage paid	**M** Monthly	**MW** Median wage paid	**TQ** Third quartile wage
ATC	Average total compensation	**D** Daily	**HR** High end range	**MCC** Median cash compensation	**MWR** Median wage range	**W** Weekly
AW	Average wage paid	**FQ** First quartile wage	**LO** Lowest wage paid	**ME** Median entry wage	**S** See annotated source	**Y** Yearly

Occupation/Type/Industry	Location	Per	Low	Mid	High	Source	Date
Nursing Instructor and Teacher							
Postsecondary	Colorado	Y	47110 FQ	62270 MW	84090 TQ	USBLS	5/15
Postsecondary	Denver-Aurora-Lakewood MSA, CO	Y	47170 FQ	68620 MW	91500 TQ	USBLS	5/15
Postsecondary	Connecticut	Y		78735 MW		CTBLS	1/16-3/16
Postsecondary	Bridgeport-Stamford-Norwalk MSA, CT	Y	67870 FQ	81180 MW	97680 TQ	USBLS	5/15
Postsecondary	Hartford-West Hartford-East Hartford MSA, CT	Y	62040 FQ	74720 MW	91880 TQ	USBLS	5/15
Postsecondary	Delaware	Y	68550 FQ	78170 MW	96950 TQ	USBLS	5/15
Postsecondary	Wilmington PMSA, DE-MD-NJ	Y	69460 FQ	86100 MW	129250 TQ	USBLS	5/15
Postsecondary	District of Columbia	Y	50770 FQ	71340 MW	93440 TQ	USBLS	5/15
Postsecondary	Washington-Arlington-Alexandria PMSA, DC-VA-MD-WV	Y	53240 FQ	67760 MW	86760 TQ	USBLS	5/15
Postsecondary	Florida	Y	50153 AE	71855 MW	85539 AEX	FLBLS	7/16-9/16
Postsecondary	Fort Lauderdale-Pompano Beach-Deerfield Beach PMSA, FL	Y	53156 AE	73898 MW	86759 AEX	FLBLS	7/16-9/16
Postsecondary	Miami-Miami Beach-Kendall PMSA, FL	Y	63156 AE	83497 MW	94558 AEX	FLBLS	7/16-9/16
Postsecondary	Orlando-Kissimmee-Sanford MSA, FL	Y	45403 AE	65862 MW	80134 AEX	FLBLS	7/16-9/16
Postsecondary	Tampa-St. Petersburg-Clearwater MSA, FL	Y	54223 AE	71104 MW	80061 AEX	FLBLS	7/16-9/16
Postsecondary	Georgia	Y	53390 FQ	61440 MW	76540 TQ	USBLS	5/15
Postsecondary	Atlanta-Sandy Springs-Roswell MSA, GA	Y	56110 FQ	63130 MW	77200 TQ	USBLS	5/15
Postsecondary	Hawaii	Y	56610 FQ	75140 MW	92310 TQ	USBLS	5/15
Postsecondary	Urban Honolulu MSA, HI	Y	54610 FQ	72650 MW	91110 TQ	USBLS	5/15
Postsecondary	Idaho	Y	44380 FQ	54780 MW	63690 TQ	USBLS	5/15
Postsecondary	Boise City MSA, ID	Y	19480 FQ	53380 MW	63280 TQ	USBLS	5/15
Postsecondary	Illinois	Y	50480 FQ	66230 MW	88730 TQ	USBLS	5/15
Postsecondary	Chicago-Naperville-Arlington Heights PMSA, IL	Y	50330 FQ	66750 MW	87680 TQ	USBLS	5/15
Postsecondary	Indiana	Y	52540 FQ	63700 MW	80200 TQ	USBLS	5/15
Postsecondary	Gary PMSA, IN	Y	52640 FQ	63640 MW	80560 TQ	USBLS	5/15
Postsecondary	Indianapolis-Carmel-Anderson MSA, IN	Y	54340 FQ	70000 MW	85830 TQ	USBLS	5/15
Postsecondary	Iowa	Y	50210 FQ	61600 MW	77020 TQ	USBLS	5/15
Postsecondary	Des Moines-West Des Moines MSA, IA	Y	49280 FQ	63040 MW	73080 TQ	USBLS	5/15
Postsecondary	Kansas	Y	43920 FQ	49770 MW	61540 TQ	USBLS	5/15
Postsecondary	Wichita MSA, KS	Y	47250 FQ	55020 MW	60680 TQ	USBLS	5/15
Postsecondary	Kentucky	Y	51170 FQ	65010 MW	83680 TQ	USBLS	5/15
Postsecondary	Louisville-Jefferson County MSA, KY-IN	Y	51760 FQ	60660 MW	73660 TQ	USBLS	5/15
Postsecondary	Louisiana	Y	48200 FQ	58230 MW	71050 TQ	USBLS	5/15
Postsecondary	Baton Rouge MSA, LA	Y	51620 FQ	60970 MW	73890 TQ	USBLS	5/15
Postsecondary	New Orleans-Metairie MSA, LA	Y	43030 FQ	57680 MW	74950 TQ	USBLS	5/15
Postsecondary	Maine	Y	53600 FQ	66110 MW	79400 TQ	USBLS	5/15
Postsecondary	Portland-South Portland MSA, ME	Y	54840 FQ	67460 MW	83060 TQ	USBLS	5/15
Postsecondary	Maryland	Y	44867 AE	71624 MW	85003 AEX	MDBLS	4/16
Postsecondary	Baltimore-Columbia-Towson MSA, MD	Y	65160 FQ	76990 MW	96020 TQ	USBLS	5/15
Postsecondary	Salisbury MSA, MD-DE	Y	55710 FQ	69920 MW	79280 TQ	USBLS	5/15
Postsecondary	Massachusetts	Y	60920 FQ	76280 MW	105970 TQ	USBLS	5/15
Postsecondary	Boston-Cambridge-Newton NECTA, MA	Y	61000 FQ	76110 MW	108020 TQ	USBLS	5/15
Postsecondary	Worcester MSA, MA-CT	Y	65750 FQ	82290 MW	108650 TQ	USBLS	5/15
Postsecondary	Michigan	Y	39380 FQ	66580 MW	87090 TQ	USBLS	5/15
Postsecondary	Detroit-Dearborn-Livonia PMSA, MI	Y	77240 FQ	88400 MW	99120 TQ	USBLS	5/15
Postsecondary	Grand Rapids-Wyoming MSA, MI	Y	46800 FQ	67960 MW	82890 TQ	USBLS	5/15
Postsecondary	Minnesota	Y	55040 FQ	70211 MW	91057 TQ	MNBLS	1/16-3/16
Postsecondary	Minneapolis-St. Paul-Bloomington MSA, MN-WI	Y	56310 FQ	71793 MW	90523 TQ	MNBLS	1/16-3/16
Postsecondary	Mississippi	Y	58690 FQ	70130 MW	80030 TQ	USBLS	5/15

Occupation/Type/Industry	Location	Per	Low	Mid	High	Source	Date
Nursing Instructor and Teacher							
Postsecondary	Jackson MSA, MS	Y	63060 FQ	73890 MW	87640 TQ	USBLS	5/15
Postsecondary	Missouri	Y	56000 FQ	70580 MW	88550 TQ	USBLS	5/15
Postsecondary	Kansas City MSA, MO-KS	Y	57130 FQ	71560 MW	90930 TQ	USBLS	5/15
Postsecondary	St. Louis MSA, MO-IL	Y	56300 FQ	70880 MW	87600 TQ	USBLS	5/15
Postsecondary	Montana	Y	51790 FQ	58920 MW	69050 TQ	USBLS	5/15
Postsecondary	Nebraska	Y	53605 FQ	62760 MW	79785 TQ	NEBLS	7/16-9/16
Postsecondary	Omaha-Council Bluffs MSA, NE-IA	Y	53245 FQ	64255 MW	83315 TQ	NEBLS	7/16-9/16
Postsecondary	Nevada	Y	50230 FQ	72570 MW	96340 TQ	USBLS	5/15
Postsecondary	Las Vegas-Henderson-Paradise MSA, NV	Y	44880 FQ	72160 MW	101880 TQ	USBLS	5/15
Postsecondary	New Hampshire	Y	53939 AE	71904 MW	86578 AEX	NHBLS	6/16
Postsecondary	Manchester NECTA, NH	Y	55623 AE	68017 MW	74787 AEX	NHBLS	6/16
Postsecondary	New Jersey	Y	70990 FQ	87720 MW	106140 TQ	USBLS	5/15
Postsecondary	Camden PMSA, NJ	Y	70180 FQ	85760 MW	100880 TQ	USBLS	5/15
Postsecondary	Newark PMSA, NJ-PA	Y	72860 FQ	89970 MW	109240 TQ	USBLS	5/15
Postsecondary	Trenton MSA, NJ	Y	64920 FQ	75530 MW	90340 TQ	USBLS	5/15
Postsecondary	New Mexico	Y	56390 FQ	66840 MW	76640 TQ	USBLS	5/15
Postsecondary	Albuquerque MSA, NM	Y	65830 FQ	73460 MW	81060 TQ	USBLS	5/15
Postsecondary	New York	Y	46370 AE	82370 MW	111180 AEX	NYBLS	1/16-3/16
Postsecondary	Buffalo-Cheektowaga-Niagara Falls MSA, NY	Y	40800 FQ	70340 MW	90220 TQ	USBLS	5/15
Postsecondary	Nassau County-Suffolk County PMSA, NY	Y	57210 FQ	90500 MW	132440 TQ	USBLS	5/15
Postsecondary	New York-Jersey City-White Plains PMSA, NY-NJ	Y	67240 FQ	92090 MW	123510 TQ	USBLS	5/15
Postsecondary	Rochester MSA, NY	Y	55470 FQ	81610 MW	115330 TQ	USBLS	5/15
Postsecondary	North Carolina	Y	53260 FQ	61520 MW	74440 TQ	USBLS	5/15
Postsecondary	Charlotte-Concord-Gastonia MSA, NC-SC	Y	54010 FQ	61220 MW	72250 TQ	USBLS	5/15
Postsecondary	Raleigh MSA, NC	Y	60040 FQ	76460 MW	100870 TQ	USBLS	5/15
Postsecondary	North Dakota	Y	53440 FQ	69930 MW	94100 TQ	USBLS	5/15
Postsecondary	Fargo MSA, ND-MN	Y	54130 FQ	67850 MW	92620 TQ	USBLS	5/15
Postsecondary	Ohio	Y	53950 FQ	65820 MW	80280 TQ	USBLS	5/15
Postsecondary	Cincinnati MSA, OH-KY-IN	Y	56930 FQ	69430 MW	79670 TQ	USBLS	5/15
Postsecondary	Cleveland-Elyria MSA, OH	Y	54890 FQ	67070 MW	79850 TQ	USBLS	5/15
Postsecondary	Columbus MSA, OH	Y	57190 FQ	73190 MW	103900 TQ	USBLS	5/15
Postsecondary	Oklahoma	Y	46620 FQ	56820 MW	70090 TQ	USBLS	5/15
Postsecondary	Oklahoma City MSA, OK	Y	45750 FQ	56740 MW	73210 TQ	USBLS	5/15
Postsecondary	Tulsa MSA, OK	Y	47510 FQ	56410 MW	63090 TQ	USBLS	5/15
Postsecondary	Oregon	Y	69735 FQ	87068 MW	101760 TQ	ORBLS	2016
Postsecondary	Portland-Vancouver-Hillsboro MSA, OR-WA	Y	68670 FQ	85970 MW	100670 TQ	USBLS	5/15
Postsecondary	Pennsylvania	Y	52450 FQ	66930 MW	84910 TQ	USBLS	5/15
Postsecondary	Allentown-Bethlehem-Easton MSA, PA-NJ	Y	54400 FQ	64540 MW	82620 TQ	USBLS	5/15
Postsecondary	Harrisburg-Carlisle MSA, PA	Y	47420 FQ	58780 MW	82260 TQ	USBLS	5/15
Postsecondary	Montgomery County-Bucks County-Chester County PMSA, PA	Y	37540 FQ	53800 MW	66090 TQ	USBLS	5/15
Postsecondary	Philadelphia PMSA, PA	Y	56970 FQ	73120 MW	91850 TQ	USBLS	5/15
Postsecondary	Pittsburgh MSA, PA	Y	53260 FQ	67920 MW	83390 TQ	USBLS	5/15
Postsecondary	South Carolina	Y	57340 FQ	69200 MW	79200 TQ	USBLS	5/15
Postsecondary	Columbia MSA, SC	Y	54470 FQ	68420 MW	80780 TQ	USBLS	5/15
Postsecondary	Greenville-Anderson-Mauldin MSA, SC	Y	66730 FQ	72870 MW	79080 TQ	USBLS	5/15
Postsecondary	South Dakota	Y	48500 FQ	58630 MW	72370 TQ	USBLS	5/15
Postsecondary	Tennessee	Y	51460 FQ	61110 MW	75280 TQ	USBLS	5/15
Postsecondary	Knoxville MSA, TN	Y	54070 FQ	60000 MW	72930 TQ	USBLS	5/15
Postsecondary	Memphis MSA, TN-MS-AR	Y	54280 FQ	65330 MW	78840 TQ	USBLS	5/15
Postsecondary	Nashville-Davidson–Murfreesboro–Franklin MSA, TN	Y	54640 FQ	66940 MW	78450 TQ	USBLS	5/15
Postsecondary	Texas	Y	51510 FQ	60980 MW	75080 TQ	USBLS	5/15
Postsecondary	Austin-Round Rock MSA, TX	Y	52540 FQ	61600 MW	76190 TQ	USBLS	5/15
Postsecondary	Dallas-Plano-Irving PMSA, TX	Y	52060 FQ	61960 MW	75860 TQ	USBLS	5/15
Postsecondary	Fort Worth-Arlington PMSA, TX	Y	49150 FQ	56620 MW	63990 TQ	USBLS	5/15
Postsecondary	Houston-The Woodlands-Sugar Land MSA, TX	Y	57890 FQ	71520 MW	86830 TQ	USBLS	5/15

Occupation/Type/Industry	Location	Per	Low	Mid	High	Source	Date
Nursing Instructor and Teacher							
Postsecondary	San Antonio-New Braunfels MSA, TX	Y	52210 FQ	61450 MW	75980 TQ	USBLS	5/15
Postsecondary	Utah	Y	57170 FQ	70200 MW	85800 TQ	USBLS	5/15
Postsecondary	Ogden-Clearfield MSA, UT	Y	54390 FQ	64270 MW	73950 TQ	USBLS	5/15
Postsecondary	Provo-Orem MSA, UT	Y	67000 FQ	77130 MW	93990 TQ	USBLS	5/15
Postsecondary	Salt Lake City MSA, UT	Y	57240 FQ	73080 MW	93400 TQ	USBLS	5/15
Postsecondary	Virginia	Y	47120 FQ	60630 MW	74390 TQ	USBLS	5/15
Postsecondary	Richmond MSA, VA	Y	36480 FQ	50310 MW	66460 TQ	USBLS	5/15
Postsecondary	Virginia Beach-Norfolk-Newport News MSA, VA-NC	Y	48420 FQ	61420 MW	73570 TQ	USBLS	5/15
Postsecondary	Washington	Y		67849 AW		WABLS	3/16
Postsecondary	Seattle-Bellevue-Everett PMSA, WA	Y		75722 AW		WABLS	3/16
Postsecondary	Tacoma-Lakewood PMSA, WA	Y		64613 AW		WABLS	3/16
Postsecondary	West Virginia	Y	43930 FQ	54140 MW	72630 TQ	USBLS	5/15
Postsecondary	Wisconsin	Y	55330 FQ	67410 MW	79990 TQ	USBLS	5/15
Postsecondary	Madison MSA, WI	Y	68550 FQ	74270 MW	80650 TQ	USBLS	5/15
Postsecondary	Milwaukee-Waukesha-West Allis MSA, WI	Y	57000 FQ	67650 MW	81760 TQ	USBLS	5/15
Postsecondary	Wyoming	Y	56800 FQ	64440 MW	73630 TQ	USBLS	5/15
Postsecondary	Puerto Rico	Y	27300 FQ	35750 MW	50320 TQ	USBLS	5/15
Postsecondary	San Juan-Carolina-Caguas MSA, PR	Y	28590 FQ	37070 MW	50680 TQ	USBLS	5/15
Nutrition Coordinator							
Recreation Department, Municipal Government	Kingsburg, CA	Y		10427 AW		CACIT	6/28/16
Obstetrician and Gynecologist	Alabama	Y	89599 AE	220276 AW	285604 AEX	ALBLS	6/16
	Alaska	Y	180900 FQ	221480 AW		USBLS	5/15
	Anchorage MSA, AK	Y		244580 AW		USBLS	5/15
	Arizona	Y		256150 AW		USBLS	5/15
	Phoenix-Mesa-Scottsdale MSA, AZ	Y		255310 AW		USBLS	5/15
	Tucson MSA, AZ	Y		261520 AW		USBLS	5/15
	Arkansas	Y	158790 FQ	240950 AW		USBLS	5/15
	California	H	59.45 FQ	101.99 AW		CABLS	1/16-3/16
	Anaheim-Santa Ana-Irvine PMSA, CA	H	24.25 FQ	57.91 MW		CABLS	1/16-3/16
	Los Angeles-Long Beach-Glendale PMSA, CA	H	55.54 FQ	95.37 AW		CABLS	1/16-3/16
	Riverside-San Bernardino-Ontario MSA, CA	H		125.30 AW		CABLS	1/16-3/16
	Sacramento–Roseville–Arden-Arcade MSA, CA	H	61.38 FQ	69.52 MW		CABLS	1/16-3/16
	San Diego-Carlsbad MSA, CA	H		124.81 AW		CABLS	1/16-3/16
	Colorado	Y	129390 FQ	198970 AW		USBLS	5/15
	Denver-Aurora-Lakewood MSA, CO	Y	144170 FQ	204040 AW		USBLS	5/15
	Connecticut	Y		219972 AW		CTBLS	1/16-3/16
	Bridgeport-Stamford-Norwalk MSA, CT	Y	172700 FQ	220290 AW		USBLS	5/15
	Hartford-West Hartford-East Hartford MSA, CT	Y	72730 FQ	212180 AW		USBLS	5/15
	Delaware	Y		247540 AW		USBLS	5/15
	Wilmington PMSA, DE-MD-NJ	Y		247540 AW		USBLS	5/15
	District of Columbia	Y	56100 FQ	131500 MW		USBLS	5/15
	Washington-Arlington-Alexandria PMSA, DC-VA-MD-WV	Y	156950 FQ	204250 AW		USBLS	5/15
	Florida	H		119.93 AW		FLBLS	7/16-9/16
	Miami-Miami Beach-Kendall PMSA, FL	H		126.91 AW		FLBLS	7/16-9/16
	Orlando-Kissimmee-Sanford MSA, FL	H	62.60 AE	116.91 AW	144.06 AEX	FLBLS	7/16-9/16
	Tampa-St. Petersburg-Clearwater MSA, FL	H		126.58 AW		FLBLS	7/16-9/16
	Georgia	Y		253550 AW		USBLS	5/15
	Atlanta-Sandy Springs-Roswell MSA, GA	Y		254980 AW		USBLS	5/15

AE	Average entry wage	AWR	Average wage range	H	Hourly	LR	Low end range	MTC	Median total compensation	TCC	Total cash compensation
AEX	Average experienced wage	B	Biweekly	HI	Highest wage paid	M	Monthly	MW	Median wage paid	TQ	Third quartile wage
ATC	Average total compensation	D	Daily	HR	High end range	MCC	Median cash compensation	MWR	Median wage range	W	Weekly
AW	Average wage paid	FQ	First quartile wage	LO	Lowest wage paid	ME	Median entry wage	S	See annotated source	Y	Yearly

1113

Occupation/Type/Industry	Location	Per	Low	Mid	High	Source	Date
Obstetrician and Gynecologist	Augusta-Richmond County MSA, GA-SC	Y		242090 AW		USBLS	5/15
	Hawaii	Y	124360 FQ	208010 AW		USBLS	5/15
	Illinois	Y	156910 FQ	217900 AW		USBLS	5/15
	Chicago-Naperville-Arlington Heights PMSA, IL	Y	124170 FQ	211500 AW		USBLS	5/15
	Lake County-Kenosha County PMSA, IL-WI	Y	116990 FQ	207020 AW		USBLS	5/15
	Gary PMSA, IN	Y		274290 AW		USBLS	5/15
	Kansas	Y	176820 FQ	214450 AW		USBLS	5/15
	Kentucky	Y		253220 AW		USBLS	5/15
	Louisville-Jefferson County MSA, KY-IN	Y		259320 AW		USBLS	5/15
	Louisiana	Y	100200 FQ	194580 AW		USBLS	5/15
	Maine	Y		279390 AW		USBLS	5/15
	Portland-South Portland MSA, ME	Y		275390 AW		USBLS	5/15
	Maryland	Y		255980 MW		MDBLS	4/16
	Baltimore-Columbia-Towson MSA, MD	Y		250420 AW		USBLS	5/15
	Massachusetts	Y		249510 AW		USBLS	5/15
	Boston-Cambridge-Newton NECTA, MA	Y	178560 FQ	238330 AW		USBLS	5/15
	Michigan	Y	62390 FQ	188070 AW		USBLS	5/15
	Detroit-Dearborn-Livonia PMSA, MI	Y	56930 FQ	172440 MW		USBLS	5/15
	Grand Rapids-Wyoming MSA, MI	Y	76310 FQ	198460 AW		USBLS	5/15
	Minnesota	Y	180623 FQ	230945 AW		MNBLS	1/16-3/16
	Minneapolis-St. Paul-Bloomington MSA, MN-WI	Y	179695 FQ	229140 AW		MNBLS	1/16-3/16
	Mississippi	Y		270510 AW		USBLS	5/15
	Missouri	Y	172430 FQ	229110 AW		USBLS	5/15
	Kansas City MSA, MO-KS	Y	174430 FQ	224140 AW		USBLS	5/15
	St. Louis MSA, MO-IL	Y		227300 AW		USBLS	5/15
	Montana	Y		246120 AW		USBLS	5/15
	Billings MSA, MT	Y	180710 FQ	233160 AW		USBLS	5/15
	New Hampshire	H		127.53 AW		NHBLS	6/16
	New Jersey	Y	157090 FQ	204840 AW		USBLS	5/15
	Camden PMSA, NJ	Y	184610 FQ	226020 AW		USBLS	5/15
	New Mexico	Y	159690 FQ	212270 AW		USBLS	5/15
	Albuquerque MSA, NM	Y	152650 FQ	185260 MW		USBLS	5/15
	New York	Y	100220 AE	174040 MW		NYBLS	1/16-3/16
	Buffalo-Cheektowaga-Niagara Falls MSA, NY	Y	43760 FQ	48090 MW	121740 TQ	USBLS	5/15
	Nassau County-Suffolk County PMSA, NY	Y	123340 FQ	165320 MW		USBLS	5/15
	New York-Jersey City-White Plains PMSA, NY-NJ	Y	140120 FQ	205140 AW		USBLS	5/15
	Rochester MSA, NY	Y	166440 FQ	225860 AW		USBLS	5/15
	North Carolina	Y	182130 FQ	238500 AW		USBLS	5/15
	Charlotte-Concord-Gastonia MSA, NC-SC	Y		256830 AW		USBLS	5/15
	Raleigh MSA, NC	Y	178270 FQ	240630 AW		USBLS	5/15
	North Dakota	Y		257410 AW		USBLS	5/15
	Ohio	Y	153460 FQ	226860 AW		USBLS	5/15
	Cincinnati MSA, OH-KY-IN	Y	117820 FQ	213910 AW		USBLS	5/15
	Cleveland-Elyria MSA, OH	Y		256520 AW		USBLS	5/15
	Columbus MSA, OH	Y		242740 AW		USBLS	5/15
	Oklahoma	Y		245530 AW		USBLS	5/15
	Oklahoma City MSA, OK	Y		245770 AW		USBLS	5/15
	Oregon	H	87.16 FQ	113.13 AW		ORBLS	2016
	Portland-Vancouver-Hillsboro MSA, OR-WA	Y	173180 FQ	210150 AW		USBLS	5/15
	Pennsylvania	Y	160340 FQ	222530 AW		USBLS	5/15
	Allentown-Bethlehem-Easton MSA, PA-NJ	Y	62790 FQ	190120 AW		USBLS	5/15
	Montgomery County-Bucks County-Chester County PMSA, PA	Y		255890 AW		USBLS	5/15
	Philadelphia PMSA, PA	Y	59170 FQ	186030 MW		USBLS	5/15
	South Carolina	Y	133680 FQ	213560 AW		USBLS	5/15

AE	Average entry wage	AWR	Average wage range	H	Hourly	LR	Low end range	MTC	Median total compensation	TCC	Total cash compensation
AEX	Average experienced wage	B	Biweekly	HI	Highest wage paid	M	Monthly	MW	Median wage paid	TQ	Third quartile wage
ATC	Average total compensation	D	Daily	HR	High end range	MCC	Median cash compensation	MWR	Median wage range	W	Weekly
AW	Average wage paid	FQ	First quartile wage	LO	Lowest wage paid	ME	Median entry wage	S	See annotated source	Y	Yearly

Occupation/Type/Industry	Location	Per	Low	Mid	High	Source	Date
Obstetrician and Gynecologist	Columbia MSA, SC	Y	75770 FQ	115720 MW	136630 TQ	USBLS	5/15
	South Dakota	Y		278440 AW		USBLS	5/15
	Tennessee	Y	171620 FQ	228800 AW		USBLS	5/15
	Texas	Y	47380 FQ	172070 MW		USBLS	5/15
	Houston-The Woodlands-Sugar Land MSA, TX	Y	44780 FQ	49870 MW		USBLS	5/15
	San Antonio-New Braunfels MSA, TX	Y	86710 FQ	185610 AW		USBLS	5/15
	Utah	Y		244500 AW		USBLS	5/15
	Ogden-Clearfield MSA, UT	Y		267370 AW		USBLS	5/15
	Provo-Orem MSA, UT	Y	171930 FQ	210780 AW		USBLS	5/15
	Vermont	Y	109440 FQ	196610 AW		USBLS	5/15
	Virginia	Y	163680 FQ	216030 AW		USBLS	5/15
	Richmond MSA, VA	Y	171630 FQ	231710 AW		USBLS	5/15
	Virginia Beach-Norfolk-Newport News MSA, VA-NC	Y	177970 FQ	236850 AW		USBLS	5/15
	Washington	H	83.66 FQ	111.12 AW		WABLS	3/16
	Seattle-Bellevue-Everett PMSA, WA	H	85.63 FQ	112.84 AW		WABLS	3/16
	Milwaukee-Waukesha-West Allis MSA, WI	Y		258450 AW		USBLS	5/15
	Puerto Rico	Y	58840 FQ	103110 MW	119400 TQ	USBLS	5/15
Occupational Health and Safety Specialist	Alabama	Y	46644 AE	70761 AW	82820 AEX	ALBLS	6/16
	Birmingham-Hoover MSA, AL	Y	56644 AE	78315 AW	89150 AEX	ALBLS	6/16
	Alaska	Y	68230 FQ	82490 MW	107090 TQ	USBLS	5/15
	Anchorage MSA, AK	Y	68970 FQ	81310 MW	108640 TQ	USBLS	5/15
	Arizona	Y	51320 FQ	67170 MW	84690 TQ	USBLS	5/15
	Phoenix-Mesa-Scottsdale MSA, AZ	Y	53990 FQ	69250 MW	87010 TQ	USBLS	5/15
	Tucson MSA, AZ	Y	49050 FQ	59620 MW	78730 TQ	USBLS	5/15
	Arkansas	Y	37780 FQ	55500 MW	77090 TQ	USBLS	5/15
	Little Rock-North Little Rock-Conway MSA, AR	Y	37780 FQ	59840 MW	76920 TQ	USBLS	5/15
	California	H	32.10 FQ	39.14 MW	47.22 TQ	CABLS	1/16-3/16
	Anaheim-Santa Ana-Irvine PMSA, CA	H	32.32 FQ	39.09 MW	47.18 TQ	CABLS	1/16-3/16
	Los Angeles-Long Beach-Glendale PMSA, CA	H	30.60 FQ	38.18 MW	46.31 TQ	CABLS	1/16-3/16
	Oakland-Hayward-Berkeley PMSA, CA	H	34.50 FQ	42.56 MW	52.03 TQ	CABLS	1/16-3/16
	Riverside-San Bernardino-Ontario MSA, CA	H	29.32 FQ	35.31 MW	41.38 TQ	CABLS	1/16-3/16
	Sacramento–Roseville–Arden-Arcade MSA, CA	H	30.71 FQ	38.52 MW	45.80 TQ	CABLS	1/16-3/16
	San Diego-Carlsbad MSA, CA	H	32.16 FQ	37.36 MW	44.69 TQ	CABLS	1/16-3/16
	San Francisco-Redwood City-South San Francisco PMSA, CA	H	37.18 FQ	47.75 MW	59.38 TQ	CABLS	1/16-3/16
	Colorado	Y	60190 FQ	75320 MW	92390 TQ	USBLS	5/15
	Denver-Aurora-Lakewood MSA, CO	Y	62250 FQ	76220 MW	93650 TQ	USBLS	5/15
	Connecticut	Y		77974 MW		CTBLS	1/16-3/16
	Bridgeport-Stamford-Norwalk MSA, CT	Y	65870 FQ	76350 MW	92960 TQ	USBLS	5/15
	Hartford-West Hartford-East Hartford MSA, CT	Y	66850 FQ	76200 MW	86150 TQ	USBLS	5/15
	Delaware	Y	52330 FQ	71030 MW	90860 TQ	USBLS	5/15
	Wilmington PMSA, DE-MD-NJ	Y	61510 FQ	77870 MW	95790 TQ	USBLS	5/15
	District of Columbia	Y	66700 FQ	86550 MW	106650 TQ	USBLS	5/15
	Washington-Arlington-Alexandria PMSA, DC-VA-MD-WV	Y	62200 FQ	81050 MW	97980 TQ	USBLS	5/15
	Florida	H	21.91 AE	32.31 MW	38.05 AEX	FLBLS	7/16-9/16
	Fort Lauderdale-Pompano Beach-Deerfield Beach PMSA, FL	H	24.82 AE	34.67 MW	39.44 AEX	FLBLS	7/16-9/16
	Miami-Miami Beach-Kendall PMSA, FL	H	19.62 AE	31.66 MW	35.96 AEX	FLBLS	7/16-9/16

AE Average entry wage	**AWR** Average wage range	**H** Hourly	**LR** Low end range	**MTC** Median total compensation	**TCC** Total cash compensation
AEX Average experienced wage	**B** Biweekly	**HI** Highest wage paid	**M** Monthly	**MW** Median wage paid	**TQ** Third quartile wage
ATC Average total compensation	**D** Daily	**HR** High end range	**MCC** Median cash compensation	**MWR** Median wage range	**W** Weekly
AW Average wage paid	**FQ** First quartile wage	**LO** Lowest wage paid	**ME** Median entry wage	**S** See annotated source	**Y** Yearly

Occupation/Type/Industry	Location	Per	Low	Mid	High	Source	Date
Occupational Health and Safety Specialist	Orlando-Kissimmee-Sanford MSA, FL	H	21.43 AE	31.06 MW	38.09 AEX	FLBLS	7/16-9/16
	Tampa-St. Petersburg-Clearwater MSA, FL	H	21.62 AE	34.74 MW	41.16 AEX	FLBLS	7/16-9/16
	Georgia	Y	60050 FQ	72540 MW	85590 TQ	USBLS	5/15
	Atlanta-Sandy Springs-Roswell MSA, GA	Y	55740 FQ	72750 MW	87310 TQ	USBLS	5/15
	Augusta-Richmond County MSA, GA-SC	Y	46620 FQ	68320 MW	86960 TQ	USBLS	5/15
	Hawaii	Y	65720 FQ	73690 MW	81180 TQ	USBLS	5/15
	Urban Honolulu MSA, HI	Y	66140 FQ	73710 MW	80970 TQ	USBLS	5/15
	Idaho	Y	52500 FQ	59160 MW	74400 TQ	USBLS	5/15
	Boise City MSA, ID	Y	54040 FQ	58390 MW	70190 TQ	USBLS	5/15
	Illinois	Y	51640 FQ	72600 MW	89740 TQ	USBLS	5/15
	Chicago-Naperville-Arlington Heights PMSA, IL	Y	48160 FQ	71760 MW	88850 TQ	USBLS	5/15
	Lake County-Kenosha County PMSA, IL-WI	Y	72740 FQ	92760 MW	112910 TQ	USBLS	5/15
	Indiana	Y	45920 FQ	60520 MW	76240 TQ	USBLS	5/15
	Gary PMSA, IN	Y	46120 FQ	58130 MW	77390 TQ	USBLS	5/15
	Indianapolis-Carmel-Anderson MSA, IN	Y	45940 FQ	61930 MW	76620 TQ	USBLS	5/15
	Iowa	Y	52110 FQ	65460 MW	77220 TQ	USBLS	5/15
	Des Moines-West Des Moines MSA, IA	Y	48950 FQ	65010 MW	76820 TQ	USBLS	5/15
	Kansas	Y	45520 FQ	55250 MW	74180 TQ	USBLS	5/15
	Wichita MSA, KS	Y	45570 FQ	58560 MW	79550 TQ	USBLS	5/15
	Kentucky	Y	48470 FQ	64850 MW	81900 TQ	USBLS	5/15
	Louisville-Jefferson County MSA, KY-IN	Y	45340 FQ	61470 MW	88070 TQ	USBLS	5/15
	Louisiana	Y	54340 FQ	72030 MW	91260 TQ	USBLS	5/15
	Baton Rouge MSA, LA	Y	65950 FQ	78020 MW	103690 TQ	USBLS	5/15
	New Orleans-Metairie MSA, LA	Y	52550 FQ	69970 MW	87170 TQ	USBLS	5/15
	Maine	Y	48410 FQ	64020 MW	81890 TQ	USBLS	5/15
	Portland-South Portland MSA, ME	Y	40850 FQ	63580 MW	75230 TQ	USBLS	5/15
	Maryland	Y	49994 AE	86907 MW	105364 AEX	MDBLS	4/16
	Baltimore-Columbia-Towson MSA, MD	Y	55860 FQ	73210 MW	93860 TQ	USBLS	5/15
	Salisbury MSA, MD-DE	Y	50970 FQ	74600 MW	92680 TQ	USBLS	5/15
	Massachusetts	Y	60330 FQ	74260 MW	91540 TQ	USBLS	5/15
	Boston-Cambridge-Newton NECTA, MA	Y	63660 FQ	76700 MW	95140 TQ	USBLS	5/15
	Worcester MSA, MA-CT	Y	52050 FQ	62760 MW	81760 TQ	USBLS	5/15
	Michigan	Y	58420 FQ	72550 MW	87390 TQ	USBLS	5/15
	Detroit-Dearborn-Livonia PMSA, MI	Y	66970 FQ	79240 MW	95270 TQ	USBLS	5/15
	Grand Rapids-Wyoming MSA, MI	Y	56060 FQ	69580 MW	78640 TQ	USBLS	5/15
	Minnesota	Y	60574 FQ	74808 MW	89374 TQ	MNBLS	1/16-3/16
	Minneapolis-St. Paul-Bloomington MSA, MN-WI	Y	63306 FQ	78023 MW	94505 TQ	MNBLS	1/16-3/16
	Mississippi	Y	53240 FQ	68230 MW	84240 TQ	USBLS	5/15
	Jackson MSA, MS	Y	55790 FQ	78300 MW	91260 TQ	USBLS	5/15
	Missouri	Y	51220 FQ	62140 MW	81690 TQ	USBLS	5/15
	Kansas City MSA, MO-KS	Y	56730 FQ	68680 MW	85610 TQ	USBLS	5/15
	St. Louis MSA, MO-IL	Y	50280 FQ	63550 MW	85540 TQ	USBLS	5/15
	Montana	Y	45200 FQ	59050 MW	78240 TQ	USBLS	5/15
	Billings MSA, MT	Y	45820 FQ	65850 MW	92820 TQ	USBLS	5/15
	Nebraska	Y	49545 FQ	63325 MW	77890 TQ	NEBLS	7/16-9/16
	Omaha-Council Bluffs MSA, NE-IA	Y	55505 FQ	70190 MW	81525 TQ	NEBLS	7/16-9/16
	Nevada	Y	55550 FQ	71100 MW	85570 TQ	USBLS	5/15
	Las Vegas-Henderson-Paradise MSA, NV	Y	50520 FQ	67220 MW	81900 TQ	USBLS	5/15
	New Hampshire	H	27.13 AE	36.70 MW	42.77 AEX	NHBLS	6/16
	Manchester NECTA, NH	H	24.32 AE	37.53 MW	40.60 AEX	NHBLS	6/16
	Nashua NECTA, NH-MA	Y	58160 FQ	72470 MW	96830 TQ	USBLS	5/15
	New Jersey	Y	63380 FQ	80090 MW	94250 TQ	USBLS	5/15
	Camden PMSA, NJ	Y	47100 FQ	67600 MW	81410 TQ	USBLS	5/15

AE	Average entry wage	AWR	Average wage range	H	Hourly
AEX	Average experienced wage	B	Biweekly	HI	Highest wage paid
ATC	Average total compensation	D	Daily	HR	High end range
AW	Average wage paid	FQ	First quartile wage	LO	Lowest wage paid

LR	Low end range	MTC	Median total compensation
M	Monthly	MW	Median wage paid
MCC	Median cash compensation	MWR	Median wage range
ME	Median entry wage	S	See annotated source

TCC	Total cash compensation		
TQ	Third quartile wage		
W	Weekly		
Y	Yearly		

Occupation/Type/Industry	Location	Per	Low	Mid	High	Source	Date
Occupational Health and Safety Specialist	Newark PMSA, NJ-PA	Y	62660 FQ	82480 MW	97470 TQ	USBLS	5/15
	Trenton MSA, NJ	Y	69410 FQ	84180 MW	94360 TQ	USBLS	5/15
	New Mexico	Y	52810 FQ	70490 MW	90030 TQ	USBLS	5/15
	Albuquerque MSA, NM	Y	57140 FQ	77220 MW	94590 TQ	USBLS	5/15
	New York	Y	47630 AE	71210 MW	85620 AEX	NYBLS	1/16-3/16
	Buffalo-Cheektowaga-Niagara Falls MSA, NY	Y	50670 FQ	60700 MW	77440 TQ	USBLS	5/15
	Nassau County-Suffolk County PMSA, NY	Y	63560 FQ	74110 MW	89020 TQ	USBLS	5/15
	New York-Jersey City-White Plains PMSA, NY-NJ	Y	59020 FQ	77140 MW	97320 TQ	USBLS	5/15
	Rochester MSA, NY	Y	45460 FQ	55640 MW	73270 TQ	USBLS	5/15
	North Carolina	Y	49110 FQ	62630 MW	78550 TQ	USBLS	5/15
	Charlotte-Concord-Gastonia MSA, NC-SC	Y	48270 FQ	63830 MW	84600 TQ	USBLS	5/15
	Raleigh MSA, NC	Y	50720 FQ	59030 MW	72980 TQ	USBLS	5/15
	North Dakota	Y	65940 FQ	76370 MW	94210 TQ	USBLS	5/15
	Ohio	Y	54600 FQ	69560 MW	82630 TQ	USBLS	5/15
	Cincinnati MSA, OH-KY-IN	Y	55550 FQ	68710 MW	86690 TQ	USBLS	5/15
	Cleveland-Elyria MSA, OH	Y	53740 FQ	72080 MW	88410 TQ	USBLS	5/15
	Columbus MSA, OH	Y	56350 FQ	70260 MW	79340 TQ	USBLS	5/15
	Oklahoma	Y	48530 FQ	64190 MW	82730 TQ	USBLS	5/15
	Oklahoma City MSA, OK	Y	49240 FQ	64930 MW	84240 TQ	USBLS	5/15
	Tulsa MSA, OK	Y	51220 FQ	64820 MW	79670 TQ	USBLS	5/15
	Oregon	H	27.05 FQ	32.73 MW	38.79 TQ	ORBLS	2016
	Portland-Vancouver-Hillsboro MSA, OR-WA	Y	55630 FQ	68370 MW	81690 TQ	USBLS	5/15
	Pennsylvania	Y	52790 FQ	67970 MW	83540 TQ	USBLS	5/15
	Allentown-Bethlehem-Easton MSA, PA-NJ	Y	54330 FQ	69580 MW	80430 TQ	USBLS	5/15
	Harrisburg-Carlisle MSA, PA	Y	54130 FQ	65450 MW	77170 TQ	USBLS	5/15
	Montgomery County-Bucks County-Chester County PMSA, PA	Y	43830 FQ	61280 MW	82320 TQ	USBLS	5/15
	Philadelphia PMSA, PA	Y	54170 FQ	65080 MW	80490 TQ	USBLS	5/15
	Pittsburgh MSA, PA	Y	56120 FQ	71850 MW	88350 TQ	USBLS	5/15
	Rhode Island	Y	66150 FQ	84890 MW	96640 TQ	USBLS	5/15
	Providence-Warwick MSA, RI-MA	Y	58220 FQ	79110 MW	93750 TQ	USBLS	5/15
	South Carolina	Y	36290 FQ	46720 MW	67180 TQ	USBLS	5/15
	Charleston-North Charleston MSA, SC	Y	34430 FQ	54190 MW	74020 TQ	USBLS	5/15
	Columbia MSA, SC	Y	39130 FQ	45700 MW	68320 TQ	USBLS	5/15
	Greenville-Anderson-Mauldin MSA, SC	Y	35790 FQ	44170 MW	63310 TQ	USBLS	5/15
	South Dakota	Y	48590 FQ	59290 MW	73720 TQ	USBLS	5/15
	Tennessee	Y	50600 FQ	68180 MW	82340 TQ	USBLS	5/15
	Knoxville MSA, TN	Y	53780 FQ	72900 MW	96270 TQ	USBLS	5/15
	Memphis MSA, TN-MS-AR	Y	48040 FQ	70730 MW	86520 TQ	USBLS	5/15
	Nashville-Davidson–Murfreesboro–Franklin MSA, TN	Y	53450 FQ	64820 MW	76010 TQ	USBLS	5/15
	Texas	Y	53250 FQ	70910 MW	90960 TQ	USBLS	5/15
	Austin-Round Rock MSA, TX	Y	53700 FQ	67650 MW	79980 TQ	USBLS	5/15
	Dallas-Plano-Irving PMSA, TX	Y	56320 FQ	70250 MW	86380 TQ	USBLS	5/15
	Fort Worth-Arlington PMSA, TX	Y	56280 FQ	69770 MW	85380 TQ	USBLS	5/15
	Houston-The Woodlands-Sugar Land MSA, TX	Y	58370 FQ	78850 MW	98950 TQ	USBLS	5/15
	San Antonio-New Braunfels MSA, TX	Y	29560 FQ	53180 MW	72830 TQ	USBLS	5/15
	Utah	Y	51890 FQ	65300 MW	79540 TQ	USBLS	5/15
	Ogden-Clearfield MSA, UT	Y	52800 FQ	66370 MW	77610 TQ	USBLS	5/15
	Provo-Orem MSA, UT	Y	51350 FQ	59950 MW	75100 TQ	USBLS	5/15
	Salt Lake City MSA, UT	Y	52130 FQ	65390 MW	79450 TQ	USBLS	5/15
	Vermont	Y	50390 FQ	66960 MW	80450 TQ	USBLS	5/15
	Burlington-South Burlington MSA, VT	Y	56030 FQ	71950 MW	84720 TQ	USBLS	5/15
	Virginia	Y	47210 FQ	61760 MW	79150 TQ	USBLS	5/15
	Richmond MSA, VA	Y	45430 FQ	58320 MW	69690 TQ	USBLS	5/15

AE	Average entry wage	AWR	Average wage range	H	Hourly	LR	Low end range	MTC	Median total compensation	TCC	Total cash compensation
AEX	Average experienced wage	B	Biweekly	HI	Highest wage paid	M	Monthly	MW	Median wage paid	TQ	Third quartile wage
ATC	Average total compensation	D	Daily	HR	High end range	MCC	Median cash compensation	MWR	Median wage range	W	Weekly
AW	Average wage paid	FQ	First quartile wage	LO	Lowest wage paid	ME	Median entry wage	S	See annotated source	Y	Yearly

1117

Occupation/Type/Industry	Location	Per	Low	Mid	High	Source	Date
Occupational Health and Safety Specialist							
	Virginia Beach-Norfolk-Newport News MSA, VA-NC	Y	48420 FQ	66350 MW	79550 TQ	USBLS	5/15
	Washington	H	29.26 FQ	36.63 MW	44.85 TQ	WABLS	3/16
	Seattle-Bellevue-Everett PMSA, WA	H	30.48 FQ	38.68 MW	47.05 TQ	WABLS	3/16
	Tacoma-Lakewood PMSA, WA	H	29.87 FQ	35.44 MW	42.16 TQ	WABLS	3/16
	West Virginia	Y	61310 FQ	74880 MW	84520 TQ	USBLS	5/15
	Huntington-Ashland MSA, WV-KY-OH	Y	48370 FQ	67440 MW	77210 TQ	USBLS	5/15
	Wisconsin	Y	53060 FQ	66340 MW	79540 TQ	USBLS	5/15
	Madison MSA, WI	Y	54290 FQ	68280 MW	82820 TQ	USBLS	5/15
	Milwaukee-Waukesha-West Allis MSA, WI	Y	62930 FQ	73130 MW	85880 TQ	USBLS	5/15
	Wyoming	Y	55770 FQ	70430 MW	89920 TQ	USBLS	5/15
	Cheyenne MSA, WY	Y	59130 FQ	64440 MW	77080 TQ	USBLS	5/15
	Puerto Rico	Y	27080 FQ	36120 MW	48420 TQ	USBLS	5/15
	San Juan-Carolina-Caguas MSA, PR	Y	26440 FQ	34890 MW	45990 TQ	USBLS	5/15
	Guam	Y	39480 FQ	47290 MW	59420 TQ	USBLS	5/15
Occupational Health and Safety Technician							
	Alabama	Y	25565 AE	47042 AW	57785 AEX	ALBLS	6/16
	Birmingham-Hoover MSA, AL	Y	24698 AE	43342 AW	52668 AEX	ALBLS	6/16
	Alaska	Y	53240 FQ	69040 MW	82220 TQ	USBLS	5/15
	Anchorage MSA, AK	Y	52100 FQ	68060 MW	84350 TQ	USBLS	5/15
	Arizona	Y	36640 FQ	45720 MW	59260 TQ	USBLS	5/15
	Phoenix-Mesa-Scottsdale MSA, AZ	Y	36850 FQ	46930 MW	61950 TQ	USBLS	5/15
	Arkansas	Y	29310 FQ	41710 MW	60210 TQ	USBLS	5/15
	Little Rock-North Little Rock-Conway MSA, AR	Y	43900 FQ	59080 MW	79880 TQ	USBLS	5/15
	California	H	18.51 FQ	25.40 MW	31.87 TQ	CABLS	1/16-3/16
	Anaheim-Santa Ana-Irvine PMSA, CA	H	25.11 FQ	30.46 MW	38.74 TQ	CABLS	1/16-3/16
	Los Angeles-Long Beach-Glendale PMSA, CA	H	17.41 FQ	19.70 MW	27.62 TQ	CABLS	1/16-3/16
	Oakland-Hayward-Berkeley PMSA, CA	H	18.79 FQ	26.23 MW	40.12 TQ	CABLS	1/16-3/16
	Riverside-San Bernardino-Ontario MSA, CA	H	23.65 FQ	28.79 MW	34.16 TQ	CABLS	1/16-3/16
	Sacramento–Roseville–Arden-Arcade MSA, CA	H	25.51 FQ	28.00 MW	30.48 TQ	CABLS	1/16-3/16
	San Diego-Carlsbad MSA, CA	H	21.28 FQ	25.87 MW	31.95 TQ	CABLS	1/16-3/16
	San Francisco-Redwood City-South San Francisco PMSA, CA	H	18.14 FQ	24.96 MW	34.31 TQ	CABLS	1/16-3/16
	Colorado	Y	50180 FQ	58180 MW	70270 TQ	USBLS	5/15
	Denver-Aurora-Lakewood MSA, CO	Y	50020 FQ	55890 MW	61850 TQ	USBLS	5/15
	Connecticut	Y		55229 MW		CTBLS	1/16-3/16
	Hartford-West Hartford-East Hartford MSA, CT	Y	53890 FQ	63390 MW	72910 TQ	USBLS	5/15
	Delaware	Y	36620 FQ	51400 MW	65800 TQ	USBLS	5/15
	Wilmington PMSA, DE-MD-NJ	Y	33820 FQ	50910 MW	65930 TQ	USBLS	5/15
	Washington-Arlington-Alexandria PMSA, DC-VA-MD-WV	Y	49260 FQ	74490 MW	95980 TQ	USBLS	5/15
	Florida	H	15.92 AE	22.49 MW	29.91 AEX	FLBLS	7/16-9/16
	Fort Lauderdale-Pompano Beach-Deerfield Beach PMSA, FL	H	16.82 AE	22.63 MW	27.19 AEX	FLBLS	7/16-9/16
	Miami-Miami Beach-Kendall PMSA, FL	H	18.84 AE	22.15 MW	24.42 AEX	FLBLS	7/16-9/16
	Orlando-Kissimmee-Sanford MSA, FL	H	18.82 AE	21.89 MW	23.38 AEX	FLBLS	7/16-9/16
	Tampa-St. Petersburg-Clearwater MSA, FL	H	14.02 AE	22.24 MW	29.76 AEX	FLBLS	7/16-9/16
	Georgia	Y	32680 FQ	44080 MW	58860 TQ	USBLS	5/15

AE	Average entry wage	**AWR** Average wage range	**H** Hourly	**LR** Low end range	**MTC** Median total compensation	**TCC** Total cash compensation
AEX	Average experienced wage	**B** Biweekly	**HI** Highest wage paid	**M** Monthly	**MW** Median wage paid	**TQ** Third quartile wage
ATC	Average total compensation	**D** Daily	**HR** High end range	**MCC** Median cash compensation	**MWR** Median wage range	**W** Weekly
AW	Average wage paid	**FQ** First quartile wage	**LO** Lowest wage paid	**ME** Median entry wage	**S** See annotated source	**Y** Yearly

Occupation/Type/Industry	Location	Per	Low	Mid	High	Source	Date
Occupational Health and Safety Technician							
	Atlanta-Sandy Springs-Roswell MSA, GA	Y	33010 FQ	43430 MW	60250 TQ	USBLS	5/15
	Hawaii	Y	42420 FQ	45930 MW	49430 TQ	USBLS	5/15
	Urban Honolulu MSA, HI	Y	42500 FQ	45980 MW	49450 TQ	USBLS	5/15
	Idaho	Y	32650 FQ	39820 MW	56020 TQ	USBLS	5/15
	Illinois	Y	42400 FQ	62160 MW	78210 TQ	USBLS	5/15
	Chicago-Naperville-Arlington Heights PMSA, IL	Y	41540 FQ	66600 MW	79680 TQ	USBLS	5/15
	Indiana	Y	29530 FQ	36970 MW	45340 TQ	USBLS	5/15
	Gary PMSA, IN	Y	35630 FQ	40900 MW	46280 TQ	USBLS	5/15
	Indianapolis-Carmel-Anderson MSA, IN	Y	35010 FQ	40290 MW	50920 TQ	USBLS	5/15
	Iowa	Y	40010 FQ	51150 MW	65010 TQ	USBLS	5/15
	Davenport-Moline-Rock Island MSA, IA-IL	Y	48560 FQ	62160 MW	71460 TQ	USBLS	5/15
	Des Moines-West Des Moines MSA, IA	Y	39900 FQ	47850 MW	56870 TQ	USBLS	5/15
	Kansas	Y	38500 FQ	45960 MW	57880 TQ	USBLS	5/15
	Kentucky	Y	37390 FQ	46830 MW	58980 TQ	USBLS	5/15
	Louisville-Jefferson County MSA, KY-IN	Y	31250 FQ	43360 MW	54370 TQ	USBLS	5/15
	Louisiana	Y	38000 FQ	53760 MW	67970 TQ	USBLS	5/15
	New Orleans-Metairie MSA, LA	Y	23920 FQ	30680 MW	46590 TQ	USBLS	5/15
	Maine	Y	33120 FQ	40840 MW	53410 TQ	USBLS	5/15
	Maryland	Y	30956 AE	49201 MW	58323 AEX	MDBLS	4/16
	Baltimore-Columbia-Towson MSA, MD	Y	44270 FQ	56550 MW	67580 TQ	USBLS	5/15
	Massachusetts	Y	46580 FQ	58560 MW	72950 TQ	USBLS	5/15
	Boston-Cambridge-Newton NECTA, MA	Y	49650 FQ	62150 MW	76060 TQ	USBLS	5/15
	Michigan	Y	37610 FQ	45690 MW	58320 TQ	USBLS	5/15
	Minnesota	Y	40695 FQ	50423 MW	60876 TQ	MNBLS	1/16-3/16
	Minneapolis-St. Paul-Bloomington MSA, MN-WI	Y	43840 FQ	52026 MW	62368 TQ	MNBLS	1/16-3/16
	Mississippi	Y	23140 FQ	34360 MW	44010 TQ	USBLS	5/15
	Missouri	Y	34890 FQ	39780 MW	52020 TQ	USBLS	5/15
	Kansas City MSA, MO-KS	Y	39650 FQ	48840 MW	61540 TQ	USBLS	5/15
	St. Louis MSA, MO-IL	Y	38990 FQ	47950 MW	58560 TQ	USBLS	5/15
	Montana	Y	48060 FQ	55980 MW	62070 TQ	USBLS	5/15
	Nebraska	Y	44420 FQ	61880 MW	72590 TQ	NEBLS	7/16-9/16
	Omaha-Council Bluffs MSA, NE-IA	Y	55045 FQ	67685 MW	75760 TQ	NEBLS	7/16-9/16
	Nevada	Y	46730 FQ	62280 MW	74320 TQ	USBLS	5/15
	Las Vegas-Henderson-Paradise MSA, NV	Y	41010 FQ	53910 MW	70010 TQ	USBLS	5/15
	New Hampshire	H	17.69 AE	23.58 MW	26.93 AEX	NHBLS	6/16
	New Jersey	Y	42010 FQ	54350 MW	68980 TQ	USBLS	5/15
	Newark PMSA, NJ-PA	Y	46430 FQ	55270 MW	65210 TQ	USBLS	5/15
	New Mexico	Y	36240 FQ	51440 MW	76100 TQ	USBLS	5/15
	New York	Y	44210 AE	56410 MW	62220 AEX	NYBLS	1/16-3/16
	New York-Jersey City-White Plains PMSA, NY-NJ	Y	50760 FQ	56750 MW	62730 TQ	USBLS	5/15
	Rochester MSA, NY	Y	36230 FQ	53100 MW	60090 TQ	USBLS	5/15
	North Carolina	Y	40810 FQ	48550 MW	57970 TQ	USBLS	5/15
	Charlotte-Concord-Gastonia MSA, NC-SC	Y	41110 FQ	48750 MW	55140 TQ	USBLS	5/15
	Raleigh MSA, NC	Y	42490 FQ	48750 MW	58980 TQ	USBLS	5/15
	North Dakota	Y	41520 FQ	47960 MW	68610 TQ	USBLS	5/15
	Ohio	Y	41690 FQ	51500 MW	61920 TQ	USBLS	5/15
	Cincinnati MSA, OH-KY-IN	Y	46930 FQ	55140 MW	63840 TQ	USBLS	5/15
	Cleveland-Elyria MSA, OH	Y	44880 FQ	58230 MW	69180 TQ	USBLS	5/15
	Columbus MSA, OH	Y	38160 FQ	48170 MW	63640 TQ	USBLS	5/15
	Oklahoma	Y	33570 FQ	38350 MW	50620 TQ	USBLS	5/15
	Oklahoma City MSA, OK	Y	33010 FQ	36860 MW	44120 TQ	USBLS	5/15
	Tulsa MSA, OK	Y	33070 FQ	37060 MW	56420 TQ	USBLS	5/15
	Oregon	H	19.28 FQ	27.19 MW	34.53 TQ	ORBLS	2016
	Portland-Vancouver-Hillsboro MSA, OR-WA	Y	38650 FQ	55770 MW	69790 TQ	USBLS	5/15
	Pennsylvania	Y	35350 FQ	44910 MW	55280 TQ	USBLS	5/15

AE Average entry wage	**AWR** Average wage range	**H** Hourly	**LR** Low end range	**MTC** Median total compensation	**TCC** Total cash compensation
AEX Average experienced wage	**B** Biweekly	**HI** Highest wage paid	**M** Monthly	**MW** Median wage paid	**TQ** Third quartile wage
ATC Average total compensation	**D** Daily	**HR** High end range	**MCC** Median cash compensation	**MWR** Median wage range	**W** Weekly
AW Average wage paid	**FQ** First quartile wage	**LO** Lowest wage paid	**ME** Median entry wage	**S** See annotated source	**Y** Yearly

Occupation/Type/Industry	Location	Per	Low	Mid	High	Source	Date
Occupational Health and Safety Technician	Allentown-Bethlehem-Easton MSA, PA-NJ	Y	39330 FQ	44930 MW	55590 TQ	USBLS	5/15
	Montgomery County-Bucks County-Chester County PMSA, PA	Y	44920 FQ	52690 MW	58960 TQ	USBLS	5/15
	Philadelphia PMSA, PA	Y	32450 FQ	35900 MW	40260 TQ	USBLS	5/15
	Pittsburgh MSA, PA	Y	23640 FQ	40600 MW	52380 TQ	USBLS	5/15
	Rhode Island	Y	52190 FQ	60640 MW	71680 TQ	USBLS	5/15
	Providence-Warwick MSA, RI-MA	Y	51960 FQ	60730 MW	72360 TQ	USBLS	5/15
	South Carolina	Y	33670 FQ	50180 MW	65070 TQ	USBLS	5/15
	Tennessee	Y	38350 FQ	51180 MW	65090 TQ	USBLS	5/15
	Knoxville MSA, TN	Y	37450 FQ	58130 MW	72010 TQ	USBLS	5/15
	Memphis MSA, TN-MS-AR	Y	44250 FQ	53810 MW	60470 TQ	USBLS	5/15
	Nashville-Davidson–Murfreesboro–Franklin MSA, TN	Y	35140 FQ	42400 MW	50730 TQ	USBLS	5/15
	Texas	Y	34430 FQ	42960 MW	55590 TQ	USBLS	5/15
	Austin-Round Rock MSA, TX	Y	45110 FQ	52660 MW	59950 TQ	USBLS	5/15
	Dallas-Plano-Irving PMSA, TX	Y	38670 FQ	46600 MW	56560 TQ	USBLS	5/15
	Fort Worth-Arlington PMSA, TX	Y	40580 FQ	47320 MW	56140 TQ	USBLS	5/15
	Houston-The Woodlands-Sugar Land MSA, TX	Y	33360 FQ	41010 MW	57040 TQ	USBLS	5/15
	San Antonio-New Braunfels MSA, TX	Y	34910 FQ	41470 MW	49710 TQ	USBLS	5/15
	Utah	Y	38280 FQ	47080 MW	69150 TQ	USBLS	5/15
	Salt Lake City MSA, UT	Y	39810 FQ	47810 MW	83320 TQ	USBLS	5/15
	Virginia	Y	41930 FQ	52050 MW	76260 TQ	USBLS	5/15
	Richmond MSA, VA	Y	38040 FQ	50370 MW	72060 TQ	USBLS	5/15
	Virginia Beach-Norfolk-Newport News MSA, VA-NC	Y	42320 FQ	50660 MW	62330 TQ	USBLS	5/15
	Washington	H	16.77 FQ	23.28 MW	37.99 TQ	WABLS	3/16
	Seattle-Bellevue-Everett PMSA, WA	H	24.98 FQ	30.91 MW	42.79 TQ	WABLS	3/16
	Tacoma-Lakewood PMSA, WA	H	16.57 FQ	18.00 MW	19.21 TQ	WABLS	3/16
	West Virginia	Y	40120 FQ	47060 MW	61880 TQ	USBLS	5/15
	Wisconsin	Y	36860 FQ	46690 MW	60420 TQ	USBLS	5/15
	Madison MSA, WI	Y	38580 FQ	48460 MW	59870 TQ	USBLS	5/15
	Milwaukee-Waukesha-West Allis MSA, WI	Y	44250 FQ	54480 MW	63550 TQ	USBLS	5/15
	Wyoming	Y	33950 FQ	40530 MW	57360 TQ	USBLS	5/15
	Puerto Rico	Y	20450 FQ	24890 MW	31250 TQ	USBLS	5/15
	San Juan-Carolina-Caguas MSA, PR	Y	19970 FQ	23890 MW	31120 TQ	USBLS	5/15
Occupational Health Nurse Airport, Municipal Government	Los Angeles, CA	Y			87234 HI	CACIT	6/23/16
Occupational Therapist	Alabama	Y	57052 AE	81199 AW	93268 AEX	ALBLS	6/16
	Birmingham-Hoover MSA, AL	Y	57949 AE	84104 AW	97182 AEX	ALBLS	6/16
	Alaska	Y	68580 FQ	83430 MW	96440 TQ	USBLS	5/15
	Anchorage MSA, AK	Y	66590 FQ	81840 MW	95810 TQ	USBLS	5/15
	Arizona	Y	66640 FQ	82360 MW	97110 TQ	USBLS	5/15
	Phoenix-Mesa-Scottsdale MSA, AZ	Y	69650 FQ	85750 MW	100160 TQ	USBLS	5/15
	Tucson MSA, AZ	Y	65040 FQ	78350 MW	91340 TQ	USBLS	5/15
	Arkansas	Y	66630 FQ	83650 MW	101630 TQ	USBLS	5/15
	Little Rock-North Little Rock-Conway MSA, AR	Y	66670 FQ	82080 MW	104720 TQ	USBLS	5/15
	California	H	36.58 FQ	44.71 MW	52.65 TQ	CABLS	1/16-3/16
	Anaheim-Santa Ana-Irvine PMSA, CA	H	36.80 FQ	44.23 MW	52.46 TQ	CABLS	1/16-3/16
	Los Angeles-Long Beach-Glendale PMSA, CA	H	36.86 FQ	44.33 MW	51.99 TQ	CABLS	1/16-3/16
	Oakland-Hayward-Berkeley PMSA, CA	H	35.22 FQ	44.06 MW	50.99 TQ	CABLS	1/16-3/16
	Riverside-San Bernardino-Ontario MSA, CA	H	38.22 FQ	45.82 MW	54.13 TQ	CABLS	1/16-3/16
	Sacramento–Roseville–Arden-Arcade MSA, CA	H	42.58 FQ	47.52 MW	54.54 TQ	CABLS	1/16-3/16

AE	Average entry wage	AWR	Average wage range	H	Hourly
AEX	Average experienced wage	B	Biweekly	HI	Highest wage paid
ATC	Average total compensation	D	Daily	HR	High end range
AW	Average wage paid	FQ	First quartile wage	LO	Lowest wage paid

LR	Low end range	MTC	Median total compensation	TCC	Total cash compensation
M	Monthly	MW	Median wage paid	TQ	Third quartile wage
MCC	Median cash compensation	MWR	Median wage range	W	Weekly
ME	Median entry wage	S	See annotated source	Y	Yearly

Occupation/Type/Industry	Location	Per	Low	Mid	High	Source	Date
Occupational Therapist	San Diego-Carlsbad MSA, CA	H	38.46 FQ	46.36 MW	55.39 TQ	CABLS	1/16-3/16
	San Francisco-Redwood City-South San Francisco PMSA, CA	H	38.70 FQ	49.06 MW	57.06 TQ	CABLS	1/16-3/16
	Colorado	Y	67560 FQ	80020 MW	94950 TQ	USBLS	5/15
	Denver-Aurora-Lakewood MSA, CO	Y	68080 FQ	80830 MW	94570 TQ	USBLS	5/15
	Fort Collins MSA, CO	Y	65890 FQ	75850 MW	91150 TQ	USBLS	5/15
	Connecticut	Y		87530 MW		CTBLS	1/16-3/16
	Bridgeport-Stamford-Norwalk MSA, CT	Y	76890 FQ	96560 MW	119550 TQ	USBLS	5/15
	Hartford-West Hartford-East Hartford MSA, CT	Y	70200 FQ	81880 MW	95020 TQ	USBLS	5/15
	Delaware	Y	69340 FQ	80090 MW	97120 TQ	USBLS	5/15
	Wilmington PMSA, DE-MD-NJ	Y	72110 FQ	85550 MW	102600 TQ	USBLS	5/15
	District of Columbia	Y	72730 FQ	86050 MW	100900 TQ	USBLS	5/15
	Washington-Arlington-Alexandria PMSA, DC-VA-MD-WV	Y	77220 FQ	92140 MW	110230 TQ	USBLS	5/15
	Florida	H	30.86 AE	41.27 MW	47.74 AEX	FLBLS	7/16-9/16
	Fort Lauderdale-Pompano Beach-Deerfield Beach PMSA, FL	H	39.56 AE	47.48 MW	53.63 AEX	FLBLS	7/16-9/16
	Miami-Miami Beach-Kendall PMSA, FL	H	30.95 AE	38.14 MW	42.37 AEX	FLBLS	7/16-9/16
	Orlando-Kissimmee-Sanford MSA, FL	H	29.97 AE	39.32 MW	43.29 AEX	FLBLS	7/16-9/16
	Tampa-St. Petersburg-Clearwater MSA, FL	H	31.57 AE	38.32 MW	42.54 AEX	FLBLS	7/16-9/16
	Georgia	Y	69380 FQ	80710 MW	93760 TQ	USBLS	5/15
	Atlanta-Sandy Springs-Roswell MSA, GA	Y	70110 FQ	81320 MW	92280 TQ	USBLS	5/15
	Augusta-Richmond County MSA, GA-SC	Y	56010 FQ	72240 MW	87800 TQ	USBLS	5/15
	Hawaii	Y	69450 FQ	80190 MW	89750 TQ	USBLS	5/15
	Urban Honolulu MSA, HI	Y	70660 FQ	81120 MW	90010 TQ	USBLS	5/15
	Idaho	Y	54840 FQ	71220 MW	82190 TQ	USBLS	5/15
	Boise City MSA, ID	Y	50040 FQ	69540 MW	79660 TQ	USBLS	5/15
	Illinois	Y	66080 FQ	79070 MW	97540 TQ	USBLS	5/15
	Chicago-Naperville-Arlington Heights PMSA, IL	Y	67100 FQ	80240 MW	97920 TQ	USBLS	5/15
	Lake County-Kenosha County PMSA, IL-WI	Y	67760 FQ	85200 MW	109180 TQ	USBLS	5/15
	Indiana	Y	62770 FQ	76140 MW	91920 TQ	USBLS	5/15
	Gary PMSA, IN	Y	65430 FQ	83050 MW	100720 TQ	USBLS	5/15
	Indianapolis-Carmel-Anderson MSA, IN	Y	62940 FQ	77050 MW	91530 TQ	USBLS	5/15
	Iowa	Y	63370 FQ	73130 MW	84570 TQ	USBLS	5/15
	Des Moines-West Des Moines MSA, IA	Y	64470 FQ	76370 MW	89360 TQ	USBLS	5/15
	Kansas	Y	67560 FQ	78770 MW	92850 TQ	USBLS	5/15
	Wichita MSA, KS	Y	67170 FQ	82580 MW	97030 TQ	USBLS	5/15
	Kentucky	Y	67170 FQ	80070 MW	92660 TQ	USBLS	5/15
	Louisville-Jefferson County MSA, KY-IN	Y	67550 FQ	80150 MW	92970 TQ	USBLS	5/15
	Louisiana	Y	62440 FQ	76500 MW	94650 TQ	USBLS	5/15
	Baton Rouge MSA, LA	Y	62700 FQ	82680 MW	101020 TQ	USBLS	5/15
	New Orleans-Metairie MSA, LA	Y	63120 FQ	74150 MW	87330 TQ	USBLS	5/15
	Maine	Y	54080 FQ	64420 MW	77320 TQ	USBLS	5/15
	Portland-South Portland MSA, ME	Y	54520 FQ	64040 MW	78380 TQ	USBLS	5/15
	Maryland	Y	59439 AE	83410 MW	95395 AEX	MDBLS	4/16
	Baltimore-Columbia-Towson MSA, MD	Y	63430 FQ	80220 MW	97340 TQ	USBLS	5/15
	Salisbury MSA, MD-DE	Y	73990 FQ	87490 MW	100570 TQ	USBLS	5/15
	Massachusetts	Y	68030 FQ	84070 MW	98190 TQ	USBLS	5/15
	Boston-Cambridge-Newton NECTA, MA	Y	72210 FQ	87490 MW	101450 TQ	USBLS	5/15
	Worcester MSA, MA-CT	Y	59590 FQ	73720 MW	90790 TQ	USBLS	5/15
	Michigan	Y	60370 FQ	71310 MW	83090 TQ	USBLS	5/15

Occupation/Type/Industry	Location	Per	Low	Mid	High	Source	Date
Occupational Therapist	Detroit-Dearborn-Livonia PMSA, MI	Y	61230 FQ	72260 MW	85090 TQ	USBLS	5/15
	Grand Rapids-Wyoming MSA, MI	Y	58480 FQ	68810 MW	77770 TQ	USBLS	5/15
	Minnesota	Y	63558 FQ	72106 MW	80382 TQ	MNBLS	1/16-3/16
	Minneapolis-St. Paul-Bloomington MSA, MN-WI	Y	63840 FQ	72338 MW	80735 TQ	MNBLS	1/16-3/16
	Mississippi	Y	68770 FQ	83800 MW	96600 TQ	USBLS	5/15
	Jackson MSA, MS	Y	66520 FQ	84200 MW	93670 TQ	USBLS	5/15
	Missouri	Y	62160 FQ	73520 MW	88350 TQ	USBLS	5/15
	Kansas City MSA, MO-KS	Y	65310 FQ	73700 MW	84220 TQ	USBLS	5/15
	St. Louis MSA, MO-IL	Y	57500 FQ	70270 MW	84300 TQ	USBLS	5/15
	Montana	Y	57150 FQ	68880 MW	80160 TQ	USBLS	5/15
	Billings MSA, MT	Y	55300 FQ	66770 MW	79690 TQ	USBLS	5/15
	Nebraska	Y	59715 FQ	72195 MW	88315 TQ	NEBLS	7/16-9/16
	Omaha-Council Bluffs MSA, NE-IA	Y	58890 FQ	71260 MW	88280 TQ	NEBLS	7/16-9/16
	Nevada	Y	75430 FQ	90460 MW	112020 TQ	USBLS	5/15
	Las Vegas-Henderson-Paradise MSA, NV	Y	76770 FQ	92170 MW	117870 TQ	USBLS	5/15
	New Hampshire	H	29.84 AE	37.82 MW	42.25 AEX	NHBLS	6/16
	Manchester NECTA, NH	H	30.84 AE	38.89 MW	43.32 AEX	NHBLS	6/16
	Nashua NECTA, NH-MA	Y	64420 FQ	74210 MW	87520 TQ	USBLS	5/15
	New Jersey	Y	72560 FQ	89670 MW	108620 TQ	USBLS	5/15
	Camden PMSA, NJ	Y	73120 FQ	91000 MW	106350 TQ	USBLS	5/15
	Newark PMSA, NJ-PA	Y	70530 FQ	87370 MW	106760 TQ	USBLS	5/15
	Trenton MSA, NJ	Y	79410 FQ	89930 MW	100510 TQ	USBLS	5/15
	New Mexico	Y	62070 FQ	78790 MW	98620 TQ	USBLS	5/15
	Albuquerque MSA, NM	Y	60810 FQ	80700 MW	98890 TQ	USBLS	5/15
	New York	Y	60110 AE	79910 MW	93300 AEX	NYBLS	1/16-3/16
	Buffalo-Cheektowaga-Niagara Falls MSA, NY	Y	54170 FQ	66760 MW	78640 TQ	USBLS	5/15
	Nassau County-Suffolk County PMSA, NY	Y	71450 FQ	86040 MW	104090 TQ	USBLS	5/15
	New York-Jersey City-White Plains PMSA, NY-NJ	Y	71710 FQ	86630 MW	105700 TQ	USBLS	5/15
	Rochester MSA, NY	Y	60010 FQ	74360 MW	89000 TQ	USBLS	5/15
	North Carolina	Y	63090 FQ	78660 MW	93100 TQ	USBLS	5/15
	Charlotte-Concord-Gastonia MSA, NC-SC	Y	62650 FQ	80590 MW	95800 TQ	USBLS	5/15
	Raleigh MSA, NC	Y	72210 FQ	83320 MW	93880 TQ	USBLS	5/15
	North Dakota	Y	54970 FQ	63850 MW	75340 TQ	USBLS	5/15
	Fargo MSA, ND-MN	Y	56330 FQ	67480 MW	78140 TQ	USBLS	5/15
	Ohio	Y	65540 FQ	79810 MW	95710 TQ	USBLS	5/15
	Cincinnati MSA, OH-KY-IN	Y	65030 FQ	80880 MW	97690 TQ	USBLS	5/15
	Cleveland-Elyria MSA, OH	Y	71690 FQ	83790 MW	95210 TQ	USBLS	5/15
	Columbus MSA, OH	Y	58440 FQ	71290 MW	87070 TQ	USBLS	5/15
	Oklahoma	Y	59100 FQ	81120 MW	100420 TQ	USBLS	5/15
	Oklahoma City MSA, OK	Y	70760 FQ	86890 MW	104540 TQ	USBLS	5/15
	Tulsa MSA, OK	Y	47550 FQ	72930 MW	91370 TQ	USBLS	5/15
	Oregon	H	35.54 FQ	41.37 MW	46.04 TQ	ORBLS	2016
	Portland-Vancouver-Hillsboro MSA, OR-WA	Y	73550 FQ	84760 MW	94280 TQ	USBLS	5/15
	Pennsylvania	Y	61210 FQ	74860 MW	91470 TQ	USBLS	5/15
	Allentown-Bethlehem-Easton MSA, PA-NJ	Y	62890 FQ	83700 MW	100460 TQ	USBLS	5/15
	Harrisburg-Carlisle MSA, PA	Y	62850 FQ	77760 MW	93450 TQ	USBLS	5/15
	Montgomery County-Bucks County-Chester County PMSA, PA	Y	68400 FQ	80560 MW	96010 TQ	USBLS	5/15
	Philadelphia PMSA, PA	Y	63410 FQ	75990 MW	94520 TQ	USBLS	5/15
	Pittsburgh MSA, PA	Y	57030 FQ	67910 MW	78700 TQ	USBLS	5/15
	Rhode Island	Y	66880 FQ	77440 MW	90900 TQ	USBLS	5/15
	Providence-Warwick MSA, RI-MA	Y	67050 FQ	78780 MW	94330 TQ	USBLS	5/15
	South Carolina	Y	60740 FQ	76130 MW	93830 TQ	USBLS	5/15
	Charleston-North Charleston MSA, SC	Y	69830 FQ	80920 MW	91850 TQ	USBLS	5/15
	Columbia MSA, SC	Y	51220 FQ	72290 MW	93480 TQ	USBLS	5/15
	Greenville-Anderson-Mauldin MSA, SC	Y	58750 FQ	71580 MW	87360 TQ	USBLS	5/15
	South Dakota	Y	54600 FQ	62460 MW	72860 TQ	USBLS	5/15

AE	Average entry wage	AWR	Average wage range	H	Hourly
AEX	Average experienced wage	B	Biweekly	HI	Highest wage paid
ATC	Average total compensation	D	Daily	HR	High end range
AW	Average wage paid	FQ	First quartile wage	LO	Lowest wage paid

LR	Low end range	MTC	Median total compensation	TCC	Total cash compensation
M	Monthly	MW	Median wage paid	TQ	Third quartile wage
MCC	Median cash compensation	MWR	Median wage range	W	Weekly
ME	Median entry wage	S	See annotated source	Y	Yearly

Occupation/Type/Industry	Location	Per	Low	Mid	High	Source	Date
Occupational Therapist	Sioux Falls MSA, SD	Y	54620 FQ	61320 MW	72030 TQ	USBLS	5/15
	Tennessee	Y	66970 FQ	80370 MW	94960 TQ	USBLS	5/15
	Knoxville MSA, TN	Y	63410 FQ	72550 MW	84640 TQ	USBLS	5/15
	Memphis MSA, TN-MS-AR	Y	70480 FQ	81120 MW	94790 TQ	USBLS	5/15
	Nashville-Davidson– Murfreesboro–Franklin MSA, TN	Y	69640 FQ	82310 MW	95050 TQ	USBLS	5/15
	Texas	Y	71210 FQ	89000 MW	111470 TQ	USBLS	5/15
	Austin-Round Rock MSA, TX	Y	60620 FQ	75750 MW	91890 TQ	USBLS	5/15
	Dallas-Plano-Irving PMSA, TX	Y	74320 FQ	96270 MW	124330 TQ	USBLS	5/15
	Fort Worth-Arlington PMSA, TX	Y	74260 FQ	89950 MW	104460 TQ	USBLS	5/15
	Houston-The Woodlands- Sugar Land MSA, TX	Y	67300 FQ	84170 MW	98600 TQ	USBLS	5/15
	San Antonio-New Braunfels MSA, TX	Y	71810 FQ	86650 MW	101790 TQ	USBLS	5/15
	Utah	Y	68290 FQ	81140 MW	93940 TQ	USBLS	5/15
	Ogden-Clearfield MSA, UT	Y	60830 FQ	75000 MW	90960 TQ	USBLS	5/15
	Provo-Orem MSA, UT	Y	66110 FQ	84610 MW	99110 TQ	USBLS	5/15
	Salt Lake City MSA, UT	Y	70820 FQ	82640 MW	94000 TQ	USBLS	5/15
	Vermont	Y	61230 FQ	71850 MW	84910 TQ	USBLS	5/15
	Burlington-South Burlington MSA, VT	Y	63930 FQ	72280 MW	82370 TQ	USBLS	5/15
	Virginia	Y	69400 FQ	85670 MW	100820 TQ	USBLS	5/15
	Richmond MSA, VA	Y	60260 FQ	74740 MW	94130 TQ	USBLS	5/15
	Virginia Beach-Norfolk- Newport News MSA, VA-NC	Y	65520 FQ	81360 MW	94090 TQ	USBLS	5/15
	Washington	H	33.92 FQ	40.20 MW	46.47 TQ	WABLS	3/16
	Seattle-Bellevue-Everett PMSA, WA	H	34.61 FQ	41.22 MW	47.01 TQ	WABLS	3/16
	Tacoma-Lakewood PMSA, WA	H	32.69 FQ	38.22 MW	45.62 TQ	WABLS	3/16
	West Virginia	Y	63910 FQ	77140 MW	95580 TQ	USBLS	5/15
	Huntington-Ashland MSA, WV-KY-OH	Y	68670 FQ	82830 MW	94510 TQ	USBLS	5/15
	Wisconsin	Y	57390 FQ	68280 MW	77610 TQ	USBLS	5/15
	Madison MSA, WI	Y	56800 FQ	70400 MW	81420 TQ	USBLS	5/15
	Milwaukee-Waukesha-West Allis MSA, WI	Y	57250 FQ	66990 MW	75940 TQ	USBLS	5/15
	Wyoming	Y	60500 FQ	72020 MW	85260 TQ	USBLS	5/15
	Cheyenne MSA, WY	Y	73330 FQ	84230 MW	96340 TQ	USBLS	5/15
	Puerto Rico	Y	34530 FQ	44200 MW	69140 TQ	USBLS	5/15
	San Juan-Carolina-Caguas MSA, PR	Y	34930 FQ	45330 MW	69160 TQ	USBLS	5/15
Occupational Therapy Aide	Alabama	Y	20911 AE	26584 AW	29416 AEX	ALBLS	6/16
	Birmingham-Hoover MSA, AL	Y	22425 AE	30425 AW	34430 AEX	ALBLS	6/16
	Arkansas	Y	19440 FQ	22700 MW	29580 TQ	USBLS	5/15
	California	H	12.62 FQ	15.46 MW	26.29 TQ	CABLS	1/16-3/16
	Anaheim-Santa Ana-Irvine PMSA, CA	H	11.30 FQ	14.29 MW	29.03 TQ	CABLS	1/16-3/16
	Los Angeles-Long Beach- Glendale PMSA, CA	H	12.19 FQ	14.20 MW	17.81 TQ	CABLS	1/16-3/16
	Oakland-Hayward-Berkeley PMSA, CA	H	13.61 FQ	21.55 MW	28.06 TQ	CABLS	1/16-3/16
	Riverside-San Bernardino- Ontario MSA, CA	H	12.74 FQ	13.63 MW	14.53 TQ	CABLS	1/16-3/16
	Sacramento–Roseville– Arden-Arcade MSA, CA	H	17.62 FQ	19.86 MW	23.24 TQ	CABLS	1/16-3/16
	San Diego-Carlsbad MSA, CA	H	18.31 FQ	28.21 MW	41.86 TQ	CABLS	1/16-3/16
	San Francisco-Redwood City- South San Francisco PMSA, CA	H	19.25 FQ	26.21 MW	29.05 TQ	CABLS	1/16-3/16
	Colorado	Y	25480 FQ	29160 MW	36580 TQ	USBLS	5/15
	Connecticut	Y		28420 MW		CTBLS	1/16-3/16
	District of Columbia	Y	27940 FQ	40340 MW	54950 TQ	USBLS	5/15
	Washington-Arlington- Alexandria PMSA, DC-VA- MD-WV	Y	23290 FQ	29740 MW	45620 TQ	USBLS	5/15
	Florida	H	12.72 AE	15.68 MW	24.33 AEX	FLBLS	7/16-9/16
	Georgia	Y	21940 FQ	26180 MW	30050 TQ	USBLS	5/15
	Atlanta-Sandy Springs- Roswell MSA, GA	Y	23590 FQ	27590 MW	31880 TQ	USBLS	5/15

AE Average entry wage	**AWR** Average wage range	**H** Hourly	**LR** Low end range	**MTC** Median total compensation	**TCC** Total cash compensation
AEX Average experienced wage **B** Biweekly		**HI** Highest wage paid	**M** Monthly	**MW** Median wage paid	**TQ** Third quartile wage
ATC Average total compensation **D** Daily		**HR** High end range	**MCC** Median cash compensation	**MWR** Median wage range	**W** Weekly
AW Average wage paid	**FQ** First quartile wage	**LO** Lowest wage paid	**ME** Median entry wage	**S** See annotated source	**Y** Yearly

1123

Occupation/Type/Industry	Location	Per	Low	Mid	High	Source	Date
Occupational Therapy Aide	Idaho	Y	25260 FQ	28550 MW	34730 TQ	USBLS	5/15
	Boise City MSA, ID	Y	25190 FQ	28400 MW	34400 TQ	USBLS	5/15
	Illinois	Y	20920 FQ	24310 MW	28900 TQ	USBLS	5/15
	Chicago-Naperville-Arlington Heights PMSA, IL	Y	20650 FQ	23820 MW	28260 TQ	USBLS	5/15
	Indiana	Y	21340 FQ	25290 MW	30190 TQ	USBLS	5/15
	Kansas	Y	28310 FQ	34460 MW	50820 TQ	USBLS	5/15
	Kentucky	Y	21800 FQ	26300 MW	38150 TQ	USBLS	5/15
	Louisiana	Y	25690 FQ	29430 MW	35910 TQ	USBLS	5/15
	Maryland	Y	18377 AE	29880 MW	35631 AEX	MDBLS	4/16
	Baltimore-Columbia-Towson MSA, MD	Y	18460 FQ	26380 MW	31850 TQ	USBLS	5/15
	Massachusetts	Y	23810 FQ	29010 MW	38350 TQ	USBLS	5/15
	Boston-Cambridge-Newton NECTA, MA	Y	27700 FQ	30430 MW	35720 TQ	USBLS	5/15
	Worcester MSA, MA-CT	Y	23860 FQ	29110 MW	38580 TQ	USBLS	5/15
	Michigan	Y	27260 FQ	31370 MW	37950 TQ	USBLS	5/15
	Grand Rapids-Wyoming MSA, MI	Y	28150 FQ	32710 MW	38590 TQ	USBLS	5/15
	Minnesota	Y	26570 FQ	34063 MW	44071 TQ	MNBLS	1/16-3/16
	Minneapolis-St. Paul-Bloomington MSA, MN-WI	Y	28589 FQ	33820 MW	43485 TQ	MNBLS	1/16-3/16
	Nebraska	Y	22220 FQ	26445 MW	33260 TQ	NEBLS	7/16-9/16
	Omaha-Council Bluffs MSA, NE-IA	Y	22010 FQ	24820 MW	32465 TQ	NEBLS	7/16-9/16
	New Hampshire	H	10.51 AE	13.25 MW	16.71 AEX	NHBLS	6/16
	New Jersey	Y	22710 FQ	27130 MW	30540 TQ	USBLS	5/15
	New Mexico	Y	21500 FQ	24410 MW	39480 TQ	USBLS	5/15
	New York	Y	23120 AE	33540 MW	37280 AEX	NYBLS	1/16-3/16
	Buffalo-Cheektowaga-Niagara Falls MSA, NY	Y	23240 FQ	31070 MW	35870 TQ	USBLS	5/15
	Nassau County-Suffolk County PMSA, NY	Y	34080 FQ	38020 MW	44150 TQ	USBLS	5/15
	New York-Jersey City-White Plains PMSA, NY-NJ	Y	21830 FQ	28250 MW	35490 TQ	USBLS	5/15
	North Carolina	Y	23420 FQ	27710 MW	32700 TQ	USBLS	5/15
	Charlotte-Concord-Gastonia MSA, NC-SC	Y	19710 FQ	25610 MW	30940 TQ	USBLS	5/15
	North Dakota	Y	31180 FQ	37030 MW	43240 TQ	USBLS	5/15
	Ohio	Y	23390 FQ	29390 MW	52050 TQ	USBLS	5/15
	Oklahoma	Y	23520 FQ	27770 MW	46040 TQ	USBLS	5/15
	Oregon	H	12.03 FQ	15.37 MW	18.16 TQ	ORBLS	2016
	Pennsylvania	Y	21620 FQ	25810 MW	31840 TQ	USBLS	5/15
	Allentown-Bethlehem-Easton MSA, PA-NJ	Y	22220 FQ	24600 MW	29920 TQ	USBLS	5/15
	Harrisburg-Carlisle MSA, PA	Y	25240 FQ	28910 MW	33790 TQ	USBLS	5/15
	Montgomery County-Bucks County-Chester County PMSA, PA	Y	23230 FQ	27040 MW	30190 TQ	USBLS	5/15
	Philadelphia PMSA, PA	Y	27310 FQ	38290 MW	44650 TQ	USBLS	5/15
	Pittsburgh MSA, PA	Y	21510 FQ	25560 MW	33570 TQ	USBLS	5/15
	South Carolina	Y	20080 FQ	22850 MW	27260 TQ	USBLS	5/15
	Tennessee	Y	21730 FQ	25960 MW	29980 TQ	USBLS	5/15
	Texas	Y	22400 FQ	26730 MW	30660 TQ	USBLS	5/15
	Dallas-Plano-Irving PMSA, TX	Y	21380 FQ	27180 MW	32960 TQ	USBLS	5/15
	Fort Worth-Arlington PMSA, TX	Y	21380 FQ	24040 MW	29590 TQ	USBLS	5/15
	Houston-The Woodlands-Sugar Land MSA, TX	Y	24120 FQ	27670 MW	31520 TQ	USBLS	5/15
	San Antonio-New Braunfels MSA, TX	Y	25520 FQ	27470 MW	29410 TQ	USBLS	5/15
	Utah	Y	24980 FQ	28870 MW	36570 TQ	USBLS	5/15
	Salt Lake City MSA, UT	Y	25720 FQ	28690 MW	31570 TQ	USBLS	5/15
	Virginia	Y	22320 FQ	26420 MW	34070 TQ	USBLS	5/15
	Virginia Beach-Norfolk-Newport News MSA, VA-NC	Y	21430 FQ	24210 MW	28190 TQ	USBLS	5/15
	Washington	H	12.02 FQ	14.23 MW	17.25 TQ	WABLS	3/16
	West Virginia	Y	26210 FQ	30520 MW	36020 TQ	USBLS	5/15
	Wisconsin	Y	26130 FQ	30490 MW	35440 TQ	USBLS	5/15
	Puerto Rico	Y	16560 FQ	17710 MW	18870 TQ	USBLS	5/15
	San Juan-Carolina-Caguas MSA, PR	Y	16660 FQ	17920 MW	19170 TQ	USBLS	5/15

AE	Average entry wage	AWR	Average wage range	H	Hourly	LR	Low end range	MTC	Median total compensation	TCC	Total cash compensation
AEX	Average experienced wage	B	Biweekly	HI	Highest wage paid	M	Monthly	MW	Median wage paid	TQ	Third quartile wage
ATC	Average total compensation	D	Daily	HR	High end range	MCC	Median cash compensation	MWR	Median wage range	W	Weekly
AW	Average wage paid	FQ	First quartile wage	LO	Lowest wage paid	ME	Median entry wage	S	See annotated source	Y	Yearly

Occupation/Type/Industry	Location	Per	Low	Mid	High	Source	Date
Occupational Therapy Assistant	Alabama	Y	43058 AE	57905 AW	65328 AEX	ALBLS	6/16
	Birmingham-Hoover MSA, AL	Y	43429 AE	58255 AW	65668 AEX	ALBLS	6/16
	Arizona	Y	51050 FQ	60240 MW	70040 TQ	USBLS	5/15
	Phoenix-Mesa-Scottsdale MSA, AZ	Y	53070 FQ	62530 MW	71440 TQ	USBLS	5/15
	Tucson MSA, AZ	Y	47160 FQ	54700 MW	61250 TQ	USBLS	5/15
	Arkansas	Y	53050 FQ	66040 MW	76670 TQ	USBLS	5/15
	Little Rock-North Little Rock-Conway MSA, AR	Y	54490 FQ	69620 MW	81670 TQ	USBLS	5/15
	California	H	26.27 FQ	33.48 MW	36.93 TQ	CABLS	1/16-3/16
	Anaheim-Santa Ana-Irvine PMSA, CA	H	17.53 FQ	24.61 MW	35.36 TQ	CABLS	1/16-3/16
	Los Angeles-Long Beach-Glendale PMSA, CA	H	30.03 FQ	33.73 MW	36.75 TQ	CABLS	1/16-3/16
	Oakland-Hayward-Berkeley PMSA, CA	H	17.70 FQ	31.33 MW	35.25 TQ	CABLS	1/16-3/16
	Riverside-San Bernardino-Ontario MSA, CA	H	29.74 FQ	33.17 MW	36.08 TQ	CABLS	1/16-3/16
	Sacramento–Roseville–Arden-Arcade MSA, CA	H	29.81 FQ	36.51 MW	43.98 TQ	CABLS	1/16-3/16
	San Diego-Carlsbad MSA, CA	H	31.53 FQ	34.51 MW	37.48 TQ	CABLS	1/16-3/16
	San Francisco-Redwood City-South San Francisco PMSA, CA	H	33.04 FQ	35.60 MW	38.14 TQ	CABLS	1/16-3/16
	Colorado	Y	41220 FQ	49280 MW	58600 TQ	USBLS	5/15
	Connecticut	Y		61562 MW		CTBLS	1/16-3/16
	Bridgeport-Stamford-Norwalk MSA, CT	Y	53340 FQ	59340 MW	68010 TQ	USBLS	5/15
	Hartford-West Hartford-East Hartford MSA, CT	Y	51990 FQ	59110 MW	67730 TQ	USBLS	5/15
	Delaware	Y	45440 FQ	63660 MW	75960 TQ	USBLS	5/15
	Wilmington PMSA, DE-MD-NJ	Y	55140 FQ	68190 MW	80560 TQ	USBLS	5/15
	District of Columbia	Y	51600 FQ	59780 MW	71600 TQ	USBLS	5/15
	Washington-Arlington-Alexandria PMSA, DC-VA-MD-WV	Y	52070 FQ	59700 MW	72240 TQ	USBLS	5/15
	Florida	H	25.28 AE	31.15 MW	34.01 AEX	FLBLS	7/16-9/16
	Fort Lauderdale-Pompano Beach-Deerfield Beach PMSA, FL	H	25.09 AE	31.84 MW	34.24 AEX	FLBLS	7/16-9/16
	Miami-Miami Beach-Kendall PMSA, FL	H	26.02 AE	30.26 MW	32.44 AEX	FLBLS	7/16-9/16
	Orlando-Kissimmee-Sanford MSA, FL	H	24.56 AE	28.58 MW	31.61 AEX	FLBLS	7/16-9/16
	Tampa-St. Petersburg-Clearwater MSA, FL	H	24.11 AE	31.57 MW	33.77 AEX	FLBLS	7/16-9/16
	Georgia	Y	51590 FQ	58230 MW	66500 TQ	USBLS	5/15
	Atlanta-Sandy Springs-Roswell MSA, GA	Y	52380 FQ	57680 MW	63540 TQ	USBLS	5/15
	Hawaii	Y	47190 FQ	52770 MW	58450 TQ	USBLS	5/15
	Urban Honolulu MSA, HI	Y	46460 FQ	51930 MW	57910 TQ	USBLS	5/15
	Idaho	Y	46970 FQ	55850 MW	66450 TQ	USBLS	5/15
	Boise City MSA, ID	Y	48970 FQ	57510 MW	68570 TQ	USBLS	5/15
	Illinois	Y	49640 FQ	59170 MW	70460 TQ	USBLS	5/15
	Chicago-Naperville-Arlington Heights PMSA, IL	Y	51980 FQ	61020 MW	72270 TQ	USBLS	5/15
	Lake County-Kenosha County PMSA, IL-WI	Y	45700 FQ	53000 MW	59450 TQ	USBLS	5/15
	Indiana	Y	47390 FQ	55910 MW	64070 TQ	USBLS	5/15
	Gary PMSA, IN	Y	52270 FQ	59310 MW	68290 TQ	USBLS	5/15
	Indianapolis-Carmel-Anderson MSA, IN	Y	52230 FQ	58560 MW	67650 TQ	USBLS	5/15
	Iowa	Y	45820 FQ	53830 MW	60920 TQ	USBLS	5/15
	Des Moines-West Des Moines MSA, IA	Y	48800 FQ	55490 MW	61550 TQ	USBLS	5/15
	Kansas	Y	50240 FQ	58400 MW	67900 TQ	USBLS	5/15
	Wichita MSA, KS	Y	45530 FQ	56650 MW	69680 TQ	USBLS	5/15
	Kentucky	Y	48450 FQ	58500 MW	68420 TQ	USBLS	5/15
	Louisville-Jefferson County MSA, KY-IN	Y	47460 FQ	58690 MW	69450 TQ	USBLS	5/15
	Louisiana	Y	41230 FQ	56170 MW	68310 TQ	USBLS	5/15

AE	Average entry wage	AWR	Average wage range	H	Hourly	LR	Low end range	MTC	Median total compensation	TCC	Total cash compensation
AEX	Average experienced wage	B	Biweekly	HI	Highest wage paid	M	Monthly	MW	Median wage paid	TQ	Third quartile wage
ATC	Average total compensation	D	Daily	HR	High end range	MCC	Median cash compensation	MWR	Median wage range	W	Weekly
AW	Average wage paid	FQ	First quartile wage	LO	Lowest wage paid	ME	Median entry wage	S	See annotated source	Y	Yearly

Occupational Therapy Assistant

Occupation/Type/Industry	Location	Per	Low	Mid	High	Source	Date
Occupational Therapy Assistant	New Orleans-Metairie MSA, LA	Y	27040 FQ	37530 MW	56350 TQ	USBLS	5/15
	Maine	Y	41590 FQ	48420 MW	56290 TQ	USBLS	5/15
	Maryland	Y	47069 AE	63643 MW	71930 AEX	MDBLS	4/16
	Baltimore-Columbia-Towson MSA, MD	Y	53940 FQ	62540 MW	74500 TQ	USBLS	5/15
	Massachusetts	Y	45510 FQ	55830 MW	66400 TQ	USBLS	5/15
	Boston-Cambridge-Newton NECTA, MA	Y	44150 FQ	55570 MW	69130 TQ	USBLS	5/15
	Worcester MSA, MA-CT	Y	35500 FQ	46950 MW	57480 TQ	USBLS	5/15
	Michigan	Y	40510 FQ	47660 MW	57160 TQ	USBLS	5/15
	Detroit-Dearborn-Livonia PMSA, MI	Y	43620 FQ	50410 MW	60260 TQ	USBLS	5/15
	Grand Rapids-Wyoming MSA, MI	Y	39840 FQ	45100 MW	50550 TQ	USBLS	5/15
	Minnesota	Y	38355 FQ	45454 MW	53382 TQ	MNBLS	1/16-3/16
	Minneapolis-St. Paul-Bloomington MSA, MN-WI	Y	37456 FQ	44465 MW	52281 TQ	MNBLS	1/16-3/16
	Mississippi	Y	44550 FQ	55390 MW	63410 TQ	USBLS	5/15
	Missouri	Y	47400 FQ	56200 MW	64170 TQ	USBLS	5/15
	Kansas City MSA, MO-KS	Y	50690 FQ	57120 MW	63780 TQ	USBLS	5/15
	St. Louis MSA, MO-IL	Y	43280 FQ	53960 MW	63080 TQ	USBLS	5/15
	Montana	Y	41670 FQ	51930 MW	59920 TQ	USBLS	5/15
	Nebraska	Y	41885 FQ	54245 MW	60240 TQ	NEBLS	7/16-9/16
	Omaha-Council Bluffs MSA, NE-IA	Y	36495 FQ	52910 MW	59515 TQ	NEBLS	7/16-9/16
	Nevada	Y	60080 FQ	71990 MW	91360 TQ	USBLS	5/15
	Las Vegas-Henderson-Paradise MSA, NV	Y	61510 FQ	72590 MW	93970 TQ	USBLS	5/15
	New Hampshire	H	20.57 AE	25.18 MW	28.84 AEX	NHBLS	6/16
	New Jersey	Y	61190 FQ	68180 MW	74640 TQ	USBLS	5/15
	Newark PMSA, NJ-PA	Y	55220 FQ	64510 MW	73370 TQ	USBLS	5/15
	New Mexico	Y	47460 FQ	60380 MW	71290 TQ	USBLS	5/15
	Albuquerque MSA, NM	Y	53470 FQ	65530 MW	73620 TQ	USBLS	5/15
	New York	Y	42170 AE	57910 MW	64780 AEX	NYBLS	1/16-3/16
	Buffalo-Cheektowaga-Niagara Falls MSA, NY	Y	36420 FQ	42920 MW	49780 TQ	USBLS	5/15
	Nassau County-Suffolk County PMSA, NY	Y	56050 FQ	62860 MW	71150 TQ	USBLS	5/15
	New York-Jersey City-White Plains PMSA, NY-NJ	Y	54940 FQ	63720 MW	72230 TQ	USBLS	5/15
	Rochester MSA, NY	Y	42820 FQ	50820 MW	57770 TQ	USBLS	5/15
	North Carolina	Y	50650 FQ	59760 MW	69830 TQ	USBLS	5/15
	Charlotte-Concord-Gastonia MSA, NC-SC	Y	48350 FQ	59930 MW	69230 TQ	USBLS	5/15
	Raleigh MSA, NC	Y	51500 FQ	56800 MW	62470 TQ	USBLS	5/15
	North Dakota	Y	37100 FQ	44130 MW	53310 TQ	USBLS	5/15
	Ohio	Y	50610 FQ	56820 MW	63310 TQ	USBLS	5/15
	Cincinnati MSA, OH-KY-IN	Y	49120 FQ	56440 MW	65100 TQ	USBLS	5/15
	Cleveland-Elyria MSA, OH	Y	53470 FQ	58600 MW	65650 TQ	USBLS	5/15
	Columbus MSA, OH	Y	49340 FQ	57300 MW	66850 TQ	USBLS	5/15
	Oklahoma	Y	51850 FQ	59020 MW	67990 TQ	USBLS	5/15
	Oklahoma City MSA, OK	Y	52980 FQ	58850 MW	66720 TQ	USBLS	5/15
	Tulsa MSA, OK	Y	51560 FQ	62920 MW	72320 TQ	USBLS	5/15
	Oregon	H	24.26 FQ	27.22 MW	29.91 TQ	ORBLS	2016
	Portland-Vancouver-Hillsboro MSA, OR-WA	Y	51390 FQ	56510 MW	61620 TQ	USBLS	5/15
	Pennsylvania	Y	38690 FQ	46780 MW	56480 TQ	USBLS	5/15
	Allentown-Bethlehem-Easton MSA, PA-NJ	Y	43520 FQ	50970 MW	58590 TQ	USBLS	5/15
	Harrisburg-Carlisle MSA, PA	Y	29820 FQ	47360 MW	58330 TQ	USBLS	5/15
	Montgomery County-Bucks County-Chester County PMSA, PA	Y	34250 FQ	43440 MW	51710 TQ	USBLS	5/15
	Philadelphia PMSA, PA	Y	37790 FQ	47320 MW	59260 TQ	USBLS	5/15
	Pittsburgh MSA, PA	Y	38460 FQ	45390 MW	54060 TQ	USBLS	5/15
	Rhode Island	Y	49730 FQ	58470 MW	68800 TQ	USBLS	5/15
	Providence-Warwick MSA, RI-MA	Y	50340 FQ	58730 MW	68600 TQ	USBLS	5/15
	South Carolina	Y	48540 FQ	58360 MW	76240 TQ	USBLS	5/15
	Charleston-North Charleston MSA, SC	Y	38200 FQ	49090 MW	59830 TQ	USBLS	5/15

AE	Average entry wage	AWR	Average wage range	H	Hourly	LR	Low end range	MTC	Median total compensation	TCC	Total cash compensation
AEX	Average experienced wage	B	Biweekly	HI	Highest wage paid	M	Monthly	MW	Median wage paid	TQ	Third quartile wage
ATC	Average total compensation	D	Daily	HR	High end range	MCC	Median cash compensation	MWR	Median wage range	W	Weekly
AW	Average wage paid	FQ	First quartile wage	LO	Lowest wage paid	ME	Median entry wage	S	See annotated source	Y	Yearly

Occupation/Type/Industry	Location	Per	Low	Mid	High	Source	Date
Occupational Therapy Assistant	Columbia MSA, SC	Y	57380 FQ	80940 MW	89240 TQ	USBLS	5/15
	Greenville-Anderson-Mauldin MSA, SC	Y	44650 FQ	50860 MW	56690 TQ	USBLS	5/15
	South Dakota	Y	33350 FQ	36620 MW	40390 TQ	USBLS	5/15
	Tennessee	Y	52430 FQ	59180 MW	68490 TQ	USBLS	5/15
	Knoxville MSA, TN	Y	45890 FQ	54090 MW	60890 TQ	USBLS	5/15
	Memphis MSA, TN-MS-AR	Y	53280 FQ	59600 MW	67650 TQ	USBLS	5/15
	Nashville-Davidson–Murfreesboro–Franklin MSA, TN	Y	52590 FQ	58610 MW	65090 TQ	USBLS	5/15
	Texas	Y	57480 FQ	69590 MW	82600 TQ	USBLS	5/15
	Austin-Round Rock MSA, TX	Y	46860 FQ	63660 MW	72590 TQ	USBLS	5/15
	Dallas-Plano-Irving PMSA, TX	Y	55960 FQ	66270 MW	82660 TQ	USBLS	5/15
	Fort Worth-Arlington PMSA, TX	Y	66480 FQ	81930 MW	92840 TQ	USBLS	5/15
	Houston-The Woodlands-Sugar Land MSA, TX	Y	57830 FQ	68120 MW	75330 TQ	USBLS	5/15
	San Antonio-New Braunfels MSA, TX	Y	63680 FQ	71560 MW	79450 TQ	USBLS	5/15
	Utah	Y	52240 FQ	59670 MW	68370 TQ	USBLS	5/15
	Salt Lake City MSA, UT	Y	53030 FQ	59860 MW	66810 TQ	USBLS	5/15
	Vermont	Y	45860 FQ	53150 MW	59740 TQ	USBLS	5/15
	Virginia	Y	50810 FQ	61180 MW	72300 TQ	USBLS	5/15
	Richmond MSA, VA	Y	51410 FQ	63660 MW	72420 TQ	USBLS	5/15
	Virginia Beach-Norfolk-Newport News MSA, VA-NC	Y	42540 FQ	56800 MW	72210 TQ	USBLS	5/15
	Washington	H	26.04 FQ	30.07 MW	34.75 TQ	WABLS	3/16
	Seattle-Bellevue-Everett PMSA, WA	H	22.29 FQ	28.29 MW	32.09 TQ	WABLS	3/16
	Tacoma-Lakewood PMSA, WA	H	28.23 FQ	32.72 MW	37.86 TQ	WABLS	3/16
	West Virginia	Y	47580 FQ	55530 MW	62620 TQ	USBLS	5/15
	Huntington-Ashland MSA, WV-KY-OH	Y	43420 FQ	50060 MW	60990 TQ	USBLS	5/15
	Wisconsin	Y	40590 FQ	46210 MW	53250 TQ	USBLS	5/15
	Madison MSA, WI	Y	40750 FQ	45500 MW	51310 TQ	USBLS	5/15
	Milwaukee-Waukesha-West Allis MSA, WI	Y	40460 FQ	45480 MW	50920 TQ	USBLS	5/15
	Wyoming	Y	42830 FQ	50890 MW	61080 TQ	USBLS	5/15
	Puerto Rico	Y	17400 FQ	19500 MW	24140 TQ	USBLS	5/15
Office Clerk							
General	Alabama	Y	17644 AE	24930 AW	28568 AEX	ALBLS	6/16
General	Birmingham-Hoover MSA, AL	Y	17685 AE	26115 AW	30330 AEX	ALBLS	6/16
General	Alaska	Y	35820 FQ	43870 MW	53440 TQ	USBLS	5/15
General	Anchorage MSA, AK	Y	35810 FQ	44190 MW	54550 TQ	USBLS	5/15
General	Arizona	Y	24140 FQ	31400 MW	39460 TQ	USBLS	5/15
General	Phoenix-Mesa-Scottsdale MSA, AZ	Y	24730 FQ	32000 MW	40500 TQ	USBLS	5/15
General	Tucson MSA, AZ	Y	23800 FQ	31740 MW	39340 TQ	USBLS	5/15
General	Arkansas	Y	18730 FQ	23030 MW	28930 TQ	USBLS	5/15
General	Little Rock-North Little Rock-Conway MSA, AR	Y	19440 FQ	23920 MW	30350 TQ	USBLS	5/15
General	California	H	12.10 FQ	16.15 MW	20.53 TQ	CABLS	1/16-3/16
General	Anaheim-Santa Ana-Irvine PMSA, CA	H	12.01 FQ	16.11 MW	20.42 TQ	CABLS	1/16-3/16
General	Los Angeles-Long Beach-Glendale PMSA, CA	H	11.37 FQ	15.18 MW	19.39 TQ	CABLS	1/16-3/16
General	Oakland-Hayward-Berkeley PMSA, CA	H	13.51 FQ	18.87 MW	23.30 TQ	CABLS	1/16-3/16
General	Riverside-San Bernardino-Ontario MSA, CA	H	11.74 FQ	15.34 MW	19.22 TQ	CABLS	1/16-3/16
General	Sacramento–Roseville–Arden-Arcade MSA, CA	H	13.63 FQ	17.27 MW	20.52 TQ	CABLS	1/16-3/16
General	San Diego-Carlsbad MSA, CA	H	12.08 FQ	15.87 MW	19.77 TQ	CABLS	1/16-3/16
General	San Francisco-Redwood City-South San Francisco PMSA, CA	H	15.31 FQ	20.01 MW	26.07 TQ	CABLS	1/16-3/16
General	Colorado	Y	26310 FQ	35080 MW	46420 TQ	USBLS	5/15
General	Denver-Aurora-Lakewood MSA, CO	Y	28060 FQ	36770 MW	48570 TQ	USBLS	5/15
General	Connecticut	Y		35879 MW		CTBLS	1/16-3/16

AE	Average entry wage	AWR	Average wage range	H	Hourly	LR	Low end range	MTC Median total compensation TCC Total cash compensation
AEX	Average experienced wage	B	Biweekly	HI	Highest wage paid	M	Monthly	MW Median wage paid TQ Third quartile wage
ATC	Average total compensation	D	Daily	HR	High end range	MCC Median cash compensation MWR Median wage range W Weekly
AW	Average wage paid	FQ	First quartile wage	LO	Lowest wage paid	ME Median entry wage	S See annotated source Y Yearly

Occupation/Type/Industry	Location	Per	Low	Mid	High	Source	Date
Office Clerk							
General	Bridgeport-Stamford-Norwalk MSA, CT	Y	27610 FQ	36140 MW	46030 TQ	USBLS	5/15
General	Hartford-West Hartford-East Hartford MSA, CT	Y	27530 FQ	35930 MW	45970 TQ	USBLS	5/15
General	Delaware	Y	20520 FQ	26510 MW	33780 TQ	USBLS	5/15
General	Wilmington PMSA, DE-MD-NJ	Y	20600 FQ	27360 MW	35200 TQ	USBLS	5/15
General	District of Columbia	Y	29130 FQ	38070 MW	49230 TQ	USBLS	5/15
General	Washington-Arlington-Alexandria PMSA, DC-VA-MD-WV	Y	27390 FQ	35990 MW	46450 TQ	USBLS	5/15
General	Florida	H	9.56 AE	12.93 MW	16.41 AEX	FLBLS	7/16-9/16
General	Fort Lauderdale-Pompano Beach-Deerfield Beach PMSA, FL	H	9.19 AE	12.62 MW	16.48 AEX	FLBLS	7/16-9/16
General	Miami-Miami Beach-Kendall PMSA, FL	H	9.49 AE	12.85 MW	16.80 AEX	FLBLS	7/16-9/16
General	Orlando-Kissimmee-Sanford MSA, FL	H	9.76 AE	13.44 MW	16.77 AEX	FLBLS	7/16-9/16
General	Tampa-St. Petersburg-Clearwater MSA, FL	H	9.43 AE	12.42 MW	16.13 AEX	FLBLS	7/16-9/16
General	Georgia	Y	19630 FQ	26190 MW	33560 TQ	USBLS	5/15
General	Atlanta-Sandy Springs-Roswell MSA, GA	Y	20380 FQ	27730 MW	35760 TQ	USBLS	5/15
General	Augusta-Richmond County MSA, GA-SC	Y	19700 FQ	24890 MW	31310 TQ	USBLS	5/15
General	Hawaii	Y	26080 FQ	31650 MW	38010 TQ	USBLS	5/15
General	Urban Honolulu MSA, HI	Y	26300 FQ	31790 MW	38380 TQ	USBLS	5/15
General	Idaho	Y	21820 FQ	28010 MW	35190 TQ	USBLS	5/15
General	Boise City MSA, ID	Y	22150 FQ	28460 MW	35310 TQ	USBLS	5/15
General	Illinois	Y	23890 FQ	31070 MW	40630 TQ	USBLS	5/15
General	Chicago-Naperville-Arlington Heights PMSA, IL	Y	24160 FQ	31060 MW	40390 TQ	USBLS	5/15
General	Indiana	Y	21590 FQ	27350 MW	34400 TQ	USBLS	5/15
General	Gary PMSA, IN	Y	20970 FQ	27050 MW	34300 TQ	USBLS	5/15
General	Indianapolis-Carmel-Anderson MSA, IN	Y	23300 FQ	29290 MW	36710 TQ	USBLS	5/15
General	Iowa	Y	24290 FQ	30740 MW	38610 TQ	USBLS	5/15
General	Des Moines-West Des Moines MSA, IA	Y	26960 FQ	33040 MW	39940 TQ	USBLS	5/15
General	Kansas	Y	21410 FQ	27440 MW	34520 TQ	USBLS	5/15
General	Wichita MSA, KS	Y	21010 FQ	26960 MW	33810 TQ	USBLS	5/15
General	Kentucky	Y	21540 FQ	27120 MW	34530 TQ	USBLS	5/15
General	Louisville-Jefferson County MSA, KY-IN	Y	22160 FQ	28940 MW	36770 TQ	USBLS	5/15
General	Louisiana	Y	19100 FQ	23200 MW	28990 TQ	USBLS	5/15
General	Baton Rouge MSA, LA	Y	18620 FQ	23150 MW	30010 TQ	USBLS	5/15
General	New Orleans-Metairie MSA, LA	Y	19690 FQ	23470 MW	28780 TQ	USBLS	5/15
General	Maine	Y	23250 FQ	30030 MW	37000 TQ	USBLS	5/15
General	Portland-South Portland MSA, ME	Y	25170 FQ	31270 MW	38730 TQ	USBLS	5/15
General	Maryland	Y	21192 AE	33696 MW	39947 AEX	MDBLS	4/16
General	Baltimore-Columbia-Towson MSA, MD	Y	23970 FQ	30590 MW	38060 TQ	USBLS	5/15
General	Salisbury MSA, MD-DE	Y	21430 FQ	27630 MW	34970 TQ	USBLS	5/15
General	Massachusetts	Y	26180 FQ	34000 MW	43890 TQ	USBLS	5/15
General	Boston-Cambridge-Newton NECTA, MA	Y	27640 FQ	36310 MW	47720 TQ	USBLS	5/15
General	Worcester MSA, MA-CT	Y	23600 FQ	31430 MW	40450 TQ	USBLS	5/15
General	Michigan	Y	23230 FQ	30180 MW	39030 TQ	USBLS	5/15
General	Detroit-Dearborn-Livonia PMSA, MI	Y	23830 FQ	31390 MW	40080 TQ	USBLS	5/15
General	Grand Rapids-Wyoming MSA, MI	Y	24370 FQ	31160 MW	40770 TQ	USBLS	5/15
General	Minnesota	Y	26040 FQ	33028 MW	40137 TQ	MNBLS	1/16-3/16
General	Minneapolis-St. Paul-Bloomington MSA, MN-WI	Y	27335 FQ	34636 MW	41978 TQ	MNBLS	1/16-3/16
General	Mississippi	Y	18800 FQ	23460 MW	30210 TQ	USBLS	5/15
General	Jackson MSA, MS	Y	18870 FQ	24190 MW	31050 TQ	USBLS	5/15
General	Missouri	Y	22040 FQ	27920 MW	35760 TQ	USBLS	5/15

AE	Average entry wage	AWR	Average wage range	H	Hourly	LR	Low end range	MTC	Median total compensation	TCC	Total cash compensation
AEX	Average experienced wage	B	Biweekly	HI	Highest wage paid	M	Monthly	MW	Median wage paid	TQ	Third quartile wage
ATC	Average total compensation	D	Daily	HR	High end range	MCC	Median cash compensation	MWR	Median wage range	W	Weekly
AW	Average wage paid	FQ	First quartile wage	LO	Lowest wage paid	ME	Median entry wage	S	See annotated source	Y	Yearly

Office Clerk

Occupation/Type/Industry	Location	Per	Low	Mid	High	Source	Date
General	Kansas City MSA, MO-KS	Y	24730 FQ	30030 MW	37550 TQ	USBLS	5/15
General	St. Louis MSA, MO-IL	Y	23020 FQ	29650 MW	38580 TQ	USBLS	5/15
General	Montana	Y	21120 FQ	27950 MW	35260 TQ	USBLS	5/15
General	Billings MSA, MT	Y	25810 FQ	30930 MW	37420 TQ	USBLS	5/15
General	Nebraska	Y	19475 FQ	24770 MW	30780 TQ	NEBLS	7/16-9/16
General	Omaha-Council Bluffs MSA, NE-IA	Y	21190 FQ	27550 MW	34305 TQ	NEBLS	7/16-9/16
General	Nevada	Y	23090 FQ	30600 MW	39580 TQ	USBLS	5/15
General	Las Vegas-Henderson-Paradise MSA, NV	Y	22300 FQ	29500 MW	38700 TQ	USBLS	5/15
General	New Hampshire	H	12.26 AE	17.23 MW	20.49 AEX	NHBLS	6/16
General	Manchester NECTA, NH	H	12.02 AE	17.74 MW	21.11 AEX	NHBLS	6/16
General	Nashua NECTA, NH-MA	Y	28820 FQ	35540 MW	44190 TQ	USBLS	5/15
General	New Jersey	Y	24000 FQ	31000 MW	41730 TQ	USBLS	5/15
General	Camden PMSA, NJ	Y	25190 FQ	30740 MW	39550 TQ	USBLS	5/15
General	Newark PMSA, NJ-PA	Y	23150 FQ	30950 MW	41140 TQ	USBLS	5/15
General	Trenton MSA, NJ	Y	27540 FQ	37690 MW	50670 TQ	USBLS	5/15
General	New Mexico	Y	19040 FQ	24060 MW	30030 TQ	USBLS	5/15
General	Albuquerque MSA, NM	Y	19640 FQ	24760 MW	30420 TQ	USBLS	5/15
General	New York	Y	20860 AE	30890 MW	38660 AEX	NYBLS	1/16-3/16
General	Buffalo-Cheektowaga-Niagara Falls MSA, NY	Y	21230 FQ	27690 MW	34830 TQ	USBLS	5/15
General	Nassau County-Suffolk County PMSA, NY	Y	22390 FQ	30910 MW	41040 TQ	USBLS	5/15
General	New York-Jersey City-White Plains PMSA, NY-NJ	Y	22440 FQ	31200 MW	39810 TQ	USBLS	5/15
General	Rochester MSA, NY	Y	22110 FQ	28480 MW	36920 TQ	USBLS	5/15
General	North Carolina	Y	21060 FQ	27120 MW	33780 TQ	USBLS	5/15
General	Charlotte-Concord-Gastonia MSA, NC-SC	Y	22270 FQ	28310 MW	35920 TQ	USBLS	5/15
General	Raleigh MSA, NC	Y	21830 FQ	28310 MW	36050 TQ	USBLS	5/15
General	North Dakota	Y	20360 FQ	26210 MW	31620 TQ	USBLS	5/15
General	Fargo MSA, ND-MN	Y	21430 FQ	26840 MW	32010 TQ	USBLS	5/15
General	Ohio	Y	21880 FQ	28590 MW	36720 TQ	USBLS	5/15
General	Cincinnati MSA, OH-KY-IN	Y	22960 FQ	29840 MW	38340 TQ	USBLS	5/15
General	Cleveland-Elyria MSA, OH	Y	22450 FQ	29590 MW	37380 TQ	USBLS	5/15
General	Columbus MSA, OH	Y	23430 FQ	30890 MW	38630 TQ	USBLS	5/15
General	Oklahoma	Y	19910 FQ	25810 MW	32700 TQ	USBLS	5/15
General	Oklahoma City MSA, OK	Y	20780 FQ	26850 MW	33790 TQ	USBLS	5/15
General	Tulsa MSA, OK	Y	20050 FQ	26250 MW	33750 TQ	USBLS	5/15
General	Oregon	H	12.70 FQ	15.76 MW	19.19 TQ	ORBLS	2016
General	Portland-Vancouver-Hillsboro MSA, OR-WA	Y	26660 FQ	33580 MW	41020 TQ	USBLS	5/15
General	Pennsylvania	Y	23240 FQ	29930 MW	38050 TQ	USBLS	5/15
General	Allentown-Bethlehem-Easton MSA, PA-NJ	Y	24050 FQ	30210 MW	37440 TQ	USBLS	5/15
General	Harrisburg-Carlisle MSA, PA	Y	26630 FQ	32400 MW	38390 TQ	USBLS	5/15
General	Montgomery County-Bucks County-Chester County PMSA, PA	Y	23580 FQ	31350 MW	40790 TQ	USBLS	5/15
General	Philadelphia PMSA, PA	Y	25300 FQ	33340 MW	43070 TQ	USBLS	5/15
General	Pittsburgh MSA, PA	Y	23290 FQ	29180 MW	37220 TQ	USBLS	5/15
General	Rhode Island	Y	25910 FQ	33080 MW	40910 TQ	USBLS	5/15
General	Providence-Warwick MSA, RI-MA	Y	25980 FQ	33110 MW	41220 TQ	USBLS	5/15
General	South Carolina	Y	20340 FQ	25690 MW	32800 TQ	USBLS	5/15
General	Charleston-North Charleston MSA, SC	Y	19170 FQ	25870 MW	33330 TQ	USBLS	5/15
General	Columbia MSA, SC	Y	19550 FQ	24080 MW	31400 TQ	USBLS	5/15
General	Greenville-Anderson-Mauldin MSA, SC	Y	20580 FQ	24950 MW	30640 TQ	USBLS	5/15
General	South Dakota	Y	19670 FQ	23020 MW	28180 TQ	USBLS	5/15
General	Sioux Falls MSA, SD	Y	21170 FQ	24490 MW	29280 TQ	USBLS	5/15
General	Tennessee	Y	21860 FQ	28290 MW	36340 TQ	USBLS	5/15
General	Knoxville MSA, TN	Y	20800 FQ	27400 MW	35220 TQ	USBLS	5/15
General	Memphis MSA, TN-MS-AR	Y	23170 FQ	28980 MW	37030 TQ	USBLS	5/15
General	Nashville-Davidson–Murfreesboro–Franklin MSA, TN	Y	24410 FQ	30970 MW	38980 TQ	USBLS	5/15
General	Texas	Y	22940 FQ	30130 MW	39630 TQ	USBLS	5/15
General	Austin-Round Rock MSA, TX	Y	23860 FQ	31160 MW	41130 TQ	USBLS	5/15

Occupation/Type/Industry	Location	Per	Low	Mid	High	Source	Date
Office Clerk							
General	Dallas-Plano-Irving PMSA, TX	Y	24520 FQ	32150 MW	41760 TQ	USBLS	5/15
General	Fort Worth-Arlington PMSA, TX	Y	25010 FQ	31520 MW	40200 TQ	USBLS	5/15
General	Houston-The Woodlands-Sugar Land MSA, TX	Y	25800 FQ	33380 MW	45390 TQ	USBLS	5/15
General	San Antonio-New Braunfels MSA, TX	Y	23700 FQ	30260 MW	38650 TQ	USBLS	5/15
General	Utah	Y	21110 FQ	26620 MW	33780 TQ	USBLS	5/15
General	Ogden-Clearfield MSA, UT	Y	21810 FQ	27360 MW	34260 TQ	USBLS	5/15
General	Provo-Orem MSA, UT	Y	18950 FQ	24120 MW	30570 TQ	USBLS	5/15
General	Salt Lake City MSA, UT	Y	22200 FQ	27650 MW	35420 TQ	USBLS	5/15
General	Vermont	Y	25000 FQ	30880 MW	36970 TQ	USBLS	5/15
General	Burlington-South Burlington MSA, VT	Y	25760 FQ	32500 MW	37460 TQ	USBLS	5/15
General	Virginia	Y	23260 FQ	30280 MW	38650 TQ	USBLS	5/15
General	Richmond MSA, VA	Y	22650 FQ	29600 MW	37290 TQ	USBLS	5/15
General	Virginia Beach-Norfolk-Newport News MSA, VA-NC	Y	22160 FQ	28200 MW	36050 TQ	USBLS	5/15
General	Washington	H	13.08 FQ	16.18 MW	19.57 TQ	WABLS	3/16
General	Seattle-Bellevue-Everett PMSA, WA	H	13.84 FQ	17.14 MW	21.27 TQ	WABLS	3/16
General	Tacoma-Lakewood PMSA, WA	H	13.39 FQ	16.49 MW	19.04 TQ	WABLS	3/16
General	West Virginia	Y	19620 FQ	24350 MW	31270 TQ	USBLS	5/15
General	Huntington-Ashland MSA, WV-KY-OH	Y	19660 FQ	24600 MW	33050 TQ	USBLS	5/15
General	Wisconsin	Y	24710 FQ	31540 MW	38420 TQ	USBLS	5/15
General	Madison MSA, WI	Y	26170 FQ	33130 MW	39940 TQ	USBLS	5/15
General	Milwaukee-Waukesha-West Allis MSA, WI	Y	25710 FQ	33180 MW	40520 TQ	USBLS	5/15
General	Wyoming	Y	25270 FQ	31610 MW	38970 TQ	USBLS	5/15
General	Cheyenne MSA, WY	Y	24940 FQ	31480 MW	38080 TQ	USBLS	5/15
General	Puerto Rico	Y	17170 FQ	18860 MW	23260 TQ	USBLS	5/15
General	San Juan-Carolina-Caguas MSA, PR	Y	17280 FQ	19090 MW	23950 TQ	USBLS	5/15
General	Virgin Islands	Y	19630 FQ	26060 MW	35020 TQ	USBLS	5/15
General	Guam	Y	18210 FQ	19270 MW	23310 TQ	USBLS	5/15
Office Machine Operator							
Except Computer	Alabama	Y	18613 AE	26280 AW	30124 AEX	ALBLS	6/16
Except Computer	Birmingham-Hoover MSA, AL	Y	20395 AE	29640 AW	34267 AEX	ALBLS	6/16
Except Computer	Alaska	Y	26540 FQ	38430 MW	45070 TQ	USBLS	5/15
Except Computer	Anchorage MSA, AK	Y	30590 FQ	40270 MW	45810 TQ	USBLS	5/15
Except Computer	Arizona	Y	25780 FQ	31260 MW	37370 TQ	USBLS	5/15
Except Computer	Phoenix-Mesa-Scottsdale MSA, AZ	Y	26060 FQ	31580 MW	37970 TQ	USBLS	5/15
Except Computer	Tucson MSA, AZ	Y	26520 FQ	31150 MW	35590 TQ	USBLS	5/15
Except Computer	Arkansas	Y	20320 FQ	23640 MW	29360 TQ	USBLS	5/15
Except Computer	Little Rock-North Little Rock-Conway MSA, AR	Y	21190 FQ	23630 MW	28960 TQ	USBLS	5/15
Except Computer	California	H	11.58 FQ	15.18 MW	20.43 TQ	CABLS	1/16-3/16
Except Computer	Anaheim-Santa Ana-Irvine PMSA, CA	H	13.09 FQ	15.25 MW	20.87 TQ	CABLS	1/16-3/16
Except Computer	Los Angeles-Long Beach-Glendale PMSA, CA	H	10.62 FQ	14.42 MW	20.94 TQ	CABLS	1/16-3/16
Except Computer	Oakland-Hayward-Berkeley PMSA, CA	H	10.89 FQ	14.12 MW	18.07 TQ	CABLS	1/16-3/16
Except Computer	Riverside-San Bernardino-Ontario MSA, CA	H	12.39 FQ	14.78 MW	18.47 TQ	CABLS	1/16-3/16
Except Computer	Sacramento–Roseville–Arden-Arcade MSA, CA	H	11.05 FQ	14.70 MW	19.34 TQ	CABLS	1/16-3/16
Except Computer	San Diego-Carlsbad MSA, CA	H	13.62 FQ	16.84 MW	20.68 TQ	CABLS	1/16-3/16
Except Computer	San Francisco-Redwood City-South San Francisco PMSA, CA	H	12.81 FQ	16.11 MW	21.52 TQ	CABLS	1/16-3/16
Except Computer	Colorado	Y	24080 FQ	32710 MW	39180 TQ	USBLS	5/15
Except Computer	Denver-Aurora-Lakewood MSA, CO	Y	27150 FQ	34140 MW	41010 TQ	USBLS	5/15
Except Computer	Connecticut	Y		34773 MW		CTBLS	1/16-3/16
Except Computer	Bridgeport-Stamford-Norwalk MSA, CT	Y	27430 FQ	30530 MW	41310 TQ	USBLS	5/15

AE	Average entry wage	AWR	Average wage range	H	Hourly	LR	Low end range	MTC	Median total compensation	TCC	Total cash compensation
AEX	Average experienced wage	B	Biweekly	HI	Highest wage paid	M	Monthly	MW	Median wage paid	TQ	Third quartile wage
ATC	Average total compensation	D	Daily	HR	High end range	MCC	Median cash compensation	MWR	Median wage range	W	Weekly
AW	Average wage paid	FQ	First quartile wage	LO	Lowest wage paid	ME	Median entry wage	S	See annotated source	Y	Yearly

Office Machine Operator

Occupation/Type/Industry	Location	Per	Low	Mid	High	Source	Date
Office Machine Operator							
Except Computer	Hartford-West Hartford-East Hartford MSA, CT	Y	23760 FQ	37930 MW	46020 TQ	USBLS	5/15
Except Computer	Delaware	Y	26350 FQ	31100 MW	36380 TQ	USBLS	5/15
Except Computer	Wilmington PMSA, DE-MD-NJ	Y	26180 FQ	31320 MW	36800 TQ	USBLS	5/15
Except Computer	District of Columbia	Y	29030 FQ	38980 MW	47600 TQ	USBLS	5/15
Except Computer	Washington-Arlington-Alexandria PMSA, DC-VA-MD-WV	Y	26630 FQ	31800 MW	43760 TQ	USBLS	5/15
Except Computer	Florida	H	10.09 AE	13.22 MW	15.71 AEX	FLBLS	7/16-9/16
Except Computer	Fort Lauderdale-Pompano Beach-Deerfield Beach PMSA, FL	H	10.16 AE	12.14 MW	13.98 AEX	FLBLS	7/16-9/16
Except Computer	Miami-Miami Beach-Kendall PMSA, FL	H	10.02 AE	14.09 MW	16.50 AEX	FLBLS	7/16-9/16
Except Computer	Orlando-Kissimmee-Sanford MSA, FL	H	10.69 AE	12.88 MW	15.09 AEX	FLBLS	7/16-9/16
Except Computer	Tampa-St. Petersburg-Clearwater MSA, FL	H	10.04 AE	12.32 MW	14.70 AEX	FLBLS	7/16-9/16
Except Computer	Georgia	Y	22680 FQ	28140 MW	36430 TQ	USBLS	5/15
Except Computer	Atlanta-Sandy Springs-Roswell MSA, GA	Y	23790 FQ	29270 MW	37850 TQ	USBLS	5/15
Except Computer	Hawaii	Y	24040 FQ	42530 MW	57530 TQ	USBLS	5/15
Except Computer	Urban Honolulu MSA, HI	Y	24480 FQ	43980 MW	59710 TQ	USBLS	5/15
Except Computer	Idaho	Y	19590 FQ	24570 MW	32520 TQ	USBLS	5/15
Except Computer	Boise City MSA, ID	Y	18620 FQ	23220 MW	29930 TQ	USBLS	5/15
Except Computer	Illinois	Y	25230 FQ	34280 MW	45000 TQ	USBLS	5/15
Except Computer	Chicago-Naperville-Arlington Heights PMSA, IL	Y	26810 FQ	36680 MW	46510 TQ	USBLS	5/15
Except Computer	Lake County-Kenosha County PMSA, IL-WI	Y	24300 FQ	32750 MW	41390 TQ	USBLS	5/15
Except Computer	Indiana	Y	26610 FQ	30960 MW	36550 TQ	USBLS	5/15
Except Computer	Gary PMSA, IN	Y	18320 FQ	29270 MW	36610 TQ	USBLS	5/15
Except Computer	Indianapolis-Carmel-Anderson MSA, IN	Y	26510 FQ	30200 MW	35260 TQ	USBLS	5/15
Except Computer	Iowa	Y	22980 FQ	28550 MW	36050 TQ	USBLS	5/15
Except Computer	Des Moines-West Des Moines MSA, IA	Y	24930 FQ	30230 MW	37480 TQ	USBLS	5/15
Except Computer	Kansas	Y	22130 FQ	27950 MW	33580 TQ	USBLS	5/15
Except Computer	Wichita MSA, KS	Y	25940 FQ	30350 MW	36880 TQ	USBLS	5/15
Except Computer	Kentucky	Y	22660 FQ	27200 MW	30930 TQ	USBLS	5/15
Except Computer	Louisville-Jefferson County MSA, KY-IN	Y	25110 FQ	30050 MW	36230 TQ	USBLS	5/15
Except Computer	Louisiana	Y	22880 FQ	27820 MW	36200 TQ	USBLS	5/15
Except Computer	Baton Rouge MSA, LA	Y	26240 FQ	35090 MW	42460 TQ	USBLS	5/15
Except Computer	New Orleans-Metairie MSA, LA	Y	22270 FQ	27500 MW	36200 TQ	USBLS	5/15
Except Computer	Maine	Y	22720 FQ	27670 MW	36440 TQ	USBLS	5/15
Except Computer	Maryland	Y	18692 AE	30503 MW	36408 AEX	MDBLS	4/16
Except Computer	Baltimore-Columbia-Towson MSA, MD	Y	18800 FQ	24460 MW	33160 TQ	USBLS	5/15
Except Computer	Massachusetts	Y	26640 FQ	32020 MW	41360 TQ	USBLS	5/15
Except Computer	Boston-Cambridge-Newton NECTA, MA	Y	27000 FQ	32000 MW	41570 TQ	USBLS	5/15
Except Computer	Worcester MSA, MA-CT	Y	22970 FQ	29960 MW	37540 TQ	USBLS	5/15
Except Computer	Michigan	Y	21160 FQ	26830 MW	33680 TQ	USBLS	5/15
Except Computer	Detroit-Dearborn-Livonia PMSA, MI	Y	26300 FQ	33120 MW	41060 TQ	USBLS	5/15
Except Computer	Grand Rapids-Wyoming MSA, MI	Y	20040 FQ	26920 MW	31550 TQ	USBLS	5/15
Except Computer	Minnesota	Y	28235 FQ	33716 MW	39187 TQ	MNBLS	1/16-3/16
Except Computer	Minneapolis-St. Paul-Bloomington MSA, MN-WI	Y	29327 FQ	34717 MW	40158 TQ	MNBLS	1/16-3/16
Except Computer	Mississippi	Y	20770 FQ	23600 MW	29700 TQ	USBLS	5/15
Except Computer	Jackson MSA, MS	Y	20610 FQ	23100 MW	26660 TQ	USBLS	5/15
Except Computer	Missouri	Y	23080 FQ	29050 MW	36160 TQ	USBLS	5/15
Except Computer	Kansas City MSA, MO-KS	Y	25420 FQ	29730 MW	35670 TQ	USBLS	5/15
Except Computer	St. Louis MSA, MO-IL	Y	21440 FQ	27780 MW	37590 TQ	USBLS	5/15
Except Computer	Montana	Y	21560 FQ	24500 MW	28730 TQ	USBLS	5/15
Except Computer	Billings MSA, MT	Y	20510 FQ	23410 MW	29810 TQ	USBLS	5/15
Except Computer	Nebraska	Y	28545 FQ	36870 MW	44580 TQ	NEBLS	7/16-9/16

AE	Average entry wage	AWR	Average wage range	H	Hourly
AEX	Average experienced wage	B	Biweekly	HI	Highest wage paid
ATC	Average total compensation	D	Daily	HR	High end range
AW	Average wage paid	FQ	First quartile wage	LO	Lowest wage paid

LR	Low end range	MTC	Median total compensation
M	Monthly	MW	Median wage paid
MCC	Median cash compensation	MWR	Median wage range
ME	Median entry wage	S	See annotated source

TCC	Total cash compensation
TQ	Third quartile wage
W	Weekly
Y	Yearly

Office Machine Operator

Occupation/Type/Industry	Location	Per	Low	Mid	High	Source	Date
Except Computer	Omaha-Council Bluffs MSA, NE-IA	Y	30670 FQ	40190 MW	45790 TQ	NEBLS	7/16-9/16
Except Computer	New Hampshire	H	9.28 AE	12.78 MW	15.61 AEX	NHBLS	6/16
Except Computer	Manchester NECTA, NH	H	9.01 AE	11.51 MW	13.18 AEX	NHBLS	6/16
Except Computer	Nashua NECTA, NH-MA	Y	17930 FQ	22400 MW	34800 TQ	USBLS	5/15
Except Computer	New Jersey	Y	21750 FQ	27830 MW	36040 TQ	USBLS	5/15
Except Computer	Camden PMSA, NJ	Y	24980 FQ	29530 MW	37360 TQ	USBLS	5/15
Except Computer	Newark PMSA, NJ-PA	Y	22790 FQ	29390 MW	39760 TQ	USBLS	5/15
Except Computer	Trenton MSA, NJ	Y	23390 FQ	29660 MW	43130 TQ	USBLS	5/15
Except Computer	New Mexico	Y	19240 FQ	23200 MW	28920 TQ	USBLS	5/15
Except Computer	Albuquerque MSA, NM	Y	19300 FQ	23110 MW	28960 TQ	USBLS	5/15
Except Computer	New York	Y	23450 AE	32310 MW	40750 AEX	NYBLS	1/16-3/16
Except Computer	Buffalo-Cheektowaga-Niagara Falls MSA, NY	Y	27600 FQ	35380 MW	43330 TQ	USBLS	5/15
Except Computer	Nassau County-Suffolk County PMSA, NY	Y	20760 FQ	32870 MW	45360 TQ	USBLS	5/15
Except Computer	New York-Jersey City-White Plains PMSA, NY-NJ	Y	24130 FQ	29940 MW	38670 TQ	USBLS	5/15
Except Computer	Rochester MSA, NY	Y	23480 FQ	28410 MW	34120 TQ	USBLS	5/15
Except Computer	North Carolina	Y	24210 FQ	27640 MW	30870 TQ	USBLS	5/15
Except Computer	Charlotte-Concord-Gastonia MSA, NC-SC	Y	24900 FQ	28410 MW	32830 TQ	USBLS	5/15
Except Computer	Raleigh MSA, NC	Y	22400 FQ	27710 MW	34090 TQ	USBLS	5/15
Except Computer	North Dakota	Y	21460 FQ	23950 MW	28780 TQ	USBLS	5/15
Except Computer	Fargo MSA, ND-MN	Y	20800 FQ	22900 MW	25260 TQ	USBLS	5/15
Except Computer	Ohio	Y	21980 FQ	26730 MW	33950 TQ	USBLS	5/15
Except Computer	Cincinnati MSA, OH-KY-IN	Y	22130 FQ	27130 MW	33990 TQ	USBLS	5/15
Except Computer	Cleveland-Elyria MSA, OH	Y	24380 FQ	30160 MW	38720 TQ	USBLS	5/15
Except Computer	Columbus MSA, OH	Y	21940 FQ	25530 MW	31150 TQ	USBLS	5/15
Except Computer	Oklahoma	Y	22160 FQ	27260 MW	32740 TQ	USBLS	5/15
Except Computer	Oklahoma City MSA, OK	Y	21550 FQ	25720 MW	30960 TQ	USBLS	5/15
Except Computer	Tulsa MSA, OK	Y	26060 FQ	30390 MW	35340 TQ	USBLS	5/15
Except Computer	Oregon	H	12.59 FQ	14.87 MW	19.61 TQ	ORBLS	2016
Except Computer	Portland-Vancouver-Hillsboro MSA, OR-WA	Y	26580 FQ	30600 MW	40070 TQ	USBLS	5/15
Except Computer	Pennsylvania	Y	22880 FQ	29520 MW	37020 TQ	USBLS	5/15
Except Computer	Allentown-Bethlehem-Easton MSA, PA-NJ	Y	22150 FQ	27580 MW	32270 TQ	USBLS	5/15
Except Computer	Harrisburg-Carlisle MSA, PA	Y	23410 FQ	28340 MW	33790 TQ	USBLS	5/15
Except Computer	Montgomery County-Bucks County-Chester County PMSA, PA	Y	23680 FQ	33670 MW	45040 TQ	USBLS	5/15
Except Computer	Philadelphia PMSA, PA	Y	23920 FQ	30850 MW	36620 TQ	USBLS	5/15
Except Computer	Pittsburgh MSA, PA	Y	25240 FQ	30960 MW	38130 TQ	USBLS	5/15
Except Computer	South Carolina	Y	20690 FQ	25690 MW	31190 TQ	USBLS	5/15
Except Computer	Charleston-North Charleston MSA, SC	Y	17690 FQ	19700 MW	24480 TQ	USBLS	5/15
Except Computer	Greenville-Anderson-Mauldin MSA, SC	Y	18550 FQ	26510 MW	29420 TQ	USBLS	5/15
Except Computer	South Dakota	Y	23910 FQ	27660 MW	31090 TQ	USBLS	5/15
Except Computer	Sioux Falls MSA, SD	Y	24220 FQ	27890 MW	31270 TQ	USBLS	5/15
Except Computer	Tennessee	Y	21860 FQ	24870 MW	30440 TQ	USBLS	5/15
Except Computer	Knoxville MSA, TN	Y	21190 FQ	23260 MW	26990 TQ	USBLS	5/15
Except Computer	Memphis MSA, TN-MS-AR	Y	21880 FQ	25170 MW	32420 TQ	USBLS	5/15
Except Computer	Nashville-Davidson–Murfreesboro–Franklin MSA, TN	Y	22740 FQ	26690 MW	31890 TQ	USBLS	5/15
Except Computer	Texas	Y	22160 FQ	28300 MW	36270 TQ	USBLS	5/15
Except Computer	Austin-Round Rock MSA, TX	Y	28100 FQ	33220 MW	38260 TQ	USBLS	5/15
Except Computer	Dallas-Plano-Irving PMSA, TX	Y	23740 FQ	30090 MW	39600 TQ	USBLS	5/15
Except Computer	Fort Worth-Arlington PMSA, TX	Y	18610 FQ	25820 MW	30890 TQ	USBLS	5/15
Except Computer	Houston-The Woodlands-Sugar Land MSA, TX	Y	21180 FQ	27560 MW	38410 TQ	USBLS	5/15
Except Computer	San Antonio-New Braunfels MSA, TX	Y	25550 FQ	28040 MW	30510 TQ	USBLS	5/15
Except Computer	Utah	Y	21280 FQ	26020 MW	33370 TQ	USBLS	5/15
Except Computer	Ogden-Clearfield MSA, UT	Y	22010 FQ	24400 MW	31920 TQ	USBLS	5/15
Except Computer	Provo-Orem MSA, UT	Y	18240 FQ	21500 MW	24460 TQ	USBLS	5/15
Except Computer	Salt Lake City MSA, UT	Y	21780 FQ	27930 MW	34430 TQ	USBLS	5/15
Except Computer	Vermont	Y	21850 FQ	25430 MW	32830 TQ	USBLS	5/15

AE	Average entry wage	AWR	Average wage range	H	Hourly
AEX	Average experienced wage	B	Biweekly	HI	Highest wage paid
ATC	Average total compensation	D	Daily	HR	High end range
AW	Average wage paid	FQ	First quartile wage	LO	Lowest wage paid

LR	Low end range	MTC	Median total compensation	TCC	Total cash compensation
M	Monthly	MW	Median wage paid	TQ	Third quartile wage
MCC	Median cash compensation	MWR	Median wage range	W	Weekly
ME	Median entry wage	S	See annotated source	Y	Yearly

Occupation/Type/Industry	Location	Per	Low	Mid	High	Source	Date
Office Machine Operator							
Except Computer	Burlington-South Burlington MSA, VT	Y	22260 FQ	24760 MW	29010 TQ	USBLS	5/15
Except Computer	Virginia	Y	20870 FQ	26840 MW	33140 TQ	USBLS	5/15
Except Computer	Richmond MSA, VA	Y	20780 FQ	25240 MW	33660 TQ	USBLS	5/15
Except Computer	Virginia Beach-Norfolk-Newport News MSA, VA-NC	Y	19450 FQ	22840 MW	29400 TQ	USBLS	5/15
Except Computer	Washington	H	14.59 FQ	17.49 MW	20.87 TQ	WABLS	3/16
Except Computer	Seattle-Bellevue-Everett PMSA, WA	H	14.26 FQ	17.14 MW	20.40 TQ	WABLS	3/16
Except Computer	Tacoma-Lakewood PMSA, WA	H	16.45 FQ	18.91 MW	22.12 TQ	WABLS	3/16
Except Computer	West Virginia	Y	19450 FQ	23900 MW	31850 TQ	USBLS	5/15
Except Computer	Wisconsin	Y	26280 FQ	30010 MW	36470 TQ	USBLS	5/15
Except Computer	Madison MSA, WI	Y	27090 FQ	30730 MW	36500 TQ	USBLS	5/15
Except Computer	Milwaukee-Waukesha-West Allis MSA, WI	Y	24760 FQ	29750 MW	36390 TQ	USBLS	5/15
Except Computer	Wyoming	Y	21940 FQ	26600 MW	30290 TQ	USBLS	5/15
Except Computer	Cheyenne MSA, WY	Y	21430 FQ	26100 MW	29420 TQ	USBLS	5/15
Except Computer	Puerto Rico	Y	17080 FQ	18660 MW	22150 TQ	USBLS	5/15
Except Computer	San Juan-Carolina-Caguas MSA, PR	Y	17120 FQ	18810 MW	22660 TQ	USBLS	5/15
Oil Engineer	United States	S		101000 AW		IBD01	2016
Oil Recycling Clerk							
Municipal Government	Colfax, CA	Y		1351 AW		CACIT	6/28/16
Oil-Rigger							
Municipal Government	Seattle, WA	H	24.10 LO		25.01 HI	CSSS	1/2/13
Older Adult Services Manager							
Municipal Government	Escondido, CA	Y			75646 HI	CACIT	6/28/16
On-Air Personality							
Radio, Large Market	United States	Y		70000-150000 AWR		BBRD01	2014
Radio, Medium Market	United States	Y		40000-90000 AWR		BBRD01	2014
Radio, Small Market	United States	Y		20000-50000 AWR		BBRD01	2014
Online Instructional Designer							
Entry-Level, Baccalaureate Institution	United States	Y		45320 MW		CHE02	2015-2016
Entry-Level, Master's Institution	United States	Y		49084 MW		CHE02	2015-2016
Entry-Level, Research University	United States	Y		54051 MW		CHE02	2015-2016
Online Sales Manager	United States	Y		111346 MW		CCAST01	2016
Online Technology Coordinator							
Ivy Tech Community College of Indiana	East Chicago, IN	Y			34893 HI	INDYS	2017
Open Source Officer							
Central Intelligence Agency	District of Columbia	Y	51603 LO		100736 HI	CIA05	2016
Operating Engineer and Other Construction Equipment Operator	Alabama	Y	28433 AE	38422 AW	43421 AEX	ALBLS	6/16
	Birmingham-Hoover MSA, AL	Y	33834 AE	43935 AW	48986 AEX	ALBLS	6/16
	Alaska	Y	56490 FQ	65480 MW	78250 TQ	USBLS	5/15
	Anchorage MSA, AK	Y	60990 FQ	71040 MW	84210 TQ	USBLS	5/15
	Arizona	Y	35870 FQ	43980 MW	51900 TQ	USBLS	5/15
	Phoenix-Mesa-Scottsdale MSA, AZ	Y	36140 FQ	44270 MW	51480 TQ	USBLS	5/15
	Tucson MSA, AZ	Y	34640 FQ	40760 MW	47010 TQ	USBLS	5/15
	Arkansas	Y	27730 FQ	33510 MW	39060 TQ	USBLS	5/15
	Little Rock-North Little Rock-Conway MSA, AR	Y	29410 FQ	34920 MW	40940 TQ	USBLS	5/15
	California	H	24.36 FQ	31.14 MW	40.75 TQ	CABLS	1/16-3/16
	Anaheim-Santa Ana-Irvine PMSA, CA	H	29.41 FQ	38.74 MW	44.32 TQ	CABLS	1/16-3/16
	Los Angeles-Long Beach-Glendale PMSA, CA	H	27.25 FQ	38.03 MW	44.86 TQ	CABLS	1/16-3/16

AE	Average entry wage	AWR	Average wage range	H	Hourly	LR	Low end range	MTC	Median total compensation	TCC	Total cash compensation
AEX	Average experienced wage	B	Biweekly	HI	Highest wage paid	M	Monthly	MW	Median wage paid	TQ	Third quartile wage
ATC	Average total compensation	D	Daily	HR	High end range	MCC	Median cash compensation	MWR	Median wage range	W	Weekly
AW	Average wage paid	FQ	First quartile wage	LO	Lowest wage paid	ME	Median entry wage	S	See annotated source	Y	Yearly

1133

Occupation/Type/Industry	Location	Per	Low	Mid	High	Source	Date
Operating Engineer and Other Construction Equipment Operator	Oakland-Hayward-Berkeley PMSA, CA	H	29.47 FQ	35.12 MW	40.15 TQ	CABLS	1/16-3/16
	Riverside-San Bernardino-Ontario MSA, CA	H	23.68 FQ	29.53 MW	41.78 TQ	CABLS	1/16-3/16
	Sacramento–Roseville–Arden-Arcade MSA, CA	H	24.62 FQ	31.22 MW	37.80 TQ	CABLS	1/16-3/16
	San Diego-Carlsbad MSA, CA	H	23.97 FQ	29.19 MW	42.59 TQ	CABLS	1/16-3/16
	San Francisco-Redwood City-South San Francisco PMSA, CA	H	32.52 FQ	37.87 MW	43.55 TQ	CABLS	1/16-3/16
	Colorado	Y	37810 FQ	44830 MW	52410 TQ	USBLS	5/15
	Denver-Aurora-Lakewood MSA, CO	Y	39300 FQ	45870 MW	53790 TQ	USBLS	5/15
	Connecticut	Y		63850 MW		CTBLS	1/16-3/16
	Bridgeport-Stamford-Norwalk MSA, CT	Y	54450 FQ	65940 MW	75220 TQ	USBLS	5/15
	Hartford-West Hartford-East Hartford MSA, CT	Y	51040 FQ	61850 MW	73740 TQ	USBLS	5/15
	Delaware	Y	34240 FQ	42010 MW	49680 TQ	USBLS	5/15
	Wilmington PMSA, DE-MD-NJ	Y	34400 FQ	44200 MW	55930 TQ	USBLS	5/15
	District of Columbia	Y	44910 FQ	56330 MW	67180 TQ	USBLS	5/15
	Washington-Arlington-Alexandria PMSA, DC-VA-MD-WV	Y	36050 FQ	44580 MW	54520 TQ	USBLS	5/15
	Florida	H	13.35 AE	17.24 MW	20.29 AEX	FLBLS	7/16-9/16
	Fort Lauderdale-Pompano Beach-Deerfield Beach PMSA, FL	H	15.61 AE	19.31 MW	22.52 AEX	FLBLS	7/16-9/16
	Miami-Miami Beach-Kendall PMSA, FL	H	13.19 AE	17.79 MW	20.88 AEX	FLBLS	7/16-9/16
	Orlando-Kissimmee-Sanford MSA, FL	H	13.73 AE	17.18 MW	20.29 AEX	FLBLS	7/16-9/16
	Tampa-St. Petersburg-Clearwater MSA, FL	H	13.07 AE	17.12 MW	19.54 AEX	FLBLS	7/16-9/16
	Georgia	Y	27660 FQ	32980 MW	38830 TQ	USBLS	5/15
	Atlanta-Sandy Springs-Roswell MSA, GA	Y	29880 FQ	35070 MW	41120 TQ	USBLS	5/15
	Augusta-Richmond County MSA, GA-SC	Y	28250 FQ	33300 MW	39520 TQ	USBLS	5/15
	Hawaii	Y	52110 FQ	72900 MW	89100 TQ	USBLS	5/15
	Urban Honolulu MSA, HI	Y	62460 FQ	80480 MW	92620 TQ	USBLS	5/15
	Idaho	Y	34720 FQ	40710 MW	48740 TQ	USBLS	5/15
	Boise City MSA, ID	Y	34410 FQ	39850 MW	46180 TQ	USBLS	5/15
	Illinois	Y	56110 FQ	74620 MW	89600 TQ	USBLS	5/15
	Chicago-Naperville-Arlington Heights PMSA, IL	Y	65220 FQ	84070 MW	93500 TQ	USBLS	5/15
	Lake County-Kenosha County PMSA, IL-WI	Y	62430 FQ	80510 MW	93050 TQ	USBLS	5/15
	Indiana	Y	37450 FQ	51300 MW	67810 TQ	USBLS	5/15
	Gary PMSA, IN	Y	48200 FQ	65510 MW	86000 TQ	USBLS	5/15
	Indianapolis-Carmel-Anderson MSA, IN	Y	40880 FQ	58970 MW	70810 TQ	USBLS	5/15
	Iowa	Y	36080 FQ	44790 MW	55660 TQ	USBLS	5/15
	Des Moines-West Des Moines MSA, IA	Y	40730 FQ	51810 MW	59760 TQ	USBLS	5/15
	Kansas	Y	29890 FQ	35810 MW	46890 TQ	USBLS	5/15
	Wichita MSA, KS	Y	29690 FQ	34380 MW	39450 TQ	USBLS	5/15
	Kentucky	Y	31820 FQ	38820 MW	52910 TQ	USBLS	5/15
	Louisville-Jefferson County MSA, KY-IN	Y	36840 FQ	45710 MW	56220 TQ	USBLS	5/15
	Louisiana	Y	31380 FQ	38110 MW	48290 TQ	USBLS	5/15
	Baton Rouge MSA, LA	Y	30940 FQ	36620 MW	45530 TQ	USBLS	5/15
	New Orleans-Metairie MSA, LA	Y	30440 FQ	37320 MW	46070 TQ	USBLS	5/15
	Maine	Y	29140 FQ	34790 MW	42640 TQ	USBLS	5/15
	Portland-South Portland MSA, ME	Y	30600 FQ	36170 MW	43580 TQ	USBLS	5/15
	Maryland	Y	35039 AE	47161 MW	53222 AEX	MDBLS	4/16

AE Average entry wage	AWR Average wage range	H Hourly	LR Low end range	MTC Median total compensation	TCC Total cash compensation
AEX Average experienced wage	B Biweekly	HI Highest wage paid	M Monthly	MW Median wage paid	TQ Third quartile wage
ATC Average total compensation	D Daily	HR High end range	MCC Median cash compensation	MWR Median wage range	W Weekly
AW Average wage paid	FQ First quartile wage	LO Lowest wage paid	ME Median entry wage	S See annotated source	Y Yearly

Occupation/Type/Industry	Location	Per	Low	Mid	High	Source	Date
Operating Engineer and Other Construction Equipment Operator							
	Baltimore-Columbia-Towson MSA, MD	Y	40940 FQ	47650 MW	56910 TQ	USBLS	5/15
	Salisbury MSA, MD-DE	Y	34430 FQ	40310 MW	47780 TQ	USBLS	5/15
	Massachusetts	Y	46090 FQ	63900 MW	83560 TQ	USBLS	5/15
	Boston-Cambridge-Newton NECTA, MA	Y	45710 FQ	70010 MW	90830 TQ	USBLS	5/15
	Worcester MSA, MA-CT	Y	45520 FQ	54410 MW	68670 TQ	USBLS	5/15
	Michigan	Y	38540 FQ	46240 MW	55710 TQ	USBLS	5/15
	Detroit-Dearborn-Livonia PMSA, MI	Y	40300 FQ	50240 MW	59620 TQ	USBLS	5/15
	Grand Rapids-Wyoming MSA, MI	Y	39490 FQ	45510 MW	51790 TQ	USBLS	5/15
	Minnesota	Y	44175 FQ	57292 MW	71055 TQ	MNBLS	1/16-3/16
	Minneapolis-St. Paul-Bloomington MSA, MN-WI	Y	56243 FQ	66989 MW	75616 TQ	MNBLS	1/16-3/16
	Mississippi	Y	28790 FQ	36370 MW	45300 TQ	USBLS	5/15
	Jackson MSA, MS	Y	23420 FQ	33110 MW	39510 TQ	USBLS	5/15
	Missouri	Y	37850 FQ	50070 MW	68610 TQ	USBLS	5/15
	Kansas City MSA, MO-KS	Y	41500 FQ	53740 MW	67140 TQ	USBLS	5/15
	St. Louis MSA, MO-IL	Y	46250 FQ	64450 MW	72610 TQ	USBLS	5/15
	Montana	Y	40110 FQ	46390 MW	54640 TQ	USBLS	5/15
	Billings MSA, MT	Y	40160 FQ	45700 MW	51250 TQ	USBLS	5/15
	Nebraska	Y	31540 FQ	37165 MW	46165 TQ	NEBLS	7/16-9/16
	Omaha-Council Bluffs MSA, NE-IA	Y	34645 FQ	40975 MW	50420 TQ	NEBLS	7/16-9/16
	Nevada	Y	42080 FQ	54580 MW	71450 TQ	USBLS	5/15
	Las Vegas-Henderson-Paradise MSA, NV	Y	54080 FQ	64060 MW	86610 TQ	USBLS	5/15
	New Hampshire	H	16.71 AE	21.42 MW	24.74 AEX	NHBLS	6/16
	Manchester NECTA, NH	H	17.10 AE	20.99 MW	23.54 AEX	NHBLS	6/16
	Nashua NECTA, NH-MA	Y	44520 FQ	52710 MW	61250 TQ	USBLS	5/15
	New Jersey	Y	50120 FQ	65050 MW	84530 TQ	USBLS	5/15
	Camden PMSA, NJ	Y	55800 FQ	72220 MW	87570 TQ	USBLS	5/15
	Newark PMSA, NJ-PA	Y	48230 FQ	61800 MW	85810 TQ	USBLS	5/15
	Trenton MSA, NJ	Y	51190 FQ	58130 MW	73610 TQ	USBLS	5/15
	New Mexico	Y	33570 FQ	39860 MW	51370 TQ	USBLS	5/15
	Albuquerque MSA, NM	Y	33900 FQ	38230 MW	47200 TQ	USBLS	5/15
	New York	Y	41690 AE	63640 MW	89850 AEX	NYBLS	1/16-3/16
	Buffalo-Cheektowaga-Niagara Falls MSA, NY	Y	50890 FQ	66340 MW	73960 TQ	USBLS	5/15
	Nassau County-Suffolk County PMSA, NY	Y	52510 FQ	65190 MW	108520 TQ	USBLS	5/15
	New York-Jersey City-White Plains PMSA, NY-NJ	Y	56710 FQ	77980 MW	109750 TQ	USBLS	5/15
	Rochester MSA, NY	Y	41260 FQ	51900 MW	66850 TQ	USBLS	5/15
	North Carolina	Y	30130 FQ	35100 MW	40090 TQ	USBLS	5/15
	Charlotte-Concord-Gastonia MSA, NC-SC	Y	31910 FQ	35920 MW	40840 TQ	USBLS	5/15
	Raleigh MSA, NC	Y	32270 FQ	36800 MW	43750 TQ	USBLS	5/15
	North Dakota	Y	44650 FQ	53240 MW	61220 TQ	USBLS	5/15
	Fargo MSA, ND-MN	Y	41800 FQ	47940 MW	55880 TQ	USBLS	5/15
	Ohio	Y	39740 FQ	48860 MW	66770 TQ	USBLS	5/15
	Cincinnati MSA, OH-KY-IN	Y	40500 FQ	48600 MW	60340 TQ	USBLS	5/15
	Cleveland-Elyria MSA, OH	Y	46250 FQ	61050 MW	72180 TQ	USBLS	5/15
	Columbus MSA, OH	Y	40680 FQ	50390 MW	67950 TQ	USBLS	5/15
	Oklahoma	Y	31780 FQ	36920 MW	45270 TQ	USBLS	5/15
	Oklahoma City MSA, OK	Y	32900 FQ	37050 MW	44830 TQ	USBLS	5/15
	Tulsa MSA, OK	Y	32890 FQ	37730 MW	45530 TQ	USBLS	5/15
	Oregon	H	20.06 FQ	25.03 MW	29.79 TQ	ORBLS	2016
	Portland-Vancouver-Hillsboro MSA, OR-WA	Y	48240 FQ	57650 MW	67910 TQ	USBLS	5/15
	Pennsylvania	Y	36200 FQ	43990 MW	55880 TQ	USBLS	5/15
	Allentown-Bethlehem-Easton MSA, PA-NJ	Y	35730 FQ	41290 MW	48940 TQ	USBLS	5/15
	Harrisburg-Carlisle MSA, PA	Y	35580 FQ	40280 MW	46500 TQ	USBLS	5/15
	Montgomery County-Bucks County-Chester County PMSA, PA	Y	48040 FQ	59200 MW	82180 TQ	USBLS	5/15
	Philadelphia PMSA, PA	Y	43320 FQ	54330 MW	81750 TQ	USBLS	5/15

AE	Average entry wage	AWR	Average wage range	H	Hourly
AEX	Average experienced wage	B	Biweekly	HI	Highest wage paid
ATC	Average total compensation	D	Daily	HR	High end range
AW	Average wage paid	FQ	First quartile wage	LO	Lowest wage paid

LR	Low end range	MTC	Median total compensation	TCC	Total cash compensation
M	Monthly	MW	Median wage paid	TQ	Third quartile wage
MCC	Median cash compensation	MWR	Median wage range	W	Weekly
ME	Median entry wage	S	See annotated source	Y	Yearly

Occupation/Type/Industry	Location	Per	Low	Mid	High	Source	Date
Operating Engineer and Other Construction Equipment Operator	Pittsburgh MSA, PA	Y	36700 FQ	47570 MW	57720 TQ	USBLS	5/15
	Rhode Island	Y	37560 FQ	52060 MW	60340 TQ	USBLS	5/15
	Providence-Warwick MSA, RI-MA	Y	37390 FQ	51950 MW	60730 TQ	USBLS	5/15
	South Carolina	Y	28890 FQ	34460 MW	40750 TQ	USBLS	5/15
	Charleston-North Charleston MSA, SC	Y	32190 FQ	37580 MW	45950 TQ	USBLS	5/15
	Columbia MSA, SC	Y	27390 FQ	32810 MW	38770 TQ	USBLS	5/15
	Greenville-Anderson-Mauldin MSA, SC	Y	29410 FQ	34450 MW	38920 TQ	USBLS	5/15
	South Dakota	Y	33940 FQ	38220 MW	45810 TQ	USBLS	5/15
	Sioux Falls MSA, SD	Y	35110 FQ	38990 MW	46060 TQ	USBLS	5/15
	Tennessee	Y	32570 FQ	36790 MW	44760 TQ	USBLS	5/15
	Knoxville MSA, TN	Y	32250 FQ	35890 MW	39720 TQ	USBLS	5/15
	Memphis MSA, TN-MS-AR	Y	32840 FQ	37770 MW	47710 TQ	USBLS	5/15
	Nashville-Davidson–Murfreesboro–Franklin MSA, TN	Y	33540 FQ	37790 MW	47650 TQ	USBLS	5/15
	Texas	Y	31220 FQ	36900 MW	45810 TQ	USBLS	5/15
	Austin-Round Rock MSA, TX	Y	30120 FQ	35320 MW	41010 TQ	USBLS	5/15
	Dallas-Plano-Irving PMSA, TX	Y	31920 FQ	36630 MW	44650 TQ	USBLS	5/15
	Fort Worth-Arlington PMSA, TX	Y	31090 FQ	36030 MW	42260 TQ	USBLS	5/15
	Houston-The Woodlands-Sugar Land MSA, TX	Y	32720 FQ	38730 MW	48820 TQ	USBLS	5/15
	San Antonio-New Braunfels MSA, TX	Y	28520 FQ	33570 MW	38230 TQ	USBLS	5/15
	Utah	Y	35280 FQ	42190 MW	51780 TQ	USBLS	5/15
	Ogden-Clearfield MSA, UT	Y	35600 FQ	43660 MW	55550 TQ	USBLS	5/15
	Provo-Orem MSA, UT	Y	32570 FQ	36220 MW	40870 TQ	USBLS	5/15
	Salt Lake City MSA, UT	Y	37550 FQ	44640 MW	54530 TQ	USBLS	5/15
	Vermont	Y	34410 FQ	40140 MW	46150 TQ	USBLS	5/15
	Burlington-South Burlington MSA, VT	Y	35790 FQ	41750 MW	47960 TQ	USBLS	5/15
	Virginia	Y	32110 FQ	37890 MW	47450 TQ	USBLS	5/15
	Richmond MSA, VA	Y	31830 FQ	36470 MW	44320 TQ	USBLS	5/15
	Virginia Beach-Norfolk-Newport News MSA, VA-NC	Y	31460 FQ	38010 MW	50250 TQ	USBLS	5/15
	Washington	H	22.84 FQ	28.18 MW	34.25 TQ	WABLS	3/16
	Seattle-Bellevue-Everett PMSA, WA	H	27.30 FQ	32.68 MW	36.73 TQ	WABLS	3/16
	Tacoma-Lakewood PMSA, WA	H	26.54 FQ	30.84 MW	36.23 TQ	WABLS	3/16
	West Virginia	Y	35090 FQ	44480 MW	59400 TQ	USBLS	5/15
	Huntington-Ashland MSA, WV-KY-OH	Y	38110 FQ	49460 MW	68300 TQ	USBLS	5/15
	Wisconsin	Y	42170 FQ	53150 MW	69920 TQ	USBLS	5/15
	Madison MSA, WI	Y	49750 FQ	66090 MW	73830 TQ	USBLS	5/15
	Milwaukee-Waukesha-West Allis MSA, WI	Y	54080 FQ	65780 MW	75740 TQ	USBLS	5/15
	Wyoming	Y	43680 FQ	54560 MW	68300 TQ	USBLS	5/15
	Cheyenne MSA, WY	Y	38690 FQ	44940 MW	55590 TQ	USBLS	5/15
	Puerto Rico	Y	17380 FQ	19320 MW	24040 TQ	USBLS	5/15
	San Juan-Carolina-Caguas MSA, PR	Y	17720 FQ	20300 MW	27080 TQ	USBLS	5/15
	Virgin Islands	Y	21720 FQ	24050 MW	42170 TQ	USBLS	5/15
	Guam	Y	30130 FQ	34350 MW	38090 TQ	USBLS	5/15
Operating Room Materials Manager	United States	Y		76250 AW		HPN02	2016
Operations Manager							
Airport	Detroit, MI	M	3983 LO		4375 HI	DETGOV	2016
Copier Industry	United States	Y		90037 AW		COPIER2	2016
Operations Research Analyst	Alabama	Y	62046 AE	96927 AW	114368 AEX	ALBLS	6/16
	Birmingham-Hoover MSA, AL	Y	54891 AE	88742 AW	105663 AEX	ALBLS	6/16
	Alaska	Y	48780 FQ	71100 MW	96010 TQ	USBLS	5/15
	Arizona	Y	51280 FQ	67600 MW	85940 TQ	USBLS	5/15

AE Average entry wage	**AWR** Average wage range	**H** Hourly	**LR** Low end range	**MTC** Median total compensation	**TCC** Total cash compensation
AEX Average experienced wage	**B** Biweekly	**HI** Highest wage paid	**M** Monthly	**MW** Median wage paid	**TQ** Third quartile wage
ATC Average total compensation	**D** Daily	**HR** High end range	**MCC** Median cash compensation	**MWR** Median wage range	**W** Weekly
AW Average wage paid	**FQ** First quartile wage	**LO** Lowest wage paid	**ME** Median entry wage	**S** See annotated source	**Y** Yearly

Operations Research Analyst

Occupation/Type/Industry	Location	Per	Low	Mid	High	Source	Date
Operations Research Analyst	Phoenix-Mesa-Scottsdale MSA, AZ	Y	51260 FQ	67530 MW	85440 TQ	USBLS	5/15
	Tucson MSA, AZ	Y	50330 FQ	66550 MW	87420 TQ	USBLS	5/15
	Arkansas	Y	45850 FQ	59370 MW	77130 TQ	USBLS	5/15
	Little Rock-North Little Rock-Conway MSA, AR	Y	47790 FQ	58310 MW	71520 TQ	USBLS	5/15
	California	H	32.65 FQ	44.03 MW	57.87 TQ	CABLS	1/16-3/16
	Anaheim-Santa Ana-Irvine PMSA, CA	H	31.19 FQ	40.68 MW	48.59 TQ	CABLS	1/16-3/16
	Los Angeles-Long Beach-Glendale PMSA, CA	H	29.69 FQ	41.01 MW	51.86 TQ	CABLS	1/16-3/16
	Oakland-Hayward-Berkeley PMSA, CA	H	31.94 FQ	47.92 MW	62.60 TQ	CABLS	1/16-3/16
	Riverside-San Bernardino-Ontario MSA, CA	H	31.39 FQ	38.60 MW	48.76 TQ	CABLS	1/16-3/16
	Sacramento–Roseville–Arden-Arcade MSA, CA	H	20.78 FQ	31.92 MW	44.08 TQ	CABLS	1/16-3/16
	San Diego-Carlsbad MSA, CA	H	31.04 FQ	41.47 MW	54.77 TQ	CABLS	1/16-3/16
	San Francisco-Redwood City-South San Francisco PMSA, CA	H	35.07 FQ	44.37 MW	59.71 TQ	CABLS	1/16-3/16
	Colorado	Y	67460 FQ	84970 MW	107990 TQ	USBLS	5/15
	Denver-Aurora-Lakewood MSA, CO	Y	64530 FQ	79870 MW	97010 TQ	USBLS	5/15
	Connecticut	Y		91913 MW		CTBLS	1/16-3/16
	Bridgeport-Stamford-Norwalk MSA, CT	Y	68440 FQ	89830 MW	117260 TQ	USBLS	5/15
	Hartford-West Hartford-East Hartford MSA, CT	Y	72150 FQ	88560 MW	110520 TQ	USBLS	5/15
	Delaware	Y	70780 FQ	89980 MW	110930 TQ	USBLS	5/15
	Wilmington PMSA, DE-MD-NJ	Y	71910 FQ	90690 MW	111360 TQ	USBLS	5/15
	District of Columbia	Y	89060 FQ	110640 MW	134680 TQ	USBLS	5/15
	Washington-Arlington-Alexandria PMSA, DC-VA-MD-WV	Y	83900 FQ	110230 MW	134680 TQ	USBLS	5/15
	Florida	H	19.40 AE	28.66 MW	37.53 AEX	FLBLS	7/16-9/16
	Fort Lauderdale-Pompano Beach-Deerfield Beach PMSA, FL	H	20.04 AE	28.84 MW	35.80 AEX	FLBLS	7/16-9/16
	Miami-Miami Beach-Kendall PMSA, FL	H	19.14 AE	28.17 MW	38.30 AEX	FLBLS	7/16-9/16
	Orlando-Kissimmee-Sanford MSA, FL	H	20.52 AE	30.49 MW	39.47 AEX	FLBLS	7/16-9/16
	Tampa-St. Petersburg-Clearwater MSA, FL	H	20.35 AE	29.83 MW	38.98 AEX	FLBLS	7/16-9/16
	Georgia	Y	44820 FQ	58420 MW	81850 TQ	USBLS	5/15
	Atlanta-Sandy Springs-Roswell MSA, GA	Y	45560 FQ	58400 MW	79550 TQ	USBLS	5/15
	Hawaii	Y	46950 FQ	59120 MW	74350 TQ	USBLS	5/15
	Urban Honolulu MSA, HI	Y	46770 FQ	59160 MW	74510 TQ	USBLS	5/15
	Idaho	Y	51200 FQ	61970 MW	80400 TQ	USBLS	5/15
	Boise City MSA, ID	Y	50190 FQ	60440 MW	79330 TQ	USBLS	5/15
	Illinois	Y	62690 FQ	81280 MW	109090 TQ	USBLS	5/15
	Chicago-Naperville-Arlington Heights PMSA, IL	Y	62190 FQ	79950 MW	107190 TQ	USBLS	5/15
	Lake County-Kenosha County PMSA, IL-WI	Y	53660 FQ	74740 MW	99500 TQ	USBLS	5/15
	Indiana	Y	52700 FQ	68310 MW	89500 TQ	USBLS	5/15
	Gary PMSA, IN	Y	57070 FQ	76740 MW	134250 TQ	USBLS	5/15
	Indianapolis-Carmel-Anderson MSA, IN	Y	52570 FQ	69670 MW	91310 TQ	USBLS	5/15
	Iowa	Y	55550 FQ	70580 MW	89630 TQ	USBLS	5/15
	Des Moines-West Des Moines MSA, IA	Y	51920 FQ	62810 MW	80630 TQ	USBLS	5/15
	Kansas	Y	47850 FQ	63690 MW	88820 TQ	USBLS	5/15
	Wichita MSA, KS	Y	49470 FQ	63740 MW	81580 TQ	USBLS	5/15
	Kentucky	Y	58510 FQ	72190 MW	87180 TQ	USBLS	5/15
	Louisville-Jefferson County MSA, KY-IN	Y	58540 FQ	70910 MW	80750 TQ	USBLS	5/15
	Louisiana	Y	37750 FQ	46820 MW	64310 TQ	USBLS	5/15
	Baton Rouge MSA, LA	Y	34560 FQ	41470 MW	49150 TQ	USBLS	5/15

AE	Average entry wage	AWR	Average wage range	H	Hourly	LR	Low end range	MTC	Median total compensation	TCC	Total cash compensation
AEX	Average experienced wage	B	Biweekly	HI	Highest wage paid	M	Monthly	MW	Median wage paid	TQ	Third quartile wage
ATC	Average total compensation	D	Daily	HR	High end range	MCC	Median cash compensation	MWR	Median wage range	W	Weekly
AW	Average wage paid	FQ	First quartile wage	LO	Lowest wage paid	ME	Median entry wage	S	See annotated source	Y	Yearly

Operations Research Analyst

Occupation/Type/Industry	Location	Per	Low	Mid	High	Source	Date
Operations Research Analyst	New Orleans-Metairie MSA, LA	Y	65230 FQ	72990 MW	81670 TQ	USBLS	5/15
	Maine	Y	50340 FQ	68030 MW	85240 TQ	USBLS	5/15
	Portland-South Portland MSA, ME	Y	54960 FQ	70720 MW	82910 TQ	USBLS	5/15
	Maryland	Y	56833 AE	94561 MW	113426 AEX	MDBLS	4/16
	Baltimore-Columbia-Towson MSA, MD	Y	69070 FQ	97210 MW	121470 TQ	USBLS	5/15
	Massachusetts	Y	50260 FQ	81010 MW	110270 TQ	USBLS	5/15
	Boston-Cambridge-Newton NECTA, MA	Y	42630 FQ	72820 MW	102810 TQ	USBLS	5/15
	Worcester MSA, MA-CT	Y	68930 FQ	79060 MW	99130 TQ	USBLS	5/15
	Michigan	Y	65490 FQ	84220 MW	102090 TQ	USBLS	5/15
	Detroit-Dearborn-Livonia PMSA, MI	Y	70930 FQ	86590 MW	102670 TQ	USBLS	5/15
	Grand Rapids-Wyoming MSA, MI	Y	53530 FQ	59580 MW	70490 TQ	USBLS	5/15
	Minnesota	Y	64515 FQ	81289 MW	104958 TQ	MNBLS	1/16-3/16
	Minneapolis-St. Paul-Bloomington MSA, MN-WI	Y	65009 FQ	81945 MW	106047 TQ	MNBLS	1/16-3/16
	Mississippi	Y	44600 FQ	65690 MW	90470 TQ	USBLS	5/15
	Jackson MSA, MS	Y	39200 FQ	55140 MW	87730 TQ	USBLS	5/15
	Missouri	Y	48200 FQ	60430 MW	82520 TQ	USBLS	5/15
	Kansas City MSA, MO-KS	Y	51100 FQ	64790 MW	98220 TQ	USBLS	5/15
	St. Louis MSA, MO-IL	Y	51040 FQ	68060 MW	91890 TQ	USBLS	5/15
	Montana	Y	45580 FQ	52880 MW	61270 TQ	USBLS	5/15
	Nebraska	Y	50545 FQ	65540 MW	89565 TQ	NEBLS	7/16-9/16
	Omaha-Council Bluffs MSA, NE-IA	Y	53400 FQ	69160 MW	92965 TQ	NEBLS	7/16-9/16
	Nevada	Y	56690 FQ	74830 MW	96740 TQ	USBLS	5/15
	Las Vegas-Henderson-Paradise MSA, NV	Y	55520 FQ	75060 MW	98800 TQ	USBLS	5/15
	Nashua NECTA, NH-MA	Y	56870 FQ	77020 MW	97050 TQ	USBLS	5/15
	New Jersey	Y	75530 FQ	96510 MW	122360 TQ	USBLS	5/15
	Camden PMSA, NJ	Y	63820 FQ	85470 MW	112380 TQ	USBLS	5/15
	Newark PMSA, NJ-PA	Y	79160 FQ	99390 MW	122480 TQ	USBLS	5/15
	Trenton MSA, NJ	Y	84660 FQ	97860 MW	112020 TQ	USBLS	5/15
	New Mexico	Y	58900 FQ	85480 MW	108500 TQ	USBLS	5/15
	Albuquerque MSA, NM	Y	59160 FQ	83470 MW	107730 TQ	USBLS	5/15
	New York	Y	52500 AE	85850 MW	128270 AEX	NYBLS	1/16-3/16
	Buffalo-Cheektowaga-Niagara Falls MSA, NY	Y	52640 FQ	65830 MW	88720 TQ	USBLS	5/15
	Nassau County-Suffolk County PMSA, NY	Y	68370 FQ	85510 MW	104880 TQ	USBLS	5/15
	New York-Jersey City-White Plains PMSA, NY-NJ	Y	63170 FQ	93450 MW	136360 TQ	USBLS	5/15
	Rochester MSA, NY	Y	51960 FQ	61960 MW	75110 TQ	USBLS	5/15
	North Carolina	Y	51060 FQ	65600 MW	90570 TQ	USBLS	5/15
	Charlotte-Concord-Gastonia MSA, NC-SC	Y	47780 FQ	62540 MW	88390 TQ	USBLS	5/15
	Raleigh MSA, NC	Y	57320 FQ	75870 MW	96750 TQ	USBLS	5/15
	North Dakota	Y	54770 FQ	70170 MW	91960 TQ	USBLS	5/15
	Fargo MSA, ND-MN	Y	54300 FQ	68970 MW	92670 TQ	USBLS	5/15
	Ohio	Y	59870 FQ	79420 MW	97420 TQ	USBLS	5/15
	Cincinnati MSA, OH-KY-IN	Y	69700 FQ	86010 MW	100610 TQ	USBLS	5/15
	Cleveland-Elyria MSA, OH	Y	53790 FQ	66770 MW	87670 TQ	USBLS	5/15
	Columbus MSA, OH	Y	60500 FQ	80800 MW	100370 TQ	USBLS	5/15
	Oklahoma	Y	46970 FQ	60420 MW	81680 TQ	USBLS	5/15
	Oklahoma City MSA, OK	Y	46020 FQ	58520 MW	78820 TQ	USBLS	5/15
	Tulsa MSA, OK	Y	46360 FQ	58620 MW	79090 TQ	USBLS	5/15
	Oregon	H	29.35 FQ	35.74 MW	43.01 TQ	ORBLS	2016
	Portland-Vancouver-Hillsboro MSA, OR-WA	Y	61060 FQ	74090 MW	90090 TQ	USBLS	5/15
	Pennsylvania	Y	54780 FQ	70270 MW	93530 TQ	USBLS	5/15
	Allentown-Bethlehem-Easton MSA, PA-NJ	Y	57630 FQ	67760 MW	78530 TQ	USBLS	5/15
	Harrisburg-Carlisle MSA, PA	Y	54610 FQ	63160 MW	82310 TQ	USBLS	5/15
	Montgomery County-Bucks County-Chester County PMSA, PA	Y	59770 FQ	79710 MW	102230 TQ	USBLS	5/15
	Philadelphia PMSA, PA	Y	62370 FQ	82290 MW	103320 TQ	USBLS	5/15
	Pittsburgh MSA, PA	Y	56260 FQ	72900 MW	95690 TQ	USBLS	5/15

AE	Average entry wage	AWR	Average wage range	H	Hourly
AEX	Average experienced wage	B	Biweekly	HI	Highest wage paid
ATC	Average total compensation	D	Daily	HR	High end range
AW	Average wage paid	FQ	First quartile wage	LO	Lowest wage paid

LR	Low end range	MTC	Median total compensation	TCC	Total cash compensation
M	Monthly	MW	Median wage paid	TQ	Third quartile wage
MCC	Median cash compensation	MWR	Median wage range	W	Weekly
ME	Median entry wage	S	See annotated source	Y	Yearly

Occupation/Type/Industry	Location	Per	Low	Mid	High	Source	Date
Operations Research Analyst	Rhode Island	Y	46730 FQ	64900 MW	111300 TQ	USBLS	5/15
	Providence-Warwick MSA, RI-MA	Y	47040 FQ	65820 MW	110450 TQ	USBLS	5/15
	South Carolina	Y	54760 FQ	70750 MW	89090 TQ	USBLS	5/15
	Columbia MSA, SC	Y	45900 FQ	58360 MW	78310 TQ	USBLS	5/15
	Greenville-Anderson-Mauldin MSA, SC	Y	50810 FQ	75590 MW	105370 TQ	USBLS	5/15
	Tennessee	Y	47210 FQ	61560 MW	81910 TQ	USBLS	5/15
	Knoxville MSA, TN	Y	40000 FQ	60560 MW	82890 TQ	USBLS	5/15
	Memphis MSA, TN-MS-AR	Y	46220 FQ	59190 MW	78300 TQ	USBLS	5/15
	Nashville-Davidson–Murfreesboro–Franklin MSA, TN	Y	47480 FQ	65230 MW	87420 TQ	USBLS	5/15
	Texas	Y	59200 FQ	81480 MW	104000 TQ	USBLS	5/15
	Austin-Round Rock MSA, TX	Y	51750 FQ	69450 MW	97970 TQ	USBLS	5/15
	Dallas-Plano-Irving PMSA, TX	Y	60480 FQ	80790 MW	100000 TQ	USBLS	5/15
	Fort Worth-Arlington PMSA, TX	Y	56970 FQ	83480 MW	104830 TQ	USBLS	5/15
	Houston-The Woodlands-Sugar Land MSA, TX	Y	61410 FQ	82810 MW	114520 TQ	USBLS	5/15
	San Antonio-New Braunfels MSA, TX	Y	65580 FQ	89030 MW	109770 TQ	USBLS	5/15
	Utah	Y	51150 FQ	69360 MW	97330 TQ	USBLS	5/15
	Ogden-Clearfield MSA, UT	Y	29520 FQ	67580 MW	85010 TQ	USBLS	5/15
	Provo-Orem MSA, UT	Y	55220 FQ	76980 MW	105850 TQ	USBLS	5/15
	Salt Lake City MSA, UT	Y	51470 FQ	71500 MW	100150 TQ	USBLS	5/15
	Vermont	Y	50850 FQ	72580 MW	90940 TQ	USBLS	5/15
	Burlington-South Burlington MSA, VT	Y	60330 FQ	74710 MW	91880 TQ	USBLS	5/15
	Virginia	Y	79280 FQ	105970 MW	129660 TQ	USBLS	5/15
	Richmond MSA, VA	Y	59490 FQ	84190 MW	107730 TQ	USBLS	5/15
	Virginia Beach-Norfolk-Newport News MSA, VA-NC	Y	64230 FQ	95220 MW	118260 TQ	USBLS	5/15
	Washington	H	32.77 FQ	41.66 MW	50.34 TQ	WABLS	3/16
	Seattle-Bellevue-Everett PMSA, WA	H	35.72 FQ	43.76 MW	51.51 TQ	WABLS	3/16
	Tacoma-Lakewood PMSA, WA	H	28.15 FQ	34.75 MW	46.25 TQ	WABLS	3/16
	West Virginia	Y	44320 FQ	55830 MW	73940 TQ	USBLS	5/15
	Wisconsin	Y	52320 FQ	65270 MW	81800 TQ	USBLS	5/15
	Madison MSA, WI	Y	56890 FQ	71180 MW	86520 TQ	USBLS	5/15
	Milwaukee-Waukesha-West Allis MSA, WI	Y	52690 FQ	65300 MW	78990 TQ	USBLS	5/15
	Puerto Rico	Y	29530 FQ	51840 MW	94250 TQ	USBLS	5/15
	San Juan-Carolina-Caguas MSA, PR	Y	28040 FQ	39630 MW	84000 TQ	USBLS	5/15
Ophthalmic Laboratory Technician	Alabama	Y	19300 AE	30970 AW	36800 AEX	ALBLS	6/16
	Arizona	Y	24150 FQ	29690 MW	43290 TQ	USBLS	5/15
	Arkansas	Y	22630 FQ	28030 MW	36520 TQ	USBLS	5/15
	Little Rock-North Little Rock-Conway MSA, AR	Y	22960 FQ	30750 MW	43360 TQ	USBLS	5/15
	California	H	12.40 FQ	15.60 MW	18.63 TQ	CABLS	1/16-3/16
	Anaheim-Santa Ana-Irvine PMSA, CA	H	12.27 FQ	15.37 MW	17.64 TQ	CABLS	1/16-3/16
	Los Angeles-Long Beach-Glendale PMSA, CA	H	12.10 FQ	14.45 MW	19.29 TQ	CABLS	1/16-3/16
	Oakland-Hayward-Berkeley PMSA, CA	H	13.76 FQ	17.32 MW	22.35 TQ	CABLS	1/16-3/16
	Sacramento–Roseville–Arden-Arcade MSA, CA	H	11.63 FQ	14.05 MW	17.09 TQ	CABLS	1/16-3/16
	San Diego-Carlsbad MSA, CA	H	14.23 FQ	17.93 MW	22.57 TQ	CABLS	1/16-3/16
	Colorado	Y	26200 FQ	31500 MW	38820 TQ	USBLS	5/15
	Denver-Aurora-Lakewood MSA, CO	Y	23750 FQ	29780 MW	37950 TQ	USBLS	5/15
	Connecticut	Y		37563 MW		CTBLS	1/16-3/16
	Bridgeport-Stamford-Norwalk MSA, CT	Y	37070 FQ	46310 MW	68940 TQ	USBLS	5/15
	Washington-Arlington-Alexandria PMSA, DC-VA-MD-WV	Y	33570 FQ	39080 MW	48090 TQ	USBLS	5/15
	Florida	H	10.63 AE	13.86 MW	17.19 AEX	FLBLS	7/16-9/16

AE	Average entry wage	**AWR**	Average wage range	**H**	Hourly
AEX	Average experienced wage	**B**	Biweekly	**HI**	Highest wage paid
ATC	Average total compensation	**D**	Daily	**HR**	High end range
AW	Average wage paid	**FQ**	First quartile wage	**LO**	Lowest wage paid

LR	Low end range	**MTC**	Median total compensation	**TCC**	Total cash compensation
M	Monthly	**MW**	Median wage paid	**TQ**	Third quartile wage
MCC	Median cash compensation	**MWR**	Median wage range	**W**	Weekly
ME	Median entry wage	**S**	See annotated source	**Y**	Yearly

Occupation/Type/Industry	Location	Per	Low	Mid	High	Source	Date
Ophthalmic Laboratory Technician	Fort Lauderdale-Pompano Beach-Deerfield Beach PMSA, FL	H	12.01 AE	13.86 MW	16.25 AEX	FLBLS	7/16-9/16
	Miami-Miami Beach-Kendall PMSA, FL	H	9.89 AE	12.71 MW	15.23 AEX	FLBLS	7/16-9/16
	Orlando-Kissimmee-Sanford MSA, FL	H	11.42 AE	14.02 MW	19.78 AEX	FLBLS	7/16-9/16
	Tampa-St. Petersburg-Clearwater MSA, FL	H	11.55 AE	13.99 MW	16.36 AEX	FLBLS	7/16-9/16
	Georgia	Y	23180 FQ	29550 MW	46990 TQ	USBLS	5/15
	Atlanta-Sandy Springs-Roswell MSA, GA	Y	23160 FQ	29270 MW	50240 TQ	USBLS	5/15
	Augusta-Richmond County MSA, GA-SC	Y	23360 FQ	30930 MW	42180 TQ	USBLS	5/15
	Hawaii	Y	20770 FQ	25120 MW	30380 TQ	USBLS	5/15
	Urban Honolulu MSA, HI	Y	19960 FQ	24090 MW	29720 TQ	USBLS	5/15
	Idaho	Y	27290 FQ	31290 MW	38300 TQ	USBLS	5/15
	Boise City MSA, ID	Y	27810 FQ	31860 MW	38720 TQ	USBLS	5/15
	Illinois	Y	26730 FQ	33490 MW	49130 TQ	USBLS	5/15
	Chicago-Naperville-Arlington Heights PMSA, IL	Y	29330 FQ	37100 MW	63170 TQ	USBLS	5/15
	Lake County-Kenosha County PMSA, IL-WI	Y	20210 FQ	28760 MW	38980 TQ	USBLS	5/15
	Indiana	Y	25010 FQ	28790 MW	35140 TQ	USBLS	5/15
	Indianapolis-Carmel-Anderson MSA, IN	Y	26430 FQ	36620 MW	45630 TQ	USBLS	5/15
	Iowa	Y	29390 FQ	39140 MW	61450 TQ	USBLS	5/15
	Kansas	Y	25970 FQ	30170 MW	35220 TQ	USBLS	5/15
	Kentucky	Y	22590 FQ	27460 MW	33050 TQ	USBLS	5/15
	Louisville-Jefferson County MSA, KY-IN	Y	23940 FQ	30010 MW	35410 TQ	USBLS	5/15
	Louisiana	Y	24850 FQ	29520 MW	36240 TQ	USBLS	5/15
	Baton Rouge MSA, LA	Y	27940 FQ	31510 MW	35890 TQ	USBLS	5/15
	New Orleans-Metairie MSA, LA	Y	26450 FQ	30950 MW	38770 TQ	USBLS	5/15
	Maine	Y	22620 FQ	28400 MW	35580 TQ	USBLS	5/15
	Maryland	Y	25694 AE	39219 MW	45981 AEX	MDBLS	4/16
	Baltimore-Columbia-Towson MSA, MD	Y	26300 FQ	29910 MW	34950 TQ	USBLS	5/15
	Salisbury MSA, MD-DE	Y	22490 FQ	27140 MW	32370 TQ	USBLS	5/15
	Massachusetts	Y	26620 FQ	31080 MW	37140 TQ	USBLS	5/15
	Boston-Cambridge-Newton NECTA, MA	Y	26800 FQ	33280 MW	38080 TQ	USBLS	5/15
	Worcester MSA, MA-CT	Y	28100 FQ	30950 MW	35410 TQ	USBLS	5/15
	Michigan	Y	25450 FQ	30430 MW	39330 TQ	USBLS	5/15
	Detroit-Dearborn-Livonia PMSA, MI	Y	47810 FQ	55890 MW	61570 TQ	USBLS	5/15
	Grand Rapids-Wyoming MSA, MI	Y	22040 FQ	25850 MW	34030 TQ	USBLS	5/15
	Minnesota	Y	26152 FQ	30282 MW	36256 TQ	MNBLS	1/16-3/16
	Minneapolis-St. Paul-Bloomington MSA, MN-WI	Y	27427 FQ	31538 MW	39506 TQ	MNBLS	1/16-3/16
	Mississippi	Y	22800 FQ	26820 MW	33160 TQ	USBLS	5/15
	Missouri	Y	20070 FQ	24480 MW	33850 TQ	USBLS	5/15
	Kansas City MSA, MO-KS	Y	24330 FQ	31020 MW	36260 TQ	USBLS	5/15
	St. Louis MSA, MO-IL	Y	24860 FQ	29510 MW	38140 TQ	USBLS	5/15
	Montana	Y	25550 FQ	29080 MW	33430 TQ	USBLS	5/15
	Billings MSA, MT	Y	27100 FQ	29840 MW	33150 TQ	USBLS	5/15
	Nebraska	Y	24580 FQ	29170 MW	35090 TQ	NEBLS	7/16-9/16
	Omaha-Council Bluffs MSA, NE-IA	Y	24755 FQ	29245 MW	35275 TQ	NEBLS	7/16-9/16
	Nevada	Y	23450 FQ	27670 MW	31580 TQ	USBLS	5/15
	New Hampshire	H	10.71 AE	14.79 MW	18.29 AEX	NHBLS	6/16
	Manchester NECTA, NH	H	10.66 AE	11.89 MW	13.33 AEX	NHBLS	6/16
	Nashua NECTA, NH-MA	Y	26710 FQ	34970 MW	45210 TQ	USBLS	5/15
	New Jersey	Y	22110 FQ	25900 MW	32140 TQ	USBLS	5/15
	Camden PMSA, NJ	Y	21690 FQ	24270 MW	29650 TQ	USBLS	5/15
	Newark PMSA, NJ-PA	Y	26750 FQ	31030 MW	40290 TQ	USBLS	5/15
	New Mexico	Y	24700 FQ	27520 MW	30300 TQ	USBLS	5/15
	Albuquerque MSA, NM	Y	25640 FQ	28090 MW	30550 TQ	USBLS	5/15
	New York	Y	24210 AE	33320 MW	41650 AEX	NYBLS	1/16-3/16

Occupation/Type/Industry	Location	Per	Low	Mid	High	Source	Date
Ophthalmic Laboratory Technician	Buffalo-Cheektowaga-Niagara Falls MSA, NY	Y	32340 FQ	50250 MW	56620 TQ	USBLS	5/15
	Nassau County-Suffolk County PMSA, NY	Y	27880 FQ	35460 MW	43050 TQ	USBLS	5/15
	New York-Jersey City-White Plains PMSA, NY-NJ	Y	25360 FQ	33870 MW	46770 TQ	USBLS	5/15
	Rochester MSA, NY	Y	26820 FQ	30520 MW	36560 TQ	USBLS	5/15
	North Carolina	Y	19900 FQ	23020 MW	30850 TQ	USBLS	5/15
	Charlotte-Concord-Gastonia MSA, NC-SC	Y	19420 FQ	27780 MW	34590 TQ	USBLS	5/15
	Ohio	Y	21760 FQ	26840 MW	31820 TQ	USBLS	5/15
	Cincinnati MSA, OH-KY-IN	Y	21940 FQ	25170 MW	34740 TQ	USBLS	5/15
	Cleveland-Elyria MSA, OH	Y	23260 FQ	27960 MW	33850 TQ	USBLS	5/15
	Columbus MSA, OH	Y	22490 FQ	27540 MW	33040 TQ	USBLS	5/15
	Oklahoma	Y	23910 FQ	28860 MW	35120 TQ	USBLS	5/15
	Oklahoma City MSA, OK	Y	22490 FQ	26270 MW	31650 TQ	USBLS	5/15
	Oregon	H	11.81 FQ	14.32 MW	18.76 TQ	ORBLS	2016
	Portland-Vancouver-Hillsboro MSA, OR-WA	Y	24530 FQ	29660 MW	38680 TQ	USBLS	5/15
	Pennsylvania	Y	24790 FQ	29840 MW	37290 TQ	USBLS	5/15
	Allentown-Bethlehem-Easton MSA, PA-NJ	Y	22010 FQ	26720 MW	36580 TQ	USBLS	5/15
	Harrisburg-Carlisle MSA, PA	Y	31200 FQ	37750 MW	43800 TQ	USBLS	5/15
	Montgomery County-Bucks County-Chester County PMSA, PA	Y	28780 FQ	33530 MW	37640 TQ	USBLS	5/15
	Philadelphia PMSA, PA	Y	21130 FQ	26340 MW	29700 TQ	USBLS	5/15
	Pittsburgh MSA, PA	Y	27030 FQ	31700 MW	38720 TQ	USBLS	5/15
	Rhode Island	Y	25390 FQ	32220 MW	36400 TQ	USBLS	5/15
	Providence-Warwick MSA, RI-MA	Y	25260 FQ	32060 MW	36450 TQ	USBLS	5/15
	South Carolina	Y	24560 FQ	28800 MW	34720 TQ	USBLS	5/15
	Charleston-North Charleston MSA, SC	Y	23070 FQ	27290 MW	31540 TQ	USBLS	5/15
	Columbia MSA, SC	Y	24550 FQ	29640 MW	39440 TQ	USBLS	5/15
	Greenville-Anderson-Mauldin MSA, SC	Y	24750 FQ	28530 MW	32750 TQ	USBLS	5/15
	South Dakota	Y	19270 FQ	27070 MW	32210 TQ	USBLS	5/15
	Tennessee	Y	22840 FQ	27910 MW	34500 TQ	USBLS	5/15
	Knoxville MSA, TN	Y	22690 FQ	27080 MW	34690 TQ	USBLS	5/15
	Memphis MSA, TN-MS-AR	Y	22700 FQ	27740 MW	33170 TQ	USBLS	5/15
	Nashville-Davidson–Murfreesboro–Franklin MSA, TN	Y	22960 FQ	29250 MW	36780 TQ	USBLS	5/15
	Texas	Y	23380 FQ	28040 MW	33800 TQ	USBLS	5/15
	Dallas-Plano-Irving PMSA, TX	Y	24060 FQ	28760 MW	35430 TQ	USBLS	5/15
	Fort Worth-Arlington PMSA, TX	Y	24000 FQ	27900 MW	31680 TQ	USBLS	5/15
	San Antonio-New Braunfels MSA, TX	Y	23560 FQ	27640 MW	31370 TQ	USBLS	5/15
	Utah	Y	27650 FQ	31640 MW	49250 TQ	USBLS	5/15
	Provo-Orem MSA, UT	Y	25630 FQ	28980 MW	35310 TQ	USBLS	5/15
	Virginia	Y	30820 FQ	37640 MW	45220 TQ	USBLS	5/15
	Virginia Beach-Norfolk-Newport News MSA, VA-NC	Y	23490 FQ	38350 MW	44350 TQ	USBLS	5/15
	Washington	H	12.96 FQ	15.39 MW	19.84 TQ	WABLS	3/16
	Seattle-Bellevue-Everett PMSA, WA	H	14.22 FQ	16.95 MW	21.19 TQ	WABLS	3/16
	West Virginia	Y	21510 FQ	26950 MW	34380 TQ	USBLS	5/15
	Wisconsin	Y	25370 FQ	29720 MW	35770 TQ	USBLS	5/15
	Madison MSA, WI	Y	25910 FQ	30350 MW	36280 TQ	USBLS	5/15
	Milwaukee-Waukesha-West Allis MSA, WI	Y	24770 FQ	30760 MW	37020 TQ	USBLS	5/15
	San Juan-Carolina-Caguas MSA, PR	Y	16740 FQ	18290 MW	22590 TQ	USBLS	5/15
Ophthalmic Medical Technician	Alabama	Y	24831 AE	31161 AW	34331 AEX	ALBLS	6/16
	Birmingham-Hoover MSA, AL	Y	26064 AE	33515 AW	26064 AEX	ALBLS	6/16
	Alaska	Y	33690 FQ	38660 MW	46260 TQ	USBLS	5/15
	Arizona	Y	28750 FQ	35750 MW	43380 TQ	USBLS	5/15

AE	Average entry wage	AWR	Average wage range	H	Hourly	LR	Low end range	MTC	Median total compensation	TCC	Total cash compensation
AEX	Average experienced wage	B	Biweekly	HI	Highest wage paid	M	Monthly	MW	Median wage paid	TQ	Third quartile wage
ATC	Average total compensation	D	Daily	HR	High end range	MCC	Median cash compensation	MWR	Median wage range	W	Weekly
AW	Average wage paid	FQ	First quartile wage	LO	Lowest wage paid	ME	Median entry wage	S	See annotated source	Y	Yearly

Occupation/Type/Industry	Location	Per	Low	Mid	High	Source	Date
Ophthalmic Medical Technician	Phoenix-Mesa-Scottsdale MSA, AZ	Y	29460 FQ	36910 MW	44210 TQ	USBLS	5/15
	Arkansas	Y	23230 FQ	28040 MW	34890 TQ	USBLS	5/15
	Little Rock-North Little Rock-Conway MSA, AR	Y	29530 FQ	36830 MW	43740 TQ	USBLS	5/15
	California	H	15.33 FQ	18.22 MW	23.21 TQ	CABLS	1/16-3/16
	Anaheim-Santa Ana-Irvine PMSA, CA	H	18.16 FQ	21.30 MW	23.89 TQ	CABLS	1/16-3/16
	Los Angeles-Long Beach-Glendale PMSA, CA	H	16.56 FQ	19.00 MW	25.09 TQ	CABLS	1/16-3/16
	Oakland-Hayward-Berkeley PMSA, CA	H	16.36 FQ	17.92 MW	19.97 TQ	CABLS	1/16-3/16
	Riverside-San Bernardino-Ontario MSA, CA	H	14.04 FQ	17.62 MW	21.41 TQ	CABLS	1/16-3/16
	Sacramento–Roseville–Arden-Arcade MSA, CA	H	15.83 FQ	18.98 MW	24.45 TQ	CABLS	1/16-3/16
	San Diego-Carlsbad MSA, CA	H	12.59 FQ	15.81 MW	20.69 TQ	CABLS	1/16-3/16
	San Francisco-Redwood City-South San Francisco PMSA, CA	H	17.26 FQ	28.48 MW	38.49 TQ	CABLS	1/16-3/16
	Colorado	Y	27660 FQ	34070 MW	47170 TQ	USBLS	5/15
	Denver-Aurora-Lakewood MSA, CO	Y	28810 FQ	42420 MW	56060 TQ	USBLS	5/15
	Connecticut	Y		41574 MW		CTBLS	1/16-3/16
	Bridgeport-Stamford-Norwalk MSA, CT	Y	35560 FQ	40830 MW	46980 TQ	USBLS	5/15
	Hartford-West Hartford-East Hartford MSA, CT	Y	36990 FQ	43300 MW	48970 TQ	USBLS	5/15
	Delaware	Y	32790 FQ	38410 MW	46060 TQ	USBLS	5/15
	Wilmington PMSA, DE-MD-NJ	Y	33380 FQ	39250 MW	46540 TQ	USBLS	5/15
	Washington-Arlington-Alexandria PMSA, DC-VA-MD-WV	Y	31340 FQ	42660 MW	56130 TQ	USBLS	5/15
	Florida	H	14.59 AE	17.90 MW	20.20 AEX	FLBLS	7/16-9/16
	Fort Lauderdale-Pompano Beach-Deerfield Beach PMSA, FL	H	14.56 AE	17.79 MW	19.65 AEX	FLBLS	7/16-9/16
	Miami-Miami Beach-Kendall PMSA, FL	H	16.43 AE	20.16 MW	22.98 AEX	FLBLS	7/16-9/16
	Orlando-Kissimmee-Sanford MSA, FL	H	15.43 AE	17.68 MW	18.83 AEX	FLBLS	7/16-9/16
	Tampa-St. Petersburg-Clearwater MSA, FL	H	13.96 AE	18.17 MW	20.72 AEX	FLBLS	7/16-9/16
	Georgia	Y	24260 FQ	28470 MW	34090 TQ	USBLS	5/15
	Atlanta-Sandy Springs-Roswell MSA, GA	Y	23160 FQ	26870 MW	31660 TQ	USBLS	5/15
	Augusta-Richmond County MSA, GA-SC	Y	32300 FQ	36390 MW	41250 TQ	USBLS	5/15
	Hawaii	Y	33360 FQ	41890 MW	52960 TQ	USBLS	5/15
	Urban Honolulu MSA, HI	Y	32980 FQ	42040 MW	53690 TQ	USBLS	5/15
	Idaho	Y	29740 FQ	34510 MW	38380 TQ	USBLS	5/15
	Boise City MSA, ID	Y	32510 FQ	36130 MW	39770 TQ	USBLS	5/15
	Illinois	Y	24700 FQ	33460 MW	42040 TQ	USBLS	5/15
	Chicago-Naperville-Arlington Heights PMSA, IL	Y	29100 FQ	37970 MW	46400 TQ	USBLS	5/15
	Indiana	Y	30610 FQ	35920 MW	42920 TQ	USBLS	5/15
	Indianapolis-Carmel-Anderson MSA, IN	Y	34750 FQ	39600 MW	46800 TQ	USBLS	5/15
	Iowa	Y	27310 FQ	30350 MW	36800 TQ	USBLS	5/15
	Des Moines-West Des Moines MSA, IA	Y	29280 FQ	34170 MW	37780 TQ	USBLS	5/15
	Kansas	Y	27860 FQ	33230 MW	38760 TQ	USBLS	5/15
	Wichita MSA, KS	Y	26860 FQ	30700 MW	38270 TQ	USBLS	5/15
	Kentucky	Y	30970 FQ	35620 MW	41180 TQ	USBLS	5/15
	Louisiana	Y	29300 FQ	35080 MW	41850 TQ	USBLS	5/15
	Baton Rouge MSA, LA	Y	32160 FQ	38420 MW	48040 TQ	USBLS	5/15
	Maine	Y	31020 FQ	36600 MW	43270 TQ	USBLS	5/15
	Maryland	Y	28497 AE	40441 MW	46413 AEX	MDBLS	4/16
	Baltimore-Columbia-Towson MSA, MD	Y	34220 FQ	41380 MW	47760 TQ	USBLS	5/15
	Salisbury MSA, MD-DE	Y	26610 FQ	30350 MW	36410 TQ	USBLS	5/15

AE	Average entry wage	AWR	Average wage range	H	Hourly
AEX	Average experienced wage	B	Biweekly	HI	Highest wage paid
ATC	Average total compensation	D	Daily	HR	High end range
AW	Average wage paid	FQ	First quartile wage	LO	Lowest wage paid

LR	Low end range	MTC	Median total compensation	TCC	Total cash compensation
M	Monthly	MW	Median wage paid	TQ	Third quartile wage
MCC	Median cash compensation	MWR	Median wage range	W	Weekly
ME	Median entry wage	S	See annotated source	Y	Yearly

Occupation/Type/Industry	Location	Per	Low	Mid	High	Source	Date
Ophthalmic Medical Technician	Massachusetts	Y	32310 FQ	39910 MW	51110 TQ	USBLS	5/15
	Boston-Cambridge-Newton NECTA, MA	Y	37030 FQ	47450 MW	57670 TQ	USBLS	5/15
	Worcester MSA, MA-CT	Y	37270 FQ	43080 MW	49030 TQ	USBLS	5/15
	Michigan	Y	26930 FQ	34470 MW	42350 TQ	USBLS	5/15
	Detroit-Dearborn-Livonia PMSA, MI	Y	27780 FQ	35900 MW	45980 TQ	USBLS	5/15
	Grand Rapids-Wyoming MSA, MI	Y	26190 FQ	32940 MW	38900 TQ	USBLS	5/15
	Minnesota	Y	33477 FQ	41552 MW	53346 TQ	MNBLS	1/16-3/16
	Minneapolis-St. Paul-Bloomington MSA, MN-WI	Y	35070 FQ	44203 MW	57499 TQ	MNBLS	1/16-3/16
	Mississippi	Y	26440 FQ	33880 MW	39900 TQ	USBLS	5/15
	Jackson MSA, MS	Y	26330 FQ	34600 MW	40340 TQ	USBLS	5/15
	Missouri	Y	26330 FQ	32320 MW	38020 TQ	USBLS	5/15
	Kansas City MSA, MO-KS	Y	30920 FQ	35700 MW	41370 TQ	USBLS	5/15
	St. Louis MSA, MO-IL	Y	23870 FQ	29610 MW	35710 TQ	USBLS	5/15
	Montana	Y	29860 FQ	35550 MW	44540 TQ	USBLS	5/15
	Nebraska	Y	26330 FQ	29565 MW	34555 TQ	NEBLS	7/16-9/16
	Omaha-Council Bluffs MSA, NE-IA	Y	27070 FQ	30355 MW	35675 TQ	NEBLS	7/16-9/16
	Nevada	Y	31780 FQ	35040 MW	38300 TQ	USBLS	5/15
	New Hampshire	H	13.64 AE	18.21 MW	21.30 AEX	NHBLS	6/16
	Manchester NECTA, NH	H	15.85 AE	20.15 MW	21.91 AEX	NHBLS	6/16
	New Jersey	Y	33620 FQ	37980 MW	45410 TQ	USBLS	5/15
	Camden PMSA, NJ	Y	32370 FQ	37220 MW	45520 TQ	USBLS	5/15
	Newark PMSA, NJ-PA	Y	33590 FQ	37090 MW	48160 TQ	USBLS	5/15
	Trenton MSA, NJ	Y	32220 FQ	40420 MW	46850 TQ	USBLS	5/15
	New Mexico	Y	28760 FQ	34290 MW	44810 TQ	USBLS	5/15
	Albuquerque MSA, NM	Y	28740 FQ	33930 MW	42650 TQ	USBLS	5/15
	New York	Y	29070 AE	38680 MW	44090 AEX	NYBLS	1/16-3/16
	Buffalo-Cheektowaga-Niagara Falls MSA, NY	Y	23440 FQ	34200 MW	39690 TQ	USBLS	5/15
	Nassau County-Suffolk County PMSA, NY	Y	32160 FQ	38200 MW	45610 TQ	USBLS	5/15
	New York-Jersey City-White Plains PMSA, NY-NJ	Y	35980 FQ	41570 MW	47560 TQ	USBLS	5/15
	Rochester MSA, NY	Y	31010 FQ	38270 MW	45180 TQ	USBLS	5/15
	North Carolina	Y	28780 FQ	33950 MW	39070 TQ	USBLS	5/15
	Charlotte-Concord-Gastonia MSA, NC-SC	Y	28850 FQ	34440 MW	39400 TQ	USBLS	5/15
	Raleigh MSA, NC	Y	31840 FQ	34680 MW	37530 TQ	USBLS	5/15
	North Dakota	Y	31660 FQ	36970 MW	44940 TQ	USBLS	5/15
	Fargo MSA, ND-MN	Y	33520 FQ	40790 MW	49050 TQ	USBLS	5/15
	Ohio	Y	31620 FQ	36810 MW	43530 TQ	USBLS	5/15
	Cincinnati MSA, OH-KY-IN	Y	32670 FQ	38130 MW	44600 TQ	USBLS	5/15
	Cleveland-Elyria MSA, OH	Y	35450 FQ	39890 MW	46830 TQ	USBLS	5/15
	Columbus MSA, OH	Y	31220 FQ	35470 MW	40380 TQ	USBLS	5/15
	Oklahoma	Y	25280 FQ	32170 MW	38740 TQ	USBLS	5/15
	Oklahoma City MSA, OK	Y	27560 FQ	34490 MW	40690 TQ	USBLS	5/15
	Tulsa MSA, OK	Y	25700 FQ	30490 MW	36810 TQ	USBLS	5/15
	Oregon	H	15.91 FQ	18.49 MW	22.60 TQ	ORBLS	2016
	Portland-Vancouver-Hillsboro MSA, OR-WA	Y	33160 FQ	40390 MW	49550 TQ	USBLS	5/15
	Pennsylvania	Y	29220 FQ	34120 MW	38490 TQ	USBLS	5/15
	Allentown-Bethlehem-Easton MSA, PA-NJ	Y	30580 FQ	35940 MW	43220 TQ	USBLS	5/15
	Harrisburg-Carlisle MSA, PA	Y	29580 FQ	34600 MW	38640 TQ	USBLS	5/15
	Philadelphia PMSA, PA	Y	32600 FQ	38490 MW	46960 TQ	USBLS	5/15
	Pittsburgh MSA, PA	Y	27780 FQ	31940 MW	36530 TQ	USBLS	5/15
	Providence-Warwick MSA, RI-MA	Y	27030 FQ	31970 MW	39520 TQ	USBLS	5/15
	South Carolina	Y	29330 FQ	34650 MW	39680 TQ	USBLS	5/15
	Charleston-North Charleston MSA, SC	Y	28800 FQ	33730 MW	37270 TQ	USBLS	5/15
	Greenville-Anderson-Mauldin MSA, SC	Y	29080 FQ	34680 MW	42800 TQ	USBLS	5/15
	South Dakota	Y	27400 FQ	30080 MW	36900 TQ	USBLS	5/15
	Tennessee	Y	28220 FQ	33480 MW	38120 TQ	NEBLS	5/15
	Memphis MSA, TN-MS-AR	Y	25370 FQ	33330 MW	37880 TQ	USBLS	5/15

AE Average entry wage	AWR Average wage range	H Hourly	LR Low end range	MTC Median total compensation	TCC Total cash compensation
AEX Average experienced wage	B Biweekly	HI Highest wage paid	M Monthly	MW Median wage paid	TQ Third quartile wage
ATC Average total compensation	D Daily	HR High end range	MCC Median cash compensation	MWR Median wage range	W Weekly
AW Average wage paid	FQ First quartile wage	LO Lowest wage paid	ME Median entry wage	S See annotated source	Y Yearly

Occupation/Type/Industry	Location	Per	Low	Mid	High	Source	Date
Ophthalmic Medical Technician	Nashville-Davidson–Murfreesboro–Franklin MSA, TN	Y	28240 FQ	33230 MW	38280 TQ	USBLS	5/15
	Texas	Y	26220 FQ	32930 MW	39090 TQ	USBLS	5/15
	Austin-Round Rock MSA, TX	Y	29710 FQ	34100 MW	37860 TQ	USBLS	5/15
	Dallas-Plano-Irving PMSA, TX	Y	30150 FQ	36160 MW	42910 TQ	USBLS	5/15
	Fort Worth-Arlington PMSA, TX	Y	26150 FQ	30700 MW	36950 TQ	USBLS	5/15
	Houston-The Woodlands-Sugar Land MSA, TX	Y	23490 FQ	35280 MW	45130 TQ	USBLS	5/15
	San Antonio-New Braunfels MSA, TX	Y	29330 FQ	34390 MW	38480 TQ	USBLS	5/15
	Utah	Y	29120 FQ	33690 MW	37750 TQ	USBLS	5/15
	Ogden-Clearfield MSA, UT	Y	27910 FQ	31300 MW	37330 TQ	USBLS	5/15
	Salt Lake City MSA, UT	Y	33440 FQ	36090 MW	38730 TQ	USBLS	5/15
	Vermont	Y	33590 FQ	39520 MW	46800 TQ	USBLS	5/15
	Burlington-South Burlington MSA, VT	Y	36630 FQ	43020 MW	49620 TQ	USBLS	5/15
	Virginia	Y	25690 FQ	31240 MW	42630 TQ	USBLS	5/15
	Richmond MSA, VA	Y	26150 FQ	31970 MW	48060 TQ	USBLS	5/15
	Virginia Beach-Norfolk-Newport News MSA, VA-NC	Y	25140 FQ	29480 MW	37760 TQ	USBLS	5/15
	Washington	H	16.77 FQ	19.90 MW	23.99 TQ	WABLS	3/16
	Seattle-Bellevue-Everett PMSA, WA	H	17.91 FQ	21.51 MW	26.09 TQ	WABLS	3/16
	Tacoma-Lakewood PMSA, WA	H	16.38 FQ	19.93 MW	23.36 TQ	WABLS	3/16
	West Virginia	Y	25580 FQ	31260 MW	38780 TQ	USBLS	5/15
	Huntington-Ashland MSA, WV-KY-OH	Y	33640 FQ	37830 MW	66630 TQ	USBLS	5/15
	Wisconsin	Y	33450 FQ	39750 MW	48270 TQ	USBLS	5/15
	Madison MSA, WI	Y	33400 FQ	37540 MW	43700 TQ	USBLS	5/15
	Milwaukee-Waukesha-West Allis MSA, WI	Y	33900 FQ	42150 MW	53710 TQ	USBLS	5/15
	Wyoming	Y	26850 FQ	30300 MW	40030 TQ	USBLS	5/15
	Puerto Rico	Y	21540 FQ	26380 MW	38060 TQ	USBLS	5/15
	San Juan-Carolina-Caguas MSA, PR	Y	22290 FQ	31750 MW	40010 TQ	USBLS	5/15
Optician, Dispensing	Alabama	Y	20804 AE	30570 AW	35452 AEX	ALBLS	6/16
	Birmingham-Hoover MSA, AL	Y	23536 AE	33729 AW	38836 AEX	ALBLS	6/16
	Alaska	Y	34770 FQ	43630 MW	53040 TQ	USBLS	5/15
	Anchorage MSA, AK	Y	34450 FQ	42360 MW	49810 TQ	USBLS	5/15
	Arizona	Y	29100 FQ	37330 MW	47370 TQ	USBLS	5/15
	Phoenix-Mesa-Scottsdale MSA, AZ	Y	29350 FQ	37930 MW	47790 TQ	USBLS	5/15
	Tucson MSA, AZ	Y	28170 FQ	35890 MW	46880 TQ	USBLS	5/15
	Arkansas	Y	25950 FQ	30950 MW	43430 TQ	USBLS	5/15
	Little Rock-North Little Rock-Conway MSA, AR	Y	27340 FQ	39580 MW	48990 TQ	USBLS	5/15
	California	H	15.20 FQ	19.21 MW	25.95 TQ	CABLS	1/16-3/16
	Anaheim-Santa Ana-Irvine PMSA, CA	H	15.92 FQ	19.02 MW	24.52 TQ	CABLS	1/16-3/16
	Los Angeles-Long Beach-Glendale PMSA, CA	H	15.16 FQ	18.65 MW	28.73 TQ	CABLS	1/16-3/16
	Oakland-Hayward-Berkeley PMSA, CA	H	14.15 FQ	18.33 MW	24.56 TQ	CABLS	1/16-3/16
	Riverside-San Bernardino-Ontario MSA, CA	H	13.10 FQ	17.22 MW	22.62 TQ	CABLS	1/16-3/16
	Sacramento–Roseville–Arden-Arcade MSA, CA	H	15.96 FQ	18.91 MW	23.36 TQ	CABLS	1/16-3/16
	San Diego-Carlsbad MSA, CA	H	14.48 FQ	21.04 MW	27.23 TQ	CABLS	1/16-3/16
	San Francisco-Redwood City-South San Francisco PMSA, CA	H	16.03 FQ	25.16 MW	33.06 TQ	CABLS	1/16-3/16
	Colorado	Y	27680 FQ	34860 MW	43320 TQ	USBLS	5/15
	Denver-Aurora-Lakewood MSA, CO	Y	28590 FQ	36680 MW	46050 TQ	USBLS	5/15
	Connecticut	Y		39738 MW		CTBLS	1/16-3/16
	Bridgeport-Stamford-Norwalk MSA, CT	Y	32320 FQ	38530 MW	47900 TQ	USBLS	5/15
	Hartford-West Hartford-East Hartford MSA, CT	Y	29640 FQ	44260 MW	62780 TQ	USBLS	5/15

AE	Average entry wage	AWR	Average wage range	H	Hourly	LR Low end range	MTC Median total compensation	TCC Total cash compensation
AEX	Average experienced wage	B	Biweekly	HI	Highest wage paid	M Monthly	MW Median wage paid	TQ Third quartile wage
ATC	Average total compensation	D	Daily	HR	High end range	MCC Median cash compensation	MWR Median wage range	W Weekly
AW	Average wage paid	FQ	First quartile wage	LO	Lowest wage paid	ME Median entry wage	S See annotated source	Y Yearly

Optician, Dispensing

Occupation/Type/Industry	Location	Per	Low	Mid	High	Source	Date
Optician, Dispensing	Delaware	Y	33210 FQ	38190 MW	44970 TQ	USBLS	5/15
	Wilmington PMSA, DE-MD-NJ	Y	31880 FQ	36870 MW	43660 TQ	USBLS	5/15
	District of Columbia	Y	28170 FQ	39310 MW	47080 TQ	USBLS	5/15
	Washington-Arlington-Alexandria PMSA, DC-VA-MD-WV	Y	29350 FQ	41030 MW	49750 TQ	USBLS	5/15
	Florida	H	13.44 AE	19.07 MW	22.64 AEX	FLBLS	7/16-9/16
	Fort Lauderdale-Pompano Beach-Deerfield Beach PMSA, FL	H	15.32 AE	22.02 MW	24.63 AEX	FLBLS	7/16-9/16
	Miami-Miami Beach-Kendall PMSA, FL	H	15.04 AE	19.41 MW	27.53 AEX	FLBLS	7/16-9/16
	Orlando-Kissimmee-Sanford MSA, FL	H	11.92 AE	17.14 MW	20.12 AEX	FLBLS	7/16-9/16
	Tampa-St. Petersburg-Clearwater MSA, FL	H	13.05 AE	18.53 MW	21.10 AEX	FLBLS	7/16-9/16
	Georgia	Y	24230 FQ	31810 MW	42750 TQ	USBLS	5/15
	Atlanta-Sandy Springs-Roswell MSA, GA	Y	23700 FQ	33100 MW	44140 TQ	USBLS	5/15
	Augusta-Richmond County MSA, GA-SC	Y	24900 FQ	28640 MW	34720 TQ	USBLS	5/15
	Hawaii	Y	28780 FQ	35620 MW	43970 TQ	USBLS	5/15
	Urban Honolulu MSA, HI	Y	27480 FQ	34700 MW	43630 TQ	USBLS	5/15
	Idaho	Y	26440 FQ	32410 MW	40270 TQ	USBLS	5/15
	Boise City MSA, ID	Y	27260 FQ	34160 MW	41640 TQ	USBLS	5/15
	Illinois	Y	24160 FQ	31160 MW	38960 TQ	USBLS	5/15
	Chicago-Naperville-Arlington Heights PMSA, IL	Y	24270 FQ	34800 MW	42640 TQ	USBLS	5/15
	Lake County-Kenosha County PMSA, IL-WI	Y	24400 FQ	29710 MW	38070 TQ	USBLS	5/15
	Indiana	Y	23990 FQ	29180 MW	35270 TQ	USBLS	5/15
	Gary PMSA, IN	Y	26790 FQ	32700 MW	37830 TQ	USBLS	5/15
	Indianapolis-Carmel-Anderson MSA, IN	Y	24360 FQ	30600 MW	35850 TQ	USBLS	5/15
	Iowa	Y	24050 FQ	29190 MW	36340 TQ	USBLS	5/15
	Des Moines-West Des Moines MSA, IA	Y	26650 FQ	33680 MW	41890 TQ	USBLS	5/15
	Kansas	Y	22130 FQ	26350 MW	31130 TQ	USBLS	5/15
	Wichita MSA, KS	Y	20800 FQ	25430 MW	29600 TQ	USBLS	5/15
	Kentucky	Y	27660 FQ	35720 MW	44350 TQ	USBLS	5/15
	Louisville-Jefferson County MSA, KY-IN	Y	23200 FQ	27820 MW	36030 TQ	USBLS	5/15
	Louisiana	Y	25050 FQ	30450 MW	36880 TQ	USBLS	5/15
	Baton Rouge MSA, LA	Y	25400 FQ	31660 MW	36490 TQ	USBLS	5/15
	New Orleans-Metairie MSA, LA	Y	26250 FQ	33160 MW	37980 TQ	USBLS	5/15
	Maine	Y	28030 FQ	33360 MW	39810 TQ	USBLS	5/15
	Portland-South Portland MSA, ME	Y	32890 FQ	39530 MW	52990 TQ	USBLS	5/15
	Maryland	Y	24555 AE	37870 MW	44528 AEX	MDBLS	4/16
	Baltimore-Columbia-Towson MSA, MD	Y	27180 FQ	34900 MW	43730 TQ	USBLS	5/15
	Salisbury MSA, MD-DE	Y	27160 FQ	35180 MW	41640 TQ	USBLS	5/15
	Massachusetts	Y	42910 FQ	51910 MW	60320 TQ	USBLS	5/15
	Boston-Cambridge-Newton NECTA, MA	Y	47280 FQ	55160 MW	62660 TQ	USBLS	5/15
	Worcester MSA, MA-CT	Y	34830 FQ	43330 MW	57280 TQ	USBLS	5/15
	Michigan	Y	27460 FQ	34200 MW	40950 TQ	USBLS	5/15
	Detroit-Dearborn-Livonia PMSA, MI	Y	23670 FQ	30480 MW	37990 TQ	USBLS	5/15
	Grand Rapids-Wyoming MSA, MI	Y	26940 FQ	32210 MW	38770 TQ	USBLS	5/15
	Minnesota	Y	28871 FQ	35877 MW	44647 TQ	MNBLS	1/16-3/16
	Minneapolis-St. Paul-Bloomington MSA, MN-WI	Y	33286 FQ	39495 MW	47016 TQ	MNBLS	1/16-3/16
	Mississippi	Y	22150 FQ	26610 MW	33910 TQ	USBLS	5/15
	Jackson MSA, MS	Y	22670 FQ	27480 MW	34640 TQ	USBLS	5/15
	Missouri	Y	22770 FQ	26850 MW	32020 TQ	USBLS	5/15
	Kansas City MSA, MO-KS	Y	24440 FQ	28390 MW	33960 TQ	USBLS	5/15
	St. Louis MSA, MO-IL	Y	23360 FQ	27710 MW	34370 TQ	USBLS	5/15
	Montana	Y	27130 FQ	32420 MW	37530 TQ	USBLS	5/15

AE	Average entry wage	AWR	Average wage range	H	Hourly
AEX	Average experienced wage	B	Biweekly	HI	Highest wage paid
ATC	Average total compensation	D	Daily	HR	High end range
AW	Average wage paid	FQ	First quartile wage	LO	Lowest wage paid

LR	Low end range	MTC	Median total compensation	TCC	Total cash compensation
M	Monthly	MW	Median wage paid	TQ	Third quartile wage
MCC	Median cash compensation	MWR	Median wage range	W	Weekly
ME	Median entry wage	S	See annotated source	Y	Yearly

Occupation/Type/Industry	Location	Per	Low	Mid	High	Source	Date
Optician, Dispensing	Billings MSA, MT	Y	28160 FQ	33240 MW	39350 TQ	USBLS	5/15
	Nebraska	Y	24860 FQ	29020 MW	35320 TQ	NEBLS	7/16-9/16
	Omaha-Council Bluffs MSA, NE-IA	Y	25680 FQ	30315 MW	37520 TQ	NEBLS	7/16-9/16
	Nevada	Y	31480 FQ	38380 MW	50820 TQ	USBLS	5/15
	Las Vegas-Henderson-Paradise MSA, NV	Y	31480 FQ	37680 MW	50190 TQ	USBLS	5/15
	New Hampshire	H	12.65 AE	17.89 MW	21.31 AEX	NHBLS	6/16
	Manchester NECTA, NH	H	12.26 AE	16.60 MW	20.66 AEX	NHBLS	6/16
	Nashua NECTA, NH-MA	Y	29170 FQ	40020 MW	45900 TQ	USBLS	5/15
	New Jersey	Y	40700 FQ	53820 MW	61030 TQ	USBLS	5/15
	Camden PMSA, NJ	Y	45240 FQ	53110 MW	59600 TQ	USBLS	5/15
	Newark PMSA, NJ-PA	Y	37210 FQ	51210 MW	59470 TQ	USBLS	5/15
	Trenton MSA, NJ	Y	42340 FQ	57640 MW	67360 TQ	USBLS	5/15
	New Mexico	Y	24050 FQ	31080 MW	36830 TQ	USBLS	5/15
	Albuquerque MSA, NM	Y	28990 FQ	34310 MW	38050 TQ	USBLS	5/15
	New York	Y	30690 AE	46870 MW	55840 AEX	NYBLS	1/16-3/16
	Buffalo-Cheektowaga-Niagara Falls MSA, NY	Y	39820 FQ	44660 MW	49510 TQ	USBLS	5/15
	Nassau County-Suffolk County PMSA, NY	Y	30750 FQ	47470 MW	60100 TQ	USBLS	5/15
	New York-Jersey City-White Plains PMSA, NY-NJ	Y	38850 FQ	52720 MW	61300 TQ	USBLS	5/15
	Rochester MSA, NY	Y	44550 FQ	51190 MW	57780 TQ	USBLS	5/15
	North Carolina	Y	29880 FQ	38750 MW	50320 TQ	USBLS	5/15
	Charlotte-Concord-Gastonia MSA, NC-SC	Y	27740 FQ	35070 MW	44390 TQ	USBLS	5/15
	Raleigh MSA, NC	Y	34470 FQ	43170 MW	52450 TQ	USBLS	5/15
	North Dakota	Y	23310 FQ	27650 MW	32950 TQ	USBLS	5/15
	Fargo MSA, ND-MN	Y	21320 FQ	24830 MW	32270 TQ	USBLS	5/15
	Ohio	Y	29810 FQ	36350 MW	43170 TQ	USBLS	5/15
	Cincinnati MSA, OH-KY-IN	Y	37810 FQ	43320 MW	47440 TQ	USBLS	5/15
	Cleveland-Elyria MSA, OH	Y	32410 FQ	37480 MW	43720 TQ	USBLS	5/15
	Columbus MSA, OH	Y	28240 FQ	35430 MW	42440 TQ	USBLS	5/15
	Oklahoma	Y	20630 FQ	25520 MW	31110 TQ	USBLS	5/15
	Oklahoma City MSA, OK	Y	22590 FQ	28210 MW	33370 TQ	USBLS	5/15
	Tulsa MSA, OK	Y	20220 FQ	25110 MW	32870 TQ	USBLS	5/15
	Oregon	H	13.94 FQ	16.79 MW	19.21 TQ	ORBLS	2016
	Portland-Vancouver-Hillsboro MSA, OR-WA	Y	28780 FQ	34950 MW	42460 TQ	USBLS	5/15
	Pennsylvania	Y	27710 FQ	35620 MW	45160 TQ	USBLS	5/15
	Allentown-Bethlehem-Easton MSA, PA-NJ	Y	31630 FQ	36680 MW	44110 TQ	USBLS	5/15
	Harrisburg-Carlisle MSA, PA	Y	32360 FQ	37100 MW	45820 TQ	USBLS	5/15
	Montgomery County-Bucks County-Chester County PMSA, PA	Y	24020 FQ	34960 MW	44660 TQ	USBLS	5/15
	Philadelphia PMSA, PA	Y	32270 FQ	37520 MW	45690 TQ	USBLS	5/15
	Pittsburgh MSA, PA	Y	29940 FQ	39030 MW	47800 TQ	USBLS	5/15
	Rhode Island	Y	36350 FQ	44940 MW	54430 TQ	USBLS	5/15
	Providence-Warwick MSA, RI-MA	Y	36980 FQ	45560 MW	54600 TQ	USBLS	5/15
	South Carolina	Y	26420 FQ	32680 MW	39250 TQ	USBLS	5/15
	Charleston-North Charleston MSA, SC	Y	24990 FQ	29240 MW	39560 TQ	USBLS	5/15
	Columbia MSA, SC	Y	31390 FQ	35590 MW	40850 TQ	USBLS	5/15
	Greenville-Anderson-Mauldin MSA, SC	Y	29440 FQ	34360 MW	38640 TQ	USBLS	5/15
	South Dakota	Y	26150 FQ	29830 MW	36120 TQ	USBLS	5/15
	Sioux Falls MSA, SD	Y	27010 FQ	30450 MW	36400 TQ	USBLS	5/15
	Tennessee	Y	24480 FQ	31020 MW	41680 TQ	USBLS	5/15
	Knoxville MSA, TN	Y	25990 FQ	33380 MW	42070 TQ	USBLS	5/15
	Memphis MSA, TN-MS-AR	Y	24750 FQ	33860 MW	42250 TQ	USBLS	5/15
	Nashville-Davidson–Murfreesboro–Franklin MSA, TN	Y	22250 FQ	26170 MW	35310 TQ	USBLS	5/15
	Texas	Y	23320 FQ	29360 MW	36150 TQ	USBLS	5/15
	Austin-Round Rock MSA, TX	Y	20310 FQ	28070 MW	35320 TQ	USBLS	5/15
	Dallas-Plano-Irving PMSA, TX	Y	22260 FQ	30950 MW	37110 TQ	USBLS	5/15
	Fort Worth-Arlington PMSA, TX	Y	24340 FQ	30190 MW	36580 TQ	USBLS	5/15

AE	Average entry wage	AWR	Average wage range	H	Hourly	LR	Low end range	MTC	Median total compensation	TCC	Total cash compensation
AEX	Average experienced wage	B	Biweekly	HI	Highest wage paid	M	Monthly	MW	Median wage paid	TQ	Third quartile wage
ATC	Average total compensation	D	Daily	HR	High end range	MCC	Median cash compensation	MWR	Median wage range	W	Weekly
AW	Average wage paid	FQ	First quartile wage	LO	Lowest wage paid	ME	Median entry wage	S	See annotated source	Y	Yearly

Occupation/Type/Industry	Location	Per	Low	Mid	High	Source	Date
Optician, Dispensing	Houston-The Woodlands-Sugar Land MSA, TX	Y	23890 FQ	30310 MW	36350 TQ	USBLS	5/15
	San Antonio-New Braunfels MSA, TX	Y	25120 FQ	31420 MW	37540 TQ	USBLS	5/15
	Utah	Y	26430 FQ	30350 MW	36390 TQ	USBLS	5/15
	Ogden-Clearfield MSA, UT	Y	25010 FQ	29290 MW	36210 TQ	USBLS	5/15
	Provo-Orem MSA, UT	Y	27840 FQ	32210 MW	38740 TQ	USBLS	5/15
	Salt Lake City MSA, UT	Y	26990 FQ	30720 MW	35890 TQ	USBLS	5/15
	Vermont	Y	35290 FQ	40770 MW	47100 TQ	USBLS	5/15
	Burlington-South Burlington MSA, VT	Y	34730 FQ	43770 MW	51060 TQ	USBLS	5/15
	Virginia	Y	28600 FQ	40970 MW	49840 TQ	USBLS	5/15
	Richmond MSA, VA	Y	24460 FQ	43640 MW	54510 TQ	USBLS	5/15
	Virginia Beach-Norfolk-Newport News MSA, VA-NC	Y	28380 FQ	42080 MW	48680 TQ	USBLS	5/15
	Washington	H	18.20 FQ	22.73 MW	26.94 TQ	WABLS	3/16
	Seattle-Bellevue-Everett PMSA, WA	H	22.68 FQ	25.98 MW	28.52 TQ	WABLS	3/16
	Tacoma-Lakewood PMSA, WA	H	16.94 FQ	19.33 MW	26.02 TQ	WABLS	3/16
	West Virginia	Y	24070 FQ	27970 MW	31490 TQ	USBLS	5/15
	Huntington-Ashland MSA, WV-KY-OH	Y	24840 FQ	30730 MW	37850 TQ	USBLS	5/15
	Wisconsin	Y	23130 FQ	28730 MW	36760 TQ	USBLS	5/15
	Madison MSA, WI	Y	25140 FQ	33130 MW	38040 TQ	USBLS	5/15
	Milwaukee-Waukesha-West Allis MSA, WI	Y	24000 FQ	31020 MW	42440 TQ	USBLS	5/15
	Wyoming	Y	26240 FQ	31830 MW	39220 TQ	USBLS	5/15
	Cheyenne MSA, WY	Y	24970 FQ	30020 MW	38400 TQ	USBLS	5/15
	Puerto Rico	Y	17910 FQ	20500 MW	24070 TQ	USBLS	5/15
	San Juan-Carolina-Caguas MSA, PR	Y	18050 FQ	21120 MW	24910 TQ	USBLS	5/15
Optometrist	Alabama	Y	55196 AE	97305 AW	118364 AEX	ALBLS	6/16
	Birmingham-Hoover MSA, AL	Y	56481 AE	94257 AW	113135 AEX	ALBLS	6/16
	Alaska	Y	124880 FQ	154810 MW		USBLS	5/15
	Anchorage MSA, AK	Y	122570 FQ	153180 MW		USBLS	5/15
	Arizona	Y	88270 FQ	111180 MW	132690 TQ	USBLS	5/15
	Phoenix-Mesa-Scottsdale MSA, AZ	Y	101810 FQ	115480 MW	134980 TQ	USBLS	5/15
	Tucson MSA, AZ	Y	63430 FQ	81540 MW	99290 TQ	USBLS	5/15
	Arkansas	Y	77410 FQ	99350 MW	167390 TQ	USBLS	5/15
	Little Rock-North Little Rock-Conway MSA, AR	Y	91300 FQ	133470 MW	170810 TQ	USBLS	5/15
	California	H	42.28 FQ	53.92 MW	70.16 TQ	CABLS	1/16-3/16
	Anaheim-Santa Ana-Irvine PMSA, CA	H	38.12 FQ	51.06 MW	60.19 TQ	CABLS	1/16-3/16
	Los Angeles-Long Beach-Glendale PMSA, CA	H	40.86 FQ	55.58 MW	71.33 TQ	CABLS	1/16-3/16
	Oakland-Hayward-Berkeley PMSA, CA	H	44.89 FQ	58.11 MW	71.56 TQ	CABLS	1/16-3/16
	Riverside-San Bernardino-Ontario MSA, CA	H	42.62 FQ	53.16 MW	78.16 TQ	CABLS	1/16-3/16
	Sacramento–Roseville–Arden-Arcade MSA, CA	H	36.22 FQ	52.56 MW	74.76 TQ	CABLS	1/16-3/16
	San Diego-Carlsbad MSA, CA	H	43.47 FQ	57.37 MW	81.71 TQ	CABLS	1/16-3/16
	San Francisco-Redwood City-South San Francisco PMSA, CA	H	45.98 FQ	52.77 MW	58.87 TQ	CABLS	1/16-3/16
	Colorado	Y	89760 FQ	116140 MW	143970 TQ	USBLS	5/15
	Denver-Aurora-Lakewood MSA, CO	Y	97890 FQ	119860 MW	146830 TQ	USBLS	5/15
	Connecticut	Y		156445 MW		CTBLS	1/16-3/16
	Bridgeport-Stamford-Norwalk MSA, CT	Y	112420 FQ	202490 AW		USBLS	5/15
	Hartford-West Hartford-East Hartford MSA, CT	Y	110250 FQ	205820 AW		USBLS	5/15
	Delaware	Y	88520 FQ	123050 MW	151410 TQ	USBLS	5/15
	Wilmington PMSA, DE-MD-NJ	Y	83830 FQ	98760 MW	142650 TQ	USBLS	5/15
	District of Columbia	Y	76390 FQ	113970 MW	134810 TQ	USBLS	5/15

Occupation/Type/Industry	Location	Per	Low	Mid	High	Source	Date
Optometrist	Washington-Arlington-Alexandria PMSA, DC-VA-MD-WV	Y	91500 FQ	115360 MW	144800 TQ	USBLS	5/15
	Florida	H	27.61 AE	41.96 MW	67.35 AEX	FLBLS	7/16-9/16
	Miami-Miami Beach-Kendall PMSA, FL	H	27.09 AE	40.25 MW	59.69 AEX	FLBLS	7/16-9/16
	Orlando-Kissimmee-Sanford MSA, FL	H	28.51 AE	35.35 MW	41.16 AEX	FLBLS	7/16-9/16
	Tampa-St. Petersburg-Clearwater MSA, FL	H	23.97 AE	63.99 MW	84.75 AEX	FLBLS	7/16-9/16
	Georgia	Y	63580 FQ	99190 MW	141370 TQ	USBLS	5/15
	Atlanta-Sandy Springs-Roswell MSA, GA	Y	68930 FQ	103590 MW	142450 TQ	USBLS	5/15
	Augusta-Richmond County MSA, GA-SC	Y	78510 FQ	127640 MW	165960 TQ	USBLS	5/15
	Hawaii	Y	97050 FQ	108800 MW	120240 TQ	USBLS	5/15
	Urban Honolulu MSA, HI	Y	99210 FQ	109820 MW	120630 TQ	USBLS	5/15
	Idaho	Y	64010 FQ	116340 MW	141930 TQ	USBLS	5/15
	Boise City MSA, ID	Y	108560 FQ	131670 MW	149450 TQ	USBLS	5/15
	Illinois	Y	81670 FQ	93100 MW	106850 TQ	USBLS	5/15
	Chicago-Naperville-Arlington Heights PMSA, IL	Y	82910 FQ	91980 MW	101190 TQ	USBLS	5/15
	Lake County-Kenosha County PMSA, IL-WI	Y	67980 FQ	106480 MW	129190 TQ	USBLS	5/15
	Indiana	Y	68800 FQ	88070 MW	111930 TQ	USBLS	5/15
	Gary PMSA, IN	Y	105850 FQ	114490 MW	123130 TQ	USBLS	5/15
	Indianapolis-Carmel-Anderson MSA, IN	Y	66290 FQ	77970 MW	94450 TQ	USBLS	5/15
	Iowa	Y	90180 FQ	112070 MW	148390 TQ	USBLS	5/15
	Des Moines-West Des Moines MSA, IA	Y	109580 FQ	127420 MW		USBLS	5/15
	Kansas	Y	69580 FQ	94690 MW	141390 TQ	USBLS	5/15
	Wichita MSA, KS	Y	77400 FQ	93590 MW	176470 TQ	USBLS	5/15
	Kentucky	Y	75760 FQ	95170 MW	114210 TQ	USBLS	5/15
	Louisville-Jefferson County MSA, KY-IN	Y	90610 FQ	103550 MW	119040 TQ	USBLS	5/15
	Louisiana	Y	68330 FQ	80610 MW	134710 TQ	USBLS	5/15
	Baton Rouge MSA, LA	Y	81590 FQ	94450 MW	126150 TQ	USBLS	5/15
	Lafayette MSA, LA	Y	57410 FQ	67720 MW	76150 TQ	USBLS	5/15
	New Orleans-Metairie MSA, LA	Y	80090 FQ	93190 MW	141260 TQ	USBLS	5/15
	Maine	Y	87980 FQ	105360 MW	136530 TQ	USBLS	5/15
	Portland-South Portland MSA, ME	Y	88250 FQ	102720 MW	165890 TQ	USBLS	5/15
	Maryland	Y	61716 AE	132921 MW	168524 AEX	MDBLS	4/16
	Baltimore-Columbia-Towson MSA, MD	Y	98260 FQ	118240 MW	143610 TQ	USBLS	5/15
	Salisbury MSA, MD-DE	Y	121880 FQ	152440 MW		USBLS	5/15
	Massachusetts	Y	89590 FQ	108610 MW	124070 TQ	USBLS	5/15
	Boston-Cambridge-Newton NECTA, MA	Y	91050 FQ	107230 MW	121300 TQ	USBLS	5/15
	Worcester MSA, MA-CT	Y	97580 FQ	130340 MW		USBLS	5/15
	Michigan	Y	73750 FQ	103340 MW	135920 TQ	USBLS	5/15
	Detroit-Dearborn-Livonia PMSA, MI	Y	48740 FQ	86280 MW	98600 TQ	USBLS	5/15
	Grand Rapids-Wyoming MSA, MI	Y	82550 FQ	105500 MW	139760 TQ	USBLS	5/15
	Minnesota	Y	80634 FQ	110049 MW	129817 TQ	MNBLS	1/16-3/16
	Minneapolis-St. Paul-Bloomington MSA, MN-WI	Y	82519 FQ	114898 MW	132851 TQ	MNBLS	1/16-3/16
	Mississippi	Y	48570 FQ	89650 MW	144350 TQ	USBLS	5/15
	Jackson MSA, MS	Y	27590 FQ	91270 MW	136750 TQ	USBLS	5/15
	Missouri	Y	80490 FQ	109740 MW	164500 TQ	USBLS	5/15
	Kansas City MSA, MO-KS	Y	83940 FQ	108650 MW	153980 TQ	USBLS	5/15
	St. Louis MSA, MO-IL	Y	67900 FQ	80180 MW	126190 TQ	USBLS	5/15
	Montana	Y	58360 FQ	96350 MW	139330 TQ	USBLS	5/15
	Billings MSA, MT	Y	90260 FQ	127680 MW		USBLS	5/15
	Nebraska	Y	68725 FQ	84515 MW	112950 TQ	NEBLS	7/16-9/16
	Omaha-Council Bluffs MSA, NE-IA	Y	71675 FQ	86805 MW	118010 TQ	NEBLS	7/16-9/16
	Nevada	Y	79620 FQ	92230 MW	117990 TQ	USBLS	5/15

AE	Average entry wage	AWR	Average wage range	H	Hourly	LR	Low end range	MTC	Median total compensation	TCC Total cash compensation
AEX	Average experienced wage	B	Biweekly	HI	Highest wage paid	M	Monthly	MW	Median wage paid	TQ Third quartile wage
ATC	Average total compensation	D	Daily	HR	High end range	MCC	Median cash compensation	MWR	Median wage range	W Weekly
AW	Average wage paid	FQ	First quartile wage	LO	Lowest wage paid	ME	Median entry wage	S	See annotated source	Y Yearly

Optometrist

Occupation/Type/Industry	Location	Per	Low	Mid	High	Source	Date
Optometrist	Las Vegas-Henderson-Paradise MSA, NV	Y	81600 FQ	91560 MW	114210 TQ	USBLS	5/15
	New Hampshire	H	34.90 AE	57.06 MW	66.86 AEX	NHBLS	6/16
	Manchester NECTA, NH	H	51.87 AE	66.27 MW	75.95 AEX	NHBLS	6/16
	New Jersey	Y	97390 FQ	112280 MW	124890 TQ	USBLS	5/15
	Camden PMSA, NJ	Y	104250 FQ	115420 MW	126740 TQ	USBLS	5/15
	Newark PMSA, NJ-PA	Y	85700 FQ	105680 MW	121820 TQ	USBLS	5/15
	Trenton MSA, NJ	Y	91180 FQ	123080 MW	162750 TQ	USBLS	5/15
	New Mexico	Y	74830 FQ	112900 MW		USBLS	5/15
	Albuquerque MSA, NM	Y	39010 FQ	88160 MW	159510 TQ	USBLS	5/15
	New York	Y	78430 AE	119600 MW	162800 AEX	NYBLS	1/16-3/16
	Buffalo-Cheektowaga-Niagara Falls MSA, NY	Y	84050 FQ	100400 MW	126040 TQ	USBLS	5/15
	Nassau County-Suffolk County PMSA, NY	Y	99560 FQ	128950 MW	148570 TQ	USBLS	5/15
	New York-Jersey City-White Plains PMSA, NY-NJ	Y	90170 FQ	112410 MW	132880 TQ	USBLS	5/15
	Rochester MSA, NY	Y	111340 FQ	126550 MW		USBLS	5/15
	North Carolina	Y	83560 FQ	108790 MW	147520 TQ	USBLS	5/15
	Charlotte-Concord-Gastonia MSA, NC-SC	Y	77060 FQ	104380 MW	144830 TQ	USBLS	5/15
	Raleigh MSA, NC	Y	92600 FQ	106470 MW	124610 TQ	USBLS	5/15
	North Dakota	Y	80140 FQ	108270 MW	143370 TQ	USBLS	5/15
	Fargo MSA, ND-MN	Y	84310 FQ	94420 MW	116700 TQ	USBLS	5/15
	Ohio	Y	73220 FQ	107480 MW	127450 TQ	USBLS	5/15
	Cincinnati MSA, OH-KY-IN	Y	79720 FQ	106490 MW	125890 TQ	USBLS	5/15
	Cleveland-Elyria MSA, OH	Y	77300 FQ	109280 MW	124620 TQ	USBLS	5/15
	Columbus MSA, OH	Y	67640 FQ	91660 MW	128560 TQ	USBLS	5/15
	Oklahoma	Y	64920 FQ	99240 MW		USBLS	5/15
	Tulsa MSA, OK	Y	81560 FQ	102490 MW	143110 TQ	USBLS	5/15
	Oregon	H	38.77 FQ	49.43 MW	60.56 TQ	ORBLS	2016
	Portland-Vancouver-Hillsboro MSA, OR-WA	Y	87180 FQ	109630 MW	128240 TQ	USBLS	5/15
	Pennsylvania	Y	66160 FQ	102010 MW	131730 TQ	USBLS	5/15
	Allentown-Bethlehem-Easton MSA, PA-NJ	Y	73410 FQ	105730 MW	121010 TQ	USBLS	5/15
	Montgomery County-Bucks County-Chester County PMSA, PA	Y	57270 FQ	113930 MW	181260 TQ	USBLS	5/15
	Philadelphia PMSA, PA	Y	50680 FQ	129370 MW		USBLS	5/15
	Pittsburgh MSA, PA	Y	48920 FQ	108190 MW	140800 TQ	USBLS	5/15
	Rhode Island	Y	89100 FQ	100090 MW	124470 TQ	USBLS	5/15
	Providence-Warwick MSA, RI-MA	Y	88300 FQ	100250 MW	123280 TQ	USBLS	5/15
	South Carolina	Y	54550 FQ	86900 MW	126700 TQ	USBLS	5/15
	Charleston-North Charleston MSA, SC	Y	31960 FQ	57210 MW	90370 TQ	USBLS	5/15
	Columbia MSA, SC	Y	31970 FQ	66770 MW	81520 TQ	USBLS	5/15
	Greenville-Anderson-Mauldin MSA, SC	Y	54530 FQ	81580 MW	175850 TQ	USBLS	5/15
	South Dakota	Y	84480 FQ	100410 MW	124140 TQ	USBLS	5/15
	Tennessee	Y	82280 FQ	106850 MW	140840 TQ	USBLS	5/15
	Knoxville MSA, TN	Y	70580 FQ	114020 MW	159020 TQ	USBLS	5/15
	Memphis MSA, TN-MS-AR	Y	82560 FQ	134610 MW	151800 TQ	USBLS	5/15
	Nashville-Davidson–Murfreesboro–Franklin MSA, TN	Y	64330 FQ	102950 MW	121280 TQ	USBLS	5/15
	Texas	Y	56650 FQ	91260 MW	149100 TQ	USBLS	5/15
	Austin-Round Rock MSA, TX	Y	53260 FQ	71100 MW	91260 TQ	USBLS	5/15
	Dallas-Plano-Irving PMSA, TX	Y	73100 FQ	100160 MW	127810 TQ	USBLS	5/15
	Fort Worth-Arlington PMSA, TX	Y	97530 FQ	142570 MW		USBLS	5/15
	Houston-The Woodlands-Sugar Land MSA, TX	Y	42100 FQ	59390 MW	142870 TQ	USBLS	5/15
	San Antonio-New Braunfels MSA, TX	Y	60540 FQ	104420 MW	129330 TQ	USBLS	5/15
	Utah	Y	77230 FQ	108210 MW	132490 TQ	USBLS	5/15
	Ogden-Clearfield MSA, UT	Y	78000 FQ	94410 MW	106010 TQ	USBLS	5/15
	Provo-Orem MSA, UT	Y	106120 FQ	113750 MW	121390 TQ	USBLS	5/15
	Salt Lake City MSA, UT	Y	101950 FQ	132270 MW	157070 TQ	USBLS	5/15
	Vermont	Y	91890 FQ	126020 MW	154530 TQ	USBLS	5/15

AE	Average entry wage	**AWR**	Average wage range	**H**	Hourly
AEX	Average experienced wage	**B**	Biweekly	**HI**	Highest wage paid
ATC	Average total compensation	**D**	Daily	**HR**	High end range
AW	Average wage paid	**FQ**	First quartile wage	**LO**	Lowest wage paid

LR	Low end range	**MTC**	Median total compensation	**TCC** Total cash compensation
M	Monthly	**MW**	Median wage paid	**TQ** Third quartile wage
MCC	Median cash compensation	**MWR**	Median wage range	**W** Weekly
ME	Median entry wage	**S**	See annotated source	**Y** Yearly

Occupation/Type/Industry	Location	Per	Low	Mid	High	Source	Date
Optometrist	Burlington-South Burlington						
	MSA, VT	Y	77430 FQ	108470 MW	143240 TQ	USBLS	5/15
	Virginia	Y	90750 FQ	112690 MW	140810 TQ	USBLS	5/15
	Richmond MSA, VA	Y	93120 FQ	117270 MW	137490 TQ	USBLS	5/15
	Virginia Beach-Norfolk-						
	Newport News MSA, VA-NC	Y	86910 FQ	113600 MW	145230 TQ	USBLS	5/15
	Washington	H	39.25 FQ	54.46 MW	64.81 TQ	WABLS	3/16
	Seattle-Bellevue-Everett						
	PMSA, WA	H	24.63 FQ	52.51 MW	59.03 TQ	WABLS	3/16
	Tacoma-Lakewood PMSA, WA	H	47.49 FQ	55.48 MW	90.11 TQ	WABLS	3/16
	West Virginia	Y	58840 FQ	91260 MW	113420 TQ	USBLS	5/15
	Wisconsin	Y	64870 FQ	94030 MW	123690 TQ	USBLS	5/15
	Madison MSA, WI	Y	79210 FQ	91270 MW	122050 TQ	USBLS	5/15
	Milwaukee-Waukesha-West						
	Allis MSA, WI	Y	82250 FQ	105010 MW	126680 TQ	USBLS	5/15
	Wyoming	Y	67560 FQ	91400 MW	148940 TQ	USBLS	5/15
	Puerto Rico	Y	37330 FQ	45470 MW	55100 TQ	USBLS	5/15
	San Juan-Carolina-Caguas						
	MSA, PR	Y	37740 FQ	45390 MW	53980 TQ	USBLS	5/15
Oracle Certified Associate	United States	Y		95740 AW		CERTM02	2015
Oral and Maxillofacial Surgeon	Alabama	Y	83289 AE	145998 AW	177352 AEX	ALBLS	6/16
	Arkansas	Y	162820 FQ	245090 AW		USBLS	5/15
	California	H		113.72 AW		CABLS	1/16-3/16
	Colorado	Y		262380 AW		USBLS	5/15
	Connecticut	Y		206297 AW		CTBLS	1/16-3/16
	Florida	H		126.62 AW		FLBLS	7/16-9/16
	Georgia	Y		236110 AW		USBLS	5/15
	Illinois	Y	22680 FQ	166650 AW		USBLS	5/15
	Indiana	Y		248750 AW		USBLS	5/15
	Kentucky	Y	172680 FQ	209350 AW		USBLS	5/15
	Massachusetts	Y		268670 AW		USBLS	5/15
	Michigan	Y	92880 FQ	124090 MW		USBLS	5/15
	Minnesota	Y		269402 AW		MNBLS	1/16-3/16
	Mississippi	Y		221490 AW		USBLS	5/15
	Missouri	Y		277690 AW		USBLS	5/15
	New Hampshire	H		141.31 AW		NHBLS	6/16
	New York	Y	103950 AE	215720 AW		NYBLS	1/16-3/16
	Ohio	Y	175390 FQ	225240 AW		USBLS	5/15
	Oklahoma	Y	115520 FQ	232320 MW		USBLS	5/15
	Pennsylvania	Y	57490 FQ	139940 MW		USBLS	5/15
	Tennessee	Y	146910 FQ	203850 AW		USBLS	5/15
	Texas	Y	175790 FQ	236060 AW		USBLS	5/15
	Vermont	Y	176880 FQ	203130 AW		USBLS	5/15
	Washington	H	76.76 FQ	104.19 AW		WABLS	3/16
Oral Health Specialist							
State Government	Ohio	H	29.39 LO		40.80 HI	OHGOV	2015
Order Clerk	Alabama	Y	19355 AE	31124 AW	37019 AEX	ALBLS	6/16
	Birmingham-Hoover MSA, AL	Y	22580 AE	36091 AW	42842 AEX	ALBLS	6/16
	Alaska	Y	30820 FQ	40740 MW	53810 TQ	USBLS	5/15
	Anchorage MSA, AK	Y	30830 FQ	41340 MW	54900 TQ	USBLS	5/15
	Arizona	Y	28240 FQ	35060 MW	44130 TQ	USBLS	5/15
	Phoenix-Mesa-Scottsdale						
	MSA, AZ	Y	28830 FQ	35390 MW	44470 TQ	USBLS	5/15
	Tucson MSA, AZ	Y	26260 FQ	33150 MW	42810 TQ	USBLS	5/15
	Arkansas	Y	21970 FQ	30250 MW	37060 TQ	USBLS	5/15
	Little Rock-North Little Rock-						
	Conway MSA, AR	Y	25060 FQ	31000 MW	36920 TQ	USBLS	5/15
	California	H	13.23 FQ	16.56 MW	21.22 TQ	CABLS	1/16-3/16
	Anaheim-Santa Ana-Irvine						
	PMSA, CA	H	13.61 FQ	16.08 MW	19.43 TQ	CABLS	1/16-3/16
	Los Angeles-Long Beach-						
	Glendale PMSA, CA	H	12.63 FQ	15.33 MW	19.31 TQ	CABLS	1/16-3/16
	Oakland-Hayward-Berkeley						
	PMSA, CA	H	14.64 FQ	18.48 MW	24.08 TQ	CABLS	1/16-3/16
	Riverside-San Bernardino-						
	Ontario MSA, CA	H	13.09 FQ	17.05 MW	21.56 TQ	CABLS	1/16-3/16
	Sacramento–Roseville–						
	Arden-Arcade MSA, CA	H	13.17 FQ	15.52 MW	19.59 TQ	CABLS	1/16-3/16
	San Diego-Carlsbad MSA, CA	H	12.97 FQ	17.33 MW	22.91 TQ	CABLS	1/16-3/16

AE	Average entry wage	AWR	Average wage range	H	Hourly	LR	Low end range	MTC	Median total compensation	TCC	Total cash compensation
AEX	Average experienced wage	B	Biweekly	HI	Highest wage paid	M	Monthly	MW	Median wage paid	TQ	Third quartile wage
ATC	Average total compensation	D	Daily	HR	High end range	MCC	Median cash compensation	MWR	Median wage range	W	Weekly
AW	Average wage paid	FQ	First quartile wage	LO	Lowest wage paid	ME	Median entry wage	S	See annotated source	Y	Yearly

Occupation/Type/Industry	Location	Per	Low	Mid	High	Source	Date
Order Clerk	San Francisco-Redwood City-South San Francisco PMSA, CA	H	16.80 FQ	21.47 MW	26.11 TQ	CABLS	1/16-3/16
	Colorado	Y	22840 FQ	30760 MW	40400 TQ	USBLS	5/15
	Denver-Aurora-Lakewood MSA, CO	Y	22740 FQ	32270 MW	42630 TQ	USBLS	5/15
	Connecticut	Y		38191 MW		CTBLS	1/16-3/16
	Bridgeport-Stamford-Norwalk MSA, CT	Y	34750 FQ	44310 MW	55070 TQ	USBLS	5/15
	Hartford-West Hartford-East Hartford MSA, CT	Y	31260 FQ	38840 MW	49980 TQ	USBLS	5/15
	Delaware	Y	26520 FQ	32840 MW	40590 TQ	USBLS	5/15
	Wilmington PMSA, DE-MD-NJ	Y	29080 FQ	36560 MW	43310 TQ	USBLS	5/15
	District of Columbia	Y	30650 FQ	40730 MW	45790 TQ	USBLS	5/15
	Washington-Arlington-Alexandria PMSA, DC-VA-MD-WV	Y	20460 FQ	31570 MW	40400 TQ	USBLS	5/15
	Florida	H	10.09 AE	13.64 MW	16.71 AEX	FLBLS	7/16-9/16
	Fort Lauderdale-Pompano Beach-Deerfield Beach PMSA, FL	H	11.44 AE	15.10 MW	17.32 AEX	FLBLS	7/16-9/16
	Miami-Miami Beach-Kendall PMSA, FL	H	9.82 AE	12.84 MW	15.95 AEX	FLBLS	7/16-9/16
	Orlando-Kissimmee-Sanford MSA, FL	H	9.54 AE	14.41 MW	17.52 AEX	FLBLS	7/16-9/16
	Tallahassee MSA, FL	H	10.67 AE	12.19 MW	15.84 AEX	FLBLS	7/16-9/16
	Tampa-St. Petersburg-Clearwater MSA, FL	H	10.73 AE	12.86 MW	15.37 AEX	FLBLS	7/16-9/16
	Georgia	Y	25510 FQ	30190 MW	38050 TQ	USBLS	5/15
	Atlanta-Sandy Springs-Roswell MSA, GA	Y	25910 FQ	30510 MW	38980 TQ	USBLS	5/15
	Augusta-Richmond County MSA, GA-SC	Y	26430 FQ	35140 MW	43640 TQ	USBLS	5/15
	Hawaii	Y	27830 FQ	34270 MW	39100 TQ	USBLS	5/15
	Urban Honolulu MSA, HI	Y	28070 FQ	34320 MW	39410 TQ	USBLS	5/15
	Idaho	Y	22440 FQ	31330 MW	51460 TQ	USBLS	5/15
	Boise City MSA, ID	Y	29090 FQ	49350 MW	55930 TQ	USBLS	5/15
	Illinois	Y	28420 FQ	35620 MW	44360 TQ	USBLS	5/15
	Chicago-Naperville-Arlington Heights PMSA, IL	Y	29760 FQ	36610 MW	45500 TQ	USBLS	5/15
	Lake County-Kenosha County PMSA, IL-WI	Y	23520 FQ	30560 MW	39920 TQ	USBLS	5/15
	Indiana	Y	26510 FQ	32350 MW	38930 TQ	USBLS	5/15
	Gary PMSA, IN	Y	24860 FQ	30120 MW	36450 TQ	USBLS	5/15
	Indianapolis-Carmel-Anderson MSA, IN	Y	28550 FQ	34420 MW	41460 TQ	USBLS	5/15
	Iowa	Y	22850 FQ	32260 MW	45830 TQ	USBLS	5/15
	Des Moines-West Des Moines MSA, IA	Y	29510 FQ	44260 MW	55350 TQ	USBLS	5/15
	Kansas	Y	25030 FQ	31820 MW	38330 TQ	USBLS	5/15
	Wichita MSA, KS	Y	25230 FQ	30800 MW	38470 TQ	USBLS	5/15
	Kentucky	Y	23640 FQ	30020 MW	36230 TQ	USBLS	5/15
	Louisville-Jefferson County MSA, KY-IN	Y	25800 FQ	30940 MW	38600 TQ	USBLS	5/15
	Louisiana	Y	20900 FQ	27500 MW	35720 TQ	USBLS	5/15
	Baton Rouge MSA, LA	Y	20240 FQ	28250 MW	37190 TQ	USBLS	5/15
	New Orleans-Metairie MSA, LA	Y	23460 FQ	28560 MW	37320 TQ	USBLS	5/15
	Maine	Y	23750 FQ	28200 MW	34100 TQ	USBLS	5/15
	Portland-South Portland MSA, ME	Y	28010 FQ	32540 MW	37960 TQ	USBLS	5/15
	Maryland	Y	23427 AE	35779 MW	41955 AEX	MDBLS	4/16
	Baltimore-Columbia-Towson MSA, MD	Y	27320 FQ	35600 MW	45190 TQ	USBLS	5/15
	Salisbury MSA, MD-DE	Y	23220 FQ	27780 MW	30980 TQ	USBLS	5/15
	Massachusetts	Y	29000 FQ	37200 MW	46030 TQ	USBLS	5/15
	Boston-Cambridge-Newton NECTA, MA	Y	23820 FQ	35910 MW	46220 TQ	USBLS	5/15
	Worcester MSA, MA-CT	Y	31450 FQ	36960 MW	46750 TQ	USBLS	5/15
	Michigan	Y	28570 FQ	35800 MW	43900 TQ	USBLS	5/15

AE	Average entry wage	AWR	Average wage range	H	Hourly
AEX	Average experienced wage	B	Biweekly	HI	Highest wage paid
ATC	Average total compensation	D	Daily	HR	High end range
AW	Average wage paid	FQ	First quartile wage	LO	Lowest wage paid

LR	Low end range	MTC	Median total compensation	TCC	Total cash compensation
M	Monthly	MW	Median wage paid	TQ	Third quartile wage
MCC	Median cash compensation	MWR	Median wage range	W	Weekly
ME	Median entry wage	S	See annotated source	Y	Yearly

Occupation/Type/Industry	Location	Per	Low	Mid	High	Source	Date
Order Clerk	Detroit-Dearborn-Livonia PMSA, MI	Y	33060 FQ	38170 MW	44980 TQ	USBLS	5/15
	Grand Rapids-Wyoming MSA, MI	Y	30870 FQ	39010 MW	50150 TQ	USBLS	5/15
	Minnesota	Y	27840 FQ	34505 MW	40987 TQ	MNBLS	1/16-3/16
	Minneapolis-St. Paul-Bloomington MSA, MN-WI	Y	29074 FQ	35364 MW	42382 TQ	MNBLS	1/16-3/16
	Mississippi	Y	22070 FQ	27940 MW	34340 TQ	USBLS	5/15
	Jackson MSA, MS	Y	22430 FQ	27410 MW	33700 TQ	USBLS	5/15
	Missouri	Y	23070 FQ	33110 MW	42480 TQ	USBLS	5/15
	Kansas City MSA, MO-KS	Y	26090 FQ	35620 MW	44240 TQ	USBLS	5/15
	St. Louis MSA, MO-IL	Y	27300 FQ	35740 MW	43910 TQ	USBLS	5/15
	Montana	Y	22370 FQ	28730 MW	37030 TQ	USBLS	5/15
	Billings MSA, MT	Y	23040 FQ	36040 MW	44000 TQ	USBLS	5/15
	Nebraska	Y	20935 FQ	24160 MW	31620 TQ	NEBLS	7/16-9/16
	Omaha-Council Bluffs MSA, NE-IA	Y	20905 FQ	24490 MW	38720 TQ	NEBLS	7/16-9/16
	Nevada	Y	27380 FQ	34780 MW	42260 TQ	USBLS	5/15
	Las Vegas-Henderson-Paradise MSA, NV	Y	26880 FQ	34230 MW	41490 TQ	USBLS	5/15
	New Hampshire	H	11.31 AE	16.21 MW	20.00 AEX	NHBLS	6/16
	Manchester NECTA, NH	H	12.22 AE	15.34 MW	17.71 AEX	NHBLS	6/16
	Nashua NECTA, NH-MA	Y	25700 FQ	32340 MW	40920 TQ	USBLS	5/15
	New Jersey	Y	26450 FQ	35590 MW	46700 TQ	USBLS	5/15
	Camden PMSA, NJ	Y	25040 FQ	33820 MW	43790 TQ	USBLS	5/15
	Newark PMSA, NJ-PA	Y	26440 FQ	35290 MW	47340 TQ	USBLS	5/15
	Trenton MSA, NJ	Y	22300 FQ	35800 MW	54950 TQ	USBLS	5/15
	New Mexico	Y	24040 FQ	29280 MW	36120 TQ	USBLS	5/15
	Albuquerque MSA, NM	Y	27260 FQ	31770 MW	38240 TQ	USBLS	5/15
	New York	Y	21880 AE	33480 MW	41180 AEX	NYBLS	1/16-3/16
	Buffalo-Cheektowaga-Niagara Falls MSA, NY	Y	26180 FQ	34250 MW	42880 TQ	USBLS	5/15
	Nassau County-Suffolk County PMSA, NY	Y	25370 FQ	34930 MW	45180 TQ	USBLS	5/15
	New York-Jersey City-White Plains PMSA, NY-NJ	Y	24740 FQ	34460 MW	45130 TQ	USBLS	5/15
	Rochester MSA, NY	Y	26990 FQ	33910 MW	38820 TQ	USBLS	5/15
	North Carolina	Y	24400 FQ	31010 MW	38960 TQ	USBLS	5/15
	Charlotte-Concord-Gastonia MSA, NC-SC	Y	26790 FQ	34540 MW	41660 TQ	USBLS	5/15
	Raleigh MSA, NC	Y	31250 FQ	36640 MW	43430 TQ	USBLS	5/15
	North Dakota	Y	30090 FQ	36750 MW	44610 TQ	USBLS	5/15
	Fargo MSA, ND-MN	Y	27190 FQ	35870 MW	45630 TQ	USBLS	5/15
	Ohio	Y	23740 FQ	30830 MW	38530 TQ	USBLS	5/15
	Cincinnati MSA, OH-KY-IN	Y	22490 FQ	30300 MW	37430 TQ	USBLS	5/15
	Cleveland-Elyria MSA, OH	Y	25860 FQ	33340 MW	41180 TQ	USBLS	5/15
	Columbus MSA, OH	Y	22640 FQ	26580 MW	37070 TQ	USBLS	5/15
	Oklahoma	Y	21930 FQ	27310 MW	34850 TQ	USBLS	5/15
	Oklahoma City MSA, OK	Y	22640 FQ	27290 MW	33030 TQ	USBLS	5/15
	Tulsa MSA, OK	Y	21180 FQ	31540 MW	39820 TQ	USBLS	5/15
	Oregon	H	11.89 FQ	15.83 MW	19.71 TQ	ORBLS	2016
	Portland-Vancouver-Hillsboro MSA, OR-WA	Y	28910 FQ	35180 MW	43170 TQ	USBLS	5/15
	Pennsylvania	Y	23540 FQ	30580 MW	38290 TQ	USBLS	5/15
	Allentown-Bethlehem-Easton MSA, PA-NJ	Y	23430 FQ	30190 MW	38980 TQ	USBLS	5/15
	Harrisburg-Carlisle MSA, PA	Y	31390 FQ	36770 MW	46000 TQ	USBLS	5/15
	Montgomery County-Bucks County-Chester County PMSA, PA	Y	25690 FQ	33440 MW	40240 TQ	USBLS	5/15
	Philadelphia PMSA, PA	Y	26360 FQ	33530 MW	38420 TQ	USBLS	5/15
	Pittsburgh MSA, PA	Y	24100 FQ	29150 MW	36080 TQ	USBLS	5/15
	Rhode Island	Y	25980 FQ	32970 MW	41070 TQ	USBLS	5/15
	Providence-Warwick MSA, RI-MA	Y	26830 FQ	34100 MW	41620 TQ	USBLS	5/15
	South Carolina	Y	25880 FQ	32150 MW	38980 TQ	USBLS	5/15
	Charleston-North Charleston MSA, SC	Y	27350 FQ	32530 MW	39600 TQ	USBLS	5/15
	Columbia MSA, SC	Y	29360 FQ	35650 MW	43310 TQ	USBLS	5/15
	Greenville-Anderson-Mauldin MSA, SC	Y	27130 FQ	31910 MW	38360 TQ	USBLS	5/15
	South Dakota	Y	25230 FQ	29370 MW	35960 TQ	USBLS	5/15

AE	Average entry wage	**AWR**	Average wage range	**H**	Hourly
AEX	Average experienced wage	**B**	Biweekly	**HI**	Highest wage paid
ATC	Average total compensation	**D**	Daily	**HR**	High end range
AW	Average wage paid	**FQ**	First quartile wage	**LO**	Lowest wage paid

LR	Low end range	**MTC**	Median total compensation	**TCC**	Total cash compensation
M	Monthly	**MW**	Median wage paid	**TQ**	Third quartile wage
MCC	Median cash compensation	**MWR**	Median wage range	**W**	Weekly
ME	Median entry wage	**S**	See annotated source	**Y**	Yearly

Occupation/Type/Industry	Location	Per	Low	Mid	High	Source	Date
Order Clerk	Sioux Falls MSA, SD	Y	26300 FQ	30950 MW	37550 TQ	USBLS	5/15
	Tennessee	Y	22320 FQ	29640 MW	38280 TQ	USBLS	5/15
	Knoxville MSA, TN	Y	18540 FQ	22010 MW	31580 TQ	USBLS	5/15
	Memphis MSA, TN-MS-AR	Y	24580 FQ	30430 MW	39280 TQ	USBLS	5/15
	Nashville-Davidson–Murfreesboro–Franklin MSA, TN	Y	24520 FQ	32800 MW	41200 TQ	USBLS	5/15
	Texas	Y	25790 FQ	34270 MW	44490 TQ	USBLS	5/15
	Austin-Round Rock MSA, TX	Y	25670 FQ	33170 MW	42760 TQ	USBLS	5/15
	Dallas-Plano-Irving PMSA, TX	Y	26480 FQ	35010 MW	44820 TQ	USBLS	5/15
	Fort Worth-Arlington PMSA, TX	Y	28070 FQ	35620 MW	44720 TQ	USBLS	5/15
	Houston-The Woodlands-Sugar Land MSA, TX	Y	29490 FQ	38580 MW	50180 TQ	USBLS	5/15
	San Antonio-New Braunfels MSA, TX	Y	23480 FQ	28280 MW	36130 TQ	USBLS	5/15
	Utah	Y	23210 FQ	28290 MW	36060 TQ	USBLS	5/15
	Ogden-Clearfield MSA, UT	Y	18450 FQ	21720 MW	29050 TQ	USBLS	5/15
	Provo-Orem MSA, UT	Y	25190 FQ	28780 MW	34340 TQ	USBLS	5/15
	Salt Lake City MSA, UT	Y	26470 FQ	29730 MW	40780 TQ	USBLS	5/15
	Vermont	Y	27660 FQ	33850 MW	40260 TQ	USBLS	5/15
	Burlington-South Burlington MSA, VT	Y	31150 FQ	36410 MW	43930 TQ	USBLS	5/15
	Virginia	Y	21010 FQ	27070 MW	36280 TQ	USBLS	5/15
	Richmond MSA, VA	Y	21820 FQ	30250 MW	37210 TQ	USBLS	5/15
	Virginia Beach-Norfolk-Newport News MSA, VA-NC	Y	21900 FQ	27930 MW	35760 TQ	USBLS	5/15
	Washington	H	13.87 FQ	17.41 MW	21.60 TQ	WABLS	3/16
	Seattle-Bellevue-Everett PMSA, WA	H	13.56 FQ	17.65 MW	21.63 TQ	WABLS	3/16
	Tacoma-Lakewood PMSA, WA	H	14.51 FQ	17.86 MW	23.05 TQ	WABLS	3/16
	West Virginia	Y	21560 FQ	26920 MW	33730 TQ	USBLS	5/15
	Huntington-Ashland MSA, WV-KY-OH	Y	21770 FQ	28830 MW	36010 TQ	USBLS	5/15
	Wisconsin	Y	23960 FQ	31390 MW	39470 TQ	USBLS	5/15
	Madison MSA, WI	Y	22590 FQ	32400 MW	40360 TQ	USBLS	5/15
	Milwaukee-Waukesha-West Allis MSA, WI	Y	28860 FQ	36190 MW	44620 TQ	USBLS	5/15
	Wyoming	Y	27110 FQ	31140 MW	38380 TQ	USBLS	5/15
	Puerto Rico	Y	17280 FQ	19000 MW	23270 TQ	USBLS	5/15
	San Juan-Carolina-Caguas MSA, PR	Y	17150 FQ	18720 MW	21830 TQ	USBLS	5/15
Orderly	Alabama	Y	17575 AE	21498 AW	23454 AEX	ALBLS	6/16
	Birmingham-Hoover MSA, AL	Y	17617 AE	22620 AW	25122 AEX	ALBLS	6/16
	Alaska	Y	26980 FQ	31570 MW	37070 TQ	USBLS	5/15
	Arizona	Y	21770 FQ	24390 MW	28570 TQ	USBLS	5/15
	Phoenix-Mesa-Scottsdale MSA, AZ	Y	22050 FQ	24610 MW	28740 TQ	USBLS	5/15
	Arkansas	Y	18990 FQ	22450 MW	27370 TQ	USBLS	5/15
	California	H	14.54 FQ	18.21 MW	24.00 TQ	CABLS	1/16-3/16
	Anaheim-Santa Ana-Irvine PMSA, CA	H	13.67 FQ	15.15 MW	19.01 TQ	CABLS	1/16-3/16
	Los Angeles-Long Beach-Glendale PMSA, CA	H	14.54 FQ	17.05 MW	20.36 TQ	CABLS	1/16-3/16
	Oakland-Hayward-Berkeley PMSA, CA	H	13.53 FQ	17.42 MW	26.29 TQ	CABLS	1/16-3/16
	Riverside-San Bernardino-Ontario MSA, CA	H	14.03 FQ	19.11 MW	26.43 TQ	CABLS	1/16-3/16
	Sacramento–Roseville–Arden-Arcade MSA, CA	H	17.22 FQ	20.69 MW	22.98 TQ	CABLS	1/16-3/16
	San Diego-Carlsbad MSA, CA	H	13.92 FQ	17.07 MW	21.48 TQ	CABLS	1/16-3/16
	San Francisco-Redwood City-South San Francisco PMSA, CA	H	21.22 FQ	25.20 MW	28.11 TQ	CABLS	1/16-3/16
	Colorado	Y	21170 FQ	26050 MW	31150 TQ	USBLS	5/15
	Denver-Aurora-Lakewood MSA, CO	Y	24030 FQ	28550 MW	34190 TQ	USBLS	5/15
	Connecticut	Y		29787 MW		CTBLS	1/16-3/16
	Bridgeport-Stamford-Norwalk MSA, CT	Y	23430 FQ	28170 MW	33650 TQ	USBLS	5/15

AE	Average entry wage	AWR	Average wage range	H	Hourly	LR	Low end range	MTC	Median total compensation	TCC	Total cash compensation
AEX	Average experienced wage	B	Biweekly	HI	Highest wage paid	M	Monthly	MW	Median wage paid	TQ	Third quartile wage
ATC	Average total compensation	D	Daily	HR	High end range	MCC	Median cash compensation	MWR	Median wage range	W	Weekly
AW	Average wage paid	FQ	First quartile wage	LO	Lowest wage paid	ME	Median entry wage	S	See annotated source	Y	Yearly

Occupation/Type/Industry	Location	Per	Low	Mid	High	Source	Date
Orderly	Hartford-West Hartford-East Hartford MSA, CT	Y	24880 FQ	29870 MW	36050 TQ	USBLS	5/15
	Delaware	Y	25780 FQ	27590 MW	29050 TQ	USBLS	5/15
	Wilmington PMSA, DE-MD-NJ	Y	25790 FQ	27590 MW	29190 TQ	USBLS	5/15
	District of Columbia	Y	26550 FQ	29120 MW	32780 TQ	USBLS	5/15
	Washington-Arlington-Alexandria PMSA, DC-VA-MD-WV	Y	23470 FQ	27250 MW	30530 TQ	USBLS	5/15
	Florida	H	9.45 AE	10.95 MW	12.16 AEX	FLBLS	7/16-9/16
	Fort Lauderdale-Pompano Beach-Deerfield Beach PMSA, FL	H	10.18 AE	11.29 MW	12.50 AEX	FLBLS	7/16-9/16
	Miami-Miami Beach-Kendall PMSA, FL	H	9.18 AE	10.74 MW	12.02 AEX	FLBLS	7/16-9/16
	Orlando-Kissimmee-Sanford MSA, FL	H	9.01 AE	10.00 MW	11.36 AEX	FLBLS	7/16-9/16
	Tampa-St. Petersburg-Clearwater MSA, FL	H	9.54 AE	10.94 MW	12.14 AEX	FLBLS	7/16-9/16
	Georgia	Y	21640 FQ	25840 MW	30760 TQ	USBLS	5/15
	Atlanta-Sandy Springs-Roswell MSA, GA	Y	25100 FQ	28950 MW	34120 TQ	USBLS	5/15
	Augusta-Richmond County MSA, GA-SC	Y	20870 FQ	22590 MW	24310 TQ	USBLS	5/15
	Hawaii	Y	33320 FQ	37130 MW	42100 TQ	USBLS	5/15
	Urban Honolulu MSA, HI	Y	33250 FQ	37460 MW	42990 TQ	USBLS	5/15
	Idaho	Y	21640 FQ	23890 MW	28230 TQ	USBLS	5/15
	Illinois	Y	22660 FQ	27450 MW	33750 TQ	USBLS	5/15
	Chicago-Naperville-Arlington Heights PMSA, IL	Y	23420 FQ	29050 MW	35040 TQ	USBLS	5/15
	Lake County-Kenosha County PMSA, IL-WI	Y	21150 FQ	23910 MW	28420 TQ	USBLS	5/15
	Indiana	Y	22100 FQ	25110 MW	29160 TQ	USBLS	5/15
	Gary PMSA, IN	Y	22610 FQ	25960 MW	29520 TQ	USBLS	5/15
	Indianapolis-Carmel-Anderson MSA, IN	Y	22450 FQ	25950 MW	29750 TQ	USBLS	5/15
	Iowa	Y	22670 FQ	25900 MW	29760 TQ	USBLS	5/15
	Des Moines-West Des Moines MSA, IA	Y	22380 FQ	25580 MW	29840 TQ	USBLS	5/15
	Kansas	Y	21810 FQ	24400 MW	28560 TQ	USBLS	5/15
	Kentucky	Y	21100 FQ	23670 MW	28280 TQ	USBLS	5/15
	Louisville-Jefferson County MSA, KY-IN	Y	20540 FQ	22620 MW	24990 TQ	USBLS	5/15
	Louisiana	Y	17150 FQ	18990 MW	22440 TQ	USBLS	5/15
	Baton Rouge MSA, LA	Y	17400 FQ	19350 MW	22440 TQ	USBLS	5/15
	New Orleans-Metairie MSA, LA	Y	16830 FQ	18560 MW	22040 TQ	USBLS	5/15
	Maine	Y	22430 FQ	25210 MW	29180 TQ	USBLS	5/15
	Maryland	Y	21566 AE	27301 MW	30168 AEX	MDBLS	4/16
	Baltimore-Columbia-Towson MSA, MD	Y	23360 FQ	27090 MW	30470 TQ	USBLS	5/15
	Salisbury MSA, MD-DE	Y	19030 FQ	22640 MW	29920 TQ	USBLS	5/15
	Massachusetts	Y	27610 FQ	33510 MW	42000 TQ	USBLS	5/15
	Boston-Cambridge-Newton NECTA, MA	Y	29770 FQ	36680 MW	43500 TQ	USBLS	5/15
	Michigan	Y	21440 FQ	24170 MW	29570 TQ	USBLS	5/15
	Detroit-Dearborn-Livonia PMSA, MI	Y	20670 FQ	22940 MW	25490 TQ	USBLS	5/15
	Grand Rapids-Wyoming MSA, MI	Y	21880 FQ	24380 MW	30610 TQ	USBLS	5/15
	Minnesota	Y	27438 FQ	33780 MW	40041 TQ	MNBLS	1/16-3/16
	Minneapolis-St. Paul-Bloomington MSA, MN-WI	Y	29327 FQ	35426 MW	41960 TQ	MNBLS	1/16-3/16
	Mississippi	Y	17460 FQ	19500 MW	24390 TQ	USBLS	5/15
	Jackson MSA, MS	Y	17250 FQ	19110 MW	23350 TQ	USBLS	5/15
	Missouri	Y	18360 FQ	21350 MW	25760 TQ	USBLS	5/15
	Kansas City MSA, MO-KS	Y	21580 FQ	24300 MW	29270 TQ	USBLS	5/15
	St. Louis MSA, MO-IL	Y	18170 FQ	20650 MW	24610 TQ	USBLS	5/15
	Montana	Y	20860 FQ	23290 MW	26930 TQ	USBLS	5/15
	Nebraska	Y	20410 FQ	23340 MW	27595 TQ	NEBLS	7/16-9/16
	Omaha-Council Bluffs MSA, NE-IA	Y	20945 FQ	23850 MW	28235 TQ	NEBLS	7/16-9/16

AE	Average entry wage	AWR	Average wage range	H	Hourly
AEX	Average experienced wage	B	Biweekly	HI	Highest wage paid
ATC	Average total compensation	D	Daily	HR	High end range
AW	Average wage paid	FQ	First quartile wage	LO	Lowest wage paid

LR	Low end range	MTC	Median total compensation
M	Monthly	MW	Median wage paid
MCC	Median cash compensation	MWR	Median wage range
ME	Median entry wage	S	See annotated source

TCC	Total cash compensation
TQ	Third quartile wage
W	Weekly
Y	Yearly

Occupation/Type/Industry	Location	Per	Low	Mid	High	Source	Date
Orderly	Nevada	Y	26150 FQ	30520 MW	36020 TQ	USBLS	5/15
	Las Vegas-Henderson-Paradise MSA, NV	Y	27980 FQ	32700 MW	37160 TQ	USBLS	5/15
	New Hampshire	H	11.35 AE	13.80 MW	15.12 AEX	NHBLS	6/16
	New Jersey	Y	21310 FQ	25700 MW	31430 TQ	USBLS	5/15
	Camden PMSA, NJ	Y	21770 FQ	23940 MW	27680 TQ	USBLS	5/15
	Newark PMSA, NJ-PA	Y	22860 FQ	28210 MW	33320 TQ	USBLS	5/15
	Trenton MSA, NJ	Y	22010 FQ	24220 MW	29060 TQ	USBLS	5/15
	New Mexico	Y	21590 FQ	24690 MW	29140 TQ	USBLS	5/15
	Albuquerque MSA, NM	Y	21110 FQ	24230 MW	28980 TQ	USBLS	5/15
	New York	Y	25010 AE	35020 MW	40720 AEX	NYBLS	1/16-3/16
	Buffalo-Cheektowaga-Niagara Falls MSA, NY	Y	19330 FQ	26420 MW	33410 TQ	USBLS	5/15
	Nassau County-Suffolk County PMSA, NY	Y	29730 FQ	34250 MW	38680 TQ	USBLS	5/15
	New York-Jersey City-White Plains PMSA, NY-NJ	Y	26600 FQ	33770 MW	39060 TQ	USBLS	5/15
	Rochester MSA, NY	Y	21560 FQ	25010 MW	30220 TQ	USBLS	5/15
	North Carolina	Y	20060 FQ	23100 MW	27130 TQ	USBLS	5/15
	Charlotte-Concord-Gastonia MSA, NC-SC	Y	19630 FQ	21820 MW	23910 TQ	USBLS	5/15
	North Dakota	Y	23910 FQ	28860 MW	31250 TQ	USBLS	5/15
	Ohio	Y	21860 FQ	24250 MW	28470 TQ	USBLS	5/15
	Cincinnati MSA, OH-KY-IN	Y	22110 FQ	24570 MW	29350 TQ	USBLS	5/15
	Cleveland-Elyria MSA, OH	Y	21580 FQ	23710 MW	27430 TQ	USBLS	5/15
	Columbus MSA, OH	Y	22090 FQ	24970 MW	29990 TQ	USBLS	5/15
	Oklahoma	Y	21130 FQ	22970 MW	24820 TQ	USBLS	5/15
	Oklahoma City MSA, OK	Y	20810 FQ	23070 MW	26420 TQ	USBLS	5/15
	Tulsa MSA, OK	Y	21510 FQ	23140 MW	24770 TQ	USBLS	5/15
	Oregon	H	13.41 FQ	15.02 MW	17.53 TQ	ORBLS	2016
	Portland-Vancouver-Hillsboro MSA, OR-WA	Y	28840 FQ	33220 MW	37660 TQ	USBLS	5/15
	Pennsylvania	Y	23240 FQ	28330 MW	35450 TQ	USBLS	5/15
	Allentown-Bethlehem-Easton MSA, PA-NJ	Y	22180 FQ	24710 MW	30270 TQ	USBLS	5/15
	Montgomery County-Bucks County-Chester County PMSA, PA	Y	22050 FQ	24120 MW	29010 TQ	USBLS	5/15
	Philadelphia PMSA, PA	Y	26310 FQ	31300 MW	39280 TQ	USBLS	5/15
	Pittsburgh MSA, PA	Y	23110 FQ	28020 MW	34510 TQ	USBLS	5/15
	Rhode Island	Y	26850 FQ	30210 MW	38290 TQ	USBLS	5/15
	Providence-Warwick MSA, RI-MA	Y	26520 FQ	29860 MW	36760 TQ	USBLS	5/15
	South Carolina	Y	18230 FQ	21050 MW	24040 TQ	USBLS	5/15
	Charleston-North Charleston MSA, SC	Y	17460 FQ	19450 MW	23410 TQ	USBLS	5/15
	Columbia MSA, SC	Y	18500 FQ	21170 MW	23770 TQ	USBLS	5/15
	Greenville-Anderson-Mauldin MSA, SC	Y	18600 FQ	21680 MW	24800 TQ	USBLS	5/15
	South Dakota	Y	19660 FQ	22270 MW	25150 TQ	USBLS	5/15
	Tennessee	Y	21830 FQ	25970 MW	29140 TQ	USBLS	5/15
	Knoxville MSA, TN	Y	18470 FQ	21480 MW	24460 TQ	USBLS	5/15
	Memphis MSA, TN-MS-AR	Y	20020 FQ	22710 MW	25700 TQ	USBLS	5/15
	Nashville-Davidson–Murfreesboro–Franklin MSA, TN	Y	23520 FQ	26680 MW	29580 TQ	USBLS	5/15
	Texas	Y	20330 FQ	23170 MW	27220 TQ	USBLS	5/15
	Austin-Round Rock MSA, TX	Y	24670 FQ	27090 MW	29280 TQ	USBLS	5/15
	Dallas-Plano-Irving PMSA, TX	Y	21660 FQ	23880 MW	27450 TQ	USBLS	5/15
	Fort Worth-Arlington PMSA, TX	Y	21420 FQ	24520 MW	28320 TQ	USBLS	5/15
	Houston-The Woodlands-Sugar Land MSA, TX	Y	21780 FQ	24590 MW	29030 TQ	USBLS	5/15
	San Antonio-New Braunfels MSA, TX	Y	18750 FQ	21750 MW	24780 TQ	USBLS	5/15
	Utah	Y	20810 FQ	22800 MW	24920 TQ	USBLS	5/15
	Provo-Orem MSA, UT	Y	20850 FQ	22320 MW	23800 TQ	USBLS	5/15
	Virginia	Y	21190 FQ	23780 MW	27890 TQ	USBLS	5/15
	Richmond MSA, VA	Y	20990 FQ	23550 MW	27500 TQ	USBLS	5/15
	Virginia Beach-Norfolk-Newport News MSA, VA-NC	Y	21270 FQ	22990 MW	24740 TQ	USBLS	5/15
	Washington	H	12.95 FQ	14.94 MW	18.52 TQ	WABLS	3/16

AE Average entry wage	**AWR** Average wage range	**H** Hourly	**LR** Low end range	**MTC** Median total compensation	**TCC** Total cash compensation
AEX Average experienced wage	**B** Biweekly	**HI** Highest wage paid	**M** Monthly	**MW** Median wage paid	**TQ** Third quartile wage
ATC Average total compensation	**D** Daily	**HR** High end range	**MCC** Median cash compensation	**MWR** Median wage range	**W** Weekly
AW Average wage paid	**FQ** First quartile wage	**LO** Lowest wage paid	**ME** Median entry wage	**S** See annotated source	**Y** Yearly

Occupation/Type/Industry	Location	Per	Low	Mid	High	Source	Date
Orderly	Seattle-Bellevue-Everett						
	PMSA, WA	H	13.01 FQ	14.86 MW	18.80 TQ	WABLS	3/16
	West Virginia	Y	18910 FQ	22080 MW	27060 TQ	USBLS	5/15
	Huntington-Ashland MSA,						
	WV-KY-OH	Y	20860 FQ	24870 MW	29610 TQ	USBLS	5/15
	Wisconsin	Y	22490 FQ	26390 MW	30450 TQ	USBLS	5/15
	Milwaukee-Waukesha-West						
	Allis MSA, WI	Y	23930 FQ	27260 MW	30150 TQ	USBLS	5/15
	Wyoming	Y	21270 FQ	23020 MW	25760 TQ	USBLS	5/15
	Puerto Rico	Y	16800 FQ	18170 MW	19630 TQ	USBLS	5/15
	San Juan-Carolina-Caguas						
	MSA, PR	Y	16850 FQ	18270 MW	19880 TQ	USBLS	5/15
Organist							
Religious Institution, Bachelor's in Music or CAGO	United States	Y	49842 LO		65622 HI	AGO	2015
Religious Institution, Doctorate in Music or FAGO	United States	Y	63877 LO		85235 HI	AGO	2015
Religious Institution, Master's in Music or AAGO	United States	Y	56705 LO		75721 HI	AGO	2015
Organizational Development Specialist							
Department of Public Health and Human Services, State Government	Helena, MT	H			38.20 HI	MTGOV	2016
Orientation and Mobility Specialist	United States	Y		49454-61101 AWR		EXHC02	2016
Orthodontist	Alabama	Y	120270 AE	189299 AW	223803 AEX	ALBLS	6/16
	California	H	48.52 FQ	94.74 AW		CABLS	1/16-3/16
	Colorado	Y		281470 AW		USBLS	5/15
	Florida	H		114.64 AW		FLBLS	7/16-9/16
	Georgia	Y		259400 AW		USBLS	5/15
	Idaho	Y	55360 FQ	60910 MW	98480 TQ	USBLS	5/15
	Indiana	Y	95690 FQ	197790 AW		USBLS	5/15
	Kansas	Y	183600 FQ	230390 AW		USBLS	5/15
	Kentucky	Y	89530 FQ	113850 AW		USBLS	5/15
	Louisiana	Y	120590 FQ	246600 AW		USBLS	5/15
	Maryland	Y	80858 AE	187639 MW	241030 AEX	MDBLS	4/16
	Massachusetts	Y	116230 FQ	225620 AW		USBLS	5/15
	Michigan	Y	151640 FQ	227530 AW		USBLS	5/15
	Minnesota	Y		274855 AW		MNBLS	1/16-3/16
	Mississippi	Y		272010 AW		USBLS	5/15
	Missouri	Y	166850 FQ	226630 AW		USBLS	5/15
	Nevada	Y	88440 FQ	95160 MW	101880 TQ	USBLS	5/15
	New Jersey	Y	146390 FQ	233180 AW		USBLS	5/15
	New York	Y		242920 AW		NYBLS	1/16-3/16
	North Carolina	Y		258940 AW		USBLS	5/15
	Ohio	Y	128770 FQ	221970 AW		USBLS	5/15
	Oklahoma	Y		251350 MW		USBLS	5/15
	Pennsylvania	Y		245140 AW		USBLS	5/15
	Texas	Y		265460 AW		USBLS	5/15
	Virginia	Y		242110 AW		USBLS	5/15
Orthopedic Surgeon	United States	Y		435000-586377 MWR		MHLTH03	2015
Orthotist and Prosthetist	Alabama	Y	36380 AE	75522 AW	95103 AEX	ALBLS	6/16
	Birmingham-Hoover MSA, AL	Y	46807 AE	86683 AW	106611 AEX	ALBLS	6/16
	Arizona	Y	36310 FQ	44350 MW	66320 TQ	USBLS	5/15
	Phoenix-Mesa-Scottsdale						
	MSA, AZ	Y	35570 FQ	39510 MW	56440 TQ	USBLS	5/15
	Arkansas	Y	43720 FQ	50870 MW	62930 TQ	USBLS	5/15
	California	H	23.55 FQ	31.82 MW	39.60 TQ	CABLS	1/16-3/16
	Anaheim-Santa Ana-Irvine						
	PMSA, CA	H	20.82 FQ	22.96 MW	28.57 TQ	CABLS	1/16-3/16
	Los Angeles-Long Beach-						
	Glendale PMSA, CA	H	23.27 FQ	33.57 MW	39.41 TQ	CABLS	1/16-3/16
	Oakland-Hayward-Berkeley						
	PMSA, CA	H	22.03 FQ	24.66 MW	34.94 TQ	CABLS	1/16-3/16

AE	Average entry wage	**AWR** Average wage range	**H** Hourly	**LR** Low end range	**MTC** Median total compensation	**TCC** Total cash compensation
AEX	Average experienced wage	**B** Biweekly	**HI** Highest wage paid	**M** Monthly	**MW** Median wage paid	**TQ** Third quartile wage
ATC	Average total compensation	**D** Daily	**HR** High end range	**MCC** Median cash compensation	**MWR** Median wage range	**W** Weekly
AW	Average wage paid	**FQ** First quartile wage	**LO** Lowest wage paid	**ME** Median entry wage	**S** See annotated source	**Y** Yearly

Occupation/Type/Industry	Location	Per	Low	Mid	High	Source	Date
Orthotist and Prosthetist	Riverside-San Bernardino-Ontario MSA, CA	H	31.81 FQ	39.82 MW	46.57 TQ	CABLS	1/16-3/16
	Sacramento–Roseville–Arden-Arcade MSA, CA	H	23.99 FQ	30.69 MW	40.68 TQ	CABLS	1/16-3/16
	San Diego-Carlsbad MSA, CA	H	21.08 FQ	26.47 MW	31.67 TQ	CABLS	1/16-3/16
	San Francisco-Redwood City-South San Francisco PMSA, CA	H	22.60 FQ	27.30 MW	34.94 TQ	CABLS	1/16-3/16
	Colorado	Y	46740 FQ	55400 MW	71220 TQ	USBLS	5/15
	Denver-Aurora-Lakewood MSA, CO	Y	45410 FQ	52410 MW	62070 TQ	USBLS	5/15
	Connecticut	Y		67038 MW		CTBLS	1/16-3/16
	Hartford-West Hartford-East Hartford MSA, CT	Y	38490 FQ	67280 MW	74310 TQ	USBLS	5/15
	Delaware	Y	38940 FQ	51320 MW	75330 TQ	USBLS	5/15
	Wilmington PMSA, DE-MD-NJ	Y	39630 FQ	55090 MW	77920 TQ	USBLS	5/15
	Washington-Arlington-Alexandria PMSA, DC-VA-MD-WV	Y	56110 FQ	61940 MW	106870 TQ	USBLS	5/15
	Florida	H	18.42 AE	32.67 MW	42.26 AEX	FLBLS	7/16-9/16
	Fort Lauderdale-Pompano Beach-Deerfield Beach PMSA, FL	H	21.75 AE	33.51 MW	40.14 AEX	FLBLS	7/16-9/16
	Orlando-Kissimmee-Sanford MSA, FL	H	13.63 AE	23.00 MW	33.02 AEX	FLBLS	7/16-9/16
	Tampa-St. Petersburg-Clearwater MSA, FL	H	24.23 AE	37.48 MW	44.08 AEX	FLBLS	7/16-9/16
	Georgia	Y	48950 FQ	76870 MW	92490 TQ	USBLS	5/15
	Atlanta-Sandy Springs-Roswell MSA, GA	Y	48240 FQ	75470 MW	90610 TQ	USBLS	5/15
	Idaho	Y	28970 FQ	42690 MW	64430 TQ	USBLS	5/15
	Illinois	Y	48020 FQ	66970 MW	83410 TQ	USBLS	5/15
	Indiana	Y	58830 FQ	76270 MW	98650 TQ	USBLS	5/15
	Indianapolis-Carmel-Anderson MSA, IN	Y	75220 FQ	116840 MW		USBLS	5/15
	Iowa	Y	60520 FQ	72080 MW	88790 TQ	USBLS	5/15
	Kansas	Y	43470 FQ	48140 MW	57990 TQ	USBLS	5/15
	Kentucky	Y	44940 FQ	57600 MW	74790 TQ	USBLS	5/15
	Louisville-Jefferson County MSA, KY-IN	Y	41220 FQ	55120 MW	67670 TQ	USBLS	5/15
	Louisiana	Y	54260 FQ	86630 MW	110250 TQ	USBLS	5/15
	New Orleans-Metairie MSA, LA	Y	76130 FQ	104540 MW	114130 TQ	USBLS	5/15
	Maine	Y	30080 FQ	55930 MW	74680 TQ	USBLS	5/15
	Maryland	Y	57578 AE	81624 MW	93647 AEX	MDBLS	4/16
	Baltimore-Columbia-Towson MSA, MD	Y	68140 FQ	82160 MW	98820 TQ	USBLS	5/15
	Massachusetts	Y	53400 FQ	66150 MW	80190 TQ	USBLS	5/15
	Boston-Cambridge-Newton NECTA, MA	Y	56170 FQ	69140 MW	98480 TQ	USBLS	5/15
	Michigan	Y	41750 FQ	59450 MW	75070 TQ	USBLS	5/15
	Detroit-Dearborn-Livonia PMSA, MI	Y	43030 FQ	58200 MW	73450 TQ	USBLS	5/15
	Grand Rapids-Wyoming MSA, MI	Y	40790 FQ	56550 MW	67580 TQ	USBLS	5/15
	Minnesota	Y	59788 FQ	71209 MW	82942 TQ	MNBLS	1/16-3/16
	Minneapolis-St. Paul-Bloomington MSA, MN-WI	Y	57328 FQ	69425 MW	90916 TQ	MNBLS	1/16-3/16
	Jackson MSA, MS	Y	58680 FQ	97320 MW	108700 TQ	USBLS	5/15
	Missouri	Y	45860 FQ	63520 MW	76140 TQ	USBLS	5/15
	Kansas City MSA, MO-KS	Y	44250 FQ	48420 MW	57430 TQ	USBLS	5/15
	Montana	Y	29410 FQ	45440 MW	65300 TQ	USBLS	5/15
	Nebraska	Y	46455 FQ	53305 MW	58765 TQ	NEBLS	7/16-9/16
	Omaha-Council Bluffs MSA, NE-IA	Y	51720 FQ	58445 MW	83330 TQ	NEBLS	7/16-9/16
	Nevada	Y	51870 FQ	64400 MW	83820 TQ	USBLS	5/15
	Las Vegas-Henderson-Paradise MSA, NV	Y	58280 FQ	73850 MW	88220 TQ	USBLS	5/15
	New Hampshire	H	17.65 AE	30.32 MW	38.14 AEX	NHBLS	6/16
	New Jersey	Y	61100 FQ	76770 MW	95980 TQ	USBLS	5/15
	Newark PMSA, NJ-PA	Y	65240 FQ	75280 MW	94840 TQ	USBLS	5/15

AE	Average entry wage	AWR	Average wage range	H	Hourly
AEX	Average experienced wage	B	Biweekly	HI	Highest wage paid
ATC	Average total compensation	D	Daily	HR	High end range
AW	Average wage paid	FQ	First quartile wage	LO	Lowest wage paid

LR	Low end range	MTC	Median total compensation	TCC	Total cash compensation
M	Monthly	MW	Median wage paid	TQ	Third quartile wage
HR	High end range	MCC	Median cash compensation	MWR	Median wage range	W	Weekly
ME	Median entry wage	S	See annotated source	Y	Yearly

Occupation/Type/Industry	Location	Per	Low	Mid	High	Source	Date
Orthotist and Prosthetist	New Mexico	Y	37660 FQ	68310 MW	119890 TQ	USBLS	5/15
	New York	Y	45810 AE	73630 MW	92640 AEX	NYBLS	1/16-3/16
	Nassau County-Suffolk County PMSA, NY	Y	50730 FQ	73790 MW	96880 TQ	USBLS	5/15
	New York-Jersey City-White Plains PMSA, NY-NJ	Y	59310 FQ	77750 MW	96630 TQ	USBLS	5/15
	North Carolina	Y	47150 FQ	61320 MW	79740 TQ	USBLS	5/15
	Charlotte-Concord-Gastonia MSA, NC-SC	Y	46540 FQ	68490 MW	77390 TQ	USBLS	5/15
	Raleigh MSA, NC	Y	54170 FQ	66460 MW	91010 TQ	USBLS	5/15
	Ohio	Y	40600 FQ	51840 MW	67800 TQ	USBLS	5/15
	Cleveland-Elyria MSA, OH	Y	42720 FQ	66970 MW	85200 TQ	USBLS	5/15
	Columbus MSA, OH	Y	41720 FQ	49330 MW	58660 TQ	USBLS	5/15
	Oklahoma	Y	53570 FQ	59840 MW	86250 TQ	USBLS	5/15
	Oklahoma City MSA, OK	Y	51310 FQ	57180 MW	63270 TQ	USBLS	5/15
	Oregon	H	29.64 FQ	36.54 MW	46.07 TQ	ORBLS	2016
	Portland-Vancouver-Hillsboro MSA, OR-WA	Y	59750 FQ	69860 MW	86870 TQ	USBLS	5/15
	Pennsylvania	Y	43200 FQ	59450 MW	84530 TQ	USBLS	5/15
	Philadelphia PMSA, PA	Y	55260 FQ	71560 MW	93030 TQ	USBLS	5/15
	Pittsburgh MSA, PA	Y	44100 FQ	56190 MW	71420 TQ	USBLS	5/15
	South Carolina	Y	25630 FQ	56380 MW	76080 TQ	USBLS	5/15
	Columbia MSA, SC	Y	19670 FQ	23290 MW	29340 TQ	USBLS	5/15
	South Dakota	Y	50020 FQ	59400 MW	72550 TQ	USBLS	5/15
	Sioux Falls MSA, SD	Y	55450 FQ	61310 MW	75820 TQ	USBLS	5/15
	Tennessee	Y	61440 FQ	82370 MW	128660 TQ	USBLS	5/15
	Knoxville MSA, TN	Y	80750 FQ	127750 MW	142010 TQ	USBLS	5/15
	Texas	Y	42620 FQ	63160 MW	82810 TQ	USBLS	5/15
	Dallas-Plano-Irving PMSA, TX	Y	57250 FQ	66020 MW	80130 TQ	USBLS	5/15
	Fort Worth-Arlington PMSA, TX	Y	29180 FQ	80460 MW	90230 TQ	USBLS	5/15
	Houston-The Woodlands-Sugar Land MSA, TX	Y	60020 FQ	74220 MW	86220 TQ	USBLS	5/15
	Utah	Y	62160 FQ	72390 MW	82120 TQ	USBLS	5/15
	Salt Lake City MSA, UT	Y	65430 FQ	76240 MW	88090 TQ	USBLS	5/15
	Vermont	Y	55090 FQ	64030 MW	115690 TQ	USBLS	5/15
	Virginia	Y	57950 FQ	71660 MW	100730 TQ	USBLS	5/15
	Washington	H	25.18 FQ	30.87 MW	40.55 TQ	WABLS	3/16
	Seattle-Bellevue-Everett PMSA, WA	H	24.82 FQ	28.84 MW	39.63 TQ	WABLS	3/16
	West Virginia	Y	35040 FQ	38800 MW	63210 TQ	USBLS	5/15
	Wisconsin	Y	55330 FQ	68430 MW	88830 TQ	USBLS	5/15
	Puerto Rico	Y	19570 FQ	35310 MW	72200 TQ	USBLS	5/15
	San Juan-Carolina-Caguas MSA, PR	Y	27110 FQ	37040 MW	73230 TQ	USBLS	5/15
Otorhinolaryngologist	United States	Y	330000 LO			AAMC	2016
Outdoor Power Equipment and Other Small Engine Mechanic	Alabama	Y	23920 AE	33236 AW	37894 AEX	ALBLS	6/16
	Birmingham-Hoover MSA, AL	Y	25883 AE	34701 AW	39104 AEX	ALBLS	6/16
	Alaska	Y	38880 FQ	52790 MW	60080 TQ	USBLS	5/15
	Arizona	Y	26720 FQ	31710 MW	39700 TQ	USBLS	5/15
	Phoenix-Mesa-Scottsdale MSA, AZ	Y	27550 FQ	32480 MW	40240 TQ	USBLS	5/15
	Tucson MSA, AZ	Y	26100 FQ	30920 MW	39320 TQ	USBLS	5/15
	Arkansas	Y	22320 FQ	30550 MW	41110 TQ	USBLS	5/15
	Little Rock-North Little Rock-Conway MSA, AR	Y	26090 FQ	33970 MW	41890 TQ	USBLS	5/15
	California	H	13.56 FQ	17.67 MW	22.18 TQ	CABLS	1/16-3/16
	Anaheim-Santa Ana-Irvine PMSA, CA	H	10.98 FQ	15.66 MW	21.43 TQ	CABLS	1/16-3/16
	Los Angeles-Long Beach-Glendale PMSA, CA	H	18.40 FQ	21.68 MW	24.47 TQ	CABLS	1/16-3/16
	Oakland-Hayward-Berkeley PMSA, CA	H	12.76 FQ	15.82 MW	19.97 TQ	CABLS	1/16-3/16
	Riverside-San Bernardino-Ontario MSA, CA	H	13.58 FQ	16.27 MW	20.31 TQ	CABLS	1/16-3/16
	Sacramento–Roseville–Arden-Arcade MSA, CA	H	13.95 FQ	16.68 MW	20.85 TQ	CABLS	1/16-3/16
	San Diego-Carlsbad MSA, CA	H	13.24 FQ	16.78 MW	21.22 TQ	CABLS	1/16-3/16

AE	Average entry wage	AWR	Average wage range	H	Hourly	LR	Low end range	MTC	Median total compensation	TCC	Total cash compensation
AEX	Average experienced wage	B	Biweekly	HI	Highest wage paid	M	Monthly	MW	Median wage paid	TQ	Third quartile wage
ATC	Average total compensation	D	Daily	HR	High end range	MCC	Median cash compensation	MWR	Median wage range	W	Weekly
AW	Average wage paid	FQ	First quartile wage	LO	Lowest wage paid	ME	Median entry wage	S	See annotated source	Y	Yearly

Occupation/Type/Industry	Location	Per	Low	Mid	High	Source	Date
Outdoor Power Equipment and Other Small Engine Mechanic	San Francisco-Redwood City-South San Francisco PMSA, CA	H	16.10 FQ	18.44 MW	25.51 TQ	CABLS	1/16-3/16
	Colorado	Y	29310 FQ	36180 MW	44630 TQ	USBLS	5/15
	Denver-Aurora-Lakewood MSA, CO	Y	34040 FQ	39440 MW	47850 TQ	USBLS	5/15
	Connecticut	Y		44964 MW		CTBLS	1/16-3/16
	Bridgeport-Stamford-Norwalk MSA, CT	Y	40140 FQ	46780 MW	55810 TQ	USBLS	5/15
	Hartford-West Hartford-East Hartford MSA, CT	Y	31460 FQ	46310 MW	56440 TQ	USBLS	5/15
	Delaware	Y	29800 FQ	34450 MW	38290 TQ	USBLS	5/15
	Wilmington PMSA, DE-MD-NJ	Y	29290 FQ	35020 MW	39310 TQ	USBLS	5/15
	Washington-Arlington-Alexandria PMSA, DC-VA-MD-WV	Y	32830 FQ	37690 MW	49490 TQ	USBLS	5/15
	Florida	H	11.29 AE	15.64 MW	18.76 AEX	FLBLS	7/16-9/16
	Fort Lauderdale-Pompano Beach-Deerfield Beach PMSA, FL	H	12.18 AE	16.20 MW	19.03 AEX	FLBLS	7/16-9/16
	Miami-Miami Beach-Kendall PMSA, FL	H	12.23 AE	15.77 MW	17.94 AEX	FLBLS	7/16-9/16
	Orlando-Kissimmee-Sanford MSA, FL	H	11.39 AE	16.33 MW	18.63 AEX	FLBLS	7/16-9/16
	Tampa-St. Petersburg-Clearwater MSA, FL	H	11.60 AE	15.48 MW	18.16 AEX	FLBLS	7/16-9/16
	Georgia	Y	22200 FQ	27730 MW	35690 TQ	USBLS	5/15
	Atlanta-Sandy Springs-Roswell MSA, GA	Y	22170 FQ	28040 MW	40400 TQ	USBLS	5/15
	Hawaii	Y	43170 FQ	47980 MW	56710 TQ	USBLS	5/15
	Urban Honolulu MSA, HI	Y	44780 FQ	52160 MW	61710 TQ	USBLS	5/15
	Idaho	Y	24950 FQ	34360 MW	40640 TQ	USBLS	5/15
	Boise City MSA, ID	Y	32020 FQ	38380 MW	50610 TQ	USBLS	5/15
	Illinois	Y	28210 FQ	36190 MW	46200 TQ	USBLS	5/15
	Chicago-Naperville-Arlington Heights PMSA, IL	Y	36010 FQ	43580 MW	54180 TQ	USBLS	5/15
	Lake County-Kenosha County PMSA, IL-WI	Y	29780 FQ	40080 MW	47850 TQ	USBLS	5/15
	Indiana	Y	25340 FQ	32060 MW	40240 TQ	USBLS	5/15
	Gary PMSA, IN	Y	21070 FQ	23310 MW	33690 TQ	USBLS	5/15
	Indianapolis-Carmel-Anderson MSA, IN	Y	32660 FQ	40230 MW	45920 TQ	USBLS	5/15
	Iowa	Y	26790 FQ	30710 MW	36600 TQ	USBLS	5/15
	Des Moines-West Des Moines MSA, IA	Y	19360 FQ	27210 MW	31930 TQ	USBLS	5/15
	Kansas	Y	25420 FQ	29340 MW	38780 TQ	USBLS	5/15
	Kentucky	Y	23730 FQ	29410 MW	35760 TQ	USBLS	5/15
	Louisville-Jefferson County MSA, KY-IN	Y	22930 FQ	31860 MW	38480 TQ	USBLS	5/15
	Louisiana	Y	25710 FQ	34330 MW	44080 TQ	USBLS	5/15
	Baton Rouge MSA, LA	Y	35070 FQ	43320 MW	49810 TQ	USBLS	5/15
	New Orleans-Metairie MSA, LA	Y	28930 FQ	33930 MW	38890 TQ	USBLS	5/15
	Maine	Y	27770 FQ	33610 MW	38100 TQ	USBLS	5/15
	Portland-South Portland MSA, ME	Y	32190 FQ	35880 MW	40510 TQ	USBLS	5/15
	Maryland	Y	26537 AE	39739 MW	46339 AEX	MDBLS	4/16
	Baltimore-Columbia-Towson MSA, MD	Y	28940 FQ	34600 MW	40140 TQ	USBLS	5/15
	Salisbury MSA, MD-DE	Y	29600 FQ	34320 MW	37950 TQ	USBLS	5/15
	Massachusetts	Y	33440 FQ	40390 MW	52510 TQ	USBLS	5/15
	Boston-Cambridge-Newton NECTA, MA	Y	34480 FQ	41480 MW	53580 TQ	USBLS	5/15
	Worcester MSA, MA-CT	Y	30960 FQ	35300 MW	39390 TQ	USBLS	5/15
	Michigan	Y	26000 FQ	30860 MW	36820 TQ	USBLS	5/15
	Grand Rapids-Wyoming MSA, MI	Y	30030 FQ	35380 MW	41930 TQ	USBLS	5/15
	Minnesota	Y	27425 FQ	30522 MW	37823 TQ	MNBLS	1/16-3/16
	Minneapolis-St. Paul-Bloomington MSA, MN-WI	Y	29265 FQ	34645 MW	42912 TQ	MNBLS	1/16-3/16

AE	Average entry wage	AWR Average wage range	H Hourly	LR Low end range	MTC Median total compensation	TCC Total cash compensation
AEX	Average experienced wage	B Biweekly	HI Highest wage paid	M Monthly	MCC Median cash compensation	TQ Third quartile wage
ATC	Average total compensation	D Daily	HR High end range	MCC Median cash compensation	MWR Median wage range	W Weekly
AW	Average wage paid	FQ First quartile wage	LO Lowest wage paid	ME Median entry wage	S See annotated source	Y Yearly

Occupation/Type/Industry	Location	Per	Low	Mid	High	Source	Date
Outdoor Power Equipment and Other Small Engine Mechanic	Mississippi	Y	25050 FQ	28790 MW	33780 TQ	USBLS	5/15
	Jackson MSA, MS	Y	27350 FQ	31540 MW	36600 TQ	USBLS	5/15
	Missouri	Y	27390 FQ	34060 MW	40790 TQ	USBLS	5/15
	Kansas City MSA, MO-KS	Y	27240 FQ	32500 MW	39880 TQ	USBLS	5/15
	St. Louis MSA, MO-IL	Y	29220 FQ	35030 MW	46020 TQ	USBLS	5/15
	Montana	Y	25550 FQ	37230 MW	45600 TQ	USBLS	5/15
	Nebraska	Y	24090 FQ	32625 MW	38055 TQ	NEBLS	7/16-9/16
	Omaha-Council Bluffs MSA, NE-IA	Y	26725 FQ	31680 MW	37695 TQ	NEBLS	7/16-9/16
	Nevada	Y	29580 FQ	36480 MW	45270 TQ	USBLS	5/15
	Las Vegas-Henderson-Paradise MSA, NV	Y	28770 FQ	35450 MW	44450 TQ	USBLS	5/15
	New Hampshire	H	12.81 AE	17.18 MW	19.98 AEX	NHBLS	6/16
	Manchester NECTA, NH	H	15.42 AE	19.40 MW	22.38 AEX	NHBLS	6/16
	New Jersey	Y	31460 FQ	40560 MW	52240 TQ	USBLS	5/15
	Camden PMSA, NJ	Y	31450 FQ	43240 MW	48930 TQ	USBLS	5/15
	Newark PMSA, NJ-PA	Y	31340 FQ	39270 MW	50290 TQ	USBLS	5/15
	Trenton MSA, NJ	Y	27290 FQ	29550 MW	32880 TQ	USBLS	5/15
	New Mexico	Y	26440 FQ	33640 MW	49800 TQ	USBLS	5/15
	Albuquerque MSA, NM	Y	26020 FQ	32550 MW	38610 TQ	USBLS	5/15
	New York	Y	25060 AE	35890 MW	42940 AEX	NYBLS	1/16-3/16
	Buffalo-Cheektowaga-Niagara Falls MSA, NY	Y	34480 FQ	40120 MW	45920 TQ	USBLS	5/15
	Nassau County-Suffolk County PMSA, NY	Y	30510 FQ	38580 MW	51560 TQ	USBLS	5/15
	New York-Jersey City-White Plains PMSA, NY-NJ	Y	32770 FQ	42290 MW	54550 TQ	USBLS	5/15
	Rochester MSA, NY	Y	24510 FQ	42460 MW	50660 TQ	USBLS	5/15
	North Carolina	Y	25250 FQ	30230 MW	36710 TQ	USBLS	5/15
	Charlotte-Concord-Gastonia MSA, NC-SC	Y	28470 FQ	34340 MW	39420 TQ	USBLS	5/15
	Raleigh MSA, NC	Y	28380 FQ	34680 MW	48640 TQ	USBLS	5/15
	North Dakota	Y	34060 FQ	40970 MW	47930 TQ	USBLS	5/15
	Fargo MSA, ND-MN	Y	28240 FQ	33190 MW	37070 TQ	USBLS	5/15
	Ohio	Y	20510 FQ	27570 MW	33890 TQ	USBLS	5/15
	Cincinnati MSA, OH-KY-IN	Y	27290 FQ	30960 MW	36580 TQ	USBLS	5/15
	Cleveland-Elyria MSA, OH	Y	20050 FQ	25940 MW	34280 TQ	USBLS	5/15
	Columbus MSA, OH	Y	19820 FQ	27720 MW	36440 TQ	USBLS	5/15
	Oklahoma	Y	22110 FQ	28780 MW	37630 TQ	USBLS	5/15
	Oklahoma City MSA, OK	Y	20640 FQ	24290 MW	36260 TQ	USBLS	5/15
	Tulsa MSA, OK	Y	27470 FQ	31340 MW	36800 TQ	USBLS	5/15
	Oregon	H	13.99 FQ	17.18 MW	21.17 TQ	ORBLS	2016
	Portland-Vancouver-Hillsboro MSA, OR-WA	Y	27310 FQ	31790 MW	39430 TQ	USBLS	5/15
	Pennsylvania	Y	23940 FQ	30380 MW	38730 TQ	USBLS	5/15
	Allentown-Bethlehem-Easton MSA, PA-NJ	Y	18320 FQ	24970 MW	35010 TQ	USBLS	5/15
	Harrisburg-Carlisle MSA, PA	Y	26570 FQ	28460 MW	30340 TQ	USBLS	5/15
	Montgomery County-Bucks County-Chester County PMSA, PA	Y	30170 FQ	37420 MW	44260 TQ	USBLS	5/15
	Philadelphia PMSA, PA	Y	41230 FQ	44810 MW	48390 TQ	USBLS	5/15
	Pittsburgh MSA, PA	Y	23500 FQ	31560 MW	37320 TQ	USBLS	5/15
	Rhode Island	Y	28640 FQ	34870 MW	51810 TQ	USBLS	5/15
	Providence-Warwick MSA, RI-MA	Y	27730 FQ	34070 MW	41350 TQ	USBLS	5/15
	South Carolina	Y	24950 FQ	30730 MW	36940 TQ	USBLS	5/15
	Charleston-North Charleston MSA, SC	Y	24450 FQ	29040 MW	35940 TQ	USBLS	5/15
	Columbia MSA, SC	Y	25400 FQ	29810 MW	35920 TQ	USBLS	5/15
	Greenville-Anderson-Mauldin MSA, SC	Y	27970 FQ	32180 MW	36450 TQ	USBLS	5/15
	South Dakota	Y	25530 FQ	28890 MW	33580 TQ	USBLS	5/15
	Sioux Falls MSA, SD	Y	19020 FQ	22040 MW	29580 TQ	USBLS	5/15
	Tennessee	Y	24760 FQ	28920 MW	35980 TQ	USBLS	5/15
	Johnson City MSA, TN	Y	18830 FQ	23950 MW	28860 TQ	USBLS	5/15
	Knoxville MSA, TN	Y	26110 FQ	28980 MW	34500 TQ	USBLS	5/15
	Memphis MSA, TN-MS-AR	Y	23690 FQ	30340 MW	38090 TQ	USBLS	5/15

Occupation/Type/Industry	Location	Per	Low	Mid	High	Source	Date
Outdoor Power Equipment and Other Small Engine Mechanic	Nashville-Davidson–Murfreesboro–Franklin MSA, TN	Y	26610 FQ	29710 MW	38840 TQ	USBLS	5/15
	Texas	Y	25480 FQ	32500 MW	42570 TQ	USBLS	5/15
	Austin-Round Rock MSA, TX	Y	28380 FQ	37240 MW	48940 TQ	USBLS	5/15
	Dallas-Plano-Irving PMSA, TX	Y	27890 FQ	37120 MW	47490 TQ	USBLS	5/15
	Fort Worth-Arlington PMSA, TX	Y	28110 FQ	34660 MW	44730 TQ	USBLS	5/15
	Houston-The Woodlands-Sugar Land MSA, TX	Y	29240 FQ	37060 MW	48450 TQ	USBLS	5/15
	San Antonio-New Braunfels MSA, TX	Y	32960 FQ	41200 MW	46960 TQ	USBLS	5/15
	Utah	Y	22110 FQ	26980 MW	34200 TQ	USBLS	5/15
	Ogden-Clearfield MSA, UT	Y	26480 FQ	29460 MW	34210 TQ	USBLS	5/15
	Salt Lake City MSA, UT	Y	25630 FQ	31600 MW	36790 TQ	USBLS	5/15
	Vermont	Y	28150 FQ	32820 MW	37750 TQ	USBLS	5/15
	Burlington-South Burlington MSA, VT	Y	32400 FQ	36760 MW	42710 TQ	USBLS	5/15
	Virginia	Y	28750 FQ	35100 MW	43200 TQ	USBLS	5/15
	Richmond MSA, VA	Y	29820 FQ	35330 MW	41340 TQ	USBLS	5/15
	Virginia Beach-Norfolk-Newport News MSA, VA-NC	Y	29100 FQ	37590 MW	44760 TQ	USBLS	5/15
	Washington	H	13.90 FQ	17.70 MW	22.74 TQ	WABLS	3/16
	Seattle-Bellevue-Everett PMSA, WA	H	13.85 FQ	17.34 MW	23.83 TQ	WABLS	3/16
	Tacoma-Lakewood PMSA, WA	H	13.21 FQ	16.11 MW	19.07 TQ	WABLS	3/16
	West Virginia	Y	21980 FQ	25570 MW	29790 TQ	USBLS	5/15
	Wisconsin	Y	25980 FQ	33030 MW	41060 TQ	USBLS	5/15
	Madison MSA, WI	Y	22670 FQ	29560 MW	39140 TQ	USBLS	5/15
	Milwaukee-Waukesha-West Allis MSA, WI	Y	34290 FQ	39750 MW	47490 TQ	USBLS	5/15
	Wyoming	Y	31890 FQ	35970 MW	42020 TQ	USBLS	5/15
	Puerto Rico	Y	17130 FQ	18710 MW	21190 TQ	USBLS	5/15
Outside Corporate Board Director	United States	Y		263500 MTC		LSJ02	2015
Overhaul Specialist United States Postal Service	City of Industry, CA	Y			61328 HI	APP02	1/16
Packaging and Filling Machine Operator and Tender	Alabama	Y	18755 AE	27371 AW	31679 AEX	ALBLS	6/16
	Birmingham-Hoover MSA, AL	Y	19803 AE	28769 AW	33252 AEX	ALBLS	6/16
	Alaska	Y	20110 FQ	25770 MW	31710 TQ	USBLS	5/15
	Anchorage MSA, AK	Y	25880 FQ	29400 MW	38060 TQ	USBLS	5/15
	Arizona	Y	19890 FQ	24440 MW	30020 TQ	USBLS	5/15
	Phoenix-Mesa-Scottsdale MSA, AZ	Y	20230 FQ	24630 MW	30190 TQ	USBLS	5/15
	Arkansas	Y	21420 FQ	26070 MW	31400 TQ	USBLS	5/15
	Little Rock-North Little Rock-Conway MSA, AR	Y	22300 FQ	33620 MW	39390 TQ	USBLS	5/15
	California	H	9.92 FQ	12.22 MW	16.45 TQ	CABLS	1/16-3/16
	Anaheim-Santa Ana-Irvine PMSA, CA	H	9.43 FQ	10.02 MW	13.00 TQ	CABLS	1/16-3/16
	Los Angeles-Long Beach-Glendale PMSA, CA	H	9.76 FQ	11.79 MW	15.11 TQ	CABLS	1/16-3/16
	Oakland-Hayward-Berkeley PMSA, CA	H	11.41 FQ	14.11 MW	20.53 TQ	CABLS	1/16-3/16
	Riverside-San Bernardino-Ontario MSA, CA	H	9.78 FQ	11.85 MW	14.84 TQ	CABLS	1/16-3/16
	Sacramento–Roseville–Arden-Arcade MSA, CA	H	9.95 FQ	12.63 MW	15.38 TQ	CABLS	1/16-3/16
	San Diego-Carlsbad MSA, CA	H	10.17 FQ	12.93 MW	16.44 TQ	CABLS	1/16-3/16
	San Francisco-Redwood City-South San Francisco PMSA, CA	H	10.65 FQ	14.75 MW	22.94 TQ	CABLS	1/16-3/16
	Colorado	Y	21510 FQ	26420 MW	38880 TQ	USBLS	5/15
	Denver-Aurora-Lakewood MSA, CO	Y	21970 FQ	27080 MW	40590 TQ	USBLS	5/15
	Connecticut	Y		31684 MW		CTBLS	1/16-3/16
	Bridgeport-Stamford-Norwalk MSA, CT	Y	20680 FQ	28350 MW	36030 TQ	USBLS	5/15

Packaging and Filling Machine Operator and Tender

Occupation/Type/Industry	Location	Per	Low	Mid	High	Source	Date
Packaging and Filling Machine Operator and Tender	Hartford-West Hartford-East Hartford MSA, CT	Y	26110 FQ	32350 MW	39120 TQ	USBLS	5/15
	Delaware	Y	24470 FQ	29080 MW	50030 TQ	USBLS	5/15
	Wilmington PMSA, DE-MD-NJ	Y	26220 FQ	29170 MW	38840 TQ	USBLS	5/15
	Washington-Arlington-Alexandria PMSA, DC-VA-MD-WV	Y	22940 FQ	30860 MW	45740 TQ	USBLS	5/15
	Florida	H	9.19 AE	11.61 MW	15.35 AEX	FLBLS	7/16-9/16
	Fort Lauderdale-Pompano Beach-Deerfield Beach PMSA, FL	H	9.04 AE	10.82 MW	13.69 AEX	FLBLS	7/16-9/16
	Miami-Miami Beach-Kendall PMSA, FL	H	9.01 AE	9.57 MW	11.68 AEX	FLBLS	7/16-9/16
	Orlando-Kissimmee-Sanford MSA, FL	H	9.95 AE	11.84 MW	14.96 AEX	FLBLS	7/16-9/16
	Tampa-St. Petersburg-Clearwater MSA, FL	H	9.08 AE	11.45 MW	15.08 AEX	FLBLS	7/16-9/16
	Georgia	Y	20020 FQ	25330 MW	34350 TQ	USBLS	5/15
	Atlanta-Sandy Springs-Roswell MSA, GA	Y	19520 FQ	25310 MW	32920 TQ	USBLS	5/15
	Augusta-Richmond County MSA, GA-SC	Y	19670 FQ	26480 MW	36080 TQ	USBLS	5/15
	Hawaii	Y	20430 FQ	24770 MW	32760 TQ	USBLS	5/15
	Urban Honolulu MSA, HI	Y	19080 FQ	22330 MW	26960 TQ	USBLS	5/15
	Idaho	Y	24160 FQ	31960 MW	37170 TQ	USBLS	5/15
	Boise City MSA, ID	Y	20100 FQ	34040 MW	38580 TQ	USBLS	5/15
	Illinois	Y	20380 FQ	25740 MW	35440 TQ	USBLS	5/15
	Chicago-Naperville-Arlington Heights PMSA, IL	Y	19970 FQ	25670 MW	36860 TQ	USBLS	5/15
	Lake County-Kenosha County PMSA, IL-WI	Y	20870 FQ	26040 MW	34480 TQ	USBLS	5/15
	Indiana	Y	21950 FQ	28130 MW	35750 TQ	USBLS	5/15
	Gary PMSA, IN	Y	23630 FQ	29880 MW	37890 TQ	USBLS	5/15
	Indianapolis-Carmel-Anderson MSA, IN	Y	21400 FQ	27770 MW	36780 TQ	USBLS	5/15
	Iowa	Y	25290 FQ	29470 MW	36670 TQ	USBLS	5/15
	Des Moines-West Des Moines MSA, IA	Y	25750 FQ	29470 MW	35330 TQ	USBLS	5/15
	Kansas	Y	24170 FQ	29600 MW	39630 TQ	USBLS	5/15
	Wichita MSA, KS	Y	23450 FQ	27790 MW	31500 TQ	USBLS	5/15
	Kentucky	Y	22540 FQ	28410 MW	34960 TQ	USBLS	5/15
	Louisville-Jefferson County MSA, KY-IN	Y	23830 FQ	30970 MW	36790 TQ	USBLS	5/15
	Louisiana	Y	18780 FQ	24070 MW	32610 TQ	USBLS	5/15
	Baton Rouge MSA, LA	Y	22520 FQ	28710 MW	35270 TQ	USBLS	5/15
	New Orleans-Metairie MSA, LA	Y	18300 FQ	22460 MW	30290 TQ	USBLS	5/15
	Maine	Y	23230 FQ	29360 MW	40370 TQ	USBLS	5/15
	Portland-South Portland MSA, ME	Y	23820 FQ	31160 MW	39620 TQ	USBLS	5/15
	Maryland	Y	20409 AE	29967 MW	34746 AEX	MDBLS	4/16
	Baltimore-Columbia-Towson MSA, MD	Y	22920 FQ	28620 MW	40540 TQ	USBLS	5/15
	Massachusetts	Y	21450 FQ	25930 MW	32480 TQ	USBLS	5/15
	Boston-Cambridge-Newton NECTA, MA	Y	22920 FQ	28760 MW	35600 TQ	USBLS	5/15
	Worcester MSA, MA-CT	Y	21470 FQ	26110 MW	34440 TQ	USBLS	5/15
	Michigan	Y	20110 FQ	27210 MW	35890 TQ	USBLS	5/15
	Detroit-Dearborn-Livonia PMSA, MI	Y	18570 FQ	22910 MW	32420 TQ	USBLS	5/15
	Grand Rapids-Wyoming MSA, MI	Y	19340 FQ	24110 MW	31350 TQ	USBLS	5/15
	Minnesota	Y	23317 FQ	29584 MW	39303 TQ	MNBLS	1/16-3/16
	Minneapolis-St. Paul-Bloomington MSA, MN-WI	Y	21930 FQ	27549 MW	37734 TQ	MNBLS	1/16-3/16
	Mississippi	Y	20810 FQ	25350 MW	30140 TQ	USBLS	5/15
	Jackson MSA, MS	Y	17090 FQ	19050 MW	27890 TQ	USBLS	5/15
	Missouri	Y	23390 FQ	28750 MW	37570 TQ	USBLS	5/15
	Kansas City MSA, MO-KS	Y	24460 FQ	30820 MW	41390 TQ	USBLS	5/15
	St. Louis MSA, MO-IL	Y	25880 FQ	30300 MW	41600 TQ	USBLS	5/15

AE Average entry wage	**AWR** Average wage range	**H** Hourly	**LR** Low end range	**MTC** Median total compensation	**TCC** Total cash compensation
AEX Average experienced wage	**B** Biweekly	**HI** Highest wage paid	**M** Monthly	**MW** Median wage paid	**TQ** Third quartile wage
ATC Average total compensation	**D** Daily	**HR** High end range	**MCC** Median cash compensation	**MWR** Median wage range	**W** Weekly
AW Average wage paid	**FQ** First quartile wage	**LO** Lowest wage paid	**ME** Median entry wage	**S** See annotated source	**Y** Yearly

Occupation/Type/Industry	Location	Per	Low	Mid	High	Source	Date
Packaging and Filling Machine Operator and Tender							
	Montana	Y	21310 FQ	24910 MW	31590 TQ	USBLS	5/15
	Billings MSA, MT	Y	22700 FQ	28040 MW	35750 TQ	USBLS	5/15
	Nebraska	Y	24030 FQ	28535 MW	35280 TQ	NEBLS	7/16-9/16
	Omaha-Council Bluffs MSA, NE-IA	Y	22955 FQ	27600 MW	35920 TQ	NEBLS	7/16-9/16
	Nevada	Y	23750 FQ	28560 MW	38180 TQ	USBLS	5/15
	Las Vegas-Henderson-Paradise MSA, NV	Y	21970 FQ	25180 MW	36640 TQ	USBLS	5/15
	New Hampshire	H	11.90 AE	14.54 MW	18.83 AEX	NHBLS	6/16
	Manchester NECTA, NH	H	10.59 AE	13.58 MW	16.02 AEX	NHBLS	6/16
	Nashua NECTA, NH-MA	Y	27800 FQ	36840 MW	56760 TQ	USBLS	5/15
	New Jersey	Y	19950 FQ	25470 MW	32600 TQ	USBLS	5/15
	Camden PMSA, NJ	Y	23190 FQ	28230 MW	36550 TQ	USBLS	5/15
	Newark PMSA, NJ-PA	Y	19570 FQ	25690 MW	32490 TQ	USBLS	5/15
	Trenton MSA, NJ	Y	23620 FQ	28200 MW	32330 TQ	USBLS	5/15
	New Mexico	Y	19370 FQ	23390 MW	29470 TQ	USBLS	5/15
	Albuquerque MSA, NM	Y	19350 FQ	24800 MW	31710 TQ	USBLS	5/15
	New York	Y	20580 AE	27550 MW	36490 AEX	NYBLS	1/16-3/16
	Buffalo-Cheektowaga-Niagara Falls MSA, NY	Y	22890 FQ	29690 MW	42890 TQ	USBLS	5/15
	Nassau County-Suffolk County PMSA, NY	Y	19790 FQ	24330 MW	32580 TQ	USBLS	5/15
	New York-Jersey City-White Plains PMSA, NY-NJ	Y	19610 FQ	23840 MW	31140 TQ	USBLS	5/15
	Rochester MSA, NY	Y	22720 FQ	29750 MW	37010 TQ	USBLS	5/15
	North Carolina	Y	21450 FQ	27310 MW	35710 TQ	USBLS	5/15
	Charlotte-Concord-Gastonia MSA, NC-SC	Y	21710 FQ	26500 MW	36360 TQ	USBLS	5/15
	Raleigh MSA, NC	Y	28150 FQ	34440 MW	38500 TQ	USBLS	5/15
	North Dakota	Y	22870 FQ	27550 MW	33730 TQ	USBLS	5/15
	Fargo MSA, ND-MN	Y	23500 FQ	28780 MW	36420 TQ	USBLS	5/15
	Ohio	Y	23250 FQ	29900 MW	38660 TQ	USBLS	5/15
	Cincinnati MSA, OH-KY-IN	Y	23190 FQ	30910 MW	44130 TQ	USBLS	5/15
	Cleveland-Elyria MSA, OH	Y	24060 FQ	28960 MW	35370 TQ	USBLS	5/15
	Columbus MSA, OH	Y	24140 FQ	32870 MW	44620 TQ	USBLS	5/15
	Oklahoma	Y	20810 FQ	24100 MW	29840 TQ	USBLS	5/15
	Oklahoma City MSA, OK	Y	21240 FQ	24320 MW	31070 TQ	USBLS	5/15
	Tulsa MSA, OK	Y	20610 FQ	23990 MW	29570 TQ	USBLS	5/15
	Oregon	H	11.06 FQ	13.43 MW	17.18 TQ	ORBLS	2016
	Portland-Vancouver-Hillsboro MSA, OR-WA	Y	24060 FQ	30460 MW	38910 TQ	USBLS	5/15
	Pennsylvania	Y	23900 FQ	31730 MW	41270 TQ	USBLS	5/15
	Allentown-Bethlehem-Easton MSA, PA-NJ	Y	25280 FQ	32380 MW	40810 TQ	USBLS	5/15
	Harrisburg-Carlisle MSA, PA	Y	22180 FQ	24890 MW	41600 TQ	USBLS	5/15
	Montgomery County-Bucks County-Chester County PMSA, PA	Y	24450 FQ	31350 MW	40450 TQ	USBLS	5/15
	Philadelphia PMSA, PA	Y	25360 FQ	33530 MW	45520 TQ	USBLS	5/15
	Pittsburgh MSA, PA	Y	25310 FQ	36330 MW	45930 TQ	USBLS	5/15
	Rhode Island	Y	19960 FQ	26260 MW	35050 TQ	USBLS	5/15
	Providence-Warwick MSA, RI-MA	Y	20600 FQ	26250 MW	33900 TQ	USBLS	5/15
	South Carolina	Y	21930 FQ	28050 MW	37430 TQ	USBLS	5/15
	Charleston-North Charleston MSA, SC	Y	27230 FQ	33550 MW	38980 TQ	USBLS	5/15
	Columbia MSA, SC	Y	21290 FQ	23890 MW	28480 TQ	USBLS	5/15
	Florence MSA, SC	Y	21160 FQ	26390 MW	30180 TQ	USBLS	5/15
	Greenville-Anderson-Mauldin MSA, SC	Y	22260 FQ	25730 MW	32700 TQ	USBLS	5/15
	South Dakota	Y	24970 FQ	28630 MW	33030 TQ	USBLS	5/15
	Sioux Falls MSA, SD	Y	26650 FQ	28710 MW	30770 TQ	USBLS	5/15
	Tennessee	Y	23590 FQ	28890 MW	36030 TQ	USBLS	5/15
	Knoxville MSA, TN	Y	25080 FQ	27410 MW	29740 TQ	USBLS	5/15
	Memphis MSA, TN-MS-AR	Y	23220 FQ	29060 MW	36610 TQ	USBLS	5/15
	Nashville-Davidson–Murfreesboro–Franklin MSA, TN	Y	25470 FQ	29750 MW	36290 TQ	USBLS	5/15
	Texas	Y	19180 FQ	23930 MW	30720 TQ	USBLS	5/15
	Austin-Round Rock MSA, TX	Y	20800 FQ	24080 MW	29300 TQ	USBLS	5/15
	Dallas-Plano-Irving PMSA, TX	Y	20510 FQ	25570 MW	30870 TQ	USBLS	5/15

AE	Average entry wage	AWR	Average wage range	H	Hourly
AEX	Average experienced wage	B	Biweekly	HI	Highest wage paid
ATC	Average total compensation	D	Daily	HR	High end range
AW	Average wage paid	FQ	First quartile wage	LO	Lowest wage paid

LR	Low end range	MTC	Median total compensation	TCC	Total cash compensation
M	Monthly	MW	Median wage paid	TQ	Third quartile wage
MCC	Median cash compensation	MWR	Median wage range	W	Weekly
ME	Median entry wage	S	See annotated source	Y	Yearly

Occupation/Type/Industry	Location	Per	Low	Mid	High	Source	Date
Packaging and Filling Machine Operator and Tender	Fort Worth-Arlington PMSA, TX	Y	19130 FQ	24980 MW	34370 TQ	USBLS	5/15
	Houston-The Woodlands-Sugar Land MSA, TX	Y	19170 FQ	24050 MW	31930 TQ	USBLS	5/15
	San Antonio-New Braunfels MSA, TX	Y	18390 FQ	21830 MW	28090 TQ	USBLS	5/15
	Utah	Y	21890 FQ	26750 MW	34010 TQ	USBLS	5/15
	Ogden-Clearfield MSA, UT	Y	21160 FQ	26600 MW	34360 TQ	USBLS	5/15
	Provo-Orem MSA, UT	Y	21850 FQ	25960 MW	30740 TQ	USBLS	5/15
	Salt Lake City MSA, UT	Y	21760 FQ	25650 MW	33280 TQ	USBLS	5/15
	Vermont	Y	27010 FQ	30870 MW	36380 TQ	USBLS	5/15
	Burlington-South Burlington MSA, VT	Y	26900 FQ	30230 MW	35300 TQ	USBLS	5/15
	Virginia	Y	20090 FQ	26250 MW	37940 TQ	USBLS	5/15
	Richmond MSA, VA	Y	19070 FQ	23360 MW	30520 TQ	USBLS	5/15
	Virginia Beach-Norfolk-Newport News MSA, VA-NC	Y	26210 FQ	34890 MW	62810 TQ	USBLS	5/15
	Washington	H	11.39 FQ	13.79 MW	17.55 TQ	WABLS	3/16
	Seattle-Bellevue-Everett PMSA, WA	H	12.12 FQ	14.21 MW	17.67 TQ	WABLS	3/16
	Tacoma-Lakewood PMSA, WA	H	13.57 FQ	16.62 MW	18.31 TQ	WABLS	3/16
	West Virginia	Y	21910 FQ	27320 MW	36760 TQ	USBLS	5/15
	Huntington-Ashland MSA, WV-KY-OH	Y	18490 FQ	21410 MW	27060 TQ	USBLS	5/15
	Wisconsin	Y	24550 FQ	30390 MW	37920 TQ	USBLS	5/15
	Madison MSA, WI	Y	19410 FQ	23170 MW	29610 TQ	USBLS	5/15
	Milwaukee-Waukesha-West Allis MSA, WI	Y	27140 FQ	31650 MW	38490 TQ	USBLS	5/15
	Wyoming	Y	33290 FQ	42550 MW	47760 TQ	USBLS	5/15
	Puerto Rico	Y	17680 FQ	19810 MW	25780 TQ	USBLS	5/15
	San Juan-Carolina-Caguas MSA, PR	Y	17810 FQ	20170 MW	30130 TQ	USBLS	5/15
	Guam	Y	18280 FQ	19400 MW	23150 TQ	USBLS	5/15
Packer and Packager							
Hand	Alabama	Y	17711 AE	22226 AW	24478 AEX	ALBLS	6/16
Hand	Birmingham-Hoover MSA, AL	Y	17793 AE	21434 AW	23254 AEX	ALBLS	6/16
Hand	Alaska	Y	20040 FQ	26660 MW	32410 TQ	USBLS	5/15
Hand	Anchorage MSA, AK	Y	19610 FQ	26320 MW	35450 TQ	USBLS	5/15
Hand	Arizona	Y	18150 FQ	19470 MW	26180 TQ	USBLS	5/15
Hand	Phoenix-Mesa-Scottsdale MSA, AZ	Y	18290 FQ	19860 MW	27060 TQ	USBLS	5/15
Hand	Tucson MSA, AZ	Y	17850 FQ	18840 MW	21690 TQ	USBLS	5/15
Hand	Arkansas	Y	18310 FQ	21310 MW	25110 TQ	USBLS	5/15
Hand	Little Rock-North Little Rock-Conway MSA, AR	Y	17430 FQ	19170 MW	22910 TQ	USBLS	5/15
Hand	California	H	9.47 FQ	9.88 MW	12.36 TQ	CABLS	1/16-3/16
Hand	Anaheim-Santa Ana-Irvine PMSA, CA	H	9.62 FQ	10.57 MW	13.06 TQ	CABLS	1/16-3/16
Hand	Los Angeles-Long Beach-Glendale PMSA, CA	H	9.44 FQ	9.63 MW	11.42 TQ	CABLS	1/16-3/16
Hand	Oakland-Hayward-Berkeley PMSA, CA	H	9.57 FQ	10.67 MW	13.22 TQ	CABLS	1/16-3/16
Hand	Riverside-San Bernardino-Ontario MSA, CA	H	9.53 FQ	9.94 MW	13.94 TQ	CABLS	1/16-3/16
Hand	Sacramento–Roseville–Arden-Arcade MSA, CA	H	9.62 FQ	11.46 MW	17.03 TQ	CABLS	1/16-3/16
Hand	San Diego-Carlsbad MSA, CA	H	9.57 FQ	10.44 MW	13.85 TQ	CABLS	1/16-3/16
Hand	San Francisco-Redwood City-South San Francisco PMSA, CA	H	10.25 FQ	12.14 MW	14.89 TQ	CABLS	1/16-3/16
Hand	Colorado	Y	18350 FQ	19660 MW	25810 TQ	USBLS	5/15
Hand	Denver-Aurora-Lakewood MSA, CO	Y	18310 FQ	19560 MW	26360 TQ	USBLS	5/15
Hand	Connecticut	Y		26355 MW		CTBLS	1/16-3/16
Hand	Bridgeport-Stamford-Norwalk MSA, CT	Y	19700 FQ	22030 MW	25480 TQ	USBLS	5/15
Hand	Hartford-West Hartford-East Hartford MSA, CT	Y	22360 FQ	27550 MW	35810 TQ	USBLS	5/15
Hand	Delaware	Y	24710 FQ	26960 MW	29180 TQ	USBLS	5/15

Occupation/Type/Industry	Location	Per	Low	Mid	High	Source	Date
Packer and Packager							
Hand	Wilmington PMSA, DE-MD-NJ	Y	25030 FQ	27130 MW	29230 TQ	USBLS	5/15
Hand	District of Columbia	Y	20690 FQ	23280 MW	28050 TQ	USBLS	5/15
Hand	Washington-Arlington-Alexandria PMSA, DC-VA-MD-WV	Y	17740 FQ	19550 MW	26010 TQ	USBLS	5/15
Hand	Florida	H	9.02 AE	9.58 MW	11.34 AEX	FLBLS	7/16-9/16
Hand	Fort Lauderdale-Pompano Beach-Deerfield Beach PMSA, FL	H	9.00 AE	9.57 MW	11.32 AEX	FLBLS	7/16-9/16
Hand	Miami-Miami Beach-Kendall PMSA, FL	H	9.00 AE	9.54 MW	10.75 AEX	FLBLS	7/16-9/16
Hand	Orlando-Kissimmee-Sanford MSA, FL	H	9.07 AE	9.74 MW	11.69 AEX	FLBLS	7/16-9/16
Hand	Tampa-St. Petersburg-Clearwater MSA, FL	H	9.05 AE	9.42 MW	10.06 AEX	FLBLS	7/16-9/16
Hand	Georgia	Y	17630 FQ	19670 MW	24660 TQ	USBLS	5/15
Hand	Atlanta-Sandy Springs-Roswell MSA, GA	Y	17650 FQ	19720 MW	25220 TQ	USBLS	5/15
Hand	Augusta-Richmond County MSA, GA-SC	Y	17310 FQ	19070 MW	23580 TQ	USBLS	5/15
Hand	Hawaii	Y	18630 FQ	22500 MW	28660 TQ	USBLS	5/15
Hand	Urban Honolulu MSA, HI	Y	18370 FQ	21570 MW	27260 TQ	USBLS	5/15
Hand	Idaho	Y	17840 FQ	20230 MW	28260 TQ	USBLS	5/15
Hand	Boise City MSA, ID	Y	19750 FQ	28260 MW	36540 TQ	USBLS	5/15
Hand	Illinois	Y	19270 FQ	22760 MW	29420 TQ	USBLS	5/15
Hand	Chicago-Naperville-Arlington Heights PMSA, IL	Y	19160 FQ	22360 MW	29070 TQ	USBLS	5/15
Hand	Lake County-Kenosha County PMSA, IL-WI	Y	19460 FQ	23370 MW	28930 TQ	USBLS	5/15
Hand	Indiana	Y	18320 FQ	21870 MW	27330 TQ	USBLS	5/15
Hand	Gary PMSA, IN	Y	17200 FQ	18920 MW	25090 TQ	USBLS	5/15
Hand	Indianapolis-Carmel-Anderson MSA, IN	Y	18310 FQ	21700 MW	26540 TQ	USBLS	5/15
Hand	Iowa	Y	17790 FQ	19940 MW	27110 TQ	USBLS	5/15
Hand	Des Moines-West Des Moines MSA, IA	Y	17510 FQ	19310 MW	23970 TQ	USBLS	5/15
Hand	Kansas	Y	17570 FQ	19560 MW	26050 TQ	USBLS	5/15
Hand	Wichita MSA, KS	Y	17340 FQ	19110 MW	23020 TQ	USBLS	5/15
Hand	Kentucky	Y	18040 FQ	20670 MW	24870 TQ	USBLS	5/15
Hand	Louisville-Jefferson County MSA, KY-IN	Y	18730 FQ	22040 MW	26120 TQ	USBLS	5/15
Hand	Louisiana	Y	17540 FQ	19670 MW	25730 TQ	USBLS	5/15
Hand	Baton Rouge MSA, LA	Y	17680 FQ	20510 MW	26620 TQ	USBLS	5/15
Hand	New Orleans-Metairie MSA, LA	Y	18030 FQ	21830 MW	27730 TQ	USBLS	5/15
Hand	Maine	Y	18660 FQ	22000 MW	26620 TQ	USBLS	5/15
Hand	Portland-South Portland MSA, ME	Y	18720 FQ	22210 MW	26920 TQ	USBLS	5/15
Hand	Maryland	Y	18133 AE	23269 MW	25837 AEX	MDBLS	4/16
Hand	Baltimore-Columbia-Towson MSA, MD	Y	18360 FQ	20530 MW	26050 TQ	USBLS	5/15
Hand	Salisbury MSA, MD-DE	Y	18940 FQ	22330 MW	26320 TQ	USBLS	5/15
Hand	Massachusetts	Y	19720 FQ	22580 MW	27470 TQ	USBLS	5/15
Hand	Boston-Cambridge-Newton NECTA, MA	Y	19780 FQ	22960 MW	28870 TQ	USBLS	5/15
Hand	Worcester MSA, MA-CT	Y	19950 FQ	24670 MW	29140 TQ	USBLS	5/15
Hand	Michigan	Y	18530 FQ	20180 MW	26610 TQ	USBLS	5/15
Hand	Detroit-Dearborn-Livonia PMSA, MI	Y	18320 FQ	19500 MW	26140 TQ	USBLS	5/15
Hand	Grand Rapids-Wyoming MSA, MI	Y	18630 FQ	20270 MW	24130 TQ	USBLS	5/15
Hand	Minnesota	Y	19084 FQ	22915 MW	28883 TQ	MNBLS	1/16-3/16
Hand	Minneapolis-St. Paul-Bloomington MSA, MN-WI	Y	19276 FQ	23611 MW	29367 TQ	MNBLS	1/16-3/16
Hand	Mississippi	Y	18020 FQ	20630 MW	24520 TQ	USBLS	5/15
Hand	Jackson MSA, MS	Y	18060 FQ	20990 MW	27670 TQ	USBLS	5/15
Hand	Missouri	Y	18110 FQ	20990 MW	27210 TQ	USBLS	5/15
Hand	Kansas City MSA, MO-KS	Y	17920 FQ	20240 MW	26820 TQ	USBLS	5/15
Hand	St. Louis MSA, MO-IL	Y	18210 FQ	20590 MW	27000 TQ	USBLS	5/15
Hand	Montana	Y	18290 FQ	19830 MW	23980 TQ	USBLS	5/15

AE	Average entry wage	AWR	Average wage range	H	Hourly
AEX	Average experienced wage	B	Biweekly	HI	Highest wage paid
ATC	Average total compensation	D	Daily	HR	High end range
AW	Average wage paid	FQ	First quartile wage	LO	Lowest wage paid

LR	Low end range	MTC	Median total compensation	TCC	Total cash compensation
M	Monthly	MW	Median wage paid	TQ	Third quartile wage
MCC	Median cash compensation	MWR	Median wage range	W	Weekly
ME	Median entry wage	S	See annotated source	Y	Yearly

Occupation/Type/Industry	Location	Per	Low	Mid	High	Source	Date
Packer and Packager							
Hand	Billings MSA, MT	Y	19880 FQ	24320 MW	29270 TQ	USBLS	5/15
Hand	Nebraska	Y	18710 FQ	21965 MW	27620 TQ	NEBLS	7/16-9/16
Hand	Omaha-Council Bluffs MSA, NE-IA	Y	18195 FQ	19925 MW	23880 TQ	NEBLS	7/16-9/16
Hand	Nevada	Y	17560 FQ	19750 MW	26800 TQ	USBLS	5/15
Hand	Las Vegas-Henderson-Paradise MSA, NV	Y	17610 FQ	19840 MW	28830 TQ	USBLS	5/15
Hand	New Hampshire	H	8.87 AE	11.21 MW	13.43 AEX	NHBLS	6/16
Hand	Manchester NECTA, NH	H	9.08 AE	10.88 MW	12.15 AEX	NHBLS	6/16
Hand	Nashua NECTA, NH-MA	Y	19290 FQ	23100 MW	29140 TQ	USBLS	5/15
Hand	New Jersey	Y	18530 FQ	19630 MW	23830 TQ	USBLS	5/15
Hand	Camden PMSA, NJ	Y	18680 FQ	20230 MW	25900 TQ	USBLS	5/15
Hand	Newark PMSA, NJ-PA	Y	18340 FQ	19190 MW	22620 TQ	USBLS	5/15
Hand	Trenton MSA, NJ	Y	19180 FQ	21440 MW	24410 TQ	USBLS	5/15
Hand	New Mexico	Y	17580 FQ	19100 MW	22380 TQ	USBLS	5/15
Hand	Albuquerque MSA, NM	Y	17620 FQ	19190 MW	23030 TQ	USBLS	5/15
Hand	New York	Y	19400 AE	22840 MW	29080 AEX	NYBLS	1/16-3/16
Hand	Buffalo-Cheektowaga-Niagara Falls MSA, NY	Y	19140 FQ	20870 MW	26890 TQ	USBLS	5/15
Hand	Nassau County-Suffolk County PMSA, NY	Y	19550 FQ	22960 MW	28900 TQ	USBLS	5/15
Hand	New York-Jersey City-White Plains PMSA, NY-NJ	Y	18900 FQ	20390 MW	25190 TQ	USBLS	5/15
Hand	Rochester MSA, NY	Y	20080 FQ	23390 MW	28510 TQ	USBLS	5/15
Hand	North Carolina	Y	17900 FQ	21000 MW	26540 TQ	USBLS	5/15
Hand	Charlotte-Concord-Gastonia MSA, NC-SC	Y	18630 FQ	22870 MW	28550 TQ	USBLS	5/15
Hand	Raleigh MSA, NC	Y	17820 FQ	20980 MW	26860 TQ	USBLS	5/15
Hand	North Dakota	Y	18870 FQ	23010 MW	28180 TQ	USBLS	5/15
Hand	Fargo MSA, ND-MN	Y	18450 FQ	22450 MW	27970 TQ	USBLS	5/15
Hand	Ohio	Y	18890 FQ	21950 MW	27450 TQ	USBLS	5/15
Hand	Cincinnati MSA, OH-KY-IN	Y	18540 FQ	20550 MW	24990 TQ	USBLS	5/15
Hand	Cleveland-Elyria MSA, OH	Y	19090 FQ	22470 MW	27520 TQ	USBLS	5/15
Hand	Columbus MSA, OH	Y	20090 FQ	23050 MW	27520 TQ	USBLS	5/15
Hand	Oklahoma	Y	17860 FQ	20780 MW	26410 TQ	USBLS	5/15
Hand	Oklahoma City MSA, OK	Y	18350 FQ	22090 MW	29150 TQ	USBLS	5/15
Hand	Tulsa MSA, OK	Y	17660 FQ	19650 MW	24010 TQ	USBLS	5/15
Hand	Oregon	H	9.75 FQ	11.00 MW	13.67 TQ	ORBLS	2016
Hand	Portland-Vancouver-Hillsboro MSA, OR-WA	Y	20150 FQ	23180 MW	29010 TQ	USBLS	5/15
Hand	Pennsylvania	Y	18630 FQ	23150 MW	30540 TQ	USBLS	5/15
Hand	Allentown-Bethlehem-Easton MSA, PA-NJ	Y	20050 FQ	24670 MW	34780 TQ	USBLS	5/15
Hand	Harrisburg-Carlisle MSA, PA	Y	18020 FQ	20150 MW	27610 TQ	USBLS	5/15
Hand	Montgomery County-Bucks County-Chester County PMSA, PA	Y	18260 FQ	22130 MW	29340 TQ	USBLS	5/15
Hand	Philadelphia PMSA, PA	Y	17510 FQ	19510 MW	25100 TQ	USBLS	5/15
Hand	Pittsburgh MSA, PA	Y	18310 FQ	21820 MW	27260 TQ	USBLS	5/15
Hand	Rhode Island	Y	19270 FQ	20050 MW	23920 TQ	USBLS	5/15
Hand	Providence-Warwick MSA, RI-MA	Y	19330 FQ	20430 MW	24400 TQ	USBLS	5/15
Hand	South Carolina	Y	18170 FQ	21040 MW	25610 TQ	USBLS	5/15
Hand	Charleston-North Charleston MSA, SC	Y	17540 FQ	19680 MW	24970 TQ	USBLS	5/15
Hand	Columbia MSA, SC	Y	17870 FQ	20150 MW	23800 TQ	USBLS	5/15
Hand	Greenville-Anderson-Mauldin MSA, SC	Y	18330 FQ	21890 MW	30570 TQ	USBLS	5/15
Hand	South Dakota	Y	19130 FQ	21880 MW	26830 TQ	USBLS	5/15
Hand	Sioux Falls MSA, SD	Y	19610 FQ	22850 MW	27310 TQ	USBLS	5/15
Hand	Tennessee	Y	17640 FQ	19750 MW	24780 TQ	USBLS	5/15
Hand	Knoxville MSA, TN	Y	17060 FQ	18600 MW	21080 TQ	USBLS	5/15
Hand	Memphis MSA, TN-MS-AR	Y	17520 FQ	19410 MW	24500 TQ	USBLS	5/15
Hand	Nashville-Davidson–Murfreesboro–Franklin MSA, TN	Y	18480 FQ	21870 MW	27180 TQ	USBLS	5/15
Hand	Texas	Y	17550 FQ	19560 MW	25760 TQ	USBLS	5/15
Hand	Austin-Round Rock MSA, TX	Y	19010 FQ	22730 MW	27420 TQ	USBLS	5/15
Hand	Dallas-Plano-Irving PMSA, TX	Y	17550 FQ	19600 MW	26020 TQ	USBLS	5/15
Hand	Fort Worth-Arlington PMSA, TX	Y	17690 FQ	19800 MW	28040 TQ	USBLS	5/15

AE	Average entry wage	AWR	Average wage range	H	Hourly	LR Low end range	MTC Median total compensation	TCC Total cash compensation
AEX	Average experienced wage	B	Biweekly	HI	Highest wage paid	M Monthly	MW Median wage paid	TQ Third quartile wage
ATC	Average total compensation	D	Daily	HR	High end range	MCC Median cash compensation	MWR Median wage range	W Weekly
AW	Average wage paid	FQ	First quartile wage	LO	Lowest wage paid	ME Median entry wage	S See annotated source	Y Yearly

Occupation/Type/Industry	Location	Per	Low	Mid	High	Source	Date
Packer and Packager							
Hand	Houston-The Woodlands-Sugar Land MSA, TX	Y	17720 FQ	19910 MW	28340 TQ	USBLS	5/15
Hand	San Antonio-New Braunfels MSA, TX	Y	17860 FQ	21240 MW	28570 TQ	USBLS	5/15
Hand	Utah	Y	17980 FQ	20990 MW	25460 TQ	USBLS	5/15
Hand	Ogden-Clearfield MSA, UT	Y	17730 FQ	19940 MW	24190 TQ	USBLS	5/15
Hand	Provo-Orem MSA, UT	Y	17460 FQ	19650 MW	24660 TQ	USBLS	5/15
Hand	Salt Lake City MSA, UT	Y	18090 FQ	21330 MW	26020 TQ	USBLS	5/15
Hand	Vermont	Y	20340 FQ	23390 MW	28360 TQ	USBLS	5/15
Hand	Burlington-South Burlington MSA, VT	Y	19880 FQ	22270 MW	25600 TQ	USBLS	5/15
Hand	Virginia	Y	18290 FQ	22190 MW	28560 TQ	USBLS	5/15
Hand	Virginia Beach-Norfolk-Newport News MSA, VA-NC	Y	18490 FQ	21740 MW	24870 TQ	USBLS	5/15
Hand	Washington	H	10.41 FQ	11.65 MW	14.27 TQ	WABLS	3/16
Hand	Seattle-Bellevue-Everett PMSA, WA	H	10.64 FQ	12.12 MW	14.90 TQ	WABLS	3/16
Hand	Tacoma-Lakewood PMSA, WA	H	10.56 FQ	11.77 MW	14.37 TQ	WABLS	3/16
Hand	West Virginia	Y	18340 FQ	20930 MW	33370 TQ	USBLS	5/15
Hand	Huntington-Ashland MSA, WV-KY-OH	Y	21960 FQ	34360 MW	37230 TQ	USBLS	5/15
Hand	Wisconsin	Y	19380 FQ	24100 MW	30600 TQ	USBLS	5/15
Hand	Madison MSA, WI	Y	24040 FQ	33800 MW	43660 TQ	USBLS	5/15
Hand	Milwaukee-Waukesha-West Allis MSA, WI	Y	19660 FQ	23760 MW	29450 TQ	USBLS	5/15
Hand	Wyoming	Y	19150 FQ	27880 MW	36880 TQ	USBLS	5/15
Hand	Cheyenne MSA, WY	Y	32310 FQ	36110 MW	39920 TQ	USBLS	5/15
Hand	Puerto Rico	Y	16720 FQ	17840 MW	18960 TQ	USBLS	5/15
Hand	San Juan-Carolina-Caguas MSA, PR	Y	16700 FQ	17840 MW	18970 TQ	USBLS	5/15
Hand	Virgin Islands	Y	16810 FQ	17940 MW	19080 TQ	USBLS	5/15
Hand	Guam	Y	17890 FQ	18620 MW	19370 TQ	USBLS	5/15
Painter							
Construction and Maintenance	Alabama	Y	24812 AE	33895 AW	38432 AEX	ALBLS	6/16
Construction and Maintenance	Birmingham-Hoover MSA, AL	Y	30717 AE	36117 AW	38812 AEX	ALBLS	6/16
Construction and Maintenance	Alaska	Y	39670 FQ	54650 MW	64790 TQ	USBLS	5/15
Construction and Maintenance	Anchorage MSA, AK	Y	37060 FQ	53110 MW	62030 TQ	USBLS	5/15
Construction and Maintenance	Arizona	Y	29890 FQ	34720 MW	38790 TQ	USBLS	5/15
Construction and Maintenance	Phoenix-Mesa-Scottsdale MSA, AZ	Y	31480 FQ	35200 MW	38910 TQ	USBLS	5/15
Construction and Maintenance	Tucson MSA, AZ	Y	26510 FQ	32500 MW	38150 TQ	USBLS	5/15
Construction and Maintenance	Arkansas	Y	26930 FQ	32260 MW	38840 TQ	USBLS	5/15
Construction and Maintenance	Little Rock-North Little Rock-Conway MSA, AR	Y	27190 FQ	33310 MW	39470 TQ	USBLS	5/15
Construction and Maintenance	California	H	16.56 FQ	20.74 MW	28.32 TQ	CABLS	1/16-3/16
Construction and Maintenance	Anaheim-Santa Ana-Irvine PMSA, CA	H	16.18 FQ	18.92 MW	23.68 TQ	CABLS	1/16-3/16
Construction and Maintenance	Los Angeles-Long Beach-Glendale PMSA, CA	H	15.62 FQ	22.49 MW	29.06 TQ	CABLS	1/16-3/16
Construction and Maintenance	Oakland-Hayward-Berkeley PMSA, CA	H	17.72 FQ	23.89 MW	33.44 TQ	CABLS	1/16-3/16
Construction and Maintenance	Riverside-San Bernardino-Ontario MSA, CA	H	16.41 FQ	19.20 MW	25.23 TQ	CABLS	1/16-3/16
Construction and Maintenance	Sacramento–Roseville–Arden-Arcade MSA, CA	H	16.68 FQ	18.50 MW	26.71 TQ	CABLS	1/16-3/16
Construction and Maintenance	San Diego-Carlsbad MSA, CA	H	16.06 FQ	18.38 MW	23.83 TQ	CABLS	1/16-3/16
Construction and Maintenance	San Francisco-Redwood City-South San Francisco PMSA, CA	H	21.16 FQ	29.16 MW	35.83 TQ	CABLS	1/16-3/16
Construction and Maintenance	Colorado	Y	29930 FQ	36320 MW	43600 TQ	USBLS	5/15
Construction and Maintenance	Denver-Aurora-Lakewood MSA, CO	Y	31160 FQ	38360 MW	45240 TQ	USBLS	5/15
Construction and Maintenance	Connecticut	Y		41286 MW		CTBLS	1/16-3/16
Construction and Maintenance	Bridgeport-Stamford-Norwalk MSA, CT	Y	31270 FQ	37650 MW	62130 TQ	USBLS	5/15
Construction and Maintenance	Hartford-West Hartford-East Hartford MSA, CT	Y	34360 FQ	42300 MW	48450 TQ	USBLS	5/15
Construction and Maintenance	Delaware	Y	32920 FQ	38510 MW	46740 TQ	USBLS	5/15
Construction and Maintenance	Wilmington PMSA, DE-MD-NJ	Y	35970 FQ	42120 MW	49500 TQ	USBLS	5/15

AE Average entry wage	**AWR** Average wage range	**H** Hourly	**LR** Low end range	**MTC** Median total compensation	**TCC** Total cash compensation
AEX Average experienced wage	**B** Biweekly	**HI** Highest wage paid	**M** Monthly	**MW** Median wage paid	**TQ** Third quartile wage
ATC Average total compensation	**D** Daily	**HR** High end range	**MCC** Median cash compensation	**MWR** Median wage range	**W** Weekly
AW Average wage paid	**FQ** First quartile wage	**LO** Lowest wage paid	**ME** Median entry wage	**S** See annotated source	**Y** Yearly

Occupation/Type/Industry	Location	Per	Low	Mid	High	Source	Date
Painter							
Construction and Maintenance	District of Columbia	Y	35000 FQ	48930 MW	59240 TQ	USBLS	5/15
Construction and Maintenance	Washington-Arlington-Alexandria PMSA, DC-VA-MD-WV	Y	32620 FQ	37680 MW	48600 TQ	USBLS	5/15
Construction and Maintenance	Florida	H	11.18 AE	14.68 MW	18.07 AEX	FLBLS	7/16-9/16
Construction and Maintenance	Fort Lauderdale-Pompano Beach-Deerfield Beach PMSA, FL	H	13.64 AE	17.39 MW	20.37 AEX	FLBLS	7/16-9/16
Construction and Maintenance	Miami-Miami Beach-Kendall PMSA, FL	H	11.25 AE	15.32 MW	18.15 AEX	FLBLS	7/16-9/16
Construction and Maintenance	Orlando-Kissimmee-Sanford MSA, FL	H	10.19 AE	14.51 MW	17.71 AEX	FLBLS	7/16-9/16
Construction and Maintenance	Tampa-St. Petersburg-Clearwater MSA, FL	H	11.46 AE	14.08 MW	19.74 AEX	FLBLS	7/16-9/16
Construction and Maintenance	Georgia	Y	29050 FQ	35240 MW	44930 TQ	USBLS	5/15
Construction and Maintenance	Atlanta-Sandy Springs-Roswell MSA, GA	Y	31090 FQ	35610 MW	41000 TQ	USBLS	5/15
Construction and Maintenance	Augusta-Richmond County MSA, GA-SC	Y	26970 FQ	30380 MW	39920 TQ	USBLS	5/15
Construction and Maintenance	Hawaii	Y	40680 FQ	52860 MW	67530 TQ	USBLS	5/15
Construction and Maintenance	Urban Honolulu MSA, HI	Y	38990 FQ	52430 MW	67570 TQ	USBLS	5/15
Construction and Maintenance	Idaho	Y	24600 FQ	29730 MW	36580 TQ	USBLS	5/15
Construction and Maintenance	Boise City MSA, ID	Y	19720 FQ	27100 MW	30960 TQ	USBLS	5/15
Construction and Maintenance	Illinois	Y	32590 FQ	49210 MW	82900 TQ	USBLS	5/15
Construction and Maintenance	Chicago-Naperville-Arlington Heights PMSA, IL	Y	33070 FQ	54610 MW	87170 TQ	USBLS	5/15
Construction and Maintenance	Lake County-Kenosha County PMSA, IL-WI	Y	28650 FQ	37160 MW	58020 TQ	USBLS	5/15
Construction and Maintenance	Indiana	Y	26250 FQ	35860 MW	49510 TQ	USBLS	5/15
Construction and Maintenance	Gary PMSA, IN	Y	33370 FQ	46450 MW	68060 TQ	USBLS	5/15
Construction and Maintenance	Indianapolis-Carmel-Anderson MSA, IN	Y	24390 FQ	35070 MW	48340 TQ	USBLS	5/15
Construction and Maintenance	Iowa	Y	28100 FQ	35190 MW	44500 TQ	USBLS	5/15
Construction and Maintenance	Des Moines-West Des Moines MSA, IA	Y	27660 FQ	35000 MW	46360 TQ	USBLS	5/15
Construction and Maintenance	Kansas	Y	25310 FQ	32880 MW	42180 TQ	USBLS	5/15
Construction and Maintenance	Wichita MSA, KS	Y	23860 FQ	29330 MW	36800 TQ	USBLS	5/15
Construction and Maintenance	Kentucky	Y	28540 FQ	34700 MW	41120 TQ	USBLS	5/15
Construction and Maintenance	Louisville-Jefferson County MSA, KY-IN	Y	31930 FQ	36920 MW	43140 TQ	USBLS	5/15
Construction and Maintenance	Louisiana	Y	28150 FQ	34900 MW	41100 TQ	USBLS	5/15
Construction and Maintenance	Baton Rouge MSA, LA	Y	27050 FQ	35970 MW	43070 TQ	USBLS	5/15
Construction and Maintenance	New Orleans-Metairie MSA, LA	Y	31340 FQ	35380 MW	39440 TQ	USBLS	5/15
Construction and Maintenance	Maine	Y	32550 FQ	40660 MW	46750 TQ	USBLS	5/15
Construction and Maintenance	Portland-South Portland MSA, ME	Y	28170 FQ	31230 MW	38060 TQ	USBLS	5/15
Construction and Maintenance	Maryland	Y	26608 AE	38021 MW	43728 AEX	MDBLS	4/16
Construction and Maintenance	Baltimore-Columbia-Towson MSA, MD	Y	32670 FQ	37410 MW	46260 TQ	USBLS	5/15
Construction and Maintenance	Salisbury MSA, MD-DE	Y	27340 FQ	31570 MW	37340 TQ	USBLS	5/15
Construction and Maintenance	Massachusetts	Y	33130 FQ	42730 MW	59300 TQ	USBLS	5/15
Construction and Maintenance	Boston-Cambridge-Newton NECTA, MA	Y	40270 FQ	56750 MW	87250 TQ	USBLS	5/15
Construction and Maintenance	Worcester MSA, MA-CT	Y	34090 FQ	40500 MW	49300 TQ	USBLS	5/15
Construction and Maintenance	Michigan	Y	31850 FQ	38750 MW	50030 TQ	USBLS	5/15
Construction and Maintenance	Detroit-Dearborn-Livonia PMSA, MI	Y	34600 FQ	42880 MW	56110 TQ	USBLS	5/15
Construction and Maintenance	Grand Rapids-Wyoming MSA, MI	Y	32250 FQ	37780 MW	45270 TQ	USBLS	5/15
Construction and Maintenance	Minnesota	Y	32480 FQ	38938 MW	49159 TQ	MNBLS	1/16-3/16
Construction and Maintenance	Minneapolis-St. Paul-Bloomington MSA, MN-WI	Y	34155 FQ	39725 MW	50098 TQ	MNBLS	1/16-3/16
Construction and Maintenance	Mississippi	Y	26120 FQ	32120 MW	39000 TQ	USBLS	5/15
Construction and Maintenance	Jackson MSA, MS	Y	27580 FQ	33770 MW	38030 TQ	USBLS	5/15
Construction and Maintenance	Missouri	Y	36630 FQ	52010 MW	63310 TQ	USBLS	5/15
Construction and Maintenance	Kansas City MSA, MO-KS	Y	29290 FQ	38160 MW	54320 TQ	USBLS	5/15
Construction and Maintenance	St. Louis MSA, MO-IL	Y	38700 FQ	56040 MW	66760 TQ	USBLS	5/15
Construction and Maintenance	Montana	Y	27180 FQ	32260 MW	41480 TQ	USBLS	5/15
Construction and Maintenance	Billings MSA, MT	Y	25830 FQ	29880 MW	39270 TQ	USBLS	5/15
Construction and Maintenance	Nebraska	Y	26680 FQ	32520 MW	37375 TQ	NEBLS	7/16-9/16

AE Average entry wage	**AWR** Average wage range	**H** Hourly	**LR** Low end range	**MTC** Median total compensation	**TCC** Total cash compensation
AEX Average experienced wage	**B** Biweekly	**HI** Highest wage paid	**M** Monthly	**MW** Median wage paid	**TQ** Third quartile wage
ATC Average total compensation	**D** Daily	**HR** High end range	**MCC** Median cash compensation	**MWR** Median wage range	**W** Weekly
AW Average wage paid	**FQ** First quartile wage	**LO** Lowest wage paid	**ME** Median entry wage	**S** See annotated source	**Y** Yearly

Painter

Occupation/Type/Industry	Location	Per	Low	Mid	High	Source	Date
Painter							
Construction and Maintenance	Omaha-Council Bluffs MSA, NE-IA	Y	28645 FQ	33935 MW	37775 TQ	NEBLS	7/16-9/16
Construction and Maintenance	Nevada	Y	32360 FQ	38830 MW	52590 TQ	USBLS	5/15
Construction and Maintenance	Las Vegas-Henderson-Paradise MSA, NV	Y	32930 FQ	39920 MW	53680 TQ	USBLS	5/15
Construction and Maintenance	New Hampshire	H	14.60 AE	17.83 MW	20.22 AEX	NHBLS	6/16
Construction and Maintenance	Manchester NECTA, NH	H	15.37 AE	20.72 MW	22.84 AEX	NHBLS	6/16
Construction and Maintenance	Nashua NECTA, NH-MA	Y	28770 FQ	33900 MW	39620 TQ	USBLS	5/15
Construction and Maintenance	New Jersey	Y	28480 FQ	37030 MW	52720 TQ	USBLS	5/15
Construction and Maintenance	Camden PMSA, NJ	Y	22560 FQ	42120 MW	48190 TQ	USBLS	5/15
Construction and Maintenance	Newark PMSA, NJ-PA	Y	27830 FQ	42910 MW	58470 TQ	USBLS	5/15
Construction and Maintenance	Trenton MSA, NJ	Y	34000 FQ	44870 MW	55480 TQ	USBLS	5/15
Construction and Maintenance	New Mexico	Y	25840 FQ	30070 MW	36880 TQ	USBLS	5/15
Construction and Maintenance	Albuquerque MSA, NM	Y	24680 FQ	28650 MW	35020 TQ	USBLS	5/15
Construction and Maintenance	New York	Y	28780 AE	47140 MW	65400 AEX	NYBLS	1/16-3/16
Construction and Maintenance	Buffalo-Cheektowaga-Niagara Falls MSA, NY	Y	36430 FQ	45080 MW	64380 TQ	USBLS	5/15
Construction and Maintenance	Nassau County-Suffolk County PMSA, NY	Y	36600 FQ	54830 MW	81850 TQ	USBLS	5/15
Construction and Maintenance	New York-Jersey City-White Plains PMSA, NY-NJ	Y	31970 FQ	46170 MW	70030 TQ	USBLS	5/15
Construction and Maintenance	Rochester MSA, NY	Y	29440 FQ	34700 MW	42320 TQ	USBLS	5/15
Construction and Maintenance	North Carolina	Y	26950 FQ	31260 MW	36660 TQ	USBLS	5/15
Construction and Maintenance	Charlotte-Concord-Gastonia MSA, NC-SC	Y	27280 FQ	32270 MW	36780 TQ	USBLS	5/15
Construction and Maintenance	Raleigh MSA, NC	Y	28010 FQ	32180 MW	36700 TQ	USBLS	5/15
Construction and Maintenance	North Dakota	Y	31380 FQ	37950 MW	47730 TQ	USBLS	5/15
Construction and Maintenance	Fargo MSA, ND-MN	Y	32800 FQ	37410 MW	48100 TQ	USBLS	5/15
Construction and Maintenance	Ohio	Y	28300 FQ	37210 MW	48820 TQ	USBLS	5/15
Construction and Maintenance	Cincinnati MSA, OH-KY-IN	Y	32410 FQ	40560 MW	47560 TQ	USBLS	5/15
Construction and Maintenance	Cleveland-Elyria MSA, OH	Y	26500 FQ	36140 MW	55780 TQ	USBLS	5/15
Construction and Maintenance	Columbus MSA, OH	Y	29530 FQ	39450 MW	47090 TQ	USBLS	5/15
Construction and Maintenance	Oklahoma	Y	27680 FQ	34900 MW	43230 TQ	USBLS	5/15
Construction and Maintenance	Oklahoma City MSA, OK	Y	26970 FQ	38970 MW	48210 TQ	USBLS	5/15
Construction and Maintenance	Tulsa MSA, OK	Y	29710 FQ	34200 MW	38000 TQ	USBLS	5/15
Construction and Maintenance	Oregon	H	13.17 FQ	16.39 MW	19.46 TQ	ORBLS	2016
Construction and Maintenance	Portland-Vancouver-Hillsboro MSA, OR-WA	Y	27050 FQ	33660 MW	41070 TQ	USBLS	5/15
Construction and Maintenance	Pennsylvania	Y	31150 FQ	38640 MW	51420 TQ	USBLS	5/15
Construction and Maintenance	Allentown-Bethlehem-Easton MSA, PA-NJ	Y	29030 FQ	35080 MW	43630 TQ	USBLS	5/15
Construction and Maintenance	Harrisburg-Carlisle MSA, PA	Y	30000 FQ	39690 MW	49520 TQ	USBLS	5/15
Construction and Maintenance	Montgomery County-Bucks County-Chester County PMSA, PA	Y	34500 FQ	38860 MW	49590 TQ	USBLS	5/15
Construction and Maintenance	Philadelphia PMSA, PA	Y	40490 FQ	49050 MW	64830 TQ	USBLS	5/15
Construction and Maintenance	Pittsburgh MSA, PA	Y	26620 FQ	35220 MW	53440 TQ	USBLS	5/15
Construction and Maintenance	Rhode Island	Y	31950 FQ	37650 MW	44630 TQ	USBLS	5/15
Construction and Maintenance	Providence-Warwick MSA, RI-MA	Y	32630 FQ	38320 MW	45250 TQ	USBLS	5/15
Construction and Maintenance	South Carolina	Y	25650 FQ	29950 MW	36320 TQ	USBLS	5/15
Construction and Maintenance	Charleston-North Charleston MSA, SC	Y	27230 FQ	31030 MW	36570 TQ	USBLS	5/15
Construction and Maintenance	Columbia MSA, SC	Y	23180 FQ	29680 MW	43440 TQ	USBLS	5/15
Construction and Maintenance	Greenville-Anderson-Mauldin MSA, SC	Y	25630 FQ	29710 MW	35740 TQ	NHBLS	5/15
Construction and Maintenance	South Dakota	Y	23840 FQ	28110 MW	33500 TQ	USBLS	5/15
Construction and Maintenance	Sioux Falls MSA, SD	Y	23290 FQ	27120 MW	31040 TQ	USBLS	5/15
Construction and Maintenance	Tennessee	Y	26420 FQ	30690 MW	36720 TQ	USBLS	5/15
Construction and Maintenance	Knoxville MSA, TN	Y	23950 FQ	29060 MW	35040 TQ	USBLS	5/15
Construction and Maintenance	Memphis MSA, TN-MS-AR	Y	29050 FQ	34380 MW	39510 TQ	USBLS	5/15
Construction and Maintenance	Nashville-Davidson–Murfreesboro–Franklin MSA, TN	Y	27370 FQ	30860 MW	37430 TQ	USBLS	5/15
Construction and Maintenance	Texas	Y	27510 FQ	32670 MW	38650 TQ	USBLS	5/15
Construction and Maintenance	Austin-Round Rock MSA, TX	Y	25620 FQ	28650 MW	32320 TQ	USBLS	5/15
Construction and Maintenance	Dallas-Plano-Irving PMSA, TX	Y	26700 FQ	30180 MW	35670 TQ	USBLS	5/15
Construction and Maintenance	Fort Worth-Arlington PMSA, TX	Y	27560 FQ	31630 MW	37440 TQ	USBLS	5/15
Construction and Maintenance	Houston-The Woodlands-Sugar Land MSA, TX	Y	30100 FQ	35140 MW	40040 TQ	USBLS	5/15

AE	Average entry wage	AWR	Average wage range	H	Hourly
AEX	Average experienced wage	B	Biweekly	HI	Highest wage paid
ATC	Average total compensation	D	Daily	HR	High end range
AW	Average wage paid	FQ	First quartile wage	LO	Lowest wage paid

LR	Low end range	MTC	Median total compensation	TCC	Total cash compensation
M	Monthly	MW	Median wage paid	TQ	Third quartile wage
MCC	Median cash compensation	MWR	Median wage range	W	Weekly
ME	Median entry wage	S	See annotated source	Y	Yearly

Occupation/Type/Industry	Location	Per	Low	Mid	High	Source	Date
Painter							
Construction and Maintenance	San Antonio-New Braunfels MSA, TX	Y	27110 FQ	32720 MW	43600 TQ	USBLS	5/15
Construction and Maintenance	Utah	Y	28960 FQ	35520 MW	43150 TQ	USBLS	5/15
Construction and Maintenance	Ogden-Clearfield MSA, UT	Y	29790 FQ	37170 MW	51270 TQ	USBLS	5/15
Construction and Maintenance	Provo-Orem MSA, UT	Y	31670 FQ	38560 MW	44710 TQ	USBLS	5/15
Construction and Maintenance	Salt Lake City MSA, UT	Y	30940 FQ	36140 MW	41920 TQ	USBLS	5/15
Construction and Maintenance	Vermont	Y	27000 FQ	35520 MW	43060 TQ	USBLS	5/15
Construction and Maintenance	Burlington-South Burlington MSA, VT	Y	32610 FQ	36790 MW	42510 TQ	USBLS	5/15
Construction and Maintenance	Virginia	Y	30680 FQ	36340 MW	43970 TQ	USBLS	5/15
Construction and Maintenance	Lynchburg MSA, VA	Y	26150 FQ	28640 MW	31130 TQ	USBLS	5/15
Construction and Maintenance	Richmond MSA, VA	Y	32520 FQ	37260 MW	44000 TQ	USBLS	5/15
Construction and Maintenance	Virginia Beach-Norfolk-Newport News MSA, VA-NC	Y	30100 FQ	38220 MW	45970 TQ	USBLS	5/15
Construction and Maintenance	Washington	H	16.11 FQ	19.09 MW	25.66 TQ	WABLS	3/16
Construction and Maintenance	Seattle-Bellevue-Everett PMSA, WA	H	16.41 FQ	19.75 MW	27.76 TQ	WABLS	3/16
Construction and Maintenance	Tacoma-Lakewood PMSA, WA	H	15.77 FQ	18.76 MW	23.01 TQ	WABLS	3/16
Construction and Maintenance	West Virginia	Y	27190 FQ	34980 MW	52480 TQ	USBLS	5/15
Construction and Maintenance	Huntington-Ashland MSA, WV-KY-OH	Y	29980 FQ	36970 MW	55190 TQ	USBLS	5/15
Construction and Maintenance	Wisconsin	Y	32430 FQ	39200 MW	54500 TQ	USBLS	5/15
Construction and Maintenance	Madison MSA, WI	Y	34140 FQ	49230 MW	58000 TQ	USBLS	5/15
Construction and Maintenance	Milwaukee-Waukesha-West Allis MSA, WI	Y	34450 FQ	42750 MW	60520 TQ	USBLS	5/15
Construction and Maintenance	Wyoming	Y	29390 FQ	35560 MW	42890 TQ	USBLS	5/15
Construction and Maintenance	Cheyenne MSA, WY	Y	21760 FQ	29630 MW	37970 TQ	USBLS	5/15
Construction and Maintenance	Puerto Rico	Y	17470 FQ	19660 MW	27550 TQ	USBLS	5/15
Construction and Maintenance	San Juan-Carolina-Caguas MSA, PR	Y	17620 FQ	20550 MW	28240 TQ	USBLS	5/15
Construction and Maintenance	Virgin Islands	Y	21510 FQ	28690 MW	37380 TQ	USBLS	5/15
Construction and Maintenance	Guam	Y	26600 AE	29020 MW	32000 TQ	USBLS	5/15
Transportation Equipment	Alabama	Y	28636 AE	40748 AW	46794 AEX	ALBLS	6/16
Transportation Equipment	Birmingham-Hoover MSA, AL	Y	25438 AE	37149 AW	43010 AEX	ALBLS	6/16
Transportation Equipment	Arizona	Y	30970 FQ	36660 MW	46060 TQ	USBLS	5/15
Transportation Equipment	Phoenix-Mesa-Scottsdale MSA, AZ	Y	29720 FQ	35850 MW	43220 TQ	USBLS	5/15
Transportation Equipment	Tucson MSA, AZ	Y	40360 FQ	46170 MW	54410 TQ	USBLS	5/15
Transportation Equipment	Arkansas	Y	28490 FQ	34390 MW	40020 TQ	USBLS	5/15
Transportation Equipment	Little Rock-North Little Rock-Conway MSA, AR	Y	32160 FQ	36260 MW	42170 TQ	USBLS	5/15
Transportation Equipment	California	H	15.31 FQ	20.35 MW	25.91 TQ	CABLS	1/16-3/16
Transportation Equipment	Anaheim-Santa Ana-Irvine PMSA, CA	H	13.68 FQ	18.33 MW	25.65 TQ	CABLS	1/16-3/16
Transportation Equipment	Los Angeles-Long Beach-Glendale PMSA, CA	H	14.10 FQ	19.70 MW	24.30 TQ	CABLS	1/16-3/16
Transportation Equipment	Oakland-Hayward-Berkeley PMSA, CA	H	17.93 FQ	23.64 MW	29.30 TQ	CABLS	1/16-3/16
Transportation Equipment	Riverside-San Bernardino-Ontario MSA, CA	H	13.79 FQ	19.18 MW	24.07 TQ	CABLS	1/16-3/16
Transportation Equipment	Sacramento–Roseville–Arden-Arcade MSA, CA	H	16.56 FQ	22.32 MW	30.43 TQ	CABLS	1/16-3/16
Transportation Equipment	San Diego-Carlsbad MSA, CA	H	13.15 FQ	18.75 MW	24.00 TQ	CABLS	1/16-3/16
Transportation Equipment	San Francisco-Redwood City-South San Francisco PMSA, CA	H	18.13 FQ	22.73 MW	28.79 TQ	CABLS	1/16-3/16
Transportation Equipment	Colorado	Y	30100 FQ	44580 MW	59840 TQ	USBLS	5/15
Transportation Equipment	Denver-Aurora-Lakewood MSA, CO	Y	29440 FQ	44180 MW	56080 TQ	USBLS	5/15
Transportation Equipment	Connecticut	Y		58764 MW		CTBLS	1/16-3/16
Transportation Equipment	Bridgeport-Stamford-Norwalk MSA, CT	Y	53970 FQ	57930 MW	61890 TQ	USBLS	5/15
Transportation Equipment	Hartford-West Hartford-East Hartford MSA, CT	Y	44050 FQ	50210 MW	74560 TQ	USBLS	5/15
Transportation Equipment	Delaware	Y	34420 FQ	38820 MW	52580 TQ	USBLS	5/15
Transportation Equipment	Wilmington PMSA, DE-MD-NJ	Y	35270 FQ	40240 MW	54590 TQ	USBLS	5/15
Transportation Equipment	Washington-Arlington-Alexandria PMSA, DC-VA-MD-WV	Y	41190 FQ	68120 MW	87290 TQ	USBLS	5/15
Transportation Equipment	Florida	H	13.81 AE	17.99 MW	22.02 AEX	FLBLS	7/16-9/16

AE	Average entry wage	AWR	Average wage range	H	Hourly	LR	Low end range	MTC	Median total compensation	TCC	Total cash compensation
AEX	Average experienced wage	B	Biweekly	HI	Highest wage paid	M	Monthly	MW	Median wage paid	TQ	Third quartile wage
ATC	Average total compensation	D	Daily	HR	High end range	MCC	Median cash compensation	MWR	Median wage range	W	Weekly
AW	Average wage paid	FQ	First quartile wage	LO	Lowest wage paid	ME	Median entry wage	S	See annotated source	Y	Yearly

Painter

Occupation/Type/Industry	Location	Per	Low	Mid	High	Source	Date
Painter							
Transportation Equipment	Fort Lauderdale-Pompano Beach-Deerfield Beach PMSA, FL	H	12.74 AE	18.28 MW	23.69 AEX	FLBLS	7/16-9/16
Transportation Equipment	Miami-Miami Beach-Kendall PMSA, FL	H	13.01 AE	16.84 MW	19.72 AEX	FLBLS	7/16-9/16
Transportation Equipment	Orlando-Kissimmee-Sanford MSA, FL	H	15.43 AE	18.39 MW	22.94 AEX	FLBLS	7/16-9/16
Transportation Equipment	Tampa-St. Petersburg-Clearwater MSA, FL	H	13.47 AE	16.31 MW	17.94 AEX	FLBLS	7/16-9/16
Transportation Equipment	Georgia	Y	34890 FQ	42990 MW	53330 TQ	USBLS	5/15
Transportation Equipment	Atlanta-Sandy Springs-Roswell MSA, GA	Y	37770 FQ	45700 MW	65800 TQ	USBLS	5/15
Transportation Equipment	Augusta-Richmond County MSA, GA-SC	Y	24250 FQ	35160 MW	45930 TQ	USBLS	5/15
Transportation Equipment	Hawaii	Y	33570 FQ	38460 MW	55420 TQ	USBLS	5/15
Transportation Equipment	Urban Honolulu MSA, HI	Y	33950 FQ	39300 MW	57470 TQ	USBLS	5/15
Transportation Equipment	Idaho	Y	32250 FQ	38090 MW	49230 TQ	USBLS	5/15
Transportation Equipment	Boise City MSA, ID	Y	30720 FQ	36700 MW	51970 TQ	USBLS	5/15
Transportation Equipment	Illinois	Y	33890 FQ	41950 MW	54100 TQ	USBLS	5/15
Transportation Equipment	Chicago-Naperville-Arlington Heights PMSA, IL	Y	34640 FQ	43140 MW	55620 TQ	USBLS	5/15
Transportation Equipment	Lake County-Kenosha County PMSA, IL-WI	Y	29760 FQ	37410 MW	66170 TQ	USBLS	5/15
Transportation Equipment	Peoria MSA, IL	Y	34500 FQ	38030 MW	56980 TQ	USBLS	5/15
Transportation Equipment	Indiana	Y	33710 FQ	43590 MW	56100 TQ	USBLS	5/15
Transportation Equipment	Gary PMSA, IN	Y	36790 FQ	52550 MW	61630 TQ	USBLS	5/15
Transportation Equipment	Indianapolis-Carmel-Anderson MSA, IN	Y	36570 FQ	48160 MW	65830 TQ	USBLS	5/15
Transportation Equipment	Iowa	Y	29780 FQ	34560 MW	39020 TQ	USBLS	5/15
Transportation Equipment	Des Moines-West Des Moines MSA, IA	Y	28490 FQ	35780 MW	43090 TQ	USBLS	5/15
Transportation Equipment	Kansas	Y	29940 FQ	36350 MW	49590 TQ	USBLS	5/15
Transportation Equipment	Wichita MSA, KS	Y	31010 FQ	39790 MW	61980 TQ	USBLS	5/15
Transportation Equipment	Kentucky	Y	34770 FQ	43220 MW	58340 TQ	USBLS	5/15
Transportation Equipment	Louisville-Jefferson County MSA, KY-IN	Y	42230 FQ	49990 MW	63650 TQ	USBLS	5/15
Transportation Equipment	Louisiana	Y	27840 FQ	39410 MW	53950 TQ	USBLS	5/15
Transportation Equipment	Baton Rouge MSA, LA	Y	33460 FQ	45670 MW	61660 TQ	USBLS	5/15
Transportation Equipment	New Orleans-Metairie MSA, LA	Y	23270 FQ	28410 MW	43500 TQ	USBLS	5/15
Transportation Equipment	Maine	Y	31820 FQ	37400 MW	46240 TQ	USBLS	5/15
Transportation Equipment	Portland-South Portland MSA, ME	Y	26060 FQ	38120 MW	51640 TQ	USBLS	5/15
Transportation Equipment	Maryland	Y	31177 AE	47194 MW	55202 AEX	MDBLS	4/16
Transportation Equipment	Baltimore-Columbia-Towson MSA, MD	Y	31080 FQ	39630 MW	57300 TQ	USBLS	5/15
Transportation Equipment	Salisbury MSA, MD-DE	Y	34460 FQ	39620 MW	49230 TQ	USBLS	5/15
Transportation Equipment	Massachusetts	Y	34330 FQ	46830 MW	56390 TQ	USBLS	5/15
Transportation Equipment	Boston-Cambridge-Newton NECTA, MA	Y	41420 FQ	53740 MW	59260 TQ	USBLS	5/15
Transportation Equipment	Worcester MSA, MA-CT	Y	36020 FQ	43550 MW	50130 TQ	USBLS	5/15
Transportation Equipment	Michigan	Y	34480 FQ	43960 MW	62740 TQ	USBLS	5/15
Transportation Equipment	Detroit-Dearborn-Livonia PMSA, MI	Y	43410 FQ	52290 MW	63120 TQ	USBLS	5/15
Transportation Equipment	Grand Rapids-Wyoming MSA, MI	Y	31300 FQ	38470 MW	52890 TQ	USBLS	5/15
Transportation Equipment	Minnesota	Y	36357 FQ	43890 MW	51523 TQ	MNBLS	1/16-3/16
Transportation Equipment	Minneapolis-St. Paul-Bloomington MSA, MN-WI	Y	40822 FQ	47099 MW	63946 TQ	MNBLS	1/16-3/16
Transportation Equipment	Mississippi	Y	28390 FQ	34090 MW	40960 TQ	USBLS	5/15
Transportation Equipment	Jackson MSA, MS	Y	33240 FQ	40090 MW	50740 TQ	USBLS	5/15
Transportation Equipment	Missouri	Y	33440 FQ	47500 MW	59590 TQ	USBLS	5/15
Transportation Equipment	Kansas City MSA, MO-KS	Y	35890 FQ	51170 MW	59240 TQ	USBLS	5/15
Transportation Equipment	St. Louis MSA, MO-IL	Y	35700 FQ	52920 MW	61770 TQ	USBLS	5/15
Transportation Equipment	Montana	Y	34210 FQ	41790 MW	47580 TQ	USBLS	5/15
Transportation Equipment	Billings MSA, MT	Y	41860 FQ	46670 MW	59880 TQ	USBLS	5/15
Transportation Equipment	Nebraska	Y	31100 FQ	38135 MW	47880 TQ	NEBLS	7/16-9/16
Transportation Equipment	Omaha-Council Bluffs MSA, NE-IA	Y	28345 FQ	35680 MW	47040 TQ	NEBLS	7/16-9/16
Transportation Equipment	Nevada	Y	31750 FQ	38130 MW	48330 TQ	USBLS	5/15

Occupation/Type/Industry	Location	Per	Low	Mid	High	Source	Date
Painter							
Transportation Equipment	Las Vegas-Henderson-Paradise MSA, NV	Y	31220 FQ	38090 MW	51530 TQ	USBLS	5/15
Transportation Equipment	New Hampshire	H	13.90 AE	21.09 MW	26.33 AEX	NHBLS	6/16
Transportation Equipment	New Jersey	Y	35870 FQ	45000 MW	55280 TQ	USBLS	5/15
Transportation Equipment	Camden PMSA, NJ	Y	34890 FQ	46380 MW	57610 TQ	USBLS	5/15
Transportation Equipment	Newark PMSA, NJ-PA	Y	36050 FQ	45750 MW	56110 TQ	USBLS	5/15
Transportation Equipment	New Mexico	Y	25920 FQ	34820 MW	45990 TQ	USBLS	5/15
Transportation Equipment	Albuquerque MSA, NM	Y	39900 FQ	49080 MW	59530 TQ	USBLS	5/15
Transportation Equipment	New York	Y	29740 AE	43160 MW	53540 AEX	NYBLS	1/16-3/16
Transportation Equipment	Buffalo-Cheektowaga-Niagara Falls MSA, NY	Y	30770 FQ	48190 MW	62040 TQ	USBLS	5/15
Transportation Equipment	Nassau County-Suffolk County PMSA, NY	Y	35430 FQ	53230 MW	65730 TQ	USBLS	5/15
Transportation Equipment	New York-Jersey City-White Plains PMSA, NY-NJ	Y	34760 FQ	42890 MW	53600 TQ	USBLS	5/15
Transportation Equipment	Rochester MSA, NY	Y	30040 FQ	57040 MW	63900 TQ	USBLS	5/15
Transportation Equipment	North Carolina	Y	33490 FQ	46340 MW	58500 TQ	USBLS	5/15
Transportation Equipment	Charlotte-Concord-Gastonia MSA, NC-SC	Y	39320 FQ	54700 MW	61080 TQ	USBLS	5/15
Transportation Equipment	North Dakota	Y	33640 FQ	41360 MW	49470 TQ	USBLS	5/15
Transportation Equipment	Fargo MSA, ND-MN	Y	29880 FQ	37040 MW	59670 TQ	USBLS	5/15
Transportation Equipment	Ohio	Y	34220 FQ	42490 MW	57300 TQ	USBLS	5/15
Transportation Equipment	Cincinnati MSA, OH-KY-IN	Y	34020 FQ	39770 MW	47850 TQ	USBLS	5/15
Transportation Equipment	Cleveland-Elyria MSA, OH	Y	34300 FQ	41630 MW	56770 TQ	USBLS	5/15
Transportation Equipment	Oklahoma	Y	27520 FQ	39150 MW	47680 TQ	USBLS	5/15
Transportation Equipment	Oklahoma City MSA, OK	Y	24000 FQ	34330 MW	45350 TQ	USBLS	5/15
Transportation Equipment	Tulsa MSA, OK	Y	39300 FQ	48440 MW	56580 TQ	USBLS	5/15
Transportation Equipment	Oregon	H	16.71 FQ	20.09 MW	28.96 TQ	ORBLS	2016
Transportation Equipment	Portland-Vancouver-Hillsboro MSA, OR-WA	Y	35310 FQ	44190 MW	62240 TQ	USBLS	5/15
Transportation Equipment	Pennsylvania	Y	35100 FQ	45700 MW	57190 TQ	USBLS	5/15
Transportation Equipment	Allentown-Bethlehem-Easton MSA, PA-NJ	Y	30040 FQ	41680 MW	54740 TQ	USBLS	5/15
Transportation Equipment	Harrisburg-Carlisle MSA, PA	Y	25410 FQ	29680 MW	49200 TQ	USBLS	5/15
Transportation Equipment	Montgomery County-Bucks County-Chester County PMSA, PA	Y	38260 FQ	50290 MW	58870 TQ	USBLS	5/15
Transportation Equipment	Philadelphia PMSA, PA	Y	42520 FQ	51730 MW	60210 TQ	USBLS	5/15
Transportation Equipment	Pittsburgh MSA, PA	Y	37240 FQ	44090 MW	49040 TQ	USBLS	5/15
Transportation Equipment	Rhode Island	Y	34660 FQ	39820 MW	49810 TQ	USBLS	5/15
Transportation Equipment	Providence-Warwick MSA, RI-MA	Y	34050 FQ	39510 MW	49610 TQ	USBLS	5/15
Transportation Equipment	South Carolina	Y	29220 FQ	36630 MW	47100 TQ	USBLS	5/15
Transportation Equipment	Charleston-North Charleston MSA, SC	Y	35410 FQ	41350 MW	47880 TQ	USBLS	5/15
Transportation Equipment	Columbia MSA, SC	Y	25990 FQ	32110 MW	37900 TQ	USBLS	5/15
Transportation Equipment	Greenville-Anderson-Mauldin MSA, SC	Y	24790 FQ	37710 MW	52860 TQ	USBLS	5/15
Transportation Equipment	South Dakota	Y	29260 FQ	34200 MW	41090 TQ	USBLS	5/15
Transportation Equipment	Sioux Falls MSA, SD	Y	28540 FQ	32320 MW	40510 TQ	USBLS	5/15
Transportation Equipment	Tennessee	Y	29010 FQ	36380 MW	48990 TQ	USBLS	5/15
Transportation Equipment	Knoxville MSA, TN	Y	30200 FQ	35480 MW	40360 TQ	USBLS	5/15
Transportation Equipment	Memphis MSA, TN-MS-AR	Y	30110 FQ	39240 MW	60600 TQ	USBLS	5/15
Transportation Equipment	Nashville-Davidson–Murfreesboro–Franklin MSA, TN	Y	25810 FQ	35000 MW	46930 TQ	USBLS	5/15
Transportation Equipment	Texas	Y	31800 FQ	39050 MW	50920 TQ	USBLS	5/15
Transportation Equipment	Austin-Round Rock MSA, TX	Y	29910 FQ	35630 MW	45410 TQ	USBLS	5/15
Transportation Equipment	Dallas-Plano-Irving PMSA, TX	Y	32390 FQ	43160 MW	59320 TQ	USBLS	5/15
Transportation Equipment	Fort Worth-Arlington PMSA, TX	Y	32760 FQ	45160 MW	60450 TQ	USBLS	5/15
Transportation Equipment	Houston-The Woodlands-Sugar Land MSA, TX	Y	30840 FQ	36720 MW	48500 TQ	USBLS	5/15
Transportation Equipment	San Antonio-New Braunfels MSA, TX	Y	37520 FQ	44400 MW	50200 TQ	USBLS	5/15
Transportation Equipment	Utah	Y	30040 FQ	43190 MW	57400 TQ	USBLS	5/15
Transportation Equipment	Salt Lake City MSA, UT	Y	29460 FQ	43910 MW	59630 TQ	USBLS	5/15
Transportation Equipment	Vermont	Y	31680 FQ	44080 MW	54640 TQ	USBLS	5/15
Transportation Equipment	Virginia	Y	37820 FQ	47380 MW	60790 TQ	USBLS	5/15
Transportation Equipment	Richmond MSA, VA	Y	31730 FQ	56190 MW	68440 TQ	USBLS	5/15

AE	Average entry wage	AWR	Average wage range	H	Hourly	LR	Low end range	MTC	Median total compensation	TCC	Total cash compensation
AEX	Average experienced wage	B	Biweekly	HI	Highest wage paid	M	Monthly	MW	Median wage paid	TQ	Third quartile wage
ATC	Average total compensation	D	Daily	HR	High end range	MCC	Median cash compensation	MWR	Median wage range	W	Weekly
AW	Average wage paid	FQ	First quartile wage	LO	Lowest wage paid	ME	Median entry wage	S	See annotated source	Y	Yearly

Occupation/Type/Industry	Location	Per	Low	Mid	High	Source	Date
Painter							
Transportation Equipment	Virginia Beach-Norfolk-Newport News MSA, VA-NC	Y	38650 FQ	44450 MW	49830 TQ	USBLS	5/15
Transportation Equipment	Washington	H	18.21 FQ	23.78 MW	33.84 TQ	WABLS	3/16
Transportation Equipment	Seattle-Bellevue-Everett PMSA, WA	H	21.09 FQ	27.81 MW	38.67 TQ	WABLS	3/16
Transportation Equipment	Tacoma-Lakewood PMSA, WA	H	18.04 FQ	21.30 MW	25.20 TQ	WABLS	3/16
Transportation Equipment	West Virginia	Y	33440 FQ	40980 MW	56200 TQ	USBLS	5/15
Transportation Equipment	Huntington-Ashland MSA, WV-KY-OH	Y	28000 FQ	33680 MW	38980 TQ	USBLS	5/15
Transportation Equipment	Wisconsin	Y	25870 FQ	36110 MW	47840 TQ	USBLS	5/15
Transportation Equipment	Madison MSA, WI	Y	35320 FQ	48380 MW	59090 TQ	USBLS	5/15
Transportation Equipment	Milwaukee-Waukesha-West Allis MSA, WI	Y	33900 FQ	46010 MW	59550 TQ	USBLS	5/15
Transportation Equipment	Wyoming	Y	42080 FQ	48110 MW	69820 TQ	USBLS	5/15
Transportation Equipment	Puerto Rico	Y	17710 FQ	19810 MW	22960 TQ	USBLS	5/15
Transportation Equipment	San Juan-Carolina-Caguas MSA, PR	Y	17590 FQ	19690 MW	23140 TQ	USBLS	5/15
Painting, Coating, and Decorating Worker	Alabama	Y	21449 AE	26867 AW	29571 AEX	ALBLS	6/16
	Birmingham-Hoover MSA, AL	Y	20184 AE	25232 AW	27752 AEX	ALBLS	6/16
	Arizona	Y	25360 FQ	29590 MW	36180 TQ	USBLS	5/15
	Phoenix-Mesa-Scottsdale MSA, AZ	Y	26430 FQ	30960 MW	38170 TQ	USBLS	5/15
	California	H	11.18 FQ	13.89 MW	18.42 TQ	CABLS	1/16-3/16
	Anaheim-Santa Ana-Irvine PMSA, CA	H	11.89 FQ	14.00 MW	17.64 TQ	CABLS	1/16-3/16
	Los Angeles-Long Beach-Glendale PMSA, CA	H	12.63 FQ	16.49 MW	24.84 TQ	CABLS	1/16-3/16
	Oakland-Hayward-Berkeley PMSA, CA	H	18.50 FQ	21.99 MW	24.87 TQ	CABLS	1/16-3/16
	Riverside-San Bernardino-Ontario MSA, CA	H	9.89 FQ	11.92 MW	14.77 TQ	CABLS	1/16-3/16
	Sacramento–Roseville–Arden-Arcade MSA, CA	H	9.86 FQ	11.47 MW	14.15 TQ	CABLS	1/16-3/16
	San Diego-Carlsbad MSA, CA	H	15.20 FQ	18.37 MW	22.29 TQ	CABLS	1/16-3/16
	San Francisco-Redwood City-South San Francisco PMSA, CA	H	11.76 FQ	19.02 MW	40.20 TQ	CABLS	1/16-3/16
	Colorado	Y	30750 FQ	36140 MW	43330 TQ	USBLS	5/15
	Denver-Aurora-Lakewood MSA, CO	Y	33700 FQ	37340 MW	43050 TQ	USBLS	5/15
	Connecticut	Y		34358 MW		CTBLS	1/16-3/16
	Bridgeport-Stamford-Norwalk MSA, CT	Y	27260 FQ	34160 MW	37420 TQ	USBLS	5/15
	Hartford-West Hartford-East Hartford MSA, CT	Y	32740 FQ	42520 MW	47570 TQ	USBLS	5/15
	District of Columbia	Y	54330 FQ	58430 MW	62520 TQ	USBLS	5/15
	Washington-Arlington-Alexandria PMSA, DC-VA-MD-WV	Y	50280 FQ	55740 MW	59910 TQ	USBLS	5/15
	Florida	H	11.77 AE	14.61 MW	17.72 AEX	FLBLS	7/16-9/16
	Miami-Miami Beach-Kendall PMSA, FL	H	12.44 AE	18.90 MW	23.33 AEX	FLBLS	7/16-9/16
	Orlando-Kissimmee-Sanford MSA, FL	H	11.44 AE	14.23 MW	16.41 AEX	FLBLS	7/16-9/16
	Tampa-St. Petersburg-Clearwater MSA, FL	H	10.06 AE	13.44 MW	14.79 AEX	FLBLS	7/16-9/16
	Georgia	Y	21630 FQ	29450 MW	47920 TQ	USBLS	5/15
	Atlanta-Sandy Springs-Roswell MSA, GA	Y	25730 FQ	31630 MW	47830 TQ	USBLS	5/15
	Idaho	Y	19040 FQ	24330 MW	32030 TQ	USBLS	5/15
	Boise City MSA, ID	Y	18060 FQ	21730 MW	26940 TQ	USBLS	5/15
	Illinois	Y	28910 FQ	34170 MW	38950 TQ	USBLS	5/15
	Chicago-Naperville-Arlington Heights PMSA, IL	Y	29970 FQ	34500 MW	38680 TQ	USBLS	5/15
	Indiana	Y	23130 FQ	27980 MW	35560 TQ	USBLS	5/15
	Indianapolis-Carmel-Anderson MSA, IN	Y	28740 FQ	34570 MW	39810 TQ	USBLS	5/15
	Iowa	Y	22080 FQ	28290 MW	34920 TQ	USBLS	5/15

AE Average entry wage	**AWR** Average wage range	**H** Hourly	**LR** Low end range	**MTC** Median total compensation	**TCC** Total cash compensation
AEX Average experienced wage	**B** Biweekly	**HI** Highest wage paid	**M** Monthly	**MW** Median wage paid	**TQ** Third quartile wage
ATC Average total compensation	**D** Daily	**HR** High end range	**MCC** Median cash compensation	**MWR** Median wage range	**W** Weekly
AW Average wage paid	**FQ** First quartile wage	**LO** Lowest wage paid	**ME** Median entry wage	**S** See annotated source	**Y** Yearly

Occupation/Type/Industry	Location	Per	Low	Mid	High	Source	Date
Painting, Coating, and Decorating Worker							
	Des Moines-West Des Moines MSA, IA	Y	18700 FQ	28810 MW	35000 TQ	USBLS	5/15
	Kansas	Y	20900 FQ	23850 MW	33400 TQ	USBLS	5/15
	Kentucky	Y	22430 FQ	27150 MW	31400 TQ	USBLS	5/15
	Louisville-Jefferson County MSA, KY-IN	Y	24300 FQ	31440 MW	35920 TQ	USBLS	5/15
	Louisiana	Y	22410 FQ	28540 MW	40150 TQ	USBLS	5/15
	Maine	Y	18870 FQ	22750 MW	30020 TQ	USBLS	5/15
	Baltimore-Columbia-Towson MSA, MD	Y	17950 FQ	19260 MW	29350 TQ	USBLS	5/15
	Massachusetts	Y	32120 FQ	35630 MW	39140 TQ	USBLS	5/15
	Michigan	Y	27880 FQ	33090 MW	37210 TQ	USBLS	5/15
	Detroit-Dearborn-Livonia PMSA, MI	Y	23800 FQ	30660 MW	44120 TQ	USBLS	5/15
	Grand Rapids-Wyoming MSA, MI	Y	31000 FQ	35570 MW	42440 TQ	USBLS	5/15
	Minnesota	Y	25747 FQ	33249 MW	37724 TQ	MNBLS	1/16-3/16
	Minneapolis-St. Paul-Bloomington MSA, MN-WI	Y	26121 FQ	33522 MW	37501 TQ	MNBLS	1/16-3/16
	Mississippi	Y	23700 FQ	30280 MW	35430 TQ	USBLS	5/15
	Missouri	Y	24670 FQ	30530 MW	36050 TQ	USBLS	5/15
	Kansas City MSA, MO-KS	Y	24930 FQ	30420 MW	36220 TQ	USBLS	5/15
	St. Louis MSA, MO-IL	Y	24550 FQ	32610 MW	37960 TQ	USBLS	5/15
	Nebraska	Y	25625 FQ	30445 MW	36395 TQ	NEBLS	7/16-9/16
	Omaha-Council Bluffs MSA, NE-IA	Y	32155 FQ	34955 MW	37760 TQ	NEBLS	7/16-9/16
	Nevada	Y	19220 FQ	28310 MW	35130 TQ	USBLS	5/15
	Las Vegas-Henderson-Paradise MSA, NV	Y	18780 FQ	26980 MW	32870 TQ	USBLS	5/15
	New Hampshire	H	10.83 AE	11.45 MW	13.04 AEX	NHBLS	6/16
	New Jersey	Y	21810 FQ	26230 MW	31100 TQ	USBLS	5/15
	Camden PMSA, NJ	Y	25550 FQ	29370 MW	34380 TQ	USBLS	5/15
	New Mexico	Y	23000 FQ	26090 MW	29550 TQ	USBLS	5/15
	Albuquerque MSA, NM	Y	22410 FQ	24830 MW	28620 TQ	USBLS	5/15
	New York	Y	23440 AE	31530 MW	41530 AEX	NYBLS	1/16-3/16
	Buffalo-Cheektowaga-Niagara Falls MSA, NY	Y	23580 FQ	27890 MW	33600 TQ	USBLS	5/15
	Nassau County-Suffolk County PMSA, NY	Y	22690 FQ	35020 MW	43170 TQ	USBLS	5/15
	New York-Jersey City-White Plains PMSA, NY-NJ	Y	22890 FQ	27680 MW	33810 TQ	USBLS	5/15
	Rochester MSA, NY	Y	27380 FQ	34710 MW	41680 TQ	USBLS	5/15
	North Carolina	Y	24490 FQ	29230 MW	37030 TQ	USBLS	5/15
	Charlotte-Concord-Gastonia MSA, NC-SC	Y	24450 FQ	29430 MW	36760 TQ	USBLS	5/15
	North Dakota	Y	24400 FQ	32200 MW	38540 TQ	USBLS	5/15
	Ohio	Y	24930 FQ	30750 MW	37820 TQ	USBLS	5/15
	Oklahoma	Y	18070 FQ	21200 MW	27200 TQ	USBLS	5/15
	Oklahoma City MSA, OK	Y	21760 FQ	24660 MW	34970 TQ	USBLS	5/15
	Tulsa MSA, OK	Y	16920 FQ	18270 MW	19640 TQ	USBLS	5/15
	Oregon	H	11.80 FQ	14.91 MW	18.52 TQ	ORBLS	2016
	Portland-Vancouver-Hillsboro MSA, OR-WA	Y	24970 FQ	30010 MW	37980 TQ	USBLS	5/15
	Pennsylvania	Y	22920 FQ	30480 MW	37880 TQ	USBLS	5/15
	Allentown-Bethlehem-Easton MSA, PA-NJ	Y	22080 FQ	26010 MW	34520 TQ	USBLS	5/15
	Montgomery County-Bucks County-Chester County PMSA, PA	Y	28020 FQ	32280 MW	38940 TQ	USBLS	5/15
	Philadelphia PMSA, PA	Y	34590 FQ	42350 MW	50320 TQ	USBLS	5/15
	Pittsburgh MSA, PA	Y	20910 FQ	26810 MW	30740 TQ	USBLS	5/15
	Rhode Island	Y	23330 FQ	29300 MW	36220 TQ	USBLS	5/15
	Providence-Warwick MSA, RI-MA	Y	23750 FQ	30810 MW	38230 TQ	USBLS	5/15
	South Carolina	Y	18720 FQ	23730 MW	29930 TQ	USBLS	5/15
	Charleston-North Charleston MSA, SC	Y	21590 FQ	24050 MW	31040 TQ	USBLS	5/15
	Columbia MSA, SC	Y	22340 FQ	26230 MW	30190 TQ	USBLS	5/15
	South Dakota	Y	22990 FQ	26320 MW	29730 TQ	USBLS	5/15
	Tennessee	Y	22280 FQ	26160 MW	30670 TQ	USBLS	5/15

Occupation/Type/Industry	Location	Per	Low	Mid	High	Source	Date
Painting, Coating, and Decorating Worker	Nashville-Davidson–Murfreesboro–Franklin MSA, TN	Y	21470 FQ	24800 MW	29550 TQ	USBLS	5/15
	Texas	Y	19520 FQ	23650 MW	34590 TQ	USBLS	5/15
	Austin-Round Rock MSA, TX	Y	18660 FQ	21670 MW	32360 TQ	USBLS	5/15
	Dallas-Plano-Irving PMSA, TX	Y	18800 FQ	22160 MW	27740 TQ	USBLS	5/15
	Houston-The Woodlands-Sugar Land MSA, TX	Y	20610 FQ	24400 MW	35610 TQ	USBLS	5/15
	San Antonio-New Braunfels MSA, TX	Y	20850 FQ	23620 MW	34470 TQ	USBLS	5/15
	Utah	Y	30640 FQ	37740 MW	52630 TQ	USBLS	5/15
	Salt Lake City MSA, UT	Y	30900 FQ	35180 MW	41780 TQ	USBLS	5/15
	Vermont	Y	22710 FQ	25770 MW	29090 TQ	USBLS	5/15
	Virginia	Y	20220 FQ	28960 MW	37450 TQ	USBLS	5/15
	Virginia Beach-Norfolk-Newport News MSA, VA-NC	Y	18510 FQ	25120 MW	33190 TQ	USBLS	5/15
	Washington	H	14.38 FQ	17.49 MW	22.46 TQ	WABLS	3/16
	Seattle-Bellevue-Everett PMSA, WA	H	16.19 FQ	19.03 MW	24.47 TQ	WABLS	3/16
	West Virginia	Y	24620 FQ	28340 MW	31470 TQ	USBLS	5/15
	Wisconsin	Y	25570 FQ	29680 MW	35310 TQ	USBLS	5/15
	Puerto Rico	Y	17750 FQ	19840 MW	32300 TQ	USBLS	5/15
	San Juan-Carolina-Caguas MSA, PR	Y	17520 FQ	19410 MW	30520 TQ	USBLS	5/15
PAL Coordinator Police Department, Municipal Government	Fairfield, CA	Y			62817 HI	CACIT	6/28/16
Paper Goods Machine Setter, Operator, and Tender	Alabama	Y	24914 AE	39792 AW	47226 AEX	ALBLS	6/16
	Birmingham-Hoover MSA, AL	Y	22127 AE	34147 AW	40162 AEX	ALBLS	6/16
	Arizona	Y	23000 FQ	29220 MW	36910 TQ	USBLS	5/15
	Phoenix-Mesa-Scottsdale MSA, AZ	Y	23000 FQ	29220 MW	36910 TQ	USBLS	5/15
	Arkansas	Y	33590 FQ	41590 MW	49160 TQ	USBLS	5/15
	Little Rock-North Little Rock-Conway MSA, AR	Y	28800 FQ	40520 MW	46940 TQ	USBLS	5/15
	California	H	10.89 FQ	15.90 MW	22.31 TQ	CABLS	1/16-3/16
	Anaheim-Santa Ana-Irvine PMSA, CA	H	13.60 FQ	19.23 MW	27.02 TQ	CABLS	1/16-3/16
	Los Angeles-Long Beach-Glendale PMSA, CA	H	10.69 FQ	15.79 MW	21.55 TQ	CABLS	1/16-3/16
	Oakland-Hayward-Berkeley PMSA, CA	H	13.33 FQ	16.39 MW	19.74 TQ	CABLS	1/16-3/16
	Riverside-San Bernardino-Ontario MSA, CA	H	10.91 FQ	13.07 MW	21.37 TQ	CABLS	1/16-3/16
	Sacramento–Roseville–Arden-Arcade MSA, CA	H	12.92 FQ	15.85 MW	18.47 TQ	CABLS	1/16-3/16
	San Diego-Carlsbad MSA, CA	H	9.62 FQ	10.07 MW	14.26 TQ	CABLS	1/16-3/16
	Colorado	Y	34320 FQ	40490 MW	46580 TQ	USBLS	5/15
	Denver-Aurora-Lakewood MSA, CO	Y	35170 FQ	41020 MW	46830 TQ	USBLS	5/15
	Connecticut	Y		44402 MW		CTBLS	1/16-3/16
	Bridgeport-Stamford-Norwalk MSA, CT	Y	36630 FQ	44390 MW	50370 TQ	USBLS	5/15
	Hartford-West Hartford-East Hartford MSA, CT	Y	33490 FQ	36870 MW	41010 TQ	USBLS	5/15
	Delaware	Y	43280 FQ	50900 MW	56910 TQ	USBLS	5/15
	Washington-Arlington-Alexandria PMSA, DC-VA-MD-WV	Y	38070 FQ	51670 MW	60090 TQ	USBLS	5/15
	Florida	H	10.48 AE	14.70 MW	17.66 AEX	FLBLS	7/16-9/16
	Fort Lauderdale-Pompano Beach-Deerfield Beach PMSA, FL	H	12.91 AE	17.05 MW	18.33 AEX	FLBLS	7/16-9/16
	Miami-Miami Beach-Kendall PMSA, FL	H	10.62 AE	13.59 MW	16.09 AEX	FLBLS	7/16-9/16
	Orlando-Kissimmee-Sanford MSA, FL	H	10.31 AE	12.44 MW	15.99 AEX	FLBLS	7/16-9/16

AE Average entry wage	**AWR** Average wage range	**H** Hourly	**LR** Low end range	**MTC** Median total compensation	**TCC** Total cash compensation
AEX Average experienced wage	**B** Biweekly	**HI** Highest wage paid	**M** Monthly	**MW** Median wage paid	**TQ** Third quartile wage
ATC Average total compensation	**D** Daily	**HR** High end range	**MCC** Median cash compensation	**MWR** Median wage range	**W** Weekly
AW Average wage paid	**FQ** First quartile wage	**LO** Lowest wage paid	**ME** Median entry wage	**S** See annotated source	**Y** Yearly

Occupation/Type/Industry	Location	Per	Low	Mid	High	Source	Date
Paper Goods Machine Setter, Operator, and Tender							
	Tampa-St. Petersburg-Clearwater MSA, FL	H	10.89 AE	16.48 MW	19.07 AEX	FLBLS	7/16-9/16
	Georgia	Y	26130 FQ	35270 MW	44520 TQ	USBLS	5/15
	Atlanta-Sandy Springs-Roswell MSA, GA	Y	23350 FQ	30570 MW	38360 TQ	USBLS	5/15
	Augusta-Richmond County MSA, GA-SC	Y	21600 FQ	25090 MW	37520 TQ	USBLS	5/15
	Idaho	Y	31160 FQ	39050 MW	49430 TQ	USBLS	5/15
	Illinois	Y	26380 FQ	33670 MW	39920 TQ	USBLS	5/15
	Chicago-Naperville-Arlington Heights PMSA, IL	Y	25550 FQ	32940 MW	39350 TQ	USBLS	5/15
	Indiana	Y	23560 FQ	32120 MW	38170 TQ	USBLS	5/15
	Gary PMSA, IN	Y	30020 FQ	34040 MW	37830 TQ	USBLS	5/15
	Indianapolis-Carmel-Anderson MSA, IN	Y	29380 FQ	34970 MW	40450 TQ	USBLS	5/15
	Iowa	Y	21270 FQ	29110 MW	39120 TQ	USBLS	5/15
	Des Moines-West Des Moines MSA, IA	Y	25740 FQ	31420 MW	35230 TQ	USBLS	5/15
	Kansas	Y	26930 FQ	31480 MW	38830 TQ	USBLS	5/15
	Kentucky	Y	24960 FQ	31220 MW	45580 TQ	USBLS	5/15
	Louisville-Jefferson County MSA, KY-IN	Y	25190 FQ	29090 MW	37130 TQ	USBLS	5/15
	Louisiana	Y	32260 FQ	42310 MW	52100 TQ	USBLS	5/15
	Maryland	Y	30869 AE	47399 MW	55664 AEX	MDBLS	4/16
	Baltimore-Columbia-Towson MSA, MD	Y	29340 FQ	39920 MW	52490 TQ	USBLS	5/15
	Massachusetts	Y	29830 FQ	36660 MW	45370 TQ	USBLS	5/15
	Boston-Cambridge-Newton NECTA, MA	Y	25500 FQ	34800 MW	44650 TQ	USBLS	5/15
	Worcester MSA, MA-CT	Y	29270 FQ	34630 MW	41600 TQ	USBLS	5/15
	Michigan	Y	30230 FQ	36690 MW	47380 TQ	USBLS	5/15
	Detroit-Dearborn-Livonia PMSA, MI	Y	19790 FQ	28410 MW	35030 TQ	USBLS	5/15
	Grand Rapids-Wyoming MSA, MI	Y	28860 FQ	34400 MW	39690 TQ	USBLS	5/15
	Minnesota	Y	29432 FQ	38584 MW	48668 TQ	MNBLS	1/16-3/16
	Minneapolis-St. Paul-Bloomington MSA, MN-WI	Y	29017 FQ	39070 MW	47332 TQ	MNBLS	1/16-3/16
	Mississippi	Y	25060 FQ	30340 MW	37550 TQ	USBLS	5/15
	Hattiesburg MSA, MS	Y	27990 FQ	33270 MW	37490 TQ	USBLS	5/15
	Missouri	Y	29980 FQ	41890 MW	53930 TQ	USBLS	5/15
	Kansas City MSA, MO-KS	Y	28930 FQ	35200 MW	42590 TQ	USBLS	5/15
	St. Louis MSA, MO-IL	Y	28420 FQ	37080 MW	43960 TQ	USBLS	5/15
	Nebraska	Y	28330 FQ	32550 MW	37775 TQ	NEBLS	7/16-9/16
	Omaha-Council Bluffs MSA, NE-IA	Y	27780 FQ	32990 MW	38915 TQ	NEBLS	7/16-9/16
	Nevada	Y	23600 FQ	29570 MW	36310 TQ	USBLS	5/15
	Las Vegas-Henderson-Paradise MSA, NV	Y	24290 FQ	29960 MW	36520 TQ	USBLS	5/15
	New Hampshire	H	12.98 AE	21.66 MW	24.86 AEX	NHBLS	6/16
	New Jersey	Y	27160 FQ	31640 MW	39380 TQ	USBLS	5/15
	Camden PMSA, NJ	Y	27370 FQ	32870 MW	41130 TQ	USBLS	5/15
	Newark PMSA, NJ-PA	Y	27250 FQ	30690 MW	38810 TQ	USBLS	5/15
	Trenton MSA, NJ	Y	28320 FQ	32140 MW	37390 TQ	USBLS	5/15
	New Mexico	Y	18590 FQ	20890 MW	26170 TQ	USBLS	5/15
	Albuquerque MSA, NM	Y	21990 FQ	24910 MW	29020 TQ	USBLS	5/15
	New York	Y	23420 AE	35990 MW	42370 AEX	NYBLS	1/16-3/16
	Buffalo-Cheektowaga-Niagara Falls MSA, NY	Y	28520 FQ	39800 MW	45720 TQ	USBLS	5/15
	Nassau County-Suffolk County PMSA, NY	Y	20940 FQ	25210 MW	32070 TQ	USBLS	5/15
	New York-Jersey City-White Plains PMSA, NY-NJ	Y	24880 FQ	30630 MW	38570 TQ	USBLS	5/15
	Rochester MSA, NY	Y	23550 FQ	29410 MW	38500 TQ	USBLS	5/15
	North Carolina	Y	24680 FQ	33220 MW	41480 TQ	USBLS	5/15
	Charlotte-Concord-Gastonia MSA, NC-SC	Y	26250 FQ	34040 MW	44900 TQ	USBLS	5/15
	Raleigh MSA, NC	Y	28900 FQ	34060 MW	39360 TQ	USBLS	5/15
	Ohio	Y	28590 FQ	35050 MW	41930 TQ	USBLS	5/15
	Cincinnati MSA, OH-KY-IN	Y	29270 FQ	34820 MW	40350 TQ	USBLS	5/15
	Cleveland-Elyria MSA, OH	Y	27100 FQ	36210 MW	45110 TQ	USBLS	5/15

AE	Average entry wage	AWR	Average wage range	H	Hourly
AEX	Average experienced wage	B	Biweekly	HI	Highest wage paid
ATC	Average total compensation	D	Daily	HR	High end range
AW	Average wage paid	FQ	First quartile wage	LO	Lowest wage paid

LR	Low end range	MTC	Median total compensation	TCC	Total cash compensation
M	Monthly	MW	Median wage paid	TQ	Third quartile wage
MCC	Median cash compensation	MWR	Median wage range	W	Weekly
ME	Median entry wage	S	See annotated source	Y	Yearly

Occupation/Type/Industry	Location	Per	Low	Mid	High	Source	Date
Paper Goods Machine Setter, Operator, and Tender	Columbus MSA, OH	Y	27650 FQ	33020 MW	36870 TQ	USBLS	5/15
	Oklahoma	Y	32900 FQ	43660 MW	55240 TQ	USBLS	5/15
	Oklahoma City MSA, OK	Y	17560 FQ	22090 MW	31710 TQ	USBLS	5/15
	Tulsa MSA, OK	Y	36220 FQ	47420 MW	56580 TQ	USBLS	5/15
	Oregon	H	14.20 FQ	18.43 MW	21.84 TQ	ORBLS	2016
	Portland-Vancouver-Hillsboro MSA, OR-WA	Y	34710 FQ	42580 MW	48080 TQ	USBLS	5/15
	Pennsylvania	Y	29940 FQ	37520 MW	46190 TQ	USBLS	5/15
	Allentown-Bethlehem-Easton MSA, PA-NJ	Y	29580 FQ	35300 MW	41580 TQ	USBLS	5/15
	Harrisburg-Carlisle MSA, PA	Y	25040 FQ	31440 MW	39280 TQ	USBLS	5/15
	Montgomery County-Bucks County-Chester County PMSA, PA	Y	24950 FQ	36360 MW	44050 TQ	USBLS	5/15
	Philadelphia PMSA, PA	Y	36730 FQ	50560 MW	60560 TQ	USBLS	5/15
	Pittsburgh MSA, PA	Y	21510 FQ	27270 MW	37670 TQ	USBLS	5/15
	Rhode Island	Y	23000 FQ	29140 MW	36800 TQ	USBLS	5/15
	Providence-Warwick MSA, RI-MA	Y	23120 FQ	29010 MW	36700 TQ	USBLS	5/15
	South Carolina	Y	34730 FQ	49320 MW	63060 TQ	USBLS	5/15
	Charleston-North Charleston MSA, SC	Y	30260 FQ	53090 MW	61510 TQ	USBLS	5/15
	Columbia MSA, SC	Y	53420 FQ	61890 MW	70040 TQ	USBLS	5/15
	Greenville-Anderson-Mauldin MSA, SC	Y	28510 FQ	35100 MW	44470 TQ	USBLS	5/15
	South Dakota	Y	24990 FQ	29560 MW	36090 TQ	USBLS	5/15
	Sioux Falls MSA, SD	Y	29030 FQ	33680 MW	39470 TQ	USBLS	5/15
	Tennessee	Y	27130 FQ	33050 MW	38740 TQ	USBLS	5/15
	Knoxville MSA, TN	Y	21980 FQ	25350 MW	30300 TQ	USBLS	5/15
	Memphis MSA, TN-MS-AR	Y	29480 FQ	34280 MW	38310 TQ	USBLS	5/15
	Nashville-Davidson–Murfreesboro–Franklin MSA, TN	Y	20350 FQ	28780 MW	37960 TQ	USBLS	5/15
	Texas	Y	24230 FQ	31580 MW	38890 TQ	USBLS	5/15
	Austin-Round Rock MSA, TX	Y	20090 FQ	24180 MW	28710 TQ	USBLS	5/15
	Dallas-Plano-Irving PMSA, TX	Y	25960 FQ	31660 MW	38990 TQ	USBLS	5/15
	Fort Worth-Arlington PMSA, TX	Y	22980 FQ	30540 MW	37020 TQ	USBLS	5/15
	Houston-The Woodlands-Sugar Land MSA, TX	Y	22280 FQ	33020 MW	38950 TQ	USBLS	5/15
	San Antonio-New Braunfels MSA, TX	Y	19420 FQ	22800 MW	27900 TQ	USBLS	5/15
	Utah	Y	26240 FQ	34820 MW	42650 TQ	USBLS	5/15
	Salt Lake City MSA, UT	Y	24980 FQ	30230 MW	36800 TQ	USBLS	5/15
	Vermont	Y	32180 FQ	36940 MW	43280 TQ	USBLS	5/15
	Virginia	Y	32100 FQ	39460 MW	56510 TQ	USBLS	5/15
	Richmond MSA, VA	Y	34670 FQ	50050 MW	63780 TQ	USBLS	5/15
	Virginia Beach-Norfolk-Newport News MSA, VA-NC	Y	26920 FQ	33370 MW	41060 TQ	USBLS	5/15
	Washington	H	17.69 FQ	21.98 MW	26.67 TQ	WABLS	3/16
	Seattle-Bellevue-Everett PMSA, WA	H	16.65 FQ	19.77 MW	23.43 TQ	WABLS	3/16
	Tacoma-Lakewood PMSA, WA	H	17.82 FQ	22.99 MW	28.02 TQ	WABLS	3/16
	Wisconsin	Y	31820 FQ	37450 MW	45550 TQ	USBLS	5/15
	Milwaukee-Waukesha-West Allis MSA, WI	Y	30950 FQ	35140 MW	39010 TQ	USBLS	5/15
	Puerto Rico	Y	16970 FQ	18420 MW	19910 TQ	USBLS	5/15
	San Juan-Carolina-Caguas MSA, PR	Y	16950 FQ	18390 MW	19870 TQ	USBLS	5/15
Paperhanger	Arizona	Y	18280 FQ	19690 MW	28920 TQ	USBLS	5/15
	Phoenix-Mesa-Scottsdale MSA, AZ	Y	18260 FQ	19660 MW	28740 TQ	USBLS	5/15
	California	H	13.03 FQ	18.02 MW	33.43 TQ	CABLS	1/16-3/16
	Anaheim-Santa Ana-Irvine PMSA, CA	H	11.16 FQ	12.68 MW	14.99 TQ	CABLS	1/16-3/16
	Riverside-San Bernardino-Ontario MSA, CA	H	32.26 FQ	34.55 MW	36.84 TQ	CABLS	1/16-3/16
	Colorado	Y	27170 FQ	29670 MW	35730 TQ	USBLS	5/15
	Connecticut	Y		46907 MW		CTBLS	1/16-3/16
	Delaware	Y	28820 FQ	36420 MW	46070 TQ	USBLS	5/15

AE	Average entry wage	AWR	Average wage range	H	Hourly	LR	Low end range	MTC	Median total compensation	TCC	Total cash compensation
AEX	Average experienced wage	B	Biweekly	HI	Highest wage paid	M	Monthly	MW	Median wage paid	TQ	Third quartile wage
ATC	Average total compensation	D	Daily	HR	High end range	MCC	Median cash compensation	MWR	Median wage range	W	Weekly
AW	Average wage paid	FQ	First quartile wage	LO	Lowest wage paid	ME	Median entry wage	S	See annotated source	Y	Yearly

Occupation/Type/Industry	Location	Per	Low	Mid	High	Source	Date
Paperhanger	Wilmington PMSA, DE-MD-NJ	Y	28820 FQ	36420 MW	46070 TQ	USBLS	5/15
	Florida	H	12.69 AE	17.32 MW	20.82 AEX	FLBLS	7/16-9/16
	Miami-Miami Beach-Kendall PMSA, FL	H	16.83 AE	19.08 MW	20.38 AEX	FLBLS	7/16-9/16
	Georgia	Y	27390 FQ	34160 MW	42320 TQ	USBLS	5/15
	Illinois	Y	30730 FQ	35180 MW	39980 TQ	USBLS	5/15
	Indiana	Y	30140 FQ	36780 MW	47960 TQ	USBLS	5/15
	Baltimore-Columbia-Towson MSA, MD	Y	33620 FQ	36010 MW	38390 TQ	USBLS	5/15
	Minnesota	Y	21391 FQ	22975 MW	24559 TQ	MNBLS	1/16-3/16
	Missouri	Y	26800 FQ	31420 MW	46360 TQ	USBLS	5/15
	Kansas City MSA, MO-KS	Y	39430 FQ	47920 MW	59370 TQ	USBLS	5/15
	New York	Y	27390 AE	39080 MW	53300 AEX	NYBLS	1/16-3/16
	Nassau County-Suffolk County PMSA, NY	Y	43880 FQ	48080 MW	91160 TQ	USBLS	5/15
	New York-Jersey City-White Plains PMSA, NY-NJ	Y	24430 FQ	34630 MW	56710 TQ	USBLS	5/15
	Rochester MSA, NY	Y	32690 FQ	34980 MW	37260 TQ	USBLS	5/15
	North Carolina	Y	28090 FQ	35640 MW	47740 TQ	USBLS	5/15
	Ohio	Y	26920 FQ	33820 MW	40790 TQ	USBLS	5/15
	Cincinnati MSA, OH-KY-IN	Y	29010 FQ	36400 MW	47340 TQ	USBLS	5/15
	Oregon	H	15.93 FQ	17.99 MW	23.49 TQ	ORBLS	2016
	Pennsylvania	Y	35440 FQ	42200 MW	48130 TQ	USBLS	5/15
	South Carolina	Y	28510 FQ	33880 MW	38340 TQ	USBLS	5/15
	Texas	Y	26660 FQ	29800 MW	35430 TQ	USBLS	5/15
	Utah	Y	22190 FQ	24340 MW	31400 TQ	USBLS	5/15
	Washington	H	16.17 FQ	22.62 MW	27.44 TQ	WABLS	3/16
Paralegal and Legal Assistant	Alabama	Y	30284 AE	45289 AW	52791 AEX	ALBLS	6/16
	Birmingham-Hoover MSA, AL	Y	32955 AE	49335 AW	57520 AEX	ALBLS	6/16
	Alaska	Y	50670 FQ	60610 MW	77990 TQ	USBLS	5/15
	Anchorage MSA, AK	Y	51440 FQ	62600 MW	85540 TQ	USBLS	5/15
	Arizona	Y	38710 FQ	50040 MW	60830 TQ	USBLS	5/15
	Phoenix-Mesa-Scottsdale MSA, AZ	Y	39650 FQ	51420 MW	61620 TQ	USBLS	5/15
	Tucson MSA, AZ	Y	35840 FQ	46200 MW	58010 TQ	USBLS	5/15
	Arkansas	Y	29480 FQ	36180 MW	45910 TQ	USBLS	5/15
	Little Rock-North Little Rock-Conway MSA, AR	Y	33130 FQ	39870 MW	50910 TQ	USBLS	5/15
	California	H	20.26 FQ	27.61 MW	35.96 TQ	CABLS	1/16-3/16
	Anaheim-Santa Ana-Irvine PMSA, CA	H	17.91 FQ	23.65 MW	31.71 TQ	CABLS	1/16-3/16
	Los Angeles-Long Beach-Glendale PMSA, CA	H	20.03 FQ	27.91 MW	36.02 TQ	CABLS	1/16-3/16
	Oakland-Hayward-Berkeley PMSA, CA	H	22.90 FQ	28.55 MW	33.85 TQ	CABLS	1/16-3/16
	Riverside-San Bernardino-Ontario MSA, CA	H	17.64 FQ	26.66 MW	36.12 TQ	CABLS	1/16-3/16
	Sacramento–Roseville–Arden-Arcade MSA, CA	H	18.28 FQ	25.60 MW	34.27 TQ	CABLS	1/16-3/16
	San Diego-Carlsbad MSA, CA	H	18.88 FQ	28.28 MW	35.47 TQ	CABLS	1/16-3/16
	San Francisco-Redwood City-South San Francisco PMSA, CA	H	26.96 FQ	34.46 MW	42.77 TQ	CABLS	1/16-3/16
	Colorado	Y	38550 FQ	50070 MW	65020 TQ	USBLS	5/15
	Denver-Aurora-Lakewood MSA, CO	Y	39140 FQ	51210 MW	68590 TQ	USBLS	5/15
	Connecticut	Y		51780 MW		CTBLS	1/16-3/16
	Bridgeport-Stamford-Norwalk MSA, CT	Y	46030 FQ	58090 MW	73940 TQ	USBLS	5/15
	Hartford-West Hartford-East Hartford MSA, CT	Y	37490 FQ	50420 MW	60960 TQ	USBLS	5/15
	Delaware	Y	43030 FQ	50150 MW	64660 TQ	USBLS	5/15
	Wilmington PMSA, DE-MD-NJ	Y	44000 FQ	52430 MW	68420 TQ	USBLS	5/15
	District of Columbia	Y	54420 FQ	75120 MW	93990 TQ	USBLS	5/15
	Washington-Arlington-Alexandria PMSA, DC-VA-MD-WV	Y	49130 FQ	65130 MW	85890 TQ	USBLS	5/15
	Florida	H	17.13 AE	23.31 MW	28.58 AEX	FLBLS	7/16-9/16

AE	Average entry wage	AWR	Average wage range	H	Hourly	LR	Low end range	MTC	Median total compensation	TCC	Total cash compensation
AEX	Average experienced wage	B	Biweekly	HI	Highest wage paid	M	Monthly	MW	Median wage paid	TQ	Third quartile wage
ATC	Average total compensation	D	Daily	HR	High end range	MCC	Median cash compensation	MWR	Median wage range	W	Weekly
AW	Average wage paid	FQ	First quartile wage	LO	Lowest wage paid	ME	Median entry wage	S	See annotated source	Y	Yearly

1178

Occupation/Type/Industry	Location	Per	Low	Mid	High	Source	Date
Paralegal and Legal Assistant	Fort Lauderdale-Pompano Beach-Deerfield Beach PMSA, FL	H	17.33 AE	22.93 MW	27.18 AEX	FLBLS	7/16-9/16
	Miami-Miami Beach-Kendall PMSA, FL	H	18.39 AE	28.53 MW	33.83 AEX	FLBLS	7/16-9/16
	Orlando-Kissimmee-Sanford MSA, FL	H	19.26 AE	24.06 MW	29.36 AEX	FLBLS	7/16-9/16
	Tampa-St. Petersburg-Clearwater MSA, FL	H	16.47 AE	22.84 MW	28.03 AEX	FLBLS	7/16-9/16
	Georgia	Y	39450 FQ	49980 MW	63730 TQ	USBLS	5/15
	Atlanta-Sandy Springs-Roswell MSA, GA	Y	41140 FQ	52400 MW	66920 TQ	USBLS	5/15
	Augusta-Richmond County MSA, GA-SC	Y	40050 FQ	45820 MW	53410 TQ	USBLS	5/15
	Hawaii	Y	35400 FQ	44590 MW	57160 TQ	USBLS	5/15
	Urban Honolulu MSA, HI	Y	35210 FQ	43890 MW	57000 TQ	USBLS	5/15
	Idaho	Y	33350 FQ	41260 MW	48270 TQ	USBLS	5/15
	Boise City MSA, ID	Y	37980 FQ	44550 MW	50910 TQ	USBLS	5/15
	Illinois	Y	37120 FQ	48310 MW	61410 TQ	USBLS	5/15
	Chicago-Naperville-Arlington Heights PMSA, IL	Y	37480 FQ	48870 MW	62000 TQ	USBLS	5/15
	Lake County-Kenosha County PMSA, IL-WI	Y	45850 FQ	56620 MW	67480 TQ	USBLS	5/15
	Indiana	Y	33090 FQ	40760 MW	54140 TQ	USBLS	5/15
	Gary PMSA, IN	Y	30990 FQ	37590 MW	52780 TQ	USBLS	5/15
	Indianapolis-Carmel-Anderson MSA, IN	Y	36020 FQ	47210 MW	60370 TQ	USBLS	5/15
	Iowa	Y	35480 FQ	46300 MW	52650 TQ	USBLS	5/15
	Des Moines-West Des Moines MSA, IA	Y	40050 FQ	51110 MW	59680 TQ	USBLS	5/15
	Kansas	Y	35720 FQ	42010 MW	50010 TQ	USBLS	5/15
	Wichita MSA, KS	Y	40350 FQ	46590 MW	55250 TQ	USBLS	5/15
	Kentucky	Y	34850 FQ	45200 MW	56580 TQ	USBLS	5/15
	Louisville-Jefferson County MSA, KY-IN	Y	40330 FQ	46160 MW	55350 TQ	USBLS	5/15
	Louisiana	Y	32850 FQ	41380 MW	51890 TQ	USBLS	5/15
	Baton Rouge MSA, LA	Y	33110 FQ	39990 MW	49770 TQ	USBLS	5/15
	New Orleans-Metairie MSA, LA	Y	37400 FQ	46590 MW	56070 TQ	USBLS	5/15
	Maine	Y	37120 FQ	44400 MW	53170 TQ	USBLS	5/15
	Portland-South Portland MSA, ME	Y	37720 FQ	48410 MW	58160 TQ	USBLS	5/15
	Maryland	Y	35646 AE	52882 MW	61500 AEX	MDBLS	4/16
	Baltimore-Columbia-Towson MSA, MD	Y	43060 FQ	53740 MW	61970 TQ	USBLS	5/15
	Salisbury MSA, MD-DE	Y	37170 FQ	43260 MW	49030 TQ	USBLS	5/15
	Massachusetts	Y	37190 FQ	48870 MW	65720 TQ	USBLS	5/15
	Boston-Cambridge-Newton NECTA, MA	Y	36350 FQ	49180 MW	68380 TQ	USBLS	5/15
	Worcester MSA, MA-CT	Y	43690 FQ	53560 MW	61750 TQ	USBLS	5/15
	Michigan	Y	37400 FQ	47610 MW	60190 TQ	USBLS	5/15
	Detroit-Dearborn-Livonia PMSA, MI	Y	46520 FQ	59160 MW	73040 TQ	USBLS	5/15
	Grand Rapids-Wyoming MSA, MI	Y	36500 FQ	47150 MW	63050 TQ	USBLS	5/15
	Minnesota	Y	42237 FQ	53074 MW	65624 TQ	MNBLS	1/16-3/16
	Minneapolis-St. Paul-Bloomington MSA, MN-WI	Y	44425 FQ	55765 MW	68185 TQ	MNBLS	1/16-3/16
	Mississippi	Y	30580 FQ	41660 MW	56550 TQ	USBLS	5/15
	Jackson MSA, MS	Y	35180 FQ	53190 MW	62450 TQ	USBLS	5/15
	Missouri	Y	33440 FQ	44350 MW	58090 TQ	USBLS	5/15
	Kansas City MSA, MO-KS	Y	37600 FQ	45540 MW	57370 TQ	USBLS	5/15
	St. Louis MSA, MO-IL	Y	30600 FQ	48410 MW	60030 TQ	USBLS	5/15
	Montana	Y	34110 FQ	41840 MW	51850 TQ	USBLS	5/15
	Billings MSA, MT	Y	37900 FQ	51430 MW	62950 TQ	USBLS	5/15
	Nebraska	Y	35220 FQ	43315 MW	55920 TQ	NEBLS	7/16-9/16
	Omaha-Council Bluffs MSA, NE-IA	Y	36205 FQ	45885 MW	58420 TQ	NEBLS	7/16-9/16
	Nevada	Y	42000 FQ	50280 MW	61090 TQ	USBLS	5/15
	Las Vegas-Henderson-Paradise MSA, NV	Y	41860 FQ	50310 MW	61160 TQ	USBLS	5/15
	New Hampshire	H	18.10 AE	23.74 MW	28.17 AEX	NHBLS	6/16

AE	Average entry wage	AWR	Average wage range	H	Hourly	LR	Low end range	MTC	Median total compensation	TCC	Total cash compensation
AEX	Average experienced wage	B	Biweekly	HI	Highest wage paid	M	Monthly	MW	Median wage paid	TQ	Third quartile wage
ATC	Average total compensation	D	Daily	HR	High end range	MCC	Median cash compensation	MWR	Median wage range	W	Weekly
AW	Average wage paid	FQ	First quartile wage	LO	Lowest wage paid	ME	Median entry wage	S	See annotated source	Y	Yearly

1179

Occupation/Type/Industry	Location	Per	Low	Mid	High	Source	Date
Paralegal and Legal Assistant	Manchester NECTA, NH	H	18.77 AE	26.18 MW	29.73 AEX	NHBLS	6/16
	Nashua NECTA, NH-MA	Y	39600 FQ	43850 MW	48010 TQ	USBLS	5/15
	New Jersey	Y	43040 FQ	55300 MW	69060 TQ	USBLS	5/15
	Camden PMSA, NJ	Y	41750 FQ	52270 MW	65630 TQ	USBLS	5/15
	Newark PMSA, NJ-PA	Y	45600 FQ	60490 MW	76210 TQ	USBLS	5/15
	Trenton MSA, NJ	Y	50610 FQ	63280 MW	74610 TQ	USBLS	5/15
	New Mexico	Y	33760 FQ	41660 MW	48120 TQ	USBLS	5/15
	Albuquerque MSA, NM	Y	33030 FQ	41560 MW	47380 TQ	USBLS	5/15
	New York	Y	38620 AE	52850 MW	68830 AEX	NYBLS	1/16-3/16
	Buffalo-Cheektowaga-Niagara Falls MSA, NY	Y	35550 FQ	45450 MW	57090 TQ	USBLS	5/15'
	Nassau County-Suffolk County PMSA, NY	Y	37830 FQ	47860 MW	62250 TQ	USBLS	5/15
	New York-Jersey City-White Plains PMSA, NY-NJ	Y	44200 FQ	55040 MW	73650 TQ	USBLS	5/15
	Rochester MSA, NY	Y	31300 FQ	42710 MW	57800 TQ	USBLS	5/15
	North Carolina	Y	32300 FQ	40330 MW	51060 TQ	USBLS	5/15
	Charlotte-Concord-Gastonia MSA, NC-SC	Y	33990 FQ	42400 MW	54770 TQ	USBLS	5/15
	Raleigh MSA, NC	Y	38110 FQ	48720 MW	60210 TQ	USBLS	5/15
	North Dakota	Y	32370 FQ	42630 MW	53230 TQ	USBLS	5/15
	Fargo MSA, ND-MN	Y	35140 FQ	41800 MW	50490 TQ	USBLS	5/15
	Ohio	Y	33250 FQ	43450 MW	57120 TQ	USBLS	5/15
	Cincinnati MSA, OH-KY-IN	Y	31900 FQ	40970 MW	60380 TQ	USBLS	5/15
	Cleveland-Elyria MSA, OH	Y	34720 FQ	48370 MW	60880 TQ	USBLS	5/15
	Columbus MSA, OH	Y	36640 FQ	46970 MW	59180 TQ	USBLS	5/15
	Oklahoma	Y	28840 FQ	39900 MW	53490 TQ	USBLS	5/15
	Oklahoma City MSA, OK	Y	32490 FQ	43190 MW	56600 TQ	USBLS	5/15
	Tulsa MSA, OK	Y	28260 FQ	40700 MW	54720 TQ	USBLS	5/15
	Oregon	H	20.40 FQ	25.70 MW	32.20 TQ	ORBLS	2016
	Portland-Vancouver-Hillsboro MSA, OR-WA	Y	43520 FQ	55600 MW	69560 TQ	USBLS	5/15
	Pennsylvania	Y	38730 FQ	50660 MW	64560 TQ	USBLS	5/15
	Allentown-Bethlehem-Easton MSA, PA-NJ	Y	37230 FQ	44570 MW	51680 TQ	USBLS	5/15
	Harrisburg-Carlisle MSA, PA	Y	36870 FQ	46010 MW	55580 TQ	USBLS	5/15
	Montgomery County-Bucks County-Chester County PMSA, PA	Y	48570 FQ	58850 MW	71720 TQ	USBLS	5/15
	Philadelphia PMSA, PA	Y	43070 FQ	54800 MW	67850 TQ	USBLS	5/15
	Pittsburgh MSA, PA	Y	43230 FQ	56210 MW	68240 TQ	USBLS	5/15
	Rhode Island	Y	45250 FQ	52790 MW	61100 TQ	USBLS	5/15
	Providence-Warwick MSA, RI-MA	Y	45060 FQ	52520 MW	60910 TQ	USBLS	5/15
	South Carolina	Y	33230 FQ	40850 MW	49360 TQ	USBLS	5/15
	Charleston-North Charleston MSA, SC	Y	36240 FQ	42520 MW	49400 TQ	USBLS	5/15
	Columbia MSA, SC	Y	34820 FQ	42210 MW	49080 TQ	USBLS	5/15
	Greenville-Anderson-Mauldin MSA, SC	Y	30390 FQ	45210 MW	59800 TQ	USBLS	5/15
	South Dakota	Y	33800 FQ	39170 MW	50910 TQ	USBLS	5/15
	Sioux Falls MSA, SD	Y	38120 FQ	46150 MW	55940 TQ	USBLS	5/15
	Tennessee	Y	37000 FQ	46850 MW	59500 TQ	USBLS	5/15
	Knoxville MSA, TN	Y	28500 FQ	43520 MW	60380 TQ	USBLS	5/15
	Memphis MSA, TN-MS-AR	Y	31930 FQ	44010 MW	53440 TQ	USBLS	5/15
	Nashville-Davidson–Murfreesboro–Franklin MSA, TN	Y	43650 FQ	51980 MW	65700 TQ	USBLS	5/15
	Texas	Y	39080 FQ	49700 MW	64700 TQ	USBLS	5/15
	Austin-Round Rock MSA, TX	Y	37390 FQ	47230 MW	62700 TQ	USBLS	5/15
	Dallas-Plano-Irving PMSA, TX	Y	45390 FQ	58460 MW	73530 TQ	USBLS	5/15
	Fort Worth-Arlington PMSA, TX	Y	42260 FQ	52160 MW	68090 TQ	USBLS	5/15
	Houston-The Woodlands-Sugar Land MSA, TX	Y	42430 FQ	54190 MW	67170 TQ	USBLS	5/15
	San Antonio-New Braunfels MSA, TX	Y	32080 FQ	44150 MW	55250 TQ	USBLS	5/15
	Utah	Y	31820 FQ	42270 MW	54480 TQ	USBLS	5/15
	Ogden-Clearfield MSA, UT	Y	27520 FQ	34390 MW	38600 TQ	USBLS	5/15
	Provo-Orem MSA, UT	Y	36300 FQ	45310 MW	64470 TQ	USBLS	5/15
	Salt Lake City MSA, UT	Y	31900 FQ	44230 MW	55710 TQ	USBLS	5/15
	Vermont	Y	42660 FQ	49010 MW	59190 TQ	USBLS	5/15

AE	Average entry wage	AWR	Average wage range	H	Hourly
AEX	Average experienced wage	B	Biweekly	HI	Highest wage paid
ATC	Average total compensation	D	Daily	HR	High end range
AW	Average wage paid	FQ	First quartile wage	LO	Lowest wage paid

LR	Low end range	MTC	Median total compensation	TCC	Total cash compensation
M	Monthly	MW	Median wage paid	TQ	Third quartile wage
MCC	Median cash compensation	MWR	Median wage range	W	Weekly
ME	Median entry wage	S	See annotated source	Y	Yearly

Occupation/Type/Industry	Location	Per	Low	Mid	High	Source	Date
Paralegal and Legal Assistant	Burlington-South Burlington						
	MSA, VT	Y	40430 FQ	50130 MW	59040 TQ	USBLS	5/15
	Virginia	Y	37260 FQ	49520 MW	60900 TQ	USBLS	5/15
	Richmond MSA, VA	Y	40750 FQ	49410 MW	58440 TQ	USBLS	5/15
	Virginia Beach-Norfolk-						
	Newport News MSA, VA-NC	Y	33350 FQ	43860 MW	54990 TQ	USBLS	5/15
	Washington	H	22.09 FQ	27.35 MW	32.67 TQ	WABLS	3/16
	Seattle-Bellevue-Everett						
	PMSA, WA	H	25.02 FQ	29.65 MW	36.10 TQ	WABLS	3/16
	Tacoma-Lakewood PMSA, WA	H	21.96 FQ	25.34 MW	29.02 TQ	WABLS	3/16
	West Virginia	Y	33860 FQ	39620 MW	51180 TQ	USBLS	5/15
	Huntington-Ashland MSA,						
	WV-KY-OH	Y	34570 FQ	39790 MW	52020 TQ	USBLS	5/15
	Wisconsin	Y	35800 FQ	44980 MW	56310 TQ	USBLS	5/15
	Madison MSA, WI	Y	38890 FQ	49670 MW	58220 TQ	USBLS	5/15
	Milwaukee-Waukesha-West						
	Allis MSA, WI	Y	40830 FQ	49520 MW	61270 TQ	USBLS	5/15
	Wyoming	Y	37850 FQ	46760 MW	54020 TQ	USBLS	5/15
	Cheyenne MSA, WY	Y	45300 FQ	48930 MW	56580 TQ	USBLS	5/15
	Puerto Rico	Y	26070 FQ	34650 MW	46320 TQ	USBLS	5/15
	San Juan-Carolina-Caguas						
	MSA, PR	Y	27520 FQ	36140 MW	46770 TQ	USBLS	5/15
	Virgin Islands	Y	40340 FQ	51790 MW	61080 TQ	USBLS	5/15
	Guam	Y	39560 FQ	49490 MW	60150 TQ	USBLS	5/15
Paramedic Coordinator							
Fire Department, Municipal Government	Pacifica, CA	Y			165738 HI	CACIT	6/28/16
Fire Department, Municipal Government	Vallejo, CA	Y			126215 HI	CACIT	6/28/16
Paramilitary Operations Officer/							
Specialized Skills Officer							
Central Intelligence Agency	District of Columbia	Y	60805 LO		100736 HI	CIA07	2016
Park Enforcement Investigator							
Municipal Government	Detroit, MI	M	2700 LO		2817 HI	DETGOV	2016
Park Horticulturist							
Municipal Government	Seattle, WA	H	40.75 LO		47.39 HI	CSSS	1/13/16
Park Manager							
Municipal Government	Belmont, CA	Y			124686 HI	CACIT	6/28/16
Municipal Government	Rowe, MA	Y			45393 HI	FRCOG	2016
Park Naturalist							
County Government	Oakland County, MI	B	1740 LO		2265 HI	MIOAK2	10/1/16
Municipal Government	Long Beach, CA	Y		52953 AW		CACIT	6/28/16
Park Planner							
Municipal Government	Carlsbad, CA	H	34.23 LO	39.50 MW	44.77 HI	CCCA01	6/28/16
Park Ranger							
Municipal Government	Fairfield, CA	Y			56874 HI	CACIT	6/28/16
National Parks	United States	Y	25621 LO		55666 HI	WSJ03	2016
Park Specialist							
Park Maintenance, Municipal Government	Lake Elsinore, CA	Y			67852 HI	CACIT	6/28/16
Parking Analyst							
Municipal Government	Burbank, CA	Y			81265 HI	CACIT	6/28/16
Municipal Government	West Hollywood, CA	Y			90101 HI	CACIT	6/28/16
Parking Coordinator							
Michigan State University	East Lansing, MI	Y	53775 LO		56021 HI	MSUSAL	10/1/14-9/30/15
Waterfront, Municipal Government	Santa Barbara, CA	Y			63098 HI	CACIT	6/28/16
Parking Enforcement Worker	Alabama	Y	22435 AE	28335 AW	31279 AEX	ALBLS	6/16
	Arizona	Y	23290 FQ	28080 MW	39330 TQ	USBLS	5/15
	Arkansas	Y	19110 FQ	24310 MW	29730 TQ	USBLS	5/15
	California	H	19.87 FQ	23.66 MW	27.97 TQ	CABLS	1/16-3/16
	Anaheim-Santa Ana-Irvine						
	PMSA, CA	H	24.90 FQ	27.15 MW	29.40 TQ	CABLS	1/16-3/16
	Los Angeles-Long Beach-						
	Glendale PMSA, CA	H	19.32 FQ	22.03 MW	24.83 TQ	CABLS	1/16-3/16

AE	Average entry wage	AWR	Average wage range	H	Hourly	LR	Low end range	MTC	Median total compensation	TCC	Total cash compensation
AEX	Average experienced wage	B	Biweekly	HI	Highest wage paid	M	Monthly	MW	Median wage paid	TQ	Third quartile wage
ATC	Average total compensation	D	Daily	HR	High end range	MCC	Median cash compensation	MWR	Median wage range	W	Weekly
AW	Average wage paid	FQ	First quartile wage	LO	Lowest wage paid	ME	Median entry wage	S	See annotated source	Y	Yearly

Parking Enforcement Worker

Occupation/Type/Industry	Location	Per	Low	Mid	High	Source	Date
Parking Enforcement Worker	Oakland-Hayward-Berkeley PMSA, CA	H	21.04 FQ	24.74 MW	28.22 TQ	CABLS	1/16-3/16
	Riverside-San Bernardino-Ontario MSA, CA	H	18.76 FQ	21.06 MW	23.04 TQ	CABLS	1/16-3/16
	Sacramento–Roseville–Arden-Arcade MSA, CA	H	16.61 FQ	23.07 MW	33.47 TQ	CABLS	1/16-3/16
	San Diego-Carlsbad MSA, CA	H	19.40 FQ	21.57 MW	23.77 TQ	CABLS	1/16-3/16
	San Francisco-Redwood City-South San Francisco PMSA, CA	H	25.23 FQ	27.49 MW	29.76 TQ	CABLS	1/16-3/16
	Colorado	Y	34920 FQ	41010 MW	47070 TQ	USBLS	5/15
	Denver-Aurora-Lakewood MSA, CO	Y	36440 FQ	42160 MW	47250 TQ	USBLS	5/15
	Connecticut	Y		48407 MW		CTBLS	1/16-3/16
	Bridgeport-Stamford-Norwalk MSA, CT	Y	50130 FQ	54810 MW	59340 TQ	USBLS	5/15
	District of Columbia	Y	42920 FQ	51090 MW	52510 TQ	USBLS	5/15
	Washington-Arlington-Alexandria PMSA, DC-VA-MD-WV	Y	36230 FQ	47010 MW	52500 TQ	USBLS	5/15
	Florida	H	13.13 AE	17.95 MW	23.26 AEX	FLBLS	7/16-9/16
	Fort Lauderdale-Pompano Beach-Deerfield Beach PMSA, FL	H	14.75 AE	18.19 MW	21.58 AEX	FLBLS	7/16-9/16
	Miami-Miami Beach-Kendall PMSA, FL	H	15.60 AE	26.08 MW	29.91 AEX	FLBLS	7/16-9/16
	Orlando-Kissimmee-Sanford MSA, FL	H	13.79 AE	14.94 MW	17.61 AEX	FLBLS	7/16-9/16
	Tampa-St. Petersburg-Clearwater MSA, FL	H	12.90 AE	17.34 MW	19.65 AEX	FLBLS	7/16-9/16
	Georgia	Y	24690 FQ	32860 MW	41840 TQ	USBLS	5/15
	Atlanta-Sandy Springs-Roswell MSA, GA	Y	31520 FQ	36920 MW	45860 TQ	USBLS	5/15
	Illinois	Y	30440 FQ	42620 MW	53340 TQ	USBLS	5/15
	Chicago-Naperville-Arlington Heights PMSA, IL	Y	31410 FQ	43680 MW	54530 TQ	USBLS	5/15
	Indiana	Y	25480 FQ	31580 MW	36230 TQ	USBLS	5/15
	Iowa	Y	38450 FQ	43500 MW	48090 TQ	USBLS	5/15
	Kansas	Y	27590 FQ	30780 MW	36350 TQ	USBLS	5/15
	Kentucky	Y	25900 FQ	29560 MW	35590 TQ	USBLS	5/15
	Louisiana	Y	18490 FQ	20660 MW	23080 TQ	USBLS	5/15
	Maine	Y	26740 FQ	30270 MW	42920 TQ	USBLS	5/15
	Maryland	Y	25342 AE	34287 MW	38759 AEX	MDBLS	4/16
	Baltimore-Columbia-Towson MSA, MD	Y	24250 FQ	29810 MW	35800 TQ	USBLS	5/15
	Massachusetts	Y	32770 FQ	41230 MW	49780 TQ	USBLS	5/15
	Boston-Cambridge-Newton NECTA, MA	Y	38760 FQ	46420 MW	55490 TQ	USBLS	5/15
	Michigan	Y	25890 FQ	29480 MW	35450 TQ	USBLS	5/15
	Detroit-Dearborn-Livonia PMSA, MI	Y	26180 FQ	28550 MW	30910 TQ	USBLS	5/15
	Minnesota	Y	32013 FQ	34881 MW	37739 TQ	MNBLS	1/16-3/16
	Minneapolis-St. Paul-Bloomington MSA, MN-WI	Y	32609 FQ	35113 MW	37618 TQ	MNBLS	1/16-3/16
	Mississippi	Y	23440 FQ	26920 MW	29810 TQ	USBLS	5/15
	Missouri	Y	29370 FQ	34870 MW	39770 TQ	USBLS	5/15
	Kansas City MSA, MO-KS	Y	28420 FQ	33300 MW	38730 TQ	USBLS	5/15
	Nevada	Y	34410 FQ	43520 MW	52710 TQ	USBLS	5/15
	Las Vegas-Henderson-Paradise MSA, NV	Y	36060 FQ	43970 MW	52370 TQ	USBLS	5/15
	New Hampshire	H	13.58 AE	17.16 MW	20.41 AEX	NHBLS	6/16
	New Jersey	Y	28310 FQ	34900 MW	40780 TQ	USBLS	5/15
	Newark PMSA, NJ-PA	Y	27370 FQ	34230 MW	39570 TQ	USBLS	5/15
	New York	Y	29790 AE	38630 MW	47430 AEX	NYBLS	1/16-3/16
	Nassau County-Suffolk County PMSA, NY	Y	29840 FQ	38920 MW	47020 TQ	USBLS	5/15
	New York-Jersey City-White Plains PMSA, NY-NJ	Y	32350 FQ	37310 MW	46300 TQ	USBLS	5/15
	Rochester MSA, NY	Y	28110 FQ	34880 MW	42620 TQ	USBLS	5/15
	North Carolina	Y	26130 FQ	29990 MW	36760 TQ	USBLS	5/15
	Ohio	Y	27930 FQ	35650 MW	43110 TQ	USBLS	5/15
	Cincinnati MSA, OH-KY-IN	Y	32300 FQ	38610 MW	44440 TQ	USBLS	5/15

AE	Average entry wage	AWR	Average wage range	H	Hourly
AEX	Average experienced wage	B	Biweekly	HI	Highest wage paid
ATC	Average total compensation	D	Daily	HR	High end range
AW	Average wage paid	FQ	First quartile wage	LO	Lowest wage paid

LR Low end range · MTC Median total compensation · TCC Total cash compensation · M Monthly · MW Median wage paid · TQ Third quartile wage · MCC Median cash compensation · MWR Median wage range · W Weekly · ME Median entry wage · S See annotated source · Y Yearly

Occupation/Type/Industry	Location	Per	Low	Mid	High	Source	Date
Parking Enforcement Worker	Cleveland-Elyria MSA, OH	Y	28620 FQ	33350 MW	37510 TQ	USBLS	5/15
	Oklahoma	Y	18940 FQ	26890 MW	32690 TQ	USBLS	5/15
	Oregon	H	19.88 FQ	24.79 MW	27.98 TQ	ORBLS	2016
	Portland-Vancouver-Hillsboro MSA, OR-WA	Y	49380 FQ	54470 MW	59100 TQ	USBLS	5/15
	Pennsylvania	Y	22400 FQ	26730 MW	32960 TQ	USBLS	5/15
	Allentown-Bethlehem-Easton MSA, PA-NJ	Y	23420 FQ	33730 MW	46660 TQ	USBLS	5/15
	Montgomery County-Bucks County-Chester County PMSA, PA	Y	24960 FQ	32890 MW	38940 TQ	USBLS	5/15
	Philadelphia PMSA, PA	Y	21900 FQ	24130 MW	28360 TQ	USBLS	5/15
	Pittsburgh MSA, PA	Y	21650 FQ	23850 MW	27560 TQ	USBLS	5/15
	Rhode Island	Y	27410 FQ	33520 MW	37190 TQ	USBLS	5/15
	Providence-Warwick MSA, RI-MA	Y	28400 FQ	33660 MW	37160 TQ	USBLS	5/15
	South Carolina	Y	24980 FQ	30430 MW	36000 TQ	USBLS	5/15
	Charleston-North Charleston MSA, SC	Y	21680 FQ	24040 MW	31370 TQ	USBLS	5/15
	Columbia MSA, SC	Y	27730 FQ	31160 MW	36530 TQ	USBLS	5/15
	Texas	Y	25860 FQ	30550 MW	37100 TQ	USBLS	5/15
	Dallas-Plano-Irving PMSA, TX	Y	26130 FQ	30550 MW	37050 TQ	USBLS	5/15
	Utah	Y	26660 FQ	31530 MW	41720 TQ	USBLS	5/15
	Salt Lake City MSA, UT	Y	27360 FQ	33470 MW	43220 TQ	USBLS	5/15
	Vermont	Y	33860 FQ	37180 MW	41530 TQ	USBLS	5/15
	Virginia	Y	22050 FQ	24600 MW	37740 TQ	USBLS	5/15
	Richmond MSA, VA	Y	21030 FQ	22560 MW	24100 TQ	USBLS	5/15
	Virginia Beach-Norfolk-Newport News MSA, VA-NC	Y	21390 FQ	23390 MW	27180 TQ	USBLS	5/15
	Washington	H	22.37 FQ	26.32 MW	28.70 TQ	WABLS	3/16
	Seattle-Bellevue-Everett PMSA, WA	H	25.42 FQ	27.32 MW	29.22 TQ	WABLS	3/16
	Tacoma-Lakewood PMSA, WA	H	15.38 FQ	22.30 MW	27.04 TQ	WABLS	3/16
	West Virginia	Y	18810 FQ	22030 MW	27550 TQ	USBLS	5/15
	Wisconsin	Y	35330 FQ	42980 MW	48420 TQ	USBLS	5/15
Parking Lot Attendant	Alabama	Y	17670 AE	21269 AW	23069 AEX	ALBLS	6/16
	Birmingham-Hoover MSA, AL	Y	17690 AE	21177 AW	22915 AEX	ALBLS	6/16
	Alaska	Y	20040 FQ	22820 MW	26350 TQ	USBLS	5/15
	Anchorage MSA, AK	Y	19960 FQ	22930 MW	26640 TQ	USBLS	5/15
	Arizona	Y	19000 FQ	21800 MW	26070 TQ	USBLS	5/15
	Phoenix-Mesa-Scottsdale MSA, AZ	Y	19120 FQ	22060 MW	27450 TQ	USBLS	5/15
	Tucson MSA, AZ	Y	18740 FQ	21330 MW	24100 TQ	USBLS	5/15
	Arkansas	Y	17560 FQ	19500 MW	22750 TQ	USBLS	5/15
	Little Rock-North Little Rock-Conway MSA, AR	Y	17740 FQ	20020 MW	23060 TQ	USBLS	5/15
	California	H	9.62 FQ	10.79 MW	12.57 TQ	CABLS	1/16-3/16
	Anaheim-Santa Ana-Irvine PMSA, CA	H	9.73 FQ	10.87 MW	12.16 TQ	CABLS	1/16-3/16
	Los Angeles-Long Beach-Glendale PMSA, CA	H	9.61 FQ	10.48 MW	11.86 TQ	CABLS	1/16-3/16
	Oakland-Hayward-Berkeley PMSA, CA	H	9.79 FQ	11.59 MW	15.67 TQ	CABLS	1/16-3/16
	Riverside-San Bernardino-Ontario MSA, CA	H	9.43 FQ	9.66 MW	11.49 TQ	CABLS	1/16-3/16
	Sacramento–Roseville–Arden-Arcade MSA, CA	H	9.63 FQ	10.64 MW	12.73 TQ	CABLS	1/16-3/16
	San Diego-Carlsbad MSA, CA	H	9.36 FQ	10.76 MW	13.05 TQ	CABLS	1/16-3/16
	San Francisco-Redwood City-South San Francisco PMSA, CA	H	11.17 FQ	13.27 MW	15.10 TQ	CABLS	1/16-3/16
	Colorado	Y	18850 FQ	21710 MW	26720 TQ	USBLS	5/15
	Denver-Aurora-Lakewood MSA, CO	Y	18770 FQ	21340 MW	25190 TQ	USBLS	5/15
	Connecticut	Y		22758 MW		CTBLS	1/16-3/16
	Bridgeport-Stamford-Norwalk MSA, CT	Y	20780 FQ	24430 MW	28490 TQ	USBLS	5/15
	Hartford-West Hartford-East Hartford MSA, CT	Y	19420 FQ	21860 MW	25980 TQ	USBLS	5/15
	Delaware	Y	17990 FQ	19660 MW	23840 TQ	USBLS	5/15

AE	Average entry wage	AWR	Average wage range	
AEX	Average experienced wage	B	Biweekly	
ATC	Average total compensation	D	Daily	
AW	Average wage paid	FQ	First quartile wage	

H	Hourly	LR	Low end range	MTC Median total compensation TCC Total cash compensation
HI	Highest wage paid	M	Monthly	MW Median wage paid TQ Third quartile wage
HR	High end range	MCC	Median cash compensation	MWR Median wage range W Weekly
LO	Lowest wage paid	ME	Median entry wage	S See annotated source Y Yearly

Occupation/Type/Industry	Location	Per	Low	Mid	High	Source	Date
Parking Lot Attendant	Wilmington PMSA, DE-MD-NJ	Y	18150 FQ	20190 MW	24170 TQ	USBLS	5/15
	District of Columbia	Y	20130 FQ	20320 MW	23330 TQ	USBLS	5/15
	Washington-Arlington-Alexandria PMSA, DC-VA-MD-WV	Y	20080 FQ	20450 MW	23530 TQ	USBLS	5/15
	Florida	H	8.99 AE	9.41 MW	10.51 AEX	FLBLS	7/16-9/16
	Fort Lauderdale-Pompano Beach-Deerfield Beach PMSA, FL	H	8.89 AE	9.28 MW	10.14 AEX	FLBLS	7/16-9/16
	Miami-Miami Beach-Kendall PMSA, FL	H	9.03 AE	9.36 MW	10.57 AEX	FLBLS	7/16-9/16
	Orlando-Kissimmee-Sanford MSA, FL	H	9.03 AE	9.42 MW	9.98 AEX	FLBLS	7/16-9/16
	Tampa-St. Petersburg-Clearwater MSA, FL	H	9.05 AE	9.65 MW	10.81 AEX	FLBLS	7/16-9/16
	Georgia	Y	17500 FQ	19400 MW	23740 TQ	USBLS	5/15
	Atlanta-Sandy Springs-Roswell MSA, GA	Y	17670 FQ	19720 MW	24060 TQ	USBLS	5/15
	Augusta-Richmond County MSA, GA-SC	Y	17430 FQ	19240 MW	26390 TQ	USBLS	5/15
	Hawaii	Y	18220 FQ	20270 MW	26450 TQ	USBLS	5/15
	Urban Honolulu MSA, HI	Y	18340 FQ	20520 MW	27000 TQ	USBLS	5/15
	Idaho	Y	17320 FQ	19010 MW	23810 TQ	USBLS	5/15
	Boise City MSA, ID	Y	17510 FQ	19480 MW	24480 TQ	USBLS	5/15
	Illinois	Y	19220 FQ	22090 MW	28260 TQ	USBLS	5/15
	Chicago-Naperville-Arlington Heights PMSA, IL	Y	19290 FQ	22380 MW	28550 TQ	USBLS	5/15
	Lake County-Kenosha County PMSA, IL-WI	Y	18510 FQ	19550 MW	22970 TQ	USBLS	5/15
	Indiana	Y	16990 FQ	18490 MW	20850 TQ	USBLS	5/15
	Gary PMSA, IN	Y	17020 FQ	18200 MW	19380 TQ	USBLS	5/15
	Indianapolis-Carmel-Anderson MSA, IN	Y	16730 FQ	18110 MW	19670 TQ	USBLS	5/15
	Iowa	Y	17760 FQ	20510 MW	25500 TQ	USBLS	5/15
	Des Moines-West Des Moines MSA, IA	Y	18250 FQ	21890 MW	26240 TQ	USBLS	5/15
	Kansas	Y	17460 FQ	19380 MW	23450 TQ	USBLS	5/15
	Wichita MSA, KS	Y	17660 FQ	20200 MW	41800 TQ	USBLS	5/15
	Kentucky	Y	17310 FQ	19010 MW	22550 TQ	USBLS	5/15
	Louisville-Jefferson County MSA, KY-IN	Y	17140 FQ	18710 MW	21350 TQ	USBLS	5/15
	Louisiana	Y	17230 FQ	18870 MW	21410 TQ	USBLS	5/15
	Baton Rouge MSA, LA	Y	17620 FQ	19520 MW	22250 TQ	USBLS	5/15
	New Orleans-Metairie MSA, LA	Y	17300 FQ	19000 MW	21650 TQ	USBLS	5/15
	Maine	Y	20980 FQ	25500 MW	34400 TQ	USBLS	5/15
	Portland-South Portland MSA, ME	Y	24560 FQ	33740 MW	36960 TQ	USBLS	5/15
	Maryland	Y	18018 AE	20688 MW	22023 AEX	MDBLS	4/16
	Baltimore-Columbia-Towson MSA, MD	Y	17650 FQ	18670 MW	20900 TQ	USBLS	5/15
	Worcester MSA, MA-CT	Y	21110 FQ	24730 MW	29510 TQ	USBLS	5/15
	Michigan	Y	18360 FQ	19530 MW	23530 TQ	USBLS	5/15
	Detroit-Dearborn-Livonia PMSA, MI	Y	18350 FQ	19510 MW	23330 TQ	USBLS	5/15
	Grand Rapids-Wyoming MSA, MI	Y	18390 FQ	19550 MW	21970 TQ	USBLS	5/15
	Minnesota	Y	19225 FQ	21796 MW	24609 TQ	MNBLS	1/16-3/16
	Minneapolis-St. Paul-Bloomington MSA, MN-WI	Y	19286 FQ	21887 MW	24669 TQ	MNBLS	1/16-3/16
	Mississippi	Y	17250 FQ	18670 MW	20160 TQ	USBLS	5/15
	Jackson MSA, MS	Y	17070 FQ	18250 MW	19440 TQ	USBLS	5/15
	Missouri	Y	17230 FQ	18500 MW	20190 TQ	USBLS	5/15
	Kansas City MSA, MO-KS	Y	17340 FQ	18840 MW	21530 TQ	USBLS	5/15
	St. Louis MSA, MO-IL	Y	17260 FQ	18550 MW	20530 TQ	USBLS	5/15
	Montana	Y	18390 FQ	20150 MW	23750 TQ	USBLS	5/15
	Nebraska	Y	17725 FQ	18805 MW	29410 TQ	NEBLS	7/16-9/16
	Omaha-Council Bluffs MSA, NE-IA	Y	17700 FQ	19050 MW	28020 TQ	NEBLS	7/16-9/16
	Nevada	Y	19590 FQ	22380 MW	25180 TQ	USBLS	5/15

AE	Average entry wage	AWR	Average wage range	H	Hourly	LR	Low end range	MTC	Median total compensation	TCC Total cash compensation
AEX	Average experienced wage	B	Biweekly	HI	Highest wage paid	M	Monthly	MW	Median wage paid	TQ Third quartile wage
ATC	Average total compensation	D	Daily	HR	High end range	MCC	Median cash compensation	MWR	Median wage range	W Weekly
AW	Average wage paid	FQ	First quartile wage	LO	Lowest wage paid	ME	Median entry wage	S	See annotated source	Y Yearly

Occupation/Type/Industry	Location	Per	Low	Mid	High	Source	Date
Parking Lot Attendant	Las Vegas-Henderson-Paradise						
	MSA, NV	Y	20390 FQ	22810 MW	25670 TQ	USBLS	5/15
	New Hampshire	H	9.78 AE	12.39 MW	13.59 AEX	NHBLS	6/16
	Manchester NECTA, NH	H	11.07 AE	12.87 MW	13.57 AEX	NHBLS	6/16
	Nashua NECTA, NH-MA	Y	21390 FQ	23450 MW	27270 TQ	USBLS	5/15
	New Jersey	Y	18980 FQ	21150 MW	24880 TQ	USBLS	5/15
	Camden PMSA, NJ	Y	18720 FQ	20080 MW	24240 TQ	USBLS	5/15
	Newark PMSA, NJ-PA	Y	19510 FQ	22040 MW	25550 TQ	USBLS	5/15
	Trenton MSA, NJ	Y	19560 FQ	22320 MW	26200 TQ	USBLS	5/15
	New Mexico	Y	18400 FQ	21750 MW	25860 TQ	USBLS	5/15
	Albuquerque MSA, NM	Y	18300 FQ	21530 MW	25310 TQ	USBLS	5/15
	New York	Y	19350 AE	21290 MW	25420 AEX	NYBLS	1/16-3/16
	Buffalo-Cheektowaga-Niagara						
	Falls MSA, NY	Y	18800 FQ	19420 MW	20150 TQ	USBLS	5/15
	Nassau County-Suffolk County						
	PMSA, NY	Y	19230 FQ	22300 MW	29150 TQ	USBLS	5/15
	New York-Jersey City-White						
	Plains PMSA, NY-NJ	Y	19170 FQ	21100 MW	24370 TQ	USBLS	5/15
	Rochester MSA, NY	Y	19250 FQ	20590 MW	24500 TQ	USBLS	5/15
	North Carolina	Y	18800 FQ	21440 MW	23930 TQ	USBLS	5/15
	Charlotte-Concord-Gastonia						
	MSA, NC-SC	Y	19460 FQ	21770 MW	24070 TQ	USBLS	5/15
	Raleigh MSA, NC	Y	17580 FQ	20020 MW	23130 TQ	USBLS	5/15
	North Dakota	Y	17870 FQ	20310 MW	24700 TQ	USBLS	5/15
	Fargo MSA, ND-MN	Y	16970 FQ	18430 MW	21140 TQ	USBLS	5/15
	Ohio	Y	18100 FQ	19190 MW	22470 TQ	USBLS	5/15
	Cincinnati MSA, OH-KY-IN	Y	17900 FQ	19040 MW	25150 TQ	USBLS	5/15
	Cleveland-Elyria MSA, OH	Y	18220 FQ	19470 MW	25770 TQ	USBLS	5/15
	Columbus MSA, OH	Y	17960 FQ	18880 MW	19850 TQ	USBLS	5/15
	Oklahoma	Y	17660 FQ	20040 MW	23930 TQ	USBLS	5/15
	Oklahoma City MSA, OK	Y	17800 FQ	20060 MW	23430 TQ	USBLS	5/15
	Tulsa MSA, OK	Y	17440 FQ	19730 MW	22480 TQ	USBLS	5/15
	Oregon	H	9.72 FQ	10.17 MW	11.43 TQ	ORBLS	2016
	Portland-Vancouver-Hillsboro						
	MSA, OR-WA	Y	19910 FQ	21000 MW	23490 TQ	USBLS	5/15
	Pennsylvania	Y	18040 FQ	20890 MW	24570 TQ	USBLS	5/15
	Allentown-Bethlehem-Easton						
	MSA, PA-NJ	Y	19340 FQ	21820 MW	24320 TQ	USBLS	5/15
	Harrisburg-Carlisle MSA, PA	Y	17080 FQ	18840 MW	22950 TQ	USBLS	5/15
	Montgomery County-Bucks						
	County-Chester County						
	PMSA, PA	Y	18500 FQ	21510 MW	24790 TQ	USBLS	5/15
	Philadelphia PMSA, PA	Y	17930 FQ	20510 MW	24220 TQ	USBLS	5/15
	Pittsburgh MSA, PA	Y	18330 FQ	21790 MW	26390 TQ	USBLS	5/15
	Rhode Island	Y	19190 FQ	21470 MW	26620 TQ	USBLS	5/15
	Providence-Warwick MSA, RI-						
	MA	Y	19210 FQ	21600 MW	26720 TQ	USBLS	5/15
	South Carolina	Y	18620 FQ	22130 MW	27020 TQ	USBLS	5/15
	Charleston-North Charleston						
	MSA, SC	Y	17530 FQ	19570 MW	25730 TQ	USBLS	5/15
	Columbia MSA, SC	Y	20940 FQ	25600 MW	34080 TQ	USBLS	5/15
	Greenville-Anderson-Mauldin						
	MSA, SC	Y	19650 FQ	22990 MW	27130 TQ	USBLS	5/15
	South Dakota	Y	20050 FQ	21940 MW	23800 TQ	USBLS	5/15
	Tennessee	Y	17520 FQ	19510 MW	23830 TQ	USBLS	5/15
	Memphis MSA, TN-MS-AR	Y	17160 FQ	18830 MW	22520 TQ	USBLS	5/15
	Nashville-Davidson–						
	Murfreesboro–Franklin						
	MSA, TN	Y	17420 FQ	19370 MW	24040 TQ	USBLS	5/15
	Texas	Y	18040 FQ	20630 MW	24030 TQ	USBLS	5/15
	Austin-Round Rock MSA, TX	Y	19050 FQ	21530 MW	23950 TQ	USBLS	5/15
	Dallas-Plano-Irving PMSA, TX	Y	18780 FQ	21910 MW	25160 TQ	USBLS	5/15
	Fort Worth-Arlington PMSA,						
	TX	Y	17690 FQ	19630 MW	22760 TQ	USBLS	5/15
	Houston-The Woodlands-						
	Sugar Land MSA, TX	Y	17480 FQ	19390 MW	23300 TQ	USBLS	5/15
	San Antonio-New Braunfels						
	MSA, TX	Y	18300 FQ	20910 MW	23670 TQ	USBLS	5/15
	Utah	Y	18350 FQ	21400 MW	24060 TQ	USBLS	5/15
	Provo-Orem MSA, UT	Y	18050 FQ	20380 MW	23030 TQ	USBLS	5/15
	Salt Lake City MSA, UT	Y	18330 FQ	21460 MW	24140 TQ	USBLS	5/15
	Vermont	Y	19520 FQ	21920 MW	26340 TQ	USBLS	5/15

AE	Average entry wage	**AWR**	Average wage range	**H**	Hourly	**LR**	Low end range	**MTC**	Median total compensation	**TCC**	Total cash compensation
AEX	Average experienced wage	**B**	Biweekly	**HI**	Highest wage paid	**M**	Monthly	**MW**	Median wage paid	**TQ**	Third quartile wage
ATC	Average total compensation	**D**	Daily	**HR**	High end range	**MCC**	Median cash compensation	**MWR**	Median wage range	**W**	Weekly
AW	Average wage paid	**FQ**	First quartile wage	**LO**	Lowest wage paid	**ME**	Median entry wage	**S**	See annotated source	**Y**	Yearly

Occupation/Type/Industry	Location	Per	Low	Mid	High	Source	Date
Parking Lot Attendant	Burlington-South Burlington MSA, VT	Y	19430 FQ	20790 MW	23440 TQ	USBLS	5/15
	Virginia	Y	18050 FQ	20360 MW	23730 TQ	USBLS	5/15
	Richmond MSA, VA	Y	17680 FQ	19630 MW	23720 TQ	USBLS	5/15
	Virginia Beach-Norfolk-Newport News MSA, VA-NC	Y	17110 FQ	18810 MW	22210 TQ	USBLS	5/15
	Washington	H	10.45 FQ	11.36 MW	12.64 TQ	WABLS	3/16
	Seattle-Bellevue-Everett PMSA, WA	H	10.45 FQ	11.35 MW	12.68 TQ	WABLS	3/16
	Tacoma-Lakewood PMSA, WA	H	10.52 FQ	11.34 MW	12.20 TQ	WABLS	3/16
	West Virginia	Y	18240 FQ	20120 MW	24730 TQ	USBLS	5/15
	Wisconsin	Y	17750 FQ	20120 MW	23580 TQ	USBLS	5/15
	Madison MSA, WI	Y	20470 FQ	22580 MW	24690 TQ	USBLS	5/15
	Milwaukee-Waukesha-West Allis MSA, WI	Y	17470 FQ	19440 MW	22640 TQ	USBLS	5/15
	Wyoming	Y	19860 FQ	23960 MW	32160 TQ	USBLS	5/15
	Puerto Rico	Y	16510 FQ	17590 MW	18670 TQ	USBLS	5/15
	San Juan-Carolina-Caguas MSA, PR	Y	16500 FQ	17570 MW	18650 TQ	USBLS	5/15
	Guam	Y	17980 FQ	18800 MW	19610 TQ	USBLS	5/15
Parking Meter Collector							
Municipal Government	Seattle, WA	H	19.44 LO		22.61 HI	CSSS	1/13/16
Parking Meter Technician							
Municipal Government	Santa Monica, CA	Y		66321 AW		CACIT	6/28/16
Parliamentarian							
United States House of Representatives	United States	Y			172500 HI	CRS01	2016
United States Senate	United States	Y			171315 HI	CRS01	2016
Particle Physicist	United States	Y		117000 AW		SKU01	2016
Parts Salesperson	Alabama	Y	19113 AE	31121 AW	37119 AEX	ALBLS	6/16
	Birmingham-Hoover MSA, AL	Y	19372 AE	32672 AW	39333 AEX	ALBLS	6/16
	Alaska	Y	28080 FQ	36340 MW	45680 TQ	USBLS	5/15
	Anchorage MSA, AK	Y	28280 FQ	36690 MW	46880 TQ	USBLS	5/15
	Arizona	Y	19680 FQ	25340 MW	35900 TQ	USBLS	5/15
	Phoenix-Mesa-Scottsdale MSA, AZ	Y	19400 FQ	24850 MW	35560 TQ	USBLS	5/15
	Tucson MSA, AZ	Y	20700 FQ	28750 MW	38240 TQ	USBLS	5/15
	Arkansas	Y	18960 FQ	25420 MW	33010 TQ	USBLS	5/15
	Little Rock-North Little Rock-Conway MSA, AR	Y	19220 FQ	26790 MW	35630 TQ	USBLS	5/15
	California	H	11.12 FQ	14.51 MW	20.99 TQ	CABLS	1/16-3/16
	Anaheim-Santa Ana-Irvine PMSA, CA	H	11.86 FQ	17.38 MW	24.68 TQ	CABLS	1/16-3/16
	Los Angeles-Long Beach-Glendale PMSA, CA	H	10.71 FQ	13.42 MW	18.71 TQ	CABLS	1/16-3/16
	Oakland-Hayward-Berkeley PMSA, CA	H	12.65 FQ	15.83 MW	22.70 TQ	CABLS	1/16-3/16
	Riverside-San Bernardino-Ontario MSA, CA	H	12.77 FQ	16.99 MW	24.82 TQ	CABLS	1/16-3/16
	Sacramento–Roseville–Arden-Arcade MSA, CA	H	10.55 FQ	14.42 MW	21.36 TQ	CABLS	1/16-3/16
	San Diego-Carlsbad MSA, CA	H	10.54 FQ	14.27 MW	20.37 TQ	CABLS	1/16-3/16
	San Francisco-Redwood City-South San Francisco PMSA, CA	H	12.46 FQ	17.86 MW	28.51 TQ	CABLS	1/16-3/16
	Colorado	Y	21850 FQ	28960 MW	42890 TQ	USBLS	5/15
	Denver-Aurora-Lakewood MSA, CO	Y	22050 FQ	29700 MW	44840 TQ	USBLS	5/15
	Connecticut	Y		34420 MW		CTBLS	1/16-3/16
	Bridgeport-Stamford-Norwalk MSA, CT	Y	28320 FQ	40030 MW	48680 TQ	USBLS	5/15
	Hartford-West Hartford-East Hartford MSA, CT	Y	22990 FQ	31510 MW	39910 TQ	USBLS	5/15
	Delaware	Y	23330 FQ	32080 MW	38820 TQ	USBLS	5/15
	Wilmington PMSA, DE-MD-NJ	Y	23530 FQ	33640 MW	45930 TQ	USBLS	5/15

AE	Average entry wage	AWR	Average wage range	H	Hourly
AEX	Average experienced wage	B	Biweekly	HI	Highest wage paid
ATC	Average total compensation	D	Daily	HR	High end range
AW	Average wage paid	FQ	First quartile wage	LO	Lowest wage paid

LR	Low end range	MTC	Median total compensation	TCC	Total cash compensation
M	Monthly	MW	Median wage paid	TQ	Third quartile wage
MCC	Median cash compensation	MWR	Median wage range	W	Weekly
ME	Median entry wage	S	See annotated source	Y	Yearly

Occupation/Type/Industry	Location	Per	Low	Mid	High	Source	Date
Parts Salesperson	Washington-Arlington-Alexandria PMSA, DC-VA-MD-WV	Y	23160 FQ	29590 MW	39810 TQ	USBLS	5/15
	Florida	H	9.89 AE	13.94 MW	17.94 AEX	FLBLS	7/16-9/16
	Fort Lauderdale-Pompano Beach-Deerfield Beach PMSA, FL	H	10.85 AE	15.40 MW	20.57 AEX	FLBLS	7/16-9/16
	Miami-Miami Beach-Kendall PMSA, FL	H	9.52 AE	13.63 MW	16.89 AEX	FLBLS	7/16-9/16
	Orlando-Kissimmee-Sanford MSA, FL	H	9.70 AE	13.65 MW	17.94 AEX	FLBLS	7/16-9/16
	Tampa-St. Petersburg-Clearwater MSA, FL	H	9.81 AE	13.74 MW	17.43 AEX	FLBLS	7/16-9/16
	Georgia	Y	20820 FQ	28570 MW	41400 TQ	USBLS	5/15
	Atlanta-Sandy Springs-Roswell MSA, GA	Y	24320 FQ	31750 MW	49000 TQ	USBLS	5/15
	Augusta-Richmond County MSA, GA-SC	Y	26100 FQ	31030 MW	37780 TQ	USBLS	5/15
	Hawaii	Y	28420 FQ	34900 MW	44350 TQ	USBLS	5/15
	Urban Honolulu MSA, HI	Y	28340 FQ	35440 MW	45700 TQ	USBLS	5/15
	Idaho	Y	22480 FQ	31290 MW	38030 TQ	USBLS	5/15
	Boise City MSA, ID	Y	19940 FQ	30660 MW	37770 TQ	USBLS	5/15
	Illinois	Y	24170 FQ	31320 MW	40550 TQ	USBLS	5/15
	Chicago-Naperville-Arlington Heights PMSA, IL	Y	24820 FQ	32640 MW	42470 TQ	USBLS	5/15
	Lake County-Kenosha County PMSA, IL-WI	Y	25600 FQ	30140 MW	40180 TQ	USBLS	5/15
	Indiana	Y	21990 FQ	28420 MW	36860 TQ	USBLS	5/15
	Gary PMSA, IN	Y	19670 FQ	25640 MW	35710 TQ	USBLS	5/15
	Indianapolis-Carmel-Anderson MSA, IN	Y	21180 FQ	26510 MW	32310 TQ	USBLS	5/15
	Iowa	Y	22960 FQ	32690 MW	43040 TQ	USBLS	5/15
	Des Moines-West Des Moines MSA, IA	Y	28800 FQ	39040 MW	48410 TQ	USBLS	5/15
	Kansas	Y	20040 FQ	28850 MW	39050 TQ	USBLS	5/15
	Wichita MSA, KS	Y	23210 FQ	33170 MW	42690 TQ	USBLS	5/15
	Kentucky	Y	19380 FQ	25000 MW	34610 TQ	USBLS	5/15
	Louisville-Jefferson County MSA, KY-IN	Y	21050 FQ	29580 MW	40130 TQ	USBLS	5/15
	Louisiana	Y	19850 FQ	26440 MW	35630 TQ	USBLS	5/15
	Baton Rouge MSA, LA	Y	23650 FQ	30230 MW	37590 TQ	USBLS	5/15
	New Orleans-Metairie MSA, LA	Y	19930 FQ	24690 MW	35160 TQ	USBLS	5/15
	Maine	Y	25060 FQ	29670 MW	36630 TQ	USBLS	5/15
	Portland-South Portland MSA, ME	Y	23680 FQ	28980 MW	35510 TQ	USBLS	5/15
	Maryland	Y	21381 AE	33955	40243 AEX	MDBLS	4/16
	Baltimore-Columbia-Towson MSA, MD	Y	27200 FQ	34970 MW	44550 TQ	USBLS	5/15
	Salisbury MSA, MD-DE	Y	23920 FQ	30860 MW	36860 TQ	USBLS	5/15
	Massachusetts	Y	26910 FQ	35620 MW	46660 TQ	USBLS	5/15
	Boston-Cambridge-Newton NECTA, MA	Y	27890 FQ	38810 MW	49230 TQ	USBLS	5/15
	Worcester MSA, MA-CT	Y	24540 FQ	30650 MW	39760 TQ	USBLS	5/15
	Michigan	Y	24650 FQ	31230 MW	38980 TQ	USBLS	5/15
	Detroit-Dearborn-Livonia PMSA, MI	Y	21300 FQ	31770 MW	39770 TQ	USBLS	5/15
	Grand Rapids-Wyoming MSA, MI	Y	27140 FQ	32340 MW	38730 TQ	USBLS	5/15
	Minnesota	Y	24019 FQ	31259 MW	40475 TQ	MNBLS	1/16-3/16
	Minneapolis-St. Paul-Bloomington MSA, MN-WI	Y	24211 FQ	33034 MW	41332 TQ	MNBLS	1/16-3/16
	Mississippi	Y	21430 FQ	28660 MW	37980 TQ	USBLS	5/15
	Jackson MSA, MS	Y	22090 FQ	31200 MW	45190 TQ	USBLS	5/15
	Missouri	Y	19970 FQ	26520 MW	36790 TQ	USBLS	5/15
	Kansas City MSA, MO-KS	Y	20300 FQ	28550 MW	38210 TQ	USBLS	5/15
	St. Louis MSA, MO-IL	Y	19810 FQ	29400 MW	41620 TQ	USBLS	5/15
	Montana	Y	22760 FQ	28830 MW	39290 TQ	USBLS	5/15
	Billings MSA, MT	Y	27210 FQ	34880 MW	43580 TQ	USBLS	5/15
	Nebraska	Y	27515 FQ	35395 MW	45205 TQ	NEBLS	7/16-9/16
	Omaha-Council Bluffs MSA, NE-IA	Y	30350 FQ	39215 MW	52040 TQ	NEBLS	7/16-9/16

AE Average entry wage	**AWR** Average wage range	**H** Hourly	**LR** Low end range	**MTC** Median total compensation	**TCC** Total cash compensation
AEX Average experienced wage	**B** Biweekly	**HI** Highest wage paid	**M** Monthly	**MW** Median wage paid	**TQ** Third quartile wage
ATC Average total compensation	**D** Daily	**HR** High end range	**MCC** Median cash compensation	**MWR** Median wage range	**W** Weekly
AW Average wage paid	**FQ** First quartile wage	**LO** Lowest wage paid	**ME** Median entry wage	**S** See annotated source	**Y** Yearly

Parts Salesperson

Occupation/Type/Industry	Location	Per	Low	Mid	High	Source	Date
Parts Salesperson	Nevada	Y	23610 FQ	32520 MW	47010 TQ	USBLS	5/15
	Las Vegas-Henderson-Paradise MSA, NV	Y	22780 FQ	29850 MW	39540 TQ	USBLS	5/15
	New Hampshire	H	10.26 AE	14.76 MW	18.01 AEX	NHBLS	6/16
	Manchester NECTA, NH	H	10.33 AE	14.94 MW	18.21 AEX	NHBLS	6/16
	Nashua NECTA, NH-MA	Y	21950 FQ	28180 MW	37890 TQ	USBLS	5/15
	New Jersey	Y	23490 FQ	30100 MW	42410 TQ	USBLS	5/15
	Camden PMSA, NJ	Y	23800 FQ	29320 MW	38030 TQ	USBLS	5/15
	Newark PMSA, NJ-PA	Y	23750 FQ	31140 MW	45680 TQ	USBLS	5/15
	Trenton MSA, NJ	Y	22880 FQ	29050 MW	39080 TQ	USBLS	5/15
	New Mexico	Y	20100 FQ	28100 MW	42690 TQ	USBLS	5/15
	Albuquerque MSA, NM	Y	19240 FQ	37210 MW	49000 TQ	USBLS	5/15
	New York	Y	22030 AE	32400 MW	43180 AEX	NYBLS	1/16-3/16
	Buffalo-Cheektowaga-Niagara Falls MSA, NY	Y	21730 FQ	32340 MW	42490 TQ	USBLS	5/15
	Nassau County-Suffolk County PMSA, NY	Y	23440 FQ	34890 MW	56280 TQ	USBLS	5/15
	New York-Jersey City-White Plains PMSA, NY-NJ	Y	23200 FQ	31360 MW	45290 TQ	USBLS	5/15
	Rochester MSA, NY	Y	24020 FQ	32330 MW	38500 TQ	USBLS	5/15
	North Carolina	Y	21310 FQ	29230 MW	38820 TQ	USBLS	5/15
	Charlotte-Concord-Gastonia MSA, NC-SC	Y	21590 FQ	29430 MW	41990 TQ	USBLS	5/15
	Raleigh MSA, NC	Y	24210 FQ	33820 MW	45590 TQ	USBLS	5/15
	North Dakota	Y	29250 FQ	38380 MW	47600 TQ	USBLS	5/15
	Fargo MSA, ND-MN	Y	26870 FQ	36520 MW	49850 TQ	USBLS	5/15
	Ohio	Y	20870 FQ	27370 MW	36180 TQ	USBLS	5/15
	Cincinnati MSA, OH-KY-IN	Y	21130 FQ	28610 MW	36780 TQ	USBLS	5/15
	Cleveland-Elyria MSA, OH	Y	20790 FQ	27050 MW	35380 TQ	USBLS	5/15
	Columbus MSA, OH	Y	24160 FQ	28970 MW	35580 TQ	USBLS	5/15
	Oklahoma	Y	21520 FQ	29190 MW	41240 TQ	USBLS	5/15
	Oklahoma City MSA, OK	Y	20450 FQ	27100 MW	39120 TQ	USBLS	5/15
	Tulsa MSA, OK	Y	24610 FQ	35040 MW	47450 TQ	USBLS	5/15
	Oregon	H	11.78 FQ	15.89 MW	20.75 TQ	ORBLS	2016
	Portland-Vancouver-Hillsboro MSA, OR-WA	Y	24040 FQ	33300 MW	42350 TQ	USBLS	5/15
	Pennsylvania	Y	24150 FQ	30170 MW	38550 TQ	USBLS	5/15
	Allentown-Bethlehem-Easton MSA, PA-NJ	Y	24480 FQ	30880 MW	38740 TQ	USBLS	5/15
	Harrisburg-Carlisle MSA, PA	Y	24220 FQ	31800 MW	38390 TQ	USBLS	5/15
	Montgomery County-Bucks County-Chester County PMSA, PA	Y	26650 FQ	34490 MW	45850 TQ	USBLS	5/15
	Philadelphia PMSA, PA	Y	23030 FQ	29110 MW	40250 TQ	USBLS	5/15
	Pittsburgh MSA, PA	Y	25320 FQ	30120 MW	37510 TQ	USBLS	5/15
	Rhode Island	Y	27070 FQ	33130 MW	41740 TQ	USBLS	5/15
	Providence-Warwick MSA, RI-MA	Y	27790 FQ	34330 MW	42140 TQ	USBLS	5/15
	South Carolina	Y	19600 FQ	26340 MW	36850 TQ	USBLS	5/15
	Charleston-North Charleston MSA, SC	Y	22070 FQ	31060 MW	39270 TQ	USBLS	5/15
	Columbia MSA, SC	Y	19680 FQ	29300 MW	43760 TQ	USBLS	5/15
	Greenville-Anderson-Mauldin MSA, SC	Y	19410 FQ	24680 MW	34440 TQ	USBLS	5/15
	South Dakota	Y	26030 FQ	30930 MW	39050 TQ	USBLS	5/15
	Sioux Falls MSA, SD	Y	28810 FQ	35070 MW	43070 TQ	USBLS	5/15
	Tennessee	Y	22270 FQ	28500 MW	37470 TQ	USBLS	5/15
	Knoxville MSA, TN	Y	21480 FQ	25890 MW	34060 TQ	USBLS	5/15
	Memphis MSA, TN-MS-AR	Y	25610 FQ	31330 MW	41170 TQ	USBLS	5/15
	Nashville-Davidson-Murfreesboro-Franklin MSA, TN	Y	22420 FQ	28960 MW	38100 TQ	USBLS	5/15
	Texas	Y	20210 FQ	28140 MW	40160 TQ	USBLS	5/15
	Austin-Round Rock MSA, TX	Y	21480 FQ	29210 MW	40990 TQ	USBLS	5/15
	Dallas-Plano-Irving PMSA, TX	Y	19450 FQ	25000 MW	39270 TQ	USBLS	5/15
	Fort Worth-Arlington PMSA, TX	Y	21260 FQ	27750 MW	38600 TQ	USBLS	5/15
	Houston-The Woodlands-Sugar Land MSA, TX	Y	23890 FQ	33540 MW	45790 TQ	USBLS	5/15
	San Antonio-New Braunfels MSA, TX	Y	22220 FQ	28010 MW	35840 TQ	USBLS	5/15
	Utah	Y	25370 FQ	30430 MW	39360 TQ	USBLS	5/15

AE	Average entry wage	AWR	Average wage range	H	Hourly
AEX	Average experienced wage	B	Biweekly	HI	Highest wage paid
ATC	Average total compensation	D	Daily	HR	High end range
AW	Average wage paid	FQ	First quartile wage	LO	Lowest wage paid

LR	Low end range	MTC	Median total compensation	TCC	Total cash compensation
M	Monthly	MW	Median wage paid	TQ	Third quartile wage
MCC	Median cash compensation	MWR	Median wage range	W	Weekly
ME	Median entry wage	S	See annotated source	Y	Yearly

Occupation/Type/Industry	Location	Per	Low	Mid	High	Source	Date
Parts Salesperson	Ogden-Clearfield MSA, UT	Y	23980 FQ	29920 MW	35650 TQ	USBLS	5/15
	Provo-Orem MSA, UT	Y	23290 FQ	29350 MW	36560 TQ	USBLS	5/15
	Salt Lake City MSA, UT	Y	27080 FQ	33170 MW	46710 TQ	USBLS	5/15
	Vermont	Y	26680 FQ	30590 MW	37320 TQ	USBLS	5/15
	Burlington-South Burlington MSA, VT	Y	25360 FQ	31060 MW	39040 TQ	USBLS	5/15
	Virginia	Y	23640 FQ	30460 MW	39910 TQ	USBLS	5/15
	Richmond MSA, VA	Y	22900 FQ	30670 MW	43540 TQ	USBLS	5/15
	Virginia Beach-Norfolk-Newport News MSA, VA-NC	Y	25790 FQ	31330 MW	39320 TQ	USBLS	5/15
	Washington	H	11.80 FQ	15.00 MW	19.92 TQ	WABLS	3/16
	Seattle-Bellevue-Everett PMSA, WA	H	12.78 FQ	17.75 MW	22.92 TQ	WABLS	3/16
	Tacoma-Lakewood PMSA, WA	H	12.98 FQ	16.70 MW	19.92 TQ	WABLS	3/16
	West Virginia	Y	20640 FQ	25790 MW	31350 TQ	USBLS	5/15
	Huntington-Ashland MSA, WV-KY-OH	Y	22580 FQ	28880 MW	36080 TQ	USBLS	5/15
	Wisconsin	Y	24130 FQ	31010 MW	38460 TQ	USBLS	5/15
	Madison MSA, WI	Y	21500 FQ	27620 MW	36750 TQ	USBLS	5/15
	Milwaukee-Waukesha-West Allis MSA, WI	Y	25590 FQ	31010 MW	38560 TQ	USBLS	5/15
	Wyoming	Y	26760 FQ	34870 MW	44490 TQ	USBLS	5/15
	Cheyenne MSA, WY	Y	24580 FQ	32230 MW	44940 TQ	USBLS	5/15
	Puerto Rico	Y	16950 FQ	18400 MW	20230 TQ	USBLS	5/15
	San Juan-Carolina-Caguas MSA, PR	Y	17190 FQ	18860 MW	22960 TQ	USBLS	5/15
	Guam	Y	18340 FQ	19700 MW	23390 TQ	USBLS	5/15
Passenger and Tugboat Operator							
Municipal Government	Seattle, WA	H	28.07 LO		31.43 HI	CSSS	3/9/16
Passenger Boarding Attendant	United States	H		10.00 AW		AVJOB02	2016
Pastry Line Cook	Chicago, IL	H	10.00 LO		15.00 HI	NYT04	2016
Patent Attorney	United States	Y		170000 MW		USN01	2013
Pathologist							
County Government	Oakland County, MI	B			4912 HI	MIOAK2	10/1/16
Patient Care Assistant							
Department of Public Health, Acute Care, Forensics	San Francisco, CA	B	1814 LO		2204 HI	SFGOV	2016-2018
Patternmaker							
Metals and Plastics	Alabama	Y	28348 AE	38702 AW	43874 AEX	ALBLS	6/16
Metals and Plastics	Birmingham-Hoover MSA, AL	Y	29613 AE	39011 AW	43720 AEX	ALBLS	6/16
Metals and Plastics	Arkansas	Y	24880 FQ	39190 MW	50160 TQ	USBLS	5/15
Metals and Plastics	California	H	9.94 FQ	11.77 MW	23.26 TQ	CABLS	1/16-3/16
Metals and Plastics	Los Angeles-Long Beach-Glendale PMSA, CA	H	9.70 FQ	11.94 MW	23.58 TQ	CABLS	1/16-3/16
Metals and Plastics	Oakland-Hayward-Berkeley PMSA, CA	H	14.65 FQ	22.94 MW	51.22 TQ	CABLS	1/16-3/16
Metals and Plastics	Connecticut	Y		47638 MW		CTBLS	1/16-3/16
Metals and Plastics	Florida	H	13.20 AE	16.58 MW	18.95 AEX	FLBLS	7/16-9/16
Metals and Plastics	Georgia	Y	39350 FQ	50870 MW	60750 TQ	USBLS	5/15
Metals and Plastics	Illinois	Y	41160 FQ	51450 MW	58800 TQ	USBLS	5/15
Metals and Plastics	Indiana	Y	28600 FQ	42690 MW	49980 TQ	USBLS	5/15
Metals and Plastics	Iowa	Y	41860 FQ	51440 MW	57490 TQ	USBLS	5/15
Metals and Plastics	Kansas	Y	38860 FQ	53610 MW	59070 TQ	USBLS	5/15
Metals and Plastics	Massachusetts	Y	19790 FQ	32540 MW	36420 TQ	USBLS	5/15
Metals and Plastics	Michigan	Y	44320 FQ	53280 MW	59000 TQ	USBLS	5/15
Metals and Plastics	Minnesota	Y	40478 FQ	45874 MW	51817 TQ	MNBLS	1/16-3/16
Metals and Plastics	Minneapolis-St. Paul-Bloomington MSA, MN-WI	Y	37116 FQ	42027 MW	47565 TQ	MNBLS	1/16-3/16
Metals and Plastics	Missouri	Y	23540 FQ	32250 MW	39610 TQ	USBLS	5/15
Metals and Plastics	New York	Y	31710 AE	42380 MW	48580 AEX	NYBLS	1/16-3/16
Metals and Plastics	North Carolina	Y	27960 FQ	35390 MW	45460 TQ	USBLS	5/15
Metals and Plastics	Ohio	Y	31560 FQ	40230 MW	53990 TQ	USBLS	5/15
Metals and Plastics	Cincinnati MSA, OH-KY-IN	Y	36210 FQ	44280 MW	52800 TQ	USBLS	5/15
Metals and Plastics	Cleveland-Elyria MSA, OH	Y	31870 FQ	37470 MW	50510 TQ	USBLS	5/15
Metals and Plastics	Oklahoma	Y	29620 FQ	40820 MW	45380 TQ	USBLS	5/15
Metals and Plastics	Oregon	H	20.19 FQ	25.93 MW	29.55 TQ	ORBLS	2016

Occupation/Type/Industry	Location	Per	Low	Mid	High	Source	Date
Patternmaker							
Metals and Plastics	Portland-Vancouver-Hillsboro MSA, OR-WA	Y	41640 FQ	54180 MW	61030 TQ	USBLS	5/15
Metals and Plastics	Pennsylvania	Y	29740 FQ	39100 MW	47090 TQ	USBLS	5/15
Metals and Plastics	Pittsburgh MSA, PA	Y	24770 FQ	29530 MW	39970 TQ	USBLS	5/15
Metals and Plastics	Texas	Y	24430 FQ	31030 MW	41870 TQ	USBLS	5/15
Metals and Plastics	Dallas-Plano-Irving PMSA, TX	Y	24220 FQ	29860 MW	45210 TQ	USBLS	5/15
Metals and Plastics	Houston-The Woodlands-Sugar Land MSA, TX	Y	35190 FQ	40750 MW	49250 TQ	USBLS	5/15
Metals and Plastics	Virginia	Y	33320 FQ	36920 MW	43040 TQ	USBLS	5/15
Metals and Plastics	Washington	H	17.75 FQ	24.43 MW	29.65 TQ	WABLS	3/16
Metals and Plastics	Wisconsin	Y	39110 FQ	50220 MW	56760 TQ	USBLS	5/15
Wood	Alabama	Y	23011 AE	33170 AW	38250 AEX	ALBLS	6/16
Wood	California	H	12.80 FQ	16.13 MW	21.76 TQ	CABLS	1/16-3/16
Wood	Michigan	Y	36470 FQ	47380 MW	65090 TQ	USBLS	5/15
Wood	New York	Y	27860 AE	41890 MW	51110 AEX	NYBLS	1/16-3/16
Wood	North Carolina	Y	32410 FQ	37530 MW	47110 TQ	USBLS	5/15
Wood	Oklahoma	Y	37890 FQ	42700 MW	46890 TQ	USBLS	5/15
Wood	Oregon	H	16.18 FQ	21.15 MW	24.06 TQ	ORBLS	2016
Wood	Pennsylvania	Y	25820 FQ	35100 MW	48440 TQ	USBLS	5/15
Wood	Tennessee	Y	21410 FQ	23050 MW	24690 TQ	USBLS	5/15
Wood	Texas	Y	29610 FQ	40240 MW	49670 TQ	USBLS	5/15
Wood	Wisconsin	Y	35210 FQ	39120 MW	59110 TQ	USBLS	5/15
Paving, Surfacing, and Tamping Equipment Operator	Alabama	Y	23279 AE	31005 AW	34873 AEX	ALBLS	6/16
	Birmingham-Hoover MSA, AL	Y	23310 AE	32836 AW	37588 AEX	ALBLS	6/16
	Alaska	Y	46820 FQ	79160 MW	90050 TQ	USBLS	5/15
	Arizona	Y	25720 FQ	34530 MW	40500 TQ	USBLS	5/15
	Phoenix-Mesa-Scottsdale MSA, AZ	Y	26470 FQ	35170 MW	41960 TQ	USBLS	5/15
	Tucson MSA, AZ	Y	22300 FQ	30140 MW	35790 TQ	USBLS	5/15
	Arkansas	Y	26770 FQ	30840 MW	38910 TQ	USBLS	5/15
	Little Rock-North Little Rock-Conway MSA, AR	Y	27910 FQ	34430 MW	44520 TQ	USBLS	5/15
	California	H	21.80 FQ	26.72 MW	31.62 TQ	CABLS	1/16-3/16
	Anaheim-Santa Ana-Irvine PMSA, CA	H	22.00 FQ	27.53 MW	33.20 TQ	CABLS	1/16-3/16
	Los Angeles-Long Beach-Glendale PMSA, CA	H	21.10 FQ	26.69 MW	31.19 TQ	CABLS	1/16-3/16
	Oakland-Hayward-Berkeley PMSA, CA	H	22.93 FQ	25.94 MW	29.57 TQ	CABLS	1/16-3/16
	Riverside-San Bernardino-Ontario MSA, CA	H	27.77 FQ	40.49 MW	45.16 TQ	CABLS	1/16-3/16
	Sacramento–Roseville–Arden-Arcade MSA, CA	H	22.27 FQ	26.10 MW	30.96 TQ	CABLS	1/16-3/16
	San Diego-Carlsbad MSA, CA	H	21.30 FQ	25.71 MW	28.62 TQ	CABLS	1/16-3/16
	San Francisco-Redwood City-South San Francisco PMSA, CA	H	30.03 FQ	36.58 MW	47.72 TQ	CABLS	1/16-3/16
	Colorado	Y	34010 FQ	38600 MW	46390 TQ	USBLS	5/15
	Denver-Aurora-Lakewood MSA, CO	Y	33930 FQ	37590 MW	44950 TQ	USBLS	5/15
	Connecticut	Y		43705 MW		CTBLS	1/16-3/16
	Bridgeport-Stamford-Norwalk MSA, CT	Y	33770 FQ	40740 MW	48200 TQ	USBLS	5/15
	Hartford-West Hartford-East Hartford MSA, CT	Y	33320 FQ	41840 MW	46720 TQ	USBLS	5/15
	Delaware	Y	36880 FQ	43900 MW	49510 TQ	USBLS	5/15
	Wilmington PMSA, DE-MD-NJ	Y	41020 FQ	45850 MW	51280 TQ	USBLS	5/15
	District of Columbia	Y	43280 FQ	53290 MW	63900 TQ	USBLS	5/15
	Washington-Arlington-Alexandria PMSA, DC-VA-MD-WV	Y	29730 FQ	35230 MW	44870 TQ	USBLS	5/15
	Florida	H	12.00 AE	15.01 MW	17.63 AEX	FLBLS	7/16-9/16
	Fort Lauderdale-Pompano Beach-Deerfield Beach PMSA, FL	H	12.83 AE	15.21 MW	16.99 AEX	FLBLS	7/16-9/16
	Miami-Miami Beach-Kendall PMSA, FL	H	12.20 AE	15.06 MW	17.76 AEX	FLBLS	7/16-9/16

AE	Average entry wage	AWR	Average wage range	H	Hourly
AEX	Average experienced wage	B	Biweekly	HI	Highest wage paid
ATC	Average total compensation	D	Daily	HR	High end range
AW	Average wage paid	FQ	First quartile wage	LO	Lowest wage paid

LR	Low end range	MTC	Median total compensation	TCC	Total cash compensation
M	Monthly	MW	Median wage paid	TQ	Third quartile wage
MCC	Median cash compensation	MWR	Median wage range	W	Weekly
ME	Median entry wage	S	See annotated source	Y	Yearly

Occupation/Type/Industry	Location	Per	Low	Mid	High	Source	Date
Paving, Surfacing, and Tamping Equipment Operator							
	Orlando-Kissimmee-Sanford MSA, FL	H	12.46 AE	15.61 MW	18.50 AEX	FLBLS	7/16-9/16
	Tampa-St. Petersburg-Clearwater MSA, FL	H	10.87 AE	14.00 MW	17.02 AEX	FLBLS	7/16-9/16
	Georgia	Y	26810 FQ	30240 MW	35590 TQ	USBLS	5/15
	Atlanta-Sandy Springs-Roswell MSA, GA	Y	27930 FQ	31720 MW	36840 TQ	USBLS	5/15
	Augusta-Richmond County MSA, GA-SC	Y	26410 FQ	29500 MW	34860 TQ	USBLS	5/15
	Hawaii	Y	39980 FQ	48250 MW	70310 TQ	USBLS	5/15
	Urban Honolulu MSA, HI	Y	40940 FQ	48440 MW	70230 TQ	USBLS	5/15
	Idaho	Y	35950 FQ	41710 MW	46020 TQ	USBLS	5/15
	Boise City MSA, ID	Y	39590 FQ	42980 MW	46380 TQ	USBLS	5/15
	Illinois	Y	54840 FQ	70600 MW	81400 TQ	USBLS	5/15
	Chicago-Naperville-Arlington Heights PMSA, IL	Y	65220 FQ	74160 MW	83260 TQ	USBLS	5/15
	Lake County-Kenosha County PMSA, IL-WI	Y	83280 FQ	89920 MW	96560 TQ	USBLS	5/15
	Indiana	Y	34490 FQ	44200 MW	68550 TQ	USBLS	5/15
	Gary PMSA, IN	Y	35490 FQ	40260 MW	60610 TQ	USBLS	5/15
	Indianapolis-Carmel-Anderson MSA, IN	Y	40220 FQ	67210 MW	74370 TQ	USBLS	5/15
	Iowa	Y	32540 FQ	36920 MW	44450 TQ	USBLS	5/15
	Kansas	Y	29370 FQ	35890 MW	46710 TQ	USBLS	5/15
	Wichita MSA, KS	Y	23440 FQ	31620 MW	37310 TQ	USBLS	5/15
	Kentucky	Y	27830 FQ	34820 MW	44270 TQ	USBLS	5/15
	Louisville-Jefferson County MSA, KY-IN	Y	28770 FQ	35750 MW	42380 TQ	USBLS	5/15
	Louisiana	Y	25310 FQ	33470 MW	41400 TQ	USBLS	5/15
	New Orleans-Metairie MSA, LA	Y	28480 FQ	34760 MW	41440 TQ	USBLS	5/15
	Maine	Y	27740 FQ	34190 MW	43300 TQ	USBLS	5/15
	Portland-South Portland MSA, ME	Y	29210 FQ	36390 MW	43800 TQ	USBLS	5/15
	Maryland	Y	27414 AE	36647 MW	41263 AEX	MDBLS	4/16
	Baltimore-Columbia-Towson MSA, MD	Y	27880 FQ	31460 MW	43090 TQ	USBLS	5/15
	Salisbury MSA, MD-DE	Y	33450 FQ	40520 MW	46240 TQ	USBLS	5/15
	Massachusetts	Y	42300 FQ	49360 MW	67160 TQ	USBLS	5/15
	Boston-Cambridge-Newton NECTA, MA	Y	42200 FQ	52320 MW	67900 TQ	USBLS	5/15
	Worcester MSA, MA-CT	Y	52590 FQ	59140 MW	84640 TQ	USBLS	5/15
	Michigan	Y	35270 FQ	42880 MW	49060 TQ	USBLS	5/15
	Detroit-Dearborn-Livonia PMSA, MI	Y	32600 FQ	38540 MW	45120 TQ	USBLS	5/15
	Grand Rapids-Wyoming MSA, MI	Y	32190 FQ	38550 MW	47450 TQ	USBLS	5/15
	Minnesota	Y	40129 FQ	48110 MW	58018 TQ	MNBLS	1/16-3/16
	Minneapolis-St. Paul-Bloomington MSA, MN-WI	Y	42691 FQ	50410 MW	59784 TQ	MNBLS	1/16-3/16
	Mississippi	Y	26550 FQ	32240 MW	37340 TQ	USBLS	5/15
	Jackson MSA, MS	Y	23170 FQ	29310 MW	35170 TQ	USBLS	5/15
	Missouri	Y	30030 FQ	36220 MW	44780 TQ	USBLS	5/15
	Kansas City MSA, MO-KS	Y	33650 FQ	41330 MW	53900 TQ	USBLS	5/15
	St. Louis MSA, MO-IL	Y	29880 FQ	41830 MW	59200 TQ	USBLS	5/15
	Montana	Y	34280 FQ	42050 MW	49340 TQ	USBLS	5/15
	Billings MSA, MT	Y	36950 FQ	43050 MW	48100 TQ	USBLS	5/15
	Nebraska	Y	26225 FQ	31190 MW	38295 TQ	NEBLS	7/16-9/16
	Omaha-Council Bluffs MSA, NE-IA	Y	26795 FQ	30955 MW	38860 TQ	NEBLS	7/16-9/16
	Nevada	Y	45740 FQ	58750 MW	86830 TQ	USBLS	5/15
	Las Vegas-Henderson-Paradise MSA, NV	Y	54290 FQ	81770 MW	92780 TQ	USBLS	5/15
	New Hampshire	H	14.74 AE	19.45 MW	21.76 AEX	NHBLS	6/16
	Nashua NECTA, NH-MA	Y	23740 FQ	38210 MW	45900 TQ	USBLS	5/15
	New Jersey	Y	43290 FQ	55830 MW	70900 TQ	USBLS	5/15
	Camden PMSA, NJ	Y	35690 FQ	42640 MW	57760 TQ	USBLS	5/15
	Newark PMSA, NJ-PA	Y	44720 FQ	57560 MW	74160 TQ	USBLS	5/15
	Trenton MSA, NJ	Y	38300 FQ	50630 MW	58350 TQ	USBLS	5/15
	New Mexico	Y	32700 FQ	39640 MW	45660 TQ	USBLS	5/15
	Albuquerque MSA, NM	Y	31860 FQ	37220 MW	43750 TQ	USBLS	5/15

AE Average entry wage	**AWR** Average wage range	**H** Hourly	**LR** Low end range	**MTC** Median total compensation	**TCC** Total cash compensation
AEX Average experienced wage	**B** Biweekly	**HI** Highest wage paid	**M** Monthly	**MW** Median wage	**TQ** Third quartile wage
ATC Average total compensation	**D** Daily	**HR** High end range	**MCC** Median cash compensation	**MWR** Median wage range	**W** Weekly
AW Average wage paid	**FQ** First quartile wage	**LO** Lowest wage paid	**ME** Median entry wage	**S** See annotated source	**Y** Yearly

Occupation/Type/Industry	Location	Per	Low	Mid	High	Source	Date
Paving, Surfacing, and Tamping Equipment Operator							
	New York	Y	34810 AE	58590 MW	80710 AEX	NYBLS	1/16-3/16
	Buffalo-Cheektowaga-Niagara Falls MSA, NY	Y	37640 FQ	52340 MW	58520 TQ	USBLS	5/15
	Nassau County-Suffolk County PMSA, NY	Y	46220 FQ	54340 MW	70880 TQ	USBLS	5/15
	New York-Jersey City-White Plains PMSA, NY-NJ	Y	43240 FQ	65470 MW	93690 TQ	USBLS	5/15
	Rochester MSA, NY	Y	40060 FQ	46150 MW	58710 TQ	USBLS	5/15
	North Carolina	Y	28260 FQ	33150 MW	38330 TQ	USBLS	5/15
	Charlotte-Concord-Gastonia MSA, NC-SC	Y	29190 FQ	34270 MW	39360 TQ	USBLS	5/15
	Raleigh MSA, NC	Y	29180 FQ	34170 MW	39130 TQ	USBLS	5/15
	North Dakota	Y	35090 FQ	51710 MW	60110 TQ	USBLS	5/15
	Fargo MSA, ND-MN	Y	31810 FQ	39420 MW	54560 TQ	USBLS	5/15
	Ohio	Y	34190 FQ	40610 MW	54770 TQ	USBLS	5/15
	Cincinnati MSA, OH-KY-IN	Y	35050 FQ	41550 MW	53430 TQ	USBLS	5/15
	Cleveland-Elyria MSA, OH	Y	36640 FQ	51650 MW	61200 TQ	USBLS	5/15
	Columbus MSA, OH	Y	34490 FQ	41870 MW	60900 TQ	USBLS	5/15
	Oklahoma	Y	30050 FQ	35320 MW	41750 TQ	USBLS	5/15
	Oklahoma City MSA, OK	Y	32290 FQ	36780 MW	43840 TQ	USBLS	5/15
	Tulsa MSA, OK	Y	33490 FQ	40820 MW	47240 TQ	USBLS	5/15
	Oregon	H	19.00 FQ	23.01 MW	27.13 TQ	ORBLS	2016
	Portland-Vancouver-Hillsboro MSA, OR-WA	Y	36310 FQ	51980 MW	58990 TQ	USBLS	5/15
	Pennsylvania	Y	32770 FQ	45030 MW	56630 TQ	USBLS	5/15
	Allentown-Bethlehem-Easton MSA, PA-NJ	Y	29090 FQ	37070 MW	50060 TQ	USBLS	5/15
	Harrisburg-Carlisle MSA, PA	Y	23950 FQ	35950 MW	83810 TQ	USBLS	5/15
	Montgomery County-Bucks County-Chester County PMSA, PA	Y	46510 FQ	57020 MW	71760 TQ	USBLS	5/15
	Philadelphia PMSA, PA	Y	53940 FQ	61620 MW	74800 TQ	USBLS	5/15
	Pittsburgh MSA, PA	Y	43430 FQ	53290 MW	59480 TQ	USBLS	5/15
	Rhode Island	Y	31870 FQ	36650 MW	44340 TQ	USBLS	5/15
	Providence-Warwick MSA, RI-MA	Y	32490 FQ	37890 MW	51170 TQ	USBLS	5/15
	South Carolina	Y	25790 FQ	30690 MW	36090 TQ	USBLS	5/15
	Charleston-North Charleston MSA, SC	Y	25570 FQ	32140 MW	37260 TQ	USBLS	5/15
	South Dakota	Y	29890 FQ	35460 MW	42600 TQ	USBLS	5/15
	Sioux Falls MSA, SD	Y	30510 FQ	35200 MW	39610 TQ	USBLS	5/15
	Tennessee	Y	28680 FQ	32980 MW	37560 TQ	USBLS	5/15
	Knoxville MSA, TN	Y	28540 FQ	32640 MW	37030 TQ	USBLS	5/15
	Memphis MSA, TN-MS-AR	Y	30970 FQ	34060 MW	37150 TQ	USBLS	5/15
	Nashville-Davidson–Murfreesboro–Franklin MSA, TN	Y	29260 FQ	35430 MW	43890 TQ	USBLS	5/15
	Texas	Y	29010 FQ	34490 MW	39440 TQ	USBLS	5/15
	Austin-Round Rock MSA, TX	Y	25670 FQ	33550 MW	38970 TQ	USBLS	5/15
	Dallas-Plano-Irving PMSA, TX	Y	31330 FQ	35870 MW	41500 TQ	USBLS	5/15
	Fort Worth-Arlington PMSA, TX	Y	30810 FQ	35830 MW	42880 TQ	USBLS	5/15
	Houston-The Woodlands-Sugar Land MSA, TX	Y	31420 FQ	35370 MW	39310 TQ	USBLS	5/15
	San Antonio-New Braunfels MSA, TX	Y	27390 FQ	31610 MW	36270 TQ	USBLS	5/15
	Utah	Y	35780 FQ	43410 MW	51640 TQ	USBLS	5/15
	Ogden-Clearfield MSA, UT	Y	34130 FQ	41890 MW	47730 TQ	USBLS	5/15
	Salt Lake City MSA, UT	Y	35250 FQ	42580 MW	52400 TQ	USBLS	5/15
	Vermont	Y	30280 FQ	34760 MW	38880 TQ	USBLS	5/15
	Virginia	Y	28340 FQ	33030 MW	37510 TQ	USBLS	5/15
	Richmond MSA, VA	Y	29300 FQ	34000 MW	38250 TQ	USBLS	5/15
	Virginia Beach-Norfolk-Newport News MSA, VA-NC	Y	27220 FQ	31510 MW	35880 TQ	USBLS	5/15
	Washington	H	18.67 FQ	25.41 MW	33.33 TQ	WABLS	3/16
	Seattle-Bellevue-Everett PMSA, WA	H	21.08 FQ	25.09 MW	34.17 TQ	WABLS	3/16
	West Virginia	Y	22740 FQ	33290 MW	51500 TQ	USBLS	5/15
	Huntington-Ashland MSA, WV-KY-OH	Y	21000 FQ	31180 MW	38090 TQ	USBLS	5/15
	Wisconsin	Y	42460 FQ	49030 MW	74120 TQ	USBLS	5/15

AE	Average entry wage	AWR Average wage range	H Hourly	LR Low end range	MTC Median total compensation TCC Total cash compensation
AEX	Average experienced wage	B Biweekly	HI Highest wage paid	M Monthly	MW Median wage paid TQ Third quartile wage
ATC	Average total compensation	D Daily	HR High end range	MCC Median cash compensation	MWR Median wage range W Weekly
AW	Average wage paid	FQ First quartile wage	LO Lowest wage paid	ME Median entry wage	S See annotated source Y Yearly

Occupation/Type/Industry	Location	Per	Low	Mid	High	Source	Date
Paving, Surfacing, and Tamping Equipment Operator	Madison MSA, WI	Y	42400 FQ	47490 MW	70530 TQ	USBLS	5/15
	Milwaukee-Waukesha-West Allis MSA, WI	Y	48090 FQ	57380 MW	77300 TQ	USBLS	5/15
	Wyoming	Y	33050 FQ	38940 MW	47760 TQ	USBLS	5/15
	Puerto Rico	Y	17480 FQ	20050 MW	27250 TQ	USBLS	5/15
	San Juan-Carolina-Caguas MSA, PR	Y	17980 FQ	21170 MW	25960 TQ	USBLS	5/15
Paymaster							
Municipal Government	Detroit, MI	M	3383 LO		3567 HI	DETGOV	2016
Payroll and Timekeeping Clerk	Alabama	Y	27197 AE	39101 AW	45058 AEX	ALBLS	6/16
	Birmingham-Hoover MSA, AL	Y	30124 AE	42347 AW	48469 AEX	ALBLS	6/16
	Alaska	Y	38890 FQ	48550 MW	58270 TQ	USBLS	5/15
	Anchorage MSA, AK	Y	38260 FQ	47450 MW	57010 TQ	USBLS	5/15
	Arizona	Y	31110 FQ	37450 MW	45920 TQ	USBLS	5/15
	Phoenix-Mesa-Scottsdale MSA, AZ	Y	33250 FQ	39370 MW	47980 TQ	USBLS	5/15
	Tucson MSA, AZ	Y	27260 FQ	33350 MW	39520 TQ	USBLS	5/15
	Arkansas	Y	27560 FQ	33230 MW	39620 TQ	USBLS	5/15
	Little Rock-North Little Rock-Conway MSA, AR	Y	29360 FQ	34190 MW	39690 TQ	USBLS	5/15
	California	H	17.82 FQ	22.30 MW	27.35 TQ	CABLS	1/16-3/16
	Anaheim-Santa Ana-Irvine PMSA, CA	H	18.80 FQ	22.74 MW	27.67 TQ	CABLS	1/16-3/16
	Los Angeles-Long Beach-Glendale PMSA, CA	H	17.60 FQ	22.21 MW	26.93 TQ	CABLS	1/16-3/16
	Oakland-Hayward-Berkeley PMSA, CA	H	18.74 FQ	23.66 MW	29.30 TQ	CABLS	1/16-3/16
	Riverside-San Bernardino-Ontario MSA, CA	H	16.77 FQ	20.16 MW	24.57 TQ	CABLS	1/16-3/16
	Sacramento–Roseville–Arden-Arcade MSA, CA	H	18.28 FQ	22.74 MW	25.58 TQ	CABLS	1/16-3/16
	San Diego-Carlsbad MSA, CA	H	17.98 FQ	22.06 MW	26.38 TQ	CABLS	1/16-3/16
	San Francisco-Redwood City-South San Francisco PMSA, CA	H	23.07 FQ	28.98 MW	37.19 TQ	CABLS	1/16-3/16
	Colorado	Y	33910 FQ	42740 MW	51760 TQ	USBLS	5/15
	Denver-Aurora-Lakewood MSA, CO	Y	34700 FQ	44030 MW	52910 TQ	USBLS	5/15
	Connecticut	Y		47627 MW		CTBLS	1/16-3/16
	Bridgeport-Stamford-Norwalk MSA, CT	Y	38980 FQ	46720 MW	55520 TQ	USBLS	5/15
	Hartford-West Hartford-East Hartford MSA, CT	Y	41930 FQ	46880 MW	53430 TQ	USBLS	5/15
	Delaware	Y	36240 FQ	44490 MW	52900 TQ	USBLS	5/15
	Wilmington PMSA, DE-MD-NJ	Y	40040 FQ	46310 MW	54950 TQ	USBLS	5/15
	District of Columbia	Y	48600 FQ	57020 MW	66920 TQ	USBLS	5/15
	Washington-Arlington-Alexandria PMSA, DC-VA-MD-WV	Y	42510 FQ	51830 MW	61390 TQ	USBLS	5/15
	Florida	H	14.64 AE	18.97 MW	22.35 AEX	FLBLS	7/16-9/16
	Fort Lauderdale-Pompano Beach-Deerfield Beach PMSA, FL	H	16.43 AE	20.21 MW	23.46 AEX	FLBLS	7/16-9/16
	Miami-Miami Beach-Kendall PMSA, FL	H	16.02 AE	21.97 MW	26.55 AEX	FLBLS	7/16-9/16
	Orlando-Kissimmee-Sanford MSA, FL	H	13.15 AE	17.85 MW	20.82 AEX	FLBLS	7/16-9/16
	Tampa-St. Petersburg-Clearwater MSA, FL	H	14.93 AE	19.10 MW	21.98 AEX	FLBLS	7/16-9/16
	Georgia	Y	33330 FQ	41430 MW	49560 TQ	USBLS	5/15
	Atlanta-Sandy Springs-Roswell MSA, GA	Y	36310 FQ	44090 MW	51540 TQ	USBLS	5/15
	Augusta-Richmond County MSA, GA-SC	Y	29070 FQ	35640 MW	44230 TQ	USBLS	5/15
	Hawaii	Y	32700 FQ	38940 MW	48300 TQ	USBLS	5/15
	Urban Honolulu MSA, HI	Y	33760 FQ	39440 MW	49260 TQ	USBLS	5/15
	Idaho	Y	29830 FQ	36680 MW	44250 TQ	USBLS	5/15
	Boise City MSA, ID	Y	30270 FQ	36960 MW	45130 TQ	USBLS	5/15

AE	Average entry wage	**AWR** Average wage range	**H** Hourly	**LR** Low end range	**MTC** Median total compensation	**TCC** Total cash compensation
AEX	Average experienced wage	**B** Biweekly	**HI** Highest wage paid	**M** Monthly	**MW** Median wage paid	**TQ** Third quartile wage
ATC	Average total compensation	**D** Daily	**HR** High end range	**MCC** Median cash compensation	**MWR** Median wage range	**W** Weekly
AW	Average wage paid	**FQ** First quartile wage	**LO** Lowest wage paid	**ME** Median entry wage	**S** See annotated source	**Y** Yearly

Occupation/Type/Industry	Location	Per	Low	Mid	High	Source	Date
Payroll and Timekeeping Clerk	Illinois	Y	35280 FQ	43630 MW	50940 TQ	USBLS	5/15
	Chicago-Naperville-Arlington Heights PMSA, IL	Y	37930 FQ	45080 MW	52980 TQ	USBLS	5/15
	Lake County-Kenosha County PMSA, IL-WI	Y	36190 FQ	44230 MW	51740 TQ	USBLS	5/15
	Indiana	Y	32090 FQ	38320 MW	45590 TQ	USBLS	5/15
	Gary PMSA, IN	Y	30630 FQ	36150 MW	43330 TQ	USBLS	5/15
	Indianapolis-Carmel-Anderson MSA, IN	Y	34580 FQ	40980 MW	46570 TQ	USBLS	5/15
	Iowa	Y	34210 FQ	38980 MW	46130 TQ	USBLS	5/15
	Des Moines-West Des Moines MSA, IA	Y	35480 FQ	40260 MW	46900 TQ	USBLS	5/15
	Kansas	Y	32000 FQ	39450 MW	47660 TQ	USBLS	5/15
	Wichita MSA, KS	Y	27300 FQ	36290 MW	46270 TQ	USBLS	5/15
	Kentucky	Y	32090 FQ	38130 MW	45390 TQ	USBLS	5/15
	Louisville-Jefferson County MSA, KY-IN	Y	33100 FQ	40170 MW	46810 TQ	USBLS	5/15
	Louisiana	Y	29130 FQ	35810 MW	43590 TQ	USBLS	5/15
	Baton Rouge MSA, LA	Y	31900 FQ	40130 MW	50120 TQ	USBLS	5/15
	New Orleans-Metairie MSA, LA	Y	29430 FQ	35760 MW	42350 TQ	USBLS	5/15
	Maine	Y	33170 FQ	39800 MW	47540 TQ	USBLS	5/15
	Portland-South Portland MSA, ME	Y	35620 FQ	42420 MW	50190 TQ	USBLS	5/15
	Maryland	Y	29554 AE	44235 MW	51575 AEX	MDBLS	4/16
	Baltimore-Columbia-Towson MSA, MD	Y	33210 FQ	43880 MW	51530 TQ	USBLS	5/15
	Salisbury MSA, MD-DE	Y	31430 FQ	37190 MW	45230 TQ	USBLS	5/15
	Massachusetts	Y	40310 FQ	47530 MW	56560 TQ	USBLS	5/15
	Boston-Cambridge-Newton NECTA, MA	Y	42190 FQ	49180 MW	57990 TQ	USBLS	5/15
	Worcester MSA, MA-CT	Y	36930 FQ	45140 MW	54150 TQ	USBLS	5/15
	Michigan	Y	32890 FQ	39550 MW	47040 TQ	USBLS	5/15
	Detroit-Dearborn-Livonia PMSA, MI	Y	32370 FQ	39010 MW	47360 TQ	USBLS	5/15
	Grand Rapids-Wyoming MSA, MI	Y	34310 FQ	41240 MW	47970 TQ	USBLS	5/15
	Minnesota	Y	36295 FQ	43839 MW	50584 TQ	MNBLS	1/16-3/16
	Minneapolis-St. Paul-Bloomington MSA, MN-WI	Y	38742 FQ	45477 MW	52495 TQ	MNBLS	1/16-3/16
	Mississippi	Y	28500 FQ	34690 MW	41730 TQ	USBLS	5/15
	Jackson MSA, MS	Y	30080 FQ	36140 MW	44410 TQ	USBLS	5/15
	Missouri	Y	32140 FQ	38380 MW	46280 TQ	USBLS	5/15
	Kansas City MSA, MO-KS	Y	34710 FQ	41170 MW	48840 TQ	USBLS	5/15
	St. Louis MSA, MO-IL	Y	33770 FQ	41230 MW	48150 TQ	USBLS	5/15
	Montana	Y	29930 FQ	36020 MW	44670 TQ	USBLS	5/15
	Billings MSA, MT	Y	33080 FQ	37780 MW	45880 TQ	USBLS	5/15
	Nebraska	Y	29575 FQ	36520 MW	44585 TQ	NEBLS	7/16-9/16
	Omaha-Council Bluffs MSA, NE-IA	Y	30930 FQ	37360 MW	45505 TQ	NEBLS	7/16-9/16
	Nevada	Y	30580 FQ	38370 MW	48520 TQ	USBLS	5/15
	Las Vegas-Henderson-Paradise MSA, NV	Y	29410 FQ	37410 MW	47380 TQ	USBLS	5/15
	New Hampshire	H	14.88 AE	21.69 MW	25.01 AEX	NHBLS	6/16
	Manchester NECTA, NH	H	16.70 AE	21.92 MW	24.88 AEX	NHBLS	6/16
	Nashua NECTA, NH-MA	Y	32560 FQ	42560 MW	48550 TQ	USBLS	5/15
	New Jersey	Y	37810 FQ	46150 MW	56030 TQ	USBLS	5/15
	Camden PMSA, NJ	Y	35000 FQ	42890 MW	51050 TQ	USBLS	5/15
	Newark PMSA, NJ-PA	Y	40670 FQ	49770 MW	58720 TQ	USBLS	5/15
	Trenton MSA, NJ	Y	38340 FQ	46030 MW	54850 TQ	USBLS	5/15
	New Mexico	Y	28790 FQ	35510 MW	43910 TQ	USBLS	5/15
	Albuquerque MSA, NM	Y	29900 FQ	35900 MW	43820 TQ	USBLS	5/15
	New York	Y	31130 AE	44840 MW	53560 AEX	NYBLS	1/16-3/16
	Buffalo-Cheektowaga-Niagara Falls MSA, NY	Y	32900 FQ	39720 MW	47170 TQ	USBLS	5/15
	Nassau County-Suffolk County PMSA, NY	Y	38320 FQ	47960 MW	59280 TQ	USBLS	5/15
	New York-Jersey City-White Plains PMSA, NY-NJ	Y	37310 FQ	46290 MW	57180 TQ	USBLS	5/15
	Rochester MSA, NY	Y	29420 FQ	37560 MW	45590 TQ	USBLS	5/15
	North Carolina	Y	31420 FQ	37620 MW	45700 TQ	USBLS	5/15

AE	Average entry wage	AWR	Average wage range	H	Hourly
AEX	Average experienced wage	B	Biweekly	HI	Highest wage paid
ATC	Average total compensation	D	Daily	HR	High end range
AW	Average wage paid	FQ	First quartile wage	LO	Lowest wage paid

LR	Low end range	MTC	Median total compensation	TCC	Total cash compensation
M	Monthly	MW	Median wage paid	TQ	Third quartile wage
MCC	Median cash compensation	MWR	Median wage range	W	Weekly
ME	Median entry wage	S	See annotated source	Y	Yearly

Occupation/Type/Industry	Location	Per	Low	Mid	High	Source	Date
Payroll and Timekeeping Clerk	Charlotte-Concord-Gastonia						
	MSA, NC-SC	Y	33550 FQ	40120 MW	48790 TQ	USBLS	5/15
	Raleigh MSA, NC	Y	32490 FQ	37810 MW	46230 TQ	USBLS	5/15
	North Dakota	Y	34600 FQ	39380 MW	46110 TQ	USBLS	5/15
	Fargo MSA, ND-MN	Y	34770 FQ	39820 MW	46230 TQ	USBLS	5/15
	Ohio	Y	32890 FQ	39810 MW	47320 TQ	USBLS	5/15
	Cincinnati MSA, OH-KY-IN	Y	32180 FQ	42350 MW	49300 TQ	USBLS	5/15
	Cleveland-Elyria MSA, OH	Y	36540 FQ	41970 MW	47130 TQ	USBLS	5/15
	Columbus MSA, OH	Y	32710 FQ	40640 MW	49340 TQ	USBLS	5/15
	Oklahoma	Y	28910 FQ	36160 MW	44840 TQ	USBLS	5/15
	Oklahoma City MSA, OK	Y	29520 FQ	36430 MW	45360 TQ	USBLS	5/15
	Tulsa MSA, OK	Y	30830 FQ	37440 MW	45820 TQ	USBLS	5/15
	Oregon	H	17.25 FQ	20.90 MW	24.22 TQ	ORBLS	2016
	Portland-Vancouver-Hillsboro						
	MSA, OR-WA	Y	37700 FQ	44500 MW	51090 TQ	USBLS	5/15
	Pennsylvania	Y	32300 FQ	39140 MW	47410 TQ	USBLS	5/15
	Allentown-Bethlehem-Easton						
	MSA, PA-NJ	Y	34130 FQ	39420 MW	46250 TQ	USBLS	5/15
	Harrisburg-Carlisle MSA, PA	Y	34690 FQ	42220 MW	49120 TQ	USBLS	5/15
	Montgomery County-Bucks						
	County-Chester County						
	PMSA, PA	Y	33210 FQ	42110 MW	51130 TQ	USBLS	5/15
	Philadelphia PMSA, PA	Y	35010 FQ	41900 MW	49500 TQ	USBLS	5/15
	Pittsburgh MSA, PA	Y	33080 FQ	39940 MW	47310 TQ	USBLS	5/15
	Rhode Island	Y	34750 FQ	42520 MW	48430 TQ	USBLS	5/15
	Providence-Warwick MSA, RI-						
	MA	Y	35460 FQ	43000 MW	48790 TQ	USBLS	5/15
	South Carolina	Y	32100 FQ	37760 MW	45700 TQ	USBLS	5/15
	Charleston-North Charleston						
	MSA, SC	Y	35470 FQ	41690 MW	47880 TQ	USBLS	5/15
	Columbia MSA, SC	Y	32550 FQ	38930 MW	47660 TQ	USBLS	5/15
	Greenville-Anderson-Mauldin						
	MSA, SC	Y	31580 FQ	36240 MW	42680 TQ	USBLS	5/15
	South Dakota	Y	29620 FQ	33960 MW	37720 TQ	USBLS	5/15
	Sioux Falls MSA, SD	Y	32440 FQ	35350 MW	38250 TQ	USBLS	5/15
	Tennessee	Y	31060 FQ	37550 MW	46780 TQ	USBLS	5/15
	Knoxville MSA, TN	Y	30900 FQ	38970 MW	48220 TQ	USBLS	5/15
	Memphis MSA, TN-MS-AR	Y	33890 FQ	39840 MW	48530 TQ	USBLS	5/15
	Nashville-Davidson–						
	Murfreesboro–Franklin						
	MSA, TN	Y	31230 FQ	38480 MW	47960 TQ	USBLS	5/15
	Texas	Y	31620 FQ	38840 MW	47930 TQ	USBLS	5/15
	Austin-Round Rock MSA, TX	Y	36180 FQ	43430 MW	50910 TQ	USBLS	5/15
	Dallas-Plano-Irving PMSA, TX	Y	33920 FQ	42070 MW	50260 TQ	USBLS	5/15
	Fort Worth-Arlington PMSA,						
	TX	Y	32270 FQ	40530 MW	48630 TQ	USBLS	5/15
	Houston-The Woodlands-						
	Sugar Land MSA, TX	Y	34160 FQ	43130 MW	52450 TQ	USBLS	5/15
	San Antonio-New Braunfels						
	MSA, TX	Y	31220 FQ	35510 MW	40390 TQ	USBLS	5/15
	Utah	Y	31500 FQ	38100 MW	46700 TQ	USBLS	5/15
	Ogden-Clearfield MSA, UT	Y	28080 FQ	37390 MW	45550 TQ	USBLS	5/15
	Provo-Orem MSA, UT	Y	31310 FQ	38100 MW	47310 TQ	USBLS	5/15
	Salt Lake City MSA, UT	Y	33720 FQ	39960 MW	48150 TQ	USBLS	5/15
	Vermont	Y	33100 FQ	38650 MW	46890 TQ	USBLS	5/15
	Burlington-South Burlington						
	MSA, VT	Y	35470 FQ	42210 MW	49130 TQ	USBLS	5/15
	Virginia	Y	34360 FQ	42220 MW	50650 TQ	USBLS	5/15
	Richmond MSA, VA	Y	36330 FQ	42980 MW	49040 TQ	USBLS	5/15
	Virginia Beach-Norfolk-						
	Newport News MSA, VA-NC	Y	34560 FQ	40940 MW	49070 TQ	USBLS	5/15
	Washington	H	18.38 FQ	22.08 MW	26.22 TQ	WABLS	3/16
	Seattle-Bellevue-Everett						
	PMSA, WA	H	20.48 FQ	23.66 MW	28.00 TQ	WABLS	3/16
	Tacoma-Lakewood PMSA, WA	H	18.33 FQ	21.21 MW	24.33 TQ	WABLS	3/16
	West Virginia	Y	25380 FQ	31310 MW	39280 TQ	USBLS	5/15
	Huntington-Ashland MSA,						
	WV-KY-OH	Y	28880 FQ	35570 MW	43790 TQ	USBLS	5/15
	Wisconsin	Y	33350 FQ	40760 MW	47450 TQ	USBLS	5/15
	Madison MSA, WI	Y	35750 FQ	43020 MW	49050 TQ	USBLS	5/15
	Milwaukee-Waukesha-West						
	Allis MSA, WI	Y	36790 FQ	43930 MW	50610 TQ	USBLS	5/15

AE	Average entry wage	AWR	Average wage range	H	Hourly	LR	Low end range	MTC	Median total compensation	TCC	Total cash compensation
AEX	Average experienced wage	B	Biweekly	HI	Highest wage paid	M	Monthly	MW	Median wage paid	TQ	Third quartile wage
ATC	Average total compensation	D	Daily	HR	High end range	MCC	Median cash compensation	MWR	Median wage range	W	Weekly
AW	Average wage paid	FQ	First quartile wage	LO	Lowest wage paid	ME	Median entry wage	S	See annotated source	Y	Yearly

Occupation/Type/Industry	Location	Per	Low	Mid	High	Source	Date
Payroll and Timekeeping Clerk	Wyoming	Y	34810 FQ	41820 MW	49760 TQ	USBLS	5/15
	Puerto Rico	Y	18270 FQ	22440 MW	29470 TQ	USBLS	5/15
	San Juan-Carolina-Caguas MSA, PR	Y	18570 FQ	23550 MW	30240 TQ	USBLS	5/15
	Virgin Islands	Y	26410 FQ	30740 MW	38860 TQ	USBLS	5/15
	Guam	Y	21000 FQ	27450 MW	35150 TQ	USBLS	5/15
Payroll/Insurance Technician							
County Government	Berrien County, GA	Y	27000 LO		35000 HI	GACTY04	2016
County Government	Dougherty County, GA	Y	26413 LO		39204 HI	GACTY04	2016
County Government	Douglas County, GA	Y	36933 LO		75580 HI	GACTY04	2016
Payroll Specialist							
Municipal Government	Hemet, CA	Y			67705 HI	CACIT	6/28/16
Municipal Government	Tulare, CA	Y			51066 HI	CACIT	6/28/16
Pediatrician							
General	Alabama	Y	130830 AE	193712 AW	225158 AEX	ALBLS	6/16
General	Birmingham-Hoover MSA, AL	Y	136294 AE	207779 AW	243527 AEX	ALBLS	6/16
General	Alaska	Y	126270 FQ	175750 MW		USBLS	5/15
General	Arizona	Y	107800 FQ	144350 MW	180390 TQ	USBLS	5/15
General	Phoenix-Mesa-Scottsdale MSA, AZ	Y	86190 FQ	147220 MW	181750 TQ	USBLS	5/15
General	Tucson MSA, AZ	Y	115170 FQ	126150 MW	157080 TQ	USBLS	5/15
General	Arkansas	Y	128730 FQ	181310 MW		USBLS	5/15
General	California	H	68.52 FQ	96.48 AW		CABLS	1/16-3/16
General	Anaheim-Santa Ana-Irvine PMSA, CA	H	72.80 FQ	105.88 AW		CABLS	1/16-3/16
General	Los Angeles-Long Beach-Glendale PMSA, CA	H	75.33 FQ	96.76 AW		CABLS	1/16-3/16
General	Oakland-Hayward-Berkeley PMSA, CA	H	62.47 FQ	84.81 MW		CABLS	1/16-3/16
General	Riverside-San Bernardino-Ontario MSA, CA	H	69.74 FQ	100.35 AW		CABLS	1/16-3/16
General	Sacramento–Roseville–Arden-Arcade MSA, CA	H	74.31 FQ	105.06 AW		CABLS	1/16-3/16
General	San Diego-Carlsbad MSA, CA	H	68.14 FQ	82.37 MW		CABLS	1/16-3/16
General	Colorado	Y	160370 FQ	207950 AW		USBLS	5/15
General	Denver-Aurora-Lakewood MSA, CO	Y	172640 FQ	210830 AW		USBLS	5/15
General	Connecticut	Y		145377 MW		CTBLS	1/16-3/16
General	Bridgeport-Stamford-Norwalk MSA, CT	Y	106520 FQ	162120 MW		USBLS	5/15
General	Hartford-West Hartford-East Hartford MSA, CT	Y	62120 FQ	150020 MW		USBLS	5/15
General	Delaware	Y	123270 FQ	148270 MW	176530 TQ	USBLS	5/15
General	Wilmington PMSA, DE-MD-NJ	Y	138830 FQ	165900 MW		USBLS	5/15
General	District of Columbia	Y	58570 FQ	76440 MW	135720 TQ	USBLS	5/15
General	Washington-Arlington-Alexandria PMSA, DC-VA-MD-WV	Y	74820 FQ	129310 MW	166290 TQ	USBLS	5/15
General	Florida	H	46.77 AE	79.72 MW	114.39 AEX	FLBLS	7/16-9/16
General	Fort Lauderdale-Pompano Beach-Deerfield Beach PMSA, FL	H	22.27 AE	87.94 MW	120.33 AEX	FLBLS	7/16-9/16
General	Miami-Miami Beach-Kendall PMSA, FL	H	27.46 AE	67.26 MW	88.28 AEX	FLBLS	7/16-9/16
General	Orlando-Kissimmee-Sanford MSA, FL	H	68.86 AE	89.60 MW	122.25 AEX	FLBLS	7/16-9/16
General	Tampa-St. Petersburg-Clearwater MSA, FL	H	59.47 AE	70.34 MW	82.93 AEX	FLBLS	7/16-9/16
General	Georgia	Y	127810 FQ	165910 MW		USBLS	5/15
General	Atlanta-Sandy Springs-Roswell MSA, GA	Y	130340 FQ	170040 MW		USBLS	5/15
General	Augusta-Richmond County MSA, GA-SC	Y	98890 FQ	142190 MW	175460 TQ	USBLS	5/15
General	Hawaii	Y	139660 FQ	166450 MW		USBLS	5/15
General	Urban Honolulu MSA, HI	Y	150600 FQ	177420 MW		USBLS	5/15
General	Idaho	Y	133550 FQ	152250 MW		USBLS	5/15
General	Illinois	Y	88700 FQ	146400 MW	179920 TQ	USBLS	5/15

AE	Average entry wage	AWR	Average wage range	H	Hourly	LR	Low end range	MTC	Median total compensation	TCC	Total cash compensation
AEX	Average experienced wage	B	Biweekly	HI	Highest wage paid	M	Monthly	MW	Median wage paid	TQ	Third quartile wage
ATC	Average total compensation	D	Daily	HR	High end range	MCC	Median cash compensation	MWR	Median wage range	W	Weekly
AW	Average wage paid	FQ	First quartile wage	LO	Lowest wage paid	ME	Median entry wage	S	See annotated source	Y	Yearly

Pediatrician

Occupation/Type/Industry	Location	Per	Low	Mid	High	Source	Date
Pediatrician							
General	Chicago-Naperville-Arlington Heights PMSA, IL	Y	70940 FQ	142830 MW	169180 TQ	USBLS	5/15
General	Lake County-Kenosha County PMSA, IL-WI	Y	64280 FQ	147000 MW	163160 TQ	USBLS	5/15
General	Indiana	Y	169520 FQ	222320 AW		USBLS	5/15
General	Indianapolis-Carmel-Anderson MSA, IN	Y	177290 FQ	235440 AW		USBLS	5/15
General	Iowa	Y	109550 FQ	160730 MW		USBLS	5/15
General	Des Moines-West Des Moines MSA, IA	Y	102000 FQ	142730 MW		USBLS	5/15
General	Kansas	Y	98700 FQ	153170 MW		USBLS	5/15
General	Wichita MSA, KS	Y	154120 FQ	235160 AW		USBLS	5/15
General	Kentucky	Y	124380 FQ	166850 MW		USBLS	5/15
General	Louisville-Jefferson County MSA, KY-IN	Y	122290 FQ	148610 MW		USBLS	5/15
General	Louisiana	Y	106260	126170 MW		USBLS	5/15
General	New Orleans-Metairie MSA, LA	Y	101040 FQ	113170 MW	126680 TQ	USBLS	5/15
General	Maine	Y	156210 FQ	176010 MW		USBLS	5/15
General	Portland-South Portland MSA, ME	Y	156500 FQ	176130 MW		USBLS	5/15
General	Maryland	Y	112597 AE	183207 MW	218512 AEX	MDBLS	4/16
General	Baltimore-Columbia-Towson MSA, MD	Y	147280 FQ	196020 AW		USBLS	5/15
General	Massachusetts	Y	164350 FQ	222480 AW		USBLS	5/15
General	Boston-Cambridge-Newton NECTA, MA	Y	180210 FQ	239940 AW		USBLS	5/15
General	Worcester MSA, MA-CT	Y	135650 FQ	195750 AW		USBLS	5/15
General	Michigan	Y	130910 FQ	176150 MW		USBLS	5/15
General	Detroit-Dearborn-Livonia PMSA, MI	Y	140360 FQ	183600 MW		USBLS	5/15
General	Grand Rapids-Wyoming MSA, MI	Y	162850 FQ	222750 AW		USBLS	5/15
General	Minnesota	Y	167951 FQ	211439 AW		MNBLS	1/16-3/16
General	Minneapolis-St. Paul-Bloomington MSA, MN-WI	Y	168324 FQ	209302 AW		MNBLS	1/16-3/16
General	Mississippi	Y		266040 AW		USBLS	5/15
General	Jackson MSA, MS	Y	179580 FQ	249850 AW		USBLS	5/15
General	Missouri	Y	167460 FQ	217520 AW		USBLS	5/15
General	Montana	Y	184560 FQ	235440 MW		USBLS	5/15
General	Nevada	Y	169640 FQ	184390 MW		USBLS	5/15
General	Las Vegas-Henderson-Paradise MSA, NV	Y	163940 FQ	179900 MW		USBLS	5/15
General	New Hampshire	H	60.91 AE	86.98 MW	108.50 AEX	NHBLS	6/16
General	Manchester NECTA, NH	H	60.44 AE	86.09 MW	111.71 AEX	NHBLS	6/16
General	New Jersey	Y	140020 FQ	159140 MW		USBLS	5/15
General	Camden PMSA, NJ	Y	134860 FQ	164680 MW		USBLS	5/15
General	Newark PMSA, NJ-PA	Y	143310 FQ	163610 MW		USBLS	5/15
General	Trenton MSA, NJ	Y	140020 FQ	154820 MW	173940 TQ	USBLS	5/15
General	New Mexico	Y	135130 FQ	173390 MW		USBLS	5/15
General	New York	Y	87830 AE	151840 MW		NYBLS	1/16-3/16
General	Buffalo-Cheektowaga-Niagara Falls MSA, NY	Y	44610 FQ	49780 MW	154680 TQ	USBLS	5/15
General	Nassau County-Suffolk County PMSA, NY	Y	119480 FQ	142840 MW	168460 TQ	USBLS	5/15
General	New York-Jersey City-White Plains PMSA, NY-NJ	Y	124670 FQ	150240 MW	185620 TQ	USBLS	5/15
General	North Carolina	Y	142380 FQ	181850 MW		USBLS	5/15
General	Charlotte-Concord-Gastonia MSA, NC-SC	Y	182630 FQ	236940 AW		USBLS	5/15
General	Ohio	Y	131110 FQ	161980 MW		USBLS	5/15
General	Cincinnati MSA, OH-KY-IN	Y	133450 FQ	158990 MW		USBLS	5/15
General	Cleveland-Elyria MSA, OH	Y	61970 FQ	163310 MW		USBLS	5/15
General	Columbus MSA, OH	Y	134580 FQ	167860 MW	187050 TQ	USBLS	5/15
General	Oklahoma	Y	131230 FQ	182440 MW		USBLS	5/15
General	Oklahoma City MSA, OK	Y	161780 FQ	210970 AW		USBLS	5/15
General	Tulsa MSA, OK	Y	112930 FQ	121840 MW	130750 TQ	USBLS	5/15
General	Oregon	H	69.60 FQ	84.00 MW		ORBLS	2016
General	Portland-Vancouver-Hillsboro MSA, OR-WA	Y	137180 FQ	167710 MW		USBLS	5/15
General	Pennsylvania	Y	109370 FQ	153510 MW		USBLS	5/15

AE Average entry wage	**AWR** Average wage range	**H** Hourly	**LR** Low end range	**MTC** Median total compensation	**TCC** Total cash compensation
AEX Average experienced wage	**B** Biweekly	**HI** Highest wage paid	**M** Monthly	**MW** Median wage paid	**TQ** Third quartile wage
ATC Average total compensation	**D** Daily	**HR** High end range	**MCC** Median cash compensation	**MWR** Median wage range	**W** Weekly
AW Average wage paid	**FQ** First quartile wage	**LO** Lowest wage paid	**ME** Median entry wage	**S** See annotated source	**Y** Yearly

Occupation/Type/Industry	Location	Per	Low	Mid	High	Source	Date
Pediatrician							
General	Allentown-Bethlehem-Easton MSA, PA-NJ	Y	135070 FQ	152010 MW	179340 TQ	USBLS	5/15
General	Harrisburg-Carlisle MSA, PA	Y	59300 FQ	90990 MW	153510 TQ	USBLS	5/15
General	Philadelphia PMSA, PA	Y	157760 FQ	203510 AW		USBLS	5/15
General	Rhode Island	Y	119220 FQ	148580 MW		USBLS	5/15
General	Providence-Warwick MSA, RI-MA	Y	117580 FQ	147780 MW	186320 TQ	USBLS	5/15
General	South Carolina	Y	153110 FQ	181620 MW		USBLS	5/15
General	Columbia MSA, SC	Y	129040 FQ	157930 MW		USBLS	5/15
General	South Dakota	Y	169850 FQ	225780 AW		USBLS	5/15
General	Tennessee	Y	151000 FQ	204300 AW		USBLS	5/15
General	Memphis MSA, TN-MS-AR	Y	152780 FQ	220990 AW		USBLS	5/15
General	Nashville-Davidson–Murfreesboro–Franklin MSA, TN	Y	155620 FQ	184790 MW		USBLS	5/15
General	Texas	Y	140390 FQ	172970 MW		USBLS	5/15
General	Austin-Round Rock MSA, TX	Y	137080 FQ	160330 MW		USBLS	5/15
General	Dallas-Plano-Irving PMSA, TX	Y	123850 FQ	149650 MW		USBLS	5/15
General	Fort Worth-Arlington PMSA, TX	Y	136550 FQ	161600 MW		USBLS	5/15
General	Houston-The Woodlands-Sugar Land MSA, TX	Y	148140 FQ	179080 MW		USBLS	5/15
General	San Antonio-New Braunfels MSA, TX	Y	148440 FQ	168820 MW		USBLS	5/15
General	Utah	Y	158440 FQ	236630 AW		USBLS	5/15
General	Salt Lake City MSA, UT	Y	178590 FQ	250080 AW		USBLS	5/15
General	Virginia	Y	119680 FQ	157330 MW		USBLS	5/15
General	Richmond MSA, VA	Y	118780 FQ	153920 MW	186690 TQ	USBLS	5/15
General	Virginia Beach-Norfolk-Newport News MSA, VA-NC	Y	123440 FQ	194540 AW		USBLS	5/15
General	Washington	H	66.36 FQ	88.52 MW		WABLS	3/16
General	Seattle-Bellevue-Everett PMSA, WA	H	62.95 FQ	101.66 AW		WABLS	3/16
General	Huntington-Ashland MSA, WV-KY-OH	Y	134220 FQ	154170 MW		USBLS	5/15
General	Wisconsin	Y	149350 FQ	182860 MW		USBLS	5/15
General	Milwaukee-Waukesha-West Allis MSA, WI	Y	153970 FQ	181360 MW		USBLS	5/15
General	Wyoming	Y	135000 FQ	155550 MW		USBLS	5/15
General	Puerto Rico	Y	31370 FQ	57040 MW	76600 TQ	USBLS	5/15
Peer Review Nurse							
Mental Health Department, State Government	Ohio	H	26.76 LO		40.80 HI	OHGOV	2015
Pegasystems Certified Lead System Architect	United States	Y		129480 AW		CERTM02	2015
People Walker	Los Angeles, CA	S			7.00 HI	GRD01	2016
Performing Artist							
Public Library	Nashville, TN	Y		40105 AW		NTNGOV	2017
Performing Arts Manager							
Parks, Recreation and Arts, Municipal Government	Lancaster, CA	Y			25168 HI	CACIT	6/28/16
Permit Analyst							
Development Services, Municipal Government	Roseville, CA	Y			89226 HI	CACIT	6/28/16
Personal Care Aide	Alabama	Y	17493 AE	18687 AW	19285 AEX	ALBLS	6/16
	Birmingham-Hoover MSA, AL	Y	17493 AE	18945 AW	19665 AEX	ALBLS	6/16
	Alaska	Y	27050 FQ	31660 MW	35770 TQ	USBLS	5/15
	Anchorage MSA, AK	Y	26730 FQ	31070 MW	35330 TQ	USBLS	5/15
	Arizona	Y	18920 FQ	21190 MW	23630 TQ	USBLS	5/15
	Phoenix-Mesa-Scottsdale MSA, AZ	Y	19850 FQ	21930 MW	24020 TQ	USBLS	5/15
	Tucson MSA, AZ	Y	18050 FQ	19330 MW	22250 TQ	USBLS	5/15
	Arkansas	Y	16740 FQ	18160 MW	19700 TQ	USBLS	5/15

AE	Average entry wage	AWR	Average wage range	H	Hourly	LR	Low end range	MTC	Median total compensation	TCC	Total cash compensation
AEX	Average experienced wage	B	Biweekly	HI	Highest wage paid	M	Monthly	MW	Median wage paid	TQ	Third quartile wage
ATC	Average total compensation	D	Daily	HR	High end range	MCC	Median cash compensation	MWR	Median wage range	W	Weekly
AW	Average wage paid	FQ	First quartile wage	LO	Lowest wage paid	ME	Median entry wage	S	See annotated source	Y	Yearly

Personal Care Aide

Occupation/Type/Industry	Location	Per	Low	Mid	High	Source	Date
Personal Care Aide	Little Rock-North Little Rock-Conway MSA, AR	Y	17320 FQ	19170 MW	22890 TQ	USBLS	5/15
	California	H	9.55 FQ	10.68 MW	11.97 TQ	CABLS	1/16-3/16
	Anaheim-Santa Ana-Irvine PMSA, CA	H	10.00 FQ	10.83 MW	11.65 TQ	CABLS	1/16-3/16
	Los Angeles-Long Beach-Glendale PMSA, CA	H	9.44 FQ	10.19 MW	11.80 TQ	CABLS	1/16-3/16
	Oakland-Hayward-Berkeley PMSA, CA	H	9.83 FQ	11.20 MW	13.03 TQ	CABLS	1/16-3/16
	Riverside-San Bernardino-Ontario MSA, CA	H	9.45 FQ	10.15 MW	11.52 TQ	CABLS	1/16-3/16
	Sacramento-Roseville-Arden-Arcade MSA, CA	H	9.65 FQ	10.67 MW	11.72 TQ	CABLS	1/16-3/16
	San Diego-Carlsbad MSA, CA	H	9.46 FQ	10.47 MW	11.55 TQ	CABLS	1/16-3/16
	San Francisco-Redwood City-South San Francisco PMSA, CA	H	10.50 FQ	12.13 MW	14.23 TQ	CABLS	1/16-3/16
	Colorado	Y	19510 FQ	21610 MW	23700 TQ	USBLS	5/15
	Denver-Aurora-Lakewood MSA, CO	Y	19980 FQ	21700 MW	23420 TQ	USBLS	5/15
	Connecticut	Y		25962 MW		CTBLS	1/16-3/16
	Bridgeport-Stamford-Norwalk MSA, CT	Y	24050 FQ	27510 MW	30680 TQ	USBLS	5/15
	Hartford-West Hartford-East Hartford MSA, CT	Y	20880 FQ	25000 MW	29230 TQ	USBLS	5/15
	Delaware	Y	21030 FQ	22720 MW	24420 TQ	USBLS	5/15
	Wilmington PMSA, DE-MD-NJ	Y	21140 FQ	22940 MW	25200 TQ	USBLS	5/15
	District of Columbia	Y	22110 FQ	24960 MW	28060 TQ	USBLS	5/15
	Washington-Arlington-Alexandria PMSA, DC-VA-MD-WV	Y	21200 FQ	23150 MW	25620 TQ	USBLS	5/15
	Florida	H	9.01 AE	10.42 MW	11.77 AEX	FLBLS	7/16-9/16
	Fort Lauderdale-Pompano Beach-Deerfield Beach PMSA, FL	H	9.00 AE	9.55 MW	10.47 AEX	FLBLS	7/16-9/16
	Miami-Miami Beach-Kendall PMSA, FL	H	9.14 AE	10.98 MW	13.57 AEX	FLBLS	7/16-9/16
	Orlando-Kissimmee-Sanford MSA, FL	H	9.18 AE	10.65 MW	11.90 AEX	FLBLS	7/16-9/16
	Tampa-St. Petersburg-Clearwater MSA, FL	H	9.06 AE	10.50 MW	11.89 AEX	FLBLS	7/16-9/16
	Georgia	Y	17200 FQ	18980 MW	22300 TQ	USBLS	5/15
	Atlanta-Sandy Springs-Roswell MSA, GA	Y	17740 FQ	20160 MW	23480 TQ	USBLS	5/15
	Augusta-Richmond County MSA, GA-SC	Y	16890 FQ	18310 MW	19830 TQ	USBLS	5/15
	Hawaii	Y	18640 FQ	22070 MW	26750 TQ	USBLS	5/15
	Urban Honolulu MSA, HI	Y	18800 FQ	21650 MW	24170 TQ	USBLS	5/15
	Idaho	Y	17520 FQ	19630 MW	22610 TQ	USBLS	5/15
	Boise City MSA, ID	Y	17910 FQ	20320 MW	22640 TQ	USBLS	5/15
	Illinois	Y	20040 FQ	21860 MW	23670 TQ	USBLS	5/15
	Chicago-Naperville-Arlington Heights PMSA, IL	Y	20470 FQ	22130 MW	23790 TQ	USBLS	5/15
	Lake County-Kenosha County PMSA, IL-WI	Y	19270 FQ	21680 MW	24300 TQ	USBLS	5/15
	Indiana	Y	17490 FQ	19530 MW	22390 TQ	USBLS	5/15
	Gary PMSA, IN	Y	17460 FQ	19420 MW	23360 TQ	USBLS	5/15
	Indianapolis-Carmel-Anderson MSA, IN	Y	17730 FQ	19930 MW	22580 TQ	USBLS	5/15
	Iowa	Y	20420 FQ	22530 MW	24680 TQ	USBLS	5/15
	Des Moines-West Des Moines MSA, IA	Y	20410 FQ	22700 MW	25610 TQ	USBLS	5/15
	Kansas	Y	19070 FQ	21410 MW	23410 TQ	USBLS	5/15
	Wichita MSA, KS	Y	20530 FQ	22040 MW	23550 TQ	USBLS	5/15
	Kentucky	Y	17830 FQ	20450 MW	23720 TQ	USBLS	5/15
	Louisville-Jefferson County MSA, KY-IN	Y	20130 FQ	22040 MW	23950 TQ	USBLS	5/15
	Louisiana	Y	16680 FQ	17950 MW	19220 TQ	USBLS	5/15
	Baton Rouge MSA, LA	Y	16720 FQ	18040 MW	19360 TQ	USBLS	5/15
	New Orleans-Metairie MSA, LA	Y	16980 FQ	18510 MW	20700 TQ	USBLS	5/15

AE	Average entry wage	AWR	Average wage range	H	Hourly	LR	Low end range	MTC	Median total compensation	TCC	Total cash compensation
AEX	Average experienced wage	B	Biweekly	HI	Highest wage paid	M	Monthly	MW	Median wage paid	TQ	Third quartile wage
ATC	Average total compensation	D	Daily	HR	High end range	MCC	Median cash compensation	MWR	Median wage range	W	Weekly
AW	Average wage paid	FQ	First quartile wage	LO	Lowest wage paid	ME	Median entry wage	S	See annotated source	Y	Yearly

Personal Care Aide

Occupation/Type/Industry	Location	Per	Low	Mid	High	Source	Date
Personal Care Aide	Shreveport-Bossier City MSA, LA	Y	16570 FQ	17730 MW	18880 TQ	USBLS	5/15
	Maine	Y	19030 FQ	21570 MW	24120 TQ	USBLS	5/15
	Portland-South Portland MSA, ME	Y	18150 FQ	20350 MW	23310 TQ	USBLS	5/15
	Maryland	Y	19271 AE	24046 MW	26433 AEX	MDBLS	4/16
	Baltimore-Columbia-Towson MSA, MD	Y	20210 FQ	23150 MW	27310 TQ	USBLS	5/15
	Salisbury MSA, MD-DE	Y	20180 FQ	22270 MW	24310 TQ	USBLS	5/15
	Massachusetts	Y	24450 FQ	27060 MW	29610 TQ	USBLS	5/15
	Boston-Cambridge-Newton NECTA, MA	Y	24650 FQ	27280 MW	29870 TQ	USBLS	5/15
	Worcester MSA, MA-CT	Y	23140 FQ	26300 MW	29560 TQ	USBLS	5/15
	Michigan	Y	18570 FQ	20690 MW	23640 TQ	USBLS	5/15
	Detroit-Dearborn-Livonia PMSA, MI	Y	17970 FQ	18900 MW	21210 TQ	USBLS	5/15
	Grand Rapids-Wyoming MSA, MI	Y	18640 FQ	20930 MW	23920 TQ	USBLS	5/15
	Minnesota	Y	21460 FQ	23419 MW	25994 TQ	MNBLS	1/16-3/16
	Minneapolis-St. Paul-Bloomington MSA, MN-WI	Y	21591 FQ	23580 MW	26418 TQ	MNBLS	1/16-3/16
	Mississippi	Y	16620 FQ	17810 MW	18990 TQ	USBLS	5/15
	Jackson MSA, MS	Y	16670 FQ	17860 MW	19060 TQ	USBLS	5/15
	Missouri	Y	17670 FQ	19410 MW	22380 TQ	USBLS	5/15
	Kansas City MSA, MO-KS	Y	19130 FQ	21430 MW	23550 TQ	USBLS	5/15
	St. Louis MSA, MO-IL	Y	18690 FQ	20890 MW	23180 TQ	USBLS	5/15
	Montana	Y	20090 FQ	21980 MW	23870 TQ	USBLS	5/15
	Billings MSA, MT	Y	20100 FQ	21930 MW	23760 TQ	USBLS	5/15
	Omaha-Council Bluffs MSA, NE-IA	Y	20720 FQ	22670 MW	24625 TQ	NEBLS	7/16-9/16
	Nevada	Y	19880 FQ	21910 MW	23930 TQ	USBLS	5/15
	Las Vegas-Henderson-Paradise MSA, NV	Y	19910 FQ	21910 MW	23910 TQ	USBLS	5/15
	New Hampshire	H	10.13 AE	11.34 MW	12.26 AEX	NHBLS	6/16
	Manchester NECTA, NH	H	9.84 AE	11.18 MW	11.95 AEX	NHBLS	6/16
	Nashua NECTA, NH-MA	Y	21390 FQ	23650 MW	27480 TQ	USBLS	5/15
	New Jersey	Y	21290 FQ	23920 MW	32170 TQ	USBLS	5/15
	Camden PMSA, NJ	Y	20900 FQ	23670 MW	42150 TQ	USBLS	5/15
	Newark PMSA, NJ-PA	Y	21310 FQ	24270 MW	37430 TQ	USBLS	5/15
	Trenton MSA, NJ	Y	20380 FQ	22430 MW	24500 TQ	USBLS	5/15
	New Mexico	Y	17510 FQ	19080 MW	22160 TQ	USBLS	5/15
	Albuquerque MSA, NM	Y	17710 FQ	19560 MW	22700 TQ	USBLS	5/15
	New York	Y	21500 AE	23690 MW	27360 AEX	NYBLS	1/16-3/16
	Buffalo-Cheektowaga-Niagara Falls MSA, NY	Y	20110 FQ	23170 MW	28120 TQ	USBLS	5/15
	Nassau County-Suffolk County PMSA, NY	Y	22110 FQ	25140 MW	29070 TQ	USBLS	5/15
	New York-Jersey City-White Plains PMSA, NY-NJ	Y	20900 FQ	22780 MW	24690 TQ	USBLS	5/15
	Rochester MSA, NY	Y	20320 FQ	22880 MW	27600 TQ	USBLS	5/15
	Utica-Rome MSA, NY	Y	20460 FQ	22980 MW	30490 TQ	USBLS	5/15
	North Carolina	Y	17570 FQ	19710 MW	23040 TQ	USBLS	5/15
	Charlotte-Concord-Gastonia MSA, NC-SC	Y	17740 FQ	20180 MW	22930 TQ	USBLS	5/15
	Raleigh MSA, NC	Y	18500 FQ	21370 MW	24060 TQ	USBLS	5/15
	North Dakota	Y	26390 FQ	29900 MW	34810 TQ	USBLS	5/15
	Fargo MSA, ND-MN	Y	22250 FQ	25190 MW	30160 TQ	USBLS	5/15
	Ohio	Y	18430 FQ	20200 MW	23320 TQ	USBLS	5/15
	Cincinnati MSA, OH-KY-IN	Y	18550 FQ	20700 MW	23070 TQ	USBLS	5/15
	Cleveland-Elyria MSA, OH	Y	18800 FQ	20950 MW	23610 TQ	USBLS	5/15
	Columbus MSA, OH	Y	18900 FQ	21740 MW	25760 TQ	USBLS	5/15
	Oklahoma	Y	16940 FQ	18410 MW	20070 TQ	USBLS	5/15
	Oklahoma City MSA, OK	Y	17890 FQ	19950 MW	22720 TQ	USBLS	5/15
	Tulsa MSA, OK	Y	16840 FQ	18150 MW	19480 TQ	USBLS	5/15
	Oregon	H	10.27 FQ	11.19 MW	12.15 TQ	ORBLS	2016
	Portland-Vancouver-Hillsboro MSA, OR-WA	Y	21080 FQ	23080 MW	25590 TQ	USBLS	5/15
	Pennsylvania	Y	19540 FQ	21920 MW	24230 TQ	USBLS	5/15
	Allentown-Bethlehem-Easton MSA, PA-NJ	Y	20080 FQ	22130 MW	24170 TQ	USBLS	5/15
	Harrisburg-Carlisle MSA, PA	Y	20520 FQ	22230 MW	23940 TQ	USBLS	5/15

Occupation/Type/Industry	Location	Per	Low	Mid	High	Source	Date
Personal Care Aide	Montgomery County-Bucks County-Chester County PMSA, PA	Y	20780 FQ	22980 MW	25950 TQ	USBLS	5/15
	Philadelphia PMSA, PA	Y	19570 FQ	21900 MW	24120 TQ	USBLS	5/15
	Pittsburgh MSA, PA	Y	19210 FQ	21850 MW	24390 TQ	USBLS	5/15
	Rhode Island	Y	20540 FQ	22640 MW	24820 TQ	USBLS	5/15
	Providence-Warwick MSA, RI-MA	Y	20750 FQ	23010 MW	26070 TQ	USBLS	5/15
	South Carolina	Y	17140 FQ	18900 MW	21690 TQ	USBLS	5/15
	Charleston-North Charleston MSA, SC	Y	18430 FQ	20850 MW	22860 TQ	USBLS	5/15
	Columbia MSA, SC	Y	17330 FQ	19360 MW	22470 TQ	USBLS	5/15
	Greenville-Anderson-Mauldin MSA, SC	Y	16890 FQ	18350 MW	20020 TQ	USBLS	5/15
	South Dakota	Y	19230 FQ	21130 MW	23320 TQ	USBLS	5/15
	Sioux Falls MSA, SD	Y	18910 FQ	20440 MW	22610 TQ	USBLS	5/15
	Tennessee	Y	17050 FQ	18690 MW	21270 TQ	USBLS	5/15
	Knoxville MSA, TN	Y	17360 FQ	19360 MW	22390 TQ	USBLS	5/15
	Memphis MSA, TN-MS-AR	Y	16850 FQ	18290 MW	20030 TQ	USBLS	5/15
	Nashville-Davidson–Murfreesboro–Franklin MSA, TN	Y	17090 FQ	18760 MW	21420 TQ	USBLS	5/15
	Texas	Y	16670 FQ	17920 MW	19160 TQ	USBLS	5/15
	Austin-Round Rock MSA, TX	Y	17460 FQ	19390 MW	22400 TQ	USBLS	5/15
	Dallas-Plano-Irving PMSA, TX	Y	16770 FQ	18060 MW	19360 TQ	USBLS	5/15
	Fort Worth-Arlington PMSA, TX	Y	16970 FQ	18460 MW	20770 TQ	USBLS	5/15
	Houston-The Woodlands-Sugar Land MSA, TX	Y	16730 FQ	18020 MW	19320 TQ	USBLS	5/15
	San Antonio-New Braunfels MSA, TX	Y	16590 FQ	17810 MW	19040 TQ	USBLS	5/15
	Utah	Y	18040 FQ	20750 MW	23750 TQ	USBLS	5/15
	Ogden-Clearfield MSA, UT	Y	20040 FQ	21770 MW	23490 TQ	USBLS	5/15
	Provo-Orem MSA, UT	Y	16820 FQ	18250 MW	19910 TQ	USBLS	5/15
	Salt Lake City MSA, UT	Y	20160 FQ	22710 MW	26570 TQ	USBLS	5/15
	Burlington-South Burlington MSA, VT	Y	21320 FQ	23310 MW	26340 TQ	USBLS	5/15
	Virginia	Y	17030 FQ	18610 MW	21240 TQ	USBLS	5/15
	Richmond MSA, VA	Y	16850 FQ	18230 MW	19650 TQ	USBLS	5/15
	Virginia Beach-Norfolk-Newport News MSA, VA-NC	Y	16630 FQ	17840 MW	19050 TQ	USBLS	5/15
	Washington	H	10.67 FQ	11.67 MW	13.41 TQ	WABLS	3/16
	Seattle-Bellevue-Everett PMSA, WA	H	10.80 FQ	11.90 MW	13.82 TQ	WABLS	3/16
	Tacoma-Lakewood PMSA, WA	H	10.92 FQ	12.08 MW	14.01 TQ	WABLS	3/16
	West Virginia	Y	17570 FQ	18490 MW	19460 TQ	USBLS	5/15
	Huntington-Ashland MSA, WV-KY-OH	Y	17450 FQ	18330 MW	19210 TQ	USBLS	5/15
	Wisconsin	Y	19000 FQ	21470 MW	23690 TQ	USBLS	5/15
	Madison MSA, WI	Y	20030 FQ	22010 MW	23980 TQ	USBLS	5/15
	Milwaukee-Waukesha-West Allis MSA, WI	Y	18410 FQ	21070 MW	23470 TQ	USBLS	5/15
	Wyoming	Y	19970 FQ	22130 MW	24290 TQ	USBLS	5/15
	Cheyenne MSA, WY	Y	19970 FQ	21840 MW	23710 TQ	USBLS	5/15
	Puerto Rico	Y	16510 FQ	17590 MW	18670 TQ	USBLS	5/15
	San Juan-Carolina-Caguas MSA, PR	Y	16510 FQ	17590 MW	18670 TQ	USBLS	5/15
	Virgin Islands	Y	20480 FQ	22200 MW	23920 TQ	USBLS	5/15
Personal Financial Advisor	United States	Y		81060 MW		FORB01	2015
	Alabama	Y	49977 AE	125640 AW	163471 AEX	ALBLS	6/16
	Birmingham-Hoover MSA, AL	Y	52447 AE	124246 AW	160150 AEX	ALBLS	6/16
	Alaska	Y	65020 FQ	87010 MW	145390 TQ	USBLS	5/15
	Anchorage MSA, AK	Y	61290 FQ	104870 MW	150750 TQ	USBLS	5/15
	Arizona	Y	41070 FQ	67200 MW	92970 TQ	USBLS	5/15
	Phoenix-Mesa-Scottsdale MSA, AZ	Y	43370 FQ	68240 MW	92370 TQ	USBLS	5/15
	Tucson MSA, AZ	Y	38400 FQ	51370 MW	101010 TQ	USBLS	5/15
	Arkansas	Y	38820 FQ	69370 MW	118460 TQ	USBLS	5/15
	Little Rock-North Little Rock-Conway MSA, AR	Y	40930 FQ	69310 MW	140120 TQ	USBLS	5/15
	California	H	30.74 FQ	47.81 MW	87.48 TQ	CABLS	1/16-3/16

AE	Average entry wage	AWR	Average wage range	H	Hourly	LR	Low end range	MTC	Median total compensation	TCC	Total cash compensation
AEX	Average experienced wage	B	Biweekly	HI	Highest wage paid	M	Monthly	MW	Median wage paid	TQ	Third quartile wage
ATC	Average total compensation	D	Daily	HR	High end range	MCC	Median cash compensation	MWR	Median wage range	W	Weekly
AW	Average wage paid	FQ	First quartile wage	LO	Lowest wage paid	ME	Median entry wage	S	See annotated source	Y	Yearly

Occupation/Type/Industry	Location	Per	Low	Mid	High	Source	Date
Personal Financial Advisor	Anaheim-Santa Ana-Irvine PMSA, CA	H	27.80 FQ	45.83 MW	77.61 TQ	CABLS	1/16-3/16
	Los Angeles-Long Beach-Glendale PMSA, CA	H	30.94 FQ	45.94 MW	83.36 TQ	CABLS	1/16-3/16
	Oakland-Hayward-Berkeley PMSA, CA	H	36.77 FQ	61.29 MW		CABLS	1/16-3/16
	Riverside-San Bernardino-Ontario MSA, CA	H	22.54 FQ	35.53 MW	64.38 TQ	CABLS	1/16-3/16
	Sacramento–Roseville–Arden-Arcade MSA, CA	H	29.62 FQ	44.04 MW	73.87 TQ	CABLS	1/16-3/16
	San Diego-Carlsbad MSA, CA	H	33.36 FQ	58.49 MW	87.16 TQ	CABLS	1/16-3/16
	San Francisco-Redwood City-South San Francisco PMSA, CA	H	37.27 FQ	59.90 MW		CABLS	1/16-3/16
	Colorado	Y	63780 FQ	82390 MW	122420 TQ	USBLS	5/15
	Denver-Aurora-Lakewood MSA, CO	Y	68990 FQ	85410 MW	143020 TQ	USBLS	5/15
	Connecticut	Y		101997 MW		CTBLS	1/16-3/16
	Bridgeport-Stamford-Norwalk MSA, CT	Y	73160 FQ	108690 MW		USBLS	5/15
	Hartford-West Hartford-East Hartford MSA, CT	Y	58490 FQ	86010 MW	127020 TQ	USBLS	5/15
	Delaware	Y	67600 FQ	100400 MW	145860 TQ	USBLS	5/15
	Wilmington PMSA, DE-MD-NJ	Y	63260 FQ	90650 MW	138550 TQ	USBLS	5/15
	District of Columbia	Y	65480 FQ	92780 MW	143970 TQ	USBLS	5/15
	Washington-Arlington-Alexandria PMSA, DC-VA-MD-WV	Y	60350 FQ	81560 MW	150240 TQ	USBLS	5/15
	Florida	H	26.91 AE	47.36 MW	75.52 AEX	FLBLS	7/16-9/16
	Fort Lauderdale-Pompano Beach-Deerfield Beach PMSA, FL	H	26.65 AE	40.73 MW	57.44 AEX	FLBLS	7/16-9/16
	Miami-Miami Beach-Kendall PMSA, FL	H	32.90 AE	52.40 MW	81.84 AEX	FLBLS	7/16-9/16
	Orlando-Kissimmee-Sanford MSA, FL	H	27.99 AE	46.55 MW	71.54 AEX	FLBLS	7/16-9/16
	Tampa-St. Petersburg-Clearwater MSA, FL	H	24.93 AE	42.29 MW	69.67 AEX	FLBLS	7/16-9/16
	Georgia	Y	53140 FQ	86710 MW	167450 TQ	USBLS	5/15
	Atlanta-Sandy Springs-Roswell MSA, GA	Y	56420 FQ	91740 MW	175770 TQ	USBLS	5/15
	Augusta-Richmond County MSA, GA-SC	Y	37200 FQ	59450 MW	93960 TQ	USBLS	5/15
	Hawaii	Y	47550 FQ	73240 MW	119650 TQ	USBLS	5/15
	Urban Honolulu MSA, HI	Y	46580 FQ	73890 MW	122870 TQ	USBLS	5/15
	Idaho	Y	53780 FQ	69960 MW	114920 TQ	USBLS	5/15
	Boise City MSA, ID	Y	53280 FQ	66020 MW	94920 TQ	USBLS	5/15
	Illinois	Y	53230 FQ	79750 MW	126410 TQ	USBLS	5/15
	Chicago-Naperville-Arlington Heights PMSA, IL	Y	54470 FQ	81180 MW	128190 TQ	USBLS	5/15
	Lake County-Kenosha County PMSA, IL-WI	Y	63670 FQ	104040 MW	164070 TQ	USBLS	5/15
	Indiana	Y	47910 FQ	76400 MW	116730 TQ	USBLS	5/15
	Indianapolis-Carmel-Anderson MSA, IN	Y	53590 FQ	80790 MW	114950 TQ	USBLS	5/15
	Iowa	Y	45500 FQ	61010 MW	85720 TQ	USBLS	5/15
	Des Moines-West Des Moines MSA, IA	Y	44610 FQ	59450 MW	80960 TQ	USBLS	5/15
	Kansas	Y	52780 FQ	89950 MW	167570 TQ	USBLS	5/15
	Wichita MSA, KS	Y	50150 FQ	74640 MW		USBLS	5/15
	Kentucky	Y	40920 FQ	62410 MW	107850 TQ	USBLS	5/15
	Louisville-Jefferson County MSA, KY-IN	Y	43040 FQ	60000 MW	107760 TQ	USBLS	5/15
	Louisiana	Y	48760 FQ	69940 MW	104600 TQ	USBLS	5/15
	Baton Rouge MSA, LA	Y	45800 FQ	63040 MW	136920 TQ	USBLS	5/15
	New Orleans-Metairie MSA, LA	Y	55240 FQ	86220 MW	118580 TQ	USBLS	5/15
	Maine	Y	57020 FQ	91240 MW		USBLS	5/15
	Portland-South Portland MSA, ME	Y	66350 FQ	113980 MW		USBLS	5/15
	Maryland	Y	44357 AE	102139 MW	131030 AEX	MDBLS	4/16

AE	Average entry wage	AWR	Average wage range	H	Hourly	LR	Low end range	MTC	Median total compensation	TCC	Total cash compensation
AEX	Average experienced wage	B	Biweekly	HI	Highest wage paid	M	Monthly	MW	Median wage paid	TQ	Third quartile wage
ATC	Average total compensation	D	Daily	HR	High end range	MCC	Median cash compensation	MWR	Median wage range	W	Weekly
AW	Average wage paid	FQ	First quartile wage	LO	Lowest wage paid	ME	Median entry wage	S	See annotated source	Y	Yearly

Personal Financial Advisor

Occupation/Type/Industry	Location	Per	Low	Mid	High	Source	Date
Personal Financial Advisor	Baltimore-Columbia-Towson MSA, MD	Y	50620 FQ	73150 MW	129520 TQ	USBLS	5/15
	Salisbury MSA, MD-DE	Y	52310 FQ	60480 MW	112900 TQ	USBLS	5/15
	Massachusetts	Y	64610 FQ	94090 MW	180790 TQ	USBLS	5/15
	Boston-Cambridge-Newton NECTA, MA	Y	67770 FQ	96770 MW		USBLS	5/15
	Worcester MSA, MA-CT	Y	49500 FQ	64780 MW	126610 TQ	USBLS	5/15
	Michigan	Y	50660 FQ	66980 MW	121810 TQ	USBLS	5/15
	Detroit-Dearborn-Livonia PMSA, MI	Y	50030 FQ	69970 MW	124110 TQ	USBLS	5/15
	Grand Rapids-Wyoming MSA, MI	Y	35370 FQ	56480 MW	78660 TQ	USBLS	5/15
	Minnesota	Y	58395 FQ	88005 MW	133587 TQ	MNBLS	1/16-3/16
	Minneapolis-St. Paul-Bloomington MSA, MN-WI	Y	61322 FQ	95504 MW	145110 TQ	MNBLS	1/16-3/16
	Mississippi	Y	38400 FQ	67740 MW	100870 TQ	USBLS	5/15
	Jackson MSA, MS	Y	48310 FQ	78840 MW	111430 TQ	USBLS	5/15
	Missouri	Y	58780 FQ	84580 MW	139630 TQ	USBLS	5/15
	Kansas City MSA, MO-KS	Y	56110 FQ	85150 MW	150330 TQ	USBLS	5/15
	St, Louis MSA, MO-IL	Y	63830 FQ	90420 MW	140180 TQ	USBLS	5/15
	Montana	Y	49080 FQ	96730 MW	183910 TQ	USBLS	5/15
	Nebraska	Y	46650 FQ	86000 MW	164885 TQ	NEBLS	7/16-9/16
	Omaha-Council Bluffs MSA, NE-IA	Y	47420 FQ	86470 MW	181835 TQ	NEBLS	7/16-9/16
	Nevada	Y	40240 FQ	83270 MW	151690 TQ	USBLS	5/15
	Las Vegas-Henderson-Paradise MSA, NV	Y	39090 FQ	85140 MW	147100 TQ	USBLS	5/15
	New Hampshire	H	25.45 AE	44.59 MW	78.34 AEX	NHBLS	6/16
	Manchester NECTA, NH	H	26.93 AE	43.97 MW	77.87 AEX	NHBLS	6/16
	New Jersey	Y	66830 FQ	97490 MW	156840 TQ	USBLS	5/15
	Camden PMSA, NJ	Y	63290 FQ	97250 MW	170130 TQ	USBLS	5/15
	Newark PMSA, NJ-PA	Y	74210 FQ	104010 MW	155320 TQ	USBLS	5/15
	Trenton MSA, NJ	Y	61080 FQ	109350 MW	159660 TQ	USBLS	5/15
	New Mexico	Y	62930 FQ	95140 MW		USBLS	5/15
	Albuquerque MSA, NM	Y	66150 FQ	81750 MW	173280 TQ	USBLS	5/15
	New York	Y	66670 AE	129530 MW		NYBLS	1/16-3/16
	Buffalo-Cheektowaga-Niagara Falls MSA, NY	Y	48820 FQ	95360 MW	163590 TQ	USBLS	5/15
	Nassau County-Suffolk County PMSA, NY	Y	80520 FQ	100960 MW	155910 TQ	USBLS	5/15
	New York-Jersey City-White Plains PMSA, NY-NJ	Y	86880 FQ	130870 MW		USBLS	5/15
	Rochester MSA, NY	Y	67660 FQ	117050 MW		USBLS	5/15
	North Carolina	Y	58090 FQ	84830 MW	148970 TQ	USBLS	5/15
	Charlotte-Concord-Gastonia MSA, NC-SC	Y	59910 FQ	84520 MW	132920 TQ	USBLS	5/15
	Raleigh MSA, NC	Y	55280 FQ	86960 MW	150800 TQ	USBLS	5/15
	North Dakota	Y	37260 FQ	64570 MW	95740 TQ	USBLS	5/15
	Fargo MSA, ND-MN	Y	47480 FQ	79590 MW	134810 TQ	USBLS	5/15
	Ohio	Y	55470 FQ	79640 MW	130310 TQ	USBLS	5/15
	Cincinnati MSA, OH-KY-IN	Y	50690 FQ	91340 MW	146180 TQ	USBLS	5/15
	Cleveland-Elyria MSA, OH	Y	51160 FQ	69850 MW	116270 TQ	USBLS	5/15
	Columbus MSA, OH	Y	61130 FQ	78360 MW	135950 TQ	USBLS	5/15
	Oklahoma	Y	44830 FQ	68960 MW	96120 TQ	USBLS	5/15
	Oklahoma City MSA, OK	Y	48200 FQ	74220 MW	98450 TQ	USBLS	5/15
	Tulsa MSA, OK	Y	42070 FQ	60410 MW	90580 TQ	USBLS	5/15
	Oregon	H	18.78 FQ	34.43 MW	59.01 TQ	ORBLS	2016
	Portland-Vancouver-Hillsboro MSA, OR-WA	Y	49470 FQ	81080 MW	128990 TQ	USBLS	5/15
	Pennsylvania	Y	61550 FQ	93610 MW	162620 TQ	USBLS	5/15
	Allentown-Bethlehem-Easton MSA, PA-NJ	Y	50650 FQ	81670 MW	156960 TQ	USBLS	5/15
	Harrisburg-Carlisle MSA, PA	Y	52020 FQ	69280 MW	96930 TQ	USBLS	5/15
	Montgomery County-Bucks County-Chester County PMSA, PA	Y	71810 FQ	100910 MW		USBLS	5/15
	Philadelphia PMSA, PA	Y	57760 FQ	92290 MW	157430 TQ	USBLS	5/15
	Pittsburgh MSA, PA	Y	69120 FQ	96200 MW	153790 TQ	USBLS	5/15
	Rhode Island	Y	50830 FQ	73540 MW	142600 TQ	USBLS	5/15
	Providence-Warwick MSA, RI-MA	Y	48940 FQ	71400 MW	144070 TQ	USBLS	5/15
	South Carolina	Y	38820 FQ	59830 MW	110800 TQ	USBLS	5/15

AE	Average entry wage	AWR	Average wage range	H	Hourly	LR	Low end range	MTC	Median total compensation	TCC	Total cash compensation
AEX	Average experienced wage	B	Biweekly	HI	Highest wage paid	M	Monthly	MW	Median wage paid	TQ	Third quartile wage
ATC	Average total compensation	D	Daily	HR	High end paid	MCC	Median cash compensation	MWR	Median wage range	W	Weekly
AW	Average wage paid	FQ	First quartile wage	LO	Lowest wage paid	ME	Median entry wage	S	See annotated source	Y	Yearly

Occupation/Type/Industry	Location	Per	Low	Mid	High	Source	Date
Personal Financial Advisor	Charleston-North Charleston						
	MSA, SC	Y	38110 FQ	60570 MW	139590 TQ	USBLS	5/15
	Columbia MSA, SC	Y	44480 FQ	56090 MW	123150 TQ	USBLS	5/15
	Greenville-Anderson-Mauldin						
	MSA, SC	Y	37590 FQ	79040 MW	128220 TQ	USBLS	5/15
	South Dakota	Y	56200 FQ	71460 MW	86000 TQ	USBLS	5/15
	Sioux Falls MSA, SD	Y	55320 FQ	72280 MW	98670 TQ	USBLS	5/15
	Tennessee	Y	51490 FQ	75760 MW	152900 TQ	USBLS	5/15
	Knoxville MSA, TN	Y	36780 FQ	58400 MW	77650 TQ	USBLS	5/15
	Memphis MSA, TN-MS-AR	Y	49830 FQ	74190 MW	153440 TQ	USBLS	5/15
	Nashville-Davidson–						
	Murfreesboro–Franklin						
	MSA, TN	Y	59520 FQ	92590 MW	173380 TQ	USBLS	5/15
	Texas	Y	51170 FQ	76330 MW	130040 TQ	USBLS	5/15
	Austin-Round Rock MSA, TX	Y	51650 FQ	77770 MW	122610 TQ	USBLS	5/15
	Dallas-Plano-Irving PMSA, TX	Y	60260 FQ	88200 MW	160170 TQ	USBLS	5/15
	Fort Worth-Arlington PMSA,						
	TX	Y	46410 FQ	65620 MW	112260 TQ	USBLS	5/15
	Houston-The Woodlands-						
	Sugar Land MSA, TX	Y	46660 FQ	71630 MW	125240 TQ	USBLS	5/15
	San Antonio-New Braunfels						
	MSA, TX	Y	57040 FQ	76260 MW	113340 TQ	USBLS	5/15
	Utah	Y	46750 FQ	74340 MW	127050 TQ	USBLS	5/15
	Ogden-Clearfield MSA, UT	Y	35540 FQ	54350 MW	69350 TQ	USBLS	5/15
	Provo-Orem MSA, UT	Y	30010 FQ	54920 MW	91840 TQ	USBLS	5/15
	Salt Lake City MSA, UT	Y	48640 FQ	78780 MW	136680 TQ	USBLS	5/15
	Vermont	Y	42450 FQ	54970 MW	88160 TQ	USBLS	5/15
	Burlington-South Burlington						
	MSA, VT	Y	41710 FQ	54180 MW	86000 TQ	USBLS	5/15
	Virginia	Y	56790 FQ	85710 MW	164060 TQ	USBLS	5/15
	Richmond MSA, VA	Y	61020 FQ	93360 MW	158620 TQ	USBLS	5/15
	Virginia Beach-Norfolk-						
	Newport News MSA, VA-NC	Y	46740 FQ	63780 MW	147570 TQ	USBLS	5/15
	Washington	H	30.27 FQ	44.54 MW	82.16 TQ	WABLS	3/16
	Seattle-Bellevue-Everett						
	PMSA, WA	H	31.26 FQ	43.53 MW	82.15 TQ	WABLS	3/16
	Tacoma-Lakewood PMSA, WA	H	36.97 FQ	66.05 MW	91.32 TQ	WABLS	3/16
	West Virginia	Y	30500 FQ	43400 MW	83860 TQ	USBLS	5/15
	Huntington-Ashland MSA,						
	WV-KY-OH	Y	35240 FQ	76000 MW	123510 TQ	USBLS	5/15
	Wisconsin	Y	41540 FQ	58780 MW	106900 TQ	USBLS	5/15
	Madison MSA, WI	Y	38730 FQ	62070 MW	109840 TQ	USBLS	5/15
	Milwaukee-Waukesha-West						
	Allis MSA, WI	Y	44340 FQ	60640 MW	113150 TQ	USBLS	5/15
	Wyoming	Y	44430 FQ	66380 MW	134690 TQ	USBLS	5/15
	Puerto Rico	Y	30210 FQ	39640 MW	46920 TQ	USBLS	5/15
	San Juan-Carolina-Caguas						
	MSA, PR	Y	30120 FQ	39470 MW	46890 TQ	USBLS	5/15
Personal Protection Order Liaison							
County Government	Oakland County, MI	B	1706 LO		2221 HI	MIOAK2	10/1/16
Personnel Analyst							
County Government	Henry County, GA	Y	40843 LO		61265 HI	GACTY04	2016
County Government	Rockdale County, GA	Y	36712 LO		59754 HI	GACTY04	2016
Personnel Specialist							
City Manager's Office	Atascadero, CA	Y			58479 HI	CACIT	6/28/16
Pest Control Worker	Alabama	Y	18934 AE	30394 AW	36119 AEX	ALBLS	6/16
	Birmingham-Hoover MSA, AL	Y	17586 AE	30353 AW	36747 AEX	ALBLS	6/16
	Arizona	Y	27610 FQ	32340 MW	41550 TQ	USBLS	5/15
	Phoenix-Mesa-Scottsdale						
	MSA, AZ	Y	27900 FQ	32450 MW	42640 TQ	USBLS	5/15
	Tucson MSA, AZ	Y	27440 FQ	32970 MW	39220 TQ	USBLS	5/15
	Arkansas	Y	24370 FQ	28500 MW	34570 TQ	USBLS	5/15
	Little Rock-North Little Rock-						
	Conway MSA, AR	Y	26370 FQ	28990 MW	33140 TQ	USBLS	5/15
	California	H	13.04 FQ	16.04 MW	19.84 TQ	CABLS	1/16-3/16
	Anaheim-Santa Ana-Irvine						
	PMSA, CA	H	14.26 FQ	16.97 MW	20.00 TQ	CABLS	1/16-3/16

Occupation/Type/Industry	Location	Per	Low	Mid	High	Source	Date
Pest Control Worker	Los Angeles-Long Beach-Glendale PMSA, CA	H	11.86 FQ	15.28 MW	19.77 TQ	CABLS	1/16-3/16
	Oakland-Hayward-Berkeley PMSA, CA	H	13.29 FQ	15.36 MW	17.67 TQ	CABLS	1/16-3/16
	Riverside-San Bernardino-Ontario MSA, CA	H	10.32 FQ	12.53 MW	14.48 TQ	CABLS	1/16-3/16
	Sacramento–Roseville–Arden-Arcade MSA, CA	H	13.40 FQ	17.03 MW	23.85 TQ	CABLS	1/16-3/16
	San Diego-Carlsbad MSA, CA	H	13.97 FQ	16.23 MW	18.67 TQ	CABLS	1/16-3/16
	San Francisco-Redwood City-South San Francisco PMSA, CA	H	23.81 FQ	27.34 MW	30.29 TQ	CABLS	1/16-3/16
	Colorado	Y	26630 FQ	33060 MW	41710 TQ	USBLS	5/15
	Denver-Aurora-Lakewood MSA, CO	Y	27560 FQ	33150 MW	39860 TQ	USBLS	5/15
	Connecticut	Y		37537 MW		CTBLS	1/16-3/16
	Bridgeport-Stamford-Norwalk MSA, CT	Y	32110 FQ	35940 MW	39770 TQ	USBLS	5/15
	Hartford-West Hartford-East Hartford MSA, CT	Y	33530 FQ	43290 MW	49860 TQ	USBLS	5/15
	Delaware	Y	28170 FQ	33260 MW	40790 TQ	USBLS	5/15
	Wilmington PMSA, DE-MD-NJ	Y	28090 FQ	34350 MW	47830 TQ	USBLS	5/15
	District of Columbia	Y	38470 FQ	53850 MW	59690 TQ	USBLS	5/15
	Washington-Arlington-Alexandria PMSA, DC-VA-MD-WV	Y	27380 FQ	34480 MW	42210 TQ	USBLS	5/15
	Florida	H	11.65 AE	15.04 MW	18.35 AEX	FLBLS	7/16-9/16
	Fort Lauderdale-Pompano Beach-Deerfield Beach PMSA, FL	H	12.92 AE	16.58 MW	18.97 AEX	FLBLS	7/16-9/16
	Miami-Miami Beach-Kendall PMSA, FL	H	10.94 AE	12.63 MW	15.86 AEX	FLBLS	7/16-9/16
	Orlando-Kissimmee-Sanford MSA, FL	H	12.69 AE	14.52 MW	16.43 AEX	FLBLS	7/16-9/16
	Tampa-St. Petersburg-Clearwater MSA, FL	H	11.12 AE	17.42 MW	20.39 AEX	FLBLS	7/16-9/16
	Georgia	Y	27280 FQ	32610 MW	39590 TQ	USBLS	5/15
	Atlanta-Sandy Springs-Roswell MSA, GA	Y	27590 FQ	33110 MW	40710 TQ	USBLS	5/15
	Augusta-Richmond County MSA, GA-SC	Y	25220 FQ	32410 MW	37280 TQ	USBLS	5/15
	Hawaii	Y	30650 FQ	35860 MW	43280 TQ	USBLS	5/15
	Urban Honolulu MSA, HI	Y	32480 FQ	36300 MW	41830 TQ	USBLS	5/15
	Idaho	Y	22960 FQ	26680 MW	30420 TQ	USBLS	5/15
	Boise City MSA, ID	Y	22970 FQ	26780 MW	30730 TQ	USBLS	5/15
	Illinois	Y	25070 FQ	33390 MW	43890 TQ	USBLS	5/15
	Chicago-Naperville-Arlington Heights PMSA, IL	Y	27500 FQ	35190 MW	45550 TQ	USBLS	5/15
	Lake County-Kenosha County PMSA, IL-WI	Y	25590 FQ	39560 MW	45890 TQ	USBLS	5/15
	Indiana	Y	25360 FQ	29220 MW	35380 TQ	USBLS	5/15
	Indianapolis-Carmel-Anderson MSA, IN	Y	25520 FQ	30150 MW	37270 TQ	USBLS	5/15
	Iowa	Y	28540 FQ	35060 MW	44200 TQ	USBLS	5/15
	Des Moines-West Des Moines MSA, IA	Y	31670 FQ	39170 MW	47340 TQ	USBLS	5/15
	Kansas	Y	25230 FQ	30710 MW	36220 TQ	USBLS	5/15
	Wichita MSA, KS	Y	23410 FQ	31790 MW	37170 TQ	USBLS	5/15
	Kentucky	Y	22370 FQ	26360 MW	33000 TQ	USBLS	5/15
	Louisville-Jefferson County MSA, KY-IN	Y	22830 FQ	26280 MW	30300 TQ	USBLS	5/15
	Louisiana	Y	24640 FQ	30640 MW	37810 TQ	USBLS	5/15
	Baton Rouge MSA, LA	Y	25900 FQ	30100 MW	38080 TQ	USBLS	5/15
	New Orleans-Metairie MSA, LA	Y	30530 FQ	34920 MW	39180 TQ	USBLS	5/15
	Maine	Y	27710 FQ	32410 MW	36940 TQ	USBLS	5/15
	Maryland	Y	26317 AE	38712 MW	44910 AEX	MDBLS	4/16
	Baltimore-Columbia-Towson MSA, MD	Y	33210 FQ	39660 MW	53110 TQ	USBLS	5/15
	Salisbury MSA, MD-DE	Y	30170 FQ	35160 MW	41760 TQ	USBLS	5/15
	Massachusetts	Y	30440 FQ	42190 MW	51510 TQ	USBLS	5/15

AE Average entry wage	**AWR** Average wage range	**H** Hourly	**LR** Low end range	**MTC** Median total compensation	**TCC** Total cash compensation
AEX Average experienced wage	**B** Biweekly	**HI** Highest wage paid	**M** Monthly	**MW** Median wage paid	**TQ** Third quartile wage
ATC Average total compensation	**D** Daily	**HR** High end range	**MCC** Median cash compensation	**MWR** Median wage range	**W** Weekly
AW Average wage paid	**FQ** First quartile wage	**LO** Lowest wage paid	**ME** Median entry wage	**S** See annotated source	**Y** Yearly

Occupation/Type/Industry	Location	Per	Low	Mid	High	Source	Date
Pest Control Worker	Boston-Cambridge-Newton NECTA, MA	Y	34380 FQ	43830 MW	50600 TQ	USBLS	5/15
	Worcester MSA, MA-CT	Y	27090 FQ	33710 MW	41730 TQ	USBLS	5/15
	Michigan	Y	25870 FQ	32700 MW	43600 TQ	USBLS	5/15
	Detroit-Dearborn-Livonia PMSA, MI	Y	22170 FQ	24670 MW	42230 TQ	USBLS	5/15
	Grand Rapids-Wyoming MSA, MI	Y	27650 FQ	32560 MW	39100 TQ	USBLS	5/15
	Minnesota	Y	28741 FQ	38224 MW	45888 TQ	MNBLS	1/16-3/16
	Minneapolis-St. Paul-Bloomington MSA, MN-WI	Y	28711 FQ	37527 MW	45171 TQ	MNBLS	1/16-3/16
	Mississippi	Y	24980 FQ	29140 MW	35800 TQ	USBLS	5/15
	Jackson MSA, MS	Y	26000 FQ	30290 MW	37910 TQ	USBLS	5/15
	Missouri	Y	25000 FQ	33020 MW	41520 TQ	USBLS	5/15
	Kansas City MSA, MO-KS	Y	27380 FQ	33140 MW	37570 TQ	USBLS	5/15
	St. Louis MSA, MO-IL	Y	27580 FQ	35140 MW	42950 TQ	USBLS	5/15
	Montana	Y	24750 FQ	28440 MW	33440 TQ	USBLS	5/15
	Nebraska	Y	27835 FQ	34960 MW	42330 TQ	NEBLS	7/16-9/16
	Omaha-Council Bluffs MSA, NE-IA	Y	29970 FQ	36880 MW	43600 TQ	NEBLS	7/16-9/16
	Nevada	Y	33650 FQ	39090 MW	46890 TQ	USBLS	5/15
	Las Vegas-Henderson-Paradise MSA, NV	Y	34360 FQ	39320 MW	46620 TQ	USBLS	5/15
	New Hampshire	H	13.32 AE	19.86 MW	21.05 AEX	NHBLS	6/16
	New Jersey	Y	32160 FQ	38540 MW	50430 TQ	USBLS	5/15
	Camden PMSA, NJ	Y	36060 FQ	41540 MW	47570 TQ	USBLS	5/15
	Newark PMSA, NJ-PA	Y	35880 FQ	43680 MW	54600 TQ	USBLS	5/15
	New Mexico	Y	21160 FQ	28420 MW	34940 TQ	USBLS	5/15
	Albuquerque MSA, NM	Y	21990 FQ	30100 MW	36350 TQ	USBLS	5/15
	New York	Y	24410 AE	34840 MW	41160 AEX	NYBLS	1/16-3/16
	Buffalo-Cheektowaga-Niagara Falls MSA, NY	Y	30070 FQ	37690 MW	58120 TQ	USBLS	5/15
	Nassau County-Suffolk County PMSA, NY	Y	27790 FQ	36390 MW	46560 TQ	USBLS	5/15
	New York-Jersey City-White Plains PMSA, NY-NJ	Y	27180 FQ	34630 MW	38910 TQ	USBLS	5/15
	Rochester MSA, NY	Y	26930 FQ	29420 MW	33630 TQ	USBLS	5/15
	North Carolina	Y	26300 FQ	30830 MW	37920 TQ	USBLS	5/15
	Charlotte-Concord-Gastonia MSA, NC-SC	Y	28080 FQ	33690 MW	38610 TQ	USBLS	5/15
	Raleigh MSA, NC	Y	26300 FQ	29510 MW	47210 TQ	USBLS	5/15
	North Dakota	Y	24310 FQ	49740 MW	55910 TQ	USBLS	5/15
	Ohio	Y	25280 FQ	29840 MW	37280 TQ	USBLS	5/15
	Cincinnati MSA, OH-KY-IN	Y	25840 FQ	30070 MW	36360 TQ	USBLS	5/15
	Cleveland-Elyria MSA, OH	Y	21640 FQ	32690 MW	42090 TQ	USBLS	5/15
	Columbus MSA, OH	Y	25400 FQ	29380 MW	37810 TQ	USBLS	5/15
	Oklahoma	Y	25690 FQ	30030 MW	37270 TQ	USBLS	5/15
	Oklahoma City MSA, OK	Y	27780 FQ	33680 MW	43260 TQ	USBLS	5/15
	Tulsa MSA, OK	Y	25220 FQ	28770 MW	33180 TQ	USBLS	5/15
	Oregon	H	15.05 FQ	17.81 MW	22.03 TQ	ORBLS	2016
	Portland-Vancouver-Hillsboro MSA, OR-WA	Y	32470 FQ	36540 MW	43410 TQ	USBLS	5/15
	Pennsylvania	Y	26000 FQ	32760 MW	41180 TQ	USBLS	5/15
	Allentown-Bethlehem-Easton MSA, PA-NJ	Y	23470 FQ	29270 MW	47740 TQ	USBLS	5/15
	Harrisburg-Carlisle MSA, PA	Y	28800 FQ	36390 MW	43590 TQ	USBLS	5/15
	Montgomery County-Bucks County-Chester County PMSA, PA	Y	25630 FQ	30040 MW	36130 TQ	USBLS	5/15
	Philadelphia PMSA, PA	Y	27720 FQ	37740 MW	52850 TQ	USBLS	5/15
	Pittsburgh MSA, PA	Y	20080 FQ	25930 MW	33540 TQ	USBLS	5/15
	Rhode Island	Y	28170 FQ	31650 MW	39270 TQ	USBLS	5/15
	Providence-Warwick MSA, RI-MA	Y	28100 FQ	31550 MW	38530 TQ	USBLS	5/15
	South Carolina	Y	24860 FQ	31120 MW	38280 TQ	USBLS	5/15
	Charleston-North Charleston MSA, SC	Y	25960 FQ	31300 MW	37590 TQ	USBLS	5/15
	Columbia MSA, SC	Y	27550 FQ	34850 MW	42370 TQ	USBLS	5/15
	Greenville-Anderson-Mauldin MSA, SC	Y	21220 FQ	24280 MW	29950 TQ	USBLS	5/15
	South Dakota	Y	30390 FQ	43260 MW	49180 TQ	USBLS	5/15
	Tennessee	Y	26100 FQ	30090 MW	38020 TQ	USBLS	5/15

AE Average entry wage	AWR Average wage range	H Hourly	LR Low end range	MTC Median total compensation	TCC Total cash compensation
AEX Average experienced wage	B Biweekly	HI Highest wage paid	M Monthly	MW Median wage paid	TQ Third quartile wage
ATC Average total compensation	D Daily	HR High end range	MCC Median cash compensation	MWR Median wage range	W Weekly
AW Average wage paid	FQ First quartile wage	LO Lowest wage paid	ME Median entry wage	S See annotated source	Y Yearly

Occupation/Type/Industry	Location	Per	Low	Mid	High	Source	Date
Pest Control Worker	Knoxville MSA, TN	Y	27300 FQ	32900 MW	41970 TQ	USBLS	5/15
	Memphis MSA, TN-MS-AR	Y	26610 FQ	30770 MW	37010 TQ	USBLS	5/15
	Nashville-Davidson–Murfreesboro–Franklin MSA, TN	Y	26190 FQ	29510 MW	37650 TQ	USBLS	5/15
	Texas	Y	26820 FQ	32660 MW	38080 TQ	USBLS	5/15
	Austin-Round Rock MSA, TX	Y	31510 FQ	35270 MW	39040 TQ	USBLS	5/15
	Dallas-Plano-Irving PMSA, TX	Y	27150 FQ	30970 MW	37870 TQ	USBLS	5/15
	Fort Worth-Arlington PMSA, TX	Y	29360 FQ	35080 MW	41160 TQ	USBLS	5/15
	Houston-The Woodlands-Sugar Land MSA, TX	Y	30880 FQ	34620 MW	38260 TQ	USBLS	5/15
	San Antonio-New Braunfels MSA, TX	Y	24760 FQ	28610 MW	34450 TQ	USBLS	5/15
	Utah	Y	24510 FQ	30190 MW	37570 TQ	USBLS	5/15
	Ogden-Clearfield MSA, UT	Y	27830 FQ	32790 MW	43860 TQ	USBLS	5/15
	Provo-Orem MSA, UT	Y	19000 FQ	25000 MW	29110 TQ	USBLS	5/15
	Salt Lake City MSA, UT	Y	29910 FQ	34990 MW	39790 TQ	USBLS	5/15
	Vermont	Y	41340 FQ	46260 MW	54030 TQ	USBLS	5/15
	Virginia	Y	26040 FQ	31310 MW	39200 TQ	USBLS	5/15
	Richmond MSA, VA	Y	28490 FQ	34890 MW	41320 TQ	USBLS	5/15
	Virginia Beach-Norfolk-Newport News MSA, VA-NC	Y	26450 FQ	29360 MW	39790 TQ	USBLS	5/15
	Washington	H	17.26 FQ	20.92 MW	27.50 TQ	WABLS	3/16
	Seattle-Bellevue-Everett PMSA, WA	H	17.38 FQ	21.55 MW	27.89 TQ	WABLS	3/16
	Tacoma-Lakewood PMSA, WA	H	18.70 FQ	21.98 MW	26.44 TQ	WABLS	3/16
	West Virginia	Y	18340 FQ	21200 MW	29990 TQ	USBLS	5/15
	Wisconsin	Y	24160 FQ	33900 MW	47170 TQ	USBLS	5/15
	Madison MSA, WI	Y	39170 FQ	46470 MW	58760 TQ	USBLS	5/15
	Milwaukee-Waukesha-West Allis MSA, WI	Y	23270 FQ	31220 MW	49180 TQ	USBLS	5/15
	Wyoming	Y	28870 FQ	53440 MW	58650 TQ	USBLS	5/15
	Puerto Rico	Y	17500 FQ	19530 MW	27520 TQ	USBLS	5/15
	San Juan-Carolina-Caguas MSA, PR	Y	17560 FQ	19650 MW	28440 TQ	USBLS	5/15
	Virgin Islands	Y	22310 FQ	25610 MW	30800 TQ	USBLS	5/15
Pesticide Handler, Sprayer, and Applicator							
Vegetation	Alabama	Y	26039 AE	33740 AW	37591 AEX	ALBLS	6/16
Vegetation	Birmingham-Hoover MSA, AL	Y	35171 AE	40947 AW	43841 AEX	ALBLS	6/16
Vegetation	Arizona	Y	26950 FQ	34260 MW	42760 TQ	USBLS	5/15
Vegetation	Phoenix-Mesa-Scottsdale MSA, AZ	Y	26220 FQ	33170 MW	41970 TQ	USBLS	5/15
Vegetation	Tucson MSA, AZ	Y	28270 FQ	32290 MW	37650 TQ	USBLS	5/15
Vegetation	Arkansas	Y	22530 FQ	25920 MW	29140 TQ	USBLS	5/15
Vegetation	Little Rock-North Little Rock-Conway MSA, AR	Y	22840 FQ	25810 MW	29150 TQ	USBLS	5/15
Vegetation	California	H	14.40 FQ	18.44 MW	24.12 TQ	CABLS	1/16-3/16
Vegetation	Anaheim-Santa Ana-Irvine PMSA, CA	H	13.51 FQ	14.79 MW	16.89 TQ	CABLS	1/16-3/16
Vegetation	Los Angeles-Long Beach-Glendale PMSA, CA	H	13.39 FQ	14.61 MW	19.57 TQ	CABLS	1/16-3/16
Vegetation	Oakland-Hayward-Berkeley PMSA, CA	H	22.01 FQ	34.18 MW	38.53 TQ	CABLS	1/16-3/16
Vegetation	Riverside-San Bernardino-Ontario MSA, CA	H	19.31 FQ	21.43 MW	23.57 TQ	CABLS	1/16-3/16
Vegetation	Sacramento–Roseville–Arden-Arcade MSA, CA	H	15.97 FQ	18.56 MW	22.86 TQ	CABLS	1/16-3/16
Vegetation	San Diego-Carlsbad MSA, CA	H	16.42 FQ	18.84 MW	24.01 TQ	CABLS	1/16-3/16
Vegetation	San Francisco-Redwood City-South San Francisco PMSA, CA	H	18.32 FQ	22.87 MW	28.10 TQ	CABLS	1/16-3/16
Vegetation	Colorado	Y	24320 FQ	34020 MW	47050 TQ	USBLS	5/15
Vegetation	Denver-Aurora-Lakewood MSA, CO	Y	39060 FQ	46330 MW	55420 TQ	USBLS	5/15
Vegetation	Connecticut	Y		36007 MW		CTBLS	1/16-3/16
Vegetation	Washington-Arlington-Alexandria PMSA, DC-VA-MD-WV	Y	29190 FQ	34760 MW	40280 TQ	USBLS	5/15
Vegetation	Florida	H	12.46 AE	15.85 MW	18.52 AEX	FLBLS	7/16-9/16

AE	Average entry wage	AWR	Average wage range	H	Hourly
AEX	Average experienced wage	B	Biweekly	HI	Highest wage paid
ATC	Average total compensation	D	Daily	HR	High end range
AW	Average wage paid	FQ	First quartile wage	LO	Lowest wage paid

LR	Low end range	MTC	Median total compensation	TCC	Total cash compensation
M	Monthly	MW	Median wage paid	TQ	Third quartile wage
MCC	Median cash compensation	MWR	Median wage range	W	Weekly
ME	Median entry wage	S	See annotated source	Y	Yearly

Pesticide Handler, Sprayer, and Applicator

Occupation/Type/Industry	Location	Per	Low	Mid	High	Source	Date
Vegetation	Fort Lauderdale-Pompano Beach-Deerfield Beach PMSA, FL	H	13.15 AE	18.22 MW	20.73 AEX	FLBLS	7/16-9/16
Vegetation	Miami-Miami Beach-Kendall PMSA, FL	H	13.73 AE	14.68 MW	18.20 AEX	FLBLS	7/16-9/16
Vegetation	Orlando-Kissimmee-Sanford MSA, FL	H	13.18 AE	15.91 MW	18.47 AEX	FLBLS	7/16-9/16
Vegetation	Tampa-St. Petersburg-Clearwater MSA, FL	H	13.58 AE	15.42 MW	18.02 AEX	FLBLS	7/16-9/16
Vegetation	Georgia	Y	26980 FQ	31300 MW	36340 TQ	USBLS	5/15
Vegetation	Atlanta-Sandy Springs-Roswell MSA, GA	Y	27280 FQ	31730 MW	36170 TQ	USBLS	5/15
Vegetation	Augusta-Richmond County MSA, GA-SC	Y	21210 FQ	24520 MW	31210 TQ	USBLS	5/15
Vegetation	Hawaii	Y	35320 FQ	40140 MW	45500 TQ	USBLS	5/15
Vegetation	Idaho	Y	23580 FQ	28020 MW	34060 TQ	USBLS	5/15
Vegetation	Boise City MSA, ID	Y	23240 FQ	27140 MW	31560 TQ	USBLS	5/15
Vegetation	Illinois	Y	30310 FQ	35430 MW	44770 TQ	USBLS	5/15
Vegetation	Chicago-Naperville-Arlington Heights PMSA, IL	Y	35820 FQ	59220 MW	81500 TQ	USBLS	5/15
Vegetation	Lake County-Kenosha County PMSA, IL-WI	Y	33800 FQ	36310 MW	38810 TQ	USBLS	5/15
Vegetation	Indiana	Y	28740 FQ	33300 MW	37330 TQ	USBLS	5/15
Vegetation	Indianapolis-Carmel-Anderson MSA, IN	Y	27060 FQ	29520 MW	34280 TQ	USBLS	5/15
Vegetation	Iowa	Y	23420 FQ	29520 MW	35560 TQ	USBLS	5/15
Vegetation	Des Moines-West Des Moines MSA, IA	Y	30300 FQ	35220 MW	40940 TQ	USBLS	5/15
Vegetation	Kansas	Y	27320 FQ	35090 MW	43800 TQ	USBLS	5/15
Vegetation	Wichita MSA, KS	Y	29600 FQ	40620 MW	46550 TQ	USBLS	5/15
Vegetation	Kentucky	Y	26500 FQ	30080 MW	34760 TQ	USBLS	5/15
Vegetation	Louisiana	Y	22680 FQ	29620 MW	38790 TQ	USBLS	5/15
Vegetation	Baton Rouge MSA, LA	Y	28480 FQ	32500 MW	37100 TQ	USBLS	5/15
Vegetation	New Orleans-Metairie MSA, LA	Y	35230 FQ	41110 MW	48400 TQ	USBLS	5/15
Vegetation	Maine	Y	29040 FQ	39550 MW	56820 TQ	USBLS	5/15
Vegetation	Maryland	Y	26255 AE	34867 MW	39173 AEX	MDBLS	4/16
Vegetation	Baltimore-Columbia-Towson MSA, MD	Y	28180 FQ	34340 MW	42600 TQ	USBLS	5/15
Vegetation	Massachusetts	Y	31890 FQ	35450 MW	39020 TQ	USBLS	5/15
Vegetation	Michigan	Y	26910 FQ	31380 MW	37170 TQ	USBLS	5/15
Vegetation	Detroit-Dearborn-Livonia PMSA, MI	Y	27340 FQ	30270 MW	35210 TQ	USBLS	5/15
Vegetation	Grand Rapids-Wyoming MSA, MI	Y	27550 FQ	33010 MW	38710 TQ	USBLS	5/15
Vegetation	Minnesota	Y	28488 FQ	32881 MW	37779 TQ	MNBLS	1/16-3/16
Vegetation	Minneapolis-St. Paul-Bloomington MSA, MN-WI	Y	28175 FQ	32215 MW	37072 TQ	MNBLS	1/16-3/16
Vegetation	Mississippi	Y	18280 FQ	25100 MW	28460 TQ	USBLS	5/15
Vegetation	Missouri	Y	27160 FQ	30290 MW	36010 TQ	USBLS	5/15
Vegetation	Kansas City MSA, MO-KS	Y	25630 FQ	32990 MW	36980 TQ	USBLS	5/15
Vegetation	St. Louis MSA, MO-IL	Y	27970 FQ	31320 MW	37140 TQ	USBLS	5/15
Vegetation	Montana	Y	22590 FQ	27230 MW	33110 TQ	USBLS	5/15
Vegetation	Billings MSA, MT	Y	22400 FQ	26830 MW	33680 TQ	USBLS	5/15
Vegetation	Nebraska	Y	27005 FQ	32485 MW	37050 TQ	NEBLS	7/16-9/16
Vegetation	Omaha-Council Bluffs MSA, NE-IA	Y	29185 FQ	33435 MW	37480 TQ	NEBLS	7/16-9/16
Vegetation	Nevada	Y	27230 FQ	29770 MW	37140 TQ	USBLS	5/15
Vegetation	New Jersey	Y	29800 FQ	36760 MW	47510 TQ	USBLS	5/15
Vegetation	Newark PMSA, NJ-PA	Y	30660 FQ	36070 MW	44070 TQ	USBLS	5/15
Vegetation	New Mexico	Y	25860 FQ	31020 MW	43770 TQ	USBLS	5/15
Vegetation	New York	Y	27470 AE	30440 MW	36180 AEX	NYBLS	1/16-3/16
Vegetation	Nassau County-Suffolk County PMSA, NY	Y	26510 FQ	28550 MW	30590 TQ	USBLS	5/15
Vegetation	New York-Jersey City-White Plains PMSA, NY-NJ	Y	27890 FQ	34350 MW	43190 TQ	USBLS	5/15
Vegetation	Rochester MSA, NY	Y	26160 FQ	28710 MW	32100 TQ	USBLS	5/15
Vegetation	North Carolina	Y	24960 FQ	29100 MW	34700 TQ	USBLS	5/15
Vegetation	Raleigh MSA, NC	Y	27900 FQ	32090 MW	35850 TQ	USBLS	5/15
Vegetation	North Dakota	Y	28520 FQ	34080 MW	42070 TQ	USBLS	5/15

AE	Average entry wage	AWR	Average wage range	H	Hourly
AEX	Average experienced wage	B	Biweekly	HI	Highest wage paid
ATC	Average total compensation	D	Daily	HR	High end range
AW	Average wage paid	FQ	First quartile wage	LO	Lowest wage paid

LR	Low end range	MTC	Median total compensation
M	Monthly	MW	Median wage paid
MCC	Median cash compensation	MWR	Median wage range
ME	Median entry wage	S	See annotated source

TCC	Total cash compensation
TQ	Third quartile wage
W	Weekly
Y	Yearly

Occupation/Type/Industry	Location	Per	Low	Mid	High	Source	Date
Pesticide Handler, Sprayer, and Applicator							
Vegetation	Fargo MSA, ND-MN	Y	26570 FQ	28650 MW	30730 TQ	USBLS	5/15
Vegetation	Ohio	Y	27340 FQ	31940 MW	36910 TQ	USBLS	5/15
Vegetation	Cincinnati MSA, OH-KY-IN	Y	26670 FQ	29200 MW	32990 TQ	USBLS	5/15
Vegetation	Columbus MSA, OH	Y	25790 FQ	29810 MW	35190 TQ	USBLS	5/15
Vegetation	Oklahoma	Y	23040 FQ	29410 MW	41460 TQ	USBLS	5/15
Vegetation	Oklahoma City MSA, OK	Y	21800 FQ	23820 MW	30110 TQ	USBLS	5/15
Vegetation	Tulsa MSA, OK	Y	25050 FQ	29700 MW	36610 TQ	USBLS	5/15
Vegetation	Oregon	H	14.06 FQ	17.60 MW	21.38 TQ	ORBLS	2016
Vegetation	Portland-Vancouver-Hillsboro MSA, OR-WA	Y	30930 FQ	38220 MW	46820 TQ	USBLS	5/15
Vegetation	Pennsylvania	Y	32360 FQ	36700 MW	43110 TQ	USBLS	5/15
Vegetation	Allentown-Bethlehem-Easton MSA, PA-NJ	Y	27360 FQ	31100 MW	35460 TQ	USBLS	5/15
Vegetation	Harrisburg-Carlisle MSA, PA	Y	27060 FQ	30030 MW	38790 TQ	USBLS	5/15
Vegetation	Montgomery County-Bucks County-Chester County PMSA, PA	Y	33650 FQ	37040 MW	43110 TQ	USBLS	5/15
Vegetation	Philadelphia PMSA, PA	Y	36300 FQ	41670 MW	64800 TQ	USBLS	5/15
Vegetation	Pittsburgh MSA, PA	Y	33860 FQ	38300 MW	44510 TQ	USBLS	5/15
Vegetation	South Carolina	Y	18350 FQ	28100 MW	35580 TQ	USBLS	5/15
Vegetation	Charleston-North Charleston MSA, SC	Y	18520 FQ	28520 MW	38500 TQ	USBLS	5/15
Vegetation	Columbia MSA, SC	Y	17130 FQ	18760 MW	33200 TQ	USBLS	5/15
Vegetation	South Dakota	Y	26800 FQ	29500 MW	33730 TQ	USBLS	5/15
Vegetation	Sioux Falls MSA, SD	Y	28900 FQ	32550 MW	36110 TQ	USBLS	5/15
Vegetation	Tennessee	Y	23830 FQ	28490 MW	37450 TQ	USBLS	5/15
Vegetation	Memphis MSA, TN-MS-AR	Y	25140 FQ	29460 MW	39850 TQ	USBLS	5/15
Vegetation	Nashville-Davidson–Murfreesboro–Franklin MSA, TN	Y	21160 FQ	23050 MW	26440 TQ	USBLS	5/15
Vegetation	Texas	Y	28000 FQ	33530 MW	41730 TQ	USBLS	5/15
Vegetation	Austin-Round Rock MSA, TX	Y	34220 FQ	38610 MW	44220 TQ	USBLS	5/15
Vegetation	Dallas-Plano-Irving PMSA, TX	Y	27490 FQ	30170 MW	38500 TQ	USBLS	5/15
Vegetation	Fort Worth-Arlington PMSA, TX	Y	24620 FQ	27480 MW	30270 TQ	USBLS	5/15
Vegetation	Houston-The Woodlands-Sugar Land MSA, TX	Y	28440 FQ	33750 MW	41200 TQ	USBLS	5/15
Vegetation	San Antonio-New Braunfels MSA, TX	Y	25730 FQ	32590 MW	40140 TQ	USBLS	5/15
Vegetation	Utah	Y	24800 FQ	31670 MW	36810 TQ	USBLS	5/15
Vegetation	Ogden-Clearfield MSA, UT	Y	24360 FQ	29890 MW	35210 TQ	USBLS	5/15
Vegetation	Virginia	Y	27560 FQ	34080 MW	38650 TQ	USBLS	5/15
Vegetation	Richmond MSA, VA	Y	27840 FQ	34380 MW	42390 TQ	USBLS	5/15
Vegetation	Virginia Beach-Norfolk-Newport News MSA, VA-NC	Y	31230 FQ	36040 MW	42380 TQ	USBLS	5/15
Vegetation	Washington	H	14.39 FQ	16.77 MW	19.07 TQ	WABLS	3/16
Vegetation	Seattle-Bellevue-Everett PMSA, WA	H	16.54 FQ	18.10 MW	20.65 TQ	WABLS	3/16
Vegetation	Tacoma-Lakewood PMSA, WA	H	13.26 FQ	16.07 MW	18.84 TQ	WABLS	3/16
Vegetation	West Virginia	Y	28340 FQ	35190 MW	42400 TQ	USBLS	5/15
Vegetation	Wisconsin	Y	30650 FQ	35650 MW	41580 TQ	USBLS	5/15
Vegetation	Madison MSA, WI	Y	34190 FQ	40490 MW	46390 TQ	USBLS	5/15
Vegetation	Milwaukee-Waukesha-West Allis MSA, WI	Y	31640 FQ	34960 MW	38270 TQ	USBLS	5/15
Vegetation	Wyoming	Y	24750 FQ	28180 MW	33030 TQ	USBLS	5/15
Pet Detective	United States	Y		54000 AW		SKU01	2016
Pet License Canvasser							
Municipal Government	Seattle, WA	H			18.36 HI	CSSS	1/13/16
Petroleum Engineer	Alabama	Y	84247 AE	143205 AW	172694 AEX	ALBLS	6/16
	Alaska	Y	107770 FQ	138090 MW	165640 TQ	USBLS	5/15
	Arizona	Y	92560 FQ	106770 MW	122680 TQ	USBLS	5/15
	California	H	49.17 FQ	59.18 MW	75.60 TQ	CABLS	1/16-3/16
	Colorado	Y	106660 FQ	138570 MW		USBLS	5/15
	Georgia	Y	72000 FQ	94970 MW	151890 TQ	USBLS	5/15
	Indiana	Y	75790 FQ	111250 MW	167570 TQ	USBLS	5/15
	Louisiana	Y	91360 FQ	121810 MW	171310 TQ	USBLS	5/15
	Michigan	Y	94070 FQ	117270 MW	160930 TQ	USBLS	5/15

AE	Average entry wage	AWR	Average wage range	H	Hourly
AEX	Average experienced wage	B	Biweekly	HI	Highest wage paid
ATC	Average total compensation	D	Daily	HR	High end range
AW	Average wage paid	FQ	First quartile wage	LO	Lowest wage paid

LR	Low end range	MTC	Median total compensation	TCC	Total cash compensation
M	Monthly	MW	Median wage paid	TQ	Third quartile wage
MCC	Median cash compensation	MWR	Median wage range	W	Weekly
ME	Median entry wage	S	See annotated source	Y	Yearly

Occupation/Type/Industry	Location	Per	Low	Mid	High	Source	Date
Petroleum Engineer	Mississippi	Y	90910 FQ	115100 MW	141540 TQ	USBLS	5/15
	Montana	Y	81980 FQ	108240 MW	138360 TQ	USBLS	5/15
	New Mexico	Y	70400 FQ	81830 MW	113030 TQ	USBLS	5/15
	North Dakota	Y	80990 FQ	92740 MW	123890 TQ	USBLS	5/15
	Ohio	Y	84540 FQ	109580 MW	128660 TQ	USBLS	5/15
	Oklahoma	Y	84600 FQ	117580 MW	163860 TQ	USBLS	5/15
	Pennsylvania	Y	73660 FQ	105580 MW	137010 TQ	USBLS	5/15
	Texas	Y	108700 FQ	146140 MW		USBLS	5/15
	Utah	Y	87960 FQ	110220 MW	154950 TQ	USBLS	5/15
	Virginia	Y	108810 FQ	122840 MW	141910 TQ	USBLS	5/15
	Washington	H	52.79 FQ	64.63 MW	79.72 TQ	WABLS	3/16
	West Virginia	Y	81420 FQ	105630 MW	167300 TQ	USBLS	5/15
	Wyoming	Y	79280 FQ	99740 MW	129580 TQ	USBLS	5/15
Petroleum Geologist	United States	Y		103900–230600 AWR		AAPG	2015
Petroleum Pump System Operator, Refinery Operator, and Gauger	Alabama	Y	35946 AE	48758 AW	55164 AEX	ALBLS	6/16
	Birmingham-Hoover MSA, AL	Y	36049 AE	45735 AW	50578 AEX	ALBLS	6/16
	Alaska	Y	64880 FQ	75650 MW	87400 TQ	USBLS	5/15
	Anchorage MSA, AK	Y	64500 FQ	80100 MW	91520 TQ	USBLS	5/15
	Arizona	Y	40880 FQ	48430 MW	54330 TQ	USBLS	5/15
	Phoenix-Mesa-Scottsdale MSA, AZ	Y	40640 FQ	48230 MW	55390 TQ	USBLS	5/15
	Arkansas	Y	44720 FQ	54050 MW	62880 TQ	USBLS	5/15
	Fort Smith MSA, AR-OK	Y	56020 FQ	62770 MW	74770 TQ	USBLS	5/15
	Little Rock-North Little Rock-Conway MSA, AR	Y	38730 FQ	55580 MW	75650 TQ	USBLS	5/15
	California	H	30.79 FQ	38.99 MW	44.67 TQ	CABLS	1/16-3/16
	Anaheim-Santa Ana-Irvine PMSA, CA	H	31.37 FQ	38.98 MW	44.55 TQ	CABLS	1/16-3/16
	Los Angeles-Long Beach-Glendale PMSA, CA	H	33.18 FQ	39.88 MW	44.91 TQ	CABLS	1/16-3/16
	Oakland-Hayward-Berkeley PMSA, CA	H	31.57 FQ	40.98 MW	45.68 TQ	CABLS	1/16-3/16
	Sacramento–Roseville–Arden-Arcade MSA, CA	H	25.50 FQ	29.36 MW	33.97 TQ	CABLS	1/16-3/16
	San Francisco-Redwood City-South San Francisco PMSA, CA	H	27.98 FQ	35.21 MW	47.07 TQ	CABLS	1/16-3/16
	Colorado	Y	67430 FQ	77050 MW	91440 TQ	USBLS	5/15
	Denver-Aurora-Lakewood MSA, CO	Y	68600 FQ	77720 MW	90400 TQ	USBLS	5/15
	Connecticut	Y		58550 MW		CTBLS	1/16-3/16
	Washington-Arlington-Alexandria PMSA, DC-VA-MD-WV	Y	51580 FQ	55800 MW	60030 TQ	USBLS	5/15
	Florida	H	17.20 AE	23.95 MW	26.20 AEX	FLBLS	7/16-9/16
	Miami-Miami Beach-Kendall PMSA, FL	H	13.95 AE	16.31 MW	17.68 AEX	FLBLS	7/16-9/16
	Tampa-St. Petersburg-Clearwater MSA, FL	H	21.06 AE	26.64 MW	28.05 AEX	FLBLS	7/16-9/16
	Georgia	Y	43040 FQ	52860 MW	67800 TQ	USBLS	5/15
	Atlanta-Sandy Springs-Roswell MSA, GA	Y	40660 FQ	55490 MW	69810 TQ	USBLS	5/15
	Hawaii	Y	50300 FQ	59570 MW	64170 TQ	USBLS	5/15
	Urban Honolulu MSA, HI	Y	49930 FQ	59560 MW	64170 TQ	USBLS	5/15
	Idaho	Y	48020 FQ	57690 MW	70330 TQ	USBLS	5/15
	Illinois	Y	43770 FQ	56860 MW	68380 TQ	USBLS	5/15
	Chicago-Naperville-Arlington Heights PMSA, IL	Y	52390 FQ	58430 MW	75340 TQ	USBLS	5/15
	Indiana	Y	38970 FQ	47770 MW	57550 TQ	USBLS	5/15
	Gary PMSA, IN	Y	38160 FQ	45950 MW	56170 TQ	USBLS	5/15
	Indianapolis-Carmel-Anderson MSA, IN	Y	51980 FQ	57170 MW	62640 TQ	USBLS	5/15
	Iowa	Y	46160 FQ	66840 MW	80420 TQ	USBLS	5/15
	Kansas	Y	52910 FQ	63910 MW	72180 TQ	USBLS	5/15
	Wichita MSA, KS	Y	63610 FQ	68510 MW	73390 TQ	USBLS	5/15
	Kentucky	Y	64780 FQ	75140 MW	89670 TQ	USBLS	5/15
	Louisiana	Y	52310 FQ	66770 MW	77870 TQ	USBLS	5/15

AE	Average entry wage	AWR	Average wage range	H	Hourly	LR	Low end range	MTC	Median total compensation	TCC	Total cash compensation
AEX	Average experienced wage	B	Biweekly	HI	Highest wage paid	M	Monthly	MW	Median wage paid	TQ	Third quartile wage
ATC	Average total compensation	D	Daily	HR	High end range	MCC	Median cash compensation	MWR	Median wage range	W	Weekly
AW	Average wage paid	FQ	First quartile wage	LO	Lowest wage paid	ME	Median entry wage	S	See annotated source	Y	Yearly

Occupation/Type/Industry	Location	Per	Low	Mid	High	Source	Date
Petroleum Pump System Operator, Refinery Operator, and Gauger	Baton Rouge MSA, LA	Y	57130 FQ	70550 MW	81250 TQ	USBLS	5/15
	New Orleans-Metairie MSA, LA	Y	53860 FQ	69240 MW	80190 TQ	USBLS	5/15
	Maine	Y	29210 FQ	43430 MW	70610 TQ	USBLS	5/15
	Maryland	Y	45084 AE	57034 MW	63009 AEX	MDBLS	4/16
	Baltimore-Columbia-Towson MSA, MD	Y	44940 FQ	49890 MW	55460 TQ	USBLS	5/15
	Massachusetts	Y	58640 FQ	65460 MW	73240 TQ	USBLS	5/15
	Boston-Cambridge-Newton NECTA, MA	Y	58530 FQ	66660 MW	73850 TQ	USBLS	5/15
	Michigan	Y	50980 FQ	55880 MW	60830 TQ	USBLS	5/15
	Minnesota	Y	54024 FQ	58894 MW	64868 TQ	MNBLS	1/16-3/16
	Minneapolis-St. Paul-Bloomington MSA, MN-WI	Y	53346 FQ	57882 MW	62458 TQ	MNBLS	1/16-3/16
	Mississippi	Y	54990 FQ	82250 MW	93250 TQ	USBLS	5/15
	Missouri	Y	41170 FQ	47840 MW	57540 TQ	USBLS	5/15
	Kansas City MSA, MO-KS	Y	44500 FQ	50190 MW	59300 TQ	USBLS	5/15
	St. Louis MSA, MO-IL	Y	38480 FQ	56170 MW	70050 TQ	USBLS	5/15
	Montana	Y	53660 FQ	72170 MW	89640 TQ	USBLS	5/15
	Billings MSA, MT	Y	54100 FQ	82420 MW	93480 TQ	USBLS	5/15
	Nebraska	Y	41190 FQ	65695 MW	73115 TQ	NEBLS	7/16-9/16
	Nevada	Y	54870 FQ	66540 MW	74420 TQ	USBLS	5/15
	New Hampshire	H	22.23 AE	26.09 MW	28.71 AEX	NHBLS	6/16
	New Jersey	Y	54480 FQ	59190 MW	64530 TQ	USBLS	5/15
	Camden PMSA, NJ	Y	53900 FQ	59040 MW	66560 TQ	USBLS	5/15
	New Mexico	Y	58280 FQ	67320 MW	75870 TQ	USBLS	5/15
	New York	Y	43820 AE	56280 MW	65480 AEX	NYBLS	1/16-3/16
	New York-Jersey City-White Plains PMSA, NY-NJ	Y	55620 FQ	61240 MW	68610 TQ	USBLS	5/15
	North Carolina	Y	43980 FQ	56960 MW	66560 TQ	USBLS	5/15
	North Dakota	Y	53770 FQ	64240 MW	76840 TQ	USBLS	5/15
	Ohio	Y	52820 FQ	61590 MW	72340 TQ	USBLS	5/15
	Cleveland-Elyria MSA, OH	Y	53010 FQ	58060 MW	63180 TQ	USBLS	5/15
	Columbus MSA, OH	Y	55610 FQ	67900 MW	75500 TQ	USBLS	5/15
	Oklahoma	Y	52970 FQ	65430 MW	77860 TQ	USBLS	5/15
	Oklahoma City MSA, OK	Y	47120 FQ	54880 MW	61810 TQ	USBLS	5/15
	Tulsa MSA, OK	Y	62490 FQ	86200 MW	117520 TQ	USBLS	5/15
	Oregon	H	24.47 FQ	27.60 MW	32.77 TQ	ORBLS	2016
	Portland-Vancouver-Hillsboro MSA, OR-WA	Y	49190 FQ	55060 MW	65050 TQ	USBLS	5/15
	Pennsylvania	Y	50610 FQ	60630 MW	74770 TQ	USBLS	5/15
	Allentown-Bethlehem-Easton MSA, PA-NJ	Y	56090 FQ	64630 MW	81660 TQ	USBLS	5/15
	Montgomery County-Bucks County-Chester County PMSA, PA	Y	55060 FQ	59930 MW	73260 TQ	USBLS	5/15
	Philadelphia PMSA, PA	Y	67630 FQ	76920 MW	91250 TQ	USBLS	5/15
	Pittsburgh MSA, PA	Y	52240 FQ	58270 MW	64640 TQ	USBLS	5/15
	Rhode Island	Y	53260 FQ	58030 MW	62800 TQ	USBLS	5/15
	Providence-Warwick MSA, RI-MA	Y	53260 FQ	58030 MW	62800 TQ	USBLS	5/15
	South Carolina	Y	40740 FQ	50440 MW	59950 TQ	USBLS	5/15
	Charleston-North Charleston MSA, SC	Y	38900 FQ	49630 MW	55670 TQ	USBLS	5/15
	Tennessee	Y	52500 FQ	58010 MW	67880 TQ	USBLS	5/15
	Texas	Y	47870 FQ	67040 MW	79740 TQ	USBLS	5/15
	Dallas-Plano-Irving PMSA, TX	Y	40440 FQ	59240 MW	75390 TQ	USBLS	5/15
	Fort Worth-Arlington PMSA, TX	Y	30030 FQ	42010 MW	56710 TQ	USBLS	5/15
	Houston-The Woodlands-Sugar Land MSA, TX	Y	54850 FQ	68270 MW	77330 TQ	USBLS	5/15
	San Antonio-New Braunfels MSA, TX	Y	44160 FQ	54920 MW	69210 TQ	USBLS	5/15
	Utah	Y	57250 FQ	69250 MW	78340 TQ	USBLS	5/15
	Ogden-Clearfield MSA, UT	Y	47830 FQ	59660 MW	74270 TQ	USBLS	5/15
	Salt Lake City MSA, UT	Y	65840 FQ	72670 MW	79710 TQ	USBLS	5/15
	Virginia	Y	42520 FQ	49310 MW	58490 TQ	USBLS	5/15
	Richmond MSA, VA	Y	36410 FQ	42000 MW	48980 TQ	USBLS	5/15
	Washington	H	19.12 FQ	33.01 MW	44.81 TQ	WABLS	3/16

AE	Average entry wage	AWR	Average wage range	H	Hourly	LR Low end range	MTC Median total compensation	TCC Total cash compensation
AEX	Average experienced wage	B	Biweekly	HI	Highest wage paid	M Monthly	MW Median wage paid	TQ Third quartile wage
ATC	Average total compensation	D	Daily	HR	High end range	MCC Median cash compensation	MWR Median wage range	W Weekly
AW	Average wage paid	FQ	First quartile wage	LO	Lowest wage paid	ME Median entry wage	S See annotated source	Y Yearly

Occupation/Type/Industry	Location	Per	Low	Mid	High	Source	Date
Petroleum Pump System Operator, Refinery Operator, and Gauger	Tacoma-Lakewood PMSA, WA	H	16.56 FQ	18.23 MW	27.81 TQ	WABLS	3/16
	West Virginia	Y	47200 FQ	54030 MW	60980 TQ	USBLS	5/15
	Wisconsin	Y	47230 FQ	58080 MW	71350 TQ	USBLS	5/15
	Wyoming	Y	56660 FQ	68440 MW	77840 TQ	USBLS	5/15
	Cheyenne MSA, WY	Y	63110 FQ	75550 MW	87490 TQ	USBLS	5/15
Pharmacist	Alabama	Y	96948 AE	123899 AW	137374 AEX	ALBLS	6/16
	Birmingham-Hoover MSA, AL	Y	93309 AE	114246 AW	124714 AEX	ALBLS	6/16
	Alaska	Y	129180 FQ	141390 MW	153800 TQ	USBLS	5/15
	Anchorage MSA, AK	Y	125140 FQ	138090 MW	151860 TQ	USBLS	5/15
	Arizona	Y	110590 FQ	123970 MW	139590 TQ	USBLS	5/15
	Phoenix-Mesa-Scottsdale MSA, AZ	Y	110690 FQ	123680 MW	139050 TQ	USBLS	5/15
	Tucson MSA, AZ	Y	108790 FQ	121580 MW	135260 TQ	USBLS	5/15
	Arkansas	Y	106490 FQ	119760 MW	135930 TQ	USBLS	5/15
	Little Rock-North Little Rock-Conway MSA, AR	Y	104830 FQ	114940 MW	125760 TQ	USBLS	5/15
	California	H	61.23 FQ	68.88 MW	76.09 TQ	CABLS	1/16-3/16
	Anaheim-Santa Ana-Irvine PMSA, CA	H	60.95 FQ	68.27 MW	75.03 TQ	CABLS	1/16-3/16
	Los Angeles-Long Beach-Glendale PMSA, CA	H	57.22 FQ	68.40 MW	77.54 TQ	CABLS	1/16-3/16
	Oakland-Hayward-Berkeley PMSA, CA	H	64.54 FQ	70.16 MW	75.88 TQ	CABLS	1/16-3/16
	Riverside-San Bernardino-Ontario MSA, CA	H	61.30 FQ	68.99 MW	76.39 TQ	CABLS	1/16-3/16
	Sacramento–Roseville–Arden-Arcade MSA, CA	H	63.86 FQ	69.90 MW	75.88 TQ	CABLS	1/16-3/16
	San Diego-Carlsbad MSA, CA	H	57.98 FQ	66.12 MW	73.32 TQ	CABLS	1/16-3/16
	San Francisco-Redwood City-South San Francisco PMSA, CA	H	64.10 FQ	70.12 MW	76.78 TQ	CABLS	1/16-3/16
	Colorado	Y	107630 FQ	120800 MW	137540 TQ	USBLS	5/15
	Boulder MSA, CO	Y	111680 FQ	127420 MW	143210 TQ	USBLS	5/15
	Denver-Aurora-Lakewood MSA, CO	Y	107530 FQ	120590 MW	137560 TQ	USBLS	5/15
	Connecticut	Y		121861 MW		CTBLS	1/16-3/16
	Bridgeport-Stamford-Norwalk MSA, CT	Y	110400 FQ	126310 MW	144710 TQ	USBLS	5/15
	Hartford-West Hartford-East Hartford MSA, CT	Y	104540 FQ	118220 MW	132690 TQ	USBLS	5/15
	Delaware	Y	105670 FQ	118870 MW	133890 TQ	USBLS	5/15
	Wilmington PMSA, DE-MD-NJ	Y	110590 FQ	121260 MW	135690 TQ	USBLS	5/15
	District of Columbia	Y	107320 FQ	116850 MW	128360 TQ	USBLS	5/15
	Washington-Arlington-Alexandria PMSA, DC-VA-MD-WV	Y	105740 FQ	118810 MW	134110 TQ	USBLS	5/15
	Florida	H	46.28 AE	58.33 MW	62.62 AEX	FLBLS	7/16-9/16
	Fort Lauderdale-Pompano Beach-Deerfield Beach PMSA, FL	H	51.29 AE	60.52 MW	69.54 AEX	FLBLS	7/16-9/16
	Miami-Miami Beach-Kendall PMSA, FL	H	51.29 AE	58.47 MW	60.61 AEX	FLBLS	7/16-9/16
	Orlando-Kissimmee-Sanford MSA, FL	H	48.38 AE	59.76 MW	62.87 AEX	FLBLS	7/16-9/16
	Tampa-St. Petersburg-Clearwater MSA, FL	H	44.51 AE	57.48 MW	61.63 AEX	FLBLS	7/16-9/16
	Georgia	Y	106300 FQ	118300 MW	131460 TQ	USBLS	5/15
	Atlanta-Sandy Springs-Roswell MSA, GA	Y	106760 FQ	118220 MW	130850 TQ	USBLS	5/15
	Augusta-Richmond County MSA, GA-SC	Y	105270 FQ	116440 MW	129230 TQ	USBLS	5/15
	Hawaii	Y	108710 FQ	118920 MW	129630 TQ	USBLS	5/15
	Urban Honolulu MSA, HI	Y	108980 FQ	118770 MW	129140 TQ	USBLS	5/15
	Idaho	Y	105610 FQ	115900 MW	127040 TQ	USBLS	5/15
	Boise City MSA, ID	Y	108820 FQ	118580 MW	129250 TQ	USBLS	5/15
	Illinois	Y	106230 FQ	121360 MW	137500 TQ	USBLS	5/15

AE	Average entry wage	AWR	Average wage range	H	Hourly	LR	Low end range	MTC	Median total compensation	TCC	Total cash compensation
AEX	Average experienced wage	B	Biweekly	HI	Highest wage paid	M	Monthly	MW	Median wage paid	TQ	Third quartile wage
ATC	Average total compensation	D	Daily	HR	High end range	MCC	Median cash compensation	MWR	Median wage range	W	Weekly
AW	Average wage paid	FQ	First quartile wage	LO	Lowest wage paid	ME	Median entry wage	S	See annotated source	Y	Yearly

Pharmacist

Occupation/Type/Industry	Location	Per	Low	Mid	High	Source	Date
Pharmacist	Chicago-Naperville-Arlington Heights PMSA, IL	Y	104590 FQ	120230 MW	136640 TQ	USBLS	5/15
	Lake County-Kenosha County PMSA, IL-WI	Y	105570 FQ	120390 MW	136220 TQ	USBLS	5/15
	Indiana	Y	108240 FQ	119080 MW	130000 TQ	USBLS	5/15
	Gary PMSA, IN	Y	109820 FQ	120120 MW	129970 TQ	USBLS	5/15
	Indianapolis-Carmel-Anderson MSA, IN	Y	107660 FQ	118280 MW	128650 TQ	USBLS	5/15
	Iowa	Y	98750 FQ	112610 MW	124510 TQ	USBLS	5/15
	Des Moines-West Des Moines MSA, IA	Y	56650 FQ	107110 MW	122080 TQ	USBLS	5/15
	Kansas	Y	107740 FQ	120830 MW	136990 TQ	USBLS	5/15
	Wichita MSA, KS	Y	110360 FQ	122120 MW	136630 TQ	USBLS	5/15
	Kentucky	Y	110000 FQ	123330 MW	140130 TQ	USBLS	5/15
	Louisville-Jefferson County MSA, KY-IN	Y	111240 FQ	123330 MW	139690 TQ	USBLS	5/15
	Louisiana	Y	100800 FQ	115230 MW	129070 TQ	USBLS	5/15
	Baton Rouge MSA, LA	Y	99730 FQ	114300 MW	128090 TQ	USBLS	5/15
	New Orleans-Metairie MSA, LA	Y	99820 FQ	113810 MW	127130 TQ	USBLS	5/15
	Maine	Y	110340 FQ	127480 MW	145730 TQ	USBLS	5/15
	Portland-South Portland MSA, ME	Y	105340 FQ	126890 MW	146090 TQ	USBLS	5/15
	Maryland	Y	96997 AE	119778 MW	131168 AEX	MDBLS	4/16
	Baltimore-Columbia-Towson MSA, MD	Y	108420 FQ	120790 MW	135530 TQ	USBLS	5/15
	Salisbury MSA, MD-DE	Y	81160 FQ	113670 MW	130210 TQ	USBLS	5/15
	Massachusetts	Y	106530 FQ	117430 MW	129100 TQ	USBLS	5/15
	Boston-Cambridge-Newton NECTA, MA	Y	106490 FQ	116960 MW	128210 TQ	USBLS	5/15
	Worcester MSA, MA-CT	Y	106020 FQ	119690 MW	136420 TQ	USBLS	5/15
	Michigan	Y	106510 FQ	116570 MW	126820 TQ	USBLS	5/15
	Detroit-Dearborn-Livonia PMSA, MI	Y	107120 FQ	116380 MW	125290 TQ	USBLS	5/15
	Grand Rapids-Wyoming MSA, MI	Y	106290 FQ	117120 MW	128710 TQ	USBLS	5/15
	Minnesota	Y	113325 FQ	128103 MW	144565 TQ	MNBLS	1/16-3/16
	Minneapolis-St. Paul-Bloomington MSA, MN-WI	Y	112368 FQ	126954 MW	143506 TQ	MNBLS	1/16-3/16
	Mississippi	Y	108700 FQ	121530 MW	137270 TQ	USBLS	5/15
	Jackson MSA, MS	Y	110140 FQ	122990 MW	137630 TQ	USBLS	5/15
	Missouri	Y	110300 FQ	122970 MW	138780 TQ	USBLS	5/15
	Kansas City MSA, MO-KS	Y	108110 FQ	121580 MW	137750 TQ	USBLS	5/15
	St. Louis MSA, MO-IL	Y	108360 FQ	119560 MW	131470 TQ	USBLS	5/15
	Montana	Y	103300 FQ	113500 MW	123750 TQ	USBLS	5/15
	Billings MSA, MT	Y	109130 FQ	117920 MW	128460 TQ	USBLS	5/15
	Nebraska	Y	91825 FQ	109550 MW	121270 TQ	NEBLS	7/16-9/16
	Omaha-Council Bluffs MSA, NE-IA	Y	87160 FQ	107800 MW	119955 TQ	NEBLS	7/16-9/16
	Nevada	Y	109590 FQ	124230 MW	142270 TQ	USBLS	5/15
	Las Vegas-Henderson-Paradise MSA, NV	Y	109230 FQ	123570 MW	141740 TQ	USBLS	5/15
	New Hampshire	H	53.07 AE	63.30 MW	67.92 AEX	NHBLS	6/16
	Manchester NECTA, NH	H	51.04 AE	62.30 MW	65.70 AEX	NHBLS	6/16
	Nashua NECTA, NH-MA	Y	114240 FQ	130660 MW	150380 TQ	USBLS	5/15
	New Jersey	Y	105090 FQ	116940 MW	129530 TQ	USBLS	5/15
	Camden PMSA, NJ	Y	109130 FQ	119480 MW	131340 TQ	USBLS	5/15
	Newark PMSA, NJ-PA	Y	106820 FQ	117300 MW	128610 TQ	USBLS	5/15
	Trenton MSA, NJ	Y	105150 FQ	115070 MW	125090 TQ	USBLS	5/15
	New Mexico	Y	105850 FQ	119660 MW	137210 TQ	USBLS	5/15
	Albuquerque MSA, NM	Y	105500 FQ	116840 MW	129140 TQ	USBLS	5/15
	New York	Y	89800 AE	119650 MW	134040 AEX	NYBLS	1/16-3/16
	Buffalo-Cheektowaga-Niagara Falls MSA, NY	Y	109380 FQ	120190 MW	134140 TQ	USBLS	5/15
	Nassau County-Suffolk County PMSA, NY	Y	111070 FQ	123910 MW	141920 TQ	USBLS	5/15
	New York-Jersey City-White Plains PMSA, NY-NJ	Y	95190 FQ	112840 MW	128380 TQ	USBLS	5/15
	Rochester MSA, NY	Y	108020 FQ	119830 MW	132110 TQ	USBLS	5/15
	North Carolina	Y	110840 FQ	124600 MW	141570 TQ	USBLS	5/15
	Charlotte-Concord-Gastonia MSA, NC-SC	Y	109370 FQ	123070 MW	139650 TQ	USBLS	5/15

AE	Average entry wage	**AWR**	Average wage range	**H**	Hourly
AEX	Average experienced wage	**B**	Biweekly	**HI**	Highest wage paid
ATC	Average total compensation	**D**	Daily	**HR**	High end range
AW	Average wage paid	**FQ**	First quartile wage	**LO**	Lowest wage paid

LR	Low end range	**MTC**	Median total compensation	**TCC**	Total cash compensation
M	Monthly	**MW**	Median wage paid	**TQ**	Third quartile wage
MCC	Median cash compensation	**MWR**	Median wage range	**W**	Weekly
ME	Median entry wage	**S**	See annotated source	**Y**	Yearly

Occupation/Type/Industry	Location	Per	Low	Mid	High	Source	Date
Pharmacist	Raleigh MSA, NC	Y	109270 FQ	121800 MW	136100 TQ	USBLS	5/15
	North Dakota	Y	103050 FQ	114200 MW	125130 TQ	USBLS	5/15
	Fargo MSA, ND-MN	Y	102400 FQ	114210 MW	125420 TQ	USBLS	5/15
	Ohio	Y	106660 FQ	118670 MW	131790 TQ	USBLS	5/15
	Cincinnati MSA, OH-KY-IN	Y	108260 FQ	121870 MW	139210 TQ	USBLS	5/15
	Cleveland-Elyria MSA, OH	Y	108460 FQ	118190 MW	127930 TQ	USBLS	5/15
	Columbus MSA, OH	Y	96420 FQ	113850 MW	127300 TQ	USBLS	5/15
	Oklahoma	Y	105080 FQ	115610 MW	126650 TQ	USBLS	5/15
	Oklahoma City MSA, OK	Y	105820 FQ	115880 MW	125970 TQ	USBLS	5/15
	Tulsa MSA, OK	Y	108790 FQ	118330 MW	128560 TQ	USBLS	5/15
	Oregon	H	53.99 FQ	60.61 MW	68.73 TQ	ORBLS	2016
	Portland-Vancouver-Hillsboro MSA, OR-WA	Y	111230 FQ	125130 MW	142410 TQ	USBLS	5/15
	Pennsylvania	Y	103810 FQ	115510 MW	127510 TQ	USBLS	5/15
	Allentown-Bethlehem-Easton MSA, PA-NJ	Y	103630 FQ	114980 MW	126700 TQ	USBLS	5/15
	Harrisburg-Carlisle MSA, PA	Y	108360 FQ	117770 MW	127960 TQ	USBLS	5/15
	Montgomery County-Bucks County-Chester County PMSA, PA	Y	109150 FQ	120210 MW	131710 TQ	USBLS	5/15
	Philadelphia PMSA, PA	Y	104690 FQ	117650 MW	131860 TQ	USBLS	5/15
	Pittsburgh MSA, PA	Y	93810 FQ	109800 MW	121480 TQ	USBLS	5/15
	Rhode Island	Y	107190 FQ	117980 MW	129570 TQ	USBLS	5/15
	Providence-Warwick MSA, RI-MA	Y	107530 FQ	118180 MW	129550 TQ	USBLS	5/15
	South Carolina	Y	108190 FQ	121940 MW	140190 TQ	USBLS	5/15
	Charleston-North Charleston MSA, SC	Y	108380 FQ	119980 MW	136290 TQ	USBLS	5/15
	Columbia MSA, SC	Y	101310 FQ	117440 MW	133140 TQ	USBLS	5/15
	Greenville-Anderson-Mauldin MSA, SC	Y	110580 FQ	123350 MW	142450 TQ	USBLS	5/15
	South Dakota	Y	102660 FQ	112760 MW	122890 TQ	USBLS	5/15
	Sioux Falls MSA, SD	Y	104260 FQ	113180 MW	122630 TQ	USBLS	5/15
	Tennessee	Y	108360 FQ	120920 MW	135210 TQ	USBLS	5/15
	Knoxville MSA, TN	Y	108550 FQ	122080 MW	140460 TQ	USBLS	5/15
	Memphis MSA, TN-MS-AR	Y	105490 FQ	124480 MW	140240 TQ	USBLS	5/15
	Nashville-Davidson– Murfreesboro–Franklin MSA, TN	Y	108840 FQ	119120 MW	130280 TQ	USBLS	5/15
	Texas	Y	108910 FQ	122590 MW	140420 TQ	USBLS	5/15
	Austin-Round Rock MSA, TX	Y	100650 FQ	120490 MW	139230 TQ	USBLS	5/15
	Dallas-Plano-Irving PMSA, TX	Y	108100 FQ	121680 MW	139090 TQ	USBLS	5/15
	Fort Worth-Arlington PMSA, TX	Y	110830 FQ	122880 MW	139310 TQ	USBLS	5/15
	Houston-The Woodlands-Sugar Land MSA, TX	Y	107460 FQ	118020 MW	129750 TQ	USBLS	5/15
	San Antonio-New Braunfels MSA, TX	Y	108500 FQ	125980 MW	144570 TQ	USBLS	5/15
	Utah	Y	107100 FQ	120960 MW	136900 TQ	USBLS	5/15
	Ogden-Clearfield MSA, UT	Y	109980 FQ	121640 MW	132710 TQ	USBLS	5/15
	Provo-Orem MSA, UT	Y	106100 FQ	119670 MW	134780 TQ	USBLS	5/15
	Salt Lake City MSA, UT	Y	105340 FQ	120500 MW	138120 TQ	USBLS	5/15
	Vermont	Y	110470 FQ	130890 MW	146190 TQ	USBLS	5/15
	Burlington-South Burlington MSA, VT	Y	120990 FQ	135720 MW	148150 TQ	USBLS	5/15
	Virginia	Y	107310 FQ	122560 MW	139290 TQ	USBLS	5/15
	Richmond MSA, VA	Y	103970 FQ	120940 MW	138390 TQ	USBLS	5/15
	Virginia Beach-Norfolk-Newport News MSA, VA-NC	Y	113550 FQ	127530 MW	143020 TQ	USBLS	5/15
	Washington	H	53.68 FQ	59.74 MW	67.64 TQ	WABLS	3/16
	Seattle-Bellevue-Everett PMSA, WA	H	53.51 FQ	59.99 MW	68.61 TQ	WABLS	3/16
	Tacoma-Lakewood PMSA, WA	H	53.44 FQ	57.94 MW	63.18 TQ	WABLS	3/16
	West Virginia	Y	109280 FQ	124780 MW	142640 TQ	USBLS	5/15
	Huntington-Ashland MSA, WV-KY-OH	Y	103900 FQ	122850 MW	144260 TQ	USBLS	5/15
	Wisconsin	Y	109750 FQ	126880 MW	144760 TQ	USBLS	5/15
	Madison MSA, WI	Y	102010 FQ	117240 MW	134370 TQ	USBLS	5/15
	Milwaukee-Waukesha-West Allis MSA, WI	Y	112960 FQ	130400 MW	149430 TQ	USBLS	5/15
	Wyoming	Y	106200 FQ	118340 MW	129770 TQ	USBLS	5/15
	Cheyenne MSA, WY	Y	109550 FQ	120180 MW	125000 TQ	USBLS	5/15

AE	Average entry wage	**AWR**	Average wage range	**H**	Hourly
AEX	Average experienced wage	**B**	Biweekly	**HI**	Highest wage paid
ATC	Average total compensation	**D**	Daily	**HR**	High end range
AW	Average wage paid	**FQ**	First quartile wage	**LO**	Lowest wage paid

LR	Low end range	**MTC**	Median total compensation	**TCC**	Total cash compensation
M	Monthly	**MW**	Median wage paid	**TQ**	Third quartile wage
MCC	Median cash compensation	**MWR**	Median wage range	**W**	Weekly
ME	Median entry wage	**S**	See annotated source	**Y**	Yearly

Occupation/Type/Industry	Location	Per	Low	Mid	High	Source	Date
Pharmacist	Puerto Rico	Y	58160 FQ	87510 MW	103430 TQ	USBLS	5/15
	San Juan-Carolina-Caguas MSA, PR	Y	64570 FQ	88330 MW	103560 TQ	USBLS	5/15
	Virgin Islands	Y	98870 FQ	111410 MW	121320 TQ	USBLS	5/15
	Guam	Y	86310 FQ	107290 MW	121980 TQ	USBLS	5/15
Pharmacologist							
Medicaid, State Government	Ohio	H	50.08 LO		54.33 HI	OHGOV	2015
Pharmacy Aide	Alabama	Y	17565 AE	23465 AW	26420 AEX	ALBLS	6/16
	Birmingham-Hoover MSA, AL	Y	17617 AE	22898 AW	25545 AEX	ALBLS	6/16
	Alaska	Y	32690 FQ	38950 MW	49740 TQ	USBLS	5/15
	Anchorage MSA, AK	Y	33960 FQ	40320 MW	51490 TQ	USBLS	5/15
	Arizona	Y	25530 FQ	28620 MW	33090 TQ	USBLS	5/15
	Phoenix-Mesa-Scottsdale MSA, AZ	Y	26090 FQ	28940 MW	33410 TQ	USBLS	5/15
	Arkansas	Y	17630 FQ	19600 MW	23210 TQ	USBLS	5/15
	Little Rock-North Little Rock-Conway MSA, AR	Y	17890 FQ	20130 MW	23200 TQ	USBLS	5/15
	California	H	11.39 FQ	14.41 MW	20.17 TQ	CABLS	1/16-3/16
	Anaheim-Santa Ana-Irvine PMSA, CA	H	12.18 FQ	16.39 MW	22.49 TQ	CABLS	1/16-3/16
	Los Angeles-Long Beach-Glendale PMSA, CA	H	11.80 FQ	16.52 MW	24.50 TQ	CABLS	1/16-3/16
	Oakland-Hayward-Berkeley PMSA, CA	H	11.03 FQ	14.30 MW	25.49 TQ	CABLS	1/16-3/16
	Riverside-San Bernardino-Ontario MSA, CA	H	10.66 FQ	12.16 MW	17.48 TQ	CABLS	1/16-3/16
	Sacramento–Roseville–Arden-Arcade MSA, CA	H	10.93 FQ	12.77 MW	15.97 TQ	CABLS	1/16-3/16
	San Diego-Carlsbad MSA, CA	H	10.92 FQ	13.24 MW	19.60 TQ	CABLS	1/16-3/16
	San Francisco-Redwood City-South San Francisco PMSA, CA	H	13.41 FQ	15.75 MW	20.03 TQ	CABLS	1/16-3/16
	Colorado	Y	23560 FQ	33570 MW	39900 TQ	USBLS	5/15
	Denver-Aurora-Lakewood MSA, CO	Y	33790 FQ	37410 MW	43240 TQ	USBLS	5/15
	Connecticut	Y		23209 MW		CTBLS	1/16-3/16
	Delaware	Y	17180 FQ	18120 MW	19060 TQ	USBLS	5/15
	Washington-Arlington-Alexandria PMSA, DC-VA-MD-WV	Y	22690 FQ	26560 MW	39160 TQ	USBLS	5/15
	Florida	H	9.00 AE	10.87 MW	15.15 AEX	FLBLS	7/16-9/16
	Fort Lauderdale-Pompano Beach-Deerfield Beach PMSA, FL	H	9.57 AE	11.30 MW	13.39 AEX	FLBLS	7/16-9/16
	Miami-Miami Beach-Kendall PMSA, FL	H	8.97 AE	13.21 MW	21.15 AEX	FLBLS	7/16-9/16
	Orlando-Kissimmee-Sanford MSA, FL	H	9.67 AE	12.04 MW	14.86 AEX	FLBLS	7/16-9/16
	Tampa-St. Petersburg-Clearwater MSA, FL	H	9.00 AE	9.48 MW	11.47 AEX	FLBLS	7/16-9/16
	Georgia	Y	20170 FQ	26510 MW	32850 TQ	USBLS	5/15
	Atlanta-Sandy Springs-Roswell MSA, GA	Y	24250 FQ	30230 MW	35830 TQ	USBLS	5/15
	Hawaii	Y	30600 FQ	38110 MW	43940 TQ	USBLS	5/15
	Idaho	Y	22820 FQ	27200 MW	30660 TQ	USBLS	5/15
	Illinois	Y	20820 FQ	24140 MW	29110 TQ	USBLS	5/15
	Chicago-Naperville-Arlington Heights PMSA, IL	Y	20850 FQ	23850 MW	30260 TQ	USBLS	5/15
	Indiana	Y	18320 FQ	21930 MW	27340 TQ	USBLS	5/15
	Indianapolis-Carmel-Anderson MSA, IN	Y	18480 FQ	23300 MW	31880 TQ	USBLS	5/15
	Iowa	Y	18470 FQ	21350 MW	24070 TQ	USBLS	5/15
	Kansas	Y	18310 FQ	21790 MW	26570 TQ	USBLS	5/15
	Wichita MSA, KS	Y	17130 FQ	18750 MW	21270 TQ	USBLS	5/15
	Kentucky	Y	18210 FQ	21190 MW	24430 TQ	USBLS	5/15
	Louisville-Jefferson County MSA, KY-IN	Y	17880 FQ	20240 MW	22580 TQ	USBLS	5/15
	Louisiana	Y	18950 FQ	22800 MW	27450 TQ	USBLS	5/15
	Baton Rouge MSA, LA	Y	19080 FQ	21940 MW	24600 TQ	USBLS	5/15

Pharmacy Aide

Occupation/Type/Industry	Location	Per	Low	Mid	High	Source	Date
Pharmacy Aide	New Orleans-Metairie MSA, LA	Y	18220 FQ	22920 MW	28210 TQ	USBLS	5/15
	Maine	Y	19120 FQ	22370 MW	26170 TQ	USBLS	5/15
	Maryland	Y	18440 AE	26037 MW	29835 AEX	MDBLS	4/16
	Baltimore-Columbia-Towson MSA, MD	Y	21260 FQ	24250 MW	35230 TQ	USBLS	5/15
	Massachusetts	Y	21920 FQ	24650 MW	33610 TQ	USBLS	5/15
	Boston-Cambridge-Newton NECTA, MA	Y	22270 FQ	24750 MW	35330 TQ	USBLS	5/15
	Michigan	Y	19650 FQ	22230 MW	24920 TQ	USBLS	5/15
	Detroit-Dearborn-Livonia PMSA, MI	Y	19060 FQ	21200 MW	23580 TQ	USBLS	5/15
	Grand Rapids-Wyoming MSA, MI	Y	22410 FQ	29120 MW	36930 TQ	USBLS	5/15
	Minnesota	Y	22167 FQ	25742 MW	29377 TQ	MNBLS	1/16-3/16
	Minneapolis-St. Paul-Bloomington MSA, MN-WI	Y	23136 FQ	26570 MW	29670 TQ	MNBLS	1/16-3/16
	Mississippi	Y	19390 FQ	26070 MW	34090 TQ	USBLS	5/15
	Jackson MSA, MS	Y	31520 FQ	34110 MW	36700 TQ	USBLS	5/15
	Missouri	Y	19580 FQ	22980 MW	27870 TQ	USBLS	5/15
	Kansas City MSA, MO-KS	Y	19100 FQ	23900 MW	28120 TQ	USBLS	5/15
	St. Louis MSA, MO-IL	Y	19810 FQ	23350 MW	28040 TQ	USBLS	5/15
	Montana	Y	22320 FQ	25820 MW	29600 TQ	USBLS	5/15
	Nebraska	Y	20505 FQ	23780 MW	28380 TQ	NEBLS	7/16-9/16
	Omaha-Council Bluffs MSA, NE-IA	Y	20660 FQ	24710 MW	29155 TQ	NEBLS	7/16-9/16
	Nevada	Y	20370 FQ	30620 MW	38050 TQ	USBLS	5/15
	Las Vegas-Henderson-Paradise MSA, NV	Y	21540 FQ	33100 MW	38810 TQ	USBLS	5/15
	New Hampshire	H	10.29 AE	12.46 MW	14.52 AEX	NHBLS	6/16
	Nashua NECTA, NH-MA	Y	22470 FQ	27110 MW	31170 TQ	USBLS	5/15
	New Jersey	Y	21450 FQ	24200 MW	28810 TQ	USBLS	5/15
	Camden PMSA, NJ	Y	21240 FQ	23020 MW	25180 TQ	USBLS	5/15
	Newark PMSA, NJ-PA	Y	19630 FQ	21900 MW	24290 TQ	USBLS	5/15
	New Mexico	Y	20980 FQ	27730 MW	39920 TQ	USBLS	5/15
	Albuquerque MSA, NM	Y	23100 FQ	28880 MW	37060 TQ	USBLS	5/15
	New York	Y	20480 AE	26640 MW	32160 AEX	NYBLS	1/16-3/16
	Buffalo-Cheektowaga-Niagara Falls MSA, NY	Y	18900 FQ	19850 MW	31680 TQ	USBLS	5/15
	Nassau County-Suffolk County PMSA, NY	Y	23460 FQ	31510 MW	37610 TQ	USBLS	5/15
	New York-Jersey City-White Plains PMSA, NY-NJ	Y	21190 FQ	25920 MW	29890 TQ	USBLS	5/15
	Rochester MSA, NY	Y	18850 FQ	19500 MW	29410 TQ	USBLS	5/15
	North Carolina	Y	17550 FQ	19550 MW	23940 TQ	USBLS	5/15
	Charlotte-Concord-Gastonia MSA, NC-SC	Y	20910 FQ	23500 MW	28850 TQ	USBLS	5/15
	Raleigh MSA, NC	Y	21010 FQ	23390 MW	27170 TQ	USBLS	5/15
	North Dakota	Y	20830 FQ	22660 MW	24510 TQ	USBLS	5/15
	Fargo MSA, ND-MN	Y	20930 FQ	22400 MW	23870 TQ	USBLS	5/15
	Ohio	Y	20000 FQ	24160 MW	30010 TQ	USBLS	5/15
	Cincinnati MSA, OH-KY-IN	Y	19860 FQ	24000 MW	30230 TQ	USBLS	5/15
	Cleveland-Elyria MSA, OH	Y	21460 FQ	23680 MW	29570 TQ	USBLS	5/15
	Columbus MSA, OH	Y	19340 FQ	21660 MW	24230 TQ	USBLS	5/15
	Oklahoma	Y	17820 FQ	20230 MW	23570 TQ	USBLS	5/15
	Oklahoma City MSA, OK	Y	21140 FQ	23950 MW	27880 TQ	USBLS	5/15
	Tulsa MSA, OK	Y	17720 FQ	20030 MW	22860 TQ	USBLS	5/15
	Oregon	H	10.96 FQ	13.41 MW	18.25 TQ	ORBLS	2016
	Portland-Vancouver-Hillsboro MSA, OR-WA	Y	22150 FQ	25790 MW	32420 TQ	USBLS	5/15
	Pennsylvania	Y	18140 FQ	21780 MW	26720 TQ	USBLS	5/15
	Allentown-Bethlehem-Easton MSA, PA-NJ	Y	18150 FQ	21110 MW	24340 TQ	USBLS	5/15
	Harrisburg-Carlisle MSA, PA	Y	17840 FQ	20180 MW	22730 TQ	USBLS	5/15
	Montgomery County-Bucks County-Chester County PMSA, PA	Y	17880 FQ	20890 MW	25720 TQ	USBLS	5/15
	Philadelphia PMSA, PA	Y	16880 FQ	18570 MW	27430 TQ	USBLS	5/15
	Pittsburgh MSA, PA	Y	21800 FQ	26660 MW	29410 TQ	USBLS	5/15
	Providence-Warwick MSA, RI-MA	Y	19670 FQ	23680 MW	29340 TQ	USBLS	5/15
	South Carolina	Y	18790 FQ	21930 MW	25160 TQ	USBLS	5/15

AE	Average entry wage	AWR	Average wage range	H	Hourly	LR	Low end range	MTC	Median total compensation	TCC	Total cash compensation
AEX	Average experienced wage	B	Biweekly	HI	Highest wage paid	M	Monthly	MW	Median wage paid	TQ	Third quartile wage
ATC	Average total compensation	D	Daily	HR	High end range	MCC	Median cash compensation	MWR	Median wage range	W	Weekly
AW	Average wage paid	FQ	First quartile wage	LO	Lowest wage paid	ME	Median entry wage	S	See annotated source	Y	Yearly

Occupation/Type/Industry	Location	Per	Low	Mid	High	Source	Date
Pharmacy Aide	Tennessee	Y	19760 FQ	22420 MW	26590 TQ	USBLS	5/15
	Knoxville MSA, TN	Y	18200 FQ	26710 MW	32350 TQ	USBLS	5/15
	Memphis MSA, TN-MS-AR	Y	19980 FQ	23400 MW	30610 TQ	USBLS	5/15
	Nashville-Davidson–Murfreesboro–Franklin MSA, TN	Y	20650 FQ	22300 MW	23950 TQ	USBLS	5/15
	Texas	Y	18540 FQ	23010 MW	30990 TQ	USBLS	5/15
	Austin-Round Rock MSA, TX	Y	22480 FQ	29390 MW	35210 TQ	USBLS	5/15
	Dallas-Plano-Irving PMSA, TX	Y	18720 FQ	22470 MW	28630 TQ	USBLS	5/15
	Fort Worth-Arlington PMSA, TX	Y	19920 FQ	27030 MW	37710 TQ	USBLS	5/15
	Houston-The Woodlands-Sugar Land MSA, TX	Y	20790 FQ	25350 MW	33980 TQ	USBLS	5/15
	San Antonio-New Braunfels MSA, TX	Y	22010 FQ	28900 MW	35160 TQ	USBLS	5/15
	Utah	Y	25190 FQ	28820 MW	35290 TQ	USBLS	5/15
	Ogden-Clearfield MSA, UT	Y	24620 FQ	27650 MW	30390 TQ	USBLS	5/15
	Provo-Orem MSA, UT	Y	26660 FQ	30190 MW	36230 TQ	USBLS	5/15
	Salt Lake City MSA, UT	Y	26720 FQ	31130 MW	42320 TQ	USBLS	5/15
	Vermont	Y	21130 FQ	22880 MW	24730 TQ	USBLS	5/15
	Burlington-South Burlington MSA, VT	Y	20870 FQ	22640 MW	24400 TQ	USBLS	5/15
	Virginia	Y	20270 FQ	22720 MW	25720 TQ	USBLS	5/15
	Richmond MSA, VA	Y	20230 FQ	23260 MW	27180 TQ	USBLS	5/15
	Virginia Beach-Norfolk-Newport News MSA, VA-NC	Y	18830 FQ	21100 MW	23170 TQ	USBLS	5/15
	Washington	H	12.35 FQ	14.16 MW	17.00 TQ	WABLS	3/16
	Seattle-Bellevue-Everett PMSA, WA	H	12.71 FQ	14.40 MW	16.92 TQ	WABLS	3/16
	Tacoma-Lakewood PMSA, WA	H	12.35 FQ	13.94 MW	19.79 TQ	WABLS	3/16
	West Virginia	Y	17680 FQ	18720 MW	21160 TQ	USBLS	5/15
	Huntington-Ashland MSA, WV-KY-OH	Y	19210 FQ	21750 MW	24020 TQ	USBLS	5/15
	Wisconsin	Y	17560 FQ	19750 MW	24490 TQ	USBLS	5/15
	Madison MSA, WI	Y	21330 FQ	23450 MW	34310 TQ	USBLS	5/15
	Milwaukee-Waukesha-West Allis MSA, WI	Y	16840 FQ	18220 MW	19620 TQ	USBLS	5/15
	Wyoming	Y	21010 FQ	23480 MW	28220 TQ	USBLS	5/15
	Puerto Rico	Y	16930 FQ	18290 MW	19660 TQ	USBLS	5/15
	San Juan-Carolina-Caguas MSA, PR	Y	16960 FQ	18330 MW	19690 TQ	USBLS	5/15
Pharmacy Technician	Alabama	Y	21131 AE	28052 AW	31507 AEX	ALBLS	6/16
	Birmingham-Hoover MSA, AL	Y	21630 AE	27573 AW	21630 AEX	ALBLS	6/16
	Alaska	Y	32640 FQ	39580 MW	46350 TQ	USBLS	5/15
	Anchorage MSA, AK	Y	32220 FQ	39780 MW	46200 TQ	USBLS	5/15
	Arizona	Y	25680 FQ	32040 MW	37730 TQ	USBLS	5/15
	Phoenix-Mesa-Scottsdale MSA, AZ	Y	25400 FQ	32000 MW	37900 TQ	USBLS	5/15
	Tucson MSA, AZ	Y	27230 FQ	33010 MW	37670 TQ	USBLS	5/15
	Arkansas	Y	22690 FQ	27020 MW	32220 TQ	USBLS	5/15
	Little Rock-North Little Rock-Conway MSA, AR	Y	24290 FQ	29330 MW	36370 TQ	USBLS	5/15
	California	H	15.18 FQ	18.75 MW	23.54 TQ	CABLS	1/16-3/16
	Anaheim-Santa Ana-Irvine PMSA, CA	H	14.93 FQ	17.81 MW	22.69 TQ	CABLS	1/16-3/16
	Los Angeles-Long Beach-Glendale PMSA, CA	H	14.19 FQ	18.24 MW	23.67 TQ	CABLS	1/16-3/16
	Oakland-Hayward-Berkeley PMSA, CA	H	17.41 FQ	22.79 MW	29.37 TQ	CABLS	1/16-3/16
	Riverside-San Bernardino-Ontario MSA, CA	H	15.24 FQ	18.17 MW	22.07 TQ	CABLS	1/16-3/16
	Sacramento–Roseville–Arden-Arcade MSA, CA	H	16.38 FQ	19.84 MW	24.21 TQ	CABLS	1/16-3/16
	San Diego-Carlsbad MSA, CA	H	13.26 FQ	17.46 MW	21.42 TQ	CABLS	1/16-3/16
	San Francisco-Redwood City-South San Francisco PMSA, CA	H	19.51 FQ	23.38 MW	28.43 TQ	CABLS	1/16-3/16
	Colorado	Y	28070 FQ	33440 MW	38790 TQ	USBLS	5/15
	Denver-Aurora-Lakewood MSA, CO	Y	28840 FQ	34410 MW	40160 TQ	USBLS	5/15
	Connecticut	Y		31774 MW		CTBLS	1/16-3/16

AE Average entry wage	**AWR** Average wage range	**H** Hourly	**LR** Low end range	**MTC** Median total compensation	**TCC** Total cash compensation
AEX Average experienced wage	**B** Biweekly	**HI** Highest wage paid	**M** Monthly	**MW** Median wage paid	**TQ** Third quartile wage
ATC Average total compensation	**D** Daily	**HR** High end range	**MCC** Median cash compensation	**MWR** Median wage range	**W** Weekly
AW Average wage paid	**FQ** First quartile wage	**LO** Lowest wage paid	**ME** Median entry wage	**S** See annotated source	**Y** Yearly

Occupation/Type/Industry	Location	Per	Low	Mid	High	Source	Date
Pharmacy Technician	Bridgeport-Stamford-Norwalk MSA, CT	Y	24220 FQ	29800 MW	37550 TQ	USBLS	5/15
	Hartford-West Hartford-East Hartford MSA, CT	Y	23760 FQ	28980 MW	36670 TQ	USBLS	5/15
	Delaware	Y	22830 FQ	27470 MW	35770 TQ	USBLS	5/15
	Wilmington PMSA, DE-MD-NJ	Y	23100 FQ	29210 MW	39010 TQ	USBLS	5/15
	District of Columbia	Y	24870 FQ	33420 MW	42720 TQ	USBLS	5/15
	Washington-Arlington-Alexandria PMSA, DC-VA-MD-WV	Y	24530 FQ	31220 MW	38560 TQ	USBLS	5/15
	Florida	H	11.05 AE	14.33 MW	16.41 AEX	FLBLS	7/16-9/16
	Fort Lauderdale-Pompano Beach-Deerfield Beach PMSA, FL	H	12.22 AE	15.72 MW	17.98 AEX	FLBLS	7/16-9/16
	Miami-Miami Beach-Kendall PMSA, FL	H	11.60 AE	14.95 MW	16.91 AEX	FLBLS	7/16-9/16
	Orlando-Kissimmee-Sanford MSA, FL	H	10.64 AE	13.38 MW	15.37 AEX	FLBLS	7/16-9/16
	Tampa-St. Petersburg-Clearwater MSA, FL	H	11.22 AE	14.39 MW	16.22 AEX	FLBLS	7/16-9/16
	Georgia	Y	22090 FQ	27270 MW	34110 TQ	USBLS	5/15
	Atlanta-Sandy Springs-Roswell MSA, GA	Y	21870 FQ	27000 MW	34640 TQ	USBLS	5/15
	Augusta-Richmond County MSA, GA-SC	Y	23140 FQ	28850 MW	35290 TQ	USBLS	5/15
	Brunswick MSA, GA	Y	26110 FQ	29840 MW	34720 TQ	USBLS	5/15
	Hawaii	Y	29370 FQ	35920 MW	42730 TQ	USBLS	5/15
	Urban Honolulu MSA, HI	Y	28800 FQ	35740 MW	42410 TQ	USBLS	5/15
	Idaho	Y	26990 FQ	32280 MW	37790 TQ	USBLS	5/15
	Boise City MSA, ID	Y	28120 FQ	32780 MW	37390 TQ	USBLS	5/15
	Illinois	Y	22560 FQ	28810 MW	36240 TQ	USBLS	5/15
	Chicago-Naperville-Arlington Heights PMSA, IL	Y	21960 FQ	29330 MW	36630 TQ	USBLS	5/15
	Lake County-Kenosha County PMSA, IL-WI	Y	25950 FQ	30690 MW	38640 TQ	USBLS	5/15
	Indiana	Y	23760 FQ	28470 MW	34180 TQ	USBLS	5/15
	Gary PMSA, IN	Y	23840 FQ	28220 MW	33380 TQ	USBLS	5/15
	Indianapolis-Carmel-Anderson MSA, IN	Y	24230 FQ	30140 MW	36270 TQ	USBLS	5/15
	Iowa	Y	24570 FQ	28700 MW	34140 TQ	USBLS	5/15
	Des Moines-West Des Moines MSA, IA	Y	26190 FQ	29510 MW	34540 TQ	USBLS	5/15
	Kansas	Y	24270 FQ	29130 MW	35090 TQ	USBLS	5/15
	Wichita MSA, KS	Y	22390 FQ	26440 MW	32530 TQ	USBLS	5/15
	Kentucky	Y	22180 FQ	26710 MW	32830 TQ	USBLS	5/15
	Louisville-Jefferson County MSA, KY-IN	Y	24360 FQ	29770 MW	35420 TQ	USBLS	5/15
	Louisiana	Y	24590 FQ	29330 MW	35330 TQ	USBLS	5/15
	Baton Rouge MSA, LA	Y	24070 FQ	29760 MW	36650 TQ	USBLS	5/15
	New Orleans-Metairie MSA, LA	Y	25470 FQ	29600 MW	35100 TQ	USBLS	5/15
	Maine	Y	25420 FQ	29270 MW	34810 TQ	USBLS	5/15
	Portland-South Portland MSA, ME	Y	26700 FQ	30620 MW	36700 TQ	USBLS	5/15
	Maryland	Y	23347 AE	31834 MW	36077 AEX	MDBLS	4/16
	Baltimore-Columbia-Towson MSA, MD	Y	25270 FQ	30550 MW	36740 TQ	USBLS	5/15
	Salisbury MSA, MD-DE	Y	23470 FQ	27840 MW	32090 TQ	USBLS	5/15
	Massachusetts	Y	23960 FQ	30040 MW	37750 TQ	USBLS	5/15
	Boston-Cambridge-Newton NECTA, MA	Y	24430 FQ	31970 MW	39280 TQ	USBLS	5/15
	Worcester MSA, MA-CT	Y	24370 FQ	29110 MW	37080 TQ	USBLS	5/15
	Michigan	Y	24320 FQ	29740 MW	35600 TQ	USBLS	5/15
	Detroit-Dearborn-Livonia PMSA, MI	Y	23730 FQ	30270 MW	35730 TQ	USBLS	5/15
	Grand Rapids-Wyoming MSA, MI	Y	26180 FQ	30820 MW	36110 TQ	USBLS	5/15
	Minnesota	Y	26391 FQ	33427 MW	39546 TQ	MNBLS	1/16-3/16
	Minneapolis-St. Paul-Bloomington MSA, MN-WI	Y	26451 FQ	34072 MW	41078 TQ	MNBLS	1/16-3/16
	Mississippi	Y	22830 FQ	27650 MW	33490 TQ	USBLS	5/15

AE Average entry wage	**AWR** Average wage range	**H** Hourly	**LR** Low end range	**MTC** Median total compensation	**TCC** Total cash compensation
AEX Average experienced wage	**B** Biweekly	**HI** Highest wage paid	**M** Monthly	**MW** Median wage paid	**TQ** Third quartile wage
ATC Average total compensation	**D** Daily	**HR** High end range	**MCC** Median cash compensation	**MWR** Median wage range	**W** Weekly
AW Average wage paid	**FQ** First quartile wage	**LO** Lowest wage paid	**ME** Median entry wage	**S** See annotated source	**Y** Yearly

Occupation/Type/Industry	Location	Per	Low	Mid	High	Source	Date
Pharmacy Technician	Jackson MSA, MS	Y	23150 FQ	27690 MW	32750 TQ	USBLS	5/15
	Missouri	Y	23260 FQ	28050 MW	34090 TQ	USBLS	5/15
	Kansas City MSA, MO-KS	Y	24590 FQ	29940 MW	35800 TQ	USBLS	5/15
	St. Louis MSA, MO-IL	Y	24280 FQ	28970 MW	35390 TQ	USBLS	5/15
	Montana	Y	28400 FQ	33110 MW	37330 TQ	USBLS	5/15
	Billings MSA, MT	Y	28750 FQ	33320 MW	37570 TQ	USBLS	5/15
	Nebraska	Y	24370 FQ	28640 MW	33970 TQ	NEBLS	7/16-9/16
	Omaha-Council Bluffs MSA, NE-IA	Y	26140 FQ	30120 MW	35760 TQ	NEBLS	7/16-9/16
	Nevada	Y	27930 FQ	33050 MW	38100 TQ	USBLS	5/15
	Las Vegas-Henderson-Paradise MSA, NV	Y	28070 FQ	32990 MW	37800 TQ	USBLS	5/15
	New Hampshire	H	10.91 AE	14.31 MW	16.65 AEX	NHBLS	6/16
	Manchester NECTA, NH	H	11.95 AE	14.85 MW	17.70 AEX	NHBLS	6/16
	Nashua NECTA, NH-MA	Y	24410 FQ	28370 MW	33140 TQ	USBLS	5/15
	New Jersey	Y	25140 FQ	30380 MW	37520 TQ	USBLS	5/15
	Camden PMSA, NJ	Y	23510 FQ	29510 MW	36400 TQ	USBLS	5/15
	Newark PMSA, NJ-PA	Y	26940 FQ	30900 MW	39050 TQ	USBLS	5/15
	Trenton MSA, NJ	Y	20660 FQ	25220 MW	35410 TQ	USBLS	5/15
	New Mexico	Y	26230 FQ	30690 MW	36670 TQ	USBLS	5/15
	Albuquerque MSA, NM	Y	26430 FQ	30950 MW	36590 TQ	USBLS	5/15
	New York	Y	22660 AE	30550 MW	37250 AEX	NYBLS	1/16-3/16
	Buffalo-Cheektowaga-Niagara Falls MSA, NY	Y	22910 FQ	27890 MW	34480 TQ	USBLS	5/15
	Nassau County-Suffolk County PMSA, NY	Y	24720 FQ	31590 MW	38320 TQ	USBLS	5/15
	New York-Jersey City-White Plains PMSA, NY-NJ	Y	25040 FQ	31950 MW	40610 TQ	USBLS	5/15
	Rochester MSA, NY	Y	22400 FQ	26920 MW	30750 TQ	USBLS	5/15
	North Carolina	Y	22960 FQ	28670 MW	34990 TQ	USBLS	5/15
	Charlotte-Concord-Gastonia MSA, NC-SC	Y	24980 FQ	30980 MW	36260 TQ	USBLS	5/15
	Raleigh MSA, NC	Y	22100 FQ	26970 MW	33340 TQ	USBLS	5/15
	North Dakota	Y	31540 FQ	36060 MW	41460 TQ	USBLS	5/15
	Fargo MSA, ND-MN	Y	23860 FQ	31780 MW	36870 TQ	USBLS	5/15
	Ohio	Y	22780 FQ	27480 MW	33510 TQ	USBLS	5/15
	Cincinnati MSA, OH-KY-IN	Y	23390 FQ	28670 MW	35160 TQ	USBLS	5/15
	Cleveland-Elyria MSA, OH	Y	23240 FQ	28720 MW	35810 TQ	USBLS	5/15
	Columbus MSA, OH	Y	24330 FQ	28630 MW	33860 TQ	USBLS	5/15
	Oklahoma	Y	23360 FQ	28460 MW	34840 TQ	USBLS	5/15
	Oklahoma City MSA, OK	Y	25240 FQ	30950 MW	36920 TQ	USBLS	5/15
	Tulsa MSA, OK	Y	22250 FQ	25990 MW	30540 TQ	USBLS	5/15
	Oregon	H	15.64 FQ	17.83 MW	20.60 TQ	ORBLS	2016
	Portland-Vancouver-Hillsboro MSA, OR-WA	Y	32820 FQ	37640 MW	43960 TQ	USBLS	5/15
	Pennsylvania	Y	23650 FQ	28880 MW	35510 TQ	USBLS	5/15
	Allentown-Bethlehem-Easton MSA, PA-NJ	Y	22990 FQ	27660 MW	32330 TQ	USBLS	5/15
	Harrisburg-Carlisle MSA, PA	Y	22460 FQ	29140 MW	37060 TQ	USBLS	5/15
	Montgomery County-Bucks County-Chester County PMSA, PA	Y	23960 FQ	29510 MW	36230 TQ	USBLS	5/15
	Philadelphia PMSA, PA	Y	27850 FQ	33580 MW	39320 TQ	USBLS	5/15
	Pittsburgh MSA, PA	Y	23190 FQ	27790 MW	32670 TQ	USBLS	5/15
	Rhode Island	Y	25460 FQ	30110 MW	39660 TQ	USBLS	5/15
	Providence-Warwick MSA, RI-MA	Y	24990 FQ	29770 MW	38350 TQ	USBLS	5/15
	South Carolina	Y	23820 FQ	28950 MW	35490 TQ	USBLS	5/15
	Charleston-North Charleston MSA, SC	Y	25940 FQ	29810 MW	37390 TQ	USBLS	5/15
	Columbia MSA, SC	Y	25170 FQ	31300 MW	36920 TQ	USBLS	5/15
	Greenville-Anderson-Mauldin MSA, SC	Y	23820 FQ	29040 MW	35280 TQ	USBLS	5/15
	South Dakota	Y	26590 FQ	29810 MW	35150 TQ	USBLS	5/15
	Sioux Falls MSA, SD	Y	26780 FQ	29470 MW	33870 TQ	USBLS	5/15
	Tennessee	Y	24510 FQ	29090 MW	35300 TQ	USBLS	5/15
	Knoxville MSA, TN	Y	23120 FQ	27730 MW	32520 TQ	USBLS	5/15
	Memphis MSA, TN-MS-AR	Y	26870 FQ	34170 MW	39720 TQ	USBLS	5/15
	Nashville-Davidson–Murfreesboro–Franklin MSA, TN	Y	26070 FQ	29310 MW	34590 TQ	USBLS	5/15
	Texas	Y	26810 FQ	32480 MW	37670 TQ	USBLS	5/15

AE	Average entry wage	AWR	Average wage range	H	Hourly	LR	Low end range	MTC	Median total compensation	TCC	Total cash compensation
AEX	Average experienced wage	B	Biweekly	HI	Highest wage paid	M	Monthly	MW	Median wage paid	TQ	Third quartile wage
ATC	Average total compensation	D	Daily	HR	High end range	MCC	Median cash compensation	MWR	Median wage range	W	Weekly
AW	Average wage paid	FQ	First quartile wage	LO	Lowest wage paid	ME	Median entry wage	S	See annotated source	Y	Yearly

Occupation/Type/Industry	Location	Per	Low	Mid	High	Source	Date
Pharmacy Technician	Austin-Round Rock MSA, TX	Y	26060 FQ	31160 MW	36340 TQ	USBLS	5/15
	Dallas-Plano-Irving PMSA, TX	Y	26920 FQ	32710 MW	38740 TQ	USBLS	5/15
	Fort Worth-Arlington PMSA, TX	Y	26580 FQ	32110 MW	37580 TQ	USBLS	5/15
	Houston-The Woodlands-Sugar Land MSA, TX	Y	28910 FQ	34200 MW	38370 TQ	USBLS	5/15
	San Antonio-New Braunfels MSA, TX	Y	27950 FQ	33310 MW	38100 TQ	USBLS	5/15
	Utah	Y	28980 FQ	33910 MW	38620 TQ	USBLS	5/15
	Ogden-Clearfield MSA, UT	Y	29220 FQ	34210 MW	38990 TQ	USBLS	5/15
	Provo-Orem MSA, UT	Y	27960 FQ	31630 MW	38860 TQ	USBLS	5/15
	Salt Lake City MSA, UT	Y	30200 FQ	34780 MW	38880 TQ	USBLS	5/15
	Vermont	Y	27410 FQ	33450 MW	38990 TQ	USBLS	5/15
	Burlington-South Burlington MSA, VT	Y	28860 FQ	36090 MW	43220 TQ	USBLS	5/15
	Virginia	Y	23310 FQ	28250 MW	35040 TQ	USBLS	5/15
	Richmond MSA, VA	Y	23540 FQ	28680 MW	35780 TQ	USBLS	5/15
	Virginia Beach-Norfolk-Newport News MSA, VA-NC	Y	22640 FQ	27540 MW	34470 TQ	USBLS	5/15
	Washington	H	17.13 FQ	20.13 MW	22.93 TQ	WABLS	3/16
	Seattle-Bellevue-Everett PMSA, WA	H	17.89 FQ	20.81 MW	23.42 TQ	WABLS	3/16
	Tacoma-Lakewood PMSA, WA	H	17.16 FQ	19.96 MW	22.63 TQ	WABLS	3/16
	West Virginia	Y	21570 FQ	25790 MW	30430 TQ	USBLS	5/15
	Huntington-Ashland MSA, WV-KY-OH	Y	21670 FQ	26540 MW	32960 TQ	USBLS	5/15
	Wisconsin	Y	24900 FQ	29960 MW	36330 TQ	USBLS	5/15
	Madison MSA, WI	Y	27230 FQ	31940 MW	38840 TQ	USBLS	5/15
	Milwaukee-Waukesha-West Allis MSA, WI	Y	25430 FQ	31440 MW	38160 TQ	USBLS	5/15
	Wyoming	Y	30030 FQ	35300 MW	39620 TQ	USBLS	5/15
	Cheyenne MSA, WY	Y	29750 FQ	35830 MW	40360 TQ	USBLS	5/15
	Puerto Rico	Y	17720 FQ	20590 MW	26310 TQ	USBLS	5/15
	San Juan-Carolina-Caguas MSA, PR	Y	18580 FQ	22980 MW	29180 TQ	USBLS	5/15
	Virgin Islands	Y	24960 FQ	30540 MW	34990 TQ	USBLS	5/15
	Guam	Y	22160 FQ	27490 MW	31550 TQ	USBLS	5/15
Philosophy and Religion Teacher							
Postsecondary	Alabama	Y	47898 AE	74054 AW	87132 AEX	ALBLS	6/16
Postsecondary	Birmingham-Hoover MSA, AL	Y	49325 AE	79100 AW	93982 AEX	ALBLS	6/16
Postsecondary	Arizona	Y	36190 FQ	56970 MW	75280 TQ	USBLS	5/15
Postsecondary	Phoenix-Mesa-Scottsdale MSA, AZ	Y	34740 FQ	54160 MW	68170 TQ	USBLS	5/15
Postsecondary	Arkansas	Y	47430 FQ	60130 MW	77330 TQ	USBLS	5/15
Postsecondary	Little Rock-North Little Rock-Conway MSA, AR	Y	51460 FQ	61840 MW	80180 TQ	USBLS	5/15
Postsecondary	California	Y		93425 AW		CABLS	1/16-3/16
Postsecondary	Anaheim-Santa Ana-Irvine PMSA, CA	Y		105213 AW		CABLS	1/16-3/16
Postsecondary	Los Angeles-Long Beach-Glendale PMSA, CA	Y		98507 AW		CABLS	1/16-3/16
Postsecondary	Riverside-San Bernardino-Ontario MSA, CA	Y		98781 AW		CABLS	1/16-3/16
Postsecondary	Sacramento–Roseville–Arden-Arcade MSA, CA	Y		85654 AW		CABLS	1/16-3/16
Postsecondary	San Diego-Carlsbad MSA, CA	Y		83675 AW		CABLS	1/16-3/16
Postsecondary	San Francisco-Redwood City-South San Francisco PMSA, CA	Y		114019 AW		CABLS	1/16-3/16
Postsecondary	Colorado	Y	28780 FQ	41210 MW	68060 TQ	USBLS	5/15
Postsecondary	Denver-Aurora-Lakewood MSA, CO	Y	36430 FQ	55520 MW	69720 TQ	USBLS	5/15
Postsecondary	Connecticut	Y		79354 MW		CTBLS	1/16-3/16
Postsecondary	Bridgeport-Stamford-Norwalk MSA, CT	Y	68660 FQ	86880 MW	119440 TQ	USBLS	5/15
Postsecondary	Hartford-West Hartford-East Hartford MSA, CT	Y	66600 FQ	84590 MW	122560 TQ	USBLS	5/15
Postsecondary	District of Columbia	Y	56540 FQ	78240 MW	95850 TQ	USBLS	5/15
Postsecondary	Washington-Arlington-Alexandria PMSA, DC-VA-MD-WV	Y	54250 FQ	71940 MW	94090 TQ	USBLS	5/15

Occupation/Type/Industry	Location	Per	Low	Mid	High	Source	Date
Philosophy and Religion Teacher							
Postsecondary	Florida	Y	35796 AE	64524 MW	87392 AEX	FLBLS	7/16-9/16
Postsecondary	Miami-Miami Beach-Kendall PMSA, FL	Y	56703 AE	79242 MW	92597 AEX	FLBLS	7/16-9/16
Postsecondary	Tampa-St. Petersburg-Clearwater MSA, FL	Y	40134 AE	70291 MW	92001 AEX	FLBLS	7/16-9/16
Postsecondary	Georgia	Y	43270 FQ	68900 MW	88090 TQ	USBLS	5/15
Postsecondary	Atlanta-Sandy Springs-Roswell MSA, GA	Y	44560 FQ	70620 MW	91470 TQ	USBLS	5/15
Postsecondary	Hawaii	Y	41950 FQ	67080 MW	86860 TQ	USBLS	5/15
Postsecondary	Urban Honolulu MSA, HI	Y	41950 FQ	68940 MW	88150 TQ	USBLS	5/15
Postsecondary	Idaho	Y	19240 FQ	52230 MW	69600 TQ	USBLS	5/15
Postsecondary	Boise City MSA, ID	Y	17950 FQ	43790 MW	58970 TQ	USBLS	5/15
Postsecondary	Illinois	Y	50850 FQ	67940 MW	91000 TQ	USBLS	5/15
Postsecondary	Chicago-Naperville-Arlington Heights PMSA, IL	Y	52630 FQ	69010 MW	89790 TQ	USBLS	5/15
Postsecondary	Indiana	Y	49250 FQ	64470 MW	85920 TQ	USBLS	5/15
Postsecondary	Indianapolis-Carmel-Anderson MSA, IN	Y	48540 FQ	66280 MW	89740 TQ	USBLS	5/15
Postsecondary	Iowa	Y	53700 FQ	64360 MW	80660 TQ	USBLS	5/15
Postsecondary	Des Moines-West Des Moines MSA, IA	Y	41220 FQ	53330 MW	64970 TQ	USBLS	5/15
Postsecondary	Kansas	Y	41510 FQ	52540 MW	65800 TQ	USBLS	5/15
Postsecondary	Kentucky	Y	49440 FQ	63870 MW	89320 TQ	USBLS	5/15
Postsecondary	Louisville-Jefferson County MSA, KY-IN	Y	55510 FQ	70090 MW	91450 TQ	USBLS	5/15
Postsecondary	Louisiana	Y	48070 FQ	84900 MW	98210 TQ	USBLS	5/15
Postsecondary	Maine	Y	48080 FQ	72030 MW	97530 TQ	USBLS	5/15
Postsecondary	Portland-South Portland MSA, ME	Y	38120 FQ	51940 MW	78220 TQ	USBLS	5/15
Postsecondary	Maryland	Y	52478 AE	84691 MW	100797 AEX	MDBLS	4/16
Postsecondary	Baltimore-Columbia-Towson MSA, MD	Y	56370 FQ	71410 MW	93410 TQ	USBLS	5/15
Postsecondary	Massachusetts	Y	65280 FQ	86220 MW	122550 TQ	USBLS	5/15
Postsecondary	Boston-Cambridge-Newton NECTA, MA	Y	69340 FQ	92740 MW	131790 TQ	USBLS	5/15
Postsecondary	Worcester MSA, MA-CT	Y	56270 FQ	73290 MW	92210 TQ	USBLS	5/15
Postsecondary	Michigan	Y	51550 FQ	66790 MW	89790 TQ	USBLS	5/15
Postsecondary	Detroit-Dearborn-Livonia PMSA, MI	Y	67790 FQ	83580 MW	96990 TQ	USBLS	5/15
Postsecondary	Grand Rapids-Wyoming MSA, MI	Y	54370 FQ	62320 MW	82880 TQ	USBLS	5/15
Postsecondary	Minnesota	Y	55513 FQ	70483 MW	87186 TQ	MNBLS	1/16-3/16
Postsecondary	Minneapolis-St. Paul-Bloomington MSA, MN-WI	Y	55503 FQ	70463 MW	86662 TQ	MNBLS	1/16-3/16
Postsecondary	Mississippi	Y	49150 FQ	59200 MW	76260 TQ	USBLS	5/15
Postsecondary	Missouri	Y	46540 FQ	63880 MW	88000 TQ	USBLS	5/15
Postsecondary	Kansas City MSA, MO-KS	Y	51580 FQ	68800 MW	89580 TQ	USBLS	5/15
Postsecondary	St. Louis MSA, MO-IL	Y	42980 FQ	58690 MW	84710 TQ	USBLS	5/15
Postsecondary	Montana	Y	34660 FQ	51700 MW	72630 TQ	USBLS	5/15
Postsecondary	Nebraska	Y	44820 FQ	60220 MW	81380 TQ	NEBLS	7/16-9/16
Postsecondary	New Hampshire	Y	58443 AE	85093 MW	108413 AEX	NHBLS	6/16
Postsecondary	New Jersey	Y	53270 FQ	75970 MW	109610 TQ	USBLS	5/15
Postsecondary	Newark PMSA, NJ-PA	Y	56300 FQ	83050 MW	118470 TQ	USBLS	5/15
Postsecondary	New Mexico	Y	56380 FQ	84030 MW	97190 TQ	USBLS	5/15
Postsecondary	New York	Y	44010 AE	69150 MW	105260 AEX	NYBLS	1/16-3/16
Postsecondary	Buffalo-Cheektowaga-Niagara Falls MSA, NY	Y	48900 FQ	71900 MW	100010 TQ	USBLS	5/15
Postsecondary	Nassau County-Suffolk County PMSA, NY	Y	46140 FQ	57670 MW	84420 TQ	USBLS	5/15
Postsecondary	New York-Jersey City-White Plains PMSA, NY-NJ	Y	48100 FQ	67140 MW	95700 TQ	USBLS	5/15
Postsecondary	Rochester MSA, NY	Y	53560 FQ	79810 MW	125760 TQ	USBLS	5/15
Postsecondary	North Carolina	Y	49270 FQ	60510 MW	78030 TQ	USBLS	5/15
Postsecondary	Charlotte-Concord-Gastonia MSA, NC-SC	Y	48030 FQ	58080 MW	72830 TQ	USBLS	5/15
Postsecondary	Raleigh MSA, NC	Y	48790 FQ	57740 MW	70040 TQ	USBLS	5/15
Postsecondary	Ohio	Y	50440 FQ	67060 MW	87740 TQ	USBLS	5/15
Postsecondary	Cincinnati MSA, OH-KY-IN	Y	55000 FQ	66510 MW	82180 TQ	USBLS	5/15
Postsecondary	Columbus MSA, OH	Y	48850 FQ	68420 MW	89190 TQ	USBLS	5/15
Postsecondary	Oklahoma	Y	36670 FQ	48680 MW	66870 TQ	USBLS	5/15
Postsecondary	Oklahoma City MSA, OK	Y	31320 FQ	44660 MW	56260 TQ	USBLS	5/15

AE	Average entry wage	AWR	Average wage range	H	Hourly	LR	Low end range	MTC	Median total compensation	TCC	Total cash compensation
AEX	Average experienced wage	B	Biweekly	HI	Highest wage paid	M	Monthly	MW	Median wage paid	TQ	Third quartile wage
ATC	Average total compensation	D	Daily	HR	High end range	MCC	Median cash compensation	MWR	Median wage range	W	Weekly
AW	Average wage paid	FQ	First quartile wage	LO	Lowest wage paid	ME	Median entry wage	S	See annotated source	Y	Yearly

Occupation/Type/Industry	Location	Per	Low	Mid	High	Source	Date
Philosophy and Religion Teacher							
Postsecondary	Oregon	Y	50531 FQ	70297 MW	93759 TQ	ORBLS	2016
Postsecondary	Portland-Vancouver-Hillsboro MSA, OR-WA	Y	49320 FQ	65430 MW	89550 TQ	USBLS	5/15
Postsecondary	Pennsylvania	Y	51720 FQ	68370 MW	91160 TQ	USBLS	5/15
Postsecondary	Allentown-Bethlehem-Easton MSA, PA-NJ	Y	58160 FQ	78000 MW	108960 TQ	USBLS	5/15
Postsecondary	Montgomery County-Bucks County-Chester County PMSA, PA	Y	48710 FQ	60210 MW	78370 TQ	USBLS	5/15
Postsecondary	Philadelphia PMSA, PA	Y	49870 FQ	65420 MW	90370 TQ	USBLS	5/15
Postsecondary	Pittsburgh MSA, PA	Y	53610 FQ	72030 MW	95200 TQ	USBLS	5/15
Postsecondary	Rhode Island	Y	67140 FQ	77120 MW	114620 TQ	USBLS	5/15
Postsecondary	Providence-Warwick MSA, RI-MA	Y	67140 FQ	77120 MW	114620 TQ	USBLS	5/15
Postsecondary	South Carolina	Y	50460 FQ	62620 MW	87570 TQ	USBLS	5/15
Postsecondary	Columbia MSA, SC	Y	46830 FQ	54490 MW	63000 TQ	USBLS	5/15
Postsecondary	Greenville-Anderson-Mauldin MSA, SC	Y	52540 FQ	64540 MW	75860 TQ	USBLS	5/15
Postsecondary	South Dakota	Y	46020 FQ	54600 MW	67860 TQ	USBLS	5/15
Postsecondary	Tennessee	Y	34420 FQ	49430 MW	71890 TQ	USBLS	5/15
Postsecondary	Knoxville MSA, TN	Y	35560 FQ	44210 MW	65190 TQ	USBLS	5/15
Postsecondary	Memphis MSA, TN-MS-AR	Y	30810 FQ	48660 MW	69010 TQ	USBLS	5/15
Postsecondary	Nashville-Davidson–Murfreesboro–Franklin MSA, TN	Y	36970 FQ	49340 MW	78580 TQ	USBLS	5/15
Postsecondary	Texas	Y	38390 FQ	63040 MW	89590 TQ	USBLS	5/15
Postsecondary	Austin-Round Rock MSA, TX	Y	21920 FQ	34900 MW	57760 TQ	USBLS	5/15
Postsecondary	Dallas-Plano-Irving PMSA, TX	Y	41380 FQ	66460 MW	91670 TQ	USBLS	5/15
Postsecondary	Fort Worth-Arlington PMSA, TX	Y	48400 FQ	64060 MW	81070 TQ	USBLS	5/15
Postsecondary	Houston-The Woodlands-Sugar Land MSA, TX	Y	56080 FQ	73680 MW	97690 TQ	USBLS	5/15
Postsecondary	San Antonio-New Braunfels MSA, TX	Y	21800 FQ	51030 MW	74530 TQ	USBLS	5/15
Postsecondary	Utah	Y	60740 FQ	78930 MW	97200 TQ	USBLS	5/15
Postsecondary	Vermont	Y	43480 FQ	54270 MW	80400 TQ	USBLS	5/15
Postsecondary	Burlington-South Burlington MSA, VT	Y	41820 FQ	48170 MW	71270 TQ	USBLS	5/15
Postsecondary	Virginia	Y	43030 FQ	56620 MW	74270 TQ	USBLS	5/15
Postsecondary	Richmond MSA, VA	Y	37170 FQ	51230 MW	76950 TQ	USBLS	5/15
Postsecondary	Virginia Beach-Norfolk-Newport News MSA, VA-NC	Y	43940 FQ	55910 MW	75120 TQ	USBLS	5/15
Postsecondary	Washington	Y		65272 AW		WABLS	3/16
Postsecondary	Seattle-Bellevue-Everett PMSA, WA	Y		73104 AW		WABLS	3/16
Postsecondary	Tacoma-Lakewood PMSA, WA	Y		67910 AW		WABLS	3/16
Postsecondary	Wisconsin	Y	46770 FQ	57810 MW	73350 TQ	USBLS	5/15
Postsecondary	Milwaukee-Waukesha-West Allis MSA, WI	Y	46890 FQ	59910 MW	77740 TQ	USBLS	5/15
Postsecondary	Puerto Rico	Y	21030 FQ	39620 MW	50940 TQ	USBLS	5/15
Phlebotomist	Alabama	Y	21519 AE	28252 AW	31619 AEX	ALBLS	6/16
	Birmingham-Hoover MSA, AL	Y	24494 AE	29838 AW	32505 AEX	ALBLS	6/16
	Alaska	Y	31830 FQ	35870 MW	40530 TQ	USBLS	5/15
	Anchorage MSA, AK	Y	30460 FQ	34960 MW	39060 TQ	USBLS	5/15
	Arizona	Y	26140 FQ	29540 MW	34250 TQ	USBLS	5/15
	Phoenix-Mesa-Scottsdale MSA, AZ	Y	26090 FQ	29670 MW	34450 TQ	USBLS	5/15
	Tucson MSA, AZ	Y	26310 FQ	29110 MW	33080 TQ	USBLS	5/15
	Arkansas	Y	23000 FQ	27320 MW	30970 TQ	USBLS	5/15
	Little Rock-North Little Rock-Conway MSA, AR	Y	22460 FQ	26660 MW	30280 TQ	USBLS	5/15
	California	H	15.84 FQ	18.40 MW	22.29 TQ	CABLS	1/16-3/16
	Anaheim-Santa Ana-Irvine PMSA, CA	H	14.68 FQ	17.69 MW	21.77 TQ	CABLS	1/16-3/16
	Los Angeles-Long Beach-Glendale PMSA, CA	H	15.56 FQ	18.08 MW	21.95 TQ	CABLS	1/16-3/16
	Oakland-Hayward-Berkeley PMSA, CA	H	17.06 FQ	20.52 MW	26.49 TQ	CABLS	1/16-3/16
	Riverside-San Bernardino-Ontario MSA, CA	H	16.02 FQ	17.98 MW	20.74 TQ	CABLS	1/16-3/16

AE	Average entry wage	AWR	Average wage range	H	Hourly	LR	Low end range	MTC	Median total compensation	TCC	Total cash compensation
AEX	Average experienced wage	B	Biweekly	HI	Highest wage paid	M	Monthly	MW	Median wage paid	TQ	Third quartile wage
ATC	Average total compensation	D	Daily	HR	High end range	MCC	Median cash compensation	MWR	Median wage range	W	Weekly
AW	Average wage paid	FQ	First quartile wage	LO	Lowest wage paid	ME	Median entry wage	S	See annotated source	Y	Yearly

1222

Occupation/Type/Industry	Location	Per	Low	Mid	High	Source	Date
Phlebotomist	Sacramento–Roseville–Arden-Arcade MSA, CA	H	16.07 FQ	20.35 MW	24.43 TQ	CABLS	1/16-3/16
	San Diego-Carlsbad MSA, CA	H	16.08 FQ	18.08 MW	21.22 TQ	CABLS	1/16-3/16
	San Francisco-Redwood City-South San Francisco PMSA, CA	H	15.62 FQ	19.96 MW	23.97 TQ	CABLS	1/16-3/16
	Colorado	Y	30250 FQ	34620 MW	38710 TQ	USBLS	5/15
	Denver-Aurora-Lakewood MSA, CO	Y	31580 FQ	35390 MW	39240 TQ	USBLS	5/15
	Connecticut	Y		37730 MW		CTBLS	1/16-3/16
	Bridgeport-Stamford-Norwalk MSA, CT	Y	35000 FQ	40540 MW	46110 TQ	USBLS	5/15
	Hartford-West Hartford-East Hartford MSA, CT	Y	31240 FQ	35640 MW	40710 TQ	USBLS	5/15
	Delaware	Y	31620 FQ	35400 MW	39230 TQ	USBLS	5/15
	Wilmington PMSA, DE-MD-NJ	Y	32280 FQ	35790 MW	39470 TQ	USBLS	5/15
	District of Columbia	Y	34400 FQ	38740 MW	45370 TQ	USBLS	5/15
	Washington-Arlington-Alexandria PMSA, DC-VA-MD-WV	Y	30730 FQ	35700 MW	42170 TQ	USBLS	5/15
	Florida	H	11.99 AE	14.31 MW	16.13 AEX	FLBLS	7/16-9/16
	Fort Lauderdale-Pompano Beach-Deerfield Beach PMSA, FL	H	12.60 AE	14.32 MW	16.15 AEX	FLBLS	7/16-9/16
	Miami-Miami Beach-Kendall PMSA, FL	H	11.56 AE	13.97 MW	15.85 AEX	FLBLS	7/16-9/16
	Orlando-Kissimmee-Sanford MSA, FL	H	11.41 AE	14.18 MW	15.85 AEX	FLBLS	7/16-9/16
	Tampa-St. Petersburg-Clearwater MSA, FL	H	12.00 AE	14.60 MW	16.73 AEX	FLBLS	7/16-9/16
	Georgia	Y	25200 FQ	29640 MW	35170 TQ	USBLS	5/15
	Atlanta-Sandy Springs-Roswell MSA, GA	Y	27280 FQ	32010 MW	37110 TQ	USBLS	5/15
	Augusta-Richmond County MSA, GA-SC	Y	24670 FQ	28420 MW	33180 TQ	USBLS	5/15
	Hawaii	Y	28730 FQ	33780 MW	38640 TQ	USBLS	5/15
	Urban Honolulu MSA, HI	Y	28450 FQ	33590 MW	38840 TQ	USBLS	5/15
	Idaho	Y	26090 FQ	29310 MW	33860 TQ	USBLS	5/15
	Boise City MSA, ID	Y	26150 FQ	28870 MW	31550 TQ	USBLS	5/15
	Illinois	Y	28490 FQ	34260 MW	39390 TQ	USBLS	5/15
	Chicago-Naperville-Arlington Heights PMSA, IL	Y	30380 FQ	35260 MW	39700 TQ	USBLS	5/15
	Lake County-Kenosha County PMSA, IL-WI	Y	26790 FQ	31070 MW	36830 TQ	USBLS	5/15
	Indiana	Y	25520 FQ	29130 MW	34420 TQ	USBLS	5/15
	Gary PMSA, IN	Y	26710 FQ	30340 MW	35770 TQ	USBLS	5/15
	Indianapolis-Carmel-Anderson MSA, IN	Y	25860 FQ	29210 MW	34030 TQ	USBLS	5/15
	Iowa	Y	25260 FQ	28490 MW	32550 TQ	USBLS	5/15
	Des Moines-West Des Moines MSA, IA	Y	25110 FQ	28410 MW	33400 TQ	USBLS	5/15
	Kansas	Y	23830 FQ	28310 MW	33780 TQ	USBLS	5/15
	Wichita MSA, KS	Y	25120 FQ	29100 MW	34260 TQ	USBLS	5/15
	Kentucky	Y	23430 FQ	28380 MW	34580 TQ	USBLS	5/15
	Louisville-Jefferson County MSA, KY-IN	Y	26770 FQ	33260 MW	37610 TQ	USBLS	5/15
	Louisiana	Y	22780 FQ	27900 MW	34120 TQ	USBLS	5/15
	Baton Rouge MSA, LA	Y	23160 FQ	27740 MW	33000 TQ	USBLS	5/15
	New Orleans-Metairie MSA, LA	Y	24140 FQ	30450 MW	36220 TQ	USBLS	5/15
	Maine	Y	25820 FQ	29820 MW	34660 TQ	USBLS	5/15
	Portland-South Portland MSA, ME	Y	28990 FQ	33550 MW	36790 TQ	USBLS	5/15
	Maryland	Y	31873 AE	37723 MW	40648 AEX	MDBLS	4/16
	Baltimore-Columbia-Towson MSA, MD	Y	33330 FQ	36700 MW	41290 TQ	USBLS	5/15
	Salisbury MSA, MD-DE	Y	25970 FQ	31140 MW	36700 TQ	USBLS	5/15
	Massachusetts	Y	32870 FQ	37020 MW	43210 TQ	USBLS	5/15
	Boston-Cambridge-Newton NECTA, MA	Y	33490 FQ	37640 MW	44530 TQ	USBLS	5/15
	Worcester MSA, MA-CT	Y	36480 FQ	41880 MW	47050 TQ	USBLS	5/15

AE	Average entry wage	AWR	Average wage range	H	Hourly
AEX	Average experienced wage	B	Biweekly	HI	Highest wage paid
ATC	Average total compensation	D	Daily	HR	High end range
AW	Average wage paid	FQ	First quartile wage	LO	Lowest wage paid

LR	Low end range	MTC	Median total compensation
M	Monthly	MW	Median wage paid
MCC	Median cash compensation	MWR	Median wage range
ME	Median entry wage	S	See annotated source

TCC	Total cash compensation
TQ	Third quartile wage
W	Weekly
Y	Yearly

Occupation/Type/Industry	Location	Per	Low	Mid	High	Source	Date
Phlebotomist	Michigan	Y	25920 FQ	29270 MW	34210 TQ	USBLS	5/15
	Detroit-Dearborn-Livonia PMSA, MI	Y	24660 FQ	28240 MW	32180 TQ	USBLS	5/15
	Grand Rapids-Wyoming MSA, MI	Y	25680 FQ	28600 MW	32390 TQ	USBLS	5/15
	Minnesota	Y	29357 FQ	34376 MW	40223 TQ	MNBLS	1/16-3/16
	Minneapolis-St. Paul-Bloomington MSA, MN-WI	Y	29125 FQ	34103 MW	39880 TQ	MNBLS	1/16-3/16
	Mississippi	Y	21720 FQ	24930 MW	29740 TQ	USBLS	5/15
	Jackson MSA, MS	Y	23640 FQ	26970 MW	29960 TQ	USBLS	5/15
	Missouri	Y	23610 FQ	28140 MW	33420 TQ	USBLS	5/15
	Kansas City MSA, MO-KS	Y	26700 FQ	31070 MW	35930 TQ	USBLS	5/15
	St. Louis MSA, MO-IL	Y	26960 FQ	31670 MW	36840 TQ	USBLS	5/15
	Montana	Y	25050 FQ	28620 MW	34250 TQ	USBLS	5/15
	Billings MSA, MT	Y	25200 FQ	28100 MW	31000 TQ	USBLS	5/15
	Nebraska	Y	25825 FQ	28765 MW	32890 TQ	NEBLS	7/16-9/16
	Omaha-Council Bluffs MSA, NE-IA	Y	27220 FQ	30025 MW	36605 TQ	NEBLS	7/16-9/16
	Nevada	Y	29180 FQ	34160 MW	39330 TQ	USBLS	5/15
	Las Vegas-Henderson-Paradise MSA, NV	Y	29260 FQ	34230 MW	39340 TQ	USBLS	5/15
	New Hampshire	H	13.68 AE	17.02 MW	19.21 AEX	NHBLS	6/16
	Manchester NECTA, NH	H	14.30 AE	17.34 MW	19.29 AEX	NHBLS	6/16
	Nashua NECTA, NH-MA	Y	32580 FQ	35980 MW	39400 TQ	USBLS	5/15
	New Jersey	Y	31440 FQ	35440 MW	39540 TQ	USBLS	5/15
	Camden PMSA, NJ	Y	30890 FQ	34330 MW	37580 TQ	USBLS	5/15
	Newark PMSA, NJ-PA	Y	32410 FQ	36340 MW	41440 TQ	USBLS	5/15
	Trenton MSA, NJ	Y	31560 FQ	35260 MW	38950 TQ	USBLS	5/15
	New Mexico	Y	24660 FQ	28550 MW	33980 TQ	USBLS	5/15
	Albuquerque MSA, NM	Y	23830 FQ	30300 MW	36640 TQ	USBLS	5/15
	New York	Y	28490 AE	38280 MW	44030 AEX	NYBLS	1/16-3/16
	Buffalo-Cheektowaga-Niagara Falls MSA, NY	Y	28210 FQ	32700 MW	36840 TQ	USBLS	5/15
	Nassau County-Suffolk County PMSA, NY	Y	34200 FQ	41250 MW	46830 TQ	USBLS	5/15
	New York-Jersey City-White Plains PMSA, NY-NJ	Y	31870 FQ	37180 MW	44430 TQ	USBLS	5/15
	Rochester MSA, NY	Y	28180 FQ	32750 MW	37850 TQ	USBLS	5/15
	North Carolina	Y	24640 FQ	28520 MW	33410 TQ	USBLS	5/15
	Charlotte-Concord-Gastonia MSA, NC-SC	Y	26050 FQ	29400 MW	34060 TQ	USBLS	5/15
	Raleigh MSA, NC	Y	28820 FQ	32930 MW	36880 TQ	USBLS	5/15
	North Dakota	Y	23020 FQ	26710 MW	30410 TQ	USBLS	5/15
	Fargo MSA, ND-MN	Y	23000 FQ	26880 MW	30880 TQ	USBLS	5/15
	Ohio	Y	26500 FQ	30260 MW	35300 TQ	USBLS	5/15
	Cincinnati MSA, OH-KY-IN	Y	28920 FQ	33030 MW	36810 TQ	USBLS	5/15
	Cleveland-Elyria MSA, OH	Y	27740 FQ	31520 MW	36200 TQ	USBLS	5/15
	Columbus MSA, OH	Y	24050 FQ	27990 MW	32510 TQ	USBLS	5/15
	Oklahoma	Y	25030 FQ	29090 MW	34460 TQ	USBLS	5/15
	Oklahoma City MSA, OK	Y	26520 FQ	31260 MW	36370 TQ	USBLS	5/15
	Tulsa MSA, OK	Y	25600 FQ	28620 MW	32150 TQ	USBLS	5/15
	Oregon	H	15.02 FQ	17.36 MW	19.70 TQ	ORBLS	2016
	Portland-Vancouver-Hillsboro MSA, OR-WA	Y	32730 FQ	37180 MW	42910 TQ	USBLS	5/15
	Pennsylvania	Y	26930 FQ	30890 MW	36470 TQ	USBLS	5/15
	Allentown-Bethlehem-Easton MSA, PA-NJ	Y	27360 FQ	30630 MW	35820 TQ	USBLS	5/15
	Harrisburg-Carlisle MSA, PA	Y	31070 FQ	35280 MW	39660 TQ	USBLS	5/15
	Montgomery County-Bucks County-Chester County PMSA, PA	Y	26600 FQ	29770 MW	35560 TQ	USBLS	5/15
	Philadelphia PMSA, PA	Y	31350 FQ	34750 MW	38140 TQ	USBLS	5/15
	Pittsburgh MSA, PA	Y	25720 FQ	29510 MW	34670 TQ	USBLS	5/15
	Rhode Island	Y	31640 FQ	36730 MW	43320 TQ	USBLS	5/15
	Providence-Warwick MSA, RI-MA	Y	31550 FQ	36540 MW	43030 TQ	USBLS	5/15
	South Carolina	Y	22470 FQ	26760 MW	30420 TQ	USBLS	5/15
	Charleston-North Charleston MSA, SC	Y	26880 FQ	29620 MW	34060 TQ	USBLS	5/15
	Columbia MSA, SC	Y	19110 FQ	25680 MW	29990 TQ	USBLS	5/15
	Greenville-Anderson-Mauldin MSA, SC	Y	24740 FQ	27970 MW	31340 TQ	USBLS	5/15

Occupation/Type/Industry	Location	Per	Low	Mid	High	Source	Date
Phlebotomist	Sioux Falls MSA, SD	Y	22450 FQ	25270 MW	29170 TQ	USBLS	5/15
	Tennessee	Y	22420 FQ	25860 MW	30890 TQ	USBLS	5/15
	Knoxville MSA, TN	Y	23260 FQ	27460 MW	33370 TQ	USBLS	5/15
	Memphis MSA, TN-MS-AR	Y	23790 FQ	27840 MW	31980 TQ	USBLS	5/15
	Nashville-Davidson–Murfreesboro–Franklin MSA, TN	Y	22280 FQ	24700 MW	30820 TQ	USBLS	5/15
	Texas	Y	25870 FQ	29560 MW	35040 TQ	USBLS	5/15
	Austin-Round Rock MSA, TX	Y	26310 FQ	30190 MW	35360 TQ	USBLS	5/15
	Dallas-Plano-Irving PMSA, TX	Y	27250 FQ	31270 MW	36390 TQ	USBLS	5/15
	Fort Worth-Arlington PMSA, TX	Y	26530 FQ	29490 MW	34600 TQ	USBLS	5/15
	Houston-The Woodlands-Sugar Land MSA, TX	Y	27370 FQ	31050 MW	36640 TQ	USBLS	5/15
	San Antonio-New Braunfels MSA, TX	Y	25310 FQ	30030 MW	37590 TQ	USBLS	5/15
	Utah	Y	22950 FQ	26250 MW	29850 TQ	USBLS	5/15
	Ogden-Clearfield MSA, UT	Y	22680 FQ	25630 MW	29350 TQ	USBLS	5/15
	Provo-Orem MSA, UT	Y	22020 FQ	24320 MW	28060 TQ	USBLS	5/15
	Salt Lake City MSA, UT	Y	23670 FQ	27130 MW	30410 TQ	USBLS	5/15
	Vermont	Y	28010 FQ	32230 MW	36820 TQ	USBLS	5/15
	Virginia	Y	26170 FQ	30850 MW	36700 TQ	USBLS	5/15
	Richmond MSA, VA	Y	24190 FQ	29130 MW	35040 TQ	USBLS	5/15
	Virginia Beach-Norfolk-Newport News MSA, VA-NC	Y	26340 FQ	31260 MW	36490 TQ	USBLS	5/15
	Washington	H	14.88 FQ	17.14 MW	19.43 TQ	WABLS	3/16
	Seattle-Bellevue-Everett PMSA, WA	H	15.64 FQ	17.61 MW	20.03 TQ	WABLS	3/16
	Tacoma-Lakewood PMSA, WA	H	14.07 FQ	16.25 MW	18.71 TQ	WABLS	3/16
	West Virginia	Y	23590 FQ	27980 MW	33270 TQ	USBLS	5/15
	Huntington-Ashland MSA, WV-KY-OH	Y	23830 FQ	28210 MW	34270 TQ	USBLS	5/15
	Wisconsin	Y	27990 FQ	32260 MW	37620 TQ	USBLS	5/15
	Madison MSA, WI	Y	29850 FQ	35300 MW	41440 TQ	USBLS	5/15
	Milwaukee-Waukesha-West Allis MSA, WI	Y	29080 FQ	33680 MW	38550 TQ	USBLS	5/15
	Wyoming	Y	26800 FQ	30340 MW	35960 TQ	USBLS	5/15
	Cheyenne MSA, WY	Y	26820 FQ	29320 MW	33480 TQ	USBLS	5/15
	Puerto Rico	Y	16960 FQ	18590 MW	23760 TQ	USBLS	5/15
	San Juan-Carolina-Caguas MSA, PR	Y	17680 FQ	19950 MW	26460 TQ	USBLS	5/15
Photographer	Alabama	Y	19377 AE	35615 AW	43729 AEX	ALBLS	6/16
	Birmingham-Hoover MSA, AL	Y	21059 AE	31630 AW	36910 AEX	ALBLS	6/16
	Alaska	Y	31120 FQ	37760 MW	47680 TQ	USBLS	5/15
	Anchorage MSA, AK	Y	30870 FQ	39660 MW	49140 TQ	USBLS	5/15
	Arizona	Y	21260 FQ	33790 MW	52560 TQ	USBLS	5/15
	Phoenix-Mesa-Scottsdale MSA, AZ	Y	22160 FQ	40000 MW	54690 TQ	USBLS	5/15
	Tucson MSA, AZ	Y	19160 FQ	23090 MW	37980 TQ	USBLS	5/15
	Arkansas	Y	19830 FQ	28730 MW	35310 TQ	USBLS	5/15
	Little Rock-North Little Rock-Conway MSA, AR	Y	26300 FQ	33200 MW	38150 TQ	USBLS	5/15
	California	H	11.60 FQ	19.09 MW	33.98 TQ	CABLS	1/16-3/16
	Los Angeles-Long Beach-Glendale PMSA, CA	H	15.47 FQ	27.48 MW	42.58 TQ	CABLS	1/16-3/16
	Oakland-Hayward-Berkeley PMSA, CA	H	12.98 FQ	16.90 MW	24.71 TQ	CABLS	1/16-3/16
	Riverside-San Bernardino-Ontario MSA, CA	H	10.87 FQ	12.37 MW	24.73 TQ	CABLS	1/16-3/16
	Sacramento–Roseville–Arden-Arcade MSA, CA	H	11.08 FQ	16.77 MW	22.59 TQ	CABLS	1/16-3/16
	San Diego-Carlsbad MSA, CA	H	10.04 FQ	11.86 MW	17.36 TQ	CABLS	1/16-3/16
	San Francisco-Redwood City-South San Francisco PMSA, CA	H	14.71 FQ	21.46 MW	28.85 TQ	CABLS	1/16-3/16
	Colorado	Y	19860 FQ	27130 MW	42470 TQ	USBLS	5/15
	Denver-Aurora-Lakewood MSA, CO	Y	20930 FQ	28980 MW	46320 TQ	USBLS	5/15
	Connecticut	Y		40042 MW		CTBLS	1/16-3/16
	Bridgeport-Stamford-Norwalk MSA, CT	Y	32330 FQ	44450 MW	60640 TQ	USBLS	5/15

AE	Average entry wage	AWR	Average wage range	H	Hourly	LR	Low end range	MTC	Median total compensation	TCC	Total cash compensation
AEX	Average experienced wage	B	Biweekly	HI	Highest wage paid	M	Monthly	MW	Median wage paid	TQ	Third quartile wage
ATC	Average total compensation	D	Daily	HR	High end range	MCC	Median cash compensation	MWR	Median wage range	W	Weekly
AW	Average wage paid	FQ	First quartile wage	LO	Lowest wage paid	ME	Median entry wage	S	See annotated source	Y	Yearly

Occupation/Type/Industry	Location	Per	Low	Mid	High	Source	Date
Photographer	Hartford-West Hartford-East Hartford MSA, CT	Y	33740 FQ	37970 MW	55200 TQ	USBLS	5/15
	Delaware	Y	26660 FQ	41830 MW	57140 TQ	USBLS	5/15
	Wilmington PMSA, DE-MD-NJ	Y	28450 FQ	45850 MW	58960 TQ	USBLS	5/15
	District of Columbia	Y	39680 FQ	56570 MW	84030 TQ	USBLS	5/15
	Washington-Arlington-Alexandria PMSA, DC-VA-MD-WV	Y	28130 FQ	41680 MW	58740 TQ	USBLS	5/15
	Florida	H	9.42 AE	13.20 MW	19.98 AEX	FLBLS	7/16-9/16
	Fort Lauderdale-Pompano Beach-Deerfield Beach PMSA, FL	H	12.07 AE	17.25 MW	23.00 AEX	FLBLS	7/16-9/16
	Miami-Miami Beach-Kendall PMSA, FL	H	11.07 AE	18.64 MW	30.51 AEX	FLBLS	7/16-9/16
	Orlando-Kissimmee-Sanford MSA, FL	H	9.52 AE	11.18 MW	17.14 AEX	FLBLS	7/16-9/16
	Tampa-St. Petersburg-Clearwater MSA, FL	H	11.29 AE	14.60 MW	22.18 AEX	FLBLS	7/16-9/16
	Georgia	Y	22130 FQ	33940 MW	48410 TQ	USBLS	5/15
	Atlanta-Sandy Springs-Roswell MSA, GA	Y	22750 FQ	34620 MW	48730 TQ	USBLS	5/15
	Augusta-Richmond County MSA, GA-SC	Y	21240 FQ	25870 MW	35570 TQ	USBLS	5/15
	Urban Honolulu MSA, HI	Y	26370 FQ	35550 MW	56310 TQ	USBLS	5/15
	Idaho	Y	21970 FQ	26990 MW	34660 TQ	USBLS	5/15
	Boise City MSA, ID	Y	21270 FQ	24410 MW	30720 TQ	USBLS	5/15
	Illinois	Y	25420 FQ	31250 MW	43200 TQ	USBLS	5/15
	Chicago-Naperville-Arlington Heights PMSA, IL	Y	25600 FQ	30990 MW	42540 TQ	USBLS	5/15
	Lake County-Kenosha County PMSA, IL-WI	Y	24760 FQ	31110 MW	43590 TQ	USBLS	5/15
	Indiana	Y	21630 FQ	28370 MW	36920 TQ	USBLS	5/15
	Gary PMSA, IN	Y	25590 FQ	30740 MW	35950 TQ	USBLS	5/15
	Indianapolis-Carmel-Anderson MSA, IN	Y	20790 FQ	28440 MW	38410 TQ	USBLS	5/15
	Iowa	Y	19050 FQ	26110 MW	30950 TQ	USBLS	5/15
	Des Moines-West Des Moines MSA, IA	Y	26770 FQ	30980 MW	42990 TQ	USBLS	5/15
	Kansas	Y	23940 FQ	30280 MW	39170 TQ	USBLS	5/15
	Wichita MSA, KS	Y	23170 FQ	30890 MW	37400 TQ	USBLS	5/15
	Kentucky	Y	21110 FQ	28780 MW	42300 TQ	USBLS	5/15
	Louisville-Jefferson County MSA, KY-IN	Y	19100 FQ	22780 MW	34090 TQ	USBLS	5/15
	Louisiana	Y	20340 FQ	25170 MW	30720 TQ	USBLS	5/15
	Baton Rouge MSA, LA	Y	20320 FQ	29250 MW	42680 TQ	USBLS	5/15
	New Orleans-Metairie MSA, LA	Y	19870 FQ	25970 MW	30590 TQ	USBLS	5/15
	Maine	Y	28880 FQ	42020 MW	49280 TQ	USBLS	5/15
	Maryland	Y	19013 AE	37295 MW	46436 AEX	MDBLS	4/16
	Baltimore-Columbia-Towson MSA, MD	Y	21090 FQ	27110 MW	41470 TQ	USBLS	5/15
	Massachusetts	Y	31660 FQ	45980 MW	63920 TQ	USBLS	5/15
	Boston-Cambridge-Newton NECTA, MA	Y	41860 FQ	51040 MW	76460 TQ	USBLS	5/15
	Worcester MSA, MA-CT	Y	36310 FQ	50150 MW	57210 TQ	USBLS	5/15
	Michigan	Y	21140 FQ	29160 MW	55270 TQ	USBLS	5/15
	Detroit-Dearborn-Livonia PMSA, MI	Y	23960 FQ	46310 MW	67180 TQ	USBLS	5/15
	Grand Rapids-Wyoming MSA, MI	Y	26260 FQ	29630 MW	48970 TQ	USBLS	5/15
	Minnesota	Y	29475 FQ	37963 MW	62066 TQ	MNBLS	1/16-3/16
	Minneapolis-St. Paul-Bloomington MSA, MN-WI	Y	30867 FQ	38699 MW	68134 TQ	MNBLS	1/16-3/16
	Mississippi	Y	18720 FQ	28910 MW	38250 TQ	USBLS	5/15
	Jackson MSA, MS	Y	18690 FQ	29410 MW	38290 TQ	USBLS	5/15
	Missouri	Y	22070 FQ	30190 MW	39600 TQ	USBLS	5/15
	Kansas City MSA, MO-KS	Y	26420 FQ	33110 MW	46160 TQ	USBLS	5/15
	St. Louis MSA, MO-IL	Y	25270 FQ	33580 MW	47440 TQ	USBLS	5/15
	Montana	Y	18040 FQ	19240 MW	26660 TQ	USBLS	5/15
	Billings MSA, MT	Y	18230 FQ	19600 MW	28830 TQ	USBLS	5/15
	Nebraska	Y	20825 FQ	24985 MW	30815 TQ	NEBLS	7/16-9/16

Photographer

Occupation/Type/Industry	Location	Per	Low	Mid	High	Source	Date
Photographer	Omaha-Council Bluffs MSA, NE-IA	Y	19425 FQ	23955 MW	29295 TQ	NEBLS	7/16-9/16
	Nevada	Y	28670 FQ	34570 MW	41450 TQ	USBLS	5/15
	Las Vegas-Henderson-Paradise MSA, NV	Y	29640 FQ	35220 MW	41610 TQ	USBLS	5/15
	New Hampshire	H	8.89 AE	12.86 MW	19.01 AEX	NHBLS	6/16
	Nashua NECTA, NH-MA	Y	19310 FQ	26340 MW	30660 TQ	USBLS	5/15
	New Jersey	Y	23540 FQ	29610 MW	39000 TQ	USBLS	5/15
	Camden PMSA, NJ	Y	22400 FQ	26080 MW	35100 TQ	USBLS	5/15
	Newark PMSA, NJ-PA	Y	23390 FQ	28210 MW	35860 TQ	USBLS	5/15
	Trenton MSA, NJ	Y	24960 FQ	29210 MW	47740 TQ	USBLS	5/15
	New Mexico	Y	22900 FQ	29590 MW	46300 TQ	USBLS	5/15
	Albuquerque MSA, NM	Y	21980 FQ	26170 MW	42420 TQ	USBLS	5/15
	New York	Y	25590 AE	54660 MW	78110 AEX	NYBLS	1/16-3/16
	Buffalo-Cheektowaga-Niagara Falls MSA, NY	Y	19760 FQ	30850 MW	53250 TQ	USBLS	5/15
	Nassau County-Suffolk County PMSA, NY	Y	28080 FQ	33880 MW	54780 TQ	USBLS	5/15
	New York-Jersey City-White Plains PMSA, NY-NJ	Y	33290 FQ	56670 MW	78630 TQ	USBLS	5/15
	Rochester MSA, NY	Y	26760 FQ	31120 MW	50680 TQ	USBLS	5/15
	North Carolina	Y	19700 FQ	26060 MW	37030 TQ	USBLS	5/15
	Charlotte-Concord-Gastonia MSA, NC-SC	Y	21210 FQ	27080 MW	36020 TQ	USBLS	5/15
	Raleigh MSA, NC	Y	21910 FQ	30790 MW	46650 TQ	USBLS	5/15
	North Dakota	Y	27990 FQ	34620 MW	40560 TQ	USBLS	5/15
	Fargo MSA, ND-MN	Y	32510 FQ	37550 MW	44920 TQ	USBLS	5/15
	Ohio	Y	19350 FQ	27150 MW	39170 TQ	USBLS	5/15
	Cincinnati MSA, OH-KY-IN	Y	19690 FQ	26250 MW	38120 TQ	USBLS	5/15
	Cleveland-Elyria MSA, OH	Y	25230 FQ	32960 MW	41510 TQ	USBLS	5/15
	Columbus MSA, OH	Y	21880 FQ	34910 MW	47880 TQ	USBLS	5/15
	Oklahoma	Y	24250 FQ	30170 MW	38430 TQ	USBLS	5/15
	Oklahoma City MSA, OK	Y	23780 FQ	32360 MW	43070 TQ	USBLS	5/15
	Tulsa MSA, OK	Y	23730 FQ	29080 MW	35370 TQ	USBLS	5/15
	Oregon	H	14.27 FQ	18.85 MW	25.87 TQ	ORBLS	2016
	Portland-Vancouver-Hillsboro MSA, OR-WA	Y	30760 FQ	41680 MW	61040 TQ	USBLS	5/15
	Pennsylvania	Y	20020 FQ	29090 MW	39250 TQ	USBLS	5/15
	Allentown-Bethlehem-Easton MSA, PA-NJ	Y	18570 FQ	30210 MW	43350 TQ	USBLS	5/15
	Harrisburg-Carlisle MSA, PA	Y	17350 FQ	19200 MW	35190 TQ	USBLS	5/15
	Montgomery County-Bucks County-Chester County PMSA, PA	Y	25640 FQ	31450 MW	41010 TQ	USBLS	5/15
	Philadelphia PMSA, PA	Y	27640 FQ	31040 MW	45990 TQ	USBLS	5/15
	Pittsburgh MSA, PA	Y	26760 FQ	34180 MW	40800 TQ	USBLS	5/15
	Rhode Island	Y	39240 FQ	49200 MW	60260 TQ	USBLS	5/15
	Providence-Warwick MSA, RI-MA	Y	31750 FQ	46980 MW	58640 TQ	USBLS	5/15
	South Carolina	Y	25980 FQ	31330 MW	40730 TQ	USBLS	5/15
	Charleston-North Charleston MSA, SC	Y	27180 FQ	29420 MW	31830 TQ	USBLS	5/15
	Columbia MSA, SC	Y	23240 FQ	35960 MW	47780 TQ	USBLS	5/15
	Greenville-Anderson-Mauldin MSA, SC	Y	32790 FQ	37570 MW	47990 TQ	USBLS	5/15
	South Dakota	Y	23200 FQ	27730 MW	37160 TQ	USBLS	5/15
	Sioux Falls MSA, SD	Y	23960 FQ	34250 MW	43120 TQ	USBLS	5/15
	Tennessee	Y	21040 FQ	29420 MW	43740 TQ	USBLS	5/15
	Knoxville MSA, TN	Y	24410 FQ	29630 MW	38570 TQ	USBLS	5/15
	Memphis MSA, TN-MS-AR	Y	20570 FQ	25900 MW	35130 TQ	USBLS	5/15
	Nashville-Davidson–Murfreesboro–Franklin MSA, TN	Y	23290 FQ	32390 MW	46440 TQ	USBLS	5/15
	Texas	Y	22300 FQ	29470 MW	43320 TQ	USBLS	5/15
	Austin-Round Rock MSA, TX	Y	25120 FQ	32820 MW	43240 TQ	USBLS	5/15
	Dallas-Plano-Irving PMSA, TX	Y	24720 FQ	32770 MW	43890 TQ	USBLS	5/15
	Fort Worth-Arlington PMSA, TX	Y	19810 FQ	27980 MW	45550 TQ	USBLS	5/15
	Utah	Y	20860 FQ	27760 MW	38610 TQ	USBLS	5/15
	Ogden-Clearfield MSA, UT	Y	17770 FQ	24420 MW	31300 TQ	USBLS	5/15
	Provo-Orem MSA, UT	Y	17990 FQ	23560 MW	49430 TQ	USBLS	5/15
	Salt Lake City MSA, UT	Y	25230 FQ	29530 MW	39810 TQ	USBLS	5/15

AE	Average entry wage	AWR	Average wage range	H	Hourly
AEX	Average experienced wage	B	Biweekly	HI	Highest wage paid
ATC	Average total compensation	D	Daily	HR	High end range
AW	Average wage paid	FQ	First quartile wage	LO	Lowest wage paid

LR	Low end range	MTC	Median total compensation	TCC	Total cash compensation
M	Monthly	MW	Median wage paid	TQ	Third quartile wage
MCC	Median cash compensation	MWR	Median wage range	W	Weekly
ME	Median entry wage	S	See annotated source	Y	Yearly

Occupation/Type/Industry	Location	Per	Low	Mid	High	Source	Date
Photographer	Vermont	Y	27950 FQ	36140 MW	46350 TQ	USBLS	5/15
	Burlington-South Burlington MSA, VT	Y	20190 FQ	34410 MW	43800 TQ	USBLS	5/15
	Virginia	Y	21760 FQ	31560 MW	45980 TQ	USBLS	5/15
	Richmond MSA, VA	Y	24930 FQ	35340 MW	42780 TQ	USBLS	5/15
	Virginia Beach-Norfolk-Newport News MSA, VA-NC	Y	17580 FQ	19620 MW	32130 TQ	USBLS	5/15
	Washington	H	12.08 FQ	17.07 MW	26.26 TQ	WABLS	3/16
	Seattle-Bellevue-Everett PMSA, WA	H	12.65 FQ	17.84 MW	27.39 TQ	WABLS	3/16
	Tacoma-Lakewood PMSA, WA	H	10.92 FQ	15.15 MW	18.73 TQ	WABLS	3/16
	West Virginia	Y	22890 FQ	34460 MW	43100 TQ	USBLS	5/15
	Wisconsin	Y	24220 FQ	36670 MW	50550 TQ	USBLS	5/15
	Madison MSA, WI	Y	24210 FQ	36480 MW	49250 TQ	USBLS	5/15
	Milwaukee-Waukesha-West Allis MSA, WI	Y	25400 FQ	40140 MW	54120 TQ	USBLS	5/15
	Wyoming	Y	20170 FQ	26180 MW	38880 TQ	USBLS	5/15
	Puerto Rico	Y	26610 FQ	36290 MW	44050 TQ	USBLS	5/15
	San Juan-Carolina-Caguas MSA, PR	Y	27550 FQ	37220 MW	44290 TQ	USBLS	5/15
Photographic Process Worker and Processing Machine Operator	Alabama	Y	19094 AE	26281 AW	29870 AEX	ALBLS	6/16
	Alaska	Y	33250 FQ	37970 MW	50380 TQ	USBLS	5/15
	Anchorage MSA, AK	Y	33000 FQ	37750 MW	49200 TQ	USBLS	5/15
	Arizona	Y	21150 FQ	24520 MW	35320 TQ	USBLS	5/15
	Phoenix-Mesa-Scottsdale MSA, AZ	Y	21110 FQ	24380 MW	36730 TQ	USBLS	5/15
	Tucson MSA, AZ	Y	20340 FQ	23790 MW	31220 TQ	USBLS	5/15
	Arkansas	Y	22440 FQ	26690 MW	32960 TQ	USBLS	5/15
	California	H	11.32 FQ	14.29 MW	19.49 TQ	CABLS	1/16-3/16
	Anaheim-Santa Ana-Irvine PMSA, CA	H	12.24 FQ	16.30 MW	21.24 TQ	CABLS	1/16-3/16
	Los Angeles-Long Beach-Glendale PMSA, CA	H	11.33 FQ	14.39 MW	20.12 TQ	CABLS	1/16-3/16
	Oakland-Hayward-Berkeley PMSA, CA	H	11.53 FQ	16.35 MW	19.72 TQ	CABLS	1/16-3/16
	Riverside-San Bernardino-Ontario MSA, CA	H	10.40 FQ	13.14 MW	17.52 TQ	CABLS	1/16-3/16
	Sacramento–Roseville–Arden-Arcade MSA, CA	H	12.65 FQ	14.35 MW	19.20 TQ	CABLS	1/16-3/16
	San Diego-Carlsbad MSA, CA	H	12.14 FQ	18.88 MW	21.85 TQ	CABLS	1/16-3/16
	San Francisco-Redwood City-South San Francisco PMSA, CA	H	11.26 FQ	14.40 MW	20.48 TQ	CABLS	1/16-3/16
	Colorado	Y	21930 FQ	25600 MW	31840 TQ	USBLS	5/15
	Denver-Aurora-Lakewood MSA, CO	Y	21440 FQ	25580 MW	29870 TQ	USBLS	5/15
	Connecticut	Y		30724 MW		CTBLS	1/16-3/16
	Bridgeport-Stamford-Norwalk MSA, CT	Y	24250 FQ	28910 MW	52470 TQ	USBLS	5/15
	Hartford-West Hartford-East Hartford MSA, CT	Y	23450 FQ	30580 MW	39560 TQ	USBLS	5/15
	Delaware	Y	21330 FQ	23850 MW	27510 TQ	USBLS	5/15
	Wilmington PMSA, DE-MD-NJ	Y	20800 FQ	22560 MW	24320 TQ	USBLS	5/15
	District of Columbia	Y	20050 FQ	24320 MW	42790 TQ	USBLS	5/15
	Washington-Arlington-Alexandria PMSA, DC-VA-MD-WV	Y	20020 FQ	25210 MW	31220 TQ	USBLS	5/15
	Florida	H	10.12 AE	12.07 MW	14.79 AEX	FLBLS	7/16-9/16
	Fort Lauderdale-Pompano Beach-Deerfield Beach PMSA, FL	H	9.58 AE	11.24 MW	12.56 AEX	FLBLS	7/16-9/16
	Miami-Miami Beach-Kendall PMSA, FL	H	10.77 AE	13.53 MW	15.98 AEX	FLBLS	7/16-9/16
	Orlando-Kissimmee-Sanford MSA, FL	H	10.45 AE	11.47 MW	13.70 AEX	FLBLS	7/16-9/16
	Tampa-St. Petersburg-Clearwater MSA, FL	H	10.38 AE	11.72 MW	13.47 AEX	FLBLS	7/16-9/16
	Georgia	Y	20690 FQ	23610 MW	28150 TQ	USBLS	5/15

AE	Average entry wage	AWR	Average wage range	H	Hourly	LR	Low end range	MTC	Median total compensation	TCC	Total cash compensation
AEX	Average experienced wage	B	Biweekly	HI	Highest wage paid	M	Monthly	MW	Median wage paid	TQ	Third quartile wage
ATC	Average total compensation	D	Daily	HR	High end range	MCC	Median cash compensation	MWR	Median wage range	W	Weekly
AW	Average wage paid	FQ	First quartile wage	LO	Lowest wage paid	ME	Median entry wage	S	See annotated source	Y	Yearly

Occupation/Type/Industry	Location	Per	Low	Mid	High	Source	Date
Photographic Process Worker and Processing Machine Operator	Atlanta-Sandy Springs-						
	Roswell MSA, GA	Y	21080 FQ	23890 MW	28670 TQ	USBLS	5/15
	Hawaii	Y	23080 FQ	27310 MW	34250 TQ	USBLS	5/15
	Urban Honolulu MSA, HI	Y	22420 FQ	25910 MW	30500 TQ	USBLS	5/15
	Idaho	Y	22350 FQ	27100 MW	38900 TQ	USBLS	5/15
	Boise City MSA, ID	Y	23220 FQ	27320 MW	44480 TQ	USBLS	5/15
	Illinois	Y	21280 FQ	27470 MW	36470 TQ	USBLS	5/15
	Chicago-Naperville-Arlington						
	Heights PMSA, IL	Y	20170 FQ	26980 MW	36780 TQ	USBLS	5/15
	Indiana	Y	21000 FQ	24040 MW	29800 TQ	USBLS	5/15
	Indianapolis-Carmel-Anderson						
	MSA, IN	Y	21760 FQ	24250 MW	30650 TQ	USBLS	5/15
	Iowa	Y	20850 FQ	24770 MW	31010 TQ	USBLS	5/15
	Des Moines-West Des Moines						
	MSA, IA	Y	22660 FQ	27460 MW	36040 TQ	USBLS	5/15
	Kansas	Y	21530 FQ	28930 MW	42270 TQ	USBLS	5/15
	Wichita MSA, KS	Y	18600 FQ	24560 MW	40750 TQ	USBLS	5/15
	Kentucky	Y	23050 FQ	27040 MW	32070 TQ	USBLS	5/15
	Louisville-Jefferson County						
	MSA, KY-IN	Y	23590 FQ	27100 MW	30180 TQ	USBLS	5/15
	Louisiana	Y	20140 FQ	23730 MW	29200 TQ	USBLS	5/15
	New Orleans-Metairie MSA,						
	LA	Y	21860 FQ	24170 MW	28230 TQ	USBLS	5/15
	Maryland	Y	20252 AE	27109 MW	30537 AEX	MDBLS	4/16
	Baltimore-Columbia-Towson						
	MSA, MD	Y	20630 FQ	22610 MW	24700 TQ	USBLS	5/15
	Massachusetts	Y	22780 FQ	28690 MW	46920 TQ	USBLS	5/15
	Worcester MSA, MA-CT	Y	23070 FQ	32160 MW	37470 TQ	USBLS	5/15
	Michigan	Y	21160 FQ	26490 MW	33820 TQ	USBLS	5/15
	Detroit-Dearborn-Livonia						
	PMSA, MI	Y	29730 FQ	42310 MW	47850 TQ	USBLS	5/15
	Grand Rapids-Wyoming MSA,						
	MI	Y	27110 FQ	30730 MW	36110 TQ	USBLS	5/15
	Minnesota	Y	21363 FQ	26050 MW	35223 TQ	MNBLS	1/16-3/16
	Minneapolis-St. Paul-						
	Bloomington MSA, MN-WI	Y	22071 FQ	27184 MW	35375 TQ	MNBLS	1/16-3/16
	Kansas City MSA, MO-KS	Y	42380 FQ	47870 MW	68180 TQ	USBLS	5/15
	St. Louis MSA, MO-IL	Y	23160 FQ	27350 MW	30660 TQ	USBLS	5/15
	Montana	Y	17850 FQ	18930 MW	22220 TQ	USBLS	5/15
	Nebraska	Y	21665 FQ	26920 MW	32190 TQ	NEBLS	7/16-9/16
	Omaha-Council Bluffs MSA,						
	NE-IA	Y	24390 FQ	32935 MW	40690 TQ	NEBLS	7/16-9/16
	Nevada	Y	24150 FQ	29430 MW	42910 TQ	USBLS	5/15
	Las Vegas-Henderson-Paradise						
	MSA, NV	Y	24520 FQ	29100 MW	38230 TQ	USBLS	5/15
	New Hampshire	H	8.46 AE	10.63 MW	14.46 AEX	NHBLS	6/16
	Manchester NECTA, NH	H	8.45 AE	9.15 MW	9.67 AEX	NHBLS	6/16
	Nashua NECTA, NH-MA	Y	17820 FQ	20770 MW	45010 TQ	USBLS	5/15
	New Jersey	Y	20800 FQ	23980 MW	32210 TQ	USBLS	5/15
	Camden PMSA, NJ	Y	21800 FQ	30050 MW	46990 TQ	USBLS	5/15
	Newark PMSA, NJ-PA	Y	21440 FQ	23400 MW	26830 TQ	USBLS	5/15
	Trenton MSA, NJ	Y	23080 FQ	28960 MW	37790 TQ	USBLS	5/15
	New Mexico	Y	24950 FQ	35490 MW	48490 TQ	USBLS	5/15
	Albuquerque MSA, NM	Y	24640 FQ	38450 MW	53460 TQ	USBLS	5/15
	New York	Y	21680 AE	33380 MW	46470 AEX	NYBLS	1/16-3/16
	Buffalo-Cheektowaga-Niagara						
	Falls MSA, NY	Y	21540 FQ	26160 MW	30070 TQ	USBLS	5/15
	Nassau County-Suffolk County						
	PMSA, NY	Y	22310 FQ	29540 MW	40430 TQ	USBLS	5/15
	New York-Jersey City-White						
	Plains PMSA, NY-NJ	Y	21850 FQ	30070 MW	45000 TQ	USBLS	5/15
	Rochester MSA, NY	Y	22810 FQ	32670 MW	43910 TQ	USBLS	5/15
	North Carolina	Y	20370 FQ	23790 MW	29880 TQ	USBLS	5/15
	Charlotte-Concord-Gastonia						
	MSA, NC-SC	Y	21490 FQ	24440 MW	29740 TQ	USBLS	5/15
	Raleigh MSA, NC	Y	21190 FQ	24450 MW	30030 TQ	USBLS	5/15
	North Dakota	Y	21320 FQ	25350 MW	29330 TQ	USBLS	5/15
	Ohio	Y	19620 FQ	24020 MW	31200 TQ	USBLS	5/15
	Cincinnati MSA, OH-KY-IN	Y	18350 FQ	19790 MW	35470 TQ	USBLS	5/15
	Cleveland-Elyria MSA, OH	Y	23100 FQ	27340 MW	35700 TQ	USBLS	5/15
	Columbus MSA, OH	Y	21480 FQ	25140 MW	30790 TQ	USBLS	5/15

AE	Average entry wage	AWR	Average wage range	H	Hourly	LR	Low end range	MTC	Median total compensation	TCC	Total cash compensation
AEX	Average experienced wage	B	Biweekly	HI	Highest wage paid	M	Monthly	MW	Median wage paid	TQ	Third quartile wage
ATC	Average total compensation	D	Daily	HR	High end range	MCC	Median cash compensation	MWR	Median wage range	W	Weekly
AW	Average wage paid	FQ	First quartile wage	LO	Lowest wage paid	ME	Median entry wage	S	See annotated source	Y	Yearly

1229

Occupation/Type/Industry	Location	Per	Low	Mid	High	Source	Date
Photographic Process Worker and Processing Machine Operator	Oklahoma	Y	20210 FQ	24020 MW	28990 TQ	USBLS	5/15
	Oklahoma City MSA, OK	Y	21450 FQ	25470 MW	30260 TQ	USBLS	5/15
	Tulsa MSA, OK	Y	17880 FQ	20450 MW	27060 TQ	USBLS	5/15
	Oregon	H	11.61 FQ	14.69 MW	19.48 TQ	ORBLS	2016
	Portland-Vancouver-Hillsboro MSA, OR-WA	Y	26860 FQ	34530 MW	43420 TQ	USBLS	5/15
	Pennsylvania	Y	19730 FQ	24220 MW	28910 TQ	USBLS	5/15
	Allentown-Bethlehem-Easton MSA, PA-NJ	Y	21190 FQ	24840 MW	29590 TQ	USBLS	5/15
	Harrisburg-Carlisle MSA, PA	Y	18860 FQ	23100 MW	35870 TQ	USBLS	5/15
	Montgomery County-Bucks County-Chester County PMSA, PA	Y	18480 FQ	24040 MW	28780 TQ	USBLS	5/15
	Philadelphia PMSA, PA	Y	21870 FQ	26200 MW	29970 TQ	USBLS	5/15
	Pittsburgh MSA, PA	Y	18970 FQ	23560 MW	27890 TQ	USBLS	5/15
	Rhode Island	Y	21830 FQ	26070 MW	30370 TQ	USBLS	5/15
	Providence-Warwick MSA, RI-MA	Y	21890 FQ	26230 MW	30430 TQ	USBLS	5/15
	South Carolina	Y	20330 FQ	23850 MW	29440 TQ	USBLS	5/15
	South Dakota	Y	22560 FQ	25830 MW	30940 TQ	USBLS	5/15
	Tennessee	Y	22710 FQ	28510 MW	36750 TQ	USBLS	5/15
	Knoxville MSA, TN	Y	20220 FQ	24560 MW	33560 TQ	USBLS	5/15
	Memphis MSA, TN-MS-AR	Y	20230 FQ	24180 MW	29430 TQ	USBLS	5/15
	Nashville-Davidson–Murfreesboro–Franklin MSA, TN	Y	23670 FQ	31470 MW	44920 TQ	USBLS	5/15
	Texas	Y	21710 FQ	25380 MW	36230 TQ	USBLS	5/15
	Austin-Round Rock MSA, TX	Y	21740 FQ	24010 MW	27740 TQ	USBLS	5/15
	Dallas-Plano-Irving PMSA, TX	Y	22030 FQ	25340 MW	35650 TQ	USBLS	5/15
	Fort Worth-Arlington PMSA, TX	Y	20810 FQ	24010 MW	29590 TQ	USBLS	5/15
	Houston-The Woodlands-Sugar Land MSA, TX	Y	25100 FQ	36510 MW	45960 TQ	USBLS	5/15
	Utah	Y	21980 FQ	27790 MW	36280 TQ	USBLS	5/15
	Ogden-Clearfield MSA, UT	Y	19260 FQ	24390 MW	40510 TQ	USBLS	5/15
	Provo-Orem MSA, UT	Y	22970 FQ	27920 MW	34090 TQ	USBLS	5/15
	Salt Lake City MSA, UT	Y	23090 FQ	29360 MW	37020 TQ	USBLS	5/15
	Vermont	Y	30280 FQ	37600 MW	55320 TQ	USBLS	5/15
	Virginia	Y	22390 FQ	27520 MW	40120 TQ	USBLS	5/15
	Richmond MSA, VA	Y	26540 FQ	28730 MW	30920 TQ	USBLS	5/15
	Washington	H	13.23 FQ	18.17 MW	23.69 TQ	WABLS	3/16
	Seattle-Bellevue-Everett PMSA, WA	H	14.55 FQ	22.34 MW	27.18 TQ	WABLS	3/16
	Tacoma-Lakewood PMSA, WA	H	21.02 FQ	22.64 MW	24.27 TQ	WABLS	3/16
	West Virginia	Y	20730 FQ	24940 MW	28620 TQ	USBLS	5/15
	Wisconsin	Y	22630 FQ	27950 MW	35680 TQ	USBLS	5/15
	Madison MSA, WI	Y	26060 FQ	30100 MW	38590 TQ	USBLS	5/15
	Milwaukee-Waukesha-West Allis MSA, WI	Y	22320 FQ	26330 MW	32660 TQ	USBLS	5/15
	Puerto Rico	Y	21410 FQ	25200 MW	28370 TQ	USBLS	5/15
Photojournalist Public Safety Department, State Government	Ohio	H			23.02 HI	OHGOV	2015
Physical Therapist	Alabama	Y	63453 AE	88936 AW	101688 AEX	ALBLS	6/16
	Birmingham-Hoover MSA, AL	Y	61771 AE	86846 AW	99374 AEX	ALBLS	6/16
	Alaska	Y	81830 FQ	96780 MW	116540 TQ	USBLS	5/15
	Anchorage MSA, AK	Y	82010 FQ	98400 MW	120790 TQ	USBLS	5/15
	Arizona	Y	67510 FQ	83440 MW	98100 TQ	USBLS	5/15
	Phoenix-Mesa-Scottsdale MSA, AZ	Y	66470 FQ	83930 MW	99710 TQ	USBLS	5/15
	Tucson MSA, AZ	Y	72610 FQ	84540 MW	94490 TQ	USBLS	5/15
	Arkansas	Y	49300 FQ	76630 MW	94600 TQ	USBLS	5/15
	Little Rock-North Little Rock-Conway MSA, AR	Y	62480 FQ	80350 MW	97090 TQ	USBLS	5/15
	California	H	39.21 FQ	45.94 MW	54.47 TQ	CABLS	1/16-3/16
	Anaheim-Santa Ana-Irvine PMSA, CA	H	36.47 FQ	43.69 MW	50.82 TQ	CABLS	1/16-3/16
	Los Angeles-Long Beach-Glendale PMSA, CA	H	38.25 FQ	45.27 MW	53.86 TQ	CABLS	1/16-3/16

AE Average entry wage	**AWR** Average wage range	**H** Hourly	**LR** Low end range	**MTC** Median total compensation	**TCC** Total cash compensation
AEX Average experienced wage	**B** Biweekly	**HI** Highest wage paid	**M** Monthly	**MW** Median wage paid	**TQ** Third quartile wage
ATC Average total compensation	**D** Daily	**HR** High end range	**MCC** Median cash compensation	**MWR** Median wage range	**W** Weekly
AW Average wage paid	**FQ** First quartile wage	**LO** Lowest wage paid	**ME** Median entry wage	**S** See annotated source	**Y** Yearly

Occupation/Type/Industry	Location	Per	Low	Mid	High	Source	Date
Physical Therapist	Oakland-Hayward-Berkeley PMSA, CA	H	41.60 FQ	49.04 MW	56.31 TQ	CABLS	1/16-3/16
	Riverside-San Bernardino-Ontario MSA, CA	H	36.06 FQ	43.17 MW	49.44 TQ	CABLS	1/16-3/16
	Sacramento–Roseville–Arden-Arcade MSA, CA	H	40.65 FQ	48.51 MW	56.36 TQ	CABLS	1/16-3/16
	San Diego-Carlsbad MSA, CA	H	37.01 FQ	44.20 MW	52.75 TQ	CABLS	1/16-3/16
	San Francisco-Redwood City-South San Francisco PMSA, CA	H	45.03 FQ	50.92 MW	58.36 TQ	CABLS	1/16-3/16
	Colorado	Y	64230 FQ	74630 MW	88860 TQ	USBLS	5/15
	Denver-Aurora-Lakewood MSA, CO	Y	63370 FQ	74410 MW	88270 TQ	USBLS	5/15
	Connecticut	Y		86455 MW		CTBLS	1/16-3/16
	Bridgeport-Stamford-Norwalk MSA, CT	Y	71660 FQ	90400 MW	112110 TQ	USBLS	5/15
	Hartford-West Hartford-East Hartford MSA, CT	Y	69120 FQ	83310 MW	94730 TQ	USBLS	5/15
	Delaware	Y	70650 FQ	81240 MW	95500 TQ	USBLS	5/15
	Wilmington PMSA, DE-MD-NJ	Y	71220 FQ	83540 MW	100880 TQ	USBLS	5/15
	District of Columbia	Y	69820 FQ	82600 MW	99170 TQ	USBLS	5/15
	Washington-Arlington-Alexandria PMSA, DC-VA-MD-WV	Y	70620 FQ	85740 MW	101350 TQ	USBLS	5/15
	Florida	H	29.38 AE	41.15 MW	48.17 AEX	FLBLS	7/16-9/16
	Fort Lauderdale-Pompano Beach-Deerfield Beach PMSA, FL	H	28.94 AE	41.81 MW	49.38 AEX	FLBLS	7/16-9/16
	Miami-Miami Beach-Kendall PMSA, FL	H	27.18 AE	36.57 MW	42.08 AEX	FLBLS	7/16-9/16
	Orlando-Kissimmee-Sanford MSA, FL	H	31.20 AE	42.08 MW	48.76 AEX	FLBLS	7/16-9/16
	Tampa-St. Petersburg-Clearwater MSA, FL	H	27.73 AE	40.30 MW	43.53 AEX	FLBLS	7/16-9/16
	Georgia	Y	70150 FQ	80970 MW	95880 TQ	USBLS	5/15
	Atlanta-Sandy Springs-Roswell MSA, GA	Y	70750 FQ	79790 MW	93350 TQ	USBLS	5/15
	Augusta-Richmond County MSA, GA-SC	Y	66800 FQ	81780 MW	96910 TQ	USBLS	5/15
	Hawaii	Y	73290 FQ	84640 MW	94580 TQ	USBLS	5/15
	Urban Honolulu MSA, HI	Y	73980 FQ	84210 MW	93090 TQ	USBLS	5/15
	Idaho	Y	63340 FQ	78210 MW	91260 TQ	USBLS	5/15
	Boise City MSA, ID	Y	48990 FQ	71700 MW	88290 TQ	USBLS	5/15
	Illinois	Y	70030 FQ	86000 MW	102250 TQ	USBLS	5/15
	Chicago-Naperville-Arlington Heights PMSA, IL	Y	71090 FQ	87510 MW	104580 TQ	USBLS	5/15
	Lake County-Kenosha County PMSA, IL-WI	Y	68180 FQ	85520 MW	99930 TQ	USBLS	5/15
	Indiana	Y	67440 FQ	83020 MW	95860 TQ	USBLS	5/15
	Gary PMSA, IN	Y	80020 FQ	94020 MW	122970 TQ	USBLS	5/15
	Indianapolis-Carmel-Anderson MSA, IN	Y	71510 FQ	84810 MW	96300 TQ	USBLS	5/15
	Iowa	Y	67790 FQ	77140 MW	90230 TQ	USBLS	5/15
	Des Moines-West Des Moines MSA, IA	Y	69060 FQ	82890 MW	92970 TQ	USBLS	5/15
	Kansas	Y	68820 FQ	79610 MW	93000 TQ	USBLS	5/15
	Wichita MSA, KS	Y	67080 FQ	75080 MW	85930 TQ	USBLS	5/15
	Kentucky	Y	70630 FQ	83910 MW	94960 TQ	USBLS	5/15
	Louisville-Jefferson County MSA, KY-IN	Y	66710 FQ	82910 MW	93820 TQ	USBLS	5/15
	Louisiana	Y	57370 FQ	78850 MW	99160 TQ	USBLS	5/15
	Baton Rouge MSA, LA	Y	65400 FQ	83980 MW	107900 TQ	USBLS	5/15
	New Orleans-Metairie MSA, LA	Y	56810 FQ	76490 MW	91770 TQ	USBLS	5/15
	Maine	Y	66500 FQ	74260 MW	85130 TQ	USBLS	5/15
	Portland-South Portland MSA, ME	Y	66080 FQ	74170 MW	85150 TQ	USBLS	5/15
	Maryland	Y	60087 AE	89462 MW	104150 AEX	MDBLS	4/16
	Baltimore-Columbia-Towson MSA, MD	Y	69460 FQ	86660 MW	101340 TQ	USBLS	5/15
	Salisbury MSA, MD-DE	Y	67420 FQ	81540 MW	96610 TQ	USBLS	5/15

AE	Average entry wage	AWR	Average wage range	H	Hourly
AEX	Average experienced wage	B	Biweekly	HI	Highest wage paid
ATC	Average total compensation	D	Daily	HR	High end range
AW	Average wage paid	FQ	First quartile wage	LO	Lowest wage paid

LR	Low end range	MTC	Median total compensation	TCC	Total cash compensation
M	Monthly	MW	Median wage paid	TQ	Third quartile wage
MCC	Median cash compensation	MWR	Median wage range	W	Weekly
ME	Median entry wage	S	See annotated source	Y	Yearly

Occupation/Type/Industry	Location	Per	Low	Mid	High	Source	Date
Physical Therapist	Massachusetts	Y	70030 FQ	82980 MW	96460 TQ	USBLS	5/15
	Boston-Cambridge-Newton NECTA, MA	Y	70990 FQ	82880 MW	96600 TQ	USBLS	5/15
	Worcester MSA, MA-CT	Y	68300 FQ	78830 MW	91460 TQ	USBLS	5/15
	Michigan	Y	67850 FQ	81530 MW	95880 TQ	USBLS	5/15
	Detroit-Dearborn-Livonia PMSA, MI	Y	70790 FQ	83880 MW	96140 TQ	USBLS	5/15
	Grand Rapids-Wyoming MSA, MI	Y	70270 FQ	81990 MW	96320 TQ	USBLS	5/15
	Minnesota	Y	69223 FQ	77892 MW	89414 TQ	MNBLS	1/16-3/16
	Minneapolis-St. Paul-Bloomington MSA, MN-WI	Y	68658 FQ	77136 MW	88477 TQ	MNBLS	1/16-3/16
	Mississippi	Y	73410 FQ	89530 MW	106630 TQ	USBLS	5/15
	Jackson MSA, MS	Y	78910 FQ	90560 MW	100690 TQ	USBLS	5/15
	Missouri	Y	64330 FQ	76460 MW	90070 TQ	USBLS	5/15
	Kansas City MSA, MO-KS	Y	67380 FQ	76690 MW	88380 TQ	USBLS	5/15
	St. Louis MSA, MO-IL	Y	63060 FQ	74730 MW	88480 TQ	USBLS	5/15
	Montana	Y	63710 FQ	73080 MW	85970 TQ	USBLS	5/15
	Billings MSA, MT	Y	62970 FQ	73100 MW	84770 TQ	USBLS	5/15
	Nebraska	Y	61715 FQ	73540 MW	87610 TQ	NEBLS	7/16-9/16
	Omaha-Council Bluffs MSA, NE-IA	Y	60650 FQ	73455 MW	87550 TQ	NEBLS	7/16-9/16
	Nevada	Y	80230 FQ	95950 MW	126280 TQ	USBLS	5/15
	Las Vegas-Henderson-Paradise MSA, NV	Y	84110 FQ	104510 MW	168940 TQ	USBLS	5/15
	New Hampshire	H	32.57 AE	39.85 MW	43.27 AEX	NHBLS	6/16
	Manchester NECTA, NH	H	32.99 AE	39.58 MW	42.42 AEX	NHBLS	6/16
	Nashua NECTA, NH-MA	Y	71490 FQ	80570 MW	98420 TQ	USBLS	5/15
	New Jersey	Y	78840 FQ	93500 MW	111930 TQ	USBLS	5/15
	Camden PMSA, NJ	Y	78150 FQ	90940 MW	103080 TQ	USBLS	5/15
	Newark PMSA, NJ-PA	Y	78020 FQ	92130 MW	108720 TQ	USBLS	5/15
	Trenton MSA, NJ	Y	73610 FQ	87630 MW	102610 TQ	USBLS	5/15
	New Mexico	Y	71680 FQ	87930 MW	101440 TQ	USBLS	5/15
	Albuquerque MSA, NM	Y	70790 FQ	88520 MW	100940 TQ	USBLS	5/15
	New York	Y	61990 AE	82880 MW	98550 AEX	NYBLS	1/16-3/16
	Buffalo-Cheektowaga-Niagara Falls MSA, NY	Y	60580 FQ	72320 MW	85870 TQ	USBLS	5/15
	Nassau County-Suffolk County PMSA, NY	Y	72750 FQ	89930 MW	106390 TQ	USBLS	5/15
	New York-Jersey City-White Plains PMSA, NY-NJ	Y	73320 FQ	89710 MW	109850 TQ	USBLS	5/15
	Rochester MSA, NY	Y	65790 FQ	77630 MW	91520 TQ	USBLS	5/15
	North Carolina	Y	68290 FQ	80810 MW	94230 TQ	USBLS	5/15
	Charlotte-Concord-Gastonia MSA, NC-SC	Y	71490 FQ	83850 MW	95140 TQ	USBLS	5/15
	Raleigh MSA, NC	Y	63170 FQ	75740 MW	89480 TQ	USBLS	5/15
	North Dakota	Y	64020 FQ	73010 MW	82820 TQ	USBLS	5/15
	Fargo MSA, ND-MN	Y	63710 FQ	73230 MW	82520 TQ	USBLS	5/15
	Ohio	Y	69210 FQ	81910 MW	95830 TQ	USBLS	5/15
	Cincinnati MSA, OH-KY-IN	Y	69910 FQ	84850 MW	100410 TQ	USBLS	5/15
	Cleveland-Elyria MSA, OH	Y	71210 FQ	84180 MW	95690 TQ	USBLS	5/15
	Columbus MSA, OH	Y	65070 FQ	75200 MW	88410 TQ	USBLS	5/15
	Oklahoma	Y	68810 FQ	84150 MW	99120 TQ	USBLS	5/15
	Oklahoma City MSA, OK	Y	66160 FQ	81880 MW	96620 TQ	USBLS	5/15
	Tulsa MSA, OK	Y	72700 FQ	86810 MW	99740 TQ	USBLS	5/15
	Oregon	H	34.39 FQ	39.78 MW	45.53 TQ	ORBLS	2016
	Portland-Vancouver-Hillsboro MSA, OR-WA	Y	72320 FQ	83320 MW	94830 TQ	USBLS	5/15
	Pennsylvania	Y	66740 FQ	81590 MW	99780 TQ	USBLS	5/15
	Allentown-Bethlehem-Easton MSA, PA-NJ	Y	71820 FQ	85710 MW	103490 TQ	USBLS	5/15
	Harrisburg-Carlisle MSA, PA	Y	73080 FQ	88280 MW	105910 TQ	USBLS	5/15
	Montgomery County-Bucks County-Chester County PMSA, PA	Y	67370 FQ	81540 MW	102230 TQ	USBLS	5/15
	Philadelphia PMSA, PA	Y	68880 FQ	86180 MW	106810 TQ	USBLS	5/15
	Pittsburgh MSA, PA	Y	64170 FQ	79480 MW	97150 TQ	USBLS	5/15
	Rhode Island	Y	68810 FQ	78120 MW	91230 TQ	USBLS	5/15
	Providence-Warwick MSA, RI-MA	Y	68040 FQ	78750 MW	94330 TQ	USBLS	5/15
	South Carolina	Y	65720 FQ	80720 MW	95410 TQ	USBLS	5/15

AE Average entry wage	**AWR** Average wage range	**H** Hourly	**LR** Low end range	**MTC** Median total compensation **TCC** Total cash compensation
AEX Average experienced wage	**B** Biweekly	**HI** Highest wage paid	**M** Monthly	**MW** Median wage paid **TQ** Third quartile wage
ATC Average total compensation	**D** Daily	**HR** High end range	**MCC** Median cash compensation	**MWR** Median wage range **W** Weekly
AW Average wage paid	**FQ** First quartile wage	**LO** Lowest wage paid	**ME** Median entry wage	**S** See annotated source **Y** Yearly

Occupation/Type/Industry	Location	Per	Low	Mid	High	Source	Date
Physical Therapist	Charleston-North Charleston						
	MSA, SC	Y	67000 FQ	78590 MW	90900 TQ	USBLS	5/15
	Columbia MSA, SC	Y	47990 FQ	72340 MW	90170 TQ	USBLS	5/15
	Greenville-Anderson-Mauldin						
	MSA, SC	Y	75970 FQ	88760 MW	99940 TQ	USBLS	5/15
	South Dakota	Y	61080 FQ	71690 MW	82030 TQ	USBLS	5/15
	Sioux Falls MSA, SD	Y	60360 FQ	70990 MW	80370 TQ	USBLS	5/15
	Tennessee	Y	71700 FQ	84770 MW	98160 TQ	USBLS	5/15
	Knoxville MSA, TN	Y	67740 FQ	80170 MW	91570 TQ	USBLS	5/15
	Memphis MSA, TN-MS-AR	Y	77060 FQ	87150 MW	97140 TQ	USBLS	5/15
	Nashville-Davidson–						
	Murfreesboro–Franklin						
	MSA, TN	Y	70840 FQ	83090 MW	96600 TQ	USBLS	5/15
	Texas	Y	74980 FQ	91100 MW	113870 TQ	USBLS	5/15
	Austin-Round Rock MSA, TX	Y	64420 FQ	86030 MW	108770 TQ	USBLS	5/15
	Dallas-Plano-Irving PMSA, TX	Y	77930 FQ	98630 MW	129860 TQ	USBLS	5/15
	Fort Worth-Arlington PMSA,						
	TX	Y	70130 FQ	81730 MW	98900 TQ	USBLS	5/15
	Houston-The Woodlands-						
	Sugar Land MSA, TX	Y	75200 FQ	88820 MW	101980 TQ	USBLS	5/15
	San Antonio-New Braunfels						
	MSA, TX	Y	71970 FQ	86130 MW	97020 TQ	USBLS	5/15
	Utah	Y	65490 FQ	79660 MW	95540 TQ	USBLS	5/15
	Ogden-Clearfield MSA, UT	Y	69270 FQ	88090 MW	109760 TQ	USBLS	5/15
	Provo-Orem MSA, UT	Y	67410 FQ	84110 MW	97630 TQ	USBLS	5/15
	Salt Lake City MSA, UT	Y	60790 FQ	77340 MW	92070 TQ	USBLS	5/15
	Vermont	Y	64930 FQ	74430 MW	86720 TQ	USBLS	5/15
	Burlington-South Burlington						
	MSA, VT	Y	65290 FQ	75040 MW	89100 TQ	USBLS	5/15
	Virginia	Y	69670 FQ	84300 MW	98690 TQ	USBLS	5/15
	Richmond MSA, VA	Y	67460 FQ	81350 MW	96510 TQ	USBLS	5/15
	Virginia Beach-Norfolk-						
	Newport News MSA, VA-NC	Y	67830 FQ	82510 MW	95220 TQ	USBLS	5/15
	Washington	H	35.49 FQ	41.67 MW	48.52 TQ	WABLS	3/16
	Seattle-Bellevue-Everett						
	PMSA, WA	H	36.54 FQ	42.74 MW	48.84 TQ	WABLS	3/16
	Tacoma-Lakewood PMSA, WA	H	33.73 FQ	37.97 MW	45.94 TQ	WABLS	3/16
	West Virginia	Y	63850 FQ	78210 MW	95460 TQ	USBLS	5/15
	Huntington-Ashland MSA,						
	WV-KY-OH	Y	72920 FQ	85430 MW	97220 TQ	USBLS	5/15
	Wisconsin	Y	66560 FQ	80190 MW	92700 TQ	USBLS	5/15
	Madison MSA, WI	Y	67210 FQ	78210 MW	90420 TQ	USBLS	5/15
	Milwaukee-Waukesha-West						
	Allis MSA, WI	Y	65050 FQ	79850 MW	92290 TQ	USBLS	5/15
	Wyoming	Y	68720 FQ	79420 MW	93360 TQ	USBLS	5/15
	Cheyenne MSA, WY	Y	72540 FQ	85570 MW	97690 TQ	USBLS	5/15
	Puerto Rico	Y	24480 FQ	40650 MW	52120 TQ	USBLS	5/15
	San Juan-Carolina-Caguas						
	MSA, PR	Y	26050 FQ	41760 MW	54880 TQ	USBLS	5/15
Hospital	United States	H		38.97 AW		MLTCN02	2016
Long-Term Care Facility	United States	H		42.30 AW		MLTCN02	2016
Physical Therapist Aide	Alabama	Y	17637 AE	25308 AW	29138 AEX	ALBLS	6/16
	Birmingham-Hoover MSA, AL	Y	17771 AE	24258 AW	27501 AEX	ALBLS	6/16
	Alaska	Y	30100 FQ	36860 MW	43780 TQ	USBLS	5/15
	Arizona	Y	22820 FQ	26880 MW	30830 TQ	USBLS	5/15
	Phoenix-Mesa-Scottsdale						
	MSA, AZ	Y	23280 FQ	27290 MW	31110 TQ	USBLS	5/15
	Tucson MSA, AZ	Y	22910 FQ	26900 MW	30270 TQ	USBLS	5/15
	Arkansas	Y	18530 FQ	22240 MW	27260 TQ	USBLS	5/15
	Little Rock-North Little Rock-						
	Conway MSA, AR	Y	22440 FQ	26500 MW	29080 TQ	USBLS	5/15
	California	H	11.47 FQ	13.48 MW	16.00 TQ	CABLS	1/16-3/16
	Anaheim-Santa Ana-Irvine						
	PMSA, CA	H	10.81 FQ	12.57 MW	15.22 TQ	CABLS	1/16-3/16
	Los Angeles-Long Beach-						
	Glendale PMSA, CA	H	12.25 FQ	13.74 MW	15.56 TQ	CABLS	1/16-3/16
	Oakland-Hayward-Berkeley						
	PMSA, CA	H	10.81 FQ	13.17 MW	15.95 TQ	CABLS	1/16-3/16
	Riverside-San Bernardino-						
	Ontario MSA, CA	H	11.50 FQ	13.36 MW	15.17 TQ	CABLS	1/16-3/16

AE	Average entry wage	AWR	Average wage range	H	Hourly
AEX	Average experienced wage	B	Biweekly	HI	Highest wage paid
ATC	Average total compensation	D	Daily	HR	High end range
AW	Average wage paid	FQ	First quartile wage	LO	Lowest wage paid

LR	Low end range	MTC	Median total compensation	TCC	Total cash compensation
M	Monthly	MW	Median wage paid	TQ	Third quartile wage
MCC	Median cash compensation	MWR	Median wage range	W	Weekly
ME	Median entry wage	S	See annotated source	Y	Yearly

Occupation/Type/Industry	Location	Per	Low	Mid	High	Source	Date
Physical Therapist Aide	Sacramento–Roseville– Arden-Arcade MSA, CA	H	11.20 FQ	14.62 MW	19.12 TQ	CABLS	1/16-3/16
	San Diego-Carlsbad MSA, CA	H	10.96 FQ	12.82 MW	16.33 TQ	CABLS	1/16-3/16
	San Francisco-Redwood City-South San Francisco PMSA, CA	H	12.74 FQ	14.13 MW	16.63 TQ	CABLS	1/16-3/16
	Colorado	Y	25140 FQ	29420 MW	36230 TQ	USBLS	5/15
	Denver-Aurora-Lakewood MSA, CO	Y	26250 FQ	30210 MW	37640 TQ	USBLS	5/15
	Connecticut	Y		29552 MW		CTBLS	1/16-3/16
	Bridgeport-Stamford-Norwalk MSA, CT	Y	24590 FQ	30370 MW	37220 TQ	USBLS	5/15
	Hartford-West Hartford-East Hartford MSA, CT	Y	26400 FQ	30840 MW	37670 TQ	USBLS	5/15
	Delaware	Y	20200 FQ	22780 MW	26410 TQ	USBLS	5/15
	Wilmington PMSA, DE-MD-NJ	Y	19420 FQ	22250 MW	25230 TQ	USBLS	5/15
	District of Columbia	Y	27700 FQ	31490 MW	36480 TQ	USBLS	5/15
	Washington-Arlington-Alexandria PMSA, DC-VA-MD-WV	Y	21790 FQ	26100 MW	32280 TQ	USBLS	5/15
	Florida	H	10.43 AE	12.47 MW	14.10 AEX	FLBLS	7/16-9/16
	Fort Lauderdale-Pompano Beach-Deerfield Beach PMSA, FL	H	10.41 AE	13.91 MW	15.66 AEX	FLBLS	7/16-9/16
	Miami-Miami Beach-Kendall PMSA, FL	H	10.22 AE	11.44 MW	12.63 AEX	FLBLS	7/16-9/16
	Orlando-Kissimmee-Sanford MSA, FL	H	10.81 AE	12.93 MW	15.46 AEX	FLBLS	7/16-9/16
	Tampa-St. Petersburg-Clearwater MSA, FL	H	10.39 AE	12.66 MW	13.95 AEX	FLBLS	7/16-9/16
	Georgia	Y	19790 FQ	22920 MW	27130 TQ	USBLS	5/15
	Atlanta-Sandy Springs-Roswell MSA, GA	Y	20180 FQ	22860 MW	26590 TQ	USBLS	5/15
	Augusta-Richmond County MSA, GA-SC	Y	22390 FQ	28750 MW	38190 TQ	USBLS	5/15
	Hawaii	Y	18410 FQ	26080 MW	33690 TQ	USBLS	5/15
	Urban Honolulu MSA, HI	Y	17970 FQ	23030 MW	31220 TQ	USBLS	5/15
	Idaho	Y	20670 FQ	23500 MW	28100 TQ	USBLS	5/15
	Boise City MSA, ID	Y	22010 FQ	24490 MW	29830 TQ	USBLS	5/15
	Illinois	Y	24420 FQ	35330 MW	54400 TQ	USBLS	5/15
	Chicago-Naperville-Arlington Heights PMSA, IL	Y	24420 FQ	33950 MW	45680 TQ	USBLS	5/15
	Lake County-Kenosha County PMSA, IL-WI	Y	21060 FQ	33140 MW	57470 TQ	USBLS	5/15
	Indiana	Y	21370 FQ	24390 MW	28550 TQ	USBLS	5/15
	Gary PMSA, IN	Y	20090 FQ	24660 MW	29310 TQ	USBLS	5/15
	Indianapolis-Carmel-Anderson MSA, IN	Y	22050 FQ	24490 MW	28080 TQ	USBLS	5/15
	Iowa	Y	22160 FQ	26980 MW	34090 TQ	USBLS	5/15
	Kansas	Y	18300 FQ	24010 MW	29320 TQ	USBLS	5/15
	Wichita MSA, KS	Y	16610 FQ	18090 MW	21340 TQ	USBLS	5/15
	Kentucky	Y	18460 FQ	22340 MW	27960 TQ	USBLS	5/15
	Louisville-Jefferson County MSA, KY-IN	Y	19930 FQ	27000 MW	36490 TQ	USBLS	5/15
	Louisiana	Y	19300 FQ	22250 MW	25630 TQ	USBLS	5/15
	Baton Rouge MSA, LA	Y	19310 FQ	22260 MW	25930 TQ	USBLS	5/15
	New Orleans-Metairie MSA, LA	Y	20960 FQ	23120 MW	26020 TQ	USBLS	5/15
	Maine	Y	22040 FQ	25080 MW	29740 TQ	USBLS	5/15
	Maryland	Y	19023 AE	26289 MW	29922 AEX	MDBLS	4/16
	Baltimore-Columbia-Towson MSA, MD	Y	19060 FQ	22500 MW	27760 TQ	USBLS	5/15
	Salisbury MSA, MD-DE	Y	21200 FQ	23260 MW	26900 TQ	USBLS	5/15
	Massachusetts	Y	25860 FQ	28940 MW	33820 TQ	USBLS	5/15
	Boston-Cambridge-Newton NECTA, MA	Y	26170 FQ	28660 MW	31950 TQ	USBLS	5/15
	Worcester MSA, MA-CT	Y	22340 FQ	24820 MW	30110 TQ	USBLS	5/15
	Michigan	Y	20240 FQ	23020 MW	28000 TQ	USBLS	5/15
	Detroit-Dearborn-Livonia PMSA, MI	Y	20370 FQ	23450 MW	28160 TQ	USBLS	5/15

AE	Average entry wage	AWR	Average wage range	H	Hourly	LR	Low end range
AEX	Average experienced wage	B	Biweekly	HI	Highest wage paid	M	Monthly
ATC	Average total compensation	D	Daily	HR	High end range	MCC	Median cash compensation
AW	Average wage paid	FQ	First quartile wage	LO	Lowest wage paid	ME	Median entry wage

MTC	Median total compensation	TCC	Total cash compensation
MW	Median wage paid	TQ	Third quartile wage
MWR	Median wage range	W	Weekly
S	See annotated source	Y	Yearly

Occupation/Type/Industry	Location	Per	Low	Mid	High	Source	Date
Physical Therapist Aide	Grand Rapids-Wyoming MSA, MI	Y	23240 FQ	27530 MW	34220 TQ	USBLS	5/15
	Minnesota	Y	26923 FQ	32669 MW	41374 TQ	MNBLS	1/16-3/16
	Minneapolis-St. Paul-Bloomington MSA, MN-WI	Y	24802 FQ	31336 MW	40566 TQ	MNBLS	1/16-3/16
	Missouri	Y	18120 FQ	21180 MW	26480 TQ	USBLS	5/15
	Kansas City MSA, MO-KS	Y	18290 FQ	25050 MW	29940 TQ	USBLS	5/15
	St. Louis MSA, MO-IL	Y	19120 FQ	23730 MW	50300 TQ	USBLS	5/15
	Montana	Y	25400 FQ	28960 MW	34160 TQ	USBLS	5/15
	Nebraska	Y	19580 FQ	22240 MW	24940 TQ	NEBLS	7/16-9/16
	Omaha-Council Bluffs MSA, NE-IA	Y	19780 FQ	22050 MW	24295 TQ	NEBLS	7/16-9/16
	Nevada	Y	19910 FQ	27750 MW	34780 TQ	USBLS	5/15
	Las Vegas-Henderson-Paradise MSA, NV	Y	25550 FQ	29300 MW	38020 TQ	USBLS	5/15
	New Hampshire	H	11.86 AE	14.89 MW	16.27 AEX	NHBLS	6/16
	Manchester NECTA, NH	H	15.88 AE	17.15 MW	17.66 AEX	NHBLS	6/16
	New Jersey	Y	21960 FQ	25760 MW	30640 TQ	USBLS	5/15
	Camden PMSA, NJ	Y	21620 FQ	25560 MW	29760 TQ	USBLS	5/15
	Newark PMSA, NJ-PA	Y	22730 FQ	26590 MW	32910 TQ	USBLS	5/15
	Trenton MSA, NJ	Y	20370 FQ	23400 MW	27830 TQ	USBLS	5/15
	New Mexico	Y	24060 FQ	27680 MW	31100 TQ	USBLS	5/15
	New York	Y	21670 AE	27030 MW	31430 AEX	NYBLS	1/16-3/16
	Buffalo-Cheektowaga-Niagara Falls MSA, NY	Y	24860 FQ	29670 MW	35220 TQ	USBLS	5/15
	Nassau County-Suffolk County PMSA, NY	Y	25870 FQ	28430 MW	31050 TQ	USBLS	5/15
	New York-Jersey City-White Plains PMSA, NY-NJ	Y	21510 FQ	24570 MW	30590 TQ	USBLS	5/15
	Rochester MSA, NY	Y	25760 FQ	29370 MW	33880 TQ	USBLS	5/15
	North Carolina	Y	21490 FQ	24640 MW	28900 TQ	USBLS	5/15
	Charlotte-Concord-Gastonia MSA, NC-SC	Y	20420 FQ	22900 MW	26280 TQ	USBLS	5/15
	Raleigh MSA, NC	Y	22410 FQ	26050 MW	29720 TQ	USBLS	5/15
	North Dakota	Y	22260 FQ	24890 MW	31290 TQ	USBLS	5/15
	Fargo MSA, ND-MN	Y	21620 FQ	23690 MW	31040 TQ	USBLS	5/15
	Ohio	Y	21250 FQ	24380 MW	28600 TQ	USBLS	5/15
	Cincinnati MSA, OH-KY-IN	Y	21700 FQ	24200 MW	28540 TQ	USBLS	5/15
	Cleveland-Elyria MSA, OH	Y	21970 FQ	24420 MW	28710 TQ	USBLS	5/15
	Columbus MSA, OH	Y	22120 FQ	25830 MW	28930 TQ	USBLS	5/15
	Oklahoma	Y	19960 FQ	22980 MW	27930 TQ	USBLS	5/15
	Oklahoma City MSA, OK	Y	18390 FQ	21780 MW	26630 TQ	USBLS	5/15
	Tulsa MSA, OK	Y	22280 FQ	26130 MW	29930 TQ	USBLS	5/15
	Oregon	H	11.50 FQ	13.47 MW	15.38 TQ	ORBLS	2016
	Portland-Vancouver-Hillsboro MSA, OR-WA	Y	25360 FQ	28530 MW	32760 TQ	USBLS	5/15
	Pennsylvania	Y	21860 FQ	27340 MW	35160 TQ	USBLS	5/15
	Allentown-Bethlehem-Easton MSA, PA-NJ	Y	22280 FQ	25590 MW	29220 TQ	USBLS	5/15
	Harrisburg-Carlisle MSA, PA	Y	20110 FQ	24360 MW	31630 TQ	USBLS	5/15
	Montgomery County-Bucks County-Chester County PMSA, PA	Y	22490 FQ	27340 MW	32500 TQ	USBLS	5/15
	Philadelphia PMSA, PA	Y	26220 FQ	33320 MW	44050 TQ	USBLS	5/15
	Pittsburgh MSA, PA	Y	24870 FQ	31650 MW	39420 TQ	USBLS	5/15
	Rhode Island	Y	23080 FQ	26630 MW	30470 TQ	USBLS	5/15
	Providence-Warwick MSA, RI-MA	Y	23660 FQ	27130 MW	30610 TQ	USBLS	5/15
	South Carolina	Y	17550 FQ	20310 MW	26250 TQ	USBLS	5/15
	Charleston-North Charleston MSA, SC	Y	17930 FQ	25800 MW	29100 TQ	USBLS	5/15
	Columbia MSA, SC	Y	17270 FQ	19150 MW	23060 TQ	USBLS	5/15
	Greenville-Anderson-Mauldin MSA, SC	Y	17480 FQ	19670 MW	24090 TQ	USBLS	5/15
	South Dakota	Y	22200 FQ	26020 MW	29850 TQ	USBLS	5/15
	Sioux Falls MSA, SD	Y	24060 FQ	27810 MW	30960 TQ	USBLS	5/15
	Tennessee	Y	18590 FQ	22090 MW	26650 TQ	USBLS	5/15
	Knoxville MSA, TN	Y	17440 FQ	19780 MW	23380 TQ	USBLS	5/15
	Memphis MSA, TN-MS-AR	Y	19660 FQ	23530 MW	28030 TQ	USBLS	5/15
	Nashville-Davidson–Murfreesboro–Franklin MSA, TN	Y	18830 FQ	22530 MW	27940 TQ	USBLS	5/15

AE	Average entry wage	AWR	Average wage range	H	Hourly
AEX	Average experienced wage	B	Biweekly	HI	Highest wage paid
ATC	Average total compensation	D	Daily	HR	High end range
AW	Average wage paid	FQ	First quartile wage	LO	Lowest wage paid

LR	Low end range	MTC	Median total compensation
M	Monthly	MW	Median wage paid
MCC	Median cash compensation	MWR	Median wage range
ME	Median entry wage	S	See annotated source

TCC	Total cash compensation	
TQ	Third quartile wage	
W	Weekly	
Y	Yearly	

Occupation/Type/Industry	Location	Per	Low	Mid	High	Source	Date
Physical Therapist Aide	Texas	Y	20590 FQ	23650 MW	27610 TQ	USBLS	5/15
	Austin-Round Rock MSA, TX	Y	24550 FQ	27320 MW	29470 TQ	USBLS	5/15
	Dallas-Plano-Irving PMSA, TX	Y	21090 FQ	24550 MW	28300 TQ	USBLS	5/15
	Fort Worth-Arlington PMSA, TX	Y	18440 FQ	22470 MW	27970 TQ	USBLS	5/15
	Houston-The Woodlands-Sugar Land MSA, TX	Y	21680 FQ	24140 MW	29540 TQ	USBLS	5/15
	San Antonio-New Braunfels MSA, TX	Y	21190 FQ	23670 MW	26810 TQ	USBLS	5/15
	Utah	Y	19500 FQ	21840 MW	24070 TQ	USBLS	5/15
	Ogden-Clearfield MSA, UT	Y	18610 FQ	21430 MW	24160 TQ	USBLS	5/15
	Provo-Orem MSA, UT	Y	20100 FQ	21830 MW	23560 TQ	USBLS	5/15
	Salt Lake City MSA, UT	Y	19810 FQ	21890 MW	23970 TQ	USBLS	5/15
	Virginia	Y	21620 FQ	24320 MW	28760 TQ	USBLS	5/15
	Richmond MSA, VA	Y	21070 FQ	22710 MW	24350 TQ	USBLS	5/15
	Virginia Beach-Norfolk-Newport News MSA, VA-NC	Y	20710 FQ	22730 MW	25110 TQ	USBLS	5/15
	Washington	H	11.18 FQ	12.90 MW	15.11 TQ	WABLS	3/16
	Seattle-Bellevue-Everett PMSA, WA	H	12.44 FQ	13.85 MW	15.25 TQ	WABLS	3/16
	Tacoma-Lakewood PMSA, WA	H	11.73 FQ	14.87 MW	27.99 TQ	WABLS	3/16
	West Virginia	Y	18920 FQ	22050 MW	26830 TQ	USBLS	5/15
	Huntington-Ashland MSA, WV-KY-OH	Y	18350 FQ	20770 MW	23460 TQ	USBLS	5/15
	Wisconsin	Y	20360 FQ	25800 MW	30430 TQ	USBLS	5/15
	Madison MSA, WI	Y	24190 FQ	28040 MW	32580 TQ	USBLS	5/15
	Milwaukee-Waukesha-West Allis MSA, WI	Y	23230 FQ	27800 MW	31210 TQ	USBLS	5/15
	Wyoming	Y	21590 FQ	24990 MW	30470 TQ	USBLS	5/15
	Puerto Rico	Y	17240 FQ	19160 MW	32620 TQ	USBLS	5/15
	San Juan-Carolina-Caguas MSA, PR	Y	18010 FQ	24590 MW	36120 TQ	USBLS	5/15
Physical Therapist Assistant	Alabama	Y	41339 AE	54075 AW	60448 AEX	ALBLS	6/16
	Birmingham-Hoover MSA, AL	Y	38415 AE	49596 AW	55187 AEX	ALBLS	6/16
	Alaska	Y	52310 FQ	65290 MW	78320 TQ	USBLS	5/15
	Anchorage MSA, AK	Y	61940 FQ	73280 MW	83580 TQ	USBLS	5/15
	Arizona	Y	27450 FQ	43050 MW	59300 TQ	USBLS	5/15
	Phoenix-Mesa-Scottsdale MSA, AZ	Y	27120 FQ	40120 MW	59580 TQ	USBLS	5/15
	Tucson MSA, AZ	Y	30610 FQ	48450 MW	57940 TQ	USBLS	5/15
	Arkansas	Y	41560 FQ	53460 MW	62240 TQ	USBLS	5/15
	Little Rock-North Little Rock-Conway MSA, AR	Y	48390 FQ	55960 MW	63300 TQ	USBLS	5/15
	California	H	25.82 FQ	32.39 MW	36.63 TQ	CABLS	1/16-3/16
	Anaheim-Santa Ana-Irvine PMSA, CA	H	21.60 FQ	28.99 MW	35.17 TQ	CABLS	1/16-3/16
	Los Angeles-Long Beach-Glendale PMSA, CA	H	28.93 FQ	33.44 MW	36.56 TQ	CABLS	1/16-3/16
	Oakland-Hayward-Berkeley PMSA, CA	H	31.07 FQ	34.79 MW	38.61 TQ	CABLS	1/16-3/16
	Riverside-San Bernardino-Ontario MSA, CA	H	26.32 FQ	31.25 MW	35.86 TQ	CABLS	1/16-3/16
	Sacramento–Roseville–Arden-Arcade MSA, CA	H	28.82 FQ	33.31 MW	37.13 TQ	CABLS	1/16-3/16
	San Diego-Carlsbad MSA, CA	H	24.59 FQ	32.33 MW	37.13 TQ	CABLS	1/16-3/16
	San Francisco-Redwood City-South San Francisco PMSA, CA	H	28.71 FQ	33.74 MW	37.74 TQ	CABLS	1/16-3/16
	Colorado	Y	41210 FQ	51480 MW	59090 TQ	USBLS	5/15
	Denver-Aurora-Lakewood MSA, CO	Y	45380 FQ	54040 MW	60190 TQ	USBLS	5/15
	Connecticut	Y		56524 MW		CTBLS	1/16-3/16
	Bridgeport-Stamford-Norwalk MSA, CT	Y	50420 FQ	60530 MW	71680 TQ	USBLS	5/15
	Hartford-West Hartford-East Hartford MSA, CT	Y	29390 FQ	54660 MW	65200 TQ	USBLS	5/15
	Delaware	Y	48520 FQ	56980 MW	66430 TQ	USBLS	5/15
	Wilmington PMSA, DE-MD-NJ	Y	51390 FQ	59600 MW	71680 TQ	USBLS	5/15
	District of Columbia	Y	33230 FQ	38200 MW	53310 TQ	USBLS	5/15

AE	Average entry wage	AWR	Average wage range	H	Hourly
AEX	Average experienced wage	B	Biweekly	HI	Highest wage paid
ATC	Average total compensation	D	Daily	HR	High end range
AW	Average wage paid	FQ	First quartile wage	LO	Lowest wage paid

LR	Low end range	MTC	Median total compensation	TCC	Total cash compensation
M	Monthly	MW	Median wage paid	TQ	Third quartile wage
MCC	Median cash compensation	MWR	Median wage range	W	Weekly
ME	Median entry wage	S	See annotated source	Y	Yearly

Physical Therapist Assistant

Occupation/Type/Industry	Location	Per	Low	Mid	High	Source	Date
Physical Therapist Assistant	Washington-Arlington-Alexandria PMSA, DC-VA-MD-WV	Y	31270 FQ	52330 MW	65540 TQ	USBLS	5/15
	Florida	H	23.88 AE	30.32 MW	34.24 AEX	FLBLS	7/16-9/16
	Fort Lauderdale-Pompano Beach-Deerfield Beach PMSA, FL	H	25.39 AE	31.30 MW	33.38 AEX	FLBLS	7/16-9/16
	Miami-Miami Beach-Kendall PMSA, FL	H	17.31 AE	28.17 MW	33.35 AEX	FLBLS	7/16-9/16
	Orlando-Kissimmee-Sanford MSA, FL	H	24.82 AE	29.00 MW	33.17 AEX	FLBLS	7/16-9/16
	Tampa-St. Petersburg-Clearwater MSA, FL	H	20.93 AE	28.94 MW	32.37 AEX	FLBLS	7/16-9/16
	Georgia	Y	45650 FQ	56160 MW	65760 TQ	USBLS	5/15
	Atlanta-Sandy Springs-Roswell MSA, GA	Y	42420 FQ	53000 MW	62300 TQ	USBLS	5/15
	Augusta-Richmond County MSA, GA-SC	Y	44470 FQ	51190 MW	63790 TQ	USBLS	5/15
	Hawaii	Y	24040 FQ	39320 MW	49950 TQ	USBLS	5/15
	Urban Honolulu MSA, HI	Y	23650 FQ	37450 MW	48600 TQ	USBLS	5/15
	Idaho	Y	35900 FQ	52180 MW	63170 TQ	USBLS	5/15
	Boise City MSA, ID	Y	32800 FQ	38660 MW	54930 TQ	USBLS	5/15
	Illinois	Y	41940 FQ	54180 MW	66020 TQ	USBLS	5/15
	Chicago-Naperville-Arlington Heights PMSA, IL	Y	42780 FQ	56570 MW	68890 TQ	USBLS	5/15
	Lake County-Kenosha County PMSA, IL-WI	Y	37800 FQ	53290 MW	63140 TQ	USBLS	5/15
	Indiana	Y	47860 FQ	55680 MW	62540 TQ	USBLS	5/15
	Gary PMSA, IN	Y	40150 FQ	53810 MW	61400 TQ	USBLS	5/15
	Indianapolis-Carmel-Anderson MSA, IN	Y	51450 FQ	58260 MW	66970 TQ	USBLS	5/15
	Iowa	Y	38260 FQ	45780 MW	55190 TQ	USBLS	5/15
	Des Moines-West Des Moines MSA, IA	Y	39850 FQ	48150 MW	59180 TQ	USBLS	5/15
	Kansas	Y	45850 FQ	54540 MW	62360 TQ	USBLS	5/15
	Wichita MSA, KS	Y	47780 FQ	55910 MW	64150 TQ	USBLS	5/15
	Kentucky	Y	44340 FQ	54390 MW	63240 TQ	USBLS	5/15
	Louisville-Jefferson County MSA, KY-IN	Y	48280 FQ	58520 MW	68870 TQ	USBLS	5/15
	Louisiana	Y	31910 FQ	43520 MW	57160 TQ	USBLS	5/15
	Baton Rouge MSA, LA	Y	38520 FQ	56220 MW	68800 TQ	USBLS	5/15
	New Orleans-Metairie MSA, LA	Y	40840 FQ	47550 MW	57930 TQ	USBLS	5/15
	Maine	Y	43860 FQ	51230 MW	58220 TQ	USBLS	5/15
	Portland-South Portland MSA, ME	Y	44930 FQ	52120 MW	59810 TQ	USBLS	5/15
	Maryland	Y	39252 AE	57734 MW	66975 AEX	MDBLS	4/16
	Baltimore-Columbia-Towson MSA, MD	Y	51810 FQ	58350 MW	67140 TQ	USBLS	5/15
	Salisbury MSA, MD-DE	Y	44050 FQ	54440 MW	62720 TQ	USBLS	5/15
	Massachusetts	Y	49700 FQ	57820 MW	67290 TQ	USBLS	5/15
	Boston-Cambridge-Newton NECTA, MA	Y	50440 FQ	59030 MW	69740 TQ	USBLS	5/15
	Worcester MSA, MA-CT	Y	39450 FQ	52840 MW	60740 TQ	USBLS	5/15
	Michigan	Y	37230 FQ	46130 MW	55640 TQ	USBLS	5/15
	Detroit-Dearborn-Livonia PMSA, MI	Y	39110 FQ	46230 MW	55040 TQ	USBLS	5/15
	Grand Rapids-Wyoming MSA, MI	Y	38350 FQ	45240 MW	51920 TQ	USBLS	5/15
	Minnesota	Y	43495 FQ	51473 MW	58784 TQ	MNBLS	1/16-3/16
	Minneapolis-St. Paul-Bloomington MSA, MN-WI	Y	44818 FQ	53271 MW	59633 TQ	MNBLS	1/16-3/16
	Mississippi	Y	27180 FQ	50820 MW	61890 TQ	USBLS	5/15
	Jackson MSA, MS	Y	23830 FQ	39740 MW	57120 TQ	USBLS	5/15
	Missouri	Y	41210 FQ	51610 MW	59970 TQ	USBLS	5/15
	Kansas City MSA, MO-KS	Y	45500 FQ	53490 MW	59500 TQ	USBLS	5/15
	St. Louis MSA, MO-IL	Y	39840 FQ	50000 MW	59860 TQ	USBLS	5/15
	Montana	Y	40770 FQ	45020 MW	49280 TQ	USBLS	5/15
	Nebraska	Y	41800 FQ	49895 MW	59795 TQ	NEBLS	7/16-9/16
	Omaha-Council Bluffs MSA, NE-IA	Y	41690 FQ	51095 MW	62695 TQ	NEBLS	7/16-9/16
	Nevada	Y	34800 FQ	55210 MW	68980 TQ	USBLS	5/15

AE	Average entry wage	AWR	Average wage range	H	Hourly	LR	Low end range	MTC Median total compensation	TCC Total cash compensation
AEX	Average experienced wage	B	Biweekly	HI	Highest wage paid	M	Monthly	MW Median wage paid	TQ Third quartile wage
ATC	Average total compensation	D	Daily	HR	High end range	MCC Median cash compensation	MWR Median wage range	W Weekly
AW	Average wage paid	FQ	First quartile wage	LO	Lowest wage paid	ME Median entry wage	S See annotated source	Y Yearly

Occupation/Type/Industry	Location	Per	Low	Mid	High	Source	Date
Physical Therapist Assistant	Las Vegas-Henderson-Paradise MSA, NV	Y	43660 FQ	59720 MW	70920 TQ	USBLS	5/15
	New Hampshire	H	22.54 AE	27.55 MW	30.10 AEX	NHBLS	6/16
	Manchester NECTA, NH	H	24.55 AE	28.78 MW	31.36 AEX	NHBLS	6/16
	Nashua NECTA, NH-MA	Y	45570 FQ	51810 MW	59990 TQ	USBLS	5/15
	New Jersey	Y	55220 FQ	63020 MW	71770 TQ	USBLS	5/15
	Camden PMSA, NJ	Y	53280 FQ	59300 MW	68220 TQ	USBLS	5/15
	Newark PMSA, NJ-PA	Y	53830 FQ	62020 MW	71410 TQ	USBLS	5/15
	Trenton MSA, NJ	Y	47840 FQ	58510 MW	72360 TQ	USBLS	5/15
	New Mexico	Y	35760 FQ	48570 MW	58780 TQ	USBLS	5/15
	Albuquerque MSA, NM	Y	38340 FQ	55130 MW	61400 TQ	USBLS	5/15
	New York	Y	39170 AE	53930 MW	60720 AEX	NYBLS	1/16-3/16
	Buffalo-Cheektowaga-Niagara Falls MSA, NY	Y	40060 FQ	45370 MW	50840 TQ	USBLS	5/15
	Nassau County-Suffolk County PMSA, NY	Y	53230 FQ	59500 MW	67230 TQ	USBLS	5/15
	New York-Jersey City-White Plains PMSA, NY-NJ	Y	49600 FQ	58890 MW	68830 TQ	USBLS	5/15
	Rochester MSA, NY	Y	38680 FQ	47830 MW	56110 TQ	USBLS	5/15
	North Carolina	Y	51200 FQ	59700 MW	69190 TQ	USBLS	5/15
	Charlotte-Concord-Gastonia MSA, NC-SC	Y	52770 FQ	59780 MW	68600 TQ	USBLS	5/15
	Raleigh MSA, NC	Y	50530 FQ	58640 MW	67940 TQ	USBLS	5/15
	North Dakota	Y	37520 FQ	43860 MW	49920 TQ	USBLS	5/15
	Ohio	Y	47730 FQ	55700 MW	63190 TQ	USBLS	5/15
	Cincinnati MSA, OH-KY-IN	Y	43910 FQ	52830 MW	63030 TQ	USBLS	5/15
	Cleveland-Elyria MSA, OH	Y	54010 FQ	60160 MW	70490 TQ	USBLS	5/15
	Columbus MSA, OH	Y	47110 FQ	53930 MW	59490 TQ	USBLS	5/15
	Oklahoma	Y	47710 FQ	56640 MW	65110 TQ	USBLS	5/15
	Oklahoma City MSA, OK	Y	47950 FQ	55850 MW	63000 TQ	USBLS	5/15
	Tulsa MSA, OK	Y	49100 FQ	57380 MW	65170 TQ	USBLS	5/15
	Oregon	H	23.86 FQ	26.78 MW	29.33 TQ	ORBLS	2016
	Portland-Vancouver-Hillsboro MSA, OR-WA	Y	48620 FQ	54640 MW	59790 TQ	USBLS	5/15
	Pennsylvania	Y	37570 FQ	46360 MW	57900 TQ	USBLS	5/15
	Allentown-Bethlehem-Easton MSA, PA-NJ	Y	43260 FQ	48750 MW	56710 TQ	USBLS	5/15
	Harrisburg-Carlisle MSA, PA	Y	44740 FQ	51610 MW	59550 TQ	USBLS	5/15
	Montgomery County-Bucks County-Chester County PMSA, PA	Y	33550 FQ	47870 MW	67950 TQ	USBLS	5/15
	Philadelphia PMSA, PA	Y	35040 FQ	47570 MW	60280 TQ	USBLS	5/15
	Pittsburgh MSA, PA	Y	37180 FQ	45750 MW	57370 TQ	USBLS	5/15
	Rhode Island	Y	43690 FQ	53290 MW	64770 TQ	USBLS	5/15
	Providence-Warwick MSA, RI-MA	Y	43650 FQ	54840 MW	66380 TQ	USBLS	5/15
	South Carolina	Y	45160 FQ	54620 MW	65200 TQ	USBLS	5/15
	Charleston-North Charleston MSA, SC	Y	37500 FQ	50700 MW	59990 TQ	USBLS	5/15
	Columbia MSA, SC	Y	50110 FQ	69540 MW	90620 TQ	USBLS	5/15
	Greenville-Anderson-Mauldin MSA, SC	Y	46120 FQ	53330 MW	59030 TQ	USBLS	5/15
	South Dakota	Y	31430 FQ	35050 MW	38650 TQ	USBLS	5/15
	Sioux Falls MSA, SD	Y	32810 FQ	35640 MW	38460 TQ	USBLS	5/15
	Tennessee	Y	48030 FQ	56100 MW	63440 TQ	USBLS	5/15
	Knoxville MSA, TN	Y	42830 FQ	49720 MW	57550 TQ	USBLS	5/15
	Memphis MSA, TN-MS-AR	Y	51820 FQ	59080 MW	67960 TQ	USBLS	5/15
	Nashville-Davidson–Murfreesboro–Franklin MSA, TN	Y	51500 FQ	56660 MW	61810 TQ	USBLS	5/15
	Texas	Y	55520 FQ	70860 MW	90130 TQ	USBLS	5/15
	Austin-Round Rock MSA, TX	Y	51020 FQ	66900 MW	76480 TQ	USBLS	5/15
	Dallas-Plano-Irving PMSA, TX	Y	62360 FQ	82770 MW	98500 TQ	USBLS	5/15
	Fort Worth-Arlington PMSA, TX	Y	53950 FQ	69500 MW	87870 TQ	USBLS	5/15
	Houston-The Woodlands-Sugar Land MSA, TX	Y	56210 FQ	65520 MW	74750 TQ	USBLS	5/15
	Killeen-Temple MSA, TX	Y	53510 FQ	65960 MW	79660 TQ	USBLS	5/15
	San Antonio-New Braunfels MSA, TX	Y	53550 FQ	70980 MW	94500 TQ	USBLS	5/15
	Utah	Y	39610 FQ	49460 MW	59830 TQ	USBLS	5/15
	Ogden-Clearfield MSA, UT	Y	46120 FQ	55140 MW	63500 TQ	USBLS	5/15

Occupation/Type/Industry	Location	Per	Low	Mid	High	Source	Date
Physical Therapist Assistant	Provo-Orem MSA, UT	Y	17900 FQ	41450 MW	56160 TQ	USBLS	5/15
	Salt Lake City MSA, UT	Y	29560 FQ	45410 MW	56210 TQ	USBLS	5/15
	Vermont	Y	45880 FQ	52120 MW	58320 TQ	USBLS	5/15
	Virginia	Y	38930 FQ	54230 MW	66470 TQ	USBLS	5/15
	Richmond MSA, VA	Y	23300 FQ	38580 MW	59360 TQ	USBLS	5/15
	Virginia Beach-Norfolk-Newport News MSA, VA-NC	Y	41720 FQ	53790 MW	67130 TQ	USBLS	5/15
	Washington	H	24.07 FQ	28.26 MW	33.19 TQ	WABLS	3/16
	Seattle-Bellevue-Everett PMSA, WA	H	25.01 FQ	28.73 MW	33.55 TQ	WABLS	3/16
	Tacoma-Lakewood PMSA, WA	H	24.95 FQ	30.64 MW	39.03 TQ	WABLS	3/16
	West Virginia	Y	41320 FQ	49280 MW	60100 TQ	USBLS	5/15
	Huntington-Ashland MSA, WV-KY-OH	Y	41910 FQ	51850 MW	62090 TQ	USBLS	5/15
	Wisconsin	Y	42980 FQ	51110 MW	58670 TQ	USBLS	5/15
	Madison MSA, WI	Y	38780 FQ	45800 MW	55760 TQ	USBLS	5/15
	Milwaukee-Waukesha-West Allis MSA, WI	Y	44280 FQ	51340 MW	58070 TQ	USBLS	5/15
	Wyoming	Y	43360 FQ	49990 MW	58860 TQ	USBLS	5/15
	Cheyenne MSA, WY	Y	46120 FQ	54020 MW	62480 TQ	USBLS	5/15
	Puerto Rico	Y	17760 FQ	20530 MW	27230 TQ	USBLS	5/15
	San Juan-Carolina-Caguas MSA, PR	Y	18580 FQ	23410 MW	29250 TQ	USBLS	5/15
Physician Assistant	Alabama	Y	65879 AE	95042 AW	109618 AEX	ALBLS	6/16
	Birmingham-Hoover MSA, AL	Y	67102 AE	94420 AW	108079 AEX	ALBLS	6/16
	Alaska	Y	93330 FQ	109110 MW	123930 TQ	USBLS	5/15
	Anchorage MSA, AK	Y	98760 FQ	111300 MW	125980 TQ	USBLS	5/15
	Arizona	Y	84470 FQ	97990 MW	116740 TQ	USBLS	5/15
	Phoenix-Mesa-Scottsdale MSA, AZ	Y	84710 FQ	97860 MW	115700 TQ	USBLS	5/15
	Tucson MSA, AZ	Y	83310 FQ	91290 MW	100760 TQ	USBLS	5/15
	Arkansas	Y	40510 FQ	74080 MW	98720 TQ	USBLS	5/15
	Little Rock-North Little Rock-Conway MSA, AR	Y	45420 FQ	74780 MW	100540 TQ	USBLS	5/15
	California	H	41.90 FQ	53.34 MW	62.85 TQ	CABLS	1/16-3/16
	Anaheim-Santa Ana-Irvine PMSA, CA	H	47.56 FQ	55.32 MW	63.58 TQ	CABLS	1/16-3/16
	Los Angeles-Long Beach-Glendale PMSA, CA	H	21.09 FQ	44.23 MW	58.40 TQ	CABLS	1/16-3/16
	Oakland-Hayward-Berkeley PMSA, CA	H	52.11 FQ	57.06 MW	62.02 TQ	CABLS	1/16-3/16
	Riverside-San Bernardino-Ontario MSA, CA	H	43.30 FQ	50.76 MW	60.87 TQ	CABLS	1/16-3/16
	Sacramento–Roseville–Arden-Arcade MSA, CA	H	49.45 FQ	57.27 MW	67.50 TQ	CABLS	1/16-3/16
	San Diego-Carlsbad MSA, CA	H	39.16 FQ	51.03 MW	62.84 TQ	CABLS	1/16-3/16
	San Francisco-Redwood City-South San Francisco PMSA, CA	H	52.66 FQ	62.58 MW	73.68 TQ	CABLS	1/16-3/16
	Colorado	Y	83450 FQ	96630 MW	113120 TQ	USBLS	5/15
	Denver-Aurora-Lakewood MSA, CO	Y	81990 FQ	96890 MW	113280 TQ	USBLS	5/15
	Connecticut	Y		113096 MW		CTBLS	1/16-3/16
	Bridgeport-Stamford-Norwalk MSA, CT	Y	87230 FQ	107270 MW	122430 TQ	USBLS	5/15
	Hartford-West Hartford-East Hartford MSA, CT	Y	97500 FQ	111800 MW	124760 TQ	USBLS	5/15
	Delaware	Y	91900 FQ	105630 MW	126630 TQ	USBLS	5/15
	Wilmington PMSA, DE-MD-NJ	Y	90400 FQ	101920 MW	118480 TQ	USBLS	5/15
	District of Columbia	Y	84360 FQ	103730 MW	120810 TQ	USBLS	5/15
	Washington-Arlington-Alexandria PMSA, DC-VA-MD-WV	Y	79360 FQ	96640 MW	115770 TQ	USBLS	5/15
	Florida	H	37.75 AE	47.96 MW	56.07 AEX	FLBLS	7/16-9/16
	Fort Lauderdale-Pompano Beach-Deerfield Beach PMSA, FL	H	42.84 AE	48.29 MW	56.58 AEX	FLBLS	7/16-9/16
	Miami-Miami Beach-Kendall PMSA, FL	H	41.05 AE	50.79 MW	57.86 AEX	FLBLS	7/16-9/16

Occupation/Type/Industry	Location	Per	Low	Mid	High	Source	Date
Physician Assistant	Orlando-Kissimmee-Sanford MSA, FL	H	35.70 AE	47.38 MW	54.26 AEX	FLBLS	7/16-9/16
	Palm Bay-Melbourne-Titusville MSA, FL	H	39.95 AE	52.46 MW	58.38 AEX	FLBLS	7/16-9/16
	Tampa-St. Petersburg-Clearwater MSA, FL	H	34.47 AE	45.13 MW	54.75 AEX	FLBLS	7/16-9/16
	Georgia	Y	83360 FQ	95720 MW	114820 TQ	USBLS	5/15
	Atlanta-Sandy Springs-Roswell MSA, GA	Y	84720 FQ	97210 MW	116180 TQ	USBLS	5/15
	Augusta-Richmond County MSA, GA-SC	Y	39410 FQ	82930 MW	94050 TQ	USBLS	5/15
	Hawaii	Y	76120 FQ	92190 MW	104950 TQ	USBLS	5/15
	Urban Honolulu MSA, HI	Y	82380 FQ	95490 MW	107730 TQ	USBLS	5/15
	Idaho	Y	84060 FQ	93980 MW	108200 TQ	USBLS	5/15
	Boise City MSA, ID	Y	85710 FQ	94280 MW	103100 TQ	USBLS	5/15
	Illinois	Y	63040 FQ	90640 MW	108290 TQ	USBLS	5/15
	Chicago-Naperville-Arlington Heights PMSA, IL	Y	56420 FQ	88040 MW	103610 TQ	USBLS	5/15
	Lake County-Kenosha County PMSA, IL-WI	Y	81030 FQ	98790 MW	138590 TQ	USBLS	5/15
	Indiana	Y	84190 FQ	94670 MW	112620 TQ	USBLS	5/15
	Gary PMSA, IN	Y	80540 FQ	88830 MW	96660 TQ	USBLS	5/15
	Indianapolis-Carmel-Anderson MSA, IN	Y	84980 FQ	94280 MW	105150 TQ	USBLS	5/15
	Iowa	Y	82210 FQ	95280 MW	112010 TQ	USBLS	5/15
	Des Moines-West Des Moines MSA, IA	Y	59680 FQ	94590 MW	108430 TQ	USBLS	5/15
	Kansas	Y	81570 FQ	95090 MW	112640 TQ	USBLS	5/15
	Wichita MSA, KS	Y	74330 FQ	85940 MW	96560 TQ	USBLS	5/15
	Kentucky	Y	85540 FQ	94760 MW	110230 TQ	USBLS	5/15
	Louisville-Jefferson County MSA, KY-IN	Y	86380 FQ	94360 MW	104010 TQ	USBLS	5/15
	Louisiana	Y	61630 FQ	88970 MW	113390 TQ	USBLS	5/15
	Baton Rouge MSA, LA	Y	81770 FQ	106290 MW	122500 TQ	USBLS	5/15
	New Orleans-Metairie MSA, LA	Y	60480 FQ	88840 MW	115600 TQ	USBLS	5/15
	Maine	Y	88290 FQ	101180 MW	118200 TQ	USBLS	5/15
	Portland-South Portland MSA, ME	Y	87580 FQ	100840 MW	118010 TQ	USBLS	5/15
	Maryland	Y	56519 AE	90354 MW	107271 AEX	MDBLS	4/16
	Baltimore-Columbia-Towson MSA, MD	Y	69690 FQ	91320 MW	106640 TQ	USBLS	5/15
	Salisbury MSA, MD-DE	Y	73320 FQ	91550 MW	111760 TQ	USBLS	5/15
	Massachusetts	Y	87260 FQ	103990 MW	122680 TQ	USBLS	5/15
	Boston-Cambridge-Newton NECTA, MA	Y	88630 FQ	104710 MW	122560 TQ	USBLS	5/15
	Worcester MSA, MA-CT	Y	85170 FQ	99770 MW	116040 TQ	USBLS	5/15
	Michigan	Y	80180 FQ	95300 MW	115800 TQ	USBLS	5/15
	Detroit-Dearborn-Livonia PMSA, MI	Y	84540 FQ	96320 MW	112610 TQ	USBLS	5/15
	Grand Rapids-Wyoming MSA, MI	Y	91180 FQ	108370 MW	136840 TQ	USBLS	5/15
	Minnesota	Y	91985 FQ	106531 MW	122519 TQ	MNBLS	1/16-3/16
	Minneapolis-St. Paul-Bloomington MSA, MN-WI	Y	89797 FQ	103406 MW	121188 TQ	MNBLS	1/16-3/16
	Mississippi	Y	28410 FQ	33660 MW	55240 TQ	USBLS	5/15
	Jackson MSA, MS	Y	27350 FQ	30080 MW	37810 TQ	USBLS	5/15
	Missouri	Y	70310 FQ	93030 MW	128760 TQ	USBLS	5/15
	Kansas City MSA, MO-KS	Y	86580 FQ	103180 MW	124530 TQ	USBLS	5/15
	St. Louis MSA, MO-IL	Y	41930 FQ	95270 MW	137220 TQ	USBLS	5/15
	Montana	Y	83650 FQ	95250 MW	114500 TQ	USBLS	5/15
	Billings MSA, MT	Y	85560 FQ	95620 MW	108110 TQ	USBLS	5/15
	Nebraska	Y	80165 FQ	92370 MW	107065 TQ	NEBLS	7/16-9/16
	Omaha-Council Bluffs MSA, NE-IA	Y	79400 FQ	91255 MW	103015 TQ	NEBLS	7/16-9/16
	Nevada	Y	88610 FQ	103960 MW	137020 TQ	USBLS	5/15
	Las Vegas-Henderson-Paradise MSA, NV	Y	90550 FQ	111200 MW	148650 TQ	USBLS	5/15
	New Hampshire	H	42.17 AE	53.88 MW	62.03 AEX	NHBLS	6/16
	Manchester NECTA, NH	H	42.11 AE	52.73 MW	59.59 AEX	NHBLS	6/16
	Nashua NECTA, NH-MA	Y	98440 FQ	113590 MW	132830 TQ	USBLS	5/15
	New Jersey	Y	90710 FQ	108370 MW	130060 TQ	USBLS	5/15

AE	Average entry wage	AWR	Average wage range	H	Hourly
AEX	Average experienced wage	B	Biweekly	HI	Highest wage paid
ATC	Average total compensation	D	Daily	HR	High end range
AW	Average wage paid	FQ	First quartile wage	LO	Lowest wage paid

LR	Low end range	MTC	Median total compensation
M	Monthly	MW	Median wage paid
MCC	Median cash compensation	MWR	Median wage range
ME	Median entry wage	S	See annotated source

TCC	Total cash compensation		
TQ	Third quartile wage		
W	Weekly		
Y	Yearly		

Physician Assistant

Occupation/Type/Industry	Location	Per	Low	Mid	High	Source	Date
Physician Assistant	Camden PMSA, NJ	Y	89180 FQ	102850 MW	120050 TQ	USBLS	5/15
	Newark PMSA, NJ-PA	Y	90040 FQ	101400 MW	121630 TQ	USBLS	5/15
	Trenton MSA, NJ	Y	83260 FQ	97960 MW	119170 TQ	USBLS	5/15
	New Mexico	Y	83340 FQ	98560 MW	121140 TQ	USBLS	5/15
	Albuquerque MSA, NM	Y	81980 FQ	96170 MW	116080 TQ	USBLS	5/15
	New York	Y	81710 AE	102500 MW	114390 AEX	NYBLS	1/16-3/16
	Buffalo-Cheektowaga-Niagara Falls MSA, NY	Y	84680 FQ	93300 MW	104340 TQ	USBLS	5/15
	Nassau County-Suffolk County PMSA, NY	Y	88090 FQ	106390 MW	121680 TQ	USBLS	5/15
	New York-Jersey City-White Plains PMSA, NY-NJ	Y	89700 FQ	104520 MW	121260 TQ	USBLS	5/15
	Rochester MSA, NY	Y	83970 FQ	93630 MW	109160 TQ	USBLS	5/15
	North Carolina	Y	84960 FQ	95530 MW	112580 TQ	USBLS	5/15
	Charlotte-Concord-Gastonia MSA, NC-SC	Y	85010 FQ	93950 MW	103700 TQ	USBLS	5/15
	Raleigh MSA, NC	Y	85620 FQ	97100 MW	114340 TQ	USBLS	5/15
	North Dakota	Y	88140 FQ	99490 MW	124320 TQ	USBLS	5/15
	Ohio	Y	87800 FQ	101190 MW	121020 TQ	USBLS	5/15
	Cincinnati MSA, OH-KY-IN	Y	82080 FQ	93420 MW	108870 TQ	USBLS	5/15
	Cleveland-Elyria MSA, OH	Y	93370 FQ	108580 MW	124830 TQ	USBLS	5/15
	Columbus MSA, OH	Y	90290 FQ	102650 MW	124990 TQ	USBLS	5/15
	Oklahoma	Y	86800 FQ	102920 MW	124170 TQ	USBLS	5/15
	Oklahoma City MSA, OK	Y	83870 FQ	98590 MW	119930 TQ	USBLS	5/15
	Tulsa MSA, OK	Y	89500 FQ	106880 MW	122990 TQ	USBLS	5/15
	Oregon	H	43.48 FQ	50.74 MW	59.67 TQ	ORBLS	2016
	Portland-Vancouver-Hillsboro MSA, OR-WA	Y	91800 FQ	110730 MW	129910 TQ	USBLS	5/15
	Pennsylvania	Y	72970 FQ	88130 MW	102320 TQ	USBLS	5/15
	Allentown-Bethlehem-Easton MSA, PA-NJ	Y	74080 FQ	89230 MW	102760 TQ	USBLS	5/15
	Harrisburg-Carlisle MSA, PA	Y	68590 FQ	86190 MW	100500 TQ	USBLS	5/15
	Montgomery County-Bucks County-Chester County PMSA, PA	Y	77290 FQ	99060 MW	119280 TQ	USBLS	5/15
	Philadelphia PMSA, PA	Y	60970 FQ	78090 MW	97340 TQ	USBLS	5/15
	Pittsburgh MSA, PA	Y	74000 FQ	86000 MW	96280 TQ	USBLS	5/15
	Rhode Island	Y	87430 FQ	108720 MW	140270 TQ	USBLS	5/15
	Providence-Warwick MSA, RI-MA	Y	85500 FQ	105010 MW	138180 TQ	USBLS	5/15
	South Carolina	Y	66620 FQ	87390 MW	101190 TQ	USBLS	5/15
	Charleston-North Charleston MSA, SC	Y	69790 FQ	86230 MW	104110 TQ	USBLS	5/15
	Columbia MSA, SC	Y	59310 FQ	89490 MW	98230 TQ	USBLS	5/15
	Greenville-Anderson-Mauldin MSA, SC	Y	74890 FQ	89240 MW	100740 TQ	USBLS	5/15
	South Dakota	Y	85140 FQ	94950 MW	109960 TQ	USBLS	5/15
	Sioux Falls MSA, SD	Y	86170 FQ	96580 MW	112900 TQ	USBLS	5/15
	Tennessee	Y	68180 FQ	87080 MW	103020 TQ	USBLS	5/15
	Knoxville MSA, TN	Y	80690 FQ	94480 MW	112740 TQ	USBLS	5/15
	Memphis MSA, TN-MS-AR	Y	38000 FQ	67920 MW	87770 TQ	USBLS	5/15
	Nashville-Davidson–Murfreesboro–Franklin MSA, TN	Y	62590 FQ	79820 MW	100450 TQ	USBLS	5/15
	Texas	Y	82580 FQ	101010 MW	119550 TQ	USBLS	5/15
	Austin-Round Rock MSA, TX	Y	83170 FQ	95110 MW	115070 TQ	USBLS	5/15
	Dallas-Plano-Irving PMSA, TX	Y	81740 FQ	103340 MW	118150 TQ	USBLS	5/15
	Fort Worth-Arlington PMSA, TX	Y	70650 FQ	92040 MW	111520 TQ	USBLS	5/15
	Houston-The Woodlands-Sugar Land MSA, TX	Y	84980 FQ	102880 MW	119540 TQ	USBLS	5/15
	San Antonio-New Braunfels MSA, TX	Y	59870 FQ	93860 MW	113090 TQ	USBLS	5/15
	Utah	Y	81340 FQ	94830 MW	117340 TQ	USBLS	5/15
	Ogden-Clearfield MSA, UT	Y	96800 FQ	119000 MW	159040 TQ	USBLS	5/15
	Provo-Orem MSA, UT	Y	35230 FQ	88580 MW	100940 TQ	USBLS	5/15
	Salt Lake City MSA, UT	Y	76970 FQ	92530 MW	114540 TQ	USBLS	5/15
	Vermont	Y	90390 FQ	104780 MW	123190 TQ	USBLS	5/15
	Burlington-South Burlington MSA, VT	Y	90790 FQ	105890 MW	121410 TQ	USBLS	5/15
	Virginia	Y	75210 FQ	90670 MW	104990 TQ	USBLS	5/15
	Richmond MSA, VA	Y	87370 FQ	102970 MW	117990 TQ	USBLS	5/15

AE	Average entry wage	AWR	Average wage range	H	Hourly
AEX	Average experienced wage	B	Biweekly	HI	Highest wage paid
ATC	Average total compensation	D	Daily	HR	High end range
AW	Average wage paid	FQ	First quartile wage	LO	Lowest wage paid

LR	Low end range	MTC	Median total compensation
M	Monthly	MW	Median wage paid
MCC	Median cash compensation	MWR	Median wage range
ME	Median entry wage	S	See annotated source

TCC	Total cash compensation		
TQ	Third quartile wage		
W	Weekly		
Y	Yearly		

Occupation/Type/Industry	Location	Per	Low	Mid	High	Source	Date
Physician Assistant	Virginia Beach-Norfolk- Newport News MSA, VA-NC	Y	70690 FQ	86250 MW	96760 TQ	USBLS	5/15
	Washington	H	44.26 FQ	52.48 MW	62.44 TQ	WABLS	3/16
	Seattle-Bellevue-Everett PMSA, WA	H	48.33 FQ	55.66 MW	64.00 TQ	WABLS	3/16
	Tacoma-Lakewood PMSA, WA	H	39.71 FQ	46.70 MW	55.78 TQ	WABLS	3/16
	West Virginia	Y	78240 FQ	90210 MW	103930 TQ	USBLS	5/15
	Huntington-Ashland MSA, WV-KY-OH	Y	82330 FQ	95550 MW	112990 TQ	USBLS	5/15
	Wisconsin	Y	79030 FQ	93070 MW	107860 TQ	USBLS	5/15
	Madison MSA, WI	Y	88000 FQ	98290 MW	114210 TQ	USBLS	5/15
	Milwaukee-Waukesha-West Allis MSA, WI	Y	73430 FQ	87030 MW	99350 TQ	USBLS	5/15
	Wyoming	Y	88810 FQ	100820 MW	120830 TQ	USBLS	5/15
	Cheyenne MSA, WY	Y	92300 FQ	107710 MW	120800 TQ	USBLS	5/15
	Puerto Rico	Y	40960 FQ	43890 MW	46830 TQ	USBLS	5/15
	San Juan-Carolina-Caguas MSA, PR	Y	41090 FQ	43980 MW	46870 TQ	USBLS	5/15
Physician Specialist							
Police Department, Municipal Government	San Francisco, CA	Y			211597 HI	CACIT	6/28/16
Physicist	Alabama	Y	76694 AE	128792 AW	154845 AEX	ALBLS	6/16
	Birmingham-Hoover MSA, AL	Y	56430 AE	154203 AW	203090 AEX	ALBLS	6/16
	Arizona	Y	58390 FQ	89060 MW	151630 TQ	USBLS	5/15
	Phoenix-Mesa-Scottsdale MSA, AZ	Y	76950 FQ	123140 MW		USBLS	5/15
	Tucson MSA, AZ	Y	56240 FQ	78150 MW	137380 TQ	USBLS	5/15
	California	H	37.77 FQ	52.92 MW	68.15 TQ	CABLS	1/16-3/16
	Anaheim-Santa Ana-Irvine PMSA, CA	H	41.79 FQ	55.88 MW	69.43 TQ	CABLS	1/16-3/16
	Los Angeles-Long Beach- Glendale PMSA, CA	H	28.36 FQ	40.10 MW	60.06 TQ	CABLS	1/16-3/16
	Oakland-Hayward-Berkeley PMSA, CA	H	51.84 FQ	62.04 MW	74.92 TQ	CABLS	1/16-3/16
	Riverside-San Bernardino- Ontario MSA, CA	H	39.60 FQ	48.39 MW	55.26 TQ	CABLS	1/16-3/16
	San Diego-Carlsbad MSA, CA	H	24.43 FQ	38.49 MW	57.57 TQ	CABLS	1/16-3/16
	San Francisco-Redwood City- South San Francisco PMSA, CA	H	45.69 FQ	55.23 MW	66.50 TQ	CABLS	1/16-3/16
	Colorado	Y	59190 FQ	88090 MW	127770 TQ	USBLS	5/15
	Wilmington PMSA, DE-MD- NJ	Y	55550 FQ	88760 MW	127500 TQ	USBLS	5/15
	District of Columbia	Y	110670 FQ	118310 MW	158690 TQ	USBLS	5/15
	Washington-Arlington- Alexandria PMSA, DC-VA- MD-WV	Y	109360 FQ	130460 MW	158690 TQ	USBLS	5/15
	Florida	H	42.15 AE	53.42 MW	89.20 AEX	FLBLS	7/16-9/16
	Orlando-Kissimmee-Sanford MSA, FL	H	44.94 AE	94.38 MW	122.33 AEX	FLBLS	7/16-9/16
	Tampa-St. Petersburg- Clearwater MSA, FL	H	43.73 AE	48.64 MW	73.05 AEX	FLBLS	7/16-9/16
	Georgia	Y	89720 FQ	120660 MW	176550 TQ	USBLS	5/15
	Atlanta-Sandy Springs- Roswell MSA, GA	Y	109000 FQ	142890 MW	174420 TQ	USBLS	5/15
	Hawaii	Y	81800 FQ	92200 MW	96540 TQ	USBLS	5/15
	Urban Honolulu MSA, HI	Y	81190 FQ	92090 MW	95590 TQ	USBLS	5/15
	Idaho	Y	73530 FQ	86250 MW	114760 TQ	USBLS	5/15
	Illinois	Y	97870 FQ	115570 MW	142280 TQ	USBLS	5/15
	Chicago-Naperville-Arlington Heights PMSA, IL	Y	98680 FQ	116170 MW	144530 TQ	USBLS	5/15
	Indiana	Y	58340 FQ	72150 MW	118790 TQ	USBLS	5/15
	Kansas	Y	130200 FQ	143470 MW	155720 TQ	USBLS	5/15
	Maryland	Y	83906 AE	126803 MW	148252 AEX	MDBLS	4/16
	Baltimore-Columbia-Towson MSA, MD	Y	89050 FQ	115220 MW	154520 TQ	USBLS	5/15
	Massachusetts	Y	56000 FQ	77400 MW	128420 TQ	USBLS	5/15
	Boston-Cambridge-Newton NECTA, MA	Y	54840 FQ	71450 MW	118810 TQ	USBLS	5/15
	Michigan	Y	68590 FQ	92320 MW	147170 TQ	USBLS	5/15

AE	Average entry wage	AWR	Average wage range	H Hourly
AEX	Average experienced wage	B	Biweekly	HI Highest wage paid
ATC	Average total compensation	D	Daily	HR High end range
AW	Average wage paid	FQ	First quartile wage	LO Lowest wage paid

LR	Low end range	MTC	Median total compensation	TCC Total cash compensation
M	Monthly	MW	Median wage paid	TQ Third quartile wage
MCC	Median cash compensation	MWR	Median wage range	W Weekly
ME	Median entry wage	S	See annotated source	Y Yearly

Occupation/Type/Industry	Location	Per	Low	Mid	High	Source	Date
Physicist	Detroit-Dearborn-Livonia						
	PMSA, MI	Y	107580 FQ	141980 MW	158870 TQ	USBLS	5/15
	Minnesota	Y	53457 FQ	92710 MW	144262 TQ	MNBLS	1/16-3/16
	Minneapolis-St. Paul-						
	Bloomington MSA, MN-WI	Y	49899 FQ	70312 MW	111934 TQ	MNBLS	1/16-3/16
	Mississippi	Y	69390 FQ	94680 MW	115080 TQ	USBLS	5/15
	Missouri	Y	88010 FQ	100320 MW	124650 TQ	USBLS	5/15
	Kansas City MSA, MO-KS	Y	88160 FQ	101580 MW	140540 TQ	USBLS	5/15
	St. Louis MSA, MO-IL	Y	101160 FQ	117270 MW	160790 TQ	USBLS	5/15
	Nebraska	Y	68100 FQ	85955 MW	108500 TQ	NEBLS	7/16-9/16
	New Hampshire	H	24.90 AE	35.52 MW	53.29 AEX	NHBLS	6/16
	Newark PMSA, NJ-PA	Y	100170 FQ	133840 MW		USBLS	5/15
	New Mexico	Y	123880 FQ	134990 MW	146420 TQ	USBLS	5/15
	New York	Y	65740 AE	116790 MW	154250 AEX	NYBLS	1/16-3/16
	Buffalo-Cheektowaga-Niagara						
	Falls MSA, NY	Y	88030 FQ	112190 MW		USBLS	5/15
	Nassau County-Suffolk County						
	PMSA, NY	Y	105070 FQ	134260 MW	160850 TQ	USBLS	5/15
	New York-Jersey City-White						
	Plains PMSA, NY-NJ	Y	71420 FQ	122370 MW		USBLS	5/15
	North Carolina	Y	52170 FQ	107190 MW	165160 TQ	USBLS	5/15
	Raleigh MSA, NC	Y	60310 FQ	102820 MW	161470 TQ	USBLS	5/15
	North Dakota	Y	87870 FQ	109330 MW	130070 TQ	USBLS	5/15
	Ohio	Y	85780 FQ	116080 MW	174710 TQ	USBLS	5/15
	Cincinnati MSA, OH-KY-IN	Y	109790 FQ	158830 MW		USBLS	5/15
	Cleveland-Elyria MSA, OH	Y	106130 FQ	134150 MW	176620 TQ	USBLS	5/15
	Oklahoma	Y	104730 FQ	153000 MW		USBLS	5/15
	Oregon	H	35.94 FQ	71.49 MW	88.93 TQ	ORBLS	2016
	Portland-Vancouver-Hillsboro						
	MSA, OR-WA	Y	71580 FQ	136530 MW	176340 TQ	USBLS	5/15
	Pennsylvania	Y	96440 FQ	128410 MW	173800 TQ	USBLS	5/15
	Philadelphia PMSA, PA	Y	66330 FQ	129000 MW	176800 TQ	USBLS	5/15
	Pittsburgh MSA, PA	Y	111310 FQ	153710 MW	185430 TQ	USBLS	5/15
	Providence-Warwick MSA, RI-						
	MA	Y	61490 FQ	118610 MW	156730 TQ	USBLS	5/15
	South Carolina	Y	107150 FQ	121280 MW	165870 TQ	USBLS	5/15
	Tennessee	Y	77980 FQ	101840 MW	135280 TQ	USBLS	5/15
	Knoxville MSA, TN	Y	75220 FQ	99960 MW	135430 TQ	USBLS	5/15
	Texas	Y	62530 FQ	94270 MW	125000 TQ	USBLS	5/15
	Austin-Round Rock MSA, TX	Y	52260 FQ	59700 MW	72510 TQ	USBLS	5/15
	Dallas-Plano-Irving PMSA, TX	Y	88600 FQ	96250 MW	103080 TQ	USBLS	5/15
	Houston-The Woodlands-						
	Sugar Land MSA, TX	Y	69520 FQ	100560 MW	135560 TQ	USBLS	5/15
	San Antonio-New Braunfels						
	MSA, TX	Y	123830 FQ	143950 MW	154780 TQ	USBLS	5/15
	Virginia	Y	84230 FQ	108860 MW	141620 TQ	USBLS	5/15
	Virginia Beach-Norfolk-						
	Newport News MSA, VA-NC	Y	71060 FQ	80800 MW	96260 TQ	USBLS	5/15
	Washington	H	41.71 FQ	53.57 MW	77.22 TQ	WABLS	3/16
	Seattle-Bellevue-Everett						
	PMSA, WA	H	44.96 FQ	66.13 MW	89.18 TQ	WABLS	3/16
	Wisconsin	Y	54450 FQ	73710 MW	144710 TQ	USBLS	5/15
	Madison MSA, WI	Y	58530 FQ	76450 MW	141980 TQ	USBLS	5/15
	Milwaukee-Waukesha-West						
	Allis MSA, WI	Y	56390 FQ	72910 MW	126690 TQ	USBLS	5/15
Physics Teacher							
Postsecondary	Alabama	Y	53678 AE	92361 AW	111708 AEX	ALBLS	6/16
Postsecondary	Birmingham-Hoover MSA, AL	Y	52302 AE	91912 AW	111718 AEX	ALBLS	6/16
Postsecondary	Arizona	Y	58090 FQ	80830 MW	109080 TQ	USBLS	5/15
Postsecondary	Phoenix-Mesa-Scottsdale						
	MSA, AZ	Y	55780 FQ	70420 MW	98040 TQ	USBLS	5/15
Postsecondary	Arkansas	Y	47110 FQ	65120 MW	92990 TQ	USBLS	5/15
Postsecondary	California	Y		110752 AW		CABLS	1/16-3/16
Postsecondary	Anaheim-Santa Ana-Irvine						
	PMSA, CA	Y		112588 AW		CABLS	1/16-3/16
Postsecondary	Los Angeles-Long Beach-						
	Glendale PMSA, CA	Y		126355 AW		CABLS	1/16-3/16
Postsecondary	Riverside-San Bernardino-						
	Ontario MSA, CA	Y		89255 AW		CABLS	1/16-3/16
Postsecondary	Sacramento–Roseville–						
	Arden-Arcade MSA, CA	Y		110610 AW		CABLS	1/16-3/16

AE	Average entry wage	AWR	Average wage range	H	Hourly	LR	Low end range	MTC	Median total compensation	TCC	Total cash compensation
AEX	Average experienced wage	B	Biweekly	HI	Highest wage paid	M	Monthly	MW	Median wage paid	TQ	Third quartile wage
ATC	Average total compensation	D	Daily	HR	High end range	MCC	Median cash compensation	MWR	Median wage range	W	Weekly
AW	Average wage paid	FQ	First quartile wage	LO	Lowest wage paid	ME	Median entry wage	S	See annotated source	Y	Yearly

Occupation/Type/Industry	Location	Per	Low	Mid	High	Source	Date
Physics Teacher							
Postsecondary	San Diego-Carlsbad MSA, CA	Y		127004 AW		CABLS	1/16-3/16
Postsecondary	San Francisco-Redwood City- South San Francisco PMSA, CA	Y		102362 AW		CABLS	1/16-3/16
Postsecondary	Colorado	Y	51440 FQ	80490 MW	109080 TQ	USBLS	5/15
Postsecondary	Denver-Aurora-Lakewood MSA, CO	Y	39110 FQ	69570 MW	101700 TQ	USBLS	5/15
Postsecondary	Connecticut	Y		81078 MW		CTBLS	1/16-3/16
Postsecondary	Hartford-West Hartford-East Hartford MSA, CT	Y	64280 FQ	89240 MW	113570 TQ	USBLS	5/15
Postsecondary	District of Columbia	Y	60490 FQ	89400 MW	120350 TQ	USBLS	5/15
Postsecondary	Washington-Arlington- Alexandria PMSA, DC-VA- MD-WV	Y	61000 FQ	95300 MW	147670 TQ	USBLS	5/15
Postsecondary	Florida	Y	57738 AE	86906 MW	117380 AEX	FLBLS	7/16-9/16
Postsecondary	Miami-Miami Beach-Kendall PMSA, FL	Y	72552 AE	113796 MW	124231 AEX	FLBLS	7/16-9/16
Postsecondary	Orlando-Kissimmee-Sanford MSA, FL	Y	60465 AE	92063 MW	118431 AEX	FLBLS	7/16-9/16
Postsecondary	Tampa-St. Petersburg- Clearwater MSA, FL	Y	53555 AE	90262 MW	138706 AEX	FLBLS	7/16-9/16
Postsecondary	Georgia	Y	53050 FQ	69190 MW	93650 TQ	USBLS	5/15
Postsecondary	Atlanta-Sandy Springs- Roswell MSA, GA	Y	51830 FQ	67120 MW	91600 TQ	USBLS	5/15
Postsecondary	Hawaii	Y	59670 FQ	85280 MW	110000 TQ	USBLS	5/15
Postsecondary	Urban Honolulu MSA, HI	Y	64690 FQ	92860 MW	123770 TQ	USBLS	5/15
Postsecondary	Idaho	Y	48710 FQ	71610 MW	99980 TQ	USBLS	5/15
Postsecondary	Illinois	Y	59730 FQ	82310 MW	111120 TQ	USBLS	5/15
Postsecondary	Chicago-Naperville-Arlington Heights PMSA, IL	Y	57870 FQ	79890 MW	105190 TQ	USBLS	5/15
Postsecondary	Indiana	Y	60640 FQ	85120 MW	113820 TQ	USBLS	5/15
Postsecondary	Indianapolis-Carmel-Anderson MSA, IN	Y	60210 FQ	78020 MW	96800 TQ	USBLS	5/15
Postsecondary	Iowa	Y	66120 FQ	85450 MW	112240 TQ	USBLS	5/15
Postsecondary	Kansas	Y	49040 FQ	59970 MW	73140 TQ	USBLS	5/15
Postsecondary	Kentucky	Y	57270 FQ	76830 MW	105330 TQ	USBLS	5/15
Postsecondary	Louisiana	Y	53590 FQ	70280 MW	91740 TQ	USBLS	5/15
Postsecondary	Maine	Y	61750 FQ	77900 MW	103670 TQ	USBLS	5/15
Postsecondary	Maryland	Y	51727 AE	104380 MW	130706 AEX	MDBLS	4/16
Postsecondary	Baltimore-Columbia-Towson MSA, MD	Y	61700 FQ	78970 MW	99880 TQ	USBLS	5/15
Postsecondary	Massachusetts	Y	75020 FQ	100430 MW	145730 TQ	USBLS	5/15
Postsecondary	Boston-Cambridge-Newton NECTA, MA	Y	86870 FQ	118960 MW	164540 TQ	USBLS	5/15
Postsecondary	Worcester MSA, MA-CT	Y	60800 FQ	92870 MW	128950 TQ	USBLS	5/15
Postsecondary	Michigan	Y	61820 FQ	84760 MW	118080 TQ	USBLS	5/15
Postsecondary	Detroit-Dearborn-Livonia PMSA, MI	Y	50570 FQ	73380 MW	89280 TQ	USBLS	5/15
Postsecondary	Minnesota	Y	56259 FQ	75886 MW	100362 TQ	MNBLS	1/16-3/16
Postsecondary	Minneapolis-St. Paul- Bloomington MSA, MN-WI	Y	55443 FQ	76390 MW	108093 TQ	MNBLS	1/16-3/16
Postsecondary	Mississippi	Y	54900 FQ	67630 MW	84390 TQ	USBLS	5/15
Postsecondary	Missouri	Y	61030 FQ	78820 MW	106520 TQ	USBLS	5/15
Postsecondary	St. Louis MSA, MO-IL	Y	55730 FQ	71580 MW	89570 TQ	USBLS	5/15
Postsecondary	Montana	Y	66340 FQ	80600 MW	99480 TQ	USBLS	5/15
Postsecondary	Nebraska	Y	60965 FQ	74755 MW	93190 TQ	NEBLS	7/16-9/16
Postsecondary	New Hampshire	Y	70433 AE	119075 MW	138351 AEX	NHBLS	6/16
Postsecondary	New Jersey	Y	66200 FQ	90200 MW	125660 TQ	USBLS	5/15
Postsecondary	Camden PMSA, NJ	Y	64350 FQ	81080 MW	111600 TQ	USBLS	5/15
Postsecondary	Newark PMSA, NJ-PA	Y	64330 FQ	85480 MW	125420 TQ	USBLS	5/15
Postsecondary	New Mexico	Y	75870 FQ	94220 MW	120610 TQ	USBLS	5/15
Postsecondary	New York	Y	57180 AE	99170 MW	140910 AEX	NYBLS	1/16-3/16
Postsecondary	Buffalo-Cheektowaga-Niagara Falls MSA, NY	Y	57700 FQ	83730 MW	96760 TQ	USBLS	5/15
Postsecondary	Nassau County-Suffolk County PMSA, NY	Y	60440 FQ	91930 MW	124190 TQ	USBLS	5/15
Postsecondary	New York-Jersey City-White Plains PMSA, NY-NJ	Y	77520 FQ	112540 MW	146220 TQ	USBLS	5/15
Postsecondary	Rochester MSA, NY	Y	68870 FQ	130040 MW		USBLS	5/15
Postsecondary	North Carolina	Y	57660 FQ	77730 MW	107110 TQ	USBLS	5/15

AE	Average entry wage	AWR	Average wage range	H	Hourly	LR	Low end range	MTC	Median total compensation	TCC	Total cash compensation
AEX	Average experienced wage	B	Biweekly	HI	Highest wage paid	M	Monthly	MW	Median wage paid	TQ	Third quartile wage
ATC	Average total compensation	D	Daily	HR	High end range	MCC	Median cash compensation	MWR	Median wage range	W	Weekly
AW	Average wage paid	FQ	First quartile wage	LO	Lowest wage paid	ME	Median entry wage	S	See annotated source	Y	Yearly

Occupation/Type/Industry	Location	Per	Low	Mid	High	Source	Date
Physics Teacher							
Postsecondary	Charlotte-Concord-Gastonia MSA, NC-SC	Y	62060 FQ	86460 MW	101900 TQ	USBLS	5/15
Postsecondary	Raleigh MSA, NC	Y	65740 FQ	87230 MW	117550 TQ	USBLS	5/15
Postsecondary	Ohio	Y	61080 FQ	89600 MW	123050 TQ	USBLS	5/15
Postsecondary	Columbus MSA, OH	Y	72790 FQ	102110 MW	127370 TQ	USBLS	5/15
Postsecondary	Oklahoma	Y	47100 FQ	65620 MW	78820 TQ	USBLS	5/15
Postsecondary	Oklahoma City MSA, OK	Y	40650 FQ	53430 MW	76460 TQ	USBLS	5/15
Postsecondary	Oregon	Y	69815 FQ	87270 MW	108374 TQ	ORBLS	2016
Postsecondary	Portland-Vancouver-Hillsboro MSA, OR-WA	Y	59300 FQ	84090 MW	100720 TQ	USBLS	5/15
Postsecondary	Pennsylvania	Y	63500 FQ	83780 MW	110340 TQ	USBLS	5/15
Postsecondary	Allentown-Bethlehem-Easton MSA, PA-NJ	Y	84140 FQ	115370 MW	176220 TQ	USBLS	5/15
Postsecondary	Montgomery County-Bucks County-Chester County PMSA, PA	Y	54610 FQ	72970 MW	98230 TQ	USBLS	5/15
Postsecondary	Philadelphia PMSA, PA	Y	70060 FQ	94850 MW	123470 TQ	USBLS	5/15
Postsecondary	Pittsburgh MSA, PA	Y	60980 FQ	80770 MW	107280 TQ	USBLS	5/15
Postsecondary	Rhode Island	Y	60370 FQ	79720 MW	111620 TQ	USBLS	5/15
Postsecondary	Providence-Warwick MSA, RI-MA	Y	59230 FQ	78620 MW	110920 TQ	USBLS	5/15
Postsecondary	South Carolina	Y	53890 FQ	69220 MW	88830 TQ	USBLS	5/15
Postsecondary	Columbia MSA, SC	Y	51900 FQ	68800 MW	83120 TQ	USBLS	5/15
Postsecondary	Greenville-Anderson-Mauldin MSA, SC	Y	64590 FQ	84900 MW	107540 TQ	USBLS	5/15
Postsecondary	South Dakota	Y	62050 FQ	71440 MW	81060 TQ	USBLS	5/15
Postsecondary	Tennessee	Y	51850 FQ	71140 MW	97240 TQ	USBLS	5/15
Postsecondary	Knoxville MSA, TN	Y	73720 FQ	94380 MW	127430 TQ	USBLS	5/15
Postsecondary	Memphis MSA, TN-MS-AR	Y	58950 FQ	73510 MW	95110 TQ	USBLS	5/15
Postsecondary	Nashville-Davidson–Murfreesboro–Franklin MSA, TN	Y	50170 FQ	70620 MW	99510 TQ	USBLS	5/15
Postsecondary	Texas	Y	53850 FQ	75650 MW	104000 TQ	USBLS	5/15
Postsecondary	Austin-Round Rock MSA, TX	Y	50610 FQ	81050 MW	122290 TQ	USBLS	5/15
Postsecondary	Dallas-Plano-Irving PMSA, TX	Y	56870 FQ	77110 MW	104080 TQ	USBLS	5/15
Postsecondary	Houston-The Woodlands-Sugar Land MSA, TX	Y	55460 FQ	81700 MW	107770 TQ	USBLS	5/15
Postsecondary	San Antonio-New Braunfels MSA, TX	Y	24850 FQ	60800 MW	89540 TQ	USBLS	5/15
Postsecondary	Utah	Y	62590 FQ	83860 MW	104190 TQ	USBLS	5/15
Postsecondary	Salt Lake City MSA, UT	Y	58950 FQ	82450 MW	98850 TQ	USBLS	5/15
Postsecondary	Vermont	Y	66220 FQ	82630 MW	105300 TQ	USBLS	5/15
Postsecondary	Virginia	Y	52930 FQ	74540 MW	103350 TQ	USBLS	5/15
Postsecondary	Richmond MSA, VA	Y	60210 FQ	83100 MW	111330 TQ	USBLS	5/15
Postsecondary	Virginia Beach-Norfolk-Newport News MSA, VA-NC	Y	50370 FQ	73630 MW	102490 TQ	USBLS	5/15
Postsecondary	Washington	Y		77741 AW		WABLS	3/16
Postsecondary	Seattle-Bellevue-Everett PMSA, WA	Y		87632 AW		WABLS	3/16
Postsecondary	Tacoma-Lakewood PMSA, WA	Y		70000 AW		WABLS	3/16
Postsecondary	West Virginia	Y	57500 FQ	72980 MW	97650 TQ	USBLS	5/15
Postsecondary	Wisconsin	Y	50530 FQ	65970 MW	91830 TQ	USBLS	5/15
Postsecondary	Milwaukee-Waukesha-West Allis MSA, WI	Y	48580 FQ	82380 MW	98850 TQ	USBLS	5/15
Postsecondary	Wyoming	Y	62000 FQ	71300 MW	80130 TQ	USBLS	5/15
Postsecondary	Puerto Rico	Y	65540 FQ	77850 MW	89560 TQ	USBLS	5/15
Postsecondary	San Juan-Carolina-Caguas MSA, PR	Y	71010 FQ	83300 MW	93410 TQ	USBLS	5/15
Piano Technician							
California State University	California	Y	33192 LO		70860 HI	CALST	2016-2017
Piano Tuner Assistant							
Michigan State University	East Lansing, MI	Y			47258 HI	MSUSAL	10/1/14-9/30/15
Pier Manager							
Municipal Government	Santa Monica, CA	Y			165302 HI	CACIT	6/28/16
Pile-Driver Operator							
	Alabama	Y	33751 AE	52000 AW	61135 AEX	ALBLS	6/16
	Alaska	Y	38780 FQ	60160 MW	75150 TQ	USBLS	5/15
	Anchorage MSA, AK	Y	49820 FQ	67690 MW	80350 TQ	USBLS	5/15

AE	Average entry wage	AWR	Average wage range	H	Hourly	LR	Low end range	MTC	Median total compensation	TCC	Total cash compensation
AEX	Average experienced wage	B	Biweekly	HI	Highest wage paid	M	Monthly	MW	Median wage paid	TQ	Third quartile wage
ATC	Average total compensation	D	Daily	HR	High end range	MCC	Median cash compensation	MWR	Median wage range	W	Weekly
AW	Average wage paid	FQ	First quartile wage	LO	Lowest wage paid	ME	Median entry wage	S	See annotated source	Y	Yearly

Occupation/Type/Industry	Location	Per	Low	Mid	High	Source	Date
Pile-Driver Operator	California	H	27.61 FQ	40.09 MW	45.17 TQ	CABLS	1/16-3/16
	Los Angeles-Long Beach-Glendale PMSA, CA	H	24.38 FQ	30.19 MW	44.39 TQ	CABLS	1/16-3/16
	Oakland-Hayward-Berkeley PMSA, CA	H	37.77 FQ	42.22 MW	46.12 TQ	CABLS	1/16-3/16
	Sacramento–Roseville–Arden-Arcade MSA, CA	H	27.10 FQ	38.97 MW	44.03 TQ	CABLS	1/16-3/16
	Colorado	Y	37270 FQ	41870 MW	45800 TQ	USBLS	5/15
	Florida	H	15.84 AE	23.14 MW	28.91 AEX	FLBLS	7/16-9/16
	Miami-Miami Beach-Kendall PMSA, FL	H	22.45 AE	29.00 MW	32.95 AEX	FLBLS	7/16-9/16
	Kentucky	Y	26820 FQ	29580 MW	37830 TQ	USBLS	5/15
	Louisiana	Y	28860 FQ	36590 MW	45800 TQ	USBLS	5/15
	Maryland	Y	36827 AE	52197 MW	59882 AEX	MDBLS	4/16
	Baltimore-Columbia-Towson MSA, MD	Y	37460 FQ	43880 MW	50530 TQ	USBLS	5/15
	Massachusetts	Y	43470 FQ	86000 MW	94640 TQ	USBLS	5/15
	Minnesota	Y	50219 FQ	72064 MW	87018 TQ	MNBLS	1/16-3/16
	Minneapolis-St. Paul-Bloomington MSA, MN-WI	Y	50976 FQ	73123 MW	87976 TQ	MNBLS	1/16-3/16
	Mississippi	Y	29330 FQ	34320 MW	39290 TQ	USBLS	5/15
	Missouri	Y	43760 FQ	67980 MW	75680 TQ	USBLS	5/15
	New Jersey	Y	45930 FQ	80830 MW	94020 TQ	USBLS	5/15
	Newark PMSA, NJ-PA	Y	61020 FQ	88500 MW	96690 TQ	USBLS	5/15
	New York	Y	37550 AE	57960 MW	78150 AEX	NYBLS	1/16-3/16
	New York-Jersey City-White Plains PMSA, NY-NJ	Y	30770 FQ	63220 MW	93800 TQ	USBLS	5/15
	North Carolina	Y	28440 FQ	34710 MW	44200 TQ	USBLS	5/15
	Charlotte-Concord-Gastonia MSA, NC-SC	Y	41300 FQ	44490 MW	47680 TQ	USBLS	5/15
	Oklahoma	Y	33520 FQ	40070 MW	46070 TQ	USBLS	5/15
	Oregon	H	17.42 FQ	32.23 MW	36.04 TQ	ORBLS	2016
	Pennsylvania	Y	48020 FQ	57990 MW	69290 TQ	USBLS	5/15
	Pittsburgh MSA, PA	Y	31160 FQ	54160 MW	66340 TQ	USBLS	5/15
	South Carolina	Y	41670 FQ	44810 MW	47960 TQ	USBLS	5/15
	Texas	Y	34290 FQ	43670 MW	58180 TQ	USBLS	5/15
	Houston-The Woodlands-Sugar Land MSA, TX	Y	33230 FQ	42020 MW	53860 TQ	USBLS	5/15
	Virginia	Y	37720 FQ	43610 MW	48830 TQ	USBLS	5/15
	Virginia Beach-Norfolk-Newport News MSA, VA-NC	Y	36260 FQ	42110 MW	47540 TQ	USBLS	5/15
	Washington	H	29.19 FQ	39.35 MW	43.85 TQ	WABLS	3/16
	Wisconsin	Y	60590 FQ	68790 MW	75380 TQ	USBLS	5/15
Pipelayer	Alabama	Y	23814 AE	35531 AW	41394 AEX	ALBLS	6/16
	Birmingham-Hoover MSA, AL	Y	26160 AE	39008 AW	45437 AEX	ALBLS	6/16
	Montgomery MSA, AL	Y	20893 AE	27517 AW	30830 AEX	ALBLS	6/16
	Alaska	Y	38290 FQ	47810 MW	73110 TQ	USBLS	5/15
	Arizona	Y	34890 FQ	39640 MW	48180 TQ	USBLS	5/15
	Phoenix-Mesa-Scottsdale MSA, AZ	Y	34650 FQ	39350 MW	48120 TQ	USBLS	5/15
	Tucson MSA, AZ	Y	35280 FQ	39280 MW	46350 TQ	USBLS	5/15
	Arkansas	Y	25230 FQ	29510 MW	38690 TQ	USBLS	5/15
	Little Rock-North Little Rock-Conway MSA, AR	Y	28250 FQ	32740 MW	36800 TQ	USBLS	5/15
	California	H	20.25 FQ	25.81 MW	32.12 TQ	CABLS	1/16-3/16
	Anaheim-Santa Ana-Irvine PMSA, CA	H	14.40 FQ	21.28 MW	29.04 TQ	CABLS	1/16-3/16
	Los Angeles-Long Beach-Glendale PMSA, CA	H	23.08 FQ	27.53 MW	32.44 TQ	CABLS	1/16-3/16
	Oakland-Hayward-Berkeley PMSA, CA	H	24.62 FQ	30.56 MW	34.49 TQ	CABLS	1/16-3/16
	Riverside-San Bernardino-Ontario MSA, CA	H	20.20 FQ	26.64 MW	34.55 TQ	CABLS	1/16-3/16
	Sacramento–Roseville–Arden-Arcade MSA, CA	H	25.27 FQ	29.64 MW	34.23 TQ	CABLS	1/16-3/16
	San Diego-Carlsbad MSA, CA	H	20.34 FQ	23.95 MW	30.01 TQ	CABLS	1/16-3/16
	San Francisco-Redwood City-South San Francisco PMSA, CA	H	21.49 FQ	23.67 MW	27.28 TQ	CABLS	1/16-3/16
	Colorado	Y	32540 FQ	37050 MW	44710 TQ	USBLS	5/15

Pipelayer

Occupation/Type/Industry	Location	Per	Low	Mid	High	Source	Date
Pipelayer	Denver-Aurora-Lakewood MSA, CO	Y	33550 FQ	37940 MW	45860 TQ	USBLS	5/15
	Connecticut	Y		57355 MW		CTBLS	1/16-3/16
	Bridgeport-Stamford-Norwalk MSA, CT	Y	52380 FQ	55960 MW	59540 TQ	USBLS	5/15
	Hartford-West Hartford-East Hartford MSA, CT	Y	56020 FQ	67220 MW	88650 TQ	USBLS	5/15
	Delaware	Y	31910 FQ	36320 MW	43760 TQ	USBLS	5/15
	Wilmington PMSA, DE-MD-NJ	Y	31520 FQ	36770 MW	45330 TQ	USBLS	5/15
	District of Columbia	Y	37000 FQ	49190 MW	59070 TQ	USBLS	5/15
	Washington-Arlington-Alexandria PMSA, DC-VA-MD-WV	Y	33840 FQ	38280 MW	49160 TQ	USBLS	5/15
	Florida	H	13.33 AE	17.15 MW	20.80 AEX	FLBLS	7/16-9/16
	Fort Lauderdale-Pompano Beach-Deerfield Beach PMSA, FL	H	15.63 AE	18.05 MW	19.94 AEX	FLBLS	7/16-9/16
	Miami-Miami Beach-Kendall PMSA, FL	H	16.20 AE	23.94 MW	27.20 AEX	FLBLS	7/16-9/16
	Orlando-Kissimmee-Sanford MSA, FL	H	14.88 AE	17.40 MW	19.17 AEX	FLBLS	7/16-9/16
	Tampa-St. Petersburg-Clearwater MSA, FL	H	13.53 AE	16.33 MW	18.37 AEX	FLBLS	7/16-9/16
	Georgia	Y	28440 FQ	34030 MW	39230 TQ	USBLS	5/15
	Atlanta-Sandy Springs-Roswell MSA, GA	Y	29590 FQ	33890 MW	37710 TQ	USBLS	5/15
	Augusta-Richmond County MSA, GA-SC	Y	25970 FQ	30710 MW	39640 TQ	USBLS	5/15
	Hawaii	Y	42380 FQ	46030 MW	49690 TQ	USBLS	5/15
	Urban Honolulu MSA, HI	Y	41740 FQ	44850 MW	47960 TQ	USBLS	5/15
	Idaho	Y	29710 FQ	35810 MW	44090 TQ	USBLS	5/15
	Boise City MSA, ID	Y	26920 FQ	31320 MW	38600 TQ	USBLS	5/15
	Illinois	Y	41900 FQ	53060 MW	67410 TQ	USBLS	5/15
	Chicago-Naperville-Arlington Heights PMSA, IL	Y	41520 FQ	51190 MW	62070 TQ	USBLS	5/15
	Lake County-Kenosha County PMSA, IL-WI	Y	40930 FQ	49810 MW	60770 TQ	USBLS	5/15
	Indiana	Y	35400 FQ	43810 MW	54660 TQ	USBLS	5/15
	Gary PMSA, IN	Y	46430 FQ	60850 MW	71860 TQ	USBLS	5/15
	Indianapolis-Carmel-Anderson MSA, IN	Y	36230 FQ	45980 MW	55260 TQ	USBLS	5/15
	Iowa	Y	31270 FQ	43590 MW	56810 TQ	USBLS	5/15
	Des Moines-West Des Moines MSA, IA	Y	50170 FQ	56370 MW	62390 TQ	USBLS	5/15
	Kansas	Y	28340 FQ	38870 MW	58440 TQ	USBLS	5/15
	Wichita MSA, KS	Y	28470 FQ	42600 MW	60340 TQ	USBLS	5/15
	Kentucky	Y	24580 FQ	39880 MW	63250 TQ	USBLS	5/15
	Louisville-Jefferson County MSA, KY-IN	Y	32010 FQ	35750 MW	39550 TQ	USBLS	5/15
	Louisiana	Y	31360 FQ	39170 MW	56910 TQ	USBLS	5/15
	Baton Rouge MSA, LA	Y	24080 FQ	35390 MW	68470 TQ	USBLS	5/15
	New Orleans-Metairie MSA, LA	Y	35230 FQ	41170 MW	53760 TQ	USBLS	5/15
	Maine	Y	36370 FQ	43330 MW	48950 TQ	USBLS	5/15
	Portland-South Portland MSA, ME	Y	38500 FQ	44610 MW	50250 TQ	USBLS	5/15
	Maryland	Y	33607 AE	42768 MW	47348 AEX	MDBLS	4/16
	Baltimore-Columbia-Towson MSA, MD	Y	34490 FQ	38510 MW	46860 TQ	USBLS	5/15
	Massachusetts	Y	49520 FQ	67610 MW	93770 TQ	USBLS	5/15
	Boston-Cambridge-Newton NECTA, MA	Y	58660 FQ	79090 MW	110380 TQ	USBLS	5/15
	Worcester MSA, MA-CT	Y	69280 FQ	85820 MW	133210 TQ	USBLS	5/15
	Michigan	Y	35210 FQ	41480 MW	46830 TQ	USBLS	5/15
	Grand Rapids-Wyoming MSA, MI	Y	31820 FQ	37350 MW	44770 TQ	USBLS	5/15
	Minnesota	Y	45153 FQ	59865 MW	70510 TQ	MNBLS	1/16-3/16
	Minneapolis-St. Paul-Bloomington MSA, MN-WI	Y	48786 FQ	63296 MW	71681 TQ	MNBLS	1/16-3/16
	Mississippi	Y	25070 FQ	31240 MW	39460 TQ	USBLS	5/15
	Jackson MSA, MS	Y	19150 FQ	24660 MW	34230 TQ	USBLS	5/15

AE Average entry wage	**AWR** Average wage range	**H** Hourly	**LR** Low end range	**MTC** Median total compensation	**TCC** Total cash compensation
AEX Average experienced wage	**B** Biweekly	**HI** Highest wage paid	**M** Monthly	**MW** Median wage paid	**TQ** Third quartile wage
ATC Average total compensation	**D** Daily	**HR** High end range	**MCC** Median cash compensation	**MWR** Median wage range	**W** Weekly
AW Average wage paid	**FQ** First quartile wage	**LO** Lowest wage paid	**ME** Median entry wage	**S** See annotated source	**Y** Yearly

Occupation/Type/Industry	Location	Per	Low	Mid	High	Source	Date
Pipelayer	Missouri	Y	37480 FQ	63140 MW	72530 TQ	USBLS	5/15
	Kansas City MSA, MO-KS	Y	37870 FQ	60220 MW	76040 TQ	USBLS	5/15
	St. Louis MSA, MO-IL	Y	52040 FQ	67030 MW	73350 TQ	USBLS	5/15
	Montana	Y	35350 FQ	50520 MW	57690 TQ	USBLS	5/15
	Nebraska	Y	31530 FQ	35875 MW	40760 TQ	NEBLS	7/16-9/16
	Omaha-Council Bluffs MSA, NE-IA	Y	33665 FQ	38395 MW	48530 TQ	NEBLS	7/16-9/16
	Nevada	Y	37920 FQ	50250 MW	63610 TQ	USBLS	5/15
	Las Vegas-Henderson-Paradise MSA, NV	Y	42590 FQ	56530 MW	68070 TQ	USBLS	5/15
	New Hampshire	H	18.08 AE	22.43 MW	23.97 AEX	NHBLS	6/16
	New Jersey	Y	47050 FQ	61680 MW	71190 TQ	USBLS	5/15
	Newark PMSA, NJ-PA	Y	57130 FQ	67350 MW	74270 TQ	USBLS	5/15
	New Mexico	Y	32430 FQ	35560 MW	38680 TQ	USBLS	5/15
	Albuquerque MSA, NM	Y	33100 FQ	35700 MW	38310 TQ	USBLS	5/15
	New York	Y	32840 AE	43240 MW	54870 AEX	NYBLS	1/16-3/16
	Buffalo-Cheektowaga-Niagara Falls MSA, NY	Y	38650 FQ	46670 MW	55900 TQ	USBLS	5/15
	New York-Jersey City-White Plains PMSA, NY-NJ	Y	34850 FQ	43170 MW	60900 TQ	USBLS	5/15
	Rochester MSA, NY	Y	41430 FQ	51350 MW	59980 TQ	USBLS	5/15
	North Carolina	Y	26430 FQ	30600 MW	36640 TQ	USBLS	5/15
	Charlotte-Concord-Gastonia MSA, NC-SC	Y	25710 FQ	30110 MW	36310 TQ	USBLS	5/15
	Raleigh MSA, NC	Y	29160 FQ	34270 MW	38510 TQ	USBLS	5/15
	North Dakota	Y	32830 FQ	37790 MW	48750 TQ	USBLS	5/15
	Fargo MSA, ND-MN	Y	33150 FQ	36210 MW	39270 TQ	USBLS	5/15
	Ohio	Y	37860 FQ	43890 MW	49720 TQ	USBLS	5/15
	Cincinnati MSA, OH-KY-IN	Y	48660 FQ	58070 MW	67940 TQ	USBLS	5/15
	Cleveland-Elyria MSA, OH	Y	41250 FQ	44580 MW	47910 TQ	USBLS	5/15
	Columbus MSA, OH	Y	40680 FQ	45180 MW	49700 TQ	USBLS	5/15
	Oklahoma	Y	27890 FQ	31710 MW	38110 TQ	USBLS	5/15
	Oklahoma City MSA, OK	Y	27490 FQ	30530 MW	37550 TQ	USBLS	5/15
	Tulsa MSA, OK	Y	26980 FQ	29910 MW	34710 TQ	USBLS	5/15
	Oregon	H	21.26 FQ	24.41 MW	28.09 TQ	ORBLS	2016
	Portland-Vancouver-Hillsboro MSA, OR-WA	Y	44600 FQ	52010 MW	58660 TQ	USBLS	5/15
	Pennsylvania	Y	39660 FQ	47610 MW	62080 TQ	USBLS	5/15
	Harrisburg-Carlisle MSA, PA	Y	38830 FQ	43450 MW	47740 TQ	USBLS	5/15
	Montgomery County-Bucks County-Chester County PMSA, PA	Y	43750 FQ	52740 MW	70070 TQ	USBLS	5/15
	Philadelphia PMSA, PA	Y	44850 FQ	53130 MW	60460 TQ	USBLS	5/15
	Pittsburgh MSA, PA	Y	43390 FQ	50380 MW	67990 TQ	USBLS	5/15
	Providence-Warwick MSA, RI-MA	Y	22840 FQ	32560 MW	36730 TQ	USBLS	5/15
	South Carolina	Y	27780 FQ	32510 MW	40390 TQ	USBLS	5/15
	Charleston-North Charleston MSA, SC	Y	27270 FQ	29750 MW	36240 TQ	USBLS	5/15
	Columbia MSA, SC	Y	25880 FQ	29540 MW	34700 TQ	USBLS	5/15
	Greenville-Anderson-Mauldin MSA, SC	Y	27290 FQ	32270 MW	39110 TQ	USBLS	5/15
	South Dakota	Y	29660 FQ	34330 MW	39380 TQ	USBLS	5/15
	Sioux Falls MSA, SD	Y	31400 FQ	41950 MW	59510 TQ	USBLS	5/15
	Tennessee	Y	27740 FQ	33280 MW	39260 TQ	USBLS	5/15
	Knoxville MSA, TN	Y	28220 FQ	33550 MW	38660 TQ	USBLS	5/15
	Memphis MSA, TN-MS-AR	Y	32320 FQ	35980 MW	40890 TQ	USBLS	5/15
	Nashville-Davidson–Murfreesboro–Franklin MSA, TN	Y	29810 FQ	35940 MW	43130 TQ	USBLS	5/15
	Texas	Y	27110 FQ	30830 MW	37390 TQ	USBLS	5/15
	Austin-Round Rock MSA, TX	Y	27690 FQ	31940 MW	37440 TQ	USBLS	5/15
	Dallas-Plano-Irving PMSA, TX	Y	26350 FQ	29050 MW	32570 TQ	USBLS	5/15
	Fort Worth-Arlington PMSA, TX	Y	28160 FQ	32250 MW	37890 TQ	USBLS	5/15
	Houston-The Woodlands-Sugar Land MSA, TX	Y	28260 FQ	32930 MW	39440 TQ	USBLS	5/15
	San Antonio-New Braunfels MSA, TX	Y	27160 FQ	30590 MW	37290 TQ	USBLS	5/15
	Utah	Y	28640 FQ	33950 MW	40180 TQ	USBLS	5/15
	Ogden-Clearfield MSA, UT	Y	27900 FQ	33120 MW	37280 TQ	USBLS	5/15
	Provo-Orem MSA, UT	Y	26850 FQ	29330 MW	33520 TQ	USBLS	5/15

AE Average entry wage	AWR Average wage range	H Hourly	LR Low end range	MTC Median total compensation	TCC Total cash compensation
AEX Average experienced wage	B Biweekly	HI Highest wage paid	M Monthly	MW Median wage paid	TQ Third quartile wage
ATC Average total compensation	D Daily	HR High end range	MCC Median cash compensation	MWR Median wage range	W Weekly
AW Average wage paid	FQ First quartile wage	LO Lowest wage paid	ME Median entry wage	S See annotated source	Y Yearly

Occupation/Type/Industry	Location	Per	Low	Mid	High	Source	Date
Pipelayer	Salt Lake City MSA, UT	Y	32820 FQ	38440 MW	45270 TQ	USBLS	5/15
	Vermont	Y	32830 FQ	35710 MW	38600 TQ	USBLS	5/15
	Burlington-South Burlington MSA, VT	Y	32180 FQ	35230 MW	38280 TQ	USBLS	5/15
	Virginia	Y	28420 FQ	33800 MW	39410 TQ	USBLS	5/15
	Richmond MSA, VA	Y	28380 FQ	33710 MW	43740 TQ	USBLS	5/15
	Virginia Beach-Norfolk-Newport News MSA, VA-NC	Y	26330 FQ	29700 MW	37440 TQ	USBLS	5/15
	Washington	H	21.99 FQ	27.29 MW	32.76 TQ	WABLS	3/16
	Seattle-Bellevue-Everett PMSA, WA	H	22.18 FQ	28.04 MW	34.22 TQ	WABLS	3/16
	Tacoma-Lakewood PMSA, WA	H	27.41 FQ	31.39 MW	35.12 TQ	WABLS	3/16
	West Virginia	Y	32320 FQ	39110 MW	56330 TQ	USBLS	5/15
	Huntington-Ashland MSA, WV-KY-OH	Y	34010 FQ	46680 MW	57060 TQ	USBLS	5/15
	Wisconsin	Y	40470 FQ	55290 MW	68130 TQ	USBLS	5/15
	Madison MSA, WI	Y	53140 FQ	60250 MW	69060 TQ	USBLS	5/15
	Milwaukee-Waukesha-West Allis MSA, WI	Y	61630 FQ	69100 MW	74930 TQ	USBLS	5/15
	Wyoming	Y	33280 FQ	37890 MW	62360 TQ	USBLS	5/15
	Puerto Rico	Y	18550 FQ	27400 MW	34040 TQ	USBLS	5/15
	San Juan-Carolina-Caguas MSA, PR	Y	19010 FQ	28560 MW	34400 TQ	USBLS	5/15
Placement Interviewer							
California State University	California	Y	30888 LO		51744 HI	CALST	2016-2017
Plan Check Engineer							
Municipal Government	Culver City, CA	Y			96141 HI	CACIT	6/28/16
Plan Check Specialist							
Municipal Government	Hawthorne, CA	Y			86703 HI	CACIT	6/28/16
Planetarium Manager							
Michigan State University	East Lansing, MI	Y			61000 HI	MSUSAL	10/1/14-9/30/15
Planner							
Federal Government	United States	Y		95000 MW		APA01	1/1/16
Private Consulting Firm	United States	Y		84000 MW		APA01	1/1/16
State Government	United States	Y		71500 MW		APA01	1/1/16
Planning Commissioner							
Municipal Government	Fillmore, CA	Y		283 AW		CACIT	7/18/16
Plant Ecologist							
Municipal Government	Seattle, WA	H	30.03 LO		35.05 HI	CSSS	1/13/16
Plasterer and Stucco Mason	Alabama	Y	27343 AE	29729 AW	30912 AEX	ALBLS	6/16
	Arizona	Y	27780 FQ	32840 MW	38440 TQ	USBLS	5/15
	Phoenix-Mesa-Scottsdale MSA, AZ	Y	28550 FQ	33530 MW	38870 TQ	USBLS	5/15
	Tucson MSA, AZ	Y	26750 FQ	31050 MW	37990 TQ	USBLS	5/15
	Arkansas	Y	33650 FQ	35990 MW	38340 TQ	USBLS	5/15
	California	H	15.76 FQ	18.88 MW	25.43 TQ	CABLS	1/16-3/16
	Anaheim-Santa Ana-Irvine PMSA, CA	H	15.52 FQ	18.95 MW	25.84 TQ	CABLS	1/16-3/16
	Los Angeles-Long Beach-Glendale PMSA, CA	H	14.88 FQ	18.80 MW	26.36 TQ	CABLS	1/16-3/16
	Oakland-Hayward-Berkeley PMSA, CA	H	11.77 FQ	23.20 MW	32.11 TQ	CABLS	1/16-3/16
	Riverside-San Bernardino-Ontario MSA, CA	H	15.45 FQ	17.43 MW	19.51 TQ	CABLS	1/16-3/16
	Sacramento-Roseville-Arden-Arcade MSA, CA	H	16.14 FQ	18.21 MW	23.02 TQ	CABLS	1/16-3/16
	San Diego-Carlsbad MSA, CA	H	17.65 FQ	23.68 MW	29.58 TQ	CABLS	1/16-3/16
	San Francisco-Redwood City-South San Francisco PMSA, CA	H	15.54 FQ	17.84 MW	21.56 TQ	CABLS	1/16-3/16
	Colorado	Y	32420 FQ	37600 MW	43690 TQ	USBLS	5/15
	Denver-Aurora-Lakewood MSA, CO	Y	35420 FQ	39280 MW	44350 TQ	USBLS	5/15
	District of Columbia	Y	54880 FQ	58940 MW	62260 TQ	USBLS	5/15

AE	Average entry wage	**AWR** Average wage range	**H** Hourly	**LR** Low end range	**MTC** Median total compensation	**TCC** Total cash compensation
AEX	Average experienced wage	**B** Biweekly	**HI** Highest wage paid	**M** Monthly	**MW** Median wage	**TQ** Third quartile wage
ATC	Average total compensation	**D** Daily	**HR** High end range	**MCC** Median cash compensation	**MWR** Median wage range	**W** Weekly
AW	Average wage paid	**FQ** First quartile wage	**LO** Lowest wage paid	**ME** Median entry wage	**S** See annotated source	**Y** Yearly

Occupation/Type/Industry	Location	Per	Low	Mid	High	Source	Date
Plasterer and Stucco Mason	Washington-Arlington-Alexandria PMSA, DC-VA-MD-WV	Y	54700 FQ	58580 MW	62080 TQ	USBLS	5/15
	Florida	H	14.21 AE	17.06 MW	18.40 AEX	FLBLS	7/16-9/16
	Fort Lauderdale-Pompano Beach-Deerfield Beach PMSA, FL	H	12.71 AE	16.19 MW	17.15 AEX	FLBLS	7/16-9/16
	Miami-Miami Beach-Kendall PMSA, FL	H	17.43 AE	19.64 MW	23.93 AEX	FLBLS	7/16-9/16
	Orlando-Kissimmee-Sanford MSA, FL	H	13.63 AE	16.86 MW	19.38 AEX	FLBLS	7/16-9/16
	Tampa-St. Petersburg-Clearwater MSA, FL	H	13.15 AE	16.85 MW	17.49 AEX	FLBLS	7/16-9/16
	Georgia	Y	32840 FQ	35700 MW	38550 TQ	USBLS	5/15
	Hawaii	Y	34370 FQ	63800 MW	80090 TQ	USBLS	5/15
	Idaho	Y	26010 FQ	29280 MW	33990 TQ	USBLS	5/15
	Boise City MSA, ID	Y	25210 FQ	28120 MW	31020 TQ	USBLS	5/15
	Illinois	Y	55710 FQ	83260 MW	92310 TQ	USBLS	5/15
	Chicago-Naperville-Arlington Heights PMSA, IL	Y	80680 FQ	87950 MW	94610 TQ	USBLS	5/15
	Indiana	Y	43420 FQ	53410 MW	59740 TQ	USBLS	5/15
	Indianapolis-Carmel-Anderson MSA, IN	Y	52230 FQ	57610 MW	62540 TQ	USBLS	5/15
	Iowa	Y	35960 FQ	42840 MW	47850 TQ	USBLS	5/15
	Des Moines-West Des Moines MSA, IA	Y	36740 FQ	42590 MW	47590 TQ	USBLS	5/15
	Kansas	Y	33410 FQ	40320 MW	49190 TQ	USBLS	5/15
	Kentucky	Y	33810 FQ	36610 MW	39400 TQ	USBLS	5/15
	Louisiana	Y	26440 FQ	30320 MW	37940 TQ	USBLS	5/15
	Baton Rouge MSA, LA	Y	25880 FQ	28140 MW	30410 TQ	USBLS	5/15
	Baltimore-Columbia-Towson MSA, MD	Y	33860 FQ	37250 MW	43760 TQ	USBLS	5/15
	Massachusetts	Y	38740 FQ	53590 MW	62790 TQ	USBLS	5/15
	Boston-Cambridge-Newton NECTA, MA	Y	32730 FQ	49930 MW	65360 TQ	USBLS	5/15
	Michigan	Y	50130 FQ	56520 MW	62720 TQ	USBLS	5/15
	Detroit-Dearborn-Livonia PMSA, MI	Y	49940 FQ	54690 MW	59220 TQ	USBLS	5/15
	Minnesota	Y	50511 FQ	55334 MW	60248 TQ	MNBLS	1/16-3/16
	Minneapolis-St. Paul-Bloomington MSA, MN-WI	Y	51601 FQ	56132 MW	60743 TQ	MNBLS	1/16-3/16
	Mississippi	Y	24740 FQ	33610 MW	37100 TQ	USBLS	5/15
	Missouri	Y	35900 FQ	43560 MW	50320 TQ	USBLS	5/15
	Kansas City MSA, MO-KS	Y	41540 FQ	47880 MW	55970 TQ	USBLS	5/15
	St. Louis MSA, MO-IL	Y	44120 FQ	48550 MW	57450 TQ	USBLS	5/15
	Montana	Y	33000 FQ	41550 MW	48080 TQ	USBLS	5/15
	Omaha-Council Bluffs MSA, NE-IA	Y	33745 FQ	36200 MW	38650 TQ	NEBLS	7/16-9/16
	Nevada	Y	28280 FQ	34450 MW	44830 TQ	USBLS	5/15
	Las Vegas-Henderson-Paradise MSA, NV	Y	28080 FQ	34020 MW	44720 TQ	USBLS	5/15
	New Jersey	Y	27450 FQ	42090 MW	57780 TQ	USBLS	5/15
	Newark PMSA, NJ-PA	Y	24610 FQ	29080 MW	46570 TQ	USBLS	5/15
	New Mexico	Y	26080 FQ	29180 MW	34430 TQ	USBLS	5/15
	Albuquerque MSA, NM	Y	25400 FQ	27980 MW	30560 TQ	USBLS	5/15
	New York-Jersey City-White Plains PMSA, NY-NJ	Y	62370 FQ	87720 MW	95750 TQ	USBLS	5/15
	North Carolina	Y	17470 FQ	19430 MW	31810 TQ	USBLS	5/15
	Ohio	Y	34950 FQ	41290 MW	55770 TQ	USBLS	5/15
	Cincinnati MSA, OH-KY-IN	Y	39570 FQ	43680 MW	47820 TQ	USBLS	5/15
	Cleveland-Elyria MSA, OH	Y	54440 FQ	58490 MW	62380 TQ	USBLS	5/15
	Oklahoma	Y	37100 FQ	42060 MW	45640 TQ	USBLS	5/15
	Oregon	H	16.01 FQ	18.62 MW	22.26 TQ	ORBLS	2016
	Portland-Vancouver-Hillsboro MSA, OR-WA	Y	31380 FQ	36660 MW	44520 TQ	USBLS	5/15
	Pennsylvania	Y	23800 FQ	46450 MW	58490 TQ	USBLS	5/15
	Montgomery County-Bucks County-Chester County PMSA, PA	Y	49700 FQ	61040 MW	74080 TQ	USBLS	5/15
	Pittsburgh MSA, PA	Y	22140 FQ	24170 MW	47720 TQ	USBLS	5/15
	South Carolina	Y	33850 FQ	37760 MW	43100 TQ	USBLS	5/15
	Tennessee	Y	30880 FQ	34530 MW	38010 TQ	USBLS	5/15

Occupation/Type/Industry	Location	Per	Low	Mid	High	Source	Date
Plasterer and Stucco Mason	Memphis MSA, TN-MS-AR	Y	27020 FQ	29090 MW	31140 TQ	USBLS	5/15
	Nashville-Davidson–Murfreesboro–Franklin MSA, TN	Y	33140 FQ	36080 MW	39060 TQ	USBLS	5/15
	Texas	Y	28170 FQ	33950 MW	39420 TQ	USBLS	5/15
	Dallas-Plano-Irving PMSA, TX	Y	28470 FQ	33310 MW	37350 TQ	USBLS	5/15
	Fort Worth-Arlington PMSA, TX	Y	35610 FQ	41320 MW	47930 TQ	USBLS	5/15
	Houston-The Woodlands-Sugar Land MSA, TX	Y	27190 FQ	32270 MW	42670 TQ	USBLS	5/15
	San Antonio-New Braunfels MSA, TX	Y	18000 FQ	30450 MW	35590 TQ	USBLS	5/15
	Utah	Y	28750 FQ	34140 MW	38900 TQ	USBLS	5/15
	Ogden-Clearfield MSA, UT	Y	31050 FQ	34530 MW	37620 TQ	USBLS	5/15
	Salt Lake City MSA, UT	Y	26390 FQ	29500 MW	35920 TQ	USBLS	5/15
	Virginia	Y	31830 FQ	38140 MW	45410 TQ	USBLS	5/15
	Washington	H	16.37 FQ	24.79 MW	35.38 TQ	WABLS	3/16
	Seattle-Bellevue-Everett PMSA, WA	H	31.80 FQ	34.64 MW	37.46 TQ	WABLS	3/16
	Wisconsin	Y	35910 FQ	42220 MW	50780 TQ	USBLS	5/15
Plastic Surgeon	United States	Y		355000 AW		MED02	2016
Plat Engineer							
County Government	Oakland County, MI	H			33.91 HI	MIOAK2	10/1/16
Plating and Coating Machine Setter, Operator, and Tender							
Metals and Plastics	Alabama	Y	24893 AE	36008 AW	41571 AEX	ALBLS	6/16
Metals and Plastics	Birmingham-Hoover MSA, AL	Y	25870 AE	33489 AW	37304 AEX	ALBLS	6/16
Metals and Plastics	Arizona	Y	24890 FQ	30270 MW	41530 TQ	USBLS	5/15
Metals and Plastics	Phoenix-Mesa-Scottsdale MSA, AZ	Y	24600 FQ	29470 MW	40190 TQ	USBLS	5/15
Metals and Plastics	Tucson MSA, AZ	Y	33370 FQ	41210 MW	46390 TQ	USBLS	5/15
Metals and Plastics	Arkansas	Y	25370 FQ	28900 MW	33590 TQ	USBLS	5/15
Metals and Plastics	Little Rock-North Little Rock-Conway MSA, AR	Y	24380 FQ	33060 MW	36750 TQ	USBLS	5/15
Metals and Plastics	California	H	11.64 FQ	14.54 MW	19.03 TQ	CABLS	1/16-3/16
Metals and Plastics	Anaheim-Santa Ana-Irvine PMSA, CA	H	10.99 FQ	13.11 MW	17.63 TQ	CABLS	1/16-3/16
Metals and Plastics	Los Angeles-Long Beach-Glendale PMSA, CA	H	12.24 FQ	14.95 MW	20.55 TQ	CABLS	1/16-3/16
Metals and Plastics	Oakland-Hayward-Berkeley PMSA, CA	H	12.70 FQ	16.46 MW	19.35 TQ	CABLS	1/16-3/16
Metals and Plastics	Riverside-San Bernardino-Ontario MSA, CA	H	11.24 FQ	14.22 MW	17.84 TQ	CABLS	1/16-3/16
Metals and Plastics	Sacramento–Roseville–Arden-Arcade MSA, CA	H	12.38 FQ	14.40 MW	17.70 TQ	CABLS	1/16-3/16
Metals and Plastics	San Diego-Carlsbad MSA, CA	H	10.85 FQ	12.58 MW	15.91 TQ	CABLS	1/16-3/16
Metals and Plastics	San Francisco-Redwood City-South San Francisco PMSA, CA	H	15.69 FQ	24.50 MW	43.45 TQ	CABLS	1/16-3/16
Metals and Plastics	Colorado	Y	26580 FQ	32110 MW	40510 TQ	USBLS	5/15
Metals and Plastics	Denver-Aurora-Lakewood MSA, CO	Y	25970 FQ	31420 MW	40500 TQ	USBLS	5/15
Metals and Plastics	Connecticut	Y		31408 MW		CTBLS	1/16-3/16
Metals and Plastics	Bridgeport-Stamford-Norwalk MSA, CT	Y	27820 FQ	31150 MW	39090 TQ	USBLS	5/15
Metals and Plastics	Hartford-West Hartford-East Hartford MSA, CT	Y	25720 FQ	29810 MW	35830 TQ	USBLS	5/15
Metals and Plastics	Delaware	Y	28410 FQ	34570 MW	43550 TQ	USBLS	5/15
Metals and Plastics	Wilmington PMSA, DE-MD-NJ	Y	28410 FQ	34570 MW	43550 TQ	USBLS	5/15
Metals and Plastics	Washington-Arlington-Alexandria PMSA, DC-VA-MD-WV	Y	31940 FQ	36630 MW	43010 TQ	USBLS	5/15
Metals and Plastics	Florida	H	10.32 AE	13.91 MW	16.28 AEX	FLBLS	7/16-9/16
Metals and Plastics	Fort Lauderdale-Pompano Beach-Deerfield Beach PMSA, FL	H	10.37 AE	11.76 MW	14.21 AEX	FLBLS	7/16-9/16
Metals and Plastics	Miami-Miami Beach-Kendall PMSA, FL	H	10.61 AE	13.49 MW	14.49 AEX	FLBLS	7/16-9/16

Occupation/Type/Industry	Location	Per	Low	Mid	High	Source	Date
Plating and Coating Machine Setter, Operator, and Tender							
Metals and Plastics	Orlando-Kissimmee-Sanford MSA, FL	H	11.45 AE	13.86 MW	15.34 AEX	FLBLS	7/16-9/16
Metals and Plastics	Tampa-St. Petersburg-Clearwater MSA, FL	H	10.20 AE	13.30 MW	15.47 AEX	FLBLS	7/16-9/16
Metals and Plastics	Georgia	Y	27770 FQ	31270 MW	39070 TQ	USBLS	5/15
Metals and Plastics	Atlanta-Sandy Springs-Roswell MSA, GA	Y	29690 FQ	34760 MW	39940 TQ	USBLS	5/15
Metals and Plastics	Augusta-Richmond County MSA, GA-SC	Y	26910 FQ	30000 MW	35390 TQ	USBLS	5/15
Metals and Plastics	Idaho	Y	25290 FQ	29580 MW	37210 TQ	USBLS	5/15
Metals and Plastics	Boise City MSA, ID	Y	26140 FQ	29200 MW	34130 TQ	USBLS	5/15
Metals and Plastics	Illinois	Y	23790 FQ	31840 MW	43810 TQ	USBLS	5/15
Metals and Plastics	Chicago-Naperville-Arlington Heights PMSA, IL	Y	22990 FQ	30780 MW	51520 TQ	USBLS	5/15
Metals and Plastics	Lake County-Kenosha County PMSA, IL-WI	Y	26470 FQ	32550 MW	48770 TQ	USBLS	5/15
Metals and Plastics	Indiana	Y	23660 FQ	29750 MW	37640 TQ	USBLS	5/15
Metals and Plastics	Gary PMSA, IN	Y	28550 FQ	36460 MW	47600 TQ	USBLS	5/15
Metals and Plastics	Indianapolis-Carmel-Anderson MSA, IN	Y	26950 FQ	31500 MW	40390 TQ	USBLS	5/15
Metals and Plastics	Iowa	Y	25080 FQ	29580 MW	36290 TQ	USBLS	5/15
Metals and Plastics	Kansas	Y	27150 FQ	30530 MW	36210 TQ	USBLS	5/15
Metals and Plastics	Kentucky	Y	26760 FQ	31540 MW	37440 TQ	USBLS	5/15
Metals and Plastics	Louisville-Jefferson County MSA, KY-IN	Y	22790 FQ	25550 MW	31390 TQ	USBLS	5/15
Metals and Plastics	Louisiana	Y	26560 FQ	31940 MW	37100 TQ	USBLS	5/15
Metals and Plastics	Maine	Y	32330 FQ	36230 MW	40960 TQ	USBLS	5/15
Metals and Plastics	Portland-South Portland MSA, ME	Y	32190 FQ	36010 MW	39850 TQ	USBLS	5/15
Metals and Plastics	Maryland	Y	24719 AE	33282 MW	37563 AEX	MDBLS	4/16
Metals and Plastics	Baltimore-Columbia-Towson MSA, MD	Y	26030 FQ	33110 MW	37940 TQ	USBLS	5/15
Metals and Plastics	Massachusetts	Y	28280 FQ	34480 MW	42040 TQ	USBLS	5/15
Metals and Plastics	Boston-Cambridge-Newton NECTA, MA	Y	28500 FQ	35020 MW	45740 TQ	USBLS	5/15
Metals and Plastics	Worcester MSA, MA-CT	Y	30490 FQ	37790 MW	45070 TQ	USBLS	5/15
Metals and Plastics	Michigan	Y	22350 FQ	27820 MW	34710 TQ	USBLS	5/15
Metals and Plastics	Detroit-Dearborn-Livonia PMSA, MI	Y	20330 FQ	27240 MW	35380 TQ	USBLS	5/15
Metals and Plastics	Grand Rapids-Wyoming MSA, MI	Y	20340 FQ	26020 MW	30150 TQ	USBLS	5/15
Metals and Plastics	Minnesota	Y	24724 FQ	30961 MW	39030 TQ	MNBLS	1/16-3/16
Metals and Plastics	Minneapolis-St. Paul-Bloomington MSA, MN-WI	Y	21697 FQ	29351 MW	37805 TQ	MNBLS	1/16-3/16
Metals and Plastics	Jackson MSA, MS	Y	29860 FQ	35810 MW	52390 TQ	USBLS	5/15
Metals and Plastics	Missouri	Y	24040 FQ	29970 MW	36890 TQ	USBLS	5/15
Metals and Plastics	Kansas City MSA, MO-KS	Y	27390 FQ	32480 MW	51900 TQ	USBLS	5/15
Metals and Plastics	St. Louis MSA, MO-IL	Y	20310 FQ	26290 MW	34750 TQ	USBLS	5/15
Metals and Plastics	Nebraska	Y	26345 FQ	30460 MW	40315 TQ	NEBLS	7/16-9/16
Metals and Plastics	Nevada	Y	27060 FQ	30510 MW	51130 TQ	USBLS	5/15
Metals and Plastics	New Hampshire	H	11.89 AE	14.65 MW	16.71 AEX	NHBLS	6/16
Metals and Plastics	Nashua NECTA, NH-MA	Y	25600 FQ	29720 MW	35930 TQ	USBLS	5/15
Metals and Plastics	New Jersey	Y	21830 FQ	28250 MW	35740 TQ	USBLS	5/15
Metals and Plastics	Camden PMSA, NJ	Y	27530 FQ	30450 MW	41460 TQ	USBLS	5/15
Metals and Plastics	Newark PMSA, NJ-PA	Y	21810 FQ	26910 MW	30650 TQ	USBLS	5/15
Metals and Plastics	New Mexico	Y	32130 FQ	35470 MW	38810 TQ	USBLS	5/15
Metals and Plastics	Albuquerque MSA, NM	Y	23180 FQ	33180 MW	37620 TQ	USBLS	5/15
Metals and Plastics	New York	Y	23510 AE	31960 MW	41080 AEX	NYBLS	1/16-3/16
Metals and Plastics	Buffalo-Cheektowaga-Niagara Falls MSA, NY	Y	26550 FQ	32800 MW	39780 TQ	USBLS	5/15
Metals and Plastics	Nassau County-Suffolk County PMSA, NY	Y	26220 FQ	32310 MW	45420 TQ	USBLS	5/15
Metals and Plastics	New York-Jersey City-White Plains PMSA, NY-NJ	Y	20940 FQ	31370 MW	40740 TQ	USBLS	5/15
Metals and Plastics	Rochester MSA, NY	Y	22610 FQ	29180 MW	38730 TQ	USBLS	5/15
Metals and Plastics	North Carolina	Y	24500 FQ	30420 MW	38130 TQ	USBLS	5/15
Metals and Plastics	Charlotte-Concord-Gastonia MSA, NC-SC	Y	27450 FQ	32850 MW	38510 TQ	USBLS	5/15
Metals and Plastics	Raleigh MSA, NC	Y	20120 FQ	24120 MW	32380 TQ	USBLS	5/15
Metals and Plastics	North Dakota	Y	32840 FQ	39840 MW	48520 TQ	USBLS	5/15

AE	Average entry wage	AWR	Average wage range	H	Hourly	LR	Low end range	MTC	Median total compensation	TCC	Total cash compensation
AEX	Average experienced wage	B	Biweekly	HI	Highest wage paid	M	Monthly	MW	Median wage paid	TQ	Third quartile wage
ATC	Average total compensation	D	Daily	HR	High end range	MCC	Median cash compensation	MWR	Median wage range	W	Weekly
AW	Average wage paid	FQ	First quartile wage	LO	Lowest wage paid	ME	Median entry wage	S	See annotated source	Y	Yearly

Occupation/Type/Industry	Location	Per	Low	Mid	High	Source	Date
Plating and Coating Machine							
Setter, Operator, and Tender							
Metals and Plastics	Ohio	Y	23210 FQ	28470 MW	35400 TQ	USBLS	5/15
Metals and Plastics	Cincinnati MSA, OH-KY-IN	Y	27190 FQ	32730 MW	40130 TQ	USBLS	5/15
Metals and Plastics	Cleveland-Elyria MSA, OH	Y	22730 FQ	27510 MW	33850 TQ	USBLS	5/15
Metals and Plastics	Columbus MSA, OH	Y	25800 FQ	31450 MW	36830 TQ	USBLS	5/15
Metals and Plastics	Oklahoma	Y	28720 FQ	35440 MW	47990 TQ	USBLS	5/15
Metals and Plastics	Oklahoma City MSA, OK	Y	31510 FQ	43030 MW	53330 TQ	USBLS	5/15
Metals and Plastics	Tulsa MSA, OK	Y	28460 FQ	33820 MW	45880 TQ	USBLS	5/15
Metals and Plastics	Oregon	H	14.61 FQ	17.24 MW	19.57 TQ	ORBLS	2016
Metals and Plastics	Portland-Vancouver-Hillsboro MSA, OR-WA	Y	30970 FQ	35720 MW	41160 TQ	USBLS	5/15
Metals and Plastics	Pennsylvania	Y	28680 FQ	35370 MW	44500 TQ	USBLS	5/15
Metals and Plastics	Allentown-Bethlehem-Easton MSA, PA-NJ	Y	25500 FQ	29020 MW	34840 TQ	USBLS	5/15
Metals and Plastics	Montgomery County-Bucks County-Chester County PMSA, PA	Y	33390 FQ	39990 MW	48780 TQ	USBLS	5/15
Metals and Plastics	Philadelphia PMSA, PA	Y	31080 FQ	41110 MW	48030 TQ	USBLS	5/15
Metals and Plastics	Pittsburgh MSA, PA	Y	31740 FQ	36880 MW	44940 TQ	USBLS	5/15
Metals and Plastics	Rhode Island	Y	23700 FQ	28790 MW	35910 TQ	USBLS	5/15
Metals and Plastics	Providence-Warwick MSA, RI-MA	Y	24630 FQ	29810 MW	37470 TQ	USBLS	5/15
Metals and Plastics	South Carolina	Y	28130 FQ	34120 MW	39400 TQ	USBLS	5/15
Metals and Plastics	Greenville-Anderson-Mauldin MSA, SC	Y	30440 FQ	34020 MW	37240 TQ	USBLS	5/15
Metals and Plastics	Tennessee	Y	21570 FQ	25890 MW	30490 TQ	USBLS	5/15
Metals and Plastics	Knoxville MSA, TN	Y	20570 FQ	24070 MW	32020 TQ	USBLS	5/15
Metals and Plastics	Memphis MSA, TN-MS-AR	Y	23900 FQ	30530 MW	37900 TQ	USBLS	5/15
Metals and Plastics	Nashville-Davidson–Murfreesboro–Franklin MSA, TN	Y	21810 FQ	26320 MW	29240 TQ	USBLS	5/15
Metals and Plastics	Texas	Y	22430 FQ	26680 MW	33790 TQ	USBLS	5/15
Metals and Plastics	Austin-Round Rock MSA, TX	Y	22080 FQ	24940 MW	34810 TQ	USBLS	5/15
Metals and Plastics	Dallas-Plano-Irving PMSA, TX	Y	22080 FQ	25810 MW	33680 TQ	USBLS	5/15
Metals and Plastics	Fort Worth-Arlington PMSA, TX	Y	23220 FQ	27780 MW	34240 TQ	USBLS	5/15
Metals and Plastics	Houston-The Woodlands-Sugar Land MSA, TX	Y	22610 FQ	26390 MW	33320 TQ	USBLS	5/15
Metals and Plastics	San Antonio-New Braunfels MSA, TX	Y	23340 FQ	28050 MW	35920 TQ	USBLS	5/15
Metals and Plastics	Utah	Y	27550 FQ	34590 MW	44900 TQ	USBLS	5/15
Metals and Plastics	Salt Lake City MSA, UT	Y	28910 FQ	34020 MW	38080 TQ	USBLS	5/15
Metals and Plastics	Vermont	Y	28980 FQ	33580 MW	37640 TQ	USBLS	5/15
Metals and Plastics	Virginia	Y	25650 FQ	32570 MW	39780 TQ	USBLS	5/15
Metals and Plastics	Richmond MSA, VA	Y	27920 FQ	32460 MW	38090 TQ	USBLS	5/15
Metals and Plastics	Virginia Beach-Norfolk-Newport News MSA, VA-NC	Y	24340 FQ	35680 MW	48700 TQ	USBLS	5/15
Metals and Plastics	Washington	H	13.97 FQ	17.37 MW	22.78 TQ	WABLS	3/16
Metals and Plastics	Seattle-Bellevue-Everett PMSA, WA	H	13.94 FQ	17.01 MW	22.99 TQ	WABLS	3/16
Metals and Plastics	Tacoma-Lakewood PMSA, WA	H	13.22 FQ	14.80 MW	17.58 TQ	WABLS	3/16
Metals and Plastics	West Virginia	Y	33170 FQ	37520 MW	47500 TQ	USBLS	5/15
Metals and Plastics	Wisconsin	Y	25610 FQ	30960 MW	39320 TQ	USBLS	5/15
Metals and Plastics	Milwaukee-Waukesha-West Allis MSA, WI	Y	24750 FQ	30400 MW	41070 TQ	USBLS	5/15
Metals and Plastics	Puerto Rico	Y	16860 FQ	18070 MW	19280 TQ	USBLS	5/15
Metals and Plastics	San Juan-Carolina-Caguas MSA, PR	Y	16860 FQ	18070 MW	19280 TQ	USBLS	5/15
Playground Equipment							
Supervisor							
Municipal Government	Los Angeles, CA	Y			83970 HI	CACIT	6/23/16
Plumber, Pipefitter, and							
Steamfitter	Alabama	Y	30429 AE	42094 AW	47937 AEX	ALBLS	6/16
	Birmingham-Hoover MSA, AL	Y	34574 AE	43668 AW	48215 AEX	ALBLS	6/16
	Alaska	Y	55160 FQ	69600 MW	85230 TQ	USBLS	5/15
	Anchorage MSA, AK	Y	51450 FQ	66030 MW	81890 TQ	USBLS	5/15
	Arizona	Y	37530 FQ	46700 MW	64120 TQ	USBLS	5/15

AE	Average entry wage	AWR	Average wage range	H	Hourly	LR	Low end range	MTC	Median total compensation	TCC	Total cash compensation
AEX	Average experienced wage	B	Biweekly	HI	Highest wage paid	M	Monthly	MW	Median wage paid	TQ	Third quartile wage
ATC	Average total compensation	D	Daily	HR	High end range	MCC	Median cash compensation	MWR	Median wage range	W	Weekly
AW	Average wage paid	FQ	First quartile wage	LO	Lowest wage paid	ME	Median entry wage	S	See annotated source	Y	Yearly

Occupation/Type/Industry	Location	Per	Low	Mid	High	Source	Date
Plumber, Pipefitter, and Steamfitter	Phoenix-Mesa-Scottsdale MSA, AZ	Y	38790 FQ	48090 MW	65990 TQ	USBLS	5/15
	Tucson MSA, AZ	Y	33850 FQ	39940 MW	47910 TQ	USBLS	5/15
	Arkansas	Y	27680 FQ	35360 MW	44500 TQ	USBLS	5/15
	Little Rock-North Little Rock-Conway MSA, AR	Y	29600 FQ	39710 MW	46460 TQ	USBLS	5/15
	California	H	19.23 FQ	26.65 MW	36.32 TQ	CABLS	1/16-3/16
	Anaheim-Santa Ana-Irvine PMSA, CA	H	18.80 FQ	27.60 MW	38.05 TQ	CABLS	1/16-3/16
	Los Angeles-Long Beach-Glendale PMSA, CA	H	17.75 FQ	25.15 MW	33.44 TQ	CABLS	1/16-3/16
	Oakland-Hayward-Berkeley PMSA, CA	H	26.01 FQ	34.52 MW	51.12 TQ	CABLS	1/16-3/16
	Riverside-San Bernardino-Ontario MSA, CA	H	17.28 FQ	24.22 MW	30.16 TQ	CABLS	1/16-3/16
	Sacramento–Roseville–Arden-Arcade MSA, CA	H	19.27 FQ	24.84 MW	37.91 TQ	CABLS	1/16-3/16
	San Diego-Carlsbad MSA, CA	H	20.33 FQ	26.65 MW	33.06 TQ	CABLS	1/16-3/16
	San Francisco-Redwood City-South San Francisco PMSA, CA	H	17.91 FQ	27.80 MW	46.50 TQ	CABLS	1/16-3/16
	Colorado	Y	37610 FQ	47700 MW	60800 TQ	USBLS	5/15
	Denver-Aurora-Lakewood MSA, CO	Y	37140 FQ	48100 MW	64310 TQ	USBLS	5/15
	Connecticut	Y		58565 MW		CTBLS	1/16-3/16
	Bridgeport-Stamford-Norwalk MSA, CT	Y	34000 FQ	52170 MW	62820 TQ	USBLS	5/15
	Hartford-West Hartford-East Hartford MSA, CT	Y	46590 FQ	57990 MW	71550 TQ	USBLS	5/15
	Delaware	Y	46790 FQ	57120 MW	68560 TQ	USBLS	5/15
	Wilmington PMSA, DE-MD-NJ	Y	48180 FQ	58170 MW	68880 TQ	USBLS	5/15
	District of Columbia	Y	53370 FQ	64960 MW	82380 TQ	USBLS	5/15
	Washington-Arlington-Alexandria PMSA, DC-VA-MD-WV	Y	40430 FQ	54250 MW	68540 TQ	USBLS	5/15
	Florida	H	13.29 AE	18.49 MW	22.43 AEX	FLBLS	7/16-9/16
	Fort Lauderdale-Pompano Beach-Deerfield Beach PMSA, FL	H	14.68 AE	20.11 MW	23.53 AEX	FLBLS	7/16-9/16
	Miami-Miami Beach-Kendall PMSA, FL	H	13.92 AE	19.82 MW	23.53 AEX	FLBLS	7/16-9/16
	Orlando-Kissimmee-Sanford MSA, FL	H	12.37 AE	17.19 MW	20.55 AEX	FLBLS	7/16-9/16
	Tampa-St. Petersburg-Clearwater MSA, FL	H	12.28 AE	18.22 MW	21.60 AEX	FLBLS	7/16-9/16
	Georgia	Y	33020 FQ	42240 MW	53320 TQ	USBLS	5/15
	Atlanta-Sandy Springs-Roswell MSA, GA	Y	35450 FQ	44260 MW	56350 TQ	USBLS	5/15
	Augusta-Richmond County MSA, GA-SC	Y	29440 FQ	40330 MW	58350 TQ	USBLS	5/15
	Hawaii	Y	50190 FQ	65320 MW	80820 TQ	USBLS	5/15
	Urban Honolulu MSA, HI	Y	49140 FQ	62810 MW	79870 TQ	USBLS	5/15
	Idaho	Y	35490 FQ	48340 MW	58210 TQ	USBLS	5/15
	Boise City MSA, ID	Y	42800 FQ	52660 MW	59630 TQ	USBLS	5/15
	Illinois	Y	54590 FQ	76040 MW	92660 TQ	USBLS	5/15
	Chicago-Naperville-Arlington Heights PMSA, IL	Y	60030 FQ	82730 MW	96200 TQ	USBLS	5/15
	Lake County-Kenosha County PMSA, IL-WI	Y	38570 FQ	59710 MW	90210 TQ	USBLS	5/15
	Indiana	Y	42700 FQ	58020 MW	73770 TQ	USBLS	5/15
	Gary PMSA, IN	Y	79270 FQ	88430 MW	97220 TQ	USBLS	5/15
	Indianapolis-Carmel-Anderson MSA, IN	Y	40670 FQ	53550 MW	63630 TQ	USBLS	5/15
	Iowa	Y	35150 FQ	46880 MW	58930 TQ	USBLS	5/15
	Des Moines-West Des Moines MSA, IA	Y	42520 FQ	54000 MW	67850 TQ	USBLS	5/15
	Kansas	Y	36640 FQ	49380 MW	60620 TQ	USBLS	5/15
	Wichita MSA, KS	Y	37050 FQ	44910 MW	54930 TQ	USBLS	5/15
	Kentucky	Y	32270 FQ	46660 MW	65500 TQ	USBLS	5/15

AE	Average entry wage	AWR	Average wage range	H	Hourly	LR	Low end range	MTC	Median total compensation	TCC	Total cash compensation
AEX	Average experienced wage	B	Biweekly	HI	Highest wage paid	M	Monthly	MW	Median wage paid	TQ	Third quartile wage
ATC	Average total compensation	D	Daily	HR	High end range	MCC	Median cash compensation	MWR	Median wage range	W	Weekly
AW	Average wage paid	FQ	First quartile wage	LO	Lowest wage paid	ME	Median entry wage	S	See annotated source	Y	Yearly

Occupation/Type/Industry	Location	Per	Low	Mid	High	Source	Date
Plumber, Pipefitter, and Steamfitter	Louisville-Jefferson County MSA, KY-IN	Y	34280 FQ	46940 MW	64920 TQ	USBLS	5/15
	Louisiana	Y	38400 FQ	46360 MW	56040 TQ	USBLS	5/15
	Baton Rouge MSA, LA	Y	39360 FQ	46900 MW	56660 TQ	USBLS	5/15
	New Orleans-Metairie MSA, LA	Y	40480 FQ	47270 MW	56770 TQ	USBLS	5/15
	Maine	Y	41640 FQ	49590 MW	56570 TQ	USBLS	5/15
	Portland-South Portland MSA, ME	Y	41720 FQ	49120 MW	56600 TQ	USBLS	5/15
	Maryland	Y	36134 AE	54414 MW	63554 AEX	MDBLS	4/16
	Baltimore-Columbia-Towson MSA, MD	Y	41020 FQ	51040 MW	60930 TQ	USBLS	5/15
	Salisbury MSA, MD-DE	Y	36600 FQ	43930 MW	52870 TQ	USBLS	5/15
	Massachusetts	Y	48140 FQ	63320 MW	92110 TQ	USBLS	5/15
	Boston-Cambridge-Newton NECTA, MA	Y	54130 FQ	74160 MW	106680 TQ	USBLS	5/15
	Worcester MSA, MA-CT	Y	31970 FQ	49610 MW	82550 TQ	USBLS	5/15
	Michigan	Y	40080 FQ	56200 MW	72830 TQ	USBLS	5/15
	Detroit-Dearborn-Livonia PMSA, MI	Y	44740 FQ	60190 MW	72090 TQ	USBLS	5/15
	Grand Rapids-Wyoming MSA, MI	Y	36210 FQ	45760 MW	56290 TQ	USBLS	5/15
	Minnesota	Y	51934 FQ	68805 MW	83930 TQ	MNBLS	1/16-3/16
	Minneapolis-St. Paul-Bloomington MSA, MN-WI	Y	57918 FQ	74435 MW	88440 TQ	MNBLS	1/16-3/16
	Mississippi	Y	31110 FQ	40360 MW	53620 TQ	USBLS	5/15
	Jackson MSA, MS	Y	27590 FQ	33850 MW	42900 TQ	USBLS	5/15
	Missouri	Y	43470 FQ	63640 MW	86230 TQ	USBLS	5/15
	Kansas City MSA, MO-KS	Y	46440 FQ	60220 MW	79670 TQ	USBLS	5/15
	St. Louis MSA, MO-IL	Y	59210 FQ	75820 MW	89870 TQ	USBLS	5/15
	Montana	Y	45090 FQ	57010 MW	69540 TQ	USBLS	5/15
	Billings MSA, MT	Y	52350 FQ	66480 MW	73990 TQ	USBLS	5/15
	Nebraska	Y	39835 FQ	52750 MW	69315 TQ	NEBLS	7/16-9/16
	Omaha-Council Bluffs MSA, NE-IA	Y	46960 FQ	62890 MW	73525 TQ	NEBLS	7/16-9/16
	Nevada	Y	38410 FQ	47320 MW	60300 TQ	USBLS	5/15
	Las Vegas-Henderson-Paradise MSA, NV	Y	38760 FQ	47640 MW	60850 TQ	USBLS	5/15
	New Hampshire	H	18.72 AE	26.23 MW	29.26 AEX	NHBLS	6/16
	Manchester NECTA, NH	H	17.48 AE	26.07 MW	28.83 AEX	NHBLS	6/16
	Nashua NECTA, NH-MA	Y	45560 FQ	55270 MW	61950 TQ	USBLS	5/15
	New Jersey	Y	48270 FQ	62450 MW	86490 TQ	USBLS	5/15
	Camden PMSA, NJ	Y	44850 FQ	58070 MW	89880 TQ	USBLS	5/15
	Newark PMSA, NJ-PA	Y	52230 FQ	60820 MW	75910 TQ	USBLS	5/15
	Trenton MSA, NJ	Y	62050 FQ	83460 MW	93530 TQ	USBLS	5/15
	New Mexico	Y	34060 FQ	43050 MW	56020 TQ	USBLS	5/15
	Albuquerque MSA, NM	Y	36510 FQ	45830 MW	58690 TQ	USBLS	5/15
	New York	Y	40870 AE	66180 MW	90060 AEX	NYBLS	1/16-3/16
	Buffalo-Cheektowaga-Niagara Falls MSA, NY	Y	40520 FQ	57150 MW	72020 TQ	USBLS	5/15
	Nassau County-Suffolk County PMSA, NY	Y	55050 FQ	77330 MW	118650 TQ	USBLS	5/15
	New York-Jersey City-White Plains PMSA, NY-NJ	Y	46560 FQ	67130 MW	101150 TQ	USBLS	5/15
	Rochester MSA, NY	Y	39470 FQ	54980 MW	70260 TQ	USBLS	5/15
	North Carolina	Y	33170 FQ	39600 MW	47480 TQ	USBLS	5/15
	Charlotte-Concord-Gastonia MSA, NC-SC	Y	32160 FQ	37850 MW	45950 TQ	USBLS	5/15
	Raleigh MSA, NC	Y	36980 FQ	44450 MW	53580 TQ	USBLS	5/15
	North Dakota	Y	38730 FQ	51150 MW	60040 TQ	USBLS	5/15
	Fargo MSA, ND-MN	Y	34630 FQ	44420 MW	55090 TQ	USBLS	5/15
	Ohio	Y	38760 FQ	51780 MW	67330 TQ	USBLS	5/15
	Cincinnati MSA, OH-KY-IN	Y	36490 FQ	51000 MW	62300 TQ	USBLS	5/15
	Cleveland-Elyria MSA, OH	Y	40320 FQ	53700 MW	66490 TQ	USBLS	5/15
	Columbus MSA, OH	Y	37290 FQ	49010 MW	70090 TQ	USBLS	5/15
	Oklahoma	Y	32960 FQ	43400 MW	60180 TQ	USBLS	5/15
	Oklahoma City MSA, OK	Y	32390 FQ	44870 MW	64700 TQ	USBLS	5/15
	Tulsa MSA, OK	Y	38740 FQ	47180 MW	61390 TQ	USBLS	5/15
	Oregon	H	27.38 FQ	35.48 MW	44.65 TQ	ORBLS	2016
	Portland-Vancouver-Hillsboro MSA, OR-WA	Y	60350 FQ	76480 MW	94280 TQ	USBLS	5/15

AE Average entry wage	**AWR** Average wage range	**H** Hourly	**LR** Low end range	**MTC** Median total compensation	**TCC** Total cash compensation
AEX Average experienced wage	**B** Biweekly	**HI** Highest wage paid	**M** Monthly	**MW** Median wage paid	**TQ** Third quartile wage
ATC Average total compensation	**D** Daily	**HR** High end range	**MCC** Median cash compensation	**MWR** Median wage range	**W** Weekly
AW Average wage paid	**FQ** First quartile wage	**LO** Lowest wage paid	**ME** Median entry wage	**S** See annotated source	**Y** Yearly

Occupation/Type/Industry	Location	Per	Low	Mid	High	Source	Date
Plumber, Pipefitter, and Steamfitter	Pennsylvania	Y	40510 FQ	52080 MW	71600 TQ	USBLS	5/15
	Allentown-Bethlehem-Easton MSA, PA-NJ	Y	42220 FQ	53910 MW	83820 TQ	USBLS	5/15
	Harrisburg-Carlisle MSA, PA	Y	36060 FQ	42910 MW	52430 TQ	USBLS	5/15
	Montgomery County-Bucks County-Chester County PMSA, PA	Y	47880 FQ	62420 MW	90450 TQ	USBLS	5/15
	Philadelphia PMSA, PA	Y	46820 FQ	61040 MW	86740 TQ	USBLS	5/15
	Pittsburgh MSA, PA	Y	44500 FQ	61070 MW	75400 TQ	USBLS	5/15
	Rhode Island	Y	39190 FQ	48970 MW	62020 TQ	USBLS	5/15
	Providence-Warwick MSA, RI-MA	Y	39060 FQ	48590 MW	61570 TQ	USBLS	5/15
	South Carolina	Y	34210 FQ	42300 MW	48910 TQ	USBLS	5/15
	Charleston-North Charleston MSA, SC	Y	38910 FQ	44190 MW	49050 TQ	USBLS	5/15
	Columbia MSA, SC	Y	35090 FQ	43950 MW	54980 TQ	USBLS	5/15
	Greenville-Anderson-Mauldin MSA, SC	Y	30490 FQ	41600 MW	48170 TQ	USBLS	5/15
	South Dakota	Y	35050 FQ	42480 MW	49930 TQ	USBLS	5/15
	Sioux Falls MSA, SD	Y	40190 FQ	46310 MW	56040 TQ	USBLS	5/15
	Tennessee	Y	36340 FQ	46060 MW	58380 TQ	USBLS	5/15
	Knoxville MSA, TN	Y	34100 FQ	39950 MW	48250 TQ	USBLS	5/15
	Memphis MSA, TN-MS-AR	Y	40440 FQ	52970 MW	60350 TQ	USBLS	5/15
	Nashville-Davidson–Murfreesboro–Franklin MSA, TN	Y	38850 FQ	48460 MW	70400 TQ	USBLS	5/15
	Texas	Y	33850 FQ	44580 MW	56070 TQ	USBLS	5/15
	Austin-Round Rock MSA, TX	Y	34990 FQ	44730 MW	55760 TQ	USBLS	5/15
	Dallas-Plano-Irving PMSA, TX	Y	29730 FQ	41110 MW	52770 TQ	USBLS	5/15
	Fort Worth-Arlington PMSA, TX	Y	38410 FQ	47460 MW	58490 TQ	USBLS	5/15
	Houston-The Woodlands-Sugar Land MSA, TX	Y	37560 FQ	49250 MW	60530 TQ	USBLS	5/15
	San Antonio-New Braunfels MSA, TX	Y	38970 FQ	44880 MW	50350 TQ	USBLS	5/15
	Utah	Y	35840 FQ	50480 MW	58900 TQ	USBLS	5/15
	Ogden-Clearfield MSA, UT	Y	35470 FQ	46720 MW	56540 TQ	USBLS	5/15
	Provo-Orem MSA, UT	Y	40710 FQ	51710 MW	57390 TQ	USBLS	5/15
	Salt Lake City MSA, UT	Y	35720 FQ	52320 MW	61040 TQ	USBLS	5/15
	Vermont	Y	40080 FQ	48830 MW	58370 TQ	USBLS	5/15
	Burlington-South Burlington MSA, VT	Y	43300 FQ	51660 MW	60230 TQ	USBLS	5/15
	Virginia	Y	35810 FQ	44170 MW	53540 TQ	USBLS	5/15
	Richmond MSA, VA	Y	40550 FQ	47790 MW	57960 TQ	USBLS	5/15
	Virginia Beach-Norfolk-Newport News MSA, VA-NC	Y	36060 FQ	45050 MW	52580 TQ	USBLS	5/15
	Washington	H	21.64 FQ	29.75 MW	41.56 TQ	WABLS	3/16
	Seattle-Bellevue-Everett PMSA, WA	H	21.23 FQ	31.13 MW	44.44 TQ	WABLS	3/16
	Tacoma-Lakewood PMSA, WA	H	27.86 FQ	34.56 MW	43.50 TQ	WABLS	3/16
	West Virginia	Y	32500 FQ	45030 MW	62730 TQ	USBLS	5/15
	Huntington-Ashland MSA, WV-KY-OH	Y	36090 FQ	59740 MW	72950 TQ	USBLS	5/15
	Wisconsin	Y	51170 FQ	68230 MW	81530 TQ	USBLS	5/15
	Madison MSA, WI	Y	60110 FQ	77630 MW	89530 TQ	USBLS	5/15
	Milwaukee-Waukesha-West Allis MSA, WI	Y	63850 FQ	74860 MW	87740 TQ	USBLS	5/15
	Wyoming	Y	33770 FQ	43720 MW	56540 TQ	USBLS	5/15
	Cheyenne MSA, WY	Y	34470 FQ	43680 MW	53520 TQ	USBLS	5/15
	Puerto Rico	Y	17320 FQ	19150 MW	23430 TQ	USBLS	5/15
	San Juan-Carolina-Caguas MSA, PR	Y	17440 FQ	19380 MW	24520 TQ	USBLS	5/15
	Virgin Islands	Y	29160 FQ	42180 MW	46480 TQ	USBLS	5/15
	Guam	Y	28970 FQ	33390 MW	37980 TQ	USBLS	5/15
Podiatrist	Alabama	Y	59416 AE	124327 AW	156792 AEX	ALBLS	6/16
	Arizona	Y	73040 FQ	100320 MW	150840 TQ	USBLS	5/15
	Phoenix-Mesa-Scottsdale MSA, AZ	Y	75180 FQ	101800 MW	157120 TQ	USBLS	5/15
	Arkansas	Y	71920 FQ	113300 MW		USBLS	5/15
	California	H	25.40 FQ	49.58 MW	75.27 TQ	CABLS	1/16-3/16

AE	Average entry wage	AWR	Average wage range	H	Hourly	LR	Low end range	MTC	Median total compensation	TCC	Total cash compensation
AEX	Average experienced wage	B	Biweekly	HI	Highest wage paid	M	Monthly	MW	Median wage paid	TQ	Third quartile wage
ATC	Average total compensation	D	Daily	HR	High end range	MCC	Median cash compensation	MWR	Median wage range	W	Weekly
AW	Average wage paid	FQ	First quartile wage	LO	Lowest wage paid	ME	Median entry wage	S	See annotated source	Y	Yearly

Occupation/Type/Industry	Location	Per	Low	Mid	High	Source	Date
Podiatrist	Anaheim-Santa Ana-Irvine PMSA, CA	H	46.17 FQ	54.42 MW	66.63 TQ	CABLS	1/16-3/16
	Los Angeles-Long Beach-Glendale PMSA, CA	H	19.97 FQ	25.93 MW	50.97 TQ	CABLS	1/16-3/16
	Oakland-Hayward-Berkeley PMSA, CA	H	67.42 FQ	75.24 MW	83.22 TQ	CABLS	1/16-3/16
	Riverside-San Bernardino-Ontario MSA, CA	H	41.33 FQ	62.51 MW	89.60 TQ	CABLS	1/16-3/16
	Sacramento–Roseville–Arden-Arcade MSA, CA	H	56.65 FQ	97.13 AW		CABLS	1/16-3/16
	San Diego-Carlsbad MSA, CA	H	23.08 FQ	59.74 MW	75.45 TQ	CABLS	1/16-3/16
	San Francisco-Redwood City-South San Francisco PMSA, CA	H	28.25 FQ	57.06 MW	79.95 TQ	CABLS	1/16-3/16
	Colorado	Y	54580 FQ	61040 MW	107450 TQ	USBLS	5/15
	Denver-Aurora-Lakewood MSA, CO	Y	53920 FQ	57760 MW	61600 TQ	USBLS	5/15
	Connecticut	Y		144910 MW		CTBLS	1/16-3/16
	Delaware	Y	130060 FQ	153620 MW	183630 TQ	USBLS	5/15
	Wilmington PMSA, DE-MD-NJ	Y	120220 FQ	147970 MW	167580 TQ	USBLS	5/15
	District of Columbia	Y	108440 FQ	125210 MW	149250 TQ	USBLS	5/15
	Washington-Arlington-Alexandria PMSA, DC-VA-MD-WV	Y	107640 FQ	127800 MW	171150 TQ	USBLS	5/15
	Florida	H	26.31 AE	52.75 MW	70.25 AEX	FLBLS	7/16-9/16
	Fort Lauderdale-Pompano Beach-Deerfield Beach PMSA, FL	H	33.31 AE	61.94 MW	80.89 AEX	FLBLS	7/16-9/16
	Miami-Miami Beach-Kendall PMSA, FL	H	23.54 AE	53.09 MW	61.71 AEX	FLBLS	7/16-9/16
	Tampa-St. Petersburg-Clearwater MSA, FL	H	27.22 AE	43.56 MW	55.84 AEX	FLBLS	7/16-9/16
	Georgia	Y	82850 FQ	141580 MW		USBLS	5/15
	Atlanta-Sandy Springs-Roswell MSA, GA	Y	93370 FQ	157620 MW		USBLS	5/15
	Hawaii	Y		268140 AW		USBLS	5/15
	Urban Honolulu MSA, HI	Y		282600 AW		USBLS	5/15
	Idaho	Y	70060 FQ	93270 MW	152890 TQ	USBLS	5/15
	Illinois	Y	80840 FQ	144140 MW		USBLS	5/15
	Chicago-Naperville-Arlington Heights PMSA, IL	Y	92420 FQ	158700 MW		USBLS	5/15
	Indiana	Y	65060 FQ	97810 MW	156590 TQ	USBLS	5/15
	Indianapolis-Carmel-Anderson MSA, IN	Y	68290 FQ	96870 MW	173200 TQ	USBLS	5/15
	Iowa	Y	63930 FQ	128820 MW	152200 TQ	USBLS	5/15
	Des Moines-West Des Moines MSA, IA	Y	61720 FQ	131080 MW	144490 TQ	USBLS	5/15
	Kansas	Y	86800 FQ	109240 MW	146970 TQ	USBLS	5/15
	Kentucky	Y	85940 FQ	119910 MW	177780 TQ	USBLS	5/15
	Louisville-Jefferson County MSA, KY-IN	Y	74110 FQ	98110 MW	177150 TQ	USBLS	5/15
	Louisiana	Y	94310 FQ	128860 MW	179740 TQ	USBLS	5/15
	New Orleans-Metairie MSA, LA	Y	89560 FQ	125140 MW	170270 TQ	USBLS	5/15
	Maryland	Y	67434 AE	166201 MW	215585 AEX	MDBLS	4/16
	Baltimore-Columbia-Towson MSA, MD	Y	64920 FQ	79090 MW	158700 TQ	USBLS	5/15
	Massachusetts	Y	101650 FQ	149440 MW		USBLS	5/15
	Boston-Cambridge-Newton NECTA, MA	Y	89840 FQ	163180 MW		USBLS	5/15
	Worcester MSA, MA-CT	Y	113580 FQ	126370 MW	173650 TQ	USBLS	5/15
	Michigan	Y	51830 FQ	103970 MW	126420 TQ	USBLS	5/15
	Detroit-Dearborn-Livonia PMSA, MI	Y	44800 FQ	53400 MW	134940 TQ	USBLS	5/15
	Minnesota	Y	120674 FQ	171591 MW		MNBLS	1/16-3/16
	Minneapolis-St. Paul-Bloomington MSA, MN-WI	Y	144565 FQ	175764 MW		MNBLS	1/16-3/16
	Missouri	Y	106200 FQ	134070 MW		USBLS	5/15
	Kansas City MSA, MO-KS	Y	76710 FQ	112210 MW	150190 TQ	USBLS	5/15
	St. Louis MSA, MO-IL	Y	116280 FQ	196510 AW		USBLS	5/15
	Nebraska	Y	106470 FQ	150835 MW		NEBLS	7/16-9/16

AE	Average entry wage	**AWR**	Average wage range	**H**	Hourly	**LR**	Low end range	**MTC** Median total compensation	**TCC** Total cash compensation
AEX	Average experienced wage	**B**	Biweekly	**HI**	Highest wage paid	**M**	Monthly	**MW** Median wage paid	**TQ** Third quartile wage
ATC	Average total compensation	**D**	Daily	**HR**	High end range	**MCC**	Median cash compensation	**MWR** Median wage range	**W** Weekly
AW	Average wage paid	**FQ**	First quartile wage	**LO**	Lowest wage paid	**ME**	Median entry wage	**S** See annotated source	**Y** Yearly

1257

Occupation/Type/Industry	Location	Per	Low	Mid	High	Source	Date
Podiatrist	Omaha-Council Bluffs MSA, NE-IA	Y	93765 FQ	103330 MW	115340 TQ	NEBLS	7/16-9/16
	Nevada	Y	118360 FQ	138000 MW	150840 TQ	USBLS	5/15
	New Jersey	Y	87890 FQ	131430 MW	172100 TQ	USBLS	5/15
	Camden PMSA, NJ	Y	86230 FQ	99850 MW	123410 TQ	USBLS	5/15
	Newark PMSA, NJ-PA	Y	71080 FQ	97060 MW		USBLS	5/15
	New Mexico	Y	97370 FQ	141030 MW		USBLS	5/15
	Albuquerque MSA, NM	Y	43380 FQ	134820 MW		USBLS	5/15
	New York	Y	81130 AE	124930 MW	177090 AEX	NYBLS	1/16-3/16
	Buffalo-Cheektowaga-Niagara Falls MSA, NY	Y	115870 FQ	154560 MW		USBLS	5/15
	Nassau County-Suffolk County PMSA, NY	Y	91430 FQ	120850 MW		USBLS	5/15
	New York-Jersey City-White Plains PMSA, NY-NJ	Y	95020 FQ	126350 MW	161830 TQ	USBLS	5/15
	North Carolina	Y	108070 FQ	148130 MW		USBLS	5/15
	Charlotte-Concord-Gastonia MSA, NC-SC	Y	118660 FQ	159460 MW		USBLS	5/15
	Ohio	Y	85440 FQ	117310 MW	166230 TQ	USBLS	5/15
	Cincinnati MSA, OH-KY-IN	Y	57710 FQ	73290 MW	141570 TQ	USBLS	5/15
	Cleveland-Elyria MSA, OH	Y	59280 FQ	116590 MW	185730 TQ	USBLS	5/15
	Columbus MSA, OH	Y	106580 FQ	117170 MW	128140 TQ	USBLS	5/15
	Oklahoma	Y	30850 FQ	123100 MW	153390 TQ	USBLS	5/15
	Oregon	H	33.79 FQ	50.16 MW	77.41 TQ	ORBLS	2016
	Pennsylvania	Y	78760 FQ	116300 MW	172400 TQ	USBLS	5/15
	Montgomery County-Bucks County-Chester County PMSA, PA	Y	39250 FQ	92010 MW	127330 TQ	USBLS	5/15
	Philadelphia PMSA, PA	Y	62130 FQ	150060 MW		USBLS	5/15
	Pittsburgh MSA, PA	Y	81940 FQ	117300 MW	175780 TQ	USBLS	5/15
	Rhode Island	Y	84770 FQ	97060 MW	118570 TQ	USBLS	5/15
	Providence-Warwick MSA, RI-MA	Y	79530 FQ	94890 MW	119120 TQ	USBLS	5/15
	South Carolina	Y	87970 FQ	127430 MW	167740 TQ	USBLS	5/15
	Tennessee	Y	90820 FQ	120670 MW	153530 TQ	USBLS	5/15
	Nashville-Davidson–Murfreesboro–Franklin MSA, TN	Y	96850 FQ	127580 MW		USBLS	5/15
	Texas	Y	68700 FQ	150830 MW		USBLS	5/15
	Houston-The Woodlands-Sugar Land MSA, TX	Y	86610 FQ	155380 MW		USBLS	5/15
	San Antonio-New Braunfels MSA, TX	Y	68050 FQ	191370 AW		USBLS	5/15
	Utah	Y	64710 FQ	93680 MW	132210 TQ	USBLS	5/15
	Ogden-Clearfield MSA, UT	Y	85750 FQ	92820 MW	109170 TQ	USBLS	5/15
	Virginia	Y	73130 FQ	109390 MW		USBLS	5/15
	Washington	H	47.50 FQ	61.26 MW	70.78 TQ	WABLS	3/16
	Seattle-Bellevue-Everett PMSA, WA	H	56.99 FQ	64.48 MW	71.07 TQ	WABLS	3/16
	Wisconsin	Y	109360 FQ	177680 MW		USBLS	5/15
	Milwaukee-Waukesha-West Allis MSA, WI	Y	119820 FQ	160050 MW		USBLS	5/15
Poet Laureate	Lansing, MI	Y			2000 HI	LSJ19	2017
Police, Fire, and Ambulance Dispatcher	Alabama	Y	24108 AE	33680 AW	38462 AEX	ALBLS	6/16
	Birmingham-Hoover MSA, AL	Y	29774 AE	40100 AW	45264 AEX	ALBLS	6/16
	Alaska	Y	45800 FQ	52950 MW	58390 TQ	USBLS	5/15
	Anchorage MSA, AK	Y	51530 FQ	55470 MW	59650 TQ	USBLS	5/15
	Arizona	Y	35330 FQ	43180 MW	51980 TQ	USBLS	5/15
	Phoenix-Mesa-Scottsdale MSA, AZ	Y	40610 FQ	48140 MW	55690 TQ	USBLS	5/15
	Tucson MSA, AZ	Y	33410 FQ	37210 MW	43220 TQ	USBLS	5/15
	Arkansas	Y	21730 FQ	26700 MW	30890 TQ	USBLS	5/15
	Little Rock-North Little Rock-Conway MSA, AR	Y	25310 FQ	28920 MW	33500 TQ	USBLS	5/15
	California	H	23.08 FQ	28.12 MW	32.97 TQ	CABLS	1/16-3/16
	Anaheim-Santa Ana-Irvine PMSA, CA	H	28.90 FQ	33.89 MW	37.54 TQ	CABLS	1/16-3/16
	Los Angeles-Long Beach-Glendale PMSA, CA	H	22.23 FQ	27.78 MW	31.03 TQ	CABLS	1/16-3/16

AE	Average entry wage	AWR	Average wage range	H	Hourly
AEX	Average experienced wage	B	Biweekly	HI	Highest wage paid
ATC	Average total compensation	D	Daily	HR	High end range
AW	Average wage paid	FQ	First quartile wage	LO	Lowest wage paid

LR	Low end range	MTC	Median total compensation
M	Monthly	MW	Median wage paid
MCC	Median cash compensation	MWR	Median wage range
ME	Median entry wage	S	See annotated source

TCC	Total cash compensation
TQ	Third quartile wage
W	Weekly
Y	Yearly

Police, Fire, and Ambulance Dispatcher

Occupation/Type/Industry	Location	Per	Low	Mid	High	Source	Date
Police, Fire, and Ambulance Dispatcher							
	Oakland-Hayward-Berkeley PMSA, CA	H	29.64 FQ	35.08 MW	39.45 TQ	CABLS	1/16-3/16
	Riverside-San Bernardino-Ontario MSA, CA	H	22.97 FQ	27.38 MW	29.56 TQ	CABLS	1/16-3/16
	Sacramento–Roseville–Arden-Arcade MSA, CA	H	24.92 FQ	28.13 MW	31.03 TQ	CABLS	1/16-3/16
	San Diego-Carlsbad MSA, CA	H	22.48 FQ	26.55 MW	30.83 TQ	CABLS	1/16-3/16
	San Francisco-Redwood City-South San Francisco PMSA, CA	H	26.44 FQ	30.88 MW	36.94 TQ	CABLS	1/16-3/16
	Colorado	Y	41050 FQ	47710 MW	54610 TQ	USBLS	5/15
	Denver-Aurora-Lakewood MSA, CO	Y	44650 FQ	50190 MW	57460 TQ	USBLS	5/15
	Connecticut	Y		51546 MW		CTBLS	1/16-3/16
	Bridgeport-Stamford-Norwalk MSA, CT	Y	43880 FQ	52250 MW	60440 TQ	USBLS	5/15
	Hartford-West Hartford-East Hartford MSA, CT	Y	43220 FQ	50960 MW	58330 TQ	USBLS	5/15
	Delaware	Y	35160 FQ	41250 MW	48750 TQ	USBLS	5/15
	Wilmington PMSA, DE-MD-NJ	Y	34910 FQ	40380 MW	48090 TQ	USBLS	5/15
	District of Columbia	Y	47770 FQ	65870 MW	70360 TQ	USBLS	5/15
	Washington-Arlington-Alexandria PMSA, DC-VA-MD-WV	Y	39260 FQ	47240 MW	58620 TQ	USBLS	5/15
	Florida	H	13.82 AE	18.31 MW	22.40 AEX	FLBLS	7/16-9/16
	Fort Lauderdale-Pompano Beach-Deerfield Beach PMSA, FL	H	17.75 AE	24.13 MW	26.49 AEX	FLBLS	7/16-9/16
	Miami-Miami Beach-Kendall PMSA, FL	H	17.06 AE	24.31 MW	28.23 AEX	FLBLS	7/16-9/16
	Orlando-Kissimmee-Sanford MSA, FL	H	13.73 AE	17.14 MW	20.22 AEX	FLBLS	7/16-9/16
	Tampa-St. Petersburg-Clearwater MSA, FL	H	15.00 AE	17.98 MW	20.15 AEX	FLBLS	7/16-9/16
	Georgia	Y	25010 FQ	29310 MW	35060 TQ	USBLS	5/15
	Atlanta-Sandy Springs-Roswell MSA, GA	Y	28740 FQ	33700 MW	38280 TQ	USBLS	5/15
	Augusta-Richmond County MSA, GA-SC	Y	21760 FQ	26080 MW	32640 TQ	USBLS	5/15
	Hawaii	Y	40230 FQ	45380 MW	50540 TQ	USBLS	5/15
	Urban Honolulu MSA, HI	Y	41030 FQ	45800 MW	50570 TQ	USBLS	5/15
	Idaho	Y	30730 FQ	35320 MW	41400 TQ	USBLS	5/15
	Boise City MSA, ID	Y	33240 FQ	36750 MW	44080 TQ	USBLS	5/15
	Illinois	Y	35810 FQ	46840 MW	61710 TQ	USBLS	5/15
	Chicago-Naperville-Arlington Heights PMSA, IL	Y	38490 FQ	50360 MW	65630 TQ	USBLS	5/15
	Lake County-Kenosha County PMSA, IL-WI	Y	45110 FQ	54860 MW	62840 TQ	USBLS	5/15
	Indiana	Y	27990 FQ	33820 MW	38460 TQ	USBLS	5/15
	Gary PMSA, IN	Y	31750 FQ	34770 MW	37790 TQ	USBLS	5/15
	Indianapolis-Carmel-Anderson MSA, IN	Y	31800 FQ	36030 MW	41070 TQ	USBLS	5/15
	Iowa	Y	33140 FQ	38790 MW	47370 TQ	USBLS	5/15
	Des Moines-West Des Moines MSA, IA	Y	43380 FQ	52020 MW	58250 TQ	USBLS	5/15
	Kansas	Y	25350 FQ	30130 MW	36230 TQ	USBLS	5/15
	Wichita MSA, KS	Y	28470 FQ	33050 MW	37850 TQ	USBLS	5/15
	Kentucky	Y	24020 FQ	30970 MW	39530 TQ	USBLS	5/15
	Louisville-Jefferson County MSA, KY-IN	Y	30630 FQ	38250 MW	45730 TQ	USBLS	5/15
	Louisiana	Y	23890 FQ	28990 MW	36240 TQ	USBLS	5/15
	Baton Rouge MSA, LA	Y	24970 FQ	35900 MW	44920 TQ	USBLS	5/15
	New Orleans-Metairie MSA, LA	Y	25710 FQ	29480 MW	35280 TQ	USBLS	5/15
	Maine	Y	33040 FQ	38210 MW	45290 TQ	USBLS	5/15
	Portland-South Portland MSA, ME	Y	34310 FQ	41550 MW	47740 TQ	USBLS	5/15
	Maryland	Y	32322 AE	43075 MW	48452 AEX	MDBLS	4/16
	Baltimore-Columbia-Towson MSA, MD	Y	38080 FQ	45240 MW	53910 TQ	USBLS	5/15

AE Average entry wage	**AWR** Average wage range	**H** Hourly	**LR** Low end range	**MTC** Median total compensation	**TCC** Total cash compensation
AEX Average experienced wage	**B** Biweekly	**HI** Highest wage paid	**M** Monthly	**MW** Median wage paid	**TQ** Third quartile wage
ATC Average total compensation	**D** Daily	**HR** High end range	**MCC** Median cash compensation	**MWR** Median wage range	**W** Weekly
AW Average wage paid	**FQ** First quartile wage	**LO** Lowest wage paid	**ME** Median entry wage	**S** See annotated source	**Y** Yearly

Occupation/Type/Industry	Location	Per	Low	Mid	High	Source	Date
Police, Fire, and Ambulance Dispatcher	Salisbury MSA, MD-DE	Y	30550 FQ	35360 MW	39810 TQ	USBLS	5/15
	Massachusetts	Y	36500 FQ	44210 MW	52030 TQ	USBLS	5/15
	Boston-Cambridge-Newton NECTA, MA	Y	38270 FQ	47630 MW	58080 TQ	USBLS	5/15
	Worcester MSA, MA-CT	Y	34810 FQ	41820 MW	48750 TQ	USBLS	5/15
	Michigan	Y	33880 FQ	40410 MW	46850 TQ	USBLS	5/15
	Detroit-Dearborn-Livonia PMSA, MI	Y	34230 FQ	39900 MW	46770 TQ	USBLS	5/15
	Grand Rapids-Wyoming MSA, MI	Y	33100 FQ	41510 MW	49000 TQ	USBLS	5/15
	Minnesota	Y	42837 FQ	49208 MW	58057 TQ	MNBLS	1/16-3/16
	Minneapolis-St. Paul-Bloomington MSA, MN-WI	Y	46569 FQ	54133 MW	61364 TQ	MNBLS	1/16-3/16
	Mississippi	Y	20630 FQ	24310 MW	29020 TQ	USBLS	5/15
	Jackson MSA, MS	Y	20210 FQ	25740 MW	28570 TQ	USBLS	5/15
	Missouri	Y	24830 FQ	32680 MW	40390 TQ	USBLS	5/15
	Kansas City MSA, MO-KS	Y	29970 FQ	36470 MW	44610 TQ	USBLS	5/15
	St. Louis MSA, MO-IL	Y	32110 FQ	37900 MW	47120 TQ	USBLS	5/15
	Montana	Y	29030 FQ	34100 MW	39440 TQ	USBLS	5/15
	Billings MSA, MT	Y	41650 FQ	45080 MW	48510 TQ	USBLS	5/15
	Nebraska	Y	26995 FQ	32480 MW	38940 TQ	NEBLS	7/16-9/16
	Omaha-Council Bluffs MSA, NE-IA	Y	33565 FQ	37575 MW	44335 TQ	NEBLS	7/16-9/16
	Nevada	Y	46870 FQ	58150 MW	69670 TQ	USBLS	5/15
	Las Vegas-Henderson-Paradise MSA, NV	Y	51960 FQ	62670 MW	72790 TQ	USBLS	5/15
	New Hampshire	H	16.40 AE	20.51 MW	22.61 AEX	NHBLS	6/16
	Manchester NECTA, NH	H	17.59 AE	21.88 MW	24.28 AEX	NHBLS	6/16
	Nashua NECTA, NH-MA	Y	35470 FQ	40790 MW	48240 TQ	USBLS	5/15
	New Jersey	Y	33500 FQ	43610 MW	54860 TQ	USBLS	5/15
	Camden PMSA, NJ	Y	29840 FQ	45560 MW	54650 TQ	USBLS	5/15
	Newark PMSA, NJ-PA	Y	38220 FQ	45810 MW	54880 TQ	USBLS	5/15
	Trenton MSA, NJ	Y	44930 FQ	54210 MW	61920 TQ	USBLS	5/15
	New Mexico	Y	27620 FQ	33170 MW	38630 TQ	USBLS	5/15
	New York	Y	32930 AE	45360 MW	52720 AEX	NYBLS	1/16-3/16
	Nassau County-Suffolk County PMSA, NY	Y	39510 FQ	49670 MW	61130 TQ	USBLS	5/15
	New York-Jersey City-White Plains PMSA, NY-NJ	Y	33110 FQ	42290 MW	53490 TQ	USBLS	5/15
	Rochester MSA, NY	Y	36520 FQ	44510 MW	50610 TQ	USBLS	5/15
	North Carolina	Y	28250 FQ	32790 MW	37410 TQ	USBLS	5/15
	Charlotte-Concord-Gastonia MSA, NC-SC	Y	30500 FQ	34650 MW	38540 TQ	USBLS	5/15
	Raleigh MSA, NC	Y	33600 FQ	36500 MW	41610 TQ	USBLS	5/15
	North Dakota	Y	30110 FQ	35830 MW	44570 TQ	USBLS	5/15
	Ohio	Y	33120 FQ	41420 MW	47250 TQ	USBLS	5/15
	Cincinnati MSA, OH-KY-IN	Y	38070 FQ	44110 MW	49850 TQ	USBLS	5/15
	Cleveland-Elyria MSA, OH	Y	37310 FQ	43420 MW	48460 TQ	USBLS	5/15
	Columbus MSA, OH	Y	35140 FQ	42930 MW	48450 TQ	USBLS	5/15
	Oklahoma	Y	22500 FQ	28070 MW	35770 TQ	USBLS	5/15
	Oklahoma City MSA, OK	Y	27440 FQ	34650 MW	45290 TQ	USBLS	5/15
	Tulsa MSA, OK	Y	23460 FQ	28260 MW	34520 TQ	USBLS	5/15
	Oregon	H	22.15 FQ	26.39 MW	30.27 TQ	ORBLS	2016
	Portland-Vancouver-Hillsboro MSA, OR-WA	Y	51100 FQ	59980 MW	70760 TQ	USBLS	5/15
	Pennsylvania	Y	29060 FQ	36690 MW	43530 TQ	USBLS	5/15
	Allentown-Bethlehem-Easton MSA, PA-NJ	Y	34670 FQ	38990 MW	45920 TQ	USBLS	5/15
	Harrisburg-Carlisle MSA, PA	Y	31990 FQ	38130 MW	45040 TQ	USBLS	5/15
	Montgomery County-Bucks County-Chester County PMSA, PA	Y	36570 FQ	43640 MW	51980 TQ	USBLS	5/15
	Philadelphia PMSA, PA	Y	33160 FQ	36760 MW	42760 TQ	USBLS	5/15
	Pittsburgh MSA, PA	Y	18280 FQ	30430 MW	43510 TQ	USBLS	5/15
	Rhode Island	Y	36080 FQ	42350 MW	47310 TQ	USBLS	5/15
	Providence-Warwick MSA, RI-MA	Y	36060 FQ	42450 MW	47730 TQ	USBLS	5/15
	South Carolina	Y	25060 FQ	30070 MW	35650 TQ	USBLS	5/15
	Columbia MSA, SC	Y	25960 FQ	30790 MW	36050 TQ	USBLS	5/15
	Greenville-Anderson-Mauldin MSA, SC	Y	23390 FQ	27420 MW	33470 TQ	USBLS	5/15

AE	Average entry wage	AWR	Average wage range	H	Hourly
AEX	Average experienced wage	B	Biweekly	HI	Highest paid
ATC	Average total compensation	D	Daily	HR	High end range
AW	Average wage paid	FQ	First quartile wage	LO	Lowest wage paid

LR	Low end range	MTC	Median total compensation	TCC	Total cash compensation
M	Monthly	MW	Median wage paid	TQ	Third quartile wage
MCC	Median cash compensation	MWR	Median wage range	W	Weekly
ME	Median entry wage	S	See annotated source	Y	Yearly

Occupation/Type/Industry	Location	Per	Low	Mid	High	Source	Date
Police, Fire, and Ambulance Dispatcher	South Dakota	Y	27400 FQ	31230 MW	36850 TQ	USBLS	5/15
	Tennessee	Y	26650 FQ	32190 MW	39020 TQ	USBLS	5/15
	Knoxville MSA, TN	Y	23580 FQ	30640 MW	36060 TQ	USBLS	5/15
	Memphis MSA, TN-MS-AR	Y	28100 FQ	37220 MW	49060 TQ	USBLS	5/15
	Nashville-Davidson–Murfreesboro–Franklin MSA, TN	Y	29210 FQ	34660 MW	41020 TQ	USBLS	5/15
	Texas	Y	28880 FQ	34710 MW	40900 TQ	USBLS	5/15
	Austin-Round Rock MSA, TX	Y	33050 FQ	38150 MW	45500 TQ	USBLS	5/15
	Dallas-Plano-Irving PMSA, TX	Y	32180 FQ	38030 MW	45490 TQ	USBLS	5/15
	Fort Worth-Arlington PMSA, TX	Y	32930 FQ	36380 MW	40820 TQ	USBLS	5/15
	Houston-The Woodlands-Sugar Land MSA, TX	Y	29400 FQ	35610 MW	43150 TQ	USBLS	5/15
	San Antonio-New Braunfels MSA, TX	Y	31750 FQ	36620 MW	42890 TQ	USBLS	5/15
	Utah	Y	30360 FQ	35150 MW	40300 TQ	USBLS	5/15
	Ogden-Clearfield MSA, UT	Y	30940 FQ	36040 MW	42460 TQ	USBLS	5/15
	Provo-Orem MSA, UT	Y	32140 FQ	36080 MW	42010 TQ	USBLS	5/15
	Vermont	Y	33790 FQ	39510 MW	47130 TQ	USBLS	5/15
	Burlington-South Burlington MSA, VT	Y	34080 FQ	39900 MW	46860 TQ	USBLS	5/15
	Virginia	Y	30940 FQ	36310 MW	44220 TQ	USBLS	5/15
	Richmond MSA, VA	Y	32830 FQ	37470 MW	43890 TQ	USBLS	5/15
	Virginia Beach-Norfolk-Newport News MSA, VA-NC	Y	31980 FQ	36060 MW	41400 TQ	USBLS	5/15
	Washington	H	21.83 FQ	26.56 MW	31.57 TQ	WABLS	3/16
	Seattle-Bellevue-Everett PMSA, WA	H	24.91 FQ	28.90 MW	33.74 TQ	WABLS	3/16
	Tacoma-Lakewood PMSA, WA	H	22.59 FQ	32.73 MW	36.50 TQ	WABLS	3/16
	West Virginia	Y	21960 FQ	25230 MW	30820 TQ	USBLS	5/15
	Huntington-Ashland MSA, WV-KY-OH	Y	22110 FQ	25960 MW	30300 TQ	USBLS	5/15
	Wisconsin	Y	36520 FQ	43010 MW	48430 TQ	USBLS	5/15
	Madison MSA, WI	Y	40970 FQ	45690 MW	51900 TQ	USBLS	5/15
	Milwaukee-Waukesha-West Allis MSA, WI	Y	36760 FQ	43480 MW	49070 TQ	USBLS	5/15
	Wyoming	Y	33180 FQ	38050 MW	45990 TQ	USBLS	5/15
	Puerto Rico	Y	17270 FQ	19150 MW	23600 TQ	USBLS	5/15
	San Juan-Carolina-Caguas MSA, PR	Y	17450 FQ	19480 MW	24090 TQ	USBLS	5/15
Police Agent Municipal Government	Brawley, CA	Y		62193 AW		CACIT	6/28/16
Police Analyst Municipal Government	Morgan Hill, CA	Y			107333 HI	CACIT	6/28/16
Police and Sheriff's Patrol Officer	Alabama	Y	30281 AE	43655 AW	50337 AEX	ALBLS	6/16
	Birmingham-Hoover MSA, AL	Y	34636 AE	49534 AW	56978 AEX	ALBLS	6/16
	Alaska	Y	64330 FQ	77900 MW	90270 TQ	USBLS	5/15
	Anchorage MSA, AK	Y	65990 FQ	81840 MW	91220 TQ	USBLS	5/15
	Arizona	Y	50550 FQ	63800 MW	71510 TQ	USBLS	5/15
	Phoenix-Mesa-Scottsdale MSA, AZ	Y	57300 FQ	66290 MW	73620 TQ	USBLS	5/15
	Tucson MSA, AZ	Y	46380 FQ	55240 MW	64410 TQ	USBLS	5/15
	Arkansas	Y	28880 FQ	35950 MW	45280 TQ	USBLS	5/15
	Little Rock-North Little Rock-Conway MSA, AR	Y	34450 FQ	43340 MW	53370 TQ	USBLS	5/15
	California	H	37.73 FQ	46.52 MW	54.36 TQ	CABLS	1/16-3/16
	Anaheim-Santa Ana-Irvine PMSA, CA	H	41.61 FQ	47.16 MW	54.43 TQ	CABLS	1/16-3/16
	Los Angeles-Long Beach-Glendale PMSA, CA	H	40.71 FQ	47.81 MW	56.11 TQ	CABLS	1/16-3/16
	Oakland-Hayward-Berkeley PMSA, CA	H	42.15 FQ	48.55 MW	55.31 TQ	CABLS	1/16-3/16
	Riverside-San Bernardino-Ontario MSA, CA	H	35.10 FQ	44.17 MW	51.20 TQ	CABLS	1/16-3/16
	Sacramento–Roseville–Arden-Arcade MSA, CA	H	34.97 FQ	44.63 MW	52.13 TQ	CABLS	1/16-3/16
	San Diego-Carlsbad MSA, CA	H	32.02 FQ	37.26 MW	45.60 TQ	CABLS	1/16-3/16

AE	Average entry wage	AWR	Average wage range	H	Hourly	LR	Low end range	MTC	Median total compensation	TCC	Total cash compensation
AEX	Average experienced wage	B	Biweekly	HI	Highest wage paid	M	Monthly	MW	Median wage paid	TQ	Third quartile wage
ATC	Average total compensation	D	Daily	HR	High end range	MCC	Median cash compensation	MWR	Median wage range	W	Weekly
AW	Average wage paid	FQ	First quartile wage	LO	Lowest wage paid	ME	Median entry wage	S	See annotated source	Y	Yearly

Occupation/Type/Industry	Location	Per	Low	Mid	High	Source	Date
Police and Sheriff's Patrol Officer	San Francisco-Redwood City-South San Francisco PMSA, CA	H	45.49 FQ	52.71 MW	60.82 TQ	CABLS	1/16-3/16
	Colorado	Y	54490 FQ	67330 MW	77220 TQ	USBLS	5/15
	Denver-Aurora-Lakewood MSA, CO	Y	64120 FQ	72730 MW	82620 TQ	USBLS	5/15
	Connecticut	Y		68853 MW		CTBLS	1/16-3/16
	Bridgeport-Stamford-Norwalk MSA, CT	Y	61540 FQ	70030 MW	77510 TQ	USBLS	5/15
	Hartford-West Hartford-East Hartford MSA, CT	Y	58380 FQ	69350 MW	77840 TQ	USBLS	5/15
	Delaware	Y	53000 FQ	65500 MW	77390 TQ	USBLS	5/15
	Wilmington PMSA, DE-MD-NJ	Y	52940 FQ	65720 MW	76500 TQ	USBLS	5/15
	District of Columbia	Y	60270 FQ	70790 MW	84970 TQ	USBLS	5/15
	Washington-Arlington-Alexandria PMSA, DC-VA-MD-WV	Y	55210 FQ	66770 MW	80360 TQ	USBLS	5/15
	Florida	H	19.67 AE	27.51 MW	33.21 AEX	FLBLS	7/16-9/16
	Fort Lauderdale-Pompano Beach-Deerfield Beach PMSA, FL	H	23.68 AE	34.55 MW	38.54 AEX	FLBLS	7/16-9/16
	Miami-Miami Beach-Kendall PMSA, FL	H	27.59 AE	38.22 MW	41.19 AEX	FLBLS	7/16-9/16
	Orlando-Kissimmee-Sanford MSA, FL	H	20.17 AE	23.96 MW	27.93 AEX	FLBLS	7/16-9/16
	Tampa-St. Petersburg-Clearwater MSA, FL	H	20.72 AE	26.57 MW	30.84 AEX	FLBLS	7/16-9/16
	Georgia	Y	32350 FQ	38430 MW	46240 TQ	USBLS	5/15
	Atlanta-Sandy Springs-Roswell MSA, GA	Y	36380 FQ	42870 MW	48770 TQ	USBLS	5/15
	Augusta-Richmond County MSA, GA-SC	Y	28110 FQ	32840 MW	41730 TQ	USBLS	5/15
	Hawaii	Y	55890 FQ	65770 MW	74420 TQ	USBLS	5/15
	Urban Honolulu MSA, HI	Y	56470 FQ	67030 MW	75330 TQ	USBLS	5/15
	Idaho	Y	39670 FQ	48400 MW	61500 TQ	USBLS	5/15
	Boise City MSA, ID	Y	45070 FQ	62070 MW	70420 TQ	USBLS	5/15
	Illinois	Y	57060 FQ	73140 MW	86810 TQ	USBLS	5/15
	Chicago-Naperville-Arlington Heights PMSA, IL	Y	66270 FQ	77290 MW	89820 TQ	USBLS	5/15
	Lake County-Kenosha County PMSA, IL-WI	Y	62870 FQ	76150 MW	89080 TQ	USBLS	5/15
	Indiana	Y	40590 FQ	47710 MW	57960 TQ	USBLS	5/15
	Gary PMSA, IN	Y	44070 FQ	50000 MW	58580 TQ	USBLS	5/15
	Indianapolis-Carmel-Anderson MSA, IN	Y	42940 FQ	52770 MW	65760 TQ	USBLS	5/15
	Iowa	Y	44350 FQ	54170 MW	65100 TQ	USBLS	5/15
	Des Moines-West Des Moines MSA, IA	Y	53680 FQ	64790 MW	73240 TQ	USBLS	5/15
	Kansas	Y	35710 FQ	43950 MW	53560 TQ	USBLS	5/15
	Wichita MSA, KS	Y	36950 FQ	44710 MW	53550 TQ	USBLS	5/15
	Kentucky	Y	34450 FQ	42200 MW	48800 TQ	USBLS	5/15
	Louisville-Jefferson County MSA, KY-IN	Y	38750 FQ	46480 MW	55170 TQ	USBLS	5/15
	Louisiana	Y	31520 FQ	37940 MW	45470 TQ	USBLS	5/15
	Baton Rouge MSA, LA	Y	34550 FQ	42780 MW	51210 TQ	USBLS	5/15
	New Orleans-Metairie MSA, LA	Y	34430 FQ	39860 MW	45450 TQ	USBLS	5/15
	Maine	Y	35110 FQ	43430 MW	52590 TQ	USBLS	5/15
	Portland-South Portland MSA, ME	Y	42990 FQ	51390 MW	57510 TQ	USBLS	5/15
	Maryland	Y	44325 AE	61605 MW	70244 AEX	MDBLS	4/16
	Baltimore-Columbia-Towson MSA, MD	Y	49420 FQ	61890 MW	73110 TQ	USBLS	5/15
	Salisbury MSA, MD-DE	Y	42960 FQ	51960 MW	63930 TQ	USBLS	5/15
	Massachusetts	Y	52790 FQ	62850 MW	75570 TQ	USBLS	5/15
	Boston-Cambridge-Newton NECTA, MA	Y	56360 FQ	68000 MW	80460 TQ	USBLS	5/15
	Worcester MSA, MA-CT	Y	45420 FQ	55000 MW	67050 TQ	USBLS	5/15
	Michigan	Y	46470 FQ	58230 MW	68550 TQ	USBLS	5/15
	Detroit-Dearborn-Livonia PMSA, MI	Y	53830 FQ	63550 MW	73390 TQ	USBLS	5/15

AE	Average entry wage	AWR	Average wage range	H	Hourly
AEX	Average experienced wage	B	Biweekly	HI	Highest wage paid
ATC	Average total compensation	D	Daily	HR	High end range
AW	Average wage paid	FQ	First quartile wage	LO	Lowest wage paid

LR	Low end range	MTC	Median total compensation	TCC	Total cash compensation
M	Monthly	MW	Median wage paid	TQ	Third quartile wage
MCC	Median cash compensation	MWR	Median wage range	W	Weekly
ME	Median entry wage	S	See annotated source	Y	Yearly

Occupation/Type/Industry	Location	Per	Low	Mid	High	Source	Date
Police and Sheriff's Patrol Officer	Grand Rapids-Wyoming MSA, MI	Y	52390 FQ	63420 MW	71350 TQ	USBLS	5/15
	Minnesota	Y	49817 FQ	61935 MW	72095 TQ	MNBLS	1/16-3/16
	Minneapolis-St. Paul-Bloomington MSA, MN-WI	Y	56704 FQ	68237 MW	75377 TQ	MNBLS	1/16-3/16
	Mississippi	Y	26820 FQ	33430 MW	39100 TQ	USBLS	5/15
	Jackson MSA, MS	Y	29610 FQ	34330 MW	38190 TQ	USBLS	5/15
	Missouri	Y	33500 FQ	43790 MW	57170 TQ	USBLS	5/15
	Cape Girardeau MSA, MO-IL	Y	32510 FQ	36820 MW	45640 TQ	USBLS	5/15
	Kansas City MSA, MO-KS	Y	39910 FQ	49330 MW	67520 TQ	USBLS	5/15
	St. Louis MSA, MO-IL	Y	41770 FQ	50930 MW	62100 TQ	USBLS	5/15
	Montana	Y	42170 FQ	49370 MW	57010 TQ	USBLS	5/15
	Billings MSA, MT	Y	49350 FQ	56110 MW	62470 TQ	USBLS	5/15
	Nebraska	Y	41180 FQ	54455 MW	66595 TQ	NEBLS	7/16-9/16
	Omaha-Council Bluffs MSA, NE-IA	Y	52045 FQ	62465 MW	71625 TQ	NEBLS	7/16-9/16
	Nevada	Y	59150 FQ	72010 MW	85710 TQ	USBLS	5/15
	Las Vegas-Henderson-Paradise MSA, NV	Y	65980 FQ	78960 MW	90730 TQ	USBLS	5/15
	New Hampshire	H	19.45 AE	25.97 MW	29.82 AEX	NHBLS	6/16
	Manchester NECTA, NH	H	19.18 AE	26.11 MW	30.38 AEX	NHBLS	6/16
	Nashua NECTA, NH-MA	Y	51530 FQ	60650 MW	71430 TQ	USBLS	5/15
	New Jersey	Y	70660 FQ	93590 MW	111070 TQ	USBLS	5/15
	Camden PMSA, NJ	Y	57380 FQ	82170 MW	94650 TQ	USBLS	5/15
	Newark PMSA, NJ-PA	Y	75550 FQ	92900 MW	108140 TQ	USBLS	5/15
	Trenton MSA, NJ	Y	72150 FQ	90680 MW	113360 TQ	USBLS	5/15
	New Mexico	Y	40340 FQ	49490 MW	57130 TQ	USBLS	5/15
	Albuquerque MSA, NM	Y	47140 FQ	54050 MW	59100 TQ	USBLS	5/15
	New York	Y	45310 AE	70510 MW	83100 AEX	NYBLS	1/16-3/16
	Buffalo-Cheektowaga-Niagara Falls MSA, NY	Y	52780 FQ	64010 MW	75210 TQ	USBLS	5/15
	Elmira MSA, NY	Y	49140 FQ	62420 MW	74860 TQ	USBLS	5/15
	Nassau County-Suffolk County PMSA, NY	Y	84750 FQ	108740 MW	119960 TQ	USBLS	5/15
	New York-Jersey City-White Plains PMSA, NY-NJ	Y	51690 FQ	72290 MW	91370 TQ	USBLS	5/15
	Rochester MSA, NY	Y	54580 FQ	68880 MW	77990 TQ	USBLS	5/15
	North Carolina	Y	34700 FQ	41260 MW	49350 TQ	USBLS	5/15
	Charlotte-Concord-Gastonia MSA, NC-SC	Y	37690 FQ	45200 MW	57320 TQ	USBLS	5/15
	Raleigh MSA, NC	Y	37100 FQ	45250 MW	56570 TQ	USBLS	5/15
	North Dakota	Y	42220 FQ	50740 MW	60120 TQ	USBLS	5/15
	Fargo MSA, ND-MN	Y	48120 FQ	57040 MW	67600 TQ	USBLS	5/15
	Ohio	Y	45220 FQ	57410 MW	69020 TQ	USBLS	5/15
	Cincinnati MSA, OH-KY-IN	Y	48760 FQ	64050 MW	71900 TQ	USBLS	5/15
	Cleveland-Elyria MSA, OH	Y	51680 FQ	58810 MW	68730 TQ	USBLS	5/15
	Columbus MSA, OH	Y	55350 FQ	68310 MW	78050 TQ	USBLS	5/15
	Oklahoma	Y	31140 FQ	40510 MW	55590 TQ	USBLS	5/15
	Oklahoma City MSA, OK	Y	35230 FQ	45510 MW	60090 TQ	USBLS	5/15
	Tulsa MSA, OK	Y	37340 FQ	48860 MW	64600 TQ	USBLS	5/15
	Oregon	H	28.73 FQ	33.43 MW	36.72 TQ	ORBLS	2016
	Portland-Vancouver-Hillsboro MSA, OR-WA	Y	65130 FQ	70320 MW	75810 TQ	USBLS	5/15
	Pennsylvania	Y	47200 FQ	66790 MW	78990 TQ	USBLS	5/15
	Allentown-Bethlehem-Easton MSA, PA-NJ	Y	48290 FQ	60410 MW	76380 TQ	USBLS	5/15
	Harrisburg-Carlisle MSA, PA	Y	40120 FQ	63250 MW	81520 TQ	USBLS	5/15
	Montgomery County-Bucks County-Chester County PMSA, PA	Y	66600 FQ	82080 MW	92310 TQ	USBLS	5/15
	Philadelphia PMSA, PA	Y	63790 FQ	69790 MW	75770 TQ	USBLS	5/15
	Pittsburgh MSA, PA	Y	37500 FQ	58180 MW	77920 TQ	USBLS	5/15
	Rhode Island	Y	49150 FQ	55820 MW	62310 TQ	USBLS	5/15
	Providence-Warwick MSA, RI-MA	Y	50320 FQ	56530 MW	62970 TQ	USBLS	5/15
	South Carolina	Y	32090 FQ	38000 MW	46540 TQ	USBLS	5/15
	Charleston-North Charleston MSA, SC	Y	36740 FQ	43230 MW	49320 TQ	USBLS	5/15
	Columbia MSA, SC	Y	32780 FQ	38500 MW	53830 TQ	USBLS	5/15
	Greenville-Anderson-Mauldin MSA, SC	Y	30810 FQ	35820 MW	42730 TQ	USBLS	5/15
	South Dakota	Y	34960 FQ	42330 MW	50440 TQ	USBLS	5/15

AE	Average entry wage	AWR	Average wage range	H	Hourly
AEX	Average experienced wage	B	Biweekly	HI	Highest wage paid
ATC	Average total compensation	D	Daily	HR	High end range
AW	Average wage paid	FQ	First quartile wage	LO	Lowest wage paid

LR	Low end range	MTC	Median total compensation
M	Monthly	MW	Median wage paid
MCC	Median cash compensation	MWR	Median wage range
ME	Median entry wage	S	See annotated source

TCC	Total cash compensation		
TQ	Third quartile wage		
W	Weekly		
Y	Yearly		

Occupation/Type/Industry	Location	Per	Low	Mid	High	Source	Date
Police and Sheriff's Patrol Officer	Sioux Falls MSA, SD	Y	42730 FQ	56090 MW	68530 TQ	USBLS	5/15
	Tennessee	Y	34440 FQ	42310 MW	52490 TQ	USBLS	5/15
	Knoxville MSA, TN	Y	32440 FQ	39700 MW	48680 TQ	USBLS	5/15
	Memphis MSA, TN-MS-AR	Y	39150 FQ	50800 MW	56850 TQ	USBLS	5/15
	Nashville-Davidson–Murfreesboro–Franklin MSA, TN	Y	37390 FQ	44770 MW	54450 TQ	USBLS	5/15
	Texas	Y	45380 FQ	58520 MW	71580 TQ	USBLS	5/15
	Austin-Round Rock MSA, TX	Y	54020 FQ	68010 MW	78480 TQ	USBLS	5/15
	Dallas-Plano-Irving PMSA, TX	Y	49880 FQ	62500 MW	75600 TQ	USBLS	5/15
	Fort Worth-Arlington PMSA, TX	Y	54490 FQ	66670 MW	75660 TQ	USBLS	5/15
	Houston-The Woodlands-Sugar Land MSA, TX	Y	50710 FQ	62610 MW	72490 TQ	USBLS	5/15
	San Antonio-New Braunfels MSA, TX	Y	44560 FQ	55610 MW	69770 TQ	USBLS	5/15
	Utah	Y	39870 FQ	47950 MW	56940 TQ	USBLS	5/15
	Ogden-Clearfield MSA, UT	Y	37560 FQ	44050 MW	51110 TQ	USBLS	5/15
	Provo-Orem MSA, UT	Y	39380 FQ	46360 MW	54730 TQ	USBLS	5/15
	Salt Lake City MSA, UT	Y	44060 FQ	53380 MW	60260 TQ	USBLS	5/15
	Vermont	Y	37740 FQ	46020 MW	54710 TQ	USBLS	5/15
	Burlington-South Burlington MSA, VT	Y	42290 FQ	47210 MW	56120 TQ	USBLS	5/15
	Virginia	Y	41890 FQ	49860 MW	62190 TQ	USBLS	5/15
	Richmond MSA, VA	Y	41110 FQ	47560 MW	57890 TQ	USBLS	5/15
	Virginia Beach-Norfolk-Newport News MSA, VA-NC	Y	41930 FQ	47260 MW	55910 TQ	USBLS	5/15
	Washington	H	31.63 FQ	36.74 MW	42.98 TQ	WABLS	3/16
	Seattle-Bellevue-Everett PMSA, WA	H	35.32 FQ	41.03 MW	45.85 TQ	WABLS	3/16
	Tacoma-Lakewood PMSA, WA	H	32.11 FQ	37.15 MW	42.77 TQ	WABLS	3/16
	West Virginia	Y	33760 FQ	41100 MW	48000 TQ	USBLS	5/15
	Huntington-Ashland MSA, WV-KY-OH	Y	32430 FQ	40830 MW	47290 TQ	USBLS	5/15
	Wisconsin	Y	43430 FQ	54750 MW	65980 TQ	USBLS	5/15
	Madison MSA, WI	Y	45990 FQ	56590 MW	66750 TQ	USBLS	5/15
	Milwaukee-Waukesha-West Allis MSA, WI	Y	47830 FQ	65110 MW	72190 TQ	USBLS	5/15
	Wyoming	Y	44450 FQ	52890 MW	61870 TQ	USBLS	5/15
	Cheyenne MSA, WY	Y	43040 FQ	50000 MW	59720 TQ	USBLS	5/15
	Puerto Rico	Y	27080 FQ	32370 MW	35850 TQ	USBLS	5/15
	San Juan-Carolina-Caguas MSA, PR	Y	28530 FQ	32880 MW	36100 TQ	USBLS	5/15
Police Cadet	San Francisco, CA	B	1320 LO		1600 HI	SFGOV	2016-2018
Police Chief							
Municipal Government	Albany, CA	Y			186624 HI	CACIT	6/28/16
Municipal Government	Antioch, CA	Y			214740 HI	CACIT	6/28/16
Municipal Government	Seaside, CA	Y			182818 HI	CACIT	6/28/16
Municipal Government	Colorado Springs, CO	Y	142288 LO		195647 HI	COSPRS	2017
Municipal Government	Loganville, GA	Y	56867 LO		80413 HI	GACTY01	2016
Municipal Government	Royston, GA	Y	45066 LO		52936 HI	GACTY01	2016
Municipal Government	Smyrna, GA	Y	85950 LO		124522 HI	GACTY01	2016
Municipal Government	Buckland, MA	Y			60187 HI	FRCOG	2016
Municipal Government	Conway, MA	Y			65681 HI	FRCOG	2016
Municipal Government	Detroit, MI	M	6233 LO		10408 HI	DETGOV	2016
Police Commander							
Municipal Government	Arroyo Grande, CA	Y			117194 HI	CACIT	6/28/16
Municipal Government	Greenfield, CA	Y			90053 HI	CACIT	6/28/16
Municipal Government	Colorado Springs, CO	M			10082 HI	COSPRS	2017
Police Communications Supervisor							
Municipal Government	Antioch, CA	Y			87795 HI	CACIT	6/28/16
Police Data Specialist							
Municipal Government	Chula Vista, CA	Y		46693 AW		CACIT	6/28/16
Police Data Transcriptionist							
Municipal Government	Fresno, CA	Y		38980 AW		CACIT	6/28/16

AE	Average entry wage	AWR	Average wage range	H	Hourly
AEX	Average experienced wage	B	Biweekly	HI	Highest wage paid
ATC	Average total compensation	D	Daily	HR	High end range
AW	Average wage paid	FQ	First quartile wage	LO	Lowest wage paid

LR	Low end range	MTC	Median total compensation
M	Monthly	MW	Median wage paid
MCC	Median cash compensation	MWR	Median wage range
ME	Median entry wage	S	See annotated source

TCC	Total cash compensation	
TQ	Third quartile wage	
W	Weekly	
Y	Yearly	

Occupation/Type/Industry	Location	Per	Low	Mid	High	Source	Date
Police Evidence Technician							
Municipal Government	Fontana, CA	Y		61611 AW		CACIT	6/28/16
Police Fleet Coordinator							
Municipal Government	Laguna Beach, CA	Y			73044 HI	CACIT	6/28/16
Police Lieutenant							
Bomb Squad, Municipal Government	Seattle, WA	H	59.20 LO		66.71 HI	CSSS	11/19/14
Police Maintenance Technician							
Municipal Government	Alameda, CA	Y			59447 HI	CACIT	6/28/16
Police Officer							
Baccalaureate Institution	United States	Y		43931 MW		CHE01	2015-2016
Master's Institution	United States	Y		37024 MW		CHE01	2015-2016
Research University	United States	Y		43846 MW		CHE01	2015-2016
SWAT, Municipal Government	Seattle, WA	H	34.46 LO		44.73 HI	CSSS	1/1/14
Police Programs Analyst							
Municipal Government	Hayward, CA	Y			65246 HI	CACIT	6/28/16
Police Projects Specialist							
Municipal Government	Escondido, CA	Y			44110 HI	CACIT	6/28/16
Police Property Room Specialist							
Municipal Government	Daly City, CA	Y			58542 HI	CACIT	6/28/16
Police Records Specialist							
Municipal Government	Arcata, CA	Y			10306 HI	CACIT	6/28/16
Municipal Government	Foster City, CA	Y			57888 HI	CACIT	6/28/16
Police Recruit							
Municipal Government	San Jose, CA	H			34.59 HI	SJPD	2016
Municipal Government	Colorado Springs, CO	M			4166 HI	COSPRS	2017
State Police	Michigan	Y	44000 LO			MDAY02	2016
Police Services Manager							
Municipal Government	Escalon, CA	Y		41720 AW		CACIT	6/28/16
Police Services Technician							
Municipal Government	Gonzales, CA	Y			28620 HI	CACIT	7/5/16
Police Training Assistant							
Municipal Government	Fullerton, CA	Y			49634 HI	CACIT	6/28/16
Political Science Teacher							
Postsecondary	Alabama	Y	55176 AE	82586 AW	96285 AEX	ALBLS	6/16
Postsecondary	Birmingham-Hoover MSA, AL	Y	55900 AE	86551 AW	101871 AEX	ALBLS	6/16
Postsecondary	Arizona	Y	51280 FQ	72740 MW	98590 TQ	USBLS	5/15
Postsecondary	Phoenix-Mesa-Scottsdale MSA, AZ	Y	48810 FQ	70110 MW	98870 TQ	USBLS	5/15
Postsecondary	Tucson MSA, AZ	Y	66750 FQ	78990 MW	100660 TQ	USBLS	5/15
Postsecondary	Arkansas	Y	52840 FQ	62020 MW	79610 TQ	USBLS	5/15
Postsecondary	Little Rock-North Little Rock-Conway MSA, AR	Y	55170 FQ	62900 MW	83370 TQ	USBLS	5/15
Postsecondary	California	Y		106572 AW		CABLS	1/16-3/16
Postsecondary	Anaheim-Santa Ana-Irvine PMSA, CA	Y		124610 AW		CABLS	1/16-3/16
Postsecondary	Los Angeles-Long Beach-Glendale PMSA, CA	Y		110164 AW		CABLS	1/16-3/16
Postsecondary	Riverside-San Bernardino-Ontario MSA, CA	Y		95981 AW		CABLS	1/16-3/16
Postsecondary	Sacramento–Roseville–Arden-Arcade MSA, CA	Y		105822 AW		CABLS	1/16-3/16
Postsecondary	San Diego-Carlsbad MSA, CA	Y		124935 AW		CABLS	1/16-3/16
Postsecondary	San Francisco-Redwood City-South San Francisco PMSA, CA	Y		93567 AW		CABLS	1/16-3/16
Postsecondary	Colorado	Y	48950 FQ	67930 MW	93300 TQ	USBLS	5/15
Postsecondary	Denver-Aurora-Lakewood MSA, CO	Y	51530 FQ	70850 MW	96810 TQ	USBLS	5/15
Postsecondary	Connecticut	Y		93820 MW		CTBLS	1/16-3/16

AE	Average entry wage	AWR	Average wage range	H	Hourly
AEX	Average experienced wage	B	Biweekly	HI	Highest wage paid
ATC	Average total compensation	D	Daily	HR	High end range
AW	Average wage paid	FQ	First quartile wage	LO	Lowest wage paid

LR	Low end range	MTC	Median total compensation
M	Monthly	MW	Median wage paid
MCC	Median cash compensation	MWR	Median wage range
ME	Median entry wage	S	See annotated source

TCC	Total cash compensation
TQ	Third quartile wage
W	Weekly
Y	Yearly

Occupation/Type/Industry	Location	Per	Low	Mid	High	Source	Date
Political Science Teacher							
Postsecondary	Hartford-West Hartford-East Hartford MSA, CT	Y	60560 FQ	79620 MW	114880 TQ	USBLS	5/15
Postsecondary	District of Columbia	Y	63780 FQ	85390 MW	120600 TQ	USBLS	5/15
Postsecondary	Washington-Arlington-Alexandria PMSA, DC-VA-MD-WV	Y	63750 FQ	85520 MW	121540 TQ	USBLS	5/15
Postsecondary	Florida	Y	52990 AE	81601 MW	104337 AEX	FLBLS	7/16-9/16
Postsecondary	Fort Lauderdale-Pompano Beach-Deerfield Beach PMSA, FL	Y	48450 AE	65137 MW	73369 AEX	FLBLS	7/16-9/16
Postsecondary	Miami-Miami Beach-Kendall PMSA, FL	Y	74774 AE	95891 MW	115856 AEX	FLBLS	7/16-9/16
Postsecondary	Orlando-Kissimmee-Sanford MSA, FL	Y	56235 AE	84170 MW	99865 AEX	FLBLS	7/16-9/16
Postsecondary	Tampa-St. Petersburg-Clearwater MSA, FL	Y	55643 AE	87877 MW	117710 AEX	FLBLS	7/16-9/16
Postsecondary	Georgia	Y	49270 FQ	63640 MW	84310 TQ	USBLS	5/15
Postsecondary	Atlanta-Sandy Springs-Roswell MSA, GA	Y	49060 FQ	60960 MW	78270 TQ	USBLS	5/15
Postsecondary	Hawaii	Y	64870 FQ	84630 MW	101280 TQ	USBLS	5/15
Postsecondary	Urban Honolulu MSA, HI	Y	71290 FQ	88500 MW	104530 TQ	USBLS	5/15
Postsecondary	Idaho	Y	44600 FQ	62770 MW	87320 TQ	USBLS	5/15
Postsecondary	Illinois	Y	56720 FQ	75690 MW	100870 TQ	USBLS	5/15
Postsecondary	Chicago-Naperville-Arlington Heights PMSA, IL	Y	56170 FQ	74000 MW	98220 TQ	USBLS	5/15
Postsecondary	Indiana	Y	54960 FQ	75900 MW	105850 TQ	USBLS	5/15
Postsecondary	Iowa	Y	57610 FQ	71120 MW	93950 TQ	USBLS	5/15
Postsecondary	Kansas	Y	40280 FQ	48650 MW	63690 TQ	USBLS	5/15
Postsecondary	Kentucky	Y	57660 FQ	75470 MW	106470 TQ	USBLS	5/15
Postsecondary	Louisville-Jefferson County MSA, KY-IN	Y	56680 FQ	74710 MW	100230 TQ	USBLS	5/15
Postsecondary	Louisiana	Y	58950 FQ	70380 MW	83250 TQ	USBLS	5/15
Postsecondary	Maine	Y	53840 FQ	78200 MW	103770 TQ	USBLS	5/15
Postsecondary	Maryland	Y	52903 AE	95295 MW	116491 AEX	MDBLS	4/16
Postsecondary	Baltimore-Columbia-Towson MSA, MD	Y	60420 FQ	80740 MW	101230 TQ	USBLS	5/15
Postsecondary	Massachusetts	Y	74710 FQ	106810 MW	155660 TQ	USBLS	5/15
Postsecondary	Boston-Cambridge-Newton NECTA, MA	Y	81630 FQ	119420 MW	174910 TQ	USBLS	5/15
Postsecondary	Worcester MSA, MA-CT	Y	60960 FQ	81270 MW	111390 TQ	USBLS	5/15
Postsecondary	Michigan	Y	57530 FQ	89050 MW	119440 TQ	USBLS	5/15
Postsecondary	Detroit-Dearborn-Livonia PMSA, MI	Y	46530 FQ	80740 MW	95990 TQ	USBLS	5/15
Postsecondary	Minnesota	Y	63296 FQ	85926 MW	114212 TQ	MNBLS	1/16-3/16
Postsecondary	Minneapolis-St. Paul-Bloomington MSA, MN-WI	Y	63003 FQ	91017 MW	124666 TQ	MNBLS	1/16-3/16
Postsecondary	Mississippi	Y	54230 FQ	62540 MW	78090 TQ	USBLS	5/15
Postsecondary	Missouri	Y	42210 FQ	57020 MW	81850 TQ	USBLS	5/15
Postsecondary	Kansas City MSA, MO-KS	Y	69300 FQ	89670 MW	111880 TQ	USBLS	5/15
Postsecondary	St. Louis MSA, MO-IL	Y	52170 FQ	72160 MW	100200 TQ	USBLS	5/15
Postsecondary	Montana	Y	43490 FQ	55840 MW	68900 TQ	USBLS	5/15
Postsecondary	Nebraska	Y	53550 FQ	67350 MW	82670 TQ	NEBLS	7/16-9/16
Postsecondary	New Hampshire	Y	65949 AE	93522 MW	118291 AEX	NHBLS	6/16
Postsecondary	New Jersey	Y	63760 FQ	85350 MW	121860 TQ	USBLS	5/15
Postsecondary	Newark PMSA, NJ-PA	Y	66870 FQ	87390 MW	121750 TQ	USBLS	5/15
Postsecondary	New Mexico	Y	69610 FQ	88490 MW	108450 TQ	USBLS	5/15
Postsecondary	New York	Y	41520 AE	82100 MW	120270 AEX	NYBLS	1/16-3/16
Postsecondary	Buffalo-Cheektowaga-Niagara Falls MSA, NY	Y	39930 FQ	67360 MW	88500 TQ	USBLS	5/15
Postsecondary	Nassau County-Suffolk County PMSA, NY	Y	51380 FQ	65190 MW	82780 TQ	USBLS	5/15
Postsecondary	New York-Jersey City-White Plains PMSA, NY-NJ	Y	53270 FQ	89120 MW	134930 TQ	USBLS	5/15
Postsecondary	Rochester MSA, NY	Y	60110 FQ	87900 MW	176360 TQ	USBLS	5/15
Postsecondary	North Carolina	Y	57660 FQ	78080 MW	122990 TQ	USBLS	5/15
Postsecondary	Charlotte-Concord-Gastonia MSA, NC-SC	Y	54290 FQ	72900 MW	112830 TQ	USBLS	5/15
Postsecondary	Ohio	Y	55340 FQ	78340 MW	108050 TQ	USBLS	5/15
Postsecondary	Columbus MSA, OH	Y	61150 FQ	85850 MW	111650 TQ	USBLS	5/15
Postsecondary	Oklahoma	Y	41800 FQ	49470 MW	72150 TQ	USBLS	5/15
Postsecondary	Oklahoma City MSA, OK	Y	39540 FQ	44820 MW	50170 TQ	USBLS	5/15

AE	Average entry wage	AWR	Average wage range	H	Hourly	LR	Low end range	MTC	Median total compensation	TCC	Total cash compensation
AEX	Average experienced wage	B	Biweekly	HI	Highest wage paid	M	Monthly	MW	Median wage paid	TQ	Third quartile wage
ATC	Average total compensation	D	Daily	HR	High end range	MCC	Median cash compensation	MWR	Median wage range	W	Weekly
AW	Average wage paid	FQ	First quartile wage	LO	Lowest wage paid	ME	Median entry wage	S	See annotated source	Y	Yearly

1266

Occupation/Type/Industry	Location	Per	Low	Mid	High	Source	Date
Political Science Teacher							
Postsecondary	Oregon	Y	65999 FQ	79372 MW	101233 TQ	ORBLS	2016
Postsecondary	Portland-Vancouver-Hillsboro MSA, OR-WA	Y	59760 FQ	75050 MW	97730 TQ	USBLS	5/15
Postsecondary	Pennsylvania	Y	62630 FQ	82200 MW	108430 TQ	USBLS	5/15
Postsecondary	Allentown-Bethlehem-Easton MSA, PA-NJ	Y	71520 FQ	96220 MW	120580 TQ	USBLS	5/15
Postsecondary	Montgomery County-Bucks County-Chester County PMSA, PA	Y	49640 FQ	73050 MW	98490 TQ	USBLS	5/15
Postsecondary	Philadelphia PMSA, PA	Y	65520 FQ	86300 MW	116910 TQ	USBLS	5/15
Postsecondary	Pittsburgh MSA, PA	Y	64820 FQ	83330 MW	111700 TQ	USBLS	5/15
Postsecondary	Rhode Island	Y	69510 FQ	86590 MW	120560 TQ	USBLS	5/15
Postsecondary	Providence-Warwick MSA, RI-MA	Y	69510 FQ	86590 MW	120560 TQ	USBLS	5/15
Postsecondary	South Carolina	Y	59330 FQ	71470 MW	84140 TQ	USBLS	5/15
Postsecondary	Greenville-Anderson-Mauldin MSA, SC	Y	67300 FQ	79520 MW	105240 TQ	USBLS	5/15
Postsecondary	South Dakota	Y	55770 FQ	71690 MW	92920 TQ	USBLS	5/15
Postsecondary	Tennessee	Y	33550 FQ	50190 MW	75710 TQ	USBLS	5/15
Postsecondary	Knoxville MSA, TN	Y	37650 FQ	51190 MW	76940 TQ	USBLS	5/15
Postsecondary	Memphis MSA, TN-MS-AR	Y	41020 FQ	54530 MW	77190 TQ	USBLS	5/15
Postsecondary	Nashville-Davidson–Murfreesboro–Franklin MSA, TN	Y	35080 FQ	47540 MW	89840 TQ	USBLS	5/15
Postsecondary	Texas	Y	49750 FQ	68580 MW	99880 TQ	USBLS	5/15
Postsecondary	Austin-Round Rock MSA, TX	Y	55530 FQ	72440 MW	105620 TQ	USBLS	5/15
Postsecondary	Dallas-Plano-Irving PMSA, TX	Y	51510 FQ	66130 MW	92060 TQ	USBLS	5/15
Postsecondary	San Antonio-New Braunfels MSA, TX	Y	25170 FQ	61110 MW	87810 TQ	USBLS	5/15
Postsecondary	Utah	Y	56490 FQ	78110 MW	100500 TQ	USBLS	5/15
Postsecondary	Vermont	Y	58470 FQ	97290 MW	120110 TQ	USBLS	5/15
Postsecondary	Virginia	Y	48090 FQ	66550 MW	96480 TQ	USBLS	5/15
Postsecondary	Virginia Beach-Norfolk-Newport News MSA, VA-NC	Y	54010 FQ	64440 MW	89660 TQ	USBLS	5/15
Postsecondary	Washington	Y		76300 AW		WABLS	3/16
Postsecondary	Seattle-Bellevue-Everett PMSA, WA	Y		86597 AW		WABLS	3/16
Postsecondary	Tacoma-Lakewood PMSA, WA	Y		65313 AW		WABLS	3/16
Postsecondary	West Virginia	Y	50080 FQ	61430 MW	76520 TQ	USBLS	5/15
Postsecondary	Wisconsin	Y	53200 FQ	65850 MW	91390 TQ	USBLS	5/15
Postsecondary	Milwaukee-Waukesha-West Allis MSA, WI	Y	58510 FQ	73940 MW	97270 TQ	USBLS	5/15
Postsecondary	Wyoming	Y	44710 FQ	65200 MW	77980 TQ	USBLS	5/15
Political Scientist	Arizona	Y	83870 FQ	93210 MW	102380 TQ	USBLS	5/15
	California	H	22.84 FQ	34.49 MW	71.58 TQ	CABLS	1/16-3/16
	District of Columbia	Y	76590 FQ	110890 MW	140480 TQ	USBLS	5/15
	Florida	H	32.60 AE	38.03 MW	51.64 AEX	FLBLS	7/16-9/16
	Georgia	Y	46710 FQ	72200 MW	93610 TQ	USBLS	5/15
	Illinois	Y	56900 FQ	66180 MW	75800 TQ	USBLS	5/15
	Maine	Y	54170 FQ	64040 MW	76830 TQ	USBLS	5/15
	Maryland	Y	72158 AE	107181 MW	124693 AEX	MDBLS	4/16
	Massachusetts	Y	49060 FQ	83000 MW	97320 TQ	USBLS	5/15
	Michigan	Y	49930 FQ	63730 MW	114610 TQ	USBLS	5/15
	New York	Y	58590 FQ	101770 MW	142900 AEX	NYBLS	1/16-3/16
	Ohio	Y	59620 FQ	84990 MW	99110 TQ	USBLS	5/15
	Texas	Y	40320 FQ	74870 MW	91820 TQ	USBLS	5/15
	Virginia	Y	105970 FQ	131500 MW	154690 TQ	USBLS	5/15
	Washington	H	25.51 FQ	32.68 MW	42.48 TQ	WABLS	3/16
Polygraph Examiner							
Attorney General's Office, State Government	Ohio	H	30.50 LO		41.25 HI	OHGOV	2015
Pool Maintenance Technician							
Municipal Government	El Segundo, CA	Y			54010 HI	CACIT	6/28/16
Port Commercial Appraiser							
Harbor, Municipal Government	Long Beach, CA	Y			119331 HI	CACIT	6/28/16

AE	Average entry wage	AWR	Average wage range	H	Hourly	LR	Low end range	MTC	Median total compensation	TCC	Total cash compensation
AEX	Average experienced wage	B	Biweekly	HI	Highest wage paid	M	Monthly	MW	Median wage paid	TQ	Third quartile wage
ATC	Average total compensation	D	Daily	HR	High end range	MCC	Median cash compensation	MWR	Median wage range	W	Weekly
AW	Average wage paid	FQ	First quartile wage	LO	Lowest wage paid	ME	Median entry wage	S	See annotated source	Y	Yearly

Occupation/Type/Industry	Location	Per	Low	Mid	High	Source	Date
Port Director							
Municipal Government	Richmond, CA	Y			207582 HI	CACIT	6/28/16
Municipal Government	San Francisco, CA	Y			266651 HI	CACIT	6/28/16
Port Marketing Manager							
Harbor, Municipal Government	Los Angeles, CA	Y		116352 AW		CACIT	6/23/16
Port Trade Analyst							
Harbor, Municipal Government	Long Beach, CA	Y			53775 HI	CACIT	6/28/16
Portfolio Manager							
Office/Industrial Real Estate	United States	Y	99300 FQ	124000 MW	144400 TQ	IREM	2016
Residential Real Estate	United States	Y	100300 FQ	113600 MW	131300 TQ	IREM	2016
Retail Real Estate	United States	Y	100700 FQ	122700 MW	151800 TQ	IREM	2016
Post Adoption Services Program Manager							
Department of Public Health and Human Services, State Government	Helena, MT	H			20.50 HI	MTGOV	2016
Postal Service Clerk	Alabama	Y	33938 AE	49293 AW	56971 AEX	ALBLS	6/16
	Birmingham-Hoover MSA, AL	Y	36030 AE	50942 AW	58394 AEX	ALBLS	6/16
	Alaska	Y	25220 FQ	39800 MW	56800 TQ	USBLS	5/15
	Anchorage MSA, AK	Y	56790 FQ	56800 MW	56800 TQ	USBLS	5/15
	Arizona	Y	56780 FQ	56790 MW	56800 TQ	USBLS	5/15
	Phoenix-Mesa-Scottsdale MSA, AZ	Y	56790 FQ	56800 MW	56800 TQ	USBLS	5/15
	Tucson MSA, AZ	Y	55860 FQ	56790 MW	56800 TQ	USBLS	5/15
	Arkansas	Y	32520 FQ	39800 MW	56800 TQ	USBLS	5/15
	Little Rock-North Little Rock-Conway MSA, AR	Y	32520 FQ	55870 MW	56800 TQ	USBLS	5/15
	California	H	27.50 FQ	27.95 MW	28.52 TQ	CABLS	1/16-3/16
	Anaheim-Santa Ana-Irvine PMSA, CA	H	27.94 FQ	27.95 MW	27.95 TQ	CABLS	1/16-3/16
	Los Angeles-Long Beach-Glendale PMSA, CA	H	27.94 FQ	27.95 MW	28.52 TQ	CABLS	1/16-3/16
	Oakland-Hayward-Berkeley PMSA, CA	H	27.94 FQ	27.95 MW	27.95 TQ	CABLS	1/16-3/16
	Riverside-San Bernardino-Ontario MSA, CA	H	27.94 FQ	27.95 MW	27.95 TQ	CABLS	1/16-3/16
	Sacramento–Roseville–Arden-Arcade MSA, CA	H	19.59 FQ	27.94 MW	27.95 TQ	CABLS	1/16-3/16
	San Diego-Carlsbad MSA, CA	H	27.94 FQ	27.95 MW	27.95 TQ	CABLS	1/16-3/16
	San Francisco-Redwood City-South San Francisco PMSA, CA	H	27.94 FQ	27.95 MW	27.95 TQ	CABLS	1/16-3/16
	Colorado	Y	39800 FQ	56790 MW	56800 TQ	USBLS	5/15
	Denver-Aurora-Lakewood MSA, CO	Y	56790 FQ	56790 MW	56800 TQ	USBLS	5/15
	Connecticut	Y		58126 MW		CTBLS	1/16-3/16
	Bridgeport-Stamford-Norwalk MSA, CT	Y	56790 FQ	56800 MW	57970 TQ	USBLS	5/15
	Hartford-West Hartford-East Hartford MSA, CT	Y	40450 FQ	56790 MW	56940 TQ	USBLS	5/15
	Delaware	Y	39790 FQ	56790 MW	57970 TQ	USBLS	5/15
	Wilmington PMSA, DE-MD-NJ	Y	32530 FQ	56790 MW	56800 TQ	USBLS	5/15
	District of Columbia	Y	53090 FQ	56790 MW	57970 TQ	USBLS	5/15
	Washington-Arlington-Alexandria PMSA, DC-VA-MD-WV	Y	56780 FQ	56790 MW	56800 TQ	USBLS	5/15
	Florida	H	20.28 AE	28.29 MW	28.55 AEX	FLBLS	7/16-9/16
	Fort Lauderdale-Pompano Beach-Deerfield Beach PMSA, FL	H	21.64 AE	28.30 MW	28.55 AEX	FLBLS	7/16-9/16
	Miami-Miami Beach-Kendall PMSA, FL	H	22.14 AE	28.29 MW	28.44 AEX	FLBLS	7/16-9/16
	Orlando-Kissimmee-Sanford MSA, FL	H	21.45 AE	28.30 MW	28.56 AEX	FLBLS	7/16-9/16
	Tampa-St. Petersburg-Clearwater MSA, FL	H	19.85 AE	28.29 MW	28.55 AEX	FLBLS	7/16-9/16
	Georgia	Y	39810 FQ	56790 MW	57970 TQ	USBLS	5/15

AE	Average entry wage	AWR	Average wage range	H	Hourly
AEX	Average experienced wage	B	Biweekly	HI	Highest wage paid
ATC	Average total compensation	D	Daily	HR	High end range
AW	Average wage paid	FQ	First quartile wage	LO	Lowest wage paid

LR	Low end range	MTC	Median total compensation	TCC	Total cash compensation
M	Monthly	MW	Median wage paid	TQ	Third quartile wage
MCC	Median cash compensation	MWR	Median wage range	W	Weekly
ME	Median entry wage	S	See annotated source	Y	Yearly

Occupation/Type/Industry	Location	Per	Low	Mid	High	Source	Date
Postal Service Clerk	Atlanta-Sandy Springs-Roswell MSA, GA	Y	56790 FQ	56800 MW	56800 TQ	USBLS	5/15
	Augusta-Richmond County MSA, GA-SC	Y	40760 FQ	56800 MW	57980 TQ	USBLS	5/15
	Hawaii	Y	56190 FQ	56790 MW	57150 TQ	USBLS	5/15
	Urban Honolulu MSA, HI	Y	56790 FQ	56790 MW	56800 TQ	USBLS	5/15
	Idaho	Y	35660 FQ	40760 MW	56800 TQ	USBLS	5/15
	Boise City MSA, ID	Y	39800 FQ	56790 MW	57970 TQ	USBLS	5/15
	Illinois	Y	35670 FQ	56790 MW	56800 TQ	USBLS	5/15
	Chicago-Naperville-Arlington Heights PMSA, IL	Y	56790 FQ	56800 MW	57970 TQ	USBLS	5/15
	Lake County-Kenosha County PMSA, IL-WI	Y	39800 FQ	56790 MW	56800 TQ	USBLS	5/15
	Indiana	Y	39790 FQ	56790 MW	56800 TQ	USBLS	5/15
	Gary PMSA, IN	Y	54020 FQ	56790 MW	56810 TQ	USBLS	5/15
	Indianapolis-Carmel-Anderson MSA, IN	Y	56010 FQ	56790 MW	56800 TQ	USBLS	5/15
	Iowa	Y	32520 FQ	39800 MW	56800 TQ	USBLS	5/15
	Des Moines-West Des Moines MSA, IA	Y	32530 FQ	40760 MW	56800 TQ	USBLS	5/15
	Kansas	Y	32530 FQ	54480 MW	57110 TQ	USBLS	5/15
	Wichita MSA, KS	Y	43090 FQ	56800 MW	57980 TQ	USBLS	5/15
	Kentucky	Y	33300 FQ	55880 MW	56800 TQ	USBLS	5/15
	Louisville-Jefferson County MSA, KY-IN	Y	39800 FQ	56790 MW	56810 TQ	USBLS	5/15
	Louisiana	Y	39790 FQ	56790 MW	56810 TQ	USBLS	5/15
	Baton Rouge MSA, LA	Y	39790 FQ	56790 MW	57970 TQ	USBLS	5/15
	Hammond MSA, LA	Y	39800 FQ	56800 MW	58110 TQ	USBLS	5/15
	New Orleans-Metairie MSA, LA	Y	39790 FQ	56790 MW	56800 TQ	USBLS	5/15
	Maine	Y	32530 FQ	39810 MW	56800 TQ	USBLS	5/15
	Portland-South Portland MSA, ME	Y	39800 FQ	56790 MW	56800 TQ	USBLS	5/15
	Maryland	Y	38328 AE	51023 MW	57371 AEX	MDBLS	4/16
	Baltimore-Columbia-Towson MSA, MD	Y	38250 FQ	56790 MW	56800 TQ	USBLS	5/15
	Salisbury MSA, MD-DE	Y	39200 FQ	56790 MW	57970 TQ	USBLS	5/15
	Massachusetts	Y	39810 FQ	56790 MW	56800 TQ	USBLS	5/15
	Boston-Cambridge-Newton NECTA, MA	Y	39810 FQ	56790 MW	56800 TQ	USBLS	5/15
	Worcester MSA, MA-CT	Y	39800 FQ	56790 MW	56800 TQ	USBLS	5/15
	Michigan	Y	39800 FQ	56790 MW	57970 TQ	USBLS	5/15
	Detroit-Dearborn-Livonia PMSA, MI	Y	56790 FQ	56790 MW	56800 TQ	USBLS	5/15
	Grand Rapids-Wyoming MSA, MI	Y	39800 FQ	56790 MW	56800 TQ	USBLS	5/15
	Minnesota	Y	32897 FQ	56813 MW	57440 TQ	MNBLS	1/16-3/16
	Minneapolis-St. Paul-Bloomington MSA, MN-WI	Y	40259 FQ	57430 MW	57440 TQ	MNBLS	1/16-3/16
	Mississippi	Y	32530 FQ	56780 MW	56800 TQ	USBLS	5/15
	Jackson MSA, MS	Y	38230 FQ	56790 MW	56800 TQ	USBLS	5/15
	Missouri	Y	32520 FQ	40760 MW	56800 TQ	USBLS	5/15
	Kansas City MSA, MO-KS	Y	39180 FQ	56790 MW	56800 TQ	USBLS	5/15
	St. Louis MSA, MO-IL	Y	32530 FQ	56790 MW	56800 TQ	USBLS	5/15
	Montana	Y	32510 FQ	39800 MW	56790 TQ	USBLS	5/15
	Billings MSA, MT	Y	32520 FQ	56790 MW	56800 TQ	USBLS	5/15
	Nebraska	Y	32520 FQ	39800 MW	56795 TQ	NEBLS	7/16-9/16
	Omaha-Council Bluffs MSA, NE-IA	Y	39805 FQ	56795 MW	57985 TQ	NEBLS	7/16-9/16
	Nevada	Y	39790 FQ	56790 MW	56800 TQ	USBLS	5/15
	Las Vegas-Henderson-Paradise MSA, NV	Y	54940 FQ	56790 MW	56800 TQ	USBLS	5/15
	New Hampshire	H	18.00 AE	28.14 MW	28.51 AEX	NHBLS	6/16
	Manchester NECTA, NH	H	21.71 AE	28.15 MW	28.63 AEX	NHBLS	6/16
	Nashua NECTA, NH-MA	Y	41230 FQ	56800 MW	57970 TQ	USBLS	5/15
	New Jersey	Y	56790 FQ	56800 MW	57110 TQ	USBLS	5/15
	Camden PMSA, NJ	Y	56780 FQ	56800 MW	57970 TQ	USBLS	5/15
	Newark PMSA, NJ-PA	Y	39810 FQ	56790 MW	56800 TQ	USBLS	5/15
	Trenton MSA, NJ	Y	56780 FQ	56790 MW	56800 TQ	USBLS	5/15
	New Mexico	Y	32530 FQ	56790 MW	56800 TQ	USBLS	5/15
	Albuquerque MSA, NM	Y	56790 FQ	56800 MW	57970 TQ	USBLS	5/15
	New York	Y	37350 AE	58120 MW	58550 AEX	NYBLS	1/16-3/16

AE	Average entry wage	AWR	Average wage range	H	Hourly
AEX	Average experienced wage	B	Biweekly	HI	Highest wage paid
ATC	Average total compensation	D	Daily	HR	High end range
AW	Average wage paid	FQ	First quartile wage	LO	Lowest wage paid

LR	Low end range	MTC	Median total compensation
M	Monthly	MW	Median wage paid
MCC	Median cash compensation	MWR	Median wage range
ME	Median entry wage	S	See annotated source

TCC	Total cash compensation	
TQ	Third quartile wage	
W	Weekly	
Y	Yearly	

Occupation/Type/Industry	Location	Per	Low	Mid	High	Source	Date
Postal Service Clerk	Buffalo-Cheektowaga-Niagara Falls MSA, NY	Y	39790 FQ	56790 MW	57970 TQ	USBLS	5/15
	Nassau County-Suffolk County PMSA, NY	Y	56790 FQ	56790 MW	56800 TQ	USBLS	5/15
	New York-Jersey City-White Plains PMSA, NY-NJ	Y	56790 FQ	56790 MW	56800 TQ	USBLS	5/15
	Rochester MSA, NY	Y	39790 FQ	56790 MW	56800 TQ	USBLS	5/15
	North Carolina	Y	39810 FQ	56790 MW	56800 TQ	USBLS	5/15
	Charlotte-Concord-Gastonia MSA, NC-SC	Y	54940 FQ	56790 MW	56800 TQ	USBLS	5/15
	New Bern MSA, NC	Y	39560 FQ	56790 MW	56800 TQ	USBLS	5/15
	Raleigh MSA, NC	Y	56790 FQ	56800 MW	57970 TQ	USBLS	5/15
	North Dakota	Y	32510 FQ	39190 MW	41720 TQ	USBLS	5/15
	Fargo MSA, ND-MN	Y	32530 FQ	55770 MW	56800 TQ	USBLS	5/15
	Ohio	Y	39790 FQ	56790 MW	56800 TQ	USBLS	5/15
	Cincinnati MSA, OH-KY-IN	Y	39790 FQ	56790 MW	57970 TQ	USBLS	5/15
	Cleveland-Elyria MSA, OH	Y	56790 FQ	56800 MW	56800 TQ	USBLS	5/15
	Columbus MSA, OH	Y	38260 FQ	56790 MW	56800 TQ	USBLS	5/15
	Oklahoma	Y	32520 FQ	39810 MW	56800 TQ	USBLS	5/15
	Oklahoma City MSA, OK	Y	38260 FQ	56790 MW	56800 TQ	USBLS	5/15
	Tulsa MSA, OK	Y	39170 FQ	56790 MW	56800 TQ	USBLS	5/15
	Oregon	H	19.58 FQ	27.94 MW	28.52 TQ	ORBLS	2016
	Portland-Vancouver-Hillsboro MSA, OR-WA	Y	53080 FQ	56790 MW	57970 TQ	USBLS	5/15
	Pennsylvania	Y	38250 FQ	56790 MW	56800 TQ	USBLS	5/15
	Allentown-Bethlehem-Easton MSA, PA-NJ	Y	39810 FQ	56800 MW	57990 TQ	USBLS	5/15
	Harrisburg-Carlisle MSA, PA	Y	43820 FQ	56790 MW	56810 TQ	USBLS	5/15
	Montgomery County-Bucks County-Chester County PMSA, PA	Y	56790 FQ	56800 MW	57530 TQ	USBLS	5/15
	Philadelphia PMSA, PA	Y	56790 FQ	56790 MW	56800 TQ	USBLS	5/15
	Pittsburgh MSA, PA	Y	32530 FQ	56790 MW	56800 TQ	USBLS	5/15
	Rhode Island	Y	54000 FQ	56800 MW	57970 TQ	USBLS	5/15
	Providence-Warwick MSA, RI-MA	Y	56780 FQ	56800 MW	57970 TQ	USBLS	5/15
	South Carolina	Y	39800 FQ	56790 MW	56800 TQ	USBLS	5/15
	Charleston-North Charleston MSA, SC	Y	40110 FQ	56790 MW	56800 TQ	USBLS	5/15
	Columbia MSA, SC	Y	39800 FQ	56790 MW	57970 TQ	USBLS	5/15
	Greenville-Anderson-Mauldin MSA, SC	Y	56790 FQ	56790 MW	56800 TQ	USBLS	5/15
	South Dakota	Y	32520 FQ	39790 MW	56790 TQ	USBLS	5/15
	Sioux Falls MSA, SD	Y	32530 FQ	39810 MW	56800 TQ	USBLS	5/15
	Tennessee	Y	38240 FQ	56790 MW	56800 TQ	USBLS	5/15
	Knoxville MSA, TN	Y	32530 FQ	56790 MW	56800 TQ	USBLS	5/15
	Memphis MSA, TN-MS-AR	Y	32530 FQ	56790 MW	56800 TQ	USBLS	5/15
	Nashville-Davidson–Murfreesboro–Franklin MSA, TN	Y	39790 FQ	56790 MW	56800 TQ	USBLS	5/15
	Texas	Y	39790 FQ	56790 MW	56800 TQ	USBLS	5/15
	Austin-Round Rock MSA, TX	Y	40770 FQ	56790 MW	56800 TQ	USBLS	5/15
	Dallas-Plano-Irving PMSA, TX	Y	56790 FQ	56790 MW	56800 TQ	USBLS	5/15
	Fort Worth-Arlington PMSA, TX	Y	56790 FQ	56800 MW	57030 TQ	USBLS	5/15
	Houston-The Woodlands-Sugar Land MSA, TX	Y	56790 FQ	56800 MW	56810 TQ	USBLS	5/15
	San Antonio-New Braunfels MSA, TX	Y	39170 FQ	56790 MW	56800 TQ	USBLS	5/15
	Utah	Y	38260 FQ	56790 MW	56800 TQ	USBLS	5/15
	Ogden-Clearfield MSA, UT	Y	35670 FQ	56790 MW	56800 TQ	USBLS	5/15
	Provo-Orem MSA, UT	Y	32530 FQ	56790 MW	56800 TQ	USBLS	5/15
	Salt Lake City MSA, UT	Y	53090 FQ	56790 MW	56800 TQ	USBLS	5/15
	Vermont	Y	35650 FQ	40760 MW	56800 TQ	USBLS	5/15
	Burlington-South Burlington MSA, VT	Y	39800 FQ	56790 MW	57980 TQ	USBLS	5/15
	Virginia	Y	39790 FQ	56790 MW	56800 TQ	USBLS	5/15
	Richmond MSA, VA	Y	39800 FQ	56790 MW	57970 TQ	USBLS	5/15
	Virginia Beach-Norfolk-Newport News MSA, VA-NC	Y	39800 FQ	56790 MW	57970 TQ	USBLS	5/15
	Washington	H	19.58 FQ	27.94 MW	27.95 TQ	WABLS	3/16

AE	Average entry wage	AWR	Average wage range	H	Hourly	LR	Low end range	MTC	Median total compensation	TCC	Total cash compensation
AEX	Average experienced wage	B	Biweekly	HI	Highest wage paid	M	Monthly	MW	Median wage paid	TQ	Third quartile wage
ATC	Average total compensation	D	Daily	HR	High end range	MCC	Median cash compensation	MWR	Median wage range	W	Weekly
AW	Average wage paid	FQ	First quartile wage	LO	Lowest wage paid	ME	Median entry wage	S	See annotated source	Y	Yearly

Occupation/Type/Industry	Location	Per	Low	Mid	High	Source	Date
Postal Service Clerk	Seattle-Bellevue-Everett						
	PMSA, WA	H	26.13 FQ	27.94 MW	27.95 TQ	WABLS	3/16
	Tacoma-Lakewood PMSA, WA	H	19.58 FQ	27.94 MW	28.12 TQ	WABLS	3/16
	West Virginia	Y	32520 FQ	39800 MW	56790 TQ	USBLS	5/15
	Huntington-Ashland MSA,						
	WV-KY-OH	Y	38260 FQ	53340 MW	56800 TQ	USBLS	5/15
	Wisconsin	Y	32530 FQ	56790 MW	56800 TQ	USBLS	5/15
	Madison MSA, WI	Y	32530 FQ	56790 MW	56800 TQ	USBLS	5/15
	Milwaukee-Waukesha-West						
	Allis MSA, WI	Y	32530 FQ	56790 MW	56800 TQ	USBLS	5/15
	Wyoming	Y	32530 FQ	40750 MW	56790 TQ	USBLS	5/15
	Puerto Rico	Y	55860 FQ	56790 MW	56800 TQ	USBLS	5/15
	Virgin Islands	Y	56790 FQ	56800 MW	56800 TQ	USBLS	5/15
	Guam	Y	32530 FQ	56790 MW	56800 TQ	USBLS	5/15
Postal Service Mail Carrier	Alabama	Y	37823 AE	52086 AW	59218 AEX	ALBLS	6/16
	Birmingham-Hoover MSA, AL	Y	38369 AE	52643 AW	59785 AEX	ALBLS	6/16
	Alaska	Y	37220 FQ	59280 MW	59290 TQ	USBLS	5/15
	Anchorage MSA, AK	Y	37650 FQ	59280 MW	59290 TQ	USBLS	5/15
	Arizona	Y	40470 FQ	58900 MW	59300 TQ	USBLS	5/15
	Phoenix-Mesa-Scottsdale						
	MSA, AZ	Y	39680 FQ	59280 MW	59300 TQ	USBLS	5/15
	Tucson MSA, AZ	Y	41890 FQ	59280 MW	59300 TQ	USBLS	5/15
	Arkansas	Y	41490 FQ	54050 MW	59290 TQ	USBLS	5/15
	Little Rock-North Little Rock-						
	Conway MSA, AR	Y	39720 FQ	57950 MW	59300 TQ	USBLS	5/15
	California	H	22.54 FQ	29.17 MW	29.18 TQ	CABLS	1/16-3/16
	Anaheim-Santa Ana-Irvine						
	PMSA, CA	H	28.01 FQ	29.17 MW	29.18 TQ	CABLS	1/16-3/16
	Los Angeles-Long Beach-						
	Glendale PMSA, CA	H	27.81 FQ	29.17 MW	29.18 TQ	CABLS	1/16-3/16
	Oakland-Hayward-Berkeley						
	PMSA, CA	H	28.10 FQ	29.17 MW	29.18 TQ	CABLS	1/16-3/16
	Riverside-San Bernardino-						
	Ontario MSA, CA	H	20.60 FQ	29.17 MW	29.18 TQ	CABLS	1/16-3/16
	Sacramento–Roseville–						
	Arden-Arcade MSA, CA	H	20.61 FQ	29.17 MW	29.18 TQ	CABLS	1/16-3/16
	San Diego-Carlsbad MSA, CA	H	18.74 FQ	29.17 MW	29.18 TQ	CABLS	1/16-3/16
	San Francisco-Redwood City-						
	South San Francisco PMSA,						
	CA	H	28.79 FQ	29.17 MW	29.18 TQ	CABLS	1/16-3/16
	Colorado	Y	37780 FQ	59280 MW	59290 TQ	USBLS	5/15
	Denver-Aurora-Lakewood						
	MSA, CO	Y	38090 FQ	59280 MW	59300 TQ	USBLS	5/15
	Connecticut	Y		60664 MW		CTBLS	1/16-3/16
	Bridgeport-Stamford-Norwalk						
	MSA, CT	Y	41880 FQ	59290 MW	59290 TQ	USBLS	5/15
	Hartford-West Hartford-East						
	Hartford MSA, CT	Y	41220 FQ	59280 MW	59300 TQ	USBLS	5/15
	Delaware	Y	41210 FQ	58320 MW	59290 TQ	USBLS	5/15
	Wilmington PMSA, DE-MD-						
	NJ	Y	41220 FQ	59280 MW	59290 TQ	USBLS	5/15
	District of Columbia	Y	40560 FQ	59280 MW	59290 TQ	USBLS	5/15
	Washington-Arlington-						
	Alexandria PMSA, DC-VA-						
	MD-WV	Y	38090 FQ	58810 MW	59290 TQ	USBLS	5/15
	Florida	H	17.98 AE	29.53 MW	29.57 AEX	FLBLS	7/16-9/16
	Fort Lauderdale-Pompano						
	Beach-Deerfield Beach						
	PMSA, FL	H	19.19 AE	29.53 MW	29.67 AEX	FLBLS	7/16-9/16
	Miami-Miami Beach-Kendall						
	PMSA, FL	H	18.47 AE	29.53 MW	29.64 AEX	FLBLS	7/16-9/16
	Orlando-Kissimmee-Sanford						
	MSA, FL	H	17.85 AE	29.53 MW	29.75 AEX	FLBLS	7/16-9/16
	Tampa-St. Petersburg-						
	Clearwater MSA, FL	H	17.83 AE	28.80 MW	29.26 AEX	FLBLS	7/16-9/16
	Georgia	Y	41870 FQ	57730 MW	59300 TQ	USBLS	5/15
	Atlanta-Sandy Springs-						
	Roswell MSA, GA	Y	41220 FQ	59280 MW	59300 TQ	USBLS	5/15
	Augusta-Richmond County						
	MSA, GA-SC	Y	41210 FQ	57730 MW	59300 TQ	USBLS	5/15
	Hawaii	Y	56540 FQ	59290 MW	59300 TQ	USBLS	5/15

AE	Average entry wage	**AWR**	Average wage range	**H**	Hourly
AEX	Average experienced wage	**B**	Biweekly	**HI**	Highest wage paid
ATC	Average total compensation	**D**	Daily	**HR**	High end range
AW	Average wage paid	**FQ**	First quartile wage	**LO**	Lowest wage paid

LR	Low end range	**MTC**	Median total compensation	**TCC**	Total cash compensation
M	Monthly	**MW**	Median wage paid	**TQ**	Third quartile wage
MCC	Median cash compensation	**MWR**	Median wage range	**W**	Weekly
ME	Median entry wage	**S**	See annotated source	**Y**	Yearly

Occupation/Type/Industry	Location	Per	Low	Mid	High	Source	Date
Postal Service Mail Carrier	Urban Honolulu MSA, HI	Y	57350 FQ	59290 MW	59300 TQ	USBLS	5/15
	Idaho	Y	35350 FQ	55750 MW	59300 TQ	USBLS	5/15
	Boise City MSA, ID	Y	36470 FQ	56700 MW	59300 TQ	USBLS	5/15
	Illinois	Y	40560 FQ	59280 MW	59290 TQ	USBLS	5/15
	Chicago-Naperville-Arlington Heights PMSA, IL	Y	41870 FQ	59280 MW	59290 TQ	USBLS	5/15
	Lake County-Kenosha County PMSA, IL-WI	Y	41880 FQ	59280 MW	59290 TQ	USBLS	5/15
	Indiana	Y	38100 FQ	56550 MW	59290 TQ	USBLS	5/15
	Gary PMSA, IN	Y	37220 FQ	57880 MW	59290 TQ	USBLS	5/15
	Indianapolis-Carmel-Anderson MSA, IN	Y	38100 FQ	58510 MW	59300 TQ	USBLS	5/15
	Lafayette-West Lafayette MSA, IN	Y	38110 FQ	57340 MW	59300 TQ	USBLS	5/15
	Iowa	Y	38100 FQ	56150 MW	59290 TQ	USBLS	5/15
	Des Moines-West Des Moines MSA, IA	Y	38090 FQ	59280 MW	59300 TQ	USBLS	5/15
	Kansas	Y	36480 FQ	54510 MW	59290 TQ	USBLS	5/15
	Wichita MSA, KS	Y	40520 FQ	57810 MW	59290 TQ	USBLS	5/15
	Kentucky	Y	39420 FQ	55740 MW	59290 TQ	USBLS	5/15
	Louisville-Jefferson County MSA, KY-IN	Y	41870 FQ	57730 MW	59290 TQ	USBLS	5/15
	Louisiana	Y	38090 FQ	56940 MW	59290 TQ	USBLS	5/15
	Baton Rouge MSA, LA	Y	41870 FQ	57330 MW	59300 TQ	USBLS	5/15
	New Orleans-Metairie MSA, LA	Y	38090 FQ	58490 MW	59290 TQ	USBLS	5/15
	Maine	Y	36470 FQ	52550 MW	59290 TQ	USBLS	5/15
	Portland-South Portland MSA, ME	Y	38620 FQ	57630 MW	59300 TQ	USBLS	5/15
	Maryland	Y	36455 AE	51539 MW	59081 AEX	MDBLS	4/16
	Baltimore-Columbia-Towson MSA, MD	Y	41870 FQ	58490 MW	59290 TQ	USBLS	5/15
	Salisbury MSA, MD-DE	Y	41870 FQ	54260 MW	59300 TQ	USBLS	5/15
	Massachusetts	Y	41880 FQ	59280 MW	59290 TQ	USBLS	5/15
	Boston-Cambridge-Newton NECTA, MA	Y	56940 FQ	59290 MW	59300 TQ	USBLS	5/15
	Worcester MSA, MA-CT	Y	36470 FQ	57420 MW	59290 TQ	USBLS	5/15
	Michigan	Y	41870 FQ	58390 MW	59290 TQ	USBLS	5/15
	Detroit-Dearborn-Livonia PMSA, MI	Y	40550 FQ	59290 MW	59290 TQ	USBLS	5/15
	Grand Rapids-Wyoming MSA, MI	Y	41880 FQ	57810 MW	59300 TQ	USBLS	5/15
	Minnesota	Y	38529 FQ	56985 MW	59958 TQ	MNBLS	1/16-3/16
	Minneapolis-St. Paul-Bloomington MSA, MN-WI	Y	38529 FQ	59352 MW	59958 TQ	MNBLS	1/16-3/16
	Mississippi	Y	41870 FQ	52690 MW	59300 TQ	USBLS	5/15
	Jackson MSA, MS	Y	38100 FQ	56540 MW	59300 TQ	USBLS	5/15
	Missouri	Y	38100 FQ	56150 MW	59290 TQ	USBLS	5/15
	Kansas City MSA, MO-KS	Y	37220 FQ	57740 MW	59290 TQ	USBLS	5/15
	St. Louis MSA, MO-IL	Y	38880 FQ	57950 MW	59290 TQ	USBLS	5/15
	Montana	Y	34650 FQ	54110 MW	59290 TQ	USBLS	5/15
	Billings MSA, MT	Y	36470 FQ	58020 MW	59290 TQ	USBLS	5/15
	Nebraska	Y	38100 FQ	53550 MW	59290 TQ	NEBLS	7/16-9/16
	Omaha-Council Bluffs MSA, NE-IA	Y	41875 FQ	59285 MW	59300 TQ	NEBLS	7/16-9/16
	Nevada	Y	37230 FQ	59280 MW	59290 TQ	USBLS	5/15
	Las Vegas-Henderson-Paradise MSA, NV	Y	37230 FQ	59280 MW	59290 TQ	USBLS	5/15
	New Hampshire	H	18.04 AE	27.62 MW	28.61 AEX	NHBLS	6/16
	Manchester NECTA, NH	H	18.88 AE	29.37 MW	29.62 AEX	NHBLS	6/16
	Nashua NECTA, NH-MA	Y	40660 FQ	55740 MW	59300 TQ	USBLS	5/15
	New Jersey	Y	41870 FQ	59280 MW	59290 TQ	USBLS	5/15
	Camden PMSA, NJ	Y	41880 FQ	59280 MW	59290 TQ	USBLS	5/15
	Newark PMSA, NJ-PA	Y	38880 FQ	59280 MW	59290 TQ	USBLS	5/15
	Trenton MSA, NJ	Y	41880 FQ	59280 MW	59290 TQ	USBLS	5/15
	New Mexico	Y	38100 FQ	58110 MW	59300 TQ	USBLS	5/15
	Albuquerque MSA, NM	Y	41870 FQ	58930 MW	59300 TQ	USBLS	5/15
	New York	Y	37290 AE	60660 MW	60320 AEX	NYBLS	1/16-3/16
	Buffalo-Cheektowaga-Niagara Falls MSA, NY	Y	38100 FQ	59280 MW	59290 TQ	USBLS	5/15
	Nassau County-Suffolk County PMSA, NY	Y	51750 FQ	59280 MW	59290 TQ	USBLS	5/15

Occupation/Type/Industry	Location	Per	Low	Mid	High	Source	Date
Postal Service Mail Carrier	New York-Jersey City-White						
	Plains PMSA, NY-NJ	Y	40540 FQ	59280 MW	59290 TQ	USBLS	5/15
	Rochester MSA, NY	Y	38100 FQ	57340 MW	59290 TQ	USBLS	5/15
	North Carolina	Y	41870 FQ	56360 MW	59300 TQ	USBLS	5/15
	Charlotte-Concord-Gastonia						
	MSA, NC-SC	Y	41870 FQ	57120 MW	59300 TQ	USBLS	5/15
	Raleigh MSA, NC	Y	41880 FQ	57820 MW	59300 TQ	USBLS	5/15
	North Dakota	Y	38100 FQ	48590 MW	59290 TQ	USBLS	5/15
	Fargo MSA, ND-MN	Y	37230 FQ	54430 MW	59290 TQ	USBLS	5/15
	Ohio	Y	37220 FQ	57820 MW	59290 TQ	USBLS	5/15
	Cincinnati MSA, OH-KY-IN	Y	40550 FQ	59280 MW	59300 TQ	USBLS	5/15
	Cleveland-Elyria MSA, OH	Y	38090 FQ	59280 MW	59290 TQ	USBLS	5/15
	Columbus MSA, OH	Y	36460 FQ	57290 MW	59290 TQ	USBLS	5/15
	Oklahoma	Y	36470 FQ	55160 MW	59290 TQ	USBLS	5/15
	Oklahoma City MSA, OK	Y	36470 FQ	57740 MW	59300 TQ	USBLS	5/15
	Tulsa MSA, OK	Y	38090 FQ	58110 MW	59300 TQ	USBLS	5/15
	Oregon	H	17.95 FQ	28.21 MW	29.18 TQ	ORBLS	2016
	Portland-Vancouver-Hillsboro						
	MSA, OR-WA	Y	38090 FQ	58810 MW	59290 TQ	USBLS	5/15
	Pennsylvania	Y	38100 FQ	58110 MW	59290 TQ	USBLS	5/15
	Allentown-Bethlehem-Easton						
	MSA, PA-NJ	Y	41870 FQ	58420 MW	59290 TQ	USBLS	5/15
	Harrisburg-Carlisle MSA, PA	Y	39160 FQ	58860 MW	59290 TQ	USBLS	5/15
	Montgomery County-Bucks						
	County-Chester County						
	PMSA, PA	Y	40900 FQ	59280 MW	59290 TQ	USBLS	5/15
	Philadelphia PMSA, PA	Y	55750 FQ	59290 MW	59290 TQ	USBLS	5/15
	Pittsburgh MSA, PA	Y	38100 FQ	57810 MW	59290 TQ	USBLS	5/15
	Rhode Island	Y	38100 FQ	59280 MW	59290 TQ	USBLS	5/15
	Providence-Warwick MSA, RI-						
	MA	Y	38100 FQ	59280 MW	59290 TQ	USBLS	5/15
	South Carolina	Y	41870 FQ	54880 MW	59300 TQ	USBLS	5/15
	Charleston-North Charleston						
	MSA, SC	Y	40530 FQ	54470 MW	59290 TQ	USBLS	5/15
	Columbia MSA, SC	Y	39160 FQ	56150 MW	59290 TQ	USBLS	5/15
	Greenville-Anderson-Mauldin						
	MSA, SC	Y	38100 FQ	56360 MW	59290 TQ	USBLS	5/15
	South Dakota	Y	38020 FQ	48610 MW	59290 TQ	USBLS	5/15
	Sioux Falls MSA, SD	Y	41870 FQ	58110 MW	59300 TQ	USBLS	5/15
	Tennessee	Y	41870 FQ	56360 MW	59300 TQ	USBLS	5/15
	Knoxville MSA, TN	Y	41880 FQ	57300 MW	59300 TQ	USBLS	5/15
	Memphis MSA, TN-MS-AR	Y	41870 FQ	57990 MW	59300 TQ	USBLS	5/15
	Nashville-Davidson–						
	Murfreesboro–Franklin						
	MSA, TN	Y	41880 FQ	57810 MW	59300 TQ	USBLS	5/15
	Texas	Y	37220 FQ	58110 MW	59300 TQ	USBLS	5/15
	Austin-Round Rock MSA, TX	Y	36480 FQ	59280 MW	59300 TQ	USBLS	5/15
	Dallas-Plano-Irving PMSA, TX	Y	41870 FQ	59280 MW	59300 TQ	USBLS	5/15
	Fort Worth-Arlington PMSA,						
	TX	Y	38090 FQ	59280 MW	59300 TQ	USBLS	5/15
	Houston-The Woodlands-						
	Sugar Land MSA, TX	Y	36480 FQ	59280 MW	59300 TQ	USBLS	5/15
	San Antonio-New Braunfels						
	MSA, TX	Y	38090 FQ	58810 MW	59300 TQ	USBLS	5/15
	Utah	Y	40530 FQ	59280 MW	59300 TQ	USBLS	5/15
	Ogden-Clearfield MSA, UT	Y	41870 FQ	58590 MW	59300 TQ	USBLS	5/15
	Provo-Orem MSA, UT	Y	36480 FQ	59060 MW	59300 TQ	USBLS	5/15
	Salt Lake City MSA, UT	Y	41870 FQ	59280 MW	59300 TQ	USBLS	5/15
	Vermont	Y	40750 FQ	51470 MW	59290 TQ	USBLS	5/15
	Burlington-South Burlington						
	MSA, VT	Y	41880 FQ	56360 MW	59290 TQ	USBLS	5/15
	Virginia	Y	37220 FQ	56360 MW	59290 TQ	USBLS	5/15
	Richmond MSA, VA	Y	36480 FQ	56160 MW	59290 TQ	USBLS	5/15
	Virginia Beach-Norfolk-						
	Newport News MSA, VA-NC	Y	37220 FQ	57740 MW	59290 TQ	USBLS	5/15
	Washington	H	18.91 FQ	28.98 MW	29.18 TQ	WABLS	3/16
	Seattle-Bellevue-Everett						
	PMSA, WA	H	18.75 FQ	29.17 MW	29.18 TQ	WABLS	3/16
	Tacoma-Lakewood PMSA, WA	H	20.60 FQ	29.17 MW	29.18 TQ	WABLS	3/16
	West Virginia	Y	36470 FQ	54710 MW	59290 TQ	USBLS	5/15
	Huntington-Ashland MSA,						
	WV-KY-OH	Y	34650 FQ	50870 MW	59290 TQ	USBLS	5/15

Occupation/Type/Industry	Location	Per	Low	Mid	High	Source	Date
Postal Service Mail Carrier	Wisconsin	Y	40530 FQ	56190 MW	59290 TQ	USBLS	5/15
	Madison MSA, WI	Y	38890 FQ	56360 MW	59290 TQ	USBLS	5/15
	Milwaukee-Waukesha-West Allis MSA, WI	Y	38090 FQ	59280 MW	59290 TQ	USBLS	5/15
	Wyoming	Y	36470 FQ	56990 MW	59290 TQ	USBLS	5/15
	Cheyenne MSA, WY	Y	38880 FQ	59280 MW	59290 TQ	USBLS	5/15
	Puerto Rico	Y	40540 FQ	58890 MW	59290 TQ	USBLS	5/15
	Virgin Islands	Y	59280 FQ	59290 MW	59300 TQ	USBLS	5/15
Postal Service Mail Sorter, Processor, and Processing Machine Operator	Alabama	Y	36236 AE	50953 AW	58321 AEX	ALBLS	6/16
	Birmingham-Hoover MSA, AL	Y	34855 AE	49644 AW	57043 AEX	ALBLS	6/16
	Alaska	Y	32530 FQ	56760 MW	56800 TQ	USBLS	5/15
	Anchorage MSA, AK	Y	32530 FQ	56750 MW	56800 TQ	USBLS	5/15
	Arizona	Y	33370 FQ	55880 MW	56790 TQ	USBLS	5/15
	Phoenix-Mesa-Scottsdale MSA, AZ	Y	33380 FQ	55860 MW	56790 TQ	USBLS	5/15
	Tucson MSA, AZ	Y	35370 FQ	56750 MW	56800 TQ	USBLS	5/15
	Arkansas	Y	39180 FQ	56760 MW	56800 TQ	USBLS	5/15
	Little Rock-North Little Rock-Conway MSA, AR	Y	39180 FQ	56760 MW	56800 TQ	USBLS	5/15
	California	H	26.30 FQ	27.49 MW	27.95 TQ	CABLS	1/16-3/16
	Anaheim-Santa Ana-Irvine PMSA, CA	H	16.01 FQ	27.41 MW	27.94 TQ	CABLS	1/16-3/16
	Los Angeles-Long Beach-Glendale PMSA, CA	H	25.68 FQ	27.41 MW	27.95 TQ	CABLS	1/16-3/16
	Oakland-Hayward-Berkeley PMSA, CA	H	26.62 FQ	27.92 MW	27.95 TQ	CABLS	1/16-3/16
	Riverside-San Bernardino-Ontario MSA, CA	H	16.01 FQ	27.40 MW	27.94 TQ	CABLS	1/16-3/16
	Sacramento–Roseville–Arden-Arcade MSA, CA	H	26.31 FQ	27.41 MW	27.95 TQ	CABLS	1/16-3/16
	San Diego-Carlsbad MSA, CA	H	25.84 FQ	27.41 MW	27.94 TQ	CABLS	1/16-3/16
	San Francisco-Redwood City-South San Francisco PMSA, CA	H	27.40 FQ	27.94 MW	27.95 TQ	CABLS	1/16-3/16
	Colorado	Y	52510 FQ	56740 MW	56790 TQ	USBLS	5/15
	Denver-Aurora-Lakewood MSA, CO	Y	41330 FQ	55700 MW	56790 TQ	USBLS	5/15
	Connecticut	Y		58075 MW		CTBLS	1/16-3/16
	Bridgeport-Stamford-Norwalk MSA, CT	Y	55700 FQ	56790 MW	56800 TQ	USBLS	5/15
	Hartford-West Hartford-East Hartford MSA, CT	Y	39180 FQ	55700 MW	56790 TQ	USBLS	5/15
	Delaware	Y	55690 FQ	56760 MW	56800 TQ	USBLS	5/15
	Wilmington PMSA, DE-MD-NJ	Y	55690 FQ	56760 MW	56800 TQ	USBLS	5/15
	District of Columbia	Y	55680 FQ	56760 MW	56800 TQ	USBLS	5/15
	Washington-Arlington-Alexandria PMSA, DC-VA-MD-WV	Y	55680 FQ	56750 MW	56790 TQ	USBLS	5/15
	Florida	H	20.49 AE	28.27 MW	28.27 AEX	FLBLS	7/16-9/16
	Fort Lauderdale-Pompano Beach-Deerfield Beach PMSA, FL	H	26.18 AE	28.59 MW	28.73 AEX	FLBLS	7/16-9/16
	Miami-Miami Beach-Kendall PMSA, FL	H	19.07 AE	28.27 MW	28.28 AEX	FLBLS	7/16-9/16
	Orlando-Kissimmee-Sanford MSA, FL	H	21.93 AE	27.75 MW	28.22 AEX	FLBLS	7/16-9/16
	Tampa-St. Petersburg-Clearwater MSA, FL	H	21.41 AE	28.28 MW	28.27 AEX	FLBLS	7/16-9/16
	Georgia	Y	55680 FQ	56760 MW	56800 TQ	USBLS	5/15
	Atlanta-Sandy Springs-Roswell MSA, GA	Y	55680 FQ	56760 MW	56800 TQ	USBLS	5/15
	Augusta-Richmond County MSA, GA-SC	Y	38240 FQ	56750 MW	56800 TQ	USBLS	5/15
	Hawaii	Y	54930 FQ	56790 MW	56800 TQ	USBLS	5/15
	Urban Honolulu MSA, HI	Y	54930 FQ	56790 MW	56800 TQ	USBLS	5/15
	Idaho	Y	54940 FQ	56790 MW	56800 TQ	USBLS	5/15
	Boise City MSA, ID	Y	54950 FQ	56790 MW	56800 TQ	USBLS	5/15

AE	Average entry wage	AWR	Average wage range	H	Hourly	LR	Low end range	MTC	Median total compensation	TCC	Total cash compensation
AEX	Average experienced wage	B	Biweekly	HI	Highest wage paid	M	Monthly	MW	Median wage paid	TQ	Third quartile wage
ATC	Average total compensation	D	Daily	HR	High end range	MCC	Median cash compensation	MWR	Median wage range	W	Weekly
AW	Average wage paid	FQ	First quartile wage	LO	Lowest wage paid	ME	Median entry wage	S	See annotated source	Y	Yearly

Occupation/Type/Industry	Location	Per	Low	Mid	High	Source	Date
Postal Service Mail Sorter, Processor, and Processing Machine Operator	Illinois	Y	40110 FQ	55700 MW	56790 TQ	USBLS	5/15
	Chicago-Naperville-Arlington Heights PMSA, IL	Y	40110 FQ	55700 MW	56790 TQ	USBLS	5/15
	Lake County-Kenosha County PMSA, IL-WI	Y	56790 FQ	56800 MW	56800 TQ	USBLS	5/15
	Indiana	Y	32530 FQ	55700 MW	56790 TQ	USBLS	5/15
	Gary PMSA, IN	Y	55690 FQ	56790 MW	56800 TQ	USBLS	5/15
	Indianapolis-Carmel-Anderson MSA, IN	Y	32530 FQ	55690 MW	56790 TQ	USBLS	5/15
	Iowa	Y	39180 FQ	55700 MW	56790 TQ	USBLS	5/15
	Des Moines-West Des Moines MSA, IA	Y	40110 FQ	55700 MW	56790 TQ	USBLS	5/15
	Kansas	Y	32520 FQ	55680 MW	56790 TQ	USBLS	5/15
	Wichita MSA, KS	Y	42880 FQ	56750 MW	56800 TQ	USBLS	5/15
	Kentucky	Y	52190 FQ	56760 MW	56800 TQ	USBLS	5/15
	Louisville-Jefferson County MSA, KY-IN	Y	39180 FQ	56750 MW	56790 TQ	USBLS	5/15
	Louisiana	Y	39180 FQ	56760 MW	56800 TQ	USBLS	5/15
	Baton Rouge MSA, LA	Y	55690 FQ	56790 MW	56800 TQ	USBLS	5/15
	New Orleans-Metairie MSA, LA	Y	39170 FQ	56760 MW	56800 TQ	USBLS	5/15
	Maine	Y	52510 FQ	55700 MW	56790 TQ	USBLS	5/15
	Portland-South Portland MSA, ME	Y	53150 FQ	55700 MW	56790 TQ	USBLS	5/15
	Maryland	Y	40982 AE	51490 MW	56744 AEX	MDBLS	4/16
	Baltimore-Columbia-Towson MSA, MD	Y	52510 FQ	56760 MW	56800 TQ	USBLS	5/15
	Massachusetts	Y	54100 FQ	55700 MW	56790 TQ	USBLS	5/15
	Boston-Cambridge-Newton NECTA, MA	Y	55680 FQ	55700 MW	56790 TQ	USBLS	5/15
	Worcester MSA, MA-CT	Y	39190 FQ	55700 MW	56790 TQ	USBLS	5/15
	Michigan	Y	39170 FQ	56750 MW	56800 TQ	USBLS	5/15
	Detroit-Dearborn-Livonia PMSA, MI	Y	55690 FQ	56780 MW	56800 TQ	USBLS	5/15
	Grand Rapids-Wyoming MSA, MI	Y	38240 FQ	55690 MW	56790 TQ	USBLS	5/15
	Minnesota	Y	40249 FQ	57430 MW	57440 TQ	MNBLS	1/16-3/16
	Minneapolis-St. Paul-Bloomington MSA, MN-WI	Y	53102 FQ	57430 MW	57440 TQ	MNBLS	1/16-3/16
	Mississippi	Y	39170 FQ	56750 MW	56800 TQ	USBLS	5/15
	Jackson MSA, MS	Y	39170 FQ	55700 MW	56790 TQ	USBLS	5/15
	Missouri	Y	52510 FQ	56740 MW	56790 TQ	USBLS	5/15
	Kansas City MSA, MO-KS	Y	38240 FQ	55700 MW	56790 TQ	USBLS	5/15
	St. Louis MSA, MO-IL	Y	41310 FQ	55700 MW	56790 TQ	USBLS	5/15
	Montana	Y	38230 FQ	55700 MW	56800 TQ	USBLS	5/15
	Billings MSA, MT	Y	33380 FQ	55700 MW	56790 TQ	USBLS	5/15
	Nebraska	Y	38245 FQ	56750 MW	56795 TQ	NEBLS	7/16-9/16
	Omaha-Council Bluffs MSA, NE-IA	Y	38245 FQ	56745 MW	56795 TQ	NEBLS	7/16-9/16
	Nevada	Y	53770 FQ	56760 MW	56800 TQ	USBLS	5/15
	Las Vegas-Henderson-Paradise MSA, NV	Y	53470 FQ	56750 MW	56790 TQ	USBLS	5/15
	New Hampshire	H	19.60 AE	27.60 MW	27.99 AEX	NHBLS	6/16
	Manchester NECTA, NH	H	21.44 AE	28.11 MW	28.06 AEX	NHBLS	6/16
	Nashua NECTA, NH-MA	Y	38700 FQ	55690 MW	56750 TQ	USBLS	5/15
	New Jersey	Y	54100 FQ	55730 MW	56790 TQ	USBLS	5/15
	Camden PMSA, NJ	Y	55370 FQ	56750 MW	56800 TQ	USBLS	5/15
	Newark PMSA, NJ-PA	Y	56760 FQ	56790 MW	56800 TQ	USBLS	5/15
	Trenton MSA, NJ	Y	55690 FQ	56750 MW	56800 TQ	USBLS	5/15
	New Mexico	Y	53160 FQ	56750 MW	56800 TQ	USBLS	5/15
	Albuquerque MSA, NM	Y	53470 FQ	56400 MW	56800 TQ	USBLS	5/15
	New York	Y	40940 AE	57000 MW	57920 AEX	NYBLS	1/16-3/16
	Buffalo-Cheektowaga-Niagara Falls MSA, NY	Y	55690 FQ	56750 MW	56800 TQ	USBLS	5/15
	Nassau County-Suffolk County PMSA, NY	Y	53460 FQ	55700 MW	56790 TQ	USBLS	5/15
	New York-Jersey City-White Plains PMSA, NY-NJ	Y	54090 FQ	55700 MW	56790 TQ	USBLS	5/15
	Rochester MSA, NY	Y	38240 FQ	55680 MW	56790 TQ	USBLS	5/15

AE Average entry wage	**AWR** Average wage range	**H** Hourly	**LR** Low end range	**MTC** Median total compensation	**TCC** Total cash compensation
AEX Average experienced wage	**B** Biweekly	**HI** Highest wage paid	**M** Monthly	**MW** Median wage paid	**TQ** Third quartile wage
ATC Average total compensation	**D** Daily	**HR** High end range	**MCC** Median cash compensation	**MWR** Median wage range	**W** Weekly
AW Average wage paid	**FQ** First quartile wage	**LO** Lowest wage paid	**ME** Median entry wage	**S** See annotated source	**Y** Yearly

Occupation/Type/Industry	Location	Per	Low	Mid	High	Source	Date
Postal Service Mail Sorter, Processor, and Processing Machine Operator	North Carolina	Y	41320 FQ	56750 MW	56790 TQ	USBLS	5/15
	Charlotte-Concord-Gastonia MSA, NC-SC	Y	53780 FQ	56760 MW	56800 TQ	USBLS	5/15
	Raleigh MSA, NC	Y	53470 FQ	56750 MW	56800 TQ	USBLS	5/15
	North Dakota	Y	32530 FQ	41630 MW	56790 TQ	USBLS	5/15
	Fargo MSA, ND-MN	Y	33380 FQ	55690 MW	56790 TQ	USBLS	5/15
	Ohio	Y	39190 FQ	56750 MW	56790 TQ	USBLS	5/15
	Cincinnati MSA, OH-KY-IN	Y	55060 FQ	56750 MW	56790 TQ	USBLS	5/15
	Cleveland-Elyria MSA, OH	Y	32530 FQ	55700 MW	56790 TQ	USBLS	5/15
	Columbus MSA, OH	Y	40120 FQ	56760 MW	56800 TQ	USBLS	5/15
	Oklahoma	Y	40110 FQ	56760 MW	56800 TQ	USBLS	5/15
	Oklahoma City MSA, OK	Y	39190 FQ	56750 MW	56800 TQ	USBLS	5/15
	Tulsa MSA, OK	Y	40100 FQ	56760 MW	56800 TQ	USBLS	5/15
	Oregon	H	18.81 FQ	27.41 MW	27.94 TQ	ORBLS	2016
	Portland-Vancouver-Hillsboro MSA, OR-WA	Y	39170 FQ	55700 MW	56790 TQ	USBLS	5/15
	Pennsylvania	Y	53780 FQ	55870 MW	56790 TQ	USBLS	5/15
	Allentown-Bethlehem-Easton MSA, PA-NJ	Y	52510 FQ	56750 MW	56790 TQ	USBLS	5/15
	Harrisburg-Carlisle MSA, PA	Y	38250 FQ	55690 MW	56790 TQ	USBLS	5/15
	Montgomery County-Bucks County-Chester County PMSA, PA	Y	56780 FQ	56800 MW	57980 TQ	USBLS	5/15
	Philadelphia PMSA, PA	Y	55690 FQ	56750 MW	56790 TQ	USBLS	5/15
	Pittsburgh MSA, PA	Y	52660 FQ	55700 MW	56790 TQ	USBLS	5/15
	Rhode Island	Y	48960 FQ	55700 MW	56790 TQ	USBLS	5/15
	Providence-Warwick MSA, RI-MA	Y	47960 FQ	55700 MW	56790 TQ	USBLS	5/15
	South Carolina	Y	32530 FQ	55690 MW	56790 TQ	USBLS	5/15
	Charleston-North Charleston MSA, SC	Y	39170 FQ	56400 MW	56800 TQ	USBLS	5/15
	Columbia MSA, SC	Y	32530 FQ	55700 MW	56790 TQ	USBLS	5/15
	Greenville-Anderson-Mauldin MSA, SC	Y	32530 FQ	54430 MW	56790 TQ	USBLS	5/15
	South Dakota	Y	38230 FQ	55700 MW	56790 TQ	USBLS	5/15
	Sioux Falls MSA, SD	Y	33370 FQ	55690 MW	56790 TQ	USBLS	5/15
	Tennessee	Y	41320 FQ	56750 MW	56800 TQ	USBLS	5/15
	Knoxville MSA, TN	Y	34800 FQ	56750 MW	56800 TQ	USBLS	5/15
	Memphis MSA, TN-MS-AR	Y	53780 FQ	56750 MW	56790 TQ	USBLS	5/15
	Nashville-Davidson–Murfreesboro–Franklin MSA, TN	Y	52500 FQ	56750 MW	56800 TQ	USBLS	5/15
	Texas	Y	53480 FQ	56750 MW	56800 TQ	USBLS	5/15
	Austin-Round Rock MSA, TX	Y	53470 FQ	56760 MW	56800 TQ	USBLS	5/15
	Dallas-Plano-Irving PMSA, TX	Y	55690 FQ	56750 MW	56800 TQ	USBLS	5/15
	Fort Worth-Arlington PMSA, TX	Y	55680 FQ	56780 MW	56800 TQ	USBLS	5/15
	Houston-The Woodlands-Sugar Land MSA, TX	Y	32530 FQ	56750 MW	56800 TQ	USBLS	5/15
	San Antonio-New Braunfels MSA, TX	Y	53790 FQ	56760 MW	56800 TQ	USBLS	5/15
	Utah	Y	38700 FQ	55700 MW	56800 TQ	USBLS	5/15
	Provo-Orem MSA, UT	Y	39170 FQ	55690 MW	56790 TQ	USBLS	5/15
	Salt Lake City MSA, UT	Y	39170 FQ	55700 MW	56800 TQ	USBLS	5/15
	Vermont	Y	55680 FQ	55700 MW	56790 TQ	USBLS	5/15
	Burlington-South Burlington MSA, VT	Y	55680 FQ	56760 MW	56800 TQ	USBLS	5/15
	Virginia	Y	41970 FQ	55700 MW	56790 TQ	USBLS	5/15
	Richmond MSA, VA	Y	34810 FQ	55690 MW	56790 TQ	USBLS	5/15
	Virginia Beach-Norfolk-Newport News MSA, VA-NC	Y	55050 FQ	56750 MW	56800 TQ	USBLS	5/15
	Washington	H	26.58 FQ	27.93 MW	27.95 TQ	WABLS	3/16
	Seattle-Bellevue-Everett PMSA, WA	H	27.40 FQ	27.93 MW	27.95 TQ	WABLS	3/16
	Tacoma-Lakewood PMSA, WA	H	18.82 FQ	27.41 MW	27.95 TQ	WABLS	3/16
	West Virginia	Y	32520 FQ	53460 MW	56790 TQ	USBLS	5/15
	Wisconsin	Y	55680 FQ	56790 MW	56800 TQ	USBLS	5/15
	Madison MSA, WI	Y	55690 FQ	56790 MW	56800 TQ	USBLS	5/15

AE	Average entry wage	AWR	Average wage range	H	Hourly	LR	Low end range	MTC Median total compensation	TCC Total cash compensation
AEX	Average experienced wage	B	Biweekly	HI	Highest wage paid	M	Monthly	MW Median wage paid	TQ Third quartile wage
ATC	Average total compensation	D	Daily	HR	High end range	MCC Median cash compensation	MWR Median wage range	W Weekly
AW	Average wage paid	FQ	First quartile wage	LO	Lowest wage paid	ME	Median entry wage	S See annotated source	Y Yearly

Occupation/Type/Industry	Location	Per	Low	Mid	High	Source	Date
Postal Service Mail Sorter, Processor, and Processing Machine Operator	Milwaukee-Waukesha-West Allis MSA, WI	Y	55680 FQ	56750 MW	56800 TQ	USBLS	5/15
	Wyoming	Y	39180 FQ	55770 MW	56800 TQ	USBLS	5/15
	Cheyenne MSA, WY	Y	53150 FQ	55700 MW	56790 TQ	USBLS	5/15
	Puerto Rico	Y	32530 FQ	55680 MW	56790 TQ	USBLS	5/15
	Virgin Islands	Y	56790 FQ	56790 MW	56800 TQ	USBLS	5/15
Postdoc							
Life Sciences	United States	Y		48907 AW		TSCI	2016
Postmaster and Mail Superintendent	Alabama	Y	61231 AE	74894 AW	81730 AEX	ALBLS	6/16
	Birmingham-Hoover MSA, AL	Y	61252 AE	76001 AW	83380 AEX	ALBLS	6/16
	Alaska	Y	32500 FQ	43520 MW	59710 TQ	USBLS	5/15
	Arizona	Y	63580 FQ	74860 MW	84750 TQ	USBLS	5/15
	Phoenix-Mesa-Scottsdale MSA, AZ	Y	78710 FQ	87450 MW	96070 TQ	USBLS	5/15
	Arkansas	Y	61420 FQ	70470 MW	79800 TQ	USBLS	5/15
	California	H	31.45 FQ	37.27 MW	41.92 TQ	CABLS	1/16-3/16
	Anaheim-Santa Ana-Irvine PMSA, CA	H	39.55 FQ	43.22 MW	45.86 TQ	CABLS	1/16-3/16
	Los Angeles-Long Beach-Glendale PMSA, CA	H	38.66 FQ	42.82 MW	46.35 TQ	CABLS	1/16-3/16
	Oakland-Hayward-Berkeley PMSA, CA	H	37.87 FQ	42.65 MW	47.68 TQ	CABLS	1/16-3/16
	Riverside-San Bernardino-Ontario MSA, CA	H	33.24 FQ	39.17 MW	43.45 TQ	CABLS	1/16-3/16
	Sacramento–Roseville–Arden-Arcade MSA, CA	H	30.22 FQ	36.40 MW	41.24 TQ	CABLS	1/16-3/16
	San Diego-Carlsbad MSA, CA	H	33.21 FQ	41.90 MW	47.61 TQ	CABLS	1/16-3/16
	San Francisco-Redwood City-South San Francisco PMSA, CA	H	36.19 FQ	41.82 MW	47.60 TQ	CABLS	1/16-3/16
	Colorado	Y	60860 FQ	67690 MW	79200 TQ	USBLS	5/15
	Denver-Aurora-Lakewood MSA, CO	Y	62660 FQ	71960 MW	83360 TQ	USBLS	5/15
	Connecticut	Y		78133 MW		CTBLS	1/16-3/16
	Hartford-West Hartford-East Hartford MSA, CT	Y	67550 FQ	79190 MW	83390 TQ	USBLS	5/15
	Delaware	Y	64370 FQ	75450 MW	83310 TQ	USBLS	5/15
	Washington-Arlington-Alexandria PMSA, DC-VA-MD-WV	Y	63580 FQ	73350 MW	84390 TQ	USBLS	5/15
	Florida	H	30.55 AE	39.60 MW	43.52 AEX	FLBLS	7/16-9/16
	Orlando-Kissimmee-Sanford MSA, FL	H	31.30 AE	39.94 MW	42.67 AEX	FLBLS	7/16-9/16
	Tampa-St. Petersburg-Clearwater MSA, FL	H	36.98 AE	45.21 MW	48.37 AEX	FLBLS	7/16-9/16
	Georgia	Y	65590 FQ	75470 MW	80390 TQ	USBLS	5/15
	Atlanta-Sandy Springs-Roswell MSA, GA	Y	67750 FQ	77370 MW	87790 TQ	USBLS	5/15
	Hawaii	Y	63420 FQ	75900 MW	80450 TQ	USBLS	5/15
	Illinois	Y	61050 FQ	69030 MW	79000 TQ	USBLS	5/15
	Chicago-Naperville-Arlington Heights PMSA, IL	Y	68470 FQ	76790 MW	87790 TQ	USBLS	5/15
	Lake County-Kenosha County PMSA, IL-WI	Y	64810 FQ	71630 MW	80380 TQ	USBLS	5/15
	Indiana	Y	62070 FQ	70880 MW	79600 TQ	USBLS	5/15
	Indianapolis-Carmel-Anderson MSA, IN	Y	66570 FQ	74090 MW	83560 TQ	USBLS	5/15
	Iowa	Y	59420 FQ	62740 MW	74610 TQ	USBLS	5/15
	Des Moines-West Des Moines MSA, IA	Y	62950 FQ	75830 MW	84280 TQ	USBLS	5/15
	Kansas	Y	61110 FQ	66560 MW	74460 TQ	USBLS	5/15
	Kentucky	Y	61380 FQ	69130 MW	79200 TQ	USBLS	5/15
	Louisville-Jefferson County MSA, KY-IN	Y	62980 FQ	72170 MW	84130 TQ	USBLS	5/15
	Louisiana	Y	62990 FQ	70980 MW	80380 TQ	USBLS	5/15
	Baton Rouge MSA, LA	Y	62660 FQ	67880 MW	72110 TQ	USBLS	5/15

AE	Average entry wage	AWR	Average wage range	H	Hourly	LR	Low end range	MTC	Median total compensation	TCC	Total cash compensation
AEX	Average experienced wage	B	Biweekly	HI	Highest wage paid	M	Monthly	MW	Median wage paid	TQ	Third quartile wage
ATC	Average total compensation	D	Daily	HR	High end range	MCC	Median cash compensation	MWR	Median wage range	W	Weekly
AW	Average wage paid	FQ	First quartile wage	LO	Lowest wage paid	ME	Median entry wage	S	See annotated source	Y	Yearly

1277

Occupation/Type/Industry	Location	Per	Low	Mid	High	Source	Date
Postmaster and Mail Superintendent	New Orleans-Metairie MSA, LA	Y	63000 FQ	75890 MW	90150 TQ	USBLS	5/15
	Maine	Y	60010 FQ	65390 MW	74450 TQ	USBLS	5/15
	Portland-South Portland MSA, ME	Y	60800 FQ	75550 MW	80890 TQ	USBLS	5/15
	Maryland	Y	55849 AE	70013 MW	77094 AEX	MDBLS	4/16
	Baltimore-Columbia-Towson MSA, MD	Y	63120 FQ	70270 MW	79200 TQ	USBLS	5/15
	Salisbury MSA, MD-DE	Y	63800 FQ	74270 MW	79600 TQ	USBLS	5/15
	Massachusetts	Y	66570 FQ	76580 MW	82430 TQ	USBLS	5/15
	Boston-Cambridge-Newton NECTA, MA	Y	73020 FQ	79200 MW	87870 TQ	USBLS	5/15
	Worcester MSA, MA-CT	Y	62660 FQ	72680 MW	79450 TQ	USBLS	5/15
	Michigan	Y	66540 FQ	74990 MW	80490 TQ	USBLS	5/15
	Grand Rapids-Wyoming MSA, MI	Y	69850 FQ	79590 MW	88300 TQ	USBLS	5/15
	Minnesota	Y	62399 FQ	68648 MW	79693 TQ	MNBLS	1/16-3/16
	Minneapolis-St. Paul-Bloomington MSA, MN-WI	Y	63628 FQ	75293 MW	81685 TQ	MNBLS	1/16-3/16
	Mississippi	Y	66430 FQ	74800 MW	81980 TQ	USBLS	5/15
	Missouri	Y	60820 FQ	69460 MW	77970 TQ	USBLS	5/15
	Kansas City MSA, MO-KS	Y	60830 FQ	73650 MW	80380 TQ	USBLS	5/15
	St. Louis MSA, MO-IL	Y	63900 FQ	70920 MW	80280 TQ	USBLS	5/15
	Montana	Y	44790 FQ	59710 MW	67790 TQ	USBLS	5/15
	Nebraska	Y	60285 FQ	62320 MW	74830 TQ	NEBLS	7/16-9/16
	Omaha-Council Bluffs MSA, NE-IA	Y	61410 FQ	72810 MW	87870 TQ	NEBLS	7/16-9/16
	Nevada	Y	48310 FQ	61040 MW	79380 TQ	USBLS	5/15
	New Hampshire	H	29.19 AE	34.64 MW	37.54 AEX	NHBLS	6/16
	New Jersey	Y	69440 FQ	76970 MW	83570 TQ	USBLS	5/15
	Camden PMSA, NJ	Y	70560 FQ	75550 MW	84330 TQ	USBLS	5/15
	Newark PMSA, NJ-PA	Y	68050 FQ	76580 MW	82360 TQ	USBLS	5/15
	New Mexico	Y	55330 FQ	62850 MW	70050 TQ	USBLS	5/15
	New York	Y	60490 AE	74210 MW	81010 AEX	NYBLS	1/16-3/16
	Buffalo-Cheektowaga-Niagara Falls MSA, NY	Y	64050 FQ	78550 MW	88080 TQ	USBLS	5/15
	Nassau County-Suffolk County PMSA, NY	Y	72910 FQ	79610 MW	86930 TQ	USBLS	5/15
	New York-Jersey City-White Plains PMSA, NY-NJ	Y	70290 FQ	78050 MW	84900 TQ	USBLS	5/15
	Rochester MSA, NY	Y	63490 FQ	73020 MW	79590 TQ	USBLS	5/15
	North Carolina	Y	62630 FQ	72080 MW	79970 TQ	USBLS	5/15
	Charlotte-Concord-Gastonia MSA, NC-SC	Y	68690 FQ	78780 MW	84400 TQ	USBLS	5/15
	North Dakota	Y	48310 FQ	60680 MW	63740 TQ	USBLS	5/15
	Ohio	Y	64850 FQ	72440 MW	79590 TQ	USBLS	5/15
	Cincinnati MSA, OH-KY-IN	Y	65530 FQ	69770 MW	79200 TQ	USBLS	5/15
	Cleveland-Elyria MSA, OH	Y	69720 FQ	76310 MW	84310 TQ	USBLS	5/15
	Columbus MSA, OH	Y	64060 FQ	71780 MW	79960 TQ	USBLS	5/15
	Oklahoma	Y	61730 FQ	67880 MW	79040 TQ	USBLS	5/15
	Oklahoma City MSA, OK	Y	67870 FQ	74970 MW	80380 TQ	USBLS	5/15
	Tulsa MSA, OK	Y	64100 FQ	76120 MW	83810 TQ	USBLS	5/15
	Oregon	H	29.66 FQ	33.23 MW	38.29 TQ	ORBLS	2016
	Portland-Vancouver-Hillsboro MSA, OR-WA	Y	66260 FQ	73640 MW	83750 TQ	USBLS	5/15
	Pennsylvania	Y	61420 FQ	68940 MW	78970 TQ	USBLS	5/15
	Allentown-Bethlehem-Easton MSA, PA-NJ	Y	61740 FQ	71500 MW	76780 TQ	USBLS	5/15
	Harrisburg-Carlisle MSA, PA	Y	61990 FQ	68230 MW	79600 TQ	USBLS	5/15
	Montgomery County-Bucks County-Chester County PMSA, PA	Y	60870 FQ	73080 MW	80730 TQ	USBLS	5/15
	Philadelphia PMSA, PA	Y	65280 FQ	79590 MW	87460 TQ	USBLS	5/15
	Pittsburgh MSA, PA	Y	62060 FQ	70310 MW	79650 TQ	USBLS	5/15
	Rhode Island	Y	70650 FQ	79310 MW	89060 TQ	USBLS	5/15
	Providence-Warwick MSA, RI-MA	Y	72080 FQ	79950 MW	88310 TQ	USBLS	5/15
	South Carolina	Y	64870 FQ	74450 MW	82770 TQ	USBLS	5/15
	South Dakota	Y	53100 FQ	61470 MW	74460 TQ	USBLS	5/15
	Tennessee	Y	68460 FQ	76710 MW	81740 TQ	USBLS	5/15
	Knoxville MSA, TN	Y	72730 FQ	80040 MW	84130 TQ	USBLS	5/15

AE	Average entry wage	AWR	Average wage range	H	Hourly	LR	Low end range	MTC	Median total compensation	TCC	Total cash compensation
AEX	Average experienced wage	B	Biweekly	HI	Highest wage paid	M	Monthly	MW	Median wage paid	TQ	Third quartile wage
ATC	Average total compensation	D	Daily	HR	High end range	MCC	Median cash compensation	MWR	Median wage range	W	Weekly
AW	Average wage paid	FQ	First quartile wage	LO	Lowest wage paid	ME	Median entry wage	S	See annotated source	Y	Yearly

Occupation/Type/Industry	Location	Per	Low	Mid	High	Source	Date
Postmaster and Mail Superintendent	Memphis MSA, TN-MS-AR	Y	67160 FQ	78000 MW	81560 TQ	USBLS	5/15
	Nashville-Davidson–Murfreesboro–Franklin MSA, TN	Y	72890 FQ	79960 MW	88310 TQ	USBLS	5/15
	Texas	Y	62050 FQ	72650 MW	80380 TQ	USBLS	5/15
	Dallas-Plano-Irving PMSA, TX	Y	72890 FQ	79930 MW	89640 TQ	USBLS	5/15
	Fort Worth-Arlington PMSA, TX	Y	68690 FQ	77760 MW	88320 TQ	USBLS	5/15
	Houston-The Woodlands-Sugar Land MSA, TX	Y	71260 FQ	80380 MW	87870 TQ	USBLS	5/15
	San Antonio-New Braunfels MSA, TX	Y	65950 FQ	75560 MW	81170 TQ	USBLS	5/15
	Utah	Y	60860 FQ	68670 MW	80390 TQ	USBLS	5/15
	Vermont	Y	59710 FQ	62020 MW	70870 TQ	USBLS	5/15
	Virginia	Y	61120 FQ	68570 MW	79200 TQ	USBLS	5/15
	Richmond MSA, VA	Y	63680 FQ	72890 MW	84220 TQ	USBLS	5/15
	Virginia Beach-Norfolk-Newport News MSA, VA-NC	Y	48320 FQ	65930 MW	72640 TQ	USBLS	5/15
	Washington	H	30.07 FQ	34.01 MW	39.39 TQ	WABLS	3/16
	Seattle-Bellevue-Everett PMSA, WA	H	34.00 FQ	39.15 MW	46.45 TQ	WABLS	3/16
	Tacoma-Lakewood PMSA, WA	H	31.00 FQ	39.46 MW	40.73 TQ	WABLS	3/16
	West Virginia	Y	54240 FQ	62000 MW	72440 TQ	USBLS	5/15
	Huntington-Ashland MSA, WV-KY-OH	Y	65610 FQ	74420 MW	80380 TQ	USBLS	5/15
	Wisconsin	Y	62510 FQ	71590 MW	79960 TQ	USBLS	5/15
	Milwaukee-Waukesha-West Allis MSA, WI	Y	73520 FQ	81230 MW	90520 TQ	USBLS	5/15
	Wyoming	Y	39370 FQ	59120 MW	66900 TQ	USBLS	5/15
	Puerto Rico	Y	69270 FQ	75930 MW	83770 TQ	USBLS	5/15
Poultry Technician California State University	California	Y	33708 LO		65664 HI	CALST	2016-2017
Pourer and Caster							
Metals	Alabama	Y	27824 AE	41406 AW	48203 AEX	ALBLS	6/16
Metals	Birmingham-Hoover MSA, AL	Y	29345 AE	39401 AW	44429 AEX	ALBLS	6/16
Metals	Arkansas	Y	32310 FQ	40590 MW	47340 TQ	USBLS	5/15
Metals	California	H	10.36 FQ	12.72 MW	17.12 TQ	CABLS	1/16-3/16
Metals	Anaheim-Santa Ana-Irvine PMSA, CA	H	10.35 FQ	11.24 MW	12.13 TQ	CABLS	1/16-3/16
Metals	Los Angeles-Long Beach-Glendale PMSA, CA	H	9.71 FQ	11.60 MW	16.39 TQ	CABLS	1/16-3/16
Metals	Oakland-Hayward-Berkeley PMSA, CA	H	16.01 FQ	20.12 MW	22.35 TQ	CABLS	1/16-3/16
Metals	Riverside-San Bernardino-Ontario MSA, CA	H	11.33 FQ	13.35 MW	15.65 TQ	CABLS	1/16-3/16
Metals	Colorado	Y	28340 FQ	32800 MW	41570 TQ	USBLS	5/15
Metals	Connecticut	Y		31633 MW		CTBLS	1/16-3/16
Metals	Tampa-St. Petersburg-Clearwater MSA, FL	H	16.05 AE	21.31 MW	22.23 AEX	FLBLS	7/16-9/16
Metals	Georgia	Y	28040 FQ	32750 MW	42310 TQ	USBLS	5/15
Metals	Illinois	Y	28720 FQ	36050 MW	46660 TQ	USBLS	5/15
Metals	Indiana	Y	24800 FQ	29870 MW	39040 TQ	USBLS	5/15
Metals	Indianapolis-Carmel-Anderson MSA, IN	Y	29930 FQ	44010 MW	50270 TQ	USBLS	5/15
Metals	Iowa	Y	27050 FQ	37350 MW	47000 TQ	USBLS	5/15
Metals	Kansas	Y	22520 FQ	27730 MW	31760 TQ	USBLS	5/15
Metals	Kentucky	Y	32330 FQ	37580 MW	45010 TQ	USBLS	5/15
Metals	Louisiana	Y	25610 FQ	36870 MW	46500 TQ	USBLS	5/15
Metals	Massachusetts	Y	33050 FQ	35600 MW	38150 TQ	USBLS	5/15
Metals	Michigan	Y	28500 FQ	34780 MW	44560 TQ	USBLS	5/15
Metals	Grand Rapids-Wyoming MSA, MI	Y	37900 FQ	45060 MW	52040 TQ	USBLS	5/15
Metals	Minnesota	Y	28551 FQ	35588 MW	47372 TQ	MNBLS	1/16-3/16
Metals	Minneapolis-St. Paul-Bloomington MSA, MN-WI	Y	32641 FQ	42462 MW	52222 TQ	MNBLS	1/16-3/16
Metals	Missouri	Y	26170 FQ	30150 MW	36470 TQ	USBLS	5/15
Metals	St. Louis MSA, MO-IL	Y	26610 FQ	29620 MW	34550 TQ	USBLS	5/15
Metals	Nevada	Y	25850 FQ	29520 MW	40350 TQ	USBLS	5/15
Metals	New Hampshire	H	16.06 AE	21.89 MW	23.56 AEX	NHBLS	6/16

AE	Average entry wage	AWR	Average wage range	H	Hourly
AEX	Average experienced wage	B	Biweekly	HI	Highest wage paid
ATC	Average total compensation	D	Daily	HR	High end range
AW	Average wage paid	FQ	First quartile wage	LO	Lowest wage paid

LR	Low end range	MTC	Median total compensation	TCC	Total cash compensation
M	Monthly	MW	Median wage paid	TQ	Third quartile wage
MCC	Median cash compensation	MWR	Median wage range	W	Weekly
ME	Median entry wage	S	See annotated source	Y	Yearly

Occupation/Type/Industry	Location	Per	Low	Mid	High	Source	Date
Pourer and Caster							
Metals	New Jersey	Y	27230 FQ	30190 MW	50500 TQ	USBLS	5/15
Metals	New York	Y	30450 AE	43630 MW	48330 AEX	NYBLS	1/16-3/16
Metals	New York-Jersey City-White Plains PMSA, NY-NJ	Y	28100 FQ	35100 MW	55790 TQ	USBLS	5/15
Metals	North Carolina	Y	25770 FQ	28810 MW	33060 TQ	USBLS	5/15
Metals	Charlotte-Concord-Gastonia MSA, NC-SC	Y	28390 FQ	32800 MW	55870 TQ	USBLS	5/15
Metals	Ohio	Y	28820 FQ	35030 MW	44460 TQ	USBLS	5/15
Metals	Cincinnati MSA, OH-KY-IN	Y	33470 FQ	37060 MW	42130 TQ	USBLS	5/15
Metals	Cleveland-Elyria MSA, OH	Y	31670 FQ	36760 MW	43870 TQ	USBLS	5/15
Metals	Oklahoma	Y	21410 FQ	26260 MW	30030 TQ	USBLS	5/15
Metals	Oregon	H	12.36 FQ	15.43 MW	19.45 TQ	ORBLS	2016
Metals	Portland-Vancouver-Hillsboro MSA, OR-WA	Y	24780 FQ	30870 MW	39480 TQ	USBLS	5/15
Metals	Pennsylvania	Y	30640 FQ	35890 MW	43370 TQ	USBLS	5/15
Metals	Allentown-Bethlehem-Easton MSA, PA-NJ	Y	32220 FQ	37100 MW	43130 TQ	USBLS	5/15
Metals	Montgomery County-Bucks County-Chester County PMSA, PA	Y	32280 FQ	38560 MW	49410 TQ	USBLS	5/15
Metals	Pittsburgh MSA, PA	Y	30190 FQ	36290 MW	43590 TQ	USBLS	5/15
Metals	Rhode Island	Y	27270 FQ	29280 MW	31290 TQ	USBLS	5/15
Metals	Providence-Warwick MSA, RI-MA	Y	27370 FQ	29500 MW	31580 TQ	USBLS	5/15
Metals	Tennessee	Y	19020 FQ	29750 MW	42980 TQ	USBLS	5/15
Metals	Knoxville MSA, TN	Y	42370 FQ	45590 MW	48810 TQ	USBLS	5/15
Metals	Texas	Y	23130 FQ	29330 MW	37680 TQ	USBLS	5/15
Metals	Dallas-Plano-Irving PMSA, TX	Y	22570 FQ	28820 MW	42550 TQ	USBLS	5/15
Metals	Fort Worth-Arlington PMSA, TX	Y	25110 FQ	28910 MW	33380 TQ	USBLS	5/15
Metals	Houston-The Woodlands-Sugar Land MSA, TX	Y	25320 FQ	29570 MW	35620 TQ	USBLS	5/15
Metals	Utah	Y	24490 FQ	28980 MW	33930 TQ	USBLS	5/15
Metals	Provo-Orem MSA, UT	Y	20760 FQ	25930 MW	31070 TQ	USBLS	5/15
Metals	Washington	H	15.85 FQ	17.45 MW	19.05 TQ	WABLS	3/16
Metals	Seattle-Bellevue-Everett PMSA, WA	H	16.23 FQ	19.28 MW	23.32 TQ	WABLS	3/16
Metals	West Virginia	Y	24640 FQ	28970 MW	35770 TQ	USBLS	5/15
Metals	Wisconsin	Y	33140 FQ	38000 MW	44500 TQ	USBLS	5/15
Metals	Milwaukee-Waukesha-West Allis MSA, WI	Y	33450 FQ	40270 MW	47040 TQ	USBLS	5/15
Power Analyst							
Municipal Government	Seattle, WA	H	37.92 LO		44.25 HI	CSSS	1/13/16
Power Distributor and Dispatcher	Alabama	Y	64006 AE	84293 AW	94442 AEX	ALBLS	6/16
	Arizona	Y	80060 FQ	88130 MW	95870 TQ	USBLS	5/15
	Arkansas	Y	73130 FQ	87670 MW	99280 TQ	USBLS	5/15
	California	H	34.01 FQ	38.50 MW	53.62 TQ	CABLS	1/16-3/16
	Colorado	Y	82690 FQ	89630 MW	97190 TQ	USBLS	5/15
	Florida	H	23.46 AE	32.59 MW	38.05 AEX	FLBLS	7/16-9/16
	Georgia	Y	68020 FQ	81900 MW	90140 TQ	USBLS	5/15
	Idaho	Y	74680 FQ	90530 MW	99540 TQ	USBLS	5/15
	Illinois	Y	68340 FQ	80900 MW	94370 TQ	USBLS	5/15
	Indiana	Y	63070 FQ	78240 MW	93560 TQ	USBLS	5/15
	Iowa	Y	67190 FQ	76170 MW	90270 TQ	USBLS	5/15
	Kansas	Y	80860 FQ	89160 MW	97420 TQ	USBLS	5/15
	Kentucky	Y	67470 FQ	82450 MW	94980 TQ	USBLS	5/15
	Maine	Y	58850 FQ	68800 MW	68800 TQ	USBLS	5/15
	Maryland	Y	65002 AE	72982 MW	76971 AEX	MDBLS	4/16
	Massachusetts	Y	82340 FQ	95520 MW	109120 TQ	USBLS	5/15
	Michigan	Y	69620 FQ	76580 MW	86610 TQ	USBLS	5/15
	Minnesota	Y	74283 FQ	87992 MW	101943 TQ	MNBLS	1/16-3/16
	Mississippi	Y	45860 FQ	64440 MW	80200 TQ	USBLS	5/15
	Missouri	Y	73790 FQ	86720 MW	95650 TQ	USBLS	5/15
	Montana	Y	72520 FQ	81360 MW	91490 TQ	USBLS	5/15
	Nebraska	Y	70140 FQ	78270 MW	95265 TQ	NEBLS	7/16-9/16
	Nevada	Y	81610 FQ	92740 MW	102060 TQ	USBLS	5/15
	New Jersey	Y	82910 FQ	91090 MW	99280 TQ	USBLS	5/15
	New York	Y	75390 AE	94050 MW	101780 AEX	NYBLS	1/16-3/16
	North Carolina	Y	61060 FQ	82360 MW	92550 TQ	USBLS	5/15

Occupation/Type/Industry	Location	Per	Low	Mid	High	Source	Date
Power Distributor and Dispatcher	North Dakota	Y	86490 FQ	92720 MW	102990 TQ	USBLS	5/15
	Ohio	Y	63620 FQ	75000 MW	88430 TQ	USBLS	5/15
	Oklahoma	Y	66670 FQ	82170 MW	93880 TQ	USBLS	5/15
	Oregon	H	42.31 FQ	43.51 MW	50.42 TQ	ORBLS	2016
	Pennsylvania	Y	60570 FQ	71790 MW	81870 TQ	USBLS	5/15
	Tennessee	Y	57400 FQ	64690 MW	75570 TQ	USBLS	5/15
	Texas	Y	53030 FQ	65850 MW	89930 TQ	USBLS	5/15
	Utah	Y	66770 FQ	89660 MW	100750 TQ	USBLS	5/15
	Virginia	Y	64220 FQ	75350 MW	89500 TQ	USBLS	5/15
	Washington	H	42.33 FQ	48.58 MW	56.32 TQ	WABLS	3/16
	West Virginia	Y	71430 FQ	81520 MW	92820 TQ	USBLS	5/15
	Wisconsin	Y	74710 FQ	84560 MW	92170 TQ	USBLS	5/15
	Wyoming	Y	86430 FQ	93580 MW	108110 TQ	USBLS	5/15
Power Marketer							
Municipal Government	Seattle, WA	H	40.54 LO		70.54 HI	CSSS	1/1/14
Power Plant Operator	Alabama	Y	49231 AE	67153 AW	76119 AEX	ALBLS	6/16
	Alaska	Y	46670 FQ	67440 MW	87030 TQ	USBLS	5/15
	Anchorage MSA, AK	Y	74960 FQ	85350 MW	96890 TQ	USBLS	5/15
	Arkansas	Y	66470 FQ	72850 MW	79510 TQ	USBLS	5/15
	California	H	33.00 FQ	41.71 MW	52.27 TQ	CABLS	1/16-3/16
	Anaheim-Santa Ana-Irvine PMSA, CA	H	33.12 FQ	39.51 MW	48.07 TQ	CABLS	1/16-3/16
	Los Angeles-Long Beach-Glendale PMSA, CA	H	36.39 FQ	45.90 MW	56.19 TQ	CABLS	1/16-3/16
	Oakland-Hayward-Berkeley PMSA, CA	H	42.82 FQ	49.56 MW	56.76 TQ	CABLS	1/16-3/16
	Riverside-San Bernardino-Ontario MSA, CA	H	31.49 FQ	34.91 MW	38.36 TQ	CABLS	1/16-3/16
	Sacramento–Roseville–Arden-Arcade MSA, CA	H	43.51 FQ	51.76 MW	60.24 TQ	CABLS	1/16-3/16
	San Diego-Carlsbad MSA, CA	H	22.48 FQ	26.09 MW	30.33 TQ	CABLS	1/16-3/16
	San Francisco-Redwood City-South San Francisco PMSA, CA	H	37.92 FQ	51.31 MW	57.62 TQ	CABLS	1/16-3/16
	Colorado	Y	57570 FQ	67810 MW	78530 TQ	USBLS	5/15
	Denver-Aurora-Lakewood MSA, CO	Y	56100 FQ	66190 MW	80680 TQ	USBLS	5/15
	Connecticut	Y		71401 MW		CTBLS	1/16-3/16
	Bridgeport-Stamford-Norwalk MSA, CT	Y	63780 FQ	71210 MW	78320 TQ	USBLS	5/15
	Hartford-West Hartford-East Hartford MSA, CT	Y	63770 FQ	69930 MW	75710 TQ	USBLS	5/15
	Wilmington PMSA, DE-MD-NJ	Y	65360 FQ	76380 MW	89450 TQ	USBLS	5/15
	Washington-Arlington-Alexandria PMSA, DC-VA-MD-WV	Y	69020 FQ	78650 MW	90550 TQ	USBLS	5/15
	Florida	H	26.13 AE	34.31 MW	37.85 AEX	FLBLS	7/16-9/16
	Miami-Miami Beach-Kendall PMSA, FL	H	20.94 AE	28.36 MW	32.74 AEX	FLBLS	7/16-9/16
	Orlando-Kissimmee-Sanford MSA, FL	H	26.39 AE	33.39 MW	38.27 AEX	FLBLS	7/16-9/16
	Georgia	Y	65640 FQ	72660 MW	79970 TQ	USBLS	5/15
	Atlanta-Sandy Springs-Roswell MSA, GA	Y	63600 FQ	71250 MW	79220 TQ	USBLS	5/15
	Hawaii	Y	67140 FQ	79290 MW	91750 TQ	USBLS	5/15
	Urban Honolulu MSA, HI	Y	65270 FQ	75840 MW	89770 TQ	USBLS	5/15
	Idaho	Y	57210 FQ	71800 MW	83630 TQ	USBLS	5/15
	Illinois	Y	62780 FQ	72650 MW	84240 TQ	USBLS	5/15
	Chicago-Naperville-Arlington Heights PMSA, IL	Y	66690 FQ	79680 MW	92230 TQ	USBLS	5/15
	Lake County-Kenosha County PMSA, IL-WI	Y	61650 FQ	77080 MW	88670 TQ	USBLS	5/15
	Indiana	Y	52700 FQ	64920 MW	81560 TQ	USBLS	5/15
	Indianapolis-Carmel-Anderson MSA, IN	Y	54990 FQ	67550 MW	84910 TQ	USBLS	5/15
	Iowa	Y	44490 FQ	64720 MW	74610 TQ	USBLS	5/15
	Des Moines-West Des Moines MSA, IA	Y	42170 FQ	51130 MW	60310 TQ	USBLS	5/15
	Kansas	Y	44630 FQ	62690 MW	77230 TQ	USBLS	5/15

AE	Average entry wage	AWR	Average wage range	H	Hourly
AEX	Average experienced wage	B	Biweekly	HI	Highest wage paid
ATC	Average total compensation	D	Daily	HR	High end range
AW	Average wage paid	FQ	First quartile wage	LO	Lowest wage paid

LR	Low end range	MTC	Median total compensation	TCC	Total cash compensation
M	Monthly	MW	Median wage paid	TQ	Third quartile wage
MCC	Median cash compensation	MWR	Median wage range	W	Weekly
ME	Median entry wage	S	See annotated source	Y	Yearly

Occupation/Type/Industry	Location	Per	Low	Mid	High	Source	Date
Power Plant Operator	Wichita MSA, KS	Y	35400 FQ	43600 MW	73810 TQ	USBLS	5/15
	Kentucky	Y	58930 FQ	72690 MW	81840 TQ	USBLS	5/15
	Louisville-Jefferson County MSA, KY-IN	Y	64270 FQ	80020 MW	89660 TQ	USBLS	5/15
	Louisiana	Y	40110 FQ	57630 MW	78110 TQ	USBLS	5/15
	New Orleans-Metairie MSA, LA	Y	49980 FQ	81600 MW	90410 TQ	USBLS	5/15
	Maine	Y	48990 FQ	59900 MW	79580 TQ	USBLS	5/15
	Maryland	Y	60559 AE	72497 MW	78466 AEX	MDBLS	4/16
	Massachusetts	Y	66420 FQ	79320 MW	89370 TQ	USBLS	5/15
	Boston-Cambridge-Newton NECTA, MA	Y	71140 FQ	82450 MW	91010 TQ	USBLS	5/15
	Worcester MSA, MA-CT	Y	70390 FQ	81270 MW	90340 TQ	USBLS	5/15
	Michigan	Y	63180 FQ	71210 MW	79190 TQ	USBLS	5/15
	Detroit-Dearborn-Livonia PMSA, MI	Y	65460 FQ	72650 MW	81140 TQ	USBLS	5/15
	Grand Rapids-Wyoming MSA, MI	Y	60050 FQ	69830 MW	77740 TQ	USBLS	5/15
	Minnesota	Y	57406 FQ	72765 MW	89116 TQ	MNBLS	1/16-3/16
	Minneapolis-St. Paul-Bloomington MSA, MN-WI	Y	66528 FQ	80328 MW	95484 TQ	MNBLS	1/16-3/16
	Mississippi	Y	52250 FQ	68720 MW	85740 TQ	USBLS	5/15
	Jackson MSA, MS	Y	63890 FQ	74230 MW	86110 TQ	USBLS	5/15
	Missouri	Y	51990 FQ	71070 MW	87960 TQ	USBLS	5/15
	Kansas City MSA, MO-KS	Y	64080 FQ	77020 MW	89270 TQ	USBLS	5/15
	St. Louis MSA, MO-IL	Y	53100 FQ	62320 MW	80200 TQ	USBLS	5/15
	Montana	Y	67240 FQ	76490 MW	89000 TQ	USBLS	5/15
	Nebraska	Y	52460 FQ	71375 MW	82090 TQ	NEBLS	7/16-9/16
	Nevada	Y	53450 FQ	69720 MW	85540 TQ	USBLS	5/15
	Las Vegas-Henderson-Paradise MSA, NV	Y	54390 FQ	75340 MW	92070 TQ	USBLS	5/15
	New Hampshire	H	19.80 AE	29.94 MW	34.21 AEX	NHBLS	6/16
	New Jersey	Y	69250 FQ	83000 MW	93790 TQ	USBLS	5/15
	Camden PMSA, NJ	Y	53390 FQ	62110 MW	74500 TQ	USBLS	5/15
	Newark PMSA, NJ-PA	Y	71350 FQ	82230 MW	93730 TQ	USBLS	5/15
	New York	Y	52540 AE	77440 MW	90790 AEX	NYBLS	1/16-3/16
	Buffalo-Cheektowaga-Niagara Falls MSA, NY	Y	53610 FQ	63790 MW	82980 TQ	USBLS	5/15
	Nassau County-Suffolk County PMSA, NY	Y	72820 FQ	85430 MW	108860 TQ	USBLS	5/15
	New York-Jersey City-White Plains PMSA, NY-NJ	Y	64690 FQ	80520 MW	94910 TQ	USBLS	5/15
	North Carolina	Y	63150 FQ	78260 MW	90050 TQ	USBLS	5/15
	Charlotte-Concord-Gastonia MSA, NC-SC	Y	65940 FQ	70540 MW	75150 TQ	USBLS	5/15
	North Dakota	Y	60600 FQ	82720 MW	92050 TQ	USBLS	5/15
	Ohio	Y	59750 FQ	69490 MW	77390 TQ	USBLS	5/15
	Cincinnati MSA, OH-KY-IN	Y	63260 FQ	70570 MW	77530 TQ	USBLS	5/15
	Columbus MSA, OH	Y	59830 FQ	71660 MW	88510 TQ	USBLS	5/15
	Oklahoma	Y	53330 FQ	63990 MW	74330 TQ	USBLS	5/15
	Oklahoma City MSA, OK	Y	52870 FQ	60310 MW	70510 TQ	USBLS	5/15
	Tulsa MSA, OK	Y	53380 FQ	60510 MW	71490 TQ	USBLS	5/15
	Oregon	H	29.56 FQ	36.11 MW	42.69 TQ	ORBLS	2016
	Portland-Vancouver-Hillsboro MSA, OR-WA	Y	63520 FQ	76260 MW	89600 TQ	USBLS	5/15
	Pennsylvania	Y	58430 FQ	70580 MW	80560 TQ	USBLS	5/15
	Montgomery County-Bucks County-Chester County PMSA, PA	Y	55120 FQ	71000 MW	82490 TQ	USBLS	5/15
	Pittsburgh MSA, PA	Y	62280 FQ	70690 MW	78350 TQ	USBLS	5/15
	Rhode Island	Y	47650 FQ	62910 MW	78120 TQ	USBLS	5/15
	Providence-Warwick MSA, RI-MA	Y	51610 FQ	65170 MW	78450 TQ	USBLS	5/15
	South Carolina	Y	52840 FQ	58730 MW	67120 TQ	USBLS	5/15
	Charleston-North Charleston MSA, SC	Y	52240 FQ	56470 MW	64130 TQ	USBLS	5/15
	Tennessee	Y	54890 FQ	79620 MW	87140 TQ	USBLS	5/15
	Knoxville MSA, TN	Y	79900 FQ	81840 MW	81850 TQ	USBLS	5/15
	Nashville-Davidson–Murfreesboro–Franklin MSA, TN	Y	32980 FQ	63520 MW	86700 TQ	USBLS	5/15
	Texas	Y	52520 FQ	69180 MW	81190 TQ	USBLS	5/15

AE	Average entry wage	AWR	Average wage range	H	Hourly
AEX	Average experienced wage	B	Biweekly	HI	Highest wage paid
ATC	Average total compensation	D	Daily	HR	High end range
AW	Average wage paid	FQ	First quartile wage	LO	Lowest wage paid

LR	Low end range	MTC	Median total compensation
M	Monthly	MW	Median wage paid
MCC	Median cash compensation	MWR	Median wage range
ME	Median entry wage	S	See annotated source

TCC	Total cash compensation
TQ	Third quartile wage
W	Weekly
Y	Yearly

Occupation/Type/Industry	Location	Per	Low	Mid	High	Source	Date
Power Plant Operator	Austin-Round Rock MSA, TX	Y	43720 FQ	56300 MW	82950 TQ	USBLS	5/15
	Dallas-Plano-Irving PMSA, TX	Y	51220 FQ	66240 MW	82170 TQ	USBLS	5/15
	Houston-The Woodlands-Sugar Land MSA, TX	Y	42580 FQ	59730 MW	75990 TQ	USBLS	5/15
	San Antonio-New Braunfels MSA, TX	Y	65370 FQ	81200 MW	92380 TQ	USBLS	5/15
	Utah	Y	56010 FQ	70790 MW	84990 TQ	USBLS	5/15
	Provo-Orem MSA, UT	Y	64590 FQ	70600 MW	76600 TQ	USBLS	5/15
	Vermont	Y	55760 FQ	71470 MW	82310 TQ	USBLS	5/15
	Virginia	Y	36700 FQ	47700 MW	82470 TQ	USBLS	5/15
	Richmond MSA, VA	Y	35560 FQ	40640 MW	48780 TQ	USBLS	5/15
	Washington	H	40.88 FQ	44.39 MW	47.90 TQ	WABLS	3/16
	Seattle-Bellevue-Everett PMSA, WA	H	42.16 FQ	45.27 MW	48.39 TQ	WABLS	3/16
	West Virginia	Y	64770 FQ	71510 MW	78250 TQ	USBLS	5/15
	Wisconsin	Y	50490 FQ	70440 MW	85580 TQ	USBLS	5/15
	Madison MSA, WI	Y	59000 FQ	72520 MW	84190 TQ	USBLS	5/15
Preacher							
Church of Christ	United States	Y		53082 AW		ACU	2/16-3/16
Prepress Technician and Worker	Alabama	Y	18909 AE	31145 AW	37252 AEX	ALBLS	6/16
	Birmingham-Hoover MSA, AL	Y	17624 AE	31782 AW	38856 AEX	ALBLS	6/16
	Arizona	Y	28050 FQ	35410 MW	45080 TQ	USBLS	5/15
	Phoenix-Mesa-Scottsdale MSA, AZ	Y	28850 FQ	37490 MW	46360 TQ	USBLS	5/15
	Tucson MSA, AZ	Y	24130 FQ	32890 MW	37230 TQ	USBLS	5/15
	Arkansas	Y	24580 FQ	33580 MW	44160 TQ	USBLS	5/15
	Little Rock-North Little Rock-Conway MSA, AR	Y	27740 FQ	34610 MW	42670 TQ	USBLS	5/15
	California	H	14.48 FQ	20.75 MW	27.37 TQ	CABLS	1/16-3/16
	Anaheim-Santa Ana-Irvine PMSA, CA	H	14.70 FQ	20.86 MW	28.10 TQ	CABLS	1/16-3/16
	Los Angeles-Long Beach-Glendale PMSA, CA	H	13.51 FQ	20.62 MW	27.96 TQ	CABLS	1/16-3/16
	Oakland-Hayward-Berkeley PMSA, CA	H	16.19 FQ	22.79 MW	27.63 TQ	CABLS	1/16-3/16
	Riverside-San Bernardino-Ontario MSA, CA	H	11.54 FQ	17.15 MW	26.14 TQ	CABLS	1/16-3/16
	Sacramento–Roseville–Arden-Arcade MSA, CA	H	16.00 FQ	21.00 MW	25.74 TQ	CABLS	1/16-3/16
	San Diego-Carlsbad MSA, CA	H	14.36 FQ	19.35 MW	26.82 TQ	CABLS	1/16-3/16
	San Francisco-Redwood City-South San Francisco PMSA, CA	H	17.16 FQ	23.72 MW	29.10 TQ	CABLS	1/16-3/16
	Colorado	Y	32780 FQ	37860 MW	46610 TQ	USBLS	5/15
	Denver-Aurora-Lakewood MSA, CO	Y	33140 FQ	37550 MW	46170 TQ	USBLS	5/15
	Connecticut	Y		48812 MW		CTBLS	1/16-3/16
	Bridgeport-Stamford-Norwalk MSA, CT	Y	38420 FQ	53400 MW	59570 TQ	USBLS	5/15
	Hartford-West Hartford-East Hartford MSA, CT	Y	37810 FQ	49750 MW	56990 TQ	USBLS	5/15
	Delaware	Y	28810 FQ	36480 MW	46730 TQ	USBLS	5/15
	Wilmington PMSA, DE-MD-NJ	Y	35600 FQ	41550 MW	50810 TQ	USBLS	5/15
	District of Columbia	Y	76070 FQ	76080 MW	76090 TQ	USBLS	5/15
	Washington-Arlington-Alexandria PMSA, DC-VA-MD-WV	Y	29510 FQ	48460 MW	76070 TQ	USBLS	5/15
	Florida	H	11.39 AE	15.75 MW	19.43 AEX	FLBLS	7/16-9/16
	Fort Lauderdale-Pompano Beach-Deerfield Beach PMSA, FL	H	13.88 AE	18.04 MW	20.56 AEX	FLBLS	7/16-9/16
	Miami-Miami Beach-Kendall PMSA, FL	H	12.56 AE	16.50 MW	20.29 AEX	FLBLS	7/16-9/16
	Orlando-Kissimmee-Sanford MSA, FL	H	9.26 AE	14.03 MW	17.16 AEX	FLBLS	7/16-9/16
	Tampa-St. Petersburg-Clearwater MSA, FL	H	11.94 AE	18.03 MW	20.82 AEX	FLBLS	7/16-9/16
	Georgia	Y	30440 FQ	40630 MW	50060 TQ	USBLS	5/15

Occupation/Type/Industry	Location	Per	Low	Mid	High	Source	Date
Prepress Technician and Worker	Atlanta-Sandy Springs-Roswell MSA, GA	Y	30270 FQ	40630 MW	50190 TQ	USBLS	5/15
	Hawaii	Y	29470 FQ	34340 MW	38840 TQ	USBLS	5/15
	Urban Honolulu MSA, HI	Y	30260 FQ	34550 MW	38690 TQ	USBLS	5/15
	Idaho	Y	23170 FQ	29890 MW	36960 TQ	USBLS	5/15
	Boise City MSA, ID	Y	25090 FQ	32830 MW	37580 TQ	USBLS	5/15
	Illinois	Y	31170 FQ	39670 MW	49120 TQ	USBLS	5/15
	Chicago-Naperville-Arlington Heights PMSA, IL	Y	32980 FQ	41540 MW	50810 TQ	USBLS	5/15
	Lake County-Kenosha County PMSA, IL-WI	Y	26140 FQ	31970 MW	44170 TQ	USBLS	5/15
	Indiana	Y	29130 FQ	35420 MW	44110 TQ	USBLS	5/15
	Gary PMSA, IN	Y	28090 FQ	34510 MW	38990 TQ	USBLS	5/15
	Indianapolis-Carmel-Anderson MSA, IN	Y	30990 FQ	36490 MW	46040 TQ	USBLS	5/15
	Iowa	Y	27220 FQ	33930 MW	39610 TQ	USBLS	5/15
	Des Moines-West Des Moines MSA, IA	Y	33430 FQ	36570 MW	40970 TQ	USBLS	5/15
	Kansas	Y	27130 FQ	32610 MW	41620 TQ	USBLS	5/15
	Wichita MSA, KS	Y	31530 FQ	38280 MW	47430 TQ	USBLS	5/15
	Kentucky	Y	31240 FQ	39230 MW	50460 TQ	USBLS	5/15
	Louisville-Jefferson County MSA, KY-IN	Y	31940 FQ	39220 MW	49610 TQ	USBLS	5/15
	Louisiana	Y	26460 FQ	32500 MW	41710 TQ	USBLS	5/15
	New Orleans-Metairie MSA, LA	Y	24560 FQ	29050 MW	36920 TQ	USBLS	5/15
	Maine	Y	27350 FQ	33070 MW	43030 TQ	USBLS	5/15
	Maryland	Y	29701 AE	40847 MW	46420 AEX	MDBLS	4/16
	Baltimore-Columbia-Towson MSA, MD	Y	34500 FQ	41120 MW	46630 TQ	USBLS	5/15
	Massachusetts	Y	36040 FQ	44910 MW	55450 TQ	USBLS	5/15
	Boston-Cambridge-Newton NECTA, MA	Y	43000 FQ	50780 MW	63230 TQ	USBLS	5/15
	Worcester MSA, MA-CT	Y	40410 FQ	47250 MW	55720 TQ	USBLS	5/15
	Michigan	Y	23430 FQ	33590 MW	43170 TQ	USBLS	5/15
	Detroit-Dearborn-Livonia PMSA, MI	Y	23580 FQ	28560 MW	35600 TQ	USBLS	5/15
	Grand Rapids-Wyoming MSA, MI	Y	23340 FQ	30760 MW	44910 TQ	USBLS	5/15
	Minnesota	Y	36813 FQ	46168 MW	56160 TQ	MNBLS	1/16-3/16
	Minneapolis-St. Paul-Bloomington MSA, MN-WI	Y	40164 FQ	49367 MW	58084 TQ	MNBLS	1/16-3/16
	Mississippi	Y	25230 FQ	31810 MW	41390 TQ	USBLS	5/15
	Missouri	Y	32420 FQ	39990 MW	51630 TQ	USBLS	5/15
	Kansas City MSA, MO-KS	Y	31650 FQ	40000 MW	50130 TQ	USBLS	5/15
	St. Louis MSA, MO-IL	Y	33790 FQ	41050 MW	49070 TQ	USBLS	5/15
	Montana	Y	20060 FQ	26990 MW	34610 TQ	USBLS	5/15
	Nebraska	Y	29005 FQ	36740 MW	44075 TQ	NEBLS	7/16-9/16
	Omaha-Council Bluffs MSA, NE-IA	Y	33795 FQ	39085 MW	45675 TQ	NEBLS	7/16-9/16
	Nevada	Y	30880 FQ	36960 MW	46870 TQ	USBLS	5/15
	Las Vegas-Henderson-Paradise MSA, NV	Y	28990 FQ	36510 MW	45480 TQ	USBLS	5/15
	New Hampshire	H	16.64 AE	21.52 MW	25.76 AEX	NHBLS	6/16
	Manchester NECTA, NH	H	19.66 AE	22.29 MW	25.61 AEX	NHBLS	6/16
	New Jersey	Y	30330 FQ	39200 MW	51430 TQ	USBLS	5/15
	Camden PMSA, NJ	Y	28730 FQ	37080 MW	51720 TQ	USBLS	5/15
	Newark PMSA, NJ-PA	Y	20150 FQ	37800 MW	47800 TQ	USBLS	5/15
	Trenton MSA, NJ	Y	34910 FQ	38690 MW	46200 TQ	USBLS	5/15
	New Mexico	Y	28090 FQ	33940 MW	38850 TQ	USBLS	5/15
	Albuquerque MSA, NM	Y	31330 FQ	34960 MW	38690 TQ	USBLS	5/15
	New York	Y	25850 AE	43220 MW	56130 AEX	NYBLS	1/16-3/16
	Buffalo-Cheektowaga-Niagara Falls MSA, NY	Y	23450 FQ	29700 MW	44080 TQ	USBLS	5/15
	Nassau County-Suffolk County PMSA, NY	Y	24060 FQ	34670 MW	49150 TQ	USBLS	5/15
	New York-Jersey City-White Plains PMSA, NY-NJ	Y	36440 FQ	49230 MW	62990 TQ	USBLS	5/15
	Rochester MSA, NY	Y	32700 FQ	39410 MW	54450 TQ	USBLS	5/15
	North Carolina	Y	31820 FQ	38150 MW	46140 TQ	USBLS	5/15
	Charlotte-Concord-Gastonia MSA, NC-SC	Y	34520 FQ	41800 MW	49000 TQ	USBLS	5/15

AE	Average entry wage	AWR	Average wage range	H	Hourly	LR	Low end range	MTC	Median total compensation	TCC	Total cash compensation
AEX	Average experienced wage	B	Biweekly	HI	Highest wage paid	M	Monthly	MW	Median wage paid	TQ	Third quartile wage
ATC	Average total compensation	D	Daily	HR	High end range	MCC	Median cash compensation	MWR	Median wage range	W	Weekly
AW	Average wage paid	FQ	First quartile wage	LO	Lowest wage paid	ME	Median entry wage	S	See annotated source	Y	Yearly

Occupation/Type/Industry	Location	Per	Low	Mid	High	Source	Date
Prepress Technician and Worker	Raleigh MSA, NC	Y	34780 FQ	44110 MW	53360 TQ	USBLS	5/15
	North Dakota	Y	21540 FQ	27060 MW	37260 TQ	USBLS	5/15
	Fargo MSA, ND-MN	Y	20980 FQ	24370 MW	41610 TQ	USBLS	5/15
	Ohio	Y	31940 FQ	37410 MW	44750 TQ	USBLS	5/15
	Cincinnati MSA, OH-KY-IN	Y	33820 FQ	41020 MW	48700 TQ	USBLS	5/15
	Cleveland-Elyria MSA, OH	Y	33780 FQ	38510 MW	45410 TQ	USBLS	5/15
	Columbus MSA, OH	Y	33060 FQ	39720 MW	49830 TQ	USBLS	5/15
	Oklahoma	Y	23760 FQ	34680 MW	44300 TQ	USBLS	5/15
	Oklahoma City MSA, OK	Y	24900 FQ	37240 MW	46450 TQ	USBLS	5/15
	Tulsa MSA, OK	Y	27060 FQ	36460 MW	44480 TQ	USBLS	5/15
	Oregon	H	15.16 FQ	19.38 MW	25.79 TQ	ORBLS	2016
	Portland-Vancouver-Hillsboro MSA, OR-WA	Y	33700 FQ	42720 MW	58160 TQ	USBLS	5/15
	Pennsylvania	Y	26150 FQ	35020 MW	43670 TQ	USBLS	5/15
	Allentown-Bethlehem-Easton MSA, PA-NJ	Y	21080 FQ	36780 MW	48380 TQ	USBLS	5/15
	Harrisburg-Carlisle MSA, PA	Y	28260 FQ	32330 MW	40700 TQ	USBLS	5/15
	Montgomery County-Bucks County-Chester County PMSA, PA	Y	27790 FQ	36360 MW	45110 TQ	USBLS	5/15
	Philadelphia PMSA, PA	Y	33310 FQ	37820 MW	46590 TQ	USBLS	5/15
	Pittsburgh MSA, PA	Y	24730 FQ	37890 MW	46810 TQ	USBLS	5/15
	Rhode Island	Y	41320 FQ	48120 MW	58440 TQ	USBLS	5/15
	Providence-Warwick MSA, RI-MA	Y	41080 FQ	46980 MW	55860 TQ	USBLS	5/15
	South Carolina	Y	26220 FQ	33390 MW	39190 TQ	USBLS	5/15
	Columbia MSA, SC	Y	23640 FQ	29950 MW	36150 TQ	USBLS	5/15
	Greenville-Anderson-Mauldin MSA, SC	Y	28290 FQ	34050 MW	39070 TQ	USBLS	5/15
	South Dakota	Y	26110 FQ	30620 MW	37010 TQ	USBLS	5/15
	Sioux Falls MSA, SD	Y	30750 FQ	35380 MW	40120 TQ	USBLS	5/15
	Tennessee	Y	25960 FQ	35040 MW	45250 TQ	USBLS	5/15
	Knoxville MSA, TN	Y	17100 FQ	19120 MW	38960 TQ	USBLS	5/15
	Memphis MSA, TN-MS-AR	Y	32830 FQ	39590 MW	47890 TQ	USBLS	5/15
	Nashville-Davidson–Murfreesboro–Franklin MSA, TN	Y	30660 FQ	37530 MW	46890 TQ	USBLS	5/15
	Texas	Y	31810 FQ	39060 MW	51100 TQ	USBLS	5/15
	Austin-Round Rock MSA, TX	Y	31990 FQ	37070 MW	43190 TQ	USBLS	5/15
	Dallas-Plano-Irving PMSA, TX	Y	32470 FQ	44230 MW	58080 TQ	USBLS	5/15
	Fort Worth-Arlington PMSA, TX	Y	34380 FQ	41780 MW	54850 TQ	USBLS	5/15
	Houston-The Woodlands-Sugar Land MSA, TX	Y	32280 FQ	38650 MW	46930 TQ	USBLS	5/15
	San Antonio-New Braunfels MSA, TX	Y	34160 FQ	42320 MW	51560 TQ	USBLS	5/15
	Utah	Y	30270 FQ	37430 MW	47520 TQ	USBLS	5/15
	Ogden-Clearfield MSA, UT	Y	22420 FQ	35740 MW	47160 TQ	USBLS	5/15
	Provo-Orem MSA, UT	Y	22420 FQ	32400 MW	38260 TQ	USBLS	5/15
	Salt Lake City MSA, UT	Y	31680 FQ	38290 MW	50000 TQ	USBLS	5/15
	Vermont	Y	31690 FQ	37700 MW	46010 TQ	USBLS	5/15
	Virginia	Y	27580 FQ	36020 MW	45280 TQ	USBLS	5/15
	Richmond MSA, VA	Y	33690 FQ	42850 MW	49320 TQ	USBLS	5/15
	Virginia Beach-Norfolk-Newport News MSA, VA-NC	Y	24130 FQ	31140 MW	38900 TQ	USBLS	5/15
	Washington	H	16.76 FQ	20.55 MW	26.27 TQ	WABLS	3/16
	Seattle-Bellevue-Everett PMSA, WA	H	17.70 FQ	21.76 MW	27.39 TQ	WABLS	3/16
	Tacoma-Lakewood PMSA, WA	H	17.15 FQ	22.67 MW	27.53 TQ	WABLS	3/16
	West Virginia	Y	22540 FQ	29030 MW	39470 TQ	USBLS	5/15
	Wisconsin	Y	32700 FQ	39950 MW	47280 TQ	USBLS	5/15
	Madison MSA, WI	Y	33900 FQ	41360 MW	47130 TQ	USBLS	5/15
	Milwaukee-Waukesha-West Allis MSA, WI	Y	34130 FQ	41220 MW	47730 TQ	USBLS	5/15
	Wyoming	Y	26100 FQ	28090 MW	30080 TQ	USBLS	5/15
	Puerto Rico	Y	18520 FQ	22770 MW	28800 TQ	USBLS	5/15
	San Juan-Carolina-Caguas MSA, PR	Y	18720 FQ	23970 MW	29910 TQ	USBLS	5/15
Preschool Aide							
Public Schools	Baldwin County, AL	Y	20493 LO		25850 HI	BCPSSS	2016-2017

AE	Average entry wage	AWR	Average wage range	H	Hourly	LR	Low end range	MTC	Median total compensation	TCC	Total cash compensation
AEX	Average experienced wage	B	Biweekly	HI	Highest wage paid	M	Monthly	MW	Median wage paid	TQ	Third quartile wage
ATC	Average total compensation	D	Daily	HR	High end range	MCC	Median cash compensation	MWR	Median wage range	W	Weekly
AW	Average wage paid	FQ	First quartile wage	LO	Lowest wage paid	ME	Median entry wage	S	See annotated source	Y	Yearly

Preschool Teacher

Occupation/Type/Industry	Location	Per	Low	Mid	High	Source	Date
Preschool Teacher							
Except Special Education	Alabama	Y	19785 AE	28949 AW	33526 AEX	ALBLS	6/16
Except Special Education	Birmingham-Hoover MSA, AL	Y	20753 AE	27389 AW	30702 AEX	ALBLS	6/16
Except Special Education	Alaska	Y	29100 FQ	36410 MW	45580 TQ	USBLS	5/15
Except Special Education	Anchorage MSA, AK	Y	27490 FQ	35040 MW	40840 TQ	USBLS	5/15
Except Special Education	Arizona	Y	19740 FQ	23560 MW	31740 TQ	USBLS	5/15
Except Special Education	Phoenix-Mesa-Scottsdale MSA, AZ	Y	19840 FQ	23410 MW	31570 TQ	USBLS	5/15
Except Special Education	Tucson MSA, AZ	Y	19230 FQ	23080 MW	30130 TQ	USBLS	5/15
Except Special Education	Arkansas	Y	19900 FQ	28170 MW	38550 TQ	USBLS	5/15
Except Special Education	Little Rock-North Little Rock-Conway MSA, AR	Y	19380 FQ	27800 MW	38060 TQ	USBLS	5/15
Except Special Education	California	H	12.68 FQ	15.47 MW	19.22 TQ	CABLS	1/16-3/16
Except Special Education	Anaheim-Santa Ana-Irvine PMSA, CA	H	12.36 FQ	15.34 MW	18.30 TQ	CABLS	1/16-3/16
Except Special Education	Los Angeles-Long Beach-Glendale PMSA, CA	H	11.93 FQ	14.49 MW	18.49 TQ	CABLS	1/16-3/16
Except Special Education	Oakland-Hayward-Berkeley PMSA, CA	H	14.75 FQ	17.12 MW	19.56 TQ	CABLS	1/16-3/16
Except Special Education	Riverside-San Bernardino-Ontario MSA, CA	H	12.05 FQ	14.05 MW	17.68 TQ	CABLS	1/16-3/16
Except Special Education	Sacramento–Roseville–Arden-Arcade MSA, CA	H	11.49 FQ	13.34 MW	15.08 TQ	CABLS	1/16-3/16
Except Special Education	San Diego-Carlsbad MSA, CA	H	13.39 FQ	16.24 MW	19.76 TQ	CABLS	1/16-3/16
Except Special Education	San Francisco-Redwood City-South San Francisco PMSA, CA	H	15.74 FQ	18.85 MW	22.30 TQ	CABLS	1/16-3/16
Except Special Education	Colorado	Y	22120 FQ	27260 MW	34390 TQ	USBLS	5/15
Except Special Education	Denver-Aurora-Lakewood MSA, CO	Y	21950 FQ	26810 MW	32370 TQ	USBLS	5/15
Except Special Education	Connecticut	Y		32078 MW		CTBLS	1/16-3/16
Except Special Education	Bridgeport-Stamford-Norwalk MSA, CT	Y	28860 FQ	38620 MW	53440 TQ	USBLS	5/15
Except Special Education	Hartford-West Hartford-East Hartford MSA, CT	Y	23570 FQ	28430 MW	34750 TQ	USBLS	5/15
Except Special Education	Delaware	Y	21760 FQ	25450 MW	29940 TQ	USBLS	5/15
Except Special Education	Wilmington PMSA, DE-MD-NJ	Y	21960 FQ	25760 MW	29930 TQ	USBLS	5/15
Except Special Education	District of Columbia	Y	21150 FQ	39940 MW	54570 TQ	USBLS	5/15
Except Special Education	Washington-Arlington-Alexandria PMSA, DC-VA-MD-WV	Y	24350 FQ	33400 MW	42840 TQ	USBLS	5/15
Except Special Education	Florida	H	9.86 AE	11.94 MW	15.09 AEX	FLBLS	7/16-9/16
Except Special Education	Fort Lauderdale-Pompano Beach-Deerfield Beach PMSA, FL	H	9.67 AE	12.03 MW	16.82 AEX	FLBLS	7/16-9/16
Except Special Education	Miami-Miami Beach-Kendall PMSA, FL	H	10.11 AE	12.97 MW	16.91 AEX	FLBLS	7/16-9/16
Except Special Education	Orlando-Kissimmee-Sanford MSA, FL	H	10.28 AE	11.92 MW	14.27 AEX	FLBLS	7/16-9/16
Except Special Education	Tampa-St. Petersburg-Clearwater MSA, FL	H	10.15 AE	11.93 MW	13.89 AEX	FLBLS	7/16-9/16
Except Special Education	Georgia	Y	22390 FQ	28190 MW	35290 TQ	USBLS	5/15
Except Special Education	Atlanta-Sandy Springs-Roswell MSA, GA	Y	23130 FQ	28040 MW	33930 TQ	USBLS	5/15
Except Special Education	Augusta-Richmond County MSA, GA-SC	Y	20950 FQ	28400 MW	39180 TQ	USBLS	5/15
Except Special Education	Hawaii	Y	26580 FQ	33690 MW	41890 TQ	USBLS	5/15
Except Special Education	Urban Honolulu MSA, HI	Y	26330 FQ	33240 MW	41210 TQ	USBLS	5/15
Except Special Education	Idaho	Y	18140 FQ	21930 MW	28340 TQ	USBLS	5/15
Except Special Education	Boise City MSA, ID	Y	19260 FQ	23860 MW	28920 TQ	USBLS	5/15
Except Special Education	Illinois	Y	23300 FQ	28670 MW	37470 TQ	USBLS	5/15
Except Special Education	Chicago-Naperville-Arlington Heights PMSA, IL	Y	24880 FQ	29260 MW	37600 TQ	USBLS	5/15
Except Special Education	Lake County-Kenosha County PMSA, IL-WI	Y	24020 FQ	29210 MW	41580 TQ	USBLS	5/15
Except Special Education	Indiana	Y	20380 FQ	24530 MW	30920 TQ	USBLS	5/15
Except Special Education	Gary PMSA, IN	Y	18390 FQ	23380 MW	28370 TQ	USBLS	5/15
Except Special Education	Indianapolis-Carmel-Anderson MSA, IN	Y	21180 FQ	23900 MW	30110 TQ	USBLS	5/15
Except Special Education	Iowa	Y	20730 FQ	24040 MW	30990 TQ	USBLS	5/15

AE	Average entry wage	AWR	Average wage range	H	Hourly	LR	Low end range	MTC	Median total compensation	TCC	Total cash compensation
AEX	Average experienced wage	B	Biweekly	HI	Highest wage paid	M	Monthly	MW	Median wage paid	TQ	Third quartile wage
ATC	Average total compensation	D	Daily	HR	High end range	MCC	Median cash compensation	MWR	Median wage range	W	Weekly
AW	Average wage paid	FQ	First quartile wage	LO	Lowest wage paid	ME	Median entry wage	S	See annotated source	Y	Yearly

Occupation/Type/Industry	Location	Per	Low	Mid	High	Source	Date
Preschool Teacher							
Except Special Education	Des Moines-West Des Moines MSA, IA	Y	20920 FQ	23640 MW	28890 TQ	USBLS	5/15
Except Special Education	Kansas	Y	19820 FQ	24570 MW	36510 TQ	USBLS	5/15
Except Special Education	Wichita MSA, KS	Y	17860 FQ	21990 MW	33330 TQ	USBLS	5/15
Except Special Education	Kentucky	Y	24770 FQ	37640 MW	49540 TQ	USBLS	5/15
Except Special Education	Louisville-Jefferson County MSA, KY-IN	Y	27220 FQ	41570 MW	54440 TQ	USBLS	5/15
Except Special Education	Louisiana	Y	25100 FQ	39970 MW	47610 TQ	USBLS	5/15
Except Special Education	Baton Rouge MSA, LA	Y	27300 FQ	39430 MW	47710 TQ	USBLS	5/15
Except Special Education	New Orleans-Metairie MSA, LA	Y	22590 FQ	39840 MW	48330 TQ	USBLS	5/15
Except Special Education	Maine	Y	26170 FQ	29620 MW	35210 TQ	USBLS	5/15
Except Special Education	Portland-South Portland MSA, ME	Y	25900 FQ	28810 MW	32580 TQ	USBLS	5/15
Except Special Education	Maryland	Y	21552 AE	31120 MW	35903 AEX	MDBLS	4/16
Except Special Education	Baltimore-Columbia-Towson MSA, MD	Y	23120 FQ	27360 MW	32070 TQ	USBLS	5/15
Except Special Education	Salisbury MSA, MD-DE	Y	21370 FQ	25190 MW	35250 TQ	USBLS	5/15
Except Special Education	Massachusetts	Y	26230 FQ	31580 MW	41540 TQ	USBLS	5/15
Except Special Education	Boston-Cambridge-Newton NECTA, MA	Y	28170 FQ	35960 MW	46070 TQ	USBLS	5/15
Except Special Education	Worcester MSA, MA-CT	Y	26590 FQ	30970 MW	37930 TQ	USBLS	5/15
Except Special Education	Michigan	Y	22020 FQ	27740 MW	35540 TQ	USBLS	5/15
Except Special Education	Detroit-Dearborn-Livonia PMSA, MI	Y	23310 FQ	30800 MW	36680 TQ	USBLS	5/15
Except Special Education	Grand Rapids-Wyoming MSA, MI	Y	21190 FQ	24780 MW	35200 TQ	USBLS	5/15
Except Special Education	Minnesota	Y	26935 FQ	32389 MW	41018 TQ	MNBLS	1/16-3/16
Except Special Education	Minneapolis-St. Paul-Bloomington MSA, MN-WI	Y	26653 FQ	31381 MW	39637 TQ	MNBLS	1/16-3/16
Except Special Education	Mississippi	Y	19760 FQ	24970 MW	35220 TQ	USBLS	5/15
Except Special Education	Jackson MSA, MS	Y	19200 FQ	23520 MW	38590 TQ	USBLS	5/15
Except Special Education	Missouri	Y	19540 FQ	25070 MW	30220 TQ	USBLS	5/15
Except Special Education	Kansas City MSA, MO-KS	Y	18850 FQ	22690 MW	29920 TQ	USBLS	5/15
Except Special Education	St. Louis MSA, MO-IL	Y	19590 FQ	24770 MW	29780 TQ	USBLS	5/15
Except Special Education	Montana	Y	21090 FQ	25900 MW	30120 TQ	USBLS	5/15
Except Special Education	Billings MSA, MT	Y	18890 FQ	22700 MW	32950 TQ	USBLS	5/15
Except Special Education	Nebraska	Y	19470 FQ	31840 MW	45800 TQ	NEBLS	7/16-9/16
Except Special Education	Omaha-Council Bluffs MSA, NE-IA	Y	23405 FQ	34145 MW	45955 TQ	NEBLS	7/16-9/16
Except Special Education	Nevada	Y	20720 FQ	24640 MW	32690 TQ	USBLS	5/15
Except Special Education	Las Vegas-Henderson-Paradise MSA, NV	Y	20650 FQ	24560 MW	32700 TQ	USBLS	5/15
Except Special Education	New Hampshire	H	10.59 AE	13.49 MW	16.35 AEX	NHBLS	6/16
Except Special Education	Manchester NECTA, NH	H	9.59 AE	12.12 MW	13.90 AEX	NHBLS	6/16
Except Special Education	Nashua NECTA, NH-MA	Y	25220 FQ	29450 MW	35870 TQ	USBLS	5/15
Except Special Education	New Jersey	Y	25800 FQ	35160 MW	54140 TQ	USBLS	5/15
Except Special Education	Camden PMSA, NJ	Y	22690 FQ	29070 MW	57810 TQ	USBLS	5/15
Except Special Education	Newark PMSA, NJ-PA	Y	28380 FQ	36670 MW	52330 TQ	USBLS	5/15
Except Special Education	Trenton MSA, NJ	Y	28560 FQ	39690 MW	52330 TQ	USBLS	5/15
Except Special Education	New Mexico	Y	20410 FQ	26670 MW	36710 TQ	USBLS	5/15
Except Special Education	Albuquerque MSA, NM	Y	19380 FQ	23600 MW	33640 TQ	USBLS	5/15
Except Special Education	New York	Y	21600 AE	31560 MW	47040 AEX	NYBLS	1/16-3/16
Except Special Education	Buffalo-Cheektowaga-Niagara Falls MSA, NY	Y	19710 FQ	23740 MW	29480 TQ	USBLS	5/15
Except Special Education	Nassau County-Suffolk County PMSA, NY	Y	22720 FQ	28430 MW	38260 TQ	USBLS	5/15
Except Special Education	New York-Jersey City-White Plains PMSA, NY-NJ	Y	26510 FQ	36360 MW	53320 TQ	USBLS	5/15
Except Special Education	Rochester MSA, NY	Y	22790 FQ	27650 MW	37510 TQ	USBLS	5/15
Except Special Education	North Carolina	Y	21370 FQ	25970 MW	31910 TQ	USBLS	5/15
Except Special Education	Charlotte-Concord-Gastonia MSA, NC-SC	Y	21370 FQ	25110 MW	30590 TQ	USBLS	5/15
Except Special Education	Raleigh MSA, NC	Y	24380 FQ	28080 MW	32700 TQ	USBLS	5/15
Except Special Education	North Dakota	Y	24250 FQ	35410 MW	49500 TQ	USBLS	5/15
Except Special Education	Fargo MSA, ND-MN	Y	22920 FQ	28230 MW	38850 TQ	USBLS	5/15
Except Special Education	Ohio	Y	20030 FQ	23690 MW	29470 TQ	USBLS	5/15
Except Special Education	Cincinnati MSA, OH-KY-IN	Y	19940 FQ	23700 MW	29880 TQ	USBLS	5/15
Except Special Education	Cleveland-Elyria MSA, OH	Y	21870 FQ	25490 MW	31830 TQ	USBLS	5/15
Except Special Education	Columbus MSA, OH	Y	20700 FQ	24130 MW	28700 TQ	USBLS	5/15
Except Special Education	Oklahoma	Y	22120 FQ	32030 MW	38190 TQ	USBLS	5/15

AE Average entry wage	**AWR** Average wage range	**H** Hourly	**LR** Low end range	**MTC** Median total compensation	**TCC** Total cash compensation
AEX Average experienced wage	**B** Biweekly	**HI** Highest wage paid	**M** Monthly	**MW** Median wage paid	**TQ** Third quartile wage
ATC Average total compensation	**D** Daily	**HR** High end range	**MCC** Median cash compensation	**MWR** Median wage range	**W** Weekly
AW Average wage paid	**FQ** First quartile wage	**LO** Lowest wage paid	**ME** Median entry wage	**S** See annotated source	**Y** Yearly

Occupation/Type/Industry	Location	Per	Low	Mid	High	Source	Date

Preschool Teacher

Occupation/Type/Industry	Location	Per	Low	Mid	High	Source	Date
Except Special Education	Oklahoma City MSA, OK	Y	20260 FQ	24300 MW	35210 TQ	USBLS	5/15
Except Special Education	Tulsa MSA, OK	Y	27550 FQ	34250 MW	39590 TQ	USBLS	5/15
Except Special Education	Oregon	H	11.35 FQ	13.50 MW	16.42 TQ	ORBLS	2016
Except Special Education	Portland-Vancouver-Hillsboro MSA, OR-WA	Y	23320 FQ	27820 MW	34550 TQ	USBLS	5/15
Except Special Education	Pennsylvania	Y	21610 FQ	25970 MW	32390 TQ	USBLS	5/15
Except Special Education	Allentown-Bethlehem-Easton MSA, PA-NJ	Y	21160 FQ	25550 MW	44430 TQ	USBLS	5/15
Except Special Education	Harrisburg-Carlisle MSA, PA	Y	20480 FQ	22930 MW	26120 TQ	USBLS	5/15
Except Special Education	Montgomery County-Bucks County-Chester County PMSA, PA	Y	22670 FQ	26110 MW	29720 TQ	USBLS	5/15
Except Special Education	Philadelphia PMSA, PA	Y	22790 FQ	28570 MW	35610 TQ	USBLS	5/15
Except Special Education	Pittsburgh MSA, PA	Y	20810 FQ	24640 MW	32590 TQ	USBLS	5/15
Except Special Education	Rhode Island	Y	27070 FQ	32900 MW	42330 TQ	USBLS	5/15
Except Special Education	Providence-Warwick MSA, RI-MA	Y	26090 FQ	31230 MW	39220 TQ	USBLS	5/15
Except Special Education	South Carolina	Y	18620 FQ	24620 MW	37740 TQ	USBLS	5/15
Except Special Education	Charleston-North Charleston MSA, SC	Y	20280 FQ	28130 MW	35860 TQ	USBLS	5/15
Except Special Education	Columbia MSA, SC	Y	18200 FQ	24850 MW	46030 TQ	USBLS	5/15
Except Special Education	Greenville-Anderson-Mauldin MSA, SC	Y	17530 FQ	19560 MW	28830 TQ	USBLS	5/15
Except Special Education	South Dakota	Y	25600 FQ	28710 MW	32750 TQ	USBLS	5/15
Except Special Education	Sioux Falls MSA, SD	Y	26650 FQ	29740 MW	34850 TQ	USBLS	5/15
Except Special Education	Tennessee	Y	18480 FQ	23840 MW	40810 TQ	USBLS	5/15
Except Special Education	Knoxville MSA, TN	Y	18160 FQ	21680 MW	30660 TQ	USBLS	5/15
Except Special Education	Memphis MSA, TN-MS-AR	Y	19020 FQ	25660 MW	43380 TQ	USBLS	5/15
Except Special Education	Nashville-Davidson–Murfreesboro–Franklin MSA, TN	Y	18060 FQ	21850 MW	40490 TQ	USBLS	5/15
Except Special Education	Texas	Y	22020 FQ	30990 MW	51890 TQ	USBLS	5/15
Except Special Education	Austin-Round Rock MSA, TX	Y	22900 FQ	29950 MW	49270 TQ	USBLS	5/15
Except Special Education	Dallas-Plano-Irving PMSA, TX	Y	24040 FQ	30450 MW	49910 TQ	USBLS	5/15
Except Special Education	Fort Worth-Arlington PMSA, TX	Y	27930 FQ	50890 MW	57760 TQ	USBLS	5/15
Except Special Education	Houston-The Woodlands-Sugar Land MSA, TX	Y	19800 FQ	23970 MW	45720 TQ	USBLS	5/15
Except Special Education	San Antonio-New Braunfels MSA, TX	Y	22070 FQ	36180 MW	54700 TQ	USBLS	5/15
Except Special Education	Utah	Y	18670 FQ	23030 MW	30660 TQ	USBLS	5/15
Except Special Education	Ogden-Clearfield MSA, UT	Y	18940 FQ	26980 MW	35370 TQ	USBLS	5/15
Except Special Education	Provo-Orem MSA, UT	Y	17580 FQ	19420 MW	27050 TQ	USBLS	5/15
Except Special Education	Salt Lake City MSA, UT	Y	18320 FQ	21390 MW	27270 TQ	USBLS	5/15
Except Special Education	Vermont	Y	26150 FQ	29390 MW	35080 TQ	USBLS	5/15
Except Special Education	Burlington-South Burlington MSA, VT	Y	23650 FQ	27190 MW	30810 TQ	USBLS	5/15
Except Special Education	Virginia	Y	22790 FQ	32490 MW	44240 TQ	USBLS	5/15
Except Special Education	Richmond MSA, VA	Y	22840 FQ	35860 MW	53450 TQ	USBLS	5/15
Except Special Education	Virginia Beach-Norfolk-Newport News MSA, VA-NC	Y	19300 FQ	23560 MW	39460 TQ	USBLS	5/15
Except Special Education	Washington	H	11.25 FQ	13.56 MW	16.98 TQ	WABLS	3/16
Except Special Education	Seattle-Bellevue-Everett PMSA, WA	H	12.36 FQ	14.76 MW	17.92 TQ	WABLS	3/16
Except Special Education	Tacoma-Lakewood PMSA, WA	H	10.68 FQ	12.10 MW	15.95 TQ	WABLS	3/16
Except Special Education	West Virginia	Y	20780 FQ	30640 MW	42520 TQ	USBLS	5/15
Except Special Education	Huntington-Ashland MSA, WV-KY-OH	Y	23600 FQ	29480 MW	41610 TQ	USBLS	5/15
Except Special Education	Wisconsin	Y	20870 FQ	23890 MW	29320 TQ	USBLS	5/15
Except Special Education	Madison MSA, WI	Y	22620 FQ	26690 MW	30800 TQ	USBLS	5/15
Except Special Education	Milwaukee-Waukesha-West Allis MSA, WI	Y	21240 FQ	23980 MW	29400 TQ	USBLS	5/15
Except Special Education	Wyoming	Y	21320 FQ	26130 MW	34570 TQ	USBLS	5/15
Except Special Education	Cheyenne MSA, WY	Y	22350 FQ	26650 MW	29340 TQ	USBLS	5/15
Except Special Education	Puerto Rico	Y	18760 FQ	22010 MW	25380 TQ	USBLS	5/15
Except Special Education	San Juan-Carolina-Caguas MSA, PR	Y	18750 FQ	22070 MW	26540 TQ	USBLS	5/15
Except Special Education	Virgin Islands	Y	19270 FQ	25850 MW	30320 TQ	USBLS	5/15
Except Special Education	Guam	Y	22240 FQ	30390 MW	38690 TQ	USBLS	5/15

Occupation/Type/Industry	Location	Per	Low	Mid	High	Source	Date
President							
Michigan State University	East Lansing, MI	Y			750000 HI	TC01	2015
Private College	United States	Y		513000 AW		CBS01	2014
Public College	United States	Y		431000 MTC		LSJ03	2015
University of Michigan	Ann Arbor, MI	Y			795675 HI	MLV01	2016
Wayne State University	Detroit, MI	Y			497000 HI	FREEP06	2016
Western Michigan University	Kalamazoo, MI	Y			398240 HI	FREEP05	2016
President of the United States	United States	Y			400000 HI	BUSIN	2017
President Pro Tempore of the Senate	United States	Y			174000 HI	OPM01	2017
Presiding Judge							
Harness Racing	Maryland	D			353 HI	MDGOV	2016
Presser							
Textile, Garment, and Related Materials	Alabama	Y	17603 AE	21325 AW	23186 AEX	ALBLS	6/16
Textile, Garment, and Related Materials	Birmingham-Hoover MSA, AL	Y	17942 AE	21233 AW	22878 AEX	ALBLS	6/16
Textile, Garment, and Related Materials	Arizona	Y	18270 FQ	19740 MW	22520 TQ	USBLS	5/15
Textile, Garment, and Related Materials	Phoenix-Mesa-Scottsdale MSA, AZ	Y	18410 FQ	19970 MW	22750 TQ	USBLS	5/15
Textile, Garment, and Related Materials	Tucson MSA, AZ	Y	18130 FQ	19540 MW	22270 TQ	USBLS	5/15
Textile, Garment, and Related Materials	Arkansas	Y	17010 FQ	18340 MW	19750 TQ	USBLS	5/15
Textile, Garment, and Related Materials	Little Rock-North Little Rock-Conway MSA, AR	Y	17100 FQ	18510 MW	20140 TQ	USBLS	5/15
Textile, Garment, and Related Materials	California	H	9.64 FQ	10.83 MW	12.34 TQ	CABLS	1/16-3/16
Textile, Garment, and Related Materials	Anaheim-Santa Ana-Irvine PMSA, CA	H	9.46 FQ	9.67 MW	11.21 TQ	CABLS	1/16-3/16
Textile, Garment, and Related Materials	Los Angeles-Long Beach-Glendale PMSA, CA	H	9.54 FQ	10.22 MW	11.45 TQ	CABLS	1/16-3/16
Textile, Garment, and Related Materials	Oakland-Hayward-Berkeley PMSA, CA	H	9.87 FQ	11.77 MW	13.57 TQ	CABLS	1/16-3/16
Textile, Garment, and Related Materials	Riverside-San Bernardino-Ontario MSA, CA	H	9.60 FQ	10.66 MW	12.24 TQ	CABLS	1/16-3/16
Textile, Garment, and Related Materials	Sacramento–Roseville–Arden-Arcade MSA, CA	H	10.02 FQ	11.45 MW	13.28 TQ	CABLS	1/16-3/16
Textile, Garment, and Related Materials	San Diego-Carlsbad MSA, CA	H	9.99 FQ	11.37 MW	13.07 TQ	CABLS	1/16-3/16
Textile, Garment, and Related Materials	San Francisco-Redwood City-South San Francisco PMSA, CA	H	11.25 FQ	13.64 MW	16.52 TQ	CABLS	1/16-3/16
Textile, Garment, and Related Materials	Colorado	Y	21180 FQ	23570 MW	28240 TQ	USBLS	5/15
Textile, Garment, and Related Materials	Denver-Aurora-Lakewood MSA, CO	Y	21680 FQ	23960 MW	29100 TQ	USBLS	5/15
Textile, Garment, and Related Materials	Connecticut	Y		23589 MW		CTBLS	1/16-3/16
Textile, Garment, and Related Materials	Bridgeport-Stamford-Norwalk MSA, CT	Y	19870 FQ	24950 MW	29850 TQ	USBLS	5/15
Textile, Garment, and Related Materials	Hartford-West Hartford-East Hartford MSA, CT	Y	20700 FQ	22600 MW	24500 TQ	USBLS	5/15
Textile, Garment, and Related Materials	Delaware	Y	17680 FQ	18860 MW	20530 TQ	USBLS	5/15
Textile, Garment, and Related Materials	District of Columbia	Y	20000 FQ	20000 MW	21670 TQ	USBLS	5/15
Textile, Garment, and Related Materials	Washington-Arlington-Alexandria PMSA, DC-VA-MD-WV	Y	18180 FQ	20000 MW	22510 TQ	USBLS	5/15
Textile, Garment, and Related Materials	Florida	H	9.02 AE	10.26 MW	11.80 AEX	FLBLS	7/16-9/16
Textile, Garment, and Related Materials	Fort Lauderdale-Pompano Beach-Deerfield Beach PMSA, FL	H	9.00 AE	10.94 MW	12.31 AEX	FLBLS	7/16-9/16
Textile, Garment, and Related Materials	Miami-Miami Beach-Kendall PMSA, FL	H	9.00 AE	10.16 MW	11.74 AEX	FLBLS	7/16-9/16
Textile, Garment, and Related Materials	Orlando-Kissimmee-Sanford MSA, FL	H	9.01 AE	10.35 MW	12.07 AEX	FLBLS	7/16-9/16
Textile, Garment, and Related Materials	Tampa-St. Petersburg-Clearwater MSA, FL	H	9.09 AE	9.93 MW	11.39 AEX	FLBLS	7/16-9/16
Textile, Garment, and Related Materials	Georgia	Y	18040 FQ	20360 MW	23080 TQ	USBLS	5/15
Textile, Garment, and Related Materials	Atlanta-Sandy Springs-Roswell MSA, GA	Y	18270 FQ	20630 MW	23060 TQ	USBLS	5/15
Textile, Garment, and Related Materials	Augusta-Richmond County MSA, GA-SC	Y	18660 FQ	21420 MW	23710 TQ	USBLS	5/15
Textile, Garment, and Related Materials	Hawaii	Y	19860 FQ	22180 MW	24670 TQ	USBLS	5/15
Textile, Garment, and Related Materials	Idaho	Y	17290 FQ	19270 MW	23110 TQ	USBLS	5/15
Textile, Garment, and Related Materials	Boise City MSA, ID	Y	17130 FQ	19040 MW	22700 TQ	USBLS	5/15

1289

Occupation/Type/Industry	Location	Per	Low	Mid	High	Source	Date
Presser							
Textile, Garment, and Related Materials	Illinois	Y	18930 FQ	20250 MW	23450 TQ	USBLS	5/15
Textile, Garment, and Related Materials	Chicago-Naperville-Arlington Heights PMSA, IL	Y	18920 FQ	20150 MW	23410 TQ	USBLS	5/15
Textile, Garment, and Related Materials	Lake County-Kenosha County PMSA, IL-WI	Y	19350 FQ	20720 MW	23690 TQ	USBLS	5/15
Textile, Garment, and Related Materials	Indiana	Y	17590 FQ	19650 MW	24200 TQ	USBLS	5/15
Textile, Garment, and Related Materials	Gary PMSA, IN	Y	17290 FQ	19270 MW	22150 TQ	USBLS	5/15
Textile, Garment, and Related Materials	Indianapolis-Carmel-Anderson MSA, IN	Y	17200 FQ	18810 MW	24120 TQ	USBLS	5/15
Textile, Garment, and Related Materials	Iowa	Y	18630 FQ	21500 MW	24280 TQ	USBLS	5/15
Textile, Garment, and Related Materials	Des Moines-West Des Moines MSA, IA	Y	20960 FQ	23030 MW	25120 TQ	USBLS	5/15
Textile, Garment, and Related Materials	Kansas	Y	18070 FQ	20270 MW	22810 TQ	USBLS	5/15
Textile, Garment, and Related Materials	Kentucky	Y	17380 FQ	19120 MW	22140 TQ	USBLS	5/15
Textile, Garment, and Related Materials	Louisville-Jefferson County MSA, KY-IN	Y	17280 FQ	19020 MW	21700 TQ	USBLS	5/15
Textile, Garment, and Related Materials	Louisiana	Y	17670 FQ	19950 MW	23620 TQ	USBLS	5/15
Textile, Garment, and Related Materials	Baton Rouge MSA, LA	Y	20000 FQ	22000 MW	23970 TQ	USBLS	5/15
Textile, Garment, and Related Materials	New Orleans-Metairie MSA, LA	Y	17780 FQ	20660 MW	24930 TQ	USBLS	5/15
Textile, Garment, and Related Materials	Maine	Y	20840 FQ	22750 MW	24680 TQ	USBLS	5/15
Textile, Garment, and Related Materials	Portland-South Portland MSA, ME	Y	20960 FQ	22520 MW	24090 TQ	USBLS	5/15
Textile, Garment, and Related Materials	Maryland	Y	18412 AE	24818 MW	28021 AEX	MDBLS	4/16
Textile, Garment, and Related Materials	Baltimore-Columbia-Towson MSA, MD	Y	19210 FQ	24150 MW	33380 TQ	USBLS	5/15
Textile, Garment, and Related Materials	Massachusetts	Y	21410 FQ	25920 MW	32980 TQ	USBLS	5/15
Textile, Garment, and Related Materials	Boston-Cambridge-Newton NECTA, MA	Y	23790 FQ	27660 MW	31070 TQ	USBLS	5/15
Textile, Garment, and Related Materials	Worcester MSA, MA-CT	Y	20650 FQ	22290 MW	23930 TQ	USBLS	5/15
Textile, Garment, and Related Materials	Michigan	Y	18620 FQ	20090 MW	23060 TQ	USBLS	5/15
Textile, Garment, and Related Materials	Detroit-Dearborn-Livonia PMSA, MI	Y	18500 FQ	19850 MW	22360 TQ	USBLS	5/15
Textile, Garment, and Related Materials	Grand Rapids-Wyoming MSA, MI	Y	18590 FQ	19970 MW	22520 TQ	USBLS	5/15
Textile, Garment, and Related Materials	Minnesota	Y	20279 FQ	24127 MW	28106 TQ	MNBLS	1/16-3/16
Textile, Garment, and Related Materials	Minneapolis-St. Paul-Bloomington MSA, MN-WI	Y	20117 FQ	23823 MW	27974 TQ	MNBLS	1/16-3/16
Textile, Garment, and Related Materials	Mississippi	Y	17130 FQ	18670 MW	20740 TQ	USBLS	5/15
Textile, Garment, and Related Materials	Jackson MSA, MS	Y	17690 FQ	19920 MW	23100 TQ	USBLS	5/15
Textile, Garment, and Related Materials	Missouri	Y	18570 FQ	21850 MW	30930 TQ	USBLS	5/15
Textile, Garment, and Related Materials	Kansas City MSA, MO-KS	Y	19160 FQ	21080 MW	23200 TQ	USBLS	5/15
Textile, Garment, and Related Materials	St. Louis MSA, MO-IL	Y	19880 FQ	23680 MW	34600 TQ	USBLS	5/15
Textile, Garment, and Related Materials	Montana	Y	20090 FQ	21990 MW	23890 TQ	USBLS	5/15
Textile, Garment, and Related Materials	Nebraska	Y	20275 FQ	21885 MW	23485 TQ	NEBLS	7/16-9/16
Textile, Garment, and Related Materials	Omaha-Council Bluffs MSA, NE-IA	Y	18655 FQ	20825 MW	23060 TQ	NEBLS	7/16-9/16
Textile, Garment, and Related Materials	Nevada	Y	17710 FQ	19750 MW	23250 TQ	USBLS	5/15
Textile, Garment, and Related Materials	Las Vegas-Henderson-Paradise MSA, NV	Y	17730 FQ	19760 MW	23100 TQ	USBLS	5/15
Textile, Garment, and Related Materials	New Hampshire	H	8.45 AE	10.35 MW	11.43 AEX	NHBLS	6/16
Textile, Garment, and Related Materials	New Jersey	Y	18990 FQ	21250 MW	24800 TQ	USBLS	5/15
Textile, Garment, and Related Materials	Camden PMSA, NJ	Y	18900 FQ	22750 MW	28670 TQ	USBLS	5/15
Textile, Garment, and Related Materials	Newark PMSA, NJ-PA	Y	18500 FQ	19640 MW	29710 TQ	USBLS	5/15
Textile, Garment, and Related Materials	Trenton MSA, NJ	Y	21130 FQ	23330 MW	31340 TQ	USBLS	5/15
Textile, Garment, and Related Materials	New Mexico	Y	18510 FQ	21010 MW	23160 TQ	USBLS	5/15
Textile, Garment, and Related Materials	Albuquerque MSA, NM	Y	19510 FQ	21500 MW	23400 TQ	USBLS	5/15
Textile, Garment, and Related Materials	New York	Y	19330 AE	20540 MW	24430 AEX	NYBLS	1/16-3/16
Textile, Garment, and Related Materials	Buffalo-Cheektowaga-Niagara Falls MSA, NY	Y	21700 FQ	25070 MW	31650 TQ	USBLS	5/15
Textile, Garment, and Related Materials	Nassau County-Suffolk County PMSA, NY	Y	18890 FQ	19910 MW	23510 TQ	USBLS	5/15
Textile, Garment, and Related Materials	New York-Jersey City-White Plains PMSA, NY-NJ	Y	18900 FQ	19800 MW	22980 TQ	USBLS	5/15
Textile, Garment, and Related Materials	Rochester MSA, NY	Y	19810 FQ	22720 MW	26130 TQ	USBLS	5/15
Textile, Garment, and Related Materials	North Carolina	Y	17570 FQ	19760 MW	22740 TQ	USBLS	5/15
Textile, Garment, and Related Materials	Charlotte-Concord-Gastonia MSA, NC-SC	Y	17790 FQ	20150 MW	22860 TQ	USBLS	5/15
Textile, Garment, and Related Materials	Raleigh MSA, NC	Y	17620 FQ	19540 MW	22220 TQ	USBLS	5/15
Textile, Garment, and Related Materials	North Dakota	Y	20190 FQ	22310 MW	24430 TQ	USBLS	5/15
Textile, Garment, and Related Materials	Ohio	Y	18180 FQ	19660 MW	24440 TQ	USBLS	5/15

AE Average entry wage	AWR Average wage range	H Hourly	LR Low end range	MTC Median total compensation	TCC Total cash compensation
AEX Average experienced wage	B Biweekly	HI Highest wage paid	M Monthly	MCC Median cash compensation	TQ Third quartile wage
ATC Average total compensation	D Daily	HR High end range	MCC Median cash compensation	MWR Median wage range	W Weekly
AW Average wage paid	FQ First quartile wage	LO Lowest wage paid	ME Median entry wage	S See annotated source	Y Yearly

Presser

Occupation/Type/Industry	Location	Per	Low	Mid	High	Source	Date
Textile, Garment, and Related Materials	Cincinnati MSA, OH-KY-IN	Y	17960 FQ	19090 MW	23910 TQ	USBLS	5/15
Textile, Garment, and Related Materials	Cleveland-Elyria MSA, OH	Y	18360 FQ	21010 MW	24830 TQ	USBLS	5/15
Textile, Garment, and Related Materials	Columbus MSA, OH	Y	22160 FQ	26280 MW	29090 TQ	USBLS	5/15
Textile, Garment, and Related Materials	Oklahoma	Y	17800 FQ	20050 MW	22740 TQ	USBLS	5/15
Textile, Garment, and Related Materials	Oklahoma City MSA, OK	Y	20090 FQ	21790 MW	23460 TQ	USBLS	5/15
Textile, Garment, and Related Materials	Tulsa MSA, OK	Y	17230 FQ	18950 MW	22040 TQ	USBLS	5/15
Textile, Garment, and Related Materials	Oregon	H	9.93 FQ	10.76 MW	11.59 TQ	ORBLS	2016
Textile, Garment, and Related Materials	Portland-Vancouver-Hillsboro MSA, OR-WA	Y	20580 FQ	22140 MW	23690 TQ	USBLS	5/15
Textile, Garment, and Related Materials	Pennsylvania	Y	18520 FQ	21520 MW	25120 TQ	USBLS	5/15
Textile, Garment, and Related Materials	Allentown-Bethlehem-Easton MSA, PA-NJ	Y	18660 FQ	24060 MW	29770 TQ	USBLS	5/15
Textile, Garment, and Related Materials	Harrisburg-Carlisle MSA, PA	Y	23010 FQ	26070 MW	28920 TQ	USBLS	5/15
Textile, Garment, and Related Materials	Montgomery County-Bucks County-Chester County PMSA, PA	Y	21210 FQ	23520 MW	27130 TQ	USBLS	5/15
Textile, Garment, and Related Materials	Philadelphia PMSA, PA	Y	19390 FQ	21760 MW	24030 TQ	USBLS	5/15
Textile, Garment, and Related Materials	Pittsburgh MSA, PA	Y	17940 FQ	20470 MW	24710 TQ	USBLS	5/15
Textile, Garment, and Related Materials	Rhode Island	Y	20210 FQ	23220 MW	26530 TQ	USBLS	5/15
Textile, Garment, and Related Materials	Providence-Warwick MSA, RI-MA	Y	20280 FQ	23410 MW	26880 TQ	USBLS	5/15
Textile, Garment, and Related Materials	South Carolina	Y	17870 FQ	20030 MW	22740 TQ	USBLS	5/15
Textile, Garment, and Related Materials	Charleston-North Charleston MSA, SC	Y	16930 FQ	18170 MW	19410 TQ	USBLS	5/15
Textile, Garment, and Related Materials	Columbia MSA, SC	Y	17600 FQ	19570 MW	22380 TQ	USBLS	5/15
Textile, Garment, and Related Materials	Greenville-Anderson-Mauldin MSA, SC	Y	19070 FQ	20990 MW	23130 TQ	USBLS	5/15
Textile, Garment, and Related Materials	South Dakota	Y	18860 FQ	20290 MW	23500 TQ	USBLS	5/15
Textile, Garment, and Related Materials	Tennessee	Y	17590 FQ	19790 MW	24170 TQ	USBLS	5/15
Textile, Garment, and Related Materials	Knoxville MSA, TN	Y	18570 FQ	20840 MW	23280 TQ	USBLS	5/15
Textile, Garment, and Related Materials	Memphis MSA, TN-MS-AR	Y	17870 FQ	20140 MW	22750 TQ	USBLS	5/15
Textile, Garment, and Related Materials	Nashville-Davidson–Murfreesboro–Franklin MSA, TN	Y	17690 FQ	20340 MW	24250 TQ	USBLS	5/15
Textile, Garment, and Related Materials	Texas	Y	17040 FQ	18540 MW	20690 TQ	USBLS	5/15
Textile, Garment, and Related Materials	Austin-Round Rock MSA, TX	Y	20580 FQ	22690 MW	24920 TQ	USBLS	5/15
Textile, Garment, and Related Materials	Dallas-Plano-Irving PMSA, TX	Y	17330 FQ	19090 MW	22120 TQ	USBLS	5/15
Textile, Garment, and Related Materials	Fort Worth-Arlington PMSA, TX	Y	16960 FQ	18410 MW	20370 TQ	USBLS	5/15
Textile, Garment, and Related Materials	Houston-The Woodlands-Sugar Land MSA, TX	Y	16830 FQ	18090 MW	19360 TQ	USBLS	5/15
Textile, Garment, and Related Materials	San Antonio-New Braunfels MSA, TX	Y	17150 FQ	18770 MW	23030 TQ	USBLS	5/15
Textile, Garment, and Related Materials	Utah	Y	17660 FQ	19870 MW	23320 TQ	USBLS	5/15
Textile, Garment, and Related Materials	Salt Lake City MSA, UT	Y	19120 FQ	21650 MW	24160 TQ	USBLS	5/15
Textile, Garment, and Related Materials	Vermont	Y	21570 FQ	23320 MW	25070 TQ	USBLS	5/15
Textile, Garment, and Related Materials	Burlington-South Burlington MSA, VT	Y	21770 FQ	23600 MW	25560 TQ	USBLS	5/15
Textile, Garment, and Related Materials	Virginia	Y	17490 FQ	19430 MW	22390 TQ	USBLS	5/15
Textile, Garment, and Related Materials	Richmond MSA, VA	Y	18610 FQ	20980 MW	23240 TQ	USBLS	5/15
Textile, Garment, and Related Materials	Virginia Beach-Norfolk-Newport News MSA, VA-NC	Y	17340 FQ	19050 MW	22030 TQ	USBLS	5/15
Textile, Garment, and Related Materials	Washington	H	11.30 FQ	13.65 MW	16.80 TQ	WABLS	3/16
Textile, Garment, and Related Materials	Seattle-Bellevue-Everett PMSA, WA	H	12.65 FQ	15.74 MW	17.76 TQ	WABLS	3/16
Textile, Garment, and Related Materials	Tacoma-Lakewood PMSA, WA	H	10.16 FQ	11.02 MW	11.88 TQ	WABLS	3/16
Textile, Garment, and Related Materials	West Virginia	Y	18210 FQ	19750 MW	22420 TQ	USBLS	5/15
Textile, Garment, and Related Materials	Huntington-Ashland MSA, WV-KY-OH	Y	18290 FQ	19830 MW	22210 TQ	USBLS	5/15
Textile, Garment, and Related Materials	Wisconsin	Y	18110 FQ	20880 MW	23870 TQ	USBLS	5/15
Textile, Garment, and Related Materials	Madison MSA, WI	Y	18200 FQ	21300 MW	25180 TQ	USBLS	5/15
Textile, Garment, and Related Materials	Milwaukee-Waukesha-West Allis MSA, WI	Y	19080 FQ	21370 MW	23550 TQ	USBLS	5/15
Textile, Garment, and Related Materials	Wyoming	Y	17990 FQ	20400 MW	23600 TQ	USBLS	5/15
Textile, Garment, and Related Materials	Puerto Rico	Y	16640 FQ	17730 MW	18820 TQ	USBLS	5/15
Textile, Garment, and Related Materials	San Juan-Carolina-Caguas MSA, PR	Y	16630 FQ	17730 MW	18830 TQ	USBLS	5/15

Pretrial Release Case Agent

Occupation/Type/Industry	Location	Per	Low	Mid	High	Source	Date
State Government	Maryland	Y	36557 LO		57808 HI	MDGOV	2016

AE	Average entry wage	AWR	Average wage range	H	Hourly
AEX	Average experienced wage	B	Biweekly	HI	Highest wage paid
ATC	Average total compensation	D	Daily	HR	High end range
AW	Average wage paid	FQ	First quartile wage	LO	Lowest wage paid

LR	Low end range	MTC	Median total compensation
M	Monthly	MW	Median wage paid
MCC	Median cash compensation	MWR	Median wage range
ME	Median entry wage	S	See annotated source

TCC	Total cash compensation		
TQ	Third quartile wage		
W	Weekly		
Y	Yearly		

Occupation/Type/Industry	Location	Per	Low	Mid	High	Source	Date
Pretrial Screener							
Full-Time, Sheriff's Office, Municipal Government	Nashville, TN	Y		47410 AW		NTNGOV	2017
Previs Artist	United States	W		2168.41 MW		TAG01	2016
Print Binding and Finishing Worker							
	Alabama	Y	19433 AE	27587 AW	31669 AEX	ALBLS	6/16
	Birmingham-Hoover MSA, AL	Y	18570 AE	26209 AW	30024 AEX	ALBLS	6/16
	Alaska	Y	35210 FQ	51190 MW	57940 TQ	USBLS	5/15
	Arizona	Y	22190 FQ	27700 MW	34270 TQ	USBLS	5/15
	Phoenix-Mesa-Scottsdale MSA, AZ	Y	22550 FQ	27990 MW	35550 TQ	USBLS	5/15
	Tucson MSA, AZ	Y	23740 FQ	28180 MW	33560 TQ	USBLS	5/15
	Arkansas	Y	24530 FQ	28270 MW	32610 TQ	USBLS	5/15
	Little Rock-North Little Rock-Conway MSA, AR	Y	24800 FQ	28050 MW	31280 TQ	USBLS	5/15
	California	H	11.12 FQ	14.31 MW	19.14 TQ	CABLS	1/16-3/16
	Anaheim-Santa Ana-Irvine PMSA, CA	H	9.55 FQ	12.62 MW	17.01 TQ	CABLS	1/16-3/16
	Los Angeles-Long Beach-Glendale PMSA, CA	H	10.68 FQ	13.22 MW	15.60 TQ	CABLS	1/16-3/16
	Oakland-Hayward-Berkeley PMSA, CA	H	13.43 FQ	18.12 MW	23.92 TQ	CABLS	1/16-3/16
	Riverside-San Bernardino-Ontario MSA, CA	H	9.86 FQ	16.03 MW	23.11 TQ	CABLS	1/16-3/16
	Sacramento–Roseville–Arden-Arcade MSA, CA	H	16.67 FQ	22.65 MW	26.44 TQ	CABLS	1/16-3/16
	San Diego-Carlsbad MSA, CA	H	12.92 FQ	16.38 MW	21.57 TQ	CABLS	1/16-3/16
	San Francisco-Redwood City-South San Francisco PMSA, CA	H	13.46 FQ	24.45 MW	28.20 TQ	CABLS	1/16-3/16
	Colorado	Y	25740 FQ	31680 MW	39490 TQ	USBLS	5/15
	Denver-Aurora-Lakewood MSA, CO	Y	26930 FQ	34140 MW	41570 TQ	USBLS	5/15
	Connecticut	Y		35604 MW		CTBLS	1/16-3/16
	Bridgeport-Stamford-Norwalk MSA, CT	Y	27930 FQ	35720 MW	45170 TQ	USBLS	5/15
	Hartford-West Hartford-East Hartford MSA, CT	Y	25170 FQ	39010 MW	56720 TQ	USBLS	5/15
	Delaware	Y	18900 FQ	24270 MW	43800 TQ	USBLS	5/15
	Wilmington PMSA, DE-MD-NJ	Y	18690 FQ	27080 MW	45310 TQ	USBLS	5/15
	District of Columbia	Y	48560 FQ	75310 MW	82170 TQ	USBLS	5/15
	Washington-Arlington-Alexandria PMSA, DC-VA-MD-WV	Y	31300 FQ	45320 MW	60270 TQ	USBLS	5/15
	Florida	H	10.57 AE	14.13 MW	16.87 AEX	FLBLS	7/16-9/16
	Fort Lauderdale-Pompano Beach-Deerfield Beach PMSA, FL	H	11.58 AE	14.01 MW	15.83 AEX	FLBLS	7/16-9/16
	Miami-Miami Beach-Kendall PMSA, FL	H	9.81 AE	12.26 MW	15.98 AEX	FLBLS	7/16-9/16
	Orlando-Kissimmee-Sanford MSA, FL	H	10.85 AE	14.09 MW	17.30 AEX	FLBLS	7/16-9/16
	Tampa-St. Petersburg-Clearwater MSA, FL	H	11.49 AE	15.61 MW	17.86 AEX	FLBLS	7/16-9/16
	Georgia	Y	22440 FQ	28420 MW	39030 TQ	USBLS	5/15
	Atlanta-Sandy Springs-Roswell MSA, GA	Y	22150 FQ	27190 MW	39460 TQ	USBLS	5/15
	Hawaii	Y	22330 FQ	30110 MW	38350 TQ	USBLS	5/15
	Urban Honolulu MSA, HI	Y	22280 FQ	26230 MW	39250 TQ	USBLS	5/15
	Idaho	Y	21550 FQ	28550 MW	35660 TQ	USBLS	5/15
	Boise City MSA, ID	Y	19470 FQ	25170 MW	35130 TQ	USBLS	5/15
	Illinois	Y	22200 FQ	32160 MW	39280 TQ	USBLS	5/15
	Chicago-Naperville-Arlington Heights PMSA, IL	Y	19650 FQ	30590 MW	38780 TQ	USBLS	5/15
	Lake County-Kenosha County PMSA, IL-WI	Y	27030 FQ	34750 MW	45540 TQ	USBLS	5/15
	Indiana	Y	22810 FQ	30660 MW	40440 TQ	USBLS	5/15
	Indianapolis-Carmel-Anderson MSA, IN	Y	23580 FQ	31680 MW	41450 TQ	USBLS	5/15

Print Binding and Finishing Worker

Occupation/Type/Industry	Location	Per	Low	Mid	High	Source	Date
Print Binding and Finishing Worker							
	Iowa	Y	27340 FQ	33030 MW	38740 TQ	USBLS	5/15
	Des Moines-West Des Moines MSA, IA	Y	33690 FQ	37350 MW	42680 TQ	USBLS	5/15
	Kansas	Y	20880 FQ	24650 MW	31430 TQ	USBLS	5/15
	Wichita MSA, KS	Y	19740 FQ	25320 MW	31070 TQ	USBLS	5/15
	Kentucky	Y	26970 FQ	36560 MW	44720 TQ	USBLS	,5/15
	Louisville-Jefferson County MSA, KY-IN	Y	23790 FQ	30320 MW	41630 TQ	USBLS	5/15
	Louisiana	Y	23120 FQ	27840 MW	34250 TQ	USBLS	5/15
	Baton Rouge MSA, LA	Y	24700 FQ	28970 MW	35980 TQ	USBLS	5/15
	New Orleans-Metairie MSA, LA	Y	22660 FQ	27580 MW	36630 TQ	USBLS	5/15
	Maine	Y	26050 FQ	32810 MW	38090 TQ	USBLS	5/15
	Portland-South Portland MSA, ME	Y	22530 FQ	32410 MW	36430 TQ	USBLS	5/15
	Maryland	Y	23598 AE	34441 MW	39863 AEX	MDBLS	4/16
	Baltimore-Columbia-Towson MSA, MD	Y	23300 FQ	32050 MW	41030 TQ	USBLS	5/15
	Massachusetts	Y	28700 FQ	36390 MW	44120 TQ	USBLS	5/15
	Boston-Cambridge-Newton NECTA, MA	Y	31630 FQ	37350 MW	44540 TQ	USBLS	5/15
	Worcester MSA, MA-CT	Y	34880 FQ	41480 MW	47860 TQ	USBLS	5/15
	Michigan	Y	25530 FQ	30800 MW	37600 TQ	USBLS	5/15
	Detroit-Dearborn-Livonia PMSA, MI	Y	26580 FQ	29940 MW	37610 TQ	USBLS	5/15
	Grand Rapids-Wyoming MSA, MI	Y	22150 FQ	27140 MW	34160 TQ	USBLS	5/15
	Minnesota	Y	30019 FQ	37268 MW	47140 TQ	MNBLS	1/16-3/16
	Minneapolis-St. Paul-Bloomington MSA, MN-WI	Y	30748 FQ	38007 MW	48233 TQ	MNBLS	1/16-3/16
	Mississippi	Y	21070 FQ	27240 MW	34380 TQ	USBLS	5/15
	Missouri	Y	23340 FQ	31580 MW	38270 TQ	USBLS	5/15
	Kansas City MSA, MO-KS	Y	23030 FQ	30260 MW	38300 TQ	USBLS	5/15
	St. Louis MSA, MO-IL	Y	23300 FQ	32060 MW	38460 TQ	USBLS	5/15
	Montana	Y	22330 FQ	26800 MW	32310 TQ	USBLS	5/15
	Nebraska	Y	19055 FQ	26410 MW	34705 TQ	NEBLS	7/16-9/16
	Omaha-Council Bluffs MSA, NE-IA	Y	32235 FQ	36420 MW	40710 TQ	NEBLS	7/16-9/16
	Nevada	Y	19510 FQ	25870 MW	36080 TQ	USBLS	5/15
	Las Vegas-Henderson-Paradise MSA, NV	Y	18760 FQ	23720 MW	33980 TQ	USBLS	5/15
	New Hampshire	H	10.19 AE	16.05 MW	17.95 AEX	NHBLS	6/16
	New Jersey	Y	21640 FQ	27170 MW	36130 TQ	USBLS	5/15
	Camden PMSA, NJ	Y	25150 FQ	29060 MW	36180 TQ	USBLS	5/15
	Newark PMSA, NJ-PA	Y	19600 FQ	25900 MW	35610 TQ	USBLS	5/15
	Trenton MSA, NJ	Y	31960 FQ	39000 MW	45400 TQ	USBLS	5/15
	New Mexico	Y	19960 FQ	24880 MW	33910 TQ	USBLS	5/15
	New York	Y	23310 AE	33870 MW	41350 AEX	NYBLS	1/16-3/16
	Buffalo-Cheektowaga-Niagara Falls MSA, NY	Y	22930 FQ	27250 MW	32870 TQ	USBLS	5/15
	Nassau County-Suffolk County PMSA, NY	Y	28570 FQ	40280 MW	51100 TQ	USBLS	5/15
	New York-Jersey City-White Plains PMSA, NY-NJ	Y	23290 FQ	30600 MW	38640 TQ	USBLS	5/15
	Rochester MSA, NY	Y	22730 FQ	27720 MW	34510 TQ	USBLS	5/15
	North Carolina	Y	21220 FQ	25360 MW	31750 TQ	USBLS	5/15
	Charlotte-Concord-Gastonia MSA, NC-SC	Y	23260 FQ	31360 MW	41240 TQ	USBLS	5/15
	Raleigh MSA, NC	Y	25250 FQ	28620 MW	33720 TQ	USBLS	5/15
	North Dakota	Y	22010 FQ	26020 MW	38770 TQ	USBLS	5/15
	Fargo MSA, ND-MN	Y	21100 FQ	23660 MW	30310 TQ	USBLS	5/15
	Ohio	Y	21560 FQ	25760 MW	32140 TQ	USBLS	5/15
	Cincinnati MSA, OH-KY-IN	Y	22490 FQ	28910 MW	40680 TQ	USBLS	5/15
	Cleveland-Elyria MSA, OH	Y	22980 FQ	28890 MW	36560 TQ	USBLS	5/15
	Columbus MSA, OH	Y	21240 FQ	24410 MW	32870 TQ	USBLS	5/15
	Oklahoma	Y	19900 FQ	26330 MW	34440 TQ	USBLS	5/15
	Oklahoma City MSA, OK	Y	18820 FQ	25290 MW	33840 TQ	USBLS	5/15
	Tulsa MSA, OK	Y	23370 FQ	27100 MW	32240 TQ	USBLS	5/15
	Oregon	H	11.66 FQ	14.62 MW	18.39 TQ	ORBLS	2016
	Portland-Vancouver-Hillsboro MSA, OR-WA	Y	23660 FQ	30630 MW	38010 TQ	USBLS	5/15

AE	Average entry wage	AWR	Average wage range	H	Hourly
AEX	Average experienced wage	B	Biweekly	HI	Highest wage paid
ATC	Average total compensation	D	Daily	HR	High end range
AW	Average wage paid	FQ	First quartile wage	LO	Lowest wage paid

LR	Low end range	MTC	Median total compensation	TCC	Total cash compensation
M	Monthly	MW	Median wage paid	TQ	Third quartile wage
MCC	Median cash compensation	MWR	Median wage range	W	Weekly
ME	Median entry wage	S	See annotated source	Y	Yearly

Occupation/Type/Industry	Location	Per	Low	Mid	High	Source	Date
Print Binding and Finishing Worker	Pennsylvania	Y	25480 FQ	32310 MW	40110 TQ	USBLS	5/15
	Allentown-Bethlehem-Easton MSA, PA-NJ	Y	27410 FQ	33990 MW	38280 TQ	USBLS	5/15
	Harrisburg-Carlisle MSA, PA	Y	21700 FQ	26360 MW	32680 TQ	USBLS	5/15
	Montgomery County-Bucks County-Chester County PMSA, PA	Y	29650 FQ	36820 MW	44810 TQ	USBLS	5/15
	Philadelphia PMSA, PA	Y	26730 FQ	35150 MW	45810 TQ	USBLS	5/15
	Pittsburgh MSA, PA	Y	21080 FQ	31560 MW	40650 TQ	USBLS	5/15
	Rhode Island	Y	27460 FQ	31410 MW	39090 TQ	USBLS	5/15
	Providence-Warwick MSA, RI-MA	Y	27770 FQ	32840 MW	40610 TQ	USBLS	5/15
	South Carolina	Y	23950 FQ	30760 MW	41590 TQ	USBLS	5/15
	Columbia MSA, SC	Y	22650 FQ	27890 MW	41240 TQ	USBLS	5/15
	Greenville-Anderson-Mauldin MSA, SC	Y	26450 FQ	30160 MW	35890 TQ	USBLS	5/15
	South Dakota	Y	23080 FQ	28840 MW	36900 TQ	USBLS	5/15
	Sioux Falls MSA, SD	Y	23440 FQ	31640 MW	38230 TQ	USBLS	5/15
	Tennessee	Y	26090 FQ	33240 MW	39300 TQ	USBLS	5/15
	Memphis MSA, TN-MS-AR	Y	25970 FQ	35670 MW	43200 TQ	USBLS	5/15
	Nashville-Davidson–Murfreesboro–Franklin MSA, TN	Y	26470 FQ	33340 MW	38800 TQ	USBLS	5/15
	Texas	Y	20770 FQ	27830 MW	36210 TQ	USBLS	5/15
	Austin-Round Rock MSA, TX	Y	24140 FQ	29420 MW	35410 TQ	USBLS	5/15
	Dallas-Plano-Irving PMSA, TX	Y	19410 FQ	27370 MW	37810 TQ	USBLS	5/15
	Fort Worth-Arlington PMSA, TX	Y	22260 FQ	31120 MW	40820 TQ	USBLS	5/15
	Houston-The Woodlands-Sugar Land MSA, TX	Y	21600 FQ	28120 MW	36020 TQ	USBLS	5/15
	San Antonio-New Braunfels MSA, TX	Y	23840 FQ	28900 MW	34900 TQ	USBLS	5/15
	Utah	Y	22760 FQ	27170 MW	31540 TQ	USBLS	5/15
	Ogden-Clearfield MSA, UT	Y	19420 FQ	24780 MW	33070 TQ	USBLS	5/15
	Provo-Orem MSA, UT	Y	25890 FQ	28510 MW	31140 TQ	USBLS	5/15
	Salt Lake City MSA, UT	Y	22320 FQ	26110 MW	31660 TQ	USBLS	5/15
	Vermont	Y	26690 FQ	33240 MW	39630 TQ	USBLS	5/15
	Burlington-South Burlington MSA, VT	Y	26510 FQ	33330 MW	39380 TQ	USBLS	5/15
	Virginia	Y	24330 FQ	33250 MW	41390 TQ	USBLS	5/15
	Richmond MSA, VA	Y	31940 FQ	36000 MW	40090 TQ	USBLS	5/15
	Virginia Beach-Norfolk-Newport News MSA, VA-NC	Y	18740 FQ	24970 MW	39750 TQ	USBLS	5/15
	Washington	H	12.81 FQ	14.95 MW	18.24 TQ	WABLS	3/16
	Seattle-Bellevue-Everett PMSA, WA	H	12.70 FQ	14.67 MW	18.36 TQ	WABLS	3/16
	West Virginia	Y	19040 FQ	24350 MW	32530 TQ	USBLS	5/15
	Wisconsin	Y	23830 FQ	30280 MW	38300 TQ	USBLS	5/15
	Madison MSA, WI	Y	18940 FQ	27320 MW	40490 TQ	USBLS	5/15
	Milwaukee-Waukesha-West Allis MSA, WI	Y	24600 FQ	30640 MW	38470 TQ	USBLS	5/15
	Wyoming	Y	18340 FQ	22580 MW	33920 TQ	USBLS	5/15
	Puerto Rico	Y	17040 FQ	18470 MW	20000 TQ	USBLS	5/15
	San Juan-Carolina-Caguas MSA, PR	Y	17060 FQ	18520 MW	20290 TQ	USBLS	5/15
Print Newspaper Reporter	United States	Y		36390 MW		CBS02	2016
Printer/Bookbinder							
Baccalaureate Institution	United States	Y		34870 MW		CHE01	2015-2016
Master's Institution	United States	Y		34507 MW		CHE01	2015-2016
Research University	United States	Y		36673 MW		CHE01	2015-2016
Printing Press Operator	Alabama	Y	20276 AE	30631 AW	35813 AEX	ALBLS	6/16
	Birmingham-Hoover MSA, AL	Y	19845 AE	30199 AW	35381 AEX	ALBLS	6/16
	Alaska	Y	31720 FQ	43900 MW	54600 TQ	USBLS	5/15
	Anchorage MSA, AK	Y	34540 FQ	45720 MW	55450 TQ	USBLS	5/15
	Arizona	Y	26610 FQ	32740 MW	38670 TQ	USBLS	5/15
	Phoenix-Mesa-Scottsdale MSA, AZ	Y	26430 FQ	32320 MW	38520 TQ	USBLS	5/15
	Tucson MSA, AZ	Y	27260 FQ	33750 MW	40220 TQ	USBLS	5/15

Occupation/Type/Industry	Location	Per	Low	Mid	High	Source	Date
Printing Press Operator	Arkansas	Y	22180 FQ	28480 MW	36770 TQ	USBLS	5/15
	Little Rock-North Little Rock-Conway MSA, AR	Y	22240 FQ	28640 MW	36660 TQ	USBLS	5/15
	California	H	12.13 FQ	16.43 MW	22.30 TQ	CABLS	1/16-3/16
	Anaheim-Santa Ana-Irvine PMSA, CA	H	11.40 FQ	15.19 MW	19.62 TQ	CABLS	1/16-3/16
	Los Angeles-Long Beach-Glendale PMSA, CA	H	11.43 FQ	15.51 MW	22.10 TQ	CABLS	1/16-3/16
	Oakland-Hayward-Berkeley PMSA, CA	H	15.15 FQ	19.37 MW	23.78 TQ	CABLS	1/16-3/16
	Riverside-San Bernardino-Ontario MSA, CA	H	11.35 FQ	14.19 MW	20.40 TQ	CABLS	1/16-3/16
	Sacramento–Roseville–Arden-Arcade MSA, CA	H	14.30 FQ	19.84 MW	23.21 TQ	CABLS	1/16-3/16
	San Diego-Carlsbad MSA, CA	H	12.35 FQ	15.42 MW	21.66 TQ	CABLS	1/16-3/16
	San Francisco-Redwood City-South San Francisco PMSA, CA	H	15.12 FQ	19.16 MW	26.43 TQ	CABLS	1/16-3/16
	Colorado	Y	27520 FQ	34620 MW	42600 TQ	USBLS	5/15
	Denver-Aurora-Lakewood MSA, CO	Y	28840 FQ	36030 MW	44240 TQ	USBLS	5/15
	Connecticut	Y		36778 MW		CTBLS	1/16-3/16
	Bridgeport-Stamford-Norwalk MSA, CT	Y	23690 FQ	29700 MW	40330 TQ	USBLS	5/15
	Hartford-West Hartford-East Hartford MSA, CT	Y	27980 FQ	36970 MW	49550 TQ	USBLS	5/15
	Delaware	Y	29600 FQ	41740 MW	55280 TQ	USBLS	5/15
	Wilmington PMSA, DE-MD-NJ	Y	30960 FQ	46300 MW	57230 TQ	USBLS	5/15
	District of Columbia	Y	53870 FQ	89130 MW	104380 TQ	USBLS	5/15
	Washington-Arlington-Alexandria PMSA, DC-VA-MD-WV	Y	30290 FQ	44590 MW	60360 TQ	USBLS	5/15
	Florida	H	9.99 AE	14.89 MW	18.42 AEX	FLBLS	7/16-9/16
	Fort Lauderdale-Pompano Beach-Deerfield Beach PMSA, FL	H	11.93 AE	16.15 MW	19.44 AEX	FLBLS	7/16-9/16
	Miami-Miami Beach-Kendall PMSA, FL	H	9.65 AE	13.84 MW	17.30 AEX	FLBLS	7/16-9/16
	Orlando-Kissimmee-Sanford MSA, FL	H	11.58 AE	17.88 MW	21.51 AEX	FLBLS	7/16-9/16
	Tampa-St. Petersburg-Clearwater MSA, FL	H	9.18 AE	13.30 MW	17.29 AEX	FLBLS	7/16-9/16
	Georgia	Y	25020 FQ	33940 MW	44090 TQ	USBLS	5/15
	Atlanta-Sandy Springs-Roswell MSA, GA	Y	29260 FQ	37730 MW	46720 TQ	USBLS	5/15
	Augusta-Richmond County MSA, GA-SC	Y	26140 FQ	33010 MW	37920 TQ	USBLS	5/15
	Hawaii	Y	21760 FQ	29340 MW	40130 TQ	USBLS	5/15
	Urban Honolulu MSA, HI	Y	19710 FQ	27400 MW	35990 TQ	USBLS	5/15
	Idaho	Y	24360 FQ	30330 MW	39350 TQ	USBLS	5/15
	Boise City MSA, ID	Y	26530 FQ	31560 MW	41760 TQ	USBLS	5/15
	Illinois	Y	26810 FQ	37960 MW	49570 TQ	USBLS	5/15
	Chicago-Naperville-Arlington Heights PMSA, IL	Y	25660 FQ	38400 MW	50340 TQ	USBLS	5/15
	Decatur MSA, IL	Y	23280 FQ	32290 MW	37160 TQ	USBLS	5/15
	Lake County-Kenosha County PMSA, IL-WI	Y	28070 FQ	36850 MW	50550 TQ	USBLS	5/15
	Indiana	Y	27610 FQ	35780 MW	45240 TQ	USBLS	5/15
	Gary PMSA, IN	Y	25800 FQ	33650 MW	41420 TQ	USBLS	5/15
	Indianapolis-Carmel-Anderson MSA, IN	Y	28150 FQ	37870 MW	47730 TQ	USBLS	5/15
	Iowa	Y	25880 FQ	34590 MW	44070 TQ	USBLS	5/15
	Des Moines-West Des Moines MSA, IA	Y	31730 FQ	38070 MW	46240 TQ	USBLS	5/15
	Kansas	Y	30240 FQ	39460 MW	51740 TQ	USBLS	5/15
	Wichita MSA, KS	Y	25540 FQ	31850 MW	39180 TQ	USBLS	5/15
	Kentucky	Y	27220 FQ	35690 MW	44530 TQ	USBLS	5/15
	Louisville-Jefferson County MSA, KY-IN	Y	30870 FQ	37370 MW	46430 TQ	USBLS	5/15
	Louisiana	Y	26190 FQ	32690 MW	39950 TQ	USBLS	5/15
	Baton Rouge MSA, LA	Y	30160 FQ	36330 MW	50260 TQ	USBLS	5/15

AE	Average entry wage	AWR	Average wage range	H	Hourly	LR	Low end range	MTC	Median total compensation	TCC	Total cash compensation
AEX	Average experienced wage	B	Biweekly	HI	Highest wage paid	M	Monthly	MW	Median wage paid	TQ	Third quartile wage
ATC	Average total compensation	D	Daily	HR	High end range	MCC	Median cash compensation	MWR	Median wage range	W	Weekly
AW	Average wage paid	FQ	First quartile wage	LO	Lowest wage paid	ME	Median entry wage	S	See annotated source	Y	Yearly

Occupation/Type/Industry	Location	Per	Low	Mid	High	Source	Date
Printing Press Operator	Houma-Thibodaux MSA, LA	Y	23240 FQ	31990 MW	39320 TQ	USBLS	5/15
	New Orleans-Metairie MSA, LA	Y	26000 FQ	29860 MW	35460 TQ	USBLS	5/15
	Maine	Y	26440 FQ	31470 MW	37800 TQ	USBLS	5/15
	Portland-South Portland MSA, ME	Y	30480 FQ	34480 MW	38080 TQ	USBLS	5/15
	Maryland	Y	26993 AE	41082 MW	48127 AEX	MDBLS	4/16
	Baltimore-Columbia-Towson MSA, MD	Y	32740 FQ	39220 MW	49600 TQ	USBLS	5/15
	Salisbury MSA, MD-DE	Y	23630 FQ	33460 MW	39760 TQ	USBLS	5/15
	Massachusetts	Y	33660 FQ	42270 MW	52010 TQ	USBLS	5/15
	Boston-Cambridge-Newton NECTA, MA	Y	35680 FQ	44600 MW	55490 TQ	USBLS	5/15
	Worcester MSA, MA-CT	Y	30040 FQ	36070 MW	44120 TQ	USBLS	5/15
	Michigan	Y	25920 FQ	34030 MW	42080 TQ	USBLS	5/15
	Detroit-Dearborn-Livonia PMSA, MI	Y	25210 FQ	33940 MW	44730 TQ	USBLS	5/15
	Grand Rapids-Wyoming MSA, MI	Y	26460 FQ	32740 MW	41490 TQ	USBLS	5/15
	Minnesota	Y	31983 FQ	41551 MW	52101 TQ	MNBLS	1/16-3/16
	Minneapolis-St. Paul-Bloomington MSA, MN-WI	Y	33006 FQ	43414 MW	54490 TQ	MNBLS	1/16-3/16
	Mississippi	Y	24000 FQ	28660 MW	34610 TQ	USBLS	5/15
	Jackson MSA, MS	Y	25670 FQ	29590 MW	35060 TQ	USBLS	5/15
	Missouri	Y	27250 FQ	33770 MW	46450 TQ	USBLS	5/15
	Kansas City MSA, MO-KS	Y	28640 FQ	38080 MW	53950 TQ	USBLS	5/15
	St. Louis MSA, MO-IL	Y	28170 FQ	34100 MW	45030 TQ	USBLS	5/15
	Montana	Y	23650 FQ	30410 MW	41120 TQ	USBLS	5/15
	Billings MSA, MT	Y	24280 FQ	30640 MW	45400 TQ	USBLS	5/15
	Nebraska	Y	25595 FQ	32865 MW	40065 TQ	NEBLS	7/16-9/16
	Omaha-Council Bluffs MSA, NE-IA	Y	25930 FQ	32905 MW	39720 TQ	NEBLS	7/16-9/16
	Nevada	Y	28960 FQ	35120 MW	41470 TQ	USBLS	5/15
	Las Vegas-Henderson-Paradise MSA, NV	Y	27790 FQ	35050 MW	42170 TQ	USBLS	5/15
	New Hampshire	H	11.35 AE	18.49 MW	21.97 AEX	NHBLS	6/16
	Manchester NECTA, NH	H	8.57 AE	12.65 MW	16.85 AEX	NHBLS	6/16
	Nashua NECTA, NH-MA	Y	39910 FQ	47420 MW	55930 TQ	USBLS	5/15
	New Jersey	Y	30720 FQ	42270 MW	57570 TQ	USBLS	5/15
	Camden PMSA, NJ	Y	33610 FQ	46370 MW	56310 TQ	USBLS	5/15
	Newark PMSA, NJ-PA	Y	32800 FQ	43390 MW	56130 TQ	USBLS	5/15
	Trenton MSA, NJ	Y	39700 FQ	49430 MW	58320 TQ	USBLS	5/15
	New Mexico	Y	22580 FQ	27850 MW	34710 TQ	USBLS	5/15
	Albuquerque MSA, NM	Y	22800 FQ	27660 MW	34330 TQ	USBLS	5/15
	New York	Y	24660 AE	39010 MW	48370 AEX	NYBLS	1/16-3/16
	Buffalo-Cheektowaga-Niagara Falls MSA, NY	Y	30400 FQ	36120 MW	43260 TQ	USBLS	5/15
	Nassau County-Suffolk County PMSA, NY	Y	23320 FQ	40000 MW	56650 TQ	USBLS	5/15
	New York-Jersey City-White Plains PMSA, NY-NJ	Y	27870 FQ	40270 MW	53420 TQ	USBLS	5/15
	Rochester MSA, NY	Y	26890 FQ	32780 MW	39350 TQ	USBLS	5/15
	North Carolina	Y	25460 FQ	32890 MW	41400 TQ	USBLS	5/15
	Charlotte-Concord-Gastonia MSA, NC-SC	Y	23320 FQ	30200 MW	38130 TQ	USBLS	5/15
	Raleigh MSA, NC	Y	34070 FQ	42300 MW	47660 TQ	USBLS	5/15
	North Dakota	Y	29450 FQ	35130 MW	40610 TQ	USBLS	5/15
	Fargo MSA, ND-MN	Y	28420 FQ	34660 MW	41580 TQ	USBLS	5/15
	Ohio	Y	27020 FQ	35400 MW	43930 TQ	USBLS	5/15
	Cincinnati MSA, OH-KY-IN	Y	27550 FQ	36650 MW	47020 TQ	USBLS	5/15
	Cleveland-Elyria MSA, OH	Y	26290 FQ	35790 MW	44880 TQ	USBLS	5/15
	Columbus MSA, OH	Y	32380 FQ	38180 MW	45370 TQ	USBLS	5/15
	Oklahoma	Y	24710 FQ	30670 MW	37860 TQ	USBLS	5/15
	Oklahoma City MSA, OK	Y	24320 FQ	32220 MW	39130 TQ	USBLS	5/15
	Tulsa MSA, OK	Y	26750 FQ	31240 MW	38080 TQ	USBLS	5/15
	Oregon	H	13.39 FQ	17.18 MW	22.20 TQ	ORBLS	2016
	Portland-Vancouver-Hillsboro MSA, OR-WA	Y	27280 FQ	34760 MW	46400 TQ	USBLS	5/15
	Pennsylvania	Y	28180 FQ	36540 MW	46230 TQ	USBLS	5/15
	Allentown-Bethlehem-Easton MSA, PA-NJ	Y	30060 FQ	41020 MW	46840 TQ	USBLS	5/15
	Harrisburg-Carlisle MSA, PA	Y	28710 FQ	34000 MW	38050 TQ	USBLS	5/15

AE	Average entry wage	AWR	Average wage range	
AEX	Average experienced wage	B	Biweekly	
ATC	Average total compensation	D	Daily	
AW	Average wage paid	FQ	First quartile wage	

H	Hourly
HI	Highest wage paid
HR	High end range
LO	Lowest wage paid

LR	Low end range
M	Monthly
MCC	Median cash compensation
ME	Median entry wage

MTC	Median total compensation
MW	Median wage paid
MWR	Median wage range
S	See annotated source

TCC	Total cash compensation
TQ	Third quartile wage
W	Weekly
Y	Yearly

Occupation/Type/Industry	Location	Per	Low	Mid	High	Source	Date
Printing Press Operator	Montgomery County-Bucks County-Chester County PMSA, PA	Y	30820 FQ	39610 MW	49850 TQ	USBLS	5/15
	Philadelphia PMSA, PA	Y	28670 FQ	40200 MW	55860 TQ	USBLS	5/15
	Pittsburgh MSA, PA	Y	23580 FQ	31510 MW	41110 TQ	USBLS	5/15
	Rhode Island	Y	29390 FQ	39040 MW	54450 TQ	USBLS	5/15
	Providence-Warwick MSA, RI-MA	Y	30190 FQ	38520 MW	52490 TQ	USBLS	5/15
	South Carolina	Y	24190 FQ	32550 MW	42010 TQ	USBLS	5/15
	Charleston-North Charleston MSA, SC	Y	27870 FQ	34340 MW	38560 TQ	USBLS	5/15
	Columbia MSA, SC	Y	25610 FQ	33080 MW	41720 TQ	USBLS	5/15
	Greenville-Anderson-Mauldin MSA, SC	Y	29000 FQ	35790 MW	47570 TQ	USBLS	5/15
	South Dakota	Y	25720 FQ	31000 MW	38890 TQ	USBLS	5/15
	Sioux Falls MSA, SD	Y	28440 FQ	33790 MW	42200 TQ	USBLS	5/15
	Tennessee	Y	25800 FQ	33020 MW	39830 TQ	USBLS	5/15
	Knoxville MSA, TN	Y	31430 FQ	35330 MW	39040 TQ	USBLS	5/15
	Memphis MSA, TN-MS-AR	Y	26800 FQ	34770 MW	39830 TQ	USBLS	5/15
	Nashville-Davidson–Murfreesboro–Franklin MSA, TN	Y	26330 FQ	33420 MW	42130 TQ	USBLS	5/15
	Texas	Y	26130 FQ	34500 MW	43850 TQ	USBLS	5/15
	Austin-Round Rock MSA, TX	Y	27560 FQ	33160 MW	38920 TQ	USBLS	5/15
	Dallas-Plano-Irving PMSA, TX	Y	29470 FQ	38650 MW	48730 TQ	USBLS	5/15
	Fort Worth-Arlington PMSA, TX	Y	25600 FQ	35570 MW	51270 TQ	USBLS	5/15
	Houston-The Woodlands-Sugar Land MSA, TX	Y	26410 FQ	35240 MW	42570 TQ	USBLS	5/15
	San Antonio-New Braunfels MSA, TX	Y	24110 FQ	31310 MW	38870 TQ	USBLS	5/15
	Utah	Y	24970 FQ	31260 MW	42040 TQ	USBLS	5/15
	Ogden-Clearfield MSA, UT	Y	22450 FQ	29980 MW	43070 TQ	USBLS	5/15
	Provo-Orem MSA, UT	Y	21980 FQ	25680 MW	34470 TQ	USBLS	5/15
	Salt Lake City MSA, UT	Y	26760 FQ	32410 MW	43640 TQ	USBLS	5/15
	Vermont	Y	30860 FQ	36770 MW	44450 TQ	USBLS	5/15
	Burlington-South Burlington MSA, VT	Y	29580 FQ	37550 MW	46880 TQ	USBLS	5/15
	Virginia	Y	25910 FQ	35450 MW	45660 TQ	USBLS	5/15
	Richmond MSA, VA	Y	30310 FQ	40080 MW	47660 TQ	USBLS	5/15
	Virginia Beach-Norfolk-Newport News MSA, VA-NC	Y	20790 FQ	31740 MW	39100 TQ	USBLS	5/15
	Washington	H	15.52 FQ	18.59 MW	22.90 TQ	WABLS	3/16
	Seattle-Bellevue-Everett PMSA, WA	H	17.13 FQ	20.35 MW	24.04 TQ	WABLS	3/16
	Tacoma-Lakewood PMSA, WA	H	14.73 FQ	16.85 MW	18.71 TQ	WABLS	3/16
	West Virginia	Y	23520 FQ	29050 MW	35730 TQ	USBLS	5/15
	Huntington-Ashland MSA, WV-KY-OH	Y	22760 FQ	28850 MW	35360 TQ	USBLS	5/15
	Wisconsin	Y	29350 FQ	38120 MW	47850 TQ	USBLS	5/15
	Madison MSA, WI	Y	26960 FQ	37470 MW	48220 TQ	USBLS	5/15
	Milwaukee-Waukesha-West Allis MSA, WI	Y	29600 FQ	38710 MW	50320 TQ	USBLS	5/15
	Wyoming	Y	24210 FQ	32540 MW	38460 TQ	USBLS	5/15
	Cheyenne MSA, WY	Y	33140 FQ	36430 MW	38790 TQ	USBLS	5/15
	Puerto Rico	Y	17430 FQ	19290 MW	25020 TQ	USBLS	5/15
	San Juan-Carolina-Caguas MSA, PR	Y	17540 FQ	19500 MW	27250 TQ	USBLS	5/15
Printing Technician							
Municipal Government	Colorado Springs, CO	Y	35857 LO		49304 HI	COSPRS	2017
Private							
U.S. Army, Active Duty, Pay Grade E-2	United States	M		1793 AW		DOD1	2017
Private 1st Class							
U.S. Army, Active Duty, Pay Grade E-3	United States	M	1886 LO		2126 HI	DOD1	2017
U.S. Marines, Active Duty, Pay Grade E-2	United States	M		1793 AW		DOD1	2017
Private Detective and Investigator	Alabama	Y	32463 AE	67233 AW	84623 AEX	ALBLS	6/16
	Birmingham-Hoover MSA, AL	Y	30209 AE	79393 AW	103990 AEX	ALBLS	6/16
	Arizona	Y	35030 FQ	42920 MW	57090 TQ	USBLS	5/15

AE Average entry wage	**AWR** Average wage range	**H** Hourly	**LR** Low end range	**MTC** Median total compensation	**TCC** Total cash compensation
AEX Average experienced wage	**B** Biweekly	**HI** Highest wage paid	**M** Monthly	**MW** Median wage paid	**TQ** Third quartile wage
ATC Average total compensation	**D** Daily	**HR** High end range	**MCC** Median cash compensation	**MWR** Median wage range	**W** Weekly
AW Average wage paid	**FQ** First quartile wage	**LO** Lowest wage paid	**ME** Median entry wage	**S** See annotated source	**Y** Yearly

Private Detective and Investigator

Occupation/Type/Industry	Location	Per	Low	Mid	High	Source	Date
Private Detective and Investigator	Phoenix-Mesa-Scottsdale MSA, AZ	Y	34880 FQ	42330 MW	55840 TQ	USBLS	5/15
	Arkansas	Y	29100 FQ	37590 MW	71620 TQ	USBLS	5/15
	California	H	18.40 FQ	22.93 MW	33.96 TQ	CABLS	1/16-3/16
	Los Angeles-Long Beach-Glendale PMSA, CA	H	18.24 FQ	27.15 MW	40.50 TQ	CABLS	1/16-3/16
	Oakland-Hayward-Berkeley PMSA, CA	H	19.26 FQ	22.98 MW	30.29 TQ	CABLS	1/16-3/16
	Riverside-San Bernardino-Ontario MSA, CA	H	19.21 FQ	23.29 MW	30.35 TQ	CABLS	1/16-3/16
	Sacramento–Roseville–Arden-Arcade MSA, CA	H	9.40 FQ	9.54 MW	11.46 TQ	CABLS	1/16-3/16
	San Diego-Carlsbad MSA, CA	H	18.72 FQ	22.34 MW	30.84 TQ	CABLS	1/16-3/16
	San Francisco-Redwood City-South San Francisco PMSA, CA	H	21.61 FQ	38.73 MW	53.15 TQ	CABLS	1/16-3/16
	Colorado	Y	36060 FQ	44250 MW	59890 TQ	USBLS	5/15
	Denver-Aurora-Lakewood MSA, CO	Y	35910 FQ	43780 MW	66600 TQ	USBLS	5/15
	Connecticut	Y		60532 MW		CTBLS	1/16-3/16
	Bridgeport-Stamford-Norwalk MSA, CT	Y	37500 FQ	58040 MW	69640 TQ	USBLS	5/15
	Hartford-West Hartford-East Hartford MSA, CT	Y	56160 FQ	65290 MW	73920 TQ	USBLS	5/15
	Delaware	Y	39730 FQ	48560 MW	57460 TQ	USBLS	5/15
	Wilmington PMSA, DE-MD-NJ	Y	36220 FQ	45830 MW	55350 TQ	USBLS	5/15
	Washington-Arlington-Alexandria PMSA, DC-VA-MD-WV	Y	43380 FQ	56690 MW	79300 TQ	USBLS	5/15
	Florida	H	16.52 AE	21.72 MW	25.65 AEX	FLBLS	7/16-9/16
	Fort Lauderdale-Pompano Beach-Deerfield Beach PMSA, FL	H	20.07 AE	22.24 MW	22.75 AEX	FLBLS	7/16-9/16
	Miami-Miami Beach-Kendall PMSA, FL	H	15.92 AE	19.25 MW	28.37 AEX	FLBLS	7/16-9/16
	Orlando-Kissimmee-Sanford MSA, FL	H	15.54 AE	19.30 MW	25.01 AEX	FLBLS	7/16-9/16
	Tampa-St. Petersburg-Clearwater MSA, FL	H	17.80 AE	26.27 MW	28.92 AEX	FLBLS	7/16-9/16
	Georgia	Y	31670 FQ	37590 MW	48850 TQ	USBLS	5/15
	Atlanta-Sandy Springs-Roswell MSA, GA	Y	31570 FQ	36860 MW	46400 TQ	USBLS	5/15
	Augusta-Richmond County MSA, GA-SC	Y	42130 FQ	48090 MW	61860 TQ	USBLS	5/15
	Hawaii	Y	38510 FQ	52860 MW	65950 TQ	USBLS	5/15
	Urban Honolulu MSA, HI	Y	38210 FQ	53040 MW	67370 TQ	USBLS	5/15
	Idaho	Y	39180 FQ	47130 MW	55490 TQ	USBLS	5/15
	Boise City MSA, ID	Y	39300 FQ	47080 MW	55380 TQ	USBLS	5/15
	Illinois	Y	26200 FQ	43850 MW	59640 TQ	USBLS	5/15
	Chicago-Naperville-Arlington Heights PMSA, IL	Y	24670 FQ	37100 MW	56170 TQ	USBLS	5/15
	Indianapolis-Carmel-Anderson MSA, IN	Y	23850 FQ	27230 MW	30470 TQ	USBLS	5/15
	Iowa	Y	32750 FQ	40490 MW	59520 TQ	USBLS	5/15
	Des Moines-West Des Moines MSA, IA	Y	34820 FQ	38510 MW	56620 TQ	USBLS	5/15
	Kansas	Y	32500 FQ	38250 MW	53720 TQ	USBLS	5/15
	Kentucky	Y	38280 FQ	46760 MW	64290 TQ	USBLS	5/15
	Louisville-Jefferson County MSA, KY-IN	Y	40280 FQ	46660 MW	61520 TQ	USBLS	5/15
	Louisiana	Y	31880 FQ	38550 MW	47220 TQ	USBLS	5/15
	Baton Rouge MSA, LA	Y	23700 FQ	32640 MW	57400 TQ	USBLS	5/15
	New Orleans-Metairie MSA, LA	Y	33650 FQ	36360 MW	39080 TQ	USBLS	5/15
	Maryland	Y	38044 AE	52545 MW	59795 AEX	MDBLS	4/16
	Baltimore-Columbia-Towson MSA, MD	Y	42770 FQ	48330 MW	63350 TQ	USBLS	5/15
	Salisbury MSA, MD-DE	Y	31820 FQ	47700 MW	59390 TQ	USBLS	5/15
	Massachusetts	Y	31040 FQ	42040 MW	62650 TQ	USBLS	5/15
	Boston-Cambridge-Newton NECTA, MA	Y	35420 FQ	45640 MW	67820 TQ	USBLS	5/15

AE	Average entry wage	AWR	Average wage range	H	Hourly
AEX	Average experienced wage	B	Biweekly	HI	Highest wage paid
ATC	Average total compensation	D	Daily	HR	High end range
AW	Average wage paid	FQ	First quartile wage	LO	Lowest wage paid

LR	Low end range	MTC	Median total compensation	TCC	Total cash compensation
M	Monthly	MW	Median wage paid	TQ	Third quartile wage
MCC	Median cash compensation	MWR	Median wage range	W	Weekly
ME	Median entry wage	S	See annotated source	Y	Yearly

Occupation/Type/Industry	Location	Per	Low	Mid	High	Source	Date
Private Detective and Investigator	Michigan	Y	31670 FQ	42970 MW	48930 TQ	USBLS	5/15
	Grand Rapids-Wyoming MSA, MI	Y	22990 FQ	32120 MW	60500 TQ	USBLS	5/15
	Mississippi	Y	22520 FQ	25960 MW	37000 TQ	USBLS	5/15
	Jackson MSA, MS	Y	27100 FQ	34300 MW	39840 TQ	USBLS	5/15
	Missouri	Y	41720 FQ	45770 MW	59530 TQ	USBLS	5/15
	Kansas City MSA, MO-KS	Y	39990 FQ	43940 MW	47900 TQ	USBLS	5/15
	Montana	Y	33060 FQ	39280 MW	67170 TQ	USBLS	5/15
	Nebraska	Y	57945 FQ	68445 MW	75925 TQ	NEBLS	7/16-9/16
	Omaha-Council Bluffs MSA, NE-IA	Y	19755 FQ	60550 MW	72380 TQ	NEBLS	7/16-9/16
	Nevada	Y	30430 FQ	44270 MW	52110 TQ	USBLS	5/15
	Las Vegas-Henderson-Paradise MSA, NV	Y	30620 FQ	43980 MW	49750 TQ	USBLS	5/15
	New Hampshire	H	16.71 AE	21.59 MW	24.82 AEX	NHBLS	6/16
	Manchester NECTA, NH	H	14.68 AE	17.59 MW	20.70 AEX	NHBLS	6/16
	New Jersey	Y	50990 FQ	65260 MW	76150 TQ	USBLS	5/15
	Camden PMSA, NJ	Y	54480 FQ	68180 MW	79100 TQ	USBLS	5/15
	Newark PMSA, NJ-PA	Y	59010 FQ	68970 MW	78500 TQ	USBLS	5/15
	Trenton MSA, NJ	Y	44790 FQ	67140 MW	80460 TQ	USBLS	5/15
	New Mexico	Y	22530 FQ	27780 MW	42340 TQ	USBLS	5/15
	Albuquerque MSA, NM	Y	20900 FQ	27310 MW	59960 TQ	USBLS	5/15
	New York	Y	39730 AE	56310 MW	71010 AEX	NYBLS	1/16-3/16
	Buffalo-Cheektowaga-Niagara Falls MSA, NY	Y	49150 FQ	53620 MW	58200 TQ	USBLS	5/15
	Nassau County-Suffolk County PMSA, NY	Y	38660 FQ	54100 MW	70920 TQ	USBLS	5/15
	New York-Jersey City-White Plains PMSA, NY-NJ	Y	47120 FQ	58120 MW	72330 TQ	USBLS	5/15
	Rochester MSA, NY	Y	24570 FQ	33690 MW	44360 TQ	USBLS	5/15
	North Carolina	Y	27940 FQ	33250 MW	46420 TQ	USBLS	5/15
	Charlotte-Concord-Gastonia MSA, NC-SC	Y	43660 FQ	48870 MW	59440 TQ	USBLS	5/15
	Ohio	Y	31430 FQ	41740 MW	49430 TQ	USBLS	5/15
	Cincinnati MSA, OH-KY-IN	Y	41050 FQ	44760 MW	48480 TQ	USBLS	5/15
	Cleveland-Elyria MSA, OH	Y	28740 FQ	35960 MW	48730 TQ	USBLS	5/15
	Columbus MSA, OH	Y	28500 FQ	37510 MW	50600 TQ	USBLS	5/15
	Oklahoma	Y	21460 FQ	29860 MW	54050 TQ	USBLS	5/15
	Oklahoma City MSA, OK	Y	28540 FQ	55160 MW	87590 TQ	USBLS	5/15
	Tulsa MSA, OK	Y	17790 FQ	20070 MW	30100 TQ	USBLS	5/15
	Oregon	H	18.70 FQ	21.04 MW	23.09 TQ	ORBLS	2016
	Portland-Vancouver-Hillsboro MSA, OR-WA	Y	39260 FQ	43150 MW	47050 TQ	USBLS	5/15
	Pennsylvania	Y	32440 FQ	39530 MW	58790 TQ	USBLS	5/15
	Allentown-Bethlehem-Easton MSA, PA-NJ	Y	37300 FQ	56420 MW	69620 TQ	USBLS	5/15
	Harrisburg-Carlisle MSA, PA	Y	33710 FQ	36640 MW	39920 TQ	USBLS	5/15
	Montgomery County-Bucks County-Chester County PMSA, PA	Y	50520 FQ	63470 MW	75330 TQ	USBLS	5/15
	Philadelphia PMSA, PA	Y	32910 FQ	43690 MW	61590 TQ	USBLS	5/15
	Pittsburgh MSA, PA	Y	29860 FQ	39040 MW	55360 TQ	USBLS	5/15
	Rhode Island	Y	39690 FQ	47520 MW	56600 TQ	USBLS	5/15
	Providence-Warwick MSA, RI-MA	Y	40080 FQ	46940 MW	55980 TQ	USBLS	5/15
	South Carolina	Y	41120 FQ	45400 MW	49730 TQ	USBLS	5/15
	Tennessee	Y	32600 FQ	46760 MW	61730 TQ	USBLS	5/15
	Knoxville MSA, TN	Y	52210 FQ	58100 MW	63950 TQ	USBLS	5/15
	Nashville-Davidson–Murfreesboro–Franklin MSA, TN	Y	46740 FQ	63300 MW	72720 TQ	USBLS	5/15
	Texas	Y	33480 FQ	43480 MW	65630 TQ	USBLS	5/15
	Austin-Round Rock MSA, TX	Y	41450 FQ	58590 MW	79570 TQ	USBLS	5/15
	Dallas-Plano-Irving PMSA, TX	Y	33790 FQ	38930 MW	66190 TQ	USBLS	5/15
	Fort Worth-Arlington PMSA, TX	Y	36470 FQ	56360 MW	74570 TQ	USBLS	5/15
	Houston-The Woodlands-Sugar Land MSA, TX	Y	37420 FQ	49040 MW	77950 TQ	USBLS	5/15
	Utah	Y	40840 FQ	45540 MW	50740 TQ	USBLS	5/15
	Provo-Orem MSA, UT	Y	41470 FQ	44780 MW	48100 TQ	USBLS	5/15
	Virginia	Y	41400 FQ	51110 MW	71350 TQ	USBLS	5/15
	Richmond MSA, VA	Y	37430 FQ	54650 MW	73350 TQ	USBLS	5/15

AE	Average entry wage	AWR	Average wage range	H	Hourly	LR	Low end range	MTC	Median total compensation	TCC	Total cash compensation
AEX	Average experienced wage	B	Biweekly	HI	Highest wage paid	M	Monthly	MW	Median wage paid	TQ	Third quartile wage
ATC	Average total compensation	D	Daily	HR	High end range	MCC	Median cash compensation	MWR	Median wage range	W	Weekly
AW	Average wage paid	FQ	First quartile wage	LO	Lowest wage paid	ME	Median entry wage	S	See annotated source	Y	Yearly

Occupation/Type/Industry	Location	Per	Low	Mid	High	Source	Date
Private Detective and Investigator	Virginia Beach-Norfolk- Newport News MSA, VA-NC	Y	36520 FQ	54790 MW	73020 TQ	USBLS	5/15
	Washington	H	17.04 FQ	23.85 MW	36.13 TQ	WABLS	3/16
	Seattle-Bellevue-Everett PMSA, WA	H	15.34 FQ	23.73 MW	32.17 TQ	WABLS	3/16
	Wisconsin	Y	27590 FQ	37440 MW	55070 TQ	USBLS	5/15
	Milwaukee-Waukesha-West Allis MSA, WI	Y	27650 FQ	37250 MW	58030 TQ	USBLS	5/15
	Puerto Rico	Y	27470 FQ	38080 MW	45410 TQ	USBLS	5/15
	San Juan-Carolina-Caguas MSA, PR	Y	20890 FQ	28700 MW	42830 TQ	USBLS	5/15
Probation Officer and **Correctional Treatment** **Specialist**	Alabama	Y	32180 AE	47042 AW	54473 AEX	ALBLS	6/16
	Birmingham-Hoover MSA, AL	Y	37919 AE	50253 AW	56409 AEX	ALBLS	6/16
	Alaska	Y	53080 FQ	61170 MW	71980 TQ	USBLS	5/15
	Anchorage MSA, AK	Y	51410 FQ	61160 MW	68550 TQ	USBLS	5/15
	Arizona	Y	44200 FQ	54470 MW	63970 TQ	USBLS	5/15
	Phoenix-Mesa-Scottsdale MSA, AZ	Y	51050 FQ	58990 MW	69230 TQ	USBLS	5/15
	Tucson MSA, AZ	Y	38220 FQ	44460 MW	51430 TQ	USBLS	5/15
	Arkansas	Y	31860 FQ	35470 MW	40920 TQ	USBLS	5/15
	Little Rock-North Little Rock- Conway MSA, AR	Y	33540 FQ	36290 MW	44970 TQ	USBLS	5/15
	California	H	33.28 FQ	41.15 MW	47.14 TQ	CABLS	1/16-3/16
	Anaheim-Santa Ana-Irvine PMSA, CA	H	41.90 FQ	45.05 MW	47.37 TQ	CABLS	1/16-3/16
	Los Angeles-Long Beach- Glendale PMSA, CA	H	32.43 FQ	40.18 MW	46.54 TQ	CABLS	1/16-3/16
	Oakland-Hayward-Berkeley PMSA, CA	H	33.06 FQ	38.80 MW	46.54 TQ	CABLS	1/16-3/16
	Riverside-San Bernardino- Ontario MSA, CA	H	32.87 FQ	37.60 MW	47.00 TQ	CABLS	1/16-3/16
	Sacramento–Roseville– Arden-Arcade MSA, CA	H	43.47 FQ	47.47 MW	53.26 TQ	CABLS	1/16-3/16
	San Diego-Carlsbad MSA, CA	H	20.97 FQ	46.56 MW	48.85 TQ	CABLS	1/16-3/16
	Colorado	Y	47000 FQ	54050 MW	67960 TQ	USBLS	5/15
	Denver-Aurora-Lakewood MSA, CO	Y	46990 FQ	54610 MW	68680 TQ	USBLS	5/15
	Wilmington PMSA, DE-MD- NJ	Y	36310 FQ	44080 MW	48550 TQ	USBLS	5/15
	District of Columbia	Y	47300 FQ	68180 MW	75410 TQ	USBLS	5/15
	Washington-Arlington- Alexandria PMSA, DC-VA- MD-WV	Y	45520 FQ	53340 MW	64180 TQ	USBLS	5/15
	Florida	H	16.05 AE	18.81 MW	21.16 AEX	FLBLS	7/16-9/16
	Fort Lauderdale-Pompano Beach-Deerfield Beach PMSA, FL	H	16.29 AE	21.39 MW	24.66 AEX	FLBLS	7/16-9/16
	Orlando-Kissimmee-Sanford MSA, FL	H	16.02 AE	18.64 MW	20.92 AEX	FLBLS	7/16-9/16
	Georgia	Y	31060 FQ	35200 MW	39370 TQ	USBLS	5/15
	Atlanta-Sandy Springs- Roswell MSA, GA	Y	31310 FQ	35420 MW	39740 TQ	USBLS	5/15
	Augusta-Richmond County MSA, GA-SC	Y	31290 FQ	35630 MW	41240 TQ	USBLS	5/15
	Hawaii	Y	50160 FQ	58420 MW	68930 TQ	USBLS	5/15
	Idaho	Y	34790 FQ	38040 MW	43570 TQ	USBLS	5/15
	Boise City MSA, ID	Y	36300 FQ	38030 MW	41750 TQ	USBLS	5/15
	Illinois	Y	51520 FQ	65890 MW	76230 TQ	USBLS	5/15
	Chicago-Naperville-Arlington Heights PMSA, IL	Y	62640 FQ	71480 MW	79920 TQ	USBLS	5/15
	Lake County-Kenosha County PMSA, IL-WI	Y	49270 FQ	55320 MW	65920 TQ	USBLS	5/15
	Indiana	Y	23860 FQ	36790 MW	47480 TQ	USBLS	5/15
	Gary PMSA, IN	Y	32100 FQ	42470 MW	51340 TQ	USBLS	5/15
	Indianapolis-Carmel-Anderson MSA, IN	Y	23850 FQ	35640 MW	46920 TQ	USBLS	5/15
	Iowa	Y	55560 FQ	69170 MW	78630 TQ	USBLS	5/15

AE	Average entry wage	AWR	Average wage range	H	Hourly
AEX	Average experienced wage	B	Biweekly	HI	Highest wage paid
ATC	Average total compensation	D	Daily	HR	High end range
AW	Average wage paid	FQ	First quartile wage	LO	Lowest wage paid

LR	Low end range	MTC	Median total compensation	TCC	Total cash compensation
M	Monthly	MW	Median wage paid	TQ	Third quartile wage
MCC	Median cash compensation	MWR	Median wage range	W	Weekly
ME	Median entry wage	S	See annotated source	Y	Yearly

Occupation/Type/Industry	Location	Per	Low	Mid	High	Source	Date
Probation Officer and Correctional Treatment Specialist	Des Moines-West Des Moines MSA, IA	Y	58850 FQ	68540 MW	76810 TQ	USBLS	5/15
	Kansas	Y	34850 FQ	38430 MW	44460 TQ	USBLS	5/15
	Wichita MSA, KS	Y	34860 FQ	38560 MW	44560 TQ	USBLS	5/15
	Kentucky	Y	33410 FQ	36350 MW	39280 TQ	USBLS	5/15
	Louisville-Jefferson County MSA, KY-IN	Y	33590 FQ	36700 MW	41150 TQ	USBLS	5/15
	Louisiana	Y	35950 FQ	44900 MW	58730 TQ	USBLS	5/15
	Baton Rouge MSA, LA	Y	36480 FQ	44290 MW	59270 TQ	USBLS	5/15
	New Orleans-Metairie MSA, LA	Y	36370 FQ	46510 MW	60710 TQ	USBLS	5/15
	Maine	Y	32860 FQ	37880 MW	47620 TQ	USBLS	5/15
	Portland-South Portland MSA, ME	Y	29160 FQ	35870 MW	42070 TQ	USBLS	5/15
	Maryland	Y	44987 AE	56084 MW	61633 AEX	MDBLS	4/16
	Baltimore-Columbia-Towson MSA, MD	Y	49970 FQ	55460 MW	64560 TQ	USBLS	5/15
	Michigan	Y	51760 FQ	60500 MW	63870 TQ	USBLS	5/15
	Detroit-Dearborn-Livonia PMSA, MI	Y	53720 FQ	63860 MW	63870 TQ	USBLS	5/15
	Grand Rapids-Wyoming MSA, MI	Y	54360 FQ	63450 MW	63870 TQ	USBLS	5/15
	Saginaw MSA, MI	Y	55270 FQ	63860 MW	63870 TQ	USBLS	5/15
	Minnesota	Y	45624 FQ	60594 MW	75009 TQ	MNBLS	1/16-3/16
	Minneapolis-St. Paul-Bloomington MSA, MN-WI	Y	45231 FQ	63638 MW	77045 TQ	MNBLS	1/16-3/16
	Mississippi	Y	27400 FQ	28940 MW	31430 TQ	USBLS	5/15
	Jackson MSA, MS	Y	27400 FQ	28920 MW	31580 TQ	USBLS	5/15
	Missouri	Y	35000 FQ	36280 MW	40440 TQ	USBLS	5/15
	Kansas City MSA, MO-KS	Y	34690 FQ	36660 MW	40450 TQ	USBLS	5/15
	St. Louis MSA, MO-IL	Y	36260 FQ	37590 MW	42010 TQ	USBLS	5/15
	Montana	Y	36340 FQ	41790 MW	48780 TQ	USBLS	5/15
	Omaha-Council Bluffs MSA, NE-IA	Y	36730 FQ	42820 MW	48850 TQ	NEBLS	7/16-9/16
	Nevada	Y	47990 FQ	57540 MW	69070 TQ	USBLS	5/15
	Las Vegas-Henderson-Paradise MSA, NV	Y	47760 FQ	57960 MW	69590 TQ	USBLS	5/15
	New Hampshire	H	24.02 AE	29.17 MW	31.45 AEX	NHBLS	6/16
	New Jersey	Y	59250 FQ	73800 MW	91480 TQ	USBLS	5/15
	Camden PMSA, NJ	Y	60460 FQ	75330 MW	90790 TQ	USBLS	5/15
	Newark PMSA, NJ-PA	Y	59720 FQ	72410 MW	91250 TQ	USBLS	5/15
	Trenton MSA, NJ	Y	61720 FQ	78930 MW	97110 TQ	USBLS	5/15
	New Mexico	Y	37460 FQ	41440 MW	47000 TQ	USBLS	5/15
	Albuquerque MSA, NM	Y	38500 FQ	41890 MW	47640 TQ	USBLS	5/15
	New York	Y	51110 AE	68290 MW	76150 AEX	NYBLS	1/16-3/16
	Buffalo-Cheektowaga-Niagara Falls MSA, NY	Y	49260 FQ	59770 MW	71120 TQ	USBLS	5/15
	Dutchess County-Putnam County PMSA, NY	Y	67150 FQ	73480 MW	79810 TQ	USBLS	5/15
	Nassau County-Suffolk County PMSA, NY	Y	67770 FQ	75150 MW	86480 TQ	USBLS	5/15
	New York-Jersey City-White Plains PMSA, NY-NJ	Y	57720 FQ	70410 MW	85480 TQ	USBLS	5/15
	Rochester MSA, NY	Y	49800 FQ	58360 MW	69200 TQ	USBLS	5/15
	North Carolina	Y	38550 FQ	39200 MW	42140 TQ	USBLS	5/15
	Charlotte-Concord-Gastonia MSA, NC-SC	Y	37190 FQ	39780 MW	44070 TQ	USBLS	5/15
	North Dakota	Y	47740 FQ	51530 MW	59350 TQ	USBLS	5/15
	Fargo MSA, ND-MN	Y	36800 FQ	47920 MW	59710 TQ	USBLS	5/15
	Ohio	Y	37940 FQ	46680 MW	55730 TQ	USBLS	5/15
	Cincinnati MSA, OH-KY-IN	Y	37590 FQ	45690 MW	55180 TQ	USBLS	5/15
	Cleveland-Elyria MSA, OH	Y	41990 FQ	51450 MW	58960 TQ	USBLS	5/15
	Columbus MSA, OH	Y	36820 FQ	46350 MW	55980 TQ	USBLS	5/15
	Oklahoma	Y	31950 FQ	37790 MW	46170 TQ	USBLS	5/15
	Oklahoma City MSA, OK	Y	30210 FQ	36560 MW	45330 TQ	USBLS	5/15
	Tulsa MSA, OK	Y	28840 FQ	34520 MW	42350 TQ	USBLS	5/15
	Oregon	H	22.91 FQ	27.12 MW	33.33 TQ	ORBLS	2016
	Portland-Vancouver-Hillsboro MSA, OR-WA	Y	54430 FQ	62990 MW	71940 TQ	USBLS	5/15

AE	Average entry wage	AWR	Average wage range	H	Hourly
AEX	Average experienced wage	B	Biweekly	HI	Highest wage paid
ATC	Average total compensation	D	Daily	HR	High end range
AW	Average wage paid	FQ	First quartile wage	LO	Lowest wage paid

LR	Low end range	MTC	Median total compensation
M	Monthly	MW	Median wage paid
MCC	Median cash compensation	MWR	Median wage range
ME	Median entry wage	S	See annotated source

TCC	Total cash compensation
TQ	Third quartile wage
W	Weekly
Y	Yearly

Occupation/Type/Industry	Location	Per	Low	Mid	High	Source	Date
Probation Officer and Correctional Treatment Specialist	Pennsylvania	Y	42100 FQ	51720 MW	61450 TQ	USBLS	5/15
	Allentown-Bethlehem-Easton MSA, PA-NJ	Y	49160 FQ	59170 MW	72600 TQ	USBLS	5/15
	Harrisburg-Carlisle MSA, PA	Y	44200 FQ	52340 MW	61940 TQ	USBLS	5/15
	Montgomery County-Bucks County-Chester County PMSA, PA	Y	44920 FQ	58330 MW	72560 TQ	USBLS	5/15
	Philadelphia PMSA, PA	Y	44500 FQ	52380 MW	58910 TQ	USBLS	5/15
	Pittsburgh MSA, PA	Y	45670 FQ	55080 MW	66590 TQ	USBLS	5/15
	South Carolina	Y	32950 FQ	37700 MW	45290 TQ	USBLS	5/15
	South Dakota	Y	35190 FQ	41150 MW	46630 TQ	USBLS	5/15
	Tennessee	Y	32520 FQ	37190 MW	44590 TQ	USBLS	5/15
	Knoxville MSA, TN	Y	29120 FQ	35430 MW	42740 TQ	USBLS	5/15
	Memphis MSA, TN-MS-AR	Y	33250 FQ	36710 MW	43630 TQ	USBLS	5/15
	Nashville-Davidson– Murfreesboro–Franklin MSA, TN	Y	33940 FQ	38990 MW	47400 TQ	USBLS	5/15
	Texas	Y	36690 FQ	40810 MW	48160 TQ	USBLS	5/15
	Austin-Round Rock MSA, TX	Y	38260 FQ	43500 MW	50900 TQ	USBLS	5/15
	Dallas-Plano-Irving PMSA, TX	Y	39620 FQ	44470 MW	51730 TQ	USBLS	5/15
	Fort Worth-Arlington PMSA, TX	Y	37400 FQ	40810 MW	46840 TQ	USBLS	5/15
	Houston-The Woodlands- Sugar Land MSA, TX	Y	38910 FQ	42490 MW	48640 TQ	USBLS	5/15
	San Antonio-New Braunfels MSA, TX	Y	36520 FQ	40570 MW	47480 TQ	USBLS	5/15
	Utah	Y	43190 FQ	48090 MW	52160 TQ	USBLS	5/15
	Salt Lake City MSA, UT	Y	38700 FQ	46770 MW	50120 TQ	USBLS	5/15
	Vermont	Y	54210 FQ	58000 MW	63290 TQ	USBLS	5/15
	Burlington-South Burlington MSA, VT	Y	54210 FQ	59780 MW	62870 TQ	USBLS	5/15
	Virginia	Y	37090 FQ	42560 MW	51590 TQ	USBLS	5/15
	Richmond MSA, VA	Y	36780 FQ	41300 MW	47700 TQ	USBLS	5/15
	Virginia Beach-Norfolk- Newport News MSA, VA-NC	Y	36120 FQ	40110 MW	46780 TQ	USBLS	5/15
	Washington	H	24.67 FQ	26.21 MW	28.40 TQ	WABLS	3/16
	Seattle-Bellevue-Everett PMSA, WA	H	25.31 FQ	26.89 MW	32.47 TQ	WABLS	3/16
	Tacoma-Lakewood PMSA, WA	H	25.58 FQ	26.88 MW	31.31 TQ	WABLS	3/16
	West Virginia	Y	30130 FQ	36370 MW	44470 TQ	USBLS	5/15
	Huntington-Ashland MSA, WV-KY-OH	Y	30590 FQ	36660 MW	45440 TQ	USBLS	5/15
	Wisconsin	Y	46290 FQ	49620 MW	54750 TQ	USBLS	5/15
	Madison MSA, WI	Y	42800 FQ	47940 MW	54200 TQ	USBLS	5/15
	Milwaukee-Waukesha-West Allis MSA, WI	Y	47930 FQ	50990 MW	54760 TQ	USBLS	5/15
	Wyoming	Y	43260 FQ	47450 MW	49780 TQ	USBLS	5/15
	Puerto Rico	Y	27370 FQ	31910 MW	35780 TQ	USBLS	5/15
	San Juan-Carolina-Caguas MSA, PR	Y	27350 FQ	31900 MW	35750 TQ	USBLS	5/15
Probationary Police Sergeant Municipal Government	San Fernando, CA	Y			86704 HI	CACIT	6/28/16
Process Improvement Analyst State Government	New Mexico	H	24.47 LO		42.56 HI	NMGOV	7/30/16
Procurement Clerk	Alabama	Y	26332 AE	38709 AW	44903 AEX	ALBLS	6/16
	Birmingham-Hoover MSA, AL	Y	28290 AE	39812 AW	45563 AEX	ALBLS	6/16
	Alaska	Y	40780 FQ	47520 MW	54200 TQ	USBLS	5/15
	Anchorage MSA, AK	Y	40150 FQ	46110 MW	53310 TQ	USBLS	5/15
	Arizona	Y	31610 FQ	38140 MW	45490 TQ	USBLS	5/15
	Phoenix-Mesa-Scottsdale MSA, AZ	Y	32870 FQ	38720 MW	45670 TQ	USBLS	5/15
	Tucson MSA, AZ	Y	25290 FQ	33560 MW	43010 TQ	USBLS	5/15
	Arkansas	Y	31900 FQ	39340 MW	47690 TQ	USBLS	5/15
	Little Rock-North Little Rock- Conway MSA, AR	Y	34560 FQ	42210 MW	50990 TQ	USBLS	5/15
	California	H	16.69 FQ	21.70 MW	26.29 TQ	CABLS	1/16-3/16

AE	Average entry wage	AWR	Average wage range	H	Hourly	LR	Low end range	MTC	Median total compensation	TCC	Total cash compensation
AEX	Average experienced wage	B	Biweekly	HI	Highest wage paid	M	Monthly	MW	Median wage paid	TQ	Third quartile wage
ATC	Average total compensation	D	Daily	HR	High end range	MCC	Median cash compensation	MWR	Median wage range	W	Weekly
AW	Average wage paid	FQ	First quartile wage	LO	Lowest wage paid	ME	Median entry wage	S	See annotated source	Y	Yearly

Procurement Clerk

Occupation/Type/Industry	Location	Per	Low	Mid	High	Source	Date
Procurement Clerk	Anaheim-Santa Ana-Irvine PMSA, CA	H	17.05 FQ	21.85 MW	26.74 TQ	CABLS	1/16-3/16
	Los Angeles-Long Beach-Glendale PMSA, CA	H	15.99 FQ	20.69 MW	25.66 TQ	CABLS	1/16-3/16
	Oakland-Hayward-Berkeley PMSA, CA	H	19.81 FQ	23.79 MW	29.77 TQ	CABLS	1/16-3/16
	Riverside-San Bernardino-Ontario MSA, CA	H	15.40 FQ	20.89 MW	25.30 TQ	CABLS	1/16-3/16
	Sacramento–Roseville–Arden-Arcade MSA, CA	H	19.92 FQ	22.85 MW	25.71 TQ	CABLS	1/16-3/16
	San Diego-Carlsbad MSA, CA	H	17.04 FQ	21.43 MW	24.20 TQ	CABLS	1/16-3/16
	San Francisco-Redwood City-South San Francisco PMSA, CA	H	20.72 FQ	24.19 MW	27.77 TQ	CABLS	1/16-3/16
	Colorado	Y	36110 FQ	43670 MW	52230 TQ	USBLS	5/15
	Denver-Aurora-Lakewood MSA, CO	Y	37720 FQ	45440 MW	54890 TQ	USBLS	5/15
	Connecticut	Y		43636 MW		CTBLS	1/16-3/16
	Bridgeport-Stamford-Norwalk MSA, CT	Y	35210 FQ	42550 MW	50970 TQ	USBLS	5/15
	Hartford-West Hartford-East Hartford MSA, CT	Y	33420 FQ	40050 MW	48210 TQ	USBLS	5/15
	Delaware	Y	30910 FQ	39390 MW	51120 TQ	USBLS	5/15
	Wilmington PMSA, DE-MD-NJ	Y	34690 FQ	44690 MW	53550 TQ	USBLS	5/15
	District of Columbia	Y	45200 FQ	52130 MW	60670 TQ	USBLS	5/15
	Washington-Arlington-Alexandria PMSA, DC-VA-MD-WV	Y	43070 FQ	50370 MW	57090 TQ	USBLS	5/15
	Florida	H	14.78 AE	19.39 MW	21.97 AEX	FLBLS	7/16-9/16
	Fort Lauderdale-Pompano Beach-Deerfield Beach PMSA, FL	H	13.41 AE	17.37 MW	19.92 AEX	FLBLS	7/16-9/16
	Miami-Miami Beach-Kendall PMSA, FL	H	15.94 AE	21.07 MW	23.33 AEX	FLBLS	7/16-9/16
	Orlando-Kissimmee-Sanford MSA, FL	H	14.92 AE	19.20 MW	23.81 AEX	FLBLS	7/16-9/16
	Tampa-St. Petersburg-Clearwater MSA, FL	H	14.29 AE	18.81 MW	21.08 AEX	FLBLS	7/16-9/16
	Georgia	Y	33180 FQ	40520 MW	46290 TQ	USBLS	5/15
	Atlanta-Sandy Springs-Roswell MSA, GA	Y	33490 FQ	41170 MW	48270 TQ	USBLS	5/15
	Augusta-Richmond County MSA, GA-SC	Y	32540 FQ	39070 MW	44650 TQ	USBLS	5/15
	Hawaii	Y	36940 FQ	42370 MW	47250 TQ	USBLS	5/15
	Urban Honolulu MSA, HI	Y	37550 FQ	42390 MW	47570 TQ	USBLS	5/15
	Idaho	Y	33990 FQ	40890 MW	46410 TQ	USBLS	5/15
	Boise City MSA, ID	Y	34690 FQ	41380 MW	46700 TQ	USBLS	5/15
	Illinois	Y	36320 FQ	43870 MW	51430 TQ	USBLS	5/15
	Chicago-Naperville-Arlington Heights PMSA, IL	Y	37810 FQ	45680 MW	55360 TQ	USBLS	5/15
	Lake County-Kenosha County PMSA, IL-WI	Y	38050 FQ	45410 MW	52270 TQ	USBLS	5/15
	Indiana	Y	30260 FQ	37800 MW	45350 TQ	USBLS	5/15
	Gary PMSA, IN	Y	34370 FQ	40900 MW	47980 TQ	USBLS	5/15
	Indianapolis-Carmel-Anderson MSA, IN	Y	30990 FQ	39740 MW	47290 TQ	USBLS	5/15
	Iowa	Y	32000 FQ	39080 MW	46490 TQ	USBLS	5/15
	Des Moines-West Des Moines MSA, IA	Y	33020 FQ	40880 MW	46440 TQ	USBLS	5/15
	Kansas	Y	29790 FQ	36800 MW	44380 TQ	USBLS	5/15
	Wichita MSA, KS	Y	29710 FQ	34450 MW	38860 TQ	USBLS	5/15
	Kentucky	Y	32780 FQ	40500 MW	46740 TQ	USBLS	5/15
	Louisville-Jefferson County MSA, KY-IN	Y	33040 FQ	39970 MW	47470 TQ	USBLS	5/15
	Louisiana	Y	33530 FQ	40890 MW	48200 TQ	USBLS	5/15
	Baton Rouge MSA, LA	Y	35980 FQ	43830 MW	50190 TQ	USBLS	5/15
	New Orleans-Metairie MSA, LA	Y	37260 FQ	42740 MW	47720 TQ	USBLS	5/15
	Maine	Y	29530 FQ	35510 MW	40880 TQ	USBLS	5/15
	Portland-South Portland MSA, ME	Y	28570 FQ	33170 MW	38650 TQ	USBLS	5/15

AE Average entry wage	**AWR** Average wage range	**H** Hourly	**LR** Low end range	**MTC** Median total compensation	**TCC** Total cash compensation
AEX Average experienced wage	**B** Biweekly	**HI** Highest wage paid	**M** Monthly	**MW** Median wage paid	**TQ** Third quartile wage
ATC Average total compensation	**D** Daily	**HR** High end range	**MCC** Median cash compensation	**MWR** Median wage range	**W** Weekly
AW Average wage paid	**FQ** First quartile wage	**LO** Lowest wage paid	**ME** Median entry wage	**S** See annotated source	**Y** Yearly

Occupation/Type/Industry	Location	Per	Low	Mid	High	Source	Date
Procurement Clerk	Maryland	Y	34300 AE	48021 MW	54881 AEX	MDBLS	4/16
	Baltimore-Columbia-Towson						
	MSA, MD	Y	39300 FQ	46960 MW	54840 TQ	USBLS	5/15
	Salisbury MSA, MD-DE	Y	25910 FQ	32690 MW	37810 TQ	USBLS	5/15
	Massachusetts	Y	37560 FQ	46140 MW	54590 TQ	USBLS	5/15
	Boston-Cambridge-Newton						
	NECTA, MA	Y	38280 FQ	47930 MW	56130 TQ	USBLS	5/15
	Worcester MSA, MA-CT	Y	36470 FQ	46630 MW	56720 TQ	USBLS	5/15
	Michigan	Y	30530 FQ	36850 MW	45970 TQ	USBLS	5/15
	Detroit-Dearborn-Livonia						
	PMSA, MI	Y	34050 FQ	38230 MW	50370 TQ	USBLS	5/15
	Grand Rapids-Wyoming MSA,						
	MI	Y	27930 FQ	33160 MW	42520 TQ	USBLS	5/15
	Minnesota	Y	31329 FQ	38428 MW	46690 TQ	MNBLS	1/16-3/16
	Minneapolis-St. Paul-						
	Bloomington MSA, MN-WI	Y	33534 FQ	40208 MW	48288 TQ	MNBLS	1/16-3/16
	Mississippi	Y	32380 FQ	41670 MW	48270 TQ	USBLS	5/15
	Jackson MSA, MS	Y	41170 FQ	44710 MW	48070 TQ	USBLS	5/15
	Missouri	Y	31790 FQ	38410 MW	45720 TQ	USBLS	5/15
	Kansas City MSA, MO-KS	Y	36390 FQ	42650 MW	48390 TQ	USBLS	5/15
	St. Louis MSA, MO-IL	Y	30690 FQ	38550 MW	46300 TQ	USBLS	5/15
	Montana	Y	31900 FQ	39560 MW	44140 TQ	USBLS	5/15
	Nebraska	Y	27265 FQ	34100 MW	42210 TQ	NEBLS	7/16-9/16
	Omaha-Council Bluffs MSA,						
	NE-IA	Y	29550 FQ	36470 MW	44075 TQ	NEBLS	7/16-9/16
	Nevada	Y	30350 FQ	38100 MW	45690 TQ	USBLS	5/15
	Las Vegas-Henderson-Paradise						
	MSA, NV	Y	29980 FQ	37680 MW	44840 TQ	USBLS	5/15
	New Hampshire	H	13.11 AE	18.09 MW	20.91 AEX	NHBLS	6/16
	Manchester NECTA, NH	H	13.30 AE	18.87 MW	20.81 AEX	NHBLS	6/16
	Nashua NECTA, NH-MA	Y	31430 FQ	38120 MW	48530 TQ	USBLS	5/15
	New Jersey	Y	35430 FQ	43550 MW	51420 TQ	USBLS	5/15
	Camden PMSA, NJ	Y	35300 FQ	42350 MW	48010 TQ	USBLS	5/15
	Newark PMSA, NJ-PA	Y	34890 FQ	43830 MW	52440 TQ	USBLS	5/15
	Trenton MSA, NJ	Y	38280 FQ	44630 MW	51340 TQ	USBLS	5/15
	New Mexico	Y	31550 FQ	39180 MW	46160 TQ	USBLS	5/15
	Albuquerque MSA, NM	Y	31940 FQ	38690 MW	44830 TQ	USBLS	5/15
	New York	Y	29760 AE	41820 MW	47940 AEX	NYBLS	1/16-3/16
	Buffalo-Cheektowaga-Niagara						
	Falls MSA, NY	Y	30170 FQ	40560 MW	46240 TQ	USBLS	5/15
	Nassau County-Suffolk County						
	PMSA, NY	Y	36140 FQ	44160 MW	51140 TQ	USBLS	5/15
	New York-Jersey City-White						
	Plains PMSA, NY-NJ	Y	34880 FQ	43080 MW	51600 TQ	USBLS	5/15
	Rochester MSA, NY	Y	32940 FQ	38370 MW	47280 TQ	USBLS	5/15
	North Carolina	Y	32870 FQ	39560 MW	46280 TQ	USBLS	5/15
	Charlotte-Concord-Gastonia						
	MSA, NC-SC	Y	33670 FQ	41480 MW	49510 TQ	USBLS	5/15
	Raleigh MSA, NC	Y	32910 FQ	37630 MW	42790 TQ	USBLS	5/15
	North Dakota	Y	31540 FQ	38940 MW	46160 TQ	USBLS	5/15
	Fargo MSA, ND-MN	Y	35340 FQ	41450 MW	47720 TQ	USBLS	5/15
	Ohio	Y	31310 FQ	38460 MW	46990 TQ	USBLS	5/15
	Cincinnati MSA, OH-KY-IN	Y	29040 FQ	37990 MW	46900 TQ	USBLS	5/15
	Cleveland-Elyria MSA, OH	Y	31570 FQ	37020 MW	44050 TQ	USBLS	5/15
	Columbus MSA, OH	Y	35290 FQ	42400 MW	49730 TQ	USBLS	5/15
	Oklahoma	Y	29700 FQ	38670 MW	46290 TQ	USBLS	5/15
	Oklahoma City MSA, OK	Y	32780 FQ	40990 MW	47470 TQ	USBLS	5/15
	Tulsa MSA, OK	Y	32580 FQ	40800 MW	51450 TQ	USBLS	5/15
	Oregon	H	15.31 FQ	18.55 MW	22.36 TQ	ORBLS	2016
	Portland-Vancouver-Hillsboro						
	MSA, OR-WA	Y	31650 FQ	38650 MW	46770 TQ	USBLS	5/15
	Pennsylvania	Y	30610 FQ	39170 MW	47790 TQ	USBLS	5/15
	Allentown-Bethlehem-Easton						
	MSA, PA-NJ	Y	32310 FQ	38260 MW	45170 TQ	USBLS	5/15
	Harrisburg-Carlisle MSA, PA	Y	28990 FQ	38140 MW	45010 TQ	USBLS	5/15
	Montgomery County-Bucks						
	County-Chester County						
	PMSA, PA	Y	33940 FQ	41250 MW	50880 TQ	USBLS	5/15
	Philadelphia PMSA, PA	Y	37990 FQ	46440 MW	53050 TQ	USBLS	5/15
	Pittsburgh MSA, PA	Y	28410 FQ	35240 MW	44190 TQ	USBLS	5/15
	Rhode Island	Y	36630 FQ	43350 MW	48470 TQ	USBLS	5/15

Occupation/Type/Industry	Location	Per	Low	Mid	High	Source	Date
Procurement Clerk	Providence-Warwick MSA, RI-MA	Y	35190 FQ	42410 MW	48010 TQ	USBLS	5/15
	South Carolina	Y	28690 FQ	37040 MW	45600 TQ	USBLS	5/15
	Charleston-North Charleston MSA, SC	Y	30160 FQ	39570 MW	47190 TQ	USBLS	5/15
	Columbia MSA, SC	Y	31210 FQ	40360 MW	46280 TQ	USBLS	5/15
	Greenville-Anderson-Mauldin MSA, SC	Y	27910 FQ	33940 MW	42820 TQ	USBLS	5/15
	South Dakota	Y	29510 FQ	36100 MW	40880 TQ	USBLS	5/15
	Sioux Falls MSA, SD	Y	27940 FQ	30800 MW	37600 TQ	USBLS	5/15
	Tennessee	Y	29800 FQ	37470 MW	45860 TQ	USBLS	5/15
	Knoxville MSA, TN	Y	25290 FQ	33810 MW	43530 TQ	USBLS	5/15
	Memphis MSA, TN-MS-AR	Y	32270 FQ	38960 MW	46530 TQ	USBLS	5/15
	Nashville-Davidson–Murfreesboro–Franklin MSA, TN	Y	33380 FQ	39100 MW	47470 TQ	USBLS	5/15
	Texas	Y	32440 FQ	40650 MW	48040 TQ	USBLS	5/15
	Austin-Round Rock MSA, TX	Y	40210 FQ	44350 MW	48550 TQ	USBLS	5/15
	Dallas-Plano-Irving PMSA, TX	Y	33490 FQ	42420 MW	48660 TQ	USBLS	5/15
	Fort Worth-Arlington PMSA, TX	Y	29910 FQ	37620 MW	47780 TQ	USBLS	5/15
	Houston-The Woodlands-Sugar Land MSA, TX	Y	32190 FQ	39360 MW	50100 TQ	USBLS	5/15
	San Antonio-New Braunfels MSA, TX	Y	38190 FQ	43920 MW	50110 TQ	USBLS	5/15
	Utah	Y	31650 FQ	39570 MW	46930 TQ	USBLS	5/15
	Ogden-Clearfield MSA, UT	Y	33840 FQ	42220 MW	48210 TQ	USBLS	5/15
	Provo-Orem MSA, UT	Y	28630 FQ	39730 MW	49580 TQ	USBLS	5/15
	Salt Lake City MSA, UT	Y	32060 FQ	39180 MW	46170 TQ	USBLS	5/15
	Vermont	Y	33800 FQ	39570 MW	46160 TQ	USBLS	5/15
	Burlington-South Burlington MSA, VT	Y	33680 FQ	39410 MW	43410 TQ	USBLS	5/15
	Virginia	Y	36030 FQ	42730 MW	48950 TQ	USBLS	5/15
	Richmond MSA, VA	Y	36100 FQ	41710 MW	47240 TQ	USBLS	5/15
	Virginia Beach-Norfolk-Newport News MSA, VA-NC	Y	36210 FQ	42220 MW	48020 TQ	USBLS	5/15
	Washington	H	18.70 FQ	22.12 MW	24.93 TQ	WABLS	3/16
	Seattle-Bellevue-Everett PMSA, WA	H	18.44 FQ	21.86 MW	25.79 TQ	WABLS	3/16
	Tacoma-Lakewood PMSA, WA	H	19.00 FQ	21.81 MW	24.30 TQ	WABLS	3/16
	West Virginia	Y	28560 FQ	35920 MW	43530 TQ	USBLS	5/15
	Huntington-Ashland MSA, WV-KY-OH	Y	30370 FQ	35220 MW	39380 TQ	USBLS	5/15
	Wisconsin	Y	32170 FQ	38530 MW	45900 TQ	USBLS	5/15
	Madison MSA, WI	Y	29930 FQ	35930 MW	43520 TQ	USBLS	5/15
	Milwaukee-Waukesha-West Allis MSA, WI	Y	35400 FQ	42230 MW	47890 TQ	USBLS	5/15
	Wyoming	Y	34610 FQ	39580 MW	44360 TQ	USBLS	5/15
	Cheyenne MSA, WY	Y	39170 FQ	42210 MW	43530 TQ	USBLS	5/15
	Puerto Rico	Y	17740 FQ	20360 MW	30520 TQ	USBLS	5/15
	San Juan-Carolina-Caguas MSA, PR	Y	18370 FQ	22160 MW	31930 TQ	USBLS	5/15
	Guam	Y	28540 FQ	39400 MW	41520 TQ	USBLS	5/15
Producer and Director	Alabama	Y	28327 AE	46848 AW	56114 AEX	ALBLS	6/16
	Birmingham-Hoover MSA, AL	Y	31222 AE	50416 AW	60018 AEX	ALBLS	6/16
	Alaska	Y	39850 FQ	49730 MW	68130 TQ	USBLS	5/15
	Anchorage MSA, AK	Y	38780 FQ	50520 MW	76710 TQ	USBLS	5/15
	Arizona	Y	37200 FQ	48490 MW	65190 TQ	USBLS	5/15
	Phoenix-Mesa-Scottsdale MSA, AZ	Y	38200 FQ	49470 MW	68420 TQ	USBLS	5/15
	Tucson MSA, AZ	Y	33610 FQ	43700 MW	56460 TQ	USBLS	5/15
	Arkansas	Y	34340 FQ	44150 MW	54180 TQ	USBLS	5/15
	Little Rock-North Little Rock-Conway MSA, AR	Y	42890 FQ	47650 MW	54300 TQ	USBLS	5/15
	California	H	30.95 FQ	43.85 MW	80.05 TQ	CABLS	1/16-3/16
	Anaheim-Santa Ana-Irvine PMSA, CA	H	25.89 FQ	31.87 MW	51.05 TQ	CABLS	1/16-3/16
	Los Angeles-Long Beach-Glendale PMSA, CA	H	32.91 FQ	46.87 MW		CABLS	1/16-3/16
	Oakland-Hayward-Berkeley PMSA, CA	H	13.90 FQ	31.14 MW	46.32 TQ	CABLS	1/16-3/16

AE	Average entry wage	AWR	Average wage range	H	Hourly
AEX	Average experienced wage	B	Biweekly	HI	Highest wage paid
ATC	Average total compensation	D	Daily	HR	High end range
AW	Average wage paid	FQ	First quartile wage	LO	Lowest wage paid

LR	Low end range	MTC	Median total compensation	TCC	Total cash compensation
M	Monthly	MW	Median wage paid	TQ	Third quartile wage
MCC	Median cash compensation	MWR	Median wage range	W	Weekly
ME	Median entry wage	S	See annotated source	Y	Yearly

Occupation/Type/Industry	Location	Per	Low	Mid	High	Source	Date
Producer and Director	Riverside-San Bernardino-Ontario MSA, CA	H	20.14 FQ	36.92 MW	43.27 TQ	CABLS	1/16-3/16
	Sacramento–Roseville–Arden-Arcade MSA, CA	H	19.42 FQ	27.28 MW	35.61 TQ	CABLS	1/16-3/16
	San Diego-Carlsbad MSA, CA	H	23.23 FQ	30.87 MW	46.40 TQ	CABLS	1/16-3/16
	San Francisco-Redwood City-South San Francisco PMSA, CA	H	28.46 FQ	40.37 MW	69.96 TQ	CABLS	1/16-3/16
	Colorado	Y	41670 FQ	55140 MW	72580 TQ	USBLS	5/15
	Denver-Aurora-Lakewood MSA, CO	Y	44330 FQ	56840 MW	74750 TQ	USBLS	5/15
	Connecticut	Y		66297 MW		CTBLS	1/16-3/16
	Bridgeport-Stamford-Norwalk MSA, CT	Y	51580 FQ	60820 MW	78220 TQ	USBLS	5/15
	Hartford-West Hartford-East Hartford MSA, CT	Y	49340 FQ	69470 MW	84890 TQ	USBLS	5/15
	Delaware	Y	55500 FQ	65270 MW	73170 TQ	USBLS	5/15
	Wilmington PMSA, DE-MD-NJ	Y	56960 FQ	65130 MW	72970 TQ	USBLS	5/15
	District of Columbia	Y	55750 FQ	83260 MW	102920 TQ	USBLS	5/15
	Washington-Arlington-Alexandria PMSA, DC-VA-MD-WV	Y	55890 FQ	80340 MW	100100 TQ	USBLS	5/15
	Florida	H	19.47 AE	31.69 MW	47.84 AEX	FLBLS	7/16-9/16
	Fort Lauderdale-Pompano Beach-Deerfield Beach PMSA, FL	H	20.78 AE	38.96 MW	53.76 AEX	FLBLS	7/16-9/16
	Miami-Miami Beach-Kendall PMSA, FL	H	22.84 AE	35.22 MW	53.86 AEX	FLBLS	7/16-9/16
	Orlando-Kissimmee-Sanford MSA, FL	H	22.35 AE	33.56 MW	47.32 AEX	FLBLS	7/16-9/16
	Tampa-St. Petersburg-Clearwater MSA, FL	H	18.28 AE	30.66 MW	43.64 AEX	FLBLS	7/16-9/16
	Georgia	Y	41610 FQ	57040 MW	77160 TQ	USBLS	5/15
	Atlanta-Sandy Springs-Roswell MSA, GA	Y	45060 FQ	57990 MW	77060 TQ	USBLS	5/15
	Augusta-Richmond County MSA, GA-SC	Y	30780 FQ	38330 MW	46980 TQ	USBLS	5/15
	Hawaii	Y	35960 FQ	49570 MW	67370 TQ	USBLS	5/15
	Urban Honolulu MSA, HI	Y	35180 FQ	49990 MW	67810 TQ	USBLS	5/15
	Idaho	Y	32820 FQ	44520 MW	55520 TQ	USBLS	5/15
	Boise City MSA, ID	Y	36430 FQ	49100 MW	57660 TQ	USBLS	5/15
	Illinois	Y	42920 FQ	68400 MW	99130 TQ	USBLS	5/15
	Chicago-Naperville-Arlington Heights PMSA, IL	Y	46360 FQ	73020 MW	104820 TQ	USBLS	5/15
	Lake County-Kenosha County PMSA, IL-WI	Y	38450 FQ	66700 MW	101990 TQ	USBLS	5/15
	Indiana	Y	38250 FQ	53940 MW	85180 TQ	USBLS	5/15
	Indianapolis-Carmel-Anderson MSA, IN	Y	43240 FQ	68980 MW	92620 TQ	USBLS	5/15
	Iowa	Y	31910 FQ	40780 MW	54520 TQ	USBLS	5/15
	Des Moines-West Des Moines MSA, IA	Y	34300 FQ	43620 MW	59740 TQ	USBLS	5/15
	Kansas	Y	32850 FQ	43220 MW	61090 TQ	USBLS	5/15
	Wichita MSA, KS	Y	32120 FQ	36960 MW	47270 TQ	USBLS	5/15
	Kentucky	Y	32740 FQ	42780 MW	58730 TQ	USBLS	5/15
	Louisville-Jefferson County MSA, KY-IN	Y	35210 FQ	44920 MW	62330 TQ	USBLS	5/15
	Louisiana	Y	41200 FQ	52680 MW	76010 TQ	USBLS	5/15
	Baton Rouge MSA, LA	Y	43650 FQ	59610 MW	102720 TQ	USBLS	5/15
	New Orleans-Metairie MSA, LA	Y	41370 FQ	49390 MW	66100 TQ	USBLS	5/15
	Maine	Y	28340 FQ	36070 MW	45120 TQ	USBLS	5/15
	Portland-South Portland MSA, ME	Y	30480 FQ	36780 MW	44950 TQ	USBLS	5/15
	Maryland	Y	36933 AE	75134 MW	94235 AEX	MDBLS	4/16
	Baltimore-Columbia-Towson MSA, MD	Y	41650 FQ	61720 MW	89110 TQ	USBLS	5/15
	Massachusetts	Y	45770 FQ	63070 MW	82850 TQ	USBLS	5/15
	Boston-Cambridge-Newton NECTA, MA	Y	47090 FQ	65000 MW	85640 TQ	USBLS	5/15
	Worcester MSA, MA-CT	Y	42630 FQ	47360 MW	58020 TQ	USBLS	5/15

AE	Average entry wage	AWR	Average wage range	H	Hourly	LR	Low end range	MTC	Median total compensation	TCC	Total cash compensation
AEX	Average experienced wage	B	Biweekly	HI	Highest wage paid	M	Monthly	MW	Median wage paid	TQ	Third quartile wage
ATC	Average total compensation	D	Daily	HR	High end range	MCC	Median cash compensation	MWR	Median wage range	W	Weekly
AW	Average wage paid	FQ	First quartile wage	LO	Lowest wage paid	ME	Median entry wage	S	See annotated source	Y	Yearly

Occupation/Type/Industry	Location	Per	Low	Mid	High	Source	Date
Producer and Director	Michigan	Y	42910 FQ	60130 MW	80790 TQ	USBLS	5/15
	Detroit-Dearborn-Livonia PMSA, MI	Y	43110 FQ	70360 MW	91700 TQ	USBLS	5/15
	Grand Rapids-Wyoming MSA, MI	Y	39040 FQ	53350 MW	72230 TQ	USBLS	5/15
	Minnesota	Y	48376 FQ	62842 MW	80029 TQ	MNBLS	1/16-3/16
	Minneapolis-St. Paul- Bloomington MSA, MN-WI	Y	52772 FQ	66219 MW	81894 TQ	MNBLS	1/16-3/16
	Mississippi	Y	32170 FQ	40690 MW	59340 TQ	USBLS	5/15
	Jackson MSA, MS	Y	36450 FQ	43840 MW	76130 TQ	USBLS	5/15
	Missouri	Y	41070 FQ	52270 MW	82510 TQ	USBLS	5/15
	Kansas City MSA, MO-KS	Y	43660 FQ	64020 MW	94730 TQ	USBLS	5/15
	St. Louis MSA, MO-IL	Y	42570 FQ	51580 MW	71740 TQ	USBLS	5/15
	Montana	Y	28060 FQ	41800 MW	60990 TQ	USBLS	5/15
	Nebraska	Y	31715 FQ	45150 MW	61190 TQ	NEBLS	7/16-9/16
	Omaha-Council Bluffs MSA, NE-IA	Y	31945 FQ	43835 MW	61445 TQ	NEBLS	7/16-9/16
	Nevada	Y	43130 FQ	63400 MW	84200 TQ	USBLS	5/15
	Las Vegas-Henderson-Paradise MSA, NV	Y	44720 FQ	63580 MW	84500 TQ	USBLS	5/15
	New Hampshire	H	10.02 AE	17.85 MW	36.58 AEX	NHBLS	6/16
	New Jersey	Y	47220 FQ	70440 MW	103470 TQ	USBLS	5/15
	Camden PMSA, NJ	Y	62690 FQ	82930 MW	121880 TQ	USBLS	5/15
	Newark PMSA, NJ-PA	Y	53100 FQ	81860 MW	108690 TQ	USBLS	5/15
	Trenton MSA, NJ	Y	70040 FQ	85360 MW	106960 TQ	USBLS	5/15
	New Mexico	Y	41220 FQ	64910 MW	97210 TQ	USBLS	5/15
	Albuquerque MSA, NM	Y	45760 FQ	70840 MW	109370 TQ	USBLS	5/15
	New York	Y	45010 AE	93190 MW	143800 AEX	NYBLS	1/16-3/16
	Buffalo-Cheektowaga-Niagara Falls MSA, NY	Y	35490 FQ	52390 MW	64250 TQ	USBLS	5/15
	Nassau County-Suffolk County PMSA, NY	Y	52170 FQ	80730 MW	101710 TQ	USBLS	5/15
	New York-Jersey City-White Plains PMSA, NY-NJ	Y	59260 FQ	95090 MW	146560 TQ	USBLS	5/15
	Rochester MSA, NY	Y	32570 FQ	51900 MW	63350 TQ	USBLS	5/15
	North Carolina	Y	35490 FQ	48370 MW	69820 TQ	USBLS	5/15
	Charlotte-Concord-Gastonia MSA, NC-SC	Y	40190 FQ	54190 MW	77490 TQ	USBLS	5/15
	Raleigh MSA, NC	Y	39040 FQ	46390 MW	62060 TQ	USBLS	5/15
	North Dakota	Y	27870 FQ	33620 MW	50080 TQ	USBLS	5/15
	Fargo MSA, ND-MN	Y	26750 FQ	29360 MW	36410 TQ	USBLS	5/15
	Ohio	Y	36180 FQ	48430 MW	63480 TQ	USBLS	5/15
	Cincinnati MSA, OH-KY-IN	Y	33060 FQ	48190 MW	65190 TQ	USBLS	5/15
	Cleveland-Elyria MSA, OH	Y	37060 FQ	51020 MW	62360 TQ	USBLS	5/15
	Columbus MSA, OH	Y	41650 FQ	49210 MW	63420 TQ	USBLS	5/15
	Oklahoma	Y	21040 FQ	39160 MW	59990 TQ	USBLS	5/15
	Oklahoma City MSA, OK	Y	18320 FQ	34130 MW	54970 TQ	USBLS	5/15
	Tulsa MSA, OK	Y	29560 FQ	44480 MW	66970 TQ	USBLS	5/15
	Oregon	H	20.45 FQ	24.90 MW	35.79 TQ	ORBLS	2016
	Portland-Vancouver-Hillsboro MSA, OR-WA	Y	43380 FQ	53860 MW	79940 TQ	USBLS	5/15
	Pennsylvania	Y	37950 FQ	54150 MW	76480 TQ	USBLS	5/15
	Allentown-Bethlehem-Easton MSA, PA-NJ	Y	34580 FQ	43400 MW	62310 TQ	USBLS	5/15
	Harrisburg-Carlisle MSA, PA	Y	33240 FQ	43560 MW	62300 TQ	USBLS	5/15
	Montgomery County-Bucks County-Chester County PMSA, PA	Y	41310 FQ	59580 MW	77260 TQ	USBLS	5/15
	Philadelphia PMSA, PA	Y	42170 FQ	55850 MW	77110 TQ	USBLS	5/15
	Pittsburgh MSA, PA	Y	47090 FQ	66460 MW	100340 TQ	USBLS	5/15
	Rhode Island	Y	40330 FQ	48890 MW	68540 TQ	USBLS	5/15
	Providence-Warwick MSA, RI-MA	Y	39990 FQ	47920 MW	63770 TQ	USBLS	5/15
	South Carolina	Y	28700 FQ	38990 MW	62470 TQ	USBLS	5/15
	Charleston-North Charleston MSA, SC	Y	28190 FQ	34720 MW	57330 TQ	USBLS	5/15
	Columbia MSA, SC	Y	25530 FQ	40090 MW	62060 TQ	USBLS	5/15
	Greenville-Anderson-Mauldin MSA, SC	Y	28060 FQ	43050 MW	84560 TQ	USBLS	5/15
	South Dakota	Y	41520 FQ	52530 MW	67910 TQ	USBLS	5/15
	Sioux Falls MSA, SD	Y	41980 FQ	54730 MW	71680 TQ	USBLS	5/15
	Tennessee	Y	32010 FQ	42350 MW	73510 TQ	USBLS	5/15

AE Average entry wage	AWR Average wage range	H Hourly	LR Low end range	MTC Median total compensation	TCC Total cash compensation
AEX Average experienced wage	B Biweekly	HI Highest wage paid	M Monthly	MW Median wage paid	TQ Third quartile wage
ATC Average total compensation	D Daily	HR High end range	MCC Median cash compensation	MWR Median wage range	W Weekly
AW Average wage paid	FQ First quartile wage	LO Lowest wage paid	ME Median entry wage	S See annotated source	Y Yearly

Occupation/Type/Industry	Location	Per	Low	Mid	High	Source	Date
Producer and Director	Knoxville MSA, TN	Y	32190 FQ	43090 MW	61880 TQ	USBLS	5/15
	Memphis MSA, TN-MS-AR	Y	31120 FQ	37590 MW	71900 TQ	USBLS	5/15
	Nashville-Davidson– Murfreesboro–Franklin MSA, TN	Y	33040 FQ	45590 MW	82300 TQ	USBLS	5/15
	Texas	Y	35580 FQ	51480 MW	75680 TQ	USBLS	5/15
	Austin-Round Rock MSA, TX	Y	32520 FQ	46980 MW	63630 TQ	USBLS	5/15
	Dallas-Plano-Irving PMSA, TX	Y	43100 FQ	70320 MW	93990 TQ	USBLS	5/15
	Fort Worth-Arlington PMSA, TX	Y	41580 FQ	55530 MW	74650 TQ	USBLS	5/15
	Houston-The Woodlands- Sugar Land MSA, TX	Y	36550 FQ	57840 MW	76010 TQ	USBLS	5/15
	San Antonio-New Braunfels MSA, TX	Y	35570 FQ	46060 MW	60930 TQ	USBLS	5/15
	Utah	Y	33540 FQ	49920 MW	70990 TQ	USBLS	5/15
	Ogden-Clearfield MSA, UT	Y	57620 FQ	70280 MW	79560 TQ	USBLS	5/15
	Provo-Orem MSA, UT	Y	45660 FQ	66050 MW	93100 TQ	USBLS	5/15
	Salt Lake City MSA, UT	Y	31030 FQ	45180 MW	66460 TQ	USBLS	5/15
	Vermont	Y	35910 FQ	46790 MW	63750 TQ	USBLS	5/15
	Burlington-South Burlington MSA, VT	Y	41650 FQ	57680 MW	75450 TQ	USBLS	5/15
	Virginia	Y	47210 FQ	62290 MW	86960 TQ	USBLS	5/15
	Richmond MSA, VA	Y	45050 FQ	58930 MW	85420 TQ	USBLS	5/15
	Virginia Beach-Norfolk- Newport News MSA, VA-NC	Y	48080 FQ	57240 MW	73140 TQ	USBLS	5/15
	Washington	H	21.97 FQ	29.59 MW	43.23 TQ	WABLS	3/16
	Seattle-Bellevue-Everett PMSA, WA	H	23.72 FQ	30.32 MW	44.05 TQ	WABLS	3/16
	Tacoma-Lakewood PMSA, WA	H	17.49 FQ	26.51 MW	37.63 TQ	WABLS	3/16
	West Virginia	Y	32400 FQ	53540 MW	82750 TQ	USBLS	5/15
	Huntington-Ashland MSA, WV-KY-OH	Y	27460 FQ	39360 MW	58070 TQ	USBLS	5/15
	Wisconsin	Y	36020 FQ	47160 MW	60140 TQ	USBLS	5/15
	Madison MSA, WI	Y	37510 FQ	49100 MW	60030 TQ	USBLS	5/15
	Milwaukee-Waukesha-West Allis MSA, WI	Y	38820 FQ	50310 MW	63040 TQ	USBLS	5/15
	Wyoming	Y	34470 FQ	42760 MW	59700 TQ	USBLS	5/15
	Puerto Rico	Y	20850 FQ	35980 MW	59000 TQ	USBLS	5/15
	San Juan-Carolina-Caguas MSA, PR	Y	20430 FQ	37210 MW	60650 TQ	USBLS	5/15
Product Manager	United States	Y		107000 MW		CNBC02	2016
	Silicon Valley, CA	Y	105000 LO			FORB02	2016
Pharmaceutical, Medical Device, and Healthcare Industries	United States	Y		95500 AW		MMM01	7/16
Product Marketing Manager	United States	Y		115000 MW		TDY01	2016
Production, Planning, and Expediting Clerk	Alabama	Y	31392 AE	49376 AW	58363 AEX	ALBLS	6/16
	Birmingham-Hoover MSA, AL	Y	32629 AE	51602 AW	61083 AEX	ALBLS	6/16
	Alaska	Y	40290 FQ	52870 MW	65050 TQ	USBLS	5/15
	Anchorage MSA, AK	Y	39650 FQ	53450 MW	66990 TQ	USBLS	5/15
	Arizona	Y	32200 FQ	40610 MW	56470 TQ	USBLS	5/15
	Phoenix-Mesa-Scottsdale MSA, AZ	Y	32070 FQ	40330 MW	56120 TQ	USBLS	5/15
	Tucson MSA, AZ	Y	34150 FQ	46300 MW	60700 TQ	USBLS	5/15
	Arkansas	Y	24450 FQ	38670 MW	52600 TQ	USBLS	5/15
	Little Rock-North Little Rock- Conway MSA, AR	Y	35510 FQ	44490 MW	55710 TQ	USBLS	5/15
	California	H	17.76 FQ	23.71 MW	30.41 TQ	CABLS	1/16-3/16
	Anaheim-Santa Ana-Irvine PMSA, CA	H	18.62 FQ	24.44 MW	30.81 TQ	CABLS	1/16-3/16
	Los Angeles-Long Beach- Glendale PMSA, CA	H	16.69 FQ	21.85 MW	28.70 TQ	CABLS	1/16-3/16
	Oakland-Hayward-Berkeley PMSA, CA	H	21.34 FQ	26.83 MW	31.75 TQ	CABLS	1/16-3/16
	Riverside-San Bernardino- Ontario MSA, CA	H	15.81 FQ	19.54 MW	24.42 TQ	CABLS	1/16-3/16
	Sacramento–Roseville– Arden-Arcade MSA, CA	H	18.53 FQ	23.93 MW	28.53 TQ	CABLS	1/16-3/16
	San Diego-Carlsbad MSA, CA	H	16.36 FQ	22.76 MW	30.21 TQ	CABLS	1/16-3/16

Occupation/Type/Industry	Location	Per	Low	Mid	High	Source	Date
Production, Planning, and Expediting Clerk	San Francisco-Redwood City-South San Francisco PMSA, CA	H	23.13 FQ	28.33 MW	35.54 TQ	CABLS	1/16-3/16
	Colorado	Y	37880 FQ	48440 MW	59880 TQ	USBLS	5/15
	Denver-Aurora-Lakewood MSA, CO	Y	37770 FQ	48450 MW	59180 TQ	USBLS	5/15
	Pueblo MSA, CO	Y	39690 FQ	47470 MW	59200 TQ	USBLS	5/15
	Connecticut	Y		49407 MW		CTBLS	1/16-3/16
	Bridgeport-Stamford-Norwalk MSA, CT	Y	41040 FQ	52010 MW	62430 TQ	USBLS	5/15
	Hartford-West Hartford-East Hartford MSA, CT	Y	36900 FQ	46090 MW	58040 TQ	USBLS	5/15
	Delaware	Y	40960 FQ	51920 MW	61160 TQ	USBLS	5/15
	Wilmington PMSA, DE-MD-NJ	Y	41210 FQ	51850 MW	62180 TQ	USBLS	5/15
	District of Columbia	Y	46170 FQ	56260 MW	64830 TQ	USBLS	5/15
	Washington-Arlington-Alexandria PMSA, DC-VA-MD-WV	Y	39020 FQ	52540 MW	63620 TQ	USBLS	5/15
	Florida	H	13.60 AE	20.30 MW	25.37 AEX	FLBLS	7/16-9/16
	Fort Lauderdale-Pompano Beach-Deerfield Beach PMSA, FL	H	14.18 AE	21.16 MW	26.32 AEX	FLBLS	7/16-9/16
	Miami-Miami Beach-Kendall PMSA, FL	H	12.80 AE	21.01 MW	25.89 AEX	FLBLS	7/16-9/16
	Orlando-Kissimmee-Sanford MSA, FL	H	13.75 AE	20.41 MW	25.87 AEX	FLBLS	7/16-9/16
	Tampa-St. Petersburg-Clearwater MSA, FL	H	12.27 AE	18.80 MW	24.26 AEX	FLBLS	7/16-9/16
	Georgia	Y	32600 FQ	45410 MW	60280 TQ	USBLS	5/15
	Atlanta-Sandy Springs-Roswell MSA, GA	Y	31210 FQ	43310 MW	57980 TQ	USBLS	5/15
	Augusta-Richmond County MSA, GA-SC	Y	29580 FQ	38220 MW	50240 TQ	USBLS	5/15
	Hawaii	Y	41140 FQ	49390 MW	58810 TQ	USBLS	5/15
	Urban Honolulu MSA, HI	Y	41050 FQ	49620 MW	59450 TQ	USBLS	5/15
	Idaho	Y	30150 FQ	38020 MW	49980 TQ	USBLS	5/15
	Boise City MSA, ID	Y	31390 FQ	38040 MW	48760 TQ	USBLS	5/15
	Illinois	Y	34410 FQ	46200 MW	58710 TQ	USBLS	5/15
	Chicago-Naperville-Arlington Heights PMSA, IL	Y	35890 FQ	48680 MW	60530 TQ	USBLS	5/15
	Lake County-Kenosha County PMSA, IL-WI	Y	33580 FQ	44510 MW	57490 TQ	USBLS	5/15
	Indiana	Y	34120 FQ	44830 MW	56950 TQ	USBLS	5/15
	Gary PMSA, IN	Y	42230 FQ	52960 MW	59670 TQ	USBLS	5/15
	Indianapolis-Carmel-Anderson MSA, IN	Y	30810 FQ	43000 MW	57970 TQ	USBLS	5/15
	Iowa	Y	34680 FQ	43650 MW	55470 TQ	USBLS	5/15
	Des Moines-West Des Moines MSA, IA	Y	40110 FQ	52380 MW	60100 TQ	USBLS	5/15
	Kansas	Y	37800 FQ	49260 MW	59440 TQ	USBLS	5/15
	Wichita MSA, KS	Y	41610 FQ	54180 MW	61710 TQ	USBLS	5/15
	Kentucky	Y	34850 FQ	44470 MW	56620 TQ	USBLS	5/15
	Louisville-Jefferson County MSA, KY-IN	Y	34230 FQ	43840 MW	55480 TQ	USBLS	5/15
	Louisiana	Y	34580 FQ	48600 MW	63120 TQ	USBLS	5/15
	Baton Rouge MSA, LA	Y	32660 FQ	50560 MW	69820 TQ	USBLS	5/15
	New Orleans-Metairie MSA, LA	Y	38180 FQ	53270 MW	70650 TQ	USBLS	5/15
	Maine	Y	42190 FQ	57970 MW	69020 TQ	USBLS	5/15
	Portland-South Portland MSA, ME	Y	34990 FQ	52950 MW	59320 TQ	USBLS	5/15
	Maryland	Y	33258 AE	49709 MW	57935 AEX	MDBLS	4/16
	Baltimore-Columbia-Towson MSA, MD	Y	37050 FQ	46760 MW	58630 TQ	USBLS	5/15
	Hagerstown-Martinsburg MSA, MD-WV	Y	35360 FQ	43010 MW	55410 TQ	USBLS	5/15
	Salisbury MSA, MD-DE	Y	29900 FQ	39480 MW	50180 TQ	USBLS	5/15
	Massachusetts	Y	40200 FQ	51410 MW	62230 TQ	USBLS	5/15
	Boston-Cambridge-Newton NECTA, MA	Y	40150 FQ	51100 MW	62320 TQ	USBLS	5/15

AE Average entry wage	**AWR** Average wage range	**H** Hourly	**LR** Low end range	**MTC** Median total compensation	**TCC** Total cash compensation
AEX Average experienced wage	**B** Biweekly	**HI** Highest wage paid	**M** Monthly	**MW** Median wage paid	**TQ** Third quartile wage
ATC Average total compensation	**D** Daily	**HR** High end range	**MCC** Median cash compensation	**MWR** Median wage range	**W** Weekly
AW Average wage paid	**FQ** First quartile wage	**LO** Lowest wage paid	**ME** Median entry wage	**S** See annotated source	**Y** Yearly

Production, Planning, and Expediting Clerk

Occupation/Type/Industry	Location	Per	Low	Mid	High	Source	Date
Production, Planning, and Expediting Clerk	Worcester MSA, MA-CT	Y	40480 FQ	52170 MW	60820 TQ	USBLS	5/15
	Michigan	Y	34920 FQ	45540 MW	57580 TQ	USBLS	5/15
	Detroit-Dearborn-Livonia PMSA, MI	Y	32310 FQ	46960 MW	57990 TQ	USBLS	5/15
	Grand Rapids-Wyoming MSA, MI	Y	37290 FQ	46210 MW	57140 TQ	USBLS	5/15
	Minnesota	Y	36729 FQ	46761 MW	57946 TQ	MNBLS	1/16-3/16
	Minneapolis-St. Paul-Bloomington MSA, MN-WI	Y	37225 FQ	47894 MW	58623 TQ	MNBLS	1/16-3/16
	Mississippi	Y	31800 FQ	42430 MW	57290 TQ	USBLS	5/15
	Jackson MSA, MS	Y	31410 FQ	39390 MW	55540 TQ	USBLS	5/15
	Missouri	Y	36630 FQ	48580 MW	58820 TQ	USBLS	5/15
	Kansas City MSA, MO-KS	Y	37120 FQ	46620 MW	57990 TQ	USBLS	5/15
	St. Louis MSA, MO-IL	Y	39100 FQ	52200 MW	60420 TQ	USBLS	5/15
	Montana	Y	33420 FQ	45620 MW	57990 TQ	USBLS	5/15
	Billings MSA, MT	Y	34870 FQ	41330 MW	57970 TQ	USBLS	5/15
	Nebraska	Y	26705 FQ	38345 MW	50085 TQ	NEBLS	7/16-9/16
	Omaha-Council Bluffs MSA, NE-IA	Y	23405 FQ	34320 MW	48970 TQ	NEBLS	7/16-9/16
	Nevada	Y	33150 FQ	39720 MW	51620 TQ	USBLS	5/15
	Las Vegas-Henderson-Paradise MSA, NV	Y	32150 FQ	38310 MW	48700 TQ	USBLS	5/15
	New Hampshire	H	18.16 AE	25.28 MW	29.12 AEX	NHBLS	6/16
	Manchester NECTA, NH	H	15.67 AE	26.72 MW	28.75 AEX	NHBLS	6/16
	Nashua NECTA, NH-MA	Y	39980 FQ	48940 MW	59710 TQ	USBLS	5/15
	New Jersey	Y	34360 FQ	45680 MW	57970 TQ	USBLS	5/15
	Camden PMSA, NJ	Y	39700 FQ	51820 MW	60920 TQ	USBLS	5/15
	Newark PMSA, NJ-PA	Y	33790 FQ	43870 MW	56880 TQ	USBLS	5/15
	Trenton MSA, NJ	Y	46040 FQ	56370 MW	61770 TQ	USBLS	5/15
	New Mexico	Y	39230 FQ	56630 MW	72500 TQ	USBLS	5/15
	Albuquerque MSA, NM	Y	36640 FQ	51870 MW	65480 TQ	USBLS	5/15
	New York	Y	34680 AE	53080 MW	63230 AEX	NYBLS	1/16-3/16
	Buffalo-Cheektowaga-Niagara Falls MSA, NY	Y	36660 FQ	47950 MW	58580 TQ	USBLS	5/15
	Nassau County-Suffolk County PMSA, NY	Y	39860 FQ	52110 MW	63570 TQ	USBLS	5/15
	New York-Jersey City-White Plains PMSA, NY-NJ	Y	39110 FQ	52070 MW	63140 TQ	USBLS	5/15
	Rochester MSA, NY	Y	34990 FQ	45990 MW	61330 TQ	USBLS	5/15
	North Carolina	Y	31360 FQ	40870 MW	53230 TQ	USBLS	5/15
	Charlotte-Concord-Gastonia MSA, NC-SC	Y	31780 FQ	42970 MW	56070 TQ	USBLS	5/15
	Raleigh MSA, NC	Y	29230 FQ	37460 MW	49170 TQ	USBLS	5/15
	North Dakota	Y	33880 FQ	39470 MW	51300 TQ	USBLS	5/15
	Fargo MSA, ND-MN	Y	32740 FQ	36560 MW	43050 TQ	USBLS	5/15
	Ohio	Y	34350 FQ	44240 MW	56590 TQ	USBLS	5/15
	Cincinnati MSA, OH-KY-IN	Y	36100 FQ	46570 MW	60270 TQ	USBLS	5/15
	Cleveland-Elyria MSA, OH	Y	33800 FQ	43610 MW	56490 TQ	USBLS	5/15
	Columbus MSA, OH	Y	36590 FQ	46680 MW	57980 TQ	USBLS	5/15
	Oklahoma	Y	36300 FQ	46570 MW	58560 TQ	USBLS	5/15
	Oklahoma City MSA, OK	Y	37830 FQ	47530 MW	58550 TQ	USBLS	5/15
	Tulsa MSA, OK	Y	36600 FQ	46830 MW	60450 TQ	USBLS	5/15
	Oregon	H	17.17 FQ	21.92 MW	27.81 TQ	ORBLS	2016
	Portland-Vancouver-Hillsboro MSA, OR-WA	Y	36360 FQ	46240 MW	57980 TQ	USBLS	5/15
	Pennsylvania	Y	36360 FQ	46620 MW	57990 TQ	USBLS	5/15
	Allentown-Bethlehem-Easton MSA, PA-NJ	Y	36090 FQ	45740 MW	56860 TQ	USBLS	5/15
	Harrisburg-Carlisle MSA, PA	Y	34080 FQ	43960 MW	55000 TQ	USBLS	5/15
	Montgomery County-Bucks County-Chester County PMSA, PA	Y	38760 FQ	48650 MW	60260 TQ	USBLS	5/15
	Philadelphia PMSA, PA	Y	40800 FQ	51450 MW	58870 TQ	USBLS	5/15
	Pittsburgh MSA, PA	Y	35620 FQ	46200 MW	57990 TQ	USBLS	5/15
	Rhode Island	Y	37820 FQ	48590 MW	57990 TQ	USBLS	5/15
	Providence-Warwick MSA, RI-MA	Y	37220 FQ	47940 MW	57990 TQ	USBLS	5/15
	South Carolina	Y	34020 FQ	43980 MW	57980 TQ	USBLS	5/15
	Charleston-North Charleston MSA, SC	Y	37190 FQ	45430 MW	56690 TQ	USBLS	5/15
	Columbia MSA, SC	Y	35090 FQ	52380 MW	60130 TQ	USBLS	5/15

AE	Average entry wage	AWR	Average wage range	H	Hourly	LR	Low end range	MTC	Median total compensation	TCC	Total cash compensation
AEX	Average experienced wage	B	Biweekly	HI	Highest wage paid	M	Monthly	MW	Median wage paid	TQ	Third quartile wage
ATC	Average total compensation	D	Daily	HR	High end range	MCC	Median cash compensation	MWR	Median wage range	W	Weekly
AW	Average wage paid	FQ	First quartile wage	LO	Lowest wage paid	ME	Median entry wage	S	See annotated source	Y	Yearly

Occupation/Type/Industry	Location	Per	Low	Mid	High	Source	Date
Production, Planning, and Expediting Clerk	Greenville-Anderson-Mauldin MSA, SC	Y	34320 FQ	43240 MW	56790 TQ	USBLS	5/15
	South Dakota	Y	31410 FQ	36990 MW	45520 TQ	USBLS	5/15
	Sioux Falls MSA, SD	Y	31850 FQ	36740 MW	44570 TQ	USBLS	5/15
	Tennessee	Y	34760 FQ	47170 MW	61050 TQ	USBLS	5/15
	Knoxville MSA, TN	Y	37560 FQ	55660 MW	87350 TQ	USBLS	5/15
	Memphis MSA, TN-MS-AR	Y	31010 FQ	41990 MW	57140 TQ	USBLS	5/15
	Nashville-Davidson–Murfreesboro–Franklin MSA, TN	Y	36940 FQ	48080 MW	60260 TQ	USBLS	5/15
	Texas	Y	32540 FQ	44020 MW	58120 TQ	USBLS	5/15
	Austin-Round Rock MSA, TX	Y	33590 FQ	45190 MW	58870 TQ	USBLS	5/15
	Dallas-Plano-Irving PMSA, TX	Y	35630 FQ	46500 MW	58070 TQ	USBLS	5/15
	Fort Worth-Arlington PMSA, TX	Y	30900 FQ	44160 MW	61020 TQ	USBLS	5/15
	Houston-The Woodlands-Sugar Land MSA, TX	Y	34700 FQ	46180 MW	62100 TQ	USBLS	5/15
	San Antonio-New Braunfels MSA, TX	Y	28190 FQ	35230 MW	48820 TQ	USBLS	5/15
	Utah	Y	34150 FQ	42030 MW	53200 TQ	USBLS	5/15
	Ogden-Clearfield MSA, UT	Y	35920 FQ	43240 MW	51440 TQ	USBLS	5/15
	Provo-Orem MSA, UT	Y	28950 FQ	37200 MW	47080 TQ	USBLS	5/15
	Salt Lake City MSA, UT	Y	34890 FQ	43750 MW	55560 TQ	USBLS	5/15
	Vermont	Y	32050 FQ	42120 MW	56450 TQ	USBLS	5/15
	Burlington-South Burlington MSA, VT	Y	29550 FQ	38740 MW	55160 TQ	USBLS	5/15
	Virginia	Y	36250 FQ	49200 MW	61280 TQ	USBLS	5/15
	Richmond MSA, VA	Y	35160 FQ	44300 MW	56290 TQ	USBLS	5/15
	Virginia Beach-Norfolk-Newport News MSA, VA-NC	Y	43230 FQ	56460 MW	68790 TQ	USBLS	5/15
	Washington	H	18.11 FQ	22.92 MW	30.73 TQ	WABLS	3/16
	Seattle-Bellevue-Everett PMSA, WA	H	18.45 FQ	23.34 MW	32.40 TQ	WABLS	3/16
	Tacoma-Lakewood PMSA, WA	H	18.93 FQ	23.69 MW	29.67 TQ	WABLS	3/16
	West Virginia	Y	36550 FQ	46150 MW	57550 TQ	USBLS	5/15
	Huntington-Ashland MSA, WV-KY-OH	Y	33200 FQ	39350 MW	50660 TQ	USBLS	5/15
	Wisconsin	Y	35180 FQ	43820 MW	54900 TQ	USBLS	5/15
	Madison MSA, WI	Y	32700 FQ	39680 MW	51050 TQ	USBLS	5/15
	Milwaukee-Waukesha-West Allis MSA, WI	Y	37690 FQ	48150 MW	57970 TQ	USBLS	5/15
	Wyoming	Y	43650 FQ	54700 MW	68190 TQ	USBLS	5/15
	Cheyenne MSA, WY	Y	36680 FQ	48160 MW	55550 TQ	USBLS	5/15
	Puerto Rico	Y	19080 FQ	26460 MW	39990 TQ	USBLS	5/15
	San Juan-Carolina-Caguas MSA, PR	Y	18610 FQ	24320 MW	38830 TQ	USBLS	5/15
	Guam	Y	29180 FQ	41700 MW	49110 TQ	USBLS	5/15
Professional Time-Killer	United States	S			25.00 HI	NWSR01	2015
Professor							
Accounting	United States	Y		156900 AW		AACSB	2014-2015
Entrepreneurship	United States	Y		156000 AW		AACSB	2014-2015
Female, 2-Year For-Profit Institution	United States	Y		23078 AW		CHE03	2014-2015
Female, 2-Year Private Institution	United States	Y		39235 AW		CHE03	2014-2015
Female, 2-Year Public Institution	United States	Y		68676 AW		CHE03	2014-2015
Female, 4-Year For-Profit Institution	United States	Y		54705 AW		CHE03	2014-2015
Female, 4-Year Private Institution	United States	Y		106940 AW		CHE03	2014-2015
Female, 4-Year Public Institution	United States	Y		100887 AW		CHE03	2014-2015
Female, Life Sciences	United States	Y		143640 AW		TSCI	2016
Male, 2-Year For-Profit Institution	United States	Y		20650 AW		CHE03	2014-2015
Male, 2-Year Private Institution	United States	Y		35917 AW		CHE03	2014-2015
Male, 2-Year Public Institution	United States	Y		71890 AW		CHE03	2014-2015
Male, 4-Year For-Profit Institution	United States	Y		55054 AW		CHE03	2014-2015
Male, 4-Year Private Institution	United States	Y		124610 AW		CHE03	2014-2015
Male, 4-Year Public Institution	United States	Y		115362 AW		CHE03	2014-2015
Male, Life Sciences	United States	Y		156915 AW		TSCI	2016
Non-Tenure-Track	United States	Y		75712 AW		APAC02	2014-2015
Tenured/Tenure-Track	United States	Y		92568 AW		APAC02	2014-2015
Tenured/Tenure-Track, Research University	United States	Y		115379 AW		APAC02	2014-2015

AE Average entry wage	**AWR** Average wage range	**H** Hourly	**LR** Low end range	**MTC** Median total compensation	**TCC** Total cash compensation
AEX Average experienced wage	**B** Biweekly	**HI** Highest wage paid	**M** Monthly	**MW** Median wage paid	**TQ** Third quartile wage
ATC Average total compensation	**D** Daily	**HR** High end range	**MCC** Median cash compensation	**MWR** Median wage range	**W** Weekly
AW Average wage paid	**FQ** First quartile wage	**LO** Lowest wage paid	**ME** Median entry wage	**S** See annotated source	**Y** Yearly

Occupation/Type/Industry	Location	Per	Low	Mid	High	Source	Date
Program Director							
Nonprofit Organization	Maine	Y		36088-72800 MWR		MENP	2016
Program Integrity Specialist							
Community and Economic Development, Municipal Government	Anaheim, CA	Y			68932 HI	CACIT	6/28/16
Programmer							
Entry-Level, Digital/Streaming Music Firm	United States	Y		120000-150000 AWR		BBRD01	2014
Project Leader							
Information Technology	United States	Y		108000 MW		INFOW02	10/15-2/16
Project Manager	United States	Y		104468 AW		CWRLD2	2016
Proofreader and Copy Marker	Alabama	Y	22281 AE	32526 AW	37637 AEX	ALBLS	6/16
	Phoenix-Mesa-Scottsdale MSA, AZ	Y	29750 FQ	35860 MW	44930 TQ	USBLS	5/15
	Arkansas	Y	24270 FQ	30700 MW	41730 TQ	USBLS	5/15
	Little Rock-North Little Rock-Conway MSA, AR	Y	25420 FQ	30370 MW	38120 TQ	USBLS	5/15
	California	H	13.02 FQ	17.36 MW	23.90 TQ	CABLS	1/16-3/16
	Anaheim-Santa Ana-Irvine PMSA, CA	H	11.77 FQ	14.64 MW	19.56 TQ	CABLS	1/16-3/16
	Los Angeles-Long Beach-Glendale PMSA, CA	H	12.70 FQ	16.56 MW	23.78 TQ	CABLS	1/16-3/16
	Oakland-Hayward-Berkeley PMSA, CA	H	14.32 FQ	17.85 MW	21.91 TQ	CABLS	1/16-3/16
	Riverside-San Bernardino-Ontario MSA, CA	H	11.47 FQ	13.94 MW	21.62 TQ	CABLS	1/16-3/16
	Sacramento–Roseville–Arden-Arcade MSA, CA	H	19.96 FQ	24.98 MW	30.24 TQ	CABLS	1/16-3/16
	San Diego-Carlsbad MSA, CA	H	13.59 FQ	19.32 MW	26.01 TQ	CABLS	1/16-3/16
	San Francisco-Redwood City-South San Francisco PMSA, CA	H	15.76 FQ	19.47 MW	25.12 TQ	CABLS	1/16-3/16
	Colorado	Y	33870 FQ	38850 MW	47810 TQ	USBLS	5/15
	Denver-Aurora-Lakewood MSA, CO	Y	33350 FQ	39620 MW	49480 TQ	USBLS	5/15
	Connecticut	Y		37659 MW		CTBLS	1/16-3/16
	Hartford-West Hartford-East Hartford MSA, CT	Y	31830 FQ	39370 MW	46670 TQ	USBLS	5/15
	District of Columbia	Y	41380 FQ	46840 MW	55110 TQ	USBLS	5/15
	Washington-Arlington-Alexandria PMSA, DC-VA-MD-WV	Y	31800 FQ	37360 MW	45270 TQ	USBLS	5/15
	Florida	H	11.66 AE	16.27 MW	19.04 AEX	FLBLS	7/16-9/16
	Fort Lauderdale-Pompano Beach-Deerfield Beach PMSA, FL	H	12.11 AE	18.47 MW	22.26 AEX	FLBLS	7/16-9/16
	Miami-Miami Beach-Kendall PMSA, FL	H	11.05 AE	14.98 MW	16.93 AEX	FLBLS	7/16-9/16
	Orlando-Kissimmee-Sanford MSA, FL	H	15.69 AE	19.94 MW	21.71 AEX	FLBLS	7/16-9/16
	Tampa-St. Petersburg-Clearwater MSA, FL	H	10.00 AE	13.85 MW	17.03 AEX	FLBLS	7/16-9/16
	Georgia	Y	22040 FQ	28970 MW	40950 TQ	USBLS	5/15
	Atlanta-Sandy Springs-Roswell MSA, GA	Y	22790 FQ	30350 MW	43460 TQ	USBLS	5/15
	Idaho	Y	22090 FQ	27460 MW	36760 TQ	USBLS	5/15
	Illinois	Y	33110 FQ	40460 MW	53240 TQ	USBLS	5/15
	Chicago-Naperville-Arlington Heights PMSA, IL	Y	34810 FQ	42440 MW	54410 TQ	USBLS	5/15
	Indiana	Y	25850 FQ	33060 MW	38460 TQ	USBLS	5/15
	Indianapolis-Carmel-Anderson MSA, IN	Y	27720 FQ	34210 MW	38980 TQ	USBLS	5/15
	Iowa	Y	24710 FQ	34260 MW	43570 TQ	USBLS	5/15
	Kansas	Y	25810 FQ	29140 MW	39850 TQ	USBLS	5/15
	Kentucky	Y	28190 FQ	34660 MW	43380 TQ	USBLS	5/15

AE	Average entry wage	AWR	Average wage range	H	Hourly	LR	Low end range	MTC	Median total compensation	TCC	Total cash compensation
AEX	Average experienced wage	B	Biweekly	HI	Highest wage paid	M	Monthly	MW	Median wage paid	TQ	Third quartile wage
ATC	Average total compensation	D	Daily	HR	High end range	MCC	Median cash compensation	MWR	Median wage range	W	Weekly
AW	Average wage paid	FQ	First quartile wage	LO	Lowest wage paid	ME	Median entry wage	S	See annotated source	Y	Yearly

Occupation/Type/Industry	Location	Per	Low	Mid	High	Source	Date
Proofreader and Copy Marker	Louisville-Jefferson County MSA, KY-IN	Y	30920 FQ	35910 MW	43040 TQ	USBLS	5/15
	Louisiana	Y	31800 FQ	41150 MW	46220 TQ	USBLS	5/15
	Maryland	Y	24808 AE	38659 MW	45584 AEX	MDBLS	4/16
	Baltimore-Columbia-Towson MSA, MD	Y	30990 FQ	42940 MW	50370 TQ	USBLS	5/15
	Massachusetts	Y	37630 FQ	46810 MW	55600 TQ	USBLS	5/15
	Boston-Cambridge-Newton NECTA, MA	Y	40140 FQ	48340 MW	56460 TQ	USBLS	5/15
	Michigan	Y	27130 FQ	33040 MW	43140 TQ	USBLS	5/15
	Grand Rapids-Wyoming MSA, MI	Y	27240 FQ	29900 MW	34730 TQ	USBLS	5/15
	Minnesota	Y	26323 FQ	31218 MW	50543 TQ	MNBLS	1/16-3/16
	Minneapolis-St. Paul-Bloomington MSA, MN-WI	Y	23633 FQ	34464 MW	57582 TQ	MNBLS	1/16-3/16
	Mississippi	Y	23090 FQ	27370 MW	33630 TQ	USBLS	5/15
	Missouri	Y	25530 FQ	34720 MW	49560 TQ	USBLS	5/15
	Kansas City MSA, MO-KS	Y	32420 FQ	44150 MW	53020 TQ	USBLS	5/15
	St. Louis MSA, MO-IL	Y	23810 FQ	30580 MW	41330 TQ	USBLS	5/15
	Nebraska	Y	19810 FQ	31880 MW	38970 TQ	NEBLS	7/16-9/16
	Omaha-Council Bluffs MSA, NE-IA	Y	32090 FQ	36890 MW	46075 TQ	NEBLS	7/16-9/16
	Nevada	Y	22880 FQ	36430 MW	48940 TQ	USBLS	5/15
	New Hampshire	H	13.42 AE	17.71 MW	22.59 AEX	NHBLS	6/16
	New Jersey	Y	27220 FQ	37780 MW	48060 TQ	USBLS	5/15
	Camden PMSA, NJ	Y	28000 FQ	37770 MW	45610 TQ	USBLS	5/15
	Newark PMSA, NJ-PA	Y	28040 FQ	38610 MW	48490 TQ	USBLS	5/15
	Trenton MSA, NJ	Y	33380 FQ	41460 MW	47390 TQ	USBLS	5/15
	New Mexico	Y	17470 FQ	18720 MW	20120 TQ	USBLS	5/15
	New York	Y	28780 AE	43710 MW	51280 AEX	NYBLS	1/16-3/16
	Buffalo-Cheektowaga-Niagara Falls MSA, NY	Y	22270 FQ	26790 MW	30230 TQ	USBLS	5/15
	Nassau County-Suffolk County PMSA, NY	Y	39500 FQ	46430 MW	53860 TQ	USBLS	5/15
	New York-Jersey City-White Plains PMSA, NY-NJ	Y	30810 FQ	41670 MW	54470 TQ	USBLS	5/15
	Rochester MSA, NY	Y	31480 FQ	47230 MW	57540 TQ	USBLS	5/15
	North Carolina	Y	34650 FQ	43770 MW	49470 TQ	USBLS	5/15
	North Dakota	Y	20590 FQ	23860 MW	33790 TQ	USBLS	5/15
	Ohio	Y	21180 FQ	28790 MW	39970 TQ	USBLS	5/15
	Cincinnati MSA, OH-KY-IN	Y	19970 FQ	29040 MW	37450 TQ	USBLS	5/15
	Cleveland-Elyria MSA, OH	Y	24390 FQ	29310 MW	45810 TQ	USBLS	5/15
	Columbus MSA, OH	Y	27690 FQ	33920 MW	38810 TQ	USBLS	5/15
	Oklahoma	Y	24770 FQ	31140 MW	40600 TQ	USBLS	5/15
	Oklahoma City MSA, OK	Y	29060 FQ	37160 MW	45830 TQ	USBLS	5/15
	Oregon	H	16.07 FQ	19.34 MW	24.98 TQ	ORBLS	2016
	Pennsylvania	Y	27240 FQ	31900 MW	39640 TQ	USBLS	5/15
	Montgomery County-Bucks County-Chester County PMSA, PA	Y	28470 FQ	34380 MW	43850 TQ	USBLS	5/15
	Philadelphia PMSA, PA	Y	28370 FQ	33270 MW	38780 TQ	USBLS	5/15
	Pittsburgh MSA, PA	Y	25670 FQ	31100 MW	41980 TQ	USBLS	5/15
	Tennessee	Y	26700 FQ	31430 MW	39920 TQ	USBLS	5/15
	Nashville-Davidson–Murfreesboro–Franklin MSA, TN	Y	27270 FQ	31170 MW	39010 TQ	USBLS	5/15
	Texas	Y	24600 FQ	34360 MW	39520 TQ	USBLS	5/15
	Dallas-Plano-Irving PMSA, TX	Y	32190 FQ	35800 MW	39410 TQ	USBLS	5/15
	Houston-The Woodlands-Sugar Land MSA, TX	Y	30920 FQ	35990 MW	43120 TQ	USBLS	5/15
	Utah	Y	23470 FQ	36280 MW	46510 TQ	USBLS	5/15
	Salt Lake City MSA, UT	Y	24210 FQ	36430 MW	46700 TQ	USBLS	5/15
	Virginia	Y	28190 FQ	36690 MW	45200 TQ	USBLS	5/15
	Virginia Beach-Norfolk-Newport News MSA, VA-NC	Y	21860 FQ	24170 MW	30210 TQ	USBLS	5/15
	Washington	H	13.80 FQ	17.50 MW	21.57 TQ	WABLS	3/16
	Seattle-Bellevue-Everett PMSA, WA	H	16.01 FQ	18.52 MW	22.30 TQ	WABLS	3/16
	Wisconsin	Y	24130 FQ	36210 MW	46520 TQ	USBLS	5/15
	Madison MSA, WI	Y	17920 FQ	40390 MW	46400 TQ	USBLS	5/15
	Milwaukee-Waukesha-West Allis MSA, WI	Y	24650 FQ	37490 MW	50270 TQ	USBLS	5/15

Occupation/Type/Industry	Location	Per	Low	Mid	High	Source	Date
Proofreader and Copy Marker	Wyoming	Y	17380 FQ	19440 MW	25460 TQ	USBLS	5/15
Prop Designer	United States	W		1875.00 MW		TAG01	2016
Property, Real Estate, and Community Association Manager							
	Alabama	Y	48399 AE	74914 AW	88167 AEX	ALBLS	6/16
	Birmingham-Hoover MSA, AL	Y	49936 AE	86025 AW	104074 AEX	ALBLS	6/16
	Alaska	Y	46970 FQ	62100 MW	85330 TQ	USBLS	5/15
	Anchorage MSA, AK	Y	43570 FQ	60800 MW	80990 TQ	USBLS	5/15
	Arizona	Y	33590 FQ	48700 MW	73950 TQ	USBLS	5/15
	Phoenix-Mesa-Scottsdale MSA, AZ	Y	37600 FQ	51830 MW	79620 TQ	USBLS	5/15
	Tucson MSA, AZ	Y	31410 FQ	38870 MW	57220 TQ	USBLS	5/15
	Arkansas	Y	23390 FQ	31550 MW	48790 TQ	USBLS	5/15
	Little Rock-North Little Rock-Conway MSA, AR	Y	26720 FQ	34320 MW	48270 TQ	USBLS	5/15
	California	H	21.44 FQ	29.61 MW	44.20 TQ	CABLS	1/16-3/16
	Anaheim-Santa Ana-Irvine PMSA, CA	H	25.31 FQ	34.03 MW	45.26 TQ	CABLS	1/16-3/16
	Los Angeles-Long Beach-Glendale PMSA, CA	H	21.12 FQ	28.54 MW	41.99 TQ	CABLS	1/16-3/16
	Oakland-Hayward-Berkeley PMSA, CA	H	23.10 FQ	30.70 MW	46.93 TQ	CABLS	1/16-3/16
	Riverside-San Bernardino-Ontario MSA, CA	H	18.38 FQ	25.89 MW	36.12 TQ	CABLS	1/16-3/16
	Sacramento–Roseville–Arden-Arcade MSA, CA	H	17.72 FQ	23.73 MW	35.55 TQ	CABLS	1/16-3/16
	San Diego-Carlsbad MSA, CA	H	18.72 FQ	25.17 MW	38.23 TQ	CABLS	1/16-3/16
	San Francisco-Redwood City-South San Francisco PMSA, CA	H	32.19 FQ	52.32 MW	72.67 TQ	CABLS	1/16-3/16
	Colorado	Y	48120 FQ	72460 MW	101870 TQ	USBLS	5/15
	Denver-Aurora-Lakewood MSA, CO	Y	50400 FQ	82270 MW	104640 TQ	USBLS	5/15
	Connecticut	Y		62987 MW		CTBLS	1/16-3/16
	Bridgeport-Stamford-Norwalk MSA, CT	Y	55710 FQ	64000 MW	96820 TQ	USBLS	5/15
	Hartford-West Hartford-East Hartford MSA, CT	Y	52450 FQ	67340 MW	97220 TQ	USBLS	5/15
	Delaware	Y	45630 FQ	57940 MW	78060 TQ	USBLS	5/15
	Wilmington PMSA, DE-MD-NJ	Y	48510 FQ	57820 MW	76570 TQ	USBLS	5/15
	District of Columbia	Y	49700 FQ	72910 MW	95090 TQ	USBLS	5/15
	Washington-Arlington-Alexandria PMSA, DC-VA-MD-WV	Y	52950 FQ	77980 MW	101320 TQ	USBLS	5/15
	Florida	H	14.34 AE	23.87 MW	34.60 AEX	FLBLS	7/16-9/16
	Fort Lauderdale-Pompano Beach-Deerfield Beach PMSA, FL	H	19.14 AE	26.96 MW	36.97 AEX	FLBLS	7/16-9/16
	Miami-Miami Beach-Kendall PMSA, FL	H	14.11 AE	21.87 MW	32.27 AEX	FLBLS	7/16-9/16
	Orlando-Kissimmee-Sanford MSA, FL	H	16.19 AE	24.65 MW	36.52 AEX	FLBLS	7/16-9/16
	Tampa-St. Petersburg-Clearwater MSA, FL	H	12.27 AE	21.05 MW	29.64 AEX	FLBLS	7/16-9/16
	Georgia	Y	44730 FQ	58650 MW	80840 TQ	USBLS	5/15
	Atlanta-Sandy Springs-Roswell MSA, GA	Y	48030 FQ	61390 MW	90210 TQ	USBLS	5/15
	Augusta-Richmond County MSA, GA-SC	Y	42100 FQ	53740 MW	74640 TQ	USBLS	5/15
	Hawaii	Y	31890 FQ	49350 MW	65800 TQ	USBLS	5/15
	Urban Honolulu MSA, HI	Y	30540 FQ	46160 MW	64240 TQ	USBLS	5/15
	Idaho	Y	22630 FQ	29250 MW	41440 TQ	USBLS	5/15
	Boise City MSA, ID	Y	25680 FQ	30320 MW	42960 TQ	USBLS	5/15
	Illinois	Y	40460 FQ	58760 MW	80420 TQ	USBLS	5/15
	Chicago-Naperville-Arlington Heights PMSA, IL	Y	45620 FQ	63360 MW	86850 TQ	USBLS	5/15
	Lake County-Kenosha County PMSA, IL-WI	Y	38160 FQ	56100 MW	69710 TQ	USBLS	5/15
	Indiana	Y	34370 FQ	44330 MW	60060 TQ	USBLS	5/15

Occupation/Type/Industry	Location	Per	Low	Mid	High	Source	Date
Property, Real Estate, and Community Association Manager							
	Gary PMSA, IN	Y	43850 FQ	55040 MW	67200 TQ	USBLS	5/15
	Indianapolis-Carmel-Anderson MSA, IN	Y	35570 FQ	44190 MW	61130 TQ	USBLS	5/15
	Iowa	Y	31810 FQ	44260 MW	61540 TQ	USBLS	5/15
	Des Moines-West Des Moines MSA, IA	Y	39740 FQ	49230 MW	70850 TQ	USBLS	5/15
	Kansas	Y	37290 FQ	52120 MW	65140 TQ	USBLS	5/15
	Wichita MSA, KS	Y	42450 FQ	57550 MW	73820 TQ	USBLS	5/15
	Kentucky	Y	32610 FQ	43600 MW	60300 TQ	USBLS	5/15
	Louisville-Jefferson County MSA, KY-IN	Y	38760 FQ	52320 MW	72820 TQ	USBLS	5/15
	Louisiana	Y	28980 FQ	38930 MW	50810 TQ	USBLS	5/15
	Baton Rouge MSA, LA	Y	36160 FQ	45190 MW	56400 TQ	USBLS	5/15
	New Orleans-Metairie MSA, LA	Y	28470 FQ	38560 MW	52990 TQ	USBLS	5/15
	Maine	Y	41070 FQ	50000 MW	65350 TQ	USBLS	5/15
	Portland-South Portland MSA, ME	Y	44710 FQ	53870 MW	66790 TQ	USBLS	5/15
	Maryland	Y	45534 AE	89674 MW	111743 AEX	MDBLS	4/16
	Baltimore-Columbia-Towson MSA, MD	Y	56660 FQ	78650 MW	118620 TQ	USBLS	5/15
	Salisbury MSA, MD-DE	Y	40930 FQ	57350 MW	75650 TQ	USBLS	5/15
	Massachusetts	Y	56610 FQ	74690 MW	101810 TQ	USBLS	5/15
	Boston-Cambridge-Newton NECTA, MA	Y	61340 FQ	82320 MW	115860 TQ	USBLS	5/15
	Worcester MSA, MA-CT	Y	47920 FQ	62830 MW	78650 TQ	USBLS	5/15
	Michigan	Y	33410 FQ	45350 MW	64030 TQ	USBLS	5/15
	Detroit-Dearborn-Livonia PMSA, MI	Y	36840 FQ	48480 MW	72880 TQ	USBLS	5/15
	Grand Rapids-Wyoming MSA, MI	Y	30860 FQ	37810 MW	52210 TQ	USBLS	5/15
	Minnesota	Y	42951 FQ	57288 MW	73657 TQ	MNBLS	1/16-3/16
	Minneapolis-St. Paul-Bloomington MSA, MN-WI	Y	46598 FQ	59493 MW	75425 TQ	MNBLS	1/16-3/16
	Mississippi	Y	30030 FQ	38650 MW	48260 TQ	USBLS	5/15
	Jackson MSA, MS	Y	22030 FQ	41100 MW	50420 TQ	USBLS	5/15
	Missouri	Y	29050 FQ	42290 MW	62160 TQ	USBLS	5/15
	Kansas City MSA, MO-KS	Y	34610 FQ	48610 MW	65590 TQ	USBLS	5/15
	St. Louis MSA, MO-IL	Y	30680 FQ	43620 MW	63080 TQ	USBLS	5/15
	Montana	Y	32440 FQ	38060 MW	51470 TQ	USBLS	5/15
	Billings MSA, MT	Y	33170 FQ	36970 MW	41760 TQ	USBLS	5/15
	Nebraska	Y	38910 FQ	53460 MW	89510 TQ	NEBLS	7/16-9/16
	Omaha-Council Bluffs MSA, NE-IA	Y	31680 FQ	50690 MW	90080 TQ	NEBLS	7/16-9/16
	Nevada	Y	34990 FQ	46970 MW	63870 TQ	USBLS	5/15
	Las Vegas-Henderson-Paradise MSA, NV	Y	36710 FQ	48550 MW	68410 TQ	USBLS	5/15
	New Hampshire	H	19.16 AE	27.69 MW	44.78 AEX	NHBLS	6/16
	Manchester NECTA, NH	H	19.65 AE	26.42 MW	32.06 AEX	NHBLS	6/16
	New Jersey	Y	52710 FQ	67170 MW	90300 TQ	USBLS	5/15
	Camden PMSA, NJ	Y	51090 FQ	68620 MW	89270 TQ	USBLS	5/15
	Newark PMSA, NJ-PA	Y	53450 FQ	67200 MW	85540 TQ	USBLS	5/15
	Trenton MSA, NJ	Y	50380 FQ	66000 MW	78310 TQ	USBLS	5/15
	New Mexico	Y	28170 FQ	40070 MW	58110 TQ	USBLS	5/15
	Albuquerque MSA, NM	Y	29390 FQ	42640 MW	63230 TQ	USBLS	5/15
	New York	Y	62310 AE	91290 MW	134520 AEX	NYBLS	1/16-3/16
	Nassau County-Suffolk County PMSA, NY	Y	76280 FQ	98930 MW	142860 TQ	USBLS	5/15
	New York-Jersey City-White Plains PMSA, NY-NJ	Y	61520 FQ	83010 MW	120300 TQ	USBLS	5/15
	Rochester MSA, NY	Y	58060 FQ	71880 MW	97660 TQ	USBLS	5/15
	North Carolina	Y	45730 FQ	57840 MW	76910 TQ	USBLS	5/15
	Charlotte-Concord-Gastonia MSA, NC-SC	Y	45900 FQ	57040 MW	75570 TQ	USBLS	5/15
	Raleigh MSA, NC	Y	43440 FQ	61530 MW	78420 TQ	USBLS	5/15
	North Dakota	Y	35470 FQ	53770 MW	75290 TQ	USBLS	5/15
	Fargo MSA, ND-MN	Y	32830 FQ	39780 MW	71490 TQ	USBLS	5/15
	Ohio	Y	35610 FQ	48920 MW	73840 TQ	USBLS	5/15
	Cincinnati MSA, OH-KY-IN	Y	34580 FQ	50900 MW	78100 TQ	USBLS	5/15

AE	Average entry wage	AWR	Average wage range	H	Hourly
AEX	Average experienced wage	B	Biweekly	HI	Highest wage paid
ATC	Average total compensation	D	Daily	HR	High end range
AW	Average wage paid	FQ	First quartile wage	LO	Lowest wage paid

LR	Low end range	MTC	Median total compensation
M	Monthly	MW	Median wage paid
MCC	Median cash compensation	MWR	Median wage range
ME	Median entry wage	S	See annotated source

TCC	Total cash compensation		
TQ	Third quartile wage		
W	Weekly		
Y	Yearly		

Occupation/Type/Industry	Location	Per	Low	Mid	High	Source	Date
Property, Real Estate, and Community Association Manager							
	Cleveland-Elyria MSA, OH	Y	37790 FQ	54530 MW	78090 TQ	USBLS	5/15
	Columbus MSA, OH	Y	34540 FQ	47050 MW	75680 TQ	USBLS	5/15
	Oklahoma	Y	34600 FQ	48830 MW	71950 TQ	USBLS	5/15
	Oklahoma City MSA, OK	Y	40410 FQ	51420 MW	75200 TQ	USBLS	5/15
	Tulsa MSA, OK	Y	31260 FQ	45790 MW	63590 TQ	USBLS	5/15
	Oregon	H	20.77 FQ	28.29 MW	40.77 TQ	ORBLS	2016
	Portland-Vancouver-Hillsboro MSA, OR-WA	Y	47430 FQ	60260 MW	88880 TQ	USBLS	5/15
	Pennsylvania	Y	45820 FQ	61910 MW	92180 TQ	USBLS	5/15
	Allentown-Bethlehem-Easton MSA, PA-NJ	Y	45460 FQ	62870 MW	93500 TQ	USBLS	5/15
	Harrisburg-Carlisle MSA, PA	Y	37630 FQ	52600 MW	66090 TQ	USBLS	5/15
	Montgomery County-Bucks County-Chester County PMSA, PA	Y	55100 FQ	77080 MW	97410 TQ	USBLS	5/15
	Philadelphia PMSA, PA	Y	56860 FQ	70000 MW	110650 TQ	USBLS	5/15
	Pittsburgh MSA, PA	Y	45360 FQ	62120 MW	107580 TQ	USBLS	5/15
	Rhode Island	Y	47340 FQ	66320 MW	104340 TQ	USBLS	5/15
	Providence-Warwick MSA, RI-MA	Y	47110 FQ	65790 MW	101670 TQ	USBLS	5/15
	South Carolina	Y	34620 FQ	46010 MW	67770 TQ	USBLS	5/15
	Charleston-North Charleston MSA, SC	Y	36990 FQ	53140 MW	77870 TQ	USBLS	5/15
	Columbia MSA, SC	Y	47230 FQ	60330 MW	81700 TQ	USBLS	5/15
	Greenville-Anderson-Mauldin MSA, SC	Y	32650 FQ	38930 MW	58320 TQ	USBLS	5/15
	South Dakota	Y	27740 FQ	33150 MW	39330 TQ	USBLS	5/15
	Sioux Falls MSA, SD	Y	29490 FQ	35240 MW	43490 TQ	USBLS	5/15
	Tennessee	Y	32440 FQ	43370 MW	60190 TQ	USBLS	5/15
	Knoxville MSA, TN	Y	30950 FQ	47130 MW	69900 TQ	USBLS	5/15
	Memphis MSA, TN-MS-AR	Y	30190 FQ	38260 MW	54620 TQ	USBLS	5/15
	Nashville-Davidson–Murfreesboro–Franklin MSA, TN	Y	35650 FQ	47520 MW	60620 TQ	USBLS	5/15
	Texas	Y	46040 FQ	62550 MW	112050 TQ	USBLS	5/15
	Austin-Round Rock MSA, TX	Y	48870 FQ	64120 MW	108730 TQ	USBLS	5/15
	Dallas-Plano-Irving PMSA, TX	Y	50860 FQ	75820 MW	141810 TQ	USBLS	5/15
	Fort Worth-Arlington PMSA, TX	Y	43570 FQ	54690 MW	89020 TQ	USBLS	5/15
	Houston-The Woodlands-Sugar Land MSA, TX	Y	48860 FQ	63870 MW	124830 TQ	USBLS	5/15
	San Antonio-New Braunfels MSA, TX	Y	43480 FQ	59580 MW	81740 TQ	USBLS	5/15
	Utah	Y	29020 FQ	39760 MW	59410 TQ	USBLS	5/15
	Ogden-Clearfield MSA, UT	Y	32670 FQ	37920 MW	48210 TQ	USBLS	5/15
	Provo-Orem MSA, UT	Y	18630 FQ	32740 MW	57270 TQ	USBLS	5/15
	Salt Lake City MSA, UT	Y	30680 FQ	43050 MW	67000 TQ	USBLS	5/15
	Vermont	Y	42490 FQ	56960 MW	78570 TQ	USBLS	5/15
	Burlington-South Burlington MSA, VT	Y	38400 FQ	59950 MW	81540 TQ	USBLS	5/15
	Virginia	Y	52800 FQ	77930 MW	104020 TQ	USBLS	5/15
	Richmond MSA, VA	Y	50780 FQ	76550 MW	121420 TQ	USBLS	5/15
	Virginia Beach-Norfolk-Newport News MSA, VA-NC	Y	39640 FQ	58150 MW	80350 TQ	USBLS	5/15
	Washington	H	23.44 FQ	31.78 MW	47.30 TQ	WABLS	3/16
	Seattle-Bellevue-Everett PMSA, WA	H	27.08 FQ	35.24 MW	53.50 TQ	WABLS	3/16
	Tacoma-Lakewood PMSA, WA	H	22.65 FQ	31.07 MW	40.78 TQ	WABLS	3/16
	West Virginia	Y	26650 FQ	32810 MW	59290 TQ	USBLS	5/15
	Huntington-Ashland MSA, WV-KY-OH	Y	27360 FQ	36280 MW	55600 TQ	USBLS	5/15
	Wisconsin	Y	38670 FQ	48560 MW	66980 TQ	USBLS	5/15
	Madison MSA, WI	Y	38590 FQ	49690 MW	68350 TQ	USBLS	5/15
	Milwaukee-Waukesha-West Allis MSA, WI	Y	40550 FQ	51870 MW	74070 TQ	USBLS	5/15
	Wyoming	Y	37970 FQ	47560 MW	65470 TQ	USBLS	5/15
	Cheyenne MSA, WY	Y	51180 FQ	60360 MW	72630 TQ	USBLS	5/15
	Puerto Rico	Y	23310 FQ	30380 MW	79960 TQ	USBLS	5/15

AE Average entry wage	**AWR** Average wage range	**H** Hourly	**LR** Low end range	**MTC** Median total compensation	**TCC** Total cash compensation
AEX Average experienced wage	**B** Biweekly	**HI** Highest wage paid	**M** Monthly	**MW** Median wage paid	**TQ** Third quartile wage
ATC Average total compensation	**D** Daily	**HR** High end range	**MCC** Median cash compensation	**MWR** Median wage range	**W** Weekly
AW Average wage paid	**FQ** First quartile wage	**LO** Lowest wage paid	**ME** Median entry wage	**S** See annotated source	**Y** Yearly

Occupation/Type/Industry	Location	Per	Low	Mid	High	Source	Date
Property, Real Estate, and Community Association Manager	San Juan-Carolina-Caguas MSA, PR	Y	20710 FQ	31690 MW	85210 TQ	USBLS	5/15
	Guam	Y	30020 FQ	45950 MW	67330 TQ	USBLS	5/15
Property Management Specialist							
Natural Resources Department, State Government	Ohio	H			18.16 HI	OHGOV	2015
Property Room Supervisor							
Police Department, Municipal Government	Bakersfield, CA	Y			67305 HI	CACIT	6/28/16
Property Security Officer							
State Police	Michigan	Y	32700 LO		53000 HI	MSP01	2017
Property Tax Specialist							
County Government	Bartow County, GA	H	13.39 LO		18.74 HI	GACTY04	2016
County Government	Greene County, GA	H	14.99 LO		20.39 HI	GACTY04	2016
County Government	Jackson County, GA	H	15.01 LO		21.02 HI	GACTY04	2016
Prosecuting Attorney							
County Government	Ingham County, MI	Y			132000 HI	TC06	2016
County Government	Oakland County, MI	B			6331 HI	MIOAK1	10/1/16
Prosthodontist	California	H	37.95 FQ	45.21 MW		CABLS	1/16-3/16
	Florida	H	54.17 AE	58.71 MW	78.28 AEX	FLBLS	7/16-9/16
	Texas	Y	116560 FQ	130770 MW		USBLS	5/15
Psychiatric Aide	Alabama	Y	20108 AE	25050 AW	27532 AEX	ALBLS	6/16
	Birmingham-Hoover MSA, AL	Y	18234 AE	23115 AW	25555 AEX	ALBLS	6/16
	Alaska	Y	33720 FQ	41550 MW	47920 TQ	USBLS	5/15
	Anchorage MSA, AK	Y	33720 FQ	41550 MW	47920 TQ	USBLS	5/15
	Arizona	Y	25790 FQ	27920 MW	30060 TQ	USBLS	5/15
	Phoenix-Mesa-Scottsdale MSA, AZ	Y	26390 FQ	28070 MW	29740 TQ	USBLS	5/15
	Arkansas	Y	18050 FQ	20910 MW	26950 TQ	USBLS	5/15
	Little Rock-North Little Rock-Conway MSA, AR	Y	25260 FQ	27830 MW	30410 TQ	USBLS	5/15
	California	H	12.39 FQ	13.85 MW	15.36 TQ	CABLS	1/16-3/16
	Anaheim-Santa Ana-Irvine PMSA, CA	H	11.61 FQ	14.70 MW	17.36 TQ	CABLS	1/16-3/16
	Los Angeles-Long Beach-Glendale PMSA, CA	H	12.62 FQ	13.92 MW	15.22 TQ	CABLS	1/16-3/16
	Riverside-San Bernardino-Ontario MSA, CA	H	12.28 FQ	13.67 MW	15.07 TQ	CABLS	1/16-3/16
	Sacramento–Roseville–Arden-Arcade MSA, CA	H	12.46 FQ	14.00 MW	15.94 TQ	CABLS	1/16-3/16
	San Diego-Carlsbad MSA, CA	H	13.05 FQ	14.19 MW	15.63 TQ	CABLS	1/16-3/16
	Colorado	Y	24560 FQ	27720 MW	30790 TQ	USBLS	5/15
	Denver-Aurora-Lakewood MSA, CO	Y	26610 FQ	28620 MW	30620 TQ	USBLS	5/15
	Connecticut	Y		36058 MW		CTBLS	1/16-3/16
	Bridgeport-Stamford-Norwalk MSA, CT	Y	27610 FQ	38760 MW	61390 TQ	USBLS	5/15
	Hartford-West Hartford-East Hartford MSA, CT	Y	33990 FQ	38400 MW	46640 TQ	USBLS	5/15
	Delaware	Y	27040 FQ	29130 MW	31220 TQ	USBLS	5/15
	Wilmington PMSA, DE-MD-NJ	Y	27040 FQ	29130 MW	31220 TQ	USBLS	5/15
	District of Columbia	Y	25120 FQ	27520 MW	29920 TQ	USBLS	5/15
	Washington-Arlington-Alexandria PMSA, DC-VA-MD-WV	Y	25970 FQ	29110 MW	33190 TQ	USBLS	5/15
	Florida	H	10.43 AE	12.57 MW	14.14 AEX	FLBLS	7/16-9/16
	Georgia	Y	21210 FQ	24610 MW	30230 TQ	USBLS	5/15
	Atlanta-Sandy Springs-Roswell MSA, GA	Y	21660 FQ	24820 MW	30600 TQ	USBLS	5/15
	Hawaii	Y	33510 FQ	36310 MW	39110 TQ	USBLS	5/15
	Urban Honolulu MSA, HI	Y	33540 FQ	36430 MW	39330 TQ	USBLS	5/15
	Illinois	Y	21700 FQ	26670 MW	31250 TQ	USBLS	5/15
	Indiana	Y	21810 FQ	24400 MW	29030 TQ	USBLS	5/15

AE	Average entry wage	AWR	Average wage range	H	Hourly	LR	Low end range	MTC	Median total compensation	TCC	Total cash compensation
AEX	Average experienced wage	B	Biweekly	HI	Highest wage paid	M	Monthly	MW	Median wage paid	TQ	Third quartile wage
ATC	Average total compensation	D	Daily	HR	High end range	MCC	Median cash compensation	MWR	Median wage range	W	Weekly
AW	Average wage paid	FQ	First quartile wage	LO	Lowest wage paid	ME	Median entry wage	S	See annotated source	Y	Yearly

Occupation/Type/Industry	Location	Per	Low	Mid	High	Source	Date
Psychiatric Aide	Indianapolis-Carmel-Anderson						
	MSA, IN	Y	21600 FQ	23970 MW	28300 TQ	USBLS	5/15
	Iowa	Y	27170 FQ	31050 MW	37010 TQ	USBLS	5/15
	Kansas	Y	24400 FQ	27450 MW	30030 TQ	USBLS	5/15
	Wichita MSA, KS	Y	21960 FQ	25330 MW	29890 TQ	USBLS	5/15
	Kentucky	Y	21950 FQ	25690 MW	29760 TQ	USBLS	5/15
	Louisiana	Y	18140 FQ	21990 MW	27560 TQ	USBLS	5/15
	New Orleans-Metairie MSA,						
	LA	Y	21620 FQ	25640 MW	29830 TQ	USBLS	5/15
	Maine	Y	22190 FQ	24780 MW	30710 TQ	USBLS	5/15
	Portland-South Portland MSA,						
	ME	Y	22290 FQ	24600 MW	30290 TQ	USBLS	5/15
	Maryland	Y	26361 AE	29883 MW	31643 AEX	MDBLS	4/16
	Baltimore-Columbia-Towson						
	MSA, MD	Y	26400 FQ	28680 MW	30980 TQ	USBLS	5/15
	Massachusetts	Y	22990 FQ	27210 MW	31730 TQ	USBLS	5/15
	Worcester MSA, MA-CT	Y	26170 FQ	28050 MW	29930 TQ	USBLS	5/15
	Michigan	Y	23990 FQ	36090 MW	43910 TQ	USBLS	5/15
	Detroit-Dearborn-Livonia						
	PMSA, MI	Y	36500 FQ	41000 MW	43030 TQ	USBLS	5/15
	Minnesota	Y	31367 FQ	35547 MW	39819 TQ	MNBLS	1/16-3/16
	Mississippi	Y	17510 FQ	17530 MW	19620 TQ	USBLS	5/15
	Jackson MSA, MS	Y	17320 FQ	17990 MW	19670 TQ	USBLS	5/15
	Missouri	Y	22690 FQ	26280 MW	30650 TQ	USBLS	5/15
	Kansas City MSA, MO-KS	Y	22300 FQ	25380 MW	28810 TQ	USBLS	5/15
	St. Louis MSA, MO-IL	Y	22680 FQ	23370 MW	27860 TQ	USBLS	5/15
	Montana	Y	21400 FQ	24990 MW	27760 TQ	USBLS	5/15
	Nebraska	Y	26750 FQ	28965 MW	31380 TQ	NEBLS	7/16-9/16
	Omaha-Council Bluffs MSA,						
	NE-IA	Y	37025 FQ	50770 MW	56300 TQ	NEBLS	7/16-9/16
	Nevada	Y	27140 FQ	29940 MW	35740 TQ	USBLS	5/15
	Las Vegas-Henderson-Paradise						
	MSA, NV	Y	26990 FQ	29930 MW	35840 TQ	USBLS	5/15
	New Jersey	Y	28520 FQ	33660 MW	38730 TQ	USBLS	5/15
	Camden PMSA, NJ	Y	30000 FQ	34600 MW	38330 TQ	USBLS	5/15
	Newark PMSA, NJ-PA	Y	28590 FQ	34220 MW	40420 TQ	USBLS	5/15
	Trenton MSA, NJ	Y	29070 FQ	34460 MW	43500 TQ	USBLS	5/15
	New Mexico	Y	19890 FQ	23030 MW	28610 TQ	USBLS	5/15
	New York	Y	31650 AE	42710 MW	46660 AEX	NYBLS	1/16-3/16
	Buffalo-Cheektowaga-Niagara						
	Falls MSA, NY	Y	35650 FQ	41620 MW	46460 TQ	USBLS	5/15
	New York-Jersey City-White						
	Plains PMSA, NY-NJ	Y	31770 FQ	40930 MW	46920 TQ	USBLS	5/15
	Rochester MSA, NY	Y	31410 FQ	40570 MW	49000 TQ	USBLS	5/15
	North Carolina	Y	25330 FQ	27750 MW	30150 TQ	USBLS	5/15
	North Dakota	Y	23610 FQ	28040 MW	33570 TQ	USBLS	5/15
	Ohio	Y	29430 FQ	33920 MW	37450 TQ	USBLS	5/15
	Cincinnati MSA, OH-KY-IN	Y	32830 FQ	35390 MW	37960 TQ	USBLS	5/15
	Columbus MSA, OH	Y	29950 FQ	34330 MW	38410 TQ	USBLS	5/15
	Oklahoma	Y	18550 FQ	22010 MW	26330 TQ	USBLS	5/15
	Oklahoma City MSA, OK	Y	20930 FQ	25150 MW	28540 TQ	USBLS	5/15
	Tulsa MSA, OK	Y	18310 FQ	21750 MW	26070 TQ	USBLS	5/15
	Oregon	H	15.60 FQ	16.93 MW	19.20 TQ	ORBLS	2016
	Portland-Vancouver-Hillsboro						
	MSA, OR-WA	Y	30860 FQ	34510 MW	39560 TQ	USBLS	5/15
	Pennsylvania	Y	25880 FQ	32160 MW	38560 TQ	USBLS	5/15
	Montgomery County-Bucks						
	County-Chester County						
	PMSA, PA	Y	31320 FQ	36060 MW	41910 TQ	USBLS	5/15
	Philadelphia PMSA, PA	Y	28570 FQ	33410 MW	36940 TQ	USBLS	5/15
	Pittsburgh MSA, PA	Y	23260 FQ	31060 MW	42820 TQ	USBLS	5/15
	South Carolina	Y	19220 FQ	21600 MW	23770 TQ	USBLS	5/15
	Greenville-Anderson-Mauldin						
	MSA, SC	Y	17780 FQ	20240 MW	22770 TQ	USBLS	5/15
	Tennessee	Y	17770 FQ	20580 MW	23240 TQ	USBLS	5/15
	Knoxville MSA, TN	Y	16770 FQ	18240 MW	20290 TQ	USBLS	5/15
	Memphis MSA, TN-MS-AR	Y	17610 FQ	21140 MW	23460 TQ	USBLS	5/15
	Nashville-Davidson–						
	Murfreesboro–Franklin						
	MSA, TN	Y	18120 FQ	21090 MW	23490 TQ	USBLS	5/15
	Texas	Y	22700 FQ	23530 MW	26600 TQ	USBLS	5/15
	Austin-Round Rock MSA, TX	Y	24100 FQ	26140 MW	28060 TQ	USBLS	5/15

AE	Average entry wage	AWR	Average wage range	H	Hourly	LR	Low end range	MTC	Median total compensation	TCC	Total cash compensation
AEX	Average experienced wage	B	Biweekly	HI	Highest wage paid	M	Monthly	MW	Median wage paid	TQ	Third quartile wage
ATC	Average total compensation	D	Daily	HR	High end range	MCC	Median cash compensation	MWR	Median wage range	W	Weekly
AW	Average wage paid	FQ	First quartile wage	LO	Lowest wage paid	ME	Median entry wage	S	See annotated source	Y	Yearly

1318

Occupation/Type/Industry	Location	Per	Low	Mid	High	Source	Date
Psychiatric Aide	Dallas-Plano-Irving PMSA, TX	Y	22700 FQ	23110 MW	27310 TQ	USBLS	5/15
	Fort Worth-Arlington PMSA, TX	Y	23740 FQ	27180 MW	30340 TQ	USBLS	5/15
	Houston-The Woodlands-Sugar Land MSA, TX	Y	21610 FQ	23520 MW	27350 TQ	USBLS	5/15
	San Antonio-New Braunfels MSA, TX	Y	22700 FQ	22750 MW	25030 TQ	USBLS	5/15
	Utah	Y	20940 FQ	23590 MW	28230 TQ	USBLS	5/15
	Salt Lake City MSA, UT	Y	20840 FQ	23410 MW	27920 TQ	USBLS	5/15
	Vermont	Y	20030 FQ	22680 MW	26840 TQ	USBLS	5/15
	Virginia	Y	22680 FQ	26710 MW	30990 TQ	USBLS	5/15
	Virginia Beach-Norfolk-Newport News MSA, VA-NC	Y	23490 FQ	27110 MW	30340 TQ	USBLS	5/15
	Washington	H	11.10 FQ	14.42 MW	17.44 TQ	WABLS	3/16
	Seattle-Bellevue-Everett PMSA, WA	H	9.67 FQ	11.76 MW	15.94 TQ	WABLS	3/16
	Tacoma-Lakewood PMSA, WA	H	12.41 FQ	13.71 MW	15.01 TQ	WABLS	3/16
	West Virginia	Y	17640 FQ	18640 MW	19860 TQ	USBLS	5/15
	Huntington-Ashland MSA, WV-KY-OH	Y	18270 FQ	19840 MW	22390 TQ	USBLS	5/15
	Wisconsin	Y	27890 FQ	31530 MW	36790 TQ	USBLS	5/15
	Wyoming	Y	21270 FQ	23320 MW	26780 TQ	USBLS	5/15
Psychiatric Technician	Alabama	Y	18980 AE	27297 AW	31456 AEX	ALBLS	6/16
	Birmingham-Hoover MSA, AL	Y	22252 AE	29571 AW	22252 AEX	ALBLS	6/16
	Alaska	Y	26330 FQ	33990 MW	49730 TQ	USBLS	5/15
	Anchorage MSA, AK	Y	25290 FQ	29780 MW	38460 TQ	USBLS	5/15
	Arizona	Y	22790 FQ	26990 MW	30610 TQ	USBLS	5/15
	Phoenix-Mesa-Scottsdale MSA, AZ	Y	22170 FQ	26460 MW	30270 TQ	USBLS	5/15
	Tucson MSA, AZ	Y	25920 FQ	28840 MW	33960 TQ	USBLS	5/15
	Arkansas	Y	20220 FQ	24270 MW	30060 TQ	USBLS	5/15
	Little Rock-North Little Rock-Conway MSA, AR	Y	24420 FQ	28530 MW	33310 TQ	USBLS	5/15
	California	H	25.31 FQ	28.78 MW	32.38 TQ	CABLS	1/16-3/16
	Anaheim-Santa Ana-Irvine PMSA, CA	H	24.87 FQ	28.43 MW	32.86 TQ	CABLS	1/16-3/16
	Los Angeles-Long Beach-Glendale PMSA, CA	H	20.83 FQ	27.36 MW	31.67 TQ	CABLS	1/16-3/16
	Oakland-Hayward-Berkeley PMSA, CA	H	15.94 FQ	18.20 MW	26.01 TQ	CABLS	1/16-3/16
	Riverside-San Bernardino-Ontario MSA, CA	H	26.83 FQ	29.81 MW	33.37 TQ	CABLS	1/16-3/16
	Sacramento–Roseville–Arden-Arcade MSA, CA	H	22.13 FQ	28.39 MW	31.48 TQ	CABLS	1/16-3/16
	San Francisco-Redwood City-South San Francisco PMSA, CA	H	25.24 FQ	31.17 MW	36.00 TQ	CABLS	1/16-3/16
	Colorado	Y	33680 FQ	35010 MW	41950 TQ	USBLS	5/15
	Denver-Aurora-Lakewood MSA, CO	Y	32620 FQ	36230 MW	42610 TQ	USBLS	5/15
	Connecticut	Y		52683 MW		CTBLS	1/16-3/16
	Bridgeport-Stamford-Norwalk MSA, CT	Y	45380 FQ	55810 MW	66180 TQ	USBLS	5/15
	Hartford-West Hartford-East Hartford MSA, CT	Y	41170 FQ	49540 MW	58930 TQ	USBLS	5/15
	District of Columbia	Y	31080 FQ	35180 MW	39160 TQ	USBLS	5/15
	Washington-Arlington-Alexandria PMSA, DC-VA-MD-WV	Y	28320 FQ	32770 MW	38130 TQ	USBLS	5/15
	Florida	H	10.35 AE	12.82 MW	14.52 AEX	FLBLS	7/16-9/16
	Fort Lauderdale-Pompano Beach-Deerfield Beach PMSA, FL	H	12.81 AE	14.47 MW	16.28 AEX	FLBLS	7/16-9/16
	Miami-Miami Beach-Kendall PMSA, FL	H	10.60 AE	13.46 MW	16.19 AEX	FLBLS	7/16-9/16
	Orlando-Kissimmee-Sanford MSA, FL	H	9.50 AE	11.85 MW	13.48 AEX	FLBLS	7/16-9/16
	Tampa-St. Petersburg-Clearwater MSA, FL	H	10.60 AE	11.47 MW	12.73 AEX	FLBLS	7/16-9/16
	Georgia	Y	23880 FQ	28010 MW	33020 TQ	USBLS	5/15

Occupation/Type/Industry	Location	Per	Low	Mid	High	Source	Date
Psychiatric Technician	Atlanta-Sandy Springs-						
	Roswell MSA, GA	Y	25580 FQ	29250 MW	35050 TQ	USBLS	5/15
	Idaho	Y	25730 FQ	29830 MW	34310 TQ	USBLS	5/15
	Boise City MSA, ID	Y	30530 FQ	33520 MW	38500 TQ	USBLS	5/15
	Illinois	Y	38450 FQ	47460 MW	58500 TQ	USBLS	5/15
	Chicago-Naperville-Arlington						
	Heights PMSA, IL	Y	40140 FQ	45430 MW	51170 TQ	USBLS	5/15
	Lake County-Kenosha County						
	PMSA, IL-WI	Y	36300 FQ	54590 MW	72300 TQ	USBLS	5/15
	Indiana	Y	22280 FQ	25150 MW	29610 TQ	USBLS	5/15
	Gary PMSA, IN	Y	24110 FQ	28140 MW	32750 TQ	USBLS	5/15
	Indianapolis-Carmel-Anderson						
	MSA, IN	Y	22840 FQ	26240 MW	31910 TQ	USBLS	5/15
	Iowa	Y	26040 FQ	28490 MW	30940 TQ	USBLS	5/15
	Des Moines-West Des Moines						
	MSA, IA	Y	25570 FQ	28210 MW	30840 TQ	USBLS	5/15
	Kansas	Y	24540 FQ	28380 MW	33930 TQ	USBLS	5/15
	Wichita MSA, KS	Y	22850 FQ	27060 MW	32240 TQ	USBLS	5/15
	Kentucky	Y	21580 FQ	25070 MW	32510 TQ	USBLS	5/15
	Louisiana	Y	18780 FQ	22630 MW	29090 TQ	USBLS	5/15
	Baton Rouge MSA, LA	Y	20980 FQ	23760 MW	27860 TQ	USBLS	5/15
	New Orleans-Metairie MSA,						
	LA	Y	27580 FQ	34170 MW	38640 TQ	USBLS	5/15
	Maine	Y	25500 FQ	29500 MW	35200 TQ	USBLS	5/15
	Maryland	Y	25364 AE	37696 MW	43862 AEX	MDBLS	4/16
	Baltimore-Columbia-Towson						
	MSA, MD	Y	29510 FQ	36770 MW	46220 TQ	USBLS	5/15
	Massachusetts	Y	27070 FQ	32960 MW	39360 TQ	USBLS	5/15
	Boston-Cambridge-Newton						
	NECTA, MA	Y	31940 FQ	37150 MW	45390 TQ	USBLS	5/15
	Worcester MSA, MA-CT	Y	19340 FQ	27820 MW	32580 TQ	USBLS	5/15
	Michigan	Y	32560 FQ	40510 MW	55810 TQ	USBLS	5/15
	Grand Rapids-Wyoming MSA,						
	MI	Y	31490 FQ	36620 MW	42830 TQ	USBLS	5/15
	Minnesota	Y	29435 FQ	34425 MW	39364 TQ	MNBLS	1/16-3/16
	Minneapolis-St. Paul-						
	Bloomington MSA, MN-WI	Y	28518 FQ	33145 MW	37903 TQ	MNBLS	1/16-3/16
	Mississippi	Y	19970 FQ	22670 MW	26650 TQ	USBLS	5/15
	Jackson MSA, MS	Y	23470 FQ	27630 MW	31640 TQ	USBLS	5/15
	Missouri	Y	22820 FQ	26430 MW	31330 TQ	USBLS	5/15
	Kansas City MSA, MO-KS	Y	25110 FQ	28930 MW	39610 TQ	USBLS	5/15
	St. Louis MSA, MO-IL	Y	27450 FQ	46160 MW	61190 TQ	USBLS	5/15
	Montana	Y	23200 FQ	26780 MW	29930 TQ	USBLS	5/15
	Billings MSA, MT	Y	21820 FQ	23970 MW	27680 TQ	USBLS	5/15
	Nebraska	Y	24325 FQ	27400 MW	30375 TQ	NEBLS	7/16-9/16
	Omaha-Council Bluffs MSA,						
	NE-IA	Y	25840 FQ	28135 MW	30425 TQ	NEBLS	7/16-9/16
	Nevada	Y	27750 FQ	30370 MW	35150 TQ	USBLS	5/15
	New Hampshire	H	13.74 AE	16.27 MW	17.85 AEX	NHBLS	6/16
	New Jersey	Y	36190 FQ	44700 MW	62900 TQ	USBLS	5/15
	Newark PMSA, NJ-PA	Y	33740 FQ	38280 MW	60720 TQ	USBLS	5/15
	New Mexico	Y	20810 FQ	25340 MW	29550 TQ	USBLS	5/15
	Albuquerque MSA, NM	Y	26270 FQ	27370 MW	34120 TQ	USBLS	5/15
	New York	Y	29850 AE	40860 MW	49330 AEX	NYBLS	1/16-3/16
	Nassau County-Suffolk County						
	PMSA, NY	Y	39610 FQ	52790 MW	58620 TQ	USBLS	5/15
	New York-Jersey City-White						
	Plains PMSA, NY-NJ	Y	36730 FQ	43430 MW	50280 TQ	USBLS	5/15
	Rochester MSA, NY	Y	27020 FQ	29560 MW	35340 TQ	USBLS	5/15
	North Carolina	Y	27350 FQ	30980 MW	37900 TQ	USBLS	5/15
	Charlotte-Concord-Gastonia						
	MSA, NC-SC	Y	28130 FQ	31270 MW	36940 TQ	USBLS	5/15
	Ohio	Y	27710 FQ	32450 MW	38270 TQ	USBLS	5/15
	Cincinnati MSA, OH-KY-IN	Y	31420 FQ	35510 MW	39980 TQ	USBLS	5/15
	Columbus MSA, OH	Y	26620 FQ	29820 MW	35180 TQ	USBLS	5/15
	Oklahoma	Y	23700 FQ	29190 MW	41570 TQ	USBLS	5/15
	Tulsa MSA, OK	Y	22450 FQ	24920 MW	28770 TQ	USBLS	5/15
	Oregon	H	14.28 FQ	19.44 MW	23.09 TQ	ORBLS	2016
	Portland-Vancouver-Hillsboro						
	MSA, OR-WA	Y	23980 FQ	28380 MW	36010 TQ	USBLS	5/15
	Pennsylvania	Y	27040 FQ	32010 MW	39920 TQ	USBLS	5/15
	Harrisburg-Carlisle MSA, PA	Y	19370 FQ	28990 MW	38430 TQ	USBLS	5/15

AE	Average entry wage	**AWR** Average wage range	**H** Hourly	**LR** Low end range	**MTC** Median total compensation	**TCC** Total cash compensation
AEX	Average experienced wage	**B** Biweekly	**HI** Highest wage paid	**M** Monthly	**MW** Median wage paid	**TQ** Third quartile wage
ATC	Average total compensation	**D** Daily	**HR** High end range	**MCC** Median cash compensation	**MWR** Median wage range	**W** Weekly
AW	Average wage paid	**FQ** First quartile wage	**LO** Lowest wage paid	**ME** Median entry wage	**S** See annotated source	**Y** Yearly

Occupation/Type/Industry	Location	Per	Low	Mid	High	Source	Date
Psychiatric Technician	Montgomery County-Bucks County-Chester County						
	PMSA, PA	Y	27740 FQ	32990 MW	38180 TQ	USBLS	5/15
	Philadelphia PMSA, PA	Y	27700 FQ	37200 MW	44800 TQ	USBLS	5/15
	Pittsburgh MSA, PA	Y	27060 FQ	29610 MW	33780 TQ	USBLS	5/15
	Rhode Island	Y	39900 FQ	44620 MW	49200 TQ	USBLS	5/15
	Providence-Warwick MSA, RI-MA	Y	35570 FQ	42110 MW	47750 TQ	USBLS	5/15
	South Carolina	Y	20690 FQ	23150 MW	26600 TQ	USBLS	5/15
	Columbia MSA, SC	Y	20930 FQ	23500 MW	27360 TQ	USBLS	5/15
	Greenville-Anderson-Mauldin MSA, SC	Y	19160 FQ	22470 MW	26540 TQ	USBLS	5/15
	Tennessee	Y	21790 FQ	23720 MW	27020 TQ	USBLS	5/15
	Nashville-Davidson–Murfreesboro–Franklin MSA, TN	Y	21780 FQ	23760 MW	27130 TQ	USBLS	5/15
	Texas	Y	24050 FQ	28760 MW	35450 TQ	USBLS	5/15
	Austin-Round Rock MSA, TX	Y	23420 FQ	27470 MW	34170 TQ	USBLS	5/15
	Dallas-Plano-Irving PMSA, TX	Y	25310 FQ	30170 MW	38540 TQ	USBLS	5/15
	Fort Worth-Arlington PMSA, TX	Y	25680 FQ	29360 MW	35420 TQ	USBLS	5/15
	Houston-The Woodlands-Sugar Land MSA, TX	Y	26100 FQ	31540 MW	36790 TQ	USBLS	5/15
	San Antonio-New Braunfels MSA, TX	Y	23840 FQ	27730 MW	32280 TQ	USBLS	5/15
	Utah	Y	22810 FQ	25860 MW	29930 TQ	USBLS	5/15
	Ogden-Clearfield MSA, UT	Y	21070 FQ	22670 MW	24270 TQ	USBLS	5/15
	Provo-Orem MSA, UT	Y	22270 FQ	24350 MW	27930 TQ	USBLS	5/15
	Salt Lake City MSA, UT	Y	26040 FQ	28910 MW	32420 TQ	USBLS	5/15
	Vermont	Y	28120 FQ	33020 MW	38400 TQ	USBLS	5/15
	Virginia	Y	22750 FQ	26460 MW	31210 TQ	USBLS	5/15
	Richmond MSA, VA	Y	24500 FQ	27760 MW	30740 TQ	USBLS	5/15
	Virginia Beach-Norfolk-Newport News MSA, VA-NC	Y	24110 FQ	27100 MW	31220 TQ	USBLS	5/15
	Washington	H	13.76 FQ	18.93 MW	23.58 TQ	WABLS	3/16
	Seattle-Bellevue-Everett PMSA, WA	H	18.35 FQ	20.64 MW	22.65 TQ	WABLS	3/16
	West Virginia	Y	17880 FQ	19120 MW	22170 TQ	USBLS	5/15
	Huntington-Ashland MSA, WV-KY-OH	Y	18250 FQ	19930 MW	23330 TQ	USBLS	5/15
	Wisconsin	Y	34830 FQ	37880 MW	41900 TQ	USBLS	5/15
	Milwaukee-Waukesha-West Allis MSA, WI	Y	28810 FQ	36320 MW	45060 TQ	USBLS	5/15
	Puerto Rico	Y	16820 FQ	18260 MW	20120 TQ	USBLS	5/15
	San Juan-Carolina-Caguas MSA, PR	Y	16810 FQ	18350 MW	22010 TQ	USBLS	5/15
Psychiatrist	Alabama	Y	137721 AE	201225 AW	232977 AEX	ALBLS	6/16
	Birmingham-Hoover MSA, AL	Y	137160 AE	176659 AW	196413 AEX	ALBLS	6/16
	Alaska	Y	179110 FQ	234130 AW		USBLS	5/15
	Arizona	Y	49680 FQ	197540 AW		USBLS	5/15
	Phoenix-Mesa-Scottsdale MSA, AZ	Y	46740 FQ	185770 MW		USBLS	5/15
	Tucson MSA, AZ	Y		277900 AW		USBLS	5/15
	Arkansas	Y	50950 FQ	59870 MW	135590 TQ	USBLS	5/15
	Little Rock-North Little Rock-Conway MSA, AR	Y	48660 FQ	54550 MW	60220 TQ	USBLS	5/15
	California	H		121.98 AW		CABLS	1/16-3/16
	Anaheim-Santa Ana-Irvine PMSA, CA	H		113.62 AW		CABLS	1/16-3/16
	Los Angeles-Long Beach-Glendale PMSA, CA	H		135.83 AW		CABLS	1/16-3/16
	Riverside-San Bernardino-Ontario MSA, CA	H		129.14 AW		CABLS	1/16-3/16
	Sacramento–Roseville–Arden-Arcade MSA, CA	H	85.11 FQ	111.61 AW		CABLS	1/16-3/16
	San Diego-Carlsbad MSA, CA	H	86.74 FQ	115.04 AW		CABLS	1/16-3/16
	San Francisco-Redwood City-South San Francisco PMSA, CA	H	57.65 FQ	95.64 AW		CABLS	1/16-3/16
	Colorado	Y	98860 FQ	205090 AW		USBLS	5/15

AE	Average entry wage	AWR	Average wage range	H	Hourly	LR	Low end range	MTC	Median total compensation	TCC	Total cash compensation
AEX	Average experienced wage	B	Biweekly	HI	Highest wage paid	M	Monthly	MW	Median wage paid	TQ	Third quartile wage
ATC	Average total compensation	D	Daily	HR	High end range	MCC	Median cash compensation	MWR	Median wage range	W	Weekly
AW	Average wage paid	FQ	First quartile wage	LO	Lowest wage paid	ME	Median entry wage	S	See annotated source	Y	Yearly

Occupation/Type/Industry	Location	Per	Low	Mid	High	Source	Date
Psychiatrist	Denver-Aurora-Lakewood MSA, CO	Y	178230 FQ	230510 AW		USBLS	5/15
	Connecticut	Y		216716 AW		CTBLS	1/16-3/16
	Bridgeport-Stamford-Norwalk MSA, CT	Y	183500 FQ	230530 AW		USBLS	5/15
	Hartford-West Hartford-East Hartford MSA, CT	Y	165900 FQ	205020 AW		USBLS	5/15
	Delaware	Y	52940 FQ	179450 MW		USBLS	5/15
	Wilmington PMSA, DE-MD-NJ	Y	52940 FQ	172370 MW		USBLS	5/15
	District of Columbia	Y	57010 FQ	140980 MW		USBLS	5/15
	Washington-Arlington-Alexandria PMSA, DC-VA-MD-WV	Y	129580 FQ	185110 MW		USBLS	5/15
	Florida	H	33.56 AE	84.32 MW	102.57 AEX	FLBLS	7/16-9/16
	Fort Lauderdale-Pompano Beach-Deerfield Beach PMSA, FL	H	40.79 AE	61.72 MW	81.22 AEX	FLBLS	7/16-9/16
	Miami-Miami Beach-Kendall PMSA, FL	H	23.04 AE	44.83 MW	77.05 AEX	FLBLS	7/16-9/16
	Orlando-Kissimmee-Sanford MSA, FL	H	22.09 AE	86.65 MW	104.30 AEX	FLBLS	7/16-9/16
	Tampa-St. Petersburg-Clearwater MSA, FL	H	73.58 AE	91.97 MW	109.33 AEX	FLBLS	7/16-9/16
	Georgia	Y	174240 FQ	224560 AW		USBLS	5/15
	Atlanta-Sandy Springs-Roswell MSA, GA	Y	168200 FQ	221980 AW		USBLS	5/15
	Hawaii	Y	58650 FQ	137690 MW		USBLS	5/15
	Urban Honolulu MSA, HI	Y	57970 FQ	131230 MW	181480 TQ	USBLS	5/15
	Boise City MSA, ID	Y	30370 FQ	91290 MW	102890 TQ	USBLS	5/15
	Illinois	Y	55410 FQ	126340 MW		USBLS	5/15
	Chicago-Naperville-Arlington Heights PMSA, IL	Y	49090 FQ	132610 MW		USBLS	5/15
	Lake County-Kenosha County PMSA, IL-WI	Y	57130 FQ	91120 MW		USBLS	5/15
	Indiana	Y		238780 AW		USBLS	5/15
	Gary PMSA, IN	Y	145880 FQ	200820 AW		USBLS	5/15
	Indianapolis-Carmel-Anderson MSA, IN	Y		255050 AW		USBLS	5/15
	Iowa	Y	152480 FQ	224860 AW		USBLS	5/15
	Kansas	Y	75920 FQ	193530 AW		USBLS	5/15
	Wichita MSA, KS	Y	65010 FQ	74520 MW	185380 TQ	USBLS	5/15
	Kentucky	Y	179430 FQ	227890 AW		USBLS	5/15
	Louisville-Jefferson County MSA, KY-IN	Y	181830 FQ	224110 AW		USBLS	5/15
	Louisiana	Y	71910	136900 MW		USBLS	5/15
	Portland-South Portland MSA, ME	Y	172510 FQ	210100 AW		USBLS	5/15
	Maryland	Y	60051 AE	186005	248982 AEX	MDBLS	4/16
	Baltimore-Columbia-Towson MSA, MD	Y	65620 FQ	186610 AW		USBLS	5/15
	Massachusetts	Y	121190 FQ	176300 MW		USBLS	5/15
	Boston-Cambridge-Newton NECTA, MA	Y	104770 FQ	169850 MW		USBLS	5/15
	Worcester MSA, MA-CT	Y	150460 FQ	192530 AW		USBLS	5/15
	Michigan	Y	120830 FQ	174180 MW		USBLS	5/15
	Detroit-Dearborn-Livonia PMSA, MI	Y	176200 FQ	224800 AW		USBLS	5/15
	Grand Rapids-Wyoming MSA, MI	Y	176850 FQ	208050 AW		USBLS	5/15
	Minnesota	Y	167810 FQ	218505 AW		MNBLS	1/16-3/16
	Minneapolis-St. Paul-Bloomington MSA, MN-WI	Y	176248 FQ	228324 AW		MNBLS	1/16-3/16
	Mississippi	Y	169490 FQ	222040 AW		USBLS	5/15
	Missouri	Y	109660 FQ	145290 MW		USBLS	5/15
	Kansas City MSA, MO-KS	Y	167190 FQ	225410 AW		USBLS	5/15
	St. Louis MSA, MO-IL	Y	108710 FQ	120810 MW		USBLS	5/15
	Montana	Y	91200 FQ	157910 MW		USBLS	5/15
	Nebraska	Y	104655 FQ	165935 MW		NEBLS	7/16-9/16
	Nevada	Y	132710 FQ	182470 MW		USBLS	5/15
	New Hampshire	H	62.92 AE	104.56 AW	125.38 AEX	NHBLS	6/16
	New Jersey	Y	172340 FQ	217690 AW		USBLS	5/15

AE Average entry wage	**AWR** Average wage range	**H** Hourly	**LR** Low end range	**MTC** Median total compensation	**TCC** Total cash compensation
AEX Average experienced wage	**B** Biweekly	**HI** Highest wage paid	**M** Monthly	**MW** Median wage paid	**TQ** Third quartile wage
ATC Average total compensation	**D** Daily	**HR** High end range	**MCC** Median cash compensation	**MWR** Median wage range	**W** Weekly
AW Average wage paid	**FQ** First quartile wage	**LO** Lowest wage paid	**ME** Median entry wage	**S** See annotated source	**Y** Yearly

Occupation/Type/Industry	Location	Per	Low	Mid	High	Source	Date
Psychiatrist	Camden PMSA, NJ	Y		246690 AW		USBLS	5/15
	Newark PMSA, NJ-PA	Y	183070 FQ	230820 AW		USBLS	5/15
	Trenton MSA, NJ	Y		268480 AW		USBLS	5/15
	New Mexico	Y	45980 FQ	61600 MW		USBLS	5/15
	Albuquerque MSA, NM	Y	44010 FQ	48120 MW		USBLS	5/15
	New York	Y	98580 AE	165550 MW		NYBLS	1/16-3/16
	Buffalo-Cheektowaga-Niagara Falls MSA, NY	Y	62820 FQ	141740 MW	161510 TQ	USBLS	5/15
	Nassau County-Suffolk County PMSA, NY	Y	113410 FQ	166760 MW		USBLS	5/15
	New York-Jersey City-White Plains PMSA, NY-NJ	Y	131370 FQ	163530 MW		USBLS	5/15
	Rochester MSA, NY	Y	160500 FQ	198250 AW		USBLS	5/15
	North Carolina	Y	167700 FQ	214300 AW		USBLS	5/15
	Charlotte-Concord-Gastonia MSA, NC-SC	Y	175110 FQ	234360 AW		USBLS	5/15
	Raleigh MSA, NC	Y	168310 FQ	215930 AW		USBLS	5/15
	North Dakota	Y	141490 FQ	214010 AW		USBLS	5/15
	Ohio	Y	160070 FQ	201740 AW		USBLS	5/15
	Cincinnati MSA, OH-KY-IN	Y	175510 FQ	211440 AW		USBLS	5/15
	Cleveland-Elyria MSA, OH	Y	111160 FQ	123850 MW		USBLS	5/15
	Columbus MSA, OH	Y	163000 FQ	204290 AW		USBLS	5/15
	Oklahoma	Y	68140 FQ	140640 MW		USBLS	5/15
	Oklahoma City MSA, OK	Y	82840 FQ	146420 MW		USBLS	5/15
	Oregon	H	73.33 FQ	100.23 AW		ORBLS	2016
	Portland-Vancouver-Hillsboro MSA, OR-WA	Y	146400 FQ	163220 MW		USBLS	5/15
	Pennsylvania	Y	89110 FQ	177220 MW		USBLS	5/15
	Allentown-Bethlehem-Easton MSA, PA-NJ	Y	167830 FQ	212070 AW		USBLS	5/15
	Harrisburg-Carlisle MSA, PA	Y	60990 FQ	190500 AW		USBLS	5/15
	Montgomery County-Bucks County-Chester County PMSA, PA	Y	92670 FQ	171350 MW		USBLS	5/15
	Philadelphia PMSA, PA	Y	62720 FQ	151650 MW		USBLS	5/15
	Pittsburgh MSA, PA	Y	103110 FQ	164760 MW		USBLS	5/15
	Rhode Island	Y	112110 FQ	199540 AW		USBLS	5/15
	Providence-Warwick MSA, RI-MA	Y	113900 FQ	200130 AW		USBLS	5/15
	South Carolina	Y	151700 FQ	180630 MW		USBLS	5/15
	South Dakota	Y	154420 FQ	240710 AW		USBLS	5/15
	Tennessee	Y	170030 FQ	194000 AW		USBLS	5/15
	Nashville-Davidson–Murfreesboro–Franklin MSA, TN	Y	174220 FQ	202820 AW		USBLS	5/15
	Texas	Y	151590 FQ	197120 AW		USBLS	5/15
	Austin-Round Rock MSA, TX	Y	125310 FQ	180000 MW		USBLS	5/15
	Dallas-Plano-Irving PMSA, TX	Y		251390 AW		USBLS	5/15
	Fort Worth-Arlington PMSA, TX	Y		242910 AW		USBLS	5/15
	Houston-The Woodlands-Sugar Land MSA, TX	Y	63050 FQ	150710 MW		USBLS	5/15
	San Antonio-New Braunfels MSA, TX	Y	58340 FQ	95410 MW		USBLS	5/15
	Utah	Y	23620 FQ	116800 MW		USBLS	5/15
	Vermont	Y	135110 FQ	206520 AW		USBLS	5/15
	Virginia	Y	126210 FQ	193920 AW		USBLS	5/15
	Richmond MSA, VA	Y	101890 FQ	197500 AW		USBLS	5/15
	Virginia Beach-Norfolk-Newport News MSA, VA-NC	Y	98100 FQ	135250 MW	187140 TQ	USBLS	5/15
	Washington	H	72.78 FQ	95.48 AW		WABLS	3/16
	Seattle-Bellevue-Everett PMSA, WA	H	51.30 FQ	91.76 AW		WABLS	3/16
	Tacoma-Lakewood PMSA, WA	H	77.18 FQ	105.09 AW		WABLS	3/16
	West Virginia	Y	108320 FQ	130490 MW	186380 TQ	USBLS	5/15
	Wisconsin	Y	157910 FQ	208550 AW		USBLS	5/15
	Madison MSA, WI	Y		223450 AW		USBLS	5/15
	Milwaukee-Waukesha-West Allis MSA, WI	Y	169760 FQ	225490 AW		USBLS	5/15
	Wyoming	Y		240890 AW		USBLS	5/15
	Puerto Rico	Y	127320 FQ	169450 MW		USBLS	5/15

AE	Average entry wage	AWR	Average wage range	H	Hourly	LR	Low end range	MTC	Median total compensation	TCC	Total cash compensation
AEX	Average experienced wage	B	Biweekly	HI	Highest wage paid	M	Monthly	MW	Median wage paid	TQ	Third quartile wage
ATC	Average total compensation	D	Daily	HR	High end range	MCC	Median cash compensation	MWR	Median wage range	W	Weekly
AW	Average wage paid	FQ	First quartile wage	LO	Lowest wage paid	ME	Median entry wage	S	See annotated source	Y	Yearly

Occupation/Type/Industry	Location	Per	Low	Mid	High	Source	Date
Psychiatrist							
Department of Corrections, State Government	Deer Lodge, MT	H			92.00 HI	MTGOV	2016
Psychologist							
Fire Department, Municipal Government	Los Angeles, CA	Y			86006 HI	CACIT	6/23/16
Police Department, Municipal Government	Colorado Springs, CO	Y	67700 LO		93088 HI	COSPRS	2017
Psychology Teacher							
Postsecondary	Alabama	Y	45248 AE	79140 AW	96092 AEX	ALBLS	6/16
Postsecondary	Birmingham-Hoover MSA, AL	Y	51822 AE	89568 AW	108446 AEX	ALBLS	6/16
Postsecondary	Arizona	Y	50070 FQ	62120 MW	87330 TQ	USBLS	5/15
Postsecondary	Phoenix-Mesa-Scottsdale MSA, AZ	Y	50700 FQ	61290 MW	84540 TQ	USBLS	5/15
Postsecondary	Tucson MSA, AZ	Y	28870 FQ	58650 MW	93320 TQ	USBLS	5/15
Postsecondary	Arkansas	Y	49210 FQ	57490 MW	71230 TQ	USBLS	5/15
Postsecondary	Little Rock-North Little Rock-Conway MSA, AR	Y	51330 FQ	59710 MW	75320 TQ	USBLS	5/15
Postsecondary	California	Y		92501 AW		CABLS	1/16-3/16
Postsecondary	Anaheim-Santa Ana-Irvine PMSA, CA	Y		113826 AW		CABLS	1/16-3/16
Postsecondary	Los Angeles-Long Beach-Glendale PMSA, CA	Y		93536 AW		CABLS	1/16-3/16
Postsecondary	Riverside-San Bernardino-Ontario MSA, CA	Y		89458 AW		CABLS	1/16-3/16
Postsecondary	Sacramento–Roseville–Arden-Arcade MSA, CA	Y		88525 AW		CABLS	1/16-3/16
Postsecondary	San Diego-Carlsbad MSA, CA	Y		96793 AW		CABLS	1/16-3/16
Postsecondary	San Francisco-Redwood City-South San Francisco PMSA, CA	Y		82245 AW		CABLS	1/16-3/16
Postsecondary	Colorado	Y	35140 FQ	56580 MW	80360 TQ	USBLS	5/15
Postsecondary	Denver-Aurora-Lakewood MSA, CO	Y	35470 FQ	51020 MW	75890 TQ	USBLS	5/15
Postsecondary	Connecticut	Y		74565 MW		CTBLS	1/16-3/16
Postsecondary	Bridgeport-Stamford-Norwalk MSA, CT	Y	62650 FQ	77410 MW	99620 TQ	USBLS	5/15
Postsecondary	Hartford-West Hartford-East Hartford MSA, CT	Y	55260 FQ	67750 MW	84420 TQ	USBLS	5/15
Postsecondary	Delaware	Y	53320 FQ	73500 MW	94900 TQ	USBLS	5/15
Postsecondary	Wilmington PMSA, DE-MD-NJ	Y	52420 FQ	74030 MW	96690 TQ	USBLS	5/15
Postsecondary	District of Columbia	Y	58330 FQ	76230 MW	98160 TQ	USBLS	5/15
Postsecondary	Washington-Arlington-Alexandria PMSA, DC-VA-MD-WV	Y	55520 FQ	73930 MW	100310 TQ	USBLS	5/15
Postsecondary	Florida	Y	48970 AE	77582 MW	102032 AEX	FLBLS	7/16-9/16
Postsecondary	Fort Lauderdale-Pompano Beach-Deerfield Beach PMSA, FL	Y	57130 AE	75929 MW	91322 AEX	FLBLS	7/16-9/16
Postsecondary	Miami-Miami Beach-Kendall PMSA, FL	Y	52118 AE	78180 MW	93636 AEX	FLBLS	7/16-9/16
Postsecondary	Orlando-Kissimmee-Sanford MSA, FL	Y	51343 AE	82326 MW	109924 AEX	FLBLS	7/16-9/16
Postsecondary	Tampa-St. Petersburg-Clearwater MSA, FL	Y	58086 AE	82985 MW	114720 AEX	FLBLS	7/16-9/16
Postsecondary	Georgia	Y	42290 FQ	60290 MW	77540 TQ	USBLS	5/15
Postsecondary	Atlanta-Sandy Springs-Roswell MSA, GA	Y	36440 FQ	59480 MW	76530 TQ	USBLS	5/15
Postsecondary	Hawaii	Y	44330 FQ	67710 MW	88750 TQ	USBLS	5/15
Postsecondary	Urban Honolulu MSA, HI	Y	44750 FQ	67350 MW	92310 TQ	USBLS	5/15
Postsecondary	Idaho	Y	42390 FQ	55040 MW	72410 TQ	USBLS	5/15
Postsecondary	Boise City MSA, ID	Y	21070 FQ	46310 MW	57500 TQ	USBLS	5/15
Postsecondary	Illinois	Y	58190 FQ	77570 MW	106220 TQ	USBLS	5/15
Postsecondary	Chicago-Naperville-Arlington Heights PMSA, IL	Y	56950 FQ	74120 MW	97350 TQ	USBLS	5/15
Postsecondary	Lake County-Kenosha County PMSA, IL-WI	Y	54470 FQ	68940 MW	93690 TQ	USBLS	5/15
Postsecondary	Indiana	Y	52730 FQ	71130 MW	97330 TQ	USBLS	5/15
Postsecondary	Indianapolis-Carmel-Anderson MSA, IN	Y	48670 FQ	58800 MW	75980 TQ	USBLS	5/15
Postsecondary	Iowa	Y	54050 FQ	69850 MW	89840 TQ	USBLS	5/15

AE Average entry wage	**AWR** Average wage range	**H** Hourly	**LR** Low end range	**MTC** Median total compensation	**TCC** Total cash compensation
AEX Average experienced wage	**B** Biweekly	**HI** Highest wage paid	**M** Monthly	**MW** Median wage paid	**TQ** Third quartile wage
ATC Average total compensation	**D** Daily	**HR** High end range	**MCC** Median cash compensation	**MWR** Median wage range	**W** Weekly
AW Average wage paid	**FQ** First quartile wage	**LO** Lowest wage paid	**ME** Median entry wage	**S** See annotated source	**Y** Yearly

1324

Occupation/Type/Industry	Location	Per	Low	Mid	High	Source	Date
Psychology Teacher							
Postsecondary	Des Moines-West Des Moines MSA, IA	Y	47000 FQ	59720 MW	80770 TQ	USBLS	5/15
Postsecondary	Kansas	Y	43950 FQ	58580 MW	76070 TQ	USBLS	5/15
Postsecondary	Kentucky	Y	53540 FQ	71360 MW	99390 TQ	USBLS	5/15
Postsecondary	Louisville-Jefferson County MSA, KY-IN	Y	52600 FQ	72390 MW	104980 TQ	USBLS	5/15
Postsecondary	Louisiana	Y	36960 FQ	57370 MW	76800 TQ	USBLS	5/15
Postsecondary	Maine	Y	50510 FQ	68840 MW	82670 TQ	USBLS	5/15
Postsecondary	Portland-South Portland MSA, ME	Y	43100 FQ	63760 MW	78310 TQ	USBLS	5/15
Postsecondary	Maryland	Y	45397 AE	90450 MW	112976 AEX	MDBLS	4/16
Postsecondary	Baltimore-Columbia-Towson MSA, MD	Y	63630 FQ	85040 MW	137980 TQ	USBLS	5/15
Postsecondary	Massachusetts	Y	60560 FQ	80100 MW	120950 TQ	USBLS	5/15
Postsecondary	Boston-Cambridge-Newton NECTA, MA	Y	65050 FQ	93590 MW	148440 TQ	USBLS	5/15
Postsecondary	Worcester MSA, MA-CT	Y	52560 FQ	62720 MW	77120 TQ	USBLS	5/15
Postsecondary	Michigan	Y	56920 FQ	80060 MW	109160 TQ	USBLS	5/15
Postsecondary	Detroit-Dearborn-Livonia PMSA, MI	Y	64900 FQ	80200 MW	97750 TQ	USBLS	5/15
Postsecondary	Grand Rapids-Wyoming MSA, MI	Y	41470 FQ	68530 MW	80310 TQ	USBLS	5/15
Postsecondary	Minnesota	Y	49465 FQ	66612 MW	84112 TQ	MNBLS	1/16-3/16
Postsecondary	Minneapolis-St. Paul-Bloomington MSA, MN-WI	Y	48911 FQ	65483 MW	83154 TQ	MNBLS	1/16-3/16
Postsecondary	Mississippi	Y	44810 FQ	58680 MW	73780 TQ	USBLS	5/15
Postsecondary	Jackson MSA, MS	Y	33660 FQ	40780 MW	47710 TQ	USBLS	5/15
Postsecondary	Missouri	Y	53360 FQ	71640 MW	94960 TQ	USBLS	5/15
Postsecondary	Kansas City MSA, MO-KS	Y	57820 FQ	73840 MW	93550 TQ	USBLS	5/15
Postsecondary	St. Louis MSA, MO-IL	Y	54810 FQ	71420 MW	93830 TQ	USBLS	5/15
Postsecondary	Montana	Y	17950 FQ	19150 MW	45470 TQ	USBLS	5/15
Postsecondary	Nebraska	Y	53575 FQ	73110 MW	96425 TQ	NEBLS	7/16-9/16
Postsecondary	Omaha-Council Bluffs MSA, NE-IA	Y	49025 FQ	75070 MW	101205 TQ	NEBLS	7/16-9/16
Postsecondary	New Hampshire	Y	54135 AE	78504 MW	100846 AEX	NHBLS	6/16
Postsecondary	New Jersey	Y	58150 FQ	76840 MW	105990 TQ	USBLS	5/15
Postsecondary	Camden PMSA, NJ	Y	55400 FQ	74880 MW	99500 TQ	USBLS	5/15
Postsecondary	Newark PMSA, NJ-PA	Y	63800 FQ	81110 MW	115710 TQ	USBLS	5/15
Postsecondary	New Mexico	Y	50260 FQ	82790 MW	100480 TQ	USBLS	5/15
Postsecondary	Albuquerque MSA, NM	Y	84230 FQ	94910 MW	108600 TQ	USBLS	5/15
Postsecondary	New York	Y	47280 AE	80530 MW	118520 AEX	NYBLS	1/16-3/16
Postsecondary	Buffalo-Cheektowaga-Niagara Falls MSA, NY	Y	45580 FQ	71030 MW	94370 TQ	USBLS	5/15
Postsecondary	Nassau County-Suffolk County PMSA, NY	Y	47600 FQ	66570 MW	95410 TQ	USBLS	5/15
Postsecondary	New York-Jersey City-White Plains PMSA, NY-NJ	Y	59880 FQ	87280 MW	132770 TQ	USBLS	5/15
Postsecondary	Rochester MSA, NY	Y	58220 FQ	77590 MW	103140 TQ	USBLS	5/15
Postsecondary	North Carolina	Y	51370 FQ	63540 MW	79750 TQ	USBLS	5/15
Postsecondary	Charlotte-Concord-Gastonia MSA, NC-SC	Y	49700 FQ	61220 MW	76460 TQ	USBLS	5/15
Postsecondary	Raleigh MSA, NC	Y	59480 FQ	73660 MW	93560 TQ	USBLS	5/15
Postsecondary	North Dakota	Y	52390 FQ	78250 MW	98010 TQ	USBLS	5/15
Postsecondary	Fargo MSA, ND-MN	Y	74240 FQ	89400 MW	104050 TQ	USBLS	5/15
Postsecondary	Ohio	Y	54370 FQ	75080 MW	102970 TQ	USBLS	5/15
Postsecondary	Cincinnati MSA, OH-KY-IN	Y	60480 FQ	83460 MW	110150 TQ	USBLS	5/15
Postsecondary	Columbus MSA, OH	Y	53010 FQ	70440 MW	93750 TQ	USBLS	5/15
Postsecondary	Oregon	Y	66064 FQ	81683 MW	103809 TQ	ORBLS	2016
Postsecondary	Portland-Vancouver-Hillsboro MSA, OR-WA	Y	61810 FQ	78910 MW	100240 TQ	USBLS	5/15
Postsecondary	Pennsylvania	Y	53880 FQ	71910 MW	94160 TQ	USBLS	5/15
Postsecondary	Allentown-Bethlehem-Easton MSA, PA-NJ	Y	62280 FQ	79240 MW	108470 TQ	USBLS	5/15
Postsecondary	Harrisburg-Carlisle MSA, PA	Y	56800 FQ	72230 MW	93020 TQ	USBLS	5/15
Postsecondary	Montgomery County-Bucks County-Chester County PMSA, PA	Y	44600 FQ	66730 MW	91750 TQ	USBLS	5/15
Postsecondary	Philadelphia PMSA, PA	Y	51490 FQ	69780 MW	91490 TQ	USBLS	5/15
Postsecondary	Pittsburgh MSA, PA	Y	54480 FQ	70140 MW	90070 TQ	USBLS	5/15
Postsecondary	Rhode Island	Y	62250 FQ	78960 MW	111590 TQ	USBLS	5/15

Occupation/Type/Industry	Location	Per	Low	Mid	High	Source	Date
Psychology Teacher							
Postsecondary	Providence-Warwick MSA, RI-MA	Y	60350 FQ	76100 MW	107830 TQ	USBLS	5/15
Postsecondary	South Carolina	Y	54610 FQ	69700 MW	84700 TQ	USBLS	5/15
Postsecondary	Columbia MSA, SC	Y	53180 FQ	69450 MW	84290 TQ	USBLS	5/15
Postsecondary	Greenville-Anderson-Mauldin MSA, SC	Y	58820 FQ	74980 MW	100090 TQ	USBLS	5/15
Postsecondary	South Dakota	Y	54700 FQ	61740 MW	81250 TQ	USBLS	5/15
Postsecondary	Tennessee	Y	35450 FQ	53430 MW	73560 TQ	USBLS	5/15
Postsecondary	Knoxville MSA, TN	Y	36130 FQ	51480 MW	74060 TQ	USBLS	5/15
Postsecondary	Memphis MSA, TN-MS-AR	Y	41720 FQ	57960 MW	74910 TQ	USBLS	5/15
Postsecondary	Nashville-Davidson–Murfreesboro–Franklin MSA, TN	Y	36940 FQ	54940 MW	77650 TQ	USBLS	5/15
Postsecondary	Texas	Y	37780 FQ	58480 MW	80430 TQ	USBLS	5/15
Postsecondary	Austin-Round Rock MSA, TX	Y	43050 FQ	57180 MW	78540 TQ	USBLS	5/15
Postsecondary	Dallas-Plano-Irving PMSA, TX	Y	39460 FQ	60260 MW	79060 TQ	USBLS	5/15
Postsecondary	Fort Worth-Arlington PMSA, TX	Y	19200 FQ	46620 MW	68120 TQ	USBLS	5/15
Postsecondary	Houston-The Woodlands-Sugar Land MSA, TX	Y	30710 FQ	58230 MW	82450 TQ	USBLS	5/15
Postsecondary	San Antonio-New Braunfels MSA, TX	Y	25020 FQ	60810 MW	88530 TQ	USBLS	5/15
Postsecondary	Utah	Y	54260 FQ	76900 MW	96620 TQ	USBLS	5/15
Postsecondary	Salt Lake City MSA, UT	Y	43610 FQ	66650 MW	90210 TQ	USBLS	5/15
Postsecondary	Burlington-South Burlington MSA, VT	Y	39800 FQ	49960 MW	74570 TQ	USBLS	5/15
Postsecondary	Virginia	Y	49760 FQ	68210 MW	93050 TQ	USBLS	5/15
Postsecondary	Richmond MSA, VA	Y	39760 FQ	66960 MW	94320 TQ	USBLS	5/15
Postsecondary	Virginia Beach-Norfolk-Newport News MSA, VA-NC	Y	47560 FQ	65960 MW	86320 TQ	USBLS	5/15
Postsecondary	Washington	Y		66165 AW		WABLS	3/16
Postsecondary	Seattle-Bellevue-Everett PMSA, WA	Y		77203 AW		WABLS	3/16
Postsecondary	Tacoma-Lakewood PMSA, WA	Y		65678 AW		WABLS	3/16
Postsecondary	West Virginia	Y	44290 FQ	57590 MW	73880 TQ	USBLS	5/15
Postsecondary	Wisconsin	Y	48670 FQ	62490 MW	78480 TQ	USBLS	5/15
Postsecondary	Milwaukee-Waukesha-West Allis MSA, WI	Y	46080 FQ	68570 MW	86220 TQ	USBLS	5/15
Postsecondary	Wyoming	Y	64060 FQ	71410 MW	79120 TQ	USBLS	5/15
Postsecondary	Puerto Rico	Y	50150 FQ	62130 MW	71660 TQ	USBLS	5/15
Postsecondary	San Juan-Carolina-Caguas MSA, PR	Y	52450 FQ	64160 MW	73070 TQ	USBLS	5/15
Psychometrician							
State Government	North Carolina	Y	59969 LO		99446 HI	NCGOV	7/1/16
Psychometrist	United States	Y		25000-58000 AWR		EXHC07	2016
Public Address System and Other Announcer	Arizona	Y	20470 FQ	23290 MW	28290 TQ	USBLS	5/15
	Phoenix-Mesa-Scottsdale MSA, AZ	Y	21260 FQ	23480 MW	26990 TQ	USBLS	5/15
	California	H	9.68 FQ	13.30 MW	21.25 TQ	CABLS	1/16-3/16
	Los Angeles-Long Beach-Glendale PMSA, CA	H	9.60 FQ	12.80 MW	17.71 TQ	CABLS	1/16-3/16
	Oakland-Hayward-Berkeley PMSA, CA	H	12.68 FQ	13.64 MW	14.60 TQ	CABLS	1/16-3/16
	Sacramento–Roseville–Arden-Arcade MSA, CA	H	10.10 FQ	16.33 MW	26.77 TQ	CABLS	1/16-3/16
	San Diego-Carlsbad MSA, CA	H	9.53 FQ	12.74 MW	15.37 TQ	CABLS	1/16-3/16
	San Francisco-Redwood City-South San Francisco PMSA, CA	H	9.85 FQ	12.30 MW	14.66 TQ	CABLS	1/16-3/16
	Colorado	Y	22820 FQ	31190 MW	57260 TQ	USBLS	5/15
	Denver-Aurora-Lakewood MSA, CO	Y	26680 FQ	54860 MW	66090 TQ	USBLS	5/15
	Washington-Arlington-Alexandria PMSA, DC-VA-MD-WV	Y	28130 FQ	53250 MW	61140 TQ	USBLS	5/15
	Florida	H	9.04 AE	14.02 MW	19.96 AEX	FLBLS	7/16-9/16

AE	Average entry wage	AWR	Average wage range	H	Hourly	LR	Low end range	MTC	Median total compensation	TCC	Total cash compensation
AEX	Average experienced wage	B	Biweekly	HI	Highest wage paid	M	Monthly	MW	Median wage paid	TQ	Third quartile wage
ATC	Average total compensation	D	Daily	HR	High end range	MCC	Median cash compensation	MWR	Median wage range	W	Weekly
AW	Average wage paid	FQ	First quartile wage	LO	Lowest wage paid	ME	Median entry wage	S	See annotated source	Y	Yearly

Occupation/Type/Industry	Location	Per	Low	Mid	High	Source	Date
Public Address System and Other Announcer							
	Fort Lauderdale-Pompano Beach-Deerfield Beach PMSA, FL	H	8.86 AE	9.30 MW	10.18 AEX	FLBLS	7/16-9/16
	Miami-Miami Beach-Kendall PMSA, FL	H	11.07 AE	31.19 MW	32.49 AEX	FLBLS	7/16-9/16
	Orlando-Kissimmee-Sanford MSA, FL	H	10.11 AE	11.77 MW	13.84 AEX	FLBLS	7/16-9/16
	Tampa-St. Petersburg-Clearwater MSA, FL	H	8.83 AE	9.13 MW	12.77 AEX	FLBLS	7/16-9/16
	Georgia	Y	16900 FQ	18490 MW	32810 TQ	USBLS	5/15
	Illinois	Y	20860 FQ	39100 MW	59210 TQ	USBLS	5/15
	Chicago-Naperville-Arlington Heights PMSA, IL	Y	24050 FQ	53430 MW	60240 TQ	USBLS	5/15
	Indiana	Y	18200 FQ	31960 MW	38130 TQ	USBLS	5/15
	Iowa	Y	18070 FQ	24580 MW	36210 TQ	USBLS	5/15
	Kentucky	Y	19340 FQ	23440 MW	45350 TQ	USBLS	5/15
	Louisville-Jefferson County MSA, KY-IN	Y	20580 FQ	31160 MW	39280 TQ	USBLS	5/15
	Louisiana	Y	18520 FQ	26670 MW	39380 TQ	USBLS	5/15
	New Orleans-Metairie MSA, LA	Y	20850 FQ	27570 MW	31190 TQ	USBLS	5/15
	Massachusetts	Y	24920 FQ	54280 MW	59740 TQ	USBLS	5/15
	Boston-Cambridge-Newton NECTA, MA	Y	52580 FQ	56810 MW	61040 TQ	USBLS	5/15
	Michigan	Y	18630 FQ	21250 MW	39940 TQ	USBLS	5/15
	Detroit-Dearborn-Livonia PMSA, MI	Y	19590 FQ	23300 MW	44310 TQ	USBLS	5/15
	Grand Rapids-Wyoming MSA, MI	Y	18820 FQ	36850 MW	58110 TQ	USBLS	5/15
	Minnesota	Y	23135 FQ	29012 MW	46068 TQ	MNBLS	1/16-3/16
	Minneapolis-St. Paul-Bloomington MSA, MN-WI	Y	23014 FQ	28457 MW	42348 TQ	MNBLS	1/16-3/16
	Missouri	Y	25040 FQ	30990 MW	56550 TQ	USBLS	5/15
	St. Louis MSA, MO-IL	Y	19470 FQ	54490 MW	63040 TQ	USBLS	5/15
	Montana	Y	18700 FQ	24020 MW	32710 TQ	USBLS	5/15
	Nebraska	Y	18865 FQ	23385 MW	34655 TQ	NEBLS	7/16-9/16
	Omaha-Council Bluffs MSA, NE-IA	Y	18775 FQ	23530 MW	34970 TQ	NEBLS	7/16-9/16
	Nevada	Y	18080 FQ	28440 MW	45080 TQ	USBLS	5/15
	Las Vegas-Henderson-Paradise MSA, NV	Y	17540 FQ	20050 MW	44400 TQ	USBLS	5/15
	New Jersey	Y	20340 FQ	43090 MW	58020 TQ	USBLS	5/15
	New Mexico	Y	18730 FQ	25250 MW	28730 TQ	USBLS	5/15
	New York	Y	24770 AE	32430 MW	60990 AEX	NYBLS	1/16-3/16
	Nassau County-Suffolk County PMSA, NY	Y	28030 FQ	34570 MW	55930 TQ	USBLS	5/15
	New York-Jersey City-White Plains PMSA, NY-NJ	Y	27130 FQ	44440 MW	56760 TQ	USBLS	5/15
	North Carolina	Y	17420 FQ	19570 MW	34820 TQ	USBLS	5/15
	Charlotte-Concord-Gastonia MSA, NC-SC	Y	16890 FQ	18460 MW	22370 TQ	USBLS	5/15
	North Dakota	Y	20050 FQ	24600 MW	36790 TQ	USBLS	5/15
	Fargo MSA, ND-MN	Y	20140 FQ	24490 MW	32070 TQ	USBLS	5/15
	Ohio	Y	18400 FQ	20890 MW	46450 TQ	USBLS	5/15
	Columbus MSA, OH	Y	17920 FQ	18990 MW	22820 TQ	USBLS	5/15
	Oregon	H	9.55 FQ	10.65 MW	11.79 TQ	ORBLS	2016
	Portland-Vancouver-Hillsboro MSA, OR-WA	Y	21230 FQ	22890 MW	24650 TQ	USBLS	5/15
	Pennsylvania	Y	19250 FQ	31270 MW	110820 TQ	USBLS	5/15
	South Carolina	Y	18930 FQ	22980 MW	34880 TQ	USBLS	5/15
	South Dakota	Y	18910 FQ	21590 MW	26670 TQ	USBLS	5/15
	Sioux Falls MSA, SD	Y	18640 FQ	20040 MW	27830 TQ	USBLS	5/15
	Tennessee	Y	16880 FQ	18220 MW	19570 TQ	USBLS	5/15
	Knoxville MSA, TN	Y	16850 FQ	18180 MW	19510 TQ	USBLS	5/15
	Memphis MSA, TN-MS-AR	Y	17290 FQ	18970 MW	26980 TQ	USBLS	5/15
	Texas	Y	17910 FQ	21180 MW	36170 TQ	USBLS	5/15
	Fort Worth-Arlington PMSA, TX	Y	17070 FQ	18620 MW	23710 TQ	USBLS	5/15
	Houston-The Woodlands-Sugar Land MSA, TX	Y	18300 FQ	22060 MW	36430 TQ	USBLS	5/15

AE	Average entry wage	AWR	Average wage range	H	Hourly	LR	Low end range	MTC	Median total compensation	TCC	Total cash compensation
AEX	Average experienced wage	B	Biweekly	HI	Highest wage paid	M	Monthly	MW	Median wage paid	TQ	Third quartile wage
ATC	Average total compensation	D	Daily	HR	High end range	MCC	Median cash compensation	MWR	Median wage range	W	Weekly
AW	Average wage paid	FQ	First quartile wage	LO	Lowest wage paid	ME	Median entry wage	S	See annotated source	Y	Yearly

Occupation/Type/Industry	Location	Per	Low	Mid	High	Source	Date
Public Address System and Other Announcer	San Antonio-New Braunfels MSA, TX	Y	17310 FQ	18830 MW	20690 TQ	USBLS	5/15
	Wisconsin	Y	19100 FQ	30030 MW	48650 TQ	USBLS	5/15
	Milwaukee-Waukesha-West Allis MSA, WI	Y	18490 FQ	27220 MW	49690 TQ	USBLS	5/15
Public Affairs Manager							
Police Department, Municipal Government	Fremont, CA	Y			121422 HI	CACIT	6/28/16
Public Defender							
Municipal Government	San Francisco, CA	Y			231056 HI	CACIT	6/28/16
State Government	New Mexico	H	19.08 LO		42.56 HI	NMGOV	7/30/16
State Government	Ohio	H			72.45 HI	OHGOV	2015
Public Fiduciary							
County Government	Gila County, AZ	Y			70385 HI	AZGOV	2017
County Government	Navajo County, AZ	Y			55744 HI	AZGOV	2017
Public Health Nurse	San Francisco, CA	B	4479 LO		5884 HI	SFGOV	2016-2018
Public Health Physician							
Municipal Government	Long Beach, CA	Y			158693 HI	CACIT	6/28/16
Public Health Veterinarian							
State Government	Ohio	H			28.11 HI	OHGOV	2015
Public Information Officer							
Police Department, Municipal Government	Clovis, CA	Y			86919 HI	CACIT	9/5/16
Public Information Specialist							
Baccalaureate Institution	United States	Y		44376 MW		CHE02	2015-2016
Master's Institution	United States	Y		46876 MW		CHE02	2015-2016
Research University	United States	Y		51036 MW		CHE02	2015-2016
Public Relations and Fundraising Manager	Alabama	Y	62820 AE	96572 AW	113453 AEX	ALBLS	6/16
	Birmingham-Hoover MSA, AL	Y	67340 AE	110614 AW	132240 AEX	ALBLS	6/16
	Alaska	Y	78890 FQ	107740 MW	132770 TQ	USBLS	5/15
	Anchorage MSA, AK	Y	83530 FQ	110380 MW	130930 TQ	USBLS	5/15
	Arizona	Y	71030 FQ	89160 MW	114630 TQ	USBLS	5/15
	Phoenix-Mesa-Scottsdale MSA, AZ	Y	74410 FQ	91840 MW	118620 TQ	USBLS	5/15
	Tucson MSA, AZ	Y	63010 FQ	77570 MW	96100 TQ	USBLS	5/15
	Arkansas	Y	40540 FQ	69760 MW	97560 TQ	USBLS	5/15
	Little Rock-North Little Rock-Conway MSA, AR	Y	37860 FQ	64680 MW	85280 TQ	USBLS	5/15
	California	H	42.04 FQ	57.70 MW	77.13 TQ	CABLS	1/16-3/16
	Anaheim-Santa Ana-Irvine PMSA, CA	H	53.92 FQ	67.52 MW	79.37 TQ	CABLS	1/16-3/16
	Los Angeles-Long Beach-Glendale PMSA, CA	H	42.21 FQ	54.68 MW	77.37 TQ	CABLS	1/16-3/16
	Oakland-Hayward-Berkeley PMSA, CA	H	42.71 FQ	56.88 MW	75.06 TQ	CABLS	1/16-3/16
	Riverside-San Bernardino-Ontario MSA, CA	H	33.95 FQ	45.34 MW	58.45 TQ	CABLS	1/16-3/16
	Sacramento–Roseville–Arden-Arcade MSA, CA	H	40.51 FQ	56.07 MW	75.27 TQ	CABLS	1/16-3/16
	San Diego-Carlsbad MSA, CA	H	43.10 FQ	56.44 MW	75.80 TQ	CABLS	1/16-3/16
	San Francisco-Redwood City-South San Francisco PMSA, CA	H	47.94 FQ	64.75 MW	82.15 TQ	CABLS	1/16-3/16
	Colorado	Y	90850 FQ	120560 MW	160150 TQ	USBLS	5/15
	Denver-Aurora-Lakewood MSA, CO	Y	93750 FQ	123480 MW	163110 TQ	USBLS	5/15
	Connecticut	Y		113121 MW		CTBLS	1/16-3/16
	Bridgeport-Stamford-Norwalk MSA, CT	Y	88210 FQ	114550 MW	151680 TQ	USBLS	5/15
	Hartford-West Hartford-East Hartford MSA, CT	Y	78210 FQ	109350 MW	141940 TQ	USBLS	5/15
	Delaware	Y	102710 FQ	136060 MW	169020 TQ	USBLS	5/15

AE	Average entry wage	AWR	Average wage range	H	Hourly	LR	Low end range	MTC	Median total compensation	TCC	Total cash compensation
AEX	Average experienced wage	B	Biweekly	HI	Highest wage paid	M	Monthly	MW	Median wage paid	TQ	Third quartile wage
ATC	Average total compensation	D	Daily	HR	High end range	MCC	Median cash compensation	MWR	Median wage range	W	Weekly
AW	Average wage paid	FQ	First quartile wage	LO	Lowest wage paid	ME	Median entry wage	S	See annotated source	Y	Yearly

Public Relations and Fundraising Manager

Occupation/Type/Industry	Location	Per	Low	Mid	High	Source	Date
Public Relations and Fundraising Manager	Wilmington PMSA, DE-MD-NJ	Y	103670 FQ	136870 MW	169140 TQ	USBLS	5/15
	District of Columbia	Y	92220 FQ	138880 MW		USBLS	5/15
	Washington-Arlington-Alexandria PMSA, DC-VA-MD-WV	Y	96380 FQ	140590 MW		USBLS	5/15
	Florida	H	37.37 AE	54.07 MW	69.95 AEX	FLBLS	7/16-9/16
	Fort Lauderdale-Pompano Beach-Deerfield Beach PMSA, FL	H	38.96 AE	60.41 MW	74.58 AEX	FLBLS	7/16-9/16
	Miami-Miami Beach-Kendall PMSA, FL	H	42.02 AE	62.23 MW	79.63 AEX	FLBLS	7/16-9/16
	Orlando-Kissimmee-Sanford MSA, FL	H	37.35 AE	50.40 MW	65.63 AEX	FLBLS	7/16-9/16
	Tampa-St. Petersburg-Clearwater MSA, FL	H	36.78 AE	51.85 MW	67.21 AEX	FLBLS	7/16-9/16
	Georgia	Y	73970 FQ	103850 MW	138810 TQ	USBLS	5/15
	Atlanta-Sandy Springs-Roswell MSA, GA	Y	75020 FQ	106940 MW	142380 TQ	USBLS	5/15
	Hawaii	Y	60810 FQ	80620 MW	110640 TQ	USBLS	5/15
	Urban Honolulu MSA, HI	Y	60560 FQ	79490 MW	110120 TQ	USBLS	5/15
	Idaho	Y	47890 FQ	69420 MW	89730 TQ	USBLS	5/15
	Boise City MSA, ID	Y	53970 FQ	72260 MW	92110 TQ	USBLS	5/15
	Illinois	Y	66870 FQ	94440 MW	136860 TQ	USBLS	5/15
	Chicago-Naperville-Arlington Heights PMSA, IL	Y	70840 FQ	97140 MW	141100 TQ	USBLS	5/15
	Lake County-Kenosha County PMSA, IL-WI	Y	70780 FQ	115950 MW	160530 TQ	USBLS	5/15
	Indiana	Y	65250 FQ	86680 MW	115680 TQ	USBLS	5/15
	Gary PMSA, IN	Y	54540 FQ	66170 MW	103580 TQ	USBLS	5/15
	Indianapolis-Carmel-Anderson MSA, IN	Y	65650 FQ	88350 MW	122390 TQ	USBLS	5/15
	Iowa	Y	59900 FQ	78050 MW	102490 TQ	USBLS	5/15
	Des Moines-West Des Moines MSA, IA	Y	60920 FQ	81820 MW	103670 TQ	USBLS	5/15
	Kansas	Y	62860 FQ	83880 MW	111460 TQ	USBLS	5/15
	Wichita MSA, KS	Y	53310 FQ	62870 MW	91530 TQ	USBLS	5/15
	Kentucky	Y	56810 FQ	74220 MW	101570 TQ	USBLS	5/15
	Louisville-Jefferson County MSA, KY-IN	Y	56590 FQ	76250 MW	109290 TQ	USBLS	5/15
	Louisiana	Y	52520 FQ	71260 MW	97870 TQ	USBLS	5/15
	Baton Rouge MSA, LA	Y	60090 FQ	74170 MW	99170 TQ	USBLS	5/15
	New Orleans-Metairie MSA, LA	Y	57880 FQ	75100 MW	112430 TQ	USBLS	5/15
	Maine	Y	66370 FQ	81170 MW	97710 TQ	USBLS	5/15
	Portland-South Portland MSA, ME	Y	67930 FQ	80410 MW	113520 TQ	USBLS	5/15
	Maryland	Y	74337 AE	117317 MW	138807 AEX	MDBLS	4/16
	Baltimore-Columbia-Towson MSA, MD	Y	80260 FQ	107930 MW	140030 TQ	USBLS	5/15
	Massachusetts	Y	80720 FQ	110270 MW	149200 TQ	USBLS	5/15
	Boston-Cambridge-Newton NECTA, MA	Y	83300 FQ	113960 MW	151340 TQ	USBLS	5/15
	Worcester MSA, MA-CT	Y	72240 FQ	96330 MW	129190 TQ	USBLS	5/15
	Michigan	Y	69570 FQ	95610 MW	129520 TQ	USBLS	5/15
	Detroit-Dearborn-Livonia PMSA, MI	Y	86240 FQ	118800 MW	162560 TQ	USBLS	5/15
	Grand Rapids-Wyoming MSA, MI	Y	63000 FQ	76800 MW	106980 TQ	USBLS	5/15
	Minnesota	Y	81979 FQ	100452 MW	130661 TQ	MNBLS	1/16-3/16
	Minneapolis-St. Paul-Bloomington MSA, MN-WI	Y	84276 FQ	102860 MW	134136 TQ	MNBLS	1/16-3/16
	Mississippi	Y	45440 FQ	61970 MW	88390 TQ	USBLS	5/15
	Jackson MSA, MS	Y	47440 FQ	60960 MW	87030 TQ	USBLS	5/15
	Missouri	Y	76730 FQ	99670 MW	136660 TQ	USBLS	5/15
	Kansas City MSA, MO-KS	Y	78430 FQ	95830 MW	131590 TQ	USBLS	5/15
	St. Louis MSA, MO-IL	Y	77320 FQ	105130 MW	143700 TQ	USBLS	5/15
	Montana	Y	56790 FQ	75470 MW	110250 TQ	USBLS	5/15
	Billings MSA, MT	Y	51120 FQ	81940 MW	119960 TQ	USBLS	5/15
	Nebraska	Y	61525 FQ	78555 MW	99225 TQ	NEBLS	7/16-9/16

Occupation/Type/Industry	Location	Per	Low	Mid	High	Source	Date
Public Relations and Fundraising Manager	Omaha-Council Bluffs MSA, NE-IA	Y	65180 FQ	81170 MW	99940 TQ	NEBLS	7/16-9/16
	Nevada	Y	65250 FQ	84250 MW	123670 TQ	USBLS	5/15
	Las Vegas-Henderson-Paradise MSA, NV	Y	64430 FQ	83640 MW	124190 TQ	USBLS	5/15
	New Hampshire	H	32.21 AE	47.57 MW	65.32 AEX	NHBLS	6/16
	Manchester NECTA, NH	H	28.15 AE	39.90 MW	57.38 AEX	NHBLS	6/16
	New Jersey	Y	100120 FQ	132360 MW	175630 TQ	USBLS	5/15
	Camden PMSA, NJ	Y	75620 FQ	97020 MW	139710 TQ	USBLS	5/15
	Newark PMSA, NJ-PA	Y	106770 FQ	145060 MW		USBLS	5/15
	Trenton MSA, NJ	Y	83260 FQ	97270 MW	126260 TQ	USBLS	5/15
	New Mexico	Y	61580 FQ	89150 MW	115890 TQ	USBLS	5/15
	Albuquerque MSA, NM	Y	54680 FQ	87110 MW	118550 TQ	USBLS	5/15
	New York	Y	86410 AE	144030 MW		NYBLS	1/16-3/16
	Buffalo-Cheektowaga-Niagara Falls MSA, NY	Y	68700 FQ	87790 MW	109930 TQ	USBLS	5/15
	Nassau County-Suffolk County PMSA, NY	Y	84480 FQ	101160 MW	135360 TQ	USBLS	5/15
	New York-Jersey City-White Plains PMSA, NY-NJ	Y	115700 FQ	152220 MW		USBLS	5/15
	Rochester MSA, NY	Y	75340 FQ	92640 MW	123320 TQ	USBLS	5/15
	North Carolina	Y	77980 FQ	99540 MW	136030 TQ	USBLS	5/15
	Charlotte-Concord-Gastonia MSA, NC-SC	Y	76680 FQ	96020 MW	127610 TQ	USBLS	5/15
	Raleigh MSA, NC	Y	76680 FQ	100280 MW	138050 TQ	USBLS	5/15
	North Dakota	Y	58800 FQ	79410 MW	101040 TQ	USBLS	5/15
	Fargo MSA, ND-MN	Y	72010 FQ	95500 MW	119810 TQ	USBLS	5/15
	Ohio	Y	72460 FQ	93250 MW	122690 TQ	USBLS	5/15
	Cincinnati MSA, OH-KY-IN	Y	69490 FQ	90020 MW	120230 TQ	USBLS	5/15
	Cleveland-Elyria MSA, OH	Y	76210 FQ	102060 MW	136600 TQ	USBLS	5/15
	Columbus MSA, OH	Y	76950 FQ	97950 MW	129090 TQ	USBLS	5/15
	Oklahoma	Y	52120 FQ	72760 MW	106750 TQ	USBLS	5/15
	Oklahoma City MSA, OK	Y	51940 FQ	77740 MW	116870 TQ	USBLS	5/15
	Tulsa MSA, OK	Y	57040 FQ	74420 MW	99670 TQ	USBLS	5/15
	Oregon	H	28.99 FQ	37.98 MW	48.59 TQ	ORBLS	2016
	Portland-Vancouver-Hillsboro MSA, OR-WA	Y	64450 FQ	78840 MW	100880 TQ	USBLS	5/15
	Pennsylvania	Y	78630 FQ	107050 MW	144050 TQ	USBLS	5/15
	Allentown-Bethlehem-Easton MSA, PA-NJ	Y	83930 FQ	113470 MW	160900 TQ	USBLS	5/15
	Harrisburg-Carlisle MSA, PA	Y	82370 FQ	96050 MW	120660 TQ	USBLS	5/15
	Montgomery County-Bucks County-Chester County PMSA, PA	Y	96170 FQ	123370 MW	159860 TQ	USBLS	5/15
	Philadelphia PMSA, PA	Y	96950 FQ	123760 MW	157870 TQ	USBLS	5/15
	Pittsburgh MSA, PA	Y	62890 FQ	90560 MW	128260 TQ	USBLS	5/15
	Rhode Island	Y	93990 FQ	124220 MW	178180 TQ	USBLS	5/15
	Providence-Warwick MSA, RI-MA	Y	91490 FQ	121100 MW	171700 TQ	USBLS	5/15
	South Carolina	Y	56020 FQ	72050 MW	94400 TQ	USBLS	5/15
	Charleston-North Charleston MSA, SC	Y	62490 FQ	85060 MW	108680 TQ	USBLS	5/15
	Columbia MSA, SC	Y	55650 FQ	70430 MW	90120 TQ	USBLS	5/15
	Greenville-Anderson-Mauldin MSA, SC	Y	56310 FQ	70020 MW	90970 TQ	USBLS	5/15
	Tennessee	Y	60040 FQ	81620 MW	106060 TQ	USBLS	5/15
	Knoxville MSA, TN	Y	46470 FQ	58890 MW	87480 TQ	USBLS	5/15
	Memphis MSA, TN-MS-AR	Y	74880 FQ	92000 MW	114890 TQ	USBLS	5/15
	Nashville-Davidson–Murfreesboro–Franklin MSA, TN	Y	67970 FQ	84220 MW	113140 TQ	USBLS	5/15
	Texas	Y	83510 FQ	114840 MW	160920 TQ	USBLS	5/15
	Austin-Round Rock MSA, TX	Y	78450 FQ	104200 MW	139920 TQ	USBLS	5/15
	Dallas-Plano-Irving PMSA, TX	Y	89170 FQ	119750 MW	165760 TQ	USBLS	5/15
	Fort Worth-Arlington PMSA, TX	Y	77390 FQ	99660 MW	168810 TQ	USBLS	5/15
	Houston-The Woodlands-Sugar Land MSA, TX	Y	92960 FQ	122770 MW	163500 TQ	USBLS	5/15
	San Antonio-New Braunfels MSA, TX	Y	80830 FQ	112490 MW	157890 TQ	USBLS	5/15
	Utah	Y	64130 FQ	87540 MW	114400 TQ	USBLS	5/15

AE	Average entry wage	AWR	Average wage range	H	Hourly
AEX	Average experienced wage	B	Biweekly	HI	Highest wage paid
ATC	Average total compensation	D	Daily	HR	High end range
AW	Average wage paid	FQ	First quartile wage	LO	Lowest wage paid

LR	Low end range	MTC	Median total compensation	TCC	Total cash compensation
M	Monthly	MW	Median wage paid	TQ	Third quartile wage
MCC	Median cash compensation	MWR	Median wage range	W	Weekly
ME	Median entry wage	S	See annotated source	Y	Yearly

Occupation/Type/Industry	Location	Per	Low	Mid	High	Source	Date
Public Relations and Fundraising Manager	Provo-Orem MSA, UT	Y	81830 FQ	106790 MW	124400 TQ	USBLS	5/15
	Salt Lake City MSA, UT	Y	65200 FQ	85910 MW	111370 TQ	USBLS	5/15
	Vermont	Y	63210 FQ	86660 MW	127340 TQ	USBLS	5/15
	Burlington-South Burlington MSA, VT	Y	61760 FQ	85970 MW	103610 TQ	USBLS	5/15
	Virginia	Y	98080 FQ	130510 MW	164870 TQ	USBLS	5/15
	Richmond MSA, VA	Y	81280 FQ	99010 MW	127320 TQ	USBLS	5/15
	Virginia Beach-Norfolk-Newport News MSA, VA-NC	Y	75660 FQ	102370 MW	124250 TQ	USBLS	5/15
	Washington	H	37.70 FQ	47.33 MW	62.05 TQ	WABLS	3/16
	Seattle-Bellevue-Everett PMSA, WA	H	39.13 FQ	49.02 MW	64.71 TQ	WABLS	3/16
	Tacoma-Lakewood PMSA, WA	H	40.21 FQ	46.17 MW	55.01 TQ	WABLS	3/16
	West Virginia	Y	50150 FQ	62450 MW	82130 TQ	USBLS	5/15
	Wisconsin	Y	66150 FQ	87210 MW	116120 TQ	USBLS	5/15
	Madison MSA, WI	Y	79760 FQ	94440 MW	121860 TQ	USBLS	5/15
	Milwaukee-Waukesha-West Allis MSA, WI	Y	63120 FQ	82620 MW	114230 TQ	USBLS	5/15
	Puerto Rico	Y	41280 FQ	55350 MW	80540 TQ	USBLS	5/15
	San Juan-Carolina-Caguas MSA, PR	Y	43530 FQ	58400 MW	83330 TQ	USBLS	5/15
Public Relations Executive Senior Level	United States	Y		201250 MW		CNBC06	2016
Public Relations Professional	Central	Y		75000 MW		PRWK	2016
	Mid-Atlantic	Y		97500 MW		PRWK	2016
	Midwest	Y		85000 MW		PRWK	2016
	Northeast	Y		105000 MW		PRWK	2016
	Northwest	Y		134500 MW		PRWK	2016
	Plains	Y		93000 MW		PRWK	2016
	Southeast	Y		80000 MW		PRWK	2016
	West	Y		89000 MW		PRWK	2016
Public Relations Specialist	Alabama	Y	30213 AE	51629 AW	62332 AEX	ALBLS	6/16
	Birmingham-Hoover MSA, AL	Y	37195 AE	56664 AW	66399 AEX	ALBLS	6/16
	Alaska	Y	46910 FQ	61490 MW	78020 TQ	USBLS	5/15
	Anchorage MSA, AK	Y	49590 FQ	61690 MW	78890 TQ	USBLS	5/15
	Arizona	Y	37210 FQ	50120 MW	67270 TQ	USBLS	5/15
	Phoenix-Mesa-Scottsdale MSA, AZ	Y	38590 FQ	51990 MW	69400 TQ	USBLS	5/15
	Tucson MSA, AZ	Y	30310 FQ	40170 MW	50850 TQ	USBLS	5/15
	Arkansas	Y	31090 FQ	41290 MW	59520 TQ	USBLS	5/15
	Little Rock-North Little Rock-Conway MSA, AR	Y	36140 FQ	46140 MW	59990 TQ	USBLS	5/15
	California	H	22.26 FQ	31.79 MW	45.75 TQ	CABLS	1/16-3/16
	Anaheim-Santa Ana-Irvine PMSA, CA	H	23.03 FQ	34.56 MW	48.50 TQ	CABLS	1/16-3/16
	Los Angeles-Long Beach-Glendale PMSA, CA	H	20.81 FQ	29.63 MW	41.93 TQ	CABLS	1/16-3/16
	Oakland-Hayward-Berkeley PMSA, CA	H	23.18 FQ	35.06 MW	48.16 TQ	CABLS	1/16-3/16
	Riverside-San Bernardino-Ontario MSA, CA	H	17.64 FQ	25.83 MW	30.36 TQ	CABLS	1/16-3/16
	Sacramento–Roseville–Arden-Arcade MSA, CA	H	20.80 FQ	32.06 MW	44.23 TQ	CABLS	1/16-3/16
	San Diego-Carlsbad MSA, CA	H	20.52 FQ	29.26 MW	42.02 TQ	CABLS	1/16-3/16
	San Francisco-Redwood City-South San Francisco PMSA, CA	H	27.12 FQ	38.59 MW	55.90 TQ	CABLS	1/16-3/16
	Colorado	Y	40910 FQ	52780 MW	75180 TQ	USBLS	5/15
	Denver-Aurora-Lakewood MSA, CO	Y	43180 FQ	55190 MW	77850 TQ	USBLS	5/15
	Connecticut	Y		68123 MW		CTBLS	1/16-3/16
	Bridgeport-Stamford-Norwalk MSA, CT	Y	46940 FQ	62710 MW	87820 TQ	USBLS	5/15
	Hartford-West Hartford-East Hartford MSA, CT	Y	56150 FQ	72410 MW	88610 TQ	USBLS	5/15
	Delaware	Y	45920 FQ	58550 MW	74510 TQ	USBLS	5/15
	Wilmington PMSA, DE-MD-NJ	Y	46890 FQ	59530 MW	76420 TQ	USBLS	5/15

Occupation/Type/Industry	Location	Per	Low	Mid	High	Source	Date
Public Relations Specialist	District of Columbia	Y	55230 FQ	81430 MW	122110 TQ	USBLS	5/15
	Washington-Arlington-Alexandria PMSA, DC-VA-MD-WV	Y	55640 FQ	80460 MW	119310 TQ	USBLS	5/15
	Florida	H	17.49 AE	26.40 MW	35.34 AEX	FLBLS	7/16-9/16
	Fort Lauderdale-Pompano Beach-Deerfield Beach PMSA, FL	H	19.12 AE	27.59 MW	37.84 AEX	FLBLS	7/16-9/16
	Miami-Miami Beach-Kendall PMSA, FL	H	18.58 AE	27.74 MW	34.51 AEX	FLBLS	7/16-9/16
	Orlando-Kissimmee-Sanford MSA, FL	H	15.57 AE	25.48 MW	34.84 AEX	FLBLS	7/16-9/16
	Tampa-St. Petersburg-Clearwater MSA, FL	H	18.63 AE	28.75 MW	39.98 AEX	FLBLS	7/16-9/16
	Georgia	Y	39570 FQ	53200 MW	70570 TQ	USBLS	5/15
	Atlanta-Sandy Springs-Roswell MSA, GA	Y	42880 FQ	55850 MW	73350 TQ	USBLS	5/15
	Augusta-Richmond County MSA, GA-SC	Y	27510 FQ	40610 MW	68500 TQ	USBLS	5/15
	Hawaii	Y	44040 FQ	54140 MW	70130 TQ	USBLS	5/15
	Urban Honolulu MSA, HI	Y	43950 FQ	53310 MW	70290 TQ	USBLS	5/15
	Idaho	Y	43000 FQ	58810 MW	78460 TQ	USBLS	5/15
	Boise City MSA, ID	Y	44000 FQ	60150 MW	81060 TQ	USBLS	5/15
	Illinois	Y	42180 FQ	60280 MW	78730 TQ	USBLS	5/15
	Chicago-Naperville-Arlington Heights PMSA, IL	Y	42130 FQ	61040 MW	80720 TQ	USBLS	5/15
	Lake County-Kenosha County PMSA, IL-WI	Y	49230 FQ	62140 MW	79160 TQ	USBLS	5/15
	Indiana	Y	34680 FQ	47090 MW	61990 TQ	USBLS	5/15
	Gary PMSA, IN	Y	26500 FQ	39230 MW	51680 TQ	USBLS	5/15
	Indianapolis-Carmel-Anderson MSA, IN	Y	38130 FQ	51450 MW	69510 TQ	USBLS	5/15
	Iowa	Y	40470 FQ	52020 MW	65130 TQ	USBLS	5/15
	Des Moines-West Des Moines MSA, IA	Y	42230 FQ	57580 MW	74370 TQ	USBLS	5/15
	Kansas	Y	35230 FQ	47190 MW	64260 TQ	USBLS	5/15
	Wichita MSA, KS	Y	32310 FQ	45380 MW	61230 TQ	USBLS	5/15
	Kentucky	Y	35360 FQ	47150 MW	60650 TQ	USBLS	5/15
	Louisville-Jefferson County MSA, KY-IN	Y	36130 FQ	50700 MW	61830 TQ	USBLS	5/15
	Louisiana	Y	34360 FQ	43560 MW	54870 TQ	USBLS	5/15
	Baton Rouge MSA, LA	Y	35350 FQ	42820 MW	49400 TQ	USBLS	5/15
	New Orleans-Metairie MSA, LA	Y	36520 FQ	47070 MW	72180 TQ	USBLS	5/15
	Maine	Y	41570 FQ	49610 MW	61470 TQ	USBLS	5/15
	Portland-South Portland MSA, ME	Y	40460 FQ	49820 MW	62000 TQ	USBLS	5/15
	Maryland	Y	33985 AE	67585 MW	84384 AEX	MDBLS	4/16
	Baltimore-Columbia-Towson MSA, MD	Y	38330 FQ	54540 MW	76140 TQ	USBLS	5/15
	Salisbury MSA, MD-DE	Y	29390 FQ	50630 MW	64270 TQ	USBLS	5/15
	Massachusetts	Y	45650 FQ	59370 MW	78150 TQ	USBLS	5/15
	Boston-Cambridge-Newton NECTA, MA	Y	46830 FQ	60150 MW	78960 TQ	USBLS	5/15
	Worcester MSA, MA-CT	Y	49020 FQ	59080 MW	72200 TQ	USBLS	5/15
	Michigan	Y	39940 FQ	55340 MW	76010 TQ	USBLS	5/15
	Detroit-Dearborn-Livonia PMSA, MI	Y	43180 FQ	65530 MW	81310 TQ	USBLS	5/15
	Grand Rapids-Wyoming MSA, MI	Y	38610 FQ	49940 MW	64450 TQ	USBLS	5/15
	Minnesota	Y	44687 FQ	56501 MW	71219 TQ	MNBLS	1/16-3/16
	Minneapolis-St. Paul-Bloomington MSA, MN-WI	Y	45957 FQ	58517 MW	73114 TQ	MNBLS	1/16-3/16
	Mississippi	Y	31270 FQ	36610 MW	42790 TQ	USBLS	5/15
	Jackson MSA, MS	Y	32170 FQ	36600 MW	40340 TQ	USBLS	5/15
	Missouri	Y	38690 FQ	49880 MW	66630 TQ	USBLS	5/15
	Kansas City MSA, MO-KS	Y	39470 FQ	53910 MW	73900 TQ	USBLS	5/15
	St. Louis MSA, MO-IL	Y	44680 FQ	56690 MW	76130 TQ	USBLS	5/15
	Montana	Y	33190 FQ	41780 MW	57300 TQ	USBLS	5/15
	Billings MSA, MT	Y	38570 FQ	51670 MW	62150 TQ	USBLS	5/15
	Nebraska	Y	33905 FQ	46020 MW	61490 TQ	NEBLS	7/16-9/16

AE Average entry wage	**AWR** Average wage range	**H** Hourly	**LR** Low end range	**MTC** Median total compensation	**TCC** Total cash compensation
AEX Average experienced wage	**B** Biweekly	**HI** Highest wage paid	**M** Monthly	**MW** Median wage paid	**TQ** Third quartile wage
ATC Average total compensation	**D** Daily	**HR** High end range	**MCC** Median cash compensation	**MWR** Median wage range	**W** Weekly
AW Average wage paid	**FQ** First quartile wage	**LO** Lowest wage paid	**ME** Median entry wage	**S** See annotated source	**Y** Yearly

Occupation/Type/Industry	Location	Per	Low	Mid	High	Source	Date
Public Relations Specialist	Omaha-Council Bluffs MSA, NE-IA	Y	39845 FQ	51780 MW	70740 TQ	NEBLS	7/16-9/16
	Nevada	Y	35540 FQ	51990 MW	69040 TQ	USBLS	5/15
	Las Vegas-Henderson-Paradise MSA, NV	Y	34150 FQ	53220 MW	68990 TQ	USBLS	5/15
	New Hampshire	H	18.33 AE	26.72 MW	37.84 AEX	NHBLS	6/16
	Manchester NECTA, NH	H	17.74 AE	26.89 MW	30.87 AEX	NHBLS	6/16
	Nashua NECTA, NH-MA	Y	34600 FQ	43850 MW	54570 TQ	NHBLS	5/15
	New Jersey	Y	45410 FQ	65210 MW	82020 TQ	USBLS	5/15
	Camden PMSA, NJ	Y	36230 FQ	60800 MW	79030 TQ	USBLS	5/15
	Newark PMSA, NJ-PA	Y	41840 FQ	65500 MW	84160 TQ	USBLS	5/15
	Trenton MSA, NJ	Y	48500 FQ	66030 MW	81400 TQ	USBLS	5/15
	New Mexico	Y	39460 FQ	54510 MW	74800 TQ	USBLS	5/15
	Albuquerque MSA, NM	Y	36680 FQ	52400 MW	67640 TQ	USBLS	5/15
	New York	Y	37690 AE	62040 MW	89470 AEX	NYBLS	1/16-3/16
	Buffalo-Cheektowaga-Niagara Falls MSA, NY	Y	36470 FQ	48260 MW	66130 TQ	USBLS	5/15
	Nassau County-Suffolk County PMSA, NY	Y	51200 FQ	66230 MW	87670 TQ	USBLS	5/15
	New York-Jersey City-White Plains PMSA, NY-NJ	Y	45340 FQ	64230 MW	90270 TQ	USBLS	5/15
	Rochester MSA, NY	Y	36700 FQ	50470 MW	65040 TQ	USBLS	5/15
	North Carolina	Y	41120 FQ	52060 MW	68830 TQ	USBLS	5/15
	Charlotte-Concord-Gastonia MSA, NC-SC	Y	41450 FQ	53500 MW	71740 TQ	USBLS	5/15
	Greenville MSA, NC	Y	38220 FQ	46270 MW	54720 TQ	USBLS	5/15
	Raleigh MSA, NC	Y	41380 FQ	52730 MW	67060 TQ	USBLS	5/15
	North Dakota	Y	38790 FQ	50220 MW	67040 TQ	USBLS	5/15
	Fargo MSA, ND-MN	Y	38490 FQ	52350 MW	63930 TQ	USBLS	5/15
	Ohio	Y	38860 FQ	49520 MW	63860 TQ	USBLS	5/15
	Cincinnati MSA, OH-KY-IN	Y	39340 FQ	50060 MW	65790 TQ	USBLS	5/15
	Cleveland-Elyria MSA, OH	Y	39280 FQ	51540 MW	62470 TQ	USBLS	5/15
	Columbus MSA, OH	Y	42500 FQ	52900 MW	68910 TQ	USBLS	5/15
	Oklahoma	Y	34680 FQ	46190 MW	64020 TQ	USBLS	5/15
	Oklahoma City MSA, OK	Y	36250 FQ	47410 MW	65390 TQ	USBLS	5/15
	Tulsa MSA, OK	Y	35560 FQ	45720 MW	66850 TQ	USBLS	5/15
	Oregon	H	18.33 FQ	26.31 MW	36.76 TQ	ORBLS	2016
	Portland-Vancouver-Hillsboro MSA, OR-WA	Y	37250 FQ	53290 MW	72460 TQ	USBLS	5/15
	Pennsylvania	Y	39910 FQ	53140 MW	70120 TQ	USBLS	5/15
	Allentown-Bethlehem-Easton MSA, PA-NJ	Y	42510 FQ	56690 MW	70290 TQ	USBLS	5/15
	Harrisburg-Carlisle MSA, PA	Y	39980 FQ	53660 MW	69580 TQ	USBLS	5/15
	Montgomery County-Bucks County-Chester County PMSA, PA	Y	42910 FQ	56310 MW	77930 TQ	USBLS	5/15
	Philadelphia PMSA, PA	Y	43970 FQ	57510 MW	74750 TQ	USBLS	5/15
	Pittsburgh MSA, PA	Y	37940 FQ	49840 MW	63140 TQ	USBLS	5/15
	Providence-Warwick MSA, RI-MA	Y	46760 FQ	64320 MW	78860 TQ	USBLS	5/15
	South Carolina	Y	34120 FQ	45290 MW	59400 TQ	USBLS	5/15
	Charleston-North Charleston MSA, SC	Y	43610 FQ	54580 MW	63510 TQ	USBLS	5/15
	Columbia MSA, SC	Y	36190 FQ	45530 MW	58560 TQ	USBLS	5/15
	Greenville-Anderson-Mauldin MSA, SC	Y	30830 FQ	42420 MW	56940 TQ	NHBLS	5/15
	South Dakota	Y	35440 FQ	43380 MW	55790 TQ	USBLS	5/15
	Sioux Falls MSA, SD	Y	39310 FQ	48190 MW	57590 TQ	USBLS	5/15
	Tennessee	Y	37210 FQ	50880 MW	68360 TQ	USBLS	5/15
	Knoxville MSA, TN	Y	36180 FQ	47590 MW	66460 TQ	USBLS	5/15
	Memphis MSA, TN-MS-AR	Y	27410 FQ	52320 MW	71750 TQ	USBLS	5/15
	Nashville-Davidson–Murfreesboro–Franklin MSA, TN	Y	40900 FQ	52610 MW	66360 TQ	USBLS	5/15
	Texas	Y	40350 FQ	54950 MW	75240 TQ	USBLS	5/15
	Austin-Round Rock MSA, TX	Y	42720 FQ	56810 MW	75860 TQ	USBLS	5/15
	Dallas-Plano-Irving PMSA, TX	Y	46210 FQ	60680 MW	83820 TQ	USBLS	5/15
	Fort Worth-Arlington PMSA, TX	Y	42820 FQ	56230 MW	75890 TQ	USBLS	5/15
	Houston-The Woodlands-Sugar Land MSA, TX	Y	38550 FQ	53890 MW	75490 TQ	USBLS	5/15

AE	Average entry wage	AWR	Average wage range	H	Hourly
AEX	Average experienced wage	B	Biweekly	HI	Highest wage paid
ATC	Average total compensation	D	Daily	HR	High end range
AW	Average wage paid	FQ	First quartile wage	LO	Lowest wage paid

LR	Low end range	MTC	Median total compensation	TCC	Total cash compensation
M	Monthly	MW	Median wage paid	TQ	Third quartile wage
MCC	Median cash compensation	MWR	Median wage range	W	Weekly
ME	Median entry wage	S	See annotated source	Y	Yearly

Occupation/Type/Industry	Location	Per	Low	Mid	High	Source	Date
Public Relations Specialist	San Antonio-New Braunfels						
	MSA, TX	Y	40740 FQ	54550 MW	72170 TQ	USBLS	5/15
	Utah	Y	37580 FQ	52100 MW	69920 TQ	USBLS	5/15
	Ogden-Clearfield MSA, UT	Y	17840 FQ	34480 MW	58560 TQ	USBLS	5/15
	Provo-Orem MSA, UT	Y	33670 FQ	45280 MW	67630 TQ	USBLS	5/15
	Salt Lake City MSA, UT	Y	42410 FQ	55660 MW	73560 TQ	USBLS	5/15
	Vermont	Y	40140 FQ	49900 MW	66300 TQ	USBLS	5/15
	Burlington-South Burlington						
	MSA, VT	Y	41070 FQ	48390 MW	67410 TQ	USBLS	5/15
	Virginia	Y	48360 FQ	66520 MW	95700 TQ	USBLS	5/15
	Richmond MSA, VA	Y	44450 FQ	56150 MW	73860 TQ	USBLS	5/15
	Virginia Beach-Norfolk-						
	Newport News MSA, VA-NC	Y	42410 FQ	57670 MW	77450 TQ	USBLS	5/15
	Washington	H	23.74 FQ	30.54 MW	38.91 TQ	WABLS	3/16
	Seattle-Bellevue-Everett						
	PMSA, WA	H	23.92 FQ	32.17 MW	40.47 TQ	WABLS	3/16
	Tacoma-Lakewood PMSA, WA	H	22.46 FQ	29.65 MW	36.78 TQ	WABLS	3/16
	West Virginia	Y	37700 FQ	49150 MW	68710 TQ	USBLS	5/15
	Wisconsin	Y	38640 FQ	50260 MW	67320 TQ	USBLS	5/15
	Madison MSA, WI	Y	43690 FQ	53840 MW	71680 TQ	USBLS	5/15
	Milwaukee-Waukesha-West						
	Allis MSA, WI	Y	37530 FQ	52950 MW	71460 TQ	USBLS	5/15
	Wyoming	Y	39310 FQ	52220 MW	61020 TQ	USBLS	5/15
	Cheyenne MSA, WY	Y	47910 FQ	56240 MW	69650 TQ	USBLS	5/15
	Puerto Rico	Y	19460 FQ	27690 MW	36330 TQ	USBLS	5/15
	San Juan-Carolina-Caguas						
	MSA, PR	Y	20290 FQ	28220 MW	37110 TQ	USBLS	5/15
	Virgin Islands	Y	31540 FQ	43530 MW	52020 TQ	USBLS	5/15
Public Works Superintendent							
Municipal Government	Canton, GA	Y	65025 LO		97537 HI	GACTY02	2016
Municipal Government	Dacula, GA	Y	33112 LO		46000 HI	GACTY02	2016
Municipal Government	Roswell, GA	Y	89067 LO		142507 HI	GACTY02	2016
Publications Specialist							
Public Library	Detroit, MI	M	3112 LO		3517 HI	DETGOV	2016
Publicist	United States	M		500-10000 AWR		BBRD01	2014
Community Services Department, Municipal Government	Beverly Hills, CA	Y			34781 HI	CACIT	6/28/16
Publisher							
Pharmaceutical, Medical Device, and Healthcare Industries	United States	Y		200000 AW		MMM01	7/16
Publishing Professional							
Female	United States	Y		61000 AW		PW01	2015
Male	United States	Y		96000 AW		PW01	2015
Pulmonary Function Technician							
Female	United States	Y		57720 AW		AHNRSP	2016
Male	United States	Y		62345 AW		AHNRSP	2016
Pump Operator							
Except Wellhead Pumpers	Alabama	Y	36460 AE	42559 AW	45604 AEX	ALBLS	6/16
Except Wellhead Pumpers	Arizona	Y	35430 FQ	39340 MW	49100 TQ	USBLS	5/15
Except Wellhead Pumpers	Arkansas	Y	32510 FQ	49250 MW	72650 TQ	USBLS	5/15
Except Wellhead Pumpers	California	H	16.53 FQ	23.71 MW	31.63 TQ	CABLS	1/16-3/16
Except Wellhead Pumpers	Colorado	Y	43640 FQ	56010 MW	70320 TQ	USBLS	5/15
Except Wellhead Pumpers	Florida	H	15.54 AE	19.79 MW	23.83 AEX	FLBLS	7/16-9/16
Except Wellhead Pumpers	Georgia	Y	42920 FQ	59670 MW	78390 TQ	USBLS	5/15
Except Wellhead Pumpers	Illinois	Y	41850 FQ	50740 MW	58000 TQ	USBLS	5/15
Except Wellhead Pumpers	Indiana	Y	27580 FQ	30060 MW	34810 TQ	USBLS	5/15
Except Wellhead Pumpers	Kansas	Y	35300 FQ	49970 MW	58860 TQ	USBLS	5/15
Except Wellhead Pumpers	Kentucky	Y	29680 FQ	41370 MW	46260 TQ	USBLS	5/15
Except Wellhead Pumpers	Maine	Y	39180 FQ	48430 MW	69040 TQ	USBLS	5/15
Except Wellhead Pumpers	Maryland	Y	39040 AE	49433 MW	54630 AEX	MDBLS	4/16
Except Wellhead Pumpers	Massachusetts	Y	28210 FQ	35170 MW	49360 TQ	USBLS	5/15
Except Wellhead Pumpers	Michigan	Y	32610 FQ	37980 MW	48100 TQ	USBLS	5/15
Except Wellhead Pumpers	Minnesota	Y	36071 AE	48673 MW	71306 TQ	MNBLS	1/16-3/16
Except Wellhead Pumpers	Mississippi	Y	21290 FQ	23130 MW	32600 TQ	USBLS	5/15
Except Wellhead Pumpers	Missouri	Y	30430 FQ	51520 MW	64760 TQ	USBLS	5/15

AE Average entry wage	**AWR** Average wage range	**H** Hourly	**LR** Low end range	**MTC** Median total compensation	**TCC** Total cash compensation
AEX Average experienced wage	**B** Biweekly	**HI** Highest wage paid	**M** Monthly	**MW** Median wage paid	**TQ** Third quartile wage
ATC Average total compensation	**D** Daily	**HR** High end range	**MCC** Median cash compensation	**MWR** Median wage range	**W** Weekly
AW Average wage paid	**FQ** First quartile wage	**LO** Lowest wage paid	**ME** Median entry wage	**S** See annotated source	**Y** Yearly

Occupation/Type/Industry	Location	Per	Low	Mid	High	Source	Date
Pump Operator							
Except Wellhead Pumpers	Montana	Y	53750 FQ	59930 MW	68840 TQ	USBLS	5/15
Except Wellhead Pumpers	Nebraska	Y	29630 FQ	47030 MW	58325 TQ	NEBLS	7/16-9/16
Except Wellhead Pumpers	Nevada	Y	33660 FQ	46460 MW	67780 TQ	USBLS	5/15
Except Wellhead Pumpers	New Hampshire	H	17.07 AE	21.87 MW	24.45 AEX	NHBLS	6/16
Except Wellhead Pumpers	New Jersey	Y	34180 FQ	42760 MW	50550 TQ	USBLS	5/15
Except Wellhead Pumpers	New Mexico	Y	34360 FQ	47020 MW	57690 TQ	USBLS	5/15
Except Wellhead Pumpers	New York	Y	30670 AE	46150 MW	54970 AEX	NYBLS	1/16-3/16
Except Wellhead Pumpers	North Carolina	Y	31350 FQ	36010 MW	41660 TQ	USBLS	5/15
Except Wellhead Pumpers	North Dakota	Y	39370 FQ	49180 MW	58340 TQ	USBLS	5/15
Except Wellhead Pumpers	Ohio	Y	27870 FQ	42810 MW	70300 TQ	USBLS	5/15
Except Wellhead Pumpers	Oklahoma	Y	34780 FQ	51510 MW	64300 TQ	USBLS	5/15
Except Wellhead Pumpers	Oregon	H	12.71 FQ	15.62 MW	18.67 TQ	ORBLS	2016
Except Wellhead Pumpers	Pennsylvania	Y	31600 FQ	38600 MW	56900 TQ	USBLS	5/15
Except Wellhead Pumpers	Tennessee	Y	30370 FQ	34650 MW	39920 TQ	USBLS	5/15
Except Wellhead Pumpers	Texas	Y	28660 FQ	37290 MW	55170 TQ	USBLS	5/15
Except Wellhead Pumpers	Virginia	Y	33100 FQ	44500 MW	54340 TQ	USBLS	5/15
Except Wellhead Pumpers	West Virginia	Y	31580 FQ	38050 MW	55840 TQ	USBLS	5/15
Except Wellhead Pumpers	Wisconsin	Y	36500 FQ	56710 MW	73820 TQ	USBLS	5/15
Except Wellhead Pumpers	Puerto Rico	Y	17260 FQ	19550 MW	27930 TQ	USBLS	5/15
Puppeteer							
Parks, Recreation and Neighborhood Services, Municipal Government	San Jose, CA	Y		8245 AW		CACIT	6/28/16
Purchasing Agent							
Except Wholesale, Retail, and Farm	Alabama	Y	40834 AE	67576 AW	80941 AEX	ALBLS	6/16
Except Wholesale, Retail, and Farm	Birmingham-Hoover MSA, AL	Y	36950 AE	60903 AW	72875 AEX	ALBLS	6/16
Except Wholesale, Retail, and Farm	Alaska	Y	56500 FQ	71070 MW	89460 TQ	USBLS	5/15
Except Wholesale, Retail, and Farm	Anchorage MSA, AK	Y	58590 FQ	75520 MW	94560 TQ	USBLS	5/15
Except Wholesale, Retail, and Farm	Arizona	Y	47470 FQ	60320 MW	76570 TQ	USBLS	5/15
Except Wholesale, Retail, and Farm	Phoenix-Mesa-Scottsdale MSA, AZ	Y	48420 FQ	60960 MW	76790 TQ	USBLS	5/15
Except Wholesale, Retail, and Farm	Tucson MSA, AZ	Y	48240 FQ	61340 MW	76470 TQ	USBLS	5/15
Except Wholesale, Retail, and Farm	Arkansas	Y	37580 FQ	48430 MW	64420 TQ	USBLS	5/15
Except Wholesale, Retail, and Farm	Little Rock-North Little Rock-Conway MSA, AR	Y	37660 FQ	52810 MW	71570 TQ	USBLS	5/15
Except Wholesale, Retail, and Farm	California	H	25.22 FQ	33.41 MW	43.60 TQ	CABLS	1/16-3/16
Except Wholesale, Retail, and Farm	Anaheim-Santa Ana-Irvine PMSA, CA	H	23.84 FQ	30.64 MW	40.13 TQ	CABLS	1/16-3/16
Except Wholesale, Retail, and Farm	Los Angeles-Long Beach-Glendale PMSA, CA	H	24.79 FQ	33.27 MW	43.34 TQ	CABLS	1/16-3/16
Except Wholesale, Retail, and Farm	Oakland-Hayward-Berkeley PMSA, CA	H	27.99 FQ	36.40 MW	46.34 TQ	CABLS	1/16-3/16
Except Wholesale, Retail, and Farm	Riverside-San Bernardino-Ontario MSA, CA	H	20.88 FQ	26.48 MW	33.84 TQ	CABLS	1/16-3/16
Except Wholesale, Retail, and Farm	Sacramento–Roseville–Arden-Arcade MSA, CA	H	25.01 FQ	32.91 MW	43.96 TQ	CABLS	1/16-3/16
Except Wholesale, Retail, and Farm	San Diego-Carlsbad MSA, CA	H	23.93 FQ	32.88 MW	44.37 TQ	CABLS	1/16-3/16
Except Wholesale, Retail, and Farm	San Francisco-Redwood City-South San Francisco PMSA, CA	H	31.81 FQ	39.40 MW	50.60 TQ	CABLS	1/16-3/16
Except Wholesale, Retail, and Farm	Colorado	Y	51490 FQ	64950 MW	84100 TQ	USBLS	5/15
Except Wholesale, Retail, and Farm	Denver-Aurora-Lakewood MSA, CO	Y	52900 FQ	66790 MW	85650 TQ	USBLS	5/15
Except Wholesale, Retail, and Farm	Connecticut	Y		66426 MW		CTBLS	1/16-3/16
Except Wholesale, Retail, and Farm	Bridgeport-Stamford-Norwalk MSA, CT	Y	52150 FQ	61950 MW	83910 TQ	USBLS	5/15
Except Wholesale, Retail, and Farm	Hartford-West Hartford-East Hartford MSA, CT	Y	56280 FQ	71880 MW	87690 TQ	USBLS	5/15
Except Wholesale, Retail, and Farm	Delaware	Y	51370 FQ	66980 MW	86450 TQ	USBLS	5/15
Except Wholesale, Retail, and Farm	Wilmington PMSA, DE-MD-NJ	Y	56830 FQ	72110 MW	90630 TQ	USBLS	5/15
Except Wholesale, Retail, and Farm	District of Columbia	Y	76380 FQ	90830 MW	102930 TQ	USBLS	5/15
Except Wholesale, Retail, and Farm	Washington-Arlington-Alexandria PMSA, DC-VA-MD-WV	Y	66970 FQ	87450 MW	102920 TQ	USBLS	5/15
Except Wholesale, Retail, and Farm	Florida	H	18.86 AE	27.66 MW	34.74 AEX	FLBLS	7/16-9/16
Except Wholesale, Retail, and Farm	Fort Lauderdale-Pompano Beach-Deerfield Beach PMSA, FL	H	18.97 AE	25.96 MW	30.93 AEX	FLBLS	7/16-9/16

Occupation/Type/Industry	Location	Per	Low	Mid	High	Source	Date
Purchasing Agent							
Except Wholesale, Retail, and Farm	Miami-Miami Beach-Kendall PMSA, FL	H	17.99 AE	27.69 MW	33.74 AEX	FLBLS	7/16-9/16
Except Wholesale, Retail, and Farm	Orlando-Kissimmee-Sanford MSA, FL	H	19.53 AE	29.10 MW	37.18 AEX	FLBLS	7/16-9/16
Except Wholesale, Retail, and Farm	Tampa-St. Petersburg-Clearwater MSA, FL	H	19.10 AE	28.00 MW	35.97 AEX	FLBLS	7/16-9/16
Except Wholesale, Retail, and Farm	Georgia	Y	44760 FQ	59100 MW	77440 TQ	USBLS	5/15
Except Wholesale, Retail, and Farm	Atlanta-Sandy Springs-Roswell MSA, GA	Y	45650 FQ	60200 MW	79340 TQ	USBLS	5/15
Except Wholesale, Retail, and Farm	Augusta-Richmond County MSA, GA-SC	Y	43270 FQ	60260 MW	83470 TQ	USBLS	5/15
Except Wholesale, Retail, and Farm	Hawaii	Y	46850 FQ	59770 MW	81200 TQ	USBLS	5/15
Except Wholesale, Retail, and Farm	Urban Honolulu MSA, HI	Y	48040 FQ	62330 MW	85190 TQ	USBLS	5/15
Except Wholesale, Retail, and Farm	Idaho	Y	39640 FQ	51000 MW	72530 TQ	USBLS	5/15
Except Wholesale, Retail, and Farm	Boise City MSA, ID	Y	40820 FQ	53240 MW	74880 TQ	USBLS	5/15
Except Wholesale, Retail, and Farm	Illinois	Y	48120 FQ	63490 MW	79970 TQ	USBLS	5/15
Except Wholesale, Retail, and Farm	Chicago-Naperville-Arlington Heights PMSA, IL	Y	48350 FQ	63080 MW	79540 TQ	USBLS	5/15
Except Wholesale, Retail, and Farm	Lake County-Kenosha County PMSA, IL-WI	Y	46360 FQ	60190 MW	79390 TQ	USBLS	5/15
Except Wholesale, Retail, and Farm	Indiana	Y	41660 FQ	53120 MW	68760 TQ	USBLS	5/15
Except Wholesale, Retail, and Farm	Gary PMSA, IN	Y	41940 FQ	49450 MW	67300 TQ	USBLS	5/15
Except Wholesale, Retail, and Farm	Indianapolis-Carmel-Anderson MSA, IN	Y	41090 FQ	54290 MW	72100 TQ	USBLS	5/15
Except Wholesale, Retail, and Farm	Iowa	Y	42540 FQ	54810 MW	67870 TQ	USBLS	5/15
Except Wholesale, Retail, and Farm	Des Moines-West Des Moines MSA, IA	Y	43800 FQ	55990 MW	70180 TQ	USBLS	5/15
Except Wholesale, Retail, and Farm	Kansas	Y	44390 FQ	58560 MW	74730 TQ	USBLS	5/15
Except Wholesale, Retail, and Farm	Wichita MSA, KS	Y	46460 FQ	60690 MW	78080 TQ	USBLS	5/15
Except Wholesale, Retail, and Farm	Kentucky	Y	42570 FQ	54860 MW	70280 TQ	USBLS	5/15
Except Wholesale, Retail, and Farm	Louisville-Jefferson County MSA, KY-IN	Y	40600 FQ	51860 MW	66930 TQ	USBLS	5/15
Except Wholesale, Retail, and Farm	Louisiana	Y	41290 FQ	53160 MW	69320 TQ	USBLS	5/15
Except Wholesale, Retail, and Farm	Baton Rouge MSA, LA	Y	47080 FQ	58490 MW	72500 TQ	USBLS	5/15
Except Wholesale, Retail, and Farm	New Orleans-Metairie MSA, LA	Y	43900 FQ	54490 MW	75670 TQ	USBLS	5/15
Except Wholesale, Retail, and Farm	Maine	Y	43880 FQ	54240 MW	71110 TQ	USBLS	5/15
Except Wholesale, Retail, and Farm	Portland-South Portland MSA, ME	Y	43910 FQ	51760 MW	61900 TQ	USBLS	5/15
Except Wholesale, Retail, and Farm	Maryland	Y	51084 AE	77403 MW	90562 AEX	MDBLS	4/16
Except Wholesale, Retail, and Farm	Baltimore-Columbia-Towson MSA, MD	Y	55740 FQ	72240 MW	90830 TQ	USBLS	5/15
Except Wholesale, Retail, and Farm	Salisbury MSA, MD-DE	Y	36570 FQ	47100 MW	59640 TQ	USBLS	5/15
Except Wholesale, Retail, and Farm	Massachusetts	Y	54930 FQ	70440 MW	87730 TQ	USBLS	5/15
Except Wholesale, Retail, and Farm	Boston-Cambridge-Newton NECTA, MA	Y	58820 FQ	74750 MW	92100 TQ	USBLS	5/15
Except Wholesale, Retail, and Farm	Worcester MSA, MA-CT	Y	47570 FQ	59640 MW	74660 TQ	USBLS	5/15
Except Wholesale, Retail, and Farm	Michigan	Y	48180 FQ	63680 MW	82630 TQ	USBLS	5/15
Except Wholesale, Retail, and Farm	Detroit-Dearborn-Livonia PMSA, MI	Y	50310 FQ	68300 MW	95670 TQ	USBLS	5/15
Except Wholesale, Retail, and Farm	Grand Rapids-Wyoming MSA, MI	Y	44380 FQ	56310 MW	71970 TQ	USBLS	5/15
Except Wholesale, Retail, and Farm	Minnesota	Y	49007 FQ	60915 MW	75100 TQ	MNBLS	1/16-3/16
Except Wholesale, Retail, and Farm	Minneapolis-St. Paul-Bloomington MSA, MN-WI	Y	52654 FQ	64035 MW	77762 TQ	MNBLS	1/16-3/16
Except Wholesale, Retail, and Farm	Mississippi	Y	41940 FQ	55170 MW	74730 TQ	USBLS	5/15
Except Wholesale, Retail, and Farm	Jackson MSA, MS	Y	38140 FQ	53690 MW	72040 TQ	USBLS	5/15
Except Wholesale, Retail, and Farm	Missouri	Y	44410 FQ	59060 MW	77520 TQ	USBLS	5/15
Except Wholesale, Retail, and Farm	Kansas City MSA, MO-KS	Y	46500 FQ	60000 MW	77220 TQ	USBLS	5/15
Except Wholesale, Retail, and Farm	St. Louis MSA, MO-IL	Y	52440 FQ	68400 MW	84240 TQ	USBLS	5/15
Except Wholesale, Retail, and Farm	Montana	Y	38390 FQ	48310 MW	64650 TQ	USBLS	5/15
Except Wholesale, Retail, and Farm	Billings MSA, MT	Y	41000 FQ	49730 MW	73830 TQ	USBLS	5/15
Except Wholesale, Retail, and Farm	Nebraska	Y	44915 FQ	56020 MW	71010 TQ	NEBLS	7/16-9/16
Except Wholesale, Retail, and Farm	Omaha-Council Bluffs MSA, NE-IA	Y	46745 FQ	58565 MW	74945 TQ	NEBLS	7/16-9/16
Except Wholesale, Retail, and Farm	Nevada	Y	40730 FQ	51420 MW	67290 TQ	USBLS	5/15
Except Wholesale, Retail, and Farm	Las Vegas-Henderson-Paradise MSA, NV	Y	40060 FQ	49960 MW	64290 TQ	USBLS	5/15
Except Wholesale, Retail, and Farm	Nashua NECTA, NH-MA	Y	51340 FQ	63380 MW	77120 TQ	USBLS	5/15
Except Wholesale, Retail, and Farm	New Jersey	Y	57820 FQ	72940 MW	92990 TQ	USBLS	5/15
Except Wholesale, Retail, and Farm	Camden PMSA, NJ	Y	55750 FQ	70970 MW	91670 TQ	USBLS	5/15

AE	Average entry wage	AWR	Average wage range	H	Hourly
AEX	Average experienced wage	B	Biweekly	HI	Highest wage paid
ATC	Average total compensation	D	Daily	HR	High end range
AW	Average wage paid	FQ	First quartile wage	LO	Lowest wage paid

LR	Low end range	MTC	Median total compensation	TCC	Total cash compensation
M	Monthly	MW	Median wage paid	TQ	Third quartile wage
MCC	Median cash compensation	MWR	Median wage range	W	Weekly
ME	Median entry wage	S	See annotated source	Y	Yearly

Occupation/Type/Industry	Location	Per	Low	Mid	High	Source	Date
Purchasing Agent							
Except Wholesale, Retail, and Farm	Newark PMSA, NJ-PA	Y	59890 FQ	75450 MW	95430 TQ	USBLS	5/15
Except Wholesale, Retail, and Farm	Trenton MSA, NJ	Y	58970 FQ	73320 MW	89860 TQ	USBLS	5/15
Except Wholesale, Retail, and Farm	New Mexico	Y	41800 FQ	55970 MW	77230 TQ	USBLS	5/15
Except Wholesale, Retail, and Farm	Albuquerque MSA, NM	Y	45200 FQ	59670 MW	84220 TQ	USBLS	5/15
Except Wholesale, Retail, and Farm	New York	Y	46370 AE	65980 MW	82470 AEX	NYBLS	1/16-3/16
Except Wholesale, Retail, and Farm	Buffalo-Cheektowaga-Niagara Falls MSA, NY	Y	44130 FQ	53980 MW	67100 TQ	USBLS	5/15
Except Wholesale, Retail, and Farm	Kingston MSA, NY	Y	43310 FQ	48500 MW	62780 TQ	USBLS	5/15
Except Wholesale, Retail, and Farm	Nassau County-Suffolk County PMSA, NY	Y	54920 FQ	69300 MW	87740 TQ	USBLS	5/15
Except Wholesale, Retail, and Farm	New York-Jersey City-White Plains PMSA, NY-NJ	Y	54670 FQ	69770 MW	90370 TQ	USBLS	5/15
Except Wholesale, Retail, and Farm	Rochester MSA, NY	Y	49230 FQ	62580 MW	79730 TQ	USBLS	5/15
Except Wholesale, Retail, and Farm	North Carolina	Y	44470 FQ	57630 MW	75940 TQ	USBLS	5/15
Except Wholesale, Retail, and Farm	Charlotte-Concord-Gastonia MSA, NC-SC	Y	46330 FQ	58840 MW	76240 TQ	USBLS	5/15
Except Wholesale, Retail, and Farm	Raleigh MSA, NC	Y	46590 FQ	58720 MW	80720 TQ	USBLS	5/15
Except Wholesale, Retail, and Farm	North Dakota	Y	44050 FQ	54130 MW	64430 TQ	USBLS	5/15
Except Wholesale, Retail, and Farm	Fargo MSA, ND-MN	Y	41100 FQ	48410 MW	59880 TQ	USBLS	5/15
Except Wholesale, Retail, and Farm	Ohio	Y	48620 FQ	61070 MW	77990 TQ	USBLS	5/15
Except Wholesale, Retail, and Farm	Cincinnati MSA, OH-KY-IN	Y	51150 FQ	62170 MW	77990 TQ	USBLS	5/15
Except Wholesale, Retail, and Farm	Cleveland-Elyria MSA, OH	Y	49120 FQ	60040 MW	74690 TQ	USBLS	5/15
Except Wholesale, Retail, and Farm	Columbus MSA, OH	Y	51360 FQ	65490 MW	79230 TQ	USBLS	5/15
Except Wholesale, Retail, and Farm	Oklahoma	Y	41310 FQ	55150 MW	74400 TQ	USBLS	5/15
Except Wholesale, Retail, and Farm	Oklahoma City MSA, OK	Y	43570 FQ	61660 MW	79550 TQ	USBLS	5/15
Except Wholesale, Retail, and Farm	Tulsa MSA, OK	Y	42800 FQ	54570 MW	66970 TQ	USBLS	5/15
Except Wholesale, Retail, and Farm	Oregon	H	22.92 FQ	28.63 MW	35.76 TQ	ORBLS	2016
Except Wholesale, Retail, and Farm	Portland-Vancouver-Hillsboro MSA, OR-WA	Y	48120 FQ	59670 MW	74160 TQ	USBLS	5/15
Except Wholesale, Retail, and Farm	Pennsylvania	Y	46940 FQ	60820 MW	79490 TQ	USBLS	5/15
Except Wholesale, Retail, and Farm	Allentown-Bethlehem-Easton MSA, PA-NJ	Y	43900 FQ	56610 MW	76400 TQ	USBLS	5/15
Except Wholesale, Retail, and Farm	Harrisburg-Carlisle MSA, PA	Y	47270 FQ	59290 MW	80490 TQ	USBLS	5/15
Except Wholesale, Retail, and Farm	Montgomery County-Bucks County-Chester County PMSA, PA	Y	49890 FQ	63250 MW	80480 TQ	USBLS	5/15
Except Wholesale, Retail, and Farm	Philadelphia PMSA, PA	Y	60290 FQ	77390 MW	91640 TQ	USBLS	5/15
Except Wholesale, Retail, and Farm	Pittsburgh MSA, PA	Y	46130 FQ	58470 MW	75670 TQ	USBLS	5/15
Except Wholesale, Retail, and Farm	Rhode Island	Y	52270 FQ	67720 MW	82040 TQ	USBLS	5/15
Except Wholesale, Retail, and Farm	Providence-Warwick MSA, RI-MA	Y	51260 FQ	66250 MW	80510 TQ	USBLS	5/15
Except Wholesale, Retail, and Farm	South Carolina	Y	43270 FQ	56310 MW	74770 TQ	USBLS	5/15
Except Wholesale, Retail, and Farm	Charleston-North Charleston MSA, SC	Y	46740 FQ	62470 MW	80070 TQ	USBLS	5/15
Except Wholesale, Retail, and Farm	Columbia MSA, SC	Y	39550 FQ	47860 MW	61530 TQ	USBLS	5/15
Except Wholesale, Retail, and Farm	Greenville-Anderson-Mauldin MSA, SC	Y	49800 FQ	61000 MW	86050 TQ	USBLS	5/15
Except Wholesale, Retail, and Farm	South Dakota	Y	44710 FQ	53240 MW	62950 TQ	USBLS	5/15
Except Wholesale, Retail, and Farm	Sioux Falls MSA, SD	Y	44920 FQ	51570 MW	61400 TQ	USBLS	5/15
Except Wholesale, Retail, and Farm	Tennessee	Y	39250 FQ	50720 MW	66220 TQ	USBLS	5/15
Except Wholesale, Retail, and Farm	Knoxville MSA, TN	Y	38390 FQ	53550 MW	75570 TQ	USBLS	5/15
Except Wholesale, Retail, and Farm	Memphis MSA, TN-MS-AR	Y	40480 FQ	51750 MW	64230 TQ	USBLS	5/15
Except Wholesale, Retail, and Farm	Nashville-Davidson–Murfreesboro–Franklin MSA, TN	Y	42060 FQ	53570 MW	70190 TQ	USBLS	5/15
Except Wholesale, Retail, and Farm	Texas	Y	47290 FQ	62430 MW	81750 TQ	USBLS	5/15
Except Wholesale, Retail, and Farm	Austin-Round Rock MSA, TX	Y	47180 FQ	58490 MW	72480 TQ	USBLS	5/15
Except Wholesale, Retail, and Farm	Dallas-Plano-Irving PMSA, TX	Y	47930 FQ	62850 MW	84080 TQ	USBLS	5/15
Except Wholesale, Retail, and Farm	Fort Worth-Arlington PMSA, TX	Y	45880 FQ	60040 MW	79130 TQ	USBLS	5/15
Except Wholesale, Retail, and Farm	Houston-The Woodlands-Sugar Land MSA, TX	Y	52580 FQ	68710 MW	90510 TQ	USBLS	5/15
Except Wholesale, Retail, and Farm	San Antonio-New Braunfels MSA, TX	Y	51140 FQ	69740 MW	86450 TQ	USBLS	5/15
Except Wholesale, Retail, and Farm	Utah	Y	49250 FQ	61640 MW	78070 TQ	USBLS	5/15
Except Wholesale, Retail, and Farm	Ogden-Clearfield MSA, UT	Y	57290 FQ	74120 MW	86870 TQ	USBLS	5/15
Except Wholesale, Retail, and Farm	Provo-Orem MSA, UT	Y	43010 FQ	55320 MW	67700 TQ	USBLS	5/15
Except Wholesale, Retail, and Farm	Salt Lake City MSA, UT	Y	48200 FQ	59560 MW	74990 TQ	USBLS	5/15
Except Wholesale, Retail, and Farm	Vermont	Y	42620 FQ	53970 MW	69230 TQ	USBLS	5/15
Except Wholesale, Retail, and Farm	Burlington-South Burlington MSA, VT	Y	47690 FQ	59050 MW	74930 TQ	USBLS	5/15

Occupation/Type/Industry	Location	Per	Low	Mid	High	Source	Date
Purchasing Agent							
Except Wholesale, Retail, and Farm	Virginia	Y	54680 FQ	72990 MW	93230 TQ	USBLS	5/15
Except Wholesale, Retail, and Farm	Richmond MSA, VA	Y	53340 FQ	67700 MW	81170 TQ	USBLS	5/15
Except Wholesale, Retail, and Farm	Virginia Beach-Norfolk- Newport News MSA, VA-NC	Y	50890 FQ	67450 MW	83460 TQ	USBLS	5/15
Except Wholesale, Retail, and Farm	Washington	H	25.52 FQ	33.07 MW	43.20 TQ	WABLS	3/16
Except Wholesale, Retail, and Farm	Tacoma-Lakewood PMSA, WA	H	21.76 FQ	26.88 MW	35.55 TQ	WABLS	3/16
Except Wholesale, Retail, and Farm	West Virginia	Y	47690 FQ	60230 MW	74870 TQ	USBLS	5/15
Except Wholesale, Retail, and Farm	Huntington-Ashland MSA, WV-KY-OH	Y	41710 FQ	51740 MW	69910 TQ	USBLS	5/15
Except Wholesale, Retail, and Farm	Wisconsin	Y	43090 FQ	53940 MW	66130 TQ	USBLS	5/15
Except Wholesale, Retail, and Farm	Madison MSA, WI	Y	47040 FQ	57420 MW	68240 TQ	USBLS	5/15
Except Wholesale, Retail, and Farm	Milwaukee-Waukesha-West Allis MSA, WI	Y	45050 FQ	56530 MW	70550 TQ	USBLS	5/15
Except Wholesale, Retail, and Farm	Wyoming	Y	45050 FQ	56150 MW	71580 TQ	USBLS	5/15
Except Wholesale, Retail, and Farm	Cheyenne MSA, WY	Y	47500 FQ	56380 MW	69710 TQ	USBLS	5/15
Except Wholesale, Retail, and Farm	Puerto Rico	Y	24280 FQ	33510 MW	46040 TQ	USBLS	5/15
Except Wholesale, Retail, and Farm	San Juan-Carolina-Caguas MSA, PR	Y	24070 FQ	31180 MW	44270 TQ	USBLS	5/15
Except Wholesale, Retail, and Farm	Virgin Islands	Y	30170 FQ	44970 MW	64130 TQ	USBLS	5/15
Except Wholesale, Retail, and Farm	Guam	Y	29040 FQ	41610 MW	77210 TQ	USBLS	5/15
Purchasing Manager	Alabama	Y	75765 AE	112520 AW	130898 AEX	ALBLS	6/16
	Birmingham-Hoover MSA, AL	Y	70302 AE	113156 AW	134577 AEX	ALBLS	6/16
	Alaska	Y	80990 FQ	110050 MW	131570 TQ	USBLS	5/15
	Anchorage MSA, AK	Y	87290 FQ	117470 MW	142420 TQ	USBLS	5/15
	Arizona	Y	70850 FQ	99180 MW	129430 TQ	USBLS	5/15
	Phoenix-Mesa-Scottsdale MSA, AZ	Y	74590 FQ	102960 MW	133610 TQ	USBLS	5/15
	Tucson MSA, AZ	Y	54580 FQ	69710 MW	100340 TQ	USBLS	5/15
	Arkansas	Y	59280 FQ	92020 MW	160710 TQ	USBLS	5/15
	Little Rock-North Little Rock- Conway MSA, AR	Y	50230 FQ	61240 MW	82810 TQ	USBLS	5/15
	California	H	39.70 FQ	54.61 MW	71.82 TQ	CABLS	1/16-3/16
	Anaheim-Santa Ana-Irvine PMSA, CA	H	41.20 FQ	51.75 MW	71.40 TQ	CABLS	1/16-3/16
	Los Angeles-Long Beach- Glendale PMSA, CA	H	31.53 FQ	49.20 MW	67.25 TQ	CABLS	1/16-3/16
	Oakland-Hayward-Berkeley PMSA, CA	H	43.73 FQ	59.99 MW	77.67 TQ	CABLS	1/16-3/16
	Riverside-San Bernardino- Ontario MSA, CA	H	34.98 FQ	46.45 MW	59.83 TQ	CABLS	1/16-3/16
	Sacramento–Roseville– Arden-Arcade MSA, CA	H	38.82 FQ	53.67 MW	62.49 TQ	CABLS	1/16-3/16
	San Diego-Carlsbad MSA, CA	H	44.15 FQ	57.10 MW	71.85 TQ	CABLS	1/16-3/16
	San Francisco-Redwood City- South San Francisco PMSA, CA	H	49.64 FQ	64.90 MW	85.66 TQ	CABLS	1/16-3/16
	Colorado	Y	104610 FQ	124350 MW	148960 TQ	USBLS	5/15
	Denver-Aurora-Lakewood MSA, CO	Y	106570 FQ	124530 MW	148940 TQ	USBLS	5/15
	Connecticut	Y		116222 MW		CTBLS	1/16-3/16
	Bridgeport-Stamford-Norwalk MSA, CT	Y	79670 FQ	117490 MW	170010 TQ	USBLS	5/15
	Hartford-West Hartford-East Hartford MSA, CT	Y	98110 FQ	120050 MW	145390 TQ	USBLS	5/15
	Delaware	Y	118240 FQ	140880 MW	158060 TQ	USBLS	5/15
	Wilmington PMSA, DE-MD- NJ	Y	119620 FQ	141110 MW	158060 TQ	USBLS	5/15
	District of Columbia	Y	118050 FQ	128790 MW	147290 TQ	USBLS	5/15
	Washington-Arlington- Alexandria PMSA, DC-VA- MD-WV	Y	118050 FQ	130450 MW	147820 TQ	USBLS	5/15
	Florida	H	35.84 AE	55.03 MW	70.52 AEX	FLBLS	7/16-9/16
	Fort Lauderdale-Pompano Beach-Deerfield Beach PMSA, FL	H	38.64 AE	54.70 MW	62.81 AEX	FLBLS	7/16-9/16
	Miami-Miami Beach-Kendall PMSA, FL	H	32.50 AE	54.15 MW	70.90 AEX	FLBLS	7/16-9/16
	Orlando-Kissimmee-Sanford MSA, FL	H	35.54 AE	51.96 MW	63.41 AEX	FLBLS	7/16-9/16

AE	Average entry wage	AWR	Average wage range	H	Hourly	LR	Low end range	MTC	Median total compensation	TCC	Total cash compensation
AEX	Average experienced wage	B	Biweekly	HI	Highest wage paid	M	Monthly	MW	Median wage paid	TQ	Third quartile wage
ATC	Average total compensation	D	Daily	HR	High end range	MCC	Median cash compensation	MWR	Median wage range	W	Weekly
AW	Average wage paid	FQ	First quartile wage	LO	Lowest wage paid	ME	Median entry wage	S	See annotated source	Y	Yearly

Occupation/Type/Industry	Location	Per	Low	Mid	High	Source	Date
Purchasing Manager	Tampa-St. Petersburg-						
	Clearwater MSA, FL	H	33.52 AE	54.69 MW	73.32 AEX	FLBLS	7/16-9/16
	Georgia	Y,	79770 FQ	108510 MW	134170 TQ	USBLS	5/15
	Atlanta-Sandy Springs-						
	Roswell MSA, GA	Y	83360 FQ	111500 MW	138570 TQ	USBLS	5/15
	Augusta-Richmond County						
	MSA, GA-SC	Y	76500 FQ	98830 MW	124930 TQ	USBLS	5/15
	Hawaii	Y	67510 FQ	90240 MW	114660 TQ	USBLS	5/15
	Urban Honolulu MSA, HI	Y	73150 FQ	96790 MW	117860 TQ	USBLS	5/15
	Idaho	Y	55540 FQ	74360 MW	101620 TQ	USBLS	5/15
	Boise City MSA, ID	Y	57080 FQ	75960 MW	105730 TQ	USBLS	5/15
	Illinois	Y	72390 FQ	97380 MW	130790 TQ	USBLS	5/15
	Chicago-Naperville-Arlington						
	Heights PMSA, IL	Y	74990 FQ	98620 MW	130330 TQ	USBLS	5/15
	Lake County-Kenosha County						
	PMSA, IL-WI	Y	74380 FQ	101010 MW	141500 TQ	USBLS	5/15
	Indiana	Y	71690 FQ	92480 MW	118910 TQ	USBLS	5/15
	Gary PMSA, IN	Y	68820 FQ	85470 MW	109820 TQ	USBLS	5/15
	Indianapolis-Carmel-Anderson						
	MSA, IN	Y	76360 FQ	97310 MW	126520 TQ	USBLS	5/15
	Iowa	Y	66950 FQ	85230 MW	107390 TQ	USBLS	5/15
	Des Moines-West Des Moines						
	MSA, IA	Y	70030 FQ	83320 MW	96460 TQ	USBLS	5/15
	Kansas	Y	69970 FQ	93830 MW	124070 TQ	USBLS	5/15
	Wichita MSA, KS	Y	70010 FQ	86470 MW	106240 TQ	USBLS	5/15
	Kentucky	Y	70420 FQ	92230 MW	117090 TQ	USBLS	5/15
	Louisville-Jefferson County						
	MSA, KY-IN	Y	70030 FQ	93570 MW	119210 TQ	USBLS	5/15
	Louisiana	Y	57330 FQ	75740 MW	101670 TQ	USBLS	5/15
	Baton Rouge MSA, LA	Y	61040 FQ	82790 MW	112030 TQ	USBLS	5/15
	New Orleans-Metairie MSA,						
	LA	Y	60440 FQ	84180 MW	108500 TQ	USBLS	5/15
	Maine	Y	75870 FQ	92510 MW	111730 TQ	USBLS	5/15
	Portland-South Portland MSA,						
	ME	Y	78620 FQ	98510 MW	119190 TQ	USBLS	5/15
	Maryland	Y	100003 AE	129605 MW	144406 AEX	MDBLS	4/16
	Baltimore-Columbia-Towson						
	MSA, MD	Y	107320 FQ	126250 MW	148260 TQ	USBLS	5/15
	Salisbury MSA, MD-DE	Y	84970 FQ	105320 MW	137720 TQ	USBLS	5/15
	Massachusetts	Y	82080 FQ	112540 MW	143180 TQ	USBLS	5/15
	Boston-Cambridge-Newton						
	NECTA, MA	Y	90890 FQ	120370 MW	152490 TQ	USBLS	5/15
	Worcester MSA, MA-CT	Y	67900 FQ	82020 MW	101960 TQ	USBLS	5/15
	Michigan	Y	73240 FQ	96740 MW	129390 TQ	USBLS	5/15
	Detroit-Dearborn-Livonia						
	PMSA, MI	Y	84040 FQ	121420 MW	157280 TQ	USBLS	5/15
	Grand Rapids-Wyoming MSA,						
	MI	Y	55530 FQ	78850 MW	100450 TQ	USBLS	5/15
	Minnesota	Y	85800 FQ	104760 MW	133211 TQ	MNBLS	1/16-3/16
	Minneapolis-St. Paul-						
	Bloomington MSA, MN-WI	Y	89448 FQ	110318 MW	141096 TQ	MNBLS	1/16-3/16
	Mississippi	Y	57380 FQ	76780 MW	105190 TQ	USBLS	5/15
	Jackson MSA, MS	Y	57610 FQ	80980 MW	108450 TQ	USBLS	5/15
	Missouri	Y	93160 FQ	118370 MW	155410 TQ	USBLS	5/15
	Kansas City MSA, MO-KS	Y	84870 FQ	107890 MW	135860 TQ	USBLS	5/15
	St. Louis MSA, MO-IL	Y	93820 FQ	121690 MW	158640 TQ	USBLS	5/15
	Montana	Y	65780 FQ	80340 MW	97280 TQ	USBLS	5/15
	Nebraska	Y	82605 FQ	101315 MW	125640 TQ	NEBLS	7/16-9/16
	Omaha-Council Bluffs MSA,						
	NE-IA	Y	85730 FQ	106075 MW	133235 TQ	NEBLS	7/16-9/16
	Nevada	Y	69840 FQ	89500 MW	109610 TQ	USBLS	5/15
	Las Vegas-Henderson-Paradise						
	MSA, NV	Y	72760 FQ	90730 MW	111050 TQ	USBLS	5/15
	New Hampshire	H	37.79 AE	48.53 MW	59.40 AEX	NHBLS	6/16
	Manchester NECTA, NH	H	37.50 AE	47.51 MW	52.40 AEX	NHBLS	6/16
	Nashua NECTA, NH-MA	Y	83530 FQ	97190 MW	122670 TQ	USBLS	5/15
	New Jersey	Y	102200 FQ	126050 MW	163130 TQ	USBLS	5/15
	Camden PMSA, NJ	Y	86320 FQ	105820 MW	129880 TQ	USBLS	5/15
	Newark PMSA, NJ-PA	Y	108070 FQ	136170 MW	178450 TQ	USBLS	5/15
	Trenton MSA, NJ	Y	102400 FQ	120540 MW	141670 TQ	USBLS	5/15
	New Mexico	Y	56470 FQ	84710 MW	112430 TQ	USBLS	5/15
	Albuquerque MSA, NM	Y	59870 FQ	94920 MW	116220 TQ	USBLS	5/15

AE	Average entry wage	AWR	Average wage range	H	Hourly	LR	Low end range	MTC	Median total compensation	TCC	Total cash compensation
AEX	Average experienced wage	B	Biweekly	HI	Highest wage paid	M	Monthly	MW	Median wage paid	TQ	Third quartile wage
ATC	Average total compensation	D	Daily	HR	High end range	MCC	Median cash compensation	MWR	Median wage range	W	Weekly
AW	Average wage paid	FQ	First quartile wage	LO	Lowest wage paid	ME	Median entry wage	S	See annotated source	Y	Yearly

Purchasing Manager

Occupation/Type/Industry	Location	Per	Low	Mid	High	Source	Date
Purchasing Manager	New York	Y	76860 AE	122050 MW	159640 AEX	NYBLS	1/16-3/16
	Buffalo-Cheektowaga-Niagara Falls MSA, NY	Y	78840 FQ	98480 MW	129690 TQ	USBLS	5/15
	Nassau County-Suffolk County PMSA, NY	Y	90100 FQ	119970 MW	151030 TQ	USBLS	5/15
	New York-Jersey City-White Plains PMSA, NY-NJ	Y	101080 FQ	132380 MW	168680 TQ	USBLS	5/15
	Rochester MSA, NY	Y	85610 FQ	109420 MW	130100 TQ	USBLS	5/15
	North Carolina	Y	83710 FQ	104830 MW	134220 TQ	USBLS	5/15
	Charlotte-Concord-Gastonia MSA, NC-SC	Y	85210 FQ	105240 MW	137830 TQ	USBLS	5/15
	Raleigh MSA, NC	Y	90950 FQ	112450 MW	136990 TQ	USBLS	5/15
	North Dakota	Y	65470 FQ	86870 MW	106510 TQ	USBLS	5/15
	Fargo MSA, ND-MN	Y	71170 FQ	96550 MW	122400 TQ	USBLS	5/15
	Ohio	Y	84380 FQ	107130 MW	128590 TQ	USBLS	5/15
	Cincinnati MSA, OH-KY-IN	Y	89570 FQ	110370 MW	127860 TQ	USBLS	5/15
	Cleveland-Elyria MSA, OH	Y	75920 FQ	101260 MW	123030 TQ	USBLS	5/15
	Columbus MSA, OH	Y	89760 FQ	114280 MW	145910 TQ	USBLS	5/15
	Oklahoma	Y	57070 FQ	76110 MW	112010 TQ	USBLS	5/15
	Oklahoma City MSA, OK	Y	66570 FQ	86580 MW	124930 TQ	USBLS	5/15
	Tulsa MSA, OK	Y	53200 FQ	78130 MW	110730 TQ	USBLS	5/15
	Oregon	H	32.45 FQ	43.70 MW	58.28 TQ	ORBLS	2016
	Portland-Vancouver-Hillsboro MSA, OR-WA	Y	70530 FQ	93440 MW	127390 TQ	USBLS	5/15
	Pennsylvania	Y	86880 FQ	113660 MW	140860 TQ	USBLS	5/15
	Allentown-Bethlehem-Easton MSA, PA-NJ	Y	88960 FQ	101870 MW	132460 TQ	USBLS	5/15
	Harrisburg-Carlisle MSA, PA	Y	95290 FQ	121440 MW	156580 TQ	USBLS	5/15
	Montgomery County-Bucks County-Chester County PMSA, PA	Y	87670 FQ	116810 MW	143940 TQ	USBLS	5/15
	Philadelphia PMSA, PA	Y	107130 FQ	127920 MW	154330 TQ	USBLS	5/15
	Pittsburgh MSA, PA	Y	90810 FQ	115090 MW	141280 TQ	USBLS	5/15
	Rhode Island	Y	96840 FQ	123130 MW	152250 TQ	USBLS	5/15
	Providence-Warwick MSA, RI-MA	Y	90030 FQ	116080 MW	147860 TQ	USBLS	5/15
	South Carolina	Y	67830 FQ	90210 MW	122670 TQ	USBLS	5/15
	Charleston-North Charleston MSA, SC	Y	67280 FQ	91100 MW	120640 TQ	USBLS	5/15
	Columbia MSA, SC	Y	61960 FQ	74090 MW	98890 TQ	USBLS	5/15
	Greenville-Anderson-Mauldin MSA, SC	Y	71430 FQ	93000 MW	119380 TQ	USBLS	5/15
	South Dakota	Y	79780 FQ	93470 MW	110820 TQ	USBLS	5/15
	Tennessee	Y	57960 FQ	76490 MW	101880 TQ	USBLS	5/15
	Knoxville MSA, TN	Y	59910 FQ	74630 MW	97390 TQ	USBLS	5/15
	Memphis MSA, TN-MS-AR	Y	61730 FQ	81700 MW	103780 TQ	USBLS	5/15
	Nashville-Davidson–Murfreesboro–Franklin MSA, TN	Y	60790 FQ	78520 MW	102930 TQ	USBLS	5/15
	Texas	Y	91150 FQ	121620 MW	156780 TQ	USBLS	5/15
	Austin-Round Rock MSA, TX	Y	86200 FQ	113130 MW	146050 TQ	USBLS	5/15
	Dallas-Plano-Irving PMSA, TX	Y	89530 FQ	118800 MW	146090 TQ	USBLS	5/15
	Fort Worth-Arlington PMSA, TX	Y	88030 FQ	113080 MW	134900 TQ	USBLS	5/15
	Houston-The Woodlands-Sugar Land MSA, TX	Y	100200 FQ	139890 MW	187110 TQ	USBLS	5/15
	San Antonio-New Braunfels MSA, TX	Y	95160 FQ	115640 MW	137820 TQ	USBLS	5/15
	Utah	Y	76110 FQ	102500 MW	128120 TQ	USBLS	5/15
	Ogden-Clearfield MSA, UT	Y	82010 FQ	111790 MW	126580 TQ	USBLS	5/15
	Provo-Orem MSA, UT	Y	73850 FQ	91910 MW	123950 TQ	USBLS	5/15
	Salt Lake City MSA, UT	Y	80100 FQ	101810 MW	130670 TQ	USBLS	5/15
	Vermont	Y	74440 FQ	93750 MW	113720 TQ	USBLS	5/15
	Burlington-South Burlington MSA, VT	Y	85530 FQ	98900 MW	116930 TQ	USBLS	5/15
	Virginia	Y	107320 FQ	125200 MW	147290 TQ	USBLS	5/15
	Richmond MSA, VA	Y	86420 FQ	109360 MW	127470 TQ	USBLS	5/15
	Virginia Beach-Norfolk-Newport News MSA, VA-NC	Y	103990 FQ	115080 MW	128440 TQ	USBLS	5/15
	Washington	H	43.27 FQ	58.47 MW	74.71 TQ	WABLS	3/16
	Seattle-Bellevue-Everett PMSA, WA	H	47.47 FQ	61.75 MW	78.37 TQ	WABLS	3/16

Occupation/Type/Industry	Location	Per	Low	Mid	High	Source	Date
Purchasing Manager	Tacoma-Lakewood PMSA, WA	H	32.72 FQ	38.47 MW	49.19 TQ	WABLS	3/16
	West Virginia	Y	101930 FQ	112130 MW	123740 TQ	USBLS	5/15
	Wisconsin	Y	73240 FQ	89520 MW	112580 TQ	USBLS	5/15
	Madison MSA, WI	Y	69430 FQ	84280 MW	99600 TQ	USBLS	5/15
	Milwaukee-Waukesha-West Allis MSA, WI	Y	76100 FQ	95810 MW	127080 TQ	USBLS	5/15
	Wyoming	Y	75250 FQ	103660 MW	121060 TQ	USBLS	5/15
	Puerto Rico	Y	46400 FQ	64300 MW	89960 TQ	USBLS	5/15
	San Juan-Carolina-Caguas MSA, PR	Y	49570 FQ	66090 MW	93770 TQ	USBLS	5/15
	Guam	Y	34320 FQ	47670 MW	60600 TQ	USBLS	5/15
Quality Assurance Manager	United States	Y		85000 MW		TDY01	2016
Quality Assurance Specialist	United States	Y		82741 AW		CWRLD3	2016
Racing Inspector							
State Government	Ohio	H	16.49 LO		19.78 HI	OHGOV	2015
Radiation Oncologist	United States	Y		361667-570529 MWR		MHLTH03	2015
Radiation Safety Officer							
California State University	California	Y	51816 LO		100932 HI	CALST	2016-2017
Radiation Therapist	Alabama	Y	60843 AE	79130 AW	88273 AEX	ALBLS	6/16
	Birmingham-Hoover MSA, AL	Y	63147 AE	79986 AW	88416 AEX	ALBLS	6/16
	Arizona	Y	63680 FQ	78570 MW	96300 TQ	USBLS	5/15
	Phoenix-Mesa-Scottsdale MSA, AZ	Y	62500 FQ	77060 MW	94550 TQ	USBLS	5/15
	Arkansas	Y	57200 FQ	72130 MW	92970 TQ	USBLS	5/15
	Little Rock-North Little Rock-Conway MSA, AR	Y	56790 FQ	79400 MW	99090 TQ	USBLS	5/15
	California	H	43.19 FQ	53.03 MW	62.41 TQ	CABLS	1/16-3/16
	Los Angeles-Long Beach-Glendale PMSA, CA	H	39.07 FQ	47.97 MW	58.26 TQ	CABLS	1/16-3/16
	Oakland-Hayward-Berkeley PMSA, CA	H	46.75 FQ	55.89 MW	65.76 TQ	CABLS	1/16-3/16
	Riverside-San Bernardino-Ontario MSA, CA	H	43.28 FQ	51.19 MW	58.74 TQ	CABLS	1/16-3/16
	Sacramento–Roseville–Arden-Arcade MSA, CA	H	56.40 FQ	64.58 MW	76.50 TQ	CABLS	1/16-3/16
	San Diego-Carlsbad MSA, CA	H	45.60 FQ	56.06 MW	74.67 TQ	CABLS	1/16-3/16
	San Francisco-Redwood City-South San Francisco PMSA, CA	H	51.75 FQ	66.66 MW	76.57 TQ	CABLS	1/16-3/16
	Colorado	Y	73220 FQ	88180 MW	103140 TQ	USBLS	5/15
	Denver-Aurora-Lakewood MSA, CO	Y	71710 FQ	86690 MW	101760 TQ	USBLS	5/15
	Connecticut	Y		92928 MW		CTBLS	1/16-3/16
	Delaware	Y	72140 FQ	91830 MW	108460 TQ	USBLS	5/15
	District of Columbia	Y	65290 FQ	75870 MW	90470 TQ	USBLS	5/15
	Washington-Arlington-Alexandria PMSA, DC-VA-MD-WV	Y	68870 FQ	81390 MW	99500 TQ	USBLS	5/15
	Florida	H	30.42 AE	39.51 MW	53.23 AEX	FLBLS	7/16-9/16
	Fort Lauderdale-Pompano Beach-Deerfield Beach PMSA, FL	H	30.07 AE	40.81 MW	44.47 AEX	FLBLS	7/16-9/16
	Miami-Miami Beach-Kendall PMSA, FL	H	33.93 AE	40.32 MW	45.67 AEX	FLBLS	7/16-9/16
	Orlando-Kissimmee-Sanford MSA, FL	H	28.87 AE	37.25 MW	48.27 AEX	FLBLS	7/16-9/16
	Tampa-St. Petersburg-Clearwater MSA, FL	H	30.62 AE	44.11 MW	67.71 AEX	FLBLS	7/16-9/16
	Georgia	Y	59200 FQ	72080 MW	89000 TQ	USBLS	5/15
	Atlanta-Sandy Springs-Roswell MSA, GA	Y	64420 FQ	74930 MW	95540 TQ	USBLS	5/15
	Augusta-Richmond County MSA, GA-SC	Y	54720 FQ	62430 MW	77670 TQ	USBLS	5/15
	Idaho	Y	69920 FQ	79990 MW	97600 TQ	USBLS	5/15
	Illinois	Y	64260 FQ	80760 MW	96330 TQ	USBLS	5/15

Occupation/Type/Industry	Location	Per	Low	Mid	High	Source	Date
Radiation Therapist	Chicago-Naperville-Arlington Heights PMSA, IL	Y	73130 FQ	87630 MW	99670 TQ	USBLS	5/15
	Indiana	Y	67430 FQ	79750 MW	94410 TQ	USBLS	5/15
	Gary PMSA, IN	Y	79770 FQ	89700 MW	98870 TQ	USBLS	5/15
	Indianapolis-Carmel-Anderson MSA, IN	Y	66680 FQ	77470 MW	91840 TQ	USBLS	5/15
	Iowa	Y	58740 FQ	67430 MW	78640 TQ	USBLS	5/15
	Kansas	Y	59830 FQ	72330 MW	90230 TQ	USBLS	5/15
	Kentucky	Y	62880 FQ	78430 MW	92270 TQ	USBLS	5/15
	Louisville-Jefferson County MSA, KY-IN	Y	71020 FQ	85090 MW	96060 TQ	USBLS	5/15
	Louisiana	Y	56220 FQ	66950 MW	76680 TQ	USBLS	5/15
	Baton Rouge MSA, LA	Y	55000 FQ	60880 MW	74410 TQ	USBLS	5/15
	New Orleans-Metairie MSA, LA	Y	66250 FQ	73240 MW	80280 TQ	USBLS	5/15
	Maine	Y	59790 FQ	69670 MW	78590 TQ	USBLS	5/15
	Maryland	Y	58944 AE	82732 MW	94626 AEX	MDBLS	4/16
	Baltimore-Columbia-Towson MSA, MD	Y	61370 FQ	75920 MW	96010 TQ	USBLS	5/15
	Massachusetts	Y	71650 FQ	88910 MW	108150 TQ	USBLS	5/15
	Boston-Cambridge-Newton NECTA, MA	Y	72870 FQ	89430 MW	108980 TQ	USBLS	5/15
	Michigan	Y	61760 FQ	72440 MW	85360 TQ	USBLS	5/15
	Detroit-Dearborn-Livonia PMSA, MI	Y	61160 FQ	73020 MW	86450 TQ	USBLS	5/15
	Minnesota	Y	67136 FQ	79213 MW	95674 TQ	MNBLS	1/16-3/16
	Minneapolis-St. Paul-Bloomington MSA, MN-WI	Y	65675 FQ	75271 MW	91642 TQ	MNBLS	1/16-3/16
	Mississippi	Y	60140 FQ	75690 MW	93030 TQ	USBLS	5/15
	Jackson MSA, MS	Y	70400 FQ	86330 MW	97190 TQ	USBLS	5/15
	Missouri	Y	66940 FQ	80180 MW	94880 TQ	USBLS	5/15
	Kansas City MSA, MO-KS	Y	65270 FQ	76870 MW	96880 TQ	USBLS	5/15
	St. Louis MSA, MO-IL	Y	65120 FQ	76850 MW	92100 TQ	USBLS	5/15
	Montana	Y	59440 FQ	80790 MW	104570 TQ	USBLS	5/15
	Nebraska	Y	61215 FQ	75110 MW	98165 TQ	NEBLS	7/16-9/16
	Omaha-Council Bluffs MSA, NE-IA	Y	60210 FQ	73800 MW	101325 TQ	NEBLS	7/16-9/16
	Nevada	Y	55560 FQ	61640 MW	88880 TQ	USBLS	5/15
	Las Vegas-Henderson-Paradise MSA, NV	Y	53800 FQ	57810 MW	61820 TQ	USBLS	5/15
	New Hampshire	H	30.03 AE	39.13 MW	45.58 AEX	NHBLS	6/16
	New Jersey	Y	86390 FQ	98240 MW	116080 TQ	USBLS	5/15
	Camden PMSA, NJ	Y	87970 FQ	97710 MW	113500 TQ	USBLS	5/15
	Newark PMSA, NJ-PA	Y	86820 FQ	97690 MW	115500 TQ	USBLS	5/15
	New Mexico	Y	68620 FQ	79190 MW	96420 TQ	USBLS	5/15
	New York	Y	60240 AE	88740 MW	106020 AEX	NYBLS	1/16-3/16
	Buffalo-Cheektowaga-Niagara Falls MSA, NY	Y	53310 FQ	59290 MW	68270 TQ	USBLS	5/15
	Nassau County-Suffolk County PMSA, NY	Y	88400 FQ	101310 MW	117130 TQ	USBLS	5/15
	New York-Jersey City-White Plains PMSA, NY-NJ	Y	78640 FQ	95660 MW	116350 TQ	USBLS	5/15
	Rochester MSA, NY	Y	55330 FQ	66220 MW	77960 TQ	USBLS	5/15
	North Carolina	Y	62680 FQ	74810 MW	89900 TQ	USBLS	5/15
	Charlotte-Concord-Gastonia MSA, NC-SC	Y	60270 FQ	73500 MW	89260 TQ	USBLS	5/15
	Durham-Chapel Hill MSA, NC	Y	64430 FQ	74200 MW	91790 TQ	USBLS	5/15
	Raleigh MSA, NC	Y	65800 FQ	80160 MW	91340 TQ	USBLS	5/15
	Ohio	Y	62510 FQ	70840 MW	79100 TQ	USBLS	5/15
	Cincinnati MSA, OH-KY-IN	Y	63370 FQ	70580 MW	77600 TQ	USBLS	5/15
	Cleveland-Elyria MSA, OH	Y	60700 FQ	70300 MW	79130 TQ	USBLS	5/15
	Columbus MSA, OH	Y	62400 FQ	74040 MW	92470 TQ	USBLS	5/15
	Oklahoma	Y	64100 FQ	79990 MW	96870 TQ	USBLS	5/15
	Oklahoma City MSA, OK	Y	64930 FQ	81750 MW	95320 TQ	USBLS	5/15
	Tulsa MSA, OK	Y	67900 FQ	83960 MW	103210 TQ	USBLS	5/15
	Oregon	H	41.09 FQ	45.68 MW	51.10 TQ	ORBLS	2016
	Portland-Vancouver-Hillsboro MSA, OR-WA	Y	83910 FQ	93120 MW	103190 TQ	USBLS	5/15
	Pennsylvania	Y	66400 FQ	79650 MW	97260 TQ	USBLS	5/15
	Allentown-Bethlehem-Easton MSA, PA-NJ	Y	62400 FQ	74770 MW	90020 TQ	USBLS	5/15

AE	Average entry wage	AWR	Average wage range	H	Hourly
AEX	Average experienced wage	B	Biweekly	HI	Highest wage paid
ATC	Average total compensation	D	Daily	HR	High end range
AW	Average wage paid	FQ	First quartile wage	LO	Lowest wage paid

LR	Low end range	MTC	Median total compensation
M	Monthly	MW	Median wage paid
MCC	Median cash compensation	MWR	Median wage range
ME	Median entry wage	S	See annotated source

TCC	Total cash compensation
TQ	Third quartile wage
W	Weekly
Y	Yearly

Occupation/Type/Industry	Location	Per	Low	Mid	High	Source	Date
Radiation Therapist	Montgomery County-Bucks County-Chester County PMSA, PA	Y	67020 FQ	77290 MW	92950 TQ	USBLS	5/15
	Philadelphia PMSA, PA	Y	81770 FQ	94890 MW	111030 TQ	USBLS	5/15
	Pittsburgh MSA, PA	Y	53590 FQ	63080 MW	81170 TQ	USBLS	5/15
	Rhode Island	Y	73070 FQ	94820 MW	113220 TQ	USBLS	5/15
	Providence-Warwick MSA, RI-MA	Y	63490 FQ	84920 MW	108070 TQ	USBLS	5/15
	South Carolina	Y	57360 FQ	71700 MW	90420 TQ	USBLS	5/15
	Greenville-Anderson-Mauldin MSA, SC	Y	64140 FQ	81650 MW	104440 TQ	USBLS	5/15
	Tennessee	Y	58220 FQ	69530 MW	79450 TQ	USBLS	5/15
	Knoxville MSA, TN	Y	60870 FQ	69890 MW	78110 TQ	USBLS	5/15
	Memphis MSA, TN-MS-AR	Y	54560 FQ	67710 MW	78810 TQ	USBLS	5/15
	Nashville-Davidson–Murfreesboro–Franklin MSA, TN	Y	65280 FQ	72440 MW	79590 TQ	USBLS	5/15
	Texas	Y	55820 FQ	73860 MW	93460 TQ	USBLS	5/15
	Dallas-Plano-Irving PMSA, TX	Y	45850 FQ	52490 MW	64910 TQ	USBLS	5/15
	Fort Worth-Arlington PMSA, TX	Y	61080 FQ	78090 MW	95000 TQ	USBLS	5/15
	Houston-The Woodlands-Sugar Land MSA, TX	Y	76450 FQ	90680 MW	105630 TQ	USBLS	5/15
	San Antonio-New Braunfels MSA, TX	Y	65070 FQ	77280 MW	90760 TQ	USBLS	5/15
	Utah	Y	65040 FQ	75000 MW	88460 TQ	USBLS	5/15
	Salt Lake City MSA, UT	Y	65010 FQ	74480 MW	87830 TQ	USBLS	5/15
	Vermont	Y	76840 FQ	88590 MW	101880 TQ	USBLS	5/15
	Virginia	Y	62120 FQ	78160 MW	96780 TQ	USBLS	5/15
	Richmond MSA, VA	Y	66860 FQ	77640 MW	94730 TQ	USBLS	5/15
	Virginia Beach-Norfolk-Newport News MSA, VA-NC	Y	80410 FQ	90090 MW	99410 TQ	USBLS	5/15
	Washington	H	36.14 FQ	44.12 MW	54.28 TQ	WABLS	3/16
	Seattle-Bellevue-Everett PMSA, WA	H	42.36 FQ	50.31 MW	59.01 TQ	WABLS	3/16
	West Virginia	Y	62940 FQ	72330 MW	86400 TQ	USBLS	5/15
	Wisconsin	Y	69030 FQ	80900 MW	93950 TQ	USBLS	5/15
	Madison MSA, WI	Y	68490 FQ	76380 MW	90180 TQ	USBLS	5/15
	Milwaukee-Waukesha-West Allis MSA, WI	Y	82670 FQ	91280 MW	100030 TQ	USBLS	5/15
Radio and Television Announcer	Alabama	Y	17451 AE	33128 AW	40967 AEX	ALBLS	6/16
	Birmingham-Hoover MSA, AL	Y	20560 AE	50161 AW	64962 AEX	ALBLS	6/16
	Alaska	Y	31680 FQ	39180 MW	54520 TQ	USBLS	5/15
	Anchorage MSA, AK	Y	36070 FQ	52790 MW	61640 TQ	USBLS	5/15
	Phoenix-Mesa-Scottsdale MSA, AZ	Y	28620 FQ	54250 MW	113670 TQ	USBLS	5/15
	Tucson MSA, AZ	Y	22910 FQ	32340 MW	44960 TQ	USBLS	5/15
	Arkansas	Y	17810 FQ	21090 MW	31960 TQ	USBLS	5/15
	California	H	13.39 FQ	20.58 MW	33.99 TQ	CABLS	1/16-3/16
	Anaheim-Santa Ana-Irvine PMSA, CA	H	10.49 FQ	16.44 MW	23.04 TQ	CABLS	1/16-3/16
	Los Angeles-Long Beach-Glendale PMSA, CA	H	14.33 FQ	21.33 MW	39.20 TQ	CABLS	1/16-3/16
	Riverside-San Bernardino-Ontario MSA, CA	H	9.64 FQ	12.18 MW	21.28 TQ	CABLS	1/16-3/16
	Sacramento–Roseville–Arden-Arcade MSA, CA	H	12.82 FQ	20.78 MW	28.96 TQ	CABLS	1/16-3/16
	San Francisco-Redwood City-South San Francisco PMSA, CA	H	17.71 FQ	23.20 MW	37.22 TQ	CABLS	1/16-3/16
	Colorado	Y	23810 FQ	37900 MW	66720 TQ	USBLS	5/15
	Denver-Aurora-Lakewood MSA, CO	Y	27400 FQ	51890 MW	81450 TQ	USBLS	5/15
	Connecticut	Y		26854 MW		CTBLS	1/16-3/16
	Hartford-West Hartford-East Hartford MSA, CT	Y	22440 FQ	25760 MW	35740 TQ	USBLS	5/15
	District of Columbia	Y	37790 FQ	55030 MW	72340 TQ	USBLS	5/15
	Washington-Arlington-Alexandria PMSA, DC-VA-MD-WV	Y	31530 FQ	52680 MW	68290 TQ	USBLS	5/15
	Florida	H	9.38 AE	14.23 MW	26.64 AEX	FLBLS	7/16-9/16

Occupation/Type/Industry	Location	Per	Low	Mid	High	Source	Date
Radio and Television Announcer	Fort Lauderdale-Pompano Beach-Deerfield Beach PMSA, FL	H	11.85 AE	20.81 MW	33.89 AEX	FLBLS	7/16-9/16
	Miami-Miami Beach-Kendall PMSA, FL	H	10.20 AE	16.52 MW	19.89 AEX	FLBLS	7/16-9/16
	Orlando-Kissimmee-Sanford MSA, FL	H	10.08 AE	17.41 MW	24.79 AEX	FLBLS	7/16-9/16
	Georgia	Y	19600 FQ	31110 MW	49430 TQ	USBLS	5/15
	Atlanta-Sandy Springs-Roswell MSA, GA	Y	31170 FQ	46210 MW	96670 TQ	USBLS	5/15
	Augusta-Richmond County MSA, GA-SC	Y	17270 FQ	19090 MW	30280 TQ	USBLS	5/15
	Hawaii	Y	25290 FQ	33220 MW	47060 TQ	USBLS	5/15
	Urban Honolulu MSA, HI	Y	26780 FQ	34290 MW	49630 TQ	USBLS	5/15
	Idaho	Y	20140 FQ	23050 MW	28160 TQ	USBLS	5/15
	Illinois	Y	20310 FQ	27630 MW	44170 TQ	USBLS	5/15
	Chicago-Naperville-Arlington Heights PMSA, IL	Y	22170 FQ	32650 MW	49330 TQ	USBLS	5/15
	Indiana	Y	18760 FQ	27320 MW	39750 TQ	USBLS	5/15
	Indianapolis-Carmel-Anderson MSA, IN	Y	18340 FQ	26360 MW	36120 TQ	USBLS	5/15
	Iowa	Y	19200 FQ	24620 MW	34790 TQ	USBLS	5/15
	Des Moines-West Des Moines MSA, IA	Y	30920 FQ	36530 MW	46740 TQ	USBLS	5/15
	Kansas	Y	18770 FQ	23620 MW	33220 TQ	USBLS	5/15
	Kentucky	Y	17850 FQ	21160 MW	27690 TQ	USBLS	5/15
	Louisville-Jefferson County MSA, KY-IN	Y	19270 FQ	27010 MW	34440 TQ	USBLS	5/15
	Louisiana	Y	21600 FQ	26770 MW	39280 TQ	USBLS	5/15
	Baton Rouge MSA, LA	Y	30230 FQ	39760 MW	61290 TQ	USBLS	5/15
	New Orleans-Metairie MSA, LA	Y	22950 FQ	27250 MW	31100 TQ	USBLS	5/15
	Maine	Y	21360 FQ	28220 MW	36710 TQ	USBLS	5/15
	Maryland	Y	24250 AE	76154 MW	102106 AEX	MDBLS	4/16
	Baltimore-Columbia-Towson MSA, MD	Y	33900 FQ	47970 MW	80340 TQ	USBLS	5/15
	Worcester MSA, MA-CT	Y	27680 FQ	40320 MW	48710 TQ	USBLS	5/15
	Michigan	Y	19040 FQ	25810 MW	36270 TQ	USBLS	5/15
	Detroit-Dearborn-Livonia PMSA, MI	Y	19720 FQ	29190 MW	35450 TQ	USBLS	5/15
	Minnesota	Y	23286 FQ	33669 MW	45463 TQ	MNBLS	1/16-3/16
	Minneapolis-St. Paul-Bloomington MSA, MN-WI	Y	30201 FQ	45181 MW	76803 TQ	MNBLS	1/16-3/16
	Mississippi	Y	18030 FQ	21620 MW	28570 TQ	USBLS	5/15
	Jackson MSA, MS	Y	20250 FQ	22690 MW	27560 TQ	USBLS	5/15
	Missouri	Y	19580 FQ	24690 MW	38400 TQ	USBLS	5/15
	Kansas City MSA, MO-KS	Y	19430 FQ	26090 MW	37890 TQ	USBLS	5/15
	St. Louis MSA, MO-IL	Y	20280 FQ	29610 MW	44070 TQ	USBLS	5/15
	Montana	Y	19810 FQ	26990 MW	35060 TQ	USBLS	5/15
	Nebraska	Y	20260 FQ	27615 MW	39330 TQ	NEBLS	7/16-9/16
	Omaha-Council Bluffs MSA, NE-IA	Y	27075 FQ	44940 MW	67485 TQ	NEBLS	7/16-9/16
	Nevada	Y	23850 FQ	36930 MW	48120 TQ	USBLS	5/15
	Las Vegas-Henderson-Paradise MSA, NV	Y	25400 FQ	37130 MW	60170 TQ	USBLS	5/15
	New Hampshire	H	9.03 AE	12.82 MW	18.82 AEX	NHBLS	6/16
	New Jersey	Y	26820 FQ	31420 MW	48480 TQ	USBLS	5/15
	Newark PMSA, NJ-PA	Y	28340 FQ	42020 MW	50870 TQ	USBLS	5/15
	New Mexico	Y	20590 FQ	27860 MW	40200 TQ	USBLS	5/15
	Albuquerque MSA, NM	Y	24580 FQ	31180 MW	50570 TQ	USBLS	5/15
	New York	Y	30410 AE	50410 MW	90810 AEX	NYBLS	1/16-3/16
	Buffalo-Cheektowaga-Niagara Falls MSA, NY	Y	25950 FQ	35970 MW	53700 TQ	USBLS	5/15
	Nassau County-Suffolk County PMSA, NY	Y	20140 FQ	40120 MW	53210 TQ	USBLS	5/15
	New York-Jersey City-White Plains PMSA, NY-NJ	Y	44340 FQ	56490 MW	95650 TQ	USBLS	5/15
	Rochester MSA, NY	Y	26190 FQ	34740 MW	57480 TQ	USBLS	5/15
	North Carolina	Y	17890 FQ	22160 MW	44310 TQ	USBLS	5/15
	Charlotte-Concord-Gastonia MSA, NC-SC	Y	18450 FQ	45470 MW	72850 TQ	USBLS	5/15
	North Dakota	Y	22910 FQ	28020 MW	35110 TQ	USBLS	5/15

AE	Average entry wage	AWR	Average wage range	H	Hourly
AEX	Average experienced wage	B	Biweekly	HI	Highest wage paid
ATC	Average total compensation	D	Daily	HR	High end range
AW	Average wage paid	FQ	First quartile wage	LO	Lowest wage paid

LR	Low end range	MTC	Median total compensation	TCC	Total cash compensation
M	Monthly	MW	Median wage paid	TQ	Third quartile wage
MCC	Median cash compensation	MWR	Median wage range	W	Weekly
ME	Median entry wage	S	See annotated source	Y	Yearly

Occupation/Type/Industry	Location	Per	Low	Mid	High	Source	Date
Radio and Television Announcer	Ohio	Y	20990 FQ	31840 MW	39610 TQ	USBLS	5/15
	Cincinnati MSA, OH-KY-IN	Y	21910 FQ	35360 MW	62280 TQ	USBLS	5/15
	Cleveland-Elyria MSA, OH	Y	24300 FQ	34010 MW	40090 TQ	USBLS	5/15
	Columbus MSA, OH	Y	22510 FQ	29180 MW	38980 TQ	USBLS	5/15
	Oklahoma	Y	19240 FQ	25620 MW	52970 TQ	USBLS	5/15
	Oklahoma City MSA, OK	Y	19550 FQ	37950 MW	58840 TQ	USBLS	5/15
	Tulsa MSA, OK	Y	24940 FQ	29980 MW	54840 TQ	USBLS	5/15
	Oregon	H	13.13 FQ	18.95 MW	49.61 TQ	ORBLS	2016
	Portland-Vancouver-Hillsboro MSA, OR-WA	Y	40060 FQ	81320 MW	139300 TQ	USBLS	5/15
	Pennsylvania	Y	18040 FQ	21960 MW	39740 TQ	USBLS	5/15
	Allentown-Bethlehem-Easton MSA, PA-NJ	Y	17790 FQ	20290 MW	46610 TQ	USBLS	5/15
	Harrisburg-Carlisle MSA, PA	Y	18460 FQ	26520 MW	45100 TQ	USBLS	5/15
	Montgomery County-Bucks County-Chester County PMSA, PA	Y	21970 FQ	36470 MW	59890 TQ	USBLS	5/15
	Philadelphia PMSA, PA	Y	17770 FQ	20130 MW	30550 TQ	USBLS	5/15
	Pittsburgh MSA, PA	Y	18290 FQ	24640 MW	66000 TQ	USBLS	5/15
	Rhode Island	Y	21240 FQ	28160 MW	42530 TQ	USBLS	5/15
	Providence-Warwick MSA, RI-MA	Y	21240 FQ	28160 MW	42530 TQ	USBLS	5/15
	South Carolina	Y	21360 FQ	24820 MW	46400 TQ	USBLS	5/15
	Charleston-North Charleston MSA, SC	Y	24330 FQ	43020 MW	62160 TQ	USBLS	5/15
	Columbia MSA, SC	Y	32830 FQ	47680 MW	70710 TQ	USBLS	5/15
	Greenville-Anderson-Mauldin MSA, SC	Y	21370 FQ	23390 MW	31690 TQ	USBLS	5/15
	South Dakota	Y	23680 FQ	29330 MW	36010 TQ	USBLS	5/15
	Sioux Falls MSA, SD	Y	25970 FQ	32000 MW	38950 TQ	USBLS	5/15
	Tennessee	Y	18250 FQ	23790 MW	36590 TQ	USBLS	5/15
	Knoxville MSA, TN	Y	19930 FQ	37760 MW	110980 TQ	USBLS	5/15
	Memphis MSA, TN-MS-AR	Y	20610 FQ	31420 MW	37870 TQ	USBLS	5/15
	Nashville-Davidson–Murfreesboro–Franklin MSA, TN	Y	18140 FQ	23500 MW	34990 TQ	USBLS	5/15
	Texas	Y	22160 FQ	36040 MW	59780 TQ	USBLS	5/15
	Austin-Round Rock MSA, TX	Y	26090 FQ	44260 MW	67300 TQ	USBLS	5/15
	Dallas-Plano-Irving PMSA, TX	Y	23980 FQ	38890 MW	68010 TQ	USBLS	5/15
	Houston-The Woodlands-Sugar Land MSA, TX	Y	32230 FQ	53550 MW	69790 TQ	USBLS	5/15
	San Antonio-New Braunfels MSA, TX	Y	26920 FQ	52280 MW	71310 TQ	USBLS	5/15
	Utah	Y	29790 FQ	44220 MW	57350 TQ	USBLS	5/15
	Salt Lake City MSA, UT	Y	28330 FQ	46790 MW	60440 TQ	USBLS	5/15
	Vermont	Y	21500 FQ	29230 MW	39370 TQ	USBLS	5/15
	Burlington-South Burlington MSA, VT	Y	23180 FQ	34830 MW	45750 TQ	USBLS	5/15
	Virginia	Y	20020 FQ	30610 MW	51060 TQ	USBLS	5/15
	Richmond MSA, VA	Y	21800 FQ	29890 MW	44340 TQ	USBLS	5/15
	Virginia Beach-Norfolk-Newport News MSA, VA-NC	Y	19480 FQ	33030 MW	55800 TQ	USBLS	5/15
	Washington	H	11.47 FQ	16.42 MW	23.90 TQ	WABLS	3/16
	Seattle-Bellevue-Everett PMSA, WA	H	11.69 FQ	17.22 MW	25.42 TQ	WABLS	3/16
	Tacoma-Lakewood PMSA, WA	H	19.43 FQ	24.94 MW	30.11 TQ	WABLS	3/16
	West Virginia	Y	18320 FQ	20100 MW	30980 TQ	USBLS	5/15
	Huntington-Ashland MSA, WV-KY-OH	Y	17750 FQ	18850 MW	19960 TQ	USBLS	5/15
	Wisconsin	Y	19100 FQ	25450 MW	38690 TQ	USBLS	5/15
	Madison MSA, WI	Y	22210 FQ	30240 MW	45630 TQ	USBLS	5/15
	Milwaukee-Waukesha-West Allis MSA, WI	Y	21000 FQ	27250 MW	46580 TQ	USBLS	5/15
	Wyoming	Y	19770 FQ	27240 MW	30030 TQ	USBLS	5/15
	Puerto Rico	Y	16900 FQ	18240 MW	19580 TQ	USBLS	5/15
	San Juan-Carolina-Caguas MSA, PR	Y	16930 FQ	18400 MW	20970 TQ	USBLS	5/15
Radio Field Engineer							
Municipal Government	Colorado Springs, CO	Y	62111 LO		85402 HI	COSPRS	2017
Radio Operator	District of Columbia	Y	51480 FQ	55520 MW	57020 TQ	USBLS	5/15

AE	Average entry wage	AWR	Average wage range	H	Hourly	LR	Low end range	MTC	Median total compensation	TCC	Total cash compensation
AEX	Average experienced wage	B	Biweekly	HI	Highest wage paid	M	Monthly	MW	Median wage paid	TQ	Third quartile wage
ATC	Average total compensation	D	Daily	HR	High end range	MCC	Median cash compensation	MWR	Median wage range	W	Weekly
AW	Average wage paid	FQ	First quartile wage	LO	Lowest wage paid	ME	Median entry wage	S	See annotated source	Y	Yearly

Occupation/Type/Industry	Location	Per	Low	Mid	High	Source	Date
Radio Operator	Indiana	Y	32230 FQ	36490 MW	46130 TQ	USBLS	5/15
	Michigan	Y	48680 FQ	57230 MW	57760 TQ	USBLS	5/15
	Minnesota	Y	43548 FQ	50342 MW	55120 TQ	MNBLS	1/16-3/16
	New York	Y	50150 AE	63610 MW	70050 AEX	NYBLS	1/16-3/16
	Ohio	Y	34500 FQ	36970 MW	43520 TQ	USBLS	5/15
	Puerto Rico	Y	16830 FQ	18190 MW	19590 TQ	USBLS	5/15
Radio Station Manager							
Michigan State University	East Lansing, MI	Y			96120 HI	MSUSAL	10/1/14-9/30/15
Radiologic Technologist	Alabama	Y	34616 AE	47878 AW	54503 AEX	ALBLS	6/16
	Birmingham-Hoover MSA, AL	Y	40426 AE	52006 AW	40426 AEX	ALBLS	6/16
	Alaska	Y	60430 FQ	70070 MW	79460 TQ	USBLS	5/15
	Anchorage MSA, AK	Y	60270 FQ	71920 MW	84240 TQ	USBLS	5/15
	Arizona	Y	51180 FQ	60950 MW	73520 TQ	USBLS	5/15
	Phoenix-Mesa-Scottsdale MSA, AZ	Y	51530 FQ	63380 MW	75580 TQ	USBLS	5/15
	Tucson MSA, AZ	Y	48270 FQ	56020 MW	63330 TQ	USBLS	5/15
	Arkansas	Y	37690 FQ	46090 MW	56970 TQ	USBLS	5/15
	Little Rock-North Little Rock-Conway MSA, AR	Y	40170 FQ	49600 MW	64160 TQ	USBLS	5/15
	California	H	27.60 FQ	36.57 MW	46.75 TQ	CABLS	1/16-3/16
	Anaheim-Santa Ana-Irvine PMSA, CA	H	21.36 FQ	31.31 MW	42.88 TQ	CABLS	1/16-3/16
	Los Angeles-Long Beach-Glendale PMSA, CA	H	26.97 FQ	34.61 MW	41.98 TQ	CABLS	1/16-3/16
	Oakland-Hayward-Berkeley PMSA, CA	H	30.93 FQ	46.56 MW	57.23 TQ	CABLS	1/16-3/16
	Riverside-San Bernardino-Ontario MSA, CA	H	23.11 FQ	31.70 MW	37.64 TQ	CABLS	1/16-3/16
	Sacramento–Roseville–Arden-Arcade MSA, CA	H	38.19 FQ	44.24 MW	49.51 TQ	CABLS	1/16-3/16
	San Diego-Carlsbad MSA, CA	H	26.43 FQ	33.85 MW	41.54 TQ	CABLS	1/16-3/16
	San Francisco-Redwood City-South San Francisco PMSA, CA	H	37.21 FQ	46.25 MW	55.36 TQ	CABLS	1/16-3/16
	Colorado	Y	50080 FQ	60800 MW	74400 TQ	USBLS	5/15
	Denver-Aurora-Lakewood MSA, CO	Y	52030 FQ	63450 MW	76770 TQ	USBLS	5/15
	Connecticut	Y		63984 MW		CTBLS	1/16-3/16
	Bridgeport-Stamford-Norwalk MSA, CT	Y	52570 FQ	63120 MW	76670 TQ	USBLS	5/15
	Hartford-West Hartford-East Hartford MSA, CT	Y	55430 FQ	65090 MW	75970 TQ	USBLS	5/15
	Delaware	Y	50250 FQ	58750 MW	69550 TQ	USBLS	5/15
	Wilmington PMSA, DE-MD-NJ	Y	50740 FQ	59560 MW	70620 TQ	USBLS	5/15
	District of Columbia	Y	64530 FQ	75390 MW	88490 TQ	USBLS	5/15
	Washington-Arlington-Alexandria PMSA, DC-VA-MD-WV	Y	57510 FQ	68490 MW	80720 TQ	USBLS	5/15
	Florida	H	18.31 AE	25.27 MW	29.03 AEX	FLBLS	7/16-9/16
	Fort Lauderdale-Pompano Beach-Deerfield Beach PMSA, FL	H	17.18 AE	24.23 MW	29.65 AEX	FLBLS	7/16-9/16
	Miami-Miami Beach-Kendall PMSA, FL	H	18.50 AE	26.25 MW	30.52 AEX	FLBLS	7/16-9/16
	Orlando-Kissimmee-Sanford MSA, FL	H	16.67 AE	23.32 MW	27.09 AEX	FLBLS	7/16-9/16
	Tampa-St. Petersburg-Clearwater MSA, FL	H	18.28 AE	26.55 MW	29.74 AEX	FLBLS	7/16-9/16
	Georgia	Y	42510 FQ	50440 MW	60640 TQ	USBLS	5/15
	Atlanta-Sandy Springs-Roswell MSA, GA	Y	44730 FQ	53660 MW	63090 TQ	USBLS	5/15
	Augusta-Richmond County MSA, GA-SC	Y	44600 FQ	51730 MW	59250 TQ	USBLS	5/15
	Hawaii	Y	59630 FQ	69860 MW	78630 TQ	USBLS	5/15
	Urban Honolulu MSA, HI	Y	64490 FQ	72210 MW	80500 TQ	USBLS	5/15
	Idaho	Y	43680 FQ	50850 MW	59890 TQ	USBLS	5/15
	Boise City MSA, ID	Y	43740 FQ	50510 MW	59880 TQ	USBLS	5/15
	Illinois	Y	48500 FQ	59490 MW	72720 TQ	USBLS	5/15

AE	Average entry wage	AWR	Average wage range	H	Hourly
AEX	Average experienced wage	B	Biweekly	HI	Highest wage paid
ATC	Average total compensation	D	Daily	HR	High end range
AW	Average wage paid	FQ	First quartile wage	LO	Lowest wage paid

LR	Low end range	MTC	Median total compensation	TCC	Total cash compensation
M	Monthly	MW	Median wage paid	TQ	Third quartile wage
MCC	Median cash compensation	MWR	Median wage range	W	Weekly
ME	Median entry wage	S	See annotated source	Y	Yearly

Occupation/Type/Industry	Location	Per	Low	Mid	High	Source	Date
Radiologic Technologist	Chicago-Naperville-Arlington Heights PMSA, IL	Y	52930 FQ	62770 MW	75410 TQ	USBLS	5/15
	Lake County-Kenosha County PMSA, IL-WI	Y	53890 FQ	64440 MW	74890 TQ	USBLS	5/15
	Indiana	Y	44630 FQ	53150 MW	62980 TQ	USBLS	5/15
	Gary PMSA, IN	Y	42840 FQ	53940 MW	65810 TQ	USBLS	5/15
	Indianapolis-Carmel-Anderson MSA, IN	Y	47710 FQ	57310 MW	68940 TQ	USBLS	5/15
	Iowa	Y	42000 FQ	48800 MW	58060 TQ	USBLS	5/15
	Des Moines-West Des Moines MSA, IA	Y	45720 FQ	53480 MW	62570 TQ	USBLS	5/15
	Kansas	Y	42970 FQ	49950 MW	58530 TQ	USBLS	5/15
	Wichita MSA, KS	Y	41680 FQ	47640 MW	55560 TQ	USBLS	5/15
	Kentucky	Y	41090 FQ	49210 MW	58520 TQ	USBLS	5/15
	Louisville-Jefferson County MSA, KY-IN	Y	41560 FQ	51820 MW	59920 TQ	USBLS	5/15
	Louisiana	Y	40140 FQ	46950 MW	55840 TQ	USBLS	5/15
	Baton Rouge MSA, LA	Y	41810 FQ	47820 MW	57320 TQ	USBLS	5/15
	New Orleans-Metairie MSA, LA	Y	44630 FQ	52430 MW	59700 TQ	USBLS	5/15
	Maine	Y	47610 FQ	55630 MW	63620 TQ	USBLS	5/15
	Portland-South Portland MSA, ME	Y	46100 FQ	55210 MW	66230 TQ	USBLS	5/15
	Maryland	Y	48272 AE	64025 MW	71901 AEX	MDBLS	4/16
	Baltimore-Columbia-Towson MSA, MD	Y	53950 FQ	63200 MW	73930 TQ	USBLS	5/15
	Salisbury MSA, MD-DE	Y	47360 FQ	56350 MW	67440 TQ	USBLS	5/15
	Massachusetts	Y	57320 FQ	70650 MW	86960 TQ	USBLS	5/15
	Boston-Cambridge-Newton NECTA, MA	Y	58780 FQ	73480 MW	89400 TQ	USBLS	5/15
	Worcester MSA, MA-CT	Y	66410 FQ	80280 MW	96460 TQ	USBLS	5/15
	Michigan	Y	44420 FQ	52530 MW	60820 TQ	USBLS	5/15
	Detroit-Dearborn-Livonia PMSA, MI	Y	46630 FQ	55190 MW	62580 TQ	USBLS	5/15
	Grand Rapids-Wyoming MSA, MI	Y	43070 FQ	48200 MW	56470 TQ	USBLS	5/15
	Minnesota	Y	53890 FQ	63376 MW	73527 TQ	MNBLS	1/16-3/16
	Minneapolis-St. Paul-Bloomington MSA, MN-WI	Y	55403 FQ	64798 MW	74062 TQ	MNBLS	1/16-3/16
	Mississippi	Y	39200 FQ	46030 MW	54830 TQ	USBLS	5/15
	Jackson MSA, MS	Y	40330 FQ	47350 MW	56980 TQ	USBLS	5/15
	Missouri	Y	42720 FQ	50320 MW	59720 TQ	USBLS	5/15
	Kansas City MSA, MO-KS	Y	45940 FQ	54180 MW	62100 TQ	USBLS	5/15
	St. Louis MSA, MO-IL	Y	43770 FQ	51500 MW	60800 TQ	USBLS	5/15
	Montana	Y	43800 FQ	51350 MW	60800 TQ	USBLS	5/15
	Billings MSA, MT	Y	43200 FQ	50460 MW	59750 TQ	USBLS	5/15
	Nebraska	Y	43900 FQ	52515 MW	60595 TQ	NEBLS	7/16-9/16
	Omaha-Council Bluffs MSA, NE-IA	Y	44385 FQ	53295 MW	60550 TQ	NEBLS	7/16-9/16
	Nevada	Y	55350 FQ	66420 MW	78450 TQ	USBLS	5/15
	Las Vegas-Henderson-Paradise MSA, NV	Y	54750 FQ	65710 MW	79870 TQ	USBLS	5/15
	New Hampshire	H	23.65 AE	30.40 MW	34.12 AEX	NHBLS	6/16
	Manchester NECTA, NH	H	24.19 AE	31.08 MW	34.32 AEX	NHBLS	6/16
	Nashua NECTA, NH-MA	Y	54260 FQ	67730 MW	82850 TQ	USBLS	5/15
	New Jersey	Y	55340 FQ	65010 MW	75130 TQ	USBLS	5/15
	Camden PMSA, NJ	Y	57360 FQ	66100 MW	73960 TQ	USBLS	5/15
	Newark PMSA, NJ-PA	Y	56780 FQ	66780 MW	76150 TQ	USBLS	5/15
	Trenton MSA, NJ	Y	58220 FQ	66760 MW	75730 TQ	USBLS	5/15
	New Mexico	Y	49360 FQ	57590 MW	67640 TQ	USBLS	5/15
	Albuquerque MSA, NM	Y	52510 FQ	60090 MW	70150 TQ	USBLS	5/15
	New York	Y	49780 AE	67420 MW	76490 AEX	NYBLS	1/16-3/16
	Buffalo-Cheektowaga-Niagara Falls MSA, NY	Y	49600 FQ	57120 MW	64610 TQ	USBLS	5/15
	Nassau County-Suffolk County PMSA, NY	Y	62360 FQ	70430 MW	78050 TQ	USBLS	5/15
	New York-Jersey City-White Plains PMSA, NY-NJ	Y	58180 FQ	69940 MW	80950 TQ	USBLS	5/15
	Rochester MSA, NY	Y	44630 FQ	51650 MW	59670 TQ	USBLS	5/15
	North Carolina	Y	45610 FQ	54490 MW	63200 TQ	USBLS	5/15
	Charlotte-Concord-Gastonia MSA, NC-SC	Y	46000 FQ	54710 MW	63060 TQ	USBLS	5/15

AE Average entry wage	**AWR** Average wage range	**H** Hourly	**LR** Low end range	**MTC** Median total compensation	**TCC** Total cash compensation
AEX Average experienced wage	**B** Biweekly	**HI** Highest wage paid	**M** Monthly	**MW** Median wage paid	**TQ** Third quartile wage
ATC Average total compensation	**D** Daily	**HR** High end range	**MCC** Median cash compensation	**MWR** Median wage range	**W** Weekly
AW Average wage paid	**FQ** First quartile wage	**LO** Lowest wage paid	**ME** Median entry wage	**S** See annotated source	**Y** Yearly

Occupation/Type/Industry	Location	Per	Low	Mid	High	Source	Date
Radiologic Technologist	Raleigh MSA, NC	Y	46810 FQ	56070 MW	64570 TQ	USBLS	5/15
	North Dakota	Y	41680 FQ	49100 MW	58080 TQ	USBLS	5/15
	Fargo MSA, ND-MN	Y	43030 FQ	49630 MW	58120 TQ	USBLS	5/15
	Ohio	Y	44780 FQ	53120 MW	60370 TQ	USBLS	5/15
	Cincinnati MSA, OH-KY-IN	Y	43550 FQ	53140 MW	61080 TQ	USBLS	5/15
	Cleveland-Elyria MSA, OH	Y	47090 FQ	55110 MW	61500 TQ	USBLS	5/15
	Columbus MSA, OH	Y	47570 FQ	55520 MW	63620 TQ	USBLS	5/15
	Oklahoma	Y	42280 FQ	49920 MW	60760 TQ	USBLS	5/15
	Oklahoma City MSA, OK	Y	44020 FQ	52590 MW	62730 TQ	USBLS	5/15
	Tulsa MSA, OK	Y	41260 FQ	47730 MW	56910 TQ	USBLS	5/15
	Oregon	H	27.27 FQ	32.39 MW	37.56 TQ	ORBLS	2016
	Portland-Vancouver-Hillsboro MSA, OR-WA	Y	58050 FQ	68750 MW	78850 TQ	USBLS	5/15
	Pennsylvania	Y	44350 FQ	54970 MW	67210 TQ	USBLS	5/15
	Allentown-Bethlehem-Easton MSA, PA-NJ	Y	52240 FQ	58990 MW	70900 TQ	USBLS	5/15
	Harrisburg-Carlisle MSA, PA	Y	46220 FQ	54570 MW	67150 TQ	USBLS	5/15
	Montgomery County-Bucks County-Chester County PMSA, PA	Y	49240 FQ	58680 MW	69720 TQ	USBLS	5/15
	Philadelphia PMSA, PA	Y	51310 FQ	65770 MW	76330 TQ	USBLS	5/15
	Pittsburgh MSA, PA	Y	41410 FQ	48790 MW	58450 TQ	USBLS	5/15
	Rhode Island	Y	55490 FQ	67130 MW	78330 TQ	USBLS	5/15
	Providence-Warwick MSA, RI-MA	Y	56540 FQ	68380 MW	79780 TQ	USBLS	5/15
	South Carolina	Y	40030 FQ	48700 MW	58980 TQ	USBLS	5/15
	Charleston-North Charleston MSA, SC	Y	45760 FQ	54830 MW	63180 TQ	USBLS	5/15
	Columbia MSA, SC	Y	37580 FQ	47430 MW	57950 TQ	USBLS	5/15
	Greenville-Anderson-Mauldin MSA, SC	Y	38420 FQ	48320 MW	58760 TQ	USBLS	5/15
	South Dakota	Y	40690 FQ	47590 MW	56310 TQ	USBLS	5/15
	Tennessee	Y	41670 FQ	49640 MW	58870 TQ	USBLS	5/15
	Knoxville MSA, TN	Y	39540 FQ	45880 MW	53370 TQ	USBLS	5/15
	Memphis MSA, TN-MS-AR	Y	46050 FQ	54450 MW	61980 TQ	USBLS	5/15
	Nashville-Davidson–Murfreesboro–Franklin MSA, TN	Y	43220 FQ	51840 MW	61000 TQ	USBLS	5/15
	Texas	Y	45170 FQ	55430 MW	65710 TQ	USBLS	5/15
	Austin-Round Rock MSA, TX	Y	39360 FQ	54080 MW	62170 TQ	USBLS	5/15
	Dallas-Plano-Irving PMSA, TX	Y	46740 FQ	58720 MW	71440 TQ	USBLS	5/15
	Fort Worth-Arlington PMSA, TX	Y	51900 FQ	61140 MW	71970 TQ	USBLS	5/15
	Houston-The Woodlands-Sugar Land MSA, TX	Y	49560 FQ	57450 MW	66590 TQ	USBLS	5/15
	San Antonio-New Braunfels MSA, TX	Y	45460 FQ	54430 MW	61980 TQ	USBLS	5/15
	Utah	Y	44750 FQ	53000 MW	62970 TQ	USBLS	5/15
	Ogden-Clearfield MSA, UT	Y	43920 FQ	51910 MW	61770 TQ	USBLS	5/15
	Provo-Orem MSA, UT	Y	44710 FQ	53970 MW	62770 TQ	USBLS	5/15
	Salt Lake City MSA, UT	Y	45070 FQ	52620 MW	62400 TQ	USBLS	5/15
	Vermont	Y	47530 FQ	57330 MW	69570 TQ	USBLS	5/15
	Virginia	Y	45520 FQ	55820 MW	67530 TQ	USBLS	5/15
	Richmond MSA, VA	Y	45810 FQ	54780 MW	63890 TQ	USBLS	5/15
	Virginia Beach-Norfolk-Newport News MSA, VA-NC	Y	45940 FQ	54050 MW	62320 TQ	USBLS	5/15
	Washington	H	27.50 FQ	32.11 MW	37.75 TQ	WABLS	3/16
	Seattle-Bellevue-Everett PMSA, WA	H	28.52 FQ	33.43 MW	39.24 TQ	WABLS	3/16
	Tacoma-Lakewood PMSA, WA	H	29.59 FQ	33.78 MW	37.95 TQ	WABLS	3/16
	West Virginia	Y	37610 FQ	45820 MW	55050 TQ	USBLS	5/15
	Huntington-Ashland MSA, WV-KY-OH	Y	42480 FQ	49610 MW	59970 TQ	USBLS	5/15
	Wisconsin	Y	46850 FQ	55520 MW	63950 TQ	USBLS	5/15
	Madison MSA, WI	Y	46050 FQ	55940 MW	63600 TQ	USBLS	5/15
	Milwaukee-Waukesha-West Allis MSA, WI	Y	49800 FQ	57850 MW	68390 TQ	USBLS	5/15
	Wyoming	Y	43180 FQ	50080 MW	59440 TQ	USBLS	5/15
	Cheyenne MSA, WY	Y	42400 FQ	49270 MW	57570 TQ	USBLS	5/15
	Puerto Rico	Y	20460 FQ	24740 MW	29420 TQ	USBLS	5/15
	San Juan-Carolina-Caguas MSA, PR	Y	21490 FQ	25610 MW	30120 TQ	USBLS	5/15

AE Average entry wage	AWR Average wage range	H Hourly	LR Low end range	MTC Median total compensation	TCC Total cash compensation
AEX Average experienced wage	B Biweekly	HI Highest wage paid	M Monthly	MW Median wage paid	TQ Third quartile wage
ATC Average total compensation	D Daily	HR High end range	MCC Median cash compensation	MWR Median wage range	W Weekly
AW Average wage paid	FQ First quartile wage	LO Lowest wage paid	ME Median entry wage	S See annotated source	Y Yearly

Occupation/Type/Industry	Location	Per	Low	Mid	High	Source	Date
Radiologic Technologist	Guam	Y	30700 FQ	40240 MW	49340 TQ	USBLS	5/15
Rail Car Repairer	Alabama	Y	26636 AE	44393 AW	53271 AEX	ALBLS	6/16
	Arizona	Y	39850 FQ	51280 MW	62180 TQ	USBLS	5/15
	Arkansas	Y	46310 FQ	59700 MW	71800 TQ	USBLS	5/15
	California	H	18.41 FQ	27.31 MW	33.55 TQ	CABLS	1/16-3/16
	Colorado	Y	45210 FQ	55610 MW	62950 TQ	USBLS	5/15
	Florida	H	17.75 AE	25.58 MW	27.63 AEX	FLBLS	7/16-9/16
	Georgia	Y	38630 FQ	45040 MW	52600 TQ	USBLS	5/15
	Idaho	Y	34800 FQ	54810 MW	67720 TQ	USBLS	5/15
	Illinois	Y	55690 FQ	64650 MW	72390 TQ	USBLS	5/15
	Indiana	Y	33370 FQ	45620 MW	55860 TQ	USBLS	5/15
	Iowa	Y	41170 FQ	49010 MW	58060 TQ	USBLS	5/15
	Kansas	Y	36860 FQ	50300 MW	59220 TQ	USBLS	5/15
	Kentucky	Y	51720 FQ	56060 MW	60410 TQ	USBLS	5/15
	Louisiana	Y	49530 FQ	58480 MW	67050 TQ	USBLS	5/15
	Maryland	Y	50737 AE	64315 MW	71104 AEX	MDBLS	4/16
	Michigan	Y	52510 FQ	62580 MW	71490 TQ	USBLS	5/15
	Minnesota	Y	39965 FQ	58269 MW	85492 TQ	MNBLS	1/16-3/16
	Mississippi	Y	43010 FQ	51830 MW	59210 TQ	USBLS	5/15
	Missouri	Y	29770 FQ	39260 MW	55550 TQ	USBLS	5/15
	Montana	Y	46210 FQ	52950 MW	58110 TQ	USBLS	5/15
	Nebraska	Y	28980 FQ	41095 MW	49730 TQ	NEBLS	7/16-9/16
	Nevada	Y	42040 FQ	47930 MW	58400 TQ	USBLS	5/15
	New Jersey	Y	51810 FQ	56350 MW	60880 TQ	USBLS	5/15
	New Mexico	Y	53620 FQ	58660 MW	63710 TQ	USBLS	5/15
	New York	Y	48180 AE	63870 MW	68970 AEX	NYBLS	1/16-3/16
	North Carolina	Y	51420 FQ	55600 MW	59780 TQ	USBLS	5/15
	Ohio	Y	35330 FQ	44760 MW	55850 TQ	USBLS	5/15
	Oklahoma	Y	46370 FQ	55270 MW	61120 TQ	USBLS	5/15
	Pennsylvania	Y	37380 FQ	47730 MW	59800 TQ	USBLS	5/15
	South Carolina	Y	30600 FQ	37040 MW	46410 TQ	USBLS	5/15
	Tennessee	Y	51960 FQ	56070 MW	60170 TQ	USBLS	5/15
	Texas	Y	38740 FQ	53820 MW	61630 TQ	USBLS	5/15
	Utah	Y	29480 FQ	46090 MW	63510 TQ	USBLS	5/15
	Virginia	Y	55530 FQ	63990 MW	76660 TQ	USBLS	5/15
	Washington	H	23.71 FQ	27.00 MW	29.31 TQ	WABLS	3/16
	West Virginia	Y	44370 FQ	52350 MW	57990 TQ	USBLS	5/15
	Wisconsin	Y	50280 FQ	56910 MW	63690 TQ	USBLS	5/15
	Wyoming	Y	42780 FQ	49350 MW	61710 TQ	USBLS	5/15
Rail-Track Laying and Maintenance Equipment Operator	Alabama	Y	35932 AE	51033 AW	58594 AEX	ALBLS	6/16
	Arizona	Y	29700 FQ	41760 MW	56070 TQ	USBLS	5/15
	Arkansas	Y	47110 FQ	55360 MW	61960 TQ	USBLS	5/15
	California	H	27.08 FQ	30.05 MW	42.19 TQ	CABLS	1/16-3/16
	Colorado	Y	48250 FQ	57420 MW	68070 TQ	USBLS	5/15
	Delaware	Y	51120 FQ	57290 MW	63610 TQ	USBLS	5/15
	Florida	H	16.73 AE	24.22 MW	30.03 AEX	FLBLS	7/16-9/16
	Georgia	Y	31410 FQ	41220 MW	54130 TQ	USBLS	5/15
	Illinois	Y	45980 FQ	54920 MW	61930 TQ	USBLS	5/15
	Indiana	Y	46590 FQ	52880 MW	58430 TQ	USBLS	5/15
	Iowa	Y	38600 FQ	48130 MW	59980 TQ	USBLS	5/15
	Kansas	Y	42500 FQ	52750 MW	58610 TQ	USBLS	5/15
	Kentucky	Y	31520 FQ	44380 MW	56300 TQ	USBLS	5/15
	Louisiana	Y	44650 FQ	52960 MW	59250 TQ	USBLS	5/15
	Maine	Y	36910 FQ	43900 MW	50610 TQ	USBLS	5/15
	Maryland	Y	41136 AE	54294 MW	60873 AEX	MDBLS	4/16
	Massachusetts	Y	52100 FQ	55890 MW	59670 TQ	USBLS	5/15
	Michigan	Y	41850 FQ	51120 MW	60760 TQ	USBLS	5/15
	Minnesota	Y	48382 FQ	60309 MW	83839 TQ	MNBLS	1/16-3/16
	Mississippi	Y	31420 FQ	45850 MW	56950 TQ	USBLS	5/15
	Missouri	Y	37860 FQ	44180 MW	51450 TQ	USBLS	5/15
	Montana	Y	44230 FQ	52710 MW	58710 TQ	USBLS	5/15
	Nevada	Y	44660 FQ	54590 MW	59610 TQ	USBLS	5/15
	New Jersey	Y	41560 FQ	46830 MW	54490 TQ	USBLS	5/15
	New Mexico	Y	42040 FQ	50070 MW	58390 TQ	USBLS	5/15
	New York	Y	51860 AE	59500 MW	63420 AEX	NYBLS	1/16-3/16
	North Carolina	Y	35180 FQ	41380 MW	52100 TQ	USBLS	5/15
	Ohio	Y	35820 FQ	50170 MW	59400 TQ	USBLS	5/15
	Oklahoma	Y	29860 FQ	33860 MW	37530 TQ	USBLS	5/15

Occupation/Type/Industry	Location	Per	Low	Mid	High	Source	Date
Rail-Track Laying and Maintenance Equipment Operator	Oregon	H	14.55 FQ	17.74 MW	25.82 TQ	ORBLS	2016
	Pennsylvania	Y	38840 FQ	53450 MW	61050 TQ	USBLS	5/15
	South Carolina	Y	30940 FQ	45800 MW	55960 TQ	USBLS	5/15
	South Dakota	Y	40820 FQ	45890 MW	50770 TQ	USBLS	5/15
	Tennessee	Y	24150 FQ	36320 MW	52350 TQ	USBLS	5/15
	Texas	Y	31690 FQ	46580 MW	57720 TQ	USBLS	5/15
	Utah	Y	46970 FQ	53680 MW	58710 TQ	USBLS	5/15
	Virginia	Y	36510 FQ	46950 MW	58190 TQ	USBLS	5/15
	Washington	H	20.12 FQ	22.56 MW	25.21 TQ	WABLS	3/16
	West Virginia	Y	32440 FQ	44430 MW	53930 TQ	USBLS	5/15
	Wisconsin	Y	45170 FQ	53460 MW	59660 TQ	USBLS	5/15
	Wyoming	Y	38240 FQ	50230 MW	58810 TQ	USBLS	5/15
Rail Yard Engineer, Dinkey Operator, and Hostler	Alabama	Y	36923 AE	50643 AW	57504 AEX	ALBLS	6/16
	California	H	13.12 FQ	18.80 MW	23.44 TQ	CABLS	1/16-3/16
	Colorado	Y	27210 FQ	34600 MW	46250 TQ	USBLS	5/15
	Florida	H	23.61 AE	27.25 MW	28.60 AEX	FLBLS	7/16-9/16
	Illinois	Y	36850 FQ	42480 MW	47530 TQ	USBLS	5/15
	Iowa	Y	31380 FQ	36460 MW	49070 TQ	USBLS	5/15
	Kentucky	Y	35800 FQ	50610 MW	58180 TQ	USBLS	5/15
	Michigan	Y	39220 FQ	49460 MW	58290 TQ	USBLS	5/15
	Minnesota	Y	51526 FQ	55710 MW	59884 TQ	MNBLS	1/16-3/16
	New York	Y	44960 AE	50270 MW	61170 AEX	NYBLS	1/16-3/16
	Ohio	Y	49050 FQ	55840 MW	61760 TQ	USBLS	5/15
	Oregon	H	21.45 FQ	24.25 MW	32.28 TQ	ORBLS	2016
	Pennsylvania	Y	41730 FQ	47650 MW	56170 TQ	USBLS	5/15
	South Carolina	Y	42800 FQ	48330 MW	56100 TQ	USBLS	5/15
	Tennessee	Y	42280 FQ	47250 MW	54360 TQ	USBLS	5/15
	Texas	Y	34740 FQ	41870 MW	46950 TQ	USBLS	5/15
	Washington	H	23.68 FQ	27.24 MW	29.88 TQ	WABLS	3/16
Railroad Brake, Signal, and Switch Operator	Alabama	Y	24890 AE	38610 AW	45470 AEX	ALBLS	6/16
	Arizona	Y	46890 FQ	54750 MW	61810 TQ	USBLS	5/15
	Arkansas	Y	48440 FQ	56120 MW	61170 TQ	USBLS	5/15
	California	H	25.88 FQ	27.91 MW	29.95 TQ	CABLS	1/16-3/16
	Colorado	Y	44310 FQ	50500 MW	59240 TQ	USBLS	5/15
	Georgia	Y	47070 FQ	65160 MW	72970 TQ	USBLS	5/15
	Idaho	Y	47700 FQ	55310 MW	61880 TQ	USBLS	5/15
	Illinois	Y	45990 FQ	55380 MW	63590 TQ	USBLS	5/15
	Indiana	Y	45620 FQ	53860 MW	59700 TQ	USBLS	5/15
	Iowa	Y	35650 FQ	59110 MW	71870 TQ	USBLS	5/15
	Kansas	Y	43380 FQ	48420 MW	60290 TQ	USBLS	5/15
	Kentucky	Y	36990 FQ	45350 MW	64900 TQ	USBLS	5/15
	Louisiana	Y	47480 FQ	56180 MW	62670 TQ	USBLS	5/15
	Massachusetts	Y	55760 FQ	65710 MW	73400 TQ	USBLS	5/15
	Michigan	Y	52830 FQ	57470 MW	62120 TQ	USBLS	5/15
	Minnesota	Y	50619 FQ	59601 MW	71004 TQ	MNBLS	1/16-3/16
	Mississippi	Y	43220 FQ	54390 MW	60940 TQ	USBLS	5/15
	Missouri	Y	44750 FQ	52850 MW	61550 TQ	USBLS	5/15
	New Jersey	Y	40580 FQ	62280 MW	71720 TQ	USBLS	5/15
	New Mexico	Y	46450 FQ	55430 MW	63380 TQ	USBLS	5/15
	New York	Y	51080 AE	73770 MW	81670 AEX	NYBLS	1/16-3/16
	North Carolina	Y	41400 FQ	52610 MW	59000 TQ	USBLS	5/15
	Ohio	Y	42350 FQ	51120 MW	64010 TQ	USBLS	5/15
	Oklahoma	Y	42720 FQ	46310 MW	52470 TQ	USBLS	5/15
	Oregon	H	25.42 FQ	27.75 MW	30.09 TQ	ORBLS	2016
	Pennsylvania	Y	44710 FQ	50400 MW	58760 TQ	USBLS	5/15
	South Carolina	Y	42910 FQ	49840 MW	57920 TQ	USBLS	5/15
	South Dakota	Y	37020 FQ	42980 MW	47970 TQ	USBLS	5/15
	Tennessee	Y	43170 FQ	48070 MW	60770 TQ	USBLS	5/15
	Texas	Y	42440 FQ	52910 MW	60740 TQ	USBLS	5/15
	Utah	Y	42360 FQ	46130 MW	49780 TQ	USBLS	5/15
	Virginia	Y	50080 FQ	56370 MW	61460 TQ	USBLS	5/15
	Washington	H	21.76 FQ	26.68 MW	30.66 TQ	WABLS	3/16
	Wisconsin	Y	53770 FQ	58520 MW	63240 TQ	USBLS	5/15
	Wyoming	Y	42590 FQ	51450 MW	60160 TQ	USBLS	5/15

AE	Average entry wage	AWR	Average wage range	H	Hourly	LR	Low end range	MTC	Median total compensation	TCC	Total cash compensation
AEX	Average experienced wage	B	Biweekly	HI	Highest wage paid	M	Monthly	MW	Median wage paid	TQ	Third quartile wage
ATC	Average total compensation	D	Daily	HR	High end range	MCC	Median cash compensation	MWR	Median wage range	W	Weekly
AW	Average wage paid	FQ	First quartile wage	LO	Lowest wage paid	ME	Median entry wage	S	See annotated source	Y	Yearly

Occupation/Type/Industry	Location	Per	Low	Mid	High	Source	Date
Railroad Conductor and Yardmaster							
	Alabama	Y	42487 AE	55724 AW	62337 AEX	ALBLS	6/16
	Arizona	Y	47090 FQ	59730 MW	72490 TQ	USBLS	5/15
	Arkansas	Y	43180 FQ	52630 MW	64850 TQ	USBLS	5/15
	California	H	21.71 FQ	25.35 MW	32.51 TQ	CABLS	1/16-3/16
	Colorado	Y	26360 FQ	39870 MW	52670 TQ	USBLS	5/15
	Florida	H	21.98 AE	24.40 MW	28.99 AEX	FLBLS	7/16-9/16
	Georgia	Y	43720 FQ	54920 MW	66720 TQ	USBLS	5/15
	Idaho	Y	44800 FQ	53890 MW	65160 TQ	USBLS	5/15
	Illinois	Y	46680 FQ	57450 MW	69970 TQ	USBLS	5/15
	Indiana	Y	46190 FQ	56490 MW	70310 TQ	USBLS	5/15
	Iowa	Y	49920 FQ	58020 MW	67950 TQ	USBLS	5/15
	Kansas	Y	43180 FQ	50600 MW	61360 TQ	USBLS	5/15
	Kentucky	Y	50340 FQ	62130 MW	72920 TQ	USBLS	5/15
	Louisiana	Y	45640 FQ	56500 MW	70050 TQ	USBLS	5/15
	Maine	Y	47300 FQ	55240 MW	61550 TQ	USBLS	5/15
	Massachusetts	Y	40660 FQ	44910 MW	49160 TQ	USBLS	5/15
	Michigan	Y	45990 FQ	59180 MW	72000 TQ	USBLS	5/15
	Minnesota	Y	48008 FQ	62414 MW	74754 TQ	MNBLS	1/16-3/16
	Mississippi	Y	52750 FQ	67040 MW	74840 TQ	USBLS	5/15
	Missouri	Y	43990 FQ	52460 MW	62280 TQ	USBLS	5/15
	Montana	Y	43640 FQ	51220 MW	61410 TQ	USBLS	5/15
	New Hampshire	H	9.76 FQ	17.90 MW	22.61 AEX	NHBLS	6/16
	New Mexico	Y	55560 FQ	69490 MW	79690 TQ	USBLS	5/15
	New York	Y	54010 AE	62220 MW	66950 AEX	NYBLS	1/16-3/16
	North Carolina	Y	42080 FQ	46770 MW	55830 TQ	USBLS	5/15
	Ohio	Y	42250 FQ	47430 MW	59090 TQ	USBLS	5/15
	Oklahoma	Y	44360 FQ	53150 MW	61420 TQ	USBLS	5/15
	Oregon	H	21.87 FQ	26.53 MW	31.44 TQ	ORBLS	2016
	Pennsylvania	Y	42590 FQ	50810 MW	61730 TQ	USBLS	5/15
	South Carolina	Y	46210 FQ	57550 MW	73680 TQ	USBLS	5/15
	South Dakota	Y	50810 FQ	56430 MW	61810 TQ	USBLS	5/15
	Tennessee	Y	45120 FQ	53530 MW	61870 TQ	USBLS	5/15
	Texas	Y	40090 FQ	53360 MW	67350 TQ	USBLS	5/15
	Virginia	Y	44540 FQ	53650 MW	63580 TQ	USBLS	5/15
	Washington	H	20.64 FQ	26.62 MW	33.50 TQ	WABLS	3/16
	West Virginia	Y	43390 FQ	49630 MW	60050 TQ	USBLS	5/15
	Wisconsin	Y	49090 FQ	58680 MW	69400 TQ	USBLS	5/15
	Wyoming	Y	46610 FQ	58580 MW	71800 TQ	USBLS	5/15
Ranch Supervisor							
Department of Corrections, State Government	Deer Lodge, MT	H	18.08 LO		24.96 HI	MTGOV	2016
Rangemaster/Armorer							
Police Department, Municipal Government	Fresno, CA	Y			27148 HI	CACIT	6/28/16
Real Estate Broker							
	Alabama	Y	26353 AE	71188 AW	93600 AEX	ALBLS	6/16
	Alaska	Y	53760 FQ	62050 MW	79220 TQ	USBLS	5/15
	Arizona	Y	27890 FQ	31210 MW	118150 TQ	USBLS	5/15
	Phoenix-Mesa-Scottsdale MSA, AZ	Y	27760 FQ	30670 MW	130600 TQ	USBLS	5/15
	Tucson MSA, AZ	Y	30990 FQ	46220 MW	118500 TQ	USBLS	5/15
	Arkansas	Y	25520 FQ	39130 MW	95910 TQ	USBLS	5/15
	Little Rock-North Little Rock-Conway MSA, AR	Y	24550 FQ	47000 MW	113060 TQ	USBLS	5/15
	California	H	17.55 FQ	28.21 MW	54.65 TQ	CABLS	1/16-3/16
	Los Angeles-Long Beach-Glendale PMSA, CA	H	20.03 FQ	27.34 MW	41.05 TQ	CABLS	1/16-3/16
	Oakland-Hayward-Berkeley PMSA, CA	H	19.88 FQ	36.86 MW	69.08 TQ	CABLS	1/16-3/16
	Riverside-San Bernardino-Ontario MSA, CA	H	11.08 FQ	26.09 MW	39.33 TQ	CABLS	1/16-3/16
	Sacramento–Roseville–Arden-Arcade MSA, CA	H	54.83 FQ	61.76 MW	71.05 TQ	CABLS	1/16-3/16
	San Diego-Carlsbad MSA, CA	H	17.03 FQ	31.26 MW	58.47 TQ	CABLS	1/16-3/16
	San Francisco-Redwood City-South San Francisco PMSA, CA	H	17.50 FQ	26.23 MW	33.88 TQ	CABLS	1/16-3/16
	Colorado	Y	33890 FQ	52610 MW	87330 TQ	USBLS	5/15
	Denver-Aurora-Lakewood MSA, CO	Y	35170 FQ	47470 MW	75980 TQ	USBLS	5/15

Occupation/Type/Industry	Location	Per	Low	Mid	High	Source	Date
Real Estate Broker	Connecticut	Y		65605 MW		CTBLS	1/16-3/16
	Hartford-West Hartford-East Hartford MSA, CT	Y	54580 FQ	83820 MW	136140 TQ	USBLS	5/15
	Delaware	Y	44050 FQ	49590 MW	77260 TQ	USBLS	5/15
	Wilmington PMSA, DE-MD-NJ	Y	43710 FQ	47540 MW	51250 TQ	USBLS	5/15
	District of Columbia	Y	70310 FQ	119720 MW		USBLS	5/15
	Washington-Arlington-Alexandria PMSA, DC-VA-MD-WV	Y	34140 FQ	65530 MW	123750 TQ	USBLS	5/15
	Florida	H	13.25 AE	27.57 MW	58.09 AEX	FLBLS	7/16-9/16
	Fort Lauderdale-Pompano Beach-Deerfield Beach PMSA, FL	H	12.09 AE	20.35 MW	47.41 AEX	FLBLS	7/16-9/16
	Orlando-Kissimmee-Sanford MSA, FL	H	19.57 AE	52.91 MW	81.91 AEX	FLBLS	7/16-9/16
	Tampa-St. Petersburg-Clearwater MSA, FL	H	9.60 AE	21.86 MW	34.32 AEX	FLBLS	7/16-9/16
	Georgia	Y	41410 FQ	76410 MW	115520 TQ	USBLS	5/15
	Atlanta-Sandy Springs-Roswell MSA, GA	Y	70820 FQ	92090 MW	138120 TQ	USBLS	5/15
	Augusta-Richmond County MSA, GA-SC	Y	17820 FQ	19890 MW	74690 TQ	USBLS	5/15
	Hawaii	Y	62540 FQ	74770 MW	141720 TQ	USBLS	5/15
	Urban Honolulu MSA, HI	Y	75430 FQ	134880 MW		USBLS	5/15
	Idaho	Y	28380 FQ	38090 MW	59780 TQ	USBLS	5/15
	Boise City MSA, ID	Y	36040 FQ	53230 MW	59680 TQ	USBLS	5/15
	Illinois	Y	27310 FQ	52700 MW	94200 TQ	USBLS	5/15
	Chicago-Naperville-Arlington Heights PMSA, IL	Y	26700 FQ	52130 MW	94900 TQ	USBLS	5/15
	Lake County-Kenosha County PMSA, IL-WI	Y	37020 FQ	66860 MW	107650 TQ	USBLS	5/15
	Indiana	Y	19450 FQ	34210 MW	58170 TQ	USBLS	5/15
	Gary PMSA, IN	Y	29020 FQ	44950 MW	85700 TQ	USBLS	5/15
	Indianapolis-Carmel-Anderson MSA, IN	Y	17960 FQ	22660 MW	60890 TQ	USBLS	5/15
	Kansas	Y	22360 FQ	42910 MW	61930 TQ	USBLS	5/15
	Wichita MSA, KS	Y	22000 FQ	24400 MW	58630 TQ	USBLS	5/15
	Kentucky	Y	18570 FQ	23660 MW	55560 TQ	USBLS	5/15
	Louisville-Jefferson County MSA, KY-IN	Y	22850 FQ	31350 MW	43780 TQ	USBLS	5/15
	Louisiana	Y	30440 FQ	52820 MW	69730 TQ	USBLS	5/15
	Maine	Y	36950 FQ	52030 MW	65180 TQ	USBLS	5/15
	Portland-South Portland MSA, ME	Y	46220 FQ	54200 MW	65030 TQ	USBLS	5/15
	Maryland	Y	31616 AE	90872 MW	120500 AEX	MDBLS	4/16
	Salisbury MSA, MD-DE	Y	33710 FQ	102650 MW	141250 TQ	USBLS	5/15
	Massachusetts	Y	58530 FQ	91200 MW	145360 TQ	USBLS	5/15
	Boston-Cambridge-Newton NECTA, MA	Y	65240 FQ	107610 MW	171110 TQ	USBLS	5/15
	Michigan	Y	32520 FQ	57450 MW	77370 TQ	USBLS	5/15
	Detroit-Dearborn-Livonia PMSA, MI	Y	44400 FQ	70900 MW	109430 TQ	USBLS	5/15
	Grand Rapids-Wyoming MSA, MI	Y	30240 FQ	72630 MW	114720 TQ	USBLS	5/15
	Minnesota	Y	26641 FQ	65220 MW	78228 TQ	MNBLS	1/16-3/16
	Mississippi	Y	34770 FQ	84170 MW	130000 TQ	USBLS	5/15
	Jackson MSA, MS	Y	89230 FQ	102650 MW	140630 TQ	USBLS	5/15
	Missouri	Y	17560 FQ	19180 MW	41390 TQ	USBLS	5/15
	St. Louis MSA, MO-IL	Y	18030 FQ	20730 MW	45510 TQ	USBLS	5/15
	Montana	Y	22000 FQ	34520 MW	65740 TQ	USBLS	5/15
	Billings MSA, MT	Y	23570 FQ	32160 MW	37300 TQ	USBLS	5/15
	Nebraska	Y	24700 FQ	32965 MW	55335 TQ	NEBLS	7/16-9/16
	Omaha-Council Bluffs MSA, NE-IA	Y	22950 FQ	27675 MW	54940 TQ	NEBLS	7/16-9/16
	Nevada	Y	54520 FQ	75850 MW		USBLS	5/15
	Las Vegas-Henderson-Paradise MSA, NV	Y	54150 FQ	75310 MW		USBLS	5/15
	New Hampshire	H	31.32 AE	48.32 MW	83.25 AEX	NHBLS	6/16
	Manchester NECTA, NH	H	34.13 AE	50.44 MW	93.55 AEX	NHBLS	6/16
	New Jersey	Y	77520 FQ	94680 MW	123850 TQ	USBLS	5/15
	Newark PMSA, NJ-PA	Y	85810 FQ	93670 MW	112480 TQ	USBLS	5/15

AE	Average entry wage	AWR	Average wage range	H	Hourly	LR	Low end range	MTC Median total compensation TCC Total cash compensation
AEX	Average experienced wage	B	Biweekly	HI	Highest wage paid	M	Monthly	MW Median wage paid TQ Third quartile wage
ATC	Average total compensation	D	Daily	HR	High end range	MCC	Median cash compensation	MWR Median wage range W Weekly
AW	Average wage paid	FQ	First quartile wage	LO	Lowest wage paid	ME	Median entry wage	S See annotated source Y Yearly

Occupation/Type/Industry	Location	Per	Low	Mid	High	Source	Date
Real Estate Broker	New York	Y	51390 AE	80510 MW	137340 AEX	NYBLS	1/16-3/16
	Nassau County-Suffolk County PMSA, NY	Y	75520 FQ	127170 MW	147150 TQ	USBLS	5/15
	New York-Jersey City-White Plains PMSA, NY-NJ	Y	57970 FQ	79070 MW	118530 TQ	USBLS	5/15
	North Carolina	Y	29530 FQ	39440 MW	68970 TQ	USBLS	5/15
	Charlotte-Concord-Gastonia MSA, NC-SC	Y	32510 FQ	43170 MW	93240 TQ	USBLS	5/15
	Goldsboro MSA, NC	Y	28300 FQ	55670 MW	81030 TQ	USBLS	5/15
	Raleigh MSA, NC	Y	34120 FQ	44130 MW	63230 TQ	USBLS	5/15
	Ohio	Y	58040 FQ	84640 MW	158450 TQ	USBLS	5/15
	Cincinnati MSA, OH-KY-IN	Y	81910 FQ	97030 MW		USBLS	5/15
	Columbus MSA, OH	Y	64720 FQ	77550 MW	145350 TQ	USBLS	5/15
	Oklahoma	Y	19080 FQ	24110 MW	38920 TQ	USBLS	5/15
	Oklahoma City MSA, OK	Y	18720 FQ	22700 MW	35150 TQ	USBLS	5/15
	Tulsa MSA, OK	Y	18810 FQ	23230 MW	38090 TQ	USBLS	5/15
	Oregon	H	16.92 FQ	23.85 MW	34.36 TQ	ORBLS	2016
	Portland-Vancouver-Hillsboro MSA, OR-WA	Y	42790 FQ	56030 MW	118160 TQ	USBLS	5/15
	Pennsylvania	Y	50700 FQ	60250 MW	106970 TQ	USBLS	5/15
	Montgomery County-Bucks County-Chester County PMSA, PA	Y	54140 FQ	61440 MW	97730 TQ	USBLS	5/15
	Philadelphia PMSA, PA	Y	37900 FQ	57700 MW	107800 TQ	USBLS	5/15
	Pittsburgh MSA, PA	Y	58840 FQ	96980 MW	185880 TQ	USBLS	5/15
	Rhode Island	Y	43160 FQ	60400 MW	94620 TQ	USBLS	5/15
	Providence-Warwick MSA, RI-MA	Y	46520 FQ	61180 MW	93650 TQ	USBLS	5/15
	South Carolina	Y	47550 FQ	60560 MW	76250 TQ	USBLS	5/15
	Charleston-North Charleston MSA, SC	Y	36700 FQ	50790 MW	73970 TQ	USBLS	5/15
	Columbia MSA, SC	Y	45750 FQ	65430 MW	79170 TQ	USBLS	5/15
	South Dakota	Y	35670 FQ	39680 MW	46230 TQ	USBLS	5/15
	Tennessee	Y	32090 FQ	40910 MW	65780 TQ	USBLS	5/15
	Knoxville MSA, TN	Y	19510 FQ	53120 MW	66870 TQ	USBLS	5/15
	Memphis MSA, TN-MS-AR	Y	31160 FQ	38220 MW	48050 TQ	USBLS	5/15
	Nashville-Davidson–Murfreesboro–Franklin MSA, TN	Y	35120 FQ	44660 MW	71240 TQ	USBLS	5/15
	Texas	Y	47950 FQ	76420 MW	149280 TQ	USBLS	5/15
	Austin-Round Rock MSA, TX	Y	60710 FQ	76450 MW	143970 TQ	USBLS	5/15
	Dallas-Plano-Irving PMSA, TX	Y	70210 FQ	96680 MW		USBLS	5/15
	Fort Worth-Arlington PMSA, TX	Y	43980 FQ	48320 MW	60770 TQ	USBLS	5/15
	Houston-The Woodlands-Sugar Land MSA, TX	Y	45980 FQ	73450 MW	166570 TQ	USBLS	5/15
	San Antonio-New Braunfels MSA, TX	Y	32010 FQ	37440 MW	86490 TQ	USBLS	5/15
	Utah	Y	33490 FQ	49970 MW	78820 TQ	USBLS	5/15
	Ogden-Clearfield MSA, UT	Y	32130 FQ	53950 MW	62120 TQ	USBLS	5/15
	Vermont	Y	30560 FQ	55150 MW	63890 TQ	USBLS	5/15
	Virginia	Y	36610 FQ	64580 MW	100830 TQ	USBLS	5/15
	Richmond MSA, VA	Y	55530 FQ	73250 MW	128260 TQ	USBLS	5/15
	Virginia Beach-Norfolk-Newport News MSA, VA-NC	Y	37420 FQ	59280 MW	94110 TQ	USBLS	5/15
	Washington	H	22.72 FQ	33.92 MW	67.21 TQ	WABLS	3/16
	Seattle-Bellevue-Everett PMSA, WA	H	25.46 FQ	32.97 MW	54.03 TQ	WABLS	3/16
	Tacoma-Lakewood PMSA, WA	H	20.78 FQ	96.81 AW		WABLS	3/16
	West Virginia	Y	21600 FQ	34880 MW	105470 TQ	USBLS	5/15
	Wisconsin	Y	41990 FQ	60860 MW	135890 TQ	USBLS	5/15
	Milwaukee-Waukesha-West Allis MSA, WI	Y	53140 FQ	125740 MW	169210 TQ	USBLS	5/15
	Wyoming	Y	33360 FQ	42080 MW	62420 TQ	USBLS	5/15
	Puerto Rico	Y	19440 FQ	40390 MW	48520 TQ	USBLS	5/15
	San Juan-Carolina-Caguas MSA, PR	Y	18630 FQ	28980 MW	49410 TQ	USBLS	5/15
Real Estate Sales Agent	Alabama	Y	36323 AE	63224 AW	76669 AEX	ALBLS	6/16
	Birmingham-Hoover MSA, AL	Y	36240 AE	60359 AW	72408 AEX	ALBLS	6/16
	Alaska	Y	52860 FQ	63980 MW	76960 TQ	USBLS	5/15
	Anchorage MSA, AK	Y	50500 FQ	63960 MW	76190 TQ	USBLS	5/15

AE	Average entry wage	AWR	Average wage range	H	Hourly	LR	Low end range	MTC	Median total compensation	TCC	Total cash compensation
AEX	Average experienced wage	B	Biweekly	HI	Highest wage paid	M	Monthly	MW	Median wage paid	TQ	Third quartile wage
ATC	Average total compensation	D	Daily	HR	High end range	MCC	Median cash compensation	MWR	Median wage range	W	Weekly
AW	Average wage paid	FQ	First quartile wage	LO	Lowest wage paid	ME	Median entry wage	S	See annotated source	Y	Yearly

Occupation/Type/Industry	Location	Per	Low	Mid	High	Source	Date
Real Estate Sales Agent	Arizona	Y	23190 FQ	40990 MW	64740 TQ	USBLS	5/15
	Phoenix-Mesa-Scottsdale MSA, AZ	Y	23200 FQ	33250 MW	64470 TQ	USBLS	5/15
	Tucson MSA, AZ	Y	23450 FQ	49950 MW	72050 TQ	USBLS	5/15
	Arkansas	Y	21240 FQ	30180 MW	42250 TQ	USBLS	5/15
	Little Rock-North Little Rock-Conway MSA, AR	Y	18930 FQ	33440 MW	52720 TQ	USBLS	5/15
	California	H	16.84 FQ	25.63 MW	34.76 TQ	CABLS	1/16-3/16
	Anaheim-Santa Ana-Irvine PMSA, CA	H	17.80 FQ	27.41 MW	37.99 TQ	CABLS	1/16-3/16
	Los Angeles-Long Beach-Glendale PMSA, CA	H	16.09 FQ	21.74 MW	31.54 TQ	CABLS	1/16-3/16
	Oakland-Hayward-Berkeley PMSA, CA	H	17.84 FQ	29.31 MW	45.61 TQ	CABLS	1/16-3/16
	Riverside-San Bernardino-Ontario MSA, CA	H	18.16 FQ	28.41 MW	35.13 TQ	CABLS	1/16-3/16
	Sacramento–Roseville–Arden-Arcade MSA, CA	H	14.68 FQ	18.18 MW	34.50 TQ	CABLS	1/16-3/16
	San Diego-Carlsbad MSA, CA	H	12.53 FQ	21.80 MW	29.79 TQ	CABLS	1/16-3/16
	San Francisco-Redwood City-South San Francisco PMSA, CA	H	22.27 FQ	29.09 MW	43.19 TQ	CABLS	1/16-3/16
	Colorado	Y	36790 FQ	54810 MW	104270 TQ	USBLS	5/15
	Denver-Aurora-Lakewood MSA, CO	Y	41180 FQ	75900 MW	121570 TQ	USBLS	5/15
	Connecticut	Y		44801 MW		CTBLS	1/16-3/16
	Bridgeport-Stamford-Norwalk MSA, CT	Y	43690 FQ	48730 MW	75620 TQ	USBLS	5/15
	Hartford-West Hartford-East Hartford MSA, CT	Y	34830 FQ	43260 MW	49990 TQ	USBLS	5/15
	Delaware	Y	33170 FQ	41880 MW	65660 TQ	USBLS	5/15
	Wilmington PMSA, DE-MD-NJ	Y	32350 FQ	39920 MW	68740 TQ	USBLS	5/15
	District of Columbia	Y	33580 FQ	63720 MW	96810 TQ	USBLS	5/15
	Washington-Arlington-Alexandria PMSA, DC-VA-MD-WV	Y	32590 FQ	58250 MW	98800 TQ	USBLS	5/15
	Florida	H	11.26 AE	17.66 MW	34.39 AEX	FLBLS	7/16-9/16
	Fort Lauderdale-Pompano Beach-Deerfield Beach PMSA, FL	H	13.29 AE	19.33 MW	46.19 AEX	FLBLS	7/16-9/16
	Miami-Miami Beach-Kendall PMSA, FL	H	11.05 AE	17.06 MW	34.37 AEX	FLBLS	7/16-9/16
	Orlando-Kissimmee-Sanford MSA, FL	H	10.84 AE	19.27 MW	34.93 AEX	FLBLS	7/16-9/16
	Tampa-St. Petersburg-Clearwater MSA, FL	H	13.60 AE	17.65 MW	30.88 AEX	FLBLS	7/16-9/16
	Georgia	Y	26470 FQ	34900 MW	50270 TQ	USBLS	5/15
	Atlanta-Sandy Springs-Roswell MSA, GA	Y	28200 FQ	36040 MW	53790 TQ	USBLS	5/15
	Augusta-Richmond County MSA, GA-SC	Y	25500 FQ	34480 MW	134180 TQ	USBLS	5/15
	Hawaii	Y	50750 FQ	62420 MW	113710 TQ	USBLS	5/15
	Urban Honolulu MSA, HI	Y	53670 FQ	78530 MW	119890 TQ	USBLS	5/15
	Idaho	Y	22040 FQ	31620 MW	56040 TQ	USBLS	5/15
	Boise City MSA, ID	Y	19380 FQ	30670 MW	53990 TQ	USBLS	5/15
	Illinois	Y	31500 FQ	46640 MW	92300 TQ	USBLS	5/15
	Chicago-Naperville-Arlington Heights PMSA, IL	Y	31480 FQ	45770 MW	89240 TQ	USBLS	5/15
	Lake County-Kenosha County PMSA, IL-WI	Y	43500 FQ	59760 MW	131200 TQ	USBLS	5/15
	Indiana	Y	23810 FQ	45430 MW	104030 TQ	USBLS	5/15
	Gary PMSA, IN	Y	24960 FQ	28760 MW	49900 TQ	USBLS	5/15
	Indianapolis-Carmel-Anderson MSA, IN	Y	27470 FQ	82940 MW	145310 TQ	USBLS	5/15
	Iowa	Y	24860 FQ	34920 MW	53490 TQ	USBLS	5/15
	Des Moines-West Des Moines MSA, IA	Y	28380 FQ	35760 MW	45030 TQ	USBLS	5/15
	Kansas	Y	29750 FQ	57570 MW	76340 TQ	USBLS	5/15
	Wichita MSA, KS	Y	22580 FQ	26020 MW	65210 TQ	USBLS	5/15
	Kentucky	Y	24530 FQ	34300 MW	47450 TQ	USBLS	5/15

AE	Average entry wage	AWR	Average wage range	H	Hourly
AEX	Average experienced wage	B	Biweekly	HI	Highest wage paid
ATC	Average total compensation	D	Daily	HR	High end range
AW	Average wage paid	FQ	First quartile wage	LO	Lowest wage paid

LR	Low end range	MTC	Median total compensation
M	Monthly	MW	Median wage paid
MCC	Median cash compensation	MWR	Median wage range
ME	Median entry wage	S	See annotated source

TCC	Total cash compensation
TQ	Third quartile wage
W	Weekly
Y	Yearly

Occupation/Type/Industry	Location	Per	Low	Mid	High	Source	Date
Real Estate Sales Agent	Louisville-Jefferson County						
	MSA, KY-IN	Y	23480 FQ	31630 MW	48380 TQ	USBLS	5/15
	Louisiana	Y	25570 FQ	33820 MW	46840 TQ	USBLS	5/15
	Baton Rouge MSA, LA	Y	37850 FQ	47190 MW	111940 TQ	USBLS	5/15
	New Orleans-Metairie MSA,						
	LA	Y	24510 FQ	32180 MW	44180 TQ	USBLS	5/15
	Maine	Y	29570 FQ	37170 MW	51730 TQ	USBLS	5/15
	Portland-South Portland MSA,						
	ME	Y	32750 FQ	39270 MW	51600 TQ	USBLS	5/15
	Maryland	Y	25559 AE	51107 MW	63881 AEX	MDBLS	4/16
	Baltimore-Columbia-Towson						
	MSA, MD	Y	28230 FQ	38740 MW	52340 TQ	USBLS	5/15
	Salisbury MSA, MD-DE	Y	32690 FQ	45690 MW	66520 TQ	USBLS	5/15
	Massachusetts	Y	39610 FQ	62590 MW	90610 TQ	USBLS	5/15
	Boston-Cambridge-Newton						
	NECTA, MA	Y	43560 FQ	66870 MW	110340 TQ	USBLS	5/15
	Worcester MSA, MA-CT	Y	37030 FQ	50810 MW	58140 TQ	USBLS	5/15
	Michigan	Y	26830 FQ	37670 MW	54310 TQ	USBLS	5/15
	Detroit-Dearborn-Livonia						
	PMSA, MI	Y	21560 FQ	39930 MW	53640 TQ	USBLS	5/15
	Grand Rapids-Wyoming MSA,						
	MI	Y	31190 FQ	40390 MW	56380 TQ	USBLS	5/15
	Minnesota	Y	28073 FQ	37723 MW	66924 TQ	MNBLS	1/16-3/16
	Minneapolis-St. Paul-						
	Bloomington MSA, MN-WI	Y	28002 FQ	37965 MW	67671 TQ	MNBLS	1/16-3/16
	Mississippi	Y	20090 FQ	32210 MW	49670 TQ	USBLS	5/15
	Jackson MSA, MS	Y	20170 FQ	49340 MW	63800 TQ	USBLS	5/15
	Missouri	Y	27690 FQ	38280 MW	84900 TQ	USBLS	5/15
	Kansas City MSA, MO-KS	Y	29420 FQ	48410 MW	65870 TQ	USBLS	5/15
	St. Louis MSA, MO-IL	Y	28780 FQ	62130 MW	93480 TQ	USBLS	5/15
	Montana	Y	23030 FQ	51640 MW	68320 TQ	USBLS	5/15
	Billings MSA, MT	Y	51630 FQ	58570 MW	71380 TQ	USBLS	5/15
	Nebraska	Y	30070 FQ	39070 MW	47950 TQ	NEBLS	7/16-9/16
	Omaha-Council Bluffs MSA,						
	NE-IA	Y	32425 FQ	39620 MW	49405 TQ	NEBLS	7/16-9/16
	Nevada	Y	43300 FQ	56530 MW	73990 TQ	USBLS	5/15
	Las Vegas-Henderson-Paradise						
	MSA, NV	Y	43370 FQ	56260 MW	72990 TQ	USBLS	5/15
	New Hampshire	H	12.20 AE	19.30 MW	26.08 AEX	NHBLS	6/16
	Nashua NECTA, NH-MA	Y	23620 FQ	34900 MW	64140 TQ	USBLS	5/15
	New Jersey	Y	33280 FQ	52430 MW	77840 TQ	USBLS	5/15
	Camden PMSA, NJ	Y	28890 FQ	41950 MW	63270 TQ	USBLS	5/15
	Newark PMSA, NJ-PA	Y	34980 FQ	51570 MW	76780 TQ	USBLS	5/15
	Trenton MSA, NJ	Y	28760 FQ	38260 MW	71190 TQ	USBLS	5/15
	New Mexico	Y	28930 FQ	41470 MW	62400 TQ	USBLS	5/15
	Albuquerque MSA, NM	Y	25130 FQ	39540 MW	59790 TQ	USBLS	5/15
	New York	Y	41420 AE	81110 MW	131060 AEX	NYBLS	1/16-3/16
	Buffalo-Cheektowaga-Niagara						
	Falls MSA, NY	Y	33460 FQ	45130 MW	79770 TQ	USBLS	5/15
	Nassau County-Suffolk County						
	PMSA, NY	Y	45520 FQ	60200 MW	87340 TQ	USBLS	5/15
	New York-Jersey City-White						
	Plains PMSA, NY-NJ	Y	48660 FQ	87020 MW	141270 TQ	USBLS	5/15
	Rochester MSA, NY	Y	34130 FQ	54450 MW	62530 TQ	USBLS	5/15
	North Carolina	Y	30560 FQ	48000 MW	71640 TQ	USBLS	5/15
	Charlotte-Concord-Gastonia						
	MSA, NC-SC	Y	31850 FQ	49750 MW	81000 TQ	USBLS	5/15
	Raleigh MSA, NC	Y	30030 FQ	47680 MW	71590 TQ	USBLS	5/15
	North Dakota	Y	30420 FQ	48800 MW	64860 TQ	USBLS	5/15
	Fargo MSA, ND-MN	Y	28560 FQ	40070 MW	65650 TQ	USBLS	5/15
	Ohio	Y	24470 FQ	31350 MW	42320 TQ	USBLS	5/15
	Cincinnati MSA, OH-KY-IN	Y	27910 FQ	35430 MW	45650 TQ	USBLS	5/15
	Cleveland-Elyria MSA, OH	Y	23360 FQ	29230 MW	44230 TQ	USBLS	5/15
	Columbus MSA, OH	Y	24560 FQ	30430 MW	37980 TQ	USBLS	5/15
	Oklahoma	Y	28780 FQ	45900 MW	76350 TQ	USBLS	5/15
	Oklahoma City MSA, OK	Y	26010 FQ	47250 MW	76870 TQ	USBLS	5/15
	Tulsa MSA, OK	Y	32030 FQ	53580 MW	84750 TQ	USBLS	5/15
	Oregon	H	11.48 FQ	15.59 MW	28.46 TQ	ORBLS	2016
	Portland-Vancouver-Hillsboro						
	MSA, OR-WA	Y	24130 FQ	31950 MW	48440 TQ	USBLS	5/15
	Pennsylvania	Y	34790 FQ	51120 MW	70790 TQ	USBLS	5/15

Occupation/Type/Industry	Location	Per	Low	Mid	High	Source	Date
Real Estate Sales Agent	Allentown-Bethlehem-Easton MSA, PA-NJ	Y	38080 FQ	58540 MW	79970 TQ	USBLS	5/15
	Harrisburg-Carlisle MSA, PA	Y	30820 FQ	43890 MW	63790 TQ	USBLS	5/15
	Montgomery County-Bucks County-Chester County PMSA, PA	Y	27400 FQ	45590 MW	61810 TQ	USBLS	5/15
	Philadelphia PMSA, PA	Y	41340 FQ	52570 MW	70970 TQ	USBLS	5/15
	Pittsburgh MSA, PA	Y	45700 FQ	64130 MW	77770 TQ	USBLS	5/15
	Rhode Island	Y	34250 FQ	42050 MW	52510 TQ	USBLS	5/15
	Providence-Warwick MSA, RI-MA	Y	35810 FQ	44750 MW	66830 TQ	USBLS	5/15
	South Carolina	Y	25980 FQ	34550 MW	49920 TQ	USBLS	5/15
	Charleston-North Charleston MSA, SC	Y	24170 FQ	33940 MW	51840 TQ	USBLS	5/15
	Columbia MSA, SC	Y	26240 FQ	32730 MW	38400 TQ	USBLS	5/15
	Greenville-Anderson-Mauldin MSA, SC	Y	25280 FQ	31090 MW	47190 TQ	USBLS	5/15
	South Dakota	Y	41820 FQ	51630 MW	66160 TQ	USBLS	5/15
	Sioux Falls MSA, SD	Y	56930 FQ	69510 MW	101190 TQ	USBLS	5/15
	Tennessee	Y	25650 FQ	29920 MW	56470 TQ	USBLS	5/15
	Knoxville MSA, TN	Y	25620 FQ	28940 MW	36660 TQ	USBLS	5/15
	Memphis MSA, TN-MS-AR	Y	23490 FQ	29190 MW	49630 TQ	USBLS	5/15
	Nashville-Davidson–Murfreesboro–Franklin MSA, TN	Y	26310 FQ	29930 MW	65860 TQ	USBLS	5/15
	Texas	Y	29680 FQ	57390 MW	87300 TQ	USBLS	5/15
	Austin-Round Rock MSA, TX	Y	44110 FQ	65310 MW	95710 TQ	USBLS	5/15
	Brownsville-Harlingen MSA, TX	Y	29120 FQ	48680 MW	68430 TQ	USBLS	5/15
	Dallas-Plano-Irving PMSA, TX	Y	27710 FQ	35410 MW	88050 TQ	USBLS	5/15
	Fort Worth-Arlington PMSA, TX	Y	40590 FQ	57920 MW	87760 TQ	USBLS	5/15
	Houston-The Woodlands-Sugar Land MSA, TX	Y	27990 FQ	63130 MW	83260 TQ	USBLS	5/15
	San Antonio-New Braunfels MSA, TX	Y	46640 FQ	73080 MW	96480 TQ	USBLS	5/15
	Utah	Y	23700 FQ	37630 MW	60820 TQ	USBLS	5/15
	Ogden-Clearfield MSA, UT	Y	27440 FQ	37590 MW	67940 TQ	USBLS	5/15
	Provo-Orem MSA, UT	Y	24200 FQ	36530 MW	45340 TQ	USBLS	5/15
	Salt Lake City MSA, UT	Y	22390 FQ	36180 MW	64130 TQ	USBLS	5/15
	Virginia	Y	30630 FQ	47440 MW	74660 TQ	USBLS	5/15
	Richmond MSA, VA	Y	36580 FQ	44990 MW	55880 TQ	USBLS	5/15
	Virginia Beach-Norfolk-Newport News MSA, VA-NC	Y	28040 FQ	46800 MW	75800 TQ	USBLS	5/15
	Washington	H	15.26 FQ	21.36 MW	29.63 TQ	WABLS	3/16
	Seattle-Bellevue-Everett PMSA, WA	H	15.78 FQ	22.09 MW	29.36 TQ	WABLS	3/16
	Tacoma-Lakewood PMSA, WA	H	13.93 FQ	18.38 MW	25.41 TQ	WABLS	3/16
	West Virginia	Y	20000 FQ	33930 MW	60520 TQ	USBLS	5/15
	Huntington-Ashland MSA, WV-KY-OH	Y	28770 FQ	35560 MW	44840 TQ	USBLS	5/15
	Wisconsin	Y	25890 FQ	39830 MW	64420 TQ	USBLS	5/15
	Madison MSA, WI	Y	24720 FQ	49530 MW	73650 TQ	USBLS	5/15
	Milwaukee-Waukesha-West Allis MSA, WI	Y	26480 FQ	35380 MW	72170 TQ	USBLS	5/15
	Wyoming	Y	36360 FQ	57980 MW	79400 TQ	USBLS	5/15
	Puerto Rico	Y	19790 FQ	26720 MW	35500 TQ	USBLS	5/15
	San Juan-Carolina-Caguas MSA, PR	Y	19360 FQ	26830 MW	39100 TQ	USBLS	5/15
Real Property Analyst Public Utilities, Municipal Government	Anaheim, CA	Y			55019 HI	CACIT	6/28/16
Realtime Captioner Full Year, California State University	California	Y	48336 LO		125592 HI	CALST	2016-2017
Receptionist and Information Clerk	Alabama	Y	19190 AE	25425 AW	28548 AEX	ALBLS	6/16
	Birmingham-Hoover MSA, AL	Y	20488 AE	27486 AW	30990 AEX	ALBLS	6/16
	Alaska	Y	26820 FQ	31850 MW	37930 TQ	USBLS	5/15
	Anchorage MSA, AK	Y	26920 FQ	32820 MW	38110 TQ	USBLS	5/15
	Arizona	Y	21640 FQ	26580 MW	31780 TQ	USBLS	5/15

AE Average entry wage	**AWR** Average wage range	**H** Hourly	**LR** Low end range	**MTC** Median total compensation	**TCC** Total cash compensation
AEX Average experienced wage	**B** Biweekly	**HI** Highest wage paid	**M** Monthly	**MW** Median wage paid	**TQ** Third quartile wage
ATC Average total compensation	**D** Daily	**HR** High end range	**MCC** Median cash compensation	**MWR** Median wage range	**W** Weekly
AW Average wage paid	**FQ** First quartile wage	**LO** Lowest wage paid	**ME** Median entry wage	**S** See annotated source	**Y** Yearly

Occupation/Type/Industry	Location	Per	Low	Mid	High	Source	Date
Receptionist and Information Clerk							
	Phoenix-Mesa-Scottsdale MSA, AZ	Y	21800 FQ	27170 MW	33110 TQ	USBLS	5/15
	Tucson MSA, AZ	Y	22000 FQ	25960 MW	30020 TQ	USBLS	5/15
	Arkansas	Y	19170 FQ	22760 MW	27430 TQ	USBLS	5/15
	Little Rock-North Little Rock-Conway MSA, AR	Y	19590 FQ	22890 MW	27360 TQ	USBLS	5/15
	California	H	11.83 FQ	14.52 MW	18.15 TQ	CABLS	1/16-3/16
	Anaheim-Santa Ana-Irvine PMSA, CA	H	11.93 FQ	14.38 MW	17.89 TQ	CABLS	1/16-3/16
	Los Angeles-Long Beach-Glendale PMSA, CA	H	11.35 FQ	13.96 MW	17.47 TQ	CABLS	1/16-3/16
	Oakland-Hayward-Berkeley PMSA, CA	H	13.00 FQ	16.36 MW	21.11 TQ	CABLS	1/16-3/16
	Riverside-San Bernardino-Ontario MSA, CA	H	10.76 FQ	13.33 MW	17.23 TQ	CABLS	1/16-3/16
	Sacramento–Roseville–Arden-Arcade MSA, CA	H	11.21 FQ	14.42 MW	18.58 TQ	CABLS	1/16-3/16
	San Diego-Carlsbad MSA, CA	H	12.45 FQ	14.91 MW	17.62 TQ	CABLS	1/16-3/16
	San Francisco-Redwood City-South San Francisco PMSA, CA	H	14.19 FQ	17.62 MW	21.93 TQ	CABLS	1/16-3/16
	Colorado	Y	24250 FQ	29260 MW	35720 TQ	USBLS	5/15
	Denver-Aurora-Lakewood MSA, CO	Y	25110 FQ	30560 MW	37210 TQ	USBLS	5/15
	Connecticut	Y		32962 MW		CTBLS	1/16-3/16
	Bridgeport-Stamford-Norwalk MSA, CT	Y	27850 FQ	33390 MW	39120 TQ	USBLS	5/15
	Hartford-West Hartford-East Hartford MSA, CT	Y	28200 FQ	33720 MW	39010 TQ	USBLS	5/15
	Delaware	Y	21350 FQ	24650 MW	29530 TQ	USBLS	5/15
	Wilmington PMSA, DE-MD-NJ	Y	21600 FQ	25710 MW	30810 TQ	USBLS	5/15
	District of Columbia	Y	26070 FQ	33520 MW	39910 TQ	USBLS	5/15
	Washington-Arlington-Alexandria PMSA, DC-VA-MD-WV	Y	24070 FQ	30640 MW	37760 TQ	USBLS	5/15
	Florida	H	10.23 AE	13.14 MW	15.12 AEX	FLBLS	7/16-9/16
	Fort Lauderdale-Pompano Beach-Deerfield Beach PMSA, FL	H	10.55 AE	13.04 MW	15.10 AEX	FLBLS	7/16-9/16
	Miami-Miami Beach-Kendall PMSA, FL	H	10.25 AE	13.08 MW	15.21 AEX	FLBLS	7/16-9/16
	Orlando-Kissimmee-Sanford MSA, FL	H	10.23 AE	13.13 MW	14.93 AEX	FLBLS	7/16-9/16
	Tampa-St. Petersburg-Clearwater MSA, FL	H	10.11 AE	13.04 MW	14.88 AEX	FLBLS	7/16-9/16
	Georgia	Y	21490 FQ	26870 MW	32910 TQ	USBLS	5/15
	Atlanta-Sandy Springs-Roswell MSA, GA	Y	22670 FQ	28380 MW	35360 TQ	USBLS	5/15
	Augusta-Richmond County MSA, GA-SC	Y	20110 FQ	24390 MW	30070 TQ	USBLS	5/15
	Hawaii	Y	25110 FQ	29730 MW	36840 TQ	USBLS	5/15
	Urban Honolulu MSA, HI	Y	24330 FQ	28850 MW	35320 TQ	USBLS	5/15
	Idaho	Y	21460 FQ	26120 MW	30260 TQ	USBLS	5/15
	Boise City MSA, ID	Y	21910 FQ	26570 MW	30360 TQ	USBLS	5/15
	Illinois	Y	22490 FQ	27540 MW	34170 TQ	USBLS	5/15
	Chicago-Naperville-Arlington Heights PMSA, IL	Y	23190 FQ	28490 MW	35600 TQ	USBLS	5/15
	Lake County-Kenosha County PMSA, IL-WI	Y	22330 FQ	28000 MW	35320 TQ	USBLS	5/15
	Indiana	Y	21210 FQ	25990 MW	30970 TQ	USBLS	5/15
	Gary PMSA, IN	Y	19770 FQ	25560 MW	29590 TQ	USBLS	5/15
	Indianapolis-Carmel-Anderson MSA, IN	Y	22540 FQ	27440 MW	33370 TQ	USBLS	5/15
	Iowa	Y	22470 FQ	27240 MW	32250 TQ	USBLS	5/15
	Des Moines-West Des Moines MSA, IA	Y	24040 FQ	28490 MW	34050 TQ	USBLS	5/15
	Kansas	Y	21180 FQ	25340 MW	30750 TQ	USBLS	5/15
	Wichita MSA, KS	Y	20600 FQ	25120 MW	29960 TQ	USBLS	5/15
	Kentucky	Y	20760 FQ	24760 MW	29760 TQ	USBLS	5/15

AE	Average entry wage	AWR	Average wage range	H	Hourly
AEX	Average experienced wage	B	Biweekly	HI	Highest wage paid
ATC	Average total compensation	D	Daily	HR	High end range
AW	Average wage paid	FQ	First quartile wage	LO	Lowest wage paid

LR	Low end range	MTC	Median total compensation
M	Monthly	MW	Median wage paid
MCC	Median cash compensation	MWR	Median wage range
ME	Median entry wage	S	See annotated source

TCC	Total cash compensation
TQ	Third quartile wage
W	Weekly
Y	Yearly

Occupation/Type/Industry	Location	Per	Low	Mid	High	Source	Date
Receptionist and Information Clerk							
	Louisville-Jefferson County MSA, KY-IN	Y	22850 FQ	27380 MW	31370 TQ	USBLS	5/15
	Louisiana	Y	18920 FQ	22510 MW	27370 TQ	USBLS	5/15
	Baton Rouge MSA, LA	Y	18830 FQ	22900 MW	28810 TQ	USBLS	5/15
	New Orleans-Metairie MSA, LA	Y	20940 FQ	24380 MW	29680 TQ	USBLS	5/15
	Maine	Y	24080 FQ	28360 MW	33220 TQ	USBLS	5/15
	Portland-South Portland MSA, ME	Y	25870 FQ	31050 MW	36250 TQ	USBLS	5/15
	Maryland	Y	19522 AE	27639 MW	31698 AEX	MDBLS	4/16
	Baltimore-Columbia-Towson MSA, MD	Y	21300 FQ	27080 MW	33000 TQ	USBLS	5/15
	Salisbury MSA, MD-DE	Y	21190 FQ	24920 MW	29070 TQ	USBLS	5/15
	Massachusetts	Y	24660 FQ	30500 MW	37260 TQ	USBLS	5/15
	Boston-Cambridge-Newton NECTA, MA	Y	26890 FQ	32970 MW	38910 TQ	USBLS	5/15
	Worcester MSA, MA-CT	Y	23490 FQ	31110 MW	37480 TQ	USBLS	5/15
	Michigan	Y	22020 FQ	26950 MW	32020 TQ	USBLS	5/15
	Detroit-Dearborn-Livonia PMSA, MI	Y	21570 FQ	27430 MW	34400 TQ	USBLS	5/15
	Grand Rapids-Wyoming MSA, MI	Y	23930 FQ	28850 MW	35190 TQ	USBLS	5/15
	Minnesota	Y	23330 FQ	29236 MW	35597 TQ	MNBLS	1/16-3/16
	Minneapolis-St. Paul-Bloomington MSA, MN-WI	Y	23815 FQ	30267 MW	36527 TQ	MNBLS	1/16-3/16
	Mississippi	Y	20590 FQ	24300 MW	29790 TQ	USBLS	5/15
	Jackson MSA, MS	Y	21610 FQ	26800 MW	33050 TQ	USBLS	5/15
	Missouri	Y	20190 FQ	24920 MW	30600 TQ	USBLS	5/15
	Kansas City MSA, MO-KS	Y	22880 FQ	28190 MW	34750 TQ	USBLS	5/15
	St. Louis MSA, MO-IL	Y	20380 FQ	24910 MW	30230 TQ	USBLS	5/15
	Montana	Y	22780 FQ	27140 MW	31120 TQ	USBLS	5/15
	Billings MSA, MT	Y	24860 FQ	28280 MW	32110 TQ	USBLS	5/15
	Nebraska	Y	21765 FQ	26440 MW	30770 TQ	NEBLS	7/16-9/16
	Omaha-Council Bluffs MSA, NE-IA	Y	22160 FQ	27115 MW	31930 TQ	NEBLS	7/16-9/16
	Nevada	Y	22710 FQ	27050 MW	31240 TQ	USBLS	5/15
	Las Vegas-Henderson-Paradise MSA, NV	Y	22480 FQ	26690 MW	30760 TQ	USBLS	5/15
	New Hampshire	H	9.70 AE	13.85 MW	16.24 AEX	NHBLS	6/16
	Manchester NECTA, NH	H	10.43 AE	14.70 MW	16.92 AEX	NHBLS	6/16
	Nashua NECTA, NH-MA	Y	19160 FQ	24330 MW	31950 TQ	USBLS	5/15
	New Jersey	Y	24170 FQ	29540 MW	35960 TQ	USBLS	5/15
	Camden PMSA, NJ	Y	23360 FQ	28390 MW	34190 TQ	USBLS	5/15
	Newark PMSA, NJ-PA	Y	24980 FQ	31820 MW	37900 TQ	USBLS	5/15
	Trenton MSA, NJ	Y	26070 FQ	32080 MW	38270 TQ	USBLS	5/15
	New Mexico	Y	20740 FQ	24370 MW	29890 TQ	USBLS	5/15
	Albuquerque MSA, NM	Y	21460 FQ	25150 MW	30780 TQ	USBLS	5/15
	New York	Y	22730 AE	30390 MW	36560 AEX	NYBLS	1/16-3/16
	Buffalo-Cheektowaga-Niagara Falls MSA, NY	Y	23040 FQ	28310 MW	34970 TQ	USBLS	5/15
	Nassau County-Suffolk County PMSA, NY	Y	24490 FQ	31380 MW	38330 TQ	USBLS	5/15
	New York-Jersey City-White Plains PMSA, NY-NJ	Y	24490 FQ	29740 MW	36890 TQ	USBLS	5/15
	Rochester MSA, NY	Y	22560 FQ	26790 MW	31950 TQ	USBLS	5/15
	North Carolina	Y	21770 FQ	26610 MW	31320 TQ	USBLS	5/15
	Charlotte-Concord-Gastonia MSA, NC-SC	Y	22430 FQ	27590 MW	33620 TQ	USBLS	5/15
	Raleigh MSA, NC	Y	21820 FQ	27560 MW	33800 TQ	USBLS	5/15
	North Dakota	Y	21600 FQ	26820 MW	31770 TQ	USBLS	5/15
	Fargo MSA, ND-MN	Y	20110 FQ	26430 MW	30650 TQ	USBLS	5/15
	Ohio	Y	19950 FQ	23970 MW	29320 TQ	USBLS	5/15
	Cincinnati MSA, OH-KY-IN	Y	21450 FQ	25840 MW	30610 TQ	USBLS	5/15
	Cleveland-Elyria MSA, OH	Y	19960 FQ	24250 MW	29990 TQ	USBLS	5/15
	Columbus MSA, OH	Y	21030 FQ	24630 MW	30670 TQ	USBLS	5/15
	Oklahoma	Y	20710 FQ	25290 MW	30040 TQ	USBLS	5/15
	Oklahoma City MSA, OK	Y	20680 FQ	25150 MW	29950 TQ	USBLS	5/15
	Tulsa MSA, OK	Y	22940 FQ	27300 MW	31150 TQ	USBLS	5/15
	Oregon	H	11.46 FQ	13.62 MW	16.19 TQ	ORBLS	2016
	Portland-Vancouver-Hillsboro MSA, OR-WA	Y	24160 FQ	28480 MW	34320 TQ	USBLS	5/15

AE	Average entry wage	AWR	Average wage range	H	Hourly
AEX	Average experienced wage	B	Biweekly	HI	Highest wage paid
ATC	Average total compensation	D	Daily	HR	High end range
AW	Average wage paid	FQ	First quartile wage	LO	Lowest wage paid

LR	Low end range	MTC	Median total compensation	TCC	Total cash compensation
M	Monthly	MW	Median wage paid	TQ	Third quartile wage
MCC	Median cash compensation	MWR	Median wage range	W	Weekly
ME	Median entry wage	S	See annotated source	Y	Yearly

Occupation/Type/Industry	Location	Per	Low	Mid	High	Source	Date
Receptionist and Information Clerk							
	Pennsylvania	Y	21430 FQ	26280 MW	31200 TQ	USBLS	5/15
	Allentown-Bethlehem-Easton MSA, PA-NJ	Y	23250 FQ	28050 MW	33600 TQ	USBLS	5/15
	Harrisburg-Carlisle MSA, PA	Y	22930 FQ	27260 MW	31170 TQ	USBLS	5/15
	Montgomery County-Bucks County-Chester County PMSA, PA	Y	20490 FQ	26370 MW	32910 TQ	USBLS	5/15
	Philadelphia PMSA, PA	Y	22590 FQ	28090 MW	34750 TQ	USBLS	5/15
	Pittsburgh MSA, PA	Y	21510 FQ	25870 MW	29970 TQ	USBLS	5/15
	Rhode Island	Y	25150 FQ	29800 MW	36200 TQ	USBLS	5/15
	Providence-Warwick MSA, RI-MA	Y	24130 FQ	29180 MW	35570 TQ	USBLS	5/15
	South Carolina	Y	21490 FQ	26020 MW	31020 TQ	USBLS	5/15
	Charleston-North Charleston MSA, SC	Y	22970 FQ	27520 MW	32490 TQ	USBLS	5/15
	Columbia MSA, SC	Y	21470 FQ	25940 MW	30940 TQ	USBLS	5/15
	Greenville-Anderson-Mauldin MSA, SC	Y	20980 FQ	25810 MW	30940 TQ	USBLS	5/15
	South Dakota	Y	21220 FQ	24300 MW	28770 TQ	USBLS	5/15
	Sioux Falls MSA, SD	Y	22040 FQ	26070 MW	30250 TQ	USBLS	5/15
	Tennessee	Y	21180 FQ	26040 MW	30850 TQ	USBLS	5/15
	Knoxville MSA, TN	Y	21920 FQ	26030 MW	30110 TQ	USBLS	5/15
	Memphis MSA, TN-MS-AR	Y	21400 FQ	26260 MW	30210 TQ	USBLS	5/15
	Nashville-Davidson– Murfreesboro–Franklin MSA, TN	Y	23350 FQ	28600 MW	34290 TQ	USBLS	5/15
	Texas	Y	20820 FQ	25190 MW	30500 TQ	USBLS	5/15
	Austin-Round Rock MSA, TX	Y	22720 FQ	26920 MW	31220 TQ	USBLS	5/15
	Dallas-Plano-Irving PMSA, TX	Y	21290 FQ	26640 MW	33150 TQ	USBLS	5/15
	Fort Worth-Arlington PMSA, TX	Y	21360 FQ	24970 MW	30170 TQ	USBLS	5/15
	Houston-The Woodlands-Sugar Land MSA, TX	Y	22280 FQ	27070 MW	31670 TQ	USBLS	5/15
	San Antonio-New Braunfels MSA, TX	Y	19830 FQ	24140 MW	29580 TQ	USBLS	5/15
	Utah	Y	21090 FQ	24770 MW	29740 TQ	USBLS	5/15
	Ogden-Clearfield MSA, UT	Y	19520 FQ	23580 MW	28580 TQ	USBLS	5/15
	Provo-Orem MSA, UT	Y	21280 FQ	24000 MW	28660 TQ	USBLS	5/15
	Salt Lake City MSA, UT	Y	22070 FQ	26230 MW	30850 TQ	USBLS	5/15
	Vermont	Y	25080 FQ	29130 MW	34830 TQ	USBLS	5/15
	Burlington-South Burlington MSA, VT	Y.	26040 FQ	31020 MW	36900 TQ	USBLS	5/15
	Virginia	Y	22060 FQ	27540 MW	34280 TQ	USBLS	5/15
	Richmond MSA, VA	Y	22310 FQ	27940 MW	34240 TQ	USBLS	5/15
	Virginia Beach-Norfolk-Newport News MSA, VA-NC	Y	20570 FQ	25420 MW	30170 TQ	USBLS	5/15
	Washington	H	12.63 FQ	14.93 MW	18.05 TQ	WABLS	3/16
	Seattle-Bellevue-Everett PMSA, WA	H	13.39 FQ	16.05 MW	19.05 TQ	WABLS	3/16
	Tacoma-Lakewood PMSA, WA	H	11.83 FQ	14.31 MW	17.65 TQ	WABLS	3/16
	West Virginia	Y	19310 FQ	22660 MW	27340 TQ	USBLS	5/15
	Huntington-Ashland MSA, WV-KY-OH	Y	19600 FQ	23160 MW	28350 TQ	USBLS	5/15
	Wisconsin	Y	21730 FQ	26850 MW	31690 TQ	USBLS	5/15
	Madison MSA, WI	Y	22180 FQ	27750 MW	33540 TQ	USBLS	5/15
	Milwaukee-Waukesha-West Allis MSA, WI	Y	22620 FQ	27650 MW	33640 TQ	USBLS	5/15
	Wyoming	Y	23150 FQ	27600 MW	31860 TQ	USBLS	5/15
	Cheyenne MSA, WY	Y	23510 FQ	27900 MW	32010 TQ	USBLS	5/15
	Puerto Rico	Y	16810 FQ	18110 MW	19440 TQ	USBLS	5/15
	San Juan-Carolina-Caguas MSA, PR	Y	16830 FQ	18150 MW	19520 TQ	USBLS	5/15
	Virgin Islands	Y	18650 FQ	23330 MW	28920 TQ	USBLS	5/15
	Guam	Y	18260 FQ	19370 MW	23070 TQ	USBLS	5/15
Record Retention Specialist							
County Government	Oakland County, MI	B	1439 LO		1874 HI	MIOAK2	10/1/16
Records Management Analyst							
Municipal Government	Seattle, WA	H	33.00 LO		38.44 HI	CSSS	1/13/16

AE Average entry wage	**AWR** Average wage range	**H** Hourly	**LR** Low end range	**MTC** Median total compensation	**TCC** Total cash compensation
AEX Average experienced wage	**B** Biweekly	**HI** Highest wage paid	**M** Monthly	**MW** Median wage paid	**TQ** Third quartile wage
ATC Average total compensation	**D** Daily	**HR** High end range	**MCC** Median cash compensation	**MWR** Median wage range	**W** Weekly
AW Average wage paid	**FQ** First quartile wage	**LO** Lowest wage paid	**ME** Median entry wage	**S** See annotated source	**Y** Yearly

Occupation/Type/Industry	Location	Per	Low	Mid	High	Source	Date
Records Manager							
Police Department, Municipal Government	Burbank, CA	Y			94301 HI	CACIT	6/28/16
Police Department, Municipal Government	Concord, CA	Y			80207 HI	CACIT	6/28/16
Police Department, Municipal Government	Colorado Springs, CO	Y	74528 LO		102473 HI	COSPRS	2017
Recreation and Fitness Studies							
Teacher							
Postsecondary	Alabama	Y	33577 AE	61904 AW	76072 AEX	ALBLS	6/16
Postsecondary	Birmingham-Hoover MSA, AL	Y	21477 AE	53046 AW	68825 AEX	ALBLS	6/16
Postsecondary	Arizona	Y	33130 FQ	48750 MW	82760 TQ	USBLS	5/15
Postsecondary	Phoenix-Mesa-Scottsdale MSA, AZ	Y	43170 FQ	82810 MW	92870 TQ	USBLS	5/15
Postsecondary	Arkansas	Y	35990 FQ	50430 MW	64670 TQ	USBLS	5/15
Postsecondary	Little Rock-North Little Rock-Conway MSA, AR	Y	38430 FQ	49200 MW	62640 TQ	USBLS	5/15
Postsecondary	California	Y		89062 AW		CABLS	1/16-3/16
Postsecondary	Anaheim-Santa Ana-Irvine PMSA, CA	Y		109890 AW		CABLS	1/16-3/16
Postsecondary	Riverside-San Bernardino-Ontario MSA, CA	Y		101713 AW		CABLS	1/16-3/16
Postsecondary	Sacramento–Roseville–Arden-Arcade MSA, CA	Y		68093 AW		CABLS	1/16-3/16
Postsecondary	San Diego-Carlsbad MSA, CA	Y		80957 AW		CABLS	1/16-3/16
Postsecondary	Colorado	Y	33130 FQ	46090 MW	59390 TQ	USBLS	5/15
Postsecondary	Denver-Aurora-Lakewood MSA, CO	Y	29910 FQ	35330 MW	44640 TQ	USBLS	5/15
Postsecondary	Connecticut	Y		71035 MW		CTBLS	1/16-3/16
Postsecondary	District of Columbia	Y	43790 FQ	57610 MW	75520 TQ	USBLS	5/15
Postsecondary	Washington-Arlington-Alexandria PMSA, DC-VA-MD-WV	Y	40700 FQ	54690 MW	73140 TQ	USBLS	5/15
Postsecondary	Florida	Y	38315 AE	69360 MW	93776 AEX	FLBLS	7/16-9/16
Postsecondary	Pensacola-Ferry Pass-Brent MSA, FL	Y	31510 AE	50627 MW	69986 AEX	FLBLS	7/16-9/16
Postsecondary	Tampa-St. Petersburg-Clearwater MSA, FL	Y	42505 AE	60909 MW	75699 AEX	FLBLS	7/16-9/16
Postsecondary	Georgia	Y	37880 FQ	48930 MW	63800 TQ	USBLS	5/15
Postsecondary	Hawaii	Y	38530 FQ	57040 MW	70380 TQ	USBLS	5/15
Postsecondary	Idaho	Y	19100 FQ	45220 MW	59380 TQ	USBLS	5/15
Postsecondary	Boise City MSA, ID	Y	18350 FQ	42030 MW	54660 TQ	USBLS	5/15
Postsecondary	Illinois	Y	39610 FQ	58900 MW	80120 TQ	USBLS	5/15
Postsecondary	Chicago-Naperville-Arlington Heights PMSA, IL	Y	45100 FQ	59990 MW	79470 TQ	USBLS	5/15
Postsecondary	Lake County-Kenosha County PMSA, IL-WI	Y	23720 FQ	43120 MW	68990 TQ	USBLS	5/15
Postsecondary	Indiana	Y	42970 FQ	55140 MW	69370 TQ	USBLS	5/15
Postsecondary	Indianapolis-Carmel-Anderson MSA, IN	Y	43790 FQ	56440 MW	72100 TQ	USBLS	5/15
Postsecondary	Iowa	Y	46780 FQ	60690 MW	81110 TQ	USBLS	5/15
Postsecondary	Kansas	Y	29110 FQ	37960 MW	56620 TQ	USBLS	5/15
Postsecondary	Kentucky	Y	51370 FQ	63770 MW	76390 TQ	USBLS	5/15
Postsecondary	Louisiana	Y	19310 FQ	47410 MW	61130 TQ	USBLS	5/15
Postsecondary	New Orleans-Metairie MSA, LA	Y	17210 FQ	18770 MW	24850 TQ	USBLS	5/15
Postsecondary	Maine	Y	44880 FQ	59470 MW	75660 TQ	USBLS	5/15
Postsecondary	Maryland	Y	30450 AE	62937 MW	79181 AEX	MDBLS	4/16
Postsecondary	Massachusetts	Y	46740 FQ	63420 MW	81280 TQ	USBLS	5/15
Postsecondary	Boston-Cambridge-Newton NECTA, MA	Y	32780 FQ	61760 MW	78950 TQ	USBLS	5/15
Postsecondary	Michigan	Y	36260 FQ	66030 MW	108150 TQ	USBLS	5/15
Postsecondary	Minnesota	Y	46058 FQ	60423 MW	77378 TQ	MNBLS	1/16-3/16
Postsecondary	Minneapolis-St. Paul-Bloomington MSA, MN-WI	Y	46310 FQ	63578 MW	84152 TQ	MNBLS	1/16-3/16
Postsecondary	Mississippi	Y	48460 FQ	59780 MW	74390 TQ	USBLS	5/15
Postsecondary	Missouri	Y	51440 FQ	64510 MW	87500 TQ	USBLS	5/15
Postsecondary	St. Louis MSA, MO-IL	Y	46280 FQ	62880 MW	85100 TQ	USBLS	5/15
Postsecondary	Nebraska	Y	33070 FQ	51825 MW	72140 TQ	NEBLS	7/16-9/16
Postsecondary	New Hampshire	Y	49836 AE	71213 MW	87339 AEX	NHBLS	6/16
Postsecondary	New Jersey	Y	45570 FQ	62350 MW	83180 TQ	USBLS	5/15
Postsecondary	Newark PMSA, NJ-PA	Y	54350 FQ	69000 MW	97100 TQ	USBLS	5/15
Postsecondary	New Mexico	Y	50650 FQ	65230 MW	81270 TQ	USBLS	5/15
Postsecondary	New York	Y	39200 AE	61890 MW	92180 AEX	NYBLS	1/16-3/16

AE Average entry wage	**AWR** Average wage range	**H** Hourly	**LR** Low end range	**MTC** Median total compensation	**TCC** Total cash compensation
AEX Average experienced wage	**B** Biweekly	**HI** Highest wage paid	**M** Monthly	**MW** Median wage paid	**TQ** Third quartile wage
ATC Average total compensation	**D** Daily	**HR** High end range	**MCC** Median cash compensation	**MWR** Median wage range	**W** Weekly
AW Average wage paid	**FQ** First quartile wage	**LO** Lowest wage paid	**ME** Median entry wage	**S** See annotated source	**Y** Yearly

Occupation/Type/Industry	Location	Per	Low	Mid	High	Source	Date
Recreation and Fitness Studies							
Teacher							
Postsecondary	Buffalo-Cheektowaga-Niagara Falls MSA, NY	Y	54570 FQ	66040 MW	86400 TQ	USBLS	5/15
Postsecondary	Nassau County-Suffolk County PMSA, NY	Y	49210 FQ	61940 MW	80640 TQ	USBLS	5/15
Postsecondary	New York-Jersey City-White Plains PMSA, NY-NJ	Y	53470 FQ	84110 MW	137620 TQ	USBLS	5/15
Postsecondary	Rochester MSA, NY	Y	48500 FQ	63640 MW	82490 TQ	USBLS	5/15
Postsecondary	North Carolina	Y	45450 FQ	57020 MW	70840 TQ	USBLS	5/15
Postsecondary	Charlotte-Concord-Gastonia MSA, NC-SC	Y	44150 FQ	51260 MW	61060 TQ	USBLS	5/15
Postsecondary	Raleigh MSA, NC	Y	41940 FQ	50390 MW	59940 TQ	USBLS	5/15
Postsecondary	Ohio	Y	36960 FQ	57640 MW	83990 TQ	USBLS	5/15
Postsecondary	Columbus MSA, OH	Y	40750 FQ	59570 MW	103990 TQ	USBLS	5/15
Postsecondary	Oklahoma	Y	32470 FQ	38930 MW	54800 TQ	USBLS	5/15
Postsecondary	Oklahoma City MSA, OK	Y	31090 FQ	35410 MW	39400 TQ	USBLS	5/15
Postsecondary	Oregon	Y	36163 FQ	57707 MW	81405 TQ	ORBLS	2016
Postsecondary	Portland-Vancouver-Hillsboro MSA, OR-WA	Y	42780 FQ	54760 MW	82240 TQ	USBLS	5/15
Postsecondary	Pennsylvania	Y	51410 FQ	61370 MW	82700 TQ	USBLS	5/15
Postsecondary	Allentown-Bethlehem-Easton MSA, PA-NJ	Y	44220 FQ	71210 MW	101350 TQ	USBLS	5/15
Postsecondary	Harrisburg-Carlisle MSA, PA	Y	66490 FQ	80160 MW	98670 TQ	USBLS	5/15
Postsecondary	Montgomery County-Bucks County-Chester County PMSA, PA	Y	49300 FQ	54850 MW	60020 TQ	USBLS	5/15
Postsecondary	Philadelphia PMSA, PA	Y	51350 FQ	66880 MW	86870 TQ	USBLS	5/15
Postsecondary	Pittsburgh MSA, PA	Y	48990 FQ	64520 MW	87900 TQ	USBLS	5/15
Postsecondary	South Carolina	Y	41710 FQ	48390 MW	68530 TQ	USBLS	5/15
Postsecondary	Greenville-Anderson-Mauldin MSA, SC	Y	63310 FQ	78840 MW	93590 TQ	USBLS	5/15
Postsecondary	South Dakota	Y	43390 FQ	53580 MW	66460 TQ	USBLS	5/15
Postsecondary	Sioux Falls MSA, SD	Y	49560 FQ	56820 MW	63550 TQ	USBLS	5/15
Postsecondary	Tennessee	Y	26830 FQ	31480 MW	59370 TQ	USBLS	5/15
Postsecondary	Knoxville MSA, TN	Y	38330 FQ	52230 MW	69140 TQ	USBLS	5/15
Postsecondary	Nashville-Davidson–Murfreesboro–Franklin MSA, TN	Y	26430 FQ	29830 MW	55490 TQ	USBLS	5/15
Postsecondary	Texas	Y	37630 FQ	59880 MW	78110 TQ	USBLS	5/15
Postsecondary	Austin-Round Rock MSA, TX	Y	44680 FQ	60820 MW	75750 TQ	USBLS	5/15
Postsecondary	Dallas-Plano-Irving PMSA, TX	Y	37460 FQ	59390 MW	77120 TQ	USBLS	5/15
Postsecondary	Fort Worth-Arlington PMSA, TX	Y	26940 FQ	51820 MW	68050 TQ	USBLS	5/15
Postsecondary	Houston-The Woodlands-Sugar Land MSA, TX	Y	47260 FQ	66910 MW	79010 TQ	USBLS	5/15
Postsecondary	San Antonio-New Braunfels MSA, TX	Y	22050 FQ	24980 MW	76440 TQ	USBLS	5/15
Postsecondary	Utah	Y	51650 FQ	61400 MW	79170 TQ	USBLS	5/15
Postsecondary	Ogden-Clearfield MSA, UT	Y	50570 FQ	60940 MW	75080 TQ	USBLS	5/15
Postsecondary	Provo-Orem MSA, UT	Y	55760 FQ	73420 MW	91450 TQ	USBLS	5/15
Postsecondary	Salt Lake City MSA, UT	Y	50370 FQ	59020 MW	72930 TQ	USBLS	5/15
Postsecondary	Vermont	Y	32090 FQ	36860 MW	56740 TQ	USBLS	5/15
Postsecondary	Virginia	Y	38930 FQ	53410 MW	71130 TQ	USBLS	5/15
Postsecondary	Richmond MSA, VA	Y	30390 FQ	38160 MW	56030 TQ	USBLS	5/15
Postsecondary	Virginia Beach-Norfolk-Newport News MSA, VA-NC	Y	37200 FQ	50370 MW	67900 TQ	USBLS	5/15
Postsecondary	Washington	Y		49558 AW		WABLS	3/16
Postsecondary	Seattle-Bellevue-Everett PMSA, WA	Y		53626 AW		WABLS	3/16
Postsecondary	Tacoma-Lakewood PMSA, WA	Y		54620 AW		WABLS	3/16
Postsecondary	West Virginia	Y	43390 FQ	50640 MW	61450 TQ	USBLS	5/15
Postsecondary	Wisconsin	Y	43770 FQ	51130 MW	64760 TQ	USBLS	5/15
Postsecondary	Wyoming	Y	46210 FQ	58370 MW	71280 TQ	USBLS	5/15
Postsecondary	Puerto Rico	Y	40320 FQ	64800 MW	80620 TQ	USBLS	5/15
Postsecondary	San Juan-Carolina-Caguas MSA, PR	Y	52870 FQ	69950 MW	83810 TQ	USBLS	5/15
Recreation and Trails Planner							
County Government	Oakland County, MI	B	1913 LO		2490 HI	MIOAK2	10/1/16

AE	Average entry wage	AWR	Average wage range	H	Hourly	LR	Low end range	MTC	Median total compensation	TCC	Total cash compensation
AEX	Average experienced wage	B	Biweekly	HI	Highest wage paid	M	Monthly	MW	Median wage paid	TQ	Third quartile wage
ATC	Average total compensation	D	Daily	HR	High end range	MCC	Median cash compensation	MWR	Median wage range	W	Weekly
AW	Average wage paid	FQ	First quartile wage	LO	Lowest wage paid	ME	Median entry wage	S	See annotated source	Y	Yearly

Occupation/Type/Industry	Location	Per	Low	Mid	High	Source	Date
Recreation Coordinator							
Municipal Government	Bakersfield, CA	Y			39186 HI	CACIT	6/28/16
Recreation Director							
County Government	Taylor County, GA	Y	31175 LO		47436 HI	GACTY04	2016
Municipal Government	Gilroy, CA	Y			116307 HI	CACIT	6/28/16
Recreation Programmer							
Municipal Government	Seattle, WA	H	23.05 LO		26.78 HI	CSSS	1/13/16
Recreation Specialist							
County Government	Carroll County, GA	Y	33390 LO		60260 HI	GACTY04	2016
County Government	Fannin County, GA	Y	20520 LO		36390 HI	GACTY04	2016
County Government	Peach County, GA	Y	34806 LO		52183 HI	GACTY04	2016
Recreation Worker	Alabama	Y	17483 AE	24463 AW	27954 AEX	ALBLS	6/16
	Birmingham-Hoover MSA, AL	Y	17524 AE	25061 AW	28829 AEX	ALBLS	6/16
	Alaska	Y	32980 FQ	38490 MW	52020 TQ	USBLS	5/15
	Anchorage MSA, AK	Y	33920 FQ	41090 MW	54150 TQ	USBLS	5/15
	Arizona	Y	18560 FQ	22120 MW	28780 TQ	USBLS	5/15
	Flagstaff MSA, AZ	Y	18140 FQ	22000 MW	39690 TQ	USBLS	5/15
	Phoenix-Mesa-Scottsdale MSA, AZ	Y	19400 FQ	23880 MW	29500 TQ	USBLS	5/15
	Tucson MSA, AZ	Y	17690 FQ	18620 MW	21240 TQ	USBLS	5/15
	Arkansas	Y	17440 FQ	19280 MW	25300 TQ	USBLS	5/15
	Little Rock-North Little Rock-Conway MSA, AR	Y	17630 FQ	19840 MW	26550 TQ	USBLS	5/15
	California	H	10.32 FQ	12.45 MW	15.85 TQ	CABLS	1/16-3/16
	Anaheim-Santa Ana-Irvine PMSA, CA	H	9.99 FQ	11.75 MW	14.96 TQ	CABLS	1/16-3/16
	Los Angeles-Long Beach-Glendale PMSA, CA	H	10.49 FQ	12.82 MW	15.15 TQ	CABLS	1/16-3/16
	Oakland-Hayward-Berkeley PMSA, CA	H	11.27 FQ	14.04 MW	17.89 TQ	CABLS	1/16-3/16
	Riverside-San Bernardino-Ontario MSA, CA	H	9.59 FQ	10.89 MW	13.13 TQ	CABLS	1/16-3/16
	Sacramento–Roseville–Arden-Arcade MSA, CA	H	9.52 FQ	10.49 MW	11.99 TQ	CABLS	1/16-3/16
	San Diego-Carlsbad MSA, CA	H	10.40 FQ	12.00 MW	14.51 TQ	CABLS	1/16-3/16
	San Francisco-Redwood City-South San Francisco PMSA, CA	H	14.02 FQ	16.92 MW	19.20 TQ	CABLS	1/16-3/16
	Colorado	Y	19940 FQ	25070 MW	30350 TQ	USBLS	5/15
	Denver-Aurora-Lakewood MSA, CO	Y	19560 FQ	24440 MW	29010 TQ	USBLS	5/15
	Connecticut	Y		26615 MW		CTBLS	1/16-3/16
	Bridgeport-Stamford-Norwalk MSA, CT	Y	21300 FQ	26980 MW	35520 TQ	USBLS	5/15
	Hartford-West Hartford-East Hartford MSA, CT	Y	19700 FQ	27190 MW	38330 TQ	USBLS	5/15
	Delaware	Y	20760 FQ	25180 MW	29680 TQ	USBLS	5/15
	Wilmington PMSA, DE-MD-NJ	Y	20230 FQ	25280 MW	29760 TQ	USBLS	5/15
	District of Columbia	Y	36550 FQ	47100 MW	60870 TQ	USBLS	5/15
	Washington-Arlington-Alexandria PMSA, DC-VA-MD-WV	Y	21370 FQ	29740 MW	40290 TQ	USBLS	5/15
	Florida	H	9.02 AE	10.82 MW	13.90 AEX	FLBLS	7/16-9/16
	Fort Lauderdale-Pompano Beach-Deerfield Beach PMSA, FL	H	9.16 AE	11.14 MW	13.81 AEX	FLBLS	7/16-9/16
	Miami-Miami Beach-Kendall PMSA, FL	H	9.02 AE	10.01 MW	13.59 AEX	FLBLS	7/16-9/16
	Orlando-Kissimmee-Sanford MSA, FL	H	9.04 AE	10.78 MW	13.36 AEX	FLBLS	7/16-9/16
	Tampa-St. Petersburg-Clearwater MSA, FL	H	8.99 AE	9.96 MW	13.19 AEX	FLBLS	7/16-9/16
	Georgia	Y	18010 FQ	21590 MW	31060 TQ	USBLS	5/15
	Atlanta-Sandy Springs-Roswell MSA, GA	Y	18160 FQ	21970 MW	32640 TQ	USBLS	5/15
	Augusta-Richmond County MSA, GA-SC	Y	23330 FQ	39970 MW	44740 TQ	USBLS	5/15

Occupation/Type/Industry	Location	Per	Low	Mid	High	Source	Date
Recreation Worker	Hawaii	Y	25510 FQ	32410 MW	41300 TQ	USBLS	5/15
	Urban Honolulu MSA, HI	Y	24410 FQ	29850 MW	38460 TQ	USBLS	5/15
	Idaho	Y	17870 FQ	20790 MW	27430 TQ	USBLS	5/15
	Boise City MSA, ID	Y	17720 FQ	20040 MW	25010 TQ	USBLS	5/15
	Illinois	Y	18990 FQ	22200 MW	28880 TQ	USBLS	5/15
	Chicago-Naperville-Arlington Heights PMSA, IL	Y	19120 FQ	22750 MW	29610 TQ	USBLS	5/15
	Lake County-Kenosha County PMSA, IL-WI	Y	18960 FQ	22120 MW	27270 TQ	USBLS	5/15
	Indiana	Y	18100 FQ	21700 MW	28520 TQ	USBLS	5/15
	Gary PMSA, IN	Y	17570 FQ	19990 MW	29450 TQ	USBLS	5/15
	Indianapolis-Carmel-Anderson MSA, IN	Y	18800 FQ	22620 MW	29760 TQ	USBLS	5/15
	Iowa	Y	18600 FQ	22430 MW	29750 TQ	USBLS	5/15
	Des Moines-West Des Moines MSA, IA	Y	18390 FQ	23290 MW	30310 TQ	USBLS	5/15
	Kansas	Y	18570 FQ	23280 MW	29310 TQ	USBLS	5/15
	Wichita MSA, KS	Y	21180 FQ	26290 MW	30200 TQ	USBLS	5/15
	Kentucky	Y	18210 FQ	22410 MW	30850 TQ	USBLS	5/15
	Louisville-Jefferson County MSA, KY-IN	Y	18360 FQ	23690 MW	34350 TQ	USBLS	5/15
	Louisiana	Y	17330 FQ	19270 MW	25210 TQ	USBLS	5/15
	Baton Rouge MSA, LA	Y	17220 FQ	19060 MW	23200 TQ	USBLS	5/15
	New Orleans-Metairie MSA, LA	Y	17260 FQ	19060 MW	27830 TQ	USBLS	5/15
	Maine	Y	19480 FQ	23340 MW	31850 TQ	USBLS	5/15
	Portland-South Portland MSA, ME	Y	20640 FQ	23770 MW	31550 TQ	USBLS	5/15
	Maryland	Y	18131 AE	26933 MW	31334 AEX	MDBLS	4/16
	Baltimore-Columbia-Towson MSA, MD	Y	19010 FQ	24500 MW	30510 TQ	USBLS	5/15
	Salisbury MSA, MD-DE	Y	21570 FQ	26560 MW	30570 TQ	USBLS	5/15
	Massachusetts	Y	19630 FQ	24460 MW	30990 TQ	USBLS	5/15
	Barnstable Town MSA, MA	Y	21610 FQ	24860 MW	32360 TQ	USBLS	5/15
	Boston-Cambridge-Newton NECTA, MA	Y	19570 FQ	25400 MW	32050 TQ	USBLS	5/15
	Worcester MSA, MA-CT	Y	20380 FQ	24930 MW	31260 TQ	USBLS	5/15
	Michigan	Y	18640 FQ	21240 MW	26950 TQ	USBLS	5/15
	Detroit-Dearborn-Livonia PMSA, MI	Y	18490 FQ	20860 MW	28190 TQ	USBLS	5/15
	Grand Rapids-Wyoming MSA, MI	Y	18570 FQ	21100 MW	30410 TQ	USBLS	5/15
	Minnesota	Y	19692 FQ	24419 MW	31377 TQ	MNBLS	1/16-3/16
	Minneapolis-St. Paul-Bloomington MSA, MN-WI	Y	21056 FQ	26448 MW	33972 TQ	MNBLS	1/16-3/16
	Mississippi	Y	18370 FQ	22050 MW	28180 TQ	USBLS	5/15
	Jackson MSA, MS	Y	21760 FQ	27150 MW	35620 TQ	USBLS	5/15
	Missouri	Y	17960 FQ	21120 MW	28690 TQ	USBLS	5/15
	Kansas City MSA, MO-KS	Y	20000 FQ	24140 MW	32200 TQ	USBLS	5/15
	St. Louis MSA, MO-IL	Y	18070 FQ	19610 MW	26320 TQ	USBLS	5/15
	Montana	Y	18450 FQ	21310 MW	27690 TQ	USBLS	5/15
	Billings MSA, MT	Y	18220 FQ	19670 MW	26160 TQ	USBLS	5/15
	Omaha-Council Bluffs MSA, NE-IA	Y	18510 FQ	21250 MW	25790 TQ	NEBLS	7/16-9/16
	Nevada	Y	21520 FQ	28370 MW	36950 TQ	USBLS	5/15
	Las Vegas-Henderson-Paradise MSA, NV	Y	22070 FQ	30370 MW	37100 TQ	USBLS	5/15
	New Hampshire	H	9.19 AE	12.63 MW	15.95 AEX	NHBLS	6/16
	Manchester NECTA, NH	H	8.44 AE	12.17 MW	15.71 AEX	NHBLS	6/16
	Nashua NECTA, NH-MA	Y	19110 FQ	25670 MW	35640 TQ	USBLS	5/15
	New Jersey	Y	19480 FQ	23760 MW	30650 TQ	USBLS	5/15
	Camden PMSA, NJ	Y	18890 FQ	21380 MW	26920 TQ	USBLS	5/15
	Newark PMSA, NJ-PA	Y	19630 FQ	24320 MW	31760 TQ	USBLS	5/15
	Trenton MSA, NJ	Y	21470 FQ	27150 MW	34930 TQ	USBLS	5/15
	New Mexico	Y	17530 FQ	19450 MW	25290 TQ	USBLS	5/15
	Albuquerque MSA, NM	Y	17170 FQ	18670 MW	23170 TQ	USBLS	5/15
	New York	Y	20140 AE	26160 MW	35000 AEX	NYBLS	1/16-3/16
	Buffalo-Cheektowaga-Niagara Falls MSA, NY	Y	18800 FQ	19430 MW	23470 TQ	USBLS	5/15
	Nassau County-Suffolk County PMSA, NY	Y	20390 FQ	25610 MW	33150 TQ	USBLS	5/15

AE	Average entry wage	AWR	Average wage range	H	Hourly
AEX	Average experienced wage	B	Biweekly	HI	Highest wage paid
ATC	Average total compensation	D	Daily	HR	High end range
AW	Average wage paid	FQ	First quartile wage	LO	Lowest wage paid

LR	Low end range	MTC	Median total compensation
M	Monthly	MW	Median wage paid
MCC	Median cash compensation	MWR	Median wage range
ME	Median entry wage	S	See annotated source

TCC	Total cash compensation		
TQ	Third quartile wage		
W	Weekly		
Y	Yearly		

Occupation/Type/Industry	Location	Per	Low	Mid	High	Source	Date
Recreation Worker	New York-Jersey City-White Plains PMSA, NY-NJ	Y	21310 FQ	27460 MW	37150 TQ	USBLS	5/15
	Rochester MSA, NY	Y	19160 FQ	24110 MW	32620 TQ	USBLS	5/15
	North Carolina	Y	18410 FQ	23440 MW	33480 TQ	USBLS	5/15
	Charlotte-Concord-Gastonia MSA, NC-SC	Y	17890 FQ	21360 MW	31910 TQ	USBLS	5/15
	Raleigh MSA, NC	Y	18750 FQ	23910 MW	38640 TQ	USBLS	5/15
	North Dakota	Y	22500 FQ	29000 MW	35630 TQ	USBLS	5/15
	Fargo MSA, ND-MN	Y	20020 FQ	23740 MW	30700 TQ	USBLS	5/15
	Ohio	Y	18810 FQ	22310 MW	29210 TQ	USBLS	5/15
	Cincinnati MSA, OH-KY-IN	Y	18670 FQ	21760 MW	28480 TQ	USBLS	5/15
	Cleveland-Elyria MSA, OH	Y	18830 FQ	23130 MW	31260 TQ	USBLS	5/15
	Columbus MSA, OH	Y	18980 FQ	22610 MW	28770 TQ	USBLS	5/15
	Oklahoma	Y	17850 FQ	21310 MW	28810 TQ	USBLS	5/15
	Oklahoma City MSA, OK	Y	18130 FQ	22270 MW	29770 TQ	USBLS	5/15
	Tulsa MSA, OK	Y	17730 FQ	20210 MW	31850 TQ	USBLS	5/15
	Oregon	H	10.37 FQ	11.88 MW	14.50 TQ	ORBLS	2016
	Portland-Vancouver-Hillsboro MSA, OR-WA	Y	20960 FQ	23860 MW	28890 TQ	USBLS	5/15
	Pennsylvania	Y	18580 FQ	23060 MW	30820 TQ	USBLS	5/15
	Allentown-Bethlehem-Easton MSA, PA-NJ	Y	19340 FQ	23380 MW	29220 TQ	USBLS	5/15
	Harrisburg-Carlisle MSA, PA	Y	19090 FQ	24000 MW	32870 TQ	USBLS	5/15
	Montgomery County-Bucks County-Chester County PMSA, PA	Y	20320 FQ	26200 MW	35620 TQ	USBLS	5/15
	Philadelphia PMSA, PA	Y	19810 FQ	27800 MW	36690 TQ	USBLS	5/15
	Pittsburgh MSA, PA	Y	17580 FQ	19780 MW	26080 TQ	USBLS	5/15
	Rhode Island	Y	19650 FQ	22390 MW	27290 TQ	USBLS	5/15
	Providence-Warwick MSA, RI-MA	Y	19510 FQ	22260 MW	27180 TQ	USBLS	5/15
	South Carolina	Y	17820 FQ	21460 MW	30410 TQ	USBLS	5/15
	Charleston-North Charleston MSA, SC	Y	18120 FQ	21890 MW	29530 TQ	USBLS	5/15
	Columbia MSA, SC	Y	17220 FQ	19170 MW	26530 TQ	USBLS	5/15
	Greenville-Anderson-Mauldin MSA, SC	Y	19600 FQ	30810 MW	37900 TQ	USBLS	5/15
	South Dakota	Y	22180 FQ	26950 MW	31930 TQ	USBLS	5/15
	Sioux Falls MSA, SD	Y	22340 FQ	27310 MW	32660 TQ	USBLS	5/15
	Tennessee	Y	17740 FQ	20800 MW	27500 TQ	USBLS	5/15
	Knoxville MSA, TN	Y	17980 FQ	20820 MW	24330 TQ	USBLS	5/15
	Memphis MSA, TN-MS-AR	Y	18290 FQ	23960 MW	28310 TQ	USBLS	5/15
	Nashville-Davidson–Murfreesboro–Franklin MSA, TN	Y	17500 FQ	20120 MW	28760 TQ	USBLS	5/15
	Texas	Y	18270 FQ	22130 MW	29550 TQ	USBLS	5/15
	Austin-Round Rock MSA, TX	Y	17630 FQ	19840 MW	30030 TQ	USBLS	5/15
	Dallas-Plano-Irving PMSA, TX	Y	19300 FQ	22720 MW	29090 TQ	USBLS	5/15
	Fort Worth-Arlington PMSA, TX	Y	18030 FQ	22060 MW	29430 TQ	USBLS	5/15
	Houston-The Woodlands-Sugar Land MSA, TX	Y	19510 FQ	23430 MW	29700 TQ	USBLS	5/15
	San Antonio-New Braunfels MSA, TX	Y	18230 FQ	24510 MW	33580 TQ	USBLS	5/15
	Utah	Y	17890 FQ	21490 MW	29370 TQ	USBLS	5/15
	Ogden-Clearfield MSA, UT	Y	17110 FQ	19040 MW	25210 TQ	USBLS	5/15
	Provo-Orem MSA, UT	Y	17130 FQ	19060 MW	23790 TQ	USBLS	5/15
	Salt Lake City MSA, UT	Y	19070 FQ	23140 MW	32750 TQ	USBLS	5/15
	Vermont	Y	23080 FQ	29420 MW	41980 TQ	USBLS	5/15
	Burlington-South Burlington MSA, VT	Y	21910 FQ	27090 MW	34940 TQ	USBLS	5/15
	Virginia	Y	18630 FQ	23660 MW	32400 TQ	USBLS	5/15
	Richmond MSA, VA	Y	20410 FQ	23830 MW	31600 TQ	USBLS	5/15
	Virginia Beach-Norfolk-Newport News MSA, VA-NC	Y	17380 FQ	20040 MW	26240 TQ	USBLS	5/15
	Washington	H	10.88 FQ	12.61 MW	16.50 TQ	WABLS	3/16
	Seattle-Bellevue-Everett PMSA, WA	H	10.93 FQ	12.86 MW	17.49 TQ	WABLS	3/16
	Tacoma-Lakewood PMSA, WA	H	10.88 FQ	12.10 MW	14.75 TQ	WABLS	3/16
	West Virginia	Y	18440 FQ	21540 MW	28290 TQ	USBLS	5/15
	Huntington-Ashland MSA, WV-KY-OH	Y	18250 FQ	21100 MW	26840 TQ	USBLS	5/15

AE Average entry wage	**AWR** Average wage range	**H** Hourly	**LR** Low end range	**MTC** Median total compensation	**TCC** Total cash compensation
AEX Average experienced wage	**B** Biweekly	**HI** Highest wage paid	**M** Monthly	**MW** Median wage paid	**TQ** Third quartile wage
ATC Average total compensation	**D** Daily	**HR** High end range	**MCC** Median cash compensation	**MWR** Median wage range	**W** Weekly
AW Average wage paid	**FQ** First quartile wage	**LO** Lowest wage paid	**ME** Median entry wage	**S** See annotated source	**Y** Yearly

Occupation/Type/Industry	Location	Per	Low	Mid	High	Source	Date
Recreation Worker	Wisconsin	Y	17950 FQ	21260 MW	27130 TQ	USBLS	5/15
	Madison MSA, WI	Y	20460 FQ	25570 MW	30140 TQ	USBLS	5/15
	Milwaukee-Waukesha-West Allis MSA, WI	Y	17850 FQ	21370 MW	27190 TQ	USBLS	5/15
	Wyoming	Y	17960 FQ	20890 MW	28640 TQ	USBLS	5/15
	Cheyenne MSA, WY	Y	17020 FQ	18420 MW	19900 TQ	USBLS	5/15
	Puerto Rico	Y	16680 FQ	17890 MW	19100 TQ	USBLS	5/15
	San Juan-Carolina-Caguas MSA, PR	Y	16710 FQ	17930 MW	19150 TQ	USBLS	5/15
	Virgin Islands	Y	21950 FQ	25730 MW	30890 TQ	USBLS	5/15
	Guam	Y	18030 FQ	18900 MW	22130 TQ	USBLS	5/15
Recreational Therapist	Alabama	Y	30865 AE	44361 AW	51109 AEX	ALBLS	6/16
	Birmingham-Hoover MSA, AL	Y	30508 AE	43678 AW	50273 AEX	ALBLS	6/16
	Arizona	Y	51220 FQ	56080 MW	60880 TQ	USBLS	5/15
	Phoenix-Mesa-Scottsdale MSA, AZ	Y	51330 FQ	56030 MW	60730 TQ	USBLS	5/15
	Arkansas	Y	30400 FQ	47130 MW	62170 TQ	USBLS	5/15
	Little Rock-North Little Rock-Conway MSA, AR	Y	44350 FQ	56510 MW	66400 TQ	USBLS	5/15
	California	H	24.92 FQ	33.58 MW	37.65 TQ	CABLS	1/16-3/16
	Anaheim-Santa Ana-Irvine PMSA, CA	H	14.26 FQ	21.16 MW	34.23 TQ	CABLS	1/16-3/16
	Los Angeles-Long Beach-Glendale PMSA, CA	H	18.85 FQ	30.49 MW	36.26 TQ	CABLS	1/16-3/16
	Oakland-Hayward-Berkeley PMSA, CA	H	21.39 FQ	27.25 MW	32.72 TQ	CABLS	1/16-3/16
	Riverside-San Bernardino-Ontario MSA, CA	H	33.08 FQ	35.60 MW	38.11 TQ	CABLS	1/16-3/16
	Sacramento–Roseville–Arden-Arcade MSA, CA	H	27.52 FQ	33.52 MW	37.70 TQ	CABLS	1/16-3/16
	San Diego-Carlsbad MSA, CA	H	16.83 FQ	20.80 MW	34.45 TQ	CABLS	1/16-3/16
	San Francisco-Redwood City-South San Francisco PMSA, CA	H	33.24 FQ	37.38 MW	40.58 TQ	CABLS	1/16-3/16
	Colorado	Y	37160 FQ	46790 MW	60300 TQ	USBLS	5/15
	Denver-Aurora-Lakewood MSA, CO	Y	41540 FQ	49590 MW	62930 TQ	USBLS	5/15
	Connecticut	Y		55188 MW		CTBLS	1/16-3/16
	Bridgeport-Stamford-Norwalk MSA, CT	Y	39570 FQ	46390 MW	57500 TQ	USBLS	5/15
	Hartford-West Hartford-East Hartford MSA, CT	Y	51120 FQ	68190 MW	78080 TQ	USBLS	5/15
	Delaware	Y	32200 FQ	36430 MW	42720 TQ	USBLS	5/15
	Wilmington PMSA, DE-MD-NJ	Y	32460 FQ	36850 MW	47050 TQ	USBLS	5/15
	District of Columbia	Y	39570 FQ	52440 MW	67200 TQ	USBLS	5/15
	Washington-Arlington-Alexandria PMSA, DC-VA-MD-WV	Y	39200 FQ	49390 MW	61980 TQ	USBLS	5/15
	Florida	H	17.78 AE	25.00 MW	29.10 AEX	FLBLS	7/16-9/16
	Fort Lauderdale-Pompano Beach-Deerfield Beach PMSA, FL	H	19.32 AE	24.30 MW	28.07 AEX	FLBLS	7/16-9/16
	Miami-Miami Beach-Kendall PMSA, FL	H	16.92 AE	26.03 MW	29.97 AEX	FLBLS	7/16-9/16
	Orlando-Kissimmee-Sanford MSA, FL	H	14.24 AE	20.83 MW	24.72 AEX	FLBLS	7/16-9/16
	Tampa-St. Petersburg-Clearwater MSA, FL	H	16.26 AE	23.34 MW	27.66 AEX	FLBLS	7/16-9/16
	Georgia	Y	32940 FQ	41320 MW	53300 TQ	USBLS	5/15
	Atlanta-Sandy Springs-Roswell MSA, GA	Y	35260 FQ	42790 MW	51520 TQ	USBLS	5/15
	Augusta-Richmond County MSA, GA-SC	Y	27120 FQ	36040 MW	53310 TQ	USBLS	5/15
	Hawaii	Y	24570 FQ	40920 MW	58650 TQ	USBLS	5/15
	Urban Honolulu MSA, HI	Y	23640 FQ	50540 MW	62410 TQ	USBLS	5/15
	Idaho	Y	44240 FQ	50120 MW	58810 TQ	USBLS	5/15
	Illinois	Y	32640 FQ	43540 MW	59710 TQ	USBLS	5/15
	Chicago-Naperville-Arlington Heights PMSA, IL	Y	39240 FQ	49550 MW	61520 TQ	USBLS	5/15

AE	Average entry wage	AWR	Average wage range	H	Hourly	LR	Low end range	MTC	Median total compensation	TCC	Total cash compensation
AEX	Average experienced wage	B	Biweekly	HI	Highest wage paid	M	Monthly	MW	Median wage paid	TQ	Third quartile wage
ATC	Average total compensation	D	Daily	HR	High end range	MCC	Median cash compensation	MWR	Median wage range	W	Weekly
AW	Average wage paid	FQ	First quartile wage	LO	Lowest wage paid	ME	Median entry wage	S	See annotated source	Y	Yearly

Occupation/Type/Industry	Location	Per	Low	Mid	High	Source	Date
Recreational Therapist	Lake County-Kenosha County						
	PMSA, IL-WI	Y	35990 FQ	46110 MW	59210 TQ	USBLS	5/15
	Indiana	Y	28530 FQ	37320 MW	46680 TQ	USBLS	5/15
	Indianapolis-Carmel-Anderson						
	MSA, IN	Y	28790 FQ	38460 MW	46860 TQ	USBLS	5/15
	Iowa	Y	34820 FQ	42900 MW	57990 TQ	USBLS	5/15
	Des Moines-West Des Moines						
	MSA, IA	Y	32350 FQ	36460 MW	40160 TQ	USBLS	5/15
	Kansas	Y	27010 FQ	34160 MW	42220 TQ	USBLS	5/15
	Wichita MSA, KS	Y	26420 FQ	33510 MW	40610 TQ	USBLS	5/15
	Kentucky	Y	31810 FQ	39020 MW	47360 TQ	USBLS	5/15
	Louisville-Jefferson County						
	MSA, KY-IN	Y	33450 FQ	38780 MW	46360 TQ	USBLS	5/15
	Louisiana	Y	33750 FQ	39240 MW	47910 TQ	USBLS	5/15
	Baton Rouge MSA, LA	Y	35560 FQ	40960 MW	46970 TQ	USBLS	5/15
	New Orleans-Metairie MSA,						
	LA	Y	41740 FQ	46640 MW	52660 TQ	USBLS	5/15
	Maine	Y	34190 FQ	38410 MW	47010 TQ	USBLS	5/15
	Maryland	Y	29698 AE	48691 MW	58188 AEX	MDBLS	4/16
	Baltimore-Columbia-Towson						
	MSA, MD	Y	37980 FQ	47510 MW	57840 TQ	USBLS	5/15
	Massachusetts	Y	33630 FQ	40480 MW	49710 TQ	USBLS	5/15
	Boston-Cambridge-Newton						
	NECTA, MA	Y	34280 FQ	39420 MW	50830 TQ	USBLS	5/15
	Worcester MSA, MA-CT	Y	26420 FQ	32520 MW	41400 TQ	USBLS	5/15
	Michigan	Y	38640 FQ	47370 MW	55950 TQ	USBLS	5/15
	Detroit-Dearborn-Livonia						
	PMSA, MI	Y	41430 FQ	51050 MW	59260 TQ	USBLS	5/15
	Grand Rapids-Wyoming MSA,						
	MI	Y	33820 FQ	39830 MW	51710 TQ	USBLS	5/15
	Minnesota	Y	36683 FQ	44374 MW	52993 TQ	MNBLS	1/16-3/16
	Minneapolis-St. Paul-						
	Bloomington MSA, MN-WI	Y	35574 FQ	43024 MW	50433 TQ	MNBLS	1/16-3/16
	Mississippi	Y	26600 FQ	30650 MW	39100 TQ	USBLS	5/15
	Jackson MSA, MS	Y	27640 FQ	32140 MW	39430 TQ	USBLS	5/15
	Missouri	Y	34180 FQ	41270 MW	48010 TQ	USBLS	5/15
	Kansas City MSA, MO-KS	Y	34650 FQ	42430 MW	49630 TQ	USBLS	5/15
	St. Louis MSA, MO-IL	Y	34200 FQ	42000 MW	49200 TQ	USBLS	5/15
	Montana	Y	35790 FQ	38930 MW	50930 TQ	USBLS	5/15
	Nebraska	Y	33440 FQ	37610 MW	44895 TQ	NEBLS	7/16-9/16
	Omaha-Council Bluffs MSA,						
	NE-IA	Y	37750 FQ	44885 MW	53355 TQ	NEBLS	7/16-9/16
	Nevada	Y	24570 FQ	43040 MW	56920 TQ	USBLS	5/15
	Las Vegas-Henderson-Paradise						
	MSA, NV	Y	41010 FQ	50870 MW	62120 TQ	USBLS	5/15
	New Hampshire	H	18.87 AE	22.55 MW	24.65 AEX	NHBLS	6/16
	New Jersey	Y	45520 FQ	54240 MW	61560 TQ	USBLS	5/15
	Camden PMSA, NJ	Y	43880 FQ	51280 MW	58350 TQ	USBLS	5/15
	Newark PMSA, NJ-PA	Y	47370 FQ	55330 MW	63630 TQ	USBLS	5/15
	New Mexico	Y	32080 FQ	36100 MW	45070 TQ	USBLS	5/15
	New York	Y	38660 AE	53360 MW	60960 AEX	NYBLS	1/16-3/16
	Buffalo-Cheektowaga-Niagara						
	Falls MSA, NY	Y	43470 FQ	54140 MW	61890 TQ	USBLS	5/15
	Nassau County-Suffolk County						
	PMSA, NY	Y	41090 FQ	49490 MW	59530 TQ	USBLS	5/15
	New York-Jersey City-White						
	Plains PMSA, NY-NJ	Y	44780 FQ	55320 MW	64200 TQ	USBLS	5/15
	Rochester MSA, NY	Y	40220 FQ	46460 MW	56740 TQ	USBLS	5/15
	North Carolina	Y	34170 FQ	42070 MW	51450 TQ	USBLS	5/15
	Charlotte-Concord-Gastonia						
	MSA, NC-SC	Y	24300 FQ	31060 MW	42620 TQ	USBLS	5/15
	Raleigh MSA, NC	Y	39750 FQ	43280 MW	47080 TQ	USBLS	5/15
	North Dakota	Y	28270 FQ	35130 MW	46710 TQ	USBLS	5/15
	Ohio	Y	40170 FQ	47430 MW	57800 TQ	USBLS	5/15
	Cincinnati MSA, OH-KY-IN	Y	36950 FQ	47650 MW	58790 TQ	USBLS	5/15
	Cleveland-Elyria MSA, OH	Y	43260 FQ	50320 MW	59930 TQ	USBLS	5/15
	Columbus MSA, OH	Y	41470 FQ	49330 MW	56970 TQ	USBLS	5/15
	Oklahoma	Y	29290 FQ	36360 MW	44550 TQ	USBLS	5/15
	Oklahoma City MSA, OK	Y	30400 FQ	36640 MW	44950 TQ	USBLS	5/15
	Tulsa MSA, OK	Y	34390 FQ	40460 MW	46690 TQ	USBLS	5/15
	Oregon	H	21.94 FQ	25.65 MW	29.76 TQ	ORBLS	2016

AE	Average entry wage	AWR	Average wage range	H	Hourly	LR	Low end range	MTC	Median total compensation	TCC	Total cash compensation
AEX	Average experienced wage	B	Biweekly	HI	Highest wage paid	M	Monthly	MW	Median wage paid	TQ	Third quartile wage
ATC	Average total compensation	D	Daily	HR	High end range	MCC	Median cash compensation	MWR	Median wage range	W	Weekly
AW	Average wage paid	FQ	First quartile wage	LO	Lowest wage paid	ME	Median entry wage	S	See annotated source	Y	Yearly

Occupation/Type/Industry	Location	Per	Low	Mid	High	Source	Date
Recreational Therapist	Portland-Vancouver-Hillsboro						
	MSA, OR-WA	Y	40470 FQ	50470 MW	59990 TQ	USBLS	5/15
	Pennsylvania	Y	31910 FQ	41460 MW	52060 TQ	USBLS	5/15
	Allentown-Bethlehem-Easton						
	MSA, PA-NJ	Y	30250 FQ	36720 MW	44570 TQ	USBLS	5/15
	Harrisburg-Carlisle MSA, PA	Y	34570 FQ	38380 MW	49540 TQ	USBLS	5/15
	Montgomery County-Bucks						
	County-Chester County						
	PMSA, PA	Y	32990 FQ	41450 MW	51530 TQ	USBLS	5/15
	Philadelphia PMSA, PA	Y	30350 FQ	36820 MW	48450 TQ	USBLS	5/15
	Pittsburgh MSA, PA	Y	31470 FQ	42470 MW	49960 TQ	USBLS	5/15
	Rhode Island	Y	30060 FQ	36920 MW	50590 TQ	USBLS	5/15
	Providence-Warwick MSA, RI-MA	Y	31490 FQ	37830 MW	50030 TQ	USBLS	5/15
	South Carolina	Y	28420 FQ	37070 MW	46600 TQ	USBLS	5/15
	Columbia MSA, SC	Y	26880 FQ	37200 MW	46080 TQ	USBLS	5/15
	Greenville-Anderson-Mauldin						
	MSA, SC	Y	31920 FQ	38980 MW	47480 TQ	USBLS	5/15
	South Dakota	Y	34050 FQ	37480 MW	43950 TQ	USBLS	5/15
	Tennessee	Y	30550 FQ	39540 MW	53980 TQ	USBLS	5/15
	Memphis MSA, TN-MS-AR	Y	34580 FQ	39130 MW	50560 TQ	USBLS	5/15
	Nashville-Davidson–						
	Murfreesboro–Franklin						
	MSA, TN	Y	39810 FQ	49050 MW	66650 TQ	USBLS	5/15
	Texas	Y	33220 FQ	48420 MW	58620 TQ	USBLS	5/15
	Austin-Round Rock MSA, TX	Y	39230 FQ	51000 MW	57390 TQ	USBLS	5/15
	Dallas-Plano-Irving PMSA, TX	Y	37830 FQ	50180 MW	58370 TQ	USBLS	5/15
	Fort Worth-Arlington PMSA,						
	TX	Y	33730 FQ	49230 MW	58220 TQ	USBLS	5/15
	Houston-The Woodlands-						
	Sugar Land MSA, TX	Y	39340 FQ	49500 MW	61520 TQ	USBLS	5/15
	Utah	Y	31330 FQ	39810 MW	49530 TQ	USBLS	5/15
	Ogden-Clearfield MSA, UT	Y	30940 FQ	42800 MW	55450 TQ	USBLS	5/15
	Provo-Orem MSA, UT	Y	31160 FQ	36320 MW	44680 TQ	USBLS	5/15
	Salt Lake City MSA, UT	Y	32940 FQ	44070 MW	52510 TQ	USBLS	5/15
	Vermont	Y	32190 FQ	39570 MW	48840 TQ	USBLS	5/15
	Virginia	Y	34260 FQ	41890 MW	52070 TQ	USBLS	5/15
	Richmond MSA, VA	Y	36680 FQ	43280 MW	49550 TQ	USBLS	5/15
	Virginia Beach-Norfolk-						
	Newport News MSA, VA-NC	Y	31970 FQ	39230 MW	53730 TQ	USBLS	5/15
	Washington	H	18.57 FQ	23.50 MW	30.69 TQ	WABLS	3/16
	Seattle-Bellevue-Everett						
	PMSA, WA	H	23.76 FQ	32.32 MW	37.58 TQ	WABLS	3/16
	Tacoma-Lakewood PMSA, WA	H	21.21 FQ	24.00 MW	30.52 TQ	WABLS	3/16
	West Virginia	Y	43170 FQ	48820 MW	58620 TQ	USBLS	5/15
	Wisconsin	Y	29280 FQ	37230 MW	52950 TQ	USBLS	5/15
	Madison MSA, WI	Y	28780 FQ	32870 MW	40900 TQ	USBLS	5/15
	Milwaukee-Waukesha-West						
	Allis MSA, WI	Y	28950 FQ	35260 MW	53880 TQ	USBLS	5/15
	Wyoming	Y	43560 FQ	46250 MW	49910 TQ	USBLS	5/15
	Puerto Rico	Y	21620 FQ	27480 MW	41480 TQ	USBLS	5/15
	San Juan-Carolina-Caguas						
	MSA, PR	Y	22200 FQ	26700 MW	37550 TQ	USBLS	5/15
Department of Corrections, State Government	Deer Lodge, MT	H			23.10 HI	MTGOV	2016
Municipal Government	Detroit, MI	M	2625 LO		3000 HI	DETGOV	2016
Recreation Senior Bureau, Municipal Government	Gardena, CA	Y			23117 HI	CACIT	6/22/16
Recreational Vehicle Service Technician	Alabama	Y	29666 AE	46661 AW	55163 AEX	ALBLS	6/16
	Arizona	Y	26360 FQ	32220 MW	38260 TQ	USBLS	5/15
	Phoenix-Mesa-Scottsdale						
	MSA, AZ	Y	22570 FQ	29940 MW	38340 TQ	USBLS	5/15
	Tucson MSA, AZ	Y	26820 FQ	32500 MW	41300 TQ	USBLS	5/15
	Arkansas	Y	30560 FQ	36610 MW	43880 TQ	USBLS	5/15
	Little Rock-North Little Rock-						
	Conway MSA, AR	Y	31970 FQ	35900 MW	39840 TQ	USBLS	5/15
	California	H	15.71 FQ	19.07 MW	23.72 TQ	CABLS	1/16-3/16
	Riverside-San Bernardino-						
	Ontario MSA, CA	H	14.06 FQ	17.84 MW	26.64 TQ	CABLS	1/16-3/16

AE	Average entry wage	**AWR**	Average wage range	**H** Hourly
AEX	Average experienced wage	**B**	Biweekly	**HI** Highest wage paid
ATC	Average total compensation	**D**	Daily	**HR** High end range
AW	Average wage paid	**FQ**	First quartile wage	**LO** Lowest wage paid

LR Low end range   **MTC** Median total compensation   **TCC** Total cash compensation
M Monthly   **MW** Median wage paid   **TQ** Third quartile wage
MCC Median cash compensation   **MWR** Median wage range   **W** Weekly
ME Median entry wage   **S** See annotated source   **Y** Yearly

Occupation/Type/Industry	Location	Per	Low	Mid	High	Source	Date
Recreational Vehicle Service Technician							
	Sacramento–Roseville–Arden-Arcade MSA, CA	H	16.44 FQ	19.35 MW	22.31 TQ	CABLS	1/16-3/16
	San Diego-Carlsbad MSA, CA	H	16.32 FQ	18.74 MW	22.11 TQ	CABLS	1/16-3/16
	Colorado	Y	31630 FQ	39330 MW	58240 TQ	USBLS	5/15
	Denver-Aurora-Lakewood MSA, CO	Y	33880 FQ	53670 MW	59550 TQ	USBLS	5/15
	Connecticut	Y		36783 MW		CTBLS	1/16-3/16
	Delaware	Y	29150 FQ	34810 MW	38920 TQ	USBLS	5/15
	Florida	H	12.64 AE	18.27 MW	22.81 AEX	FLBLS	7/16-9/16
	Georgia	Y	23100 FQ	31790 MW	40110 TQ	USBLS	5/15
	Idaho	Y	28130 FQ	34240 MW	43490 TQ	USBLS	5/15
	Boise City MSA, ID	Y	33810 FQ	40790 MW	52620 TQ	USBLS	5/15
	Illinois	Y	26390 FQ	33470 MW	38930 TQ	USBLS	5/15
	Indiana	Y	29500 FQ	35070 MW	39450 TQ	USBLS	5/15
	Indianapolis-Carmel-Anderson MSA, IN	Y	31880 FQ	36540 MW	41970 TQ	USBLS	5/15
	Iowa	Y	27570 FQ	34280 MW	42900 TQ	USBLS	5/15
	Kansas	Y	23030 FQ	29330 MW	34970 TQ	USBLS	5/15
	Wichita MSA, KS	Y	27480 FQ	32410 MW	35920 TQ	USBLS	5/15
	Kentucky	Y	28390 FQ	34230 MW	39270 TQ	USBLS	5/15
	Louisville-Jefferson County MSA, KY-IN	Y	29210 FQ	33290 MW	36940 TQ	USBLS	5/15
	Louisiana	Y	30320 FQ	34930 MW	38520 TQ	USBLS	5/15
	Maine	Y	31190 FQ	34740 MW	38300 TQ	USBLS	5/15
	Maryland	Y	26279 AE	43211 MW	51676 AEX	MDBLS	4/16
	Massachusetts	Y	36700 FQ	41850 MW	48130 TQ	USBLS	5/15
	Worcester MSA, MA-CT	Y	43000 FQ	46850 MW	51640 TQ	USBLS	5/15
	Michigan	Y	26330 FQ	34660 MW	43720 TQ	USBLS	5/15
	Minnesota	Y	29446 FQ	34736 MW	39533 TQ	MNBLS	1/16-3/16
	Minneapolis-St. Paul-Bloomington MSA, MN-WI	Y	31216 FQ	35993 MW	41082 TQ	MNBLS	1/16-3/16
	Mississippi	Y	17620 FQ	22310 MW	29360 TQ	USBLS	5/15
	Missouri	Y	26840 FQ	34110 MW	42260 TQ	USBLS	5/15
	Kansas City MSA, MO-KS	Y	25230 FQ	35360 MW	42320 TQ	USBLS	5/15
	St. Louis MSA, MO-IL	Y	30760 FQ	35370 MW	39690 TQ	USBLS	5/15
	Montana	Y	19650 FQ	28290 MW	38450 TQ	USBLS	5/15
	Nebraska	Y	26340 FQ	29695 MW	35340 TQ	NEBLS	7/16-9/16
	Omaha-Council Bluffs MSA, NE-IA	Y	26965 FQ	29300 MW	32060 TQ	NEBLS	7/16-9/16
	Nevada	Y	32350 FQ	38250 MW	47460 TQ	USBLS	5/15
	Las Vegas-Henderson-Paradise MSA, NV	Y	32610 FQ	37620 MW	47740 TQ	USBLS	5/15
	New Hampshire	H	13.73 AE	17.30 MW	19.40 AEX	NHBLS	6/16
	New Jersey	Y	29750 FQ	35920 MW	43090 TQ	USBLS	5/15
	Newark PMSA, NJ-PA	Y	29390 FQ	40560 MW	45240 TQ	USBLS	5/15
	New Mexico	Y	26910 FQ	34970 MW	44330 TQ	USBLS	5/15
	Albuquerque MSA, NM	Y	26040 FQ	33340 MW	41380 TQ	USBLS	5/15
	New York	Y	22870 AE	34590 MW	41400 AEX	NYBLS	1/16-3/16
	New York-Jersey City-White Plains PMSA, NY-NJ	Y	26490 FQ	31430 MW	41310 TQ	USBLS	5/15
	North Carolina	Y	24550 FQ	33100 MW	43350 TQ	USBLS	5/15
	North Dakota	Y	31740 FQ	40580 MW	47970 TQ	USBLS	5/15
	Ohio	Y	26980 FQ	31920 MW	37450 TQ	USBLS	5/15
	Oklahoma	Y	29440 FQ	35770 MW	41580 TQ	USBLS	5/15
	Oklahoma City MSA, OK	Y	23340 FQ	32060 MW	36480 TQ	USBLS	5/15
	Tulsa MSA, OK	Y	33240 FQ	39410 MW	49280 TQ	USBLS	5/15
	Oregon	H	15.58 FQ	18.09 MW	21.45 TQ	ORBLS	2016
	Portland-Vancouver-Hillsboro MSA, OR-WA	Y	33410 FQ	37950 MW	45360 TQ	USBLS	5/15
	Pennsylvania	Y	27890 FQ	33330 MW	41770 TQ	USBLS	5/15
	Allentown-Bethlehem-Easton MSA, PA-NJ	Y	30330 FQ	38300 MW	55940 TQ	USBLS	5/15
	South Carolina	Y	26750 FQ	30390 MW	35480 TQ	USBLS	5/15
	South Dakota	Y	25940 FQ	29900 MW	35470 TQ	USBLS	5/15
	Tennessee	Y	29450 FQ	35340 MW	39780 TQ	USBLS	5/15
	Memphis MSA, TN-MS-AR	Y	16880 FQ	18620 MW	32000 TQ	USBLS	5/15
	Texas	Y	31070 FQ	36200 MW	44840 TQ	USBLS	5/15
	Dallas-Plano-Irving PMSA, TX	Y	32580 FQ	37250 MW	49970 TQ	USBLS	5/15
	Fort Worth-Arlington PMSA, TX	Y	35120 FQ	41400 MW	49380 TQ	USBLS	5/15

AE Average entry wage	**AWR** Average wage range	**H** Hourly	**LR** Low end range	**MTC** Median total compensation	**TCC** Total cash compensation
AEX Average experienced wage	**B** Biweekly	**HI** Highest wage paid	**M** Monthly	**MW** Median wage paid	**TQ** Third quartile wage
ATC Average total compensation	**D** Daily	**HR** High end range	**MCC** Median cash compensation	**MWR** Median wage range	**W** Weekly
AW Average wage paid	**FQ** First quartile wage	**LO** Lowest wage paid	**ME** Median entry wage	**S** See annotated source	**Y** Yearly

Occupation/Type/Industry	Location	Per	Low	Mid	High	Source	Date
Recreational Vehicle Service Technician	San Antonio-New Braunfels MSA, TX	Y	32650 FQ	35540 MW	38430 TQ	USBLS	5/15
	Utah	Y	32660 FQ	42610 MW	50390 TQ	USBLS	5/15
	Salt Lake City MSA, UT	Y	27200 FQ	33790 MW	45550 TQ	USBLS	5/15
	Vermont	Y	31880 FQ	35570 MW	39260 TQ	USBLS	5/15
	Virginia	Y	22760 FQ	29920 MW	38900 TQ	USBLS	5/15
	Richmond MSA, VA	Y	22430 FQ	28770 MW	43150 TQ	USBLS	5/15
	Virginia Beach-Norfolk-Newport News MSA, VA-NC	Y	27230 FQ	32880 MW	38760 TQ	USBLS	5/15
	Washington	H	15.58 FQ	19.84 MW	25.49 TQ	WABLS	3/16
	Seattle-Bellevue-Everett PMSA, WA	H	19.62 FQ	24.95 MW	27.93 TQ	WABLS	3/16
	Tacoma-Lakewood PMSA, WA	H	15.30 FQ	17.50 MW	20.61 TQ	WABLS	3/16
	West Virginia	Y	23540 FQ	28260 MW	34210 TQ	USBLS	5/15
	Wisconsin	Y	29280 FQ	34980 MW	41570 TQ	USBLS	5/15
	Wyoming	Y	26160 FQ	33890 MW	41310 TQ	USBLS	5/15
Recycling Coordinator Municipal Government	Glendale, CA	Y			79063 HI	CACIT	6/28/16
Recycling Program Manager Municipal Government	Berkeley, CA	Y			110600 HI	CACIT	6/28/16
Recycling Specialist Municipal Government	Burbank, CA	Y			17160 HI	CACIT	6/28/16
Red Hat Certified Engineer	United States	Y		125350 AW		CERTM02	2015
Reference Librarian Public Library	Carlsbad, CA	H	21.50 LO		28.00 HI	CCCA02	1/1/16
Refractory Materials Repairer							
Except Brickmasons	Alabama	Y	43549 AE	65801 AW	76937 AEX	ALBLS	6/16
Except Brickmasons	Florida	H	19.95 AE	22.04 MW	23.49 AEX	FLBLS	7/16-9/16
Except Brickmasons	Indiana	Y	36680 FQ	42640 MW	49720 TQ	USBLS	5/15
Except Brickmasons	New York	Y	39800 AE	46230 MW	51190 AEX	NYBLS	1/16-3/16
Except Brickmasons	North Carolina	Y	38340 FQ	52830 MW	58160 TQ	USBLS	5/15
Except Brickmasons	Ohio	Y	40730 FQ	47960 MW	57350 TQ	USBLS	5/15
Except Brickmasons	Oklahoma	Y	36230 FQ	41090 MW	46130 TQ	USBLS	5/15
Except Brickmasons	Oregon	H	17.33 FQ	21.33 MW	24.23 TQ	ORBLS	2016
Except Brickmasons	Pennsylvania	Y	35410 FQ	43110 MW	48390 TQ	USBLS	5/15
Except Brickmasons	Tennessee	Y	41420 FQ	47760 MW	56050 TQ	USBLS	5/15
Except Brickmasons	Texas	Y	37270 FQ	51190 MW	59500 TQ	USBLS	5/15
Except Brickmasons	Virginia	Y	42500 FQ	50940 MW	59840 TQ	USBLS	5/15
Except Brickmasons	Washington	H	21.40 FQ	24.67 MW	30.08 TQ	WABLS	3/16
Except Brickmasons	Wisconsin	Y	35490 FQ	44980 MW	53610 TQ	USBLS	5/15
Refuse and Recyclable Material Collector	Alabama	Y	21167 AE	30197 AW	34702 AEX	ALBLS	6/16
	Birmingham-Hoover MSA, AL	Y	24838 AE	34136 AW	38785 AEX	ALBLS	6/16
	Alaska	Y	30240 FQ	36640 MW	47220 TQ	USBLS	5/15
	Anchorage MSA, AK	Y	37430 FQ	47220 MW	55450 TQ	USBLS	5/15
	Arizona	Y	33050 FQ	38650 MW	45840 TQ	USBLS	5/15
	Phoenix-Mesa-Scottsdale MSA, AZ	Y	35530 FQ	41700 MW	47860 TQ	USBLS	5/15
	Tucson MSA, AZ	Y	31270 FQ	34920 MW	38600 TQ	USBLS	5/15
	Arkansas	Y	20690 FQ	24620 MW	30290 TQ	USBLS	5/15
	Little Rock-North Little Rock-Conway MSA, AR	Y	21960 FQ	26500 MW	33740 TQ	USBLS	5/15
	Pine Bluff MSA, AR	Y	20880 FQ	22870 MW	24860 TQ	USBLS	5/15
	California	H	17.75 FQ	22.55 MW	27.22 TQ	CABLS	1/16-3/16
	Anaheim-Santa Ana-Irvine PMSA, CA	H	9.67 FQ	16.80 MW	22.50 TQ	CABLS	1/16-3/16
	Los Angeles-Long Beach-Glendale PMSA, CA	H	20.53 FQ	23.17 MW	29.01 TQ	CABLS	1/16-3/16
	Oakland-Hayward-Berkeley PMSA, CA	H	21.34 FQ	27.57 MW	34.17 TQ	CABLS	1/16-3/16
	Riverside-San Bernardino-Ontario MSA, CA	H	20.42 FQ	22.14 MW	23.85 TQ	CABLS	1/16-3/16
	Sacramento–Roseville–Arden-Arcade MSA, CA	H	15.94 FQ	22.20 MW	28.41 TQ	CABLS	1/16-3/16

AE	Average entry wage	**AWR**	Average wage range	**H**	Hourly	**LR**	Low end range	**MTC**	Median total compensation	**TCC**	Total cash compensation
AEX	Average experienced wage	**B**	Biweekly	**HI**	Highest wage paid	**M**	Monthly	**MW**	Median wage paid	**TQ**	Third quartile wage
ATC	Average total compensation	**D**	Daily	**HR**	High end range	**MCC**	Median cash compensation	**MWR**	Median wage range	**W**	Weekly
AW	Average wage paid	**FQ**	First quartile wage	**LO**	Lowest wage paid	**ME**	Median entry wage	**S**	See annotated source	**Y**	Yearly

Occupation/Type/Industry	Location	Per	Low	Mid	High	Source	Date
Refuse and Recyclable Material Collector	San Diego-Carlsbad MSA, CA	H	14.44 FQ	21.36 MW	24.55 TQ	CABLS	1/16-3/16
	San Francisco-Redwood City-South San Francisco PMSA, CA	H	19.63 FQ	22.87 MW	26.50 TQ	CABLS	1/16-3/16
	Colorado	Y	26800 FQ	35290 MW	44660 TQ	USBLS	5/15
	Denver-Aurora-Lakewood MSA, CO	Y	23920 FQ	34900 MW	45260 TQ	USBLS	5/15
	Connecticut	Y		39751 MW		CTBLS	1/16-3/16
	Bridgeport-Stamford-Norwalk MSA, CT	Y	32620 FQ	44060 MW	52960 TQ	USBLS	5/15
	Hartford-West Hartford-East Hartford MSA, CT	Y	31320 FQ	37180 MW	44270 TQ	USBLS	5/15
	Delaware	Y	30650 FQ	38580 MW	46290 TQ	USBLS	5/15
	Wilmington PMSA, DE-MD-NJ	Y	31680 FQ	38790 MW	46140 TQ	USBLS	5/15
	District of Columbia	Y	33210 FQ	42130 MW	47550 TQ	USBLS	5/15
	Washington-Arlington-Alexandria PMSA, DC-VA-MD-WV	Y	25110 FQ	33310 MW	43430 TQ	USBLS	5/15
	Florida	H	11.60 AE	15.89 MW	18.77 AEX	FLBLS	7/16-9/16
	Fort Lauderdale-Pompano Beach-Deerfield Beach PMSA, FL	H	12.90 AE	18.04 MW	20.77 AEX	FLBLS	7/16-9/16
	Miami-Miami Beach-Kendall PMSA, FL	H	12.19 AE	18.08 MW	20.86 AEX	FLBLS	7/16-9/16
	Orlando-Kissimmee-Sanford MSA, FL	H	11.68 AE	15.69 MW	18.04 AEX	FLBLS	7/16-9/16
	Tampa-St. Petersburg-Clearwater MSA, FL	H	12.55 AE	17.02 MW	20.24 AEX	FLBLS	7/16-9/16
	Georgia	Y	21860 FQ	28490 MW	35510 TQ	USBLS	5/15
	Atlanta-Sandy Springs-Roswell MSA, GA	Y	27390 FQ	31730 MW	38020 TQ	USBLS	5/15
	Augusta-Richmond County MSA, GA-SC	Y	18770 FQ	27750 MW	39140 TQ	USBLS	5/15
	Hawaii	Y	36060 FQ	42970 MW	47180 TQ	USBLS	5/15
	Urban Honolulu MSA, HI	Y	37370 FQ	43110 MW	47030 TQ	USBLS	5/15
	Idaho	Y	27910 FQ	33630 MW	37480 TQ	USBLS	5/15
	Boise City MSA, ID	Y	31350 FQ	34650 MW	37530 TQ	USBLS	5/15
	Illinois	Y	35140 FQ	45300 MW	67500 TQ	USBLS	5/15
	Chicago-Naperville-Arlington Heights PMSA, IL	Y	37140 FQ	48350 MW	71380 TQ	USBLS	5/15
	Lake County-Kenosha County PMSA, IL-WI	Y	35530 FQ	43890 MW	49110 TQ	USBLS	5/15
	Indiana	Y	25930 FQ	32660 MW	37340 TQ	USBLS	5/15
	Gary PMSA, IN	Y	27990 FQ	35330 MW	42720 TQ	USBLS	5/15
	Indianapolis-Carmel-Anderson MSA, IN	Y	25330 FQ	30520 MW	36080 TQ	USBLS	5/15
	Iowa	Y	21820 FQ	28650 MW	38950 TQ	USBLS	5/15
	Des Moines-West Des Moines MSA, IA	Y	21870 FQ	24850 MW	54100 TQ	USBLS	5/15
	Kansas	Y	21700 FQ	27050 MW	33700 TQ	USBLS	5/15
	Wichita MSA, KS	Y	25440 FQ	32950 MW	37120 TQ	USBLS	5/15
	Kentucky	Y	20550 FQ	26580 MW	34590 TQ	USBLS	5/15
	Louisville-Jefferson County MSA, KY-IN	Y	23970 FQ	31530 MW	36890 TQ	USBLS	5/15
	Louisiana	Y	19210 FQ	25230 MW	30090 TQ	USBLS	5/15
	Baton Rouge MSA, LA	Y	20000 FQ	24890 MW	28480 TQ	USBLS	5/15
	New Orleans-Metairie MSA, LA	Y	18220 FQ	24210 MW	35560 TQ	USBLS	5/15
	Maine	Y	21300 FQ	26600 MW	32660 TQ	USBLS	5/15
	Portland-South Portland MSA, ME	Y	25230 FQ	30290 MW	35720 TQ	USBLS	5/15
	Maryland	Y	21193 AE	31464 MW	36599 AEX	MDBLS	4/16
	Baltimore-Columbia-Towson MSA, MD	Y	24310 FQ	29290 MW	36990 TQ	USBLS	5/15
	Salisbury MSA, MD-DE	Y	23540 FQ	30880 MW	40480 TQ	USBLS	5/15
	Massachusetts	Y	30480 FQ	36940 MW	44620 TQ	USBLS	5/15
	Boston-Cambridge-Newton NECTA, MA	Y	30160 FQ	38120 MW	46630 TQ	USBLS	5/15
	Worcester MSA, MA-CT	Y	34080 FQ	39280 MW	45130 TQ	USBLS	5/15
	Michigan	Y	28490 FQ	35920 MW	44270 TQ	USBLS	5/15

AE	Average entry wage	AWR	Average wage range	H	Hourly	LR	Low end range	MTC	Median total compensation	TCC	Total cash compensation
AEX	Average experienced wage	B	Biweekly	HI	Highest wage paid	M	Monthly	MW	Median wage paid	TQ	Third quartile wage
ATC	Average total compensation	D	Daily	HR	High end range	MCC	Median cash compensation	MWR	Median wage range	W	Weekly
AW	Average wage paid	FQ	First quartile wage	LO	Lowest wage paid	ME	Median entry wage	S	See annotated source	Y	Yearly

1370

Occupation/Type/Industry	Location	Per	Low	Mid	High	Source	Date
Refuse and Recyclable Material Collector							
	Detroit-Dearborn-Livonia PMSA, MI	Y	26590 FQ	36520 MW	46150 TQ	USBLS	5/15
	Grand Rapids-Wyoming MSA, MI	Y	30600 FQ	37660 MW	45190 TQ	USBLS	5/15
	Minnesota	Y	34237 FQ	41344 MW	49863 TQ	MNBLS	1/16-3/16
	Minneapolis-St. Paul-Bloomington MSA, MN-WI	Y	37967 FQ	45810 MW	54440 TQ	MNBLS	1/16-3/16
	Mississippi	Y	21950 FQ	26260 MW	31260 TQ	USBLS	5/15
	Jackson MSA, MS	Y	21300 FQ	25020 MW	30390 TQ	USBLS	5/15
	Missouri	Y	20790 FQ	28880 MW	37190 TQ	USBLS	5/15
	Kansas City MSA, MO-KS	Y	21920 FQ	28220 MW	35820 TQ	USBLS	5/15
	St. Louis MSA, MO-IL	Y	19090 FQ	34550 MW	44980 TQ	USBLS	5/15
	Montana	Y	32050 FQ	35750 MW	39510 TQ	USBLS	5/15
	Billings MSA, MT	Y	34310 FQ	38550 MW	44760 TQ	USBLS	5/15
	Nebraska	Y	25050 FQ	28340 MW	32680 TQ	NEBLS	7/16-9/16
	Omaha-Council Bluffs MSA, NE-IA	Y	25905 FQ	28075 MW	30250 TQ	NEBLS	7/16-9/16
	Nevada	Y	31680 FQ	42030 MW	51230 TQ	USBLS	5/15
	Las Vegas-Henderson-Paradise MSA, NV	Y	23920 FQ	34260 MW	44460 TQ	USBLS	5/15
	New Hampshire	H	10.50 AE	14.70 MW	18.26 AEX	NHBLS	6/16
	Manchester NECTA, NH	H	9.32 AE	15.30 MW	18.86 AEX	NHBLS	6/16
	Nashua NECTA, NH-MA	Y	22000 FQ	25290 MW	32220 TQ	USBLS	5/15
	New Jersey	Y	27750 FQ	38780 MW	50000 TQ	USBLS	5/15
	Camden PMSA, NJ	Y	26170 FQ	36310 MW	45360 TQ	USBLS	5/15
	Newark PMSA, NJ-PA	Y	22790 FQ	34680 MW	46860 TQ	USBLS	5/15
	Trenton MSA, NJ	Y	35210 FQ	42670 MW	48060 TQ	USBLS	5/15
	New Mexico	Y	23010 FQ	32050 MW	37670 TQ	USBLS	5/15
	Albuquerque MSA, NM	Y	32610 FQ	35880 MW	39460 TQ	USBLS	5/15
	New York	Y	31480 AE	53220 MW	64200 AEX	NYBLS	1/16-3/16
	Buffalo-Cheektowaga-Niagara Falls MSA, NY	Y	33400 FQ	41600 MW	51800 TQ	USBLS	5/15
	Nassau County-Suffolk County PMSA, NY	Y	42110 FQ	54820 MW	69730 TQ	USBLS	5/15
	New York-Jersey City-White Plains PMSA, NY-NJ	Y	37040 FQ	59820 MW	72260 TQ	USBLS	5/15
	Rochester MSA, NY	Y	26410 FQ	30300 MW	36860 TQ	USBLS	5/15
	North Carolina	Y	21280 FQ	26620 MW	31550 TQ	USBLS	5/15
	Charlotte-Concord-Gastonia MSA, NC-SC	Y	23490 FQ	28590 MW	34510 TQ	USBLS	5/15
	Raleigh MSA, NC	Y	25700 FQ	29110 MW	34230 TQ	USBLS	5/15
	North Dakota	Y	25410 FQ	30300 MW	37720 TQ	USBLS	5/15
	Fargo MSA, ND-MN	Y	27070 FQ	32850 MW	37780 TQ	USBLS	5/15
	Ohio	Y	25640 FQ	33470 MW	42020 TQ	USBLS	5/15
	Cincinnati MSA, OH-KY-IN	Y	24470 FQ	33570 MW	42710 TQ	USBLS	5/15
	Cleveland-Elyria MSA, OH	Y	31250 FQ	37520 MW	45780 TQ	USBLS	5/15
	Columbus MSA, OH	Y	25590 FQ	34660 MW	43740 TQ	USBLS	5/15
	Oklahoma	Y	23370 FQ	28910 MW	36560 TQ	USBLS	5/15
	Oklahoma City MSA, OK	Y	26090 FQ	35400 MW	41740 TQ	USBLS	5/15
	Tulsa MSA, OK	Y	21950 FQ	27460 MW	34730 TQ	USBLS	5/15
	Oregon	H	15.94 FQ	21.20 MW	24.26 TQ	ORBLS	2016
	Portland-Vancouver-Hillsboro MSA, OR-WA	Y	37170 FQ	45910 MW	53770 TQ	USBLS	5/15
	Pennsylvania	Y	24200 FQ	31990 MW	41540 TQ	USBLS	5/15
	Allentown-Bethlehem-Easton MSA, PA-NJ	Y	23620 FQ	28430 MW	36550 TQ	USBLS	5/15
	Harrisburg-Carlisle MSA, PA	Y	29320 FQ	35140 MW	41850 TQ	USBLS	5/15
	Montgomery County-Bucks County-Chester County PMSA, PA	Y	26600 FQ	35840 MW	48330 TQ	USBLS	5/15
	Philadelphia PMSA, PA	Y	27110 FQ	35980 MW	46840 TQ	USBLS	5/15
	Pittsburgh MSA, PA	Y	26210 FQ	34630 MW	42790 TQ	USBLS	5/15
	Rhode Island	Y	32340 FQ	43740 MW	54880 TQ	USBLS	5/15
	Providence-Warwick MSA, RI-MA	Y	29490 FQ	39460 MW	51700 TQ	USBLS	5/15
	South Carolina	Y	18500 FQ	22820 MW	29280 TQ	USBLS	5/15
	Charleston-North Charleston MSA, SC	Y	23070 FQ	26890 MW	29970 TQ	USBLS	5/15
	Columbia MSA, SC	Y	18260 FQ	23060 MW	33510 TQ	USBLS	5/15
	Greenville-Anderson-Mauldin MSA, SC	Y	18120 FQ	20160 MW	25210 TQ	USBLS	5/15

AE Average entry wage	**AWR** Average wage range	**H** Hourly	**LR** Low end range	**MTC** Median total compensation	**TCC** Total cash compensation
AEX Average experienced wage	**B** Biweekly	**HI** Highest wage paid	**M** Monthly	**MW** Median wage paid	**TQ** Third quartile wage
ATC Average total compensation	**D** Daily	**HR** High end range	**MCC** Median cash compensation	**MWR** Median wage range	**W** Weekly
AW Average wage paid	**FQ** First quartile wage	**LO** Lowest wage paid	**ME** Median entry wage	**S** See annotated source	**Y** Yearly

Occupation/Type/Industry	Location	Per	Low	Mid	High	Source	Date
Refuse and Recyclable Material Collector	South Dakota	Y	21540 FQ	24310 MW	28510 TQ	USBLS	5/15
	Sioux Falls MSA, SD	Y	25310 FQ	27870 MW	30460 TQ	USBLS	5/15
	Tennessee	Y	19460 FQ	24570 MW	32150 TQ	USBLS	5/15
	Knoxville MSA, TN	Y	19810 FQ	24080 MW	31570 TQ	USBLS	5/15
	Memphis MSA, TN-MS-AR	Y	23150 FQ	30610 MW	36530 TQ	USBLS	5/15
	Nashville-Davidson– Murfreesboro–Franklin MSA, TN	Y	19470 FQ	23670 MW	31720 TQ	USBLS	5/15
	Texas	Y	24560 FQ	30660 MW	37010 TQ	USBLS	5/15
	Austin-Round Rock MSA, TX	Y	27750 FQ	32130 MW	40890 TQ	USBLS	5/15
	Dallas-Plano-Irving PMSA, TX	Y	22250 FQ	26610 MW	35290 TQ	USBLS	5/15
	Fort Worth-Arlington PMSA, TX	Y	22670 FQ	27160 MW	36270 TQ	USBLS	5/15
	Houston-The Woodlands- Sugar Land MSA, TX	Y	26070 FQ	32140 MW	37640 TQ	USBLS	5/15
	San Antonio-New Braunfels MSA, TX	Y	24010 FQ	32220 MW	37020 TQ	USBLS	5/15
	Utah	Y	24560 FQ	33680 MW	40650 TQ	USBLS	5/15
	Ogden-Clearfield MSA, UT	Y	25690 FQ	30330 MW	41280 TQ	USBLS	5/15
	Provo-Orem MSA, UT	Y	17970 FQ	29640 MW	37950 TQ	USBLS	5/15
	Salt Lake City MSA, UT	Y	27250 FQ	35580 MW	42560 TQ	USBLS	5/15
	Vermont	Y	28410 FQ	33270 MW	37390 TQ	USBLS	5/15
	Burlington-South Burlington MSA, VT	Y	31950 FQ	35220 MW	38490 TQ	USBLS	5/15
	Virginia	Y	20590 FQ	26620 MW	34000 TQ	USBLS	5/15
	Charlottesville MSA, VA	Y	23520 FQ	28730 MW	35310 TQ	USBLS	5/15
	Richmond MSA, VA	Y	20390 FQ	24900 MW	32650 TQ	USBLS	5/15
	Virginia Beach-Norfolk- Newport News MSA, VA-NC	Y	18670 FQ	24670 MW	30530 TQ	USBLS	5/15
	Washington	H	19.59 FQ	23.92 MW	28.63 TQ	WABLS	3/16
	Seattle-Bellevue-Everett PMSA, WA	H	17.89 FQ	23.30 MW	29.26 TQ	WABLS	3/16
	Tacoma-Lakewood PMSA, WA	H	22.09 FQ	26.45 MW	30.09 TQ	WABLS	3/16
	West Virginia	Y	18890 FQ	22890 MW	28140 TQ	USBLS	5/15
	Huntington-Ashland MSA, WV-KY-OH	Y	19360 FQ	23950 MW	32660 TQ	USBLS	5/15
	Wisconsin	Y	22310 FQ	27170 MW	37360 TQ	USBLS	5/15
	Madison MSA, WI	Y	20420 FQ	23800 MW	34330 TQ	USBLS	5/15
	Milwaukee-Waukesha-West Allis MSA, WI	Y	25500 FQ	30490 MW	44540 TQ	USBLS	5/15
	Wyoming	Y	27460 FQ	34220 MW	41330 TQ	USBLS	5/15
	Cheyenne MSA, WY	Y	25300 FQ	28910 MW	35270 TQ	USBLS	5/15
	Puerto Rico	Y	16930 FQ	18240 MW	19540 TQ	USBLS	5/15
	San Juan-Carolina-Caguas MSA, PR	Y	16910 FQ	18190 MW	19460 TQ	USBLS	5/15
Refuse and Recycling Collection Supervisor							
Municipal Government	Blakely, GA	H	17.00 LO		20.34 HI	GACTY02	2016
Municipal Government	Newnan, GA	H	19.60 LO		30.39 HI	GACTY02	2016
Refuse Collection Packer Operator							
Municipal Government	Detroit, MI	M	2037 LO		2579 HI	DETGOV	2016
Regional Sales Manager							
Aviation Industry	United States	Y		62500 AW		AVJOB04	2016
Registered Nurse	Alabama	Y	44014 AE	57989 AW	64982 AEX	ALBLS	6/16
	Birmingham-Hoover MSA, AL	Y	47072 AE	60171 AW	66715 AEX	ALBLS	6/16
	Alaska	Y	73960 FQ	88130 MW	103010 TQ	USBLS	5/15
	Anchorage MSA, AK	Y	74020 FQ	88940 MW	104930 TQ	USBLS	5/15
	Arizona	Y	60660 FQ	71510 MW	83120 TQ	USBLS	5/15
	Phoenix-Mesa-Scottsdale MSA, AZ	Y	62280 FQ	73400 MW	86780 TQ	USBLS	5/15
	Tucson MSA, AZ	Y	58660 FQ	67590 MW	75610 TQ	USBLS	5/15
	Arkansas	Y	46110 FQ	55660 MW	65800 TQ	USBLS	5/15
	Little Rock-North Little Rock- Conway MSA, AR	Y	50710 FQ	60690 MW	72180 TQ	USBLS	5/15
	California	H	38.43 FQ	48.97 MW	60.19 TQ	CABLS	1/16-3/16

AE Average entry wage	**AWR** Average wage range	**H** Hourly	**LR** Low end range	**MTC** Median total compensation	**TCC** Total cash compensation
AEX Average experienced wage	**B** Biweekly	**HI** Highest wage paid	**M** Monthly	**MW** Median wage paid	**TQ** Third quartile wage
ATC Average total compensation	**D** Daily	**HR** High end range	**MCC** Median cash compensation	**MWR** Median wage range	**W** Weekly
AW Average wage paid	**FQ** First quartile wage	**LO** Lowest wage paid	**ME** Median entry wage	**S** See annotated source	**Y** Yearly

Occupation/Type/Industry	Location	Per	Low	Mid	High	Source	Date
Registered Nurse	Anaheim-Santa Ana-Irvine PMSA, CA	H	34.54 FQ	43.20 MW	52.03 TQ	CABLS	1/16-3/16
	Los Angeles-Long Beach-Glendale PMSA, CA	H	38.50 FQ	47.99 MW	57.07 TQ	CABLS	1/16-3/16
	Oakland-Hayward-Berkeley PMSA, CA	H	51.95 FQ	62.63 MW	72.74 TQ	CABLS	1/16-3/16
	Riverside-San Bernardino-Ontario MSA, CA	H	37.40 FQ	45.90 MW	55.41 TQ	CABLS	1/16-3/16
	Sacramento–Roseville–Arden-Arcade MSA, CA	H	45.91 FQ	56.91 MW	67.06 TQ	CABLS	1/16-3/16
	San Diego-Carlsbad MSA, CA	H	33.65 FQ	41.69 MW	51.43 TQ	CABLS	1/16-3/16
	San Francisco-Redwood City-South San Francisco PMSA, CA	H	58.50 FQ	67.75 MW	75.27 TQ	CABLS	1/16-3/16
	Colorado	Y	57680 FQ	68540 MW	80650 TQ	USBLS	5/15
	Denver-Aurora-Lakewood MSA, CO	Y	58880 FQ	70580 MW	83100 TQ	USBLS	5/15
	Connecticut	Y		77568 MW		CTBLS	1/16-3/16
	Bridgeport-Stamford-Norwalk MSA, CT	Y	66290 FQ	75830 MW	90750 TQ	USBLS	5/15
	Hartford-West Hartford-East Hartford MSA, CT	Y	65960 FQ	76020 MW	88510 TQ	USBLS	5/15
	Delaware	Y	61600 FQ	71060 MW	81140 TQ	USBLS	5/15
	Wilmington PMSA, DE-MD-NJ	Y	63550 FQ	72460 MW	82460 TQ	USBLS	5/15
	District of Columbia	Y	64520 FQ	79630 MW	93030 TQ	USBLS	5/15
	Washington-Arlington-Alexandria PMSA, DC-VA-MD-WV	Y	63210 FQ	76060 MW	91140 TQ	USBLS	5/15
	Florida	H	24.67 AE	30.59 MW	34.90 AEX	FLBLS	7/16-9/16
	Fort Lauderdale-Pompano Beach-Deerfield Beach PMSA, FL	H	26.00 AE	33.59 MW	38.03 AEX	FLBLS	7/16-9/16
	Miami-Miami Beach-Kendall PMSA, FL	H	25.61 AE	31.33 MW	37.01 AEX	FLBLS	7/16-9/16
	Orlando-Kissimmee-Sanford MSA, FL	H	23.33 AE	30.31 MW	33.85 AEX	FLBLS	7/16-9/16
	Tampa-St. Petersburg-Clearwater MSA, FL	H	25.68 AE	31.01 MW	35.39 AEX	FLBLS	7/16-9/16
	Georgia	Y	53270 FQ	63140 MW	73660 TQ	USBLS	5/15
	Atlanta-Sandy Springs-Roswell MSA, GA	Y	56510 FQ	67010 MW	75510 TQ	USBLS	5/15
	Augusta-Richmond County MSA, GA-SC	Y	55740 FQ	65910 MW	76650 TQ	USBLS	5/15
	Hawaii	Y	77180 FQ	92290 MW	106280 TQ	USBLS	5/15
	Urban Honolulu MSA, HI	Y	77710 FQ	93970 MW	109540 TQ	USBLS	5/15
	Idaho	Y	52650 FQ	60960 MW	71490 TQ	USBLS	5/15
	Boise City MSA, ID	Y	53720 FQ	61760 MW	72070 TQ	USBLS	5/15
	Illinois	Y	54850 FQ	67140 MW	82940 TQ	USBLS	5/15
	Chicago-Naperville-Arlington Heights PMSA, IL	Y	60150 FQ	73220 MW	89780 TQ	USBLS	5/15
	Lake County-Kenosha County PMSA, IL-WI	Y	61410 FQ	72890 MW	87250 TQ	USBLS	5/15
	Indiana	Y	47910 FQ	57890 MW	69840 TQ	USBLS	5/15
	Gary PMSA, IN	Y	54700 FQ	63970 MW	75100 TQ	USBLS	5/15
	Indianapolis-Carmel-Anderson MSA, IN	Y	49820 FQ	61450 MW	73440 TQ	USBLS	5/15
	Iowa	Y	45490 FQ	53910 MW	62590 TQ	USBLS	5/15
	Des Moines-West Des Moines MSA, IA	Y	47270 FQ	56420 MW	65960 TQ	USBLS	5/15
	Kansas	Y	47020 FQ	56320 MW	66990 TQ	USBLS	5/15
	Wichita MSA, KS	Y	44740 FQ	51440 MW	61620 TQ	USBLS	5/15
	Kentucky	Y	48940 FQ	57970 MW	68440 TQ	USBLS	5/15
	Louisville-Jefferson County MSA, KY-IN	Y	52050 FQ	61510 MW	72110 TQ	USBLS	5/15
	Louisiana	Y	50550 FQ	59780 MW	72110 TQ	USBLS	5/15
	Baton Rouge MSA, LA	Y	48080 FQ	56830 MW	67620 TQ	USBLS	5/15
	New Orleans-Metairie MSA, LA	Y	55980 FQ	66140 MW	77830 TQ	USBLS	5/15
	Maine	Y	53770 FQ	62840 MW	74680 TQ	USBLS	5/15
	Portland-South Portland MSA, ME	Y	55330 FQ	64470 MW	77980 TQ	USBLS	5/15

AE	Average entry wage	AWR	Average wage range	H	Hourly
AEX	Average experienced wage	B	Biweekly	HI	Highest wage paid
ATC	Average total compensation	D	Daily	HR	High end range
AW	Average wage paid	FQ	First quartile wage	LO	Lowest wage paid

LR	Low end range	MTC	Median total compensation
M	Monthly	MW	Median wage paid
MCC	Median cash compensation	MWR	Median wage range
ME	Median entry wage	S	See annotated source

TCC	Total cash compensation
TQ	Third quartile wage
W	Weekly
Y	Yearly

Occupation/Type/Industry	Location	Per	Low	Mid	High	Source	Date
Registered Nurse	Maryland	Y	55451 AE	73198 MW	82072 AEX	MDBLS	4/16
	Baltimore-Columbia-Towson MSA, MD	Y	60980 FQ	72460 MW	86400 TQ	USBLS	5/15
	Salisbury MSA, MD-DE	Y	55620 FQ	65170 MW	77940 TQ	USBLS	5/15
	Massachusetts	Y	67100 FQ	83950 MW	109920 TQ	USBLS	5/15
	Boston-Cambridge-Newton NECTA, MA	Y	71950 FQ	92190 MW	120820 TQ	USBLS	5/15
	Worcester MSA, MA-CT	Y	63760 FQ	82700 MW	122540 TQ	USBLS	5/15
	Michigan	Y	56420 FQ	65830 MW	76070 TQ	USBLS	5/15
	Detroit-Dearborn-Livonia PMSA, MI	Y	58080 FQ	67420 MW	75670 TQ	USBLS	5/15
	Grand Rapids-Wyoming MSA, MI	Y	53670 FQ	60180 MW	69220 TQ	USBLS	5/15
	Minnesota	Y	58144 FQ	72711 MW	88819 TQ	MNBLS	1/16-3/16
	Minneapolis-St. Paul-Bloomington MSA, MN-WI	Y	64989 FQ	78023 MW	92317 TQ	MNBLS	1/16-3/16
	Mississippi	Y	46190 FQ	55620 MW	66530 TQ	USBLS	5/15
	Jackson MSA, MS	Y	48480 FQ	60990 MW	74850 TQ	USBLS	5/15
	Missouri	Y	47410 FQ	57770 MW	70410 TQ	USBLS	5/15
	Kansas City MSA, MO-KS	Y	53230 FQ	63260 MW	73640 TQ	USBLS	5/15
	St. Louis MSA, MO-IL	Y	48570 FQ	59020 MW	72440 TQ	USBLS	5/15
	Montana	Y	53970 FQ	60720 MW	71830 TQ	USBLS	5/15
	Billings MSA, MT	Y	55490 FQ	62670 MW	75420 TQ	USBLS	5/15
	Nebraska	Y	49200 FQ	57955 MW	68450 TQ	NEBLS	7/16-9/16
	Omaha-Council Bluffs MSA, NE-IA	Y	50715 FQ	59630 MW	71200 TQ	NEBLS	7/16-9/16
	Nevada	Y	68770 FQ	81370 MW	94690 TQ	USBLS	5/15
	Las Vegas-Henderson-Paradise MSA, NV	Y	71110 FQ	84080 MW	96570 TQ	USBLS	5/15
	New Hampshire	H	24.90 AE	32.07 MW	36.94 AEX	NHBLS	6/16
	Manchester NECTA, NH	H	24.75 AE	33.27 MW	37.85 AEX	NHBLS	6/16
	Nashua NECTA, NH-MA	Y	53900 FQ	63890 MW	78180 TQ	USBLS	5/15
	New Jersey	Y	67500 FQ	79230 MW	92980 TQ	USBLS	5/15
	Camden PMSA, NJ	Y	67940 FQ	78090 MW	90260 TQ	USBLS	5/15
	Newark PMSA, NJ-PA	Y	68670 FQ	81250 MW	94170 TQ	USBLS	5/15
	Trenton MSA, NJ	Y	62090 FQ	71710 MW	80830 TQ	USBLS	5/15
	New Mexico	Y	56120 FQ	64710 MW	75490 TQ	USBLS	5/15
	Albuquerque MSA, NM	Y	57450 FQ	66430 MW	76550 TQ	USBLS	5/15
	New York	Y	57400 AE	79110 MW	91440 AEX	NYBLS	1/16-3/16
	Buffalo-Cheektowaga-Niagara Falls MSA, NY	Y	59010 FQ	70090 MW	81300 TQ	USBLS	5/15
	Nassau County-Suffolk County PMSA, NY	Y	69640 FQ	85700 MW	98010 TQ	USBLS	5/15
	New York-Jersey City-White Plains PMSA, NY-NJ	Y	72210 FQ	86520 MW	100070 TQ	USBLS	5/15
	Rochester MSA, NY	Y	53500 FQ	60760 MW	70820 TQ	USBLS	5/15
	North Carolina	Y	50240 FQ	58950 MW	70370 TQ	USBLS	5/15
	Charlotte-Concord-Gastonia MSA, NC-SC	Y	50970 FQ	59750 MW	70700 TQ	USBLS	5/15
	Raleigh MSA, NC	Y	52290 FQ	60090 MW	70590 TQ	USBLS	5/15
	North Dakota	Y	50780 FQ	57880 MW	66380 TQ	USBLS	5/15
	Fargo MSA, ND-MN	Y	51620 FQ	58380 MW	67130 TQ	USBLS	5/15
	Ohio	Y	53770 FQ	61280 MW	72300 TQ	USBLS	5/15
	Cincinnati MSA, OH-KY-IN	Y	54160 FQ	62580 MW	73720 TQ	USBLS	5/15
	Cleveland-Elyria MSA, OH	Y	57030 FQ	65220 MW	74480 TQ	USBLS	5/15
	Columbus MSA, OH	Y	53610 FQ	61330 MW	75690 TQ	USBLS	5/15
	Oklahoma	Y	50040 FQ	58460 MW	68480 TQ	USBLS	5/15
	Oklahoma City MSA, OK	Y	51010 FQ	60220 MW	70910 TQ	USBLS	5/15
	Tulsa MSA, OK	Y	50900 FQ	58820 MW	68490 TQ	USBLS	5/15
	Oregon	H	34.83 FQ	41.55 MW	47.21 TQ	ORBLS	2016
	Portland-Vancouver-Hillsboro MSA, OR-WA	Y	71840 FQ	86940 MW	98870 TQ	USBLS	5/15
	Pennsylvania	Y	55450 FQ	65690 MW	78270 TQ	USBLS	5/15
	Allentown-Bethlehem-Easton MSA, PA-NJ	Y	55990 FQ	63980 MW	75110 TQ	USBLS	5/15
	Harrisburg-Carlisle MSA, PA	Y	56070 FQ	64360 MW	78610 TQ	USBLS	5/15
	Montgomery County-Bucks County-Chester County PMSA, PA	Y	59990 FQ	71700 MW	83030 TQ	USBLS	5/15
	Philadelphia PMSA, PA	Y	66940 FQ	80950 MW	94610 TQ	USBLS	5/15
	Pittsburgh MSA, PA	Y	54230 FQ	61520 MW	72110 TQ	USBLS	5/15
	Rhode Island	Y	64650 FQ	76300 MW	89420 TQ	USBLS	5/15

AE	Average entry wage	AWR	Average wage range	H	Hourly	LR Low end range	MTC Median total compensation	TCC Total cash compensation
AEX	Average experienced wage	B	Biweekly	HI	Highest wage paid	M Monthly	MW Median wage paid	TQ Third quartile wage
ATC	Average total compensation	D	Daily	HR	High end range	MCC Median cash compensation	MWR Median wage range	W Weekly
AW	Average wage paid	FQ	First quartile wage	LO	Lowest wage paid	ME Median entry wage	S See annotated source	Y Yearly

Occupation/Type/Industry	Location	Per	Low	Mid	High	Source	Date
Registered Nurse	Providence-Warwick MSA, RI-MA	Y	63900 FQ	76050 MW	90050 TQ	USBLS	5/15
	South Carolina	Y	50750 FQ	59340 MW	70820 TQ	USBLS	5/15
	Charleston-North Charleston MSA, SC	Y	55810 FQ	65020 MW	77430 TQ	USBLS	5/15
	Columbia MSA, SC	Y	46830 FQ	57080 MW	68330 TQ	USBLS	5/15
	Greenville-Anderson-Mauldin MSA, SC	Y	49530 FQ	57960 MW	68300 TQ	USBLS	5/15
	South Dakota	Y	45340 FQ	53420 MW	63320 TQ	USBLS	5/15
	Tennessee	Y	48010 FQ	56840 MW	66630 TQ	USBLS	5/15
	Knoxville MSA, TN	Y	46150 FQ	54240 MW	61660 TQ	USBLS	5/15
	Memphis MSA, TN-MS-AR	Y	52910 FQ	60500 MW	71200 TQ	USBLS	5/15
	Nashville-Davidson–Murfreesboro–Franklin MSA, TN	Y	48760 FQ	58810 MW	70350 TQ	USBLS	5/15
	Texas	Y	57220 FQ	68590 MW	80890 TQ	USBLS	5/15
	Austin-Round Rock MSA, TX	Y	56910 FQ	66340 MW	76520 TQ	USBLS	5/15
	Dallas-Plano-Irving PMSA, TX	Y	60510 FQ	71680 MW	83770 TQ	USBLS	5/15
	Fort Worth-Arlington PMSA, TX	Y	61030 FQ	72490 MW	86000 TQ	USBLS	5/15
	Houston-The Woodlands-Sugar Land MSA, TX	Y	64760 FQ	76670 MW	90170 TQ	USBLS	5/15
	San Antonio-New Braunfels MSA, TX	Y	54950 FQ	65450 MW	76870 TQ	USBLS	5/15
	Utah	Y	51470 FQ	59670 MW	70610 TQ	USBLS	5/15
	Ogden-Clearfield MSA, UT	Y	48360 FQ	57090 MW	67310 TQ	USBLS	5/15
	Provo-Orem MSA, UT	Y	50680 FQ	58130 MW	67830 TQ	USBLS	5/15
	Salt Lake City MSA, UT	Y	53290 FQ	61730 MW	73120 TQ	USBLS	5/15
	Vermont	Y	54320 FQ	62770 MW	77090 TQ	USBLS	5/15
	Virginia	Y	51620 FQ	63640 MW	76180 TQ	USBLS	5/15
	Richmond MSA, VA	Y	52790 FQ	64510 MW	75230 TQ	USBLS	5/15
	Virginia Beach-Norfolk-Newport News MSA, VA-NC	Y	50030 FQ	61350 MW	72230 TQ	USBLS	5/15
	Washington	H	30.35 FQ	37.57 MW	45.81 TQ	WABLS	3/16
	Seattle-Bellevue-Everett PMSA, WA	H	32.72 FQ	39.70 MW	47.77 TQ	WABLS	3/16
	Tacoma-Lakewood PMSA, WA	H	31.78 FQ	38.97 MW	45.73 TQ	WABLS	3/16
	West Virginia	Y	47530 FQ	56710 MW	67140 TQ	USBLS	5/15
	Huntington-Ashland MSA, WV-KY-OH	Y	45750 FQ	55600 MW	65860 TQ	USBLS	5/15
	Wisconsin	Y	55780 FQ	65150 MW	76490 TQ	USBLS	5/15
	Madison MSA, WI	Y	64320 FQ	73910 MW	87510 TQ	USBLS	5/15
	Milwaukee-Waukesha-West Allis MSA, WI	Y	57730 FQ	67980 MW	78430 TQ	USBLS	5/15
	Wyoming	Y	52520 FQ	60780 MW	72210 TQ	USBLS	5/15
	Cheyenne MSA, WY	Y	55440 FQ	64100 MW	75650 TQ	USBLS	5/15
	Puerto Rico	Y	27510 FQ	32130 MW	37750 TQ	USBLS	5/15
	San Juan-Carolina-Caguas MSA, PR	Y	28530 FQ	33620 MW	38860 TQ	USBLS	5/15
	Virgin Islands	Y	30980 FQ	48820 MW	59440 TQ	USBLS	5/15
	Guam	Y	40490 FQ	52310 MW	65180 TQ	USBLS	5/15
Corrections Department, State Government	Chelsea, MI	H	22.36 LO		31.70 HI	MIGOV	2016
Staff, Skilled Nursing Facility	United States	H		27.19 AW		MLTCN03	2016
Wound Care Specialist, Home for Veterans	Grand Rapids, MI	H	24.33 LO		32.02 HI	MIGOV	2016
Registered Polysomnographic Technologist	East North Central	Y		51000 MW		SLEEP	2015
	East South Central	Y		47500 MW		SLEEP	2015
	Mid-Atlantic	Y		53500 MW		SLEEP	2015
	Mountain	Y		51272 MW		SLEEP	2015
	New England	Y		58500 MW		SLEEP	2015
	Pacific	Y		63000 MW		SLEEP	2015
	South Atlantic	Y		52000 MW		SLEEP	2015
	West North Central	Y		56081 MW		SLEEP	2015
	West South Central	Y		53500 MW		SLEEP	2015
Regulatory Specialist							
Port, Municipal Government	San Francisco, CA	Y			106116 HI	CACIT	6/28/16
Rehabilitation Counselor	Alabama	Y	20621 AE	37032 AW	45238 AEX	ALBLS	6/16
	Birmingham-Hoover MSA, AL	Y	25187 AE	38816 AW	45635 AEX	ALBLS	6/16
	Alaska	Y	45070 FQ	55200 MW	65190 TQ	USBLS	5/15

AE	Average entry wage	AWR	Average wage range	H	Hourly	LR	Low end range	MTC	Median total compensation	TCC	Total cash compensation
AEX	Average experienced wage	B	Biweekly	HI	Highest wage paid	M	Monthly	MW	Median wage paid	TQ	Third quartile wage
ATC	Average total compensation	D	Daily	HR	High end range	MCC	Median cash compensation	MWR	Median wage range	W	Weekly
AW	Average wage paid	FQ	First quartile wage	LO	Lowest wage paid	ME	Median entry wage	S	See annotated source	Y	Yearly

Occupation/Type/Industry	Location	Per	Low	Mid	High	Source	Date
Rehabilitation Counselor	Anchorage MSA, AK	Y	50560 FQ	58250 MW	67680 TQ	USBLS	5/15
	Arizona	Y	26700 FQ	35410 MW	38610 TQ	USBLS	5/15
	Phoenix-Mesa-Scottsdale MSA, AZ	Y	25500 FQ	32120 MW	37540 TQ	USBLS	5/15
	Tucson MSA, AZ	Y	23940 FQ	37520 MW	39780 TQ	USBLS	5/15
	Arkansas	Y	32950 FQ	37050 MW	45310 TQ	USBLS	5/15
	Little Rock-North Little Rock-Conway MSA, AR	Y	34530 FQ	38060 MW	45490 TQ	USBLS	5/15
	California	H	11.46 FQ	15.00 MW	21.71 TQ	CABLS	1/16-3/16
	Anaheim-Santa Ana-Irvine PMSA, CA	H	11.08 FQ	13.69 MW	18.44 TQ	CABLS	1/16-3/16
	Los Angeles-Long Beach-Glendale PMSA, CA	H	10.90 FQ	13.83 MW	19.23 TQ	CABLS	1/16-3/16
	Oakland-Hayward-Berkeley PMSA, CA	H	16.22 FQ	19.06 MW	23.64 TQ	CABLS	1/16-3/16
	Riverside-San Bernardino-Ontario MSA, CA	H	9.65 FQ	11.94 MW	20.51 TQ	CABLS	1/16-3/16
	Sacramento–Roseville–Arden-Arcade MSA, CA	H	13.64 FQ	20.91 MW	27.30 TQ	CABLS	1/16-3/16
	San Diego-Carlsbad MSA, CA	H	11.51 FQ	13.95 MW	18.42 TQ	CABLS	1/16-3/16
	San Francisco-Redwood City-South San Francisco PMSA, CA	H	12.36 FQ	14.91 MW	19.54 TQ	CABLS	1/16-3/16
	Colorado	Y	27160 FQ	36460 MW	51920 TQ	USBLS	5/15
	Denver-Aurora-Lakewood MSA, CO	Y	28850 FQ	37410 MW	53590 TQ	USBLS	5/15
	Connecticut	Y		41584 MW		CTBLS	1/16-3/16
	Bridgeport-Stamford-Norwalk MSA, CT	Y	29860 FQ	39390 MW	67430 TQ	USBLS	5/15
	Hartford-West Hartford-East Hartford MSA, CT	Y	29890 FQ	38880 MW	61940 TQ	USBLS	5/15
	Delaware	Y	30510 FQ	34550 MW	39190 TQ	USBLS	5/15
	Wilmington PMSA, DE-MD-NJ	Y	29880 FQ	34630 MW	38830 TQ	USBLS	5/15
	District of Columbia	Y	28600 FQ	40090 MW	57620 TQ	USBLS	5/15
	Washington-Arlington-Alexandria PMSA, DC-VA-MD-WV	Y	30780 FQ	42170 MW	55940 TQ	USBLS	5/15
	Florida	H	12.81 AE	17.20 MW	20.51 AEX	FLBLS	7/16-9/16
	Fort Lauderdale-Pompano Beach-Deerfield Beach PMSA, FL	H	12.04 AE	16.82 MW	20.73 AEX	FLBLS	7/16-9/16
	Miami-Miami Beach-Kendall PMSA, FL	H	13.14 AE	16.54 MW	19.25 AEX	FLBLS	7/16-9/16
	Orlando-Kissimmee-Sanford MSA, FL	H	13.98 AE	16.95 MW	18.96 AEX	FLBLS	7/16-9/16
	Tampa-St. Petersburg-Clearwater MSA, FL	H	14.36 AE	17.89 MW	20.37 AEX	FLBLS	7/16-9/16
	Georgia	Y	32490 FQ	39370 MW	48910 TQ	USBLS	5/15
	Atlanta-Sandy Springs-Roswell MSA, GA	Y	34310 FQ	42050 MW	56160 TQ	USBLS	5/15
	Augusta-Richmond County MSA, GA-SC	Y	24740 FQ	34770 MW	39100 TQ	USBLS	5/15
	Hawaii	Y	29290 FQ	34080 MW	38860 TQ	USBLS	5/15
	Urban Honolulu MSA, HI	Y	29680 FQ	34190 MW	38270 TQ	USBLS	5/15
	Idaho	Y	24530 FQ	36890 MW	47260 TQ	USBLS	5/15
	Boise City MSA, ID	Y	19330 FQ	33780 MW	43850 TQ	USBLS	5/15
	Illinois	Y	25470 FQ	34660 MW	51490 TQ	USBLS	5/15
	Chicago-Naperville-Arlington Heights PMSA, IL	Y	28300 FQ	36960 MW	54650 TQ	USBLS	5/15
	Lake County-Kenosha County PMSA, IL-WI	Y	23290 FQ	30710 MW	53900 TQ	USBLS	5/15
	Indiana	Y	25120 FQ	31410 MW	39420 TQ	USBLS	5/15
	Gary PMSA, IN	Y	26160 FQ	63220 MW	71750 TQ	USBLS	5/15
	Indianapolis-Carmel-Anderson MSA, IN	Y	32080 FQ	37990 MW	44980 TQ	USBLS	5/15
	Iowa	Y	23990 FQ	30120 MW	44650 TQ	USBLS	5/15
	Des Moines-West Des Moines MSA, IA	Y	30680 FQ	39890 MW	56390 TQ	USBLS	5/15
	Kansas	Y	22650 FQ	29610 MW	37090 TQ	USBLS	5/15
	Wichita MSA, KS	Y	20060 FQ	23620 MW	31020 TQ	USBLS	5/15
	Kentucky	Y	27620 FQ	33760 MW	41720 TQ	USBLS	5/15

AE	Average entry wage	AWR	Average wage range	H	Hourly	LR	Low end range	MTC	Median total compensation	TCC	Total cash compensation
AEX	Average experienced wage	B	Biweekly	HI	Highest wage paid	M	Monthly	MW	Median wage paid	TQ	Third quartile wage
ATC	Average total compensation	D	Daily	HR	High end range	MCC	Median cash compensation	MWR	Median wage range	W	Weekly
AW	Average wage paid	FQ	First quartile wage	LO	Lowest wage paid	ME	Median entry wage	S	See annotated source	Y	Yearly

Rehabilitation Counselor

Occupation/Type/Industry	Location	Per	Low	Mid	High	Source	Date
Rehabilitation Counselor	Louisville-Jefferson County MSA, KY-IN	Y	25120 FQ	29750 MW	37540 TQ	USBLS	5/15
	Louisiana	Y	32990 FQ	42780 MW	55640 TQ	USBLS	5/15
	New Orleans-Metairie MSA, LA	Y	35610 FQ	45240 MW	60440 TQ	USBLS	5/15
	Maine	Y	31370 FQ	36480 MW	43890 TQ	USBLS	5/15
	Portland-South Portland MSA, ME	Y	33880 FQ	37740 MW	56090 TQ	USBLS	5/15
	Maryland	Y	24548 AE	34681 MW	39747 AEX	MDBLS	4/16
	Baltimore-Columbia-Towson MSA, MD	Y	26350 FQ	29720 MW	38800 TQ	USBLS	5/15
	Salisbury MSA, MD-DE	Y	31200 FQ	33890 MW	37910 TQ	USBLS	5/15
	Massachusetts	Y	26800 FQ	31170 MW	38250 TQ	USBLS	5/15
	Boston-Cambridge-Newton NECTA, MA	Y	26680 FQ	32240 MW	37680 TQ	USBLS	5/15
	Worcester MSA, MA-CT	Y	27340 FQ	30310 MW	38050 TQ	USBLS	5/15
	Michigan	Y	25570 FQ	36290 MW	49230 TQ	USBLS	5/15
	Detroit-Dearborn-Livonia PMSA, MI	Y	21710 FQ	33640 MW	44590 TQ	USBLS	5/15
	Grand Rapids-Wyoming MSA, MI	Y	31700 FQ	37030 MW	47760 TQ	USBLS	5/15
	Minnesota	Y	27863 FQ	34143 MW	44889 TQ	MNBLS	1/16-3/16
	Minneapolis-St. Paul-Bloomington MSA, MN-WI	Y	27762 FQ	33709 MW	44042 TQ	MNBLS	1/16-3/16
	Mississippi	Y	29760 FQ	33970 MW	39790 TQ	USBLS	5/15
	Jackson MSA, MS	Y	31240 FQ	38270 MW	45990 TQ	USBLS	5/15
	Missouri	Y	30020 FQ	31800 MW	40740 TQ	USBLS	5/15
	Kansas City MSA, MO-KS	Y	28160 FQ	31050 MW	38300 TQ	USBLS	5/15
	St. Louis MSA, MO-IL	Y	29150 FQ	34000 MW	45690 TQ	USBLS	5/15
	Montana	Y	28580 FQ	36300 MW	43540 TQ	USBLS	5/15
	Billings MSA, MT	Y	23450 FQ	29490 MW	37200 TQ	USBLS	5/15
	Omaha-Council Bluffs MSA, NE-IA	Y	31635 FQ	36855 MW	46035 TQ	NEBLS	7/16-9/16
	Nevada	Y	33080 FQ	38690 MW	48300 TQ	USBLS	5/15
	Las Vegas-Henderson-Paradise MSA, NV	Y	32900 FQ	37490 MW	46870 TQ	USBLS	5/15
	Nashua NECTA, NH-MA	Y	35240 FQ	41450 MW	46930 TQ	USBLS	5/15
	New Jersey	Y	27810 FQ	40420 MW	67260 TQ	USBLS	5/15
	Camden PMSA, NJ	Y	37010 FQ	57030 MW	75230 TQ	USBLS	5/15
	Newark PMSA, NJ-PA	Y	24780 FQ	34300 MW	55800 TQ	USBLS	5/15
	Trenton MSA, NJ	Y	46610 FQ	69160 MW	84040 TQ	USBLS	5/15
	New Mexico	Y	18520 FQ	31940 MW	43160 TQ	USBLS	5/15
	Albuquerque MSA, NM	Y	17930 FQ	24150 MW	40710 TQ	USBLS	5/15
	New York	Y	25210 AE	33810 MW	41400 AEX	NYBLS	1/16-3/16
	Buffalo-Cheektowaga-Niagara Falls MSA, NY	Y	25590 FQ	32040 MW	38580 TQ	USBLS	5/15
	Nassau County-Suffolk County PMSA, NY	Y	28710 FQ	34440 MW	43150 TQ	USBLS	5/15
	New York-Jersey City-White Plains PMSA, NY-NJ	Y	27630 FQ	34710 MW	43650 TQ	USBLS	5/15
	Rochester MSA, NY	Y	25830 FQ	33930 MW	38490 TQ	USBLS	5/15
	North Carolina	Y	23750 FQ	35030 MW	44470 TQ	USBLS	5/15
	Charlotte-Concord-Gastonia MSA, NC-SC	Y	25720 FQ	31490 MW	45040 TQ	USBLS	5/15
	Raleigh MSA, NC	Y	34280 FQ	38790 MW	47230 TQ	USBLS	5/15
	North Dakota	Y	34300 FQ	44920 MW	50990 TQ	USBLS	5/15
	Fargo MSA, ND-MN	Y	29780 FQ	41290 MW	52170 TQ	USBLS	5/15
	Ohio	Y	26710 FQ	35840 MW	49230 TQ	USBLS	5/15
	Cincinnati MSA, OH-KY-IN	Y	28280 FQ	35630 MW	48640 TQ	USBLS	5/15
	Cleveland-Elyria MSA, OH	Y	33970 FQ	40510 MW	56690 TQ	USBLS	5/15
	Columbus MSA, OH	Y	32530 FQ	38210 MW	49420 TQ	USBLS	5/15
	Oklahoma	Y	18510 FQ	25110 MW	36910 TQ	USBLS	5/15
	Oklahoma City MSA, OK	Y	20890 FQ	28860 MW	41960 TQ	USBLS	5/15
	Tulsa MSA, OK	Y	22990 FQ	33270 MW	37380 TQ	USBLS	5/15
	Oregon	H	13.83 FQ	17.59 MW	23.86 TQ	ORBLS	2016
	Portland-Vancouver-Hillsboro MSA, OR-WA	Y	31240 FQ	36390 MW	46340 TQ	USBLS	5/15
	Pennsylvania	Y	28380 FQ	35600 MW	47500 TQ	USBLS	5/15
	Allentown-Bethlehem-Easton MSA, PA-NJ	Y	27190 FQ	32280 MW	44790 TQ	USBLS	5/15
	Harrisburg-Carlisle MSA, PA	Y	31950 FQ	48130 MW	61910 TQ	USBLS	5/15

AE Average entry wage	**AWR** Average wage range	**H** Hourly	**LR** Low end range	**MTC** Median total compensation	**TCC** Total cash compensation
AEX Average experienced wage	**B** Biweekly	**HI** Highest wage paid	**M** Monthly	**MW** Median wage paid	**TQ** Third quartile wage
ATC Average total compensation	**D** Daily	**HR** High end range	**MCC** Median cash compensation	**MWR** Median wage range	**W** Weekly
AW Average wage paid	**FQ** First quartile wage	**LO** Lowest wage paid	**ME** Median entry wage	**S** See annotated source	**Y** Yearly

Occupation/Type/Industry	Location	Per	Low	Mid	High	Source	Date
Rehabilitation Counselor	Montgomery County-Bucks County-Chester County						
	PMSA, PA	Y	30450 FQ	36080 MW	45530 TQ	USBLS	5/15
	Philadelphia PMSA, PA	Y	32490 FQ	36180 MW	40650 TQ	USBLS	5/15
	Pittsburgh MSA, PA	Y	25550 FQ	29840 MW	39280 TQ	USBLS	5/15
	Rhode Island	Y	30760 FQ	42140 MW	64360 TQ	USBLS	5/15
	Providence-Warwick MSA, RI-MA	Y	28860 FQ	36560 MW	50720 TQ	USBLS	5/15
	South Carolina	Y	22500 FQ	26360 MW	36420 TQ	USBLS	5/15
	Charleston-North Charleston MSA, SC	Y	30590 FQ	35960 MW	47810 TQ	USBLS	5/15
	Columbia MSA, SC	Y	21700 FQ	23740 MW	28230 TQ	USBLS	5/15
	Greenville-Anderson-Mauldin MSA, SC	Y	22730 FQ	33020 MW	40730 TQ	USBLS	5/15
	South Dakota	Y	33530 FQ	38970 MW	46400 TQ	USBLS	5/15
	Sioux Falls MSA, SD	Y	36080 FQ	48370 MW	69220 TQ	USBLS	5/15
	Tennessee	Y	17070 FQ	18750 MW	23300 TQ	USBLS	5/15
	Knoxville MSA, TN	Y	17350 FQ	19410 MW	23820 TQ	USBLS	5/15
	Memphis MSA, TN-MS-AR	Y	17520 FQ	19440 MW	30650 TQ	USBLS	5/15
	Nashville-Davidson–Murfreesboro–Franklin MSA, TN	Y	16800 FQ	18310 MW	28810 TQ	USBLS	5/15
	Texas	Y	32080 FQ	39320 MW	49610 TQ	USBLS	5/15
	Austin-Round Rock MSA, TX	Y	42400 FQ	49630 MW	56990 TQ	USBLS	5/15
	Dallas-Plano-Irving PMSA, TX	Y	36390 FQ	43060 MW	50850 TQ	USBLS	5/15
	Fort Worth-Arlington PMSA, TX	Y	34340 FQ	40830 MW	50750 TQ	USBLS	5/15
	Houston-The Woodlands-Sugar Land MSA, TX	Y	34280 FQ	40520 MW	48890 TQ	USBLS	5/15
	San Antonio-New Braunfels MSA, TX	Y	34790 FQ	38610 MW	51280 TQ	USBLS	5/15
	Utah	Y	30330 FQ	44540 MW	54000 TQ	USBLS	5/15
	Ogden-Clearfield MSA, UT	Y	31180 FQ	45150 MW	54000 TQ	USBLS	5/15
	Provo-Orem MSA, UT	Y	31490 FQ	38690 MW	49800 TQ	USBLS	5/15
	Salt Lake City MSA, UT	Y	39810 FQ	47160 MW	58380 TQ	USBLS	5/15
	Vermont	Y	30650 FQ	40030 MW	50790 TQ	USBLS	5/15
	Virginia	Y	30990 FQ	39190 MW	49820 TQ	USBLS	5/15
	Richmond MSA, VA	Y	29860 FQ	37480 MW	46680 TQ	USBLS	5/15
	Virginia Beach-Norfolk-Newport News MSA, VA-NC	Y	26940 FQ	39320 MW	48290 TQ	USBLS	5/15
	Washington	H	14.37 FQ	17.73 MW	24.71 TQ	WABLS	3/16
	Seattle-Bellevue-Everett PMSA, WA	H	14.43 FQ	17.91 MW	26.22 TQ	WABLS	3/16
	Tacoma-Lakewood PMSA, WA	H	14.04 FQ	16.96 MW	20.47 TQ	WABLS	3/16
	West Virginia	Y	30830 FQ	35920 MW	42720 TQ	USBLS	5/15
	Huntington-Ashland MSA, WV-KY-OH	Y	26560 FQ	33670 MW	44590 TQ	USBLS	5/15
	Wisconsin	Y	26220 FQ	32280 MW	43010 TQ	USBLS	5/15
	Madison MSA, WI	Y	29940 FQ	38350 MW	46450 TQ	USBLS	5/15
	Milwaukee-Waukesha-West Allis MSA, WI	Y	26420 FQ	30270 MW	38820 TQ	USBLS	5/15
	Wyoming	Y	24990 FQ	32070 MW	50840 TQ	USBLS	5/15
	Cheyenne MSA, WY	Y	29330 FQ	34110 MW	42640 TQ	USBLS	5/15
	Puerto Rico	Y	26700 FQ	30490 MW	37170 TQ	USBLS	5/15
	San Juan-Carolina-Caguas MSA, PR	Y	26850 FQ	30580 MW	37210 TQ	USBLS	5/15
	Guam	Y	32450 FQ	35240 MW	38030 TQ	USBLS	5/15
Rehabilitation Grant Specialist							
Community Development, Municipal Government	La Puente, CA	Y			56010 HI	CACIT	6/28/16
Reinforcing Iron and Rebar Worker							
	Arizona	Y	34570 FQ	38620 MW	55650 TQ	USBLS	5/15
	Phoenix-Mesa-Scottsdale MSA, AZ	Y	34090 FQ	37540 MW	45980 TQ	USBLS	5/15
	Tucson MSA, AZ	Y	36540 FQ	53220 MW	69410 TQ	USBLS	5/15
	California	H	16.42 FQ	25.46 MW	34.61 TQ	CABLS	1/16-3/16
	Anaheim-Santa Ana-Irvine PMSA, CA	H	14.59 FQ	17.39 MW	22.24 TQ	CABLS	1/16-3/16
	Los Angeles-Long Beach-Glendale PMSA, CA	H	17.17 FQ	26.93 MW	32.79 TQ	CABLS	1/16-3/16

AE	Average entry wage	AWR	Average wage range	H	Hourly	LR	Low end range	MTC	Median total compensation	TCC	Total cash compensation
AEX	Average experienced wage	B	Biweekly	HI	Highest wage paid	M	Monthly	MW	Median wage paid	TQ	Third quartile wage
ATC	Average total compensation	D	Daily	HR	High end range	MCC	Median cash compensation	MWR	Median wage range	W	Weekly
AW	Average wage paid	FQ	First quartile wage	LO	Lowest wage paid	ME	Median entry wage	S	See annotated source	Y	Yearly

Occupation/Type/Industry	Location	Per	Low	Mid	High	Source	Date
Reinforcing Iron and Rebar Worker							
	Oakland-Hayward-Berkeley PMSA, CA	H	15.08 FQ	21.80 MW	33.93 TQ	CABLS	1/16-3/16
	Riverside-San Bernardino-Ontario MSA, CA	H	15.35 FQ	32.57 MW	36.90 TQ	CABLS	1/16-3/16
	Sacramento–Roseville–Arden-Arcade MSA, CA	H	15.93 FQ	25.39 MW	32.14 TQ	CABLS	1/16-3/16
	San Diego-Carlsbad MSA, CA	H	22.77 FQ	30.57 MW	35.84 TQ	CABLS	1/16-3/16
	San Francisco-Redwood City-South San Francisco PMSA, CA	H	33.11 FQ	36.15 MW	40.14 TQ	CABLS	1/16-3/16
	Colorado	Y	32760 FQ	41000 MW	52690 TQ	USBLS	5/15
	Denver-Aurora-Lakewood MSA, CO	Y	36250 FQ	41290 MW	48250 TQ	USBLS	5/15
	Connecticut	Y		66137 MW		CTBLS	1/16-3/16
	District of Columbia	Y	42390 FQ	47760 MW	56730 TQ	USBLS	5/15
	Washington-Arlington-Alexandria PMSA, DC-VA-MD-WV	Y	39860 FQ	48220 MW	62210 TQ	USBLS	5/15
	Florida	H	14.67 AE	18.72 MW	23.14 AEX	FLBLS	7/16-9/16
	Fort Lauderdale-Pompano Beach-Deerfield Beach PMSA, FL	H	16.65 AE	18.18 MW	19.48 AEX	FLBLS	7/16-9/16
	Orlando-Kissimmee-Sanford MSA, FL	H	17.32 AE	25.05 MW	28.00 AEX	FLBLS	7/16-9/16
	Georgia	Y	32740 FQ	36160 MW	39940 TQ	USBLS	5/15
	Atlanta-Sandy Springs-Roswell MSA, GA	Y	32150 FQ	35920 MW	41150 TQ	USBLS	5/15
	Augusta-Richmond County MSA, GA-SC	Y	34780 FQ	39200 MW	56470 TQ	USBLS	5/15
	Hawaii	Y	40690 FQ	71100 MW	87990 TQ	USBLS	5/15
	Urban Honolulu MSA, HI	Y	41080 FQ	71350 MW	88000 TQ	USBLS	5/15
	Idaho	Y	33220 FQ	49670 MW	63250 TQ	USBLS	5/15
	Illinois	Y	65040 FQ	83410 MW	91550 TQ	USBLS	5/15
	Chicago-Naperville-Arlington Heights PMSA, IL	Y	80680 FQ	86870 MW	93170 TQ	USBLS	5/15
	Indiana	Y	43670 FQ	81630 MW	91720 TQ	USBLS	5/15
	Iowa	Y	32260 FQ	37780 MW	61760 TQ	USBLS	5/15
	Kansas	Y	36780 FQ	64610 MW	72220 TQ	USBLS	5/15
	Kentucky	Y	47100 FQ	55770 MW	65220 TQ	USBLS	5/15
	Louisiana	Y	43030 FQ	51800 MW	63300 TQ	USBLS	5/15
	Baton Rouge MSA, LA	Y	52930 FQ	61610 MW	70010 TQ	USBLS	5/15
	New Orleans-Metairie MSA, LA	Y	40690 FQ	45250 MW	49800 TQ	USBLS	5/15
	Maryland	Y	37686 AE	51021 MW	57688 AEX	MDBLS	4/16
	Baltimore-Columbia-Towson MSA, MD	Y	40680 FQ	45220 MW	49770 TQ	USBLS	5/15
	Massachusetts	Y	61560 FQ	72700 MW	84480 TQ	USBLS	5/15
	Boston-Cambridge-Newton NECTA, MA	Y	58220 FQ	83310 MW	91330 TQ	USBLS	5/15
	Michigan	Y	62420 FQ	68560 MW	74890 TQ	USBLS	5/15
	Minnesota	Y	32995 FQ	50572 MW	69128 TQ	MNBLS	1/16-3/16
	Mississippi	Y	32090 FQ	42320 MW	52310 TQ	USBLS	5/15
	Missouri	Y	45330 FQ	55620 MW	61090 TQ	USBLS	5/15
	Kansas City MSA, MO-KS	Y	33840 FQ	62370 MW	70330 TQ	USBLS	5/15
	St. Louis MSA, MO-IL	Y	50920 FQ	56540 MW	62170 TQ	USBLS	5/15
	Nebraska	Y	29095 FQ	41645 MW	47190 TQ	NEBLS	7/16-9/16
	Omaha-Council Bluffs MSA, NE-IA	Y	21840 FQ	27690 MW	50615 TQ	NEBLS	7/16-9/16
	Nevada	Y	43270 FQ	48840 MW	73890 TQ	USBLS	5/15
	Las Vegas-Henderson-Paradise MSA, NV	Y	41990 FQ	45990 MW	63600 TQ	USBLS	5/15
	New Jersey	Y	67710 FQ	78430 MW	92190 TQ	USBLS	5/15
	Newark PMSA, NJ-PA	Y	70860 FQ	82920 MW	93180 TQ	USBLS	5/15
	New Mexico	Y	31630 FQ	37440 MW	53520 TQ	USBLS	5/15
	Albuquerque MSA, NM	Y	31700 FQ	37310 MW	52910 TQ	USBLS	5/15
	New York	Y	62500 AE	97110 MW	110530 AEX	NYBLS	1/16-3/16
	Nassau County-Suffolk County PMSA, NY	Y	86500 FQ	98970 MW	130830 TQ	USBLS	5/15
	New York-Jersey City-White Plains PMSA, NY-NJ	Y	69150 FQ	89010 MW	108620 TQ	USBLS	5/15
	North Carolina	Y	30620 FQ	35630 MW	42200 TQ	USBLS	5/15

AE	Average entry wage	AWR	Average wage range	H	Hourly
AEX	Average experienced wage	B	Biweekly	HI	Highest wage paid
ATC	Average total compensation	D	Daily	HR	High end range
AW	Average wage paid	FQ	First quartile wage	LO	Lowest wage paid

LR	Low end range	MTC	Median total compensation	TCC	Total cash compensation
M	Monthly	MW	Median wage paid	TQ	Third quartile wage
MCC	Median cash compensation	MWR	Median wage range	W	Weekly
ME	Median entry wage	S	See annotated source	Y	Yearly

Occupation/Type/Industry	Location	Per	Low	Mid	High	Source	Date
Reinforcing Iron and Rebar Worker	North Dakota	Y	48760 FQ	54150 MW	59090 TQ	USBLS	5/15
	Ohio	Y	54560 FQ	63570 MW	71830 TQ	USBLS	5/15
	Oklahoma	Y	29310 FQ	33760 MW	37460 TQ	USBLS	5/15
	Oklahoma City MSA, OK	Y	28940 FQ	33350 MW	36930 TQ	USBLS	5/15
	Oregon	H	14.15 FQ	22.07 MW	38.31 TQ	ORBLS	2016
	Pennsylvania	Y	41420 FQ	59790 MW	75110 TQ	USBLS	5/15
	Pittsburgh MSA, PA	Y	42150 FQ	48650 MW	67470 TQ	USBLS	5/15
	South Carolina	Y	43850 FQ	54930 MW	60220 TQ	USBLS	5/15
	Charleston-North Charleston MSA, SC	Y	28000 FQ	33270 MW	43260 TQ	USBLS	5/15
	Columbia MSA, SC	Y	53160 FQ	56840 MW	60530 TQ	USBLS	5/15
	South Dakota	Y	27090 FQ	31080 MW	36690 TQ	USBLS	5/15
	Sioux Falls MSA, SD	Y	26840 FQ	30730 MW	36480 TQ	USBLS	5/15
	Tennessee	Y	33160 FQ	38440 MW	57010 TQ	USBLS	5/15
	Memphis MSA, TN-MS-AR	Y	33730 FQ	38220 MW	60180 TQ	USBLS	5/15
	Texas	Y	29160 FQ	34920 MW	44270 TQ	USBLS	5/15
	Austin-Round Rock MSA, TX	Y	27950 FQ	32780 MW	36870 TQ	USBLS	5/15
	Dallas-Plano-Irving PMSA, TX	Y	27210 FQ	32040 MW	36340 TQ	USBLS	5/15
	Fort Worth-Arlington PMSA, TX	Y	32280 FQ	36250 MW	41720 TQ	USBLS	5/15
	Houston-The Woodlands-Sugar Land MSA, TX	Y	29010 FQ	35510 MW	50370 TQ	USBLS	5/15
	Utah	Y	35710 FQ	43830 MW	60060 TQ	USBLS	5/15
	Salt Lake City MSA, UT	Y	35710 FQ	43830 MW	60060 TQ	USBLS	5/15
	Virginia	Y	35370 FQ	42460 MW	54020 TQ	USBLS	5/15
	Washington	H	22.34 FQ	31.39 MW	37.18 TQ	WABLS	3/16
	Seattle-Bellevue-Everett PMSA, WA	H	22.23 FQ	30.75 MW	36.03 TQ	WABLS	3/16
	West Virginia	Y	38390 FQ	67610 MW	74200 TQ	USBLS	5/15
	Wisconsin	Y	35970 FQ	44760 MW	58810 TQ	USBLS	5/15
	Milwaukee-Waukesha-West Allis MSA, WI	Y	36130 FQ	41450 MW	46570 TQ	USBLS	5/15
	Puerto Rico	Y	19030 FQ	21670 MW	23750 TQ	USBLS	5/15
	San Juan-Carolina-Caguas MSA, PR	Y	20150 FQ	22050 MW	23940 TQ	USBLS	5/15
	Guam	Y	26320 FQ	28290 MW	30260 TQ	USBLS	5/15
Render Wrangler	United States	H		15.00 AW		NYFA	2015
Renewable Energy Specialist Department of Environmental Quality, State Government	Helena, MT	H			29.31 HI	MTGOV	2016
Rental Inspection Coordinator Municipal Government	Coralville, IA	Y			56181 HI	ICPC	2014
Reporter and Correspondent	Alabama	Y	25402 AE	40029 AW	47337 AEX	ALBLS	6/16
	Birmingham-Hoover MSA, AL	Y	24922 AE	38581 AW	45411 AEX	ALBLS	6/16
	Alaska	Y	34880 FQ	39680 MW	55940 TQ	USBLS	5/15
	Anchorage MSA, AK	Y	36450 FQ	44680 MW	63190 TQ	USBLS	5/15
	Arizona	Y	28840 FQ	37960 MW	54850 TQ	USBLS	5/15
	Phoenix-Mesa-Scottsdale MSA, AZ	Y	30770 FQ	41970 MW	59320 TQ	USBLS	5/15
	Tucson MSA, AZ	Y	28750 FQ	36200 MW	49230 TQ	USBLS	5/15
	Arkansas	Y	21580 FQ	27500 MW	37780 TQ	USBLS	5/15
	Little Rock-North Little Rock-Conway MSA, AR	Y	29800 FQ	38080 MW	49370 TQ	USBLS	5/15
	California	H	15.57 FQ	19.21 MW	28.37 TQ	CABLS	1/16-3/16
	Anaheim-Santa Ana-Irvine PMSA, CA	H	15.45 FQ	22.40 MW	33.81 TQ	CABLS	1/16-3/16
	Los Angeles-Long Beach-Glendale PMSA, CA	H	15.93 FQ	18.90 MW	27.64 TQ	CABLS	1/16-3/16
	Oakland-Hayward-Berkeley PMSA, CA	H	14.21 FQ	18.37 MW	23.88 TQ	CABLS	1/16-3/16
	Riverside-San Bernardino-Ontario MSA, CA	H	15.84 FQ	19.67 MW	24.43 TQ	CABLS	1/16-3/16
	Sacramento–Roseville–Arden-Arcade MSA, CA	H	15.31 FQ	19.20 MW	35.22 TQ	CABLS	1/16-3/16
	San Diego-Carlsbad MSA, CA	H	15.66 FQ	19.26 MW	27.06 TQ	CABLS	1/16-3/16

Occupation/Type/Industry	Location	Per	Low	Mid	High	Source	Date
Reporter and Correspondent	San Francisco-Redwood City-South San Francisco PMSA, CA	H	15.72 FQ	22.50 MW	35.49 TQ	CABLS	1/16-3/16
	Colorado	Y	30370 FQ	38750 MW	63000 TQ	USBLS	5/15
	Denver-Aurora-Lakewood MSA, CO	Y	33540 FQ	43110 MW	69580 TQ	USBLS	5/15
	Connecticut	Y		37120 MW		CTBLS	1/16-3/16
	Hartford-West Hartford-East Hartford MSA, CT	Y	31110 FQ	39540 MW	56380 TQ	USBLS	5/15
	Delaware	Y	25230 FQ	37490 MW	59320 TQ	USBLS	5/15
	District of Columbia	Y	48500 FQ	71850 MW	101710 TQ	USBLS	5/15
	Washington-Arlington-Alexandria PMSA, DC-VA-MD-WV	Y	45910 FQ	68600 MW	98620 TQ	USBLS	5/15
	Florida	H	11.94 AE	18.72 MW	26.64 AEX	FLBLS	7/16-9/16
	Fort Lauderdale-Pompano Beach-Deerfield Beach PMSA, FL	H	13.19 AE	20.48 MW	30.15 AEX	FLBLS	7/16-9/16
	Miami-Miami Beach-Kendall PMSA, FL	H	11.74 AE	18.36 MW	28.17 AEX	FLBLS	7/16-9/16
	Orlando-Kissimmee-Sanford MSA, FL	H	14.03 AE	23.58 MW	34.32 AEX	FLBLS	7/16-9/16
	Tampa-St. Petersburg-Clearwater MSA, FL	H	11.76 AE	18.82 MW	24.70 AEX	FLBLS	7/16-9/16
	Georgia	Y	29730 FQ	40450 MW	68060 TQ	USBLS	5/15
	Atlanta-Sandy Springs-Roswell MSA, GA	Y	36950 FQ	51170 MW	77080 TQ	USBLS	5/15
	Hawaii	Y	34070 FQ	46230 MW	58310 TQ	USBLS	5/15
	Urban Honolulu MSA, HI	Y	30400 FQ	44480 MW	57650 TQ	USBLS	5/15
	Idaho	Y	23920 FQ	28630 MW	37060 TQ	USBLS	5/15
	Boise City MSA, ID	Y	24290 FQ	29880 MW	48790 TQ	USBLS	5/15
	Illinois	Y	25950 FQ	30470 MW	46720 TQ	USBLS	5/15
	Chicago-Naperville-Arlington Heights PMSA, IL	Y	25900 FQ	31010 MW	52160 TQ	USBLS	5/15
	Indiana	Y	27640 FQ	34750 MW	46270 TQ	USBLS	5/15
	Gary PMSA, IN	Y	25570 FQ	29510 MW	35910 TQ	USBLS	5/15
	Indianapolis-Carmel-Anderson MSA, IN	Y	36500 FQ	45460 MW	58810 TQ	USBLS	5/15
	Iowa	Y	25770 FQ	31940 MW	36940 TQ	USBLS	5/15
	Des Moines-West Des Moines MSA, IA	Y	28650 FQ	35750 MW	50270 TQ	USBLS	5/15
	Kansas	Y	22420 FQ	27740 MW	39500 TQ	USBLS	5/15
	Wichita MSA, KS	Y	22910 FQ	29970 MW	52610 TQ	USBLS	5/15
	Kentucky	Y	23510 FQ	30340 MW	49470 TQ	USBLS	5/15
	Louisville-Jefferson County MSA, KY-IN	Y	28590 FQ	44200 MW	63690 TQ	USBLS	5/15
	Louisiana	Y	24520 FQ	31690 MW	51070 TQ	USBLS	5/15
	Baton Rouge MSA, LA	Y	20330 FQ	30700 MW	46990 TQ	USBLS	5/15
	New Orleans-Metairie MSA, LA	Y	30840 FQ	47320 MW	70450 TQ	USBLS	5/15
	Maine	Y	25070 FQ	31000 MW	41140 TQ	USBLS	5/15
	Portland-South Portland MSA, ME	Y	27020 FQ	32460 MW	40860 TQ	USBLS	5/15
	Maryland	Y	30204 AE	57486 MW	71127 AEX	MDBLS	4/16
	Baltimore-Columbia-Towson MSA, MD	Y	33960 FQ	49040 MW	66990 TQ	USBLS	5/15
	Massachusetts	Y	30840 FQ	39700 MW	70740 TQ	USBLS	5/15
	Boston-Cambridge-Newton NECTA, MA	Y	30970 FQ	50930 MW	84390 TQ	USBLS	5/15
	Michigan	Y	26020 FQ	33510 MW	60900 TQ	USBLS	5/15
	Detroit-Dearborn-Livonia PMSA, MI	Y	42130 FQ	68200 MW	87670 TQ	USBLS	5/15
	Grand Rapids-Wyoming MSA, MI	Y	26110 FQ	30740 MW	39060 TQ	USBLS	5/15
	Minnesota	Y	29254 FQ	38618 MW	69727 TQ	MNBLS	1/16-3/16
	Minneapolis-St. Paul-Bloomington MSA, MN-WI	Y	33316 FQ	59334 MW	75241 TQ	MNBLS	1/16-3/16
	Mississippi	Y	23070 FQ	29510 MW	39070 TQ	USBLS	5/15
	Jackson MSA, MS	Y	27710 FQ	33370 MW	41930 TQ	USBLS	5/15
	Missouri	Y	23100 FQ	29540 MW	47970 TQ	USBLS	5/15
	Kansas City MSA, MO-KS	Y	24180 FQ	32860 MW	59980 TQ	USBLS	5/15
	St. Louis MSA, MO-IL	Y	27360 FQ	36890 MW	54240 TQ	USBLS	5/15

AE	Average entry wage	AWR	Average wage range	H	Hourly
AEX	Average experienced wage	B	Biweekly	HI	Highest wage paid
ATC	Average total compensation	D	Daily	HR	High end range
AW	Average wage paid	FQ	First quartile wage	LO	Lowest wage paid

LR	Low end range	MTC	Median total compensation	TCC	Total cash compensation
M	Monthly	MW	Median wage paid	TQ	Third quartile wage
MCC	Median cash compensation	MWR	Median wage range	W	Weekly
ME	Median entry wage	S	See annotated source	Y	Yearly

Occupation/Type/Industry	Location	Per	Low	Mid	High	Source	Date
Reporter and Correspondent	Montana	Y	22180 FQ	26870 MW	31530 TQ	USBLS	5/15
	Nebraska	Y	19090 FQ	25945 MW	36555 TQ	NEBLS	7/16-9/16
	Omaha-Council Bluffs MSA, NE-IA	Y	28860 FQ	39550 MW	60385 TQ	NEBLS	7/16-9/16
	Nevada	Y	31510 FQ	46050 MW	61820 TQ	USBLS	5/15
	Las Vegas-Henderson-Paradise MSA, NV	Y	41700 FQ	51570 MW	70270 TQ	USBLS	5/15
	New Hampshire	H	13.10 AE	15.44 MW	20.37 AEX	NHBLS	6/16
	Nashua NECTA, NH-MA	Y	28180 FQ	31190 MW	37990 TQ	USBLS	5/15
	New Jersey	Y	29560 FQ	42360 MW	68800 TQ	USBLS	5/15
	Camden PMSA, NJ	Y	33530 FQ	41160 MW	50420 TQ	USBLS	5/15
	Newark PMSA, NJ-PA	Y	27340 FQ	38980 MW	72610 TQ	USBLS	5/15
	Trenton MSA, NJ	Y	29870 FQ	47730 MW	73100 TQ	USBLS	5/15
	New Mexico	Y	24860 FQ	30480 MW	43110 TQ	USBLS	5/15
	Albuquerque MSA, NM	Y	29260 FQ	40670 MW	46630 TQ	USBLS	5/15
	New York	Y	28500 AE	48470 MW	81580 AEX	NYBLS	1/16-3/16
	Buffalo-Cheektowaga-Niagara Falls MSA, NY	Y	27170 FQ	30440 MW	46110 TQ	USBLS	5/15
	Nassau County-Suffolk County PMSA, NY	Y	26330 FQ	31660 MW	42410 TQ	USBLS	5/15
	New York-Jersey City-White Plains PMSA, NY-NJ	Y	36270 FQ	57440 MW	77100 TQ	USBLS	5/15
	Rochester MSA, NY	Y	32110 FQ	41550 MW	50870 TQ	USBLS	5/15
	North Carolina	Y	26260 FQ	31290 MW	46010 TQ	USBLS	5/15
	Charlotte-Concord-Gastonia MSA, NC-SC	Y	32480 FQ	42950 MW	56270 TQ	USBLS	5/15
	Raleigh MSA, NC	Y	26890 FQ	39190 MW	60320 TQ	USBLS	5/15
	North Dakota	Y	17550 FQ	19590 MW	29020 TQ	USBLS	5/15
	Ohio	Y	22850 FQ	29390 MW	40330 TQ	USBLS	5/15
	Cincinnati MSA, OH-KY-IN	Y	29740 FQ	38510 MW	59280 TQ	USBLS	5/15
	Cleveland-Elyria MSA, OH	Y	25070 FQ	33840 MW	48520 TQ	USBLS	5/15
	Columbus MSA, OH	Y	25380 FQ	30110 MW	39040 TQ	USBLS	5/15
	Oklahoma	Y	22550 FQ	29220 MW	43010 TQ	USBLS	5/15
	Oklahoma City MSA, OK	Y	23760 FQ	33850 MW	47450 TQ	USBLS	5/15
	Tulsa MSA, OK	Y	27480 FQ	34300 MW	56010 TQ	USBLS	5/15
	Oregon	H	14.40 FQ	18.88 MW	30.55 TQ	ORBLS	2016
	Portland-Vancouver-Hillsboro MSA, OR-WA	Y	32130 FQ	52880 MW	69270 TQ	USBLS	5/15
	Pennsylvania	Y	25440 FQ	34430 MW	47300 TQ	USBLS	5/15
	Allentown-Bethlehem-Easton MSA, PA-NJ	Y	28490 FQ	36630 MW	51220 TQ	USBLS	5/15
	Harrisburg-Carlisle MSA, PA	Y	22120 FQ	29280 MW	38030 TQ	USBLS	5/15
	Montgomery County-Bucks County-Chester County PMSA, PA	Y	31740 FQ	40860 MW	50180 TQ	USBLS	5/15
	Philadelphia PMSA, PA	Y	35130 FQ	46540 MW	66590 TQ	USBLS	5/15
	Pittsburgh MSA, PA	Y	28890 FQ	36440 MW	48690 TQ	USBLS	5/15
	Providence-Warwick MSA, RI-MA	Y	30670 FQ	47330 MW	70710 TQ	USBLS	5/15
	South Carolina	Y	27750 FQ	35250 MW	47400 TQ	USBLS	5/15
	Charleston-North Charleston MSA, SC	Y	22790 FQ	30390 MW	43840 TQ	USBLS	5/15
	Columbia MSA, SC	Y	27730 FQ	35800 MW	51790 TQ	USBLS	5/15
	Greenville-Anderson-Mauldin MSA, SC	Y	34560 FQ	43530 MW	55040 TQ	USBLS	5/15
	South Dakota	Y	22510 FQ	27700 MW	34910 TQ	USBLS	5/15
	Sioux Falls MSA, SD	Y	19570 FQ	30970 MW	39080 TQ	USBLS	5/15
	Tennessee	Y	23750 FQ	30850 MW	43290 TQ	USBLS	5/15
	Knoxville MSA, TN	Y	32140 FQ	40260 MW	47030 TQ	USBLS	5/15
	Memphis MSA, TN-MS-AR	Y	24490 FQ	35530 MW	56220 TQ	USBLS	5/15
	Nashville-Davidson–Murfreesboro–Franklin MSA, TN	Y	27590 FQ	35770 MW	50660 TQ	USBLS	5/15
	Texas	Y	23680 FQ	30440 MW	46290 TQ	USBLS	5/15
	Austin-Round Rock MSA, TX	Y	24640 FQ	38040 MW	48680 TQ	USBLS	5/15
	Dallas-Plano-Irving PMSA, TX	Y	22510 FQ	30610 MW	62430 TQ	USBLS	5/15
	Fort Worth-Arlington PMSA, TX	Y	30380 FQ	43910 MW	56570 TQ	USBLS	5/15
	Houston-The Woodlands-Sugar Land MSA, TX	Y	26230 FQ	37830 MW	56750 TQ	USBLS	5/15
	San Antonio-New Braunfels MSA, TX	Y	21350 FQ	26570 MW	39320 TQ	USBLS	5/15

AE	Average entry wage	AWR	Average wage range	H	Hourly
AEX	Average experienced wage	B	Biweekly	HI	Highest wage paid
ATC	Average total compensation	D	Daily	HR	High end range
AW	Average wage paid	FQ	First quartile wage	LO	Lowest wage paid

LR	Low end range	MTC	Median total compensation	TCC	Total cash compensation
M	Monthly	MW	Median wage paid	TQ	Third quartile wage
MCC	Median cash compensation	MWR	Median wage range	W	Weekly
ME	Median entry wage	S	See annotated source	Y	Yearly

Occupation/Type/Industry	Location	Per	Low	Mid	High	Source	Date
Reporter and Correspondent	Utah	Y	20020 FQ	33080 MW	61490 TQ	USBLS	5/15
	Salt Lake City MSA, UT	Y	18640 FQ	30090 MW	54650 TQ	USBLS	5/15
	Vermont	Y	28090 FQ	32330 MW	39050 TQ	USBLS	5/15
	Burlington-South Burlington MSA, VT	Y	30580 FQ	38100 MW	51600 TQ	USBLS	5/15
	Virginia	Y	29820 FQ	43580 MW	64970 TQ	USBLS	5/15
	Richmond MSA, VA	Y	27560 FQ	40700 MW	75470 TQ	USBLS	5/15
	Washington	H	12.80 FQ	16.82 MW	26.64 TQ	WABLS	3/16
	Seattle-Bellevue-Everett PMSA, WA	H	13.45 FQ	19.73 MW	31.36 TQ	WABLS	3/16
	Tacoma-Lakewood PMSA, WA	H	13.18 FQ	14.88 MW	25.40 TQ	WABLS	3/16
	West Virginia	Y	24480 FQ	31210 MW	39700 TQ	USBLS	5/15
	Huntington-Ashland MSA, WV-KY-OH	Y	31100 FQ	36030 MW	47460 TQ	USBLS	5/15
	Wisconsin	Y	26390 FQ	31560 MW	41480 TQ	USBLS	5/15
	Madison MSA, WI	Y	25760 FQ	30960 MW	44130 TQ	USBLS	5/15
	Milwaukee-Waukesha-West Allis MSA, WI	Y	27300 FQ	34060 MW	42510 TQ	USBLS	5/15
	Wyoming	Y	20650 FQ	26960 MW	30830 TQ	USBLS	5/15
	Cheyenne MSA, WY	Y	26680 FQ	32140 MW	38170 TQ	USBLS	5/15
	Puerto Rico	Y	23970 FQ	36160 MW	44970 TQ	USBLS	5/15
	San Juan-Carolina-Caguas MSA, PR	Y	24870 FQ	36800 MW	45190 TQ	USBLS	5/15
	Guam	Y	20800 FQ	25710 MW	30160 TQ	USBLS	5/15
Representative							
United States House of Representatives	United States	Y			174000 HI	OPM01	2017
Reprographics Specialist							
Municipal Government	Brea, CA	Y			75554 HI	CACIT	6/28/16
Rescue Specialist							
State Government	Texas	Y	36976-48278 LR		58399-78953 HR	TXGOV	9/1/15-8/31/17
Research Analyst							
Pharmaceutical, Medical Device, and Healthcare Industries	United States	Y		81800 AW		MMM01	7/16
Research Assistant							
Life Sciences, Female	United States	Y		60051 AW		TSCI	2016
Life Sciences, Male	United States	Y		60979 AW		TSCI	2016
Research Biologist	United States	Y	93000 LO		110000 HI	CNBC04	2015
Research Fellow							
California State University	California	Y	2265 LO		16773 HI	CALST	2016-2017
Research Historian							
State Government	North Carolina	Y	36761 LO		58006 HI	NCGOV	7/1/16
Research Integrity Officer							
Michigan State University	East Lansing, MI	Y			147600 HI	MSUSAL	10/1/14-9/30/15
Research Psychologist							
Public Health Department, Municipal Government	San Francisco, CA	Y		111306 AW		CACIT	6/28/16
Research Vessel Operator							
Natural Resources Department, State Government	Ohio	H	21.33 LO		24.98 HI	OHGOV	2015
Reservation and Transportation Ticket Agent and Travel Clerk	Alabama	Y	22972 AE	37174 AW	44274 AEX	ALBLS	6/16
	Birmingham-Hoover MSA, AL	Y	22725 AE	38503 AW	46387 AEX	ALBLS	6/16
	Alaska	Y	26900 FQ	32140 MW	40670 TQ	USBLS	5/15
	Anchorage MSA, AK	Y	26310 FQ	30870 MW	41600 TQ	USBLS	5/15
	Arizona	Y	24380 FQ	34260 MW	45670 TQ	USBLS	5/15
	Phoenix-Mesa-Scottsdale MSA, AZ	Y	24970 FQ	35030 MW	45640 TQ	USBLS	5/15
	Tucson MSA, AZ	Y	20270 FQ	30150 MW	44680 TQ	USBLS	5/15
	Arkansas	Y	22720 FQ	28550 MW	43900 TQ	USBLS	5/15

Occupation/Type/Industry	Location	Per	Low	Mid	High	Source	Date
Reservation and Transportation Ticket Agent and Travel Clerk	Little Rock-North Little Rock-Conway MSA, AR	Y	24890 FQ	35360 MW	51740 TQ	USBLS	5/15
	California	H	14.65 FQ	19.17 MW	23.96 TQ	CABLS	1/16-3/16
	Anaheim-Santa Ana-Irvine PMSA, CA	H	13.72 FQ	18.79 MW	24.17 TQ	CABLS	1/16-3/16
	Los Angeles-Long Beach-Glendale PMSA, CA	H	15.63 FQ	19.88 MW	23.57 TQ	CABLS	1/16-3/16
	Oakland-Hayward-Berkeley PMSA, CA	H	12.10 FQ	16.09 MW	22.18 TQ	CABLS	1/16-3/16
	Riverside-San Bernardino-Ontario MSA, CA	H	13.73 FQ	17.35 MW	22.53 TQ	CABLS	1/16-3/16
	Sacramento–Roseville–Arden-Arcade MSA, CA	H	13.18 FQ	14.65 MW	19.80 TQ	CABLS	1/16-3/16
	San Diego-Carlsbad MSA, CA	H	13.66 FQ	18.52 MW	26.20 TQ	CABLS	1/16-3/16
	San Francisco-Redwood City-South San Francisco PMSA, CA	H	14.34 FQ	17.59 MW	22.19 TQ	CABLS	1/16-3/16
	Colorado	Y	24370 FQ	31060 MW	46020 TQ	USBLS	5/15
	Connecticut	Y		36748 MW		CTBLS	1/16-3/16
	Bridgeport-Stamford-Norwalk MSA, CT	Y	31650 FQ	42430 MW	49500 TQ	USBLS	5/15
	District of Columbia	Y	35360 FQ	46190 MW	56730 TQ	USBLS	5/15
	Washington-Arlington-Alexandria PMSA, DC-VA-MD-WV	Y	27290 FQ	36660 MW	53470 TQ	USBLS	5/15
	Florida	H	10.54 AE	15.25 MW	20.31 AEX	FLBLS	7/16-9/16
	Fort Lauderdale-Pompano Beach-Deerfield Beach PMSA, FL	H	9.82 AE	17.13 MW	22.78 AEX	FLBLS	7/16-9/16
	Miami-Miami Beach-Kendall PMSA, FL	H	10.65 AE	17.19 MW	20.09 AEX	FLBLS	7/16-9/16
	Orlando-Kissimmee-Sanford MSA, FL	H	10.80 AE	14.11 MW	18.31 AEX	FLBLS	7/16-9/16
	Tampa-St. Petersburg-Clearwater MSA, FL	H	10.74 AE	15.40 MW	21.48 AEX	FLBLS	7/16-9/16
	Hawaii	Y	25750 FQ	31310 MW	43560 TQ	USBLS	5/15
	Urban Honolulu MSA, HI	Y	25810 FQ	32050 MW	43820 TQ	USBLS	5/15
	Idaho	Y	25500 FQ	34760 MW	43530 TQ	USBLS	5/15
	Boise City MSA, ID	Y	26730 FQ	36130 MW	44780 TQ	USBLS	5/15
	Illinois	Y	28230 FQ	40190 MW	53070 TQ	USBLS	5/15
	Chicago-Naperville-Arlington Heights PMSA, IL	Y	28290 FQ	39830 MW	52800 TQ	USBLS	5/15
	Indiana	Y	26860 FQ	37410 MW	49110 TQ	USBLS	5/15
	Indianapolis-Carmel-Anderson MSA, IN	Y	29810 FQ	40360 MW	50690 TQ	USBLS	5/15
	Iowa	Y	19230 FQ	24940 MW	37820 TQ	USBLS	5/15
	Kansas	Y	22080 FQ	26230 MW	35970 TQ	USBLS	5/15
	Wichita MSA, KS	Y	22520 FQ	26680 MW	35540 TQ	USBLS	5/15
	Louisville-Jefferson County MSA, KY-IN	Y	22970 FQ	29420 MW	50230 TQ	USBLS	5/15
	Louisiana	Y	29250 FQ	37340 MW	51380 TQ	USBLS	5/15
	New Orleans-Metairie MSA, LA	Y	32020 FQ	38080 MW	51110 TQ	USBLS	5/15
	Maine	Y	22900 FQ	26440 MW	31130 TQ	USBLS	5/15
	Portland-South Portland MSA, ME	Y	22700 FQ	25710 MW	30390 TQ	USBLS	5/15
	Maryland	Y	24072 AE	37232 MW	43812 AEX	MDBLS	4/16
	Baltimore-Columbia-Towson MSA, MD	Y	28510 FQ	36600 MW	46630 TQ	USBLS	5/15
	Salisbury MSA, MD-DE	Y	23990 FQ	40750 MW	46260 TQ	USBLS	5/15
	Massachusetts	Y	30580 FQ	39200 MW	47690 TQ	USBLS	5/15
	Boston-Cambridge-Newton NECTA, MA	Y	32700 FQ	42090 MW	49520 TQ	USBLS	5/15
	Michigan	Y	26470 FQ	45660 MW	55960 TQ	USBLS	5/15
	Grand Rapids-Wyoming MSA, MI	Y	19680 FQ	24390 MW	39530 TQ	USBLS	5/15
	Minnesota	Y	33807 FQ	51575 MW	57410 TQ	MNBLS	1/16-3/16
	Minneapolis-St. Paul-Bloomington MSA, MN-WI	Y	35334 FQ	52141 MW	57693 TQ	MNBLS	1/16-3/16
	Mississippi	Y	19270 FQ	23430 MW	30970 TQ	USBLS	5/15
	Jackson MSA, MS	Y	22580 FQ	26060 MW	35790 TQ	USBLS	5/15

AE	Average entry wage	AWR	Average wage range	H	Hourly	LR	Low end range	MTC	Median total compensation	TCC	Total cash compensation
AEX	Average experienced wage	B	Biweekly	HI	Highest wage paid	M	Monthly	MW	Median wage paid	TQ	Third quartile wage
ATC	Average total compensation	D	Daily	HR	High end range	MCC	Median cash compensation	MWR	Median wage range	W	Weekly
AW	Average wage paid	FQ	First quartile wage	LO	Lowest wage paid	ME	Median entry wage	S	See annotated source	Y	Yearly

Occupation/Type/Industry	Location	Per	Low	Mid	High	Source	Date
Reservation and Transportation Ticket Agent and Travel Clerk							
	Missouri	Y	26760 FQ	35790 MW	50220 TQ	USBLS	5/15
	Kansas City MSA, MO-KS	Y	27290 FQ	37560 MW	51540 TQ	USBLS	5/15
	St. Louis MSA, MO-IL	Y	27990 FQ	36910 MW	49580 TQ	USBLS	5/15
	Montana	Y	19010 FQ	22300 MW	28890 TQ	USBLS	5/15
	Nebraska	Y	22150 FQ	25060 MW	31700 TQ	NEBLS	7/16-9/16
	Omaha-Council Bluffs MSA, NE-IA	Y	22315 FQ	25215 MW	31975 TQ	NEBLS	7/16-9/16
	Nevada	Y	25060 FQ	32470 MW	39800 TQ	USBLS	5/15
	Las Vegas-Henderson-Paradise MSA, NV	Y	26670 FQ	33620 MW	40460 TQ	USBLS	5/15
	New Hampshire	H	10.81 AE	13.01 MW	16.69 AEX	NHBLS	6/16
	New Jersey	Y	29070 FQ	40520 MW	47010 TQ	USBLS	5/15
	Newark PMSA, NJ-PA	Y	33220 FQ	42090 MW	47070 TQ	USBLS	5/15
	New Mexico	Y	30290 FQ	43220 MW	51070 TQ	USBLS	5/15
	Albuquerque MSA, NM	Y	34580 FQ	44530 MW	51620 TQ	USBLS	5/15
	New York	Y	22840 AE	34130 MW	42370 AEX	NYBLS	1/16-3/16
	Buffalo-Cheektowaga-Niagara Falls MSA, NY	Y	26130 FQ	39030 MW	46980 TQ	USBLS	5/15
	Nassau County-Suffolk County PMSA, NY	Y	27810 FQ	34700 MW	43000 TQ	USBLS	5/15
	New York-Jersey City-White Plains PMSA, NY-NJ	Y	24290 FQ	32580 MW	45070 TQ	USBLS	5/15
	Rochester MSA, NY	Y	28770 FQ	33700 MW	50650 TQ	USBLS	5/15
	North Carolina	Y	22580 FQ	31060 MW	42720 TQ	USBLS	5/15
	Charlotte-Concord-Gastonia MSA, NC-SC	Y	25300 FQ	34720 MW	44070 TQ	USBLS	5/15
	Raleigh MSA, NC	Y	20550 FQ	28840 MW	42110 TQ	USBLS	5/15
	Ohio	Y	23500 FQ	30530 MW	50970 TQ	USBLS	5/15
	Cleveland-Elyria MSA, OH	Y	22370 FQ	24870 MW	38120 TQ	USBLS	5/15
	Columbus MSA, OH	Y	22630 FQ	28860 MW	46010 TQ	USBLS	5/15
	Oklahoma	Y	38500 FQ	52840 MW	57980 TQ	USBLS	5/15
	Oklahoma City MSA, OK	Y	26220 FQ	42940 MW	54560 TQ	USBLS	5/15
	Tulsa MSA, OK	Y	40680 FQ	53360 MW	58230 TQ	USBLS	5/15
	Oregon	H	12.95 FQ	16.86 MW	25.44 TQ	ORBLS	2016
	Portland-Vancouver-Hillsboro MSA, OR-WA	Y	29270 FQ	39380 MW	54270 TQ	USBLS	5/15
	Pennsylvania	Y	25060 FQ	33980 MW	43870 TQ	USBLS	5/15
	Allentown-Bethlehem-Easton MSA, PA-NJ	Y	19970 FQ	28130 MW	35550 TQ	USBLS	5/15
	Montgomery County-Bucks County-Chester County PMSA, PA	Y	27130 FQ	31890 MW	44220 TQ	USBLS	5/15
	Philadelphia PMSA, PA	Y	24870 FQ	33360 MW	42380 TQ	USBLS	5/15
	Pittsburgh MSA, PA	Y	25940 FQ	35450 MW	45410 TQ	USBLS	5/15
	Rhode Island	Y	30010 FQ	36460 MW	43500 TQ	USBLS	5/15
	Providence-Warwick MSA, RI-MA	Y	32430 FQ	37080 MW	43120 TQ	USBLS	5/15
	South Carolina	Y	20800 FQ	26730 MW	39410 TQ	USBLS	5/15
	Charleston-North Charleston MSA, SC	Y	24890 FQ	30120 MW	45680 TQ	USBLS	5/15
	South Dakota	Y	20310 FQ	23440 MW	28540 TQ	USBLS	5/15
	Tennessee	Y	23210 FQ	37480 MW	46540 TQ	USBLS	5/15
	Knoxville MSA, TN	Y	19080 FQ	24090 MW	50250 TQ	USBLS	5/15
	Memphis MSA, TN-MS-AR	Y	33890 FQ	42940 MW	46880 TQ	USBLS	5/15
	Nashville-Davidson–Murfreesboro–Franklin MSA, TN	Y	24940 FQ	32610 MW	46670 TQ	USBLS	5/15
	Texas	Y	24500 FQ	39890 MW	50350 TQ	USBLS	5/15
	Austin-Round Rock MSA, TX	Y	24270 FQ	28510 MW	39190 TQ	USBLS	5/15
	Dallas-Plano-Irving PMSA, TX	Y	21910 FQ	24520 MW	30810 TQ	USBLS	5/15
	Fort Worth-Arlington PMSA, TX	Y	30300 FQ	44640 MW	50580 TQ	USBLS	5/15
	Houston-The Woodlands-Sugar Land MSA, TX	Y	27020 FQ	50200 MW	56780 TQ	USBLS	5/15
	San Antonio-New Braunfels MSA, TX	Y	23010 FQ	29180 MW	44170 TQ	USBLS	5/15
	Utah	Y	22030 FQ	24930 MW	41180 TQ	USBLS	5/15
	Salt Lake City MSA, UT	Y	22090 FQ	24950 MW	41620 TQ	USBLS	5/15
	Vermont	Y	20080 FQ	23950 MW	29880 TQ	USBLS	5/15
	Burlington-South Burlington MSA, VT	Y	22520 FQ	26290 MW	33420 TQ	USBLS	5/15

AE Average entry wage	**AWR** Average wage range	**H** Hourly	**LR** Low end range	**MTC** Median total compensation	**TCC** Total cash compensation
AEX Average experienced wage	**B** Biweekly	**HI** Highest wage paid	**M** Monthly	**MW** Median wage paid	**TQ** Third quartile wage
ATC Average total compensation	**D** Daily	**HR** High end range	**MCC** Median cash compensation	**MWR** Median wage range	**W** Weekly
AW Average wage paid	**FQ** First quartile wage	**LO** Lowest wage paid	**ME** Median entry wage	**S** See annotated source	**Y** Yearly

Occupation/Type/Industry	Location	Per	Low	Mid	High	Source	Date
Reservation and Transportation Ticket Agent and Travel Clerk	Virginia	Y	24540 FQ	31250 MW	48480 TQ	USBLS	5/15
	Richmond MSA, VA	Y	22760 FQ	29460 MW	45260 TQ	USBLS	5/15
	Virginia Beach-Norfolk-Newport News MSA, VA-NC	Y	22360 FQ	25710 MW	30860 TQ	USBLS	5/15
	Washington	H	12.19 FQ	16.10 MW	21.24 TQ	WABLS	3/16
	Seattle-Bellevue-Everett PMSA, WA	H	12.23 FQ	15.73 MW	20.78 TQ	WABLS	3/16
	West Virginia	Y	21630 FQ	25170 MW	30750 TQ	USBLS	5/15
	Wisconsin	Y	23370 FQ	29900 MW	42420 TQ	USBLS	5/15
	Madison MSA, WI	Y	20230 FQ	21750 MW	23260 TQ	USBLS	5/15
	Milwaukee-Waukesha-West Allis MSA, WI	Y	26710 FQ	31990 MW	46110 TQ	USBLS	5/15
	Wyoming	Y	24330 FQ	28020 MW	31260 TQ	USBLS	5/15
	Puerto Rico	Y	16760 FQ	18130 MW	19570 TQ	USBLS	5/15
	San Juan-Carolina-Caguas MSA, PR	Y	16790 FQ	18180 MW	19760 TQ	USBLS	5/15
	Virgin Islands	Y	17860 FQ	22340 MW	31570 TQ	USBLS	5/15
Reserve Police Officer							
Municipal Government	Erving, MA	H			15.87 HI	FRCOG	2016
Municipal Government	Shelburne, MA	H			17.95 HI	FRCOG	2016
Reservoir Engineer	United States	Y		143000 MW		CNBC05	2016
Reservoir Keeper							
Municipal Government	San Diego, CA	Y		44046 AW		CACIT	6/28/16
Residential Advisor	Alabama	Y	17575 AE	23166 AW	25967 AEX	ALBLS	6/16
	Birmingham-Hoover MSA, AL	Y	17822 AE	25277 AW	29014 AEX	ALBLS	6/16
	Alaska	Y	34030 FQ	40770 MW	47700 TQ	USBLS	5/15
	Anchorage MSA, AK	Y	32330 FQ	36960 MW	48200 TQ	USBLS	5/15
	Arizona	Y	25180 FQ	30090 MW	37240 TQ	USBLS	5/15
	Phoenix-Mesa-Scottsdale MSA, AZ	Y	26940 FQ	30720 MW	38010 TQ	USBLS	5/15
	Tucson MSA, AZ	Y	25860 FQ	33380 MW	38610 TQ	USBLS	5/15
	Arkansas	Y	19300 FQ	22760 MW	29200 TQ	USBLS	5/15
	Little Rock-North Little Rock-Conway MSA, AR	Y	20060 FQ	22540 MW	26640 TQ	USBLS	5/15
	California	H	12.37 FQ	14.84 MW	18.36 TQ	CABLS	1/16-3/16
	Anaheim-Santa Ana-Irvine PMSA, CA	H	13.03 FQ	14.68 MW	17.62 TQ	CABLS	1/16-3/16
	Los Angeles-Long Beach-Glendale PMSA, CA	H	12.48 FQ	16.02 MW	20.36 TQ	CABLS	1/16-3/16
	Oakland-Hayward-Berkeley PMSA, CA	H	12.02 FQ	15.47 MW	21.59 TQ	CABLS	1/16-3/16
	Riverside-San Bernardino-Ontario MSA, CA	H	13.45 FQ	15.63 MW	18.82 TQ	CABLS	1/16-3/16
	Sacramento–Roseville–Arden-Arcade MSA, CA	H	9.58 FQ	11.48 MW	14.44 TQ	CABLS	1/16-3/16
	San Diego-Carlsbad MSA, CA	H	13.95 FQ	15.98 MW	18.45 TQ	CABLS	1/16-3/16
	San Francisco-Redwood City-South San Francisco PMSA, CA	H	12.96 FQ	14.46 MW	16.86 TQ	CABLS	1/16-3/16
	Colorado	Y	21240 FQ	25370 MW	31230 TQ	USBLS	5/15
	Denver-Aurora-Lakewood MSA, CO	Y	26470 FQ	31490 MW	42610 TQ	USBLS	5/15
	Connecticut	Y		28389 MW		CTBLS	1/16-3/16
	Bridgeport-Stamford-Norwalk MSA, CT	Y	21330 FQ	28550 MW	37780 TQ	USBLS	5/15
	Hartford-West Hartford-East Hartford MSA, CT	Y	22200 FQ	26150 MW	36150 TQ	USBLS	5/15
	Delaware	Y	21050 FQ	23690 MW	29750 TQ	USBLS	5/15
	Wilmington PMSA, DE-MD-NJ	Y	21600 FQ	24090 MW	30140 TQ	USBLS	5/15
	District of Columbia	Y	25940 FQ	29490 MW	35390 TQ	USBLS	5/15
	Washington-Arlington-Alexandria PMSA, DC-VA-MD-WV	Y	22160 FQ	26800 MW	35640 TQ	USBLS	5/15
	Florida	H	9.02 AE	10.86 MW	13.63 AEX	FLBLS	7/16-9/16

AE	Average entry wage	AWR	Average wage range	H	Hourly	LR	Low end range
AEX	Average experienced wage	B	Biweekly	HI	Highest wage paid	M	Monthly
ATC	Average total compensation	D	Daily	HR	High end range	MCC	Median cash compensation
AW	Average wage paid	FQ	First quartile wage	LO	Lowest wage paid	ME	Median entry wage

MTC	Median total compensation	TCC	Total cash compensation
MW	Median wage paid	TQ	Third quartile wage
MWR	Median wage range	W	Weekly
S	See annotated source	Y	Yearly

Residential Advisor

Occupation/Type/Industry	Location	Per	Low	Mid	High	Source	Date
Residential Advisor	Fort Lauderdale-Pompano Beach-Deerfield Beach PMSA, FL	H	11.48 AE	15.12 MW	17.20 AEX	FLBLS	7/16-9/16
	Miami-Miami Beach-Kendall PMSA, FL	H	10.42 AE	11.99 MW	14.75 AEX	FLBLS	7/16-9/16
	Orlando-Kissimmee-Sanford MSA, FL	H	9.03 AE	9.36 MW	10.91 AEX	FLBLS	7/16-9/16
	Tampa-St. Petersburg-Clearwater MSA, FL	H	9.01 AE	10.27 MW	12.27 AEX	FLBLS	7/16-9/16
	Georgia	Y	18330 FQ	22060 MW	27760 TQ	USBLS	5/15
	Atlanta-Sandy Springs-Roswell MSA, GA	Y	20840 FQ	23930 MW	30030 TQ	USBLS	5/15
	Augusta-Richmond County MSA, GA-SC	Y	18030 FQ	20880 MW	27420 TQ	USBLS	5/15
	Hawaii	Y	18490 FQ	25410 MW	32680 TQ	USBLS	5/15
	Urban Honolulu MSA, HI	Y	18140 FQ	24580 MW	34870 TQ	USBLS	5/15
	Idaho	Y	17390 FQ	19260 MW	26430 TQ	USBLS	5/15
	Boise City MSA, ID	Y	16810 FQ	18080 MW	19360 TQ	USBLS	5/15
	Illinois	Y	21230 FQ	24480 MW	30950 TQ	USBLS	5/15
	Chicago-Naperville-Arlington Heights PMSA, IL	Y	22050 FQ	24970 MW	33210 TQ	USBLS	5/15
	Lake County-Kenosha County PMSA, IL-WI	Y	20730 FQ	25410 MW	33230 TQ	USBLS	5/15
	Indiana	Y	19980 FQ	24910 MW	29790 TQ	USBLS	5/15
	Gary PMSA, IN	Y	23400 FQ	28930 MW	35700 TQ	USBLS	5/15
	Indianapolis-Carmel-Anderson MSA, IN	Y	20300 FQ	24770 MW	28670 TQ	USBLS	5/15
	Iowa	Y	20360 FQ	24350 MW	30670 TQ	USBLS	5/15
	Des Moines-West Des Moines MSA, IA	Y	20980 FQ	23430 MW	27770 TQ	USBLS	5/15
	Kansas	Y	19430 FQ	24120 MW	28370 TQ	USBLS	5/15
	Wichita MSA, KS	Y	18630 FQ	22820 MW	26930 TQ	USBLS	5/15
	Kentucky	Y	18400 FQ	21450 MW	24520 TQ	USBLS	5/15
	Louisville-Jefferson County MSA, KY-IN	Y	19030 FQ	22090 MW	25320 TQ	USBLS	5/15
	Louisiana	Y	18340 FQ	21400 MW	25970 TQ	USBLS	5/15
	Baton Rouge MSA, LA	Y	18840 FQ	22570 MW	27930 TQ	USBLS	5/15
	New Orleans-Metairie MSA, LA	Y	19750 FQ	22100 MW	24540 TQ	USBLS	5/15
	Maine	Y	24420 FQ	28010 MW	32290 TQ	USBLS	5/15
	Portland-South Portland MSA, ME	Y	24620 FQ	28630 MW	34910 TQ	USBLS	5/15
	Maryland	Y	20679 AE	28656 MW	32644 AEX	MDBLS	4/16
	Baltimore-Columbia-Towson MSA, MD	Y	21970 FQ	27080 MW	34050 TQ	USBLS	5/15
	Salisbury MSA, MD-DE	Y	23360 FQ	35540 MW	41610 TQ	USBLS	5/15
	Massachusetts	Y	25460 FQ	28230 MW	31170 TQ	USBLS	5/15
	Boston-Cambridge-Newton NECTA, MA	Y	26140 FQ	28480 MW	30810 TQ	USBLS	5/15
	Worcester MSA, MA-CT	Y	23980 FQ	27320 MW	31210 TQ	USBLS	5/15
	Michigan	Y	20950 FQ	24840 MW	30640 TQ	USBLS	5/15
	Ann Arbor MSA, MI	Y	24140 FQ	32120 MW	38600 TQ	USBLS	5/15
	Detroit-Dearborn-Livonia PMSA, MI	Y	20810 FQ	24760 MW	29470 TQ	USBLS	5/15
	Grand Rapids-Wyoming MSA, MI	Y	19830 FQ	23650 MW	29040 TQ	USBLS	5/15
	Minnesota	Y	27832 FQ	34022 MW	39607 TQ	MNBLS	1/16-3/16
	Minneapolis-St. Paul-Bloomington MSA, MN-WI	Y	27973 FQ	35739 MW	43384 TQ	MNBLS	1/16-3/16
	Mississippi	Y	18510 FQ	22170 MW	28280 TQ	USBLS	5/15
	Jackson MSA, MS	Y	18510 FQ	21210 MW	24550 TQ	USBLS	5/15
	Missouri	Y	20220 FQ	24390 MW	31840 TQ	USBLS	5/15
	Kansas City MSA, MO-KS	Y	20030 FQ	24090 MW	29500 TQ	USBLS	5/15
	St. Louis MSA, MO-IL	Y	21590 FQ	26830 MW	35380 TQ	USBLS	5/15
	Montana	Y	19560 FQ	24530 MW	29230 TQ	USBLS	5/15
	Omaha-Council Bluffs MSA, NE-IA	Y	25120 FQ	29750 MW	36455 TQ	NEBLS	7/16-9/16
	Nevada	Y	22120 FQ	26210 MW	30590 TQ	USBLS	5/15
	Las Vegas-Henderson-Paradise MSA, NV	Y	22250 FQ	25510 MW	30870 TQ	USBLS	5/15
	New Hampshire	H	10.85 AE	15.08 MW	17.43 AEX	NHBLS	6/16
	Manchester NECTA, NH	H	12.95 AE	14.63 MW	15.83 AEX	NHBLS	6/16

AE Average entry wage	**AWR** Average wage range	**H** Hourly	**LR** Low end range	**MTC** Median total compensation	**TCC** Total cash compensation
AEX Average experienced wage	**B** Biweekly	**HI** Highest wage paid	**M** Monthly	**MW** Median wage paid	**TQ** Third quartile wage
ATC Average total compensation	**D** Daily	**HR** High end range	**MCC** Median cash compensation	**MWR** Median wage range	**W** Weekly
AW Average wage paid	**FQ** First quartile wage	**LO** Lowest wage paid	**ME** Median entry wage	**S** See annotated source	**Y** Yearly

Occupation/Type/Industry	Location	Per	Low	Mid	High	Source	Date
Residential Advisor	New Jersey	Y	25920 FQ	29440 MW	37930 TQ	USBLS	5/15
	Camden PMSA, NJ	Y	28470 FQ	40320 MW	48180 TQ	USBLS	5/15
	Newark PMSA, NJ-PA	Y	26090 FQ	28700 MW	31520 TQ	USBLS	5/15
	Trenton MSA, NJ	Y	39770 FQ	45270 MW	51640 TQ	USBLS	5/15
	New Mexico	Y	20680 FQ	23900 MW	28680 TQ	USBLS	5/15
	Albuquerque MSA, NM	Y	21950 FQ	24430 MW	28330 TQ	USBLS	5/15
	New York	Y	24530 AE	33710 MW	38800 AEX	NYBLS	1/16-3/16
	Buffalo-Cheektowaga-Niagara Falls MSA, NY	Y	28240 FQ	33920 MW	37550 TQ	USBLS	5/15
	Nassau County-Suffolk County PMSA, NY	Y	28990 FQ	35150 MW	41440 TQ	USBLS	5/15
	New York-Jersey City-White Plains PMSA, NY-NJ	Y	25790 FQ	32090 MW	39460 TQ	USBLS	5/15
	Rochester MSA, NY	Y	30600 FQ	34500 MW	38190 TQ	USBLS	5/15
	North Carolina	Y	19660 FQ	25520 MW	34350 TQ	USBLS	5/15
	Charlotte-Concord-Gastonia MSA, NC-SC	Y	21160 FQ	24260 MW	31190 TQ	USBLS	5/15
	Raleigh MSA, NC	Y	22430 FQ	28660 MW	35390 TQ	USBLS	5/15
	North Dakota	Y	22190 FQ	26580 MW	36710 TQ	USBLS	5/15
	Fargo MSA, ND-MN	Y	21640 FQ	24210 MW	34450 TQ	USBLS	5/15
	Ohio	Y	24370 FQ	29220 MW	35740 TQ	USBLS	5/15
	Cincinnati MSA, OH-KY-IN	Y	22330 FQ	25130 MW	32090 TQ	USBLS	5/15
	Cleveland-Elyria MSA, OH	Y	26030 FQ	30780 MW	39380 TQ	USBLS	5/15
	Columbus MSA, OH	Y	23900 FQ	28810 MW	34590 TQ	USBLS	5/15
	Oklahoma	Y	17700 FQ	20160 MW	25190 TQ	USBLS	5/15
	Oklahoma City MSA, OK	Y	17630 FQ	19710 MW	25970 TQ	USBLS	5/15
	Tulsa MSA, OK	Y	20660 FQ	23120 MW	28190 TQ	USBLS	5/15
	Oregon	H	10.89 FQ	14.22 MW	17.86 TQ	ORBLS	2016
	Portland-Vancouver-Hillsboro MSA, OR-WA	Y	30740 FQ	35600 MW	41070 TQ	USBLS	5/15
	Pennsylvania	Y	21190 FQ	24180 MW	29750 TQ	USBLS	5/15
	Allentown-Bethlehem-Easton MSA, PA-NJ	Y	21750 FQ	23760 MW	30250 TQ	USBLS	5/15
	Montgomery County-Bucks County-Chester County PMSA, PA	Y	19420 FQ	22570 MW	26970 TQ	USBLS	5/15
	Philadelphia PMSA, PA	Y	21760 FQ	24310 MW	28820 TQ	USBLS	5/15
	Pittsburgh MSA, PA	Y	21330 FQ	24440 MW	28570 TQ	USBLS	5/15
	Rhode Island	Y	22490 FQ	26620 MW	34780 TQ	USBLS	5/15
	Providence-Warwick MSA, RI-MA	Y	23000 FQ	26570 MW	30250 TQ	USBLS	5/15
	South Carolina	Y	20170 FQ	23200 MW	28370 TQ	USBLS	5/15
	Charleston-North Charleston MSA, SC	Y	21120 FQ	24350 MW	31830 TQ	USBLS	5/15
	Columbia MSA, SC	Y	20550 FQ	23510 MW	28170 TQ	USBLS	5/15
	Greenville-Anderson-Mauldin MSA, SC	Y	18160 FQ	22280 MW	28830 TQ	USBLS	5/15
	South Dakota	Y	21590 FQ	23700 MW	27220 TQ	USBLS	5/15
	Sioux Falls MSA, SD	Y	21800 FQ	23950 MW	27810 TQ	USBLS	5/15
	Tennessee	Y	17120 FQ	18800 MW	21900 TQ	USBLS	5/15
	Knoxville MSA, TN	Y	18480 FQ	21120 MW	23890 TQ	USBLS	5/15
	Memphis MSA, TN-MS-AR	Y	16910 FQ	18330 MW	19910 TQ	USBLS	5/15
	Nashville-Davidson–Murfreesboro–Franklin MSA, TN	Y	17130 FQ	18920 MW	22960 TQ	USBLS	5/15
	Texas	Y	19270 FQ	23950 MW	29890 TQ	USBLS	5/15
	Austin-Round Rock MSA, TX	Y	22580 FQ	26860 MW	30930 TQ	USBLS	5/15
	Dallas-Plano-Irving PMSA, TX	Y	20600 FQ	26920 MW	32750 TQ	USBLS	5/15
	Fort Worth-Arlington PMSA, TX	Y	17880 FQ	20700 MW	28250 TQ	USBLS	5/15
	Houston-The Woodlands-Sugar Land MSA, TX	Y	21630 FQ	27140 MW	35570 TQ	USBLS	5/15
	San Antonio-New Braunfels MSA, TX	Y	19820 FQ	24220 MW	28420 TQ	USBLS	5/15
	Utah	Y	21120 FQ	24040 MW	28510 TQ	USBLS	5/15
	Ogden-Clearfield MSA, UT	Y	24540 FQ	27420 MW	30400 TQ	USBLS	5/15
	Provo-Orem MSA, UT	Y	21140 FQ	23290 MW	27260 TQ	USBLS	5/15
	Salt Lake City MSA, UT	Y	22160 FQ	26260 MW	29350 TQ	USBLS	5/15
	Vermont	Y	22930 FQ	27720 MW	34120 TQ	USBLS	5/15
	Burlington-South Burlington MSA, VT	Y	22790 FQ	27700 MW	35120 TQ	USBLS	5/15
	Virginia	Y	22750 FQ	27260 MW	33720 TQ	USBLS	5/15

AE	Average entry wage	AWR	Average wage range	H	Hourly
AEX	Average experienced wage	B	Biweekly	HI	Highest wage paid
ATC	Average total compensation	D	Daily	HR	High end range
AW	Average wage paid	FQ	First quartile wage	LO	Lowest wage paid

LR	Low end range	MTC	Median total compensation	TCC	Total cash compensation
M	Monthly	MW	Median wage paid	TQ	Third quartile wage
MCC	Median cash compensation	MWR	Median wage range	W	Weekly
ME	Median entry wage	S	See annotated source	Y	Yearly

Occupation/Type/Industry	Location	Per	Low	Mid	High	Source	Date
Residential Advisor	Richmond MSA, VA	Y	22850 FQ	26080 MW	29760 TQ	USBLS	5/15
	Virginia Beach-Norfolk-Newport News MSA, VA-NC	Y	25670 FQ	32540 MW	37260 TQ	USBLS	5/15
	Washington	H	11.69 FQ	13.45 MW	15.08 TQ	WABLS	3/16
	Seattle-Bellevue-Everett PMSA, WA	H	11.69 FQ	13.34 MW	14.82 TQ	WABLS	3/16
	Tacoma-Lakewood PMSA, WA	H	13.04 FQ	16.81 MW	26.10 TQ	WABLS	3/16
	West Virginia	Y	20080 FQ	25910 MW	37500 TQ	USBLS	5/15
	Huntington-Ashland MSA, WV-KY-OH	Y	18100 FQ	20180 MW	25200 TQ	USBLS	5/15
	Wisconsin	Y	20670 FQ	23940 MW	28860 TQ	USBLS	5/15
	Madison MSA, WI	Y	18060 FQ	21480 MW	27170 TQ	USBLS	5/15
	Milwaukee-Waukesha-West Allis MSA, WI	Y	24130 FQ	27380 MW	30340 TQ	USBLS	5/15
	Wyoming	Y	18370 FQ	23860 MW	30300 TQ	USBLS	5/15
	Puerto Rico	Y	17840 FQ	24880 MW	29430 TQ	USBLS	5/15
Residential Construction Specialist							
Municipal Government	Santa Ana, CA	Y			77432 HI	CACIT	6/28/16
Resource Specialist							
Community Development and Housing, Municipal Government	Glendale, CA	Y			85028 HI	CACIT	6/28/16
Respiratory Therapist	Alabama	Y	38163 AE	47837 AW	52668 AEX	ALBLS	6/16
	Birmingham-Hoover MSA, AL	Y	40070 AE	48612 AW	52872 AEX	ALBLS	6/16
	Alaska	Y	64570 FQ	71220 MW	77860 TQ	USBLS	5/15
	Anchorage MSA, AK	Y	64040 FQ	71430 MW	79380 TQ	USBLS	5/15
	Arizona	Y	47620 FQ	55240 MW	61600 TQ	USBLS	5/15
	Phoenix-Mesa-Scottsdale MSA, AZ	Y	50020 FQ	56480 MW	62350 TQ	USBLS	5/15
	Tucson MSA, AZ	Y	43760 FQ	48620 MW	56300 TQ	USBLS	5/15
	Arkansas	Y	40530 FQ	47440 MW	56870 TQ	USBLS	5/15
	Little Rock-North Little Rock-Conway MSA, AR	Y	40710 FQ	48120 MW	57960 TQ	USBLS	5/15
	California	H	32.19 FQ	38.76 MW	45.75 TQ	CABLS	1/16-3/16
	Anaheim-Santa Ana-Irvine PMSA, CA	H	31.33 FQ	38.09 MW	45.47 TQ	CABLS	1/16-3/16
	Los Angeles-Long Beach-Glendale PMSA, CA	H	31.03 FQ	36.50 MW	42.83 TQ	CABLS	1/16-3/16
	Oakland-Hayward-Berkeley PMSA, CA	H	36.96 FQ	43.32 MW	49.44 TQ	CABLS	1/16-3/16
	Riverside-San Bernardino-Ontario MSA, CA	H	29.51 FQ	34.38 MW	39.27 TQ	CABLS	1/16-3/16
	Sacramento–Roseville–Arden-Arcade MSA, CA	H	41.24 FQ	44.57 MW	47.89 TQ	CABLS	1/16-3/16
	San Diego-Carlsbad MSA, CA	H	28.91 FQ	35.69 MW	42.83 TQ	CABLS	1/16-3/16
	San Francisco-Redwood City-South San Francisco PMSA, CA	H	42.88 FQ	48.32 MW	55.21 TQ	CABLS	1/16-3/16
	Colorado	Y	50970 FQ	58200 MW	67140 TQ	USBLS	5/15
	Denver-Aurora-Lakewood MSA, CO	Y	51850 FQ	58480 MW	66780 TQ	USBLS	5/15
	Connecticut	Y		65607 MW		CTBLS	1/16-3/16
	Bridgeport-Stamford-Norwalk MSA, CT	Y	59640 FQ	70690 MW	80750 TQ	USBLS	5/15
	Hartford-West Hartford-East Hartford MSA, CT	Y	53390 FQ	61490 MW	70900 TQ	USBLS	5/15
	Delaware	Y	51900 FQ	60370 MW	70710 TQ	USBLS	5/15
	Wilmington PMSA, DE-MD-NJ	Y	53990 FQ	62450 MW	72530 TQ	USBLS	5/15
	District of Columbia	Y	53880 FQ	67280 MW	77550 TQ	USBLS	5/15
	Washington-Arlington-Alexandria PMSA, DC-VA-MD-WV	Y	58770 FQ	68360 MW	76180 TQ	USBLS	5/15
	Florida	H	21.36 AE	26.96 MW	29.72 AEX	FLBLS	7/16-9/16
	Cape Coral-Fort Myers MSA, FL	Y	51830 FQ	55730 MW	59630 TQ	USBLS	5/15
	Fort Lauderdale-Pompano Beach-Deerfield Beach PMSA, FL	H	22.24 AE	28.34 MW	31.91 AEX	FLBLS	7/16-9/16

AE	Average entry wage	AWR	Average wage range	H	Hourly
AEX	Average experienced wage	B	Biweekly	HI	Highest wage paid
ATC	Average total compensation	D	Daily	HR	High end range
AW	Average wage paid	FQ	First quartile wage	LO	Lowest wage paid

LR	Low end range	MTC	Median total compensation	TCC	Total cash compensation
M	Monthly	MW	Median wage paid	TQ	Third quartile wage
MCC	Median cash compensation	MWR	Median wage range	W	Weekly
ME	Median entry wage	S	See annotated source	Y	Yearly

Respiratory Therapist

Occupation/Type/Industry	Location	Per	Low	Mid	High	Source	Date
Respiratory Therapist	Miami-Miami Beach-Kendall PMSA, FL	H	20.83 AE	25.98 MW	28.69 AEX	FLBLS	7/16-9/16
	Orlando-Kissimmee-Sanford MSA, FL	H	21.65 AE	27.09 MW	30.25 AEX	FLBLS	7/16-9/16
	Tampa-St. Petersburg-Clearwater MSA, FL	H	24.16 AE	27.89 MW	30.02 AEX	FLBLS	7/16-9/16
	Georgia	Y	45980 FQ	53550 MW	60590 TQ	USBLS	5/15
	Atlanta-Sandy Springs-Roswell MSA, GA	Y	48800 FQ	55860 MW	62160 TQ	USBLS	5/15
	Augusta-Richmond County MSA, GA-SC	Y	46440 FQ	53310 MW	60290 TQ	USBLS	5/15
	Hawaii	Y	62980 FQ	69340 MW	75260 TQ	USBLS	5/15
	Urban Honolulu MSA, HI	Y	64370 FQ	69950 MW	75550 TQ	USBLS	5/15
	Idaho	Y	47860 FQ	54470 MW	60490 TQ	USBLS	5/15
	Boise City MSA, ID	Y	47300 FQ	53950 MW	60170 TQ	USBLS	5/15
	Illinois	Y	45630 FQ	54200 MW	62250 TQ	USBLS	5/15
	Chicago-Naperville-Arlington Heights PMSA, IL	Y	46860 FQ	55430 MW	63110 TQ	USBLS	5/15
	Lake County-Kenosha County PMSA, IL-WI	Y	47080 FQ	57670 MW	68620 TQ	USBLS	5/15
	Indiana	Y	46240 FQ	54000 MW	61170 TQ	USBLS	5/15
	Gary PMSA, IN	Y	51060 FQ	57650 MW	64510 TQ	USBLS	5/15
	Indianapolis-Carmel-Anderson MSA, IN	Y	46310 FQ	53910 MW	61260 TQ	USBLS	5/15
	Iowa	Y	43660 FQ	49370 MW	57590 TQ	USBLS	5/15
	Des Moines-West Des Moines MSA, IA	Y	44860 FQ	50910 MW	58050 TQ	USBLS	5/15
	Kansas	Y	43080 FQ	50110 MW	58610 TQ	USBLS	5/15
	Wichita MSA, KS	Y	44850 FQ	51240 MW	59230 TQ	USBLS	5/15
	Kentucky	Y	41160 FQ	47270 MW	55270 TQ	USBLS	5/15
	Louisville-Jefferson County MSA, KY-IN	Y	42640 FQ	48750 MW	56610 TQ	USBLS	5/15
	Louisiana	Y	44320 FQ	51950 MW	59670 TQ	USBLS	5/15
	Baton Rouge MSA, LA	Y	42810 FQ	49080 MW	57260 TQ	USBLS	5/15
	New Orleans-Metairie MSA, LA	Y	49640 FQ	56190 MW	62380 TQ	USBLS	5/15
	Maine	Y	49020 FQ	56250 MW	63580 TQ	USBLS	5/15
	Portland-South Portland MSA, ME	Y	48250 FQ	58210 MW	69230 TQ	USBLS	5/15
	Maryland	Y	53701 AE	65902 MW	72002 AEX	MDBLS	4/16
	Baltimore-Columbia-Towson MSA, MD	Y	57990 FQ	66290 MW	74410 TQ	USBLS	5/15
	Salisbury MSA, MD-DE	Y	51230 FQ	58890 MW	68200 TQ	USBLS	5/15
	Massachusetts	Y	59400 FQ	69310 MW	78920 TQ	USBLS	5/15
	Boston-Cambridge-Newton NECTA, MA	Y	61410 FQ	71640 MW	82940 TQ	USBLS	5/15
	Worcester MSA, MA-CT	Y	61690 FQ	71900 MW	83260 TQ	USBLS	5/15
	Michigan	Y	47800 FQ	54390 MW	60060 TQ	USBLS	5/15
	Detroit-Dearborn-Livonia PMSA, MI	Y	46410 FQ	53650 MW	59800 TQ	USBLS	5/15
	Grand Rapids-Wyoming MSA, MI	Y	46450 FQ	52890 MW	59020 TQ	USBLS	5/15
	Minnesota	Y	57640 FQ	66189 MW	74495 TQ	MNBLS	1/16-3/16
	Minneapolis-St. Paul-Bloomington MSA, MN-WI	Y	58487 FQ	66844 MW	74102 TQ	MNBLS	1/16-3/16
	Mississippi	Y	41520 FQ	47590 MW	55640 TQ	USBLS	5/15
	Jackson MSA, MS	Y	45210 FQ	51390 MW	58390 TQ	USBLS	5/15
	Missouri	Y	43580 FQ	49770 MW	58390 TQ	USBLS	5/15
	Kansas City MSA, MO-KS	Y	44430 FQ	51010 MW	59210 TQ	USBLS	5/15
	St. Louis MSA, MO-IL	Y	43490 FQ	49300 MW	58880 TQ	USBLS	5/15
	Montana	Y	45900 FQ	52600 MW	59100 TQ	USBLS	5/15
	Billings MSA, MT	Y	45760 FQ	51330 MW	60020 TQ	USBLS	5/15
	Nebraska	Y	44580 FQ	50445 MW	57985 TQ	NEBLS	7/16-9/16
	Omaha-Council Bluffs MSA, NE-IA	Y	43865 FQ	49180 MW	57240 TQ	NEBLS	7/16-9/16
	Nevada	Y	60220 FQ	69880 MW	79020 TQ	USBLS	5/15
	Las Vegas-Henderson-Paradise MSA, NV	Y	59150 FQ	69180 MW	78650 TQ	USBLS	5/15
	New Hampshire	H	26.25 AE	30.58 MW	32.69 AEX	NHBLS	6/16
	Manchester NECTA, NH	H	27.53 AE	32.26 MW	34.12 AEX	NHBLS	6/16
	Nashua NECTA, NH-MA	Y	54840 FQ	60830 MW	68380 TQ	USBLS	5/15
	New Jersey	Y	64370 FQ	71390 MW	78400 TQ	USBLS	5/15

AE	Average entry wage	AWR	Average wage range	
AEX	Average experienced wage	B	Biweekly	
ATC	Average total compensation	D	Daily	
AW	Average wage paid	FQ	First quartile wage	

H	Hourly
HI	Highest wage paid
HR	High end range
LO	Lowest wage paid
ME	Median entry wage

LR	Low end range
M	Monthly
MCC	Median cash compensation

MTC	Median total compensation
MW	Median wage paid
MWR	Median wage range
S	See annotated source

TCC	Total cash compensation
TQ	Third quartile wage
W	Weekly
Y	Yearly

Respiratory Therapist

Occupation/Type/Industry	Location	Per	Low	Mid	High	Source	Date
Respiratory Therapist	Camden PMSA, NJ	Y	60530 FQ	68910 MW	76230 TQ	USBLS	5/15
	Newark PMSA, NJ-PA	Y	64770 FQ	71330 MW	77960 TQ	USBLS	5/15
	Trenton MSA, NJ	Y	64970 FQ	70980 MW	76990 TQ	USBLS	5/15
	New Mexico	Y	46360 FQ	53730 MW	59850 TQ	USBLS	5/15
	Albuquerque MSA, NM	Y	50650 FQ	56110 MW	61470 TQ	USBLS	5/15
	New York	Y	56580 AE	71630 MW	77610 AEX	NYBLS	1/16-3/16
	Buffalo-Cheektowaga-Niagara Falls MSA, NY	Y	51690 FQ	58520 MW	67830 TQ	USBLS	5/15
	Nassau County-Suffolk County PMSA, NY	Y	68030 FQ	73800 MW	79850 TQ	USBLS	5/15
	New York-Jersey City-White Plains PMSA, NY-NJ	Y	67320 FQ	73840 MW	80870 TQ	USBLS	5/15
	Rochester MSA, NY	Y	46940 FQ	54470 MW	61220 TQ	USBLS	5/15
	North Carolina	Y	46290 FQ	53390 MW	59900 TQ	USBLS	5/15
	Charlotte-Concord-Gastonia MSA, NC-SC	Y	48680 FQ	55440 MW	61590 TQ	USBLS	5/15
	Raleigh MSA, NC	Y	49550 FQ	56070 MW	61840 TQ	USBLS	5/15
	North Dakota	Y	44220 FQ	49660 MW	57530 TQ	USBLS	5/15
	Fargo MSA, ND-MN	Y	44810 FQ	50270 MW	58730 TQ	USBLS	5/15
	Ohio	Y	46760 FQ	53900 MW	60280 TQ	USBLS	5/15
	Cincinnati MSA, OH-KY-IN	Y	47070 FQ	54800 MW	62600 TQ	USBLS	5/15
	Cleveland-Elyria MSA, OH	Y	49750 FQ	55670 MW	61160 TQ	USBLS	5/15
	Columbus MSA, OH	Y	45430 FQ	53010 MW	60210 TQ	USBLS	5/15
	Oklahoma	Y	44650 FQ	51270 MW	59210 TQ	USBLS	5/15
	Oklahoma City MSA, OK	Y	45560 FQ	52760 MW	60280 TQ	USBLS	5/15
	Tulsa MSA, OK	Y	44770 FQ	50900 MW	58790 TQ	USBLS	5/15
	Oregon	H	27.41 FQ	32.08 MW	35.99 TQ	ORBLS	2016
	Portland-Vancouver-Hillsboro MSA, OR-WA	Y	61370 FQ	69160 MW	76110 TQ	USBLS	5/15
	Pennsylvania	Y	48630 FQ	57390 MW	67740 TQ	USBLS	5/15
	Allentown-Bethlehem-Easton MSA, PA-NJ	Y	50390 FQ	59940 MW	70930 TQ	USBLS	5/15
	Harrisburg-Carlisle MSA, PA	Y	52850 FQ	62470 MW	71660 TQ	USBLS	5/15
	Montgomery County-Bucks County-Chester County PMSA, PA	Y	49660 FQ	59530 MW	70290 TQ	USBLS	5/15
	Philadelphia PMSA, PA	Y	59880 FQ	68750 MW	76460 TQ	USBLS	5/15
	Pittsburgh MSA, PA	Y	45510 FQ	52590 MW	59830 TQ	USBLS	5/15
	Rhode Island	Y	54810 FQ	64380 MW	72020 TQ	USBLS	5/15
	Providence-Warwick MSA, RI-MA	Y	53920 FQ	63840 MW	71970 TQ	USBLS	5/15
	South Carolina	Y	44950 FQ	53080 MW	61170 TQ	USBLS	5/15
	Charleston-North Charleston MSA, SC	Y	52070 FQ	59100 MW	68940 TQ	USBLS	5/15
	Greenville-Anderson-Mauldin MSA, SC	Y	44010 FQ	49850 MW	57510 TQ	USBLS	5/15
	South Dakota	Y	43110 FQ	48940 MW	57770 TQ	USBLS	5/15
	Tennessee	Y	42840 FQ	48490 MW	56600 TQ	USBLS	5/15
	Knoxville MSA, TN	Y	41510 FQ	46860 MW	54020 TQ	USBLS	5/15
	Memphis MSA, TN-MS-AR	Y	43510 FQ	48410 MW	55900 TQ	USBLS	5/15
	Nashville-Davidson–Murfreesboro–Franklin MSA, TN	Y	44010 FQ	49480 MW	57570 TQ	USBLS	5/15
	Texas	Y	48850 FQ	56260 MW	63590 TQ	USBLS	5/15
	Austin-Round Rock MSA, TX	Y	50900 FQ	56800 MW	62780 TQ	USBLS	5/15
	Dallas-Plano-Irving PMSA, TX	Y	50980 FQ	58720 MW	68120 TQ	USBLS	5/15
	Fort Worth-Arlington PMSA, TX	Y	52650 FQ	58700 MW	66950 TQ	USBLS	5/15
	Houston-The Woodlands-Sugar Land MSA, TX	Y	51520 FQ	57540 MW	64200 TQ	USBLS	5/15
	San Antonio-New Braunfels MSA, TX	Y	44160 FQ	51820 MW	59160 TQ	USBLS	5/15
	Utah	Y	48230 FQ	57770 MW	68590 TQ	USBLS	5/15
	Ogden-Clearfield MSA, UT	Y	46000 FQ	53800 MW	62240 TQ	USBLS	5/15
	Provo-Orem MSA, UT	Y	49870 FQ	59670 MW	69610 TQ	USBLS	5/15
	Salt Lake City MSA, UT	Y	49190 FQ	59230 MW	70130 TQ	USBLS	5/15
	Vermont	Y	52360 FQ	58920 MW	68330 TQ	USBLS	5/15
	Virginia	Y	49090 FQ	58520 MW	69330 TQ	USBLS	5/15
	Richmond MSA, VA	Y	48400 FQ	56520 MW	64430 TQ	USBLS	5/15
	Virginia Beach-Norfolk-Newport News MSA, VA-NC	Y	48840 FQ	56970 MW	66170 TQ	USBLS	5/15
	Washington	H	28.11 FQ	32.91 MW	37.60 TQ	WABLS	3/16

AE	Average entry wage	AWR	Average wage range	H	Hourly	LR	Low end range	MTC	Median total compensation	TCC	Total cash compensation
AEX	Average experienced wage	B	Biweekly	HI	Highest wage paid	M	Monthly	MW	Median wage paid	TQ	Third quartile wage
ATC	Average total compensation	D	Daily	HR	High end range	MCC	Median cash compensation	MWR	Median wage range	W	Weekly
AW	Average wage paid	FQ	First quartile wage	LO	Lowest wage paid	ME	Median entry wage	S	See annotated source	Y	Yearly

Occupation/Type/Industry	Location	Per	Low	Mid	High	Source	Date
Respiratory Therapist	Seattle-Bellevue-Everett						
	PMSA, WA	H	30.05 FQ	34.67 MW	38.92 TQ	WABLS	3/16
	Tacoma-Lakewood PMSA, WA	H	27.01 FQ	29.93 MW	35.74 TQ	WABLS	3/16
	West Virginia	Y	41780 FQ	47720 MW	56030 TQ	USBLS	5/15
	Huntington-Ashland MSA,						
	WV-KY-OH	Y	42910 FQ	50450 MW	59260 TQ	USBLS	5/15
	Wisconsin	Y	51790 FQ	58670 MW	67250 TQ	USBLS	5/15
	Madison MSA, WI	Y	52340 FQ	59190 MW	68430 TQ	USBLS	5/15
	Milwaukee-Waukesha-West						
	Allis MSA, WI	Y	54290 FQ	61580 MW	70810 TQ	USBLS	5/15
	Wyoming	Y	49360 FQ	56220 MW	62730 TQ	USBLS	5/15
	Cheyenne MSA, WY	Y	52690 FQ	57600 MW	62530 TQ	USBLS	5/15
	Puerto Rico	Y	18040 FQ	21240 MW	27440 TQ	USBLS	5/15
	San Juan-Carolina-Caguas						
	MSA, PR	Y	18180 FQ	21800 MW	28140 TQ	USBLS	5/15
Respiratory Therapy Technician	Alabama	Y	31823 AE	42598 AW	47980 AEX	ALBLS	6/16
	Arizona	Y	40410 FQ	54500 MW	63930 TQ	USBLS	5/15
	Phoenix-Mesa-Scottsdale						
	MSA, AZ	Y	42630 FQ	54660 MW	63040 TQ	USBLS	5/15
	Arkansas	Y	32150 FQ	39690 MW	48110 TQ	USBLS	5/15
	Little Rock-North Little Rock-						
	Conway MSA, AR	Y	28820 FQ	38330 MW	49150 TQ	USBLS	5/15
	California	H	26.76 FQ	32.89 MW	40.04 TQ	CABLS	1/16-3/16
	Anaheim-Santa Ana-Irvine						
	PMSA, CA	H	27.52 FQ	30.76 MW	36.06 TQ	CABLS	1/16-3/16
	Los Angeles-Long Beach-						
	Glendale PMSA, CA	H	30.44 FQ	37.41 MW	44.28 TQ	CABLS	1/16-3/16
	Riverside-San Bernardino-						
	Ontario MSA, CA	H	26.88 FQ	32.24 MW	41.06 TQ	CABLS	1/16-3/16
	Sacramento–Roseville–						
	Arden-Arcade MSA, CA	H	20.51 FQ	26.53 MW	41.27 TQ	CABLS	1/16-3/16
	San Diego-Carlsbad MSA, CA	H	23.34 FQ	34.42 MW	41.35 TQ	CABLS	1/16-3/16
	Colorado	Y	34360 FQ	40620 MW	56650 TQ	USBLS	5/15
	Connecticut	Y		50512 MW		CTBLS	1/16-3/16
	Florida	H	16.68 AE	22.12 MW	24.89 AEX	FLBLS	7/16-9/16
	Fort Lauderdale-Pompano						
	Beach-Deerfield Beach						
	PMSA, FL	H	15.95 AE	21.44 MW	23.65 AEX	FLBLS	7/16-9/16
	Miami-Miami Beach-Kendall						
	PMSA, FL	H	17.44 AE	22.24 MW	25.06 AEX	FLBLS	7/16-9/16
	Orlando-Kissimmee-Sanford						
	MSA, FL	H	20.58 AE	27.40 MW	30.13 AEX	FLBLS	7/16-9/16
	Georgia	Y	29960 FQ	36750 MW	45950 TQ	USBLS	5/15
	Atlanta-Sandy Springs-						
	Roswell MSA, GA	Y	26720 FQ	33350 MW	38740 TQ	USBLS	5/15
	Hawaii	Y	43640 FQ	55810 MW	63560 TQ	USBLS	5/15
	Urban Honolulu MSA, HI	Y	36170 FQ	50350 MW	62740 TQ	USBLS	5/15
	Illinois	Y	35510 FQ	44480 MW	54670 TQ	USBLS	5/15
	Chicago-Naperville-Arlington						
	Heights PMSA, IL	Y	34100 FQ	43890 MW	55780 TQ	USBLS	5/15
	Indiana	Y	38910 FQ	49110 MW	57240 TQ	USBLS	5/15
	Indianapolis-Carmel-Anderson						
	MSA, IN	Y	34750 FQ	39700 MW	55730 TQ	USBLS	5/15
	Iowa	Y	39800 FQ	43670 MW	47440 TQ	USBLS	5/15
	Kansas	Y	31780 FQ	41040 MW	50090 TQ	USBLS	5/15
	Wichita MSA, KS	Y	25830 FQ	36070 MW	49660 TQ	USBLS	5/15
	Kentucky	Y	29360 FQ	36770 MW	46330 TQ	USBLS	5/15
	Louisiana	Y	37690 FQ	45050 MW	52770 TQ	USBLS	5/15
	New Orleans-Metairie MSA,						
	LA	Y	37780 FQ	46670 MW	55000 TQ	USBLS	5/15
	Maine	Y	24830 FQ	48270 MW	62370 TQ	USBLS	5/15
	Maryland	Y	47949 AE	57883 MW	62849 AEX	MDBLS	4/16
	Baltimore-Columbia-Towson						
	MSA, MD	Y	53190 FQ	58560 MW	63940 TQ	USBLS	5/15
	Massachusetts	Y	42690 FQ	53900 MW	66870 TQ	USBLS	5/15
	Boston-Cambridge-Newton						
	NECTA, MA	Y	41470 FQ	51840 MW	70250 TQ	USBLS	5/15
	Michigan	Y	34740 FQ	43140 MW	49710 TQ	USBLS	5/15
	Minnesota	Y	44919 FQ	52671 MW	69082 TQ	MNBLS	1/16-3/16
	Minneapolis-St. Paul-						
	Bloomington MSA, MN-WI	Y	41088 FQ	45080 MW	49082 TQ	MNBLS	1/16-3/16

AE	Average entry wage	AWR	Average wage range	H	Hourly
AEX	Average experienced wage	B	Biweekly	HI	Highest wage paid
ATC	Average total compensation	D	Daily	HR	High end range
AW	Average wage paid	FQ	First quartile wage	LO	Lowest wage paid

LR	Low end range	MTC	Median total compensation
M	Monthly	MW	Median wage paid
MCC	Median cash compensation	MWR	Median wage range
ME	Median entry wage	S	See annotated source

TCC	Total cash compensation
TQ	Third quartile wage
W	Weekly
Y	Yearly

Occupation/Type/Industry	Location	Per	Low	Mid	High	Source	Date
Respiratory Therapy Technician	Mississippi	Y	39470 FQ	48300 MW	57460 TQ	USBLS	5/15
	Missouri	Y	40780 FQ	50850 MW	59530 TQ	USBLS	5/15
	Kansas City MSA, MO-KS	Y	44990 FQ	53820 MW	60910 TQ	USBLS	5/15
	St. Louis MSA, MO-IL	Y	42110 FQ	50970 MW	59580 TQ	USBLS	5/15
	Omaha-Council Bluffs MSA, NE-IA	Y	44760 FQ	50850 MW	65125 TQ	NEBLS	7/16-9/16
	Nevada	Y	54300 FQ	64410 MW	75320 TQ	USBLS	5/15
	Las Vegas-Henderson-Paradise MSA, NV	Y	64240 FQ	75700 MW	88780 TQ	USBLS	5/15
	New Jersey	Y	50780 FQ	62370 MW	72560 TQ	USBLS	5/15
	Newark PMSA, NJ-PA	Y	46270 FQ	59950 MW	72160 TQ	USBLS	5/15
	New Mexico	Y	31730 FQ	40830 MW	55420 TQ	USBLS	5/15
	New York	Y	42980 AE	56650 MW	65430 AEX	NYBLS	1/16-3/16
	Nassau County-Suffolk County PMSA, NY	Y	54420 FQ	65780 MW	73430 TQ	USBLS	5/15
	New York-Jersey City-White Plains PMSA, NY-NJ	Y	51190 FQ	62930 MW	72740 TQ	USBLS	5/15
	North Carolina	Y	34620 FQ	41990 MW	48060 TQ	USBLS	5/15
	Ohio	Y	34810 FQ	44080 MW	55020 TQ	USBLS	5/15
	Cincinnati MSA, OH-KY-IN	Y	32360 FQ	38420 MW	50670 TQ	USBLS	5/15
	Columbus MSA, OH	Y	30520 FQ	38080 MW	54080 TQ	USBLS	5/15
	Oklahoma	Y	32440 FQ	43040 MW	51100 TQ	USBLS	5/15
	Oklahoma City MSA, OK	Y	28200 FQ	42140 MW	50350 TQ	USBLS	5/15
	Pennsylvania	Y	41730 FQ	49300 MW	66450 TQ	USBLS	5/15
	Montgomery County-Bucks County-Chester County PMSA, PA	Y	44960 FQ	66720 MW	73500 TQ	USBLS	5/15
	Philadelphia PMSA, PA	Y	45360 FQ	58070 MW	69520 TQ	USBLS	5/15
	Pittsburgh MSA, PA	Y	39970 FQ	45810 MW	58530 TQ	USBLS	5/15
	Rhode Island	Y	47090 FQ	57560 MW	69410 TQ	USBLS	5/15
	Providence-Warwick MSA, RI-MA	Y	46540 FQ	57860 MW	70340 TQ	USBLS	5/15
	South Carolina	Y	42130 FQ	47950 MW	57500 TQ	USBLS	5/15
	Tennessee	Y	33150 FQ	42040 MW	48380 TQ	USBLS	5/15
	Memphis MSA, TN-MS-AR	Y	39560 FQ	43620 MW	47580 TQ	USBLS	5/15
	Nashville-Davidson–Murfreesboro–Franklin MSA, TN	Y	32110 FQ	39750 MW	55760 TQ	USBLS	5/15
	Texas	Y	41100 FQ	49880 MW	58910 TQ	USBLS	5/15
	Dallas-Plano-Irving PMSA, TX	Y	45050 FQ	54270 MW	62730 TQ	USBLS	5/15
	Fort Worth-Arlington PMSA, TX	Y	42910 FQ	53370 MW	60000 TQ	USBLS	5/15
	Houston-The Woodlands-Sugar Land MSA, TX	Y	43170 FQ	52970 MW	60590 TQ	USBLS	5/15
	San Antonio-New Braunfels MSA, TX	Y	40700 FQ	46490 MW	54080 TQ	USBLS	5/15
	Vermont	Y	42860 FQ	50120 MW	58120 TQ	USBLS	5/15
	Virginia	Y	37980 FQ	44870 MW	50590 TQ	USBLS	5/15
	Washington	H	21.16 FQ	26.44 MW	33.04 TQ	WABLS	3/16
	Seattle-Bellevue-Everett PMSA, WA	H	18.98 FQ	24.54 MW	29.43 TQ	WABLS	3/16
	West Virginia	Y	36180 FQ	45830 MW	56530 TQ	USBLS	5/15
	Wisconsin	Y	36210 FQ	45370 MW	61940 TQ	USBLS	5/15
	Puerto Rico	Y	17190 FQ	19000 MW	22510 TQ	USBLS	5/15
	San Juan-Carolina-Caguas MSA, PR	Y	17500 FQ	19720 MW	23310 TQ	USBLS	5/15
Retail Salesperson	Alabama	Y	17686 AE	26880 AW	31472 AEX	ALBLS	6/16
	Birmingham-Hoover MSA, AL	Y	17748 AE	27801 AW	32827 AEX	ALBLS	6/16
	Alaska	Y	21750 FQ	25340 MW	30480 TQ	USBLS	5/15
	Anchorage MSA, AK	Y	21350 FQ	24800 MW	30140 TQ	USBLS	5/15
	Arizona	Y	18730 FQ	21550 MW	27230 TQ	USBLS	5/15
	Phoenix-Mesa-Scottsdale MSA, AZ	Y	18770 FQ	21680 MW	27650 TQ	USBLS	5/15
	Tucson MSA, AZ	Y	18650 FQ	21280 MW	25390 TQ	USBLS	5/15
	Arkansas	Y	17590 FQ	19540 MW	25260 TQ	USBLS	5/15
	Little Rock-North Little Rock-Conway MSA, AR	Y	17680 FQ	19910 MW	28230 TQ	USBLS	5/15
	California	H	9.58 FQ	11.31 MW	14.73 TQ	CABLS	1/16-3/16
	Anaheim-Santa Ana-Irvine PMSA, CA	H	9.61 FQ	11.15 MW	14.24 TQ	CABLS	1/16-3/16

AE	Average entry wage	AWR	Average wage range	H Hourly
AEX	Average experienced wage	B	Biweekly	HI Highest wage paid
ATC	Average total compensation	D	Daily	HR High end range
AW	Average wage paid	FQ	First quartile wage	LO Lowest wage paid

LR Low end range — MTC Median total compensation — TCC Total cash compensation
M Monthly — MW Median wage paid — TQ Third quartile wage
MCC Median cash compensation — MWR Median wage range — W Weekly
ME Median entry wage — S See annotated source — Y Yearly

Retail Salesperson

Occupation/Type/Industry	Location	Per	Low	Mid	High	Source	Date
Retail Salesperson	Los Angeles-Long Beach-Glendale PMSA, CA	H	9.53 FQ	11.19 MW	14.71 TQ	CABLS	1/16-3/16
	Oakland-Hayward-Berkeley PMSA, CA	H	9.71 FQ	11.67 MW	15.19 TQ	CABLS	1/16-3/16
	Riverside-San Bernardino-Ontario MSA, CA	H	9.45 FQ	10.59 MW	13.82 TQ	CABLS	1/16-3/16
	Sacramento–Roseville–Arden-Arcade MSA, CA	H	9.56 FQ	11.29 MW	14.61 TQ	CABLS	1/16-3/16
	San Diego-Carlsbad MSA, CA	H	9.52 FQ	11.03 MW	14.80 TQ	CABLS	1/16-3/16
	San Francisco-Redwood City-South San Francisco PMSA, CA	H	11.23 FQ	13.53 MW	17.12 TQ	CABLS	1/16-3/16
	Colorado	Y	19230 FQ	22990 MW	30440 TQ	USBLS	5/15
	Denver-Aurora-Lakewood MSA, CO	Y	18950 FQ	22210 MW	29140 TQ	USBLS	5/15
	Connecticut	Y		23270 MW		CTBLS	1/16-3/16
	Bridgeport-Stamford-Norwalk MSA, CT	Y	20150 FQ	23940 MW	34650 TQ	USBLS	5/15
	Hartford-West Hartford-East Hartford MSA, CT	Y	19760 FQ	22890 MW	29700 TQ	USBLS	5/15
	Delaware	Y	18380 FQ	21330 MW	27830 TQ	USBLS	5/15
	Wilmington PMSA, DE-MD-NJ	Y	18280 FQ	20890 MW	27290 TQ	USBLS	5/15
	District of Columbia	Y	21060 FQ	24860 MW	34560 TQ	USBLS	5/15
	Washington-Arlington-Alexandria PMSA, DC-VA-MD-WV	Y	18780 FQ	22100 MW	28150 TQ	USBLS	5/15
	Florida	H	8.92 AE	10.24 MW	14.15 AEX	FLBLS	7/16-9/16
	Fort Lauderdale-Pompano Beach-Deerfield Beach PMSA, FL	H	8.90 AE	10.22 MW	15.09 AEX	FLBLS	7/16-9/16
	Miami-Miami Beach-Kendall PMSA, FL	H	8.92 AE	9.82 MW	12.98 AEX	FLBLS	7/16-9/16
	Orlando-Kissimmee-Sanford MSA, FL	H	8.92 AE	10.07 MW	13.83 AEX	FLBLS	7/16-9/16
	Tampa-St. Petersburg-Clearwater MSA, FL	H	8.90 AE	10.22 MW	14.28 AEX	FLBLS	7/16-9/16
	Georgia	Y	17590 FQ	19770 MW	26070 TQ	USBLS	5/15
	Atlanta-Sandy Springs-Roswell MSA, GA	Y	17640 FQ	19940 MW	26600 TQ	USBLS	5/15
	Augusta-Richmond County MSA, GA-SC	Y	17630 FQ	20070 MW	27820 TQ	USBLS	5/15
	Hawaii	Y	19840 FQ	23830 MW	30020 TQ	USBLS	5/15
	Urban Honolulu MSA, HI	Y	19430 FQ	23360 MW	29170 TQ	USBLS	5/15
	Idaho	Y	18370 FQ	22260 MW	29660 TQ	USBLS	5/15
	Boise City MSA, ID	Y	18320 FQ	21980 MW	29010 TQ	USBLS	5/15
	Illinois	Y	19130 FQ	21990 MW	28570 TQ	USBLS	5/15
	Chicago-Naperville-Arlington Heights PMSA, IL	Y	19310 FQ	22370 MW	29160 TQ	USBLS	5/15
	Lake County-Kenosha County PMSA, IL-WI	Y	18690 FQ	21050 MW	27910 TQ	USBLS	5/15
	Indiana	Y	17670 FQ	19980 MW	26590 TQ	USBLS	5/15
	Gary PMSA, IN	Y	17520 FQ	19740 MW	27300 TQ	USBLS	5/15
	Indianapolis-Carmel-Anderson MSA, IN	Y	17760 FQ	20040 MW	26980 TQ	USBLS	5/15
	Iowa	Y	17910 FQ	21000 MW	28530 TQ	USBLS	5/15
	Des Moines-West Des Moines MSA, IA	Y	18200 FQ	22220 MW	30080 TQ	USBLS	5/15
	Kansas	Y	18030 FQ	21380 MW	28820 TQ	USBLS	5/15
	Wichita MSA, KS	Y	18220 FQ	22000 MW	31610 TQ	USBLS	5/15
	Kentucky	Y	17600 FQ	19860 MW	26100 TQ	USBLS	5/15
	Louisville-Jefferson County MSA, KY-IN	Y	17710 FQ	20010 MW	25160 TQ	USBLS	5/15
	Louisiana	Y	18030 FQ	21280 MW	27360 TQ	USBLS	5/15
	Baton Rouge MSA, LA	Y	17790 FQ	20590 MW	26710 TQ	USBLS	5/15
	New Orleans-Metairie MSA, LA	Y	18850 FQ	22620 MW	29000 TQ	USBLS	5/15
	Maine	Y	18720 FQ	22280 MW	28660 TQ	USBLS	5/15
	Portland-South Portland MSA, ME	Y	19350 FQ	22860 MW	29510 TQ	USBLS	5/15
	Maryland	Y	18083 AE	26222 MW	30291 AEX	MDBLS	4/16

AE	Average entry wage	**AWR**	Average wage range		
AEX	Average experienced wage	**B**	Biweekly		
ATC	Average total compensation	**D**	Daily		
AW	Average wage paid	**FQ**	First quartile wage		

H	Hourly
HI	Highest wage paid
HR	High end range
LO	Lowest wage paid

LR	Low end range
M	Monthly
MCC	Median cash compensation
ME	Median entry wage

MTC	Median total compensation
MW	Median wage paid
MWR	Median wage range
S	See annotated source

TCC	Total cash compensation
TQ	Third quartile wage
W	Weekly
Y	Yearly

Retail Salesperson

Occupation/Type/Industry	Location	Per	Low	Mid	High	Source	Date
Retail Salesperson	Baltimore-Columbia-Towson MSA, MD	Y	18400 FQ	21080 MW	28060 TQ	USBLS	5/15
	Salisbury MSA, MD-DE	Y	18770 FQ	22270 MW	29080 TQ	USBLS	5/15
	Massachusetts	Y	19680 FQ	22890 MW	29160 TQ	USBLS	5/15
	Boston-Cambridge-Newton NECTA, MA	Y	20180 FQ	23430 MW	29490 TQ	USBLS	5/15
	Lowell-Billerica-Chelmsford NECTA, MA-NH	Y	19560 FQ	22830 MW	31130 TQ	USBLS	5/15
	Worcester MSA, MA-CT	Y	19400 FQ	21450 MW	25970 TQ	USBLS	5/15
	Michigan	Y	18550 FQ	20930 MW	27180 TQ	USBLS	5/15
	Detroit-Dearborn-Livonia PMSA, MI	Y	18370 FQ	20080 MW	24790 TQ	USBLS	5/15
	Grand Rapids-Wyoming MSA, MI	Y	19000 FQ	22300 MW	29280 TQ	USBLS	5/15
	Minnesota	Y	18695 FQ	21417 MW	28083 TQ	MNBLS	1/16-3/16
	Minneapolis-St. Paul-Bloomington MSA, MN-WI	Y	18776 FQ	21569 MW	28335 TQ	MNBLS	1/16-3/16
	Mississippi	Y	17830 FQ	20530 MW	27460 TQ	USBLS	5/15
	Jackson MSA, MS	Y	18320 FQ	21930 MW	30000 TQ	USBLS	5/15
	Missouri	Y	18140 FQ	20890 MW	27460 TQ	USBLS	5/15
	Kansas City MSA, MO-KS	Y	18100 FQ	21020 MW	26440 TQ	USBLS	5/15
	St. Louis MSA, MO-IL	Y	18530 FQ	21520 MW	29610 TQ	USBLS	5/15
	Montana	Y	19050 FQ	22460 MW	28860 TQ	USBLS	5/15
	Billings MSA, MT	Y	18950 FQ	22100 MW	27850 TQ	USBLS	5/15
	Nebraska	Y	18545 FQ	21680 MW	29630 TQ	NEBLS	7/16-9/16
	Omaha-Council Bluffs MSA, NE-IA	Y	18690 FQ	22370 MW	31095 TQ	NEBLS	7/16-9/16
	Nevada	Y	18780 FQ	22240 MW	27000 TQ	USBLS	5/15
	Las Vegas-Henderson-Paradise MSA, NV	Y	18730 FQ	22140 MW	26490 TQ	USBLS	5/15
	New Hampshire	H	8.54 AE	11.19 MW	15.35 AEX	NHBLS	6/16
	Manchester NECTA, NH	H	8.47 AE	10.49 MW	14.67 AEX	NHBLS	6/16
	Nashua NECTA, NH-MA	Y	18540 FQ	22240 MW	29020 TQ	USBLS	5/15
	New Jersey	Y	19050 FQ	22300 MW	29200 TQ	USBLS	5/15
	Camden PMSA, NJ	Y	18930 FQ	21930 MW	29120 TQ	USBLS	5/15
	Newark PMSA, NJ-PA	Y	19060 FQ	22430 MW	30090 TQ	USBLS	5/15
	Trenton MSA, NJ	Y	19100 FQ	22260 MW	29080 TQ	USBLS	5/15
	New Mexico	Y	18600 FQ	22100 MW	28020 TQ	USBLS	5/15
	Albuquerque MSA, NM	Y	18610 FQ	22170 MW	28010 TQ	USBLS	5/15
	New York	Y	19140 AE	21530 MW	31590 AEX	NYBLS	1/16-3/16
	Buffalo-Cheektowaga-Niagara Falls MSA, NY	Y	18940 FQ	19990 MW	24730 TQ	USBLS	5/15
	Nassau County-Suffolk County PMSA, NY	Y	19210 FQ	22510 MW	32210 TQ	USBLS	5/15
	New York-Jersey City-White Plains PMSA, NY-NJ	Y	19030 FQ	21430 MW	29290 TQ	USBLS	5/15
	Rochester MSA, NY	Y	19020 FQ	20840 MW	29620 TQ	USBLS	5/15
	North Carolina	Y	17880 FQ	20840 MW	28060 TQ	USBLS	5/15
	Charlotte-Concord-Gastonia MSA, NC-SC	Y	17890 FQ	20930 MW	29150 TQ	USBLS	5/15
	Raleigh MSA, NC	Y	17770 FQ	20440 MW	27350 TQ	USBLS	5/15
	North Dakota	Y	20250 FQ	24970 MW	33840 TQ	USBLS	5/15
	Fargo MSA, ND-MN	Y	18690 FQ	22180 MW	29480 TQ	USBLS	5/15
	Ohio	Y	18460 FQ	20640 MW	27530 TQ	USBLS	5/15
	Cincinnati MSA, OH-KY-IN	Y	18460 FQ	21320 MW	28900 TQ	USBLS	5/15
	Cleveland-Elyria MSA, OH	Y	18500 FQ	20800 MW	27630 TQ	USBLS	5/15
	Columbus MSA, OH	Y	18490 FQ	20740 MW	26500 TQ	USBLS	5/15
	Oklahoma	Y	17890 FQ	20760 MW	27310 TQ	USBLS	5/15
	Oklahoma City MSA, OK	Y	18050 FQ	21200 MW	28570 TQ	USBLS	5/15
	Tulsa MSA, OK	Y	17830 FQ	20630 MW	25060 TQ	USBLS	5/15
	Oregon	H	10.09 FQ	11.54 MW	14.47 TQ	ORBLS	2016
	Portland-Vancouver-Hillsboro MSA, OR-WA	Y	21210 FQ	24220 MW	30470 TQ	USBLS	5/15
	Pennsylvania	Y	18210 FQ	21890 MW	29110 TQ	USBLS	5/15
	Allentown-Bethlehem-Easton MSA, PA-NJ	Y	18240 FQ	21670 MW	29170 TQ	USBLS	5/15
	Harrisburg-Carlisle MSA, PA	Y	18590 FQ	22460 MW	30250 TQ	USBLS	5/15
	Montgomery County-Bucks County-Chester County PMSA, PA	Y	18940 FQ	23120 MW	30260 TQ	USBLS	5/15
	Philadelphia PMSA, PA	Y	18000 FQ	21110 MW	28260 TQ	USBLS	5/15
	Pittsburgh MSA, PA	Y	18010 FQ	21550 MW	29080 TQ	USBLS	5/15

AE	Average entry wage	AWR	Average wage range	H	Hourly	LR Low end range	MTC Median total compensation	TCC Total cash compensation
AEX	Average experienced wage	B	Biweekly	HI	Highest wage paid	M Monthly	MW Median wage paid	TQ Third quartile wage
ATC	Average total compensation	D	Daily	HR	High end range	MCC Median cash compensation	MWR Median wage range	W Weekly
AW	Average wage paid	FQ	First quartile wage	LO	Lowest wage paid	ME Median entry wage	S See annotated source	Y Yearly

Occupation/Type/Industry	Location	Per	Low	Mid	High	Source	Date
Retail Salesperson	Rhode Island	Y	19650 FQ	23210 MW	31450 TQ	USBLS	5/15
	Providence-Warwick MSA, RI-MA	Y	19500 FQ	22390 MW	29760 TQ	USBLS	5/15
	South Carolina	Y	17790 FQ	20480 MW	26770 TQ	USBLS	5/15
	Charleston-North Charleston MSA, SC	Y	17560 FQ	19780 MW	25330 TQ	USBLS	5/15
	Columbia MSA, SC	Y	17910 FQ	20760 MW	26760 TQ	USBLS	5/15
	Greenville-Anderson-Mauldin MSA, SC	Y	18170 FQ	21440 MW	27450 TQ	USBLS	5/15
	South Dakota	Y	19170 FQ	22740 MW	30920 TQ	USBLS	5/15
	Sioux Falls MSA, SD	Y	19350 FQ	23990 MW	35330 TQ	USBLS	5/15
	Tennessee	Y	17990 FQ	21250 MW	28240 TQ	USBLS	5/15
	Knoxville MSA, TN	Y	17600 FQ	20030 MW	27130 TQ	USBLS	5/15
	Memphis MSA, TN-MS-AR	Y	18290 FQ	22410 MW	31810 TQ	USBLS	5/15
	Nashville-Davidson–Murfreesboro–Franklin MSA, TN	Y	18200 FQ	21760 MW	28570 TQ	USBLS	5/15
	Texas	Y	18100 FQ	21570 MW	28930 TQ	USBLS	5/15
	Austin-Round Rock MSA, TX	Y	19150 FQ	23230 MW	30830 TQ	USBLS	5/15
	Dallas-Plano-Irving PMSA, TX	Y	18360 FQ	22340 MW	30100 TQ	USBLS	5/15
	Fort Worth-Arlington PMSA, TX	Y	18050 FQ	21250 MW	28280 TQ	USBLS	5/15
	Houston-The Woodlands-Sugar Land MSA, TX	Y	18300 FQ	22070 MW	29130 TQ	USBLS	5/15
	San Antonio-New Braunfels MSA, TX	Y	18270 FQ	22100 MW	30550 TQ	USBLS	5/15
	Utah	Y	17910 FQ	20930 MW	28340 TQ	USBLS	5/15
	Ogden-Clearfield MSA, UT	Y	17950 FQ	20680 MW	26490 TQ	USBLS	5/15
	Provo-Orem MSA, UT	Y	17760 FQ	20510 MW	25600 TQ	USBLS	5/15
	Salt Lake City MSA, UT	Y	17800 FQ	20560 MW	29480 TQ	USBLS	5/15
	Vermont	Y	20530 FQ	23940 MW	30980 TQ	USBLS	5/15
	Burlington-South Burlington MSA, VT	Y	20460 FQ	23570 MW	30180 TQ	USBLS	5/15
	Virginia	Y	18010 FQ	20960 MW	26870 TQ	USBLS	5/15
	Richmond MSA, VA	Y	17910 FQ	20530 MW	26630 TQ	USBLS	5/15
	Virginia Beach-Norfolk-Newport News MSA, VA-NC	Y	17590 FQ	19700 MW	25010 TQ	USBLS	5/15
	Washington	H	10.58 FQ	12.01 MW	15.18 TQ	WABLS	3/16
	Seattle-Bellevue-Everett PMSA, WA	H	10.69 FQ	12.29 MW	15.55 TQ	WABLS	3/16
	Tacoma-Lakewood PMSA, WA	H	10.61 FQ	11.97 MW	15.84 TQ	WABLS	3/16
	West Virginia	Y	18080 FQ	19590 MW	24370 TQ	USBLS	5/15
	Huntington-Ashland MSA, WV-KY-OH	Y	17740 FQ	19050 MW	23260 TQ	USBLS	5/15
	Wisconsin	Y	17810 FQ	20530 MW	27370 TQ	USBLS	5/15
	Madison MSA, WI	Y	18140 FQ	21600 MW	27990 TQ	USBLS	5/15
	Milwaukee-Waukesha-West Allis MSA, WI	Y	17810 FQ	20540 MW	28000 TQ	USBLS	5/15
	Wyoming	Y	19290 FQ	23380 MW	30900 TQ	USBLS	5/15
	Cheyenne MSA, WY	Y	17750 FQ	20190 MW	26650 TQ	USBLS	5/15
	Puerto Rico	Y	16760 FQ	18010 MW	19260 TQ	USBLS	5/15
	San Juan-Carolina-Caguas MSA, PR	Y	16770 FQ	18030 MW	19300 TQ	USBLS	5/15
	Virgin Islands	Y	17720 FQ	19950 MW	23970 TQ	USBLS	5/15
	Guam	Y	18250 FQ	19390 MW	23280 TQ	USBLS	5/15
Retirement Specialist Municipal Government	Seattle, WA	H	26.29 LO		30.59 HI	CSSS	1/13/16
Revenue Collector Municipal Government	Detroit, MI	M	2442 LO		3150 HI	DETGOV	2016
Revenue-Cycle Executive Healthcare System	United States	Y		302000 MCC		MHLTH01	2015
Revenue Manager Municipal Government	Garden Grove, CA	Y			116492 HI	CACIT	6/28/16
Revenue Protection Coordinator Municipal Government	Glendale, CA	Y			77058 HI	CACIT	6/28/16
Rheumatologist	United States	Y		234000 AW		MED02	2016

AE	Average entry wage	AWR	Average wage range	H	Hourly	LR	Low end range	MTC	Median total compensation	TCC	Total cash compensation
AEX	Average experienced wage	B	Biweekly	HI	Highest wage paid	M	Monthly	MW	Median wage paid	TQ	Third quartile wage
ATC	Average total compensation	D	Daily	HR	High end range	MCC	Median cash compensation	MWR	Median wage range	W	Weekly
AW	Average wage paid	FQ	First quartile wage	LO	Lowest wage paid	ME	Median entry wage	S	See annotated source	Y	Yearly

Occupation/Type/Industry	Location	Per	Low	Mid	High	Source	Date
Ride On Mechanic	United States	Y		47500 AW		AVJOB06	2016
Rigger	Alabama	Y	31589 AE	42481 AW	47932 AEX	ALBLS	6/16
	Alaska	Y	34910 FQ	40710 MW	56570 TQ	USBLS	5/15
	Anchorage MSA, AK	Y	34910 FQ	42390 MW	56820 TQ	USBLS	5/15
	Arizona	Y	26860 FQ	29270 MW	36410 TQ	USBLS	5/15
	Arkansas	Y	22780 FQ	25420 MW	30620 TQ	USBLS	5/15
	California	H	18.45 FQ	25.64 MW	32.26 TQ	CABLS	1/16-3/16
	Los Angeles-Long Beach-Glendale PMSA, CA	H	18.41 FQ	28.28 MW	41.63 TQ	CABLS	1/16-3/16
	San Diego-Carlsbad MSA, CA	H	22.02 FQ	26.14 MW	30.96 TQ	CABLS	1/16-3/16
	San Francisco-Redwood City-South San Francisco PMSA, CA	H	17.62 FQ	20.58 MW	23.42 TQ	CABLS	1/16-3/16
	Colorado	Y	30360 FQ	46190 MW	61910 TQ	USBLS	5/15
	Denver-Aurora-Lakewood MSA, CO	Y	26980 FQ	30750 MW	54580 TQ	USBLS	5/15
	Connecticut	Y		49172 MW		CTBLS	1/16-3/16
	Hartford-West Hartford-East Hartford MSA, CT	Y	40720 FQ	48530 MW	57030 TQ	USBLS	5/15
	District of Columbia	Y	55650 FQ	62010 MW	70140 TQ	USBLS	5/15
	Washington-Arlington-Alexandria PMSA, DC-VA-MD-WV	Y	46250 FQ	62130 MW	74730 TQ	USBLS	5/15
	Florida	H	13.25 AE	18.59 MW	22.87 AEX	FLBLS	7/16-9/16
	Orlando-Kissimmee-Sanford MSA, FL	H	15.99 AE	20.04 MW	23.55 AEX	FLBLS	7/16-9/16
	Tampa-St. Petersburg-Clearwater MSA, FL	H	13.73 AE	16.75 MW	20.87 AEX	FLBLS	7/16-9/16
	Georgia	Y	42290 FQ	50760 MW	54950 TQ	USBLS	5/15
	Atlanta-Sandy Springs-Roswell MSA, GA	Y	44980 FQ	52170 MW	58090 TQ	USBLS	5/15
	Hawaii	Y	57350 FQ	70330 MW	70340 TQ	USBLS	5/15
	Urban Honolulu MSA, HI	Y	57350 FQ	70330 MW	70340 TQ	USBLS	5/15
	Illinois	Y	35010 FQ	39470 MW	64040 TQ	USBLS	5/15
	Chicago-Naperville-Arlington Heights PMSA, IL	Y	39030 FQ	61140 MW	75720 TQ	USBLS	5/15
	Lake County-Kenosha County PMSA, IL-WI	Y	36830 FQ	44170 MW	53020 TQ	USBLS	5/15
	Indiana	Y	32340 FQ	37960 MW	63550 TQ	USBLS	5/15
	Indianapolis-Carmel-Anderson MSA, IN	Y	36130 FQ	47720 MW	67270 TQ	USBLS	5/15
	Kentucky	Y	35260 FQ	53120 MW	59780 TQ	USBLS	5/15
	Louisville-Jefferson County MSA, KY-IN	Y	43810 FQ	54640 MW	60050 TQ	USBLS	5/15
	Louisiana	Y	28710 FQ	34900 MW	47150 TQ	USBLS	5/15
	Baton Rouge MSA, LA	Y	27930 FQ	34630 MW	54100 TQ	USBLS	5/15
	New Orleans-Metairie MSA, LA	Y	28700 FQ	34760 MW	43620 TQ	USBLS	5/15
	Maryland	Y	37760 AE	55724 MW	64705 AEX	MDBLS	4/16
	Baltimore-Columbia-Towson MSA, MD	Y	45630 FQ	54150 MW	60970 TQ	USBLS	5/15
	Massachusetts	Y	40770 FQ	46510 MW	59040 TQ	USBLS	5/15
	Boston-Cambridge-Newton NECTA, MA	Y	40300 FQ	44820 MW	49770 TQ	USBLS	5/15
	Michigan	Y	37220 FQ	51330 MW	61580 TQ	USBLS	5/15
	Detroit-Dearborn-Livonia PMSA, MI	Y	54860 FQ	63920 MW	72670 TQ	USBLS	5/15
	Minnesota	Y	39533 FQ	61990 MW	89887 TQ	MNBLS	1/16-3/16
	Minneapolis-St. Paul-Bloomington MSA, MN-WI	Y	45798 FQ	82355 MW	93628 TQ	MNBLS	1/16-3/16
	Mississippi	Y	27370 FQ	40320 MW	46870 TQ	USBLS	5/15
	Missouri	Y	32380 FQ	38720 MW	62940 TQ	USBLS	5/15
	Kansas City MSA, MO-KS	Y	36150 FQ	45910 MW	64430 TQ	USBLS	5/15
	Montana	Y	41420 FQ	46390 MW	52940 TQ	USBLS	5/15
	Nebraska	Y	24415 FQ	30485 MW	39115 TQ	NEBLS	7/16-9/16
	Nevada	Y	28410 FQ	38980 MW	78800 TQ	USBLS	5/15
	Las Vegas-Henderson-Paradise MSA, NV	Y	33170 FQ	45500 MW	81730 TQ	USBLS	5/15
	New Hampshire	H	12.44 AE	18.63 MW	22.16 AEX	NHBLS	6/16
	New Jersey	Y	50910 FQ	66120 MW	73060 TQ	USBLS	5/15
	New York	Y	41370 AE	56010 MW	67400 AEX	NYBLS	1/16-3/16

AE	Average entry wage	AWR	Average wage range	H	Hourly
AEX	Average experienced wage	B	Biweekly	HI	Highest wage paid
ATC	Average total compensation	D	Daily	HR	High end range
AW	Average wage paid	FQ	First quartile wage	LO	Lowest wage paid

LR	Low end range	MTC	Median total compensation	TCC	Total cash compensation
M	Monthly	MW	Median wage paid	TQ	Third quartile wage
MCC	Median cash compensation	MWR	Median wage range	W	Weekly
ME	Median entry wage	S	See annotated source	Y	Yearly

Occupation/Type/Industry	Location	Per	Low	Mid	High	Source	Date
Rigger	Nassau County-Suffolk County						
	PMSA, NY	Y	42730 FQ	63170 MW	79470 TQ	USBLS	5/15
	New York-Jersey City-White						
	Plains PMSA, NY-NJ	Y	49310 FQ	63850 MW	71590 TQ	USBLS	5/15
	North Carolina	Y	32930 FQ	41890 MW	74390 TQ	USBLS	5/15
	Charlotte-Concord-Gastonia						
	MSA, NC-SC	Y	28730 FQ	35980 MW	60190 TQ	USBLS	5/15
	Ohio	Y	37960 FQ	52870 MW	66600 TQ	USBLS	5/15
	Cincinnati MSA, OH-KY-IN	Y	42820 FQ	57100 MW	72260 TQ	USBLS	5/15
	Oklahoma	Y	36590 FQ	44280 MW	54800 TQ	USBLS	5/15
	Oklahoma City MSA, OK	Y	37810 FQ	44450 MW	50730 TQ	USBLS	5/15
	Tulsa MSA, OK	Y	35590 FQ	42440 MW	48650 TQ	USBLS	5/15
	Oregon	H	20.05 FQ	26.48 MW	42.04 TQ	ORBLS	2016
	Portland-Vancouver-Hillsboro						
	MSA, OR-WA	Y	37240 FQ	45850 MW	61770 TQ	USBLS	5/15
	Pennsylvania	Y	41430 FQ	48570 MW	64900 TQ	USBLS	5/15
	Pittsburgh MSA, PA	Y	29770 FQ	44480 MW	53700 TQ	USBLS	5/15
	Rhode Island	Y	33950 FQ	37570 MW	44780 TQ	USBLS	5/15
	Providence-Warwick MSA, RI-						
	MA	Y	34190 FQ	37980 MW	45330 TQ	USBLS	5/15
	South Carolina	Y	31700 FQ	51140 MW	57580 TQ	USBLS	5/15
	Columbia MSA, SC	Y	51740 FQ	55950 MW	60150 TQ	USBLS	5/15
	Tennessee	Y	27940 FQ	34330 MW	45120 TQ	USBLS	5/15
	Knoxville MSA, TN	Y	27870 FQ	49870 MW	72990 TQ	USBLS	5/15
	Nashville-Davidson–						
	Murfreesboro–Franklin						
	MSA, TN ,	Y	28010 FQ	34620 MW	43590 TQ	USBLS	5/15
	Texas	Y	32290 FQ	42810 MW	56700 TQ	USBLS	5/15
	Dallas-Plano-Irving PMSA, TX	Y	29170 FQ	40170 MW	48820 TQ	USBLS	5/15
	Fort Worth-Arlington PMSA,						
	TX	Y	35520 FQ	42840 MW	61060 TQ	USBLS	5/15
	Houston-The Woodlands-						
	Sugar Land MSA, TX	Y	32960 FQ	44220 MW	57430 TQ	USBLS	5/15
	San Antonio-New Braunfels						
	MSA, TX	Y	28970 FQ	36770 MW	45520 TQ	USBLS	5/15
	Utah	Y	33780 FQ	43840 MW	56240 TQ	USBLS	5/15
	Salt Lake City MSA, UT	Y	33500 FQ	45590 MW	57650 TQ	USBLS	5/15
	Virginia	Y	40100 FQ	48010 MW	52740 TQ	USBLS	5/15
	Richmond MSA, VA	Y	44570 FQ	51970 MW	61010 TQ	USBLS	5/15
	Virginia Beach-Norfolk-						
	Newport News MSA, VA-NC	Y	40950 FQ	48020 MW	52710 TQ	USBLS	5/15
	Washington	H	19.63 FQ	26.18 MW	31.10 TQ	WABLS	3/16
	Seattle-Bellevue-Everett						
	PMSA, WA	H	25.14 FQ	27.45 MW	29.58 TQ	WABLS	3/16
	Wisconsin	Y	28550 FQ	34410 MW	42640 TQ	USBLS	5/15
	Wyoming	Y	33690 FQ	36780 MW	40240 TQ	USBLS	5/15
Risk Analyst							
Municipal Government	Detroit, MI	M	4333 LO		4658 HI	DETGOV	2016
Risk Management Analyst							
Municipal Government	Orange, CA	Y			79180 HI	CACIT	6/28/16
Municipal Government	Seattle, WA	H	33.00 LO		38.44 HI	CSSS	1/13/16
Risk Manager							
City Attorney's Office	Alameda, CA	Y			136513 HI	CACIT	6/28/16
City Attorney's Office	Compton, CA	Y			115946 HI	CACIT	8/12/16
Riverboat Operator							
United States Department of Interior,							
Bureau of Reclamation	Yuma, AZ	Y	52613 LO		56683 HI	APP01	2015
Roadie							
Club-Level Touring Band	United States	W		700-1000 AWR		BBRD01	2014
Roads and Bridges							
Superintendent							
Municipal Government	Loganville, GA	Y	30680 LO		52811 HI	GACTY02	2016
Municipal Government	Marietta, GA	Y	46574 LO		70481 HI	GACTY02	2016
Municipal Government	Soperton, GA	Y			39150 HI	GACTY02	2016
Robotics Engineer	United States	Y	47640 LO		121970 HI	BUZZ02	2015

AE	Average entry wage	AWR	Average wage range	H	Hourly	LR	Low end range	MTC	Median total compensation	TCC	Total cash compensation
AEX	Average experienced wage	B	Biweekly	HI	Highest wage paid	M	Monthly	MW	Median wage paid	TQ	Third quartile wage
ATC	Average total compensation	D	Daily	HR	High end range	MCC	Median cash compensation	MWR	Median wage range	W	Weekly
AW	Average wage paid	FQ	First quartile wage	LO	Lowest wage paid	ME	Median entry wage	S	See annotated source	Y	Yearly

Occupation/Type/Industry	Location	Per	Low	Mid	High	Source	Date
Rock Splitter							
Quarry	Arizona	Y	27920 FQ	33710 MW	37350 TQ	USBLS	5/15
Quarry	Arkansas	Y	29410 FQ	34570 MW	38900 TQ	USBLS	5/15
Quarry	California	H	11.93 FQ	15.71 MW	19.89 TQ	CABLS	1/16-3/16
Quarry	Colorado	Y	33820 FQ	44080 MW	54430 TQ	USBLS	5/15
Quarry	Georgia	Y	29790 FQ	34250 MW	38350 TQ	USBLS	5/15
Quarry	Illinois	Y	27060 FQ	30590 MW	41660 TQ	USBLS	5/15
Quarry	Indiana	Y	27320 FQ	34160 MW	40670 TQ	USBLS	5/15
Quarry	Iowa	Y	27900 FQ	31810 MW	38640 TQ	USBLS	5/15
Quarry	Kansas	Y	26590 FQ	32650 MW	39080 TQ	USBLS	5/15
Quarry	Kentucky	Y	26060 FQ	30030 MW	36590 TQ	USBLS	5/15
Quarry	Maryland	Y	24792 AE	33413 MW	37723 AEX	MDBLS	4/16
Quarry	Massachusetts	Y	42050 FQ	46100 MW	50060 TQ	USBLS	5/15
Quarry	Minnesota	Y	33631 FQ	37878 MW	45315 TQ	MNBLS	1/16-3/16
Quarry	Missouri	Y	24090 FQ	30110 MW	36810 TQ	USBLS	5/15
Quarry	Montana	Y	26150 FQ	29220 MW	35620 TQ	USBLS	5/15
Quarry	Nebraska	Y	18725 FQ	22260 MW	43220 TQ	NEBLS	7/16-9/16
Quarry	New York	Y	26590 AE	34760 MW	49140 AEX	NYBLS	1/16-3/16
Quarry	North Carolina	Y	27610 FQ	34640 MW	41510 TQ	USBLS	5/15
Quarry	Ohio	Y	26550 FQ	36170 MW	45650 TQ	USBLS	5/15
Quarry	Oklahoma	Y	25520 FQ	28210 MW	32210 TQ	USBLS	5/15
Quarry	Pennsylvania	Y	28350 FQ	34760 MW	41610 TQ	USBLS	5/15
Quarry	Tennessee	Y	30890 FQ	34700 MW	38500 TQ	USBLS	5/15
Quarry	Texas	Y	17550 FQ	19870 MW	29500 TQ	USBLS	5/15
Quarry	Utah	Y	34150 FQ	37930 MW	45830 TQ	USBLS	5/15
Quarry	Vermont	Y	36290 FQ	44200 MW	54510 TQ	USBLS	5/15
Quarry	Virginia	Y	33780 FQ	38460 MW	44280 TQ	USBLS	5/15
Quarry	Washington	H	18.74 FQ	22.18 MW	26.62 TQ	WABLS	3/16
Quarry	West Virginia	Y	27880 FQ	32900 MW	41950 TQ	USBLS	5/15
Quarry	Wisconsin	Y	27290 FQ	31330 MW	37240 TQ	USBLS	5/15
Rolling Machine Setter, Operator, and Tender							
Metals and Plastics	Alabama	Y	26014 AE	49056 AW	60582 AEX	ALBLS	6/16
Metals and Plastics	Birmingham-Hoover MSA, AL	Y	22590 AE	31906 AW	36574 AEX	ALBLS	6/16
Metals and Plastics	Arizona	Y	29500 FQ	35610 MW	42770 TQ	USBLS	5/15
Metals and Plastics	Phoenix-Mesa-Scottsdale MSA, AZ	Y	28420 FQ	34360 MW	41450 TQ	USBLS	5/15
Metals and Plastics	Arkansas	Y	29130 FQ	38400 MW	47700 TQ	USBLS	5/15
Metals and Plastics	California	H	12.82 FQ	14.84 MW	19.29 TQ	CABLS	1/16-3/16
Metals and Plastics	Anaheim-Santa Ana-Irvine PMSA, CA	H	11.62 FQ	13.58 MW	16.08 TQ	CABLS	1/16-3/16
Metals and Plastics	Los Angeles-Long Beach-Glendale PMSA, CA	H	12.22 FQ	14.36 MW	17.72 TQ	CABLS	1/16-3/16
Metals and Plastics	Oakland-Hayward-Berkeley PMSA, CA	H	14.73 FQ	18.39 MW	25.25 TQ	CABLS	1/16-3/16
Metals and Plastics	Riverside-San Bernardino-Ontario MSA, CA	H	13.24 FQ	14.87 MW	19.71 TQ	CABLS	1/16-3/16
Metals and Plastics	San Diego-Carlsbad MSA, CA	H	18.48 FQ	23.30 MW	27.36 TQ	CABLS	1/16-3/16
Metals and Plastics	Colorado	Y	28440 FQ	39590 MW	45970 TQ	USBLS	5/15
Metals and Plastics	Denver-Aurora-Lakewood MSA, CO	Y	26330 FQ	28220 MW	30110 TQ	USBLS	5/15
Metals and Plastics	Connecticut	Y		40473 MW		CTBLS	1/16-3/16
Metals and Plastics	Bridgeport-Stamford-Norwalk MSA, CT	Y	35200 FQ	38730 MW	44930 TQ	USBLS	5/15
Metals and Plastics	Hartford-West Hartford-East Hartford MSA, CT	Y	31640 FQ	38310 MW	48130 TQ	USBLS	5/15
Metals and Plastics	Delaware	Y	32120 FQ	38950 MW	66160 TQ	USBLS	5/15
Metals and Plastics	Florida	H	13.08 AE	18.76 MW	21.21 AEX	FLBLS	7/16-9/16
Metals and Plastics	Miami-Miami Beach-Kendall PMSA, FL	H	17.59 AE	22.06 MW	22.38 AEX	FLBLS	7/16-9/16
Metals and Plastics	Tampa-St. Petersburg-Clearwater MSA, FL	H	17.58 AE	20.55 MW	23.83 AEX	FLBLS	7/16-9/16
Metals and Plastics	Georgia	Y	26400 FQ	31580 MW	38900 TQ	USBLS	5/15
Metals and Plastics	Atlanta-Sandy Springs-Roswell MSA, GA	Y	26150 FQ	30600 MW	38300 TQ	USBLS	5/15
Metals and Plastics	Idaho	Y	25340 FQ	30410 MW	38630 TQ	USBLS	5/15
Metals and Plastics	Illinois	Y	28530 FQ	40710 MW	45760 TQ	USBLS	5/15
Metals and Plastics	Chicago-Naperville-Arlington Heights PMSA, IL	Y	26670 FQ	31870 MW	41680 TQ	USBLS	5/15
Metals and Plastics	Lake County-Kenosha County PMSA, IL-WI	Y	33150 FQ	35530 MW	37920 TQ	USBLS	5/15

AE Average entry wage	**AWR** Average wage range	**H** Hourly	**LR** Low end range	**MTC** Median total compensation	**TCC** Total cash compensation
AEX Average experienced wage	**B** Biweekly	**HI** Highest wage paid	**M** Monthly	**MW** Median wage paid	**TQ** Third quartile wage
ATC Average total compensation	**D** Daily	**HR** High end range	**MCC** Median cash compensation	**MWR** Median wage range	**W** Weekly
AW Average wage paid	**FQ** First quartile wage	**LO** Lowest wage paid	**ME** Median entry wage	**S** See annotated source	**Y** Yearly

Rolling Machine Setter, Operator, and Tender

Occupation/Type/Industry	Location	Per	Low	Mid	High	Source	Date
Metals and Plastics	Indiana	Y	42130 FQ	52760 MW	61140 TQ	USBLS	5/15
Metals and Plastics	Gary PMSA, IN	Y	49740 FQ	56990 MW	63660 TQ	USBLS	5/15
Metals and Plastics	Indianapolis-Carmel-Anderson MSA, IN	Y	40750 FQ	49650 MW	59080 TQ	USBLS	5/15
Metals and Plastics	Iowa	Y	32680 FQ	40700 MW	47400 TQ	USBLS	5/15
Metals and Plastics	Kansas	Y	28980 FQ	36180 MW	42650 TQ	USBLS	5/15
Metals and Plastics	Kentucky	Y	31250 FQ	37070 MW	43970 TQ	USBLS	5/15
Metals and Plastics	Louisville-Jefferson County MSA, KY-IN	Y	31620 FQ	36380 MW	42410 TQ	USBLS	5/15
Metals and Plastics	Louisiana	Y	27510 FQ	34850 MW	43540 TQ	USBLS	5/15
Metals and Plastics	Maryland	Y	24325 AE	38122 MW	45020 AEX	MDBLS	4/16
Metals and Plastics	Baltimore-Columbia-Towson MSA, MD	Y	30910 FQ	38270 MW	53970 TQ	USBLS	5/15
Metals and Plastics	Massachusetts	Y	36360 FQ	45040 MW	53370 TQ	USBLS	5/15
Metals and Plastics	Boston-Cambridge-Newton NECTA, MA	Y	33190 FQ	44190 MW	55830 TQ	USBLS	5/15
Metals and Plastics	Worcester MSA, MA-CT	Y	26700 FQ	36610 MW	47470 TQ	USBLS	5/15
Metals and Plastics	Michigan	Y	31260 FQ	42840 MW	50160 TQ	USBLS	5/15
Metals and Plastics	Detroit-Dearborn-Livonia PMSA, MI	Y	41320 FQ	46520 MW	53500 TQ	USBLS	5/15
Metals and Plastics	Grand Rapids-Wyoming MSA, MI	Y	25010 FQ	27850 MW	30700 TQ	USBLS	5/15
Metals and Plastics	Minnesota	Y	26800 FQ	33006 MW	43485 TQ	MNBLS	1/16-3/16
Metals and Plastics	Minneapolis-St. Paul-Bloomington MSA, MN-WI	Y	24400 FQ	31153 MW	42300 TQ	MNBLS	1/16-3/16
Metals and Plastics	Mississippi	Y	32890 FQ	40730 MW	45700 TQ	USBLS	5/15
Metals and Plastics	Missouri	Y	28550 FQ	36400 MW	45330 TQ	USBLS	5/15
Metals and Plastics	Kansas City MSA, MO-KS	Y	33100 FQ	40850 MW	47350 TQ	USBLS	5/15
Metals and Plastics	Nebraska	Y	27945 FQ	31055 MW	36920 TQ	NEBLS	7/16-9/16
Metals and Plastics	Omaha-Council Bluffs MSA, NE-IA	Y	35215 FQ	41600 MW	45955 TQ	NEBLS	7/16-9/16
Metals and Plastics	New Hampshire	H	14.74 AE	18.00 MW	19.88 AEX	NHBLS	6/16
Metals and Plastics	New Jersey	Y	26630 FQ	30810 MW	41230 TQ	USBLS	5/15
Metals and Plastics	Newark PMSA, NJ-PA	Y	26620 FQ	29250 MW	34570 TQ	USBLS	5/15
Metals and Plastics	New York	Y	30600 AE	41430 MW	45870 AEX	NYBLS	1/16-3/16
Metals and Plastics	Buffalo-Cheektowaga-Niagara Falls MSA, NY	Y	38660 FQ	46600 MW	54600 TQ	USBLS	5/15
Metals and Plastics	New York-Jersey City-White Plains PMSA, NY-NJ	Y	26670 FQ	36270 MW	47940 TQ	USBLS	5/15
Metals and Plastics	Rochester MSA, NY	Y	30300 FQ	37750 MW	44950 TQ	USBLS	5/15
Metals and Plastics	North Carolina	Y	29030 FQ	35700 MW	44190 TQ	USBLS	5/15
Metals and Plastics	Charlotte-Concord-Gastonia MSA, NC-SC	Y	34140 FQ	41060 MW	48140 TQ	USBLS	5/15
Metals and Plastics	Ohio	Y	33170 FQ	41540 MW	48760 TQ	USBLS	5/15
Metals and Plastics	Cincinnati MSA, OH-KY-IN	Y	40250 FQ	47120 MW	54800 TQ	USBLS	5/15
Metals and Plastics	Cleveland-Elyria MSA, OH	Y	29490 FQ	35770 MW	42590 TQ	USBLS	5/15
Metals and Plastics	Columbus MSA, OH	Y	38500 FQ	51650 MW	57330 TQ	USBLS	5/15
Metals and Plastics	Oklahoma	Y	26740 FQ	34410 MW	39970 TQ	USBLS	5/15
Metals and Plastics	Oklahoma City MSA, OK	Y	19240 FQ	24450 MW	31230 TQ	USBLS	5/15
Metals and Plastics	Tulsa MSA, OK	Y	32480 FQ	36990 MW	42900 TQ	USBLS	5/15
Metals and Plastics	Oregon	H	15.55 FQ	19.36 MW	26.09 TQ	ORBLS	2016
Metals and Plastics	Portland-Vancouver-Hillsboro MSA, OR-WA	Y	36060 FQ	43950 MW	53060 TQ	USBLS	5/15
Metals and Plastics	Pennsylvania	Y	34050 FQ	42390 MW	51110 TQ	USBLS	5/15
Metals and Plastics	Allentown-Bethlehem-Easton MSA, PA-NJ	Y	32040 FQ	40960 MW	46010 TQ	USBLS	5/15
Metals and Plastics	Montgomery County-Bucks County-Chester County PMSA, PA	Y	37780 FQ	48750 MW	58040 TQ	USBLS	5/15
Metals and Plastics	Philadelphia PMSA, PA	Y	38500 FQ	45000 MW	51420 TQ	USBLS	5/15
Metals and Plastics	Pittsburgh MSA, PA	Y	35180 FQ	42760 MW	53850 TQ	USBLS	5/15
Metals and Plastics	Rhode Island	Y	36480 FQ	42180 MW	47320 TQ	USBLS	5/15
Metals and Plastics	Providence-Warwick MSA, RI-MA	Y	38260 FQ	43920 MW	48700 TQ	USBLS	5/15
Metals and Plastics	South Carolina	Y	41350 FQ	47050 MW	55290 TQ	USBLS	5/15
Metals and Plastics	Columbia MSA, SC	Y	35510 FQ	41410 MW	46780 TQ	USBLS	5/15
Metals and Plastics	Greenville-Anderson-Mauldin MSA, SC	Y	19760 FQ	52550 MW	58850 TQ	USBLS	5/15
Metals and Plastics	South Dakota	Y	27550 FQ	35210 MW	43290 TQ	USBLS	5/15
Metals and Plastics	Tennessee	Y	29090 FQ	37160 MW	45670 TQ	USBLS	5/15

AE	Average entry wage	AWR	Average wage range	H	Hourly	LR	Low end range	MTC	Median total compensation	TCC	Total cash compensation
AEX	Average experienced wage	B	Biweekly	HI	Highest wage paid	M	Monthly	MW	Median wage paid	TQ	Third quartile wage
ATC	Average total compensation	D	Daily	HR	High end range	MCC	Median cash compensation	MWR	Median wage range	W	Weekly
AW	Average wage paid	FQ	First quartile wage	LO	Lowest wage paid	ME	Median entry wage	S	See annotated source	Y	Yearly

Occupation/Type/Industry	Location	Per	Low	Mid	High	Source	Date
Rolling Machine Setter, Operator, and Tender							
Metals and Plastics	Knoxville MSA, TN	Y	40620 FQ	44990 MW	49370 TQ	USBLS	5/15
Metals and Plastics	Memphis MSA, TN-MS-AR	Y	27800 FQ	34480 MW	42830 TQ	USBLS	5/15
Metals and Plastics	Nashville-Davidson–Murfreesboro–Franklin MSA, TN	Y	28150 FQ	36130 MW	51420 TQ	USBLS	5/15
Metals and Plastics	Texas	Y	27260 FQ	32000 MW	40420 TQ	USBLS	5/15
Metals and Plastics	Dallas-Plano-Irving PMSA, TX	Y	28900 FQ	33910 MW	39950 TQ	USBLS	5/15
Metals and Plastics	Fort Worth-Arlington PMSA, TX	Y	27700 FQ	31240 MW	37500 TQ	USBLS	5/15
Metals and Plastics	Houston-The Woodlands-Sugar Land MSA, TX	Y	27980 FQ	33660 MW	40940 TQ	USBLS	5/15
Metals and Plastics	San Antonio-New Braunfels MSA, TX	Y	25840 FQ	28540 MW	31240 TQ	USBLS	5/15
Metals and Plastics	Utah	Y	27690 FQ	31720 MW	37840 TQ	USBLS	5/15
Metals and Plastics	Ogden-Clearfield MSA, UT	Y	25700 FQ	30110 MW	39400 TQ	USBLS	5/15
Metals and Plastics	Salt Lake City MSA, UT	Y	28940 FQ	33140 MW	37410 TQ	USBLS	5/15
Metals and Plastics	Virginia	Y	33560 FQ	38120 MW	45750 TQ	USBLS	5/15
Metals and Plastics	Richmond MSA, VA	Y	37100 FQ	48590 MW	57890 TQ	USBLS	5/15
Metals and Plastics	Washington	H	15.53 FQ	18.78 MW	22.86 TQ	WABLS	3/16
Metals and Plastics	Seattle-Bellevue-Everett PMSA, WA	H	15.45 FQ	18.28 MW	22.61 TQ	WABLS	3/16
Metals and Plastics	Tacoma-Lakewood PMSA, WA	H	17.09 FQ	19.67 MW	24.54 TQ	WABLS	3/16
Metals and Plastics	West Virginia	Y	43240 FQ	47450 MW	53320 TQ	USBLS	5/15
Metals and Plastics	Huntington-Ashland MSA, WV-KY-OH	Y	40590 FQ	45360 MW	50120 TQ	USBLS	5/15
Metals and Plastics	Wisconsin	Y	31820 FQ	38250 MW	47920 TQ	USBLS	5/15
Metals and Plastics	Milwaukee-Waukesha-West Allis MSA, WI	Y	32830 FQ	38290 MW	45500 TQ	USBLS	5/15
Metals and Plastics	Puerto Rico	Y	19570 FQ	22460 MW	25340 TQ	USBLS	5/15
Roof Bolter							
Mining	Colorado	Y	55300 FQ	61130 MW	70100 TQ	USBLS	5/15
Mining	Illinois	Y	45490 FQ	53930 MW	61400 TQ	USBLS	5/15
Mining	Indiana	Y	43840 FQ	47640 MW	51550 TQ	USBLS	5/15
Mining	Kentucky	Y	44960 FQ	50680 MW	57600 TQ	USBLS	5/15
Mining	Pennsylvania	Y	47660 FQ	54730 MW	61420 TQ	USBLS	5/15
Mining	Utah	Y	54250 FQ	57690 MW	61140 TQ	USBLS	5/15
Mining	West Virginia	Y	49400 FQ	55000 MW	60720 TQ	USBLS	5/15
Mining	Wyoming	Y	71120 FQ	84900 MW	94920 TQ	USBLS	5/15
Roofer							
	Alabama	Y	25172 AE	31581 AW	34790 AEX	ALBLS	6/16
	Birmingham-Hoover MSA, AL	Y	25573 AE	32291 AW	35654 AEX	ALBLS	6/16
	Alaska	Y	46630 FQ	56860 MW	67690 TQ	USBLS	5/15
	Anchorage MSA, AK	Y	43250 FQ	54480 MW	63640 TQ	USBLS	5/15
	Arizona	Y	29840 FQ	35070 MW	39740 TQ	USBLS	5/15
	Phoenix-Mesa-Scottsdale MSA, AZ	Y	29280 FQ	34850 MW	39530 TQ	USBLS	5/15
	Tucson MSA, AZ	Y	33380 FQ	36370 MW	39420 TQ	USBLS	5/15
	Arkansas	Y	25900 FQ	30650 MW	38450 TQ	USBLS	5/15
	Little Rock-North Little Rock-Conway MSA, AR	Y	27690 FQ	32740 MW	42170 TQ	USBLS	5/15
	California	H	18.93 FQ	24.37 MW	28.81 TQ	CABLS	1/16-3/16
	Anaheim-Santa Ana-Irvine PMSA, CA	H	19.40 FQ	22.43 MW	27.52 TQ	CABLS	1/16-3/16
	Los Angeles-Long Beach-Glendale PMSA, CA	H	18.08 FQ	25.59 MW	31.38 TQ	CABLS	1/16-3/16
	Oakland-Hayward-Berkeley PMSA, CA	H	19.50 FQ	23.72 MW	27.45 TQ	CABLS	1/16-3/16
	Riverside-San Bernardino-Ontario MSA, CA	H	18.38 FQ	24.90 MW	28.18 TQ	CABLS	1/16-3/16
	Sacramento–Roseville–Arden-Arcade MSA, CA	H	20.79 FQ	24.25 MW	28.52 TQ	CABLS	1/16-3/16
	San Diego-Carlsbad MSA, CA	H	16.42 FQ	18.76 MW	26.78 TQ	CABLS	1/16-3/16
	San Francisco-Redwood City-South San Francisco PMSA, CA	H	27.47 FQ	32.93 MW	37.43 TQ	CABLS	1/16-3/16
	Colorado	Y	29420 FQ	36240 MW	46060 TQ	USBLS	5/15
	Denver-Aurora-Lakewood MSA, CO	Y	29230 FQ	35560 MW	45070 TQ	USBLS	5/15
	Connecticut	Y		48319 MW		CTBLS	1/16-3/16

AE	Average entry wage	**AWR**	Average wage range	**H**	Hourly	**LR**	Low end range	
AEX	Average experienced wage	**B**	Biweekly	**HI**	Highest wage paid	**M**	Monthly	
ATC	Average total compensation	**D**	Daily	**HR**	High end range	**MCC**	Median cash compensation	
AW	Average wage paid	**FQ**	First quartile wage	**LO**	Lowest wage paid	**ME**	Median entry wage	

MTC	Median total compensation	**TCC**	Total cash compensation	
MW	Median wage paid	**TQ**	Third quartile wage	
MWR	Median wage range	**W**	Weekly	
S	See annotated source	**Y**	Yearly	

Occupation/Type/Industry	Location	Per	Low	Mid	High	Source	Date
Roofer	Bridgeport-Stamford-Norwalk MSA, CT	Y	33030 FQ	36120 MW	39220 TQ	USBLS	5/15
	Hartford-West Hartford-East Hartford MSA, CT	Y	41490 FQ	49200 MW	56680 TQ	USBLS	5/15
	Delaware	Y	28450 FQ	36330 MW	48590 TQ	USBLS	5/15
	Wilmington PMSA, DE-MD-NJ	Y	32700 FQ	39870 MW	51220 TQ	USBLS	5/15
	District of Columbia	Y	31690 FQ	37670 MW	62870 TQ	USBLS	5/15
	Washington-Arlington-Alexandria PMSA, DC-VA-MD-WV	Y	38890 FQ	48650 MW	62420 TQ	USBLS	5/15
	Florida	H	11.80 AE	15.45 MW	17.77 AEX	FLBLS	7/16-9/16
	Fort Lauderdale-Pompano Beach-Deerfield Beach PMSA, FL	H	13.34 AE	17.49 MW	19.50 AEX	FLBLS	7/16-9/16
	Miami-Miami Beach-Kendall PMSA, FL	H	9.39 AE	12.79 MW	14.97 AEX	FLBLS	7/16-9/16
	Orlando-Kissimmee-Sanford MSA, FL	H	10.93 AE	14.77 MW	17.65 AEX	FLBLS	7/16-9/16
	Tampa-St. Petersburg-Clearwater MSA, FL	H	12.63 AE	16.25 MW	18.69 AEX	FLBLS	7/16-9/16
	Georgia	Y	27110 FQ	30660 MW	37410 TQ	USBLS	5/15
	Atlanta-Sandy Springs-Roswell MSA, GA	Y	27640 FQ	30460 MW	37010 TQ	USBLS	5/15
	Augusta-Richmond County MSA, GA-SC	Y	26280 FQ	28790 MW	31230 TQ	USBLS	5/15
	Hawaii	Y	36520 FQ	48060 MW	61280 TQ	USBLS	5/15
	Urban Honolulu MSA, HI	Y	36540 FQ	48360 MW	62580 TQ	USBLS	5/15
	Idaho	Y	27750 FQ	34220 MW	40380 TQ	USBLS	5/15
	Boise City MSA, ID	Y	26370 FQ	31810 MW	37890 TQ	USBLS	5/15
	Illinois	Y	32760 FQ	41890 MW	55760 TQ	USBLS	5/15
	Chicago-Naperville-Arlington Heights PMSA, IL	Y	33710 FQ	42730 MW	53380 TQ	USBLS	5/15
	Lake County-Kenosha County PMSA, IL-WI	Y	33620 FQ	42910 MW	56280 TQ	USBLS	5/15
	Indiana	Y	28770 FQ	35330 MW	44720 TQ	USBLS	5/15
	Gary PMSA, IN	Y	26960 FQ	33930 MW	46040 TQ	USBLS	5/15
	Indianapolis-Carmel-Anderson MSA, IN	Y	32250 FQ	38540 MW	46800 TQ	USBLS	5/15
	Iowa	Y	26930 FQ	33370 MW	41860 TQ	USBLS	5/15
	Des Moines-West Des Moines MSA, IA	Y	34210 FQ	42740 MW	50140 TQ	USBLS	5/15
	Kansas	Y	26970 FQ	33520 MW	51130 TQ	USBLS	5/15
	Wichita MSA, KS	Y	25000 FQ	28960 MW	34710 TQ	USBLS	5/15
	Kentucky	Y	27720 FQ	33100 MW	37400 TQ	USBLS	5/15
	Louisville-Jefferson County MSA, KY-IN	Y	30010 FQ	34120 MW	37480 TQ	USBLS	5/15
	Louisiana	Y	29400 FQ	36100 MW	43760 TQ	USBLS	5/15
	Baton Rouge MSA, LA	Y	32090 FQ	38800 MW	45030 TQ	USBLS	5/15
	New Orleans-Metairie MSA, LA	Y	31670 FQ	36680 MW	43320 TQ	USBLS	5/15
	Maine	Y	29770 FQ	35700 MW	42610 TQ	USBLS	5/15
	Portland-South Portland MSA, ME	Y	34190 FQ	40860 MW	46390 TQ	USBLS	5/15
	Maryland	Y	29255 AE	42165 MW	48620 AEX	MDBLS	4/16
	Baltimore-Columbia-Towson MSA, MD	Y	32940 FQ	38520 MW	47110 TQ	USBLS	5/15
	Massachusetts	Y	38160 FQ	46340 MW	56020 TQ	USBLS	5/15
	Boston-Cambridge-Newton NECTA, MA	Y	43540 FQ	52520 MW	60020 TQ	USBLS	5/15
	Worcester MSA, MA-CT	Y	34580 FQ	45910 MW	64000 TQ	USBLS	5/15
	Michigan	Y	30550 FQ	40240 MW	56560 TQ	USBLS	5/15
	Detroit-Dearborn-Livonia PMSA, MI	Y	29880 FQ	41010 MW	53610 TQ	USBLS	5/15
	Grand Rapids-Wyoming MSA, MI	Y	27760 FQ	34760 MW	40390 TQ	USBLS	5/15
	Minnesota	Y	39836 FQ	60238 MW	72225 TQ	MNBLS	1/16-3/16
	Minneapolis-St. Paul-Bloomington MSA, MN-WI	Y	55990 FQ	67846 MW	75152 TQ	MNBLS	1/16-3/16
	Mississippi	Y	22730 FQ	28410 MW	34280 TQ	USBLS	5/15
	Jackson MSA, MS	Y	28560 FQ	32370 MW	36200 TQ	USBLS	5/15
	Missouri	Y	28680 FQ	35980 MW	49670 TQ	USBLS	5/15

Roofer

Occupation/Type/Industry	Location	Per	Low	Mid	High	Source	Date
Roofer	Kansas City MSA, MO-KS	Y	35800 FQ	51970 MW	68030 TQ	USBLS	5/15
	St. Louis MSA, MO-IL	Y	33240 FQ	39700 MW	58260 TQ	USBLS	5/15
	Montana	Y	30660 FQ	35300 MW	39610 TQ	USBLS	5/15
	Billings MSA, MT	Y	28260 FQ	32060 MW	37430 TQ	USBLS	5/15
	Nebraska	Y	26115 FQ	30260 MW	36445 TQ	NEBLS	7/16-9/16
	Omaha-Council Bluffs MSA, NE-IA	Y	27545 FQ	31880 MW	36790 TQ	NEBLS	7/16-9/16
	Nevada	Y	31440 FQ	36510 MW	44170 TQ	USBLS	5/15
	Las Vegas-Henderson-Paradise MSA, NV	Y	31060 FQ	36200 MW	44950 TQ	USBLS	5/15
	New Hampshire	H	14.27 AE	18.35 MW	25.04 AEX	NHBLS	6/16
	New Jersey	Y	40520 FQ	54570 MW	72360 TQ	USBLS	5/15
	Camden PMSA, NJ	Y	48650 FQ	67670 MW	81500 TQ	USBLS	5/15
	Newark PMSA, NJ-PA	Y	40410 FQ	47200 MW	68550 TQ	USBLS	5/15
	Trenton MSA, NJ	Y	33410 FQ	40120 MW	71840 TQ	USBLS	5/15
	New Mexico	Y	27760 FQ	32890 MW	36930 TQ	USBLS	5/15
	Albuquerque MSA, NM	Y	27850 FQ	32980 MW	37310 TQ	USBLS	5/15
	New York	Y	31390 AE	44640 MW	73010 AEX	NYBLS	1/16-3/16
	Buffalo-Cheektowaga-Niagara Falls MSA, NY	Y	32160 FQ	36270 MW	43060 TQ	USBLS	5/15
	Nassau County-Suffolk County PMSA, NY	Y	37920 FQ	55890 MW	84640 TQ	USBLS	5/15
	New York-Jersey City-White Plains PMSA, NY-NJ	Y	39130 FQ	63070 MW	93420 TQ	USBLS	5/15
	Rochester MSA, NY	Y	30420 FQ	35820 MW	43690 TQ	USBLS	5/15
	North Carolina	Y	26230 FQ	30340 MW	35860 TQ	USBLS	5/15
	Charlotte-Concord-Gastonia MSA, NC-SC	Y	26400 FQ	31610 MW	37500 TQ	USBLS	5/15
	Raleigh MSA, NC	Y	27070 FQ	30230 MW	34980 TQ	USBLS	5/15
	North Dakota	Y	32750 FQ	37500 MW	45010 TQ	USBLS	5/15
	Fargo MSA, ND-MN	Y	31240 FQ	37290 MW	46770 TQ	USBLS	5/15
	Ohio	Y	30570 FQ	37120 MW	48340 TQ	USBLS	5/15
	Cincinnati MSA, OH-KY-IN	Y	32980 FQ	40610 MW	53380 TQ	USBLS	5/15
	Cleveland-Elyria MSA, OH	Y	30020 FQ	35530 MW	42010 TQ	USBLS	5/15
	Columbus MSA, OH	Y	36960 FQ	46430 MW	55970 TQ	USBLS	5/15
	Oklahoma	Y	25960 FQ	31210 MW	37070 TQ	USBLS	5/15
	Oklahoma City MSA, OK	Y	26470 FQ	30690 MW	36560 TQ	USBLS	5/15
	Tulsa MSA, OK	Y	32230 FQ	35540 MW	38850 TQ	USBLS	5/15
	Oregon	H	14.77 FQ	19.07 MW	26.74 TQ	ORBLS	2016
	Portland-Vancouver-Hillsboro MSA, OR-WA	Y	34010 FQ	48600 MW	59930 TQ	USBLS	5/15
	Pennsylvania	Y	29010 FQ	36530 MW	51030 TQ	USBLS	5/15
	Allentown-Bethlehem-Easton MSA, PA-NJ	Y	27390 FQ	30900 MW	38010 TQ	USBLS	5/15
	Harrisburg-Carlisle MSA, PA	Y	30940 FQ	36240 MW	43180 TQ	USBLS	5/15
	Montgomery County-Bucks County-Chester County PMSA, PA	Y	36140 FQ	55100 MW	68730 TQ	USBLS	5/15
	Philadelphia PMSA, PA	Y	45130 FQ	54190 MW	59190 TQ	USBLS	5/15
	Pittsburgh MSA, PA	Y	28230 FQ	35330 MW	47410 TQ	USBLS	5/15
	Rhode Island	Y	33000 FQ	39440 MW	49440 TQ	USBLS	5/15
	Providence-Warwick MSA, RI-MA	Y	36110 FQ	45430 MW	54510 TQ	USBLS	5/15
	South Carolina	Y	23790 FQ	28540 MW	35520 TQ	USBLS	5/15
	Charleston-North Charleston MSA, SC	Y	22780 FQ	28160 MW	35070 TQ	USBLS	5/15
	Columbia MSA, SC	Y	25850 FQ	28420 MW	31010 TQ	USBLS	5/15
	Greenville-Anderson-Mauldin MSA, SC	Y	22000 FQ	26140 MW	39800 TQ	USBLS	5/15
	South Dakota	Y	24600 FQ	28440 MW	33070 TQ	USBLS	5/15
	Sioux Falls MSA, SD	Y	26320 FQ	29540 MW	34160 TQ	USBLS	5/15
	Tennessee	Y	25780 FQ	32620 MW	39080 TQ	USBLS	5/15
	Knoxville MSA, TN	Y	28600 FQ	34440 MW	39350 TQ	USBLS	5/15
	Memphis MSA, TN-MS-AR	Y	31080 FQ	35940 MW	43510 TQ	USBLS	5/15
	Nashville-Davidson–Murfreesboro–Franklin MSA, TN	Y	30740 FQ	36020 MW	42820 TQ	USBLS	5/15
	Texas	Y	26670 FQ	32360 MW	38350 TQ	USBLS	5/15
	Austin-Round Rock MSA, TX	Y	26530 FQ	33360 MW	37870 TQ	USBLS	5/15
	Dallas-Plano-Irving PMSA, TX	Y	28820 FQ	34750 MW	41100 TQ	USBLS	5/15
	Fort Worth-Arlington PMSA, TX	Y	30830 FQ	35540 MW	40970 TQ	USBLS	5/15

AE	Average entry wage	AWR	Average wage range	H	Hourly	LR	Low end range	MTC	Median total compensation	TCC	Total cash compensation
AEX	Average experienced wage	B	Biweekly	HI	Highest wage paid	M	Monthly	MW	Median wage paid	TQ	Third quartile wage
ATC	Average total compensation	D	Daily	HR	High end range	MCC	Median cash compensation	MWR	Median wage range	W	Weekly
AW	Average wage paid	FQ	First quartile wage	LO	Lowest wage paid	ME	Median entry wage	S	See annotated source	Y	Yearly

Occupation/Type/Industry	Location	Per	Low	Mid	High	Source	Date
Roofer	Houston-The Woodlands-Sugar Land MSA, TX	Y	29090 FQ	34350 MW	39520 TQ	USBLS	5/15
	San Antonio-New Braunfels MSA, TX	Y	27090 FQ	30970 MW	37510 TQ	USBLS	5/15
	Utah	Y	28880 FQ	34310 MW	39360 TQ	USBLS	5/15
	Ogden-Clearfield MSA, UT	Y	27710 FQ	32520 MW	37280 TQ	USBLS	5/15
	Provo-Orem MSA, UT	Y	31180 FQ	43560 MW	54200 TQ	USBLS	5/15
	Salt Lake City MSA, UT	Y	30850 FQ	35390 MW	39890 TQ	USBLS	5/15
	Vermont	Y	31240 FQ	36030 MW	41940 TQ	USBLS	5/15
	Burlington-South Burlington MSA, VT	Y	29170 FQ	34210 MW	41160 TQ	USBLS	5/15
	Virginia	Y	30640 FQ	37940 MW	47410 TQ	USBLS	5/15
	Richmond MSA, VA	Y	31800 FQ	36270 MW	43230 TQ	USBLS	5/15
	Virginia Beach-Norfolk-Newport News MSA, VA-NC	Y	29060 FQ	36840 MW	45030 TQ	USBLS	5/15
	Washington	H	17.36 FQ	23.37 MW	28.76 TQ	WABLS	3/16
	Seattle-Bellevue-Everett PMSA, WA	H	19.44 FQ	25.75 MW	29.29 TQ	WABLS	3/16
	Tacoma-Lakewood PMSA, WA	H	19.24 FQ	24.64 MW	32.77 TQ	WABLS	3/16
	West Virginia	Y	25830 FQ	31940 MW	37050 TQ	USBLS	5/15
	Huntington-Ashland MSA, WV-KY-OH	Y	22430 FQ	28790 MW	36030 TQ	USBLS	5/15
	Wisconsin	Y	29320 FQ	37110 MW	47270 TQ	USBLS	5/15
	Madison MSA, WI	Y	35320 FQ	41110 MW	50210 TQ	USBLS	5/15
	Milwaukee-Waukesha-West Allis MSA, WI	Y	30800 FQ	42790 MW	55300 TQ	USBLS	5/15
	Wyoming	Y	23880 FQ	30170 MW	42440 TQ	USBLS	5/15
	Cheyenne MSA, WY	Y	20800 FQ	30910 MW	46240 TQ	USBLS	5/15
	Puerto Rico	Y	16720 FQ	17920 MW	19120 TQ	USBLS	5/15
	San Juan-Carolina-Caguas MSA, PR	Y	16750 FQ	17960 MW	19170 TQ	USBLS	5/15
	Guam	Y	25630 FQ	27600 MW	29570 TQ	USBLS	5/15
Rosarian							
Municipal Government	Berkeley, CA	Y			66639 HI	CACIT	6/28/16
Rotary Drill Operator							
Oil and Gas	Alabama	Y	27394 AE	42104 AW	49459 AEX	ALBLS	6/16
Oil and Gas	Alaska	Y	58060 FQ	71550 MW	89950 TQ	USBLS	5/15
Oil and Gas	Arizona	Y	30060 FQ	42350 MW	55600 TQ	USBLS	5/15
Oil and Gas	Arkansas	Y	48700 FQ	53820 MW	58330 TQ	USBLS	5/15
Oil and Gas	California	H	25.54 FQ	35.26 MW	43.24 TQ	CABLS	1/16-3/16
Oil and Gas	Colorado	Y	52330 FQ	59950 MW	69650 TQ	USBLS	5/15
Oil and Gas	Florida	H	16.87 AE	23.60 MW	30.06 AEX	FLBLS	7/16-9/16
Oil and Gas	Georgia	Y	24210 FQ	39680 MW	67200 TQ	USBLS	5/15
Oil and Gas	Illinois	Y	34720 FQ	42740 MW	61550 TQ	USBLS	5/15
Oil and Gas	Indiana	Y	35970 FQ	53970 MW	71330 TQ	USBLS	5/15
Oil and Gas	Kansas	Y	35490 FQ	42080 MW	55300 TQ	USBLS	5/15
Oil and Gas	Kentucky	Y	32150 FQ	36480 MW	50550 TQ	USBLS	5/15
Oil and Gas	Louisiana	Y	40340 FQ	53820 MW	67760 TQ	USBLS	5/15
Oil and Gas	Maryland	Y	35374 AE	43338 MW	47320 AEX	MDBLS	4/16
Oil and Gas	Michigan	Y	28770 FQ	37500 MW	48460 TQ	USBLS	5/15
Oil and Gas	Minnesota	Y	44366 FQ	54658 MW	61752 TQ	MNBLS	1/16-3/16
Oil and Gas	Mississippi	Y	55840 FQ	84290 MW	96250 TQ	USBLS	5/15
Oil and Gas	Montana	Y	40970 FQ	47850 MW	60500 TQ	USBLS	5/15
Oil and Gas	Nebraska	Y	34615 FQ	41495 MW	46330 TQ	NEBLS	7/16-9/16
Oil and Gas	New Mexico	Y	29840 FQ	44270 MW	71050 TQ	USBLS	5/15
Oil and Gas	New York	Y	35040 AE	54200 MW	55970 AEX	NYBLS	1/16-3/16
Oil and Gas	North Dakota	Y	49680 FQ	59870 MW	81060 TQ	USBLS	5/15
Oil and Gas	Ohio	Y	29520 FQ	40980 MW	49770 TQ	USBLS	5/15
Oil and Gas	Oklahoma	Y	36680 FQ	53150 MW	63970 TQ	USBLS	5/15
Oil and Gas	Pennsylvania	Y	39790 FQ	51670 MW	60910 TQ	USBLS	5/15
Oil and Gas	Texas	Y	39270 FQ	54320 MW	76560 TQ	USBLS	5/15
Oil and Gas	Utah	Y	43890 FQ	53150 MW	67710 TQ	USBLS	5/15
Oil and Gas	Virginia	Y	35320 FQ	41390 MW	50390 TQ	USBLS	5/15
Oil and Gas	Washington	H	16.55 FQ	18.02 MW	20.80 TQ	WABLS	3/16
Oil and Gas	West Virginia	Y	35090 FQ	43100 MW	63450 TQ	USBLS	5/15
Oil and Gas	Wyoming	Y	47750 FQ	61920 MW	80100 TQ	USBLS	5/15
Roustabout							
Oil and Gas	Alabama	Y	25542 AE	36745 AW	42341 AEX	ALBLS	6/16
Oil and Gas	Alaska	Y	36500 FQ	52330 MW	63640 TQ	USBLS	5/15

Occupation/Type/Industry	Location	Per	Low	Mid	High	Source	Date
Roustabout							
Oil and Gas	Arkansas	Y	31100 FQ	37850 MW	48580 TQ	USBLS	5/15
Oil and Gas	California	H	13.96 FQ	18.23 MW	26.76 TQ	CABLS	1/16-3/16
Oil and Gas	Colorado	Y	32350 FQ	37650 MW	50020 TQ	USBLS	5/15
Oil and Gas	Florida	H	12.78 AE	17.15 MW	19.91 AEX	FLBLS	7/16-9/16
Oil and Gas	Georgia	Y	28120 FQ	31330 MW	51400 TQ	USBLS	5/15
Oil and Gas	Illinois	Y	24990 FQ	31310 MW	38790 TQ	USBLS	5/15
Oil and Gas	Indiana	Y	30540 FQ	36010 MW	42190 TQ	USBLS	5/15
Oil and Gas	Kansas	Y	31040 FQ	38120 MW	47740 TQ	USBLS	5/15
Oil and Gas	Kentucky	Y	21600 FQ	29270 MW	38430 TQ	USBLS	5/15
Oil and Gas	Louisiana	Y	29830 FQ	37330 MW	47680 TQ	USBLS	5/15
Oil and Gas	Michigan	Y	33990 FQ	39660 MW	53430 TQ	USBLS	5/15
Oil and Gas	Mississippi	Y	29270 FQ	35630 MW	44390 TQ	USBLS	5/15
Oil and Gas	Montana	Y	37180 FQ	47750 MW	55670 TQ	USBLS	5/15
Oil and Gas	Nebraska	Y	27820 FQ	31010 MW	41560 TQ	NEBLS	7/16-9/16
Oil and Gas	New Mexico	Y	27380 FQ	34910 MW	41220 TQ	USBLS	5/15
Oil and Gas	New York	Y	28260 AE	29260 MW	38950 AEX	NYBLS	1/16-3/16
Oil and Gas	North Dakota	Y	36580 FQ	44600 MW	53930 TQ	USBLS	5/15
Oil and Gas	Ohio	Y	25910 FQ	30510 MW	38520 TQ	USBLS	5/15
Oil and Gas	Oklahoma	Y	29840 FQ	35790 MW	43330 TQ	USBLS	5/15
Oil and Gas	Pennsylvania	Y	30780 FQ	38210 MW	48180 TQ	USBLS	5/15
Oil and Gas	Texas	Y	28770 FQ	35030 MW	42710 TQ	USBLS	5/15
Oil and Gas	Utah	Y	31070 FQ	37670 MW	47890 TQ	USBLS	5/15
Oil and Gas	Virginia	Y	30690 FQ	35060 MW	39150 TQ	USBLS	5/15
Oil and Gas	Washington	H	16.80 FQ	22.04 MW	27.23 TQ	WABLS	3/16
Oil and Gas	West Virginia	Y	24860 FQ	29560 MW	37240 TQ	USBLS	5/15
Oil and Gas	Wyoming	Y	35510 FQ	42550 MW	50350 TQ	USBLS	5/15
Russian Community Outreach Coordinator							
Public Safety Administration, Municipal Government	West Hollywood, CA	Y			95078 HI	CACIT	6/28/16
Safe Place Manager							
Michigan State University	East Lansing, MI	Y			63996 HI	MSUSAL	10/1/14-9/30/15
Safety Analyst							
Workers' Compensation Program	San Francisco, CA	B	3851 LO		4681 HI	SFGOV	2016-2018
Safety Director							
Construction Management Firm	United States	Y		114201 AW		ENR02	2015
General Contractor	United States	Y		106387 AW		ENR02	2015
Safety Engineer							
	United States	Y		98000 AW		ASSE	1/1/15
Safety Manager							
Human Resources Department, Municipal Government	Anaheim, CA	Y			126415 HI	CACIT	6/28/16
Sage Grouse Stewardship Manager							
Department of Natural Resources and Conservation, State Government	Helena, MT	H			35.79 HI	MTGOV	2016
Sailor and Marine Oiler	Alabama	Y	30197 AE	40945 AW	46324 AEX	ALBLS	6/16
	Alaska	Y	38000 FQ	48110 MW	54550 TQ	USBLS	5/15
	Anchorage MSA, AK	Y	44600 FQ	51270 MW	57500 TQ	USBLS	5/15
	Little Rock-North Little Rock-Conway MSA, AR	Y	25790 FQ	31280 MW	44450 TQ	USBLS	5/15
	California	H	10.01 FQ	15.84 MW	22.27 TQ	CABLS	1/16-3/16
	Anaheim-Santa Ana-Irvine PMSA, CA	H	13.18 FQ	14.23 MW	15.27 TQ	CABLS	1/16-3/16
	Los Angeles-Long Beach-Glendale PMSA, CA	H	9.64 FQ	15.31 MW	21.97 TQ	CABLS	1/16-3/16
	Oakland-Hayward-Berkeley PMSA, CA	H	14.20 FQ	20.28 MW	25.03 TQ	CABLS	1/16-3/16
	San Diego-Carlsbad MSA, CA	H	13.96 FQ	17.50 MW	19.94 TQ	CABLS	1/16-3/16
	San Francisco-Redwood City-South San Francisco PMSA, CA	H	13.95 FQ	18.16 MW	22.70 TQ	CABLS	1/16-3/16
	Connecticut	Y		30898 MW		CTBLS	1/16-3/16

Sailor and Marine Oiler

Occupation/Type/Industry	Location	Per	Low	Mid	High	Source	Date
Sailor and Marine Oiler	Bridgeport-Stamford-Norwalk MSA, CT	Y	26450 FQ	30220 MW	44280 TQ	USBLS	5/15
	Delaware	Y	29380 FQ	38250 MW	49840 TQ	USBLS	5/15
	Wilmington PMSA, DE-MD-NJ	Y	44350 FQ	56930 MW	67080 TQ	USBLS	5/15
	Washington-Arlington-Alexandria PMSA, DC-VA-MD-WV	Y	20420 FQ	27100 MW	34070 TQ	USBLS	5/15
	Florida	H	11.24 AE	15.07 MW	25.61 AEX	FLBLS	7/16-9/16
	Fort Lauderdale-Pompano Beach-Deerfield Beach PMSA, FL	H	10.20 AE	18.34 MW	23.14 AEX	FLBLS	7/16-9/16
	Hawaii	Y	27520 FQ	30040 MW	36670 TQ	USBLS	5/15
	Urban Honolulu MSA, HI	Y	27110 FQ	29190 MW	31250 TQ	USBLS	5/15
	Illinois	Y	30120 FQ	62440 MW	75960 TQ	USBLS	5/15
	Chicago-Naperville-Arlington Heights PMSA, IL	Y	19730 FQ	30910 MW	55130 TQ	USBLS	5/15
	Gary PMSA, IN	Y	24550 FQ	34980 MW	45320 TQ	USBLS	5/15
	Iowa	Y	25370 FQ	29510 MW	39670 TQ	USBLS	5/15
	Kentucky	Y	24540 FQ	30210 MW	42150 TQ	USBLS	5/15
	Louisiana	Y	32030 FQ	42110 MW	56450 TQ	USBLS	5/15
	Baton Rouge MSA, LA	Y	29330 FQ	35400 MW	44080 TQ	USBLS	5/15
	New Orleans-Metairie MSA, LA	Y	29530 FQ	42530 MW	57830 TQ	USBLS	5/15
	Maine	Y	22860 FQ	32410 MW	40420 TQ	USBLS	5/15
	Portland-South Portland MSA, ME	Y	24850 FQ	36330 MW	43620 TQ	USBLS	5/15
	Maryland	Y	33007 AE	49856 MW	58281 AEX	MDBLS	4/16
	Baltimore-Columbia-Towson MSA, MD	Y	42810 FQ	47880 MW	64160 TQ	USBLS	5/15
	Massachusetts	Y	21000 FQ	31070 MW	48150 TQ	USBLS	5/15
	Boston-Cambridge-Newton NECTA, MA	Y	20030 FQ	23360 MW	36740 TQ	USBLS	5/15
	Michigan	Y	32300 FQ	42400 MW	59380 TQ	USBLS	5/15
	Mississippi	Y	30630 FQ	36480 MW	40810 TQ	USBLS	5/15
	Missouri	Y	30340 FQ	38800 MW	46190 TQ	USBLS	5/15
	St. Louis MSA, MO-IL	Y	31140 FQ	42630 MW	55390 TQ	USBLS	5/15
	New Jersey	Y	24140 FQ	36300 MW	58380 TQ	USBLS	5/15
	New York	Y	24660 AE	44190 MW	54470 AEX	NYBLS	1/16-3/16
	Buffalo-Cheektowaga-Niagara Falls MSA, NY	Y	22530 FQ	24860 MW	37440 TQ	USBLS	5/15
	Nassau County-Suffolk County PMSA, NY	Y	23310 FQ	30480 MW	40690 TQ	USBLS	5/15
	New York-Jersey City-White Plains PMSA, NY-NJ	Y	34720 FQ	48380 MW	61230 TQ	USBLS	5/15
	North Carolina	Y	23790 FQ	28350 MW	35500 TQ	USBLS	5/15
	Ohio	Y	28090 FQ	34750 MW	45460 TQ	USBLS	5/15
	Cincinnati MSA, OH-KY-IN	Y	25890 FQ	28570 MW	31420 TQ	USBLS	5/15
	Cleveland-Elyria MSA, OH	Y	40860 FQ	49080 MW	62520 TQ	USBLS	5/15
	Oregon	H	20.82 FQ	27.30 MW	33.63 TQ	ORBLS	2016
	Portland-Vancouver-Hillsboro MSA, OR-WA	Y	53030 FQ	59160 MW	67690 TQ	USBLS	5/15
	Pennsylvania	Y	27760 FQ	32410 MW	40210 TQ	USBLS	5/15
	Montgomery County-Bucks County-Chester County PMSA, PA	Y	29030 FQ	50990 MW	70790 TQ	USBLS	5/15
	Philadelphia PMSA, PA	Y	28180 FQ	31830 MW	61510 TQ	USBLS	5/15
	Pittsburgh MSA, PA	Y	28450 FQ	32970 MW	37960 TQ	USBLS	5/15
	Rhode Island	Y	27510 FQ	33190 MW	37350 TQ	USBLS	5/15
	Providence-Warwick MSA, RI-MA	Y	28000 FQ	33640 MW	37850 TQ	USBLS	5/15
	South Carolina	Y	20050 FQ	25830 MW	34770 TQ	USBLS	5/15
	Charleston-North Charleston MSA, SC	Y	26100 FQ	30930 MW	39500 TQ	USBLS	5/15
	Tennessee	Y	33710 FQ	40780 MW	47310 TQ	USBLS	5/15
	Memphis MSA, TN-MS-AR	Y	29340 FQ	37560 MW	44460 TQ	USBLS	5/15
	Nashville-Davidson–Murfreesboro–Franklin MSA, TN	Y	36570 FQ	42800 MW	48870 TQ	USBLS	5/15
	Texas	Y	24740 FQ	39090 MW	64360 TQ	USBLS	5/15
	Austin-Round Rock MSA, TX	Y	19630 FQ	23830 MW	38630 TQ	USBLS	5/15
	Dallas-Plano-Irving PMSA, TX	Y	31670 FQ	37250 MW	46220 TQ	USBLS	5/15

AE Average entry wage	**AWR** Average wage range	**H** Hourly	**LR** Low end range	**MTC** Median total compensation	**TCC** Total cash compensation
AEX Average experienced wage	**B** Biweekly	**HI** Highest wage paid	**M** Monthly	**MW** Median wage paid	**TQ** Third quartile wage
ATC Average total compensation	**D** Daily	**HR** High end range	**MCC** Median cash compensation	**MWR** Median wage range	**W** Weekly
AW Average wage paid	**FQ** First quartile wage	**LO** Lowest wage paid	**ME** Median entry wage	**S** See annotated source	**Y** Yearly

Occupation/Type/Industry	Location	Per	Low	Mid	High	Source	Date
Sailor and Marine Oiler	Houston-The Woodlands-Sugar Land MSA, TX	Y	24930 FQ	41210 MW	67950 TQ	USBLS	5/15
	Virginia	Y	35200 FQ	39520 MW	45230 TQ	USBLS	5/15
	Virginia Beach-Norfolk-Newport News MSA, VA-NC	Y	35200 FQ	39520 MW	45230 TQ	USBLS	5/15
	Washington	H	22.97 FQ	24.60 MW	26.11 TQ	WABLS	3/16
	Seattle-Bellevue-Everett PMSA, WA	H	22.97 FQ	24.60 MW	26.10 TQ	WABLS	3/16
	Tacoma-Lakewood PMSA, WA	H	16.26 FQ	18.71 MW	19.93 TQ	WABLS	3/16
	Huntington-Ashland MSA, WV-KY-OH	Y	22540 FQ	24760 MW	34360 TQ	USBLS	5/15
	Wisconsin	Y	27310 FQ	30790 MW	38490 TQ	USBLS	5/15
	Puerto Rico	Y	18280 FQ	24230 MW	41440 TQ	USBLS	5/15
	San Juan-Carolina-Caguas MSA, PR	Y	18150 FQ	21950 MW	40640 TQ	USBLS	5/15
	Virgin Islands	Y	18560 FQ	25910 MW	28790 TQ	USBLS	5/15
	Guam	Y	18770 FQ	23640 MW	29890 TQ	USBLS	5/15
Sales Agronomist							
Entry-Level, Full-Time	United States	Y		46742 AW		AGPRO	2016
Sales and Distribution Worker							
Solar Industry	United States	H		45.26 MW		SOLF	2016
Sales Engineer	Alabama	Y	64093 AE	97789 AW	114637 AEX	ALBLS	6/16
	Birmingham-Hoover MSA, AL	Y	60328 AE	93848 AW	110613 AEX	ALBLS	6/16
	Alaska	Y	79310 FQ	105560 MW	130510 TQ	USBLS	5/15
	Anchorage MSA, AK	Y	76040 FQ	102390 MW	126910 TQ	USBLS	5/15
	Arizona	Y	78780 FQ	103130 MW	132400 TQ	USBLS	5/15
	Phoenix-Mesa-Scottsdale MSA, AZ	Y	80720 FQ	104180 MW	131030 TQ	USBLS	5/15
	Tucson MSA, AZ	Y	65920 FQ	94680 MW	139260 TQ	USBLS	5/15
	Arkansas	Y	64330 FQ	88610 MW	110120 TQ	USBLS	5/15
	Little Rock-North Little Rock-Conway MSA, AR	Y	62470 FQ	91840 MW	112910 TQ	USBLS	5/15
	California	H	39.34 FQ	51.65 MW	70.62 TQ	CABLS	1/16-3/16
	Anaheim-Santa Ana-Irvine PMSA, CA	H	33.98 FQ	44.35 MW	60.05 TQ	CABLS	1/16-3/16
	Los Angeles-Long Beach-Glendale PMSA, CA	H	38.83 FQ	47.30 MW	61.83 TQ	CABLS	1/16-3/16
	Oakland-Hayward-Berkeley PMSA, CA	H	40.34 FQ	55.66 MW	75.37 TQ	CABLS	1/16-3/16
	Riverside-San Bernardino-Ontario MSA, CA	H	32.47 FQ	39.23 MW	51.09 TQ	CABLS	1/16-3/16
	Sacramento–Roseville–Arden-Arcade MSA, CA	H	34.66 FQ	49.29 MW	67.81 TQ	CABLS	1/16-3/16
	San Diego-Carlsbad MSA, CA	H	33.90 FQ	44.48 MW	59.46 TQ	CABLS	1/16-3/16
	San Francisco-Redwood City-South San Francisco PMSA, CA	H	45.49 FQ	63.41 MW	79.39 TQ	CABLS	1/16-3/16
	Colorado	Y	77700 FQ	106670 MW	129220 TQ	USBLS	5/15
	Denver-Aurora-Lakewood MSA, CO	Y	82220 FQ	110100 MW	131550 TQ	USBLS	5/15
	Connecticut	Y		89886 MW		CTBLS	1/16-3/16
	Bridgeport-Stamford-Norwalk MSA, CT	Y	70760 FQ	86530 MW	121980 TQ	USBLS	5/15
	Hartford-West Hartford-East Hartford MSA, CT	Y	74290 FQ	89390 MW	101480 TQ	USBLS	5/15
	Delaware	Y	126250 FQ	142780 MW	155450 TQ	USBLS	5/15
	Wilmington PMSA, DE-MD-NJ	Y	120510 FQ	143020 MW	156510 TQ	USBLS	5/15
	District of Columbia	Y	101010 FQ	113350 MW	125150 TQ	USBLS	5/15
	Washington-Arlington-Alexandria PMSA, DC-VA-MD-WV	Y	105980 FQ	124090 MW	150170 TQ	USBLS	5/15
	Florida	H	31.32 AE	52.53 MW	68.94 AEX	FLBLS	7/16-9/16
	Fort Lauderdale-Pompano Beach-Deerfield Beach PMSA, FL	H	23.60 AE	34.35 MW	48.02 AEX	FLBLS	7/16-9/16
	Miami-Miami Beach-Kendall PMSA, FL	H	26.39 AE	52.74 MW	84.51 AEX	FLBLS	7/16-9/16

AE Average entry wage	**AWR** Average wage range	**H** Hourly	**LR** Low end range	**MTC** Median total compensation	**TCC** Total cash compensation
AEX Average experienced wage	**B** Biweekly	**HI** Highest wage paid	**M** Monthly	**MW** Median wage paid	**TQ** Third quartile wage
ATC Average total compensation	**D** Daily	**HR** High end range	**MCC** Median cash compensation	**MWR** Median wage range	**W** Weekly
AW Average wage paid	**FQ** First quartile wage	**LO** Lowest wage paid	**ME** Median entry wage	**S** See annotated source	**Y** Yearly

Occupation/Type/Industry	Location	Per	Low	Mid	High	Source	Date
Sales Engineer	Orlando-Kissimmee-Sanford MSA, FL	H	29.60 AE	48.48 MW	55.52 AEX	FLBLS	7/16-9/16
	Tampa-St. Petersburg-Clearwater MSA, FL	H	33.65 AE	56.33 MW	72.72 AEX	FLBLS	7/16-9/16
	Georgia	Y	67040 FQ	101050 MW	132960 TQ	USBLS	5/15
	Atlanta-Sandy Springs-Roswell MSA, GA	Y	66540 FQ	101180 MW	134370 TQ	USBLS	5/15
	Hawaii	Y	70400 FQ	79970 MW	122150 TQ	USBLS	5/15
	Idaho	Y	49910 FQ	93930 MW	114070 TQ	USBLS	5/15
	Boise City MSA, ID	Y	48030 FQ	89160 MW	111000 TQ	USBLS	5/15
	Illinois	Y	64880 FQ	90920 MW	123420 TQ	USBLS	5/15
	Chicago-Naperville-Arlington Heights PMSA, IL	Y	70670 FQ	98060 MW	128990 TQ	USBLS	5/15
	Lake County-Kenosha County PMSA, IL-WI	Y	47160 FQ	70370 MW	102520 TQ	USBLS	5/15
	Indiana	Y	57460 FQ	76570 MW	99770 TQ	USBLS	5/15
	Gary PMSA, IN	Y	46700 FQ	56690 MW	73340 TQ	USBLS	5/15
	Indianapolis-Carmel-Anderson MSA, IN	Y	56000 FQ	75770 MW	100130 TQ	USBLS	5/15
	Iowa	Y	72780 FQ	89420 MW	113360 TQ	USBLS	5/15
	Des Moines-West Des Moines MSA, IA	Y	71180 FQ	84510 MW	118180 TQ	USBLS	5/15
	Kansas	Y	63350 FQ	77750 MW	102000 TQ	USBLS	5/15
	Wichita MSA, KS	Y	65610 FQ	75860 MW	92630 TQ	USBLS	5/15
	Kentucky	Y	56800 FQ	74200 MW	97160 TQ	USBLS	5/15
	Louisville-Jefferson County MSA, KY-IN	Y	51040 FQ	66600 MW	87640 TQ	USBLS	5/15
	Louisiana	Y	65430 FQ	89540 MW	131720 TQ	USBLS	5/15
	Baton Rouge MSA, LA	Y	48480 FQ	68170 MW	78100 TQ	USBLS	5/15
	New Orleans-Metairie MSA, LA	Y	76720 FQ	92310 MW	104830 TQ	USBLS	5/15
	Maine	Y	61220 FQ	72330 MW	85770 TQ	USBLS	5/15
	Portland-South Portland MSA, ME	Y	61440 FQ	75640 MW	96600 TQ	USBLS	5/15
	Maryland	Y	60983 AE	119869 MW	149312 AEX	MDBLS	4/16
	Baltimore-Columbia-Towson MSA, MD	Y	66560 FQ	81240 MW	120290 TQ	USBLS	5/15
	Massachusetts	Y	81700 FQ	104120 MW	134890 TQ	USBLS	5/15
	Boston-Cambridge-Newton NECTA, MA	Y	84320 FQ	107280 MW	140010 TQ	USBLS	5/15
	Worcester MSA, MA-CT	Y	81150 FQ	92500 MW	106990 TQ	USBLS	5/15
	Michigan	Y	69030 FQ	90140 MW	117520 TQ	USBLS	5/15
	Detroit-Dearborn-Livonia PMSA, MI	Y	70400 FQ	91800 MW	114900 TQ	USBLS	5/15
	Grand Rapids-Wyoming MSA, MI	Y	57310 FQ	72980 MW	94250 TQ	USBLS	5/15
	Minnesota	Y	71482 FQ	93091 MW	130612 TQ	MNBLS	1/16-3/16
	Minneapolis-St. Paul-Bloomington MSA, MN-WI	Y	72763 FQ	94654 MW	133143 TQ	MNBLS	1/16-3/16
	Mississippi	Y	65250 FQ	78300 MW	110900 TQ	USBLS	5/15
	Missouri	Y	66720 FQ	82520 MW	114220 TQ	USBLS	5/15
	Kansas City MSA, MO-KS	Y	64360 FQ	80550 MW	99330 TQ	USBLS	5/15
	St. Louis MSA, MO-IL	Y	71950 FQ	94820 MW	129010 TQ	USBLS	5/15
	Montana	Y	52750 FQ	61110 MW	80770 TQ	USBLS	5/15
	Nebraska	Y	65650 FQ	84500 MW	98125 TQ	NEBLS	7/16-9/16
	Omaha-Council Bluffs MSA, NE-IA	Y	56445 FQ	82980 MW	98160 TQ	NEBLS	7/16-9/16
	Nevada	Y	85390 FQ	96340 MW	112040 TQ	USBLS	5/15
	Las Vegas-Henderson-Paradise MSA, NV	Y	86650 FQ	98010 MW	114000 TQ	USBLS	5/15
	New Hampshire	H	31.38 AE	52.75 MW	74.85 AEX	NHBLS	6/16
	Manchester NECTA, NH	H	31.72 AE	52.19 MW	57.19 AEX	NHBLS	6/16
	Nashua NECTA, NH-MA	Y	88770 FQ	117080 MW		USBLS	5/15
	New Jersey	Y	67150 FQ	94340 MW	123690 TQ	USBLS	5/15
	Camden PMSA, NJ	Y	57630 FQ	71910 MW	90730 TQ	USBLS	5/15
	Newark PMSA, NJ-PA	Y	66940 FQ	94180 MW	119690 TQ	USBLS	5/15
	Trenton MSA, NJ	Y	66340 FQ	88790 MW	125480 TQ	USBLS	5/15
	New Mexico	Y	57080 FQ	92150 MW	145870 TQ	USBLS	5/15
	New York	Y	66480 AE	101400 MW	132060 AEX	NYBLS	1/16-3/16
	Buffalo-Cheektowaga-Niagara Falls MSA, NY	Y	62030 FQ	74710 MW	95390 TQ	USBLS	5/15

AE Average entry wage	**AWR** Average wage range	**H** Hourly	**LR** Low end range	**MTC** Median total compensation	**TCC** Total cash compensation
AEX Average experienced wage	**B** Biweekly	**HI** Highest wage paid	**M** Monthly	**MW** Median wage paid	**TQ** Third quartile wage
ATC Average total compensation	**D** Daily	**HR** High end range	**MCC** Median cash compensation	**MWR** Median wage range	**W** Weekly
AW Average wage paid	**FQ** First quartile wage	**LO** Lowest wage paid	**ME** Median entry wage	**S** See annotated source	**Y** Yearly

Occupation/Type/Industry	Location	Per	Low	Mid	High	Source	Date
Sales Engineer	Nassau County-Suffolk County						
	PMSA, NY	Y	75720 FQ	94640 MW	126590 TQ	USBLS	5/15
	New York-Jersey City-White						
	Plains PMSA, NY-NJ	Y	80740 FQ	112710 MW	145070 TQ	USBLS	5/15
	Rochester MSA, NY	Y	71650 FQ	91400 MW	114190 TQ	USBLS	5/15
	North Carolina	Y	66550 FQ	96940 MW	127440 TQ	USBLS	5/15
	Charlotte-Concord-Gastonia						
	MSA, NC-SC	Y	73800 FQ	111230 MW	147900 TQ	USBLS	5/15
	Raleigh MSA, NC	Y	51240 FQ	86980 MW	119010 TQ	USBLS	5/15
	North Dakota	Y	79040 FQ	95340 MW	125980 TQ	USBLS	5/15
	Fargo MSA, ND-MN	Y	82230 FQ	96890 MW	130790 TQ	USBLS	5/15
	Ohio	Y	68980 FQ	93040 MW	128670 TQ	USBLS	5/15
	Cincinnati MSA, OH-KY-IN	Y	65930 FQ	91890 MW	132930 TQ	USBLS	5/15
	Cleveland-Elyria MSA, OH	Y	79550 FQ	109190 MW	142450 TQ	USBLS	5/15
	Columbus MSA, OH	Y	71140 FQ	89790 MW	109830 TQ	USBLS	5/15
	Oklahoma	Y	62810 FQ	86490 MW	116590 TQ	USBLS	5/15
	Oklahoma City MSA, OK	Y	76310 FQ	94520 MW	117920 TQ	USBLS	5/15
	Tulsa MSA, OK	Y	59680 FQ	79650 MW	102720 TQ	USBLS	5/15
	Oregon	H	37.22 FQ	51.35 MW	71.62 TQ	ORBLS	2016
	Portland-Vancouver-Hillsboro						
	MSA, OR-WA	Y	77150 FQ	108640 MW	150770 TQ	USBLS	5/15
	Pennsylvania	Y	63690 FQ	82310 MW	108950 TQ	USBLS	5/15
	Allentown-Bethlehem-Easton						
	MSA, PA-NJ	Y	68510 FQ	80420 MW	96540 TQ	USBLS	5/15
	Harrisburg-Carlisle MSA, PA	Y	59110 FQ	70560 MW	108780 TQ	USBLS	5/15
	Montgomery County-Bucks						
	County-Chester County						
	PMSA, PA	Y	70090 FQ	95630 MW	131720 TQ	USBLS	5/15
	Philadelphia PMSA, PA	Y	66540 FQ	86790 MW	114180 TQ	USBLS	5/15
	Pittsburgh MSA, PA	Y	61510 FQ	80760 MW	98470 TQ	USBLS	5/15
	Rhode Island	Y	87160 FQ	112220 MW	173950 TQ	USBLS	5/15
	Providence-Warwick MSA, RI-						
	MA	Y	87330 FQ	110040 MW	153570 TQ	USBLS	5/15
	South Carolina	Y	57150 FQ	84890 MW	113400 TQ	USBLS	5/15
	Charleston-North Charleston						
	MSA, SC	Y	77560 FQ	109370 MW	120720 TQ	USBLS	5/15
	Columbia MSA, SC	Y	45230 FQ	63040 MW	78740 TQ	USBLS	5/15
	Greenville-Anderson-Mauldin						
	MSA, SC	Y	57010 FQ	91440 MW	114940 TQ	USBLS	5/15
	South Dakota	Y	106040 FQ	152550 MW		USBLS	5/15
	Sioux Falls MSA, SD	Y	132750 FQ	162130 MW		USBLS	5/15
	Tennessee	Y	58540 FQ	83320 MW	105450 TQ	USBLS	5/15
	Knoxville MSA, TN	Y	62960 FQ	82610 MW	101200 TQ	USBLS	5/15
	Memphis MSA, TN-MS-AR	Y	67360 FQ	86430 MW	102340 TQ	USBLS	5/15
	Nashville-Davidson–						
	Murfreesboro–Franklin						
	MSA, TN	Y	48840 FQ	73630 MW	116030 TQ	USBLS	5/15
	Texas	Y	76600 FQ	99490 MW	132130 TQ	USBLS	5/15
	Austin-Round Rock MSA, TX	Y	93770 FQ	115040 MW	131360 TQ	USBLS	5/15
	Dallas-Plano-Irving PMSA, TX	Y	82600 FQ	101450 MW	141270 TQ	USBLS	5/15
	Fort Worth-Arlington PMSA,						
	TX	Y	66490 FQ	86390 MW	130940 TQ	USBLS	5/15
	Houston-The Woodlands-						
	Sugar Land MSA, TX	Y	71000 FQ	91600 MW	125350 TQ	USBLS	5/15
	San Antonio-New Braunfels						
	MSA, TX	Y	82310 FQ	101860 MW	145410 TQ	USBLS	5/15
	Utah	Y	64300 FQ	91780 MW	117440 TQ	USBLS	5/15
	Provo-Orem MSA, UT	Y	63960 FQ	84470 MW	104810 TQ	USBLS	5/15
	Salt Lake City MSA, UT	Y	65850 FQ	96170 MW	120880 TQ	USBLS	5/15
	Vermont	Y	59010 FQ	76300 MW	97860 TQ	USBLS	5/15
	Burlington-South Burlington						
	MSA, VT	Y	55130 FQ	73790 MW	98900 TQ	USBLS	5/15
	Virginia	Y	92610 FQ	117660 MW	145830 TQ	USBLS	5/15
	Richmond MSA, VA	Y	73680 FQ	96080 MW	128360 TQ	USBLS	5/15
	Virginia Beach-Norfolk-						
	Newport News MSA, VA-NC	Y	99980 FQ	159430 MW	179660 TQ	USBLS	5/15
	Washington	H	37.20 FQ	53.87 MW	69.49 TQ	WABLS	3/16
	Seattle-Bellevue-Everett						
	PMSA, WA	H	42.44 FQ	56.50 MW	70.09 TQ	WABLS	3/16
	Tacoma-Lakewood PMSA, WA	H	32.60 FQ	34.79 MW	36.99 TQ	WABLS	3/16
	West Virginia	Y	59480 FQ	81300 MW	102240 TQ	USBLS	5/15
	Wisconsin	Y	66370 FQ	87670 MW	115860 TQ	USBLS	5/15

AE	Average entry wage	**AWR**	Average wage range	**H**	Hourly	**LR** Low end range	**MTC** Median total compensation **TCC** Total cash compensation
AEX	Average experienced wage	**B**	Biweekly	**HI**	Highest wage paid	**M** Monthly	**MW** Median wage paid **TQ** Third quartile wage
ATC	Average total compensation	**D**	Daily	**HR**	High end range	**MCC** Median cash compensation	**MWR** Median wage range **W** Weekly
AW	Average wage paid	**FQ**	First quartile wage	**LO**	Lowest wage paid	**ME** Median entry wage	**S** See annotated source **Y** Yearly

1409

Occupation/Type/Industry	Location	Per	Low	Mid	High	Source	Date
Sales Engineer	Madison MSA, WI	Y	70310 FQ	104150 MW	122760 TQ	USBLS	5/15
	Milwaukee-Waukesha-West Allis MSA, WI	Y	68390 FQ	88950 MW	115600 TQ	USBLS	5/15
Sales Manager	Alabama	Y	72639 AE	127075 AW	154297 AEX	ALBLS	6/16
	Birmingham-Hoover MSA, AL	Y	83268 AE	139231 AW	167212 AEX	ALBLS	6/16
	Alaska	Y	66810 FQ	80080 MW	114560 TQ	USBLS	5/15
	Anchorage MSA, AK	Y	65820 FQ	79210 MW	115850 TQ	USBLS	5/15
	Arizona	Y	65360 FQ	94540 MW	137580 TQ	USBLS	5/15
	Phoenix-Mesa-Scottsdale MSA, AZ	Y	67370 FQ	97110 MW	141150 TQ	USBLS	5/15
	Tucson MSA, AZ	Y	59940 FQ	86910 MW	122290 TQ	USBLS	5/15
	Arkansas	Y	64010 FQ	95240 MW	147250 TQ	USBLS	5/15
	Little Rock-North Little Rock-Conway MSA, AR	Y	63170 FQ	92060 MW	121950 TQ	USBLS	5/15
	California	H	34.28 FQ	55.05 MW	83.41 TQ	CABLS	1/16-3/16
	Anaheim-Santa Ana-Irvine PMSA, CA	H	35.80 FQ	56.09 MW	79.65 TQ	CABLS	1/16-3/16
	Los Angeles-Long Beach-Glendale PMSA, CA	H	33.10 FQ	54.09 MW	81.09 TQ	CABLS	1/16-3/16
	Oakland-Hayward-Berkeley PMSA, CA	H	42.66 FQ	62.13 MW		CABLS	1/16-3/16
	Riverside-San Bernardino-Ontario MSA, CA	H	27.60 FQ	44.08 MW	66.49 TQ	CABLS	1/16-3/16
	Sacramento–Roseville–Arden-Arcade MSA, CA	H	28.83 FQ	44.93 MW	71.37 TQ	CABLS	1/16-3/16
	San Diego-Carlsbad MSA, CA	H	34.23 FQ	53.18 MW	77.22 TQ	CABLS	1/16-3/16
	San Francisco-Redwood City-South San Francisco PMSA, CA	H	46.12 FQ	71.46 MW		CABLS	1/16-3/16
	Colorado	Y	83520 FQ	126740 MW	174810 TQ	USBLS	5/15
	Denver-Aurora-Lakewood MSA, CO	Y	90350 FQ	132480 MW	181400 TQ	USBLS	5/15
	Connecticut	Y		134386 MW		CTBLS	1/16-3/16
	Bridgeport-Stamford-Norwalk MSA, CT	Y	106510 FQ	152910 MW		USBLS	5/15
	Hartford-West Hartford-East Hartford MSA, CT	Y	93430 FQ	124110 MW	174560 TQ	USBLS	5/15
	Delaware	Y	117860 FQ	152950 MW		USBLS	5/15
	Wilmington PMSA, DE-MD-NJ	Y	116860 FQ	153250 MW		USBLS	5/15
	District of Columbia	Y	71820 FQ	109950 MW	155560 TQ	USBLS	5/15
	Washington-Arlington-Alexandria PMSA, DC-VA-MD-WV	Y	92590 FQ	149290 MW		USBLS	5/15
	Florida	H	34.85 AE	58.95 MW	81.74 AEX	FLBLS	7/16-9/16
	Fort Lauderdale-Pompano Beach-Deerfield Beach PMSA, FL	H	39.68 AE	65.40 MW	86.54 AEX	FLBLS	7/16-9/16
	Miami-Miami Beach-Kendall PMSA, FL	H	32.18 AE	59.05 MW	89.72 AEX	FLBLS	7/16-9/16
	Orlando-Kissimmee-Sanford MSA, FL	H	33.33 AE	54.85 MW	73.61 AEX	FLBLS	7/16-9/16
	Tampa-St. Petersburg-Clearwater MSA, FL	H	36.66 AE	59.10 MW	84.21 AEX	FLBLS	7/16-9/16
	Georgia	Y	72530 FQ	110780 MW	158000 TQ	USBLS	5/15
	Atlanta-Sandy Springs-Roswell MSA, GA	Y	75100 FQ	115760 MW	161240 TQ	USBLS	5/15
	Augusta-Richmond County MSA, GA-SC	Y	72160 FQ	99470 MW	139790 TQ	USBLS	5/15
	Hawaii	Y	53950 FQ	67950 MW	92920 TQ	USBLS	5/15
	Urban Honolulu MSA, HI	Y	54610 FQ	68750 MW	96040 TQ	USBLS	5/15
	Idaho	Y	62940 FQ	90570 MW	129600 TQ	USBLS	5/15
	Boise City MSA, ID	Y	61660 FQ	90600 MW	123130 TQ	USBLS	5/15
	Illinois	Y	74030 FQ	106310 MW	152480 TQ	USBLS	5/15
	Chicago-Naperville-Arlington Heights PMSA, IL	Y	77740 FQ	111200 MW	157390 TQ	USBLS	5/15
	Lake County-Kenosha County PMSA, IL-WI	Y	80870 FQ	113100 MW	164180 TQ	USBLS	5/15
	Indiana	Y	68890 FQ	97600 MW	136240 TQ	USBLS	5/15
	Gary PMSA, IN	Y	69340 FQ	106780 MW	133960 TQ	USBLS	5/15

Sales Manager

Occupation/Type/Industry	Location	Per	Low	Mid	High	Source	Date
Sales Manager	Indianapolis-Carmel-Anderson MSA, IN	Y	74850 FQ	102640 MW	141990 TQ	USBLS	5/15
	Iowa	Y	68780 FQ	93260 MW	128810 TQ	USBLS	5/15
	Des Moines-West Des Moines MSA, IA	Y	75080 FQ	101540 MW	151370 TQ	USBLS	5/15
	Kansas	Y	72730 FQ	104080 MW	156960 TQ	USBLS	5/15
	Wichita MSA, KS	Y	64970 FQ	87220 MW	129080 TQ	USBLS	5/15
	Kentucky	Y	66030 FQ	93730 MW	133980 TQ	USBLS	5/15
	Louisville-Jefferson County MSA, KY-IN	Y	60880 FQ	91410 MW	127740 TQ	USBLS	5/15
	Louisiana	Y	62050 FQ	87510 MW	129180 TQ	USBLS	5/15
	Baton Rouge MSA, LA	Y	58430 FQ	95090 MW	155950 TQ	USBLS	5/15
	New Orleans-Metairie MSA, LA	Y	61090 FQ	85770 MW	121280 TQ	USBLS	5/15
	Maine	Y	83700 FQ	107020 MW	135250 TQ	USBLS	5/15
	Portland-South Portland MSA, ME	Y	87910 FQ	110410 MW	141870 TQ	USBLS	5/15
	Maryland	Y	73753 AE	139054 MW	171705 AEX	MDBLS	4/16
	Baltimore-Columbia-Towson MSA, MD	Y	91260 FQ	128240 MW	173690 TQ	USBLS	5/15
	Salisbury MSA, MD-DE	Y	87550 FQ	122250 MW	165680 TQ	USBLS	5/15
	Massachusetts	Y	92320 FQ	130550 MW	183720 TQ	USBLS	5/15
	Boston-Cambridge-Newton NECTA, MA	Y	98610 FQ	141300 MW		USBLS	5/15
	Worcester MSA, MA-CT	Y	80400 FQ	109800 MW	139040 TQ	USBLS	5/15
	Michigan	Y	81400 FQ	115150 MW	152240 TQ	USBLS	5/15
	Detroit-Dearborn-Livonia PMSA, MI	Y	104570 FQ	127580 MW	158020 TQ	USBLS	5/15
	Grand Rapids-Wyoming MSA, MI	Y	79710 FQ	110660 MW	148460 TQ	USBLS	5/15
	Minnesota	Y	81989 FQ	114992 MW	162048 TQ	MNBLS	1/16-3/16
	Minneapolis-St. Paul-Bloomington MSA, MN-WI	Y	88807 FQ	121800 MW	172118 TQ	MNBLS	1/16-3/16
	Mississippi	Y	51320 FQ	71010 MW	110220 TQ	USBLS	5/15
	Jackson MSA, MS	Y	54910 FQ	70590 MW	101320 TQ	USBLS	5/15
	Missouri	Y	71720 FQ	108200 MW	155430 TQ	USBLS	5/15
	Kansas City MSA, MO-KS	Y	72500 FQ	108020 MW	154420 TQ	USBLS	5/15
	St. Louis MSA, MO-IL	Y	81590 FQ	120250 MW	175640 TQ	USBLS	5/15
	Montana	Y	66580 FQ	81120 MW	120010 TQ	USBLS	5/15
	Billings MSA, MT	Y	64430 FQ	77520 MW	120610 TQ	USBLS	5/15
	Nebraska	Y	72395 FQ	105405 MW	153090 TQ	NEBLS	7/16-9/16
	Omaha-Council Bluffs MSA, NE-IA	Y	74315 FQ	106165 MW	146020 TQ	NEBLS	7/16-9/16
	Nevada	Y	63730 FQ	85580 MW	130060 TQ	USBLS	5/15
	Las Vegas-Henderson-Paradise MSA, NV	Y	58360 FQ	78370 MW	120900 TQ	USBLS	5/15
	New Hampshire	H	37.99 AE	60.85 MW	80.56 AEX	NHBLS	6/16
	Manchester NECTA, NH	H	39.05 AE	61.14 MW	78.80 AEX	NHBLS	6/16
	Nashua NECTA, NH-MA	Y	96770 FQ	125250 MW	155180 TQ	USBLS	5/15
	New Jersey	Y	103250 FQ	140930 MW		USBLS	5/15
	Camden PMSA, NJ	Y	96700 FQ	128300 MW	176960 TQ	USBLS	5/15
	Newark PMSA, NJ-PA	Y	109340 FQ	143980 MW		USBLS	5/15
	Trenton MSA, NJ	Y	111130 FQ	142070 MW		USBLS	5/15
	New Mexico	Y	60900 FQ	82420 MW	120270 TQ	USBLS	5/15
	Albuquerque MSA, NM	Y	61770 FQ	86820 MW	123680 TQ	USBLS	5/15
	New York	Y	91820 AE	176690 MW		NYBLS	1/16-3/16
	Buffalo-Cheektowaga-Niagara Falls MSA, NY	Y	82350 FQ	102590 MW	134430 TQ	USBLS	5/15
	Nassau County-Suffolk County PMSA, NY	Y	102700 FQ	156550 MW		USBLS	5/15
	New York-Jersey City-White Plains PMSA, NY-NJ	Y	118290 FQ	177510 MW		USBLS	5/15
	Rochester MSA, NY	Y	79260 FQ	115390 MW	159010 TQ	USBLS	5/15
	North Carolina	Y	82760 FQ	119820 MW	164550 TQ	USBLS	5/15
	Charlotte-Concord-Gastonia MSA, NC-SC	Y	89420 FQ	126610 MW	172130 TQ	USBLS	5/15
	Raleigh MSA, NC	Y	84760 FQ	119350 MW	165320 TQ	USBLS	5/15
	North Dakota	Y	70960 FQ	94730 MW	130100 TQ	USBLS	5/15
	Fargo MSA, ND-MN	Y	70460 FQ	91930 MW	122480 TQ	USBLS	5/15
	Ohio	Y	81420 FQ	111860 MW	153160 TQ	USBLS	5/15
	Cincinnati MSA, OH-KY-IN	Y	84540 FQ	117930 MW	167820 TQ	USBLS	5/15
	Cleveland-Elyria MSA, OH	Y	85550 FQ	122120 MW	168770 TQ	USBLS	5/15

AE	Average entry wage	AWR	Average wage range	H	Hourly
AEX	Average experienced wage	B	Biweekly	HI	Highest wage paid
ATC	Average total compensation	D	Daily	HR	High end range
AW	Average wage paid	FQ	First quartile wage	LO	Lowest wage paid

LR	Low end range	MTC	Median total compensation	TCC	Total cash compensation
M	Monthly	MW	Median wage paid	TQ	Third quartile wage
MCC	Median cash compensation	MWR	Median wage range	W	Weekly
ME	Median entry wage	S	See annotated source	Y	Yearly

Occupation/Type/Industry	Location	Per	Low	Mid	High	Source	Date
Sales Manager	Columbus MSA, OH	Y	80640 FQ	103570 MW	139320 TQ	USBLS	5/15
	Oklahoma	Y	59470 FQ	82280 MW	118270 TQ	USBLS	5/15
	Oklahoma City MSA, OK	Y	61300 FQ	84340 MW	114670 TQ	USBLS	5/15
	Tulsa MSA, OK	Y	64730 FQ	90050 MW	126260 TQ	USBLS	5/15
	Oregon	H	33.42 FQ	48.74 MW	68.40 TQ	ORBLS	2016
	Portland-Vancouver-Hillsboro MSA, OR-WA	Y	72520 FQ	107060 MW	146590 TQ	USBLS	5/15
	Pennsylvania	Y	86950 FQ	127960 MW	179220 TQ	USBLS	5/15
	Allentown-Bethlehem-Easton MSA, PA-NJ	Y	80910 FQ	123210 MW	160310 TQ	USBLS	5/15
	Harrisburg-Carlisle MSA, PA	Y	66820 FQ	95600 MW	134300 TQ	USBLS	5/15
	Montgomery County-Bucks County-Chester County PMSA, PA	Y	106910 FQ	148060 MW		USBLS	5/15
	Philadelphia PMSA, PA	Y	105410 FQ	145870 MW		USBLS	5/15
	Pittsburgh MSA, PA	Y	83220 FQ	129360 MW	175250 TQ	USBLS	5/15
	Rhode Island	Y	87640 FQ	126020 MW	158350 TQ	USBLS	5/15
	Providence-Warwick MSA, RI-MA	Y	81810 FQ	119510 MW	156820 TQ	USBLS	5/15
	South Carolina	Y	66140 FQ	91590 MW	122680 TQ	USBLS	5/15
	Charleston-North Charleston MSA, SC	Y	59810 FQ	88250 MW	118820 TQ	USBLS	5/15
	Columbia MSA, SC	Y	70200 FQ	95670 MW	125470 TQ	USBLS	5/15
	Greenville-Anderson-Mauldin MSA, SC	Y	70770 FQ	95100 MW	124240 TQ	USBLS	5/15
	South Dakota	Y	88120 FQ	115210 MW	146940 TQ	USBLS	5/15
	Sioux Falls MSA, SD	Y	90930 FQ	114440 MW	135330 TQ	USBLS	5/15
	Tennessee	Y	61170 FQ	86760 MW	127310 TQ	USBLS	5/15
	Knoxville MSA, TN	Y	64430 FQ	90480 MW	123250 TQ	USBLS	5/15
	Memphis MSA, TN-MS-AR	Y	59290 FQ	90510 MW	134050 TQ	USBLS	5/15
	Nashville-Davidson–Murfreesboro–Franklin MSA, TN	Y	63670 FQ	85700 MW	132880 TQ	USBLS	5/15
	Texas	Y	88940 FQ	126290 MW	174330 TQ	USBLS	5/15
	Austin-Round Rock MSA, TX	Y	88750 FQ	126690 MW	183780 TQ	USBLS	5/15
	Dallas-Plano-Irving PMSA, TX	Y	92170 FQ	133950 MW	175650 TQ	USBLS	5/15
	Fort Worth-Arlington PMSA, TX	Y	87100 FQ	119470 MW	162510 TQ	USBLS	5/15
	Houston-The Woodlands-Sugar Land MSA, TX	Y	95560 FQ	131350 MW	181280 TQ	USBLS	5/15
	San Antonio-New Braunfels MSA, TX	Y	79600 FQ	122870 MW	176310 TQ	USBLS	5/15
	Utah	Y	64710 FQ	96440 MW	147660 TQ	USBLS	5/15
	Ogden-Clearfield MSA, UT	Y	50840 FQ	63330 MW	112820 TQ	USBLS	5/15
	Provo-Orem MSA, UT	Y	64930 FQ	101930 MW	149330 TQ	USBLS	5/15
	Salt Lake City MSA, UT	Y	69070 FQ	102450 MW	154390 TQ	USBLS	5/15
	Vermont	Y	74710 FQ	100230 MW	151860 TQ	USBLS	5/15
	Virginia	Y	86860 FQ	146040 MW		USBLS	5/15
	Richmond MSA, VA	Y	88520 FQ	136590 MW		USBLS	5/15
	Virginia Beach-Norfolk-Newport News MSA, VA-NC	Y	71220 FQ	95130 MW	156990 TQ	USBLS	5/15
	Washington	H	38.24 FQ	53.41 MW	74.67 TQ	WABLS	3/16
	Seattle-Bellevue-Everett PMSA, WA	H	41.04 FQ	57.93 MW	78.08 TQ	WABLS	3/16
	Tacoma-Lakewood PMSA, WA	H	36.39 FQ	46.26 MW	67.85 TQ	WABLS	3/16
	West Virginia	Y	61390 FQ	77230 MW	100270 TQ	USBLS	5/15
	Huntington-Ashland MSA, WV-KY-OH	Y	70770 FQ	90990 MW	123340 TQ	USBLS	5/15
	Wisconsin	Y	78790 FQ	108310 MW	143690 TQ	USBLS	5/15
	Madison MSA, WI	Y	90360 FQ	119010 MW	148850 TQ	USBLS	5/15
	Milwaukee-Waukesha-West Allis MSA, WI	Y	83760 FQ	115110 MW	153990 TQ	USBLS	5/15
	Wyoming	Y	73190 FQ	95220 MW	117670 TQ	USBLS	5/15
	Puerto Rico	Y	47030 FQ	70700 MW	103960 TQ	USBLS	5/15
	San Juan-Carolina-Caguas MSA, PR	Y	47060 FQ	72410 MW	106030 TQ	USBLS	5/15
	Virgin Islands	Y	49720 FQ	68320 MW	87410 TQ	USBLS	5/15
	Guam	Y	33910 FQ	43960 MW	57980 TQ	USBLS	5/15
Copier Industry	United States	Y		152557 ATC		COPIER	2016

Occupation/Type/Industry	Location	Per	Low	Mid	High	Source	Date
Sales Representative							
Consumer Packaged Goods	United States	Y		55730-76190 AWR		MST01	2016
Livestock Feed	United States	Y		54410 MW		SKU02	2016
Medical Devices	United States	Y		87916 AW		MST01	2016
Pet Products	United States	Y		79000 AW		BAL01	2011
Wholesale and Manufacturing	Alabama	Y	32496 AE	65096 AW	81396 AEX	ALBLS	6/16
Wholesale and Manufacturing	Birmingham-Hoover MSA, AL	Y	35227 AE	71777 AW	90052 AEX	ALBLS	6/16
Wholesale and Manufacturing	Alaska	Y	45240 FQ	57910 MW	73720 TQ	USBLS	5/15
Wholesale and Manufacturing	Anchorage MSA, AK	Y	47230 FQ	60370 MW	75220 TQ	USBLS	5/15
Wholesale and Manufacturing	Arizona	Y	34650 FQ	48940 MW	73700 TQ	USBLS	5/15
Wholesale and Manufacturing	Phoenix-Mesa-Scottsdale MSA, AZ	Y	35520 FQ	50370 MW	76420 TQ	USBLS	5/15
Wholesale and Manufacturing	Tucson MSA, AZ	Y	30650 FQ	41420 MW	57300 TQ	USBLS	5/15
Wholesale and Manufacturing	Arkansas	Y	33180 FQ	48170 MW	71850 TQ	USBLS	5/15
Wholesale and Manufacturing	Little Rock-North Little Rock-Conway MSA, AR	Y	36820 FQ	50450 MW	72090 TQ	USBLS	5/15
Wholesale and Manufacturing	California	H	17.55 FQ	26.05 MW	38.65 TQ	CABLS	1/16-3/16
Wholesale and Manufacturing	Anaheim-Santa Ana-Irvine PMSA, CA	H	17.62 FQ	26.25 MW	39.58 TQ	CABLS	1/16-3/16
Wholesale and Manufacturing	Los Angeles-Long Beach-Glendale PMSA, CA	H	15.25 FQ	23.31 MW	36.27 TQ	CABLS	1/16-3/16
Wholesale and Manufacturing	Oakland-Hayward-Berkeley PMSA, CA	H	19.15 FQ	28.12 MW	42.56 TQ	CABLS	1/16-3/16
Wholesale and Manufacturing	Riverside-San Bernardino-Ontario MSA, CA	H	18.98 FQ	26.84 MW	38.90 TQ	CABLS	1/16-3/16
Wholesale and Manufacturing	Sacramento–Roseville–Arden-Arcade MSA, CA	H	20.08 FQ	28.67 MW	41.05 TQ	CABLS	1/16-3/16
Wholesale and Manufacturing	San Diego-Carlsbad MSA, CA	H	16.82 FQ	25.23 MW	37.36 TQ	CABLS	1/16-3/16
Wholesale and Manufacturing	San Francisco-Redwood City-South San Francisco PMSA, CA	H	19.68 FQ	27.15 MW	37.80 TQ	CABLS	1/16-3/16
Wholesale and Manufacturing	Colorado	Y	40220 FQ	57830 MW	83100 TQ	USBLS	5/15
Wholesale and Manufacturing	Denver-Aurora-Lakewood MSA, CO	Y	41700 FQ	58720 MW	81830 TQ	USBLS	5/15
Wholesale and Manufacturing	Connecticut	Y		63280 MW		CTBLS	1/16-3/16
Wholesale and Manufacturing	Bridgeport-Stamford-Norwalk MSA, CT	Y	49960 FQ	68750 MW	93410 TQ	USBLS	5/15
Wholesale and Manufacturing	Hartford-West Hartford-East Hartford MSA, CT	Y	45020 FQ	60400 MW	92030 TQ	USBLS	5/15
Wholesale and Manufacturing	Delaware	Y	42550 FQ	56910 MW	77960 TQ	USBLS	5/15
Wholesale and Manufacturing	Wilmington PMSA, DE-MD-NJ	Y	45510 FQ	58230 MW	77820 TQ	USBLS	5/15
Wholesale and Manufacturing	District of Columbia	Y	34200 FQ	52480 MW	74870 TQ	USBLS	5/15
Wholesale and Manufacturing	Washington-Arlington-Alexandria PMSA, DC-VA-MD-WV	Y	44790 FQ	60820 MW	90650 TQ	USBLS	5/15
Wholesale and Manufacturing	Florida	H	12.42 AE	23.39 MW	36.45 AEX	FLBLS	7/16-9/16
Wholesale and Manufacturing	Fort Lauderdale-Pompano Beach-Deerfield Beach PMSA, FL	H	13.52 AE	24.42 MW	36.32 AEX	FLBLS	7/16-9/16
Wholesale and Manufacturing	Miami-Miami Beach-Kendall PMSA, FL	H	10.88 AE	19.50 MW	33.03 AEX	FLBLS	7/16-9/16
Wholesale and Manufacturing	Orlando-Kissimmee-Sanford MSA, FL	H	12.93 AE	25.09 MW	38.03 AEX	FLBLS	7/16-9/16
Wholesale and Manufacturing	Tampa-St. Petersburg-Clearwater MSA, FL	H	14.43 AE	25.85 MW	38.91 AEX	FLBLS	7/16-9/16
Wholesale and Manufacturing	Georgia	Y	36770 FQ	53870 MW	77430 TQ	USBLS	5/15
Wholesale and Manufacturing	Atlanta-Sandy Springs-Roswell MSA, GA	Y	40530 FQ	56700 MW	80610 TQ	USBLS	5/15
Wholesale and Manufacturing	Augusta-Richmond County MSA, GA-SC	Y	29460 FQ	46140 MW	68900 TQ	USBLS	5/15
Wholesale and Manufacturing	Hawaii	Y	30340 FQ	42700 MW	58070 TQ	USBLS	5/15
Wholesale and Manufacturing	Urban Honolulu MSA, HI	Y	31500 FQ	44190 MW	58840 TQ	USBLS	5/15
Wholesale and Manufacturing	Idaho	Y	38880 FQ	56040 MW	76460 TQ	USBLS	5/15
Wholesale and Manufacturing	Boise City MSA, ID	Y	40140 FQ	57840 MW	78590 TQ	USBLS	5/15
Wholesale and Manufacturing	Illinois	Y	40610 FQ	58830 MW	85760 TQ	USBLS	5/15
Wholesale and Manufacturing	Chicago-Naperville-Arlington Heights PMSA, IL	Y	43140 FQ	61420 MW	88520 TQ	USBLS	5/15
Wholesale and Manufacturing	Lake County-Kenosha County PMSA, IL-WI	Y	38520 FQ	58280 MW	90180 TQ	USBLS	5/15
Wholesale and Manufacturing	Indiana	Y	38300 FQ	56110 MW	80700 TQ	USBLS	5/15

AE Average entry wage	**AWR** Average wage range	**H** Hourly	**LR** Low end range	**MTC** Median total compensation	**TCC** Total cash compensation
AEX Average experienced wage	**B** Biweekly	**HI** Highest wage paid	**M** Monthly	**MW** Median wage paid	**TQ** Third quartile wage
ATC Average total compensation	**D** Daily	**HR** High end range	**MCC** Median cash compensation	**MWR** Median wage range	**W** Weekly
AW Average wage paid	**FQ** First quartile wage	**LO** Lowest wage paid	**ME** Median entry wage	**S** See annotated source	**Y** Yearly

Occupation/Type/Industry	Location	Per	Low	Mid	High	Source	Date
Sales Representative							
Wholesale and Manufacturing	Gary PMSA, IN	Y	44270 FQ	60890 MW	87440 TQ	USBLS	5/15
Wholesale and Manufacturing	Indianapolis-Carmel-Anderson MSA, IN	Y	40740 FQ	59150 MW	84760 TQ	USBLS	5/15
Wholesale and Manufacturing	Iowa	Y	40770 FQ	54600 MW	74270 TQ	USBLS	5/15
Wholesale and Manufacturing	Des Moines-West Des Moines MSA, IA	Y	44610 FQ	59040 MW	79950 TQ	USBLS	5/15
Wholesale and Manufacturing	Kansas	Y	41110 FQ	58310 MW	84650 TQ	USBLS	5/15
Wholesale and Manufacturing	Wichita MSA, KS	Y	41000 FQ	57710 MW	83180 TQ	USBLS	5/15
Wholesale and Manufacturing	Kentucky	Y	36090 FQ	53430 MW	79450 TQ	USBLS	5/15
Wholesale and Manufacturing	Louisville-Jefferson County MSA, KY-IN	Y	38260 FQ	56910 MW	88400 TQ	USBLS	5/15
Wholesale and Manufacturing	Louisiana	Y	37380 FQ	49740 MW	69490 TQ	USBLS	5/15
Wholesale and Manufacturing	Baton Rouge MSA, LA	Y	34720 FQ	50150 MW	71190 TQ	USBLS	5/15
Wholesale and Manufacturing	New Orleans-Metairie MSA, LA	Y	39770 FQ	50700 MW	70980 TQ	USBLS	5/15
Wholesale and Manufacturing	Maine	Y	40970 FQ	54970 MW	75830 TQ	USBLS	5/15
Wholesale and Manufacturing	Portland-South Portland MSA, ME	Y	44750 FQ	58280 MW	75380 TQ	USBLS	5/15
Wholesale and Manufacturing	Maryland	Y	32954 AE	68965 MW	86970 AEX	MDBLS	4/16
Wholesale and Manufacturing	Baltimore-Columbia-Towson MSA, MD	Y	40890 FQ	59100 MW	84710 TQ	USBLS	5/15
Wholesale and Manufacturing	Salisbury MSA, MD-DE	Y	35850 FQ	53080 MW	75430 TQ	USBLS	5/15
Wholesale and Manufacturing	Massachusetts	Y	48800 FQ	65300 MW	94040 TQ	USBLS	5/15
Wholesale and Manufacturing	Boston-Cambridge-Newton NECTA, MA	Y	50440 FQ	66780 MW	97060 TQ	USBLS	5/15
Wholesale and Manufacturing	Worcester MSA, MA-CT	Y	46420 FQ	63040 MW	93440 TQ	USBLS	5/15
Wholesale and Manufacturing	Michigan	Y	37460 FQ	55080 MW	80490 TQ	USBLS	5/15
Wholesale and Manufacturing	Detroit-Dearborn-Livonia PMSA, MI	Y	43440 FQ	62080 MW	90130 TQ	USBLS	5/15
Wholesale and Manufacturing	Grand Rapids-Wyoming MSA, MI	Y	37970 FQ	54760 MW	82200 TQ	USBLS	5/15
Wholesale and Manufacturing	Minnesota	Y	45396 FQ	62215 MW	87797 TQ	MNBLS	1/16-3/16
Wholesale and Manufacturing	Minneapolis-St. Paul-Bloomington MSA, MN-WI	Y	49097 FQ	66491 MW	93505 TQ	MNBLS	1/16-3/16
Wholesale and Manufacturing	Mississippi	Y	32170 FQ	47470 MW	65050 TQ	USBLS	5/15
Wholesale and Manufacturing	Jackson MSA, MS	Y	37590 FQ	51470 MW	65370 TQ	USBLS	5/15
Wholesale and Manufacturing	Missouri	Y	35900 FQ	53240 MW	75260 TQ	USBLS	5/15
Wholesale and Manufacturing	Kansas City MSA, MO-KS	Y	41410 FQ	58460 MW	85100 TQ	USBLS	5/15
Wholesale and Manufacturing	St. Louis MSA, MO-IL	Y	38560 FQ	58390 MW	80770 TQ	USBLS	5/15
Wholesale and Manufacturing	Montana	Y	32010 FQ	45400 MW	64100 TQ	USBLS	5/15
Wholesale and Manufacturing	Billings MSA, MT	Y	29930 FQ	45050 MW	62450 TQ	USBLS	5/15
Wholesale and Manufacturing	Nebraska	Y	36450 FQ	50265 MW	69680 TQ	NEBLS	7/16-9/16
Wholesale and Manufacturing	Omaha-Council Bluffs MSA, NE-IA	Y	39945 FQ	53135 MW	71525 TQ	NEBLS	7/16-9/16
Wholesale and Manufacturing	Nevada	Y	39550 FQ	55040 MW	81060 TQ	USBLS	5/15
Wholesale and Manufacturing	Las Vegas-Henderson-Paradise MSA, NV	Y	39950 FQ	54640 MW	81990 TQ	USBLS	5/15
Wholesale and Manufacturing	New Hampshire	H	19.74 AE	31.47 MW	46.47 AEX	NHBLS	6/16
Wholesale and Manufacturing	Manchester NECTA, NH	H	21.00 AE	33.16 MW	46.24 AEX	NHBLS	6/16
Wholesale and Manufacturing	Nashua NECTA, NH-MA	Y	50660 FQ	68790 MW	94250 TQ	USBLS	5/15
Wholesale and Manufacturing	New Jersey	Y	45000 FQ	65180 MW	92500 TQ	USBLS	5/15
Wholesale and Manufacturing	Camden PMSA, NJ	Y	49670 FQ	72080 MW	98380 TQ	USBLS	5/15
Wholesale and Manufacturing	Newark PMSA, NJ-PA	Y	44440 FQ	65070 MW	93670 TQ	USBLS	5/15
Wholesale and Manufacturing	Trenton MSA, NJ	Y	45310 FQ	71430 MW	99620 TQ	USBLS	5/15
Wholesale and Manufacturing	New Mexico	Y	31050 FQ	46040 MW	62920 TQ	USBLS	5/15
Wholesale and Manufacturing	Albuquerque MSA, NM	Y	31630 FQ	46200 MW	64260 TQ	USBLS	5/15
Wholesale and Manufacturing	New York	Y	31870 AE	59430 MW	93030 AEX	NYBLS	1/16-3/16
Wholesale and Manufacturing	Buffalo-Cheektowaga-Niagara Falls MSA, NY	Y	38070 FQ	54560 MW	75280 TQ	USBLS	5/15
Wholesale and Manufacturing	Nassau County-Suffolk County PMSA, NY	Y	42930 FQ	65530 MW	101610 TQ	USBLS	5/15
Wholesale and Manufacturing	New York-Jersey City-White Plains PMSA, NY-NJ	Y	40120 FQ	61120 MW	91960 TQ	USBLS	5/15
Wholesale and Manufacturing	Rochester MSA, NY	Y	39950 FQ	55720 MW	76940 TQ	USBLS	5/15
Wholesale and Manufacturing	North Carolina	Y	39480 FQ	57500 MW	82820 TQ	USBLS	5/15
Wholesale and Manufacturing	Charlotte-Concord-Gastonia MSA, NC-SC	Y	44990 FQ	64480 MW	90450 TQ	USBLS	5/15
Wholesale and Manufacturing	Raleigh MSA, NC	Y	41950 FQ	58910 MW	81880 TQ	USBLS	5/15
Wholesale and Manufacturing	North Dakota	Y	43920 FQ	57970 MW	78310 TQ	USBLS	5/15
Wholesale and Manufacturing	Fargo MSA, ND-MN	Y	42720 FQ	57480 MW	83580 TQ	USBLS	5/15
Wholesale and Manufacturing	Ohio	Y	39420 FQ	55220 MW	78870 TQ	USBLS	5/15

AE	Average entry wage	AWR	Average wage range	H	Hourly
AEX	Average experienced wage	B	Biweekly	HI	Highest wage paid
ATC	Average total compensation	D	Daily	HR	High end range
AW	Average wage paid	FQ	First quartile wage	LO	Lowest wage paid

LR	Low end range	MTC	Median total compensation
M	Monthly	MW	Median wage paid
MCC	Median cash compensation	MWR	Median wage range
ME	Median entry wage	S	See annotated source

TCC	Total cash compensation
TQ	Third quartile wage
W	Weekly
Y	Yearly

Occupation/Type/Industry	Location	Per	Low	Mid	High	Source	Date
Sales Representative							
Wholesale and Manufacturing	Cincinnati MSA, OH-KY-IN	Y	43610 FQ	61450 MW	87360 TQ	USBLS	5/15
Wholesale and Manufacturing	Cleveland-Elyria MSA, OH	Y	42780 FQ	59110 MW	85370 TQ	USBLS	5/15
Wholesale and Manufacturing	Columbus MSA, OH	Y	40680 FQ	55980 MW	80730 TQ	USBLS	5/15
Wholesale and Manufacturing	Oklahoma	Y	35160 FQ	49680 MW	73360 TQ	USBLS	5/15
Wholesale and Manufacturing	Oklahoma City MSA, OK	Y	34560 FQ	49100 MW	73600 TQ	USBLS	5/15
Wholesale and Manufacturing	Tulsa MSA, OK	Y	37490 FQ	51980 MW	75660 TQ	USBLS	5/15
Wholesale and Manufacturing	Oregon	H	19.23 FQ	26.08 MW	37.10 TQ	ORBLS	2016
Wholesale and Manufacturing	Portland-Vancouver-Hillsboro MSA, OR-WA	Y	42810 FQ	58640 MW	82950 TQ	USBLS	5/15
Wholesale and Manufacturing	Pennsylvania	Y	41510 FQ	57850 MW	80150 TQ	USBLS	5/15
Wholesale and Manufacturing	Allentown-Bethlehem-Easton MSA, PA-NJ	Y	43340 FQ	59760 MW	77580 TQ	USBLS	5/15
Wholesale and Manufacturing	Harrisburg-Carlisle MSA, PA	Y	36760 FQ	50250 MW	70890 TQ	USBLS	5/15
Wholesale and Manufacturing	Montgomery County-Bucks County-Chester County PMSA, PA	Y	44170 FQ	60640 MW	88750 TQ	USBLS	5/15
Wholesale and Manufacturing	Philadelphia PMSA, PA	Y	43730 FQ	59120 MW	81050 TQ	USBLS	5/15
Wholesale and Manufacturing	Pittsburgh MSA, PA	Y	44170 FQ	60660 MW	79710 TQ	USBLS	5/15
Wholesale and Manufacturing	Rhode Island	Y	43180 FQ	59590 MW	79470 TQ	USBLS	5/15
Wholesale and Manufacturing	Providence-Warwick MSA, RI-MA	Y	42770 FQ	58900 MW	78780 TQ	USBLS	5/15
Wholesale and Manufacturing	South Carolina	Y	37220 FQ	52460 MW	78010 TQ	USBLS	5/15
Wholesale and Manufacturing	Charleston-North Charleston MSA, SC	Y	37230 FQ	53020 MW	72540 TQ	USBLS	5/15
Wholesale and Manufacturing	Columbia MSA, SC	Y	37830 FQ	54630 MW	78870 TQ	USBLS	5/15
Wholesale and Manufacturing	Greenville-Anderson-Mauldin MSA, SC	Y	39610 FQ	51120 MW	76130 TQ	USBLS	5/15
Wholesale and Manufacturing	South Dakota	Y	42000 FQ	53080 MW	68040 TQ	USBLS	5/15
Wholesale and Manufacturing	Sioux Falls MSA, SD	Y	43610 FQ	55550 MW	71430 TQ	USBLS	5/15
Wholesale and Manufacturing	Tennessee	Y	34570 FQ	50920 MW	72300 TQ	USBLS	5/15
Wholesale and Manufacturing	Knoxville MSA, TN	Y	32910 FQ	48740 MW	72600 TQ	USBLS	5/15
Wholesale and Manufacturing	Memphis MSA, TN-MS-AR	Y	37210 FQ	54220 MW	79080 TQ	USBLS	5/15
Wholesale and Manufacturing	Nashville-Davidson–Murfreesboro–Franklin MSA, TN	Y	37030 FQ	52830 MW	73940 TQ	USBLS	5/15
Wholesale and Manufacturing	Texas	Y	38440 FQ	57410 MW	86670 TQ	USBLS	5/15
Wholesale and Manufacturing	Austin-Round Rock MSA, TX	Y	34940 FQ	53360 MW	85380 TQ	USBLS	5/15
Wholesale and Manufacturing	Dallas-Plano-Irving PMSA, TX	Y	41450 FQ	61390 MW	91600 TQ	USBLS	5/15
Wholesale and Manufacturing	Fort Worth-Arlington PMSA, TX	Y	39750 FQ	54950 MW	79780 TQ	USBLS	5/15
Wholesale and Manufacturing	Houston-The Woodlands-Sugar Land MSA, TX	Y	39810 FQ	61720 MW	93010 TQ	USBLS	5/15
Wholesale and Manufacturing	San Antonio-New Braunfels MSA, TX	Y	37850 FQ	54360 MW	79320 TQ	USBLS	5/15
Wholesale and Manufacturing	Utah	Y	38640 FQ	55790 MW	86660 TQ	USBLS	5/15
Wholesale and Manufacturing	Ogden-Clearfield MSA, UT	Y	35410 FQ	55990 MW	86540 TQ	USBLS	5/15
Wholesale and Manufacturing	Provo-Orem MSA, UT	Y	35790 FQ	50850 MW	82760 TQ	USBLS	5/15
Wholesale and Manufacturing	Salt Lake City MSA, UT	Y	41100 FQ	58100 MW	90140 TQ	USBLS	5/15
Wholesale and Manufacturing	Vermont	Y	41240 FQ	57320 MW	74820 TQ	USBLS	5/15
Wholesale and Manufacturing	Burlington-South Burlington MSA, VT	Y	42030 FQ	54400 MW	68110 TQ	USBLS	5/15
Wholesale and Manufacturing	Virginia	Y	39890 FQ	57640 MW	84420 TQ	USBLS	5/15
Wholesale and Manufacturing	Richmond MSA, VA	Y	42940 FQ	65890 MW	89680 TQ	USBLS	5/15
Wholesale and Manufacturing	Virginia Beach-Norfolk-Newport News MSA, VA-NC	Y	36690 FQ	50680 MW	76440 TQ	USBLS	5/15
Wholesale and Manufacturing	Washington	H	19.35 FQ	29.16 MW	42.88 TQ	WABLS	3/16
Wholesale and Manufacturing	Seattle-Bellevue-Everett PMSA, WA	H	20.96 FQ	31.48 MW	45.54 TQ	WABLS	3/16
Wholesale and Manufacturing	Tacoma-Lakewood PMSA, WA	H	17.86 FQ	27.41 MW	39.93 TQ	WABLS	3/16
Wholesale and Manufacturing	West Virginia	Y	29290 FQ	45820 MW	61610 TQ	USBLS	5/15
Wholesale and Manufacturing	Huntington-Ashland MSA, WV-KY-OH	Y	34020 FQ	48530 MW	67680 TQ	USBLS	5/15
Wholesale and Manufacturing	Wisconsin	Y	41380 FQ	57370 MW	80360 TQ	USBLS	5/15
Wholesale and Manufacturing	Madison MSA, WI	Y	40570 FQ	56030 MW	76620 TQ	USBLS	5/15
Wholesale and Manufacturing	Milwaukee-Waukesha-West Allis MSA, WI	Y	45120 FQ	60930 MW	86460 TQ	USBLS	5/15
Wholesale and Manufacturing	Wyoming	Y	42050 FQ	56740 MW	77100 TQ	USBLS	5/15
Wholesale and Manufacturing	Cheyenne MSA, WY	Y	38770 FQ	60430 MW	78710 TQ	USBLS	5/15
Wholesale and Manufacturing	Puerto Rico	Y	18300 FQ	23600 MW	36020 TQ	USBLS	5/15
Wholesale and Manufacturing	San Juan-Carolina-Caguas MSA, PR	Y	18410 FQ	24270 MW	37510 TQ	USBLS	5/15

AE Average entry wage	**AWR** Average wage range	**H** Hourly	**LR** Low end range	**MTC** Median total compensation	**TCC** Total cash compensation
AEX Average experienced wage **B**	Biweekly	**HI** Highest wage paid	**M** Monthly	**MW** Median wage paid	**TQ** Third quartile wage
ATC Average total compensation **D**	Daily	**HR** High end range	**MCC** Median cash compensation	**MWR** Median wage range	**W** Weekly
AW Average wage paid	**FQ** First quartile wage	**LO** Lowest wage paid	**ME** Median entry wage	**S** See annotated source	**Y** Yearly

Sales Representative

Occupation/Type/Industry	Location	Per	Low	Mid	High	Source	Date
Wholesale and Manufacturing	Virgin Islands	Y	25460 FQ	36550 MW	48500 TQ	USBLS	5/15
Wholesale and Manufacturing	Guam	Y	18800 FQ	21890 MW	31870 TQ	USBLS	5/15
Wholesale and Manufacturing, Technical and Scientific Products	Alabama	Y	45083 AE	87332 AW	108452 AEX	ALBLS	6/16
Wholesale and Manufacturing, Technical and Scientific Products	Birmingham-Hoover MSA, AL	Y	43925 AE	91087 AW	114668 AEX	ALBLS	6/16
Wholesale and Manufacturing, Technical and Scientific Products	Alaska	Y	42340 FQ	73620 MW	108660 TQ	USBLS	5/15
Wholesale and Manufacturing, Technical and Scientific Products	Anchorage MSA, AK	Y	39860 FQ	66960 MW	110330 TQ	USBLS	5/15
Wholesale and Manufacturing, Technical and Scientific Products	Arizona	Y	50400 FQ	69190 MW	113380 TQ	USBLS	5/15
Wholesale and Manufacturing, Technical and Scientific Products	Phoenix-Mesa-Scottsdale MSA, AZ	Y	51980 FQ	70140 MW	113670 TQ	USBLS	5/15
Wholesale and Manufacturing, Technical and Scientific Products	Tucson MSA, AZ	Y	44930 FQ	61210 MW	106050 TQ	USBLS	5/15
Wholesale and Manufacturing, Technical and Scientific Products	Arkansas	Y	51230 FQ	60680 MW	81300 TQ	USBLS	5/15
Wholesale and Manufacturing, Technical and Scientific Products	Little Rock-North Little Rock-Conway MSA, AR	Y	52640 FQ	59420 MW	71670 TQ	USBLS	5/15
Wholesale and Manufacturing, Technical and Scientific Products	California	H	26.82 FQ	39.03 MW	57.73 TQ	CABLS	1/16-3/16
Wholesale and Manufacturing, Technical and Scientific Products	Anaheim-Santa Ana-Irvine PMSA, CA	H	23.36 FQ	35.90 MW	53.92 TQ	CABLS	1/16-3/16
Wholesale and Manufacturing, Technical and Scientific Products	Los Angeles-Long Beach-Glendale PMSA, CA	H	24.25 FQ	35.20 MW	51.13 TQ	CABLS	1/16-3/16
Wholesale and Manufacturing, Technical and Scientific Products	Oakland-Hayward-Berkeley PMSA, CA	H	30.47 FQ	44.76 MW	60.60 TQ	CABLS	1/16-3/16
Wholesale and Manufacturing, Technical and Scientific Products	Riverside-San Bernardino-Ontario MSA, CA	H	23.15 FQ	29.64 MW	40.16 TQ	CABLS	1/16-3/16
Wholesale and Manufacturing, Technical and Scientific Products	Sacramento–Roseville–Arden-Arcade MSA, CA	H	25.13 FQ	35.29 MW	52.37 TQ	CABLS	1/16-3/16
Wholesale and Manufacturing, Technical and Scientific Products	San Diego-Carlsbad MSA, CA	H	22.43 FQ	32.06 MW	48.35 TQ	CABLS	1/16-3/16
Wholesale and Manufacturing, Technical and Scientific Products	San Francisco-Redwood City-South San Francisco PMSA, CA	H	34.78 FQ	47.14 MW	69.23 TQ	CABLS	1/16-3/16
Wholesale and Manufacturing, Technical and Scientific Products	Colorado	Y	62790 FQ	97390 MW	127410 TQ	USBLS	5/15
Wholesale and Manufacturing, Technical and Scientific Products	Denver-Aurora-Lakewood MSA, CO	Y	74230 FQ	104420 MW	137200 TQ	USBLS	5/15
Wholesale and Manufacturing, Technical and Scientific Products	Connecticut	Y		87581 MW		CTBLS	1/16-3/16
Wholesale and Manufacturing, Technical and Scientific Products	Bridgeport-Stamford-Norwalk MSA, CT	Y	64740 FQ	82940 MW	117650 TQ	USBLS	5/15
Wholesale and Manufacturing, Technical and Scientific Products	Hartford-West Hartford-East Hartford MSA, CT	Y	71610 FQ	93560 MW	117780 TQ	USBLS	5/15
Wholesale and Manufacturing, Technical and Scientific Products	Delaware	Y	70640 FQ	94620 MW	140110 TQ	USBLS	5/15
Wholesale and Manufacturing, Technical and Scientific Products	Wilmington PMSA, DE-MD-NJ	Y	70070 FQ	94780 MW	141170 TQ	USBLS	5/15
Wholesale and Manufacturing, Technical and Scientific Products	District of Columbia	Y	51510 FQ	72240 MW	104880 TQ	USBLS	5/15
Wholesale and Manufacturing, Technical and Scientific Products	Washington-Arlington-Alexandria PMSA, DC-VA-MD-WV	Y	70140 FQ	107610 MW	148960 TQ	USBLS	5/15

AE	Average entry wage	AWR	Average wage range	H	Hourly	LR	Low end range	MTC	Median total compensation	TCC	Total cash compensation
AEX	Average experienced wage	B	Biweekly	HI	Highest wage paid	M	Monthly	MW	Median wage paid	TQ	Third quartile wage
ATC	Average total compensation	D	Daily	HR	High end range	MCC	Median cash compensation	MWR	Median wage range	W	Weekly
AW	Average wage paid	FQ	First quartile wage	LO	Lowest wage paid	ME	Median entry wage	S	See annotated source	Y	Yearly

Sales Representative

Occupation/Type/Industry	Location	Per	Low	Mid	High	Source	Date
Sales Representative							
Wholesale and Manufacturing, Technical and Scientific Products	Florida	H	19.16 AE	34.19 MW	50.71 AEX	FLBLS	7/16-9/16
Wholesale and Manufacturing, Technical and Scientific Products	Fort Lauderdale-Pompano Beach-Deerfield Beach PMSA, FL	H	24.92 AE	43.68 MW	57.86 AEX	FLBLS	7/16-9/16
Wholesale and Manufacturing, Technical and Scientific Products	Miami-Miami Beach-Kendall PMSA, FL	H	16.12 AE	29.40 MW	49.36 AEX	FLBLS	7/16-9/16
Wholesale and Manufacturing, Technical and Scientific Products	Orlando-Kissimmee-Sanford MSA, FL	H	18.90 AE	31.80 MW	48.16 AEX	FLBLS	7/16-9/16
Wholesale and Manufacturing, Technical and Scientific Products	Tampa-St. Petersburg-Clearwater MSA, FL	H	18.34 AE	31.36 MW	47.56 AEX	FLBLS	7/16-9/16
Wholesale and Manufacturing, Technical and Scientific Products	Georgia	Y	46600 FQ	64710 MW	97720 TQ	USBLS	5/15
Wholesale and Manufacturing, Technical and Scientific Products	Atlanta-Sandy Springs-Roswell MSA, GA	Y	47760 FQ	66960 MW	98860 TQ	USBLS	5/15
Wholesale and Manufacturing, Technical and Scientific Products	Augusta-Richmond County MSA, GA-SC	Y	37420 FQ	47500 MW	91660 TQ	USBLS	5/15
Wholesale and Manufacturing, Technical and Scientific Products	Hawaii	Y	46170 FQ	61520 MW	76810 TQ	USBLS	5/15
Wholesale and Manufacturing, Technical and Scientific Products	Urban Honolulu MSA, HI	Y	45580 FQ	61730 MW	77410 TQ	USBLS	5/15
Wholesale and Manufacturing, Technical and Scientific Products	Idaho	Y	42950 FQ	58370 MW	95450 TQ	USBLS	5/15
Wholesale and Manufacturing, Technical and Scientific Products	Boise City MSA, ID	Y	39550 FQ	55980 MW	86200 TQ	USBLS	5/15
Wholesale and Manufacturing, Technical and Scientific Products	Illinois	Y	48050 FQ	65400 MW	95500 TQ	USBLS	5/15
Wholesale and Manufacturing, Technical and Scientific Products	Chicago-Naperville-Arlington Heights PMSA, IL	Y	46450 FQ	63440 MW	92530 TQ	USBLS	5/15
Wholesale and Manufacturing, Technical and Scientific Products	Lake County-Kenosha County PMSA, IL-WI	Y	56550 FQ	73500 MW	103880 TQ	USBLS	5/15
Wholesale and Manufacturing, Technical and Scientific Products	Indiana	Y	55770 FQ	77590 MW	112890 TQ	USBLS	5/15
Wholesale and Manufacturing, Technical and Scientific Products	Gary PMSA, IN	Y	54800 FQ	70770 MW	96680 TQ	USBLS	5/15
Wholesale and Manufacturing, Technical and Scientific Products	Indianapolis-Carmel-Anderson MSA, IN	Y	58390 FQ	81330 MW	123130 TQ	USBLS	5/15
Wholesale and Manufacturing, Technical and Scientific Products	Iowa	Y	42610 FQ	61140 MW	87350 TQ	USBLS	5/15
Wholesale and Manufacturing, Technical and Scientific Products	Des Moines-West Des Moines MSA, IA	Y	42210 FQ	60390 MW	94040 TQ	USBLS	5/15
Wholesale and Manufacturing, Technical and Scientific Products	Kansas	Y	53460 FQ	73870 MW	113700 TQ	USBLS	5/15
Wholesale and Manufacturing, Technical and Scientific Products	Wichita MSA, KS	Y	50300 FQ	68770 MW	88010 TQ	USBLS	5/15
Wholesale and Manufacturing, Technical and Scientific Products	Kentucky	Y	55610 FQ	78690 MW	112090 TQ	USBLS	5/15
Wholesale and Manufacturing, Technical and Scientific Products	Louisville-Jefferson County MSA, KY-IN	Y	68040 FQ	90790 MW	123570 TQ	USBLS	5/15
Wholesale and Manufacturing, Technical and Scientific Products	Louisiana	Y	55550 FQ	76320 MW	97650 TQ	USBLS	5/15
Wholesale and Manufacturing, Technical and Scientific Products	Baton Rouge MSA, LA	Y	49220 FQ	69720 MW	94030 TQ	USBLS	5/15
Wholesale and Manufacturing, Technical and Scientific Products	New Orleans-Metairie MSA, LA	Y	62970 FQ	86740 MW	110100 TQ	USBLS	5/15
Wholesale and Manufacturing, Technical and Scientific Products	Maine	Y	52690 FQ	80190 MW	101250 TQ	USBLS	5/15

AE	Average entry wage	AWR	Average wage range	H	Hourly
AEX	Average experienced wage	B	Biweekly	HI	Highest wage paid
ATC	Average total compensation	D	Daily	HR	High end range
AW	Average wage paid	FQ	First quartile wage	LO	Lowest wage paid

LR	Low end range	MTC	Median total compensation	TCC	Total cash compensation
M	Monthly	MW	Median wage paid	TQ	Third quartile wage
MCC	Median cash compensation	MWR	Median wage range	W	Weekly
ME	Median entry wage	S	See annotated source	Y	Yearly

Occupation/Type/Industry	Location	Per	Low	Mid	High	Source	Date
Sales Representative							
Wholesale and Manufacturing, Technical and Scientific Products	Portland-South Portland MSA, ME	Y	44970 FQ	66870 MW	95190 TQ	USBLS	5/15
Wholesale and Manufacturing, Technical and Scientific Products	Maryland	Y	45469 AE	98604 MW	125171 AEX	MDBLS	4/16
Wholesale and Manufacturing, Technical and Scientific Products	Baltimore-Columbia-Towson MSA, MD	Y	57080 FQ	81390 MW	125200 TQ	USBLS	5/15
Wholesale and Manufacturing, Technical and Scientific Products	Salisbury MSA, MD-DE	Y	56710 FQ	79550 MW	102970 TQ	USBLS	5/15
Wholesale and Manufacturing, Technical and Scientific Products	Massachusetts	Y	64010 FQ	89040 MW	123300 TQ	USBLS	5/15
Wholesale and Manufacturing, Technical and Scientific Products	Boston-Cambridge-Newton NECTA, MA	Y	69040 FQ	95210 MW	127330 TQ	USBLS	5/15
Wholesale and Manufacturing, Technical and Scientific Products	Worcester MSA, MA-CT	Y	57370 FQ	77750 MW	110870 TQ	USBLS	5/15
Wholesale and Manufacturing, Technical and Scientific Products	Michigan	Y	55620 FQ	76690 MW	108780 TQ	USBLS	5/15
Wholesale and Manufacturing, Technical and Scientific Products	Detroit-Dearborn-Livonia PMSA, MI	Y	60600 FQ	82470 MW	105450 TQ	USBLS	5/15
Wholesale and Manufacturing, Technical and Scientific Products	Grand Rapids-Wyoming MSA, MI	Y	50510 FQ	72290 MW	104400 TQ	USBLS	5/15
Wholesale and Manufacturing, Technical and Scientific Products	Minnesota	Y	68740 FQ	105756 MW	149751 TQ	MNBLS	1/16-3/16
Wholesale and Manufacturing, Technical and Scientific Products	Minneapolis-St. Paul-Bloomington MSA, MN-WI	Y	72238 FQ	113329 MW	153492 TQ	MNBLS	1/16-3/16
Wholesale and Manufacturing, Technical and Scientific Products	Mississippi	Y	39050 FQ	59450 MW	86480 TQ	USBLS	5/15
Wholesale and Manufacturing, Technical and Scientific Products	Jackson MSA, MS	Y	31320 FQ	45630 MW	79780 TQ	USBLS	5/15
Wholesale and Manufacturing, Technical and Scientific Products	Missouri	Y	49040 FQ	66130 MW	88140 TQ	USBLS	5/15
Wholesale and Manufacturing, Technical and Scientific Products	Kansas City MSA, MO-KS	Y	53580 FQ	73020 MW	115980 TQ	USBLS	5/15
Wholesale and Manufacturing, Technical and Scientific Products	St. Louis MSA, MO-IL	Y	51640 FQ	66760 MW	90800 TQ	USBLS	5/15
Wholesale and Manufacturing, Technical and Scientific Products	Montana	Y	42130 FQ	62630 MW	88530 TQ	USBLS	5/15
Wholesale and Manufacturing, Technical and Scientific Products	Nebraska	Y	41270 FQ	59230 MW	94025 TQ	NEBLS	7/16-9/16
Wholesale and Manufacturing, Technical and Scientific Products	Omaha-Council Bluffs MSA, NE-IA	Y	43370 FQ	60000 MW	96380 TQ	NEBLS	7/16-9/16
Wholesale and Manufacturing, Technical and Scientific Products	Nevada	Y	53520 FQ	71970 MW	97370 TQ	USBLS	5/15
Wholesale and Manufacturing, Technical and Scientific Products	Las Vegas-Henderson-Paradise MSA, NV	Y	52280 FQ	69120 MW	93060 TQ	USBLS	5/15
Wholesale and Manufacturing, Technical and Scientific Products	New Hampshire	H	22.89 AE	41.54 MW	62.06 AEX	NHBLS	6/16
Wholesale and Manufacturing, Technical and Scientific Products	Manchester NECTA, NH	H	27.05 AE	40.55 MW	58.84 AEX	NHBLS	6/16
Wholesale and Manufacturing, Technical and Scientific Products	Nashua NECTA, NH-MA	Y	52740 FQ	80930 MW	133800 TQ	USBLS	5/15
Wholesale and Manufacturing, Technical and Scientific Products	New Jersey	Y	72140 FQ	99300 MW	135760 TQ	USBLS	5/15
Wholesale and Manufacturing, Technical and Scientific Products	Camden PMSA, NJ	Y	72820 FQ	115750 MW	161880 TQ	USBLS	5/15
Wholesale and Manufacturing, Technical and Scientific Products	Newark PMSA, NJ-PA	Y	63470 FQ	86710 MW	126860 TQ	USBLS	5/15
Wholesale and Manufacturing, Technical and Scientific Products	Trenton MSA, NJ	Y	81860 FQ	97330 MW	123930 TQ	USBLS	5/15
Wholesale and Manufacturing, Technical and Scientific Products	New Mexico	Y	46520 FQ	57420 MW	74370 TQ	USBLS	5/15
Wholesale and Manufacturing, Technical and Scientific Products	Albuquerque MSA, NM	Y	47850 FQ	58090 MW	74310 TQ	USBLS	5/15

AE Average entry wage	**AWR** Average wage range	**H** Hourly	**LR** Low end range	**MTC** Median total compensation	**TCC** Total cash compensation
AEX Average experienced wage	**B** Biweekly	**HI** Highest wage paid	**M** Monthly	**MW** Median wage paid	**TQ** Third quartile wage
ATC Average total compensation	**D** Daily	**HR** High end range	**MCC** Median cash compensation	**MWR** Median wage range	**W** Weekly
AW Average wage paid	**FQ** First quartile wage	**LO** Lowest wage paid	**ME** Median entry wage	**S** See annotated source	**Y** Yearly

Sales Representative

Occupation/Type/Industry	Location	Per	Low	Mid	High	Source	Date
Wholesale and Manufacturing, Technical and Scientific Products	New York	Y	51860 AE	85020 MW	117880 AEX	NYBLS	1/16-3/16
Wholesale and Manufacturing, Technical and Scientific Products	Buffalo-Cheektowaga-Niagara Falls MSA, NY	Y	51890 FQ	66250 MW	92240 TQ	USBLS	5/15
Wholesale and Manufacturing, Technical and Scientific Products	Nassau County-Suffolk County PMSA, NY	Y	48580 FQ	74890 MW	114460 TQ	USBLS	5/15
Wholesale and Manufacturing, Technical and Scientific Products	New York-Jersey City-White Plains PMSA, NY-NJ	Y	72700 FQ	96360 MW	128840 TQ	USBLS	5/15
Wholesale and Manufacturing, Technical and Scientific Products	Rochester MSA, NY	Y	59500 FQ	74910 MW	101520 TQ	USBLS	5/15
Wholesale and Manufacturing, Technical and Scientific Products	North Carolina	Y	59920 FQ	85300 MW	119550 TQ	USBLS	5/15
Wholesale and Manufacturing, Technical and Scientific Products	Charlotte-Concord-Gastonia MSA, NC-SC	Y	57570 FQ	82780 MW	111100 TQ	USBLS	5/15
Wholesale and Manufacturing, Technical and Scientific Products	Raleigh MSA, NC	Y	68150 FQ	95690 MW	127710 TQ	USBLS	5/15
Wholesale and Manufacturing, Technical and Scientific Products	North Dakota	Y	56590 FQ	76780 MW	103570 TQ	USBLS	5/15
Wholesale and Manufacturing, Technical and Scientific Products	Fargo MSA, ND-MN	Y	55200 FQ	73340 MW	97810 TQ	USBLS	5/15
Wholesale and Manufacturing, Technical and Scientific Products	Ohio	Y	48980 FQ	68370 MW	96250 TQ	USBLS	5/15
Wholesale and Manufacturing, Technical and Scientific Products	Cincinnati MSA, OH-KY-IN	Y	49620 FQ	74090 MW	105070 TQ	USBLS	5/15
Wholesale and Manufacturing, Technical and Scientific Products	Cleveland-Elyria MSA, OH	Y	53200 FQ	70730 MW	96460 TQ	USBLS	5/15
Wholesale and Manufacturing, Technical and Scientific Products	Columbus MSA, OH	Y	53290 FQ	71310 MW	102610 TQ	USBLS	5/15
Wholesale and Manufacturing, Technical and Scientific Products	Oklahoma	Y	41310 FQ	55830 MW	83700 TQ	USBLS	5/15
Wholesale and Manufacturing, Technical and Scientific Products	Oklahoma City MSA, OK	Y	41410 FQ	53220 MW	84020 TQ	USBLS	5/15
Wholesale and Manufacturing, Technical and Scientific Products	Tulsa MSA, OK	Y	44040 FQ	58980 MW	84990 TQ	USBLS	5/15
Wholesale and Manufacturing, Technical and Scientific Products	Oregon	H	22.54 FQ	34.66 MW	51.90 TQ	ORBLS	2016
Wholesale and Manufacturing, Technical and Scientific Products	Portland-Vancouver-Hillsboro MSA, OR-WA	Y	46520 FQ	70850 MW	109180 TQ	USBLS	5/15
Wholesale and Manufacturing, Technical and Scientific Products	Pennsylvania	Y	58370 FQ	80050 MW	114050 TQ	USBLS	5/15
Wholesale and Manufacturing, Technical and Scientific Products	Allentown-Bethlehem-Easton MSA, PA-NJ	Y	69240 FQ	93020 MW	121940 TQ	USBLS	5/15
Wholesale and Manufacturing, Technical and Scientific Products	Harrisburg-Carlisle MSA, PA	Y	47530 FQ	62270 MW	80910 TQ	USBLS	5/15
Wholesale and Manufacturing, Technical and Scientific Products	Montgomery County-Bucks County-Chester County PMSA, PA	Y	61620 FQ	86890 MW	126120 TQ	USBLS	5/15
Wholesale and Manufacturing, Technical and Scientific Products	Philadelphia PMSA, PA	Y	65190 FQ	81070 MW	112060 TQ	USBLS	5/15
Wholesale and Manufacturing, Technical and Scientific Products	Pittsburgh MSA, PA	Y	52910 FQ	76700 MW	113900 TQ	USBLS	5/15
Wholesale and Manufacturing, Technical and Scientific Products	Rhode Island	Y	47210 FQ	67490 MW	109780 TQ	USBLS	5/15
Wholesale and Manufacturing, Technical and Scientific Products	Providence-Warwick MSA, RI-MA	Y	46000 FQ	64300 MW	101840 TQ	USBLS	5/15
Wholesale and Manufacturing, Technical and Scientific Products	South Carolina	Y	44510 FQ	66300 MW	98870 TQ	USBLS	5/15
Wholesale and Manufacturing, Technical and Scientific Products	Charleston-North Charleston MSA, SC	Y	47210 FQ	70430 MW	94450 TQ	USBLS	5/15
Wholesale and Manufacturing, Technical and Scientific Products	Columbia MSA, SC	Y	55180 FQ	88740 MW	134120 TQ	USBLS	5/15

AE	Average entry wage	AWR	Average wage range	H	Hourly
AEX	Average experienced wage	B	Biweekly	HI	Highest wage paid
ATC	Average total compensation	D	Daily	HR	High end range
AW	Average wage paid	FQ	First quartile wage	LO	Lowest wage paid

LR	Low end range	MTC	Median total compensation	TCC	Total cash compensation
M	Monthly	MW	Median wage paid	TQ	Third quartile wage
MCC	Median cash compensation	MWR	Median wage range	W	Weekly
ME	Median entry wage	S	See annotated source	Y	Yearly

Occupation/Type/Industry	Location	Per	Low	Mid	High	Source	Date
Sales Representative							
Wholesale and Manufacturing, Technical and Scientific Products	Greenville-Anderson-Mauldin MSA, SC	Y	42410 FQ	54880 MW	80840 TQ	USBLS	5/15
Wholesale and Manufacturing, Technical and Scientific Products	South Dakota	Y	55770 FQ	72990 MW	99470 TQ	USBLS	5/15
Wholesale and Manufacturing, Technical and Scientific Products	Sioux Falls MSA, SD	Y	65360 FQ	84550 MW	119960 TQ	USBLS	5/15
Wholesale and Manufacturing, Technical and Scientific Products	Tennessee	Y	47280 FQ	67960 MW	91750 TQ	USBLS	5/15
Wholesale and Manufacturing, Technical and Scientific Products	Knoxville MSA, TN	Y	54280 FQ	71370 MW	94220 TQ	USBLS	5/15
Wholesale and Manufacturing, Technical and Scientific Products	Memphis MSA, TN-MS-AR	Y	51430 FQ	69250 MW	95970 TQ	USBLS	5/15
Wholesale and Manufacturing, Technical and Scientific Products	Nashville-Davidson–Murfreesboro–Franklin MSA, TN	Y	44920 FQ	65680 MW	82980 TQ	USBLS	5/15
Wholesale and Manufacturing, Technical and Scientific Products	Texas	Y	53700 FQ	73200 MW	103890 TQ	USBLS	5/15
Wholesale and Manufacturing, Technical and Scientific Products	Austin-Round Rock MSA, TX	Y	50160 FQ	63820 MW	94970 TQ	USBLS	5/15
Wholesale and Manufacturing, Technical and Scientific Products	Dallas-Plano-Irving PMSA, TX	Y	54840 FQ	73200 MW	95190 TQ	USBLS	5/15
Wholesale and Manufacturing, Technical and Scientific Products	Fort Worth-Arlington PMSA, TX	Y	51040 FQ	71770 MW	93650 TQ	USBLS	5/15
Wholesale and Manufacturing, Technical and Scientific Products	Houston-The Woodlands-Sugar Land MSA, TX	Y	56990 FQ	85370 MW	129810 TQ	USBLS	5/15
Wholesale and Manufacturing, Technical and Scientific Products	San Antonio-New Braunfels MSA, TX	Y	49940 FQ	66500 MW	102850 TQ	USBLS	5/15
Wholesale and Manufacturing, Technical and Scientific Products	Utah	Y	51270 FQ	80810 MW	117290 TQ	USBLS	5/15
Wholesale and Manufacturing, Technical and Scientific Products	Ogden-Clearfield MSA, UT	Y	56520 FQ	80740 MW	114300 TQ	USBLS	5/15
Wholesale and Manufacturing, Technical and Scientific Products	Provo-Orem MSA, UT	Y	45750 FQ	67860 MW	92830 TQ	USBLS	5/15
Wholesale and Manufacturing, Technical and Scientific Products	Salt Lake City MSA, UT	Y	54230 FQ	89940 MW	131950 TQ	USBLS	5/15
Wholesale and Manufacturing, Technical and Scientific Products	Vermont	Y	65460 FQ	81810 MW	103660 TQ	USBLS	5/15
Wholesale and Manufacturing, Technical and Scientific Products	Burlington-South Burlington MSA, VT	Y	67610 FQ	78800 MW	100070 TQ	USBLS	5/15
Wholesale and Manufacturing, Technical and Scientific Products	Virginia	Y	68580 FQ	98160 MW	138880 TQ	USBLS	5/15
Wholesale and Manufacturing, Technical and Scientific Products	Richmond MSA, VA	Y	66750 FQ	78840 MW	119420 TQ	USBLS	5/15
Wholesale and Manufacturing, Technical and Scientific Products	Virginia Beach-Norfolk-Newport News MSA, VA-NC	Y	74960 FQ	104720 MW	123710 TQ	USBLS	5/15
Wholesale and Manufacturing, Technical and Scientific Products	Washington	H	23.56 FQ	39.75 MW	58.06 TQ	WABLS	3/16
Wholesale and Manufacturing, Technical and Scientific Products	Seattle-Bellevue-Everett PMSA, WA	H	23.36 FQ	41.28 MW	58.95 TQ	WABLS	3/16
Wholesale and Manufacturing, Technical and Scientific Products	Tacoma-Lakewood PMSA, WA	H	28.63 FQ	40.37 MW	48.94 TQ	WABLS	3/16
Wholesale and Manufacturing, Technical and Scientific Products	West Virginia	Y	44870 FQ	74900 MW	135810 TQ	USBLS	5/15
Wholesale and Manufacturing, Technical and Scientific Products	Huntington-Ashland MSA, WV-KY-OH	Y	52560 FQ	102500 MW	156080 TQ	USBLS	5/15
Wholesale and Manufacturing, Technical and Scientific Products	Wisconsin	Y	52350 FQ	71560 MW	101320 TQ	USBLS	5/15
Wholesale and Manufacturing, Technical and Scientific Products	Madison MSA, WI	Y	50850 FQ	63780 MW	95390 TQ	USBLS	5/15

Occupation/Type/Industry	Location	Per	Low	Mid	High	Source	Date
Sales Representative							
Wholesale and Manufacturing, Technical and Scientific Products	Milwaukee-Waukesha-West Allis MSA, WI	Y	55790 FQ	74830 MW	107660 TQ	USBLS	5/15
Wholesale and Manufacturing, Technical and Scientific Products	Wyoming	Y	59720 FQ	102900 MW		USBLS	5/15
Wholesale and Manufacturing, Technical and Scientific Products	Puerto Rico	Y	28800 FQ	44480 MW	69760 TQ	USBLS	5/15
Wholesale and Manufacturing, Technical and Scientific Products	San Juan-Carolina-Caguas MSA, PR	Y	30790 FQ	45970 MW	71420 TQ	USBLS	5/15
Sales Tax Manager							
Municipal Government	Colorado Springs, CO	Y	74526 LO		102473 HI	COSPRS	2017
Sandblast Operator							
Public Works - Sanitation, Municipal Government	Los Angeles, CA	Y			60210 HI	CACIT	6/23/16
Sawing Machine Setter, Operator, and Tender, Wood	Alabama	Y	17696 AE	26507 AW	30918 AEX	ALBLS	6/16
	Birmingham-Hoover MSA, AL	Y	22456 AE	29109 AW	32430 AEX	ALBLS	6/16
	Florence-Muscle Shoals MSA, AL	Y	18120 FQ	21110 MW	24190 TQ	USBLS	5/15
	Alaska	Y	41960 FQ	50700 MW	57070 TQ	USBLS	5/15
	Arizona	Y	22900 FQ	27110 MW	31070 TQ	USBLS	5/15
	Phoenix-Mesa-Scottsdale MSA, AZ	Y	22380 FQ	26650 MW	30620 TQ	USBLS	5/15
	Arkansas	Y	20560 FQ	24640 MW	30650 TQ	USBLS	5/15
	Little Rock-North Little Rock-Conway MSA, AR	Y	22210 FQ	32600 MW	36890 TQ	USBLS	5/15
	California	H	10.61 FQ	12.26 MW	17.38 TQ	CABLS	1/16-3/16
	Anaheim-Santa Ana-Irvine PMSA, CA	H	10.14 FQ	11.27 MW	12.87 TQ	CABLS	1/16-3/16
	Los Angeles-Long Beach-Glendale PMSA, CA	H	11.60 FQ	15.75 MW	19.31 TQ	CABLS	1/16-3/16
	Oakland-Hayward-Berkeley PMSA, CA	H	9.33 FQ	9.64 MW	11.79 TQ	CABLS	1/16-3/16
	Riverside-San Bernardino-Ontario MSA, CA	H	10.59 FQ	12.03 MW	17.19 TQ	CABLS	1/16-3/16
	Sacramento–Roseville–Arden-Arcade MSA, CA	H	10.76 FQ	12.01 MW	14.99 TQ	CABLS	1/16-3/16
	San Diego-Carlsbad MSA, CA	H	10.42 FQ	12.58 MW	18.46 TQ	CABLS	1/16-3/16
	Colorado	Y	26010 FQ	31040 MW	37980 TQ	USBLS	5/15
	Denver-Aurora-Lakewood MSA, CO	Y	22350 FQ	30560 MW	38750 TQ	USBLS	5/15
	Connecticut	Y		34144 MW		CTBLS	1/16-3/16
	Bridgeport-Stamford-Norwalk MSA, CT	Y	29670 FQ	34710 MW	39360 TQ	USBLS	5/15
	Washington-Arlington-Alexandria PMSA, DC-VA-MD-WV	Y	21890 FQ	28560 MW	38420 TQ	USBLS	5/15
	Florida	H	10.73 AE	14.01 MW	16.58 AEX	FLBLS	7/16-9/16
	Miami-Miami Beach-Kendall PMSA, FL	H	10.66 AE	13.19 MW	15.13 AEX	FLBLS	7/16-9/16
	Orlando-Kissimmee-Sanford MSA, FL	H	11.18 AE	16.90 MW	18.76 AEX	FLBLS	7/16-9/16
	Tampa-St. Petersburg-Clearwater MSA, FL	H	10.20 AE	12.05 MW	14.07 AEX	FLBLS	7/16-9/16
	Georgia	Y	20790 FQ	28010 MW	35200 TQ	USBLS	5/15
	Atlanta-Sandy Springs-Roswell MSA, GA	Y	20900 FQ	29710 MW	37030 TQ	USBLS	5/15
	Idaho	Y	26740 FQ	33640 MW	42050 TQ	USBLS	5/15
	Boise City MSA, ID	Y	21510 FQ	26520 MW	30770 TQ	USBLS	5/15
	Illinois	Y	27940 FQ	33230 MW	37710 TQ	USBLS	5/15
	Chicago-Naperville-Arlington Heights PMSA, IL	Y	28360 FQ	32590 MW	36270 TQ	USBLS	5/15
	Indiana	Y	23980 FQ	29340 MW	36200 TQ	USBLS	5/15
	Indianapolis-Carmel-Anderson MSA, IN	Y	23970 FQ	28310 MW	36350 TQ	USBLS	5/15
	Iowa	Y	21740 FQ	26550 MW	30920 TQ	USBLS	5/15
	Kansas	Y	21460 FQ	25660 MW	30600 TQ	USBLS	5/15

AE Average entry wage	**AWR** Average wage range	**H** Hourly	**LR** Low end range	**MTC** Median total compensation	**TCC** Total cash compensation
AEX Average experienced wage	**B** Biweekly	**HI** Highest wage paid	**M** Monthly	**MW** Median wage paid	**TQ** Third quartile wage
ATC Average total compensation	**D** Daily	**HR** High end range	**MCC** Median cash compensation	**MWR** Median wage range	**W** Weekly
AW Average wage paid	**FQ** First quartile wage	**LO** Lowest wage paid	**ME** Median entry wage	**S** See annotated source	**Y** Yearly

Occupation/Type/Industry	Location	Per	Low	Mid	High	Source	Date
Sawing Machine Setter, Operator, and Tender, Wood	Wichita MSA, KS	Y	21810 FQ	25940 MW	30380 TQ	USBLS	5/15
	Kentucky	Y	20030 FQ	23600 MW	29690 TQ	USBLS	5/15
	Louisville-Jefferson County MSA, KY-IN	Y	21630 FQ	24490 MW	28780 TQ	USBLS	5/15
	Louisiana	Y	25340 FQ	32040 MW	37210 TQ	USBLS	5/15
	Baton Rouge MSA, LA	Y	33820 FQ	36180 MW	38540 TQ	USBLS	5/15
	Maine	Y	23470 FQ	28520 MW	34980 TQ	USBLS	5/15
	Portland-South Portland MSA, ME	Y	24130 FQ	30470 MW	36780 TQ	USBLS	5/15
	Maryland	Y	25584 AE	33137 MW	36913 AEX	MDBLS	4/16
	Baltimore-Columbia-Towson MSA, MD	Y	27440 FQ	31130 MW	37340 TQ	USBLS	5/15
	Massachusetts	Y	22410 FQ	26830 MW	31050 TQ	USBLS	5/15
	Boston-Cambridge-Newton NECTA, MA	Y	26720 FQ	28480 MW	30250 TQ	USBLS	5/15
	Worcester MSA, MA-CT	Y	21530 FQ	23510 MW	31600 TQ	USBLS	5/15
	Michigan	Y	24850 FQ	29150 MW	35000 TQ	USBLS	5/15
	Detroit-Dearborn-Livonia PMSA, MI	Y	33490 FQ	41500 MW	48660 TQ	USBLS	5/15
	Grand Rapids-Wyoming MSA, MI	Y	24200 FQ	27800 MW	31520 TQ	USBLS	5/15
	Minnesota	Y	23823 FQ	29989 MW	36954 TQ	MNBLS	1/16-3/16
	Minneapolis-St. Paul-Bloomington MSA, MN-WI	Y	26891 FQ	32398 MW	37693 TQ	MNBLS	1/16-3/16
	Mississippi	Y	18830 FQ	23940 MW	31300 TQ	USBLS	5/15
	Jackson MSA, MS	Y	17680 FQ	19930 MW	24890 TQ	USBLS	5/15
	Missouri	Y	20830 FQ	24290 MW	29200 TQ	USBLS	5/15
	Kansas City MSA, MO-KS	Y	20770 FQ	23740 MW	29010 TQ	USBLS	5/15
	St. Louis MSA, MO-IL	Y	22290 FQ	26100 MW	30100 TQ	USBLS	5/15
	Montana	Y	22780 FQ	28090 MW	39290 TQ	USBLS	5/15
	Nebraska	Y	22485 FQ	25710 MW	30950 TQ	NEBLS	7/16-9/16
	Omaha-Council Bluffs MSA, NE-IA	Y	22500 FQ	25705 MW	29265 TQ	NEBLS	7/16-9/16
	Nevada	Y	23110 FQ	28010 MW	35150 TQ	USBLS	5/15
	New Hampshire	H	11.34 AE	14.34 MW	16.17 AEX	NHBLS	6/16
	New Jersey	Y	24400 FQ	34030 MW	45910 TQ	USBLS	5/15
	Camden PMSA, NJ	Y	21590 FQ	23440 MW	28610 TQ	USBLS	5/15
	Newark PMSA, NJ-PA	Y	26370 FQ	32950 MW	43280 TQ	USBLS	5/15
	New Mexico	Y	21760 FQ	24620 MW	29430 TQ	USBLS	5/15
	New York	Y	21420 AE	27840 MW	34990 AEX	NYBLS	1/16-3/16
	Buffalo-Cheektowaga-Niagara Falls MSA, NY	Y	22000 FQ	24110 MW	28750 TQ	USBLS	5/15
	Nassau County-Suffolk County PMSA, NY	Y	35720 FQ	51230 MW	57430 TQ	USBLS	5/15
	New York-Jersey City-White Plains PMSA, NY-NJ	Y	22890 FQ	35290 MW	45180 TQ	USBLS	5/15
	North Carolina	Y	21700 FQ	27670 MW	34460 TQ	USBLS	5/15
	Charlotte-Concord-Gastonia MSA, NC-SC	Y	18980 FQ	29410 MW	35890 TQ	USBLS	5/15
	Raleigh MSA, NC	Y	23090 FQ	27540 MW	33190 TQ	USBLS	5/15
	North Dakota	Y	27000 FQ	29690 MW	33510 TQ	USBLS	5/15
	Ohio	Y	24320 FQ	29460 MW	35480 TQ	USBLS	5/15
	Cincinnati MSA, OH-KY-IN	Y	24660 FQ	28250 MW	31690 TQ	USBLS	5/15
	Columbus MSA, OH	Y	22100 FQ	25890 MW	30020 TQ	USBLS	5/15
	Oklahoma	Y	20810 FQ	25870 MW	35250 TQ	USBLS	5/15
	Oklahoma City MSA, OK	Y	31100 FQ	40250 MW	45970 TQ	USBLS	5/15
	Tulsa MSA, OK	Y	19560 FQ	27920 MW	34050 TQ	USBLS	5/15
	Oregon	H	14.07 FQ	17.24 MW	20.43 TQ	ORBLS	2016
	Portland-Vancouver-Hillsboro MSA, OR-WA	Y	26910 FQ	33380 MW	39390 TQ	USBLS	5/15
	Pennsylvania	Y	23840 FQ	28220 MW	34070 TQ	USBLS	5/15
	Allentown-Bethlehem-Easton MSA, PA-NJ	Y	22570 FQ	32020 MW	35950 TQ	USBLS	5/15
	Harrisburg-Carlisle MSA, PA	Y	31720 FQ	36150 MW	41620 TQ	USBLS	5/15
	Montgomery County-Bucks County-Chester County PMSA, PA	Y	26960 FQ	29770 MW	45260 TQ	USBLS	5/15
	Pittsburgh MSA, PA	Y	23460 FQ	28920 MW	35910 TQ	USBLS	5/15
	Rhode Island	Y	21340 FQ	23000 MW	24670 TQ	USBLS	5/15
	Providence-Warwick MSA, RI-MA	Y	20930 FQ	23390 MW	28140 TQ	USBLS	5/15

AE Average entry wage   AWR Average wage range   H Hourly   LR Low end range   MTC Median total compensation   TCC Total cash compensation
AEX Average experienced wage   B Biweekly   HI Highest wage paid   M Monthly   MW Median wage paid   TQ Third quartile wage
ATC Average total compensation   D Daily   HR High end range   MCC Median cash compensation   MWR Median wage range   W Weekly
AW Average wage paid   FQ First quartile wage   LO Lowest wage paid   ME Median entry wage   S See annotated source   Y Yearly

Occupation/Type/Industry	Location	Per	Low	Mid	High	Source	Date
Sawing Machine Setter, Operator, and Tender, Wood	South Carolina	Y	21640 FQ	26280 MW	33040 TQ	USBLS	5/15
	Charleston-North Charleston MSA, SC	Y	31330 FQ	34820 MW	38290 TQ	USBLS	5/15
	Columbia MSA, SC	Y	22610 FQ	28230 MW	36740 TQ	USBLS	5/15
	Greenville-Anderson-Mauldin MSA, SC	Y	18630 FQ	21670 MW	25790 TQ	USBLS	5/15
	South Dakota	Y	25780 FQ	29260 MW	34650 TQ	USBLS	5/15
	Sioux Falls MSA, SD	Y	26420 FQ	30310 MW	36960 TQ	USBLS	5/15
	Tennessee	Y	21510 FQ	25050 MW	30040 TQ	USBLS	5/15
	Knoxville MSA, TN	Y	18120 FQ	22040 MW	28920 TQ	USBLS	5/15
	Memphis MSA, TN-MS-AR	Y	22310 FQ	25300 MW	28700 TQ	USBLS	5/15
	Nashville-Davidson–Murfreesboro–Franklin MSA, TN	Y	21770 FQ	24380 MW	33090 TQ	USBLS	5/15
	Texas	Y	18260 FQ	21950 MW	28890 TQ	USBLS	5/15
	Austin-Round Rock MSA, TX	Y	17420 FQ	19800 MW	27850 TQ	USBLS	5/15
	Dallas-Plano-Irving PMSA, TX	Y	18370 FQ	22200 MW	29500 TQ	USBLS	5/15
	Fort Worth-Arlington PMSA, TX	Y	20860 FQ	26140 MW	31160 TQ	USBLS	5/15
	Houston-The Woodlands-Sugar Land MSA, TX	Y	18660 FQ	26180 MW	34310 TQ	USBLS	5/15
	Utah	Y	22830 FQ	26630 MW	31250 TQ	USBLS	5/15
	Salt Lake City MSA, UT	Y	22510 FQ	25360 MW	30420 TQ	USBLS	5/15
	Vermont	Y	26870 FQ	30430 MW	41260 TQ	USBLS	5/15
	Virginia	Y	21700 FQ	25980 MW	32800 TQ	USBLS	5/15
	Richmond MSA, VA	Y	20450 FQ	23460 MW	30780 TQ	USBLS	5/15
	Virginia Beach-Norfolk-Newport News MSA, VA-NC	Y	21480 FQ	26460 MW	34770 TQ	USBLS	5/15
	Washington	H	14.11 FQ	17.68 MW	21.66 TQ	WABLS	3/16
	Seattle-Bellevue-Everett PMSA, WA	H	15.66 FQ	17.94 MW	21.09 TQ	WABLS	3/16
	Tacoma-Lakewood PMSA, WA	H	14.85 FQ	17.62 MW	21.11 TQ	WABLS	3/16
	West Virginia	Y	22720 FQ	27960 MW	34830 TQ	USBLS	5/15
	Wisconsin	Y	24810 FQ	28800 MW	34270 TQ	USBLS	5/15
	Madison MSA, WI	Y	24750 FQ	27330 MW	29840 TQ	USBLS	5/15
	Milwaukee-Waukesha-West Allis MSA, WI	Y	26650 FQ	38790 MW	53260 TQ	USBLS	5/15
	Wyoming	Y	27150 FQ	29960 MW	36040 TQ	USBLS	5/15
Scale House Attendant							
Municipal Government	Fitzgerald, GA	H	10.48 LO		12.72 HI	GACTY02	2016
Municipal Government	Savannah, GA	H	12.19 LO		18.32 HI	GACTY02	2016
Scenic Artist							
Made for Television Motion Picture	United States	W	1582 LO			MPEG01	7/31/16-7/29/17
School Breakfast/AmeriCorps Specialist							
Department of Public Health and Human Services, State Government	Helena, MT	H			20.69 HI	MTGOV	2016
School Bus Transportation Specialist							
State Government	New Mexico	H	12.61 LO		21.95 HI	NMGOV	7/30/16
School Business Manager	Narragansett, RI	Y			108782 HI	RIGOV	2017
	New Shoreham, RI	Y			56570 HI	RIGOV	2017
School Principal	United States	Y		90219 MW		CCAST01	2016
School Resource Officer							
Municipal Government	Coalinga, CA	Y			59441 HI	CACIT	6/28/16
Municipal Government	Commerce, GA	Y	35948 LO		53485 HI	GACTY01	2016
Municipal Government	Greensboro, GA	Y	28746 LO		39499 HI	GACTY01	2016
Municipal Government	Valdosta, GA	Y	26059 LO		46111 HI	GACTY01	2016
Script Supervisor	Alaska	Y		29000 AW		BUZZ04	2015
	Idaho	Y		26000 AW		BUZZ04	2015
	Iowa	Y		39000 AW		BUZZ04	2015
	Pennsylvania	Y		38000 AW		BUZZ04	2015

AE	Average entry wage	AWR	Average wage range	H	Hourly	LR	Low end range	MTC	Median total compensation	TCC	Total cash compensation
AEX	Average experienced wage	B	Biweekly	HI	Highest wage paid	M	Monthly	MW	Median wage paid	TQ	Third quartile wage
ATC	Average total compensation	D	Daily	HR	High end range	MCC	Median cash compensation	MWR	Median wage range	W	Weekly
AW	Average wage paid	FQ	First quartile wage	LO	Lowest wage paid	ME	Median entry wage	S	See annotated source	Y	Yearly

Occupation/Type/Industry	Location	Per	Low	Mid	High	Source	Date
Scrum Master	United States	Y		100000 MW		HCHRON1	2017
Seaman							
U.S. Navy, Active Duty, Pay Grade E-2	United States	M		1793 AW		DOD1	2017
U.S. Navy, Active Duty, Pay Grade E-3	United States	M	1886 LO		2126 HI	DOD1	2017
Secondary School Teacher							
Except Special and Career/Technical Education	Alabama	Y	41140 AE	50925 AW	55818 AEX	ALBLS	6/16
Except Special and Career/Technical Education	Birmingham-Hoover MSA, AL	Y	41731 AE	52118 AW	57306 AEX	ALBLS	6/16
Except Special and Career/Technical Education	Alaska	Y	65470 FQ	78890 MW	97510 TQ	USBLS	5/15
Except Special and Career/Technical Education	Anchorage MSA, AK	Y	71490 FQ	88240 MW	109020 TQ	USBLS	5/15
Except Special and Career/Technical Education	Arizona	Y	37190 FQ	44970 MW	55620 TQ	USBLS	5/15
Except Special and Career/Technical Education	Phoenix-Mesa-Scottsdale MSA, AZ	Y	39810 FQ	47530 MW	58730 TQ	USBLS	5/15
Except Special and Career/Technical Education	Tucson MSA, AZ	Y	33920 FQ	37690 MW	44320 TQ	USBLS	5/15
Except Special and Career/Technical Education	Arkansas	Y	40740 FQ	47250 MW	56490 TQ	USBLS	5/15
Except Special and Career/Technical Education	Little Rock-North Little Rock-Conway MSA, AR	Y	42100 FQ	48830 MW	58070 TQ	USBLS	5/15
Except Special and Career/Technical Education	California	Y		75854 AW		CABLS	1/16-3/16
Except Special and Career/Technical Education	Anaheim-Santa Ana-Irvine PMSA, CA	Y		80987 AW		CABLS	1/16-3/16
Except Special and Career/Technical Education	Los Angeles-Long Beach-Glendale PMSA, CA	Y		77822 AW		CABLS	1/16-3/16
Except Special and Career/Technical Education	Oakland-Hayward-Berkeley PMSA, CA	Y		74991 AW		CABLS	1/16-3/16
Except Special and Career/Technical Education	Riverside-San Bernardino-Ontario MSA, CA	Y		74565 AW		CABLS	1/16-3/16
Except Special and Career/Technical Education	Sacramento–Roseville–Arden-Arcade MSA, CA	Y		71167 AW		CABLS	1/16-3/16
Except Special and Career/Technical Education	San Diego-Carlsbad MSA, CA	Y		75996 AW		CABLS	1/16-3/16
Except Special and Career/Technical Education	San Francisco-Redwood City-South San Francisco PMSA, CA	Y		76939 AW		CABLS	1/16-3/16
Except Special and Career/Technical Education	Colorado	Y	41110 FQ	50000 MW	63260 TQ	USBLS	5/15
Except Special and Career/Technical Education	Denver-Aurora-Lakewood MSA, CO	Y	44250 FQ	55110 MW	69410 TQ	USBLS	5/15
Except Special and Career/Technical Education	Connecticut	Y		76422 MW		CTBLS	1/16-3/16
Except Special and Career/Technical Education	Bridgeport-Stamford-Norwalk MSA, CT	Y	64050 FQ	82330 MW	97670 TQ	USBLS	5/15
Except Special and Career/Technical Education	Hartford-West Hartford-East Hartford MSA, CT	Y	56360 FQ	73900 MW	90340 TQ	USBLS	5/15
Except Special and Career/Technical Education	Delaware	Y	47210 FQ	57610 MW	70460 TQ	USBLS	5/15
Except Special and Career/Technical Education	Wilmington PMSA, DE-MD-NJ	Y	45280 FQ	57940 MW	75140 TQ	USBLS	5/15
Except Special and Career/Technical Education	District of Columbia	Y	38850 FQ	60050 MW	77800 TQ	USBLS	5/15

AE Average entry wage	**AWR** Average wage range	**H** Hourly	**LR** Low end range	**MTC** Median total compensation	**TCC** Total cash compensation
AEX Average experienced wage	**B** Biweekly	**HI** Highest wage paid	**M** Monthly	**MW** Median wage paid	**TQ** Third quartile wage
ATC Average total compensation	**D** Daily	**HR** High end range	**MCC** Median cash compensation	**MWR** Median wage range	**W** Weekly
AW Average wage paid	**FQ** First quartile wage	**LO** Lowest wage paid	**ME** Median entry wage	**S** See annotated source	**Y** Yearly

Occupation/Type/Industry	Location	Per	Low	Mid	High	Source	Date
Secondary School Teacher							
Except Special and Career/Technical Education	Washington-Arlington-Alexandria PMSA, DC-VA-MD-WV	Y	53770 FQ	69740 MW	90640 TQ	USBLS	5/15
Except Special and Career/Technical Education	Florida	Y	40382 AE	49112 MW	57465 AEX	FLBLS	7/16-9/16
Except Special and Career/Technical Education	Fort Lauderdale-Pompano Beach-Deerfield Beach PMSA, FL	Y	42991 AE	52520 MW	62374 AEX	FLBLS	7/16-9/16
Except Special and Career/Technical Education	Miami-Miami Beach-Kendall PMSA, FL	Y	44227 AE	57661 MW	67092 AEX	FLBLS	7/16-9/16
Except Special and Career/Technical Education	Orlando-Kissimmee-Sanford MSA, FL	Y	38842 AE	46994 MW	52807 AEX	FLBLS	7/16-9/16
Except Special and Career/Technical Education	Tampa-St. Petersburg-Clearwater MSA, FL	Y	38264 AE	46820 MW	53986 AEX	FLBLS	7/16-9/16
Except Special and Career/Technical Education	Georgia	Y	44920 FQ	54810 MW	64700 TQ	USBLS	5/15
Except Special and Career/Technical Education	Atlanta-Sandy Springs-Roswell MSA, GA	Y	45980 FQ	55780 MW	66630 TQ	USBLS	5/15
Except Special and Career/Technical Education	Augusta-Richmond County MSA, GA-SC	Y	41490 FQ	49730 MW	59650 TQ	USBLS	5/15
Except Special and Career/Technical Education	Hawaii	Y	47680 FQ	56180 MW	64210 TQ	USBLS	5/15
Except Special and Career/Technical Education	Urban Honolulu MSA, HI	Y	47040 FQ	55790 MW	64170 TQ	USBLS	5/15
Except Special and Career/Technical Education	Idaho	Y	35190 FQ	41860 MW	54030 TQ	USBLS	5/15
Except Special and Career/Technical Education	Boise City MSA, ID	Y	35430 FQ	42900 MW	55290 TQ	USBLS	5/15
Except Special and Career/Technical Education	Illinois	Y	50700 FQ	66260 MW	87320 TQ	USBLS	5/15
Except Special and Career/Technical Education	Chicago-Naperville-Arlington Heights PMSA, IL	Y	56310 FQ	73990 MW	93650 TQ	USBLS	5/15
Except Special and Career/Technical Education	Lake County-Kenosha County PMSA, IL-WI	Y	50270 FQ	66010 MW	84260 TQ	USBLS	5/15
Except Special and Career/Technical Education	Indiana	Y	40190 FQ	49770 MW	61820 TQ	USBLS	5/15
Except Special and Career/Technical Education	Gary PMSA, IN	Y	39080 FQ	47860 MW	60510 TQ	USBLS	5/15
Except Special and Career/Technical Education	Indianapolis-Carmel-Anderson MSA, IN	Y	42780 FQ	53300 MW	66130 TQ	USBLS	5/15
Except Special and Career/Technical Education	Iowa	Y	40440 FQ	50950 MW	60880 TQ	USBLS	5/15
Except Special and Career/Technical Education	Des Moines-West Des Moines MSA, IA	Y	42740 FQ	57080 MW	70430 TQ	USBLS	5/15
Except Special and Career/Technical Education	Kansas	Y	40790 FQ	46690 MW	55050 TQ	USBLS	5/15
Except Special and Career/Technical Education	Wichita MSA, KS	Y	41160 FQ	46950 MW	54940 TQ	USBLS	5/15
Except Special and Career/Technical Education	Kentucky	Y	44540 FQ	53040 MW	61220 TQ	USBLS	5/15
Except Special and Career/Technical Education	Louisville-Jefferson County MSA, KY-IN	Y	45960 FQ	56740 MW	69440 TQ	USBLS	5/15
Except Special and Career/Technical Education	Louisiana	Y	43520 FQ	48470 MW	55940 TQ	USBLS	5/15
Except Special and Career/Technical Education	Baton Rouge MSA, LA	Y	44770 FQ	50820 MW	58170 TQ	USBLS	5/15

AE	Average entry wage	**AWR**	Average wage range	**H**	Hourly	**LR**	Low end range	**MTC**	Median total compensation	**TCC**	Total cash compensation
AEX	Average experienced wage	**B**	Biweekly	**HI**	Highest wage paid	**M**	Monthly	**MW**	Median wage	**TQ**	Third quartile wage
ATC	Average total compensation	**D**	Daily	**HR**	High end range	**MCC**	Median cash compensation	**MWR**	Median wage range	**W**	Weekly
AW	Average wage paid	**FQ**	First quartile wage	**LO**	Lowest wage paid	**ME**	Median entry wage	**S**	See annotated source	**Y**	Yearly

Occupation/Type/Industry	Location	Per	Low	Mid	High	Source	Date
Secondary School Teacher							
Except Special and Career/Technical Education	New Orleans-Metairie MSA, LA	Y	44290 FQ	49780 MW	57520 TQ	USBLS	5/15
Except Special and Career/Technical Education	Maine	Y	40960 FQ	52050 MW	61110 TQ	USBLS	5/15
Except Special and Career/Technical Education	Portland-South Portland MSA, ME	Y	48850 FQ	57480 MW	65910 TQ	USBLS	5/15
Except Special and Career/Technical Education	Maryland	Y	45644 AE	66085 MW	76305 AEX	MDBLS	4/16
Except Special and Career/Technical Education	Baltimore-Columbia-Towson MSA, MD	Y	49610 FQ	61660 MW	77850 TQ	USBLS	5/15
Except Special and Career/Technical Education	Salisbury MSA, MD-DE	Y	47120 FQ	58960 MW	73410 TQ	USBLS	5/15
Except Special and Career/Technical Education	Massachusetts	Y	58170 FQ	71570 MW	85430 TQ	USBLS	5/15
Except Special and Career/Technical Education	Boston-Cambridge-Newton NECTA, MA	Y	60310 FQ	74770 MW	89630 TQ	USBLS	5/15
Except Special and Career/Technical Education	Worcester MSA, MA-CT	Y	60210 FQ	70920 MW	80330 TQ	USBLS	5/15
Except Special and Career/Technical Education	Michigan	Y	46140 FQ	59600 MW	73680 TQ	USBLS	5/15
Except Special and Career/Technical Education	Detroit-Dearborn-Livonia PMSA, MI	Y	43130 FQ	62490 MW	83720 TQ	USBLS	5/15
Except Special and Career/Technical Education	Grand Rapids-Wyoming MSA, MI	Y	45280 FQ	57280 MW	69510 TQ	USBLS	5/15
Except Special and Career/Technical Education	Minnesota	Y	49001 FQ	60513 MW	75503 TQ	MNBLS	1/16-3/16
Except Special and Career/Technical Education	Minneapolis-St. Paul-Bloomington MSA, MN-WI	Y	51068 FQ	64999 MW	79868 TQ	MNBLS	1/16-3/16
Except Special and Career/Technical Education	Mississippi	Y	35930 FQ	41920 MW	48790 TQ	USBLS	5/15
Except Special and Career/Technical Education	Jackson MSA, MS	Y	35670 FQ	41830 MW	48930 TQ	USBLS	5/15
Except Special and Career/Technical Education	Missouri	Y	36730 FQ	44220 MW	55390 TQ	USBLS	5/15
Except Special and Career/Technical Education	Kansas City MSA, MO-KS	Y	38490 FQ	45180 MW	53360 TQ	USBLS	5/15
Except Special and Career/Technical Education	St. Louis MSA, MO-IL	Y	42690 FQ	53740 MW	68750 TQ	USBLS	5/15
Except Special and Career/Technical Education	Montana	Y	37460 FQ	48460 MW	59860 TQ	USBLS	5/15
Except Special and Career/Technical Education	Billings MSA, MT	Y	42030 FQ	53180 MW	63040 TQ	USBLS	5/15
Except Special and Career/Technical Education	Nebraska	Y	42980 FQ	51300 MW	59450 TQ	NEBLS	7/16-9/16
Except Special and Career/Technical Education	Omaha-Council Bluffs MSA, NE-IA	Y	42145 FQ	49515 MW	57755 TQ	NEBLS	7/16-9/16
Except Special and Career/Technical Education	Nevada	Y	44270 FQ	53380 MW	64010 TQ	USBLS	5/15
Except Special and Career/Technical Education	Las Vegas-Henderson-Paradise MSA, NV	Y	44010 FQ	52680 MW	63700 TQ	USBLS	5/15
Except Special and Career/Technical Education	New Hampshire	Y	40822 AE	57640 MW	66504 AEX	NHBLS	6/16
Except Special and Career/Technical Education	Manchester NECTA, NH	Y	43926 AE	60629 MW	66158 AEX	NHBLS	6/16
Except Special and Career/Technical Education	Nashua NECTA, NH-MA	Y	47880 FQ	57820 MW	68730 TQ	USBLS	5/15
Except Special and Career/Technical Education	New Jersey	Y	58310 FQ	71560 MW	89760 TQ	USBLS	5/15
Except Special and Career/Technical Education	Camden PMSA, NJ	Y	57460 FQ	68530 MW	85650 TQ	USBLS	5/15

AE	Average entry wage	AWR	Average wage range	H	Hourly	LR	Low end range	MTC	Median total compensation	TCC	Total cash compensation
AEX	Average experienced wage	B	Biweekly	HI	Highest wage paid	M	Monthly	MCC	Median cash compensation	MWR	Median wage range	TQ	Third quartile wage
ATC	Average total compensation	D	Daily	HR	High end range	MCC	Median cash compensation	MWR	Median wage range	W	Weekly
AW	Average wage paid	FQ	First quartile wage	LO	Lowest wage paid	ME	Median entry wage	S	See annotated source	Y	Yearly

Secondary School Teacher

Occupation/Type/Industry	Location	Per	Low	Mid	High	Source	Date
Secondary School Teacher							
Except Special and Career/Technical Education	Newark PMSA, NJ-PA	Y	59300 FQ	71820 MW	88160 TQ	USBLS	5/15
Except Special and Career/Technical Education	Trenton MSA, NJ	Y	57180 FQ	70140 MW	87540 TQ	USBLS	5/15
Except Special and Career/Technical Education	New Mexico	Y	43520 FQ	52920 MW	63120 TQ	USBLS	5/15
Except Special and Career/Technical Education	Albuquerque MSA, NM	Y	41800 FQ	49440 MW	59030 TQ	USBLS	5/15
Except Special and Career/Technical Education	New York	Y	52080 AE	77740 MW	95270 AEX	NYBLS	1/16-3/16
Except Special and Career/Technical Education	Buffalo-Cheektowaga-Niagara Falls MSA, NY	Y	51160 FQ	61600 MW	78470 TQ	USBLS	5/15
Except Special and Career/Technical Education	Nassau County-Suffolk County PMSA, NY	Y	86680 FQ	105190 MW	121020 TQ	USBLS	5/15
Except Special and Career/Technical Education	New York-Jersey City-White Plains PMSA, NY-NJ	Y	63690 FQ	79620 MW	98930 TQ	USBLS	5/15
Except Special and Career/Technical Education	Rochester MSA, NY	Y	47990 FQ	57280 MW	69480 TQ	USBLS	5/15
Except Special and Career/Technical Education	North Carolina	Y	36560 FQ	43090 MW	50760 TQ	USBLS	5/15
Except Special and Career/Technical Education	Charlotte-Concord-Gastonia MSA, NC-SC	Y	37750 FQ	45080 MW	54220 TQ	USBLS	5/15
Except Special and Career/Technical Education	Raleigh MSA, NC	Y	37400 FQ	45390 MW	56540 TQ	USBLS	5/15
Except Special and Career/Technical Education	North Dakota	Y	40280 FQ	46920 MW	56240 TQ	USBLS	5/15
Except Special and Career/Technical Education	Fargo MSA, ND-MN	Y	38490 FQ	45840 MW	55010 TQ	USBLS	5/15
Except Special and Career/Technical Education	Ohio	Y	46800 FQ	58850 MW	72340 TQ	USBLS	5/15
Except Special and Career/Technical Education	Cincinnati MSA, OH-KY-IN	Y	46600 FQ	57680 MW	69900 TQ	USBLS	5/15
Except Special and Career/Technical Education	Cleveland-Elyria MSA, OH	Y	45750 FQ	60720 MW	73820 TQ	USBLS	5/15
Except Special and Career/Technical Education	Columbus MSA, OH	Y	49430 FQ	63640 MW	79330 TQ	USBLS	5/15
Except Special and Career/Technical Education	Oklahoma	Y	35470 FQ	41280 MW	48250 TQ	USBLS	5/15
Except Special and Career/Technical Education	Oklahoma City MSA, OK	Y	34800 FQ	39310 MW	46480 TQ	USBLS	5/15
Except Special and Career/Technical Education	Tulsa MSA, OK	Y	36340 FQ	43820 MW	54830 TQ	USBLS	5/15
Except Special and Career/Technical Education	Oregon	Y	48199 FQ	60637 MW	74499 TQ	ORBLS	2016
Except Special and Career/Technical Education	Portland-Vancouver-Hillsboro MSA, OR-WA	Y	48620 FQ	61920 MW	72830 TQ	USBLS	5/15
Except Special and Career/Technical Education	Pennsylvania	Y	49800 FQ	62560 MW	78100 TQ	USBLS	5/15
Except Special and Career/Technical Education	Allentown-Bethlehem-Easton MSA, PA-NJ	Y	49740 FQ	61790 MW	77660 TQ	USBLS	5/15
Except Special and Career/Technical Education	Harrisburg-Carlisle MSA, PA	Y	45830 FQ	57340 MW	69210 TQ	USBLS	5/15
Except Special and Career/Technical Education	Montgomery County-Bucks County-Chester County PMSA, PA	Y	53690 FQ	69120 MW	89190 TQ	USBLS	5/15
Except Special and Career/Technical Education	Philadelphia PMSA, PA	Y	48950 FQ	66110 MW	83020 TQ	USBLS	5/15
Except Special and Career/Technical Education	Pittsburgh MSA, PA	Y	51530 FQ	60870 MW	76840 TQ	USBLS	5/15
Except Special and Career/Technical Education	Rhode Island	Y	53270 FQ	67930 MW	79130 TQ	USBLS	5/15

AE	Average entry wage	AWR	Average wage range	H	Hourly
AEX	Average experienced wage	B	Biweekly	HI	Highest wage paid
ATC	Average total compensation	D	Daily	HR	High end range
AW	Average wage paid	FQ	First quartile wage	LO	Lowest wage paid

LR	Low end range	MTC	Median total compensation	TCC	Total cash compensation
M	Monthly	MW	Median wage paid	TQ	Third quartile wage
MCC	Median cash compensation	MWR	Median wage range	W	Weekly
ME	Median entry wage	S	See annotated source	Y	Yearly

Occupation/Type/Industry	Location	Per	Low	Mid	High	Source	Date
Secondary School Teacher							
Except Special and Career/Technical Education	Providence-Warwick MSA, RI-MA	Y	53740 FQ	68240 MW	79470 TQ	USBLS	5/15
Except Special and Career/Technical Education	South Carolina	Y	41420 FQ	50430 MW	60620 TQ	USBLS	5/15
Except Special and Career/Technical Education	Charleston-North Charleston MSA, SC	Y	39640 FQ	49880 MW	61300 TQ	USBLS	5/15
Except Special and Career/Technical Education	Columbia MSA, SC	Y	41730 FQ	48600 MW	58440 TQ	USBLS	5/15
Except Special and Career/Technical Education	Greenville-Anderson-Mauldin MSA, SC	Y	40050 FQ	49950 MW	60600 TQ	USBLS	5/15
Except Special and Career/Technical Education	South Dakota	Y	35220 FQ	41510 MW	49680 TQ	USBLS	5/15
Except Special and Career/Technical Education	Sioux Falls MSA, SD	Y	35390 FQ	43230 MW	53610 TQ	USBLS	5/15
Except Special and Career/Technical Education	Tennessee	Y	41950 FQ	49520 MW	59260 TQ	USBLS	5/15
Except Special and Career/Technical Education	Knoxville MSA, TN	Y	42590 FQ	49200 MW	58680 TQ	USBLS	5/15
Except Special and Career/Technical Education	Memphis MSA, TN-MS-AR	Y	44130 FQ	53070 MW	61810 TQ	USBLS	5/15
Except Special and Career/Technical Education	Nashville-Davidson–Murfreesboro–Franklin MSA, TN	Y	40760 FQ	49530 MW	59990 TQ	USBLS	5/15
Except Special and Career/Technical Education	Texas	Y	45620 FQ	53310 MW	60570 TQ	USBLS	5/15
Except Special and Career/Technical Education	Austin-Round Rock MSA, TX	Y	44570 FQ	51110 MW	59880 TQ	USBLS	5/15
Except Special and Career/Technical Education	Dallas-Plano-Irving PMSA, TX	Y	47230 FQ	54700 MW	61660 TQ	USBLS	5/15
Except Special and Career/Technical Education	Fort Worth-Arlington PMSA, TX	Y	50970 FQ	56310 MW	61650 TQ	USBLS	5/15
Except Special and Career/Technical Education	Houston-The Woodlands-Sugar Land MSA, TX	Y	49630 FQ	56600 MW	63450 TQ	USBLS	5/15
Except Special and Career/Technical Education	San Antonio-New Braunfels MSA, TX	Y	49420 FQ	54670 MW	59820 TQ	USBLS	5/15
Except Special and Career/Technical Education	Utah	Y	43300 FQ	55690 MW	67810 TQ	USBLS	5/15
Except Special and Career/Technical Education	Ogden-Clearfield MSA, UT	Y	43980 FQ	55370 MW	63370 TQ	USBLS	5/15
Except Special and Career/Technical Education	Provo-Orem MSA, UT	Y	51920 FQ	61340 MW	76800 TQ	USBLS	5/15
Except Special and Career/Technical Education	Salt Lake City MSA, UT	Y	43750 FQ	57050 MW	72490 TQ	USBLS	5/15
Except Special and Career/Technical Education	Vermont	Y	42810 FQ	54050 MW	64260 TQ	USBLS	5/15
Except Special and Career/Technical Education	Burlington-South Burlington MSA, VT	Y	49000 FQ	62510 MW	74270 TQ	USBLS	5/15
Except Special and Career/Technical Education	Virginia	Y	48010 FQ	59830 MW	76770 TQ	USBLS	5/15
Except Special and Career/Technical Education	Richmond MSA, VA	Y	51820 FQ	58020 MW	64390 TQ	USBLS	5/15
Except Special and Career/Technical Education	Virginia Beach-Norfolk-Newport News MSA, VA-NC	Y	48170 FQ	58710 MW	72700 TQ	USBLS	5/15
Except Special and Career/Technical Education	Washington	Y		62817 AW		WABLS	3/16
Except Special and Career/Technical Education	Mount Vernon-Anacortes MSA, WA	Y		65019 AW		WABLS	3/16
Except Special and Career/Technical Education	Seattle-Bellevue-Everett PMSA, WA	Y		65648 AW		WABLS	3/16

AE	Average entry wage	AWR	Average wage range	H	Hourly	LR	Low end range	MTC	Median total compensation	TCC	Total cash compensation
AEX	Average experienced wage	B	Biweekly	HI	Highest wage paid	M	Monthly	MW	Median wage paid	TQ	Third quartile wage
ATC	Average total compensation	D	Daily	HR	High end range	MCC	Median cash compensation	MWR	Median wage range	W	Weekly
AW	Average wage paid	FQ	First quartile wage	LO	Lowest wage paid	ME	Median entry wage	S	See annotated source	Y	Yearly

Occupation/Type/Industry	Location	Per	Low	Mid	High	Source	Date
Secondary School Teacher							
Except Special and Career/Technical Education	Tacoma-Lakewood PMSA, WA	Y		63172 AW		WABLS	3/16
Except Special and Career/Technical Education	West Virginia	Y	36840 FQ	44070 MW	52500 TQ	USBLS	5/15
Except Special and Career/Technical Education	Huntington-Ashland MSA, WV-KY-OH	Y	37750 FQ	47350 MW	57540 TQ	USBLS	5/15
Except Special and Career/Technical Education	Wisconsin	Y	44400 FQ	54810 MW	65560 TQ	USBLS	5/15
Except Special and Career/Technical Education	Madison MSA, WI	Y	42830 FQ	53860 MW	63110 TQ	USBLS	5/15
Except Special and Career/Technical Education	Milwaukee-Waukesha-West Allis MSA, WI	Y	49160 FQ	62710 MW	74730 TQ	USBLS	5/15
Except Special and Career/Technical Education	Wyoming	Y	50410 FQ	58380 MW	68130 TQ	USBLS	5/15
Except Special and Career/Technical Education	Cheyenne MSA, WY	Y	53090 FQ	60600 MW	69850 TQ	USBLS	5/15
Except Special and Career/Technical Education	Puerto Rico	Y	28380 FQ	35010 MW	42770 TQ	USBLS	5/15
Except Special and Career/Technical Education	San Juan-Carolina-Caguas MSA, PR	Y	27790 FQ	34270 MW	42440 TQ	USBLS	5/15
Except Special and Career/Technical Education	Virgin Islands	Y	33660 FQ	41720 MW	49410 TQ	USBLS	5/15
Except Special and Career/Technical Education	Guam	Y	32840 FQ	40940 MW	52380 TQ	USBLS	5/15
Secretary and Administrative Assistant							
Except Legal, Medical, and Executive	Alabama	Y	25281 AE	34741 AW	39472 AEX	ALBLS	6/16
Except Legal, Medical, and Executive	Birmingham-Hoover MSA, AL	Y	26806 AE	36988 AW	42079 AEX	ALBLS	6/16
Except Legal, Medical, and Executive	Alaska	Y	30230 FQ	36630 MW	44810 TQ	USBLS	5/15
Except Legal, Medical, and Executive	Anchorage MSA, AK	Y	28880 FQ	35520 MW	43500 TQ	USBLS	5/15
Except Legal, Medical, and Executive	Arizona	Y	26340 FQ	32820 MW	40060 TQ	USBLS	5/15
Except Legal, Medical, and Executive	Phoenix-Mesa-Scottsdale MSA, AZ	Y	27260 FQ	34010 MW	41850 TQ	USBLS	5/15
Except Legal, Medical, and Executive	Tucson MSA, AZ	Y	26000 FQ	31530 MW	38400 TQ	USBLS	5/15
Except Legal, Medical, and Executive	Arkansas	Y	21600 FQ	27340 MW	35110 TQ	USBLS	5/15
Except Legal, Medical, and Executive	Little Rock-North Little Rock-Conway MSA, AR	Y	22450 FQ	29370 MW	36840 TQ	USBLS	5/15
Except Legal, Medical, and Executive	California	H	14.94 FQ	18.86 MW	23.83 TQ	CABLS	1/16-3/16
Except Legal, Medical, and Executive	Anaheim-Santa Ana-Irvine PMSA, CA	H	14.92 FQ	18.81 MW	23.44 TQ	CABLS	1/16-3/16
Except Legal, Medical, and Executive	Los Angeles-Long Beach-Glendale PMSA, CA	H	14.79 FQ	18.81 MW	24.04 TQ	CABLS	1/16-3/16
Except Legal, Medical, and Executive	Oakland-Hayward-Berkeley PMSA, CA	H	16.60 FQ	20.92 MW	26.32 TQ	CABLS	1/16-3/16
Except Legal, Medical, and Executive	Riverside-San Bernardino-Ontario MSA, CA	H	14.84 FQ	18.35 MW	22.42 TQ	CABLS	1/16-3/16
Except Legal, Medical, and Executive	Sacramento–Roseville–Arden-Arcade MSA, CA	H	14.22 FQ	17.66 MW	22.28 TQ	CABLS	1/16-3/16
Except Legal, Medical, and Executive	San Diego-Carlsbad MSA, CA	H	14.80 FQ	18.77 MW	23.73 TQ	CABLS	1/16-3/16
Except Legal, Medical, and Executive	San Francisco-Redwood City-South San Francisco PMSA, CA	H	17.06 FQ	21.89 MW	28.01 TQ	CABLS	1/16-3/16
Except Legal, Medical, and Executive	Colorado	Y	28380 FQ	35650 MW	44490 TQ	USBLS	5/15
Except Legal, Medical, and Executive	Denver-Aurora-Lakewood MSA, CO	Y	30240 FQ	37460 MW	46610 TQ	USBLS	5/15
Except Legal, Medical, and Executive	Connecticut	Y		42019 MW		CTBLS	1/16-3/16
Except Legal, Medical, and Executive	Bridgeport-Stamford-Norwalk MSA, CT	Y	33170 FQ	41200 MW	53250 TQ	USBLS	5/15
Except Legal, Medical, and Executive	Hartford-West Hartford-East Hartford MSA, CT	Y	33720 FQ	42980 MW	53670 TQ	USBLS	5/15
Except Legal, Medical, and Executive	Delaware	Y	30360 FQ	36520 MW	44510 TQ	USBLS	5/15
Except Legal, Medical, and Executive	Wilmington PMSA, DE-MD-NJ	Y	30230 FQ	36440 MW	45100 TQ	USBLS	5/15
Except Legal, Medical, and Executive	District of Columbia	Y	36870 FQ	45980 MW	56920 TQ	USBLS	5/15

AE	Average entry wage	AWR	Average wage range	H	Hourly
AEX	Average experienced wage	B	Biweekly	HI	Highest wage paid
ATC	Average total compensation	D	Daily	HR	High end range
AW	Average wage paid	FQ	First quartile wage	LO	Lowest wage paid

LR	Low end range	MTC	Median total compensation	TCC	Total cash compensation
M	Monthly	MW	Median wage paid	TQ	Third quartile wage
MCC	Median cash compensation	MWR	Median wage range	W	Weekly
ME	Median entry wage	S	See annotated source	Y	Yearly

Occupation/Type/Industry	Location	Per	Low	Mid	High	Source	Date
Secretary and Administrative Assistant							
Except Legal, Medical, and Executive	Washington-Arlington-Alexandria PMSA, DC-VA-MD-WV	Y	33900 FQ	42740 MW	52520 TQ	USBLS	5/15
Except Legal, Medical, and Executive	Florida	H	11.15 AE	15.26 MW	18.39 AEX	FLBLS	7/16-9/16
Except Legal, Medical, and Executive	Fort Lauderdale-Pompano Beach-Deerfield Beach PMSA, FL	H	11.55 AE	15.88 MW	19.13 AEX	FLBLS	7/16-9/16
Except Legal, Medical, and Executive	Miami-Miami Beach-Kendall PMSA, FL	H	11.41 AE	15.48 MW	18.97 AEX	FLBLS	7/16-9/16
Except Legal, Medical, and Executive	Orlando-Kissimmee-Sanford MSA, FL	H	11.72 AE	15.41 MW	18.77 AEX	FLBLS	7/16-9/16
Except Legal, Medical, and Executive	Tampa-St. Petersburg-Clearwater MSA, FL	H	11.16 AE	15.50 MW	18.15 AEX	FLBLS	7/16-9/16
Except Legal, Medical, and Executive	Georgia	Y	25880 FQ	32850 MW	41030 TQ	USBLS	5/15
Except Legal, Medical, and Executive	Atlanta-Sandy Springs-Roswell MSA, GA	Y	27710 FQ	35050 MW	44340 TQ	USBLS	5/15
Except Legal, Medical, and Executive	Augusta-Richmond County MSA, GA-SC	Y	23920 FQ	31040 MW	38860 TQ	USBLS	5/15
Except Legal, Medical, and Executive	Hawaii	Y	31600 FQ	38340 MW	47460 TQ	USBLS	5/15
Except Legal, Medical, and Executive	Urban Honolulu MSA, HI	Y	32130 FQ	39560 MW	48510 TQ	USBLS	5/15
Except Legal, Medical, and Executive	Idaho	Y	23500 FQ	29100 MW	35740 TQ	USBLS	5/15
Except Legal, Medical, and Executive	Boise City MSA, ID	Y	25080 FQ	29960 MW	36110 TQ	USBLS	5/15
Except Legal, Medical, and Executive	Illinois	Y	25830 FQ	33270 MW	42920 TQ	USBLS	5/15
Except Legal, Medical, and Executive	Chicago-Naperville-Arlington Heights PMSA, IL	Y	27800 FQ	35660 MW	46110 TQ	USBLS	5/15
Except Legal, Medical, and Executive	Lake County-Kenosha County PMSA, IL-WI	Y	27970 FQ	35920 MW	45440 TQ	USBLS	5/15
Except Legal, Medical, and Executive	Indiana	Y	25490 FQ	31270 MW	38070 TQ	USBLS	5/15
Except Legal, Medical, and Executive	Gary PMSA, IN	Y	18590 FQ	28290 MW	36100 TQ	USBLS	5/15
Except Legal, Medical, and Executive	Indianapolis-Carmel-Anderson MSA, IN	Y	28100 FQ	34690 MW	42200 TQ	USBLS	5/15
Except Legal, Medical, and Executive	Iowa	Y	24690 FQ	30560 MW	37890 TQ	USBLS	5/15
Except Legal, Medical, and Executive	Des Moines-West Des Moines MSA, IA	Y	29380 FQ	35700 MW	42660 TQ	USBLS	5/15
Except Legal, Medical, and Executive	Kansas	Y	24740 FQ	30310 MW	37090 TQ	USBLS	5/15
Except Legal, Medical, and Executive	Wichita MSA, KS	Y	25880 FQ	30610 MW	37440 TQ	USBLS	5/15
Except Legal, Medical, and Executive	Kentucky	Y	23300 FQ	29480 MW	37140 TQ	USBLS	5/15
Except Legal, Medical, and Executive	Louisville-Jefferson County MSA, KY-IN	Y	25520 FQ	31620 MW	39450 TQ	USBLS	5/15
Except Legal, Medical, and Executive	Louisiana	Y	23130 FQ	28420 MW	35010 TQ	USBLS	5/15
Except Legal, Medical, and Executive	Baton Rouge MSA, LA	Y	23200 FQ	28590 MW	35600 TQ	USBLS	5/15
Except Legal, Medical, and Executive	New Orleans-Metairie MSA, LA	Y	26440 FQ	31310 MW	37670 TQ	USBLS	5/15
Except Legal, Medical, and Executive	Maine	Y	27400 FQ	33190 MW	38420 TQ	USBLS	5/15
Except Legal, Medical, and Executive	Portland-South Portland MSA, ME	Y	29070 FQ	35520 MW	42230 TQ	USBLS	5/15
Except Legal, Medical, and Executive	Maryland	Y	25625 AE	38491 MW	44924 AEX	MDBLS	4/16
Except Legal, Medical, and Executive	Baltimore-Columbia-Towson MSA, MD	Y	30240 FQ	37840 MW	46550 TQ	USBLS	5/15
Except Legal, Medical, and Executive	Salisbury MSA, MD-DE	Y	26870 FQ	32650 MW	40010 TQ	USBLS	5/15
Except Legal, Medical, and Executive	Massachusetts	Y	34120 FQ	42790 MW	52550 TQ	USBLS	5/15
Except Legal, Medical, and Executive	Boston-Cambridge-Newton NECTA, MA	Y	36590 FQ	45850 MW	56050 TQ	USBLS	5/15
Except Legal, Medical, and Executive	Brockton-Bridgewater-Easton NECTA, MA	Y	33190 FQ	40090 MW	48030 TQ	USBLS	5/15
Except Legal, Medical, and Executive	Worcester MSA, MA-CT	Y	33660 FQ	40450 MW	48220 TQ	USBLS	5/15
Except Legal, Medical, and Executive	Michigan	Y	26240 FQ	33100 MW	40690 TQ	USBLS	5/15
Except Legal, Medical, and Executive	Detroit-Dearborn-Livonia PMSA, MI	Y	27010 FQ	34600 MW	42970 TQ	USBLS	5/15
Except Legal, Medical, and Executive	Grand Rapids-Wyoming MSA, MI	Y	25160 FQ	31210 MW	38750 TQ	USBLS	5/15
Except Legal, Medical, and Executive	Minnesota	Y	32118 FQ	38317 MW	46519 TQ	MNBLS	1/16-3/16
Except Legal, Medical, and Executive	Minneapolis-St. Paul-Bloomington MSA, MN-WI	Y	33979 FQ	40785 MW	48592 TQ	MNBLS	1/16-3/16
Except Legal, Medical, and Executive	Mississippi	Y	22870 FQ	28810 MW	35830 TQ	USBLS	5/15
Except Legal, Medical, and Executive	Jackson MSA, MS	Y	23830 FQ	29650 MW	37320 TQ	USBLS	5/15
Except Legal, Medical, and Executive	Missouri	Y	23980 FQ	30620 MW	38130 TQ	USBLS	5/15
Except Legal, Medical, and Executive	Kansas City MSA, MO-KS	Y	26680 FQ	33650 MW	40160 TQ	USBLS	5/15
Except Legal, Medical, and Executive	St. Louis MSA, MO-IL	Y	26140 FQ	33520 MW	40870 TQ	USBLS	5/15
Except Legal, Medical, and Executive	Montana	Y	23800 FQ	29260 MW	35980 TQ	USBLS	5/15

AE	Average entry wage	AWR	Average wage range	H	Hourly	LR	Low end range	MTC	Median total compensation	TCC	Total cash compensation
AEX	Average experienced wage	B	Biweekly	HI	Highest wage paid	M	Monthly	MW	Median wage paid	TQ	Third quartile wage
ATC	Average total compensation	D	Daily	HR	High end range	MCC	Median cash compensation	MWR	Median wage range	W	Weekly
AW	Average wage paid	FQ	First quartile wage	LO	Lowest wage paid	ME	Median entry wage	S	See annotated source	Y	Yearly

Occupation/Type/Industry	Location	Per	Low	Mid	High	Source	Date
Secretary and Administrative Assistant							
Except Legal, Medical, and Executive	Billings MSA, MT	Y	24900 FQ	29690 MW	36190 TQ	USBLS	5/15
Except Legal, Medical, and Executive	Nebraska	Y	26370 FQ	31555 MW	37480 TQ	NEBLS	7/16-9/16
Except Legal, Medical, and Executive	Omaha-Council Bluffs MSA, NE-IA	Y	27305 FQ	33290 MW	39150 TQ	NEBLS	7/16-9/16
Except Legal, Medical, and Executive	Nevada	Y	29030 FQ	35740 MW	44400 TQ	USBLS	5/15
Except Legal, Medical, and Executive	Las Vegas-Henderson-Paradise MSA, NV	Y	29070 FQ	35880 MW	44620 TQ	USBLS	5/15
Except Legal, Medical, and Executive	New Hampshire	H	11.87 AE	16.69 MW	19.25 AEX	NHBLS	6/16
Except Legal, Medical, and Executive	Manchester NECTA, NH	H	11.73 AE	16.41 MW	19.35 AEX	NHBLS	6/16
Except Legal, Medical, and Executive	Nashua NECTA, NH-MA	Y	26050 FQ	33680 MW	41190 TQ	USBLS	5/15
Except Legal, Medical, and Executive	New Jersey	Y	31970 FQ	39780 MW	49440 TQ	USBLS	5/15
Except Legal, Medical, and Executive	Camden PMSA, NJ	Y	32180 FQ	38610 MW	47100 TQ	USBLS	5/15
Except Legal, Medical, and Executive	Newark PMSA, NJ-PA	Y	32490 FQ	40890 MW	50230 TQ	USBLS	5/15
Except Legal, Medical, and Executive	Trenton MSA, NJ	Y	37070 FQ	46540 MW	56210 TQ	USBLS	5/15
Except Legal, Medical, and Executive	New Mexico	Y	24460 FQ	30400 MW	37790 TQ	USBLS	5/15
Except Legal, Medical, and Executive	Albuquerque MSA, NM	Y	25180 FQ	31000 MW	38450 TQ	USBLS	5/15
Except Legal, Medical, and Executive	New York	Y	27280 AE	39190 MW	46040 AEX	NYBLS	1/16-3/16
Except Legal, Medical, and Executive	Buffalo-Cheektowaga-Niagara Falls MSA, NY	Y	26970 FQ	33520 MW	42200 TQ	USBLS	5/15
Except Legal, Medical, and Executive	Nassau County-Suffolk County PMSA, NY	Y	30020 FQ	38770 MW	48020 TQ	USBLS	5/15
Except Legal, Medical, and Executive	New York-Jersey City-White Plains PMSA, NY-NJ	Y	32260 FQ	40580 MW	49630 TQ	USBLS	5/15
Except Legal, Medical, and Executive	Rochester MSA, NY	Y	28240 FQ	34290 MW	42420 TQ	USBLS	5/15
Except Legal, Medical, and Executive	North Carolina	Y	27750 FQ	33560 MW	39280 TQ	USBLS	5/15
Except Legal, Medical, and Executive	Charlotte-Concord-Gastonia MSA, NC-SC	Y	28010 FQ	34560 MW	41380 TQ	USBLS	5/15
Except Legal, Medical, and Executive	Raleigh MSA, NC	Y	29540 FQ	34640 MW	39380 TQ	USBLS	5/15
Except Legal, Medical, and Executive	North Dakota	Y	29560 FQ	35530 MW	42850 TQ	USBLS	5/15
Except Legal, Medical, and Executive	Fargo MSA, ND-MN	Y	28630 FQ	34580 MW	40670 TQ	USBLS	5/15
Except Legal, Medical, and Executive	Ohio	Y	25910 FQ	32620 MW	39460 TQ	USBLS	5/15
Except Legal, Medical, and Executive	Cincinnati MSA, OH-KY-IN	Y	27660 FQ	34390 MW	41580 TQ	USBLS	5/15
Except Legal, Medical, and Executive	Cleveland-Elyria MSA, OH	Y	27310 FQ	33870 MW	40730 TQ	USBLS	5/15
Except Legal, Medical, and Executive	Columbus MSA, OH	Y	26970 FQ	34610 MW	41800 TQ	USBLS	5/15
Except Legal, Medical, and Executive	Oklahoma	Y	22870 FQ	29290 MW	36520 TQ	USBLS	5/15
Except Legal, Medical, and Executive	Oklahoma City MSA, OK	Y	24480 FQ	31340 MW	37970 TQ	USBLS	5/15
Except Legal, Medical, and Executive	Tulsa MSA, OK	Y	24700 FQ	30430 MW	37570 TQ	USBLS	5/15
Except Legal, Medical, and Executive	Oregon	H	13.54 FQ	16.97 MW	20.87 TQ	ORBLS	2016
Except Legal, Medical, and Executive	Portland-Vancouver-Hillsboro MSA, OR-WA	Y	29770 FQ	36650 MW	44840 TQ	USBLS	5/15
Except Legal, Medical, and Executive	Pennsylvania	Y	26410 FQ	33230 MW	40790 TQ	USBLS	5/15
Except Legal, Medical, and Executive	Allentown-Bethlehem-Easton MSA, PA-NJ	Y	26970 FQ	33210 MW	39960 TQ	USBLS	5/15
Except Legal, Medical, and Executive	Harrisburg-Carlisle MSA, PA	Y	27590 FQ	34690 MW	43170 TQ	USBLS	5/15
Except Legal, Medical, and Executive	Montgomery County-Bucks County-Chester County PMSA, PA	Y	28900 FQ	36160 MW	45020 TQ	USBLS	5/15
Except Legal, Medical, and Executive	Philadelphia PMSA, PA	Y	30890 FQ	37030 MW	45290 TQ	USBLS	5/15
Except Legal, Medical, and Executive	Pittsburgh MSA, PA	Y	26180 FQ	32940 MW	40890 TQ	USBLS	5/15
Except Legal, Medical, and Executive	Rhode Island	Y	32000 FQ	39570 MW	47620 TQ	USBLS	5/15
Except Legal, Medical, and Executive	Providence-Warwick MSA, RI-MA	Y	31310 FQ	39000 MW	47190 TQ	USBLS	5/15
Except Legal, Medical, and Executive	South Carolina	Y	24450 FQ	30140 MW	37400 TQ	USBLS	5/15
Except Legal, Medical, and Executive	Charleston-North Charleston MSA, SC	Y	26280 FQ	32930 MW	39100 TQ	USBLS	5/15
Except Legal, Medical, and Executive	Columbia MSA, SC	Y	25700 FQ	30870 MW	37320 TQ	USBLS	5/15
Except Legal, Medical, and Executive	Greenville-Anderson-Mauldin MSA, SC	Y	24830 FQ	30320 MW	37680 TQ	USBLS	5/15
Except Legal, Medical, and Executive	South Dakota	Y	23060 FQ	26930 MW	30440 TQ	USBLS	5/15
Except Legal, Medical, and Executive	Sioux Falls MSA, SD	Y	24860 FQ	28310 MW	32450 TQ	USBLS	5/15
Except Legal, Medical, and Executive	Tennessee	Y	23180 FQ	29290 MW	37170 TQ	USBLS	5/15
Except Legal, Medical, and Executive	Knoxville MSA, TN	Y	23320 FQ	29020 MW	37250 TQ	USBLS	5/15
Except Legal, Medical, and Executive	Memphis MSA, TN-MS-AR	Y	25610 FQ	31880 MW	39120 TQ	USBLS	5/15
Except Legal, Medical, and Executive	Nashville-Davidson–Murfreesboro–Franklin MSA, TN	Y	24320 FQ	31120 MW	39170 TQ	USBLS	5/15
Except Legal, Medical, and Executive	Texas	Y	24380 FQ	31300 MW	39160 TQ	USBLS	5/15
Except Legal, Medical, and Executive	Austin-Round Rock MSA, TX	Y	26680 FQ	32990 MW	39460 TQ	USBLS	5/15
Except Legal, Medical, and Executive	Dallas-Plano-Irving PMSA, TX	Y	27410 FQ	34710 MW	43660 TQ	USBLS	5/15

AE Average entry wage	**AWR** Average wage range	**H** Hourly	**LR** Low end range	**MTC** Median total compensation	**TCC** Total cash compensation
AEX Average experienced wage	**B** Biweekly	**HI** Highest wage paid	**M** Monthly	**MW** Median wage paid	**TQ** Third quartile wage
ATC Average total compensation	**D** Daily	**HR** High end range	**MCC** Median cash compensation	**MWR** Median wage range	**W** Weekly
AW Average wage paid	**FQ** First quartile wage	**LO** Lowest wage paid	**ME** Median entry wage	**S** See annotated source	**Y** Yearly

Occupation/Type/Industry	Location	Per	Low	Mid	High	Source	Date
Secretary and Administrative Assistant							
Except Legal, Medical, and Executive	Fort Worth-Arlington PMSA, TX	Y	23420 FQ	29680 MW	37730 TQ	USBLS	5/15
Except Legal, Medical, and Executive	Houston-The Woodlands-Sugar Land MSA, TX	Y	25780 FQ	34100 MW	44190 TQ	USBLS	5/15
Except Legal, Medical, and Executive	San Antonio-New Braunfels MSA, TX	Y	25910 FQ	31670 MW	38360 TQ	USBLS	5/15
Except Legal, Medical, and Executive	Utah	Y	24870 FQ	30660 MW	37620 TQ	USBLS	5/15
Except Legal, Medical, and Executive	Ogden-Clearfield MSA, UT	Y	24170 FQ	29690 MW	36150 TQ	USBLS	5/15
Except Legal, Medical, and Executive	Provo-Orem MSA, UT	Y	22430 FQ	28920 MW	35460 TQ	USBLS	5/15
Except Legal, Medical, and Executive	Salt Lake City MSA, UT	Y	26740 FQ	33040 MW	39710 TQ	USBLS	5/15
Except Legal, Medical, and Executive	Vermont	Y	28340 FQ	33630 MW	38800 TQ	USBLS	5/15
Except Legal, Medical, and Executive	Burlington-South Burlington MSA, VT	Y	31160 FQ	36030 MW	41750 TQ	USBLS	5/15
Except Legal, Medical, and Executive	Virginia	Y	27600 FQ	35090 MW	43910 TQ	USBLS	5/15
Except Legal, Medical, and Executive	Richmond MSA, VA	Y	28060 FQ	35120 MW	44100 TQ	USBLS	5/15
Except Legal, Medical, and Executive	Virginia Beach-Norfolk-Newport News MSA, VA-NC	Y	26400 FQ	32540 MW	39300 TQ	USBLS	5/15
Except Legal, Medical, and Executive	Washington	H	15.85 FQ	18.91 MW	23.03 TQ	WABLS	3/16
Except Legal, Medical, and Executive	Seattle-Bellevue-Everett PMSA, WA	H	16.84 FQ	20.58 MW	24.45 TQ	WABLS	3/16
Except Legal, Medical, and Executive	Tacoma-Lakewood PMSA, WA	H	15.95 FQ	19.37 MW	23.29 TQ	WABLS	3/16
Except Legal, Medical, and Executive	West Virginia	Y	22510 FQ	28630 MW	35670 TQ	USBLS	5/15
Except Legal, Medical, and Executive	Huntington-Ashland MSA, WV-KY-OH	Y	21070 FQ	26930 MW	34390 TQ	USBLS	5/15
Except Legal, Medical, and Executive	Wisconsin	Y	30070 FQ	35700 MW	42390 TQ	USBLS	5/15
Except Legal, Medical, and Executive	Madison MSA, WI	Y	31350 FQ	36570 MW	43730 TQ	USBLS	5/15
Except Legal, Medical, and Executive	Milwaukee-Waukesha-West Allis MSA, WI	Y	32730 FQ	39110 MW	46290 TQ	USBLS	5/15
Except Legal, Medical, and Executive	Wyoming	Y	27840 FQ	34190 MW	41540 TQ	USBLS	5/15
Except Legal, Medical, and Executive	Cheyenne MSA, WY	Y	27680 FQ	33290 MW	38790 TQ	USBLS	5/15
Except Legal, Medical, and Executive	Puerto Rico	Y	17240 FQ	18970 MW	23250 TQ	USBLS	5/15
Except Legal, Medical, and Executive	San Juan-Carolina-Caguas MSA, PR	Y	17460 FQ	19440 MW	24370 TQ	USBLS	5/15
Except Legal, Medical, and Executive	Virgin Islands	Y	22540 FQ	28190 MW	35500 TQ	USBLS	5/15
Except Legal, Medical, and Executive	Guam	Y	21740 FQ	28720 MW	37040 TQ	USBLS	5/15
Secretary of State							
Federal Government	United States	Y			203700 HI	CNNM01	2016
Securities, Commodities, and Financial Services Sales Agent	Alabama	Y	33282 AE	80982 AW	104832 AEX	ALBLS	6/16
	Anniston-Oxford-Jacksonville MSA, AL	Y	34310 FQ	37640 MW	46870 TQ	USBLS	5/15
	Birmingham-Hoover MSA, AL	Y	36933 AE	97509 AW	127803 AEX	ALBLS	6/16
	Alaska	Y	44430 FQ	63310 MW	82460 TQ	USBLS	5/15
	Anchorage MSA, AK	Y	44390 FQ	66330 MW	104890 TQ	USBLS	5/15
	Arizona	Y	35470 FQ	49740 MW	87270 TQ	USBLS	5/15
	Phoenix-Mesa-Scottsdale MSA, AZ	Y	36880 FQ	54500 MW	93690 TQ	USBLS	5/15
	Tucson MSA, AZ	Y	33110 FQ	38160 MW	62700 TQ	USBLS	5/15
	Arkansas	Y	34100 FQ	50710 MW	87950 TQ	USBLS	5/15
	Little Rock-North Little Rock-Conway MSA, AR	Y	33410 FQ	46980 MW	78850 TQ	USBLS	5/15
	California	H	18.51 FQ	26.69 MW	49.41 TQ	CABLS	1/16-3/16
	Anaheim-Santa Ana-Irvine PMSA, CA	H	17.87 FQ	24.21 MW	48.69 TQ	CABLS	1/16-3/16
	Los Angeles-Long Beach-Glendale PMSA, CA	H	18.92 FQ	31.40 MW	55.74 TQ	CABLS	1/16-3/16
	Oakland-Hayward-Berkeley PMSA, CA	H	19.53 FQ	25.26 MW	44.60 TQ	CABLS	1/16-3/16
	Riverside-San Bernardino-Ontario MSA, CA	H	17.32 FQ	20.32 MW	24.68 TQ	CABLS	1/16-3/16
	Sacramento–Roseville–Arden-Arcade MSA, CA	H	17.26 FQ	21.39 MW	42.76 TQ	CABLS	1/16-3/16
	San Diego-Carlsbad MSA, CA	H	17.98 FQ	24.55 MW	41.90 TQ	CABLS	1/16-3/16
	San Francisco-Redwood City-South San Francisco PMSA, CA	H	21.66 FQ	38.21 MW		CABLS	1/16-3/16
	Colorado	Y	36050 FQ	48470 MW	81700 TQ	USBLS	5/15

AE Average entry wage	**AWR** Average wage range	**H** Hourly	**LR** Low end range	**MTC** Median total compensation	**TCC** Total cash compensation
AEX Average experienced wage	**B** Biweekly	**HI** Highest wage paid	**M** Monthly	**MW** Median wage paid	**TQ** Third quartile wage
ATC Average total compensation	**D** Daily	**HR** High end range	**MCC** Median cash compensation	**MWR** Median wage range	**W** Weekly
AW Average wage paid	**FQ** First quartile wage	**LO** Lowest wage paid	**ME** Median entry wage	**S** See annotated source	**Y** Yearly

Occupation/Type/Industry	Location	Per	Low	Mid	High	Source	Date
Securities, Commodities, and Financial Services Sales Agent	Denver-Aurora-Lakewood MSA, CO	Y	37170 FQ	49880 MW	80210 TQ	USBLS	5/15
	Connecticut	Y		103189 MW		CTBLS	1/16-3/16
	Bridgeport-Stamford-Norwalk MSA, CT	Y	65720 FQ	111330 MW		USBLS	5/15
	Hartford-West Hartford-East Hartford MSA, CT	Y	51830 FQ	82250 MW	147100 TQ	USBLS	5/15
	Delaware	Y	54340 FQ	75450 MW	115120 TQ	USBLS	5/15
	Wilmington PMSA, DE-MD-NJ	Y	54840 FQ	75520 MW	113620 TQ	USBLS	5/15
	District of Columbia	Y	45110 FQ	74040 MW	138990 TQ	USBLS	5/15
	Washington-Arlington-Alexandria PMSA, DC-VA-MD-WV	Y	47730 FQ	76140 MW	135340 TQ	USBLS	5/15
	Florida	H	17.37 AE	28.82 MW	55.84 AEX	FLBLS	7/16-9/16
	Fort Lauderdale-Pompano Beach-Deerfield Beach PMSA, FL	H	16.13 AE	24.13 MW	46.00 AEX	FLBLS	7/16-9/16
	Miami-Miami Beach-Kendall PMSA, FL	H	18.73 AE	35.91 MW	65.17 AEX	FLBLS	7/16-9/16
	North Port-Sarasota-Bradenton MSA, FL	H	14.40 AE	23.27 MW	42.66 AEX	FLBLS	7/16-9/16
	Orlando-Kissimmee-Sanford MSA, FL	H	15.66 AE	21.68 MW	42.08 AEX	FLBLS	7/16-9/16
	Tampa-St. Petersburg-Clearwater MSA, FL	H	17.87 AE	27.66 MW	47.96 AEX	FLBLS	7/16-9/16
	Georgia	Y	40180 FQ	66460 MW	110780 TQ	USBLS	5/15
	Atlanta-Sandy Springs-Roswell MSA, GA	Y	41180 FQ	69000 MW	114330 TQ	USBLS	5/15
	Hawaii	Y	47680 FQ	67480 MW	110400 TQ	USBLS	5/15
	Urban Honolulu MSA, HI	Y	53190 FQ	70790 MW	112220 TQ	USBLS	5/15
	Idaho	Y	31970 FQ	41950 MW	75420 TQ	USBLS	5/15
	Boise City MSA, ID	Y	31500 FQ	44390 MW	61290 TQ	USBLS	5/15
	Illinois	Y	44010 FQ	72580 MW	133470 TQ	USBLS	5/15
	Chicago-Naperville-Arlington Heights PMSA, IL	Y	48440 FQ	74510 MW	140180 TQ	USBLS	5/15
	Lake County-Kenosha County PMSA, IL-WI	Y	37950 FQ	74120 MW	122010 TQ	USBLS	5/15
	Indiana	Y	36700 FQ	51670 MW	121440 TQ	USBLS	5/15
	Gary PMSA, IN	Y	38380 FQ	47700 MW	103540 TQ	USBLS	5/15
	Indianapolis-Carmel-Anderson MSA, IN	Y	37650 FQ	61030 MW	141280 TQ	USBLS	5/15
	Iowa	Y	36220 FQ	55190 MW	95270 TQ	USBLS	5/15
	Des Moines-West Des Moines MSA, IA	Y	42520 FQ	67710 MW	101440 TQ	USBLS	5/15
	Sioux City MSA, IA-NE-SD	Y	40240 FQ	54070 MW	62530 TQ	USBLS	5/15
	Kansas	Y	54650 FQ	89700 MW	139590 TQ	USBLS	5/15
	Wichita MSA, KS	Y	53260 FQ	69070 MW	122650 TQ	USBLS	5/15
	Kentucky	Y	29570 FQ	46530 MW	92040 TQ	USBLS	5/15
	Louisville-Jefferson County MSA, KY-IN	Y	33210 FQ	50810 MW	101350 TQ	USBLS	5/15
	Louisiana	Y	33690 FQ	49570 MW	123090 TQ	USBLS	5/15
	Baton Rouge MSA, LA	Y	32240 FQ	43810 MW	91240 TQ	USBLS	5/15
	New Orleans-Metairie MSA, LA	Y	37690 FQ	76170 MW	155500 TQ	USBLS	5/15
	Maine	Y	51170 FQ	69230 MW	95000 TQ	USBLS	5/15
	Portland-South Portland MSA, ME	Y	48310 FQ	68700 MW	99090 TQ	USBLS	5/15
	Maryland	Y	33067 AE	87964 MW	115413 AEX	MDBLS	4/16
	Baltimore-Columbia-Towson MSA, MD	Y	35660 FQ	53050 MW	121780 TQ	USBLS	5/15
	Salisbury MSA, MD-DE	Y	37030 FQ	64460 MW	111580 TQ	USBLS	5/15
	Massachusetts	Y	71630 FQ	99660 MW	168740 TQ	USBLS	5/15
	Boston-Cambridge-Newton NECTA, MA	Y	74320 FQ	101520 MW	170200 TQ	USBLS	5/15
	Worcester MSA, MA-CT	Y	42190 FQ	77260 MW	171890 TQ	USBLS	5/15
	Michigan	Y	36770 FQ	55630 MW	101960 TQ	USBLS	5/15
	Detroit-Dearborn-Livonia PMSA, MI	Y	34860 FQ	39030 MW	71520 TQ	USBLS	5/15
	Grand Rapids-Wyoming MSA, MI	Y	39440 FQ	62300 MW	100180 TQ	USBLS	5/15

AE	Average entry wage	AWR	Average wage range	H	Hourly
AEX	Average experienced wage	B	Biweekly	HI	Highest wage paid
ATC	Average total compensation	D	Daily	HR	High end range
AW	Average wage paid	FQ	First quartile wage	LO	Lowest wage paid

LR	Low end range	MTC	Median total compensation
M	Monthly	MW	Median wage paid
MCC	Median cash compensation	MWR	Median wage range
ME	Median entry wage	S	See annotated source

TCC	Total cash compensation		
TQ	Third quartile wage		
W	Weekly		
Y	Yearly		

Occupation/Type/Industry	Location	Per	Low	Mid	High	Source	Date
Securities, Commodities, and Financial Services Sales Agent	Minnesota	Y	38227 FQ	74830 MW	121134 TQ	MNBLS	1/16-3/16
	Minneapolis-St. Paul-Bloomington MSA, MN-WI	Y	41615 FQ	84228 MW	127365 TQ	MNBLS	1/16-3/16
	Mississippi	Y	49610 FQ	80380 MW	122670 TQ	USBLS	5/15
	Jackson MSA, MS	Y	58590 FQ	103050 MW	161900 TQ	USBLS	5/15
	Missouri	Y	35070 FQ	58990 MW	103190 TQ	USBLS	5/15
	Kansas City MSA, MO-KS	Y	46630 FQ	83580 MW	127540 TQ	USBLS	5/15
	St. Louis MSA, MO-IL	Y	36290 FQ	66550 MW	117530 TQ	USBLS	5/15
	Montana	Y	35870 FQ	55290 MW	96210 TQ	USBLS	5/15
	Billings MSA, MT	Y	38550 FQ	75630 MW	101140 TQ	USBLS	5/15
	Nebraska	Y	37645 FQ	55215 MW	88950 TQ	NEBLS	7/16-9/16
	Omaha-Council Bluffs MSA, NE-IA	Y	41495 FQ	57990 MW	90380 TQ	NEBLS	7/16-9/16
	Nevada	Y	33560 FQ	41460 MW	70030 TQ	USBLS	5/15
	Las Vegas-Henderson-Paradise MSA, NV	Y	32240 FQ	38840 MW	65650 TQ	USBLS	5/15
	New Hampshire	H	23.14 AE	62.90 MW	100.13 AEX	NHBLS	6/16
	Manchester NECTA, NH	H	25.89 AE	60.14 MW	96.74 AEX	NHBLS	6/16
	New Jersey	Y	48200 FQ	82000 MW	142030 TQ	USBLS	5/15
	Camden PMSA, NJ	Y	40780 FQ	74270 MW	109490 TQ	USBLS	5/15
	Newark PMSA, NJ-PA	Y	45290 FQ	80630 MW	154870 TQ	USBLS	5/15
	Trenton PMSA, NJ	Y	55580 FQ	82450 MW	132180 TQ	USBLS	5/15
	New Mexico	Y	33310 FQ	45230 MW	74920 TQ	USBLS	5/15
	Albuquerque MSA, NM	Y	35580 FQ	48910 MW	72780 TQ	USBLS	5/15
	New York	Y	55310 AE	130630 MW		NYBLS	1/16-3/16
	Buffalo-Cheektowaga-Niagara Falls MSA, NY	Y	42400 FQ	92200 MW	144270 TQ	USBLS	5/15
	Nassau County-Suffolk County PMSA, NY	Y	41670 FQ	53530 MW	84940 TQ	USBLS	5/15
	New York-Jersey City-White Plains PMSA, NY-NJ	Y	82020 FQ	137860 MW		USBLS	5/15
	Rochester MSA, NY	Y	29840 FQ	37290 MW	119820 TQ	USBLS	5/15
	North Carolina	Y	43790 FQ	78160 MW	139860 TQ	USBLS	5/15
	Charlotte-Concord-Gastonia MSA, NC-SC	Y	53960 FQ	93950 MW	165310 TQ	USBLS	5/15
	Raleigh MSA, NC	Y	40070 FQ	74280 MW	135860 TQ	USBLS	5/15
	North Dakota	Y	40010 FQ	62730 MW	105580 TQ	USBLS	5/15
	Fargo MSA, ND-MN	Y	43180 FQ	60730 MW	91900 TQ	USBLS	5/15
	Ohio	Y	36690 FQ	59990 MW	113220 TQ	USBLS	5/15
	Cincinnati MSA, OH-KY-IN	Y	37080 FQ	66010 MW	115500 TQ	USBLS	5/15
	Cleveland-Elyria MSA, OH	Y	41510 FQ	65330 MW	121880 TQ	USBLS	5/15
	Columbus MSA, OH	Y	41330 FQ	76270 MW	107280 TQ	USBLS	5/15
	Oklahoma	Y	38670 FQ	61060 MW	123810 TQ	USBLS	5/15
	Oklahoma City MSA, OK	Y	38800 FQ	58180 MW	132490 TQ	USBLS	5/15
	Tulsa MSA, OK	Y	43130 FQ	80470 MW	121750 TQ	USBLS	5/15
	Oregon	H	16.97 FQ	24.52 MW	39.86 TQ	ORBLS	2016
	Portland-Vancouver-Hillsboro MSA, OR-WA	Y	36890 FQ	54070 MW	88610 TQ	USBLS	5/15
	Pennsylvania	Y	50580 FQ	74230 MW	120640 TQ	USBLS	5/15
	Allentown-Bethlehem-Easton MSA, PA-NJ	Y	50400 FQ	63050 MW	81040 TQ	USBLS	5/15
	Harrisburg-Carlisle MSA, PA	Y	42700 FQ	68700 MW	127490 TQ	USBLS	5/15
	Montgomery County-Bucks County-Chester County PMSA, PA	Y	55440 FQ	84960 MW	130680 TQ	USBLS	5/15
	Philadelphia PMSA, PA	Y	59050 FQ	83800 MW	131060 TQ	USBLS	5/15
	Pittsburgh MSA, PA	Y	51770 FQ	75010 MW	123780 TQ	USBLS	5/15
	South Carolina	Y	39030 FQ	61440 MW	123540 TQ	USBLS	5/15
	Charleston-North Charleston MSA, SC	Y	36410 FQ	82690 MW	141340 TQ	USBLS	5/15
	Columbia MSA, SC	Y	40670 FQ	58550 MW	123920 TQ	USBLS	5/15
	Greenville-Anderson-Mauldin MSA, SC	Y	47380 FQ	69500 MW	115170 TQ	USBLS	5/15
	South Dakota	Y	35800 FQ	60750 MW	122000 TQ	USBLS	5/15
	Sioux Falls MSA, SD	Y	46500 FQ	67830 MW	108200 TQ	USBLS	5/15
	Tennessee	Y	36710 FQ	58110 MW	102750 TQ	USBLS	5/15
	Knoxville MSA, TN	Y	30290 FQ	35860 MW	46690 TQ	USBLS	5/15
	Memphis MSA, TN-MS-AR	Y	45330 FQ	80940 MW	146630 TQ	USBLS	5/15

AE	Average entry wage	AWR	Average wage range	H	Hourly
AEX	Average experienced wage	B	Biweekly	HI	Highest wage paid
ATC	Average total compensation	D	Daily	HR	High end range
AW	Average wage paid	FQ	First quartile wage	LO	Lowest wage paid

LR	Low end range	MTC	Median total compensation	TCC	Total cash compensation
M	Monthly	MW	Median wage paid	TQ	Third quartile wage
MCC	Median cash compensation	MWR	Median wage range	W	Weekly
ME	Median entry wage	S	See annotated source	Y	Yearly

Occupation/Type/Industry	Location	Per	Low	Mid	High	Source	Date
Securities, Commodities, and Financial Services Sales Agent	Nashville-Davidson–Murfreesboro–Franklin MSA, TN	Y	42030 FQ	62260 MW	97300 TQ	USBLS	5/15
	Texas	Y	36620 FQ	57970 MW	116780 TQ	USBLS	5/15
	Austin-Round Rock MSA, TX	Y	33900 FQ	42840 MW	71100 TQ	USBLS	5/15
	Dallas-Plano-Irving PMSA, TX	Y	41370 FQ	75530 MW	141280 TQ	USBLS	5/15
	Fort Worth-Arlington PMSA, TX	Y	35510 FQ	44740 MW	79550 TQ	USBLS	5/15
	Houston-The Woodlands-Sugar Land MSA, TX	Y	35980 FQ	57490 MW	126470 TQ	USBLS	5/15
	San Antonio-New Braunfels MSA, TX	Y	36350 FQ	56380 MW	102600 TQ	USBLS	5/15
	Utah	Y	36300 FQ	51020 MW	94110 TQ	USBLS	5/15
	Ogden-Clearfield MSA, UT	Y	32920 FQ	45570 MW	68400 TQ	USBLS	5/15
	Provo-Orem MSA, UT	Y	32490 FQ	36790 MW	70620 TQ	USBLS	5/15
	Salt Lake City MSA, UT	Y	37840 FQ	57520 MW	111160 TQ	USBLS	5/15
	Vermont	Y	51610 FQ	66620 MW	108270 TQ	USBLS	5/15
	Burlington-South Burlington MSA, VT	Y	67050 FQ	99760 MW	142670 TQ	USBLS	5/15
	Virginia	Y	48950 FQ	75290 MW	133340 TQ	USBLS	5/15
	Richmond MSA, VA	Y	61030 FQ	77850 MW	129440 TQ	USBLS	5/15
	Virginia Beach-Norfolk-Newport News MSA, VA-NC	Y	38190 FQ	56990 MW	123940 TQ	USBLS	5/15
	Washington	H	17.95 FQ	28.68 MW	57.77 TQ	WABLS	3/16
	Seattle-Bellevue-Everett PMSA, WA	H	20.02 FQ	34.40 MW	72.97 TQ	WABLS	3/16
	Tacoma-Lakewood PMSA, WA	H	16.49 FQ	19.63 MW	33.99 TQ	WABLS	3/16
	West Virginia	Y	36670 FQ	63830 MW	96210 TQ	USBLS	5/15
	Huntington-Ashland MSA, WV-KY-OH	Y	33190 FQ	38020 MW	89710 TQ	USBLS	5/15
	Wisconsin	Y	39120 FQ	59260 MW	101520 TQ	USBLS	5/15
	Madison MSA, WI	Y	47280 FQ	82220 MW	111620 TQ	USBLS	5/15
	Milwaukee-Waukesha-West Allis MSA, WI	Y	38810 FQ	59190 MW	101070 TQ	USBLS	5/15
	Wyoming	Y	36720 FQ	52900 MW	81410 TQ	USBLS	5/15
	Cheyenne MSA, WY	Y	39240 FQ	67970 MW	79780 TQ	USBLS	5/15
	Puerto Rico	Y	28520 FQ	44810 MW	71170 TQ	USBLS	5/15
	San Juan-Carolina-Caguas MSA, PR	Y	28240 FQ	40090 MW	73280 TQ	USBLS	5/15
Security and Fire Alarm Systems Installer	Alabama	Y	24510 AE	38504 AW	45491 AEX	ALBLS	6/16
	Birmingham-Hoover MSA, AL	Y	28426 AE	41108 AW	47444 AEX	ALBLS	6/16
	Alaska	Y	41570 FQ	57210 MW	75950 TQ	USBLS	5/15
	Anchorage MSA, AK	Y	44200 FQ	65560 MW	80840 TQ	USBLS	5/15
	Arizona	Y	41370 FQ	53230 MW	62300 TQ	USBLS	5/15
	Phoenix-Mesa-Scottsdale MSA, AZ	Y	45670 FQ	55840 MW	63790 TQ	USBLS	5/15
	Tucson MSA, AZ	Y	22300 FQ	30820 MW	45120 TQ	USBLS	5/15
	Arkansas	Y	27050 FQ	31940 MW	37440 TQ	USBLS	5/15
	Little Rock-North Little Rock-Conway MSA, AR	Y	33140 FQ	36140 MW	39170 TQ	USBLS	5/15
	California	H	17.53 FQ	23.16 MW	29.27 TQ	CABLS	1/16-3/16
	Anaheim-Santa Ana-Irvine PMSA, CA	H	17.68 FQ	22.66 MW	31.20 TQ	CABLS	1/16-3/16
	Los Angeles-Long Beach-Glendale PMSA, CA	H	16.62 FQ	22.91 MW	28.33 TQ	CABLS	1/16-3/16
	Oakland-Hayward-Berkeley PMSA, CA	H	23.38 FQ	27.38 MW	30.62 TQ	CABLS	1/16-3/16
	Riverside-San Bernardino-Ontario MSA, CA	H	19.94 FQ	24.73 MW	29.07 TQ	CABLS	1/16-3/16
	Sacramento–Roseville–Arden-Arcade MSA, CA	H	16.69 FQ	21.49 MW	27.00 TQ	CABLS	1/16-3/16
	San Diego-Carlsbad MSA, CA	H	17.51 FQ	22.21 MW	28.18 TQ	CABLS	1/16-3/16
	San Francisco-Redwood City-South San Francisco PMSA, CA	H	15.96 FQ	17.79 MW	22.20 TQ	CABLS	1/16-3/16
	Colorado	Y	35220 FQ	42650 MW	55150 TQ	USBLS	5/15
	Denver-Aurora-Lakewood MSA, CO	Y	34810 FQ	40580 MW	53360 TQ	USBLS	5/15

AE	Average entry wage	AWR	Average wage range	H	Hourly	LR	Low end range	MTC	Median total compensation	TCC	Total cash compensation
AEX	Average experienced wage	B	Biweekly	HI	Highest wage paid	M	Monthly	MW	Median wage paid	TQ	Third quartile wage
ATC	Average total compensation	D	Daily	HR	High end range	MCC	Median cash compensation	MWR	Median wage range	W	Weekly
AW	Average wage paid	FQ	First quartile wage	LO	Lowest wage paid	ME	Median entry wage	S	See annotated source	Y	Yearly

Occupation/Type/Industry	Location	Per	Low	Mid	High	Source	Date
Security and Fire Alarm Systems Installer							
	Connecticut	Y		55189 MW		CTBLS	1/16-3/16
	Bridgeport-Stamford-Norwalk MSA, CT	Y	43990 FQ	56160 MW	62390 TQ	USBLS	5/15
	Hartford-West Hartford-East Hartford MSA, CT	Y	43400 FQ	52340 MW	60990 TQ	USBLS	5/15
	Delaware	Y	41350 FQ	47500 MW	57170 TQ	USBLS	5/15
	Wilmington PMSA, DE-MD-NJ	Y	40470 FQ	47110 MW	57140 TQ	USBLS	5/15
	Washington-Arlington-Alexandria PMSA, DC-VA-MD-WV	Y	35650 FQ	44310 MW	53950 TQ	USBLS	5/15
	Florida	H	14.52 AE	20.04 MW	22.74 AEX	FLBLS	7/16-9/16
	Fort Lauderdale-Pompano Beach-Deerfield Beach PMSA, FL	H	14.34 AE	20.81 MW	22.87 AEX	FLBLS	7/16-9/16
	Miami-Miami Beach-Kendall PMSA, FL	H	13.63 AE	18.57 MW	21.05 AEX	FLBLS	7/16-9/16
	Orlando-Kissimmee-Sanford MSA, FL	H	13.45 AE	20.14 MW	22.67 AEX	FLBLS	7/16-9/16
	Tampa-St. Petersburg-Clearwater MSA, FL	H	15.52 AE	20.21 MW	22.79 AEX	FLBLS	7/16-9/16
	Georgia	Y	29280 FQ	37110 MW	46440 TQ	USBLS	5/15
	Atlanta-Sandy Springs-Roswell MSA, GA	Y	30370 FQ	38280 MW	47020 TQ	USBLS	5/15
	Augusta-Richmond County MSA, GA-SC	Y	24950 FQ	28670 MW	34970 TQ	USBLS	5/15
	Hawaii	Y	35500 FQ	43030 MW	53440 TQ	USBLS	5/15
	Urban Honolulu MSA, HI	Y	35760 FQ	43550 MW	53780 TQ	USBLS	5/15
	Idaho	Y	32810 FQ	42860 MW	48440 TQ	USBLS	5/15
	Boise City MSA, ID	Y	40510 FQ	44400 MW	48280 TQ	USBLS	5/15
	Illinois	Y	34370 FQ	46060 MW	59740 TQ	USBLS	5/15
	Chicago-Naperville-Arlington Heights PMSA, IL	Y	33290 FQ	44860 MW	57960 TQ	USBLS	5/15
	Indiana	Y	35820 FQ	43790 MW	49720 TQ	USBLS	5/15
	Gary PMSA, IN	Y	44390 FQ	55390 MW	67590 TQ	USBLS	5/15
	Indianapolis-Carmel-Anderson MSA, IN	Y	40370 FQ	44710 MW	49050 TQ	USBLS	5/15
	Iowa	Y	35190 FQ	42100 MW	50020 TQ	USBLS	5/15
	Des Moines-West Des Moines MSA, IA	Y	36700 FQ	44530 MW	53490 TQ	USBLS	5/15
	Kansas	Y	37380 FQ	46250 MW	63710 TQ	USBLS	5/15
	Wichita MSA, KS	Y	33680 FQ	40220 MW	50040 TQ	USBLS	5/15
	Kentucky	Y	29210 FQ	36090 MW	44100 TQ	USBLS	5/15
	Louisville-Jefferson County MSA, KY-IN	Y	33430 FQ	41470 MW	47760 TQ	USBLS	5/15
	Louisiana	Y	30620 FQ	36520 MW	44010 TQ	USBLS	5/15
	Baton Rouge MSA, LA	Y	33760 FQ	37630 MW	45520 TQ	USBLS	5/15
	New Orleans-Metairie MSA, LA	Y	32730 FQ	38790 MW	45040 TQ	USBLS	5/15
	Maine	Y	40190 FQ	47400 MW	56410 TQ	USBLS	5/15
	Portland-South Portland MSA, ME	Y	42720 FQ	49570 MW	57600 TQ	USBLS	5/15
	Maryland	Y	31786 AE	49221 MW	57938 AEX	MDBLS	4/16
	Baltimore-Columbia-Towson MSA, MD	Y	41540 FQ	51420 MW	62800 TQ	USBLS	5/15
	Salisbury MSA, MD-DE	Y	25540 FQ	34250 MW	38130 TQ	USBLS	5/15
	Massachusetts	Y	43260 FQ	56110 MW	69480 TQ	USBLS	5/15
	Boston-Cambridge-Newton NECTA, MA	Y	47730 FQ	60770 MW	72120 TQ	USBLS	5/15
	Worcester MSA, MA-CT	Y	37210 FQ	54290 MW	65690 TQ	USBLS	5/15
	Michigan	Y	36990 FQ	46130 MW	55270 TQ	USBLS	5/15
	Detroit-Dearborn-Livonia PMSA, MI	Y	43970 FQ	51140 MW	57400 TQ	USBLS	5/15
	Grand Rapids-Wyoming MSA, MI	Y	35030 FQ	42590 MW	48740 TQ	USBLS	5/15
	Minnesota	Y	39513 FQ	48966 MW	58349 TQ	MNBLS	1/16-3/16
	Minneapolis-St. Paul-Bloomington MSA, MN-WI	Y	42178 FQ	50877 MW	59083 TQ	MNBLS	1/16-3/16
	Mississippi	Y	26710 FQ	29690 MW	35220 TQ	USBLS	5/15
	Jackson MSA, MS	Y	26970 FQ	29210 MW	31890 TQ	USBLS	5/15
	Missouri	Y	30970 FQ	40500 MW	49630 TQ	USBLS	5/15

AE	Average entry wage	**AWR**	Average wage range	**H**	Hourly	**LR**	Low end range	**MTC**	Median total compensation	**TCC**	Total cash compensation
AEX	Average experienced wage	**B**	Biweekly	**HI**	Highest wage paid	**M**	Monthly	**MW**	Median wage paid	**TQ**	Third quartile wage
ATC	Average total compensation	**D**	Daily	**HR**	High end range	**MCC**	Median cash compensation	**MWR**	Median wage range	**W**	Weekly
AW	Average wage paid	**FQ**	First quartile wage	**LO**	Lowest wage paid	**ME**	Median entry wage	**S**	See annotated source	**Y**	Yearly

Occupation/Type/Industry	Location	Per	Low	Mid	High	Source	Date
Security and Fire Alarm Systems Installer							
	Kansas City MSA, MO-KS	Y	35130 FQ	45140 MW	57210 TQ	USBLS	5/15
	St. Louis MSA, MO-IL	Y	31040 FQ	40740 MW	50100 TQ	USBLS	5/15
	Montana	Y	33960 FQ	43200 MW	52440 TQ	USBLS	5/15
	Nebraska	Y	27780 FQ	35485 MW	44470 TQ	NEBLS	7/16-9/16
	Omaha-Council Bluffs MSA, NE-IA	Y	31280 FQ	38210 MW	46935 TQ	NEBLS	7/16-9/16
	Nevada	Y	38040 FQ	46090 MW	59690 TQ	USBLS	5/15
	Las Vegas-Henderson-Paradise MSA, NV	Y	37690 FQ	45490 MW	60300 TQ	USBLS	5/15
	New Hampshire	H	13.55 AE	25.21 MW	29.01 AEX	NHBLS	6/16
	Manchester NECTA, NH	H	12.82 AE	25.15 MW	29.45 AEX	NHBLS	6/16
	New Jersey	Y	38230 FQ	46700 MW	57810 TQ	USBLS	5/15
	Camden PMSA, NJ	Y	38290 FQ	51370 MW	58330 TQ	USBLS	5/15
	Newark PMSA, NJ-PA	Y	41210 FQ	46200 MW	55730 TQ	USBLS	5/15
	New Mexico	Y	27420 FQ	36400 MW	46280 TQ	USBLS	5/15
	Albuquerque MSA, NM	Y	27110 FQ	35250 MW	45750 TQ	USBLS	5/15
	New York	Y	30090 AE	45980 MW	57670 AEX	NYBLS	1/16-3/16
	Buffalo-Cheektowaga-Niagara Falls MSA, NY	Y	41000 FQ	47520 MW	69090 TQ	USBLS	5/15
	Nassau County-Suffolk County PMSA, NY	Y	36930 FQ	44520 MW	53720 TQ	USBLS	5/15
	New York-Jersey City-White Plains PMSA, NY-NJ	Y	31870 FQ	47250 MW	62900 TQ	USBLS	5/15
	Rochester MSA, NY	Y	42570 FQ	48390 MW	61370 TQ	USBLS	5/15
	North Carolina	Y	33160 FQ	41200 MW	48860 TQ	USBLS	5/15
	Charlotte-Concord-Gastonia MSA, NC-SC	Y	37070 FQ	43530 MW	48910 TQ	USBLS	5/15
	Raleigh MSA, NC	Y	35520 FQ	43900 MW	52290 TQ	USBLS	5/15
	North Dakota	Y	34980 FQ	43500 MW	56420 TQ	USBLS	5/15
	Ohio	Y	34350 FQ	42720 MW	52170 TQ	USBLS	5/15
	Cincinnati MSA, OH-KY-IN	Y	36360 FQ	45840 MW	58150 TQ	USBLS	5/15
	Cleveland-Elyria MSA, OH	Y	22380 FQ	38420 MW	48320 TQ	USBLS	5/15
	Columbus MSA, OH	Y	35590 FQ	44070 MW	53250 TQ	USBLS	5/15
	Oklahoma	Y	27430 FQ	35800 MW	46970 TQ	USBLS	5/15
	Oklahoma City MSA, OK	Y	29440 FQ	37050 MW	47530 TQ	USBLS	5/15
	Tulsa MSA, OK	Y	29530 FQ	40290 MW	50890 TQ	USBLS	5/15
	Oregon	H	17.85 FQ	22.91 MW	27.78 TQ	ORBLS	2016
	Portland-Vancouver-Hillsboro MSA, OR-WA	Y	35770 FQ	43550 MW	55990 TQ	USBLS	5/15
	Pennsylvania	Y	36800 FQ	45120 MW	54180 TQ	USBLS	5/15
	Allentown-Bethlehem-Easton MSA, PA-NJ	Y	39480 FQ	44530 MW	49570 TQ	USBLS	5/15
	Harrisburg-Carlisle MSA, PA	Y	40050 FQ	44490 MW	48920 TQ	USBLS	5/15
	Montgomery County-Bucks County-Chester County PMSA, PA	Y	42000 FQ	49550 MW	58330 TQ	USBLS	5/15
	Philadelphia PMSA, PA	Y	40990 FQ	47040 MW	55110 TQ	USBLS	5/15
	Pittsburgh MSA, PA	Y	35480 FQ	42080 MW	49700 TQ	USBLS	5/15
	Rhode Island	Y	39730 FQ	48020 MW	58300 TQ	USBLS	5/15
	Providence-Warwick MSA, RI-MA	Y	40790 FQ	48560 MW	60610 TQ	USBLS	5/15
	South Carolina	Y	26830 FQ	34940 MW	42080 TQ	USBLS	5/15
	Charleston-North Charleston MSA, SC	Y	27880 FQ	37900 MW	53720 TQ	USBLS	5/15
	Columbia MSA, SC	Y	25340 FQ	30830 MW	36860 TQ	USBLS	5/15
	Greenville-Anderson-Mauldin MSA, SC	Y	32870 FQ	36800 MW	42960 TQ	USBLS	5/15
	South Dakota	Y	36150 FQ	53430 MW	60600 TQ	USBLS	5/15
	Sioux Falls MSA, SD	Y	35710 FQ	52860 MW	60060 TQ	USBLS	5/15
	Tennessee	Y	32510 FQ	40340 MW	49270 TQ	USBLS	5/15
	Knoxville MSA, TN	Y	34090 FQ	38700 MW	45880 TQ	USBLS	5/15
	Memphis MSA, TN-MS-AR	Y	31680 FQ	39100 MW	47700 TQ	USBLS	5/15
	Nashville-Davidson–Murfreesboro–Franklin MSA, TN	Y	36170 FQ	45420 MW	57190 TQ	USBLS	5/15
	Texas	Y	34590 FQ	42200 MW	50880 TQ	USBLS	5/15
	Austin-Round Rock MSA, TX	Y	35450 FQ	43570 MW	52560 TQ	USBLS	5/15
	Dallas-Plano-Irving PMSA, TX	Y	34770 FQ	42720 MW	50770 TQ	USBLS	5/15
	Fort Worth-Arlington PMSA, TX	Y	33950 FQ	41850 MW	51130 TQ	USBLS	5/15

AE Average entry wage	**AWR** Average wage range	**H** Hourly	**LR** Low end range	**MTC** Median total compensation	**TCC** Total cash compensation
AEX Average experienced wage	**B** Biweekly	**HI** Highest wage paid	**M** Monthly	**MW** Median wage paid	**W** Weekly
ATC Average total compensation	**D** Daily	**HR** High end range	**MCC** Median cash compensation	**MWR** Median wage range	**Y** Yearly
AW Average wage paid	**FQ** First quartile wage	**LO** Lowest wage paid	**ME** Median entry wage	**S** See annotated source	

Occupation/Type/Industry	Location	Per	Low	Mid	High	Source	Date
Security and Fire Alarm Systems Installer	Houston-The Woodlands-Sugar Land MSA, TX	Y	37540 FQ	45990 MW	55450 TQ	USBLS	5/15
	San Antonio-New Braunfels MSA, TX	Y	35500 FQ	41840 MW	49640 TQ	USBLS	5/15
	Utah	Y	36230 FQ	43620 MW	49230 TQ	USBLS	5/15
	Ogden-Clearfield MSA, UT	Y	32850 FQ	42280 MW	49590 TQ	USBLS	5/15
	Provo-Orem MSA, UT	Y	39870 FQ	43960 MW	47840 TQ	USBLS	5/15
	Salt Lake City MSA, UT	Y	37800 FQ	44080 MW	49510 TQ	USBLS	5/15
	Vermont	Y	35680 FQ	46580 MW	59140 TQ	USBLS	5/15
	Burlington-South Burlington MSA, VT	Y	33930 FQ	44740 MW	58870 TQ	USBLS	5/15
	Virginia	Y	35460 FQ	42820 MW	50270 TQ	USBLS	5/15
	Richmond MSA, VA	Y	37080 FQ	43240 MW	48730 TQ	USBLS	5/15
	Virginia Beach-Norfolk-Newport News MSA, VA-NC	Y	34410 FQ	41490 MW	52920 TQ	USBLS	5/15
	Washington	H	18.54 FQ	23.42 MW	28.76 TQ	WABLS	3/16
	Seattle-Bellevue-Everett PMSA, WA	H	16.59 FQ	23.33 MW	28.05 TQ	WABLS	3/16
	Tacoma-Lakewood PMSA, WA	H	21.92 FQ	26.07 MW	32.34 TQ	WABLS	3/16
	West Virginia	Y	29260 FQ	40340 MW	49890 TQ	USBLS	5/15
	Huntington-Ashland MSA, WV-KY-OH	Y	30120 FQ	41110 MW	46200 TQ	USBLS	5/15
	Wisconsin	Y	33200 FQ	38160 MW	47270 TQ	USBLS	5/15
	Madison MSA, WI	Y	36650 FQ	44000 MW	53380 TQ	USBLS	5/15
	Milwaukee-Waukesha-West Allis MSA, WI	Y	28240 FQ	31320 MW	38480 TQ	USBLS	5/15
	Wyoming	Y	32320 FQ	43950 MW	55280 TQ	USBLS	5/15
	Puerto Rico	Y	17440 FQ	19280 MW	23620 TQ	USBLS	5/15
	San Juan-Carolina-Caguas MSA, PR	Y	17340 FQ	19060 MW	23680 TQ	USBLS	5/15
	Guam	Y	22080 FQ	27810 MW	34710 TQ	USBLS	5/15
Security Architect	United States	Y		116500 MW		GLKN	2016
Security Guard	Alabama	Y	17452 AE	24309 AW	27738 AEX	ALBLS	6/16
	Birmingham-Hoover MSA, AL	Y	17421 AE	22888 AW	25617 AEX	ALBLS	6/16
	Alaska	Y	29850 FQ	36470 MW	44420 TQ	USBLS	5/15
	Anchorage MSA, AK	Y	28160 FQ	33980 MW	39330 TQ	USBLS	5/15
	Arizona	Y	20810 FQ	24030 MW	30780 TQ	USBLS	5/15
	Phoenix-Mesa-Scottsdale MSA, AZ	Y	21240 FQ	24320 MW	31290 TQ	USBLS	5/15
	Tucson MSA, AZ	Y	18840 FQ	21870 MW	26400 TQ	USBLS	5/15
	Arkansas	Y	18150 FQ	21830 MW	28910 TQ	USBLS	5/15
	Little Rock-North Little Rock-Conway MSA, AR	Y	18800 FQ	23340 MW	30210 TQ	USBLS	5/15
	California	H	10.22 FQ	12.05 MW	15.08 TQ	CABLS	1/16-3/16
	Anaheim-Santa Ana-Irvine PMSA, CA	H	9.87 FQ	11.34 MW	13.81 TQ	CABLS	1/16-3/16
	Los Angeles-Long Beach-Glendale PMSA, CA	H	9.80 FQ	11.64 MW	14.43 TQ	CABLS	1/16-3/16
	Oakland-Hayward-Berkeley PMSA, CA	H	11.80 FQ	14.03 MW	17.26 TQ	CABLS	1/16-3/16
	Riverside-San Bernardino-Ontario MSA, CA	H	9.96 FQ	11.22 MW	13.28 TQ	CABLS	1/16-3/16
	Sacramento–Roseville–Arden-Arcade MSA, CA	H	10.44 FQ	12.26 MW	14.61 TQ	CABLS	1/16-3/16
	San Diego-Carlsbad MSA, CA	H	10.55 FQ	12.03 MW	16.23 TQ	CABLS	1/16-3/16
	San Francisco-Redwood City-South San Francisco PMSA, CA	H	12.80 FQ	15.86 MW	19.46 TQ	CABLS	1/16-3/16
	Colorado	Y	22400 FQ	26720 MW	31110 TQ	USBLS	5/15
	Denver-Aurora-Lakewood MSA, CO	Y	22690 FQ	26630 MW	30420 TQ	USBLS	5/15
	Connecticut	Y		27523 MW		CTBLS	1/16-3/16
	Bridgeport-Stamford-Norwalk MSA, CT	Y	22710 FQ	27170 MW	33790 TQ	USBLS	5/15
	Hartford-West Hartford-East Hartford MSA, CT	Y	22180 FQ	25630 MW	35750 TQ	USBLS	5/15
	Delaware	Y	20720 FQ	23440 MW	27990 TQ	USBLS	5/15
	Wilmington PMSA, DE-MD-NJ	Y	20700 FQ	23360 MW	27870 TQ	USBLS	5/15

AE Average entry wage	**AWR** Average wage range	**H** Hourly	**LR** Low end range	**MTC** Median total compensation	**TCC** Total cash compensation
AEX Average experienced wage	**B** Biweekly	**HI** Highest wage paid	**M** Monthly	**MW** Median wage paid	**TQ** Third quartile wage
ATC Average total compensation	**D** Daily	**HR** High end range	**MCC** Median cash compensation	**MWR** Median wage range	**W** Weekly
AW Average wage paid	**FQ** First quartile wage	**LO** Lowest wage paid	**ME** Median entry wage	**S** See annotated source	**Y** Yearly

Occupation/Type/Industry	Location	Per	Low	Mid	High	Source	Date
Security Guard	District of Columbia	Y	27820 FQ	36760 MW	50110 TQ	USBLS	5/15
	Washington-Arlington-Alexandria PMSA, DC-VA-MD-WV	Y	27310 FQ	35640 MW	48060 TQ	USBLS	5/15
	Florida	H	9.05 AE	10.84 MW	12.76 AEX	FLBLS	7/16-9/16
	Fort Lauderdale-Pompano Beach-Deerfield Beach PMSA, FL	H	9.02 AE	10.70 MW	12.63 AEX	FLBLS	7/16-9/16
	Miami-Miami Beach-Kendall PMSA, FL	H	9.06 AE	10.74 MW	12.35 AEX	FLBLS	7/16-9/16
	Orlando-Kissimmee-Sanford MSA, FL	H	9.05 AE	10.72 MW	12.45 AEX	FLBLS	7/16-9/16
	Tampa-St. Petersburg-Clearwater MSA, FL	H	9.07 AE	10.82 MW	12.41 AEX	FLBLS	7/16-9/16
	The Villages MSA, FL	H	10.53 AE	11.16 MW	11.67 AEX	FLBLS	7/16-9/16
	Georgia	Y	18680 FQ	23260 MW	31170 TQ	USBLS	5/15
	Atlanta-Sandy Springs-Roswell MSA, GA	Y	18480 FQ	22900 MW	30690 TQ	USBLS	5/15
	Augusta-Richmond County MSA, GA-SC	Y	22670 FQ	30500 MW	42860 TQ	USBLS	5/15
	Hawaii	Y	21660 FQ	26910 MW	35470 TQ	USBLS	5/15
	Urban Honolulu MSA, HI	Y	21240 FQ	25630 MW	34290 TQ	USBLS	5/15
	Idaho	Y	20740 FQ	25400 MW	38210 TQ	USBLS	5/15
	Boise City MSA, ID	Y	20540 FQ	23890 MW	30020 TQ	USBLS	5/15
	Illinois	Y	22500 FQ	28190 MW	36020 TQ	USBLS	5/15
	Chicago-Naperville-Arlington Heights PMSA, IL	Y	23160 FQ	28700 MW	36170 TQ	USBLS	5/15
	Lake County-Kenosha County PMSA, IL-WI	Y	22620 FQ	30500 MW	37610 TQ	USBLS	5/15
	Indiana	Y	18610 FQ	22830 MW	32130 TQ	USBLS	5/15
	Gary PMSA, IN	Y	19530 FQ	23740 MW	31980 TQ	USBLS	5/15
	Indianapolis-Carmel-Anderson MSA, IN	Y	18180 FQ	21930 MW	29630 TQ	USBLS	5/15
	Iowa	Y	20560 FQ	24040 MW	34960 TQ	USBLS	5/15
	Des Moines-West Des Moines MSA, IA	Y	20150 FQ	22840 MW	30330 TQ	USBLS	5/15
	Kansas	Y	20180 FQ	24100 MW	31810 TQ	USBLS	5/15
	Wichita MSA, KS	Y	19880 FQ	24570 MW	33700 TQ	USBLS	5/15
	Kentucky	Y	18060 FQ	21370 MW	26420 TQ	USBLS	5/15
	Louisville-Jefferson County MSA, KY-IN	Y	19010 FQ	22880 MW	28420 TQ	USBLS	5/15
	Louisiana	Y	19490 FQ	23180 MW	30310 TQ	USBLS	5/15
	Baton Rouge MSA, LA	Y	21380 FQ	24030 MW	29310 TQ	USBLS	5/15
	New Orleans-Metairie MSA, LA	Y	19420 FQ	23860 MW	40350 TQ	USBLS	5/15
	Maine	Y	21920 FQ	25040 MW	30110 TQ	USBLS	5/15
	Portland-South Portland MSA, ME	Y	22480 FQ	25730 MW	29830 TQ	USBLS	5/15
	Maryland	Y	20434 AE	31859 MW	37572 AEX	MDBLS	4/16
	Baltimore-Columbia-Towson MSA, MD	Y	20970 FQ	24090 MW	35220 TQ	USBLS	5/15
	Salisbury MSA, MD-DE	Y	19800 FQ	24340 MW	30740 TQ	USBLS	5/15
	Massachusetts	Y	23390 FQ	28060 MW	34980 TQ	USBLS	5/15
	Boston-Cambridge-Newton NECTA, MA	Y	24200 FQ	28540 MW	35300 TQ	USBLS	5/15
	Worcester MSA, MA-CT	Y	21740 FQ	25790 MW	35520 TQ	USBLS	5/15
	Michigan	Y	19590 FQ	23680 MW	30840 TQ	USBLS	5/15
	Detroit-Dearborn-Livonia PMSA, MI	Y	21260 FQ	24270 MW	32240 TQ	USBLS	5/15
	Grand Rapids-Wyoming MSA, MI	Y	19270 FQ	22870 MW	28600 TQ	USBLS	5/15
	Minnesota	Y	25913 FQ	30225 MW	39284 TQ	MNBLS	1/16-3/16
	Minneapolis-St. Paul-Bloomington MSA, MN-WI	Y	26135 FQ	30336 MW	39536 TQ	MNBLS	1/16-3/16
	Mississippi	Y	18070 FQ	21320 MW	26980 TQ	USBLS	5/15
	Jackson MSA, MS	Y	17700 FQ	20030 MW	27010 TQ	USBLS	5/15
	Missouri	Y	20420 FQ	24130 MW	30440 TQ	USBLS	5/15
	Kansas City MSA, MO-KS	Y	21590 FQ	25200 MW	31160 TQ	USBLS	5/15
	St. Louis MSA, MO-IL	Y	20380 FQ	23730 MW	30170 TQ	USBLS	5/15
	Montana	Y	20610 FQ	23600 MW	28190 TQ	USBLS	5/15
	Billings MSA, MT	Y	21250 FQ	23840 MW	27590 TQ	USBLS	5/15
	Nebraska	Y	21615 FQ	26680 MW	37770 TQ	NEBLS	7/16-9/16

AE	Average entry wage	AWR	Average wage range	H	Hourly
AEX	Average experienced wage	B	Biweekly	HI	Highest wage paid
ATC	Average total compensation	D	Daily	HR	High end range
AW	Average wage paid	FQ	First quartile wage	LO	Lowest wage paid

LR	Low end range	MTC	Median total compensation	TCC	Total cash compensation
M	Monthly	MW	Median wage paid	TQ	Third quartile wage
MCC	Median cash compensation	MWR	Median wage range	W	Weekly
ME	Median entry wage	S	See annotated source	Y	Yearly

Security Guard

Occupation/Type/Industry	Location	Per	Low	Mid	High	Source	Date
Security Guard	Omaha-Council Bluffs MSA, NE-IA	Y	22150 FQ	26660 MW	36825 TQ	NEBLS	7/16-9/16
	Nevada	Y	21040 FQ	25180 MW	32040 TQ	USBLS	5/15
	Las Vegas-Henderson-Paradise MSA, NV	Y	20990 FQ	25700 MW	32600 TQ	USBLS	5/15
	New Hampshire	H	10.72 AE	13.97 MW	18.40 AEX	NHBLS	6/16
	Manchester NECTA, NH	H	10.57 AE	12.11 MW	15.33 AEX	NHBLS	6/16
	Nashua NECTA, NH-MA	Y	22780 FQ	26740 MW	33770 TQ	USBLS	5/15
	New Jersey	Y	21370 FQ	26280 MW	34780 TQ	USBLS	5/15
	Camden PMSA, NJ	Y	21560 FQ	26760 MW	36580 TQ	USBLS	5/15
	Newark PMSA, NJ-PA	Y	21550 FQ	25420 MW	33530 TQ	USBLS	5/15
	Trenton MSA, NJ	Y	27390 FQ	37900 MW	48300 TQ	USBLS	5/15
	New Mexico	Y	21080 FQ	25060 MW	34340 TQ	USBLS	5/15
	Albuquerque MSA, NM	Y	20380 FQ	24150 MW	30550 TQ	USBLS	5/15
	New York	Y	20310 AE	30420 MW	39090 AEX	NYBLS	1/16-3/16
	Buffalo-Cheektowaga-Niagara Falls MSA, NY	Y	19190 FQ	22020 MW	27180 TQ	USBLS	5/15
	Nassau County-Suffolk County PMSA, NY	Y	22320 FQ	32390 MW	38700 TQ	USBLS	5/15
	New York-Jersey City-White Plains PMSA, NY-NJ	Y	20150 FQ	29200 MW	40660 TQ	USBLS	5/15
	Rochester MSA, NY	Y	22860 FQ	27870 MW	36300 TQ	USBLS	5/15
	North Carolina	Y	19480 FQ	23150 MW	29810 TQ	USBLS	5/15
	Charlotte-Concord-Gastonia MSA, NC-SC	Y	19800 FQ	23000 MW	28280 TQ	USBLS	5/15
	Raleigh MSA, NC	Y	19950 FQ	23070 MW	28180 TQ	USBLS	5/15
	North Dakota	Y	22500 FQ	28300 MW	35420 TQ	USBLS	5/15
	Fargo MSA, ND-MN	Y	19790 FQ	23250 MW	28660 TQ	USBLS	5/15
	Ohio	Y	19690 FQ	23320 MW	32110 TQ	USBLS	5/15
	Cincinnati MSA, OH-KY-IN	Y	20450 FQ	23180 MW	29440 TQ	USBLS	5/15
	Cleveland-Elyria MSA, OH	Y	19410 FQ	23540 MW	35400 TQ	USBLS	5/15
	Columbus MSA, OH	Y	20110 FQ	22850 MW	28160 TQ	USBLS	5/15
	Oklahoma	Y	20820 FQ	24340 MW	33290 TQ	USBLS	5/15
	Oklahoma City MSA, OK	Y	19590 FQ	24240 MW	38770 TQ	USBLS	5/15
	Tulsa MSA, OK	Y	21520 FQ	24470 MW	31440 TQ	USBLS	5/15
	Oregon	H	10.70 FQ	12.84 MW	17.84 TQ	ORBLS	2016
	Portland-Vancouver-Hillsboro MSA, OR-WA	Y	22120 FQ	27890 MW	39420 TQ	USBLS	5/15
	Pennsylvania	Y	19710 FQ	23450 MW	29540 TQ	USBLS	5/15
	Allentown-Bethlehem-Easton MSA, PA-NJ	Y	20020 FQ	23020 MW	28090 TQ	USBLS	5/15
	Harrisburg-Carlisle MSA, PA	Y	22440 FQ	27770 MW	32520 TQ	USBLS	5/15
	Montgomery County-Bucks County-Chester County PMSA, PA	Y	21040 FQ	24860 MW	31320 TQ	USBLS	5/15
	Philadelphia PMSA, PA	Y	19990 FQ	23220 MW	28940 TQ	USBLS	5/15
	Pittsburgh MSA, PA	Y	18500 FQ	22070 MW	27310 TQ	USBLS	5/15
	Rhode Island	Y	23070 FQ	26910 MW	30850 TQ	USBLS	5/15
	Providence-Warwick MSA, RI-MA	Y	22790 FQ	26670 MW	30950 TQ	USBLS	5/15
	South Carolina	Y	19570 FQ	23520 MW	31710 TQ	USBLS	5/15
	Charleston-North Charleston MSA, SC	Y	21060 FQ	24100 MW	35730 TQ	USBLS	5/15
	Columbia MSA, SC	Y	18680 FQ	22910 MW	31460 TQ	USBLS	5/15
	Greenville-Anderson-Mauldin MSA, SC	Y	20010 FQ	23740 MW	30100 TQ	USBLS	5/15
	South Dakota	Y	21440 FQ	23560 MW	27400 TQ	USBLS	5/15
	Sioux Falls MSA, SD	Y	22000 FQ	25080 MW	29280 TQ	USBLS	5/15
	Tennessee	Y	18840 FQ	22560 MW	29740 TQ	USBLS	5/15
	Memphis MSA, TN-MS-AR	Y	18110 FQ	20850 MW	24060 TQ	USBLS	5/15
	Nashville-Davidson–Murfreesboro–Franklin MSA, TN	Y	19800 FQ	23720 MW	32620 TQ	USBLS	5/15
	Texas	Y	20020 FQ	23800 MW	30080 TQ	USBLS	5/15
	Austin-Round Rock MSA, TX	Y	22680 FQ	27460 MW	34360 TQ	USBLS	5/15
	Dallas-Plano-Irving PMSA, TX	Y	20470 FQ	24410 MW	30170 TQ	USBLS	5/15
	Fort Worth-Arlington PMSA, TX	Y	18240 FQ	21970 MW	30380 TQ	USBLS	5/15
	Houston-The Woodlands-Sugar Land MSA, TX	Y	20620 FQ	23650 MW	29100 TQ	USBLS	5/15
	San Antonio-New Braunfels MSA, TX	Y	18640 FQ	22440 MW	28620 TQ	USBLS	5/15

AE Average entry wage
AEX Average experienced wage
ATC Average total compensation
AW Average wage paid
AWR Average wage range
B Biweekly
D Daily
FQ First quartile wage
H Hourly
HI Highest wage paid
HR High end range
LO Lowest wage paid
LR Low end range
M Monthly
MCC Median cash compensation
ME Median entry wage
MTC Median total compensation
MW Median wage paid
MWR Median wage range
S See annotated source
TCC Total cash compensation
TQ Third quartile wage
W Weekly
Y Yearly

Occupation/Type/Industry	Location	Per	Low	Mid	High	Source	Date
Security Guard	Utah	Y	21800 FQ	26500 MW	34940 TQ	USBLS	5/15
	Ogden-Clearfield MSA, UT	Y	25280 FQ	30840 MW	41830 TQ	USBLS	5/15
	Provo-Orem MSA, UT	Y	22030 FQ	26150 MW	32290 TQ	USBLS	5/15
	Salt Lake City MSA, UT	Y	21670 FQ	25610 MW	34980 TQ	USBLS	5/15
	Vermont	Y	21820 FQ	25360 MW	32780 TQ	USBLS	5/15
	Burlington-South Burlington MSA, VT	Y	21130 FQ	24350 MW	29990 TQ	USBLS	5/15
	Virginia	Y	22370 FQ	29640 MW	41140 TQ	USBLS	5/15
	Richmond MSA, VA	Y	18760 FQ	22930 MW	30690 TQ	USBLS	5/15
	Virginia Beach-Norfolk-Newport News MSA, VA-NC	Y	22290 FQ	26910 MW	32290 TQ	USBLS	5/15
	Washington	H	11.96 FQ	14.80 MW	19.91 TQ	WABLS	3/16
	Seattle-Bellevue-Everett PMSA, WA	H	12.41 FQ	14.90 MW	20.51 TQ	WABLS	3/16
	Tacoma-Lakewood PMSA, WA	H	11.71 FQ	14.71 MW	18.95 TQ	WABLS	3/16
	Walla Walla MSA, WA	H	14.04 FQ	17.64 MW	21.74 TQ	WABLS	3/16
	West Virginia	Y	18460 FQ	21430 MW	29030 TQ	USBLS	5/15
	Huntington-Ashland MSA, WV-KY-OH	Y	17850 FQ	19290 MW	24110 TQ	USBLS	5/15
	Wisconsin	Y	20690 FQ	23850 MW	29900 TQ	USBLS	5/15
	Madison MSA, WI	Y	20140 FQ	22990 MW	28640 TQ	USBLS	5/15
	Milwaukee-Waukesha-West Allis MSA, WI	Y	21150 FQ	24070 MW	30270 TQ	USBLS	5/15
	Oshkosh-Neenah MSA, WI	Y	20050 FQ	22450 MW	25570 TQ	USBLS	5/15
	Wyoming	Y	24110 FQ	28680 MW	35060 TQ	USBLS	5/15
	Cheyenne MSA, WY	Y	26130 FQ	32180 MW	39780 TQ	USBLS	5/15
	Puerto Rico	Y	16610 FQ	17750 MW	18890 TQ	USBLS	5/15
	San Juan-Carolina-Caguas MSA, PR	Y	16590 FQ	17710 MW	18830 TQ	USBLS	5/15
	Virgin Islands	Y	17200 FQ	19090 MW	27240 TQ	USBLS	5/15
	Guam	Y	17920 FQ	18680 MW	19440 TQ	USBLS	5/15
Security Specialist Information Technology	United States	Y		103000 MW		INFOW02	10/15-2/16
Seed Analyst State Government	North Carolina	Y	29826 LO		45099 HI	NCGOV	7/1/16
Segmental Paver	Florida	H	10.68 AE	12.49 MW	15.38 AEX	FLBLS	7/16-9/16
	Nevada	Y	24220 FQ	33620 MW	36910 TQ	USBLS	5/15
	Texas	Y	24300 FQ	27570 MW	30640 TQ	USBLS	5/15
	Wisconsin	Y	31490 FQ	35640 MW	39840 TQ	USBLS	5/15
Self-Enrichment Education Teacher	Alabama	Y	17991 AE	37511 AW	47266 AEX	ALBLS	6/16
	Birmingham-Hoover MSA, AL	Y	19999 AE	37073 AW	45615 AEX	ALBLS	6/16
	Alaska	Y	35230 FQ	44570 MW	55800 TQ	USBLS	5/15
	Anchorage MSA, AK	Y	37110 FQ	45170 MW	53240 TQ	USBLS	5/15
	Arizona	Y	24220 FQ	34640 MW	46240 TQ	USBLS	5/15
	Phoenix-Mesa-Scottsdale MSA, AZ	Y	25740 FQ	37790 MW	48330 TQ	USBLS	5/15
	Tucson MSA, AZ	Y	20370 FQ	28170 MW	35600 TQ	USBLS	5/15
	Arkansas	Y	18890 FQ	33680 MW	45110 TQ	USBLS	5/15
	Little Rock-North Little Rock-Conway MSA, AR	Y	19280 FQ	33920 MW	45040 TQ	USBLS	5/15
	California	H	13.30 FQ	18.28 MW	27.73 TQ	CABLS	1/16-3/16
	Anaheim-Santa Ana-Irvine PMSA, CA	H	13.28 FQ	16.75 MW	22.41 TQ	CABLS	1/16-3/16
	Los Angeles-Long Beach-Glendale PMSA, CA	H	13.46 FQ	17.75 MW	25.22 TQ	CABLS	1/16-3/16
	Oakland-Hayward-Berkeley PMSA, CA	H	13.27 FQ	22.54 MW	35.78 TQ	CABLS	1/16-3/16
	Riverside-San Bernardino-Ontario MSA, CA	H	9.58 FQ	13.12 MW	19.92 TQ	CABLS	1/16-3/16
	Sacramento–Roseville–Arden-Arcade MSA, CA	H	13.29 FQ	17.21 MW	24.20 TQ	CABLS	1/16-3/16
	San Diego-Carlsbad MSA, CA	H	15.62 FQ	20.01 MW	27.01 TQ	CABLS	1/16-3/16
	San Francisco-Redwood City-South San Francisco PMSA, CA	H	15.80 FQ	21.89 MW	34.82 TQ	CABLS	1/16-3/16
	Colorado	Y	26370 FQ	36370 MW	50690 TQ	USBLS	5/15

AE	Average entry wage	AWR	Average wage range	H	Hourly
AEX	Average experienced wage	B	Biweekly	HI	Highest wage paid
ATC	Average total compensation	D	Daily	HR	High end range
AW	Average wage paid	FQ	First quartile wage	LO	Lowest wage paid

LR	Low end range
M	Monthly
MCC	Median cash compensation
ME	Median entry wage

MTC	Median total compensation	TCC	Total cash compensation
MW	Median wage paid	TQ	Third quartile wage
MWR	Median wage range	W	Weekly
S	See annotated source	Y	Yearly

Occupation/Type/Industry	Location	Per	Low	Mid	High	Source	Date
Self-Enrichment Education Teacher							
	Denver-Aurora-Lakewood MSA, CO	Y	31660 FQ	38360 MW	53830 TQ	USBLS	5/15
	Connecticut	Y	.	41665 MW		CTBLS	1/16-3/16
	Bridgeport-Stamford-Norwalk MSA, CT	Y	26890 FQ	44060 MW	55530 TQ	USBLS	5/15
	Hartford-West Hartford-East Hartford MSA, CT	Y	27530 FQ	36900 MW	62830 TQ	USBLS	5/15
	Delaware	Y	22980 FQ	38860 MW	67990 TQ	USBLS	5/15
	Wilmington PMSA, DE-MD-NJ	Y	22710 FQ	36470 MW	65400 TQ	USBLS	5/15
	District of Columbia	Y	35020 FQ	55850 MW	74470 TQ	USBLS	5/15
	Washington-Arlington-Alexandria PMSA, DC-VA-MD-WV	Y	31170 FQ	41280 MW	49890 TQ	USBLS	5/15
	Florida	H	10.11 AE	15.52 MW	22.40 AEX	FLBLS	7/16-9/16
	Fort Lauderdale-Pompano Beach-Deerfield Beach PMSA, FL	H	11.15 AE	17.05 MW	21.57 AEX	FLBLS	7/16-9/16
	Miami-Miami Beach-Kendall PMSA, FL	H	10.17 AE	19.01 MW	25.68 AEX	FLBLS	7/16-9/16
	Orlando-Kissimmee-Sanford MSA, FL	H	10.50 AE	14.87 MW	20.02 AEX	FLBLS	7/16-9/16
	Tampa-St. Petersburg-Clearwater MSA, FL	H	9.73 AE	14.76 MW	21.34 AEX	FLBLS	7/16-9/16
	Georgia	Y	23110 FQ	34070 MW	50370 TQ	USBLS	5/15
	Atlanta-Sandy Springs-Roswell MSA, GA	Y	24740 FQ	36160 MW	51470 TQ	USBLS	5/15
	Augusta-Richmond County MSA, GA-SC	Y	18250 FQ	23910 MW	46340 TQ	USBLS	5/15
	Hawaii	Y	31590 FQ	39310 MW	60960 TQ	USBLS	5/15
	Urban Honolulu MSA, HI	Y	32170 FQ	40140 MW	66390 TQ	USBLS	5/15
	Idaho	Y	19040 FQ	26760 MW	43160 TQ	USBLS	5/15
	Boise City MSA, ID	Y	23760 FQ	39790 MW	47660 TQ	USBLS	5/15
	Illinois	Y	22300 FQ	33000 MW	50530 TQ	USBLS	5/15
	Chicago-Naperville-Arlington Heights PMSA, IL	Y	24250 FQ	34600 MW	51410 TQ	USBLS	5/15
	Lake County-Kenosha County PMSA, IL-WI	Y	26970 FQ	44550 MW	66200 TQ	USBLS	5/15
	Indiana	Y	25770 FQ	36480 MW	47480 TQ	USBLS	5/15
	Gary PMSA, IN	Y	28790 FQ	38710 MW	52400 TQ	USBLS	5/15
	Indianapolis-Carmel-Anderson MSA, IN	Y	27920 FQ	37670 MW	48390 TQ	USBLS	5/15
	Iowa	Y	24600 FQ	39270 MW	49100 TQ	USBLS	5/15
	Des Moines-West Des Moines MSA, IA	Y	22730 FQ	40110 MW	47020 TQ	USBLS	5/15
	Kansas	Y	22410 FQ	34080 MW	46000 TQ	USBLS	5/15
	Wichita MSA, KS	Y	32570 FQ	38340 MW	51520 TQ	USBLS	5/15
	Kentucky	Y	21880 FQ	31050 MW	37610 TQ	USBLS	5/15
	Louisville-Jefferson County MSA, KY-IN	Y	27840 FQ	33510 MW	39300 TQ	USBLS	5/15
	Louisiana	Y	22510 FQ	30090 MW	41480 TQ	USBLS	5/15
	Baton Rouge MSA, LA	Y	17640 FQ	22810 MW	50720 TQ	USBLS	5/15
	New Orleans-Metairie MSA, LA	Y	25970 FQ	32750 MW	43640 TQ	USBLS	5/15
	Maine	Y	29400 FQ	37640 MW	53380 TQ	USBLS	5/15
	Portland-South Portland MSA, ME	Y	29990 FQ	38770 MW	51710 TQ	USBLS	5/15
	Maryland	Y	22505 AE	45391 MW	56834 AEX	MDBLS	4/16
	Baltimore-Columbia-Towson MSA, MD	Y	24750 FQ	34020 MW	47300 TQ	USBLS	5/15
	Salisbury MSA, MD-DE	Y	32530 FQ	49490 MW	60130 TQ	USBLS	5/15
	Massachusetts	Y	26220 FQ	39710 MW	60300 TQ	USBLS	5/15
	Boston-Cambridge-Newton NECTA, MA	Y	24180 FQ	42780 MW	63850 TQ	USBLS	5/15
	Worcester MSA, MA-CT	Y	42530 FQ	57050 MW	68590 TQ	USBLS	5/15
	Michigan	Y	20920 FQ	34420 MW	45800 TQ	USBLS	5/15
	Detroit-Dearborn-Livonia PMSA, MI	Y	22620 FQ	33100 MW	38460 TQ	USBLS	5/15
	Grand Rapids-Wyoming MSA, MI	Y	20770 FQ	32020 MW	46220 TQ	USBLS	5/15
	Minnesota	Y	22147 FQ	31754 MW	43225 TQ	MNBLS	1/16-3/16

AE	Average entry wage	AWR	Average wage range	H	Hourly	LR	Low end range	MTC	Median total compensation	TCC	Total cash compensation
AEX	Average experienced wage	B	Biweekly	HI	Highest wage paid	M	Monthly	MW	Median wage paid	TQ	Third quartile wage
ATC	Average total compensation	D	Daily	HR	High end range	MCC	Median cash compensation	MWR	Median wage range	W	Weekly
AW	Average wage paid	FQ	First quartile wage	LO	Lowest wage paid	ME	Median entry wage	S	See annotated source	Y	Yearly

Occupation/Type/Industry	Location	Per	Low	Mid	High	Source	Date
Self-Enrichment Education Teacher	Minneapolis-St. Paul-Bloomington MSA, MN-WI	Y	22086 FQ	32096 MW	42499 TQ	MNBLS	1/16-3/16
	Mississippi	Y	26890 FQ	37670 MW	49230 TQ	USBLS	5/15
	Jackson MSA, MS	Y	28740 FQ	39730 MW	49040 TQ	USBLS	5/15
	Missouri	Y	19300 FQ	29240 MW	46740 TQ	USBLS	5/15
	Kansas City MSA, MO-KS	Y	18750 FQ	34620 MW	53700 TQ	USBLS	5/15
	St. Louis MSA, MO-IL	Y	21760 FQ	30100 MW	46230 TQ	USBLS	5/15
	Montana	Y	23430 FQ	30420 MW	38180 TQ	USBLS	5/15
	Billings MSA, MT	Y	31540 FQ	35600 MW	40510 TQ	USBLS	5/15
	Nebraska	Y	20065 FQ	27175 MW	37745 TQ	NEBLS	7/16-9/16
	Omaha-Council Bluffs MSA, NE-IA	Y	19245 FQ	26565 MW	39030 TQ	NEBLS	7/16-9/16
	Nevada	Y	18650 FQ	31000 MW	56150 TQ	USBLS	5/15
	Las Vegas-Henderson-Paradise MSA, NV	Y	25990 FQ	47690 MW	63470 TQ	USBLS	5/15
	New Hampshire	H	11.42 AE	19.32 MW	25.97 AEX	NHBLS	6/16
	Manchester NECTA, NH	H	13.67 AE	19.18 MW	27.56 AEX	NHBLS	6/16
	Nashua NECTA, NH-MA	Y	33740 FQ	46460 MW	60020 TQ	USBLS	5/15
	New Jersey	Y	35810 FQ	50400 MW	66000 TQ	USBLS	5/15
	Camden PMSA, NJ	Y	39280 FQ	52140 MW	65520 TQ	USBLS	5/15
	Newark PMSA, NJ-PA	Y	39740 FQ	49450 MW	65000 TQ	USBLS	5/15
	Trenton MSA, NJ	Y	22510 FQ	42340 MW	56590 TQ	USBLS	5/15
	New Mexico	Y	24630 FQ	33790 MW	51540 TQ	USBLS	5/15
	Albuquerque MSA, NM	Y	24130 FQ	30890 MW	53990 TQ	USBLS	5/15
	New York	Y	25970 AE	46150 MW	68630 AEX	NYBLS	1/16-3/16
	Buffalo-Cheektowaga-Niagara Falls MSA, NY	Y	24790 FQ	36960 MW	46950 TQ	USBLS	5/15
	Nassau County-Suffolk County PMSA, NY	Y	25020 FQ	38350 MW	49240 TQ	USBLS	5/15
	New York-Jersey City-White Plains PMSA, NY-NJ	Y	34660 FQ	54780 MW	79640 TQ	USBLS	5/15
	Rochester MSA, NY	Y	29750 FQ	41320 MW	54490 TQ	USBLS	5/15
	North Carolina	Y	20700 FQ	29800 MW	46650 TQ	USBLS	5/15
	Charlotte-Concord-Gastonia MSA, NC-SC	Y	23850 FQ	30770 MW	45530 TQ	USBLS	5/15
	Raleigh MSA, NC	Y	20820 FQ	38400 MW	61100 TQ	USBLS	5/15
	North Dakota	Y	18530 FQ	23040 MW	33350 TQ	USBLS	5/15
	Fargo MSA, ND-MN	Y	18560 FQ	31440 MW	36260 TQ	USBLS	5/15
	Ohio	Y	21710 FQ	29000 MW	41160 TQ	USBLS	5/15
	Cincinnati MSA, OH-KY-IN	Y	22670 FQ	27760 MW	33350 TQ	USBLS	5/15
	Cleveland-Elyria MSA, OH	Y	20760 FQ	26620 MW	46040 TQ	USBLS	5/15
	Columbus MSA, OH	Y	27600 FQ	37480 MW	50110 TQ	USBLS	5/15
	Oklahoma	Y	21260 FQ	34500 MW	48940 TQ	USBLS	5/15
	Oklahoma City MSA, OK	Y	22850 FQ	36780 MW	70190 TQ	USBLS	5/15
	Tulsa MSA, OK	Y	19080 FQ	31040 MW	42990 TQ	USBLS	5/15
	Oregon	H	13.91 FQ	19.94 MW	26.75 TQ	ORBLS	2016
	Portland-Vancouver-Hillsboro MSA, OR-WA	Y	31180 FQ	43650 MW	54490 TQ	USBLS	5/15
	Pennsylvania	Y	22220 FQ	32440 MW	48810 TQ	USBLS	5/15
	Allentown-Bethlehem-Easton MSA, PA-NJ	Y	20330 FQ	27440 MW	40060 TQ	USBLS	5/15
	Harrisburg-Carlisle MSA, PA	Y	30470 FQ	36200 MW	44460 TQ	USBLS	5/15
	Montgomery County-Bucks County-Chester County PMSA, PA	Y	25620 FQ	33900 MW	52660 TQ	USBLS	5/15
	Philadelphia PMSA, PA	Y	22980 FQ	36820 MW	55900 TQ	USBLS	5/15
	Pittsburgh MSA, PA	Y	20190 FQ	33280 MW	42780 TQ	USBLS	5/15
	Rhode Island	Y	22730 FQ	39140 MW	51910 TQ	USBLS	5/15
	Providence-Warwick MSA, RI-MA	Y	19670 FQ	36130 MW	50470 TQ	USBLS	5/15
	South Carolina	Y	23700 FQ	38510 MW	55410 TQ	USBLS	5/15
	Charleston-North Charleston MSA, SC	Y	33810 FQ	45020 MW	54590 TQ	USBLS	5/15
	Columbia MSA, SC	Y	21560 FQ	36290 MW	54330 TQ	USBLS	5/15
	Greenville-Anderson-Mauldin MSA, SC	Y	27230 FQ	40660 MW	56610 TQ	USBLS	5/15
	South Dakota	Y	26760 FQ	28980 MW	31230 TQ	USBLS	5/15
	Sioux Falls MSA, SD	Y	27390 FQ	29690 MW	32710 TQ	USBLS	5/15
	Tennessee	Y	19500 FQ	25400 MW	42860 TQ	USBLS	5/15
	Knoxville MSA, TN	Y	21470 FQ	27520 MW	40940 TQ	USBLS	5/15
	Memphis MSA, TN-MS-AR	Y	19010 FQ	24640 MW	32060 TQ	USBLS	5/15

AE	Average entry wage	AWR	Average wage range	H	Hourly	LR	Low end range	MTC	Median total compensation	TCC	Total cash compensation
AEX	Average experienced wage	B	Biweekly	HI	Highest wage paid	M	Monthly	MW	Median wage paid	TQ	Third quartile wage
ATC	Average total compensation	D	Daily	HR	High end range	MCC	Median cash compensation	MWR	Median wage range	W	Weekly
AW	Average wage paid	FQ	First quartile wage	LO	Lowest wage paid	ME	Median entry wage	S	See annotated source	Y	Yearly

Occupation/Type/Industry	Location	Per	Low	Mid	High	Source	Date
Self-Enrichment Education Teacher	Nashville-Davidson–Murfreesboro–Franklin MSA, TN	Y	21360 FQ	30510 MW	48350 TQ	USBLS	5/15
	Texas	Y	23340 FQ	35100 MW	51620 TQ	USBLS	5/15
	Austin-Round Rock MSA, TX	Y	27360 FQ	38660 MW	52990 TQ	USBLS	5/15
	Dallas-Plano-Irving PMSA, TX	Y	23280 FQ	36190 MW	54320 TQ	USBLS	5/15
	Fort Worth-Arlington PMSA, TX	Y	24740 FQ	41560 MW	61230 TQ	USBLS	5/15
	Houston-The Woodlands-Sugar Land MSA, TX	Y	24230 FQ	37130 MW	56050 TQ	USBLS	5/15
	San Antonio-New Braunfels MSA, TX	Y	22470 FQ	30070 MW	41430 TQ	USBLS	5/15
	Utah	Y	21560 FQ	31290 MW	51000 TQ	USBLS	5/15
	Ogden-Clearfield MSA, UT	Y	19070 FQ	24420 MW	40130 TQ	USBLS	5/15
	Provo-Orem MSA, UT	Y	18240 FQ	25270 MW	36590 TQ	USBLS	5/15
	Salt Lake City MSA, UT	Y	26070 FQ	33010 MW	57110 TQ	USBLS	5/15
	Vermont	Y	29640 FQ	42780 MW	53200 TQ	USBLS	5/15
	Burlington-South Burlington MSA, VT	Y	28380 FQ	41910 MW	57100 TQ	USBLS	5/15
	Virginia	Y	23830 FQ	37340 MW	48210 TQ	USBLS	5/15
	Richmond MSA, VA	Y	19550 FQ	28910 MW	42290 TQ	USBLS	5/15
	Virginia Beach-Norfolk-Newport News MSA, VA-NC	Y	27120 FQ	38530 MW	55190 TQ	USBLS	5/15
	Washington	H	15.11 FQ	19.81 MW	26.16 TQ	WABLS	3/16
	Seattle-Bellevue-Everett PMSA, WA	H	15.19 FQ	20.11 MW	26.80 TQ	WABLS	3/16
	Tacoma-Lakewood PMSA, WA	H	15.88 FQ	21.07 MW	26.09 TQ	WABLS	3/16
	West Virginia	Y	18580 FQ	22730 MW	33490 TQ	USBLS	5/15
	Huntington-Ashland MSA, WV-KY-OH	Y	22200 FQ	29010 MW	36790 TQ	USBLS	5/15
	Wisconsin	Y	19210 FQ	30570 MW	42830 TQ	USBLS	5/15
	Madison MSA, WI	Y	18990 FQ	33900 MW	42770 TQ	USBLS	5/15
	Milwaukee-Waukesha-West Allis MSA, WI	Y	18780 FQ	31180 MW	47550 TQ	USBLS	5/15
	Wyoming	Y	29300 FQ	42610 MW	54890 TQ	USBLS	5/15
	Puerto Rico	Y	19870 FQ	23240 MW	29990 TQ	USBLS	5/15
Semiconductor Processor	Arizona	Y	33770 FQ	42020 MW	55800 TQ	USBLS	5/15
	Phoenix-Mesa-Scottsdale MSA, AZ	Y	34800 FQ	44680 MW	56600 TQ	USBLS	5/15
	California	H	13.91 FQ	17.30 MW	21.58 TQ	CABLS	1/16-3/16
	Anaheim-Santa Ana-Irvine PMSA, CA	H	13.40 FQ	16.14 MW	20.25 TQ	CABLS	1/16-3/16
	Los Angeles-Long Beach-Glendale PMSA, CA	H	13.32 FQ	16.21 MW	19.15 TQ	CABLS	1/16-3/16
	Oakland-Hayward-Berkeley PMSA, CA	H	14.96 FQ	18.03 MW	21.78 TQ	CABLS	1/16-3/16
	Colorado	Y	26700 FQ	30120 MW	35010 TQ	USBLS	5/15
	Connecticut	Y		30847 MW		CTBLS	1/16-3/16
	Florida	H	13.28 AE	18.80 MW	25.59 AEX	FLBLS	7/16-9/16
	Orlando-Kissimmee-Sanford MSA, FL	H	11.70 AE	14.02 MW	16.60 AEX	FLBLS	7/16-9/16
	Maine	Y	31170 FQ	35720 MW	39930 TQ	USBLS	5/15
	Massachusetts	Y	27570 FQ	33960 MW	42290 TQ	USBLS	5/15
	Boston-Cambridge-Newton NECTA, MA	Y	31660 FQ	38810 MW	52270 TQ	USBLS	5/15
	Missouri	Y	26630 FQ	30410 MW	42010 TQ	USBLS	5/15
	New Hampshire	H	16.72 AE	22.14 MW	24.95 AEX	NHBLS	6/16
	New Jersey	Y	33970 FQ	41000 MW	53050 TQ	USBLS	5/15
	Newark PMSA, NJ-PA	Y	36230 FQ	43910 MW	56590 TQ	USBLS	5/15
	New Mexico	Y	30930 FQ	36450 MW	44380 TQ	USBLS	5/15
	Albuquerque MSA, NM	Y	30930 FQ	36450 MW	44380 TQ	USBLS	5/15
	New York	Y	27650 AE	37650 MW	50350 AEX	NYBLS	1/16-3/16
	New York-Jersey City-White Plains PMSA, NY-NJ	Y	28700 FQ	33680 MW	41730 TQ	USBLS	5/15
	Ohio	Y	33540 FQ	40440 MW	60430 TQ	USBLS	5/15
	Oregon	H	13.84 FQ	16.67 MW	19.97 TQ	ORBLS	2016
	Portland-Vancouver-Hillsboro MSA, OR-WA	Y	29630 FQ	35510 MW	41910 TQ	USBLS	5/15
	Pennsylvania	Y	32120 FQ	38640 MW	45200 TQ	USBLS	5/15
	Pittsburgh MSA, PA	Y	33170 FQ	39090 MW	44860 TQ	USBLS	5/15

Occupation/Type/Industry	Location	Per	Low	Mid	High	Source	Date
Semiconductor Processor	Rhode Island	Y	28930 FQ	34490 MW	40690 TQ	USBLS	5/15
	Providence-Warwick MSA, RI-MA	Y	26510 FQ	31820 MW	38200 TQ	USBLS	5/15
	Texas	Y	28880 FQ	34580 MW	41650 TQ	USBLS	5/15
	Austin-Round Rock MSA, TX	Y	28560 FQ	36430 MW	47380 TQ	USBLS	5/15
	Dallas-Plano-Irving PMSA, TX	Y	29600 FQ	34740 MW	40570 TQ	USBLS	5/15
	Fort Worth-Arlington PMSA, TX	Y	31270 FQ	35330 MW	39340 TQ	USBLS	5/15
	Houston-The Woodlands-Sugar Land MSA, TX	Y	28680 FQ	34020 MW	39620 TQ	USBLS	5/15
	Salt Lake City MSA, UT	Y	23440 FQ	26750 MW	30550 TQ	USBLS	5/15
	Washington	H	16.34 FQ	18.36 MW	21.21 TQ	WABLS	3/16
	Seattle-Bellevue-Everett PMSA, WA	H	14.36 FQ	17.46 MW	23.96 TQ	WABLS	3/16
Senator							
United States Senate	United States	Y			174000 HI	OPM01	2017
Senior Analytical Chemist							
Municipal Government	Detroit, MI	M	4183 LO		4517 HI	DETGOV	2016
Senior Biomedical Statistician							
Municipal Government	Detroit, MI	M	3517 LO		3825 HI	DETGOV	2016
Senior Chief Petty Officer							
U.S. Navy, Active Duty, Pay Grade E-8	United States	M	4136 LO		5899 HI	DOD1	2017
Senior Community Health Specialist							
Municipal Government	Berkeley, CA	Y			66636 HI	CACIT	6/28/16
Senior Master Sergeant							
U.S. Air Force, Active Duty, Pay Grade E-8	United States	M	4136 LO		5899 HI	DOD1	2017
Senior Medical Writer	United States	Y	110000 LO		115000 HI	CNBC04	2015
Senior Pastor							
Full-Time, Southern Baptist Convention	United States	Y		64743 AW		LWAY01	2016
Senior Substance Abuse Counselor							
Municipal Government	Detroit, MI	M	2550 LO		2625 HI	DETGOV	2016
Senior Wildfire Mitigation Specialist							
County Government	Douglas County, CO	Y			82828 HI	DCOGOV	2016
SEO Analyst	United States	Y		94000 MW		LH01	2016
SEO Specialist	United States	Y	62250 LO		87750 HI	RH02	2017
Separating, Filtering, Clarifying, Precipitating, and Still Machine Setter, Operator, and Tender	Alabama	Y	26734 AE	37550 AW	42959 AEX	ALBLS	6/16
	Birmingham-Hoover MSA, AL	Y	28204 AE	36255 AW	40285 AEX	ALBLS	6/16
	Alaska	Y	36340 FQ	48930 MW	56880 TQ	USBLS	5/15
	Anchorage MSA, AK	Y	24190 FQ	35590 MW	47210 TQ	USBLS	5/15
	Arizona	Y	29140 FQ	38570 MW	53020 TQ	USBLS	5/15
	Phoenix-Mesa-Scottsdale MSA, AZ	Y	28100 FQ	36750 MW	47870 TQ	USBLS	5/15
	Tucson MSA, AZ	Y	32140 FQ	39100 MW	45610 TQ	USBLS	5/15
	Arkansas	Y	31900 FQ	35310 MW	38720 TQ	USBLS	5/15
	Little Rock-North Little Rock-Conway MSA, AR	Y	40880 FQ	44440 MW	47990 TQ	USBLS	5/15
	California	H	14.32 FQ	18.48 MW	23.56 TQ	CABLS	1/16-3/16
	Anaheim-Santa Ana-Irvine PMSA, CA	H	16.79 FQ	19.00 MW	21.94 TQ	CABLS	1/16-3/16
	Los Angeles-Long Beach-Glendale PMSA, CA	H	12.92 FQ	18.33 MW	26.51 TQ	CABLS	1/16-3/16
	Oakland-Hayward-Berkeley PMSA, CA	H	16.20 FQ	21.00 MW	26.38 TQ	CABLS	1/16-3/16

AE	Average entry wage	AWR	Average wage range	H	Hourly
AEX	Average experienced wage	B	Biweekly	HI	Highest wage paid
ATC	Average total compensation	D	Daily	HR	High end range
AW	Average wage paid	FQ	First quartile wage	LO	Lowest wage paid

LR	Low end range	MTC	Median total compensation	TCC	Total cash compensation
M	Monthly	MW	Median wage paid	TQ	Third quartile wage
MCC	Median cash compensation	MWR	Median wage range	W	Weekly
ME	Median entry wage	S	See annotated source	Y	Yearly

Occupation/Type/Industry	Location	Per	Low	Mid	High	Source	Date
Separating, Filtering, Clarifying, Precipitating, and Still Machine Setter, Operator, and Tender							
	Riverside-San Bernardino-Ontario MSA, CA	H	11.86 FQ	15.87 MW	19.66 TQ	CABLS	1/16-3/16
	Sacramento–Roseville–Arden-Arcade MSA, CA	H	14.31 FQ	17.86 MW	22.94 TQ	CABLS	1/16-3/16
	San Diego-Carlsbad MSA, CA	H	15.37 FQ	17.57 MW	21.68 TQ	CABLS	1/16-3/16
	Colorado	Y	28720 FQ	42160 MW	56940 TQ	USBLS	5/15
	Denver-Aurora-Lakewood MSA, CO	Y	26020 FQ	44600 MW	60970 TQ	USBLS	5/15
	Connecticut	Y		19639 MW		CTBLS	1/16-3/16
	Hartford-West Hartford-East Hartford MSA, CT	Y	19110 FQ	19180 MW	30830 TQ	USBLS	5/15
	Delaware	Y	29360 FQ	33760 MW	38730 TQ	USBLS	5/15
	Wilmington PMSA, DE-MD-NJ	Y	29330 FQ	37850 MW	68310 TQ	USBLS	5/15
	Washington-Arlington-Alexandria PMSA, DC-VA-MD-WV	Y	38760 FQ	46850 MW	58360 TQ	USBLS	5/15
	Florida	H	12.02 AE	18.04 MW	23.03 AEX	FLBLS	7/16-9/16
	Fort Lauderdale-Pompano Beach-Deerfield Beach PMSA, FL	H	9.67 AE	14.60 MW	18.10 AEX	FLBLS	7/16-9/16
	Miami-Miami Beach-Kendall PMSA, FL	H	12.53 AE	18.30 MW	23.04 AEX	FLBLS	7/16-9/16
	Orlando-Kissimmee-Sanford MSA, FL	H	9.68 AE	13.76 MW	17.69 AEX	FLBLS	7/16-9/16
	Tampa-St. Petersburg-Clearwater MSA, FL	H	11.52 AE	16.56 MW	19.38 AEX	FLBLS	7/16-9/16
	Georgia	Y	30110 FQ	43730 MW	60960 TQ	USBLS	5/15
	Atlanta-Sandy Springs-Roswell MSA, GA	Y	27340 FQ	37420 MW	47900 TQ	USBLS	5/15
	Augusta-Richmond County MSA, GA-SC	Y	30230 FQ	38060 MW	45710 TQ	USBLS	5/15
	Hawaii	Y	32650 FQ	39160 MW	50340 TQ	USBLS	5/15
	Urban Honolulu MSA, HI	Y	40880 FQ	50390 MW	56140 TQ	USBLS	5/15
	Idaho	Y	28550 FQ	36010 MW	43590 TQ	USBLS	5/15
	Boise City MSA, ID	Y	22950 FQ	33390 MW	39520 TQ	USBLS	5/15
	Illinois	Y	33920 FQ	42210 MW	56050 TQ	USBLS	5/15
	Chicago-Naperville-Arlington Heights PMSA, IL	Y	35620 FQ	46970 MW	58100 TQ	USBLS	5/15
	Indiana	Y	26630 FQ	37600 MW	51800 TQ	USBLS	5/15
	Indianapolis-Carmel-Anderson MSA, IN	Y	22340 FQ	27710 MW	42470 TQ	USBLS	5/15
	Iowa	Y	30060 FQ	35940 MW	43170 TQ	USBLS	5/15
	Des Moines-West Des Moines MSA, IA	Y	32370 FQ	35810 MW	39240 TQ	USBLS	5/15
	Kansas	Y	28560 FQ	34070 MW	38250 TQ	USBLS	5/15
	Wichita MSA, KS	Y	26770 FQ	36690 MW	47210 TQ	USBLS	5/15
	Kentucky	Y	31900 FQ	38820 MW	50080 TQ	USBLS	5/15
	Louisville-Jefferson County MSA, KY-IN	Y	33870 FQ	39140 MW	54740 TQ	USBLS	5/15
	Louisiana	Y	26920 FQ	32290 MW	39710 TQ	CABLS	5/15
	Baton Rouge MSA, LA	Y	29160 FQ	36680 MW	53100 TQ	USBLS	5/15
	New Orleans-Metairie MSA, LA	Y	29130 FQ	35570 MW	46240 TQ	USBLS	5/15
	Maine	Y	31640 FQ	49560 MW	62920 TQ	USBLS	5/15
	Portland-South Portland MSA, ME	Y	27840 FQ	31760 MW	37830 TQ	USBLS	5/15
	Maryland	Y	27697 AE	41492 MW	48389 AEX	MDBLS	4/16
	Baltimore-Columbia-Towson MSA, MD	Y	32700 FQ	38070 MW	49250 TQ	USBLS	5/15
	Salisbury MSA, MD-DE	Y	29510 FQ	36270 MW	43620 TQ	USBLS	5/15
	Massachusetts	Y	32060 FQ	37310 MW	44440 TQ	USBLS	5/15
	Boston-Cambridge-Newton NECTA, MA	Y	30550 FQ	36140 MW	43410 TQ	USBLS	5/15
	Michigan	Y	25170 FQ	35610 MW	46410 TQ	USBLS	5/15
	Detroit-Dearborn-Livonia PMSA, MI	Y	27580 FQ	35810 MW	46420 TQ	USBLS	5/15
	Grand Rapids-Wyoming MSA, MI	Y	26850 FQ	41260 MW	47430 TQ	USBLS	5/15

AE	Average entry wage	AWR	Average wage range	H	Hourly
AEX	Average experienced wage	B	Biweekly	HI	Highest wage paid
ATC	Average total compensation	D	Daily	HR	High end range
AW	Average wage paid	FQ	First quartile wage	LO	Lowest wage paid

LR	Low end range	MTC	Median total compensation	TCC	Total cash compensation
M	Monthly	MW	Median wage paid	TQ	Third quartile wage
MCC	Median cash compensation	MWR	Median wage range	W	Weekly
ME	Median entry wage	S	See annotated source	Y	Yearly

Occupation/Type/Industry	Location	Per	Low	Mid	High	Source	Date
Separating, Filtering, Clarifying, Precipitating, and Still Machine Setter, Operator, and Tender	Minnesota	Y	38372 FQ	45783 MW	53720 TQ	MNBLS	1/16-3/16
	Minneapolis-St. Paul-Bloomington MSA, MN-WI	Y	39546 FQ	47423 MW	55492 TQ	MNBLS	1/16-3/16
	Mississippi	Y	25630 FQ	35840 MW	48750 TQ	USBLS	5/15
	Missouri	Y	24350 FQ	35080 MW	46660 TQ	USBLS	5/15
	Kansas City MSA, MO-KS	Y	32650 FQ	38030 MW	47090 TQ	USBLS	5/15
	St. Louis MSA, MO-IL	Y	33030 FQ	41720 MW	48670 TQ	USBLS	5/15
	Montana	Y	29290 FQ	36260 MW	45150 TQ	USBLS	5/15
	Billings MSA, MT	Y	29060 FQ	39090 MW	48890 TQ	USBLS	5/15
	Nebraska	Y	26970 FQ	31625 MW	41430 TQ	NEBLS	7/16-9/16
	Omaha-Council Bluffs MSA, NE-IA	Y	29450 FQ	39400 MW	46265 TQ	NEBLS	7/16-9/16
	Nevada	Y	34200 FQ	50830 MW	61300 TQ	USBLS	5/15
	Las Vegas-Henderson-Paradise MSA, NV	Y	28300 FQ	34740 MW	40290 TQ	USBLS	5/15
	New Hampshire	H	13.49 AE	21.89 MW	25.43 AEX	NHBLS	6/16
	Nashua NECTA, NH-MA	Y	27210 FQ	51220 MW	57760 TQ	USBLS	5/15
	New Jersey	Y	28670 FQ	37230 MW	55290 TQ	USBLS	5/15
	Camden PMSA, NJ	Y	27690 FQ	31880 MW	37920 TQ	USBLS	5/15
	Newark PMSA, NJ-PA	Y	27950 FQ	41040 MW	57510 TQ	USBLS	5/15
	New Mexico	Y	24090 FQ	32810 MW	42760 TQ	USBLS	5/15
	Albuquerque MSA, NM	Y	23170 FQ	30900 MW	44100 TQ	USBLS	5/15
	New York	Y	25460 AE	35060 MW	44060 AEX	NYBLS	1/16-3/16
	Buffalo-Cheektowaga-Niagara Falls MSA, NY	Y	25570 FQ	32200 MW	36540 TQ	USBLS	5/15
	Nassau County-Suffolk County PMSA, NY	Y	26870 FQ	32100 MW	44820 TQ	USBLS	5/15
	New York-Jersey City-White Plains PMSA, NY-NJ	Y	25790 FQ	33680 MW	49900 TQ	USBLS	5/15
	Rochester MSA, NY	Y	27930 FQ	33920 MW	37120 TQ	USBLS	5/15
	North Carolina	Y	41130 FQ	54090 MW	65300 TQ	USBLS	5/15
	Charlotte-Concord-Gastonia MSA, NC-SC	Y	31080 FQ	35520 MW	40090 TQ	USBLS	5/15
	Raleigh MSA, NC	Y	49570 FQ	56280 MW	63560 TQ	USBLS	5/15
	North Dakota	Y	29160 FQ	36850 MW	48270 TQ	USBLS	5/15
	Ohio	Y	31370 FQ	41030 MW	47040 TQ	USBLS	5/15
	Cincinnati MSA, OH-KY-IN	Y	32410 FQ	38950 MW	48270 TQ	USBLS	5/15
	Cleveland-Elyria MSA, OH	Y	29750 FQ	37100 MW	44940 TQ	USBLS	5/15
	Columbus MSA, OH	Y	31620 FQ	42530 MW	48460 TQ	USBLS	5/15
	Oklahoma	Y	21860 FQ	27330 MW	34030 TQ	USBLS	5/15
	Oklahoma City MSA, OK	Y	24210 FQ	29450 MW	34920 TQ	USBLS	5/15
	Tulsa MSA, OK	Y	20490 FQ	26930 MW	32530 TQ	USBLS	5/15
	Oregon	H	12.58 FQ	16.62 MW	22.04 TQ	ORBLS	2016
	Portland-Vancouver-Hillsboro MSA, OR-WA	Y	25080 FQ	39090 MW	51860 TQ	USBLS	5/15
	Pennsylvania	Y	32030 FQ	39700 MW	49570 TQ	USBLS	5/15
	Allentown-Bethlehem-Easton MSA, PA-NJ	Y	25110 FQ	32150 MW	36800 TQ	USBLS	5/15
	Montgomery County-Bucks County-Chester County PMSA, PA	Y	32460 FQ	40070 MW	48360 TQ	USBLS	5/15
	Philadelphia PMSA, PA	Y	39540 FQ	45840 MW	54110 TQ	USBLS	5/15
	Pittsburgh MSA, PA	Y	35450 FQ	44910 MW	63820 TQ	USBLS	5/15
	Rhode Island	Y	19470 FQ	28510 MW	33520 TQ	USBLS	5/15
	Providence-Warwick MSA, RI-MA	Y	19640 FQ	28690 MW	33990 TQ	USBLS	5/15
	South Carolina	Y	23920 FQ	30650 MW	44190 TQ	USBLS	5/15
	Charleston-North Charleston MSA, SC	Y	29070 FQ	41520 MW	50130 TQ	USBLS	5/15
	South Dakota	Y	25730 FQ	30350 MW	40490 TQ	USBLS	5/15
	Tennessee	Y	27280 FQ	39190 MW	51890 TQ	USBLS	5/15
	Knoxville MSA, TN	Y	35920 FQ	42820 MW	47410 TQ	USBLS	5/15
	Memphis MSA, TN-MS-AR	Y	31740 FQ	39940 MW	54200 TQ	USBLS	5/15
	Nashville-Davidson–Murfreesboro–Franklin MSA, TN	Y	23270 FQ	41860 MW	48500 TQ	USBLS	5/15
	Texas	Y	29330 FQ	37830 MW	59500 TQ	USBLS	5/15
	Austin-Round Rock MSA, TX	Y	28980 FQ	35510 MW	54420 TQ	USBLS	5/15
	Dallas-Plano-Irving PMSA, TX	Y	30780 FQ	37110 MW	54400 TQ	USBLS	5/15

AE	Average entry wage	AWR	Average wage range	H	Hourly
AEX	Average experienced wage	B	Biweekly	HI	Highest wage paid
ATC	Average total compensation	D	Daily	HR	High end range
AW	Average wage paid	FQ	First quartile wage	LO	Lowest wage paid

LR	Low end range	MTC	Median total compensation
M	Monthly	MW	Median wage paid
MCC	Median cash compensation	MWR	Median wage range
ME	Median entry wage	S	See annotated source

TCC	Total cash compensation
TQ	Third quartile wage
W	Weekly
Y	Yearly

Occupation/Type/Industry	Location	Per	Low	Mid	High	Source	Date
Separating, Filtering, Clarifying, Precipitating, and Still Machine Setter, Operator, and Tender	Fort Worth-Arlington PMSA, TX	Y	27870 FQ	30910 MW	48370 TQ	USBLS	5/15
	Houston-The Woodlands-Sugar Land MSA, TX	Y	32270 FQ	38860 MW	57050 TQ	USBLS	5/15
	San Antonio-New Braunfels MSA, TX	Y	24630 FQ	33210 MW	37430 TQ	USBLS	5/15
	Utah	Y	37420 FQ	48980 MW	57040 TQ	USBLS	5/15
	Salt Lake City MSA, UT	Y	35710 FQ	51330 MW	57540 TQ	USBLS	5/15
	Vermont	Y	31730 FQ	37460 MW	45990 TQ	USBLS	5/15
	Burlington-South Burlington MSA, VT	Y	27770 FQ	30510 MW	36220 TQ	USBLS	5/15
	Virginia	Y	29490 FQ	38560 MW	51200 TQ	USBLS	5/15
	Richmond MSA, VA	Y	32570 FQ	39430 MW	55710 TQ	USBLS	5/15
	Virginia Beach-Norfolk-Newport News MSA, VA-NC	Y	28170 FQ	36310 MW	68350 TQ	USBLS	5/15
	Washington	H	14.07 FQ	17.56 MW	23.28 TQ	WABLS	3/16
	Seattle-Bellevue-Everett PMSA, WA	H	13.69 FQ	16.67 MW	21.35 TQ	WABLS	3/16
	West Virginia	Y	19400 FQ	42320 MW	47570 TQ	USBLS	5/15
	Wisconsin	Y	29130 FQ	35770 MW	44780 TQ	USBLS	5/15
	Madison MSA, WI	Y	33340 FQ	37610 MW	45790 TQ	USBLS	5/15
	Milwaukee-Waukesha-West Allis MSA, WI	Y	34690 FQ	40530 MW	47530 TQ	USBLS	5/15
	Wyoming	Y	59420 FQ	71460 MW	80490 TQ	USBLS	5/15
	Puerto Rico	Y	18080 FQ	26530 MW	38410 TQ	USBLS	5/15
	San Juan-Carolina-Caguas MSA, PR	Y	19310 FQ	30270 MW	40320 TQ	USBLS	5/15
Septic Tank Servicer and Sewer Pipe Cleaner	Alabama	Y	18208 AE	28824 AW	34132 AEX	ALBLS	6/16
	Alaska	Y	36520 FQ	42480 MW	48340 TQ	USBLS	5/15
	Arizona	Y	24640 FQ	32750 MW	37760 TQ	USBLS	5/15
	Phoenix-Mesa-Scottsdale MSA, AZ	Y	23320 FQ	29540 MW	35440 TQ	USBLS	5/15
	Tucson MSA, AZ	Y	34330 FQ	39070 MW	69730 TQ	USBLS	5/15
	Arkansas	Y	23160 FQ	28540 MW	35750 TQ	USBLS	5/15
	California	H	17.30 FQ	22.87 MW	30.28 TQ	CABLS	1/16-3/16
	Anaheim-Santa Ana-Irvine PMSA, CA	H	24.56 FQ	33.82 MW	38.93 TQ	CABLS	1/16-3/16
	Los Angeles-Long Beach-Glendale PMSA, CA	H	16.23 FQ	18.40 MW	26.82 TQ	CABLS	1/16-3/16
	Oakland-Hayward-Berkeley PMSA, CA	H	20.70 FQ	25.60 MW	31.61 TQ	CABLS	1/16-3/16
	Riverside-San Bernardino-Ontario MSA, CA	H	25.22 FQ	28.66 MW	33.37 TQ	CABLS	1/16-3/16
	Sacramento–Roseville–Arden-Arcade MSA, CA	H	16.32 FQ	17.79 MW	19.25 TQ	CABLS	1/16-3/16
	San Diego-Carlsbad MSA, CA	H	21.25 FQ	23.60 MW	27.13 TQ	CABLS	1/16-3/16
	Colorado	Y	31850 FQ	36480 MW	45610 TQ	USBLS	5/15
	Denver-Aurora-Lakewood MSA, CO	Y	32550 FQ	36930 MW	47470 TQ	USBLS	5/15
	Connecticut	Y		37220 MW		CTBLS	1/16-3/16
	Bridgeport-Stamford-Norwalk MSA, CT	Y	50740 FQ	55280 MW	59470 TQ	USBLS	5/15
	Hartford-West Hartford-East Hartford MSA, CT	Y	30410 FQ	34290 MW	37870 TQ	USBLS	5/15
	Delaware	Y	33160 FQ	38660 MW	48290 TQ	USBLS	5/15
	Wilmington PMSA, DE-MD-NJ	Y	32390 FQ	37980 MW	45710 TQ	USBLS	5/15
	Washington-Arlington-Alexandria PMSA, DC-VA-MD-WV	Y	33220 FQ	42860 MW	64050 TQ	USBLS	5/15
	Florida	H	10.15 AE	13.73 MW	17.51 AEX	FLBLS	7/16-9/16
	Fort Lauderdale-Pompano Beach-Deerfield Beach PMSA, FL	H	9.81 AE	12.89 MW	16.62 AEX	FLBLS	7/16-9/16
	Miami-Miami Beach-Kendall PMSA, FL	H	10.28 AE	13.94 MW	18.55 AEX	FLBLS	7/16-9/16

AE	Average entry wage	AWR	Average wage range	H	Hourly	LR	Low end range	MTC Median total compensation TCC Total cash compensation
AEX	Average experienced wage	B	Biweekly	HI	Highest wage paid	M	Monthly	MW Median wage paid TQ Third quartile wage
ATC	Average total compensation	D	Daily	HR	High end range	MCC	Median cash compensation	MWR Median wage range W Weekly
AW	Average wage paid	FQ	First quartile wage	LO	Lowest wage paid	ME	Median entry wage	S See annotated source Y Yearly

Occupation/Type/Industry	Location	Per	Low	Mid	High	Source	Date
Septic Tank Servicer and Sewer Pipe Cleaner	Orlando-Kissimmee-Sanford MSA, FL	H	9.36 AE	12.71 MW	14.15 AEX	FLBLS	7/16-9/16
	Tampa-St. Petersburg-Clearwater MSA, FL	H	11.79 AE	14.54 MW	18.48 AEX	FLBLS	7/16-9/16
	Georgia	Y	25270 FQ	33110 MW	41570 TQ	USBLS	5/15
	Atlanta-Sandy Springs-Roswell MSA, GA	Y	31550 FQ	40070 MW	45880 TQ	USBLS	5/15
	Augusta-Richmond County MSA, GA-SC	Y	24890 FQ	33610 MW	37520 TQ	USBLS	5/15
	Hawaii	Y	36090 FQ	43910 MW	52200 TQ	USBLS	5/15
	Idaho	Y	25910 FQ	33830 MW	39090 TQ	USBLS	5/15
	Boise City MSA, ID	Y	27380 FQ	32730 MW	39580 TQ	USBLS	5/15
	Illinois	Y	35200 FQ	49470 MW	62630 TQ	USBLS	5/15
	Chicago-Naperville-Arlington Heights PMSA, IL	Y	35500 FQ	50320 MW	64660 TQ	USBLS	5/15
	Indiana	Y	28420 FQ	34690 MW	44330 TQ	USBLS	5/15
	Gary PMSA, IN	Y	40340 FQ	46120 MW	52130 TQ	USBLS	5/15
	Indianapolis-Carmel-Anderson MSA, IN	Y	36430 FQ	42340 MW	47030 TQ	USBLS	5/15
	Iowa	Y	25430 FQ	30130 MW	38950 TQ	USBLS	5/15
	Des Moines-West Des Moines MSA, IA	Y	37510 FQ	48730 MW	60750 TQ	USBLS	5/15
	Kansas	Y	27810 FQ	35380 MW	49160 TQ	USBLS	5/15
	Wichita MSA, KS	Y	33410 FQ	38680 MW	56520 TQ	USBLS	5/15
	Kentucky	Y	23210 FQ	27400 MW	33350 TQ	USBLS	5/15
	Louisville-Jefferson County MSA, KY-IN	Y	23800 FQ	27680 MW	31940 TQ	USBLS	5/15
	Louisiana	Y	28300 FQ	35340 MW	49560 TQ	USBLS	5/15
	Maine	Y	27480 FQ	32180 MW	38640 TQ	USBLS	5/15
	Portland-South Portland MSA, ME	Y	30450 FQ	40550 MW	49320 TQ	USBLS	5/15
	Maryland	Y	26338 AE	38086 MW	43960 AEX	MDBLS	4/16
	Baltimore-Columbia-Towson MSA, MD	Y	31230 FQ	36640 MW	45830 TQ	USBLS	5/15
	Massachusetts	Y	32930 FQ	37460 MW	45390 TQ	USBLS	5/15
	Worcester MSA, MA-CT	Y	33830 FQ	36900 MW	44970 TQ	USBLS	5/15
	Michigan	Y	28050 FQ	36690 MW	46000 TQ	USBLS	5/15
	Detroit-Dearborn-Livonia PMSA, MI	Y	34200 FQ	38730 MW	44380 TQ	USBLS	5/15
	Grand Rapids-Wyoming MSA, MI	Y	22030 FQ	24650 MW	41510 TQ	USBLS	5/15
	Minnesota	Y	31592 FQ	43721 MW	56081 TQ	MNBLS	1/16-3/16
	Minneapolis-St. Paul-Bloomington MSA, MN-WI	Y	34407 FQ	48796 MW	57786 TQ	MNBLS	1/16-3/16
	Mississippi	Y	23090 FQ	29740 MW	40010 TQ	USBLS	5/15
	Missouri	Y	31080 FQ	36950 MW	45690 TQ	USBLS	5/15
	Kansas City MSA, MO-KS	Y	29750 FQ	35350 MW	43330 TQ	USBLS	5/15
	St. Louis MSA, MO-IL	Y	33430 FQ	40340 MW	50230 TQ	USBLS	5/15
	Montana	Y	27160 FQ	33310 MW	38950 TQ	USBLS	5/15
	Billings MSA, MT	Y	32560 FQ	36160 MW	39750 TQ	USBLS	5/15
	Nebraska	Y	27220 FQ	29865 MW	35400 TQ	NEBLS	7/16-9/16
	Omaha-Council Bluffs MSA, NE-IA	Y	26715 FQ	31165 MW	36620 TQ	NEBLS	7/16-9/16
	Nevada	Y	32830 FQ	41040 MW	48170 TQ	USBLS	5/15
	New Hampshire	H	11.57 AE	16.93 MW	19.49 AEX	NHBLS	6/16
	Manchester NECTA, NH	H	15.95 AE	18.31 MW	19.53 AEX	NHBLS	6/16
	New Jersey	Y	38340 FQ	51090 MW	68060 TQ	USBLS	5/15
	Camden PMSA, NJ	Y	42210 FQ	46900 MW	54400 TQ	USBLS	5/15
	Newark PMSA, NJ-PA	Y	38020 FQ	59930 MW	71600 TQ	USBLS	5/15
	Trenton MSA, NJ	Y	40940 FQ	51250 MW	57990 TQ	USBLS	5/15
	New Mexico	Y	26020 FQ	30610 MW	35530 TQ	USBLS	5/15
	Albuquerque MSA, NM	Y	24700 FQ	32530 MW	37240 TQ	USBLS	5/15
	New York	Y	26680 AE	40540 MW	47100 AEX	NYBLS	1/16-3/16
	Buffalo-Cheektowaga-Niagara Falls MSA, NY	Y	44080 FQ	50930 MW	57200 TQ	USBLS	5/15
	Nassau County-Suffolk County PMSA, NY	Y	40700 FQ	46490 MW	54500 TQ	USBLS	5/15
	New York-Jersey City-White Plains PMSA, NY-NJ	Y	36000 FQ	44060 MW	52600 TQ	USBLS	5/15
	Rochester MSA, NY	Y	18730 FQ	19250 MW	19780 TQ	USBLS	5/15
	North Carolina	Y	23590 FQ	29770 MW	35750 TQ	USBLS	5/15

AE	Average entry wage	AWR	Average wage range	H	Hourly
AEX	Average experienced wage	B	Biweekly	HI	Highest wage paid
ATC	Average total compensation	D	Daily	HR	High end range
AW	Average wage paid	FQ	First quartile wage	LO	Lowest wage paid

LR	Low end range	MTC	Median total compensation	TCC	Total cash compensation
M	Monthly	MW	Median wage paid	TQ	Third quartile wage
MCC	Median cash compensation	MWR	Median wage range	W	Weekly
ME	Median entry wage	S	See annotated source	Y	Yearly

Occupation/Type/Industry	Location	Per	Low	Mid	High	Source	Date
Septic Tank Servicer and Sewer Pipe Cleaner	Charlotte-Concord-Gastonia MSA, NC-SC	Y	25000 FQ	31430 MW	36600 TQ	USBLS	5/15
	North Dakota	Y	33880 FQ	41810 MW	48910 TQ	USBLS	5/15
	Ohio	Y	26820 FQ	36700 MW	46140 TQ	USBLS	5/15
	Cincinnati MSA, OH-KY-IN	Y	30650 FQ	39320 MW	45800 TQ	USBLS	5/15
	Cleveland-Elyria MSA, OH	Y	39310 FQ	45810 MW	53700 TQ	USBLS	5/15
	Columbus MSA, OH	Y	27510 FQ	35570 MW	42090 TQ	USBLS	5/15
	Oklahoma	Y	26970 FQ	31830 MW	37990 TQ	USBLS	5/15
	Oklahoma City MSA, OK	Y	28200 FQ	32770 MW	39790 TQ	USBLS	5/15
	Tulsa MSA, OK	Y	22830 FQ	26470 MW	30610 TQ	USBLS	5/15
	Oregon	H	15.16 FQ	20.17 MW	25.66 TQ	ORBLS	2016
	Portland-Vancouver-Hillsboro MSA, OR-WA	Y	33510 FQ	44430 MW	55460 TQ	USBLS	5/15
	Pennsylvania	Y	33360 FQ	41360 MW	48420 TQ	USBLS	5/15
	Allentown-Bethlehem-Easton MSA, PA-NJ	Y	42870 FQ	46260 MW	49720 TQ	USBLS	5/15
	Harrisburg-Carlisle MSA, PA	Y	28660 FQ	34910 MW	39440 TQ	USBLS	5/15
	Montgomery County-Bucks County-Chester County PMSA, PA	Y	35100 FQ	43390 MW	52560 TQ	USBLS	5/15
	Philadelphia PMSA, PA	Y	40790 FQ	46200 MW	54820 TQ	USBLS	5/15
	Pittsburgh MSA, PA	Y	33850 FQ	41790 MW	52100 TQ	USBLS	5/15
	Rhode Island	Y	27500 FQ	33310 MW	47390 TQ	USBLS	5/15
	Providence-Warwick MSA, RI-MA	Y	28310 FQ	40140 MW	49130 TQ	USBLS	5/15
	South Carolina	Y	22450 FQ	28270 MW	36260 TQ	USBLS	5/15
	Charleston-North Charleston MSA, SC	Y	25310 FQ	30700 MW	37120 TQ	USBLS	5/15
	Greenville-Anderson-Mauldin MSA, SC	Y	26620 FQ	32580 MW	43330 TQ	USBLS	5/15
	South Dakota	Y	22360 FQ	25880 MW	30950 TQ	USBLS	5/15
	Sioux Falls MSA, SD	Y	24040 FQ	29550 MW	40510 TQ	USBLS	5/15
	Tennessee	Y	26850 FQ	32150 MW	37930 TQ	USBLS	5/15
	Knoxville MSA, TN	Y	26280 FQ	33040 MW	38460 TQ	USBLS	5/15
	Memphis MSA, TN-MS-AR	Y	30330 FQ	34580 MW	38540 TQ	USBLS	5/15
	Nashville-Davidson–Murfreesboro–Franklin MSA, TN	Y	29280 FQ	34160 MW	38250 TQ	USBLS	5/15
	Texas	Y	24680 FQ	29250 MW	36920 TQ	USBLS	5/15
	Austin-Round Rock MSA, TX	Y	28360 FQ	40680 MW	49730 TQ	USBLS	5/15
	Dallas-Plano-Irving PMSA, TX	Y	27190 FQ	31910 MW	40820 TQ	USBLS	5/15
	Fort Worth-Arlington PMSA, TX	Y	28110 FQ	31270 MW	39990 TQ	USBLS	5/15
	Houston-The Woodlands-Sugar Land MSA, TX	Y	26030 FQ	28800 MW	32950 TQ	USBLS	5/15
	San Antonio-New Braunfels MSA, TX	Y	25750 FQ	29720 MW	35710 TQ	USBLS	5/15
	Utah	Y	27270 FQ	34000 MW	40840 TQ	USBLS	5/15
	Ogden-Clearfield MSA, UT	Y	25970 FQ	32100 MW	36460 TQ	USBLS	5/15
	Provo-Orem MSA, UT	Y	20070 FQ	35450 MW	44660 TQ	USBLS	5/15
	Salt Lake City MSA, UT	Y	30100 FQ	35390 MW	40000 TQ	USBLS	5/15
	Vermont	Y	28440 FQ	32720 MW	38530 TQ	USBLS	5/15
	Virginia	Y	27490 FQ	36000 MW	48550 TQ	USBLS	5/15
	Richmond MSA, VA	Y	30320 FQ	38150 MW	46010 TQ	USBLS	5/15
	Virginia Beach-Norfolk-Newport News MSA, VA-NC	Y	26220 FQ	34350 MW	46160 TQ	USBLS	5/15
	Washington	H	13.56 FQ	17.90 MW	23.89 TQ	WABLS	3/16
	Seattle-Bellevue-Everett PMSA, WA	H	12.66 FQ	18.38 MW	25.56 TQ	WABLS	3/16
	Tacoma-Lakewood PMSA, WA	H	18.55 FQ	22.97 MW	31.50 TQ	WABLS	3/16
	West Virginia	Y	27830 FQ	30980 MW	37420 TQ	USBLS	5/15
	Huntington-Ashland MSA, WV-KY-OH	Y	27320 FQ	30390 MW	35660 TQ	USBLS	5/15
	Wisconsin	Y	27970 FQ	34970 MW	41860 TQ	USBLS	5/15
	Madison MSA, WI	Y	26810 FQ	32740 MW	37210 TQ	USBLS	5/15
	Milwaukee-Waukesha-West Allis MSA, WI	Y	37540 FQ	43370 MW	49100 TQ	USBLS	5/15
	Wyoming	Y	31700 FQ	35140 MW	38570 TQ	USBLS	5/15
Sergeant							
U.S. Marines, Active Duty, Pay Grade E-4	United States	M	2089 LO		2354 HI	DOD1	2017

AE	Average entry wage	AWR	Average wage range	H	Hourly	LR	Low end range	MTC	Median total compensation	TCC	Total cash compensation
AEX	Average experienced wage	B	Biweekly	HI	Highest wage paid	M	Monthly	MW	Median wage paid	TQ	Third quartile wage
ATC	Average total compensation	D	Daily	HR	High end range	MCC	Median cash compensation	MWR	Median wage range	W	Weekly
AW	Average wage paid	FQ	First quartile wage	LO	Lowest wage paid	ME	Median entry wage	S	See annotated source	Y	Yearly

Occupation/Type/Industry	Location	Per	Low	Mid	High	Source	Date
Sergeant							
U.S. Marines, Active Duty, Pay Grade E-5	United States	M	2278 LO		3233 HI	DOD1	2017
Sergeant, Specialist 4							
U.S. Army, Active Duty, Pay Grade E-4	United States	M	2089 LO		2354 HI	DOD1	2017
Sergeant, Specialist 5							
U.S. Army, Active Duty, Pay Grade E-5	United States	M	2278 LO		3233 HI	DOD1	2017
Sergeant 1st Class							
U.S. Army, Active Duty, Pay Grade E-7	United States	M	2875 LO		5168 HI	DOD1	2017
Sergeant at Arms							
Municipal Government	Detroit, MI	M			274 HI	DETGOV	2016
Sergeant Major							
U.S. Army, Active Duty, Pay Grade E-9	United States	M	5053 LO		7845 HI	DOD1	2017
U.S. Marines, Active Duty, Pay Grade E-9	United States	M	5053 LO		7845 HI	DOD1	2017
Service Advisor							
Luxury Automotive Dealership	United States	Y		78327 AW		AUTON1	2015
Nonluxury Automotive Dealership	United States	Y		59499 AW		AUTON1	2015
Service Manager							
Copier Industry	United States	Y		77411 AW		COPIER2	2016
Service/Repair Person							
Home Healthcare Industry	United States	H		17.00 AW		HCARE2	2015
Service Technician							
Automotive Dealership	United States	Y		59484 AW		AUTON	2015
Copier Industry	United States	Y		45121 AW		COPIER3	2016
Service Unit Operator							
Oil, Gas, and Mining	Alabama	Y	26273 AE	46702 AW	56917 AEX	ALBLS	6/16
Oil, Gas, and Mining	Alaska	Y	67000 FQ	72420 MW	77830 TQ	USBLS	5/15
Oil, Gas, and Mining	Arkansas	Y	35200 FQ	47250 MW	56920 TQ	USBLS	5/15
Oil, Gas, and Mining	California	H	21.01 FQ	26.89 MW	30.45 TQ	CABLS	1/16-3/16
Oil, Gas, and Mining	Colorado	Y	37020 FQ	44000 MW	50890 TQ	USBLS	5/15
Oil, Gas, and Mining	Florida	H	16.41 AE	21.12 MW	25.02 AEX	FLBLS	7/16-9/16
Oil, Gas, and Mining	Illinois	Y	21090 FQ	24330 MW	38370 TQ	USBLS	5/15
Oil, Gas, and Mining	Indiana	Y	21850 FQ	24310 MW	42810 TQ	USBLS	5/15
Oil, Gas, and Mining	Kansas	Y	32620 FQ	39770 MW	58390 TQ	USBLS	5/15
Oil, Gas, and Mining	Kentucky	Y	29750 FQ	39040 MW	57060 TQ	USBLS	5/15
Oil, Gas, and Mining	Louisiana	Y	36340 FQ	47570 MW	62850 TQ	USBLS	5/15
Oil, Gas, and Mining	Michigan	Y	33320 FQ	38960 MW	53250 TQ	USBLS	5/15
Oil, Gas, and Mining	Mississippi	Y	36200 FQ	43340 MW	49020 TQ	USBLS	5/15
Oil, Gas, and Mining	Montana	Y	43060 FQ	50600 MW	59540 TQ	USBLS	5/15
Oil, Gas, and Mining	Nevada	Y	40040 FQ	45390 MW	55110 TQ	USBLS	5/15
Oil, Gas, and Mining	New Mexico	Y	35830 FQ	44070 MW	57830 TQ	USBLS	5/15
Oil, Gas, and Mining	New York	Y	28680 AE	40170 MW	52240 AEX	NYBLS	1/16-3/16
Oil, Gas, and Mining	North Dakota	Y	40130 FQ	47810 MW	58570 TQ	USBLS	5/15
Oil, Gas, and Mining	Ohio	Y	27170 FQ	34280 MW	43070 TQ	USBLS	5/15
Oil, Gas, and Mining	Oklahoma	Y	34720 FQ	42510 MW	51760 TQ	USBLS	5/15
Oil, Gas, and Mining	Pennsylvania	Y	34530 FQ	42360 MW	53960 TQ	USBLS	5/15
Oil, Gas, and Mining	Tennessee	Y	28600 FQ	33240 MW	37380 TQ	USBLS	5/15
Oil, Gas, and Mining	Texas	Y	35090 FQ	43800 MW	56890 TQ	USBLS	5/15
Oil, Gas, and Mining	Utah	Y	44170 FQ	53530 MW	61820 TQ	USBLS	5/15
Oil, Gas, and Mining	Virginia	Y	36220 FQ	43580 MW	65360 TQ	USBLS	5/15
Oil, Gas, and Mining	West Virginia	Y	30030 FQ	36950 MW	49790 TQ	USBLS	5/15
Oil, Gas, and Mining	Wyoming	Y	43400 FQ	52220 MW	60890 TQ	USBLS	5/15
Session Musician	United States	D		100-2500 AWR		BBRD01	2014
Set and Exhibit Designer	Alabama	Y	23159 AE	45176 AW	56175 AEX	ALBLS	6/16
	Arizona	Y	27720 FQ	33550 MW	48600 TQ	USBLS	5/15
	Phoenix-Mesa-Scottsdale MSA, AZ	Y	27070 FQ	31260 MW	43700 TQ	USBLS	5/15
	California	H	17.05 FQ	23.97 MW	40.09 TQ	CABLS	1/16-3/16
	Los Angeles-Long Beach-Glendale PMSA, CA	H	17.25 FQ	24.03 MW	41.42 TQ	CABLS	1/16-3/16
	Oakland-Hayward-Berkeley PMSA, CA	H	17.10 FQ	19.17 MW	30.29 TQ	CABLS	1/16-3/16

AE	Average entry wage	AWR	Average wage range	H	Hourly	LR Low end range	MTC Median total compensation	TCC Total cash compensation
AEX	Average experienced wage	B	Biweekly	HI	Highest wage paid	M Monthly	MW Median wage paid	TQ Third quartile wage
ATC	Average total compensation	D	Daily	HR	High end range	MCC Median cash compensation	MWR Median wage range	W Weekly
AW	Average wage paid	FQ	First quartile wage	LO	Lowest wage paid	ME Median entry wage	S See annotated source	Y Yearly

Occupation/Type/Industry	Location	Per	Low	Mid	High	Source	Date
Set and Exhibit Designer	Riverside-San Bernardino-Ontario MSA, CA	H	19.19 FQ	21.51 MW	23.82 TQ	CABLS	1/16-3/16
	Sacramento–Roseville–Arden-Arcade MSA, CA	H	17.62 FQ	23.03 MW	28.77 TQ	CABLS	1/16-3/16
	San Diego-Carlsbad MSA, CA	H	13.98 FQ	18.82 MW	26.16 TQ	CABLS	1/16-3/16
	San Francisco-Redwood City-South San Francisco PMSA, CA	H	19.21 FQ	28.85 MW	37.24 TQ	CABLS	1/16-3/16
	Colorado	Y	33780 FQ	38370 MW	53660 TQ	USBLS	5/15
	Denver-Aurora-Lakewood MSA, CO	Y	33210 FQ	36690 MW	45390 TQ	USBLS	5/15
	Connecticut	Y		66733 MW		CTBLS	1/16-3/16
	Hartford-West Hartford-East Hartford MSA, CT	Y	27580 FQ	36150 MW	51400 TQ	USBLS	5/15
	District of Columbia	Y	51790 FQ	70100 MW	82830 TQ	USBLS	5/15
	Washington-Arlington-Alexandria PMSA, DC-VA-MD-WV	Y	41130 FQ	66120 MW	81050 TQ	USBLS	5/15
	Florida	H	10.47 AE	18.42 MW	23.75 AEX	FLBLS	7/16-9/16
	Fort Lauderdale-Pompano Beach-Deerfield Beach PMSA, FL	H	9.88 AE	13.86 MW	21.13 AEX	FLBLS	7/16-9/16
	Miami-Miami Beach-Kendall PMSA, FL	H	17.59 AE	22.66 MW	27.39 AEX	FLBLS	7/16-9/16
	Orlando-Kissimmee-Sanford MSA, FL	H	9.05 AE	12.36 MW	21.17 AEX	FLBLS	7/16-9/16
	Tampa-St. Petersburg-Clearwater MSA, FL	H	16.25 AE	19.87 MW	24.98 AEX	FLBLS	7/16-9/16
	Georgia	Y	36010 FQ	55230 MW	72700 TQ	USBLS	5/15
	Atlanta-Sandy Springs-Roswell MSA, GA	Y	34330 FQ	50750 MW	74220 TQ	USBLS	5/15
	Hawaii	Y	29790 FQ	40350 MW	50790 TQ	USBLS	5/15
	Urban Honolulu MSA, HI	Y	30540 FQ	40600 MW	49540 TQ	USBLS	5/15
	Illinois	Y	34420 FQ	45250 MW	66090 TQ	USBLS	5/15
	Chicago-Naperville-Arlington Heights PMSA, IL	Y	34530 FQ	45200 MW	66790 TQ	USBLS	5/15
	Indiana	Y	37630 FQ	45220 MW	55950 TQ	USBLS	5/15
	Indianapolis-Carmel-Anderson MSA, IN	Y	39680 FQ	45980 MW	57250 TQ	USBLS	5/15
	Kansas	Y	32340 FQ	41650 MW	102000 TQ	USBLS	5/15
	Louisiana	Y	33480 FQ	37490 MW	67100 TQ	USBLS	5/15
	New Orleans-Metairie MSA, LA	Y	33470 FQ	37480 MW	67290 TQ	USBLS	5/15
	Maryland	Y	30280 AE	57898 MW	71706 AEX	MDBLS	4/16
	Baltimore-Columbia-Towson MSA, MD	Y	46980 FQ	58040 MW	73880 TQ	USBLS	5/15
	Massachusetts	Y	36120 FQ	47180 MW	62150 TQ	USBLS	5/15
	Boston-Cambridge-Newton NECTA, MA	Y	39250 FQ	48170 MW	61300 TQ	USBLS	5/15
	Michigan	Y	20900 FQ	26000 MW	45370 TQ	USBLS	5/15
	Minnesota	Y	51169 FQ	55886 MW	60584 TQ	MNBLS	1/16-3/16
	Minneapolis-St. Paul-Bloomington MSA, MN-WI	Y	51249 FQ	55836 MW	60423 TQ	MNBLS	1/16-3/16
	Missouri	Y	40370 FQ	52300 MW	62570 TQ	USBLS	5/15
	Kansas City MSA, MO-KS	Y	43980 FQ	66580 MW	81270 TQ	USBLS	5/15
	St. Louis MSA, MO-IL	Y	41240 FQ	51350 MW	60060 TQ	USBLS	5/15
	Nebraska	Y	51045 FQ	60880 MW	76300 TQ	NEBLS	7/16-9/16
	Omaha-Council Bluffs MSA, NE-IA	Y	19325 FQ	73265 MW	86835 TQ	NEBLS	7/16-9/16
	Nevada	Y	35170 FQ	46620 MW	61940 TQ	USBLS	5/15
	Las Vegas-Henderson-Paradise MSA, NV	Y	35120 FQ	46390 MW	61760 TQ	USBLS	5/15
	New Jersey	Y	46000 FQ	59090 MW	70040 TQ	USBLS	5/15
	Newark PMSA, NJ-PA	Y	47570 FQ	66230 MW	72460 TQ	USBLS	5/15
	New Mexico	Y	35900 FQ	52150 MW	69110 TQ	USBLS	5/15
	Albuquerque MSA, NM	Y	41320 FQ	56460 MW	76540 TQ	USBLS	5/15
	New York	Y	35600 AE	62750 MW	81290 AEX	NYBLS	1/16-3/16
	Buffalo-Cheektowaga-Niagara Falls MSA, NY	Y	38320 FQ	44270 MW	49670 TQ	USBLS	5/15
	Nassau County-Suffolk County PMSA, NY	Y	46330 FQ	67840 MW	77460 TQ	USBLS	5/15

AE	Average entry wage	AWR	Average wage range	H	Hourly
AEX	Average experienced wage	B	Biweekly	HI	Highest wage paid
ATC	Average total compensation	D	Daily	HR	High end range
AW	Average wage paid	FQ	First quartile wage	LO	Lowest wage paid

LR	Low end range	MTC	Median total compensation
M	Monthly	MW	Median wage paid
MCC	Median cash compensation	MWR	Median wage range
ME	Median entry wage	S	See annotated source

TCC	Total cash compensation
TQ	Third quartile wage
W	Weekly
Y	Yearly

Occupation/Type/Industry	Location	Per	Low	Mid	High	Source	Date
Set and Exhibit Designer	New York-Jersey City-White Plains PMSA, NY-NJ	Y	43720 FQ	61960 MW	85440 TQ	USBLS	5/15
	North Carolina	Y	35240 FQ	44760 MW	59480 TQ	USBLS	5/15
	Charlotte-Concord-Gastonia MSA, NC-SC	Y	34370 FQ	37510 MW	42620 TQ	USBLS	5/15
	Ohio	Y	27100 FQ	38600 MW	56030 TQ	USBLS	5/15
	Cincinnati MSA, OH-KY-IN	Y	28230 FQ	36070 MW	46190 TQ	USBLS	5/15
	Cleveland-Elyria MSA, OH	Y	42060 FQ	51500 MW	62040 TQ	USBLS	5/15
	Columbus MSA, OH	Y	29860 FQ	37840 MW	50450 TQ	USBLS	5/15
	Oklahoma	Y	30220 FQ	34390 MW	37900 TQ	USBLS	5/15
	Oklahoma City MSA, OK	Y	31890 FQ	35040 MW	38190 TQ	USBLS	5/15
	Oregon	H	25.24 FQ	27.81 MW	30.82 TQ	ORBLS	2016
	Pennsylvania	Y	34690 FQ	43890 MW	56440 TQ	USBLS	5/15
	Montgomery County-Bucks County-Chester County PMSA, PA	Y	40120 FQ	48020 MW	70920 TQ	USBLS	5/15
	Philadelphia PMSA, PA	Y	30930 FQ	37260 MW	50860 TQ	USBLS	5/15
	Pittsburgh MSA, PA	Y	41550 FQ	45630 MW	50170 TQ	USBLS	5/15
	South Carolina	Y	22250 FQ	24740 MW	30660 TQ	USBLS	5/15
	Tennessee	Y	41500 FQ	52770 MW	61780 TQ	USBLS	5/15
	Nashville-Davidson–Murfreesboro–Franklin MSA, TN	Y	44290 FQ	53580 MW	62030 TQ	USBLS	5/15
	Texas	Y	22130 FQ	36030 MW	50270 TQ	USBLS	5/15
	Austin-Round Rock MSA, TX	Y	24440 FQ	33630 MW	39190 TQ	USBLS	5/15
	Dallas-Plano-Irving PMSA, TX	Y	38480 FQ	45570 MW	56980 TQ	USBLS	5/15
	Fort Worth-Arlington PMSA, TX	Y	31600 FQ	47640 MW	62520 TQ	USBLS	5/15
	Houston-The Woodlands-Sugar Land MSA, TX	Y	21590 FQ	32820 MW	54620 TQ	USBLS	5/15
	Utah	Y	27950 FQ	32200 MW	42350 TQ	USBLS	5/15
	Salt Lake City MSA, UT	Y	28550 FQ	34160 MW	44180 TQ	USBLS	5/15
	Vermont	Y	41270 FQ	44880 MW	48490 TQ	USBLS	5/15
	Virginia	Y	31160 FQ	41030 MW	58420 TQ	USBLS	5/15
	Richmond MSA, VA	Y	27090 FQ	32620 MW	42550 TQ	USBLS	5/15
	Virginia Beach-Norfolk-Newport News MSA, VA-NC	Y	35380 FQ	44820 MW	54860 TQ	USBLS	5/15
	Washington	H	20.11 FQ	24.49 MW	30.91 TQ	WABLS	3/16
	Seattle-Bellevue-Everett PMSA, WA	H	21.01 FQ	26.35 MW	32.62 TQ	WABLS	3/16
	Wisconsin	Y	26830 FQ	36880 MW	49610 TQ	USBLS	5/15
	Milwaukee-Waukesha-West Allis MSA, WI	Y	28320 FQ	37350 MW	55850 TQ	USBLS	5/15
Sewer							
Hand	Alabama	Y	18621 AE	23166 AW	25438 AEX	ALBLS	6/16
Hand	Arkansas	Y	21260 FQ	22550 MW	23850 TQ	USBLS	5/15
Hand	California	H	10.07 FQ	11.16 MW	12.39 TQ	CABLS	1/16-3/16
Hand	Anaheim-Santa Ana-Irvine PMSA, CA	H	10.16 FQ	11.11 MW	12.07 TQ	CABLS	1/16-3/16
Hand	Los Angeles-Long Beach-Glendale PMSA, CA	H	9.95 FQ	10.88 MW	11.81 TQ	CABLS	1/16-3/16
Hand	Oakland-Hayward-Berkeley PMSA, CA	H	13.22 FQ	14.37 MW	15.64 TQ	CABLS	1/16-3/16
Hand	Riverside-San Bernardino-Ontario MSA, CA	H	9.51 FQ	9.72 MW	10.66 TQ	CABLS	1/16-3/16
Hand	Sacramento–Roseville–Arden-Arcade MSA, CA	H	11.15 FQ	13.82 MW	17.09 TQ	CABLS	1/16-3/16
Hand	San Diego-Carlsbad MSA, CA	H	10.43 FQ	11.31 MW	12.22 TQ	CABLS	1/16-3/16
Hand	San Francisco-Redwood City-South San Francisco PMSA, CA	H	11.23 FQ	13.46 MW	15.59 TQ	CABLS	1/16-3/16
Hand	Florida	H	9.32 AE	11.34 MW	13.23 AEX	FLBLS	7/16-9/16
Hand	Georgia	Y	17020 FQ	18590 MW	23400 TQ	USBLS	5/15
Hand	Illinois	Y	18230 FQ	19590 MW	28810 TQ	USBLS	5/15
Hand	Chicago-Naperville-Arlington Heights PMSA, IL	Y	18180 FQ	19200 MW	28940 TQ	USBLS	5/15
Hand	Indiana	Y	21240 FQ	24170 MW	29630 TQ	USBLS	5/15
Hand	Kentucky	Y	19680 FQ	24650 MW	27730 TQ	USBLS	5/15
Hand	Louisiana	Y	17270 FQ	19200 MW	28470 TQ	USBLS	5/15
Hand	Massachusetts	Y	23930 FQ	32090 MW	41070 TQ	USBLS	5/15

AE	Average entry wage	AWR	Average wage range	H	Hourly	LR Low end range	MTC Median total compensation	TCC Total cash compensation
AEX	Average experienced wage	B	Biweekly	HI	Highest wage paid	M Monthly	MW Median wage paid	TQ Third quartile wage
ATC	Average total compensation	D	Daily	HR	High end range	MCC Median cash compensation	MWR Median wage range	W Weekly
AW	Average wage paid	FQ	First quartile wage	LO	Lowest wage paid	ME Median entry wage	S See annotated source	Y Yearly

Occupation/Type/Industry	Location	Per	Low	Mid	High	Source	Date
Sewer							
Hand	Boston-Cambridge-Newton NECTA, MA	Y	24090 FQ	30440 MW	42170 TQ	USBLS	5/15
Hand	Michigan	Y	19410 FQ	25650 MW	31240 TQ	USBLS	5/15
Hand	Grand Rapids-Wyoming MSA, MI	Y	20650 FQ	27660 MW	32870 TQ	USBLS	5/15
Hand	Minnesota	Y	20917 FQ	23580 MW	27832 TQ	MNBLS	1/16-3/16
Hand	Minneapolis-St. Paul-Bloomington MSA, MN-WI	Y	25210 FQ	27994 MW	30708 TQ	MNBLS	1/16-3/16
Hand	Kansas City MSA, MO-KS	Y	22430 FQ	25550 MW	33430 TQ	USBLS	5/15
Hand	Montana	Y	21530 FQ	23430 MW	26000 TQ	USBLS	5/15
Hand	Nebraska	Y	19100 FQ	21660 MW	24085 TQ	NEBLS	7/16-9/16
Hand	New Jersey	Y	20350 FQ	27440 MW	37370 TQ	USBLS	5/15
Hand	Camden PMSA, NJ	Y	19200 FQ	21830 MW	31520 TQ	USBLS	5/15
Hand	New Mexico	Y	22260 FQ	26010 MW	28900 TQ	USBLS	5/15
Hand	New York	Y	20040 AE	24870 MW	29870 AEX	NYBLS	1/16-3/16
Hand	Nassau County-Suffolk County PMSA, NY	Y	21670 FQ	25660 MW	37800 TQ	USBLS	5/15
Hand	New York-Jersey City-White Plains PMSA, NY-NJ	Y	19150 FQ	22790 MW	31810 TQ	USBLS	5/15
Hand	North Carolina	Y	19830 FQ	27010 MW	29790 TQ	USBLS	5/15
Hand	Charlotte-Concord-Gastonia MSA, NC-SC	Y	25780 FQ	27690 MW	29590 TQ	USBLS	5/15
Hand	Ohio	Y	18740 FQ	21330 MW	25540 TQ	USBLS	5/15
Hand	Oklahoma	Y	17460 FQ	19250 MW	24710 TQ	USBLS	5/15
Hand	Oregon	H	10.87 FQ	12.94 MW	15.68 TQ	ORBLS	2016
Hand	Pennsylvania	Y	23150 FQ	27380 MW	30980 TQ	USBLS	5/15
Hand	Rhode Island	Y	20700 FQ	22140 MW	23580 TQ	USBLS	5/15
Hand	Providence-Warwick MSA, RI-MA	Y	20800 FQ	22330 MW	23860 TQ	USBLS	5/15
Hand	Tennessee	Y	20570 FQ	22810 MW	25180 TQ	USBLS	5/15
Hand	Texas	Y	20080 FQ	24520 MW	28430 TQ	USBLS	5/15
Hand	Austin-Round Rock MSA, TX	Y	24980 FQ	27030 MW	29070 TQ	USBLS	5/15
Hand	Fort Worth-Arlington PMSA, TX	Y	19180 FQ	21870 MW	24940 TQ	USBLS	5/15
Hand	Houston-The Woodlands-Sugar Land MSA, TX	Y	20120 FQ	26050 MW	29220 TQ	USBLS	5/15
Hand	San Antonio-New Braunfels MSA, TX	Y	22050 FQ	24420 MW	27760 TQ	USBLS	5/15
Hand	Utah	Y	20970 FQ	26950 MW	32560 TQ	USBLS	5/15
Hand	Virginia	Y	20040 FQ	28350 MW	34190 TQ	USBLS	5/15
Hand	Washington	H	10.54 FQ	12.24 MW	15.26 TQ	WABLS	3/16
Hand	Puerto Rico	Y	17350 FQ	19120 MW	21810 TQ	USBLS	5/15
Hand	San Juan-Carolina-Caguas MSA, PR	Y	18770 FQ	20760 MW	22840 TQ	USBLS	5/15
Sewer Camera Truck Operator							
Public Works Department, Municipal Government	Antioch, CA	Y			56186 HI	CACIT	6/28/16
Sewer System Supervisor							
Municipal Government	Baxley, GA	Y	34900 LO		45891 HI	GACTY02	2016
Municipal Government	Pooler, GA	Y	47941 LO		71911 HI	GACTY02	2016
Sewing Machine Operator	Alabama	Y	17706 AE	22477 AW	24862 AEX	ALBLS	6/16
	Birmingham-Hoover MSA, AL	Y	22415 AE	26867 AW	29099 AEX	ALBLS	6/16
	Alaska	Y	32460 FQ	40710 MW	46290 TQ	USBLS	5/15
	Arizona	Y	19800 FQ	23400 MW	28950 TQ	USBLS	5/15
	Phoenix-Mesa-Scottsdale MSA, AZ	Y	20260 FQ	23850 MW	30160 TQ	USBLS	5/15
	Tucson MSA, AZ	Y	17810 FQ	18870 MW	21960 TQ	USBLS	5/15
	Arkansas	Y	18510 FQ	21870 MW	26310 TQ	USBLS	5/15
	Little Rock-North Little Rock-Conway MSA, AR	Y	18220 FQ	21520 MW	26770 TQ	USBLS	5/15
	California	H	9.50 FQ	9.80 MW	12.46 TQ	CABLS	1/16-3/16
	Anaheim-Santa Ana-Irvine PMSA, CA	H	9.56 FQ	10.47 MW	13.89 TQ	CABLS	1/16-3/16
	Los Angeles-Long Beach-Glendale PMSA, CA	H	9.47 FQ	9.70 MW	11.66 TQ	CABLS	1/16-3/16
	Oakland-Hayward-Berkeley PMSA, CA	H	9.49 FQ	10.99 MW	14.42 TQ	CABLS	1/16-3/16

AE Average entry wage	AWR Average wage range	H Hourly	LR Low end range	MTC Median total compensation	TCC Total cash compensation
AEX Average experienced wage	B Biweekly	HI Highest wage paid	M Monthly	MW Median wage paid	TQ Third quartile wage
ATC Average total compensation	D Daily	HR High end range	MCC Median cash compensation	MWR Median wage range	W Weekly
AW Average wage paid	FQ First quartile wage	LO Lowest wage paid	ME Median entry wage	S See annotated source	Y Yearly

Occupation/Type/Industry	Location	Per	Low	Mid	High	Source	Date
Sewing Machine Operator	Riverside-San Bernardino-Ontario MSA, CA	H	9.70 FQ	10.99 MW	12.73 TQ	CABLS	1/16-3/16
	Sacramento–Roseville–Arden-Arcade MSA, CA	H	10.53 FQ	12.14 MW	14.88 TQ	CABLS	1/16-3/16
	San Diego-Carlsbad MSA, CA	H	10.16 FQ	11.53 MW	13.81 TQ	CABLS	1/16-3/16
	San Francisco-Redwood City-South San Francisco PMSA, CA	H	11.16 FQ	12.41 MW	15.77 TQ	CABLS	1/16-3/16
	Colorado	Y	19070 FQ	22610 MW	29510 TQ	USBLS	5/15
	Denver-Aurora-Lakewood MSA, CO	Y	18920 FQ	21560 MW	27650 TQ	USBLS	5/15
	Connecticut	Y		28714 MW		CTBLS	1/16-3/16
	Bridgeport-Stamford-Norwalk MSA, CT	Y	24870 FQ	30090 MW	37270 TQ	USBLS	5/15
	Hartford-West Hartford-East Hartford MSA, CT	Y	24510 FQ	28590 MW	33990 TQ	USBLS	5/15
	Delaware	Y	24510 FQ	32800 MW	36460 TQ	USBLS	5/15
	Wilmington PMSA, DE-MD-NJ	Y	24170 FQ	31010 MW	35730 TQ	USBLS	5/15
	District of Columbia	Y	20000 FQ	27650 MW	36320 TQ	USBLS	5/15
	Washington-Arlington-Alexandria PMSA, DC-VA-MD-WV	Y	21670 FQ	25850 MW	33070 TQ	USBLS	5/15
	Florida	H	9.02 AE	10.79 MW	13.14 AEX	FLBLS	7/16-9/16
	Fort Lauderdale-Pompano Beach-Deerfield Beach PMSA, FL	H	9.07 AE	10.48 MW	12.82 AEX	FLBLS	7/16-9/16
	Miami-Miami Beach-Kendall PMSA, FL	H	8.95 AE	9.98 MW	11.77 AEX	FLBLS	7/16-9/16
	Orlando-Kissimmee-Sanford MSA, FL	H	9.28 AE	11.86 MW	14.85 AEX	FLBLS	7/16-9/16
	Tampa-St. Petersburg-Clearwater MSA, FL	H	9.00 AE	10.82 MW	12.55 AEX	FLBLS	7/16-9/16
	Georgia	Y	20050 FQ	26130 MW	31770 TQ	USBLS	5/15
	Atlanta-Sandy Springs-Roswell MSA, GA	Y	22270 FQ	27230 MW	31150 TQ	USBLS	5/15
	Augusta-Richmond County MSA, GA-SC	Y	17030 FQ	18570 MW	21190 TQ	USBLS	5/15
	Hawaii	Y	18630 FQ	23210 MW	29730 TQ	USBLS	5/15
	Urban Honolulu MSA, HI	Y	18540 FQ	22880 MW	29560 TQ	USBLS	5/15
	Idaho	Y	18020 FQ	20740 MW	23930 TQ	USBLS	5/15
	Boise City MSA, ID	Y	18030 FQ	20860 MW	23710 TQ	USBLS	5/15
	Illinois	Y	21480 FQ	24570 MW	30400 TQ	USBLS	5/15
	Chicago-Naperville-Arlington Heights PMSA, IL	Y	21780 FQ	24600 MW	30530 TQ	USBLS	5/15
	Lake County-Kenosha County PMSA, IL-WI	Y	22500 FQ	26310 MW	33980 TQ	USBLS	5/15
	Indiana	Y	20750 FQ	24210 MW	29270 TQ	USBLS	5/15
	Gary PMSA, IN	Y	18440 FQ	21160 MW	23850 TQ	USBLS	5/15
	Indianapolis-Carmel-Anderson MSA, IN	Y	21020 FQ	24820 MW	31000 TQ	USBLS	5/15
	Iowa	Y	21240 FQ	25200 MW	30210 TQ	USBLS	5/15
	Des Moines-West Des Moines MSA, IA	Y	23000 FQ	26620 MW	29960 TQ	USBLS	5/15
	Kansas	Y	20270 FQ	25230 MW	31500 TQ	USBLS	5/15
	Wichita MSA, KS	Y	17900 FQ	21440 MW	27570 TQ	USBLS	5/15
	Kentucky	Y	17920 FQ	20710 MW	25270 TQ	USBLS	5/15
	Louisville-Jefferson County MSA, KY-IN	Y	20130 FQ	26360 MW	33330 TQ	USBLS	5/15
	Louisiana	Y	18220 FQ	22430 MW	27710 TQ	USBLS	5/15
	Baton Rouge MSA, LA	Y	21300 FQ	28090 MW	34980 TQ	USBLS	5/15
	New Orleans-Metairie MSA, LA	Y	18250 FQ	21340 MW	24280 TQ	USBLS	5/15
	Maine	Y	21220 FQ	26750 MW	30300 TQ	USBLS	5/15
	Portland-South Portland MSA, ME	Y	26120 FQ	30050 MW	36050 TQ	USBLS	5/15
	Maryland	Y	18111 AE	25012 MW	28463 AEX	MDBLS	4/16
	Baltimore-Columbia-Towson MSA, MD	Y	18660 FQ	21920 MW	28420 TQ	USBLS	5/15
	Salisbury MSA, MD-DE	Y	18160 FQ	19940 MW	23530 TQ	USBLS	5/15
	Massachusetts	Y	21640 FQ	27100 MW	34080 TQ	USBLS	5/15

AE	Average entry wage	AWR	Average wage range	H	Hourly	LR	Low end range	MTC	Median total compensation	TCC	Total cash compensation
AEX	Average experienced wage	B	Biweekly	HI	Highest wage paid	M	Monthly	MW	Median wage paid	TQ	Third quartile wage
ATC	Average total compensation	D	Daily	HR	High end range	MCC	Median cash compensation	MWR	Median wage range	W	Weekly
AW	Average wage paid	FQ	First quartile wage	LO	Lowest wage paid	ME	Median entry wage	S	See annotated source	Y	Yearly

Sewing Machine Operator

Occupation/Type/Industry	Location	Per	Low	Mid	High	Source	Date
Sewing Machine Operator	Boston-Cambridge-Newton NECTA, MA	Y	20030 FQ	26790 MW	31170 TQ	USBLS	5/15
	Worcester MSA, MA-CT	Y	20590 FQ	23630 MW	28090 TQ	USBLS	5/15
	Michigan	Y	19440 FQ	23150 MW	29680 TQ	USBLS	5/15
	Detroit-Dearborn-Livonia PMSA, MI	Y	19450 FQ	24260 MW	30590 TQ	USBLS	5/15
	Grand Rapids-Wyoming MSA, MI	Y	20870 FQ	23540 MW	29470 TQ	USBLS	5/15
	Minnesota	Y	23266 FQ	27832 MW	33279 TQ	MNBLS	1/16-3/16
	Minneapolis-St. Paul-Bloomington MSA, MN-WI	Y	25595 FQ	29756 MW	35831 TQ	MNBLS	1/16-3/16
	Mississippi	Y	19320 FQ	25560 MW	30120 TQ	USBLS	5/15
	Missouri	Y	17930 FQ	20380 MW	25000 TQ	USBLS	5/15
	Kansas City MSA, MO-KS	Y	19710 FQ	24260 MW	35710 TQ	USBLS	5/15
	St. Louis MSA, MO-IL	Y	19500 FQ	24080 MW	29810 TQ	USBLS	5/15
	Montana	Y	21590 FQ	24760 MW	28700 TQ	USBLS	5/15
	Billings MSA, MT	Y	19520 FQ	22440 MW	25670 TQ	USBLS	5/15
	Nebraska	Y	20175 FQ	24660 MW	29570 TQ	NEBLS	7/16-9/16
	Omaha-Council Bluffs MSA, NE-IA	Y	23230 FQ	27315 MW	30630 TQ	NEBLS	7/16-9/16
	Nevada	Y	22590 FQ	28260 MW	35940 TQ	USBLS	5/15
	Las Vegas-Henderson-Paradise MSA, NV	Y	23010 FQ	29250 MW	37240 TQ	USBLS	5/15
	New Hampshire	H	10.60 AE	14.15 MW	16.27 AEX	NHBLS	6/16
	Manchester NECTA, NH	H	12.66 AE	15.82 MW	17.23 AEX	NHBLS	6/16
	Nashua NECTA, NH-MA	Y	25760 FQ	28090 MW	30420 TQ	USBLS	5/15
	New Jersey	Y	19690 FQ	23510 MW	28770 TQ	USBLS	5/15
	Camden PMSA, NJ	Y	20340 FQ	24740 MW	30460 TQ	USBLS	5/15
	Newark PMSA, NJ-PA	Y	19760 FQ	23780 MW	29190 TQ	USBLS	5/15
	Trenton MSA, NJ	Y	21150 FQ	26450 MW	41100 TQ	USBLS	5/15
	New Mexico	Y	18940 FQ	21090 MW	23490 TQ	USBLS	5/15
	Albuquerque MSA, NM	Y	20860 FQ	22850 MW	25550 TQ	USBLS	5/15
	New York	Y	19380 AE	20650 MW	28740 AEX	NYBLS	1/16-3/16
	Buffalo-Cheektowaga-Niagara Falls MSA, NY	Y	19750 FQ	26920 MW	35300 TQ	USBLS	5/15
	Nassau County-Suffolk County PMSA, NY	Y	21350 FQ	25450 MW	30940 TQ	USBLS	5/15
	New York-Jersey City-White Plains PMSA, NY-NJ	Y	18960 FQ	19970 MW	27630 TQ	USBLS	5/15
	Rochester MSA, NY	Y	21690 FQ	24060 MW	28220 TQ	USBLS	5/15
	North Carolina	Y	19190 FQ	23100 MW	29330 TQ	USBLS	5/15
	Charlotte-Concord-Gastonia MSA, NC-SC	Y	19790 FQ	23840 MW	28930 TQ	USBLS	5/15
	Raleigh MSA, NC	Y	18890 FQ	23760 MW	31890 TQ	USBLS	5/15
	North Dakota	Y	23280 FQ	28780 MW	34810 TQ	USBLS	5/15
	Fargo MSA, ND-MN	Y	32310 FQ	34740 MW	37020 TQ	USBLS	5/15
	Ohio	Y	21170 FQ	24550 MW	29450 TQ	USBLS	5/15
	Cincinnati MSA, OH-KY-IN	Y	22160 FQ	26250 MW	30590 TQ	USBLS	5/15
	Cleveland-Elyria MSA, OH	Y	21050 FQ	22970 MW	24890 TQ	USBLS	5/15
	Columbus MSA, OH	Y	23090 FQ	27340 MW	31500 TQ	USBLS	5/15
	Oklahoma	Y	19100 FQ	22520 MW	26890 TQ	USBLS	5/15
	Oklahoma City MSA, OK	Y	20100 FQ	24330 MW	28850 TQ	USBLS	5/15
	Tulsa MSA, OK	Y	21220 FQ	23310 MW	26210 TQ	USBLS	5/15
	Oregon	H	10.59 FQ	11.99 MW	16.33 TQ	ORBLS	2016
	Portland-Vancouver-Hillsboro MSA, OR-WA	Y	21370 FQ	23880 MW	33140 TQ	USBLS	5/15
	Pennsylvania	Y	19570 FQ	22970 MW	27720 TQ	USBLS	5/15
	Allentown-Bethlehem-Easton MSA, PA-NJ	Y	20590 FQ	22990 MW	26160 TQ	USBLS	5/15
	Harrisburg-Carlisle MSA, PA	Y	23990 FQ	29710 MW	36690 TQ	USBLS	5/15
	Montgomery County-Bucks County-Chester County PMSA, PA	Y	19540 FQ	22700 MW	27360 TQ	USBLS	5/15
	Philadelphia PMSA, PA	Y	17870 FQ	20410 MW	26130 TQ	USBLS	5/15
	Pittsburgh MSA, PA	Y	21010 FQ	24730 MW	29060 TQ	USBLS	5/15
	Rhode Island	Y	19650 FQ	26280 MW	32690 TQ	USBLS	5/15
	Providence-Warwick MSA, RI-MA	Y	20160 FQ	25060 MW	32920 TQ	USBLS	5/15
	South Carolina	Y	17950 FQ	21050 MW	24790 TQ	USBLS	5/15
	Charleston-North Charleston MSA, SC	Y	18550 FQ	22070 MW	25620 TQ	USBLS	5/15
	Columbia MSA, SC	Y	26480 FQ	32900 MW	36620 TQ	USBLS	5/15

AE	Average entry wage	AWR	Average wage range	H	Hourly	LR	Low end range	MTC	Median total compensation	TCC	Total cash compensation
AEX	Average experienced wage	B	Biweekly	HI	Highest wage paid	M	Monthly	MW	Median wage paid	TQ	Third quartile wage
ATC	Average total compensation	D	Daily	HR	High end range	MCC	Median cash compensation	MWR	Median wage range	W	Weekly
AW	Average wage paid	FQ	First quartile wage	LO	Lowest wage paid	ME	Median entry wage	S	See annotated source	Y	Yearly

Occupation/Type/Industry	Location	Per	Low	Mid	High	Source	Date
Sewing Machine Operator	Greenville-Anderson-Mauldin						
	MSA, SC	Y	17820 FQ	20550 MW	23580 TQ	USBLS	5/15
	South Dakota	Y	18980 FQ	21270 MW	26280 TQ	USBLS	5/15
	Sioux Falls MSA, SD	Y	23060 FQ	26030 MW	29200 TQ	USBLS	5/15
	Tennessee	Y	18120 FQ	21280 MW	26830 TQ	USBLS	5/15
	Knoxville MSA, TN	Y	18470 FQ	22440 MW	28320 TQ	USBLS	5/15
	Memphis MSA, TN-MS-AR	Y	19970 FQ	22200 MW	24360 TQ	USBLS	5/15
	Nashville-Davidson–						
	Murfreesboro–Franklin						
	MSA, TN	Y	18830 FQ	22380 MW	28060 TQ	USBLS	5/15
	Texas	Y	18320 FQ	21770 MW	26690 TQ	USBLS	5/15
	Austin-Round Rock MSA, TX	Y	18100 FQ	21700 MW	27000 TQ	USBLS	5/15
	Dallas-Plano-Irving PMSA, TX	Y	18070 FQ	21080 MW	25220 TQ	USBLS	5/15
	Fort Worth-Arlington PMSA,						
	TX	Y	17590 FQ	19870 MW	24100 TQ	USBLS	5/15
	Houston-The Woodlands-						
	Sugar Land MSA, TX	Y	20570 FQ	23240 MW	28230 TQ	USBLS	5/15
	San Antonio-New Braunfels						
	MSA, TX	Y	25910 FQ	28410 MW	30920 TQ	USBLS	5/15
	Utah	Y	18910 FQ	22570 MW	27890 TQ	USBLS	5/15
	Ogden-Clearfield MSA, UT	Y	20360 FQ	23200 MW	27030 TQ	USBLS	5/15
	Provo-Orem MSA, UT	Y	18120 FQ	21080 MW	23810 TQ	USBLS	5/15
	Salt Lake City MSA, UT	Y	19370 FQ	23500 MW	31380 TQ	USBLS	5/15
	Vermont	Y	20550 FQ	23570 MW	27620 TQ	USBLS	5/15
	Burlington-South Burlington						
	MSA, VT	Y	23100 FQ	27470 MW	31750 TQ	USBLS	5/15
	Virginia	Y	19020 FQ	22340 MW	26800 TQ	USBLS	5/15
	Richmond MSA, VA	Y	20860 FQ	23720 MW	28070 TQ	USBLS	5/15
	Virginia Beach-Norfolk-						
	Newport News MSA, VA-NC	Y	19590 FQ	22310 MW	25060 TQ	USBLS	5/15
	Washington	H	11.65 FQ	13.95 MW	17.06 TQ	WABLS	3/16
	Seattle-Bellevue-Everett						
	PMSA, WA	H	11.71 FQ	13.92 MW	16.94 TQ	WABLS	3/16
	Tacoma-Lakewood PMSA, WA	H	11.19 FQ	13.18 MW	17.25 TQ	WABLS	3/16
	West Virginia	Y	18810 FQ	21610 MW	26490 TQ	USBLS	5/15
	Wisconsin	Y	22050 FQ	26260 MW	30690 TQ	USBLS	5/15
	Madison MSA, WI	Y	23590 FQ	27780 MW	32390 TQ	USBLS	5/15
	Milwaukee-Waukesha-West						
	Allis MSA, WI	Y	22530 FQ	25550 MW	30420 TQ	USBLS	5/15
	Wyoming	Y	21940 FQ	26880 MW	30620 TQ	USBLS	5/15
	Puerto Rico	Y	16530 FQ	17600 MW	18680 TQ	USBLS	5/15
	San Juan-Carolina-Caguas						
	MSA, PR	Y	16760 FQ	17870 MW	18970 TQ	USBLS	5/15
Sex Registrant Specialist							
Police Department, Municipal Government	Oxnard, CA	Y			36284 HI	CACIT	6/28/16
Sexual Assault Safety Program Coordinator							
Michigan State University	East Lansing, MI	Y			60177 HI	MSUSAL	10/1/14-9/30/15
Shampooer	Alabama	Y	17544 AE	18564 AW	19079 AEX	ALBLS	6/16
	California	H	9.59 FQ	10.47 MW	12.06 TQ	CABLS	1/16-3/16
	Los Angeles-Long Beach-						
	Glendale PMSA, CA	H	9.62 FQ	10.68 MW	12.44 TQ	CABLS	1/16-3/16
	Connecticut	Y		20140 MW		CTBLS	1/16-3/16
	Bridgeport-Stamford-Norwalk						
	MSA, CT	Y	20750 FQ	23560 MW	27190 TQ	USBLS	5/15
	Delaware	Y	17370 FQ	18350 MW	19350 TQ	USBLS	5/15
	Wilmington PMSA, DE-MD-						
	NJ	Y	17360 FQ	18260 MW	19140 TQ	USBLS	5/15
	District of Columbia	Y	19920 FQ	19940 MW	23090 TQ	USBLS	5/15
	Washington-Arlington-						
	Alexandria PMSA, DC-VA-						
	MD-WV	Y	17630 FQ	19210 MW	21310 TQ	USBLS	5/15
	Florida	H	9.00 AE	9.93 MW	10.94 AEX	FLBLS	7/16-9/16
	Fort Lauderdale-Pompano						
	Beach-Deerfield Beach						
	PMSA, FL	H	9.05 AE	9.73 MW	11.64 AEX	FLBLS	7/16-9/16
	Tampa-St. Petersburg-						
	Clearwater MSA, FL	H	9.77 AE	10.88 MW	11.45 AEX	FLBLS	7/16-9/16
	Georgia	Y	17320 FQ	19010 MW	21220 TQ	USBLS	5/15

AE	Average entry wage	AWR	Average wage range	H	Hourly	LR	Low end range	MTC	Median total compensation	TCC Total cash compensation
AEX	Average experienced wage	B	Biweekly	HI	Highest wage paid	M	Monthly	MCC	Median cash compensation	TQ Third quartile wage
ATC	Average total compensation	D	Daily	HR	High end range	MW	Median wage paid	ME	Median entry wage	W Weekly
AW	Average wage paid	FQ	First quartile wage	LO	Lowest wage paid	ME	Median entry wage	S	See annotated source	Y Yearly

Occupation/Type/Industry	Location	Per	Low	Mid	High	Source	Date
Shampooer	Atlanta-Sandy Springs- Roswell MSA, GA	Y	17400 FQ	19150 MW	21440 TQ	USBLS	5/15
	Hawaii	Y	17510 FQ	18900 MW	22030 TQ	USBLS	5/15
	Urban Honolulu MSA, HI	Y	17510 FQ	18900 MW	22030 TQ	USBLS	5/15
	Illinois	Y	18310 FQ	19010 MW	19830 TQ	USBLS	5/15
	Chicago-Naperville-Arlington Heights PMSA, IL	Y	18280 FQ	18940 MW	19650 TQ	USBLS	5/15
	Lake County-Kenosha County PMSA, IL-WI	Y	18410 FQ	19370 MW	23590 TQ	USBLS	5/15
	Indiana	Y	16640 FQ	17740 MW	18840 TQ	USBLS	5/15
	Louisiana	Y	16790 FQ	18120 MW	19500 TQ	USBLS	5/15
	Maryland	Y	18009 AE	19269 MW	19899 AEX	MDBLS	4/16
	Baltimore-Columbia-Towson MSA, MD	Y	17750 FQ	18860 MW	21280 TQ	USBLS	5/15
	Salisbury MSA, MD-DE	Y	17620 FQ	18750 MW	20510 TQ	USBLS	5/15
	Massachusetts	Y	19240 FQ	20450 MW	23210 TQ	USBLS	5/15
	Boston-Cambridge-Newton NECTA, MA	Y	19330 FQ	20670 MW	23270 TQ	USBLS	5/15
	Michigan	Y	18450 FQ	19870 MW	23120 TQ	USBLS	5/15
	Detroit-Dearborn-Livonia PMSA, MI	Y	17960 FQ	18850 MW	19730 TQ	USBLS	5/15
	St. Louis MSA, MO-IL	Y	17320 FQ	18270 MW	19080 TQ	USBLS	5/15
	New Jersey	Y	18230 FQ	18950 MW	19970 TQ	USBLS	5/15
	Camden PMSA, NJ	Y	18060 FQ	18630 MW	19200 TQ	USBLS	5/15
	Newark PMSA, NJ-PA	Y	18080 FQ	18670 MW	19260 TQ	USBLS	5/15
	New York	Y	19240 AE	20130 MW	22730 AEX	NYBLS	1/16-3/16
	Buffalo-Cheektowaga-Niagara Falls MSA, NY	Y	18710 FQ	19220 MW	19730 TQ	USBLS	5/15
	Nassau County-Suffolk County PMSA, NY	Y	18730 FQ	19270 MW	21770 TQ	USBLS	5/15
	New York-Jersey City-White Plains PMSA, NY-NJ	Y	18720 FQ	19640 MW	22620 TQ	USBLS	5/15
	Rochester MSA, NY	Y	18610 FQ	19010 MW	19410 TQ	USBLS	5/15
	North Carolina	Y	16670 FQ	17900 MW	19140 TQ	USBLS	5/15
	Charlotte-Concord-Gastonia MSA, NC-SC	Y	16600 FQ	17790 MW	18980 TQ	USBLS	5/15
	Ohio	Y	17580 FQ	18300 MW	19020 TQ	USBLS	5/15
	Pennsylvania	Y	17020 FQ	18560 MW	20600 TQ	USBLS	5/15
	Allentown-Bethlehem-Easton MSA, PA-NJ	Y	18160 FQ	20380 MW	22440 TQ	USBLS	5/15
	Montgomery County-Bucks County-Chester County PMSA, PA	Y	17440 FQ	19380 MW	22180 TQ	USBLS	5/15
	Philadelphia PMSA, PA	Y	16820 FQ	18030 MW	19230 TQ	USBLS	5/15
	Pittsburgh MSA, PA	Y	16530 FQ	17600 MW	18670 TQ	USBLS	5/15
	Tennessee	Y	23070 FQ	31110 MW	39840 TQ	USBLS	5/15
	Memphis MSA, TN-MS-AR	Y	27450 FQ	32730 MW	39960 TQ	USBLS	5/15
	Nashville-Davidson– Murfreesboro–Franklin MSA, TN	Y	21120 FQ	33630 MW	43930 TQ	USBLS	5/15
	Texas	Y	17160 FQ	18930 MW	22650 TQ	USBLS	5/15
	Fort Worth-Arlington PMSA, TX	Y	17920 FQ	24810 MW	28000 TQ	USBLS	5/15
	Houston-The Woodlands- Sugar Land MSA, TX	Y	16990 FQ	18580 MW	21200 TQ	USBLS	5/15
	San Antonio-New Braunfels MSA, TX	Y	19570 FQ	21260 MW	22970 TQ	USBLS	5/15
	Virginia	Y	17170 FQ	18830 MW	21730 TQ	USBLS	5/15
	Richmond MSA, VA	Y	17140 FQ	18790 MW	21740 TQ	USBLS	5/15
	Virginia Beach-Norfolk- Newport News MSA, VA-NC	Y	17020 FQ	18570 MW	20970 TQ	USBLS	5/15
	Washington	H	10.33 FQ	11.02 MW	11.72 TQ	WABLS	3/16
	Seattle-Bellevue-Everett PMSA, WA	H	10.33 FQ	11.02 MW	11.72 TQ	WABLS	3/16
	Wisconsin	Y	16450 FQ	17510 MW	18570 TQ	USBLS	5/15
	Milwaukee-Waukesha-West Allis MSA, WI	Y	16450 FQ	17510 MW	18570 TQ	USBLS	5/15
Sheet Metal Worker	Alabama	Y	28392 AE	40417 AW	46425 AEX	ALBLS	6/16
	Birmingham-Hoover MSA, AL	Y	32291 AE	39749 AW	43472 AEX	ALBLS	6/16
	Alaska	Y	54690 FQ	74790 MW	90330 TQ	USBLS	5/15
	Anchorage MSA, AK	Y	57060 FQ	80450 MW	91960 TQ	USBLS	5/15

AE Average entry wage	**AWR** Average wage range	**H** Hourly	**LR** Low end range	**MTC** Median total compensation	**TCC** Total cash compensation
AEX Average experienced wage	**B** Biweekly	**HI** Highest wage paid	**M** Monthly	**MW** Median wage paid	**TQ** Third quartile wage
ATC Average total compensation	**D** Daily	**HR** High end range	**MCC** Median cash compensation	**MWR** Median wage range	**W** Weekly
AW Average wage paid	**FQ** First quartile wage	**LO** Lowest wage paid	**ME** Median entry wage	**S** See annotated source	**Y** Yearly

Occupation/Type/Industry	Location	Per	Low	Mid	High	Source	Date
Sheet Metal Worker	Arizona	Y	34330 FQ	43310 MW	54640 TQ	USBLS	5/15
	Phoenix-Mesa-Scottsdale MSA, AZ	Y	34930 FQ	43360 MW	54190 TQ	USBLS	5/15
	Tucson MSA, AZ	Y	33860 FQ	49270 MW	57440 TQ	USBLS	5/15
	Arkansas	Y	27440 FQ	34110 MW	42160 TQ	USBLS	5/15
	Little Rock-North Little Rock-Conway MSA, AR	Y	28520 FQ	35650 MW	43760 TQ	USBLS	5/15
	California	H	19.09 FQ	27.46 MW	38.43 TQ	CABLS	1/16-3/16
	Anaheim-Santa Ana-Irvine PMSA, CA	H	16.59 FQ	23.49 MW	34.46 TQ	CABLS	1/16-3/16
	Los Angeles-Long Beach-Glendale PMSA, CA	H	17.42 FQ	28.80 MW	42.44 TQ	CABLS	1/16-3/16
	Oakland-Hayward-Berkeley PMSA, CA	H	20.45 FQ	26.68 MW	35.08 TQ	CABLS	1/16-3/16
	Riverside-San Bernardino-Ontario MSA, CA	H	17.47 FQ	26.62 MW	34.66 TQ	CABLS	1/16-3/16
	Sacramento–Roseville–Arden-Arcade MSA, CA	H	23.90 FQ	33.00 MW	42.12 TQ	CABLS	1/16-3/16
	San Diego-Carlsbad MSA, CA	H	19.92 FQ	27.04 MW	32.41 TQ	CABLS	1/16-3/16
	San Francisco-Redwood City-South San Francisco PMSA, CA	H	25.19 FQ	36.99 MW	47.50 TQ	CABLS	1/16-3/16
	Colorado	Y	34010 FQ	43520 MW	53630 TQ	USBLS	5/15
	Denver-Aurora-Lakewood MSA, CO	Y	38380 FQ	45200 MW	53860 TQ	USBLS	5/15
	Connecticut	Y		52151 MW		CTBLS	1/16-3/16
	Bridgeport-Stamford-Norwalk MSA, CT	Y	38030 FQ	47270 MW	56140 TQ	USBLS	5/15
	Hartford-West Hartford-East Hartford MSA, CT	Y	43190 FQ	53340 MW	60350 TQ	USBLS	5/15
	Delaware	Y	39890 FQ	52620 MW	61260 TQ	USBLS	5/15
	Wilmington PMSA, DE-MD-NJ	Y	37820 FQ	51940 MW	63070 TQ	USBLS	5/15
	District of Columbia	Y	53590 FQ	57550 MW	61580 TQ	USBLS	5/15
	Washington-Arlington-Alexandria PMSA, DC-VA-MD-WV	Y	38350 FQ	49170 MW	63500 TQ	USBLS	5/15
	Florida	H	12.53 AE	17.31 MW	20.40 AEX	FLBLS	7/16-9/16
	Fort Lauderdale-Pompano Beach-Deerfield Beach PMSA, FL	H	13.34 AE	16.46 MW	19.66 AEX	FLBLS	7/16-9/16
	Miami-Miami Beach-Kendall PMSA, FL	H	12.34 AE	17.09 MW	20.04 AEX	FLBLS	7/16-9/16
	Orlando-Kissimmee-Sanford MSA, FL	H	13.57 AE	18.11 MW	20.33 AEX	FLBLS	7/16-9/16
	Tampa-St. Petersburg-Clearwater MSA, FL	H	11.86 AE	15.10 MW	17.69 AEX	FLBLS	7/16-9/16
	Georgia	Y	30900 FQ	42720 MW	54630 TQ	USBLS	5/15
	Atlanta-Sandy Springs-Roswell MSA, GA	Y	27790 FQ	36270 MW	52530 TQ	USBLS	5/15
	Augusta-Richmond County MSA, GA-SC	Y	36840 FQ	51110 MW	59180 TQ	USBLS	5/15
	Hawaii	Y	48430 FQ	68700 MW	81780 TQ	USBLS	5/15
	Urban Honolulu MSA, HI	Y	48680 FQ	68610 MW	82070 TQ	USBLS	5/15
	Idaho	Y	30780 FQ	47070 MW	55920 TQ	USBLS	5/15
	Boise City MSA, ID	Y	30020 FQ	49540 MW	56260 TQ	USBLS	5/15
	Illinois	Y	54860 FQ	77340 MW	91120 TQ	USBLS	5/15
	Chicago-Naperville-Arlington Heights PMSA, IL	Y	65480 FQ	86490 MW	94890 TQ	USBLS	5/15
	Lake County-Kenosha County PMSA, IL-WI	Y	53490 FQ	67310 MW	79490 TQ	USBLS	5/15
	Indiana	Y	31500 FQ	47980 MW	66900 TQ	USBLS	5/15
	Gary PMSA, IN	Y	34020 FQ	52450 MW	87950 TQ	USBLS	5/15
	Indianapolis-Carmel-Anderson MSA, IN	Y	30820 FQ	46900 MW	63650 TQ	USBLS	5/15
	Iowa	Y	35110 FQ	47910 MW	64060 TQ	USBLS	5/15
	Des Moines-West Des Moines MSA, IA	Y	39010 FQ	57110 MW	68100 TQ	USBLS	5/15
	Kansas	Y	31300 FQ	39090 MW	62210 TQ	USBLS	5/15
	Wichita MSA, KS	Y	28290 FQ	34920 MW	44880 TQ	USBLS	5/15
	Kentucky	Y	29350 FQ	39690 MW	53940 TQ	USBLS	5/15

AE Average entry wage	**AWR** Average wage range	**H** Hourly	**LR** Low end range	**MTC** Median total compensation	**TCC** Total cash compensation
AEX Average experienced wage	**B** Biweekly	**HI** Highest wage paid	**M** Monthly	**MW** Median wage paid	**TQ** Third quartile wage
ATC Average total compensation	**D** Daily	**HR** High end range	**MCC** Median cash compensation	**MWR** Median wage range	**W** Weekly
AW Average wage paid	**FQ** First quartile wage	**LO** Lowest wage paid	**ME** Median entry wage	**S** See annotated source	**Y** Yearly

Occupation/Type/Industry	Location	Per	Low	Mid	High	Source	Date
Sheet Metal Worker	Louisville-Jefferson County MSA, KY-IN	Y	39330 FQ	46050 MW	59630 TQ	USBLS	5/15
	Louisiana	Y	31990 FQ	39410 MW	51630 TQ	USBLS	5/15
	Baton Rouge MSA, LA	Y	31000 FQ	38980 MW	48790 TQ	USBLS	5/15
	New Orleans-Metairie MSA, LA	Y	34340 FQ	43890 MW	56210 TQ	USBLS	5/15
	Maine	Y	37720 FQ	48220 MW	55960 TQ	USBLS	5/15
	Portland-South Portland MSA, ME	Y	36290 FQ	43580 MW	53400 TQ	USBLS	5/15
	Maryland	Y	32909 AE	49323 MW	57530 AEX	MDBLS	4/16
	Baltimore-Columbia-Towson MSA, MD	Y	41400 FQ	49770 MW	62450 TQ	USBLS	5/15
	Salisbury MSA, MD-DE	Y	35470 FQ	40690 MW	47010 TQ	USBLS	5/15
	Massachusetts	Y	38000 FQ	54290 MW	78250 TQ	USBLS	5/15
	Boston-Cambridge-Newton NECTA, MA	Y	45500 FQ	75710 MW	90320 TQ	USBLS	5/15
	Worcester MSA, MA-CT	Y	40300 FQ	48620 MW	61530 TQ	USBLS	5/15
	Michigan	Y	37970 FQ	50550 MW	60130 TQ	USBLS	5/15
	Detroit-Dearborn-Livonia PMSA, MI	Y	42170 FQ	49130 MW	58280 TQ	USBLS	5/15
	Grand Rapids-Wyoming MSA, MI	Y	31950 FQ	40840 MW	56650 TQ	USBLS	5/15
	Minnesota	Y	47212 FQ	63225 MW	78824 TQ	MNBLS	1/16-3/16
	Minneapolis-St. Paul-Bloomington MSA, MN-WI	Y	55203 FQ	70641 MW	86130 TQ	MNBLS	1/16-3/16
	Mississippi	Y	26810 FQ	34470 MW	46600 TQ	USBLS	5/15
	Jackson MSA, MS	Y	28280 FQ	35400 MW	44390 TQ	USBLS	5/15
	Missouri	Y	37080 FQ	55100 MW	81080 TQ	USBLS	5/15
	Kansas City MSA, MO-KS	Y	39180 FQ	73350 MW	90620 TQ	USBLS	5/15
	St. Louis MSA, MO-IL	Y	41360 FQ	62610 MW	82510 TQ	USBLS	5/15
	Montana	Y	39770 FQ	53170 MW	60660 TQ	USBLS	5/15
	Billings MSA, MT	Y	49820 FQ	56820 MW	62980 TQ	USBLS	5/15
	Nebraska	Y	31170 FQ	41420 MW	61975 TQ	NEBLS	7/16-9/16
	Omaha-Council Bluffs MSA, NE-IA	Y	39685 FQ	55430 MW	70370 TQ	NEBLS	7/16-9/16
	Nevada	Y	28900 FQ	43900 MW	59560 TQ	USBLS	5/15
	Las Vegas-Henderson-Paradise MSA, NV	Y	27420 FQ	43170 MW	62660 TQ	USBLS	5/15
	New Hampshire	H	14.79 AE	21.31 MW	24.80 AEX	NHBLS	6/16
	Manchester NECTA, NH	H	15.13 AE	23.30 MW	26.65 AEX	NHBLS	6/16
	Nashua NECTA, NH-MA	Y	31450 FQ	41160 MW	52520 TQ	USBLS	5/15
	New Jersey	Y	34450 FQ	57580 MW	89100 TQ	USBLS	5/15
	Camden PMSA, NJ	Y	33810 FQ	53590 MW	87070 TQ	USBLS	5/15
	Newark PMSA, NJ-PA	Y	30880 FQ	55180 MW	90350 TQ	USBLS	5/15
	Trenton MSA, NJ	Y	54830 FQ	82110 MW	90570 TQ	USBLS	5/15
	New Mexico	Y	32810 FQ	42310 MW	57810 TQ	USBLS	5/15
	Albuquerque MSA, NM	Y	40180 FQ	52350 MW	60560 TQ	USBLS	5/15
	New York	Y	36980 AE	63260 MW	88090 AEX	NYBLS	1/16-3/16
	Buffalo-Cheektowaga-Niagara Falls MSA, NY	Y	36670 FQ	50960 MW	70190 TQ	USBLS	5/15
	Nassau County-Suffolk County PMSA, NY	Y	42340 FQ	74850 MW	112240 TQ	USBLS	5/15
	New York-Jersey City-White Plains PMSA, NY-NJ	Y	51050 FQ	74130 MW	103190 TQ	USBLS	5/15
	Rochester MSA, NY	Y	29310 FQ	43780 MW	62350 TQ	USBLS	5/15
	North Carolina	Y	27320 FQ	35410 MW	44810 TQ	USBLS	5/15
	Charlotte-Concord-Gastonia MSA, NC-SC	Y	25860 FQ	33930 MW	40500 TQ	USBLS	5/15
	Raleigh MSA, NC	Y	31530 FQ	35920 MW	42260 TQ	USBLS	5/15
	North Dakota	Y	29780 FQ	42180 MW	52240 TQ	USBLS	5/15
	Fargo MSA, ND-MN	Y	29590 FQ	44560 MW	53040 TQ	USBLS	5/15
	Ohio	Y	31900 FQ	44940 MW	59440 TQ	USBLS	5/15
	Cincinnati MSA, OH-KY-IN	Y	30790 FQ	41900 MW	49880 TQ	USBLS	5/15
	Cleveland-Elyria MSA, OH	Y	32990 FQ	49370 MW	68280 TQ	USBLS	5/15
	Columbus MSA, OH	Y	37440 FQ	52400 MW	58720 TQ	USBLS	5/15
	Oklahoma	Y	33960 FQ	49920 MW	55860 TQ	USBLS	5/15
	Oklahoma City MSA, OK	Y	45230 FQ	53720 MW	55860 TQ	USBLS	5/15
	Tulsa MSA, OK	Y	33840 FQ	44910 MW	55220 TQ	USBLS	5/15
	Oregon	H	17.52 FQ	23.00 MW	32.40 TQ	ORBLS	2016
	Portland-Vancouver-Hillsboro MSA, OR-WA	Y	35960 FQ	47230 MW	67780 TQ	USBLS	5/15
	Pennsylvania	Y	37090 FQ	52060 MW	69870 TQ	USBLS	5/15

AE	Average entry wage	AWR	Average wage range	H	Hourly	LR	Low end range	MTC	Median total compensation	TCC	Total cash compensation
AEX	Average experienced wage	B	Biweekly	HI	Highest wage paid	M	Monthly	MW	Median wage paid	TQ	Third quartile wage
ATC	Average total compensation	D	Daily	HR	High end range	MCC	Median cash compensation	MWR	Median wage range	W	Weekly
AW	Average wage paid	FQ	First quartile wage	LO	Lowest wage paid	ME	Median entry wage	S	See annotated source	Y	Yearly

Occupation/Type/Industry	Location	Per	Low	Mid	High	Source	Date
Sheet Metal Worker	Allentown-Bethlehem-Easton						
	MSA, PA-NJ	Y	49450 FQ	69750 MW	76320 TQ	USBLS	5/15
	Harrisburg-Carlisle MSA, PA	Y	39110 FQ	45950 MW	53300 TQ	USBLS	5/15
	Montgomery County-Bucks County-Chester County						
	PMSA, PA	Y	30810 FQ	39320 MW	78080 TQ	USBLS	5/15
	Philadelphia PMSA, PA	Y	34450 FQ	57150 MW	83590 TQ	USBLS	5/15
	Pittsburgh MSA, PA	Y	51460 FQ	68990 MW	75590 TQ	USBLS	5/15
	Rhode Island	Y	35230 FQ	43750 MW	54750 TQ	USBLS	5/15
	Providence-Warwick MSA, RI-MA	Y	35060 FQ	43630 MW	54850 TQ	USBLS	5/15
	South Carolina	Y	25670 FQ	35130 MW	43790 TQ	USBLS	5/15
	Charleston-North Charleston MSA, SC	Y	28390 FQ	35070 MW	42060 TQ	USBLS	5/15
	Columbia MSA, SC	Y	29400 FQ	34830 MW	40830 TQ	USBLS	5/15
	Greenville-Anderson-Mauldin MSA, SC	Y	21250 FQ	23380 MW	35160 TQ	USBLS	5/15
	South Dakota	Y	31140 FQ	36250 MW	46550 TQ	USBLS	5/15
	Sioux Falls MSA, SD	Y	32850 FQ	36810 MW	49510 TQ	USBLS	5/15
	Tennessee	Y	31520 FQ	38110 MW	48230 TQ	USBLS	5/15
	Knoxville MSA, TN	Y	31070 FQ	36060 MW	42930 TQ	USBLS	5/15
	Memphis MSA, TN-MS-AR	Y	27670 FQ	33470 MW	45050 TQ	USBLS	5/15
	Nashville-Davidson–Murfreesboro–Franklin MSA, TN	Y	32870 FQ	40880 MW	49830 TQ	USBLS	5/15
	Texas	Y	26970 FQ	36150 MW	47460 TQ	USBLS	5/15
	Austin-Round Rock MSA, TX	Y	29520 FQ	38180 MW	53050 TQ	USBLS	5/15
	Dallas-Plano-Irving PMSA, TX	Y	25260 FQ	32920 MW	40120 TQ	USBLS	5/15
	Fort Worth-Arlington PMSA, TX	Y	27270 FQ	34970 MW	41990 TQ	USBLS	5/15
	Houston-The Woodlands-Sugar Land MSA, TX	Y	28610 FQ	39050 MW	49880 TQ	USBLS	5/15
	San Antonio-New Braunfels MSA, TX	Y	30190 FQ	36410 MW	44330 TQ	USBLS	5/15
	Utah	Y	32580 FQ	42700 MW	56550 TQ	USBLS	5/15
	Ogden-Clearfield MSA, UT	Y	37160 FQ	52550 MW	56550 TQ	USBLS	5/15
	Provo-Orem MSA, UT	Y	27900 FQ	34880 MW	43030 TQ	USBLS	5/15
	Salt Lake City MSA, UT	Y	32610 FQ	39920 MW	58510 TQ	USBLS	5/15
	Vermont	Y	36120 FQ	44660 MW	55060 TQ	USBLS	5/15
	Burlington-South Burlington MSA, VT	Y	39260 FQ	50450 MW	59570 TQ	USBLS	5/15
	Virginia	Y	34770 FQ	43240 MW	51710 TQ	USBLS	5/15
	Richmond MSA, VA	Y	32990 FQ	41510 MW	51120 TQ	USBLS	5/15
	Virginia Beach-Norfolk-Newport News MSA, VA-NC	Y	39680 FQ	46140 MW	52540 TQ	USBLS	5/15
	Washington	H	21.09 FQ	28.44 MW	37.93 TQ	WABLS	3/16
	Seattle-Bellevue-Everett PMSA, WA	H	21.15 FQ	28.12 MW	36.91 TQ	WABLS	3/16
	Tacoma-Lakewood PMSA, WA	H	26.32 FQ	31.82 MW	42.57 TQ	WABLS	3/16
	West Virginia	Y	29620 FQ	59640 MW	69930 TQ	USBLS	5/15
	Huntington-Ashland MSA, WV-KY-OH	Y	22920 FQ	29710 MW	53390 TQ	USBLS	5/15
	Wisconsin	Y	39570 FQ	49310 MW	64250 TQ	USBLS	5/15
	Madison MSA, WI	Y	40240 FQ	47550 MW	62730 TQ	USBLS	5/15
	Milwaukee-Waukesha-West Allis MSA, WI	Y	43450 FQ	54330 MW	71100 TQ	USBLS	5/15
	Wyoming	Y	30410 FQ	40140 MW	54790 TQ	USBLS	5/15
	Cheyenne MSA, WY	Y	38190 FQ	48300 MW	54870 TQ	USBLS	5/15
	Puerto Rico	Y	18880 FQ	24490 MW	49160 TQ	USBLS	5/15
	San Juan-Carolina-Caguas MSA, PR	Y	21580 FQ	26730 MW	53240 TQ	USBLS	5/15
	Guam	Y	27440 FQ	30820 MW	36220 TQ	USBLS	5/15
Shelter Veterinarian							
Animal Welfare Program	San Francisco, CA	B	3799 LO		4961 HI	SFGOV	2016-2018
Sheriff							
County Government	Liberty County, GA	Y			86008 HI	GACTY03	2016
County Government	Pike County, GA	Y			71102 HI	GACTY03	2016
County Government	Ingham County, MI	Y			124935 HI	LSJ14	2017
County Government	Oakland County, MI	B			5636 HI	MIOAK1	10/1/16

Occupation/Type/Industry	Location	Per	Low	Mid	High	Source	Date
Sheriff's Aide							
Forensic Services Division, County Government	Contra Costa County, CA	M	3336 LO		4055 HI	CAC	10/14
Ship Carpenter							
Harbor, Municipal Government	Los Angeles, CA	Y		80719 AW		CACIT	6/23/16
Ship Engineer	Alaska	Y	50020 FQ	63150 MW	76460 TQ	USBLS	5/15
	California	H	22.30 FQ	31.09 MW	39.10 TQ	CABLS	1/16-3/16
	Connecticut	Y		62713 MW		CTBLS	1/16-3/16
	Florida	H	23.70 AE	37.08 MW	48.23 AEX	FLBLS	7/16-9/16
	Indiana	Y	66220 FQ	72600 MW	79020 TQ	USBLS	5/15
	Kentucky	Y	46900 FQ	68610 MW	84060 TQ	USBLS	5/15
	Louisiana	Y	64810 FQ	101370 MW	134950 TQ	USBLS	5/15
	Maine	Y	46530 FQ	46540 MW	77010 TQ	USBLS	5/15
	Massachusetts	Y	80980 FQ	92660 MW	115580 TQ	USBLS	5/15
	Mississippi	Y	53650 FQ	73490 MW	93390 TQ	USBLS	5/15
	New Jersey	Y	53630 FQ	73230 MW	87480 TQ	USBLS	5/15
	New York	Y	54250 AE	83440 MW	101790 AEX	NYBLS	1/16-3/16
	Ohio	Y	78710 FQ	96260 MW	116580 TQ	USBLS	5/15
	Oregon	H	12.29 FQ	26.16 MW	43.66 TQ	ORBLS	2016
	Pennsylvania	Y	47980 FQ	58870 MW	70610 TQ	USBLS	5/15
	South Carolina	Y	47130 FQ	61180 MW	82230 TQ	USBLS	5/15
	Tennessee	Y	53810 FQ	60690 MW	76040 TQ	USBLS	5/15
	Texas	Y	51670 FQ	77310 MW	104020 TQ	USBLS	5/15
	Virginia	Y	44240 FQ	57780 MW	87510 TQ	USBLS	5/15
	Washington	H	33.68 FQ	38.86 MW	43.81 TQ	WABLS	3/16
Shipping, Receiving, and Traffic Clerk	Alabama	Y	20777 AE	31289 AW	36545 AEX	ALBLS	6/16
	Birmingham-Hoover MSA, AL	Y	21900 AE	31299 AW	35999 AEX	ALBLS	6/16
	Alaska	Y	29770 FQ	36430 MW	48120 TQ	USBLS	5/15
	Anchorage MSA, AK	Y	30180 FQ	35940 MW	47240 TQ	USBLS	5/15
	Arizona	Y	24090 FQ	29470 MW	36810 TQ	USBLS	5/15
	Phoenix-Mesa-Scottsdale MSA, AZ	Y	24550 FQ	29930 MW	37250 TQ	USBLS	5/15
	Tucson MSA, AZ	Y	24700 FQ	28990 MW	35360 TQ	USBLS	5/15
	Arkansas	Y	22890 FQ	28300 MW	35530 TQ	USBLS	5/15
	Little Rock-North Little Rock-Conway MSA, AR	Y	22740 FQ	27360 MW	34490 TQ	USBLS	5/15
	California	H	12.02 FQ	15.05 MW	19.22 TQ	CABLS	1/16-3/16
	Anaheim-Santa Ana-Irvine PMSA, CA	H	12.36 FQ	15.10 MW	19.25 TQ	CABLS	1/16-3/16
	Los Angeles-Long Beach-Glendale PMSA, CA	H	11.33 FQ	14.05 MW	17.90 TQ	CABLS	1/16-3/16
	Oakland-Hayward-Berkeley PMSA, CA	H	13.78 FQ	17.09 MW	21.35 TQ	CABLS	1/16-3/16
	Riverside-San Bernardino-Ontario MSA, CA	H	11.54 FQ	14.51 MW	18.66 TQ	CABLS	1/16-3/16
	Sacramento–Roseville–Arden-Arcade MSA, CA	H	11.82 FQ	14.88 MW	18.88 TQ	CABLS	1/16-3/16
	San Diego-Carlsbad MSA, CA	H	12.46 FQ	15.77 MW	19.51 TQ	CABLS	1/16-3/16
	San Francisco-Redwood City-South San Francisco PMSA, CA	H	15.37 FQ	18.67 MW	23.11 TQ	CABLS	1/16-3/16
	Colorado	Y	25440 FQ	30850 MW	38940 TQ	USBLS	5/15
	Denver-Aurora-Lakewood MSA, CO	Y	26260 FQ	31250 MW	39920 TQ	USBLS	5/15
	Connecticut	Y		34599 MW		CTBLS	1/16-3/16
	Bridgeport-Stamford-Norwalk MSA, CT	Y	27930 FQ	34950 MW	42890 TQ	USBLS	5/15
	Hartford-West Hartford-East Hartford MSA, CT	Y	27020 FQ	34490 MW	42750 TQ	USBLS	5/15
	Delaware	Y	26040 FQ	28660 MW	31760 TQ	USBLS	5/15
	Wilmington PMSA, DE-MD-NJ	Y	26160 FQ	28670 MW	31550 TQ	USBLS	5/15
	District of Columbia	Y	29700 FQ	45200 MW	53870 TQ	USBLS	5/15
	Washington-Arlington-Alexandria PMSA, DC-VA-MD-WV	Y	27140 FQ	35590 MW	44780 TQ	USBLS	5/15
	Florida	H	10.29 AE	13.95 MW	17.01 AEX	FLBLS	7/16-9/16

AE	Average entry wage	AWR	Average wage range	H	Hourly
AEX	Average experienced wage	B	Biweekly	HI	Highest wage paid
ATC	Average total compensation	D	Daily	HR	High end range
AW	Average wage paid	FQ	First quartile wage	LO	Lowest wage paid

LR	Low end range	MTC	Median total compensation	TCC	Total cash compensation
M	Monthly	MW	Median wage paid	TQ	Third quartile wage
MCC	Median cash compensation	MWR	Median wage range	W	Weekly
ME	Median entry wage	S	See annotated source	Y	Yearly

Occupation/Type/Industry	Location	Per	Low	Mid	High	Source	Date
Shipping, Receiving, and Traffic Clerk							
	Fort Lauderdale-Pompano Beach-Deerfield Beach PMSA, FL	H	10.23 AE	14.28 MW	17.48 AEX	FLBLS	7/16-9/16
	Miami-Miami Beach-Kendall PMSA, FL	H	10.09 AE	13.32 MW	16.65 AEX	FLBLS	7/16-9/16
	Orlando-Kissimmee-Sanford MSA, FL	H	10.40 AE	13.98 MW	16.80 AEX	FLBLS	7/16-9/16
	Tampa-St. Petersburg-Clearwater MSA, FL	H	10.36 AE	13.71 MW	16.14 AEX	FLBLS	7/16-9/16
	Georgia	Y	23150 FQ	28680 MW	35670 TQ	USBLS	5/15
	Atlanta-Sandy Springs-Roswell MSA, GA	Y	22920 FQ	28240 MW	34510 TQ	USBLS	5/15
	Augusta-Richmond County MSA, GA-SC	Y	25090 FQ	30440 MW	40940 TQ	USBLS	5/15
	Hawaii	Y	24510 FQ	33320 MW	46110 TQ	USBLS	5/15
	Urban Honolulu MSA, HI	Y	25660 FQ	34840 MW	47570 TQ	USBLS	5/15
	Idaho	Y	21970 FQ	27010 MW	34480 TQ	USBLS	5/15
	Boise City MSA, ID	Y	21970 FQ	26890 MW	34680 TQ	USBLS	5/15
	Illinois	Y	25180 FQ	31550 MW	39530 TQ	USBLS	5/15
	Chicago-Naperville-Arlington Heights PMSA, IL	Y	25370 FQ	32300 MW	40330 TQ	USBLS	5/15
	Lake County-Kenosha County PMSA, IL-WI	Y	24090 FQ	29570 MW	38390 TQ	USBLS	5/15
	Indiana	Y	24440 FQ	29870 MW	37200 TQ	USBLS	5/15
	Gary PMSA, IN	Y	23140 FQ	31250 MW	39200 TQ	USBLS	5/15
	Indianapolis-Carmel-Anderson MSA, IN	Y	23730 FQ	28660 MW	35730 TQ	USBLS	5/15
	Iowa	Y	25450 FQ	31610 MW	37840 TQ	USBLS	5/15
	Des Moines-West Des Moines MSA, IA	Y	28670 FQ	35690 MW	42940 TQ	USBLS	5/15
	Kansas	Y	24420 FQ	29970 MW	37490 TQ	USBLS	5/15
	Wichita MSA, KS	Y	25080 FQ	29680 MW	37360 TQ	USBLS	5/15
	Kentucky	Y	23530 FQ	29310 MW	37190 TQ	USBLS	5/15
	Louisville-Jefferson County MSA, KY-IN	Y	25320 FQ	30390 MW	38350 TQ	USBLS	5/15
	Louisiana	Y	23680 FQ	29620 MW	37980 TQ	USBLS	5/15
	Baton Rouge MSA, LA	Y	21660 FQ	27810 MW	35360 TQ	USBLS	5/15
	New Orleans-Metairie MSA, LA	Y	25680 FQ	30490 MW	38410 TQ	USBLS	5/15
	Maine	Y	26460 FQ	33940 MW	44170 TQ	USBLS	5/15
	Portland-South Portland MSA, ME	Y	27340 FQ	33080 MW	39710 TQ	USBLS	5/15
	Maryland	Y	23652 AE	34394 MW	39765 AEX	MDBLS	4/16
	Baltimore-Columbia-Towson MSA, MD	Y	26400 FQ	32540 MW	42050 TQ	USBLS	5/15
	Salisbury MSA, MD-DE	Y	23170 FQ	27640 MW	30990 TQ	USBLS	5/15
	Massachusetts	Y	28070 FQ	35430 MW	43530 TQ	USBLS	5/15
	Boston-Cambridge-Newton NECTA, MA	Y	28550 FQ	36440 MW	44870 TQ	USBLS	5/15
	Worcester MSA, MA-CT	Y	28860 FQ	35340 MW	42950 TQ	USBLS	5/15
	Michigan	Y	25480 FQ	31270 MW	38540 TQ	USBLS	5/15
	Detroit-Dearborn-Livonia PMSA, MI	Y	26770 FQ	33590 MW	47920 TQ	USBLS	5/15
	Grand Rapids-Wyoming MSA, MI	Y	24950 FQ	30350 MW	36740 TQ	USBLS	5/15
	Kalamazoo-Portage MSA, MI	Y	24550 FQ	30140 MW	37430 TQ	USBLS	5/15
	Minnesota	Y	27557 FQ	33675 MW	40491 TQ	MNBLS	1/16-3/16
	Minneapolis-St. Paul-Bloomington MSA, MN-WI	Y	28275 FQ	34656 MW	41948 TQ	MNBLS	1/16-3/16
	Mississippi	Y	22230 FQ	27380 MW	33730 TQ	USBLS	5/15
	Jackson MSA, MS	Y	23040 FQ	28940 MW	36850 TQ	USBLS	5/15
	Missouri	Y	24400 FQ	30760 MW	37920 TQ	USBLS	5/15
	Kansas City MSA, MO-KS	Y	24210 FQ	30390 MW	38250 TQ	USBLS	5/15
	St. Louis MSA, MO-IL	Y	26150 FQ	33140 MW	39490 TQ	USBLS	5/15
	Montana	Y	23090 FQ	28790 MW	37280 TQ	USBLS	5/15
	Billings MSA, MT	Y	23020 FQ	28070 MW	36350 TQ	USBLS	5/15
	Nebraska	Y	24820 FQ	30705 MW	37455 TQ	NEBLS	7/16-9/16
	Omaha-Council Bluffs MSA, NE-IA	Y	23635 FQ	30015 MW	37815 TQ	NEBLS	7/16-9/16
	Nevada	Y	25540 FQ	30490 MW	38220 TQ	USBLS	5/15

AE Average entry wage	**AWR** Average wage range	**H** Hourly	**LR** Low end range	**MTC** Median total compensation	**TCC** Total cash compensation
AEX Average experienced wage	**B** Biweekly	**HI** Highest wage paid	**M** Monthly	**MW** Median wage paid	**TQ** Third quartile wage
ATC Average total compensation	**D** Daily	**HR** High end range	**MCC** Median cash compensation	**MWR** Median wage range	**W** Weekly
AW Average wage paid	**FQ** First quartile wage	**LO** Lowest wage paid	**ME** Median entry wage	**S** See annotated source	**Y** Yearly

Occupation/Type/Industry	Location	Per	Low	Mid	High	Source	Date
Shipping, Receiving, and Traffic Clerk	Las Vegas-Henderson-Paradise MSA, NV	Y	24150 FQ	30740 MW	41610 TQ	USBLS	5/15
	New Hampshire	H	12.22 AE	15.56 MW	18.40 AEX	NHBLS	6/16
	Manchester NECTA, NH	H	12.24 AE	15.10 MW	17.76 AEX	NHBLS	6/16
	Nashua NECTA, NH-MA	Y	26590 FQ	31700 MW	38920 TQ	USBLS	5/15
	New Jersey	Y	24840 FQ	33190 MW	44030 TQ	USBLS	5/15
	Camden PMSA, NJ	Y	27580 FQ	35200 MW	45410 TQ	USBLS	5/15
	Newark PMSA, NJ-PA	Y	25230 FQ	32870 MW	43210 TQ	USBLS	5/15
	Trenton MSA, NJ	Y	29180 FQ	37670 MW	46190 TQ	USBLS	5/15
	New Mexico	Y	21740 FQ	27260 MW	35050 TQ	USBLS	5/15
	Albuquerque MSA, NM	Y	22100 FQ	27680 MW	35270 TQ	USBLS	5/15
	New York	Y	23420 AE	33270 MW	41940 AEX	NYBLS	1/16-3/16
	Buffalo-Cheektowaga-Niagara Falls MSA, NY	Y	25390 FQ	30620 MW	38250 TQ	USBLS	5/15
	Nassau County-Suffolk County PMSA, NY	Y	27510 FQ	35710 MW	47360 TQ	USBLS	5/15
	New York-Jersey City-White Plains PMSA, NY-NJ	Y	23970 FQ	32550 MW	44230 TQ	USBLS	5/15
	Rochester MSA, NY	Y	24500 FQ	29840 MW	37540 TQ	USBLS	5/15
	North Carolina	Y	24550 FQ	29930 MW	36930 TQ	USBLS	5/15
	Charlotte-Concord-Gastonia MSA, NC-SC	Y	25680 FQ	30640 MW	37270 TQ	USBLS	5/15
	Raleigh MSA, NC	Y	24520 FQ	29740 MW	36440 TQ	USBLS	5/15
	North Dakota	Y	26200 FQ	31850 MW	37800 TQ	USBLS	5/15
	Fargo MSA, ND-MN	Y	26790 FQ	30840 MW	36620 TQ	USBLS	5/15
	Ohio	Y	24530 FQ	30190 MW	37090 TQ	USBLS	5/15
	Cincinnati MSA, OH-KY-IN	Y.	25750 FQ	32440 MW	39470 TQ	USBLS	5/15
	Cleveland-Elyria MSA, OH	Y	25480 FQ	31220 MW	38000 TQ	USBLS	5/15
	Columbus MSA, OH	Y	21430 FQ	27800 MW	34210 TQ	USBLS	5/15
	Oklahoma	Y	25120 FQ	30550 MW	38150 TQ	USBLS	5/15
	Oklahoma City MSA, OK	Y	25380 FQ	30530 MW	39530 TQ	USBLS	5/15
	Tulsa MSA, OK	Y	26310 FQ	32030 MW	38310 TQ	USBLS	5/15
	Oregon	H	12.78 FQ	15.41 MW	18.93 TQ	ORBLS	2016
	Portland-Vancouver-Hillsboro MSA, OR-WA	Y	26180 FQ	31830 MW	38970 TQ	USBLS	5/15
	Pennsylvania	Y	26180 FQ	32220 MW	39180 TQ	USBLS	5/15
	Allentown-Bethlehem-Easton MSA, PA-NJ	Y	27430 FQ	32500 MW	39130 TQ	USBLS	5/15
	Harrisburg-Carlisle MSA, PA	Y	24620 FQ	32270 MW	39220 TQ	USBLS	5/15
	Montgomery County-Bucks County-Chester County PMSA, PA	Y	26080 FQ	32280 MW	39290 TQ	USBLS	5/15
	Philadelphia PMSA, PA	Y	26200 FQ	33240 MW	42750 TQ	USBLS	5/15
	Pittsburgh MSA, PA	Y	26280 FQ	30910 MW	38530 TQ	USBLS	5/15
	Rhode Island	Y	25870 FQ	32210 MW	39360 TQ	USBLS	5/15
	Providence-Warwick MSA, RI-MA	Y	25750 FQ	31610 MW	38890 TQ	USBLS	5/15
	South Carolina	Y	24490 FQ	30110 MW	37680 TQ	USBLS	5/15
	Charleston-North Charleston MSA, SC	Y	24590 FQ	30670 MW	37940 TQ	USBLS	5/15
	Columbia MSA, SC	Y	24150 FQ	30060 MW	37460 TQ	USBLS	5/15
	Greenville-Anderson-Mauldin MSA, SC	Y	25250 FQ	31610 MW	38420 TQ	USBLS	5/15
	South Dakota	Y	26310 FQ	30730 MW	36350 TQ	USBLS	5/15
	Sioux Falls MSA, SD	Y	26830 FQ	30340 MW	35120 TQ	USBLS	5/15
	Tennessee	Y	23520 FQ	28940 MW	35470 TQ	USBLS	5/15
	Knoxville MSA, TN	Y	21860 FQ	26820 MW	31460 TQ	USBLS	5/15
	Memphis MSA, TN-MS-AR	Y	23360 FQ	28380 MW	34840 TQ	USBLS	5/15
	Nashville-Davidson–Murfreesboro–Franklin MSA, TN	Y	24550 FQ	29670 MW	35710 TQ	USBLS	5/15
	Texas	Y	22280 FQ	28340 MW	35650 TQ	USBLS	5/15
	Austin-Round Rock MSA, TX	Y	24660 FQ	30760 MW	36870 TQ	USBLS	5/15
	Dallas-Plano-Irving PMSA, TX	Y	21780 FQ	27460 MW	34800 TQ	USBLS	5/15
	Fort Worth-Arlington PMSA, TX	Y	23460 FQ	28680 MW	35700 TQ	USBLS	5/15
	Houston-The Woodlands-Sugar Land MSA, TX	Y	24350 FQ	30060 MW	37110 TQ	USBLS	5/15
	San Antonio-New Braunfels MSA, TX	Y	22110 FQ	27640 MW	34760 TQ	USBLS	5/15
	Utah	Y	22780 FQ	28820 MW	36300 TQ	USBLS	5/15

Occupation/Type/Industry	Location	Per	Low	Mid	High	Source	Date
Shipping, Receiving, and Traffic Clerk	Ogden-Clearfield MSA, UT	Y	22400 FQ	29330 MW	36670 TQ	USBLS	5/15
	Provo-Orem MSA, UT	Y	22260 FQ	26650 MW	31770 TQ	USBLS	5/15
	Salt Lake City MSA, UT	Y	23210 FQ	29600 MW	37120 TQ	USBLS	5/15
	Vermont	Y	25440 FQ	30500 MW	37340 TQ	USBLS	5/15
	Burlington-South Burlington MSA, VT	Y	25110 FQ	30440 MW	37360 TQ	USBLS	5/15
	Virginia	Y	25250 FQ	30070 MW	38480 TQ	USBLS	5/15
	Richmond MSA, VA	Y	25920 FQ	28780 MW	33770 TQ	USBLS	5/15
	Virginia Beach-Norfolk-Newport News MSA, VA-NC	Y	23990 FQ	31550 MW	39460 TQ	USBLS	5/15
	Washington	H	13.83 FQ	17.09 MW	21.34 TQ	WABLS	3/16
	Seattle-Bellevue-Everett PMSA, WA	H	14.10 FQ	17.48 MW	21.77 TQ	WABLS	3/16
	Tacoma-Lakewood PMSA, WA	H	13.60 FQ	16.66 MW	20.71 TQ	WABLS	3/16
	West Virginia	Y	21300 FQ	29390 MW	39980 TQ	USBLS	5/15
	Huntington-Ashland MSA, WV-KY-OH	Y	22340 FQ	29250 MW	36100 TQ	USBLS	5/15
	Wisconsin	Y	26610 FQ	32230 MW	38300 TQ	USBLS	5/15
	Madison MSA, WI	Y	26960 FQ	31850 MW	37440 TQ	USBLS	5/15
	Milwaukee-Waukesha-West Allis MSA, WI	Y	28420 FQ	34110 MW	39060 TQ	USBLS	5/15
	Wyoming	Y	25470 FQ	32950 MW	38700 TQ	USBLS	5/15
	Cheyenne MSA, WY	Y	20750 FQ	26660 MW	33610 TQ	USBLS	5/15
	Puerto Rico	Y	16960 FQ	18450 MW	21160 TQ	USBLS	5/15
	San Juan-Carolina-Caguas MSA, PR	Y	16940 FQ	18410 MW	20830 TQ	USBLS	5/15
	Virgin Islands	Y	21900 FQ	31320 MW	41180 TQ	USBLS	5/15
	Guam	Y	18160 FQ	19170 MW	34060 TQ	USBLS	5/15
Shoe and Leather Worker and Repairer	Alabama	Y	18066 AE	23083 AW	25592 AEX	ALBLS	6/16
	Arizona	Y	24870 FQ	28790 MW	33470 TQ	USBLS	5/15
	California	H	10.34 FQ	11.61 MW	13.72 TQ	CABLS	1/16-3/16
	Anaheim-Santa Ana-Irvine PMSA, CA	H	10.73 FQ	12.89 MW	25.49 TQ	CABLS	1/16-3/16
	Los Angeles-Long Beach-Glendale PMSA, CA	H	10.04 FQ	11.10 MW	12.13 TQ	CABLS	1/16-3/16
	Colorado	Y	18840 FQ	21970 MW	24940 TQ	USBLS	5/15
	Washington-Arlington-Alexandria PMSA, DC-VA-MD-WV	Y	26160 FQ	34460 MW	45420 TQ	USBLS	5/15
	Florida	H	9.13 AE	11.40 MW	13.39 AEX	FLBLS	7/16-9/16
	Miami-Miami Beach-Kendall PMSA, FL	H	8.95 AE	10.11 MW	11.10 AEX	FLBLS	7/16-9/16
	Tampa-St. Petersburg-Clearwater MSA, FL	H	9.19 AE	13.08 MW	13.67 AEX	FLBLS	7/16-9/16
	Georgia	Y	17950 FQ	20540 MW	23130 TQ	USBLS	5/15
	Atlanta-Sandy Springs-Roswell MSA, GA	Y	18700 FQ	21270 MW	23250 TQ	USBLS	5/15
	Illinois	Y	25400 FQ	28570 MW	32210 TQ	USBLS	5/15
	Chicago-Naperville-Arlington Heights PMSA, IL	Y	26710 FQ	29420 MW	36430 TQ	USBLS	5/15
	Indiana	Y	20990 FQ	23260 MW	33040 TQ	USBLS	5/15
	Kansas	Y	21690 FQ	25260 MW	35400 TQ	USBLS	5/15
	Kentucky	Y	18840 FQ	23310 MW	27460 TQ	USBLS	5/15
	Maine	Y	21770 FQ	24920 MW	29880 TQ	USBLS	5/15
	Baltimore-Columbia-Towson MSA, MD	Y	21070 FQ	25810 MW	30580 TQ	USBLS	5/15
	Massachusetts	Y	22750 FQ	25230 MW	43960 TQ	USBLS	5/15
	Michigan	Y	20430 FQ	25810 MW	30560 TQ	USBLS	5/15
	Minnesota	Y	22952 FQ	26688 MW	35031 TQ	MNBLS	1/16-3/16
	Minneapolis-St. Paul-Bloomington MSA, MN-WI	Y	22851 FQ	26152 MW	34231 TQ	MNBLS	1/16-3/16
	Mississippi	Y	21440 FQ	23090 MW	24740 TQ	USBLS	5/15
	Missouri	Y	18270 FQ	21730 MW	31960 TQ	USBLS	5/15
	Montana	Y	26470 FQ	28290 MW	30110 TQ	USBLS	5/15
	Nebraska	Y	18280 FQ	21115 MW	28980 TQ	NEBLS	7/16-9/16
	Nevada	Y	18340 FQ	21130 MW	24320 TQ	USBLS	5/15
	New Jersey	Y	21210 FQ	26800 MW	34770 TQ	USBLS	5/15
	Newark PMSA, NJ-PA	Y	20860 FQ	25040 MW	30880 TQ	USBLS	5/15

AE	Average entry wage	AWR	Average wage range	H	Hourly
AEX	Average experienced wage	B	Biweekly	HI	Highest wage paid
ATC	Average total compensation	D	Daily	HR	High end range
AW	Average wage paid	FQ	First quartile wage	LO	Lowest wage paid
LR	Low end range	MTC	Median total compensation	TCC	Total cash compensation
M	Monthly	MW	Median wage paid	TQ	Third quartile wage
MCC	Median cash compensation	MWR	Median wage range	W	Weekly
ME	Median entry wage	S	See annotated source	Y	Yearly

Occupation/Type/Industry	Location	Per	Low	Mid	High	Source	Date
Shoe and Leather Worker and Repairer	New York	Y	19320 AE	23060 MW	27530 AEX	NYBLS	1/16-3/16
	New York-Jersey City-White Plains PMSA, NY-NJ	Y	18900 FQ	20070 MW	26500 TQ	USBLS	5/15
	Ohio	Y	18340 FQ	20890 MW	25340 TQ	USBLS	5/15
	Cincinnati MSA, OH-KY-IN	Y	18960 FQ	22450 MW	25000 TQ	USBLS	5/15
	Oklahoma	Y	20310 FQ	22410 MW	24520 TQ	USBLS	5/15
	Oregon	H	9.45 FQ	11.05 MW	13.66 TQ	ORBLS	2016
	Pennsylvania	Y	18510 FQ	22790 MW	27640 TQ	USBLS	5/15
	Tennessee	Y	19420 FQ	21690 MW	23990 TQ	USBLS	5/15
	Texas	Y	18820 FQ	22550 MW	27290 TQ	USBLS	5/15
	Dallas-Plano-Irving PMSA, TX	Y	17320 FQ	19670 MW	24980 TQ	USBLS	5/15
	Fort Worth-Arlington PMSA, TX	Y	21000 FQ	25320 MW	30270 TQ	USBLS	5/15
	Houston-The Woodlands-Sugar Land MSA, TX	Y	20840 FQ	23770 MW	28300 TQ	USBLS	5/15
	Utah	Y	22180 FQ	26760 MW	30400 TQ	USBLS	5/15
	Washington	H	11.48 FQ	13.28 MW	14.81 TQ	WABLS	3/16
	Wisconsin	Y	18300 FQ	22200 MW	28470 TQ	USBLS	5/15
Shoe Machine Operator and Tender	Arkansas	Y	18260 FQ	21010 MW	24020 TQ	USBLS	5/15
	California	H	9.44 FQ	10.29 MW	11.73 TQ	CABLS	1/16-3/16
	Georgia	Y	22670 FQ	26800 MW	30090 TQ	USBLS	5/15
	Massachusetts	Y	27000 FQ	30510 MW	35140 TQ	USBLS	5/15
	Wisconsin	Y	17850 FQ	24520 MW	28390 TQ	USBLS	5/15
Shooting Range Attendant Natural Resources Department, State Government	Ohio	H	16.01 LO		18.21 HI	OHGOV	2015
Showband/Orchestra Musician Cruise Ship	United States	M	1800 LO		2700 HI	CRU02	2016
Sign Language Interpreter Central Intelligence Agency	District of Columbia	Y	77490 LO		119794 HI	CIA06	2016
Sign Painter Department of Water and Power, Municipal Government	Los Angeles, CA	Y			87959 HI	CACIT	6/23/16
Sign Shop Technician Airport, Municipal Government	San Jose, CA	Y			74220 HI	CACIT	6/28/16
Sign Writer Made for Television Motion Picture	United States	H	46.61 LO			MPEG01	7/31/16-7/29/17
Signal and Track Switch Repairer	Arizona	Y	55290 FQ	61880 MW	71830 TQ	USBLS	5/15
	Arkansas	Y	55520 FQ	65230 MW	74360 TQ	USBLS	5/15
	California	H	27.29 FQ	33.91 MW	38.74 TQ	CABLS	1/16-3/16
	Colorado	Y	49910 FQ	54980 MW	59840 TQ	USBLS	5/15
	Florida	H	15.50 AE	26.66 MW	30.98 AEX	FLBLS	7/16-9/16
	Georgia	Y	51680 FQ	64270 MW	72260 TQ	USBLS	5/15
	Idaho	Y	39690 FQ	52910 MW	61650 TQ	USBLS	5/15
	Illinois	Y	58680 FQ	68480 MW	75740 TQ	USBLS	5/15
	Indiana	Y	51740 FQ	56280 MW	60820 TQ	USBLS	5/15
	Iowa	Y	54090 FQ	60580 MW	70890 TQ	USBLS	5/15
	Kansas	Y	47660 FQ	56070 MW	67050 TQ	USBLS	5/15
	Kentucky	Y	61140 FQ	70080 MW	76570 TQ	USBLS	5/15
	Louisiana	Y	32000 FQ	40110 MW	52280 TQ	USBLS	5/15
	Minnesota	Y	49338 FQ	62523 MW	86116 TQ	MNBLS	1/16-3/16
	Missouri	Y	50130 FQ	57650 MW	67840 TQ	USBLS	5/15
	Nebraska	Y	51650 FQ	56085 MW	60520 TQ	NEBLS	7/16-9/16
	New York	Y	66940 AE	73670 MW	74090 AEX	NYBLS	1/16-3/16
	Ohio	Y	52730 FQ	59010 MW	68720 TQ	USBLS	5/15
	Pennsylvania	Y	51620 FQ	61240 MW	71770 TQ	USBLS	5/15
	Texas	Y	44000 FQ	50820 MW	66200 TQ	USBLS	5/15
	Utah	Y	54380 FQ	59280 MW	64470 TQ	USBLS	5/15
	Virginia	Y	59680 FQ	69460 MW	76810 TQ	USBLS	5/15
	Washington	H	28.04 FQ	33.20 MW	38.12 TQ	WABLS	3/16
	Wisconsin	Y	58590 FQ	67000 MW	74530 TQ	USBLS	5/15

AE	Average entry wage	AWR	Average wage range	H	Hourly	LR	Low end range	MTC	Median total compensation	TCC	Total cash compensation
AEX	Average experienced wage	B	Biweekly	HI	Highest wage paid	M	Monthly	MW	Median wage paid	TQ	Third quartile wage
ATC	Average total compensation	D	Daily	HR	High end range	MCC	Median cash compensation	MWR	Median wage range	W	Weekly
AW	Average wage paid	FQ	First quartile wage	LO	Lowest wage paid	ME	Median entry wage	S	See annotated source	Y	Yearly

Occupation/Type/Industry	Location	Per	Low	Mid	High	Source	Date
Site Reliability Engineer	United States	Y		140000 MW		HCHRON1	2017
Skate Park Attendant							
Municipal Government	Campbell, CA	Y		4591 AW		CACIT	6/28/16
Ski Instructor	United States	H		13.00 AW		MST04	2017
Skincare Specialist	Alabama	Y	25874 AE	36695 AW	42111 AEX	ALBLS	6/16
	Birmingham-Hoover MSA, AL	Y	29725 AE	36438 AW	39805 AEX	ALBLS	6/16
	Alaska	Y	26410 FQ	28380 MW	30360 TQ	USBLS	5/15
	Anchorage MSA, AK	Y	26190 FQ	27940 MW	29690 TQ	USBLS	5/15
	Arizona	Y	19260 FQ	29190 MW	44570 TQ	USBLS	5/15
	Phoenix-Mesa-Scottsdale MSA, AZ	Y	19030 FQ	27070 MW	38510 TQ	USBLS	5/15
	Tucson MSA, AZ	Y	23500 FQ	50410 MW	57060 TQ	USBLS	5/15
	Arkansas	Y	28630 FQ	42210 MW	58870 TQ	USBLS	5/15
	California	H	11.05 FQ	15.19 MW	19.09 TQ	CABLS	1/16-3/16
	Anaheim-Santa Ana-Irvine PMSA, CA	H	12.64 FQ	14.86 MW	20.20 TQ	CABLS	1/16-3/16
	Los Angeles-Long Beach-Glendale PMSA, CA	H	12.13 FQ	16.89 MW	21.71 TQ	CABLS	1/16-3/16
	Oakland-Hayward-Berkeley PMSA, CA	H	11.93 FQ	16.27 MW	19.68 TQ	CABLS	1/16-3/16
	Riverside-San Bernardino-Ontario MSA, CA	H	9.39 FQ	12.57 MW	16.44 TQ	CABLS	1/16-3/16
	Sacramento–Roseville–Arden-Arcade MSA, CA	H	9.46 FQ	11.20 MW	22.57 TQ	CABLS	1/16-3/16
	San Diego-Carlsbad MSA, CA	H	9.96 FQ	11.67 MW	17.29 TQ	CABLS	1/16-3/16
	San Francisco-Redwood City-South San Francisco PMSA, CA	H	10.88 FQ	12.41 MW	16.99 TQ	CABLS	1/16-3/16
	San Jose-Sunnyvale-Santa Clara MSA, CA	Y	26620 FQ	32470 MW	37200 TQ	USBLS	5/15
	Colorado	Y	19770 FQ	27930 MW	44560 TQ	USBLS	5/15
	Denver-Aurora-Lakewood MSA, CO	Y	18890 FQ	26670 MW	40330 TQ	USBLS	5/15
	Connecticut	Y		35038 MW		CTBLS	1/16-3/16
	Bridgeport-Stamford-Norwalk MSA, CT	Y	28280 FQ	43390 MW	69810 TQ	USBLS	5/15
	Hartford-West Hartford-East Hartford MSA, CT	Y	23090 FQ	29500 MW	38620 TQ	USBLS	5/15
	Delaware	Y	22890 FQ	28950 MW	35210 TQ	USBLS	5/15
	Wilmington PMSA, DE-MD-NJ	Y	22520 FQ	31110 MW	37070 TQ	USBLS	5/15
	District of Columbia	Y	21790 FQ	33040 MW	47020 TQ	USBLS	5/15
	Washington-Arlington-Alexandria PMSA, DC-VA-MD-WV	Y	26990 FQ	51900 MW	71200 TQ	USBLS	5/15
	Florida	H	9.99 AE	14.53 MW	20.59 AEX	FLBLS	7/16-9/16
	Fort Lauderdale-Pompano Beach-Deerfield Beach PMSA, FL	H	11.13 AE	16.91 MW	22.09 AEX	FLBLS	7/16-9/16
	Miami-Miami Beach-Kendall PMSA, FL	H	11.11 AE	14.70 MW	22.06 AEX	FLBLS	7/16-9/16
	Orlando-Kissimmee-Sanford MSA, FL	H	10.28 AE	16.58 MW	24.42 AEX	FLBLS	7/16-9/16
	Tampa-St. Petersburg-Clearwater MSA, FL	H	9.90 AE	12.78 MW	17.88 AEX	FLBLS	7/16-9/16
	Georgia	Y	18460 FQ	32460 MW	37940 TQ	USBLS	5/15
	Atlanta-Sandy Springs-Roswell MSA, GA	Y	18630 FQ	33360 MW	38310 TQ	USBLS	5/15
	Hawaii	Y	18170 FQ	21210 MW	34860 TQ	USBLS	5/15
	Urban Honolulu MSA, HI	Y	17910 FQ	19760 MW	29630 TQ	USBLS	5/15
	Idaho	Y	19190 FQ	30220 MW	46680 TQ	USBLS	5/15
	Boise City MSA, ID	Y	26640 FQ	42100 MW	62550 TQ	USBLS	5/15
	Illinois	Y	22070 FQ	27690 MW	39860 TQ	USBLS	5/15
	Chicago-Naperville-Arlington Heights PMSA, IL	Y	22020 FQ	26980 MW	41380 TQ	USBLS	5/15
	Lake County-Kenosha County PMSA, IL-WI	Y	26320 FQ	30480 MW	37240 TQ	USBLS	5/15
	Indiana	Y	17010 FQ	18570 MW	21940 TQ	USBLS	5/15
	Gary PMSA, IN	Y	16630 FQ	18030 MW	19580 TQ	USBLS	5/15

AE Average entry wage	**AWR** Average wage range	**H** Hourly	**LR** Low end range	**MTC** Median total compensation	**TCC** Total cash compensation
AEX Average experienced wage	**B** Biweekly	**HI** Highest wage paid	**M** Monthly	**MW** Median wage paid	**TQ** Third quartile wage
ATC Average total compensation	**D** Daily	**HR** High end range	**MCC** Median cash compensation	**MWR** Median wage range	**W** Weekly
AW Average wage paid	**FQ** First quartile wage	**LO** Lowest wage paid	**ME** Median entry wage	**S** See annotated source	**Y** Yearly

Skincare Specialist

Occupation/Type/Industry	Location	Per	Low	Mid	High	Source	Date
Skincare Specialist	Indianapolis-Carmel-Anderson MSA, IN	Y	16950 FQ	18330 MW	19770 TQ	USBLS	5/15
	Iowa	Y	20690 FQ	28350 MW	35690 TQ	USBLS	5/15
	Des Moines-West Des Moines MSA, IA	Y	25220 FQ	29620 MW	37020 TQ	USBLS	5/15
	Kansas	Y	22490 FQ	27640 MW	41740 TQ	USBLS	5/15
	Wichita MSA, KS	Y	21570 FQ	23960 MW	29380 TQ	USBLS	5/15
	Kentucky	Y	19510 FQ	32320 MW	40950 TQ	USBLS	5/15
	Louisville-Jefferson County MSA, KY-IN	Y	19180 FQ	33670 MW	39200 TQ	USBLS	5/15
	Louisiana	Y	17580 FQ	19840 MW	29880 TQ	USBLS	5/15
	Baton Rouge MSA, LA	Y	18260 FQ	27430 MW	35350 TQ	USBLS	5/15
	Maine	Y	19440 FQ	30860 MW	39150 TQ	USBLS	5/15
	Portland-South Portland MSA, ME	Y	27130 FQ	33640 MW	42130 TQ	USBLS	5/15
	Maryland	Y	23460 AE	40212 MW	48588 AEX	MDBLS	4/16
	Baltimore-Columbia-Towson MSA, MD	Y	27220 FQ	38330 MW	46820 TQ	USBLS	5/15
	Massachusetts	Y	33150 FQ	45750 MW	54190 TQ	USBLS	5/15
	Boston-Cambridge-Newton NECTA, MA	Y	40560 FQ	49580 MW	57200 TQ	USBLS	5/15
	Worcester MSA, MA-CT	Y	41170 FQ	45130 MW	49100 TQ	USBLS	5/15
	Michigan	Y	20290 FQ	27570 MW	36120 TQ	USBLS	5/15
	Detroit-Dearborn-Livonia PMSA, MI	Y	24870 FQ	28930 MW	36510 TQ	USBLS	5/15
	Grand Rapids-Wyoming MSA, MI	Y	18460 FQ	21500 MW	31360 TQ	USBLS	5/15
	Minnesota	Y	24287 FQ	31326 MW	42324 TQ	MNBLS	1/16-3/16
	Minneapolis-St. Paul-Bloomington MSA, MN-WI	Y	22944 FQ	31033 MW	43030 TQ	MNBLS	1/16-3/16
	Mississippi	Y	20740 FQ	25660 MW	29450 TQ	USBLS	5/15
	Jackson MSA, MS	Y	25010 FQ	27120 MW	29230 TQ	USBLS	5/15
	Missouri	Y	19340 FQ	29070 MW	46790 TQ	USBLS	5/15
	Kansas City MSA, MO-KS	Y	19640 FQ	32430 MW	45590 TQ	USBLS	5/15
	St. Louis MSA, MO-IL	Y	19150 FQ	27040 MW	43540 TQ	USBLS	5/15
	Montana	Y	25860 FQ	28900 MW	35700 TQ	USBLS	5/15
	Billings MSA, MT	Y	26580 FQ	28500 MW	30430 TQ	USBLS	5/15
	Omaha-Council Bluffs MSA, NE-IA	Y	25890 FQ	33385 MW	38495 TQ	NEBLS	7/16-9/16
	Nevada	Y	18760 FQ	23530 MW	49370 TQ	USBLS	5/15
	Las Vegas-Henderson-Paradise MSA, NV	Y	18650 FQ	24020 MW	50550 TQ	USBLS	5/15
	New Hampshire	H	9.47 AE	12.77 MW	17.36 AEX	NHBLS	6/16
	Manchester NECTA, NH	H	12.52 AE	14.93 MW	16.80 AEX	NHBLS	6/16
	Nashua NECTA, NH-MA	Y	21200 FQ	23760 MW	30430 TQ	USBLS	5/15
	New Jersey	Y	25910 FQ	37490 MW	47900 TQ	USBLS	5/15
	Camden PMSA, NJ	Y	21920 FQ	27930 MW	36330 TQ	USBLS	5/15
	Newark PMSA, NJ-PA	Y	22820 FQ	35670 MW	45940 TQ	USBLS	5/15
	Trenton MSA, NJ	Y	40250 FQ	45140 MW	50030 TQ	USBLS	5/15
	New Mexico	Y	31730 FQ	42750 MW	64950 TQ	USBLS	5/15
	Albuquerque MSA, NM	Y	33540 FQ	43930 MW	68770 TQ	USBLS	5/15
	New York	Y	24860 AE	33910 MW	48500 AEX	NYBLS	1/16-3/16
	Buffalo-Cheektowaga-Niagara Falls MSA, NY	Y	19230 FQ	29040 MW	36500 TQ	USBLS	5/15
	Nassau County-Suffolk County PMSA, NY	Y	26570 FQ	50290 MW	66550 TQ	USBLS	5/15
	New York-Jersey City-White Plains PMSA, NY-NJ	Y	27830 FQ	35700 MW	47430 TQ	USBLS	5/15
	Rochester MSA, NY	Y	25800 FQ	36050 MW	47500 TQ	USBLS	5/15
	North Carolina	Y	23820 FQ	31620 MW	41170 TQ	USBLS	5/15
	Charlotte-Concord-Gastonia MSA, NC-SC	Y	23760 FQ	31300 MW	40950 TQ	USBLS	5/15
	Raleigh MSA, NC	Y	20120 FQ	31260 MW	42490 TQ	USBLS	5/15
	North Dakota	Y	23670 FQ	33810 MW	38800 TQ	USBLS	5/15
	Ohio	Y	19260 FQ	30310 MW	61080 TQ	USBLS	5/15
	Cincinnati MSA, OH-KY-IN	Y	23700 FQ	38590 MW	72060 TQ	USBLS	5/15
	Cleveland-Elyria MSA, OH	Y	27650 FQ	39150 MW	55060 TQ	USBLS	5/15
	Oklahoma	Y	17500 FQ	19330 MW	27590 TQ	USBLS	5/15
	Oklahoma City MSA, OK	Y	17500 FQ	19330 MW	26680 TQ	USBLS	5/15
	Tulsa MSA, OK	Y	17160 FQ	18640 MW	20880 TQ	USBLS	5/15
	Oregon	H	10.67 FQ	27.61 MW	36.31 TQ	ORBLS	2016

Occupation/Type/Industry	Location	Per	Low	Mid	High	Source	Date
Skincare Specialist	Portland-Vancouver-Hillsboro MSA, OR-WA	Y	24580 FQ	64360 MW	76530 TQ	USBLS	5/15
	Pennsylvania	Y	21130 FQ	27490 MW	39620 TQ	USBLS	5/15
	Allentown-Bethlehem-Easton MSA, PA-NJ	Y	24980 FQ	32250 MW	38110 TQ	USBLS	5/15
	Harrisburg-Carlisle MSA, PA	Y	27620 FQ	46600 MW	57050 TQ	USBLS	5/15
	Montgomery County-Bucks County-Chester County PMSA, PA	Y	19220 FQ	27530 MW	39000 TQ	USBLS	5/15
	Philadelphia PMSA, PA	Y	19170 FQ	28560 MW	51680 TQ	USBLS	5/15
	Pittsburgh MSA, PA	Y	20930 FQ	23890 MW	27840 TQ	USBLS	5/15
	Rhode Island	Y	21320 FQ	33270 MW	43560 TQ	USBLS	5/15
	Providence-Warwick MSA, RI-MA	Y	22800 FQ	36660 MW	44520 TQ	USBLS	5/15
	South Carolina	Y	19390 FQ	27150 MW	35700 TQ	USBLS	5/15
	Charleston-North Charleston MSA, SC	Y	21410 FQ	28800 MW	34310 TQ	USBLS	5/15
	Columbia MSA, SC	Y	20360 FQ	26040 MW	28810 TQ	USBLS	5/15
	Greenville-Anderson-Mauldin MSA, SC	Y	17800 FQ	26860 MW	41760 TQ	USBLS	5/15
	Tennessee	Y	27340 FQ	34880 MW	45540 TQ	USBLS	5/15
	Knoxville MSA, TN	Y	30660 FQ	34560 MW	37880 TQ	USBLS	5/15
	Memphis MSA, TN-MS-AR	Y	26600 FQ	34140 MW	41010 TQ	USBLS	5/15
	Nashville-Davidson–Murfreesboro–Franklin MSA, TN	Y	19900 FQ	30350 MW	41140 TQ	USBLS	5/15
	Texas	Y	19160 FQ	26930 MW	38660 TQ	USBLS	5/15
	Austin-Round Rock MSA, TX	Y	19570 FQ	31430 MW	38800 TQ	USBLS	5/15
	Dallas-Plano-Irving PMSA, TX	Y	21830 FQ	25040 MW	46940 TQ	USBLS	5/15
	Fort Worth-Arlington PMSA, TX	Y	16970 FQ	18720 MW	29340 TQ	USBLS	5/15
	Houston-The Woodlands-Sugar Land MSA, TX	Y	18020 FQ	28440 MW	41700 TQ	USBLS	5/15
	San Antonio-New Braunfels MSA, TX	Y	18460 FQ	26090 MW	32740 TQ	USBLS	5/15
	Utah	Y	21050 FQ	26960 MW	33610 TQ	USBLS	5/15
	Ogden-Clearfield MSA, UT	Y	25500 FQ	32630 MW	36770 TQ	USBLS	5/15
	Provo-Orem MSA, UT	Y	23460 FQ	28530 MW	33820 TQ	USBLS	5/15
	Salt Lake City MSA, UT	Y	18500 FQ	22140 MW	27560 TQ	USBLS	5/15
	Vermont	Y	31580 FQ	55920 MW	72240 TQ	USBLS	5/15
	Burlington-South Burlington MSA, VT	Y	47510 FQ	69040 MW	75570 TQ	USBLS	5/15
	Virginia	Y	20090 FQ	34570 MW	63120 TQ	USBLS	5/15
	Richmond MSA, VA	Y	21780 FQ	27420 MW	33330 TQ	USBLS	5/15
	Virginia Beach-Norfolk-Newport News MSA, VA-NC	Y	19610 FQ	42670 MW	59520 TQ	USBLS	5/15
	Washington	H	11.32 FQ	13.91 MW	18.93 TQ	WABLS	3/16
	Seattle-Bellevue-Everett PMSA, WA	H	11.19 FQ	13.33 MW	16.73 TQ	WABLS	3/16
	Tacoma-Lakewood PMSA, WA	H	17.09 FQ	19.94 MW	30.37 TQ	WABLS	3/16
	West Virginia	Y	26890 FQ	40310 MW	71870 TQ	USBLS	5/15
	Wisconsin	Y	20850 FQ	27960 MW	38140 TQ	USBLS	5/15
	Madison MSA, WI	Y	24440 FQ	33480 MW	47620 TQ	USBLS	5/15
	Milwaukee-Waukesha-West Allis MSA, WI	Y	23940 FQ	31070 MW	38070 TQ	USBLS	5/15
	Wyoming	Y	48010 FQ	60760 MW	71520 TQ	USBLS	5/15
	Puerto Rico	Y	17190 FQ	18970 MW	24770 TQ	USBLS	5/15
	San Juan-Carolina-Caguas MSA, PR	Y	17170 FQ	18980 MW	24850 TQ	USBLS	5/15
Slaughterer and Meat Packer	Alabama	Y	20338 AE	24235 AW	26189 AEX	ALBLS	6/16
	Arizona	Y	20930 FQ	26480 MW	29890 TQ	USBLS	5/15
	Phoenix-Mesa-Scottsdale MSA, AZ	Y	21320 FQ	26720 MW	29980 TQ	USBLS	5/15
	Arkansas	Y	20720 FQ	22670 MW	24640 TQ	USBLS	5/15
	California	H	10.05 FQ	11.76 MW	14.37 TQ	CABLS	1/16-3/16
	Anaheim-Santa Ana-Irvine PMSA, CA	H	9.62 FQ	11.05 MW	12.52 TQ	CABLS	1/16-3/16
	Los Angeles-Long Beach-Glendale PMSA, CA	H	9.75 FQ	11.47 MW	13.69 TQ	CABLS	1/16-3/16
	Riverside-San Bernardino-Ontario MSA, CA	H	9.53 FQ	10.51 MW	13.32 TQ	CABLS	1/16-3/16

AE	Average entry wage	AWR	Average wage range	H	Hourly	
AEX	Average experienced wage	B	Biweekly	HI	Highest wage paid	
ATC	Average total compensation	D	Daily	HR	High end range	
AW	Average wage paid	FQ	First quartile wage	LO	Lowest wage paid	
LR	Low end range	MTC	Median total compensation	TCC	Total cash compensation
M	Monthly	MW	Median wage	TQ	Third quartile wage
MCC	Median cash compensation	MWR	Median wage range	W	Weekly
ME	Median entry wage	S	See annotated source	Y	Yearly

Occupation/Type/Industry	Location	Per	Low	Mid	High	Source	Date
Slaughterer and Meat Packer	Colorado	Y	30000 FQ	34420 MW	37290 TQ	USBLS	5/15
	Denver-Aurora-Lakewood MSA, CO	Y	27820 FQ	32980 MW	37950 TQ	USBLS	5/15
	Connecticut	Y		26468 MW		CTBLS	1/16-3/16
	Hartford-West Hartford-East Hartford MSA, CT	Y	24640 FQ	27670 MW	30220 TQ	USBLS	5/15
	Delaware	Y	20330 FQ	22860 MW	25670 TQ	USBLS	5/15
	Wilmington PMSA, DE-MD-NJ	Y	26670 FQ	28430 MW	30190 TQ	USBLS	5/15
	Florida	H	8.98 AE	10.34 MW	12.28 AEX	FLBLS	7/16-9/16
	Miami-Miami Beach-Kendall PMSA, FL	H	8.97 AE	9.75 MW	11.27 AEX	FLBLS	7/16-9/16
	Georgia	Y	19770 FQ	22090 MW	24470 TQ	USBLS	5/15
	Atlanta-Sandy Springs-Roswell MSA, GA	Y	19940 FQ	22170 MW	24390 TQ	USBLS	5/15
	Augusta-Richmond County MSA, GA-SC	Y	17310 FQ	18950 MW	23240 TQ	USBLS	5/15
	Hawaii	Y	18990 FQ	27210 MW	32330 TQ	USBLS	5/15
	Urban Honolulu MSA, HI	Y	17720 FQ	19330 MW	25330 TQ	USBLS	5/15
	Idaho	Y	18350 FQ	25350 MW	42320 TQ	USBLS	5/15
	Illinois	Y	22540 FQ	26120 MW	30030 TQ	USBLS	5/15
	Chicago-Naperville-Arlington Heights PMSA, IL	Y	22970 FQ	27060 MW	30670 TQ	USBLS	5/15
	Indiana	Y	21790 FQ	25100 MW	28960 TQ	USBLS	5/15
	Iowa	Y	26220 FQ	30490 MW	34870 TQ	USBLS	5/15
	Kansas	Y	24140 FQ	27910 MW	31350 TQ	USBLS	5/15
	Kentucky	Y	24070 FQ	27780 MW	30950 TQ	USBLS	5/15
	Louisiana	Y	18100 FQ	20690 MW	23370 TQ	USBLS	5/15
	New Orleans-Metairie MSA, LA	Y	17700 FQ	20100 MW	22820 TQ	USBLS	5/15
	Maine	Y	20700 FQ	26030 MW	30010 TQ	USBLS	5/15
	Maryland	Y	19988 AE	24608 MW	26917 AEX	MDBLS	4/16
	Baltimore-Columbia-Towson MSA, MD	Y	20040 FQ	22860 MW	26720 TQ	USBLS	5/15
	Salisbury MSA, MD-DE	Y	20520 FQ	22960 MW	25690 TQ	USBLS	5/15
	Massachusetts	Y	23110 FQ	28820 MW	34960 TQ	USBLS	5/15
	Michigan	Y	22470 FQ	26910 MW	33320 TQ	USBLS	5/15
	Detroit-Dearborn-Livonia PMSA, MI	Y	22390 FQ	26780 MW	34280 TQ	USBLS	5/15
	Grand Rapids-Wyoming MSA, MI	Y	23240 FQ	28530 MW	33930 TQ	USBLS	5/15
	Minnesota	Y	23914 FQ	28389 MW	33380 TQ	MNBLS	1/16-3/16
	Minneapolis-St. Paul-Bloomington MSA, MN-WI	Y	31345 FQ	37056 MW	55067 TQ	MNBLS	1/16-3/16
	Mississippi	Y	18480 FQ	21400 MW	25070 TQ	USBLS	5/15
	Missouri	Y	22140 FQ	26120 MW	29550 TQ	USBLS	5/15
	Kansas City MSA, MO-KS	Y	22240 FQ	26480 MW	29880 TQ	USBLS	5/15
	St. Louis MSA, MO-IL	Y	21030 FQ	23470 MW	27740 TQ	USBLS	5/15
	Montana	Y	22320 FQ	28100 MW	34450 TQ	USBLS	5/15
	Nebraska	Y	24380 FQ	29445 MW	34845 TQ	NEBLS	7/16-9/16
	Omaha-Council Bluffs MSA, NE-IA	Y	23310 FQ	26910 MW	30065 TQ	NEBLS	7/16-9/16
	New Jersey	Y	19630 FQ	23410 MW	29500 TQ	USBLS	5/15
	Camden PMSA, NJ	Y	21170 FQ	23180 MW	25500 TQ	USBLS	5/15
	Newark PMSA, NJ-PA	Y	19350 FQ	21550 MW	24100 TQ	USBLS	5/15
	New York	Y	19270 AE	20440 MW	25380 AEX	NYBLS	1/16-3/16
	New York-Jersey City-White Plains PMSA, NY-NJ	Y	18830 FQ	19790 MW	24160 TQ	USBLS	5/15
	Rochester MSA, NY	Y	22320 FQ	33240 MW	36800 TQ	USBLS	5/15
	North Carolina	Y	22010 FQ	25140 MW	28300 TQ	USBLS	5/15
	North Dakota	Y	24790 FQ	36540 MW	43980 TQ	USBLS	5/15
	Ohio	Y	20790 FQ	23280 MW	27070 TQ	USBLS	5/15
	Cincinnati MSA, OH-KY-IN	Y	21590 FQ	23820 MW	27340 TQ	USBLS	5/15
	Cleveland-Elyria MSA, OH	Y	20400 FQ	24510 MW	29030 TQ	USBLS	5/15
	Columbus MSA, OH	Y	18630 FQ	20590 MW	23980 TQ	USBLS	5/15
	Oklahoma	Y	19810 FQ	22080 MW	24240 TQ	USBLS	5/15
	Oklahoma City MSA, OK	Y	21050 FQ	22620 MW	24200 TQ	USBLS	5/15
	Oregon	H	9.64 FQ	12.76 MW	15.25 TQ	ORBLS	2016
	Portland-Vancouver-Hillsboro MSA, OR-WA	Y	26470 FQ	30900 MW	35780 TQ	USBLS	5/15
	Pennsylvania	Y	21400 FQ	24500 MW	30210 TQ	USBLS	5/15

Occupation/Type/Industry	Location	Per	Low	Mid	High	Source	Date
Slaughterer and Meat Packer	Montgomery County-Bucks County-Chester County PMSA, PA	Y	23310 FQ	29380 MW	35230 TQ	USBLS	5/15
	Philadelphia PMSA, PA	Y	21640 FQ	25950 MW	30080 TQ	USBLS	5/15
	Pittsburgh MSA, PA	Y	21530 FQ	24780 MW	33850 TQ	USBLS	5/15
	South Carolina	Y	17270 FQ	19060 MW	23200 TQ	USBLS	5/15
	Columbia MSA, SC	Y	17900 FQ	19890 MW	22740 TQ	USBLS	5/15
	Tennessee	Y	21600 FQ	24430 MW	28120 TQ	USBLS	5/15
	Memphis MSA, TN-MS-AR	Y	18340 FQ	23510 MW	34320 TQ	USBLS	5/15
	Texas	Y	20170 FQ	24260 MW	29280 TQ	USBLS	5/15
	Dallas-Plano-Irving PMSA, TX	Y	17660 FQ	20020 MW	24060 TQ	USBLS	5/15
	Fort Worth-Arlington PMSA, TX	Y	21440 FQ	24950 MW	30270 TQ	USBLS	5/15
	San Antonio-New Braunfels MSA, TX	Y	19580 FQ	22250 MW	25160 TQ	USBLS	5/15
	Utah	Y	25340 FQ	27840 MW	30340 TQ	USBLS	5/15
	Ogden-Clearfield MSA, UT	Y	18520 FQ	25000 MW	34110 TQ	USBLS	5/15
	Salt Lake City MSA, UT	Y	24730 FQ	26980 MW	29250 TQ	USBLS	5/15
	Vermont	Y	22670 FQ	26810 MW	35190 TQ	USBLS	5/15
	Virginia	Y	21470 FQ	24420 MW	29070 TQ	USBLS	5/15
	Washington	H	12.24 FQ	13.63 MW	15.05 TQ	WABLS	3/16
	Seattle-Bellevue-Everett PMSA, WA	H	11.05 FQ	12.21 MW	13.92 TQ	WABLS	3/16
	West Virginia	Y	18110 FQ	19580 MW	24300 TQ	USBLS	5/15
	Huntington-Ashland MSA, WV-KY-OH	Y	17810 FQ	19050 MW	21780 TQ	USBLS	5/15
	Wisconsin	Y	24400 FQ	28690 MW	33230 TQ	USBLS	5/15
	Madison MSA, WI	Y	22650 FQ	26580 MW	32250 TQ	USBLS	5/15
	Puerto Rico	Y	17070 FQ	18570 MW	20680 TQ	USBLS	5/15
	San Juan-Carolina-Caguas MSA, PR	Y	17220 FQ	18840 MW	21590 TQ	USBLS	5/15
Sleep Facility Manager							
Female	United States	Y		64206 AW		AHNRSP	2016
Male	United States	Y		67308 AW		AHNRSP	2016
Sleep Technician							
Female	United States	Y		50008 AW		AHNRSP	2016
Male	United States	Y		55192 AW		AHNRSP	2016
Slot Supervisor	Alabama	Y	21313 AE	34554 AW	41174 AEX	ALBLS	6/16
	Birmingham-Hoover MSA, AL	Y	22209 AE	25215 AW	26718 AEX	ALBLS	6/16
	Arizona	Y	22880 FQ	31270 MW	43960 TQ	USBLS	5/15
	California	H	15.44 FQ	19.50 MW	24.80 TQ	CABLS	1/16-3/16
	Riverside-San Bernardino-Ontario MSA, CA	H	15.81 FQ	19.46 MW	27.09 TQ	CABLS	1/16-3/16
	San Diego-Carlsbad MSA, CA	H	16.38 FQ	20.38 MW	25.39 TQ	CABLS	1/16-3/16
	Colorado	Y	33180 FQ	42860 MW	53220 TQ	USBLS	5/15
	Denver-Aurora-Lakewood MSA, CO	Y	31910 FQ	40660 MW	50520 TQ	USBLS	5/15
	Delaware	Y	36280 FQ	43370 MW	49490 TQ	USBLS	5/15
	Florida	H	10.27 AE	15.68 MW	19.51 AEX	FLBLS	7/16-9/16
	Miami-Miami Beach-Kendall PMSA, FL	H	11.78 AE	19.59 MW	21.81 AEX	FLBLS	7/16-9/16
	Tampa-St. Petersburg-Clearwater MSA, FL	H	10.95 AE	17.18 MW	19.77 AEX	FLBLS	7/16-9/16
	Illinois	Y	22920 FQ	29940 MW	39520 TQ	USBLS	5/15
	Chicago-Naperville-Arlington Heights PMSA, IL	Y	21770 FQ	23520 MW	32680 TQ	USBLS	5/15
	Indiana	Y	33800 FQ	42100 MW	48350 TQ	USBLS	5/15
	Iowa	Y	22170 FQ	27370 MW	36830 TQ	USBLS	5/15
	Kansas	Y	22970 FQ	32800 MW	38320 TQ	USBLS	5/15
	Kentucky	Y	28440 FQ	35870 MW	45190 TQ	USBLS	5/15
	Louisiana	Y	24620 FQ	34500 MW	40220 TQ	USBLS	5/15
	Maryland	Y	27513 AE	40901 MW	47594 AEX	MDBLS	4/16
	Baltimore-Columbia-Towson MSA, MD	Y	28770 FQ	38970 MW	48270 TQ	USBLS	5/15
	Michigan	Y	28780 FQ	36100 MW	49230 TQ	USBLS	5/15
	Detroit-Dearborn-Livonia PMSA, MI	Y	32080 FQ	35770 MW	41200 TQ	USBLS	5/15
	Minnesota	Y	25227 FQ	36305 MW	47181 TQ	MNBLS	1/16-3/16
	Mississippi	Y	29980 FQ	39070 MW	47130 TQ	USBLS	5/15

AE	Average entry wage	AWR	Average wage range	H	Hourly
AEX	Average experienced wage	B	Biweekly	HI	Highest paid
ATC	Average total compensation	D	Daily	HR	High end range
AW	Average wage paid	FQ	First quartile wage	LO	Lowest wage paid

LR	Low end range	MTC	Median total compensation	TCC	Total cash compensation
M	Monthly	MW	Median wage paid	TQ	Third quartile wage
MCC	Median cash compensation	MWR	Median wage range	W	Weekly
ME	Median entry wage	S	See annotated source	Y	Yearly

Occupation/Type/Industry	Location	Per	Low	Mid	High	Source	Date
Slot Supervisor	Missouri	Y	25100 FQ	34830 MW	44170 TQ	USBLS	5/15
	Kansas City MSA, MO-KS	Y	21760 FQ	24440 MW	42730 TQ	USBLS	5/15
	St. Louis MSA, MO-IL	Y	23820 FQ	33240 MW	43480 TQ	USBLS	5/15
	Nevada	Y	27760 FQ	35700 MW	45850 TQ	USBLS	5/15
	Las Vegas-Henderson-Paradise MSA, NV	Y	30450 FQ	37580 MW	47760 TQ	USBLS	5/15
	New Mexico	Y	20540 FQ	24960 MW	39970 TQ	USBLS	5/15
	Albuquerque MSA, NM	Y	17130 FQ	18650 MW	44480 TQ	USBLS	5/15
	New York	Y	21940 AE	34280 MW	43540 AEX	NYBLS	1/16-3/16
	North Dakota	Y	23870 FQ	31160 MW	37620 TQ	USBLS	5/15
	Ohio	Y	24200 FQ	36400 MW	45240 TQ	USBLS	5/15
	Cleveland-Elyria MSA, OH	Y	23240 FQ	30780 MW	42790 TQ	USBLS	5/15
	Columbus MSA, OH	Y	40670 FQ	44630 MW	48590 TQ	USBLS	5/15
	Oklahoma	Y	19920 FQ	25750 MW	31420 TQ	USBLS	5/15
	Tulsa MSA, OK	Y	21620 FQ	27280 MW	34170 TQ	USBLS	5/15
	Oregon	H	16.62 FQ	20.59 MW	23.78 TQ	ORBLS	2016
	Pennsylvania	Y	36860 FQ	49190 MW	57790 TQ	USBLS	5/15
	Memphis MSA, TN-MS-AR	Y	37020 FQ	43920 MW	50170 TQ	USBLS	5/15
	Washington	H	15.94 FQ	18.99 MW	25.59 TQ	WABLS	3/16
	West Virginia	Y	22920 FQ	28350 MW	41640 TQ	USBLS	5/15
	Wisconsin	Y	25450 FQ	34020 MW	46190 TQ	USBLS	5/15
	Puerto Rico	Y	21860 FQ	25730 MW	31150 TQ	USBLS	5/15
	San Juan-Carolina-Caguas MSA, PR	Y	21990 FQ	26920 MW	33220 TQ	USBLS	5/15
Slot Technician							
Cruise Ship	United States	M	2500 LO		3000 HI	CRU03	2016
Small Business Counselor							
County Government	Oakland County, MI	B	2014 LO		2628 HI	MIOAK2	10/1/16
Snow Plow Driver							
County Road Commission	Wayne County, MI	H			15.00 HI	LSJ12	2016
Soccer Player							
U.S. Women's Soccer Team	United States	Y	72000 LO			NYT02	2016
Social and Community Service Manager	Alabama	Y	41603 AE	66868 AW	79506 AEX	ALBLS	6/16
	Birmingham-Hoover MSA, AL	Y	44893 AE	71624 AW	85000 AEX	ALBLS	6/16
	Alaska	Y	53260 FQ	80020 MW	97150 TQ	USBLS	5/15
	Anchorage MSA, AK	Y	55150 FQ	79980 MW	98980 TQ	USBLS	5/15
	Arizona	Y	48580 FQ	62750 MW	81790 TQ	USBLS	5/15
	Phoenix-Mesa-Scottsdale MSA, AZ	Y	53330 FQ	69490 MW	89160 TQ	USBLS	5/15
	Tucson MSA, AZ	Y	44610 FQ	55250 MW	72140 TQ	USBLS	5/15
	Arkansas	Y	36780 FQ	46300 MW	62920 TQ	USBLS	5/15
	Little Rock-North Little Rock-Conway MSA, AR	Y	41820 FQ	51870 MW	68120 TQ	USBLS	5/15
	California	H	24.89 FQ	32.97 MW	45.52 TQ	CABLS	1/16-3/16
	Anaheim-Santa Ana-Irvine PMSA, CA	H	23.71 FQ	29.77 MW	39.40 TQ	CABLS	1/16-3/16
	Los Angeles-Long Beach-Glendale PMSA, CA	H	27.92 FQ	35.74 MW	46.60 TQ	CABLS	1/16-3/16
	Oakland-Hayward-Berkeley PMSA, CA	H	25.13 FQ	33.93 MW	58.21 TQ	CABLS	1/16-3/16
	Riverside-San Bernardino-Ontario MSA, CA	H	22.42 FQ	30.58 MW	42.83 TQ	CABLS	1/16-3/16
	Sacramento–Roseville–Arden-Arcade MSA, CA	H	18.15 FQ	30.31 MW	40.83 TQ	CABLS	1/16-3/16
	San Diego-Carlsbad MSA, CA	H	23.53 FQ	32.20 MW	42.44 TQ	CABLS	1/16-3/16
	San Francisco-Redwood City-South San Francisco PMSA, CA	H	24.36 FQ	32.80 MW	47.33 TQ	CABLS	1/16-3/16
	Colorado	Y	52630 FQ	65370 MW	86970 TQ	USBLS	5/15
	Denver-Aurora-Lakewood MSA, CO	Y	51260 FQ	60480 MW	81650 TQ	USBLS	5/15
	Connecticut	Y		66354 MW		CTBLS	1/16-3/16
	Bridgeport-Stamford-Norwalk MSA, CT	Y	48080 FQ	67680 MW	93330 TQ	USBLS	5/15
	Hartford-West Hartford-East Hartford MSA, CT	Y	52410 FQ	67140 MW	84520 TQ	USBLS	5/15

AE	Average entry wage	AWR	Average wage range	H	Hourly	LR	Low end range	MTC	Median total compensation	TCC	Total cash compensation
AEX	Average experienced wage	B	Biweekly	HI	Highest wage paid	M	Monthly	MW	Median wage paid	TQ	Third quartile wage
ATC	Average total compensation	D	Daily	HR	High end range	MCC	Median cash compensation	MWR	Median wage range	W	Weekly
AW	Average wage paid	FQ	First quartile wage	LO	Lowest wage paid	ME	Median entry wage	S	See annotated source	Y	Yearly

Occupation/Type/Industry	Location	Per	Low	Mid	High	Source	Date
Social and Community Service Manager	Delaware	Y	54540 FQ	62590 MW	74490 TQ	USBLS	5/15
	Wilmington PMSA, DE-MD-NJ	Y	56510 FQ	66450 MW	76990 TQ	USBLS	5/15
	District of Columbia	Y	67000 FQ	88870 MW	120350 TQ	USBLS	5/15
	Washington-Arlington-Alexandria PMSA, DC-VA-MD-WV	Y	69350 FQ	95260 MW	121110 TQ	USBLS	5/15
	Florida	H	24.90 AE	34.35 MW	44.33 AEX	FLBLS	7/16-9/16
	Fort Lauderdale-Pompano Beach-Deerfield Beach PMSA, FL	H	29.69 AE	43.02 MW	54.03 AEX	FLBLS	7/16-9/16
	Miami-Miami Beach-Kendall PMSA, FL	H	26.43 AE	36.37 MW	47.08 AEX	FLBLS	7/16-9/16
	Orlando-Kissimmee-Sanford MSA, FL	H	24.05 AE	31.15 MW	41.77 AEX	FLBLS	7/16-9/16
	Tampa-St. Petersburg-Clearwater MSA, FL	H	25.94 AE	35.20 MW	45.44 AEX	FLBLS	7/16-9/16
	Georgia	Y	47370 FQ	62420 MW	85110 TQ	USBLS	5/15
	Atlanta-Sandy Springs-Roswell MSA, GA	Y	50430 FQ	69060 MW	89100 TQ	USBLS	5/15
	Augusta-Richmond County MSA, GA-SC	Y	43240 FQ	58730 MW	89320 TQ	USBLS	5/15
	Hawaii	Y	47000 FQ	59040 MW	74560 TQ	USBLS	5/15
	Urban Honolulu MSA, HI	Y	46790 FQ	58550 MW	72640 TQ	USBLS	5/15
	Idaho	Y	36020 FQ	46950 MW	61030 TQ	USBLS	5/15
	Boise City MSA, ID	Y	39580 FQ	47370 MW	62640 TQ	USBLS	5/15
	Illinois	Y	43540 FQ	56790 MW	77040 TQ	USBLS	5/15
	Chicago-Naperville-Arlington Heights PMSA, IL	Y	45140 FQ	60990 MW	81360 TQ	USBLS	5/15
	Lake County-Kenosha County PMSA, IL-WI	Y	44220 FQ	51060 MW	70270 TQ	USBLS	5/15
	Indiana	Y	38510 FQ	48750 MW	61770 TQ	USBLS	5/15
	Gary PMSA, IN	Y	40950 FQ	49330 MW	62070 TQ	USBLS	5/15
	Indianapolis-Carmel-Anderson MSA, IN	Y	44360 FQ	56220 MW	72660 TQ	USBLS	5/15
	Iowa	Y	38890 FQ	49010 MW	65050 TQ	USBLS	5/15
	Des Moines-West Des Moines MSA, IA	Y	39440 FQ	54360 MW	71880 TQ	USBLS	5/15
	Kansas	Y	43830 FQ	54170 MW	69220 TQ	USBLS	5/15
	Wichita MSA, KS	Y	44480 FQ	55320 MW	72360 TQ	USBLS	5/15
	Kentucky	Y	41720 FQ	52890 MW	68200 TQ	USBLS	5/15
	Elizabethtown-Fort Knox MSA, KY	Y	42460 FQ	50650 MW	72420 TQ	USBLS	5/15
	Louisville-Jefferson County MSA, KY-IN	Y	46380 FQ	58260 MW	73340 TQ	USBLS	5/15
	Louisiana	Y	49740 FQ	62960 MW	78170 TQ	USBLS	5/15
	Baton Rouge MSA, LA	Y	56540 FQ	70280 MW	84450 TQ	USBLS	5/15
	New Orleans-Metairie MSA, LA	Y	49590 FQ	60730 MW	76220 TQ	USBLS	5/15
	Maine	Y	45850 FQ	55280 MW	63430 TQ	USBLS	5/15
	Portland-South Portland MSA, ME	Y	45140 FQ	55360 MW	63420 TQ	USBLS	5/15
	Maryland	Y	48200 AE	76976 MW	91364 AEX	MDBLS	4/16
	Baltimore-Columbia-Towson MSA, MD	Y	58590 FQ	70430 MW	88630 TQ	USBLS	5/15
	Salisbury MSA, MD-DE	Y	47690 FQ	57860 MW	66230 TQ	USBLS	5/15
	Massachusetts	Y	48570 FQ	61510 MW	79460 TQ	USBLS	5/15
	Boston-Cambridge-Newton NECTA, MA	Y	52540 FQ	64890 MW	85890 TQ	USBLS	5/15
	Worcester MSA, MA-CT	Y	43410 FQ	55370 MW	73120 TQ	USBLS	5/15
	Michigan	Y	47950 FQ	61290 MW	77410 TQ	USBLS	5/15
	Detroit-Dearborn-Livonia PMSA, MI	Y	51090 FQ	62340 MW	82370 TQ	USBLS	5/15
	Grand Rapids-Wyoming MSA, MI	Y	47920 FQ	59560 MW	72680 TQ	USBLS	5/15
	Minnesota	Y	56384 FQ	71483 MW	90616 TQ	MNBLS	1/16-3/16
	Minneapolis-St. Paul-Bloomington MSA, MN-WI	Y	58548 FQ	75466 MW	93573 TQ	MNBLS	1/16-3/16
	Mississippi	Y	32870 FQ	40930 MW	50310 TQ	USBLS	5/15
	Jackson MSA, MS	Y	36860 FQ	43630 MW	58440 TQ	USBLS	5/15
	Missouri	Y	44220 FQ	54980 MW	68800 TQ	USBLS	5/15

AE	Average entry wage	AWR	Average wage range	H	Hourly
AEX	Average experienced wage	B	Biweekly	HI	Highest wage paid
ATC	Average total compensation	D	Daily	HR	High end range
AW	Average wage paid	FQ	First quartile wage	LO	Lowest wage paid

LR	Low end range	MTC	Median total compensation	TCC	Total cash compensation
M	Monthly	MW	Median wage paid	TQ	Third quartile wage
MCC	Median cash compensation	MWR	Median wage range	W	Weekly
ME	Median entry wage	S	See annotated source	Y	Yearly

Occupation/Type/Industry	Location	Per	Low	Mid	High	Source	Date
Social and Community Service Manager							
	Kansas City MSA, MO-KS	Y	48270 FQ	59530 MW	78540 TQ	USBLS	5/15
	St. Louis MSA, MO-IL	Y	48680 FQ	58310 MW	72950 TQ	USBLS	5/15
	Montana	Y	37660 FQ	49300 MW	62450 TQ	USBLS	5/15
	Billings MSA, MT	Y	38930 FQ	55520 MW	74060 TQ	USBLS	5/15
	Nebraska	Y	42430 FQ	55435 MW	70160 TQ	NEBLS	7/16-9/16
	Omaha-Council Bluffs MSA, NE-IA	Y	38885 FQ	51300 MW	67200 TQ	NEBLS	7/16-9/16
	Nevada	Y	46560 FQ	60380 MW	78550 TQ	USBLS	5/15
	Las Vegas-Henderson-Paradise MSA, NV	Y	44980 FQ	59230 MW	77740 TQ	USBLS	5/15
	New Hampshire	H	20.62 AE	29.01 MW	35.94 AEX	NHBLS	6/16
	Manchester NECTA, NH	H	19.77 AE	33.20 MW	43.41 AEX	NHBLS	6/16
	Nashua NECTA, NH-MA	Y	48140 FQ	65850 MW	79010 TQ	USBLS	5/15
	New Jersey	Y	63250 FQ	77050 MW	98220 TQ	USBLS	5/15
	Camden PMSA, NJ	Y	66420 FQ	77120 MW	102040 TQ	USBLS	5/15
	Newark PMSA, NJ-PA	Y	59330 FQ	74680 MW	95690 TQ	USBLS	5/15
	Trenton MSA, NJ	Y	66830 FQ	87450 MW	107730 TQ	USBLS	5/15
	New Mexico	Y	48030 FQ	63580 MW	75220 TQ	USBLS	5/15
	Albuquerque MSA, NM	Y	45920 FQ	65020 MW	74620 TQ	USBLS	5/15
	New York	Y	59510 AE	86880 MW	104150 AEX	NYBLS	1/16-3/16
	Buffalo-Cheektowaga-Niagara Falls MSA, NY	Y	50380 FQ	69900 MW	86750 TQ	USBLS	5/15
	Nassau County-Suffolk County PMSA, NY	Y	69390 FQ	86510 MW	103400 TQ	USBLS	5/15
	New York-Jersey City-White Plains PMSA, NY-NJ	Y	69980 FQ	88580 MW	108780 TQ	USBLS	5/15
	Rochester MSA, NY	Y	58060 FQ	72210 MW	91830 TQ	USBLS	5/15
	North Carolina	Y	47420 FQ	62330 MW	80820 TQ	USBLS	5/15
	Charlotte-Concord-Gastonia MSA, NC-SC	Y	50370 FQ	69400 MW	89030 TQ	USBLS	5/15
	Raleigh MSA, NC	Y	55990 FQ	71150 MW	89160 TQ	USBLS	5/15
	North Dakota	Y	53340 FQ	62830 MW	72690 TQ	USBLS	5/15
	Fargo MSA, ND-MN	Y	49020 FQ	60880 MW	75890 TQ	USBLS	5/15
	Ohio	Y	52280 FQ	64170 MW	79230 TQ	USBLS	5/15
	Cincinnati MSA, OH-KY-IN	Y	52510 FQ	62310 MW	76090 TQ	USBLS	5/15
	Cleveland-Elyria MSA, OH	Y	54180 FQ	65170 MW	79490 TQ	USBLS	5/15
	Columbus MSA, OH	Y	57630 FQ	71740 MW	82930 TQ	USBLS	5/15
	Oklahoma	Y	39880 FQ	51520 MW	64750 TQ	USBLS	5/15
	Oklahoma City MSA, OK	Y	42970 FQ	53310 MW	62900 TQ	USBLS	5/15
	Tulsa MSA, OK	Y	44240 FQ	59680 MW	77680 TQ	USBLS	5/15
	Oregon	H	22.32 FQ	29.01 MW	37.26 TQ	ORBLS	2016
	Portland-Vancouver-Hillsboro MSA, OR-WA	Y	48670 FQ	61180 MW	77890 TQ	USBLS	5/15
	Pennsylvania	Y	48210 FQ	61390 MW	79630 TQ	USBLS	5/15
	Allentown-Bethlehem-Easton MSA, PA-NJ	Y	44630 FQ	59220 MW	77440 TQ	USBLS	5/15
	Harrisburg-Carlisle MSA, PA	Y	53210 FQ	70550 MW	89900 TQ	USBLS	5/15
	Montgomery County-Bucks County-Chester County PMSA, PA	Y	50770 FQ	64640 MW	84820 TQ	USBLS	5/15
	Philadelphia PMSA, PA	Y	54540 FQ	65320 MW	83610 TQ	USBLS	5/15
	Pittsburgh MSA, PA	Y	47090 FQ	63080 MW	82380 TQ	USBLS	5/15
	Rhode Island	Y	49380 FQ	71060 MW	105760 TQ	USBLS	5/15
	Providence-Warwick MSA, RI-MA	Y	47780 FQ	66630 MW	96800 TQ	USBLS	5/15
	South Carolina	Y	43350 FQ	56120 MW	72700 TQ	USBLS	5/15
	Charleston-North Charleston MSA, SC	Y	37200 FQ	49980 MW	75000 TQ	USBLS	5/15
	Columbia MSA, SC	Y	43060 FQ	52240 MW	69320 TQ	USBLS	5/15
	Greenville-Anderson-Mauldin MSA, SC	Y	49890 FQ	57670 MW	69500 TQ	USBLS	5/15
	South Dakota	Y	56160 FQ	65930 MW	76990 TQ	USBLS	5/15
	Sioux Falls MSA, SD	Y	57770 FQ	68690 MW	80830 TQ	USBLS	5/15
	Tennessee	Y	42720 FQ	55630 MW	71450 TQ	USBLS	5/15
	Knoxville MSA, TN	Y	43400 FQ	50780 MW	61770 TQ	USBLS	5/15
	Memphis MSA, TN-MS-AR	Y	37570 FQ	51730 MW	72640 TQ	USBLS	5/15
	Nashville-Davidson–Murfreesboro–Franklin MSA, TN	Y	45680 FQ	59740 MW	78530 TQ	USBLS	5/15
	Texas	Y	51040 FQ	66390 MW	91250 TQ	USBLS	5/15
	Austin-Round Rock MSA, TX	Y	55360 FQ	70500 MW	90760 TQ	USBLS	5/15

AE	Average entry wage	AWR	Average wage range	H	Hourly	LR	Low end range	MTC	Median total compensation	TCC	Total cash compensation
AEX	Average experienced wage	B	Biweekly	HI	Highest wage paid	M	Monthly	MW	Median wage paid	TQ	Third quartile wage
ATC	Average total compensation	D	Daily	HR	High end range	MCC	Median cash compensation	MWR	Median wage range	W	Weekly
AW	Average wage paid	FQ	First quartile wage	LO	Lowest wage paid	ME	Median entry wage	S	See annotated source	Y	Yearly

Occupation/Type/Industry	Location	Per	Low	Mid	High	Source	Date
Social and Community Service Manager	Dallas-Plano-Irving PMSA, TX	Y	56660 FQ	77740 MW	108830 TQ	USBLS	5/15
	Fort Worth-Arlington PMSA, TX	Y	52210 FQ	63340 MW	85880 TQ	USBLS	5/15
	Houston-The Woodlands-Sugar Land MSA, TX	Y	51540 FQ	69360 MW	100110 TQ	USBLS	5/15
	San Antonio-New Braunfels MSA, TX	Y	61050 FQ	74300 MW	94590 TQ	USBLS	5/15
	Utah	Y	44510 FQ	55260 MW	70470 TQ	USBLS	5/15
	Ogden-Clearfield MSA, UT	Y	41100 FQ	48250 MW	59610 TQ	USBLS	5/15
	Provo-Orem MSA, UT	Y	43930 FQ	56080 MW	69800 TQ	USBLS	5/15
	Salt Lake City MSA, UT	Y	47710 FQ	59810 MW	75580 TQ	USBLS	5/15
	Vermont	Y	53500 FQ	65550 MW	81030 TQ	USBLS	5/15
	Burlington-South Burlington MSA, VT	Y	55810 FQ	67480 MW	81030 TQ	USBLS	5/15
	Virginia	Y	58510 FQ	73490 MW	94850 TQ	USBLS	5/15
	Richmond MSA, VA	Y	56640 FQ	73070 MW	88630 TQ	USBLS	5/15
	Virginia Beach-Norfolk-Newport News MSA, VA-NC	Y	59240 FQ	71220 MW	82490 TQ	USBLS	5/15
	Washington	H	24.17 FQ	30.69 MW	39.05 TQ	WABLS	3/16
	Seattle-Bellevue-Everett PMSA, WA	H	25.68 FQ	32.38 MW	43.20 TQ	WABLS	3/16
	Tacoma-Lakewood PMSA, WA	H	21.44 FQ	30.69 MW	38.83 TQ	WABLS	3/16
	West Virginia	Y	41690 FQ	56150 MW	71740 TQ	USBLS	5/15
	Huntington-Ashland MSA, WV-KY-OH	Y	50400 FQ	60880 MW	76050 TQ	USBLS	5/15
	Wisconsin	Y	45510 FQ	58080 MW	73910 TQ	USBLS	5/15
	Madison MSA, WI	Y	45460 FQ	58560 MW	76930 TQ	USBLS	5/15
	Milwaukee-Waukesha-West Allis MSA, WI	Y	45800 FQ	58140 MW	75970 TQ	USBLS	5/15
	Wyoming	Y	44420 FQ	57020 MW	71940 TQ	USBLS	5/15
	Cheyenne MSA, WY	Y	60910 FQ	70990 MW	79040 TQ	USBLS	5/15
	Puerto Rico	Y	28570 FQ	37360 MW	64990 TQ	USBLS	5/15
	San Juan-Carolina-Caguas MSA, PR	Y	29810 FQ	40110 MW	67590 TQ	USBLS	5/15
	Virgin Islands	Y	47950 FQ	64960 MW	75200 TQ	USBLS	5/15
Social and Human Service Assistant	Alabama	Y	17522 AE	26472 AW	30947 AEX	ALBLS	6/16
	Birmingham-Hoover MSA, AL	Y	21579 AE	31436 AW	36369 AEX	ALBLS	6/16
	Alaska	Y	27930 FQ	33450 MW	43200 TQ	USBLS	5/15
	Anchorage MSA, AK	Y	28550 FQ	33370 MW	42630 TQ	USBLS	5/15
	Arizona	Y	23910 FQ	28150 MW	34180 TQ	USBLS	5/15
	Phoenix-Mesa-Scottsdale MSA, AZ	Y	23890 FQ	27920 MW	33410 TQ	USBLS	5/15
	Tucson MSA, AZ	Y	23150 FQ	27970 MW	34800 TQ	USBLS	5/15
	Arkansas	Y	20000 FQ	25030 MW	32370 TQ	USBLS	5/15
	Little Rock-North Little Rock-Conway MSA, AR	Y	23430 FQ	28900 MW	38060 TQ	USBLS	5/15
	California	H	13.67 FQ	17.59 MW	23.51 TQ	CABLS	1/16-3/16
	Anaheim-Santa Ana-Irvine PMSA, CA	H	11.57 FQ	15.68 MW	18.95 TQ	CABLS	1/16-3/16
	Los Angeles-Long Beach-Glendale PMSA, CA	H	14.98 FQ	19.68 MW	27.70 TQ	CABLS	1/16-3/16
	Oakland-Hayward-Berkeley PMSA, CA	H	15.11 FQ	18.02 MW	22.31 TQ	CABLS	1/16-3/16
	Riverside-San Bernardino-Ontario MSA, CA	H	13.76 FQ	17.28 MW	22.77 TQ	CABLS	1/16-3/16
	Sacramento–Roseville–Arden-Arcade MSA, CA	H	11.71 FQ	15.29 MW	22.88 TQ	CABLS	1/16-3/16
	San Diego-Carlsbad MSA, CA	H	12.73 FQ	15.98 MW	19.35 TQ	CABLS	1/16-3/16
	San Francisco-Redwood City-South San Francisco PMSA, CA	H	14.11 FQ	18.64 MW	23.86 TQ	CABLS	1/16-3/16
	Colorado	Y	26610 FQ	32590 MW	38890 TQ	USBLS	5/15
	Denver-Aurora-Lakewood MSA, CO	Y	25900 FQ	32230 MW	38720 TQ	USBLS	5/15
	Connecticut	Y		38216 MW		CTBLS	1/16-3/16
	Bridgeport-Stamford-Norwalk MSA, CT	Y	35490 FQ	46960 MW	51650 TQ	USBLS	5/15

AE	Average entry wage	AWR	Average wage range	H	Hourly	LR	Low end range	MTC	Median total compensation	TCC	Total cash compensation
AEX	Average experienced wage	B	Biweekly	HI	Highest wage paid	M	Monthly	MW	Median wage paid	TQ	Third quartile wage
ATC	Average total compensation	D	Daily	HR	High end range	MCC	Median cash compensation	MWR	Median wage range	W	Weekly
AW	Average wage paid	FQ	First quartile wage	LO	Lowest wage paid	ME	Median entry wage	S	See annotated source	Y	Yearly

Occupation/Type/Industry	Location	Per	Low	Mid	High	Source	Date
Social and Human Service Assistant							
	Hartford-West Hartford-East Hartford MSA, CT	Y	32370 FQ	38140 MW	49480 TQ	USBLS	5/15
	Delaware	Y	26950 FQ	30560 MW	35590 TQ	USBLS	5/15
	Wilmington PMSA, DE-MD-NJ	Y	27530 FQ	33910 MW	45370 TQ	USBLS	5/15
	District of Columbia	Y	29660 FQ	36360 MW	44520 TQ	USBLS	5/15
	Washington-Arlington-Alexandria PMSA, DC-VA-MD-WV	Y	29760 FQ	38280 MW	46660 TQ	USBLS	5/15
	Florida	H	11.91 AE	14.79 MW	17.62 AEX	FLBLS	7/16-9/16
	Fort Lauderdale-Pompano Beach-Deerfield Beach PMSA, FL	H	12.83 AE	16.19 MW	19.27 AEX	FLBLS	7/16-9/16
	Miami-Miami Beach-Kendall PMSA, FL	H	12.55 AE	15.41 MW	18.67 AEX	FLBLS	7/16-9/16
	Orlando-Kissimmee-Sanford MSA, FL	H	12.55 AE	15.80 MW	18.92 AEX	FLBLS	7/16-9/16
	Tampa-St. Petersburg-Clearwater MSA, FL	H	11.94 AE	14.23 MW	16.30 AEX	FLBLS	7/16-9/16
	Georgia	Y	20580 FQ	26450 MW	32830 TQ	USBLS	5/15
	Atlanta-Sandy Springs-Roswell MSA, GA	Y	21590 FQ	27450 MW	33510 TQ	USBLS	5/15
	Augusta-Richmond County MSA, GA-SC	Y	18990 FQ	24530 MW	31790 TQ	USBLS	5/15
	Hawaii	Y	26290 FQ	33140 MW	39660 TQ	USBLS	5/15
	Urban Honolulu MSA, HI	Y	24540 FQ	32860 MW	41490 TQ	USBLS	5/15
	Idaho	Y	19950 FQ	31930 MW	38760 TQ	USBLS	5/15
	Boise City MSA, ID	Y	19930 FQ	31330 MW	37250 TQ	USBLS	5/15
	Illinois	Y	23440 FQ	30370 MW	41010 TQ	USBLS	5/15
	Chicago-Naperville-Arlington Heights PMSA, IL	Y	24300 FQ	31490 MW	41830 TQ	USBLS	5/15
	Lake County-Kenosha County PMSA, IL-WI	Y	23510 FQ	28130 MW	34590 TQ	USBLS	5/15
	Indiana	Y	23230 FQ	28290 MW	34120 TQ	USBLS	5/15
	Gary PMSA, IN	Y	20680 FQ	25260 MW	31230 TQ	USBLS	5/15
	Indianapolis-Carmel-Anderson MSA, IN	Y	27330 FQ	31810 MW	37110 TQ	USBLS	5/15
	Iowa	Y	21940 FQ	27330 MW	35860 TQ	USBLS	5/15
	Des Moines-West Des Moines MSA, IA	Y	24130 FQ	29840 MW	38530 TQ	USBLS	5/15
	Kansas	Y	25990 FQ	30870 MW	34990 TQ	USBLS	5/15
	Wichita MSA, KS	Y	25140 FQ	30190 MW	34160 TQ	USBLS	5/15
	Kentucky	Y	21060 FQ	27050 MW	34140 TQ	USBLS	5/15
	Louisville-Jefferson County MSA, KY-IN	Y	23310 FQ	28330 MW	34760 TQ	USBLS	5/15
	Louisiana	Y	20940 FQ	26630 MW	32740 TQ	USBLS	5/15
	Baton Rouge MSA, LA	Y	19370 FQ	24550 MW	32730 TQ	USBLS	5/15
	New Orleans-Metairie MSA, LA	Y	23830 FQ	28460 MW	33960 TQ	USBLS	5/15
	Maine	Y	26370 FQ	31770 MW	36670 TQ	USBLS	5/15
	Portland-South Portland MSA, ME	Y	26470 FQ	31360 MW	36720 TQ	USBLS	5/15
	Maryland	Y	21183 AE	34240 MW	40768 AEX	MDBLS	4/16
	Baltimore-Columbia-Towson MSA, MD	Y	22130 FQ	27760 MW	38670 TQ	USBLS	5/15
	Salisbury MSA, MD-DE	Y	23810 FQ	30350 MW	36340 TQ	USBLS	5/15
	Massachusetts	Y	25140 FQ	30490 MW	40810 TQ	USBLS	5/15
	Boston-Cambridge-Newton NECTA, MA	Y	25320 FQ	31460 MW	43830 TQ	USBLS	5/15
	Worcester MSA, MA-CT	Y	23050 FQ	29220 MW	38730 TQ	USBLS	5/15
	Michigan	Y	21280 FQ	26280 MW	34350 TQ	USBLS	5/15
	Detroit-Dearborn-Livonia PMSA, MI	Y	20670 FQ	25680 MW	33630 TQ	USBLS	5/15
	Grand Rapids-Wyoming MSA, MI	Y	22060 FQ	26570 MW	34890 TQ	USBLS	5/15
	Minnesota	Y	26421 FQ	32641 MW	42247 TQ	MNBLS	1/16-3/16
	Minneapolis-St. Paul-Bloomington MSA, MN-WI	Y	26955 FQ	32147 MW	41008 TQ	MNBLS	1/16-3/16
	Mississippi	Y	18600 FQ	23570 MW	31690 TQ	USBLS	5/15
	Jackson MSA, MS	Y	19880 FQ	24400 MW	30220 TQ	USBLS	5/15
	Missouri	Y	21550 FQ	28490 MW	35380 TQ	USBLS	5/15

AE	Average entry wage	**AWR**	Average wage range	**H**	Hourly
AEX	Average experienced wage	**B**	Biweekly	**HI**	Highest wage paid
ATC	Average total compensation	**D**	Daily	**HR**	High end range
AW	Average wage paid	**FQ**	First quartile wage	**LO**	Lowest wage paid

LR	Low end range	**MTC**	Median total compensation	**TCC**	Total cash compensation
M	Monthly	**MW**	Median wage paid	**TQ**	Third quartile wage
MCC	Median cash compensation	**MWR**	Median wage range	**W**	Weekly
ME	Median entry wage	**S**	See annotated source	**Y**	Yearly

Social and Human Service Assistant

Occupation/Type/Industry	Location	Per	Low	Mid	High	Source	Date
Social and Human Service Assistant	Kansas City MSA, MO-KS	Y	26280 FQ	32860 MW	37310 TQ	USBLS	5/15
	St. Louis MSA, MO-IL	Y	21140 FQ	28550 MW	36350 TQ	USBLS	5/15
	Montana	Y	20920 FQ	25480 MW	31950 TQ	USBLS	5/15
	Billings MSA, MT	Y	22700 FQ	26910 MW	31990 TQ	USBLS	5/15
	Omaha-Council Bluffs MSA, NE-IA	Y	22370 FQ	26405 MW	30705 TQ	NEBLS	7/16-9/16
	Nevada	Y	27450 FQ	35020 MW	44440 TQ	USBLS	5/15
	Las Vegas-Henderson-Paradise MSA, NV	Y	28260 FQ	35550 MW	44900 TQ	USBLS	5/15
	New Hampshire	H	10.51 AE	13.77 MW	16.70 AEX	NHBLS	6/16
	Manchester NECTA, NH	H	10.64 AE	13.17 MW	16.29 AEX	NHBLS	6/16
	Nashua NECTA, NH-MA	Y	24880 MW	29510 MW	35750 TQ	USBLS	5/15
	New Jersey	Y	26800 FQ	34160 MW	43620 TQ	USBLS	5/15
	Camden PMSA, NJ	Y	25600 FQ	31300 MW	38620 TQ	USBLS	5/15
	Newark PMSA, NJ-PA	Y	26400 FQ	33420 MW	42530 TQ	USBLS	5/15
	Trenton MSA, NJ	Y	31150 FQ	40620 MW	46470 TQ	USBLS	5/15
	New Mexico	Y	26660 FQ	32480 MW	36950 TQ	USBLS	5/15
	Albuquerque MSA, NM	Y	24820 FQ	32190 MW	34820 TQ	USBLS	5/15
	New York	Y	24530 AE	34390 MW	41800 AEX	NYBLS	1/16-3/16
	Buffalo-Cheektowaga-Niagara Falls MSA, NY	Y	24130 FQ	28940 MW	35410 TQ	USBLS	5/15
	Nassau County-Suffolk County PMSA, NY	Y	29940 FQ	36900 MW	46690 TQ	USBLS	5/15
	New York-Jersey City-White Plains PMSA, NY-NJ	Y	27700 FQ	34780 MW	43160 TQ	USBLS	5/15
	Rochester MSA, NY	Y	25280 FQ	33000 MW	42030 TQ	USBLS	5/15
	North Carolina	Y	22770 FQ	27590 MW	33800 TQ	USBLS	5/15
	Charlotte-Concord-Gastonia MSA, NC-SC	Y	24940 FQ	28590 MW	33350 TQ	USBLS	5/15
	Raleigh MSA, NC	Y	22210 FQ	25770 MW	30170 TQ	USBLS	5/15
	North Dakota	Y	26220 FQ	32870 MW	39380 TQ	USBLS	5/15
	Fargo MSA, ND-MN	Y	29040 FQ	33410 MW	37330 TQ	USBLS	5/15
	Ohio	Y	22670 FQ	29070 MW	37360 TQ	USBLS	5/15
	Cincinnati MSA, OH-KY-IN	Y	24050 FQ	31130 MW	39120 TQ	USBLS	5/15
	Cleveland-Elyria MSA, OH	Y	22680 FQ	28640 MW	35820 TQ	USBLS	5/15
	Columbus MSA, OH	Y	23880 FQ	30220 MW	41260 TQ	USBLS	5/15
	Oklahoma	Y	20570 FQ	26470 MW	34140 TQ	USBLS	5/15
	Oklahoma City MSA, OK	Y	22990 FQ	27930 MW	34080 TQ	USBLS	5/15
	Tulsa MSA, OK	Y	21100 FQ	26790 MW	34420 TQ	USBLS	5/15
	Oregon	H	12.68 FQ	16.30 MW	19.20 TQ	ORBLS	2016
	Portland-Vancouver-Hillsboro MSA, OR-WA	Y	25030 FQ	31880 MW	38090 TQ	USBLS	5/15
	Pennsylvania	Y	24070 FQ	29700 MW	35800 TQ	USBLS	5/15
	Allentown-Bethlehem-Easton MSA, PA-NJ	Y	24510 FQ	29130 MW	35760 TQ	USBLS	5/15
	Harrisburg-Carlisle MSA, PA	Y	23310 FQ	29620 MW	36810 TQ	USBLS	5/15
	Montgomery County-Bucks County-Chester County PMSA, PA	Y	25320 FQ	29920 MW	37650 TQ	USBLS	5/15
	Philadelphia PMSA, PA	Y	24820 FQ	29370 MW	35930 TQ	USBLS	5/15
	Pittsburgh MSA, PA	Y	23860 FQ	29060 MW	36400 TQ	USBLS	5/15
	Rhode Island	Y	24590 FQ	30880 MW	37010 TQ	USBLS	5/15
	Providence-Warwick MSA, RI-MA	Y	24040 FQ	29770 MW	37180 TQ	USBLS	5/15
	South Carolina	Y	20900 FQ	23560 MW	29320 TQ	USBLS	5/15
	Charleston-North Charleston MSA, SC	Y	21790 FQ	27220 MW	36710 TQ	USBLS	5/15
	Columbia MSA, SC	Y	21280 FQ	23760 MW	29860 TQ	USBLS	5/15
	Greenville-Anderson-Mauldin MSA, SC	Y	20590 FQ	23100 MW	30210 TQ	USBLS	5/15
	South Dakota	Y	20810 FQ	22990 MW	25890 TQ	USBLS	5/15
	Sioux Falls MSA, SD	Y	20670 FQ	22440 MW	24220 TQ	USBLS	5/15
	Tennessee	Y	21880 FQ	28500 MW	35260 TQ	USBLS	5/15
	Knoxville MSA, TN	Y	18560 FQ	24020 MW	30970 TQ	USBLS	5/15
	Memphis MSA, TN-MS-AR	Y	18940 FQ	29090 MW	36140 TQ	USBLS	5/15
	Nashville-Davidson–Murfreesboro–Franklin MSA, TN	Y	25970 FQ	30230 MW	37480 TQ	USBLS	5/15
	Texas	Y	24460 FQ	31280 MW	38120 TQ	USBLS	5/15
	Austin-Round Rock MSA, TX	Y	29600 FQ	36110 MW	42890 TQ	USBLS	5/15
	Dallas-Plano-Irving PMSA, TX	Y	24830 FQ	32700 MW	38690 TQ	USBLS	5/15

AE	Average entry wage	AWR	Average wage range	H	Hourly
AEX	Average experienced wage	B	Biweekly	HI	Highest wage paid
ATC	Average total compensation	D	Daily	HR	High end range
AW	Average wage paid	FQ	First quartile wage	LO	Lowest wage paid

LR	Low end range	MTC	Median total compensation
M	Monthly	MW	Median wage paid
MCC	Median cash compensation	MWR	Median wage range
ME	Median entry wage	S	See annotated source

TCC	Total cash compensation		
TQ	Third quartile wage		
W	Weekly		
Y	Yearly		

Occupation/Type/Industry	Location	Per	Low	Mid	High	Source	Date
Social and Human Service Assistant	Fort Worth-Arlington PMSA, TX	Y	23970 FQ	29300 MW	36980 TQ	USBLS	5/15
	Houston-The Woodlands-Sugar Land MSA, TX	Y	26890 FQ	32420 MW	38770 TQ	USBLS	5/15
	San Antonio-New Braunfels MSA, TX	Y	17820 FQ	26340 MW	35460 TQ	USBLS	5/15
	Utah	Y	21440 FQ	25440 MW	31780 TQ	USBLS	5/15
	Ogden-Clearfield MSA, UT	Y	19810 FQ	25840 MW	31480 TQ	USBLS	5/15
	Provo-Orem MSA, UT	Y	21120 FQ	23600 MW	28830 TQ	USBLS	5/15
	Salt Lake City MSA, UT	Y	22980 FQ	29260 MW	35480 TQ	USBLS	5/15
	Vermont	Y	26970 FQ	31350 MW	38350 TQ	USBLS	5/15
	Burlington-South Burlington MSA, VT	Y	28940 FQ	33780 MW	38410 TQ	USBLS	5/15
	Virginia	Y	24000 FQ	29330 MW	37130 TQ	USBLS	5/15
	Richmond MSA, VA	Y	25260 FQ	29110 MW	35490 TQ	USBLS	5/15
	Virginia Beach-Norfolk-Newport News MSA, VA-NC	Y	22550 FQ	27750 MW	33360 TQ	USBLS	5/15
	Washington	H	12.10 FQ	15.44 MW	18.92 TQ	WABLS	3/16
	Seattle-Bellevue-Everett PMSA, WA	H	14.10 FQ	16.66 MW	19.33 TQ	WABLS	3/16
	Tacoma-Lakewood PMSA, WA	H	11.48 FQ	15.59 MW	21.51 TQ	WABLS	3/16
	West Virginia	Y	21420 FQ	26860 MW	33920 TQ	USBLS	5/15
	Wisconsin	Y	23410 FQ	31170 MW	39890 TQ	USBLS	5/15
	Madison MSA, WI	Y	23180 FQ	29260 MW	41730 TQ	USBLS	5/15
	Milwaukee-Waukesha-West Allis MSA, WI	Y	26100 FQ	33430 MW	38110 TQ	USBLS	5/15
	Wyoming	Y	25580 FQ	31870 MW	37810 TQ	USBLS	5/15
	Cheyenne MSA, WY	Y	27870 FQ	32980 MW	37570 TQ	USBLS	5/15
	Puerto Rico	Y	18390 FQ	22580 MW	27740 TQ	USBLS	5/15
	San Juan-Carolina-Caguas MSA, PR	Y	18510 FQ	22940 MW	27920 TQ	USBLS	5/15
	Guam	Y	28100 FQ	38020 MW	47560 TQ	USBLS	5/15
Social Fundraiser	United States	Y		57000 AW		SKU01	2016
Social Media Manager	United States	Y		55680 MW		CCAST01	2016
Social Media Professional							
Nonprofit Organization, $2 Million-$5 Million Budget	District of Columbia	Y		40000-50000 AWR		PNP01	2016
Nonprofit Organization, More Than $50 Million Budget	District of Columbia	Y		60000-70000 AWR		PNP01	2016
Social Media Specialist	United States	Y	54000 LO		77750 HI	RH02	2017
Social Media Strategist	United States	Y		50000 MW		LH03	2016
Social Science Research Assistant	Alabama	Y	26207 AE	34096 AW	38041 AEX	ALBLS	6/16
	Alaska	Y	41680 FQ	50610 MW	59140 TQ	USBLS	5/15
	Arizona	Y	39510 FQ	43560 MW	47640 TQ	USBLS	5/15
	Phoenix-Mesa-Scottsdale MSA, AZ	Y	26750 FQ	34740 MW	47260 TQ	USBLS	5/15
	Tucson MSA, AZ	Y	40510 FQ	44090 MW	47680 TQ	USBLS	5/15
	Arkansas	Y	30250 FQ	40980 MW	50460 TQ	USBLS	5/15
	California	H	17.36 FQ	24.82 MW	31.43 TQ	CABLS	1/16-3/16
	Anaheim-Santa Ana-Irvine PMSA, CA	H	17.96 FQ	23.89 MW	30.50 TQ	CABLS	1/16-3/16
	Los Angeles-Long Beach-Glendale PMSA, CA	H	16.65 FQ	23.75 MW	33.88 TQ	CABLS	1/16-3/16
	Oakland-Hayward-Berkeley PMSA, CA	H	20.30 FQ	26.55 MW	30.06 TQ	CABLS	1/16-3/16
	Riverside-San Bernardino-Ontario MSA, CA	H	17.64 FQ	26.89 MW	30.97 TQ	CABLS	1/16-3/16
	Sacramento–Roseville–Arden-Arcade MSA, CA	H	16.54 FQ	18.07 MW	19.55 TQ	CABLS	1/16-3/16
	San Diego-Carlsbad MSA, CA	H	18.64 FQ	25.53 MW	37.19 TQ	CABLS	1/16-3/16
	San Francisco-Redwood City-South San Francisco PMSA, CA	H	17.93 FQ	24.87 MW	32.57 TQ	CABLS	1/16-3/16
	Colorado	Y	29120 FQ	41330 MW	50480 TQ	USBLS	5/15

AE Average entry wage	**AWR** Average wage range	**H** Hourly	**LR** Low end range	**MTC** Median total compensation	**TCC** Total cash compensation
AEX Average experienced wage	**B** Biweekly	**HI** Highest wage paid	**M** Monthly	**MW** Median wage paid	**TQ** Third quartile wage
ATC Average total compensation	**D** Daily	**HR** High end range	**MCC** Median cash compensation	**MWR** Median wage range	**W** Weekly
AW Average wage paid	**FQ** First quartile wage	**LO** Lowest wage paid	**ME** Median entry wage	**S** See annotated source	**Y** Yearly

Occupation/Type/Industry	Location	Per	Low	Mid	High	Source	Date
Social Science Research Assistant	Denver-Aurora-Lakewood MSA, CO	Y	28940 FQ	40680 MW	48970 TQ	USBLS	5/15
	Connecticut	Y		47712 MW		CTBLS	1/16-3/16
	District of Columbia	Y	34690 FQ	43570 MW	54530 TQ	USBLS	5/15
	Washington-Arlington-Alexandria PMSA, DC-VA-MD-WV	Y	35220 FQ	44820 MW	57150 TQ	USBLS	5/15
	Florida	H	12.63 AE	17.02 MW	19.38 AEX	FLBLS	7/16-9/16
	Fort Lauderdale-Pompano Beach-Deerfield Beach PMSA, FL	H	13.09 AE	20.73 MW	22.38 AEX	FLBLS	7/16-9/16
	Tampa-St. Petersburg-Clearwater MSA, FL	H	17.41 AE	18.99 MW	21.46 AEX	FLBLS	7/16-9/16
	Georgia	Y	33660 FQ	42000 MW	56040 TQ	USBLS	5/15
	Atlanta-Sandy Springs-Roswell MSA, GA	Y	35760 FQ	46410 MW	62400 TQ	USBLS	5/15
	Augusta-Richmond County MSA, GA-SC	Y	30330 FQ	37550 MW	48000 TQ	USBLS	5/15
	Hawaii	Y	37550 FQ	45850 MW	54080 TQ	USBLS	5/15
	Urban Honolulu MSA, HI	Y	33370 FQ	46310 MW	55610 TQ	USBLS	5/15
	Illinois	Y	25900 FQ	40520 MW	62320 TQ	USBLS	5/15
	Chicago-Naperville-Arlington Heights PMSA, IL	Y	27080 FQ	40960 MW	61900 TQ	USBLS	5/15
	Lake County-Kenosha County PMSA, IL-WI	Y	46900 FQ	63980 MW	78520 TQ	USBLS	5/15
	Indiana	Y	30420 FQ	39080 MW	51320 TQ	USBLS	5/15
	Indianapolis-Carmel-Anderson MSA, IN	Y	30860 FQ	38500 MW	51800 TQ	USBLS	5/15
	Iowa	Y	29690 FQ	37210 MW	44390 TQ	USBLS	5/15
	Kansas	Y	39390 FQ	53780 MW	59290 TQ	USBLS	5/15
	Kentucky	Y	19190 FQ	39360 MW	56210 TQ	USBLS	5/15
	Louisiana	Y	17170 FQ	19090 MW	37430 TQ	USBLS	5/15
	New Orleans-Metairie MSA, LA	Y	27130 FQ	40440 MW	72860 TQ	USBLS	5/15
	Maine	Y	36140 FQ	41240 MW	48710 TQ	USBLS	5/15
	Portland-South Portland MSA, ME	Y	36320 FQ	44500 MW	58240 TQ	USBLS	5/15
	Maryland	Y	30385 AE	48592 MW	57695 AEX	MDBLS	4/16
	Baltimore-Columbia-Towson MSA, MD	Y	32880 FQ	42310 MW	55560 TQ	USBLS	5/15
	Massachusetts	Y	38700 FQ	48320 MW	62440 TQ	USBLS	5/15
	Boston-Cambridge-Newton NECTA, MA	Y	38540 FQ	48270 MW	62830 TQ	USBLS	5/15
	Michigan	Y	25990 FQ	32980 MW	43540 TQ	USBLS	5/15
	Detroit-Dearborn-Livonia PMSA, MI	Y	27800 FQ	34490 MW	58050 TQ	USBLS	5/15
	Minnesota	Y	35020 FQ	45211 MW	55977 TQ	MNBLS	1/16-3/16
	Minneapolis-St. Paul-Bloomington MSA, MN-WI	Y	34435 FQ	45524 MW	56864 TQ	MNBLS	1/16-3/16
	Missouri	Y	30200 FQ	37830 MW	49640 TQ	USBLS	5/15
	Kansas City MSA, MO-KS	Y	30490 FQ	39180 MW	55640 TQ	USBLS	5/15
	St. Louis MSA, MO-IL	Y	24840 FQ	34070 MW	41420 TQ	USBLS	5/15
	Omaha-Council Bluffs MSA, NE-IA	Y	32645 FQ	42475 MW	55760 TQ	NEBLS	7/16-9/16
	Nevada	Y	40920 FQ	44930 MW	48950 TQ	USBLS	5/15
	New Jersey	Y	42780 FQ	52620 MW	66810 TQ	USBLS	5/15
	Newark PMSA, NJ-PA	Y	50250 FQ	59460 MW	72240 TQ	USBLS	5/15
	Trenton MSA, NJ	Y	31960 FQ	38400 MW	71550 TQ	USBLS	5/15
	New York	Y	20530 AE	41940 MW	57400 AEX	NYBLS	1/16-3/16
	Albany-Schenectady-Troy MSA, NY	Y	26770 FQ	40720 MW	52030 TQ	USBLS	5/15
	Buffalo-Cheektowaga-Niagara Falls MSA, NY	Y	19510 FQ	40720 MW	63490 TQ	USBLS	5/15
	Nassau County-Suffolk County PMSA, NY	Y	18750 FQ	19310 MW	19890 TQ	USBLS	5/15
	New York-Jersey City-White Plains PMSA, NY-NJ	Y	39500 FQ	50410 MW	64370 TQ	USBLS	5/15
	Rochester MSA, NY	Y	47250 FQ	58320 MW	68990 TQ	USBLS	5/15
	North Carolina	Y	36630 FQ	43910 MW	52570 TQ	USBLS	5/15
	Charlotte-Concord-Gastonia MSA, NC-SC	Y	37620 FQ	45090 MW	54800 TQ	USBLS	5/15
	Raleigh MSA, NC	Y	40100 FQ	48020 MW	66760 TQ	USBLS	5/15

AE Average entry wage	**AWR** Average wage range	**H** Hourly	**LR** Low end range	**MTC** Median total compensation	**TCC** Total cash compensation
AEX Average experienced wage	**B** Biweekly	**HI** Highest wage paid	**M** Monthly	**MW** Median wage paid	**TQ** Third quartile wage
ATC Average total compensation	**D** Daily	**HR** High end range	**MCC** Median cash compensation	**MWR** Median wage range	**W** Weekly
AW Average wage paid	**FQ** First quartile wage	**LO** Lowest wage paid	**ME** Median entry wage	**S** See annotated source	**Y** Yearly

Occupation/Type/Industry	Location	Per	Low	Mid	High	Source	Date
Social Science Research Assistant	Ohio	Y	29320 FQ	35670 MW	46660 TQ	USBLS	5/15
	Cincinnati MSA, OH-KY-IN	Y	29720 FQ	37610 MW	59170 TQ	USBLS	5/15
	Cleveland-Elyria MSA, OH	Y	33780 FQ	39240 MW	53230 TQ	USBLS	5/15
	Columbus MSA, OH	Y	27610 FQ	30670 MW	36880 TQ	USBLS	5/15
	Oklahoma	Y	33760 FQ	36790 MW	39880 TQ	USBLS	5/15
	Oregon	H	17.34 FQ	22.36 MW	28.31 TQ	ORBLS	2016
	Portland-Vancouver-Hillsboro MSA, OR-WA	Y	39450 FQ	49570 MW	61440 TQ	USBLS	5/15
	Pennsylvania	Y	32490 FQ	40500 MW	52060 TQ	USBLS	5/15
	Allentown-Bethlehem-Easton MSA, PA-NJ	Y	32450 FQ	40290 MW	59960 TQ	USBLS	5/15
	Montgomery County-Bucks County-Chester County PMSA, PA	Y	31970 FQ	36820 MW	43730 TQ	USBLS	5/15
	Philadelphia PMSA, PA	Y	32690 FQ	40100 MW	51120 TQ	USBLS	5/15
	Pittsburgh MSA, PA	Y	33640 FQ	44540 MW	59000 TQ	USBLS	5/15
	South Carolina	Y	26200 FQ	35660 MW	51280 TQ	USBLS	5/15
	Columbia MSA, SC	Y	26430 FQ	37640 MW	55260 TQ	USBLS	5/15
	Tennessee	Y	23950 FQ	35420 MW	51900 TQ	USBLS	5/15
	Texas	Y	21100 FQ	34350 MW	43690 TQ	USBLS	5/15
	Austin-Round Rock MSA, TX	Y	32620 FQ	39740 MW	50360 TQ	USBLS	5/15
	Dallas-Plano-Irving PMSA, TX	Y	27460 FQ	35870 MW	43170 TQ	USBLS	5/15
	Houston-The Woodlands-Sugar Land MSA, TX	Y	17790 FQ	23840 MW	40390 TQ	USBLS	5/15
	Utah	Y	32630 FQ	43930 MW	57340 TQ	USBLS	5/15
	Provo-Orem MSA, UT	Y	36820 FQ	45150 MW	53900 TQ	USBLS	5/15
	Salt Lake City MSA, UT	Y	33080 FQ	45010 MW	59950 TQ	USBLS	5/15
	Virginia	Y	35860 FQ	48080 MW	67750 TQ	USBLS	5/15
	Virginia Beach-Norfolk-Newport News MSA, VA-NC	Y	28700 FQ	36370 MW	48350 TQ	USBLS	5/15
	Washington	H	16.36 FQ	18.37 MW	22.13 TQ	WABLS	3/16
	Seattle-Bellevue-Everett PMSA, WA	H	16.27 FQ	18.03 MW	21.01 TQ	WABLS	3/16
	West Virginia	Y	34550 FQ	44800 MW	57700 TQ	USBLS	5/15
	Wisconsin	Y	25740 FQ	35500 MW	44410 TQ	USBLS	5/15
	Wyoming	Y	31880 FQ	34920 MW	37960 TQ	USBLS	5/15
Social Work Teacher							
Postsecondary	Alabama	Y	44942 AE	74400 AW	89130 AEX	ALBLS	6/16
Postsecondary	Arizona	Y	51290 FQ	67640 MW	87570 TQ	USBLS	5/15
Postsecondary	Phoenix-Mesa-Scottsdale MSA, AZ	Y	51290 FQ	67800 MW	87450 TQ	USBLS	5/15
Postsecondary	Arkansas	Y	52950 FQ	60640 MW	75030 TQ	USBLS	5/15
Postsecondary	California	Y		90168 AW		CABLS	1/16-3/16
Postsecondary	Anaheim-Santa Ana-Irvine PMSA, CA	Y		124904 AW		CABLS	1/16-3/16
Postsecondary	Colorado	Y	37190 FQ	55710 MW	77680 TQ	USBLS	5/15
Postsecondary	Denver-Aurora-Lakewood MSA, CO	Y	36240 FQ	56110 MW	82300 TQ	USBLS	5/15
Postsecondary	Connecticut	Y		72719 MW		CTBLS	1/16-3/16
Postsecondary	Hartford-West Hartford-East Hartford MSA, CT	Y	54950 FQ	72210 MW	93290 TQ	USBLS	5/15
Postsecondary	Delaware	Y	65330 FQ	72760 MW	81150 TQ	USBLS	5/15
Postsecondary	Wilmington PMSA, DE-MD-NJ	Y	63680 FQ	72080 MW	84620 TQ	USBLS	5/15
Postsecondary	Washington-Arlington-Alexandria PMSA, DC-VA-MD-WV	Y	55440 FQ	70870 MW	89630 TQ	USBLS	5/15
Postsecondary	Florida	Y	46355 AE	76321 MW	99063 AEX	FLBLS	7/16-9/16
Postsecondary	Miami-Miami Beach-Kendall PMSA, FL	Y	56406 AE	84530 MW	111975 AEX	FLBLS	7/16-9/16
Postsecondary	Tampa-St. Petersburg-Clearwater MSA, FL	Y	48932 AE	75764 MW	90797 AEX	FLBLS	7/16-9/16
Postsecondary	Atlanta-Sandy Springs-Roswell MSA, GA	Y	44780 FQ	51340 MW	64830 TQ	USBLS	5/15
Postsecondary	Idaho	Y	50880 FQ	57200 MW	63820 TQ	USBLS	5/15
Postsecondary	Boise City MSA, ID	Y	53550 FQ	59530 MW	68390 TQ	USBLS	5/15
Postsecondary	Illinois	Y	43500 FQ	58210 MW	77000 TQ	USBLS	5/15
Postsecondary	Chicago-Naperville-Arlington Heights PMSA, IL	Y	43790 FQ	57080 MW	73410 TQ	USBLS	5/15
Postsecondary	Indiana	Y	57030 FQ	65200 MW	76870 TQ	USBLS	5/15

AE	Average entry wage	AWR	Average wage range	H	Hourly	LR	Low end range	MTC	Median total compensation	TCC	Total cash compensation
AEX	Average experienced wage	B	Biweekly	HI	Highest wage paid	M	Monthly	MW	Median wage paid	TQ	Third quartile wage
ATC	Average total compensation	D	Daily	HR	High end range	MCC	Median cash compensation	MWR	Median wage range	W	Weekly
AW	Average wage paid	FQ	First quartile wage	LO	Lowest wage paid	ME	Median entry wage	S	See annotated source	Y	Yearly

Occupation/Type/Industry	Location	Per	Low	Mid	High	Source	Date
Social Work Teacher							
Postsecondary	Indianapolis-Carmel-Anderson MSA, IN	Y	56910 FQ	65250 MW	76800 TQ	USBLS	5/15
Postsecondary	Iowa	Y	51870 FQ	64520 MW	79240 TQ	USBLS	5/15
Postsecondary	Kentucky	Y	48420 FQ	62250 MW	84460 TQ	USBLS	5/15
Postsecondary	Louisville-Jefferson County MSA, KY-IN	Y	59150 FQ	74920 MW	107190 TQ	USBLS	5/15
Postsecondary	Louisiana	Y	55370 FQ	67910 MW	76550 TQ	USBLS	5/15
Postsecondary	Maine	Y	29750 FQ	59050 MW	84940 TQ	USBLS	5/15
Postsecondary	Maryland	Y	46993 AE	69617 MW	80929 AEX	MDBLS	4/16
Postsecondary	Baltimore-Columbia-Towson MSA, MD	Y	51160 FQ	60200 MW	91720 TQ	USBLS	5/15
Postsecondary	Massachusetts	Y	43900 FQ	67460 MW	90860 TQ	USBLS	5/15
Postsecondary	Boston-Cambridge-Newton NECTA, MA	Y	39540 FQ	67110 MW	92590 TQ	USBLS	5/15
Postsecondary	Michigan	Y	47300 FQ	75760 MW	99450 TQ	USBLS	5/15
Postsecondary	Grand Rapids-Wyoming MSA, MI	Y	48850 FQ	68040 MW	81540 TQ	USBLS	5/15
Postsecondary	Minnesota	Y	47761 FQ	63548 MW	80211 TQ	MNBLS	1/16-3/16
Postsecondary	Minneapolis-St. Paul-Bloomington MSA, MN-WI	Y	47893 FQ	63921 MW	82630 TQ	MNBLS	1/16-3/16
Postsecondary	Mississippi	Y	50110 FQ	60530 MW	74350 TQ	USBLS	5/15
Postsecondary	Missouri	Y	45710 FQ	60260 MW	74950 TQ	USBLS	5/15
Postsecondary	St. Louis MSA, MO-IL	Y	37830 FQ	53050 MW	74180 TQ	USBLS	5/15
Postsecondary	Nebraska	Y	28640 FQ	48690 MW	66080 TQ	NEBLS	7/16-9/16
Postsecondary	New Jersey	Y	62710 FQ	79910 MW	100200 TQ	USBLS	5/15
Postsecondary	Newark PMSA, NJ-PA	Y	68930 FQ	82670 MW	140920 TQ	USBLS	5/15
Postsecondary	New Mexico	Y	53690 FQ	60500 MW	70440 TQ	USBLS	5/15
Postsecondary	New York	Y	34650 AE	59440 MW	92830 AEX	NYBLS	1/16-3/16
Postsecondary	Nassau County-Suffolk County PMSA, NY	Y	50830 FQ	58440 MW	90520 TQ	USBLS	5/15
Postsecondary	New York-Jersey City-White Plains PMSA, NY-NJ	Y	43090 FQ	67820 MW	111830 TQ	USBLS	5/15
Postsecondary	North Carolina	Y	53930 FQ	64480 MW	78570 TQ	USBLS	5/15
Postsecondary	Charlotte-Concord-Gastonia MSA, NC-SC	Y	53560 FQ	62490 MW	76560 TQ	USBLS	5/15
Postsecondary	Raleigh MSA, NC	Y	38090 FQ	52930 MW	64900 TQ	USBLS	5/15
Postsecondary	North Dakota	Y	60820 FQ	81270 MW	100350 TQ	USBLS	5/15
Postsecondary	Ohio	Y	41850 FQ	55120 MW	75750 TQ	USBLS	5/15
Postsecondary	Cincinnati MSA, OH-KY-IN	Y	45170 FQ	60620 MW	78890 TQ	USBLS	5/15
Postsecondary	Columbus MSA, OH	Y	43480 FQ	51550 MW	74160 TQ	USBLS	5/15
Postsecondary	Oklahoma	Y	38970 FQ	50670 MW	72730 TQ	USBLS	5/15
Postsecondary	Oregon	Y	58605 FQ	69144 MW	84881 TQ	ORBLS	2016
Postsecondary	Pennsylvania	Y	46860 FQ	61390 MW	88040 TQ	USBLS	5/15
Postsecondary	Harrisburg-Carlisle MSA, PA	Y	46640 FQ	65220 MW	85770 TQ	USBLS	5/15
Postsecondary	Montgomery County-Bucks County-Chester County PMSA, PA	Y	44870 FQ	57000 MW	92350 TQ	USBLS	5/15
Postsecondary	Philadelphia PMSA, PA	Y	47790 FQ	68340 MW	94300 TQ	USBLS	5/15
Postsecondary	Pittsburgh MSA, PA	Y	45160 FQ	59150 MW	89650 TQ	USBLS	5/15
Postsecondary	Rhode Island	Y	56340 FQ	69690 MW	81460 TQ	USBLS	5/15
Postsecondary	Providence-Warwick MSA, RI-MA	Y	56200 FQ	68670 MW	80210 TQ	USBLS	5/15
Postsecondary	South Carolina	Y	40370 FQ	62210 MW	83690 TQ	USBLS	5/15
Postsecondary	Columbia MSA, SC	Y	37640 FQ	59880 MW	80470 TQ	USBLS	5/15
Postsecondary	South Dakota	Y	46520 FQ	57420 MW	80790 TQ	USBLS	5/15
Postsecondary	Tennessee	Y	30940 FQ	56500 MW	72140 TQ	USBLS	5/15
Postsecondary	Texas	Y	28960 FQ	55300 MW	76920 TQ	USBLS	5/15
Postsecondary	Austin-Round Rock MSA, TX	Y	35150 FQ	54990 MW	88810 TQ	USBLS	5/15
Postsecondary	Dallas-Plano-Irving PMSA, TX	Y	39530 FQ	60830 MW	80370 TQ	USBLS	5/15
Postsecondary	Houston-The Woodlands-Sugar Land MSA, TX	Y	30500 FQ	57240 MW	76600 TQ	USBLS	5/15
Postsecondary	San Antonio-New Braunfels MSA, TX	Y	23160 FQ	45610 MW	73810 TQ	USBLS	5/15
Postsecondary	Utah	Y	56630 FQ	71370 MW	92390 TQ	USBLS	5/15
Postsecondary	Virginia	Y	38780 FQ	54950 MW	74160 TQ	USBLS	5/15
Postsecondary	Virginia Beach-Norfolk-Newport News MSA, VA-NC	Y	40010 FQ	57900 MW	73630 TQ	USBLS	5/15
Postsecondary	Washington	Y		80601 AW		WABLS	3/16
Postsecondary	West Virginia	Y	40590 FQ	63210 MW	74940 TQ	USBLS	5/15
Postsecondary	Wisconsin	Y	38300 FQ	53450 MW	69800 TQ	USBLS	5/15
Postsecondary	Puerto Rico	Y	19040 FQ	34990 MW	71680 TQ	USBLS	5/15

AE Average entry wage	**AWR** Average wage range	**H** Hourly	**LR** Low end range	**MTC** Median total compensation	**TCC** Total cash compensation
AEX Average experienced wage	**B** Biweekly	**HI** Highest wage paid	**M** Monthly	**MW** Median wage paid	**TQ** Third quartile wage
ATC Average total compensation	**D** Daily	**HR** High end range	**MCC** Median cash compensation	**MWR** Median wage range	**W** Weekly
AW Average wage paid	**FQ** First quartile wage	**LO** Lowest wage paid	**ME** Median entry wage	**S** See annotated source	**Y** Yearly

Occupation/Type/Industry	Location	Per	Low	Mid	High	Source	Date
Social Work Teacher							
Postsecondary	San Juan-Carolina-Caguas MSA, PR	Y	18490 FQ	30040 MW	79450 TQ	USBLS	5/15
Sociologist	Arizona	Y	47970 FQ	64710 MW	77820 TQ	USBLS	5/15
	California	H	37.13 FQ	48.40 MW	64.27 TQ	CABLS	1/16-3/16
	Los Angeles-Long Beach-Glendale PMSA, CA	H	42.51 FQ	59.78 MW	76.43 TQ	CABLS	1/16-3/16
	Oakland-Hayward-Berkeley PMSA, CA	H	34.85 FQ	41.86 MW	53.92 TQ	CABLS	1/16-3/16
	Sacramento–Roseville–Arden-Arcade MSA, CA	H	23.99 FQ	35.56 MW	42.94 TQ	CABLS	1/16-3/16
	San Diego-Carlsbad MSA, CA	H	41.44 FQ	47.13 MW	54.38 TQ	CABLS	1/16-3/16
	San Francisco-Redwood City-South San Francisco PMSA, CA	H	39.68 FQ	50.45 MW	61.94 TQ	CABLS	1/16-3/16
	District of Columbia	Y	67180 FQ	79760 MW	124710 TQ	USBLS	5/15
	Washington-Arlington-Alexandria PMSA, DC-VA-MD-WV	Y	71420 FQ	103780 MW	146310 TQ	USBLS	5/15
	Florida	H	21.51 AE	30.23 MW	38.55 AEX	FLBLS	7/16-9/16
	Michigan	Y	40820 FQ	60830 MW	88030 TQ	USBLS	5/15
	New Jersey	Y	86140 FQ	153000 MW	186930 TQ	USBLS	5/15
	New York	Y	44180 AE	69590 MW	89050 AEX	NYBLS	1/16-3/16
	New York-Jersey City-White Plains PMSA, NY-NJ	Y	50400 FQ	67440 MW	90630 TQ	USBLS	5/15
	North Carolina	Y	52940 FQ	75490 MW	100800 TQ	USBLS	5/15
	Oregon	H	27.56 FQ	40.07 MW	47.84 TQ	ORBLS	2016
	Pennsylvania	Y	67730 FQ	88450 MW	115780 TQ	USBLS	5/15
	Philadelphia PMSA, PA	Y	63620 FQ	78060 MW	91120 TQ	USBLS	5/15
	Texas	Y	21700 FQ	33450 MW	38950 TQ	USBLS	5/15
	Washington	H	26.31 FQ	33.55 MW	35.59 TQ	WABLS	3/16
	Wisconsin	Y	36240 FQ	49190 MW	61530 TQ	USBLS	5/15
	Madison MSA, WI	Y	28040 FQ	37880 MW	52750 TQ	USBLS	5/15
	Milwaukee-Waukesha-West Allis MSA, WI	Y	43870 FQ	53850 MW	63180 TQ	USBLS	5/15
Sociology Teacher							
Postsecondary	Alabama	Y	43199 AE	66776 AW	78559 AEX	ALBLS	6/16
Postsecondary	Birmingham-Hoover MSA, AL	Y	49305 AE	74767 AW	87499 AEX	ALBLS	6/16
Postsecondary	Arizona	Y	49670 FQ	68330 MW	90120 TQ	USBLS	5/15
Postsecondary	Phoenix-Mesa-Scottsdale MSA, AZ	Y	51660 FQ	68450 MW	89480 TQ	USBLS	5/15
Postsecondary	Arkansas	Y	41820 FQ	48720 MW	72020 TQ	USBLS	5/15
Postsecondary	Little Rock-North Little Rock-Conway MSA, AR	Y	44480 FQ	54510 MW	74460 TQ	USBLS	5/15
Postsecondary	California	Y		92917 AW		CABLS	1/16-3/16
Postsecondary	Anaheim-Santa Ana-Irvine PMSA, CA	Y		120816 AW		CABLS	1/16-3/16
Postsecondary	Los Angeles-Long Beach-Glendale PMSA, CA	Y		93628 AW		CABLS	1/16-3/16
Postsecondary	Riverside-San Bernardino-Ontario MSA, CA	Y		103549 AW		CABLS	1/16-3/16
Postsecondary	Sacramento–Roseville–Arden-Arcade MSA, CA	Y		90888 AW		CABLS	1/16-3/16
Postsecondary	San Diego-Carlsbad MSA, CA	Y		94551 AW		CABLS	1/16-3/16
Postsecondary	San Francisco-Redwood City-South San Francisco PMSA, CA	Y		87480 AW		CABLS	1/16-3/16
Postsecondary	Colorado	Y	35950 FQ	55320 MW	75770 TQ	USBLS	5/15
Postsecondary	Denver-Aurora-Lakewood MSA, CO	Y	35000 FQ	54040 MW	74370 TQ	USBLS	5/15
Postsecondary	Connecticut	Y		78319 MW		CTBLS	1/16-3/16
Postsecondary	Bridgeport-Stamford-Norwalk MSA, CT	Y	67730 FQ	77700 MW	101110 TQ	USBLS	5/15
Postsecondary	Hartford-West Hartford-East Hartford MSA, CT	Y	60280 FQ	73400 MW	95910 TQ	USBLS	5/15
Postsecondary	Delaware	Y	66510 FQ	71350 MW	76200 TQ	USBLS	5/15
Postsecondary	Wilmington PMSA, DE-MD-NJ	Y	65540 FQ	71160 MW	76790 TQ	USBLS	5/15
Postsecondary	District of Columbia	Y	62610 FQ	78140 MW	102150 TQ	USBLS	5/15

Occupation/Type/Industry	Location	Per	Low	Mid	High	Source	Date
Sociology Teacher							
Postsecondary	Washington-Arlington-Alexandria PMSA, DC-VA-MD-WV	Y	55650 FQ	70330 MW	93710 TQ	USBLS	5/15
Postsecondary	Florida	Y	42381 AE	81147 MW	100296 AEX	FLBLS	7/16-9/16
Postsecondary	Fort Lauderdale-Pompano Beach-Deerfield Beach PMSA, FL	Y	43961 AE	67230 MW	77200 AEX	FLBLS	7/16-9/16
Postsecondary	Miami-Miami Beach-Kendall PMSA, FL	Y	56919 AE	88993 MW	105807 AEX	FLBLS	7/16-9/16
Postsecondary	Orlando-Kissimmee-Sanford MSA, FL	Y	28754 AE	56076 MW	82514 AEX	FLBLS	7/16-9/16
Postsecondary	Georgia	Y	51960 FQ	64940 MW	78340 TQ	USBLS	5/15
Postsecondary	Atlanta-Sandy Springs-Roswell MSA, GA	Y	56870 FQ	68130 MW	77690 TQ	USBLS	5/15
Postsecondary	Hawaii	Y	35650 FQ	66090 MW	93870 TQ	USBLS	5/15
Postsecondary	Urban Honolulu MSA, HI	Y	36150 FQ	69130 MW	96850 TQ	USBLS	5/15
Postsecondary	Idaho	Y	43010 FQ	51340 MW	62950 TQ	USBLS	5/15
Postsecondary	Illinois	Y	54720 FQ	71910 MW	94420 TQ	USBLS	5/15
Postsecondary	Chicago-Naperville-Arlington Heights PMSA, IL	Y	54900 FQ	69680 MW	89180 TQ	USBLS	5/15
Postsecondary	Indiana	Y	53490 FQ	69730 MW	88130 TQ	USBLS	5/15
Postsecondary	Iowa	Y	55910 FQ	70300 MW	91300 TQ	USBLS	5/15
Postsecondary	Kansas	Y	44470 FQ	55070 MW	68280 TQ	USBLS	5/15
Postsecondary	Kentucky	Y	52930 FQ	66140 MW	88610 TQ	USBLS	5/15
Postsecondary	Louisville-Jefferson County MSA, KY-IN	Y	48460 FQ	61270 MW	75070 TQ	USBLS	5/15
Postsecondary	Louisiana	Y	49870 FQ	58560 MW	72600 TQ	USBLS	5/15
Postsecondary	Maine	Y	58740 FQ	74650 MW	97430 TQ	USBLS	5/15
Postsecondary	Maryland	Y	38774 AE	77889 MW	97446 AEX	MDBLS	4/16
Postsecondary	Baltimore-Columbia-Towson MSA, MD	Y	50130 FQ	84250 MW	106190 TQ	USBLS	5/15
Postsecondary	Salisbury MSA, MD-DE	Y	38190 FQ	67770 MW	76050 TQ	USBLS	5/15
Postsecondary	Massachusetts	Y	55690 FQ	71970 MW	97710 TQ	USBLS	5/15
Postsecondary	Boston-Cambridge-Newton NECTA, MA	Y	59870 FQ	79310 MW	114520 TQ	USBLS	5/15
Postsecondary	Worcester MSA, MA-CT	Y	51740 FQ	62040 MW	76980 TQ	USBLS	5/15
Postsecondary	Michigan	Y	56520 FQ	75200 MW	97760 TQ	USBLS	5/15
Postsecondary	Detroit-Dearborn-Livonia PMSA, MI	Y	53660 FQ	73450 MW	94340 TQ	USBLS	5/15
Postsecondary	Minnesota	Y	54485 FQ	70654 MW	94081 TQ	MNBLS	1/16-3/16
Postsecondary	Minneapolis-St. Paul-Bloomington MSA, MN-WI	Y	49778 FQ	66511 MW	93547 TQ	MNBLS	1/16-3/16
Postsecondary	Mississippi	Y	47610 FQ	58440 MW	71220 TQ	USBLS	5/15
Postsecondary	Missouri	Y	53160 FQ	66880 MW	81040 TQ	USBLS	5/15
Postsecondary	Kansas City MSA, MO-KS	Y	51860 FQ	64170 MW	73590 TQ	USBLS	5/15
Postsecondary	St. Louis MSA, MO-IL	Y	52550 FQ	66390 MW	78220 TQ	USBLS	5/15
Postsecondary	Montana	Y	46630 FQ	59290 MW	72750 TQ	USBLS	5/15
Postsecondary	Nebraska	Y	53365 FQ	64825 MW	77475 TQ	NEBLS	7/16-9/16
Postsecondary	Nevada	Y	37450 FQ	58870 MW	81980 TQ	USBLS	5/15
Postsecondary	New Hampshire	Y	63248 AE	89264 MW	112434 AEX	NHBLS	6/16
Postsecondary	New Jersey	Y	57350 FQ	74490 MW	99560 TQ	USBLS	5/15
Postsecondary	Camden PMSA, NJ	Y	52940 FQ	73160 MW	96280 TQ	USBLS	5/15
Postsecondary	Newark PMSA, NJ-PA	Y	64950 FQ	76650 MW	103410 TQ	USBLS	5/15
Postsecondary	New Mexico	Y	60630 FQ	81420 MW	96460 TQ	USBLS	5/15
Postsecondary	New York	Y	45490 AE	78650 MW	111170 AEX	NYBLS	1/16-3/16
Postsecondary	Buffalo-Cheektowaga-Niagara Falls MSA, NY	Y	40800 FQ	63720 MW	77980 TQ	USBLS	5/15
Postsecondary	Nassau County-Suffolk County PMSA, NY	Y	47820 FQ	61620 MW	83760 TQ	USBLS	5/15
Postsecondary	New York-Jersey City-White Plains PMSA, NY-NJ	Y	64530 FQ	91930 MW	136570 TQ	USBLS	5/15
Postsecondary	Rochester MSA, NY	Y	53220 FQ	67290 MW	82020 TQ	USBLS	5/15
Postsecondary	North Carolina	Y	50620 FQ	63000 MW	77610 TQ	USBLS	5/15
Postsecondary	Charlotte-Concord-Gastonia MSA, NC-SC	Y	46170 FQ	58140 MW	74970 TQ	USBLS	5/15
Postsecondary	Raleigh MSA, NC	Y	46980 FQ	59550 MW	78380 TQ	USBLS	5/15
Postsecondary	North Dakota	Y	53730 FQ	74790 MW	96490 TQ	USBLS	5/15
Postsecondary	Ohio	Y	48480 FQ	67300 MW	90760 TQ	USBLS	5/15
Postsecondary	Columbus MSA, OH	Y	51230 FQ	63860 MW	94880 TQ	USBLS	5/15
Postsecondary	Oklahoma	Y	42630 FQ	56010 MW	70000 TQ	USBLS	5/15
Postsecondary	Oregon	Y	59373 FQ	76602 MW	97937 TQ	ORBLS	2016

AE	Average entry wage	AWR	Average wage range	H	Hourly	LR	Low end range	MTC	Median total compensation	TCC	Total cash compensation
AEX	Average experienced wage	B	Biweekly	HI	Highest wage paid	M	Monthly	MW	Median wage paid	TQ	Third quartile wage
ATC	Average total compensation	D	Daily	HR	High end range	MCC	Median cash compensation	MWR	Median wage range	W	Weekly
AW	Average wage paid	FQ	First quartile wage	LO	Lowest wage paid	ME	Median entry wage	S	See annotated source	Y	Yearly

Occupation/Type/Industry	Location	Per	Low	Mid	High	Source	Date
Sociology Teacher							
Postsecondary	Portland-Vancouver-Hillsboro MSA, OR-WA	Y	54200 FQ	63390 MW	87810 TQ	USBLS	5/15
Postsecondary	Pennsylvania	Y	56430 FQ	72650 MW	95220 TQ	USBLS	5/15
Postsecondary	Allentown-Bethlehem-Easton MSA, PA-NJ	Y	65290 FQ	87130 MW	113420 TQ	USBLS	5/15
Postsecondary	Harrisburg-Carlisle MSA, PA	Y	57450 FQ	74410 MW	96450 TQ	USBLS	5/15
Postsecondary	Montgomery County-Bucks County-Chester County PMSA, PA	Y	55430 FQ	69960 MW	91510 TQ	USBLS	5/15
Postsecondary	Philadelphia PMSA, PA	Y	56060 FQ	71600 MW	94080 TQ	USBLS	5/15
Postsecondary	Pittsburgh MSA, PA	Y	58420 FQ	74170 MW	96190 TQ	USBLS	5/15
Postsecondary	Rhode Island	Y	88220 FQ	138870 MW	154760 TQ	USBLS	5/15
Postsecondary	Providence-Warwick MSA, RI-MA	Y	76710 FQ	136050 MW	153350 TQ	USBLS	5/15
Postsecondary	South Carolina	Y	46510 FQ	58610 MW	72910 TQ	USBLS	5/15
Postsecondary	Columbia MSA, SC	Y	50380 FQ	67970 MW	78760 TQ	USBLS	5/15
Postsecondary	Greenville-Anderson-Mauldin MSA, SC	Y	45200 FQ	55960 MW	67140 TQ	USBLS	5/15
Postsecondary	South Dakota	Y	48960 FQ	57520 MW	68290 TQ	USBLS	5/15
Postsecondary	Tennessee	Y	32650 FQ	48820 MW	70200 TQ	USBLS	5/15
Postsecondary	Knoxville MSA, TN	Y	37090 FQ	48730 MW	73730 TQ	USBLS	5/15
Postsecondary	Memphis MSA, TN-MS-AR	Y	31150 FQ	55590 MW	73430 TQ	USBLS	5/15
Postsecondary	Nashville-Davidson–Murfreesboro–Franklin MSA, TN	Y	37100 FQ	51780 MW	80320 TQ	USBLS	5/15
Postsecondary	Texas	Y	42370 FQ	65240 MW	81990 TQ	USBLS	5/15
Postsecondary	Austin-Round Rock MSA, TX	Y	50300 FQ	66590 MW	100550 TQ	USBLS	5/15
Postsecondary	Dallas-Plano-Irving PMSA, TX	Y	45910 FQ	67250 MW	89870 TQ	USBLS	5/15
Postsecondary	Fort Worth-Arlington PMSA, TX	Y	39870 FQ	59690 MW	73480 TQ	USBLS	5/15
Postsecondary	Houston-The Woodlands-Sugar Land MSA, TX	Y	42500 FQ	61600 MW	86200 TQ	USBLS	5/15
Postsecondary	San Antonio-New Braunfels MSA, TX	Y	23410 FQ	49110 MW	76990 TQ	USBLS	5/15
Postsecondary	Utah	Y	45770 FQ	67100 MW	86050 TQ	USBLS	5/15
Postsecondary	Salt Lake City MSA, UT	Y	35880 FQ	54060 MW	73090 TQ	USBLS	5/15
Postsecondary	Vermont	Y	45670 FQ	71840 MW	95190 TQ	USBLS	5/15
Postsecondary	Burlington-South Burlington MSA, VT	Y	42760 FQ	69700 MW	95990 TQ	USBLS	5/15
Postsecondary	Virginia	Y	44620 FQ	59000 MW	75350 TQ	USBLS	5/15
Postsecondary	Richmond MSA, VA	Y	34850 FQ	50140 MW	74310 TQ	USBLS	5/15
Postsecondary	Virginia Beach-Norfolk-Newport News MSA, VA-NC	Y	43770 FQ	55130 MW	71270 TQ	USBLS	5/15
Postsecondary	Washington	Y		64897 AW		WABLS	3/16
Postsecondary	Seattle-Bellevue-Everett PMSA, WA	Y		81007 AW		WABLS	3/16
Postsecondary	Tacoma-Lakewood PMSA, WA	Y		60636 AW		WABLS	3/16
Postsecondary	West Virginia	Y	50930 FQ	58390 MW	68130 TQ	USBLS	5/15
Postsecondary	Wisconsin	Y	54800 FQ	72690 MW	108610 TQ	USBLS	5/15
Postsecondary	Milwaukee-Waukesha-West Allis MSA, WI	Y	59400 FQ	72670 MW	91450 TQ	USBLS	5/15
Postsecondary	Puerto Rico	Y	50680 FQ	66450 MW	82350 TQ	USBLS	5/15
Postsecondary	San Juan-Carolina-Caguas MSA, PR	Y	19470 FQ	61010 MW	85670 TQ	USBLS	5/15
Software Developer							
Applications	Alabama	Y	62209 AE	96326 AW	113390 AEX	ALBLS	6/16
Applications	Birmingham-Hoover MSA, AL	Y	57898 AE	86592 AW	100944 AEX	ALBLS	6/16
Applications	Arizona	Y	69400 FQ	89400 MW	111140 TQ	USBLS	5/15
Applications	Phoenix-Mesa-Scottsdale MSA, AZ	Y	70430 FQ	91040 MW	113480 TQ	USBLS	5/15
Applications	Tucson MSA, AZ	Y	67390 FQ	83060 MW	101690 TQ	USBLS	5/15
Applications	Arkansas	Y	64600 FQ	79930 MW	97470 TQ	USBLS	5/15
Applications	Little Rock-North Little Rock-Conway MSA, AR	Y	57820 FQ	74490 MW	90780 TQ	USBLS	5/15
Applications	California	H	45.87 FQ	58.40 MW	72.98 TQ	CABLS	1/16-3/16
Applications	Anaheim-Santa Ana-Irvine PMSA, CA	H	40.78 FQ	51.52 MW	62.15 TQ	CABLS	1/16-3/16
Applications	Los Angeles-Long Beach-Glendale PMSA, CA	H	42.58 FQ	53.42 MW	64.34 TQ	CABLS	1/16-3/16

Software Developer

Occupation/Type/Industry	Location	Per	Low	Mid	High	Source	Date
Applications	Oakland-Hayward-Berkeley PMSA, CA	H	45.91 FQ	59.06 MW	72.42 TQ	CABLS	1/16-3/16
Applications	Riverside-San Bernardino-Ontario MSA, CA	H	39.74 FQ	47.12 MW	58.26 TQ	CABLS	1/16-3/16
Applications	Sacramento–Roseville–Arden-Arcade MSA, CA	H	42.09 FQ	50.56 MW	60.22 TQ	CABLS	1/16-3/16
Applications	San Diego-Carlsbad MSA, CA	H	40.13 FQ	49.75 MW	61.85 TQ	CABLS	1/16-3/16
Applications	San Francisco-Redwood City-South San Francisco PMSA, CA	H	44.14 FQ	56.24 MW	70.27 TQ	CABLS	1/16-3/16
Applications	Colorado	Y	80990 FQ	102200 MW	124390 TQ	USBLS	5/15
Applications	Denver-Aurora-Lakewood MSA, CO	Y	81810 FQ	103380 MW	124520 TQ	USBLS	5/15
Applications	Connecticut	Y		94926 MW		CTBLS	1/16-3/16
Applications	Bridgeport-Stamford-Norwalk MSA, CT	Y	74740 FQ	97510 MW	134140 TQ	USBLS	5/15
Applications	Hartford-West Hartford-East Hartford MSA, CT	Y	77030 FQ	92940 MW	111190 TQ	USBLS	5/15
Applications	Delaware	Y	78800 FQ	95590 MW	116050 TQ	USBLS	5/15
Applications	Wilmington PMSA, DE-MD-NJ	Y	78380 FQ	95990 MW	116750 TQ	USBLS	5/15
Applications	District of Columbia	Y	73620 FQ	100640 MW	123230 TQ	USBLS	5/15
Applications	Washington-Arlington-Alexandria PMSA, DC-VA-MD-WV	Y	83280 FQ	110460 MW	137880 TQ	USBLS	5/15
Applications	Florida	H	26.81 AE	40.97 MW	50.06 AEX	FLBLS	7/16-9/16
Applications	Fort Lauderdale-Pompano Beach-Deerfield Beach PMSA, FL	H	25.49 AE	40.19 MW	48.08 AEX	FLBLS	7/16-9/16
Applications	Miami-Miami Beach-Kendall PMSA, FL	H	27.27 AE	31.77 MW	41.50 AEX	FLBLS	7/16-9/16
Applications	Orlando-Kissimmee-Sanford MSA, FL	H	29.03 AE	41.77 MW	51.57 AEX	FLBLS	7/16-9/16
Applications	Tampa-St. Petersburg-Clearwater MSA, FL	H	26.12 AE	43.25 MW	52.25 AEX	FLBLS	7/16-9/16
Applications	Georgia	Y	68090 FQ	92340 MW	116110 TQ	USBLS	5/15
Applications	Atlanta-Sandy Springs-Roswell MSA, GA	Y	70330 FQ	94030 MW	117480 TQ	USBLS	5/15
Applications	Augusta-Richmond County MSA, GA-SC	Y	55620 FQ	73600 MW	100050 TQ	USBLS	5/15
Applications	Hawaii	Y	62370 FQ	81580 MW	107680 TQ	USBLS	5/15
Applications	Urban Honolulu MSA, HI	Y	61710 FQ	80750 MW	104070 TQ	USBLS	5/15
Applications	Idaho	Y	56730 FQ	74980 MW	95340 TQ	USBLS	5/15
Applications	Boise City MSA, ID	Y	57510 FQ	76220 MW	95630 TQ	USBLS	5/15
Applications	Illinois	Y	70060 FQ	91340 MW	114000 TQ	USBLS	5/15
Applications	Chicago-Naperville-Arlington Heights PMSA, IL	Y	69710 FQ	91810 MW	115440 TQ	USBLS	5/15
Applications	Lake County-Kenosha County PMSA, IL-WI	Y	82390 FQ	95360 MW	115060 TQ	USBLS	5/15
Applications	Indiana	Y	63430 FQ	78790 MW	96720 TQ	USBLS	5/15
Applications	Gary PMSA, IN	Y	47990 FQ	69680 MW	85260 TQ	USBLS	5/15
Applications	Indianapolis-Carmel-Anderson MSA, IN	Y	64620 FQ	80000 MW	97380 TQ	USBLS	5/15
Applications	Iowa	Y	64780 FQ	80410 MW	96910 TQ	USBLS	5/15
Applications	Des Moines-West Des Moines MSA, IA	Y	66160 FQ	85600 MW	98790 TQ	USBLS	5/15
Applications	Kansas	Y	68960 FQ	90640 MW	111520 TQ	USBLS	5/15
Applications	Wichita MSA, KS	Y	69370 FQ	88590 MW	106360 TQ	USBLS	5/15
Applications	Kentucky	Y	56740 FQ	71710 MW	89580 TQ	USBLS	5/15
Applications	Louisville-Jefferson County MSA, KY-IN	Y	56740 FQ	73130 MW	91960 TQ	USBLS	5/15
Applications	Louisiana	Y	59780 FQ	78120 MW	95120 TQ	USBLS	5/15
Applications	Baton Rouge MSA, LA	Y	38520 FQ	63600 MW	79940 TQ	USBLS	5/15
Applications	New Orleans-Metairie MSA, LA	Y	71890 FQ	87860 MW	102900 TQ	USBLS	5/15
Applications	Maine	Y	68250 FQ	84960 MW	101090 TQ	USBLS	5/15
Applications	Portland-South Portland MSA, ME	Y	68450 FQ	84360 MW	101590 TQ	USBLS	5/15
Applications	Maryland	Y	66254 AE	108187 MW	129154 AEX	MDBLS	4/16
Applications	Baltimore-Columbia-Towson MSA, MD	Y	75100 FQ	102940 MW	136800 TQ	USBLS	5/15

AE	Average entry wage	AWR	Average wage range	H	Hourly	LR	Low end range
AEX	Average experienced wage	B	Biweekly	HI	Highest wage paid	M	Monthly
ATC	Average total compensation	D	Daily	HR	High end range	MCC	Median cash compensation
AW	Average wage paid	FQ	First quartile wage	LO	Lowest wage paid	ME	Median entry wage

MTC	Median total compensation	TCC	Total cash compensation
MW	Median wage paid	TQ	Third quartile wage
MWR	Median wage range	W	Weekly
S	See annotated source	Y	Yearly

Occupation/Type/Industry	Location	Per	Low	Mid	High	Source	Date
Software Developer							
Applications	Salisbury MSA, MD-DE	Y	83380 FQ	94920 MW	108990 TQ	USBLS	5/15
Applications	Massachusetts	Y	80740 FQ	105650 MW	130130 TQ	USBLS	5/15
Applications	Boston-Cambridge-Newton NECTA, MA	Y	79840 FQ	106410 MW	132600 TQ	USBLS	5/15
Applications	Worcester MSA, MA-CT	Y	76350 FQ	100750 MW	122380 TQ	USBLS	5/15
Applications	Michigan	Y	64280 FQ	81240 MW	105200 TQ	USBLS	5/15
Applications	Detroit-Dearborn-Livonia PMSA, MI	Y	71750 FQ	92960 MW	116920 TQ	USBLS	5/15
Applications	Grand Rapids-Wyoming MSA, MI	Y	58060 FQ	72410 MW	89280 TQ	USBLS	5/15
Applications	Minnesota	Y	72015 FQ	91168 MW	113003 TQ	MNBLS	1/16-3/16
Applications	Minneapolis-St. Paul-Bloomington MSA, MN-WI	Y	72882 FQ	92015 MW	113890 TQ	MNBLS	1/16-3/16
Applications	Mississippi	Y	66120 FQ	85190 MW	105310 TQ	USBLS	5/15
Applications	Jackson MSA, MS	Y	65950 FQ	89270 MW	111190 TQ	USBLS	5/15
Applications	Missouri	Y	72390 FQ	91310 MW	112740 TQ	USBLS	5/15
Applications	Kansas City MSA, MO-KS	Y	75910 FQ	92660 MW	111500 TQ	USBLS	5/15
Applications	St. Louis MSA, MO-IL	Y	75450 FQ	93970 MW	116560 TQ	USBLS	5/15
Applications	Montana	Y	55160 FQ	72170 MW	94830 TQ	USBLS	5/15
Applications	Billings MSA, MT	Y	76300 FQ	85700 MW	93090 TQ	USBLS	5/15
Applications	Nebraska	Y	63450 FQ	78950 MW	98390 TQ	NEBLS	7/16-9/16
Applications	Omaha-Council Bluffs MSA, NE-IA	Y	67480 FQ	84085 MW	103195 TQ	NEBLS	7/16-9/16
Applications	Nevada	Y	73730 FQ	90960 MW	108790 TQ	USBLS	5/15
Applications	Las Vegas-Henderson-Paradise MSA, NV	Y	77810 FQ	92170 MW	107080 TQ	USBLS	5/15
Applications	New Hampshire	H	30.64 AE	45.65 MW	54.17 AEX	NHBLS	6/16
Applications	Manchester NECTA, NH	H	29.36 AE	44.15 MW	52.42 AEX	NHBLS	6/16
Applications	Nashua NECTA, NH-MA	Y	71250 FQ	93700 MW	121180 TQ	USBLS	5/15
Applications	New Jersey	Y	74260 FQ	94970 MW	119680 TQ	USBLS	5/15
Applications	Camden PMSA, NJ	Y	62630 FQ	84760 MW	106380 TQ	USBLS	5/15
Applications	Newark PMSA, NJ-PA	Y	76280 FQ	98210 MW	121800 TQ	USBLS	5/15
Applications	Trenton MSA, NJ	Y	82930 FQ	100210 MW	123070 TQ	USBLS	5/15
Applications	New Mexico	Y	59360 FQ	77590 MW	104510 TQ	USBLS	5/15
Applications	Albuquerque MSA, NM	Y	59800 FQ	80080 MW	109100 TQ	USBLS	5/15
Applications	New York	Y	69040 AE	106650 MW	133680 AEX	NYBLS	1/16-3/16
Applications	Buffalo-Cheektowaga-Niagara Falls MSA, NY	Y	68750 FQ	85410 MW	100350 TQ	USBLS	5/15
Applications	Nassau County-Suffolk County PMSA, NY	Y	70170 FQ	92330 MW	121410 TQ	USBLS	5/15
Applications	New York-Jersey City-White Plains PMSA, NY-NJ	Y	79740 FQ	105650 MW	135810 TQ	USBLS	5/15
Applications	Rochester MSA, NY	Y	64230 FQ	80720 MW	101490 TQ	USBLS	5/15
Applications	North Carolina	Y	72720 FQ	92380 MW	116370 TQ	USBLS	5/15
Applications	Charlotte-Concord-Gastonia MSA, NC-SC	Y	72460 FQ	92830 MW	116830 TQ	USBLS	5/15
Applications	Raleigh MSA, NC	Y	74630 FQ	92980 MW	115590 TQ	USBLS	5/15
Applications	North Dakota	Y	55420 FQ	66350 MW	78830 TQ	USBLS	5/15
Applications	Fargo MSA, ND-MN	Y	54420 FQ	67180 MW	79290 TQ	USBLS	5/15
Applications	Ohio	Y	66530 FQ	84920 MW	101010 TQ	USBLS	5/15
Applications	Cincinnati MSA, OH-KY-IN	Y	63910 FQ	82940 MW	102110 TQ	USBLS	5/15
Applications	Cleveland-Elyria MSA, OH	Y	65460 FQ	84620 MW	99920 TQ	USBLS	5/15
Applications	Columbus MSA, OH	Y	73530 FQ	89060 MW	102440 TQ	USBLS	5/15
Applications	Oklahoma	Y	56210 FQ	75800 MW	98040 TQ	USBLS	5/15
Applications	Oklahoma City MSA, OK	Y	63500 FQ	80160 MW	100150 TQ	USBLS	5/15
Applications	Tulsa MSA, OK	Y	49780 FQ	68920 MW	96830 TQ	USBLS	5/15
Applications	Oregon	H	37.61 FQ	46.97 MW	57.48 TQ	ORBLS	2016
Applications	Portland-Vancouver-Hillsboro MSA, OR-WA	Y	80560 FQ	98910 MW	120300 TQ	USBLS	5/15
Applications	Pennsylvania	Y	71540 FQ	91670 MW	114850 TQ	USBLS	5/15
Applications	Allentown-Bethlehem-Easton MSA, PA-NJ	Y	72280 FQ	91530 MW	119130 TQ	USBLS	5/15
Applications	Harrisburg-Carlisle MSA, PA	Y	60200 FQ	74720 MW	91280 TQ	USBLS	5/15
Applications	Montgomery County-Bucks County-Chester County PMSA, PA	Y	80220 FQ	98400 MW	120910 TQ	USBLS	5/15
Applications	Philadelphia PMSA, PA	Y	81580 FQ	100840 MW	123750 TQ	USBLS	5/15
Applications	Pittsburgh MSA, PA	Y	67210 FQ	86540 MW	104990 TQ	USBLS	5/15
Applications	Rhode Island	Y	73360 FQ	90680 MW	109850 TQ	USBLS	5/15
Applications	Providence-Warwick MSA, RI-MA	Y	72840 FQ	90270 MW	109330 TQ	USBLS	5/15

AE	Average entry wage	AWR	Average wage range	H	Hourly
AEX	Average experienced wage	B	Biweekly	HI	Highest wage paid
ATC	Average total compensation	D	Daily	HR	High end range
AW	Average wage paid	FQ	First quartile wage	LO	Lowest wage paid

LR	Low end range	MTC	Median total compensation
M	Monthly	MW	Median wage paid
MCC	Median cash compensation	MWR	Median wage range
ME	Median entry wage	S	See annotated source

TCC	Total cash compensation	
TQ	Third quartile wage	
W	Weekly	
Y	Yearly	

Occupation/Type/Industry	Location	Per	Low	Mid	High	Source	Date
Software Developer							
Applications	South Carolina	Y	61740 FQ	78950 MW	100690 TQ	USBLS	5/15
Applications	Charleston-North Charleston MSA, SC	Y	67650 FQ	83960 MW	113190 TQ	USBLS	5/15
Applications	Columbia MSA, SC	Y	65070 FQ	80850 MW	96790 TQ	USBLS	5/15
Applications	Greenville-Anderson-Mauldin MSA, SC	Y	61210 FQ	78000 MW	100790 TQ	USBLS	5/15
Applications	South Dakota	Y	62240 FQ	75320 MW	93770 TQ	USBLS	5/15
Applications	Sioux Falls MSA, SD	Y	60800 FQ	81330 MW	99490 TQ	USBLS	5/15
Applications	Tennessee	Y	64090 FQ	81710 MW	99820 TQ	USBLS	5/15
Applications	Knoxville MSA, TN	Y	63310 FQ	80890 MW	99660 TQ	USBLS	5/15
Applications	Memphis MSA, TN-MS-AR	Y	67030 FQ	83620 MW	100720 TQ	USBLS	5/15
Applications	Nashville-Davidson–Murfreesboro–Franklin MSA, TN	Y	66400 FQ	83800 MW	102170 TQ	USBLS	5/15
Applications	Texas	Y	76060 FQ	99340 MW	122400 TQ	USBLS	5/15
Applications	Austin-Round Rock MSA, TX	Y	69670 FQ	99420 MW	121770 TQ	USBLS	5/15
Applications	Dallas-Plano-Irving PMSA, TX	Y	79370 FQ	101270 MW	122860 TQ	USBLS	5/15
Applications	Fort Worth-Arlington PMSA, TX	Y	84320 FQ	105090 MW	126850 TQ	USBLS	5/15
Applications	Houston-The Woodlands-Sugar Land MSA, TX	Y	80350 FQ	101020 MW	125310 TQ	USBLS	5/15
Applications	San Antonio-New Braunfels MSA, TX	Y	74620 FQ	92640 MW	116750 TQ	USBLS	5/15
Applications	Utah	Y	69620 FQ	91440 MW	116940 TQ	USBLS	5/15
Applications	Ogden-Clearfield MSA, UT	Y	45480 FQ	73920 MW	94800 TQ	USBLS	5/15
Applications	Provo-Orem MSA, UT	Y	74890 FQ	98210 MW	119540 TQ	USBLS	5/15
Applications	Salt Lake City MSA, UT	Y	73040 FQ	92680 MW	118520 TQ	USBLS	5/15
Applications	Vermont	Y	66900 FQ	77610 MW	97610 TQ	USBLS	5/15
Applications	Burlington-South Burlington MSA, VT	Y	66330 FQ	77060 MW	95970 TQ	USBLS	5/15
Applications	Virginia	Y	78570 FQ	103490 MW	132540 TQ	USBLS	5/15
Applications	Richmond MSA, VA	Y	68680 FQ	89600 MW	107390 TQ	USBLS	5/15
Applications	Virginia Beach-Norfolk-Newport News MSA, VA-NC	Y	63870 FQ	83600 MW	109650 TQ	USBLS	5/15
Applications	Washington	H	48.74 FQ	57.72 MW	69.61 TQ	WABLS	3/16
Applications	Seattle-Bellevue-Everett PMSA, WA	H	49.85 FQ	58.48 MW	70.25 TQ	WABLS	3/16
Applications	Tacoma-Lakewood PMSA, WA	H	38.03 FQ	46.35 MW	57.34 TQ	WABLS	3/16
Applications	West Virginia	Y	69030 FQ	86630 MW	103480 TQ	USBLS	5/15
Applications	Huntington-Ashland MSA, WV-KY-OH	Y	54890 FQ	73490 MW	96930 TQ	USBLS	5/15
Applications	Wisconsin	Y	66500 FQ	82010 MW	98380 TQ	USBLS	5/15
Applications	Madison MSA, WI	Y	66410 FQ	83220 MW	102320 TQ	USBLS	5/15
Applications	Milwaukee-Waukesha-West Allis MSA, WI	Y	69320 FQ	84010 MW	100650 TQ	USBLS	5/15
Applications	Wyoming	Y	54960 FQ	62880 MW	72760 TQ	USBLS	5/15
Applications	Cheyenne MSA, WY	Y	59380 FQ	63030 MW	70190 TQ	USBLS	5/15
Applications	Puerto Rico	Y	42490 FQ	52820 MW	62660 TQ	USBLS	5/15
Applications	San Juan-Carolina-Caguas MSA, PR	Y	42860 FQ	52970 MW	62860 TQ	USBLS	5/15
C++	United States	Y		91739 AW		STOF1	2015
Objective-C	United States	Y		98828 AW		STOF1	2015
Python	United States	Y		88966 AW		STOF1	2015
Systems Software	Alabama	Y	66806 AE	101698 AW	119139 AEX	ALBLS	6/16
Systems Software	Birmingham-Hoover MSA, AL	Y	65094 AE	90913 AW	103818 AEX	ALBLS	6/16
Systems Software	Anchorage MSA, AK	Y	69460 FQ	93620 MW	146160 TQ	USBLS	5/15
Systems Software	Arizona	Y	72960 FQ	96150 MW	118790 TQ	USBLS	5/15
Systems Software	Phoenix-Mesa-Scottsdale MSA, AZ	Y	71460 FQ	97760 MW	120910 TQ	USBLS	5/15
Systems Software	Tucson MSA, AZ	Y	78880 FQ	92390 MW	109530 TQ	USBLS	5/15
Systems Software	Arkansas	Y	55940 FQ	68500 MW	81840 TQ	USBLS	5/15
Systems Software	Little Rock-North Little Rock-Conway MSA, AR	Y	59200 FQ	71510 MW	83910 TQ	USBLS	5/15
Systems Software	California	H	47.90 FQ	60.56 MW	74.88 TQ	CABLS	1/16-3/16
Systems Software	Anaheim-Santa Ana-Irvine PMSA, CA	H	42.39 FQ	56.00 MW	71.25 TQ	CABLS	1/16-3/16
Systems Software	Los Angeles-Long Beach-Glendale PMSA, CA	H	43.50 FQ	57.01 MW	71.25 TQ	CABLS	1/16-3/16
Systems Software	Oakland-Hayward-Berkeley PMSA, CA	H	47.44 FQ	59.45 MW	73.16 TQ	CABLS	1/16-3/16

AE	Average entry wage	AWR	Average wage range	H	Hourly	
AEX	Average experienced wage	B	Biweekly	HI	Highest wage paid	
ATC	Average total compensation	D	Daily	HR	High end range	
AW	Average wage paid	FQ	First quartile wage	LO	Lowest wage paid	

LR   Low end range
M   Monthly
MCC Median cash compensation
ME   Median entry wage

MTC Median total compensation
MW   Median wage paid
MWR Median wage range
S   See annotated source

TCC Total cash compensation
TQ   Third quartile wage
W   Weekly
Y   Yearly

Occupation/Type/Industry	Location	Per	Low	Mid	High	Source	Date
Software Developer							
Systems Software	Riverside-San Bernardino-Ontario MSA, CA	H	40.96 FQ	50.84 MW	60.41 TQ	CABLS	1/16-3/16
Systems Software	Sacramento–Roseville–Arden-Arcade MSA, CA	H	40.21 FQ	44.73 MW	50.93 TQ	CABLS	1/16-3/16
Systems Software	San Diego-Carlsbad MSA, CA	H	45.86 FQ	56.20 MW	68.83 TQ	CABLS	1/16-3/16
Systems Software	San Francisco-Redwood City-South San Francisco PMSA, CA	H	52.43 FQ	63.75 MW	75.13 TQ	CABLS	1/16-3/16
Systems Software	Colorado	Y	87230 FQ	108280 MW	129820 TQ	USBLS	5/15
Systems Software	Denver-Aurora-Lakewood MSA, CO	Y	85870 FQ	105980 MW	127550 TQ	USBLS	5/15
Systems Software	Connecticut	Y		100922 MW		CTBLS	1/16-3/16
Systems Software	Bridgeport-Stamford-Norwalk MSA, CT	Y	84670 FQ	100790 MW	124760 TQ	USBLS	5/15
Systems Software	Hartford-West Hartford-East Hartford MSA, CT	Y	84250 FQ	103290 MW	123930 TQ	USBLS	5/15
Systems Software	Delaware	Y	98890 FQ	114400 MW	128520 TQ	USBLS	5/15
Systems Software	Wilmington PMSA, DE-MD-NJ	Y	98200 FQ	114260 MW	128690 TQ	USBLS	5/15
Systems Software	District of Columbia	Y	79920 FQ	106310 MW	132420 TQ	USBLS	5/15
Systems Software	Washington-Arlington-Alexandria PMSA, DC-VA-MD-WV	Y	88000 FQ	114850 MW	143000 TQ	USBLS	5/15
Systems Software	Florida	H	30.30 AE	45.98 MW	56.68 AEX	FLBLS	7/16-9/16
Systems Software	Fort Lauderdale-Pompano Beach-Deerfield Beach PMSA, FL	H	30.41 AE	38.70 MW	48.28 AEX	FLBLS	7/16-9/16
Systems Software	Miami-Miami Beach-Kendall PMSA, FL	H	28.76 AE	40.91 MW	50.01 AEX	FLBLS	7/16-9/16
Systems Software	Orlando-Kissimmee-Sanford MSA, FL	H	33.78 AE	49.05 MW	63.22 AEX	FLBLS	7/16-9/16
Systems Software	Tampa-St. Petersburg-Clearwater MSA, FL	H	26.20 AE	43.77 MW	53.14 AEX	FLBLS	7/16-9/16
Systems Software	Georgia	Y	73350 FQ	94360 MW	116400 TQ	USBLS	5/15
Systems Software	Atlanta-Sandy Springs-Roswell MSA, GA	Y	74920 FQ	95780 MW	117750 TQ	USBLS	5/15
Systems Software	Augusta-Richmond County MSA, GA-SC	Y	67860 FQ	85980 MW	104860 TQ	USBLS	5/15
Systems Software	Hawaii	Y	78780 FQ	91950 MW	106080 TQ	USBLS	5/15
Systems Software	Urban Honolulu MSA, HI	Y	78350 FQ	91010 MW	103320 TQ	USBLS	5/15
Systems Software	Illinois	Y	82950 FQ	101950 MW	123790 TQ	USBLS	5/15
Systems Software	Chicago-Naperville-Arlington Heights PMSA, IL	Y	84110 FQ	103030 MW	123960 TQ	USBLS	5/15
Systems Software	Lake County-Kenosha County PMSA, IL-WI	Y	87800 FQ	109740 MW	133410 TQ	USBLS	5/15
Systems Software	Indiana	Y	60660 FQ	76000 MW	96400 TQ	USBLS	5/15
Systems Software	Gary PMSA, IN	Y	45080 FQ	65730 MW	86130 TQ	USBLS	5/15
Systems Software	Indianapolis-Carmel-Anderson MSA, IN	Y	59000 FQ	73150 MW	93250 TQ	USBLS	5/15
Systems Software	Iowa	Y	70590 FQ	85590 MW	101640 TQ	USBLS	5/15
Systems Software	Des Moines-West Des Moines MSA, IA	Y	71550 FQ	89610 MW	107880 TQ	USBLS	5/15
Systems Software	Kansas	Y	76870 FQ	95430 MW	117570 TQ	USBLS	5/15
Systems Software	Wichita MSA, KS	Y	76860 FQ	98160 MW	142660 TQ	USBLS	5/15
Systems Software	Kentucky	Y	67910 FQ	84560 MW	100810 TQ	USBLS	5/15
Systems Software	Louisville-Jefferson County MSA, KY-IN	Y	76030 FQ	89550 MW	100470 TQ	USBLS	5/15
Systems Software	Louisiana	Y	55680 FQ	70730 MW	88160 TQ	USBLS	5/15
Systems Software	Baton Rouge MSA, LA	Y	62580 FQ	73160 MW	87300 TQ	USBLS	5/15
Systems Software	New Orleans-Metairie MSA, LA	Y	48110 FQ	69580 MW	91570 TQ	USBLS	5/15
Systems Software	Maine	Y	80890 FQ	104390 MW	117160 TQ	USBLS	5/15
Systems Software	Portland-South Portland MSA, ME	Y	81540 FQ	104540 MW	115560 TQ	USBLS	5/15
Systems Software	Maryland	Y	71547 AE	118955 MW	142659 AEX	MDBLS	4/16
Systems Software	Baltimore-Columbia-Towson MSA, MD	Y	89860 FQ	123970 MW	156400 TQ	USBLS	5/15
Systems Software	Massachusetts	Y	90420 FQ	112780 MW	136950 TQ	USBLS	5/15
Systems Software	Boston-Cambridge-Newton NECTA, MA	Y	92040 FQ	114160 MW	138090 TQ	USBLS	5/15
Systems Software	Pittsfield MSA, MA	Y	74510 FQ	89410 MW	106480 TQ	USBLS	5/15

AE	Average entry wage	AWR	Average wage range	H	Hourly
AEX	Average experienced wage	B	Biweekly	HI	Highest wage paid
ATC	Average total compensation	D	Daily	HR	High end range
AW	Average wage paid	FQ	First quartile wage	LO	Lowest wage paid

LR Low end range   MTC Median total compensation   TCC Total cash compensation
M Monthly   MW Median wage paid   TQ Third quartile wage
MCC Median cash compensation   MWR Median wage range   W Weekly
ME Median entry wage   S See annotated source   Y Yearly

Occupation/Type/Industry	Location	Per	Low	Mid	High	Source	Date
Software Developer							
Systems Software	Worcester MSA, MA-CT	Y	72710 FQ	93230 MW	117630 TQ	USBLS	5/15
Systems Software	Michigan	Y	70270 FQ	88340 MW	106960 TQ	USBLS	5/15
Systems Software	Detroit-Dearborn-Livonia PMSA, MI	Y	65910 FQ	86130 MW	100700 TQ	USBLS	5/15
Systems Software	Grand Rapids-Wyoming MSA, MI	Y	66470 FQ	82550 MW	105960 TQ	USBLS	5/15
Systems Software	Minnesota	Y	84807 FQ	105724 MW	127025 TQ	MNBLS	1/16-3/16
Systems Software	Minneapolis-St. Paul-Bloomington MSA, MN-WI	Y	85755 FQ	106702 MW	130412 TQ	MNBLS	1/16-3/16
Systems Software	Mississippi	Y	56170 FQ	73260 MW	94060 TQ	USBLS	5/15
Systems Software	Jackson MSA, MS	Y	62280 FQ	78010 MW	93160 TQ	USBLS	5/15
Systems Software	Missouri	Y	81450 FQ	100940 MW	120120 TQ	USBLS	5/15
Systems Software	Kansas City MSA, MO-KS	Y	77230 FQ	96290 MW	116030 TQ	USBLS	5/15
Systems Software	St. Louis MSA, MO-IL	Y	85780 FQ	103820 MW	124120 TQ	USBLS	5/15
Systems Software	Montana	Y	61850 FQ	74580 MW	93410 TQ	USBLS	5/15
Systems Software	Billings MSA, MT	Y	69660 FQ	82030 MW	103480 TQ	USBLS	5/15
Systems Software	Nebraska	Y	63905 FQ	81900 MW	100455 TQ	NEBLS	7/16-9/16
Systems Software	Omaha-Council Bluffs MSA, NE-IA	Y	68020 FQ	85920 MW	103630 TQ	NEBLS	7/16-9/16
Systems Software	Nevada	Y	61260 FQ	83570 MW	110510 TQ	USBLS	5/15
Systems Software	Las Vegas-Henderson-Paradise MSA, NV	Y	61510 FQ	89090 MW	114380 TQ	USBLS	5/15
Systems Software	New Hampshire	H	41.61 AE	58.16 MW	67.48 AEX	NHBLS	6/16
Systems Software	Manchester NECTA, NH	H	41.22 AE	53.56 MW	59.07 AEX	NHBLS	6/16
Systems Software	Nashua NECTA, NH-MA	Y	106040 FQ	128620 MW	151800 TQ	USBLS	5/15
Systems Software	New Jersey	Y	84240 FQ	109420 MW	133820 TQ	USBLS	5/15
Systems Software	Camden PMSA, NJ	Y	81390 FQ	99390 MW	121760 TQ	USBLS	5/15
Systems Software	Newark PMSA, NJ-PA	Y	92740 FQ	118260 MW	148080 TQ	USBLS	5/15
Systems Software	Trenton MSA, NJ	Y	87640 FQ	108260 MW	129280 TQ	USBLS	5/15
Systems Software	New Mexico	Y	74480 FQ	94590 MW	122120 TQ	USBLS	5/15
Systems Software	Albuquerque MSA, NM	Y	75470 FQ	93550 MW	116730 TQ	USBLS	5/15
Systems Software	New York	Y	71030 AE	107740 MW	132460 AEX	NYBLS	1/16-3/16
Systems Software	Buffalo-Cheektowaga-Niagara Falls MSA, NY	Y	64390 FQ	84370 MW	119710 TQ	USBLS	5/15
Systems Software	Nassau County-Suffolk County PMSA, NY	Y	84620 FQ	109660 MW	134400 TQ	USBLS	5/15
Systems Software	New York-Jersey City-White Plains PMSA, NY-NJ	Y	82850 FQ	112340 MW	141940 TQ	USBLS	5/15
Systems Software	Rochester MSA, NY	Y	76290 FQ	94450 MW	114120 TQ	USBLS	5/15
Systems Software	North Carolina	Y	86130 FQ	106950 MW	127330 TQ	USBLS	5/15
Systems Software	Charlotte-Concord-Gastonia MSA, NC-SC	Y	87020 FQ	109310 MW	127160 TQ	USBLS	5/15
Systems Software	Raleigh MSA, NC	Y	84680 FQ	103740 MW	126360 TQ	USBLS	5/15
Systems Software	North Dakota	Y	54080 FQ	63000 MW	83910 TQ	USBLS	5/15
Systems Software	Fargo MSA, ND-MN	Y	53610 FQ	60730 MW	77290 TQ	USBLS	5/15
Systems Software	Ohio	Y	75650 FQ	92570 MW	112910 TQ	USBLS	5/15
Systems Software	Cincinnati MSA, OH-KY-IN	Y	72980 FQ	90310 MW	108070 TQ	USBLS	5/15
Systems Software	Cleveland-Elyria MSA, OH	Y	70160 FQ	87040 MW	103470 TQ	USBLS	5/15
Systems Software	Columbus MSA, OH	Y	85120 FQ	106010 MW	122060 TQ	USBLS	5/15
Systems Software	Oklahoma	Y	53470 FQ	70490 MW	92790 TQ	USBLS	5/15
Systems Software	Oklahoma City MSA, OK	Y	52330 FQ	67500 MW	89960 TQ	USBLS	5/15
Systems Software	Tulsa MSA, OK	Y	57140 FQ	77240 MW	98960 TQ	USBLS	5/15
Systems Software	Oregon	H	39.52 FQ	50.18 MW	60.78 TQ	ORBLS	2016
Systems Software	Portland-Vancouver-Hillsboro MSA, OR-WA	Y	81420 FQ	102530 MW	124020 TQ	USBLS	5/15
Systems Software	Pennsylvania	Y	73080 FQ	92010 MW	113430 TQ	USBLS	5/15
Systems Software	Allentown-Bethlehem-Easton MSA, PA-NJ	Y	65300 FQ	89860 MW	114410 TQ	USBLS	5/15
Systems Software	Harrisburg-Carlisle MSA, PA	Y	75550 FQ	91160 MW	113350 TQ	USBLS	5/15
Systems Software	Montgomery County-Bucks County-Chester County PMSA, PA	Y	81760 FQ	99800 MW	118890 TQ	USBLS	5/15
Systems Software	Philadelphia PMSA, PA	Y	75190 FQ	92190 MW	114060 TQ	USBLS	5/15
Systems Software	Pittsburgh MSA, PA	Y	64320 FQ	78300 MW	97380 TQ	USBLS	5/15
Systems Software	Rhode Island	Y	85250 FQ	106500 MW	129830 TQ	USBLS	5/15
Systems Software	Providence-Warwick MSA, RI-MA	Y	86870 FQ	108230 MW	130180 TQ	USBLS	5/15
Systems Software	South Carolina	Y	59390 FQ	77450 MW	96520 TQ	USBLS	5/15
Systems Software	Charleston-North Charleston MSA, SC	Y	59230 FQ	77540 MW	94180 TQ	USBLS	5/15
Systems Software	Columbia MSA, SC	Y	51460 FQ	68740 MW	87090 TQ	USBLS	5/15

AE Average entry wage	**AWR** Average wage range	**H** Hourly	**LR** Low end range	**MTC** Median total compensation	**TCC** Total cash compensation
AEX Average experienced wage	**B** Biweekly	**HI** Highest wage paid	**M** Monthly	**MW** Median wage paid	**TQ** Third quartile wage
ATC Average total compensation	**D** Daily	**HR** High end range	**MCC** Median cash compensation	**MWR** Median wage range	**W** Weekly
AW Average wage paid	**FQ** First quartile wage	**LO** Lowest wage paid	**ME** Median entry wage	**S** See annotated source	**Y** Yearly

Occupation/Type/Industry	Location	Per	Low	Mid	High	Source	Date
Software Developer							
Systems Software	Greenville-Anderson-Mauldin MSA, SC	Y	63080 FQ	84140 MW	98550 TQ	USBLS	5/15
Systems Software	South Dakota	Y	64750 FQ	82180 MW	98220 TQ	USBLS	5/15
Systems Software	Sioux Falls MSA, SD	Y	60410 FQ	77410 MW	96700 TQ	USBLS	5/15
Systems Software	Tennessee	Y	66350 FQ	83370 MW	105470 TQ	USBLS	5/15
Systems Software	Knoxville MSA, TN	Y	68340 FQ	84950 MW	100460 TQ	USBLS	5/15
Systems Software	Memphis MSA, TN-MS-AR	Y	66520 FQ	78050 MW	100210 TQ	USBLS	5/15
Systems Software	Nashville-Davidson– Murfreesboro–Franklin MSA, TN	Y	65940 FQ	86730 MW	110020 TQ	USBLS	5/15
Systems Software	Texas	Y	80900 FQ	101310 MW	124430 TQ	USBLS	5/15
Systems Software	Austin-Round Rock MSA, TX	Y	74720 FQ	98960 MW	123560 TQ	USBLS	5/15
Systems Software	Dallas-Plano-Irving PMSA, TX	Y	83440 FQ	99790 MW	121290 TQ	USBLS	5/15
Systems Software	Fort Worth-Arlington PMSA, TX	Y	85120 FQ	111290 MW	136920 TQ	USBLS	5/15
Systems Software	Houston-The Woodlands- Sugar Land MSA, TX	Y	85060 FQ	105170 MW	127770 TQ	USBLS	5/15
Systems Software	Utah	Y	73230 FQ	92840 MW	113300 TQ	USBLS	5/15
Systems Software	Ogden-Clearfield MSA, UT	Y	74440 FQ	92910 MW	117390 TQ	USBLS	5/15
Systems Software	Provo-Orem MSA, UT	Y	73450 FQ	93990 MW	115070 TQ	USBLS	5/15
Systems Software	Salt Lake City MSA, UT	Y	73490 FQ	92930 MW	112660 TQ	USBLS	5/15
Systems Software	Vermont	Y	80280 FQ	96960 MW	143710 TQ	USBLS	5/15
Systems Software	Burlington-South Burlington MSA, VT	Y	74300 FQ	91450 MW	127690 TQ	USBLS	5/15
Systems Software	Virginia	Y	86020 FQ	110950 MW	138910 TQ	USBLS	5/15
Systems Software	Richmond MSA, VA	Y	79950 FQ	97640 MW	115940 TQ	USBLS	5/15
Systems Software	Virginia Beach-Norfolk- Newport News MSA, VA-NC	Y	78340 FQ	95730 MW	120500 TQ	USBLS	5/15
Systems Software	Washington	H	45.55 FQ	55.63 MW	66.32 TQ	WABLS	3/16
Systems Software	Seattle-Bellevue-Everett PMSA, WA	H	47.18 FQ	56.76 MW	67.48 TQ	WABLS	3/16
Systems Software	Tacoma-Lakewood PMSA, WA	H	38.39 FQ	53.60 MW	63.72 TQ	WABLS	3/16
Systems Software	West Virginia	Y	55060 FQ	76300 MW	97310 TQ	USBLS	5/15
Systems Software	Wisconsin	Y	68950 FQ	84780 MW	99610 TQ	USBLS	5/15
Systems Software	Madison MSA, WI	Y	62700 FQ	80000 MW	97430 TQ	USBLS	5/15
Systems Software	Milwaukee-Waukesha-West Allis MSA, WI	Y	72220 FQ	88160 MW	102250 TQ	USBLS	5/15
Systems Software	Wyoming	Y	73270 FQ	100300 MW	117230 TQ	USBLS	5/15
Systems Software	Puerto Rico	Y	47650 FQ	65000 MW	79140 TQ	USBLS	5/15
Systems Software	San Juan-Carolina-Caguas MSA, PR	Y	47400 FQ	64820 MW	79640 TQ	USBLS	5/15
Software Engineer							
Major Corporation, Female	United States	Y		119456 AW		QTZ01	2016
Major Corporation, Male	United States	Y		126456 AW		QTZ01	2016
Seed-Stage Company, Female	United States	Y		113036 AW		QTZ01	2016
Seed-Stage Company, Male	United States	Y		120021 AW		QTZ01	2016
Soil and Plant Scientist	Alabama	Y	43647 AE	63076 AW	72790 AEX	ALBLS	6/16
	Alaska	Y	58150 FQ	68730 MW	77810 TQ	USBLS	5/15
	Arizona	Y	44150 FQ	64200 MW	75460 TQ	USBLS	5/15
	Phoenix-Mesa-Scottsdale MSA, AZ	Y	52030 FQ	68110 MW	75950 TQ	USBLS	5/15
	Arkansas	Y	48380 FQ	62480 MW	91260 TQ	USBLS	5/15
	California	H	24.83 FQ	32.62 MW	44.73 TQ	CABLS	1/16-3/16
	Anaheim-Santa Ana-Irvine PMSA, CA	H	21.65 FQ	36.40 MW	51.97 TQ	CABLS	1/16-3/16
	Los Angeles-Long Beach- Glendale PMSA, CA	H	24.26 FQ	36.07 MW	43.67 TQ	CABLS	1/16-3/16
	Oakland-Hayward-Berkeley PMSA, CA	H	33.08 FQ	36.15 MW	39.80 TQ	CABLS	1/16-3/16
	Riverside-San Bernardino- Ontario MSA, CA	H	17.79 FQ	21.51 MW	36.07 TQ	CABLS	1/16-3/16
	Sacramento–Roseville– Arden-Arcade MSA, CA	H	27.54 FQ	32.56 MW	47.75 TQ	CABLS	1/16-3/16
	San Diego-Carlsbad MSA, CA	H	22.03 FQ	25.59 MW	29.27 TQ	CABLS	1/16-3/16
	Colorado	Y	36560 FQ	51240 MW	71220 TQ	USBLS	5/15
	Denver-Aurora-Lakewood MSA, CO	Y	29390 FQ	34310 MW	39800 TQ	USBLS	5/15
	Connecticut	Y		70051 MW		CTBLS	1/16-3/16
	Delaware	Y	43120 FQ	48110 MW	57020 TQ	USBLS	5/15

AE	Average entry wage	AWR	Average wage range	H	Hourly	LR	Low end range
AEX	Average experienced wage	B	Biweekly	HI	Highest wage paid	M	Monthly
ATC	Average total compensation	D	Daily	HR	High end range	MCC	Median cash compensation
AW	Average wage paid	FQ	First quartile wage	LO	Lowest wage paid	ME	Median entry wage

MTC	Median total compensation	TCC	Total cash compensation
MW	Median wage paid	TQ	Third quartile wage
MWR	Median wage range	W	Weekly
S	See annotated source	Y	Yearly

Occupation/Type/Industry	Location	Per	Low	Mid	High	Source	Date
Soil and Plant Scientist	Wilmington PMSA, DE-MD-NJ	Y	43150 FQ	49730 MW	59830 TQ	USBLS	5/15
	District of Columbia	Y	63720 FQ	78590 MW	91660 TQ	USBLS	5/15
	Washington-Arlington-Alexandria PMSA, DC-VA-MD-WV	Y	67960 FQ	82830 MW	110250 TQ	USBLS	5/15
	Florida	H	19.19 AE	25.18 MW	34.11 AEX	FLBLS	7/16-9/16
	Miami-Miami Beach-Kendall PMSA, FL	H	16.67 AE	27.87 MW	33.96 AEX	FLBLS	7/16-9/16
	Orlando-Kissimmee-Sanford MSA, FL	H	20.55 AE	24.01 MW	30.52 AEX	FLBLS	7/16-9/16
	Tampa-St. Petersburg-Clearwater MSA, FL	H	18.92 AE	29.06 MW	43.14 AEX	FLBLS	7/16-9/16
	Georgia	Y	43490 FQ	50870 MW	66360 TQ	USBLS	5/15
	Atlanta-Sandy Springs-Roswell MSA, GA	Y	38980 FQ	47060 MW	58730 TQ	USBLS	5/15
	Hawaii	Y	51960 FQ	60660 MW	74420 TQ	USBLS	5/15
	Urban Honolulu MSA, HI	Y	51940 FQ	60600 MW	75700 TQ	USBLS	5/15
	Idaho	Y	58560 FQ	71230 MW	82200 TQ	USBLS	5/15
	Boise City MSA, ID	Y	65230 FQ	73620 MW	82160 TQ	USBLS	5/15
	Illinois	Y	45310 FQ	64230 MW	76130 TQ	USBLS	5/15
	Chicago-Naperville-Arlington Heights PMSA, IL	Y	57750 FQ	69070 MW	78330 TQ	USBLS	5/15
	Indiana	Y	40820 FQ	51670 MW	72540 TQ	USBLS	5/15
	Indianapolis-Carmel-Anderson MSA, IN	Y	36910 FQ	44450 MW	62740 TQ	USBLS	5/15
	Iowa	Y	49760 FQ	63270 MW	84130 TQ	USBLS	5/15
	Des Moines-West Des Moines MSA, IA	Y	57260 FQ	72900 MW	96710 TQ	USBLS	5/15
	Kansas	Y	48870 FQ	61840 MW	72610 TQ	USBLS	5/15
	Kentucky	Y	33880 FQ	46750 MW	58570 TQ	USBLS	5/15
	Louisiana	Y	42240 FQ	59620 MW	77220 TQ	USBLS	5/15
	Maryland	Y	51045 AE	88483 MW	107203 AEX	MDBLS	4/16
	Massachusetts	Y	50320 FQ	67730 MW	83810 TQ	USBLS	5/15
	Boston-Cambridge-Newton NECTA, MA	Y	49270 FQ	68300 MW	85400 TQ	USBLS	5/15
	Michigan	Y	43570 FQ	50710 MW	59370 TQ	USBLS	5/15
	Minnesota	Y	47338 FQ	61824 MW	82731 TQ	MNBLS	1/16-3/16
	Minneapolis-St. Paul-Bloomington MSA, MN-WI	Y	41280 FQ	56673 MW	85160 TQ	MNBLS	1/16-3/16
	Mississippi	Y	59180 FQ	76150 MW	102940 TQ	USBLS	5/15
	Missouri	Y	39810 FQ	46510 MW	60300 TQ	USBLS	5/15
	Kansas City MSA, MO-KS	Y	49720 FQ	68570 MW	76070 TQ	USBLS	5/15
	St. Louis MSA, MO-IL	Y	40170 FQ	45740 MW	64520 TQ	USBLS	5/15
	Montana	Y	52590 FQ	61310 MW	76140 TQ	USBLS	5/15
	Nebraska	Y	44130 FQ	58575 MW	82440 TQ	NEBLS	7/16-9/16
	Omaha-Council Bluffs MSA, NE-IA	Y	52185 FQ	62720 MW	80720 TQ	NEBLS	7/16-9/16
	Nevada	Y	61170 FQ	68100 MW	76940 TQ	USBLS	5/15
	New Hampshire	H	31.34 AE	42.18 MW	51.61 AEX	NHBLS	6/16
	New Jersey	Y	62710 FQ	73030 MW	79940 TQ	USBLS	5/15
	New Mexico	Y	45540 FQ	58560 MW	70620 TQ	USBLS	5/15
	New York	Y	43330 AE	62650 MW	88340 AEX	NYBLS	1/16-3/16
	New York-Jersey City-White Plains PMSA, NY-NJ	Y	54490 FQ	68930 MW	85310 TQ	USBLS	5/15
	North Carolina	Y	41370 FQ	54090 MW	82110 TQ	USBLS	5/15
	Charlotte-Concord-Gastonia MSA, NC-SC	Y	30080 FQ	41720 MW	73020 TQ	USBLS	5/15
	Raleigh MSA, NC	Y	43150 FQ	49760 MW	65210 TQ	USBLS	5/15
	North Dakota	Y	43560 FQ	64820 MW	78240 TQ	USBLS	5/15
	Fargo MSA, ND-MN	Y	41440 FQ	55040 MW	76650 TQ	USBLS	5/15
	Ohio	Y	47550 FQ	66360 MW	76120 TQ	USBLS	5/15
	Cincinnati MSA, OH-KY-IN	Y	45480 FQ	54000 MW	72720 TQ	USBLS	5/15
	Columbus MSA, OH	Y	35110 FQ	41280 MW	48860 TQ	USBLS	5/15
	Oklahoma	Y	36650 FQ	43830 MW	66360 TQ	USBLS	5/15
	Oregon	H	19.81 FQ	29.12 MW	35.22 TQ	ORBLS	2016
	Portland-Vancouver-Hillsboro MSA, OR-WA	Y	33760 FQ	59960 MW	71380 TQ	USBLS	5/15
	Pennsylvania	Y	37290 FQ	50060 MW	69070 TQ	USBLS	5/15
	Harrisburg-Carlisle MSA, PA	Y	29300 FQ	49550 MW	60820 TQ	USBLS	5/15
	South Dakota	Y	45930 FQ	54320 MW	63340 TQ	USBLS	5/15
	Sioux Falls MSA, SD	Y	54400 FQ	59440 MW	64660 TQ	USBLS	5/15

AE	Average entry wage	AWR	Average wage range	H	Hourly
AEX	Average experienced wage	B	Biweekly	HI	Highest wage paid
ATC	Average total compensation	D	Daily	HR	High end range
AW	Average wage paid	FQ	First quartile wage	LO	Lowest wage paid

LR	Low end range	MTC	Median total compensation	TCC	Total cash compensation
M	Monthly	MW	Median wage paid	TQ	Third quartile wage
MCC	Median cash compensation	MWR	Median wage range	W	Weekly
ME	Median entry wage	S	See annotated source	Y	Yearly

Occupation/Type/Industry	Location	Per	Low	Mid	High	Source	Date
Soil and Plant Scientist	Tennessee	Y	42420 FQ	54410 MW	76150 TQ	USBLS	5/15
	Memphis MSA, TN-MS-AR	Y	56160 FQ	74290 MW	90790 TQ	USBLS	5/15
	Nashville-Davidson–Murfreesboro–Franklin MSA, TN	Y	43720 FQ	49750 MW	72210 TQ	USBLS	5/15
	Texas	Y	44070 FQ	55390 MW	76140 TQ	USBLS	5/15
	Dallas-Plano-Irving PMSA, TX	Y	44340 FQ	50160 MW	64630 TQ	USBLS	5/15
	Fort Worth-Arlington PMSA, TX	Y	39590 FQ	52320 MW	78890 TQ	USBLS	5/15
	Houston-The Woodlands-Sugar Land MSA, TX	Y	52260 FQ	71270 MW	87380 TQ	USBLS	5/15
	San Antonio-New Braunfels MSA, TX	Y	51450 FQ	72820 MW	87770 TQ	USBLS	5/15
	Utah	Y	53240 FQ	61960 MW	72220 TQ	USBLS	5/15
	Virginia	Y	43960 FQ	56300 MW	75430 TQ	USBLS	5/15
	Richmond MSA, VA	Y	41560 FQ	51720 MW	67140 TQ	USBLS	5/15
	Washington	H	30.81 FQ	37.82 MW	53.89 TQ	WABLS	3/16
	Seattle-Bellevue-Everett PMSA, WA	H	31.47 FQ	36.22 MW	43.91 TQ	WABLS	3/16
	Wisconsin	Y	45570 FQ	55060 MW	66360 TQ	USBLS	5/15
	Madison MSA, WI	Y	49930 FQ	59190 MW	70480 TQ	USBLS	5/15
	Milwaukee-Waukesha-West Allis MSA, WI	Y	43530 FQ	48130 MW	55140 TQ	USBLS	5/15
	San Juan-Carolina-Caguas MSA, PR	Y	29700 FQ	35000 MW	40630 TQ	USBLS	5/15
Solar Photovoltaic Installer	United States	H		24.90 MW		SOLF	2016
	Arizona	Y	31480 FQ	39130 MW	48030 TQ	USBLS	5/15
	Phoenix-Mesa-Scottsdale MSA, AZ	Y	31800 FQ	39350 MW	47870 TQ	USBLS	5/15
	California	H	16.42 FQ	20.24 MW	24.35 TQ	CABLS	1/16-3/16
	Anaheim-Santa Ana-Irvine PMSA, CA	H	15.78 FQ	19.62 MW	24.24 TQ	CABLS	1/16-3/16
	Oakland-Hayward-Berkeley PMSA, CA	H	16.39 FQ	19.01 MW	23.42 TQ	CABLS	1/16-3/16
	Riverside-San Bernardino-Ontario MSA, CA	H	15.77 FQ	21.10 MW	25.20 TQ	CABLS	1/16-3/16
	Sacramento–Roseville–Arden-Arcade MSA, CA	H	16.14 FQ	18.65 MW	24.58 TQ	CABLS	1/16-3/16
	Colorado	Y	41790 FQ	44540 MW	47300 TQ	USBLS	5/15
	Connecticut	Y		36743 MW		CTBLS	1/16-3/16
	Florida	H	12.29 AE	14.43 MW	17.00 AEX	FLBLS	7/16-9/16
	Hawaii	Y	40910 FQ	50070 MW	59710 TQ	USBLS	5/15
	Urban Honolulu MSA, HI	Y	41890 FQ	48140 MW	56880 TQ	USBLS	5/15
	Idaho	Y	29320 FQ	36360 MW	54810 TQ	USBLS	5/15
	Louisiana	Y	38300 FQ	43690 MW	47980 TQ	USBLS	5/15
	Massachusetts	Y	35790 FQ	40650 MW	52440 TQ	USBLS	5/15
	New Jersey	Y	34030 FQ	42360 MW	54600 TQ	USBLS	5/15
	Newark PMSA, NJ-PA	Y	32720 FQ	42530 MW	58500 TQ	USBLS	5/15
	New Mexico	Y	31640 FQ	36700 MW	43180 TQ	USBLS	5/15
	New York	Y	32300 AE	36150 MW	38570 AEX	NYBLS	1/16-3/16
	New York-Jersey City-White Plains PMSA, NY-NJ	Y	34810 FQ	42150 MW	50830 TQ	USBLS	5/15
	North Carolina	Y	31770 FQ	34330 MW	36900 TQ	USBLS	5/15
	Ohio	Y	33490 FQ	37660 MW	43630 TQ	USBLS	5/15
	Oregon	H	16.91 FQ	18.67 MW	21.89 TQ	ORBLS	2016
	Portland-Vancouver-Hillsboro MSA, OR-WA	Y	34350 FQ	37640 MW	43220 TQ	USBLS	5/15
	Texas	Y	29390 FQ	33610 MW	37670 TQ	USBLS	5/15
	Vermont	Y	33990 FQ	38820 MW	45580 TQ	USBLS	5/15
	Burlington-South Burlington MSA, VT	Y	31300 FQ	36550 MW	44780 TQ	USBLS	5/15
Solicitor							
State Court	Charlton County, GA	Y			26931 HI	GACTY03	2016
State Court	Fulton County, GA	Y			158412 HI	GACTY03	2016
State Court	Thomas County, GA	Y			38192 HI	GACTY03	2016
Solid Waste Manager							
Municipal Government	East Point, GA	Y	29145 LO		45547 HI	GACTY02	2016
Municipal Government	Tifton, GA	Y	52478 LO		78718 HI	GACTY02	2016

AE	Average entry wage	AWR	Average wage range	H	Hourly	LR	Low end range	MTC	Median total compensation	TCC	Total cash compensation
AEX	Average experienced wage	B	Biweekly	HI	Highest wage paid	M	Monthly	MW	Median wage paid	TQ	Third quartile wage
ATC	Average total compensation	D	Daily	HR	High end range	MCC	Median cash compensation	MWR	Median wage range	W	Weekly
AW	Average wage paid	FQ	First quartile wage	LO	Lowest wage paid	ME	Median entry wage	S	See annotated source	Y	Yearly

Occupation/Type/Industry	Location	Per	Low	Mid	High	Source	Date
Solutions Architect	United States	Y		125000 MW		CNBC08	2017
Sonographer							
State Government	North Carolina	Y	42667 LO		69177 HI	NCGOV	7/1/16
Sound Effects Editor							
Subscription Video on Demand, High Budget	United States	H	41.85 LO			MPEG01	7/31/16-7/29/17
Sound Engineering Technician	Alabama	Y	21936 AE	44932 AW	56430 AEX	ALBLS	6/16
	Birmingham-Hoover MSA, AL	Y	22140 AE	45472 AW	57133 AEX	ALBLS	6/16
	Arizona	Y	28720 FQ	38860 MW	62840 TQ	USBLS	5/15
	Phoenix-Mesa-Scottsdale MSA, AZ	Y	32680 FQ	42970 MW	64330 TQ	USBLS	5/15
	Arkansas	Y	37680 FQ	47580 MW	66860 TQ	USBLS	5/15
	California	H	20.47 FQ	30.13 MW	47.02 TQ	CABLS	1/16-3/16
	Anaheim-Santa Ana-Irvine PMSA, CA	H	21.88 FQ	30.78 MW	51.80 TQ	CABLS	1/16-3/16
	Los Angeles-Long Beach-Glendale PMSA, CA	H	20.98 FQ	30.53 MW	47.40 TQ	CABLS	1/16-3/16
	Riverside-San Bernardino-Ontario MSA, CA	H	14.75 FQ	21.67 MW	42.38 TQ	CABLS	1/16-3/16
	Sacramento–Roseville–Arden-Arcade MSA, CA	H	16.61 FQ	20.77 MW	23.76 TQ	CABLS	1/16-3/16
	San Diego-Carlsbad MSA, CA	H	21.67 FQ	31.42 MW	44.37 TQ	CABLS	1/16-3/16
	San Francisco-Redwood City-South San Francisco PMSA, CA	H	24.54 FQ	40.01 MW	47.84 TQ	CABLS	1/16-3/16
	Colorado	Y	36100 FQ	50960 MW	83060 TQ	USBLS	5/15
	Denver-Aurora-Lakewood MSA, CO	Y	38080 FQ	57760 MW	92440 TQ	USBLS	5/15
	Hartford-West Hartford-East Hartford MSA, CT	Y	36890 FQ	48660 MW	73640 TQ	USBLS	5/15
	District of Columbia	Y	38390 FQ	51730 MW	71450 TQ	USBLS	5/15
	Washington-Arlington-Alexandria PMSA, DC-VA-MD-WV	Y	38290 FQ	49780 MW	69900 TQ	USBLS	5/15
	Florida	H	11.17 AE	14.93 MW	21.60 AEX	FLBLS	7/16-9/16
	Fort Lauderdale-Pompano Beach-Deerfield Beach PMSA, FL	H	12.85 AE	19.18 MW	25.16 AEX	FLBLS	7/16-9/16
	Miami-Miami Beach-Kendall PMSA, FL	H	11.01 AE	15.18 MW	23.32 AEX	FLBLS	7/16-9/16
	Orlando-Kissimmee-Sanford MSA, FL	H	12.50 AE	19.88 MW	23.26 AEX	FLBLS	7/16-9/16
	Tampa-St. Petersburg-Clearwater MSA, FL	H	10.68 AE	16.56 MW	22.38 AEX	FLBLS	7/16-9/16
	Georgia	Y	31990 FQ	38690 MW	59880 TQ	USBLS	5/15
	Atlanta-Sandy Springs-Roswell MSA, GA	Y	32030 FQ	38160 MW	57370 TQ	USBLS	5/15
	Illinois	Y	30530 FQ	48690 MW	65820 TQ	USBLS	5/15
	Chicago-Naperville-Arlington Heights PMSA, IL	Y	37790 FQ	57130 MW	71350 TQ	USBLS	5/15
	Indiana	Y	32650 FQ	45080 MW	71630 TQ	USBLS	5/15
	Indianapolis-Carmel-Anderson MSA, IN	Y	35730 FQ	46740 MW	85560 TQ	USBLS	5/15
	Iowa	Y	33540 FQ	50800 MW	61310 TQ	USBLS	5/15
	Kentucky	Y	30420 FQ	36980 MW	53700 TQ	USBLS	5/15
	Portland-South Portland MSA, ME	Y	32950 FQ	35630 MW	38310 TQ	USBLS	5/15
	Maryland	Y	34289 AE	52915 MW	62228 AEX	MDBLS	4/16
	Baltimore-Columbia-Towson MSA, MD	Y	36080 FQ	52880 MW	59670 TQ	USBLS	5/15
	Massachusetts	Y	41520 FQ	54860 MW	77520 TQ	USBLS	5/15
	Boston-Cambridge-Newton NECTA, MA	Y	42900 FQ	57010 MW	77270 TQ	USBLS	5/15
	Michigan	Y	30220 FQ	42420 MW	56200 TQ	USBLS	5/15
	Minnesota	Y	35766 FQ	50524 MW	61612 TQ	MNBLS	1/16-3/16
	Minneapolis-St. Paul-Bloomington MSA, MN-WI	Y	37419 FQ	52751 MW	62600 TQ	MNBLS	1/16-3/16
	Missouri	Y	43050 FQ	65810 MW	74450 TQ	USBLS	5/15
	Kansas City MSA, MO-KS	Y	43770 FQ	54200 MW	72880 TQ	USBLS	5/15

AE Average entry wage	**AWR** Average wage range	**H** Hourly	**LR** Low end range	**MTC** Median total compensation	**TCC** Total cash compensation
AEX Average experienced wage	**B** Biweekly	**HI** Highest wage paid	**M** Monthly	**MW** Median wage paid	**TQ** Third quartile wage
ATC Average total compensation	**D** Daily	**HR** High end range	**MCC** Median cash compensation	**MWR** Median wage range	**W** Weekly
AW Average wage paid	**FQ** First quartile wage	**LO** Lowest wage paid	**ME** Median entry wage	**S** See annotated source	**Y** Yearly

Occupation/Type/Industry	Location	Per	Low	Mid	High	Source	Date
Sound Engineering Technician	St. Louis MSA, MO-IL	Y	47460 FQ	68660 MW	75700 TQ	USBLS	5/15
	Nevada	Y	60990 FQ	70170 MW	77200 TQ	USBLS	5/15
	Las Vegas-Henderson-Paradise MSA, NV	Y	64590 FQ	71150 MW	77700 TQ	USBLS	5/15
	Newark PMSA, NJ-PA	Y	29040 FQ	45420 MW	59650 TQ	USBLS	5/15
	New Mexico	Y	43350 FQ	54960 MW	70190 TQ	USBLS	5/15
	Albuquerque MSA, NM	Y	46310 FQ	58610 MW	71510 TQ	USBLS	5/15
	New York	Y	34280 AE	65750 MW	99970 AEX	NYBLS	1/16-3/16
	Buffalo-Cheektowaga-Niagara Falls MSA, NY	Y	20900 FQ	23290 MW	66070 TQ	USBLS	5/15
	Nassau County-Suffolk County PMSA, NY	Y	34400 FQ	55660 MW	72920 TQ	USBLS	5/15
	New York-Jersey City-White Plains PMSA, NY-NJ	Y	42410 FQ	67450 MW	104650 TQ	USBLS	5/15
	Rochester MSA, NY	Y	34700 FQ	54400 MW	93140 TQ	USBLS	5/15
	North Carolina	Y	32990 FQ	39370 MW	50160 TQ	USBLS	5/15
	Charlotte-Concord-Gastonia MSA, NC-SC	Y	23760 FQ	36920 MW	53730 TQ	USBLS	5/15
	Ohio	Y	24720 FQ	48440 MW	58400 TQ	USBLS	5/15
	Cincinnati MSA, OH-KY-IN	Y	34470 FQ	42410 MW	56570 TQ	USBLS	5/15
	Cleveland-Elyria MSA, OH	Y	37670 FQ	48740 MW	59640 TQ	USBLS	5/15
	Oklahoma	Y	24120 FQ	34520 MW	47880 TQ	USBLS	5/15
	Oregon	H	15.84 FQ	28.44 MW	39.11 TQ	ORBLS	2016
	Portland-Vancouver-Hillsboro MSA, OR-WA	Y	37780 FQ	62990 MW	86600 TQ	USBLS	5/15
	Pennsylvania	Y	33520 FQ	39370 MW	56840 TQ	USBLS	5/15
	Philadelphia PMSA, PA	Y	34010 FQ	39720 MW	73700 TQ	USBLS	5/15
	Pittsburgh MSA, PA	Y	35630 FQ	40830 MW	55480 TQ	USBLS	5/15
	Tennessee	Y	39460 FQ	49230 MW	72970 TQ	USBLS	5/15
	Knoxville MSA, TN	Y	19020 FQ	31720 MW	48870 TQ	USBLS	5/15
	Memphis MSA, TN-MS-AR	Y	40140 FQ	46380 MW	61780 TQ	USBLS	5/15
	Nashville-Davidson–Murfreesboro–Franklin MSA, TN	Y	41150 FQ	53960 MW	76610 TQ	USBLS	5/15
	Texas	Y	19460 FQ	37040 MW	56950 TQ	USBLS	5/15
	Austin-Round Rock MSA, TX	Y	35800 FQ	45940 MW	60210 TQ	USBLS	5/15
	Dallas-Plano-Irving PMSA, TX	Y	32920 FQ	41430 MW	66330 TQ	USBLS	5/15
	Houston-The Woodlands-Sugar Land MSA, TX	Y	17950 FQ	30610 MW	59770 TQ	USBLS	5/15
	Utah	Y	17060 FQ	18450 MW	19870 TQ	USBLS	5/15
	Salt Lake City MSA, UT	Y	17040 FQ	18410 MW	19780 TQ	USBLS	5/15
	Virginia	Y	21590 FQ	39230 MW	58590 TQ	USBLS	5/15
	Richmond MSA, VA	Y	33100 FQ	49040 MW	59690 TQ	USBLS	5/15
	Virginia Beach-Norfolk-Newport News MSA, VA-NC	Y	19160 FQ	23520 MW	46750 TQ	USBLS	5/15
	Washington	H	22.16 FQ	32.24 MW	39.23 TQ	WABLS	3/16
	Seattle-Bellevue-Everett PMSA, WA	H	23.20 FQ	34.97 MW	51.51 TQ	WABLS	3/16
	Wisconsin	Y	41690 FQ	46770 MW	67260 TQ	USBLS	5/15
	Milwaukee-Waukesha-West Allis MSA, WI	Y	48060 FQ	71780 MW	79950 TQ	USBLS	5/15
	Puerto Rico	Y	17930 FQ	22050 MW	31510 TQ	USBLS	5/15
	San Juan-Carolina-Caguas MSA, PR	Y	18190 FQ	23700 MW	32740 TQ	USBLS	5/15
Sound Mixer							
Made for Television Motion Picture	United States	W	1832 LO			MPEG01	7/31/16-7/29/17
Speaker of the House							
United States House of Representatives	United States	Y			223500 HI	OPM01	2017
Special Education Teacher							
Kindergarten and Elementary	Alabama	Y	41639 AE	51374 AW	56246 AEX	ALBLS	6/16
Kindergarten and Elementary	Birmingham-Hoover MSA, AL	Y	43943 AE	52974 AW	57490 AEX	ALBLS	6/16
Kindergarten and Elementary	Alaska	Y	58890 FQ	72920 MW	89190 TQ	USBLS	5/15
Kindergarten and Elementary	Anchorage MSA, AK	Y	67550 FQ	79220 MW	94280 TQ	USBLS	5/15
Kindergarten and Elementary	Arizona	Y	36490 FQ	43270 MW	51170 TQ	USBLS	5/15
Kindergarten and Elementary	Phoenix-Mesa-Scottsdale MSA, AZ	Y	37430 FQ	44470 MW	53160 TQ	USBLS	5/15
Kindergarten and Elementary	Tucson MSA, AZ	Y	35010 FQ	39390 MW	47000 TQ	USBLS	5/15
Kindergarten and Elementary	Arkansas	Y	39380 FQ	45050 MW	51250 TQ	USBLS	5/15

AE	Average entry wage	AWR	Average wage range	H	Hourly	LR	Low end range	MTC	Median total compensation	TCC	Total cash compensation
AEX	Average experienced wage	B	Biweekly	HI	Highest wage paid	M	Monthly	MW	Median wage paid	TQ	Third quartile wage
ATC	Average total compensation	D	Daily	HR	High end range	MCC	Median cash compensation	MWR	Median wage range	W	Weekly
AW	Average wage paid	FQ	First quartile wage	LO	Lowest wage paid	ME	Median entry wage	S	See annotated source	Y	Yearly

Occupation/Type/Industry	Location	Per	Low	Mid	High	Source	Date
Special Education Teacher							
Kindergarten and Elementary	Little Rock-North Little Rock-Conway MSA, AR	Y	41790 FQ	46590 MW	54240 TQ	USBLS	5/15
Kindergarten and Elementary	California	Y		69686 AW		CABLS	1/16-3/16
Kindergarten and Elementary	Anaheim-Santa Ana-Irvine PMSA, CA	Y		73936 AW		CABLS	1/16-3/16
Kindergarten and Elementary	Los Angeles-Long Beach-Glendale PMSA, CA	Y		72830 AW		CABLS	1/16-3/16
Kindergarten and Elementary	Oakland-Hayward-Berkeley PMSA, CA	Y		65465 AW		CABLS	1/16-3/16
Kindergarten and Elementary	Riverside-San Bernardino-Ontario MSA, CA	Y		77933 AW		CABLS	1/16-3/16
Kindergarten and Elementary	Sacramento–Roseville–Arden-Arcade MSA, CA	Y		61022 AW		CABLS	1/16-3/16
Kindergarten and Elementary	San Diego-Carlsbad MSA, CA	Y		66338 AW		CABLS	1/16-3/16
Kindergarten and Elementary	San Francisco-Redwood City-South San Francisco PMSA, CA	Y		61762 AW		CABLS	1/16-3/16
Kindergarten and Elementary	Colorado	Y	40920 FQ	48800 MW	61470 TQ	USBLS	5/15
Kindergarten and Elementary	Denver-Aurora-Lakewood MSA, CO	Y	43370 FQ	52120 MW	66510 TQ	USBLS	5/15
Kindergarten and Elementary	Connecticut	Y		80104 MW		CTBLS	1/16-3/16
Kindergarten and Elementary	Bridgeport-Stamford-Norwalk MSA, CT	Y	63890 FQ	83110 MW	100010 TQ	USBLS	5/15
Kindergarten and Elementary	Hartford-West Hartford-East Hartford MSA, CT	Y	50110 FQ	72890 MW	90050 TQ	USBLS	5/15
Kindergarten and Elementary	Delaware	Y	52650 FQ	61930 MW	75030 TQ	USBLS	5/15
Kindergarten and Elementary	Wilmington PMSA, DE-MD-NJ	Y	52940 FQ	63450 MW	76920 TQ	USBLS	5/15
Kindergarten and Elementary	District of Columbia	Y	48400 FQ	59050 MW	76400 TQ	USBLS	5/15
Kindergarten and Elementary	Washington-Arlington-Alexandria PMSA, DC-VA-MD-WV	Y	52220 FQ	66160 MW	82960 TQ	USBLS	5/15
Kindergarten and Elementary	Florida	Y	40859 AE	49380 MW	58009 AEX	FLBLS	7/16-9/16
Kindergarten and Elementary	Fort Lauderdale-Pompano Beach-Deerfield Beach PMSA, FL	Y	43278 AE	53579 MW	63462 AEX	FLBLS	7/16-9/16
Kindergarten and Elementary	Miami-Miami Beach-Kendall PMSA, FL	Y	38404 AE	46208 MW	51010 AEX	FLBLS	7/16-9/16
Kindergarten and Elementary	Orlando-Kissimmee-Sanford MSA, FL	Y	42540 AE	48779 MW	55429 AEX	FLBLS	7/16-9/16
Kindergarten and Elementary	Tampa-St. Petersburg-Clearwater MSA, FL	Y	37796 AE	45572 MW	48837 AEX	FLBLS	7/16-9/16
Kindergarten and Elementary	Georgia	Y	44740 FQ	53170 MW	61850 TQ	USBLS	5/15
Kindergarten and Elementary	Atlanta-Sandy Springs-Roswell MSA, GA	Y	45020 FQ	53180 MW	62700 TQ	USBLS	5/15
Kindergarten and Elementary	Augusta-Richmond County MSA, GA-SC	Y	43230 FQ	52050 MW	60720 TQ	USBLS	5/15
Kindergarten and Elementary	Hawaii	Y	40280 FQ	47780 MW	57340 TQ	USBLS	5/15
Kindergarten and Elementary	Urban Honolulu MSA, HI	Y	31460 FQ	46600 MW	56070 TQ	USBLS	5/15
Kindergarten and Elementary	Idaho	Y	36190 FQ	43350 MW	53060 TQ	USBLS	5/15
Kindergarten and Elementary	Boise City MSA, ID	Y	34990 FQ	39560 MW	49220 TQ	USBLS	5/15
Kindergarten and Elementary	Illinois	Y	45330 FQ	56680 MW	72920 TQ	USBLS	5/15
Kindergarten and Elementary	Chicago-Naperville-Arlington Heights PMSA, IL	Y	49180 FQ	60350 MW	78880 TQ	USBLS	5/15
Kindergarten and Elementary	Lake County-Kenosha County PMSA, IL-WI	Y	40360 FQ	56300 MW	73260 TQ	USBLS	5/15
Kindergarten and Elementary	Indiana	Y	38750 FQ	49060 MW	60950 TQ	USBLS	5/15
Kindergarten and Elementary	Gary PMSA, IN	Y	39410 FQ	50580 MW	63970 TQ	USBLS	5/15
Kindergarten and Elementary	Indianapolis-Carmel-Anderson MSA, IN	Y	39690 FQ	47600 MW	60880 TQ	USBLS	5/15
Kindergarten and Elementary	South Bend-Mishawaka MSA, IN-MI	Y	40190 FQ	48910 MW	59240 TQ	USBLS	5/15
Kindergarten and Elementary	Iowa	Y	41130 FQ	50470 MW	60920 TQ	USBLS	5/15
Kindergarten and Elementary	Des Moines-West Des Moines MSA, IA	Y	47480 FQ	58180 MW	71040 TQ	USBLS	5/15
Kindergarten and Elementary	Kansas	Y	42930 FQ	50370 MW	61030 TQ	USBLS	5/15
Kindergarten and Elementary	Wichita MSA, KS	Y	42590 FQ	52830 MW	67420 TQ	USBLS	5/15
Kindergarten and Elementary	Kentucky	Y	44640 FQ	52040 MW	59780 TQ	USBLS	5/15
Kindergarten and Elementary	Louisville-Jefferson County MSA, KY-IN	Y	46860 FQ	57890 MW	69590 TQ	USBLS	5/15
Kindergarten and Elementary	Louisiana	Y	43170 FQ	47860 MW	55050 TQ	USBLS	5/15

AE	Average entry wage	AWR	Average wage range	H	Hourly	LR	Low end range	MTC	Median total compensation	TCC	Total cash compensation
AEX	Average experienced wage	B	Biweekly	HI	Highest wage paid	M	Monthly	MW	Median wage paid	TQ	Third quartile wage
ATC	Average total compensation	D	Daily	HR	High end range	MCC	Median cash compensation	MWR	Median wage range	W	Weekly
AW	Average wage paid	FQ	First quartile wage	LO	Lowest wage paid	ME	Median entry wage	S	See annotated source	Y	Yearly

Occupation/Type/Industry	Location	Per	Low	Mid	High	Source	Date
Special Education Teacher							
Kindergarten and Elementary	Baton Rouge MSA, LA	Y	46940 FQ	53880 MW	60200 TQ	USBLS	5/15
Kindergarten and Elementary	New Orleans-Metairie MSA, LA	Y	43900 FQ	49530 MW	58110 TQ	USBLS	5/15
Kindergarten and Elementary	Maine	Y	40400 FQ	51220 MW	59880 TQ	USBLS	5/15
Kindergarten and Elementary	Portland-South Portland MSA, ME	Y	45460 FQ	55230 MW	64320 TQ	USBLS	5/15
Kindergarten and Elementary	Maryland	Y	38591 AE	55952 MW	64632 AEX	MDBLS	4/16
Kindergarten and Elementary	Baltimore-Columbia-Towson MSA, MD	Y	41810 FQ	52480 MW	70310 TQ	USBLS	5/15
Kindergarten and Elementary	Salisbury MSA, MD-DE	Y	50070 FQ	57100 MW	66710 TQ	USBLS	5/15
Kindergarten and Elementary	Massachusetts	Y	52670 FQ	67070 MW	80360 TQ	USBLS	5/15
Kindergarten and Elementary	Boston-Cambridge-Newton NECTA, MA	Y	51510 FQ	68330 MW	86910 TQ	USBLS	5/15
Kindergarten and Elementary	Worcester MSA, MA-CT	Y	59270 FQ	68330 MW	75270 TQ	USBLS	5/15
Kindergarten and Elementary	Michigan	Y	47120 FQ	58720 MW	71020 TQ	USBLS	5/15
Kindergarten and Elementary	Detroit-Dearborn-Livonia PMSA, MI	Y	52380 FQ	62490 MW	73700 TQ	USBLS	5/15
Kindergarten and Elementary	Grand Rapids-Wyoming MSA, MI	Y	48240 FQ	63230 MW	74500 TQ	USBLS	5/15
Kindergarten and Elementary	Monroe MSA, MI	Y	51650 FQ	65840 MW	76210 TQ	USBLS	5/15
Kindergarten and Elementary	Minnesota	Y	41713 FQ	54122 MW	70352 TQ	MNBLS	1/16-3/16
Kindergarten and Elementary	Minneapolis-St. Paul-Bloomington MSA, MN-WI	Y	40120 FQ	55050 MW	73729 TQ	MNBLS	1/16-3/16
Kindergarten and Elementary	Mississippi	Y	36920 FQ	43370 MW	50600 TQ	USBLS	5/15
Kindergarten and Elementary	Jackson MSA, MS	Y	35980 FQ	41320 MW	48030 TQ	USBLS	5/15
Kindergarten and Elementary	Missouri	Y	36420 FQ	45560 MW	59450 TQ	USBLS	5/15
Kindergarten and Elementary	Kansas City MSA, MO-KS	Y	38530 FQ	47680 MW	60720 TQ	USBLS	5/15
Kindergarten and Elementary	St. Louis MSA, MO-IL	Y	38990 FQ	50270 MW	65070 TQ	USBLS	5/15
Kindergarten and Elementary	Montana	Y	42020 FQ	52030 MW	61630 TQ	USBLS	5/15
Kindergarten and Elementary	Billings MSA, MT	Y	42630 FQ	52430 MW	62050 TQ	USBLS	5/15
Kindergarten and Elementary	Nebraska	Y	42795 FQ	51105 MW	58960 TQ	NEBLS	7/16-9/16
Kindergarten and Elementary	Omaha-Council Bluffs MSA, NE-IA	Y	40995 FQ	47545 MW	55905 TQ	NEBLS	7/16-9/16
Kindergarten and Elementary	Nevada	Y	42960 FQ	50000 MW	60810 TQ	USBLS	5/15
Kindergarten and Elementary	Las Vegas-Henderson-Paradise MSA, NV	Y	43120 FQ	49870 MW	61030 TQ	USBLS	5/15
Kindergarten and Elementary	New Hampshire	Y	40776 AE	58183 MW	65376 AEX	NHBLS	6/16
Kindergarten and Elementary	Manchester NECTA, NH	Y	40546 AE	60767 MW	66574 AEX	NHBLS	6/16
Kindergarten and Elementary	Nashua NECTA, NH-MA	Y	46300 FQ	56480 MW	67880 TQ	USBLS	5/15
Kindergarten and Elementary	New Jersey	Y	55370 FQ	62710 MW	79580 TQ	USBLS	5/15
Kindergarten and Elementary	Camden PMSA, NJ	Y	54490 FQ	60940 MW	75660 TQ	USBLS	5/15
Kindergarten and Elementary	Newark PMSA, NJ-PA	Y	55530 FQ	62630 MW	77640 TQ	USBLS	5/15
Kindergarten and Elementary	Trenton MSA, NJ	Y	56210 FQ	66980 MW	81840 TQ	USBLS	5/15
Kindergarten and Elementary	New Mexico	Y	45970 FQ	56110 MW	73800 TQ	USBLS	5/15
Kindergarten and Elementary	Albuquerque MSA, NM	Y	47620 FQ	57510 MW	75560 TQ	USBLS	5/15
Kindergarten and Elementary	New York	Y	46870 AE	67670 MW	84670 AEX	NYBLS	1/16-3/16
Kindergarten and Elementary	Buffalo-Cheektowaga-Niagara Falls MSA, NY	Y	45800 FQ	56780 MW	75960 TQ	USBLS	5/15
Kindergarten and Elementary	Nassau County-Suffolk County PMSA, NY	Y	61810 FQ	90820 MW	112960 TQ	USBLS	5/15
Kindergarten and Elementary	New York-Jersey City-White Plains PMSA, NY-NJ	Y	54300 FQ	66610 MW	87490 TQ	USBLS	5/15
Kindergarten and Elementary	Rochester MSA, NY	Y	50630 FQ	60290 MW	73270 TQ	USBLS	5/15
Kindergarten and Elementary	North Carolina	Y	36830 FQ	43630 MW	52100 TQ	USBLS	5/15
Kindergarten and Elementary	Charlotte-Concord-Gastonia MSA, NC-SC	Y	36970 FQ	44130 MW	52320 TQ	USBLS	5/15
Kindergarten and Elementary	Raleigh MSA, NC	Y	38180 FQ	47960 MW	60070 TQ	USBLS	5/15
Kindergarten and Elementary	North Dakota	Y	43360 FQ	49660 MW	59370 TQ	USBLS	5/15
Kindergarten and Elementary	Fargo MSA, ND-MN	Y	42980 FQ	46810 MW	51120 TQ	USBLS	5/15
Kindergarten and Elementary	Ohio	Y	45190 FQ	56420 MW	69150 TQ	USBLS	5/15
Kindergarten and Elementary	Cincinnati MSA, OH-KY-IN	Y	44750 FQ	54060 MW	66190 TQ	USBLS	5/15
Kindergarten and Elementary	Cleveland-Elyria MSA, OH	Y	46330 FQ	58760 MW	70870 TQ	USBLS	5/15
Kindergarten and Elementary	Columbus MSA, OH	Y	47550 FQ	61170 MW	75540 TQ	USBLS	5/15
Kindergarten and Elementary	Oklahoma	Y	35210 FQ	40410 MW	48290 TQ	USBLS	5/15
Kindergarten and Elementary	Oklahoma City MSA, OK	Y	34680 FQ	38600 MW	45750 TQ	USBLS	5/15
Kindergarten and Elementary	Tulsa MSA, OK	Y	36530 FQ	44060 MW	53720 TQ	USBLS	5/15
Kindergarten and Elementary	Oregon	Y	49677 FQ	61938 MW	76375 TQ	ORBLS	2016
Kindergarten and Elementary	Portland-Vancouver-Hillsboro MSA, OR-WA	Y	50860 FQ	63750 MW	77810 TQ	USBLS	5/15
Kindergarten and Elementary	Pennsylvania	Y	48840 FQ	61200 MW	75790 TQ	USBLS	5/15

Occupation/Type/Industry	Location	Per	Low	Mid	High	Source	Date

Special Education Teacher

Occupation/Type/Industry	Location	Per	Low	Mid	High	Source	Date
Kindergarten and Elementary	Allentown-Bethlehem-Easton MSA, PA-NJ	Y	50150 FQ	61260 MW	81230 TQ	USBLS	5/15
Kindergarten and Elementary	Harrisburg-Carlisle MSA, PA	Y	33060 FQ	48040 MW	63200 TQ	USBLS	5/15
Kindergarten and Elementary	Montgomery County-Bucks County-Chester County PMSA, PA	Y	49040 FQ	67930 MW	89500 TQ	USBLS	5/15
Kindergarten and Elementary	Philadelphia PMSA, PA	Y	54020 FQ	63900 MW	79850 TQ	USBLS	5/15
Kindergarten and Elementary	Pittsburgh MSA, PA	Y	49780 FQ	61630 MW	74340 TQ	USBLS	5/15
Kindergarten and Elementary	Rhode Island	Y	59030 FQ	70970 MW	80540 TQ	USBLS	5/15
Kindergarten and Elementary	Providence-Warwick MSA, RI-MA	Y	59610 FQ	71580 MW	82220 TQ	USBLS	5/15
Kindergarten and Elementary	South Carolina	Y	44740 FQ	55170 MW	64830 TQ	USBLS	5/15
Kindergarten and Elementary	Charleston-North Charleston MSA, SC	Y	42130 FQ	53070 MW	61570 TQ	USBLS	5/15
Kindergarten and Elementary	Columbia MSA, SC	Y	37860 FQ	47390 MW	57210 TQ	USBLS	5/15
Kindergarten and Elementary	Greenville-Anderson-Mauldin MSA, SC	Y	44060 FQ	51890 MW	59350 TQ	USBLS	5/15
Kindergarten and Elementary	South Dakota	Y	35380 FQ	40810 MW	49930 TQ	USBLS	5/15
Kindergarten and Elementary	Sioux Falls MSA, SD	Y	36070 FQ	43640 MW	54290 TQ	USBLS	5/15
Kindergarten and Elementary	Tennessee	Y	42500 FQ	50190 MW	60280 TQ	USBLS	5/15
Kindergarten and Elementary	Knoxville MSA, TN	Y	41530 FQ	47850 MW	56590 TQ	USBLS	5/15
Kindergarten and Elementary	Memphis MSA, TN-MS-AR	Y	46570 FQ	55460 MW	63700 TQ	USBLS	5/15
Kindergarten and Elementary	Nashville-Davidson–Murfreesboro–Franklin MSA, TN	Y	42440 FQ	50560 MW	61130 TQ	USBLS	5/15
Kindergarten and Elementary	Texas	Y	45890 FQ	53180 MW	60140 TQ	USBLS	5/15
Kindergarten and Elementary	Austin-Round Rock MSA, TX	Y	45060 FQ	50890 MW	60190 TQ	USBLS	5/15
Kindergarten and Elementary	Dallas-Plano-Irving PMSA, TX	Y	47650 FQ	54530 MW	60920 TQ	USBLS	5/15
Kindergarten and Elementary	Fort Worth-Arlington PMSA, TX	Y	40980 FQ	50850 MW	57610 TQ	USBLS	5/15
Kindergarten and Elementary	Houston-The Woodlands-Sugar Land MSA, TX	Y	51220 FQ	57830 MW	66290 TQ	USBLS	5/15
Kindergarten and Elementary	McAllen-Edinburg-Mission MSA, TX	Y	44450 FQ	49120 MW	60830 TQ	USBLS	5/15
Kindergarten and Elementary	San Antonio-New Braunfels MSA, TX	Y	51060 FQ	55180 MW	59310 TQ	USBLS	5/15
Kindergarten and Elementary	Utah	Y	26800 FQ	36680 MW	57560 TQ	USBLS	5/15
Kindergarten and Elementary	Ogden-Clearfield MSA, UT	Y	39300 FQ	55360 MW	79870 TQ	USBLS	5/15
Kindergarten and Elementary	Provo-Orem MSA, UT	Y	29900 FQ	42080 MW	51240 TQ	USBLS	5/15
Kindergarten and Elementary	Salt Lake City MSA, UT	Y	23770 FQ	34340 MW	63010 TQ	USBLS	5/15
Kindergarten and Elementary	Vermont	Y	43910 FQ	52970 MW	63970 TQ	USBLS	5/15
Kindergarten and Elementary	Burlington-South Burlington MSA, VT	Y	51350 FQ	62300 MW	77450 TQ	USBLS	5/15
Kindergarten and Elementary	Virginia	Y	47880 FQ	60010 MW	75830 TQ	USBLS	5/15
Kindergarten and Elementary	Richmond MSA, VA	Y	46880 FQ	56520 MW	65490 TQ	USBLS	5/15
Kindergarten and Elementary	Virginia Beach-Norfolk-Newport News MSA, VA-NC	Y	48790 FQ	59340 MW	73570 TQ	USBLS	5/15
Kindergarten and Elementary	Washington	Y		59733 AW		WABLS	3/16
Kindergarten and Elementary	Seattle-Bellevue-Everett PMSA, WA	Y		61346 AW		WABLS	3/16
Kindergarten and Elementary	Tacoma-Lakewood PMSA, WA	Y		60799 AW		WABLS	3/16
Kindergarten and Elementary	West Virginia	Y	33850 FQ	40450 MW	48900 TQ	USBLS	5/15
Kindergarten and Elementary	Huntington-Ashland MSA, WV-KY-OH	Y	35070 FQ	41160 MW	50430 TQ	USBLS	5/15
Kindergarten and Elementary	Wisconsin	Y	40610 FQ	51560 MW	63240 TQ	USBLS	5/15
Kindergarten and Elementary	Madison MSA, WI	Y	43560 FQ	53500 MW	62710 TQ	USBLS	5/15
Kindergarten and Elementary	Milwaukee-Waukesha-West Allis MSA, WI	Y	42950 FQ	55820 MW	68910 TQ	USBLS	5/15
Kindergarten and Elementary	Wyoming	Y	51630 FQ	58450 MW	66680 TQ	USBLS	5/15
Kindergarten and Elementary	Puerto Rico	Y	28480 FQ	33820 MW	42820 TQ	USBLS	5/15
Kindergarten and Elementary	San Juan-Carolina-Caguas MSA, PR	Y	28420 FQ	33710 MW	42640 TQ	USBLS	5/15
Middle School	Alabama	Y	40732 AE	49702 AW	54187 AEX	ALBLS	6/16
Middle School	Birmingham-Hoover MSA, AL	Y	41018 AE	49926 AW	54371 AEX	ALBLS	6/16
Middle School	Alaska	Y	56390 FQ	65520 MW	84380 TQ	USBLS	5/15
Middle School	Arizona	Y	34360 FQ	39590 MW	47170 TQ	USBLS	5/15
Middle School	Phoenix-Mesa-Scottsdale MSA, AZ	Y	34430 FQ	39960 MW	47560 TQ	USBLS	5/15
Middle School	Tucson MSA, AZ	Y	33810 FQ	37900 MW	45390 TQ	USBLS	5/15
Middle School	Arkansas	Y	42340 FQ	48350 MW	56630 TQ	USBLS	5/15

AE	Average entry wage	AWR	Average wage range	H	Hourly	LR	Low end range	MTC	Median total compensation	TCC	Total cash compensation
AEX	Average experienced wage	B	Biweekly	HI	Highest wage paid	M	Monthly	MW	Median wage paid	TQ	Third quartile wage
ATC	Average total compensation	D	Daily	HR	High end range	MCC	Median cash compensation	MWR	Median wage range	W	Weekly
AW	Average wage paid	FQ	First quartile wage	LO	Lowest wage paid	ME	Median entry wage	S	See annotated source	Y	Yearly

Special Education Teacher

Occupation/Type/Industry	Location	Per	Low	Mid	High	Source	Date
Middle School	Little Rock-North Little Rock-Conway MSA, AR	Y	43150 FQ	50540 MW	58160 TQ	USBLS	5/15
Middle School	California	Y		67088 AW		CABLS	1/16-3/16
Middle School	Anaheim-Santa Ana-Irvine PMSA, CA	Y		69462 AW		CABLS	1/16-3/16
Middle School	Los Angeles-Long Beach-Glendale PMSA, CA	Y		67920 AW		CABLS	1/16-3/16
Middle School	Oakland-Hayward-Berkeley PMSA, CA	Y		67180 AW		CABLS	1/16-3/16
Middle School	Riverside-San Bernardino-Ontario MSA, CA	Y		65891 AW		CABLS	1/16-3/16
Middle School	Sacramento–Roseville–Arden-Arcade MSA, CA	Y		66175 AW		CABLS	1/16-3/16
Middle School	San Diego-Carlsbad MSA, CA	Y		68438 AW		CABLS	1/16-3/16
Middle School	San Francisco-Redwood City-South San Francisco PMSA, CA	Y		74119 AW		CABLS	1/16-3/16
Middle School	Colorado	Y	40680 FQ	48400 MW	60450 TQ	USBLS	5/15
Middle School	Denver-Aurora-Lakewood MSA, CO	Y	42830 FQ	51050 MW	63180 TQ	USBLS	5/15
Middle School	Connecticut	Y		72993 MW		CTBLS	1/16-3/16
Middle School	Bridgeport-Stamford-Norwalk MSA, CT	Y	59840 FQ	78070 MW	97180 TQ	USBLS	5/15
Middle School	Hartford-West Hartford-East Hartford MSA, CT	Y	56320 FQ	71610 MW	88460 TQ	USBLS	5/15
Middle School	Delaware	Y	47660 FQ	69750 MW	88190 TQ	USBLS	5/15
Middle School	Wilmington PMSA, DE-MD-NJ	Y	52400 FQ	63760 MW	85010 TQ	USBLS	5/15
Middle School	District of Columbia	Y	50970 FQ	60430 MW	76700 TQ	USBLS	5/15
Middle School	Washington-Arlington-Alexandria PMSA, DC-VA-MD-WV	Y	58700 FQ	72000 MW	87380 TQ	USBLS	5/15
Middle School	Florida	Y	40755 AE	48333 MW	56325 AEX	FLBLS	7/16-9/16
Middle School	Fort Lauderdale-Pompano Beach-Deerfield Beach PMSA, FL	Y	40836 AE	53807 MW	65217 AEX	FLBLS	7/16-9/16
Middle School	Orlando-Kissimmee-Sanford MSA, FL	Y	43676 AE	48172 MW	54542 AEX	FLBLS	7/16-9/16
Middle School	Tampa-St. Petersburg-Clearwater MSA, FL	Y	37088 AE	45206 MW	51415 AEX	FLBLS	7/16-9/16
Middle School	Georgia	Y	42910 FQ	51360 MW	60560 TQ	USBLS	5/15
Middle School	Atlanta-Sandy Springs-Roswell MSA, GA	Y	43130 FQ	50900 MW	61280 TQ	USBLS	5/15
Middle School	Augusta-Richmond County MSA, GA-SC	Y	42470 FQ	49730 MW	57020 TQ	USBLS	5/15
Middle School	Idaho	Y	37460 FQ	51020 MW	59560 TQ	USBLS	5/15
Middle School	Boise City MSA, ID	Y	36890 FQ	49620 MW	58640 TQ	USBLS	5/15
Middle School	Illinois	Y	48780 FQ	60650 MW	81630 TQ	USBLS	5/15
Middle School	Chicago-Naperville-Arlington Heights PMSA, IL	Y	52870 FQ	63990 MW	86080 TQ	USBLS	5/15
Middle School	Lake County-Kenosha County PMSA, IL-WI	Y	47900 FQ	59710 MW	81030 TQ	USBLS	5/15
Middle School	Indiana	Y	40600 FQ	51130 MW	63590 TQ	USBLS	5/15
Middle School	Gary PMSA, IN	Y	39390 FQ	47500 MW	59480 TQ	USBLS	5/15
Middle School	Indianapolis-Carmel-Anderson MSA, IN	Y	41100 FQ	51670 MW	63190 TQ	USBLS	5/15
Middle School	Iowa	Y	43600 FQ	56100 MW	70170 TQ	USBLS	5/15
Middle School	Des Moines-West Des Moines MSA, IA	Y	52040 FQ	61950 MW	77280 TQ	USBLS	5/15
Middle School	Kansas	Y	42560 FQ	48340 MW	57470 TQ	USBLS	5/15
Middle School	Lawrence MSA, KS	Y	44250 FQ	49350 MW	56420 TQ	USBLS	5/15
Middle School	Wichita MSA, KS	Y	43970 FQ	49500 MW	56930 TQ	USBLS	5/15
Middle School	Kentucky	Y	44050 FQ	51010 MW	59090 TQ	USBLS	5/15
Middle School	Louisville-Jefferson County MSA, KY-IN	Y	44550 FQ	53520 MW	64660 TQ	USBLS	5/15
Middle School	Louisiana	Y	43170 FQ	47190 MW	52780 TQ	USBLS	5/15
Middle School	Baton Rouge MSA, LA	Y	43710 FQ	48380 MW	56320 TQ	USBLS	5/15
Middle School	New Orleans-Metairie MSA, LA	Y	42670 FQ	46080 MW	49480 TQ	USBLS	5/15
Middle School	Maine	Y	40470 FQ	48580 MW	59370 TQ	USBLS	5/15

AE	Average entry wage	AWR	Average wage range	H	Hourly
AEX	Average experienced wage	B	Biweekly	HI	Highest wage paid
ATC	Average total compensation	D	Daily	HR	High end range
AW	Average wage paid	FQ	First quartile wage	LO	Lowest wage paid

LR	Low end range	MTC	Median total compensation	TCC	Total cash compensation
M	Monthly	MW	Median wage paid	TQ	Third quartile wage
MCC	Median cash compensation	MWR	Median wage range	W	Weekly
ME	Median entry wage	S	See annotated source	Y	Yearly

Special Education Teacher

Occupation/Type/Industry	Location	Per	Low	Mid	High	Source	Date
Special Education Teacher							
Middle School	Portland-South Portland MSA, ME	Y	42090 FQ	51780 MW	62260 TQ	USBLS	5/15
Middle School	Maryland	Y	46340 AE	66015 MW	75852 AEX	MDBLS	4/16
Middle School	Baltimore-Columbia-Towson MSA, MD	Y	51100 FQ	63210 MW	78420 TQ	USBLS	5/15
Middle School	Salisbury MSA, MD-DE	Y	48960 FQ	62660 MW	72160 TQ	USBLS	5/15
Middle School	Massachusetts	Y	52700 FQ	66940 MW	79920 TQ	USBLS	5/15
Middle School	Boston-Cambridge-Newton NECTA, MA	Y	54680 FQ	69370 MW	87670 TQ	USBLS	5/15
Middle School	Worcester MSA, MA-CT	Y	60080 FQ	70130 MW	78930 TQ	USBLS	5/15
Middle School	Michigan	Y	49950 FQ	62530 MW	75780 TQ	USBLS	5/15
Middle School	Detroit-Dearborn-Livonia PMSA, MI	Y	49170 FQ	64300 MW	82280 TQ	USBLS	5/15
Middle School	Grand Rapids-Wyoming MSA, MI	Y	51670 FQ	65710 MW	76090 TQ	USBLS	5/15
Middle School	Minnesota	Y	49636 FQ	60886 MW	74818 TQ	MNBLS	1/16-3/16
Middle School	Minneapolis-St. Paul-Bloomington MSA, MN-WI	Y	50392 FQ	64052 MW	77600 TQ	MNBLS	1/16-3/16
Middle School	Mississippi	Y	36300 FQ	42030 MW	48580 TQ	USBLS	5/15
Middle School	Jackson MSA, MS	Y	37520 FQ	43510 MW	49160 TQ	USBLS	5/15
Middle School	Missouri	Y	40000 FQ	49810 MW	61920 TQ	USBLS	5/15
Middle School	Kansas City MSA, MO-KS	Y	42350 FQ	49120 MW	60380 TQ	USBLS	5/15
Middle School	St. Louis MSA, MO-IL	Y	43920 FQ	53750 MW	65820 TQ	USBLS	5/15
Middle School	Montana	Y	40980 FQ	49400 MW	59370 TQ	USBLS	5/15
Middle School	Nebraska	Y	43075 FQ	50080 MW	58925 TQ	NEBLS	7/16-9/16
Middle School	Omaha-Council Bluffs MSA, NE-IA	Y	44450 FQ	53225 MW	60860 TQ	NEBLS	7/16-9/16
Middle School	Nevada	Y	44050 FQ	51780 MW	61310 TQ	USBLS	5/15
Middle School	Las Vegas-Henderson-Paradise MSA, NV	Y	44060 FQ	52370 MW	63410 TQ	USBLS	5/15
Middle School	New Hampshire	Y	39476 AE	57196 MW	65549 AEX	NHBLS	6/16
Middle School	Manchester NECTA, NH	Y	42989 AE	57392 MW	64084 AEX	NHBLS	6/16
Middle School	Nashua NECTA, NH-MA	Y	46390 FQ	59580 MW	70000 TQ	USBLS	5/15
Middle School	New Jersey	Y	55790 FQ	63350 MW	80000 TQ	USBLS	5/15
Middle School	Camden PMSA, NJ	Y	55440 FQ	61870 MW	78130 TQ	USBLS	5/15
Middle School	Newark PMSA, NJ-PA	Y	56780 FQ	65320 MW	80530 TQ	USBLS	5/15
Middle School	Trenton MSA, NJ	Y	51520 FQ	65100 MW	84840 TQ	USBLS	5/15
Middle School	New Mexico	Y	41390 FQ	48140 MW	60860 TQ	USBLS	5/15
Middle School	Albuquerque MSA, NM	Y	40120 FQ	46020 MW	55450 TQ	USBLS	5/15
Middle School	New York	Y	53440 AE	75640 MW	92410 AEX	NYBLS	1/16-3/16
Middle School	Buffalo-Cheektowaga-Niagara Falls MSA, NY	Y	51660 FQ	63870 MW	77330 TQ	USBLS	5/15
Middle School	Nassau County-Suffolk County PMSA, NY	Y	83120 FQ	101470 MW	119180 TQ	USBLS	5/15
Middle School	New York-Jersey City-White Plains PMSA, NY-NJ	Y	58530 FQ	71900 MW	92060 TQ	USBLS	5/15
Middle School	Rochester MSA, NY	Y	47330 FQ	57480 MW	69780 TQ	USBLS	5/15
Middle School	North Carolina	Y	36130 FQ	42180 MW	49850 TQ	USBLS	5/15
Middle School	Charlotte-Concord-Gastonia MSA, NC-SC	Y	36910 FQ	43580 MW	51000 TQ	USBLS	5/15
Middle School	Raleigh MSA, NC	Y	39250 FQ	49020 MW	62360 TQ	USBLS	5/15
Middle School	North Dakota	Y	44700 FQ	53070 MW	61560 TQ	USBLS	5/15
Middle School	Fargo MSA, ND-MN	Y	43320 FQ	53310 MW	61890 TQ	USBLS	5/15
Middle School	Ohio	Y	45610 FQ	57660 MW	70640 TQ	USBLS	5/15
Middle School	Cincinnati MSA, OH-KY-IN	Y	44750 FQ	54650 MW	67860 TQ	USBLS	5/15
Middle School	Cleveland-Elyria MSA, OH	Y	52010 FQ	64460 MW	75510 TQ	USBLS	5/15
Middle School	Columbus MSA, OH	Y	45620 FQ	59130 MW	72970 TQ	USBLS	5/15
Middle School	Oklahoma	Y	36680 FQ	43050 MW	50030 TQ	USBLS	5/15
Middle School	Oklahoma City MSA, OK	Y	36180 FQ	41920 MW	48190 TQ	USBLS	5/15
Middle School	Tulsa MSA, OK	Y	38210 FQ	48510 MW	61540 TQ	USBLS	5/15
Middle School	Oregon	Y	50072 FQ	60924 MW	78154 TQ	ORBLS	2016
Middle School	Portland-Vancouver-Hillsboro MSA, OR-WA	Y	55010 FQ	68060 MW	89320 TQ	USBLS	5/15
Middle School	Pennsylvania	Y	50500 FQ	61250 MW	74770 TQ	USBLS	5/15
Middle School	Allentown-Bethlehem-Easton MSA, PA-NJ	Y	55910 FQ	66600 MW	78300 TQ	USBLS	5/15
Middle School	Harrisburg-Carlisle MSA, PA	Y	50100 FQ	57930 MW	67520 TQ	USBLS	5/15
Middle School	Montgomery County-Bucks County-Chester County PMSA, PA	Y	45870 FQ	58560 MW	74200 TQ	USBLS	5/15
Middle School	Philadelphia PMSA, PA	Y	52760 FQ	65260 MW	78220 TQ	USBLS	5/15

AE	Average entry wage	AWR	Average wage range	H	Hourly	LR	Low end range	MTC	Median total compensation	TCC	Total cash compensation
AEX	Average experienced wage	B	Biweekly	HI	Highest wage paid	M	Monthly	MW	Median wage paid	TQ	Third quartile wage
ATC	Average total compensation	D	Daily	HR	High end range	MCC	Median cash compensation	MWR	Median wage range	W	Weekly
AW	Average wage paid	FQ	First quartile wage	LO	Lowest wage paid	ME	Median entry wage	S	See annotated source	Y	Yearly

Special Education Teacher

Occupation/Type/Industry	Location	Per	Low	Mid	High	Source	Date
Middle School	Pittsburgh MSA, PA	Y	52690 FQ	62360 MW	73400 TQ	USBLS	5/15
Middle School	Rhode Island	Y	58120 FQ	71090 MW	81190 TQ	USBLS	5/15
Middle School	Providence-Warwick MSA, RI-MA	Y	57880 FQ	70920 MW	81990 TQ	USBLS	5/15
Middle School	South Carolina	Y	43250 FQ	52610 MW	61250 TQ	USBLS	5/15
Middle School	Charleston-North Charleston MSA, SC	Y	49020 FQ	55380 MW	61690 TQ	USBLS	5/15
Middle School	Columbia MSA, SC	Y	41180 FQ	49220 MW	58060 TQ	USBLS	5/15
Middle School	Greenville-Anderson-Mauldin MSA, SC	Y	37690 FQ	47060 MW	57460 TQ	USBLS	5/15
Middle School	South Dakota	Y	36400 FQ	43020 MW	51310 TQ	USBLS	5/15
Middle School	Sioux Falls MSA, SD	Y	36370 FQ	44720 MW	54310 TQ	USBLS	5/15
Middle School	Tennessee	Y	43480 FQ	52340 MW	63060 TQ	USBLS	5/15
Middle School	Knoxville MSA, TN	Y	41140 FQ	49260 MW	56520 TQ	USBLS	5/15
Middle School	Memphis MSA, TN-MS-AR	Y	36890 FQ	42840 MW	49410 TQ	USBLS	5/15
Middle School	Nashville-Davidson–Murfreesboro–Franklin MSA, TN	Y	46430 FQ	57290 MW	70570 TQ	USBLS	5/15
Middle School	Texas	Y	46750 FQ	53940 MW	60870 TQ	USBLS	5/15
Middle School	Austin-Round Rock MSA, TX	Y	45400 FQ	51340 MW	59820 TQ	USBLS	5/15
Middle School	Dallas-Plano-Irving PMSA, TX	Y	49330 FQ	55750 MW	62020 TQ	USBLS	5/15
Middle School	Fort Worth-Arlington PMSA, TX	Y	48350 FQ	54070 MW	59440 TQ	USBLS	5/15
Middle School	Houston-The Woodlands-Sugar Land MSA, TX	Y	50680 FQ	58000 MW	68380 TQ	USBLS	5/15
Middle School	San Antonio-New Braunfels MSA, TX	Y	51300 FQ	55540 MW	59770 TQ	USBLS	5/15
Middle School	Utah	Y	25610 FQ	38330 MW	54480 TQ	USBLS	5/15
Middle School	Provo-Orem MSA, UT	Y	41190 FQ	46080 MW	52630 TQ	USBLS	5/15
Middle School	Salt Lake City MSA, UT	Y	24350 FQ	31480 MW	54740 TQ	USBLS	5/15
Middle School	Vermont	Y	47080 FQ	57350 MW	69560 TQ	USBLS	5/15
Middle School	Burlington-South Burlington MSA, VT	Y	57370 FQ	69200 MW	81340 TQ	USBLS	5/15
Middle School	Virginia	Y	48090 FQ	60030 MW	75000 TQ	USBLS	5/15
Middle School	Richmond MSA, VA	Y	47970 FQ	57030 MW	65170 TQ	USBLS	5/15
Middle School	Virginia Beach-Norfolk-Newport News MSA, VA-NC	Y	49230 FQ	58600 MW	71630 TQ	USBLS	5/15
Middle School	Washington	Y		60180 AW		WABLS	3/16
Middle School	Seattle-Bellevue-Everett PMSA, WA	Y		62097 AW		WABLS	3/16
Middle School	Tacoma-Lakewood PMSA, WA	Y		62077 AW		WABLS	3/16
Middle School	West Virginia	Y	34170 FQ	40430 MW	49380 TQ	USBLS	5/15
Middle School	Huntington-Ashland MSA, WV-KY-OH	Y	36970 FQ	43510 MW	50420 TQ	USBLS	5/15
Middle School	Wisconsin	Y	44510 FQ	56840 MW	68920 TQ	USBLS	5/15
Middle School	Madison MSA, WI	Y	42230 FQ	52400 MW	58720 TQ	USBLS	5/15
Middle School	Milwaukee-Waukesha-West Allis MSA, WI	Y	50040 FQ	65120 MW	72420 TQ	USBLS	5/15
Middle School	Wyoming	Y	52860 FQ	59130 MW	67180 TQ	USBLS	5/15
Preschool	Alabama	Y	23332 AE	40753 AW	49468 AEX	ALBLS	6/16
Preschool	Alaska	Y	55460 FQ	70580 MW	84780 TQ	USBLS	5/15
Preschool	Anchorage MSA, AK	Y	63080 FQ	72930 MW	84980 TQ	USBLS	5/15
Preschool	Arizona	Y	37490 FQ	44750 MW	53790 TQ	USBLS	5/15
Preschool	Phoenix-Mesa-Scottsdale MSA, AZ	Y	38990 FQ	45800 MW	55310 TQ	USBLS	5/15
Preschool	Arkansas	Y	23890 FQ	31410 MW	42310 TQ	USBLS	5/15
Preschool	Little Rock-North Little Rock-Conway MSA, AR	Y	22780 FQ	27650 MW	37470 TQ	USBLS	5/15
Preschool	California	Y		68772 AW		CABLS	1/16-3/16
Preschool	Anaheim-Santa Ana-Irvine PMSA, CA	Y		62554 AW		CABLS	1/16-3/16
Preschool	Los Angeles-Long Beach-Glendale PMSA, CA	Y		74078 AW		CABLS	1/16-3/16
Preschool	Riverside-San Bernardino-Ontario MSA, CA	Y		45003 AW		CABLS	1/16-3/16
Preschool	Sacramento–Roseville–Arden-Arcade MSA, CA	Y		66814 AW		CABLS	1/16-3/16
Preschool	San Diego-Carlsbad MSA, CA	Y		81941 AW		CABLS	1/16-3/16
Preschool	Colorado	Y	43890 FQ	52390 MW	60240 TQ	USBLS	5/15
Preschool	Denver-Aurora-Lakewood MSA, CO	Y	47960 FQ	54830 MW	60990 TQ	USBLS	5/15

AE	Average entry wage	AWR	Average wage range	H	Hourly	LR	Low end range	MTC	Median total compensation	TCC	Total cash compensation
AEX	Average experienced wage	B	Biweekly	HI	Highest wage paid	M	Monthly	MW	Median wage paid	TQ	Third quartile wage
ATC	Average total compensation	D	Daily	HR	High end range	MCC	Median cash compensation	MWR	Median wage range	W	Weekly
AW	Average wage paid	FQ	First quartile wage	LO	Lowest wage paid	ME	Median entry wage	S	See annotated source	Y	Yearly

Special Education Teacher

Occupation/Type/Industry	Location	Per	Low	Mid	High	Source	Date
Special Education Teacher							
Preschool	Connecticut	Y		71207 MW		CTBLS	1/16-3/16
Preschool	Hartford-West Hartford-East Hartford MSA, CT	Y	59370 FQ	76740 MW	92470 TQ	USBLS	5/15
Preschool	Washington-Arlington-Alexandria PMSA, DC-VA-MD-WV	Y	60170 FQ	79450 MW	109560 TQ	USBLS	5/15
Preschool	Florida	Y	39735 AE	47992 MW	54844 AEX	FLBLS	7/16-9/16
Preschool	Miami-Miami Beach-Kendall PMSA, FL	Y	44448 AE	48937 MW	54190 AEX	FLBLS	7/16-9/16
Preschool	Orlando-Kissimmee-Sanford MSA, FL	Y	44922 AE	51816 MW	58925 AEX	FLBLS	7/16-9/16
Preschool	Tampa-St. Petersburg-Clearwater MSA, FL	Y	36785 AE	46074 MW	53042 AEX	FLBLS	7/16-9/16
Preschool	Georgia	Y	41460 FQ	48300 MW	61070 TQ	USBLS	5/15
Preschool	Atlanta-Sandy Springs-Roswell MSA, GA	Y	41200 FQ	46790 MW	59380 TQ	USBLS	5/15
Preschool	Urban Honolulu MSA, HI	Y	48990 FQ	56650 MW	63590 TQ	USBLS	5/15
Preschool	Idaho	Y	33700 FQ	38280 MW	46270 TQ	USBLS	5/15
Preschool	Illinois	Y	49180 FQ	78530 MW	93760 TQ	USBLS	5/15
Preschool	Chicago-Naperville-Arlington Heights PMSA, IL	Y	60710 FQ	83250 MW	96180 TQ	USBLS	5/15
Preschool	Indiana	Y	35420 FQ	48570 MW	61260 TQ	USBLS	5/15
Preschool	Iowa	Y	45050 FQ	58120 MW	70310 TQ	USBLS	5/15
Preschool	Des Moines-West Des Moines MSA, IA	Y	46310 FQ	58380 MW	69330 TQ	USBLS	5/15
Preschool	Kansas	Y	38210 FQ	44680 MW	50930 TQ	USBLS	5/15
Preschool	Wichita MSA, KS	Y	27550 FQ	43160 MW	50120 TQ	USBLS	5/15
Preschool	Kentucky	Y	40400 FQ	46550 MW	55390 TQ	USBLS	5/15
Preschool	Louisiana	Y	43420 FQ	48230 MW	55400 TQ	USBLS	5/15
Preschool	Baton Rouge MSA, LA	Y	44450 FQ	49590 MW	58290 TQ	USBLS	5/15
Preschool	New Orleans-Metairie MSA, LA	Y	43430 FQ	47990 MW	54460 TQ	USBLS	5/15
Preschool	Maine	Y	27680 FQ	32480 MW	40770 TQ	USBLS	5/15
Preschool	Maryland	Y	33832 AE	64434 MW	79735 AEX	MDBLS	4/16
Preschool	Baltimore-Columbia-Towson MSA, MD	Y	35010 FQ	38900 MW	68720 TQ	USBLS	5/15
Preschool	Massachusetts	Y	37480 FQ	55860 MW	73980 TQ	USBLS	5/15
Preschool	Boston-Cambridge-Newton NECTA, MA	Y	39850 FQ	63190 MW	81760 TQ	USBLS	5/15
Preschool	Worcester MSA, MA-CT	Y	29900 FQ	36590 MW	59350 TQ	USBLS	5/15
Preschool	Michigan	Y	40470 FQ	51320 MW	67010 TQ	USBLS	5/15
Preschool	Detroit-Dearborn-Livonia PMSA, MI	Y	35570 FQ	46320 MW	73040 TQ	USBLS	5/15
Preschool	Minnesota	Y	46058 FQ	57207 MW	72902 TQ	MNBLS	1/16-3/16
Preschool	Minneapolis-St. Paul-Bloomington MSA, MN-WI	Y	46239 FQ	57923 MW	74505 TQ	MNBLS	1/16-3/16
Preschool	Mississippi	Y	31900 FQ	35600 MW	39780 TQ	USBLS	5/15
Preschool	Missouri	Y	39590 FQ	47360 MW	59220 TQ	USBLS	5/15
Preschool	Kansas City MSA, MO-KS	Y	40580 FQ	47300 MW	55710 TQ	USBLS	5/15
Preschool	St. Louis MSA, MO-IL	Y	42740 FQ	47830 MW	56420 TQ	USBLS	5/15
Preschool	Nebraska	Y	43770 FQ	51650 MW	60825 TQ	NEBLS	7/16-9/16
Preschool	Omaha-Council Bluffs MSA, NE-IA	Y	40755 FQ	47655 MW	56465 TQ	NEBLS	7/16-9/16
Preschool	Nevada	Y	44190 FQ	51950 MW	61950 TQ	USBLS	5/15
Preschool	Las Vegas-Henderson-Paradise MSA, NV	Y	44070 FQ	51700 MW	61990 TQ	USBLS	5/15
Preschool	New Hampshire	Y	34350 AE	49878 MW	57616 AEX	NHBLS	6/16
Preschool	New Jersey	Y	52960 FQ	62700 MW	83710 TQ	USBLS	5/15
Preschool	Camden PMSA, NJ	Y	58540 FQ	71090 MW	90470 TQ	USBLS	5/15
Preschool	Newark PMSA, NJ-PA	Y	56530 FQ	68220 MW	86610 TQ	USBLS	5/15
Preschool	New Mexico	Y	53110 FQ	61420 MW	72550 TQ	USBLS	5/15
Preschool	New York	Y	37170 AE	58210 MW	78780 AEX	NYBLS	1/16-3/16
Preschool	Buffalo-Cheektowaga-Niagara Falls MSA, NY	Y	41170 FQ	47600 MW	64660 TQ	USBLS	5/15
Preschool	Nassau County-Suffolk County PMSA, NY	Y	47360 FQ	67440 MW	96430 TQ	USBLS	5/15
Preschool	New York-Jersey City-White Plains PMSA, NY-NJ	Y	41550 FQ	59350 MW	85560 TQ	USBLS	5/15
Preschool	Rochester MSA, NY	Y	39960 FQ	46290 MW	56940 TQ	USBLS	5/15
Preschool	North Carolina	Y	40250 FQ	49520 MW	61020 TQ	USBLS	5/15

AE	Average entry wage	AWR	Average wage range	H	Hourly
AEX	Average experienced wage	B	Biweekly	HI	Highest wage paid
ATC	Average total compensation	D	Daily	HR	High end range
AW	Average wage paid	FQ	First quartile wage	LO	Lowest wage paid

LR	Low end range	MTC	Median total compensation	TCC	Total cash compensation
M	Monthly	MW	Median wage paid	TQ	Third quartile wage
MCC	Median cash compensation	MWR	Median wage range	W	Weekly
ME	Median entry wage	S	See annotated source	Y	Yearly

Special Education Teacher

Occupation/Type/Industry	Location	Per	Low	Mid	High	Source	Date
Preschool	Charlotte-Concord-Gastonia MSA, NC-SC	Y	42980 FQ	51250 MW	58000 TQ	USBLS	5/15
Preschool	Raleigh MSA, NC	Y	37190 FQ	47360 MW	60380 TQ	USBLS	5/15
Preschool	Ohio	Y	39410 FQ	52240 MW	66540 TQ	USBLS	5/15
Preschool	Cincinnati MSA, OH-KY-IN	Y	37710 FQ	50440 MW	62810 TQ	USBLS	5/15
Preschool	Cleveland-Elyria MSA, OH	Y	47300 FQ	63600 MW	73240 TQ	USBLS	5/15
Preschool	Columbus MSA, OH	Y	27590 FQ	35990 MW	60550 TQ	USBLS	5/15
Preschool	Oklahoma	Y	22310 FQ	33200 MW	43090 TQ	USBLS	5/15
Preschool	Oregon	Y	56152 FQ	68832 MW	86057 TQ	ORBLS	2016
Preschool	Portland-Vancouver-Hillsboro MSA, OR-WA	Y	59300 FQ	70910 MW	85940 TQ	USBLS	5/15
Preschool	Allentown-Bethlehem-Easton MSA, PA-NJ	Y	56650 FQ	63390 MW	71740 TQ	USBLS	5/15
Preschool	Montgomery County-Bucks County-Chester County PMSA, PA	Y	58400 FQ	81750 MW	102220 TQ	USBLS	5/15
Preschool	Philadelphia PMSA, PA	Y	23680 FQ	34100 MW	46340 TQ	USBLS	5/15
Preschool	Pittsburgh MSA, PA	Y	37310 FQ	43620 MW	47880 TQ	USBLS	5/15
Preschool	Rhode Island	Y	60650 FQ	72030 MW	81380 TQ	USBLS	5/15
Preschool	Providence-Warwick MSA, RI-MA	Y	44970 FQ	61580 MW	76410 TQ	USBLS	5/15
Preschool	South Carolina	Y	40580 FQ	47650 MW	60060 TQ	USBLS	5/15
Preschool	South Dakota	Y	35180 FQ	39130 MW	51600 TQ	USBLS	5/15
Preschool	Tennessee	Y	35760 FQ	42930 MW	49750 TQ	USBLS	5/15
Preschool	Nashville-Davidson–Murfreesboro–Franklin MSA, TN	Y	33650 FQ	40010 MW	47150 TQ	USBLS	5/15
Preschool	Texas	Y	48430 FQ	55180 MW	61350 TQ	USBLS	5/15
Preschool	Austin-Round Rock MSA, TX	Y	48430 FQ	56090 MW	64770 TQ	USBLS	5/15
Preschool	Dallas-Plano-Irving PMSA, TX	Y	50660 FQ	57520 MW	65470 TQ	USBLS	5/15
Preschool	Fort Worth-Arlington PMSA, TX	Y	51200 FQ	55450 MW	59700 TQ	USBLS	5/15
Preschool	Houston-The Woodlands-Sugar Land MSA, TX	Y	51280 FQ	59380 MW	70640 TQ	USBLS	5/15
Preschool	San Antonio-New Braunfels MSA, TX	Y	52830 FQ	56240 MW	59640 TQ	USBLS	5/15
Preschool	Utah	Y	40080 FQ	64090 MW	82870 TQ	USBLS	5/15
Preschool	Provo-Orem MSA, UT	Y	24050 FQ	50550 MW	67470 TQ	USBLS	5/15
Preschool	Vermont	Y	41970 FQ	52560 MW	65850 TQ	USBLS	5/15
Preschool	Burlington-South Burlington MSA, VT	Y	37190 FQ	47870 MW	62270 TQ	USBLS	5/15
Preschool	Virginia	Y	50370 FQ	62290 MW	76860 TQ	USBLS	5/15
Preschool	Richmond MSA, VA	Y	54330 FQ	61110 MW	69740 TQ	USBLS	5/15
Preschool	Virginia Beach-Norfolk-Newport News MSA, VA-NC	Y	49350 FQ	56860 MW	63250 TQ	USBLS	5/15
Preschool	Washington	Y		60677 AW		WABLS	3/16
Preschool	Seattle-Bellevue-Everett PMSA, WA	Y		61083 AW		WABLS	3/16
Preschool	Tacoma-Lakewood PMSA, WA	Y		62533 AW		WABLS	3/16
Preschool	Wisconsin	Y	32010 FQ	38250 MW	48040 TQ	USBLS	5/15
Preschool	Wyoming	Y	40760 FQ	47900 MW	56600 TQ	USBLS	5/15
Secondary School	Alabama	Y	43484 AE	52138 AW	56471 AEX	ALBLS	6/16
Secondary School	Birmingham-Hoover MSA, AL	Y	38775 AE	46247 AW	49988 AEX	ALBLS	6/16
Secondary School	Alaska	Y	64360 FQ	76470 MW	91810 TQ	USBLS	5/15
Secondary School	Arizona	Y	36670 FQ	44930 MW	57100 TQ	USBLS	5/15
Secondary School	Phoenix-Mesa-Scottsdale MSA, AZ	Y	37530 FQ	46950 MW	59370 TQ	USBLS	5/15
Secondary School	Tucson MSA, AZ	Y	34410 FQ	38640 MW	46920 TQ	USBLS	5/15
Secondary School	Arkansas	Y	42820 FQ	48420 MW	57480 TQ	USBLS	5/15
Secondary School	Little Rock-North Little Rock-Conway MSA, AR	Y	43300 FQ	51460 MW	59910 TQ	USBLS	5/15
Secondary School	California	Y		75438 AW		CABLS	1/16-3/16
Secondary School	Anaheim-Santa Ana-Irvine PMSA, CA	Y		77629 AW		CABLS	1/16-3/16
Secondary School	Fresno MSA, CA	Y		84183 AW		CABLS	1/16-3/16
Secondary School	Los Angeles-Long Beach-Glendale PMSA, CA	Y		73693 AW		CABLS	1/16-3/16
Secondary School	Oakland-Hayward-Berkeley PMSA, CA	Y		85288 AW		CABLS	1/16-3/16
Secondary School	Riverside-San Bernardino-Ontario MSA, CA	Y		75833 AW		CABLS	1/16-3/16

AE	Average entry wage	AWR	Average wage range	H	Hourly	LR	Low end range	MTC Median total compensation TCC Total cash compensation
AEX	Average experienced wage	B	Biweekly	HI	Highest wage paid	M	Monthly	MW Median wage paid TQ Third quartile wage
ATC	Average total compensation	D	Daily	HR	High end range	MCC	Median cash compensation	MWR Median wage range W Weekly
AW	Average wage paid	FQ	First quartile wage	LO	Lowest wage paid	ME	Median entry wage	S See annotated source Y Yearly

Occupation/Type/Industry	Location	Per	Low	Mid	High	Source	Date
Special Education Teacher							
Secondary School	Sacramento–Roseville–Arden-Arcade MSA, CA	Y		79719 AW		CABLS	1/16-3/16
Secondary School	San Diego-Carlsbad MSA, CA	Y		72932 AW		CABLS	1/16-3/16
Secondary School	San Francisco-Redwood City-South San Francisco PMSA, CA	Y		72455 AW		CABLS	1/16-3/16
Secondary School	Colorado	Y	42380 FQ	51650 MW	64720 TQ	USBLS	5/15
Secondary School	Denver-Aurora-Lakewood MSA, CO	Y	44860 FQ	56600 MW	70000 TQ	USBLS	5/15
Secondary School	Connecticut	Y		78045 MW		CTBLS	1/16-3/16
Secondary School	Bridgeport-Stamford-Norwalk MSA, CT	Y	64310 FQ	76830 MW	92110 TQ	USBLS	5/15
Secondary School	Hartford-West Hartford-East Hartford MSA, CT	Y	66690 FQ	82560 MW	93770 TQ	USBLS	5/15
Secondary School	Delaware	Y	53740 FQ	61840 MW	72340 TQ	USBLS	5/15
Secondary School	Wilmington PMSA, DE-MD-NJ	Y	51750 FQ	59280 MW	72230 TQ	USBLS	5/15
Secondary School	District of Columbia	Y	55970 FQ	64270 MW	82110 TQ	USBLS	5/15
Secondary School	Washington-Arlington-Alexandria PMSA, DC-VA-MD-WV	Y	56800 FQ	71680 MW	93480 TQ	USBLS	5/15
Secondary School	Florida	Y	42439 AE	50089 MW	59352 AEX	FLBLS	7/16-9/16
Secondary School	Miami-Miami Beach-Kendall PMSA, FL	Y	41389 AE	49486 MW	58823 AEX	FLBLS	7/16-9/16
Secondary School	Orlando-Kissimmee-Sanford MSA, FL	Y	43624 AE	48401 MW	54252 AEX	FLBLS	7/16-9/16
Secondary School	Tampa-St. Petersburg-Clearwater MSA, FL	Y	40220 AE	46688 MW	51666 AEX	FLBLS	7/16-9/16
Secondary School	Georgia	Y	46440 FQ	55750 MW	64980 TQ	USBLS	5/15
Secondary School	Atlanta-Sandy Springs-Roswell MSA, GA	Y	47210 FQ	57680 MW	69680 TQ	USBLS	5/15
Secondary School	Augusta-Richmond County MSA, GA-SC	Y	39930 FQ	49910 MW	57130 TQ	USBLS	5/15
Secondary School	Hawaii	Y	46120 FQ	54180 MW	61440 TQ	USBLS	5/15
Secondary School	Urban Honolulu MSA, HI	Y	45420 FQ	53560 MW	61690 TQ	USBLS	5/15
Secondary School	Idaho	Y	38940 FQ	46220 MW	57220 TQ	USBLS	5/15
Secondary School	Boise City MSA, ID	Y	36900 FQ	45090 MW	58930 TQ	USBLS	5/15
Secondary School	Illinois	Y	48930 FQ	62460 MW	83420 TQ	USBLS	5/15
Secondary School	Chicago-Naperville-Arlington Heights PMSA, IL	Y	54400 FQ	70140 MW	90480 TQ	USBLS	5/15
Secondary School	Lake County-Kenosha County PMSA, IL-WI	Y	46620 FQ	61920 MW	82890 TQ	USBLS	5/15
Secondary School	Indiana	Y	42710 FQ	52890 MW	63370 TQ	USBLS	5/15
Secondary School	Gary PMSA, IN	Y	43040 FQ	53000 MW	62060 TQ	USBLS	5/15
Secondary School	Indianapolis-Carmel-Anderson MSA, IN	Y	43240 FQ	53200 MW	65140 TQ	USBLS	5/15
Secondary School	Iowa	Y	44270 FQ	53310 MW	63250 TQ	USBLS	5/15
Secondary School	Des Moines-West Des Moines MSA, IA	Y	48070 FQ	56430 MW	67200 TQ	USBLS	5/15
Secondary School	Kansas	Y	42830 FQ	47910 MW	56530 TQ	USBLS	5/15
Secondary School	Wichita MSA, KS	Y	44830 FQ	50860 MW	57930 TQ	USBLS	5/15
Secondary School	Kentucky	Y	45360 FQ	52880 MW	59950 TQ	USBLS	5/15
Secondary School	Louisville-Jefferson County MSA, KY-IN	Y	47580 FQ	57160 MW	69070 TQ	USBLS	5/15
Secondary School	Louisiana	Y	43730 FQ	49050 MW	56760 TQ	USBLS	5/15
Secondary School	Baton Rouge MSA, LA	Y	47630 FQ	54690 MW	60920 TQ	USBLS	5/15
Secondary School	New Orleans-Metairie MSA, LA	Y	43050 FQ	49770 MW	57970 TQ	USBLS	5/15
Secondary School	Maine	Y	38100 FQ	48480 MW	59290 TQ	USBLS	5/15
Secondary School	Portland-South Portland MSA, ME	Y	39410 FQ	53570 MW	63040 TQ	USBLS	5/15
Secondary School	Maryland	Y	45430 AE	65082 MW	74907 AEX	MDBLS	4/16
Secondary School	Baltimore-Columbia-Towson MSA, MD	Y	52760 FQ	65630 MW	80440 TQ	USBLS	5/15
Secondary School	Salisbury MSA, MD-DE	Y	52900 FQ	59910 MW	69320 TQ	USBLS	5/15
Secondary School	Massachusetts	Y	51510 FQ	64810 MW	78160 TQ	USBLS	5/15
Secondary School	Boston-Cambridge-Newton NECTA, MA	Y	52910 FQ	66910 MW	86030 TQ	USBLS	5/15
Secondary School	Worcester MSA, MA-CT	Y	57760 FQ	68530 MW	78230 TQ	USBLS	5/15
Secondary School	Michigan	Y	52420 FQ	65970 MW	76640 TQ	USBLS	5/15

AE	Average entry wage	AWR	Average wage range	H	Hourly	LR	Low end range	MTC	Median total compensation	TCC	Total cash compensation
AEX	Average experienced wage	B	Biweekly	HI	Highest wage paid	M	Monthly	MW	Median wage paid	TQ	Third quartile wage
ATC	Average total compensation	D	Daily	HR	High end range	MCC	Median cash compensation	MWR	Median wage range	W	Weekly
AW	Average wage paid	FQ	First quartile wage	LO	Lowest wage paid	ME	Median entry wage	S	See annotated source	Y	Yearly

Occupation/Type/Industry	Location	Per	Low	Mid	High	Source	Date
Special Education Teacher							
Secondary School	Detroit-Dearborn-Livonia PMSA, MI	Y	56380 FQ	70760 MW	81840 TQ	USBLS	5/15
Secondary School	Grand Rapids-Wyoming MSA, MI	Y	55250 FQ	67310 MW	75450 TQ	USBLS	5/15
Secondary School	Minnesota	Y	47499 FQ	61663 MW	77469 TQ	MNBLS	1/16-3/16
Secondary School	Minneapolis-St. Paul-Bloomington MSA, MN-WI	Y	46895 FQ	64515 MW	78920 TQ	MNBLS	1/16-3/16
Secondary School	Mississippi	Y	37090 FQ	43630 MW	50960 TQ	USBLS	5/15
Secondary School	Jackson MSA, MS	Y	36630 FQ	42940 MW	50320 TQ	USBLS	5/15
Secondary School	Missouri	Y	38150 FQ	47310 MW	65590 TQ	USBLS	5/15
Secondary School	Kansas City MSA, MO-KS	Y	41880 FQ	47710 MW	58940 TQ	USBLS	5/15
Secondary School	St. Louis MSA, MO-IL	Y	46310 FQ	60640 MW	79460 TQ	USBLS	5/15
Secondary School	Montana	Y	32980 FQ	38880 MW	56600 TQ	USBLS	5/15
Secondary School	Billings MSA, MT	Y	32240 FQ	36300 MW	47210 TQ	USBLS	5/15
Secondary School	Nebraska	Y	44140 FQ	52235 MW	60200 TQ	NEBLS	7/16-9/16
Secondary School	Omaha-Council Bluffs MSA, NE-IA	Y	43735 FQ	51950 MW	60290 TQ	NEBLS	7/16-9/16
Secondary School	Nevada	Y	46130 FQ	54820 MW	64140 TQ	USBLS	5/15
Secondary School	Las Vegas-Henderson-Paradise MSA, NV	Y	44770 FQ	54100 MW	66340 TQ	USBLS	5/15
Secondary School	New Hampshire	Y	43221 AE	58446 MW	66375 AEX	NHBLS	6/16
Secondary School	Manchester NECTA, NH	Y	49564 AE	61799 MW	67898 AEX	NHBLS	6/16
Secondary School	Nashua NECTA, NH-MA	Y	53580 FQ	59460 MW	67840 TQ	USBLS	5/15
Secondary School	New Jersey	Y	57950 FQ	70450 MW	88200 TQ	USBLS	5/15
Secondary School	Camden PMSA, NJ	Y	57640 FQ	71210 MW	88410 TQ	USBLS	5/15
Secondary School	Newark PMSA, NJ-PA	Y	58450 FQ	70480 MW	87580 TQ	USBLS	5/15
Secondary School	Trenton MSA, NJ	Y	57450 FQ	74730 MW	90490 TQ	USBLS	5/15
Secondary School	New Mexico	Y	43520 FQ	51050 MW	66930 TQ	USBLS	5/15
Secondary School	Albuquerque MSA, NM	Y	41260 FQ	46760 MW	54560 TQ	USBLS	5/15
Secondary School	New York	Y	52390 AE	76930 MW	94060 AEX	NYBLS	1/16-3/16
Secondary School	Buffalo-Cheektowaga-Niagara Falls MSA, NY	Y	45920 FQ	56770 MW	71230 TQ	USBLS	5/15
Secondary School	Nassau County-Suffolk County PMSA, NY	Y	82210 FQ	103050 MW	119820 TQ	USBLS	5/15
Secondary School	New York-Jersey City-White Plains PMSA, NY-NJ	Y	60630 FQ	78080 MW	97250 TQ	USBLS	5/15
Secondary School	Rochester MSA, NY	Y	48770 FQ	58640 MW	72680 TQ	USBLS	5/15
Secondary School	North Carolina	Y	37920 FQ	45040 MW	53730 TQ	USBLS	5/15
Secondary School	Charlotte-Concord-Gastonia MSA, NC-SC	Y	37720 FQ	45240 MW	54410 TQ	USBLS	5/15
Secondary School	Raleigh MSA, NC	Y	39450 FQ	51560 MW	60760 TQ	USBLS	5/15
Secondary School	North Dakota	Y	44410 FQ	50440 MW	59560 TQ	USBLS	5/15
Secondary School	Ohio	Y	44170 FQ	55290 MW	67820 TQ	USBLS	5/15
Secondary School	Cincinnati MSA, OH-KY-IN	Y	43370 FQ	54570 MW	66260 TQ	USBLS	5/15
Secondary School	Cleveland-Elyria MSA, OH	Y	51060 FQ	64630 MW	74800 TQ	USBLS	5/15
Secondary School	Columbus MSA, OH	Y	43280 FQ	55080 MW	70810 TQ	USBLS	5/15
Secondary School	Oklahoma	Y	35800 FQ	42910 MW	50900 TQ	USBLS	5/15
Secondary School	Oklahoma City MSA, OK	Y	35450 FQ	41140 MW	47870 TQ	USBLS	5/15
Secondary School	Tulsa MSA, OK	Y	38970 FQ	48230 MW	67030 TQ	USBLS	5/15
Secondary School	Oregon	Y	50757 FQ	61457 MW	73963 TQ	ORBLS	2016
Secondary School	Portland-Vancouver-Hillsboro MSA, OR-WA	Y	53360 FQ	63100 MW	73050 TQ	USBLS	5/15
Secondary School	Pennsylvania	Y	50900 FQ	62330 MW	79140 TQ	USBLS	5/15
Secondary School	Allentown-Bethlehem-Easton MSA, PA-NJ	Y	52440 FQ	61020 MW	75310 TQ	USBLS	5/15
Secondary School	Harrisburg-Carlisle MSA, PA	Y	44640 FQ	54810 MW	62540 TQ	USBLS	5/15
Secondary School	Montgomery County-Bucks County-Chester County PMSA, PA	Y	55640 FQ	73670 MW	95350 TQ	USBLS	5/15
Secondary School	Philadelphia PMSA, PA	Y	59430 FQ	73900 MW	86990 TQ	USBLS	5/15
Secondary School	Pittsburgh MSA, PA	Y	48480 FQ	57130 MW	69140 TQ	USBLS	5/15
Secondary School	Rhode Island	Y	59770 FQ	71630 MW	82040 TQ	USBLS	5/15
Secondary School	Providence-Warwick MSA, RI-MA	Y	58450 FQ	70750 MW	81050 TQ	USBLS	5/15
Secondary School	South Carolina	Y	44920 FQ	54820 MW	64000 TQ	USBLS	5/15
Secondary School	Charleston-North Charleston MSA, SC	Y	49270 FQ	57830 MW	67710 TQ	USBLS	5/15
Secondary School	Columbia MSA, SC	Y	40710 FQ	51840 MW	62430 TQ	USBLS	5/15
Secondary School	Greenville-Anderson-Mauldin MSA, SC	Y	50340 FQ	57400 MW	66880 TQ	USBLS	5/15
Secondary School	South Dakota	Y	35610 FQ	41340 MW	47890 TQ	USBLS	5/15

AE	Average entry wage	AWR	Average wage range	H	Hourly
AEX	Average experienced wage	B	Biweekly	HI	Highest wage paid
ATC	Average total compensation	D	Daily	HR	High end range
AW	Average wage paid	FQ	First quartile wage	LO	Lowest wage paid

LR	Low end range	MTC	Median total compensation
M	Monthly	MW	Median wage paid
MCC	Median cash compensation	MWR	Median wage range
ME	Median entry wage	S	See annotated source

TCC	Total cash compensation
TQ	Third quartile wage
W	Weekly
Y	Yearly

Occupation/Type/Industry	Location	Per	Low	Mid	High	Source	Date
Special Education Teacher							
Secondary School	Sioux Falls MSA, SD	Y	36350 FQ	44480 MW	53690 TQ	USBLS	5/15
Secondary School	Tennessee	Y	40010 FQ	47010 MW	57270 TQ	USBLS	5/15
Secondary School	Knoxville MSA, TN	Y	41610 FQ	48520 MW	56700 TQ	USBLS	5/15
Secondary School	Memphis MSA, TN-MS-AR	Y	33090 FQ	41180 MW	49430 TQ	USBLS	5/15
Secondary School	Nashville-Davidson–Murfreesboro–Franklin MSA, TN	Y	40940 FQ	49150 MW	61420 TQ	USBLS	5/15
Secondary School	Texas	Y	47130 FQ	54640 MW	61620 TQ	USBLS	5/15
Secondary School	Austin-Round Rock MSA, TX	Y	45320 FQ	51510 MW	60430 TQ	USBLS	5/15
Secondary School	Dallas-Plano-Irving PMSA, TX	Y	50080 FQ	56480 MW	62930 TQ	USBLS	5/15
Secondary School	Fort Worth-Arlington PMSA, TX	Y	51660 FQ	58170 MW	68340 TQ	USBLS	5/15
Secondary School	Houston-The Woodlands-Sugar Land MSA, TX	Y	51370 FQ	58110 MW	67420 TQ	USBLS	5/15
Secondary School	San Antonio-New Braunfels MSA, TX	Y	51180 FQ	55670 MW	60170 TQ	USBLS	5/15
Secondary School	Utah	Y	28780 FQ	38690 MW	57800 TQ	USBLS	5/15
Secondary School	Ogden-Clearfield MSA, UT	Y	36100 FQ	41700 MW	49500 TQ	USBLS	5/15
Secondary School	Provo-Orem MSA, UT	Y	35360 FQ	44390 MW	56080 TQ	USBLS	5/15
Secondary School	Salt Lake City MSA, UT	Y	24140 FQ	39680 MW	64870 TQ	USBLS	5/15
Secondary School	Vermont	Y	48680 FQ	59080 MW	70800 TQ	USBLS	5/15
Secondary School	Burlington-South Burlington MSA, VT	Y	52090 FQ	64180 MW	77280 TQ	USBLS	5/15
Secondary School	Virginia	Y	47260 FQ	58860 MW	77900 TQ	USBLS	5/15
Secondary School	Richmond MSA, VA	Y	48090 FQ	56800 MW	64490 TQ	USBLS	5/15
Secondary School	Virginia Beach-Norfolk-Newport News MSA, VA-NC	Y	47420 FQ	58340 MW	73730 TQ	USBLS	5/15
Secondary School	Washington	Y		61732 AW		WABLS	3/16
Secondary School	Seattle-Bellevue-Everett PMSA, WA	Y		62828 AW		WABLS	3/16
Secondary School	Tacoma-Lakewood PMSA, WA	Y		63659 AW		WABLS	3/16
Secondary School	West Virginia	Y	38310 FQ	45240 MW	52850 TQ	USBLS	5/15
Secondary School	Huntington-Ashland MSA, WV-KY-OH	Y	40030 FQ	47590 MW	55880 TQ	USBLS	5/15
Secondary School	Wisconsin	Y	42140 FQ	52060 MW	63300 TQ	USBLS	5/15
Secondary School	Madison MSA, WI	Y	43010 FQ	49460 MW	61300 TQ	USBLS	5/15
Secondary School	Milwaukee-Waukesha-West Allis MSA, WI	Y	41730 FQ	54770 MW	68580 TQ	USBLS	5/15
Secondary School	Wyoming	Y	50950 FQ	57650 MW	65430 TQ	USBLS	5/15
Special Events Coordinator							
Municipal Government	Chula Vista, CA	Y			99337 HI	CACIT	6/28/16
Special Events Manager							
Municipal Government	Rocklin, CA	Y			65227 HI	CACIT	6/28/16
Special Events Supervisor							
Municipal Government	Colorado Springs, CO	Y	65794 LO		90467 HI	COSPRS	2017
Specialist 6							
U.S. Army, Active Duty, Pay Grade E-6	United States	M	2487 LO		3852 HI	DOD1	2017
Specimen Processing Assistant							
Michigan State University	East Lansing, MI	Y	30035 LO		38376 HI	MSUSAL	10/1/14-9/30/15
Speech-Language Pathologist	Alabama	Y	50385 AE	69161 AW	78549 AEX	ALBLS	6/16
	Birmingham-Hoover MSA, AL	Y	52546 AE	68611 AW	76643 AEX	ALBLS	6/16
	Alaska	Y	72000 FQ	87050 MW	102470 TQ	USBLS	5/15
	Anchorage MSA, AK	Y	79080 FQ	90500 MW	102080 TQ	USBLS	5/15
	Arizona	Y	53700 FQ	68690 MW	84800 TQ	USBLS	5/15
	Phoenix-Mesa-Scottsdale MSA, AZ	Y	55970 FQ	72010 MW	88060 TQ	USBLS	5/15
	Tucson MSA, AZ	Y	50380 FQ	62020 MW	75860 TQ	USBLS	5/15
	Arkansas	Y	50470 FQ	67400 MW	96920 TQ	USBLS	5/15
	Little Rock-North Little Rock-Conway MSA, AR	Y	53740 FQ	70980 MW	95260 TQ	USBLS	5/15
	California	H	34.08 FQ	42.83 MW	50.74 TQ	CABLS	1/16-3/16
	Anaheim-Santa Ana-Irvine PMSA, CA	H	36.09 FQ	43.91 MW	50.33 TQ	CABLS	1/16-3/16
	Los Angeles-Long Beach-Glendale PMSA, CA	H	32.53 FQ	41.25 MW	48.60 TQ	CABLS	1/16-3/16

AE	Average entry wage	AWR	Average wage range	H	Hourly
AEX	Average experienced wage	B	Biweekly	HI	Highest wage paid
ATC	Average total compensation	D	Daily	HR	High end range
AW	Average wage paid	FQ	First quartile wage	LO	Lowest wage paid

LR	Low end range	MTC	Median total compensation
M	Monthly	MW	Median wage paid
MCC	Median cash compensation	MWR	Median wage range
ME	Median entry wage	S	See annotated source

TCC	Total cash compensation
TQ	Third quartile wage
W	Weekly
Y	Yearly

Occupation/Type/Industry	Location	Per	Low	Mid	High	Source	Date
Speech-Language Pathologist	Oakland-Hayward-Berkeley PMSA, CA	H	35.16 FQ	43.63 MW	52.88 TQ	CABLS	1/16-3/16
	Riverside-San Bernardino-Ontario MSA, CA	H	34.84 FQ	42.60 MW	49.75 TQ	CABLS	1/16-3/16
	Sacramento–Roseville–Arden-Arcade MSA, CA	H	33.83 FQ	45.31 MW	55.85 TQ	CABLS	1/16-3/16
	San Diego-Carlsbad MSA, CA	H	33.83 FQ	42.92 MW	53.15 TQ	CABLS	1/16-3/16
	San Francisco-Redwood City-South San Francisco PMSA, CA	H	36.62 FQ	44.34 MW	52.49 TQ	CABLS	1/16-3/16
	Colorado	Y	67890 FQ	82740 MW	100290 TQ	USBLS	5/15
	Denver-Aurora-Lakewood MSA, CO	Y	71620 FQ	86720 MW	104130 TQ	USBLS	5/15
	Connecticut	Y		89894 MW		CTBLS	1/16-3/16
	Bridgeport-Stamford-Norwalk MSA, CT	Y	72100 FQ	91790 MW	111670 TQ	USBLS	5/15
	Hartford-West Hartford-East Hartford MSA, CT	Y	74430 FQ	89860 MW	103580 TQ	USBLS	5/15
	Delaware	Y	54160 FQ	68390 MW	85070 TQ	USBLS	5/15
	Wilmington PMSA, DE-MD-NJ	Y	54610 FQ	69000 MW	89650 TQ	USBLS	5/15
	District of Columbia	Y	67090 FQ	86560 MW	109080 TQ	USBLS	5/15
	Washington-Arlington-Alexandria PMSA, DC-VA-MD-WV	Y	68190 FQ	84090 MW	106480 TQ	USBLS	5/15
	Florida	H	26.37 AE	38.02 MW	45.00 AEX	FLBLS	7/16-9/16
	Fort Lauderdale-Pompano Beach-Deerfield Beach PMSA, FL	H	33.64 AE	41.18 MW	49.47 AEX	FLBLS	7/16-9/16
	Miami-Miami Beach-Kendall PMSA, FL	H	32.49 AE	39.54 MW	42.84 AEX	FLBLS	7/16-9/16
	Orlando-Kissimmee-Sanford MSA, FL	H	23.62 AE	34.40 MW	39.23 AEX	FLBLS	7/16-9/16
	Tampa-St. Petersburg-Clearwater MSA, FL	H	24.66 AE	34.94 MW	44.60 AEX	FLBLS	7/16-9/16
	Georgia	Y	56310 FQ	70230 MW	86300 TQ	USBLS	5/15
	Atlanta-Sandy Springs-Roswell MSA, GA	Y	57030 FQ	71370 MW	85420 TQ	USBLS	5/15
	Augusta-Richmond County MSA, GA-SC	Y	51790 FQ	67440 MW	81900 TQ	USBLS	5/15
	Hawaii	Y	65030 FQ	74620 MW	83860 TQ	USBLS	5/15
	Urban Honolulu MSA, HI	Y	65570 FQ	75370 MW	84500 TQ	USBLS	5/15
	Idaho	Y	53930 FQ	67640 MW	79800 TQ	USBLS	5/15
	Boise City MSA, ID	Y	51660 FQ	66250 MW	77730 TQ	USBLS	5/15
	Illinois	Y	56950 FQ	73880 MW	94920 TQ	USBLS	5/15
	Chicago-Naperville-Arlington Heights PMSA, IL	Y	59340 FQ	76970 MW	97260 TQ	USBLS	5/15
	Lake County-Kenosha County PMSA, IL-WI	Y	61340 FQ	74460 MW	91790 TQ	USBLS	5/15
	Indiana	Y	52840 FQ	71710 MW	91800 TQ	USBLS	5/15
	Gary PMSA, IN	Y	56420 FQ	75300 MW	103320 TQ	USBLS	5/15
	Indianapolis-Carmel-Anderson MSA, IN	Y	57840 FQ	79890 MW	96130 TQ	USBLS	5/15
	Iowa	Y	59050 FQ	70320 MW	82750 TQ	USBLS	5/15
	Des Moines-West Des Moines MSA, IA	Y	55830 FQ	66770 MW	79810 TQ	USBLS	5/15
	Kansas	Y	50650 FQ	65970 MW	86200 TQ	USBLS	5/15
	Wichita MSA, KS	Y	47660 FQ	56010 MW	63970 TQ	USBLS	5/15
	Kentucky	Y	54040 FQ	64360 MW	86710 TQ	USBLS	5/15
	Louisville-Jefferson County MSA, KY-IN	Y	64720 FQ	82790 MW	96840 TQ	USBLS	5/15
	Louisiana	Y	49240 FQ	58210 MW	72980 TQ	USBLS	5/15
	Baton Rouge MSA, LA	Y	49570 FQ	59520 MW	77250 TQ	USBLS	5/15
	New Orleans-Metairie MSA, LA	Y	52240 FQ	59900 MW	73890 TQ	USBLS	5/15
	Maine	Y	52450 FQ	63170 MW	74960 TQ	USBLS	5/15
	Portland-South Portland MSA, ME	Y	54500 FQ	63420 MW	77770 TQ	USBLS	5/15
	Maryland	Y	54064 AE	80601 MW	93870 AEX	MDBLS	4/16
	Baltimore-Columbia-Towson MSA, MD	Y	60240 FQ	77130 MW	96520 TQ	USBLS	5/15
	Salisbury MSA, MD-DE	Y	69700 FQ	79850 MW	94690 TQ	USBLS	5/15

AE	Average entry wage	AWR	Average wage range	H	Hourly
AEX	Average experienced wage	B	Biweekly	HI	Highest wage paid
ATC	Average total compensation	D	Daily	HR	High end range
AW	Average wage paid	FQ	First quartile wage	LO	Lowest wage paid

LR	Low end range	MTC	Median total compensation	TCC Total cash compensation
M	Monthly	MW	Median wage paid	TQ Third quartile wage
MCC	Median cash compensation	MWR	Median wage range	W Weekly
ME	Median entry wage	S	See annotated source	Y Yearly

Occupation/Type/Industry	Location	Per	Low	Mid	High	Source	Date
Speech-Language Pathologist	Massachusetts	Y	64620 FQ	80370 MW	96680 TQ	USBLS	5/15
	Boston-Cambridge-Newton NECTA, MA	Y	68200 FQ	85190 MW	100020 TQ	USBLS	5/15
	Worcester MSA, MA-CT	Y	61140 FQ	72900 MW	87090 TQ	USBLS	5/15
	Michigan	Y	59550 FQ	71940 MW	85590 TQ	USBLS	5/15
	Detroit-Dearborn-Livonia PMSA, MI	Y	56340 FQ	71860 MW	87310 TQ	USBLS	5/15
	Grand Rapids-Wyoming MSA, MI	Y	59590 FQ	69640 MW	77550 TQ	USBLS	5/15
	Minnesota	Y	54636 FQ	68295 MW	82479 TQ	MNBLS	1/16-3/16
	Minneapolis-St. Paul-Bloomington MSA, MN-WI	Y	55241 FQ	71582 MW	89394 TQ	MNBLS	1/16-3/16
	Mississippi	Y	45460 FQ	57850 MW	78200 TQ	USBLS	5/15
	Jackson MSA, MS	Y	51900 FQ	65780 MW	89350 TQ	USBLS	5/15
	Missouri	Y	48800 FQ	66650 MW	84460 TQ	USBLS	5/15
	Kansas City MSA, MO-KS	Y	51810 FQ	68410 MW	83470 TQ	USBLS	5/15
	St. Louis MSA, MO-IL	Y	52510 FQ	70610 MW	88880 TQ	USBLS	5/15
	Montana	Y	54710 FQ	66170 MW	77860 TQ	USBLS	5/15
	Billings MSA, MT	Y	55610 FQ	66470 MW	79940 TQ	USBLS	5/15
	Nebraska	Y	50170 FQ	60330 MW	74905 TQ	NEBLS	7/16-9/16
	Omaha-Council Bluffs MSA, NE-IA	Y	47930 FQ	59050 MW	75660 TQ	NEBLS	7/16-9/16
	Nevada	Y	52320 FQ	69850 MW	91270 TQ	USBLS	5/15
	Las Vegas-Henderson-Paradise MSA, NV	Y	54300 FQ	73060 MW	98990 TQ	USBLS	5/15
	New Hampshire	H	25.35 AE	34.98 MW	40.69 AEX	NHBLS	6/16
	Manchester NECTA, NH	H	29.31 AE	38.16 MW	42.06 AEX	NHBLS	6/16
	Nashua NECTA, NH-MA	Y	57970 FQ	68690 MW	78520 TQ	USBLS	5/15
	New Jersey	Y	64780 FQ	81930 MW	102880 TQ	USBLS	5/15
	Camden PMSA, NJ	Y	61150 FQ	76450 MW	92250 TQ	USBLS	5/15
	Newark PMSA, NJ-PA	Y	64200 FQ	83400 MW	106570 TQ	USBLS	5/15
	Trenton MSA, NJ	Y	62360 FQ	79550 MW	95330 TQ	USBLS	5/15
	New Mexico	Y	57850 FQ	74120 MW	95060 TQ	USBLS	5/15
	Albuquerque MSA, NM	Y	55460 FQ	72540 MW	91720 TQ	USBLS	5/15
	New York	Y	51840 AE	81090 MW	107450 AEX	NYBLS	1/16-3/16
	Buffalo-Cheektowaga-Niagara Falls MSA, NY	Y	50540 FQ	70750 MW	91520 TQ	USBLS	5/15
	Nassau County-Suffolk County PMSA, NY	Y	73810 FQ	104050 MW	125110 TQ	USBLS	5/15
	New York-Jersey City-White Plains PMSA, NY-NJ	Y	68540 FQ	89160 MW	113150 TQ	USBLS	5/15
	Rochester MSA, NY	Y	51190 FQ	61220 MW	77340 TQ	USBLS	5/15
	North Carolina	Y	53830 FQ	65840 MW	86820 TQ	USBLS	5/15
	Charlotte-Concord-Gastonia MSA, NC-SC	Y	54050 FQ	64930 MW	83110 TQ	USBLS	5/15
	Raleigh MSA, NC	Y	55950 FQ	70610 MW	97910 TQ	USBLS	5/15
	North Dakota	Y	49790 FQ	59420 MW	71750 TQ	USBLS	5/15
	Fargo MSA, ND-MN	Y	47330 FQ	58310 MW	71300 TQ	USBLS	5/15
	Ohio	Y	57160 FQ	71840 MW	89040 TQ	USBLS	5/15
	Canton-Massillon MSA, OH	Y	53770 FQ	69760 MW	80460 TQ	USBLS	5/15
	Cincinnati MSA, OH-KY-IN	Y	58720 FQ	73300 MW	88950 TQ	USBLS	5/15
	Cleveland-Elyria MSA, OH	Y	65380 FQ	77200 MW	92380 TQ	USBLS	5/15
	Columbus MSA, OH	Y	54240 FQ	66860 MW	90000 TQ	USBLS	5/15
	Oklahoma	Y	46240 FQ	59910 MW	84750 TQ	USBLS	5/15
	Oklahoma City MSA, OK	Y	45310 FQ	60510 MW	84140 TQ	USBLS	5/15
	Tulsa MSA, OK	Y	48290 FQ	61500 MW	88840 TQ	USBLS	5/15
	Oregon	H	31.17 FQ	37.92 MW	44.49 TQ	ORBLS	2016
	Portland-Vancouver-Hillsboro MSA, OR-WA	Y	67430 FQ	83460 MW	94160 TQ	USBLS	5/15
	Pennsylvania	Y	58590 FQ	72730 MW	92400 TQ	USBLS	5/15
	Allentown-Bethlehem-Easton MSA, PA-NJ	Y	66350 FQ	79230 MW	114540 TQ	USBLS	5/15
	Harrisburg-Carlisle MSA, PA	Y	56530 FQ	67790 MW	80440 TQ	USBLS	5/15
	Montgomery County-Bucks County-Chester County PMSA, PA	Y	61140 FQ	77100 MW	96660 TQ	USBLS	5/15
	Philadelphia PMSA, PA	Y	63110 FQ	83650 MW	100760 TQ	USBLS	5/15
	Pittsburgh MSA, PA	Y	55990 FQ	70590 MW	89550 TQ	USBLS	5/15
	Rhode Island	Y	66540 FQ	77270 MW	89540 TQ	USBLS	5/15
	Providence-Warwick MSA, RI-MA	Y	65560 FQ	77290 MW	91030 TQ	USBLS	5/15
	South Carolina	Y	52150 FQ	64830 MW	84800 TQ	USBLS	5/15

AE	Average entry wage	AWR	Average wage range	H	Hourly
AEX	Average experienced wage	B	Biweekly	HI	Highest wage paid
ATC	Average total compensation	D	Daily	HR	High end range
AW	Average wage paid	FQ	First quartile wage	LO	Lowest wage paid

LR	Low end range	MTC	Median total compensation
M	Monthly	MW	Median wage paid
MCC	Median cash compensation	MWR	Median wage range
ME	Median entry wage	S	See annotated source

TCC	Total cash compensation		
TQ	Third quartile wage		
W	Weekly		
Y	Yearly		

Occupation/Type/Industry	Location	Per	Low	Mid	High	Source	Date
Speech-Language Pathologist	Charleston-North Charleston						
	MSA, SC	Y	54240 FQ	72910 MW	87760 TQ	USBLS	5/15
	Columbia MSA, SC	Y	48110 FQ	59110 MW	74800 TQ	USBLS	5/15
	Greenville-Anderson-Mauldin						
	MSA, SC	Y	55720 FQ	70010 MW	91980 TQ	USBLS	5/15
	South Dakota	Y	44780 FQ	54620 MW	65570 TQ	USBLS	5/15
	Sioux Falls MSA, SD	Y	47740 FQ	57740 MW	69140 TQ	USBLS	5/15
	Tennessee	Y	51570 FQ	66650 MW	87940 TQ	USBLS	5/15
	Knoxville MSA, TN	Y	49780 FQ	60850 MW	78800 TQ	USBLS	5/15
	Memphis MSA, TN-MS-AR	Y	56250 FQ	69400 MW	86150 TQ	USBLS	5/15
	Nashville-Davidson–						
	Murfreesboro–Franklin						
	MSA, TN	Y	49710 FQ	63700 MW	85030 TQ	USBLS	5/15
	Texas	Y	56250 FQ	71090 MW	96460 TQ	USBLS	5/15
	Austin-Round Rock MSA, TX	Y	53810 FQ	61580 MW	76140 TQ	USBLS	5/15
	Dallas-Plano-Irving PMSA, TX	Y	60200 FQ	76420 MW	112550 TQ	USBLS	5/15
	Fort Worth-Arlington PMSA,						
	TX	Y	53100 FQ	65550 MW	86820 TQ	USBLS	5/15
	Houston-The Woodlands-						
	Sugar Land MSA, TX	Y	58170 FQ	75030 MW	108140 TQ	USBLS	5/15
	San Antonio-New Braunfels						
	MSA, TX	Y	57540 FQ	72370 MW	89310 TQ	USBLS	5/15
	Utah	Y	51590 FQ	66210 MW	83790 TQ	USBLS	5/15
	Ogden-Clearfield MSA, UT	Y	57950 FQ	70360 MW	85380 TQ	USBLS	5/15
	Provo-Orem MSA, UT	Y	43240 FQ	57940 MW	73500 TQ	USBLS	5/15
	Salt Lake City MSA, UT	Y	58150 FQ	76600 MW	90690 TQ	USBLS	5/15
	Vermont	Y	54780 FQ	66700 MW	79580 TQ	USBLS	5/15
	Burlington-South Burlington						
	MSA, VT	Y	60870 FQ	72530 MW	87450 TQ	USBLS	5/15
	Virginia	Y	62500 FQ	76390 MW	95900 TQ	USBLS	5/15
	Richmond MSA, VA	Y	59650 FQ	72300 MW	87070 TQ	USBLS	5/15
	Virginia Beach-Norfolk-						
	Newport News MSA, VA-NC	Y	58640 FQ	74280 MW	90550 TQ	USBLS	5/15
	Washington	H	30.42 FQ	35.55 MW	42.11 TQ	WABLS	3/16
	Bellingham MSA, WA	H	30.20 FQ	35.24 MW	41.32 TQ	WABLS	3/16
	Seattle-Bellevue-Everett						
	PMSA, WA	H	31.96 FQ	37.39 MW	45.34 TQ	WABLS	3/16
	Tacoma-Lakewood PMSA, WA	H	30.32 FQ	34.68 MW	38.51 TQ	WABLS	3/16
	West Virginia	Y	48750 FQ	58640 MW	72320 TQ	USBLS	5/15
	Huntington-Ashland MSA,						
	WV-KY-OH	Y	49420 FQ	60170 MW	84240 TQ	USBLS	5/15
	Wisconsin	Y	54370 FQ	66060 MW	77320 TQ	USBLS	5/15
	Madison MSA, WI	Y	53970 FQ	64500 MW	76480 TQ	USBLS	5/15
	Milwaukee-Waukesha-West						
	Allis MSA, WI	Y	61940 FQ	70840 MW	78910 TQ	USBLS	5/15
	Wyoming	Y	57180 FQ	67870 MW	78670 TQ	USBLS	5/15
	Cheyenne MSA, WY	Y	63830 FQ	73370 MW	84660 TQ	USBLS	5/15
	Puerto Rico	Y	35550 FQ	46650 MW	58760 TQ	USBLS	5/15
	San Juan-Carolina-Caguas						
	MSA, PR	Y	38960 FQ	49670 MW	60460 TQ	USBLS	5/15
Speechwriter							
United States Postal Service	District of Columbia	Y	107396 LO		112236 HI	APP02	1/16
Spill Response Coordinator							
Department of Environmental Quality,							
State Government	Helena, MT	H			24.10 HI	MTGOV	2016
Sports Anchor							
Radio	United States	Y		34700 MW		RTDNA	2016
Television	United States	Y		48500 MW		RTDNA	2016
Sports Coordinator							
Municipal Government	Hanford, CA	Y			41600 HI	CACIT	6/28/16
Sports Facility Coordinator							
Municipal Government	Fullerton, CA	Y			51326 HI	CACIT	6/28/16
Sports Management Manager	United States	Y		127130 MW		ABS01	2016-2017
Sports Scout	United States	Y		40000 AW		SKU01	2016

AE	Average entry wage	AWR	Average wage range	H	Hourly	LR	Low end range	MTC	Median total compensation	TCC	Total cash compensation
AEX	Average experienced wage	B	Biweekly	HI	Highest wage paid	M	Monthly	MW	Median wage paid	TQ	Third quartile wage
ATC	Average total compensation	D	Daily	HR	High end range	MCC	Median cash compensation	MWR	Median wage range	W	Weekly
AW	Average wage paid	FQ	First quartile wage	LO	Lowest wage paid	ME	Median entry wage	S	See annotated source	Y	Yearly

Occupation/Type/Industry	Location	Per	Low	Mid	High	Source	Date
Sprinkler Technician							
Municipal Government	Fountain Valley, CA	Y		56700 AW		CACIT	6/28/16
Stable Attendant							
Municipal Government	Detroit, MI	M	1621 LO		2167 HI	DETGOV	2016
Police Department, Municipal Government	San Francisco, CA	Y		42566 AW		CACIT	6/28/16
Staff Sergeant							
U.S. Air Force, Active Duty, Pay Grade E-4	United States	M	2089 LO		2354 HI	DOD1	2017
U.S. Air Force, Active Duty, Pay Grade E-5	United States	M	2278 LO		3233 HI	DOD1	2017
U.S. Army, Active Duty, Pay Grade E-6	United States	M	2487 LO		3852 HI	DOD1	2017
U.S. Marines, Active Duty, Pay Grade E-6	United States	M	2487 LO		3852 HI	DOD1	2017
Stage Technician							
Municipal Government	Seattle, WA	H			29.68 HI	CSSS	3/9/16
Stamp Supply Clerk							
United States Postal Service	United States	Y			57987 HI	APP02	1/16
State Court Administrator	United States	Y		143163 MW		NCSC	1/1/17
State Demographer							
State Government	North Carolina	Y	59969 LO		99446 HI	NCGOV	7/1/16
State Fair Manager							
State Government	North Carolina	Y	62696 LO		104089 HI	NCGOV	7/1/16
State Veterinarian							
Agriculture Department, State Government	Ohio	H			59.14 HI	OHGOV	2015
Stationary Engineer and Boiler Operator	Alabama	Y	29911 AE	45663 AW	53539 AEX	ALBLS	6/16
	Birmingham-Hoover MSA, AL	Y	39617 AE	44902 AW	47534 AEX	ALBLS	6/16
	Alaska	Y	65650 FQ	74970 MW	84320 TQ	USBLS	5/15
	Arizona	Y	41300 FQ	46780 MW	55490 TQ	USBLS	5/15
	Phoenix-Mesa-Scottsdale MSA, AZ	Y	38470 FQ	45760 MW	56850 TQ	USBLS	5/15
	Tucson MSA, AZ	Y	41900 FQ	45020 MW	48150 TQ	USBLS	5/15
	Arkansas	Y	40170 FQ	48770 MW	57190 TQ	USBLS	5/15
	Little Rock-North Little Rock-Conway MSA, AR	Y	34110 FQ	39970 MW	50790 TQ	USBLS	5/15
	California	H	30.81 FQ	36.51 MW	44.31 TQ	CABLS	1/16-3/16
	Anaheim-Santa Ana-Irvine PMSA, CA	H	29.96 FQ	37.57 MW	43.99 TQ	CABLS	1/16-3/16
	Los Angeles-Long Beach-Glendale PMSA, CA	H	32.13 FQ	37.82 MW	44.45 TQ	CABLS	1/16-3/16
	Oakland-Hayward-Berkeley PMSA, CA	H	30.81 FQ	41.15 MW	46.06 TQ	CABLS	1/16-3/16
	Riverside-San Bernardino-Ontario MSA, CA	H	25.25 FQ	29.87 MW	33.88 TQ	CABLS	1/16-3/16
	Sacramento–Roseville–Arden-Arcade MSA, CA	H	30.81 FQ	33.89 MW	42.89 TQ	CABLS	1/16-3/16
	San Diego-Carlsbad MSA, CA	H	28.74 FQ	33.88 MW	39.84 TQ	CABLS	1/16-3/16
	San Francisco-Redwood City-South San Francisco PMSA, CA	H	41.75 FQ	45.24 MW	48.77 TQ	CABLS	1/16-3/16
	Colorado	Y	40960 FQ	52000 MW	61680 TQ	USBLS	5/15
	Denver-Aurora-Lakewood MSA, CO	Y	45490 FQ	55350 MW	66420 TQ	USBLS	5/15
	Connecticut	Y		57989 MW		CTBLS	1/16-3/16
	Bridgeport-Stamford-Norwalk MSA, CT	Y	50150 FQ	55340 MW	62020 TQ	USBLS	5/15
	Hartford-West Hartford-East Hartford MSA, CT	Y	48240 FQ	56310 MW	61740 TQ	USBLS	5/15
	Delaware	Y	55530 FQ	64120 MW	71290 TQ	USBLS	5/15
	Wilmington PMSA, DE-MD-NJ	Y	52090 FQ	64110 MW	70250 TQ	USBLS	5/15
	District of Columbia	Y	59980 FQ	70900 MW	81290 TQ	USBLS	5/15
	Washington-Arlington-Alexandria PMSA, DC-VA-MD-WV	Y	58090 FQ	68210 MW	78990 TQ	USBLS	5/15
	Florida	H	19.14 AE	27.24 MW	31.16 AEX	FLBLS	7/16-9/16

Occupation/Type/Industry	Location	Per	Low	Mid	High	Source	Date
Stationary Engineer and Boiler Operator							
	Fort Lauderdale-Pompano Beach-Deerfield Beach PMSA, FL	H	16.76 AE	25.31 MW	26.79 AEX	FLBLS	7/16-9/16
	Orlando-Kissimmee-Sanford MSA, FL	H	26.64 AE	35.14 MW	37.09 AEX	FLBLS	7/16-9/16
	Tampa-St. Petersburg-Clearwater MSA, FL	H	16.30 AE	19.78 MW	23.54 AEX	FLBLS	7/16-9/16
	Georgia	Y	39630 FQ	54640 MW	68080 TQ	USBLS	5/15
	Atlanta-Sandy Springs-Roswell MSA, GA	Y	42820 FQ	54960 MW	69830 TQ	USBLS	5/15
	Augusta-Richmond County MSA, GA-SC	Y	46130 FQ	57530 MW	69590 TQ	USBLS	5/15
	Hawaii	Y	64750 FQ	73010 MW	81010 TQ	USBLS	5/15
	Idaho	Y	39850 FQ	47260 MW	57790 TQ	USBLS	5/15
	Illinois	Y	68530 FQ	80590 MW	94690 TQ	USBLS	5/15
	Chicago-Naperville-Arlington Heights PMSA, IL	Y	70220 FQ	81060 MW	93780 TQ	USBLS	5/15
	Lake County-Kenosha County PMSA, IL-WI	Y	62370 FQ	74160 MW	94960 TQ	USBLS	5/15
	Indiana	Y	34410 FQ	50110 MW	62030 TQ	USBLS	5/15
	Gary PMSA, IN	Y	30420 FQ	54410 MW	60220 TQ	USBLS	5/15
	Indianapolis-Carmel-Anderson MSA, IN	Y	35320 FQ	50510 MW	67970 TQ	USBLS	5/15
	Iowa	Y	44720 FQ	53480 MW	59960 TQ	USBLS	5/15
	Des Moines-West Des Moines MSA, IA	Y	43910 FQ	52890 MW	60580 TQ	USBLS	5/15
	Kansas	Y	54900 FQ	61720 MW	70010 TQ	USBLS	5/15
	Kentucky	Y	32640 FQ	43310 MW	63400 TQ	USBLS	5/15
	Louisville-Jefferson County MSA, KY-IN	Y	37790 FQ	46100 MW	58970 TQ	USBLS	5/15
	Louisiana	Y	34680 FQ	40290 MW	48850 TQ	USBLS	5/15
	New Orleans-Metairie MSA, LA	Y	34860 FQ	41230 MW	48860 TQ	USBLS	5/15
	Maine	Y	34560 FQ	44470 MW	57770 TQ	USBLS	5/15
	Portland-South Portland MSA, ME	Y	28430 FQ	41310 MW	52270 TQ	USBLS	5/15
	Maryland	Y	43619 AE	57703 MW	64745 AEX	MDBLS	4/16
	Baltimore-Columbia-Towson MSA, MD	Y	50410 FQ	56930 MW	63390 TQ	USBLS	5/15
	Massachusetts	Y	52010 FQ	59700 MW	71450 TQ	USBLS	5/15
	Boston-Cambridge-Newton NECTA, MA	Y	56110 FQ	65950 MW	75230 TQ	USBLS	5/15
	Worcester MSA, MA-CT	Y	51540 FQ	60820 MW	74400 TQ	USBLS	5/15
	Michigan	Y	52050 FQ	61410 MW	71090 TQ	USBLS	5/15
	Detroit-Dearborn-Livonia PMSA, MI	Y	52770 FQ	59390 MW	67930 TQ	USBLS	5/15
	Grand Rapids-Wyoming MSA, MI	Y	59180 FQ	66090 MW	73060 TQ	USBLS	5/15
	Minnesota	Y	50228 FQ	57467 MW	65303 TQ	MNBLS	1/16-3/16
	Minneapolis-St. Paul-Bloomington MSA, MN-WI	Y	54237 FQ	61364 MW	70780 TQ	MNBLS	1/16-3/16
	Mississippi	Y	38430 FQ	44780 MW	50410 TQ	USBLS	5/15
	Missouri	Y	35660 FQ	51030 MW	62750 TQ	USBLS	5/15
	Kansas City MSA, MO-KS	Y	55580 FQ	65340 MW	71690 TQ	USBLS	5/15
	St. Louis MSA, MO-IL	Y	54920 FQ	65490 MW	76930 TQ	USBLS	5/15
	Montana	Y	36720 FQ	53120 MW	75540 TQ	USBLS	5/15
	Nebraska	Y	37725 FQ	44420 MW	50825 TQ	NEBLS	7/16-9/16
	Omaha-Council Bluffs MSA, NE-IA	Y	39890 FQ	44590 MW	49110 TQ	NEBLS	7/16-9/16
	Las Vegas-Henderson-Paradise MSA, NV	Y	50560 FQ	56440 MW	62100 TQ	USBLS	5/15
	New Hampshire	H	22.37 AE	26.96 MW	30.63 AEX	NHBLS	6/16
	New Jersey	Y	45390 FQ	55350 MW	63280 TQ	USBLS	5/15
	Camden PMSA, NJ	Y	46240 FQ	54350 MW	59840 TQ	USBLS	5/15
	Newark PMSA, NJ-PA	Y	40680 FQ	53350 MW	63290 TQ	USBLS	5/15
	Trenton MSA, NJ	Y	46300 FQ	54740 MW	62600 TQ	USBLS	5/15
	New Mexico	Y	31140 FQ	38180 MW	52250 TQ	USBLS	5/15
	New York	Y	49030 AE	64610 MW	84870 AEX	NYBLS	1/16-3/16
	Buffalo-Cheektowaga-Niagara Falls MSA, NY	Y	43830 FQ	52060 MW	58570 TQ	USBLS	5/15

Stationary Engineer and Boiler Operator

Occupation/Type/Industry	Location	Per	Low	Mid	High	Source	Date
Stationary Engineer and Boiler Operator	Nassau County-Suffolk County PMSA, NY	Y	53910 FQ	61070 MW	70850 TQ	USBLS	5/15
	New York-Jersey City-White Plains PMSA, NY-NJ	Y	60020 FQ	78440 MW	105780 TQ	USBLS	5/15
	Rochester MSA, NY	Y	51520 FQ	57250 MW	64020 TQ	USBLS	5/15
	North Carolina	Y	37150 FQ	48050 MW	58570 TQ	USBLS	5/15
	Charlotte-Concord-Gastonia MSA, NC-SC	Y	22430 FQ	30490 MW	46830 TQ	USBLS	5/15
	Raleigh MSA, NC	Y	34150 FQ	42710 MW	49130 TQ	USBLS	5/15
	North Dakota	Y	42230 FQ	51770 MW	68300 TQ	USBLS	5/15
	Fargo MSA, ND-MN	Y	43980 FQ	50130 MW	57090 TQ	USBLS	5/15
	Ohio	Y	44820 FQ	53020 MW	61390 TQ	USBLS	5/15
	Cincinnati MSA, OH-KY-IN	Y	45680 FQ	52460 MW	58790 TQ	USBLS	5/15
	Cleveland-Elyria MSA, OH	Y	46250 FQ	58040 MW	69400 TQ	USBLS	5/15
	Columbus MSA, OH	Y	43380 FQ	51010 MW	58190 TQ	USBLS	5/15
	Oklahoma	Y	42300 FQ	51930 MW	58400 TQ	USBLS	5/15
	Oklahoma City MSA, OK	Y	43490 FQ	49060 MW	56390 TQ	USBLS	5/15
	Tulsa MSA, OK	Y	45370 FQ	54100 MW	59080 TQ	USBLS	5/15
	Oregon	H	21.73 FQ	26.45 MW	32.66 TQ	ORBLS	2016
	Portland-Vancouver-Hillsboro MSA, OR-WA	Y	55800 FQ	67070 MW	74500 TQ	USBLS	5/15
	Pennsylvania	Y	42770 FQ	53260 MW	60330 TQ	USBLS	5/15
	Allentown-Bethlehem-Easton MSA, PA-NJ	Y	41250 FQ	48710 MW	56490 TQ	USBLS	5/15
	Harrisburg-Carlisle MSA, PA	Y	35870 FQ	39530 MW	44950 TQ	USBLS	5/15
	Montgomery County-Bucks County-Chester County PMSA, PA	Y	45610 FQ	53660 MW	60430 TQ	USBLS	5/15
	Philadelphia PMSA, PA	Y	52240 FQ	57880 MW	62430 TQ	USBLS	5/15
	Pittsburgh MSA, PA	Y	43670 FQ	54530 MW	60120 TQ	USBLS	5/15
	Rhode Island	Y	44510 FQ	50770 MW	62200 TQ	USBLS	5/15
	Providence-Warwick MSA, RI-MA	Y	44980 FQ	52070 MW	61600 TQ	USBLS	5/15
	South Carolina	Y	46820 FQ	55210 MW	62310 TQ	USBLS	5/15
	Greenville-Anderson-Mauldin MSA, SC	Y	38000 FQ	47850 MW	59940 TQ	USBLS	5/15
	South Dakota	Y	34250 FQ	42150 MW	50090 TQ	USBLS	5/15
	Tennessee	Y	41250 FQ	55370 MW	62280 TQ	USBLS	5/15
	Memphis MSA, TN-MS-AR	Y	52050 FQ	56360 MW	59950 TQ	USBLS	5/15
	Nashville-Davidson–Murfreesboro–Franklin MSA, TN	Y	51660 FQ	59010 MW	70190 TQ	USBLS	5/15
	Texas	Y	29610 FQ	40900 MW	55520 TQ	USBLS	5/15
	Austin-Round Rock MSA, TX	Y	35900 FQ	42260 MW	49840 TQ	USBLS	5/15
	Dallas-Plano-Irving PMSA, TX	Y	31650 FQ	43050 MW	49560 TQ	USBLS	5/15
	Fort Worth-Arlington PMSA, TX	Y	37660 FQ	57140 MW	70600 TQ	USBLS	5/15
	Houston-The Woodlands-Sugar Land MSA, TX	Y	26310 FQ	35840 MW	51440 TQ	USBLS	5/15
	San Antonio-New Braunfels MSA, TX	Y	35220 FQ	45790 MW	79500 TQ	USBLS	5/15
	Utah	Y	41700 FQ	52560 MW	58930 TQ	USBLS	5/15
	Ogden-Clearfield MSA, UT	Y	50500 FQ	54530 MW	56550 TQ	USBLS	5/15
	Salt Lake City MSA, UT	Y	40330 FQ	48310 MW	58350 TQ	USBLS	5/15
	Vermont	Y	31900 FQ	41500 MW	54710 TQ	USBLS	5/15
	Virginia	Y	42760 FQ	52970 MW	64320 TQ	USBLS	5/15
	Richmond MSA, VA	Y	30230 FQ	41560 MW	51630 TQ	USBLS	5/15
	Virginia Beach-Norfolk-Newport News MSA, VA-NC	Y	46170 FQ	51710 MW	57080 TQ	USBLS	5/15
	Washington	H	25.82 FQ	31.38 MW	37.00 TQ	WABLS	3/16
	Seattle-Bellevue-Everett PMSA, WA	H	27.22 FQ	33.43 MW	38.73 TQ	WABLS	3/16
	Tacoma-Lakewood PMSA, WA	H	25.74 FQ	30.82 MW	34.48 TQ	WABLS	3/16
	West Virginia	Y	42240 FQ	49410 MW	62120 TQ	USBLS	5/15
	Huntington-Ashland MSA, WV-KY-OH	Y	42070 FQ	49000 MW	60160 TQ	USBLS	5/15
	Wisconsin	Y	45430 FQ	52750 MW	61050 TQ	USBLS	5/15
	Madison MSA, WI	Y	41410 FQ	45740 MW	50370 TQ	USBLS	5/15
	Milwaukee-Waukesha-West Allis MSA, WI	Y	41660 FQ	50210 MW	61700 TQ	USBLS	5/15
	Puerto Rico	Y	27930 FQ	37860 MW	42880 TQ	USBLS	5/15

AE	Average entry wage	AWR	Average wage range	H	Hourly
AEX	Average experienced wage	B	Biweekly	HI	Highest wage paid
ATC	Average total compensation	D	Daily	HR	High end range
AW	Average wage paid	FQ	First quartile wage	LO	Lowest wage paid

LR	Low end range	MTC	Median total compensation	TCC	Total cash compensation
M	Monthly	MW	Median wage paid	TQ	Third quartile wage
MCC	Median cash compensation	MWR	Median wage range	W	Weekly
ME	Median entry wage	S	See annotated source	Y	Yearly

Occupation/Type/Industry	Location	Per	Low	Mid	High	Source	Date
Stationary Engineer and Boiler Operator	San Juan-Carolina-Caguas MSA, PR	Y	27620 FQ	37700 MW	42540 TQ	USBLS	5/15
Statistical Assistant	Alabama	Y	24374 AE	37988 AW	44800 AEX	ALBLS	6/16
	Arizona	Y	28010 FQ	36300 MW	48370 TQ	USBLS	5/15
	Phoenix-Mesa-Scottsdale MSA, AZ	Y	27970 FQ	34550 MW	44610 TQ	USBLS	5/15
	Tucson MSA, AZ	Y	36130 FQ	45770 MW	56950 TQ	USBLS	5/15
	Arkansas	Y	36430 FQ	47000 MW	54860 TQ	USBLS	5/15
	California	H	20.35 FQ	25.04 MW	30.18 TQ	CABLS	1/16-3/16
	Anaheim-Santa Ana-Irvine PMSA, CA	H	22.81 FQ	26.53 MW	30.76 TQ	CABLS	1/16-3/16
	Los Angeles-Long Beach-Glendale PMSA, CA	H	17.09 FQ	19.32 MW	24.75 TQ	CABLS	1/16-3/16
	Oakland-Hayward-Berkeley PMSA, CA	H	23.59 FQ	27.49 MW	31.99 TQ	CABLS	1/16-3/16
	Sacramento–Roseville–Arden-Arcade MSA, CA	H	20.18 FQ	23.56 MW	26.88 TQ	CABLS	1/16-3/16
	San Diego-Carlsbad MSA, CA	H	20.41 FQ	22.87 MW	25.84 TQ	CABLS	1/16-3/16
	San Francisco-Redwood City-South San Francisco PMSA, CA	H	24.07 FQ	28.57 MW	35.06 TQ	CABLS	1/16-3/16
	Colorado	Y	41140 FQ	49790 MW	56970 TQ	USBLS	5/15
	Denver-Aurora-Lakewood MSA, CO	Y	41030 FQ	50950 MW	57280 TQ	USBLS	5/15
	Connecticut	Y		61432 MW		CTBLS	1/16-3/16
	District of Columbia	Y	42600 FQ	49420 MW	58600 TQ	USBLS	5/15
	Washington-Arlington-Alexandria PMSA, DC-VA-MD-WV	Y	43580 FQ	50360 MW	58170 TQ	USBLS	5/15
	Florida	H	12.11 AE	17.76 MW	22.37 AEX	FLBLS	7/16-9/16
	Miami-Miami Beach-Kendall PMSA, FL	H	13.98 AE	15.67 MW	23.89 AEX	FLBLS	7/16-9/16
	Orlando-Kissimmee-Sanford MSA, FL	H	16.69 AE	26.52 MW	29.59 AEX	FLBLS	7/16-9/16
	Tampa-St. Petersburg-Clearwater MSA, FL	H	11.29 AE	16.52 MW	19.67 AEX	FLBLS	7/16-9/16
	Georgia	Y	22480 FQ	25730 MW	30140 TQ	USBLS	5/15
	Atlanta-Sandy Springs-Roswell MSA, GA	Y	22510 FQ	26000 MW	31570 TQ	USBLS	5/15
	Augusta-Richmond County MSA, GA-SC	Y	21440 FQ	23380 MW	26360 TQ	USBLS	5/15
	Hawaii	Y	34210 FQ	40960 MW	48130 TQ	USBLS	5/15
	Illinois	Y	40020 FQ	52370 MW	62440 TQ	USBLS	5/15
	Chicago-Naperville-Arlington Heights PMSA, IL	Y	19600 FQ	47220 MW	62470 TQ	USBLS	5/15
	Lake County-Kenosha County PMSA, IL-WI	Y	39060 FQ	52020 MW	60010 TQ	USBLS	5/15
	Indiana	Y	31410 FQ	34270 MW	37260 TQ	USBLS	5/15
	Indianapolis-Carmel-Anderson MSA, IN	Y	35710 FQ	46380 MW	61240 TQ	USBLS	5/15
	Iowa	Y	39880 FQ	52130 MW	64540 TQ	USBLS	5/15
	Des Moines-West Des Moines MSA, IA	Y	46240 FQ	58450 MW	69920 TQ	USBLS	5/15
	Kansas	Y	33150 FQ	37790 MW	45840 TQ	USBLS	5/15
	Kentucky	Y	43730 FQ	52850 MW	59730 TQ	USBLS	5/15
	Louisiana	Y	33700 FQ	43510 MW	60090 TQ	USBLS	5/15
	New Orleans-Metairie MSA, LA	Y	34500 FQ	40930 MW	61310 TQ	USBLS	5/15
	Maine	Y	31650 FQ	37110 MW	46710 TQ	USBLS	5/15
	Portland-South Portland MSA, ME	Y	37090 FQ	46810 MW	68580 TQ	USBLS	5/15
	Maryland	Y	31346 AE	46874 MW	54638 AEX	MDBLS	4/16
	Baltimore-Columbia-Towson MSA, MD	Y	36440 FQ	43150 MW	50660 TQ	USBLS	5/15
	Massachusetts	Y	44470 FQ	54260 MW	65880 TQ	USBLS	5/15
	Boston-Cambridge-Newton NECTA, MA	Y	45310 FQ	55040 MW	66280 TQ	USBLS	5/15
	Michigan	Y	42040 FQ	46880 MW	52730 TQ	USBLS	5/15
	Grand Rapids-Wyoming MSA, MI	Y	42130 FQ	45310 MW	48480 TQ	USBLS	5/15

AE	Average entry wage	AWR	Average wage range	H	Hourly	LR	Low end range	MTC	Median total compensation	TCC	Total cash compensation
AEX	Average experienced wage	B	Biweekly	HI	Highest wage paid	M	Monthly	MW	Median wage paid	TQ	Third quartile wage
ATC	Average total compensation	D	Daily	HR	High end range	MCC	Median cash compensation	MWR	Median wage range	W	Weekly
AW	Average wage paid	FQ	First quartile wage	LO	Lowest wage paid	ME	Median entry wage	S	See annotated source	Y	Yearly

Occupation/Type/Industry	Location	Per	Low	Mid	High	Source	Date
Statistical Assistant	Minnesota	Y	38843 FQ	54083 MW	64175 TQ	MNBLS	1/16-3/16
	Minneapolis-St. Paul-Bloomington MSA, MN-WI	Y	37882 FQ	54285 MW	66279 TQ	MNBLS	1/16-3/16
	Mississippi	Y	21110 FQ	23040 MW	39240 TQ	USBLS	5/15
	Missouri	Y	39810 FQ	48810 MW	58060 TQ	USBLS	5/15
	Kansas City MSA, MO-KS	Y	34300 FQ	38280 MW	56880 TQ	USBLS	5/15
	St. Louis MSA, MO-IL	Y	38660 FQ	46940 MW	55500 TQ	USBLS	5/15
	Montana	Y	49890 FQ	53990 MW	58600 TQ	USBLS	5/15
	Nebraska	Y	33670 FQ	44560 MW	51515 TQ	NEBLS	7/16-9/16
	Omaha-Council Bluffs MSA, NE-IA	Y	40180 FQ	46405 MW	53180 TQ	NEBLS	7/16-9/16
	Nevada	Y	43080 FQ	48850 MW	57010 TQ	USBLS	5/15
	Las Vegas-Henderson-Paradise MSA, NV	Y	43080 FQ	48850 MW	57010 TQ	USBLS	5/15
	New Hampshire	H	17.56 AE	23.35 MW	26.59 AEX	NHBLS	6/16
	New Jersey	Y	42200 FQ	50690 MW	61420 TQ	USBLS	5/15
	Newark PMSA, NJ-PA	Y	31750 FQ	52320 MW	58770 TQ	USBLS	5/15
	New York	Y	40710 AE	51700 MW	60080 AEX	NYBLS	1/16-3/16
	Nassau County-Suffolk County PMSA, NY	Y	44560 FQ	53610 MW	60620 TQ	USBLS	5/15
	New York-Jersey City-White Plains PMSA, NY-NJ	Y	44300 FQ	50860 MW	65600 TQ	USBLS	5/15
	North Carolina	Y	32970 FQ	38300 MW	48780 TQ	USBLS	5/15
	Charlotte-Concord-Gastonia MSA, NC-SC	Y	34130 FQ	40480 MW	55260 TQ	USBLS	5/15
	Raleigh MSA, NC	Y	39440 FQ	53710 MW	59820 TQ	USBLS	5/15
	Ohio	Y	34380 FQ	41490 MW	48300 TQ	USBLS	5/15
	Cincinnati MSA, OH-KY-IN	Y	35930 FQ	42700 MW	48230 TQ	USBLS	5/15
	Cleveland-Elyria MSA, OH	Y	33490 FQ	38300 MW	45730 TQ	USBLS	5/15
	Columbus MSA, OH	Y	33790 FQ	41910 MW	50670 TQ	USBLS	5/15
	Oklahoma	Y	39590 FQ	47780 MW	59870 TQ	USBLS	5/15
	Oregon	H	19.13 FQ	21.79 MW	24.19 TQ	ORBLS	2016
	Portland-Vancouver-Hillsboro MSA, OR-WA	Y	40340 FQ	45190 MW	50580 TQ	USBLS	5/15
	Harrisburg-Carlisle MSA, PA	Y	38130 FQ	40890 MW	50200 TQ	USBLS	5/15
	Philadelphia PMSA, PA	Y	41510 FQ	54390 MW	60000 TQ	USBLS	5/15
	Pittsburgh MSA, PA	Y	36520 FQ	43180 MW	53920 TQ	USBLS	5/15
	Rhode Island	Y	39290 FQ	44120 MW	48960 TQ	USBLS	5/15
	Providence-Warwick MSA, RI-MA	Y	38370 FQ	43500 MW	48460 TQ	USBLS	5/15
	South Carolina	Y	29000 FQ	35370 MW	42040 TQ	USBLS	5/15
	Charleston-North Charleston MSA, SC	Y	28530 FQ	33660 MW	39280 TQ	USBLS	5/15
	Texas	Y	41370 FQ	47860 MW	56960 TQ	USBLS	5/15
	Austin-Round Rock MSA, TX	Y	41470 FQ	46710 MW	55970 TQ	USBLS	5/15
	Dallas-Plano-Irving PMSA, TX	Y	44360 FQ	52440 MW	62300 TQ	USBLS	5/15
	Houston-The Woodlands-Sugar Land MSA, TX	Y	40540 FQ	48830 MW	57540 TQ	USBLS	5/15
	San Antonio-New Braunfels MSA, TX	Y	29220 FQ	41830 MW	47210 TQ	USBLS	5/15
	Utah	Y	38460 FQ	45310 MW	52630 TQ	USBLS	5/15
	Salt Lake City MSA, UT	Y	38350 FQ	45040 MW	51210 TQ	USBLS	5/15
	Virginia	Y	45190 FQ	52680 MW	57940 TQ	USBLS	5/15
	Washington	H	18.59 FQ	23.79 MW	29.52 TQ	WABLS	3/16
	Seattle-Bellevue-Everett PMSA, WA	H	20.80 FQ	26.86 MW	31.53 TQ	WABLS	3/16
	Tacoma-Lakewood PMSA, WA	H	19.76 FQ	23.56 MW	27.68 TQ	WABLS	3/16
	West Virginia	Y	19180 FQ	42110 MW	51110 TQ	USBLS	5/15
	Wisconsin	Y	36140 FQ	45580 MW	58420 TQ	USBLS	5/15
	Milwaukee-Waukesha-West Allis MSA, WI	Y	33440 FQ	41360 MW	54290 TQ	USBLS	5/15
	Puerto Rico	Y	21270 FQ	25790 MW	29460 TQ	USBLS	5/15
	San Juan-Carolina-Caguas MSA, PR	Y	21610 FQ	25980 MW	29550 TQ	USBLS	5/15
Statistical Manager							
Fire Department, Municipal Government	Los Angeles, CA	Y			102775 HI	CACIT	6/23/16
Statistician	Alabama	Y	41170 AE	63963 AW	75359 AEX	ALBLS	6/16
	Birmingham-Hoover MSA, AL	Y	45584 AE	69324 AW	81189 AEX	ALBLS	6/16
	Arizona	Y	57780 FQ	76250 MW	93720 TQ	USBLS	5/15

AE	Average entry wage	**AWR**	Average wage range	**H**	Hourly	**LR**	Low end range	**MTC**	Median total compensation	**TCC** Total cash compensation
AEX	Average experienced wage	**B**	Biweekly	**HI**	Highest wage paid	**M**	Monthly	**MW**	Median wage paid	**TQ** Third quartile wage
ATC	Average total compensation	**D**	Daily	**HR**	High end range	**MCC**	Median cash compensation	**MWR**	Median wage range	**W** Weekly
AW	Average wage paid	**FQ**	First quartile wage	**LO**	Lowest wage paid	**ME**	Median entry wage	**S**	See annotated source	**Y** Yearly

Occupation/Type/Industry	Location	Per	Low	Mid	High	Source	Date
Statistician	Phoenix-Mesa-Scottsdale MSA, AZ	Y	57450 FQ	75430 MW	93330 TQ	USBLS	5/15
	Tucson MSA, AZ	Y	54670 FQ	71180 MW	91910 TQ	USBLS	5/15
	Arkansas	Y	36250 FQ	49740 MW	72550 TQ	USBLS	5/15
	Little Rock-North Little Rock-Conway MSA, AR	Y	34810 FQ	43680 MW	60270 TQ	USBLS	5/15
	California	H	33.55 FQ	40.12 MW	56.16 TQ	CABLS	1/16-3/16
	Anaheim-Santa Ana-Irvine PMSA, CA	H	35.49 FQ	43.62 MW	52.27 TQ	CABLS	1/16-3/16
	Los Angeles-Long Beach-Glendale PMSA, CA	H	28.39 FQ	37.76 MW	49.53 TQ	CABLS	1/16-3/16
	Oakland-Hayward-Berkeley PMSA, CA	H	23.97 FQ	41.88 MW	62.18 TQ	CABLS	1/16-3/16
	Riverside-San Bernardino-Ontario MSA, CA	H	26.34 FQ	29.40 MW	35.84 TQ	CABLS	1/16-3/16
	Sacramento–Roseville–Arden-Arcade MSA, CA	H	32.29 FQ	34.93 MW	39.57 TQ	CABLS	1/16-3/16
	San Diego-Carlsbad MSA, CA	H	35.37 FQ	45.25 MW	66.36 TQ	CABLS	1/16-3/16
	San Francisco-Redwood City-South San Francisco PMSA, CA	H	46.34 FQ	59.11 MW	71.31 TQ	CABLS	1/16-3/16
	Colorado	Y	65170 FQ	79910 MW	97160 TQ	USBLS	5/15
	Denver-Aurora-Lakewood MSA, CO	Y	63030 FQ	77690 MW	94140 TQ	USBLS	5/15
	Connecticut	Y		101135 MW		CTBLS	1/16-3/16
	Hartford-West Hartford-East Hartford MSA, CT	Y	80340 FQ	93720 MW	111220 TQ	USBLS	5/15
	Delaware	Y	76880 FQ	97570 MW	134300 TQ	USBLS	5/15
	Wilmington PMSA, DE-MD-NJ	Y	81240 FQ	99980 MW	134300 TQ	USBLS	5/15
	District of Columbia	Y	90690 FQ	105960 MW	122650 TQ	USBLS	5/15
	Washington-Arlington-Alexandria PMSA, DC-VA-MD-WV	Y	84020 FQ	99290 MW	118050 TQ	USBLS	5/15
	Florida	H	19.05 AE	27.66 MW	37.32 AEX	FLBLS	7/16-9/16
	Fort Lauderdale-Pompano Beach-Deerfield Beach PMSA, FL	H	21.32 AE	39.24 MW	40.81 AEX	FLBLS	7/16-9/16
	Miami-Miami Beach-Kendall PMSA, FL	H	19.60 AE	29.00 MW	37.55 AEX	FLBLS	7/16-9/16
	Orlando-Kissimmee-Sanford MSA, FL	H	20.50 AE	26.39 MW	39.37 AEX	FLBLS	7/16-9/16
	Tampa-St. Petersburg-Clearwater MSA, FL	H	17.21 AE	26.10 MW	36.24 AEX	FLBLS	7/16-9/16
	Georgia	Y	59930 FQ	85690 MW	107560 TQ	USBLS	5/15
	Atlanta-Sandy Springs-Roswell MSA, GA	Y	65180 FQ	91450 MW	109930 TQ	USBLS	5/15
	Hawaii	Y	52790 FQ	61190 MW	73680 TQ	USBLS	5/15
	Urban Honolulu MSA, HI	Y	53520 FQ	61780 MW	74280 TQ	USBLS	5/15
	Idaho	Y	49750 FQ	59450 MW	91260 TQ	USBLS	5/15
	Boise City MSA, ID	Y	52890 FQ	67000 MW	91270 TQ	USBLS	5/15
	Illinois	Y	62450 FQ	76930 MW	101010 TQ	USBLS	5/15
	Chicago-Naperville-Arlington Heights PMSA, IL	Y	59410 FQ	73590 MW	96450 TQ	USBLS	5/15
	Lake County-Kenosha County PMSA, IL-WI	Y	74880 FQ	95540 MW	119360 TQ	USBLS	5/15
	Indiana	Y	41960 FQ	52880 MW	79420 TQ	USBLS	5/15
	Indianapolis-Carmel-Anderson MSA, IN	Y	39600 FQ	47840 MW	59200 TQ	USBLS	5/15
	Iowa	Y	53180 FQ	64240 MW	76810 TQ	USBLS	5/15
	Des Moines-West Des Moines MSA, IA	Y	51750 FQ	66490 MW	74870 TQ	USBLS	5/15
	Kansas	Y	56870 FQ	65710 MW	84300 TQ	USBLS	5/15
	Kentucky	Y	62600 FQ	76700 MW	94580 TQ	USBLS	5/15
	Louisville-Jefferson County MSA, KY-IN	Y	70200 FQ	79560 MW	91260 TQ	USBLS	5/15
	Louisiana	Y	49860 FQ	73830 MW	86590 TQ	USBLS	5/15
	Maryland	Y	67891 AE	97940 MW	112964 AEX	MDBLS	4/16
	Baltimore-Columbia-Towson MSA, MD	Y	71020 FQ	88910 MW	111410 TQ	USBLS	5/15
	Massachusetts	Y	62260 FQ	79180 MW	100020 TQ	USBLS	5/15

AE	Average entry wage	AWR	Average wage range	H	Hourly	LR	Low end range	MTC	Median total compensation	TCC	Total cash compensation
AEX	Average experienced wage	B	Biweekly	HI	Highest wage paid	M	Monthly	MW	Median wage paid	TQ	Third quartile wage
ATC	Average total compensation	D	Daily	HR	High end range	MCC	Median cash compensation	MWR	Median wage range	W	Weekly
AW	Average wage paid	FQ	First quartile wage	LO	Lowest wage paid	ME	Median entry wage	S	See annotated source	Y	Yearly

Occupation/Type/Industry	Location	Per	Low	Mid	High	Source	Date
Statistician	Boston-Cambridge-Newton NECTA, MA	Y	62470 FQ	79020 MW	98340 TQ	USBLS	5/15
	Worcester MSA, MA-CT	Y	58990 FQ	71700 MW	85900 TQ	USBLS	5/15
	Michigan	Y	63750 FQ	84560 MW	101390 TQ	USBLS	5/15
	Detroit-Dearborn-Livonia PMSA, MI	Y	44670 FQ	60310 MW	94430 TQ	USBLS	5/15
	Grand Rapids-Wyoming MSA, MI	Y	84120 FQ	92520 MW	100920 TQ	USBLS	5/15
	Minnesota	Y	61169 FQ	83336 MW	107025 TQ	MNBLS	1/16-3/16
	Minneapolis-St. Paul-Bloomington MSA, MN-WI	Y	57106 FQ	83184 MW	105190 TQ	MNBLS	1/16-3/16
	Mississippi	Y	42140 FQ	55730 MW	81450 TQ	USBLS	5/15
	Jackson MSA, MS	Y	43520 FQ	55690 MW	69490 TQ	USBLS	5/15
	Missouri	Y	46980 FQ	62480 MW	91830 TQ	USBLS	5/15
	Kansas City MSA, MO-KS	Y	58770 FQ	74200 MW	95770 TQ	USBLS	5/15
	St. Louis MSA, MO-IL	Y	63700 FQ	81710 MW	102950 TQ	USBLS	5/15
	Montana	Y	29170 FQ	43850 MW	55740 TQ	USBLS	5/15
	Billings MSA, MT	Y	27140 FQ	29410 MW	34700 TQ	USBLS	5/15
	Nebraska	Y	38875 FQ	50510 MW	70185 TQ	NEBLS	7/16-9/16
	Omaha-Council Bluffs MSA, NE-IA	Y	48160 FQ	58680 MW	73150 TQ	NEBLS	7/16-9/16
	Las Vegas-Henderson-Paradise MSA, NV	Y	60250 FQ	84940 MW	94950 TQ	USBLS	5/15
	New Hampshire	H	23.45 AE	31.14 MW	39.09 AEX	NHBLS	6/16
	New Jersey	Y	76880 FQ	107940 MW	133770 TQ	USBLS	5/15
	Newark PMSA, NJ-PA	Y	78220 FQ	112000 MW	136970 TQ	USBLS	5/15
	Trenton MSA, NJ	Y	90250 FQ	107910 MW	133610 TQ	USBLS	5/15
	New Mexico	Y	38630 FQ	64600 MW	87100 TQ	USBLS	5/15
	Albuquerque MSA, NM	Y	54260 FQ	72530 MW	89470 TQ	USBLS	5/15
	New York	Y	55830 AE	78630 MW	93540 AEX	NYBLS	1/16-3/16
	Nassau County-Suffolk County PMSA, NY	Y	61510 FQ	71990 MW	85470 TQ	USBLS	5/15
	New York-Jersey City-White Plains PMSA, NY-NJ	Y	65270 FQ	81300 MW	100020 TQ	USBLS	5/15
	North Carolina	Y	72590 FQ	96030 MW	124220 TQ	USBLS	5/15
	Charlotte-Concord-Gastonia MSA, NC-SC	Y	58980 FQ	77270 MW	111790 TQ	USBLS	5/15
	Raleigh MSA, NC	Y	94040 FQ	113410 MW	134580 TQ	USBLS	5/15
	North Dakota	Y	50720 FQ	57800 MW	70130 TQ	USBLS	5/15
	Ohio	Y	59160 FQ	79690 MW	100750 TQ	USBLS	5/15
	Cincinnati MSA, OH-KY-IN	Y	60370 FQ	82880 MW	100720 TQ	USBLS	5/15
	Cleveland-Elyria MSA, OH	Y	62160 FQ	78580 MW	95790 TQ	USBLS	5/15
	Columbus MSA, OH	Y	66180 FQ	85290 MW	109150 TQ	USBLS	5/15
	Oklahoma	Y	42670 FQ	52250 MW	70120 TQ	USBLS	5/15
	Oklahoma City MSA, OK	Y	41890 FQ	49770 MW	62760 TQ	USBLS	5/15
	Oregon	H	27.04 FQ	32.72 MW	39.61 TQ	ORBLS	2016
	Portland-Vancouver-Hillsboro MSA, OR-WA	Y	56110 FQ	69750 MW	84700 TQ	USBLS	5/15
	Pennsylvania	Y	51480 FQ	68830 MW	93100 TQ	USBLS	5/15
	Allentown-Bethlehem-Easton MSA, PA-NJ	Y	58890 FQ	75150 MW	121740 TQ	USBLS	5/15
	Harrisburg-Carlisle MSA, PA	Y	50290 FQ	60020 MW	74400 TQ	USBLS	5/15
	Montgomery County-Bucks County-Chester County PMSA, PA	Y	62760 FQ	89040 MW	130860 TQ	USBLS	5/15
	Philadelphia PMSA, PA	Y	61170 FQ	74820 MW	92310 TQ	USBLS	5/15
	Pittsburgh MSA, PA	Y	43120 FQ	54610 MW	73930 TQ	USBLS	5/15
	Rhode Island	Y	69370 FQ	79830 MW	94520 TQ	USBLS	5/15
	Providence-Warwick MSA, RI-MA	Y	69370 FQ	79830 MW	94520 TQ	USBLS	5/15
	South Carolina	Y	47630 FQ	59840 MW	76720 TQ	USBLS	5/15
	Charleston-North Charleston MSA, SC	Y	47970 FQ	63950 MW	76900 TQ	USBLS	5/15
	Columbia MSA, SC	Y	41090 FQ	49750 MW	64380 TQ	USBLS	5/15
	Greenville-Anderson-Mauldin MSA, SC	Y	52420 FQ	60820 MW	71620 TQ	USBLS	5/15
	Tennessee	Y	45880 FQ	58430 MW	76940 TQ	USBLS	5/15
	Knoxville MSA, TN	Y	43450 FQ	47100 MW	50720 TQ	USBLS	5/15
	Memphis MSA, TN-MS-AR	Y	55860 FQ	76070 MW	93830 TQ	USBLS	5/15
	Nashville-Davidson–Murfreesboro–Franklin MSA, TN	Y	46340 FQ	59520 MW	74870 TQ	USBLS	5/15

Occupation/Type/Industry	Location	Per	Low	Mid	High	Source	Date
Statistician	Texas	Y	54070 FQ	74960 MW	97420 TQ	USBLS	5/15
	Austin-Round Rock MSA, TX	Y	55080 FQ	76680 MW	106470 TQ	USBLS	5/15
	Dallas-Plano-Irving PMSA, TX	Y	54480 FQ	73090 MW	102140 TQ	USBLS	5/15
	Fort Worth-Arlington PMSA, TX	Y	56680 FQ	77080 MW	102400 TQ	USBLS	5/15
	Houston-The Woodlands-Sugar Land MSA, TX	Y	67800 FQ	84200 MW	97560 TQ	USBLS	5/15
	San Antonio-New Braunfels MSA, TX	Y	46130 FQ	60630 MW	86380 TQ	USBLS	5/15
	Utah	Y	62480 FQ	73830 MW	92720 TQ	USBLS	5/15
	Salt Lake City MSA, UT	Y	63390 FQ	73820 MW	91260 TQ	USBLS	5/15
	Vermont	Y	49360 FQ	57620 MW	73830 TQ	USBLS	5/15
	Virginia	Y	59290 FQ	86130 MW	115170 TQ	USBLS	5/15
	Richmond MSA, VA	Y	54290 FQ	78460 MW	100580 TQ	USBLS	5/15
	Virginia Beach-Norfolk-Newport News MSA, VA-NC	Y	21940 FQ	24050 MW	53290 TQ	USBLS	5/15
	Washington	H	32.46 FQ	42.30 MW	49.86 TQ	WABLS	3/16
	Seattle-Bellevue-Everett PMSA, WA	H	35.22 FQ	43.93 MW	51.13 TQ	WABLS	3/16
	Tacoma-Lakewood PMSA, WA	H	35.41 FQ	41.71 MW	47.76 TQ	WABLS	3/16
	West Virginia	Y	31860 FQ	61930 MW	100910 TQ	USBLS	5/15
	Wisconsin	Y	58730 FQ	71580 MW	90510 TQ	USBLS	5/15
	Madison MSA, WI	Y	65180 FQ	82960 MW	105710 TQ	USBLS	5/15
	Milwaukee-Waukesha-West Allis MSA, WI	Y	60170 FQ	71730 MW	85080 TQ	USBLS	5/15
	Puerto Rico	Y	29610 FQ	34840 MW	39350 TQ	USBLS	5/15
	San Juan-Carolina-Caguas MSA, PR	Y	29330 FQ	34970 MW	41560 TQ	USBLS	5/15
Still Photographer							
Made for Television Motion Picture	United States	W	1576 LO			MPEG01	7/31/16-7/29/17
Stock Clerk and Order Filler	Alabama	Y	17592 AE	24868 AW	28506 AEX	ALBLS	6/16
	Birmingham-Hoover MSA, AL	Y	17757 AE	25425 AW	29259 AEX	ALBLS	6/16
	Alaska	Y	22670 FQ	28550 MW	38380 TQ	USBLS	5/15
	Anchorage MSA, AK	Y	22620 FQ	27950 MW	36330 TQ	USBLS	5/15
	Arizona	Y	19140 FQ	23610 MW	30120 TQ	USBLS	5/15
	Phoenix-Mesa-Scottsdale MSA, AZ	Y	19100 FQ	23800 MW	30450 TQ	USBLS	5/15
	Tucson MSA, AZ	Y	19420 FQ	23500 MW	29640 TQ	USBLS	5/15
	Arkansas	Y	17900 FQ	20440 MW	26750 TQ	USBLS	5/15
	Little Rock-North Little Rock-Conway MSA, AR	Y	18090 FQ	21880 MW	28630 TQ	USBLS	5/15
	California	H	9.78 FQ	11.77 MW	15.37 TQ	CABLS	1/16-3/16
	Anaheim-Santa Ana-Irvine PMSA, CA	H	9.91 FQ	11.75 MW	14.54 TQ	CABLS	1/16-3/16
	Los Angeles-Long Beach-Glendale PMSA, CA	H	9.64 FQ	11.26 MW	14.63 TQ	CABLS	1/16-3/16
	Oakland-Hayward-Berkeley PMSA, CA	H	9.97 FQ	12.03 MW	16.54 TQ	CABLS	1/16-3/16
	Riverside-San Bernardino-Ontario MSA, CA	H	9.65 FQ	11.46 MW	14.89 TQ	CABLS	1/16-3/16
	Sacramento–Roseville–Arden-Arcade MSA, CA	H	9.65 FQ	11.81 MW	17.21 TQ	CABLS	1/16-3/16
	San Diego-Carlsbad MSA, CA	H	9.83 FQ	11.56 MW	14.61 TQ	CABLS	1/16-3/16
	San Francisco-Redwood City-South San Francisco PMSA, CA	H	12.26 FQ	14.98 MW	19.78 TQ	CABLS	1/16-3/16
	Colorado	Y	20520 FQ	25520 MW	34360 TQ	USBLS	5/15
	Denver-Aurora-Lakewood MSA, CO	Y	20340 FQ	25230 MW	34730 TQ	USBLS	5/15
	Connecticut	Y		24325 MW		CTBLS	1/16-3/16
	Bridgeport-Stamford-Norwalk MSA, CT	Y	20230 FQ	23530 MW	30190 TQ	USBLS	5/15
	Hartford-West Hartford-East Hartford MSA, CT	Y	20430 FQ	24020 MW	32730 TQ	USBLS	5/15
	Delaware	Y	18820 FQ	22700 MW	28640 TQ	USBLS	5/15
	Wilmington PMSA, DE-MD-NJ	Y	18790 FQ	22130 MW	27980 TQ	USBLS	5/15
	District of Columbia	Y	22750 FQ	28760 MW	37870 TQ	USBLS	5/15

AE	Average entry wage	AWR	Average wage range	H	Hourly	LR	Low end range	MTC	Median total compensation	TCC	Total cash compensation
AEX	Average experienced wage	B	Biweekly	HI	Highest wage paid	M	Monthly	MW	Median wage paid	TQ	Third quartile wage
ATC	Average total compensation	D	Daily	HR	High end range	MCC	Median cash compensation	MWR	Median wage range	W	Weekly
AW	Average wage paid	FQ	First quartile wage	LO	Lowest wage paid	ME	Median entry wage	S	See annotated source	Y	Yearly

Occupation/Type/Industry	Location	Per	Low	Mid	High	Source	Date
Stock Clerk and Order Filler	Washington-Arlington-Alexandria PMSA, DC-VA-MD-WV	Y	19770 FQ	24010 MW	33930 TQ	USBLS	5/15
	Florida	H	9.33 AE	11.38 MW	13.74 AEX	FLBLS	7/16-9/16
	Fort Lauderdale-Pompano Beach-Deerfield Beach PMSA, FL	H	9.56 AE	11.70 MW	14.28 AEX	FLBLS	7/16-9/16
	Miami-Miami Beach-Kendall PMSA, FL	H	9.10 AE	11.07 MW	13.41 AEX	FLBLS	7/16-9/16
	Orlando-Kissimmee-Sanford MSA, FL	H	9.47 AE	11.33 MW	14.07 AEX	FLBLS	7/16-9/16
	Tampa-St. Petersburg-Clearwater MSA, FL	H	9.16 AE	11.28 MW	13.52 AEX	FLBLS	7/16-9/16
	Georgia	Y	18400 FQ	22350 MW	28600 TQ	USBLS	5/15
	Atlanta-Sandy Springs-Roswell MSA, GA	Y	18730 FQ	23000 MW	29250 TQ	USBLS	5/15
	Augusta-Richmond County MSA, GA-SC	Y	17820 FQ	20740 MW	25950 TQ	USBLS	5/15
	Hawaii	Y	20920 FQ	27200 MW	35540 TQ	USBLS	5/15
	Urban Honolulu MSA, HI	Y	20580 FQ	26080 MW	34720 TQ	USBLS	5/15
	Idaho	Y	18730 FQ	22780 MW	29160 TQ	USBLS	5/15
	Boise City MSA, ID	Y	19160 FQ	23740 MW	29980 TQ	USBLS	5/15
	Illinois	Y	19780 FQ	23680 MW	30740 TQ	USBLS	5/15
	Chicago-Naperville-Arlington Heights PMSA, IL	Y	19910 FQ	23560 MW	30450 TQ	USBLS	5/15
	Lake County-Kenosha County PMSA, IL-WI	Y	20070 FQ	25100 MW	34820 TQ	USBLS	5/15
	Indiana	Y	18520 FQ	22770 MW	29340 TQ	USBLS	5/15
	Gary PMSA, IN	Y	17840 FQ	20510 MW	27170 TQ	USBLS	5/15
	Indianapolis-Carmel-Anderson MSA, IN	Y	19080 FQ	23580 MW	29890 TQ	USBLS	5/15
	Iowa	Y	19150 FQ	23740 MW	30420 TQ	USBLS	5/15
	Des Moines-West Des Moines MSA, IA	Y	19720 FQ	24140 MW	30910 TQ	USBLS	5/15
	Kansas	Y	18560 FQ	22650 MW	28990 TQ	USBLS	5/15
	Wichita MSA, KS	Y	18640 FQ	22850 MW	28500 TQ	USBLS	5/15
	Kentucky	Y	18490 FQ	22710 MW	30320 TQ	USBLS	5/15
	Louisiana	Y	17900 FQ	20710 MW	25920 TQ	USBLS	5/15
	Baton Rouge MSA, LA	Y	17830 FQ	20230 MW	24890 TQ	USBLS	5/15
	New Orleans-Metairie MSA, LA	Y	18670 FQ	22300 MW	27870 TQ	USBLS	5/15
	Maine	Y	19290 FQ	23410 MW	29630 TQ	USBLS	5/15
	Portland-South Portland MSA, ME	Y	20290 FQ	24750 MW	31010 TQ	USBLS	5/15
	Maryland	Y	18107 AE	26338 MW	30454 AEX	MDBLS	4/16
	Baltimore-Columbia-Towson MSA, MD	Y	18830 FQ	22750 MW	31620 TQ	USBLS	5/15
	Salisbury MSA, MD-DE	Y	18600 FQ	22570 MW	28540 TQ	USBLS	5/15
	Massachusetts	Y	19850 FQ	23720 MW	31610 TQ	USBLS	5/15
	Boston-Cambridge-Newton NECTA, MA	Y	19980 FQ	23910 MW	32640 TQ	USBLS	5/15
	Worcester MSA, MA-CT	Y	20220 FQ	24020 MW	31010 TQ	USBLS	5/15
	Michigan	Y	18680 FQ	21500*MW	28190 TQ	USBLS	5/15
	Detroit-Dearborn-Livonia PMSA, MI	Y	18580 FQ	20960 MW	27950 TQ	USBLS	5/15
	Grand Rapids-Wyoming MSA, MI	Y	18820 FQ	21780 MW	27580 TQ	USBLS	5/15
	Minnesota	Y	20033 FQ	24898 MW	33018 TQ	MNBLS	1/16-3/16
	Minneapolis-St. Paul-Bloomington MSA, MN-WI	Y	20954 FQ	26283 MW	34950 TQ	MNBLS	1/16-3/16
	Mississippi	Y	17900 FQ	20800 MW	27620 TQ	USBLS	5/15
	Jackson MSA, MS	Y	18030 FQ	21170 MW	27470 TQ	USBLS	5/15
	Missouri	Y	18970 FQ	23520 MW	30230 TQ	USBLS	5/15
	Kansas City MSA, MO-KS	Y	19710 FQ	23770 MW	30280 TQ	USBLS	5/15
	St. Louis MSA, MO-IL	Y	19830 FQ	25130 MW	33170 TQ	USBLS	5/15
	Montana	Y	20000 FQ	23500 MW	28720 TQ	USBLS	5/15
	Billings MSA, MT	Y	19440 FQ	22600 MW	27470 TQ	USBLS	5/15
	Nebraska	Y	18560 FQ	21315 MW	26800 TQ	NEBLS	7/16-9/16
	Omaha-Council Bluffs MSA, NE-IA	Y	18770 FQ	21980 MW	27260 TQ	NEBLS	7/16-9/16
	Nevada	Y	20830 FQ	25950 MW	34340 TQ	USBLS	5/15

AE Average entry wage	**AWR** Average wage range	**H** Hourly	**LR** Low end range	**MTC** Median total compensation	**TCC** Total cash compensation
AEX Average experienced wage	**B** Biweekly	**HI** Highest wage paid	**M** Monthly	**MW** Median wage paid	**TQ** Third quartile wage
ATC Average total compensation	**D** Daily	**HR** High end range	**MCC** Median cash compensation	**MWR** Median wage range	**W** Weekly
AW Average wage paid	**FQ** First quartile wage	**LO** Lowest wage paid	**ME** Median entry wage	**S** See annotated source	**Y** Yearly

Occupation/Type/Industry	Location	Per	Low	Mid	High	Source	Date
Stock Clerk and Order Filler	Las Vegas-Henderson-Paradise MSA, NV	Y	20200 FQ	25490 MW	34140 TQ	USBLS	5/15
	New Hampshire	H	9.10 AE	12.09 MW	15.06 AEX	NHBLS	6/16
	Manchester NECTA, NH	H	9.28 AE	12.09 MW	15.17 AEX	NHBLS	6/16
	Nashua NECTA, NH-MA	Y	19740 FQ	24350 MW	32630 TQ	USBLS	5/15
	New Jersey	Y	19220 FQ	22790 MW	30280 TQ	USBLS	5/15
	Camden PMSA, NJ	Y	19040 FQ	22770 MW	30200 TQ	USBLS	5/15
	Newark PMSA, NJ-PA	Y	19170 FQ	22230 MW	29090 TQ	USBLS	5/15
	Trenton MSA, NJ	Y	20780 FQ	26220 MW	35610 TQ	USBLS	5/15
	New Mexico	Y	19340 FQ	23410 MW	29650 TQ	USBLS	5/15
	Albuquerque MSA, NM	Y	20030 FQ	24150 MW	30590 TQ	USBLS	5/15
	New York	Y	19490 AE	23010 MW	30330 AEX	NYBLS	1/16-3/16
	Buffalo-Cheektowaga-Niagara Falls MSA, NY	Y	19270 FQ	22090 MW	28630 TQ	USBLS	5/15
	Nassau County-Suffolk County PMSA, NY	Y	19400 FQ	22820 MW	30510 TQ	USBLS	5/15
	New York-Jersey City-White Plains PMSA, NY-NJ	Y	19230 FQ	22430 MW	30040 TQ	USBLS	5/15
	Rochester MSA, NY	Y	19390 FQ	22560 MW	29190 TQ	USBLS	5/15
	North Carolina	Y	18300 FQ	22100 MW	28420 TQ	USBLS	5/15
	Charlotte-Concord-Gastonia MSA, NC-SC	Y	18500 FQ	22250 MW	28530 TQ	USBLS	5/15
	Raleigh MSA, NC	Y	18610 FQ	22370 MW	28170 TQ	USBLS	5/15
	North Dakota	Y	22100 FQ	27130 MW	33380 TQ	USBLS	5/15
	Fargo MSA, ND-MN	Y	20540 FQ	24100 MW	28960 TQ	USBLS	5/15
	Ohio	Y	19160 FQ	23410 MW	30710 TQ	USBLS	5/15
	Cincinnati MSA, OH-KY-IN	Y	19670 FQ	24040 MW	30760 TQ	USBLS	5/15
	Cleveland-Elyria MSA, OH	Y	19490 FQ	23680 MW	31600 TQ	USBLS	5/15
	Columbus MSA, OH	Y	19090 FQ	23290 MW	31330 TQ	USBLS	5/15
	Oklahoma	Y	18510 FQ	22520 MW	29140 TQ	USBLS	5/15
	Oklahoma City MSA, OK	Y	18910 FQ	23380 MW	30050 TQ	USBLS	5/15
	Tulsa MSA, OK	Y	19150 FQ	22990 MW	29210 TQ	USBLS	5/15
	Oregon	H	11.19 FQ	13.76 MW	17.45 TQ	ORBLS	2016
	Portland-Vancouver-Hillsboro MSA, OR-WA	Y	23190 FQ	28820 MW	36250 TQ	USBLS	5/15
	Pennsylvania	Y	18240 FQ	22030 MW	28300 TQ	USBLS	5/15
	Allentown-Bethlehem-Easton MSA, PA-NJ	Y	18590 FQ	21840 MW	26820 TQ	USBLS	5/15
	Harrisburg-Carlisle MSA, PA	Y	18770 FQ	23860 MW	33180 TQ	USBLS	5/15
	Montgomery County-Bucks County-Chester County PMSA, PA	Y	18890 FQ	22910 MW	29050 TQ	USBLS	5/15
	Philadelphia PMSA, PA	Y	17960 FQ	21560 MW	27830 TQ	USBLS	5/15
	Pittsburgh MSA, PA	Y	18220 FQ	21700 MW	27380 TQ	USBLS	5/15
	Rhode Island	Y	19720 FQ	23330 MW	33830 TQ	USBLS	5/15
	Providence-Warwick MSA, RI-MA	Y	19580 FQ	22930 MW	32050 TQ	USBLS	5/15
	South Carolina	Y	17960 FQ	21170 MW	27070 TQ	USBLS	5/15
	Charleston-North Charleston MSA, SC	Y	18180 FQ	21830 MW	28280 TQ	USBLS	5/15
	Columbia MSA, SC	Y	17620 FQ	19980 MW	25580 TQ	USBLS	5/15
	Greenville-Anderson-Mauldin MSA, SC	Y	18700 FQ	22820 MW	29450 TQ	USBLS	5/15
	South Dakota	Y	18950 FQ	21550 MW	27270 TQ	USBLS	5/15
	Sioux Falls MSA, SD	Y	19210 FQ	22420 MW	27950 TQ	USBLS	5/15
	Tennessee	Y	18550 FQ	22630 MW	28990 TQ	USBLS	5/15
	Knoxville MSA, TN	Y	18430 FQ	22720 MW	28430 TQ	USBLS	5/15
	Memphis MSA, TN-MS-AR	Y	19320 FQ	23610 MW	30700 TQ	USBLS	5/15
	Nashville-Davidson–Murfreesboro–Franklin MSA, TN	Y	18960 FQ	23560 MW	30120 TQ	USBLS	5/15
	Texas	Y	19320 FQ	23670 MW	29980 TQ	USBLS	5/15
	Austin-Round Rock MSA, TX	Y	20150 FQ	24180 MW	30360 TQ	USBLS	5/15
	Dallas-Plano-Irving PMSA, TX	Y	19590 FQ	24280 MW	30330 TQ	USBLS	5/15
	Fort Worth-Arlington PMSA, TX	Y	19300 FQ	23600 MW	30260 TQ	USBLS	5/15
	Houston-The Woodlands-Sugar Land MSA, TX	Y	20040 FQ	24400 MW	30890 TQ	USBLS	5/15
	San Antonio-New Braunfels MSA, TX	Y	20100 FQ	24440 MW	29950 TQ	USBLS	5/15
	Utah	Y	19560 FQ	24250 MW	30660 TQ	USBLS	5/15
	Ogden-Clearfield MSA, UT	Y	21010 FQ	26710 MW	33300 TQ	USBLS	5/15

AE	Average entry wage	AWR	Average wage range	H	Hourly	LR	Low end range	MTC	Median total compensation	TCC	Total cash compensation
AEX	Average experienced wage	B	Biweekly	HI	Highest wage paid	M	Monthly	MW	Median wage paid	TQ	Third quartile wage
ATC	Average total compensation	D	Daily	HR	High end range	MCC	Median cash compensation	MWR	Median wage range	W	Weekly
AW	Average wage paid	FQ	First quartile wage	LO	Lowest wage paid	ME	Median entry wage	S	See annotated source	Y	Yearly

Occupation/Type/Industry	Location	Per	Low	Mid	High	Source	Date
Stock Clerk and Order Filler	Provo-Orem MSA, UT	Y	19080 FQ	23550 MW	30440 TQ	USBLS	5/15
	Salt Lake City MSA, UT	Y	19510 FQ	24100 MW	30270 TQ	USBLS	5/15
	Vermont	Y	20870 FQ	24090 MW	30650 TQ	USBLS	5/15
	Burlington-South Burlington MSA, VT	Y	20720 FQ	23640 MW	30260 TQ	USBLS	5/15
	Virginia	Y	18850 FQ	23240 MW	31320 TQ	USBLS	5/15
	Richmond MSA, VA	Y	18360 FQ	22540 MW	31670 TQ	USBLS	5/15
	Virginia Beach-Norfolk-Newport News MSA, VA-NC	Y	18820 FQ	23530 MW	31560 TQ	USBLS	5/15
	Washington	H	11.46 FQ	14.23 MW	19.52 TQ	WABLS	3/16
	Seattle-Bellevue-Everett PMSA, WA	H	11.77 FQ	14.94 MW	20.61 TQ	WABLS	3/16
	Tacoma-Lakewood PMSA, WA	H	11.71 FQ	15.05 MW	20.78 TQ	WABLS	3/16
	West Virginia	Y	18420 FQ	21180 MW	27930 TQ	USBLS	5/15
	Beckley MSA, WV	Y	18320 FQ	20280 MW	27360 TQ	USBLS	5/15
	Huntington-Ashland MSA, WV-KY-OH	Y	18340 FQ	21230 MW	28020 TQ	USBLS	5/15
	Wisconsin	Y	18070 FQ	21610 MW	28740 TQ	USBLS	5/15
	Madison MSA, WI	Y	19150 FQ	23410 MW	29690 TQ	USBLS	5/15
	Milwaukee-Waukesha-West Allis MSA, WI	Y	18190 FQ	22070 MW	29830 TQ	USBLS	5/15
	Wyoming	Y	20080 FQ	24440 MW	32670 TQ	USBLS	5/15
	Cheyenne MSA, WY	Y	19120 FQ	22820 MW	30020 TQ	USBLS	5/15
	Puerto Rico	Y	16800 FQ	18090 MW	19400 TQ	USBLS	5/15
	San Juan-Carolina-Caguas MSA, PR	Y	16820 FQ	18140 MW	19470 TQ	USBLS	5/15
	Virgin Islands	Y	16970 FQ	18560 MW	22380 TQ	USBLS	5/15
	Guam	Y	18140 FQ	19120 MW	23420 TQ	USBLS	5/15
Stock Plan Administration Manager							
10 or More Years of Experience	United States	Y		120000 MW		CNBC07	2016-2017
Stonemason	Alabama	Y	26592 AE	32846 AW	35963 AEX	ALBLS	6/16
	Arizona	Y	18470 FQ	29420 MW	44720 TQ	USBLS	5/15
	Phoenix-Mesa-Scottsdale MSA, AZ	Y	18390 FQ	40990 MW	46110 TQ	USBLS	5/15
	Arkansas	Y	32540 FQ	35970 MW	39420 TQ	USBLS	5/15
	California	H	14.65 FQ	18.60 MW	25.16 TQ	CABLS	1/16-3/16
	Anaheim-Santa Ana-Irvine PMSA, CA	H	16.46 FQ	18.79 MW	22.11 TQ	CABLS	1/16-3/16
	Los Angeles-Long Beach-Glendale PMSA, CA	H	11.01 FQ	12.95 MW	18.74 TQ	CABLS	1/16-3/16
	Riverside-San Bernardino-Ontario MSA, CA	H	15.93 FQ	18.47 MW	23.05 TQ	CABLS	1/16-3/16
	Sacramento–Roseville–Arden-Arcade MSA, CA	H	17.98 FQ	24.18 MW	27.86 TQ	CABLS	1/16-3/16
	San Diego-Carlsbad MSA, CA	H	14.12 FQ	21.50 MW	26.75 TQ	CABLS	1/16-3/16
	San Francisco-Redwood City-South San Francisco PMSA, CA	H	18.18 FQ	23.66 MW	35.10 TQ	CABLS	1/16-3/16
	Colorado	Y	20410 FQ	33970 MW	39850 TQ	USBLS	5/15
	Denver-Aurora-Lakewood MSA, CO	Y	23230 FQ	33540 MW	36750 TQ	USBLS	5/15
	Connecticut	Y		61614 MW		CTBLS	1/16-3/16
	Delaware	Y	30130 FQ	37550 MW	50970 TQ	USBLS	5/15
	District of Columbia	Y	31580 FQ	40400 MW	66210 TQ	USBLS	5/15
	Washington-Arlington-Alexandria PMSA, DC-VA-MD-WV	Y	41220 FQ	56280 MW	68970 TQ	USBLS	5/15
	Florida	H	11.94 AE	19.43 MW	21.78 AEX	FLBLS	7/16-9/16
	Tampa-St. Petersburg-Clearwater MSA, FL	H	15.01 AE	21.38 MW	23.63 AEX	FLBLS	7/16-9/16
	Hawaii	Y	48200 FQ	65270 MW	73750 TQ	USBLS	5/15
	Idaho	Y	40090 FQ	49890 MW	56600 TQ	USBLS	5/15
	Illinois	Y	24820 FQ	55830 MW	85270 TQ	USBLS	5/15
	Lake County-Kenosha County PMSA, IL-WI	Y	52920 FQ	56960 MW	61000 TQ	USBLS	5/15
	Indiana	Y	40100 FQ	50260 MW	59500 TQ	USBLS	5/15
	Kansas	Y	19580 FQ	35320 MW	46800 TQ	USBLS	5/15
	Kentucky	Y	28030 FQ	35660 MW	42380 TQ	USBLS	5/15
	Louisiana	Y	23900 FQ	28660 MW	35350 TQ	USBLS	5/15

AE Average entry wage	**AWR** Average wage range	**H** Hourly	**LR** Low end range	**MTC** Median total compensation	**TCC** Total cash compensation
AEX Average experienced wage	**B** Biweekly	**HI** Highest wage paid	**M** Monthly	**MW** Median wage paid	**TQ** Third quartile wage
ATC Average total compensation	**D** Daily	**HR** High end range	**MCC** Median cash compensation	**MWR** Median wage range	**W** Weekly
AW Average wage paid	**FQ** First quartile wage	**LO** Lowest wage paid	**ME** Median entry wage	**S** See annotated source	**Y** Yearly

Occupation/Type/Industry	Location	Per	Low	Mid	High	Source	Date
Stonemason	Maine	Y	37250 FQ	43450 MW	48640 TQ	USBLS	5/15
	Portland-South Portland MSA, ME	Y	38690 FQ	43170 MW	47010 TQ	USBLS	5/15
	Maryland	Y	32657 AE	46127 MW	52862 AEX	MDBLS	4/16
	Baltimore-Columbia-Towson MSA, MD	Y	36030 FQ	41410 MW	47130 TQ	USBLS	5/15
	Massachusetts	Y	49360 FQ	82550 MW	102660 TQ	USBLS	5/15
	Boston-Cambridge-Newton NECTA, MA	Y	107550 FQ	119870 MW	134240 TQ	USBLS	5/15
	Michigan	Y	32220 FQ	34860 MW	37510 TQ	USBLS	5/15
	Minnesota	Y	25811 FQ	32944 MW	39987 TQ	MNBLS	1/16-3/16
	Missouri	Y	29510 FQ	40170 MW	48630 TQ	USBLS	5/15
	Kansas City MSA, MO-KS	Y	22030 FQ	39210 MW	46620 TQ	USBLS	5/15
	St. Louis MSA, MO-IL	Y	27840 FQ	33200 MW	42360 TQ	USBLS	5/15
	Montana	Y	37560 FQ	44150 MW	49980 TQ	USBLS	5/15
	Nebraska	Y	26525 FQ	33970 MW	41875 TQ	NEBLS	7/16-9/16
	Omaha-Council Bluffs MSA, NE-IA	Y	26250 FQ	33355 MW	41080 TQ	NEBLS	7/16-9/16
	Nevada	Y	27890 FQ	36880 MW	50780 TQ	USBLS	5/15
	Las Vegas-Henderson-Paradise MSA, NV	Y	27060 FQ	35710 MW	54010 TQ	USBLS	5/15
	New Hampshire	H	13.71 AE	20.95 MW	23.92 AEX	NHBLS	6/16
	New Jersey	Y	29610 FQ	44370 MW	56410 TQ	USBLS	5/15
	Camden PMSA, NJ	Y	26680 FQ	28490 MW	30300 TQ	USBLS	5/15
	New York	Y	33050 AE	45370 MW	63080 AEX	NYBLS	1/16-3/16
	Nassau County-Suffolk County PMSA, NY	Y	38070 FQ	58350 MW	86550 TQ	USBLS	5/15
	New York-Jersey City-White Plains PMSA, NY-NJ	Y	34720 FQ	40880 MW	51420 TQ	USBLS	5/15
	North Carolina	Y	28200 FQ	35090 MW	42120 TQ	USBLS	5/15
	Raleigh MSA, NC	Y	35160 FQ	39110 MW	45500 TQ	USBLS	5/15
	Ohio	Y	21390 FQ	23400 MW	30300 TQ	USBLS	5/15
	Columbus MSA, OH	Y	27060 FQ	29740 MW	36110 TQ	USBLS	5/15
	Oklahoma	Y	29000 FQ	34240 MW	39380 TQ	USBLS	5/15
	Oregon	H	9.48 FQ	9.53 MW	9.58 TQ	ORBLS	2016
	Allentown-Bethlehem-Easton MSA, PA-NJ	Y	34140 FQ	36680 MW	39190 TQ	USBLS	5/15
	Montgomery County-Bucks County-Chester County PMSA, PA	Y	57510 FQ	72200 MW	93210 TQ	USBLS	5/15
	South Carolina	Y	25010 FQ	28390 MW	36450 TQ	USBLS	5/15
	Tennessee	Y	23350 FQ	32570 MW	37060 TQ	USBLS	5/15
	Nashville-Davidson–Murfreesboro–Franklin MSA, TN	Y	33570 FQ	35750 MW	37940 TQ	USBLS	5/15
	Texas	Y	25020 FQ	28970 MW	35560 TQ	USBLS	5/15
	Dallas-Plano-Irving PMSA, TX	Y	25560 FQ	28500 MW	31790 TQ	USBLS	5/15
	Fort Worth-Arlington PMSA, TX	Y	27010 FQ	32760 MW	40690 TQ	USBLS	5/15
	Houston-The Woodlands-Sugar Land MSA, TX	Y	26050 FQ	32750 MW	39120 TQ	USBLS	5/15
	Utah	Y	32820 FQ	35840 MW	38860 TQ	USBLS	5/15
	Ogden-Clearfield MSA, UT	Y	33360 FQ	35750 MW	38150 TQ	USBLS	5/15
	Salt Lake City MSA, UT	Y	31110 FQ	35510 MW	40670 TQ	USBLS	5/15
	Vermont	Y	30040 FQ	39400 MW	55120 TQ	USBLS	5/15
	Burlington-South Burlington MSA, VT	Y	42330 FQ	53310 MW	59010 TQ	USBLS	5/15
	Virginia	Y	44180 FQ	56690 MW	67410 TQ	USBLS	5/15
	Washington	H	16.17 FQ	21.01 MW	26.53 TQ	WABLS	3/16
	Seattle-Bellevue-Everett PMSA, WA	H	16.59 FQ	22.39 MW	27.38 TQ	WABLS	3/16
	Wisconsin	Y	34410 FQ	40030 MW	47440 TQ	USBLS	5/15
Stop Motion Animator	United States	Y		60000 AW		NYFA	2015
Storm Drain Maintenance Worker							
Municipal Government	Carlsbad, CA	H	20.61 LO	23.79 MW	26.96 HI	CCCA01	6/28/16
Storm Water Inspector							
Municipal Government	Camarillo, CA	Y			36018 HI	CACIT	6/28/16
Strategy Manager	United States	Y		130000 MW		TSTR	2017

AE	Average entry wage	AWR	Average wage range	H	Hourly	LR	Low end range
AEX	Average experienced wage	B	Biweekly	HI	Highest wage paid	M	Monthly
ATC	Average total compensation	D	Daily	HR	High end range	MCC	Median cash compensation
AW	Average wage paid	FQ	First quartile wage	LO	Lowest wage paid	ME	Median entry wage

MTC	Median total compensation	TCC	Total cash compensation
MW	Median wage paid	TQ	Third quartile wage
MWR	Median wage range	W	Weekly
S	See annotated source	Y	Yearly

Occupation/Type/Industry	Location	Per	Low	Mid	High	Source	Date
Street Maintenance Manager							
Municipal Government	Fairfield, CA	Y			88412 HI	CACIT	6/28/16
Street Sweeper Operator							
Municipal Government	Anaheim, CA	Y		43517 AW		CACIT	6/28/16
Municipal Government	Belmont, CA	Y			66296 HI	CACIT	6/28/16
Street Traffic Painter							
Municipal Government	Gardena, CA	Y			59400 HI	CACIT	6/22/16
Streets Manager							
Municipal Government	Colorado Springs, CO	Y	81979 LO		112721 HI	COSPRS	2017
Strength Coach							
Football, University of Iowa	Iowa City, IA	Y			625204 TCC	USAT05	2016
Football, University of Missouri	Columbia, MO	Y			360000 TCC	USAT05	2016
Football, University of South Carolina	Columbia, SC	Y			400000 TCC	USAT05	2016
Structural Engineer							
Building Inspection Department, Municipal Government	San Francisco, CA	Y			149312 HI	CACIT	6/28/16
Structural Iron and Steel Worker	Alabama	Y	29153 AE	41014 AW	46939 AEX	ALBLS	6/16
	Birmingham-Hoover MSA, AL	Y	33762 AE	44532 AW	49922 AEX	ALBLS	6/16
	Alaska	Y	48520 FQ	65660 MW	78630 TQ	USBLS	5/15
	Anchorage MSA, AK	Y	50120 FQ	69330 MW	78180 TQ	USBLS	5/15
	Arizona	Y	32060 FQ	38000 MW	49300 TQ	USBLS	5/15
	Phoenix-Mesa-Scottsdale MSA, AZ	Y	31400 FQ	36620 MW	45100 TQ	USBLS	5/15
	Tucson MSA, AZ	Y	35330 FQ	51180 MW	57210 TQ	USBLS	5/15
	Arkansas	Y	31450 FQ	38230 MW	50680 TQ	USBLS	5/15
	Little Rock-North Little Rock-Conway MSA, AR	Y	33600 FQ	40890 MW	51790 TQ	USBLS	5/15
	California	H	21.14 FQ	32.21 MW	38.46 TQ	CABLS	1/16-3/16
	Anaheim-Santa Ana-Irvine PMSA, CA	H	31.97 FQ	35.18 MW	38.64 TQ	CABLS	1/16-3/16
	Los Angeles-Long Beach-Glendale PMSA, CA	H	22.13 FQ	33.95 MW	41.47 TQ	CABLS	1/16-3/16
	Oakland-Hayward-Berkeley PMSA, CA	H	20.32 FQ	26.65 MW	35.06 TQ	CABLS	1/16-3/16
	Riverside-San Bernardino-Ontario MSA, CA	H	30.98 FQ	35.14 MW	38.97 TQ	CABLS	1/16-3/16
	Sacramento–Roseville–Arden-Arcade MSA, CA	H	23.15 FQ	32.34 MW	38.09 TQ	CABLS	1/16-3/16
	San Diego-Carlsbad MSA, CA	H	18.88 FQ	28.40 MW	38.91 TQ	CABLS	1/16-3/16
	San Francisco-Redwood City-South San Francisco PMSA, CA	H	29.16 FQ	34.63 MW	39.17 TQ	CABLS	1/16-3/16
	Colorado	Y	32660 FQ	41380 MW	54440 TQ	USBLS	5/15
	Denver-Aurora-Lakewood MSA, CO	Y	34790 FQ	39930 MW	50350 TQ	USBLS	5/15
	Connecticut	Y		48025 MW		CTBLS	1/16-3/16
	Hartford-West Hartford-East Hartford MSA, CT	Y	43940 FQ	53210 MW	74830 TQ	USBLS	5/15
	Delaware	Y	38230 FQ	45680 MW	52020 TQ	USBLS	5/15
	Wilmington PMSA, DE-MD-NJ	Y	39110 FQ	45940 MW	52200 TQ	USBLS	5/15
	District of Columbia	Y	47430 FQ	58800 MW	71720 TQ	USBLS	5/15
	Washington-Arlington-Alexandria PMSA, DC-VA-MD-WV	Y	40590 FQ	51200 MW	60040 TQ	USBLS	5/15
	Florida	H	15.10 AE	19.30 MW	24.31 AEX	FLBLS	7/16-9/16
	Fort Lauderdale-Pompano Beach-Deerfield Beach PMSA, FL	H	16.38 AE	18.65 MW	22.43 AEX	FLBLS	7/16-9/16
	Miami-Miami Beach-Kendall PMSA, FL	H	14.58 AE	17.86 MW	21.29 AEX	FLBLS	7/16-9/16
	Orlando-Kissimmee-Sanford MSA, FL	H	16.33 AE	20.42 MW	25.75 AEX	FLBLS	7/16-9/16
	Tampa-St. Petersburg-Clearwater MSA, FL	H	16.04 AE	26.62 MW	28.07 AEX	FLBLS	7/16-9/16
	Georgia	Y	28960 FQ	35440 MW	47250 TQ	USBLS	5/15

AE	Average entry wage	AWR	Average wage range	H	Hourly
AEX	Average experienced wage	B	Biweekly	HI	Highest wage paid
ATC	Average total compensation	D	Daily	HR	High end range
AW	Average wage paid	FQ	First quartile wage	LO	Lowest wage paid

LR	Low end range	MTC	Median total compensation	TCC	Total cash compensation
M	Monthly	MW	Median wage paid	TQ	Third quartile wage
MCC	Median cash compensation	MWR	Median wage range	W	Weekly
ME	Median entry wage	S	See annotated source	Y	Yearly

Occupation/Type/Industry	Location	Per	Low	Mid	High	Source	Date
Structural Iron and Steel Worker	Atlanta-Sandy Springs-Roswell MSA, GA	Y	29200 FQ	34970 MW	44060 TQ	USBLS	5/15
	Augusta-Richmond County MSA, GA-SC	Y	26500 FQ	29820 MW	35740 TQ	USBLS	5/15
	Hawaii	Y	54750 FQ	67930 MW	76790 TQ	USBLS	5/15
	Urban Honolulu MSA, HI	Y	48040 FQ	68230 MW	76060 TQ	USBLS	5/15
	Idaho	Y	29450 FQ	36620 MW	48800 TQ	USBLS	5/15
	Boise City MSA, ID	Y	27790 FQ	30870 MW	35670 TQ	USBLS	5/15
	Illinois	Y	76720 FQ	88070 MW	95710 TQ	USBLS	5/15
	Chicago-Naperville-Arlington Heights PMSA, IL	Y	85200 FQ	91280 MW	97350 TQ	USBLS	5/15
	Lake County-Kenosha County PMSA, IL-WI	Y	47930 FQ	81470 MW	92210 TQ	USBLS	5/15
	Indiana	Y	37940 FQ	50940 MW	76060 TQ	USBLS	5/15
	Gary PMSA, IN	Y	42030 FQ	80950 MW	90280 TQ	USBLS	5/15
	Indianapolis-Carmel-Anderson MSA, IN	Y	44360 FQ	68730 MW	77820 TQ	USBLS	5/15
	Iowa	Y	44710 FQ	54650 MW	60590 TQ	USBLS	5/15
	Des Moines-West Des Moines MSA, IA	Y	53190 FQ	57530 MW	61870 TQ	USBLS	5/15
	Kansas	Y	34130 FQ	38720 MW	52830 TQ	USBLS	5/15
	Wichita MSA, KS	Y	32490 FQ	37490 MW	46070 TQ	USBLS	5/15
	Kentucky	Y	36450 FQ	49980 MW	58280 TQ	USBLS	5/15
	Louisville-Jefferson County MSA, KY-IN	Y	36630 FQ	46360 MW	55520 TQ	USBLS	5/15
	Louisiana	Y	36260 FQ	46010 MW	58860 TQ	USBLS	5/15
	Baton Rouge MSA, LA	Y	40570 FQ	51680 MW	65560 TQ	USBLS	5/15
	New Orleans-Metairie MSA, LA	Y	32750 FQ	40230 MW	48400 TQ	USBLS	5/15
	Maine	Y	31830 FQ	40800 MW	50660 TQ	USBLS	5/15
	Maryland	Y	33007 AE	48891 MW	56833 AEX	MDBLS	4/16
	Baltimore-Columbia-Towson MSA, MD	Y	38850 FQ	51690 MW	68140 TQ	USBLS	5/15
	Salisbury MSA, MD-DE	Y	32870 FQ	40820 MW	45170 TQ	USBLS	5/15
	Massachusetts	Y	55870 FQ	69390 MW	87140 TQ	USBLS	5/15
	Boston-Cambridge-Newton NECTA, MA	Y	55900 FQ	66130 MW	87770 TQ	USBLS	5/15
	Worcester MSA, MA-CT	Y	48370 FQ	65700 MW	73690 TQ	USBLS	5/15
	Michigan	Y	39790 FQ	50360 MW	60530 TQ	USBLS	5/15
	Detroit-Dearborn-Livonia PMSA, MI	Y	47670 FQ	57820 MW	66870 TQ	USBLS	5/15
	Grand Rapids-Wyoming MSA, MI	Y	39540 FQ	44280 MW	49040 TQ	USBLS	5/15
	Minnesota	Y	56878 FQ	69138 MW	76060 TQ	MNBLS	1/16-3/16
	Minneapolis-St. Paul-Bloomington MSA, MN-WI	Y	65980 FQ	71691 MW	77402 TQ	MNBLS	1/16-3/16
	Mississippi	Y	33880 FQ	40260 MW	52760 TQ	USBLS	5/15
	Jackson MSA, MS	Y	35820 FQ	41680 MW	48050 TQ	USBLS	5/15
	Missouri	Y	43990 FQ	60040 MW	72070 TQ	USBLS	5/15
	Kansas City MSA, MO-KS	Y	48100 FQ	68010 MW	74710 TQ	USBLS	5/15
	St. Louis MSA, MO-IL	Y	45140 FQ	55660 MW	70000 TQ	USBLS	5/15
	Montana	Y	51330 FQ	55210 MW	59080 TQ	USBLS	5/15
	Nebraska	Y	30830 FQ	41305 MW	55520 TQ	NEBLS	7/16-9/16
	Omaha-Council Bluffs MSA, NE-IA	Y	52735 FQ	56450 MW	60160 TQ	NEBLS	7/16-9/16
	Nevada	Y	33400 FQ	38740 MW	66140 TQ	USBLS	5/15
	Las Vegas-Henderson-Paradise MSA, NV	Y	32210 FQ	36620 MW	51120 TQ	USBLS	5/15
	New Hampshire	H	18.33 AE	22.88 MW	25.72 AEX	NHBLS	6/16
	Nashua NECTA, NH-MA	Y	41780 FQ	49420 MW	56450 TQ	USBLS	5/15
	New Jersey	Y	78040 FQ	91660 MW	108500 TQ	USBLS	5/15
	Camden PMSA, NJ	Y	82500 FQ	97680 MW	115700 TQ	USBLS	5/15
	Newark PMSA, NJ-PA	Y	82610 FQ	92770 MW	111980 TQ	USBLS	5/15
	New Mexico	Y	44480 FQ	50820 MW	57150 TQ	USBLS	5/15
	Albuquerque MSA, NM	Y	46720 FQ	52250 MW	57960 TQ	USBLS	5/15
	New York	Y	53520 AE	90810 MW	106240 AEX	NYBLS	1/16-3/16
	Buffalo-Cheektowaga-Niagara Falls MSA, NY	Y	52650 FQ	57310 MW	61980 TQ	USBLS	5/15
	Nassau County-Suffolk County PMSA, NY	Y	93920 FQ	113420 MW	129410 TQ	USBLS	5/15
	New York-Jersey City-White Plains PMSA, NY-NJ	Y	58740 FQ	87570 MW	102570 TQ	USBLS	5/15

AE Average entry wage	**AWR** Average wage range	**H** Hourly	**LR** Low end range	**MTC** Median total compensation	**TCC** Total cash compensation
AEX Average experienced wage	**B** Biweekly	**HI** Highest wage paid	**M** Monthly	**MW** Median wage paid	**TQ** Third quartile wage
ATC Average total compensation	**D** Daily	**HR** High end range	**MCC** Median cash compensation	**MWR** Median wage range	**W** Weekly
AW Average wage paid	**FQ** First quartile wage	**LO** Lowest wage paid	**ME** Median entry wage	**S** See annotated source	**Y** Yearly

Occupation/Type/Industry	Location	Per	Low	Mid	High	Source	Date
Structural Iron and Steel Worker	North Carolina	Y	32650 FQ	36780 MW	42760 TQ	USBLS	5/15
	Charlotte-Concord-Gastonia MSA, NC-SC	Y	33160 FQ	36240 MW	39320 TQ	USBLS	5/15
	Raleigh MSA, NC	Y	35750 FQ	41470 MW	46370 TQ	USBLS	5/15
	North Dakota	Y	41490 FQ	51390 MW	67120 TQ	USBLS	5/15
	Fargo MSA, ND-MN	Y	37000 FQ	44030 MW	50300 TQ	USBLS	5/15
	Ohio	Y	51750 FQ	58030 MW	66210 TQ	USBLS	5/15
	Cincinnati MSA, OH-KY-IN	Y	48750 FQ	54600 MW	59570 TQ	USBLS	5/15
	Cleveland-Elyria MSA, OH	Y	55090 FQ	62790 MW	72350 TQ	USBLS	5/15
	Columbus MSA, OH	Y	49840 FQ	55420 MW	60630 TQ	USBLS	5/15
	Oklahoma	Y	27280 FQ	39390 MW	46860 TQ	USBLS	5/15
	Oklahoma City MSA, OK	Y	22930 FQ	26480 MW	30550 TQ	USBLS	5/15
	Tulsa MSA, OK	Y	34220 FQ	42630 MW	47410 TQ	USBLS	5/15
	Oregon	H	22.11 FQ	28.23 MW	36.58 TQ	ORBLS	2016
	Portland-Vancouver-Hillsboro MSA, OR-WA	Y	46240 FQ	58820 MW	81280 TQ	USBLS	5/15
	Pennsylvania	Y	40560 FQ	51370 MW	73740 TQ	USBLS	5/15
	Allentown-Bethlehem-Easton MSA, PA-NJ	Y	47400 FQ	59200 MW	76970 TQ	USBLS	5/15
	Montgomery County-Bucks County-Chester County PMSA, PA	Y	62700 FQ	83200 MW	91810 TQ	USBLS	5/15
	Philadelphia PMSA, PA	Y	36500 FQ	48600 MW	82540 TQ	USBLS	5/15
	Pittsburgh MSA, PA	Y	41370 FQ	49400 MW	69400 TQ	USBLS	5/15
	Rhode Island	Y	67480 FQ	72120 MW	76770 TQ	USBLS	5/15
	Providence-Warwick MSA, RI-MA	Y	68200 FQ	73570 MW	78930 TQ	USBLS	5/15
	South Carolina	Y	32090 FQ	41780 MW	54910 TQ	USBLS	5/15
	Columbia MSA, SC	Y	51200 FQ	55490 MW	59780 TQ	USBLS	5/15
	Greenville-Anderson-Mauldin MSA, SC	Y	28400 FQ	34890 MW	50930 TQ	USBLS	5/15
	South Dakota	Y	28450 FQ	33910 MW	45680 TQ	USBLS	5/15
	Sioux Falls MSA, SD	Y	32940 FQ	39430 MW	56410 TQ	USBLS	5/15
	Tennessee	Y	35000 FQ	40750 MW	49500 TQ	USBLS	5/15
	Knoxville MSA, TN	Y	34840 FQ	38630 MW	45240 TQ	USBLS	5/15
	Memphis MSA, TN-MS-AR	Y	35360 FQ	40130 MW	46260 TQ	USBLS	5/15
	Nashville-Davidson–Murfreesboro–Franklin MSA, TN	Y	35680 FQ	45050 MW	57670 TQ	USBLS	5/15
	Texas	Y	30470 FQ	36510 MW	46620 TQ	USBLS	5/15
	Austin-Round Rock MSA, TX	Y	30100 FQ	34840 MW	39270 TQ	USBLS	5/15
	Dallas-Plano-Irving PMSA, TX	Y	29330 FQ	34860 MW	39670 TQ	USBLS	5/15
	Fort Worth-Arlington PMSA, TX	Y	27310 FQ	31160 MW	37910 TQ	USBLS	5/15
	Houston-The Woodlands-Sugar Land MSA, TX	Y	33600 FQ	39640 MW	49250 TQ	USBLS	5/15
	San Antonio-New Braunfels MSA, TX	Y	26550 FQ	30020 MW	35150 TQ	USBLS	5/15
	Utah	Y	35030 FQ	41810 MW	53360 TQ	USBLS	5/15
	Ogden-Clearfield MSA, UT	Y	34450 FQ	40540 MW	48510 TQ	USBLS	5/15
	Provo-Orem MSA, UT	Y	34220 FQ	37620 MW	49360 TQ	USBLS	5/15
	Salt Lake City MSA, UT	Y	36540 FQ	47700 MW	58010 TQ	USBLS	5/15
	Vermont	Y	35490 FQ	40340 MW	47870 TQ	USBLS	5/15
	Virginia	Y	36490 FQ	44790 MW	53680 TQ	USBLS	5/15
	Richmond MSA, VA	Y	36780 FQ	45490 MW	55490 TQ	USBLS	5/15
	Virginia Beach-Norfolk-Newport News MSA, VA-NC	Y	37360 FQ	43040 MW	48460 TQ	USBLS	5/15
	Washington	H	30.66 FQ	40.73 MW	45.04 TQ	WABLS	3/16
	Seattle-Bellevue-Everett PMSA, WA	H	39.94 FQ	43.10 MW	46.26 TQ	WABLS	3/16
	Tacoma-Lakewood PMSA, WA	H	34.84 FQ	40.68 MW	44.92 TQ	WABLS	3/16
	West Virginia	Y	39550 FQ	45820 MW	61400 TQ	USBLS	5/15
	Huntington-Ashland MSA, WV-KY-OH	Y	43000 FQ	53680 MW	62190 TQ	USBLS	5/15
	Wisconsin	Y	55590 FQ	67600 MW	74760 TQ	USBLS	5/15
	Madison MSA, WI	Y	50640 FQ	68780 MW	75160 TQ	USBLS	5/15
	Milwaukee-Waukesha-West Allis MSA, WI	Y	64750 FQ	70090 MW	75440 TQ	USBLS	5/15
	Wyoming	Y	31460 FQ	39610 MW	56610 TQ	USBLS	5/15
	Puerto Rico	Y	16940 FQ	18480 MW	21020 TQ	USBLS	5/15
	San Juan-Carolina-Caguas MSA, PR	Y	17200 FQ	18920 MW	21900 TQ	USBLS	5/15

AE	Average entry wage	AWR	Average wage range	H	Hourly	LR	Low end range	MTC	Median total compensation	TCC	Total cash compensation
AEX	Average experienced wage	B	Biweekly	HI	Highest wage paid	M	Monthly	MW	Median wage paid	TQ	Third quartile wage
ATC	Average total compensation	D	Daily	HR	High end range	MCC	Median cash compensation	MWR	Median wage range	W	Weekly
AW	Average wage paid	FQ	First quartile wage	LO	Lowest wage paid	ME	Median entry wage	S	See annotated source	Y	Yearly

Occupation/Type/Industry	Location	Per	Low	Mid	High	Source	Date
Structural Iron and Steel Worker	Guam	Y	26460 FQ	28350 MW	30240 TQ	USBLS	5/15
Structural Metal Fabricator and Fitter							
	Alabama	Y	24831 AE	37170 AW	43339 AEX	ALBLS	6/16
	Birmingham-Hoover MSA, AL	Y	25037 AE	34569 AW	39340 AEX	ALBLS	6/16
	Alaska	Y	29870 FQ	37310 MW	49160 TQ	USBLS	5/15
	Arizona	Y	26630 FQ	31850 MW	37120 TQ	USBLS	5/15
	Phoenix-Mesa-Scottsdale MSA, AZ	Y	26570 FQ	31740 MW	37070 TQ	USBLS	5/15
	Tucson MSA, AZ	Y	25110 FQ	29810 MW	35150 TQ	USBLS	5/15
	Arkansas	Y	26050 FQ	31880 MW	39670 TQ	USBLS	5/15
	Little Rock-North Little Rock-Conway MSA, AR	Y	25300 FQ	30450 MW	42710 TQ	USBLS	5/15
	California	H	14.32 FQ	18.57 MW	24.74 TQ	CABLS	1/16-3/16
	Anaheim-Santa Ana-Irvine PMSA, CA	H	14.30 FQ	17.89 MW	23.14 TQ	CABLS	1/16-3/16
	Los Angeles-Long Beach-Glendale PMSA, CA	H	14.91 FQ	19.95 MW	26.94 TQ	CABLS	1/16-3/16
	Oakland-Hayward-Berkeley PMSA, CA	H	16.96 FQ	20.55 MW	24.50 TQ	CABLS	1/16-3/16
	Riverside-San Bernardino-Ontario MSA, CA	H	11.88 FQ	15.77 MW	18.26 TQ	CABLS	1/16-3/16
	Sacramento–Roseville–Arden-Arcade MSA, CA	H	15.09 FQ	21.17 MW	27.20 TQ	CABLS	1/16-3/16
	San Diego-Carlsbad MSA, CA	H	13.44 FQ	19.82 MW	26.49 TQ	CABLS	1/16-3/16
	Colorado	Y	30820 FQ	37680 MW	46750 TQ	USBLS	5/15
	Denver-Aurora-Lakewood MSA, CO	Y	29500 FQ	38500 MW	50590 TQ	USBLS	5/15
	Connecticut	Y		49782 MW		CTBLS	1/16-3/16
	Bridgeport-Stamford-Norwalk MSA, CT	Y	42500 FQ	45760 MW	49010 TQ	USBLS	5/15
	Hartford-West Hartford-East Hartford MSA, CT	Y	42950 FQ	51980 MW	59750 TQ	USBLS	5/15
	Delaware	Y	33110 FQ	39430 MW	47110 TQ	USBLS	5/15
	Wilmington PMSA, DE-MD-NJ	Y	37920 FQ	44060 MW	49240 TQ	USBLS	5/15
	Washington-Arlington-Alexandria PMSA, DC-VA-MD-WV	Y	29830 FQ	36740 MW	46390 TQ	USBLS	5/15
	Florida	H	12.91 AE	17.87 MW	21.00 AEX	FLBLS	7/16-9/16
	Fort Lauderdale-Pompano Beach-Deerfield Beach PMSA, FL	H	14.94 AE	18.47 MW	20.78 AEX	FLBLS	7/16-9/16
	Miami-Miami Beach-Kendall PMSA, FL	H	10.48 AE	15.27 MW	19.92 AEX	FLBLS	7/16-9/16
	Orlando-Kissimmee-Sanford MSA, FL	H	13.34 AE	16.73 MW	21.19 AEX	FLBLS	7/16-9/16
	Tampa-St. Petersburg-Clearwater MSA, FL	H	13.37 AE	17.45 MW	20.88 AEX	FLBLS	7/16-9/16
	Georgia	Y	27920 FQ	34020 MW	40540 TQ	USBLS	5/15
	Atlanta-Sandy Springs-Roswell MSA, GA	Y	28380 FQ	34340 MW	42370 TQ	USBLS	5/15
	Augusta-Richmond County MSA, GA-SC	Y	33380 FQ	38060 MW	46860 TQ	USBLS	5/15
	Idaho	Y	28460 FQ	34500 MW	43360 TQ	USBLS	5/15
	Boise City MSA, ID	Y	28040 FQ	33670 MW	42300 TQ	USBLS	5/15
	Illinois	Y	32120 FQ	37500 MW	46400 TQ	USBLS	5/15
	Chicago-Naperville-Arlington Heights PMSA, IL	Y	32140 FQ	37550 MW	46320 TQ	USBLS	5/15
	Lake County-Kenosha County PMSA, IL-WI	Y	34060 FQ	40450 MW	47010 TQ	USBLS	5/15
	Indiana	Y	31440 FQ	36300 MW	43370 TQ	USBLS	5/15
	Gary PMSA, IN	Y	33580 FQ	39100 MW	46660 TQ	USBLS	5/15
	Indianapolis-Carmel-Anderson MSA, IN	Y	31870 FQ	36670 MW	43810 TQ	USBLS	5/15
	Iowa	Y	26610 FQ	33200 MW	39730 TQ	USBLS	5/15
	Des Moines-West Des Moines MSA, IA	Y	23210 FQ	28570 MW	35620 TQ	USBLS	5/15
	Kansas	Y	31610 FQ	36800 MW	54260 TQ	USBLS	5/15
	Wichita MSA, KS	Y	34350 FQ	38640 MW	71390 TQ	USBLS	5/15
	Kentucky	Y	27190 FQ	32890 MW	39570 TQ	USBLS	5/15

AE	Average entry wage	AWR	Average wage range	H	Hourly	LR	Low end range	MTC	Median total compensation	TCC	Total cash compensation
AEX	Average experienced wage	B	Biweekly	HI	Highest wage paid	M	Monthly	MW	Median wage paid	TQ	Third quartile wage
ATC	Average total compensation	D	Daily	HR	High end range	MCC	Median cash compensation	MWR	Median wage range	W	Weekly
AW	Average wage paid	FQ	First quartile wage	LO	Lowest wage paid	ME	Median entry wage	S	See annotated source	Y	Yearly

Occupation/Type/Industry	Location	Per	Low	Mid	High	Source	Date
Structural Metal Fabricator and Fitter	Louisville-Jefferson County MSA, KY-IN	Y	32330 FQ	38460 MW	65370 TQ	USBLS	5/15
	Louisiana	Y	35520 FQ	42190 MW	48790 TQ	USBLS	5/15
	Baton Rouge MSA, LA	Y	37040 FQ	43050 MW	48700 TQ	USBLS	5/15
	New Orleans-Metairie MSA, LA	Y	36040 FQ	42740 MW	47990 TQ	USBLS	5/15
	Maine	Y	45670 FQ	53020 MW	58060 TQ	USBLS	5/15
	Maryland	Y	31182 AE	42449 MW	48082 AEX	MDBLS	4/16
	Baltimore-Columbia-Towson MSA, MD	Y	34480 FQ	43150 MW	53360 TQ	USBLS	5/15
	Salisbury MSA, MD-DE	Y	30850 FQ	35070 MW	39070 TQ	USBLS	5/15
	Massachusetts	Y	31350 FQ	41050 MW	54400 TQ	USBLS	5/15
	Boston-Cambridge-Newton NECTA, MA	Y	31400 FQ	45910 MW	57290 TQ	USBLS	5/15
	Worcester MSA, MA-CT	Y	32120 FQ	39810 MW	48750 TQ	USBLS	5/15
	Michigan	Y	28450 FQ	34880 MW	41770 TQ	USBLS	5/15
	Detroit-Dearborn-Livonia PMSA, MI	Y	30360 FQ	40150 MW	48660 TQ	USBLS	5/15
	Grand Rapids-Wyoming MSA, MI	Y	30030 FQ	34890 MW	39770 TQ	USBLS	5/15
	Minnesota	Y	33289 FQ	41885 MW	50430 TQ	MNBLS	1/16-3/16
	Minneapolis-St. Paul-Bloomington MSA, MN-WI	Y	33664 FQ	43039 MW	53093 TQ	MNBLS	1/16-3/16
	Mississippi	Y	26080 FQ	32180 MW	44450 TQ	USBLS	5/15
	Jackson MSA, MS	Y	24820 FQ	36350 MW	44720 TQ	USBLS	5/15
	Missouri	Y	34000 FQ	43940 MW	55510 TQ	USBLS	5/15
	Kansas City MSA, MO-KS	Y	37000 FQ	52270 MW	58010 TQ	USBLS	5/15
	St. Louis MSA, MO-IL	Y	34650 FQ	41590 MW	47880 TQ	USBLS	5/15
	Montana	Y	34200 FQ	39520 MW	44810 TQ	USBLS	5/15
	Nebraska	Y	29020 FQ	35355 MW	44655 TQ	NEBLS	7/16-9/16
	Omaha-Council Bluffs MSA, NE-IA	Y	31925 FQ	38345 MW	68550 TQ	NEBLS	7/16-9/16
	Nevada	Y	32840 FQ	36160 MW	39990 TQ	USBLS	5/15
	Las Vegas-Henderson-Paradise MSA, NV	Y	33130 FQ	37060 MW	42570 TQ	USBLS	5/15
	New Hampshire	H	15.51 AE	22.07 MW	25.19 AEX	NHBLS	6/16
	Nashua NECTA, NH-MA	Y	42920 FQ	49690 MW	57460 TQ	USBLS	5/15
	New Jersey	Y	34050 FQ	44120 MW	53020 TQ	USBLS	5/15
	Camden PMSA, NJ	Y	22650 FQ	32450 MW	49520 TQ	USBLS	5/15
	Newark PMSA, NJ-PA	Y	33110 FQ	41980 MW	47610 TQ	USBLS	5/15
	Trenton MSA, NJ	Y	39470 FQ	51280 MW	56880 TQ	USBLS	5/15
	New Mexico	Y	25260 FQ	34520 MW	45970 TQ	USBLS	5/15
	Albuquerque MSA, NM	Y	24100 FQ	33070 MW	46690 TQ	USBLS	5/15
	New York	Y	31100 AE	44240 MW	56230 AEX	NYBLS	1/16-3/16
	Buffalo-Cheektowaga-Niagara Falls MSA, NY	Y	39940 FQ	43740 MW	47560 TQ	USBLS	5/15
	Nassau County-Suffolk County PMSA, NY	Y	36080 FQ	54370 MW	68130 TQ	USBLS	5/15
	New York-Jersey City-White Plains PMSA, NY-NJ	Y	34840 FQ	43500 MW	55380 TQ	USBLS	5/15
	Rochester MSA, NY	Y	33800 FQ	42150 MW	50420 TQ	USBLS	5/15
	North Carolina	Y	28740 FQ	35510 MW	43030 TQ	USBLS	5/15
	Charlotte-Concord-Gastonia MSA, NC-SC	Y	29460 FQ	36190 MW	44740 TQ	USBLS	5/15
	Raleigh MSA, NC	Y	32330 FQ	34920 MW	37520 TQ	USBLS	5/15
	North Dakota	Y	31690 FQ	38880 MW	47530 TQ	USBLS	5/15
	Fargo MSA, ND-MN	Y	32070 FQ	38750 MW	47430 TQ	USBLS	5/15
	Ohio	Y	27310 FQ	34210 MW	41590 TQ	USBLS	5/15
	Cincinnati MSA, OH-KY-IN	Y	24760 FQ	33900 MW	40910 TQ	USBLS	5/15
	Cleveland-Elyria MSA, OH	Y	26880 FQ	33090 MW	41410 TQ	USBLS	5/15
	Columbus MSA, OH	Y	28610 FQ	34710 MW	40460 TQ	USBLS	5/15
	Oklahoma	Y	27770 FQ	34670 MW	42950 TQ	USBLS	5/15
	Oklahoma City MSA, OK	Y	27520 FQ	33210 MW	37820 TQ	USBLS	5/15
	Tulsa MSA, OK	Y	29190 FQ	36340 MW	45680 TQ	USBLS	5/15
	Oregon	H	16.62 FQ	20.24 MW	24.46 TQ	ORBLS	2016
	Eugene MSA, OR	Y	31810 FQ	36750 MW	45260 TQ	USBLS	5/15
	Portland-Vancouver-Hillsboro MSA, OR-WA	Y	39550 FQ	47050 MW	55510 TQ	USBLS	5/15
	Pennsylvania	Y	33220 FQ	38820 MW	46730 TQ	USBLS	5/15
	Allentown-Bethlehem-Easton MSA, PA-NJ	Y	33020 FQ	37230 MW	43310 TQ	USBLS	5/15

AE	Average entry wage	**AWR**	Average wage range	**H**	Hourly
AEX	Average experienced wage	**B**	Biweekly	**HI**	Highest wage paid
ATC	Average total compensation	**D**	Daily	**HR**	High end range
AW	Average wage paid	**FQ**	First quartile wage	**LO**	Lowest wage paid

LR	Low end range	**MTC**	Median total compensation
M	Monthly	**MW**	Median wage paid
MCC	Median cash compensation	**MWR**	Median wage range
ME	Median entry wage	**S**	See annotated source

TCC	Total cash compensation
TQ	Third quartile wage
W	Weekly
Y	Yearly

Occupation/Type/Industry	Location	Per	Low	Mid	High	Source	Date
Structural Metal Fabricator and Fitter	Harrisburg-Carlisle MSA, PA	Y	29810 FQ	37810 MW	45770 TQ	USBLS	5/15
	Montgomery County-Bucks County-Chester County PMSA, PA	Y	35760 FQ	42360 MW	49970 TQ	USBLS	5/15
	Philadelphia PMSA, PA	Y	33120 FQ	41540 MW	48530 TQ	USBLS	5/15
	Pittsburgh MSA, PA	Y	30770 FQ	35740 MW	42090 TQ	USBLS	5/15
	Rhode Island	Y	37320 FQ	45850 MW	55740 TQ	USBLS	5/15
	Providence-Warwick MSA, RI-MA	Y	32090 FQ	41350 MW	51290 TQ	USBLS	5/15
	South Carolina	Y	27680 FQ	36510 MW	46520 TQ	USBLS	5/15
	Charleston-North Charleston MSA, SC	Y	33030 FQ	37280 MW	43990 TQ	USBLS	5/15
	Columbia MSA, SC	Y	28820 FQ	34690 MW	41020 TQ	USBLS	5/15
	Greenville-Anderson-Mauldin MSA, SC	Y	23970 FQ	32950 MW	55550 TQ	USBLS	5/15
	South Dakota	Y	28270 FQ	31720 MW	36620 TQ	USBLS	5/15
	Sioux Falls MSA, SD	Y	28430 FQ	31810 MW	36720 TQ	USBLS	5/15
	Tennessee	Y	26080 FQ	31930 MW	38700 TQ	USBLS	5/15
	Knoxville MSA, TN	Y	23030 FQ	27270 MW	32870 TQ	USBLS	5/15
	Memphis MSA, TN-MS-AR	Y	27960 FQ	32350 MW	37170 TQ	USBLS	5/15
	Nashville-Davidson–Murfreesboro–Franklin MSA, TN	Y	26670 FQ	30730 MW	37280 TQ	USBLS	5/15
	Texas	Y	28850 FQ	35590 MW	44160 TQ	USBLS	5/15
	Austin-Round Rock MSA, TX	Y	29260 FQ	34500 MW	40870 TQ	USBLS	5/15
	Dallas-Plano-Irving PMSA, TX	Y	27630 FQ	32350 MW	38730 TQ	USBLS	5/15
	Fort Worth-Arlington PMSA, TX	Y	26890 FQ	32860 MW	38630 TQ	USBLS	5/15
	Houston-The Woodlands-Sugar Land MSA, TX	Y	32570 FQ	39300 MW	48670 TQ	USBLS	5/15
	San Antonio-New Braunfels MSA, TX	Y	26550 FQ	30730 MW	39080 TQ	USBLS	5/15
	Utah	Y	31950 FQ	36750 MW	43080 TQ	USBLS	5/15
	Ogden-Clearfield MSA, UT	Y	28910 FQ	33680 MW	38490 TQ	USBLS	5/15
	Provo-Orem MSA, UT	Y	33660 FQ	37330 MW	42030 TQ	USBLS	5/15
	Salt Lake City MSA, UT	Y	35480 FQ	41470 MW	47810 TQ	USBLS	5/15
	Vermont	Y	28590 FQ	33180 MW	42740 TQ	USBLS	5/15
	Virginia	Y	26910 FQ	34710 MW	43180 TQ	USBLS	5/15
	Richmond MSA, VA	Y	26960 FQ	36090 MW	43840 TQ	USBLS	5/15
	Virginia Beach-Norfolk-Newport News MSA, VA-NC	Y	23970 FQ	32150 MW	43510 TQ	USBLS	5/15
	Washington	H	17.17 FQ	20.82 MW	26.60 TQ	WABLS	3/16
	Seattle-Bellevue-Everett PMSA, WA	H	16.88 FQ	19.47 MW	26.12 TQ	WABLS	3/16
	Tacoma-Lakewood PMSA, WA	H	14.84 FQ	20.21 MW	25.52 TQ	WABLS	3/16
	West Virginia	Y	29630 FQ	34710 MW	39510 TQ	USBLS	5/15
	Huntington-Ashland MSA, WV-KY-OH	Y	29720 FQ	34150 MW	38180 TQ	USBLS	5/15
	Wisconsin	Y	33340 FQ	40030 MW	47330 TQ	USBLS	5/15
	Madison MSA, WI	Y	31940 FQ	36680 MW	42570 TQ	USBLS	5/15
	Milwaukee-Waukesha-West Allis MSA, WI	Y	35470 FQ	41480 MW	48210 TQ	USBLS	5/15
	Wyoming	Y	34920 FQ	39670 MW	49970 TQ	USBLS	5/15
	Cheyenne MSA, WY	Y	30020 FQ	34260 MW	37290 TQ	USBLS	5/15
	Puerto Rico	Y	17250 FQ	18930 MW	23130 TQ	USBLS	5/15
	San Juan-Carolina-Caguas MSA, PR	Y	17240 FQ	18910 MW	22840 TQ	USBLS	5/15
	Guam	Y	26970 FQ	29150 MW	31340 TQ	USBLS	5/15
Student-Services Coordinator							
Baccalaureate Institution	United States	Y		35200 MW		CHE01	2015-2016
Master's Institution	United States	Y		34405 MW		CHE01	2015-2016
Research University	United States	Y		37489 MW		CHE01	2015-2016
Study-Abroad Advisor							
Baccalaureate Institution	United States	Y		47279 MW		CHE02	2015-2016
Master's Institution	United States	Y		43628 MW		CHE02	2015-2016
Research University	United States	Y		44151 MW		CHE02	2015-2016
Stunt Performer							
Film	United States	D	933 LO			AFTRA2	7/1/16-6/30/17

AE	Average entry wage	AWR	Average wage range	H	Hourly	LR	Low end range	MTC	Median total compensation	TCC	Total cash compensation
AEX	Average experienced wage	B	Biweekly	HI	Highest wage paid	M	Monthly	MW	Median wage paid	TQ	Third quartile wage
ATC	Average total compensation	D	Daily	HR	High end range	MCC	Median cash compensation	MWR	Median wage range	W	Weekly
AW	Average wage paid	FQ	First quartile wage	LO	Lowest wage paid	ME	Median entry wage	S	See annotated source	Y	Yearly

Occupation/Type/Industry	Location	Per	Low	Mid	High	Source	Date
Stunt Performer							
Television	United States	D	933 LO			AFTRA1	7/1/16-6/30/17
Substance Abuse and Behavioral							
Disorder Counselor	Alabama	Y	27960 AE	42220 AW	49356 AEX	ALBLS	6/16
	Birmingham-Hoover MSA, AL	Y	37929 AE	53423 AW	61170 AEX	ALBLS	6/16
	Alaska	Y	41130 FQ	48160 MW	59430 TQ	USBLS	5/15
	Anchorage MSA, AK	Y	37520 FQ	43730 MW	48910 TQ	USBLS	5/15
	Arizona	Y	28710 FQ	38260 MW	47730 TQ	USBLS	5/15
	Phoenix-Mesa-Scottsdale MSA, AZ	Y	29600 FQ	40700 MW	49000 TQ	USBLS	5/15
	Tucson MSA, AZ	Y	27560 FQ	32770 MW	44020 TQ	USBLS	5/15
	Arkansas	Y	26460 FQ	34300 MW	43320 TQ	USBLS	5/15
	Little Rock-North Little Rock-Conway MSA, AR	Y	23340 FQ	31380 MW	40360 TQ	USBLS	5/15
	California	H	14.37 FQ	18.10 MW	23.30 TQ	CABLS	1/16-3/16
	Anaheim-Santa Ana-Irvine PMSA, CA	H	10.62 FQ	14.14 MW	18.08 TQ	CABLS	1/16-3/16
	Los Angeles-Long Beach-Glendale PMSA, CA	H	15.51 FQ	17.80 MW	22.04 TQ	CABLS	1/16-3/16
	Oakland-Hayward-Berkeley PMSA, CA	H	16.69 FQ	19.76 MW	27.04 TQ	CABLS	1/16-3/16
	Riverside-San Bernardino-Ontario MSA, CA	H	14.43 FQ	19.63 MW	26.23 TQ	CABLS	1/16-3/16
	Sacramento–Roseville–Arden-Arcade MSA, CA	H	12.84 FQ	15.42 MW	20.27 TQ	CABLS	1/16-3/16
	San Diego-Carlsbad MSA, CA	H	14.46 FQ	18.33 MW	22.25 TQ	CABLS	1/16-3/16
	San Francisco-Redwood City-South San Francisco PMSA, CA	H	15.86 FQ	19.98 MW	22.93 TQ	CABLS	1/16-3/16
	Colorado	Y	31740 FQ	41230 MW	59070 TQ	USBLS	5/15
	Denver-Aurora-Lakewood MSA, CO	Y	33240 FQ	45570 MW	62430 TQ	USBLS	5/15
	Connecticut	Y		46890 MW		CTBLS	1/16-3/16
	Bridgeport-Stamford-Norwalk MSA, CT	Y	34490 FQ	41710 MW	53240 TQ	USBLS	5/15
	Hartford-West Hartford-East Hartford MSA, CT	Y	37380 FQ	46780 MW	57350 TQ	USBLS	5/15
	Delaware	Y	33420 FQ	38040 MW	46950 TQ	USBLS	5/15
	Wilmington PMSA, DE-MD-NJ	Y	34340 FQ	38840 MW	47420 TQ	USBLS	5/15
	District of Columbia	Y	36760 FQ	46090 MW	60220 TQ	USBLS	5/15
	Washington-Arlington-Alexandria PMSA, DC-VA-MD-WV	Y	42950 FQ	55860 MW	70830 TQ	USBLS	5/15
	Florida	H	13.82 AE	20.80 MW	26.40 AEX	FLBLS	7/16-9/16
	Fort Lauderdale-Pompano Beach-Deerfield Beach PMSA, FL	H	13.77 AE	22.83 MW	28.72 AEX	FLBLS	7/16-9/16
	Miami-Miami Beach-Kendall PMSA, FL	H	15.69 AE	29.41 MW	32.77 AEX	FLBLS	7/16-9/16
	Orlando-Kissimmee-Sanford MSA, FL	H	14.01 AE	19.21 MW	25.27 AEX	FLBLS	7/16-9/16
	Tampa-St. Petersburg-Clearwater MSA, FL	H	15.84 AE	25.07 MW	29.18 AEX	FLBLS	7/16-9/16
	Georgia	Y	31700 FQ	39240 MW	50120 TQ	USBLS	5/15
	Atlanta-Sandy Springs-Roswell MSA, GA	Y	33080 FQ	40710 MW	49330 TQ	USBLS	5/15
	Hawaii	Y	35070 FQ	41580 MW	48420 TQ	USBLS	5/15
	Urban Honolulu MSA, HI	Y	32780 FQ	39010 MW	50190 TQ	USBLS	5/15
	Idaho	Y	35880 FQ	42120 MW	48920 TQ	USBLS	5/15
	Boise City MSA, ID	Y	34200 FQ	41020 MW	46700 TQ	USBLS	5/15
	Illinois	Y	28570 FQ	34450 MW	40980 TQ	USBLS	5/15
	Chicago-Naperville-Arlington Heights PMSA, IL	Y	27380 FQ	32570 MW	38830 TQ	USBLS	5/15
	Lake County-Kenosha County PMSA, IL-WI	Y	32300 FQ	36780 MW	43650 TQ	USBLS	5/15
	Indiana	Y	29870 FQ	36330 MW	44880 TQ	USBLS	5/15
	Gary PMSA, IN	Y	28210 FQ	31700 MW	43410 TQ	USBLS	5/15
	Indianapolis-Carmel-Anderson MSA, IN	Y	32550 FQ	37060 MW	44870 TQ	USBLS	5/15
	Iowa	Y	28620 FQ	37660 MW	52610 TQ	USBLS	5/15

AE	Average entry wage	**AWR**	Average wage range	**H**	Hourly
AEX	Average experienced wage	**B**	Biweekly	**HI**	Highest wage paid
ATC	Average total compensation	**D**	Daily	**HR**	High end range
AW	Average wage paid	**FQ**	First quartile wage	**LO**	Lowest wage paid

LR	Low end range	**MTC**	Median total compensation	**TCC**	Total cash compensation
M	Monthly	**MW**	Median wage paid	**TQ**	Third quartile wage
MCC	Median cash compensation	**MWR**	Median wage range	**W**	Weekly
ME	Median entry wage	**S**	See annotated source	**Y**	Yearly

Occupation/Type/Industry	Location	Per	Low	Mid	High	Source	Date
Substance Abuse and Behavioral Disorder Counselor							
	Des Moines-West Des Moines MSA, IA	Y	30450 FQ	41830 MW	55070 TQ	USBLS	5/15
	Kansas	Y	28910 FQ	35520 MW	45050 TQ	USBLS	5/15
	Wichita MSA, KS	Y	26310 FQ	30550 MW	41510 TQ	USBLS	5/15
	Kentucky	Y	28280 FQ	34420 MW	42640 TQ	USBLS	5/15
	Louisville-Jefferson County MSA, KY-IN	Y	26230 FQ	29930 MW	41050 TQ	USBLS	5/15
	Louisiana	Y	24640 FQ	34210 MW	44000 TQ	USBLS	5/15
	Baton Rouge MSA, LA	Y	33040 FQ	37000 MW	50660 TQ	USBLS	5/15
	New Orleans-Metairie MSA, LA	Y	21500 FQ	31490 MW	40750 TQ	USBLS	5/15
	Maine	Y	34670 FQ	42840 MW	54690 TQ	USBLS	5/15
	Portland-South Portland MSA, ME	Y	39360 FQ	43510 MW	47300 TQ	USBLS	5/15
	Maryland	Y	31583 AE	44327 MW	50699 AEX	MDBLS	4/16
	Baltimore-Columbia-Towson MSA, MD	Y	34770 FQ	41970 MW	49520 TQ	USBLS	5/15
	Salisbury MSA, MD-DE	Y	31470 FQ	37930 MW	47320 TQ	USBLS	5/15
	Massachusetts	Y	30670 FQ	39570 MW	53540 TQ	USBLS	5/15
	Boston-Cambridge-Newton NECTA, MA	Y	30950 FQ	38780 MW	51220 TQ	USBLS	5/15
	Worcester MSA, MA-CT	Y	38720 FQ	53200 MW	61120 TQ	USBLS	5/15
	Michigan	Y	30080 FQ	37420 MW	49040 TQ	USBLS	5/15
	Detroit-Dearborn-Livonia PMSA, MI	Y	28360 FQ	33420 MW	38760 TQ	USBLS	5/15
	Grand Rapids-Wyoming MSA, MI	Y	43020 FQ	51040 MW	59430 TQ	USBLS	5/15
	Minnesota	Y	40705 FQ	45826 MW	51108 TQ	MNBLS	1/16-3/16
	Minneapolis-St. Paul-Bloomington MSA, MN-WI	Y	40816 FQ	45826 MW	51088 TQ	MNBLS	1/16-3/16
	Mississippi	Y	25220 FQ	27860 MW	32100 TQ	USBLS	5/15
	Jackson MSA, MS	Y	25250 FQ	28320 MW	32710 TQ	USBLS	5/15
	Missouri	Y	29020 FQ	34790 MW	40260 TQ	USBLS	5/15
	Kansas City MSA, MO-KS	Y	28460 FQ	33250 MW	41400 TQ	USBLS	5/15
	St. Louis MSA, MO-IL	Y	31450 FQ	37700 MW	45860 TQ	USBLS	5/15
	Montana	Y	23860 FQ	38550 MW	45900 TQ	USBLS	5/15
	Billings MSA, MT	Y	41150 FQ	45240 MW	49320 TQ	USBLS	5/15
	Omaha-Council Bluffs MSA, NE-IA	Y	32880 FQ	38185 MW	46490 TQ	NEBLS	7/16-9/16
	Nevada	Y	36320 FQ	44400 MW	54900 TQ	USBLS	5/15
	Las Vegas-Henderson-Paradise MSA, NV	Y	36060 FQ	43660 MW	52810 TQ	USBLS	5/15
	New Hampshire	H	19.73 AE	23.72 MW	31.34 AEX	NHBLS	6/16
	New Jersey	Y	37880 FQ	46810 MW	59410 TQ	USBLS	5/15
	Camden PMSA, NJ	Y	35010 FQ	42950 MW	57110 TQ	USBLS	5/15
	Newark PMSA, NJ-PA	Per	39390 FQ	47290 MW	57530 TQ	USBLS	5/15
	Trenton MSA, NJ	Y	39560 FQ	50400 MW	64720 TQ	USBLS	5/15
	New Mexico	Y	34410 FQ	42710 MW	55060 TQ	USBLS	5/15
	New York	Y	32630 AE	48250 MW	58160 AEX	NYBLS	1/16-3/16
	Buffalo-Cheektowaga-Niagara Falls MSA, NY	Y	31840 FQ	40780 MW	49050 TQ	USBLS	5/15
	Nassau County-Suffolk County PMSA, NY	Y	40280 FQ	49570 MW	62040 TQ	USBLS	5/15
	New York-Jersey City-White Plains PMSA, NY-NJ	Y	39670 FQ	51140 MW	61570 TQ	USBLS	5/15
	Rochester MSA, NY	Y	34480 FQ	39550 MW	48920 TQ	USBLS	5/15
	Watertown-Fort Drum MSA, NY	Y	29610 FQ	36310 MW	49980 TQ	USBLS	5/15
	North Carolina	Y	35770 FQ	42720 MW	50210 TQ	USBLS	5/15
	Charlotte-Concord-Gastonia MSA, NC-SC	Y	34360 FQ	41260 MW	50320 TQ	USBLS	5/15
	Raleigh MSA, NC	Y	40860 FQ	44660 MW	48400 TQ	USBLS	5/15
	North Dakota	Y	46580 FQ	51200 MW	56970 TQ	USBLS	5/15
	Fargo MSA, ND-MN	Y	46200 FQ	50920 MW	58510 TQ	USBLS	5/15
	Ohio	Y	33600 FQ	40890 MW	49370 TQ	USBLS	5/15
	Cincinnati MSA, OH-KY-IN	Y	31320 FQ	38680 MW	48810 TQ	USBLS	5/15
	Cleveland-Elyria MSA, OH	Y	34180 FQ	40930 MW	53080 TQ	USBLS	5/15
	Columbus MSA, OH	Y	38620 FQ	45610 MW	59700 TQ	USBLS	5/15
	Oklahoma	Y	26770 FQ	39910 MW	54920 TQ	USBLS	5/15
	Oklahoma City MSA, OK	Y	31270 FQ	38570 MW	49020 TQ	USBLS	5/15
	Tulsa MSA, OK	Y	19950 FQ	42510 MW	61060 TQ	USBLS	5/15

AE Average entry wage	**AWR** Average wage range	**H** Hourly	**LR** Low end range	**MTC** Median total compensation	**TCC** Total cash compensation
AEX Average experienced wage	**B** Biweekly	**HI** Highest wage paid	**M** Monthly	**MW** Median wage paid	**TQ** Third quartile wage
ATC Average total compensation	**D** Daily	**HR** High end range	**MCC** Median cash compensation	**MWR** Median wage range	**W** Weekly
AW Average wage paid	**FQ** First quartile wage	**LO** Lowest wage paid	**ME** Median entry wage	**S** See annotated source	**Y** Yearly

Occupation/Type/Industry	Location	Per	Low	Mid	High	Source	Date
Substance Abuse and Behavioral Disorder Counselor	Oregon	H	16.46 FQ	19.35 MW	26.16 TQ	ORBLS	2016
	Portland-Vancouver-Hillsboro MSA, OR-WA	Y	34570 FQ	41930 MW	58050 TQ	USBLS	5/15
	Pennsylvania	Y	32930 FQ	40850 MW	51470 TQ	USBLS	5/15
	Allentown-Bethlehem-Easton MSA, PA-NJ	Y	35440 FQ	44160 MW	55720 TQ	USBLS	5/15
	Harrisburg-Carlisle MSA, PA	Y	28980 FQ	37240 MW	53370 TQ	USBLS	5/15
	Montgomery County-Bucks County-Chester County PMSA, PA	Y	36050 FQ	43540 MW	52140 TQ	USBLS	5/15
	Philadelphia PMSA, PA	Y	36980 FQ	44630 MW	53800 TQ	USBLS	5/15
	Pittsburgh MSA, PA	Y	28720 FQ	34680 MW	43560 TQ	USBLS	5/15
	Rhode Island	Y	33390 FQ	37320 MW	45890 TQ	USBLS	5/15
	Providence-Warwick MSA, RI-MA	Y	28180 FQ	34530 MW	38730 TQ	USBLS	5/15
	South Carolina	Y	29530 FQ	36780 MW	45100 TQ	USBLS	5/15
	Charleston-North Charleston MSA, SC	Y	31160 FQ	36940 MW	44560 TQ	USBLS	5/15
	Columbia MSA, SC	Y	31300 FQ	37650 MW	46400 TQ	USBLS	5/15
	Greenville-Anderson-Mauldin MSA, SC	Y	33900 FQ	39760 MW	45990 TQ	USBLS	5/15
	South Dakota	Y	32370 FQ	37300 MW	44200 TQ	USBLS	5/15
	Sioux Falls MSA, SD	Y	31860 FQ	37330 MW	44550 TQ	USBLS	5/15
	Tennessee	Y	26460 FQ	34510 MW	46420 TQ	USBLS	5/15
	Knoxville MSA, TN	Y	22800 FQ	27810 MW	36870 TQ	USBLS	5/15
	Memphis MSA, TN-MS-AR	Y	35520 FQ	44900 MW	55450 TQ	USBLS	5/15
	Nashville-Davidson–Murfreesboro–Franklin MSA, TN	Y	31920 FQ	39160 MW	48630 TQ	USBLS	5/15
	Texas	Y	31610 FQ	37340 MW	46670 TQ	USBLS	5/15
	Austin-Round Rock MSA, TX	Y	30900 FQ	36530 MW	44430 TQ	USBLS	5/15
	Dallas-Plano-Irving PMSA, TX	Y	34980 FQ	43700 MW	50180 TQ	USBLS	5/15
	Fort Worth-Arlington PMSA, TX	Y	32740 FQ	38400 MW	47800 TQ	USBLS	5/15
	Houston-The Woodlands-Sugar Land MSA, TX	Y	32830 FQ	37560 MW	47050 TQ	USBLS	5/15
	San Antonio-New Braunfels MSA, TX	Y	31900 FQ	36960 MW	46550 TQ	USBLS	5/15
	Utah	Y	22740 FQ	36300 MW	46620 TQ	USBLS	5/15
	Ogden-Clearfield MSA, UT	Y	32300 FQ	36300 MW	40790 TQ	USBLS	5/15
	Provo-Orem MSA, UT	Y	39500 FQ	44820 MW	50210 TQ	USBLS	5/15
	Salt Lake City MSA, UT	Y	32200 FQ	40840 MW	49810 TQ	USBLS	5/15
	Vermont	Y	40060 FQ	50140 MW	58130 TQ	USBLS	5/15
	Burlington-South Burlington MSA, VT	Y	35890 FQ	44500 MW	55440 TQ	USBLS	5/15
	Virginia	Y	34210 FQ	41950 MW	58130 TQ	USBLS	5/15
	Richmond MSA, VA	Y	34650 FQ	39400 MW	48060 TQ	USBLS	5/15
	Virginia Beach-Norfolk-Newport News MSA, VA-NC	Y	35050 FQ	39380 MW	49240 TQ	USBLS	5/15
	Washington	H	14.58 FQ	18.48 MW	22.93 TQ	WABLS	3/16
	Seattle-Bellevue-Everett PMSA, WA	H	13.92 FQ	18.33 MW	22.65 TQ	WABLS	3/16
	Tacoma-Lakewood PMSA, WA	H	17.68 FQ	21.07 MW	23.82 TQ	WABLS	3/16
	West Virginia	Y	22640 FQ	28960 MW	35020 TQ	USBLS	5/15
	Huntington-Ashland MSA, WV-KY-OH	Y	28670 FQ	33330 MW	38090 TQ	USBLS	5/15
	Wisconsin	Y	33090 FQ	41850 MW	57290 TQ	USBLS	5/15
	Madison MSA, WI	Y	42120 FQ	50340 MW	83140 TQ	USBLS	5/15
	Milwaukee-Waukesha-West Allis MSA, WI	Y	31570 FQ	42010 MW	62830 TQ	USBLS	5/15
	Wyoming	Y	37660 FQ	45720 MW	58080 TQ	USBLS	5/15
	Puerto Rico	Y	19250 FQ	22680 MW	28500 TQ	USBLS	5/15
	San Juan-Carolina-Caguas MSA, PR	Y	18420 FQ	21520 MW	29500 TQ	USBLS	5/15
Substance Abuse Counselor Department of Corrections, State Government	Boulder, MT	H			21.45 HI	MTGOV	2016
Substitute Teacher	Alabama	Y	17461 AE	18011 AW	18297 AEX	ALBLS	6/16
	Birmingham-Hoover MSA, AL	Y	17543 AE	18062 AW	18317 AEX	ALBLS	6/16

AE Average entry wage	**AWR** Average wage range	**H** Hourly	**LR** Low end range	**MTC** Median total compensation	**TCC** Total cash compensation
AEX Average experienced wage	**B** Biweekly	**HI** Highest wage paid	**M** Monthly	**MW** Median wage paid	**TQ** Third quartile wage
ATC Average total compensation	**D** Daily	**HR** High end range	**MCC** Median cash compensation	**MWR** Median wage range	**W** Weekly
AW Average wage paid	**FQ** First quartile wage	**LO** Lowest wage paid	**ME** Median entry wage	**S** See annotated source	**Y** Yearly

Occupation/Type/Industry	Location	Per	Low	Mid	High	Source	Date
Substitute Teacher	Alaska	Y	33780 FQ	41380 MW	61230 TQ	USBLS	5/15
	Anchorage MSA, AK	Y	41040 FQ	45590 MW	50150 TQ	USBLS	5/15
	Arizona	Y	22430 FQ	25780 MW	29630 TQ	USBLS	5/15
	Phoenix-Mesa-Scottsdale MSA, AZ	Y	22970 FQ	26610 MW	29860 TQ	USBLS	5/15
	Tucson MSA, AZ	Y	22160 FQ	25230 MW	29350 TQ	USBLS	5/15
	Little Rock-North Little Rock-Conway MSA, AR	Y	18550 FQ	24290 MW	28000 TQ	USBLS	5/15
	California	H	16.28 FQ	18.44 MW	21.53 TQ	CABLS	1/16-3/16
	Anaheim-Santa Ana-Irvine PMSA, CA	H	15.90 FQ	17.31 MW	18.73 TQ	CABLS	1/16-3/16
	Los Angeles-Long Beach-Glendale PMSA, CA	H	16.79 FQ	19.80 MW	22.56 TQ	CABLS	1/16-3/16
	Oakland-Hayward-Berkeley PMSA, CA	H	17.50 FQ	20.36 MW	22.76 TQ	CABLS	1/16-3/16
	Riverside-San Bernardino-Ontario MSA, CA	H	16.87 FQ	19.34 MW	22.07 TQ	CABLS	1/16-3/16
	Sacramento–Roseville–Arden-Arcade MSA, CA	H	16.54 FQ	18.58 MW	21.61 TQ	CABLS	1/16-3/16
	San Diego-Carlsbad MSA, CA	H	16.33 FQ	17.65 MW	18.97 TQ	CABLS	1/16-3/16
	San Francisco-Redwood City-South San Francisco PMSA, CA	H	12.60 FQ	15.52 MW	19.66 TQ	CABLS	1/16-3/16
	Connecticut	Y		28913 MW		CTBLS	1/16-3/16
	Bridgeport-Stamford-Norwalk MSA, CT	Y	27710 FQ	31370 MW	36020 TQ	USBLS	5/15
	Hartford-West Hartford-East Hartford MSA, CT	Y	25030 FQ	28140 MW	31210 TQ	USBLS	5/15
	Delaware	Y	21580 FQ	24440 MW	29150 TQ	USBLS	5/15
	Wilmington PMSA, DE-MD-NJ	Y	22990 FQ	29020 MW	35340 TQ	USBLS	5/15
	District of Columbia	Y	21650 FQ	26430 MW	40530 TQ	USBLS	5/15
	Washington-Arlington-Alexandria PMSA, DC-VA-MD-WV	Y	25370 FQ	32590 MW	36600 TQ	USBLS	5/15
	Florida	H	8.93 AE	10.88 MW	13.42 AEX	FLBLS	7/16-9/16
	Fort Lauderdale-Pompano Beach-Deerfield Beach PMSA, FL	H	11.65 AE	15.16 MW	16.23 AEX	FLBLS	7/16-9/16
	Miami-Miami Beach-Kendall PMSA, FL	H	11.37 AE	13.53 MW	14.95 AEX	FLBLS	7/16-9/16
	Orlando-Kissimmee-Sanford MSA, FL	H	8.98 AE	10.47 MW	11.56 AEX	FLBLS	7/16-9/16
	Tampa-St. Petersburg-Clearwater MSA, FL	H	8.95 AE	9.23 MW	9.91 AEX	FLBLS	7/16-9/16
	Georgia	Y	17370 FQ	19230 MW	22610 TQ	USBLS	5/15
	Atlanta-Sandy Springs-Roswell MSA, GA	Y	18950 FQ	21610 MW	23890 TQ	USBLS	5/15
	Augusta-Richmond County MSA, GA-SC	Y	16790 FQ	18020 MW	19260 TQ	USBLS	5/15
	Hawaii	Y	40420 FQ	43990 MW	47560 TQ	USBLS	5/15
	Urban Honolulu MSA, HI	Y	40170 FQ	43950 MW	47720 TQ	USBLS	5/15
	Idaho	Y	17190 FQ	18910 MW	22150 TQ	USBLS	5/15
	Boise City MSA, ID	Y	17260 FQ	19660 MW	23700 TQ	USBLS	5/15
	Illinois	Y	22560 FQ	29120 MW	38540 TQ	USBLS	5/15
	Chicago-Naperville-Arlington Heights PMSA, IL	Y	27820 FQ	35560 MW	52420 TQ	USBLS	5/15
	Lake County-Kenosha County PMSA, IL-WI	Y	25370 FQ	28100 MW	30900 TQ	USBLS	5/15
	Indiana	Y	18090 FQ	20770 MW	23710 TQ	USBLS	5/15
	Indianapolis-Carmel-Anderson MSA, IN	Y	19290 FQ	21550 MW	23630 TQ	USBLS	5/15
	Iowa	Y	24860 FQ	27850 MW	30800 TQ	USBLS	5/15
	Des Moines-West Des Moines MSA, IA	Y	25930 FQ	31440 MW	35430 TQ	USBLS	5/15
	Kansas	Y	21980 FQ	27570 MW	33320 TQ	USBLS	5/15
	Wichita MSA, KS	Y	26170 FQ	28560 MW	30950 TQ	USBLS	5/15
	Kentucky	Y	18860 FQ	25940 MW	31750 TQ	USBLS	5/15
	Louisville-Jefferson County MSA, KY-IN	Y	19620 FQ	21930 MW	24250 TQ	USBLS	5/15
	Louisiana	Y	18900 FQ	23630 MW	32770 TQ	USBLS	5/15

Occupation/Type/Industry	Location	Per	Low	Mid	High	Source	Date
Substitute Teacher	New Orleans-Metairie MSA, LA	Y	19170 FQ	24870 MW	35610 TQ	USBLS	5/15
	Maine	Y	19390 FQ	21700 MW	23880 TQ	USBLS	5/15
	Portland-South Portland MSA, ME	Y	20950 FQ	23470 MW	32890 TQ	USBLS	5/15
	Maryland	Y	22079 AE	34250 MW	40335 AEX	MDBLS	4/16
	Baltimore-Columbia-Towson MSA, MD	Y	30060 FQ	34320 MW	37600 TQ	USBLS	5/15
	Salisbury MSA, MD-DE	Y	22020 FQ	24770 MW	29450 TQ	USBLS	5/15
	Massachusetts	Y	22380 FQ	26860 MW	32660 TQ	USBLS	5/15
	Boston-Cambridge-Newton NECTA, MA	Y	22780 FQ	27570 MW	32430 TQ	USBLS	5/15
	Worcester MSA, MA-CT	Y	23790 FQ	28410 MW	37140 TQ	USBLS	5/15
	Michigan	Y	20780 FQ	23390 MW	28260 TQ	USBLS	5/15
	Detroit-Dearborn-Livonia PMSA, MI	Y	21160 FQ	23530 MW	27580 TQ	USBLS	5/15
	Grand Rapids-Wyoming MSA, MI	Y	20940 FQ	23230 MW	27170 TQ	USBLS	5/15
	Minnesota	Y	27772 FQ	30836 MW	36260 TQ	MNBLS	1/16-3/16
	Minneapolis-St. Paul-Bloomington MSA, MN-WI	Y	28064 FQ	31169 MW	37187 TQ	MNBLS	1/16-3/16
	Jackson MSA, MS	Y	16610 FQ	17700 MW	18800 TQ	USBLS	5/15
	Missouri	Y	21060 FQ	23760 MW	28200 TQ	USBLS	5/15
	Kansas City MSA, MO-KS	Y	21690 FQ	24760 MW	30280 TQ	USBLS	5/15
	St. Louis MSA, MO-IL	Y	22060 FQ	26950 MW	32130 TQ	USBLS	5/15
	Montana	Y	18980 FQ	21940 MW	24920 TQ	USBLS	5/15
	Billings MSA, MT	Y	18500 FQ	20780 MW	23140 TQ	USBLS	5/15
	Nebraska	Y	27940 FQ	32055 MW	38465 TQ	NEBLS	7/16-9/16
	Omaha-Council Bluffs MSA, NE-IA	Y	29235 FQ	33085 MW	36490 TQ	NEBLS	7/16-9/16
	Nevada	Y	25780 FQ	27840 MW	29890 TQ	USBLS	5/15
	Las Vegas-Henderson-Paradise MSA, NV	Y	26780 FQ	28410 MW	30030 TQ	USBLS	5/15
	New Hampshire	H	9.89 AE	11.10 MW	12.00 AEX	NHBLS	6/16
	Manchester NECTA, NH	H	11.39 AE	13.48 MW	14.12 AEX	NHBLS	6/16
	Nashua NECTA, NH-MA	Y	20950 FQ	22440 MW	23920 TQ	USBLS	5/15
	New Jersey	Y	24580 FQ	27540 MW	30550 TQ	USBLS	5/15
	Newark PMSA, NJ-PA	Y	25810 FQ	28700 MW	39620 TQ	USBLS	5/15
	Trenton MSA, NJ	Y	24790 FQ	27230 MW	29610 TQ	USBLS	5/15
	New Mexico	Y	17980 FQ	19710 MW	23490 TQ	USBLS	5/15
	Albuquerque MSA, NM	Y	18160 FQ	20670 MW	26500 TQ	USBLS	5/15
	New York	Y	24430 AE	30990 MW	40620 AEX	NYBLS	1/16-3/16
	Buffalo-Cheektowaga-Niagara Falls MSA, NY	Y	26220 FQ	29290 MW	34000 TQ	USBLS	5/15
	Nassau County-Suffolk County PMSA, NY	Y	27980 FQ	35740 MW	43600 TQ	USBLS	5/15
	New York-Jersey City-White Plains PMSA, NY-NJ	Y	25240 FQ	29430 MW	43460 TQ	USBLS	5/15
	Rochester MSA, NY	Y	24930 FQ	29350 MW	39110 TQ	USBLS	5/15
	North Carolina	Y	20960 FQ	23200 MW	26310 TQ	USBLS	5/15
	Charlotte-Concord-Gastonia MSA, NC-SC	Y	19800 FQ	22190 MW	24920 TQ	USBLS	5/15
	Raleigh MSA, NC	Y	20670 FQ	23630 MW	27850 TQ	USBLS	5/15
	North Dakota	Y	39120 FQ	42720 MW	46320 TQ	USBLS	5/15
	Ohio	Y	21010 FQ	24550 MW	28300 TQ	USBLS	5/15
	Cincinnati MSA, OH-KY-IN	Y	18990 FQ	22240 MW	26480 TQ	USBLS	5/15
	Cleveland-Elyria MSA, OH	Y	18120 FQ	20410 MW	24430 TQ	USBLS	5/15
	Columbus MSA, OH	Y	25980 FQ	27990 MW	30010 TQ	USBLS	5/15
	Oklahoma	Y	16830 FQ	18180 MW	19580 TQ	USBLS	5/15
	Oklahoma City MSA, OK	Y	16910 FQ	18200 MW	19500 TQ	USBLS	5/15
	Tulsa MSA, OK	Y	17160 FQ	18940 MW	23180 TQ	USBLS	5/15
	Oregon	H	20.52 FQ	21.89 MW	23.26 TQ	ORBLS	2016
	Portland-Vancouver-Hillsboro MSA, OR-WA	Y	40950 FQ	44090 MW	47230 TQ	USBLS	5/15
	Pennsylvania	Y	22970 FQ	27610 MW	31330 TQ	USBLS	5/15
	Allentown-Bethlehem-Easton MSA, PA-NJ	Y	22060 FQ	27230 MW	30840 TQ	USBLS	5/15
	Harrisburg-Carlisle MSA, PA	Y	26120 FQ	28030 MW	29950 TQ	USBLS	5/15
	Montgomery County-Bucks County-Chester County PMSA, PA	Y	29480 FQ	33720 MW	37170 TQ	USBLS	5/15
	Philadelphia PMSA, PA	Y	29620 FQ	33950 MW	38220 TQ	USBLS	5/15

Occupation/Type/Industry	Location	Per	Low	Mid	High	Source	Date
Substitute Teacher	Pittsburgh MSA, PA	Y	20960 FQ	25910 MW	30020 TQ	USBLS	5/15
	Rhode Island	Y	24390 FQ	28050 MW	31670 TQ	USBLS	5/15
	Providence-Warwick MSA, RI-MA	Y	24360 FQ	28080 MW	31700 TQ	USBLS	5/15
	South Carolina	Y	17560 FQ	19540 MW	24760 TQ	USBLS	5/15
	Charleston-North Charleston MSA, SC	Y	17550 FQ	19400 MW	22150 TQ	USBLS	5/15
	Columbia MSA, SC	Y	17980 FQ	20900 MW	24310 TQ	USBLS	5/15
	Greenville-Anderson-Mauldin MSA, SC	Y	19550 FQ	23580 MW	28000 TQ	USBLS	5/15
	South Dakota	Y	25430 FQ	27690 MW	29960 TQ	USBLS	5/15
	Sioux Falls MSA, SD	Y	26160 FQ	28060 MW	29970 TQ	USBLS	5/15
	Tennessee	Y	17250 FQ	19000 MW	22300 TQ	USBLS	5/15
	Chattanooga MSA, TN-GA	Y	16760 FQ	17920 MW	19080 TQ	USBLS	5/15
	Knoxville MSA, TN	Y	16690 FQ	17790 MW	18900 TQ	USBLS	5/15
	Nashville-Davidson–Murfreesboro–Franklin MSA, TN	Y	20030 FQ	21790 MW	23620 TQ	USBLS	5/15
	Texas	Y	19010 FQ	21930 MW	24880 TQ	USBLS	5/15
	Austin-Round Rock MSA, TX	Y	20700 FQ	22160 MW	23620 TQ	USBLS	5/15
	Dallas-Plano-Irving PMSA, TX	Y	19690 FQ	22500 MW	25560 TQ	USBLS	5/15
	Fort Worth-Arlington PMSA, TX	Y	18880 FQ	21350 MW	23430 TQ	USBLS	5/15
	Houston-The Woodlands-Sugar Land MSA, TX	Y	21040 FQ	24950 MW	28610 TQ	USBLS	5/15
	San Antonio-New Braunfels MSA, TX	Y	17900 FQ	20600 MW	23820 TQ	USBLS	5/15
	Utah	Y	20140 FQ	24050 MW	30210 TQ	USBLS	5/15
	Ogden-Clearfield MSA, UT	Y	19110 FQ	24150 MW	35070 TQ	USBLS	5/15
	Provo-Orem MSA, UT	Y	19220 FQ	22860 MW	26800 TQ	USBLS	5/15
	Salt Lake City MSA, UT	Y	23450 FQ	31820 MW	35850 TQ	USBLS	5/15
	Vermont	Y	21800 FQ	24070 MW	28420 TQ	USBLS	5/15
	Burlington-South Burlington MSA, VT	Y	22760 FQ	26070 MW	30860 TQ	USBLS	5/15
	Virginia	Y	21990 FQ	28260 MW	34930 TQ	USBLS	5/15
	Richmond MSA, VA	Y	20610 FQ	24500 MW	29680 TQ	USBLS	5/15
	Virginia Beach-Norfolk-Newport News MSA, VA-NC	Y	20520 FQ	25420 MW	29770 TQ	USBLS	5/15
	Washington	H	15.71 FQ	17.57 MW	19.67 TQ	WABLS	3/16
	Seattle-Bellevue-Everett PMSA, WA	H	17.46 FQ	19.87 MW	22.25 TQ	WABLS	3/16
	Tacoma-Lakewood PMSA, WA	H	15.95 FQ	17.23 MW	18.51 TQ	WABLS	3/16
	West Virginia	Y	34380 FQ	39070 MW	44780 TQ	USBLS	5/15
	Huntington-Ashland MSA, WV-KY-OH	Y	34930 FQ	39380 MW	45220 TQ	USBLS	5/15
	Wisconsin	Y	25400 FQ	28480 MW	32160 TQ	USBLS	5/15
	Madison MSA, WI	Y	23320 FQ	27630 MW	30570 TQ	USBLS	5/15
	Milwaukee-Waukesha-West Allis MSA, WI	Y	26240 FQ	28980 MW	33700 TQ	USBLS	5/15
	Wyoming	Y	25540 FQ	27730 MW	29930 TQ	USBLS	5/15
	Guam	Y	18060 FQ	18960 MW	19860 TQ	USBLS	5/15
Overseas Elementary and Secondary School, United States Department of Defense	United States	D			105.50 HI	CPMS	2015-2016
Overseas Summer School, United States Department of Defense	United States	D			70.00 HI	CPMS	2015-2016
Subway and Streetcar Operator	California	H	25.33 FQ	28.20 MW	31.02 TQ	CABLS	1/16-3/16
	Los Angeles-Long Beach-Glendale PMSA, CA	H	21.77 FQ	24.11 MW	27.46 TQ	CABLS	1/16-3/16
	San Francisco-Redwood City-South San Francisco PMSA, CA	H	25.51 FQ	27.44 MW	29.38 TQ	CABLS	1/16-3/16
	Colorado	Y	36010 FQ	41170 MW	46020 TQ	USBLS	5/15
	Florida	H	13.35 AE	27.66 MW	31.56 AEX	FLBLS	7/16-9/16
	Illinois	Y	51820 FQ	65730 MW	72910 TQ	USBLS	5/15
	Maryland	Y	42808 AE	56373 MW	63155 AEX	MDBLS	4/16
	New Jersey	Y	53270 FQ	56600 MW	59940 TQ	USBLS	5/15
	New York	Y	74560 AE	75630 MW	74960 AEX	NYBLS	1/16-3/16
	New York-Jersey City-White Plains PMSA, NY-NJ	Y	68290 FQ	73260 MW	78230 TQ	USBLS	5/15
	Oregon	H	26.64 FQ	28.43 MW	30.23 TQ	ORBLS	2016

Occupation/Type/Industry	Location	Per	Low	Mid	High	Source	Date
Subway and Streetcar Operator	Pennsylvania	Y	42460 FQ	53850 MW	58790 TQ	USBLS	5/15
Superintendent							
Highway Department, Municipal Government	Colrain, MA	H			25.86 HI	FRCOG	2016
Highway Department, Municipal Government	Montague, MA	H	18.50 LO		21.67 HI	FRCOG	2016
Public Schools	Huntsville, AL	Y	175000 LO		250000 HI	LSJ17	2017
Public Schools	Haslett, MI	Y			131000 HI	TC04	2015-2016
Supervising Criminalist							
Department of Public Safety	Arizona	M			6829 HI	CAC	1/14
Sheriff's Office	Alameda County, CA	M	7836 LO		9531 HI	CAC	3/16
Sheriff's Office, Forensic Science Division	Washoe County, NV	M	5755 LO		7481 HI	CAC	7/15
Supervising Fingerprint Examiner							
Sheriff's Office, Forensic Services Division	Contra Costa County, CA	M	5848 LO		7109 HI	CAC	10/14
Supervising Librarian							
Public Library	San Rafael, CA	Y		50221 AW		CACIT	6/28/16
Supervising Occupational Health Nurse							
Department of Water and Power, Municipal Government	Los Angeles, CA	Y			86495 HI	CACIT	6/23/16
Supply Room Attendant							
Public Health Department, Municipal Government	San Francisco, CA	Y			50905 HI	CACIT	6/28/16
Surface/Texture Artist	United States	W		1845.42 MW		TAG01	2016
Surgeon	Alabama	Y	152450 AE	244943 AW	291190 AEX	ALBLS	6/16
	Birmingham-Hoover MSA, AL	Y	131564 AE	209736 AW	248827 AEX	ALBLS	6/16
	Arizona	Y		256760 AW		USBLS	5/15
	Phoenix-Mesa-Scottsdale MSA, AZ	Y		264310 AW		USBLS	5/15
	Tucson MSA, AZ	Y		263730 AW		USBLS	5/15
	Arkansas	Y		258790 AW		USBLS	5/15
	Little Rock-North Little Rock-Conway MSA, AR	Y	128190 FQ	230590 AW		USBLS	5/15
	California	H	84.71 FQ	116.29 AW		CABLS	1/16-3/16
	Anaheim-Santa Ana-Irvine PMSA, CA	H	50.47 FQ	75.53 MW		CABLS	1/16-3/16
	Los Angeles-Long Beach-Glendale PMSA, CA	H		125.86 AW		CABLS	1/16-3/16
	Oakland-Hayward-Berkeley PMSA, CA	H	75.06 FQ	120.21 AW		CABLS	1/16-3/16
	Riverside-San Bernardino-Ontario MSA, CA	H		132.12 AW		CABLS	1/16-3/16
	Sacramento–Roseville–Arden-Arcade MSA, CA	H		125.52 AW		CABLS	1/16-3/16
	San Diego-Carlsbad MSA, CA	H	71.71 FQ	116.74 AW		CABLS	1/16-3/16
	San Francisco-Redwood City-South San Francisco PMSA, CA	H	79.54 FQ	88.69 MW		CABLS	1/16-3/16
	Santa Rosa MSA, CA	Y		265810 AW		USBLS	5/15
	Colorado	Y		250460 AW		USBLS	5/15
	Denver-Aurora-Lakewood MSA, CO	Y		252730 AW		USBLS	5/15
	Connecticut	Y		240516 AW		CTBLS	1/16-3/16
	Bridgeport-Stamford-Norwalk MSA, CT	Y		267160 AW		USBLS	5/15
	Hartford-West Hartford-East Hartford MSA, CT	Y	173920 FQ	225840 AW		USBLS	5/15
	Delaware	Y		243920 AW		USBLS	5/15
	Wilmington PMSA, DE-MD-NJ	Y		238740 AW		USBLS	5/15
	District of Columbia	Y	61400 FQ	178330 MW		USBLS	5/15
	Washington-Arlington-Alexandria PMSA, DC-VA-MD-WV	Y	107580 FQ	207400 AW		USBLS	5/15

AE	Average entry wage	**AWR**	Average wage range	**H**	Hourly	**LR** Low end range	**MTC** Median total compensation	**TCC** Total cash compensation
AEX	Average experienced wage	**B**	Biweekly	**HI**	Highest wage paid	**M** Monthly	**MW** Median wage paid	**TQ** Third quartile surge
ATC	Average total compensation	**D**	Daily	**HR**	High end range	**MCC** Median cash compensation	**MWR** Median wage range	**W** Weekly
AW	Average wage paid	**FQ**	First quartile wage	**LO**	Lowest wage paid	**ME** Median entry wage	**S** See annotated source	**Y** Yearly

Occupation/Type/Industry	Location	Per	Low	Mid	High	Source	Date
Surgeon	Florida	H		123.53 AW		FLBLS	7/16-9/16
	Fort Lauderdale-Pompano Beach-Deerfield Beach PMSA, FL	H		111.58 AW		FLBLS	7/16-9/16
	Miami-Miami Beach-Kendall PMSA, FL	H		125.88 AW		FLBLS	7/16-9/16
	Orlando-Kissimmee-Sanford MSA, FL	H		119.12 AW		FLBLS	7/16-9/16
	Tampa-St. Petersburg-Clearwater MSA, FL	H		120.65 AW		FLBLS	7/16-9/16
	Georgia	Y		271420 AW		USBLS	5/15
	Atlanta-Sandy Springs-Roswell MSA, GA	Y		266600 AW		USBLS	5/15
	Urban Honolulu MSA, HI	Y		263770 AW		USBLS	5/15
	Illinois	Y		248420 AW		USBLS	5/15
	Chicago-Naperville-Arlington Heights PMSA, IL	Y		255580 AW		USBLS	5/15
	Lake County-Kenosha County PMSA, IL-WI	Y	63640 FQ	186910 AW		USBLS	5/15
	Iowa	Y		257350 AW		USBLS	5/15
	Des Moines-West Des Moines MSA, IA	Y	148160 FQ	232020 AW		USBLS	5/15
	Kansas	Y		240600 AW		USBLS	5/15
	Kentucky	Y		265520 AW		USBLS	5/15
	Louisville-Jefferson County MSA, KY-IN	Y		271070 AW		USBLS	5/15
	Louisiana	Y	184850 FQ	242560 AW		USBLS	5/15
	Baton Rouge MSA, LA	Y		275070 AW		USBLS	5/15
	New Orleans-Metairie MSA, LA	Y	176700 FQ	229990 AW		USBLS	5/15
	Maine	Y		262790 AW		USBLS	5/15
	Maryland	Y		264819 MW		MDBLS	4/16
	Baltimore-Columbia-Towson MSA, MD	Y		271510 AW		USBLS	5/15
	Salisbury MSA, MD-DE	Y		257090 AW		USBLS	5/15
	Massachusetts	Y	163350 FQ	232760 AW		USBLS	5/15
	Boston-Cambridge-Newton NECTA, MA	Y	144260 FQ	221420 AW		USBLS	5/15
	Michigan	Y		245150 AW		USBLS	5/15
	Detroit-Dearborn-Livonia PMSA, MI	Y	51460 FQ	191360 AW		USBLS	5/15
	Minnesota	Y		270944 AW		MNBLS	1/16-3/16
	Minneapolis-St. Paul-Bloomington MSA, MN-WI	Y		270581 AW		MNBLS	1/16-3/16
	Mississippi	Y		260140 AW		USBLS	5/15
	Jackson MSA, MS	Y	154860 FQ	242600 AW		USBLS	5/15
	Kansas City MSA, MO-KS	Y		255980 AW		USBLS	5/15
	Montana	Y	125580 FQ	225390 AW		USBLS	5/15
	Billings MSA, MT	Y		267590 AW		USBLS	5/15
	Nevada	Y		278550 AW		USBLS	5/15
	New Hampshire	H		134.31 AW		NHBLS	6/16
	Manchester NECTA, NH	H		142.92 AW		NHBLS	6/16
	New Jersey	Y		270790 AW		USBLS	5/15
	Newark PMSA, NJ-PA	Y		254860 AW		USBLS	5/15
	New York	Y		230090 AW		NYBLS	1/16-3/16
	New York-Jersey City-White Plains PMSA, NY-NJ	Y	164990 FQ	235840 AW		USBLS	5/15
	Rochester MSA, NY	Y		266480 AW		USBLS	5/15
	North Carolina	Y		269760 AW		USBLS	5/15
	Charlotte-Concord-Gastonia MSA, NC-SC	Y		256160 AW		USBLS	5/15
	Ohio	Y	174660 FQ	233100 AW		USBLS	5/15
	Cincinnati MSA, OH-KY-IN	Y	59770 FQ	159500 MW		USBLS	5/15
	Columbus MSA, OH	Y		244720 AW		USBLS	5/15
	Oklahoma	Y	80670 FQ	218340 AW		USBLS	5/15
	Oklahoma City MSA, OK	Y		223690 AW		USBLS	5/15
	Tulsa MSA, OK	Y	68820 FQ	220520 AW		USBLS	5/15
	Pennsylvania	Y	75020 FQ	203350 AW		USBLS	5/15
	Harrisburg-Carlisle MSA, PA	Y	60310 FQ	138770 MW		USBLS	5/15
	Montgomery County-Bucks County-Chester County PMSA, PA	Y		274720 AW		USBLS	5/15

Occupation/Type/Industry	Location	Per	Low	Mid	High	Source	Date
Surgeon	Philadelphia PMSA, PA	Y	59540 FQ	181680 AW		USBLS	5/15
	Pittsburgh MSA, PA	Y		244560 AW		USBLS	5/15
	Providence-Warwick MSA, RI-MA	Y		256890 AW		USBLS	5/15
	South Carolina	Y		259920 AW		USBLS	5/15
	Columbia MSA, SC	Y	168930 FQ	222600 AW		USBLS	5/15
	Tennessee	Y		239620 AW		USBLS	5/15
	Knoxville MSA, TN	Y		256360 AW		USBLS	5/15
	Memphis MSA, TN-MS-AR	Y		265790 AW		USBLS	5/15
	Nashville-Davidson–Murfreesboro–Franklin MSA, TN	Y	147910 FQ	235360 AW		USBLS	5/15
	Texas	Y		243090 AW		USBLS	5/15
	Austin-Round Rock MSA, TX	Y	173900 FQ	210920 AW		USBLS	5/15
	Dallas-Plano-Irving PMSA, TX	Y		249650 AW		USBLS	5/15
	Houston-The Woodlands-Sugar Land MSA, TX	Y	169490 FQ	221790 AW		USBLS	5/15
	San Antonio-New Braunfels MSA, TX	Y	186240 FQ	243600 AW		USBLS	5/15
	Ogden-Clearfield MSA, UT	Y		262050 AW		USBLS	5/15
	Provo-Orem MSA, UT	Y	95600 FQ	224480 AW		USBLS	5/15
	Vermont	Y	167800 FQ	232110 AW		USBLS	5/15
	Burlington-South Burlington MSA, VT	Y	85020 FQ	216390 AW		USBLS	5/15
	Virginia	Y		247800 AW		USBLS	5/15
	Richmond MSA, VA	Y		261120 AW		USBLS	5/15
	Virginia Beach-Norfolk-Newport News MSA, VA-NC	Y		250120 AW		USBLS	5/15
	Washington	Y		252335 AW		WABLS	3/16
	Seattle-Bellevue-Everett PMSA, WA	H	64.16 FQ	110.21 AW		WABLS	3/15
	West Virginia	Y		258850 AW		USBLS	5/15
	Huntington-Ashland MSA, WV-KY-OH	Y		252220 AW		USBLS	5/15
	Wisconsin	Y		245940 AW		USBLS	5/15
	Milwaukee-Waukesha-West Allis MSA, WI	Y	81830 FQ	195650 AW		USBLS	5/15
Surgical Procedures Technician Public Health Department, Municipal Government	San Francisco, CA	Y		47881 AW		CACIT	6/28/16
Surgical Technologist	Alabama	Y	26625 AE	36278 AW	41099 AEX	ALBLS	6/16
	Birmingham-Hoover MSA, AL	Y	27185 AE	36584 AW	27185 AEX	ALBLS	6/16
	Alaska	Y	44180 FQ	53370 MW	61190 TQ	USBLS	5/15
	Anchorage MSA, AK	Y	45870 FQ	53880 MW	61310 TQ	USBLS	5/15
	Arizona	Y	41300 FQ	48770 MW	58370 TQ	USBLS	5/15
	Phoenix-Mesa-Scottsdale MSA, AZ	Y	42220 FQ	49810 MW	58930 TQ	USBLS	5/15
	Tucson MSA, AZ	Y	37230 FQ	46960 MW	57800 TQ	USBLS	5/15
	Arkansas	Y	31800 FQ	38680 MW	47700 TQ	USBLS	5/15
	Little Rock-North Little Rock-Conway MSA, AR	Y	34670 FQ	43320 MW	51720 TQ	USBLS	5/15
	California	H	23.81 FQ	28.42 MW	34.49 TQ	CABLS	1/16-3/16
	Anaheim-Santa Ana-Irvine PMSA, CA	H	24.68 FQ	28.11 MW	32.92 TQ	CABLS	1/16-3/16
	Los Angeles-Long Beach-Glendale PMSA, CA	H	23.92 FQ	27.56 MW	31.59 TQ	CABLS	1/16-3/16
	Oakland-Hayward-Berkeley PMSA, CA	H	27.54 FQ	34.18 MW	40.44 TQ	CABLS	1/16-3/16
	Riverside-San Bernardino-Ontario MSA, CA	H	20.55 FQ	25.40 MW	31.20 TQ	CABLS	1/16-3/16
	Sacramento–Roseville–Arden-Arcade MSA, CA	H	24.26 FQ	30.65 MW	35.67 TQ	CABLS	1/16-3/16
	San Diego-Carlsbad MSA, CA	H	22.83 FQ	26.82 MW	31.48 TQ	CABLS	1/16-3/16
	San Francisco-Redwood City-South San Francisco PMSA, CA	H	31.74 FQ	36.69 MW	42.61 TQ	CABLS	1/16-3/16
	Colorado	Y	40850 FQ	48260 MW	57550 TQ	USBLS	5/15
	Denver-Aurora-Lakewood MSA, CO	Y	41200 FQ	47660 MW	56110 TQ	USBLS	5/15
	Connecticut	Y		53484 MW		CTBLS	1/16-3/16

AE	Average entry wage	AWR	Average wage range	H	Hourly	LR	Low end range	MTC	Median total compensation	TCC	Total cash compensation
AEX	Average experienced wage	B	Biweekly	HI	Highest wage paid	M	Monthly	MW	Median wage paid	TQ	Third quartile wage
ATC	Average total compensation	D	Daily	HR	High end range	MCC	Median cash compensation	MWR	Median wage range	W	Weekly
AW	Average wage paid	FQ	First quartile wage	LO	Lowest wage paid	ME	Median entry wage	S	See annotated source	Y	Yearly

Surgical Technologist

Occupation/Type/Industry	Location	Per	Low	Mid	High	Source	Date
Surgical Technologist	Bridgeport-Stamford-Norwalk MSA, CT	Y	42140 FQ	51520 MW	62700 TQ	USBLS	5/15
	Hartford-West Hartford-East Hartford MSA, CT	Y	50480 FQ	56850 MW	63230 TQ	USBLS	5/15
	Delaware	Y	37830 FQ	44010 MW	50410 TQ	USBLS	5/15
	Wilmington PMSA, DE-MD-NJ	Y	39910 FQ	45360 MW	52390 TQ	USBLS	5/15
	District of Columbia	Y	45830 FQ	56670 MW	65490 TQ	USBLS	5/15
	Washington-Arlington-Alexandria PMSA, DC-VA-MD-WV	Y	44460 FQ	54400 MW	62730 TQ	USBLS	5/15
	Florida	H	15.85 AE	19.97 MW	22.39 AEX	FLBLS	7/16-9/16
	Fort Lauderdale-Pompano Beach-Deerfield Beach PMSA, FL	H	16.36 AE	21.31 MW	23.86 AEX	FLBLS	7/16-9/16
	Miami-Miami Beach-Kendall PMSA, FL	H	14.68 AE	20.63 MW	23.39 AEX	FLBLS	7/16-9/16
	Orlando-Kissimmee-Sanford MSA, FL	H	15.92 AE	19.91 MW	21.71 AEX	FLBLS	7/16-9/16
	Tampa-St. Petersburg-Clearwater MSA, FL	H	16.06 AE	20.42 MW	22.54 AEX	FLBLS	7/16-9/16
	Georgia	Y	33480 FQ	39030 MW	45670 TQ	USBLS	5/15
	Atlanta-Sandy Springs-Roswell MSA, GA	Y	35650 FQ	41400 MW	47230 TQ	USBLS	5/15
	Augusta-Richmond County MSA, GA-SC	Y	34440 FQ	39050 MW	45570 TQ	USBLS	5/15
	Hawaii	Y	42010 FQ	52490 MW	68730 TQ	USBLS	5/15
	Urban Honolulu MSA, HI	Y	42020 FQ	54910 MW	69470 TQ	USBLS	5/15
	Idaho	Y	35580 FQ	42230 MW	48490 TQ	USBLS	5/15
	Boise City MSA, ID	Y	36980 FQ	43170 MW	49090 TQ	USBLS	5/15
	Illinois	Y	35940 FQ	43370 MW	52000 TQ	USBLS	5/15
	Chicago-Naperville-Arlington Heights PMSA, IL	Y	37820 FQ	45720 MW	55360 TQ	USBLS	5/15
	Lake County-Kenosha County PMSA, IL-WI	Y	39710 FQ	46460 MW	54810 TQ	USBLS	5/15
	Indiana	Y	35420 FQ	41450 MW	48310 TQ	USBLS	5/15
	Gary PMSA, IN	Y	35800 FQ	42090 MW	49020 TQ	USBLS	5/15
	Indianapolis-Carmel-Anderson MSA, IN	Y	36440 FQ	42820 MW	49520 TQ	USBLS	5/15
	Iowa	Y	33900 FQ	38770 MW	45200 TQ	USBLS	5/15
	Des Moines-West Des Moines MSA, IA	Y	35660 FQ	41630 MW	47500 TQ	USBLS	5/15
	Kansas	Y	32890 FQ	37710 MW	45740 TQ	USBLS	5/15
	Wichita MSA, KS	Y	32780 FQ	36370 MW	40810 TQ	USBLS	5/15
	Kentucky	Y	32560 FQ	38020 MW	45570 TQ	USBLS	5/15
	Louisville-Jefferson County MSA, KY-IN	Y	35740 FQ	41930 MW	47500 TQ	USBLS	5/15
	Louisiana	Y	32310 FQ	38520 MW	45680 TQ	USBLS	5/15
	Baton Rouge MSA, LA	Y	34330 FQ	39150 MW	45820 TQ	USBLS	5/15
	New Orleans-Metairie MSA, LA	Y	33340 FQ	40030 MW	46140 TQ	USBLS	5/15
	Maine	Y	36160 FQ	42080 MW	49310 TQ	USBLS	5/15
	Portland-South Portland MSA, ME	Y	36230 FQ	42140 MW	51110 TQ	USBLS	5/15
	Maryland	Y	36624 AE	51597 MW	59083 AEX	MDBLS	4/16
	Baltimore-Columbia-Towson MSA, MD	Y	39190 FQ	49920 MW	58110 TQ	USBLS	5/15
	Salisbury MSA, MD-DE	Y	34200 FQ	38770 MW	46090 TQ	USBLS	5/15
	Massachusetts	Y	40930 FQ	49180 MW	60250 TQ	USBLS	5/15
	Boston-Cambridge-Newton NECTA, MA	Y	41680 FQ	48760 MW	61040 TQ	USBLS	5/15
	Worcester MSA, MA-CT	Y	42310 FQ	50260 MW	61720 TQ	USBLS	5/15
	Michigan	Y	36440 FQ	42940 MW	48460 TQ	USBLS	5/15
	Detroit-Dearborn-Livonia PMSA, MI	Y	34690 FQ	41890 MW	47860 TQ	USBLS	5/15
	Grand Rapids-Wyoming MSA, MI	Y	35210 FQ	41340 MW	48110 TQ	USBLS	5/15
	Minnesota	Y	44304 FQ	51108 MW	58860 TQ	MNBLS	1/16-3/16
	Minneapolis-St. Paul-Bloomington MSA, MN-WI	Y	46179 FQ	52953 MW	59314 TQ	MNBLS	1/16-3/16
	Mississippi	Y	31710 FQ	37660 MW	44920 TQ	USBLS	5/15
	Jackson MSA, MS	Y	33460 FQ	39700 MW	46880 TQ	USBLS	5/15

AE	Average entry wage	AWR	Average wage range	H	Hourly	LR	Low end range	MTC	Median total compensation	TCC	Total cash compensation
AEX	Average experienced wage	B	Biweekly	HI	Highest wage paid	M	Monthly	MW	Median wage paid	TQ	Third quartile wage
ATC	Average total compensation	D	Daily	HR	High end range	MCC	Median cash compensation	MWR	Median wage range	W	Weekly
AW	Average wage paid	FQ	First quartile wage	LO	Lowest wage paid	ME	Median entry wage	S	See annotated source	Y	Yearly

Occupation/Type/Industry	Location	Per	Low	Mid	High	Source	Date
Surgical Technologist	Missouri	Y	33750 FQ	39690 MW	47990 TQ	USBLS	5/15
	Kansas City MSA, MO-KS	Y	36610 FQ	43660 MW	51040 TQ	USBLS	5/15
	St. Louis MSA, MO-IL	Y	34410 FQ	39560 MW	48240 TQ	USBLS	5/15
	Montana	Y	35640 FQ	43370 MW	50610 TQ	USBLS	5/15
	Billings MSA, MT	Y	31660 FQ	38480 MW	49410 TQ	USBLS	5/15
	Nebraska	Y	35625 FQ	40995 MW	47440 TQ	NEBLS	7/16-9/16
	Omaha-Council Bluffs MSA, NE-IA	Y	36670 FQ	42475 MW	48375 TQ	NEBLS	7/16-9/16
	Nevada	Y	52300 FQ	60970 MW	71780 TQ	USBLS	5/15
	Las Vegas-Henderson-Paradise MSA, NV	Y	53480 FQ	63340 MW	73600 TQ	USBLS	5/15
	New Hampshire	H	17.86 AE	23.45 MW	26.40 AEX	NHBLS	6/16
	Manchester NECTA, NH	H	20.55 AE	24.98 MW	27.00 AEX	NHBLS	6/16
	Nashua NECTA, NH-MA	Y	41060 FQ	52410 MW	61760 TQ	USBLS	5/15
	New Jersey	Y	41420 FQ	48940 MW	57730 TQ	USBLS	5/15
	Camden PMSA, NJ	Y	41150 FQ	47270 MW	54300 TQ	USBLS	5/15
	Newark PMSA, NJ-PA	Y	42270 FQ	48320 MW	56760 TQ	USBLS	5/15
	Trenton MSA, NJ	Y	37350 FQ	43590 MW	49150 TQ	USBLS	5/15
	New Mexico	Y	34460 FQ	41020 MW	48340 TQ	USBLS	5/15
	Albuquerque MSA, NM	Y	39950 FQ	45300 MW	51110 TQ	USBLS	5/15
	New York	Y	37480 AE	51060 MW	59680 AEX	NYBLS	1/16-3/16
	Buffalo-Cheektowaga-Niagara Falls MSA, NY	Y	44300 FQ	52640 MW	58210 TQ	USBLS	5/15
	Nassau County-Suffolk County PMSA, NY	Y	46880 FQ	55710 MW	63740 TQ	USBLS	5/15
	New York-Jersey City-White Plains PMSA, NY-NJ	Y	42400 FQ	53230 MW	65050 TQ	USBLS	5/15
	Rochester MSA, NY	Y	34320 FQ	38290 MW	44730 TQ	USBLS	5/15
	North Carolina	Y	34500 FQ	38960 MW	45770 TQ	USBLS	5/15
	Charlotte-Concord-Gastonia MSA, NC-SC	Y	35410 FQ	40150 MW	45890 TQ	USBLS	5/15
	Raleigh MSA, NC	Y	36880 FQ	42820 MW	49120 TQ	USBLS	5/15
	North Dakota	Y	34230 FQ	39090 MW	45520 TQ	USBLS	5/15
	Fargo MSA, ND-MN	Y	33960 FQ	38610 MW	44870 TQ	USBLS	5/15
	Ohio	Y	34380 FQ	40520 MW	47400 TQ	USBLS	5/15
	Cincinnati MSA, OH-KY-IN	Y	36580 FQ	43260 MW	50240 TQ	USBLS	5/15
	Cleveland-Elyria MSA, OH	Y	32620 FQ	39260 MW	47980 TQ	USBLS	5/15
	Columbus MSA, OH	Y	33830 FQ	40520 MW	46810 TQ	USBLS	5/15
	Oklahoma	Y	31700 FQ	37300 MW	45440 TQ	USBLS	5/15
	Oklahoma City MSA, OK	Y	33210 FQ	39630 MW	49070 TQ	USBLS	5/15
	Tulsa MSA, OK	Y	32360 FQ	36680 MW	42280 TQ	USBLS	5/15
	Oregon	H	20.84 FQ	23.87 MW	27.58 TQ	ORBLS	2016
	Portland-Vancouver-Hillsboro MSA, OR-WA	Y	44140 FQ	51280 MW	57820 TQ	USBLS	5/15
	Pennsylvania	Y	34810 FQ	41670 MW	48580 TQ	USBLS	5/15
	Allentown-Bethlehem-Easton MSA, PA-NJ	Y	35360 FQ	42890 MW	50110 TQ	USBLS	5/15
	Harrisburg-Carlisle MSA, PA	Y	35860 FQ	44040 MW	53320 TQ	USBLS	5/15
	Montgomery County-Bucks County-Chester County PMSA, PA	Y	34100 FQ	41710 MW	49160 TQ	USBLS	5/15
	Philadelphia PMSA, PA	Y	40350 FQ	46410 MW	53950 TQ	USBLS	5/15
	Pittsburgh MSA, PA	Y	33190 FQ	38340 MW	45380 TQ	USBLS	5/15
	Rhode Island	Y	42900 FQ	50420 MW	58600 TQ	USBLS	5/15
	Providence-Warwick MSA, RI-MA	Y	42780 FQ	51010 MW	58930 TQ	USBLS	5/15
	South Carolina	Y	32560 FQ	37200 MW	43680 TQ	USBLS	5/15
	Charleston-North Charleston MSA, SC	Y	34450 FQ	38970 MW	44960 TQ	USBLS	5/15
	Columbia MSA, SC	Y	29640 FQ	35880 MW	42550 TQ	USBLS	5/15
	Greenville-Anderson-Mauldin MSA, SC	Y	32150 FQ	36500 MW	42320 TQ	USBLS	5/15
	South Dakota	Y	33400 FQ	38280 MW	45130 TQ	USBLS	5/15
	Tennessee	Y	33450 FQ	38130 MW	45320 TQ	USBLS	5/15
	Knoxville MSA, TN	Y	32970 FQ	36580 MW	40750 TQ	USBLS	5/15
	Memphis MSA, TN-MS-AR	Y	34830 FQ	40820 MW	47350 TQ	USBLS	5/15
	Nashville-Davidson–Murfreesboro–Franklin MSA, TN	Y	35220 FQ	40740 MW	47870 TQ	USBLS	5/15
	Texas	Y	37040 FQ	44410 MW	52180 TQ	USBLS	5/15
	Austin-Round Rock MSA, TX	Y	37740 FQ	44450 MW	52330 TQ	USBLS	5/15
	Dallas-Plano-Irving PMSA, TX	Y	39140 FQ	45340 MW	52470 TQ	USBLS	5/15

AE	Average entry wage	AWR	Average wage range	H	Hourly
AEX	Average experienced wage	B	Biweekly	HI	Highest wage paid
ATC	Average total compensation	D	Daily	HR	High end range
AW	Average wage paid	FQ	First quartile wage	LO	Lowest wage paid

LR	Low end range	MTC	Median total compensation
M	Monthly	MW	Median wage paid
MCC	Median cash compensation	MWR	Median wage range
ME	Median entry wage	S	See annotated source

TCC	Total cash compensation
TQ	Third quartile wage
W	Weekly
Y	Yearly

Occupation/Type/Industry	Location	Per	Low	Mid	High	Source	Date
Surgical Technologist	Fort Worth-Arlington PMSA, TX	Y	39920 FQ	47050 MW	55090 TQ	USBLS	5/15
	Houston-The Woodlands-Sugar Land MSA, TX	Y	40450 FQ	46830 MW	54720 TQ	USBLS	5/15
	San Antonio-New Braunfels MSA, TX	Y	31210 FQ	39340 MW	46970 TQ	USBLS	5/15
	Utah	Y	31810 FQ	37540 MW	44940 TQ	USBLS	5/15
	Ogden-Clearfield MSA, UT	Y	30930 FQ	35870 MW	42200 TQ	USBLS	5/15
	Provo-Orem MSA, UT	Y	31410 FQ	37150 MW	45600 TQ	USBLS	5/15
	Salt Lake City MSA, UT	Y	32610 FQ	38650 MW	45800 TQ	USBLS	5/15
	Vermont	Y	33930 FQ	39060 MW	47320 TQ	USBLS	5/15
	Virginia	Y	38310 FQ	46060 MW	56780 TQ	USBLS	5/15
	Richmond MSA, VA	Y	37070 FQ	43660 MW	50190 TQ	USBLS	5/15
	Virginia Beach-Norfolk-Newport News MSA, VA-NC	Y	40030 FQ	46180 MW	58320 TQ	USBLS	5/15
	Washington	H	21.74 FQ	25.61 MW	29.54 TQ	WABLS	3/16
	Seattle-Bellevue-Everett PMSA, WA	H	22.29 FQ	26.45 MW	30.47 TQ	WABLS	3/16
	Tacoma-Lakewood PMSA, WA	H	22.36 FQ	26.18 MW	29.57 TQ	WABLS	3/16
	West Virginia	Y	31730 FQ	37110 MW	44500 TQ	USBLS	5/15
	Huntington-Ashland MSA, WV-KY-OH	Y	34130 FQ	39980 MW	46320 TQ	USBLS	5/15
	Wisconsin	Y	42210 FQ	49860 MW	59060 TQ	USBLS	5/15
	Madison MSA, WI	Y	42700 FQ	49550 MW	57440 TQ	USBLS	5/15
	Milwaukee-Waukesha-West Allis MSA, WI	Y	45880 FQ	56160 MW	67070 TQ	USBLS	5/15
	Wyoming	Y	37550 FQ	44990 MW	54080 TQ	USBLS	5/15
	Cheyenne MSA, WY	Y	42510 FQ	48770 MW	58930 TQ	USBLS	5/15
	Puerto Rico	Y	17080 FQ	18700 MW	22210 TQ	USBLS	5/15
	San Juan-Carolina-Caguas MSA, PR	Y	17320 FQ	19160 MW	23650 TQ	USBLS	5/15
Survey Party Chief							
Municipal Government	Seattle, WA	H	29.68 LO		34.68 HI	CSSS	1/13/16
Survey Researcher	Arizona	Y	44430 FQ	53980 MW	60780 TQ	USBLS	5/15
	Phoenix-Mesa-Scottsdale MSA, AZ	Y	44760 FQ	53990 MW	60470 TQ	USBLS	5/15
	Arkansas	Y	34730 FQ	40020 MW	48830 TQ	USBLS	5/15
	California	H	19.42 FQ	27.79 MW	40.46 TQ	CABLS	1/16-3/16
	Anaheim-Santa Ana-Irvine PMSA, CA	H	19.32 FQ	36.19 MW	45.59 TQ	CABLS	1/16-3/16
	Los Angeles-Long Beach-Glendale PMSA, CA	H	17.21 FQ	28.32 MW	44.96 TQ	CABLS	1/16-3/16
	Oakland-Hayward-Berkeley PMSA, CA	H	24.70 FQ	35.56 MW	46.28 TQ	CABLS	1/16-3/16
	Sacramento–Roseville–Arden-Arcade MSA, CA	H	19.81 FQ	24.99 MW	30.18 TQ	CABLS	1/16-3/16
	San Diego-Carlsbad MSA, CA	H	26.70 FQ	39.03 MW	44.99 TQ	CABLS	1/16-3/16
	San Francisco-Redwood City-South San Francisco PMSA, CA	H	22.62 FQ	27.35 MW	30.62 TQ	CABLS	1/16-3/16
	Colorado	Y	40000 FQ	49700 MW	81240 TQ	USBLS	5/15
	Denver-Aurora-Lakewood MSA, CO	Y	38890 FQ	46210 MW	70250 TQ	USBLS	5/15
	Connecticut	Y		69868 MW		CTBLS	1/16-3/16
	Bridgeport-Stamford-Norwalk MSA, CT	Y	47080 FQ	69280 MW	91450 TQ	USBLS	5/15
	Hartford-West Hartford-East Hartford MSA, CT	Y	23370 FQ	58500 MW	87720 TQ	USBLS	5/15
	Wilmington PMSA, DE-MD-NJ	Y	47590 FQ	60470 MW	70480 TQ	USBLS	5/15
	District of Columbia	Y	49810 FQ	73440 MW	95650 TQ	USBLS	5/15
	Washington-Arlington-Alexandria PMSA, DC-VA-MD-WV	Y	45700 FQ	67070 MW	92350 TQ	USBLS	5/15
	Florida	H	10.51 AE	18.91 MW	25.96 AEX	FLBLS	7/16-9/16
	Miami-Miami Beach-Kendall PMSA, FL	H	13.64 AE	22.17 MW	29.56 AEX	FLBLS	7/16-9/16
	Tampa-St. Petersburg-Clearwater MSA, FL	H	10.82 AE	24.88 MW	33.68 AEX	FLBLS	7/16-9/16
	Georgia	Y	23740 FQ	28910 MW	43990 TQ	USBLS	5/15

AE	Average entry wage	AWR	Average wage range	H	Hourly	LR	Low end range	MTC	Median total compensation	TCC	Total cash compensation
AEX	Average experienced wage	B	Biweekly	HI	Highest wage paid	M	Monthly	MW	Median wage paid	TQ	Third quartile wage
ATC	Average total compensation	D	Daily	HR	High end range	MCC	Median cash compensation	MWR	Median wage range	W	Weekly
AW	Average wage paid	FQ	First quartile wage	LO	Lowest wage paid	ME	Median entry wage	S	See annotated source	Y	Yearly

Occupation/Type/Industry	Location	Per	Low	Mid	High	Source	Date
Survey Researcher	Atlanta-Sandy Springs-Roswell MSA, GA	Y	19030 FQ	30700 MW	50350 TQ	USBLS	5/15
	Hawaii	Y	19540 FQ	27240 MW	42860 TQ	USBLS	5/15
	Urban Honolulu MSA, HI	Y	19270 FQ	27200 MW	43860 TQ	USBLS	5/15
	Illinois	Y	42060 FQ	51880 MW	77510 TQ	USBLS	5/15
	Chicago-Naperville-Arlington Heights PMSA, IL	Y	41980 FQ	52850 MW	79940 TQ	USBLS	5/15
	Indiana	Y	22900 FQ	36330 MW	52380 TQ	USBLS	5/15
	Indianapolis-Carmel-Anderson MSA, IN	Y	36380 FQ	45490 MW	60030 TQ	USBLS	5/15
	Kansas	Y	41330 FQ	51520 MW	62650 TQ	USBLS	5/15
	Kentucky	Y	24210 FQ	32280 MW	54740 TQ	USBLS	5/15
	Louisville-Jefferson County MSA, KY-IN	Y	38300 FQ	55520 MW	78920 TQ	USBLS	5/15
	Louisiana	Y	36490 FQ	42140 MW	50230 TQ	USBLS	5/15
	Baton Rouge MSA, LA	Y	36410 FQ	41970 MW	50140 TQ	USBLS	5/15
	Maryland	Y	56156 AE	83321 MW	96903 AEX	MDBLS	4/16
	Baltimore-Columbia-Towson MSA, MD	Y	60780 FQ	68730 MW	75370 TQ	USBLS	5/15
	Massachusetts	Y	37860 FQ	55820 MW	74010 TQ	USBLS	5/15
	Boston-Cambridge-Newton NECTA, MA	Y	41350 FQ	60950 MW	77820 TQ	USBLS	5/15
	Michigan	Y	44660 FQ	58430 MW	75980 TQ	USBLS	5/15
	Grand Rapids-Wyoming MSA, MI	Y	31660 FQ	36210 MW	43220 TQ	USBLS	5/15
	Minnesota	Y	46743 FQ	64374 MW	74505 TQ	MNBLS	1/16-3/16
	Minneapolis-St. Paul-Bloomington MSA, MN-WI	Y	49011 FQ	65745 MW	75906 TQ	MNBLS	1/16-3/16
	Missouri	Y	17720 FQ	19530 MW	42200 TQ	USBLS	5/15
	Kansas City MSA, MO-KS	Y	45010 FQ	54500 MW	63770 TQ	USBLS	5/15
	St. Louis MSA, MO-IL	Y	18190 FQ	32970 MW	45550 TQ	USBLS	5/15
	Nebraska	Y	20790 FQ	44135 MW	61685 TQ	NEBLS	7/16-9/16
	Nevada	Y	27810 FQ	35160 MW	56510 TQ	USBLS	5/15
	New Jersey	Y	45720 FQ	61060 MW	90540 TQ	USBLS	5/15
	Newark PMSA, NJ-PA	Y	37120 FQ	47520 MW	68640 TQ	USBLS	5/15
	Trenton MSA, NJ	Y	61240 FQ	82140 MW	121670 TQ	USBLS	5/15
	New York	Y	40930 AE	66570 MW	79050 AEX	NYBLS	1/16-3/16
	New York-Jersey City-White Plains PMSA, NY-NJ	Y	44300 FQ	56420 MW	74140 TQ	USBLS	5/15
	Rochester MSA, NY	Y	39660 FQ	46420 MW	67110 TQ	USBLS	5/15
	North Carolina	Y	40680 FQ	61260 MW	82770 TQ	USBLS	5/15
	Ohio	Y	42690 FQ	58180 MW	71520 TQ	USBLS	5/15
	Cincinnati MSA, OH-KY-IN	Y	32080 FQ	47820 MW	66530 TQ	USBLS	5/15
	Oklahoma	Y	31280 FQ	42200 MW	55470 TQ	USBLS	5/15
	Oregon	H	19.22 FQ	27.99 MW	35.61 TQ	ORBLS	2016
	Portland-Vancouver-Hillsboro MSA, OR-WA	Y	38740 FQ	58830 MW	77340 TQ	USBLS	5/15
	Pennsylvania	Y	29550 FQ	45430 MW	72150 TQ	USBLS	5/15
	Montgomery County-Bucks County-Chester County PMSA, PA	Y	33030 FQ	40480 MW	55980 TQ	USBLS	5/15
	Philadelphia PMSA, PA	Y	22980 FQ	42880 MW	66790 TQ	USBLS	5/15
	Pittsburgh MSA, PA	Y	37000 FQ	58560 MW	86770 TQ	USBLS	5/15
	South Carolina	Y	41540 FQ	54170 MW	68760 TQ	USBLS	5/15
	South Dakota	Y	40730 FQ	46760 MW	57840 TQ	USBLS	5/15
	Sioux Falls MSA, SD	Y	43640 FQ	48710 MW	61240 TQ	USBLS	5/15
	Tennessee	Y	63950 FQ	70550 MW	76850 TQ	USBLS	5/15
	Texas	Y	23210 FQ	43180 MW	72590 TQ	USBLS	5/15
	Austin-Round Rock MSA, TX	Y	20390 FQ	29510 MW	59030 TQ	USBLS	5/15
	Houston-The Woodlands-Sugar Land MSA, TX	Y	19890 FQ	50210 MW	75700 TQ	USBLS	5/15
	San Antonio-New Braunfels MSA, TX	Y	29690 FQ	68480 MW	89850 TQ	USBLS	5/15
	Utah	Y	43760 FQ	50940 MW	59920 TQ	USBLS	5/15
	Provo-Orem MSA, UT	Y	43360 FQ	48810 MW	57760 TQ	USBLS	5/15
	Salt Lake City MSA, UT	Y	46720 FQ	54550 MW	62010 TQ	USBLS	5/15
	Virginia	Y	54110 FQ	73700 MW	94840 TQ	USBLS	5/15
	Washington	H	20.74 FQ	27.62 MW	36.96 TQ	WABLS	3/16
	Seattle-Bellevue-Everett PMSA, WA	H	20.68 FQ	27.77 MW	37.23 TQ	WABLS	3/16
	West Virginia	Y	18050 FQ	19460 MW	31370 TQ	USBLS	5/15
	Wisconsin	Y	52090 FQ	59340 MW	76550 TQ	USBLS	5/15

AE	Average entry wage	AWR	Average wage range	H	Hourly
AEX	Average experienced wage	B	Biweekly	HI	Highest wage paid
ATC	Average total compensation	D	Daily	HR	High end range
AW	Average wage paid	FQ	First quartile wage	LO	Lowest wage paid

LR	Low end range	MTC	Median total compensation	TCC	Total cash compensation
M	Monthly	MW	Median wage paid	TQ	Third quartile wage
MCC	Median cash compensation	MWR	Median wage range	W	Weekly
ME	Median entry wage	S	See annotated source	Y	Yearly

Surveying and Mapping Technician

Occupation/Type/Industry	Location	Per	Low	Mid	High	Source	Date
Surveying and Mapping Technician	Alabama	Y	24902 AE	40620 AW	48489 AEX	ALBLS	6/16
	Birmingham-Hoover MSA, AL	Y	25177 AE	45003 AW	54911 AEX	ALBLS	6/16
	Alaska	Y	46850 FQ	59350 MW	70520 TQ	USBLS	5/15
	Anchorage MSA, AK	Y	43210 FQ	59370 MW	71400 TQ	USBLS	5/15
	Arizona	Y	37970 FQ	50380 MW	57620 TQ	USBLS	5/15
	Phoenix-Mesa-Scottsdale MSA, AZ	Y	39460 FQ	52720 MW	59140 TQ	USBLS	5/15
	Tucson MSA, AZ	Y	24570 FQ	41480 MW	53940 TQ	USBLS	5/15
	Arkansas	Y	27910 FQ	35580 MW	46630 TQ	USBLS	5/15
	Little Rock-North Little Rock-Conway MSA, AR	Y	30300 FQ	37830 MW	49360 TQ	USBLS	5/15
	California	H	24.64 FQ	30.26 MW	38.60 TQ	CABLS	1/16-3/16
	Anaheim-Santa Ana-Irvine PMSA, CA	H	27.25 FQ	32.18 MW	36.22 TQ	CABLS	1/16-3/16
	Los Angeles-Long Beach-Glendale PMSA, CA	H	27.95 FQ	36.06 MW	44.28 TQ	CABLS	1/16-3/16
	Oakland-Hayward-Berkeley PMSA, CA	H	26.41 FQ	32.03 MW	41.29 TQ	CABLS	1/16-3/16
	Riverside-San Bernardino-Ontario MSA, CA	H	24.00 FQ	28.72 MW	35.30 TQ	CABLS	1/16-3/16
	Sacramento–Roseville–Arden-Arcade MSA, CA	H	25.99 FQ	29.10 MW	36.60 TQ	CABLS	1/16-3/16
	San Diego-Carlsbad MSA, CA	H	22.80 FQ	28.62 MW	34.39 TQ	CABLS	1/16-3/16
	San Francisco-Redwood City-South San Francisco PMSA, CA	H	31.18 FQ	38.03 MW	44.47 TQ	CABLS	1/16-3/16
	Colorado	Y	36590 FQ	44710 MW	54670 TQ	USBLS	5/15
	Denver-Aurora-Lakewood MSA, CO	Y	41460 FQ	47070 MW	59130 TQ	USBLS	5/15
	Connecticut	Y		54113 MW		CTBLS	1/16-3/16
	Bridgeport-Stamford-Norwalk MSA, CT	Y	41420 FQ	51320 MW	69140 TQ	USBLS	5/15
	Hartford-West Hartford-East Hartford MSA, CT	Y	39240 FQ	56680 MW	69430 TQ	USBLS	5/15
	Delaware	Y	33600 FQ	38890 MW	46620 TQ	USBLS	5/15
	Wilmington PMSA, DE-MD-NJ	Y	35180 FQ	41990 MW	49390 TQ	USBLS	5/15
	Washington-Arlington-Alexandria PMSA, DC-VA-MD-WV	Y	36220 FQ	47450 MW	65040 TQ	USBLS	5/15
	Florida	H	13.11 AE	18.22 MW	21.91 AEX	FLBLS	7/16-9/16
	Fort Lauderdale-Pompano Beach-Deerfield Beach PMSA, FL	H	12.90 AE	17.45 MW	21.93 AEX	FLBLS	7/16-9/16
	Miami-Miami Beach-Kendall PMSA, FL	H	13.06 AE	16.99 MW	20.76 AEX	FLBLS	7/16-9/16
	Orlando-Kissimmee-Sanford MSA, FL	H	13.82 AE	19.17 MW	22.39 AEX	FLBLS	7/16-9/16
	Tampa-St. Petersburg-Clearwater MSA, FL	H	12.68 AE	17.82 MW	21.15 AEX	FLBLS	7/16-9/16
	Georgia	Y	28460 FQ	37110 MW	48640 TQ	USBLS	5/15
	Atlanta-Sandy Springs-Roswell MSA, GA	Y	29210 FQ	39010 MW	50280 TQ	USBLS	5/15
	Augusta-Richmond County MSA, GA-SC	Y	26700 FQ	34000 MW	47240 TQ	USBLS	5/15
	Hawaii	Y	36400 FQ	45350 MW	56630 TQ	USBLS	5/15
	Urban Honolulu MSA, HI	Y	35160 FQ	40680 MW	53450 TQ	USBLS	5/15
	Idaho	Y	33780 FQ	42240 MW	53000 TQ	USBLS	5/15
	Boise City MSA, ID	Y	36980 FQ	45610 MW	54430 TQ	USBLS	5/15
	Illinois	Y	37810 FQ	50150 MW	62030 TQ	USBLS	5/15
	Chicago-Naperville-Arlington Heights PMSA, IL	Y	36980 FQ	50670 MW	64070 TQ	USBLS	5/15
	Lake County-Kenosha County PMSA, IL-WI	Y	37490 FQ	51350 MW	59350 TQ	USBLS	5/15
	Indiana	Y	32620 FQ	38550 MW	47400 TQ	USBLS	5/15
	Gary PMSA, IN	Y	36010 FQ	45950 MW	62310 TQ	USBLS	5/15
	Indianapolis-Carmel-Anderson MSA, IN	Y	35340 FQ	42530 MW	52820 TQ	USBLS	5/15
	Iowa	Y	34290 FQ	41270 MW	51870 TQ	USBLS	5/15
	Kansas	Y	27920 FQ	34750 MW	43030 TQ	USBLS	5/15
	Wichita MSA, KS	Y	24650 FQ	29630 MW	35320 TQ	USBLS	5/15

AE Average entry wage	**AWR** Average wage range	**H** Hourly	**LR** Low end range	**MTC** Median total compensation	**TCC** Total cash compensation
AEX Average experienced wage	**B** Biweekly	**HI** Highest wage paid	**M** Monthly	**MW** Median wage paid	**TQ** Third quartile wage
ATC Average total compensation	**D** Daily	**HR** High end range	**MCC** Median cash compensation	**MWR** Median wage range	**W** Weekly
AW Average wage paid	**FQ** First quartile wage	**LO** Lowest wage paid	**ME** Median entry wage	**S** See annotated source	**Y** Yearly

Surveying and Mapping Technician

Occupation/Type/Industry	Location	Per	Low	Mid	High	Source	Date
Surveying and Mapping Technician	Kentucky	Y	28470 FQ	35410 MW	46650 TQ	USBLS	5/15
	Louisville-Jefferson County MSA, KY-IN	Y	33000 FQ	37110 MW	46300 TQ	USBLS	5/15
	Louisiana	Y	27730 FQ	35820 MW	46250 TQ	USBLS	5/15
	Baton Rouge MSA, LA	Y	23850 FQ	29230 MW	39160 TQ	USBLS	5/15
	Monroe MSA, LA	Y	32330 FQ	37340 MW	45940 TQ	USBLS	5/15
	New Orleans-Metairie MSA, LA	Y	34280 FQ	43310 MW	54570 TQ	USBLS	5/15
	Maine	Y	30910 FQ	39180 MW	46810 TQ	USBLS	5/15
	Portland-South Portland MSA, ME	Y	33060 FQ	40200 MW	47060 TQ	USBLS	5/15
	Maryland	Y	33450 AE	50945 MW	59692 AEX	MDBLS	4/16
	Baltimore-Columbia-Towson MSA, MD	Y	37700 FQ	48470 MW	60130 TQ	USBLS	5/15
	California-Lexington Park MSA, MD	Y	34330 FQ	57370 MW	81890 TQ	USBLS	5/15
	Salisbury MSA, MD-DE	Y	33660 FQ	38680 MW	45280 TQ	USBLS	5/15
	Massachusetts	Y	37870 FQ	50470 MW	58940 TQ	USBLS	5/15
	Boston-Cambridge-Newton NECTA, MA	Y	39220 FQ	51560 MW	58980 TQ	USBLS	5/15
	Worcester MSA, MA-CT	Y	39790 FQ	49400 MW	60060 TQ	USBLS	5/15
	Michigan	Y	31720 FQ	37330 MW	46470 TQ	USBLS	5/15
	Detroit-Dearborn-Livonia PMSA, MI	Y	32280 FQ	36120 MW	40410 TQ	USBLS	5/15
	Grand Rapids-Wyoming MSA, MI	Y	29900 FQ	35840 MW	43320 TQ	USBLS	5/15
	Minnesota	Y	42530 FQ	51441 MW	60564 TQ	MNBLS	1/16-3/16
	Minneapolis-St. Paul-Bloomington MSA, MN-WI	Y	44405 FQ	52741 MW	61038 TQ	MNBLS	1/16-3/16
	Mississippi	Y	27290 FQ	35690 MW	47470 TQ	USBLS	5/15
	Jackson MSA, MS	Y	29460 FQ	37700 MW	55990 TQ	USBLS	5/15
	Missouri	Y	30140 FQ	38500 MW	53230 TQ	USBLS	5/15
	Kansas City MSA, MO-KS	Y	33490 FQ	40510 MW	53010 TQ	USBLS	5/15
	St. Louis MSA, MO-IL	Y	32200 FQ	38370 MW	53830 TQ	USBLS	5/15
	Montana	Y	34450 FQ	43590 MW	53740 TQ	USBLS	5/15
	Billings MSA, MT	Y	37140 FQ	45640 MW	53770 TQ	USBLS	5/15
	Nebraska	Y	31555 FQ	38395 MW	46635 TQ	NEBLS	7/16-9/16
	Omaha-Council Bluffs MSA, NE-IA	Y	30400 FQ	36830 MW	45330 TQ	NEBLS	7/16-9/16
	Nevada	Y	43510 FQ	57340 MW	70930 TQ	USBLS	5/15
	Las Vegas-Henderson-Paradise MSA, NV	Y	49190 FQ	66490 MW	76770 TQ	USBLS	5/15
	New Hampshire	H	15.11 AE	19.90 MW	23.83 AEX	NHBLS	6/16
	Manchester NECTA, NH	H	17.00 AE	20.05 MW	25.02 AEX	NHBLS	6/16
	Nashua NECTA, NH-MA	Y	32640 FQ	43750 MW	54990 TQ	USBLS	5/15
	New Jersey	Y	37370 FQ	44940 MW	54030 TQ	USBLS	5/15
	Camden PMSA, NJ	Y	33840 FQ	41280 MW	46930 TQ	USBLS	5/15
	Newark PMSA, NJ-PA	Y	41380 FQ	47830 MW	59000 TQ	USBLS	5/15
	New Mexico	Y	32930 FQ	41110 MW	49620 TQ	USBLS	5/15
	Albuquerque MSA, NM	Y	35140 FQ	42850 MW	49590 TQ	USBLS	5/15
	New York	Y	31450 AE	43060 MW	52230 AEX	NYBLS	1/16-3/16
	Buffalo-Cheektowaga-Niagara Falls MSA, NY	Y	31820 FQ	37770 MW	48160 TQ	USBLS	5/15
	Nassau County-Suffolk County PMSA, NY	Y	38240 FQ	44270 MW	49530 TQ	USBLS	5/15
	New York-Jersey City-White Plains PMSA, NY-NJ	Y	33340 FQ	41500 MW	54060 TQ	USBLS	5/15
	Rochester MSA, NY	Y	33870 FQ	43680 MW	56000 TQ	USBLS	5/15
	North Carolina	Y	30990 FQ	38360 MW	47200 TQ	USBLS	5/15
	Charlotte-Concord-Gastonia MSA, NC-SC	Y	30670 FQ	39480 MW	47930 TQ	USBLS	5/15
	Raleigh MSA, NC	Y	33010 FQ	40390 MW	48030 TQ	USBLS	5/15
	North Dakota	Y	36390 FQ	43530 MW	53480 TQ	USBLS	5/15
	Ohio	Y	33710 FQ	41280 MW	49760 TQ	USBLS	5/15
	Cincinnati MSA, OH-KY-IN	Y	34030 FQ	38730 MW	46170 TQ	USBLS	5/15
	Cleveland-Elyria MSA, OH	Y	36680 FQ	44960 MW	54150 TQ	USBLS	5/15
	Columbus MSA, OH	Y	37000 FQ	44750 MW	53490 TQ	USBLS	5/15
	Oklahoma	Y	32720 FQ	50650 MW	61910 TQ	USBLS	5/15
	Oklahoma City MSA, OK	Y	29560 FQ	44660 MW	62050 TQ	USBLS	5/15
	Tulsa MSA, OK	Y	39260 FQ	55990 MW	75680 TQ	USBLS	5/15
	Oregon	H	20.16 FQ	23.14 MW	27.60 TQ	ORBLS	2016

AE	Average entry wage	AWR	Average wage range	H	Hourly
AEX	Average experienced wage	B	Biweekly	HI	Highest wage paid
ATC	Average total compensation	D	Daily	HR	High end range
AW	Average wage paid	FQ	First quartile wage	LO	Lowest wage paid

LR	Low end range	MTC	Median total compensation
M	Monthly	MW	Median wage paid
MCC	Median cash compensation	MWR	Median wage range
ME	Median entry wage	S	See annotated source

TCC	Total cash compensation
TQ	Third quartile wage
W	Weekly
Y	Yearly

Occupation/Type/Industry	Location	Per	Low	Mid	High	Source	Date
Surveying and Mapping Technician	Portland-Vancouver-Hillsboro MSA, OR-WA	Y	44000 FQ	49640 MW	59380 TQ	USBLS	5/15
	Pennsylvania	Y	34660 FQ	44290 MW	56060 TQ	USBLS	5/15
	Allentown-Bethlehem-Easton MSA, PA-NJ	Y	42660 FQ	49080 MW	56850 TQ	USBLS	5/15
	Harrisburg-Carlisle MSA, PA	Y	38370 FQ	48480 MW	59000 TQ	USBLS	5/15
	Montgomery County-Bucks County-Chester County PMSA, PA	Y	42600 FQ	52870 MW	62450 TQ	USBLS	5/15
	Philadelphia PMSA, PA	Y	34550 FQ	38560 MW	45380 TQ	USBLS	5/15
	Pittsburgh MSA, PA	Y	29720 FQ	38390 MW	54620 TQ	USBLS	5/15
	Rhode Island	Y	41840 FQ	45990 MW	50190 TQ	USBLS	5/15
	Providence-Warwick MSA, RI-MA	Y	41680 FQ	45960 MW	50270 TQ	USBLS	5/15
	South Carolina	Y	27250 FQ	34870 MW	45430 TQ	USBLS	5/15
	Charleston-North Charleston MSA, SC	Y	28990 FQ	35040 MW	43370 TQ	USBLS	5/15
	Columbia MSA, SC	Y	28980 FQ	36050 MW	45940 TQ	USBLS	5/15
	Greenville-Anderson-Mauldin MSA, SC	Y	24510 FQ	34600 MW	44310 TQ	USBLS	5/15
	South Dakota	Y	30260 FQ	36090 MW	43140 TQ	USBLS	5/15
	Tennessee	Y	30940 FQ	41330 MW	51740 TQ	USBLS	5/15
	Knoxville MSA, TN	Y	33430 FQ	45820 MW	62870 TQ	USBLS	5/15
	Memphis MSA, TN-MS-AR	Y	34310 FQ	46220 MW	59220 TQ	USBLS	5/15
	Nashville-Davidson– Murfreesboro–Franklin MSA, TN	Y	31920 FQ	42440 MW	50050 TQ	USBLS	5/15
	Texas	Y	31350 FQ	39700 MW	53020 TQ	USBLS	5/15
	Austin-Round Rock MSA, TX	Y	33240 FQ	38660 MW	49760 TQ	USBLS	5/15
	Dallas-Plano-Irving PMSA, TX	Y	31850 FQ	41100 MW	54620 TQ	USBLS	5/15
	Fort Worth-Arlington PMSA, TX	Y	33800 FQ	41380 MW	50730 TQ	USBLS	5/15
	Houston-The Woodlands-Sugar Land MSA, TX	Y	33770 FQ	44610 MW	57660 TQ	USBLS	5/15
	San Antonio-New Braunfels MSA, TX	Y	26220 FQ	32320 MW	42170 TQ	USBLS	5/15
	Utah	Y	35330 FQ	45220 MW	55330 TQ	USBLS	5/15
	Ogden-Clearfield MSA, UT	Y	42430 FQ	52330 MW	62340 TQ	USBLS	5/15
	Provo-Orem MSA, UT	Y	28210 FQ	51020 MW	60070 TQ	USBLS	5/15
	Salt Lake City MSA, UT	Y	39090 FQ	46310 MW	55280 TQ	USBLS	5/15
	Vermont	Y	36110 FQ	43780 MW	53390 TQ	USBLS	5/15
	Virginia	Y	33160 FQ	40660 MW	53250 TQ	USBLS	5/15
	Richmond MSA, VA	Y	36940 FQ	44470 MW	52210 TQ	USBLS	5/15
	Virginia Beach-Norfolk-Newport News MSA, VA-NC	Y	30170 FQ	40280 MW	49480 TQ	USBLS	5/15
	Washington	H	20.40 FQ	25.67 MW	30.83 TQ	WABLS	3/16
	Seattle-Bellevue-Everett PMSA, WA	H	22.72 FQ	27.91 MW	33.56 TQ	WABLS	3/16
	Tacoma-Lakewood PMSA, WA	H	21.32 FQ	25.96 MW	29.30 TQ	WABLS	3/16
	West Virginia	Y	24440 FQ	30220 MW	39130 TQ	USBLS	5/15
	Huntington-Ashland MSA, WV-KY-OH	Y	28010 FQ	38460 MW	48810 TQ	USBLS	5/15
	Wisconsin	Y	34020 FQ	44000 MW	54120 TQ	USBLS	5/15
	Madison MSA, WI	Y	30620 FQ	38800 MW	48370 TQ	USBLS	5/15
	Milwaukee-Waukesha-West Allis MSA, WI	Y	45990 FQ	53350 MW	59660 TQ	USBLS	5/15
	Wyoming	Y	35370 FQ	45360 MW	55880 TQ	USBLS	5/15
	Puerto Rico	Y	17380 FQ	19590 MW	27600 TQ	USBLS	5/15
	San Juan-Carolina-Caguas MSA, PR	Y	17390 FQ	19720 MW	28000 TQ	USBLS	5/15
Surveyor	Alabama	Y	32598 AE	53912 AW	64574 AEX	ALBLS	6/16
	Birmingham-Hoover MSA, AL	Y	31283 AE	54473 AW	66073 AEX	ALBLS	6/16
	Alaska	Y	71800 FQ	85420 MW	95870 TQ	USBLS	5/15
	Anchorage MSA, AK	Y	76980 FQ	88090 MW	97030 TQ	USBLS	5/15
	Arizona	Y	44970 FQ	52880 MW	62210 TQ	USBLS	5/15
	Phoenix-Mesa-Scottsdale MSA, AZ	Y	45370 FQ	52830 MW	61810 TQ	USBLS	5/15
	Tucson MSA, AZ	Y	44610 FQ	52750 MW	62910 TQ	USBLS	5/15
	Arkansas	Y	32450 FQ	43930 MW	57610 TQ	USBLS	5/15

AE	Average entry wage	**AWR**	Average wage range	**H**	Hourly	**LR**	Low end range	**MTC**	Median total compensation	**TCC**	Total cash compensation
AEX	Average experienced wage	**B**	Biweekly	**HI**	Highest wage paid	**M**	Monthly	**MW**	Median wage paid	**TQ**	Third quartile wage
ATC	Average total compensation	**D**	Daily	**HR**	High end range	**MCC**	Median cash compensation	**MWR**	Median wage range	**W**	Weekly
AW	Average wage paid	**FQ**	First quartile wage	**LO**	Lowest wage paid	**ME**	Median entry wage	**S**	See annotated source	**Y**	Yearly

Occupation/Type/Industry	Location	Per	Low	Mid	High	Source	Date
Surveyor	Little Rock-North Little Rock-Conway MSA, AR	Y	31900 FQ	44050 MW	57260 TQ	USBLS	5/15
	California	H	32.67 FQ	41.10 MW	48.09 TQ	CABLS	1/16-3/16
	Anaheim-Santa Ana-Irvine PMSA, CA	H	34.81 FQ	41.37 MW	46.17 TQ	CABLS	1/16-3/16
	Los Angeles-Long Beach-Glendale PMSA, CA	H	35.40 FQ	44.44 MW	52.57 TQ	CABLS	1/16-3/16
	Oakland-Hayward-Berkeley PMSA, CA	H	37.77 FQ	45.19 MW	53.29 TQ	CABLS	1/16-3/16
	Riverside-San Bernardino-Ontario MSA, CA	H	30.74 FQ	40.55 MW	47.59 TQ	CABLS	1/16-3/16
	Sacramento–Roseville–Arden-Arcade MSA, CA	H	36.66 FQ	45.19 MW	51.09 TQ	CABLS	1/16-3/16
	San Diego-Carlsbad MSA, CA	H	27.77 FQ	37.69 MW	45.57 TQ	CABLS	1/16-3/16
	San Francisco-Redwood City-South San Francisco PMSA, CA	H	32.17 FQ	41.49 MW	48.57 TQ	CABLS	1/16-3/16
	Colorado	Y	38240 FQ	53430 MW	66820 TQ	USBLS	5/15
	Denver-Aurora-Lakewood MSA, CO	Y	36380 FQ	52370 MW	62280 TQ	USBLS	5/15
	Connecticut	Y		59814 MW		CTBLS	1/16-3/16
	Bridgeport-Stamford-Norwalk MSA, CT	Y	52780 FQ	62410 MW	76090 TQ	USBLS	5/15
	Hartford-West Hartford-East Hartford MSA, CT	Y	51980 FQ	60300 MW	71960 TQ	USBLS	5/15
	Delaware	Y	54390 FQ	62170 MW	71830 TQ	USBLS	5/15
	Wilmington PMSA, DE-MD-NJ	Y	55480 FQ	63500 MW	73290 TQ	USBLS	5/15
	District of Columbia	Y	56580 FQ	87570 MW	120860 TQ	USBLS	5/15
	Washington-Arlington-Alexandria PMSA, DC-VA-MD-WV	Y	45730 FQ	58650 MW	76150 TQ	USBLS	5/15
	Florida	H	17.21 AE	27.24 MW	37.28 AEX	FLBLS	7/16-9/16
	Fort Lauderdale-Pompano Beach-Deerfield Beach PMSA, FL	H	17.88 AE	28.76 MW	36.43 AEX	FLBLS	7/16-9/16
	Miami-Miami Beach-Kendall PMSA, FL	H	16.73 AE	22.77 MW	42.46 AEX	FLBLS	7/16-9/16
	Orlando-Kissimmee-Sanford MSA, FL	H	15.22 AE	28.64 MW	38.14 AEX	FLBLS	7/16-9/16
	Tampa-St. Petersburg-Clearwater MSA, FL	H	22.76 AE	29.62 MW	46.13 AEX	FLBLS	7/16-9/16
	Georgia	Y	39370 FQ	50400 MW	65630 TQ	USBLS	5/15
	Atlanta-Sandy Springs-Roswell MSA, GA	Y	42280 FQ	55090 MW	71850 TQ	USBLS	5/15
	Augusta-Richmond County MSA, GA-SC	Y	34990 FQ	43110 MW	58710 TQ	USBLS	5/15
	Hawaii	Y	44450 FQ	56230 MW	68870 TQ	USBLS	5/15
	Urban Honolulu MSA, HI	Y	45000 FQ	58490 MW	73190 TQ	USBLS	5/15
	Idaho	Y	49340 FQ	62760 MW	77350 TQ	USBLS	5/15
	Boise City MSA, ID	Y	52930 FQ	64290 MW	79540 TQ	USBLS	5/15
	Illinois	Y	45690 FQ	57030 MW	73440 TQ	USBLS	5/15
	Chicago-Naperville-Arlington Heights PMSA, IL	Y	46400 FQ	56830 MW	74750 TQ	USBLS	5/15
	Lake County-Kenosha County PMSA, IL-WI	Y	38910 FQ	51940 MW	72640 TQ	USBLS	5/15
	Indiana	Y	37450 FQ	51170 MW	70040 TQ	USBLS	5/15
	Gary PMSA, IN	Y	54130 FQ	66930 MW	85680 TQ	USBLS	5/15
	Indianapolis-Carmel-Anderson MSA, IN	Y	45080 FQ	57600 MW	78370 TQ	USBLS	5/15
	Iowa	Y	45300 FQ	57050 MW	70770 TQ	USBLS	5/15
	Des Moines-West Des Moines MSA, IA	Y	30070 FQ	53100 MW	61520 TQ	USBLS	5/15
	Kansas	Y	42330 FQ	52160 MW	62410 TQ	USBLS	5/15
	Wichita MSA, KS	Y	40740 FQ	49680 MW	70820 TQ	USBLS	5/15
	Kentucky	Y	39930 FQ	49090 MW	61670 TQ	USBLS	5/15
	Louisville-Jefferson County MSA, KY-IN	Y	40480 FQ	46050 MW	54710 TQ	USBLS	5/15
	Louisiana	Y	40940 FQ	53360 MW	72910 TQ	USBLS	5/15
	Baton Rouge MSA, LA	Y	45570 FQ	59880 MW	79990 TQ	USBLS	5/15
	New Orleans-Metairie MSA, LA	Y	42080 FQ	56680 MW	74920 TQ	USBLS	5/15

AE	Average entry wage	AWR	Average wage range	H	Hourly
AEX	Average experienced wage	B	Biweekly	HI	Highest wage paid
ATC	Average total compensation	D	Daily	HR	High end range
AW	Average wage paid	FQ	First quartile wage	LO	Lowest wage paid

LR	Low end range	MTC	Median total compensation	TCC	Total cash compensation
M	Monthly	MW	Median wage paid	TQ	Third quartile wage
MCC	Median cash compensation	MWR	Median wage range	W	Weekly
ME	Median entry wage	S	See annotated source	Y	Yearly

Occupation/Type/Industry	Location	Per	Low	Mid	High	Source	Date
Surveyor	Maine	Y	37550 FQ	50810 MW	61670 TQ	USBLS	5/15
	Portland-South Portland MSA, ME	Y	36420 FQ	44260 MW	50830 TQ	USBLS	5/15
	Maryland	Y	39001 AE	63133 MW	75199 AEX	MDBLS	4/16
	Baltimore-Columbia-Towson MSA, MD	Y	46380 FQ	57850 MW	74300 TQ	USBLS	5/15
	Salisbury MSA, MD-DE	Y	44580 FQ	51440 MW	67110 TQ	USBLS	5/15
	Massachusetts	Y	44950 FQ	56990 MW	70940 TQ	USBLS	5/15
	Boston-Cambridge-Newton NECTA, MA	Y	46070 FQ	58370 MW	73460 TQ	USBLS	5/15
	Worcester MSA, MA-CT	Y	46210 FQ	55380 MW	66080 TQ	USBLS	5/15
	Michigan	Y	38610 FQ	48580 MW	62670 TQ	USBLS	5/15
	Detroit-Dearborn-Livonia PMSA, MI	Y	30210 FQ	45010 MW	55280 TQ	USBLS	5/15
	Grand Rapids-Wyoming MSA, MI	Y	28550 FQ	46400 MW	58350 TQ	USBLS	5/15
	Minnesota	Y	55201 FQ	66441 MW	88346 TQ	MNBLS	1/16-3/16
	Minneapolis-St. Paul-Bloomington MSA, MN-WI	Y	57751 FQ	71904 MW	94888 TQ	MNBLS	1/16-3/16
	Mississippi	Y	33840 FQ	44930 MW	56120 TQ	USBLS	5/15
	Jackson MSA, MS	Y	37270 FQ	56090 MW	86760 TQ	USBLS	5/15
	Missouri	Y	40500 FQ	50230 MW	62710 TQ	USBLS	5/15
	Kansas City MSA, MO-KS	Y	43260 FQ	54780 MW	62740 TQ	USBLS	5/15
	St. Louis MSA, MO-IL	Y	46960 FQ	56470 MW	74770 TQ	USBLS	5/15
	Montana	Y	44670 FQ	58190 MW	71430 TQ	USBLS	5/15
	Billings MSA, MT	Y	47270 FQ	59340 MW	70270 TQ	USBLS	5/15
	Nebraska	Y	39675 FQ	48080 MW	62465 TQ	NEBLS	7/16-9/16
	Omaha-Council Bluffs MSA, NE-IA	Y	46500 FQ	57190 MW	71210 TQ	NEBLS	7/16-9/16
	Nevada	Y	54590 FQ	68050 MW	83390 TQ	USBLS	5/15
	Las Vegas-Henderson-Paradise MSA, NV	Y	55460 FQ	68090 MW	81250 TQ	USBLS	5/15
	New Hampshire	H	17.87 AE	26.15 MW	30.63 AEX	NHBLS	6/16
	New Jersey	Y	53730 FQ	72040 MW	87580 TQ	USBLS	5/15
	Camden PMSA, NJ	Y	47900 FQ	69610 MW	88410 TQ	USBLS	5/15
	Newark PMSA, NJ-PA	Y	61190 FQ	73540 MW	88570 TQ	USBLS	5/15
	Trenton MSA, NJ	Y	57990 FQ	69510 MW	79170 TQ	USBLS	5/15
	New Mexico	Y	47290 FQ	59510 MW	77260 TQ	USBLS	5/15
	Albuquerque MSA, NM	Y	50010 FQ	61650 MW	84890 TQ	USBLS	5/15
	New York	Y	48180 AE	70260 MW	85460 AEX	NYBLS	1/16-3/16
	Buffalo-Cheektowaga-Niagara Falls MSA, NY	Y	47540 FQ	60220 MW	81470 TQ	USBLS	5/15
	Nassau County-Suffolk County PMSA, NY	Y	71120 FQ	89680 MW	103020 TQ	USBLS	5/15
	New York-Jersey City-White Plains PMSA, NY-NJ	Y	55520 FQ	72390 MW	88320 TQ	USBLS	5/15
	Rochester MSA, NY	Y	47540 FQ	58670 MW	82700 TQ	USBLS	5/15
	North Carolina	Y	44500 FQ	55390 MW	70720 TQ	USBLS	5/15
	Charlotte-Concord-Gastonia MSA, NC-SC	Y	42690 FQ	57040 MW	73210 TQ	USBLS	5/15
	Raleigh MSA, NC	Y	47650 FQ	61240 MW	79260 TQ	USBLS	5/15
	North Dakota	Y	49360 FQ	60400 MW	77050 TQ	USBLS	5/15
	Fargo MSA, ND-MN	Y	48870 FQ	63050 MW	73630 TQ	USBLS	5/15
	Ohio	Y	41800 FQ	57360 MW	71620 TQ	USBLS	5/15
	Cincinnati MSA, OH-KY-IN	Y	49400 FQ	61310 MW	72290 TQ	USBLS	5/15
	Cleveland-Elyria MSA, OH	Y	34890 FQ	48330 MW	63360 TQ	USBLS	5/15
	Columbus MSA, OH	Y	50060 FQ	58560 MW	77120 TQ	USBLS	5/15
	Oklahoma	Y	33950 FQ	47130 MW	62760 TQ	USBLS	5/15
	Oklahoma City MSA, OK	Y	29830 FQ	45360 MW	67300 TQ	USBLS	5/15
	Tulsa MSA, OK	Y	37300 FQ	50390 MW	60750 TQ	USBLS	5/15
	Oregon	H	26.06 FQ	33.26 MW	40.40 TQ	ORBLS	2016
	Portland-Vancouver-Hillsboro MSA, OR-WA	Y	57750 FQ	70980 MW	83370 TQ	USBLS	5/15
	Pennsylvania	Y	47130 FQ	58880 MW	74540 TQ	USBLS	5/15
	Allentown-Bethlehem-Easton MSA, PA-NJ	Y	50400 FQ	59320 MW	73310 TQ	USBLS	5/15
	Harrisburg-Carlisle MSA, PA	Y	47980 FQ	60990 MW	75160 TQ	USBLS	5/15
	Montgomery County-Bucks County-Chester County PMSA, PA	Y	56460 FQ	71280 MW	90680 TQ	USBLS	5/15
	Philadelphia PMSA, PA	Y	45010 FQ	57150 MW	85310 TQ	USBLS	5/15
	Pittsburgh MSA, PA	Y	48650 FQ	58710 MW	71310 TQ	USBLS	5/15

AE	Average entry wage	AWR	Average wage range	H	Hourly
AEX	Average experienced wage	B	Biweekly	HI	Highest wage paid
ATC	Average total compensation	D	Daily	HR	High end range
AW	Average wage paid	FQ	First quartile wage	LO	Lowest wage paid

LR	Low end range	MTC	Median total compensation	TCC	Total cash compensation
M	Monthly	MW	Median wage paid	TQ	Third quartile wage
MCC	Median cash compensation	MWR	Median wage range	W	Weekly
ME	Median entry wage	S	See annotated source	Y	Yearly

Occupation/Type/Industry	Location	Per	Low	Mid	High	Source	Date
Surveyor	Providence-Warwick MSA, RI-MA	Y	48400 FQ	82840 MW	97690 TQ	USBLS	5/15
	South Carolina	Y	29930 FQ	38270 MW	55690 TQ	USBLS	5/15
	Charleston-North Charleston MSA, SC	Y	33290 FQ	42600 MW	58250 TQ	USBLS	5/15
	Columbia MSA, SC	Y	30940 FQ	46320 MW	59270 TQ	USBLS	5/15
	Greenville-Anderson-Mauldin MSA, SC	Y	34670 FQ	47000 MW	73090 TQ	USBLS	5/15
	South Dakota	Y	44940 FQ	54410 MW	66720 TQ	USBLS	5/15
	Sioux Falls MSA, SD	Y	48920 FQ	61320 MW	81080 TQ	USBLS	5/15
	Tennessee	Y	31610 FQ	43070 MW	53630 TQ	USBLS	5/15
	Knoxville MSA, TN	Y	28580 FQ	38280 MW	49230 TQ	USBLS	5/15
	Memphis MSA, TN-MS-AR	Y	38320 FQ	47450 MW	61270 TQ	USBLS	5/15
	Nashville-Davidson–Murfreesboro–Franklin MSA, TN	Y	40690 FQ	47800 MW	57100 TQ	USBLS	5/15
	Texas	Y	39390 FQ	56370 MW	79190 TQ	USBLS	5/15
	Austin-Round Rock MSA, TX	Y	35390 FQ	62300 MW	80280 TQ	USBLS	5/15
	Dallas-Plano-Irving PMSA, TX	Y	42810 FQ	64340 MW	85480 TQ	USBLS	5/15
	Fort Worth-Arlington PMSA, TX	Y	39290 FQ	58350 MW	78210 TQ	USBLS	5/15
	Houston-The Woodlands-Sugar Land MSA, TX	Y	37910 FQ	54460 MW	80760 TQ	USBLS	5/15
	San Antonio-New Braunfels MSA, TX	Y	44260 FQ	53550 MW	73410 TQ	USBLS	5/15
	Utah	Y	48530 FQ	60880 MW	76150 TQ	USBLS	5/15
	Ogden-Clearfield MSA, UT	Y	47120 FQ	59840 MW	86300 TQ	USBLS	5/15
	Provo-Orem MSA, UT	Y	46810 FQ	58670 MW	78530 TQ	USBLS	5/15
	Salt Lake City MSA, UT	Y	51020 FQ	63520 MW	76680 TQ	USBLS	5/15
	Vermont	Y	40730 FQ	51640 MW	57540 TQ	USBLS	5/15
	Virginia	Y	40000 FQ	52210 MW	71670 TQ	USBLS	5/15
	Richmond MSA, VA	Y	36000 FQ	44570 MW	63260 TQ	USBLS	5/15
	Virginia Beach-Norfolk-Newport News MSA, VA-NC	Y	47580 FQ	59980 MW	83940 TQ	USBLS	5/15
	Washington	H	27.73 FQ	35.10 MW	43.01 TQ	WABLS	3/16
	Seattle-Bellevue-Everett PMSA, WA	H	28.55 FQ	37.85 MW	45.92 TQ	WABLS	3/16
	Tacoma-Lakewood PMSA, WA	H	30.79 FQ	35.96 MW	42.76 TQ	WABLS	3/16
	West Virginia	Y	37770 FQ	47100 MW	61750 TQ	USBLS	5/15
	Huntington-Ashland MSA, WV-KY-OH	Y	35260 FQ	49920 MW	59940 TQ	USBLS	5/15
	Wisconsin	Y	43780 FQ	56520 MW	69150 TQ	USBLS	5/15
	Madison MSA, WI	Y	34830 FQ	51940 MW	60810 TQ	USBLS	5/15
	Milwaukee-Waukesha-West Allis MSA, WI	Y	45460 FQ	64260 MW	77310 TQ	USBLS	5/15
	Wyoming	Y	51980 FQ	60900 MW	75170 TQ	USBLS	5/15
	Puerto Rico	Y	28170 FQ	36710 MW	45920 TQ	USBLS	5/15
	San Juan-Carolina-Caguas MSA, PR	Y	28790 FQ	36830 MW	45300 TQ	USBLS	5/15
Sustainability Analyst							
Municipal Government	Santa Monica, CA	Y		89265 AW		CACIT	6/28/16
Sustainability Coordinator							
City Manager's Office	Burlingame, CA	Y			52161 HI	CACIT	6/28/16
Swim Team Coach							
Municipal Government	Montague, MA	H	10.50 LO		11.50 HI	FRCOG	2016
Switchboard Operator							
Including Answering Service	Alabama	Y	19303 AE	25229 AW	28187 AEX	ALBLS	6/16
Including Answering Service	Birmingham-Hoover MSA, AL	Y	22003 AE	27754 AW	30629 AEX	ALBLS	6/16
Including Answering Service	Alaska	Y	26360 FQ	32710 MW	37820 TQ	USBLS	5/15
Including Answering Service	Anchorage MSA, AK	Y	24960 FQ	29980 MW	36000 TQ	USBLS	5/15
Including Answering Service	Arizona	Y	22510 FQ	26320 MW	29880 TQ	USBLS	5/15
Including Answering Service	Phoenix-Mesa-Scottsdale MSA, AZ	Y	23190 FQ	26790 MW	30000 TQ	USBLS	5/15
Including Answering Service	Tucson MSA, AZ	Y	20410 FQ	23730 MW	28560 TQ	USBLS	5/15
Including Answering Service	Arkansas	Y	21240 FQ	25110 MW	30670 TQ	USBLS	5/15
Including Answering Service	Little Rock-North Little Rock-Conway MSA, AR	Y	22200 FQ	27700 MW	34190 TQ	USBLS	5/15
Including Answering Service	California	H	11.98 FQ	14.84 MW	19.34 TQ	CABLS	1/16-3/16

Switchboard Operator

Occupation/Type/Industry	Location	Per	Low	Mid	High	Source	Date
Including Answering Service	Anaheim-Santa Ana-Irvine PMSA, CA	H	11.74 FQ	14.27 MW	17.45 TQ	CABLS	1/16-3/16
Including Answering Service	Los Angeles-Long Beach-Glendale PMSA, CA	H	12.00 FQ	14.69 MW	18.27 TQ	CABLS	1/16-3/16
Including Answering Service	Oakland-Hayward-Berkeley PMSA, CA	H	14.11 FQ	19.56 MW	26.72 TQ	CABLS	1/16-3/16
Including Answering Service	Riverside-San Bernardino-Ontario MSA, CA	H	11.17 FQ	13.36 MW	16.02 TQ	CABLS	1/16-3/16
Including Answering Service	Sacramento–Roseville–Arden-Arcade MSA, CA	H	12.70 FQ	16.19 MW	22.67 TQ	CABLS	1/16-3/16
Including Answering Service	San Diego-Carlsbad MSA, CA	H	10.96 FQ	13.27 MW	16.11 TQ	CABLS	1/16-3/16
Including Answering Service	San Francisco-Redwood City-South San Francisco PMSA, CA	H	13.57 FQ	19.90 MW	23.32 TQ	CABLS	1/16-3/16
Including Answering Service	Colorado	Y	24150 FQ	28600 MW	34140 TQ	USBLS	5/15
Including Answering Service	Denver-Aurora-Lakewood MSA, CO	Y	24570 FQ	29000 MW	35320 TQ	USBLS	5/15
Including Answering Service	Connecticut	Y		35039 MW		CTBLS	1/16-3/16
Including Answering Service	Bridgeport-Stamford-Norwalk MSA, CT	Y	24860 FQ	33270 MW	39120 TQ	USBLS	5/15
Including Answering Service	Hartford-West Hartford-East Hartford MSA, CT	Y	31960 FQ	35890 MW	39790 TQ	USBLS	5/15
Including Answering Service	Delaware	Y	22110 FQ	26810 MW	33390 TQ	USBLS	5/15
Including Answering Service	Wilmington PMSA, DE-MD-NJ	Y	22470 FQ	27880 MW	34210 TQ	USBLS	5/15
Including Answering Service	District of Columbia	Y	32030 FQ	36970 MW	43490 TQ	USBLS	5/15
Including Answering Service	Washington-Arlington-Alexandria PMSA, DC-VA-MD-WV	Y	26080 FQ	31860 MW	37790 TQ	USBLS	5/15
Including Answering Service	Florida	H	10.09 AE	12.23 MW	14.24 AEX	FLBLS	7/16-9/16
Including Answering Service	Fort Lauderdale-Pompano Beach-Deerfield Beach PMSA, FL	H	10.57 AE	13.35 MW	16.63 AEX	FLBLS	7/16-9/16
Including Answering Service	Lakeland-Winter Haven MSA, FL	H	10.37 AE	11.41 MW	13.04 AEX	FLBLS	7/16-9/16
Including Answering Service	Miami-Miami Beach-Kendall PMSA, FL	H	10.56 AE	13.29 MW	14.99 AEX	FLBLS	7/16-9/16
Including Answering Service	Orlando-Kissimmee-Sanford MSA, FL	H	9.43 AE	11.50 MW	13.50 AEX	FLBLS	7/16-9/16
Including Answering Service	Tampa-St. Petersburg-Clearwater MSA, FL	H	10.28 AE	12.75 MW	14.06 AEX	FLBLS	7/16-9/16
Including Answering Service	Georgia	Y	21040 FQ	25960 MW	30730 TQ	USBLS	5/15
Including Answering Service	Atlanta-Sandy Springs-Roswell MSA, GA	Y	22480 FQ	27480 MW	31620 TQ	USBLS	5/15
Including Answering Service	Augusta-Richmond County MSA, GA-SC	Y	19300 FQ	22640 MW	28040 TQ	USBLS	5/15
Including Answering Service	Hawaii	Y	31510 FQ	39280 MW	45090 TQ	USBLS	5/15
Including Answering Service	Urban Honolulu MSA, HI	Y	29740 FQ	37270 MW	44260 TQ	USBLS	5/15
Including Answering Service	Idaho	Y	22470 FQ	26560 MW	31050 TQ	USBLS	5/15
Including Answering Service	Boise City MSA, ID	Y	24400 FQ	28030 MW	32710 TQ	USBLS	5/15
Including Answering Service	Illinois	Y	23520 FQ	28190 MW	33680 TQ	USBLS	5/15
Including Answering Service	Chicago-Naperville-Arlington Heights PMSA, IL	Y	24860 FQ	29300 MW	35000 TQ	USBLS	5/15
Including Answering Service	Lake County-Kenosha County PMSA, IL-WI	Y	25730 FQ	30630 MW	37080 TQ	USBLS	5/15
Including Answering Service	Indiana	Y	21860 FQ	25810 MW	29770 TQ	USBLS	5/15
Including Answering Service	Gary PMSA, IN	Y	20410 FQ	23660 MW	27610 TQ	USBLS	5/15
Including Answering Service	Indianapolis-Carmel-Anderson MSA, IN	Y	23810 FQ	27610 MW	31220 TQ	USBLS	5/15
Including Answering Service	Iowa	Y	22020 FQ	25090 MW	29760 TQ	USBLS	5/15
Including Answering Service	Des Moines-West Des Moines MSA, IA	Y	24680 FQ	28090 MW	31440 TQ	USBLS	5/15
Including Answering Service	Kansas	Y	22420 FQ	26670 MW	31310 TQ	USBLS	5/15
Including Answering Service	Wichita MSA, KS	Y	23400 FQ	26860 MW	29960 TQ	USBLS	5/15
Including Answering Service	Kentucky	Y	20800 FQ	24720 MW	30940 TQ	USBLS	5/15
Including Answering Service	Louisville-Jefferson County MSA, KY-IN	Y	21250 FQ	25390 MW	33020 TQ	USBLS	5/15
Including Answering Service	Louisiana	Y	20090 FQ	23520 MW	28330 TQ	USBLS	5/15
Including Answering Service	Baton Rouge MSA, LA	Y	21680 FQ	24560 MW	29150 TQ	USBLS	5/15
Including Answering Service	New Orleans-Metairie MSA, LA	Y	19560 FQ	22730 MW	26780 TQ	USBLS	5/15

AE	Average entry wage	AWR	Average wage range	H	Hourly	LR	Low end range	MTC	Median total compensation	TCC	Total cash compensation
AEX	Average experienced wage	B	Biweekly	HI	Highest wage paid	M	Monthly	MW	Median wage paid	TQ	Third quartile wage
ATC	Average total compensation	D	Daily	HR	High end range	MCC	Median cash compensation	MWR	Median wage range	W	Weekly
AW	Average wage paid	FQ	First quartile wage	LO	Lowest wage paid	ME	Median entry wage	S	See annotated source	Y	Yearly

1546

Occupation/Type/Industry	Location	Per	Low	Mid	High	Source	Date
Switchboard Operator							
Including Answering Service	Maine	Y	22640 FQ	26870 MW	32920 TQ	USBLS	5/15
Including Answering Service	Portland-South Portland MSA, ME	Y	24250 FQ	28560 MW	32870 TQ	USBLS	5/15
Including Answering Service	Maryland	Y	22145 AE	30149 MW	34152 AEX	MDBLS	4/16
Including Answering Service	Baltimore-Columbia-Towson MSA, MD	Y	23260 FQ	27200 MW	30590 TQ	USBLS	5/15
Including Answering Service	Salisbury MSA, MD-DE	Y	21200 FQ	25970 MW	29770 TQ	USBLS	5/15
Including Answering Service	Massachusetts	Y	25500 FQ	30230 MW	36600 TQ	USBLS	5/15
Including Answering Service	Boston-Cambridge-Newton NECTA, MA	Y	27530 FQ	31940 MW	38290 TQ	USBLS	5/15
Including Answering Service	Worcester MSA, MA-CT	Y	22500 FQ	28740 MW	34240 TQ	USBLS	5/15
Including Answering Service	Michigan	Y	21610 FQ	26740 MW	32440 TQ	USBLS	5/15
Including Answering Service	Detroit-Dearborn-Livonia PMSA, MI	Y	23820 FQ	28300 MW	32560 TQ	USBLS	5/15
Including Answering Service	Grand Rapids-Wyoming MSA, MI	Y	22430 FQ	26270 MW	31260 TQ	USBLS	5/15
Including Answering Service	Minnesota	Y	25858 FQ	31107 MW	36507 TQ	MNBLS	1/16-3/16
Including Answering Service	Minneapolis-St. Paul-Bloomington MSA, MN-WI	Y	24978 FQ	31087 MW	36679 TQ	MNBLS	1/16-3/16
Including Answering Service	Mississippi	Y	19680 FQ	23010 MW	27740 TQ	USBLS	5/15
Including Answering Service	Jackson MSA, MS	Y	21200 FQ	24380 MW	29510 TQ	USBLS	5/15
Including Answering Service	Missouri	Y	21890 FQ	25440 MW	29790 TQ	USBLS	5/15
Including Answering Service	Kansas City MSA, MO-KS	Y	22930 FQ	27590 MW	32710 TQ	USBLS	5/15
Including Answering Service	St. Louis MSA, MO-IL	Y	23220 FQ	27190 MW	31270 TQ	USBLS	5/15
Including Answering Service	Montana	Y	21420 FQ	24280 MW	28250 TQ	USBLS	5/15
Including Answering Service	Billings MSA, MT	Y	21680 FQ	24810 MW	28790 TQ	USBLS	5/15
Including Answering Service	Nebraska	Y	22130 FQ	26520 MW	32465 TQ	NEBLS	7/16-9/16
Including Answering Service	Omaha-Council Bluffs MSA, NE-IA	Y	23925 FQ	29400 MW	35975 TQ	NEBLS	7/16-9/16
Including Answering Service	Nevada	Y	25130 FQ	31460 MW	36660 TQ	USBLS	5/15
Including Answering Service	Las Vegas-Henderson-Paradise MSA, NV	Y	26940 FQ	32730 MW	37160 TQ	USBLS	5/15
Including Answering Service	New Hampshire	H	10.13 AE	14.00 MW	17.02 AEX	NHBLS	6/16
Including Answering Service	Manchester NECTA, NH	H	11.80 AE	14.33 MW	16.26 AEX	NHBLS	6/16
Including Answering Service	Nashua NECTA, NH-MA	Y	19180 FQ	26770 MW	31920 TQ	USBLS	5/15
Including Answering Service	New Jersey	Y	25760 FQ	29760 MW	35310 TQ	USBLS	5/15
Including Answering Service	Camden PMSA, NJ	Y	23990 FQ	29110 MW	34910 TQ	USBLS	5/15
Including Answering Service	Newark PMSA, NJ-PA	Y	25980 FQ	30320 MW	35870 TQ	USBLS	5/15
Including Answering Service	Trenton MSA, NJ	Y	23790 FQ	29020 MW	34970 TQ	USBLS	5/15
Including Answering Service	New Mexico	Y	19830 FQ	24530 MW	29690 TQ	USBLS	5/15
Including Answering Service	Albuquerque MSA, NM	Y	20170 FQ	25440 MW	29810 TQ	USBLS	5/15
Including Answering Service	New York	Y	22400 AE	31400 MW	39100 AEX	NYBLS	1/16-3/16
Including Answering Service	Buffalo-Cheektowaga-Niagara Falls MSA, NY	Y	25090 FQ	30590 MW	37000 TQ	USBLS	5/15
Including Answering Service	Nassau County-Suffolk County PMSA, NY	Y	24630 FQ	32410 MW	38530 TQ	USBLS	5/15
Including Answering Service	New York-Jersey City-White Plains PMSA, NY-NJ	Y	26180 FQ	32810 MW	41250 TQ	USBLS	5/15
Including Answering Service	Rochester MSA, NY	Y	22470 FQ	27990 MW	37070 TQ	USBLS	5/15
Including Answering Service	North Carolina	Y	21720 FQ	26510 MW	31570 TQ	USBLS	5/15
Including Answering Service	Charlotte-Concord-Gastonia MSA, NC-SC	Y	22560 FQ	28220 MW	34470 TQ	USBLS	5/15
Including Answering Service	Raleigh MSA, NC	Y	24200 FQ	28630 MW	34640 TQ	USBLS	5/15
Including Answering Service	North Dakota	Y	22710 FQ	27350 MW	34570 TQ	USBLS	5/15
Including Answering Service	Fargo MSA, ND-MN	Y	23490 FQ	29860 MW	36400 TQ	USBLS	5/15
Including Answering Service	Ohio	Y	24010 FQ	27960 MW	32050 TQ	USBLS	5/15
Including Answering Service	Cincinnati MSA, OH-KY-IN	Y	24810 FQ	28180 MW	31530 TQ	USBLS	5/15
Including Answering Service	Cleveland-Elyria MSA, OH	Y	25930 FQ	29610 MW	35080 TQ	USBLS	5/15
Including Answering Service	Columbus MSA, OH	Y	25510 FQ	28610 MW	33170 TQ	USBLS	5/15
Including Answering Service	Oklahoma	Y	20050 FQ	24430 MW	30550 TQ	USBLS	5/15
Including Answering Service	Oklahoma City MSA, OK	Y	22160 FQ	28550 MW	35200 TQ	USBLS	5/15
Including Answering Service	Tulsa MSA, OK	Y	22380 FQ	26540 MW	30160 TQ	USBLS	5/15
Including Answering Service	Oregon	H	11.24 FQ	14.45 MW	18.15 TQ	ORBLS	2016
Including Answering Service	Portland-Vancouver-Hillsboro MSA, OR-WA	Y	23640 FQ	32440 MW	39200 TQ	USBLS	5/15
Including Answering Service	Pennsylvania	Y	22800 FQ	27650 MW	33840 TQ	USBLS	5/15
Including Answering Service	Allentown-Bethlehem-Easton MSA, PA-NJ	Y	20850 FQ	25010 MW	30700 TQ	USBLS	5/15
Including Answering Service	Harrisburg-Carlisle MSA, PA	Y	24860 FQ	28930 MW	34280 TQ	USBLS	5/15

AE	Average entry wage	AWR	Average wage range	
AEX	Average experienced wage	B	Biweekly	
ATC	Average total compensation	D	Daily	
AW	Average wage paid	FQ	First quartile wage	

H	Hourly	
HI	Highest wage paid	
HR	High end range	
LO	Lowest wage paid	

LR	Low end range
M	Monthly
MCC	Median cash compensation
ME	Median entry wage

MTC	Median total compensation
MW	Median wage paid
MWR	Median wage range
S	See annotated source

TCC	Total cash compensation
TQ	Third quartile wage
W	Weekly
Y	Yearly

Occupation/Type/Industry	Location	Per	Low	Mid	High	Source	Date
Switchboard Operator							
Including Answering Service	Montgomery County-Bucks County-Chester County PMSA, PA	Y	23620 FQ	27740 MW	32750 TQ	USBLS	5/15
Including Answering Service	Philadelphia PMSA, PA	Y	27140 FQ	33150 MW	39290 TQ	USBLS	5/15
Including Answering Service	Pittsburgh MSA, PA	Y	23700 FQ	28650 MW	36500 TQ	USBLS	5/15
Including Answering Service	Rhode Island	Y	23340 FQ	28180 MW	34300 TQ	USBLS	5/15
Including Answering Service	Providence-Warwick MSA, RI-MA	Y	22560 FQ	27160 MW	33510 TQ	USBLS	5/15
Including Answering Service	South Carolina	Y	21710 FQ	25410 MW	30230 TQ	USBLS	5/15
Including Answering Service	Charleston-North Charleston MSA, SC	Y	25160 FQ	28400 MW	32750 TQ	USBLS	5/15
Including Answering Service	Columbia MSA, SC	Y	21400 FQ	26170 MW	31520 TQ	USBLS	5/15
Including Answering Service	Greenville-Anderson-Mauldin MSA, SC	Y	21780 FQ	24800 MW	29260 TQ	USBLS	5/15
Including Answering Service	Sioux Falls MSA, SD	Y	21950 FQ	23990 MW	28090 TQ	USBLS	5/15
Including Answering Service	Tennessee	Y	21320 FQ	25980 MW	30810 TQ	USBLS	5/15
Including Answering Service	Knoxville MSA, TN	Y	22470 FQ	25620 MW	29530 TQ	USBLS	5/15
Including Answering Service	Memphis MSA, TN-MS-AR	Y	23180 FQ	27500 MW	31220 TQ	USBLS	5/15
Including Answering Service	Nashville-Davidson–Murfreesboro–Franklin MSA, TN	Y	22250 FQ	27900 MW	34140 TQ	USBLS	5/15
Including Answering Service	Texas	Y	21080 FQ	25680 MW	30870 TQ	USBLS	5/15
Including Answering Service	Austin-Round Rock MSA, TX	Y	23260 FQ	27350 MW	30880 TQ	USBLS	5/15
Including Answering Service	Dallas-Plano-Irving PMSA, TX	Y	20800 FQ	25350 MW	31060 TQ	USBLS	5/15
Including Answering Service	Fort Worth-Arlington PMSA, TX	Y	21730 FQ	26750 MW	30620 TQ	USBLS	5/15
Including Answering Service	Houston-The Woodlands-Sugar Land MSA, TX	Y	24440 FQ	29410 MW	38940 TQ	USBLS	5/15
Including Answering Service	San Antonio-New Braunfels MSA, TX	Y	20440 FQ	23630 MW	27880 TQ	USBLS	5/15
Including Answering Service	Utah	Y	21020 FQ	24260 MW	28850 TQ	USBLS	5/15
Including Answering Service	Ogden-Clearfield MSA, UT	Y	18430 FQ	23540 MW	29290 TQ	USBLS	5/15
Including Answering Service	Provo-Orem MSA, UT	Y	19620 FQ	23480 MW	28170 TQ	USBLS	5/15
Including Answering Service	Salt Lake City MSA, UT	Y	21800 FQ	24530 MW	29010 TQ	USBLS	5/15
Including Answering Service	Vermont	Y	22530 FQ	26800 MW	30690 TQ	USBLS	5/15
Including Answering Service	Burlington-South Burlington MSA, VT	Y	25530 FQ	29010 MW	33520 TQ	USBLS	5/15
Including Answering Service	Virginia	Y	21340 FQ	26040 MW	30250 TQ	USBLS	5/15
Including Answering Service	Richmond MSA, VA	Y	19560 FQ	26510 MW	32190 TQ	USBLS	5/15
Including Answering Service	Virginia Beach-Norfolk-Newport News MSA, VA-NC	Y	19910 FQ	22880 MW	25970 TQ	USBLS	5/15
Including Answering Service	Washington	H	13.49 FQ	16.13 MW	18.70 TQ	WABLS	3/16
Including Answering Service	Seattle-Bellevue-Everett PMSA, WA	H	14.77 FQ	16.84 MW	18.76 TQ	WABLS	3/16
Including Answering Service	Tacoma-Lakewood PMSA, WA	H	12.96 FQ	15.62 MW	18.06 TQ	WABLS	3/16
Including Answering Service	West Virginia	Y	19540 FQ	23660 MW	29390 TQ	USBLS	5/15
Including Answering Service	Huntington-Ashland MSA, WV-KY-OH	Y	19250 FQ	23620 MW	30650 TQ	USBLS	5/15
Including Answering Service	Wisconsin	Y	23210 FQ	28500 MW	34840 TQ	USBLS	5/15
Including Answering Service	Madison MSA, WI	Y	23880 FQ	29660 MW	37360 TQ	USBLS	5/15
Including Answering Service	Milwaukee-Waukesha-West Allis MSA, WI	Y	23650 FQ	28940 MW	35020 TQ	USBLS	5/15
Including Answering Service	Wyoming	Y	23990 FQ	26980 MW	29620 TQ	USBLS	5/15
Including Answering Service	Puerto Rico	Y	17590 FQ	19570 MW	22450 TQ	USBLS	5/15
Including Answering Service	San Juan-Carolina-Caguas MSA, PR	Y	17890 FQ	19990 MW	22700 TQ	USBLS	5/15
Including Answering Service	Virgin Islands	Y	18980 FQ	24790 MW	28760 TQ	USBLS	5/15
Including Answering Service	Guam	Y	18600 FQ	20370 MW	24070 TQ	USBLS	5/15
Tag/Tax Clerk							
County Government	Calhoun County, GA	Y			24415 HI	GACTY04	2016
County Government	Columbus/Muscogee County, GA	Y	27717 LO		44310 HI	GACTY04	2016
County Government	Cook County, GA	Y	19988 LO		24331 HI	GACTY04	2016
Tailor, Dressmaker, and Custom Sewer							
	Alabama	Y	18960 AE	26065 AW	29623 AEX	ALBLS	6/16
	Birmingham-Hoover MSA, AL	Y	22446 AE	27947 AW	30692 AEX	ALBLS	6/16
	Alaska	Y	27520 FQ	31790 MW	38260 TQ	USBLS	5/15
	Arizona	Y	24100 FQ	32970 MW	42660 TQ	USBLS	5/15

AE	Average entry wage	AWR	Average wage range	H	Hourly	LR	Low end range
AEX	Average experienced wage	B	Biweekly	HI	Highest wage paid	M	Monthly
ATC	Average total compensation	D	Daily	HR	High end range	MCC	Median cash compensation
AW	Average wage paid	FQ	First quartile wage	LO	Lowest wage paid	ME	Median entry wage

MTC	Median total compensation	TCC	Total cash compensation
MW	Median wage paid	TQ	Third quartile wage
MWR	Median wage range	W	Weekly
S	See annotated source	Y	Yearly

Occupation/Type/Industry	Location	Per	Low	Mid	High	Source	Date
Tailor, Dressmaker, and Custom Sewer	Phoenix-Mesa-Scottsdale MSA, AZ	Y	30050 FQ	36730 MW	45690 TQ	USBLS	5/15
	Tucson MSA, AZ	Y	20490 FQ	23480 MW	29700 TQ	USBLS	5/15
	Arkansas	Y	18090 FQ	20950 MW	24580 TQ	USBLS	5/15
	Little Rock-North Little Rock-Conway MSA, AR	Y	19240 FQ	22770 MW	26910 TQ	USBLS	5/15
	California	H	11.68 FQ	14.33 MW	19.26 TQ	CABLS	1/16-3/16
	Anaheim-Santa Ana-Irvine PMSA, CA	H	12.60 FQ	14.93 MW	17.43 TQ	CABLS	1/16-3/16
	Los Angeles-Long Beach-Glendale PMSA, CA	H	11.34 FQ	13.77 MW	18.22 TQ	CABLS	1/16-3/16
	Oakland-Hayward-Berkeley PMSA, CA	H	11.45 FQ	17.15 MW	21.59 TQ	CABLS	1/16-3/16
	Riverside-San Bernardino-Ontario MSA, CA	H	11.26 FQ	12.84 MW	14.99 TQ	CABLS	1/16-3/16
	Sacramento–Roseville–Arden-Arcade MSA, CA	H	13.02 FQ	13.99 MW	14.96 TQ	CABLS	1/16-3/16
	San Francisco-Redwood City-South San Francisco PMSA, CA	H	16.31 FQ	20.63 MW	22.97 TQ	CABLS	1/16-3/16
	Colorado	Y	20810 FQ	25550 MW	29290 TQ	USBLS	5/15
	Connecticut	Y		35685 MW		CTBLS	1/16-3/16
	Bridgeport-Stamford-Norwalk MSA, CT	Y	22530 FQ	26860 MW	35630 TQ	USBLS	5/15
	Delaware	Y	26730 FQ	29420 MW	33200 TQ	USBLS	5/15
	District of Columbia	Y	37420 FQ	44480 MW	51840 TQ	USBLS	5/15
	Washington-Arlington-Alexandria PMSA, DC-VA-MD-WV	Y	25180 FQ	29010 MW	39900 TQ	USBLS	5/15
	Florida	H	9.00 AE	12.32 MW	15.37 AEX	FLBLS	7/16-9/16
	Fort Lauderdale-Pompano Beach-Deerfield Beach PMSA, FL	H	10.10 AE	15.49 MW	17.11 AEX	FLBLS	7/16-9/16
	Miami-Miami Beach-Kendall PMSA, FL	H	8.91 AE	9.22 MW	10.74 AEX	FLBLS	7/16-9/16
	Tampa-St. Petersburg-Clearwater MSA, FL	H	10.48 AE	13.29 MW	15.93 AEX	FLBLS	7/16-9/16
	Georgia	Y	18140 FQ	21230 MW	32140 TQ	USBLS	5/15
	Atlanta-Sandy Springs-Roswell MSA, GA	Y	18720 FQ	22370 MW	33720 TQ	USBLS	5/15
	Hawaii	Y	18690 FQ	23230 MW	38340 TQ	USBLS	5/15
	Urban Honolulu MSA, HI	Y	18160 FQ	21040 MW	31270 TQ	USBLS	5/15
	Idaho	Y	25210 FQ	27580 MW	29960 TQ	USBLS	5/15
	Boise City MSA, ID	Y	25860 FQ	27880 MW	29890 TQ	USBLS	5/15
	Illinois	Y	23130 FQ	28680 MW	35720 TQ	USBLS	5/15
	Chicago-Naperville-Arlington Heights PMSA, IL	Y	24160 FQ	29480 MW	36920 TQ	USBLS	5/15
	Lake County-Kenosha County PMSA, IL-WI	Y	17900 FQ	20050 MW	27570 TQ	USBLS	5/15
	Indiana	Y	21040 FQ	25100 MW	31350 TQ	USBLS	5/15
	Indianapolis-Carmel-Anderson MSA, IN	Y	25130 FQ	30170 MW	35190 TQ	USBLS	5/15
	Iowa	Y	21930 FQ	23990 MW	27650 TQ	USBLS	5/15
	Des Moines-West Des Moines MSA, IA	Y	21570 FQ	23340 MW	25370 TQ	USBLS	5/15
	Kansas	Y	17480 FQ	19270 MW	23250 TQ	USBLS	5/15
	Kentucky	Y	21880 FQ	26750 MW	29480 TQ	USBLS	5/15
	Louisville-Jefferson County MSA, KY-IN	Y	25040 FQ	27440 MW	29840 TQ	USBLS	5/15
	Louisiana	Y	19570 FQ	22640 MW	26260 TQ	USBLS	5/15
	Baton Rouge MSA, LA	Y	20300 FQ	22370 MW	24430 TQ	USBLS	5/15
	Maine	Y	26440 FQ	28750 MW	31400 TQ	USBLS	5/15
	Portland-South Portland MSA, ME	Y	26520 FQ	28840 MW	31910 TQ	USBLS	5/15
	Maryland	Y	19127 AE	29599 MW	34834 AEX	MDBLS	4/16
	Baltimore-Columbia-Towson MSA, MD	Y	24970 FQ	29190 MW	38470 TQ	USBLS	5/15
	Massachusetts	Y	21560 FQ	24180 MW	35350 TQ	USBLS	5/15
	Boston-Cambridge-Newton NECTA, MA	Y	21690 FQ	31170 MW	43390 TQ	USBLS	5/15
	Michigan	Y	19140 FQ	23260 MW	30920 TQ	USBLS	5/15

AE	Average entry wage	AWR	Average wage range	H	Hourly
AEX	Average experienced wage	B	Biweekly	HI	Highest wage paid
ATC	Average total compensation	D	Daily	HR	High end range
AW	Average wage paid	FQ	First quartile wage	LO	Lowest wage paid

LR	Low end range	MTC	Median total compensation
M	Monthly	MW	Median wage paid
MCC	Median cash compensation	MWR	Median wage range
ME	Median entry wage	S	See annotated source

TCC	Total cash compensation
TQ	Third quartile wage
W	Weekly
Y	Yearly

Occupation/Type/Industry	Location	Per	Low	Mid	High	Source	Date
Tailor, Dressmaker, and Custom Sewer							
	Detroit-Dearborn-Livonia PMSA, MI	Y	22070 FQ	28840 MW	35290 TQ	USBLS	5/15
	Grand Rapids-Wyoming MSA, MI	Y	18380 FQ	19590 MW	23960 TQ	USBLS	5/15
	Minnesota	Y	27782 FQ	32469 MW	40660 TQ	MNBLS	1/16-3/16
	Minneapolis-St. Paul-Bloomington MSA, MN-WI	Y	28440 FQ	33684 MW	54541 TQ	MNBLS	1/16-3/16
	Mississippi	Y	17950 FQ	21700 MW	27100 TQ	USBLS	5/15
	Jackson MSA, MS	Y	16880 FQ	18190 MW	20310 TQ	USBLS	5/15
	Missouri	Y	21520 FQ	24020 MW	28940 TQ	USBLS	5/15
	Kansas City MSA, MO-KS	Y	17530 FQ	19350 MW	23880 TQ	USBLS	5/15
	St. Louis MSA, MO-IL	Y	22120 FQ	26100 MW	29970 TQ	USBLS	5/15
	Montana	Y	21090 FQ	24000 MW	27670 TQ	USBLS	5/15
	Nebraska	Y	20285 FQ	24290 MW	30925 TQ	NEBLS	7/16-9/16
	Omaha-Council Bluffs MSA, NE-IA	Y	23270 FQ	27805 MW	34960 TQ	NEBLS	7/16-9/16
	Nevada	Y	22080 FQ	33000 MW	39850 TQ	USBLS	5/15
	Las Vegas-Henderson-Paradise MSA, NV	Y	26980 FQ	35580 MW	46980 TQ	USBLS	5/15
	New Hampshire	H	16.78 AE	17.66 MW	18.38 AEX	NHBLS	6/16
	New Jersey	Y	27000 FQ	32360 MW	38170 TQ	USBLS	5/15
	Newark PMSA, NJ-PA	Y	27120 FQ	32460 MW	37320 TQ	USBLS	5/15
	New Mexico	Y	21660 FQ	24990 MW	29600 TQ	USBLS	5/15
	Buffalo-Cheektowaga-Niagara Falls MSA, NY	Y	19270 FQ	22170 MW	25680 TQ	USBLS	5/15
	Rochester MSA, NY	Y	23390 FQ	28060 MW	32940 TQ	USBLS	5/15
	North Carolina	Y	18090 FQ	21530 MW	26590 TQ	USBLS	5/15
	Charlotte-Concord-Gastonia MSA, NC-SC	Y	18350 FQ	23670 MW	29040 TQ	USBLS	5/15
	Raleigh MSA, NC	Y	20940 FQ	23300 MW	26650 TQ	USBLS	5/15
	Ohio	Y	25840 FQ	31870 MW	36350 TQ	USBLS	5/15
	Cincinnati MSA, OH-KY-IN	Y	20660 FQ	25020 MW	29150 TQ	USBLS	5/15
	Cleveland-Elyria MSA, OH	Y	24410 FQ	28210 MW	31550 TQ	USBLS	5/15
	Oklahoma	Y	21030 FQ	24630 MW	30060 TQ	USBLS	5/15
	Oklahoma City MSA, OK	Y	19740 FQ	26070 MW	29100 TQ	USBLS	5/15
	Oregon	H	10.67 FQ	12.38 MW	15.03 TQ	ORBLS	2016
	Portland-Vancouver-Hillsboro MSA, OR-WA	Y	23670 FQ	28480 MW	36500 TQ	USBLS	5/15
	Pennsylvania	Y	22490 FQ	26100 MW	31250 TQ	USBLS	5/15
	Montgomery County-Bucks County-Chester County PMSA, PA	Y	21140 FQ	23140 MW	28320 TQ	USBLS	5/15
	Pittsburgh MSA, PA	Y	23030 FQ	27670 MW	35660 TQ	USBLS	5/15
	South Carolina	Y	20340 FQ	23250 MW	29170 TQ	USBLS	5/15
	Greenville-Anderson-Mauldin MSA, SC	Y	19070 FQ	34990 MW	43320 TQ	USBLS	5/15
	Tennessee	Y	21910 FQ	27940 MW	37960 TQ	USBLS	5/15
	Memphis MSA, TN-MS-AR	Y	19090 FQ	22440 MW	30370 TQ	USBLS	5/15
	Nashville-Davidson–Murfreesboro–Franklin MSA, TN	Y	32210 FQ	36210 MW	40870 TQ	USBLS	5/15
	Texas	Y	19360 FQ	22320 MW	25180 TQ	USBLS	5/15
	Dallas-Plano-Irving PMSA, TX	Y	22310 FQ	27700 MW	42510 TQ	USBLS	5/15
	Fort Worth-Arlington PMSA, TX	Y	21990 FQ	25990 MW	28960 TQ	USBLS	5/15
	Houston-The Woodlands-Sugar Land MSA, TX	Y	20460 FQ	22320 MW	24190 TQ	USBLS	5/15
	San Antonio-New Braunfels MSA, TX	Y	18220 FQ	20790 MW	23190 TQ	USBLS	5/15
	Utah	Y	19920 FQ	26900 MW	31120 TQ	USBLS	5/15
	Provo-Orem MSA, UT	Y	26160 FQ	30140 MW	34690 TQ	USBLS	5/15
	Salt Lake City MSA, UT	Y	17510 FQ	19410 MW	25600 TQ	USBLS	5/15
	Virginia	Y	21420 FQ	26850 MW	30530 TQ	USBLS	5/15
	Richmond MSA, VA	Y	16800 FQ	18490 MW	26950 TQ	USBLS	5/15
	Virginia Beach-Norfolk-Newport News MSA, VA-NC	Y	20810 FQ	25110 MW	31470 TQ	USBLS	5/15
	Washington	H	12.15 FQ	13.85 MW	15.66 TQ	WABLS	3/16
	Seattle-Bellevue-Everett PMSA, WA	H	12.36 FQ	14.05 MW	16.10 TQ	WABLS	3/16
	Tacoma-Lakewood PMSA, WA	H	12.09 FQ	13.65 MW	15.14 TQ	WABLS	3/16
	West Virginia	Y	19540 FQ	21600 MW	23640 TQ	USBLS	5/15

AE	Average entry wage	AWR	Average wage range	H	Hourly	LR	Low end range	MTC	Median total compensation	TCC	Total cash compensation
AEX	Average experienced wage	B	Biweekly	HI	Highest wage paid	M	Monthly	MW	Median wage paid	TQ	Third quartile wage
ATC	Average total compensation	D	Daily	HR	High end range	MCC	Median cash compensation	MWR	Median wage range	W	Weekly
AW	Average wage paid	FQ	First quartile wage	LO	Lowest wage paid	ME	Median entry wage	S	See annotated source	Y	Yearly

Occupation/Type/Industry	Location	Per	Low	Mid	High	Source	Date
Tailor, Dressmaker, and Custom Sewer							
	Wisconsin	Y	21560 FQ	26460 MW	30340 TQ	USBLS	5/15
	Madison MSA, WI	Y	24990 FQ	28090 MW	31150 TQ	USBLS	5/15
	Milwaukee-Waukesha-West Allis MSA, WI	Y	25370 FQ	28230 MW	31070 TQ	USBLS	5/15
	Puerto Rico	Y	16410 FQ	17480 MW	18540 TQ	USBLS	5/15
	San Juan-Carolina-Caguas MSA, PR	Y	16350 FQ	17410 MW	18480 TQ	USBLS	5/15
Tank Car, Truck, and Ship Loader							
	Alabama	Y	26237 AE	35000 AW	39381 AEX	ALBLS	6/16
	Birmingham-Hoover MSA, AL	Y	43341 AE	45398 AW	46427 AEX	ALBLS	6/16
	Arizona	Y	41060 FQ	46860 MW	54040 TQ	USBLS	5/15
	Arkansas	Y	34940 FQ	42870 MW	48060 TQ	USBLS	5/15
	California	H	14.36 FQ	24.46 MW	38.91 TQ	CABLS	1/16-3/16
	Los Angeles-Long Beach-Glendale PMSA, CA	H	15.12 FQ	28.28 MW	38.23 TQ	CABLS	1/16-3/16
	Colorado	Y	27420 FQ	34080 MW	51420 TQ	USBLS	5/15
	Florida	H	13.88 AE	17.92 MW	20.20 AEX	FLBLS	7/16-9/16
	Tampa-St. Petersburg-Clearwater MSA, FL	H	19.83 AE	22.41 MW	22.70 AEX	FLBLS	7/16-9/16
	Georgia	Y	35620 FQ	45900 MW	63760 TQ	USBLS	5/15
	Atlanta-Sandy Springs-Roswell MSA, GA	Y	25370 FQ	34040 MW	42860 TQ	USBLS	5/15
	Illinois	Y	28610 FQ	35280 MW	46030 TQ	USBLS	5/15
	Chicago-Naperville-Arlington Heights PMSA, IL	Y	28580 FQ	35050 MW	42770 TQ	USBLS	5/15
	Indiana	Y	30530 FQ	38060 MW	46980 TQ	USBLS	5/15
	Gary PMSA, IN	Y	36530 FQ	43870 MW	49180 TQ	USBLS	5/15
	Iowa	Y	31990 FQ	34920 MW	37850 TQ	USBLS	5/15
	Kansas	Y	32130 FQ	37460 MW	43830 TQ	USBLS	5/15
	Kentucky	Y	26220 FQ	30170 MW	37630 TQ	USBLS	5/15
	Louisiana	Y	34870 FQ	45430 MW	65520 TQ	USBLS	5/15
	Baton Rouge MSA, LA	Y	30630 FQ	45320 MW	71240 TQ	USBLS	5/15
	Maine	Y	36810 FQ	42210 MW	46800 TQ	USBLS	5/15
	Maryland	Y	30145 AE	37364 MW	40973 AEX	MDBLS	4/16
	Baltimore-Columbia-Towson MSA, MD	Y	31500 FQ	35920 MW	41080 TQ	USBLS	5/15
	Massachusetts	Y	34910 FQ	46520 MW	64680 TQ	USBLS	5/15
	Michigan	Y	28130 FQ	34190 MW	40380 TQ	USBLS	5/15
	Minnesota	Y	19064 FQ	25052 MW	42796 TQ	MNBLS	1/16-3/16
	Minneapolis-St. Paul-Bloomington MSA, MN-WI	Y	18772 FQ	20687 MW	37846 TQ	MNBLS	1/16-3/16
	Mississippi	Y	24870 FQ	29180 MW	40220 TQ	USBLS	5/15
	Missouri	Y	27390 FQ	32530 MW	38040 TQ	USBLS	5/15
	Kansas City MSA, MO-KS	Y	33030 FQ	42390 MW	46400 TQ	USBLS	5/15
	Nevada	Y	36370 FQ	52500 MW	57840 TQ	USBLS	5/15
	New Jersey	Y	40140 FQ	49340 MW	73850 TQ	USBLS	5/15
	New Mexico	Y	29490 FQ	34410 MW	38030 TQ	USBLS	5/15
	North Carolina	Y	61930 FQ	67880 MW	73240 TQ	USBLS	5/15
	North Dakota	Y	27820 FQ	35180 MW	43640 TQ	USBLS	5/15
	Fargo MSA, ND-MN	Y	28230 FQ	39130 MW	46670 TQ	USBLS	5/15
	Ohio	Y	31730 FQ	37900 MW	49700 TQ	USBLS	5/15
	Cincinnati MSA, OH-KY-IN	Y	28170 FQ	36530 MW	48250 TQ	USBLS	5/15
	Cleveland-Elyria MSA, OH	Y	33300 FQ	37850 MW	48550 TQ	USBLS	5/15
	Columbus MSA, OH	Y	27430 FQ	29730 MW	33060 TQ	USBLS	5/15
	Oklahoma	Y	20430 FQ	29300 MW	37930 TQ	USBLS	5/15
	Tulsa MSA, OK	Y	17970 FQ	22210 MW	30410 TQ	USBLS	5/15
	Oregon	H	14.98 FQ	22.11 MW	29.02 TQ	ORBLS	2016
	Portland-Vancouver-Hillsboro MSA, OR-WA	Y	33710 FQ	45030 MW	56480 TQ	USBLS	5/15
	Pennsylvania	Y	32210 FQ	39300 MW	61820 TQ	USBLS	5/15
	Philadelphia PMSA, PA	Y	56930 FQ	67670 MW	74250 TQ	USBLS	5/15
	Tennessee	Y	26430 FQ	34290 MW	43920 TQ	USBLS	5/15
	Memphis MSA, TN-MS-AR	Y	26880 FQ	30390 MW	45050 TQ	USBLS	5/15
	Texas	Y	25090 FQ	33080 MW	39580 TQ	USBLS	5/15
	Houston-The Woodlands-Sugar Land MSA, TX	Y	25430 FQ	32810 MW	39050 TQ	USBLS	5/15
	Virginia	Y	23390 FQ	30650 MW	48810 TQ	USBLS	5/15
	Virginia Beach-Norfolk-Newport News MSA, VA-NC	Y	23420 FQ	31070 MW	49130 TQ	USBLS	5/15

AE Average entry wage	**AWR** Average wage range	**H** Hourly	**LR** Low end range	**MTC** Median total compensation	**TCC** Total cash compensation
AEX Average experienced wage	**B** Biweekly	**HI** Highest wage paid	**M** Monthly	**MW** Median wage paid	**TQ** Third quartile wage
ATC Average total compensation	**D** Daily	**HR** High end range	**MCC** Median cash compensation	**MWR** Median wage range	**W** Weekly
AW Average wage paid	**FQ** First quartile wage	**LO** Lowest wage paid	**ME** Median entry wage	**S** See annotated source	**Y** Yearly

Occupation/Type/Industry	Location	Per	Low	Mid	High	Source	Date
Tank Car, Truck, and Ship Loader	Washington	H	15.51 FQ	20.47 MW	30.54 TQ	WABLS	3/16
	Seattle-Bellevue-Everett PMSA, WA	H	16.01 FQ	21.59 MW	35.54 TQ	WABLS	3/16
	Wisconsin	Y	33940 FQ	39060 MW	47710 TQ	USBLS	5/15
	Wyoming	Y	32650 FQ	35200 MW	37750 TQ	USBLS	5/15
Tape Editor							
Television	United States	Y		30000 MW		RTDNA	2016
Taper	Alaska	Y	54000 FQ	57720 MW	61430 TQ	USBLS	5/15
	Arizona	Y	30450 FQ	35990 MW	42460 TQ	USBLS	5/15
	Phoenix-Mesa-Scottsdale MSA, AZ	Y	29520 FQ	35850 MW	42020 TQ	USBLS	5/15
	Tucson MSA, AZ	Y	29730 FQ	35800 MW	45490 TQ	USBLS	5/15
	California	H	18.93 FQ	25.76 MW	35.69 TQ	CABLS	1/16-3/16
	Anaheim-Santa Ana-Irvine PMSA, CA	H	18.05 FQ	22.60 MW	27.88 TQ	CABLS	1/16-3/16
	Los Angeles-Long Beach-Glendale PMSA, CA	H	19.24 FQ	23.83 MW	37.86 TQ	CABLS	1/16-3/16
	Oakland-Hayward-Berkeley PMSA, CA	H	32.14 FQ	40.99 MW	45.86 TQ	CABLS	1/16-3/16
	Riverside-San Bernardino-Ontario MSA, CA	H	16.17 FQ	21.84 MW	28.74 TQ	CABLS	1/16-3/16
	Sacramento–Roseville–Arden-Arcade MSA, CA	H	15.57 FQ	25.34 MW	30.08 TQ	CABLS	1/16-3/16
	San Diego-Carlsbad MSA, CA	H	17.30 FQ	23.94 MW	30.74 TQ	CABLS	1/16-3/16
	San Francisco-Redwood City-South San Francisco PMSA, CA	H	26.42 FQ	39.79 MW	45.02 TQ	CABLS	1/16-3/16
	Colorado	Y	38260 FQ	45580 MW	56650 TQ	USBLS	5/15
	Denver-Aurora-Lakewood MSA, CO	Y	38140 FQ	45710 MW	57520 TQ	USBLS	5/15
	Connecticut	Y		52771 MW		CTBLS	1/16-3/16
	Bridgeport-Stamford-Norwalk MSA, CT	Y	48410 FQ	66310 MW	87790 TQ	USBLS	5/15
	Hartford-West Hartford-East Hartford MSA, CT	Y	39290 FQ	49000 MW	59050 TQ	USBLS	5/15
	Washington-Arlington-Alexandria PMSA, DC-VA-MD-WV	Y	32300 FQ	36480 MW	42800 TQ	USBLS	5/15
	Florida	H	15.14 AE	16.94 MW	17.38 AEX	FLBLS	7/16-9/16
	Atlanta-Sandy Springs-Roswell MSA, GA	Y	35210 FQ	40570 MW	47100 TQ	USBLS	5/15
	Hawaii	Y	48550 FQ	70550 MW	89120 TQ	USBLS	5/15
	Urban Honolulu MSA, HI	Y	47970 FQ	71690 MW	89150 TQ	USBLS	5/15
	Idaho	Y	26650 FQ	32560 MW	38500 TQ	USBLS	5/15
	Boise City MSA, ID	Y	26030 FQ	31710 MW	37520 TQ	USBLS	5/15
	Illinois	Y	47350 FQ	82710 MW	92690 TQ	USBLS	5/15
	Chicago-Naperville-Arlington Heights PMSA, IL	Y	48580 FQ	83640 MW	93090 TQ	USBLS	5/15
	Indiana	Y	43220 FQ	54370 MW	60460 TQ	USBLS	5/15
	Iowa	Y	39660 FQ	47770 MW	57120 TQ	USBLS	5/15
	Kansas	Y	37500 FQ	46320 MW	58660 TQ	USBLS	5/15
	Wichita MSA, KS	Y	36020 FQ	42190 MW	48490 TQ	USBLS	5/15
	Kentucky	Y	50470 FQ	55280 MW	59710 TQ	USBLS	5/15
	Louisville-Jefferson County MSA, KY-IN	Y	44840 FQ	54620 MW	59920 TQ	USBLS	5/15
	Louisiana	Y	31500 FQ	39630 MW	62470 TQ	USBLS	5/15
	New Orleans-Metairie MSA, LA	Y	29020 FQ	33940 MW	45920 TQ	USBLS	5/15
	Maine	Y	39600 FQ	44710 MW	49970 TQ	USBLS	5/15
	Portland-South Portland MSA, ME	Y	44060 FQ	48990 MW	56150 TQ	USBLS	5/15
	Maryland	Y	32131 AE	38483 MW	41659 AEX	MDBLS	4/16
	Massachusetts	Y	61800 FQ	84380 MW	92630 TQ	USBLS	5/15
	Boston-Cambridge-Newton NECTA, MA	Y	79290 FQ	86730 MW	93660 TQ	USBLS	5/15
	Michigan	Y	44550 FQ	53400 MW	58920 TQ	USBLS	5/15
	Minnesota	Y	44215 FQ	68431 MW	74768 TQ	MNBLS	1/16-3/16
	Minneapolis-St. Paul-Bloomington MSA, MN-WI	Y	64506 FQ	70207 MW	75646 TQ	MNBLS	1/16-3/16

AE	Average entry wage	AWR	Average wage range	H	Hourly
AEX	Average experienced wage	B	Biweekly	HI	Highest wage paid
ATC	Average total compensation	D	Daily	HR	High end range
AW	Average wage paid	FQ	First quartile wage	LO	Lowest wage paid

LR	Low end range	MTC	Median total compensation	TCC	Total cash compensation
M	Monthly	MW	Median wage paid	TQ	Third quartile wage
MCC	Median cash compensation	MWR	Median wage range	W	Weekly
ME	Median entry wage	S	See annotated source	Y	Yearly

Occupation/Type/Industry	Location	Per	Low	Mid	High	Source	Date
Taper	Missouri	Y	42190 FQ	56200 MW	70360 TQ	USBLS	5/15
	Kansas City MSA, MO-KS	Y	41860 FQ	54440 MW	66440 TQ	USBLS	5/15
	St. Louis MSA, MO-IL	Y	48320 FQ	65220 MW	72960 TQ	USBLS	5/15
	Nebraska	Y	36220 FQ	44720 MW	61915 TQ	NEBLS	7/16-9/16
	Omaha-Council Bluffs MSA, NE-IA	Y	39885 FQ	46785 MW	66845 TQ	NEBLS	7/16-9/16
	Nevada	Y	31850 FQ	38810 MW	56020 TQ	USBLS	5/15
	Las Vegas-Henderson-Paradise MSA, NV	Y	31200 FQ	38000 MW	59690 TQ	USBLS	5/15
	New Hampshire	H	28.52 AE	35.29 MW	35.74 AEX	NHBLS	6/16
	New Jersey	Y	32740 FQ	63310 MW	77050 TQ	USBLS	5/15
	Camden PMSA, NJ	Y	67320 FQ	72440 MW	77560 TQ	USBLS	5/15
	Newark PMSA, NJ-PA	Y	68050 FQ	84390 MW	91380 TQ	USBLS	5/15
	New Mexico	Y	29760 FQ	40790 MW	46900 TQ	USBLS	5/15
	Albuquerque MSA, NM	Y	29930 FQ	39450 MW	46320 TQ	USBLS	5/15
	New York	Y	37280 AE	59980 MW	76650 AEX	NYBLS	1/16-3/16
	Buffalo-Cheektowaga-Niagara Falls MSA, NY	Y	31520 FQ	36510 MW	44960 TQ	USBLS	5/15
	Nassau County-Suffolk County PMSA, NY	Y	51970 FQ	82900 MW	92710 TQ	USBLS	5/15
	New York-Jersey City-White Plains PMSA, NY-NJ	Y	38570 FQ	62930 MW	84730 TQ	USBLS	5/15
	Ohio	Y	41440 FQ	49040 MW	57550 TQ	USBLS	5/15
	Oklahoma	Y	34460 FQ	38130 MW	43370 TQ	USBLS	5/15
	Tulsa MSA, OK	Y	34890 FQ	38520 MW	43790 TQ	USBLS	5/15
	Oregon	H	13.96 FQ	19.25 MW	24.08 TQ	ORBLS	2016
	Portland-Vancouver-Hillsboro MSA, OR-WA	Y.	39220 FQ	47050 MW	67980 TQ	USBLS	5/15
	Pennsylvania	Y	39970 FQ	47640 MW	63160 TQ	USBLS	5/15
	Montgomery County-Bucks County-Chester County PMSA, PA	Y	51900 FQ	67940 MW	75850 TQ	USBLS	5/15
	Pittsburgh MSA, PA	Y	40390 FQ	52550 MW	59400 TQ	USBLS	5/15
	Rhode Island	Y	43070 FQ	48190 MW	55050 TQ	USBLS	5/15
	Providence-Warwick MSA, RI-MA	Y	43070 FQ	48190 MW	55050 TQ	USBLS	5/15
	Tennessee	Y	33090 FQ	37240 MW	47960 TQ	USBLS	5/15
	Knoxville MSA, TN	Y	34050 FQ	38820 MW	55460 TQ	USBLS	5/15
	Memphis MSA, TN-MS-AR	Y	34160 FQ	37620 MW	48340 TQ	USBLS	5/15
	Nashville-Davidson–Murfreesboro–Franklin MSA, TN	Y	33430 FQ	36940 MW	44540 TQ	USBLS	5/15
	Texas	Y	30530 FQ	39390 MW	58090 TQ	USBLS	5/15
	San Antonio-New Braunfels MSA, TX	Y	41680 FQ	45790 MW	49910 TQ	USBLS	5/15
	Utah	Y	30910 FQ	36060 MW	42410 TQ	USBLS	5/15
	Ogden-Clearfield MSA, UT	Y	30410 FQ	35710 MW	41670 TQ	USBLS	5/15
	Provo-Orem MSA, UT	Y	28960 FQ	33710 MW	39050 TQ	USBLS	5/15
	Salt Lake City MSA, UT	Y	35620 FQ	41050 MW	45820 TQ	USBLS	5/15
	Vermont	Y	35810 FQ	40960 MW	47880 TQ	USBLS	5/15
	Burlington-South Burlington MSA, VT	Y	36790 FQ	42850 MW	49170 TQ	USBLS	5/15
	Washington	H	20.51 FQ	23.31 MW	33.52 TQ	WABLS	3/16
	Seattle-Bellevue-Everett PMSA, WA	H	21.22 FQ	23.51 MW	33.95 TQ	WABLS	3/16
	Tacoma-Lakewood PMSA, WA	H	14.87 FQ	21.20 MW	34.76 TQ	WABLS	3/16
	Wisconsin	Y	42680 FQ	51640 MW	59780 TQ	USBLS	5/15
	Madison MSA, WI	Y	50790 FQ	55280 MW	59710 TQ	USBLS	5/15
	Milwaukee-Waukesha-West Allis MSA, WI	Y	38640 FQ	51240 MW	88580 TQ	USBLS	5/15
Task Force Officer							
Department of Corrections, State Government	Billings, MT	H			24.35 HI	MTGOV	2016
Tasting Room Manager	United States	Y		66480 AW		WBM	2/1/16
Tax Commissioner							
County Government	Columbia County, GA	Y			102455 HI	GACTY03	2016
County Government	Grady County, GA	Y			67366 HI	GACTY03	2016
County Government	Treutlen County, GA	Y			52651 HI	GACTY03	2016

AE	Average entry wage	AWR	Average wage range	H	Hourly
AEX	Average experienced wage	B	Biweekly	HI	Highest wage paid
ATC	Average total compensation	D	Daily	HR	High end range
AW	Average wage paid	FQ	First quartile wage	LO	Lowest wage paid

LR	Low end range	MTC	Median total compensation	TCC	Total cash compensation
M	Monthly	MW	Median wage paid	TQ	Third quartile wage
MCC	Median cash compensation	MWR	Median wage range	W	Weekly
ME	Median entry wage	S	See annotated source	Y	Yearly

Occupation/Type/Industry	Location	Per	Low	Mid	High	Source	Date
Tax Examiner, Collector, and Revenue Agent	Alabama	Y	34808 AE	57377 AW	68662 AEX	ALBLS	6/16
	Birmingham-Hoover MSA, AL	Y	43889 AE	64654 AW	75037 AEX	ALBLS	6/16
	Alaska	Y	68030 FQ	79190 MW	108770 TQ	USBLS	5/15
	Anchorage MSA, AK	Y	70350 FQ	84770 MW	109390 TQ	USBLS	5/15
	Arizona	Y	42500 FQ	54470 MW	75530 TQ	USBLS	5/15
	Phoenix-Mesa-Scottsdale MSA, AZ	Y	41820 FQ	54470 MW	76390 TQ	USBLS	5/15
	Tucson MSA, AZ	Y	43020 FQ	54870 MW	79550 TQ	USBLS	5/15
	Arkansas	Y	30330 FQ	46670 MW	66360 TQ	USBLS	5/15
	Little Rock-North Little Rock-Conway MSA, AR	Y	33910 FQ	53230 MW	67560 TQ	USBLS	5/15
	California	H	21.51 FQ	28.04 MW	37.35 TQ	CABLS	1/16-3/16
	Anaheim-Santa Ana-Irvine PMSA, CA	H	30.06 FQ	36.42 MW	50.32 TQ	CABLS	1/16-3/16
	Los Angeles-Long Beach-Glendale PMSA, CA	H	28.46 FQ	36.38 MW	50.00 TQ	CABLS	1/16-3/16
	Oakland-Hayward-Berkeley PMSA, CA	H	29.67 FQ	36.76 MW	45.66 TQ	CABLS	1/16-3/16
	Riverside-San Bernardino-Ontario MSA, CA	H	28.85 FQ	35.26 MW	42.32 TQ	CABLS	1/16-3/16
	Sacramento–Roseville–Arden-Arcade MSA, CA	H	20.15 FQ	24.58 MW	29.92 TQ	CABLS	1/16-3/16
	San Francisco-Redwood City-South San Francisco PMSA, CA	H	35.03 FQ	38.91 MW	51.85 TQ	CABLS	1/16-3/16
	Colorado	Y	42930 FQ	56130 MW	74190 TQ	USBLS	5/15
	Denver-Aurora-Lakewood MSA, CO	Y	42920 FQ	55930 MW	75430 TQ	USBLS	5/15
	Connecticut	Y		83526 MW		CTBLS	1/16-3/16
	Bridgeport-Stamford-Norwalk MSA, CT	Y	62030 FQ	87050 MW	103540 TQ	USBLS	5/15
	Hartford-West Hartford-East Hartford MSA, CT	Y	66100 FQ	81310 MW	95700 TQ	USBLS	5/15
	Delaware	Y	47610 FQ	57940 MW	68730 TQ	USBLS	5/15
	Wilmington PMSA, DE-MD-NJ	Y	48450 FQ	59860 MW	74900 TQ	USBLS	5/15
	Washington-Arlington-Alexandria PMSA, DC-VA-MD-WV	Y	58040 FQ	70090 MW	90830 TQ	USBLS	5/15
	Florida	H	13.77 AE	17.99 MW	27.24 AEX	FLBLS	7/16-9/16
	Fort Lauderdale-Pompano Beach-Deerfield Beach PMSA, FL	H	15.07 AE	27.04 MW	36.54 AEX	FLBLS	7/16-9/16
	Miami-Miami Beach-Kendall PMSA, FL	H	17.84 AE	30.55 MW	37.47 AEX	FLBLS	7/16-9/16
	Orlando-Kissimmee-Sanford MSA, FL	H	13.79 AE	16.40 MW	24.29 AEX	FLBLS	7/16-9/16
	Tampa-St. Petersburg-Clearwater MSA, FL	H	13.78 AE	17.74 MW	28.13 AEX	FLBLS	7/16-9/16
	Georgia	Y	33380 FQ	46840 MW	56210 TQ	USBLS	5/15
	Atlanta-Sandy Springs-Roswell MSA, GA	Y	38780 FQ	49620 MW	58990 TQ	USBLS	5/15
	Augusta-Richmond County MSA, GA-SC	Y	31740 FQ	46520 MW	68070 TQ	USBLS	5/15
	Hawaii	Y	48180 FQ	64230 MW	93140 TQ	USBLS	5/15
	Idaho	Y	37450 FQ	46290 MW	57950 TQ	USBLS	5/15
	Boise City MSA, ID	Y	38550 FQ	49060 MW	60510 TQ	USBLS	5/15
	Illinois	Y	59700 FQ	74880 MW	94880 TQ	USBLS	5/15
	Chicago-Naperville-Arlington Heights PMSA, IL	Y	64170 FQ	80540 MW	100630 TQ	USBLS	5/15
	Indiana	Y	30010 FQ	40750 MW	65420 TQ	USBLS	5/15
	Gary PMSA, IN	Y	37060 FQ	60830 MW	74870 TQ	USBLS	5/15
	Indianapolis-Carmel-Anderson MSA, IN	Y	28110 FQ	37240 MW	60780 TQ	USBLS	5/15
	Iowa	Y	53230 FQ	61810 MW	74000 TQ	USBLS	5/15
	Des Moines-West Des Moines MSA, IA	Y	52010 FQ	61800 MW	67860 TQ	USBLS	5/15
	Kansas	Y	31650 FQ	36610 MW	42400 TQ	USBLS	5/15
	Kentucky	Y	37550 FQ	45610 MW	53410 TQ	USBLS	5/15
	Louisville-Jefferson County MSA, KY-IN	Y	36410 FQ	53230 MW	79540 TQ	USBLS	5/15

AE Average entry wage	**AWR** Average wage range	**H** Hourly	**LR** Low end range	**MTC** Median total compensation	**TCC** Total cash compensation
AEX Average experienced wage	**B** Biweekly	**HI** Highest wage paid	**M** Monthly	**MW** Median wage paid	**TQ** Third quartile wage
ATC Average total compensation	**D** Daily	**HR** High end range	**MCC** Median cash compensation	**MWR** Median wage range	**W** Weekly
AW Average wage paid	**FQ** First quartile wage	**LO** Lowest wage paid	**ME** Median entry wage	**S** See annotated source	**Y** Yearly

Occupation/Type/Industry	Location	Per	Low	Mid	High	Source	Date
Tax Examiner, Collector, and Revenue Agent	Louisiana	Y	34230 FQ	44500 MW	60330 TQ	USBLS	5/15
	Baton Rouge MSA, LA	Y	31800 FQ	41220 MW	51790 TQ	USBLS	5/15
	New Orleans-Metairie MSA, LA	Y	41520 FQ	58550 MW	84230 TQ	USBLS	5/15
	Maine	Y	36890 FQ	43550 MW	53130 TQ	USBLS	5/15
	Portland-South Portland MSA, ME	Y	43550 FQ	52620 MW	66360 TQ	USBLS	5/15
	Maryland	Y	37671 AE	63561 MW	76506 AEX	MDBLS	4/16
	Baltimore-Columbia-Towson MSA, MD	Y	40460 FQ	50800 MW	70090 TQ	USBLS	5/15
	Massachusetts	Y	49020 FQ	59080 MW	79850 TQ	USBLS	5/15
	Boston-Cambridge-Newton NECTA, MA	Y	49020 FQ	56240 MW	76830 TQ	USBLS	5/15
	Worcester MSA, MA-CT	Y	41240 FQ	56860 MW	74340 TQ	USBLS	5/15
	Michigan	Y	48800 FQ	66370 MW	94590 TQ	USBLS	5/15
	Detroit-Dearborn-Livonia PMSA, MI	Y	45150 FQ	57170 MW	78850 TQ	USBLS	5/15
	Grand Rapids-Wyoming MSA, MI	Y	53390 FQ	69800 MW	91830 TQ	USBLS	5/15
	Minnesota	Y	46344 FQ	56973 MW	73139 TQ	MNBLS	1/16-3/16
	Minneapolis-St. Paul-Bloomington MSA, MN-WI	Y	46334 FQ	54961 MW	72753 TQ	MNBLS	1/16-3/16
	Mississippi	Y	29010 FQ	37190 MW	64430 TQ	USBLS	5/15
	Jackson MSA, MS	Y	30770 FQ	51850 MW	79560 TQ	USBLS	5/15
	Missouri	Y	32520 FQ	40960 MW	50120 TQ	USBLS	5/15
	Kansas City MSA, MO-KS	Y	35150 FQ	41530 MW	48810 TQ	USBLS	5/15
	St. Louis MSA, MO-IL	Y	52530 FQ	66370 MW	91810 TQ	USBLS	5/15
	Montana	Y	40710 FQ	47850 MW	59040 TQ	USBLS	5/15
	Nebraska	Y	38460 FQ	53380 MW	71445 TQ	NEBLS	7/16-9/16
	Omaha-Council Bluffs MSA, NE-IA	Y	51425 FQ	66360 MW	89045 TQ	NEBLS	7/16-9/16
	Nevada	Y	47150 FQ	62470 MW	84240 TQ	USBLS	5/15
	Las Vegas-Henderson-Paradise MSA, NV	Y	54860 FQ	70200 MW	91820 TQ	USBLS	5/15
	New Hampshire	H	16.20 AE	24.07 MW	32.60 AEX	NHBLS	6/16
	Manchester NECTA, NH	H	19.02 AE	36.80 MW	44.81 AEX	NHBLS	6/16
	Nashua NECTA, NH-MA	Y	45430 FQ	59980 MW	83240 TQ	USBLS	5/15
	New Jersey	Y	58220 FQ	73570 MW	94260 TQ	USBLS	5/15
	Camden PMSA, NJ	Y	55740 FQ	68730 MW	81210 TQ	USBLS	5/15
	Newark PMSA, NJ-PA	Y	59390 FQ	77330 MW	100390 TQ	USBLS	5/15
	Trenton MSA, NJ	Y	49970 FQ	66640 MW	79900 TQ	USBLS	5/15
	New Mexico	Y	33700 FQ	36990 MW	46040 TQ	USBLS	5/15
	Albuquerque MSA, NM	Y	33950 FQ	37000 MW	51630 TQ	USBLS	5/15
	New York	Y	44650 AE	60950 MW	77910 AEX	NYBLS	1/16-3/16
	Buffalo-Cheektowaga-Niagara Falls MSA, NY	Y	55720 FQ	70010 MW	86150 TQ	USBLS	5/15
	Nassau County-Suffolk County PMSA, NY	Y	49070 FQ	56500 MW	64230 TQ	USBLS	5/15
	New York-Jersey City-White Plains PMSA, NY-NJ	Y	61340 FQ	77470 MW	102880 TQ	USBLS	5/15
	Rochester MSA, NY	Y	54500 FQ	68680 MW	90300 TQ	USBLS	5/15
	North Carolina	Y	39600 FQ	47530 MW	62050 TQ	USBLS	5/15
	Charlotte-Concord-Gastonia MSA, NC-SC	Y	42310 FQ	51660 MW	72550 TQ	USBLS	5/15
	Raleigh MSA, NC	Y	41640 FQ	49280 MW	64850 TQ	USBLS	5/15
	North Dakota	Y	38660 FQ	63310 MW	78350 TQ	USBLS	5/15
	Ohio	Y	42960 FQ	54140 MW	75190 TQ	USBLS	5/15
	Cincinnati MSA, OH-KY-IN	Y	43150 FQ	49320 MW	59160 TQ	USBLS	5/15
	Cleveland-Elyria MSA, OH	Y	46440 FQ	62850 MW	94860 TQ	USBLS	5/15
	Columbus MSA, OH	Y	41870 FQ	49640 MW	66190 TQ	USBLS	5/15
	Oklahoma	Y	30660 FQ	38320 MW	66360 TQ	USBLS	5/15
	Oklahoma City MSA, OK	Y	33830 FQ	46290 MW	79540 TQ	USBLS	5/15
	Tulsa MSA, OK	Y	35820 FQ	64420 MW	91260 TQ	USBLS	5/15
	Oregon	H	17.17 FQ	22.60 MW	31.54 TQ	ORBLS	2016
	Portland-Vancouver-Hillsboro MSA, OR-WA	Y	52940 FQ	61750 MW	83870 TQ	USBLS	5/15
	Pennsylvania	Y	36470 FQ	47850 MW	58000 TQ	USBLS	5/15
	Allentown-Bethlehem-Easton MSA, PA-NJ	Y	44050 FQ	58570 MW	77220 TQ	USBLS	5/15
	Harrisburg-Carlisle MSA, PA	Y	39660 FQ	46030 MW	56190 TQ	USBLS	5/15

AE Average entry wage	**AWR** Average wage range	**H** Hourly	**LR** Low end range	**MTC** Median total compensation	**TCC** Total cash compensation
AEX Average experienced wage	**B** Biweekly	**HI** Highest wage paid	**M** Monthly	**MW** Median wage paid	**TQ** Third quartile wage
ATC Average total compensation	**D** Daily	**HR** High end range	**MCC** Median cash compensation	**MWR** Median wage range	**W** Weekly
AW Average wage paid	**FQ** First quartile wage	**LO** Lowest wage paid	**ME** Median entry wage	**S** See annotated source	**Y** Yearly

Occupation/Type/Industry	Location	Per	Low	Mid	High	Source	Date
Tax Examiner, Collector, and Revenue Agent	Montgomery County-Bucks County-Chester County						
	PMSA, PA	Y	25770 FQ	57350 MW	87380 TQ	USBLS	5/15
	Philadelphia PMSA, PA	Y	44320 FQ	50650 MW	56110 TQ	USBLS	5/15
	Pittsburgh MSA, PA	Y	27100 FQ	52430 MW	81090 TQ	USBLS	5/15
	Rhode Island	Y	50220 FQ	67940 MW	83820 TQ	USBLS	5/15
	Providence-Warwick MSA, RI-MA	Y	50600 FQ	68910 MW	83810 TQ	USBLS	5/15
	South Carolina	Y	34750 FQ	46770 MW	66360 TQ	USBLS	5/15
	Charleston-North Charleston MSA, SC	Y	42730 FQ	59780 MW	70280 TQ	USBLS	5/15
	Columbia MSA, SC	Y	35550 FQ	54860 MW	72530 TQ	USBLS	5/15
	Greenville-Anderson-Mauldin MSA, SC	Y	49090 FQ	75220 MW	94590 TQ	USBLS	5/15
	South Dakota	Y	37320 FQ	43930 MW	50210 TQ	USBLS	5/15
	Sioux Falls MSA, SD	Y	37380 FQ	45110 MW	58560 TQ	USBLS	5/15
	Tennessee	Y	38650 FQ	48800 MW	60510 TQ	USBLS	5/15
	Knoxville MSA, TN	Y	42720 FQ	58570 MW	88920 TQ	USBLS	5/15
	Memphis MSA, TN-MS-AR	Y	37120 FQ	46170 MW	51440 TQ	USBLS	5/15
	Nashville-Davidson–Murfreesboro–Franklin MSA, TN	Y	43530 FQ	64420 MW	86250 TQ	USBLS	5/15
	Texas	Y	39180 FQ	48410 MW	68310 TQ	USBLS	5/15
	Austin-Round Rock MSA, TX	Y	37270 FQ	42730 MW	50110 TQ	USBLS	5/15
	Dallas-Plano-Irving PMSA, TX	Y	61380 FQ	79140 MW	99990 TQ	USBLS	5/15
	Fort Worth-Arlington PMSA, TX	Y	56280 FQ	71430 MW	94250 TQ	USBLS	5/15
	Houston-The Woodlands-Sugar Land MSA, TX	Y	60010 FQ	81780 MW	103520 TQ	USBLS	5/15
	San Antonio-New Braunfels MSA, TX	Y	40000 FQ	58480 MW	77220 TQ	USBLS	5/15
	Utah	Y	41550 FQ	47470 MW	51440 TQ	USBLS	5/15
	Ogden-Clearfield MSA, UT	Y	41550 FQ	46290 MW	51430 TQ	USBLS	5/15
	Salt Lake City MSA, UT	Y	54860 FQ	71400 MW	91820 TQ	USBLS	5/15
	Vermont	Y	42970 FQ	50570 MW	65130 TQ	USBLS	5/15
	Virginia	Y	35760 FQ	45960 MW	65000 TQ	USBLS	5/15
	Richmond MSA, VA	Y	34650 FQ	43450 MW	61030 TQ	USBLS	5/15
	Virginia Beach-Norfolk-Newport News MSA, VA-NC	Y	35440 FQ	44900 MW	59880 TQ	USBLS	5/15
	Washington	H	23.99 FQ	27.15 MW	31.47 TQ	WABLS	3/16
	Seattle-Bellevue-Everett PMSA, WA	H	25.19 FQ	29.22 MW	39.97 TQ	WABLS	3/16
	Tacoma-Lakewood PMSA, WA	H	26.47 FQ	30.69 MW	36.85 TQ	WABLS	3/16
	West Virginia	Y	27730 FQ	34810 MW	52770 TQ	USBLS	5/15
	Huntington-Ashland MSA, WV-KY-OH	Y	28780 FQ	37970 MW	59680 TQ	USBLS	5/15
	Wisconsin	Y	44050 FQ	57270 MW	77220 TQ	USBLS	5/15
	Madison MSA, WI	Y	44010 FQ	47330 MW	57270 TQ	USBLS	5/15
	Milwaukee-Waukesha-West Allis MSA, WI	Y	60840 FQ	79890 MW	97850 TQ	USBLS	5/15
	Wyoming	Y	44210 FQ	51470 MW	63800 TQ	USBLS	5/15
	Puerto Rico	Y	17100 FQ	18910 MW	23520 TQ	USBLS	5/15
	San Juan-Carolina-Caguas MSA, PR	Y	17060 FQ	18840 MW	23310 TQ	USBLS	5/15
Tax Manager	United States	Y		110000 MW		TSTR	2017
Tax Preparer	Alabama	Y	19064 AE	29929 AW	35351 AEX	ALBLS	6/16
	Birmingham-Hoover MSA, AL	Y	17773 AE	24199 AW	27418 AEX	ALBLS	6/16
	Alaska	Y	35910 FQ	52280 MW	66930 TQ	USBLS	5/15
	Anchorage MSA, AK	Y	37590 FQ	54420 MW	67520 TQ	USBLS	5/15
	Arizona	Y	24300 FQ	38740 MW	61560 TQ	USBLS	5/15
	Phoenix-Mesa-Scottsdale MSA, AZ	Y	25060 FQ	42210 MW	64380 TQ	USBLS	5/15
	Tucson MSA, AZ	Y	28210 FQ	31680 MW	62790 TQ	USBLS	5/15
	Arkansas	Y	17700 FQ	19700 MW	25480 TQ	USBLS	5/15
	Little Rock-North Little Rock-Conway MSA, AR	Y	17600 FQ	19470 MW	22150 TQ	USBLS	5/15
	California	H	15.46 FQ	24.42 MW	36.46 TQ	CABLS	1/16-3/16
	Anaheim-Santa Ana-Irvine PMSA, CA	H	16.74 FQ	23.46 MW	34.17 TQ	CABLS	1/16-3/16

AE	Average entry wage	AWR	Average wage range	H	Hourly	LR	Low end range	MTC Median total compensation	TCC Total cash compensation
AEX	Average experienced wage	B	Biweekly	HI	Highest wage paid	M	Monthly	MW Median wage paid	TQ Third quartile wage
ATC	Average total compensation	D	Daily	HR	High end range	MCC Median cash compensation	MWR Median wage range	W Weekly
AW	Average wage paid	FQ	First quartile wage	LO	Lowest wage paid	ME Median entry wage	S See annotated source	Y Yearly

Occupation/Type/Industry	Location	Per	Low	Mid	High	Source	Date
Tax Preparer	Los Angeles-Long Beach-Glendale PMSA, CA	H	15.15 FQ	22.60 MW	37.12 TQ	CABLS	1/16-3/16
	Oakland-Hayward-Berkeley PMSA, CA	H	17.47 FQ	33.62 MW	40.38 TQ	CABLS	1/16-3/16
	Riverside-San Bernardino-Ontario MSA, CA	H	9.79 FQ	13.25 MW	21.05 TQ	CABLS	1/16-3/16
	Sacramento–Roseville–Arden-Arcade MSA, CA	H	14.16 FQ	24.25 MW	31.57 TQ	CABLS	1/16-3/16
	San Diego-Carlsbad MSA, CA	H	17.17 FQ	27.84 MW	36.85 TQ	CABLS	1/16-3/16
	San Francisco-Redwood City-South San Francisco PMSA, CA	H	27.21 FQ	33.34 MW	45.28 TQ	CABLS	1/16-3/16
	Colorado	Y	23340 FQ	41020 MW	59680 TQ	USBLS	5/15
	Connecticut	Y		41087 MW		CTBLS	1/16-3/16
	Bridgeport-Stamford-Norwalk MSA, CT	Y	42880 FQ	48030 MW	62470 TQ	USBLS	5/15
	Hartford-West Hartford-East Hartford MSA, CT	Y	20440 FQ	30920 MW	53050 TQ	USBLS	5/15
	Washington-Arlington-Alexandria PMSA, DC-VA-MD-WV	Y	23890 FQ	40040 MW	54990 TQ	USBLS	5/15
	Florida	H	9.07 AE	11.34 MW	17.49 AEX	FLBLS	7/16-9/16
	Fort Lauderdale-Pompano Beach-Deerfield Beach PMSA, FL	H	10.09 AE	11.69 MW	15.15 AEX	FLBLS	7/16-9/16
	Miami-Miami Beach-Kendall PMSA, FL	H	9.98 AE	18.88 MW	26.12 AEX	FLBLS	7/16-9/16
	Orlando-Kissimmee-Sanford MSA, FL	H	9.36 AE	10.61 MW	15.29 AEX	FLBLS	7/16-9/16
	Tampa-St. Petersburg-Clearwater MSA, FL	H	9.47 AE	16.09 MW	17.87 AEX	FLBLS	7/16-9/16
	Georgia	Y	27320 FQ	36560 MW	51460 TQ	USBLS	5/15
	Atlanta-Sandy Springs-Roswell MSA, GA	Y	33670 FQ	41140 MW	59400 TQ	USBLS	5/15
	Augusta-Richmond County MSA, GA-SC	Y	19630 FQ	34210 MW	53760 TQ	USBLS	5/15
	Hawaii	Y	31220 FQ	49330 MW	70470 TQ	USBLS	5/15
	Urban Honolulu MSA, HI	Y	42790 FQ	54460 MW	76980 TQ	USBLS	5/15
	Idaho	Y	22240 FQ	28000 MW	42340 TQ	USBLS	5/15
	Boise City MSA, ID	Y	25340 FQ	30600 MW	56990 TQ	USBLS	5/15
	Illinois	Y	22660 FQ	40020 MW	61860 TQ	USBLS	5/15
	Chicago-Naperville-Arlington Heights PMSA, IL	Y	22300 FQ	41530 MW	62100 TQ	USBLS	5/15
	Indiana	Y	21370 FO	29650 MW	39050 TQ	USBLS	5/15
	Gary PMSA, IN	Y	27580 FQ	33720 MW	38230 TQ	USBLS	5/15
	Indianapolis-Carmel-Anderson MSA, IN	Y	20780 FQ	29910 MW	39290 TQ	USBLS	5/15
	Iowa	Y	23660 FQ	31800 MW	56800 TQ	USBLS	5/15
	Des Moines-West Des Moines MSA, IA	Y	29140 FQ	37210 MW	62210 TQ	USBLS	5/15
	Kansas	Y	23850 FQ	33660 MW	46630 TQ	USBLS	5/15
	Wichita MSA, KS	Y	26460 FQ	33870 MW	47160 TQ	USBLS	5/15
	Kentucky	Y	21680 FQ	29610 MW	47280 TQ	USBLS	5/15
	Louisville-Jefferson County MSA, KY-IN	Y	25520 FQ	36510 MW	59980 TQ	USBLS	5/15
	Louisiana	Y	20980 FQ	28270 MW	36260 TQ	USBLS	5/15
	Baton Rouge MSA, LA	Y	24630 FQ	29120 MW	35090 TQ	USBLS	5/15
	New Orleans-Metairie MSA, LA	Y	19300 FQ	26810 MW	33350 TQ	USBLS	5/15
	Maine	Y	28210 FQ	39340 MW	49080 TQ	USBLS	5/15
	Portland-South Portland MSA, ME	Y	34220 FQ	38110 MW	45380 TQ	USBLS	5/15
	Maryland	Y	19567 AE	47521 MW	61498 AEX	MDBLS	4/16
	Baltimore-Columbia-Towson MSA, MD	Y	19380 FQ	51450 MW	68290 TQ	USBLS	5/15
	Salisbury MSA, MD-DE	Y	22140 FQ	26890 MW	34580 TQ	USBLS	5/15
	Massachusetts	Y	35560 FQ	51800 MW	75810 TQ	USBLS	5/15
	Boston-Cambridge-Newton NECTA, MA	Y	34870 FQ	47970 MW	76420 TQ	USBLS	5/15
	Worcester MSA, MA-CT	Y	45640 FQ	58010 MW	71840 TQ	USBLS	5/15
	Michigan	Y	22730 FQ	34250 MW	49130 TQ	USBLS	5/15

AE	Average entry wage	AWR	Average wage range	H	Hourly	LR	Low end range
AEX	Average experienced wage	B	Biweekly	HI	Highest wage paid	M	Monthly
ATC	Average total compensation	D	Daily	HR	High end range	MCC	Median cash compensation
AW	Average wage paid	FQ	First quartile wage	LO	Lowest wage paid	ME	Median entry wage

MTC	Median total compensation	TCC	Total cash compensation
MW	Median wage paid	TQ	Third quartile wage
MWR	Median wage range	W	Weekly
S	See annotated source	Y	Yearly

Occupation/Type/Industry	Location	Per	Low	Mid	High	Source	Date
Tax Preparer	Detroit-Dearborn-Livonia PMSA, MI	Y	21960 FQ	25360 MW	42810 TQ	USBLS	5/15
	Grand Rapids-Wyoming MSA, MI	Y	25380 FQ	37060 MW	49210 TQ	USBLS	5/15
	Minnesota	Y	30422 FQ	41213 MW	52746 TQ	MNBLS	1/16-3/16
	Minneapolis-St. Paul-Bloomington MSA, MN-WI	Y	30696 FQ	43357 MW	58497 TQ	MNBLS	1/16-3/16
	Mississippi	Y	17940 FQ	20630 MW	34830 TQ	USBLS	5/15
	Jackson MSA, MS	Y	18940 FQ	22700 MW	36600 TQ	USBLS	5/15
	Missouri	Y	23650 FQ	32430 MW	52580 TQ	USBLS	5/15
	Kansas City MSA, MO-KS	Y	29110 FQ	41980 MW	55520 TQ	USBLS	5/15
	St. Louis MSA, MO-IL	Y	24390 FQ	36300 MW	63500 TQ	USBLS	5/15
	Montana	Y	23540 FQ	34070 MW	44020 TQ	USBLS	5/15
	Billings MSA, MT	Y	31600 FQ	37700 MW	46680 TQ	USBLS	5/15
	Nebraska	Y	26950 FQ	31735 MW	40585 TQ	NEBLS	7/16-9/16
	Omaha-Council Bluffs MSA, NE-IA	Y	24575 FQ	29855 MW	48400 TQ	NEBLS	7/16-9/16
	Nevada	Y	33270 FQ	43140 MW	61000 TQ	USBLS	5/15
	Las Vegas-Henderson-Paradise MSA, NV	Y	33010 FQ	38490 MW	60670 TQ	USBLS	5/15
	New Hampshire	H	9.43 AE	14.84 MW	21.88 AEX	NHBLS	6/16
	Nashua NECTA, NH-MA	Y	20510 FQ	27810 MW	54110 TQ	USBLS	5/15
	New Jersey	Y	24700 FQ	36950 MW	52890 TQ	USBLS	5/15
	Camden PMSA, NJ	Y	35740 FQ	41450 MW	45860 TQ	USBLS	5/15
	Newark PMSA, NJ-PA	Y	21230 FQ	28830 MW	37120 TQ	USBLS	5/15
	New Mexico	Y	23510 FQ	33390 MW	44050 TQ	USBLS	5/15
	Albuquerque MSA, NM	Y	24200 FQ	44190 MW	55740 TQ	USBLS	5/15
	New York	Y	25530 AE	53080 MW	77190 AEX	NYBLS	1/16-3/16
	Buffalo-Cheektowaga-Niagara Falls MSA, NY	Y	22170 FQ	27840 MW	43450 TQ	USBLS	5/15
	Nassau County-Suffolk County PMSA, NY	Y	28400 FQ	39220 MW	59350 TQ	USBLS	5/15
	New York-Jersey City-White Plains PMSA, NY-NJ	Y	31510 FQ	62130 MW	85410 TQ	USBLS	5/15
	Rochester MSA, NY	Y	36540 FQ	57760 MW	81460 TQ	USBLS	5/15
	North Carolina	Y	23490 FQ	31190 MW	59820 TQ	USBLS	5/15
	Charlotte-Concord-Gastonia MSA, NC-SC	Y	25770 FQ	36890 MW	71470 TQ	USBLS	5/15
	Raleigh MSA, NC	Y	24710 FQ	44980 MW	66930 TQ	USBLS	5/15
	North Dakota	Y	41080 FQ	50260 MW	65830 TQ	USBLS	5/15
	Fargo MSA, ND-MN	Y	41000 FQ	55320 MW	66540 TQ	USBLS	5/15
	Ohio	Y	21320 FQ	29170 MW	46270 TQ	USBLS	5/15
	Cincinnati MSA, OH-KY-IN	Y	19500 FQ	28430 MW	45610 TQ	USBLS	5/15
	Cleveland-Elyria MSA, OH	Y	27240 FQ	40750 MW	53960 TQ	USBLS	5/15
	Columbus MSA, OH	Y	24580 FQ	27370 MW	30280 TQ	USBLS	5/15
	Oklahoma	Y	22220 FQ	31710 MW	49420 TQ	USBLS	5/15
	Oklahoma City MSA, OK	Y	27500 FQ	33680 MW	53000 TQ	USBLS	5/15
	Tulsa MSA, OK	Y	21260 FQ	42200 MW	51400 TQ	USBLS	5/15
	Oregon	H	14.88 FQ	19.35 MW	27.53 TQ	ORBLS	2016
	Portland-Vancouver-Hillsboro MSA, OR-WA	Y	29480 FQ	39600 MW	58100 TQ	USBLS	5/15
	Pennsylvania	Y	25690 FQ	36970 MW	53500 TQ	USBLS	5/15
	Allentown-Bethlehem-Easton MSA, PA-NJ	Y	31720 FQ	36000 MW	41930 TQ	USBLS	5/15
	Harrisburg-Carlisle MSA, PA	Y	24290 FQ	33930 MW	46950 TQ	USBLS	5/15
	Montgomery County-Bucks County-Chester County PMSA, PA	Y	42640 FQ	50040 MW	62660 TQ	USBLS	5/15
	Philadelphia PMSA, PA	Y	36590 FQ	53090 MW	71140 TQ	USBLS	5/15
	Pittsburgh MSA, PA	Y	19900 FQ	29900 MW	54180 TQ	USBLS	5/15
	South Carolina	Y	18920 FQ	26160 MW	36380 TQ	USBLS	5/15
	Charleston-North Charleston MSA, SC	Y	20420 FQ	26660 MW	33230 TQ	USBLS	5/15
	Columbia MSA, SC	Y	27330 FQ	33040 MW	45420 TQ	USBLS	5/15
	Greenville-Anderson-Mauldin MSA, SC	Y	17540 FQ	22720 MW	30840 TQ	USBLS	5/15
	South Dakota	Y	28610 FQ	34460 MW	45580 TQ	USBLS	5/15
	Sioux Falls MSA, SD	Y	41510 FQ	48920 MW	61840 TQ	USBLS	5/15
	Tennessee	Y	25350 FQ	39760 MW	64060 TQ	USBLS	5/15
	Knoxville MSA, TN	Y	27810 FQ	41670 MW	61080 TQ	USBLS	5/15
	Memphis MSA, TN-MS-AR	Y	23090 FQ	28110 MW	44030 TQ	USBLS	5/15

AE Average entry wage	AWR Average wage range	H Hourly	LR Low end range	MTC Median total compensation	TCC Total cash compensation
AEX Average experienced wage	B Biweekly	HI Highest wage paid	M Monthly	MW Median wage paid	TQ Third quartile wage
ATC Average total compensation	D Daily	HR High end range	MCC Median cash compensation	MWR Median wage range	W Weekly
AW Average wage paid	FQ First quartile wage	LO Lowest wage paid	ME Median entry wage	S See annotated source	Y Yearly

Occupation/Type/Industry	Location	Per	Low	Mid	High	Source	Date
Tax Preparer	Nashville-Davidson–Murfreesboro–Franklin MSA, TN	Y	35740 FQ	48240 MW	73540 TQ	USBLS	5/15
	Texas	Y	23920 FQ	38780 MW	58080 TQ	USBLS	5/15
	Austin-Round Rock MSA, TX	Y	41940 FQ	49700 MW	59230 TQ	USBLS	5/15
	Dallas-Plano-Irving PMSA, TX	Y	28240 FQ	43440 MW	70770 TQ	USBLS	5/15
	Fort Worth-Arlington PMSA, TX	Y	32950 FQ	52350 MW	71500 TQ	USBLS	5/15
	Houston-The Woodlands-Sugar Land MSA, TX	Y	23650 FQ	41640 MW	58950 TQ	USBLS	5/15
	San Antonio-New Braunfels MSA, TX	Y	20730 FQ	24290 MW	35130 TQ	USBLS	5/15
	Utah	Y	28700 FQ	44210 MW	65140 TQ	USBLS	5/15
	Ogden-Clearfield MSA, UT	Y	27220 FQ	30370 MW	39340 TQ	USBLS	5/15
	Provo-Orem MSA, UT	Y	51730 FQ	64060 MW	82790 TQ	USBLS	5/15
	Salt Lake City MSA, UT	Y	28670 FQ	45300 MW	67990 TQ	USBLS	5/15
	Vermont	Y	40630 FQ	52290 MW	60380 TQ	USBLS	5/15
	Burlington-South Burlington MSA, VT	Y	36200 FQ	43380 MW	49220 TQ	USBLS	5/15
	Virginia	Y	22610 FQ	32330 MW	52110 TQ	USBLS	5/15
	Richmond MSA, VA	Y	22510 FQ	28950 MW	57830 TQ	USBLS	5/15
	Virginia Beach-Norfolk-Newport News MSA, VA-NC	Y	19640 FQ	37650 MW	49710 TQ	USBLS	5/15
	Washington	H	13.53 FQ	16.11 MW	21.15 TQ	WABLS	3/16
	Seattle-Bellevue-Everett PMSA, WA	H	14.18 FQ	17.12 MW	22.09 TQ	WABLS	3/16
	Tacoma-Lakewood PMSA, WA	H	14.53 FQ	20.37 MW	23.82 TQ	WABLS	3/16
	West Virginia	Y	20050 FQ	23850 MW	29410 TQ	USBLS	5/15
	Huntington-Ashland MSA, WV-KY-OH	Y	21420 FQ	26780 MW	39040 TQ	USBLS	5/15
	Wisconsin	Y	29300 FQ	36960 MW	49310 TQ	USBLS	5/15
	Madison MSA, WI	Y	39780 FQ	52720 MW	65120 TQ	USBLS	5/15
	Milwaukee-Waukesha-West Allis MSA, WI	Y	33740 FQ	38550 MW	49040 TQ	USBLS	5/15
	Wyoming	Y	18610 FQ	24540 MW	38880 TQ	USBLS	5/15
	Puerto Rico	Y	17180 FQ	18850 MW	23860 TQ	USBLS	5/15
	San Juan-Carolina-Caguas MSA, PR	Y	17190 FQ	18850 MW	23940 TQ	USBLS	5/15
	Guam	Y	28620 FQ	31960 MW	36770 TQ	USBLS	5/15
Tax Research Analyst State Government	North Carolina	Y	35474 LO		55460 HI	NCGOV	7/1/16
Tax Standards Specialist County Government	Oakland County, MI	B	1913 LO		2490 HI	MIOAK2	10/1/16
Taxi Administrator Municipal Government	Los Angeles, CA	Y			139533 HI	CACIT	6/23/16
Taxi Driver and Chauffeur	Alabama	Y	17670 AE	21928 AW	24057 AEX	ALBLS	6/16
	Birmingham-Hoover MSA, AL	Y	17721 AE	20519 AW	21928 AEX	ALBLS	6/16
	Alaska	Y	22980 FQ	27690 MW	34740 TQ	USBLS	5/15
	Anchorage MSA, AK	Y	22170 FQ	24750 MW	29080 TQ	USBLS	5/15
	Arizona	Y	19180 FQ	22660 MW	27350 TQ	USBLS	5/15
	Phoenix-Mesa-Scottsdale MSA, AZ	Y	19530 FQ	23310 MW	28020 TQ	USBLS	5/15
	Tucson MSA, AZ	Y	19200 FQ	22300 MW	25790 TQ	USBLS	5/15
	Arkansas	Y	17790 FQ	19990 MW	24520 TQ	USBLS	5/15
	Little Rock-North Little Rock-Conway MSA, AR	Y	18880 FQ	21950 MW	25840 TQ	USBLS	5/15
	California	H	10.23 FQ	12.49 MW	16.09 TQ	CABLS	1/16-3/16
	Anaheim-Santa Ana-Irvine PMSA, CA	H	9.74 FQ	12.47 MW	17.74 TQ	CABLS	1/16-3/16
	Los Angeles-Long Beach-Glendale PMSA, CA	H	9.89 FQ	12.66 MW	17.66 TQ	CABLS	1/16-3/16
	Oakland-Hayward-Berkeley PMSA, CA	H	9.98 FQ	13.24 MW	18.38 TQ	CABLS	1/16-3/16
	Riverside-San Bernardino-Ontario MSA, CA	H	10.63 FQ	11.80 MW	14.22 TQ	CABLS	1/16-3/16
	Sacramento–Roseville–Arden-Arcade MSA, CA	H	10.50 FQ	13.47 MW	17.59 TQ	CABLS	1/16-3/16
	San Diego-Carlsbad MSA, CA	H	10.47 FQ	12.29 MW	14.27 TQ	CABLS	1/16-3/16

AE	Average entry wage	AWR	Average wage range	H	Hourly	LR	Low end range	MTC	Median total compensation	TCC	Total cash compensation
AEX	Average experienced wage	B	Biweekly	HI	Highest wage paid	M	Monthly	MW	Median wage paid	TQ	Third quartile wage
ATC	Average total compensation	D	Daily	HR	High end range	MCC	Median cash compensation	MWR	Median wage range	W	Weekly
AW	Average wage paid	FQ	First quartile wage	LO	Lowest wage paid	ME	Median entry wage	S	See annotated source	Y	Yearly

Occupation/Type/Industry	Location	Per	Low	Mid	High	Source	Date
Taxi Driver and Chauffeur	San Francisco-Redwood City-South San Francisco PMSA, CA	H	11.57 FQ	13.22 MW	14.68 TQ	CABLS	1/16-3/16
	Colorado	Y	21500 FQ	25440 MW	30220 TQ	USBLS	5/15
	Denver-Aurora-Lakewood MSA, CO	Y	22810 FQ	26850 MW	30550 TQ	USBLS	5/15
	Connecticut	Y		28504 MW		CTBLS	1/16-3/16
	Bridgeport-Stamford-Norwalk MSA, CT	Y	20710 FQ	31130 MW	48230 TQ	USBLS	5/15
	Hartford-West Hartford-East Hartford MSA, CT	Y	21910 FQ	26200 MW	33210 TQ	USBLS	5/15
	Delaware	Y	22300 FQ	25660 MW	29430 TQ	USBLS	5/15
	Wilmington PMSA, DE-MD-NJ	Y	21660 FQ	25210 MW	29480 TQ	USBLS	5/15
	District of Columbia	Y	27290 FQ	30710 MW	41580 TQ	USBLS	5/15
	Washington-Arlington-Alexandria PMSA, DC-VA-MD-WV	Y	24080 FQ	28410 MW	35640 TQ	USBLS	5/15
	Florida	H	9.12 AE	10.96 MW	12.74 AEX	FLBLS	7/16-9/16
	Fort Lauderdale-Pompano Beach-Deerfield Beach PMSA, FL	H	9.66 AE	11.40 MW	12.78 AEX	FLBLS	7/16-9/16
	Miami-Miami Beach-Kendall PMSA, FL	H	9.14 AE	10.80 MW	12.21 AEX	FLBLS	7/16-9/16
	Orlando-Kissimmee-Sanford MSA, FL	H	9.03 AE	10.04 MW	12.38 AEX	FLBLS	7/16-9/16
	Tampa-St. Petersburg-Clearwater MSA, FL	H	9.23 AE	11.25 MW	12.59 AEX	FLBLS	7/16-9/16
	Georgia	Y	17910 FQ	20110 MW	26440 TQ	USBLS	5/15
	Atlanta-Sandy Springs-Roswell MSA, GA	Y	18030 FQ	20560 MW	27650 TQ	USBLS	5/15
	Augusta-Richmond County MSA, GA-SC	Y	18890 FQ	21950 MW	25110 TQ	USBLS	5/15
	Hawaii	Y	20710 FQ	24410 MW	35070 TQ	USBLS	5/15
	Urban Honolulu MSA, HI	Y	19440 FQ	23170 MW	31220 TQ	USBLS	5/15
	Idaho	Y	18430 FQ	21630 MW	24800 TQ	USBLS	5/15
	Boise City MSA, ID	Y	19180 FQ	22530 MW	26110 TQ	USBLS	5/15
	Illinois	Y	20190 FQ	23000 MW	27660 TQ	USBLS	5/15
	Chicago-Naperville-Arlington Heights PMSA, IL	Y	20750 FQ	23160 MW	27120 TQ	USBLS	5/15
	Lake County-Kenosha County PMSA, IL-WI	Y	21960 FQ	27360 MW	36650 TQ	USBLS	5/15
	Indiana	Y	18680 FQ	21630 MW	24600 TQ	USBLS	5/15
	Gary PMSA, IN	Y	20200 FQ	22990 MW	30000 TQ	USBLS	5/15
	Indianapolis-Carmel-Anderson MSA, IN	Y	19900 FQ	22600 MW	25700 TQ	USBLS	5/15
	Iowa	Y	18920 FQ	22070 MW	25400 TQ	USBLS	5/15
	Des Moines-West Des Moines MSA, IA	Y	20050 FQ	22400 MW	24760 TQ	USBLS	5/15
	Kansas	Y	17980 FQ	21060 MW	24590 TQ	USBLS	5/15
	Wichita MSA, KS	Y	20120 FQ	23740 MW	28390 TQ	USBLS	5/15
	Kentucky	Y	17370 FQ	19270 MW	23270 TQ	USBLS	5/15
	Louisville-Jefferson County MSA, KY-IN	Y	17250 FQ	19090 MW	23170 TQ	USBLS	5/15
	Louisiana	Y	18080 FQ	21380 MW	28010 TQ	USBLS	5/15
	Baton Rouge MSA, LA	Y	24140 FQ	27920 MW	31020 TQ	USBLS	5/15
	New Orleans-Metairie MSA, LA	Y	17720 FQ	19780 MW	25000 TQ	USBLS	5/15
	Maine	Y	18800 FQ	22050 MW	25420 TQ	USBLS	5/15
	Portland-South Portland MSA, ME	Y	20000 FQ	23900 MW	27960 TQ	USBLS	5/15
	Maryland	Y	19944 AE	26511 MW	29795 AEX	MDBLS	4/16
	Baltimore-Columbia-Towson MSA, MD	Y	20810 FQ	23960 MW	30100 TQ	USBLS	5/15
	Salisbury MSA, MD-DE	Y	21200 FQ	24120 MW	27880 TQ	USBLS	5/15
	Massachusetts	Y	20990 FQ	24580 MW	30630 TQ	USBLS	5/15
	Boston-Cambridge-Newton NECTA, MA	Y	21110 FQ	25400 MW	32770 TQ	USBLS	5/15
	Worcester MSA, MA-CT	Y	21940 FQ	25640 MW	30670 TQ	USBLS	5/15
	Michigan	Y	18720 FQ	21080 MW	25030 TQ	USBLS	5/15
	Detroit-Dearborn-Livonia PMSA, MI	Y	19440 FQ	23130 MW	28570 TQ	USBLS	5/15

AE	Average entry wage	AWR	Average wage range	H	Hourly	LR	Low end range	MTC	Median total compensation	TCC	Total cash compensation
AEX	Average experienced wage	B	Biweekly	HI	Highest wage paid	M	Monthly	MW	Median wage paid	TQ	Third quartile wage
ATC	Average total compensation	D	Daily	HR	High end range	MCC	Median cash compensation	MWR	Median wage range	W	Weekly
AW	Average wage paid	FQ	First quartile wage	LO	Lowest wage paid	ME	Median entry wage	S	See annotated source	Y	Yearly

Occupation/Type/Industry	Location	Per	Low	Mid	High	Source	Date
Taxi Driver and Chauffeur	Grand Rapids-Wyoming MSA, MI	Y	19040 FQ	21880 MW	24880 TQ	USBLS	5/15
	Minnesota	Y	20244 FQ	24962 MW	31101 TQ	MNBLS	1/16-3/16
	Minneapolis-St. Paul-Bloomington MSA, MN-WI	Y	21211 FQ	25980 MW	31091 TQ	MNBLS	1/16-3/16
	Mississippi	Y	17020 FQ	18570 MW	21680 TQ	USBLS	5/15
	Jackson MSA, MS	Y	17520 FQ	19380 MW	22460 TQ	USBLS	5/15
	Missouri	Y	18710 FQ	22180 MW	28450 TQ	USBLS	5/15
	Kansas City MSA, MO-KS	Y	18690 FQ	22000 MW	25470 TQ	USBLS	5/15
	St. Louis MSA, MO-IL	Y	18790 FQ	23430 MW	31800 TQ	USBLS	5/15
	Montana	Y	18450 FQ	20720 MW	25090 TQ	USBLS	5/15
	Billings MSA, MT	Y	17720 FQ	18620 MW	19520 TQ	USBLS	5/15
	Nebraska	Y	19725 FQ	23010 MW	27680 TQ	NEBLS	7/16-9/16
	Omaha-Council Bluffs MSA, NE-IA	Y	20850 FQ	24505 MW	29325 TQ	NEBLS	7/16-9/16
	Nevada	Y	21410 FQ	28490 MW	35570 TQ	USBLS	5/15
	Las Vegas-Henderson-Paradise MSA, NV	Y	21760 FQ	28920 MW	35800 TQ	USBLS	5/15
	New Hampshire	H	9.72 AE	11.93 MW	14.52 AEX	NHBLS	6/16
	Manchester NECTA, NH	H	9.85 AE	11.95 MW	15.97 AEX	NHBLS	6/16
	Nashua NECTA, NH-MA	Y	19420 FQ	21880 MW	24050 TQ	USBLS	5/15
	New Jersey	Y	20710 FQ	26450 MW	33250 TQ	USBLS	5/15
	Camden PMSA, NJ	Y	21860 FQ	27100 MW	32360 TQ	USBLS	5/15
	Newark PMSA, NJ-PA	Y	22440 FQ	26930 MW	31300 TQ	USBLS	5/15
	Trenton MSA, NJ	Y	22050 FQ	26990 MW	32980 TQ	USBLS	5/15
	New Mexico	Y	18800 FQ	22030 MW	27040 TQ	USBLS	5/15
	Albuquerque MSA, NM	Y	18570 FQ	21630 MW	26640 TQ	USBLS	5/15
	New York	Y	20960 AE	28380 MW	39010 AEX	NYBLS	1/16-3/16
	Buffalo-Cheektowaga-Niagara Falls MSA, NY	Y	19230 FQ	21390 MW	32790 TQ	USBLS	5/15
	Glens Falls MSA, NY	Y	19570 FQ	21800 MW	24180 TQ	USBLS	5/15
	Nassau County-Suffolk County PMSA, NY	Y	23540 FQ	28610 MW	40940 TQ	USBLS	5/15
	New York-Jersey City-White Plains PMSA, NY-NJ	Y	21780 FQ	29570 MW	38500 TQ	USBLS	5/15
	Rochester MSA, NY	Y	21110 FQ	24270 MW	29570 TQ	USBLS	5/15
	North Carolina	Y	18790 FQ	22520 MW	27400 TQ	USBLS	5/15
	Charlotte-Concord-Gastonia MSA, NC-SC	Y	18610 FQ	23740 MW	29230 TQ	USBLS	5/15
	Raleigh MSA, NC	Y	19390 FQ	22400 MW	25820 TQ	USBLS	5/15
	North Dakota	Y	19290 FQ	24320 MW	30510 TQ	USBLS	5/15
	Fargo MSA, ND-MN	Y	18620 FQ	21810 MW	26770 TQ	USBLS	5/15
	Ohio	Y	18360 FQ	20270 MW	24160 TQ	USBLS	5/15
	Cincinnati MSA, OH-KY-IN	Y	18280 FQ	20400 MW	24590 TQ	USBLS	5/15
	Cleveland-Elyria MSA, OH	Y	18400 FQ	20730 MW	24240 TQ	USBLS	5/15
	Columbus MSA, OH	Y	18560 FQ	20910 MW	24370 TQ	USBLS	5/15
	Oklahoma	Y	17500 FQ	19660 MW	23800 TQ	USBLS	5/15
	Oklahoma City MSA, OK	Y	17260 FQ	19180 MW	23210 TQ	USBLS	5/15
	Tulsa MSA, OK	Y	17980 FQ	20940 MW	24680 TQ	USBLS	5/15
	Oregon	H	9.92 FQ	11.37 MW	13.53 TQ	ORBLS	2016
	Portland-Vancouver-Hillsboro MSA, OR-WA	Y	20160 FQ	23130 MW	27620 TQ	USBLS	5/15
	Pennsylvania	Y	19190 FQ	22480 MW	27300 TQ	USBLS	5/15
	Allentown-Bethlehem-Easton MSA, PA-NJ	Y	21130 FQ	25700 MW	36290 TQ	USBLS	5/15
	Harrisburg-Carlisle MSA, PA	Y	19100 FQ	22360 MW	27840 TQ	USBLS	5/15
	Montgomery County-Bucks County-Chester County PMSA, PA	Y	18810 FQ	22420 MW	28320 TQ	USBLS	5/15
	Philadelphia PMSA, PA	Y	20450 FQ	23920 MW	30430 TQ	USBLS	5/15
	Pittsburgh MSA, PA	Y	18440 FQ	21580 MW	25150 TQ	USBLS	5/15
	Rhode Island	Y	19530 FQ	22880 MW	28410 TQ	USBLS	5/15
	Providence-Warwick MSA, RI-MA	Y	19340 FQ	22640 MW	28370 TQ	USBLS	5/15
	South Carolina	Y	18900 FQ	21970 MW	25120 TQ	USBLS	5/15
	Charleston-North Charleston MSA, SC	Y	20620 FQ	23720 MW	28650 TQ	USBLS	5/15
	Columbia MSA, SC	Y	18730 FQ	21540 MW	24250 TQ	USBLS	5/15
	Greenville-Anderson-Mauldin MSA, SC	Y	19280 FQ	21830 MW	24270 TQ	USBLS	5/15
	South Dakota	Y	20960 FQ	22910 MW	24850 TQ	USBLS	5/15
	Sioux Falls MSA, SD	Y	21130 FQ	23020 MW	24930 TQ	USBLS	5/15

AE Average entry wage	**AWR** Average wage range	**H** Hourly	**LR** Low end range	**MTC** Median total compensation	**TCC** Total cash compensation
AEX Average experienced wage	**B** Biweekly	**HI** Highest wage paid	**M** Monthly	**MW** Median wage paid	**TQ** Third quartile wage
ATC Average total compensation	**D** Daily	**HR** High end range	**MCC** Median cash compensation	**MWR** Median wage range	**W** Weekly
AW Average wage paid	**FQ** First quartile wage	**LO** Lowest wage paid	**ME** Median entry wage	**S** See annotated source	**Y** Yearly

Occupation/Type/Industry	Location	Per	Low	Mid	High	Source	Date
Taxi Driver and Chauffeur	Tennessee	Y	18230 FQ	21430 MW	26360 TQ	USBLS	5/15
	Knoxville MSA, TN	Y	17520 FQ	19630 MW	23070 TQ	USBLS	5/15
	Memphis MSA, TN-MS-AR	Y	18800 FQ	22750 MW	28090 TQ	USBLS	5/15
	Nashville-Davidson–Murfreesboro–Franklin MSA, TN	Y	19590 FQ	23350 MW	39780 TQ	USBLS	5/15
	Texas	Y	18580 FQ	22420 MW	28560 TQ	USBLS	5/15
	Austin-Round Rock MSA, TX	Y	17570 FQ	19540 MW	26360 TQ	USBLS	5/15
	Dallas-Plano-Irving PMSA, TX	Y	18730 FQ	23860 MW	29870 TQ	USBLS	5/15
	Fort Worth-Arlington PMSA, TX	Y	19330 FQ	24740 MW	31230 TQ	USBLS	5/15
	Houston-The Woodlands-Sugar Land MSA, TX	Y	21470 FQ	25550 MW	31510 TQ	USBLS	5/15
	San Antonio-New Braunfels MSA, TX	Y	19330 FQ	22520 MW	26420 TQ	USBLS	5/15
	Utah	Y	19840 FQ	22760 MW	26390 TQ	USBLS	5/15
	Ogden-Clearfield MSA, UT	Y	16670 FQ	17940 MW	19160 TQ	USBLS	5/15
	Provo-Orem MSA, UT	Y	20670 FQ	23200 MW	26570 TQ	USBLS	5/15
	Salt Lake City MSA, UT	Y	21310 FQ	23940 MW	29400 TQ	USBLS	5/15
	Vermont	Y	19610 FQ	22890 MW	27760 TQ	USBLS	5/15
	Burlington-South Burlington MSA, VT	Y	20520 FQ	23360 MW	27430 TQ	USBLS	5/15
	Virginia	Y	21470 FQ	25790 MW	31020 TQ	USBLS	5/15
	Richmond MSA, VA	Y	22060 FQ	25110 MW	30110 TQ	USBLS	5/15
	Virginia Beach-Norfolk-Newport News MSA, VA-NC	Y	22110 FQ	26530 MW	30410 TQ	USBLS	5/15
	Washington	H	10.83 FQ	12.25 MW	16.73 TQ	WABLS	3/16
	Seattle-Bellevue-Everett PMSA, WA	H	11.05 FQ	13.35 MW	17.54 TQ	WABLS	3/16
	Tacoma-Lakewood PMSA, WA	H	11.60 FQ	14.28 MW	17.15 TQ	WABLS	3/16
	West Virginia	Y	18280 FQ	20100 MW	24490 TQ	USBLS	5/15
	Huntington-Ashland MSA, WV-KY-OH	Y	17930 FQ	19700 MW	23260 TQ	USBLS	5/15
	Wisconsin	Y	18460 FQ	21560 MW	25460 TQ	USBLS	5/15
	Madison MSA, WI	Y	20620 FQ	24830 MW	29150 TQ	USBLS	5/15
	Milwaukee-Waukesha-West Allis MSA, WI	Y	19770 FQ	22680 MW	27580 TQ	USBLS	5/15
	Wyoming	Y	17950 FQ	21480 MW	27460 TQ	USBLS	5/15
	Cheyenne MSA, WY	Y	17070 FQ	18640 MW	21210 TQ	USBLS	5/15
	Puerto Rico	Y	17150 FQ	18680 MW	21500 TQ	USBLS	5/15
	San Juan-Carolina-Caguas MSA, PR	Y	17220 FQ	18840 MW	22570 TQ	USBLS	5/15
	Virgin Islands	Y	24340 FQ	27410 MW	30260 TQ	USBLS	5/15
	Guam	Y	17940 FQ	18710 MW	19540 TQ	USBLS	5/15
Taxi Specialist							
Municipal Government	West Hollywood, CA	Y			92998 HI	CACIT	6/28/16
Teacher	Los Angeles County, CA	Y		74100 AW		RFIN01	2015
	Orange County, CA	Y		79900 AW		RFIN01	2015
	San Joaquin County, CA	Y		67700 AW		RFIN01	2015
	Santa Cruz County, CA	Y		63800 AW		RFIN01	2015
Teacher Allotment Supervisor							
State Government	North Carolina	Y	50238 LO		82872 HI	NCGOV	7/1/16
Teacher Assistant	Alabama	Y	17359 AE	20611 AW	22231 AEX	ALBLS	6/16
	Birmingham-Hoover MSA, AL	Y	17665 AE	22333 AW	24668 AEX	ALBLS	6/16
	Alaska	Y	31210 FQ	38440 MW	47730 TQ	USBLS	5/15
	Anchorage MSA, AK	Y	31440 FQ	37340 MW	45230 TQ	USBLS	5/15
	Arizona	Y	20830 FQ	23710 MW	28000 TQ	USBLS	5/15
	Phoenix-Mesa-Scottsdale MSA, AZ	Y	21370 FQ	24170 MW	28340 TQ	USBLS	5/15
	Tucson MSA, AZ	Y	20000 FQ	22980 MW	27490 TQ	USBLS	5/15
	Arkansas	Y	17030 FQ	18390 MW	20110 TQ	USBLS	5/15
	Little Rock-North Little Rock-Conway MSA, AR	Y	17210 FQ	18740 MW	21880 TQ	USBLS	5/15
	California	Y		31672 AW		CABLS	1/16-3/16
	Anaheim-Santa Ana-Irvine PMSA, CA	Y		34645 AW		CABLS	1/16-3/16
	Los Angeles-Long Beach-Glendale PMSA, CA	Y		31439 AW		CABLS	1/16-3/16

AE	Average entry wage	AWR	Average wage range	H	Hourly
AEX	Average experienced wage	B	Biweekly	HI	Highest wage paid
ATC	Average total compensation	D	Daily	HR	High end range
AW	Average wage paid	FQ	First quartile wage	LO	Lowest wage paid

LR	Low end range	MTC	Median total compensation
M	Monthly	MW	Median wage paid
MCC	Median cash compensation	MWR	Median wage range
ME	Median entry wage	S	See annotated source

TCC	Total cash compensation
TQ	Third quartile wage
W	Weekly
Y	Yearly

Teacher Assistant

Occupation/Type/Industry	Location	Per	Low	Mid	High	Source	Date
Teacher Assistant	Oakland-Hayward-Berkeley PMSA, CA	Y		32697 AW		CABLS	1/16-3/16
	Riverside-San Bernardino-Ontario MSA, CA	Y		30496 AW		CABLS	1/16-3/16
	Sacramento–Roseville–Arden-Arcade MSA, CA	Y		32068 AW		CABLS	1/16-3/16
	San Diego-Carlsbad MSA, CA	Y		30029 AW		CABLS	1/16-3/16
	San Francisco-Redwood City-South San Francisco PMSA, CA	Y		37658 AW		CABLS	1/16-3/16
	Colorado	Y	22580 FQ	26720 MW	31390 TQ	USBLS	5/15
	Denver-Aurora-Lakewood MSA, CO	Y	23050 FQ	27430 MW	32800 TQ	USBLS	5/15
	Connecticut	Y		30161 MW		CTBLS	1/16-3/16
	Bridgeport-Stamford-Norwalk MSA, CT	Y	25850 FQ	32520 MW	39120 TQ	USBLS	5/15
	Hartford-West Hartford-East Hartford MSA, CT	Y	21240 FQ	26500 MW	32510 TQ	USBLS	5/15
	Delaware	Y	22850 FQ	28750 MW	34300 TQ	USBLS	5/15
	Wilmington PMSA, DE-MD-NJ	Y	20910 FQ	27150 MW	33080 TQ	USBLS	5/15
	District of Columbia	Y	25950 FQ	31570 MW	36240 TQ	USBLS	5/15
	Washington-Arlington-Alexandria PMSA, DC-VA-MD-WV	Y	23050 FQ	30180 MW	38360 TQ	USBLS	5/15
	Florida	Y	19283 AE	23663 MW	27825 AEX	FLBLS	7/16-9/16
	Fort Lauderdale-Pompano Beach-Deerfield Beach PMSA, FL	Y	20120 AE	23173 MW	25748 AEX	FLBLS	7/16-9/16
	Miami-Miami Beach-Kendall PMSA, FL	Y	18953 AE	23065 MW	28784 AEX	FLBLS	7/16-9/16
	Orlando-Kissimmee-Sanford MSA, FL	Y	19089 AE	23420 MW	27315 AEX	FLBLS	7/16-9/16
	Tampa-St. Petersburg-Clearwater MSA, FL	Y	18664 AE	21540 MW	26547 AEX	FLBLS	7/16-9/16
	Georgia	Y	17230 FQ	18990 MW	22800 TQ	USBLS	5/15
	Atlanta-Sandy Springs-Roswell MSA, GA	Y	17710 FQ	20160 MW	24180 TQ	USBLS	5/15
	Augusta-Richmond County MSA, GA-SC	Y	16780 FQ	18100 MW	19440 TQ	USBLS	5/15
	Hawaii	Y	24820 FQ	28000 MW	30920 TQ	USBLS	5/15
	Urban Honolulu MSA, HI	Y	24970 FQ	28020 MW	30910 TQ	USBLS	5/15
	Idaho	Y	18250 FQ	21660 MW	25990 TQ	USBLS	5/15
	Boise City MSA, ID	Y	20950 FQ	24260 MW	28210 TQ	USBLS	5/15
	Illinois	Y	19770 FQ	25700 MW	33180 TQ	USBLS	5/15
	Chicago-Naperville-Arlington Heights PMSA, IL	Y	20980 FQ	28190 MW	35240 TQ	USBLS	5/15
	Lake County-Kenosha County PMSA, IL-WI	Y	20800 FQ	26250 MW	32650 TQ	USBLS	5/15
	Indiana	Y	18650 FQ	22090 MW	26270 TQ	USBLS	5/15
	Gary PMSA, IN	Y	19330 FQ	22470 MW	26200 TQ	USBLS	5/15
	Indianapolis-Carmel-Anderson MSA, IN	Y	18970 FQ	23120 MW	28030 TQ	USBLS	5/15
	Iowa	Y	18980 FQ	22950 MW	27600 TQ	USBLS	5/15
	Des Moines-West Des Moines MSA, IA	Y	18890 FQ	22860 MW	27300 TQ	USBLS	5/15
	Kansas	Y	19830 FQ	22980 MW	27230 TQ	USBLS	5/15
	Wichita MSA, KS	Y	21330 FQ	26040 MW	29690 TQ	USBLS	5/15
	Kentucky	Y	21600 FQ	24930 MW	30450 TQ	USBLS	5/15
	Louisville-Jefferson County MSA, KY-IN	Y	22930 FQ	28740 MW	35900 TQ	USBLS	5/15
	Louisiana	Y	17340 FQ	19120 MW	22640 TQ	USBLS	5/15
	Baton Rouge MSA, LA	Y	17350 FQ	19140 MW	22060 TQ	USBLS	5/15
	New Orleans-Metairie MSA, LA	Y	20550 FQ	23940 MW	28310 TQ	USBLS	5/15
	Maine	Y	27340 FQ	32350 MW	37940 TQ	USBLS	5/15
	Portland-South Portland MSA, ME	Y	32240 FQ	36480 MW	41980 TQ	USBLS	5/15
	Maryland	Y	19637 AE	27977 MW	32147 AEX	MDBLS	4/16
	Baltimore-Columbia-Towson MSA, MD	Y	20730 FQ	25440 MW	31850 TQ	USBLS	5/15
	Salisbury MSA, MD-DE	Y	19620 FQ	24310 MW	29570 TQ	USBLS	5/15

AE Average entry wage	**AWR** Average wage range	**H** Hourly	**LR** Low end range	**MTC** Median total compensation	**TCC** Total cash compensation
AEX Average experienced wage	**B** Biweekly	**HI** Highest wage paid	**M** Monthly	**MW** Median wage paid	**TQ** Third quartile wage
ATC Average total compensation	**D** Daily	**HR** High end range	**MCC** Median cash compensation	**MWR** Median wage range	**W** Weekly
AW Average wage paid	**FQ** First quartile wage	**LO** Lowest wage paid	**ME** Median entry wage	**S** See annotated source	**Y** Yearly

Occupation/Type/Industry	Location	Per	Low	Mid	High	Source	Date
Teacher Assistant	Massachusetts	Y	22480 FQ	28810 MW	36310 TQ	USBLS	5/15
	Boston-Cambridge-Newton NECTA, MA	Y	22540 FQ	29700 MW	37820 TQ	USBLS	5/15
	Worcester MSA, MA-CT	Y	25820 FQ	29470 MW	35660 TQ	USBLS	5/15
	Michigan	Y	20220 FQ	24700 MW	30190 TQ	USBLS	5/15
	Detroit-Dearborn-Livonia PMSA, MI	Y	21240 FQ	26500 MW	32270 TQ	USBLS	5/15
	Grand Rapids-Wyoming MSA, MI	Y	20700 FQ	25110 MW	30300 TQ	USBLS	5/15
	Minnesota	Y	23971 FQ	30181 MW	36784 TQ	MNBLS	1/16-3/16
	Minneapolis-St. Paul-Bloomington MSA, MN-WI	Y	25715 FQ	32046 MW	38639 TQ	MNBLS	1/16-3/16
	Mississippi	Y	16850 FQ	18280 MW	20010 TQ	USBLS	5/15
	Jackson MSA, MS	Y	16590 FQ	17860 MW	19130 TQ	USBLS	5/15
	Missouri	Y	18580 FQ	22890 MW	28250 TQ	USBLS	5/15
	Kansas City MSA, MO-KS	Y	20270 FQ	23810 MW	27960 TQ	USBLS	5/15
	St. Louis MSA, MO-IL	Y	19200 FQ	25610 MW	31680 TQ	USBLS	5/15
	Montana	Y	20390 FQ	24160 MW	28980 TQ	USBLS	5/15
	Billings MSA, MT	Y	25570 FQ	28900 MW	33200 TQ	USBLS	5/15
	Nebraska	Y	19785 FQ	22725 MW	26395 TQ	NEBLS	7/16-9/16
	Omaha-Council Bluffs MSA, NE-IA	Y	18985 FQ	21815 MW	25625 TQ	NEBLS	7/16-9/16
	Nevada	Y	26000 FQ	31250 MW	37050 TQ	USBLS	5/15
	Las Vegas-Henderson-Paradise MSA, NV	Y	27950 FQ	32930 MW	38050 TQ	USBLS	5/15
	New Hampshire	Y	20710 AE	29348 MW	33693 AEX	NHBLS	6/16
	Manchester NECTA, NH	Y	19989 AE	25322 MW	30928 AEX	NHBLS	6/16
	Nashua NECTA, NH-MA	Y	26500 FQ	31770 MW	36180 TQ	USBLS	5/15
	New Jersey	Y	20530 FQ	25400 MW	31270 TQ	USBLS	5/15
	Camden PMSA, NJ	Y	19940 FQ	24300 MW	30300 TQ	USBLS	5/15
	Newark PMSA, NJ-PA	Y	21060 FQ	26120 MW	31040 TQ	USBLS	5/15
	Trenton MSA, NJ	Y	22720 FQ	27390 MW	32180 TQ	USBLS	5/15
	New Mexico	Y	18170 FQ	21000 MW	26460 TQ	USBLS	5/15
	Albuquerque MSA, NM	Y	17790 FQ	19560 MW	25730 TQ	USBLS	5/15
	New York	Y	20210 AE	26080 MW	32070 AEX	NYBLS	1/16-3/16
	Buffalo-Cheektowaga-Niagara Falls MSA, NY	Y	19250 FQ	21960 MW	26090 TQ	USBLS	5/15
	Nassau County-Suffolk County PMSA, NY	Y	21010 FQ	26780 MW	35620 TQ	USBLS	5/15
	New York-Jersey City-White Plains PMSA, NY-NJ	Y	21230 FQ	27410 MW	34440 TQ	USBLS	5/15
	Rochester MSA, NY	Y	19660 FQ	23500 MW	29180 TQ	USBLS	5/15
	North Carolina	Y	20750 FQ	22780 MW	24890 TQ	USBLS	5/15
	Charlotte-Concord-Gastonia MSA, NC-SC	Y	20650 FQ	23450 MW	27230 TQ	USBLS	5/15
	Raleigh MSA, NC	Y	20930 FQ	22680 MW	24430 TQ	USBLS	5/15
	North Dakota	Y	25750 FQ	29590 MW	34790 TQ	USBLS	5/15
	Fargo MSA, ND-MN	Y	25760 FQ	30150 MW	35150 TQ	USBLS	5/15
	Ohio	Y	20260 FQ	25600 MW	31420 TQ	USBLS	5/15
	Cincinnati MSA, OH-KY-IN	Y	21680 FQ	27460 MW	33550 TQ	USBLS	5/15
	Cleveland-Elyria MSA, OH	Y	21840 FQ	27600 MW	33870 TQ	USBLS	5/15
	Columbus MSA, OH	Y	22240 FQ	26770 MW	31780 TQ	USBLS	5/15
	Oklahoma	Y	17040 FQ	18620 MW	22270 TQ	USBLS	5/15
	Oklahoma City MSA, OK	Y	16710 FQ	17980 MW	19260 TQ	USBLS	5/15
	Tulsa MSA, OK	Y	18430 FQ	23320 MW	28660 TQ	USBLS	5/15
	Oregon	Y	24785 FQ	29603 MW	35498 TQ	ORBLS	2016
	Portland-Vancouver-Hillsboro MSA, OR-WA	Y	25310 FQ	30120 MW	35750 TQ	USBLS	5/15
	Pennsylvania	Y	18940 FQ	23410 MW	29090 TQ	USBLS	5/15
	Allentown-Bethlehem-Easton MSA, PA-NJ	Y	18180 FQ	21760 MW	30080 TQ	USBLS	5/15
	Harrisburg-Carlisle MSA, PA	Y	18310 FQ	21900 MW	26740 TQ	USBLS	5/15
	Montgomery County-Bucks County-Chester County PMSA, PA	Y	21610 FQ	27090 MW	33090 TQ	USBLS	5/15
	Philadelphia PMSA, PA	Y	19300 FQ	23490 MW	28140 TQ	USBLS	5/15
	Pittsburgh MSA, PA	Y	18550 FQ	22380 MW	28630 TQ	USBLS	5/15
	Rhode Island	Y	24350 FQ	33490 MW	38410 TQ	USBLS	5/15
	Providence-Warwick MSA, RI-MA	Y	24620 FQ	32770 MW	38050 TQ	USBLS	5/15
	South Carolina	Y	17790 FQ	20510 MW	25180 TQ	USBLS	5/15

AE Average entry wage	**AWR** Average wage range	**H** Hourly	**LR** Low end range	**MTC** Median total compensation	**TCC** Total cash compensation
AEX Average experienced wage	**B** Biweekly	**HI** Highest wage paid	**M** Monthly	**MW** Median wage paid	**TQ** Third quartile wage
ATC Average total compensation	**D** Daily	**HR** High end range	**MCC** Median cash compensation	**MWR** Median wage range	**W** Weekly
AW Average wage paid	**FQ** First quartile wage	**LO** Lowest wage paid	**ME** Median entry wage	**S** See annotated source	**Y** Yearly

Occupation/Type/Industry	Location	Per	Low	Mid	High	Source	Date
Teacher Assistant	Charleston-North Charleston						
	MSA, SC	Y	17690 FQ	20070 MW	24630 TQ	USBLS	5/15
	Columbia MSA, SC	Y	18590 FQ	22220 MW	27030 TQ	USBLS	5/15
	Greenville-Anderson-Mauldin						
	MSA, SC	Y	18140 FQ	21870 MW	28770 TQ	USBLS	5/15
	South Dakota	Y	19970 FQ	22320 MW	24690 TQ	USBLS	5/15
	Sioux Falls MSA, SD	Y	20680 FQ	22520 MW	24360 TQ	USBLS	5/15
	Tennessee	Y	17540 FQ	19800 MW	25570 TQ	USBLS	5/15
	Knoxville MSA, TN	Y	16910 FQ	18500 MW	21770 TQ	USBLS	5/15
	Memphis MSA, TN-MS-AR	Y	18400 FQ	25870 MW	30050 TQ	USBLS	5/15
	Nashville-Davidson–						
	Murfreesboro–Franklin						
	MSA, TN	Y	19240 FQ	23010 MW	28370 TQ	USBLS	5/15
	Texas	Y	17890 FQ	20690 MW	25510 TQ	USBLS	5/15
	Austin-Round Rock MSA, TX	Y	19360 FQ	23180 MW	27920 TQ	USBLS	5/15
	Dallas-Plano-Irving PMSA, TX	Y	19370 FQ	23370 MW	28170 TQ	USBLS	5/15
	Fort Worth-Arlington PMSA,						
	TX	Y	17090 FQ	18660 MW	21450 TQ	USBLS	5/15
	Houston-The Woodlands-						
	Sugar Land MSA, TX	Y	17900 FQ	20670 MW	25090 TQ	USBLS	5/15
	San Antonio-New Braunfels						
	MSA, TX	Y	18050 FQ	21280 MW	26470 TQ	USBLS	5/15
	Utah	Y	20430 FQ	23570 MW	27930 TQ	USBLS	5/15
	Ogden-Clearfield MSA, UT	Y	21990 FQ	25880 MW	30190 TQ	USBLS	5/15
	Provo-Orem MSA, UT	Y	19920 FQ	23490 MW	28070 TQ	USBLS	5/15
	Salt Lake City MSA, UT	Y	19930 FQ	22620 MW	25950 TQ	USBLS	5/15
	Vermont	Y	25280 FQ	29390 MW	35000 TQ	USBLS	5/15
	Burlington-South Burlington						
	MSA, VT	Y	25480 FQ	29690 MW	35540 TQ	USBLS	5/15
	Virginia	Y	19310 FQ	24840 MW	31630 TQ	USBLS	5/15
	Richmond MSA, VA	Y	19860 FQ	24080 MW	28700 TQ	USBLS	5/15
	Virginia Beach-Norfolk-						
	Newport News MSA, VA-NC	Y	19850 FQ	25840 MW	29890 TQ	USBLS	5/15
	Washington	Y		32028 AW		WABLS	3/16
	Seattle-Bellevue-Everett						
	PMSA, WA	Y		34635 AW		WABLS	3/16
	Tacoma-Lakewood PMSA, WA	Y		33174 AW		WABLS	3/16
	West Virginia	Y	20470 FQ	23640 MW	27730 TQ	USBLS	5/15
	Huntington-Ashland MSA,						
	WV-KY-OH	Y	18850 FQ	21640 MW	24810 TQ	USBLS	5/15
	Wisconsin	Y	21180 FQ	26620 MW	31420 TQ	USBLS	5/15
	Madison MSA, WI	Y	21530 FQ	26500 MW	32810 TQ	USBLS	5/15
	Milwaukee-Waukesha-West						
	Allis MSA, WI	Y	21350 FQ	27970 MW	34800 TQ	USBLS	5/15
	Wyoming	Y	22910 FQ	28130 MW	33220 TQ	USBLS	5/15
	Cheyenne MSA, WY	Y	25070 FQ	28090 MW	31110 TQ	USBLS	5/15
	Puerto Rico	Y	16780 FQ	18190 MW	19910 TQ	USBLS	5/15
	San Juan-Carolina-Caguas						
	MSA, PR	Y	16750 FQ	18180 MW	20070 TQ	USBLS	5/15
	Virgin Islands	Y	20850 FQ	25150 MW	28550 TQ	USBLS	5/15
	Guam	Y	18370 FQ	19580 MW	24260 TQ	USBLS	5/15
Teaching Elder							
Presbyterian Church	United States	Y		59374 AW		BOPP01	5/1/16
Team Assembler	Alabama	Y	21932 AE	35854 AW	42805 AEX	ALBLS	6/16
	Birmingham-Hoover MSA, AL	Y	21202 AE	29541 AW	33705 AEX	ALBLS	6/16
	Alaska	Y	23400 FQ	29610 MW	37270 TQ	USBLS	5/15
	Anchorage MSA, AK	Y	23350 FQ	29470 MW	37310 TQ	USBLS	5/15
	Arizona	Y	20110 FQ	24570 MW	31760 TQ	USBLS	5/15
	Phoenix-Mesa-Scottsdale						
	MSA, AZ	Y	20970 FQ	25260 MW	32440 TQ	USBLS	5/15
	Tucson MSA, AZ	Y	22200 FQ	27390 MW	35170 TQ	USBLS	5/15
	Arkansas	Y	21620 FQ	26850 MW	32620 TQ	USBLS	5/15
	Little Rock-North Little Rock-						
	Conway MSA, AR	Y	21300 FQ	27710 MW	35650 TQ	USBLS	5/15
	California	H	10.61 FQ	13.14 MW	17.11 TQ	CABLS	1/16-3/16
	Anaheim-Santa Ana-Irvine						
	PMSA, CA	H	10.77 FQ	12.60 MW	15.27 TQ	CABLS	1/16-3/16
	Los Angeles-Long Beach-						
	Glendale PMSA, CA	H	9.77 FQ	11.78 MW	15.21 TQ	CABLS	1/16-3/16

AE	Average entry wage	AWR	Average wage range	H	Hourly	LR	Low end range	MTC	Median total compensation	TCC	Total cash compensation
AEX	Average experienced wage	B	Biweekly	HI	Highest wage paid	M	Monthly	MW	Median wage paid	TQ	Third quartile wage
ATC	Average total compensation	D	Daily	HR	High end range	MCC	Median cash compensation	MWR	Median wage range	W	Weekly
AW	Average wage paid	FQ	First quartile wage	LO	Lowest wage paid	ME	Median entry wage	S	See annotated source	Y	Yearly

Occupation/Type/Industry	Location	Per	Low	Mid	High	Source	Date
Team Assembler	Oakland-Hayward-Berkeley PMSA, CA	H	12.24 FQ	17.16 MW	25.88 TQ	CABLS	1/16-3/16
	Riverside-San Bernardino-Ontario MSA, CA	H	10.72 FQ	13.01 MW	16.28 TQ	CABLS	1/16-3/16
	Sacramento–Roseville–Arden-Arcade MSA, CA	H	11.49 FQ	13.91 MW	17.18 TQ	CABLS	1/16-3/16
	San Diego-Carlsbad MSA, CA	H	10.45 FQ	13.12 MW	17.30 TQ	CABLS	1/16-3/16
	San Francisco-Redwood City-South San Francisco PMSA, CA	H	12.95 FQ	16.47 MW	20.68 TQ	CABLS	1/16-3/16
	Colorado	Y	22760 FQ	29070 MW	37190 TQ	USBLS	5/15
	Denver-Aurora-Lakewood MSA, CO	Y	23560 FQ	29240 MW	36960 TQ	USBLS	5/15
	Connecticut	Y		30224 MW		CTBLS	1/16-3/16
	Bridgeport-Stamford-Norwalk MSA, CT	Y	21260 FQ	26930 MW	37040 TQ	USBLS	5/15
	Hartford-West Hartford-East Hartford MSA, CT	Y	24040 FQ	31420 MW	39300 TQ	USBLS	5/15
	Delaware	Y	23470 FQ	29040 MW	36290 TQ	USBLS	5/15
	Wilmington PMSA, DE-MD-NJ	Y	22940 FQ	29150 MW	36210 TQ	USBLS	5/15
	Washington-Arlington-Alexandria PMSA, DC-VA-MD-WV	Y	20440 FQ	24220 MW	31000 TQ	USBLS	5/15
	Florida	H	9.94 AE	13.15 MW	15.93 AEX	FLBLS	7/16-9/16
	Fort Lauderdale-Pompano Beach-Deerfield Beach PMSA, FL	H	10.32 AE	13.62 MW	16.54 AEX	FLBLS	7/16-9/16
	Miami-Miami Beach-Kendall PMSA, FL	H	9.13 AE	11.25 MW	14.20 AEX	FLBLS	7/16-9/16
	Orlando-Kissimmee-Sanford MSA, FL	H	9.48 AE	12.99 MW	15.89 AEX	FLBLS	7/16-9/16
	Tampa-St. Petersburg-Clearwater MSA, FL	H	9.81 AE	13.20 MW	15.88 AEX	FLBLS	7/16-9/16
	Georgia	Y	21720 FQ	27320 MW	34310 TQ	USBLS	5/15
	Atlanta-Sandy Springs-Roswell MSA, GA	Y	20770 FQ	25530 MW	30960 TQ	USBLS	5/15
	Augusta-Richmond County MSA, GA-SC	Y	21480 FQ	25600 MW	33970 TQ	USBLS	5/15
	Hawaii	Y	18340 FQ	22780 MW	32700 TQ	USBLS	5/15
	Urban Honolulu MSA, HI	Y	18070 FQ	21380 MW	29650 TQ	USBLS	5/15
	Idaho	Y	20460 FQ	24390 MW	30680 TQ	USBLS	5/15
	Boise City MSA, ID	Y	20080 FQ	23530 MW	28920 TQ	USBLS	5/15
	Illinois	Y	21800 FQ	29440 MW	37900 TQ	USBLS	5/15
	Chicago-Naperville-Arlington Heights PMSA, IL	Y	20540 FQ	26020 MW	36010 TQ	USBLS	5/15
	Lake County-Kenosha County PMSA, IL-WI	Y	20800 FQ	24730 MW	34050 TQ	USBLS	5/15
	Rockford MSA, IL	Y	33000 FQ	37650 MW	48710 TQ	USBLS	5/15
	Indiana	Y	22460 FQ	28230 MW	38560 TQ	USBLS	5/15
	Gary PMSA, IN	Y	21490 FQ	26190 MW	32780 TQ	USBLS	5/15
	Indianapolis-Carmel-Anderson MSA, IN	Y	21120 FQ	23430 MW	27670 TQ	USBLS	5/15
	Iowa	Y	26040 FQ	30840 MW	36440 TQ	USBLS	5/15
	Des Moines-West Des Moines MSA, IA	Y	22270 FQ	29880 MW	36330 TQ	USBLS	5/15
	Kansas	Y	26000 FQ	33040 MW	39660 TQ	USBLS	5/15
	Wichita MSA, KS	Y	25030 FQ	32580 MW	37250 TQ	USBLS	5/15
	Kentucky	Y	26250 FQ	33200 MW	45000 TQ	USBLS	5/15
	Louisville-Jefferson County MSA, KY-IN	Y	26030 FQ	35130 MW	53330 TQ	USBLS	5/15
	Louisiana	Y	25120 FQ	32720 MW	41580 TQ	USBLS	5/15
	Baton Rouge MSA, LA	Y	23220 FQ	29050 MW	37250 TQ	USBLS	5/15
	New Orleans-Metairie MSA, LA	Y	21690 FQ	28590 MW	37850 TQ	USBLS	5/15
	Maine	Y	24810 FQ	30600 MW	37530 TQ	USBLS	5/15
	Portland-South Portland MSA, ME	Y	23330 FQ	28070 MW	34820 TQ	USBLS	5/15
	Maryland	Y	19985 AE	29652 MW	34486 AEX	MDBLS	4/16
	Baltimore-Columbia-Towson MSA, MD	Y	20990 FQ	27820 MW	36610 TQ	USBLS	5/15
	Salisbury MSA, MD-DE	Y	22470 FQ	26600 MW	32550 TQ	USBLS	5/15

Occupation/Type/Industry	Location	Per	Low	Mid	High	Source	Date
Team Assembler	Massachusetts	Y	23280 FQ	29400 MW	37080 TQ	USBLS	5/15
	Boston-Cambridge-Newton NECTA, MA	Y	23870 FQ	29260 MW	36930 TQ	USBLS	5/15
	Worcester MSA, MA-CT	Y	22280 FQ	28470 MW	37760 TQ	USBLS	5/15
	Michigan	Y	23820 FQ	32200 MW	44730 TQ	USBLS	5/15
	Detroit-Dearborn-Livonia PMSA, MI	Y	33690 FQ	43990 MW	56480 TQ	USBLS	5/15
	Grand Rapids-Wyoming MSA, MI	Y	22330 FQ	27780 MW	35780 TQ	USBLS	5/15
	Minnesota	Y	24380 FQ	30110 MW	37734 TQ	MNBLS	1/16-3/16
	Minneapolis-St. Paul-Bloomington MSA, MN-WI	Y	23337 FQ	29209 MW	36904 TQ	MNBLS	1/16-3/16
	Mississippi	Y	23290 FQ	30050 MW	41930 TQ	USBLS	5/15
	Jackson MSA, MS	Y	28900 FQ	52520 MW	57810 TQ	USBLS	5/15
	Missouri	Y	23990 FQ	31710 MW	39520 TQ	USBLS	5/15
	Kansas City MSA, MO-KS	Y	31450 FQ	44990 MW	56400 TQ	USBLS	5/15
	St. Louis MSA, MO-IL	Y	24400 FQ	32790 MW	38520 TQ	USBLS	5/15
	Montana	Y	22040 FQ	28010 MW	37850 TQ	USBLS	5/15
	Billings MSA, MT	Y	19220 FQ	23820 MW	29470 TQ	USBLS	5/15
	Nebraska	Y	23865 FQ	30650 MW	38045 TQ	NEBLS	7/16-9/16
	Omaha-Council Bluffs MSA, NE-IA	Y	22890 FQ	27740 MW	35050 TQ	NEBLS	7/16-9/16
	Nevada	Y	20670 FQ	24130 MW	30390 TQ	USBLS	5/15
	Las Vegas-Henderson-Paradise MSA, NV	Y	20130 FQ	24580 MW	31990 TQ	USBLS	5/15
	New Hampshire	H	12.00 AE	15.77 MW	19.58 AEX	NHBLS	6/16
	Manchester NECTA, NH	H	12.71 AE	15.80 MW	22.81 AEX	NHBLS	6/16
	Nashua NECTA, NH-MA	Y	25810 FQ	31120 MW	38030 TQ	USBLS	5/15
	New Jersey	Y	21020 FQ	24920 MW	31110 TQ	USBLS	5/15
	Camden PMSA, NJ	Y	20820 FQ	25880 MW	31720 TQ	USBLS	5/15
	Newark PMSA, NJ-PA	Y	20790 FQ	24130 MW	29880 TQ	USBLS	5/15
	Trenton MSA, NJ	Y	23420 FQ	35310 MW	43610 TQ	USBLS	5/15
	New Mexico	Y	19870 FQ	24380 MW	30500 TQ	USBLS	5/15
	Albuquerque MSA, NM	Y	19440 FQ	24000 MW	29860 TQ	USBLS	5/15
	New York	Y	21100 AE	29040 MW	36070 AEX	NYBLS	1/16-3/16
	Buffalo-Cheektowaga-Niagara Falls MSA, NY	Y	25400 FQ	33850 MW	40640 TQ	USBLS	5/15
	Nassau County-Suffolk County PMSA, NY	Y	21140 FQ	27160 MW	36470 TQ	USBLS	5/15
	New York-Jersey City-White Plains PMSA, NY-NJ	Y	19930 FQ	24620 MW	32070 TQ	USBLS	5/15
	Rochester MSA, NY	Y	21800 FQ	27290 MW	34670 TQ	USBLS	5/15
	North Carolina	Y	21370 FQ	27180 MW	34630 TQ	USBLS	5/15
	Charlotte-Concord-Gastonia MSA, NC-SC	Y	22920 FQ	29970 MW	38360 TQ	USBLS	5/15
	Raleigh MSA, NC	Y	19790 FQ	23280 MW	28340 TQ	USBLS	5/15
	North Dakota	Y	26030 FQ	30800 MW	37130 TQ	USBLS	5/15
	Fargo MSA, ND-MN	Y	25700 FQ	29560 MW	36610 TQ	USBLS	5/15
	Ohio	Y	24310 FQ	32330 MW	46340 TQ	USBLS	5/15
	Akron MSA, OH	Y	22800 FQ	27530 MW	34180 TQ	USBLS	5/15
	Cincinnati MSA, OH-KY-IN	Y	24650 FQ	30010 MW	36750 TQ	USBLS	5/15
	Cleveland-Elyria MSA, OH	Y	23400 FQ	29610 MW	37570 TQ	USBLS	5/15
	Columbus MSA, OH	Y	24260 FQ	35250 MW	51630 TQ	USBLS	5/15
	Oklahoma	Y	22640 FQ	28360 MW	35830 TQ	USBLS	5/15
	Oklahoma City MSA, OK	Y	22330 FQ	27310 MW	32820 TQ	USBLS	5/15
	Tulsa MSA, OK	Y	23010 FQ	30240 MW	37810 TQ	USBLS	5/15
	Oregon	H	11.35 FQ	13.78 MW	17.80 TQ	ORBLS	2016
	Portland-Vancouver-Hillsboro MSA, OR-WA	Y	22510 FQ	26870 MW	35030 TQ	USBLS	5/15
	Pennsylvania	Y	23610 FQ	29540 MW	37180 TQ	USBLS	5/15
	Allentown-Bethlehem-Easton MSA, PA-NJ	Y	26730 FQ	32300 MW	38020 TQ	USBLS	5/15
	Harrisburg-Carlisle MSA, PA	Y	21080 FQ	25340 MW	30730 TQ	USBLS	5/15
	Montgomery County-Bucks County-Chester County PMSA, PA	Y	26420 FQ	30600 MW	38350 TQ	USBLS	5/15
	Philadelphia PMSA, PA	Y	24370 FQ	29140 MW	36850 TQ	USBLS	5/15
	Pittsburgh MSA, PA	Y	22230 FQ	28610 MW	37210 TQ	USBLS	5/15
	Rhode Island	Y	22320 FQ	28020 MW	35380 TQ	USBLS	5/15
	Providence-Warwick MSA, RI-MA	Y	22950 FQ	28840 MW	36840 TQ	USBLS	5/15
	South Carolina	Y	22950 FQ	30190 MW	37560 TQ	USBLS	5/15

AE	Average entry wage	AWR	Average wage range	H	Hourly
AEX	Average experienced wage	B	Biweekly	HI	Highest wage paid
ATC	Average total compensation	D	Daily	HR	High end range
AW	Average wage paid	FQ	First quartile wage	LO	Lowest wage paid

LR	Low end range	MTC	Median total compensation	TCC	Total cash compensation
M	Monthly	MW	Median wage paid	TQ	Third quartile wage
MCC	Median cash compensation	MWR	Median wage range	W	Weekly
ME	Median entry wage	S	See annotated source	Y	Yearly

Occupation/Type/Industry	Location	Per	Low	Mid	High	Source	Date
Team Assembler	Charleston-North Charleston MSA, SC	Y	26980 FQ	33510 MW	39170 TQ	USBLS	5/15
	Columbia MSA, SC	Y	22790 FQ	28750 MW	37150 TQ	USBLS	5/15
	Greenville-Anderson-Mauldin MSA, SC	Y	22080 FQ	27650 MW	35000 TQ	USBLS	5/15
	South Dakota	Y	23140 FQ	27060 MW	31010 TQ	USBLS	5/15
	Sioux Falls MSA, SD	Y	23240 FQ	26760 MW	30310 TQ	USBLS	5/15
	Tennessee	Y	23030 FQ	29100 MW	37100 TQ	USBLS	5/15
	Knoxville MSA, TN	Y	24620 FQ	30190 MW	36640 TQ	USBLS	5/15
	Memphis MSA, TN-MS-AR	Y	21700 FQ	29340 MW	37790 TQ	USBLS	5/15
	Nashville-Davidson–Murfreesboro–Franklin MSA, TN	Y	25230 FQ	31750 MW	46320 TQ	USBLS	5/15
	Texas	Y	20740 FQ	26430 MW	35130 TQ	USBLS	5/15
	Austin-Round Rock MSA, TX	Y	20970 FQ	23700 MW	31260 TQ	USBLS	5/15
	Dallas-Plano-Irving PMSA, TX	Y	18720 FQ	23080 MW	30020 TQ	USBLS	5/15
	Fort Worth-Arlington PMSA, TX	Y	24020 FQ	33060 MW	44620 TQ	USBLS	5/15
	Houston-The Woodlands-Sugar Land MSA, TX	Y	22680 FQ	29460 MW	37260 TQ	USBLS	5/15
	San Antonio-New Braunfels MSA, TX	Y	20540 FQ	24910 MW	32770 TQ	USBLS	5/15
	Utah	Y	22170 FQ	27380 MW	34320 TQ	USBLS	5/15
	Ogden-Clearfield MSA, UT	Y	24630 FQ	31200 MW	36420 TQ	USBLS	5/15
	Provo-Orem MSA, UT	Y	21630 FQ	25780 MW	30470 TQ	USBLS	5/15
	Salt Lake City MSA, UT	Y	21230 FQ	25230 MW	32630 TQ	USBLS	5/15
	Vermont	Y	24930 FQ	28730 MW	34180 TQ	USBLS	5/15
	Burlington-South Burlington MSA, VT	Y	27480 FQ	30840 MW	37510 TQ	USBLS	5/15
	Virginia	Y	20870 FQ	26100 MW	35580 TQ	USBLS	5/15
	Richmond MSA, VA	Y	20950 FQ	26230 MW	36360 TQ	USBLS	5/15
	Virginia Beach-Norfolk-Newport News MSA, VA-NC	Y	21300 FQ	27080 MW	35630 TQ	USBLS	5/15
	Washington	H	12.87 FQ	15.48 MW	19.39 TQ	WABLS	3/16
	Seattle-Bellevue-Everett PMSA, WA	H	13.38 FQ	16.49 MW	20.92 TQ	WABLS	3/16
	Tacoma-Lakewood PMSA, WA	H	13.08 FQ	16.32 MW	22.00 TQ	WABLS	3/16
	West Virginia	Y	19130 FQ	22580 MW	31940 TQ	USBLS	5/15
	Huntington-Ashland MSA, WV-KY-OH	Y	19800 FQ	29560 MW	52370 TQ	USBLS	5/15
	Wisconsin	Y	22870 FQ	29040 MW	36800 TQ	USBLS	5/15
	Madison MSA, WI	Y	26620 FQ	31330 MW	37550 TQ	USBLS	5/15
	Milwaukee-Waukesha-West Allis MSA, WI	Y	22840 FQ	30520 MW	42230 TQ	USBLS	5/15
	Wyoming	Y	26270 FQ	32590 MW	39840 TQ	USBLS	5/15
	Puerto Rico	Y	17370 FQ	19230 MW	22610 TQ	USBLS	5/15
	San Juan-Carolina-Caguas MSA, PR	Y	17540 FQ	19560 MW	23550 TQ	USBLS	5/15
Technical Account Manager	United States	Y		66000 MW		TSTR	2017
Technical Communications Specialist Police Services Agency, Municipal Government	Oakland, CA	Y			90971 HI	CACIT	6/28/16
Technical Security Professional	United States	Y			233333 HI	IBD03	2015
Technical Sergeant U.S. Air Force, Active Duty, Pay Grade E-6	United States	M	2487 LO		3852 HI	DOD1	2017
Technical Trainer	United States	Y		75571 AW		CWRLD3	2016
Technical Writer	Alabama	Y	44809 AE	63504 AW	72861 AEX	ALBLS	6/16
	Birmingham-Hoover MSA, AL	Y	45931 AE	63667 AW	72535 AEX	ALBLS	6/16
	Alaska	Y	50680 FQ	59170 MW	72170 TQ	USBLS	5/15
	Anchorage MSA, AK	Y	54990 FQ	61670 MW	73220 TQ	USBLS	5/15
	Arizona	Y	52110 FQ	61920 MW	75640 TQ	USBLS	5/15
	Phoenix-Mesa-Scottsdale MSA, AZ	Y	53020 FQ	62420 MW	76260 TQ	USBLS	5/15
	Tucson MSA, AZ	Y	46280 FQ	59320 MW	72440 TQ	USBLS	5/15
	Arkansas	Y	37850 FQ	47810 MW	57300 TQ	USBLS	5/15

AE	Average entry wage	AWR	Average wage range	H	Hourly
AEX	Average experienced wage	B	Biweekly	HI	Highest wage paid
ATC	Average total compensation	D	Daily	HR	High end range
AW	Average wage paid	FQ	First quartile wage	LO	Lowest wage paid

LR	Low end range	MTC	Median total compensation	TCC	Total cash compensation
M	Monthly	MW	Median wage paid	TQ	Third quartile wage
MCC	Median cash compensation	MWR	Median wage range	W	Weekly
ME	Median entry wage	S	See annotated source	Y	Yearly

Technical Writer

Occupation/Type/Industry	Location	Per	Low	Mid	High	Source	Date
Technical Writer	Little Rock-North Little Rock-Conway MSA, AR	Y	38520 FQ	48230 MW	58090 TQ	USBLS	5/15
	California	H	31.50 FQ	41.85 MW	54.26 TQ	CABLS	1/16-3/16
	Anaheim-Santa Ana-Irvine PMSA, CA	H	31.84 FQ	40.62 MW	46.83 TQ	CABLS	1/16-3/16
	Los Angeles-Long Beach-Glendale PMSA, CA	H	29.44 FQ	36.81 MW	48.13 TQ	CABLS	1/16-3/16
	Oakland-Hayward-Berkeley PMSA, CA	H	31.56 FQ	40.59 MW	49.58 TQ	CABLS	1/16-3/16
	Riverside-San Bernardino-Ontario MSA, CA	H	28.06 FQ	36.45 MW	48.51 TQ	CABLS	1/16-3/16
	Sacramento–Roseville–Arden-Arcade MSA, CA	H	32.07 FQ	36.32 MW	49.08 TQ	CABLS	1/16-3/16
	San Diego-Carlsbad MSA, CA	H	34.13 FQ	46.35 MW	55.82 TQ	CABLS	1/16-3/16
	San Francisco-Redwood City-South San Francisco PMSA, CA	H	29.49 FQ	40.62 MW	53.92 TQ	CABLS	1/16-3/16
	Colorado	Y	55880 FQ	68330 MW	85100 TQ	USBLS	5/15
	Denver-Aurora-Lakewood MSA, CO	Y	56500 FQ	67360 MW	82330 TQ	USBLS	5/15
	Connecticut	Y		83848 MW		CTBLS	1/16-3/16
	Bridgeport-Stamford-Norwalk MSA, CT	Y	62600 FQ	78230 MW	94040 TQ	USBLS	5/15
	Hartford-West Hartford-East Hartford MSA, CT	Y	67380 FQ	81890 MW	104620 TQ	USBLS	5/15
	Delaware	Y	52570 FQ	69380 MW	82570 TQ	USBLS	5/15
	Wilmington PMSA, DE-MD-NJ	Y	53000 FQ	70690 MW	86800 TQ	USBLS	5/15
	District of Columbia	Y	70810 FQ	84660 MW	97600 TQ	USBLS	5/15
	Washington-Arlington-Alexandria PMSA, DC-VA-MD-WV	Y	65440 FQ	82350 MW	100010 TQ	USBLS	5/15
	Florida	H	21.06 AE	29.21 MW	34.53 AEX	FLBLS	7/16-9/16
	Fort Lauderdale-Pompano Beach-Deerfield Beach PMSA, FL	H	22.72 AE	29.06 MW	36.10 AEX	FLBLS	7/16-9/16
	Miami-Miami Beach-Kendall PMSA, FL	H	18.55 AE	27.50 MW	35.74 AEX	FLBLS	7/16-9/16
	Orlando-Kissimmee-Sanford MSA, FL	H	20.66 AE	28.14 MW	33.40 AEX	FLBLS	7/16-9/16
	Tampa-St. Petersburg-Clearwater MSA, FL	H	21.11 AE	29.26 MW	33.72 AEX	FLBLS	7/16-9/16
	Georgia	Y	55810 FQ	71390 MW	86360 TQ	USBLS	5/15
	Atlanta-Sandy Springs-Roswell MSA, GA	Y	60590 FQ	73480 MW	88230 TQ	USBLS	5/15
	Augusta-Richmond County MSA, GA-SC	Y	64280 FQ	73650 MW	88880 TQ	USBLS	5/15
	Hawaii	Y	24330 FQ	42210 MW	54130 TQ	USBLS	5/15
	Urban Honolulu MSA, HI	Y	23620 FQ	40830 MW	49650 TQ	USBLS	5/15
	Idaho	Y	43740 FQ	57920 MW	70150 TQ	USBLS	5/15
	Boise City MSA, ID	Y	44110 FQ	58250 MW	69950 TQ	USBLS	5/15
	Illinois	Y	53100 FQ	70240 MW	84880 TQ	USBLS	5/15
	Chicago-Naperville-Arlington Heights PMSA, IL	Y	54690 FQ	72540 MW	86930 TQ	USBLS	5/15
	Lake County-Kenosha County PMSA, IL-WI	Y	57160 FQ	70870 MW	86540 TQ	USBLS	5/15
	Indiana	Y	42360 FQ	60150 MW	73350 TQ	USBLS	5/15
	Indianapolis-Carmel-Anderson MSA, IN	Y	54740 FQ	68050 MW	77570 TQ	USBLS	5/15
	Iowa	Y	41960 FQ	49770 MW	63420 TQ	USBLS	5/15
	Des Moines-West Des Moines MSA, IA	Y	41980 FQ	48150 MW	58610 TQ	USBLS	5/15
	Kansas	Y	43510 FQ	56870 MW	70600 TQ	USBLS	5/15
	Wichita MSA, KS	Y	52260 FQ	60680 MW	72260 TQ	USBLS	5/15
	Kentucky	Y	48820 FQ	62530 MW	79490 TQ	USBLS	5/15
	Louisville-Jefferson County MSA, KY-IN	Y	44560 FQ	55160 MW	69850 TQ	USBLS	5/15
	Louisiana	Y	39100 FQ	59690 MW	75750 TQ	USBLS	5/15
	Baton Rouge MSA, LA	Y	40690 FQ	60630 MW	74130 TQ	USBLS	5/15
	New Orleans-Metairie MSA, LA	Y	55320 FQ	66360 MW	84840 TQ	USBLS	5/15
	Maine	Y	41090 FQ	49490 MW	65270 TQ	USBLS	5/15

AE Average entry wage	**AWR** Average wage range	**H** Hourly	**LR** Low end range	**MTC** Median total compensation	**TCC** Total cash compensation
AEX Average experienced wage	**B** Biweekly	**HI** Highest wage paid	**M** Monthly	**MW** Median wage paid	**TQ** Third quartile wage
ATC Average total compensation	**D** Daily	**HR** High end range	**MCC** Median cash compensation	**MWR** Median wage range	**W** Weekly
AW Average wage paid	**FQ** First quartile wage	**LO** Lowest wage paid	**ME** Median entry wage	**S** See annotated source	**Y** Yearly

Occupation/Type/Industry	Location	Per	Low	Mid	High	Source	Date
Technical Writer	Portland-South Portland MSA, ME	Y	43440 FQ	50300 MW	73080 TQ	USBLS	5/15
	Maryland	Y	53052 AE	79899 MW	93323 AEX	MDBLS	4/16
	Baltimore-Columbia-Towson MSA, MD	Y	62360 FQ	77540 MW	96320 TQ	USBLS	5/15
	Massachusetts	Y	64980 FQ	82080 MW	99120 TQ	USBLS	5/15
	Boston-Cambridge-Newton NECTA, MA	Y	63620 FQ	79160 MW	96080 TQ	USBLS	5/15
	Worcester MSA, MA-CT	Y	65520 FQ	83250 MW	97730 TQ	USBLS	5/15
	Michigan	Y	51260 FQ	65100 MW	80720 TQ	USBLS	5/15
	Detroit-Dearborn-Livonia PMSA, MI	Y	55030 FQ	67650 MW	78200 TQ	USBLS	5/15
	Grand Rapids-Wyoming MSA, MI	Y	37340 FQ	53640 MW	70430 TQ	USBLS	5/15
	Minnesota	Y	53669 FQ	66753 MW	80866 TQ	MNBLS	1/16-3/16
	Minneapolis-St. Paul-Bloomington MSA, MN-WI	Y	55100 FQ	68215 MW	82791 TQ	MNBLS	1/16-3/16
	Mississippi	Y	46080 FQ	54870 MW	62940 TQ	USBLS	5/15
	Missouri	Y	46780 FQ	64150 MW	77250 TQ	USBLS	5/15
	Kansas City MSA, MO-KS	Y	42280 FQ	57790 MW	74000 TQ	USBLS	5/15
	St. Louis MSA, MO-IL	Y	57270 FQ	69750 MW	80920 TQ	USBLS	5/15
	Montana	Y	35900 FQ	48900 MW	70210 TQ	USBLS	5/15
	Nebraska	Y	45515 FQ	60650 MW	75150 TQ	NEBLS	7/16-9/16
	Omaha-Council Bluffs MSA, NE-IA	Y	46385 FQ	60160 MW	73555 TQ	NEBLS	7/16-9/16
	Nevada	Y	52070 FQ	65050 MW	76430 TQ	USBLS	5/15
	Las Vegas-Henderson-Paradise MSA, NV	Y	52710 FQ	65440 MW	75550 TQ	USBLS	5/15
	New Hampshire	H	25.42 AE	37.33 MW	46.48 AEX	NHBLS	6/16
	Nashua NECTA, NH-MA	Y	70600 FQ	97900 MW	123910 TQ	USBLS	5/15
	New Jersey	Y	56270 FQ	81360 MW	100410 TQ	USBLS	5/15
	Camden PMSA, NJ	Y	36460 FQ	54080 MW	85850 TQ	USBLS	5/15
	Trenton MSA, NJ	Y	67370 FQ	82490 MW	99100 TQ	USBLS	5/15
	New Mexico	Y	53610 FQ	67310 MW	91260 TQ	USBLS	5/15
	Albuquerque MSA, NM	Y	54510 FQ	66830 MW	92050 TQ	USBLS	5/15
	New York	Y	49160 AE	80180 MW	98090 AEX	NYBLS	1/16-3/16
	Buffalo-Cheektowaga-Niagara Falls MSA, NY	Y	31760 FQ	50580 MW	64230 TQ	USBLS	5/15
	Nassau County-Suffolk County PMSA, NY	Y	65980 FQ	80740 MW	102430 TQ	USBLS	5/15
	New York-Jersey City-White Plains PMSA, NY-NJ	Y	59640 FQ	87600 MW	110480 TQ	USBLS	5/15
	Rochester MSA, NY	Y	49780 FQ	65230 MW	87580 TQ	USBLS	5/15
	North Carolina	Y	58110 FQ	73430 MW	93760 TQ	USBLS	5/15
	Charlotte-Concord-Gastonia MSA, NC-SC	Y	58400 FQ	70180 MW	82500 TQ	USBLS	5/15
	Raleigh MSA, NC	Y	60720 FQ	78130 MW	96040 TQ	USBLS	5/15
	North Dakota	Y	46830 FQ	61170 MW	82890 TQ	USBLS	5/15
	Fargo MSA, ND-MN	Y	44680 FQ	56120 MW	82140 TQ	USBLS	5/15
	Ohio	Y	49630 FQ	59450 MW	72800 TQ	USBLS	5/15
	Cincinnati MSA, OH-KY-IN	Y	49900 FQ	60490 MW	76450 TQ	USBLS	5/15
	Cleveland-Elyria MSA, OH	Y	52970 FQ	63590 MW	79040 TQ	USBLS	5/15
	Columbus MSA, OH	Y	52250 FQ	59360 MW	69510 TQ	USBLS	5/15
	Oklahoma	Y	43310 FQ	56850 MW	72230 TQ	USBLS	5/15
	Oklahoma City MSA, OK	Y	46160 FQ	64780 MW	75800 TQ	USBLS	5/15
	Tulsa MSA, OK	Y	43560 FQ	53410 MW	69490 TQ	USBLS	5/15
	Oregon	H	27.47 FQ	38.69 MW	49.42 TQ	ORBLS	2016
	Portland-Vancouver-Hillsboro MSA, OR-WA	Y	62570 FQ	81350 MW	101760 TQ	USBLS	5/15
	Pennsylvania	Y	50350 FQ	67170 MW	83650 TQ	USBLS	5/15
	Allentown-Bethlehem-Easton MSA, PA-NJ	Y	56200 FQ	72730 MW	89840 TQ	USBLS	5/15
	Harrisburg-Carlisle MSA, PA	Y	36860 FQ	44000 MW	64230 TQ	USBLS	5/15
	Montgomery County-Bucks County-Chester County PMSA, PA	Y	61260 FQ	75080 MW	92090 TQ	USBLS	5/15
	Philadelphia PMSA, PA	Y	65030 FQ	76160 MW	91110 TQ	USBLS	5/15
	Pittsburgh MSA, PA	Y	46660 FQ	59220 MW	74920 TQ	USBLS	5/15
	Rhode Island	Y	56220 FQ	73790 MW	89470 TQ	USBLS	5/15
	Providence-Warwick MSA, RI-MA	Y	58180 FQ	75320 MW	91180 TQ	USBLS	5/15
	South Carolina	Y	49900 FQ	66350 MW	81710 TQ	USBLS	5/15

AE	Average entry wage	AWR	Average wage range	H	Hourly	LR	Low end range	MTC	Median total compensation	TCC	Total cash compensation
AEX	Average experienced wage	B	Biweekly	HI	Highest wage paid	M	Monthly	MW	Median wage paid	TQ	Third quartile wage
ATC	Average total compensation	D	Daily	HR	High end range	MCC	Median cash compensation	MWR	Median wage range	W	Weekly
AW	Average wage paid	FQ	First quartile wage	LO	Lowest wage paid	ME	Median entry wage	S	See annotated source	Y	Yearly

Occupation/Type/Industry	Location	Per	Low	Mid	High	Source	Date
Technical Writer	Charleston-North Charleston						
	MSA, SC	Y	56010 FQ	67260 MW	76630 TQ	USBLS	5/15
	Columbia MSA, SC	Y	49500 FQ	60510 MW	76800 TQ	USBLS	5/15
	Greenville-Anderson-Mauldin						
	MSA, SC	Y	34150 FQ	50370 MW	71380 TQ	USBLS	5/15
	South Dakota	Y	35360 FQ	43350 MW	52760 TQ	USBLS	5/15
	Sioux Falls MSA, SD	Y	39210 FQ	46470 MW	55500 TQ	USBLS	5/15
	Tennessee	Y	43370 FQ	54750 MW	76790 TQ	USBLS	5/15
	Knoxville MSA, TN	Y	40820 FQ	58890 MW	90070 TQ	USBLS	5/15
	Memphis MSA, TN-MS-AR	Y	47470 FQ	67190 MW	100480 TQ	USBLS	5/15
	Nashville-Davidson–						
	Murfreesboro–Franklin						
	MSA, TN	Y	43080 FQ	50570 MW	61330 TQ	USBLS	5/15
	Texas	Y	52740 FQ	67410 MW	85490 TQ	USBLS	5/15
	Austin-Round Rock MSA, TX	Y	48680 FQ	62110 MW	85300 TQ	USBLS	5/15
	Dallas-Plano-Irving PMSA, TX	Y	56340 FQ	71410 MW	85020 TQ	USBLS	5/15
	Fort Worth-Arlington PMSA,						
	TX	Y	46560 FQ	59970 MW	74470 TQ	USBLS	5/15
	Houston-The Woodlands-						
	Sugar Land MSA, TX	Y	56740 FQ	72410 MW	95100 TQ	USBLS	5/15
	San Antonio-New Braunfels						
	MSA, TX	Y	44090 FQ	58590 MW	79190 TQ	USBLS	5/15
	Utah	Y	48780 FQ	60410 MW	76600 TQ	USBLS	5/15
	Ogden-Clearfield MSA, UT	Y	54870 FQ	66360 MW	83140 TQ	USBLS	5/15
	Provo-Orem MSA, UT	Y	49290 FQ	60260 MW	78550 TQ	USBLS	5/15
	Salt Lake City MSA, UT	Y	50600 FQ	61090 MW	77460 TQ	USBLS	5/15
	Vermont	Y	46060 FQ	57160 MW	70510 TQ	USBLS	5/15
	Burlington-South Burlington						
	MSA, VT	Y	45010 FQ	56130 MW	69450 TQ	USBLS	5/15
	Virginia	Y	58710 FQ	75750 MW	97620 TQ	USBLS	5/15
	Richmond MSA, VA	Y	55310 FQ	65840 MW	87220 TQ	USBLS	5/15
	Virginia Beach-Norfolk-						
	Newport News MSA, VA-NC	Y	47310 FQ	57880 MW	71750 TQ	USBLS	5/15
	Washington	H	30.16 FQ	37.64 MW	46.31 TQ	WABLS	3/16
	Seattle-Bellevue-Everett						
	PMSA, WA	H	31.90 FQ	39.67 MW	47.80 TQ	WABLS	3/16
	Tacoma-Lakewood PMSA, WA	H	28.39 FQ	41.10 MW	47.49 TQ	WABLS	3/16
	West Virginia	Y	45110 FQ	56370 MW	73270 TQ	USBLS	5/15
	Wisconsin	Y	46600 FQ	57110 MW	70240 TQ	USBLS	5/15
	Green Bay MSA, WI	Y	43800 FQ	49400 MW	62610 TQ	USBLS	5/15
	Madison MSA, WI	Y	47640 FQ	57310 MW	72720 TQ	USBLS	5/15
	Milwaukee-Waukesha-West						
	Allis MSA, WI	Y	51190 FQ	61230 MW	74070 TQ	USBLS	5/15
	Puerto Rico	Y	23390 FQ	30890 MW	41440 TQ	USBLS	5/15
	San Juan-Carolina-Caguas						
	MSA, PR	Y	22800 FQ	29150 MW	38570 TQ	USBLS	5/15
Aviation Industry	United States	H		23.00 AW		AVJOB05	2016
Technology Development							
Manager							
Police Department, Municipal Government	Anaheim, CA	Y			140677 HI	CACIT	6/28/16
Technology Professional							
Big Data Expertise	United States	Y		121328 AW		DICE01	10/6/15-11/25/15
COBOL Expertise	United States	Y		104878 AW		DICE01	10/6/15-11/25/15
HANA Expertise	United States	Y		154749 AW		DICE01	10/6/15-11/25/15
ITIL Intermediate Certification	United States	Y		87040 AW		CERTM01	2014
Java/J2EE Expertise	United States	Y		109245 AW		DICE01	10/6/15-11/25/15
.NET Expertise	United States	Y		102683 AW		DICE01	10/6/15-11/25/15
OpenStack Expertise	United States	Y		138579 AW		DICE01	10/6/15-11/25/15
Puppet Expertise	United States	Y		131121 AW		DICE01	10/6/15-11/25/15
Six Sigma Expertise	United States	Y		109296 AW		DICE01	10/6/15-11/25/15
Swift Expertise	United States	Y		112077 AW		DICE01	10/6/15-11/25/15
Visual C++ Expertise	United States	Y		115894 AW		DICE01	10/6/15-11/25/15
XML Expertise	United States	Y		105641 AW		DICE01	10/6/15-11/25/15
Technology Services Coordinator							
IT Department, Municipal Government	Alameda, CA	Y			89158 HI	CACIT	6/28/16
Telecommunications Equipment							
Installer and Repairer							
Except Line Installer	Alabama	Y	34833 AE	54156 AW	63818 AEX	ALBLS	6/16

AE	Average entry wage	**AWR**	Average wage range	**H**	Hourly	**LR**	Low end range	**MTC** Median total compensation	**TCC** Total cash compensation
AEX	Average experienced wage	**B**	Biweekly	**HI**	Highest wage paid	**M**	Monthly	**MW** Median wage paid	**TQ** Third quartile wage
ATC	Average total compensation	**D**	Daily	**HR**	High end range	**MCC**	Median cash compensation	**MWR** Median wage range	**W** Weekly
AW	Average wage paid	**FQ**	First quartile wage	**LO**	Lowest wage paid	**ME**	Median entry wage	**S** See annotated source	**Y** Yearly

Telecommunications Equipment
Installer and Repairer

Occupation/Type/Industry	Location	Per	Low	Mid	High	Source	Date
Except Line Installer	Birmingham-Hoover MSA, AL	Y	37538 AE	56414 AW	65852 AEX	ALBLS	6/16
Except Line Installer	Alaska	Y	54780 FQ	72770 MW	86930 TQ	USBLS	5/15
Except Line Installer	Anchorage MSA, AK	Y	44930 FQ	64970 MW	83060 TQ	USBLS	5/15
Except Line Installer	Arizona	Y	46010 FQ	63250 MW	72230 TQ	USBLS	5/15
Except Line Installer	Phoenix-Mesa-Scottsdale MSA, AZ	Y	44930 FQ	58120 MW	71290 TQ	USBLS	5/15
Except Line Installer	Tucson MSA, AZ	Y	49510 FQ	66420 MW	73240 TQ	USBLS	5/15
Except Line Installer	Arkansas	Y	38130 FQ	51540 MW	61370 TQ	USBLS	5/15
Except Line Installer	Little Rock-North Little Rock-Conway MSA, AR	Y	34420 FQ	45200 MW	60280 TQ	USBLS	5/15
Except Line Installer	California	H	20.77 FQ	29.07 MW	35.01 TQ	CABLS	1/16-3/16
Except Line Installer	Anaheim-Santa Ana-Irvine PMSA, CA	H	19.71 FQ	30.22 MW	35.41 TQ	CABLS	1/16-3/16
Except Line Installer	Los Angeles-Long Beach-Glendale PMSA, CA	H	19.79 FQ	27.13 MW	34.22 TQ	CABLS	1/16-3/16
Except Line Installer	Oakland-Hayward-Berkeley PMSA, CA	H	23.64 FQ	31.99 MW	36.03 TQ	CABLS	1/16-3/16
Except Line Installer	Riverside-San Bernardino-Ontario MSA, CA	H	19.19 FQ	28.34 MW	34.60 TQ	CABLS	1/16-3/16
Except Line Installer	Sacramento–Roseville–Arden-Arcade MSA, CA	H	20.82 FQ	29.15 MW	34.62 TQ	CABLS	1/16-3/16
Except Line Installer	San Diego-Carlsbad MSA, CA	H	18.49 FQ	27.13 MW	33.49 TQ	CABLS	1/16-3/16
Except Line Installer	San Francisco-Redwood City-South San Francisco PMSA, CA	H	25.63 FQ	33.36 MW	37.45 TQ	CABLS	1/16-3/16
Except Line Installer	Colorado	Y	51910 FQ	66270 MW	74010 TQ	USBLS	5/15
Except Line Installer	Denver-Aurora-Lakewood MSA, CO	Y	55050 FQ	67670 MW	74720 TQ	USBLS	5/15
Except Line Installer	Connecticut	Y		58607 MW		CTBLS	1/16-3/16
Except Line Installer	Bridgeport-Stamford-Norwalk MSA, CT	Y	40030 FQ	54790 MW	68730 TQ	USBLS	5/15
Except Line Installer	Hartford-West Hartford-East Hartford MSA, CT	Y	47600 FQ	59880 MW	72250 TQ	USBLS	5/15
Except Line Installer	District of Columbia	Y	53010 FQ	66490 MW	73850 TQ	USBLS	5/15
Except Line Installer	Washington-Arlington-Alexandria PMSA, DC-VA-MD-WV	Y	51000 FQ	63710 MW	73650 TQ	USBLS	5/15
Except Line Installer	Florida	H	15.39 AE	24.51 MW	29.57 AEX	FLBLS	7/16-9/16
Except Line Installer	Fort Lauderdale-Pompano Beach-Deerfield Beach PMSA, FL	H	17.58 AE	26.91 MW	31.94 AEX	FLBLS	7/16-9/16
Except Line Installer	Miami-Miami Beach-Kendall PMSA, FL	H	13.26 AE	27.71 MW	31.64 AEX	FLBLS	7/16-9/16
Except Line Installer	Orlando-Kissimmee-Sanford MSA, FL	H	14.27 AE	20.57 MW	26.12 AEX	FLBLS	7/16-9/16
Except Line Installer	Tampa-St. Petersburg-Clearwater MSA, FL	H	15.30 AE	24.43 MW	28.05 AEX	FLBLS	7/16-9/16
Except Line Installer	Georgia	Y	36870 FQ	55120 MW	71270 TQ	USBLS	5/15
Except Line Installer	Atlanta-Sandy Springs-Roswell MSA, GA	Y	37170 FQ	58090 MW	71900 TQ	USBLS	5/15
Except Line Installer	Augusta-Richmond County MSA, GA-SC	Y	28200 FQ	53740 MW	70910 TQ	USBLS	5/15
Except Line Installer	Hawaii	Y	56410 FQ	68230 MW	75240 TQ	USBLS	5/15
Except Line Installer	Urban Honolulu MSA, HI	Y	55220 FQ	67420 MW	74840 TQ	USBLS	5/15
Except Line Installer	Idaho	Y	29810 FQ	51860 MW	68060 TQ	USBLS	5/15
Except Line Installer	Boise City MSA, ID	Y	33070 FQ	59420 MW	70920 TQ	USBLS	5/15
Except Line Installer	Illinois	Y	43600 FQ	59200 MW	72400 TQ	USBLS	5/15
Except Line Installer	Chicago-Naperville-Arlington Heights PMSA, IL	Y	43840 FQ	59380 MW	72880 TQ	USBLS	5/15
Except Line Installer	Lake County-Kenosha County PMSA, IL-WI	Y	53100 FQ	62060 MW	71920 TQ	USBLS	5/15
Except Line Installer	Indiana	Y	39410 FQ	50510 MW	59010 TQ	USBLS	5/15
Except Line Installer	Gary PMSA, IN	Y	43670 FQ	58210 MW	69790 TQ	USBLS	5/15
Except Line Installer	Indianapolis-Carmel-Anderson MSA, IN	Y	40620 FQ	49860 MW	57880 TQ	USBLS	5/15
Except Line Installer	Iowa	Y	42300 FQ	55890 MW	68380 TQ	USBLS	5/15
Except Line Installer	Des Moines-West Des Moines MSA, IA	Y	47440 FQ	65310 MW	72650 TQ	USBLS	5/15
Except Line Installer	Kansas	Y	36780 FQ	46640 MW	57620 TQ	USBLS	5/15
Except Line Installer	Wichita MSA, KS	Y	42390 FQ	49950 MW	59510 TQ	USBLS	5/15

AE	Average entry wage	AWR	Average wage range	H	Hourly	LR	Low end range	MTC	Median total compensation	TCC	Total cash compensation
AEX	Average experienced wage	B	Biweekly	HI	Highest wage paid	M	Monthly	MW	Median wage paid	TQ	Third quartile wage
ATC	Average total compensation	D	Daily	HR	High end range	MCC	Median cash compensation	MWR	Median wage range	W	Weekly
AW	Average wage paid	FQ	First quartile wage	LO	Lowest wage paid	ME	Median entry wage	S	See annotated source	Y	Yearly

Occupation/Type/Industry	Location	Per	Low	Mid	High	Source	Date
Telecommunications Equipment Installer and Repairer							
Except Line Installer	Kentucky	Y	32950 FQ	47510 MW	66940 TQ	USBLS	5/15
Except Line Installer	Louisville-Jefferson County MSA, KY-IN	Y	36880 FQ	49530 MW	62080 TQ	USBLS	5/15
Except Line Installer	Louisiana	Y	36920 FQ	58560 MW	71940 TQ	USBLS	5/15
Except Line Installer	Baton Rouge MSA, LA	Y	40500 FQ	66760 MW	74410 TQ	USBLS	5/15
Except Line Installer	New Orleans-Metairie MSA, LA	Y	37400 FQ	55460 MW	71030 TQ	USBLS	5/15
Except Line Installer	Maine	Y	36910 FQ	49630 MW	65910 TQ	USBLS	5/15
Except Line Installer	Portland-South Portland MSA, ME	Y	34990 FQ	46060 MW	58270 TQ	USBLS	5/15
Except Line Installer	Maryland	Y	38103 AE	58952 MW	69376 AEX	MDBLS	4/16
Except Line Installer	Baltimore-Columbia-Towson MSA, MD	Y	41200 FQ	49440 MW	67160 TQ	USBLS	5/15
Except Line Installer	Salisbury MSA, MD-DE	Y	44130 FQ	63370 MW	71330 TQ	USBLS	5/15
Except Line Installer	Massachusetts	Y	47990 FQ	65160 MW	84270 TQ	USBLS	5/15
Except Line Installer	Boston-Cambridge-Newton NECTA, MA	Y	47780 FQ	68990 MW	87390 TQ	USBLS	5/15
Except Line Installer	Worcester MSA, MA-CT	Y	44070 FQ	59170 MW	75190 TQ	USBLS	5/15
Except Line Installer	Michigan	Y	38660 FQ	48960 MW	66180 TQ	USBLS	5/15
Except Line Installer	Detroit-Dearborn-Livonia PMSA, MI	Y	43250 FQ	60890 MW	73200 TQ	USBLS	5/15
Except Line Installer	Grand Rapids-Wyoming MSA, MI	Y	35730 FQ	48700 MW	66730 TQ	USBLS	5/15
Except Line Installer	Minnesota	Y	39885 FQ	61467 MW	72117 TQ	MNBLS	1/16-3/16
Except Line Installer	Minneapolis-St. Paul-Bloomington MSA, MN-WI	Y	45235 FQ	65429 MW	73605 TQ	MNBLS	1/16-3/16
Except Line Installer	Mississippi	Y	25620 FQ	45640 MW	68480 TQ	USBLS	5/15
Except Line Installer	Jackson MSA, MS	Y	37090 FQ	50370 MW	69120 TQ	USBLS	5/15
Except Line Installer	Missouri	Y	35840 FQ	49530 MW	59740 TQ	USBLS	5/15
Except Line Installer	Kansas City MSA, MO-KS	Y	33560 FQ	39850 MW	50240 TQ	USBLS	5/15
Except Line Installer	St. Louis MSA, MO-IL	Y	40300 FQ	54910 MW	62740 TQ	USBLS	5/15
Except Line Installer	Montana	Y	40720 FQ	58230 MW	68950 TQ	USBLS	5/15
Except Line Installer	Billings MSA, MT	Y	35010 FQ	47370 MW	61490 TQ	USBLS	5/15
Except Line Installer	Nebraska	Y	41260 FQ	52735 MW	68695 TQ	NEBLS	7/16-9/16
Except Line Installer	Omaha-Council Bluffs MSA, NE-IA	Y	45045 FQ	56310 MW	70190 TQ	NEBLS	7/16-9/16
Except Line Installer	Nevada	Y	54730 FQ	65420 MW	72980 TQ	USBLS	5/15
Except Line Installer	Las Vegas-Henderson-Paradise MSA, NV	Y	58160 FQ	66810 MW	73530 TQ	USBLS	5/15
Except Line Installer	New Hampshire	H	22.64 AE	33.42 MW	37.21 AEX	NHBLS	6/16
Except Line Installer	Manchester NECTA, NH	H	24.03 AE	33.87 MW	37.21 AEX	NHBLS	6/16
Except Line Installer	Nashua NECTA, NH-MA	Y	37340 FQ	68450 MW	77850 TQ	USBLS	5/15
Except Line Installer	New Jersey	Y	46680 FQ	63750 MW	75230 TQ	USBLS	5/15
Except Line Installer	Newark PMSA, NJ-PA	Y	56590 FQ	69170 MW	77530 TQ	USBLS	5/15
Except Line Installer	Trenton MSA, NJ	Y	36460 FQ	49000 MW	65280 TQ	USBLS	5/15
Except Line Installer	New Mexico	Y	38510 FQ	57370 MW	70020 TQ	USBLS	5/15
Except Line Installer	Albuquerque MSA, NM	Y	37420 FQ	55290 MW	70310 TQ	USBLS	5/15
Except Line Installer	New York	Y	37690 AE	70300 MW	80820 AEX	NYBLS	1/16-3/16
Except Line Installer	Buffalo-Cheektowaga-Niagara Falls MSA, NY	Y	39060 FQ	50480 MW	74810 TQ	USBLS	5/15
Except Line Installer	Nassau County-Suffolk County PMSA, NY	Y	45810 FQ	62740 MW	90720 TQ	USBLS	5/15
Except Line Installer	New York-Jersey City-White Plains PMSA, NY-NJ	Y	50460 FQ	71750 MW	86540 TQ	USBLS	5/15
Except Line Installer	Rochester MSA, NY	Y	52450 FQ	71400 MW	90630 TQ	USBLS	5/15
Except Line Installer	North Carolina	Y	37520 FQ	50780 MW	61490 TQ	USBLS	5/15
Except Line Installer	Charlotte-Concord-Gastonia MSA, NC-SC	Y	37440 FQ	49990 MW	64990 TQ	USBLS	5/15
Except Line Installer	Raleigh MSA, NC	Y	39210 FQ	51920 MW	62030 TQ	USBLS	5/15
Except Line Installer	North Dakota	Y	56640 FQ	68070 MW	76010 TQ	USBLS	5/15
Except Line Installer	Fargo MSA, ND-MN	Y	44330 FQ	67580 MW	74480 TQ	USBLS	5/15
Except Line Installer	Ohio	Y	37470 FQ	51690 MW	60930 TQ	USBLS	5/15
Except Line Installer	Cincinnati MSA, OH-KY-IN	Y	30600 FQ	40490 MW	54940 TQ	USBLS	5/15
Except Line Installer	Cleveland-Elyria MSA, OH	Y	50910 FQ	58760 MW	68570 TQ	USBLS	5/15
Except Line Installer	Columbus MSA, OH	Y	39280 FQ	51210 MW	58680 TQ	USBLS	5/15
Except Line Installer	Oklahoma	Y	33700 FQ	42490 MW	54320 TQ	USBLS	5/15
Except Line Installer	Oklahoma City MSA, OK	Y	34650 FQ	40570 MW	51640 TQ	USBLS	5/15
Except Line Installer	Tulsa MSA, OK	Y	33760 FQ	43440 MW	50920 TQ	USBLS	5/15
Except Line Installer	Oregon	H	23.02 FQ	29.21 MW	34.25 TQ	ORBLS	2016

AE	Average entry wage	AWR	Average wage range	H	Hourly
AEX	Average experienced wage	B	Biweekly	HI	Highest wage paid
ATC	Average total compensation	D	Daily	HR	High end range
AW	Average wage paid	FQ	First quartile wage	LO	Lowest wage paid

LR	Low end range	MTC	Median total compensation	TCC	Total cash compensation
M	Monthly	MW	Median wage paid	TQ	Third quartile wage
MCC	Median cash compensation	MWR	Median wage range	W	Weekly
ME	Median entry wage	S	See annotated source	Y	Yearly

Occupation/Type/Industry	Location	Per	Low	Mid	High	Source	Date
Telecommunications Equipment Installer and Repairer							
Except Line Installer	Portland-Vancouver-Hillsboro MSA, OR-WA	Y	52590 FQ	63820 MW	72470 TQ	USBLS	5/15
Except Line Installer	Pennsylvania	Y	43000 FQ	56540 MW	70670 TQ	USBLS	5/15
Except Line Installer	Allentown-Bethlehem-Easton MSA, PA-NJ	Y	53460 FQ	65690 MW	76060 TQ	USBLS	5/15
Except Line Installer	Harrisburg-Carlisle MSA, PA	Y	51630 FQ	60890 MW	71610 TQ	USBLS	5/15*
Except Line Installer	Montgomery County-Bucks County-Chester County PMSA, PA	Y	46230 FQ	62460 MW	81090 TQ	USBLS	5/15
Except Line Installer	Philadelphia PMSA, PA	Y	37030 FQ	58200 MW	71800 TQ	USBLS	5/15
Except Line Installer	Pittsburgh MSA, PA	Y	44910 FQ	55760 MW	66980 TQ	USBLS	5/15
Except Line Installer	Rhode Island	Y	56220 FQ	62770 MW	76300 TQ	USBLS	5/15
Except Line Installer	Providence-Warwick MSA, RI-MA	Y	55840 FQ	62780 MW	76970 TQ	USBLS	5/15
Except Line Installer	South Carolina	Y	35820 FQ	49350 MW	68120 TQ	USBLS	5/15
Except Line Installer	Charleston-North Charleston MSA, SC	Y	49420 FQ	66570 MW	75840 TQ	USBLS	5/15
Except Line Installer	Columbia MSA, SC	Y	37210 FQ	52470 MW	70630 TQ	USBLS	5/15
Except Line Installer	Greenville-Anderson-Mauldin MSA, SC	Y	33230 FQ	41660 MW	60660 TQ	USBLS	5/15
Except Line Installer	South Dakota	Y	46180 FQ	56840 MW	67360 TQ	USBLS	5/15
Except Line Installer	Sioux Falls MSA, SD	Y	42540 FQ	54580 MW	67510 TQ	USBLS	5/15
Except Line Installer	Tennessee	Y	30900 FQ	45590 MW	68120 TQ	USBLS	5/15
Except Line Installer	Knoxville MSA, TN	Y	23270 FQ	33220 MW	60200 TQ	USBLS	5/15
Except Line Installer	Memphis MSA, TN-MS-AR	Y	31950 FQ	43210 MW	68450 TQ	USBLS	5/15
Except Line Installer	Nashville-Davidson–Murfreesboro–Franklin MSA, TN	Y	29470 FQ	42650 MW	67100 TQ	USBLS	5/15
Except Line Installer	Texas	Y	34980 FQ	44960 MW	59080 TQ	USBLS	5/15
Except Line Installer	Austin-Round Rock MSA, TX	Y	36050 FQ	44440 MW	55000 TQ	USBLS	5/15
Except Line Installer	Dallas-Plano-Irving PMSA, TX	Y	36710 FQ	46190 MW	59830 TQ	USBLS	5/15
Except Line Installer	Fort Worth-Arlington PMSA, TX	Y	34530 FQ	45040 MW	65440 TQ	USBLS	5/15
Except Line Installer	Houston-The Woodlands-Sugar Land MSA, TX	Y	36890 FQ	46830 MW	61410 TQ	USBLS	5/15
Except Line Installer	San Antonio-New Braunfels MSA, TX	Y	33420 FQ	41310 MW	51280 TQ	USBLS	5/15
Except Line Installer	Utah	Y	36990 FQ	50990 MW	71170 TQ	USBLS	5/15
Except Line Installer	Ogden-Clearfield MSA, UT	Y	35870 FQ	43450 MW	54820 TQ	USBLS	5/15
Except Line Installer	Provo-Orem MSA, UT	Y	40120 FQ	48880 MW	71060 TQ	USBLS	5/15
Except Line Installer	Salt Lake City MSA, UT	Y	35840 FQ	56000 MW	72020 TQ	USBLS	5/15
Except Line Installer	Vermont	Y	52040 FQ	63160 MW	72710 TQ	USBLS	5/15
Except Line Installer	Burlington-South Burlington MSA, VT	Y	55140 FQ	62420 MW	73560 TQ	USBLS	5/15
Except Line Installer	Virginia	Y	49500 FQ	61730 MW	73240 TQ	USBLS	5/15
Except Line Installer	Richmond MSA, VA	Y	59760 FQ	69670 MW	77190 TQ	USBLS	5/15
Except Line Installer	Virginia Beach-Norfolk-Newport News MSA, VA-NC	Y	35910 FQ	59360 MW	72800 TQ	USBLS	5/15
Except Line Installer	Washington	H	21.15 FQ	28.07 MW	34.19 TQ	WABLS	3/16
Except Line Installer	Seattle-Bellevue-Everett PMSA, WA	H	19.22 FQ	25.91 MW	33.64 TQ	WABLS	3/16
Except Line Installer	Tacoma-Lakewood PMSA, WA	H	24.63 FQ	28.18 MW	32.66 TQ	WABLS	3/16
Except Line Installer	West Virginia	Y	35010 FQ	51800 MW	66900 TQ	USBLS	5/15
Except Line Installer	Huntington-Ashland MSA, WV-KY-OH	Y	43400 FQ	63720 MW	76730 TQ	USBLS	5/15
Except Line Installer	Wisconsin	Y	36410 FQ	48420 MW	61210 TQ	USBLS	5/15
Except Line Installer	Madison MSA, WI	Y	32240 FQ	43350 MW	56360 TQ	USBLS	5/15
Except Line Installer	Milwaukee-Waukesha-West Allis MSA, WI	Y	37640 FQ	48660 MW	64350 TQ	USBLS	5/15
Except Line Installer	Wyoming	Y	36330 FQ	48210 MW	63340 TQ	USBLS	5/15
Except Line Installer	Cheyenne MSA, WY	Y	34050 FQ	44310 MW	56610 TQ	USBLS	5/15
Except Line Installer	Puerto Rico	Y	21440 FQ	30290 MW	38500 TQ	USBLS	5/15
Except Line Installer	San Juan-Carolina-Caguas MSA, PR	Y	23030 FQ	32690 MW	39070 TQ	USBLS	5/15
Except Line Installer	Virgin Islands	Y	32630 FQ	37470 MW	57200 TQ	USBLS	5/15
Telecommunications Line Installer and Repairer	Alabama	Y	26900 AE	39806 AW	46254 AEX	ALBLS	6/16
	Birmingham-Hoover MSA, AL	Y	27917 AE	36531 AW	40843 AEX	ALBLS	6/16

AE	Average entry wage	AWR	Average wage range	H	Hourly	LR Low end range	MTC Median total compensation	TCC Total cash compensation
AEX	Average experienced wage	B	Biweekly	HI	Highest wage paid	M Monthly	MW Median wage paid	TQ Third quartile wage
ATC	Average total compensation	D	Daily	HR	High end range	MCC Median cash compensation	MWR Median wage range	W Weekly
AW	Average wage paid	FQ	First quartile wage	LO	Lowest wage paid	ME Median entry wage	S See annotated source	Y Yearly

Occupation/Type/Industry	Location	Per	Low	Mid	High	Source	Date
Telecommunications Line Installer and Repairer							
	Alaska	Y	58190 FQ	73380 MW	86430 TQ	USBLS	5/15
	Anchorage MSA, AK	Y	60810 FQ	72160 MW	82020 TQ	USBLS	5/15
	Arizona	Y	35770 FQ	44440 MW	56570 TQ	USBLS	5/15
	Phoenix-Mesa-Scottsdale MSA, AZ	Y	36460 FQ	44630 MW	57200 TQ	USBLS	5/15
	Tucson MSA, AZ	Y	44100 FQ	57210 MW	65990 TQ	USBLS	5/15
	Arkansas	Y	33210 FQ	43340 MW	67410 TQ	USBLS	5/15
	Little Rock-North Little Rock-Conway MSA, AR	Y	32250 FQ	37590 MW	47910 TQ	USBLS	5/15
	California	H	21.37 FQ	31.84 MW	36.00 TQ	CABLS	1/16-3/16
	Anaheim-Santa Ana-Irvine PMSA, CA	H	21.83 FQ	29.90 MW	35.86 TQ	CABLS	1/16-3/16
	Los Angeles-Long Beach-Glendale PMSA, CA	H	22.18 FQ	32.59 MW	36.31 TQ	CABLS	1/16-3/16
	Oakland-Hayward-Berkeley PMSA, CA	H	25.60 FQ	33.70 MW	37.31 TQ	CABLS	1/16-3/16
	Riverside-San Bernardino-Ontario MSA, CA	H	15.78 FQ	23.51 MW	31.88 TQ	CABLS	1/16-3/16
	Sacramento–Roseville–Arden-Arcade MSA, CA	H	21.32 FQ	30.59 MW	36.04 TQ	CABLS	1/16-3/16
	San Diego-Carlsbad MSA, CA	H	25.49 FQ	31.88 MW	35.88 TQ	CABLS	1/16-3/16
	San Francisco-Redwood City-South San Francisco PMSA, CA	H	23.51 FQ	31.26 MW	36.44 TQ	CABLS	1/16-3/16
	Colorado	Y	35930 FQ	45980 MW	57980 TQ	USBLS	5/15
	Denver-Aurora-Lakewood MSA, CO	Y	34610 FQ	45850 MW	58350 TQ	USBLS	5/15
	Bridgeport-Stamford-Norwalk MSA, CT	Y	19200 FQ	64650 MW	79800 TQ	USBLS	5/15
	Hartford-West Hartford-East Hartford MSA, CT	Y	38680 FQ	51970 MW	82110 TQ	USBLS	5/15
	Delaware	Y	66200 FQ	71560 MW	76920 TQ	USBLS	5/15
	Wilmington PMSA, DE-MD-NJ	Y	63620 FQ	70250 MW	76390 TQ	USBLS	5/15
	District of Columbia	Y	36940 FQ	44960 MW	64180 TQ	USBLS	5/15
	Washington-Arlington-Alexandria PMSA, DC-VA-MD-WV	Y	44950 FQ	65370 MW	73130 TQ	USBLS	5/15
	Florida	H	14.22 AE	18.97 MW	23.52 AEX	FLBLS	7/16-9/16
	Fort Lauderdale-Pompano Beach-Deerfield Beach PMSA, FL	H	14.39 AE	18.68 MW	22.31 AEX	FLBLS	7/16-9/16
	Miami-Miami Beach-Kendall PMSA, FL	H	15.29 AE	21.04 MW	26.03 AEX	FLBLS	7/16-9/16
	Orlando-Kissimmee-Sanford MSA, FL	H	11.35 AE	18.59 MW	23.33 AEX	FLBLS	7/16-9/16
	Tampa-St. Petersburg-Clearwater MSA, FL	H	15.41 AE	20.57 MW	26.10 AEX	FLBLS	7/16-9/16
	Georgia	Y	29230 FQ	36370 MW	46500 TQ	USBLS	5/15
	Atlanta-Sandy Springs-Roswell MSA, GA	Y	29690 FQ	36550 MW	46520 TQ	USBLS	5/15
	Augusta-Richmond County MSA, GA-SC	Y	28180 FQ	32930 MW	38860 TQ	USBLS	5/15
	Hawaii	Y	37990 FQ	62780 MW	71900 TQ	USBLS	5/15
	Urban Honolulu MSA, HI	Y	37390 FQ	56380 MW	70970 TQ	USBLS	5/15
	Idaho	Y	39310 FQ	46490 MW	54650 TQ	USBLS	5/15
	Boise City MSA, ID	Y	39900 FQ	46530 MW	54400 TQ	USBLS	5/15
	Illinois	Y	44530 FQ	67230 MW	82160 TQ	USBLS	5/15
	Chicago-Naperville-Arlington Heights PMSA, IL	Y	43430 FQ	66010 MW	86100 TQ	USBLS	5/15
	Lake County-Kenosha County PMSA, IL-WI	Y	59530 FQ	70960 MW	78110 TQ	USBLS	5/15
	Indiana	Y	36190 FQ	47030 MW	56720 TQ	USBLS	5/15
	Gary PMSA, IN	Y	42920 FQ	53240 MW	61770 TQ	USBLS	5/15
	Indianapolis-Carmel-Anderson MSA, IN	Y	30120 FQ	36910 MW	48500 TQ	USBLS	5/15
	Iowa	Y	34570 FQ	42810 MW	51790 TQ	USBLS	5/15
	Des Moines-West Des Moines MSA, IA	Y	28890 FQ	37020 MW	45470 TQ	USBLS	5/15
	Kansas	Y	36350 FQ	51630 MW	70030 TQ	USBLS	5/15
	Wichita MSA, KS	Y	33270 FQ	50280 MW	68720 TQ	USBLS	5/15

Occupation/Type/Industry	Location	Per	Low	Mid	High	Source	Date
Telecommunications Line Installer and Repairer							
	Kentucky	Y	32960 FQ	44890 MW	57380 TQ	USBLS	5/15
	Louisville-Jefferson County MSA, KY-IN	Y	33370 FQ	46730 MW	58020 TQ	USBLS	5/15
	Louisiana	Y	30020 FQ	36830 MW	45940 TQ	USBLS	5/15
	Baton Rouge MSA, LA	Y	28670 FQ	35630 MW	45130 TQ	USBLS	5/15
	New Orleans-Metairie MSA, LA	Y	31890 FQ	39470 MW	49790 TQ	USBLS	5/15
	Maine	Y	35370 FQ	47220 MW	69290 TQ	USBLS	5/15
	Portland-South Portland MSA, ME	Y	34820 FQ	50570 MW	71160 TQ	USBLS	5/15
	Maryland	Y	39005 AE	59814 MW	70218 AEX	MDBLS	4/16
	Baltimore-Columbia-Towson MSA, MD	Y	48490 FQ	66340 MW	74260 TQ	USBLS	5/15
	Salisbury MSA, MD-DE	Y	67990 FQ	72250 MW	76500 TQ	USBLS	5/15
	Massachusetts	Y	66580 FQ	76680 MW	88620 TQ	USBLS	5/15
	Boston-Cambridge-Newton NECTA, MA	Y	68680 FQ	78280 MW	89570 TQ	USBLS	5/15
	Worcester MSA, MA-CT	Y	56970 FQ	71030 MW	84340 TQ	USBLS	5/15
	Michigan	Y	37130 FQ	47060 MW	58400 TQ	USBLS	5/15
	Detroit-Dearborn-Livonia PMSA, MI	Y	43670 FQ	52760 MW	58630 TQ	USBLS	5/15
	Grand Rapids-Wyoming MSA, MI	Y	28500 FQ	34720 MW	45030 TQ	USBLS	5/15
	Minnesota	Y	32081 FQ	39191 MW	52727 TQ	MNBLS	1/16-3/16
	Minneapolis-St. Paul-Bloomington MSA, MN-WI	Y	31407 FQ	40720 MW	56237 TQ	MNBLS	1/16-3/16
	Mississippi	Y	32020 FQ	38710 MW	47920 TQ	USBLS	5/15
	Jackson MSA, MS	Y	32080 FQ	36680 MW	44630 TQ	USBLS	5/15
	Missouri	Y	35640 FQ	51840 MW	71710 TQ	USBLS	5/15
	Kansas City MSA, MO-KS	Y	38570 FQ	50120 MW	69660 TQ	USBLS	5/15
	St. Louis MSA, MO-IL	Y	36930 FQ	62680 MW	73480 TQ	USBLS	5/15
	Montana	Y	27580 FQ	40270 MW	59930 TQ	USBLS	5/15
	Billings MSA, MT	Y	28000 FQ	36870 MW	53040 TQ	USBLS	5/15
	Nebraska	Y	35970 FQ	46975 MW	63000 TQ	NEBLS	7/16-9/16
	Omaha-Council Bluffs MSA, NE-IA	Y	44160 FQ	54815 MW	67245 TQ	NEBLS	7/16-9/16
	Nevada	Y	35470 FQ	46880 MW	63640 TQ	USBLS	5/15
	Las Vegas-Henderson-Paradise MSA, NV	Y	35330 FQ	45450 MW	60070 TQ	USBLS	5/15
	New Hampshire	H	16.75 AE	31.50 MW	34.74 AEX	NHBLS	6/16
	Manchester NECTA, NH	H	15.36 AE	18.44 MW	22.70 AEX	NHBLS	6/16
	New Jersey	Y	44550 FQ	66730 MW	74240 TQ	USBLS	5/15
	Camden PMSA, NJ	Y	45330 FQ	66800 MW	73940 TQ	USBLS	5/15
	Newark PMSA, NJ-PA	Y	54030 FQ	67120 MW	76240 TQ	USBLS	5/15
	Trenton MSA, NJ	Y	65390 FQ	71080 MW	76770 TQ	USBLS	5/15
	New Mexico	Y	30850 FQ	43340 MW	59380 TQ	USBLS	5/15
	Albuquerque MSA, NM	Y	29240 FQ	39630 MW	57330 TQ	USBLS	5/15
	New York	Y	35860 AE	78950 MW	85750 AEX	NYBLS	1/16-3/16
	Buffalo-Cheektowaga-Niagara Falls MSA, NY	Y	48470 FQ	78320 MW	91340 TQ	USBLS	5/15
	Nassau County-Suffolk County PMSA, NY	Y	48180 FQ	82520 MW	93630 TQ	USBLS	5/15
	New York-Jersey City-White Plains PMSA, NY-NJ	Y	43430 FQ	74910 MW	89830 TQ	USBLS	5/15
	Rochester MSA, NY	Y	34720 FQ	56100 MW	76970 TQ	USBLS	5/15
	North Carolina	Y	31360 FQ	37060 MW	46580 TQ	USBLS	5/15
	Charlotte-Concord-Gastonia MSA, NC-SC	Y	31630 FQ	36880 MW	44580 TQ	USBLS	5/15
	Raleigh MSA, NC	Y	30000 FQ	36560 MW	45060 TQ	USBLS	5/15
	Wilmington MSA, NC	Y	21400 FQ	24260 MW	38150 TQ	USBLS	5/15
	North Dakota	Y	48210 FQ	63340 MW	73710 TQ	USBLS	5/15
	Fargo MSA, ND-MN	Y	49590 FQ	60990 MW	72390 TQ	USBLS	5/15
	Ohio	Y	32520 FQ	42760 MW	53540 TQ	USBLS	5/15
	Cincinnati MSA, OH-KY-IN	Y	39170 FQ	46350 MW	58930 TQ	USBLS	5/15
	Cleveland-Elyria MSA, OH	Y	35210 FQ	40090 MW	52580 TQ	USBLS	5/15
	Columbus MSA, OH	Y	33000 FQ	43650 MW	54170 TQ	USBLS	5/15
	Oklahoma	Y	36190 FQ	48910 MW	69480 TQ	USBLS	5/15
	Oklahoma City MSA, OK	Y	52330 FQ	67810 MW	74870 TQ	USBLS	5/15
	Tulsa MSA, OK	Y	34080 FQ	41940 MW	57680 TQ	USBLS	5/15
	Oregon	H	15.03 FQ	21.17 MW	30.69 TQ	ORBLS	2016

AE	Average entry wage	AWR	Average wage range	H	Hourly	LR	Low end range	MTC	Median total compensation	TCC	Total cash compensation
AEX	Average experienced wage	B	Biweekly	HI	Highest wage paid	M	Monthly	MW	Median wage paid	TQ	Third quartile wage
ATC	Average total compensation	D	Daily	HR	High end range	MCC	Median cash compensation	MWR	Median wage range	W	Weekly
AW	Average wage paid	FQ	First quartile wage	LO	Lowest wage paid	ME	Median entry wage	S	See annotated source	Y	Yearly

Occupation/Type/Industry	Location	Per	Low	Mid	High	Source	Date
Telecommunications Line Installer and Repairer							
	Portland-Vancouver-Hillsboro MSA, OR-WA	Y	29800 FQ	38230 MW	54250 TQ	USBLS	5/15
	Pennsylvania	Y	45210 FQ	65620 MW	73930 TQ	USBLS	5/15
	Allentown-Bethlehem-Easton MSA, PA-NJ	Y	54100 FQ	67760 MW	74500 TQ	USBLS	5/15
	Harrisburg-Carlisle MSA, PA	Y	38940 FQ	62380 MW	75850 TQ	USBLS	5/15
	Montgomery County-Bucks County-Chester County PMSA, PA	Y	53430 FQ	68910 MW	76360 TQ	USBLS	5/15
	Philadelphia PMSA, PA	Y	38980 FQ	63480 MW	72220 TQ	USBLS	5/15
	Pittsburgh MSA, PA	Y	56290 FQ	68350 MW	74930 TQ	USBLS	5/15
	Providence-Warwick MSA, RI-MA	Y	57090 FQ	69540 MW	80420 TQ	USBLS	5/15
	South Carolina	Y	29030 FQ	38160 MW	49650 TQ	USBLS	5/15
	Charleston-North Charleston MSA, SC	Y	28870 FQ	35780 MW	44870 TQ	USBLS	5/15
	Columbia MSA, SC	Y	30320 FQ	42980 MW	50240 TQ	USBLS	5/15
	Greenville-Anderson-Mauldin MSA, SC	Y	28370 FQ	35050 MW	48080 TQ	USBLS	5/15
	South Dakota	Y	34490 FQ	43460 MW	58120 TQ	USBLS	5/15
	Sioux Falls MSA, SD	Y	37740 FQ	48170 MW	61820 TQ	USBLS	5/15
	Tennessee	Y	29300 FQ	36230 MW	47070 TQ	USBLS	5/15
	Knoxville MSA, TN	Y	26300 FQ	32440 MW	43320 TQ	USBLS	5/15
	Memphis MSA, TN-MS-AR	Y	29850 FQ	34300 MW	38750 TQ	USBLS	5/15
	Nashville-Davidson–Murfreesboro–Franklin MSA, TN	Y	32680 FQ	39370 MW	48960 TQ	USBLS	5/15
	Texas	Y	34900 FQ	49910 MW	68820 TQ	USBLS	5/15
	Austin-Round Rock MSA, TX	Y	33970 FQ	44950 MW	62700 TQ	USBLS	5/15
	Dallas-Plano-Irving PMSA, TX	Y	35630 FQ	51390 MW	64780 TQ	USBLS	5/15
	Fort Worth-Arlington PMSA, TX	Y	44640 FQ	63830 MW	73260 TQ	USBLS	5/15
	Houston-The Woodlands-Sugar Land MSA, TX	Y	32380 FQ	49080 MW	69940 TQ	USBLS	5/15
	San Antonio-New Braunfels MSA, TX	Y	32720 FQ	40370 MW	52980 TQ	USBLS	5/15
	Utah	Y	30300 FQ	39090 MW	54870 TQ	USBLS	5/15
	Provo-Orem MSA, UT	Y	34170 FQ	42250 MW	55210 TQ	USBLS	5/15
	Salt Lake City MSA, UT	Y	30210 FQ	41290 MW	61350 TQ	USBLS	5/15
	Vermont	Y	54270 FQ	68170 MW	75250 TQ	USBLS	5/15
	Virginia	Y	43620 FQ	63710 MW	72550 TQ	USBLS	5/15
	Blacksburg-Christiansburg-Radford MSA, VA	Y	29420 FQ	36340 MW	45290 TQ	USBLS	5/15
	Richmond MSA, VA	Y	37670 FQ	48570 MW	68040 TQ	USBLS	5/15
	Virginia Beach-Norfolk-Newport News MSA, VA-NC	Y	42900 FQ	62290 MW	72140 TQ	USBLS	5/15
	Washington	H	17.77 FQ	23.76 MW	32.53 TQ	WABLS	3/16
	Seattle-Bellevue-Everett PMSA, WA	H	18.36 FQ	25.14 MW	35.40 TQ	WABLS	3/16
	Tacoma-Lakewood PMSA, WA	H	17.00 FQ	22.27 MW	32.27 TQ	WABLS	3/16
	West Virginia	Y	64780 FQ	71520 MW	78270 TQ	USBLS	5/15
	Huntington-Ashland MSA, WV-KY-OH	Y	62090 FQ	69640 MW	75520 TQ	USBLS	5/15
	Wisconsin	Y	38050 FQ	49540 MW	60080 TQ	USBLS	5/15
	Madison MSA, WI	Y	41820 FQ	61650 MW	73590 TQ	USBLS	5/15
	Milwaukee-Waukesha-West Allis MSA, WI	Y	38050 FQ	52870 MW	58800 TQ	USBLS	5/15
	Wyoming	Y	35730 FQ	46190 MW	59450 TQ	USBLS	5/15
	Cheyenne MSA, WY	Y	29790 FQ	50080 MW	65460 TQ	USBLS	5/15
	Puerto Rico	Y	18690 FQ	33050 MW	41930 TQ	USBLS	5/15
	San Juan-Carolina-Caguas MSA, PR	Y	18300 FQ	32170 MW	42050 TQ	USBLS	5/15
Telecommunications Specialist							
Municipal Government	Escondido, CA	Y			51089 HI	CACIT	6/28/16
Telemarketer							
	Alabama	Y	17551 AE	24584 AW	28101 AEX	ALBLS	6/16
	Birmingham-Hoover MSA, AL	Y	18720 AE	28297 AW	33086 AEX	ALBLS	6/16
	Alaska	Y	22560 FQ	26380 MW	33680 TQ	USBLS	5/15
	Arizona	Y	19320 FQ	23440 MW	30880 TQ	USBLS	5/15

AE	Average entry wage	AWR	Average wage range	H	Hourly	LR	Low end range	MTC	Median total compensation	TCC	Total cash compensation
AEX	Average experienced wage	B	Biweekly	HI	Highest wage paid	M	Monthly	MW	Median wage paid	TQ	Third quartile wage
ATC	Average total compensation	D	Daily	HR	High end range	MCC	Median cash compensation	MWR	Median wage range	W	Weekly
AW	Average wage paid	FQ	First quartile wage	LO	Lowest wage paid	ME	Median entry wage	S	See annotated source	Y	Yearly

Occupation/Type/Industry	Location	Per	Low	Mid	High	Source	Date
Telemarketer	Phoenix-Mesa-Scottsdale MSA, AZ	Y	19870 FQ	24340 MW	32540 TQ	USBLS	5/15
	Tucson MSA, AZ	Y	18000 FQ	19190 MW	22120 TQ	USBLS	5/15
	Arkansas	Y	17280 FQ	18940 MW	22050 TQ	USBLS	5/15
	Little Rock-North Little Rock-Conway MSA, AR	Y	17410 FQ	19210 MW	22540 TQ	USBLS	5/15
	California	H	9.87 FQ	12.45 MW	15.44 TQ	CABLS	1/16-3/16
	Anaheim-Santa Ana-Irvine PMSA, CA	H	9.96 FQ	11.39 MW	14.73 TQ	CABLS	1/16-3/16
	Los Angeles-Long Beach-Glendale PMSA, CA	H	10.53 FQ	13.13 MW	15.00 TQ	CABLS	1/16-3/16
	Oakland-Hayward-Berkeley PMSA, CA	H	10.89 FQ	13.41 MW	16.82 TQ	CABLS	1/16-3/16
	Riverside-San Bernardino-Ontario MSA, CA	H	9.32 FQ	11.01 MW	14.25 TQ	CABLS	1/16-3/16
	Sacramento–Roseville–Arden-Arcade MSA, CA	H	9.33 FQ	10.32 MW	14.06 TQ	CABLS	1/16-3/16
	San Diego-Carlsbad MSA, CA	H	9.48 FQ	11.71 MW	17.17 TQ	CABLS	1/16-3/16
	San Francisco-Redwood City-South San Francisco PMSA, CA	H	12.12 FQ	15.01 MW	23.37 TQ	CABLS	1/16-3/16
	Colorado	Y	19250 FQ	24660 MW	30610 TQ	USBLS	5/15
	Denver-Aurora-Lakewood MSA, CO	Y	23200 FQ	28010 MW	33670 TQ	USBLS	5/15
	Connecticut	Y		31610 MW		CTBLS	1/16-3/16
	Bridgeport-Stamford-Norwalk MSA, CT	Y	19940 FQ	27690 MW	56220 TQ	USBLS	5/15
	Hartford-West Hartford-East Hartford MSA, CT	Y	19580 FQ	23220 MW	34900 TQ	USBLS	5/15
	Delaware	Y	19880 FQ	25530 MW	33900 TQ	USBLS	5/15
	Wilmington PMSA, DE-MD-NJ	Y	20200 FQ	25570 MW	34010 TQ	USBLS	5/15
	District of Columbia	Y	19890 FQ	21650 MW	29190 TQ	USBLS	5/15
	Washington-Arlington-Alexandria PMSA, DC-VA-MD-WV	Y	21630 FQ	26110 MW	29400 TQ	USBLS	5/15
	Florida	H	8.94 AE	11.42 MW	14.31 AEX	FLBLS	7/16-9/16
	Fort Lauderdale-Pompano Beach-Deerfield Beach PMSA, FL	H	9.02 AE	13.08 MW	15.35 AEX	FLBLS	7/16-9/16
	Miami-Miami Beach-Kendall PMSA, FL	H	9.62 AE	11.78 MW	14.18 AEX	FLBLS	7/16-9/16
	Orlando-Kissimmee-Sanford MSA, FL	H	8.90 AE	10.45 MW	12.88 AEX	FLBLS	7/16-9/16
	Tampa-St. Petersburg-Clearwater MSA, FL	H	8.87 AE	10.52 MW	14.89 AEX	FLBLS	7/16-9/16
	Georgia	Y	19150 FQ	23140 MW	32350 TQ	USBLS	5/15
	Atlanta-Sandy Springs-Roswell MSA, GA	Y	21780 FQ	27470 MW	37540 TQ	USBLS	5/15
	Augusta-Richmond County MSA, GA-SC	Y	17690 FQ	19500 MW	23720 TQ	USBLS	5/15
	Hawaii	Y	18520 FQ	22090 MW	29020 TQ	USBLS	5/15
	Urban Honolulu MSA, HI	Y	18640 FQ	22330 MW	29200 TQ	USBLS	5/15
	Idaho	Y	18750 FQ	22000 MW	25670 TQ	USBLS	5/15
	Boise City MSA, ID	Y	19870 FQ	23700 MW	27920 TQ	USBLS	5/15
	Illinois	Y	19960 FQ	23820 MW	29420 TQ	USBLS	5/15
	Chicago-Naperville-Arlington Heights PMSA, IL	Y	20090 FQ	24190 MW	29440 TQ	USBLS	5/15
	Lake County-Kenosha County PMSA, IL-WI	Y	20540 FQ	24100 MW	39470 TQ	USBLS	5/15
	Indiana	Y	19740 FQ	23050 MW	28430 TQ	USBLS	5/15
	Gary PMSA, IN	Y	17850 FQ	20550 MW	24070 TQ	USBLS	5/15
	Indianapolis-Carmel-Anderson MSA, IN	Y	20370 FQ	23730 MW	31300 TQ	USBLS	5/15
	Iowa	Y	18830 FQ	22520 MW	28340 TQ	USBLS	5/15
	Des Moines-West Des Moines MSA, IA	Y	22220 FQ	28860 MW	34630 TQ	USBLS	5/15
	Kansas	Y	24210 FQ	28320 MW	33600 TQ	USBLS	5/15
	Wichita MSA, KS	Y	22170 FQ	26020 MW	35440 TQ	USBLS	5/15
	Kentucky	Y	19690 FQ	23060 MW	28710 TQ	USBLS	5/15
	Louisville-Jefferson County MSA, KY-IN	Y	21070 FQ	23470 MW	27160 TQ	USBLS	5/15

AE	Average entry wage	AWR	Average wage range	H	Hourly
AEX	Average experienced wage	B	Biweekly	HI	Highest wage paid
ATC	Average total compensation	D	Daily	HR	High end range
AW	Average wage paid	FQ	First quartile wage	LO	Lowest wage paid

LR	Low end range	MTC	Median total compensation
M	Monthly	MW	Median wage paid
MCC	Median cash compensation	MWR	Median wage range
ME	Median entry wage	S	See annotated source

TCC	Total cash compensation
TQ	Third quartile wage
W	Weekly
Y	Yearly

Telemarketer

Occupation/Type/Industry	Location	Per	Low	Mid	High	Source	Date
Telemarketer	Louisiana	Y	21130 FQ	25850 MW	30660 TQ	USBLS	5/15
	Baton Rouge MSA, LA	Y	18860 FQ	23960 MW	34970 TQ	USBLS	5/15
	New Orleans-Metairie MSA, LA	Y	21170 FQ	24830 MW	28970 TQ	USBLS	5/15
	Maine	Y	18930 FQ	25280 MW	29450 TQ	USBLS	5/15
	Portland-South Portland MSA, ME	Y	19230 FQ	25030 MW	31960 TQ	USBLS	5/15
	Maryland	Y	17988 AE	24859 MW	28294 AEX	MDBLS	4/16
	Baltimore-Columbia-Towson MSA, MD	Y	17870 FQ	19090 MW	25790 TQ	USBLS	5/15
	Salisbury MSA, MD-DE	Y	19950 FQ	27230 MW	35740 TQ	USBLS	5/15
	Massachusetts	Y	22970 FQ	29030 MW	38350 TQ	USBLS	5/15
	Boston-Cambridge-Newton NECTA, MA	Y	22640 FQ	28860 MW	39420 TQ	USBLS	5/15
	Worcester MSA, MA-CT	Y	22600 FQ	27480 MW	39660 TQ	USBLS	5/15
	Michigan	Y	19130 FQ	22090 MW	27560 TQ	USBLS	5/15
	Detroit-Dearborn-Livonia PMSA, MI	Y	19100 FQ	21760 MW	27080 TQ	USBLS	5/15
	Grand Rapids-Wyoming MSA, MI	Y	19080 FQ	22200 MW	25170 TQ	USBLS	5/15
	Minnesota	Y	21165 FQ	25098 MW	35040 TQ	MNBLS	1/16-3/16
	Minneapolis-St. Paul-Bloomington MSA, MN-WI	Y	21468 FQ	25400 MW	35706 TQ	MNBLS	1/16-3/16
	Mississippi	Y	17670 FQ	19830 MW	27230 TQ	USBLS	5/15
	Missouri	Y	18100 FQ	21050 MW	27300 TQ	USBLS	5/15
	Kansas City MSA, MO-KS	Y	21140 FQ	27220 MW	33020 TQ	USBLS	5/15
	St. Louis MSA, MO-IL	Y	18420 FQ	22530 MW	29050 TQ	USBLS	5/15
	Montana	Y	24950 FQ	27280 MW	29590 TQ	USBLS	5/15
	Billings MSA, MT	Y	18320 FQ	20090 MW	23760 TQ	USBLS	5/15
	Nebraska	Y	19905 FQ	22170 MW	24590 TQ	NEBLS	7/16-9/16
	Omaha-Council Bluffs MSA, NE-IA	Y	20000 FQ	22240 MW	24575 TQ	NEBLS	7/16-9/16
	Nevada	Y	19120 FQ	25760 MW	39230 TQ	USBLS	5/15
	Las Vegas-Henderson-Paradise MSA, NV	Y	18740 FQ	23460 MW	40440 TQ	USBLS	5/15
	New Hampshire	H	9.80 AE	14.16 MW	18.00 AEX	NHBLS	6/16
	Manchester NECTA, NH	H	10.83 AE	15.09 MW	17.39 AEX	NHBLS	6/16
	New Jersey	Y	19950 FQ	23740 MW	31050 TQ	USBLS	5/15
	Camden PMSA, NJ	Y	18860 FQ	22530 MW	27100 TQ	USBLS	5/15
	Newark PMSA, NJ-PA	Y	21130 FQ	24320 MW	34700 TQ	USBLS	5/15
	Trenton MSA, NJ	Y	21410 FQ	23600 MW	27240 TQ	USBLS	5/15
	New Mexico	Y	18300 FQ	20760 MW	23370 TQ	USBLS	5/15
	Albuquerque MSA, NM	Y	20150 FQ	22130 MW	24140 TQ	USBLS	5/15
	New York	Y	19250 AE	25290 MW	33510 AEX	NYBLS	1/16-3/16
	Buffalo-Cheektowaga-Niagara Falls MSA, NY	Y	19080 FQ	21820 MW	28140 TQ	USBLS	5/15
	Nassau County-Suffolk County PMSA, NY	Y	19810 FQ	26960 MW	32660 TQ	USBLS	5/15
	New York-Jersey City-White Plains PMSA, NY-NJ	Y	19060 FQ	24730 MW	32990 TQ	USBLS	5/15
	Rochester MSA, NY	Y	19090 FQ	21860 MW	24580 TQ	USBLS	5/15
	North Carolina	Y	21380 FQ	23970 MW	30220 TQ	USBLS	5/15
	Charlotte-Concord-Gastonia MSA, NC-SC	Y	22190 FQ	25040 MW	31590 TQ	USBLS	5/15
	Raleigh MSA, NC	Y	25170 FQ	34740 MW	48520 TQ	USBLS	5/15
	North Dakota	Y	17700 FQ	19760 MW	24200 TQ	USBLS	5/15
	Fargo MSA, ND-MN	Y	17610 FQ	19630 MW	23460 TQ	USBLS	5/15
	Ohio	Y	18800 FQ	22700 MW	29390 TQ	USBLS	5/15
	Cincinnati MSA, OH-KY-IN	Y	22010 FQ	26700 MW	30990 TQ	USBLS	5/15
	Cleveland-Elyria MSA, OH	Y	18970 FQ	26590 MW	35790 TQ	USBLS	5/15
	Columbus MSA, OH	Y	18890 FQ	22390 MW	27930 TQ	USBLS	5/15
	Oklahoma	Y	18000 FQ	20880 MW	24640 TQ	USBLS	5/15
	Oklahoma City MSA, OK	Y	17170 FQ	18770 MW	21860 TQ	USBLS	5/15
	Tulsa MSA, OK	Y	18630 FQ	21890 MW	25140 TQ	USBLS	5/15
	Oregon	H	10.14 FQ	11.98 MW	14.33 TQ	ORBLS	2016
	Portland-Vancouver-Hillsboro MSA, OR-WA	Y	21320 FQ	25510 MW	30320 TQ	USBLS	5/15
	Pennsylvania	Y	18200 FQ	21930 MW	29840 TQ	USBLS	5/15
	Allentown-Bethlehem-Easton MSA, PA-NJ	Y	32560 FQ	35930 MW	39320 TQ	USBLS	5/15
	Harrisburg-Carlisle MSA, PA	Y	18410 FQ	23460 MW	33450 TQ	USBLS	5/15

AE	Average entry wage	AWR	Average wage range	H	Hourly
AEX	Average experienced wage	B	Biweekly	HI	Highest wage paid
ATC	Average total compensation	D	Daily	HR	High end range
AW	Average wage paid	FQ	First quartile wage	LO	Lowest wage paid

LR	Low end range	MTC	Median total compensation	TCC	Total cash compensation
M	Monthly	MW	Median wage paid	TQ	Third quartile wage
MCC	Median cash compensation	MWR	Median wage range	W	Weekly
ME	Median entry wage	S	See annotated source	Y	Yearly

Occupation/Type/Industry	Location	Per	Low	Mid	High	Source	Date
Telemarketer	Montgomery County-Bucks County-Chester County						
	PMSA, PA	Y	19910 FQ	29370 MW	36370 TQ	USBLS	5/15
	Philadelphia PMSA, PA	Y	19080 FQ	22150 MW	28540 TQ	USBLS	5/15
	Pittsburgh MSA, PA	Y	17270 FQ	19080 MW	23990 TQ	USBLS	5/15
	Rhode Island	Y	20630 FQ	23900 MW	29890 TQ	USBLS	5/15
	Providence-Warwick MSA, RI-MA	Y	21310 FQ	25460 MW	33470 TQ	USBLS	5/15
	South Carolina	Y	19170 FQ	25530 MW	31540 TQ	USBLS	5/15
	Charleston-North Charleston MSA, SC	Y	17980 FQ	22620 MW	28290 TQ	USBLS	5/15
	Columbia MSA, SC	Y	19390 FQ	26960 MW	31770 TQ	USBLS	5/15
	Greenville-Anderson-Mauldin MSA, SC	Y	19030 FQ	25380 MW	34750 TQ	USBLS	5/15
	South Dakota	Y	22960 FQ	26970 MW	33050 TQ	USBLS	5/15
	Tennessee	Y	19640 FQ	23850 MW	29320 TQ	USBLS	5/15
	Knoxville MSA, TN	Y	20340 FQ	23040 MW	26200 TQ	USBLS	5/15
	Memphis MSA, TN-MS-AR	Y	20890 FQ	24640 MW	30020 TQ	USBLS	5/15
	Nashville-Davidson–Murfreesboro–Franklin MSA, TN	Y	19460 FQ	24210 MW	30930 TQ	USBLS	5/15
	Texas	Y	20370 FQ	23350 MW	29330 TQ	USBLS	5/15
	Austin-Round Rock MSA, TX	Y	20540 FQ	24430 MW	29110 TQ	USBLS	5/15
	Dallas-Plano-Irving PMSA, TX	Y	21870 FQ	24950 MW	35810 TQ	USBLS	5/15
	Fort Worth-Arlington PMSA, TX	Y	17590 FQ	19670 MW	28000 TQ	USBLS	5/15
	Houston-The Woodlands-Sugar Land MSA, TX	Y	19980 FQ	23320 MW	30130 TQ	USBLS	5/15
	San Antonio-New Braunfels MSA, TX	Y	21200 FQ	23200 MW	25290 TQ	USBLS	5/15
	Utah	Y	18430 FQ	23670 MW	28070 TQ	USBLS	5/15
	Ogden-Clearfield MSA, UT	Y	17500 FQ	19600 MW	24170 TQ	USBLS	5/15
	Provo-Orem MSA, UT	Y	17970 FQ	20660 MW	24770 TQ	USBLS	5/15
	Salt Lake City MSA, UT	Y	18590 FQ	25300 MW	28600 TQ	USBLS	5/15
	Vermont	Y	24020 FQ	27600 MW	30510 TQ	USBLS	5/15
	Burlington-South Burlington MSA, VT	Y	26030 FQ	28330 MW	30630 TQ	USBLS	5/15
	Virginia	Y	20400 FQ	25010 MW	30060 TQ	USBLS	5/15
	Richmond MSA, VA	Y	20720 FQ	24780 MW	30660 TQ	USBLS	5/15
	Virginia Beach-Norfolk-Newport News MSA, VA-NC	Y	18200 FQ	21950 MW	26930 TQ	USBLS	5/15
	Washington	H	10.59 FQ	11.61 MW	13.83 TQ	WABLS	3/16
	Seattle-Bellevue-Everett PMSA, WA	H	11.05 FQ	13.48 MW	16.74 TQ	WABLS	3/16
	Tacoma-Lakewood PMSA, WA	H	12.65 FQ	14.45 MW	16.95 TQ	WABLS	3/16
	West Virginia	Y	19480 FQ	22670 MW	30210 TQ	USBLS	5/15
	Huntington-Ashland MSA, WV-KY-OH	Y	19830 FQ	22010 MW	24210 TQ	USBLS	5/15
	Wisconsin	Y	20260 FQ	24510 MW	29330 TQ	USBLS	5/15
	Madison MSA, WI	Y	20260 FQ	26520 MW	35400 TQ	USBLS	5/15
	Milwaukee-Waukesha-West Allis MSA, WI	Y	21610 FQ	25930 MW	31130 TQ	USBLS	5/15
	Puerto Rico	Y	16550 FQ	17740 MW	18940 TQ	USBLS	5/15
	San Juan-Carolina-Caguas MSA, PR	Y	16550 FQ	17740 MW	18940 TQ	USBLS	5/15
Telemarketing Technician							
State Government	Helena, MT	H			14.94 HI	MTGOV	2016
Telemetry Systems Superintendent							
Water Department, Municipal Government	Long Beach, CA	Y			108717 HI	CACIT	6/28/16
Telephone Operator	Phoenix-Mesa-Scottsdale MSA, AZ	Y	22560 FQ	25280 MW	30110 TQ	USBLS	5/15
	California	H	18.35 FQ	25.73 MW	29.46 TQ	CABLS	1/16-3/16
	Oakland-Hayward-Berkeley PMSA, CA	H	18.62 FQ	26.35 MW	30.72 TQ	CABLS	1/16-3/16
	Hartford-West Hartford-East Hartford MSA, CT	Y	25480 FQ	29570 MW	35290 TQ	USBLS	5/15
	Delaware	Y	27940 FQ	31610 MW	37020 TQ	USBLS	5/15

Occupation/Type/Industry	Location	Per	Low	Mid	High	Source	Date
Telephone Operator	Wilmington PMSA, DE-MD-NJ	Y	28170 FQ	32270 MW	37450 TQ	USBLS	5/15
	District of Columbia	Y	33040 FQ	38180 MW	47540 TQ	USBLS	5/15
	Washington-Arlington-Alexandria PMSA, DC-VA-MD-WV	Y	26830 FQ	32970 MW	38370 TQ	USBLS	5/15
	Florida	H	10.57 AE	11.73 MW	14.18 AEX	FLBLS	7/16-9/16
	Fort Lauderdale-Pompano Beach-Deerfield Beach PMSA, FL	H	11.96 AE	15.14 MW	20.33 AEX	FLBLS	7/16-9/16
	Miami-Miami Beach-Kendall PMSA, FL	H	10.31 AE	11.08 MW	12.94 AEX	FLBLS	7/16-9/16
	Orlando-Kissimmee-Sanford MSA, FL	H	10.79 AE	13.96 MW	16.81 AEX	FLBLS	7/16-9/16
	Tampa-St. Petersburg-Clearwater MSA, FL	H	10.34 AE	11.27 MW	12.92 AEX	FLBLS	7/16-9/16
	Georgia	Y	39610 FQ	43590 MW	47600 TQ	USBLS	5/15
	Atlanta-Sandy Springs-Roswell MSA, GA	Y	40200 FQ	43950 MW	47710 TQ	USBLS	5/15
	Hawaii	Y	41330 FQ	44280 MW	47220 TQ	USBLS	5/15*
	Idaho	Y	21540 FQ	23490 MW	26700 TQ	USBLS	5/15
	Illinois	Y	21380 FQ	27590 MW	37410 TQ	USBLS	5/15
	Chicago-Naperville-Arlington Heights PMSA, IL	Y	21330 FQ	27070 MW	37320 TQ	USBLS	5/15
	Lake County-Kenosha County PMSA, IL-WI	Y	24490 FQ	35590 MW	45470 TQ	USBLS	5/15
	Indiana	Y	27250 FQ	33470 MW	42910 TQ	USBLS	5/15
	Indianapolis-Carmel-Anderson MSA, IN	Y	30230 FQ	38720 MW	45850 TQ	USBLS	5/15
	Iowa	Y	26780 FQ	30350 MW	39680 TQ	USBLS	5/15
	Kansas	Y	18380 FQ	24840 MW	30230 TQ	USBLS	5/15
	Maryland	Y	25709 AE	44626 MW	54085 AEX	MDBLS	4/16
	Baltimore-Columbia-Towson MSA, MD	Y	34630 FQ	52410 MW	76540 TQ	USBLS	5/15
	Massachusetts	Y	32490 FQ	42670 MW	56720 TQ	USBLS	5/15
	Boston-Cambridge-Newton NECTA, MA	Y	26860 FQ	35500 MW	49410 TQ	USBLS	5/15
	Michigan	Y	26490 FQ	29610 MW	34630 TQ	USBLS	5/15
	Minnesota	Y	39642 FQ	45386 MW	52869 TQ	MNBLS	1/16-3/16
	Mississippi	Y	21400 FQ	24440 MW	28600 TQ	USBLS	5/15
	Missouri	Y	24890 FQ	28690 MW	50330 TQ	USBLS	5/15
	Kansas City MSA, MO-KS	Y	25410 FQ	28400 MW	31630 TQ	USBLS	5/15
	New Jersey	Y	35140 FQ	44990 MW	56830 TQ	USBLS	5/15
	Newark PMSA, NJ-PA	Y	39370 FQ	42640 MW	47780 TQ	USBLS	5/15
	New York	Y	31830 AE	40120 MW	45300 AEX	NYBLS	1/16-3/16
	Nassau County-Suffolk County PMSA, NY	Y	36070 FQ	40330 MW	45630 TQ	USBLS	5/15
	New York-Jersey City-White Plains PMSA, NY-NJ	Y	35500 FQ	41140 MW	48990 TQ	USBLS	5/15
	Ohio	Y	23630 FQ	29950 MW	35230 TQ	USBLS	5/15
	Cincinnati MSA, OH-KY-IN	Y	22310 FQ	25900 MW	33870 TQ	USBLS	5/15
	Cleveland-Elyria MSA, OH	Y	24710 FQ	29230 MW	35050 TQ	USBLS	5/15
	Columbus MSA, OH	Y	31010 FQ	33410 MW	36420 TQ	USBLS	5/15
	Oklahoma	Y	19450 FQ	23830 MW	33920 TQ	USBLS	5/15
	Pennsylvania	Y	29760 FQ	38260 MW	54330 TQ	USBLS	5/15
	Philadelphia PMSA, PA	Y	29450 FQ	40170 MW	55960 TQ	USBLS	5/15
	Pittsburgh MSA, PA	Y	34670 FQ	39320 MW	48510 TQ	USBLS	5/15
	Rhode Island	Y	28310 FQ	37740 MW	44400 TQ	USBLS	5/15
	Providence-Warwick MSA, RI-MA	Y	36990 FQ	52300 MW	58680 TQ	USBLS	5/15
	South Carolina	Y	22610 FQ	27320 MW	32230 TQ	USBLS	5/15
	Tennessee	Y	25880 FQ	29860 MW	34880 TQ	USBLS	5/15
	Memphis MSA, TN-MS-AR	Y	25790 FQ	29610 MW	34260 TQ	USBLS	5/15
	Texas	Y	28280 FQ	49980 MW	56640 TQ	USBLS	5/15
	Dallas-Plano-Irving PMSA, TX	Y	44400 FQ	53360 MW	58240 TQ	USBLS	5/15
	Houston-The Woodlands-Sugar Land MSA, TX	Y	31180 FQ	53190 MW	58330 TQ	USBLS	5/15
	San Antonio-New Braunfels MSA, TX	Y	53040 FQ	56400 MW	59770 TQ	USBLS	5/15
	Utah	Y	23960 FQ	28130 MW	34230 TQ	USBLS	5/15
	Salt Lake City MSA, UT	Y	27020 FQ	30210 MW	37710 TQ	USBLS	5/15
	Virginia	Y	32980 FQ	52200 MW	59060 TQ	USBLS	5/15

AE	Average entry wage	AWR	Average wage range	H	Hourly	LR	Low end range	MTC	Median total compensation	TCC	Total cash compensation
AEX	Average experienced wage	B	Biweekly	HI	Highest wage paid	M	Monthly	MW	Median wage paid	TQ	Third quartile wage
ATC	Average total compensation	D	Daily	HR	High end range	MCC	Median cash compensation	MWR	Median wage range	W	Weekly
AW	Average wage paid	FQ	First quartile wage	LO	Lowest wage paid	ME	Median entry wage	S	See annotated source	Y	Yearly

Occupation/Type/Industry	Location	Per	Low	Mid	High	Source	Date
Telephone Operator	Washington	H	15.80 FQ	17.05 MW	18.31 TQ	WABLS	3/16
	Wisconsin	Y	26320 FQ	32860 MW	38340 TQ	USBLS	5/15
Teleprompter Operator							
Made for Television Motion Picture	United States	W	1291 LO			MPEG01	7/31/16-7/29/17
Television Station Manager							
Michigan State University	East Lansing, MI	Y			98693 HI	MSUSAL	10/1/14-9/30/15
Teller	Alabama	Y	22003 AE	27486 AW	30227 AEX	ALBLS	6/16
	Birmingham-Hoover MSA, AL	Y	22838 AE	29063 AW	32165 AEX	ALBLS	6/16
	Alaska	Y	26050 FQ	29720 MW	36510 TQ	USBLS	5/15
	Anchorage MSA, AK	Y	24630 FQ	29140 MW	36490 TQ	USBLS	5/15
	Arizona	Y	22770 FQ	26200 MW	30170 TQ	USBLS	5/15
	Phoenix-Mesa-Scottsdale MSA, AZ	Y	22650 FQ	26120 MW	30110 TQ	USBLS	5/15
	Tucson MSA, AZ	Y	23570 FQ	27040 MW	30450 TQ	USBLS	5/15
	Arkansas	Y	20540 FQ	23240 MW	27160 TQ	USBLS	5/15
	Little Rock-North Little Rock-Conway MSA, AR	Y	20280 FQ	22830 MW	26190 TQ	USBLS	5/15
	California	H	12.11 FQ	13.94 MW	16.11 TQ	CABLS	1/16-3/16
	Anaheim-Santa Ana-Irvine PMSA, CA	H	11.70 FQ	13.66 MW	15.53 TQ	CABLS	1/16-3/16
	Los Angeles-Long Beach-Glendale PMSA, CA	H	11.78 FQ	13.62 MW	15.32 TQ	CABLS	1/16-3/16
	Oakland-Hayward-Berkeley PMSA, CA	H	13.55 FQ	15.20 MW	17.91 TQ	CABLS	1/16-3/16
	Riverside-San Bernardino-Ontario MSA, CA	H	12.19 FQ	14.05 MW	16.63 TQ	CABLS	1/16-3/16
	Sacramento–Roseville–Arden-Arcade MSA, CA	H	11.85 FQ	13.73 MW	15.70 TQ	CABLS	1/16-3/16
	San Diego-Carlsbad MSA, CA	H	11.51 FQ	13.63 MW	16.05 TQ	CABLS	1/16-3/16
	San Francisco-Redwood City-South San Francisco PMSA, CA	H	13.54 FQ	15.11 MW	18.07 TQ	CABLS	1/16-3/16
	Colorado	Y	23090 FQ	27000 MW	31540 TQ	USBLS	5/15
	Denver-Aurora-Lakewood MSA, CO	Y	23000 FQ	27020 MW	32510 TQ	USBLS	5/15
	Connecticut	Y		31836 MW		CTBLS	1/16-3/16
	Bridgeport-Stamford-Norwalk MSA, CT	Y	28250 FQ	33110 MW	37720 TQ	USBLS	5/15
	Hartford-West Hartford-East Hartford MSA, CT	Y	26100 FQ	30470 MW	36020 TQ	USBLS	5/15
	Delaware	Y	24280 FQ	27880 MW	31370 TQ	USBLS	5/15
	Wilmington PMSA, DE-MD-NJ	Y	24320 FQ	28030 MW	31870 TQ	USBLS	5/15
	District of Columbia	Y	26150 FQ	29100 MW	33990 TQ	USBLS	5/15
	Washington-Arlington-Alexandria PMSA, DC-VA-MD-WV	Y	26520 FQ	30590 MW	37770 TQ	USBLS	5/15
	Florida	H	11.20 AE	14.07 MW	16.14 AEX	FLBLS	7/16-9/16
	Fort Lauderdale-Pompano Beach-Deerfield Beach PMSA, FL	H	11.23 AE	14.27 MW	16.71 AEX	FLBLS	7/16-9/16
	Miami-Miami Beach-Kendall PMSA, FL	H	10.98 AE	13.91 MW	16.31 AEX	FLBLS	7/16-9/16
	Orlando-Kissimmee-Sanford MSA, FL	H	10.83 AE	13.76 MW	15.81 AEX	FLBLS	7/16-9/16
	Tampa-St. Petersburg-Clearwater MSA, FL	H	12.06 AE	14.94 MW	16.76 AEX	FLBLS	7/16-9/16
	Georgia	Y	23600 FQ	27720 MW	32450 TQ	USBLS	5/15
	Atlanta-Sandy Springs-Roswell MSA, GA	Y	25420 FQ	29430 MW	35350 TQ	USBLS	5/15
	Augusta-Richmond County MSA, GA-SC	Y	24120 FQ	27420 MW	30520 TQ	USBLS	5/15
	Hawaii	Y	21670 FQ	25120 MW	30070 TQ	USBLS	5/15
	Urban Honolulu MSA, HI	Y	21530 FQ	24870 MW	30020 TQ	USBLS	5/15
	Idaho	Y	21980 FQ	24600 MW	28770 TQ	USBLS	5/15
	Boise City MSA, ID	Y	22140 FQ	24550 MW	28900 TQ	USBLS	5/15
	Illinois	Y	22290 FQ	25930 MW	30820 TQ	USBLS	5/15
	Chicago-Naperville-Arlington Heights PMSA, IL	Y	22690 FQ	27070 MW	32410 TQ	USBLS	5/15

AE	Average entry wage	AWR	Average wage range	H	Hourly	LR	Low end range	MTC	Median total compensation	TCC	Total cash compensation
AEX	Average experienced wage	B	Biweekly	HI	Highest wage paid	M	Monthly	MW	Median wage paid	TQ	Third quartile wage
ATC	Average total compensation	D	Daily	HR	High end range	MCC	Median cash compensation	MWR	Median wage range	W	Weekly
AW	Average wage paid	FQ	First quartile wage	LO	Lowest wage paid	ME	Median entry wage	S	See annotated source	Y	Yearly

Teller

Occupation/Type/Industry	Location	Per	Low	Mid	High	Source	Date
Teller	Lake County-Kenosha County PMSA, IL-WI	Y	22900 FQ	26500 MW	30330 TQ	USBLS	5/15
	Indiana	Y	21650 FQ	24140 MW	28300 TQ	USBLS	5/15
	Gary PMSA, IN	Y	21910 FQ	24690 MW	29150 TQ	USBLS	5/15
	Indianapolis-Carmel-Anderson MSA, IN	Y	21810 FQ	24310 MW	28410 TQ	USBLS	5/15
	Iowa	Y	21960 FQ	25500 MW	29930 TQ	USBLS	5/15
	Des Moines-West Des Moines MSA, IA	Y	21870 FQ	25750 MW	31600 TQ	USBLS	5/15
	Kansas	Y	21220 FQ	23620 MW	27490 TQ	USBLS	5/15
	Wichita MSA, KS	Y	20920 FQ	22820 MW	24730 TQ	USBLS	5/15
	Kentucky	Y	21000 FQ	24500 MW	29190 TQ	USBLS	5/15
	Louisville-Jefferson County MSA, KY-IN	Y	22220 FQ	26720 MW	30460 TQ	USBLS	5/15
	Louisiana	Y	21580 FQ	24090 MW	28160 TQ	USBLS	5/15
	Baton Rouge MSA, LA	Y	21510 FQ	23860 MW	28160 TQ	USBLS	5/15
	New Orleans-Metairie MSA, LA	Y	22100 FQ	24850 MW	28930 TQ	USBLS	5/15
	Maine	Y	22270 FQ	24890 MW	29090 TQ	USBLS	5/15
	Portland-South Portland MSA, ME	Y	23540 FQ	27840 MW	33030 TQ	USBLS	5/15
	Maryland	Y	23038 AE	29414 MW	32601 AEX	MDBLS	4/16
	Baltimore-Columbia-Towson MSA, MD	Y	25470 FQ	28960 MW	34060 TQ	USBLS	5/15
	Salisbury MSA, MD-DE	Y	22590 FQ	26820 MW	30770 TQ	USBLS	5/15
	Massachusetts	Y	26020 FQ	29540 MW	35240 TQ	USBLS	5/15
	Boston-Cambridge-Newton NECTA, MA	Y	26390 FQ	29720 MW	35850 TQ	USBLS	5/15
	Worcester MSA, MA-CT	Y	25520 FQ	30440 MW	36240 TQ	USBLS	5/15
	Michigan	Y	21630 FQ	24990 MW	30050 TQ	USBLS	5/15
	Detroit-Dearborn-Livonia PMSA, MI	Y	22440 FQ	26490 MW	30890 TQ	USBLS	5/15
	Grand Rapids-Wyoming MSA, MI	Y	22190 FQ	25200 MW	30200 TQ	USBLS	5/15
	Minnesota	Y	22481 FQ	25666 MW	30409 TQ	MNBLS	1/16-3/16
	Minneapolis-St. Paul-Bloomington MSA, MN-WI	Y	22460 FQ	25777 MW	30743 TQ	MNBLS	1/16-3/16
	Mississippi	Y	21630 FQ	24810 MW	28890 TQ	USBLS	5/15
	Jackson MSA, MS	Y	22300 FQ	26160 MW	29880 TQ	USBLS	5/15
	Missouri	Y	20220 FQ	23060 MW	26950 TQ	USBLS	5/15
	Kansas City MSA, MO-KS	Y	21490 FQ	23740 MW	27730 TQ	USBLS	5/15
	St. Louis MSA, MO-IL	Y	21860 FQ	25180 MW	29300 TQ	USBLS	5/15
	Montana	Y	21970 FQ	24790 MW	28920 TQ	USBLS	5/15
	Billings MSA, MT	Y	23330 FQ	26770 MW	30210 TQ	USBLS	5/15
	Nebraska	Y	21575 FQ	24065 MW	27980 TQ	NEBLS	7/16-9/16
	Omaha-Council Bluffs MSA, NE-IA	Y	22260 FQ	25010 MW	28800 TQ	NEBLS	7/16-9/16
	Nevada	Y	24460 FQ	27910 MW	31360 TQ	USBLS	5/15
	Las Vegas-Henderson-Paradise MSA, NV	Y	24500 FQ	28170 MW	32450 TQ	USBLS	5/15
	New Hampshire	H	11.02 AE	13.68 MW	15.36 AEX	NHBLS	6/16
	Manchester NECTA, NH	H	11.42 AE	14.05 MW	15.49 AEX	NHBLS	6/16
	Nashua NECTA, NH-MA	Y	23550 FQ	27320 MW	31010 TQ	USBLS	5/15
	New Jersey	Y	24890 FQ	28320 MW	32210 TQ	USBLS	5/15
	Camden PMSA, NJ	Y	24390 FQ	28240 MW	33730 TQ	USBLS	5/15
	Newark PMSA, NJ-PA	Y	25460 FQ	28630 MW	32360 TQ	USBLS	5/15
	Trenton MSA, NJ	Y	26090 FQ	29040 MW	32520 TQ	USBLS	5/15
	New Mexico	Y	21590 FQ	24190 MW	28320 TQ	USBLS	5/15
	Albuquerque MSA, NM	Y	22310 FQ	25090 MW	28820 TQ	USBLS	5/15
	New York	Y	23380 AE	28830 MW	32740 AEX	NYBLS	1/16-3/16
	Buffalo-Cheektowaga-Niagara Falls MSA, NY	Y	22940 FQ	27570 MW	34740 TQ	USBLS	5/15
	Nassau County-Suffolk County PMSA, NY	Y	26650 FQ	29990 MW	35700 TQ	USBLS	5/15
	New York-Jersey City-White Plains PMSA, NY-NJ	Y	24880 FQ	28270 MW	32070 TQ	USBLS	5/15
	Rochester MSA, NY	Y	23440 FQ	27350 MW	30630 TQ	USBLS	5/15
	North Carolina	Y	24720 FQ	28090 MW	31490 TQ	USBLS	5/15
	Charlotte-Concord-Gastonia MSA, NC-SC	Y	24060 FQ	27580 MW	30870 TQ	USBLS	5/15
	Raleigh MSA, NC	Y	23820 FQ	28070 MW	33440 TQ	USBLS	5/15
	North Dakota	Y	23270 FQ	27490 MW	32270 TQ	USBLS	5/15

AE	Average entry wage	AWR	Average wage range	H	Hourly	LR	Low end range	MTC	Median total compensation	TCC	Total cash compensation
AEX	Average experienced wage	B	Biweekly	HI	Highest wage paid	M	Monthly	MW	Median wage paid	TQ	Third quartile wage
ATC	Average total compensation	D	Daily	HR	High end range	MCC	Median cash compensation	MWR	Median wage range	W	Weekly
AW	Average wage paid	FQ	First quartile wage	LO	Lowest wage paid	ME	Median entry wage	S	See annotated source	Y	Yearly

Occupation/Type/Industry	Location	Per	Low	Mid	High	Source	Date
Teller	Fargo MSA, ND-MN	Y	22370 FQ	25420 MW	29870 TQ	USBLS	5/15
	Ohio	Y	21580 FQ	24210 MW	28670 TQ	USBLS	5/15
	Cincinnati MSA, OH-KY-IN	Y	21690 FQ	24150 MW	28220 TQ	USBLS	5/15
	Cleveland-Elyria MSA, OH	Y	23030 FQ	26620 MW	30860 TQ	USBLS	5/15
	Columbus MSA, OH	Y	21290 FQ	23420 MW	27010 TQ	USBLS	5/15
	Oklahoma	Y	20920 FQ	23760 MW	28000 TQ	USBLS	5/15
	Oklahoma City MSA, OK	Y	20770 FQ	23680 MW	27530 TQ	USBLS	5/15
	Tulsa MSA, OK	Y	22450 FQ	25960 MW	30020 TQ	USBLS	5/15
	Oregon	H	11.43 FQ	13.06 MW	14.66 TQ	ORBLS	2016
	Portland-Vancouver-Hillsboro MSA, OR-WA	Y	24620 FQ	27650 MW	30660 TQ	USBLS	5/15
	Pennsylvania	Y	21950 FQ	25390 MW	30030 TQ	USBLS	5/15
	Allentown-Bethlehem-Easton MSA, PA-NJ	Y	22090 FQ	25140 MW	29830 TQ	USBLS	5/15
	Harrisburg-Carlisle MSA, PA	Y	23170 FQ	26820 MW	30550 TQ	USBLS	5/15
	Montgomery County-Bucks County-Chester County PMSA, PA	Y	21970 FQ	27440 MW	32140 TQ	USBLS	5/15
	Philadelphia PMSA, PA	Y	23760 FQ	28430 MW	33540 TQ	USBLS	5/15
	Pittsburgh MSA, PA	Y	21460 FQ	23960 MW	28610 TQ	USBLS	5/15
	Rhode Island	Y	23290 FQ	27800 MW	34210 TQ	USBLS	5/15
	Providence-Warwick MSA, RI-MA	Y	23420 FQ	27740 MW	33700 TQ	USBLS	5/15
	South Carolina	Y	24000 FQ	27720 MW	31490 TQ	USBLS	5/15
	Charleston-North Charleston MSA, SC	Y	24480 FQ	28440 MW	33470 TQ	USBLS	5/15
	Columbia MSA, SC	Y	23520 FQ	27030 MW	30250 TQ	USBLS	5/15
	Greenville-Anderson-Mauldin MSA, SC	Y	25260 FQ	28820 MW	33430 TQ	USBLS	5/15
	South Dakota	Y	21870 FQ	24240 MW	28240 TQ	USBLS	5/15
	Sioux Falls MSA, SD	Y	21590 FQ	23720 MW	27020 TQ	USBLS	5/15
	Tennessee	Y	21870 FQ	24880 MW	29350 TQ	USBLS	5/15
	Knoxville MSA, TN	Y	22560 FQ	25910 MW	30060 TQ	USBLS	5/15
	Memphis MSA, TN-MS-AR	Y	22660 FQ	26250 MW	29960 TQ	USBLS	5/15
	Nashville-Davidson–Murfreesboro–Franklin MSA, TN	Y	22400 FQ	25330 MW	30140 TQ	USBLS	5/15
	Texas	Y	21560 FQ	24530 MW	29110 TQ	USBLS	5/15
	Austin-Round Rock MSA, TX	Y	23140 FQ	26550 MW	30150 TQ	USBLS	5/15
	Dallas-Plano-Irving PMSA, TX	Y	22110 FQ	25410 MW	30380 TQ	USBLS	5/15
	Fort Worth-Arlington PMSA, TX	Y	21450 FQ	24090 MW	28060 TQ	USBLS	5/15
	Houston-The Woodlands-Sugar Land MSA, TX	Y	22010 FQ	24930 MW	29370 TQ	USBLS	5/15
	San Antonio-New Braunfels MSA, TX	Y	22350 FQ	25310 MW	30660 TQ	USBLS	5/15
	Utah	Y	21500 FQ	23750 MW	27890 TQ	USBLS	5/15
	Ogden-Clearfield MSA, UT	Y	20700 FQ	23230 MW	27110 TQ	USBLS	5/15
	Provo-Orem MSA, UT	Y	21680 FQ	23860 MW	28450 TQ	USBLS	5/15
	Salt Lake City MSA, UT	Y	21610 FQ	23780 MW	27880 TQ	USBLS	5/15
	Vermont	Y	23660 FQ	27370 MW	30780 TQ	USBLS	5/15
	Burlington-South Burlington MSA, VT	Y	24800 FQ	28360 MW	33450 TQ	USBLS	5/15
	Virginia	Y	25100 FQ	29070 MW	35130 TQ	USBLS	5/15
	Richmond MSA, VA	Y	24810 FQ	28420 MW	32900 TQ	USBLS	5/15
	Virginia Beach-Norfolk-Newport News MSA, VA-NC	Y	24700 FQ	28390 MW	33690 TQ	USBLS	5/15
	Washington	H	12.58 FQ	14.16 MW	16.33 TQ	WABLS	3/16
	Seattle-Bellevue-Everett PMSA, WA	H	12.99 FQ	14.48 MW	16.91 TQ	WABLS	3/16
	Tacoma-Lakewood PMSA, WA	H	12.73 FQ	14.09 MW	15.48 TQ	WABLS	3/16
	West Virginia	Y	19800 FQ	22660 MW	26100 TQ	USBLS	5/15
	Huntington-Ashland MSA, WV-KY-OH	Y	18850 FQ	21570 MW	24520 TQ	USBLS	5/15
	Wisconsin	Y	21840 FQ	24890 MW	29770 TQ	USBLS	5/15
	Madison MSA, WI	Y	22010 FQ	25590 MW	29950 TQ	USBLS	5/15
	Milwaukee-Waukesha-West Allis MSA, WI	Y	22090 FQ	25070 MW	31510 TQ	USBLS	5/15
	Wyoming	Y	22390 FQ	25380 MW	29040 TQ	USBLS	5/15
	Cheyenne MSA, WY	Y	22140 FQ	25770 MW	29100 TQ	USBLS	5/15
	Puerto Rico	Y	16760 FQ	18030 MW	19300 TQ	USBLS	5/15

AE	Average entry wage	AWR	Average wage range	H	Hourly
AEX	Average experienced wage	B	Biweekly	HI	Highest wage paid
ATC	Average total compensation	D	Daily	HR	High end range
AW	Average wage paid	FQ	First quartile wage	LO	Lowest wage paid

LR	Low end range	MTC	Median total compensation
M	Monthly	MW	Median wage paid
MCC	Median cash compensation	MWR	Median wage range
ME	Median entry wage	S	See annotated source

TCC	Total cash compensation
TQ	Third quartile wage
W	Weekly
Y	Yearly

Occupation/Type/Industry	Location	Per	Low	Mid	High	Source	Date
Teller	San Juan-Carolina-Caguas						
	MSA, PR	Y	16750 FQ	18000 MW	19260 TQ	USBLS	5/15
	Guam	Y	20650 FQ	22890 MW	26140 TQ	USBLS	5/15
Tennis Instructor							
Municipal Government	Seattle, WA	H	20.97 LO		24.32 HI	CSSS	1/13/16
Tenprint Supervisor							
Municipal Government	Seattle, WA	H	32.35 LO		37.67 HI	CSSS	1/13/16
Terrazzo Worker and Finisher	California	H	18.05 FQ	23.56 MW	30.77 TQ	CABLS	1/16-3/16
	Anaheim-Santa Ana-Irvine						
	PMSA, CA	H	17.71 FQ	24.68 MW	33.56 TQ	CABLS	1/16-3/16
	Los Angeles-Long Beach-						
	Glendale PMSA, CA	H	20.25 FQ	25.96 MW	28.84 TQ	CABLS	1/16-3/16
	Oakland-Hayward-Berkeley						
	PMSA, CA	H	17.53 FQ	21.69 MW	34.14 TQ	CABLS	1/16-3/16
	Florida	H	14.34 AE	17.86 MW	20.40 AEX	FLBLS	7/16-9/16
	Orlando-Kissimmee-Sanford						
	MSA, FL	H	16.82 AE	18.52 MW	19.72 AEX	FLBLS	7/16-9/16
	Maryland	Y	40284 AE	58939 MW	68266 AEX	MDBLS	4/16
	Massachusetts	Y	58070 FQ	87590 MW	95130 TQ	USBLS	5/15
	Michigan	Y	40110 FQ	46820 MW	55040 TQ	USBLS	5/15
	Minnesota	Y	27597 FQ	30301 MW	35467 TQ	MNBLS	1/16-3/16
	Mississippi	Y	19920 FQ	32140 MW	35960 TQ	USBLS	5/15
	New Jersey	Y	29430 FQ	36940 MW	47140 TQ	USBLS	5/15
	New York	Y	27140 AE	57140 MW	88500 AEX	NYBLS	1/16-3/16
	North Carolina	Y	24360 FQ	32750 MW	36450 TQ	USBLS	5/15
	Pennsylvania	Y	35820 FQ	43020 MW	64310 TQ	USBLS	5/15
	Texas	Y	27680 FQ	30820 MW	40480 TQ	USBLS	5/15
	Houston-The Woodlands-						
	Sugar Land MSA, TX	Y	29090 FQ	36240 MW	45710 TQ	USBLS	5/15
	Washington	H	13.28 FQ	15.25 MW	21.89 TQ	WABLS	3/16
	Seattle-Bellevue-Everett						
	PMSA, WA	H	13.24 FQ	15.25 MW	22.07 TQ	WABLS	3/16
	Wisconsin	Y	39230 FQ	46130 MW	55820 TQ	USBLS	5/15
	Puerto Rico	Y	17060 FQ	18510 MW	20280 TQ	USBLS	5/15
	San Juan-Carolina-Caguas						
	MSA, PR	Y	16910 FQ	18260 MW	19720 TQ	USBLS	5/15
Textile Bleaching and Dyeing							
Machine Operator and Tender	Alabama	Y	22271 AE	28749 AW	31988 AEX	ALBLS	6/16
	California	H	9.62 FQ	11.35 MW	14.77 TQ	CABLS	1/16-3/16
	Florida	H	10.11 AE	12.54 MW	13.73 AEX	FLBLS	7/16-9/16
	Georgia	Y	24100 FQ	28750 MW	34750 TQ	USBLS	5/15
	Illinois	Y	26250 FQ	31180 MW	37040 TQ	USBLS	5/15
	Maine	Y	26870 FQ	28680 MW	30480 TQ	USBLS	5/15
	Massachusetts	Y	19730 FQ	32670 MW	37180 TQ	USBLS	5/15
	Michigan	Y	24000 FQ	28860 MW	33870 TQ	USBLS	5/15
	New Hampshire	H	11.78 AE	15.07 MW	17.88 AEX	NHBLS	6/16
	New Jersey	Y	22510 FQ	28700 MW	36530 TQ	USBLS	5/15
	New York	Y	23320 AE	28900 MW	31410 AEX	NYBLS	1/16-3/16
	North Carolina	Y	21940 FQ	25320 MW	29800 TQ	USBLS	5/15
	Pennsylvania	Y	23440 FQ	29050 MW	36840 TQ	USBLS	5/15
	South Carolina	Y	21210 FQ	24970 MW	30770 TQ	USBLS	5/15
	Tennessee	Y	24700 FQ	28620 MW	33480 TQ	USBLS	5/15
	Texas	Y	21570 FQ	23910 MW	28560 TQ	USBLS	5/15
	Utah	Y	22940 FQ	26670 MW	30850 TQ	USBLS	5/15
	Virginia	Y	27380 FQ	30530 MW	35340 TQ	USBLS	5/15
	Washington	H	15.60 FQ	17.01 MW	18.40 TQ	WABLS	3/16
	Wisconsin	Y	20870 FQ	24760 MW	29160 TQ	USBLS	5/15
Textile Cutting Machine Setter,							
Operator, and Tender	Alabama	Y	20533 AE	26713 AW	29798 AEX	ALBLS	6/16
	Arizona	Y	25400 FQ	28490 MW	31570 TQ	USBLS	5/15
	Phoenix-Mesa-Scottsdale						
	MSA, AZ	Y	25360 FQ	28440 MW	31520 TQ	USBLS	5/15
	Arkansas	Y	19020 FQ	22230 MW	26320 TQ	USBLS	5/15
	California	H	9.86 FQ	11.54 MW	13.85 TQ	CABLS	1/16-3/16
	Anaheim-Santa Ana-Irvine						
	PMSA, CA	H	9.34 FQ	9.92 MW	13.72 TQ	CABLS	1/16-3/16

AE	Average entry wage	AWR	Average wage range	H	Hourly
AEX	Average experienced wage	B	Biweekly	HI	Highest wage paid
ATC	Average total compensation	D	Daily	HR	High end range
AW	Average wage paid	FQ	First quartile wage	LO	Lowest wage paid

LR	Low end range	MTC	Median total compensation	TCC	Total cash compensation
M	Monthly	MW	Median wage paid	TQ	Third quartile wage
MCC	Median cash compensation	MWR	Median wage range	W	Weekly
ME	Median entry wage	S	See annotated source	Y	Yearly

Occupation/Type/Industry	Location	Per	Low	Mid	High	Source	Date
Textile Cutting Machine Setter, Operator, and Tender	Los Angeles-Long Beach-Glendale PMSA, CA	H	9.97 FQ	11.60 MW	13.81 TQ	CABLS	1/16-3/16
	Oakland-Hayward-Berkeley PMSA, CA	H	9.97 FQ	11.53 MW	16.82 TQ	CABLS	1/16-3/16
	Riverside-San Bernardino-Ontario MSA, CA	H	10.03 FQ	11.25 MW	12.76 TQ	CABLS	1/16-3/16
	Sacramento–Roseville–Arden-Arcade MSA, CA	H	9.91 FQ	10.89 MW	11.87 TQ	CABLS	1/16-3/16
	San Diego-Carlsbad MSA, CA	H	10.52 FQ	11.48 MW	13.22 TQ	CABLS	1/16-3/16
	Colorado	Y	25280 FQ	29570 MW	35270 TQ	USBLS	5/15
	Denver-Aurora-Lakewood MSA, CO	Y	27410 FQ	30700 MW	35230 TQ	USBLS	5/15
	Connecticut	Y		28264 MW		CTBLS	1/16-3/16
	Florida	H	8.97 AE	11.47 MW	13.56 AEX	FLBLS	7/16-9/16
	Miami-Miami Beach-Kendall PMSA, FL	H	8.90 AE	10.96 MW	12.82 AEX	FLBLS	7/16-9/16
	Tampa-St. Petersburg-Clearwater MSA, FL	H	9.01 AE	10.23 MW	11.76 AEX	FLBLS	7/16-9/16
	Georgia	Y	22710 FQ	28430 MW	34390 TQ	USBLS	5/15
	Atlanta-Sandy Springs-Roswell MSA, GA	Y	23100 FQ	27310 MW	32400 TQ	USBLS	5/15
	Illinois	Y	22720 FQ	26970 MW	34140 TQ	USBLS	5/15
	Chicago-Naperville-Arlington Heights PMSA, IL	Y	22730 FQ	25750 MW	32600 TQ	USBLS	5/15
	Indiana	Y	24500 FQ	29800 MW	37690 TQ	USBLS	5/15
	Iowa	Y	20070 FQ	22480 MW	25510 TQ	USBLS	5/15
	Kansas	Y	17980 FQ	23350 MW	32790 TQ	USBLS	5/15
	Wichita MSA, KS	Y	16910 FQ	18730 MW	24890 TQ	USBLS	5/15
	Kentucky	Y	17370 FQ	19280 MW	22720 TQ	USBLS	5/15
	Louisiana	Y	21940 FQ	24090 MW	28330 TQ	USBLS	5/15
	Maryland	Y	18260 AE	21221 MW	22701 AEX	MDBLS	4/16
	Baltimore-Columbia-Towson MSA, MD	Y	20100 FQ	25020 MW	32340 TQ	USBLS	5/15
	Massachusetts	Y	26170 FQ	32210 MW	38880 TQ	USBLS	5/15
	Boston-Cambridge-Newton NECTA, MA	Y	26210 FQ	30020 MW	39600 TQ	USBLS	5/15
	Worcester MSA, MA-CT	Y	34280 FQ	38100 MW	43610 TQ	USBLS	5/15
	Michigan	Y	22370 FQ	26770 MW	30450 TQ	USBLS	5/15
	Grand Rapids-Wyoming MSA, MI	Y	21930 FQ	28610 MW	33520 TQ	USBLS	5/15
	Minnesota	Y	24157 FQ	28774 MW	34251 TQ	MNBLS	1/16-3/16
	Minneapolis-St. Paul-Bloomington MSA, MN-WI	Y	24208 FQ	28399 MW	32945 TQ	MNBLS	1/16-3/16
	Mississippi	Y	22380 FQ	27180 MW	33320 TQ	USBLS	5/15
	Missouri	Y	21590 FQ	25880 MW	30910 TQ	USBLS	5/15
	Kansas City MSA, MO-KS	Y	26240 FQ	32750 MW	36810 TQ	USBLS	5/15
	St. Louis MSA, MO-IL	Y	20350 FQ	23920 MW	28120 TQ	USBLS	5/15
	New Hampshire	H	12.04 AE	16.18 MW	18.28 AEX	NHBLS	6/16
	New Jersey	Y	19540 FQ	25180 MW	34730 TQ	USBLS	5/15
	Camden PMSA, NJ	Y	23990 FQ	28030 MW	32990 TQ	USBLS	5/15
	Newark PMSA, NJ-PA	Y	21980 FQ	32370 MW	37540 TQ	USBLS	5/15
	New York	Y	22050 AE	28810 MW	34800 AEX	NYBLS	1/16-3/16
	Buffalo-Cheektowaga-Niagara Falls MSA, NY	Y	21990 FQ	25700 MW	31550 TQ	USBLS	5/15
	Nassau County-Suffolk County PMSA, NY	Y	19660 FQ	26280 MW	36340 TQ	USBLS	5/15
	New York-Jersey City-White Plains PMSA, NY-NJ	Y	21320 FQ	27660 MW	31640 TQ	USBLS	5/15
	North Carolina	Y	20690 FQ	26380 MW	34910 TQ	USBLS	5/15
	Charlotte-Concord-Gastonia MSA, NC-SC	Y	21630 FQ	26280 MW	31970 TQ	USBLS	5/15
	Ohio	Y	23100 FQ	26690 MW	29950 TQ	USBLS	5/15
	Cincinnati MSA, OH-KY-IN	Y	19460 FQ	26040 MW	29450 TQ	USBLS	5/15
	Cleveland-Elyria MSA, OH	Y	26260 FQ	28230 MW	30190 TQ	USBLS	5/15
	Oklahoma	Y	21160 FQ	23750 MW	28260 TQ	USBLS	5/15
	Oklahoma City MSA, OK	Y	20860 FQ	24220 MW	29300 TQ	USBLS	5/15
	Oregon	H	10.39 FQ	11.52 MW	13.33 TQ	ORBLS	2016
	Portland-Vancouver-Hillsboro MSA, OR-WA	Y	21730 FQ	24070 MW	28520 TQ	USBLS	5/15
	Pennsylvania	Y	21320 FQ	27510 MW	33590 TQ	USBLS	5/15

AE Average entry wage	**AWR** Average wage range	**H** Hourly	**LR** Low end range	**MTC** Median total compensation	**TCC** Total cash compensation
AEX Average experienced wage	**B** Biweekly	**HI** Highest wage paid	**M** Monthly	**MW** Median wage paid	**TQ** Third quartile wage
ATC Average total compensation	**D** Daily	**HR** High end range	**MCC** Median cash compensation	**MWR** Median wage range	**W** Weekly
AW Average wage paid	**FQ** First quartile wage	**LO** Lowest wage paid	**ME** Median entry wage	**S** See annotated source	**Y** Yearly

Occupation/Type/Industry	Location	Per	Low	Mid	High	Source	Date
Textile Cutting Machine Setter, Operator, and Tender	Allentown-Bethlehem-Easton MSA, PA-NJ	Y	17880 FQ	19860 MW	25390 TQ	USBLS	5/15
	Montgomery County-Bucks County-Chester County PMSA, PA	Y	20170 FQ	31070 MW	43640 TQ	USBLS	5/15
	Philadelphia PMSA, PA	Y	19630 FQ	27140 MW	34030 TQ	USBLS	5/15
	Pittsburgh MSA, PA	Y	24500 FQ	26820 MW	29020 TQ	USBLS	5/15
	Rhode Island	Y	19280 FQ	21780 MW	29430 TQ	USBLS	5/15
	Providence-Warwick MSA, RI-MA	Y	19350 FQ	22870 MW	29730 TQ	USBLS	5/15
	South Carolina	Y	21420 FQ	24240 MW	29630 TQ	USBLS	5/15
	Greenville-Anderson-Mauldin MSA, SC	Y	21090 FQ	23710 MW	27190 TQ	USBLS	5/15
	South Dakota	Y	25880 FQ	28720 MW	32560 TQ	USBLS	5/15
	Tennessee	Y	21130 FQ	24020 MW	29670 TQ	USBLS	5/15
	Knoxville MSA, TN	Y	21290 FQ	24160 MW	30480 TQ	USBLS	5/15
	Texas	Y	17830 FQ	20520 MW	24510 TQ	USBLS	5/15
	Dallas-Plano-Irving PMSA, TX	Y	20250 FQ	23670 MW	29370 TQ	USBLS	5/15
	Fort Worth-Arlington PMSA, TX	Y	17850 FQ	20030 MW	23540 TQ	USBLS	5/15
	Houston-The Woodlands-Sugar Land MSA, TX	Y	16930 FQ	18430 MW	20750 TQ	USBLS	5/15
	Utah	Y	22160 FQ	26240 MW	31190 TQ	USBLS	5/15
	Salt Lake City MSA, UT	Y	22740 FQ	27050 MW	31560 TQ	USBLS	5/15
	Virginia	Y	21090 FQ	27480 MW	43030 TQ	USBLS	5/15
	Washington	H	11.76 FQ	13.58 MW	15.77 TQ	WABLS	3/16
	Seattle-Bellevue-Everett PMSA, WA	H	11.18 FQ	13.93 MW	17.52 TQ	WABLS	3/16
	Wisconsin	Y	21930 FQ	26800 MW	34630 TQ	USBLS	5/15
	Puerto Rico	Y	16710 FQ	17820 MW	18930 TQ	USBLS	5/15
	San Juan-Carolina-Caguas MSA, PR	Y	16830 FQ	18060 MW	19280 TQ	USBLS	5/15
Textile Knitting and Weaving Machine Setter, Operator, and Tender	Alabama	Y	20873 AE	28276 AW	31978 AEX	ALBLS	6/16
	Arkansas	Y	26140 FQ	28180 MW	30230 TQ	USBLS	5/15
	California	H	9.47 FQ	10.33 MW	13.33 TQ	CABLS	1/16-3/16
	Florida	H	10.21 AE	13.05 MW	14.42 AEX	FLBLS	7/16-9/16
	Georgia	Y	24750 FQ	28350 MW	32640 TQ	USBLS	5/15
	Indiana	Y	26060 FQ	28200 MW	30340 TQ	USBLS	5/15
	Kentucky	Y	20630 FQ	23880 MW	28290 TQ	USBLS	5/15
	Maine	Y	25530 FQ	28200 MW	30870 TQ	USBLS	5/15
	Massachusetts	Y	29350 FQ	36410 MW	43090 TQ	USBLS	5/15
	Michigan	Y	22200 FQ	29180 MW	38960 TQ	USBLS	5/15
	Minnesota	Y	22476 FQ	26658 MW	33998 TQ	MNBLS	1/16-3/16
	Mississippi	Y	21360 FQ	31730 MW	35500 TQ	USBLS	5/15
	Missouri	Y	18390 FQ	23210 MW	29840 TQ	USBLS	5/15
	New Hampshire	H	11.96 AE	14.83 MW	18.24 AEX	NHBLS	6/16
	New Jersey	Y	20610 FQ	23780 MW	28620 TQ	USBLS	5/15
	New York	Y	19150 AE	22560 MW	29850 AEX	NYBLS	1/16-3/16
	North Carolina	Y	21210 FQ	25040 MW	30170 TQ	USBLS	5/15
	Ohio	Y	35390 FQ	42040 MW	47150 TQ	USBLS	5/15
	Pennsylvania	Y	23880 FQ	29680 MW	36430 TQ	USBLS	5/15
	Rhode Island	Y	19370 FQ	24650 MW	30980 TQ	USBLS	5/15
	South Carolina	Y	24240 FQ	28630 MW	34740 TQ	USBLS	5/15
	Tennessee	Y	21480 FQ	27500 MW	33240 TQ	USBLS	5/15
	Texas	Y	22420 FQ	27410 MW	33180 TQ	USBLS	5/15
	Utah	Y	22420 FQ	24780 MW	34280 TQ	USBLS	5/15
	Virginia	Y	25740 FQ	28380 MW	31020 TQ	USBLS	5/15
	Washington	H	12.63 FQ	14.39 MW	16.63 TQ	WABLS	3/16
	Wisconsin	Y	22760 FQ	27690 MW	31200 TQ	USBLS	5/15
Textile Winding, Twisting, and Drawing Out Machine Setter, Operator, and Tender	Alabama	Y	24945 AE	32502 AW	36275 AEX	ALBLS	6/16
	California	H	10.38 FQ	12.57 MW	14.67 TQ	CABLS	1/16-3/16
	Connecticut	Y		35553 MW		CTBLS	1/16-3/16
	Florida	H	9.25 AE	13.55 MW	15.70 AEX	FLBLS	7/16-9/16
	Georgia	Y	24700 FQ	28040 MW	31620 TQ	USBLS	5/15

AE Average entry wage	**AWR** Average wage range	**H** Hourly	**LR** Low end range	**MTC** Median total compensation	**TCC** Total cash compensation
AEX Average experienced wage	**B** Biweekly	**HI** Highest wage paid	**M** Monthly	**MW** Median wage paid	**TQ** Third quartile wage
ATC Average total compensation	**D** Daily	**HR** High end range	**MCC** Median cash compensation	**MWR** Median wage range	**W** Weekly
AW Average wage paid	**FQ** First quartile wage	**LO** Lowest wage paid	**ME** Median entry wage	**S** See annotated source	**Y** Yearly

Occupation/Type/Industry	Location	Per	Low	Mid	High	Source	Date
Textile Winding, Twisting, and Drawing Out Machine Setter, Operator, and Tender	Illinois	Y	21580 FQ	25650 MW	30850 TQ	USBLS	5/15
	Indiana	Y	22790 FQ	27070 MW	32980 TQ	USBLS	5/15
	Maine	Y	22340 FQ	27260 MW	31610 TQ	USBLS	5/15
	Massachusetts	Y	26760 FQ	30380 MW	35380 TQ	USBLS	5/15
	Michigan	Y	22980 FQ	30080 MW	35830 TQ	USBLS	5/15
	New Jersey	Y	26050 FQ	29630 MW	34490 TQ	USBLS	5/15
	New York	Y	21460 AE	24490 MW	28240 AEX	NYBLS	1/16-3/16
	North Carolina	Y	21230 FQ	24130 MW	27970 TQ	USBLS	5/15
	Ohio	Y	25320 FQ	27880 MW	30430 TQ	USBLS	5/15
	Pennsylvania	Y	22930 FQ	27290 MW	30910 TQ	USBLS	5/15
	Rhode Island	Y	20920 FQ	22570 MW	24220 TQ	USBLS	5/15
	South Carolina	Y	23030 FQ	27280 MW	30550 TQ	USBLS	5/15
	Tennessee	Y	19460 FQ	24740 MW	28450 TQ	USBLS	5/15
	Texas	Y	25410 FQ	30550 MW	37840 TQ	USBLS	5/15
	Virginia	Y	23320 FQ	28370 MW	35050 TQ	USBLS	5/15
	Washington	H	11.06 FQ	12.88 MW	15.38 TQ	WABLS	3/16
	Wisconsin	Y	25190 FQ	29590 MW	40950 TQ	USBLS	5/15
Theater Facility Manager Municipal Government	Vista, CA	Y			46601 HI	CACIT	6/28/16
Theater Specialist Municipal Government	Palo Alto, CA	Y			88290 HI	CACIT	6/28/16
Theater Technician Community Services Department, Municipal Government	Pleasanton, CA	Y			80030 HI	CACIT	6/28/16
Performing Arts Center, Municipal Government	Big Bear Lake, CA	Y			41100 HI	CACIT	6/28/16
Tile and Marble Setter	Alabama	Y	25090 AE	35438 AW	40613 AEX	ALBLS	6/16
	Birmingham-Hoover MSA, AL	Y	32630 AE	35932 AW	37578 AEX	ALBLS	6/16
	Arizona	Y	28720 FQ	35370 MW	43870 TQ	USBLS	5/15
	Phoenix-Mesa-Scottsdale MSA, AZ	Y	28040 FQ	35530 MW	44350 TQ	USBLS	5/15
	Tucson MSA, AZ	Y	29360 FQ	34520 MW	39110 TQ	USBLS	5/15
	Arkansas	Y	24980 FQ	28460 MW	33190 TQ	USBLS	5/15
	California	H	16.42 FQ	21.90 MW	28.13 TQ	CABLS	1/16-3/16
	Anaheim-Santa Ana-Irvine PMSA, CA	H	14.90 FQ	22.07 MW	30.06 TQ	CABLS	1/16-3/16
	Los Angeles-Long Beach-Glendale PMSA, CA	H	15.44 FQ	20.33 MW	26.12 TQ	CABLS	1/16-3/16
	Oakland-Hayward-Berkeley PMSA, CA	H	14.62 FQ	25.45 MW	29.58 TQ	CABLS	1/16-3/16
	Riverside-San Bernardino-Ontario MSA, CA	H	21.61 FQ	26.75 MW	31.30 TQ	CABLS	1/16-3/16
	Sacramento–Roseville–Arden-Arcade MSA, CA	H	20.72 FQ	24.92 MW	28.96 TQ	CABLS	1/16-3/16
	San Diego-Carlsbad MSA, CA	H	15.38 FQ	19.97 MW	29.65 TQ	CABLS	1/16-3/16
	San Francisco-Redwood City-South San Francisco PMSA, CA	H	18.14 FQ	22.03 MW	27.17 TQ	CABLS	1/16-3/16
	Colorado	Y	31510 FQ	37290 MW	47340 TQ	USBLS	5/15
	Denver-Aurora-Lakewood MSA, CO	Y	35090 FQ	42220 MW	50930 TQ	USBLS	5/15
	Connecticut	Y		56694 MW		CTBLS	1/16-3/16
	Hartford-West Hartford-East Hartford MSA, CT	Y	47640 FQ	53800 MW	58380 TQ	USBLS	5/15
	Delaware	Y	35180 FQ	39710 MW	45650 TQ	USBLS	5/15
	Wilmington PMSA, DE-MD-NJ	Y	35530 FQ	40080 MW	45510 TQ	USBLS	5/15
	Washington-Arlington-Alexandria PMSA, DC-VA-MD-WV	Y	36520 FQ	44280 MW	54420 TQ	USBLS	5/15
	Florida	H	10.69 AE	15.45 MW	18.47 AEX	FLBLS	7/16-9/16
	Fort Lauderdale-Pompano Beach-Deerfield Beach PMSA, FL	H	10.16 AE	14.75 MW	17.18 AEX	FLBLS	7/16-9/16
	Miami-Miami Beach-Kendall PMSA, FL	H	8.86 AE	11.95 MW	15.01 AEX	FLBLS	7/16-9/16

AE	Average entry wage	AWR	Average wage range	H	Hourly
AEX	Average experienced wage	B	Biweekly	HI	Highest wage paid
ATC	Average total compensation	D	Daily	HR	High end range
AW	Average wage paid	FQ	First quartile wage	LO	Lowest wage paid

LR	Low end range	MTC	Median total compensation
M	Monthly	MW	Median wage paid
MCC	Median cash compensation	MWR	Median wage range
ME	Median entry wage	S	See annotated source

TCC	Total cash compensation
TQ	Third quartile wage
W	Weekly
Y	Yearly

Occupation/Type/Industry	Location	Per	Low	Mid	High	Source	Date
Tile and Marble Setter	Orlando-Kissimmee-Sanford MSA, FL	H	11.46 AE	16.85 MW	20.51 AEX	FLBLS	7/16-9/16
	Tampa-St. Petersburg-Clearwater MSA, FL	H	11.20 AE	15.39 MW	16.60 AEX	FLBLS	7/16-9/16
	Georgia	Y	27070 FQ	35590 MW	44900 TQ	USBLS	5/15
	Atlanta-Sandy Springs-Roswell MSA, GA	Y	33600 FQ	40810 MW	47910 TQ	USBLS	5/15
	Augusta-Richmond County MSA, GA-SC	Y	29000 FQ	33820 MW	38750 TQ	USBLS	5/15
	Hawaii	Y	40520 FQ	62750 MW	79520 TQ	USBLS	5/15
	Urban Honolulu MSA, HI	Y	46200 FQ	65850 MW	77730 TQ	USBLS	5/15
	Idaho	Y	26510 FQ	32180 MW	37610 TQ	USBLS	5/15
	Boise City MSA, ID	Y	24370 FQ	31090 MW	35870 TQ	USBLS	5/15
	Illinois	Y	30370 FQ	47110 MW	80580 TQ	USBLS	5/15
	Chicago-Naperville-Arlington Heights PMSA, IL	Y	27330 FQ	46830 MW	83150 TQ	USBLS	5/15
	Lake County-Kenosha County PMSA, IL-WI	Y	36450 FQ	52610 MW	72370 TQ	USBLS	5/15
	Indiana	Y	27140 FQ	37220 MW	50310 TQ	USBLS	5/15
	Indianapolis-Carmel-Anderson MSA, IN	Y	31340 FQ	39970 MW	55660 TQ	USBLS	5/15
	Iowa	Y	30170 FQ	35680 MW	42610 TQ	USBLS	5/15
	Des Moines-West Des Moines MSA, IA	Y	30020 FQ	35610 MW	42650 TQ	USBLS	5/15
	Kansas	Y	41860 FQ	55700 MW	69580 TQ	USBLS	5/15
	Kentucky	Y	28990 FQ	36700 MW	45220 TQ	USBLS	5/15
	Louisville-Jefferson County MSA, KY-IN	Y	26970 FQ	37870 MW	44070 TQ	USBLS	5/15
	Louisiana	Y	27500 FQ	34240 MW	39570 TQ	USBLS	5/15
	Baton Rouge MSA, LA	Y	19000 FQ	33580 MW	40680 TQ	USBLS	5/15
	New Orleans-Metairie MSA, LA	Y	32700 FQ	39450 MW	45690 TQ	USBLS	5/15
	Maryland	Y	35047 AE	47373 MW	53536 AEX	MDBLS	4/16
	Baltimore-Columbia-Towson MSA, MD	Y	37410 FQ	42880 MW	47650 TQ	USBLS	5/15
	Salisbury MSA, MD-DE	Y	23380 FQ	33620 MW	47080 TQ	USBLS	5/15
	Massachusetts	Y	54320 FQ	85320 MW	95750 TQ	USBLS	5/15
	Boston-Cambridge-Newton NECTA, MA	Y	59050 FQ	86320 MW	95580 TQ	USBLS	5/15
	Michigan	Y	37520 FQ	44040 MW	49680 TQ	USBLS	5/15
	Grand Rapids-Wyoming MSA, MI	Y	39840 FQ	44130 MW	48240 TQ	USBLS	5/15
	Minnesota	Y	36718 FQ	43832 MW	51732 TQ	MNBLS	1/16-3/16
	Minneapolis-St. Paul-Bloomington MSA, MN-WI	Y	37868 FQ	43993 MW	49512 TQ	MNBLS	1/16-3/16
	Mississippi	Y	18870 FQ	31440 MW	49970 TQ	USBLS	5/15
	Missouri	Y	34320 FQ	47120 MW	70020 TQ	USBLS	5/15
	Kansas City MSA, MO-KS	Y	33350 FQ	46050 MW	63330 TQ	USBLS	5/15
	St. Louis MSA, MO-IL	Y	37140 FQ	66070 MW	84940 TQ	USBLS	5/15
	Montana	Y	24950 FQ	30750 MW	40450 TQ	USBLS	5/15
	Nebraska	Y	31190 FQ	38335 MW	46500 TQ	NEBLS	7/16-9/16
	Omaha-Council Bluffs MSA, NE-IA	Y	32790 FQ	41540 MW	48815 TQ	NEBLS	7/16-9/16
	Nevada	Y	31730 FQ	38350 MW	49270 TQ	USBLS	5/15
	Las Vegas-Henderson-Paradise MSA, NV	Y	31120 FQ	37060 MW	47580 TQ	USBLS	5/15
	New Hampshire	H	16.70 AE	20.56 MW	26.84 AEX	NHBLS	6/16
	New Jersey	Y	34030 FQ	44480 MW	59650 TQ	USBLS	5/15
	Camden PMSA, NJ	Y	33170 FQ	43050 MW	80040 TQ	USBLS	5/15
	Newark PMSA, NJ-PA	Y	37280 FQ	49430 MW	61520 TQ	USBLS	5/15
	New Mexico	Y	29430 FQ	34710 MW	38750 TQ	USBLS	5/15
	Albuquerque MSA, NM	Y	31460 FQ	36010 MW	49770 TQ	USBLS	5/15
	New York	Y	38930 AE	68720 MW	85860 AEX	NYBLS	1/16-3/16
	Buffalo-Cheektowaga-Niagara Falls MSA, NY	Y	37530 FQ	46410 MW	58940 TQ	USBLS	5/15
	Nassau County-Suffolk County PMSA, NY	Y	46660 FQ	70660 MW	109920 TQ	USBLS	5/15
	New York-Jersey City-White Plains PMSA, NY-NJ	Y	37920 FQ	63110 MW	91740 TQ	USBLS	5/15
	North Carolina	Y	31330 FQ	37560 MW	52470 TQ	USBLS	5/15
	North Dakota	Y	27920 FQ	34260 MW	43560 TQ	USBLS	5/15
	Ohio	Y	39940 FQ	49010 MW	57350 TQ	USBLS	5/15

AE	Average entry wage	AWR	Average wage range	H	Hourly
AEX	Average experienced wage	B	Biweekly	HI	Highest wage paid
ATC	Average total compensation	D	Daily	HR	High end range
AW	Average wage paid	FQ	First quartile wage	LO	Lowest wage paid

LR	Low end range	MTC	Median total compensation
M	Monthly	MW	Median wage paid
MCC	Median cash compensation	MWR	Median wage range
ME	Median entry wage	S	See annotated source

TCC	Total cash compensation
TQ	Third quartile wage
W	Weekly
Y	Yearly

Occupation/Type/Industry	Location	Per	Low	Mid	High	Source	Date
Tile and Marble Setter	Cincinnati MSA, OH-KY-IN	Y	28210 FQ	40690 MW	51250 TQ	USBLS	5/15
	Cleveland-Elyria MSA, OH	Y	50270 FQ	54940 MW	59560 TQ	USBLS	5/15
	Columbus MSA, OH	Y	39470 FQ	46240 MW	55290 TQ	USBLS	5/15
	Oklahoma	Y	26250 FQ	30080 MW	35830 TQ	USBLS	5/15
	Oklahoma City MSA, OK	Y	25320 FQ	28020 MW	30740 TQ	USBLS	5/15
	Tulsa MSA, OK	Y	29920 FQ	34070 MW	38350 TQ	USBLS	5/15
	Oregon	H	14.23 FQ	17.97 MW	22.56 TQ	ORBLS	2016
	Portland-Vancouver-Hillsboro MSA, OR-WA	Y	30240 FQ	40070 MW	46080 TQ	USBLS	5/15
	Pennsylvania	Y	28940 FQ	39240 MW	54790 TQ	USBLS	5/15
	Allentown-Bethlehem-Easton MSA, PA-NJ	Y	32400 FQ	41480 MW	48050 TQ	USBLS	5/15
	Montgomery County-Bucks County-Chester County PMSA, PA	Y	23620 FQ	35550 MW	63290 TQ	USBLS	5/15
	Philadelphia PMSA, PA	Y	33380 FQ	39250 MW	48630 TQ	USBLS	5/15
	Pittsburgh MSA, PA	Y	33370 FQ	44940 MW	54720 TQ	USBLS	5/15
	Rhode Island	Y	28670 FQ	36280 MW	64550 TQ	USBLS	5/15
	Providence-Warwick MSA, RI-MA	Y	28720 FQ	36550 MW	65140 TQ	USBLS	5/15
	South Carolina	Y	23510 FQ	32490 MW	41080 TQ	USBLS	5/15
	Charleston-North Charleston MSA, SC	Y	21510 FQ	31490 MW	37960 TQ	USBLS	5/15
	Columbia MSA, SC	Y	32380 FQ	37640 MW	48760 TQ	USBLS	5/15
	Greenville-Anderson-Mauldin MSA, SC	Y	20990 FQ	26770 MW	42000 TQ	USBLS	5/15
	South Dakota	Y	40460 FQ	44280 MW	48090 TQ	USBLS	5/15
	Sioux Falls MSA, SD	Y	42030 FQ	46010 MW	50250 TQ	USBLS	5/15
	Tennessee	Y	30300 FQ	35270 MW	40760 TQ	USBLS	5/15
	Memphis MSA, TN-MS-AR	Y	32770 FQ	35860 MW	38950 TQ	USBLS	5/15
	Nashville-Davidson–Murfreesboro–Franklin MSA, TN	Y	29960 FQ	35600 MW	44100 TQ	USBLS	5/15
	Texas	Y	25600 FQ	31430 MW	37570 TQ	USBLS	5/15
	Austin-Round Rock MSA, TX	Y	28080 FQ	33470 MW	37600 TQ	USBLS	5/15
	Dallas-Plano-Irving PMSA, TX	Y	25630 FQ	33360 MW	42230 TQ	USBLS	5/15
	Fort Worth-Arlington PMSA, TX	Y	25330 FQ	32200 MW	38670 TQ	USBLS	5/15
	Houston-The Woodlands-Sugar Land MSA, TX	Y	26550 FQ	32850 MW	37800 TQ	USBLS	5/15
	San Antonio-New Braunfels MSA, TX	Y	21680 FQ	24350 MW	29250 TQ	USBLS	5/15
	Utah	Y	31990 FQ	37020 MW	44280 TQ	USBLS	5/15
	Ogden-Clearfield MSA, UT	Y	35810 FQ	42230 MW	46810 TQ	USBLS	5/15
	Provo-Orem MSA, UT	Y	31360 FQ	35590 MW	40000 TQ	USBLS	5/15
	Salt Lake City MSA, UT	Y	32600 FQ	37710 MW	45510 TQ	USBLS	5/15
	Vermont	Y	33180 FQ	35950 MW	38730 TQ	USBLS	5/15
	Virginia	Y	35480 FQ	43180 MW	51360 TQ	USBLS	5/15
	Richmond MSA, VA	Y	40030 FQ	43960 MW	47890 TQ	USBLS	5/15
	Virginia Beach-Norfolk-Newport News MSA, VA-NC	Y	27210 FQ	29510 MW	36500 TQ	USBLS	5/15
	Washington	H	20.48 FQ	24.12 MW	29.26 TQ	WABLS	3/16
	Seattle-Bellevue-Everett PMSA, WA	H	21.47 FQ	24.67 MW	29.62 TQ	WABLS	3/16
	Tacoma-Lakewood PMSA, WA	H	22.33 FQ	25.74 MW	28.27 TQ	WABLS	3/16
	Wisconsin	Y	38450 FQ	48380 MW	64750 TQ	USBLS	5/15
	Madison MSA, WI	Y	51290 FQ	68200 MW	74670 TQ	USBLS	5/15
	Milwaukee-Waukesha-West Allis MSA, WI	Y	51710 FQ	59830 MW	72050 TQ	USBLS	5/15
	Wyoming	Y	24770 FQ	29410 MW	36950 TQ	USBLS	5/15
	Puerto Rico	Y	17000 FQ	18820 MW	25240 TQ	USBLS	5/15
Timing Device Assembler and Adjuster	Illinois	Y	32920 FQ	45790 MW	61770 TQ	USBLS	5/15
	Minnesota	Y	27012 FQ	31963 MW	42037 TQ	MNBLS	1/16-3/16
	Ohio	Y	21390 FQ	24000 MW	29030 TQ	USBLS	5/15
	Texas	Y	31270 FQ	42010 MW	48790 TQ	USBLS	5/15
	Virginia	Y	24570 FQ	42020 MW	58640 TQ	USBLS	5/15
	Wisconsin	Y	40440 FQ	51390 MW	57340 TQ	USBLS	5/15
Timing Director	United States	W		2000 MW		TAG01	2016

AE	Average entry wage	AWR	Average wage range	H	Hourly
AEX	Average experienced wage	B	Biweekly	HI	Highest wage paid
ATC	Average total compensation	D	Daily	HR	High end range
AW	Average wage paid	FQ	First quartile wage	LO	Lowest wage paid

LR	Low end range	MTC	Median total compensation	TCC	Total cash compensation
M	Monthly	MW	Median wage paid	TQ	Third quartile wage
MCC	Median cash compensation	MWR	Median wage range	W	Weekly
ME	Median entry wage	S	See annotated source	Y	Yearly

Occupation/Type/Industry	Location	Per	Low	Mid	High	Source	Date
Tiny Tot Instructor							
Recreation Department, Municipal Government	Alameda, CA	Y		11249 AW		CACIT	6/28/16
Tiny Tot Specialist							
Municipal Government	Chula Vista, CA	Y		8175 AW		CACIT	6/28/16
Municipal Government	Fremont, CA	Y		37610 AW		CACIT	6/28/16
Tire Builder	Alabama	Y	37026 AE	51277 AW	58392 AEX	ALBLS	6/16
	Arizona	Y	23520 FQ	41080 MW	45230 TQ	USBLS	5/15
	California	H	13.08 FQ	15.31 MW	18.01 TQ	CABLS	1/16-3/16
	Florida	H	11.79 AE	14.06 MW	15.45 AEX	FLBLS	7/16-9/16
	Georgia	Y	32820 FQ	40030 MW	44940 TQ	USBLS	5/15
	Idaho	Y	25570 FQ	28370 MW	31180 TQ	USBLS	5/15
	Illinois	Y	29140 FQ	35910 MW	47110 TQ	USBLS	5/15
	Iowa	Y	32480 FQ	42820 MW	50030 TQ	USBLS	5/15
	Kentucky	Y	22290 FQ	24510 MW	30840 TQ	USBLS	5/15
	Maine	Y	26350 FQ	29280 MW	32820 TQ	USBLS	5/15
	Minnesota	Y	26476 FQ	30039 MW	35993 TQ	MNBLS	1/16-3/16
	Missouri	Y	22730 FQ	27920 MW	35470 TQ	USBLS	5/15
	Nebraska	Y	24350 FQ	27655 MW	31100 TQ	NEBLS	7/16-9/16
	North Carolina	Y	36500 FQ	44210 MW	52380 TQ	USBLS	5/15
	Ohio	Y	31310 FQ	38270 MW	50530 TQ	USBLS	5/15
	Oklahoma	Y	19110 FQ	27620 MW	45020 TQ	USBLS	5/15
	Oregon	H	12.54 FQ	14.04 MW	15.66 TQ	ORBLS	2016
	Pennsylvania	Y	26490 FQ	29000 MW	32680 TQ	USBLS	5/15
	South Carolina	Y	29660 FQ	39570 MW	50950 TQ	USBLS	5/15
	South Dakota	Y	27530 FQ	30170 MW	33980 TQ	USBLS	5/15
	Texas	Y	23100 FQ	26990 MW	31310 TQ	USBLS	5/15
	Virginia	Y	37220 FQ	52680 MW	57620 TQ	USBLS	5/15
	Wisconsin	Y	25900 FQ	28620 MW	31740 TQ	USBLS	5/15
Tire Repairer and Changer	Alabama	Y	17910 AE	24449 AW	27714 AEX	ALBLS	6/16
	Birmingham-Hoover MSA, AL	Y	17991 AE	27754 AW	32636 AEX	ALBLS	6/16
	Alaska	Y	26150 FQ	28950 MW	31840 TQ	USBLS	5/15
	Anchorage MSA, AK	Y	26630 FQ	28960 MW	31310 TQ	USBLS	5/15
	Arizona	Y	20120 FQ	22720 MW	26410 TQ	USBLS	5/15
	Phoenix-Mesa-Scottsdale MSA, AZ	Y	20530 FQ	23170 MW	27880 TQ	USBLS	5/15
	Tucson MSA, AZ	Y	19210 FQ	21890 MW	24640 TQ	USBLS	5/15
	Arkansas	Y	18390 FQ	21760 MW	27420 TQ	USBLS	5/15
	Little Rock-North Little Rock-Conway MSA, AR	Y	18920 FQ	22290 MW	26850 TQ	USBLS	5/15
	California	H	9.97 FQ	12.52 MW	16.93 TQ	CABLS	1/16-3/16
	Anaheim-Santa Ana-Irvine PMSA, CA	H	10.02 FQ	11.85 MW	14.82 TQ	CABLS	1/16-3/16
	Los Angeles-Long Beach-Glendale PMSA, CA	H	10.26 FQ	15.20 MW	18.95 TQ	CABLS	1/16-3/16
	Oakland-Hayward-Berkeley PMSA, CA	H	11.64 FQ	14.97 MW	19.84 TQ	CABLS	1/16-3/16
	Riverside-San Bernardino-Ontario MSA, CA	H	9.54 FQ	11.52 MW	15.24 TQ	CABLS	1/16-3/16
	Sacramento–Roseville–Arden-Arcade MSA, CA	H	9.45 FQ	10.68 MW	14.70 TQ	CABLS	1/16-3/16
	San Diego-Carlsbad MSA, CA	H	10.98 FQ	12.96 MW	16.14 TQ	CABLS	1/16-3/16
	San Francisco-Redwood City-South San Francisco PMSA, CA	H	14.60 FQ	17.29 MW	20.49 TQ	CABLS	1/16-3/16
	Colorado	Y	21610 FQ	25130 MW	29420 TQ	USBLS	5/15
	Denver-Aurora-Lakewood MSA, CO	Y	21590 FQ	25360 MW	29200 TQ	USBLS	5/15
	Connecticut	Y		23959 MW		CTBLS	1/16-3/16
	Bridgeport-Stamford-Norwalk MSA, CT	Y	20090 FQ	23870 MW	27820 TQ	USBLS	5/15
	Hartford-West Hartford-East Hartford MSA, CT	Y	19740 FQ	21330 MW	23660 TQ	USBLS	5/15
	Delaware	Y	18230 FQ	20990 MW	30170 TQ	USBLS	5/15
	Wilmington PMSA, DE-MD-NJ	Y	18270 FQ	20360 MW	34500 TQ	USBLS	5/15
	Washington-Arlington-Alexandria PMSA, DC-VA-MD-WV	Y	19010 FQ	24530 MW	33120 TQ	USBLS	5/15

AE	Average entry wage	AWR	Average wage range	H	Hourly	LR	Low end range	MTC	Median total compensation	TCC	Total cash compensation
AEX	Average experienced wage	B	Biweekly	HI	Highest wage paid	M	Monthly	MW	Median wage paid	TQ	Third quartile wage
ATC	Average total compensation	D	Daily	HR	High end range	MCC	Median cash compensation	MWR	Median wage range	W	Weekly
AW	Average wage paid	FQ	First quartile wage	LO	Lowest wage paid	ME	Median entry wage	S	See annotated source	Y	Yearly

1591

Occupation/Type/Industry	Location	Per	Low	Mid	High	Source	Date
Tire Repairer and Changer	Florida	H	8.91 AE	9.43 MW	11.14 AEX	FLBLS	7/16-9/16
	Fort Lauderdale-Pompano Beach-Deerfield Beach PMSA, FL	H	8.86 AE	9.61 MW	13.11 AEX	FLBLS	7/16-9/16
	Miami-Miami Beach-Kendall PMSA, FL	H	8.90 AE	9.71 MW	10.88 AEX	FLBLS	7/16-9/16
	Orlando-Kissimmee-Sanford MSA, FL	H	8.83 AE	9.41 MW	11.47 AEX	FLBLS	7/16-9/16
	Tampa-St. Petersburg-Clearwater MSA, FL	H	8.93 AE	9.31 MW	10.33 AEX	FLBLS	7/16-9/16
	Georgia	Y	19970 FQ	22870 MW	26980 TQ	USBLS	5/15
	Atlanta-Sandy Springs-Roswell MSA, GA	Y	21140 FQ	24360 MW	29530 TQ	USBLS	5/15
	Augusta-Richmond County MSA, GA-SC	Y	20090 FQ	22260 MW	24440 TQ	USBLS	5/15
	Hawaii	Y	23020 FQ	30500 MW	42410 TQ	USBLS	5/15
	Urban Honolulu MSA, HI	Y	24390 FQ	33300 MW	43930 TQ	USBLS	5/15
	Idaho	Y	22650 FQ	27320 MW	33090 TQ	USBLS	5/15
	Boise City MSA, ID	Y	25180 FQ	29900 MW	35280 TQ	USBLS	5/15
	Illinois	Y	21720 FQ	26010 MW	32400 TQ	USBLS	5/15
	Chicago-Naperville-Arlington Heights PMSA, IL	Y	21480 FQ	25170 MW	31890 TQ	USBLS	5/15
	Lake County-Kenosha County PMSA, IL-WI	Y	19080 FQ	22910 MW	28230 TQ	USBLS	5/15
	Indiana	Y	21280 FQ	24430 MW	29220 TQ	USBLS	5/15
	Gary PMSA, IN	Y	21720 FQ	24820 MW	28770 TQ	USBLS	5/15
	Indianapolis-Carmel-Anderson MSA, IN	Y	21850 FQ	25090 MW	29940 TQ	USBLS	5/15
	Iowa	Y	22970 FQ	28190 MW	34940 TQ	USBLS	5/15
	Des Moines-West Des Moines MSA, IA	Y	25110 FQ	29990 MW	35650 TQ	USBLS	5/15
	Kansas	Y	22230 FQ	26650 MW	31390 TQ	USBLS	5/15
	Wichita MSA, KS	Y	20200 FQ	23770 MW	29690 TQ	USBLS	5/15
	Kentucky	Y	19460 FQ	22340 MW	25020 TQ	USBLS	5/15
	Louisville-Jefferson County MSA, KY-IN	Y	21780 FQ	24600 MW	30580 TQ	USBLS	5/15
	Louisiana	Y	18040 FQ	21340 MW	25150 TQ	USBLS	5/15
	Baton Rouge MSA, LA	Y	18300 FQ	21310 MW	24400 TQ	USBLS	5/15
	New Orleans-Metairie MSA, LA	Y	23080 FQ	26580 MW	29650 TQ	USBLS	5/15
	Maine	Y	19800 FQ	23480 MW	28680 TQ	USBLS	5/15
	Maryland	Y	17957 AE	24414 MW	27643 AEX	MDBLS	4/16
	Baltimore-Columbia-Towson MSA, MD	Y	18810 FQ	21970 MW	26430 TQ	USBLS	5/15
	Salisbury MSA, MD-DE	Y	20210 FQ	28580 MW	38880 TQ	USBLS	5/15
	Massachusetts	Y	21290 FQ	24570 MW	30750 TQ	USBLS	5/15
	Boston-Cambridge-Newton NECTA, MA	Y	20260 FQ	22350 MW	24430 TQ	USBLS	5/15
	Worcester MSA, MA-CT	Y	23190 FQ	28020 MW	33190 TQ	USBLS	5/15
	Michigan	Y	22020 FQ	26380 MW	29380 TQ	USBLS	5/15
	Detroit-Dearborn-Livonia PMSA, MI	Y	25820 FQ	28060 MW	30310 TQ	USBLS	5/15
	Grand Rapids-Wyoming MSA, MI	Y	21180 FQ	24630 MW	28280 TQ	USBLS	5/15
	Minnesota	Y	23332 FQ	28068 MW	34022 TQ	MNBLS	1/16-3/16
	Minneapolis-St. Paul-Bloomington MSA, MN-WI	Y	22819 FQ	27022 MW	33288 TQ	MNBLS	1/16-3/16
	Mississippi	Y	21130 FQ	24990 MW	29830 TQ	USBLS	5/15
	Jackson MSA, MS	Y	20390 FQ	22650 MW	24980 TQ	USBLS	5/15
	Missouri	Y	19020 FQ	22490 MW	28280 TQ	USBLS	5/15
	Kansas City MSA, MO-KS	Y	19910 FQ	24910 MW	33030 TQ	USBLS	5/15
	St. Louis MSA, MO-IL	Y	20950 FQ	27030 MW	34340 TQ	USBLS	5/15
	Montana	Y	23800 FQ	27510 MW	30740 TQ	USBLS	5/15
	Billings MSA, MT	Y	21990 FQ	26850 MW	35070 TQ	USBLS	5/15
	Nebraska	Y	20965 FQ	24110 MW	29765 TQ	NEBLS	7/16-9/16
	Omaha-Council Bluffs MSA, NE-IA	Y	19870 FQ	23670 MW	33540 TQ	NEBLS	7/16-9/16
	Nevada	Y	20630 FQ	23750 MW	30780 TQ	USBLS	5/15
	Las Vegas-Henderson-Paradise MSA, NV	Y	18800 FQ	21910 MW	24720 TQ	USBLS	5/15
	New Hampshire	H	9.12 AE	11.52 MW	13.61 AEX	NHBLS	6/16
	Manchester NECTA, NH	H	9.75 AE	12.03 MW	13.90 AEX	NHBLS	6/16

AE	Average entry wage	AWR	Average wage range	H	Hourly
AEX	Average experienced wage	B	Biweekly	HI	Highest wage paid
ATC	Average total compensation	D	Daily	HR	High end range
AW	Average wage paid	FQ	First quartile wage	LO	Lowest wage paid

LR	Low end range	MTC	Median total compensation	TCC	Total cash compensation
M	Monthly	MW	Median wage paid	TQ	Third quartile wage
MCC	Median cash compensation	MWR	Median wage range	W	Weekly
ME	Median entry wage	S	See annotated source	Y	Yearly

Occupation/Type/Industry	Location	Per	Low	Mid	High	Source	Date
Tire Repairer and Changer	Nashua NECTA, NH-MA	Y	17740 FQ	20300 MW	23780 TQ	USBLS	5/15
	New Jersey	Y	21510 FQ	26130 MW	30430 TQ	USBLS	5/15
	Camden PMSA, NJ	Y	22630 FQ	26510 MW	29990 TQ	USBLS	5/15
	Newark PMSA, NJ-PA	Y	22310 FQ	26620 MW	30450 TQ	USBLS	5/15
	Trenton MSA, NJ	Y	21330 FQ	27020 MW	31500 TQ	USBLS	5/15
	New Mexico	Y	19500 FQ	24110 MW	28590 TQ	USBLS	5/15
	Albuquerque MSA, NM	Y	23460 FQ	26870 MW	29720 TQ	USBLS	5/15
	New York	Y	21820 AE	28640 MW	36460 AEX	NYBLS	1/16-3/16
	Buffalo-Cheektowaga-Niagara Falls MSA, NY	Y	21370 FQ	23240 MW	25430 TQ	USBLS	5/15
	Nassau County-Suffolk County PMSA, NY	Y	28900 FQ	35180 MW	42230 TQ	USBLS	5/15
	New York-Jersey City-White Plains PMSA, NY-NJ	Y	22280 FQ	27880 MW	39690 TQ	USBLS	5/15
	Rochester MSA, NY	Y	19240 FQ	21360 MW	31540 TQ	USBLS	5/15
	North Carolina	Y	19560 FQ	23040 MW	27990 TQ	USBLS	5/15
	Charlotte-Concord-Gastonia MSA, NC-SC	Y	20670 FQ	26590 MW	30560 TQ	USBLS	5/15
	Raleigh MSA, NC	Y	19450 FQ	22160 MW	25930 TQ	USBLS	5/15
	North Dakota	Y	24970 FQ	28550 MW	33540 TQ	USBLS	5/15
	Fargo MSA, ND-MN	Y	26650 FQ	30050 MW	35970 TQ	USBLS	5/15
	Ohio	Y	19450 FQ	22420 MW	27050 TQ	USBLS	5/15
	Cincinnati MSA, OH-KY-IN	Y	18510 FQ	20260 MW	23760 TQ	USBLS	5/15
	Cleveland-Elyria MSA, OH	Y	20240 FQ	24410 MW	30290 TQ	USBLS	5/15
	Columbus MSA, OH	Y	21040 FQ	22890 MW	24770 TQ	USBLS	5/15
	Oklahoma	Y	19700 FQ	22460 MW	26290 TQ	USBLS	5/15
	Oklahoma City MSA, OK	Y	21910 FQ	24380 MW	28540 TQ	USBLS	5/15
	Tulsa MSA, OK	Y	19230 FQ	21240 MW	23460 TQ	USBLS	5/15
	Oregon	H	11.18 FQ	14.46 MW	17.47 TQ	ORBLS	2016
	Portland-Vancouver-Hillsboro MSA, OR-WA	Y	22760 FQ	30800 MW	36200 TQ	USBLS	5/15
	Pennsylvania	Y	20920 FQ	25630 MW	30840 TQ	USBLS	5/15
	Allentown-Bethlehem-Easton MSA, PA-NJ	Y	22620 FQ	27610 MW	34590 TQ	USBLS	5/15
	Harrisburg-Carlisle MSA, PA	Y	21360 FQ	25630 MW	30810 TQ	USBLS	5/15
	Montgomery County-Bucks County-Chester County PMSA, PA	Y	22140 FQ	27640 MW	33470 TQ	USBLS	5/15
	Philadelphia PMSA, PA	Y	18020 FQ	21220 MW	24480 TQ	USBLS	5/15
	Pittsburgh MSA, PA	Y	20390 FQ	25340 MW	30200 TQ	USBLS	5/15
	Rhode Island	Y	28930 FQ	33380 MW	36640 TQ	USBLS	5/15
	Providence-Warwick MSA, RI-MA	Y	24600 FQ	31110 MW	35510 TQ	USBLS	5/15
	South Carolina	Y	21300 FQ	24480 MW	29750 TQ	USBLS	5/15
	Charleston-North Charleston MSA, SC	Y	21090 FQ	23870 MW	29980 TQ	USBLS	5/15
	Columbia MSA, SC	Y	21910 FQ	24560 MW	29940 TQ	USBLS	5/15
	Greenville-Anderson-Mauldin MSA, SC	Y	22680 FQ	26620 MW	29680 TQ	USBLS	5/15
	South Dakota	Y	22250 FQ	25170 MW	29370 TQ	USBLS	5/15
	Sioux Falls MSA, SD	Y	22870 FQ	25950 MW	29630 TQ	USBLS	5/15
	Tennessee	Y	22520 FQ	29080 MW	41090 TQ	USBLS	5/15
	Knoxville MSA, TN	Y	24050 FQ	28570 MW	33820 TQ	USBLS	5/15
	Memphis MSA, TN-MS-AR	Y	21550 FQ	26320 MW	31580 TQ	USBLS	5/15
	Nashville-Davidson–Murfreesboro–Franklin MSA, TN	Y	25070 FQ	38780 MW	50780 TQ	USBLS	5/15
	Texas	Y	21350 FQ	24360 MW	29150 TQ	USBLS	5/15
	Austin-Round Rock MSA, TX	Y	21830 FQ	24580 MW	28210 TQ	USBLS	5/15
	Dallas-Plano-Irving PMSA, TX	Y	21210 FQ	23840 MW	29740 TQ	USBLS	5/15
	Fort Worth-Arlington PMSA, TX	Y	21750 FQ	24320 MW	28950 TQ	USBLS	5/15
	Houston-The Woodlands-Sugar Land MSA, TX	Y	22080 FQ	25590 MW	29700 TQ	USBLS	5/15
	San Antonio-New Braunfels MSA, TX	Y	22410 FQ	25510 MW	28980 TQ	USBLS	5/15
	Utah	Y	21360 FQ	24780 MW	31540 TQ	USBLS	5/15
	Ogden-Clearfield MSA, UT	Y	21810 FQ	25000 MW	30420 TQ	USBLS	5/15
	Provo-Orem MSA, UT	Y	21340 FQ	26060 MW	31650 TQ	USBLS	5/15
	Salt Lake City MSA, UT	Y	21540 FQ	24770 MW	33650 TQ	USBLS	5/15
	Vermont	Y	26800 FQ	29590 MW	33780 TQ	USBLS	5/15

AE Average entry wage	**AWR** Average wage range	**H** Hourly	**LR** Low end range	**MTC** Median total compensation	**TCC** Total cash compensation
AEX Average experienced wage	**B** Biweekly	**HI** Highest wage paid	**M** Monthly	**MW** Median wage paid	**TQ** Third quartile wage
ATC Average total compensation	**D** Daily	**HR** High end range	**MCC** Median cash compensation	**MWR** Median wage range	**W** Weekly
AW Average wage paid	**FQ** First quartile wage	**LO** Lowest wage paid	**ME** Median entry wage	**S** See annotated source	**Y** Yearly

Occupation/Type/Industry	Location	Per	Low	Mid	High	Source	Date
Tire Repairer and Changer	Burlington-South Burlington						
	MSA, VT	Y	27540 FQ	30060 MW	34580 TQ	USBLS	5/15
	Virginia	Y	23500 FQ	28240 MW	34870 TQ	USBLS	5/15
	Richmond MSA, VA	Y	24430 FQ	32220 MW	40550 TQ	USBLS	5/15
	Virginia Beach-Norfolk-						
	Newport News MSA, VA-NC	Y	24350 FQ	28790 MW	34440 TQ	USBLS	5/15
	Washington	H	11.55 FQ	13.80 MW	16.69 TQ	WABLS	3/16
	Seattle-Bellevue-Everett						
	PMSA, WA	H	11.61 FQ	13.80 MW	16.55 TQ	WABLS	3/16
	Tacoma-Lakewood PMSA, WA	H	11.50 FQ	14.01 MW	17.02 TQ	WABLS	3/16
	West Virginia	Y	19050 FQ	21660 MW	24590 TQ	USBLS	5/15
	Huntington-Ashland MSA,						
	WV-KY-OH	Y	18210 FQ	20020 MW	23120 TQ	USBLS	5/15
	Wisconsin	Y	21060 FQ	26950 MW	34010 TQ	USBLS	5/15
	Madison MSA, WI	Y	26940 FQ	29640 MW	34490 TQ	USBLS	5/15
	Milwaukee-Waukesha-West						
	Allis MSA, WI	Y	24830 FQ	28870 MW	34980 TQ	USBLS	5/15
	Wyoming	Y	23140 FQ	28280 MW	35360 TQ	USBLS	5/15
	Puerto Rico	Y	16800 FQ	18040 MW	19280 TQ	USBLS	5/15
	San Juan-Carolina-Caguas						
	MSA, PR	Y	16900 FQ	18150 MW	19400 TQ	USBLS	5/15
	Virgin Islands	Y	19620 FQ	23280 MW	32110 TQ	USBLS	5/15
	Guam	Y	18290 FQ	19420 MW	25560 TQ	USBLS	5/15
Title Examiner, Abstractor, and							
Searcher	Alabama	Y	22609 AE	33617 AW	39111 AEX	ALBLS	6/16
	Birmingham-Hoover MSA, AL	Y	33597 AE	42088 AW	46328 AEX	ALBLS	6/16
	Alaska	Y	50290 FQ	59980 MW	74610 TQ	USBLS	5/15
	Anchorage MSA, AK	Y	50960 FQ	62940 MW	74630 TQ	USBLS	5/15
	Arizona	Y	40780 FQ	51430 MW	60520 TQ	USBLS	5/15
	Phoenix-Mesa-Scottsdale						
	MSA, AZ	Y	40820 FQ	50680 MW	60720 TQ	USBLS	5/15
	Tucson MSA, AZ	Y	51240 FQ	56150 MW	61010 TQ	USBLS	5/15
	Arkansas	Y	28240 FQ	34810 MW	42080 TQ	USBLS	5/15
	Little Rock-North Little Rock-						
	Conway MSA, AR	Y	29780 FQ	35430 MW	41440 TQ	USBLS	5/15
	California	H	20.01 FQ	25.74 MW	35.14 TQ	CABLS	1/16-3/16
	Anaheim-Santa Ana-Irvine						
	PMSA, CA	H	23.50 FQ	28.49 MW	39.43 TQ	CABLS	1/16-3/16
	Los Angeles-Long Beach-						
	Glendale PMSA, CA	H	17.67 FQ	21.32 MW	24.81 TQ	CABLS	1/16-3/16
	Oakland-Hayward-Berkeley						
	PMSA, CA	H	17.61 FQ	24.20 MW	34.54 TQ	CABLS	1/16-3/16
	Riverside-San Bernardino-						
	Ontario MSA, CA	H	23.00 FQ	27.58 MW	34.83 TQ	CABLS	1/16-3/16
	Sacramento–Roseville–						
	Arden-Arcade MSA, CA	H	20.01 FQ	26.29 MW	32.82 TQ	CABLS	1/16-3/16
	San Diego-Carlsbad MSA, CA	H	23.64 FQ	28.25 MW	37.29 TQ	CABLS	1/16-3/16
	San Francisco-Redwood City-						
	South San Francisco PMSA,						
	CA	H	32.94 FQ	37.38 MW	42.73 TQ	CABLS	1/16-3/16
	Colorado	Y	38060 FQ	46480 MW	61440 TQ	USBLS	5/15
	Denver-Aurora-Lakewood						
	MSA, CO	Y	41100 FQ	47860 MW	68210 TQ	USBLS	5/15
	Connecticut	Y		50593 MW		CTBLS	1/16-3/16
	Bridgeport-Stamford-Norwalk						
	MSA, CT	Y	45670 FQ	55350 MW	61780 TQ	USBLS	5/15
	Hartford-West Hartford-East						
	Hartford MSA, CT	Y	44470 FQ	49220 MW	68060 TQ	USBLS	5/15
	Delaware	Y	40530 FQ	44260 MW	47990 TQ	USBLS	5/15
	Wilmington PMSA, DE-MD-						
	NJ	Y	41500 FQ	44840 MW	48180 TQ	USBLS	5/15
	District of Columbia	Y	56890 FQ	72360 MW	86050 TQ	USBLS	5/15
	Washington-Arlington-						
	Alexandria PMSA, DC-VA-						
	MD-WV	Y	36720 FQ	62890 MW	71640 TQ	USBLS	5/15
	Florida	H	15.14 AE	20.95 MW	25.72 AEX	FLBLS	7/16-9/16
	Fort Lauderdale-Pompano						
	Beach-Deerfield Beach						
	PMSA, FL	H	16.77 AE	20.70 MW	26.63 AEX	FLBLS	7/16-9/16
	Miami-Miami Beach-Kendall						
	PMSA, FL	H	16.31 AE	22.06 MW	25.48 AEX	FLBLS	7/16-9/16

AE	Average entry wage	AWR	Average wage range	H	Hourly	LR	Low end range	MTC	Median total compensation	TCC	Total cash compensation
AEX	Average experienced wage	B	Biweekly	HI	Highest wage paid	M	Monthly	MW	Median wage paid	TQ	Third quartile wage
ATC	Average total compensation	D	Daily	HR	High end range	MCC	Median cash compensation	MWR	Median wage range	W	Weekly
AW	Average wage paid	FQ	First quartile wage	LO	Lowest wage paid	ME	Median entry wage	S	See annotated source	Y	Yearly

Occupation/Type/Industry	Location	Per	Low	Mid	High	Source	Date
Title Examiner, Abstractor, and Searcher							
	Orlando-Kissimmee-Sanford MSA, FL	H	15.89 AE	23.00 MW	28.69 AEX	FLBLS	7/16-9/16
	Tampa-St. Petersburg-Clearwater MSA, FL	H	11.48 AE	16.89 MW	20.39 AEX	FLBLS	7/16-9/16
	Georgia	Y	35370 FQ	45840 MW	59780 TQ	USBLS	5/15
	Atlanta-Sandy Springs-Roswell MSA, GA	Y	39930 FQ	46970 MW	64140 TQ	USBLS	5/15
	Hawaii	Y	42210 FQ	52910 MW	62020 TQ	USBLS	5/15
	Urban Honolulu MSA, HI	Y	40690 FQ	51560 MW	61810 TQ	USBLS	5/15
	Idaho	Y	35740 FQ	46130 MW	62810 TQ	USBLS	5/15
	Boise City MSA, ID	Y	40140 FQ	53920 MW	70270 TQ	USBLS	5/15
	Illinois	Y	29450 FQ	36360 MW	46970 TQ	USBLS	5/15
	Chicago-Naperville-Arlington Heights PMSA, IL	Y	30300 FQ	37580 MW	49990 TQ	USBLS	5/15
	Lake County-Kenosha County PMSA, IL-WI	Y	26850 FQ	31160 MW	40900 TQ	USBLS	5/15
	Indiana	Y	26600 FQ	33030 MW	40440 TQ	USBLS	5/15
	Indianapolis-Carmel-Anderson MSA, IN	Y	32990 FQ	38590 MW	69000 TQ	USBLS	5/15
	Iowa	Y	27630 FQ	31160 MW	44360 TQ	USBLS	5/15
	Des Moines-West Des Moines MSA, IA	Y	29710 FQ	37290 MW	49420 TQ	USBLS	5/15
	Kansas	Y	30260 FQ	37060 MW	48080 TQ	USBLS	5/15
	Wichita MSA, KS	Y	27900 FQ	32170 MW	41370 TQ	USBLS	5/15
	Kentucky	Y	33690 FQ	37190 MW	44140 TQ	USBLS	5/15
	Louisville-Jefferson County MSA, KY-IN	Y	32200 FQ	34870 MW	37540 TQ	USBLS	5/15
	Louisiana	Y	28310 FQ	39420 MW	54670 TQ	USBLS	5/15
	Baton Rouge MSA, LA	Y	47090 FQ	57960 MW	73100 TQ	USBLS	5/15
	New Orleans-Metairie MSA, LA	Y	27630 FQ	34730 MW	55450 TQ	USBLS	5/15
	Maine	Y	36110 FQ	41870 MW	47330 TQ	USBLS	5/15
	Maryland	Y	29853 AE	45297 MW	53020 AEX	MDBLS	4/16
	Baltimore-Columbia-Towson MSA, MD	Y	36140 FQ	43070 MW	47840 TQ	USBLS	5/15
	Massachusetts	Y	43330 FQ	53910 MW	65960 TQ	USBLS	5/15
	Boston-Cambridge-Newton NECTA, MA	Y	53610 FQ	60340 MW	68710 TQ	USBLS	5/15
	Worcester MSA, MA-CT	Y	24320 FQ	47430 MW	66270 TQ	USBLS	5/15
	Michigan	Y	34070 FQ	41990 MW	49290 TQ	USBLS	5/15
	Detroit-Dearborn-Livonia PMSA, MI	Y	42090 FQ	52590 MW	66110 TQ	USBLS	5/15
	Grand Rapids-Wyoming MSA, MI	Y	34620 FQ	42740 MW	49850 TQ	USBLS	5/15
	Minnesota	Y	37792 FQ	45735 MW	57751 TQ	MNBLS	1/16-3/16
	Minneapolis-St. Paul-Bloomington MSA, MN-WI	Y	38840 FQ	46280 MW	57318 TQ	MNBLS	1/16-3/16
	Mississippi	Y	31300 FQ	40460 MW	57370 TQ	USBLS	5/15
	Jackson MSA, MS	Y	31580 FQ	39470 MW	55960 TQ	USBLS	5/15
	Missouri	Y	34600 FQ	42420 MW	48130 TQ	USBLS	5/15
	Kansas City MSA, MO-KS	Y	34630 FQ	43160 MW	53270 TQ	USBLS	5/15
	St. Louis MSA, MO-IL	Y	38780 FQ	43440 MW	47270 TQ	USBLS	5/15
	Montana	Y	27210 FQ	41090 MW	53350 TQ	USBLS	5/15
	Billings MSA, MT	Y	22200 FQ	53240 MW	60520 TQ	USBLS	5/15
	Nebraska	Y	32115 FQ	40140 MW	47015 TQ	NEBLS	7/16-9/16
	Omaha-Council Bluffs MSA, NE-IA	Y	32025 FQ	40205 MW	47260 TQ	NEBLS	7/16-9/16
	Nevada	Y	37840 FQ	53170 MW	67690 TQ	USBLS	5/15
	Las Vegas-Henderson-Paradise MSA, NV	Y	37360 FQ	49710 MW	74030 TQ	USBLS	5/15
	New Hampshire	H	16.66 AE	21.34 MW	24.21 AEX	NHBLS	6/16
	Manchester NECTA, NH	H	18.85 AE	21.86 MW	22.52 AEX	NHBLS	6/16
	New Jersey	Y	32210 FQ	37950 MW	50500 TQ	USBLS	5/15
	Camden PMSA, NJ	Y	32400 FQ	36890 MW	47550 TQ	USBLS	5/15
	Newark PMSA, NJ-PA	Y	31360 FQ	39570 MW	53630 TQ	USBLS	5/15
	Trenton MSA, NJ	Y	35110 FQ	38880 MW	64310 TQ	USBLS	5/15
	New Mexico	Y	29070 FQ	38200 MW	48540 TQ	USBLS	5/15
	Albuquerque MSA, NM	Y	31630 FQ	41910 MW	49910 TQ	USBLS	5/15
	New York	Y	33870 AE	53110 MW	59520 AEX	NYBLS	1/16-3/16
	Nassau County-Suffolk County PMSA, NY	Y	32080 FQ	53580 MW	59750 TQ	USBLS	5/15

AE	Average entry wage	AWR	Average wage range	H	Hourly
AEX	Average experienced wage	B	Biweekly	HI	Highest wage paid
ATC	Average total compensation	D	Daily	HR	High end range
AW	Average wage paid	FQ	First quartile wage	LO	Lowest wage paid

LR	Low end range	MTC	Median total compensation	TCC	Total cash compensation
M	Monthly	MW	Median wage paid	TQ	Third quartile wage
MCC	Median cash compensation	MWR	Median wage range	W	Weekly
ME	Median entry wage	S	See annotated source	Y	Yearly

Occupation/Type/Industry	Location	Per	Low	Mid	High	Source	Date
Title Examiner, Abstractor, and Searcher	New York-Jersey City-White						
	Plains PMSA, NY-NJ	Y	44080 FQ	52930 MW	60090 TQ	USBLS	5/15
	Rochester MSA, NY	Y	29120 FQ	36650 MW	47230 TQ	USBLS	5/15
	North Carolina	Y	30460 FQ	38510 MW	53230 TQ	USBLS	5/15
	Charlotte-Concord-Gastonia						
	MSA, NC-SC	Y	27910 FQ	36540 MW	53820 TQ	USBLS	5/15
	Raleigh MSA, NC	Y	35500 FQ	39100 MW	43790 TQ	USBLS	5/15
	North Dakota	Y	36090 FQ	46490 MW	56380 TQ	USBLS	5/15
	Fargo MSA, ND-MN	Y	42110 FQ	53850 MW	59030 TQ	USBLS	5/15
	Ohio	Y	30260 FQ	38310 MW	48650 TQ	USBLS	5/15
	Cincinnati MSA, OH-KY-IN	Y	32590 FQ	42230 MW	52330 TQ	USBLS	5/15
	Cleveland-Elyria MSA, OH	Y	27550 FQ	31580 MW	41420 TQ	USBLS	5/15
	Columbus MSA, OH	Y	32900 FQ	39260 MW	59790 TQ	USBLS	5/15
	Oklahoma	Y	33110 FQ	42930 MW	60010 TQ	USBLS	5/15
	Oklahoma City MSA, OK	Y	33090 FQ	38340 MW	51090 TQ	USBLS	5/15
	Tulsa MSA, OK	Y	37200 FQ	53830 MW	73470 TQ	USBLS	5/15
	Oregon	H	20.25 FQ	26.53 MW	34.54 TQ	ORBLS	2016
	Portland-Vancouver-Hillsboro						
	MSA, OR-WA	Y	46180 FQ	57630 MW	77350 TQ	USBLS	5/15
	Pennsylvania	Y	31160 FQ	39780 MW	48190 TQ	USBLS	5/15
	Harrisburg-Carlisle MSA, PA	Y	36990 FQ	46670 MW	59090 TQ	USBLS	5/15
	Montgomery County-Bucks						
	County-Chester County						
	PMSA, PA	Y	39760 FQ	45820 MW	58870 TQ	USBLS	5/15
	Philadelphia PMSA, PA	Y	35510 FQ	40300 MW	51180 TQ	USBLS	5/15
	Pittsburgh MSA, PA	Y	29760 FQ	39550 MW	46750 TQ	USBLS	5/15
	Rhode Island	Y	34070 FQ	49230 MW	59460 TQ	USBLS	5/15
	Providence-Warwick MSA, RI-						
	MA	Y	34070 FQ	49230 MW	59460 TQ	USBLS	5/15
	South Carolina	Y	29250 FQ	36330 MW	45080 TQ	USBLS	5/15
	Charleston-North Charleston						
	MSA, SC	Y	28110 FQ	35060 MW	55240 TQ	USBLS	5/15
	Columbia MSA, SC	Y	34190 FQ	40380 MW	48080 TQ	USBLS	5/15
	Greenville-Anderson-Mauldin						
	MSA, SC	Y	26320 FQ	33060 MW	47530 TQ	USBLS	5/15
	South Dakota	Y	34810 FQ	43270 MW	62360 TQ	USBLS	5/15
	Sioux Falls MSA, SD	Y	38910 FQ	55750 MW	69150 TQ	USBLS	5/15
	Tennessee	Y	28310 FQ	34610 MW	43130 TQ	USBLS	5/15
	Knoxville MSA, TN	Y	29870 FQ	38730 MW	48240 TQ	USBLS	5/15
	Memphis MSA, TN-MS-AR	Y	27850 FQ	35280 MW	46300 TQ	USBLS	5/15
	Nashville-Davidson–						
	Murfreesboro–Franklin						
	MSA, TN	Y	27880 FQ	30980 MW	39320 TQ	USBLS	5/15
	Texas	Y	36110 FQ	50580 MW	79810 TQ	USBLS	5/15
	Austin-Round Rock MSA, TX	Y	43670 FQ	50940 MW	88490 TQ	USBLS	5/15
	Dallas-Plano-Irving PMSA, TX	Y	37710 FQ	49500 MW	82090 TQ	USBLS	5/15
	Fort Worth-Arlington PMSA,						
	TX	Y	38630 FQ	53020 MW	67710 TQ	USBLS	5/15
	Houston-The Woodlands-						
	Sugar Land MSA, TX	Y	38740 FQ	66550 MW	97540 TQ	USBLS	5/15
	San Antonio-New Braunfels						
	MSA, TX	Y	41140 FQ	52550 MW	68720 TQ	USBLS	5/15
	Utah	Y	37660 FQ	45290 MW	56230 TQ	USBLS	5/15
	Ogden-Clearfield MSA, UT	Y	39750 FQ	43610 MW	47450 TQ	USBLS	5/15
	Provo-Orem MSA, UT	Y	45060 FQ	52270 MW	58780 TQ	USBLS	5/15
	Salt Lake City MSA, UT	Y	35780 FQ	50630 MW	61320 TQ	USBLS	5/15
	Vermont	Y	42680 FQ	45790 MW	48900 TQ	USBLS	5/15
	Virginia	Y	34260 FQ	41250 MW	65790 TQ	USBLS	5/15
	Richmond MSA, VA	Y	33020 FQ	35640 MW	38260 TQ	USBLS	5/15
	Virginia Beach-Norfolk-						
	Newport News MSA, VA-NC	Y	34140 FQ	36660 MW	39180 TQ	USBLS	5/15
	Washington	H	18.23 FQ	22.23 MW	27.15 TQ	WABLS	3/16
	Seattle-Bellevue-Everett						
	PMSA, WA	H	18.44 FQ	22.90 MW	28.04 TQ	WABLS	3/16
	Tacoma-Lakewood PMSA, WA	H	17.06 FQ	21.11 MW	24.14 TQ	WABLS	3/16
	West Virginia	Y	39520 FQ	46140 MW	57490 TQ	USBLS	5/15
	Wisconsin	Y	31670 FQ	38410 MW	48270 TQ	USBLS	5/15
	Madison MSA, WI	Y	40270 FQ	45410 MW	50540 TQ	USBLS	5/15
	Milwaukee-Waukesha-West						
	Allis MSA, WI	Y	35570 FQ	41360 MW	49550 TQ	USBLS	5/15
	Wyoming	Y	36820 FQ	44830 MW	54860 TQ	USBLS	5/15

AE Average entry wage	**AWR** Average wage range	**H** Hourly	**LR** Low end range	**MTC** Median total compensation	**TCC** Total cash compensation
AEX Average experienced wage	**B** Biweekly	**HI** Highest wage paid	**M** Monthly	**MW** Median wage paid	**TQ** Third quartile wage
ATC Average total compensation	**D** Daily	**HR** High end range	**MCC** Median cash compensation	**MWR** Median wage range	**W** Weekly
AW Average wage paid	**FQ** First quartile wage	**LO** Lowest wage paid	**ME** Median entry wage	**S** See annotated source	**Y** Yearly

Occupation/Type/Industry	Location	Per	Low	Mid	High	Source	Date
Title Examiner, Abstractor, and Searcher	Cheyenne MSA, WY	Y	40010 FQ	50590 MW	60520 TQ	USBLS	5/15
	Puerto Rico	Y	19540 FQ	25180 MW	38620 TQ	USBLS	5/15
	San Juan-Carolina-Caguas MSA, PR	Y	19540 FQ	25180 MW	38620 TQ	USBLS	5/15
Title IX Coordinator							
Baccalaureate Institution	United States	Y		78200 MW		CHE02	2015-2016
Master's Institution	United States	Y		69430 MW		CHE02	2015-2016
Research University	United States	Y		79500 MW		CHE02	2015-2016
Tool and Die Maker	Alabama	Y	31648 AE	47390 AW	55256 AEX	ALBLS	6/16
	Birmingham-Hoover MSA, AL	Y	34281 AE	48635 AW	55812 AEX	ALBLS	6/16
	Arizona	Y	34910 FQ	45000 MW	57750 TQ	USBLS	5/15
	Phoenix-Mesa-Scottsdale MSA, AZ	Y	35550 FQ	45630 MW	58180 TQ	USBLS	5/15
	Arkansas	Y	36880 FQ	44020 MW	49940 TQ	USBLS	5/15
	Little Rock-North Little Rock-Conway MSA, AR	Y	36570 FQ	44100 MW	51360 TQ	USBLS	5/15
	California	H	18.68 FQ	26.11 MW	33.33 TQ	CABLS	1/16-3/16
	Anaheim-Santa Ana-Irvine PMSA, CA	H	19.74 FQ	26.80 MW	33.89 TQ	CABLS	1/16-3/16
	Los Angeles-Long Beach-Glendale PMSA, CA	H	19.74 FQ	26.57 MW	34.24 TQ	CABLS	1/16-3/16
	Oakland-Hayward-Berkeley PMSA, CA	H	15.31 FQ	25.73 MW	33.77 TQ	CABLS	1/16-3/16
	Riverside-San Bernardino-Ontario MSA, CA	H	18.63 FQ	24.06 MW	30.39 TQ	CABLS	1/16-3/16
	Sacramento–Roseville–Arden-Arcade MSA, CA	H	18.77 FQ	26.10 MW	36.41 TQ	CABLS	1/16-3/16
	San Diego-Carlsbad MSA, CA	H	17.90 FQ	27.11 MW	33.35 TQ	CABLS	1/16-3/16
	San Francisco-Redwood City-South San Francisco PMSA, CA	H	26.44 FQ	36.64 MW	42.50 TQ	CABLS	1/16-3/16
	Colorado	Y	38070 FQ	50070 MW	62030 TQ	USBLS	5/15
	Denver-Aurora-Lakewood MSA, CO	Y	43970 FQ	54320 MW	64320 TQ	USBLS	5/15
	Connecticut	Y		58223 MW		CTBLS	1/16-3/16
	Bridgeport-Stamford-Norwalk MSA, CT	Y	48270 FQ	61040 MW	73960 TQ	USBLS	5/15
	Hartford-West Hartford-East Hartford MSA, CT	Y	40940 FQ	54780 MW	61850 TQ	USBLS	5/15
	Wilmington PMSA, DE-MD-NJ	Y	50570 FQ	56480 MW	62300 TQ	USBLS	5/15
	Florida	H	16.03 AE	22.52 MW	25.96 AEX	FLBLS	7/16-9/16
	Fort Lauderdale-Pompano Beach-Deerfield Beach PMSA, FL	H	16.99 AE	22.23 MW	24.46 AEX	FLBLS	7/16-9/16
	Miami-Miami Beach-Kendall PMSA, FL	H	16.25 AE	25.36 MW	26.94 AEX	FLBLS	7/16-9/16
	Orlando-Kissimmee-Sanford MSA, FL	H	15.45 AE	22.82 MW	27.01 AEX	FLBLS	7/16-9/16
	Tampa-St. Petersburg-Clearwater MSA, FL	H	16.31 AE	22.80 MW	25.78 AEX	FLBLS	7/16-9/16
	Georgia	Y	39230 FQ	46960 MW	59440 TQ	USBLS	5/15
	Atlanta-Sandy Springs-Roswell MSA, GA	Y	40080 FQ	47100 MW	72510 TQ	USBLS	5/15
	Augusta-Richmond County MSA, GA-SC	Y	34280 FQ	45580 MW	55040 TQ	USBLS	5/15
	Idaho	Y	34490 FQ	42080 MW	52420 TQ	USBLS	5/15
	Illinois	Y	42900 FQ	53160 MW	65320 AEX	ALBLS	5/15
	Chicago-Naperville-Arlington Heights PMSA, IL	Y	44040 FQ	55040 MW	67500 TQ	USBLS	5/15
	Lake County-Kenosha County PMSA, IL-WI	Y	40310 FQ	49000 MW	62160 TQ	USBLS	5/15
	Indiana	Y	40800 FQ	51150 MW	66590 TQ	USBLS	5/15
	Gary PMSA, IN	Y	36770 FQ	46870 MW	54620 TQ	USBLS	5/15
	Indianapolis-Carmel-Anderson MSA, IN	Y	31700 FQ	44820 MW	63690 TQ	USBLS	5/15
	Iowa	Y	42130 FQ	49480 MW	56850 TQ	USBLS	5/15
	Des Moines-West Des Moines MSA, IA	Y	45820 FQ	54370 MW	61560 TQ	USBLS	5/15

AE Average entry wage	**AWR** Average wage range	**H** Hourly	**LR** Low end range	**MTC** Median total compensation	**TCC** Total cash compensation
AEX Average experienced wage	**B** Biweekly	**HI** Highest wage paid	**M** Monthly	**MW** Median wage paid	**TQ** Third quartile wage
ATC Average total compensation	**D** Daily	**HR** High end range	**MCC** Median cash compensation	**MWR** Median wage range	**W** Weekly
AW Average wage paid	**FQ** First quartile wage	**LO** Lowest wage paid	**ME** Median entry wage	**S** See annotated source	**Y** Yearly

Tool and Die Maker

Occupation/Type/Industry	Location	Per	Low	Mid	High	Source	Date
Tool and Die Maker	Kansas	Y	35000 FQ	47680 MW	62860 TQ	USBLS	5/15
	Wichita MSA, KS	Y	37350 FQ	53160 MW	65520 TQ	USBLS	5/15
	Kentucky	Y	42660 FQ	51140 MW	61520 TQ	USBLS	5/15
	Louisville-Jefferson County MSA, KY-IN	Y	43110 FQ	51830 MW	62970 TQ	USBLS	5/15
	Louisiana	Y	33290 FQ	40740 MW	51670 TQ	USBLS	5/15
	Maine	Y	43150 FQ	47950 MW	61700 TQ	USBLS	5/15
	Portland-South Portland MSA, ME	Y	41700 FQ	44590 MW	47480 TQ	USBLS	5/15
	Maryland	Y	27223 AE	46823 MW	56623 AEX	MDBLS	4/16
	Baltimore-Columbia-Towson MSA, MD	Y	28170 FQ	41840 MW	57750 TQ	USBLS	5/15
	Massachusetts	Y	41220 FQ	52110 MW	61560 TQ	USBLS	5/15
	Boston-Cambridge-Newton NECTA, MA	Y	43410 FQ	55750 MW	69580 TQ	USBLS	5/15
	Worcester MSA, MA-CT	Y	40020 FQ	50930 MW	59850 TQ	USBLS	5/15
	Michigan	Y	41390 FQ	51500 MW	63910 TQ	USBLS	5/15
	Detroit-Dearborn-Livonia PMSA, MI	Y	52730 FQ	65800 MW	72810 TQ	USBLS	5/15
	Grand Rapids-Wyoming MSA, MI	Y	40190 FQ	47620 MW	57300 TQ	USBLS	5/15
	Minnesota	Y	44031 FQ	55148 MW	67358 TQ	MNBLS	1/16-3/16
	Minneapolis-St. Paul-Bloomington MSA, MN-WI	Y	47494 FQ	59491 MW	69839 TQ	MNBLS	1/16-3/16
	Mississippi	Y	37270 FQ	45660 MW	53960 TQ	USBLS	5/15
	Jackson MSA, MS	Y	49630 FQ	54340 MW	58810 TQ	USBLS	5/15
	Missouri	Y	37310 FQ	52520 MW	66580 TQ	USBLS	5/15
	Kansas City MSA, MO-KS	Y	44400 FQ	62270 MW	71300 TQ	USBLS	5/15
	St. Louis MSA, MO-IL	Y	41330 FQ	55950 MW	68960 TQ	USBLS	5/15
	Nebraska	Y	40230 FQ	48060 MW	58035 TQ	NEBLS	7/16-9/16
	Omaha-Council Bluffs MSA, NE-IA	Y	41175 FQ	47650 MW	56060 TQ	NEBLS	7/16-9/16
	Nevada	Y	42590 FQ	50480 MW	60460 TQ	USBLS	5/15
	Las Vegas-Henderson-Paradise MSA, NV	Y	39930 FQ	47000 MW	55980 TQ	USBLS	5/15
	New Hampshire	H	18.07 AE	25.83 MW	28.70 AEX	NHBLS	6/16
	Manchester NECTA, NH	H	17.42 AE	27.44 MW	30.63 AEX	NHBLS	6/16
	Nashua NECTA, NH-MA	Y	35040 FQ	46240 MW	55930 TQ	USBLS	5/15
	New Jersey	Y	45060 FQ	56400 MW	66400 TQ	USBLS	5/15
	Camden PMSA, NJ	Y	44620 FQ	53680 MW	59420 TQ	USBLS	5/15
	Newark PMSA, NJ-PA	Y	45660 FQ	56610 MW	66590 TQ	USBLS	5/15
	New York	Y	40520 AE	53190 MW	60360 AEX	NYBLS	1/16-3/16
	Buffalo-Cheektowaga-Niagara Falls MSA, NY	Y	48780 FQ	57060 MW	65870 TQ	USBLS	5/15
	Nassau County-Suffolk County PMSA, NY	Y	54280 FQ	60810 MW	75300 TQ	USBLS	5/15
	New York-Jersey City-White Plains PMSA, NY-NJ	Y	39820 FQ	54390 MW	67050 TQ	USBLS	5/15
	Rochester MSA, NY	Y	42810 FQ	48130 MW	56460 TQ	USBLS	5/15
	North Carolina	Y	36570 FQ	46030 MW	55750 TQ	USBLS	5/15
	Charlotte-Concord-Gastonia MSA, NC-SC	Y	37440 FQ	48150 MW	57550 TQ	USBLS	5/15
	Raleigh MSA, NC	Y	25170 FQ	36240 MW	44870 TQ	USBLS	5/15
	North Dakota	Y	41240 FQ	44660 MW	48080 TQ	USBLS	5/15
	Ohio	Y	40750 FQ	48800 MW	58540 TQ	USBLS	5/15
	Cincinnati MSA, OH-KY-IN	Y	43110 FQ	51350 MW	65250 TQ	USBLS	5/15
	Cleveland-Elyria MSA, OH	Y	43780 FQ	52810 MW	59830 TQ	USBLS	5/15
	Columbus MSA, OH	Y	41160 FQ	50230 MW	57940 TQ	USBLS	5/15
	Oklahoma	Y	38300 FQ	48290 MW	59630 TQ	USBLS	5/15
	Oklahoma City MSA, OK	Y	41060 FQ	54180 MW	58340 TQ	USBLS	5/15
	Tulsa MSA, OK	Y	36160 FQ	44240 MW	52790 TQ	USBLS	5/15
	Oregon	H	23.26 FQ	27.60 MW	31.49 TQ	ORBLS	2016
	Portland-Vancouver-Hillsboro MSA, OR-WA	Y	47140 FQ	56020 MW	64620 TQ	USBLS	5/15
	Pennsylvania	Y	38780 FQ	45920 MW	54520 TQ	USBLS	5/15
	Allentown-Bethlehem-Easton MSA, PA-NJ	Y	38600 FQ	48480 MW	63630 TQ	USBLS	5/15
	Harrisburg-Carlisle MSA, PA	Y	41240 FQ	45730 MW	50900 TQ	USBLS	5/15
	Montgomery County-Bucks County-Chester County PMSA, PA	Y	45390 FQ	53100 MW	60190 TQ	USBLS	5/15
	Philadelphia PMSA, PA	Y	37890 FQ	53180 MW	65780 TQ	USBLS	5/15

AE Average entry wage	**AWR** Average wage range	**H** Hourly	**LR** Low end range	**MTC** Median total compensation	**TCC** Total cash compensation
AEX Average experienced wage	**B** Biweekly	**HI** Highest wage paid	**M** Monthly	**MW** Median wage paid	**TQ** Third quartile wage
ATC Average total compensation	**D** Daily	**HR** High end range	**MCC** Median cash compensation	**MWR** Median wage range	**W** Weekly
AW Average wage paid	**FQ** First quartile wage	**LO** Lowest wage paid	**ME** Median entry wage	**S** See annotated source	**Y** Yearly

Occupation/Type/Industry	Location	Per	Low	Mid	High	Source	Date
Tool and Die Maker	Pittsburgh MSA, PA	Y	39870 FQ	45720 MW	53180 TQ	USBLS	5/15
	Rhode Island	Y	39710 FQ	46220 MW	54720 TQ	USBLS	5/15
	Providence-Warwick MSA, RI-MA	Y	39840 FQ	47710 MW	56940 TQ	USBLS	5/15
	South Carolina	Y	41240 FQ	54020 MW	61570 TQ	USBLS	5/15
	Columbia MSA, SC	Y	48900 FQ	56040 MW	62380 TQ	USBLS	5/15
	Greenville-Anderson-Mauldin MSA, SC	Y	46880 FQ	56620 MW	64880 TQ	USBLS	5/15
	South Dakota	Y	39760 FQ	44280 MW	48700 TQ	USBLS	5/15
	Sioux Falls MSA, SD	Y	40670 FQ	44920 MW	49170 TQ	USBLS	5/15
	Tennessee	Y	37530 FQ	46180 MW	56580 TQ	USBLS	5/15
	Knoxville MSA, TN	Y	39150 FQ	47590 MW	56110 TQ	USBLS	5/15
	Memphis MSA, TN-MS-AR	Y	38060 FQ	47750 MW	59320 TQ	USBLS	5/15
	Nashville-Davidson–Murfreesboro–Franklin MSA, TN	Y	42240 FQ	52370 MW	62770 TQ	USBLS	5/15
	Texas	Y	34280 FQ	44600 MW	57470 TQ	USBLS	5/15
	Austin-Round Rock MSA, TX	Y	32610 FQ	39630 MW	57100 TQ	USBLS	5/15
	Dallas-Plano-Irving PMSA, TX	Y	34590 FQ	41640 MW	49420 TQ	USBLS	5/15
	Fort Worth-Arlington PMSA, TX	Y	41240 FQ	64370 MW	73910 TQ	USBLS	5/15
	Houston-The Woodlands-Sugar Land MSA, TX	Y	33830 FQ	43310 MW	55640 TQ	USBLS	5/15
	San Antonio-New Braunfels MSA, TX	Y	40160 FQ	46060 MW	53840 TQ	USBLS	5/15
	Utah	Y	43490 FQ	56630 MW	66230 TQ	USBLS	5/15
	Ogden-Clearfield MSA, UT	Y	53510 FQ	63840 MW	66240 TQ	USBLS	5/15
	Salt Lake City MSA, UT	Y	42480 FQ	50040 MW	60630 TQ	USBLS	5/15
	Vermont	Y	44940 FQ	65380 MW	74100 TQ	USBLS	5/15
	Virginia	Y	35540 FQ	48710 MW	59080 TQ	USBLS	5/15
	Richmond MSA, VA	Y	37770 FQ	50560 MW	58650 TQ	USBLS	5/15
	Virginia Beach-Norfolk-Newport News MSA, VA-NC	Y	33640 FQ	52790 MW	62620 TQ	USBLS	5/15
	Washington	H	24.43 FQ	33.91 MW	42.20 TQ	WABLS	3/16
	Tacoma-Lakewood PMSA, WA	H	28.10 FQ	38.48 MW	43.71 TQ	WABLS	3/16
	West Virginia	Y	36790 FQ	45400 MW	54890 TQ	USBLS	5/15
	Wisconsin	Y	41470 FQ	50000 MW	58370 TQ	USBLS	5/15
	Madison MSA, WI	Y	29850 FQ	43710 MW	51490 TQ	USBLS	5/15
	Milwaukee-Waukesha-West Allis MSA, WI	Y	43320 FQ	51580 MW	59480 TQ	USBLS	5/15
	Puerto Rico	Y	21040 FQ	29250 MW	36760 TQ	USBLS	5/15
	San Juan-Carolina-Caguas MSA, PR	Y	19860 FQ	27920 MW	36010 TQ	USBLS	5/15
Tool Grinder, Filer, and Sharpener	Alabama	Y	23361 AE	32224 AW	36656 AEX	ALBLS	6/16
	Birmingham-Hoover MSA, AL	Y	25016 AE	33335 AW	37499 AEX	ALBLS	6/16
	Arizona	Y	30990 FQ	36570 MW	43740 TQ	USBLS	5/15
	Phoenix-Mesa-Scottsdale MSA, AZ	Y	30870 FQ	36480 MW	43470 TQ	USBLS	5/15
	Arkansas	Y	27920 FQ	35070 MW	42250 TQ	USBLS	5/15
	California	H	11.65 FQ	15.68 MW	20.70 TQ	CABLS	1/16-3/16
	Anaheim-Santa Ana-Irvine PMSA, CA	H	11.05 FQ	13.14 MW	18.00 TQ	CABLS	1/16-3/16
	Los Angeles-Long Beach-Glendale PMSA, CA	H	11.43 FQ	14.44 MW	20.03 TQ	CABLS	1/16-3/16
	Riverside-San Bernardino-Ontario MSA, CA	H	10.51 FQ	11.89 MW	15.49 TQ	CABLS	1/16-3/16
	Sacramento–Roseville–Arden-Arcade MSA, CA	H	14.16 FQ	18.72 MW	22.82 TQ	CABLS	1/16-3/16
	San Diego-Carlsbad MSA, CA	H	16.49 FQ	18.13 MW	25.77 TQ	CABLS	1/16-3/16
	Colorado	Y	20010 FQ	32640 MW	42210 TQ	USBLS	5/15
	Florida	H	9.08 AE	15.01 MW	18.51 AEX	FLBLS	7/16-9/16
	Georgia	Y	28970 FQ	35690 MW	44660 TQ	USBLS	5/15
	Idaho	Y	26870 FQ	35650 MW	44150 TQ	USBLS	5/15
	Boise City MSA, ID	Y	22840 FQ	25960 MW	31250 TQ	USBLS	5/15
	Illinois	Y	29840 FQ	37420 MW	45630 TQ	USBLS	5/15
	Chicago-Naperville-Arlington Heights PMSA, IL	Y	33630 FQ	39920 MW	46280 TQ	USBLS	5/15
	Lake County-Kenosha County PMSA, IL-WI	Y	33470 FQ	41230 MW	51260 TQ	USBLS	5/15
	Indiana	Y	25440 FQ	32950 MW	39970 TQ	USBLS	5/15

AE	Average entry wage	AWR	Average wage range	H	Hourly	LR	Low end range	MTC	Median total compensation	TCC	Total cash compensation
AEX	Average experienced wage	B	Biweekly	HI	Highest wage paid	M	Monthly	MW	Median wage paid	TQ	Third quartile wage
ATC	Average total compensation	D	Daily	HR	High end range	MCC	Median cash compensation	MWR	Median wage range	W	Weekly
AW	Average wage paid	FQ	First quartile wage	LO	Lowest wage paid	ME	Median entry wage	S	See annotated source	Y	Yearly

Tool Grinder, Filer, and Sharpener

Occupation/Type/Industry	Location	Per	Low	Mid	High	Source	Date
	Iowa	Y	27380 FQ	34710 MW	44120 TQ	USBLS	5/15
	Kentucky	Y	26700 FQ	33760 MW	43340 TQ	USBLS	5/15
	Louisville-Jefferson County MSA, KY-IN	Y	22640 FQ	25110 MW	29640 TQ	USBLS	5/15
	Louisiana	Y	27780 FQ	35850 MW	45740 TQ	USBLS	5/15
	Baton Rouge MSA, LA	Y	32000 FQ	37340 MW	44890 TQ	USBLS	5/15
	Maine	Y	32130 FQ	36230 MW	41600 TQ	USBLS	5/15
	Portland-South Portland MSA, ME	Y	30320 FQ	35150 MW	39360 TQ	USBLS	5/15
	Maryland	Y	27657 AE	37253 MW	42050 AEX	MDBLS	4/16
	Baltimore-Columbia-Towson MSA, MD	Y	31110 FQ	35220 MW	39360 TQ	USBLS	5/15
	Massachusetts	Y	33220 FQ	38170 MW	49260 TQ	USBLS	5/15
	Boston-Cambridge-Newton NECTA, MA	Y	26640 FQ	32410 MW	37810 TQ	USBLS	5/15
	Worcester MSA, MA-CT	Y	33380 FQ	36250 MW	39130 TQ	USBLS	5/15
	Michigan	Y	30090 FQ	38810 MW	47010 TQ	USBLS	5/15
	Detroit-Dearborn-Livonia PMSA, MI	Y	43310 FQ	47870 MW	56320 TQ	USBLS	5/15
	Grand Rapids-Wyoming MSA, MI	Y	23340 FQ	30640 MW	42310 TQ	USBLS	5/15
	Minnesota	Y	31740 FQ	40903 MW	47534 TQ	MNBLS	1/16-3/16
	Minneapolis-St. Paul-Bloomington MSA, MN-WI	Y	29088 FQ	41996 MW	48638 TQ	MNBLS	1/16-3/16
	Mississippi	Y	31610 FQ	38960 MW	45920 TQ	USBLS	5/15
	Missouri	Y	27270 FQ	32480 MW	37670 TQ	USBLS	5/15
	Kansas City MSA, MO-KS	Y	25950 FQ	30100 MW	34770 TQ	USBLS	5/15
	St. Louis MSA, MO-IL	Y	25680 FQ	33040 MW	39540 TQ	USBLS	5/15
	Montana	Y	35110 FQ	39330 MW	48270 TQ	USBLS	5/15
	Nebraska	Y	33015 FQ	36685 MW	40120 TQ	NEBLS	7/16-9/16
	Nevada	Y	24490 FQ	28280 MW	32650 TQ	USBLS	5/15
	New Hampshire	H	13.83 AE	19.75 MW	24.27 AEX	NHBLS	6/16
	New Jersey	Y	28680 FQ	40630 MW	46420 TQ	USBLS	5/15
	New York	Y	25070 AE	35280 MW	42210 AEX	NYBLS	1/16-3/16
	Buffalo-Cheektowaga-Niagara Falls MSA, NY	Y	25050 FQ	33860 MW	49100 TQ	USBLS	5/15
	Nassau County-Suffolk County PMSA, NY	Y	32210 FQ	35350 MW	38490 TQ	USBLS	5/15
	New York-Jersey City-White Plains PMSA, NY-NJ	Y	29350 FQ	41090 MW	47900 TQ	USBLS	5/15
	Rochester MSA, NY	Y	27080 FQ	36560 MW	45480 TQ	USBLS	5/15
	North Carolina	Y	25210 FQ	32410 MW	42910 TQ	USBLS	5/15
	Charlotte-Concord-Gastonia MSA, NC-SC	Y	26990 FQ	34030 MW	46890 TQ	USBLS	5/15
	Ohio	Y	27110 FQ	33920 MW	41100 TQ	USBLS	5/15
	Cincinnati MSA, OH-KY-IN	Y	27870 FQ	40640 MW	49620 TQ	USBLS	5/15
	Cleveland-Elyria MSA, OH	Y	25940 FQ	32160 MW	39830 TQ	USBLS	5/15
	Columbus MSA, OH	Y	24180 FQ	32300 MW	37850 TQ	USBLS	5/15
	Oklahoma	Y	26450 FQ	33720 MW	43680 TQ	USBLS	5/15
	Oklahoma City MSA, OK	Y	27230 FQ	34830 MW	44000 TQ	USBLS	5/15
	Tulsa MSA, OK	Y	28860 FQ	39200 MW	45870 TQ	USBLS	5/15
	Oregon	H	16.33 FQ	21.36 MW	26.37 TQ	ORBLS	2016
	Portland-Vancouver-Hillsboro MSA, OR-WA	Y	34640 FQ	46000 MW	56650 TQ	USBLS	5/15
	Pennsylvania	Y	30260 FQ	37520 MW	44880 TQ	USBLS	5/15
	Montgomery County-Bucks County-Chester County PMSA, PA	Y	30730 FQ	39120 MW	46030 TQ	USBLS	5/15
	Pittsburgh MSA, PA	Y	36050 FQ	42070 MW	47110 TQ	USBLS	5/15
	South Carolina	Y	24930 FQ	32040 MW	41570 TQ	USBLS	5/15
	South Dakota	Y	28320 FQ	34040 MW	39670 TQ	USBLS	5/15
	Tennessee	Y	25030 FQ	31110 MW	42300 TQ	USBLS	5/15
	Nashville-Davidson–Murfreesboro–Franklin MSA, TN	Y	26580 FQ	35280 MW	44350 TQ	USBLS	5/15
	Texas	Y	22440 FQ	28070 MW	37080 TQ	USBLS	5/15
	Dallas-Plano-Irving PMSA, TX	Y	19130 FQ	23930 MW	33900 TQ	USBLS	5/15
	Fort Worth-Arlington PMSA, TX	Y	21220 FQ	26400 MW	33160 TQ	USBLS	5/15
	Utah	Y	21300 FQ	23130 MW	27580 TQ	USBLS	5/15
	Salt Lake City MSA, UT	Y	21330 FQ	23200 MW	28650 TQ	USBLS	5/15

AE	Average entry wage	AWR	Average wage range	H	Hourly	LR	Low end range	MTC	Median total compensation	TCC	Total cash compensation
AEX	Average experienced wage	B	Biweekly	HI	Highest wage paid	M	Monthly	MW	Median wage paid	TQ	Third quartile wage
ATC	Average total compensation	D	Daily	HR	High end range	MCC	Median cash compensation	MWR	Median wage range	W	Weekly
AW	Average wage paid	FQ	First quartile wage	LO	Lowest wage paid	ME	Median entry wage	S	See annotated source	Y	Yearly

Occupation/Type/Industry	Location	Per	Low	Mid	High	Source	Date
Tool Grinder, Filer, and Sharpener	Vermont	Y	33080 FQ	38680 MW	45830 TQ	USBLS	5/15
	Virginia	Y	25920 FQ	29850 MW	37150 TQ	USBLS	5/15
	Washington	H	20.22 FQ	24.63 MW	31.28 TQ	WABLS	3/16
	Seattle-Bellevue-Everett PMSA, WA	H	20.14 FQ	33.55 MW	45.88 TQ	WABLS	3/16
	Tacoma-Lakewood PMSA, WA	H	16.10 FQ	20.29 MW	23.80 TQ	WABLS	3/16
	West Virginia	Y	28870 FQ	41750 MW	49150 TQ	USBLS	5/15
	Wisconsin	Y	29520 FQ	37610 MW	46780 TQ	USBLS	5/15
	Milwaukee-Waukesha-West Allis MSA, WI	Y	31410 FQ	40220 MW	50310 TQ	USBLS	5/15
Tool Lending Specialist Branch Libraries/Tool Lending/Culture Recreation Department, Municipal Government	Berkeley, CA	Y		30391 AW		CACIT	6/28/16
Tort Claims Adjuster State Government	North Carolina	Y	41125 LO		66204 HI	NCGOV	7/1/16
Tour Accountant Theater/Arena-Level Touring Band	United States	W		1500-6000 AWR		BBRD01	2014
Tour Guide and Escort	Alabama	Y	17421 AE	23907 AW	27140 AEX	ALBLS	6/16
	Birmingham-Hoover MSA, AL	Y	22991 AE	28705 AW	31568 AEX	ALBLS	6/16
	Alaska	Y	25030 FQ	29450 MW	35790 TQ	USBLS	5/15
	Anchorage MSA, AK	Y	23990 FQ	31430 MW	45810 TQ	USBLS	5/15
	Arizona	Y	21700 FQ	25600 MW	30370 TQ	USBLS	5/15
	Phoenix-Mesa-Scottsdale MSA, AZ	Y	20440 FQ	22660 MW	25130 TQ	USBLS	5/15
	Tucson MSA, AZ	Y	19970 FQ	28260 MW	34910 TQ	USBLS	5/15
	Arkansas	Y	19970 FQ	23000 MW	28540 TQ	USBLS	5/15
	California	H	10.45 FQ	14.45 MW	18.14 TQ	CABLS	1/16-3/16
	Anaheim-Santa Ana-Irvine PMSA, CA	H	9.52 FQ	10.76 MW	15.25 TQ	CABLS	1/16-3/16
	Los Angeles-Long Beach-Glendale PMSA, CA	H	9.62 FQ	14.06 MW	16.95 TQ	CABLS	1/16-3/16
	Oakland-Hayward-Berkeley PMSA, CA	H	12.15 FQ	13.32 MW	14.51 TQ	CABLS	1/16-3/16
	Riverside-San Bernardino-Ontario MSA, CA	H	9.91 FQ	13.62 MW	16.58 TQ	CABLS	1/16-3/16
	Sacramento–Roseville–Arden-Arcade MSA, CA	H	11.60 FQ	16.80 MW	20.49 TQ	CABLS	1/16-3/16
	San Diego-Carlsbad MSA, CA	H	9.63 FQ	13.17 MW	19.19 TQ	CABLS	1/16-3/16
	San Francisco-Redwood City-South San Francisco PMSA, CA	H	13.08 FQ	16.13 MW	18.55 TQ	CABLS	1/16-3/16
	Colorado	Y	21760 FQ	31240 MW	37250 TQ	USBLS	5/15
	Denver-Aurora-Lakewood MSA, CO	Y	20780 FQ	24760 MW	31150 TQ	USBLS	5/15
	Connecticut	Y		29215 MW		CTBLS	1/16-3/16
	Delaware	Y	19580 FQ	25450 MW	28750 TQ	USBLS	5/15
	Wilmington PMSA, DE-MD-NJ	Y	21770 FQ	26680 MW	29300 TQ	USBLS	5/15
	District of Columbia	Y	30490 FQ	34770 MW	38720 TQ	USBLS	5/15
	Washington-Arlington-Alexandria PMSA, DC-VA-MD-WV	Y	23390 FQ	30080 MW	35830 TQ	USBLS	5/15
	Florida	H	9.11 AE	11.40 MW	13.89 AEX	FLBLS	7/16-9/16
	Fort Lauderdale-Pompano Beach-Deerfield Beach PMSA, FL	H	9.08 AE	10.41 MW	11.89 AEX	FLBLS	7/16-9/16
	Miami-Miami Beach-Kendall PMSA, FL	H	10.03 AE	13.10 MW	14.69 AEX	FLBLS	7/16-9/16
	Orlando-Kissimmee-Sanford MSA, FL	H	9.08 AE	10.20 MW	12.76 AEX	FLBLS	7/16-9/16
	Tampa-St. Petersburg-Clearwater MSA, FL	H	9.14 AE	11.00 MW	13.11 AEX	FLBLS	7/16-9/16
	Georgia	Y	18020 FQ	21720 MW	29560 TQ	USBLS	5/15
	Atlanta-Sandy Springs-Roswell MSA, GA	Y	19640 FQ	26570 MW	34420 TQ	USBLS	5/15

AE Average entry wage	**AWR** Average wage range	**H** Hourly	**LR** Low end range	**MTC** Median total compensation	**TCC** Total cash compensation
AEX Average experienced wage	**B** Biweekly	**HI** Highest wage paid	**M** Monthly	**MW** Median wage paid	**TQ** Third quartile wage
ATC Average total compensation	**D** Daily	**HR** High end range	**MCC** Median cash compensation	**MWR** Median wage range	**W** Weekly
AW Average wage paid	**FQ** First quartile wage	**LO** Lowest wage paid	**ME** Median entry wage	**S** See annotated source	**Y** Yearly

Occupation/Type/Industry	Location	Per	Low	Mid	High	Source	Date
Tour Guide and Escort	Hawaii	Y	23200 FQ	27620 MW	31200 TQ	USBLS	5/15
	Urban Honolulu MSA, HI	Y	21650 FQ	26530 MW	29670 TQ	USBLS	5/15
	Idaho	Y	17190 FQ	19040 MW	31860 TQ	USBLS	5/15
	Boise City MSA, ID	Y	16890 FQ	18350 MW	23390 TQ	USBLS	5/15
	Illinois	Y	19400 FQ	24390 MW	33430 TQ	USBLS	5/15
	Chicago-Naperville-Arlington Heights PMSA, IL	Y	20590 FQ	26130 MW	38210 TQ	USBLS	5/15
	Lake County-Kenosha County PMSA, IL-WI	Y	17680 FQ	18910 MW	22590 TQ	USBLS	5/15
	Indiana	Y	17360 FQ	19370 MW	23020 TQ	USBLS	5/15
	Indianapolis-Carmel-Anderson MSA, IN	Y	18170 FQ	20750 MW	23330 TQ	USBLS	5/15
	Iowa	Y	17530 FQ	19510 MW	26290 TQ	USBLS	5/15
	Des Moines-West Des Moines MSA, IA	Y	21800 FQ	28600 MW	31440 TQ	USBLS	5/15
	Kansas	Y	17550 FQ	19850 MW	26400 TQ	USBLS	5/15
	Wichita MSA, KS	Y	19250 FQ	28660 MW	34840 TQ	USBLS	5/15
	Kentucky	Y	18000 FQ	21420 MW	28550 TQ	USBLS	5/15
	Louisville-Jefferson County MSA, KY-IN	Y	16840 FQ	18450 MW	25610 TQ	USBLS	5/15
	Louisiana	Y	18080 FQ	22160 MW	30330 TQ	USBLS	5/15
	Baton Rouge MSA, LA	Y	17060 FQ	18730 MW	30270 TQ	USBLS	5/15
	New Orleans-Metairie MSA, LA	Y	18830 FQ	22780 MW	29060 TQ	USBLS	5/15
	Maine	Y	17420 FQ	19200 MW	24100 TQ	USBLS	5/15
	Maryland	Y	18195 AE	23201 MW	25704 AEX	MDBLS	4/16
	Baltimore-Columbia-Towson MSA, MD	Y	18760 FQ	20900 MW	23390 TQ	USBLS	5/15
	Salisbury MSA, MD-DE	Y	18770 FQ	22030 MW	28290 TQ	USBLS	5/15
	Massachusetts	Y	19660 FQ	22760 MW	32420 TQ	USBLS	5/15
	Boston-Cambridge-Newton NECTA, MA	Y	19770 FQ	23360 MW	33930 TQ	USBLS	5/15
	Worcester MSA, MA-CT	Y	19650 FQ	21870 MW	24290 TQ	USBLS	5/15
	Michigan	Y	18230 FQ	19400 MW	24170 TQ	USBLS	5/15
	Detroit-Dearborn-Livonia PMSA, MI	Y	17950 FQ	18830 MW	19710 TQ	USBLS	5/15
	Grand Rapids-Wyoming MSA, MI	Y	18240 FQ	19770 MW	25000 TQ	USBLS	5/15
	Minnesota	Y	21904 FQ	26297 MW	29731 TQ	MNBLS	1/16-3/16
	Minneapolis-St. Paul-Bloomington MSA, MN-WI	Y	23863 FQ	27479 MW	30831 TQ	MNBLS	1/16-3/16
	Mississippi	Y	18710 FQ	24850 MW	28550 TQ	USBLS	5/15
	Missouri	Y	18460 FQ	20880 MW	23870 TQ	USBLS	5/15
	Kansas City MSA, MO-KS	Y	17880 FQ	20730 MW	28030 TQ	USBLS	5/15
	St. Louis MSA, MO-IL	Y	20380 FQ	22270 MW	24160 TQ	USBLS	5/15
	Montana	Y	25010 FQ	27480 MW	29870 TQ	USBLS	5/15
	Omaha-Council Bluffs MSA, NE-IA	Y	20895 FQ	22810 MW	24740 TQ	NEBLS	7/16-9/16
	Nevada	Y	24330 FQ	28080 MW	31930 TQ	USBLS	5/15
	Las Vegas-Henderson-Paradise MSA, NV	Y	25170 FQ	28480 MW	32080 TQ	USBLS	5/15
	New Hampshire	H	9.00 AE	13.50 MW	17.67 AEX	NHBLS	6/16
	New Jersey	Y	19740 FQ	23520 MW	32770 TQ	USBLS	5/15
	Newark PMSA, NJ-PA	Y	23280 FQ	28680 MW	34850 TQ	USBLS	5/15
	Trenton MSA, NJ	Y	18880 FQ	32010 MW	35590 TQ	USBLS	5/15
	New Mexico	Y	20440 FQ	25110 MW	31940 TQ	USBLS	5/15
	Albuquerque MSA, NM	Y	18990 FQ	23390 MW	29670 TQ	USBLS	5/15
	New York	Y	19600 AE	26000 MW	37090 AEX	NYBLS	1/16-3/16
	Buffalo-Cheektowaga-Niagara Falls MSA, NY	Y	18810 FQ	19490 MW	25840 TQ	USBLS	5/15
	Nassau County-Suffolk County PMSA, NY	Y	23090 FQ	27170 MW	30820 TQ	USBLS	5/15
	New York-Jersey City-White Plains PMSA, NY-NJ	Y	21090 FQ	29290 MW	45630 TQ	USBLS	5/15
	Rochester MSA, NY	Y	18580 FQ	18960 MW	20000 TQ	USBLS	5/15
	North Carolina	Y	19900 FQ	22950 MW	27840 TQ	USBLS	5/15
	Charlotte-Concord-Gastonia MSA, NC-SC	Y	21280 FQ	24920 MW	29590 TQ	USBLS	5/15
	Raleigh MSA, NC	Y	21100 FQ	24740 MW	28090 TQ	USBLS	5/15
	North Dakota	Y	17080 FQ	18420 MW	19960 TQ	USBLS	5/15
	Ohio	Y	18310 FQ	20150 MW	26860 TQ	USBLS	5/15
	Cincinnati MSA, OH-KY-IN	Y	18500 FQ	20650 MW	25620 TQ	USBLS	5/15

AE Average entry wage	**AWR** Average wage range	**H** Hourly	**LR** Low end range	**MTC** Median total compensation	**TCC** Total cash compensation
AEX Average experienced wage	**B** Biweekly	**HI** Highest wage paid	**M** Monthly	**MW** Median wage paid	**TQ** Third quartile wage
ATC Average total compensation	**D** Daily	**HR** High end range	**MCC** Median cash compensation	**MWR** Median wage range	**W** Weekly
AW Average wage paid	**FQ** First quartile wage	**LO** Lowest wage paid	**ME** Median entry wage	**S** See annotated source	**Y** Yearly

Occupation/Type/Industry	Location	Per	Low	Mid	High	Source	Date
Tour Guide and Escort	Cleveland-Elyria MSA, OH	Y	22040 FQ	31860 MW	36570 TQ	USBLS	5/15
	Columbus MSA, OH	Y	18840 FQ	21730 MW	25670 TQ	USBLS	5/15
	Oklahoma	Y	20520 FQ	23090 MW	30860 TQ	USBLS	5/15
	Oklahoma City MSA, OK	Y	20790 FQ	22390 MW	24000 TQ	USBLS	5/15
	Tulsa MSA, OK	Y	18720 FQ	28850 MW	34620 TQ	USBLS	5/15
	Oregon	H	9.63 FQ	11.47 MW	13.86 TQ	ORBLS	2016
	Portland-Vancouver-Hillsboro MSA, OR-WA	Y	21710 FQ	23940 MW	27950 TQ	USBLS	5/15
	Pennsylvania	Y	20920 FQ	26990 MW	34080 TQ	USBLS	5/15
	Montgomery County-Bucks County-Chester County PMSA, PA	Y	25780 FQ	32640 MW	37900 TQ	USBLS	5/15
	Philadelphia PMSA, PA	Y	22880 FQ	27920 MW	34080 TQ	USBLS	5/15
	Pittsburgh MSA, PA	Y	22000 FQ	28240 MW	34390 TQ	USBLS	5/15
	Rhode Island	Y	20620 FQ	24890 MW	30190 TQ	USBLS	5/15
	Providence-Warwick MSA, RI-MA	Y	20630 FQ	24920 MW	30180 TQ	USBLS	5/15
	South Carolina	Y	17570 FQ	20040 MW	28880 TQ	USBLS	5/15
	Charleston-North Charleston MSA, SC	Y	17350 FQ	19310 MW	27260 TQ	USBLS	5/15
	Columbia MSA, SC	Y	17250 FQ	18810 MW	21760 TQ	USBLS	5/15
	Greenville-Anderson-Mauldin MSA, SC	Y	17330 FQ	19460 MW	27480 TQ	USBLS	5/15
	South Dakota	Y	18950 FQ	21790 MW	27140 TQ	USBLS	5/15
	Sioux Falls MSA, SD	Y	18720 FQ	20160 MW	24300 TQ	USBLS	5/15
	Tennessee	Y	17480 FQ	19630 MW	26300 TQ	USBLS	5/15
	Knoxville MSA, TN	Y	17480 FQ	19400 MW	23290 TQ	USBLS	5/15
	Memphis MSA, TN-MS-AR	Y	19020 FQ	22620 MW	28960 TQ	USBLS	5/15
	Nashville-Davidson–Murfreesboro–Franklin MSA, TN	Y	18080 FQ	24450 MW	35350 TQ	USBLS	5/15
	Texas	Y	18410 FQ	21990 MW	31180 TQ	USBLS	5/15
	Austin-Round Rock MSA, TX	Y	17570 FQ	19580 MW	25730 TQ	USBLS	5/15
	Dallas-Plano-Irving PMSA, TX	Y	19620 FQ	28240 MW	44750 TQ	USBLS	5/15
	Fort Worth-Arlington PMSA, TX	Y	19730 FQ	22540 MW	29950 TQ	USBLS	5/15
	Houston-The Woodlands-Sugar Land MSA, TX	Y	18920 FQ	22900 MW	40970 TQ	USBLS	5/15
	San Antonio-New Braunfels MSA, TX	Y	17380 FQ	19330 MW	23300 TQ	USBLS	5/15
	Utah	Y	19980 FQ	24310 MW	32520 TQ	USBLS	5/15
	Salt Lake City MSA, UT	Y	19110 FQ	22440 MW	27790 TQ	USBLS	5/15
	Vermont	Y	19520 FQ	20250 MW	23350 TQ	USBLS	5/15
	Virginia	Y	19840 FQ	23510 MW	28600 TQ	USBLS	5/15
	Richmond MSA, VA	Y	19930 FQ	24130 MW	30780 TQ	USBLS	5/15
	Virginia Beach-Norfolk-Newport News MSA, VA-NC	Y	20970 FQ	23730 MW	28920 TQ	USBLS	5/15
	Washington	H	12.28 FQ	14.60 MW	22.82 TQ	WABLS	3/16
	Seattle-Bellevue-Everett PMSA, WA	H	10.85 FQ	13.71 MW	21.79 TQ	WABLS	3/16
	Tacoma-Lakewood PMSA, WA	H	12.00 FQ	25.52 MW	29.51 TQ	WABLS	3/16
	West Virginia	Y	18590 FQ	21060 MW	27030 TQ	USBLS	5/15
	Huntington-Ashland MSA, WV-KY-OH	Y	20880 FQ	25370 MW	29680 TQ	USBLS	5/15
	Wisconsin	Y	18200 FQ	22640 MW	28630 TQ	USBLS	5/15
	Madison MSA, WI	Y	19370 FQ	22360 MW	27110 TQ	USBLS	5/15
	Milwaukee-Waukesha-West Allis MSA, WI	Y	18600 FQ	23330 MW	27980 TQ	USBLS	5/15
	Wyoming	Y	26740 FQ	33230 MW	45430 TQ	USBLS	5/15
	Puerto Rico	Y	16890 FQ	18370 MW	20700 TQ	USBLS	5/15
	San Juan-Carolina-Caguas MSA, PR	Y	16850 FQ	18300 MW	20320 TQ	USBLS	5/15
	Virgin Islands	Y	20550 FQ	22220 MW	23900 TQ	USBLS	5/15
	Guam	Y	18220 FQ	19280 MW	24100 TQ	USBLS	5/15
Tourism and Marketing Manager Municipal Government	Palm Desert, CA	Y			135636 HI	CACIT	6/28/16
Town Administrator	Ashfield, MA	Y			60000 HI	FRCOG	2016
	Conway, MA	Y			54631 HI	FRCOG	2016
	Shelburne, MA	Y			63440 HI	FRCOG	2016

AE	Average entry wage	AWR	Average wage range	H	Hourly	LR	Low end range	MTC	Median total compensation	TCC	Total cash compensation
AEX	Average experienced wage	B	Biweekly	HI	Highest wage paid	M	Monthly	MW	Median wage paid	TQ	Third quartile wage
ATC	Average total compensation	D	Daily	HR	High end range	MCC	Median cash compensation	MWR	Median wage range	W	Weekly
AW	Average wage paid	FQ	First quartile wage	LO	Lowest wage paid	ME	Median entry wage	S	See annotated source	Y	Yearly

Occupation/Type/Industry	Location	Per	Low	Mid	High	Source	Date
Town Attorney	Los Gatos, CA	Y			188348 HI	CACIT	6/28/16
Town Counsel	Charlemont, MA	H			175.00 HI'	FRCOG	2016
	Erving, MA	H			100.00 HI	FRCOG	2016
	New Salem, MA	H			175.00 HI	FRCOG	2016
Town Manager	Loomis, CA	Y			127110 HI	CACIT	6/28/16
Town Marshal	Markle, IN	Y			45539 HI	HCTAB	2017
Town Nurse	Greenfield, MA	H			30.30 HI	FRCOG	2016
	Heath, MA	H			23.31 HI	FRCOG	2016
Township Manager	Delta Township, MI	Y	90000 LO		125000 HI	LSJ07	2015
	Meridian Township, MI	Y			110727 HI	TC05	8/1/15-11/1/17
Township Supervisor	Lyon Township, MI	Y			63227 HI	HTL01	2015
Toxicology Chemist							
County Government	Bexar County, TX	Y		47874 MW		TTT	6/8/16
Traffic Analyst							
Police Department, Municipal Government	Alhambra, CA	Y			51971 HI	CACIT	6/28/16
Transportation Department, State Government	Ohio	H			20.42 HI	OHGOV	2015
Traffic Engineer							
Municipal Government	Bakersfield, CA	Y			129720 HI	CACIT	6/28/16
Municipal Government	Daly City, CA	Y			111613 HI	CACIT	6/28/16
Municipal Government	El Cajon, CA	Y			111982 HI	CACIT	6/28/16
Municipal Government	Long Beach, CA	Y			33730 HI	CACIT	6/28/16
Municipal Government	Manhattan Beach, CA	Y			124616 HI	CACIT	6/28/16
Municipal Government	Walnut Creek, CA	Y			134005 HI	CACIT	6/28/16
Traffic Engineering Analyst							
Municipal Government	Fullerton, CA	Y			74729 HI	CACIT	6/28/16
Traffic Manager							
Design and Production Industries	United States	Y	54750 LO		77000 HI	RH02	2017
Traffic Safety Specialist							
State Government	Ohio	H			25.69 HI	OHGOV	2015
Traffic Signal Technician							
Municipal Government	Compton, CA	Y			61639 HI	CACIT	8/12/16
Municipal Government	Livermore, CA	Y		76914 AW		CACIT	6/28/16
Municipal Government	Santa Rosa, CA	Y		72540 AW		CACIT	6/28/16
State Government	Miles City, MT	H			26.34 HI	MTGOV	2016
Traffic Specialist							
Police Department, Municipal Government	Beverly Hills, CA	Y			70241 HI	CACIT	6/28/16
Traffic Striper Operator							
Municipal Government	San Diego, CA	Y		37996 AW		CACIT	6/28/16
Traffic Technician	Alabama	Y	31153 AE	43104 AW	49080 AEX	ALBLS	6/16
	Arizona	Y	36840 FQ	46290 MW	63000 TQ	USBLS	5/15
	Phoenix-Mesa-Scottsdale MSA, AZ	Y	37740 FQ	51550 MW	69530 TQ	USBLS	5/15
	Arkansas	Y	30800 FQ	37810 MW	46800 TQ	USBLS	5/15
	California	H	25.41 FQ	32.35 MW	37.48 TQ	CABLS	1/16-3/16
	Anaheim-Santa Ana-Irvine PMSA, CA	H	32.75 FQ	35.43 MW	38.10 TQ	CABLS	1/16-3/16
	Los Angeles-Long Beach-Glendale PMSA, CA	H	29.56 FQ	33.86 MW	37.47 TQ	CABLS	1/16-3/16
	Riverside-San Bernardino-Ontario MSA, CA	H	25.16 FQ	33.64 MW	42.26 TQ	CABLS	1/16-3/16
	Colorado	Y	43210 FQ	52520 MW	59830 TQ	USBLS	5/15
	Denver-Aurora-Lakewood MSA, CO	Y	37400 FQ	46530 MW	56720 TQ	USBLS	5/15
	Washington-Arlington-Alexandria PMSA, DC-VA-MD-WV	Y	42890 FQ	52230 MW	62430 TQ	USBLS	5/15
	Florida	H	12.25 AE	17.64 MW	20.46 AEX	FLBLS	7/16-9/16

Traffic Technician

Occupation/Type/Industry	Location	Per	Low	Mid	High	Source	Date
Traffic Technician	Tampa-St. Petersburg-Clearwater MSA, FL	H	16.45 AE	18.10 MW	19.25 AEX	FLBLS	7/16-9/16
	Georgia	Y	30340 FQ	35660 MW	42080 TQ	USBLS	5/15
	Atlanta-Sandy Springs-Roswell MSA, GA	Y	32010 FQ	36300 MW	42630 TQ	USBLS	5/15
	Hawaii	Y	41720 FQ	48310 MW	58150 TQ	USBLS	5/15
	Illinois	Y	40550 FQ	50570 MW	62140 TQ	USBLS	5/15
	Indiana	Y	31130 FQ	34870 MW	39870 TQ	USBLS	5/15
	Iowa	Y	31700 FQ	34080 MW	34080 TQ	USBLS	5/15
	Kansas	Y	34130 FQ	38160 MW	44830 TQ	USBLS	5/15
	Louisiana	Y	32290 FQ	37170 MW	46720 TQ	USBLS	5/15
	Baton Rouge MSA, LA	Y	34030 FQ	36880 MW	39740 TQ	USBLS	5/15
	New Orleans-Metairie MSA, LA	Y	31650 FQ	37470 MW	49880 TQ	USBLS	5/15
	Maryland	Y	29590 AE	42383 MW	48779 AEX	MDBLS	4/16
	Baltimore-Columbia-Towson MSA, MD	Y	35900 FQ	44970 MW	56160 TQ	USBLS	5/15
	Massachusetts	Y	32640 FQ	35270 MW	37910 TQ	USBLS	5/15
	Michigan	Y	43260 FQ	48620 MW	55280 TQ	USBLS	5/15
	Minnesota	Y	37080 FQ	47373 MW	58382 TQ	MNBLS	1/16-3/16
	Minneapolis-St. Paul-Bloomington MSA, MN-WI	Y	36969 FQ	47090 MW	59551 TQ	MNBLS	1/16-3/16
	Mississippi	Y	23570 FQ	26120 MW	35540 TQ	USBLS	5/15
	Missouri	Y	35070 FQ	41540 MW	45470 TQ	USBLS	5/15
	Kansas City MSA, MO-KS	Y	35800 FQ	40370 MW	45460 TQ	USBLS	5/15
	Nebraska	Y	27520 FQ	30130 MW	36015 TQ	NEBLS	7/16-9/16
	Omaha-Council Bluffs MSA, NE-IA	Y	29075 FQ	30115 MW	33625 TQ	NEBLS	7/16-9/16
	Nevada	Y	57880 FQ	72100 MW	82050 TQ	USBLS	5/15
	Las Vegas-Henderson-Paradise MSA, NV	Y	59330 FQ	72590 MW	82330 TQ	USBLS	5/15
	New Jersey	Y	40150 FQ	48670 MW	60660 TQ	USBLS	5/15
	New Mexico	Y	30310 FQ	34720 MW	41720 TQ	USBLS	5/15
	Albuquerque MSA, NM	Y	29930 FQ	34340 MW	40100 TQ	USBLS	5/15
	New York	Y	31420 AE	64980 MW	71580 AEX	NYBLS	1/16-3/16
	Nassau County-Suffolk County PMSA, NY	Y	51720 FQ	59560 MW	69540 TQ	USBLS	5/15
	New York-Jersey City-White Plains PMSA, NY-NJ	Y	36680 FQ	66220 MW	75540 TQ	USBLS	5/15
	Rochester MSA, NY	Y	35290 FQ	39160 MW	47870 TQ	USBLS	5/15
	North Carolina	Y	34340 FQ	40490 MW	47820 TQ	USBLS	5/15
	Ohio	Y	42240 FQ	53980 MW	63160 TQ	USBLS	5/15
	Cleveland-Elyria MSA, OH	Y	43690 FQ	65890 MW	72480 TQ	USBLS	5/15
	Oklahoma	Y	32600 FQ	40150 MW	49620 TQ	USBLS	5/15
	Oklahoma City MSA, OK	Y	36230 FQ	45220 MW	54350 TQ	USBLS	5/15
	Oregon	H	17.26 FQ	24.89 MW	29.04 TQ	ORBLS	2016
	Portland-Vancouver-Hillsboro MSA, OR-WA	Y	35890 FQ	51030 MW	58710 TQ	USBLS	5/15
	Pennsylvania	Y	43110 FQ	49060 MW	55890 TQ	USBLS	5/15
	South Carolina	Y	30850 FQ	37880 MW	49630 TQ	USBLS	5/15
	Tennessee	Y	35670 FQ	48240 MW	60900 TQ	USBLS	5/15
	Knoxville MSA, TN	Y	35030 FQ	47780 MW	60090 TQ	USBLS	5/15
	Memphis MSA, TN-MS-AR	Y	33050 FQ	37220 MW	43030 TQ	USBLS	5/15
	Nashville-Davidson–Murfreesboro–Franklin MSA, TN	Y	48730 FQ	57900 MW	66970 TQ	USBLS	5/15
	Texas	Y	32570 FQ	38880 MW	52030 TQ	USBLS	5/15
	Dallas-Plano-Irving PMSA, TX	Y	33870 FQ	39420 MW	50960 TQ	USBLS	5/15
	Fort Worth-Arlington PMSA, TX	Y	34670 FQ	38190 MW	44620 TQ	USBLS	5/15
	Houston-The Woodlands-Sugar Land MSA, TX	Y	35770 FQ	46700 MW	76830 TQ	USBLS	5/15
	Utah	Y	41350 FQ	47350 MW	54980 TQ	USBLS	5/15
	Virginia	Y	35770 FQ	45940 MW	59260 TQ	USBLS	5/15
	Virginia Beach-Norfolk-Newport News MSA, VA-NC	Y	27520 FQ	33550 MW	41760 TQ	USBLS	5/15
	Washington	H	23.18 FQ	27.45 MW	30.84 TQ	WABLS	3/16
	Seattle-Bellevue-Everett PMSA, WA	H	27.03 FQ	32.19 MW	37.52 TQ	WABLS	3/16
	Wisconsin	Y	41700 FQ	46200 MW	51620 TQ	USBLS	5/15
	Wyoming	Y	33670 FQ	40170 MW	48110 TQ	USBLS	5/15

AE	Average entry wage	AWR	Average wage range	H	Hourly
AEX	Average experienced wage	B	Biweekly	HI	Highest wage paid
ATC	Average total compensation	D	Daily	HR	High end range
AW	Average wage paid	FQ	First quartile wage	LO	Lowest wage paid

LR	Low end range	MTC	Median total compensation	TCC	Total cash compensation
M	Monthly	MW	Median wage paid	TQ	Third quartile wage
MCC	Median cash compensation	MWR	Median wage range	W	Weekly
ME	Median entry wage	S	See annotated source	Y	Yearly

Occupation/Type/Industry	Location	Per	Low	Mid	High	Source	Date
Trail Builder	United States	H	8.00 LO		20.00 HI	LH02	2016
Train Controller							
Municipal Transportation Agency	San Francisco, CA	Y		72350 AW		CACIT	6/28/16
Training and Development Manager							
	Alabama	Y	72403 AE	118239 AW	141168 AEX	ALBLS	6/16
	Birmingham-Hoover MSA, AL	Y	69882 AE	130365 AW	160601 AEX	ALBLS	6/16
	Alaska	Y	70000 FQ	88840 MW	109320 TQ	USBLS	5/15
	Anchorage MSA, AK	Y	61670 FQ	92820 MW	121710 TQ	USBLS	5/15
	Arizona	Y	63810 FQ	81250 MW	111580 TQ	USBLS	5/15
	Phoenix-Mesa-Scottsdale MSA, AZ	Y	61840 FQ	78970 MW	113820 TQ	USBLS	5/15
	Tucson MSA, AZ	Y	68710 FQ	79290 MW	98780 TQ	USBLS	5/15
	Arkansas	Y	46470 FQ	66190 MW	82560 TQ	USBLS	5/15
	Little Rock-North Little Rock-Conway MSA, AR	Y	37370 FQ	58380 MW	75310 TQ	USBLS	5/15
	California	H	43.23 FQ	58.24 MW	78.73 TQ	CABLS	1/16-3/16
	Anaheim-Santa Ana-Irvine PMSA, CA	H	37.68 FQ	54.67 MW	71.15 TQ	CABLS	1/16-3/16
	Los Angeles-Long Beach-Glendale PMSA, CA	H	41.13 FQ	55.25 MW	73.29 TQ	CABLS	1/16-3/16
	Oakland-Hayward-Berkeley PMSA, CA	H	50.49 FQ	62.66 MW	77.13 TQ	CABLS	1/16-3/16
	Riverside-San Bernardino-Ontario MSA, CA	H	35.85 FQ	46.70 MW	62.66 TQ	CABLS	1/16-3/16
	Sacramento–Roseville–Arden-Arcade MSA, CA	H	42.74 FQ	49.00 MW	58.63 TQ	CABLS	1/16-3/16
	San Diego-Carlsbad MSA, CA	H	38.73 FQ	50.03 MW	63.83 TQ	CABLS	1/16-3/16
	San Francisco-Redwood City-South San Francisco PMSA, CA	H	53.41 FQ	68.47 MW	89.67 TQ	CABLS	1/16-3/16
	Colorado	Y	85610 FQ	106780 MW	129350 TQ	USBLS	5/15
	Denver-Aurora-Lakewood MSA, CO	Y	84640 FQ	107020 MW	129360 TQ	USBLS	5/15
	Connecticut	Y		118105 MW		CTBLS	1/16-3/16
	Bridgeport-Stamford-Norwalk MSA, CT	Y	101530 FQ	120890 MW	162650 TQ	USBLS	5/15
	Hartford-West Hartford-East Hartford MSA, CT	Y	93470 FQ	112260 MW	127610 TQ	USBLS	5/15
	Delaware	Y	94820 FQ	115310 MW	145880 TQ	USBLS	5/15
	Wilmington PMSA, DE-MD-NJ	Y	108890 FQ	123610 MW	147150 TQ	USBLS	5/15
	District of Columbia	Y	91960 FQ	117110 MW	161290 TQ	USBLS	5/15
	Washington-Arlington-Alexandria PMSA, DC-VA-MD-WV	Y	95910 FQ	120100 MW	164730 TQ	USBLS	5/15
	Florida	H	29.85 AE	46.82 MW	61.10 AEX	FLBLS	7/16-9/16
	Fort Lauderdale-Pompano Beach-Deerfield Beach PMSA, FL	H	21.99 AE	37.86 MW	54.92 AEX	FLBLS	7/16-9/16
	Miami-Miami Beach-Kendall PMSA, FL	H	37.19 AE	48.88 MW	57.94 AEX	FLBLS	7/16-9/16
	Orlando-Kissimmee-Sanford MSA, FL	H	31.79 AE	41.52 MW	55.85 AEX	FLBLS	7/16-9/16
	Tampa-St. Petersburg-Clearwater MSA, FL	H	31.21 AE	48.29 MW	64.58 AEX	FLBLS	7/16-9/16
	Georgia	Y	91260 FQ	115140 MW	142550 TQ	USBLS	5/15
	Atlanta-Sandy Springs-Roswell MSA, GA	Y	97010 FQ	118980 MW	147090 TQ	USBLS	5/15
	Augusta-Richmond County MSA, GA-SC	Y	80800 FQ	100910 MW	131000 TQ	USBLS	5/15
	Hawaii	Y	72630 FQ	103650 MW	117170 TQ	USBLS	5/15
	Urban Honolulu MSA, HI	Y	70960 FQ	103670 MW	117300 TQ	USBLS	5/15
	Idaho	Y	54360 FQ	68270 MW	90220 TQ	USBLS	5/15
	Boise City MSA, ID	Y	53530 FQ	66570 MW	90060 TQ	USBLS	5/15
	Illinois	Y	55950 FQ	84150 MW	115550 TQ	USBLS	5/15
	Chicago-Naperville-Arlington Heights PMSA, IL	Y	68090 FQ	89920 MW	118570 TQ	USBLS	5/15
	Indiana	Y	62910 FQ	78290 MW	99740 TQ	USBLS	5/15
	Gary PMSA, IN	Y	60180 FQ	89560 MW	146160 TQ	USBLS	5/15

Occupation/Type/Industry	Location	Per	Low	Mid	High	Source	Date
Training and Development Manager	Indianapolis-Carmel-Anderson						
	MSA, IN	Y	67210 FQ	80450 MW	99340 TQ	USBLS	5/15
	Iowa	Y	58840 FQ	78300 MW	99520 TQ	USBLS	5/15
	Des Moines-West Des Moines						
	MSA, IA	Y	72740 FQ	92390 MW	110950 TQ	USBLS	5/15
	Kansas	Y	62960 FQ	79870 MW	126860 TQ	USBLS	5/15
	Wichita MSA, KS	Y	70670 FQ	95770 MW	125510 TQ	USBLS	5/15
	Kentucky	Y	68730 FQ	86040 MW	111160 TQ	USBLS	5/15
	Louisville-Jefferson County						
	MSA, KY-IN	Y	68990 FQ	87110 MW	112200 TQ	USBLS	5/15
	Louisiana	Y	54550 FQ	70210 MW	90770 TQ	USBLS	5/15
	Baton Rouge MSA, LA	Y	57830 FQ	71650 MW	93650 TQ	USBLS	5/15
	New Orleans-Metairie MSA,						
	LA	Y	59180 FQ	80930 MW	97220 TQ	USBLS	5/15
	Maine	Y	71570 FQ	87860 MW	102170 TQ	USBLS	5/15
	Portland-South Portland MSA,						
	ME	Y	77720 FQ	93440 MW	118510 TQ	USBLS	5/15
	Maryland	Y	73869 AE	124516 MW	149840 AEX	MDBLS	4/16
	Baltimore-Columbia-Towson						
	MSA, MD	Y	82330 FQ	108890 MW	134930 TQ	USBLS	5/15
	Massachusetts	Y	89840 FQ	117500 MW	158070 TQ	USBLS	5/15
	Boston-Cambridge-Newton						
	NECTA, MA	Y	93970 FQ	122520 MW	165090 TQ	USBLS	5/15
	Worcester MSA, MA-CT	Y	84950 FQ	94840 MW	109210 TQ	USBLS	5/15
	Michigan	Y	65170 FQ	89640 MW	122620 TQ	USBLS	5/15
	Detroit-Dearborn-Livonia						
	PMSA, MI	Y	78370 FQ	96790 MW	140530 TQ	USBLS	5/15
	Minnesota	Y	90199 FQ	115968 MW	157405 TQ	MNBLS	1/16-3/16
	Minneapolis-St. Paul-						
	Bloomington MSA, MN-WI	Y	93227 FQ	121455 MW	162658 TQ	MNBLS	1/16-3/16
	Mississippi	Y	60680 FQ	78210 MW	118590 TQ	USBLS	5/15
	Jackson MSA, MS	Y	56370 FQ	72750 MW	93370 TQ	USBLS	5/15
	Missouri	Y	75060 FQ	98310 MW	125160 TQ	USBLS	5/15
	Kansas City MSA, MO-KS	Y	64870 FQ	87270 MW	122190 TQ	USBLS	5/15
	St. Louis MSA, MO-IL	Y	77480 FQ	107060 MW	139720 TQ	USBLS	5/15
	Nebraska	Y	78430 FQ	94630 MW	118075 TQ	NEBLS	7/16-9/16
	Omaha-Council Bluffs MSA,						
	NE-IA	Y	78440 FQ	93635 MW	117510 TQ	NEBLS	7/16-9/16
	Nevada	Y	65720 FQ	81500 MW	101810 TQ	USBLS	5/15
	Las Vegas-Henderson-Paradise						
	MSA, NV	Y	64880 FQ	81800 MW	99460 TQ	USBLS	5/15
	New Hampshire	H	36.11 AE	51.68 MW	60.95 AEX	NHBLS	6/16
	New Jersey	Y	105920 FQ	124510 MW	157470 TQ	USBLS	5/15
	Camden PMSA, NJ	Y	88540 FQ	108140 MW	128220 TQ	USBLS	5/15
	Newark PMSA, NJ-PA	Y	110900 FQ	133460 MW	172560 TQ	USBLS	5/15
	Trenton MSA, NJ	Y	99740 FQ	115720 MW	137250 TQ	USBLS	5/15
	New Mexico	Y	56330 FQ	76110 MW	113130 TQ	USBLS	5/15
	Albuquerque MSA, NM	Y	59040 FQ	91350 MW	122850 TQ	USBLS	5/15
	New York	Y	80830 AE	122830 MW	167770 AEX	NYBLS	1/16-3/16
	Buffalo-Cheektowaga-Niagara						
	Falls MSA, NY	Y	75740 FQ	92240 MW	117970 TQ	USBLS	5/15
	Nassau County-Suffolk County						
	PMSA, NY	Y	90110 FQ	127950 MW	162430 TQ	USBLS	5/15
	New York-Jersey City-White						
	Plains PMSA, NY-NJ	Y	101240 FQ	126650 MW	172830 TQ	USBLS	5/15
	Rochester MSA, NY	Y	84630 FQ	100770 MW	130910 TQ	USBLS	5/15
	North Carolina	Y	89360 FQ	115100 MW	147130 TQ	USBLS	5/15
	Charlotte-Concord-Gastonia						
	MSA, NC-SC	Y	87000 FQ	119770 MW	157860 TQ	USBLS	5/15
	Raleigh MSA, NC	Y	89010 FQ	108810 MW	132740 TQ	USBLS	5/15
	North Dakota	Y	76790 FQ	93700 MW	119330 TQ	USBLS	5/15
	Fargo MSA, ND-MN	Y	73510 FQ	91390 MW	121090 TQ	USBLS	5/15
	Ohio	Y	73490 FQ	95770 MW	122090 TQ	USBLS	5/15
	Cincinnati MSA, OH-KY-IN	Y	78280 FQ	108780 MW	128550 TQ	USBLS	5/15
	Cleveland-Elyria MSA, OH	Y	77170 FQ	103790 MW	124620 TQ	USBLS	5/15
	Columbus MSA, OH	Y	77120 FQ	97390 MW	127850 TQ	USBLS	5/15
	Oklahoma	Y	62710 FQ	74390 MW	100760 TQ	USBLS	5/15
	Oklahoma City MSA, OK	Y	63740 FQ	74930 MW	119850 AEX	USBLS	5/15
	Tulsa MSA, OK	Y	64220 FQ	75290 MW	97260 TQ	USBLS	5/15
	Oregon	H	35.88 FQ	48.17 MW	61.19 TQ	ORBLS	2016

Occupation/Type/Industry	Location	Per	Low	Mid	High	Source	Date
Training and Development Manager	Portland-Vancouver-Hillsboro						
	MSA, OR-WA	Y	75290 FQ	101190 MW	130110 TQ	USBLS	5/15
	Pennsylvania	Y	83030 FQ	110220 MW	148740 TQ	USBLS	5/15
	Allentown-Bethlehem-Easton						
	MSA, PA-NJ	Y	78860 FQ	103700 MW	159770 TQ	USBLS	5/15
	Harrisburg-Carlisle MSA, PA	Y	80740 FQ	96050 MW	122260 TQ	USBLS	5/15
	Montgomery County-Bucks						
	County-Chester County						
	PMSA, PA	Y	90900 FQ	120110 MW	158670 TQ	USBLS	5/15
	Philadelphia PMSA, PA	Y	78130 FQ	101550 MW	140710 TQ	USBLS	5/15
	Pittsburgh MSA, PA	Y	89650 FQ	115910 MW	155110 TQ	USBLS	5/15
	Rhode Island	Y	92920 FQ	112670 MW	139070 TQ	USBLS	5/15
	Providence-Warwick MSA, RI-						
	MA	Y	93790 FQ	112610 MW	136350 TQ	USBLS	5/15
	South Carolina	Y	61380 FQ	88050 MW	118490 TQ	USBLS	5/15
	Charleston-North Charleston						
	MSA, SC	Y	68240 FQ	89270 MW	114780 TQ	USBLS	5/15
	Columbia MSA, SC	Y	54910 FQ	73590 MW	113590 TQ	USBLS	5/15
	Greenville-Anderson-Mauldin						
	MSA, SC	Y	68210 FQ	93580 MW	117750 TQ	USBLS	5/15
	Tennessee	Y	47860 FQ	68320 MW	97810 TQ	USBLS	5/15
	Knoxville MSA, TN	Y	62530 FQ	78270 MW	97370 TQ	USBLS	5/15
	Memphis MSA, TN-MS-AR	Y	53100 FQ	74670 MW	100000 TQ	USBLS	5/15
	Nashville-Davidson–						
	Murfreesboro–Franklin						
	MSA, TN	Y	47560 FQ	68870 MW	97480 TQ	USBLS	5/15
	Texas	Y	91960 FQ	114350 MW	142460 TQ	USBLS	5/15
	Austin-Round Rock MSA, TX	Y	67810 FQ	105580 MW	131960 TQ	USBLS	5/15
	Dallas-Plano-Irving PMSA, TX	Y	105850 FQ	123170 MW	151370 TQ	USBLS	5/15
	Fort Worth-Arlington PMSA,						
	TX	Y	90190 FQ	101640 MW	118270 TQ	USBLS	5/15
	Houston-The Woodlands-						
	Sugar Land MSA, TX	Y	96320 FQ	120230 MW	154930 TQ	USBLS	5/15
	San Antonio-New Braunfels						
	MSA, TX	Y	90590 FQ	113320 MW	140660 TQ	USBLS	5/15
	Utah	Y	57510 FQ	77410 MW	96180 TQ	USBLS	5/15
	Provo-Orem MSA, UT	Y	56600 FQ	69670 MW	100910 TQ	USBLS	5/15
	Salt Lake City MSA, UT	Y	61650 FQ	81200 MW	96230 TQ	USBLS	5/15
	Vermont	Y	75400 FQ	83440 MW	94130 TQ	USBLS	5/15
	Burlington-South Burlington						
	MSA, VT	Y	72420 FQ	80970 MW	92290 TQ	USBLS	5/15
	Virginia	Y	88990 FQ	112920 MW	143190 TQ	USBLS	5/15
	Richmond MSA, VA	Y	70450 FQ	83400 MW	114590 TQ	USBLS	5/15
	Virginia Beach-Norfolk-						
	Newport News MSA, VA-NC	Y	83310 FQ	108840 MW	124620 TQ	USBLS	5/15
	Washington	H	41.38 FQ	51.41 MW	65.91 TQ	WABLS	3/16
	Seattle-Bellevue-Everett						
	PMSA, WA	H	43.72 FQ	52.91 MW	67.60 TQ	WABLS	3/16
	Tacoma-Lakewood PMSA, WA	H	36.88 FQ	51.87 MW	64.16 TQ	WABLS	3/16
	West Virginia	Y	61590 FQ	74310 MW	87950 TQ	USBLS	5/15
	Wisconsin	Y	71840 FQ	90570 MW	116150 TQ	USBLS	5/15
	Madison MSA, WI	Y	70390 FQ	87090 MW	106340 TQ	USBLS	5/15
	Milwaukee-Waukesha-West						
	Allis MSA, WI	Y	80040 FQ	99650 MW	138410 TQ	USBLS	5/15
	Puerto Rico	Y	46720 FQ	61710 MW	93830 TQ	USBLS	5/15
	San Juan-Carolina-Caguas						
	MSA, PR	Y	48000 FQ	61720 MW	96210 TQ	USBLS	5/15
Training and Development Specialist							
	Alabama	Y	33916 AE	58689 AW	71081 AEX	ALBLS	6/16
	Birmingham-Hoover MSA, AL	Y	36181 AE	58535 AW	69718 AEX	ALBLS	6/16
	Anchorage MSA, AK	Y	60770 FQ	104700 MW	117680 TQ	USBLS	5/15
	Arizona	Y	40900 FQ	54310 MW	75170 TQ	USBLS	5/15
	Phoenix-Mesa-Scottsdale						
	MSA, AZ	Y	40810 FQ	53230 MW	74380 TQ	USBLS	5/15
	Tucson MSA, AZ	Y	36660 FQ	46470 MW	60910 TQ	USBLS	5/15
	Arkansas	Y	38370 FQ	48680 MW	61880 TQ	USBLS	5/15
	Little Rock-North Little Rock-						
	Conway MSA, AR	Y	40510 FQ	50020 MW	63660 TQ	USBLS	5/15
	California	H	24.01 FQ	33.39 MW	45.39 TQ	CABLS	1/16-3/16

AE Average entry wage	**AWR** Average wage range	**H** Hourly	**LR** Low end range	**MTC** Median total compensation	**TCC** Total cash compensation
AEX Average experienced wage	**B** Biweekly	**HI** Highest wage paid	**M** Monthly	**MW** Median wage paid	**TQ** Third quartile wage
ATC Average total compensation	**D** Daily	**HR** High end range	**MCC** Median cash compensation	**MWR** Median wage range	**W** Weekly
AW Average wage paid	**FQ** First quartile wage	**LO** Lowest wage paid	**ME** Median entry wage	**S** See annotated source	**Y** Yearly

Training and Development Specialist

Occupation/Type/Industry	Location	Per	Low	Mid	High	Source	Date
Training and Development Specialist							
	Anaheim-Santa Ana-Irvine PMSA, CA	H	24.25 FQ	32.27 MW	42.71 TQ	CABLS	1/16-3/16
	Los Angeles-Long Beach-Glendale PMSA, CA	H	21.47 FQ	29.52 MW	40.14 TQ	CABLS	1/16-3/16
	Oakland-Hayward-Berkeley PMSA, CA	H	30.16 FQ	42.62 MW	53.01 TQ	CABLS	1/16-3/16
	Riverside-San Bernardino-Ontario MSA, CA	H	21.44 FQ	28.93 MW	37.01 TQ	CABLS	1/16-3/16
	Sacramento–Roseville–Arden-Arcade MSA, CA	H	25.53 FQ	32.42 MW	41.91 TQ	CABLS	1/16-3/16
	San Diego-Carlsbad MSA, CA	H	22.97 FQ	31.52 MW	42.74 TQ	CABLS	1/16-3/16
	San Francisco-Redwood City-South San Francisco PMSA, CA	H	30.98 FQ	39.83 MW	53.14 TQ	CABLS	1/16-3/16
	Colorado	Y	49880 FQ	64470 MW	83640 TQ	USBLS	5/15
	Denver-Aurora-Lakewood MSA, CO	Y	52060 FQ	67160 MW	84240 TQ	USBLS	5/15
	Connecticut	Y		71604 MW		CTBLS	1/16-3/16
	Bridgeport-Stamford-Norwalk MSA, CT	Y	57010 FQ	77740 MW	94140 TQ	USBLS	5/15
	Hartford-West Hartford-East Hartford MSA, CT	Y	51730 FQ	67660 MW	84250 TQ	USBLS	5/15
	Delaware	Y	51080 FQ	66650 MW	87190 TQ	USBLS	5/15
	Wilmington PMSA, DE-MD-NJ	Y	50640 FQ	68360 MW	90120 TQ	USBLS	5/15
	District of Columbia	Y	58490 FQ	75080 MW	93970 TQ	USBLS	5/15
	Washington-Arlington-Alexandria PMSA, DC-VA-MD-WV	Y	54710 FQ	77460 MW	98040 TQ	USBLS	5/15
	Florida	H	17.53 AE	27.00 MW	33.88 AEX	FLBLS	7/16-9/16
	Fort Lauderdale-Pompano Beach-Deerfield Beach PMSA, FL	H	18.66 AE	29.91 MW	38.92 AEX	FLBLS	7/16-9/16
	Miami-Miami Beach-Kendall PMSA, FL	H	19.58 AE	29.38 MW	36.09 AEX	FLBLS	7/16-9/16
	Orlando-Kissimmee-Sanford MSA, FL	H	17.22 AE	25.45 MW	32.09 AEX	FLBLS	7/16-9/16
	Tampa-St. Petersburg-Clearwater MSA, FL	H	17.80 AE	27.19 MW	34.31 AEX	FLBLS	7/16-9/16
	Georgia	Y	42520 FQ	57400 MW	76780 TQ	USBLS	5/15
	Atlanta-Sandy Springs-Roswell MSA, GA	Y	45140 FQ	60320 MW	79460 TQ	USBLS	5/15
	Augusta-Richmond County MSA, GA-SC	Y	38150 FQ	51770 MW	65380 TQ	USBLS	5/15
	Hawaii	Y	43840 FQ	55810 MW	74080 TQ	USBLS	5/15
	Urban Honolulu MSA, HI	Y	45460 FQ	56900 MW	75320 TQ	USBLS	5/15
	Idaho	Y	37990 FQ	48850 MW	65510 TQ	USBLS	5/15
	Boise City MSA, ID	Y	38650 FQ	47920 MW	60130 TQ	USBLS	5/15
	Illinois	Y	36630 FQ	54400 MW	75730 TQ	USBLS	5/15
	Chicago-Naperville-Arlington Heights PMSA, IL	Y	39390 FQ	57020 MW	76570 TQ	USBLS	5/15
	Lake County-Kenosha County PMSA, IL-WI	Y	30600 FQ	51700 MW	75290 TQ	USBLS	5/15
	Indiana	Y	39450 FQ	53050 MW	70170 TQ	USBLS	5/15
	Elkhart-Goshen MSA, IN	Y	34430 FQ	43420 MW	56170 TQ	USBLS	5/15
	Gary PMSA, IN	Y	38490 FQ	46260 MW	59580 TQ	USBLS	5/15
	Indianapolis-Carmel-Anderson MSA, IN	Y	43360 FQ	59240 MW	75360 TQ	USBLS	5/15
	Iowa	Y	35160 FQ	47150 MW	63440 TQ	USBLS	5/15
	Des Moines-West Des Moines MSA, IA	Y	45300 FQ	58030 MW	72180 TQ	USBLS	5/15
	Iowa City MSA, IA	Y	36590 FQ	49270 MW	61310 TQ	USBLS	5/15
	Kansas	Y	40790 FQ	55570 MW	75600 TQ	USBLS	5/15
	Wichita MSA, KS	Y	33310 FQ	47630 MW	72910 TQ	USBLS	5/15
	Kentucky	Y	39790 FQ	51770 MW	70190 TQ	USBLS	5/15
	Louisville-Jefferson County MSA, KY-IN	Y	39880 FQ	53400 MW	69050 TQ	USBLS	5/15
	Louisiana	Y	34770 FQ	45010 MW	61500 TQ	USBLS	5/15
	Baton Rouge MSA, LA	Y	35280 FQ	44580 MW	66190 TQ	USBLS	5/15
	New Orleans-Metairie MSA, LA	Y	35140 FQ	48190 MW	61160 TQ	USBLS	5/15

AE	Average entry wage	**AWR**	Average wage range	**H**	Hourly
AEX	Average experienced wage	**B**	Biweekly	**HI**	Highest wage paid
ATC	Average total compensation	**D**	Daily	**HR**	High end range
AW	Average wage paid	**FQ**	First quartile wage	**LO**	Lowest wage paid

LR	Low end range	**MTC**	Median total compensation	**TCC**	Total cash compensation
M	Monthly	**MW**	Median wage paid	**TQ**	Third quartile wage
MCC	Median cash compensation	**MWR**	Median wage range	**W**	Weekly
ME	Median entry wage	**S**	See annotated source	**Y**	Yearly

Training and Development Specialist

Occupation/Type/Industry	Location	Per	Low	Mid	High	Source	Date
	Maine	Y	38780 FQ	52080 MW	63490 TQ	USBLS	5/15
	Portland-South Portland MSA, ME	Y	42750 FQ	55300 MW	67730 TQ	USBLS	5/15
	Maryland	Y	35863 AE	64904 MW	79424 AEX	MDBLS	4/16
	Baltimore-Columbia-Towson MSA, MD	Y	44980 FQ	60380 MW	78030 TQ	USBLS	5/15
	Salisbury MSA, MD-DE	Y	37350 FQ	54710 MW	80130 TQ	USBLS	5/15
	Massachusetts	Y	52600 FQ	70400 MW	93390 TQ	USBLS	5/15
	Boston-Cambridge-Newton NECTA, MA	Y	55090 FQ	74960 MW	97840 TQ	USBLS	5/15
	Worcester MSA, MA-CT	Y	37380 FQ	55600 MW	67990 TQ	USBLS	5/15
	Michigan	Y	37170 FQ	50420 MW	70450 TQ	USBLS	5/15
	Detroit-Dearborn-Livonia PMSA, MI	Y	41630 FQ	54350 MW	74630 TQ	USBLS	5/15
	Grand Rapids-Wyoming MSA, MI	Y	32310 FQ	50620 MW	69750 TQ	USBLS	5/15
	Minnesota	Y	44505 FQ	59483 MW	76340 TQ	MNBLS	1/16-3/16
	Minneapolis-St. Paul-Bloomington MSA, MN-WI	Y	46029 FQ	61393 MW	77529 TQ	MNBLS	1/16-3/16
	Mississippi	Y	39370 FQ	52910 MW	66620 TQ	USBLS	5/15
	Jackson MSA, MS	Y	40220 FQ	51610 MW	70980 TQ	USBLS	5/15
	Missouri	Y	39640 FQ	52560 MW	71210 TQ	USBLS	5/15
	Kansas City MSA, MO-KS	Y	44440 FQ	61080 MW	77960 TQ	USBLS	5/15
	St. Louis MSA, MO-IL	Y	44160 FQ	59270 MW	75860 TQ	USBLS	5/15
	Montana	Y	37690 FQ	47510 MW	63850 TQ	USBLS	5/15
	Billings MSA, MT	Y	37950 FQ	52230 MW	86700 TQ	USBLS	5/15
	Nebraska	Y	38545 FQ	49520 MW	67010 TQ	NEBLS	7/16-9/16
	Omaha-Council Bluffs MSA, NE-IA	Y	38055 FQ	51060 MW	68500 TQ	NEBLS	7/16-9/16
	Nevada	Y	33980 FQ	48590 MW	65770 TQ	USBLS	5/15
	Las Vegas-Henderson-Paradise MSA, NV	Y	31870 FQ	45070 MW	60930 TQ	USBLS	5/15
	New Hampshire	H	20.59 AE	32.17 MW	39.07 AEX	NHBLS	6/16
	Manchester NECTA, NH	H	24.71 AE	39.32 MW	45.16 AEX	NHBLS	6/16
	Nashua NECTA, NH-MA	Y	43710 FQ	57470 MW	78750 TQ	USBLS	5/15
	New Jersey	Y	51560 FQ	69140 MW	91070 TQ	USBLS	5/15
	Camden PMSA, NJ	Y	48590 FQ	60900 MW	78670 TQ	USBLS	5/15
	Newark PMSA, NJ-PA	Y	51780 FQ	72460 MW	93100 TQ	USBLS	5/15
	Trenton MSA, NJ	Y	53580 FQ	73890 MW	89760 TQ	USBLS	5/15
	New Mexico	Y	41650 FQ	52010 MW	71730 TQ	USBLS	5/15
	Albuquerque MSA, NM	Y	42620 FQ	55200 MW	73810 TQ	USBLS	5/15
	New York	Y	37450 AE	62740 MW	82540 AEX	NYBLS	1/16-3/16
	Buffalo-Cheektowaga-Niagara Falls MSA, NY	Y	40140 FQ	52380 MW	69330 TQ	USBLS	5/15
	Nassau County-Suffolk County PMSA, NY	Y	47990 FQ	62790 MW	84830 TQ	USBLS	5/15
	New York-Jersey City-White Plains PMSA, NY-NJ	Y	47630 FQ	65170 MW	90580 TQ	USBLS	5/15
	Rochester MSA, NY	Y	44980 FQ	58630 MW	74540 TQ	USBLS	5/15
	North Carolina	Y	44240 FQ	60570 MW	79360 TQ	USBLS	5/15
	Charlotte-Concord-Gastonia MSA, NC-SC	Y	49780 FQ	66900 MW	83900 TQ	USBLS	5/15
	Raleigh MSA, NC	Y	43140 FQ	57980 MW	78060 TQ	USBLS	5/15
	North Dakota	Y	40210 FQ	49810 MW	63190 TQ	USBLS	5/15
	Fargo MSA, ND-MN	Y	39630 FQ	48270 MW	61590 TQ	USBLS	5/15
	Ohio	Y	42590 FQ	55570 MW	71050 TQ	USBLS	5/15
	Cincinnati MSA, OH-KY-IN	Y	45260 FQ	59200 MW	78010 TQ	USBLS	5/15
	Cleveland-Elyria MSA, OH	Y	43020 FQ	55740 MW	70380 TQ	USBLS	5/15
	Columbus MSA, OH	Y	44010 FQ	57590 MW	72940 TQ	USBLS	5/15
	Oklahoma	Y	37330 FQ	51120 MW	72090 TQ	USBLS	5/15
	Oklahoma City MSA, OK	Y	41060 FQ	54440 MW	73310 TQ	USBLS	5/15
	Tulsa MSA, OK	Y	32800 FQ	50880 MW	84720 TQ	USBLS	5/15
	Oregon	H	20.11 FQ	26.78 MW	35.77 TQ	ORBLS	2016
	Portland-Vancouver-Hillsboro MSA, OR-WA	Y	43470 FQ	59640 MW	76120 TQ	USBLS	5/15
	Pennsylvania	Y	43680 FQ	57620 MW	75090 TQ	USBLS	5/15
	Allentown-Bethlehem-Easton MSA, PA-NJ	Y	42890 FQ	58900 MW	75460 TQ	USBLS	5/15
	Harrisburg-Carlisle MSA, PA	Y	45150 FQ	58060 MW	72100 TQ	USBLS	5/15

AE Average entry wage	**AWR** Average wage range	**H** Hourly	**LR** Low end range	**MTC** Median total compensation	**TCC** Total cash compensation
AEX Average experienced wage	**B** Biweekly	**HI** Highest wage paid	**M** Monthly	**MW** Median wage paid	**TQ** Third quartile wage
ATC Average total compensation	**D** Daily	**HR** High end range	**MCC** Median cash compensation	**MWR** Median wage range	**W** Weekly
AW Average wage paid	**FQ** First quartile wage	**LO** Lowest wage paid	**ME** Median entry wage	**S** See annotated source	**Y** Yearly

Occupation/Type/Industry	Location	Per	Low	Mid	High	Source	Date
Training and Development Specialist	Montgomery County-Bucks County-Chester County PMSA, PA	Y	48040 FQ	62000 MW	83730 TQ	USBLS	5/15
	Philadelphia PMSA, PA	Y	48680 FQ	60020 MW	78630 TQ	USBLS	5/15
	Pittsburgh MSA, PA	Y	42110 FQ	55800 MW	74770 TQ	USBLS	5/15
	Rhode Island	Y	57380 FQ	72770 MW	90550 TQ	USBLS	5/15
	Providence-Warwick MSA, RI-MA	Y	56290 FQ	72200 MW	90030 TQ	USBLS	5/15
	South Carolina	Y	37090 FQ	49180 MW	67550 TQ	USBLS	5/15
	Charleston-North Charleston MSA, SC	Y	40520 FQ	51760 MW	72830 TQ	USBLS	5/15
	Columbia MSA, SC	Y	37830 FQ	49020 MW	61680 TQ	USBLS	5/15
	Greenville-Anderson-Mauldin MSA, SC	Y	36740 FQ	48340 MW	72530 TQ	USBLS	5/15
	South Dakota	Y	36810 FQ	45230 MW	56430 TQ	USBLS	5/15
	Sioux Falls MSA, SD	Y	37150 FQ	44730 MW	54730 TQ	USBLS	5/15
	Tennessee	Y	36230 FQ	52240 MW	71230 TQ	USBLS	5/15
	Knoxville MSA, TN	Y	36220 FQ	52910 MW	73810 TQ	USBLS	5/15
	Memphis MSA, TN-MS-AR	Y	36220 FQ	53400 MW	69350 TQ	USBLS	5/15
	Nashville-Davidson–Murfreesboro–Franklin MSA, TN	Y	41490 FQ	56090 MW	72750 TQ	USBLS	5/15
	Texas	Y	43100 FQ	60460 MW	80730 TQ	USBLS	5/15
	Austin-Round Rock MSA, TX	Y	43460 FQ	56370 MW	73650 TQ	USBLS	5/15
	Dallas-Plano-Irving PMSA, TX	Y	45940 FQ	64400 MW	83690 TQ	USBLS	5/15
	Fort Worth-Arlington PMSA, TX	Y	41300 FQ	57370 MW	75380 TQ	USBLS	5/15
	Houston-The Woodlands-Sugar Land MSA, TX	Y	49560 FQ	69200 MW	91750 TQ	USBLS	5/15
	San Antonio-New Braunfels MSA, TX	Y	43430 FQ	56620 MW	76560 TQ	USBLS	5/15
	Utah	Y	35860 FQ	46790 MW	61630 TQ	USBLS	5/15
	Ogden-Clearfield MSA, UT	Y	31770 FQ	37310 MW	49520 TQ	USBLS	5/15
	Provo-Orem MSA, UT	Y	34110 FQ	41310 MW	57310 TQ	USBLS	5/15
	Salt Lake City MSA, UT	Y	38920 FQ	51440 MW	63630 TQ	USBLS	5/15
	Vermont	Y	38140 FQ	54140 MW	78590 TQ	USBLS	5/15
	Burlington-South Burlington MSA, VT	Y	36800 FQ	48960 MW	78490 TQ	USBLS	5/15
	Virginia	Y	48110 FQ	64870 MW	89080 TQ	USBLS	5/15
	Richmond MSA, VA	Y	44670 FQ	57980 MW	80320 TQ	USBLS	5/15
	Virginia Beach-Norfolk-Newport News MSA, VA-NC	Y	47820 FQ	59770 MW	75600 TQ	USBLS	5/15
	Washington	H	24.55 FQ	32.08 MW	41.08 TQ	WABLS	3/16
	Seattle-Bellevue-Everett PMSA, WA	H	25.67 FQ	34.39 MW	44.20 TQ	WABLS	3/16
	Tacoma-Lakewood PMSA, WA	H	23.06 FQ	29.12 MW	34.41 TQ	WABLS	3/16
	West Virginia	Y	33310 FQ	43390 MW	61150 TQ	USBLS	5/15
	Huntington-Ashland MSA, WV-KY-OH	Y	30910 FQ	40510 MW	58450 TQ	USBLS	5/15
	Wisconsin	Y	37060 FQ	50060 MW	65010 TQ	USBLS	5/15
	Madison MSA, WI	Y	37060 FQ	51170 MW	64250 TQ	USBLS	5/15
	Milwaukee-Waukesha-West Allis MSA, WI	Y	42460 FQ	57520 MW	73530 TQ	USBLS	5/15
	Wyoming	Y	44910 FQ	59110 MW	82820 TQ	USBLS	5/15
	Cheyenne MSA, WY	Y	37110 FQ	48860 MW	63110 TQ	USBLS	5/15
	Puerto Rico	Y	23900 FQ	35720 MW	47180 TQ	USBLS	5/15
	San Juan-Carolina-Caguas MSA, PR	Y	25210 FQ	36960 MW	47450 TQ	USBLS	5/15
	Guam	Y	29100 FQ	39860 MW	49260 TQ	USBLS	5/15
Training Coordinator							
Police Department, Municipal Government	Azusa, CA	Y			71955 HI	CACIT	6/28/16
Police Department, Municipal Government	National City, CA	Y			35066 HI	CACIT	6/28/16
Transcribing Typist							
Police Department, Municipal Government	Bakersfield, CA	Y		37206 AW		CACIT	6/28/16
Transfer Station Attendant							
Solid Waste Department, Municipal Government	Ashfield, MA	H			13.07 HI	FRCOG	2016

AE	Average entry wage	**AWR**	Average wage range	**H**	Hourly	**LR** Low end range	**MTC** Median total compensation	**TCC** Total cash compensation
AEX	Average experienced wage	**B**	Biweekly	**HI**	Highest wage paid	**M** Monthly	**MW** Median wage paid	**TQ** Third quartile wage
ATC	Average total compensation	**D**	Daily	**HR**	High end range	**MCC** Median cash compensation	**MWR** Median wage range	**W** Weekly
AW	Average wage paid	**FQ**	First quartile wage	**LO**	Lowest wage paid	**ME** Median entry wage	**S** See annotated source	**Y** Yearly

Occupation/Type/Industry	Location	Per	Low	Mid	High	Source	Date
Transfer Station Attendant							
Solid Waste Department, Municipal Government	Heath, MA	H			13.30 HI	FRCOG	2016
Solid Waste Department, Municipal Government	New Salem, MA	H			13.06 HI	FRCOG	2016
Transit and Railroad Police	California	H	22.25 FQ	29.83 MW	38.94 TQ	CABLS	1/16-3/16
	Florida	H	26.06 AE	32.59 MW	36.39 AEX	FLBLS	7/16-9/16
	Georgia	Y	45860 FQ	54000 MW	60040 TQ	USBLS	5/15
	Illinois	Y	51930 FQ	67970 MW	75730 TQ	USBLS	5/15
	Louisiana	Y	33660 FQ	39580 MW	48250 TQ	USBLS	5/15
	Maryland	Y	36399 AE	58982 MW	70273 AEX	MDBLS	4/16
	Minnesota	Y	57159 FQ	67712 MW	74942 TQ	MNBLS	1/16-3/16
	Missouri	Y	32280 FQ	34750 MW	37220 TQ	USBLS	5/15
	Montana	Y	30000 FQ	44520 MW	57030 TQ	USBLS	5/15
	New Jersey	Y	81710 FQ	90320 MW	98940 TQ	USBLS	5/15
	New York	Y	46260 AE	60550 MW	69070 AEX	NYBLS	1/16-3/16
	Ohio	Y	51700 FQ	58990 MW	69080 TQ	USBLS	5/15
	Pennsylvania	Y	56250 FQ	68350 MW	80200 TQ	USBLS	5/15
	Tennessee	Y	55770 FQ	60540 MW	67880 TQ	USBLS	5/15
	Texas	Y	44440 FQ	55500 MW	67050 TQ	USBLS	5/15
	Washington	H	18.64 FQ	21.47 MW	24.02 TQ	WABLS	3/16
	Wyoming	Y	35730 FQ	39820 MW	53450 TQ	USBLS	5/15
Transit Planner							
Municipal Government	Elk Grove, CA	Y		83499 AW		CACIT	6/28/16
Transit Planning Manager							
Municipal Government	Anaheim, CA	Y			131600 HI	CACIT	6/28/16
Transit Scheduler							
Municipal Government	Folsom, CA	Y			53860 HI	CACIT	6/28/16
Municipal Government	Colorado Springs, CO	Y	46996 LO		64619 HI	COSPRS	2017
Transit Secretary							
Police Department, Municipal Government	Los Angeles, CA	Y			66529 HI	CACIT	6/23/16
Transit Systems Manager							
Municipal Government	Colorado Springs, CO	Y	99194 LO		136391 HI	COSPRS	2017
Transportation, Storage, and Distribution Manager	Alabama	Y	61969 AE	93784 AW	109691 AEX	ALBLS	6/16
	Birmingham-Hoover MSA, AL	Y	60196 AE	94337 AW	111413 AEX	ALBLS	6/16
	Alaska	Y	70760 FQ	86140 MW	107460 TQ	USBLS	5/15
	Anchorage MSA, AK	Y	72110 FQ	88240 MW	110160 TQ	USBLS	5/15
	Arizona	Y	55970 FQ	72220 MW	95850 TQ	USBLS	5/15
	Phoenix-Mesa-Scottsdale MSA, AZ	Y	55900 FQ	72100 MW	94980 TQ	USBLS	5/15
	Tucson MSA, AZ	Y	59510 FQ	72120 MW	90270 TQ	USBLS	5/15
	Arkansas	Y	66670 FQ	86930 MW	118620 TQ	USBLS	5/15
	Little Rock-North Little Rock-Conway MSA, AR	Y	60630 FQ	83520 MW	100350 TQ	USBLS	5/15
	California	H	33.75 FQ	43.23 MW	57.34 TQ	CABLS	1/16-3/16
	Anaheim-Santa Ana-Irvine PMSA, CA	H	29.63 FQ	39.10 MW	55.59 TQ	CABLS	1/16-3/16
	Los Angeles-Long Beach-Glendale PMSA, CA	H	33.23 FQ	42.02 MW	54.14 TQ	CABLS	1/16-3/16
	Oakland-Hayward-Berkeley PMSA, CA	H	36.19 FQ	51.47 MW	67.92 TQ	CABLS	1/16-3/16
	Riverside-San Bernardino-Ontario MSA, CA	H	33.34 FQ	40.86 MW	48.56 TQ	CABLS	1/16-3/16
	Sacramento–Roseville–Arden-Arcade MSA, CA	H	32.84 FQ	42.47 MW	55.84 TQ	CABLS	1/16-3/16
	San Diego-Carlsbad MSA, CA	H	36.24 FQ	47.03 MW	59.50 TQ	CABLS	1/16-3/16
	San Francisco-Redwood City-South San Francisco PMSA, CA	H	40.28 FQ	54.74 MW	75.08 TQ	CABLS	1/16-3/16
	Colorado	Y	76840 FQ	102320 MW	126880 TQ	USBLS	5/15
	Denver-Aurora-Lakewood MSA, CO	Y	76050 FQ	103630 MW	131530 TQ	USBLS	5/15
	Connecticut	Y		102069 MW		CTBLS	1/16-3/16

AE Average entry wage	**AWR** Average wage range	**H** Hourly	**LR** Low end range	**MTC** Median total compensation	**TCC** Total cash compensation
AEX Average experienced wage	**B** Biweekly	**HI** Highest wage paid	**M** Monthly	**MW** Median wage paid	**TQ** Third quartile wage
ATC Average total compensation	**D** Daily	**HR** High end range	**MCC** Median cash compensation	**MWR** Median wage range	**W** Weekly
AW Average wage paid	**FQ** First quartile wage	**LO** Lowest wage paid	**ME** Median entry wage	**S** See annotated source	**Y** Yearly

Occupation/Type/Industry	Location	Per	Low	Mid	High	Source	Date
Transportation, Storage, and Distribution Manager	Bridgeport-Stamford-Norwalk MSA, CT	Y	76830 FQ	116960 MW	163560 TQ	USBLS	5/15
	Hartford-West Hartford-East Hartford MSA, CT	Y	74320 FQ	93860 MW	114980 TQ	USBLS	5/15
	Delaware	Y	104200 FQ	130320 MW	156360 TQ	USBLS	5/15
	Wilmington PMSA, DE-MD-NJ	Y	100070 FQ	126990 MW	155660 TQ	USBLS	5/15
	District of Columbia	Y	102940 FQ	128790 MW	151490 TQ	USBLS	5/15
	Washington-Arlington-Alexandria PMSA, DC-VA-MD-WV	Y	82460 FQ	108980 MW	136220 TQ	USBLS	5/15
	Florida	H	29.32 AE	45.52 MW	57.98 AEX	FLBLS	7/16-9/16
	Fort Lauderdale-Pompano Beach-Deerfield Beach PMSA, FL	H	29.79 AE	44.88 MW	56.53 AEX	FLBLS	7/16-9/16
	Miami-Miami Beach-Kendall PMSA, FL	H	26.83 AE	44.71 MW	55.77 AEX	FLBLS	7/16-9/16
	Orlando-Kissimmee-Sanford MSA, FL	H	29.18 AE	42.09 MW	53.17 AEX	FLBLS	7/16-9/16
	Tampa-St. Petersburg-Clearwater MSA, FL	H	29.68 AE	44.42 MW	59.52 AEX	FLBLS	7/16-9/16
	Georgia	Y	65180 FQ	88210 MW	114950 TQ	USBLS	5/15
	Atlanta-Sandy Springs-Roswell MSA, GA	Y	68340 FQ	92360 MW	118840 TQ	USBLS	5/15
	Augusta-Richmond County MSA, GA-SC	Y	53590 FQ	72640 MW	106600 TQ	USBLS	5/15
	Hawaii	Y	63440 FQ	81040 MW	108350 TQ	USBLS	5/15
	Urban Honolulu MSA, HI	Y	65280 FQ	87120 MW	113440 TQ	USBLS	5/15
	Idaho	Y	48640 FQ	61280 MW	80210 TQ	USBLS	5/15
	Boise City MSA, ID	Y	48590 FQ	60190 MW	77390 TQ	USBLS	5/15
	Illinois	Y	60030 FQ	81320 MW	108500 TQ	USBLS	5/15
	Chicago-Naperville-Arlington Heights PMSA, IL	Y	57230 FQ	78550 MW	103240 TQ	USBLS	5/15
	Lake County-Kenosha County PMSA, IL-WI	Y	70610 FQ	105890 MW	155440 TQ	USBLS	5/15
	Indiana	Y	58910 FQ	76830 MW	98250 TQ	USBLS	5/15
	Gary PMSA, IN	Y	47630 FQ	62630 MW	90790 TQ	USBLS	5/15
	Indianapolis-Carmel-Anderson MSA, IN	Y	60570 FQ	77570 MW	99300 TQ	USBLS	5/15
	Iowa	Y	54470 FQ	66870 MW	91420 TQ	USBLS	5/15
	Des Moines-West Des Moines MSA, IA	Y	56310 FQ	71420 MW	97220 TQ	USBLS	5/15
	Kansas	Y	67610 FQ	86330 MW	113620 TQ	USBLS	5/15
	Wichita MSA, KS	Y	63110 FQ	77680 MW	98080 TQ	USBLS	5/15
	Kentucky	Y	63630 FQ	80970 MW	104080 TQ	USBLS	5/15
	Louisville-Jefferson County MSA, KY-IN	Y	63150 FQ	83550 MW	106390 TQ	USBLS	5/15
	Louisiana	Y	61710 FQ	79510 MW	106240 TQ	USBLS	5/15
	Baton Rouge MSA, LA	Y	71280 FQ	91390 MW	126180 TQ	USBLS	5/15
	New Orleans-Metairie MSA, LA	Y	63840 FQ	80800 MW	118610 TQ	USBLS	5/15
	Maine	Y	54330 FQ	68610 MW	87590 TQ	USBLS	5/15
	Portland-South Portland MSA, ME	Y	62380 FQ	75940 MW	97130 TQ	USBLS	5/15
	Maryland	Y	64384 AE	98426 MW	115447 AEX	MDBLS	4/16
	Baltimore-Columbia-Towson MSA, MD	Y	70900 FQ	92690 MW	116770 TQ	USBLS	5/15
	Salisbury MSA, MD-DE	Y	74150 FQ	88660 MW	111180 TQ	USBLS	5/15
	Massachusetts	Y	68350 FQ	86340 MW	116730 TQ	USBLS	5/15
	Boston-Cambridge-Newton NECTA, MA	Y	72170 FQ	91050 MW	120360 TQ	USBLS	5/15
	Worcester MSA, MA-CT	Y	65830 FQ	78000 MW	103900 TQ	USBLS	5/15
	Michigan	Y	66320 FQ	90300 MW	119760 TQ	USBLS	5/15
	Detroit-Dearborn-Livonia PMSA, MI	Y	70160 FQ	92280 MW	121580 TQ	USBLS	5/15
	Grand Rapids-Wyoming MSA, MI	Y	54910 FQ	70610 MW	93060 TQ	USBLS	5/15
	Minnesota	Y	71473 FQ	89021 MW	116141 TQ	MNBLS	1/16-3/16
	Minneapolis-St. Paul-Bloomington MSA, MN-WI	Y	72316 FQ	91246 MW	119179 TQ	MNBLS	1/16-3/16
	Mississippi	Y	46260 FQ	64250 MW	88460 TQ	USBLS	5/15

Occupation/Type/Industry	Location	Per	Low	Mid	High	Source	Date
Transportation, Storage, and Distribution Manager	Jackson MSA, MS	Y	44000 FQ	62470 MW	81990 TQ	USBLS	5/15
	Missouri	Y	66270 FQ	84560 MW	106920 TQ	USBLS	5/15
	Kansas City MSA, MO-KS	Y	70130 FQ	90000 MW	113860 TQ	USBLS	5/15
	St. Louis MSA, MO-IL	Y	68140 FQ	90140 MW	111940 TQ	USBLS	5/15
	Montana	Y	68150 FQ	80560 MW	103120 TQ	USBLS	5/15
	Billings MSA, MT	Y	72080 FQ	87120 MW	108650 TQ	USBLS	5/15
	Nebraska	Y	58430 FQ	75975 MW	105165 TQ	NEBLS	7/16-9/16
	Omaha-Council Bluffs MSA, NE-IA	Y	55140 FQ	69530 MW	104975 TQ	NEBLS	7/16-9/16
	Nevada	Y	60220 FQ	72110 MW	89620 TQ	USBLS	5/15
	Las Vegas-Henderson-Paradise MSA, NV	Y	57070 FQ	69830 MW	93280 TQ	USBLS	5/15
	New Hampshire	H	33.66 AE	49.05 MW	56.57 AEX	NHBLS	6/16
	Manchester NECTA, NH	H	26.45 AE	46.47 MW	51.78 AEX	NHBLS	6/16
	Nashua NECTA, NH-MA	Y	83850 FQ	103890 MW	120340 TQ	USBLS	5/15
	New Jersey	Y	87130 FQ	109840 MW	149580 TQ	USBLS	5/15
	Camden PMSA, NJ	Y	82710 FQ	96620 MW	117670 TQ	USBLS	5/15
	Newark PMSA, NJ-PA	Y	92970 FQ	118060 MW	168900 TQ	USBLS	5/15
	Trenton MSA, NJ	Y	89820 FQ	115700 MW	145170 TQ	USBLS	5/15
	New Mexico	Y	61270 FQ	79270 MW	104470 TQ	USBLS	5/15
	Albuquerque MSA, NM	Y	65710 FQ	85700 MW	109060 TQ	USBLS	5/15
	New York	Y	70330 AE	103920 MW	139840 AEX	NYBLS	1/16-3/16
	Buffalo-Cheektowaga-Niagara Falls MSA, NY	Y	69480 FQ	89250 MW	112860 TQ	USBLS	5/15
	Nassau County-Suffolk County PMSA, NY	Y	87150 FQ	104160 MW	134780 TQ	USBLS	5/15
	New York-Jersey City-White Plains PMSA, NY-NJ	Y	85710 FQ	109710 MW	148400 TQ	USBLS	5/15
	Rochester MSA, NY	Y	69900 FQ	84050 MW	104620 TQ	USBLS	5/15
	North Carolina	Y	70230 FQ	89810 MW	116940 TQ	USBLS	5/15
	Charlotte-Concord-Gastonia MSA, NC-SC	Y	72580 FQ	93270 MW	121420 TQ	USBLS	5/15
	Raleigh MSA, NC	Y	71550 FQ	90880 MW	120360 TQ	USBLS	5/15
	North Dakota	Y	65690 FQ	75900 MW	100250 TQ	USBLS	5/15
	Fargo MSA, ND-MN	Y	67150 FQ	81880 MW	107970 TQ	USBLS	5/15
	Ohio	Y	63900 FQ	80280 MW	105090 TQ	USBLS	5/15
	Cincinnati MSA, OH-KY-IN	Y	66840 FQ	82240 MW	112330 TQ	USBLS	5/15
	Cleveland-Elyria MSA, OH	Y	67520 FQ	82850 MW	112960 TQ	USBLS	5/15
	Columbus MSA, OH	Y	66480 FQ	82930 MW	103090 TQ	USBLS	5/15
	Oklahoma	Y	53170 FQ	68840 MW	93830 TQ	USBLS	5/15
	Oklahoma City MSA, OK	Y	57140 FQ	73430 MW	96450 TQ	USBLS	5/15
	Tulsa MSA, OK	Y	48990 FQ	63330 MW	88070 TQ	USBLS	5/15
	Oregon	H	32.57 FQ	39.29 MW	50.70 TQ	ORBLS	2016
	Portland-Vancouver-Hillsboro MSA, OR-WA	Y	66080 FQ	83400 MW	112910 TQ	USBLS	5/15
	Pennsylvania	Y	74620 FQ	94820 MW	119650 TQ	USBLS	5/15
	Allentown-Bethlehem-Easton MSA, PA-NJ	Y	73400 FQ	90840 MW	116560 TQ	USBLS	5/15
	Harrisburg-Carlisle MSA, PA	Y	73950 FQ	94140 MW	114550 TQ	USBLS	5/15
	Montgomery County-Bucks County-Chester County PMSA, PA	Y	87100 FQ	107350 MW	130770 TQ	USBLS	5/15
	Philadelphia PMSA, PA	Y	80730 FQ	101780 MW	124590 TQ	USBLS	5/15
	Pittsburgh MSA, PA	Y	76910 FQ	93140 MW	116010 TQ	USBLS	5/15
	Rhode Island	Y	79440 FQ	104110 MW	120410 TQ	USBLS	5/15
	Providence-Warwick MSA, RI-MA	Y	74050 FQ	100590 MW	119390 TQ	USBLS	5/15
	South Carolina	Y	67130 FQ	85310 MW	111360 TQ	USBLS	5/15
	Charleston-North Charleston MSA, SC	Y	66800 FQ	84020 MW	124960 TQ	USBLS	5/15
	Columbia MSA, SC	Y	70490 FQ	89660 MW	108640 TQ	USBLS	5/15
	Greenville-Anderson-Mauldin MSA, SC	Y	72090 FQ	91560 MW	115910 TQ	USBLS	5/15
	South Dakota	Y	74160 FQ	88930 MW	103410 TQ	USBLS	5/15
	Sioux Falls MSA, SD	Y	75690 FQ	89330 MW	99930 TQ	USBLS	5/15
	Tennessee	Y	51430 FQ	74010 MW	100000 TQ	USBLS	5/15
	Knoxville MSA, TN	Y	50450 FQ	74070 MW	102200 TQ	USBLS	5/15
	Memphis MSA, TN-MS-AR	Y	59990 FQ	80850 MW	102650 TQ	USBLS	5/15

AE	Average entry wage	**AWR**	Average wage range	**H**	Hourly
AEX	Average experienced wage	**B**	Biweekly	**HI**	Highest wage paid
ATC	Average total compensation	**D**	Daily	**HR**	High end range
AW	Average wage paid	**FQ**	First quartile wage	**LO**	Lowest wage paid

LR	Low end range	**MTC**	Median total compensation	**TCC** Total cash compensation
M	Monthly	**MW**	Median wage paid	**TQ** Third quartile wage
MCC	Median cash compensation	**MWR**	Median wage range	**W** Weekly
ME	Median entry wage	**S**	See annotated source	**Y** Yearly

Occupation/Type/Industry	Location	Per	Low	Mid	High	Source	Date
Transportation, Storage, and Distribution Manager	Nashville-Davidson–Murfreesboro–Franklin MSA, TN	Y	50520 FQ	74670 MW	102350 TQ	USBLS	5/15
	Texas	Y	66290 FQ	87070 MW	117180 TQ	USBLS	5/15
	Austin-Round Rock MSA, TX	Y	61600 FQ	73340 MW	99430 TQ	USBLS	5/15
	Dallas-Plano-Irving PMSA, TX	Y	70320 FQ	97710 MW	125020 TQ	USBLS	5/15
	Fort Worth-Arlington PMSA, TX	Y	67400 FQ	91090 MW	118150 TQ	USBLS	5/15
	Houston-The Woodlands-Sugar Land MSA, TX	Y	70980 FQ	93290 MW	127800 TQ	USBLS	5/15
	San Antonio-New Braunfels MSA, TX	Y	63930 FQ	86680 MW	107080 TQ	USBLS	5/15
	Utah	Y	57080 FQ	77430 MW	107520 TQ	USBLS	5/15
	Ogden-Clearfield MSA, UT	Y	62120 FQ	86790 MW	111530 TQ	USBLS	5/15
	Provo-Orem MSA, UT	Y	47940 FQ	66180 MW	113580 TQ	USBLS	5/15
	Salt Lake City MSA, UT	Y	56750 FQ	75510 MW	102720 TQ	USBLS	5/15
	Vermont	Y	65130 FQ	80740 MW	101530 TQ	USBLS	5/15
	Burlington-South Burlington MSA, VT	Y	66800 FQ	84800 MW	108680 TQ	USBLS	5/15
	Virginia	Y	76290 FQ	99600 MW	123100 TQ	USBLS	5/15
	Richmond MSA, VA	Y	71360 FQ	96130 MW	118940 TQ	USBLS	5/15
	Virginia Beach-Norfolk-Newport News MSA, VA-NC	Y	79410 FQ	98920 MW	119490 TQ	USBLS	5/15
	Washington	H	35.05 FQ	46.59 MW	61.02 TQ	WABLS	3/16
	Seattle-Bellevue-Everett PMSA, WA	H	36.99 FQ	51.20 MW	65.30 TQ	WABLS	3/16
	Tacoma-Lakewood PMSA, WA	H	34.42 FQ	41.41 MW	48.66 TQ	WABLS	3/16
	West Virginia	Y	60780 FQ	75140 MW	101790 TQ	USBLS	5/15
	Huntington-Ashland MSA, WV-KY-OH	Y	51990 FQ	82260 MW	99920 TQ	USBLS	5/15
	Wisconsin	Y	65290 FQ	84050 MW	110560 TQ	USBLS	5/15
	Madison MSA, WI	Y	68770 FQ	87290 MW	103660 TQ	USBLS	5/15
	Milwaukee-Waukesha-West Allis MSA, WI	Y	71330 FQ	93350 MW	123370 TQ	USBLS	5/15
	Wyoming	Y	73620 FQ	88960 MW	104330 TQ	USBLS	5/15
	Cheyenne MSA, WY	Y	63740 FQ	78020 MW	93280 TQ	USBLS	5/15
	Puerto Rico	Y	43300 FQ	73090 MW	106500 TQ	USBLS	5/15
	San Juan-Carolina-Caguas MSA, PR	Y	47050 FQ	76810 MW	108230 TQ	USBLS	5/15
	Virgin Islands	Y	35600 FQ	60340 MW	85640 TQ	USBLS	5/15
	Guam	Y	43640 FQ	61440 MW	91830 TQ	USBLS	5/15
Transportation Analyst							
Municipal Government	Orange, CA	Y			104901 HI	CACIT	6/28/16
Transportation Attendant							
Except Flight Attendant	Alaska	Y	25550 FQ	30890 MW	48660 TQ	USBLS	5/15
Except Flight Attendant	Arizona	Y	19960 FQ	22250 MW	24530 TQ	USBLS	5/15
Except Flight Attendant	Phoenix-Mesa-Scottsdale MSA, AZ	Y	20190 FQ	22290 MW	24370 TQ	USBLS	5/15
Except Flight Attendant	Arkansas	Y	16960 FQ	18290 MW	19690 TQ	USBLS	5/15
Except Flight Attendant	California	H	12.08 FQ	15.47 MW	29.25 TQ	CABLS	1/16-3/16
Except Flight Attendant	Anaheim-Santa Ana-Irvine PMSA, CA	H	9.55 FQ	10.85 MW	14.78 TQ	CABLS	1/16-3/16
Except Flight Attendant	Los Angeles-Long Beach-Glendale PMSA, CA	H	10.21 FQ	12.69 MW	14.70 TQ	CABLS	1/16-3/16
Except Flight Attendant	Riverside-San Bernardino-Ontario MSA, CA	H	12.75 FQ	13.72 MW	14.69 TQ	CABLS	1/16-3/16
Except Flight Attendant	Sacramento–Roseville–Arden-Arcade MSA, CA	H	12.20 FQ	14.02 MW	16.91 TQ	CABLS	1/16-3/16
Except Flight Attendant	San Diego-Carlsbad MSA, CA	H	10.63 FQ	11.78 MW	13.59 TQ	CABLS	1/16-3/16
Except Flight Attendant	Connecticut	Y		21740 MW		CTBLS	1/16-3/16
Except Flight Attendant	Washington-Arlington-Alexandria PMSA, DC-VA-MD-WV	Y	27070 FQ	39910 MW	53290 TQ	USBLS	5/15
Except Flight Attendant	Florida	H	10.90 AE	20.25 MW	22.78 AEX	FLBLS	7/16-9/16
Except Flight Attendant	Fort Lauderdale-Pompano Beach-Deerfield Beach PMSA, FL	H	10.11 AE	15.14 MW	18.90 AEX	FLBLS	7/16-9/16
Except Flight Attendant	Georgia	Y	17790 FQ	20920 MW	32200 TQ	USBLS	5/15
Except Flight Attendant	Hawaii	Y	18040 FQ	20640 MW	29690 TQ	USBLS	5/15

AE Average entry wage	**AWR** Average wage range	**H** Hourly	**LR** Low end range	**MTC** Median total compensation	**TCC** Total cash compensation
AEX Average experienced wage	**B** Biweekly	**HI** Highest wage paid	**M** Monthly	**MW** Median wage paid	**TQ** Third quartile wage
ATC Average total compensation	**D** Daily	**HR** High end range	**MCC** Median cash compensation	**MWR** Median wage range	**W** Weekly
AW Average wage paid	**FQ** First quartile wage	**LO** Lowest wage paid	**ME** Median entry wage	**S** See annotated source	**Y** Yearly

Occupation/Type/Industry	Location	Per	Low	Mid	High	Source	Date
Transportation Attendant							
Except Flight Attendant	Urban Honolulu MSA, HI	Y	17620 FQ	19120 MW	27520 TQ	USBLS	5/15
Except Flight Attendant	Idaho	Y	26400 FQ	28430 MW	30450 TQ	USBLS	5/15
Except Flight Attendant	Illinois	Y	19160 FQ	21990 MW	29050 TQ	USBLS	5/15
Except Flight Attendant	Chicago-Naperville-Arlington Heights PMSA, IL	Y	19050 FQ	21460 MW	28630 TQ	USBLS	5/15
Except Flight Attendant	Iowa	Y	16900 FQ	18590 MW	24970 TQ	USBLS	5/15
Except Flight Attendant	Kansas	Y	17280 FQ	19010 MW	27780 TQ	USBLS	5/15
Except Flight Attendant	Louisiana	Y	20990 FQ	25410 MW	30420 TQ	USBLS	5/15
Except Flight Attendant	New Orleans-Metairie MSA, LA	Y	20450 FQ	22580 MW	24710 TQ	USBLS	5/15
Except Flight Attendant	Maryland	Y	18113 AE	23559 MW	26282 AEX	MDBLS	4/16
Except Flight Attendant	Baltimore-Columbia-Towson MSA, MD	Y	18140 FQ	20340 MW	22890 TQ	USBLS	5/15
Except Flight Attendant	Massachusetts	Y	22430 FQ	27910 MW	31040 TQ	USBLS	5/15
Except Flight Attendant	Boston-Cambridge-Newton NECTA, MA	Y	26200 FQ	28890 MW	31520 TQ	USBLS	5/15
Except Flight Attendant	Michigan	Y	19460 FQ	22780 MW	26770 TQ	USBLS	5/15
Except Flight Attendant	Detroit-Dearborn-Livonia PMSA, MI	Y	19090 FQ	21250 MW	23790 TQ	USBLS	5/15
Except Flight Attendant	Missouri	Y	18360 FQ	22890 MW	31580 TQ	USBLS	5/15
Except Flight Attendant	Kansas City MSA, MO-KS	Y	18100 FQ	22370 MW	32080 TQ	USBLS	5/15
Except Flight Attendant	St. Louis MSA, MO-IL	Y	19250 FQ	26620 MW	34180 TQ	USBLS	5/15
Except Flight Attendant	Nevada	Y	25280 FQ	30390 MW	35510 TQ	USBLS	5/15
Except Flight Attendant	Las Vegas-Henderson-Paradise MSA, NV	Y	25280 FQ	30390 MW	35510 TQ	USBLS	5/15
Except Flight Attendant	New Jersey	Y	20310 FQ	23950 MW	29980 TQ	USBLS	5/15
Except Flight Attendant	Newark PMSA, NJ-PA	Y	18900 FQ	20210 MW	24360 TQ	USBLS	5/15
Except Flight Attendant	New Mexico	Y	20530 FQ	23400 MW	27740 TQ	USBLS	5/15
Except Flight Attendant	New York	Y	19320 AE	22360 MW	28780 AEX	NYBLS	1/16-3/16
Except Flight Attendant	Nassau County-Suffolk County PMSA, NY	Y	20990 FQ	23040 MW	27310 TQ	USBLS	5/15
Except Flight Attendant	New York-Jersey City-White Plains PMSA, NY-NJ	Y	19300 FQ	22810 MW	32420 TQ	USBLS	5/15
Except Flight Attendant	North Dakota	Y	30690 FQ	33500 MW	36300 TQ	USBLS	5/15
Except Flight Attendant	Ohio	Y	18570 FQ	20440 MW	30200 TQ	USBLS	5/15
Except Flight Attendant	Cleveland-Elyria MSA, OH	Y	17920 FQ	18820 MW	20080 TQ	USBLS	5/15
Except Flight Attendant	Oklahoma	Y	18160 FQ	21040 MW	23820 TQ	USBLS	5/15
Except Flight Attendant	Oklahoma City MSA, OK	Y	18130 FQ	20980 MW	23970 TQ	USBLS	5/15
Except Flight Attendant	Pennsylvania	Y	16950 FQ	18330 MW	19780 TQ	USBLS	5/15
Except Flight Attendant	Montgomery County-Bucks County-Chester County PMSA, PA	Y	18360 FQ	21740 MW	31720 TQ	USBLS	5/15
Except Flight Attendant	Philadelphia PMSA, PA	Y	16720 FQ	17900 MW	19090 TQ	USBLS	5/15
Except Flight Attendant	Pittsburgh MSA, PA	Y	17570 FQ	19230 MW	21280 TQ	USBLS	5/15
Except Flight Attendant	South Carolina	Y	21140 FQ	23830 MW	28220 TQ	USBLS	5/15
Except Flight Attendant	Tennessee	Y	17130 FQ	18370 MW	19620 TQ	USBLS	5/15
Except Flight Attendant	Texas	Y	18080 FQ	21730 MW	30260 TQ	USBLS	5/15
Except Flight Attendant	Fort Worth-Arlington PMSA, TX	Y	18100 FQ	21580 MW	30130 TQ	USBLS	5/15
Except Flight Attendant	Houston-The Woodlands-Sugar Land MSA, TX	Y	17450 FQ	19370 MW	44230 TQ	USBLS	5/15
Except Flight Attendant	Utah	Y	19780 FQ	24200 MW	31770 TQ	USBLS	5/15
Except Flight Attendant	Ogden-Clearfield MSA, UT	Y	19360 FQ	21560 MW	23840 TQ	USBLS	5/15
Except Flight Attendant	Salt Lake City MSA, UT	Y	27220 FQ	31640 MW	44470 TQ	USBLS	5/15
Except Flight Attendant	Virginia	Y	17790 FQ	19100 MW	29330 TQ	USBLS	5/15
Except Flight Attendant	Richmond MSA, VA	Y	16510 FQ	17670 MW	18830 TQ	USBLS	5/15
Except Flight Attendant	Virginia Beach-Norfolk-Newport News MSA, VA-NC	Y	17280 FQ	18960 MW	22080 TQ	USBLS	5/15
Except Flight Attendant	Washington	H	12.61 FQ	13.76 MW	14.91 TQ	WABLS	3/16
Except Flight Attendant	Seattle-Bellevue-Everett PMSA, WA	H	12.93 FQ	13.97 MW	15.02 TQ	WABLS	3/16
Transportation Inspector	Alabama	Y	53564 AE	76315 AW	87690 AEX	ALBLS	6/16
	Birmingham-Hoover MSA, AL	Y	66441 AE	92174 AW	105041 AEX	ALBLS	6/16
	Alaska	Y	76660 FQ	97260 MW	115470 TQ	USBLS	5/15
	Anchorage MSA, AK	Y	76660 FQ	100290 MW	118500 TQ	USBLS	5/15
	Arizona	Y	33250 FQ	58080 MW	90140 TQ	USBLS	5/15
	Phoenix-Mesa-Scottsdale MSA, AZ	Y	27610 FQ	58550 MW	93900 TQ	USBLS	5/15
	Little Rock-North Little Rock-Conway MSA, AR	Y	42200 FQ	81910 MW	97370 TQ	USBLS	5/15

Occupation/Type/Industry	Location	Per	Low	Mid	High	Source	Date
Transportation Inspector	California	H	24.59 FQ	30.44 MW	42.64 TQ	CABLS	1/16-3/16
	Los Angeles-Long Beach-Glendale PMSA, CA	H	27.76 FQ	34.23 MW	42.17 TQ	CABLS	1/16-3/16
	Oakland-Hayward-Berkeley PMSA, CA	H	24.59 FQ	40.71 MW	58.26 TQ	CABLS	1/16-3/16
	Riverside-San Bernardino-Ontario MSA, CA	H	16.81 FQ	24.58 MW	34.98 TQ	CABLS	1/16-3/16
	Sacramento–Roseville–Arden-Arcade MSA, CA	H	28.42 FQ	37.81 MW	51.06 TQ	CABLS	1/16-3/16
	San Diego-Carlsbad MSA, CA	H	20.08 FQ	27.51 MW	34.97 TQ	CABLS	1/16-3/16
	San Francisco-Redwood City-South San Francisco PMSA, CA	H	39.61 FQ	43.69 MW	47.94 TQ	CABLS	1/16-3/16
	Colorado	Y	43730 FQ	57030 MW	98540 TQ	USBLS	5/15
	Connecticut	Y		70781 MW		CTBLS	1/16-3/16
	Hartford-West Hartford-East Hartford MSA, CT	Y	54570 FQ	63320 MW	69490 TQ	USBLS	5/15
	Delaware	Y	27820 FQ	29580 MW	51850 TQ	USBLS	5/15
	Wilmington PMSA, DE-MD-NJ	Y	27820 FQ	32710 MW	59570 TQ	USBLS	5/15
	District of Columbia	Y	60680 FQ	109630 MW	132930 TQ	USBLS	5/15
	Washington-Arlington-Alexandria PMSA, DC-VA-MD-WV	Y	57410 FQ	86750 MW	118050 TQ	USBLS	5/15
	Florida	H	29.81 AE	43.98 MW	50.00 AEX	FLBLS	7/16-9/16
	Fort Lauderdale-Pompano Beach-Deerfield Beach PMSA, FL	H	36.36 AE	49.85 MW	56.40 AEX	FLBLS	7/16-9/16
	Miami-Miami Beach-Kendall PMSA, FL	H	32.79 AE	46.10 MW	52.12 AEX	FLBLS	7/16-9/16
	Orlando-Kissimmee-Sanford MSA, FL	H	36.67 AE	46.05 MW	49.66 AEX	FLBLS	7/16-9/16
	Tampa-St. Petersburg-Clearwater MSA, FL	H	38.69 AE	48.18 MW	52.71 AEX	FLBLS	7/16-9/16
	Georgia	Y	46150 FQ	72660 MW	95930 TQ	USBLS	5/15
	Atlanta-Sandy Springs-Roswell MSA, GA	Y	47240 FQ	78240 MW	96090 TQ	USBLS	5/15
	Hawaii	Y	54340 FQ	71590 MW	107380 TQ	USBLS	5/15
	Urban Honolulu MSA, HI	Y	54970 FQ	74240 MW	107380 TQ	USBLS	5/15
	Idaho	Y	54490 FQ	60080 MW	84240 TQ	USBLS	5/15
	Illinois	Y	59250 FQ	73280 MW	98270 TQ	USBLS	5/15
	Chicago-Naperville-Arlington Heights PMSA, IL	Y	72370 FQ	91470 MW	109760 TQ	USBLS	5/15
	Indiana	Y	39820 FQ	55740 MW	95020 TQ	USBLS	5/15
	Indianapolis-Carmel-Anderson MSA, IN	Y	52670 FQ	89430 MW	105690 TQ	USBLS	5/15
	Iowa	Y	46860 FQ	79530 MW	97370 TQ	USBLS	5/15
	Kansas	Y	63710 FQ	89120 MW	109650 TQ	USBLS	5/15
	Kentucky	Y	52010 FQ	70180 MW	100170 TQ	USBLS	5/15
	Louisville-Jefferson County MSA, KY-IN	Y	77080 FQ	100160 MW	112570 TQ	CABLS	5/15
	Louisiana	Y	50440 FQ	69040 MW	88910 TQ	USBLS	5/15
	Baton Rouge MSA, LA	Y	54610 FQ	70190 MW	93750 TQ	USBLS	5/15
	New Orleans-Metairie MSA, LA	Y	43510 FQ	59670 MW	78240 TQ	USBLS	5/15
	Maine	Y	72540 FQ	102110 MW	115080 TQ	USBLS	5/15
	Maryland	Y	40121 AE	60750 MW	71064 AEX	MDBLS	4/16
	Baltimore-Columbia-Towson MSA, MD	Y	44380 FQ	50920 MW	90820 TQ	USBLS	5/15
	Massachusetts	Y	64310 FQ	71170 MW	77840 TQ	USBLS	5/15
	Boston-Cambridge-Newton NECTA, MA	Y	66310 FQ	72380 MW	78250 TQ	USBLS	5/15
	Michigan	Y	63060 FQ	91830 MW	110780 TQ	USBLS	5/15
	Detroit-Dearborn-Livonia PMSA, MI	Y	90710 FQ	105840 MW	123110 TQ	USBLS	5/15
	Minnesota	Y	84402 FQ	98082 MW	108849 TQ	MNBLS	1/16-3/16
	Minneapolis-St. Paul-Bloomington MSA, MN-WI	Y	74986 FQ	101046 MW	119404 TQ	MNBLS	1/16-3/16
	Mississippi	Y	50930 FQ	55260 MW	61870 TQ	USBLS	5/15
	Jackson MSA, MS	Y	31620 FQ	57480 MW	97380 TQ	USBLS	5/15
	Missouri	Y	39160 FQ	65470 MW	101160 TQ	USBLS	5/15
	Kansas City MSA, MO-KS	Y	33360 FQ	70200 MW	108500 TQ	USBLS	5/15

AE Average entry wage	**AWR** Average wage range	**H** Hourly	**LR** Low end range	**MTC** Median total compensation	**TCC** Total cash compensation
AEX Average experienced wage	**B** Biweekly	**HI** Highest wage paid	**M** Monthly	**MW** Median wage paid	**TQ** Third quartile wage
ATC Average total compensation	**D** Daily	**HR** High end range	**MCC** Median cash compensation	**MWR** Median wage range	**W** Weekly
AW Average wage paid	**FQ** First quartile wage	**LO** Lowest wage paid	**ME** Median entry wage	**S** See annotated source	**Y** Yearly

Occupation/Type/Industry	Location	Per	Low	Mid	High	Source	Date
Transportation Inspector	St. Louis MSA, MO-IL	Y	60400 FQ	72590 MW	94590 TQ	USBLS	5/15
	Montana	Y	44230 FQ	70200 MW	97380 TQ	USBLS	5/15
	Billings MSA, MT	Y	43350 FQ	47220 MW	70180 TQ	USBLS	5/15
	Nebraska	Y	70965 FQ	86580 MW	94595 TQ	NEBLS	7/16-9/16
	Omaha-Council Bluffs MSA, NE-IA	Y	66045 FQ	73515 MW	80670 TQ	NEBLS	7/16-9/16
	Nevada	Y	26920 FQ	51900 MW	89030 TQ	USBLS	5/15
	Las Vegas-Henderson-Paradise MSA, NV	Y	22860 FQ	35240 MW	91810 TQ	USBLS	5/15
	New Hampshire	H	21.33 AE	29.97 MW	38.89 AEX	NHBLS	6/16
	New Jersey	Y	56520 FQ	71970 MW	87140 TQ	USBLS	5/15
	Newark PMSA, NJ-PA	Y	61790 FQ	71690 MW	79950 TQ	USBLS	5/15
	New Mexico	Y	29910 FQ	40840 MW	73560 TQ	USBLS	5/15
	New York	Y	61350 AE	74020 MW	77280 AEX	NYBLS	1/16-3/16
	Buffalo-Cheektowaga-Niagara Falls MSA, NY	Y	52570 FQ	59310 MW	69720 TQ	USBLS	5/15
	Nassau County-Suffolk County PMSA, NY	Y	61000 FQ	94120 MW	111210 TQ	USBLS	5/15
	New York-Jersey City-White Plains PMSA, NY-NJ	Y	66970 FQ	72610 MW	78250 TQ	USBLS	5/15
	Charlotte-Concord-Gastonia MSA, NC-SC	Y	55770 FQ	91250 MW	97370 TQ	USBLS	5/15
	North Dakota	Y	70200 FQ	87830 MW	98160 TQ	USBLS	5/15
	Fargo MSA, ND-MN	Y	85190 FQ	92740 MW	100280 TQ	USBLS	5/15
	Ohio	Y	40300 FQ	50310 MW	88200 TQ	USBLS	5/15
	Cincinnati MSA, OH-KY-IN	Y	41790 FQ	89580 MW	101120 TQ	USBLS	5/15
	Cleveland-Elyria MSA, OH	Y	20150 FQ	41950 MW	63020 TQ	USBLS	5/15
	Columbus MSA, OH	Y	50000 FQ	73900 MW	97080 TQ	USBLS	5/15
	Oklahoma	Y	50400 FQ	92210 MW	121660 TQ	USBLS	5/15
	Oklahoma City MSA, OK	Y	52490 FQ	91480 MW	112770 TQ	USBLS	5/15
	Tulsa MSA, OK	Y	38120 FQ	48250 MW	60490 TQ	USBLS	5/15
	Oregon	H	23.73 FQ	28.55 MW	36.24 TQ	ORBLS	2016
	Portland-Vancouver-Hillsboro MSA, OR-WA	Y	50750 FQ	73950 MW	99720 TQ	USBLS	5/15
	Pennsylvania	Y	50510 FQ	71440 MW	107770 TQ	USBLS	5/15
	Montgomery County-Bucks County-Chester County PMSA, PA	Y	53650 FQ	76870 MW	106860 TQ	USBLS	5/15
	Philadelphia PMSA, PA	Y	73250 FQ	106860 MW	122770 TQ	USBLS	5/15
	Pittsburgh MSA, PA	Y	47250 FQ	85880 MW	110610 TQ	USBLS	5/15
	Providence-Warwick MSA, RI-MA	Y	43610 FQ	58090 MW	89530 TQ	USBLS	5/15
	South Carolina	Y	52880 FQ	73320 MW	94590 TQ	USBLS	5/15
	Columbia MSA, SC	Y	81800 FQ	94590 MW	108510 TQ	USBLS	5/15
	South Dakota	Y	34600 FQ	40030 MW	77210 TQ	USBLS	5/15
	Tennessee	Y	51680 FQ	70200 MW	105220 TQ	USBLS	5/15
	Memphis MSA, TN-MS-AR	Y	30590 FQ	84830 MW	105720 TQ	USBLS	5/15
	Nashville-Davidson–Murfreesboro–Franklin MSA, TN	Y	57360 FQ	79610 MW	108510 TQ	USBLS	5/15
	Texas	Y	36020 FQ	61260 MW	94840 TQ	USBLS	5/15
	Dallas-Plano-Irving PMSA, TX	Y	88080 FQ	98620 MW	114680 TQ	USBLS	5/15
	Fort Worth-Arlington PMSA, TX	Y	37860 FQ	49230 MW	85880 TQ	USBLS	5/15
	Houston-The Woodlands-Sugar Land MSA, TX	Y	26090 FQ	43360 MW	89190 TQ	USBLS	5/15
	San Antonio-New Braunfels MSA, TX	Y	88210 FQ	100360 MW	119640 TQ	USBLS	5/15
	Utah	Y	51090 FQ	107430 MW	120280 TQ	USBLS	5/15
	Salt Lake City MSA, UT	Y	94590 FQ	113940 MW	123730 TQ	USBLS	5/15
	Virginia	Y	54690 FQ	74440 MW	89880 TQ	USBLS	5/15
	Richmond MSA, VA	Y	51640 FQ	85170 MW	97390 TQ	USBLS	5/15
	Virginia Beach-Norfolk-Newport News MSA, VA-NC	Y	66430 FQ	72730 MW	78820 TQ	USBLS	5/15
	Washington	H	30.89 FQ	46.32 MW	56.55 TQ	WABLS	3/16
	Seattle-Bellevue-Everett PMSA, WA	H	43.61 FQ	53.10 MW	60.28 TQ	WABLS	3/16
	Wisconsin	Y	39090 FQ	73390 MW	100740 TQ	USBLS	5/15
	Milwaukee-Waukesha-West Allis MSA, WI	Y	76790 FQ	100740 MW	112240 TQ	USBLS	5/15
	Wyoming	Y	33360 FQ	44050 MW	71250 TQ	USBLS	5/15
	Cheyenne MSA, WY	Y	33230 FQ	34600 MW	45110 TQ	USBLS	5/15

AE	Average entry wage	AWR	Average wage range	H	Hourly	LR	Low end range	MTC	Median total compensation	TCC	Total cash compensation
AEX	Average experienced wage	B	Biweekly	HI	Highest wage paid	M	Monthly	MW	Median wage paid	TQ	Third quartile wage
ATC	Average total compensation	D	Daily	HR	High end range	MCC	Median cash compensation	MWR	Median wage range	W	Weekly
AW	Average wage paid	FQ	First quartile wage	LO	Lowest wage paid	ME	Median entry wage	S	See annotated source	Y	Yearly

Occupation/Type/Industry	Location	Per	Low	Mid	High	Source	Date
Transportation Inspector	Puerto Rico	Y	16880 FQ	18340 MW	21630 TQ	USBLS	5/15
Transportation Schedule Analyst							
Municipal Government	Detroit, MI	M	2708 LO		3183 HI	DETGOV	2016
Transportation Security Screener							
Federal	Alabama	Y	35490 AE	39959 AW	42193 AEX	ALBLS	6/16
Federal	Birmingham-Hoover MSA, AL	Y	35696 AE	40505 AW	42914 AEX	ALBLS	6/16
Federal	Anchorage MSA, AK	Y	39130 FQ	39920 MW	44500 TQ	USBLS	5/15
Federal	Arizona	Y	36650 FQ	37500 MW	40950 TQ	USBLS	5/15
Federal	Phoenix-Mesa-Scottsdale MSA, AZ	Y	36650 FQ	37570 MW	41120 TQ	USBLS	5/15
Federal	Tucson MSA, AZ	Y	36020 FQ	38530 MW	40950 TQ	USBLS	5/15
Federal	Little Rock-North Little Rock-Conway MSA, AR	Y	35830 FQ	37850 MW	41360 TQ	USBLS	5/15
Federal	California	H	19.29 FQ	19.75 MW	21.39 TQ	CABLS	1/16-3/16
Federal	Anaheim-Santa Ana-Irvine PMSA, CA	H	19.57 FQ	19.83 MW	21.72 TQ	CABLS	1/16-3/16
Federal	Los Angeles-Long Beach-Glendale PMSA, CA	H	19.56 FQ	19.67 MW	20.91 TQ	CABLS	1/16-3/16
Federal	Oakland-Hayward-Berkeley PMSA, CA	H	20.79 FQ	21.09 MW	23.53 TQ	CABLS	1/16-3/16
Federal	Riverside-San Bernardino-Ontario MSA, CA	H	19.67 FQ	20.75 MW	22.36 TQ	CABLS	1/16-3/16
Federal	Sacramento–Roseville–Arden-Arcade MSA, CA	H	18.79 FQ	18.81 MW	20.86 TQ	CABLS	1/16-3/16
Federal	San Diego-Carlsbad MSA, CA	H	19.10 FQ	19.30 MW	20.88 TQ	CABLS	1/16-3/16
Federal	San Francisco-Redwood City-South San Francisco PMSA, CA	H	23.49 FQ	25.02 MW	33.89 TQ	CABLS	1/16-3/16
Federal	Connecticut	Y		42350 MW		CTBLS	1/16-3/16
Federal	Washington-Arlington-Alexandria PMSA, DC-VA-MD-WV	Y	38980 FQ	39190 MW	42820 TQ	USBLS	5/15
Federal	Florida	H	16.36 AE	19.04 MW	20.78 AEX	FLBLS	7/16-9/16
Federal	Fort Lauderdale-Pompano Beach-Deerfield Beach PMSA, FL	H	16.59 AE	19.03 MW	20.83 AEX	FLBLS	7/16-9/16
Federal	Miami-Miami Beach-Kendall PMSA, FL	H	15.89 AE	19.32 MW	20.85 AEX	FLBLS	7/16-9/16
Federal	Orlando-Kissimmee-Sanford MSA, FL	H	17.72 AE	18.72 MW	20.48 AEX	FLBLS	7/16-9/16
Federal	Tampa-St. Petersburg-Clearwater MSA, FL	H	17.93 AE	19.11 MW	20.95 AEX	FLBLS	7/16-9/16
Federal	Georgia	Y	37460 FQ	38200 MW	41540 TQ	USBLS	5/15
Federal	Atlanta-Sandy Springs-Roswell MSA, GA	Y	37610 FQ	38210 MW	41740 TQ	USBLS	5/15
Federal	Augusta-Richmond County MSA, GA-SC	Y	35830 FQ	37090 MW	39170 TQ	USBLS	5/15
Federal	Hawaii	Y	36580 FQ	37310 MW	40730 TQ	USBLS	5/15
Federal	Urban Honolulu MSA, HI	Y	36580 FQ	38000 MW	41560 TQ	USBLS	5/15
Federal	Idaho	Y	35830 FQ	37140 MW	40950 TQ	USBLS	5/15
Federal	Boise City MSA, ID	Y	35830 FQ	36350 MW	40560 TQ	USBLS	5/15
Federal	Illinois	Y	39260 FQ	39660 MW	42700 TQ	USBLS	5/15
Federal	Chicago-Naperville-Arlington Heights PMSA, IL	Y	39260 FQ	39670 MW	42920 TQ	USBLS	5/15
Federal	Indiana	Y	35990 FQ	36870 MW	41130 TQ	USBLS	5/15
Federal	Indianapolis-Carmel-Anderson MSA, IN	Y	36000 FQ	37620 MW	41350 TQ	USBLS	5/15
Federal	Iowa	Y	35830 FQ	36190 MW	39730 TQ	USBLS	5/15
Federal	Des Moines-West Des Moines MSA, IA	Y	35820 FQ	35840 MW	39740 TQ	USBLS	5/15
Federal	Kansas	Y	35820 FQ	36450 MW	40400 TQ	USBLS	5/15
Federal	Wichita MSA, KS	Y	33630 FQ	36190 MW	40540 TQ	USBLS	5/15
Federal	Kentucky	Y	36760 FQ	38740 MW	42360 TQ	USBLS	5/15
Federal	Louisville-Jefferson County MSA, KY-IN	Y	35830 FQ	37030 MW	39630 TQ	USBLS	5/15
Federal	Louisiana	Y	35820 FQ	36190 MW	39740 TQ	USBLS	5/15
Federal	Baton Rouge MSA, LA	Y	35840 FQ	36720 MW	41150 TQ	USBLS	5/15
Federal	New Orleans-Metairie MSA, LA	Y	35820 FQ	36180 MW	39160 TQ	USBLS	5/15
Federal	Maine	Y	35830 FQ	36720 MW	40550 TQ	USBLS	5/15

AE	Average entry wage	AWR	Average wage range	H	Hourly	LR	Low end range	MTC	Median total compensation	TCC	Total cash compensation
AEX	Average experienced wage	B	Biweekly	HI	Highest wage paid	M	Monthly	MW	Median wage paid	TQ	Third quartile wage
ATC	Average total compensation	D	Daily	HR	High end range	MCC	Median cash compensation	MWR	Median wage range	W	Weekly
AW	Average wage paid	FQ	First quartile wage	LO	Lowest wage paid	ME	Median entry wage	S	See annotated source	Y	Yearly

Transportation Security Screener

Occupation/Type/Industry	Location	Per	Low	Mid	High	Source	Date
Transportation Security Screener							
Federal	Portland-South Portland MSA, ME	Y	35830 FQ	36390 MW	40960 TQ	USBLS	5/15
Federal	Maryland	Y	33241 AE	40012 MW	43398 AEX	MDBLS	4/16
Federal	Baltimore-Columbia-Towson MSA, MD	Y	34400 FQ	39410 MW	43680 TQ	USBLS	5/15
Federal	Massachusetts	Y	39170 FQ	39180 MW	42060 TQ	USBLS	5/15
Federal	Boston-Cambridge-Newton NECTA, MA	Y	39170 FQ	39180 MW	41580 TQ	USBLS	5/15
Federal	Michigan	Y	37080 FQ	39350 MW	42250 TQ	USBLS	5/15
Federal	Detroit-Dearborn-Livonia PMSA, MI	Y	38950 FQ	39940 MW	43420 TQ	USBLS	5/15
Federal	Grand Rapids-Wyoming MSA, MI	Y	35830 FQ	36560 MW	40160 TQ	USBLS	5/15
Federal	Minnesota	Y	38335 FQ	38728 MW	43455 TQ	MNBLS	1/16-3/16
Federal	Minneapolis-St. Paul-Bloomington MSA, MN-WI	Y	38345 FQ	39042 MW	43828 TQ	MNBLS	1/16-3/16
Federal	Mississippi	Y	35830 FQ	36550 MW	40760 TQ	USBLS	5/15
Federal	Jackson MSA, MS	Y	35830 FQ	36560 MW	40890 TQ	USBLS	5/15
Federal	Missouri	Y	35840 FQ	37110 MW	41160 TQ	USBLS	5/15
Federal	St. Louis MSA, MO-IL	Y	35840 FQ	36580 MW	40750 TQ	USBLS	5/15
Federal	Montana	Y	35830 FQ	36860 MW	40490 TQ	USBLS	5/15
Federal	Billings MSA, MT	Y	35820 FQ	36560 MW	40160 TQ	USBLS	5/15
Federal	Nebraska	Y	31220 FQ	36225 MW	39790 TQ	NEBLS	7/16-9/16
Federal	Omaha-Council Bluffs MSA, NE-IA	Y	31215 FQ	35940 MW	39165 TQ	NEBLS	7/16-9/16
Federal	New Hampshire	H	17.18 AE	19.53 MW	21.69 AEX	NHBLS	6/16
Federal	Manchester NECTA, NH	H	17.23 AE	19.53 MW	21.69 AEX	NHBLS	6/16
Federal	New Jersey	Y	40400 FQ	40600 MW	43460 TQ	USBLS	5/15
Federal	Newark PMSA, NJ-PA	Y	40400 FQ	40640 MW	43580 TQ	USBLS	5/15
Federal	New Mexico	Y	31210 FQ	35840 MW	39160 TQ	USBLS	5/15
Federal	Albuquerque MSA, NM	Y	35820 FQ	36190 MW	39440 TQ	USBLS	5/15
Federal	Buffalo-Cheektowaga-Niagara Falls MSA, NY	Y	36730 FQ	37460 MW	41960 TQ	USBLS	5/15
Federal	Nassau County-Suffolk County PMSA, NY	Y	40410 FQ	40840 MW	44340 TQ	USBLS	5/15
Federal	New York-Jersey City-White Plains PMSA, NY-NJ	Y	40400 FQ	40790 MW	43310 TQ	USBLS	5/15
Federal	Raleigh MSA, NC	Y	36940 FQ	38610 MW	42800 TQ	USBLS	5/15
Federal	North Dakota	Y	35900 FQ	39150 MW	43120 TQ	USBLS	5/15
Federal	Fargo MSA, ND-MN	Y	35830 FQ	36760 MW	41310 TQ	USBLS	5/15
Federal	Ohio	Y	36860 FQ	38600 MW	42440 TQ	USBLS	5/15
Federal	Cincinnati MSA, OH-KY-IN	Y	37570 FQ	40720 MW	43910 TQ	USBLS	5/15
Federal	Cleveland-Elyria MSA, OH	Y	37610 FQ	40720 MW	44930 TQ	USBLS	5/15
Federal	Columbus MSA, OH	Y	36760 FQ	37150 MW	40800 TQ	USBLS	5/15
Federal	Oklahoma	Y	35830 FQ	36230 MW	39940 TQ	USBLS	5/15
Federal	Oklahoma City MSA, OK	Y	35830 FQ	36170 MW	39740 TQ	USBLS	5/15
Federal	Tulsa MSA, OK	Y	35830 FQ	36950 MW	40620 TQ	USBLS	5/15
Federal	Oregon	H	18.44 FQ	18.68 MW	20.56 TQ	ORBLS	2016
Federal	Portland-Vancouver-Hillsboro MSA, OR-WA	Y	37780 FQ	38530 MW	42310 TQ	USBLS	5/15
Federal	Allentown-Bethlehem-Easton MSA, PA-NJ	Y	36010 FQ	37120 MW	42400 TQ	USBLS	5/15
Federal	Philadelphia PMSA, PA	Y	38220 FQ	38630 MW	42210 TQ	USBLS	5/15
Federal	Pittsburgh MSA, PA	Y	36520 FQ	38150 MW	42100 TQ	USBLS	5/15
Federal	Charleston-North Charleston MSA, SC	Y	35840 FQ	36570 MW	40240 TQ	USBLS	5/15
Federal	Columbia MSA, SC	Y	35840 FQ	37020 MW	41370 TQ	USBLS	5/15
Federal	Greenville-Anderson-Mauldin MSA, SC	Y	35840 FQ	37120 MW	39350 TQ	USBLS	5/15
Federal	South Dakota	Y	35830 FQ	36560 MW	40900 TQ	USBLS	5/15
Federal	Tennessee	Y	35830 FQ	36570 MW	40940 TQ	USBLS	5/15
Federal	Knoxville MSA, TN	Y	36170 FQ	37760 MW	42920 TQ	USBLS	5/15
Federal	Memphis MSA, TN-MS-AR	Y	35840 FQ	36760 MW	41360 TQ	USBLS	5/15
Federal	Nashville-Davidson–Murfreesboro–Franklin MSA, TN	Y	35820 FQ	36550 MW	40350 TQ	USBLS	5/15
Federal	Texas	Y	37500 FQ	40400 MW	42870 TQ	USBLS	5/15
Federal	Austin-Round Rock MSA, TX	Y	35820 FQ	35840 MW	39550 TQ	USBLS	5/15
Federal	Dallas-Plano-Irving PMSA, TX	Y	37860 FQ	38440 MW	42380 TQ	USBLS	5/15
Federal	Fort Worth-Arlington PMSA, TX	Y	37870 FQ	38640 MW	42450 TQ	USBLS	5/15

Occupation/Type/Industry	Location	Per	Low	Mid	High	Source	Date
Transportation Security Screener							
Federal	Houston-The Woodlands-Sugar Land MSA, TX	Y	40410 FQ	41440 MW	45270 TQ	USBLS	5/15
Federal	San Antonio-New Braunfels MSA, TX	Y	35830 FQ	36550 MW	40940 TQ	USBLS	5/15
Federal	Utah	Y	35830 FQ	37070 MW	40340 TQ	USBLS	5/15
Federal	Salt Lake City MSA, UT	Y	35840 FQ	37260 MW	40560 TQ	USBLS	5/15
Federal	Vermont	Y	31220 FQ	35830 MW	39730 TQ	USBLS	5/15
Federal	Burlington-South Burlington MSA, VT	Y	31220 FQ	35830 MW	39500 TQ	USBLS	5/15
Federal	Virginia	Y	36550 FQ	39000 MW	42200 TQ	USBLS	5/15
Federal	Richmond MSA, VA	Y	36560 FQ	37510 MW	40980 TQ	USBLS	5/15
Federal	Virginia Beach-Norfolk-Newport News MSA, VA-NC	Y	35820 FQ	36580 MW	40950 TQ	USBLS	5/15
Federal	West Virginia	Y	35820 FQ	37410 MW	41780 TQ	USBLS	5/15
Federal	Wisconsin	Y	37070 FQ	38190 MW	42540 TQ	USBLS	5/15
Federal	Madison MSA, WI	Y	35830 FQ	36180 MW	40150 TQ	USBLS	5/15
Federal	Milwaukee-Waukesha-West Allis MSA, WI	Y	37240 FQ	38730 MW	42160 TQ	USBLS	5/15
Federal	Virgin Islands	Y	39370 FQ	42990 MW	43330 TQ	USBLS	5/15
Federal	Guam	Y	35830 FQ	36190 MW	39740 TQ	USBLS	5/15
Transportation Specialist							
Municipal Government	La Mesa, CA	Y			41236 HI	CACIT	6/28/16
Transportation Timekeeper							
Municipal Government	Detroit, MI	M	2217 LO		2558 HI	DETGOV	2016
Travel Agent							
	Alabama	Y	29849 AE	38753 AW	43201 AEX	ALBLS	6/16
	Birmingham-Hoover MSA, AL	Y	29817 AE	41763 AW	47731 AEX	ALBLS	6/16
	Alaska	Y	29420 FQ	35250 MW	42250 TQ	USBLS	5/15
	Anchorage MSA, AK	Y	30350 FQ	36060 MW	44260 TQ	USBLS	5/15
	Arizona	Y	24750 FQ	35360 MW	45710 TQ	USBLS	5/15
	Phoenix-Mesa-Scottsdale MSA, AZ	Y	24770 FQ	35450 MW	45620 TQ	USBLS	5/15
	Tucson MSA, AZ	Y	23250 FQ	34110 MW	47560 TQ	USBLS	5/15
	Arkansas	Y	27270 FQ	34160 MW	41810 TQ	USBLS	5/15
	Little Rock-North Little Rock-Conway MSA, AR	Y	26440 FQ	32470 MW	41320 TQ	USBLS	5/15
	California	H	13.60 FQ	17.55 MW	23.67 TQ	CABLS	1/16-3/16
	Anaheim-Santa Ana-Irvine PMSA, CA	H	17.08 FQ	24.49 MW	28.01 TQ	CABLS	1/16-3/16
	Los Angeles-Long Beach-Glendale PMSA, CA	H	13.35 FQ	16.65 MW	22.48 TQ	CABLS	1/16-3/16
	Oakland-Hayward-Berkeley PMSA, CA	H	14.34 FQ	19.53 MW	24.72 TQ	CABLS	1/16-3/16
	Riverside-San Bernardino-Ontario MSA, CA	H	13.23 FQ	15.81 MW	19.29 TQ	CABLS	1/16-3/16
	Sacramento–Roseville–Arden-Arcade MSA, CA	H	14.74 FQ	20.19 MW	26.84 TQ	CABLS	1/16-3/16
	San Diego-Carlsbad MSA, CA	H	13.06 FQ	15.93 MW	21.52 TQ	CABLS	1/16-3/16
	San Francisco-Redwood City-South San Francisco PMSA, CA	H	13.76 FQ	16.89 MW	21.68 TQ	CABLS	1/16-3/16
	Colorado	Y	27750 FQ	37100 MW	47620 TQ	USBLS	5/15
	Denver-Aurora-Lakewood MSA, CO	Y	27780 FQ	36470 MW	45940 TQ	USBLS	5/15
	Connecticut	Y		38807 MW		CTBLS	1/16-3/16
	Bridgeport-Stamford-Norwalk MSA, CT	Y	32400 FQ	37540 MW	44830 TQ	USBLS	5/15
	Hartford-West Hartford-East Hartford MSA, CT	Y	32350 FQ	39920 MW	48160 TQ	USBLS	5/15
	Delaware	Y	28780 FQ	36730 MW	45320 TQ	USBLS	5/15
	Wilmington PMSA, DE-MD-NJ	Y	30300 FQ	38540 MW	46690 TQ	USBLS	5/15
	District of Columbia	Y	31620 FQ	39040 MW	49180 TQ	USBLS	5/15
	Washington-Arlington-Alexandria PMSA, DC-VA-MD-WV	Y	34300 FQ	44170 MW	57470 TQ	USBLS	5/15
	Florida	H	9.85 AE	15.48 MW	20.52 AEX	FLBLS	7/16-9/16

Occupation/Type/Industry	Location	Per	Low	Mid	High	Source	Date
Travel Agent	Fort Lauderdale-Pompano Beach-Deerfield Beach PMSA, FL	H	8.93 AE	14.26 MW	20.88 AEX	FLBLS	7/16-9/16
	Miami-Miami Beach-Kendall PMSA, FL	H	10.16 AE	16.98 MW	22.07 AEX	FLBLS	7/16-9/16
	Orlando-Kissimmee-Sanford MSA, FL	H	9.58 AE	13.17 MW	19.17 AEX	FLBLS	7/16-9/16
	Tampa-St. Petersburg-Clearwater MSA, FL	H	9.55 AE	14.39 MW	17.07 AEX	FLBLS	7/16-9/16
	Georgia	Y	27440 FQ	34710 MW	44870 TQ	USBLS	5/15
	Atlanta-Sandy Springs-Roswell MSA, GA	Y	27400 FQ	35580 MW	45000 TQ	USBLS	5/15
	Hawaii	Y	29610 FQ	35850 MW	43030 TQ	USBLS	5/15
	Urban Honolulu MSA, HI	Y	29710 FQ	35660 MW	42170 TQ	USBLS	5/15
	Idaho	Y	25200 FQ	29370 MW	38790 TQ	USBLS	5/15
	Boise City MSA, ID	Y	25840 FQ	29640 MW	41370 TQ	USBLS	5/15
	Illinois	Y	25770 FQ	34500 MW	46860 TQ	USBLS	5/15
	Chicago-Naperville-Arlington Heights PMSA, IL	Y	26900 FQ	35990 MW	47690 TQ	USBLS	5/15
	Lake County-Kenosha County PMSA, IL-WI	Y	27770 FQ	35730 MW	46290 TQ	USBLS	5/15
	Indiana	Y	27080 FQ	36150 MW	51020 TQ	USBLS	5/15
	Gary PMSA, IN	Y	18750 FQ	22260 MW	27120 TQ	USBLS	5/15
	Indianapolis-Carmel-Anderson MSA, IN	Y	36210 FQ	50120 MW	57950 TQ	USBLS	5/15
	Iowa	Y	25050 FQ	33990 MW	42940 TQ	USBLS	5/15
	Des Moines-West Des Moines MSA, IA	Y	21300 FQ	28970 MW	36850 TQ	USBLS	5/15
	Kansas	Y	27340 FQ	36050 MW	49260 TQ	USBLS	5/15
	Wichita MSA, KS	Y	32300 FQ	35280 MW	38260 TQ	USBLS	5/15
	Kentucky	Y	27250 FQ	34250 MW	40980 TQ	USBLS	5/15
	Louisville-Jefferson County MSA, KY-IN	Y	22340 FQ	28460 MW	38120 TQ	USBLS	5/15
	Louisiana	Y	24280 FQ	30380 MW	42790 TQ	USBLS	5/15
	Baton Rouge MSA, LA	Y	23560 FQ	28500 MW	36740 TQ	USBLS	5/15
	New Orleans-Metairie MSA, LA	Y	29180 FQ	40720 MW	46970 TQ	USBLS	5/15
	Maine	Y	30590 FQ	36650 MW	45810 TQ	USBLS	5/15
	Portland-South Portland MSA, ME	Y	19710 FQ	37830 MW	52090 TQ	USBLS	5/15
	Maryland	Y	23306 AE	41659 MW	50836 AEX	MDBLS	4/16
	Baltimore-Columbia-Towson MSA, MD	Y	33710 FQ	48530 MW	62180 TQ	USBLS	5/15
	Salisbury MSA, MD-DE	Y	26230 FQ	29770 MW	35980 TQ	USBLS	5/15
	Massachusetts	Y	37450 FQ	49030 MW	57380 TQ	USBLS	5/15
	Boston-Cambridge-Newton NECTA, MA	Y	40590 FQ	50880 MW	58060 TQ	USBLS	5/15
	Worcester MSA, MA-CT	Y	26400 FQ	37840 MW	47970 TQ	USBLS	5/15
	Michigan	Y	25240 FQ	30290 MW	41110 TQ	USBLS	5/15
	Detroit-Dearborn-Livonia PMSA, MI	Y	27220 FQ	31350 MW	38170 TQ	USBLS	5/15
	Grand Rapids-Wyoming MSA, MI	Y	24640 FQ	28270 MW	36350 TQ	USBLS	5/15
	Minnesota	Y	24069 FQ	30926 MW	42452 TQ	MNBLS	1/16-3/16
	Minneapolis-St. Paul-Bloomington MSA, MN-WI	Y	23606 FQ	30261 MW	42603 TQ	MNBLS	1/16-3/16
	Mississippi	Y	27270 FQ	33780 MW	37670 TQ	USBLS	5/15
	Missouri	Y	26720 FQ	34570 MW	44320 TQ	USBLS	5/15
	Kansas City MSA, MO-KS	Y	27210 FQ	35520 MW	48500 TQ	USBLS	5/15
	St. Louis MSA, MO-IL	Y	27850 FQ	35320 MW	44240 TQ	USBLS	5/15
	Montana	Y	26940 FQ	32860 MW	40910 TQ	USBLS	5/15
	Billings MSA, MT	Y	32990 FQ	35730 MW	38480 TQ	USBLS	5/15
	Nebraska	Y	29285 FQ	37995 MW	52100 TQ	NEBLS	7/16-9/16
	Omaha-Council Bluffs MSA, NE-IA	Y	28830 FQ	37450 MW	49045 TQ	NEBLS	7/16-9/16
	Nevada	Y	26510 FQ	34570 MW	43530 TQ	USBLS	5/15
	Las Vegas-Henderson-Paradise MSA, NV	Y	26210 FQ	34140 MW	42910 TQ	USBLS	5/15
	New Hampshire	H	16.23 AE	21.66 MW	26.52 AEX	NHBLS	6/16
	Manchester NECTA, NH	H	16.94 AE	21.98 MW	23.37 AEX	NHBLS	6/16
	Nashua NECTA, NH-MA	Y	37840 FQ	45300 MW	54320 TQ	USBLS	5/15
	New Jersey	Y	32420 FQ	40520 MW	49820 TQ	USBLS	5/15

AE	Average entry wage	AWR	Average wage range	H	Hourly
AEX	Average experienced wage	B	Biweekly	HI	Highest wage paid
ATC	Average total compensation	D	Daily	HR	High end range
AW	Average wage paid	FQ	First quartile wage	LO	Lowest wage paid

LR	Low end range	MTC	Median total compensation	TCC	Total cash compensation
M	Monthly	MW	Median wage paid	TQ	Third quartile wage
MCC	Median cash compensation	MWR	Median wage range	W	Weekly
ME	Median entry wage	S	See annotated source	Y	Yearly

Occupation/Type/Industry	Location	Per	Low	Mid	High	Source	Date
Travel Agent	Camden PMSA, NJ	Y	23710 FQ	31630 MW	37500 TQ	USBLS	5/15
	Newark PMSA, NJ-PA	Y	34600 FQ	42680 MW	52870 TQ	USBLS	5/15
	Trenton MSA, NJ	Y	34560 FQ	37870 MW	44050 TQ	USBLS	5/15
	New Mexico	Y	24000 FQ	33780 MW	47770 TQ	USBLS	5/15
	Albuquerque MSA, NM	Y	23640 FQ	33630 MW	44990 TQ	USBLS	5/15
	New York	Y	21590 AE	32070 MW	47300 AEX	NYBLS	1/16-3/16
	Buffalo-Cheektowaga-Niagara Falls MSA, NY	Y	26680 FQ	29940 MW	36130 TQ	USBLS	5/15
	Nassau County-Suffolk County PMSA, NY	Y	26280 FQ	34190 MW	40660 TQ	USBLS	5/15
	New York-Jersey City-White Plains PMSA, NY-NJ	Y	23560 FQ	32670 MW	53080 TQ	USBLS	5/15
	Rochester MSA, NY	Y	26250 FQ	33050 MW	37990 TQ	USBLS	5/15
	North Carolina	Y	29440 FQ	41650 MW	47800 TQ	USBLS	5/15
	Charlotte-Concord-Gastonia MSA, NC-SC	Y	27780 FQ	41620 MW	47490 TQ	USBLS	5/15
	Raleigh MSA, NC	Y	31590 FQ	42960 MW	47820 TQ	USBLS	5/15
	North Dakota	Y	29110 FQ	34320 MW	38610 TQ	USBLS	5/15
	Fargo MSA, ND-MN	Y	31820 FQ	35170 MW	38530 TQ	USBLS	5/15
	Ohio	Y	20510 FQ	27550 MW	37940 TQ	USBLS	5/15
	Cincinnati MSA, OH-KY-IN	Y	24650 FQ	31050 MW	41060 TQ	USBLS	5/15
	Cleveland-Elyria MSA, OH	Y	21170 FQ	25970 MW	39450 TQ	USBLS	5/15
	Columbus MSA, OH	Y	19100 FQ	25390 MW	36500 TQ	USBLS	5/15
	Oklahoma	Y	23640 FQ	30020 MW	38600 TQ	USBLS	5/15
	Oklahoma City MSA, OK	Y	23110 FQ	29440 MW	37010 TQ	USBLS	5/15
	Oregon	H	12.81 FQ	16.09 MW	21.45 TQ	ORBLS	2016
	Portland-Vancouver-Hillsboro MSA, OR-WA	Y	26280 FQ	33340 MW	47110 TQ	USBLS	5/15
	Pennsylvania	Y	29560 FQ	36870 MW	45420 TQ	USBLS	5/15
	Allentown-Bethlehem-Easton MSA, PA-NJ	Y	28080 FQ	36830 MW	46100 TQ	USBLS	5/15
	Harrisburg-Carlisle MSA, PA	Y	27050 FQ	29660 MW	43540 TQ	USBLS	5/15
	Montgomery County-Bucks County-Chester County PMSA, PA	Y	33280 FQ	38890 MW	47900 TQ	USBLS	5/15
	Philadelphia PMSA, PA	Y	32460 FQ	37000 MW	43970 TQ	USBLS	5/15
	Pittsburgh MSA, PA	Y	26170 FQ	33050 MW	41760 TQ	USBLS	5/15
	Rhode Island	Y	31980 FQ	35270 MW	38560 TQ	USBLS	5/15
	Providence-Warwick MSA, RI-MA	Y	31410 FQ	34900 MW	38310 TQ	USBLS	5/15
	South Carolina	Y	21640 FQ	26430 MW	36650 TQ	USBLS	5/15
	Charleston-North Charleston MSA, SC	Y	31170 FQ	40470 MW	51750 TQ	USBLS	5/15
	Columbia MSA, SC	Y	24250 FQ	28510 MW	34190 TQ	USBLS	5/15
	Greenville-Anderson-Mauldin MSA, SC	Y	18060 FQ	25980 MW	33210 TQ	USBLS	5/15
	South Dakota	Y	25500 FQ	28820 MW	33230 TQ	USBLS	5/15
	Sioux Falls MSA; SD	Y	26290 FQ	30720 MW	38030 TQ	USBLS	5/15
	Tennessee	Y	27540 FQ	36510 MW	45740 TQ	USBLS	5/15
	Knoxville MSA, TN	Y	24170 FQ	35730 MW	46360 TQ	USBLS	5/15
	Memphis MSA, TN-MS-AR	Y	27030 FQ	34660 MW	38780 TQ	USBLS	5/15
	Nashville-Davidson–Murfreesboro–Franklin MSA, TN	Y	31860 FQ	38770 MW	48450 TQ	USBLS	5/15
	Texas	Y	30710 FQ	41330 MW	51530 TQ	USBLS	5/15
	Austin-Round Rock MSA, TX	Y	24470 FQ	35980 MW	48410 TQ	USBLS	5/15
	Dallas-Plano-Irving PMSA, TX	Y	34370 FQ	43130 MW	50200 TQ	USBLS	5/15
	Fort Worth-Arlington PMSA, TX	Y	29240 FQ	41210 MW	51470 TQ	USBLS	5/15
	Houston-The Woodlands-Sugar Land MSA, TX	Y	33620 FQ	43620 MW	55660 TQ	USBLS	5/15
	San Antonio-New Braunfels MSA, TX	Y	26270 FQ	41060 MW	60890 TQ	USBLS	5/15
	Utah	Y	26860 FQ	36160 MW	48320 TQ	USBLS	5/15
	Ogden-Clearfield MSA, UT	Y	22050 FQ	64260 MW	72170 TQ	USBLS	5/15
	Salt Lake City MSA, UT	Y	26790 FQ	35400 MW	42550 TQ	USBLS	5/15
	Vermont	Y	32320 FQ	38310 MW	45680 TQ	USBLS	5/15
	Burlington-South Burlington MSA, VT	Y	30700 FQ	40850 MW	46360 TQ	USBLS	5/15
	Virginia	Y	34240 FQ	45250 MW	60550 TQ	USBLS	5/15
	Richmond MSA, VA	Y	32920 FQ	42590 MW	53940 TQ	USBLS	5/15

AE	Average entry wage	**AWR**	Average wage range	**H**	Hourly
AEX	Average experienced wage	**B**	Biweekly	**HI**	Highest wage paid
ATC	Average total compensation	**D**	Daily	**HR**	High end range
AW	Average wage paid	**FQ**	First quartile wage	**LO**	Lowest wage paid

LR	Low end range	**MTC**	Median total compensation	**TCC**	Total cash compensation
		MW	Median wage paid	**TQ**	Third quartile wage
M	Monthly	**MCC**	Median cash compensation	**MWR**	Median wage range	**W**	Weekly
ME	Median entry wage	**S**	See annotated source	**Y**	Yearly

Occupation/Type/Industry	Location	Per	Low	Mid	High	Source	Date
Travel Agent	Virginia Beach-Norfolk-Newport News MSA, VA-NC	Y	32700 FQ	38450 MW	50280 TQ	USBLS	5/15
	Washington	H	14.95 FQ	20.12 MW	24.40 TQ	WABLS	3/16
	Seattle-Bellevue-Everett PMSA, WA	H	15.40 FQ	21.35 MW	25.38 TQ	WABLS	3/16
	Tacoma-Lakewood PMSA, WA	H	15.00 FQ	16.94 MW	18.86 TQ	WABLS	3/16
	West Virginia	Y	27910 FQ	32780 MW	38340 TQ	USBLS	5/15
	Wisconsin	Y	26520 FQ	31380 MW	39230 TQ	USBLS	5/15
	Madison MSA, WI	Y	30580 FQ	40810 MW	46500 TQ	USBLS	5/15
	Milwaukee-Waukesha-West Allis MSA, WI	Y	25750 FQ	29760 MW	35680 TQ	USBLS	5/15
	Wyoming	Y	34880 FQ	42390 MW	48100 TQ	USBLS	5/15
	Puerto Rico	Y	21400 FQ	26020 MW	33620 TQ	USBLS	5/15
	San Juan-Carolina-Caguas MSA, PR	Y	22550 FQ	27260 MW	34870 TQ	USBLS	5/15
	Guam	Y	20890 FQ	26100 MW	29650 TQ	USBLS	5/15
Travel Analyst	United States	Y		72887 ATC		BTN01	2016
Travel Director	United States	Y		149320 ATC		BTN01	2016
Travel Guide	Arizona	Y	17520 FQ	18300 MW	19080 TQ	USBLS	5/15
	California	H	13.49 FQ	16.24 MW	19.15 TQ	CABLS	1/16-3/16
	Los Angeles-Long Beach-Glendale PMSA, CA	H	13.81 FQ	16.27 MW	18.61 TQ	CABLS	1/16-3/16
	San Francisco-Redwood City-South San Francisco PMSA, CA	H	15.55 FQ	17.88 MW	20.72 TQ	CABLS	1/16-3/16
	Colorado	Y	27750 FQ	33960 MW	39610 TQ	USBLS	5/15
	Denver-Aurora-Lakewood MSA, CO	Y	28360 FQ	34390 MW	39880 TQ	USBLS	5/15
	District of Columbia	Y	41700 FQ	50100 MW	61020 TQ	USBLS	5/15
	Washington-Arlington-Alexandria PMSA, DC-VA-MD-WV	Y	31050 FQ	45220 MW	57790 TQ	USBLS	5/15
	Florida	H	12.30 AE	19.32 MW	21.10 AEX	FLBLS	7/16-9/16
	Miami-Miami Beach-Kendall PMSA, FL	H	14.12 AE	20.72 MW	21.81 AEX	FLBLS	7/16-9/16
	Orlando-Kissimmee-Sanford MSA, FL	H	10.78 AE	16.60 MW	18.88 AEX	FLBLS	7/16-9/16
	Illinois	Y	26100 FQ	34940 MW	60450 TQ	USBLS	5/15
	Chicago-Naperville-Arlington Heights PMSA, IL	Y	25250 FQ	30460 MW	46610 TQ	USBLS	5/15
	Massachusetts	Y	35170 FQ	45460 MW	56590 TQ	USBLS	5/15
	Minnesota	Y	24600 FQ	29165 MW	36567 TQ	MNBLS	1/16-3/16
	Mississippi	Y	18590 FQ	20480 MW	22000 TQ	USBLS	5/15
	Montana	Y	19680 FQ	27180 MW	29850 TQ	USBLS	5/15
	New York	Y	21070 AE	28320 ATC	42590 AEX	NYBLS	1/16-3/16
	New York-Jersey City-White Plains PMSA, NY-NJ	Y	24380 FQ	29340 MW	58430 TQ	USBLS	5/15
	North Carolina	Y	39010 FQ	45150 MW	54060 TQ	USBLS	5/15
	Charlotte-Concord-Gastonia MSA, NC-SC	Y	42480 FQ	45440 MW	48400 TQ	USBLS	5/15
	Oregon	H	12.83 FQ	16.32 MW	21.61 TQ	ORBLS	2016
	Pennsylvania	Y	38150 FQ	43320 MW	47560 TQ	USBLS	5/15
	Tennessee	Y	50310 FQ	54290 MW	58270 TQ	USBLS	5/15
	Virginia	Y	25720 FQ	29750 MW	45680 TQ	USBLS	5/15
	Washington	H	17.48 FQ	25.40 MW	28.44 TQ	WABLS	3/16
	Seattle-Bellevue-Everett PMSA, WA	H	20.12 FQ	26.11 MW	28.82 TQ	WABLS	3/16
	Wisconsin	Y	33350 FQ	36180 MW	39010 TQ	USBLS	5/15
Treasurer							
County Government	Ingham County, MI	Y			99800 HI	LSJ14	2017
Municipal Government	Alturas, CA	Y			59567 HI	CACIT	6/28/16
Municipal Government	Atascadero, CA	Y			1977 HI	CACIT	6/28/16
Municipal Government	Dos Palos, CA	Y			1800 HI	CACIT	6/28/16
Municipal Government	San Francisco, CA	Y			179824 HI	CACIT	6/28/16
Municipal Government	Bernardston, MA	Y			20848 HI	FRCOG	2016
Municipal Government	Hawley, MA	Y			7570 HI	FRCOG	2016
Municipal Government	Warwick, MA	Y			18449 HI	FRCOG	2016
Municipal Government	Detroit, MI	M	5042 LO		7567 HI	DETGOV	2016
Municipal Government	Lyon Township, MI	Y			63227 HI	HTL01	2015

AE	Average entry wage	AWR	Average wage range	H	Hourly
AEX	Average experienced wage	B	Biweekly	HI	Highest wage paid
ATC	Average total compensation	D	Daily	HR	High end range
AW	Average wage paid	FQ	First quartile wage	LO	Lowest wage paid

LR	Low end range	MTC	Median total compensation	TCC	Total cash compensation
M	Monthly	MW	Median wage paid	TQ	Third quartile wage
MCC	Median cash compensation	MWR	Median wage range	W	Weekly
ME	Median entry wage	S	See annotated source	Y	Yearly

Occupation/Type/Industry	Location	Per	Low	Mid	High	Source	Date
Treasury Analyst							
Municipal Government	Fremont, CA	Y			97225 HI	CACIT	6/28/16
Municipal Government	Sacramento, CA	Y			61033 HI	CACIT	6/28/16
Treasury Cashier							
Municipal Government	Seattle, WA	H	30.03 LO		35.05 HI	CSSS	1/13/16
Treasury Manager							
Municipal Government	Escondido, CA	Y			72867 HI	CACIT	6/28/16
Tree Artisan							
Municipal Government	Detroit, MI	M	2130 LO		2375 HI	DETGOV	2016
Tree Care Specialist							
Municipal Government	Carmel-By-The-Sea, CA	Y			54825 HI	CACIT	7/8/16
Tree High Climber							
Municipal Government	Oakland, CA	Y		69166 AW		CACIT	6/28/16
Tree Surgeon							
Department of Water and Power, Municipal Government	Los Angeles, CA	Y		76463 AW		CACIT	6/23/16
Harbor, Municipal Government	Los Angeles, CA	Y		68552 AW		CACIT	6/23/16
Tree Trimmer and Pruner	Alabama	Y	26090 AE	37920 AW	43841 AEX	ALBLS	6/16
	Alaska	Y	42280 FQ	50820 MW	57410 TQ	USBLS	5/15
	Arizona	Y	27060 FQ	30500 MW	49650 TQ	USBLS	5/15
	Phoenix-Mesa-Scottsdale MSA, AZ	Y	26800 FQ	30070 MW	48210 TQ	USBLS	5/15
	Arkansas	Y	23340 FQ	29230 MW	34750 TQ	USBLS	5/15
	Little Rock-North Little Rock-Conway MSA, AR	Y	23230 FQ	27960 MW	33620 TQ	USBLS	5/15
	California	H	13.87 FQ	17.58 MW	23.30 TQ	CABLS	1/16-3/16
	Anaheim-Santa Ana-Irvine PMSA, CA	H	11.26 FQ	12.93 MW	14.93 TQ	CABLS	1/16-3/16
	Los Angeles-Long Beach-Glendale PMSA, CA	H	17.57 FQ	23.35 MW	30.40 TQ	CABLS	1/16-3/16
	Oakland-Hayward-Berkeley PMSA, CA	H	12.81 FQ	16.06 MW	18.43 TQ	CABLS	1/16-3/16
	Riverside-San Bernardino-Ontario MSA, CA	H	12.02 FQ	15.73 MW	17.65 TQ	CABLS	1/16-3/16
	Sacramento–Roseville–Arden-Arcade MSA, CA	H	19.29 FQ	24.41 MW	27.77 TQ	CABLS	1/16-3/16
	San Diego-Carlsbad MSA, CA	H	13.20 FQ	14.16 MW	15.14 TQ	CABLS	1/16-3/16
	San Francisco-Redwood City-South San Francisco PMSA, CA	H	20.89 FQ	23.09 MW	30.83 TQ	CABLS	1/16-3/16
	Colorado	Y	26650 FQ	29650 MW	39970 TQ	USBLS	5/15
	Denver-Aurora-Lakewood MSA, CO	Y	42480 FQ	46080 MW	49680 TQ	USBLS	5/15
	Connecticut	Y		40269 MW		CTBLS	1/16-3/16
	Washington-Arlington-Alexandria PMSA, DC-VA-MD-WV	Y	42070 FQ	45310 MW	48630 TQ	USBLS	5/15
	Florida	H	9.86 AE	12.98 MW	15.47 AEX	FLBLS	7/16-9/16
	Fort Lauderdale-Pompano Beach-Deerfield Beach PMSA, FL	H	10.76 AE	13.42 MW	15.50 AEX	FLBLS	7/16-9/16
	Miami-Miami Beach-Kendall PMSA, FL	H	9.28 AE	11.34 MW	15.66 AEX	FLBLS	7/16-9/16
	Orlando-Kissimmee-Sanford MSA, FL	H	11.14 AE	13.94 MW	16.23 AEX	FLBLS	7/16-9/16
	Tampa-St. Petersburg-Clearwater MSA, FL	H	9.36 AE	10.79 MW	12.43 AEX	FLBLS	7/16-9/16
	Georgia	Y	26260 FQ	32500 MW	37630 TQ	USBLS	5/15
	Atlanta-Sandy Springs-Roswell MSA, GA	Y	28830 FQ	33540 MW	37810 TQ	USBLS	5/15
	Hawaii	Y	41000 FQ	47470 MW	55420 TQ	USBLS	5/15
	Urban Honolulu MSA, HI	Y	41210 FQ	46970 MW	54700 TQ	USBLS	5/15
	Idaho	Y	29310 FQ	34870 MW	39800 TQ	USBLS	5/15
	Illinois	Y	28630 FQ	39790 MW	60310 TQ	USBLS	5/15

AE Average entry wage	**AWR** Average wage range	**H** Hourly	**LR** Low end range	**MTC** Median total compensation	**TCC** Total cash compensation
AEX Average experienced wage	**B** Biweekly	**HI** Highest wage paid	**M** Monthly	**MW** Median wage paid	**TQ** Third quartile wage
ATC Average total compensation	**D** Daily	**HR** High end range	**MCC** Median cash compensation	**MWR** Median wage range	**W** Weekly
AW Average wage paid	**FQ** First quartile wage	**LO** Lowest wage paid	**ME** Median entry wage	**S** See annotated source	**Y** Yearly

Occupation/Type/Industry	Location	Per	Low	Mid	High	Source	Date
Tree Trimmer and Pruner	Chicago-Naperville-Arlington Heights PMSA, IL	Y	30520 FQ	53320 MW	70230 TQ	USBLS	5/15
	Lake County-Kenosha County PMSA, IL-WI	Y	24150 FQ	33810 MW	40950 TQ	USBLS	5/15
	Indiana	Y	27430 FQ	30980 MW	39510 TQ	USBLS	5/15
	Iowa	Y	33580 FQ	38210 MW	45550 TQ	USBLS	5/15
	Kansas	Y	25390 FQ	28310 MW	33270 TQ	USBLS	5/15
	Wichita MSA, KS	Y	20690 FQ	28720 MW	38450 TQ	USBLS	5/15
	Kentucky	Y	25640 FQ	28210 MW	30830 TQ	USBLS	5/15
	Louisiana	Y	32960 FQ	37650 MW	44090 TQ	USBLS	5/15
	Baton Rouge MSA, LA	Y	33190 FQ	35940 MW	38680 TQ	USBLS	5/15
	Maine	Y	27460 FQ	33510 MW	38760 TQ	USBLS	5/15
	Maryland	Y	25495 AE	38181 MW	44524 AEX	MDBLS	4/16
	Baltimore-Columbia-Towson MSA, MD	Y	28360 FQ	36370 MW	50110 TQ	USBLS	5/15
	Massachusetts	Y	39940 FQ	49620 MW	57790 TQ	USBLS	5/15
	Boston-Cambridge-Newton NECTA, MA	Y	44590 FQ	54590 MW	59760 TQ	USBLS	5/15
	Worcester MSA, MA-CT	Y	37850 FQ	43720 MW	49610 TQ	USBLS	5/15
	Michigan	Y	37290 FQ	44230 MW	49450 TQ	USBLS	5/15
	Detroit-Dearborn-Livonia PMSA, MI	Y	38290 FQ	51790 MW	57940 TQ	USBLS	5/15
	Minnesota	Y	26661 FQ	38728 MW	47615 TQ	MNBLS	1/16-3/16
	Minneapolis-St. Paul-Bloomington MSA, MN-WI	Y	21137 FQ	29367 MW	39698 TQ	MNBLS	1/16-3/16
	Mississippi	Y	26140 FQ	29980 MW	38050 TQ	USBLS	5/15
	Missouri	Y	21840 FQ	30410 MW	40780 TQ	USBLS	5/15
	Kansas City MSA, MO-KS	Y	26390 FQ	28730 MW	32890 TQ	USBLS	5/15
	St. Louis MSA, MO-IL	Y	19910 FQ	30800 MW	42670 TQ	USBLS	5/15
	Montana	Y	43230 FQ	50810 MW	58260 TQ	USBLS	5/15
	Nebraska	Y	28060 FQ	31195 MW	51870 TQ	NEBLS	7/16-9/16
	New Hampshire	H	19.57 AE	21.78 MW	22.31 AEX	NHBLS	6/16
	New Jersey	Y	36240 FQ	47230 MW	57130 TQ	USBLS	5/15
	Camden PMSA, NJ	Y	45580 FQ	51350 MW	58280 TQ	USBLS	5/15
	Newark PMSA, NJ-PA	Y	39660 FQ	48640 MW	56410 TQ	USBLS	5/15
	New York	Y	31400 AE	47370 MW	52990 AEX	NYBLS	1/16-3/16
	Buffalo-Cheektowaga-Niagara Falls MSA, NY	Y	49690 FQ	53880 MW	58080 TQ	USBLS	5/15
	Nassau County-Suffolk County PMSA, NY	Y	36810 FQ	48620 MW	55850 TQ	USBLS	5/15
	New York-Jersey City-White Plains PMSA, NY-NJ	Y	27900 FQ	31220 MW	54630 TQ	USBLS	5/15
	North Carolina	Y	25970 FQ	30230 MW	36670 TQ	USBLS	5/15
	Charlotte-Concord-Gastonia MSA, NC-SC	Y	26750 FQ	30340 MW	36510 TQ	USBLS	5/15
	Raleigh MSA, NC	Y	24050 FQ	28850 MW	34070 TQ	USBLS	5/15
	Ohio	Y	19070 FQ	26930 MW	36490 TQ	USBLS	5/15
	Cincinnati MSA, OH-KY-IN	Y	27370 FQ	31760 MW	38580 TQ	USBLS	5/15
	Cleveland-Elyria MSA, OH	Y	42060 FQ	45440 MW	48820 TQ	USBLS	5/15
	Columbus MSA, OH	Y	33260 FQ	38210 MW	45740 TQ	USBLS	5/15
	Oklahoma	Y	23880 FQ	29620 MW	37880 TQ	USBLS	5/15
	Oklahoma City MSA, OK	Y	23990 FQ	29900 MW	38630 TQ	USBLS	5/15
	Tulsa MSA, OK	Y	30280 FQ	33600 MW	36440 TQ	USBLS	5/15
	Oregon	H	15.60 FQ	19.28 MW	23.80 TQ	ORBLS	2016
	Portland-Vancouver-Hillsboro MSA, OR-WA	Y	33060 FQ	42830 MW	50710 TQ	USBLS	5/15
	Pennsylvania	Y	27720 FQ	33780 MW	40600 TQ	USBLS	5/15
	Allentown-Bethlehem-Easton MSA, PA-NJ	Y	26710 FQ	36430 MW	47590 TQ	USBLS	5/15
	Montgomery County-Bucks County-Chester County PMSA, PA	Y	32780 FQ	35820 MW	38860 TQ	USBLS	5/15
	Philadelphia PMSA, PA	Y	25350 FQ	30170 MW	37750 TQ	USBLS	5/15
	Pittsburgh MSA, PA	Y	37160 FQ	43500 MW	50260 TQ	USBLS	5/15
	Rhode Island	Y	35540 FQ	43170 MW	50020 TQ	USBLS	5/15
	Providence-Warwick MSA, RI-MA	Y	36320 FQ	43430 MW	49670 TQ	USBLS	5/15
	Greenville-Anderson-Mauldin MSA, SC	Y	24850 FQ	28030 MW	31230 TQ	USBLS	5/15
	South Dakota	Y	24750 FQ	30160 MW	36380 TQ	USBLS	5/15
	Sioux Falls MSA, SD	Y	21310 FQ	30710 MW	41780 TQ	USBLS	5/15
	Tennessee	Y	29660 FQ	36270 MW	43780 TQ	USBLS	5/15

AE Average entry wage	**AWR** Average wage range	**H** Hourly	**LR** Low end range	**MTC** Median total compensation	**TCC** Total cash compensation
AEX Average experienced wage	**B** Biweekly	**HI** Highest wage paid	**M** Monthly	**MW** Median wage paid	**TQ** Third quartile wage
ATC Average total compensation	**D** Daily	**HR** High end range	**MCC** Median cash compensation	**MWR** Median wage range	**W** Weekly
AW Average wage paid	**FQ** First quartile wage	**LO** Lowest wage paid	**ME** Median entry wage	**S** See annotated source	**Y** Yearly

Occupation/Type/Industry	Location	Per	Low	Mid	High	Source	Date
Tree Trimmer and Pruner	Knoxville MSA, TN	Y	27660 FQ	40980 MW	45180 TQ	USBLS	5/15
	Memphis MSA, TN-MS-AR	Y	30070 FQ	34070 MW	37640 TQ	USBLS	5/15
	Nashville-Davidson–Murfreesboro–Franklin MSA, TN	Y	29990 FQ	34740 MW	38860 TQ	USBLS	5/15
	Texas	Y	24090 FQ	28720 MW	34310 TQ	USBLS	5/15
	Austin-Round Rock MSA, TX	Y	23540 FQ	27140 MW	30340 TQ	USBLS	5/15
	Dallas-Plano-Irving PMSA, TX	Y	25560 FQ	31080 MW	35200 TQ	USBLS	5/15
	Fort Worth-Arlington PMSA, TX	Y	22980 FQ	26890 MW	31520 TQ	USBLS	5/15
	Houston-The Woodlands-Sugar Land MSA, TX	Y	25560 FQ	29110 MW	35340 TQ	USBLS	5/15
	San Antonio-New Braunfels MSA, TX	Y	22030 FQ	24270 MW	27610 TQ	USBLS	5/15
	Utah	Y	26190 FQ	29890 MW	41370 TQ	USBLS	5/15
	Provo-Orem MSA, UT	Y	18550 FQ	31360 MW	37210 TQ	USBLS	5/15
	Salt Lake City MSA, UT	Y	27250 FQ	29990 MW	43570 TQ	USBLS	5/15
	Vermont	Y	32980 FQ	35630 MW	38270 TQ	USBLS	5/15
	Virginia	Y	27990 FQ	32840 MW	43930 TQ	USBLS	5/15
	Virginia Beach-Norfolk-Newport News MSA, VA-NC	Y	26200 FQ	28060 MW	29920 TQ	USBLS	5/15
	Washington	H	13.06 FQ	15.61 MW	22.32 TQ	WABLS	3/16
	Seattle-Bellevue-Everett PMSA, WA	H	26.30 FQ	28.29 MW	30.27 TQ	WABLS	3/16
	West Virginia	Y	27000 FQ	30110 MW	36530 TQ	USBLS	5/15
	Huntington-Ashland MSA, WV-KY-OH	Y	19120 FQ	27010 MW	43740 TQ	USBLS	5/15
	Wisconsin	Y	25200 FQ	30730 MW	47170 TQ	USBLS	5/15
	Madison MSA, WI	Y	22610 FQ	25560 MW	28810 TQ	USBLS	5/15
	Wyoming	Y	24520 FQ	29250 MW	35290 TQ	USBLS	5/15
	Puerto Rico	Y	30020 FQ	34210 MW	38130 TQ	USBLS	5/15
Tree Warden							
Highway Department, Municipal Government	Bernardston, MA	Y			3235 HI	FRCOG	2016
Tribal and Cultural Resource Officer							
Department of Environmental Quality, State Government	Helena, MT	H			26.75 HI	MTGOV	2016
Tribal Relations Program Manager							
Department of Public Health and Human Services, State Government	Helena, MT	H			38.72 HI	MTGOV	2016
Trooper							
State Police	Michigan	Y	44000 LO		66000 HI	MSP03	2017
Troubleshooter							
Electric Utility, Municipal Government	Santa Clara, CA	Y		138798 AW		CACIT	6/28/16
Truck Driver							
Dry Van	Midwest	Y		56626 MW		HDT	2015
Dry Van	Northeast	Y		59751 MW		HDT	2015
Dry Van	Southeast	Y		53691 MW		HDT	2015
Dry Van	West	Y		51663 MW		HDT	2015
Flatbed Truck	United States	Y		57000 MW		FLTO	1/16
Flatbed Truck	Midwest	Y		59283 MW		HDT	2015
Flatbed Truck	Northeast	Y		62436 MW		HDT	2015
Flatbed Truck	Southeast	Y		56687 MW		HDT	2015
Flatbed Truck	West	Y		54701 MW		HDT	2015
High-Touch Food Service	United States	Y		77000 MW		FLTO	1/16
Less Than Truckload	United States	Y		60000 MW		FLTO	1/16
Local	United States	Y		40000 MW		FLTO	1/16
Over-the-Road Truckload	United States	Y		55000 MW		FLTO	1/16
Refrigerated Truck	Midwest	Y		58327 MW		HDT	2015
Refrigerated Truck	Northeast	Y		61200 MW		HDT	2015
Refrigerated Truck	Southeast	Y		55251 MW		HDT	2015
Refrigerated Truck	West	Y		53163 MW		HDT	2015
Specialty/Permitted Long-Haul	United States	Y		70000 MW		FLTO	1/16

AE	Average entry wage	AWR	Average wage range	H	Hourly	LR	Low end range	MTC	Median total compensation	TCC	Total cash compensation
AEX	Average experienced wage	B	Biweekly	HI	Highest wage paid	M	Monthly	MW	Median wage paid	TQ	Third quartile wage
ATC	Average total compensation	D	Daily	HR	High end range	MCC	Median cash compensation	MWR	Median wage range	W	Weekly
AW	Average wage paid	FQ	First quartile wage	LO	Lowest wage paid	ME	Median entry wage	S	See annotated source	Y	Yearly

Occupation/Type/Industry	Location	Per	Low	Mid	High	Source	Date
Trustee							
Township Government	Ohio	H	40.41 LO		113.38 HI	OHGOV1	2017
Uber Driver	Denver, CO	H		13.17 AW		BF01	10/19/15-12/14/15
	Detroit, MI	H		8.77 AW		BF01	12/7/15-12/21/15
	Houston, TX	H		10.75 AW		BF01	12/7/15-12/21/15
UH 72 Aircraft Mechanic	United States	Y		78083 AW		AVJOB05	2016
UI Designer	United States	Y		80000 MW		TSTR	2017
Umpire, Referee, and Other Sports Official	Alabama	Y	17145 AE	25035 AW	28979 AEX	ALBLS	6/16
	Alaska	Y	33120 FQ	45600 MW	56680 TQ	USBLS	5/15
	Anchorage MSA, AK	Y	24280 FQ	41300 MW	54750 TQ	USBLS	5/15
	Arizona	Y	25430 FQ	28790 MW	34840 TQ	USBLS	5/15
	Phoenix-Mesa-Scottsdale MSA, AZ	Y	25600 FQ	28380 MW	31160 TQ	USBLS	5/15
	California	Y		33255 AW		CABLS	1/16-3/16
	Anaheim-Santa Ana-Irvine PMSA, CA	Y		31510 AW		CABLS	1/16-3/16
	Los Angeles-Long Beach-Glendale PMSA, CA	Y		22288 AW		CABLS	1/16-3/16
	Oakland-Hayward-Berkeley PMSA, CA	Y		40833 AW		CABLS	1/16-3/16
	Riverside-San Bernardino-Ontario MSA, CA	Y		24165 AW		CABLS	1/16-3/16
	Sacramento–Roseville–Arden-Arcade MSA, CA	Y		42406 AW		CABLS	1/16-3/16
	Colorado	Y	18780 FQ	24040 MW	34660 TQ	USBLS	5/15
	Denver-Aurora-Lakewood MSA, CO	Y	18690 FQ	22390 MW	30200 TQ	USBLS	5/15
	Connecticut	Y		22096 MW		CTBLS	1/16-3/16
	Bridgeport-Stamford-Norwalk MSA, CT	Y	21110 FQ	23140 MW	41240 TQ	USBLS	5/15
	Delaware	Y	19180 FQ	23800 MW	43030 TQ	USBLS	5/15
	Washington-Arlington-Alexandria PMSA, DC-VA-MD-WV	Y	22870 FQ	39350 MW	55860 TQ	USBLS	5/15
	Florida	Y	18658 AE	26187 MW	37972 AEX	FLBLS	7/16-9/16
	Fort Lauderdale-Pompano Beach-Deerfield Beach PMSA, FL	Y	23075 AE	25307 MW	30977 AEX	FLBLS	7/16-9/16
	Miami-Miami Beach-Kendall PMSA, FL	Y	18439 AE	23389 MW	37710 AEX	FLBLS	7/16-9/16
	Tampa-St. Petersburg-Clearwater MSA, FL	Y	18818 AE	27804 MW	36770 AEX	FLBLS	7/16-9/16
	Georgia	Y	18100 FQ	26290 MW	42470 TQ	USBLS	5/15
	Atlanta-Sandy Springs-Roswell MSA, GA	Y	20870 FQ	37170 MW	44740 TQ	USBLS	5/15
	Idaho	Y	17670 FQ	19960 MW	24870 TQ	USBLS	5/15
	Boise City MSA, ID	Y	17630 FQ	20250 MW	22670 TQ	USBLS	5/15
	Illinois	Y	20730 FQ	23240 MW	30040 TQ	USBLS	5/15
	Chicago-Naperville-Arlington Heights PMSA, IL	Y	21080 FQ	23330 MW	28890 TQ	USBLS	5/15
	Lake County-Kenosha County PMSA, IL-WI	Y	21690 FQ	23560 MW	28130 TQ	USBLS	5/15
	Indiana	Y	17750 FQ	19840 MW	27930 TQ	USBLS	5/15
	Indianapolis-Carmel-Anderson MSA, IN	Y	18170 FQ	24740 MW	29950 TQ	USBLS	5/15
	Iowa	Y	17370 FQ	19210 MW	23680 TQ	USBLS	5/15
	Des Moines-West Des Moines MSA, IA	Y	16760 FQ	17980 MW	19200 TQ	USBLS	5/15
	Kansas	Y	21570 FQ	24810 MW	33840 TQ	USBLS	5/15
	Wichita MSA, KS	Y	24140 FQ	32320 MW	42210 TQ	USBLS	5/15
	Kentucky	Y	19910 FQ	40670 MW	51230 TQ	USBLS	5/15
	Louisville-Jefferson County MSA, KY-IN	Y	18110 FQ	23620 MW	56560 TQ	USBLS	5/15
	Baton Rouge MSA, LA	Y	21100 FQ	22920 MW	24740 TQ	USBLS	5/15
	Maine	Y	17730 FQ	19550 MW	37590 TQ	USBLS	5/15
	Massachusetts	Y	19040 FQ	19390 MW	30440 TQ	USBLS	5/15

AE	Average entry wage	AWR	Average wage range	H	Hourly	LR	Low end range	MTC	Median total compensation	TCC	Total cash compensation
AEX	Average experienced wage	B	Biweekly	HI	Highest wage paid	M	Monthly	MW	Median wage paid	TQ	Third quartile wage
ATC	Average total compensation	D	Daily	HR	High end range	MCC	Median cash compensation	MWR	Median wage range	W	Weekly
AW	Average wage paid	FQ	First quartile wage	LO	Lowest wage paid	ME	Median entry wage	S	See annotated source	Y	Yearly

1628

Occupation/Type/Industry	Location	Per	Low	Mid	High	Source	Date
Umpire, Referee, and Other Sports Official	Boston-Cambridge-Newton NECTA, MA	Y	24290 FQ	29100 MW	61130 TQ	USBLS	5/15
	Michigan	Y	18810 FQ	26370 MW	41670 TQ	USBLS	5/15
	Grand Rapids-Wyoming MSA, MI	Y	19350 FQ	31510 MW	36940 TQ	USBLS	5/15
	Minnesota	Y	19314 FQ	33790 MW	42570 TQ	MNBLS	1/16-3/16
	Minneapolis-St. Paul-Bloomington MSA, MN-WI	Y	20957 FQ	29324 MW	48709 TQ	MNBLS	1/16-3/16
	Missouri	Y	18260 FQ	22500 MW	31500 TQ	USBLS	5/15
	Kansas City MSA, MO-KS	Y	19880 FQ	23620 MW	33860 TQ	USBLS	5/15
	St. Louis MSA, MO-IL	Y	18390 FQ	24930 MW	34360 TQ	USBLS	5/15
	Montana	Y	18160 FQ	19990 MW	33040 TQ	USBLS	5/15
	Nebraska	Y	18495 FQ	21395 MW	31865 TQ	NEBLS	7/16-9/16
	Newark PMSA, NJ-PA	Y	47200 FQ	83020 MW	92860 TQ	USBLS	5/15
	New Mexico	Y	18130 FQ	32400 MW	36380 TQ	USBLS	5/15
	Nassau County-Suffolk County PMSA, NY	Y	18980 FQ	19760 MW	51000 TQ	USBLS	5/15
	North Carolina	Y	25580 FQ	31420 MW	55140 TQ	USBLS	5/15
	Raleigh MSA, NC	Y	27120 FQ	31610 MW	55690 TQ	USBLS	5/15
	North Dakota	Y	20780 FQ	31030 MW	46470 TQ	USBLS	5/15
	Ohio	Y	18070 FQ	19250 MW	27820 TQ	USBLS	5/15
	Cincinnati MSA, OH-KY-IN	Y	17540 FQ	18930 MW	24390 TQ	USBLS	5/15
	Cleveland-Elyria MSA, OH	Y	18150 FQ	19440 MW	28960 TQ	USBLS	5/15
	Oklahoma	Y	22280 FQ	33540 MW	46540 TQ	USBLS	5/15
	Oregon	Y	19872 FQ	22933 MW	31184 TQ	ORBLS	2016
	Portland-Vancouver-Hillsboro MSA, OR-WA	Y	19500 FQ	20790 MW	29760 TQ	USBLS	5/15
	Pennsylvania	Y	17900 FQ	21050 MW	38160 TQ	USBLS	5/15
	Harrisburg-Carlisle MSA, PA	Y	18820 FQ	21230 MW	23910 TQ	USBLS	5/15
	Rhode Island	Y	19120 FQ	29970 MW	43780 TQ	USBLS	5/15
	Providence-Warwick MSA, RI-MA	Y	18960 FQ	19200 MW	19460 TQ	USBLS	5/15
	South Carolina	Y	18590 FQ	23840 MW	30750 TQ	USBLS	5/15
	Tennessee	Y	26900 FQ	36490 MW	43050 TQ	USBLS	5/15
	Memphis MSA, TN-MS-AR	Y	39320 FQ	43050 MW	46800 TQ	USBLS	5/15
	Texas	Y	20250 FQ	29740 MW	38210 TQ	USBLS	5/15
	Austin-Round Rock MSA, TX	Y	22280 FQ	33460 MW	41840 TQ	USBLS	5/15
	Dallas-Plano-Irving PMSA, TX	Y	20640 FQ	23400 MW	32990 TQ	USBLS	5/15
	Fort Worth-Arlington PMSA, TX	Y	32570 FQ	35570 MW	38570 TQ	USBLS	5/15
	San Antonio-New Braunfels MSA, TX	Y	19160 FQ	23050 MW	43200 TQ	USBLS	5/15
	Utah	Y	16440 FQ	17750 MW	19060 TQ	USBLS	5/15
	Provo-Orem MSA, UT	Y	16250 FQ	17420 MW	18590 TQ	USBLS	5/15
	Salt Lake City MSA, UT	Y	16560 FQ	18050 MW	20760 TQ	USBLS	5/15
	Virginia	Y	22670 FQ	36760 MW	49130 TQ	USBLS	5/15
	Richmond MSA, VA	Y	33750 FQ	36110 MW	38460 TQ	USBLS	5/15
	Virginia Beach-Norfolk-Newport News MSA, VA-NC	Y	17140 FQ	18850 MW	21780 TQ	USBLS	5/15
	Washington	Y		37851 AW		WABLS	3/16
	Seattle-Bellevue-Everett PMSA, WA	Y		44617 AW		WABLS	3/16
	Tacoma-Lakewood PMSA, WA	Y		30100 AW		WABLS	3/16
	Wisconsin	Y	21340 FQ	30320 MW	40000 TQ	USBLS	5/15
	Madison MSA, WI	Y	25250 FQ	31880 MW	38240 TQ	USBLS	5/15
	Milwaukee-Waukesha-West Allis MSA, WI	Y	27590 FQ	33150 MW	41480 TQ	USBLS	5/15
Underground Storage Tank Inspector State Government	Ohio	H	22.78 LO		26.35 HI	OHGOV	2015
University Press Editor Michigan State University	East Lansing, MI	Y	44683 LO		62363 HI	MSUSAL	10/1/14-9/30/15
Upholsterer	Alabama	Y	20266 AE	32954 AW	39309 AEX	ALBLS	6/16
	Arizona	Y	22920 FQ	29100 MW	40110 TQ	USBLS	5/15
	Phoenix-Mesa-Scottsdale MSA, AZ	Y	23200 FQ	29400 MW	40400 TQ	USBLS	5/15
	Arkansas	Y	29840 FQ	35290 MW	39820 TQ	USBLS	5/15
	California	H	11.68 FQ	15.04 MW	19.04 TQ	CABLS	1/16-3/16

AE	Average entry wage	AWR	Average wage range	H	Hourly
AEX	Average experienced wage	B	Biweekly	HI	Highest wage paid
ATC	Average total compensation	D	Daily	HR	High end range
AW	Average wage paid	FQ	First quartile wage	LO	Lowest wage paid

LR	Low end range	MTC	Median total compensation
M	Monthly	MW	Median wage paid
MCC	Median cash compensation	MWR	Median wage range
ME	Median entry wage	S	See annotated source

TCC	Total cash compensation		
TQ	Third quartile wage		
W	Weekly		
Y	Yearly		

Occupation/Type/Industry	Location	Per	Low	Mid	High	Source	Date
Upholsterer	Anaheim-Santa Ana-Irvine PMSA, CA	H	11.79 FQ	15.31 MW	17.52 TQ	CABLS	1/16-3/16
	Los Angeles-Long Beach-Glendale PMSA, CA	H	11.06 FQ	14.66 MW	19.47 TQ	CABLS	1/16-3/16
	Oakland-Hayward-Berkeley PMSA, CA	H	16.01 FQ	19.27 MW	27.97 TQ	CABLS	1/16-3/16
	Riverside-San Bernardino-Ontario MSA, CA	H	11.59 FQ	13.25 MW	14.79 TQ	CABLS	1/16-3/16
	Sacramento–Roseville–Arden-Arcade MSA, CA	H	15.48 FQ	17.37 MW	19.68 TQ	CABLS	1/16-3/16
	San Diego-Carlsbad MSA, CA	H	11.40 FQ	14.86 MW	18.46 TQ	CABLS	1/16-3/16
	San Francisco-Redwood City-South San Francisco PMSA, CA	H	17.37 FQ	20.80 MW	24.06 TQ	CABLS	1/16-3/16
	Colorado	Y	32490 FQ	36550 MW	42740 TQ	USBLS	'5/15
	Denver-Aurora-Lakewood MSA, CO	Y	33750 FQ	38240 MW	51020 TQ	USBLS	5/15
	Connecticut	Y		37084 MW		CTBLS	1/16-3/16
	Bridgeport-Stamford-Norwalk MSA, CT	Y	24910 FQ	34550 MW	53740 TQ	USBLS	5/15
	Delaware	Y	32530 FQ	36100 MW	40260 TQ	USBLS	5/15
	Wilmington PMSA, DE-MD-NJ	Y	31840 FQ	36880 MW	45090 TQ	USBLS	5/15
	Washington-Arlington-Alexandria PMSA, DC-VA-MD-WV	Y	26790 FQ	31330 MW	37190 TQ	USBLS	5/15
	Florida	H	11.27 AE	15.04 MW	18.34 AEX	FLBLS	7/16-9/16
	Fort Lauderdale-Pompano Beach-Deerfield Beach PMSA, FL	H	13.16 AE	17.22 MW	21.86 AEX	FLBLS	7/16-9/16
	Miami-Miami Beach-Kendall PMSA, FL	H	12.78 AE	15.30 MW	20.84 AEX	FLBLS	7/16-9/16
	Orlando-Kissimmee-Sanford MSA, FL	H	12.88 AE	16.17 MW	17.69 AEX	FLBLS	7/16-9/16
	Tampa-St. Petersburg-Clearwater MSA, FL	H	11.18 AE	12.29 MW	14.73 AEX	FLBLS	7/16-9/16
	Georgia	Y	19330 FQ	27020 MW	41560 TQ	USBLS	5/15
	Atlanta-Sandy Springs-Roswell MSA, GA	Y	18140 FQ	23230 MW	33510 TQ	USBLS	5/15
	Idaho	Y	18520 FQ	26450 MW	34700 TQ	USBLS	5/15
	Illinois	Y	28410 FQ	35010 MW	42750 TQ	USBLS	5/15
	Chicago-Naperville-Arlington Heights PMSA, IL	Y	29940 FQ	35940 MW	43310 TQ	USBLS	5/15
	Lake County-Kenosha County PMSA, IL-WI	Y	26710 FQ	29120 MW	34080 TQ	USBLS	5/15
	Indiana	Y	24300 FQ	29140 MW	36050 TQ	USBLS	5/15
	Indianapolis-Carmel-Anderson MSA, IN	Y	28250 FQ	32200 MW	41200 TQ	USBLS	5/15
	Iowa	Y	18140 FQ	26590 MW	31210 TQ	USBLS	5/15
	Kansas	Y	26340 FQ	29760 MW	36720 TQ	USBLS	5/15
	Wichita MSA, KS	Y	24340 FQ	29630 MW	54290 TQ	USBLS	5/15
	Kentucky	Y	22740 FQ	28760 MW	36620 TQ	USBLS	5/15
	Louisville-Jefferson County MSA, KY-IN	Y	24090 FQ	28930 MW	34850 TQ	USBLS	5/15
	Louisiana	Y	23780 FQ	31930 MW	36320 TQ	USBLS	5/15
	New Orleans-Metairie MSA, LA	Y	33190 FQ	35430 MW	37670 TQ	USBLS	5/15
	Maine	Y	18530 FQ	25630 MW	34150 TQ	USBLS	5/15
	Maryland	Y	18468 AE	28557 MW	33602 AEX	MDBLS	4/16
	Baltimore-Columbia-Towson MSA, MD	Y	26430 FQ	30920 MW	37180 TQ	USBLS	5/15
	Salisbury MSA, MD-DE	Y	33170 FQ	35750 MW	38330 TQ	USBLS	5/15
	Massachusetts	Y	27350 FQ	34020 MW	41470 TQ	USBLS	5/15
	Boston-Cambridge-Newton NECTA, MA	Y	29590 FQ	35490 MW	43480 TQ	USBLS	5/15
	Michigan	Y	25680 FQ	32240 MW	37330 TQ	USBLS	5/15
	Grand Rapids-Wyoming MSA, MI	Y	26430 FQ	30850 MW	36030 TQ	USBLS	5/15
	Mississippi	Y	27070 FQ	34060 MW	38770 TQ	USBLS	5/15
	Missouri	Y	28320 FQ	34040 MW	37430 TQ	USBLS	5/15
	Kansas City MSA, MO-KS	Y	24540 FQ	30630 MW	37650 TQ	USBLS	5/15
	St. Louis MSA, MO-IL	Y	26880 FQ	30640 MW	45240 TQ	USBLS	5/15

Upholsterer

Occupation/Type/Industry	Location	Per	Low	Mid	High	Source	Date
Upholsterer	Montana	Y	20770 FQ	24760 MW	50300 TQ	USBLS	5/15
	Nebraska	Y	29065 FQ	37910 MW	53515 TQ	NEBLS	7/16-9/16
	Omaha-Council Bluffs MSA, NE-IA	Y	24015 FQ	33850 MW	43060 TQ	NEBLS	7/16-9/16
	Nevada	Y	24680 FQ	29470 MW	36890 TQ	USBLS	5/15
	Las Vegas-Henderson-Paradise MSA, NV	Y	24620 FQ	29240 MW	36300 TQ	USBLS	5/15
	New Hampshire	H	13.79 AE	26.30 MW	27.48 AEX	NHBLS	6/16
	New Jersey	Y	32380 FQ	39010 MW	48170 TQ	USBLS	5/15
	Camden PMSA, NJ	Y	31970 FQ	34910 MW	37850 TQ	USBLS	5/15
	New Mexico	Y	22770 FQ	28580 MW	37070 TQ	USBLS	5/15
	New York	Y	23380 AE	36050 MW	45720 AEX	NYBLS	1/16-3/16
	Nassau County-Suffolk County PMSA, NY	Y	32600 FQ	42150 MW	47210 TQ	USBLS	5/15
	New York-Jersey City-White Plains PMSA, NY-NJ	Y	26290 FQ	35590 MW	48490 TQ	USBLS	5/15
	Rochester MSA, NY	Y	24150 FQ	34530 MW	42620 TQ	USBLS	5/15
	North Carolina	Y	26230 FQ	35120 MW	44640 TQ	USBLS	5/15
	Charlotte-Concord-Gastonia MSA, NC-SC	Y	20520 FQ	23900 MW	31360 TQ	USBLS	5/15
	Ohio	Y	20590 FQ	28210 MW	36460 TQ	USBLS	5/15
	Cincinnati MSA, OH-KY-IN	Y	24720 FQ	30060 MW	37470 TQ	USBLS	5/15
	Cleveland-Elyria MSA, OH	Y	18760 FQ	23140 MW	37040 TQ	USBLS	5/15
	Columbus MSA, OH	Y	26970 FQ	34260 MW	42720 TQ	USBLS	5/15
	Oklahoma	Y	19530 FQ	25480 MW	33820 TQ	USBLS	5/15
	Oklahoma City MSA, OK	Y	20750 FQ	26680 MW	36360 TQ	USBLS	5/15
	Tulsa MSA, OK	Y	17640 FQ	26660 MW	34330 TQ	USBLS	5/15
	Oregon	H	12.60 FQ	16.39 MW	21.31 TQ	ORBLS	2016
	Portland-Vancouver-Hillsboro MSA, OR-WA	Y	22580 FQ	28190 MW	40180 TQ	USBLS	5/15
	Pennsylvania	Y	25300 FQ	34240 MW	48870 TQ	USBLS	5/15
	Allentown-Bethlehem-Easton MSA, PA-NJ	Y	21760 FQ	29350 MW	37300 TQ	USBLS	5/15
	Montgomery County-Bucks County-Chester County PMSA, PA	Y	40900 FQ	50980 MW	57200 TQ	USBLS	5/15
	Philadelphia PMSA, PA	Y	23610 FQ	37810 MW	56580 TQ	USBLS	5/15
	Pittsburgh MSA, PA	Y	22740 FQ	26720 MW	54000 TQ	USBLS	5/15
	Rhode Island	Y	31500 FQ	36610 MW	50680 TQ	USBLS	5/15
	Providence-Warwick MSA, RI-MA	Y	31500 FQ	36610 MW	50680 TQ	USBLS	5/15
	South Carolina	Y	19150 FQ	22910 MW	28790 TQ	USBLS	5/15
	Charleston-North Charleston MSA, SC	Y	20210 FQ	23020 MW	29670 TQ	USBLS	5/15
	Columbia MSA, SC	Y	25580 FQ	30650 MW	35690 TQ	USBLS	5/15
	Tennessee	Y	21210 FQ	24450 MW	30060 TQ	USBLS	5/15
	Knoxville MSA, TN	Y	17550 FQ	19370 MW	23740 TQ	USBLS	5/15
	Memphis MSA, TN-MS-AR	Y	26260 FQ	28990 MW	31640 TQ	USBLS	5/15
	Nashville-Davidson–Murfreesboro–Franklin MSA, TN	Y	21030 FQ	22660 MW	24300 TQ	USBLS	5/15
	Texas	Y	22780 FQ	28490 MW	34140 TQ	USBLS	5/15
	Austin-Round Rock MSA, TX	Y	29070 FQ	35890 MW	42800 TQ	USBLS	5/15
	Dallas-Plano-Irving PMSA, TX	Y	23180 FQ	28370 MW	32760 TQ	USBLS	5/15
	Houston-The Woodlands-Sugar Land MSA, TX	Y	24310 FQ	27790 MW	30920 TQ	USBLS	5/15
	San Antonio-New Braunfels MSA, TX	Y	28900 FQ	33630 MW	37180 TQ	USBLS	5/15
	Utah	Y	26740 FQ	31810 MW	38180 TQ	USBLS	5/15
	Salt Lake City MSA, UT	Y	25340 FQ	30650 MW	37410 TQ	USBLS	5/15
	Virginia	Y	24280 FQ	29610 MW	36840 TQ	USBLS	5/15
	Richmond MSA, VA	Y	21730 FQ	23540 MW	25240 TQ	USBLS	5/15
	Virginia Beach-Norfolk-Newport News MSA, VA-NC	Y	18490 FQ	29310 MW	37370 TQ	USBLS	5/15
	Washington	H	15.11 FQ	19.24 MW	25.21 TQ	WABLS	3/16
	Seattle-Bellevue-Everett PMSA, WA	H	16.07 FQ	20.50 MW	27.60 TQ	WABLS	3/16
	Tacoma-Lakewood PMSA, WA	H	13.45 FQ	15.09 MW	21.56 TQ	WABLS	3/16
	West Virginia	Y	29560 FQ	36500 MW	43720 TQ	USBLS	5/15
	Wisconsin	Y	26760 FQ	33090 MW	39780 TQ	USBLS	5/15
	Milwaukee-Waukesha-West Allis MSA, WI	Y	24150 FQ	34620 MW	43550 TQ	USBLS	5/15

AE	Average entry wage	AWR	Average wage range	H	Hourly	LR	Low end range	MTC	Median total compensation	TCC	Total cash compensation
AEX	Average experienced wage	B	Biweekly	HI	Highest wage paid	M	Monthly	MW	Median wage paid	TQ	Third quartile wage
ATC	Average total compensation	D	Daily	HR	High end range	MCC	Median cash compensation	MWR	Median wage range	W	Weekly
AW	Average wage paid	FQ	First quartile wage	LO	Lowest wage paid	ME	Median entry wage	S	See annotated source	Y	Yearly

Occupation/Type/Industry	Location	Per	Low	Mid	High	Source	Date
Upholsterer	Puerto Rico	Y	16820 FQ	17960 MW	19100 TQ	USBLS	5/15
	San Juan-Carolina-Caguas MSA, PR	Y	16940 FQ	18130 MW	19320 TQ	USBLS	5/15
Upward Bound Instructor							
Municipal Government	Seattle, WA	H			22.91 HI	CSSS	1/13/16
Urban and Regional Planner	Alabama	Y	40916 AE	61853 AW	72321 AEX	ALBLS	6/16
	Birmingham-Hoover MSA, AL	Y	45757 AE	63626 AW	72566 AEX	ALBLS	6/16
	Alaska	Y	65820 FQ	78900 MW	92670 TQ	USBLS	5/15
	Anchorage MSA, AK	Y	68000 FQ	77410 MW	92630 TQ	USBLS	5/15
	Arizona	Y	55130 FQ	67010 MW	82040 TQ	USBLS	5/15
	Phoenix-Mesa-Scottsdale MSA, AZ	Y	58490 FQ	72060 MW	88170 TQ	USBLS	5/15
	Tucson MSA, AZ	Y	53270 FQ	60350 MW	72560 TQ	USBLS	5/15
	Arkansas	Y	28860 FQ	45530 MW	59710 TQ	USBLS	5/15
	California	H	31.67 FQ	38.43 MW	47.89 TQ	CABLS	1/16-3/16
	Anaheim-Santa Ana-Irvine PMSA, CA	H	34.93 FQ	42.36 MW	49.26 TQ	CABLS	1/16-3/16
	Los Angeles-Long Beach-Glendale PMSA, CA	H	28.92 FQ	37.26 MW	48.70 TQ	CABLS	1/16-3/16
	Oakland-Hayward-Berkeley PMSA, CA	H	33.12 FQ	41.84 MW	53.09 TQ	CABLS	1/16-3/16
	Riverside-San Bernardino-Ontario MSA, CA	H	32.42 FQ	38.83 MW	46.05 TQ	CABLS	1/16-3/16
	Sacramento–Roseville–Arden-Arcade MSA, CA	H	34.25 FQ	37.12 MW	43.51 TQ	CABLS	1/16-3/16
	San Diego-Carlsbad MSA, CA	H	31.20 FQ	36.65 MW	44.70 TQ	CABLS	1/16-3/16
	San Francisco-Redwood City-South San Francisco PMSA, CA	H	35.15 FQ	45.70 MW	58.44 TQ	CABLS	1/16-3/16
	Colorado	Y	60120 FQ	73050 MW	89910 TQ	USBLS	5/15
	Denver-Aurora-Lakewood MSA, CO	Y	61390 FQ	75320 MW	95540 TQ	USBLS	5/15
	Connecticut	Y		82468 MW		CTBLS	1/16-3/16
	Bridgeport-Stamford-Norwalk MSA, CT	Y	62490 FQ	88000 MW	113150 TQ	USBLS	5/15
	Hartford-West Hartford-East Hartford MSA, CT	Y	71650 FQ	85180 MW	96280 TQ	USBLS	5/15
	Delaware	Y	53490 FQ	60320 MW	71030 TQ	USBLS	5/15
	Wilmington PMSA, DE-MD-NJ	Y	56230 FQ	66600 MW	84160 TQ	USBLS	5/15
	District of Columbia	Y	69770 FQ	93850 MW	117970 TQ	USBLS	5/15
	Washington-Arlington-Alexandria PMSA, DC-VA-MD-WV	Y	67190 FQ	84020 MW	99560 TQ	USBLS	5/15
	Florida	H	23.49 AE	32.26 MW	38.21 AEX	FLBLS	7/16-9/16
	Fort Lauderdale-Pompano Beach-Deerfield Beach PMSA, FL	H	26.06 AE	35.34 MW	39.82 AEX	FLBLS	7/16-9/16
	Miami-Miami Beach-Kendall PMSA, FL	H	28.08 AE	36.71 MW	41.59 AEX	FLBLS	7/16-9/16
	Orlando-Kissimmee-Sanford MSA, FL	H	23.29 AE	30.68 MW	36.42 AEX	FLBLS	7/16-9/16
	Tampa-St. Petersburg-Clearwater MSA, FL	H	24.17 AE	34.07 MW	40.60 AEX	FLBLS	7/16-9/16
	Georgia	Y	43790 FQ	52030 MW	63360 TQ	USBLS	5/15
	Atlanta-Sandy Springs-Roswell MSA, GA	Y	44910 FQ	52660 MW	63500 TQ	USBLS	5/15
	Augusta-Richmond County MSA, GA-SC	Y	64200 FQ	71140 MW	78080 TQ	USBLS	5/15
	Hawaii	Y	54140 FQ	65010 MW	79570 TQ	USBLS	5/15
	Urban Honolulu MSA, HI	Y	54390 FQ	65840 MW	80050 TQ	USBLS	5/15
	Idaho	Y	46090 FQ	54960 MW	63960 TQ	USBLS	5/15
	Boise City MSA, ID	Y	50250 FQ	57760 MW	67630 TQ	USBLS	5/15
	Illinois	Y	63620 FQ	81510 MW	98850 TQ	USBLS	5/15
	Chicago-Naperville-Arlington Heights PMSA, IL	Y	68430 FQ	85120 MW	99550 TQ	USBLS	5/15
	Lake County-Kenosha County PMSA, IL-WI	Y	61050 FQ	75890 MW	93840 TQ	USBLS	5/15
	Indiana	Y	41220 FQ	50630 MW	60520 TQ	USBLS	5/15
	Gary PMSA, IN	Y	42500 FQ	46160 MW	49910 TQ	USBLS	5/15

AE	Average entry wage	AWR	Average wage range	H	Hourly	LR	Low end range	MTC	Median total compensation	TCC	Total cash compensation
AEX	Average experienced wage	B	Biweekly	HI	Highest wage paid	M	Monthly	MW	Median wage paid	TQ	Third quartile wage
ATC	Average total compensation	D	Daily	HR	High end range	MCC	Median cash compensation	MWR	Median wage range	W	Weekly
AW	Average wage paid	FQ	First quartile wage	LO	Lowest wage paid	ME	Median entry wage	S	See annotated source	Y	Yearly

1632

Urban and Regional Planner

Occupation/Type/Industry	Location	Per	Low	Mid	High	Source	Date
Urban and Regional Planner	Indianapolis-Carmel-Anderson						
	MSA, IN	Y	46250 FQ	55290 MW	62740 TQ	USBLS	5/15
	Iowa	Y	42300 FQ	60550 MW	75320 TQ	USBLS	5/15
	Des Moines-West Des Moines						
	MSA, IA	Y	59680 FQ	73450 MW	87530 TQ	USBLS	5/15
	Kansas	Y	44840 FQ	55450 MW	71150 TQ	USBLS	5/15
	Wichita MSA, KS	Y	48650 FQ	60730 MW	73130 TQ	USBLS	5/15
	Kentucky	Y	43750 FQ	53630 MW	64060 TQ	USBLS	5/15
	Louisville-Jefferson County						
	MSA, KY-IN	Y	26830 FQ	43770 MW	57930 TQ	USBLS	5/15
	Louisiana	Y	41140 FQ	49690 MW	70260 TQ	USBLS	5/15
	Maine	Y	54330 FQ	64780 MW	75130 TQ	USBLS	5/15
	Portland-South Portland MSA,						
	ME	Y	55730 FQ	65170 MW	73640 TQ	USBLS	5/15
	Maryland	Y	46652 AE	66099 MW	75822 AEX	MDBLS	4/16
	Baltimore-Columbia-Towson						
	MSA, MD	Y	49530 FQ	65310 MW	75040 TQ	USBLS	5/15
	Salisbury MSA, MD-DE	Y	44700 FQ	54380 MW	66290 TQ	USBLS	5/15
	Massachusetts	Y	59870 FQ	74000 MW	90240 TQ	USBLS	5/15
	Boston-Cambridge-Newton						
	NECTA, MA	Y	60360 FQ	76740 MW	92410 TQ	USBLS	5/15
	Worcester MSA, MA-CT	Y	61040 FQ	72070 MW	84370 TQ	USBLS	5/15
	Michigan	Y	47220 FQ	60050 MW	73260 TQ	USBLS	5/15
	Detroit-Dearborn-Livonia						
	PMSA, MI	Y	47580 FQ	56490 MW	66810 TQ	USBLS	5/15
	Grand Rapids-Wyoming MSA,						
	MI	Y	61750 FQ	69060 MW	74730 TQ	USBLS	5/15
	Minnesota	Y	58538 FQ	69908 MW	77388 TQ	MNBLS	1/16-3/16
	Minneapolis-St. Paul-						
	Bloomington MSA, MN-WI	Y	59001 FQ	71632 MW	78830 TQ	MNBLS	1/16-3/16
	Mississippi	Y	41130 FQ	57070 MW	78040 TQ	USBLS	5/15
	Jackson MSA, MS	Y	35330 FQ	44470 MW	73560 TQ	USBLS	5/15
	Missouri	Y	50830 FQ	61080 MW	79650 TQ	USBLS	5/15
	Kansas City MSA, MO-KS	Y	44750 FQ	57970 MW	76770 TQ	USBLS	5/15
	St. Louis MSA, MO-IL	Y	52220 FQ	61530 MW	86020 TQ	USBLS	5/15
	Montana	Y	49600 FQ	60670 MW	87510 TQ	USBLS	5/15
	Nebraska	Y	51325 FQ	60895 MW	74600 TQ	NEBLS	7/16-9/16
	Omaha-Council Bluffs MSA,						
	NE-IA	Y	53600 FQ	61720 MW	76320 TQ	NEBLS	7/16-9/16
	Nevada	Y	70670 FQ	84020 MW	96970 TQ	USBLS	5/15
	Las Vegas-Henderson-Paradise						
	MSA, NV	Y	72470 FQ	86330 MW	97980 TQ	USBLS	5/15
	New Hampshire	H	23.28 AE	31.11 MW	34.97 AEX	NHBLS	6/16
	Manchester NECTA, NH	H	23.49 AE	32.75 MW	38.00 AEX	NHBLS	6/16
	Nashua NECTA, NH-MA	Y	48050 FQ	63410 MW	74330 TQ	USBLS	5/15
	New Jersey	Y	61760 FQ	78290 MW	97000 TQ	USBLS	5/15
	Camden PMSA, NJ	Y	59950 FQ	80700 MW	109380 TQ	USBLS	5/15
	Newark PMSA, NJ-PA	Y	60570 FQ	75860 MW	92050 TQ	USBLS	5/15
	Trenton MSA, NJ	Y	67550 FQ	87220 MW	102580 TQ	USBLS	5/15
	New Mexico	Y	44650 FQ	54790 MW	69710 TQ	USBLS	5/15
	Albuquerque MSA, NM	Y	43050 FQ	53100 MW	62990 TQ	USBLS	5/15
	New York	Y	47820 AE	70840 MW	88400 AEX	NYBLS	1/16-3/16
	Buffalo-Cheektowaga-Niagara						
	Falls MSA, NY	Y	53780 FQ	67040 MW	77310 TQ	USBLS	5/15
	Nassau County-Suffolk County						
	PMSA, NY	Y	62680 FQ	78470 MW	101390 TQ	USBLS	5/15
	New York-Jersey City-White						
	Plains PMSA, NY-NJ	Y	59600 FQ	74120 MW	92930 TQ	USBLS	5/15
	Rochester MSA, NY	Y	54230 FQ	67620 MW	76570 TQ	USBLS	5/15
	North Carolina	Y	49980 FQ	59650 MW	72600 TQ	USBLS	5/15
	Charlotte-Concord-Gastonia						
	MSA, NC-SC	Y	54570 FQ	64750 MW	75950 TQ	USBLS	5/15
	Raleigh MSA, NC	Y	51980 FQ	61390 MW	75790 TQ	USBLS	5/15
	North Dakota	Y	37270 FQ	57710 MW	70200 TQ	USBLS	5/15
	Ohio	Y	52400 FQ	60810 MW	75940 TQ	USBLS	5/15
	Cincinnati MSA, OH-KY-IN	Y	51490 FQ	61200 MW	80740 TQ	USBLS	5/15
	Cleveland-Elyria MSA, OH	Y	52610 FQ	61390 MW	80310 TQ	USBLS	5/15
	Columbus MSA, OH	Y	53810 FQ	61530 MW	75720 TQ	USBLS	5/15
	Oklahoma	Y	51200 FQ	66290 MW	82160 TQ	USBLS	5/15
	Oklahoma City MSA, OK	Y	63930 FQ	74620 MW	89140 TQ	USBLS	5/15
	Oregon	H	32.00 FQ	37.43 MW	44.55 TQ	ORBLS	2016

AE Average entry wage	**AWR** Average wage range	**H** Hourly	**LR** Low end range	**MTC** Median total compensation	**TCC** Total cash compensation
AEX Average experienced wage	**B** Biweekly	**HI** Highest wage paid	**M** Monthly	**MW** Median wage paid	**TQ** Third quartile wage
ATC Average total compensation	**D** Daily	**HR** High end range	**MCC** Median cash compensation	**MWR** Median wage range	**W** Weekly
AW Average wage paid	**FQ** First quartile wage	**LO** Lowest wage paid	**ME** Median entry wage	**S** See annotated source	**Y** Yearly

Occupation/Type/Industry	Location	Per	Low	Mid	High	Source	Date
Urban and Regional Planner	Portland-Vancouver-Hillsboro						
	MSA, OR-WA	Y	70310 FQ	81760 MW	98160 TQ	USBLS	5/15
	Pennsylvania	Y	40920 FQ	56010 MW	72030 TQ	USBLS	5/15
	Allentown-Bethlehem-Easton						
	MSA, PA-NJ	Y	30260 FQ	55650 MW	73070 TQ	USBLS	5/15
	Harrisburg-Carlisle MSA, PA	Y	30540 FQ	47260 MW	59830 TQ	USBLS	5/15
	Montgomery County-Bucks						
	County-Chester County						
	PMSA, PA	Y	53820 FQ	60090 MW	72180 TQ	USBLS	5/15
	Philadelphia PMSA, PA	Y	54060 FQ	68990 MW	86890 TQ	USBLS	5/15
	Pittsburgh MSA, PA	Y	45780 FQ	58220 MW	80190 TQ	USBLS	5/15
	Rhode Island	Y	62490 FQ	73300 MW	83200 TQ	USBLS	5/15
	Providence-Warwick MSA, RI-						
	MA	Y	63260 FQ	73320 MW	83820 TQ	USBLS	5/15
	South Carolina	Y	47570 FQ	59490 MW	74150 TQ	USBLS	5/15
	Charleston-North Charleston						
	MSA, SC	Y	47910 FQ	58390 MW	78810 TQ	USBLS	5/15
	Columbia MSA, SC	Y	51430 FQ	65200 MW	73100 TQ	USBLS	5/15
	Greenville-Anderson-Mauldin						
	MSA, SC	Y	44790 FQ	51880 MW	60660 TQ	USBLS	5/15
	South Dakota	Y	43600 FQ	49810 MW	60230 TQ	USBLS	5/15
	Sioux Falls MSA, SD	Y	46130 FQ	58510 MW	72760 TQ	USBLS	5/15
	Tennessee	Y	43460 FQ	55800 MW	69280 TQ	USBLS	5/15
	Memphis MSA, TN-MS-AR	Y	47340 FQ	58820 MW	74470 TQ	USBLS	5/15
	Nashville-Davidson–						
	Murfreesboro–Franklin						
	MSA, TN	Y	49540 FQ	59850 MW	73480 TQ	USBLS	5/15
	Texas	Y	48670 FQ	60800 MW	78240 TQ	USBLS	5/15
	Austin-Round Rock MSA, TX	Y	49290 FQ	59630 MW	75470 TQ	USBLS	5/15
	Dallas-Plano-Irving PMSA, TX	Y	55500 FQ	64350 MW	81010 TQ	USBLS	5/15
	Fort Worth-Arlington PMSA,						
	TX	Y	57710 FQ	71570 MW	90300 TQ	USBLS	5/15
	Houston-The Woodlands-						
	Sugar Land MSA, TX	Y	51860 FQ	63320 MW	78090 TQ	USBLS	5/15
	San Antonio-New Braunfels						
	MSA, TX	Y	45230 FQ	55150 MW	76830 TQ	USBLS	5/15
	Utah	Y	50820 FQ	59170 MW	72950 TQ	USBLS	5/15
	Ogden-Clearfield MSA, UT	Y	37180 FQ	57710 MW	71770 TQ	USBLS	5/15
	Provo-Orem MSA, UT	Y	52340 FQ	64200 MW	83760 TQ	USBLS	5/15
	Salt Lake City MSA, UT	Y	52680 FQ	58590 MW	72360 TQ	USBLS	5/15
	Vermont	Y	45000 FQ	54160 MW	64060 TQ	USBLS	5/15
	Burlington-South Burlington						
	MSA, VT	Y	47700 FQ	56570 MW	67660 TQ	USBLS	5/15
	Virginia	Y	51900 FQ	67790 MW	86940 TQ	USBLS	5/15
	Richmond MSA, VA	Y	47610 FQ	56310 MW	70310 TQ	USBLS	5/15
	Washington	H	31.72 FQ	37.36 MW	44.29 TQ	WABLS	3/16
	Seattle-Bellevue-Everett						
	PMSA, WA	H	35.02 FQ	40.91 MW	47.30 TQ	WABLS	3/16
	Tacoma-Lakewood PMSA, WA	H	29.53 FQ	37.32 MW	44.33 TQ	WABLS	3/16
	West Virginia	Y	41530 FQ	48850 MW	68540 TQ	USBLS	5/15
	Wisconsin	Y	49850 FQ	61230 MW	77430 TQ	USBLS	5/15
	Madison MSA, WI	Y	54300 FQ	65140 MW	77300 TQ	USBLS	5/15
	Milwaukee-Waukesha-West						
	Allis MSA, WI	Y	52710 FQ	73510 MW	107520 TQ	USBLS	5/15
	Wyoming	Y	51940 FQ	59040 MW	74020 TQ	USBLS	5/15
Urban Forest Inspector							
Municipal Government	Beverly Hills, CA	Y		56952 AW		CACIT	6/28/16
Urban Forest Manager							
Municipal Government	West Sacramento, CA	Y			84593 HI	CACIT	6/28/16
Urban Forester							
Municipal Government	Culver City, CA	Y			68208 HI	CACIT	6/28/16
Municipal Government	Monterey, CA	Y			89456 HI	CACIT	6/28/16
Municipal Government	Santa Monica, CA	Y			99520 HI	CACIT	6/28/16
Urban Forester Coordinator							
Municipal Government	Albany, CA	Y			57078 HI	CACIT	6/28/16
Urban Initiatives Manager							
City Manager's Office	Fremont, CA	Y			124387 HI	CACIT	6/28/16

AE	Average entry wage	**AWR**	Average wage range	**H**	Hourly	**LR**	Low end range	**MTC**	Median total compensation	**TCC**	Total cash compensation
AEX	Average experienced wage	**B**	Biweekly	**HI**	Highest wage paid	**M**	Monthly	**MW**	Median wage paid	**TQ**	Third quartile wage
ATC	Average total compensation	**D**	Daily	**HR**	High end range	**MCC**	Median cash compensation	**MWR**	Median wage range	**W**	Weekly
AW	Average wage paid	**FQ**	First quartile wage	**LO**	Lowest wage paid	**ME**	Median entry wage	**S**	See annotated source	**Y**	Yearly

Occupation/Type/Industry	Location	Per	Low	Mid	High	Source	Date
User Experience Designer	United States	Y		92500 MW		CNBC08	2017
User Experience Researcher							
1 to 3 Years Experience	United States	Y	61250 LO		80500 HI	RH02	2017
Usher, Lobby Attendant, and Ticket Taker							
	Alaska	Y	18670 FQ	19130 MW	19650 TQ	USBLS	5/15
	Anchorage MSA, AK	Y	18650 FQ	19100 MW	19600 TQ	USBLS	5/15
	Arizona	Y	17650 FQ	18530 MW	19420 TQ	USBLS	5/15
	Phoenix-Mesa-Scottsdale MSA, AZ	Y	17600 FQ	18430 MW	19260 TQ	USBLS	5/15
	Tucson MSA, AZ	Y	17880 FQ	19020 MW	21780 TQ	USBLS	5/15
	Arkansas	Y	16870 FQ	18120 MW	19410 TQ	USBLS	5/15
	Little Rock-North Little Rock-Conway MSA, AR	Y	16750 FQ	17890 MW	19040 TQ	USBLS	5/15
	California	H	9.40 FQ	9.66 MW	11.80 TQ	CABLS	1/16-3/16
	Anaheim-Santa Ana-Irvine PMSA, CA	H	9.40 FQ	9.59 MW	10.80 TQ	CABLS	1/16-3/16
	Los Angeles-Long Beach-Glendale PMSA, CA	H	9.46 FQ	9.76 MW	12.47 TQ	CABLS	1/16-3/16
	Oakland-Hayward-Berkeley PMSA, CA	H	9.39 FQ	9.65 MW	13.38 TQ	CABLS	1/16-3/16
	Riverside-San Bernardino-Ontario MSA, CA	H	9.35 FQ	9.48 MW	9.71 TQ	CABLS	1/16-3/16
	Sacramento–Roseville–Arden-Arcade MSA, CA	H	9.37 FQ	9.59 MW	11.44 TQ	CABLS	1/16-3/16
	San Diego-Carlsbad MSA, CA	H	9.42 FQ	9.91 MW	11.69 TQ	CABLS	1/16-3/16
	San Francisco-Redwood City-South San Francisco PMSA, CA	H	9.99 FQ	12.84 MW	15.22 TQ	CABLS	1/16-3/16
	Colorado	Y	18100 FQ	19080 MW	21380 TQ	USBLS	5/15
	Connecticut	Y		19813 MW		CTBLS	1/16-3/16
	Bridgeport-Stamford-Norwalk MSA, CT	Y	19230 FQ	19540 MW	19990 TQ	USBLS	5/15
	Hartford-West Hartford-East Hartford MSA, CT	Y	19190 FQ	19450 MW	19990 TQ	USBLS	5/15
	Delaware	Y	17470 FQ	18660 MW	23470 TQ	USBLS	5/15
	Wilmington PMSA, DE-MD-NJ	Y	17450 FQ	18630 MW	23780 TQ	USBLS	5/15
	District of Columbia	Y	20000 FQ	25270 MW	30060 TQ	USBLS	5/15
	Washington-Arlington-Alexandria PMSA, DC-VA-MD-WV	Y	17450 FQ	19310 MW	23500 TQ	USBLS	5/15
	Florida	H	9.02 AE	9.27 MW	9.99 AEX	FLBLS	7/16-9/16
	Fort Lauderdale-Pompano Beach-Deerfield Beach PMSA, FL	H	9.00 AE	9.24 MW	10.18 AEX	FLBLS	7/16-9/16
	Miami-Miami Beach-Kendall PMSA, FL	H	9.06 AE	9.29 MW	9.83 AEX	FLBLS	7/16-9/16
	Orlando-Kissimmee-Sanford MSA, FL	H	9.06 AE	9.46 MW	10.52 AEX	FLBLS	7/16-9/16
	Tampa-St. Petersburg-Clearwater MSA, FL	H	8.99 AE	9.16 MW	9.49 AEX	FLBLS	7/16-9/16
	Georgia	Y	16610 FQ	17880 MW	19160 TQ	USBLS	5/15
	Atlanta-Sandy Springs-Roswell MSA, GA	Y	16570 FQ	17810 MW	19050 TQ	USBLS	5/15
	Augusta-Richmond County MSA, GA-SC	Y	17130 FQ	18740 MW	20850 TQ	USBLS	5/15
	Hawaii	Y	18150 FQ	20340 MW	24290 TQ	USBLS	5/15
	Urban Honolulu MSA, HI	Y	18660 FQ	21330 MW	24450 TQ	USBLS	5/15
	Idaho	Y	17120 FQ	18580 MW	20220 TQ	USBLS	5/15
	Boise City MSA, ID	Y	17210 FQ	18730 MW	20890 TQ	USBLS	5/15
	Illinois	Y	18630 FQ	19690 MW	24220 TQ	USBLS	5/15
	Chicago-Naperville-Arlington Heights PMSA, IL	Y	18550 FQ	19510 MW	24570 TQ	USBLS	5/15
	Lake County-Kenosha County PMSA, IL-WI	Y	18520 FQ	22540 MW	28680 TQ	USBLS	5/15
	Indiana	Y	16710 FQ	17980 MW	19250 TQ	USBLS	5/15
	Gary PMSA, IN	Y	16910 FQ	18230 MW	19550 TQ	USBLS	5/15
	Indianapolis-Carmel-Anderson MSA, IN	Y	16730 FQ	18190 MW	20770 TQ	USBLS	5/15
	Iowa	Y	16970 FQ	18490 MW	20700 TQ	USBLS	5/15

AE	Average entry wage	AWR	Average wage range	H	Hourly
AEX	Average experienced wage	B	Biweekly	HI	Highest wage paid
ATC	Average total compensation	D	Daily	HR	High end range
AW	Average wage paid	FQ	First quartile wage	LO	Lowest wage paid

LR	Low end range	MTC	Median total compensation
M	Monthly	MW	Median wage paid
MCC	Median cash compensation	MWR	Median wage range
ME	Median entry wage	S	See annotated source

TCC	Total cash compensation
TQ	Third quartile wage
W	Weekly
Y	Yearly

Occupation/Type/Industry	Location	Per	Low	Mid	High	Source	Date
Usher, Lobby Attendant, and Ticket Taker	Des Moines-West Des Moines MSA, IA	Y	16680 FQ	17950 MW	19230 TQ	USBLS	5/15
	Kansas	Y	16910 FQ	18470 MW	21910 TQ	USBLS	5/15
	Kentucky	Y	16630 FQ	17770 MW	18920 TQ	USBLS	5/15
	Louisville-Jefferson County MSA, KY-IN	Y	16570 FQ	17700 MW	18830 TQ	USBLS	5/15
	Louisiana	Y	16990 FQ	18610 MW	21230 TQ	USBLS	5/15
	Baton Rouge MSA, LA	Y	16840 FQ	18410 MW	20920 TQ	USBLS	5/15
	New Orleans-Metairie MSA, LA	Y	17170 FQ	18960 MW	21900 TQ	USBLS	5/15
	Maine	Y	17180 FQ	18430 MW	20000 TQ	USBLS	5/15
	Maryland	Y	18056 AE	19874 MW	20782 AEX	MDBLS	4/16
	Baltimore-Columbia-Towson MSA, MD	Y	17540 FQ	18440 MW	19350 TQ	USBLS	5/15
	Salisbury MSA, MD-DE	Y	17460 FQ	18300 MW	19130 TQ	USBLS	5/15
	Massachusetts	Y	19380 FQ	21380 MW	24420 TQ	USBLS	5/15
	Boston-Cambridge-Newton NECTA, MA	Y	19560 FQ	21770 MW	24430 TQ	USBLS	5/15
	Worcester MSA, MA-CT	Y	24060 FQ	42400 MW	46230 TQ	USBLS	5/15
	Michigan	Y	18180 FQ	19320 MW	22180 TQ	USBLS	5/15
	Detroit-Dearborn-Livonia PMSA, MI	Y	18510 FQ	20200 MW	22970 TQ	USBLS	5/15
	Grand Rapids-Wyoming MSA, MI	Y	18170 FQ	19280 MW	22440 TQ	USBLS	5/15
	Minnesota	Y	18026 FQ	19127 MW	21046 TQ	MNBLS	1/16-3/16
	Minneapolis-St. Paul-Bloomington MSA, MN-WI	Y	17996 FQ	19087 MW	20743 TQ	MNBLS	1/16-3/16
	Mississippi	Y	16540 FQ	17810 MW	19070 TQ	USBLS	5/15
	Missouri	Y	17230 FQ	18540 MW	20570 TQ	USBLS	5/15
	Kansas City MSA, MO-KS	Y	17100 FQ	18450 MW	19890 TQ	USBLS	5/15
	St. Louis MSA, MO-IL	Y	17400 FQ	18830 MW	21640 TQ	USBLS	5/15
	Montana	Y	17690 FQ	18620 MW	19880 TQ	USBLS	5/15
	Nevada	Y	19300 FQ	26870 MW	34570 TQ	USBLS	5/15
	Las Vegas-Henderson-Paradise MSA, NV	Y	20180 FQ	29260 MW	35150 TQ	USBLS	5/15
	New Hampshire	H	8.42 AE	8.77 MW	8.84 AEX	NHBLS	6/16
	Nashua NECTA, NH-MA	Y	16660 FQ	17810 MW	18960 TQ	USBLS	5/15
	New Jersey	Y	18760 FQ	22530 MW	29360 TQ	USBLS	5/15
	Camden PMSA, NJ	Y	18130 FQ	18730 MW	19350 TQ	USBLS	5/15
	Newark PMSA, NJ-PA	Y	18810 FQ	23660 MW	28770 TQ	USBLS	5/15
	New Mexico	Y	16870 FQ	17920 MW	18970 TQ	USBLS	5/15
	Albuquerque MSA, NM	Y	16900 FQ	17960 MW	19020 TQ	USBLS	5/15
	New York	Y	19240 AE	20970 MW	27720 AEX	NYBLS	1/16-3/16
	Buffalo-Cheektowaga-Niagara Falls MSA, NY	Y	19070 FQ	22840 MW	28310 TQ	USBLS	5/15
	Nassau County-Suffolk County PMSA, NY	Y	18740 FQ	19290 MW	26710 TQ	USBLS	5/15
	New York-Jersey City-White Plains PMSA, NY-NJ	Y	19070 FQ	21800 MW	29290 TQ	USBLS	5/15
	Rochester MSA, NY	Y	18840 FQ	19530 MW	30230 TQ	USBLS	5/15
	North Carolina	Y	16570 FQ	17820 MW	19080 TQ	USBLS	5/15
	Charlotte-Concord-Gastonia MSA, NC-SC	Y	16520 FQ	17660 MW	18810 TQ	USBLS	5/15
	Raleigh MSA, NC	Y	16550 FQ	17780 MW	19020 TQ	USBLS	5/15
	North Dakota	Y	17390 FQ	19290 MW	24270 TQ	USBLS	5/15
	Fargo MSA, ND-MN	Y	16670 FQ	17830 MW	18980 TQ	USBLS	5/15
	Ohio	Y	17800 FQ	18730 MW	19870 TQ	USBLS	5/15
	Cincinnati MSA, OH-KY-IN	Y	17870 FQ	18980 MW	21440 TQ	USBLS	5/15
	Cleveland-Elyria MSA, OH	Y	17720 FQ	18570 MW	19510 TQ	USBLS	5/15
	Columbus MSA, OH	Y	17740 FQ	18620 MW	19760 TQ	USBLS	5/15
	Oklahoma	Y	16690 FQ	17900 MW	19110 TQ	USBLS	5/15
	Oklahoma City MSA, OK	Y	16640 FQ	17800 MW	18950 TQ	USBLS	5/15
	Tulsa MSA, OK	Y	16910 FQ	18340 MW	19900 TQ	USBLS	5/15
	Oregon	H	9.60 FQ	9.91 MW	11.75 TQ	ORBLS	2016
	Portland-Vancouver-Hillsboro MSA, OR-WA	Y	19680 FQ	21420 MW	24960 TQ	USBLS	5/15
	Pennsylvania	Y	17390 FQ	19450 MW	22960 TQ	USBLS	5/15
	Allentown-Bethlehem-Easton MSA, PA-NJ	Y	16850 FQ	18360 MW	21140 TQ	USBLS	5/15
	Harrisburg-Carlisle MSA, PA	Y	17640 FQ	20350 MW	23360 TQ	USBLS	5/15

AE Average entry wage	**AWR** Average wage range	**H** Hourly	**LR** Low end range	**MTC** Median total compensation	**TCC** Total cash compensation
AEX Average experienced wage	**B** Biweekly	**HI** Highest wage paid	**M** Monthly	**MW** Median wage paid	**TQ** Third quartile wage
ATC Average total compensation	**D** Daily	**HR** High end range	**MCC** Median cash compensation	**MWR** Median wage range	**W** Weekly
AW Average wage paid	**FQ** First quartile wage	**LO** Lowest wage paid	**ME** Median entry wage	**S** See annotated source	**Y** Yearly

Occupation/Type/Industry	Location	Per	Low	Mid	High	Source	Date
Usher, Lobby Attendant, and Ticket Taker							
	Montgomery County-Bucks County-Chester County PMSA, PA	Y	16730 FQ	18050 MW	19390 TQ	USBLS	5/15
	Philadelphia PMSA, PA	Y	18100 FQ	20900 MW	23550 TQ	USBLS	5/15
	Pittsburgh MSA, PA	Y	17950 FQ	20510 MW	23170 TQ	USBLS	5/15
	Rhode Island	Y	19080 FQ	19700 MW	25630 TQ	USBLS	5/15
	Providence-Warwick MSA, RI-MA	Y	19080 FQ	19590 MW	23860 TQ	USBLS	5/15
	South Carolina	Y	16570 FQ	17730 MW	18900 TQ	USBLS	5/15
	Charleston-North Charleston MSA, SC	Y	16810 FQ	18040 MW	19260 TQ	USBLS	5/15
	Columbia MSA, SC	Y	16250 FQ	17350 MW	18450 TQ	USBLS	5/15
	Greenville-Anderson-Mauldin MSA, SC	Y	16680 FQ	17840 MW	18990 TQ	USBLS	5/15
	South Dakota	Y	18430 FQ	19180 MW	21450 TQ	USBLS	5/15
	Sioux Falls MSA, SD	Y	18530 FQ	19380 MW	22170 TQ	USBLS	5/15
	Tennessee	Y	16870 FQ	18200 MW	19540 TQ	USBLS	5/15
	Knoxville MSA, TN	Y	16770 FQ	17920 MW	19060 TQ	USBLS	5/15
	Memphis MSA, TN-MS-AR	Y	17000 FQ	18620 MW	21170 TQ	USBLS	5/15
	Nashville-Davidson–Murfreesboro–Franklin MSA, TN	Y	16720 FQ	18000 MW	19280 TQ	USBLS	5/15
	Texas	Y	16690 FQ	18010 MW	19350 TQ	USBLS	5/15
	Austin-Round Rock MSA, TX	Y	17060 FQ	18670 MW	23280 TQ	USBLS	5/15
	Dallas-Plano-Irving PMSA, TX	Y	16750 FQ	18070 MW	19420 TQ	USBLS	5/15
	Fort Worth-Arlington PMSA, TX	Y	16590 FQ	17850 MW	19110 TQ	USBLS	5/15
	Houston-The Woodlands-Sugar Land MSA, TX	Y	16600 FQ	17960 MW	19350 TQ	USBLS	5/15
	San Antonio-New Braunfels MSA, TX	Y	16760 FQ	18040 MW	19340 TQ	USBLS	5/15
	Utah	Y	16730 FQ	18070 MW	19460 TQ	USBLS	5/15
	Ogden-Clearfield MSA, UT	Y	16720 FQ	18090 MW	19620 TQ	USBLS	5/15
	Provo-Orem MSA, UT	Y	16480 FQ	17640 MW	18800 TQ	USBLS	5/15
	Salt Lake City MSA, UT	Y	16790 FQ	18180 MW	19690 TQ	USBLS	5/15
	Vermont	Y	19290 FQ	19560 MW	20650 TQ	USBLS	5/15
	Virginia	Y	16630 FQ	17860 MW	19090 TQ	USBLS	5/15
	Richmond MSA, VA	Y	16460 FQ	17650 MW	18840 TQ	USBLS	5/15
	Virginia Beach-Norfolk-Newport News MSA, VA-NC	Y	16590 FQ	17770 MW	18960 TQ	USBLS	5/15
	Washington	H	10.56 FQ	12.08 MW	15.73 TQ	WABLS	3/16
	Seattle-Bellevue-Everett PMSA, WA	H	10.95 FQ	12.97 MW	16.14 TQ	WABLS	3/16
	Tacoma-Lakewood PMSA, WA	H	10.50 FQ	11.36 MW	13.59 TQ	WABLS	3/16
	West Virginia	Y	17770 FQ	18910 MW	24600 TQ	USBLS	5/15
	Huntington-Ashland MSA, WV-KY-OH	Y	17350 FQ	18070 MW	18780 TQ	USBLS	5/15
	Wisconsin	Y	17030 FQ	18580 MW	21510 TQ	USBLS	5/15
	Milwaukee-Waukesha-West Allis MSA, WI	Y	17050 FQ	18540 MW	20470 TQ	USBLS	5/15
	Wyoming	Y	16420 FQ	17610 MW	18790 TQ	USBLS	5/15
	Puerto Rico	Y	16520 FQ	17650 MW	18770 TQ	USBLS	5/15
	San Juan-Carolina-Caguas MSA, PR	Y	16520 FQ	17670 MW	18810 TQ	USBLS	5/15
	Guam	Y	17700 FQ	18230 MW	18770 TQ	USBLS	5/15
Utilities Relocation Technician							
State Government	Ohio	H	21.33 LO		31.05 HI	OHGOV	2015
Utilities Troubleshooter							
Municipal Government	Anaheim, CA	Y		113858 AW		CACIT	6/28/16
Utility Arborist							
Municipal Government	Redding, CA	Y		51895 AW		CACIT	6/28/16
Utility Bookkeeper							
Public Schools	Baldwin County, AL	Y	36721 LO		44453 HI	BCPSSS	2016-2017
Utility Clerk							
Municipal Government	Markle, IN	H			13.00 HI	HCTAB	2017

AE	Average entry wage	AWR	Average wage range	H	Hourly	LR	Low end range	MTC	Median total compensation	TCC	Total cash compensation
AEX	Average experienced wage	B	Biweekly	HI	Highest wage paid	M	Monthly	MW	Median wage paid	TQ	Third quartile wage
ATC	Average total compensation	D	Daily	HR	High end range	MCC	Median cash compensation	MWR	Median wage range	W	Weekly
AW	Average wage paid	FQ	First quartile wage	LO	Lowest wage paid	ME	Median entry wage	S	See annotated source	Y	Yearly

Occupation/Type/Industry	Location	Per	Low	Mid	High	Source	Date
Utility System Modeler							
Municipal Government	Corona, CA	Y			88683 HI	CACIT	6/28/16
Utility Technology Specialist							
Municipal Government	Stockton, CA	Y			69056 HI	CACIT	6/28/16
Vaccine Supply Clerk							
County Government	Oakland County, MI	B	1243 LO		1619 HI	MIOAK2	10/1/16
Value Analysis Coordinator							
Healthcare Industry	United States	Y		84063 AW		HPN02	2016
Van Driver							
Senior Center, County Government	Douglas County, GA	Y	20565 LO		42088 HI	GACTY04	2016
Senior Center, County Government	Habersham County, GA	Y	24194 LO		36813 HI	GACTY04	2016
Vegetation Management Supervisor							
Fire Department, Municipal Government	Oakland, CA	Y			87989 HI	CACIT	6/28/16
Vehicle Abatement Officer							
Police Department, Municipal Government	Arcata, CA	Y			14834 HI	CACIT	6/28/16
Vendor Master							
County Government	Johnson County, KS	H	18.96 FQ	20.50 MW	22.04 TQ	JCOKS	2017
Vermiculturist	United States	Y		73000 AW		SKU01	2016
Veterans Services Officer							
Department of Military Affairs, State Government	Miles City, MT	H			23.17 HI	MTGOV	2016
Veterinarian	Alabama	Y	55553 AE	79507 AW	91484 AEX	ALBLS	6/16
	Birmingham-Hoover MSA, AL	Y	59213 AE	76918 AW	85766 AEX	ALBLS	6/16
	Alaska	Y	77610 FQ	90640 MW	100810 TQ	USBLS	5/15
	Anchorage MSA, AK	Y	73330 FQ	89050 MW	99280 TQ	USBLS	5/15
	Arizona	Y	65290 FQ	86000 MW	112700 TQ	USBLS	5/15
	Phoenix-Mesa-Scottsdale MSA, AZ	Y	63260 FQ	85220 MW	109850 TQ	USBLS	5/15
	Tucson MSA, AZ	Y	72900 FQ	89320 MW	131480 TQ	USBLS	5/15
	Arkansas	Y	58520 FQ	79530 MW	98500 TQ	USBLS	5/15
	Little Rock-North Little Rock-Conway MSA, AR	Y	62620 FQ	78170 MW	93110 TQ	USBLS	5/15
	California	H	39.51 FQ	50.21 MW	64.86 TQ	CABLS	1/16-3/16
	Anaheim-Santa Ana-Irvine PMSA, CA	H	42.21 FQ	56.01 MW	73.23 TQ	CABLS	1/16-3/16
	Los Angeles-Long Beach-Glendale PMSA, CA	H	39.95 FQ	52.10 MW	70.95 TQ	CABLS	1/16-3/16
	Oakland-Hayward-Berkeley PMSA, CA	H	36.98 FQ	47.18 MW	61.98 TQ	CABLS	1/16-3/16
	Riverside-San Bernardino-Ontario MSA, CA	H	33.07 FQ	41.44 MW	53.63 TQ	CABLS	1/16-3/16
	Sacramento–Roseville–Arden-Arcade MSA, CA	H	46.86 FQ	55.41 MW	69.56 TQ	CABLS	1/16-3/16
	San Diego-Carlsbad MSA, CA	H	39.35 FQ	49.81 MW	64.12 TQ	CABLS	1/16-3/16
	San Francisco-Redwood City-South San Francisco PMSA, CA	H	44.34 FQ	52.81 MW	82.10 TQ	CABLS	1/16-3/16
	Colorado	Y	59860 FQ	76610 MW	96420 TQ	USBLS	5/15
	Denver-Aurora-Lakewood MSA, CO	Y	54200 FQ	78810 MW	97250 TQ	USBLS	5/15
	Connecticut	Y		109748 MW		CTBLS	1/16-3/16
	Bridgeport-Stamford-Norwalk MSA, CT	Y	85380 FQ	123570 MW		USBLS	5/15
	Hartford-West Hartford-East Hartford MSA, CT	Y	86670 FQ	107290 MW	123240 TQ	USBLS	5/15
	Delaware	Y	74300 FQ	94440 MW	125610 TQ	USBLS	5/15
	Wilmington PMSA, DE-MD-NJ	Y	82240 FQ	107920 MW	145020 TQ	USBLS	5/15
	District of Columbia	Y	85800 FQ	96900 MW	140590 TQ	USBLS	5/15

AE	Average entry wage	AWR	Average wage range	H	Hourly	LR	Low end range	MTC	Median total compensation	TCC	Total cash compensation
AEX	Average experienced wage	B	Biweekly	HI	Highest wage paid	M	Monthly	MW	Median wage paid	TQ	Third quartile wage
ATC	Average total compensation	D	Daily	HR	High end range	MCC	Median cash compensation	MWR	Median wage range	W	Weekly
AW	Average wage paid	FQ	First quartile wage	LO	Lowest wage paid	ME	Median entry wage	S	See annotated source	Y	Yearly

1638

Occupation/Type/Industry	Location	Per	Low	Mid	High	Source	Date
Veterinarian	Washington-Arlington-Alexandria PMSA, DC-VA-MD-WV	Y	85490 FQ	98950 MW	137760 TQ	USBLS	5/15
	Florida	H	30.24 AE	45.69 MW	55.82 AEX	FLBLS	7/16-9/16
	Fort Lauderdale-Pompano Beach-Deerfield Beach PMSA, FL	H	33.04 AE	48.45 MW	57.19 AEX	FLBLS	7/16-9/16
	Miami-Miami Beach-Kendall PMSA, FL	H	41.46 AE	51.91 MW	60.40 AEX	FLBLS	7/16-9/16
	Orlando-Kissimmee-Sanford MSA, FL	H	30.80 AE	43.00 MW	51.60 AEX	FLBLS	7/16-9/16
	Tampa-St. Petersburg-Clearwater MSA, FL	H	31.21 AE	48.93 MW	53.87 AEX	FLBLS	7/16-9/16
	Georgia	Y	62080 FQ	79420 MW	97580 TQ	USBLS	5/15
	Atlanta-Sandy Springs-Roswell MSA, GA	Y	70260 FQ	84550 MW	98770 TQ	USBLS	5/15
	Augusta-Richmond County MSA, GA-SC	Y	44110 FQ	72430 MW	100110 TQ	USBLS	5/15
	Hawaii	Y	92330 FQ	198600 AW		USBLS	5/15
	Urban Honolulu MSA, HI	Y	124390 FQ	226370 AW		USBLS	5/15
	Idaho	Y	68590 FQ	82240 MW	99200 TQ	USBLS	5/15
	Boise City MSA, ID	Y	73610 FQ	89680 MW	116630 TQ	USBLS	5/15
	Illinois	Y	67520 FQ	82650 MW	103180 TQ	USBLS	5/15
	Chicago-Naperville-Arlington Heights PMSA, IL	Y	67820 FQ	80770 MW	103800 TQ	USBLS	5/15
	Lake County-Kenosha County PMSA, IL-WI	Y	83610 FQ	97190 MW	139270 TQ	USBLS	5/15
	Indiana	Y	67540 FQ	80520 MW	104550 TQ	USBLS	5/15
	Gary PMSA, IN	Y	69060 FQ	78260 MW	97320 TQ	USBLS	5/15
	Indianapolis-Carmel-Anderson MSA, IN	Y	65800 FQ	77110 MW	122810 TQ	USBLS	5/15
	Iowa	Y	64740 FQ	78040 MW	100290 TQ	USBLS	5/15
	Des Moines-West Des Moines MSA, IA	Y	71360 FQ	79740 MW	95170 TQ	USBLS	5/15
	Kansas	Y	53790 FQ	71470 MW	86590 TQ	USBLS	5/15
	Kentucky	Y	60340 FQ	77700 MW	97420 TQ	USBLS	5/15
	Louisville-Jefferson County MSA, KY-IN	Y	66430 FQ	77550 MW	92680 TQ	USBLS	5/15
	Louisiana	Y	59360 FQ	76410 MW	94900 TQ	USBLS	5/15
	Baton Rouge MSA, LA	Y	52930 FQ	58280 MW	66040 TQ	USBLS	5/15
	New Orleans-Metairie MSA, LA	Y	59830 FQ	73700 MW	87950 TQ	USBLS	5/15
	Maine	Y	69430 FQ	84160 MW	97080 TQ	USBLS	5/15
	Portland-South Portland MSA, ME	Y	75460 FQ	89360 MW	101130 TQ	USBLS	5/15
	Maryland	Y	55621 AE	113136 MW	141894 AEX	MDBLS	4/16
	Baltimore-Columbia-Towson MSA, MD	Y	64210 FQ	100410 MW	139960 TQ	USBLS	5/15
	Salisbury MSA, MD-DE	Y	66940 FQ	80310 MW	102730 TQ	USBLS	5/15
	Massachusetts	Y	77480 FQ	102630 MW	140650 TQ	USBLS	5/15
	Boston-Cambridge-Newton NECTA, MA	Y	74830 FQ	98850 MW	129570 TQ	USBLS	5/15
	Framingham NECTA, MA	Y	71690 FQ	87040 MW	136430 TQ	USBLS	5/15
	Worcester MSA, MA-CT	Y	38890 FQ	78870 MW	113980 TQ	USBLS	5/15
	Michigan	Y	68100 FQ	87150 MW	119730 TQ	USBLS	5/15
	Detroit-Dearborn-Livonia PMSA, MI	Y	70230 FQ	86450 MW	111440 TQ	USBLS	5/15
	Grand Rapids-Wyoming MSA, MI	Y	28000 FQ	55300 MW	78140 TQ	USBLS	5/15
	Minnesota	Y	68124 FQ	82096 MW	95331 TQ	MNBLS	1/16-3/16
	Minneapolis-St. Paul-Bloomington MSA, MN-WI	Y	71158 FQ	83789 MW	96077 TQ	MNBLS	1/16-3/16
	Mississippi	Y	63090 FQ	76600 MW	93960 TQ	USBLS	5/15
	Jackson MSA, MS	Y	70180 FQ	83910 MW	92300 TQ	USBLS	5/15
	Missouri	Y	67640 FQ	81070 MW	96120 TQ	USBLS	5/15
	Kansas City MSA, MO-KS	Y	65360 FQ	77200 MW	92660 TQ	USBLS	5/15
	St. Louis MSA, MO-IL	Y	68390 FQ	81250 MW	96220 TQ	USBLS	5/15
	Montana	Y	52140 FQ	66670 MW	86700 TQ	USBLS	5/15
	Billings MSA, MT	Y	57850 FQ	84220 MW	110120 TQ	USBLS	5/15
	Nebraska	Y	57290 FQ	71560 MW	90645 TQ	NEBLS	7/16-9/16
	Omaha-Council Bluffs MSA, NE-IA	Y	64865 FQ	78975 MW	106680 TQ	NEBLS	7/16-9/16

AE	Average entry wage	AWR	Average wage range	H	Hourly	LR	Low end range	MTC	Median total compensation	TCC	Total cash compensation
AEX	Average experienced wage	B	Biweekly	HI	Highest wage paid	M	Monthly	MW	Median wage paid	TQ	Third quartile wage
ATC	Average total compensation	D	Daily	HR	High end range	MCC	Median cash compensation	MWR	Median wage range	W	Weekly
AW	Average wage paid	FQ	First quartile wage	LO	Lowest wage paid	ME	Median entry wage	S	See annotated source	Y	Yearly

Occupation/Type/Industry	Location	Per	Low	Mid	High	Source	Date
Veterinarian	Nevada	Y	72640 FQ	87370 MW	102850 TQ	USBLS	5/15
	Las Vegas-Henderson-Paradise MSA, NV	Y	83460 FQ	93810 MW	108900 TQ	USBLS	5/15
	New Hampshire	H	31.56 AE	47.68 MW	55.88 AEX	NHBLS	6/16
	Manchester NECTA, NH	H	34.65 AE	48.68 MW	53.34 AEX	NHBLS	6/16
	Nashua NECTA, NH-MA	Y	85200 FQ	98090 MW	115510 TQ	USBLS	5/15
	New Jersey	Y	90310 FQ	114040 MW	153810 TQ	USBLS	5/15
	Camden PMSA, NJ	Y	84280 FQ	99670 MW	119210 TQ	USBLS	5/15
	Newark PMSA, NJ-PA	Y	91800 FQ	120840 MW	181800 TQ	USBLS	5/15
	Trenton MSA, NJ	Y	88760 FQ	113720 MW	143080 TQ	USBLS	5/15
	New Mexico	Y	67130 FQ	79370 MW	97360 TQ	USBLS	5/15
	Albuquerque MSA, NM	Y	70950 FQ	85890 MW	118870 TQ	USBLS	5/15
	New York	Y	74860 AE	117550 MW	150730 AEX	NYBLS	1/16-3/16
	Buffalo-Cheektowaga-Niagara Falls MSA, NY	Y	75670 FQ	103110 MW	174660 TQ	USBLS	5/15
	Nassau County-Suffolk County PMSA, NY	Y	102120 FQ	133300 MW	161320 TQ	USBLS	5/15
	New York-Jersey City-White Plains PMSA, NY-NJ	Y	99570 FQ	123960 MW	166110 TQ	USBLS	5/15
	Rochester MSA, NY	Y	71210 FQ	83390 MW	93340 TQ	USBLS	5/15
	North Carolina	Y	68290 FQ	83740 MW	112980 TQ	USBLS	5/15
	Charlotte-Concord-Gastonia MSA, NC-SC	Y	69510 FQ	82180 MW	110420 TQ	USBLS	5/15
	Raleigh MSA, NC	Y	58100 FQ	83430 MW	121240 TQ	USBLS	5/15
	North Dakota	Y	64780 FQ	79000 MW	101140 TQ	USBLS	5/15
	Fargo MSA, ND-MN	Y	74330 FQ	85620 MW	97560 TQ	USBLS	5/15
	Ohio	Y	64110 FQ	81700 MW	106840 TQ	USBLS	5/15
	Cincinnati MSA, OH-KY-IN	Y	66690 FQ	81530 MW	113950 TQ	USBLS	5/15
	Cleveland-Elyria MSA, OH	Y	18620 FQ	57620 MW	89760 TQ	USBLS	5/15
	Columbus MSA, OH	Y	73540 FQ	87660 MW	121030 TQ	USBLS	5/15
	Oklahoma	Y	67180 FQ	79900 MW	110390 TQ	USBLS	5/15
	Oklahoma City MSA, OK	Y	73750 FQ	87700 MW	110830 TQ	USBLS	5/15
	Oregon	H	30.84 FQ	36.26 MW	44.26 TQ	ORBLS	2016
	Portland-Vancouver-Hillsboro MSA, OR-WA	Y	61860 FQ	71490 MW	83010 TQ	USBLS	5/15
	Pennsylvania	Y	76840 FQ	102950 MW	143530 TQ	USBLS	5/15
	Harrisburg-Carlisle MSA, PA	Y	84030 FQ	105480 MW	138210 TQ	USBLS	5/15
	Montgomery County-Bucks County-Chester County PMSA, PA	Y	97720 FQ	137510 MW	153780 TQ	USBLS	5/15
	Philadelphia PMSA, PA	Y	94410 FQ	120960 MW		USBLS	5/15
	Pittsburgh MSA, PA	Y	76200 FQ	92460 MW	116490 TQ	USBLS	5/15
	Rhode Island	Y	112230 FQ	125260 MW	143070 TQ	USBLS	5/15
	Providence-Warwick MSA, RI-MA	Y	106080 FQ	121580 MW	141780 TQ	USBLS	5/15
	South Carolina	Y	75690 FQ	89120 MW	104880 TQ	USBLS	5/15
	Charleston-North Charleston MSA, SC	Y	87090 FQ	103090 MW	122590 TQ	USBLS	5/15
	Columbia MSA, SC	Y	78560 FQ	88120 MW	97570 TQ	USBLS	5/15
	Greenville-Anderson-Mauldin MSA, SC	Y	79210 FQ	89640 MW	98960 TQ	USBLS	5/15
	South Dakota	Y	64360 FQ	78250 MW	98270 TQ	USBLS	5/15
	Sioux Falls MSA, SD	Y	58460 FQ	69740 MW	92300 TQ	USBLS	5/15
	Tennessee	Y	64670 FQ	78580 MW	96130 TQ	USBLS	5/15
	Knoxville MSA, TN	Y	45000 FQ	80210 MW	91900 TQ	USBLS	5/15
	Memphis MSA, TN-MS-AR	Y	49850 FQ	65510 MW	92770 TQ	USBLS	5/15
	Nashville-Davidson–Murfreesboro–Franklin MSA, TN	Y	69660 FQ	77970 MW	102290 TQ	USBLS	5/15
	Texas	Y	74650 FQ	93310 MW	116840 TQ	USBLS	5/15
	Austin-Round Rock MSA, TX	Y	80470 FQ	98910 MW	117770 TQ	USBLS	5/15
	Dallas-Plano-Irving PMSA, TX	Y	75810 FQ	105940 MW	121090 TQ	USBLS	5/15
	Fort Worth-Arlington PMSA, TX	Y	75420 FQ	90520 MW	129660 TQ	USBLS	5/15
	Houston-The Woodlands-Sugar Land MSA, TX	Y	77070 FQ	94970 MW	114970 TQ	USBLS	5/15
	San Antonio-New Braunfels MSA, TX	Y	64210 FQ	103520 MW	153630 TQ	USBLS	5/15
	Utah	Y	69220 FQ	84480 MW	98530 TQ	USBLS	5/15
	Ogden-Clearfield MSA, UT	Y	86720 FQ	108280 MW	123200 TQ	USBLS	5/15
	Provo-Orem MSA, UT	Y	76350 FQ	84890 MW	95390 TQ	USBLS	5/15
	Salt Lake City MSA, UT	Y	71300 FQ	84900 MW	94330 TQ	USBLS	5/15

AE Average entry wage	**AWR** Average wage range	**H** Hourly	**LR** Low end range	**MTC** Median total compensation	**TCC** Total cash compensation
AEX Average experienced wage	**B** Biweekly	**HI** Highest wage paid	**M** Monthly	**MW** Median wage paid	**TQ** Third quartile wage
ATC Average total compensation	**D** Daily	**HR** High end range	**MCC** Median cash compensation	**MWR** Median wage range	**W** Weekly
AW Average wage paid	**FQ** First quartile wage	**LO** Lowest wage paid	**ME** Median entry wage	**S** See annotated source	**Y** Yearly

Occupation/Type/Industry	Location	Per	Low	Mid	High	Source	Date
Veterinarian	Vermont	Y	71450 FQ	86650 MW	109690 TQ	USBLS	5/15
	Burlington-South Burlington MSA, VT	Y	76360 FQ	93610 MW	119270 TQ	USBLS	5/15
	Virginia	Y	75190 FQ	92660 MW	121600 TQ	USBLS	5/15
	Richmond MSA, VA	Y	72100 FQ	90410 MW	112060 TQ	USBLS	5/15
	Virginia Beach-Norfolk-Newport News MSA, VA-NC	Y	70680 FQ	85010 MW	102470 TQ	USBLS	5/15
	Washington	H	34.85 FQ	41.96 MW	53.86 TQ	WABLS	3/16
	Seattle-Bellevue-Everett PMSA, WA	H	37.81 FQ	46.61 MW	59.49 TQ	WABLS	3/16
	Tacoma-Lakewood PMSA, WA	H	31.09 FQ	36.86 MW	46.60 TQ	WABLS	3/16
	West Virginia	Y	70040 FQ	80750 MW	99680 TQ	USBLS	5/15
	Huntington-Ashland MSA, WV-KY-OH	Y	67800 FQ	73890 MW	79430 TQ	USBLS	5/15
	Wisconsin	Y	64170 FQ	78600 MW	107760 TQ	USBLS	5/15
	Madison MSA, WI	Y	58970 FQ	74360 MW	92880 TQ	USBLS	5/15
	Milwaukee-Waukesha-West Allis MSA, WI	Y	75700 FQ	106160 MW	132210 TQ	USBLS	5/15
	Wyoming	Y	58070 FQ	80750 MW	117130 TQ	USBLS	5/15
	Puerto Rico	Y	37980 FQ	57860 MW	95790 TQ	USBLS	5/15
	San Juan-Carolina-Caguas MSA, PR	Y	39570 FQ	63400 MW	98840 TQ	USBLS	5/15
Animal Control, Municipal Government	Detroit, MI	M	3800 LO		5325 HI	DETGOV	2016
Practices With Seven or More Doctors	United States	Y		201667 AW		DVM01	2015
Solo Practitioners	United States	Y		87788 AW		DVM01	2015
Veterinary Acupuncturist	United States	Y		87000 AW		SKU01	2016
Veterinary Assistant and Laboratory Animal Caretaker	Alabama	Y	17977 AE	24134 AW	27212 AEX	ALBLS	6/16
	Alaska	Y	25280 FQ	28230 MW	31360 TQ	USBLS	5/15
	Anchorage MSA, AK	Y	24990 FQ	27350 MW	29720 TQ	USBLS	5/15
	Arizona	Y	20870 FQ	24310 MW	30650 TQ	USBLS	5/15
	Phoenix-Mesa-Scottsdale MSA, AZ	Y	20800 FQ	24530 MW	31330 TQ	USBLS	5/15
	Tucson MSA, AZ	Y	21320 FQ	24110 MW	28850 TQ	USBLS	5/15
	Arkansas	Y	18450 FQ	21410 MW	24570 TQ	USBLS	5/15
	Little Rock-North Little Rock-Conway MSA, AR	Y	17490 FQ	19380 MW	23940 TQ	USBLS	5/15
	California	H	11.28 FQ	13.48 MW	16.05 TQ	CABLS	1/16-3/16
	Anaheim-Santa Ana-Irvine PMSA, CA	H	10.16 FQ	12.19 MW	14.43 TQ	CABLS	1/16-3/16
	Los Angeles-Long Beach-Glendale PMSA, CA	H	11.44 FQ	13.33 MW	15.00 TQ	CABLS	1/16-3/16
	Oakland-Hayward-Berkeley PMSA, CA	H	13.32 FQ	15.23 MW	21.51 TQ	CABLS	1/16-3/16
	Riverside-San Bernardino-Ontario MSA, CA	H	10.27 FQ	12.32 MW	15.82 TQ	CABLS	1/16-3/16
	Sacramento–Roseville–Arden-Arcade MSA, CA	H	10.50 FQ	12.77 MW	16.15 TQ	CABLS	1/16-3/16
	San Diego-Carlsbad MSA, CA	H	12.25 FQ	14.20 MW	16.91 TQ	CABLS	1/16-3/16
	San Francisco-Redwood City-South San Francisco PMSA, CA	H	12.88 FQ	14.85 MW	18.73 TQ	CABLS	1/16-3/16
	Colorado	Y	20980 FQ	23670 MW	27660 TQ	USBLS	5/15
	Denver-Aurora-Lakewood MSA, CO	Y	22420 FQ	25410 MW	29180 TQ	USBLS	5/15
	Connecticut	Y		27880 MW		CTBLS	1/16-3/16
	Bridgeport-Stamford-Norwalk MSA, CT	Y	20100 FQ	23790 MW	29650 TQ	USBLS	5/15
	Hartford-West Hartford-East Hartford MSA, CT	Y	20870 FQ	24600 MW	30750 TQ	USBLS	5/15
	Delaware	Y	21010 FQ	24100 MW	29440 TQ	USBLS	5/15
	Wilmington PMSA, DE-MD-NJ	Y	20440 FQ	24430 MW	37370 TQ	USBLS	5/15
	District of Columbia	Y	27000 FQ	35900 MW	44900 TQ	USBLS	5/15
	Washington-Arlington-Alexandria PMSA, DC-VA-MD-WV	Y	23400 FQ	28550 MW	37030 TQ	USBLS	5/15
	Florida	H	9.49 AE	11.16 MW	12.66 AEX	FLBLS	7/16-9/16

AE	Average entry wage	AWR	Average wage range	H	Hourly	LR	Low end range	MTC	Median total compensation	TCC	Total cash compensation
AEX	Average experienced wage	B	Biweekly	HI	Highest wage paid	M	Monthly	MW	Median wage paid	TQ	Third quartile wage
ATC	Average total compensation	D	Daily	HR	High end range	MCC	Median cash compensation	MWR	Median wage range	W	Weekly
AW	Average wage paid	FQ	First quartile wage	LO	Lowest wage paid	ME	Median entry wage	S	See annotated source	Y	Yearly

Occupation/Type/Industry	Location	Per	Low	Mid	High	Source	Date
Veterinary Assistant and Laboratory Animal Caretaker	Fort Lauderdale-Pompano Beach-Deerfield Beach PMSA, FL	H	10.52 AE	11.29 MW	11.92 AEX	FLBLS	7/16-9/16
	Miami-Miami Beach-Kendall PMSA, FL	H	9.90 AE	11.50 MW	13.26 AEX	FLBLS	7/16-9/16
	Orlando-Kissimmee-Sanford MSA, FL	H	9.57 AE	11.35 MW	12.47 AEX	FLBLS	7/16-9/16
	Tampa-St. Petersburg-Clearwater MSA, FL	H	9.13 AE	10.69 MW	11.79 AEX	FLBLS	7/16-9/16
	Georgia	Y	19710 FQ	22520 MW	26700 TQ	USBLS	5/15
	Atlanta-Sandy Springs-Roswell MSA, GA	Y	20120 FQ	22710 MW	26980 TQ	USBLS	5/15
	Augusta-Richmond County MSA, GA-SC	Y	19980 FQ	23040 MW	27350 TQ	USBLS	5/15
	Hawaii	Y	21170 FQ	25840 MW	30680 TQ	USBLS	5/15
	Urban Honolulu MSA, HI	Y	19240 FQ	25010 MW	34310 TQ	USBLS	5/15
	Idaho	Y	20550 FQ	25440 MW	29250 TQ	USBLS	5/15
	Boise City MSA, ID	Y	21130 FQ	25930 MW	29980 TQ	USBLS	5/15
	Illinois	Y	21920 FQ	26370 MW	30230 TQ	USBLS	5/15
	Chicago-Naperville-Arlington Heights PMSA, IL	Y	25050 FQ	28170 MW	31390 TQ	USBLS	5/15
	Lake County-Kenosha County PMSA, IL-WI	Y	21700 FQ	23950 MW	27930 TQ	USBLS	5/15
	Indiana	Y	19760 FQ	23930 MW	29900 TQ	USBLS	5/15
	Gary PMSA, IN	Y	21050 FQ	24780 MW	28240 TQ	USBLS	5/15
	Indianapolis-Carmel-Anderson MSA, IN	Y	20700 FQ	25440 MW	32400 TQ	USBLS	5/15
	Iowa	Y	19700 FQ	23090 MW	27870 TQ	USBLS	5/15
	Des Moines-West Des Moines MSA, IA	Y	18250 FQ	22500 MW	27470 TQ	USBLS	5/15
	Kansas	Y	21330 FQ	25710 MW	29140 TQ	USBLS	5/15
	Wichita MSA, KS	Y	22550 FQ	25790 MW	28880 TQ	USBLS	5/15
	Kentucky	Y	17900 FQ	20730 MW	24640 TQ	USBLS	5/15
	Louisville-Jefferson County MSA, KY-IN	Y	18540 FQ	21830 MW	25430 TQ	USBLS	5/15
	Louisiana	Y	18530 FQ	22070 MW	27540 TQ	USBLS	5/15
	Baton Rouge MSA, LA	Y	18820 FQ	21950 MW	29740 TQ	USBLS	5/15
	New Orleans-Metairie MSA, LA	Y	20330 FQ	23340 MW	27440 TQ	USBLS	5/15
	Maine	Y	24460 FQ	28430 MW	34670 TQ	USBLS	5/15
	Portland-South Portland MSA, ME	Y	24460 FQ	28020 MW	31980 TQ	USBLS	5/15
	Maryland	Y	19466 AE	28077 MW	32383 AEX	MDBLS	4/16
	Baltimore-Columbia-Towson MSA, MD	Y	19770 FQ	22910 MW	29710 TQ	USBLS	5/15
	Salisbury MSA, MD-DE	Y	20700 FQ	24970 MW	30380 TQ	USBLS	5/15
	Massachusetts	Y	24410 FQ	31820 MW	40130 TQ	USBLS	5/15
	Boston-Cambridge-Newton NECTA, MA	Y	29400 FQ	36240 MW	44040 TQ	USBLS	5/15
	Worcester MSA, MA-CT	Y	23510 FQ	27920 MW	34270 TQ	USBLS	5/15
	Michigan	Y	20750 FQ	23730 MW	29060 TQ	USBLS	5/15
	Detroit-Dearborn-Livonia PMSA, MI	Y	24180 FQ	28170 MW	34430 TQ	USBLS	5/15
	Grand Rapids-Wyoming MSA, MI	Y	19790 FQ	21960 MW	24160 TQ	USBLS	5/15
	Minnesota	Y	23106 FQ	28297 MW	34073 TQ	MNBLS	1/16-3/16
	Minneapolis-St. Paul-Bloomington MSA, MN-WI	Y	25529 FQ	29155 MW	34467 TQ	MNBLS	1/16-3/16
	Mississippi	Y	18880 FQ	22170 MW	26350 TQ	USBLS	5/15
	Jackson MSA, MS	Y	18220 FQ	20900 MW	24500 TQ	USBLS	5/15
	Missouri	Y	17960 FQ	20220 MW	24590 TQ	USBLS	5/15
	Kansas City MSA, MO-KS	Y	18870 FQ	24430 MW	28730 TQ	USBLS	5/15
	St. Louis MSA, MO-IL	Y	17830 FQ	19580 MW	23150 TQ	USBLS	5/15
	Montana	Y	20690 FQ	23400 MW	27440 TQ	USBLS	5/15
	Nebraska	Y	19315 FQ	23670 MW	28795 TQ	NEBLS	7/16-9/16
	Omaha-Council Bluffs MSA, NE-IA	Y	20930 FQ	24915 MW	33745 TQ	NEBLS	7/16-9/16
	Nevada	Y	20160 FQ	23020 MW	26760 TQ	USBLS	5/15
	Las Vegas-Henderson-Paradise MSA, NV	Y	20010 FQ	22340 MW	24690 TQ	USBLS	5/15
	New Hampshire	H	8.38 AE	12.47 MW	14.60 AEX	NHBLS	6/16

AE	Average entry wage	AWR	Average wage range	H	Hourly	LR	Low end range	MTC	Median total compensation	TCC	Total cash compensation
AEX	Average experienced wage	B	Biweekly	HI	Highest wage paid	M	Monthly	MW	Median wage paid	TQ	Third quartile wage
ATC	Average total compensation	D	Daily	HR	High end range	MCC	Median cash compensation	MWR	Median wage range	W	Weekly
AW	Average wage paid	FQ	First quartile wage	LO	Lowest wage paid	ME	Median entry wage	S	See annotated source	Y	Yearly

Occupation/Type/Industry	Location	Per	Low	Mid	High	Source	Date
Veterinary Assistant and Laboratory Animal Caretaker	Nashua NECTA, NH-MA	Y	16330 FQ	17560 MW	18790 TQ	USBLS	5/15
	New Jersey	Y	19460 FQ	25470 MW	31410 TQ	USBLS	5/15
	Camden PMSA, NJ	Y	27300 FQ	30740 MW	35030 TQ	USBLS	5/15
	Newark PMSA, NJ-PA	Y	18660 FQ	20010 MW	27660 TQ	USBLS	5/15
	Trenton MSA, NJ	Y	22070 FQ	25310 MW	28970 TQ	USBLS	5/15
	New Mexico	Y	19490 FQ	23120 MW	28020 TQ	USBLS	5/15
	Albuquerque MSA, NM	Y	22200 FQ	25140 MW	29590 TQ	USBLS	5/15
	New York	Y	21460 AE	27030 MW	32490 AEX	NYBLS	1/16-3/16
	Buffalo-Cheektowaga-Niagara Falls MSA, NY	Y	20910 FQ	24980 MW	28780 TQ	USBLS	5/15
	Nassau County-Suffolk County PMSA, NY	Y	21510 FQ	24190 MW	28810 TQ	USBLS	5/15
	New York-Jersey City-White Plains PMSA, NY-NJ	Y	23500 FQ	28600 MW	35320 TQ	USBLS	5/15
	Rochester MSA, NY	Y	21930 FQ	25930 MW	29540 TQ	USBLS	5/15
	North Carolina	Y	18760 FQ	23240 MW	29140 TQ	USBLS	5/15
	Charlotte-Concord-Gastonia MSA, NC-SC	Y	20880 FQ	25730 MW	29350 TQ	USBLS	5/15
	Raleigh MSA, NC	Y	17390 FQ	19280 MW	24060 TQ	USBLS	5/15
	North Dakota	Y	21260 FQ	25090 MW	33410 TQ	USBLS	5/15
	Fargo MSA, ND-MN	Y	21450 FQ	25220 MW	33580 TQ	USBLS	5/15
	Ohio	Y	19380 FQ	22680 MW	27700 TQ	USBLS	5/15
	Cincinnati MSA, OH-KY-IN	Y	19160 FQ	26300 MW	31940 TQ	USBLS	5/15
	Cleveland-Elyria MSA, OH	Y	21330 FQ	25330 MW	29610 TQ	USBLS	5/15
	Columbus MSA, OH	Y	19520 FQ	21750 MW	24080 TQ	USBLS	5/15
	Oklahoma	Y	17950 FQ	22760 MW	28110 TQ	USBLS	5/15
	Oklahoma City MSA, OK	Y	17080 FQ	18880 MW	25940 TQ	USBLS	5/15
	Tulsa MSA, OK	Y	18790 FQ	26170 MW	28660 TQ	USBLS	5/15
	Oregon	H	10.60 FQ	13.01 MW	14.96 TQ	ORBLS	2016
	Portland-Vancouver-Hillsboro MSA, OR-WA	Y	22110 FQ	27270 MW	31090 TQ	USBLS	5/15
	Pennsylvania	Y	20050 FQ	23550 MW	29040 TQ	USBLS	5/15
	Allentown-Bethlehem-Easton MSA, PA-NJ	Y	18320 FQ	20490 MW	23340 TQ	USBLS	5/15
	Harrisburg-Carlisle MSA, PA	Y	18920 FQ	21770 MW	24540 TQ	USBLS	5/15
	Montgomery County-Bucks County-Chester County PMSA, PA	Y	24320 FQ	27480 MW	30330 TQ	USBLS	5/15
	Philadelphia PMSA, PA	Y	21530 FQ	24250 MW	30630 TQ	USBLS	5/15
	Pittsburgh MSA, PA	Y	20460 FQ	24350 MW	30260 TQ	USBLS	5/15
	Rhode Island	Y	21750 FQ	24420 MW	40110 TQ	USBLS	5/15
	Providence-Warwick MSA, RI-MA	Y	21910 FQ	24820 MW	38960 TQ	USBLS	5/15
	South Carolina	Y	19660 FQ	22980 MW	27240 TQ	USBLS	5/15
	Charleston-North Charleston MSA, SC	Y	21470 FQ	23680 MW	26700 TQ	USBLS	5/15
	Columbia MSA, SC	Y	19940 FQ	22870 MW	27990 TQ	USBLS	5/15
	Greenville-Anderson-Mauldin MSA, SC	Y	18290 FQ	21390 MW	26570 TQ	USBLS	5/15
	South Dakota	Y	20200 FQ	23710 MW	28280 TQ	USBLS	5/15
	Tennessee	Y	20360 FQ	22960 MW	26880 TQ	USBLS	5/15
	Knoxville MSA, TN	Y	17150 FQ	19060 MW	26990 TQ	USBLS	5/15
	Memphis MSA, TN-MS-AR	Y	21250 FQ	23690 MW	28340 TQ	USBLS	5/15
	Nashville-Davidson–Murfreesboro–Franklin MSA, TN	Y	21660 FQ	23810 MW	28060 TQ	USBLS	5/15
	Texas	Y	19750 FQ	23330 MW	27970 TQ	USBLS	5/15
	Austin-Round Rock MSA, TX	Y	19590 FQ	24080 MW	28390 TQ	USBLS	5/15
	Dallas-Plano-Irving PMSA, TX	Y	21490 FQ	23890 MW	28480 TQ	USBLS	5/15
	Fort Worth-Arlington PMSA, TX	Y	17620 FQ	20160 MW	23880 TQ	USBLS	5/15
	Houston-The Woodlands-Sugar Land MSA, TX	Y	20080 FQ	23570 MW	28580 TQ	USBLS	5/15
	Longview MSA, TX	Y	21570 FQ	23880 MW	29160 TQ	USBLS	5/15
	San Antonio-New Braunfels MSA, TX	Y	20270 FQ	23460 MW	27840 TQ	USBLS	5/15
	Utah	Y	17050 FQ	18790 MW	25100 TQ	USBLS	5/15
	Ogden-Clearfield MSA, UT	Y	16700 FQ	18150 MW	22780 TQ	USBLS	5/15
	Provo-Orem MSA, UT	Y	16440 FQ	17560 MW	18680 TQ	USBLS	5/15
	Salt Lake City MSA, UT	Y	17360 FQ	20650 MW	28220 TQ	USBLS	5/15
	Vermont	Y	21720 FQ	25580 MW	28490 TQ	USBLS	5/15

AE	Average entry wage	AWR	Average wage range	H	Hourly
AEX	Average experienced wage	B	Biweekly	HI	Highest wage paid
ATC	Average total compensation	D	Daily	HR	High end range
AW	Average wage paid	FQ	First quartile wage	LO	Lowest wage paid

LR	Low end range	MTC	Median total compensation	TCC	Total cash compensation
M	Monthly	MW	Median wage paid	TQ	Third quartile wage
MCC	Median cash compensation	MWR	Median wage range	W	Weekly
ME	Median entry wage	S	See annotated source	Y	Yearly

Occupation/Type/Industry	Location	Per	Low	Mid	High	Source	Date
Veterinary Assistant and Laboratory Animal Caretaker	Burlington-South Burlington MSA, VT	Y	24090 FQ	26920 MW	29130 TQ	USBLS	5/15
	Virginia	Y	20780 FQ	25130 MW	30040 TQ	USBLS	5/15
	Richmond MSA, VA	Y	21420 FQ	25760 MW	29760 TQ	USBLS	5/15
	Virginia Beach-Norfolk-Newport News MSA, VA-NC	Y	20960 FQ	23570 MW	27970 TQ	USBLS	5/15
	Washington	H	11.54 FQ	13.30 MW	14.90 TQ	WABLS	3/16
	Seattle-Bellevue-Everett PMSA, WA	H	12.67 FQ	14.25 MW	16.52 TQ	WABLS	3/16
	Tacoma-Lakewood PMSA, WA	H	10.89 FQ	13.00 MW	14.50 TQ	WABLS	3/16
	West Virginia	Y	18530 FQ	20990 MW	24290 TQ	USBLS	5/15
	Huntington-Ashland MSA, WV-KY-OH	Y	19930 FQ	22260 MW	24600 TQ	USBLS	5/15
	Wisconsin	Y	18300 FQ	22530 MW	28410 TQ	USBLS	5/15
	Madison MSA, WI	Y	18070 FQ	23730 MW	30070 TQ	USBLS	5/15
	Milwaukee-Waukesha-West Allis MSA, WI	Y	18300 FQ	24990 MW	31570 TQ	USBLS	5/15
	Wyoming	Y	23410 FQ	27440 MW	31690 TQ	USBLS	5/15
	Puerto Rico	Y	16770 FQ	18260 MW	20450 TQ	USBLS	5/15
	San Juan-Carolina-Caguas MSA, PR	Y	17080 FQ	18890 MW	21810 TQ	USBLS	5/15
Veterinary Bacteriologist Agriculture Department, State Government	Ohio	H			51.80 HI	OHGOV	2015
Veterinary Pathologist Agriculture Department, State Government	Ohio	H	41.50 LO		49.30 HI	OHGOV	2015
Veterinary Technologist and Technician	Alabama	Y	21610 AE	29744 AW	33811 AEX	ALBLS	6/16
	Birmingham-Hoover MSA, AL	Y	21681 AE	30794 AW	21681 AEX	ALBLS	6/16
	Alaska	Y	38400 FQ	43150 MW	47110 TQ	USBLS	5/15
	Anchorage MSA, AK	Y	40430 FQ	43520 MW	46840 TQ	USBLS	5/15
	Arizona	Y	23330 FQ	28790 MW	35950 TQ	USBLS	5/15
	Phoenix-Mesa-Scottsdale MSA, AZ	Y	26570 FQ	31770 MW	38030 TQ	USBLS	5/15
	Tucson MSA, AZ	Y	21100 FQ	23280 MW	28020 TQ	USBLS	5/15
	Arkansas	Y	20710 FQ	24870 MW	30310 TQ	USBLS	5/15
	Little Rock-North Little Rock-Conway MSA, AR	Y	27010 FQ	29300 MW	33320 TQ	USBLS	5/15
	California	H	14.48 FQ	18.27 MW	22.71 TQ	CABLS	1/16-3/16
	Anaheim-Santa Ana-Irvine PMSA, CA	H	13.38 FQ	15.71 MW	24.11 TQ	CABLS	1/16-3/16
	Los Angeles-Long Beach-Glendale PMSA, CA	H	16.62 FQ	18.56 MW	22.64 TQ	CABLS	1/16-3/16
	Oakland-Hayward-Berkeley PMSA, CA	H	15.98 FQ	19.22 MW	23.15 TQ	CABLS	1/16-3/16
	Riverside-San Bernardino-Ontario MSA, CA	H	15.12 FQ	17.54 MW	20.77 TQ	CABLS	1/16-3/16
	Sacramento–Roseville–Arden-Arcade MSA, CA	H	12.39 FQ	14.71 MW	21.73 TQ	CABLS	1/16-3/16
	San Diego-Carlsbad MSA, CA	H	18.87 FQ	21.53 MW	23.93 TQ	CABLS	1/16-3/16
	San Francisco-Redwood City-South San Francisco PMSA, CA	H	19.43 FQ	21.99 MW	24.87 TQ	CABLS	1/16-3/16
	Colorado	Y	25470 FQ	29890 MW	35650 TQ	USBLS	5/15
	Denver-Aurora-Lakewood MSA, CO	Y	26820 FQ	31630 MW	36480 TQ	USBLS	5/15
	Connecticut	Y		36775 MW		CTBLS	1/16-3/16
	Bridgeport-Stamford-Norwalk MSA, CT	Y	31220 FQ	38690 MW	48660 TQ	USBLS	5/15
	Hartford-West Hartford-East Hartford MSA, CT	Y	28940 FQ	34700 MW	40630 TQ	USBLS	5/15
	Delaware	Y	25390 FQ	28950 MW	35440 TQ	USBLS	5/15
	Wilmington PMSA, DE-MD-NJ	Y	24650 FQ	28470 MW	34400 TQ	USBLS	5/15
	District of Columbia	Y	23180 FQ	32820 MW	43320 TQ	USBLS	5/15
	Washington-Arlington-Alexandria PMSA, DC-VA-MD-WV	Y	29530 FQ	37200 MW	47830 TQ	USBLS	5/15
	Florida	H	11.70 AE	14.78 MW	17.00 AEX	FLBLS	7/16-9/16

AE Average entry wage	**AWR** Average wage range	**H** Hourly	**LR** Low end range	**MTC** Median total compensation	**TCC** Total cash compensation
AEX Average experienced wage	**B** Biweekly	**HI** Highest wage paid	**M** Monthly	**MW** Median wage paid	**TQ** Third quartile wage
ATC Average total compensation	**D** Daily	**HR** High end range	**MCC** Median cash compensation	**MWR** Median wage range	**W** Weekly
AW Average wage paid	**FQ** First quartile wage	**LO** Lowest wage paid	**ME** Median entry wage	**S** See annotated source	**Y** Yearly

Occupation/Type/Industry	Location	Per	Low	Mid	High	Source	Date
Veterinary Technologist and Technician	Fort Lauderdale-Pompano Beach-Deerfield Beach PMSA, FL	H	13.75 AE	17.67 MW	19.56 AEX	FLBLS	7/16-9/16
	Miami-Miami Beach-Kendall PMSA, FL	H	11.88 AE	16.23 MW	17.91 AEX	FLBLS	7/16-9/16
	Orlando-Kissimmee-Sanford MSA, FL	H	11.72 AE	14.06 MW	15.54 AEX	FLBLS	7/16-9/16
	Tampa-St. Petersburg-Clearwater MSA, FL	H	10.78 AE	13.91 MW	15.63 AEX	FLBLS	7/16-9/16
	Georgia	Y	23350 FQ	28260 MW	34560 TQ	USBLS	5/15
	Atlanta-Sandy Springs-Roswell MSA, GA	Y	23800 FQ	28590 MW	34660 TQ	USBLS	5/15
	Augusta-Richmond County MSA, GA-SC	Y	22430 FQ	27060 MW	31060 TQ	USBLS	5/15
	Hawaii	Y	26720 FQ	30170 MW	35850 TQ	USBLS	5/15
	Urban Honolulu MSA, HI	Y	26720 FQ	30170 MW	35930 TQ	USBLS	5/15
	Idaho	Y	23650 FQ	27480 MW	31160 TQ	USBLS	5/15
	Boise City MSA, ID	Y	25750 FQ	29070 MW	33470 TQ	USBLS	5/15
	Illinois	Y	27200 FQ	30320 MW	37540 TQ	USBLS	5/15
	Chicago-Naperville-Arlington Heights PMSA, IL	Y	27370 FQ	30000 MW	36800 TQ	USBLS	5/15
	Lake County-Kenosha County PMSA, IL-WI	Y	30320 FQ	35910 MW	43740 TQ	USBLS	5/15
	Indiana	Y	23730 FQ	28870 MW	35700 TQ	USBLS	5/15
	Gary PMSA, IN	Y	19100 FQ	23450 MW	30750 TQ	USBLS	5/15
	Indianapolis-Carmel-Anderson MSA, IN	Y	24740 FQ	29410 MW	36520 TQ	USBLS	5/15
	Iowa	Y	25740 FQ	29930 MW	35720 TQ	USBLS	5/15
	Des Moines-West Des Moines MSA, IA	Y	26090 FQ	29920 MW	34850 TQ	USBLS	5/15
	Kansas	Y	24180 FQ	28520 MW	34800 TQ	USBLS	5/15
	Wichita MSA, KS	Y	26580 FQ	28720 MW	32230 TQ	USBLS	5/15
	Kentucky	Y	22330 FQ	26950 MW	32990 TQ	USBLS	5/15
	Louisville-Jefferson County MSA, KY-IN	Y	21800 FQ	25400 MW	30180 TQ	USBLS	5/15
	Louisiana	Y	22720 FQ	27080 MW	30910 TQ	USBLS	5/15
	Baton Rouge MSA, LA	Y	20860 FQ	22780 MW	24700 TQ	USBLS	5/15
	New Orleans-Metairie MSA, LA	Y	25840 FQ	28710 MW	32060 TQ	USBLS	5/15
	Maine	Y	28540 FQ	33780 MW	38010 TQ	USBLS	5/15
	Portland-South Portland MSA, ME	Y	28060 FQ	33950 MW	38140 TQ	USBLS	5/15
	Maryland	Y	25439 AE	35330 MW	40276 AEX	MDBLS	4/16
	Baltimore-Columbia-Towson MSA, MD	Y	25180 FQ	31000 MW	39550 TQ	USBLS	5/15
	Salisbury MSA, MD-DE	Y	26150 FQ	29240 MW	35200 TQ	USBLS	5/15
	Massachusetts	Y	34230 FQ	40300 MW	48660 TQ	USBLS	5/15
	Boston-Cambridge-Newton NECTA, MA	Y	37790 FQ	46220 MW	55360 TQ	USBLS	5/15
	Worcester MSA, MA-CT	Y	34500 FQ	38830 MW	46790 TQ	USBLS	5/15
	Michigan	Y	24410 FQ	30600 MW	37240 TQ	USBLS	5/15
	Detroit-Dearborn-Livonia PMSA, MI	Y	28370 FQ	33470 MW	38090 TQ	USBLS	5/15
	Grand Rapids-Wyoming MSA, MI	Y	26680 FQ	30140 MW	35290 TQ	USBLS	5/15
	Minnesota	Y	28457 FQ	32913 MW	38225 TQ	MNBLS	1/16-3/16
	Minneapolis-St. Paul-Bloomington MSA, MN-WI	Y	29657 FQ	34233 MW	38618 TQ	MNBLS	1/16-3/16
	Mississippi	Y	23600 FQ	28380 MW	36010 TQ	USBLS	5/15
	Jackson MSA, MS	Y	24010 FQ	29100 MW	35900 TQ	USBLS	5/15
	Missouri	Y	29480 FQ	35310 MW	42380 TQ	USBLS	5/15
	Kansas City MSA, MO-KS	Y	31890 FQ	34920 MW	37950 TQ	USBLS	5/15
	St. Louis MSA, MO-IL	Y	28870 FQ	35590 MW	44090 TQ	USBLS	5/15
	Montana	Y	25280 FQ	28890 MW	33890 TQ	USBLS	5/15
	Billings MSA, MT	Y	28650 FQ	34760 MW	41860 TQ	USBLS	5/15
	Nebraska	Y	24320 FQ	29415 MW	35305 TQ	NEBLS	7/16-9/16
	Omaha-Council Bluffs MSA, NE-IA	Y	27975 FQ	33040 MW	38425 TQ	NEBLS	7/16-9/16
	Nevada	Y	27430 FQ	33670 MW	39250 TQ	USBLS	5/15
	Las Vegas-Henderson-Paradise MSA, NV	Y	26710 FQ	33770 MW	40030 TQ	USBLS	5/15

AE	Average entry wage	AWR	Average wage range	H	Hourly
AEX	Average experienced wage	B	Biweekly	HI	Highest wage paid
ATC	Average total compensation	D	Daily	HR	High end range
AW	Average wage paid	FQ	First quartile wage	LO	Lowest wage paid

LR	Low end range	MTC	Median total compensation	TCC	Total cash compensation
M	Monthly	MW	Median wage paid	TQ	Third quartile wage
MCC	Median cash compensation	MWR	Median wage range	W	Weekly
ME	Median entry wage	S	See annotated source	Y	Yearly

Occupation/Type/Industry	Location	Per	Low	Mid	High	Source	Date
Veterinary Technologist and Technician							
	New Hampshire	H	12.97 AE	16.41 MW	18.63 AEX	NHBLS	6/16
	Manchester NECTA, NH	H	13.66 AE	16.30 MW	18.41 AEX	NHBLS	6/16
	Nashua NECTA, NH-MA	Y	28880 FQ	34830 MW	42680 TQ	USBLS	5/15
	New Jersey	Y	27070 FQ	33120 MW	38630 TQ	USBLS	5/15
	Camden PMSA, NJ	Y	25340 FQ	29340 MW	34900 TQ	USBLS	5/15
	Newark PMSA, NJ-PA	Y	27710 FQ	36340 MW	47420 TQ	USBLS	5/15
	Trenton MSA, NJ	Y	26690 FQ	32600 MW	37980 TQ	USBLS	5/15
	New Mexico	Y	26370 FQ	32990 MW	38160 TQ	USBLS	5/15
	Albuquerque MSA, NM	Y	26360 FQ	33100 MW	38650 TQ	USBLS	5/15
	New York	Y	30010 AE	39050 MW	47090 AEX	NYBLS	1/16-3/16
	Buffalo-Cheektowaga-Niagara Falls MSA, NY	Y	29160 FQ	36100 MW	44700 TQ	USBLS	5/15
	Nassau County-Suffolk County PMSA, NY	Y	32460 FQ	38330 MW	47030 TQ	USBLS	5/15
	New York-Jersey City-White Plains PMSA, NY-NJ	Y	32130 FQ	37810 MW	48510 TQ	USBLS	5/15
	Rochester MSA, NY	Y	32620 FQ	35210 MW	37790 TQ	USBLS	5/15
	North Carolina	Y	25140 FQ	30420 MW	36170 TQ	USBLS	5/15
	Charlotte-Concord-Gastonia MSA, NC-SC	Y	28180 FQ	33510 MW	37640 TQ	USBLS	5/15
	Raleigh MSA, NC	Y	27510 FQ	32230 MW	36850 TQ	USBLS	5/15
	North Dakota	Y	26980 FQ	29770 MW	40360 TQ	USBLS	5/15
	Fargo MSA, ND-MN	Y	26930 FQ	29470 MW	33630 TQ	USBLS	5/15
	Ohio	Y	27290 FQ	31230 MW	38090 TQ	USBLS	5/15
	Cincinnati MSA, OH-KY-IN	Y	27020 FQ	30970 MW	37430 TQ	USBLS	5/15
	Cleveland-Elyria MSA, OH	Y	26360 FQ	30740 MW	37840 TQ	USBLS	5/15
	Columbus MSA, OH	Y	28230 FQ	32190 MW	39350 TQ	USBLS	5/15
	Oklahoma	Y	25800 FQ	32010 MW	36640 TQ	USBLS	5/15
	Oklahoma City MSA, OK	Y	28200 FQ	33920 MW	37740 TQ	USBLS	5/15
	Tulsa MSA, OK	Y	26130 FQ	30540 MW	35070 TQ	USBLS	5/15
	Oregon	H	13.51 FQ	16.37 MW	18.54 TQ	ORBLS	2016
	Portland-Vancouver-Hillsboro MSA, OR-WA	Y	29610 FQ	34550 MW	38480 TQ	USBLS	5/15
	Pennsylvania	Y	27180 FQ	33070 MW	39580 TQ	USBLS	5/15
	Allentown-Bethlehem-Easton MSA, PA-NJ	Y	23830 FQ	28560 MW	35630 TQ	USBLS	5/15
	Harrisburg-Carlisle MSA, PA	Y	28890 FQ	32940 MW	37680 TQ	USBLS	5/15
	Montgomery County-Bucks County-Chester County PMSA, PA	Y	29880 FQ	35660 MW	43070 TQ	USBLS	5/15
	Philadelphia PMSA, PA	Y	28430 FQ	40390 MW	46460 TQ	USBLS	5/15
	Pittsburgh MSA, PA	Y	23570 FQ	30590 MW	36730 TQ	USBLS	5/15
	Rhode Island	Y	30640 FQ	35500 MW	40190 TQ	USBLS	5/15
	Providence-Warwick MSA, RI-MA	Y	30020 FQ	34800 MW	39270 TQ	USBLS	5/15
	South Carolina	Y	24100 FQ	29230 MW	35710 TQ	USBLS	5/15
	Charleston-North Charleston MSA, SC	Y	26320 FQ	32140 MW	36440 TQ	USBLS	5/15
	Columbia MSA, SC	Y	24600 FQ	27660 MW	30660 TQ	USBLS	5/15
	Greenville-Anderson-Mauldin MSA, SC	Y	24300 FQ	31100 MW	41600 TQ	NHBLS	5/15
	South Dakota	Y	25140 FQ	28610 MW	33190 TQ	USBLS	5/15
	Sioux Falls MSA, SD	Y	28010 FQ	32810 MW	36940 TQ	USBLS	5/15
	Tennessee	Y	25520 FQ	29920 MW	37040 TQ	USBLS	5/15
	Knoxville MSA, TN	Y	27100 FQ	32570 MW	39800 TQ	USBLS	5/15
	Memphis MSA, TN-MS-AR	Y	28230 FQ	33720 MW	38950 TQ	USBLS	5/15
	Nashville-Davidson–Murfreesboro–Franklin MSA, TN	Y	26350 FQ	29570 MW	36800 TQ	USBLS	5/15
	Texas	Y	24700 FQ	28780 MW	34500 TQ	USBLS	5/15
	Austin-Round Rock MSA, TX	Y	24500 FQ	27660 MW	30770 TQ	USBLS	5/15
	Dallas-Plano-Irving PMSA, TX	Y	27130 FQ	31680 MW	38780 TQ	USBLS	5/15
	Fort Worth-Arlington PMSA, TX	Y	26720 FQ	30570 MW	36400 TQ	USBLS	5/15
	Houston-The Woodlands-Sugar Land MSA, TX	Y	23470 FQ	28650 MW	34910 TQ	USBLS	5/15
	San Antonio-New Braunfels MSA, TX	Y	25250 FQ	28230 MW	31260 TQ	USBLS	5/15
	Utah	Y	22250 FQ	26690 MW	31940 TQ	USBLS	5/15
	Ogden-Clearfield MSA, UT	Y	24190 FQ	30790 MW	36110 TQ	USBLS	5/15
	Provo-Orem MSA, UT	Y	22890 FQ	26350 MW	28840 TQ	USBLS	5/15

AE	Average entry wage	AWR	Average wage range	H	Hourly
AEX	Average experienced wage	B	Biweekly	HI	Highest wage paid
ATC	Average total compensation	D	Daily	HR	High end range
AW	Average wage paid	FQ	First quartile wage	LO	Lowest wage paid

LR	Low end range	MTC	Median total compensation
M	Monthly	MW	Median wage paid
MCC	Median cash compensation	MWR	Median wage range
ME	Median entry wage	S	See annotated source

TCC	Total cash compensation		
TQ	Third quartile wage		
W	Weekly		
Y	Yearly		

Occupation/Type/Industry	Location	Per	Low	Mid	High	Source	Date
Veterinary Technologist and Technician	Salt Lake City MSA, UT	Y	21810 FQ	25470 MW	30320 TQ	USBLS	5/15
	Vermont	Y	28560 FQ	33810 MW	38550 TQ	USBLS	5/15
	Burlington-South Burlington MSA, VT	Y	27780 FQ	32610 MW	37110 TQ	USBLS	5/15
	Virginia	Y	28480 FQ	34740 MW	41070 TQ	USBLS	5/15
	Richmond MSA, VA	Y	27750 FQ	33470 MW	38580 TQ	USBLS	5/15
	Virginia Beach-Norfolk-Newport News MSA, VA-NC	Y	24810 FQ	30640 MW	36180 TQ	USBLS	5/15
	Washington	H	15.54 FQ	17.40 MW	19.30 TQ	WABLS	3/16
	Seattle-Bellevue-Everett PMSA, WA	H	15.60 FQ	17.49 MW	19.42 TQ	WABLS	3/16
	Tacoma-Lakewood PMSA, WA	H	14.74 FQ	17.35 MW	19.91 TQ	WABLS	3/16
	West Virginia	Y	20870 FQ	26210 MW	29510 TQ	USBLS	5/15
	Huntington-Ashland MSA, WV-KY-OH	Y	25410 FQ	29310 MW	34530 TQ	USBLS	5/15
	Wisconsin	Y	25890 FQ	30900 MW	37870 TQ	USBLS	5/15
	Madison MSA, WI	Y	23310 FQ	31070 MW	38710 TQ	USBLS	5/15
	Milwaukee-Waukesha-West Allis MSA, WI	Y	30490 FQ	36980 MW	43860 TQ	USBLS	5/15
	Wyoming	Y	24910 FQ	28330 MW	32990 TQ	USBLS	5/15
	Cheyenne MSA, WY	Y	23950 FQ	27900 MW	32550 TQ	USBLS	5/15
	Puerto Rico	Y	26960 FQ	30250 MW	47820 TQ	USBLS	5/15
	San Juan-Carolina-Caguas MSA, PR	Y	27350 FQ	30320 MW	49950 TQ	USBLS	5/15
Veterinary Virologist							
Agriculture Department, State Government	Ohio	H			52.18 HI	OHGOV	2015
Vice President of Loss Prevention							
Supermarket, Large Company	United States	Y		225000 AW		SN01	2015
Supermarket, Medium Company	United States	Y		185000 AW		SN01	2015
Supermarket, Small Company	United States	Y		150000 AW		SN01	2015
Vice President of the United States	United States	Y			240100 HI	OPM01	2017
Victim Advocate							
County Government	Oakland County, MI	B	1740 LO		2265 HI	MIOAK2	10/1/16
Municipal Government	Santa Cruz, CA	Y			66924 HI	CACIT	6/28/16
Municipal Government	West Covina, CA	Y			46848 HI	CACIT	6/28/16
Municipal Government	Colorado Springs, CO	Y	40368 LO		55505 HI	COSPRS	2017
Municipal Government	Seattle, WA	H	27.81 LO		32.35 HI	CSSS	1/13/16
Victim Advocate Coordinator							
Municipal Government	Colorado Springs, CO	Y	62111 LO		85402 HI	COSPRS	2017
Victim Assistance Program Director							
County Government	Mohave County, AZ	Y			46904 HI	AZGOV	2017
Victim Services Specialist							
Police Department, Municipal Government	Oxnard, CA	Y			54756 HI	CACIT	6/28/16
Video Communications Officer							
Municipal Government	Long Beach, CA	Y			53125 HI	CACIT	6/28/16
Video Production Coordinator							
City Administration	Anaheim, CA	Y			80400 HI	CACIT	6/28/16
Recreation and Parks Department, Municipal Government	Los Angeles, CA	Y			73148 HI	CACIT	6/23/16
Video Production Specialist							
City Manager's Office	Compton, CA	Y		32700 AW		CACIT	8/12/16
Municipal Government	Hawaiian Gardens, CA	Y			63184 HI	CACIT	6/28/16
Municipal Government	Colorado Springs, CO	Y	51225 LO		70435 HI	COSPRS	2017
Videogame Actor	United States	S		825 AW		WSJ04	2016
Videography Technician							
Michigan State University	East Lansing, MI	Y	42016 LO		46987 HI	MSUSAL	10/1/14-9/30/15
Vineyard Manager	United States	Y		92234 AW		WBM	2/1/16

AE	Average entry wage	AWR	Average wage range	H	Hourly	LR	Low end range	MTC Median total compensation	TCC Total cash compensation
AEX	Average experienced wage	B	Biweekly	HI	Highest wage paid	M	Monthly	MW Median wage paid	TQ Third quartile wage
ATC	Average total compensation	D	Daily	HR	High end range	MCC Median cash compensation		MWR Median wage range	W Weekly
AW	Average wage paid	FQ	First quartile wage	LO	Lowest wage paid	ME Median entry wage		S See annotated source	Y Yearly

Occupation/Type/Industry	Location	Per	Low	Mid	High	Source	Date
Vision Rehabilitation Therapist							
Department of Public Health and Human Services, State Government	Great Falls, MT	H	16.75 LO		18.62 HI	MTGOV	2016
Visitor Center Specialist							
County Government	Oconee County, GA	Y	32813 LO		47579 HI	GACTY04	2016
Visual Journalism Producer							
Michigan State University	East Lansing, MI	Y			51278 HI	MSUSAL	10/1/14-9/30/15
Vocational Education Teacher							
Postsecondary	Alabama	Y	17573 AE	39346 AW	50232 AEX	ALBLS	6/16
Postsecondary	Birmingham-Hoover MSA, AL	Y	18226 AE	43444 AW	56053 AEX	ALBLS	6/16
Postsecondary	Alaska	Y	55600 FQ	67010 MW	82740 TQ	USBLS	5/15
Postsecondary	Anchorage MSA, AK	Y	54610 FQ	62950 MW	77920 TQ	USBLS	5/15
Postsecondary	Arizona	Y	35670 FQ	46300 MW	60010 TQ	USBLS	5/15
Postsecondary	Phoenix-Mesa-Scottsdale MSA, AZ	Y	34830 FQ	44590 MW	56620 TQ	USBLS	5/15
Postsecondary	Tucson MSA, AZ	Y	39860 FQ	60100 MW	87260 TQ	USBLS	5/15
Postsecondary	Arkansas	Y	35160 FQ	43280 MW	49860 TQ	USBLS	5/15
Postsecondary	Little Rock-North Little Rock-Conway MSA, AR	Y	34520 FQ	41840 MW	58630 TQ	USBLS	5/15
Postsecondary	California	H	20.50 FQ	28.66 MW	42.26 TQ	CABLS	1/16-3/16
Postsecondary	Anaheim-Santa Ana-Irvine PMSA, CA	H	19.64 FQ	30.54 MW	51.07 TQ	CABLS	1/16-3/16
Postsecondary	Los Angeles-Long Beach-Glendale PMSA, CA	H	21.11 FQ	27.53 MW	38.96 TQ	CABLS	1/16-3/16
Postsecondary	Oakland-Hayward-Berkeley PMSA, CA	H	20.85 FQ	31.01 MW	44.31 TQ	CABLS	1/16-3/16
Postsecondary	Riverside-San Bernardino-Ontario MSA, CA	H	20.62 FQ	28.45 MW	41.02 TQ	CABLS	1/16-3/16
Postsecondary	Sacramento–Roseville–Arden-Arcade MSA, CA	H	19.51 FQ	30.42 MW	42.58 TQ	CABLS	1/16-3/16
Postsecondary	San Diego-Carlsbad MSA, CA	H	21.27 FQ	31.02 MW	42.05 TQ	CABLS	1/16-3/16
Postsecondary	San Francisco-Redwood City-South San Francisco PMSA, CA	H	20.71 FQ	27.78 MW	41.28 TQ	CABLS	1/16-3/16
Postsecondary	Colorado	Y	35440 FQ	50170 MW	66540 TQ	USBLS	5/15
Postsecondary	Denver-Aurora-Lakewood MSA, CO	Y	40510 FQ	53950 MW	82800 TQ	USBLS	5/15
Postsecondary	Connecticut	Y		47103 MW		CTBLS	1/16-3/16
Postsecondary	Bridgeport-Stamford-Norwalk MSA, CT	Y	42590 FQ	50800 MW	59200 TQ	USBLS	5/15
Postsecondary	Hartford-West Hartford-East Hartford MSA, CT	Y	38330 FQ	45420 MW	53970 TQ	USBLS	5/15
Postsecondary	Delaware	Y	40490 FQ	53070 MW	63530 TQ	USBLS	5/15
Postsecondary	Wilmington PMSA, DE-MD-NJ	Y	40010 FQ	52190 MW	71300 TQ	USBLS	5/15
Postsecondary	District of Columbia	Y	40070 FQ	64270 MW	84720 TQ	USBLS	5/15
Postsecondary	Washington-Arlington-Alexandria PMSA, DC-VA-MD-WV	Y	41410 FQ	53560 MW	62990 TQ	USBLS	5/15
Postsecondary	Florida	H	15.01 AE	23.12 MW	31.28 AEX	FLBLS	7/16-9/16
Postsecondary	Fort Lauderdale-Pompano Beach-Deerfield Beach PMSA, FL	H	13.66 AE	21.37 MW	27.49 AEX	FLBLS	7/16-9/16
Postsecondary	Miami-Miami Beach-Kendall PMSA, FL	H	16.83 AE	29.32 MW	37.72 AEX	FLBLS	7/16-9/16
Postsecondary	Orlando-Kissimmee-Sanford MSA, FL	H	16.47 AE	26.52 MW	33.81 AEX	FLBLS	7/16-9/16
Postsecondary	Tampa-St. Petersburg-Clearwater MSA, FL	H	14.71 AE	20.47 MW	26.15 AEX	FLBLS	7/16-9/16
Postsecondary	Georgia	Y	38000 FQ	46760 MW	56530 TQ	USBLS	5/15
Postsecondary	Atlanta-Sandy Springs-Roswell MSA, GA	Y	40880 FQ	48700 MW	57350 TQ	USBLS	5/15
Postsecondary	Augusta-Richmond County MSA, GA-SC	Y	30910 FQ	42180 MW	58090 TQ	USBLS	5/15
Postsecondary	Hawaii	Y	32850 FQ	57740 MW	83270 TQ	USBLS	5/15
Postsecondary	Urban Honolulu MSA, HI	Y	34860 FQ	61750 MW	90670 TQ	USBLS	5/15
Postsecondary	Idaho	Y	28360 FQ	37260 MW	51240 TQ	USBLS	5/15
Postsecondary	Boise City MSA, ID	Y	27550 FQ	31510 MW	43260 TQ	USBLS	5/15
Postsecondary	Illinois	Y	29670 FQ	47830 MW	62950 TQ	USBLS	5/15

AE	Average entry wage	**AWR**	Average wage range	**H**	Hourly	**LR**	Low end range	**MTC** Median total compensation	**TCC** Total cash compensation
AEX	Average experienced wage	**B**	Biweekly	**HI**	Highest wage paid	**M**	Monthly	**MW** Median wage paid	**TQ** Third quartile wage
ATC	Average total compensation	**D**	Daily	**HR**	High end range	**MCC**	Median cash compensation	**MWR** Median wage range	**W** Weekly
AW	Average wage paid	**FQ**	First quartile wage	**LO**	Lowest wage paid	**ME**	Median entry wage	**S** See annotated source	**Y** Yearly

Occupation/Type/Industry	Location	Per	Low	Mid	High	Source	Date
Vocational Education Teacher							
Postsecondary	Chicago-Naperville-Arlington Heights PMSA, IL	Y	34700 FQ	48710 MW	61600 TQ	USBLS	5/15
Postsecondary	Lake County-Kenosha County PMSA, IL-WI	Y	47290 FQ	58350 MW	72480 TQ	USBLS	5/15
Postsecondary	Indiana	Y	37580 FQ	50930 MW	64280 TQ	USBLS	5/15
Postsecondary	Gary PMSA, IN	Y	40090 FQ	54680 MW	68080 TQ	USBLS	5/15
Postsecondary	Indianapolis-Carmel-Anderson MSA, IN	Y	39530 FQ	53580 MW	81120 TQ	USBLS	5/15
Postsecondary	Iowa	Y	37150 FQ	49090 MW	65210 TQ	USBLS	5/15
Postsecondary	Des Moines-West Des Moines MSA, IA	Y	41790 FQ	56520 MW	69260 TQ	USBLS	5/15
Postsecondary	Kansas	Y	35120 FQ	44690 MW	56010 TQ	USBLS	5/15
Postsecondary	Wichita MSA, KS	Y	35790 FQ	46230 MW	58290 TQ	USBLS	5/15
Postsecondary	Kentucky	Y	43020 FQ	48510 MW	57990 TQ	USBLS	5/15
Postsecondary	Louisville-Jefferson County MSA, KY-IN	Y	41940 FQ	50640 MW	58710 TQ	USBLS	5/15
Postsecondary	Louisiana	Y	31380 FQ	43280 MW	57570 TQ	USBLS	5/15
Postsecondary	New Orleans-Metairie MSA, LA	Y	40030 FQ	51840 MW	65930 TQ	USBLS	5/15
Postsecondary	Maine	Y	34280 FQ	44460 MW	56590 TQ	USBLS	5/15
Postsecondary	Portland-South Portland MSA, ME	Y	30500 FQ	37130 MW	47540 TQ	USBLS	5/15
Postsecondary	Maryland	Y	30686 AE	47679 MW	56175 AEX	MDBLS	4/16
Postsecondary	Baltimore-Columbia-Towson MSA, MD	Y	40630 FQ	49070 MW	60530 TQ	USBLS	5/15
Postsecondary	Salisbury MSA, MD-DE	Y	46430 FQ	61020 MW	70630 TQ	USBLS	5/15
Postsecondary	Massachusetts	Y	37920 FQ	50170 MW	70590 TQ	USBLS	5/15
Postsecondary	Boston-Cambridge-Newton NECTA, MA	Y	44510 FQ	57540 MW	80060 TQ	USBLS	5/15
Postsecondary	Worcester MSA, MA-CT	Y	31860 FQ	41070 MW	50180 TQ	USBLS	5/15
Postsecondary	Michigan	Y	32970 FQ	39630 MW	59700 TQ	USBLS	5/15
Postsecondary	Detroit-Dearborn-Livonia PMSA, MI	Y	36230 FQ	46480 MW	57860 TQ	USBLS	5/15
Postsecondary	Grand Rapids-Wyoming MSA, MI	Y	28100 FQ	33840 MW	40350 TQ	USBLS	5/15
Postsecondary	Minnesota	Y	36471 FQ	48638 MW	63114 TQ	MNBLS	1/16-3/16
Postsecondary	Minneapolis-St. Paul-Bloomington MSA, MN-WI	Y	37096 FQ	50987 MW	67691 TQ	MNBLS	1/16-3/16
Postsecondary	Mississippi	Y	37540 FQ	48690 MW	60390 TQ	USBLS	5/15
Postsecondary	Jackson MSA, MS	Y	38630 FQ	47920 MW	61370 TQ	USBLS	5/15
Postsecondary	Missouri	Y	32880 FQ	43340 MW	58120 TQ	USBLS	5/15
Postsecondary	Kansas City MSA, MO-KS	Y	35180 FQ	44900 MW	56520 TQ	USBLS	5/15
Postsecondary	St. Louis MSA, MO-IL	Y	23350 FQ	42220 MW	65880 TQ	USBLS	5/15
Postsecondary	Montana	Y	25790 FQ	37030 MW	50960 TQ	USBLS	5/15
Postsecondary	Billings MSA, MT	Y	19470 FQ	31640 MW	37280 TQ	USBLS	5/15
Postsecondary	Nebraska	Y	42560 FQ	56745 MW	75930 TQ	NEBLS	7/16-9/16
Postsecondary	Omaha-Council Bluffs MSA, NE-IA	Y	42960 FQ	72780 MW	104755 TQ	NEBLS	7/16-9/16
Postsecondary	Nevada	Y	36790 FQ	55870 MW	74530 TQ	USBLS	5/15
Postsecondary	Las Vegas-Henderson-Paradise MSA, NV	Y	36920 FQ	57860 MW	76220 TQ	USBLS	5/15
Postsecondary	New Hampshire	H	18.19 AE	26.17 MW	34.83 AEX	NHBLS	6/16
Postsecondary	Manchester NECTA, NH	H	16.85 AE	23.74 MW	31.16 AEX	NHBLS	6/16
Postsecondary	New Jersey	Y	45660 FQ	56050 MW	66520 TQ	USBLS	5/15
Postsecondary	Camden PMSA, NJ	Y	45580 FQ	56830 MW	69770 TQ	USBLS	5/15
Postsecondary	Newark PMSA, NJ-PA	Y	50950 FQ	58800 MW	69190 TQ	USBLS	5/15
Postsecondary	Trenton MSA, NJ	Y	53910 FQ	58270 MW	62630 TQ	USBLS	5/15
Postsecondary	New Mexico	Y	40660 FQ	55900 MW	70620 TQ	USBLS	5/15
Postsecondary	Albuquerque MSA, NM	Y	27210 FQ	51410 MW	71830 TQ	USBLS	5/15
Postsecondary	New York	Y	40310 AE	63080 MW	79130 AEX	NYBLS	1/16-3/16
Postsecondary	Buffalo-Cheektowaga-Niagara Falls MSA, NY	Y	44980 FQ	82610 MW	96970 TQ	USBLS	5/15
Postsecondary	Nassau County-Suffolk County PMSA, NY	Y	41700 FQ	52620 MW	70200 TQ	USBLS	5/15
Postsecondary	New York-Jersey City-White Plains PMSA, NY-NJ	Y	49340 FQ	64600 MW	82020 TQ	USBLS	5/15
Postsecondary	Rochester MSA, NY	Y	35630 FQ	48850 MW	65400 TQ	USBLS	5/15
Postsecondary	North Carolina	Y	41560 FQ	50760 MW	60300 TQ	USBLS	5/15
Postsecondary	Charlotte-Concord-Gastonia MSA, NC-SC	Y	48420 FQ	56770 MW	65460 TQ	USBLS	5/15
Postsecondary	Raleigh MSA, NC	Y	33350 FQ	38730 MW	54770 TQ	USBLS	5/15

AE Average entry wage	**AWR** Average wage range	**H** Hourly	**LR** Low end range	**MTC** Median total compensation	**TCC** Total cash compensation
AEX Average experienced wage	**B** Biweekly	**HI** Highest wage paid	**M** Monthly	**MW** Median wage paid	**TQ** Third quartile wage
ATC Average total compensation	**D** Daily	**HR** High end range	**MCC** Median cash compensation	**MWR** Median wage range	**W** Weekly
AW Average wage paid	**FQ** First quartile wage	**LO** Lowest wage paid	**ME** Median entry wage	**S** See annotated source	**Y** Yearly

Vocational Education Teacher

Occupation/Type/Industry	Location	Per	Low	Mid	High	Source	Date
Postsecondary	North Dakota	Y	38300 FQ	46400 MW	57070 TQ	USBLS	5/15
Postsecondary	Ohio	Y	32100 FQ	43530 MW	58630 TQ	USBLS	5/15
Postsecondary	Cincinnati MSA, OH-KY-IN	Y	30630 FQ	42940 MW	54460 TQ	USBLS	5/15
Postsecondary	Cleveland-Elyria MSA, OH	Y	23250 FQ	35960 MW	58750 TQ	USBLS	5/15
Postsecondary	Columbus MSA, OH	Y	39580 FQ	50990 MW	83740 TQ	USBLS	5/15
Postsecondary	Oklahoma	Y	44520 FQ	55370 MW	71550 TQ	USBLS	5/15
Postsecondary	Oklahoma City MSA, OK	Y	49980 FQ	67460 MW	90200 TQ	USBLS	5/15
Postsecondary	Tulsa MSA, OK	Y	40180 FQ	49490 MW	63130 TQ	USBLS	5/15
Postsecondary	Oregon	H	17.88 FQ	22.84 MW	35.72 TQ	ORBLS	2016
Postsecondary	Portland-Vancouver-Hillsboro MSA, OR-WA	Y	38330 FQ	47620 MW	78590 TQ	USBLS	5/15
Postsecondary	Pennsylvania	Y	36720 FQ	51520 MW	71590 TQ	USBLS	5/15
Postsecondary	Allentown-Bethlehem-Easton MSA, PA-NJ	Y	36950 FQ	46240 MW	59380 TQ	USBLS	5/15
Postsecondary	Harrisburg-Carlisle MSA, PA	Y	45450 FQ	63340 MW	74320 TQ	USBLS	5/15
Postsecondary	Montgomery County-Bucks County-Chester County PMSA, PA	Y	38290 FQ	45980 MW	55380 TQ	USBLS	5/15
Postsecondary	Philadelphia PMSA, PA	Y	30900 FQ	38150 MW	67370 TQ	USBLS	5/15
Postsecondary	Pittsburgh MSA, PA	Y	36930 FQ	53880 MW	85990 TQ	USBLS	5/15
Postsecondary	Rhode Island	Y	41650 FQ	59570 MW	82560 TQ	USBLS	5/15
Postsecondary	Providence-Warwick MSA, RI-MA	Y	44010 FQ	59230 MW	77810 TQ	USBLS	5/15
Postsecondary	South Carolina	Y	37130 FQ	49900 MW	64830 TQ	USBLS	5/15
Postsecondary	Charleston-North Charleston MSA, SC	Y	50340 FQ	62510 MW	72820 TQ	USBLS	5/15
Postsecondary	Columbia MSA, SC	Y	31800 FQ	38390 MW	45370 TQ	USBLS	5/15
Postsecondary	Greenville-Anderson-Mauldin MSA, SC	Y	32330 FQ	44990 MW	60450 TQ	USBLS	5/15
Postsecondary	South Dakota	Y	42680 FQ	49120 MW	58100 TQ	USBLS	5/15
Postsecondary	Tennessee	Y	31900 FQ	41070 MW	51080 TQ	USBLS	5/15
Postsecondary	Knoxville MSA, TN	Y	23210 FQ	35050 MW	46110 TQ	USBLS	5/15
Postsecondary	Memphis MSA, TN-MS-AR	Y	35470 FQ	50280 MW	58890 TQ	USBLS	5/15
Postsecondary	Nashville-Davidson–Murfreesboro–Franklin MSA, TN	Y	32420 FQ	41140 MW	47960 TQ	USBLS	5/15
Postsecondary	Texas	Y	31910 FQ	47730 MW	68430 TQ	USBLS	5/15
Postsecondary	Austin-Round Rock MSA, TX	Y	38990 FQ	49220 MW	60960 TQ	USBLS	5/15
Postsecondary	Dallas-Plano-Irving PMSA, TX	Y	29430 FQ	46980 MW	76230 TQ	USBLS	5/15
Postsecondary	Fort Worth-Arlington PMSA, TX	Y	43810 FQ	68210 MW	84360 TQ	USBLS	5/15
Postsecondary	Houston-The Woodlands-Sugar Land MSA, TX	Y	34900 FQ	55490 MW	74340 TQ	USBLS	5/15
Postsecondary	San Antonio-New Braunfels MSA, TX	Y	30040 FQ	36140 MW	46010 TQ	USBLS	5/15
Postsecondary	Utah	Y	28300 FQ	42670 MW	59090 TQ	USBLS	5/15
Postsecondary	Ogden-Clearfield MSA, UT	Y	35930 FQ	46300 MW	67340 TQ	USBLS	5/15
Postsecondary	Provo-Orem MSA, UT	Y	19210 FQ	45770 MW	70710 TQ	USBLS	5/15
Postsecondary	Salt Lake City MSA, UT	Y	24360 FQ	35420 MW	47280 TQ	USBLS	5/15
Postsecondary	Vermont	Y	37190 FQ	57350 MW	78410 TQ	USBLS	5/15
Postsecondary	Burlington-South Burlington MSA, VT	Y	35230 FQ	39510 MW	79060 TQ	USBLS	5/15
Postsecondary	Virginia	Y	39430 FQ	48090 MW	57770 TQ	USBLS	5/15
Postsecondary	Richmond MSA, VA	Y	38420 FQ	48080 MW	51500 TQ	USBLS	5/15
Postsecondary	Virginia Beach-Norfolk-Newport News MSA, VA-NC	Y	35460 FQ	45180 MW	55930 TQ	USBLS	5/15
Postsecondary	Washington	H	20.83 FQ	26.60 MW	32.97 TQ	WABLS	3/16
Postsecondary	Seattle-Bellevue-Everett PMSA, WA	H	22.56 FQ	27.78 MW	35.75 TQ	WABLS	3/16
Postsecondary	Tacoma-Lakewood PMSA, WA	H	20.75 FQ	25.94 MW	31.09 TQ	WABLS	3/16
Postsecondary	West Virginia	Y	39880 FQ	47490 MW	57350 TQ	USBLS	5/15
Postsecondary	Huntington-Ashland MSA, WV-KY-OH	Y	42380 FQ	46140 MW	49910 TQ	USBLS	5/15
Postsecondary	Wisconsin	Y	50120 FQ	66490 MW	83670 TQ	USBLS	5/15
Postsecondary	Madison MSA, WI	Y	52220 FQ	64330 MW	86700 TQ	USBLS	5/15
Postsecondary	Milwaukee-Waukesha-West Allis MSA, WI	Y	38780 FQ	80450 MW	92790 TQ	USBLS	5/15
Postsecondary	Wyoming	Y	30810 FQ	37750 MW	60830 TQ	USBLS	5/15
Postsecondary	Puerto Rico	Y	25560 FQ	29140 MW	33850 TQ	USBLS	5/15
Postsecondary	San Juan-Carolina-Caguas MSA, PR	Y	26000 FQ	29500 MW	34350 TQ	USBLS	5/15

AE	Average entry wage	AWR	Average wage range	H	Hourly
AEX	Average experienced wage	B	Biweekly	HI	Highest wage paid
ATC	Average total compensation	D	Daily	HR	High end range
AW	Average wage paid	FQ	First quartile wage	LO	Lowest wage paid

LR	Low end range	MTC	Median total compensation
M	Monthly	MW	Median wage paid
MCC	Median cash compensation	MWR	Median wage range
ME	Median entry wage	S	See annotated source

TCC	Total cash compensation
TQ	Third quartile wage
W	Weekly
Y	Yearly

Occupation/Type/Industry	Location	Per	Low	Mid	High	Source	Date
Vote Machine Mechanic							
County Government	Boone County, IN	Y			34957 HI	INDYS	2017
Voter Registration Investigator							
Municipal Government	Detroit, MI	M	2525 LO		2742 HI	DETGOV	2016
Waiter and Waitress	Alabama	Y	17483 AE	19954 AW	21189 AEX	ALBLS	6/16
	Birmingham-Hoover MSA, AL	Y	17524 AE	20582 AW	22116 AEX	ALBLS	6/16
	Alaska	Y	19320 FQ	22220	34990 TQ	USBLS	5/15
	Anchorage MSA, AK	Y	19330 FQ	22800 MW	38450 TQ	USBLS	5/15
	Arizona	Y	17760 FQ	18760 MW	20850 TQ	USBLS	5/15
	Phoenix-Mesa-Scottsdale MSA, AZ	Y	17780 FQ	18780 MW	21560 TQ	USBLS	5/15
	Tucson MSA, AZ	Y	17720 FQ	18660 MW	19760 TQ	USBLS	5/15
	Arkansas	Y	16750 FQ	17890 MW	19030 TQ	USBLS	5/15
	Little Rock-North Little Rock-Conway MSA, AR	Y	16780 FQ	17930 MW	19090 TQ	USBLS	5/15
	California	H	9.59 FQ	11.41 MW	16.30 TQ	CABLS	1/16-3/16
	Anaheim-Santa Ana-Irvine PMSA, CA	H	9.51 FQ	10.54 MW	16.52 TQ	CABLS	1/16-3/16
	Los Angeles-Long Beach-Glendale PMSA, CA	H	9.52 FQ	11.05 MW	16.43 TQ	CABLS	1/16-3/16
	Oakland-Hayward-Berkeley PMSA, CA	H	9.54 FQ	10.88 MW	14.98 TQ	CABLS	1/16-3/16
	Riverside-San Bernardino-Ontario MSA, CA	H	9.48 FQ	10.09 MW	13.39 TQ	CABLS	1/16-3/16
	Sacramento–Roseville–Arden-Arcade MSA, CA	H	9.55 FQ	11.50 MW	16.96 TQ	CABLS	1/16-3/16
	San Diego-Carlsbad MSA, CA	H	9.64 FQ	12.24 MW	19.01 TQ	CABLS	1/16-3/16
	San Francisco-Redwood City-South San Francisco PMSA, CA	H	11.21 FQ	13.38 MW	17.63 TQ	CABLS	1/16-3/16
	Colorado	Y	17940 FQ	18760 MW	19740 TQ	USBLS	5/15
	Denver-Aurora-Lakewood MSA, CO	Y	17900 FQ	18680 MW	19520 TQ	USBLS	5/15
	Connecticut	Y		19936 MW		CTBLS	1/16-3/16
	Bridgeport-Stamford-Norwalk MSA, CT	Y	19280 FQ	19660 MW	23410 TQ	USBLS	5/15
	Hartford-West Hartford-East Hartford MSA, CT	Y	19210 FQ	19520 MW	22170 TQ	USBLS	5/15
	Delaware	Y	17890 FQ	19470 MW	23430 TQ	USBLS	5/15
	Wilmington PMSA, DE-MD-NJ	Y	17910 FQ	19310 MW	23040 TQ	USBLS	5/15
	District of Columbia	Y	19910 FQ	19930 MW	24110 TQ	USBLS	5/15
	Washington-Arlington-Alexandria PMSA, DC-VA-MD-WV	Y	18750 FQ	20030 MW	27120 TQ	USBLS	5/15
	Florida	H	9.01 AE	9.67 MW	13.92 AEX	FLBLS	7/16-9/16
	Fort Lauderdale-Pompano Beach-Deerfield Beach PMSA, FL	H	9.01 AE	9.63 MW	13.87 AEX	FLBLS	7/16-9/16
	Miami-Miami Beach-Kendall PMSA, FL	H	9.01 AE	9.56 MW	12.81 AEX	FLBLS	7/16-9/16
	Orlando-Kissimmee-Sanford MSA, FL	H	9.00 AE	9.74 MW	15.42 AEX	FLBLS	7/16-9/16
	Tampa-St. Petersburg-Clearwater MSA, FL	H	9.01 AE	9.60 MW	13.18 AEX	FLBLS	7/16-9/16
	Georgia	Y	16730 FQ	18040 MW	19360 TQ	USBLS	5/15
	Atlanta-Sandy Springs-Roswell MSA, GA	Y	16760 FQ	18090 MW	19450 TQ	USBLS	5/15
	Augusta-Richmond County MSA, GA-SC	Y	16880 FQ	18340 MW	20330 TQ	USBLS	5/15
	Hawaii	Y	18320 FQ	24090 MW	44080 TQ	USBLS	5/15
	Urban Honolulu MSA, HI	Y	18240 FQ	23910 MW	40800 TQ	USBLS	5/15
	Idaho	Y	16910 FQ	18380 MW	20750 TQ	USBLS	5/15
	Boise City MSA, ID	Y	17000 FQ	18550 MW	21840 TQ	USBLS	5/15
	Illinois	Y	18230 FQ	18920 MW	19760 TQ	USBLS	5/15
	Chicago-Naperville-Arlington Heights PMSA, IL	Y	18230 FQ	18920 MW	19760 TQ	USBLS	5/15
	Lake County-Kenosha County PMSA, IL-WI	Y	18080 FQ	18840 MW	19880 TQ	USBLS	5/15
	Indiana	Y	16990 FQ	18560 MW	22000 TQ	USBLS	5/15

AE	Average entry wage	AWR	Average wage range	
AEX	Average experienced wage	B	Biweekly	
ATC	Average total compensation	D	Daily	
AW	Average wage paid	FQ	First quartile wage	

H	Hourly	LR	Low end range	
HI	Highest wage paid	M	Monthly	
HR	High end range	MCC	Median cash compensation	
LO	Lowest wage paid	ME	Median entry wage	

MTC	Median total compensation	TCC	Total cash compensation	
MW	Median wage paid	TQ	Third quartile wage	
MWR	Median wage range	W	Weekly	
S	See annotated source	Y	Yearly	

Occupation/Type/Industry	Location	Per	Low	Mid	High	Source	Date
Waiter and Waitress	Gary PMSA, IN	Y	16890 FQ	18380 MW	21110 TQ	USBLS	5/15
	Indianapolis-Carmel-Anderson MSA, IN	Y	17010 FQ	18640 MW	22750 TQ	USBLS	5/15
	Iowa	Y	16750 FQ	18090 MW	19460 TQ	USBLS	5/15
	Des Moines-West Des Moines MSA, IA	Y	16840 FQ	18210 MW	19630 TQ	USBLS	5/15
	Kansas	Y	16820 FQ	18190 MW	19640 TQ	USBLS	5/15
	Wichita MSA, KS	Y	16850 FQ	18230 MW	19660 TQ	USBLS	5/15
	Kentucky	Y	16770 FQ	18090 MW	19460 TQ	USBLS	5/15
	Louisville-Jefferson County MSA, KY-IN	Y	16850 FQ	18280 MW	19920 TQ	USBLS	5/15
	Louisiana	Y	16640 FQ	17870 MW	19100 TQ	USBLS	5/15
	Baton Rouge MSA, LA	Y	16660 FQ	17910 MW	19160 TQ	USBLS	5/15
	New Orleans-Metairie MSA, LA	Y	16640 FQ	17880 MW	19120 TQ	USBLS	5/15
	Maine	Y	17420 FQ	18850 MW	24120 TQ	USBLS	5/15
	Portland-South Portland MSA, ME	Y	17160 FQ	18380 MW	19730 TQ	USBLS	5/15
	Maryland	Y	18062 AE	22794 MW	25160 AEX	MDBLS	4/16
	Baltimore-Columbia-Towson MSA, MD	Y	17760 FQ	18890 MW	24030 TQ	USBLS	5/15
	Salisbury MSA, MD-DE	Y	17840 FQ	19150 MW	24570 TQ	USBLS	5/15
	Massachusetts	Y	19190 FQ	21650 MW	31240 TQ	USBLS	5/15
	Boston-Cambridge-Newton NECTA, MA	Y	19250 FQ	25760 MW	34520 TQ	USBLS	5/15
	Worcester MSA, MA-CT	Y	19310 FQ	21830 MW	30060 TQ	USBLS	5/15
	Michigan	Y	17960 FQ	18880 MW	21470 TQ	USBLS	5/15
	Detroit-Dearborn-Livonia PMSA, MI	Y	17920 FQ	18800 MW	21070 TQ	USBLS	5/15
	Grand Rapids-Wyoming MSA, MI	Y	18020 FQ	18990 MW	22400 TQ	USBLS	5/15
	Minnesota	Y	17854 FQ	18804 MW	19834 TQ	MNBLS	1/16-3/16
	Minneapolis-St. Paul-Bloomington MSA, MN-WI	Y	17885 FQ	18874 MW	20036 TQ	MNBLS	1/16-3/16
	Mississippi	Y	16800 FQ	18180 MW	19670 TQ	USBLS	5/15
	Jackson MSA, MS	Y	17130 FQ	18840 MW	22750 TQ	USBLS	5/15
	Missouri	Y	17120 FQ	18310 MW	19560 TQ	USBLS	5/15
	Kansas City MSA, MO-KS	Y	17150 FQ	18580 MW	21450 TQ	USBLS	5/15
	St. Louis MSA, MO-IL	Y	17310 FQ	18420 MW	19480 TQ	USBLS	5/15
	Montana	Y	17690 FQ	18600 MW	19650 TQ	USBLS	5/15
	Billings MSA, MT	Y	17800 FQ	18830 MW	22580 TQ	USBLS	5/15
	Nebraska	Y	17540 FQ	18440 MW	19360 TQ	NEBLS	7/16-9/16
	Omaha-Council Bluffs MSA, NE-IA	Y	17455 FQ	18415 MW	19400 TQ	NEBLS	7/16-9/16
	Nevada	Y	17540 FQ	19710 MW	27420 TQ	USBLS	5/15
	Las Vegas-Henderson-Paradise MSA, NV	Y	17930 FQ	21900 MW	28090 TQ	USBLS	5/15
	New Hampshire	H	8.42 AE	9.44 MW	13.59 AEX	NHBLS	6/16
	Manchester NECTA, NH	H	8.42 AE	9.71 MW	14.16 AEX	NHBLS	6/16
	Nashua NECTA, NH-MA	Y	16830 FQ	18300 MW	22090 TQ	USBLS	5/15
	New Jersey	Y	19010 FQ	21320 MW	25020 TQ	USBLS	5/15
	Camden PMSA, NJ	Y	18730 FQ	19890 MW	23040 TQ	USBLS	5/15
	Newark PMSA, NJ-PA	Y	19120 FQ	21850 MW	26660 TQ	USBLS	5/15
	Trenton MSA, NJ	Y	18340 FQ	19210 MW	23590 TQ	USBLS	5/15
	New Mexico	Y	17280 FQ	18690 MW	23310 TQ	USBLS	5/15
	Albuquerque MSA, NM	Y	17340 FQ	18780 MW	23650 TQ	USBLS	5/15
	New York	Y	19290 AE	20740 MW	33070 AEX	NYBLS	1/16-3/16
	Buffalo-Cheektowaga-Niagara Falls MSA, NY	Y	18810 FQ	19450 MW	26130 TQ	USBLS	5/15
	Nassau County-Suffolk County PMSA, NY	Y	19050 FQ	20950 MW	30750 TQ	USBLS	5/15
	New York-Jersey City-White Plains PMSA, NY-NJ	Y	19080 FQ	22160 MW	32760 TQ	USBLS	5/15
	Rochester MSA, NY	Y	19010 FQ	20340 MW	25920 TQ	USBLS	5/15
	North Carolina	Y	16890 FQ	18350 MW	20450 TQ	USBLS	5/15
	Charlotte-Concord-Gastonia MSA, NC-SC	Y	17030 FQ	18640 MW	22610 TQ	USBLS	5/15
	Raleigh MSA, NC	Y	16900 FQ	18400 MW	23250 TQ	USBLS	5/15
	North Dakota	Y	17100 FQ	18780 MW	23090 TQ	USBLS	5/15
	Fargo MSA, ND-MN	Y	16980 FQ	18330 MW	19990 TQ	USBLS	5/15
	Ohio	Y	17770 FQ	18660 MW	19670 TQ	USBLS	5/15
	Cincinnati MSA, OH-KY-IN	Y	17590 FQ	18500 MW	19460 TQ	USBLS	5/15

AE	Average entry wage	AWR	Average wage range	H	Hourly	LR	Low end range	MTC	Median total compensation	TCC	Total cash compensation
AEX	Average experienced wage	B	Biweekly	HI	Highest wage paid	M	Monthly	MW	Median wage paid	TQ	Third quartile wage
ATC	Average total compensation	D	Daily	HR	High end range	MCC	Median cash compensation	MWR	Median wage range	W	Weekly
AW	Average wage paid	FQ	First quartile wage	LO	Lowest wage paid	ME	Median entry wage	S	See annotated source	Y	Yearly

Occupation/Type/Industry	Location	Per	Low	Mid	High	Source	Date
Waiter and Waitress	Cleveland-Elyria MSA, OH	Y	17830 FQ	18790 MW	21330 TQ	USBLS	5/15
	Columbus MSA, OH	Y	17900 FQ	18910 MW	22010 TQ	USBLS	5/15
	Oklahoma	Y	17000 FQ	18560 MW	21880 TQ	USBLS	5/15
	Oklahoma City MSA, OK	Y	17280 FQ	19150 MW	23920 TQ	USBLS	5/15
	Tulsa MSA, OK	Y	16870 FQ	18280 MW	19850 TQ	USBLS	5/15
	Oregon	H	9.57 FQ	9.73 MW	11.39 TQ	ORBLS	2016
	Portland-Vancouver-Hillsboro MSA, OR-WA	Y	19570 FQ	19970 MW	23800 TQ	USBLS	5/15
	Pennsylvania	Y	17250 FQ	19070 MW	22920 TQ	USBLS	5/15
	Allentown-Bethlehem-Easton MSA, PA-NJ	Y	17600 FQ	19610 MW	23850 TQ	USBLS	5/15
	Harrisburg-Carlisle MSA, PA	Y	17120 FQ	18780 MW	21770 TQ	USBLS	5/15
	Montgomery County-Bucks County-Chester County PMSA, PA	Y	17640 FQ	19910 MW	24210 TQ	USBLS	5/15
	Philadelphia PMSA, PA	Y	17590 FQ	19760 MW	23880 TQ	USBLS	5/15
	Pittsburgh MSA, PA	Y	17120 FQ	18840 MW	22300 TQ	USBLS	5/15
	Rhode Island	Y	19040 FQ	19380 MW	20440 TQ	USBLS	5/15
	Providence-Warwick MSA, RI-MA	Y	19060 FQ	19430 MW	21460 TQ	USBLS	5/15
	South Carolina	Y	16820 FQ	18220 MW	19780 TQ	USBLS	5/15
	Charleston-North Charleston MSA, SC	Y	17170 FQ	18890 MW	26410 TQ	USBLS	5/15
	Columbia MSA, SC	Y	16680 FQ	17940 MW	19200 TQ	USBLS	5/15
	Greenville-Anderson-Mauldin MSA, SC	Y	16770 FQ	18090 MW	19430 TQ	USBLS	5/15
	South Dakota	Y	18370 FQ	19050 MW	20010 TQ	USBLS	5/15
	Sioux Falls MSA, SD	Y	18390 FQ	19110 MW	20520 TQ	USBLS	5/15
	Tennessee	Y	16710 FQ	18000 MW	19290 TQ	USBLS	5/15
	Knoxville MSA, TN	Y	16810 FQ	18140 MW	19520 TQ	USBLS	5/15
	Memphis MSA, TN-MS-AR	Y	16680 FQ	17930 MW	19180 TQ	USBLS	5/15
	Nashville-Davidson–Murfreesboro–Franklin MSA, TN	Y	16700 FQ	17980 MW	19270 TQ	USBLS	5/15
	Texas	Y	17000 FQ	18560 MW	23620 TQ	USBLS	5/15
	Austin-Round Rock MSA, TX	Y	17310 FQ	19150 MW	26850 TQ	USBLS	5/15
	Dallas-Plano-Irving PMSA, TX	Y	17150 FQ	18810 MW	28310 TQ	USBLS	5/15
	Fort Worth-Arlington PMSA, TX	Y	16850 FQ	18280 MW	19910 TQ	USBLS	5/15
	Houston-The Woodlands-Sugar Land MSA, TX	Y	17050 FQ	18640 MW	24450 TQ	USBLS	5/15
	San Antonio-New Braunfels MSA, TX	Y	17240 FQ	19030 MW	27610 TQ	USBLS	5/15
	Utah	Y	17650 FQ	20560 MW	27890 TQ	USBLS	5/15
	Ogden-Clearfield MSA, UT	Y	17430 FQ	19470 MW	24320 TQ	USBLS	5/15
	Provo-Orem MSA, UT	Y	17140 FQ	18880 MW	24550 TQ	USBLS	5/15
	Salt Lake City MSA, UT	Y	17920 FQ	21840 MW	29120 TQ	USBLS	5/15
	Vermont	Y	20700 FQ	27570 MW	36340 TQ	USBLS	5/15
	Burlington-South Burlington MSA, VT	Y	21120 FQ	25400 MW	32560 TQ	USBLS	5/15
	Virginia	Y	17850 FQ	20850 MW	26340 TQ	USBLS	5/15
	Richmond MSA, VA	Y	17520 FQ	19810 MW	23480 TQ	USBLS	5/15
	Virginia Beach-Norfolk-Newport News MSA, VA-NC	Y	18100 FQ	21680 MW	28640 TQ	USBLS	5/15
	Washington	H	10.04 FQ	11.70 MW	17.51 TQ	WABLS	3/16
	Seattle-Bellevue-Everett PMSA, WA	H	10.28 FQ	12.32 MW	18.98 TQ	WABLS	3/16
	Tacoma-Lakewood PMSA, WA	H	9.94 FQ	11.20 MW	14.32 TQ	WABLS	3/16
	West Virginia	Y	17850 FQ	19050 MW	24130 TQ	USBLS	5/15
	Huntington-Ashland MSA, WV-KY-OH	Y	17490 FQ	18640 MW	20550 TQ	USBLS	5/15
	Wisconsin	Y	16880 FQ	18330 MW	20350 TQ	USBLS	5/15
	Madison MSA, WI	Y	18210 FQ	22940 MW	34120 TQ	USBLS	5/15
	Milwaukee-Waukesha-West Allis MSA, WI	Y	16820 FQ	18210 MW	19770 TQ	USBLS	5/15
	Wyoming	Y	16810 FQ	18200 MW	19720 TQ	USBLS	5/15
	Cheyenne MSA, WY	Y	16940 FQ	18430 MW	22770 TQ	USBLS	5/15
	Puerto Rico	Y	16490 FQ	17590 MW	18690 TQ	USBLS	5/15
	San Juan-Carolina-Caguas MSA, PR	Y	16500 FQ	17590 MW	18690 TQ	USBLS	5/15
	Virgin Islands	Y	16950 FQ	18510 MW	22500 TQ	USBLS	5/15
	Guam	Y	17850 FQ	18540 MW	19220 TQ	USBLS	5/15

AE	Average entry wage	AWR	Average wage range	H	Hourly
AEX	Average experienced wage	B	Biweekly	HI	Highest wage paid
ATC	Average total compensation	D	Daily	HR	High end range
AW	Average wage paid	FQ	First quartile wage	LO	Lowest wage paid

LR	Low end range	MTC	Median total compensation
M	Monthly	MW	Median wage paid
MCC	Median cash compensation	MWR	Median wage range
ME	Median entry wage	S	See annotated source

TCC	Total cash compensation
TQ	Third quartile wage
W	Weekly
Y	Yearly

Occupation/Type/Industry	Location	Per	Low	Mid	High	Source	Date
Wardrobe Specialist							
Convention/Sports/Entertainment							
Department, Municipal Government	Anaheim, CA	Y			43851 HI	CACIT	6/28/16
Warrant Officer							
Military, Active Duty, Pay Grade W-1	United States	M	7436 LO		9731 HI	DOD1	2017
Military, Active Duty, Pay Grade W-2	United States	M	4182 LO		7790 HI	DOD1	2017
Military, Active Duty, Pay Grade W-3	United States	M	3819 LO		6699 HI	DOD1	2017
Military, Active Duty, Pay Grade W-4	United States	M	3380 LO		5641 HI	DOD1	2017
Military, Active Duty, Pay Grade W-5	United States	M	2966 LO		5126 HI	DOD1	2017
Military, Reserve, 4-Drill Pay Grade W-1	United States	S	2966 LO		5126 HI	DOD1	2017
Military, Reserve, 4-Drill Pay Grade W-2	United States	S	3380 LO		5641 HI	DOD1	2017
Military, Reserve, 4-Drill Pay Grade W-3	United States	S	3819 LO		6699 HI	DOD1	2017
Military, Reserve, 4-Drill Pay Grade W-4	United States	S	4182 LO		7790 HI	DOD1	2017
Military, Reserve, 4-Drill Pay Grade W-5	United States	S	7436 LO		9731 HI	DOD1	2017
Wastewater Reclamation Coordinator							
Public Utilities, Municipal Government	Fresno, CA	Y			52545 HI	CACIT	6/28/16
Wastewater Residuals Research Engineer							
Municipal Government	Los Angeles, CA	Y			57125 HI	CACIT	6/23/16
Watch Repairer	Alabama	Y	28476 AE	36684 AW	40793 AEX	ALBLS	6/16
	Arizona	Y	22590 FQ	25050 MW	28270 TQ	USBLS	5/15
	Phoenix-Mesa-Scottsdale MSA, AZ	Y	22750 FQ	25430 MW	28480 TQ	USBLS	5/15
	California	H	10.17 FQ	17.69 MW	24.58 TQ	CABLS	1/16-3/16
	Colorado	Y	30320 FQ	38620 MW	44810 TQ	USBLS	5/15
	Denver-Aurora-Lakewood MSA, CO	Y	32490 FQ	41480 MW	45920 TQ	USBLS	5/15
	Connecticut	Y		38188 MW		CTBLS	1/16-3/16
	Florida	H	9.13 AE	12.34 MW	18.60 AEX	FLBLS	7/16-9/16
	Orlando-Kissimmee-Sanford MSA, FL	H	11.16 AE	12.19 MW	14.16 AEX	FLBLS	7/16-9/16
	Illinois	Y	26130 FQ	34240 MW	43370 TQ	USBLS	5/15
	Michigan	Y	24020 FQ	42920 MW	55970 TQ	USBLS	5/15
	New Jersey	Y	41160 FQ	45220 MW	49280 TQ	USBLS	5/15
	New York	Y	27130 AE	37110 MW	51380 AEX	NYBLS	1/16-3/16
	New York-Jersey City-White Plains PMSA, NY-NJ	Y	31600 FQ	42090 MW	58760 TQ	USBLS	5/15
	North Carolina	Y	19100 FQ	28430 MW	42360 TQ	USBLS	5/15
	Ohio	Y	30870 FQ	35770 MW	39910 TQ	USBLS	5/15
	Oregon	H	20.42 FQ	23.95 MW	28.53 TQ	ORBLS	2016
	Pennsylvania	Y	28650 FQ	41660 MW	51270 TQ	USBLS	5/15
	Texas	Y	45530 FQ	56660 MW	76590 TQ	USBLS	5/15
	Virginia	Y	28230 FQ	38120 MW	45250 TQ	USBLS	5/15
Water and Wastewater Laboratory Technician							
Municipal Government	Buford, GA	H	12.00 LO		28.00 HI	GACTY02	2016
Municipal Government	Gainesville, GA	H	12.54 LO		19.44 HI	GACTY02	2016
Municipal Government	Lula, GA	H	15.00 LO		18.00 HI	GACTY02	2016
Water and Wastewater Treatment Plant and System Operator	Alabama	Y	33129 AE	45211 AW	51257 AEX	ALBLS	6/16
	Birmingham-Hoover MSA, AL	Y	36759 AE	46784 AW	51791 AEX	ALBLS	6/16
	Alaska	Y	44490 FQ	57860 MW	73280 TQ	USBLS	5/15
	Anchorage MSA, AK	Y	64910 FQ	76020 MW	88370 TQ	USBLS	5/15
	Arizona	Y	37980 FQ	45630 MW	55040 TQ	USBLS	5/15
	Phoenix-Mesa-Scottsdale MSA, AZ	Y	41270 FQ	49140 MW	59670 TQ	USBLS	5/15
	Tucson MSA, AZ	Y	38040 FQ	43630 MW	48620 TQ	USBLS	5/15
	Arkansas	Y	24450 FQ	31690 MW	38650 TQ	USBLS	5/15
	Little Rock-North Little Rock-Conway MSA, AR	Y	28510 FQ	36640 MW	47880 TQ	USBLS	5/15
	California	H	25.15 FQ	31.30 MW	39.04 TQ	CABLS	1/16-3/16
	Anaheim-Santa Ana-Irvine PMSA, CA	H	29.38 FQ	35.39 MW	42.44 TQ	CABLS	1/16-3/16

AE	Average entry wage	AWR	Average wage range	H	Hourly	LR	Low end range	MTC	Median total compensation	TCC	Total cash compensation
AEX	Average experienced wage	B	Biweekly	HI	Highest wage paid	M	Monthly	MCC	Median cash compensation	MWR	Median wage range	TQ	Third quartile wage
ATC	Average total compensation	D	Daily	HR	High end range	MCC	Median cash compensation	MWR	Median wage range	W	Weekly
AW	Average wage paid	FQ	First quartile wage	LO	Lowest wage paid	ME	Median entry wage	S	See annotated source	Y	Yearly

Occupation/Type/Industry	Location	Per	Low	Mid	High	Source	Date
Water and Wastewater Treatment Plant and System Operator	Los Angeles-Long Beach-Glendale PMSA, CA	H	28.90 FQ	38.06 MW	46.37 TQ	CABLS	1/16-3/16
	Oakland-Hayward-Berkeley PMSA, CA	H	33.51 FQ	42.93 MW	51.38 TQ	CABLS	1/16-3/16
	Redding MSA, CA	H	18.64 FQ	26.26 MW	33.09 TQ	CABLS	1/16-3/16
	Riverside-San Bernardino-Ontario MSA, CA	H	24.79 FQ	30.05 MW	36.63 TQ	CABLS	1/16-3/16
	Sacramento–Roseville–Arden-Arcade MSA, CA	H	27.90 FQ	32.93 MW	37.54 TQ	CABLS	1/16-3/16
	San Diego-Carlsbad MSA, CA	H	23.10 FQ	27.57 MW	32.56 TQ	CABLS	1/16-3/16
	San Francisco-Redwood City-South San Francisco PMSA, CA	H	30.20 FQ	35.43 MW	42.21 TQ	CABLS	1/16-3/16
	Colorado	Y	40180 FQ	50830 MW	61880 TQ	USBLS	5/15
	Denver-Aurora-Lakewood MSA, CO	Y	44040 FQ	54680 MW	63490 TQ	USBLS	5/15
	Connecticut	Y		62419 MW		CTBLS	1/16-3/16
	Bridgeport-Stamford-Norwalk MSA, CT	Y	52470 FQ	60790 MW	71300 TQ	USBLS	5/15
	Hartford-West Hartford-East Hartford MSA, CT	Y	54980 FQ	61350 MW	72010 TQ	USBLS	5/15
	Delaware	Y	36600 FQ	45970 MW	56130 TQ	USBLS	5/15
	Wilmington PMSA, DE-MD-NJ	Y	44980 FQ	55360 MW	67180 TQ	USBLS	5/15
	District of Columbia	Y	35440 FQ	53110 MW	62980 TQ	USBLS	5/15
	Washington-Arlington-Alexandria PMSA, DC-VA-MD-WV	Y	39990 FQ	50290 MW	62970 TQ	USBLS	5/15
	Florida	H	16.39 AE	22.48 MW	26.63 AEX	FLBLS	7/16-9/16
	Fort Lauderdale-Pompano Beach-Deerfield Beach PMSA, FL	H	19.35 AE	24.59 MW	28.64 AEX	FLBLS	7/16-9/16
	Miami-Miami Beach-Kendall PMSA, FL	H	18.61 AE	25.49 MW	30.60 AEX	FLBLS	7/16-9/16
	Orlando-Kissimmee-Sanford MSA, FL	H	16.28 AE	21.94 MW	26.57 AEX	FLBLS	7/16-9/16
	Tampa-St. Petersburg-Clearwater MSA, FL	H	16.79 AE	20.42 MW	23.44 AEX	FLBLS	7/16-9/16
	Georgia	Y	29970 FQ	36030 MW	43980 TQ	USBLS	5/15
	Atlanta-Sandy Springs-Roswell MSA, GA	Y	32100 FQ	39120 MW	47400 TQ	USBLS	5/15
	Augusta-Richmond County MSA, GA-SC	Y	45920 FQ	82790 MW	91050 TQ	USBLS	5/15
	Hawaii	Y	42950 FQ	48700 MW	56680 TQ	USBLS	5/15
	Urban Honolulu MSA, HI	Y	44040 FQ	50480 MW	59040 TQ	USBLS	5/15
	Idaho	Y	32060 FQ	38250 MW	47360 TQ	USBLS	5/15
	Boise City MSA, ID	Y	33540 FQ	38310 MW	45660 TQ	USBLS	5/15
	Illinois	Y	39410 FQ	51430 MW	62780 TQ	USBLS	5/15
	Chicago-Naperville-Arlington Heights PMSA, IL	Y	48540 FQ	61470 MW	75280 TQ	USBLS	5/15
	Lake County-Kenosha County PMSA, IL-WI	Y	48290 FQ	57550 MW	69200 TQ	USBLS	5/15
	Indiana	Y	33490 FQ	40400 MW	47840 TQ	USBLS	5/15
	Gary PMSA, IN	Y	36640 FQ	44100 MW	51130 TQ	USBLS	5/15
	Indianapolis-Carmel-Anderson MSA, IN	Y	34530 FQ	42100 MW	50340 TQ	USBLS	5/15
	Iowa	Y	35300 FQ	44050 MW	52700 TQ	USBLS	5/15
	Des Moines-West Des Moines MSA, IA	Y	50510 FQ	57430 MW	64300 TQ	USBLS	5/15
	Kansas	Y	29110 FQ	36340 MW	44510 TQ	USBLS	5/15
	Wichita MSA, KS	Y	31790 FQ	37740 MW	44510 TQ	USBLS	5/15
	Kentucky	Y	30460 FQ	36540 MW	44440 TQ	USBLS	5/15
	Louisville-Jefferson County MSA, KY-IN	Y	30370 FQ	35990 MW	43040 TQ	USBLS	5/15
	Louisiana	Y	26750 FQ	32630 MW	39910 TQ	USBLS	5/15
	Baton Rouge MSA, LA	Y	27360 FQ	33060 MW	39110 TQ	USBLS	5/15
	New Orleans-Metairie MSA, LA	Y	27540 FQ	34050 MW	42170 TQ	USBLS	5/15
	Maine	Y	40730 FQ	47200 MW	56210 TQ	USBLS	5/15
	Portland-South Portland MSA, ME	Y	42400 FQ	47750 MW	54650 TQ	USBLS	5/15

Occupation/Type/Industry	Location	Per	Low	Mid	High	Source	Date
Water and Wastewater Treatment Plant and System Operator	Maryland	Y	31631 AE	44924 MW	51571 AEX	MDBLS	4/16
	Baltimore-Columbia-Towson MSA, MD	Y	34940 FQ	42620 MW	49920 TQ	USBLS	5/15
	Salisbury MSA, MD-DE	Y	31110 FQ	38190 MW	47290 TQ	USBLS	5/15
	Massachusetts	Y	43450 FQ	50950 MW	59260 TQ	USBLS	5/15
	Boston-Cambridge-Newton NECTA, MA	Y	45490 FQ	54190 MW	61300 TQ	USBLS	5/15
	Worcester MSA, MA-CT	Y	44170 FQ	51610 MW	59470 TQ	USBLS	5/15
	Michigan	Y	40540 FQ	46390 MW	54080 TQ	USBLS	5/15
	Detroit-Dearborn-Livonia PMSA, MI	Y	42890 FQ	47070 MW	53440 TQ	USBLS	5/15
	Grand Rapids-Wyoming MSA, MI	Y	41750 FQ	47230 MW	54640 TQ	USBLS	5/15
	Minnesota	Y	43758 FQ	50825 MW	58054 TQ	MNBLS	1/16-3/16
	Minneapolis-St. Paul-Bloomington MSA, MN-WI	Y	48598 FQ	55108 MW	60301 TQ	MNBLS	1/16-3/16
	Mississippi	Y	27340 FQ	35060 MW	44020 TQ	USBLS	5/15
	Jackson MSA, MS	Y	26300 FQ	31040 MW	46270 TQ	USBLS	5/15
	Missouri	Y	32870 FQ	40500 MW	49900 TQ	USBLS	5/15
	Kansas City MSA, MO-KS	Y	34400 FQ	42470 MW	50890 TQ	USBLS	5/15
	St. Louis MSA, MO-IL	Y	34630 FQ	50050 MW	58110 TQ	USBLS	5/15
	Montana	Y	33980 FQ	42360 MW	49380 TQ	USBLS	5/15
	Billings MSA, MT	Y	41220 FQ	45870 MW	52440 TQ	USBLS	5/15
	Nebraska	Y	33005 FQ	38850 MW	47845 TQ	NEBLS	7/16-9/16
	Omaha-Council Bluffs MSA, NE-IA	Y	34620 FQ	43855 MW	51050 TQ	NEBLS	7/16-9/16
	Nevada	Y	50280 FQ	61870 MW	74020 TQ	USBLS	5/15
	Las Vegas-Henderson-Paradise MSA, NV	Y	54500 FQ	66940 MW	77700 TQ	USBLS	5/15
	New Hampshire	H	19.14 AE	23.73 MW	26.83 AEX	NHBLS	6/16
	Manchester NECTA, NH	H	20.15 AE	23.62 MW	27.86 AEX	NHBLS	6/16
	Nashua NECTA, NH-MA	Y	46450 FQ	53410 MW	58870 TQ	USBLS	5/15
	New Jersey	Y	46230 FQ	56810 MW	68150 TQ	USBLS	5/15
	Camden PMSA, NJ	Y	44570 FQ	53070 MW	63520 TQ	USBLS	5/15
	Newark PMSA, NJ-PA	Y	49610 FQ	56910 MW	63980 TQ	USBLS	5/15
	Trenton MSA, NJ	Y	45140 FQ	53260 MW	64970 TQ	USBLS	5/15
	New Mexico	Y	27880 FQ	36600 MW	48070 TQ	USBLS	5/15
	Albuquerque MSA, NM	Y	32730 FQ	39520 MW	46420 TQ	USBLS	5/15
	New York	Y	37920 AE	52000 MW	62320 AEX	NYBLS	1/16-3/16
	Buffalo-Cheektowaga-Niagara Falls MSA, NY	Y	42000 FQ	47760 MW	55830 TQ	USBLS	5/15
	Nassau County-Suffolk County PMSA, NY	Y	45420 FQ	57750 MW	72660 TQ	USBLS	5/15
	New York-Jersey City-White Plains PMSA, NY-NJ	Y	51030 FQ	64840 MW	74490 TQ	USBLS	5/15
	Rochester MSA, NY	Y	39830 FQ	48680 MW	57660 TQ	USBLS	5/15
	North Carolina	Y	32250 FQ	38070 MW	46560 TQ	USBLS	5/15
	Charlotte-Concord-Gastonia MSA, NC-SC	Y	31430 FQ	38200 MW	47250 TQ	USBLS	5/15
	Raleigh MSA, NC	Y	37410 FQ	45280 MW	54440 TQ	USBLS	5/15
	North Dakota	Y	34630 FQ	44820 MW	54940 TQ	USBLS	5/15
	Grand Forks MSA, ND-MN	Y	35140 FQ	40900 MW	50420 TQ	USBLS	5/15
	Ohio	Y	37230 FQ	45120 MW	53140 TQ	USBLS	5/15
	Cincinnati MSA, OH-KY-IN	Y	35970 FQ	43340 MW	49660 TQ	USBLS	5/15
	Cleveland-Elyria MSA, OH	Y	42840 FQ	49990 MW	58350 TQ	USBLS	5/15
	Columbus MSA, OH	Y	36950 FQ	46020 MW	55780 TQ	USBLS	5/15
	Oklahoma	Y	26580 FQ	31750 MW	39620 TQ	USBLS	5/15
	Oklahoma City MSA, OK	Y	32720 FQ	38560 MW	46940 TQ	USBLS	5/15
	Tulsa MSA, OK	Y	27650 FQ	32930 MW	38570 TQ	USBLS	5/15
	Oregon	H	22.24 FQ	26.53 MW	30.19 TQ	ORBLS	2016
	Portland-Vancouver-Hillsboro MSA, OR-WA	Y	52140 FQ	60270 MW	72730 TQ	USBLS	5/15
	Pennsylvania	Y	38380 FQ	46930 MW	57050 TQ	USBLS	5/15
	Allentown-Bethlehem-Easton MSA, PA-NJ	Y	41550 FQ	48220 MW	56580 TQ	USBLS	5/15
	Harrisburg-Carlisle MSA, PA	Y	30670 FQ	43640 MW	47960 TQ	USBLS	5/15
	Montgomery County-Bucks County-Chester County PMSA, PA	Y	44450 FQ	53240 MW	60460 TQ	USBLS	5/15
	Philadelphia PMSA, PA	Y	38640 FQ	46310 MW	58220 TQ	USBLS	5/15
	Pittsburgh MSA, PA	Y	41450 FQ	48420 MW	61030 TQ	USBLS	5/15

AE	Average entry wage	AWR	Average wage range	H	Hourly	LR	Low end range	MTC	Median total compensation	TCC	Total cash compensation
AEX	Average experienced wage	B	Biweekly	HI	Highest wage paid	M	Monthly	MW	Median wage paid	TQ	Third quartile wage
ATC	Average total compensation	D	Daily	HR	High end range	MCC	Median cash compensation	MWR	Median wage range	W	Weekly
AW	Average wage paid	FQ	First quartile wage	LO	Lowest wage paid	ME	Median entry wage	S	See annotated source	Y	Yearly

Occupation/Type/Industry	Location	Per	Low	Mid	High	Source	Date
Water and Wastewater Treatment Plant and System Operator	Rhode Island	Y	43110 FQ	49610 MW	59900 TQ	USBLS	5/15
	Providence-Warwick MSA, RI-MA	Y	43090 FQ	49040 MW	58320 TQ	USBLS	5/15
	South Carolina	Y	31770 FQ	40530 MW	53450 TQ	USBLS	5/15
	Charleston-North Charleston MSA, SC	Y	28030 FQ	35650 MW	43870 TQ	USBLS	5/15
	Columbia MSA, SC	Y	29540 FQ	35880 MW	44630 TQ	USBLS	5/15
	Greenville-Anderson-Mauldin MSA, SC	Y	33900 FQ	41290 MW	48460 TQ	USBLS	5/15
	South Dakota	Y	33270 FQ	39060 MW	47800 TQ	USBLS	5/15
	Sioux Falls MSA, SD	Y	37790 FQ	44160 MW	50710 TQ	USBLS	5/15
	Tennessee	Y	32010 FQ	38300 MW	47130 TQ	USBLS	5/15
	Knoxville MSA, TN	Y	32220 FQ	39520 MW	49750 TQ	USBLS	5/15
	Memphis MSA, TN-MS-AR	Y	33960 FQ	41810 MW	48330 TQ	USBLS	5/15
	Nashville-Davidson–Murfreesboro–Franklin MSA, TN	Y	33860 FQ	41130 MW	49270 TQ	USBLS	5/15
	Texas	Y	28590 FQ	35630 MW	44380 TQ	USBLS	5/15
	Austin-Round Rock MSA, TX	Y	33760 FQ	41420 MW	48070 TQ	USBLS	5/15
	Dallas-Plano-Irving PMSA, TX	Y	32710 FQ	39450 MW	47280 TQ	USBLS	5/15
	Fort Worth-Arlington PMSA, TX	Y	30140 FQ	37390 MW	46700 TQ	USBLS	5/15
	Houston-The Woodlands-Sugar Land MSA, TX	Y	29790 FQ	37100 MW	45100 TQ	USBLS	5/15
	San Antonio-New Braunfels MSA, TX	Y	29810 FQ	38620 MW	50900 TQ	USBLS	5/15
	Utah	Y	36070 FQ	44140 MW	53150 TQ	USBLS	5/15
	Ogden-Clearfield MSA, UT	Y	37280 FQ	46250 MW	57110 TQ	USBLS	5/15
	Provo-Orem MSA, UT	Y	32310 FQ	38050 MW	46330 TQ	USBLS	5/15
	Salt Lake City MSA, UT	Y	40000 FQ	46990 MW	55780 TQ	USBLS	5/15
	Vermont	Y	39100 FQ	45780 MW	53290 TQ	USBLS	5/15
	Burlington-South Burlington MSA, VT	Y	43070 FQ	48450 MW	56880 TQ	USBLS	5/15
	Virginia	Y	32900 FQ	40940 MW	50840 TQ	USBLS	5/15
	Richmond MSA, VA	Y	34240 FQ	41860 MW	53610 TQ	USBLS	5/15
	Virginia Beach-Norfolk-Newport News MSA, VA-NC	Y	35020 FQ	43020 MW	52390 TQ	USBLS	5/15
	Washington	H	25.51 FQ	30.68 MW	37.39 TQ	WABLS	3/16
	Seattle-Bellevue-Everett PMSA, WA	H	30.37 FQ	35.20 MW	39.96 TQ	WABLS	3/16
	Tacoma-Lakewood PMSA, WA	H	27.18 FQ	32.50 MW	36.83 TQ	WABLS	3/16
	West Virginia	Y	26870 FQ	33740 MW	41080 TQ	USBLS	5/15
	Huntington-Ashland MSA, WV-KY-OH	Y	27620 FQ	35090 MW	44230 TQ	USBLS	5/15
	Wisconsin	Y	36610 FQ	47610 MW	56540 TQ	USBLS	5/15
	Madison MSA, WI	Y	40530 FQ	45490 MW	50560 TQ	USBLS	5/15
	Milwaukee-Waukesha-West Allis MSA, WI	Y	29960 FQ	53500 MW	59960 TQ	USBLS	5/15
	Wyoming	Y	40630 FQ	51550 MW	61060 TQ	USBLS	5/15
	Puerto Rico	Y	20420 FQ	24320 MW	31860 TQ	USBLS	5/15
	San Juan-Carolina-Caguas MSA, PR	Y	20400 FQ	24290 MW	31940 TQ	USBLS	5/15
Water Biologist							
Municipal Government	Los Angeles, CA	Y		94420 AW		CACIT	6/23/16
Water Conservation Specialist							
Municipal Government	Carlsbad, CA	H	21.88 LO	25.25 MW	28.62 HI	CCCA01	6/28/16
Municipal Government	Colton, CA	Y			63284 HI	CACIT	6/28/16
Municipal Government	Grover Beach, CA	Y			17948 HI	CACIT	6/28/16
State Government	Helena, MT	H			29.98 HI	MTGOV	2016
Water Conservationist							
Municipal Government	Ceres, CA	Y		7860 AW		CACIT	6/28/16
Water Facilities Superintendent							
Wastewater Treatment Facility, Municipal Government	Greenfield, MA	Y			72992 HI	FRCOG	2016
Water Quality Analyst							
Municipal Government	Antioch, CA	Y			105408 HI	CACIT	6/28/16

AE	Average entry wage	AWR	Average wage range	H	Hourly	LR	Low end range	MTC	Median total compensation	TCC	Total cash compensation

AE   Average entry wage   AWR Average wage range   H   Hourly   LR   Low end range   MTC Median total compensation   TCC Total cash compensation
AEX Average experienced wage B Biweekly   HI Highest wage paid   M   Monthly   MW Median wage paid   TQ Third quartile wage
ATC Average total compensation D Daily   HR High end range   MCC Median cash compensation   MWR Median wage range   W   Weekly
AW   Average wage paid   FQ First quartile wage   LO Lowest wage paid   ME Median entry wage   S   See annotated source   Y   Yearly

Occupation/Type/Industry	Location	Per	Low	Mid	High	Source	Date
Water Quality Analyst							
Municipal Government	Burbank, CA	Y			75258 HI	CACIT	6/28/16
Municipal Government	Vallejo, CA	Y		61471 AW		CACIT	6/28/16
Municipal Government	Seattle, WA	H	30.55 LO		35.69 HI	CSSS	1/13/16
Water Quality Inspector							
Municipal Government	Buena Park, CA	Y			69564 HI	CACIT	6/28/16
Municipal Government	Lake Forest, CA	Y			72389 HI	CACIT	6/28/16
Water Quality Manager							
Municipal Government	Cypress, CA	Y			104793 HI	CACIT	6/28/16
Water Quality Specialist							
Municipal Government	Beverly Hills, CA	Y			89556 HI	CACIT	6/28/16
Municipal Government	Glendale, CA	Y			65689 HI	CACIT	6/28/16
Municipal Government	Los Banos, CA	Y			54170 HI	CACIT	6/28/16
Municipal Government	Victorville, CA	Y			58492 HI	CACIT	6/28/16
Water Quality Technician							
Municipal Government	Folsom, CA	Y			69730 HI	CACIT	6/28/16
Water Resource Analyst							
Wells and Tanks, Municipal Government	Modesto, CA	Y			57445 HI	CACIT	6/28/16
Water Safety Instructor							
Municipal Government	Escondido, CA	Y		3764 AW		CACIT	6/28/16
Water Service Inspector							
Airport	San Francisco, CA	B	3304 LO		4017 HI	SFGOV	2016-2018
Water Supervisor							
Municipal Government	Markle, IN	Y			43113 HI	HCTAB	2017
Water System Chemist							
Municipal Government	Detroit, MI	M	3917 LO		4133 HI	DETGOV	2016
Waterpolo Coach							
Parks and Recreation Department, Municipal Government	Commerce, CA	Y		71436 AW		CACIT	6/28/16
Watershed Inspector							
Municipal Government	Seattle, WA	H	28.06 LO		32.63 HI	CSSS	1/13/16
Watershed Keeper							
Public Utilities Commission	San Francisco, CA	B	2281 LO		2772 HI	SFGOV	2016-2018
Weatherization Coordinator							
Municipal Government	Detroit, MI	M	4592 LO		4750 HI	DETGOV	2016
Web Coordinator							
Municipal Government	Colorado Springs, CO	Y	52277 LO		71881 HI	COSPRS	2017
Web Developer	Alabama	Y	34423 AE	56939 AW	68203 AEX	ALBLS	6/16
	Birmingham-Hoover MSA, AL	Y	42383 AE	64482 AW	75542 AEX	ALBLS	6/16
	Alaska	Y	35410 FQ	55020 MW	75290 TQ	USBLS	5/15
	Anchorage MSA, AK	Y	34450 FQ	45570 MW	73510 TQ	USBLS	5/15
	Arizona	Y	46050 FQ	64170 MW	93970 TQ	USBLS	5/15
	Phoenix-Mesa-Scottsdale MSA, AZ	Y	48390 FQ	68340 MW	98450 TQ	USBLS	5/15
	Tucson MSA, AZ	Y	37110 FQ	50030 MW	62590 TQ	USBLS	5/15
	Arkansas	Y	37490 FQ	51200 MW	73970 TQ	USBLS	5/15
	Little Rock-North Little Rock-Conway MSA, AR	Y	37010 FQ	51910 MW	64710 TQ	USBLS	5/15
	California	H	25.42 FQ	37.29 MW	51.77 TQ	CABLS	1/16-3/16
	Anaheim-Santa Ana-Irvine PMSA, CA	H	26.44 FQ	34.70 MW	47.39 TQ	CABLS	1/16-3/16
	Los Angeles-Long Beach-Glendale PMSA, CA	H	22.26 FQ	31.61 MW	44.46 TQ	CABLS	1/16-3/16
	Oakland-Hayward-Berkeley PMSA, CA	H	28.61 FQ	36.74 MW	49.59 TQ	CABLS	1/16-3/16
	Riverside-San Bernardino-Ontario MSA, CA	H	15.18 FQ	27.09 MW	40.07 TQ	CABLS	1/16-3/16

AE	Average entry wage	AWR	Average wage range	H	Hourly	LR	Low end range	MTC	Median total compensation	TCC	Total cash compensation
AEX	Average experienced wage	B	Biweekly	HI	Highest wage paid	M	Monthly	MW	Median wage paid	TQ	Third quartile wage
ATC	Average total compensation	D	Daily	HR	High end range	MCC	Median cash compensation	MWR	Median wage range	W	Weekly
AW	Average wage paid	FQ	First quartile wage	LO	Lowest wage paid	ME	Median entry wage	S	See annotated source	Y	Yearly

Occupation/Type/Industry	Location	Per	Low	Mid	High	Source	Date
Web Developer	Sacramento–Roseville–Arden-Arcade MSA, CA	H	23.65 FQ	36.33 MW	53.62 TQ	CABLS	1/16-3/16
	San Diego-Carlsbad MSA, CA	H	21.79 FQ	33.92 MW	47.34 TQ	CABLS	1/16-3/16
	San Francisco-Redwood City-South San Francisco PMSA, CA	H	31.89 FQ	45.74 MW	61.75 TQ	CABLS	1/16-3/16
	Colorado	Y	42620 FQ	55540 MW	79920 TQ	USBLS	5/15
	Denver-Aurora-Lakewood MSA, CO	Y	45740 FQ	59890 MW	90530 TQ	USBLS	5/15
	Connecticut	Y		67616 MW		CTBLS	1/16-3/16
	Bridgeport-Stamford-Norwalk MSA, CT	Y	49320 FQ	67180 MW	97100 TQ	USBLS	5/15
	Hartford-West Hartford-East Hartford MSA, CT	Y	55940 FQ	71290 MW	88140 TQ	USBLS	5/15
	Delaware	Y	61690 FQ	78220 MW	96370 TQ	USBLS	5/15
	Wilmington PMSA, DE-MD-NJ	Y	65340 FQ	81420 MW	96780 TQ	USBLS	5/15
	District of Columbia	Y	63790 FQ	79770 MW	100620 TQ	USBLS	5/15
	Washington-Arlington-Alexandria PMSA, DC-VA-MD-WV	Y	66610 FQ	85610 MW	108640 TQ	USBLS	5/15
	Florida	H	18.64 AE	27.95 MW	35.65 AEX	FLBLS	7/16-9/16
	Fort Lauderdale-Pompano Beach-Deerfield Beach PMSA, FL	H	15.65 AE	25.42 MW	34.33 AEX	FLBLS	7/16-9/16
	Miami-Miami Beach-Kendall PMSA, FL	H	21.11 AE	29.17 MW	34.88 AEX	FLBLS	7/16-9/16
	Orlando-Kissimmee-Sanford MSA, FL	H	18.98 AE	27.39 MW	34.55 AEX	FLBLS	7/16-9/16
	Tampa-St. Petersburg-Clearwater MSA, FL	H	20.54 AE	29.55 MW	36.19 AEX	FLBLS	7/16-9/16
	Georgia	Y	56010 FQ	73530 MW	96020 TQ	USBLS	5/15
	Atlanta-Sandy Springs-Roswell MSA, GA	Y	59960 FQ	76280 MW	98370 TQ	USBLS	5/15
	Augusta-Richmond County MSA, GA-SC	Y	47460 FQ	59190 MW	78450 TQ	USBLS	5/15
	Idaho	Y	25790 FQ	38150 MW	55430 TQ	USBLS	5/15
	Boise City MSA, ID	Y	22920 FQ	36740 MW	52690 TQ	USBLS	5/15
	Illinois	Y	51870 FQ	69920 MW	90740 TQ	USBLS	5/15
	Chicago-Naperville-Arlington Heights PMSA, IL	Y	57160 FQ	74090 MW	94440 TQ	USBLS	5/15
	Lake County-Kenosha County PMSA, IL-WI	Y	37390 FQ	57700 MW	82990 TQ	USBLS	5/15
	Indiana	Y	41790 FQ	53220 MW	67780 TQ	USBLS	5/15
	Gary PMSA, IN	Y	36300 FQ	46890 MW	59920 TQ	USBLS	5/15
	Indianapolis-Carmel-Anderson MSA, IN	Y	43490 FQ	57420 MW	72450 TQ	USBLS	5/15
	Iowa	Y	39560 FQ	54820 MW	78830 TQ	USBLS	5/15
	Des Moines-West Des Moines MSA, IA	Y	40320 FQ	55940 MW	82860 TQ	USBLS	5/15
	Kansas	Y	39380 FQ	51950 MW	72650 TQ	USBLS	5/15
	Wichita MSA, KS	Y	38040 FQ	46450 MW	63870 TQ	USBLS	5/15
	Kentucky	Y	39230 FQ	48290 MW	62720 TQ	USBLS	5/15
	Louisville-Jefferson County MSA, KY-IN	Y	40880 FQ	47970 MW	63670 TQ	USBLS	5/15
	Louisiana	Y	41190 FQ	52280 MW	60660 TQ	USBLS	5/15
	Baton Rouge MSA, LA	Y	53320 FQ	59980 MW	79210 TQ	USBLS	5/15
	New Orleans-Metairie MSA, LA	Y	39080 FQ	48510 MW	58420 TQ	USBLS	5/15
	Maine	Y	41550 FQ	47590 MW	63920 TQ	USBLS	5/15
	Portland-South Portland MSA, ME	Y	43830 FQ	49570 MW	76700 TQ	USBLS	5/15
	Maryland	Y	36290 AE	76163 MW	96099 AEX	MDBLS	4/16
	Baltimore-Columbia-Towson MSA, MD	Y	33780 FQ	59850 MW	99900 TQ	USBLS	5/15
	Salisbury MSA, MD-DE	Y	32370 FQ	36750 MW	45400 TQ	USBLS	5/15
	Massachusetts	Y	57120 FQ	75540 MW	95230 TQ	USBLS	5/15
	Boston-Cambridge-Newton NECTA, MA	Y	60750 FQ	78200 MW	95960 TQ	USBLS	5/15
	Worcester MSA, MA-CT	Y	44120 FQ	66700 MW	88850 TQ	USBLS	5/15
	Michigan	Y	46040 FQ	59500 MW	76110 TQ	USBLS	5/15

AE	Average entry wage	**AWR**	Average wage range	**H**	Hourly
AEX	Average experienced wage	**B**	Biweekly	**HI**	Highest wage paid
ATC	Average total compensation	**D**	Daily	**HR**	High end range
AW	Average wage paid	**FQ**	First quartile wage	**LO**	Lowest wage paid

LR	Low end range	**MTC**	Median total compensation
M	Monthly	**MW**	Median wage paid
MCC	Median cash compensation	**MWR**	Median wage range
ME	Median entry wage	**S**	See annotated source

TCC	Total cash compensation
TQ	Third quartile wage
W	Weekly
Y	Yearly

Occupation/Type/Industry	Location	Per	Low	Mid	High	Source	Date
Web Developer	Detroit-Dearborn-Livonia PMSA, MI	Y	47690 FQ	59780 MW	76370 TQ	USBLS	5/15
	Grand Rapids-Wyoming MSA, MI	Y	43210 FQ	58660 MW	72620 TQ	USBLS	5/15
	Minnesota	Y	47509 FQ	63628 MW	88275 TQ	MNBLS	1/16-3/16
	Minneapolis-St. Paul-Bloomington MSA, MN-WI	Y	48659 FQ	66098 MW	89918 TQ	MNBLS	1/16-3/16
	Mississippi	Y	37830 FQ	49800 MW	67770 TQ	USBLS	5/15
	Jackson MSA, MS	Y	48360 FQ	59290 MW	76800 TQ	USBLS	5/15
	Missouri	Y	41630 FQ	55550 MW	77390 TQ	USBLS	5/15
	Kansas City MSA, MO-KS	Y	39800 FQ	54850 MW	75800 TQ	USBLS	5/15
	St. Louis MSA, MO-IL	Y	44570 FQ	60190 MW	84820 TQ	USBLS	5/15
	Montana	Y	26240 FQ	47670 MW	61450 TQ	USBLS	5/15
	Billings MSA, MT	Y	38850 FQ	45440 MW	53940 TQ	USBLS	5/15
	Nebraska	Y	40460 FQ	55750 MW	77625 TQ	NEBLS	7/16-9/16
	Omaha-Council Bluffs MSA, NE-IA	Y	46030 FQ	63975 MW	84565 TQ	NEBLS	7/16-9/16
	Nevada	Y	50840 FQ	59030 MW	71690 TQ	USBLS	5/15
	Las Vegas-Henderson-Paradise MSA, NV	Y	51210 FQ	59900 MW	74320 TQ	USBLS	5/15
	New Hampshire	H	15.25 AE	27.60 MW	35.57 AEX	NHBLS	6/16
	Manchester NECTA, NH	H	13.42 AE	26.83 MW	34.52 AEX	NHBLS	6/16
	Nashua NECTA, NH-MA	Y	22680 FQ	41600 MW	60870 TQ	USBLS	5/15
	New Jersey	Y	49880 FQ	65200 MW	87420 TQ	USBLS	5/15
	Camden PMSA, NJ	Y	40060 FQ	55270 MW	71230 TQ	USBLS	5/15
	Newark PMSA, NJ-PA	Y	49860 FQ	63370 MW	93490 TQ	USBLS	5/15
	Trenton MSA, NJ	Y	57030 FQ	72880 MW	104210 TQ	USBLS	5/15
	New Mexico	Y	39740 FQ	53360 MW	69570 TQ	USBLS	5/15
	Albuquerque MSA, NM	Y	35710 FQ	50060 MW	69970 TQ	USBLS	5/15
	New York	Y	45550 AE	72810 MW	96400 AEX	NYBLS	1/16-3/16
	Buffalo-Cheektowaga-Niagara Falls MSA, NY	Y	35100 FQ	47420 MW	61500 TQ	USBLS	5/15
	Nassau County-Suffolk County PMSA, NY	Y	54940 FQ	72180 MW	93150 TQ	USBLS	5/15
	New York-Jersey City-White Plains PMSA, NY-NJ	Y	57630 FQ	76190 MW	100700 TQ	USBLS	5/15
	Rochester MSA, NY	Y	38120 FQ	51200 MW	66400 TQ	USBLS	5/15
	North Carolina	Y	43340 FQ	61700 MW	87000 TQ	USBLS	5/15
	Charlotte-Concord-Gastonia MSA, NC-SC	Y	43700 FQ	71890 MW	95800 TQ	USBLS	5/15
	Raleigh MSA, NC	Y	46800 FQ	64320 MW	83130 TQ	USBLS	5/15
	North Dakota	Y	42150 FQ	52890 MW	71660 TQ	USBLS	5/15
	Fargo MSA, ND-MN	Y	42640 FQ	54200 MW	71380 TQ	USBLS	5/15
	Ohio	Y	43470 FQ	58710 MW	79000 TQ	USBLS	5/15
	Cincinnati MSA, OH-KY-IN	Y	42990 FQ	63060 MW	85970 TQ	USBLS	5/15
	Cleveland-Elyria MSA, OH	Y	47420 FQ	59150 MW	78340 TQ	USBLS	5/15
	Columbus MSA, OH	Y	54900 FQ	73410 MW	88720 TQ	USBLS	5/15
	Oklahoma	Y	37060 FQ	48640 MW	63820 TQ	USBLS	5/15
	Oklahoma City MSA, OK	Y	38470 FQ	51170 MW	65290 TQ	USBLS	5/15
	Tulsa MSA, OK	Y	39590 FQ	50940 MW	70600 TQ	USBLS	5/15
	Oregon	H	21.77 FQ	29.36 MW	40.70 TQ	ORBLS	2016
	Portland-Vancouver-Hillsboro MSA, OR-WA	Y	46490 FQ	62640 MW	84170 TQ	USBLS	5/15
	Pennsylvania	Y	44500 FQ	59600 MW	76500 TQ	USBLS	5/15
	Allentown-Bethlehem-Easton MSA, PA-NJ	Y	42950 FQ	59090 MW	74850 TQ	USBLS	5/15
	Harrisburg-Carlisle MSA, PA	Y	38860 FQ	52970 MW	74510 TQ	USBLS	5/15
	Montgomery County-Bucks County-Chester County PMSA, PA	Y	51050 FQ	64570 MW	81790 TQ	USBLS	5/15
	Philadelphia PMSA, PA	Y	53540 FQ	67530 MW	85190 TQ	USBLS	5/15
	Pittsburgh MSA, PA	Y	38230 FQ	54030 MW	72140 TQ	USBLS	5/15
	Rhode Island	Y	59850 FQ	79010 MW	93600 TQ	USBLS	5/15
	Providence-Warwick MSA, RI-MA	Y	56960 FQ	76540 MW	92800 TQ	USBLS	5/15
	South Carolina	Y	39960 FQ	54520 MW	74490 TQ	USBLS	5/15
	Charleston-North Charleston MSA, SC	Y	43630 FQ	70290 MW	90700 TQ	USBLS	5/15
	Columbia MSA, SC	Y	44590 FQ	56220 MW	71520 TQ	USBLS	5/15
	Greenville-Anderson-Mauldin MSA, SC	Y	43650 FQ	57570 MW	73580 TQ	USBLS	5/15
	South Dakota	Y	42350 FQ	53540 MW	69050 TQ	USBLS	5/15

AE Average entry wage	**AWR** Average wage range	**H** Hourly	**LR** Low end range	**MTC** Median total compensation	**TCC** Total cash compensation
AEX Average experienced wage	**B** Biweekly	**HI** Highest wage paid	**M** Monthly	**MW** Median wage paid	**TQ** Third quartile wage
ATC Average total compensation	**D** Daily	**HR** High end range	**MCC** Median cash compensation	**MWR** Median wage range	**W** Weekly
AW Average wage paid	**FQ** First quartile wage	**LO** Lowest wage paid	**ME** Median entry wage	**S** See annotated source	**Y** Yearly

Occupation/Type/Industry	Location	Per	Low	Mid	High	Source	Date
Web Developer	Sioux Falls MSA, SD	Y	50190 FQ	61060 MW	76480 TQ	USBLS	5/15
	Tennessee	Y	41890 FQ	55950 MW	74970 TQ	USBLS	5/15
	Knoxville MSA, TN	Y	43130 FQ	56170 MW	72720 TQ	USBLS	5/15
	Memphis MSA, TN-MS-AR	Y	39750 FQ	55340 MW	72290 TQ	USBLS	5/15
	Nashville-Davidson–Murfreesboro–Franklin MSA, TN	Y	46800 FQ	58920 MW	81910 TQ	USBLS	5/15
	Texas	Y	48300 FQ	65840 MW	85560 TQ	USBLS	5/15
	Austin-Round Rock MSA, TX	Y	51920 FQ	70590 MW	91370 TQ	USBLS	5/15
	Dallas-Plano-Irving PMSA, TX	Y	54290 FQ	71740 MW	91220 TQ	USBLS	5/15
	Fort Worth-Arlington PMSA, TX	Y	51730 FQ	70270 MW	85970 TQ	USBLS	5/15
	Houston-The Woodlands-Sugar Land MSA, TX	Y	44640 FQ	62260 MW	77890 TQ	USBLS	5/15
	San Antonio-New Braunfels MSA, TX	Y	47420 FQ	63690 MW	79680 TQ	USBLS	5/15
	Utah	Y	37850 FQ	55910 MW	77840 TQ	USBLS	5/15
	Ogden-Clearfield MSA, UT	Y	30070 FQ	46270 MW	67640 TQ	USBLS	5/15
	Provo-Orem MSA, UT	Y	37540 FQ	53270 MW	77440 TQ	USBLS	5/15
	Salt Lake City MSA, UT	Y	42040 FQ	61260 MW	80860 TQ	USBLS	5/15
	Vermont	Y	44230 FQ	60080 MW	83100 TQ	USBLS	5/15
	Burlington-South Burlington MSA, VT	Y	48300 FQ	67950 MW	88730 TQ	USBLS	5/15
	Virginia	Y	55230 FQ	78680 MW	102870 TQ	USBLS	5/15
	Richmond MSA, VA	Y	49370 FQ	64600 MW	85250 TQ	USBLS	5/15
	Virginia Beach-Norfolk-Newport News MSA, VA-NC	Y	46550 FQ	59000 MW	76880 TQ	USBLS	5/15
	Washington	H	28.16 FQ	39.62 MW	55.23 TQ	WABLS	3/16
	Seattle-Bellevue-Everett PMSA, WA	H	30.32 FQ	44.63 MW	58.47 TQ	WABLS	3/16
	Tacoma-Lakewood PMSA, WA	H	26.72 FQ	33.00 MW	39.00 TQ	WABLS	3/16
	West Virginia	Y	31070 FQ	39110 MW	51850 TQ	USBLS	5/15
	Huntington-Ashland MSA, WV-KY-OH	Y	28410 FQ	33200 MW	46260 TQ	USBLS	5/15
	Wisconsin	Y	40630 FQ	52420 MW	68510 TQ	USBLS	5/15
	Madison MSA, WI	Y	43190 FQ	55520 MW	71270 TQ	USBLS	5/15
	Milwaukee-Waukesha-West Allis MSA, WI	Y	43150 FQ	57490 MW	75320 TQ	USBLS	5/15
	Wyoming	Y	44230 FQ	54980 MW	61940 TQ	USBLS	5/15
	Puerto Rico	Y	27720 FQ	36250 MW	44390 TQ	USBLS	5/15
	San Juan-Carolina-Caguas MSA, PR	Y	28210 FQ	37360 MW	44870 TQ	USBLS	5/15
Wedding Planner	United States	Y		51000 AW		SKU01	2016
Weed Abatement Coordinator Municipal Government	San Bernardino, CA	Y			58704 HI	CACIT	6/28/16
Weed Specialist State Government	North Carolina	Y	42667 LO		69177 HI	NCGOV	7/1/16
Weigher, Measurer, Checker, and Sampler, Recordkeeping	Alabama	Y	19076 AE	29465 AW	34669 AEX	ALBLS	6/16
	Birmingham-Hoover MSA, AL	Y	22601 AE	33453 AW	38874 AEX	ALBLS	6/16
	Alaska	Y	32130 FQ	43360 MW	55330 TQ	USBLS	5/15
	Anchorage MSA, AK	Y	33620 FQ	47130 MW	56340 TQ	USBLS	5/15
	Arizona	Y	22830 FQ	29760 MW	37880 TQ	USBLS	5/15
	Phoenix-Mesa-Scottsdale MSA, AZ	Y	23600 FQ	30660 MW	38670 TQ	USBLS	5/15
	Tucson MSA, AZ	Y	21390 FQ	27040 MW	33930 TQ	USBLS	5/15
	Arkansas	Y	21140 FQ	24130 MW	30950 TQ	USBLS	5/15
	Little Rock-North Little Rock-Conway MSA, AR	Y	23390 FQ	27910 MW	32920 TQ	USBLS	5/15
	California	H	10.05 FQ	12.47 MW	16.30 TQ	CABLS	1/16-3/16
	Anaheim-Santa Ana-Irvine PMSA, CA	H	11.02 FQ	13.46 MW	16.93 TQ	CABLS	1/16-3/16
	Los Angeles-Long Beach-Glendale PMSA, CA	H	9.65 FQ	11.49 MW	14.53 TQ	CABLS	1/16-3/16
	Oakland-Hayward-Berkeley PMSA, CA	H	11.26 FQ	15.70 MW	23.19 TQ	CABLS	1/16-3/16
	Riverside-San Bernardino-Ontario MSA, CA	H	10.40 FQ	12.99 MW	16.23 TQ	CABLS	1/16-3/16

AE	Average entry wage	AWR	Average wage range	H	Hourly	LR	Low end range	MTC	Median total compensation	TCC	Total cash compensation
AEX	Average experienced wage	B	Biweekly	HI	Highest wage paid	M	Monthly	MW	Median wage paid	TQ	Third quartile wage
ATC	Average total compensation	D	Daily	HR	High end range	MCC	Median cash compensation	MWR	Median wage range	W	Weekly
AW	Average wage paid	FQ	First quartile wage	LO	Lowest wage paid	ME	Median entry wage	S	See annotated source	Y	Yearly

Occupation/Type/Industry	Location	Per	Low	Mid	High	Source	Date
Weigher, Measurer, Checker, and Sampler, Recordkeeping	Sacramento–Roseville–Arden-Arcade MSA, CA	H	9.80 FQ	11.75 MW	17.05 TQ	CABLS	1/16-3/16
	San Diego-Carlsbad MSA, CA	H	10.77 FQ	13.61 MW	17.08 TQ	CABLS	1/16-3/16
	San Francisco-Redwood City-South San Francisco PMSA, CA	H	10.14 FQ	11.97 MW	15.43 TQ	CABLS	1/16-3/16
	Colorado	Y	28820 FQ	35720 MW	43660 TQ	USBLS	5/15
	Denver-Aurora-Lakewood MSA, CO	Y	32080 FQ	36190 MW	40950 TQ	USBLS	5/15
	Connecticut	Y		37925 MW		CTBLS	1/16-3/16
	Bridgeport-Stamford-Norwalk MSA, CT	Y	27940 FQ	37570 MW	57680 TQ	USBLS	5/15
	Hartford-West Hartford-East Hartford MSA, CT	Y	27920 FQ	36190 MW	44570 TQ	USBLS	5/15
	Delaware	Y	26540 FQ	32200 MW	41640 TQ	USBLS	5/15
	Wilmington PMSA, DE-MD-NJ	Y	26800 FQ	34040 MW	40030 TQ	USBLS	5/15
	Washington-Arlington-Alexandria PMSA, DC-VA-MD-WV	Y	26680 FQ	31070 MW	37480 TQ	USBLS	5/15
	Florida	H	11.22 AE	14.82 MW	16.89 AEX	FLBLS	7/16-9/16
	Fort Lauderdale-Pompano Beach-Deerfield Beach PMSA, FL	H	9.67 AE	14.34 MW	16.48 AEX	FLBLS	7/16-9/16
	Miami-Miami Beach-Kendall PMSA, FL	H	9.18 AE	13.16 MW	15.50 AEX	FLBLS	7/16-9/16
	Orlando-Kissimmee-Sanford MSA, FL	H	11.02 AE	14.97 MW	16.75 AEX	FLBLS	7/16-9/16
	Tampa-St. Petersburg-Clearwater MSA, FL	H	11.88 AE	15.37 MW	17.12 AEX	FLBLS	7/16-9/16
	Georgia	Y	22570 FQ	27300 MW	31980 TQ	USBLS	5/15
	Atlanta-Sandy Springs-Roswell MSA, GA	Y	22920 FQ	27550 MW	31370 TQ	USBLS	5/15
	Augusta-Richmond County MSA, GA-SC	Y	24610 FQ	28600 MW	33880 TQ	USBLS	5/15
	Hawaii	Y	17510 FQ	18900 MW	23490 TQ	USBLS	5/15
	Urban Honolulu MSA, HI	Y	17470 FQ	18820 MW	22440 TQ	USBLS	5/15
	Idaho	Y	18500 FQ	25660 MW	32260 TQ	USBLS	5/15
	Boise City MSA, ID	Y	17410 FQ	19080 MW	28340 TQ	USBLS	5/15
	Illinois	Y	26080 FQ	33180 MW	41910 TQ	USBLS	5/15
	Chicago-Naperville-Arlington Heights PMSA, IL	Y	24600 FQ	30310 MW	38300 TQ	USBLS	5/15
	Lake County-Kenosha County PMSA, IL-WI	Y	23420 FQ	32190 MW	40310 TQ	USBLS	5/15
	Indiana	Y	24970 FQ	30620 MW	38860 TQ	USBLS	5/15
	Gary PMSA, IN	Y	27140 FQ	34140 MW	43320 TQ	USBLS	5/15
	Indianapolis-Carmel-Anderson MSA, IN	Y	24030 FQ	30120 MW	38100 TQ	USBLS	5/15
	Iowa	Y	22960 FQ	28410 MW	35300 TQ	USBLS	5/15
	Des Moines-West Des Moines MSA, IA	Y	23850 FQ	33160 MW	39850 TQ	USBLS	5/15
	Kansas	Y	27160 FQ	32090 MW	40420 TQ	USBLS	5/15
	Wichita MSA, KS	Y	27690 FQ	35830 MW	52930 TQ	USBLS	5/15
	Kentucky	Y	24100 FQ	29510 MW	37150 TQ	USBLS	5/15
	Louisville-Jefferson County MSA, KY-IN	Y	22500 FQ	28220 MW	38120 TQ	USBLS	5/15
	Louisiana	Y	24340 FQ	32430 MW	41870 TQ	USBLS	5/15
	Baton Rouge MSA, LA	Y	23510 FQ	28820 MW	36650 TQ	USBLS	5/15
	New Orleans-Metairie MSA, LA	Y	25160 FQ	31690 MW	43490 TQ	USBLS	5/15
	Maine	Y	18380 FQ	22080 MW	29020 TQ	USBLS	5/15
	Portland-South Portland MSA, ME	Y	18810 FQ	23790 MW	29890 TQ	USBLS	5/15
	Maryland	Y	24599 AE	35520 MW	40980 AEX	MDBLS	4/16
	Baltimore-Columbia-Towson MSA, MD	Y	28180 FQ	34420 MW	40500 TQ	USBLS	5/15
	Salisbury MSA, MD-DE	Y	23480 FQ	27230 MW	32200 TQ	USBLS	5/15
	Massachusetts	Y	25270 FQ	35520 MW	50360 TQ	USBLS	5/15
	Boston-Cambridge-Newton NECTA, MA	Y	28610 FQ	39180 MW	54250 TQ	USBLS	5/15
	Worcester MSA, MA-CT	Y	19800 FQ	31310 MW	42810 TQ	USBLS	5/15

AE	Average entry wage	AWR	Average wage range	H	Hourly	LR	Low end range	MTC	Median total compensation	TCC	Total cash compensation
AEX	Average experienced wage	B	Biweekly	HI	Highest wage paid	M	Monthly	MW	Median wage paid	TQ	Third quartile wage
ATC	Average total compensation	D	Daily	HR	High end range	MCC	Median cash compensation	MWR	Median wage range	W	Weekly
AW	Average wage paid	FQ	First quartile wage	LO	Lowest wage paid	ME	Median entry wage	S	See annotated source	Y	Yearly

Occupation/Type/Industry	Location	Per	Low	Mid	High	Source	Date
Weigher, Measurer, Checker, and Sampler, Recordkeeping	Michigan	Y	21760 FQ	27060 MW	36030 TQ	USBLS	5/15
	Detroit-Dearborn-Livonia PMSA, MI	Y	19990 FQ	25030 MW	32680 TQ	USBLS	5/15
	Grand Rapids-Wyoming MSA, MI	Y	25910 FQ	31490 MW	39830 TQ	USBLS	5/15
	Minnesota	Y	28285 FQ	35647 MW	42372 TQ	MNBLS	1/16-3/16
	Minneapolis-St. Paul-Bloomington MSA, MN-WI	Y	27921 FQ	35304 MW	41826 TQ	MNBLS	1/16-3/16
	Mississippi	Y	20350 FQ	26110 MW	38740 TQ	USBLS	5/15
	Jackson MSA, MS	Y	21570 FQ	27280 MW	43800 TQ	USBLS	5/15
	Missouri	Y	22890 FQ	28520 MW	37690 TQ	USBLS	5/15
	Kansas City MSA, MO-KS	Y	28450 FQ	36000 MW	44510 TQ	USBLS	5/15
	St. Louis MSA, MO-IL	Y	23370 FQ	30190 MW	40840 TQ	USBLS	5/15
	Montana	Y	22890 FQ	27870 MW	33010 TQ	USBLS	5/15
	Billings MSA, MT	Y	25550 FQ	29640 MW	35800 TQ	USBLS	5/15
	Nebraska	Y	27505 FQ	31520 MW	39700 TQ	NEBLS	7/16-9/16
	Omaha-Council Bluffs MSA, NE-IA	Y	28660 FQ	34275 MW	44280 TQ	NEBLS	7/16-9/16
	Nevada	Y	19110 FQ	24480 MW	32700 TQ	USBLS	5/15
	Las Vegas-Henderson-Paradise MSA, NV	Y	18700 FQ	23130 MW	31040 TQ	USBLS	5/15
	New Hampshire	H	12.87 AE	19.91 MW	22.30 AEX	NHBLS	6/16
	Nashua NECTA, NH-MA	Y	26840 FQ	34130 MW	42660 TQ	USBLS	5/15
	New Jersey	Y	26080 FQ	34100 MW	48260 TQ	USBLS	5/15
	Camden PMSA, NJ	Y	31560 FQ	37680 MW	47180 TQ	USBLS	5/15
	Newark PMSA, NJ-PA	Y	26160 FQ	35380 MW	58300 TQ	USBLS	5/15
	New Mexico	Y	22400 FQ	28810 MW	40920 TQ	USBLS	5/15
	Albuquerque MSA, NM	Y	21990 FQ	28400 MW	40560 TQ	USBLS	5/15
	New York	Y	20100 AE	27180 MW	36300 AEX	NYBLS	1/16-3/16
	Buffalo-Cheektowaga-Niagara Falls MSA, NY	Y	18730 FQ	19400 MW	33760 TQ	USBLS	5/15
	Nassau County-Suffolk County PMSA, NY	Y	19240 FQ	26230 MW	40040 TQ	USBLS	5/15
	New York-Jersey City-White Plains PMSA, NY-NJ	Y	20970 FQ	28920 MW	38510 TQ	USBLS	5/15
	Rochester MSA, NY	Y	19290 FQ	21120 MW	28940 TQ	USBLS	5/15
	North Carolina	Y	21770 FQ	27440 MW	33920 TQ	USBLS	5/15
	Charlotte-Concord-Gastonia MSA, NC-SC	Y	23920 FQ	29200 MW	35190 TQ	USBLS	5/15
	Raleigh MSA, NC	Y	23570 FQ	29300 MW	37080 TQ	USBLS	5/15
	North Dakota	Y	25810 FQ	31790 MW	46230 TQ	USBLS	5/15
	Ohio	Y	25180 FQ	30230 MW	36640 TQ	USBLS	5/15
	Cincinnati MSA, OH-KY-IN	Y	25040 FQ	28980 MW	34250 TQ	USBLS	5/15
	Cleveland-Elyria MSA, OH	Y	26070 FQ	31570 MW	36960 TQ	USBLS	5/15
	Columbus MSA, OH	Y	25550 FQ	30190 MW	35610 TQ	USBLS	5/15
	Oklahoma	Y	24800 FQ	32430 MW	38970 TQ	USBLS	5/15
	Oklahoma City MSA, OK	Y	22470 FQ	27380 MW	34240 TQ	USBLS	5/15
	Tulsa MSA, OK	Y	24480 FQ	29880 MW	39450 TQ	USBLS	5/15
	Oregon	H	11.25 FQ	13.64 MW	17.48 TQ	ORBLS	2016
	Portland-Vancouver-Hillsboro MSA, OR-WA	Y	23040 FQ	27830 MW	36450 TQ	USBLS	5/15
	Pennsylvania	Y	23840 FQ	31910 MW	43030 TQ	USBLS	5/15
	Allentown-Bethlehem-Easton MSA, PA-NJ	Y	27410 FQ	30570 MW	46390 TQ	USBLS	5/15
	Harrisburg-Carlisle MSA, PA	Y	28040 FQ	36230 MW	46090 TQ	USBLS	5/15
	Montgomery County-Bucks County-Chester County PMSA, PA	Y	21940 FQ	29770 MW	45730 TQ	USBLS	5/15
	Philadelphia PMSA, PA	Y	18490 FQ	22540 MW	32340 TQ	USBLS	5/15
	Pittsburgh MSA, PA	Y	24930 FQ	33230 MW	45690 TQ	USBLS	5/15
	Rhode Island	Y	19510 FQ	24680 MW	33690 TQ	USBLS	5/15
	Providence-Warwick MSA, RI-MA	Y	20660 FQ	27900 MW	35760 TQ	USBLS	5/15
	South Carolina	Y	21780 FQ	28860 MW	37250 TQ	USBLS	5/15
	Charleston-North Charleston MSA, SC	Y	26560 FQ	31620 MW	41660 TQ	USBLS	5/15
	Columbia MSA, SC	Y	17280 FQ	18960 MW	23830 TQ	USBLS	5/15
	Greenville-Anderson-Mauldin MSA, SC	Y	30010 FQ	42030 MW	55010 TQ	USBLS	5/15
	South Dakota	Y	26430 FQ	28740 MW	31130 TQ	USBLS	5/15
	Tennessee	Y	24460 FQ	32520 MW	40510 TQ	USBLS	5/15

AE	Average entry wage	AWR	Average wage range	H	Hourly
AEX	Average experienced wage	B	Biweekly	HI	Highest wage paid
ATC	Average total compensation	D	Daily	HR	High end range
AW	Average wage paid	FQ	First quartile wage	LO	Lowest wage paid

LR	Low end range	MTC	Median total compensation	TCC	Total cash compensation
M	Monthly	MW	Median wage paid	TQ	Third quartile wage
MCC	Median cash compensation	MWR	Median wage range	W	Weekly
ME	Median entry wage	S	See annotated source	Y	Yearly

Weigher, Measurer, Checker, and Sampler, Recordkeeping

Occupation/Type/Industry	Location	Per	Low	Mid	High	Source	Date
Weigher, Measurer, Checker, and Sampler, Recordkeeping	Knoxville MSA, TN	Y	34470 FQ	50010 MW	56910 TQ	USBLS	5/15
	Memphis MSA, TN-MS-AR	Y	22730 FQ	32010 MW	40540 TQ	USBLS	5/15
	Nashville-Davidson–Murfreesboro–Franklin MSA, TN	Y	26970 FQ	32410 MW	38120 TQ	USBLS	5/15
	Texas	Y	20340 FQ	26910 MW	35010 TQ	USBLS	5/15
	Austin-Round Rock MSA, TX	Y	18420 FQ	22260 MW	29690 TQ	USBLS	5/15
	Dallas-Plano-Irving PMSA, TX	Y	21100 FQ	28680 MW	36670 TQ	USBLS	5/15
	Fort Worth-Arlington PMSA, TX	Y	21470 FQ	28000 MW	35390 TQ	USBLS	5/15
	Houston-The Woodlands-Sugar Land MSA, TX	Y	20730 FQ	26790 MW	34860 TQ	USBLS	5/15
	San Antonio-New Braunfels MSA, TX	Y	20370 FQ	26850 MW	33820 TQ	USBLS	5/15
	Utah	Y	25930 FQ	30170 MW	37290 TQ	USBLS	5/15
	Ogden-Clearfield MSA, UT	Y	26050 FQ	31100 MW	39230 TQ	USBLS	5/15
	Provo-Orem MSA, UT	Y	25450 FQ	30260 MW	37010 TQ	USBLS	5/15
	Salt Lake City MSA, UT	Y	26290 FQ	29780 MW	36380 TQ	USBLS	5/15
	Vermont	Y	28840 FQ	35220 MW	45050 TQ	USBLS	5/15
	Burlington-South Burlington MSA, VT	Y	29820 FQ	38720 MW	51450 TQ	USBLS	5/15
	Virginia	Y	23440 FQ	29910 MW	37580 TQ	USBLS	5/15
	Richmond MSA, VA	Y	21720 FQ	28570 MW	36140 TQ	USBLS	5/15
	Virginia Beach-Norfolk-Newport News MSA, VA-NC	Y	22110 FQ	29290 MW	38180 TQ	USBLS	5/15
	Washington	H	12.22 FQ	15.95 MW	20.31 TQ	WABLS	3/16
	Seattle-Bellevue-Everett PMSA, WA	H	14.97 FQ	17.76 MW	21.09 TQ	WABLS	3/16
	Tacoma-Lakewood PMSA, WA	H	10.77 FQ	11.81 MW	17.64 TQ	WABLS	3/16
	West Virginia	Y	20670 FQ	23850 MW	30300 TQ	USBLS	5/15
	Huntington-Ashland MSA, WV-KY-OH	Y	18310 FQ	20010 MW	34080 TQ	USBLS	5/15
	Wisconsin	Y	22710 FQ	28320 MW	34950 TQ	USBLS	5/15
	Madison MSA, WI	Y	27110 FQ	31280 MW	37200 TQ	USBLS	5/15
	Milwaukee-Waukesha-West Allis MSA, WI	Y	22790 FQ	28170 MW	34490 TQ	USBLS	5/15
	Wyoming	Y	32660 FQ	36880 MW	44930 TQ	USBLS	5/15
	Cheyenne MSA, WY	Y	27240 FQ	36000 MW	42660 TQ	USBLS	5/15
	Puerto Rico	Y	17720 FQ	19900 MW	23830 TQ	USBLS	5/15
	San Juan-Carolina-Caguas MSA, PR	Y	17640 FQ	19710 MW	23710 TQ	USBLS	5/15
	Guam	Y	25540 FQ	32470 MW	37060 TQ	USBLS	5/15
Welder, Cutter, Solderer, and Brazer	Alabama	Y	26867 AE	38157 AW	43802 AEX	ALBLS	6/16
	Birmingham-Hoover MSA, AL	Y	27741 AE	37550 AW	42465 AEX	ALBLS	6/16
	Alaska	Y	56480 FQ	70410 MW	83940 TQ	USBLS	5/15
	Anchorage MSA, AK	Y	55520 FQ	70420 MW	86500 TQ	USBLS	5/15
	Arizona	Y	30880 FQ	37290 MW	48740 TQ	USBLS	5/15
	Phoenix-Mesa-Scottsdale MSA, AZ	Y	30660 FQ	36760 MW	47630 TQ	USBLS	5/15
	Tucson MSA, AZ	Y	29260 FQ	36710 MW	44960 TQ	USBLS	5/15
	Arkansas	Y	28010 FQ	33920 MW	41050 TQ	USBLS	5/15
	Little Rock-North Little Rock-Conway MSA, AR	Y	29200 FQ	34420 MW	39300 TQ	USBLS	5/15
	California	H	15.15 FQ	18.99 MW	25.65 TQ	CABLS	1/16-3/16
	Anaheim-Santa Ana-Irvine PMSA, CA	H	13.76 FQ	17.03 MW	22.28 TQ	CABLS	1/16-3/16
	Los Angeles-Long Beach-Glendale PMSA, CA	H	14.20 FQ	17.83 MW	23.33 TQ	CABLS	1/16-3/16
	Oakland-Hayward-Berkeley PMSA, CA	H	17.51 FQ	22.54 MW	28.73 TQ	CABLS	1/16-3/16
	Riverside-San Bernardino-Ontario MSA, CA	H	14.19 FQ	17.27 MW	20.52 TQ	CABLS	1/16-3/16
	Sacramento–Roseville–Arden-Arcade MSA, CA	H	16.43 FQ	20.45 MW	29.28 TQ	CABLS	1/16-3/16
	San Diego-Carlsbad MSA, CA	H	18.50 FQ	24.92 MW	28.41 TQ	CABLS	1/16-3/16
	San Francisco-Redwood City-South San Francisco PMSA, CA	H	21.42 FQ	29.36 MW	43.77 TQ	CABLS	1/16-3/16

AE	Average entry wage	AWR	Average wage range	H	Hourly
AEX	Average experienced wage	B	Biweekly	HI	Highest wage paid
ATC	Average total compensation	D	Daily	HR	High end range
AW	Average wage paid	FQ	First quartile wage	LO	Lowest wage paid

LR	Low end range	MTC	Median total compensation	TCC	Total cash compensation
M	Monthly	MW	Median wage paid	TQ	Third quartile wage
MCC	Median cash compensation	MWR	Median wage range	W	Weekly
ME	Median entry wage	S	See annotated source	Y	Yearly

Occupation/Type/Industry	Location	Per	Low	Mid	High	Source	Date
Welder, Cutter, Solderer, and Brazer							
	Colorado	Y	33730 FQ	39900 MW	50530 TQ	USBLS	5/15
	Denver-Aurora-Lakewood MSA, CO	Y	32600 FQ	37330 MW	45600 TQ	USBLS	5/15
	Connecticut	Y		42606 MW		CTBLS	1/16-3/16
	Bridgeport-Stamford-Norwalk MSA, CT	Y	31210 FQ	39230 MW	46840 TQ	USBLS	5/15
	Hartford-West Hartford-East Hartford MSA, CT	Y	36610 FQ	44360 MW	54040 TQ	USBLS	5/15
	New Haven MSA, CT	Y	33080 FQ	37710 MW	44590 TQ	USBLS	5/15
	Delaware	Y	36790 FQ	46940 MW	57340 TQ	USBLS	5/15
	Wilmington PMSA, DE-MD-NJ	Y	39810 FQ	49700 MW	61260 TQ	USBLS	5/15
	District of Columbia	Y	50840 FQ	57520 MW	66030 TQ	USBLS	5/15
	Washington-Arlington-Alexandria PMSA, DC-VA-MD-WV	Y	38530 FQ	48670 MW	60700 TQ	USBLS	5/15
	Florida	H	12.85 AE	17.66 MW	21.14 AEX	FLBLS	7/16-9/16
	Fort Lauderdale-Pompano Beach-Deerfield Beach PMSA, FL	H	15.36 AE	18.36 MW	21.94 AEX	FLBLS	7/16-9/16
	Miami-Miami Beach-Kendall PMSA, FL	H	12.65 AE	18.32 MW	21.15 AEX	FLBLS	7/16-9/16
	Orlando-Kissimmee-Sanford MSA, FL	H	12.11 AE	16.86 MW	19.81 AEX	FLBLS	7/16-9/16
	Tampa-St. Petersburg-Clearwater MSA, FL	H	13.13 AE	17.10 MW	19.52 AEX	FLBLS	7/16-9/16
	Georgia	Y	27760 FQ	34250 MW	40790 TQ	USBLS	5/15
	Atlanta-Sandy Springs-Roswell MSA, GA	Y	27570 FQ	34080 MW	40170 TQ	USBLS	5/15
	Augusta-Richmond County MSA, GA-SC	Y	33020 FQ	37920 MW	47200 TQ	USBLS	5/15
	Hawaii	Y	47410 FQ	62810 MW	72390 TQ	USBLS	5/15
	Urban Honolulu MSA, HI	Y	51000 FQ	65390 MW	74010 TQ	USBLS	5/15
	Idaho	Y	28800 FQ	34670 MW	39790 TQ	USBLS	5/15
	Boise City MSA, ID	Y	26530 FQ	32330 MW	37530 TQ	USBLS	5/15
	Illinois	Y	29500 FQ	36040 MW	44850 TQ	USBLS	5/15
	Chicago-Naperville-Arlington Heights PMSA, IL	Y	29950 FQ	36780 MW	46910 TQ	USBLS	5/15
	Lake County-Kenosha County PMSA, IL-WI	Y	29170 FQ	35780 MW	44590 TQ	USBLS	5/15
	Indiana	Y	29150 FQ	35100 MW	41600 TQ	USBLS	5/15
	Gary PMSA, IN	Y	29930 FQ	36710 MW	47300 TQ	USBLS	5/15
	Indianapolis-Carmel-Anderson MSA, IN	Y	31050 FQ	37780 MW	47440 TQ	USBLS	5/15
	Iowa	Y	30450 FQ	35660 MW	41530 TQ	USBLS	5/15
	Des Moines-West Des Moines MSA, IA	Y	31230 FQ	36110 MW	42700 TQ	USBLS	5/15
	Kansas	Y	29640 FQ	35770 MW	44050 TQ	USBLS	5/15
	Wichita MSA, KS	Y	26220 FQ	34860 MW	44700 TQ	USBLS	5/15
	Kentucky	Y	29140 FQ	35810 MW	44730 TQ	USBLS	5/15
	Louisville-Jefferson County MSA, KY-IN	Y	31910 FQ	38890 MW	47650 TQ	USBLS	5/15
	Louisiana	Y	35570 FQ	43290 MW	51240 TQ	USBLS	5/15
	Baton Rouge MSA, LA	Y	34300 FQ	39540 MW	53190 TQ	USBLS	5/15
	New Orleans-Metairie MSA, LA	Y	39820 FQ	46090 MW	54270 TQ	USBLS	5/15
	Maine	Y	36560 FQ	47390 MW	55550 TQ	USBLS	5/15
	Portland-South Portland MSA, ME	Y	40000 FQ	45300 MW	50910 TQ	USBLS	5/15
	Maryland	Y	31404 AE	45314 MW	52269 AEX	MDBLS	4/16
	Baltimore-Columbia-Towson MSA, MD	Y	38130 FQ	46380 MW	55630 TQ	USBLS	5/15
	Salisbury MSA, MD-DE	Y	28250 FQ	35830 MW	46690 TQ	USBLS	5/15
	Massachusetts	Y	34940 FQ	44870 MW	56400 TQ	USBLS	5/15
	Boston-Cambridge-Newton NECTA, MA	Y	37750 FQ	47690 MW	59620 TQ	USBLS	5/15
	Worcester MSA, MA-CT	Y	34640 FQ	42020 MW	53190 TQ	USBLS	5/15
	Michigan	Y	29590 FQ	35680 MW	43460 TQ	USBLS	5/15
	Detroit-Dearborn-Livonia PMSA, MI	Y	33020 FQ	38700 MW	50140 TQ	USBLS	5/15

AE Average entry wage	**AWR** Average wage range	**H** Hourly	**LR** Low end range	**MTC** Median total compensation **TCC** Total cash compensation
AEX Average experienced wage	**B** Biweekly	**HI** Highest wage paid	**M** Monthly	**MW** Median wage paid **TQ** Third quartile wage
ATC Average total compensation	**D** Daily	**HR** High end range	**MCC** Median cash compensation	**MWR** Median wage range **W** Weekly
AW Average wage paid	**FQ** First quartile wage	**LO** Lowest wage paid	**ME** Median entry wage	**S** See annotated source **Y** Yearly

Welder, Cutter, Solderer, and Brazer

Occupation/Type/Industry	Location	Per	Low	Mid	High	Source	Date
Welder, Cutter, Solderer, and Brazer	Grand Rapids-Wyoming MSA, MI	Y	27490 FQ	33370 MW	40010 TQ	USBLS	5/15
	Minnesota	Y	34302 FQ	41004 MW	49063 TQ	MNBLS	1/16-3/16
	Minneapolis-St. Paul-Bloomington MSA, MN-WI	Y	35800 FQ	43343 MW	50744 TQ	MNBLS	1/16-3/16
	Mississippi	Y	32470 FQ	41500 MW	50140 TQ	USBLS	5/15
	Jackson MSA, MS	Y	28170 FQ	32440 MW	38560 TQ	USBLS	5/15
	Missouri	Y	29040 FQ	36720 MW	46460 TQ	USBLS	5/15
	Kansas City MSA, MO-KS	Y	29450 FQ	38000 MW	52960 TQ	USBLS	5/15
	St. Louis MSA, MO-IL	Y	30390 FQ	39130 MW	46880 TQ	USBLS	5/15
	Montana	Y	30790 FQ	36550 MW	45440 TQ	USBLS	5/15
	Billings MSA, MT	Y	31580 FQ	36450 MW	43410 TQ	USBLS	5/15
	Nebraska	Y	30300 FQ	35690 MW	42020 TQ	NEBLS	7/16-9/16
	Omaha-Council Bluffs MSA, NE-IA	Y	32270 FQ	36635 MW	42895 TQ	NEBLS	7/16-9/16
	Nevada	Y	30580 FQ	38650 MW	58830 TQ	USBLS	5/15
	Las Vegas-Henderson-Paradise MSA, NV	Y	30830 FQ	37460 MW	52380 TQ	USBLS	5/15
	New Hampshire	H	14.94 AE	19.92 MW	23.67 AEX	NHBLS	6/16
	Manchester NECTA, NH	H	18.56 AE	24.58 MW	26.71 AEX	NHBLS	6/16
	Nashua NECTA, NH-MA	Y	30070 FQ	40560 MW	49370 TQ	USBLS	5/15
	New Jersey	Y	35270 FQ	43790 MW	54030 TQ	USBLS	5/15
	Camden PMSA, NJ	Y	33730 FQ	41560 MW	49860 TQ	USBLS	5/15
	Newark PMSA, NJ-PA	Y	37810 FQ	45460 MW	53900 TQ	USBLS	5/15
	Trenton MSA, NJ	Y	36950 FQ	45500 MW	56440 TQ	USBLS	5/15
	New Mexico	Y	33940 FQ	44930 MW	62230 TQ	USBLS	5/15
	Albuquerque MSA, NM	Y	33770 FQ	40040 MW	46460 TQ	USBLS	5/15
	New York	Y	29800 AE	40950 MW	51410 AEX	NYBLS	1/16-3/16
	Buffalo-Cheektowaga-Niagara Falls MSA, NY	Y	32490 FQ	38570 MW	46300 TQ	USBLS	5/15
	Nassau County-Suffolk County PMSA, NY	Y	34410 FQ	45990 MW	58410 TQ	USBLS	5/15
	New York-Jersey City-White Plains PMSA, NY-NJ	Y	33670 FQ	43280 MW	55890 TQ	USBLS	5/15
	Rochester MSA, NY	Y	31310 FQ	37880 MW	46460 TQ	USBLS	5/15
	North Carolina	Y	31570 FQ	37950 MW	46200 TQ	USBLS	5/15
	Charlotte-Concord-Gastonia MSA, NC-SC	Y	31970 FQ	37720 MW	45940 TQ	USBLS	5/15
	Raleigh MSA, NC	Y	32450 FQ	37920 MW	46350 TQ	USBLS	5/15
	North Dakota	Y	38230 FQ	46920 MW	61030 TQ	USBLS	5/15
	Fargo MSA, ND-MN	Y	35100 FQ	40760 MW	46860 TQ	USBLS	5/15
	Ohio	Y	30730 FQ	36340 MW	43970 TQ	USBLS	5/15
	Cincinnati MSA, OH-KY-IN	Y	30630 FQ	36810 MW	45010 TQ	USBLS	5/15
	Cleveland-Elyria MSA, OH	Y	31090 FQ	36710 MW	44650 TQ	USBLS	5/15
	Columbus MSA, OH	Y	32200 FQ	37770 MW	45850 TQ	USBLS	5/15
	Oklahoma	Y	30760 FQ	37580 MW	47370 TQ	USBLS	5/15
	Oklahoma City MSA, OK	Y	29680 FQ	35610 MW	42940 TQ	USBLS	5/15
	Tulsa MSA, OK	Y	33260 FQ	40520 MW	49080 TQ	USBLS	5/15
	Oregon	H	16.84 FQ	20.16 MW	23.76 TQ	ORBLS	2016
	Portland-Vancouver-Hillsboro MSA, OR-WA	Y	35980 FQ	42890 MW	49640 TQ	USBLS	5/15
	Pennsylvania	Y	32580 FQ	38610 MW	47180 TQ	USBLS	5/15
	Allentown-Bethlehem-Easton MSA, PA-NJ	Y	35200 FQ	41370 MW	50060 TQ	USBLS	5/15
	Harrisburg-Carlisle MSA, PA	Y	31470 FQ	39110 MW	50360 TQ	USBLS	5/15
	Montgomery County-Bucks County-Chester County PMSA, PA	Y	33540 FQ	40330 MW	48010 TQ	USBLS	5/15
	Philadelphia PMSA, PA	Y	34370 FQ	41050 MW	48390 TQ	USBLS	5/15
	Pittsburgh MSA, PA	Y	34810 FQ	40960 MW	48500 TQ	USBLS	5/15
	Rhode Island	Y	35040 FQ	40280 MW	49290 TQ	USBLS	5/15
	Providence-Warwick MSA, RI-MA	Y	34580 FQ	40080 MW	49500 TQ	USBLS	5/15
	South Carolina	Y	31180 FQ	36680 MW	45200 TQ	USBLS	5/15
	Charleston-North Charleston MSA, SC	Y	33590 FQ	37360 MW	43390 TQ	USBLS	5/15
	Columbia MSA, SC	Y	32060 FQ	38530 MW	52470 TQ	USBLS	5/15
	Greenville-Anderson-Mauldin MSA, SC	Y	32280 FQ	37200 MW	44110 TQ	USBLS	5/15
	South Dakota	Y	30020 FQ	34590 MW	38780 TQ	USBLS	5/15
	Sioux Falls MSA, SD	Y	31460 FQ	35280 MW	39110 TQ	USBLS	5/15

AE	Average entry wage	AWR	Average wage range
AEX	Average experienced wage	B	Biweekly
ATC	Average total compensation	D	Daily
AW	Average wage paid	FQ	First quartile wage

H	Hourly
HI	Highest wage paid
HR	High end range
LO	Lowest wage paid

LR	Low end range
M	Monthly
MCC	Median cash compensation
ME	Median entry wage

MTC	Median total compensation
MW	Median wage paid
MWR	Median wage range
S	See annotated source

TCC	Total cash compensation
TQ	Third quartile wage
W	Weekly
Y	Yearly

Occupation/Type/Industry	Location	Per	Low	Mid	High	Source	Date
Welder, Cutter, Solderer, and Brazer							
	Tennessee	Y	30670 FQ	36470 MW	44040 TQ	USBLS	5/15
	Knoxville MSA, TN	Y	32780 FQ	36560 MW	42100 TQ	USBLS	5/15
	Memphis MSA, TN-MS-AR	Y	33130 FQ	39480 MW	51510 TQ	USBLS	5/15
	Nashville-Davidson–Murfreesboro–Franklin MSA, TN	Y	31070 FQ	37060 MW	44840 TQ	USBLS	5/15
	Texas	Y	31830 FQ	39180 MW	50290 TQ	USBLS	5/15
	Austin-Round Rock MSA, TX	Y	29250 FQ	34540 MW	39030 TQ	USBLS	5/15
	Dallas-Plano-Irving PMSA, TX	Y	28800 FQ	35620 MW	44020 TQ	USBLS	5/15
	Fort Worth-Arlington PMSA, TX	Y	31500 FQ	36270 MW	43690 TQ	USBLS	5/15
	Houston-The Woodlands-Sugar Land MSA, TX	Y	35230 FQ	43570 MW	55430 TQ	USBLS	5/15
	San Antonio-New Braunfels MSA, TX	Y	31580 FQ	35860 MW	41450 TQ	USBLS	5/15
	Utah	Y	31860 FQ	37460 MW	47730 TQ	USBLS	5/15
	Ogden-Clearfield MSA, UT	Y	31660 FQ	37090 MW	45190 TQ	USBLS	5/15
	Provo-Orem MSA, UT	Y	28300 FQ	35010 MW	49430 TQ	USBLS	5/15
	Salt Lake City MSA, UT	Y	32690 FQ	37750 MW	47640 TQ	USBLS	5/15
	Vermont	Y	27950 FQ	33520 MW	41490 TQ	USBLS	5/15
	Burlington-South Burlington MSA, VT	Y	33360 FQ	40760 MW	49470 TQ	USBLS	5/15
	Virginia	Y	35130 FQ	43810 MW	51780 TQ	USBLS	5/15
	Richmond MSA, VA	Y	35150 FQ	43660 MW	51460 TQ	USBLS	5/15
	Virginia Beach-Norfolk-Newport News MSA, VA-NC	Y	41140 FQ	47760 MW	54510 TQ	USBLS	5/15
	Washington	H	17.79 FQ	21.88 MW	27.40 TQ	WABLS	3/16
	Seattle-Bellevue-Everett PMSA, WA	H	19.15 FQ	23.15 MW	28.43 TQ	WABLS	3/16
	Tacoma-Lakewood PMSA, WA	H	17.77 FQ	21.75 MW	26.74 TQ	WABLS	3/16
	West Virginia	Y	32410 FQ	39230 MW	51430 TQ	USBLS	5/15
	Huntington-Ashland MSA, WV-KY-OH	Y	31610 FQ	37810 MW	48180 TQ	USBLS	5/15
	Wisconsin	Y	33640 FQ	39240 MW	46170 TQ	USBLS	5/15
	Madison MSA, WI	Y	34120 FQ	39830 MW	52390 TQ	USBLS	5/15
	Milwaukee-Waukesha-West Allis MSA, WI	Y	34490 FQ	40070 MW	47430 TQ	USBLS	5/15
	Wyoming	Y	40320 FQ	54270 MW	70510 TQ	USBLS	5/15
	Cheyenne MSA, WY	Y	30770 FQ	40970 MW	52760 TQ	USBLS	5/15
	Puerto Rico	Y	18680 FQ	22170 MW	26880 TQ	USBLS	5/15
	San Juan-Carolina-Caguas MSA, PR	Y	19010 FQ	22550 MW	27410 TQ	USBLS	5/15
	Virgin Islands	Y	29560 FQ	40080 MW	46070 TQ	USBLS	5/15
	Guam	Y	31320 FQ	35310 MW	39160 TQ	USBLS	5/15
Welding, Soldering, and Brazing Machine Setter, Operator, and Tender							
	Alabama	Y	28739 AE	40501 AW	46383 AEX	ALBLS	6/16
	Birmingham-Hoover MSA, AL	Y	33222 AE	38846 AW	41663 AEX	ALBLS	6/16
	Arizona	Y	33360 FQ	36630 MW	40000 TQ	USBLS	5/15
	Phoenix-Mesa-Scottsdale MSA, AZ	Y	33460 FQ	36550 MW	39620 TQ	USBLS	5/15
	Arkansas	Y	31750 FQ	35620 MW	39480 TQ	USBLS	5/15
	Little Rock-North Little Rock-Conway MSA, AR	Y	28720 FQ	34060 MW	40250 TQ	USBLS	5/15
	California	H	13.31 FQ	17.54 MW	23.43 TQ	CABLS	1/16-3/16
	Anaheim-Santa Ana-Irvine PMSA, CA	H	12.96 FQ	15.96 MW	24.02 TQ	CABLS	1/16-3/16
	Los Angeles-Long Beach-Glendale PMSA, CA	H	11.33 FQ	14.71 MW	20.18 TQ	CABLS	1/16-3/16
	Oakland-Hayward-Berkeley PMSA, CA	H	19.00 FQ	21.98 MW	24.51 TQ	CABLS	1/16-3/16
	Riverside-San Bernardino-Ontario MSA, CA	H	13.23 FQ	16.30 MW	21.41 TQ	CABLS	1/16-3/16
	Sacramento–Roseville–Arden-Arcade MSA, CA	H	15.91 FQ	18.55 MW	22.46 TQ	CABLS	1/16-3/16
	San Diego-Carlsbad MSA, CA	H	17.89 FQ	23.53 MW	28.04 TQ	CABLS	1/16-3/16
	San Francisco-Redwood City-South San Francisco PMSA, CA	H	19.25 FQ	22.15 MW	25.73 TQ	CABLS	1/16-3/16

AE Average entry wage	**AWR** Average wage range	**H** Hourly	**LR** Low end range	**MTC** Median total compensation	**TCC** Total cash compensation
AEX Average experienced wage	**B** Biweekly	**HI** Highest wage paid	**M** Monthly	**MW** Median wage paid	**TQ** Third quartile wage
ATC Average total compensation	**D** Daily	**HR** High end range	**MCC** Median cash compensation	**MWR** Median wage range	**W** Weekly
AW Average wage paid	**FQ** First quartile wage	**LO** Lowest wage paid	**ME** Median entry wage	**S** See annotated source	**Y** Yearly

Occupation/Type/Industry	Location	Per	Low	Mid	High	Source	Date
Welding, Soldering, and Brazing Machine Setter, Operator, and Tender	Colorado	Y	25570 FQ	30640 MW	38960 TQ	USBLS	5/15
	Denver-Aurora-Lakewood MSA, CO	Y	23050 FQ	34850 MW	43700 TQ	USBLS	5/15
	Connecticut	Y		36757 MW		CTBLS	1/16-3/16
	Bridgeport-Stamford-Norwalk MSA, CT	Y	25190 FQ	31670 MW	40470 TQ	USBLS	5/15
	Hartford-West Hartford-East Hartford MSA, CT	Y	26700 FQ	37600 MW	45730 TQ	USBLS	5/15
	Florida	H	13.25 AE	17.78 MW	21.18 AEX	FLBLS	7/16-9/16
	Fort Lauderdale-Pompano Beach-Deerfield Beach PMSA, FL	H	12.70 AE	14.38 MW	16.21 AEX	FLBLS	7/16-9/16
	Orlando-Kissimmee-Sanford MSA, FL	H	13.87 AE	17.33 MW	21.36 AEX	FLBLS	7/16-9/16
	Tampa-St. Petersburg-Clearwater MSA, FL	H	12.21 AE	17.51 MW	20.26 AEX	FLBLS	7/16-9/16
	Georgia	Y	25970 FQ	33780 MW	43630 TQ	USBLS	5/15
	Atlanta-Sandy Springs-Roswell MSA, GA	Y	24650 FQ	31700 MW	40580 TQ	USBLS	5/15
	Idaho	Y	28190 FQ	33370 MW	38840 TQ	USBLS	5/15
	Boise City MSA, ID	Y	31060 FQ	35300 MW	39070 TQ	USBLS	5/15
	Illinois	Y	27960 FQ	34920 MW	42300 TQ	USBLS	5/15
	Chicago-Naperville-Arlington Heights PMSA, IL	Y	26340 FQ	32970 MW	39540 TQ	USBLS	5/15
	Lake County-Kenosha County PMSA, IL-WI	Y	24330 FQ	29590 MW	37400 TQ	USBLS	5/15
	Indiana	Y	27470 FQ	32760 MW	39650 TQ	USBLS	5/15
	Gary PMSA, IN	Y	29730 FQ	34520 MW	38680 TQ	USBLS	5/15
	Indianapolis-Carmel-Anderson MSA, IN	Y	24710 FQ	29050 MW	34550 TQ	USBLS	5/15
	Iowa	Y	31520 FQ	35420 MW	39500 TQ	USBLS	5/15
	Des Moines-West Des Moines MSA, IA	Y	34540 FQ	38080 MW	43400 TQ	USBLS	5/15
	Kansas	Y	29410 FQ	34680 MW	38900 TQ	USBLS	5/15
	Wichita MSA, KS	Y	32570 FQ	36090 MW	39610 TQ	USBLS	5/15
	Kentucky	Y	24800 FQ	31050 MW	36340 TQ	USBLS	5/15
	Louisville-Jefferson County MSA, KY-IN	Y	26770 FQ	31080 MW	35650 TQ	USBLS	5/15
	Louisiana	Y	31300 FQ	37950 MW	48200 TQ	USBLS	5/15
	New Orleans-Metairie MSA, LA	Y	35680 FQ	42950 MW	50320 TQ	USBLS	5/15
	Maine	Y	34410 FQ	41130 MW	47620 TQ	USBLS	5/15
	Portland-South Portland MSA, ME	Y	41730 FQ	45440 MW	49150 TQ	USBLS	5/15
	Maryland	Y	22256 AE	35595 MW	42265 AEX	MDBLS	4/16
	Baltimore-Columbia-Towson MSA, MD	Y	27760 FQ	36500 MW	45810 TQ	USBLS	5/15
	Massachusetts	Y	31390 FQ	37740 MW	49310 TQ	USBLS	5/15
	Boston-Cambridge-Newton NECTA, MA	Y	28100 FQ	36690 MW	49560 TQ	USBLS	5/15
	Worcester MSA, MA-CT	Y	32750 FQ	36230 MW	42120 TQ	USBLS	5/15
	Michigan	Y	27060 FQ	37030 MW	47950 TQ	USBLS	5/15
	Detroit-Dearborn-Livonia PMSA, MI	Y	33910 FQ	54520 MW	61110 TQ	USBLS	5/15
	Grand Rapids-Wyoming MSA, MI	Y	31680 FQ	40810 MW	46280 TQ	USBLS	5/15
	Minnesota	Y	32165 FQ	38878 MW	46077 TQ	MNBLS	1/16-3/16
	Minneapolis-St. Paul-Bloomington MSA, MN-WI	Y	35081 FQ	43829 MW	51696 TQ	MNBLS	1/16-3/16
	Mississippi	Y	28820 FQ	35670 MW	48940 TQ	USBLS	5/15
	Jackson MSA, MS	Y	31110 FQ	35520 MW	40330 TQ	USBLS	5/15
	Missouri	Y	26750 FQ	31930 MW	36980 TQ	USBLS	5/15
	Kansas City MSA, MO-KS	Y	32590 FQ	36410 MW	42320 TQ	USBLS	5/15
	St. Louis MSA, MO-IL	Y	27430 FQ	34070 MW	40950 TQ	USBLS	5/15
	Montana	Y	30740 FQ	35820 MW	41220 TQ	USBLS	5/15
	Nebraska	Y	30335 FQ	36205 MW	42605 TQ	NEBLS	7/16-9/16
	Omaha-Council Bluffs MSA, NE-IA	Y	34865 FQ	40715 MW	45385 TQ	NEBLS	7/16-9/16
	Nevada	Y	24320 FQ	32610 MW	37950 TQ	USBLS	5/15

Welding, Soldering, and Brazing Machine Setter, Operator, and Tender

Occupation/Type/Industry	Location	Per	Low	Mid	High	Source	Date
	Las Vegas-Henderson-Paradise MSA, NV	Y	23660 FQ	31940 MW	38140 TQ	USBLS	5/15
	New Hampshire	H	11.95 AE	15.00 MW	17.65 AEX	NHBLS	6/16
	Manchester NECTA, NH	H	9.75 AE	14.29 MW	18.07 AEX	NHBLS	6/16
	Nashua NECTA, NH-MA	Y	26340 FQ	29480 MW	35100 TQ	USBLS	5/15
	New Jersey	Y	29610 FQ	36820 MW	45040 TQ	USBLS	5/15
	Newark PMSA, NJ-PA	Y	29010 FQ	35200 MW	43790 TQ	USBLS	5/15
	New Mexico	Y	24750 FQ	32910 MW	38780 TQ	USBLS	5/15
	New York	Y	27350 AE	41360 MW	48330 AEX	NYBLS	1/16-3/16
	Buffalo-Cheektowaga-Niagara Falls MSA, NY	Y	38560 FQ	50900 MW	61240 TQ	USBLS	5/15
	Nassau County-Suffolk County PMSA, NY	Y	24040 FQ	32790 MW	43130 TQ	USBLS	5/15
	New York-Jersey City-White Plains PMSA, NY-NJ	Y	30230 FQ	41720 MW	48220 TQ	USBLS	5/15
	Rochester MSA, NY	Y	26380 FQ	34990 MW	44760 TQ	USBLS	5/15
	North Carolina	Y	26910 FQ	31640 MW	37330 TQ	USBLS	5/15
	Charlotte-Concord-Gastonia MSA, NC-SC	Y	28290 FQ	33850 MW	38020 TQ	USBLS	5/15
	Raleigh MSA, NC	Y	25430 FQ	29440 MW	34580 TQ	USBLS	5/15
	North Dakota	Y	40120 FQ	44520 MW	48820 TQ	USBLS	5/15
	Fargo MSA, ND-MN	Y	34790 FQ	39130 MW	45540 TQ	USBLS	5/15
	Ohio	Y	29610 FQ	36750 MW	47980 TQ	USBLS	5/15
	Cincinnati MSA, OH-KY-IN	Y	28860 FQ	36110 MW	45400 TQ	USBLS	5/15
	Cleveland-Elyria MSA, OH	Y	27440 FQ	32320 MW	39270 TQ	USBLS	5/15
	Oklahoma	Y	32760 FQ	40320 MW	47130 TQ	USBLS	5/15
	Oklahoma City MSA, OK	Y	27640 FQ	31040 MW	38640 TQ	USBLS	5/15
	Tulsa MSA, OK	Y	37810 FQ	43560 MW	48630 TQ	USBLS	5/15
	Oregon	H	15.31 FQ	18.54 MW	21.96 TQ	ORBLS	2016
	Portland-Vancouver-Hillsboro MSA, OR-WA	Y	30630 FQ	37390 MW	44590 TQ	USBLS	5/15
	Pennsylvania	Y	27750 FQ	34620 MW	40860 TQ	USBLS	5/15
	Montgomery County-Bucks County-Chester County PMSA, PA	Y	33950 FQ	42610 MW	50830 TQ	USBLS	5/15
	Pittsburgh MSA, PA	Y	35820 FQ	40950 MW	46080 TQ	USBLS	5/15
	Rhode Island	Y	27470 FQ	34320 MW	43830 TQ	USBLS	5/15
	Providence-Warwick MSA, RI-MA	Y	25540 FQ	34110 MW	44110 TQ	USBLS	5/15
	South Carolina	Y	26610 FQ	35240 MW	44900 TQ	USBLS	5/15
	Charleston-North Charleston MSA, SC	Y	28960 FQ	43880 MW	67000 TQ	USBLS	5/15
	Columbia MSA, SC	Y	24220 FQ	35850 MW	45040 TQ	USBLS	5/15
	Greenville-Anderson-Mauldin MSA, SC	Y	24500 FQ	30200 MW	43600 TQ	USBLS	5/15
	South Dakota	Y	34200 FQ	38610 MW	44300 TQ	USBLS	5/15
	Sioux Falls MSA, SD	Y	33730 FQ	37390 MW	42380 TQ	USBLS	5/15
	Tennessee	Y	29820 FQ	35990 MW	42790 TQ	USBLS	5/15
	Knoxville MSA, TN	Y	31810 FQ	38190 MW	48150 TQ	USBLS	5/15
	Memphis MSA, TN-MS-AR	Y	30160 FQ	35770 MW	42180 TQ	USBLS	5/15
	Nashville-Davidson–Murfreesboro–Franklin MSA, TN	Y	20010 FQ	32360 MW	36960 TQ	USBLS	5/15
	Texas	Y	31420 FQ	39260 MW	48540 TQ	USBLS	5/15
	Austin-Round Rock MSA, TX	Y	27730 FQ	34510 MW	42980 TQ	USBLS	5/15
	Dallas-Plano-Irving PMSA, TX	Y	23430 FQ	28680 MW	36940 TQ	USBLS	5/15
	Fort Worth-Arlington PMSA, TX	Y	28080 FQ	34610 MW	40790 TQ	USBLS	5/15
	Houston-The Woodlands-Sugar Land MSA, TX	Y	37190 FQ	45780 MW	54300 TQ	USBLS	5/15
	San Antonio-New Braunfels MSA, TX	Y	27960 FQ	32030 MW	36130 TQ	USBLS	5/15
	Utah	Y	33340 FQ	39620 MW	47530 TQ	USBLS	5/15
	Ogden-Clearfield MSA, UT	Y	41480 FQ	45670 MW	49770 TQ	USBLS	5/15
	Provo-Orem MSA, UT	Y	24150 FQ	34600 MW	40370 TQ	USBLS	5/15
	Salt Lake City MSA, UT	Y	33750 FQ	38310 MW	45010 TQ	USBLS	5/15
	Virginia	Y	35730 FQ	43610 MW	51240 TQ	USBLS	5/15
	Richmond MSA, VA	Y	33580 FQ	36720 MW	40560 TQ	USBLS	5/15
	Washington	H	17.63 FQ	21.94 MW	27.04 TQ	WABLS	3/16

AE	Average entry wage	AWR	Average wage range	H	Hourly
AEX	Average experienced wage	B	Biweekly	HI	Highest wage paid
ATC	Average total compensation	D	Daily	HR	High end range
AW	Average wage paid	FQ	First quartile wage	LO	Lowest wage paid

LR	Low end range	MTC	Median total compensation	TCC	Total cash compensation
M	Monthly	MW	Median wage paid	TQ	Third quartile wage
MCC	Median cash compensation	MWR	Median wage range	W	Weekly
ME	Median entry wage	S	See annotated source	Y	Yearly

Occupation/Type/Industry	Location	Per	Low	Mid	High	Source	Date
Welding, Soldering, and Brazing Machine Setter, Operator, and Tender							
	Seattle-Bellevue-Everett PMSA, WA	H	18.08 FQ	24.15 MW	28.59 TQ	WABLS	3/16
	Tacoma-Lakewood PMSA, WA	H	16.69 FQ	20.38 MW	25.15 TQ	WABLS	3/16
	Wisconsin	Y	33170 FQ	40740 MW	51110 TQ	USBLS	5/15
	Madison MSA, WI	Y	29130 FQ	34740 MW	40750 TQ	USBLS	5/15
	Milwaukee-Waukesha-West Allis MSA, WI	Y	42430 FQ	53890 MW	67920 TQ	USBLS	5/15
	Puerto Rico	Y	20690 FQ	23350 MW	27790 TQ	USBLS	5/15
	San Juan-Carolina-Caguas MSA, PR	Y	20720 FQ	23510 MW	28230 TQ	USBLS	5/15
Welfare Fraud Investigator							
Municipal Government	San Francisco, CA	Y		55463 AW		CACIT	6/28/16
Wellhead Pumper							
	Arkansas	Y	26170 FQ	42820 MW	50210 TQ	USBLS	5/15
	California	H	21.53 FQ	26.50 MW	31.79 TQ	CABLS	1/16-3/16
	Colorado	Y	50680 FQ	57610 MW	65030 TQ	USBLS	5/15
	Indiana	Y	18060 FQ	28880 MW	55250 TQ	USBLS	5/15
	Kansas	Y	32530 FQ	36710 MW	45750 TQ	USBLS	5/15
	Kentucky	Y	34150 FQ	42410 MW	49010 TQ	USBLS	5/15
	Louisiana	Y	21660 FQ	24680 MW	55900 TQ	USBLS	5/15
	Michigan	Y	35260 FQ	42170 MW	51390 TQ	USBLS	5/15
	Mississippi	Y	24530 FQ	44720 MW	56210 TQ	USBLS	5/15
	Montana	Y	51720 FQ	59920 MW	70260 TQ	USBLS	5/15
	Nebraska	Y	36585 FQ	42260 MW	47010 TQ	NEBLS	7/16-9/16
	New Mexico	Y	44140 FQ	53930 MW	63720 TQ	USBLS	5/15
	North Dakota	Y	47690 FQ	58580 MW	73120 TQ	USBLS	5/15
	Ohio	Y	28470 FQ	33850 MW	38090 TQ	USBLS	5/15
	Oklahoma	Y	41570 FQ	48580 MW	57900 TQ	USBLS	5/15
	Pennsylvania	Y	33860 FQ	41240 MW	49530 TQ	USBLS	5/15
	Texas	Y	37400 FQ	48160 MW	59930 TQ	USBLS	5/15
	Utah	Y	46100 FQ	54870 MW	61010 TQ	USBLS	5/15
	West Virginia	Y	27920 FQ	34830 MW	47220 TQ	USBLS	5/15
	Wyoming	Y	45340 FQ	54670 MW	61130 TQ	USBLS	5/15
Wellness Coach	United States	Y		40000 AW		BUZZ03	2015
Wellness Coordinator							
County Government	Oakland County, MI	B	1913 LO		2490 HI	MIOAK2	10/1/16
Police Administration, Municipal Government	El Segundo, CA	Y	69720 LO		82104 HI	CACIT	6/28/16
Wellness Director							
Municipal Government	Lindsay, CA	Y			41608 HI	CACIT	6/28/16
Wholesale and Retail Buyer							
Except Farm Products	Alabama	Y	31169 AE	52304 AW	62871 AEX	ALBLS	6/16
Except Farm Products	Birmingham-Hoover MSA, AL	Y	33332 AE	53206 AW	63148 AEX	ALBLS	6/16
Except Farm Products	Alaska	Y	34980 FQ	47800 MW	67610 TQ	USBLS	5/15
Except Farm Products	Anchorage MSA, AK	Y	38810 FQ	57010 MW	76160 TQ	USBLS	5/15
Except Farm Products	Arizona	Y	36240 FQ	46460 MW	64300 TQ	USBLS	5/15
Except Farm Products	Phoenix-Mesa-Scottsdale MSA, AZ	Y	37950 FQ	47590 MW	66320 TQ	USBLS	5/15
Except Farm Products	Tucson MSA, AZ	Y	32900 FQ	39470 MW	54340 TQ	USBLS	5/15
Except Farm Products	Little Rock-North Little Rock-Conway MSA, AR	Y	29950 FQ	39000 MW	50030 TQ	USBLS	5/15
Except Farm Products	California	H	18.71 FQ	25.76 MW	36.09 TQ	CABLS	1/16-3/16
Except Farm Products	Anaheim-Santa Ana-Irvine PMSA, CA	H	21.86 FQ	27.99 MW	36.87 TQ	CABLS	1/16-3/16
Except Farm Products	Los Angeles-Long Beach-Glendale PMSA, CA	H	17.47 FQ	25.89 MW	36.92 TQ	CABLS	1/16-3/16
Except Farm Products	Oakland-Hayward-Berkeley PMSA, CA	H	19.17 FQ	24.88 MW	34.09 TQ	CABLS	1/16-3/16
Except Farm Products	Riverside-San Bernardino-Ontario MSA, CA	H	18.36 FQ	24.34 MW	30.21 TQ	CABLS	1/16-3/16
Except Farm Products	Sacramento–Roseville–Arden-Arcade MSA, CA	H	19.07 FQ	23.35 MW	30.81 TQ	CABLS	1/16-3/16
Except Farm Products	San Diego-Carlsbad MSA, CA	H	19.91 FQ	25.37 MW	34.49 TQ	CABLS	1/16-3/16

AE Average entry wage	**AWR** Average wage range	**H** Hourly	**LR** Low end range	**MTC** Median total compensation	**TCC** Total cash compensation
AEX Average experienced wage	**B** Biweekly	**HI** Highest wage paid	**M** Monthly	**MW** Median wage paid	**TQ** Third quartile wage
ATC Average total compensation	**D** Daily	**HR** High end range	**MCC** Median cash compensation	**MWR** Median wage range	**W** Weekly
AW Average wage paid	**FQ** First quartile wage	**LO** Lowest wage paid	**ME** Median entry wage	**S** See annotated source	**Y** Yearly

Occupation/Type/Industry	Location	Per	Low	Mid	High	Source	Date
Wholesale and Retail Buyer							
Except Farm Products	San Francisco-Redwood City-South San Francisco PMSA, CA	H	25.34 FQ	32.90 MW	43.25 TQ	CABLS	1/16-3/16
Except Farm Products	Colorado	Y	38990 FQ	50050 MW	63200 TQ	USBLS	5/15
Except Farm Products	Denver-Aurora-Lakewood MSA, CO	Y	38700 FQ	50530 MW	62610 TQ	USBLS	5/15
Except Farm Products	Connecticut	Y		54115 MW		CTBLS	1/16-3/16
Except Farm Products	Bridgeport-Stamford-Norwalk MSA, CT	Y	40130 FQ	55720 MW	71460 TQ	USBLS	5/15
Except Farm Products	Hartford-West Hartford-East Hartford MSA, CT	Y	39290 FQ	52570 MW	72530 TQ	USBLS	5/15
Except Farm Products	Delaware	Y	44760 FQ	55140 MW	63250 TQ	USBLS	5/15
Except Farm Products	Wilmington PMSA, DE-MD-NJ	Y	45390 FQ	55840 MW	67500 TQ	USBLS	5/15
Except Farm Products	District of Columbia	Y	42230 FQ	50500 MW	71090 TQ	USBLS	5/15
Except Farm Products	Washington-Arlington-Alexandria PMSA, DC-VA-MD-WV	Y	44200 FQ	59660 MW	74150 TQ	USBLS	5/15
Except Farm Products	Florida	H	18.54 AE	27.77 MW	39.42 AEX	FLBLS	7/16-9/16
Except Farm Products	Fort Lauderdale-Pompano Beach-Deerfield Beach PMSA, FL	H	18.84 AE	25.72 MW	34.22 AEX	FLBLS	7/16-9/16
Except Farm Products	Miami-Miami Beach-Kendall PMSA, FL	H	18.12 AE	27.53 MW	42.68 AEX	FLBLS	7/16-9/16
Except Farm Products	Orlando-Kissimmee-Sanford MSA, FL	H	18.21 AE	28.52 MW	39.46 AEX	FLBLS	7/16-9/16
Except Farm Products	Tampa-St. Petersburg-Clearwater MSA, FL	H	17.71 AE	27.45 MW	37.11 AEX	FLBLS	7/16-9/16
Except Farm Products	Georgia	Y	41480 FQ	54260 MW	71270 TQ	USBLS	5/15
Except Farm Products	Atlanta-Sandy Springs-Roswell MSA, GA	Y	43130 FQ	56410 MW	73630 TQ	USBLS	5/15
Except Farm Products	Augusta-Richmond County MSA, GA-SC	Y	45880 FQ	61680 MW	77320 TQ	USBLS	5/15
Except Farm Products	Hawaii	Y	31570 FQ	42390 MW	54950 TQ	USBLS	5/15
Except Farm Products	Urban Honolulu MSA, HI	Y	31290 FQ	41940 MW	54190 TQ	USBLS	5/15
Except Farm Products	Idaho	Y	29940 FQ	41810 MW	56250 TQ	USBLS	5/15
Except Farm Products	Boise City MSA, ID	Y	32960 FQ	44370 MW	58020 TQ	USBLS	5/15
Except Farm Products	Illinois	Y	42460 FQ	57370 MW	74800 TQ	USBLS	5/15
Except Farm Products	Chicago-Naperville-Arlington Heights PMSA, IL	Y	41210 FQ	56680 MW	75270 TQ	USBLS	5/15
Except Farm Products	Lake County-Kenosha County PMSA, IL-WI	Y	43550 FQ	55320 MW	72190 TQ	USBLS	5/15
Except Farm Products	Indiana	Y	35900 FQ	48580 MW	60840 TQ	USBLS	5/15
Except Farm Products	Gary PMSA, IN	Y	32900 FQ	47310 MW	64360 TQ	USBLS	5/15
Except Farm Products	Indianapolis-Carmel-Anderson MSA, IN	Y	41990 FQ	52580 MW	62330 TQ	USBLS	5/15
Except Farm Products	Iowa	Y	36080 FQ	47770 MW	62520 TQ	USBLS	5/15
Except Farm Products	Des Moines-West Des Moines MSA, IA	Y	35830 FQ	50800 MW	61920 TQ	USBLS	5/15
Except Farm Products	Kansas	Y	37750 FQ	50440 MW	66000 TQ	USBLS	5/15
Except Farm Products	Wichita MSA, KS	Y	26800 FQ	38880 MW	47580 TQ	USBLS	5/15
Except Farm Products	Kentucky	Y	33860 FQ	44980 MW	60910 TQ	USBLS	5/15
Except Farm Products	Louisville-Jefferson County MSA, KY-IN	Y	37060 FQ	46620 MW	72260 TQ	USBLS	5/15
Except Farm Products	Louisiana	Y	28580 FQ	41750 MW	55220 TQ	USBLS	5/15
Except Farm Products	Baton Rouge MSA, LA	Y	34100 FQ	51800 MW	63940 TQ	USBLS	5/15
Except Farm Products	New Orleans-Metairie MSA, LA	Y	23430 FQ	35950 MW	46790 TQ	USBLS	5/15
Except Farm Products	Maine	Y	39570 FQ	53800 MW	67060 TQ	USBLS	5/15
Except Farm Products	Portland-South Portland MSA, ME	Y	46880 FQ	59640 MW	72350 TQ	USBLS	5/15
Except Farm Products	Maryland	Y	33558 AE	57859 MW	70010 AEX	MDBLS	4/16
Except Farm Products	Baltimore-Columbia-Towson MSA, MD	Y	40390 FQ	49030 MW	60590 TQ	USBLS	5/15
Except Farm Products	Salisbury MSA, MD-DE	Y	36130 FQ	52660 MW	61490 TQ	USBLS	5/15
Except Farm Products	Massachusetts	Y	44890 FQ	59730 MW	81100 TQ	USBLS	5/15
Except Farm Products	Boston-Cambridge-Newton NECTA, MA	Y	47530 FQ	61580 MW	84190 TQ	USBLS	5/15
Except Farm Products	Worcester MSA, MA-CT	Y	42560 FQ	57170 MW	86180 TQ	USBLS	5/15
Except Farm Products	Michigan	Y	35410 FQ	47660 MW	61730 TQ	USBLS	5/15

AE	Average entry wage	AWR	Average wage range	H	Hourly	LR	Low end range	MTC	Median total compensation	TCC	Total cash compensation
AEX	Average experienced wage	B	Biweekly	HI	Highest wage paid	M	Monthly	MW	Median wage paid	TQ	Third quartile wage
ATC	Average total compensation	D	Daily	HR	High end range	MCC	Median cash compensation	MWR	Median wage range	W	Weekly
AW	Average wage paid	FQ	First quartile wage	LO	Lowest wage paid	ME	Median entry wage	S	See annotated source	Y	Yearly

Occupation/Type/Industry	Location	Per	Low	Mid	High	Source	Date
Wholesale and Retail Buyer							
Except Farm Products	Detroit-Dearborn-Livonia PMSA, MI	Y	36050 FQ	48760 MW	66930 TQ	USBLS	5/15
Except Farm Products	Grand Rapids-Wyoming MSA, MI	Y	37830 FQ	46830 MW	60340 TQ	USBLS	5/15
Except Farm Products	Minnesota	Y	42026 FQ	57135 MW	78809 TQ	MNBLS	1/16-3/16
Except Farm Products	Minneapolis-St. Paul-Bloomington MSA, MN-WI	Y	43672 FQ	60621 MW	81187 TQ	MNBLS	1/16-3/16
Except Farm Products	Mississippi	Y	35260 FQ	46890 MW	60200 TQ	USBLS	5/15
Except Farm Products	Jackson MSA, MS	Y	36470 FQ	51560 MW	70850 TQ	USBLS	5/15
Except Farm Products	Missouri	Y	37600 FQ	53730 MW	72750 TQ	USBLS	5/15
Except Farm Products	Kansas City MSA, MO-KS	Y	44720 FQ	58980 MW	81860 TQ	USBLS	5/15
Except Farm Products	St. Louis MSA, MO-IL	Y	41570 FQ	55290 MW	72120 TQ	USBLS	5/15
Except Farm Products	Montana	Y	26630 FQ	36990 MW	57590 TQ	USBLS	5/15
Except Farm Products	Billings MSA, MT	Y	25110 FQ	35320 MW	46360 TQ	USBLS	5/15
Except Farm Products	Nebraska	Y	37570 FQ	49450 MW	62225 TQ	NEBLS	7/16-9/16
Except Farm Products	Omaha-Council Bluffs MSA, NE-IA	Y	40815 FQ	49990 MW	61200 TQ	NEBLS	7/16-9/16
Except Farm Products	Nevada	Y	43170 FQ	53630 MW	64590 TQ	USBLS	5/15
Except Farm Products	Las Vegas-Henderson-Paradise MSA, NV	Y	44520 FQ	54460 MW	64830 TQ	USBLS	5/15
Except Farm Products	New Hampshire	H	17.25 AE	26.30 MW	35.78 AEX	NHBLS	6/16
Except Farm Products	Manchester NECTA, NH	H	13.34 AE	22.76 MW	33.14 AEX	NHBLS	6/16
Except Farm Products	Nashua NECTA, NH-MA	Y	46550 FQ	56080 MW	70380 TQ	USBLS	5/15
Except Farm Products	New Jersey	Y	49470 FQ	66530 MW	88430 TQ	USBLS	5/15
Except Farm Products	Camden PMSA, NJ	Y	51680 FQ	61920 MW	80280 TQ	USBLS	5/15
Except Farm Products	Newark PMSA, NJ-PA	Y	59630 FQ	74700 MW	97630 TQ	USBLS	5/15
Except Farm Products	Trenton MSA, NJ	Y	58390 FQ	76810 MW	102010 TQ	USBLS	5/15
Except Farm Products	New Mexico	Y	33010 FQ	42230 MW	58400 TQ	USBLS	5/15
Except Farm Products	Albuquerque MSA, NM	Y	34330 FQ	43310 MW	58940 TQ	USBLS	5/15
Except Farm Products	New York	Y	36780 AE	60560 MW	85820 AEX	NYBLS	1/16-3/16
Except Farm Products	Buffalo-Cheektowaga-Niagara Falls MSA, NY	Y	42600 FQ	53290 MW	67140 TQ	USBLS	5/15
Except Farm Products	Nassau County-Suffolk County PMSA, NY	Y	44360 FQ	61550 MW	81440 TQ	USBLS	5/15
Except Farm Products	New York-Jersey City-White Plains PMSA, NY-NJ	Y	47150 FQ	63100 MW	88180 TQ	USBLS	5/15
Except Farm Products	Rochester MSA, NY	Y	33550 FQ	45840 MW	62410 TQ	USBLS	5/15
Except Farm Products	North Carolina	Y	40590 FQ	51940 MW	67470 TQ	USBLS	5/15
Except Farm Products	Charlotte-Concord-Gastonia MSA, NC-SC	Y	40450 FQ	52660 MW	69960 TQ	USBLS	5/15
Except Farm Products	Raleigh MSA, NC	Y	42520 FQ	52770 MW	68240 TQ	USBLS	5/15
Except Farm Products	North Dakota	Y	38400 FQ	47930 MW	63920 TQ	USBLS	5/15
Except Farm Products	Fargo MSA, ND-MN	Y	39740 FQ	48560 MW	66370 TQ	USBLS	5/15
Except Farm Products	Ohio	Y	43050 FQ	54060 MW	67830 TQ	USBLS	5/15
Except Farm Products	Cincinnati MSA, OH-KY-IN	Y	41900 FQ	52560 MW	64600 TQ	USBLS	5/15
Except Farm Products	Cleveland-Elyria MSA, OH	Y	44680 FQ	54590 MW	63620 TQ	USBLS	5/15
Except Farm Products	Columbus MSA, OH	Y	46680 FQ	58010 MW	79310 TQ	USBLS	5/15
Except Farm Products	Oklahoma	Y	37320 FQ	53580 MW	72020 TQ	USBLS	5/15
Except Farm Products	Oklahoma City MSA, OK	Y	38080 FQ	53180 MW	64730 TQ	USBLS	5/15
Except Farm Products	Tulsa MSA, OK	Y	46090 FQ	62120 MW	81620 TQ	USBLS	5/15
Except Farm Products	Oregon	H	17.69 FQ	23.03 MW	29.89 TQ	ORBLS	2016
Except Farm Products	Portland-Vancouver-Hillsboro MSA, OR-WA	Y	36840 FQ	49270 MW	63140 TQ	USBLS	5/15
Except Farm Products	Pennsylvania	Y	41150 FQ	54880 MW	68830 TQ	USBLS	5/15
Except Farm Products	Allentown-Bethlehem-Easton MSA, PA-NJ	Y	41530 FQ	50220 MW	63570 TQ	USBLS	5/15
Except Farm Products	Harrisburg-Carlisle MSA, PA	Y	39890 FQ	54720 MW	67480 TQ	USBLS	5/15
Except Farm Products	Montgomery County-Bucks County-Chester County PMSA, PA	Y	48060 FQ	57880 MW	70180 TQ	USBLS	5/15
Except Farm Products	Philadelphia PMSA, PA	Y	43140 FQ	58880 MW	75590 TQ	USBLS	5/15
Except Farm Products	Pittsburgh MSA, PA	Y	38290 FQ	53470 MW	66430 TQ	USBLS	5/15
Except Farm Products	Rhode Island	Y	36650 FQ	56190 MW	78310 TQ	USBLS	5/15
Except Farm Products	Providence-Warwick MSA, RI-MA	Y	41430 FQ	58900 MW	76190 TQ	USBLS	5/15
Except Farm Products	South Carolina	Y	39830 FQ	52030 MW	71420 TQ	USBLS	5/15
Except Farm Products	Charleston-North Charleston MSA, SC	Y	32680 FQ	43150 MW	60400 TQ	USBLS	5/15
Except Farm Products	Columbia MSA, SC	Y	41730 FQ	48560 MW	62210 TQ	USBLS	5/15
Except Farm Products	Greenville-Anderson-Mauldin MSA, SC	Y	44760 FQ	62100 MW	77930 TQ	USBLS	5/15

Occupation/Type/Industry	Location	Per	Low	Mid	High	Source	Date
Wholesale and Retail Buyer							
Except Farm Products	South Dakota	Y	41850 FQ	50960 MW	59310 TQ	USBLS	5/15
Except Farm Products	Sioux Falls MSA, SD	Y	46780 FQ	54680 MW	61800 TQ	USBLS	5/15
Except Farm Products	Tennessee	Y	36060 FQ	47580 MW	60220 TQ	USBLS	5/15
Except Farm Products	Knoxville MSA, TN	Y	31120 FQ	44070 MW	59280 TQ	USBLS	5/15
Except Farm Products	Memphis MSA, TN-MS-AR	Y	41010 FQ	48460 MW	61780 TQ	USBLS	5/15
Except Farm Products	Nashville-Davidson– Murfreesboro–Franklin MSA, TN	Y	36980 FQ	51080 MW	60140 TQ	USBLS	5/15
Except Farm Products	Texas	Y	39840 FQ	52370 MW	71280 TQ	USBLS	5/15
Except Farm Products	Austin-Round Rock MSA, TX	Y	41700 FQ	58650 MW	88920 TQ	USBLS	5/15
Except Farm Products	Dallas-Plano-Irving PMSA, TX	Y	45720 FQ	57450 MW	74520 TQ	USBLS	5/15
Except Farm Products	Fort Worth-Arlington PMSA, TX	Y	41410 FQ	48610 MW	61050 TQ	USBLS	5/15
Except Farm Products	Houston-The Woodlands- Sugar Land MSA, TX	Y	36250 FQ	53230 MW	73120 TQ	USBLS	5/15
Except Farm Products	San Antonio-New Braunfels MSA, TX	Y	40900 FQ	49940 MW	63280 TQ	USBLS	5/15
Except Farm Products	Utah	Y	36630 FQ	48230 MW	62470 TQ	USBLS	5/15
Except Farm Products	Ogden-Clearfield MSA, UT	Y	31980 FQ	38870 MW	53790 TQ	USBLS	5/15
Except Farm Products	Provo-Orem MSA, UT	Y	26610 FQ	38960 MW	57390 TQ	USBLS	5/15
Except Farm Products	Salt Lake City MSA, UT	Y	38870 FQ	51120 MW	67920 TQ	USBLS	5/15
Except Farm Products	Vermont	Y	34490 FQ	43570 MW	54630 TQ	USBLS	5/15
Except Farm Products	Burlington-South Burlington MSA, VT	Y	37630 FQ	45590 MW	55370 TQ	USBLS	5/15
Except Farm Products	Virginia	Y	38250 FQ	50360 MW	71270 TQ	USBLS	5/15
Except Farm Products	Richmond MSA, VA	Y	41930 FQ	50610 MW	74330 TQ	USBLS	5/15
Except Farm Products	Virginia Beach-Norfolk- Newport News MSA, VA-NC	Y	34230 FQ	44990 MW	58390 TQ	USBLS	5/15
Except Farm Products	Washington	H	20.71 FQ	26.64 MW	34.65 TQ	WABLS	3/16
Except Farm Products	Seattle-Bellevue-Everett PMSA, WA	H	22.29 FQ	27.84 MW	35.29 TQ	WABLS	3/16
Except Farm Products	Tacoma-Lakewood PMSA, WA	H	13.67 FQ	18.23 MW	26.25 TQ	WABLS	3/16
Except Farm Products	West Virginia	Y	35440 FQ	43420 MW	53150 TQ	USBLS	5/15
Except Farm Products	Huntington-Ashland MSA, WV-KY-OH	Y	34420 FQ	47610 MW	58880 TQ	USBLS	5/15
Except Farm Products	Wisconsin	Y	39930 FQ	49310 MW	62780 TQ	USBLS	5/15
Except Farm Products	Madison MSA, WI	Y	42640 FQ	51280 MW	60530 TQ	USBLS	5/15
Except Farm Products	Milwaukee-Waukesha-West Allis MSA, WI	Y	43810 FQ	51570 MW	67910 TQ	USBLS	5/15
Except Farm Products	Puerto Rico	Y	17290 FQ	19140 MW	23410 TQ	USBLS	5/15
Except Farm Products	San Juan-Carolina-Caguas MSA, PR	Y	17370 FQ	19290 MW	23590 TQ	USBLS	5/15
Except Farm Products	Guam	Y	24580 FQ	28110 MW	33140 TQ	USBLS	5/15
WIC Eligibility Interviewer							
State Government	New Mexico	H	11.31 LO		19.67 HI	NMGOV	7/30/16
Wilderness Guide	United States	Y	28000 LO		34000 HI	MST02	2017
Wind Turbine Service Technician	United States	Y		48800 MW		FORB01	2015
	California	H	20.77 FQ	24.29 MW	28.42 TQ	CABLS	1/16-3/16
	Riverside-San Bernardino- Ontario MSA, CA	H	21.36 FQ	25.20 MW	28.52 TQ	CABLS	1/16-3/16
	Colorado	Y	43530 FQ	52450 MW	63320 TQ	USBLS	5/15
	Illinois	Y	41640 FQ	45330 MW	49020 TQ	USBLS	5/15
	Indiana	Y	38560 FQ	47320 MW	60520 TQ	USBLS	5/15
	Iowa	Y	42510 FQ	48430 MW	59830 TQ	USBLS	5/15
	Kansas	Y	47260 FQ	55020 MW	60730 TQ	USBLS	5/15
	Minnesota	Y	42319 FQ	55302 MW	67843 TQ	MNBLS	1/16-3/16
	New York	Y	37210 AE	48480 MW	55980 AEX	NYBLS	1/16-3/16
	North Dakota	Y	52320 FQ	57700 MW	63100 TQ	USBLS	5/15
	Oregon	H	21.07 FQ	27.75 MW	34.54 TQ	ORBLS	2016
	South Dakota	Y	51870 FQ	65790 MW	73960 TQ	USBLS	5/15
	Texas	Y	44420 FQ	51760 MW	59400 TQ	USBLS	5/15
	Houston-The Woodlands- Sugar Land MSA, TX	Y	44210 FQ	51030 MW	58340 TQ	USBLS	5/15
	Washington	H	21.12 FQ	24.15 MW	28.17 TQ	WABLS	3/16
	Wisconsin	Y	36310 FQ	44230 MW	60710 TQ	USBLS	5/15
	Wyoming	Y	35140 FQ	38910 MW	47460 TQ	USBLS	5/15
Wine Club Manager	United States	Y		63708 AW		WBM	2/1/16

AE	Average entry wage	AWR	Average wage range	H	Hourly	LR	Low end range	MTC	Median total compensation	TCC	Total cash compensation
AEX	Average experienced wage	B	Biweekly	HI	Highest wage paid	M	Monthly	MW	Median wage paid	TQ	Third quartile wage
ATC	Average total compensation	D	Daily	HR	High end range	MCC	Median cash compensation	MWR	Median wage range	W	Weekly
AW	Average wage paid	FQ	First quartile wage	LO	Lowest wage paid	ME	Median entry wage	S	See annotated source	Y	Yearly

Occupation/Type/Industry	Location	Per	Low	Mid	High	Source	Date
Winemaker	United States	Y		90700-137189 MWR		WBM	2/1/16
Wireless Communications Officer							
Municipal Government	Long Beach, CA	Y			138208 HI	CACIT	6/28/16
Wireless System Technician							
Municipal Government	Glendale, CA	Y		67439 AW		CACIT	6/28/16
Woodworking Machine Setter, Operator, and Tender							
Except Sawing	Alabama	Y	20503 AE	27392 AW	30846 AEX	ALBLS	6/16
Except Sawing	Birmingham-Hoover MSA, AL	Y	21428 AE	27926 AW	31176 AEX	ALBLS	6/16
Except Sawing	Arizona	Y	19190 FQ	23120 MW	29800 TQ	USBLS	5/15
Except Sawing	Phoenix-Mesa-Scottsdale MSA, AZ	Y	18960 FQ	22890 MW	30020 TQ	USBLS	5/15
Except Sawing	Arkansas	Y	20900 FQ	24020 MW	29140 TQ	USBLS	5/15
Except Sawing	Little Rock-North Little Rock-Conway MSA, AR	Y	23500 FQ	27550 MW	32200 TQ	USBLS	5/15
Except Sawing	California	H	10.73 FQ	13.31 MW	17.20 TQ	CABLS	1/16-3/16
Except Sawing	Anaheim-Santa Ana-Irvine PMSA, CA	H	10.07 FQ	12.87 MW	17.54 TQ	CABLS	1/16-3/16
Except Sawing	Los Angeles-Long Beach-Glendale PMSA, CA	H	11.25 FQ	13.68 MW	16.98 TQ	CABLS	1/16-3/16
Except Sawing	Oakland-Hayward-Berkeley PMSA, CA	H	13.54 FQ	15.15 MW	18.54 TQ	CABLS	1/16-3/16
Except Sawing	Riverside-San Bernardino-Ontario MSA, CA	H	9.72 FQ	11.65 MW	14.63 TQ	CABLS	1/16-3/16
Except Sawing	Sacramento–Roseville–Arden-Arcade MSA, CA	H	11.39 FQ	16.12 MW	21.46 TQ	CABLS	1/16-3/16
Except Sawing	San Diego-Carlsbad MSA, CA	H	11.69 FQ	14.63 MW	18.71 TQ	CABLS	1/16-3/16
Except Sawing	Colorado	Y	23390 FQ	28750 MW	35650 TQ	USBLS	5/15
Except Sawing	Denver-Aurora-Lakewood MSA, CO	Y	23270 FQ	28600 MW	35780 TQ	USBLS	5/15
Except Sawing	Connecticut	Y		36818 MW		CTBLS	1/16-3/16
Except Sawing	Hartford-West Hartford-East Hartford MSA, CT	Y	31830 FQ	35080 MW	38330 TQ	USBLS	5/15
Except Sawing	Delaware	Y	26230 FQ	31210 MW	38480 TQ	USBLS	5/15
Except Sawing	Wilmington PMSA, DE-MD-NJ	Y	19620 FQ	26800 MW	33560 TQ	USBLS	5/15
Except Sawing	Washington-Arlington-Alexandria PMSA, DC-VA-MD-WV	Y	22410 FQ	32750 MW	41690 TQ	USBLS	5/15
Except Sawing	Florida	H	11.15 AE	14.36 MW	16.86 AEX	FLBLS	7/16-9/16
Except Sawing	Fort Lauderdale-Pompano Beach-Deerfield Beach PMSA, FL	H	11.59 AE	14.44 MW	17.04 AEX	FLBLS	7/16-9/16
Except Sawing	Miami-Miami Beach-Kendall PMSA, FL	H	10.86 AE	13.96 MW	15.60 AEX	FLBLS	7/16-9/16
Except Sawing	Orlando-Kissimmee-Sanford MSA, FL	H	13.20 AE	15.42 MW	18.63 AEX	FLBLS	7/16-9/16
Except Sawing	Tampa-St. Petersburg-Clearwater MSA, FL	H	11.04 AE	14.59 MW	18.58 AEX	FLBLS	7/16-9/16
Except Sawing	Georgia	Y	20640 FQ	26600 MW	33350 TQ	USBLS	5/15
Except Sawing	Atlanta-Sandy Springs-Roswell MSA, GA	Y	23380 FQ	29240 MW	35080 TQ	USBLS	5/15
Except Sawing	Augusta-Richmond County MSA, GA-SC	Y	22820 FQ	28180 MW	36170 TQ	USBLS	5/15
Except Sawing	Idaho	Y	23350 FQ	30570 MW	40060 TQ	USBLS	5/15
Except Sawing	Boise City MSA, ID	Y	18800 FQ	23560 MW	32010 TQ	USBLS	5/15
Except Sawing	Illinois	Y	22670 FQ	28400 MW	36190 TQ	USBLS	5/15
Except Sawing	Chicago-Naperville-Arlington Heights PMSA, IL	Y	22310 FQ	28380 MW	35630 TQ	USBLS	5/15
Except Sawing	Lake County-Kenosha County PMSA, IL-WI	Y	34310 FQ	38770 MW	45630 TQ	USBLS	5/15
Except Sawing	Indiana	Y	24390 FQ	28850 MW	34340 TQ	USBLS	5/15
Except Sawing	Indianapolis-Carmel-Anderson MSA, IN	Y	27500 FQ	32860 MW	37210 TQ	USBLS	5/15
Except Sawing	Iowa	Y	24180 FQ	29300 MW	35110 TQ	USBLS	5/15
Except Sawing	Des Moines-West Des Moines MSA, IA	Y	32910 FQ	36270 MW	39620 TQ	USBLS	5/15
Except Sawing	Kansas	Y	23070 FQ	26960 MW	30830 TQ	USBLS	5/15

Occupation/Type/Industry	Location	Per	Low	Mid	High	Source	Date
Woodworking Machine Setter, Operator, and Tender							
Except Sawing	Wichita MSA, KS	Y	24610 FQ	28690 MW	33450 TQ	USBLS	5/15
Except Sawing	Kentucky	Y	19430 FQ	23780 MW	29050 TQ	USBLS	5/15
Except Sawing	Louisville-Jefferson County MSA, KY-IN	Y	24470 FQ	29950 MW	36300 TQ	USBLS	5/15
Except Sawing	Louisiana	Y	28300 FQ	34010 MW	37850 TQ	USBLS	5/15
Except Sawing	New Orleans-Metairie MSA, LA	Y	29470 FQ	33570 MW	37570 TQ	USBLS	5/15
Except Sawing	Maine	Y	22500 FQ	28550 MW	35040 TQ	USBLS	5/15
Except Sawing	Portland-South Portland MSA, ME	Y	29820 FQ	33900 MW	37470 TQ	USBLS	5/15
Except Sawing	Maryland	Y	20593 AE	32228 MW	38046 AEX	MDBLS	4/16
Except Sawing	Baltimore-Columbia-Towson MSA, MD	Y	21090 FQ	26070 MW	38570 TQ	USBLS	5/15
Except Sawing	Salisbury MSA, MD-DE	Y	25210 FQ	30350 MW	39620 TQ	USBLS	5/15
Except Sawing	Massachusetts	Y	26470 FQ	30670 MW	37320 TQ	USBLS	5/15
Except Sawing	Boston-Cambridge-Newton NECTA, MA	Y	27690 FQ	32610 MW	38680 TQ	USBLS	5/15
Except Sawing	Worcester MSA, MA-CT	Y	26240 FQ	28860 MW	33680 TQ	USBLS	5/15
Except Sawing	Michigan	Y	21310 FQ	25640 MW	31320 TQ	USBLS	5/15
Except Sawing	Detroit-Dearborn-Livonia PMSA, MI	Y	19860 FQ	26810 MW	38640 TQ	USBLS	5/15
Except Sawing	Grand Rapids-Wyoming MSA, MI	Y	22160 FQ	26340 MW	33120 TQ	USBLS	5/15
Except Sawing	Minnesota	Y	25362 FQ	30495 MW	37714 TQ	MNBLS	1/16-3/16
Except Sawing	Minneapolis-St. Paul-Bloomington MSA, MN-WI	Y	26384 FQ	30971 MW	37531 TQ	MNBLS	1/16-3/16
Except Sawing	Mississippi	Y	20360 FQ	23830 MW	32590 TQ	USBLS	5/15
Except Sawing	Missouri	Y	22540 FQ	27220 MW	31860 TQ	USBLS	5/15
Except Sawing	Kansas City MSA, MO-KS	Y	23700 FQ	28230 MW	34540 TQ	USBLS	5/15
Except Sawing	St. Louis MSA, MO-IL	Y	24900 FQ	29470 MW	35250 TQ	USBLS	5/15
Except Sawing	Montana	Y	29990 FQ	35880 MW	41760 TQ	USBLS	5/15
Except Sawing	Billings MSA, MT	Y	24620 FQ	30040 MW	42150 TQ	USBLS	5/15
Except Sawing	Nebraska	Y	24440 FQ	33025 MW	37155 TQ	NEBLS	7/16-9/16
Except Sawing	Omaha-Council Bluffs MSA, NE-IA	Y	25655 FQ	29685 MW	37305 TQ	NEBLS	7/16-9/16
Except Sawing	Las Vegas-Henderson-Paradise MSA, NV	Y	26520 FQ	28850 MW	31160 TQ	USBLS	5/15
Except Sawing	New Hampshire	H	11.01 AE	15.23 MW	17.16 AEX	NHBLS	6/16
Except Sawing	Manchester NECTA, NH	H	14.44 AE	18.89 MW	20.56 AEX	NHBLS	6/16
Except Sawing	Nashua NECTA, NH-MA	Y	34480 FQ	37590 MW	42380 TQ	USBLS	5/15
Except Sawing	New Jersey	Y	24220 FQ	32110 MW	44070 TQ	USBLS	5/15
Except Sawing	New Mexico	Y	18880 FQ	22000 MW	26050 TQ	USBLS	5/15
Except Sawing	Albuquerque MSA, NM	Y	21000 FQ	23710 MW	29180 TQ	USBLS	5/15
Except Sawing	New York	Y	21770 AE	29430 MW	38780 AEX	NYBLS	1/16-3/16
Except Sawing	Buffalo-Cheektowaga-Niagara Falls MSA, NY	Y	27650 FQ	32460 MW	36800 TQ	USBLS	5/15
Except Sawing	Nassau County-Suffolk County PMSA, NY	Y	19640 FQ	29710 MW	52290 TQ	USBLS	5/15
Except Sawing	New York-Jersey City-White Plains PMSA, NY-NJ	Y	26310 FQ	30630 MW	44530 TQ	USBLS	5/15
Except Sawing	Rochester MSA, NY	Y	24700 FQ	27360 MW	29820 TQ	USBLS	5/15
Except Sawing	North Carolina	Y	21430 FQ	26360 MW	32440 TQ	USBLS	5/15
Except Sawing	Charlotte-Concord-Gastonia MSA, NC-SC	Y	19150 FQ	24700 MW	32690 TQ	USBLS	5/15
Except Sawing	Raleigh MSA, NC	Y	22740 FQ	27860 MW	35440 TQ	USBLS	5/15
Except Sawing	North Dakota	Y	28390 FQ	32140 MW	37210 TQ	USBLS	5/15
Except Sawing	Ohio	Y	24670 FQ	28810 MW	34190 TQ	USBLS	5/15
Except Sawing	Cincinnati MSA, OH-KY-IN	Y	20520 FQ	27500 MW	33730 TQ	USBLS	5/15
Except Sawing	Cleveland-Elyria MSA, OH	Y	25570 FQ	30350 MW	36260 TQ	USBLS	5/15
Except Sawing	Columbus MSA, OH	Y	22790 FQ	28350 MW	34520 TQ	USBLS	5/15
Except Sawing	Oklahoma	Y	24850 FQ	29170 MW	35760 TQ	USBLS	5/15
Except Sawing	Oklahoma City MSA, OK	Y	23060 FQ	27400 MW	31610 TQ	USBLS	5/15
Except Sawing	Tulsa MSA, OK	Y	27280 FQ	30700 MW	38070 TQ	USBLS	5/15
Except Sawing	Oregon	H	13.00 FQ	15.89 MW	20.51 TQ	ORBLS	2016
Except Sawing	Portland-Vancouver-Hillsboro MSA, OR-WA	Y	25920 FQ	29810 MW	38340 TQ	USBLS	5/15
Except Sawing	Pennsylvania	Y	24580 FQ	29730 MW	36340 TQ	USBLS	5/15
Except Sawing	Allentown-Bethlehem-Easton MSA, PA-NJ	Y	26410 FQ	32090 MW	36930 TQ	USBLS	5/15
Except Sawing	Harrisburg-Carlisle MSA, PA	Y	24270 FQ	27230 MW	29460 TQ	USBLS	5/15

AE	Average entry wage	AWR	Average wage range	H	Hourly
AEX	Average experienced wage	B	Biweekly	HI	Highest wage paid
ATC	Average total compensation	D	Daily	HR	High end range
AW	Average wage paid	FQ	First quartile wage	LO	Lowest wage paid

LR	Low end range	MTC	Median total compensation	TCC	Total cash compensation
M	Monthly	MW	Median wage paid	TQ	Third quartile wage
MCC	Median cash compensation	MWR	Median wage range	W	Weekly
ME	Median entry wage	S	See annotated source	Y	Yearly

Occupation/Type/Industry	Location	Per	Low	Mid	High	Source	Date
Woodworking Machine Setter, Operator, and Tender							
Except Sawing	Montgomery County-Bucks County-Chester County PMSA, PA	Y	31490 FQ	45110 MW	54440 TQ	USBLS	5/15
Except Sawing	Pittsburgh MSA, PA	Y	21550 FQ	27820 MW	35540 TQ	USBLS	5/15
Except Sawing	Rhode Island	Y	22260 FQ	31000 MW	39890 TQ	USBLS	5/15
Except Sawing	Providence-Warwick MSA, RI-MA	Y	22260 FQ	31000 MW	39890 TQ	USBLS	5/15
Except Sawing	South Carolina	Y	20620 FQ	26030 MW	34180 TQ	USBLS	5/15
Except Sawing	Charleston-North Charleston MSA, SC	Y	18740 FQ	27040 MW	34700 TQ	USBLS	5/15
Except Sawing	Columbia MSA, SC	Y	25300 FQ	28620 MW	34890 TQ	USBLS	5/15
Except Sawing	Greenville-Anderson-Mauldin MSA, SC	Y	23360 FQ	28910 MW	34870 TQ	USBLS	5/15
Except Sawing	South Dakota	Y	22940 FQ	26440 MW	30690 TQ	USBLS	5/15
Except Sawing	Sioux Falls MSA, SD	Y	22710 FQ	25960 MW	32270 TQ	USBLS	5/15
Except Sawing	Tennessee	Y	19530 FQ	23470 MW	29930 TQ	USBLS	5/15
Except Sawing	Memphis MSA, TN-MS-AR	Y	19790 FQ	21860 MW	23970 TQ	USBLS	5/15
Except Sawing	Nashville-Davidson–Murfreesboro–Franklin MSA, TN	Y	21810 FQ	30940 MW	37710 TQ	USBLS	5/15
Except Sawing	Texas	Y	20070 FQ	23570 MW	28550 TQ	USBLS	5/15
Except Sawing	Austin-Round Rock MSA, TX	Y	21520 FQ	26260 MW	29830 TQ	USBLS	5/15
Except Sawing	Dallas-Plano-Irving PMSA, TX	Y	19860 FQ	24990 MW	29750 TQ	USBLS	5/15
Except Sawing	Fort Worth-Arlington PMSA, TX	Y	20320 FQ	23480 MW	28360 TQ	USBLS	5/15
Except Sawing	Houston-The Woodlands-Sugar Land MSA, TX	Y	18820 FQ	22980 MW	28060 TQ	USBLS	5/15
Except Sawing	San Antonio-New Braunfels MSA, TX	Y	22000 FQ	26710 MW	31540 TQ	USBLS	5/15
Except Sawing	Utah	Y	21670 FQ	27310 MW	36260 TQ	USBLS	5/15
Except Sawing	Ogden-Clearfield MSA, UT	Y	21530 FQ	24340 MW	29780 TQ	USBLS	5/15
Except Sawing	Provo-Orem MSA, UT	Y	19620 FQ	24580 MW	30600 TQ	USBLS	5/15
Except Sawing	Salt Lake City MSA, UT	Y	23110 FQ	30690 MW	45530 TQ	USBLS	5/15
Except Sawing	Vermont	Y	23920 FQ	27750 MW	31970 TQ	USBLS	5/15
Except Sawing	Burlington-South Burlington MSA, VT	Y	27110 FQ	30790 MW	35880 TQ	USBLS	5/15
Except Sawing	Virginia	Y	21060 FQ	24920 MW	33250 TQ	USBLS	5/15
Except Sawing	Richmond MSA, VA	Y	22290 FQ	26520 MW	34490 TQ	USBLS	5/15
Except Sawing	Virginia Beach-Norfolk-Newport News MSA, VA-NC	Y	25230 FQ	29480 MW	35560 TQ	USBLS	5/15
Except Sawing	Washington	H	13.73 FQ	17.07 MW	21.18 TQ	WABLS	3/16
Except Sawing	Seattle-Bellevue-Everett PMSA, WA	H	13.40 FQ	16.73 MW	20.16 TQ	WABLS	3/16
Except Sawing	Tacoma-Lakewood PMSA, WA	H	14.13 FQ	17.29 MW	20.71 TQ	WABLS	3/16
Except Sawing	West Virginia	Y	21060 FQ	23610 MW	28780 TQ	USBLS	5/15
Except Sawing	Wisconsin	Y	24270 FQ	28920 MW	34770 TQ	USBLS	5/15
Except Sawing	Madison MSA, WI	Y	29070 FQ	34190 MW	37630 TQ	USBLS	5/15
Except Sawing	Milwaukee-Waukesha-West Allis MSA, WI	Y	23660 FQ	29240 MW	36980 TQ	USBLS	5/15
Except Sawing	Wyoming	Y	22450 FQ	25550 MW	30910 TQ	USBLS	5/15
Except Sawing	Puerto Rico	Y	16550 FQ	17700 MW	18850 TQ	USBLS	5/15
Except Sawing	San Juan-Carolina-Caguas MSA, PR	Y	16680 FQ	17880 MW	19080 TQ	USBLS	5/15
Word Processor and Typist	Alabama	Y	23415 AE	33020 AW	37823 AEX	ALBLS	6/16
	Birmingham-Hoover MSA, AL	Y	25445 AE	37524 AW	43553 AEX	ALBLS	6/16
	Alaska	Y	32950 FQ	37190 MW	43030 TQ	USBLS	5/15
	Anchorage MSA, AK	Y	31740 FQ	36070 MW	41880 TQ	USBLS	5/15
	Arizona	Y	25320 FQ	30500 MW	40090 TQ	USBLS	5/15
	Phoenix-Mesa-Scottsdale MSA, AZ	Y	25540 FQ	29750 MW	41960 TQ	USBLS	5/15
	Tucson MSA, AZ	Y	22190 FQ	26370 MW	35150 TQ	USBLS	5/15
	Arkansas	Y	31530 FQ	34890 MW	38240 TQ	USBLS	5/15
	Little Rock-North Little Rock-Conway MSA, AR	Y	32390 FQ	35300 MW	38050 TQ	USBLS	5/15
	California	H	18.38 FQ	21.50 MW	24.46 TQ	CABLS	1/16-3/16
	Anaheim-Santa Ana-Irvine PMSA, CA	H	20.26 FQ	22.14 MW	24.00 TQ	CABLS	1/16-3/16
	Los Angeles-Long Beach-Glendale PMSA, CA	H	19.07 FQ	21.77 MW	24.39 TQ	CABLS	1/16-3/16

AE Average entry wage	AWR Average wage range	H Hourly	LR Low end range	MTC Median total compensation	TCC Total cash compensation
AEX Average experienced wage	B Biweekly	HI Highest wage paid	M Monthly	MCC Median cash compensation	TQ Third quartile wage
ATC Average total compensation	D Daily	HR High end range	MCC Median cash compensation	MWR Median wage range	W Weekly
AW Average wage paid	FQ First quartile wage	LO Lowest wage paid	ME Median entry wage	S See annotated source	Y Yearly

Occupation/Type/Industry	Location	Per	Low	Mid	High	Source	Date
Word Processor and Typist	Oakland-Hayward-Berkeley PMSA, CA	H	16.89 FQ	18.80 MW	22.95 TQ	CABLS	1/16-3/16
	Riverside-San Bernardino-Ontario MSA, CA	H	17.65 FQ	20.34 MW	24.06 TQ	CABLS	1/16-3/16
	Sacramento–Roseville–Arden-Arcade MSA, CA	H	16.23 FQ	18.71 MW	23.92 TQ	CABLS	1/16-3/16
	San Diego-Carlsbad MSA, CA	H	16.41 FQ	19.09 MW	22.24 TQ	CABLS	1/16-3/16
	San Francisco-Redwood City-South San Francisco PMSA, CA	H	23.62 FQ	27.01 MW	29.88 TQ	CABLS	1/16-3/16
	Colorado	Y	25850 FQ	35970 MW	44190 TQ	USBLS	5/15
	Denver-Aurora-Lakewood MSA, CO	Y	23230 FQ	33390 MW	41340 TQ	USBLS	5/15
	Connecticut	Y		41057 MW		CTBLS	1/16-3/16
	Bridgeport-Stamford-Norwalk MSA, CT	Y	41870 FQ	47360 MW	54320 TQ	USBLS	5/15
	Hartford-West Hartford-East Hartford MSA, CT	Y	32650 FQ	36450 MW	42890 TQ	USBLS	5/15
	Delaware	Y	35870 FQ	44370 MW	56160 TQ	USBLS	5/15
	Wilmington PMSA, DE-MD-NJ	Y	38470 FQ	47510 MW	56800 TQ	USBLS	5/15
	District of Columbia	Y	37500 FQ	45190 MW	55960 TQ	USBLS	5/15
	Washington-Arlington-Alexandria PMSA, DC-VA-MD-WV	Y	35210 FQ	41290 MW	49090 TQ	USBLS	5/15
	Florida	H	11.07 AE	14.43 MW	17.09 AEX	FLBLS	7/16-9/16
	Fort Lauderdale-Pompano Beach-Deerfield Beach PMSA, FL	H	12.91 AE	15.49 MW	17.07 AEX	FLBLS	7/16-9/16
	Miami-Miami Beach-Kendall PMSA, FL	H	12.79 AE	15.54 MW	20.18 AEX	FLBLS	7/16-9/16
	Orlando-Kissimmee-Sanford MSA, FL	H	11.38 AE	15.07 MW	17.89 AEX	FLBLS	7/16-9/16
	Tampa-St. Petersburg-Clearwater MSA, FL	H	10.58 AE	13.74 MW	17.40 AEX	FLBLS	7/16-9/16
	Georgia	Y	24620 FQ	33090 MW	41530 TQ	USBLS	5/15
	Atlanta-Sandy Springs-Roswell MSA, GA	Y	23560 FQ	34560 MW	43710 TQ	USBLS	5/15
	Hawaii	Y	27240 FQ	30220 MW	37530 TQ	USBLS	5/15
	Urban Honolulu MSA, HI	Y	27380 FQ	30360 MW	37880 TQ	USBLS	5/15
	Idaho	Y	17490 FQ	19570 MW	28860 TQ	USBLS	5/15
	Boise City MSA, ID	Y	28890 FQ	34090 MW	39060 TQ	USBLS	5/15
	Illinois	Y	22820 FQ	35440 MW	45600 TQ	USBLS	5/15
	Chicago-Naperville-Arlington Heights PMSA, IL	Y	26550 FQ	36510 MW	45490 TQ	USBLS	5/15
	Lake County-Kenosha County PMSA, IL-WI	Y	19850 FQ	40150 MW	53400 TQ	USBLS	5/15
	Indiana	Y	26060 FQ	29380 MW	34280 TQ	USBLS	5/15
	Gary PMSA, IN	Y	24640 FQ	27050 MW	29460 TQ	USBLS	5/15
	Indianapolis-Carmel-Anderson MSA, IN	Y	26440 FQ	29910 MW	34820 TQ	USBLS	5/15
	Iowa	Y	31080 FQ	38180 MW	40110 TQ	USBLS	5/15
	Des Moines-West Des Moines MSA, IA	Y	31060 FQ	38750 MW	43370 TQ	USBLS	5/15
	Kansas	Y	26790 FQ	35230 MW	41530 TQ	USBLS	5/15
	Kentucky	Y	31420 FQ	36570 MW	41220 TQ	USBLS	5/15
	Louisville-Jefferson County MSA, KY-IN	Y	27550 FQ	32420 MW	39400 TQ	USBLS	5/15
	Louisiana	Y	27040 FQ	31940 MW	37320 TQ	USBLS	5/15
	Baton Rouge MSA, LA	Y	28770 FQ	33380 MW	38160 TQ	USBLS	5/15
	New Orleans-Metairie MSA, LA	Y	27200 FQ	31660 MW	37710 TQ	USBLS	5/15
	Maine	Y	32000 FQ	36310 MW	40070 TQ	USBLS	5/15
	Portland-South Portland MSA, ME	Y	32740 FQ	36820 MW	40520 TQ	USBLS	5/15
	Maryland	Y	29989 AE	38701 MW	43057 AEX	MDBLS	4/16
	Baltimore-Columbia-Towson MSA, MD	Y	33570 FQ	37500 MW	44000 TQ	USBLS	5/15
	Massachusetts	Y	34090 FQ	41140 MW	47940 TQ	USBLS	5/15
	Boston-Cambridge-Newton NECTA, MA	Y	37990 FQ	45650 MW	53450 TQ	USBLS	5/15
	Worcester MSA, MA-CT	Y	27430 FQ	31240 MW	37500 TQ	USBLS	5/15

AE	Average entry wage	AWR	Average wage range	H	Hourly	LR	Low end range	MTC	Median total compensation	TCC	Total cash compensation
AEX	Average experienced wage	B	Biweekly	HI	Highest wage paid	M	Monthly	MW	Median wage paid	TQ	Third quartile wage
ATC	Average total compensation	D	Daily	HR	High end range	MCC	Median cash compensation	MWR	Median wage range	W	Weekly
AW	Average wage paid	FQ	First quartile wage	LO	Lowest wage paid	ME	Median entry wage	S	See annotated source	Y	Yearly

Occupation/Type/Industry	Location	Per	Low	Mid	High	Source	Date
Word Processor and Typist	Michigan	Y	31230 FQ	37710 MW	44790 TQ	USBLS	5/15
	Detroit-Dearborn-Livonia PMSA, MI	Y	30090 FQ	36860 MW	44790 TQ	USBLS	5/15
	Grand Rapids-Wyoming MSA, MI	Y	34200 FQ	39950 MW	44800 TQ	USBLS	5/15
	Minnesota	Y	31036 FQ	41209 MW	46680 TQ	MNBLS	1/16-3/16
	Minneapolis-St. Paul-Bloomington MSA, MN-WI	Y	31825 FQ	42413 MW	47267 TQ	MNBLS	1/16-3/16
	Mississippi	Y	18280 FQ	20880 MW	34180 TQ	USBLS	5/15
	Jackson MSA, MS	Y	19240 FQ	30790 MW	41420 TQ	USBLS	5/15
	Missouri	Y	25660 FQ	30560 MW	38300 TQ	USBLS	5/15
	Kansas City MSA, MO-KS	Y	28640 FQ	36200 MW	42870 TQ	USBLS	5/15
	St. Louis MSA, MO-IL	Y	25950 FQ	30240 MW	38180 TQ	USBLS	5/15
	Montana	Y	25440 FQ	31930 MW	35150 TQ	USBLS	5/15*
	Nebraska	Y	27425 FQ	31175 MW	36825 TQ	NEBLS	7/16-9/16
	Omaha-Council Bluffs MSA, NE-IA	Y	28050 FQ	32255 MW	37815 TQ	NEBLS	7/16-9/16
	Nevada	Y	24720 FQ	28520 MW	32560 TQ	USBLS	5/15
	Las Vegas-Henderson-Paradise MSA, NV	Y	24520 FQ	28080 MW	31640 TQ	USBLS	5/15
	New Hampshire	H	14.48 AE	17.19 MW	19.00 AEX	NHBLS	6/16
	New Jersey	Y	33830 FQ	41010 MW	48360 TQ	USBLS	5/15
	Camden PMSA, NJ	Y	30680 FQ	39840 MW	48630 TQ	USBLS	5/15
	Newark PMSA, NJ-PA	Y	36450 FQ	41480 MW	49050 TQ	USBLS	5/15
	Trenton MSA, NJ	Y	37080 FQ	42960 MW	47490 TQ	USBLS	5/15
	New Mexico	Y	28540 FQ	33310 MW	37120 TQ	USBLS	5/15
	Albuquerque MSA, NM	Y	29040 FQ	33310 MW	37580 TQ	USBLS	5/15
	New York	Y	28240 AE	37990 MW	45400 AEX	NYBLS	1/16-3/16
	Buffalo-Cheektowaga-Niagara Falls MSA, NY	Y	30220 FQ	35680 MW	42590 TQ	USBLS	5/15
	Nassau County-Suffolk County PMSA, NY	Y	33670 FQ	42630 MW	52400 TQ	USBLS	5/15
	New York-Jersey City-White Plains PMSA, NY-NJ	Y	32260 FQ	38990 MW	48320 TQ	USBLS	5/15
	Rochester MSA, NY	Y	25240 FQ	32760 MW	39160 TQ	USBLS	5/15
	North Carolina	Y	27410 FQ	31940 MW	39420 TQ	USBLS	5/15
	Charlotte-Concord-Gastonia MSA, NC-SC	Y	29160 FQ	35370 MW	43700 TQ	USBLS	5/15
	Raleigh MSA, NC	Y	28020 FQ	30850 MW	39410 TQ	USBLS	5/15
	North Dakota	Y	22850 FQ	27860 MW	33010 TQ	USBLS	5/15
	Ohio	Y	29890 FQ	35250 MW	41390 TQ	USBLS	5/15
	Cincinnati MSA, OH-KY-IN	Y	33370 FQ	36360 MW	39340 TQ	USBLS	5/15
	Cleveland-Elyria MSA, OH	Y	29060 FQ	34090 MW	42070 TQ	USBLS	5/15
	Columbus MSA, OH	Y	26890 FQ	30530 MW	37520 TQ	USBLS	5/15
	Oklahoma	Y	25670 FQ	31930 MW	41540 TQ	USBLS	5/15
	Oklahoma City MSA, OK	Y	25730 FQ	30780 MW	40460 TQ	USBLS	5/15
	Tulsa MSA, OK	Y	40380 FQ	44320 MW	48120 TQ	USBLS	5/15
	Oregon	H	15.71 FQ	17.81 MW	21.53 TQ	ORBLS	2016
	Portland-Vancouver-Hillsboro MSA, OR-WA	Y	32400 FQ	37550 MW	52440 TQ	USBLS	5/15
	Pennsylvania	Y	30030 FQ	34070 MW	38970 TQ	USBLS	5/15
	Allentown-Bethlehem-Easton MSA, PA-NJ	Y	30450 FQ	34530 MW	39170 TQ	USBLS	5/15
	Harrisburg-Carlisle MSA, PA	Y	30550 FQ	35190 MW	38980 TQ	USBLS	5/15
	Montgomery County-Bucks County-Chester County PMSA, PA	Y	30550 FQ	34940 MW	39800 TQ	USBLS	5/15
	Philadelphia PMSA, PA	Y	30290 FQ	33690 MW	37730 TQ	USBLS	5/15
	Pittsburgh MSA, PA	Y	30550 FQ	35160 MW	40550 TQ	USBLS	5/15
	Rhode Island	Y	35490 FQ	39760 MW	44230 TQ	USBLS	5/15
	Providence-Warwick MSA, RI-MA	Y	34850 FQ	38990 MW	43580 TQ	USBLS	5/15
	South Carolina	Y	23830 FQ	30860 MW	40000 TQ	USBLS	5/15
	Charleston-North Charleston MSA, SC	Y	32350 FQ	39410 MW	46620 TQ	USBLS	5/15
	Tennessee	Y	29420 FQ	34030 MW	38180 TQ	USBLS	5/15
	Knoxville MSA, TN	Y	26670 FQ	34770 MW	48660 TQ	USBLS	5/15
	Memphis MSA, TN-MS-AR	Y	31000 FQ	34560 MW	37410 TQ	USBLS	5/15
	Nashville-Davidson–Murfreesboro–Franklin MSA, TN	Y	28540 FQ	32830 MW	38100 TQ	USBLS	5/15
	Texas	Y	27750 FQ	34260 MW	41720 TQ	USBLS	5/15

AE	Average entry wage	AWR	Average wage range	H	Hourly	LR	Low end range	MTC	Median total compensation	TCC	Total cash compensation
AEX	Average experienced wage	B	Biweekly	HI	Highest wage paid	M	Monthly	MW	Median wage paid	TQ	Third quartile wage
ATC	Average total compensation	D	Daily	HR	High end range	MCC	Median cash compensation	MWR	Median wage range	W	Weekly
AW	Average wage paid	FQ	First quartile wage	LO	Lowest wage paid	ME	Median entry wage	S	See annotated source	Y	Yearly

Occupation/Type/Industry	Location	Per	Low	Mid	High	Source	Date
Word Processor and Typist	Austin-Round Rock MSA, TX	Y	27980 FQ	33050 MW	39540 TQ	USBLS	5/15
	Dallas-Plano-Irving PMSA, TX	Y	30310 FQ	35830 MW	43530 TQ	USBLS	5/15
	Fort Worth-Arlington PMSA, TX	Y	29390 FQ	34930 MW	39110 TQ	USBLS	5/15
	Houston-The Woodlands-Sugar Land MSA, TX	Y	26520 FQ	33010 MW	48180 TQ	USBLS	5/15
	San Antonio-New Braunfels MSA, TX	Y	32980 FQ	37620 MW	43990 TQ	USBLS	5/15
	Utah	Y	24850 FQ	29890 MW	39100 TQ	USBLS	5/15
	Ogden-Clearfield MSA, UT	Y	18770 FQ	31920 MW	39310 TQ	USBLS	5/15
	Provo-Orem MSA, UT	Y	22420 FQ	33940 MW	39010 TQ	USBLS	5/15
	Salt Lake City MSA, UT	Y	26070 FQ	29910 MW	40140 TQ	USBLS	5/15
	Vermont	Y	30460 FQ	41230 MW	45700 TQ	USBLS	5/15
	Virginia	Y	33320 FQ	38360 MW	44020 TQ	USBLS	5/15
	Richmond MSA, VA	Y	32790 FQ	38040 MW	44750 TQ	USBLS	5/15
	Virginia Beach-Norfolk-Newport News MSA, VA-NC	Y	32360 FQ	37270 MW	41540 TQ	USBLS	5/15
	Washington	H	18.45 FQ	23.36 MW	31.27 TQ	WABLS	3/16
	Seattle-Bellevue-Everett PMSA, WA	H	21.81 FQ	27.51 MW	35.09 TQ	WABLS	3/16
	Tacoma-Lakewood PMSA, WA	H	13.24 FQ	19.01 MW	23.31 TQ	WABLS	3/16
	West Virginia	Y	29180 FQ	36740 MW	41530 TQ	USBLS	5/15
	Wisconsin	Y	33280 FQ	37420 MW	43060 TQ	USBLS	5/15
	Madison MSA, WI	Y	36810 FQ	42870 MW	48340 TQ	USBLS	5/15
	Milwaukee-Waukesha-West Allis MSA, WI	Y	33470 FQ	36980 MW	40290 TQ	USBLS	5/15
	Puerto Rico	Y	20080 FQ	26360 MW	30810 TQ	USBLS	5/15
	San Juan-Carolina-Caguas MSA, PR	Y	20540 FQ	26180 MW	30930 TQ	USBLS	5/15
	Guam	Y	25720 FQ	31930 MW	36520 TQ	USBLS	5/15
Workers' Compensation Analyst							
Human Resources Department, Municipal Government	Glendale, CA	Y			78626 HI	CACIT	6/28/16
Workers' Compensation Manager							
Human Resources Department, Municipal Government	Anaheim, CA	Y			108953 HI	CACIT	6/28/16
Worship Minister							
Church of Christ	United States	Y		40200 AW		ACU	2/16-3/16
Writer and Author	Alabama	Y	32537 AE	56797 AW	68937 AEX	ALBLS	6/16
	Birmingham-Hoover MSA, AL	Y	32221 AE	53861 AW	64686 AEX	ALBLS	6/16
	Arizona	Y	37680 FQ	47090 MW	60960 TQ	USBLS	5/15
	Phoenix-Mesa-Scottsdale MSA, AZ	Y	36840 FQ	46180 MW	60290 TQ	USBLS	5/15
	Tucson MSA, AZ	Y	42120 FQ	48430 MW	62930 TQ	USBLS	5/15
	Arkansas	Y	30540 FQ	37470 MW	51900 TQ	USBLS	5/15
	Little Rock-North Little Rock-Conway MSA, AR	Y	33970 FQ	38180 MW	56170 TQ	USBLS	5/15
	California	H	24.83 FQ	35.00 MW	48.47 TQ	CABLS	1/16-3/16
	Anaheim-Santa Ana-Irvine PMSA, CA	H	22.22 FQ	30.34 MW	38.75 TQ	CABLS	1/16-3/16
	Oakland-Hayward-Berkeley PMSA, CA	H	29.34 FQ	35.94 MW	49.23 TQ	CABLS	1/16-3/16
	Riverside-San Bernardino-Ontario MSA, CA	H	22.35 FQ	32.12 MW	43.27 TQ	CABLS	1/16-3/16
	Sacramento–Roseville–Arden-Arcade MSA, CA	H	17.32 FQ	19.70 MW	28.83 TQ	CABLS	1/16-3/16
	San Diego-Carlsbad MSA, CA	H	19.09 FQ	27.61 MW	36.57 TQ	CABLS	1/16-3/16
	San Francisco-Redwood City-South San Francisco PMSA, CA	H	23.40 FQ	30.71 MW	38.68 TQ	CABLS	1/16-3/16
	Colorado	Y	47700 FQ	62040 MW	80720 TQ	USBLS	5/15
	Denver-Aurora-Lakewood MSA, CO	Y	53570 FQ	69800 MW	86050 TQ	USBLS	5/15
	Connecticut	Y		61103 MW		CTBLS	1/16-3/16
	Bridgeport-Stamford-Norwalk MSA, CT	Y	34430 FQ	51940 MW	74330 TQ	USBLS	5/15
	Hartford-West Hartford-East Hartford MSA, CT	Y	24410 FQ	59100 MW	89630 TQ	USBLS	5/15

Occupation/Type/Industry	Location	Per	Low	Mid	High	Source	Date
Writer and Author	Delaware	Y	36000 FQ	57540 MW	91030 TQ	USBLS	5/15
	Wilmington PMSA, DE-MD-NJ	Y	35880 FQ	52030 MW	85960 TQ	USBLS	5/15
	District of Columbia	Y	65380 FQ	90250 MW	113640 TQ	USBLS	5/15
	Washington-Arlington-Alexandria PMSA, DC-VA-MD-WV	Y	61940 FQ	85120 MW	108370 TQ	USBLS	5/15
	Florida	H	14.00 AE	23.83 MW	30.62 AEX	FLBLS	7/16-9/16
	Fort Lauderdale-Pompano Beach-Deerfield Beach PMSA, FL	H	16.82 AE	22.66 MW	29.53 AEX	FLBLS	7/16-9/16
	Miami-Miami Beach-Kendall PMSA, FL	H	11.97 AE	25.56 MW	32.29 AEX	FLBLS	7/16-9/16
	Orlando-Kissimmee-Sanford MSA, FL	H	16.26 AE	25.57 MW	33.27 AEX	FLBLS	7/16-9/16
	Tampa-St. Petersburg-Clearwater MSA, FL	H	16.85 AE	25.14 MW	29.96 AEX	FLBLS	7/16-9/16
	Georgia	Y	39490 FQ	53050 MW	80680 TQ	USBLS	5/15
	Atlanta-Sandy Springs-Roswell MSA, GA	Y	39570 FQ	49440 MW	80950 TQ	USBLS	5/15
	Hawaii	Y	40290 FQ	54670 MW	72570 TQ	USBLS	5/15
	Urban Honolulu MSA, HI	Y	41650 FQ	59250 MW	77120 TQ	USBLS	5/15
	Idaho	Y	37830 FQ	61080 MW	77400 TQ	USBLS	5/15
	Boise City MSA, ID	Y	35370 FQ	66130 MW	86460 TQ	USBLS	5/15
	Illinois	Y	46840 FQ	62740 MW	82890 TQ	USBLS	5/15
	Chicago-Naperville-Arlington Heights PMSA, IL	Y	48300 FQ	63730 MW	84600 TQ	USBLS	5/15
	Lake County-Kenosha County PMSA, IL-WI	Y	53740 FQ	67970 MW	82510 TQ	USBLS	5/15
	Indiana	Y	29900 FQ	43460 MW	56550 TQ	USBLS	5/15
	Gary PMSA, IN	Y	21380 FQ	32220 MW	43030 TQ	USBLS	5/15
	Indianapolis-Carmel-Anderson MSA, IN	Y	30030 FQ	44460 MW	59420 TQ	USBLS	5/15
	Iowa	Y	29670 FQ	39800 MW	54280 TQ	USBLS	5/15
	Des Moines-West Des Moines MSA, IA	Y	30810 FQ	43890 MW	58050 TQ	USBLS	5/15
	Kansas	Y	25640 FQ	41740 MW	67310 TQ	USBLS	5/15
	Wichita MSA, KS	Y	31050 FQ	39780 MW	53410 TQ	USBLS	5/15
	Kentucky	Y	34490 FQ	46220 MW	61110 TQ	USBLS	5/15
	Louisville-Jefferson County MSA, KY-IN	Y	36480 FQ	44970 MW	59360 TQ	USBLS	5/15
	Louisiana	Y	30780 FQ	43340 MW	57620 TQ	USBLS	5/15
	Baton Rouge MSA, LA	Y	30120 FQ	47810 MW	58590 TQ	USBLS	5/15
	New Orleans-Metairie MSA, LA	Y	35550 FQ	43680 MW	52530 TQ	USBLS	5/15
	Maine	Y	26620 FQ	38680 MW	57850 TQ	USBLS	5/15
	Portland-South Portland MSA, ME	Y	27220 FQ	38570 MW	53180 TQ	USBLS	5/15
	Maryland	Y	33610 AE	72103 MW	91350 AEX	MDBLS	4/16
	Baltimore-Columbia-Towson MSA, MD	Y	44960 FQ	58540 MW	84790 TQ	USBLS	5/15
	Massachusetts	Y	50510 FQ	67800 MW	91070 TQ	USBLS	5/15
	Boston-Cambridge-Newton NECTA, MA	Y	50740 FQ	69350 MW	93580 TQ	USBLS	5/15
	Worcester MSA, MA-CT	Y	50090 FQ	58350 MW	68390 TQ	USBLS	5/15
	Michigan	Y	37300 FQ	52390 MW	70010 TQ	USBLS	5/15
	Detroit-Dearborn-Livonia PMSA, MI	Y	34940 FQ	53290 MW	74230 TQ	USBLS	5/15
	Grand Rapids-Wyoming MSA, MI	Y	36110 FQ	57020 MW	73180 TQ	USBLS	5/15
	Minnesota	Y	43487 FQ	58628 MW	76995 TQ	MNBLS	1/16-3/16
	Minneapolis-St. Paul-Bloomington MSA, MN-WI	Y	49374 FQ	64455 MW	82076 TQ	MNBLS	1/16-3/16
	Mississippi	Y	20730 FQ	38520 MW	51820 TQ	USBLS	5/15
	Jackson MSA, MS	Y	19330 FQ	38720 MW	48160 TQ	USBLS	5/15
	Missouri	Y	42290 FQ	59490 MW	80120 TQ	USBLS	5/15
	Kansas City MSA, MO-KS	Y	46120 FQ	69440 MW	90530 TQ	USBLS	5/15
	St. Louis MSA, MO-IL	Y	45150 FQ	59580 MW	75580 TQ	USBLS	5/15
	Montana	Y	19770 FQ	39410 MW	54420 TQ	USBLS	5/15
	Nebraska	Y	33790 FQ	47420 MW	68075 TQ	NEBLS	7/16-9/16
	Omaha-Council Bluffs MSA, NE-IA	Y	38935 FQ	49920 MW	70805 TQ	NEBLS	7/16-9/16

AE	Average entry wage	AWR	Average wage range	H	Hourly	LR	Low end range	MTC	Median total compensation	TCC	Total cash compensation
AEX	Average experienced wage	B	Biweekly	HI	Highest wage paid	M	Monthly	MW	Median wage paid	TQ	Third quartile wage
ATC	Average total compensation	D	Daily	HR	High end range	MCC	Median cash compensation	MWR	Median wage range	W	Weekly
AW	Average wage paid	FQ	First quartile wage	LO	Lowest wage paid	ME	Median entry wage	S	See annotated source	Y	Yearly

Occupation/Type/Industry	Location	Per	Low	Mid	High	Source	Date
Writer and Author	Nevada	Y	36550 FQ	46710 MW	61950 TQ	USBLS	5/15
	Las Vegas-Henderson-Paradise MSA, NV	Y	35420 FQ	43610 MW	57000 TQ	USBLS	5/15
	New Hampshire	H	11.55 AE	22.94 MW	34.10 AEX	NHBLS	6/16
	Manchester NECTA, NH	H	10.58 AE	17.39 MW	22.03 AEX	NHBLS	6/16
	Camden PMSA, NJ	Y	42890 FQ	64170 MW	72680 TQ	USBLS	5/15
	Trenton MSA, NJ	Y	45680 FQ	58260 MW	76730 TQ	USBLS	5/15
	New Mexico	Y	34650 FQ	54620 MW	68100 TQ	USBLS	5/15
	Albuquerque MSA, NM	Y	31450 FQ	53050 MW	64630 TQ	USBLS	5/15
	New York	Y	44420 AE	74350 MW	104920 AEX	NYBLS	1/16-3/16
	Buffalo-Cheektowaga-Niagara Falls MSA, NY	Y	27730 FQ	49520 MW	76820 TQ	USBLS	5/15
	Nassau County-Suffolk County PMSA, NY	Y	39150 FQ	56520 MW	82490 TQ	USBLS	5/15
	New York-Jersey City-White Plains PMSA, NY-NJ	Y	54990 FQ	74880 MW	101930 TQ	USBLS	5/15
	Rochester MSA, NY	Y	43660 FQ	67520 MW	101180 TQ	USBLS	5/15
	North Carolina	Y	45310 FQ	59310 MW	76460 TQ	USBLS	5/15
	Charlotte-Concord-Gastonia MSA, NC-SC	Y	44360 FQ	58460 MW	73670 TQ	USBLS	5/15
	Raleigh MSA, NC	Y	56260 FQ	73030 MW	105660 TQ	USBLS	5/15
	North Dakota	Y	32150 FQ	37790 MW	51290 TQ	USBLS	5/15
	Fargo MSA, ND-MN	Y	34300 FQ	38930 MW	58170 TQ	USBLS	5/15
	Ohio	Y	41030 FQ	53860 MW	73140 TQ	USBLS	5/15
	Cincinnati MSA, OH-KY-IN	Y	38400 FQ	49380 MW	66510 TQ	USBLS	5/15
	Cleveland-Elyria MSA, OH	Y	39770 FQ	49970 MW	86160 TQ	USBLS	5/15
	Columbus MSA, OH	Y	42430 FQ	55170 MW	66290 TQ	USBLS	5/15
	Oklahoma	Y	28080 FQ	36710 MW	54450 TQ	USBLS	5/15
	Oklahoma City MSA, OK	Y	25310 FQ	29010 MW	49010 TQ	USBLS	5/15
	Tulsa MSA, OK	Y	35810 FQ	45300 MW	62920 TQ	USBLS	5/15
	Oregon	H	20.80 FQ	31.48 MW	41.21 TQ	ORBLS	2016
	Portland-Vancouver-Hillsboro MSA, OR-WA	Y	48290 FQ	69000 MW	86720 TQ	USBLS	5/15
	Pennsylvania	Y	42230 FQ	57640 MW	78380 TQ	USBLS	5/15
	Allentown-Bethlehem-Easton MSA, PA-NJ	Y	49280 FQ	54470 MW	59600 TQ	USBLS	5/15
	Harrisburg-Carlisle MSA, PA	Y	44010 FQ	49150 MW	65490 TQ	USBLS	5/15
	Montgomery County-Bucks County-Chester County PMSA, PA	Y	46640 FQ	64610 MW	84030 TQ	USBLS	5/15
	Philadelphia PMSA, PA	Y	47120 FQ	62830 MW	79520 TQ	USBLS	5/15
	Rhode Island	Y	39730 FQ	57830 MW	70200 TQ	USBLS	5/15
	Providence-Warwick MSA, RI-MA	Y	40580 FQ	57770 MW	69890 TQ	USBLS	5/15
	South Carolina	Y	39510 FQ	50750 MW	63060 TQ	USBLS	5/15
	Charleston-North Charleston MSA, SC	Y	45680 FQ	55230 MW	62960 TQ	USBLS	5/15
	Columbia MSA, SC	Y	42930 FQ	56190 MW	70610 TQ	USBLS	5/15
	Greenville-Anderson-Mauldin MSA, SC	Y	35040 FQ	39060 MW	47900 TQ	USBLS	5/15
	South Dakota	Y	37400 FQ	44250 MW	50090 TQ	USBLS	5/15
	Sioux Falls MSA, SD	Y	34970 FQ	43460 MW	48760 TQ	USBLS	5/15
	Tennessee	Y	29770 FQ	40290 MW	57310 TQ	USBLS	5/15
	Knoxville MSA, TN	Y	28080 FQ	33470 MW	46800 TQ	USBLS	5/15
	Memphis MSA, TN-MS-AR	Y	28340 FQ	39200 MW	65770 TQ	USBLS	5/15
	Nashville-Davidson–Murfreesboro–Franklin MSA, TN	Y	34490 FQ	44340 MW	57150 TQ	USBLS	5/15
	Texas	Y	35550 FQ	54390 MW	73270 TQ	USBLS	5/15
	Austin-Round Rock MSA, TX	Y	31790 FQ	46940 MW	73280 TQ	USBLS	5/15
	Dallas-Plano-Irving PMSA, TX	Y	49320 FQ	62450 MW	77380 TQ	USBLS	5/15
	Fort Worth-Arlington PMSA, TX	Y	24190 FQ	45410 MW	65750 TQ	USBLS	5/15
	Houston-The Woodlands-Sugar Land MSA, TX	Y	42740 FQ	62580 MW	75000 TQ	USBLS	5/15
	San Antonio-New Braunfels MSA, TX	Y	42160 FQ	58840 MW	74210 TQ	USBLS	5/15
	Utah	Y	29160 FQ	37750 MW	54850 TQ	USBLS	5/15
	Ogden-Clearfield MSA, UT	Y	17410 FQ	19150 MW	43520 TQ	USBLS	5/15
	Provo-Orem MSA, UT	Y	26030 FQ	30250 MW	43930 TQ	USBLS	5/15
	Salt Lake City MSA, UT	Y	33390 FQ	41570 MW	57220 TQ	USBLS	5/15
	Vermont	Y	36030 FQ	50810 MW	60120 TQ	USBLS	5/15

AE	Average entry wage	AWR	Average wage range	H	Hourly	LR	Low end range	MTC	Median total compensation	TCC	Total cash compensation
AEX	Average experienced wage	B	Biweekly	HI	Highest wage paid	M	Monthly	MW	Median wage paid	TQ	Third quartile wage
ATC	Average total compensation	D	Daily	HR	High end range	MCC	Median cash compensation	MWR	Median wage range	W	Weekly
AW	Average wage paid	FQ	First quartile wage	LO	Lowest wage paid	ME	Median entry wage	S	See annotated source	Y	Yearly

Occupation/Type/Industry	Location	Per	Low	Mid	High	Source	Date
Writer and Author	Burlington-South Burlington						
	MSA, VT	Y	32520 FQ	36320 MW	42080 TQ	USBLS	5/15
	Virginia	Y	47910 FQ	61660 MW	85590 TQ	USBLS	5/15
	Richmond MSA, VA	Y	48210 FQ	59550 MW	77600 TQ	USBLS	5/15
	Virginia Beach-Norfolk-						
	Newport News MSA, VA-NC	Y	43340 FQ	49370 MW	64540 TQ	USBLS	5/15
	Washington	H	21.18 FQ	31.63 MW	42.40 TQ	WABLS	3/16
	Seattle-Bellevue-Everett						
	PMSA, WA	H	24.18 FQ	34.15 MW	44.37 TQ	WABLS	3/16
	Tacoma-Lakewood PMSA, WA	H	21.85 FQ	25.84 MW	32.09 TQ	WABLS	3/16
	West Virginia	Y	28980 FQ	38740 MW	59260 TQ	USBLS	5/15
	Wisconsin	Y	31510 FQ	43560 MW	55180 TQ	USBLS	5/15
	Madison MSA, WI	Y	31530 FQ	45730 MW	57600 TQ	USBLS	5/15
	Milwaukee-Waukesha-West						
	Allis MSA, WI	Y	33160 FQ	46660 MW	56180 TQ	USBLS	5/15
	Wyoming	Y	22020 FQ	39950 MW	52880 TQ	USBLS	5/15
	Puerto Rico	Y	25630 FQ	34630 MW	50560 TQ	USBLS	5/15
	San Juan-Carolina-Caguas						
	MSA, PR	Y	26880 FQ	35730 MW	51690 TQ	USBLS	5/15
X-Ray Technician							
Municipal Government	Long Beach, CA	Y			60785 HI	CACIT	6/28/16
Municipal Government	Detroit, MI	M	2108 LO		2442 HI	DETGOV	2016
Youth Counselor							
Police Department, Municipal Government	West Sacramento, CA	Y			72799 HI	CACIT	6/28/16
Youth Intervention Caseworker							
Police Services, Municipal Government	Santa Fe Springs, CA	Y			64476 HI	CACIT	6/28/16
Youth Intervention Specialist							
Police Department, Municipal Government	Davis, CA	Y			51759 HI	CACIT	6/28/16
Youth Outreach Worker							
Municipal Government	Lodi, CA	Y			42616 HI	CACIT	6/28/16
Youth Specialist							
Department of Health and Human Services, State Government	Michigan	H	17.26 LO		22.91 HI	MIGOV	2016
Youth Task Force Coordinator							
Police Department, Municipal Government	Gilroy, CA	Y			78007 HI	CACIT	6/28/16
Youth Transition Coordinator							
Child Protective Services, State Government	New Mexico	H	15.28 LO		26.59 HI	NMGOV	7/30/16
Zamboni Driver	United States	H		13.00 AW		JM03	2017
Zero Waste Coordinator							
Public Works Department, Municipal Government	Palo Alto, CA	Y		79908 AW		CACIT	6/28/16
Zoo Animal Registrar							
Municipal Government	Santa Ana, CA	Y			57780 HI	CACIT	6/28/16
Zoo Curator							
Fishes, Municipal Government	Detroit, MI	M	3800 LO		5325 HI	DETGOV	2016
Mammals, Municipal Government	Detroit, MI	M	3967 LO		5550 HI	DETGOV	2016
Zoo Endocrinologist	United States	Y		90000 AW		SKU01	2016
Zoo Horticulturist							
Municipal Government	Detroit, MI	M	3800 LO		5325 HI	DETGOV	2016
Zoo Research Director							
Municipal Government	Los Angeles, CA	Y			85509 HI	CACIT	6/23/16
Zoologist and Wildlife Biologist	Alabama	Y	44483 AE	63698 AW	73310 AEX	ALBLS	6/16
	Alaska	Y	60600 FQ	72500 MW	85680 TQ	USBLS	5/15
	Anchorage MSA, AK	Y	56830 FQ	69290 MW	84160 TQ	USBLS	5/15
	Arizona	Y	50010 FQ	59890 MW	69880 TQ	USBLS	5/15

AE	Average entry wage	AWR	Average wage range	H	Hourly	LR	Low end range	MTC	Median total compensation	TCC	Total cash compensation
AEX	Average experienced wage	B	Biweekly	HI	Highest wage paid	M	Monthly	MW	Median wage paid	TQ	Third quartile wage
ATC	Average total compensation	D	Daily	HR	High end range	MCC	Median cash compensation	MWR	Median wage range	W	Weekly
AW	Average wage paid	FQ	First quartile wage	LO	Lowest wage paid	ME	Median entry wage	S	See annotated source	Y	Yearly

Occupation/Type/Industry	Location	Per	Low	Mid	High	Source	Date
Zoologist and Wildlife Biologist	Phoenix-Mesa-Scottsdale MSA, AZ	Y	47960 FQ	57550 MW	68260 TQ	USBLS	5/15
	Tucson MSA, AZ	Y	49250 FQ	58890 MW	76150 TQ	USBLS	5/15
	Arkansas	Y	40760 FQ	50020 MW	58080 TQ	USBLS	5/15
	Little Rock-North Little Rock-Conway MSA, AR	Y	37970 FQ	42190 MW	50620 TQ	USBLS	5/15
	California	H	23.90 FQ	29.79 MW	40.24 TQ	CABLS	1/16-3/16
	Anaheim-Santa Ana-Irvine PMSA, CA	H	27.97 FQ	35.68 MW	46.07 TQ	CABLS	1/16-3/16
	Los Angeles-Long Beach-Glendale PMSA, CA	H	22.89 FQ	26.35 MW	30.16 TQ	CABLS	1/16-3/16
	Oakland-Hayward-Berkeley PMSA, CA	H	26.36 FQ	30.23 MW	40.37 TQ	CABLS	1/16-3/16
	Riverside-San Bernardino-Ontario MSA, CA	H	33.93 FQ	40.12 MW	44.49 TQ	CABLS	1/16-3/16
	Sacramento–Roseville–Arden-Arcade MSA, CA	H	24.43 FQ	29.81 MW	38.77 TQ	CABLS	1/16-3/16
	San Diego-Carlsbad MSA, CA	H	22.66 FQ	29.13 MW	39.46 TQ	CABLS	1/16-3/16
	Colorado	Y	56560 FQ	62470 MW	76140 TQ	USBLS	5/15
	Denver-Aurora-Lakewood MSA, CO	Y	49220 FQ	60410 MW	82870 TQ	USBLS	5/15
	Connecticut	Y		92877 MW		CTBLS	1/16-3/16
	Washington-Arlington-Alexandria PMSA, DC-VA-MD-WV	Y	68170 FQ	90830 MW	121620 TQ	USBLS	5/15
	Florida	H	16.85 AE	24.22 MW	29.49 AEX	FLBLS	7/16-9/16
	Fort Lauderdale-Pompano Beach-Deerfield Beach PMSA, FL	H	17.65 AE	24.24 MW	31.53 AEX	FLBLS	7/16-9/16
	Miami-Miami Beach-Kendall PMSA, FL	H	22.25 AE	36.10 MW	47.09 AEX	FLBLS	7/16-9/16
	Tampa-St. Petersburg-Clearwater MSA, FL	H	17.38 AE	25.96 MW	28.80 AEX	FLBLS	7/16-9/16
	Georgia	Y	38980 FQ	47310 MW	59070 TQ	USBLS	5/15
	Atlanta-Sandy Springs-Roswell MSA, GA	Y	35740 FQ	44690 MW	57660 TQ	USBLS	5/15
	Hawaii	Y	54600 FQ	67670 MW	93120 TQ	USBLS	5/15
	Urban Honolulu MSA, HI	Y	57460 FQ	75260 MW	93140 TQ	USBLS	5/15
	Idaho	Y	47450 FQ	58620 MW	73630 TQ	USBLS	5/15
	Boise City MSA, ID	Y	43480 FQ	59690 MW	79670 TQ	USBLS	5/15
	Illinois	Y	53230 FQ	64430 MW	76140 TQ	USBLS	5/15
	Chicago-Naperville-Arlington Heights PMSA, IL	Y	55490 FQ	66570 MW	77140 TQ	USBLS	5/15
	Indiana	Y	43360 FQ	59500 MW	71480 TQ	USBLS	5/15
	Iowa	Y	57550 FQ	70000 MW	70010 TQ	USBLS	5/15
	Kentucky	Y	36670 FQ	43780 MW	55840 TQ	USBLS	5/15
	Louisville-Jefferson County MSA, KY-IN	Y	33710 FQ	35900 MW	38100 TQ	USBLS	5/15
	Louisiana	Y	54090 FQ	69290 MW	80460 TQ	USBLS	5/15
	Maine	Y	46890 FQ	54530 MW	61990 TQ	USBLS	5/15
	Maryland	Y	63277 AE	93073 MW	107971 AEX	MDBLS	4/16
	Baltimore-Columbia-Towson MSA, MD	Y	57950 FQ	84030 MW	107130 TQ	USBLS	5/15
	Massachusetts	Y	59970 FQ	80740 MW	103860 TQ	USBLS	5/15
	Boston-Cambridge-Newton NECTA, MA	Y	57040 FQ	71490 MW	99770 TQ	USBLS	5/15
	Worcester MSA, MA-CT	Y	53490 FQ	59990 MW	72610 TQ	USBLS	5/15
	Michigan	Y	57890 FQ	69140 MW	77670 TQ	USBLS	5/15
	Minnesota	Y	49092 FQ	57610 MW	65846 TQ	MNBLS	1/16-3/16
	Minneapolis-St. Paul-Bloomington MSA, MN-WI	Y	47499 FQ	56471 MW	63336 TQ	MNBLS	1/16-3/16
	Mississippi	Y	43260 FQ	64430 MW	87330 TQ	USBLS	5/15
	Jackson MSA, MS	Y	39700 FQ	46100 MW	50220 TQ	USBLS	5/15
	Missouri	Y	41380 FQ	50010 MW	62480 TQ	USBLS	5/15
	St. Louis MSA, MO-IL	Y	41860 FQ	54800 MW	75180 TQ	USBLS	5/15
	Montana	Y	49470 FQ	58090 MW	72220 TQ	USBLS	5/15
	Nebraska	Y	46720 FQ	55505 MW	64435 TQ	NEBLS	7/16-9/16
	Nevada	Y	51820 FQ	63410 MW	73310 TQ	USBLS	5/15
	Las Vegas-Henderson-Paradise MSA, NV	Y	48330 FQ	62940 MW	82840 TQ	USBLS	5/15
	New Hampshire	H	19.72 AE	27.94 MW	30.78 AEX	NHBLS	6/16
	New Jersey	Y	54170 FQ	74730 MW	88830 TQ	USBLS	5/15

AE	Average entry wage	AWR	Average wage range	H	Hourly	LR	Low end range	MTC	Median total compensation	TCC	Total cash compensation
AEX	Average experienced wage	B	Biweekly	HI	Highest wage paid	M	Monthly	MW	Median wage paid	TQ	Third quartile wage
ATC	Average total compensation	D	Daily	HR	High end range	MCC	Median cash compensation	MWR	Median wage range	W	Weekly
AW	Average wage paid	FQ	First quartile wage	LO	Lowest wage paid	ME	Median entry wage	S	See annotated source	Y	Yearly

Occupation/Type/Industry	Location	Per	Low	Mid	High	Source	Date
Zoologist and Wildlife Biologist	Newark PMSA, NJ-PA	Y	67160 FQ	80410 MW	89690 TQ	USBLS	5/15
	New Mexico	Y	48000 FQ	58570 MW	70280 TQ	USBLS	5/15
	Albuquerque MSA, NM	Y	49800 FQ	62770 MW	72240 TQ	USBLS	5/15
	New York	Y	46160 AE	68240 MW	78420 AEX	NYBLS	1/16-3/16
	Nassau County-Suffolk County PMSA, NY	Y	59550 FQ	73950 MW	89350 TQ	USBLS	5/15
	New York-Jersey City-White Plains PMSA, NY-NJ	Y	49780 FQ	65850 MW	84040 TQ	USBLS	5/15
	North Carolina	Y	42390 FQ	50640 MW	69350 TQ	USBLS	5/15
	Raleigh MSA, NC	Y	45490 FQ	54220 MW	97480 TQ	USBLS	5/15
	North Dakota	Y	30360 FQ	57930 MW	70280 TQ	USBLS	5/15
	Ohio	Y	45300 FQ	56980 MW	65820 TQ	USBLS	5/15
	Columbus MSA, OH	Y	45300 FQ	51900 MW	62100 TQ	USBLS	5/15
	Oklahoma	Y	38120 FQ	47920 MW	61320 TQ	USBLS	5/15
	Oklahoma City MSA, OK	Y	19090 FQ	46490 MW	57480 TQ	USBLS	5/15
	Oregon	H	26.75 FQ	31.24 MW	37.13 TQ	ORBLS	2016
	Portland-Vancouver-Hillsboro MSA, OR-WA	Y	59320 FQ	71450 MW	91150 TQ	USBLS	5/15
	Pennsylvania	Y	47600 FQ	56820 MW	70500 TQ	USBLS	5/15
	Harrisburg-Carlisle MSA, PA	Y	40070 FQ	46810 MW	56550 TQ	USBLS	5/15
	Rhode Island	Y	70540 FQ	80520 MW	91650 TQ	USBLS	5/15
	Providence-Warwick MSA, RI-MA	Y	70390 FQ	80460 MW	90630 TQ	USBLS	5/15
	South Carolina	Y	39320 FQ	48930 MW	61480 TQ	USBLS	5/15
	Charleston-North Charleston MSA, SC	Y	41290 FQ	49770 MW	65690 TQ	USBLS	5/15
	Columbia MSA, SC	Y	42960 FQ	55200 MW	59960 TQ	USBLS	5/15
	South Dakota	Y	41750 FQ	51630 MW	61140 TQ	USBLS	5/15
	Tennessee	Y	52850 FQ	68200 MW	82020 TQ	USBLS	5/15
	Knoxville MSA, TN	Y	60900 FQ	80150 MW	90130 TQ	USBLS	5/15
	Texas	Y	56270 FQ	66360 MW	78120 TQ	USBLS	5/15
	Austin-Round Rock MSA, TX	Y	47910 FQ	61390 MW	74300 TQ	USBLS	5/15
	Dallas-Plano-Irving PMSA, TX	Y	56030 FQ	63610 MW	79940 TQ	USBLS	5/15
	Fort Worth-Arlington PMSA, TX	Y	63000 FQ	72590 MW	84800 TQ	USBLS	5/15
	Houston-The Woodlands-Sugar Land MSA, TX	Y	57350 FQ	73160 MW	96520 TQ	USBLS	5/15
	Utah	Y	43140 FQ	51770 MW	66370 TQ	USBLS	5/15
	Provo-Orem MSA, UT	Y	43280 FQ	48090 MW	55610 TQ	USBLS	5/15
	Salt Lake City MSA, UT	Y	43090 FQ	50440 MW	67950 TQ	USBLS	5/15
	Vermont	Y	49350 FQ	61490 MW	71050 TQ	USBLS	5/15
	Burlington-South Burlington MSA, VT	Y	47360 FQ	51860 MW	63540 TQ	USBLS	5/15
	Virginia	Y	46550 FQ	54870 MW	67480 TQ	USBLS	5/15
	Richmond MSA, VA	Y	49830 FQ	56220 MW	65110 TQ	USBLS	5/15
	Virginia Beach-Norfolk-Newport News MSA, VA-NC	Y	39320 FQ	49190 MW	60520 TQ	USBLS	5/15
	Washington	H	25.59 FQ	30.16 MW	39.97 TQ	WABLS	3/16
	Seattle-Bellevue-Everett PMSA, WA	H	27.78 FQ	36.51 MW	47.97 TQ	WABLS	3/16
	West Virginia	Y	30740 FQ	43170 MW	56480 TQ	USBLS	5/15
	Wisconsin	Y	45510 FQ	51520 MW	61240 TQ	USBLS	5/15
	Madison MSA, WI	Y	35080 FQ	47290 MW	61650 TQ	USBLS	5/15
	Wyoming	Y	48370 FQ	60870 MW	66610 TQ	USBLS	5/15

AE	Average entry wage	AWR	Average wage range	H	Hourly	LR	Low end range	MTC	Median total compensation	TCC	Total cash compensation
AEX	Average experienced wage	B	Biweekly	HI	Highest wage paid	M	Monthly	MW	Median wage paid	TQ	Third quartile wage
ATC	Average total compensation	D	Daily	HR	High end range	MCC	Median cash compensation	MWR	Median wage range	W	Weekly
AW	Average wage paid	FQ	First quartile wage	LO	Lowest wage paid	ME	Median entry wage	S	See annotated source	Y	Yearly

Appendix I

SOURCES

AACSB

"Average Full-Time Salaries," October 3, 2016.

AACSB International
777 South Harbour Island Boulevard, Suite 750
Tampa, FL 33602
Telephone: 813-769-6500
Fax: 813-769-6559
Online: http://www.aacsb.edu
Survey Period: 2014-2015

AAHS

"Public Health Careers Salary Information," October 3, 2016.

Online: http://www.allalliedhealthschools.com
Survey Period: 2016

Note: Data were downloaded on October 3, 2016 and were considered current by the source.

AAMC

"Starting Salaries for Physicians," October 31, 2016.

AAMC
Financial Information, Resources, and Tools (FIRST)
655 K Street, NW, Suite 100
Washington, DC 20001-2399
Online: https://students-residents.aamc.org
Email: first@aamc.org
Survey Period: 2016

Note: Starting salaries.

AAPG

Brian Ervin, "Salary Survey Points to Experience Gap," June 1, 2016.

American Association of Petroleum Geologists
1444 South Boulder
Tulsa, OK 74119
Telephone: 918-584-2555
Fax: 918-560-2665
Online: http://www.aapg.org
Survey Period: 2015

ABS01

"Sports Management Salary and Job Outlook," *All Business Schools*, October 3, 2016.

Online: http://www.allbusinessschools.com
Survey Period: 2016-2017

Note: Data was downloaded on October 3, 2016.

ACU

2016 Ministers' Salary Survey, May 1, 2016.

Siburt Institute for Church Ministry
ACU Box 29425
Abilene, TX 79699
Telephone: 325-674-3722
Fax: 325-674-3776
Online: http://www.acu.edu
Email: siburtinstitute@acu.edu
Survey Period: February 2016-March 2016

ADAGE01

Jack Neff, "Why Employers Can't Get Enough of Marketers," *Advertising Age*, March 2, 2015, pp. 16-17.

Survey Period: 2015

ADAGE02

Felicia Greiff, "Digital Strategy Needs and Restructuring Drive Boost in Six-Figure Salaries," *Advertising Age*, May 4, 2015.

Online: http://www.adage.com
Survey Period: 2015

AFTRA1

"SAG-AFTRA Television Agreement Wage Tables," December 11, 2015.

SAG-AFTRA
5757 Wilshire Boulevard, 7th Floor
Los Angeles, CA 90036
Telephone: 855-724-2387
Online: https://www.sagaftra.org
Survey Period: July 1, 2016-June 30, 2017

Note: Minimum wage rates.

AFTRA2

"SAG-AFTRA Theatrical Wage Table," September 9, 2014.

SAG-AFTRA
5757 Wilshire Boulevard, 7th Floor
Los Angeles, CA 90036
Telephone: 855-724-2387
Online: https://www.sagaftra.org
Survey Period: July 1, 2016-June 30, 2017

Note: Minimum wage rates.

AGO

"2015 Salary Guide for Musicians in Religious Institutions," October 3, 2016.

American Guild of Organists
475 Riverside Drive, Suite 1260
New York, NY 10115
Telephone: 212-870-2310
Fax: 212-870-2163
Online: https://www.agohq.org
Email: info@agohq.org
Survey Period: 2015

Note: Base salary. Data were downloaded on October 3, 2016.

AGPRO

Colleen Scherer, "Salary Survey 2016," *Ag Professional*, May 2016, pp. 26-28.

Online: http://www.agprofessional.com/magazine
Survey Period: 2016

AHNRSP

"2016 Salary Survey Results: Respiratory Care & Sleep Medicine," *ADVANCE for Respiratory Care and Sleep Medicine*, September 29, 2016.

Online: http://respiratory-care-sleep-medicine.advance-web.com
Survey Period: 2016

AIFS

"Program Cost," October 5, 2016.

Au Pair in America
1 High Ridge Park
Stamford, CT 06905
Telephone: 203-399-5000
Online: http://www.aupairinamerica.com/fees/
Email: aupair.info@aifs.com
Survey Period: 2016

Note: Minimum weekly stipend. Data were downloaded on October 5, 2016.

ALBLS

Occupational Wage Estimates, August 17, 2016.

Alabama Department of Labor
Labor Market Information Division
649 Monroe Street
Montgomery, AL 36131
Telephone: 334-353-8021
Online: http://www2.labor.alabama.gov
Email: David.Murphy@labor.alabama.gov
Survey Period: June 2016

Note: All data are provided by the State Employment Security Administration to the Occupational Employment Statistics (OES) survey conducted by the U.S. Department of Labor, Bureau of Labor Statistics. May 2015 Occupational Employment and Wage Estimates have been adjusted to June 2016 using the Employment Cost Index.

APA01

"APA/AICP Planners Salary Survey Summary," October 31, 2016.

American Planning Association
1030 15th Street, NW, Suite 750 W
Washington, DC 20005-1503
Telephone: 202-872-0611
Fax: 202-872-0643
Online: https://planning.org/salary/summary/
Survey Period: January 1, 2016

Note: Data were downloaded on October 31, 2016. Salary data as of January 1, 2016.

APAC01

Stacy Lu, "Median Salaries for New Psychologists Are Static," April 2016.

American Psychological Association
750 First Street, NE
Washington, DC 20002-4242
Telephone: 202-336-5500
Online: http://www.apa.org
Survey Period: 2016

APAC02

Peggy Christidis, et. al., *Psychology Faculty Salaries for the 2014-2015 Academic Year*, October 2015.

> American Psychological Association
> 750 First Street, NE
> Washington, DC 20002-4242
> **Telephone:** 202-336-5500
> **Online:** http://www.apa.org
> **Survey Period:** 2014-2015

APP01

"Federal Employees UPDATED," *DataUniverse*, October 31, 2016.

> **Online:** http://php.app.com/agent/federalemployees/search
> **Survey Period:** 2015

Note: Data were downloaded on October 31, 2016. Actual base wages for Federal fiscal year 2015. DataUniverse is maintained by Asbury Park Press.

APP02

"US Postal Employees," *DataUniverse*, October 31, 2016.

> **Online:** http://php.app.com/agent/postalemployees/search
> **Survey Period:** January 2016

Note: Data were downloaded on October 31, 2016. Actual base wages as of January 2016. DataUniverse is maintained by Asbury Park Press.

ASSE

"Salary Survey," November 2, 2016.

> The American Society of Safety Engineers
> 520 North Northwest Highway
> Park Ridge, IL 60068
> **Telephone:** 847-699-2929
> **Online:** http://www.asse.org/salarysurvey/
> **Survey Period:** January 1, 2015

Note: Salary as of January 1, 2015.

ASSEM01

Austin Weber, "Special Report: State of the Profession 2016," *ASSEMBLY*, July 1, 2016.

> **Online:** http://www.assemblymag.com
> **Survey Period:** March 2016

AUTOF

Lauren Fletcher, "Fleet Manager Salaries Moving Higher," *Automotive Fleet*, 2015, pp. 20-22.

> **Survey Period:** 2014

AUTOM

"Salary Survey Results 2016," *Automation.com*, October 2016.

> **Online:** http://www.automation.com
> **Survey Period:** July 7, 2016-August 24, 2016

AUTON

"Checking in on Paychecks," *Automotive News*, October 3, 2016, p. 40.

> **Survey Period:** 2015

AUTON1

Stephanie Hernandez McGavin, "Turning Around Turnover," *Automotive News*, November 2016, pp. 12-13.

> **Survey Period:** 2015

AVJOB01

"Airport Salaries, Wages and Pay," October 31, 2016.

Online: http://www.avjobs.com/salaries-wages-pay/
Survey Period: 2016

Note: Annual salaries are rounded to the nearest dollar. Data were downloaded on October 31, 2016 and were considered current by the source.

AVJOB02

"Ground and Ramp Salaries, Wages and Pay," October 31, 2016.

Online: http://www.avjobs.com/salaries-wages-pay/
Survey Period: 2016

Note: Data were downloaded on October 31, 2016 and were considered current by the source.

AVJOB03

"Helicopter Salaries, Wages and Pay," October 31, 2016.

Online: http://www.avjobs.com/salaries-wages-pay/
Survey Period: 2016

Note: Data were downloaded on October 31, 2016 and were considered current by the source.

AVJOB04

"Reservations & Travel Agent Salaries, Wages and Pay," October 31, 2016.

Online: http://www.avjobs.com/salaries-wages-pay/
Survey Period: 2016

Note: Data were downloaded on October 31, 2016 and were considered current by the source.

AVJOB05

"Avionics Salaries, Wages and Pay," October 31, 2016.

Online: http://www.avjobs.com/salaries-wages-pay/
Survey Period: 2016

Note: Annual salaries are rounded to the nearest dollar. Data were downloaded on October 31, 2016 and were considered current by the source.

AVJOB06

"AP Mechanic Salaries, Wages and Pay," October 31, 2016.

Online: http://www.avjobs.com/salaries-wages-pay/
Survey Period: 2016

Note: Data were downloaded on October 31, 2016 and were considered current by the source.

AZGOV

2017 Arizona County Government Salary and Benefit Survey, March 1, 2017.

Arizona Association of Counties
1910 West Jefferson
Phoenix, AZ 85009
Telephone: 602-252-6563
Online: http://www.arizona.org
Survey Period: 2017

Note: Data were downloaded on March 1, 2017. Actual salaries.

BAL01

Mary Hope Kramer, "Top Paying Animal Careers," *The Balance*, August 16, 2016.

Online: http://www.thebalance.com
Survey Period: 2011

BAL02

Mary Hope Kramer, "Top Paying Equine Careers," *The Balance*, June 5, 2016.

> **Online:** https://www.thebalance.com
> **Survey Period:** September 2011

BBRD01

"Who's Earning: Billboard Followed the Money to Determine Who's Pulling in the Largest—and Smallest—Paychecks in the Industry: From the Tens of Millions in Equity Awards Reaped by Apple Executives to a Radio-Station Mascot's Minimum Wage," *Billboard*, June 27, 2015, pp. 42+.

> **Survey Period:** 2014

Note: Salary for Radio On-Air Personality does not include bonuses for ratings.

BCPSSS

2016-2017 Salary Schedules, June 26, 2016.

> Baldwin County Public Schools
> Department of Human Resources
> 2600 North Hand Avenue
> Bay Minette, AL 36507
> **Telephone:** 251-937-0306
> **Fax:** 251-937-0318
> **Online:** http://www.bcbe.org
> **Survey Period:** 2016-2017

Note: JROTC Instructor salary is only the portion paid by the Baldwin County Board of Education. It does not include the portion of the salary funded by the United States Armed Forces.

BF01

Caroline O'Donovan and Jeremy Singer-Vine, "How Much Uber Drivers Actually Make per Hour," *BuzzFeed*, June 22, 2016.

> **Online:** http://www.buzzfeed.com
> **Survey Period:** October 19, 2015-December 21, 2015

Note: Survey in Detroit and Houston was conducted between December 7, 2015 and December 21, 2015. Survey in Denver was conducted between October 19, 2015 and December 14, 2015. Average hourly wages after expenses.

BGIE

Anuja Vaidya, "15 Statistics on Gastroenterologist Salary, Net Worth, Jobs & More," *Becker's GI & Endoscopy*, July 22, 2016.

> **Online:** http://www.beckersasc.com
> **Survey Period:** 2016

BHICR

Erin Dietsche, "CareerCast Ranks 10 Best Jobs in IT, Engineering," *Becker's Health IT & CIO Review*, October 17, 2016.

> **Online:** http://www.beckershospitalreview.com
> **Survey Period:** 2016

BHR01

Mackenzie Bean, "Supply Chain Salaries to Increase Nearly 3% in 2017," *Becker's Hospital Review*, September 15, 2016.

> **Online:** http://www.beckershospitalreview.com
> **Survey Period:** 2016

BMO01

Jeffrey M. Silber and Henry Sou Chien, "Exhibit 258. Median Salaries for Typical Sales and Marketing Positions (FY2004-2005 to FY2014-2015 School Years)," *Education and Training*, September 2015, p. 231.

> BMO Capital Markets
> **Telephone:** 212-885-4063
> **Survey Period:** 2014-2015

BOPP01

"Salaries in the Parish Ministry 2016 Salary Study," November 2, 2016.

> The Board of Pensions of the Presbyterian Church (U.S.A.)
> 2000 Market Street
> Philadelphia, PA 19103-3296
> **Telephone:** 800-773-7752
> **Fax:** 215-587-6215
> **Online:** http://www.pensions.org
> **Survey Period:** May 1, 2016

Note: Salary data as of May 1, 2016.

BSR

Laura Dyrda, "10 Updates on Neurosurgeon Pay Featured," *Becker's Spine Review*, July 20, 2016.

> **Online:** http://www.beckersspine.com
> **Survey Period:** 2014

BTN01

Chris Davis, "Summer Days: Travel Buyer Compensation Is Up & Attitudes Are Brighter," *Business Travel News*, July 18, 2016, pp. 12-20.

> **Survey Period:** 2016

Note: Data include salary, bonuses and incentives.

BUSIN

Rachel Gillett, "Trump Has Said He Does Not Want to Take a Salary, But He May Have To," *Business Insider*, November 16, 2016.

> **Online:** http://www.businessinsider.com
> **Survey Period:** 2017

Note: The salary of the President of the United States does not include a $50,000 annual expense account, a $100,000 travel account, and a $19,000 entertainment account.

BUZZ01

Kundan Pandey, "Average Salary for an Air Hostess," *Buzzle*, March 3, 2015.

> **Online:** http://www.buzzle.com
> **Survey Period:** 2015

BUZZ02

Ujwal Deshmukh, "Robotics Engineer Average Salary," *Buzzle*, May 25, 2015.

> **Online:** http://www.buzzle.com
> **Survey Period:** 2015

Note: Salary data according to the National Human Genome Research Institute.

BUZZ03

Salpriya Iyer, "Job Description and Salary of a Wellness Coach," *Buzzle*, May 7, 2015.

> **Online:** http://www.buzzle.com
> **Survey Period:** 2015

BUZZ04

Vijith Menon, "Job Description and Average Salary of a Script Supervisor," *Buzzle*, March 18, 2015.

Online: http://www.buzzle.com
Survey Period: 2015

CABLS

California OES Employment and Wages, June 2016.

Employment Development Department
Labor Market Information Division
P.O. Box 826880, MIC 57
Sacramento, CA 94280-0001
Telephone: 916-262-2162
Fax: 916-262-2352
Online: http://www.labormarketinfo.edd.ca.gov
Survey Period: January 2016-March 2016

Note: All data are provided by the State Employment Security Administration to the Occupational Employment Statistics (OES) survey conducted by the U.S. Department of Labor, Bureau of Labor Statistics. May 2015 Occupational Employment and Wage Estimates have been adjusted to the first quarter of 2016 using the Employment Cost Index.

CAC

California Association of Criminalists 2015-2016 Salary Survey, December 14, 2016.

Online: http://www.cacnews.org
Survey Period: 2014-2016

Note: Salaries became effective on the date stated in each individual record.

CACIT

"2015 City Data," November 15, 2016.

Government Compensation in California
California State Controller's Office
300 Capitol Mall, Suite 1850
Sacramento, CA 95814
Telephone: 916-445-2636
Fax: 916-322-4404
Online: http://gcc.sco.ca.gov
Survey Period: June 22, 2016-October 20, 2016

Note: Data were downloaded on November 15, 2016. Salaries were updated by the source on the date stated in each individual record. Average salaries are rounded to the nearest dollar. Non-average salaries are actual salaries. Roseville's Permit Analyst and Community Relations Analyst and Santa Barbara's Parking Coordinator salaries are rounded to the nearest dollar.

CALST

The California State University Salary Schedule, February 3, 2017.

CSU, HR-Data Operations
300 Capitol Mall, 10th Floor
Sacramento, CA 94250-5878
Telephone: 916-323-5694
Online: http://www.calstate.edu
Email: cirs@calstate.edu
Survey Period: 2016-2017

CARE

Tiffany Smith, "Leave a Comment," *Care.com*, March 24, 2015.

Online: http://www.care.com/a/how-much-should-you-pay-your-sitter-04131708
Survey Period: 2014

CBS01

"It Really Pays to Be a Private College President," *CBS News*, December 5, 2016.

Online: http://www.cbsnews.com
Survey Period: 2014

CBS02

Aimee Picchi, "5 Best and Worst Jobs for 2016," *CBS Money-Watch*, April 13, 2016.

Online: http://www.cbsnews.com
Survey Period: 2016

CBS03

"Program Trains Young Garbage Collectors Amid U.S. Shortage," *CBS News*, November 24, 2016.

Online: http://www.cbsnews.com
Survey Period: 2016

CBS04

Leif Walcutt, "The 10 Most Stressful Jobs," *CBS Money-Watch*, January 7, 2016.

Online: http://www.cbsnews.com
Survey Period: 2016

CBS05

Aimee Picchi, "America's 10 Toughest Jobs to Fill in 2017," *CBS News*, February 2, 2017.

Online: http://www.cbsnews.com
Survey Period: 2017

CCAST01

"The 2016 Jobs Rated Report," *CareerCast*, November 2, 2016.

Online: http://www.careercast.com
Survey Period: 2016

Note: Data were downloaded on November 2, 2016.

CCCA01

"Salary Schedule — General Employees," June 16, 2016.

City of Carlsbad
Human Resources
1635 Faraday Avenue
Carlsbad, CA 92008
Telephone: 760-602-2440
Fax: 760-602-8554
Online: http://www.carlsbadca.gov
Email: hr@carlsbadca.gov
Survey Period: June 28, 2016

Note: Salaries became effective on June 28, 2016.

CCCA02

"Hourly Salary Schedule," November 15, 2016.

City of Carlsbad
Human Resources
1635 Faraday Avenue
Carlsbad, CA 92008
Telephone: 760-602-2440
Fax: 760-602-8554
Online: http://www.carlsbadca.gov
Email: hr@carlsbadca.gov
Survey Period: January 1, 2016

Note: Data were downloaded on November 15, 2016. Salaries became effective on January 1, 2016.

CEN01

Andrea Widener, "Does Your Salary Stand Out?" *C&EN*, November 14, 2016, pp. 28-29.

    Online: http://cen.acs.org
    Survey Period: March 2016-April 2016

CERTM01

"Salary Survey Data: 10 Certs at the Top of Many 2015 To-Do Lists," *Certification Magazine*, September 4, 2015.

    Online: http://certmag.com
    Survey Period: 2014

CERTM02

"Salary Survey," *Certification Magazine*, September 26, 2016.

    Online: http://certmag.com/salary-survey/
    Survey Period: 2015

Note: Data were downloaded on September 26, 2016.

CHE01

"What Hourly Higher-Ed Employees Made in 2015-16," *The Chronicle*, April 25, 2016.

    The Chronicle of Higher Education
    1255 Twenty-Third Street NW, Seventh Floor
    Washington, DC 20037
    Telephone: 202-466-1000
    Fax: 202-452-1033
    Online: http://www.chronicle.com
    Survey Period: 2015-2016

CHE02

"What Higher-Education Professionals Made in 2015-16," *The Chronicle*, April 11, 2016.

    The Chronicle of Higher Education
    1255 Twenty-Third Street NW, Seventh Floor
    Washington, DC 20037
    Telephone: 202-466-1000
    Fax: 202-452-1033
    Online: http://www.chronicle.com
    Survey Period: 2015-2016

CHE03

Chronicle Data, December 1, 2016.

    The Chronicle of Higher Education
    1255 Twenty-Third Street NW, Seventh Floor
    Washington, DC 20037
    Telephone: 202-466-1000
    Fax: 202-452-1033
    Online: http://data.chronicle.com
    Survey Period: 2014-2015

Note: Data were downloaded on December 1, 2016.

CIA01

"Analytic Methodologist," November 17, 2016.

    Central Intelligence Agency
    Office of Public Affairs
    Washington, DC 20505
    Telephone: 703-482-0623
    Fax: 571-204-3800
    Online: https://www.cia.gov/careers/
    Survey Period: 2016

Note: Salary data were last updated on November 17, 2016.

CIA02

"Counterintelligence Threat Analyst," November 17, 2016.

Central Intelligence Agency
Office of Public Affairs
Washington, DC 20505
Telephone: 703-482-0623
Fax: 571-204-3800
Online: https://www.cia.gov/careers/
Survey Period: 2016

Note: Salary data were last updated on November 17, 2016.

CIA03

"Data Scientist — Central Intelligence Agency," November 17, 2016.

Central Intelligence Agency
Office of Public Affairs
Washington, DC 20505
Telephone: 703-482-0623
Fax: 571-204-3800
Online: https://www.cia.gov/careers/
Survey Period: 2016

Note: Salary data were last updated on November 17, 2016.

CIA04

"Cyber Threat Analyst," November 17, 2016.

Central Intelligence Agency
Office of Public Affairs
Washington, DC 20505
Telephone: 703-482-0623
Fax: 571-204-3800
Online: https://www.cia.gov/careers/
Survey Period: 2016

Note: Salary data were last updated on November 17, 2016.

CIA05

"Open Source Officer," November 17, 2016.

Central Intelligence Agency
Office of Public Affairs
Washington, DC 20505
Telephone: 703-482-0623
Fax: 571-204-3800
Online: https://www.cia.gov/careers/
Survey Period: 2016

Note: Salary data were last updated on November 17, 2016.

CIA06

"SL Interpreter — Central Intelligence Agency," November 17, 2016.

Central Intelligence Agency
Office of Public Affairs
Washington, DC 20505
Telephone: 703-482-0623
Fax: 571-204-3800
Online: https://www.cia.gov/careers/
Survey Period: 2016

Note: Salary data were last updated on November 17, 2016.

CIA07

"Paramilitary Operations Officer/Specialized Skills Officer," November 17, 2016.

Central Intelligence Agency
Office of Public Affairs
Washington, DC 20505
Telephone: 703-482-0623
Fax: 571-204-3800
Online: https://www.cia.gov/careers/
Survey Period: 2016

Note: Salary data were last updated on November 17, 2016.

CIA08

"Interactive Designer," November 17, 2016.

Central Intelligence Agency
Office of Public Affairs
Washington, DC 20505
Telephone: 703-482-0623
Fax: 571-204-3800
Online: https://www.cia.gov/careers/
Survey Period: 2016

Note: Salary data were last updated on November 17, 2016.

CNAV01

"10 Highly-Rated Charities With Low Paid CEOs," *Charity Navigator*, January 4, 2016.

Online: http://www.charitynavigator.org
Survey Period: 2015

Note: Data were downloaded on January 4, 2016. Average of the CEO compensation reported by the more than 7,000 charities rated by Charity Navigator.

CNBC01

Michelle Castillo, "Some People Make Seven Figures to Post on Social Media," *CNBC*, August 31, 2016.

Online: http://www.cnbc.com
Survey Period: 2016

Note: Data are based on the number of followers, from a low of less than 250,000 to a high of 7,000,000 or more. Data are per brand campaign.

CNBC02

Marguerite Ward, "The 25 Highest-Paying Jobs in America," *CNBC*, July 26, 2016.

Online: http://www.cnbc.com
Survey Period: 2016

Note: Base salaries.

CNBC03

Linda Dimyan, "Rising Pay for Truckers Is Reshaping the Industry," *CNBC*, November 1, 2015.

Online: http://www.cnbc.com
Survey Period: 2015

Note: Salary data according to the National Transportation Institute.

CNBC04

Jane Wells, "How to Make Six Figures From Home," *CNBC*, June 19, 2015.

Online: http://www.cnbc.com/id/102772816
Survey Period: 2015

CNBC05

Marguerite Ward, "11 Surprising Jobs Where You Can Earn More Than $100,000 a Year," *CNBC*, November 15, 2016.

Online: http://www.cnbc.com
Survey Period: 2016

CNBC06

Jessica Dickler, "The Highest-Paying Jobs in America," *CNBC*, November 22, 2016.

Online: http://www.cnbc.com
Survey Period: 2016

CNBC07

Kathleen Elkins, "The 15 Highest-Paying Jobs for Business Majors," *CNBC*, December 1, 2016.

Online: http://www.cnbc.com
Survey Period: 2016-2017

CNBC08

Catherine Clifford, "The 15 Best Jobs in America in 2017," *CNBC*, January 24, 2017.

Online: http://www.cnbc.com
Survey Period: 2017

Note: Base salary.

CNNM01

Jill Disis, "Big Pay Cut in Store if Exxon CEO Becomes Secretary of State," *CNNMoney*, December 12, 2016.

Online: http://money.cnn.com
Survey Period: 2016

COPIER

Twenty-Sixteen Sales Manager Salary Survey, October 24, 2016.

Online: http://copiercareers.com
Survey Period: 2016

COPIER1

"Copier Careers Sales Representative Salary Survey 2016," *Copier Careers*, November 29, 2016.

Online: http://copiercareers.com
Survey Period: 2016

COPIER2

Twenty-Sixteen Service & Operations Manager Salary Survey, October 24, 2016.

Online: http://copiercareers.com
Survey Period: 2016

COPIER3

Twenty-Sixteen Service Tech Salary Survey, October 24, 2016.

Online: http://copiercareers.com
Survey Period: 2016

COSPRS

City of Colorado Springs — 2017 Salary Schedule, November 28, 2016.

City of Colorado Springs
Human Resources Department
30 South Nevada Avenue, Suite 702
Colorado Springs, CO 80903
Telephone: 719-385-5904
Online: https://coloradosprings.gov
Survey Period: 2017

Note: Salaries took effect on January 1, 2017.

CPMS

Overseas Educators School Year 2015-2016 Salary Schedule, August 1, 2015.

Department of Defense Education Activity
4800 Mark Center Drive
Alexandria, VA 22350-1400
Online: http://www.dodea.edu
Survey Period: 2015-2016

Note: Salaries took effect on August 1, 2015.

CRS01

Ida A. Brudnick, *Congressional Salaries and Allowance: In Brief*, July 14, 2016.

Congressional Research Service
Library of Congress
101 Independence Avenue SE
Washington, DC 20540
Telephone: 202-707-5000
Online: http://www.senate.gov
Survey Period: 2016

CRU01

"Beauty, Hairdressing and Fitness Jobs on Cruise Ships," *Cruise Ship Jobs*, December 6, 2016.

Online: http://cruiseshipjob.com/beauty.htm
Survey Period: 2016

Note: Data were downloaded on December 6, 2016 and were considered current by the source.

CRU02

"Cruise Ship Entertainment Jobs," *Cruise Ship Jobs*, December 6, 2016.

Online: http://cruiseshipjob.com/entertain.htm
Survey Period: 2016

Note: Data were downloaded on December 6, 2016 and were considered current by the source.

CRU03

"Cruise Ship Slot Technician Jobs," *Cruise Ship Jobs*, December 6, 2016.

Online: http://cruiseshipjob.com/slot-technician-jobs.htm
Survey Period: 2016

Note: Data were downloaded on December 6, 2016 and were considered current by the source.

CRU04

"Culinary Jobs on Cruise Ships," *Cruise Ship Jobs*, December 6, 2016.

Online: http://cruiseshipjob.com/galley.htm
Survey Period: 2016

Note: Data were downloaded on December 6, 2016 and were considered current by the source.

CSG

Jennifer Burnett, "Governors' Salaries 2016," July 19, 2016.

The Council of State Governments
1776 Avenue of the States
Lexington, KY 40511
Telephone: 859-244-8000
Fax: 859-244-8001
Online: http://knowledgecenter.csg.org/kc/content/governors-salaries-2016
Survey Period: 2016

Note: Average Governor's salary has been rounded to the nearest dollar.

CSSS

2016 Salary Schedule and Compensation Plan, April 6, 2016.

Seattle Department of Human Resources
Seattle Municipal Tower
700 5th Avenue, Suite 5500
Seattle, WA 98124-4028
Telephone: 206-684-7999
Fax: 206-684-4157
Online: http://www.seattle.gov
Survey Period: 2013-2016

Note: Salaries took effect on the dates in the individual records.

CTBLS

State of Connecticut Occupational Employment and Wages, December 6, 2016.

> State of Connecticut Department of Labor
> Office of Research
> 200 Folly Brook Boulevard
> Wethersfield, CT 06109
> **Telephone:** 860-263-6285
> **Online:** http://www1.ctdol.state.ct.us/lmi/wages/
> **Survey Period:** January 2016-March 2016

Note: All data are provided by the State Employment Security Administration to the Occupational Employment Statistics (OES) survey conducted by the U.S. Department of Labor, Bureau of Labor Statistics. May 2015 Occupational Employment and Wage Estimates have been adjusted to the first quarter of 2016 using the Employment Cost Index. Data were downloaded on December 6, 2016.

CUMGT

Karen Bankston, "Poised to Compete," *CU Management*, August 2016.

> **Online:** http://www.cues.org
> **Survey Period:** 2016

Note: Base salaries plus bonuses.

CVENE

Michelle Russell, "Convene's 2016 Salary Survey," *PCMA Convene*, May 31, 2016.

> Professional Convention Management Association
> 35 East Wacker Drive, Suite 500
> Chicago, IL 60601-2105
> **Telephone:** 877-827-7262
> **Fax:** 312-423-7222
> **Online:** http://www.pcmaconvene.org
> **Email:** communications@pcma.org
> **Survey Period:** 2016

CWRLD1

"IT Salary Watch: 2016 Salaries: Senior IT Management," *ComputerWorld*, December 7, 2016.

> **Online:** http://www.computerworld.com
> **Survey Period:** 2016

Note: Base salaries. Data were downloaded on December 7, 2016.

CWRLD2

"IT Salary Watch: 2016 Salaries: Middle IT Management," *ComputerWorld*, December 7, 2016.

> **Online:** http://www.computerworld.com
> **Survey Period:** 2016

Note: Base salaries. Data were downloaded on December 7, 2016.

CWRLD3

"IT Salary Watch: 2016 Salaries: Staff and Entry-Level IT Positions," *ComputerWorld*, December 7, 2016.

> **Online:** http://www.computerworld.com
> **Survey Period:** 2016

Note: Base salaries. Data were downloaded on December 7, 2016.

DATAM1

Cynthia Harvey, "Top 10 Best-Paying IT Certs," *Datamation*, November 1, 2016.

> **Online:** http://www.datamation.com/careers/
> **Survey Period:** 2016

DATAM2

Cynthia Harvey, "IT Salary: 12 Best-Paying IT Jobs," *Datamation*, October 11, 2016.

Online: http://www.datamation.com/careers/
Survey Period: 2017

DCOGOV

2016 Annual Salary Publication, March 1, 2017.

Douglas County, Colorado
100 Third Street
Castle Rock, CO 80104
Telephone: 303-660-7400
Online: http://www.douglas.co.us
Survey Period: 2016

Note: Salaries have been rounded to the nearest dollar. Data were downloaded on March 1, 2017. Actual salaries.

DETGOV

Class Specifications, December 7, 2016.

City of Detroit Human Resources Department
Coleman A. Young Municipal Center
2 Woodward Avenue, Suite 314
Detroit, MI 48226
Online: https://www.governmentjobs.com/careers/detroit/
classspecs
Survey Period: 2016

Note: Data were downloaded on December 7, 2016 and were considered current by the source. Wages are rounded to the nearest dollar.

DICE01

2015-2016 Dice Salary Survey, January 26, 2016.

Dice
1040 Avenue of the Americas, Floor 8
New York, NY 10018
Telephone: 408-850-8750
Online: http://media.dice.com
Contact: Anita Lawhon
Email: dicemedia@dice.com
Survey Period: October 6, 2015-November 25, 2015

DOD1

"2017 Military Pay Tables," *Defense Finance and Accounting Service*, January 15, 2017.

Defense Finance and Accounting Service (DFAS)
8899 East 56th Street
Indianapolis, IN 46249
Telephone: 888-332-7411
Online: http://www.dfas.mil/militarymembers.html
Survey Period: 2017

Note: Salaries took effect on January 1, 2017. Data were downloaded on January 15, 2017. Salaries are rounded to the nearest dollar.

DTREND01

Mary Nichols, "Snapchat Interns Earn How Much?" *Design & Trend*, April 30, 2016.

Online: http://www.designntrend.com
Survey Period: 2016

Note: Data show monthly salaries. Salary data do not include benefits and housing allowances. According to the May 2015 National Occupational Employment and Wage Estimates, the average annual salary in the United States was $48,320 in 2015, which equates to approximately $4,000 per month.

DVM01

"State of the Veterinary Profession: The 2015 Results From This Triennial DVM360 Survey Shows That Veterinarians Are Holding Steady in Recovery," *DVM Newsmagazine*, January 2016, p. 1.

> **Survey Period:** 2015

EDES

"2016 Electronic Design Annual Salary & Career Report: Struggling to Stand Out," *Electronic Design*, October 4, 2016.

> **Online:** http://www.electronicdesign.com
> **Survey Period:** 2016

ENR01

Bruce Buckley, Mary B. Powers and Debra K. Rubin, "Labor Gaps Bring Steady Pay Raises," *ENR*, October 10, 2016, pp. 36-38.

> **Survey Period:** 2016

ENR02

Bruce Buckley, "Top Staff Getting Top Dollar," *ENR*, July 11, 2015, p. 40.

> **Survey Period:** 2015

ERI01

Executive Compensation Trends, September 2016.

> ERI Economic Research Institute
> 111 Academy Drive, Suite 270
> Irvine, CA 92617
> **Telephone:** 800-627-3697
> **Online:** http://www.erieri.com
> **Contact:** Matt Skrinjar
> **Email:** matt.skrinjar@erieri.com
> **Survey Period:** 2015

EXHC01

"Blood Bank Technology Specialist," December 12, 2016.

> American Dental Education Association
> 655 K Street, NW, Suite 800
> Washington, DC 20001
> **Telephone:** 202-289-7201
> **Online:** http://www.explorehealthcareers.org
> **Survey Period:** 2016

Note: Data were downloaded on December 12, 2016 and were considered current by the source.

EXHC02

"Orientation & Mobility Specialist," December 12, 2016.

> American Dental Education Association
> 655 K Street, NW, Suite 800
> Washington, DC 20001
> **Telephone:** 202-289-7201
> **Online:** http://www.explorehealthcareers.org
> **Survey Period:** 2016

Note: Data were downloaded on December 12, 2016 and were considered current by the source.

EXHC03

"Naturopathic Physician," December 12, 2016.

> American Dental Education Association
> 655 K Street, NW, Suite 800
> Washington, DC 20001
> **Telephone:** 202-289-7201
> **Online:** http://www.explorehealthcareers.org
> **Survey Period:** 2016

Note: Data were downloaded on December 12, 2016 and were considered current by the source.

EXHC04

"Food Safety Specialist," December 12, 2016.

American Dental Education Association
655 K Street, NW, Suite 800
Washington, DC 20001
Telephone: 202-289-7201
Online: http://www.explorehealthcareers.org
Survey Period: 2016

Note: Data were downloaded on December 12, 2016 and were considered current by the source.

EXHC05

"Dental Informaticist," December 12, 2016.

American Dental Education Association
655 K Street, NW, Suite 800
Washington, DC 20001
Telephone: 202-289-7201
Online: http://www.explorehealthcareers.org
Survey Period: 2016

Note: Data were downloaded on December 12, 2016 and were considered current by the source.

EXHC06

"Biogerontologist," December 12, 2016.

American Dental Education Association
655 K Street, NW, Suite 800
Washington, DC 20001
Telephone: 202-289-7201
Online: http://www.explorehealthcareers.org
Survey Period: 2016

Note: Data were downloaded on December 12, 2016 and were considered current by the source.

EXHC07

"Psychometrist," December 12, 2016.

American Dental Education Association
655 K Street, NW, Suite 800
Washington, DC 20001
Telephone: 202-289-7201
Online: http://www.explorehealthcareers.org
Survey Period: 2016

Note: Data were downloaded on December 12, 2016 and were considered current by the source.

EXHC08

"Disaster Medical Specialist," December 12, 2016.

American Dental Education Association
655 K Street, NW, Suite 800
Washington, DC 20001
Telephone: 202-289-7201
Online: http://www.explorehealthcareers.org
Survey Period: 2016

Note: Data were downloaded on December 12, 2016 and were considered current by the source.

FLBLS

Florida Occupational Employment Statistics and Wages, November 2016.

Florida Department of Economic Activity
Bureau of Labor Market Statistics
107 East Madison Street
Tallahassee, FL 32399-4111
Telephone: 850-245-7205
Online: http://www.floridajobs.org
Email: oes.survey@deo.myflorida.com
Survey Period: July 2016-September 2016

Note: All data are provided by the State Employment Security Administration to the Occupational Employment Statistics (OES) survey conducted by the U.S. Department of Labor, Bureau of Labor Statistics. May 2015 Occupational Employment and Wage Estimates have been adjusted to the third quarter of 2016 using the Employment Cost Index.

FLTO

Kevin Jones, "Driver Pay: Know Your Target," *Fleet Owner*, June 6, 2016.

Survey Period: January 2016

FOLIO01

Bill Mickey, "In Editorial Salaries, Males Out-Earn Females. By a Lot," *Folio:*, December 26, 2015.

Online: http://www.foliomag.com
Survey Period: April 22, 2015-May 22, 2015

FOLIO02

Michael Rondon, "In Sales, a Rare Result: Women Make More Than Men," *Folio:*, July 8, 2015.

Online: http://www.foliomag.com
Survey Period: April 22, 2015-May 22, 2015

Note: Base salary.

FOODP

Kevin T. Higgins, "2016 Salary Survey Results: Haves and Have-Nots," *Food Processing*, July 13, 2016.

Online: http://www.foodprocessing.com
Survey Period: 2016

FORB01

Katie Sola, "The 20 Fastest Growing Jobs in America," *Forbes*, July 8, 2016.

Online: http://www.forbes.com
Survey Period: 2015

FORB02

Daniel Kleinman, "The SEC Is Still the Top Coaching Destination Despite Jim Harbaugh's Salary," *Forbes*, October 26, 2016.

Online: http://www.forbes.com
Survey Period: 2016

FORB03

Karsten Strauss, "10 Part-Time Jobs That Pay $50 or More per Hour," *Forbes*, September 8, 2016.

Online: http://www.forbes.com
Survey Period: 2016

FPAT

Beth Dalbey, "You Do What for a Living? 5 Odd Jobs Paying Over $50K," *Farmington Patch*, December 27, 2015.

Online: http://www.patch.com
Survey Period: 2015

FPE

"SFPE & University of Maryland Exhibiting at USA Science & Engineering Festival," April 16, 2016.

SFPE
9711 Washingtonian Boulevard, Suite 380
Gaithersburg, MD 20878
Telephone: 301-718-2910
Fax: 240-328-6225
Online: http://sfpe.org/news/news.asp
Email: info@sfpe.org
Survey Period: 2016

Note: According to the source, the starting salary for Fire Protection Engineers is nearly $65,000.

FRCOG

Wage and Salary Survey FY2016, December 12, 2016.

Franklin Regional Council of Governments
12 Olive Street, Suite 2
Greenfield, MA 01301
Telephone: 413-774-3167
Fax: 413-774-3169
Online: http://www.frcog.org
Email: info@frcog.org
Survey Period: 2016

Note: Data were downloaded on December 12, 2016. Data are for fiscal year 2016. Salaries for Conway's and Greenfield's Fire Chief and Montague's Children's Librarian have been rounded to the nearest dollar.

FREEP01

Mark Stryker, "DIA Director Salary Could Rise to $475K by 2020," *Detroit Free Press*, October 15, 2015.

Online: http://www.freep.com
Survey Period: 2015

Note: Salary data provided by the Association of Art Museum Directors.

FREEP02

Joe Guillen, "Detroit Consultant Made $280K a Year, Plus Flights, Hotels," *Detroit Free Press*, August 14, 2016.

Online: http://www.freep.com
Survey Period: 2016

Note: Human Resources Consultant salary does not include reimbursements for travel, hotels, and meals.

FREEP03

Mark Snyder, "Coach Salary Database: Wolverines' John Beilein is Compensated Well," *Detroit Free Press*, March 30, 2016.

Online: http://www.freep.com
Survey Period: 2017

Note: Total compensation including bonuses and monies paid from sources other than the university.

FREEP04

Joe Rexrode, "Tom Izzo Tops Big Ten in Pay, Salary Database Says," *Detroit Free Press*, March 30, 2016.

Online: http://www.freep.com
Survey Period: 2016

Note: Total compensation including bonuses and monies paid from sources other than the university.

FREEP05

David Jesse, "WMU President Donates Salary Increase to School," *Detroit Free Press*, December 18, 2015.

Online: http://www.freep.com
Survey Period: 2016

Note: Base salary.

FREEP06

David Jesse, "Wayne State President Gets 2-Year Contract Extension," *Detroit Free Press*, December 15, 2015.

Online: http://www.freep.com
Survey Period: 2016

Note: Base salary.

FTIME

Millie Dent, "50 Top-Paying Careers in Health Care," *The Fiscal Times*, March 28, 2016.

   Online: http://www.thefiscaltimes.com
   Survey Period: 2016

FTUNE01

Michal Addady, "The Worst Job in America in 2016," *Fortune*, April 13, 2016.

   Online: http://fortune.com
   Survey Period: 2016

Note: Salary data from CareerCast.

FTUNE02

Anne Fisher, "Wanted: Highly Skilled Tech Workers, $100,000-Plus Salary, No College Required," *Fortune*, May 13, 2015.

   Online: http://fortune.com
   Survey Period: 2015

GACTY01

2016 Municipal Wage and Salary Survey: Public Safety Positions, November 2016.

   Georgia Department of Community Affairs
   Office of Research
   60 Executive Park South
   Atlanta, GA 30329-2231
   Telephone: 404-679-4940
   Online: http://www.dca.state.ga.us/dcawss/reports/
   Survey Period: 2016

Note: Annual salaries are rounded to the nearest dollar.

GACTY02

2016 Municipal Wage and Salary Survey: Public Works/Solid Waste Positions, November 2016.

   Georgia Department of Community Affairs
   Office of Research
   60 Executive Park South
   Atlanta, GA 30329-2231
   Telephone: 404-679-4940
   Online: http://www.dca.state.ga.us/dcawss/reports/
   Survey Period: 2016

Note: Annual salaries are rounded to the nearest dollar.

GACTY03

2016 County Wage and Salary Survey: Elected Officials, November 2016.

   Georgia Department of Community Affairs
   Office of Research
   60 Executive Park South
   Atlanta, GA 30329-2231
   Telephone: 404-679-4940
   Online: http://www.dca.state.ga.us/dcawss/reports/
   Survey Period: 2016

Note: Annual salaries do not include supplemental pay.

GACTY04

2016 County Wage and Salary Survey: General and Administrative Positions, November 2016.

   Georgia Department of Community Affairs
   Office of Research
   60 Executive Park South
   Atlanta, GA 30329-2231
   Telephone: 404-679-4940
   Online: http://www.dca.state.ga.us/dcawss/reports/
   Survey Period: 2016

Note: Annual salaries are rounded to the nearest dollar.

GLKN

2016 IT Skills and Salary Report: A Comprehensive Study from Global Knowledge, May 23, 2016.

Online: https://www.globalknowledge.com
Survey Period: 2016

GOVFL

"Charts: 2015 Salaries & Retirement Plans," *Government Fleet*, September 2015.

Online: http://www.government-fleet.com
Survey Period: 2015

Note: Average salaries based on number of staff managed.

GRD01

Rory Carroll, "'We Need Human Interaction': Meet the LA Man Who Walks People for a Living," *The Guardian*, September 14, 2016.

Online: http://www.theguardian.com
Survey Period: 2016

Note: Salary is per mile.

HCARE1

Dr. Diana Hoppe, "Health Coaching Provides Alluring Opportunities," *HomeCare*, May 4, 2016.

Online: http://www.homecaremag.com
Survey Period: 2016

HCARE2

"2016 Salary Survey," *HomeCare*, January 19, 2016.

Online: http://www.homecaremag.com
Survey Period: 2015

HCHRON1

John-Henry Perera, "LinkedIn Says These Are the 'Most Promising' Jobs of 2017," *Houston Chronicle*, January 23, 2017.

Online: http://www.chron.com
Survey Period: 2017

Note: Base salary.

HCHRON2

Rick Suttle, "What Do Ice Truckers Make?" *Houston Chronicle*, January 24, 2017.

Online: http://work.chron.com
Survey Period: 2013

Note: Data were downloaded on January 24, 2017.

HCHRON3

Will Charpentier, "The Average Salary of American Merchant Ship Captains," *Houston Chronicle*, January 24, 2017.

Online: http://work.chron.com
Survey Period: 2017

Note: Data were downloaded on January 24, 2017 and were considered current by the source.

HCHRON4

Will Charpentier, "Salaries for Harbor Pilots," *Houston Chronicle*, January 24, 2017.

Online: http://work.chron.com
Survey Period: 2017

Note: Data were downloaded on January 24, 2017 and were considered current by the source.

HCTAB

Rebecca Sandlin, "Markle TC Adopts $1.31M Budget, Salary Increases for Employees," *The Huntington County TAB*, September 26, 2016.

Online: http://www.huntingtoncountytab.com
Survey Period: 2017

HDT

"Truck Drivers and Owner-Operator Compensation," *Heavy-Duty Trucking*, August 2016, pp. 94-95.

Survey Period: 2015

HED01

"Professionals in Higher Education Salaries (Mid-Level Administrators)," *HigherEdJobs*, January 24, 2017.

Online: https://www.higheredjobs.com
Survey Period: 2015-2016

Note: Data were downloaded on January 24, 2017.

HED02

"Administrators in Higher Education Salaries," *HigherEdJobs*, January 24, 2017.

Online: https://www.higheredjobs.com
Survey Period: 2015-2016

Note: Data were downloaded on January 24, 2017.

HED03

"Non-Exempt Staff in Higher Education Salaries," *HigherEdJobs*, January 24, 2017.

Online: https://www.higheredjobs.com
Survey Period: 2015-2016

Note: Data were downloaded on January 24, 2017.

HPN01

Susan Cantrell, "Steady Numbers, Significant Trends," *Healthcare Purchasing News*, May 2016, pp. 22-25.

Online: http://www.hponline.com
Survey Period: 2016

HPN02

Rick Dana Barlow, "2016 SCM Salary Survey: Supply Chain Salaries Rebound After Two-Year Slide," *Healthcare Purchasing News*, August 2016, pp. 42, 44-45.

Online: http://www.hponline.com
Survey Period: 2016

HSCT

Sahra Santosha, et. al., "Customer Support Salary Study," *HelpScout*, October 31, 2016.

Online: http://www.helpscout.net
Survey Period: 2016

HTL01

Diane Gale Andreassi, "Wage Study Indicates Lyon Salaries About Average," *HomeTownLife*, April 3, 2015.

Online: http://www.hometownlife.com
Survey Period: 2015

Note: Actual salaries.

HVACN01

Herb Woerpel, "Will You Be Raising Your Prices in 2015?" *Air Conditioning, Heating & Refrigeration News*, March 16, 2015, pp. 1, 24-25.

Survey Period: 2015

IAI

2015 Annual Salary Survey, January 24, 2017.

The Information Architecture Institute
822 Cherry SE
Grand Rapids, MI 49506
Online: http://www.iainstitute.org
Email: info@iainstitute.org
Survey Period: April 11, 2016-May 9, 2016

IBD01

Russ Britt, "Grads Find Highest Pay Is in That Gooey Stuff," *Investor's Business Daily*, May 23, 2016, p. A12.

Survey Period: 2016

Note: Average salary for the first five years of work.

IBD02

"Where FAs Make Big Bucks," *Investor's Business Daily*, February 16, 2016, p. A7.

Survey Period: 2015

IBD03

Allison Gatlin, "Hackers Wanted, but Be Nice: Cybersecurity Jobs Hard to Fill," *Investor's Business Daily*, August 22, 2016, p. A6.

Survey Period: 2015

ICPC

"Database: Johnson County Government Employee Salaries," *Iowa City Press-Citizen*, March 1, 2017.

Online: http://db.press-citizen.com/salaries
Survey Period: 2014

Note: Salaries are for fiscal year 2014. Data were downloaded on March 1, 2017. Actual salaries.

INA

2014 INA Salary & Benefits Survey, 2015.

The International Nanny Association
P.O. Box 4109
Peachtree City, GA 30269
Telephone: 888-878-1477
Fax: 508-638-6462
Online: http://www.nanny.org
Email: info@nanny.org
Survey Period: 2014

INDWK

Laura Putre, "2016 Salary Survey: Ready, Set, Go (Slow)," *IndustryWeek*, March 2016.

Online: http://www.industryweek.com
Survey Period: 2015

INDYS

"Indiana Compensation Database," *IndyStar.com*, March 1, 2017.

Online: http://interactive.indystar.com/news/standing/
salarydatabase/
Survey Period: 2017

Note: Salaries have been rounded to the nearest dollar. Actual salaries. Data were downloaded on March 1, 2017.

INFOW01

Dawn Kawamoto, "IT Salary Outlook 2017: Starting Pay on the Rise," *InformationWeek*, September 1, 2016.

Online: http://www.informationweek.com
Survey Period: 2017

Note: Projected starting salaries for 2017.

INFOW02

Susan Nunziata, *InformationWeek Reports: Annual U.S. IT Salary Survey*, November 2016.

> **Online:** http://reg.interop.com/salary-survey
> **Survey Period:** October 2015-February 2016

INVPED

Matt Danielsson, "Internal Auditor: Job Description & Average Salary," *Investopedia*, January 11, 2016.

> **Online:** http://www.investopedia.com
> **Survey Period:** 2015

Note: Base salary.

IREM

"Compensation," January 24, 2017.

> Institute of Real Estate Management
> 430 North Michigan Avenue
> Chicago, IL 60611
> **Telephone:** 800-837-0706
> **Fax:** 800-338-4736
> **Online:** http://www.irem.org
> **Email:** getinfo@irem.org
> **Survey Period:** 2016

Note: Base salary.

IWRLD

Kelsey O'Hallaren and Taylor Palmer, "High-Paying Industries Within the Fastest-Growing US Sectors," *IBISWorld*, February 2016, pp. 1-5.

> **Survey Period:** 2016

JCOKS

"Job Description," *Johnson County Kansas Human Resources*, March 29, 2016.

> Johnson County, Kansas
> 111 South Cherry, Suite 2600
> Olathe, KS 66061
> **Telephone:** 913-715-1400
> **Online:** http://www.jocogov.org
> **Survey Period:** 2017

Note: Salaries are for fiscal year 2017.

JEMS

Jonathan D. Washko and Michael G. Ragone, "2015 JEMS Salary Survey," *Journal of Emergency Medical Services*, December 23, 2015.

> **Online:** http://www.jems.com
> **Survey Period:** 2014

Note: Salaries have been rounded to the nearest dollar.

JM01

"Avalanche Forecaster Jobs," *Job Monkey*, March 2, 2017.

> **Online:** http://www.jobmonkey.com/uniquejobs/
> **Survey Period:** 2017

Note: Data were downloaded on March 2, 2017 and were considered current by the source. Avalanche forecasters work from November to May.

JM02

"Image Consultant Jobs," *Job Monkey*, March 2, 2017.

Online: http://www.jobmonkey.com/uniquejobs/
Survey Period: 2017

Note: Data were downloaded on March 2, 2017 and were considered current by the source. Image consultants are paid per session and per session rates can vary widely. According to the source per session rates can range from $50 to $500.

JM03

"Zamboni Driver Jobs," *Job Monkey*, March 2, 2017.

Online: http://www.jobmonkey.com/uniquejobs/
Survey Period: 2017

Note: Data were downloaded on March 2, 2017 and were considered current by the source.

LAGE1

"Wages Rise for Some Workers at Life Plan Communities," *Leading Age*, July 6, 2016.

Online: http://www.leadingage.org
Survey Period: 2016

Note: Life Plan Communities were formerly known as Continuing Care Retirement Communities.

LAGE2

"Does Your Activity Director Deserve a Raise?" *Leading Age*, July 12, 2015.

Online: http://www.leadingage.org
Survey Period: 2015

Note: Life Plan Communities were formerly known as Continuing Care Retirement Communities.

LCT01

Tom Halligan, "Operator Survey Results," *Limousine, Charter & Tour*, June 2016, pp. 20-21.

Survey Period: 2016

LH01

"Top 8 High-Paying Business and Tech Jobs of 2016 — and How to Get Them!" *Lifehack*, August 16, 2016.

Online: http://www.lifehack.org
Survey Period: 2016

Note: Data were downloaded on August 16, 2016.

LH02

Jyssica Scott, "15 Weird Jobs Around the World That You Should Know About," *Lifehack*, January 4, 2016.

Online: http://www.lifehack.org
Survey Period: 2016

Note: Data were downloaded on January 14, 2016.

LH03

Al Gomez, "6 Highest Paid Jobs for the Social Media Savvy," *Lifehack*, August 2, 2016.

Online: http://www.lifehack.org
Survey Period: 2016

Note: Data were downloaded on August 2, 2016.

LI01

Ryan Sandler, "The Highest-Paying Jobs in America Based on LinkedIn Salary Data," *LinkedIn Official Blog*, January 10, 2017.

Online: http://blog.linkedin.com
Survey Period: 2017

LJ01

Suzie Allard, "Placements & Salaries 2016: Explore All the Data," *Library Journal*, October 17, 2016.

Online: http://www.libraryjournal.com
Survey Period: 2015

LKY01

"Employee Salary Search," *LouisvilleKy.com*, March 1, 2017.

Online: http://portal.louisvilleky.gov/service/data/
Survey Period: 2017

Note: Salaries have been rounded to the nearest dollar. Non-average salaries are actual salaries. Data were downloaded on March 1, 2017.

LOGMGT

Josh Bond, "How Manufacturing Employers Are Getting Lean," *Logistics Management*, October 26, 2015.

Online: http://www.logisticsmgmt.com
Survey Period: 2015

LP01

"Becoming a Flash Animator: Salary Info & Job Description," *Learning Path*, January 26, 2017.

Online: http://www.learningpath.org
Survey Period: July 2015

Note: Salary data include bonuses. Data were downloaded on January 26, 2017.

LSJ01

Brent Snavely, "Fiat Chrysler Ending Car Production in U.S.," *Lansing State Journal*, July 31, 2016, p. 5B.

Survey Period: 2016

Note: Actual hourly wage for entry-level assembly line workers hired after 2007. This wage will rise to about $29 in eight years according to the source.

LSJ02

Matt Krantz, "This Job Pays $263,500 for a Few Days' Work," *Lansing State Journal*, July 20, 2016, p. 6B.

Survey Period: 2015

Note: Median total direct compensation.

LSJ03

David Jesse, "Simon 6th on College President Pay List," *Lansing State Journal*, July 18, 2016, pp. 1A, 7A.

Survey Period: 2015

Note: Median total compensation among public-college presidents who served a full year.

LSJ04

Lori Higgins, "State Appoints E. Detroit Schools Leader," *Lansing State Journal*, June 18, 2016, p. 6A.

Survey Period: 2016

Note: Actual salary.

LSJ05

Eric Lacy, "Bernero Makes $135K Appointment," *Lansing State Journal*, April 22, 2016.

Online: http://www.lansingstatejournal.com
Survey Period: 2016

Note: Actual salary.

LSJ06

Jae Yang and Janet Loehrke, "Average Rate for Household Chores," *Lansing State Journal*, October 11, 2016, p. 4B.

Survey Period: 2016

Note: Average children's allowance for walking the family dog. According to the source, the average allowance for mowing the lawn is $6.28 and the average allowance for cleaning the garage is $5.20.

LSJ07

Rachel Greco, "Delta Twp. Gleans Manager Applicants," *Lansing State Journal*, March 1, 2015, p. 10A.

Survey Period: 2015

LSJ08

Justin A. Hinkley and Matt Mencarini, "Court-Appointed Attorneys Paid Little, Do Little, Records Show," *Lansing State Journal*, November 3, 2016.

Online: http://www.lansingstatejournal.com
Survey Period: 2015

Note: Salary for Court-Appointed Criminal Attorney is per case.

LSJ09

Virg Bernero and Bill Peduto, "Midwest No Longer 'Rust Belt,' Now the 'Production Belt'," *Lansing State Journal*, November 18, 2016, p. A4.

Survey Period: 2016

Note: Average total compensation includes wages and benefits.

LSJ10

Brent Snavely, "Magna Key Player in Backup-Camera Market," *Lansing State Journal*, November 29, 2016, p. 6A.

Survey Period: 2016

LSJ11

Justin A. Hinkley, "Attorneys Get Better Pay, More Oversight in State Program," *Lansing State Journal*, December 8, 2016, p. 1A.

Survey Period: 2016

LSJ12

John Wisely, "Housing Bust Means Lost Services," *Lansing State Journal*, December 11, 2016, p. 7A.

Survey Period: 2016

LSJ13

Eric Lacy, "CEO: Ordinance May Push Us Out," *Lansing State Journal*, December 12, 2016, pp. 1A-2A.

Survey Period: 2018

Note: Salaries based on projected expansion of employment at the Lansing, Michigan facility.

LSJ14

Beth LeBlanc, "Ingham County Officials Getting Raises," *Lansing State Journal*, December 20, 2016, p. 3A.

Survey Period: 2017

Note: Actual salaries.

LSJ15

Judy Putnam, "Engineer Is Retiring After 51-Year Career," *Lansing State Journal*, December 18, 2016, pp. 15A, 19A.

Survey Period: 2016

LSJ16

Eric Lacy, "Council Hits Impasse, Fails to Elect Leadership," *Lansing State Journal*, January 11, 2017, p. 1A.

Survey Period: 2017

LSJ17

RJ Wolcott, "Thompson Interviewed for Jobs in Michigan, Alabama," *Lansing State Journal*, January 26, 2017, p. 3A.

Survey Period: 2017

Note: Projected salary range for the new Huntsville, Alabama school district superintendent.

LSJ18

Jennifer Dixon, "Learning Skills While Behind Bars," *Lansing State Journal*, January 29, 2017, p. 4A.

Survey Period: 2017

LSJ19

Kathleen Lavey, "Wanted: One Poet Willing to Spread the Word in Lansing," *Lansing State Journal*, January 29, 2017, p. 15A.

Survey Period: 2017

LWAY01

"Compensation Summary by Position," *2016 Southern Baptist Convention Compensation Study*, March 2, 2017.

LifeWay Christian Resources
One LifeWay Plaza
Nashville, TN 37234
Telephone: 800-458-2772
Online: http://compstudy.lifeway.com/homepage.do
Email: compensationadmin@lifeway.com
Survey Period: 2016

Note: Data were downloaded on March 1, 2017.

LWAY02

"Compensation Summary for Non-Pastor Ministerial Staff," *2016 Southern Baptist Convention Compensation Study*, March 2, 2017.

LifeWay Christian Resources
One LifeWay Plaza
Nashville, TN 37234
Telephone: 800-458-2772
Online: http://compstudy.lifeway.com/homepage.do
Email: compensationadmin@lifeway.com
Survey Period: 2016

Note: Data were downloaded on March 1, 2017.

MANDC

Sarah J.F. Braley, "2016 Salary Survey," *Meetings and Conventions*, September 1, 2016.

Online: http://www.meetings-conventions.com
Survey Period: 2016

MCCS

Sam Becker, "13 Jobs With the Fastest Growing Salaries and Biggest Pay Raises," *Money & Career CheatSheet*, October 31, 2016.

Online: http://www.cheatsheet.com/money-career/
Survey Period: 2016

MDAY01

Allie Caren, "Steal This Job: Marijuana Growing Coach," *Macomb Daily*, January 9, 2017.

Online: http://www.macombdaily.com
Survey Period: 2017

Note: Actual wage of a Cannabis Coach at Buds Organic in Washington, DC. Salary is dependent on the number of clients and garden visits per year.

MDAY02

Norb Franz, "State Police Seeking Minority Applicants," *Macomb Daily*, December 1, 2016.

Online: http://www.macombdaily.com
Survey Period: 2016

MDBLS

Maryland Occupational Wage Estimates, April 2016.

Department of Labor, Licensing, and Regulation
Office of Workforce Information and Performance
1100 North Eutaw Street
Baltimore, MD 21201
Telephone: 410-767-2250
Online: http://www.dllr.state.md.us/lmi/wages/
Survey Period: April 2016

Note: All data are provided by the State Employment Security Administration to the Occupational Employment Statistics (OES) survey conducted by the U.S. Department of Labor, Bureau of Labor Statistics. May 2015 Occupational Employment and Wage Estimates have been adjusted to April 2016 using the Employment Cost Index.

MDES

Carlos Gonzalez, "Annual Salary & Career Report: Five Years of Engineering Thoughts and Opinions," *Machine Design*, October 4, 2016.

Online: http://www.machinedesign.com
Survey Period: 2016

MDGOV

"State Salary Plan," July 1, 2016.

Maryland Department of Budget and Management
42 Calvert Street
Annapolis, MD 21401
Telephone: 800-705-3493
Online: http://dbm.maryland.gov
Survey Period: 2016

Note: Salary data were last updated on July 1, 2016.

MED01

Neil Chesanow, "Residents Salary & Debt Report 2016," *Medscape*, July 20, 2016.

Online: http://www.medscape.com
Survey Period: 2016

MED02

Carol Peckham, "Medscape Physician Compensation Report 2016," *Medscape*, April 1, 2016.

Online: http://www.medscape.com
Survey Period: 2016

Note: Salary data includes bonus and profit-sharing contributions.

MENP

"Executive Summary + Key Findings," *2016 Report on Non-profit Wages + Benefits in Maine*, January 30, 2017.

> Maine Association of Nonprofits
> 565 Congress Street, #301
> Portland, ME 04101
> **Telephone:** 207-871-1885
> **Fax:** 207-780-0346
> **Online:** http://www.nonprofitmaine.org
> **Survey Period:** 2016

Note: Salaries are dependent on the nonprofit's revenue. Lower salaries are paid to Executive Directors and Program Directors employed by nonprofits with lower revenue.

MHLTH01

Modern Healthcare's by the Numbers, December 21, 2015, pp. 12-13.

> **Survey Period:** 2015

MHLTH02

Michael Sandler, "Bonus Bonanzas: Association Chief Executives Got Healthy Pay Hikes in 2013," *Modern Healthcare*, June 8, 2015, pp. 14-18.

> **Survey Period:** 2013

MHLTH03

Joseph Conn, "Competition for New Docs Pushing Pay Higher," *Modern Healthcare*, July 18, 2016, pp. 12-16.

> **Survey Period:** 2015

Note: Data include salaries and bonuses.

MIGOV

"State of Michigan Job Openings," December 12, 2016.

> Michigan Civil Service Commission
> 400 South Pine Street
> Lansing, MI 48933
> **Telephone:** 517-373-3030
> **Fax:** 517-373-7690
> **Online:** https://www.governmentjobs.com/careers/michigan
> **Survey Period:** 2016

MIOAK1

"2017 Salary Schedule for Elected Officials," October 7, 2016.

> Oakland County, Michigan
> 2100 Pontiac Lake Road, Building 41 West
> Waterford, MI 48328
> **Telephone:** 248-858-0530
> **Online:** https://www.oakgov.com/hr/
> **Email:** ocijobs@oakgov.com
> **Survey Period:** October 1, 2016

Note: Salaries took effect on October 1, 2016. Biweekly salaries have been rounded to the nearest dollar.

MIOAK2

"2017 Salary Schedule for All Classes," December 21, 2016.

> Oakland County, Michigan
> 2100 Pontiac Lake Road, Building 41 West
> Waterford, MI 48328
> **Telephone:** 248-858-0530
> **Online:** https://www.oakgov.com/hr/
> **Email:** ocijobs@oakgov.com
> **Survey Period:** October 1, 2016

Note: Salaries took effect on October 1, 2016. Biweekly salaries have been rounded to the nearest dollar.

MLEVU1

"Working in an Academic Medical Center: The Good, the Bad, and the Ugly," *MidlevelU*, January 30, 2017.

Online: http://www.midlevelu.com/blog/
Survey Period: 2015

MLEVU2

"10 Highest Paying Nurse Practitioner Specialties," *MidlevelU*, October 18, 2016.

Online: http://www.midlevelu.com/blog/
Survey Period: 2016

MLTCN01

Liza Berger, "Admins' Pay Rises to $102K, DONs' up to $90K," *McKnight's Long-Term Care News*, November 5, 2016.

Online: http://www.mcknights.com
Survey Period: 2016

MLTCN02

Emily Mongan, "Physical Therapists in LTC See Higher Wage Increases Than Those in Hospitals, Home Health," *McKnight's Long-Term Care News*, October 19, 2016.

Online: http://www.mcknights.com
Survey Period: 2016

MLTCN03

James M. Berklan, "Nursing Home Nurses Enjoying a Hot Salary Market: Survey," *McKnight's Long-Term Care News*, August 8, 2016.

Online: http://www.mcknights.com
Survey Period: 2016

MLTCN04

Elizabeth Leis Newman, "Top CCRC Posts See Salary Increases, Report Discovers," *McKnight's Long-Term Care News*, August 5, 2016.

Online: http://www.mcknights.com
Survey Period: 2016

MLV01

Martin Slagter, "Search Salaries for All 45,000 University of Michigan Employees," *MLive*, December 15, 2016.

Online: http://www.mlive.com/news/ann-arbor/
Survey Period: 2016

Note: Salary for President took effect in the Fall of 2016.

MLV02

Jeremy Allen, "Eastern Michigan University Paid Head Coaches $1.88M in Base Salary in 2015," *MLive*, January 8, 2016.

Online: http://www.mlive.com/news/ann-arbor/
Survey Period: 2015

Note: Actual salaries.

MMH01

"2016 Annual Salary Survey," *Modern Materials Handling*, November 9, 2016.

Online: http://www.mmh.com
Survey Period: September 2016

MMM01

Larry Dobrow, "Pharma Marketing Salaries Veer Off Track, Dropping 2.6% in 2016," *MM&M*, September 6, 2016.

Online: http://www.mmm-online.com
Survey Period: July 2016

MNBLS

Minnesota Occupational Employment Statistics, November 10, 2016.

> Minnesota Department of Employment and Economic Development
> 1st National Bank Building
> 322 Minnesota Street, Suite E-200
> Saint Paul, MN 55101-1351
> **Telephone:** 651-259-7114
> **Online:** http://mn.gov/deed/data/data-tools/oes/
> **Email:** deed.customerservice@state.mn.us
> **Survey Period:** January 2016-March 2016

Note: All data are provided by the State Employment Security Administration to the Occupational Employment Statistics (OES) survey conducted by the U.S. Department of Labor, Bureau of Labor Statistics. May 2015 Occupational Employment and Wage Estimates have been adjusted to the first quarter of 2016 using the Employment Cost Index. Data were downloaded on November 10, 2016.

MPEG01

"Producer - I.A.T.S.E. and M.P.T.A.A.C. Basic Agreement of 2015," January 30, 2017.

> Motion Picture Editors Guild
> 7715 Sunset Boulevard, Suite 200
> Hollywood, CA 90046
> **Telephone:** 323-876-4770
> **Online:** http://www.editorsguild.com
> **Email:** info@editorsguild.com
> **Survey Period:** July 31, 2016-July 29, 2017

Note: Data were downloaded on January 30, 2017. Weekly salaries have been rounded to the nearest dollar.

MSC

Bill Zuckerman, "What Happens to Music Majors After They Graduate College? New Study Reveals Amazing Data," *Music School Central*, March 1, 2016.

> **Online:** http://www.musicschoolcentral.com
> **Survey Period:** 2015

MSP01

"Salary and Benefits," January 30, 2017.

> **Online:** http://www.michigan.gov/msp/
> **Survey Period:** 2017

Note: Property Security Officer salary includes the starting salary for State Property Security Officer 7. Data were downloaded on January 30, 2017 and were considered current by the source.

MSP02

"Forensic Scientist," January 30, 2017.

> **Online:** http://www.michigan.gov/msp/
> **Survey Period:** 2017

Note: Data were downloaded on January 30, 2017 and were considered current by the source.

MSP03

"Salary and Benefits," January 30, 2017.

> **Online:** http://www.michigan.gov/msp/
> **Survey Period:** 2017

Note: Trooper salary includes the starting salary for Trooper 10. Data were downloaded on January 30, 2017 and were considered current by the source.

MST01

Daniel Bortz, "10 High-Paying Jobs for Natural-Born Salespeople," *Monster*, February 2017.

> **Online:** http://www.monster.com/career-advice/
> **Survey Period:** 2016

MST02

Cathie Ericson, "Love to Travel? These 5 Jobs Are for You," *Monster*, February 7, 2017.

Online: http://www.monster.com/career-advice/
Survey Period: 2017

Note: Data was downloaded on February 7, 2017 and was considered current by the source.

MST03

Elana Lyn Gross, "10 Jobs for People Who Never Confuse 'They're,' 'Their,' and 'There'," *Monster*, February 2017.

Online: http://www.monster.com/career-advice/
Survey Period: May 2015

MST04

Jon Simmons, "7 Jobs for Thrill Seekers," *Monster*, December 2016.

Online: http://www.monster.com/career-advice/
Survey Period: 2017

MSUSAL

Salary Rate of Faculty and Staff - FY15, November 10, 2016.

Michigan State University
East Lansing, MI 48824
Telephone: 517-355-1855
Online: https://msu.edu/state-transparency-reporting/
Survey Period: October 1, 2014-September 30, 2015

Note: Actual salaries. Data were downloaded on November 10, 2016.

MTGOV

"State Employee Data," January 17, 2017.

Montana Department of Administration
State Information Technology Services Division
P.O. Box 200113
Helena, MT 59620-0113
Telephone: 406-444-2000
Fax: 406-444-2701
Online: https://employeepay.mt.gov/transEmpPay/
Survey Period: 2016

NALC

"Letter Carrier Pay Schedule," February 19, 2016.

National Association of Letter Carriers
100 Indiana Ave., NW
Washington, DC 20001-2144
Telephone: 202-393-4695
Online: https://www.nalc.org
Survey Period: February 19, 2016

Note: Salaries took effect on February 19, 2016.

NALP

"First-Year Associate Salaries at Large Law Firms Have Become Less Homogenous, Though $160,000 Continues to Define the Top of the Market," April 15, 2015.

The National Association for Law Placement
1220 19th Street NW, Suite 401
Washington, DC 20036-2405
Telephone: 202-835-1001
Fax: 202-835-1112
Online: http://www.nalp.org/2015_assoc
Email: info@nalp.org
Survey Period: 2015

Note: Salary data as of April 1, 2015.

NATH

"Doula Training and Careers," *Natural Healers*, March 2, 2017.

Online: http://www.naturalhealers.com/midwifery/doula/
Survey Period: 2017

Note: Data were downloaded on March 2, 2017 and were considered current by the source. Salary data are on a weekly basis. According to the source, a doula's salary varies widely based on geographic location, training, experience and how many hours he or she works per week.

NCGOV

State of North Carolina Salary Plan, January 1, 2017.

North Carolina Office of State Human Resources
116 West Jones Street
Raleigh, NC 27603
Telephone: 919-807-4800
Online: https://oshr.nc.gov/state-employee-resources/
Email: ask_hr@nc.gov
Survey Period: July 1, 2016

Note: Salaries took effect on July 1, 2016 and were revised on January 1, 2017.

NCSC

"Survey of Judicial Salaries," January 2017.

National Center for State Courts
300 Newport Avenue
Williamsburg, VA 23185
Telephone: 800-616-6164
Fax: 757-220-0449
Online: http://www.ncsc.org
Survey Period: January 1, 2017

Note: Salary data as of January 1, 2017.

NCSL

"2016 Survey: State Legislative Compensation, Session per Diem and Mileage," *National Conference of State Legislatures*, December 8, 2016.

National Conference of State Legislatures
444 North Capitol Street, NW, Suite 515
Washington, DC 20001
Telephone: 202-624-5400
Fax: 202-737-1069
Online: http://www.ncsl.org
Survey Period: 2016

Note: Actual salaries. Annual base salaries do not include additional per diem payments that are made by some states. Data were downloaded on December 8, 2016.

NEBLS

Nebraska Employment and Wage Estimates, January 2, 2017.

Nebraska Department of Labor
Telephone: 402-471-9000
Online: http://neblswages.nwd.ne.gov/navtree.php
Survey Period: July 2016-September 2016

Note: All data are provided by the State Employment Security Administration to the Occupational Employment Statistics (OES) survey conducted by the U.S. Department of Labor, Bureau of Labor Statistics. May 2015 Occupational Employment and Wage Estimates have been adjusted to the third quarter of 2016 using the Employment Cost Index. Data were downloaded on January 2, 2017.

NHBLS

New Hampshire Occupational Employment & Wages - 2016, November 2016.

  Economic and Labor Market Information Bureau
  New Hampshire Employment Security
  45 South Fruit Street
  Concord, NH 03301
  Telephone: 603-224-3311
  Online: http://www.nhes.nh.gov/elmi/
  Email: elmi@nhes.nh.gov
  Survey Period: June 2016

Note: All data are provided by the State Employment Security Administration to the Occupational Employment Statistics (OES) survey conducted by the U.S. Department of Labor, Bureau of Labor Statistics. May 2015 Occupational Employment and Wage Estimates have been adjusted to June 2016 using the Employment Cost Index.

NHC01

Brian Stromberg and Mindy Ault, "A Snapshot of Housing Affordability for School Workers," *Paycheck to Paycheck*, September 2016.

  National Housing Conference
  1900 M Street, NW, Suite 200
  Washington, DC 20036
  Telephone: 202-466-2121
  Online: http://www.nhc.org/
  Survey Period: 2016

NLSM01

"Nail Tech Income," *Nails Magazine: 2015-2016 The Big Book*, 2016, p. 44.

  Online: http://ww.nailsmag.com/page/70218/market-
        research
  Survey Period: 2015-2016

NMGOV

"Classification & Pay Listing," July 30, 2016.

  New Mexico State Personnel Office
  2600 Cerrillos Road
  Santa Fe, NM 87505
  Telephone: 505-476-7759
  Online: http://www.spo.state.nm.us
  Survey Period: July 30, 2016

Note: Salaries took effect on July 30, 2016.

NSI

2016 Executive Compensation Study, February 2, 2016.

  Nursing Solutions, Inc.
  2055 East State Street
  East Petersburg, PA 17520
  Telephone: 717-560-3863
  Fax: 717-560-9111
  Survey Period: 2016

Note: Base salary.

NTNGOV

"General Government Employees Titles and Base Annual Salaries," January 3, 2017.

  Metropolitan Government of Nashville and Davidson
  County, Tennessee
  Human Resources Department
  404 James Robertson Parkway, Suite 1000
  Nashville, TN 37219
  Telephone: 615-862-6640
  Fax: 615-862-6659
  Online: http://data.nashville.gov
  Email: opendata@nashville.gov
  Survey Period: 2017

Note: Salaries have been rounded to the nearest dollar. Actual salary for Auditorium Manager.

NWSR01

Elizabeth Armstrong Moore, "Meet the Dudes Who Make $1K a Week Waiting in Lines," *Newser*, October 2, 2015.

Online: http://www.newser.com
Survey Period: 2015

Note: A Professional Time-Killer is someone who is paid to wait in lines for someone else. Actual salary. The professional time-killer mentioned in the source charges $25 for the first hour and $10 for every hour after that.

NYBLS

Occupational Wages for New York State, November 10, 2016.

New York State Department of Labor
Building 12, W.A. Harriman Campus
Albany, NY 12240
Telephone: 518-457-9000
Online: https://labor.ny.gov/stats/lswage2.asp
Survey Period: January 2016-March 2016

Note: All data are provided by the State Employment Security Administration to the Occupational Employment Statistics (OES) survey conducted by the U.S. Department of Labor, Bureau of Labor Statistics. May 2015 Occupational Employment and Wage Estimates have been adjusted to the first quarter of 2016 using the Employment Cost Index. Data were downloaded on November 10, 2016.

NYFA

Zeke, "Jobs in Animation: Average Salaries & Career Paths," January 16, 2015.

New York Film Academy
17 Battery Place
New York, NY 10004
Telephone: 202-674-4300
Online: http://www.nyfa.edu
Survey Period: 2015

NYT01

David Segal, "The Cage Match," *The New York Times*, March 27, 2016, pp. 1, 6-7.

Survey Period: 2016

Note: Data do not include bonuses. Entry-level fighters earn $12,000 if they win. At the highest level title matches, fighters can earn bonuses of $3,000,000 or more.

NYT02

Andrew Das, "U.S. Soccer Pay Disparity? Yes. But It's Complicated," *The New York Times*, April 22, 2016, pp. B12, B17.

Survey Period: 2016

Note: Base salary for most of the soccer players on the U.S. women's soccer team. Does not include bonuses for each game won.

NYT03

Katie Rogers, "No End in Sight to Strike by Harvard's Cafeteria Workers Over Wages," *The New York Times*, October 11, 2016.

Online: http://www.nytimes.com
Survey Period: 2016

NYT04

Noam Scheiber, "Making a Chef From Scratch," *The New York Times*, October 14, 2016, pp. B1-B2.

Survey Period: 2016

Note: Salary for Executive Pastry Chef depends on a restaurant's size and profitablilty.

OHGOV

2015 State Salary, December 5, 2016.

State Treasurer of Ohio
30 East Broad Street, 9th Floor
Columbus, OH 43215
Telephone: 614-466-2160
Online: http://www.tos.oh.gov/state_salary
Survey Period: 2015

Note: Data were downloaded on December 5, 2016.

OHGOV1

"2017 Compensation Charts," February 1, 2017.

Ohio Township Association
6500 Taylor Road, Suite A
Blacklick, OH 43004-8570
Telephone: 614-863-0045
Fax: 614-863-9751
Online: http://www.ohiotownship.org
Survey Period: 2017

Note: Salaries are dependent on the township budget. Lower salaries are paid to Fiscal Officers and Trustees employed by townships with lower budgets.

OPM01

Barack Obama, "Executive Order 13756 Adjustments of Certain Rates of Pay," December 27, 2016.

U.S. Office of Personnel Management
1900 E Street, NW
Washington, DC 20415-1000
Telephone: 202-606-1800
Online: http://www.opm.gov
Survey Period: 2017

OPM02

2017 Locality Rates of Pay: Administrative Appeals Judges, February 2, 2017.

U.S. Office of Personnel Management
1900 E Street, NW
Washington, DC 20415-1000
Telephone: 202-606-1800
Online: http://www.opm.gov
Survey Period: 2017

Note: Data were downloaded on February 2, 2017.

ORBLS

2016 Oregon Wage Information, January 3, 2017.

Oregon Employment Department
875 Union St. NE
Salem, OR 97311
Telephone: 800-262-3912
Online: https://www.qualityinfo.org/pubs
Survey Period: 2016

Note: All data are provided by the State Employment Security Administration to the Occupational Employment Statistics (OES) survey conducted by the U.S. Department of Labor, Bureau of Labor Statistics. May 2015 Occupational Employment and Wage Estimates have been adjusted to 2016 using the Employment Cost Index. Data were downloaded on January 3, 2017.

PNP01

2016-2017 Nonprofit Salaries, Staffing & Trends Report: For Greater Washington, DC Area NonProfits & Associations, November 2016.

PNP Staffing Group
515 Madison Avenue, Suite 1100
New York, NY 10022
Telephone: 646-846-4160
Online: http://pnpstaffinggroup.com
Email: info@pnpstaffinggroup.com
Survey Period: 2016

PRWK

"2016 Salary Survey: Data and Infographics," *PR Week*, February 29, 2016.

> **Online:** http://www.prweek.com
> **Survey Period:** 2016

PW01

Jim Milliot, "The PW Publishing Industry Salary Survey, 2016," *Publishers Weekly*, September 16, 2016.

> **Online:** http://www.publishersweekly.com
> **Survey Period:** 2015

QTZ01

Alice Truong, "Women in Tech are Asking for Lower Salaries Than Men for the Same Jobs," *Quartz*, April 12, 2016.

> **Online:** http://qz.com
> **Survey Period:** 2016

RFIN01

Jeffery Marino, "California Fails the Affordability Test for Teachers," *Redfin*, September 20, 2016.

> **Online:** http://www.redfin.com/blog/2016/09/
> **Survey Period:** 2015

RH01

2017 Salary Guide for the Legal Profession, October 2016.

> Robert Half Legal
> 2884 Sand Hill Road
> Menlo Park, CA 94025
> **Telephone:** 877-862-2689
> **Online:** https://www.roberthalf.com
> **Survey Period:** 2017

RH02

2017 Salary Guide, 2016.

> The Creative Group
> 1401 I Street, 4th Floor
> Washington, DC 20005
> **Telephone:** 202-626-0290
> **Fax:** 202-626-4950
> **Online:** https://www.roberthalf.com
> **Email:** washington.dc@creativegroup.com
> **Survey Period:** 2017

Note: Starting salaries unless otherwise specified.

RIGOV

Municipal Salary Survey: Fiscal Year 2017, February 2017.

> State of Rhode Island
> Division of Municipal Finance
> One Capitol Hill, 1st Floor
> Providence, RI 02908
> **Telephone:** 401-574-9900
> **Online:** http://www.municipalfinance.ri.gov
> **Survey Period:** 2017

Note: Salaries are for fiscal year 2017. Actual salaries.

RTDNA

Bob Papper, "RTDNA Research: Newsroom Salary Survey," *RTDNA*, June 27, 2016.

> **Online:** http://www.rtdna.org
> **Survey Period:** 2016

SCHAIN

2016 Salary Survey, February 2016.

> **Online:** http://www.supplychain247.com
> **Survey Period:** 2016

Note: Salary survey was conducted by Peerless Research Group for Logistics Management.

SCR01

"Top 10 Highest Paying Nursing Specialties," *Scrubs*, September 8, 2016.

> **Online:** http://www.scrubsmag.com
> **Survey Period:** 2016

SCR02

"The Nursing Specialties With the Best Salaries," *Scrubs*, April 7, 2016.

> **Online:** http://www.scrubsmag.com
> **Survey Period:** 2015

SFGOV

City and County of San Francisco Salary Ordinance, July 27, 2016.

> City and County of San Francisco
> Office of the Controller
> 1 Dr. Carlton B. Goodlett Place
> San Francisco, CA 94102
> **Telephone:** 415-554-7500
> **Fax:** 415-554-7466
> **Online:** http://sfcontroller.org
> **Email:** controller@sfgov.org
> **Survey Period:** 2016-2018

Note: Salary data are for both the city and county of San Francisco, California.

SJPD

"Salary, Benefits, and Retirement," December 1, 2016.

> **Online:** http://www.sjpd.org
> **Survey Period:** 2016

Note: Data were downloaded on December 1, 2016 and were considered current by the source. Actual wage.

SKU01

"Career Listings," December 1, 2016.

> Sokanu
> 130-319 West Pender Street
> Vancouver, BC V6B-1T3
> **Online:** http://www.sokanu.com/careers/
> **Email:** contact@sokanu.com
> **Survey Period:** 2016

Note: Data were downloaded on December 1, 2016 and were considered current by the source.

SKU02

"Livestock Feed Sales Representative Salary," December 1, 2016.

> Sokanu
> 130-319 West Pender Street
> Vancouver, BC V6B-1T3
> **Online:** http://www.sokanu.com/careers/
> **Email:** contact@sokanu.com
> **Survey Period:** 2016

Note: Data were downloaded on December 1, 2016 and were considered current by the source.

SLEEP

Mike Matson, "Sleep Review Salary Survey 2015," *Sleep Review*, August 2015.

> **Online:** http://www.sleepreviewmag.com
> **Survey Period:** 2015

SN01

"Industry Salary Table — 2015," *Supermarket News*, November 5, 2015.

Online: http://www.supermarketnews.com
Survey Period: 2015

Note: Small companies have revenues of $500 million to $1 billion. Medium companies have revenues of $2 billion to $10 billion. Large companies have revenues of more than $10 billion.

SOLF

2016 National Solar Jobs Census, January 2017.

The Solar Foundation
1717 Pennsylvania Avenue NW, Suite 750
Washington, DC 20006
Telephone: 202-469-3750
Online: http://www.thesolarfoundation.org/national/
Email: info@solarfound.org
Survey Period: 2016

Note: Installers do not include electricians. The median wage for electricians in the solar industry is $3.92 per hour more than installers.

STHE

Lucas Resetar, "Detroit Revitalization Fellows Prepare for 2015 Campaign," *The South End*, March 4, 2015.

Online: http://www.thesouthend.wayne.edu
Survey Period: 2015

Note: Base salary.

STOF1

"Stack Overflow Developer Survey 2015," *Stack Overflow*, January 25, 2017.

Online: http://www.stackoverflow.com
Survey Period: 2015

Note: Data were downloaded on January 25, 2017.

STOF2

"Stack Overflow Developer Survey 2016 Results," *Stack Overflow*, January 25, 2017.

Online: http://www.stackoverflow.com
Survey Period: 2016

Note: Average salary with five or more years of experience. Data were downloaded on January 25, 2017.

TAG01

"Member Wage Survey, 2016," September 2016.

The Animation Guild
Local 839 IATSE
1105 North Hollywood Way
Burbank, CA 91505
Telephone: 818-845-7500
Online: http://animationguild.org
Survey Period: 2016

TC01

David Jesse, "Simon 6th on State College President Pay," *The Towne Courier*, August 7, 2016, p. 5A.

Survey Period: 2015

Note: Actual salary. Does not include bonus pay.

TC02

RJ Wolcott, "High School Grads Fast Track Careers," *The Towne Courier*, July 10, 2016, p. 6A.

Survey Period: 2016

TC03

Curt Smith, "Fired Ingham IT Chief Pleads No Contest," *The Towne Courier*, April 24, 2016, p. 7A.

Survey Period: 2015

Note: Actual salary.

TC04

Curt Smith, "Duda to Retire as Haslett Schools Superintendent," *The Towne Courier*, January 10, 2016, p. 1A.

Survey Period: 2015-2016

Note: Actual salary.

TC05

Dawn Park, "Township Manager's Contract Extended," *The Towne Courier*, August 23, 2015, p. 4A.

Survey Period: August 1, 2015-November 1, 2017

Note: Actual salary.

TC06

Matt Mencarini, "Dunnings to Resign in Wake of Charges," *The Towne Courier*, April 3, 2016, p. 1A.

Survey Period: 2016

Note: According to the source, the Ingham County Prosecutor's annual salary was more than $132,000.

TC07

Eric Lacy, "Election Officials 'Plan for the Worst, Hope for the Best'," *The Towne Courier*, October 30, 2016, pp. 1A, 5A.

Survey Period: 2016

TC08

Justin A. Hinkley, "Presidential Recount Could Cost Ingham County 'Thousands'," *The Towne Courier*, December 4, 2016, p. 1A.

Survey Period: 2016

Note: Actual wage.

TDY01

Sarah Epstein, "25 Best Jobs in the US in 2016 According to Glassdoor," *Today*, January 20, 2016.

Online: http://www.today.com/money/
Survey Period: 2016

Note: Base salaries.

TIME01

Alexandra Sifferlin, "Surgeon Salary: Here's How Much Doctors Make," *Time*, July 25, 2016.

Online: http://www.time.com
Survey Period: 2016

TJN01

Joanna Hughes, "Show Me the Money: 8 Good-Paying Part-Time Jobs," *TheJobNetwork*, August 12, 2015.

Online: http://www.thejobnetwork.com
Survey Period: 2015

TJN02

Peter Jones, "11 Flexible Jobs for Working Parents," *TheJob-Network*, July 27, 2016.

Online: http://www.thejobnetwork.com
Survey Period: 2016

Note: According to the source, the average salary for a Call Center Representative is more than $28,000.

TNV

"All Salaries for 2015," *TransparentNevada*, March 1, 2017.

Online: http://transparentnevada.com/agencies/salaries
Survey Period: 2015

Note: Salaries have been rounded to the nearest dollar. Non-average salaries are actual salaries. Data were downloaded on March 1, 2017.

TRAIN

"Dip in Dollars," *Training*, November 2016-December 2016, pp. 42-51.

Online: http://trainingmag.com/digital-archives
Survey Period: 2015-2016

TSCI

Karen Zusi, "2016 Life Sciences Salary Survey," *The Scientist*, November 1, 2016.

Online: http://www.the-scientist.com
Survey Period: 2016

TSTR

Ellen Chang, "Top 50 Jobs in the U.S. for 2017," *TheStreet*, January 28, 2017.

Online: http://www.thestreet.com
Survey Period: 2017

TTT

"Government Salaries Explorer," *The Texas Tribune*, March 1, 2017.

Online: http://salaries.texastribune.org/
Survey Period: 2015-2016

Note: Salaries were updated on the dates shown in the individual records. Data were downloaded on March 1, 2017.

TXGOV

"Job Descriptions for the 2016-2017 Biennium," February 7, 2017.

Texas State Auditor's Office
1501 North Congress Avenue
Austin, TX 78701
Telephone: 512-936-9500
Fax: 512-936-9400
Online: http://www.hr.sao.texas.gov
Email: auditor@sao.texas.gov
Survey Period: September 1, 2015-August 31, 2017

Note: Data was downloaded on February 7, 2017.

UBJ01

Ashley Boncimino, "David Clayton Outlines His Vision for the Center for Manufacturing Innovation," *Upstate Business Journal*, November 11, 2015.

Online: http://www.upstatebusinessjournal.com
Survey Period: 2015

USAT01

Dan Wolken, Steve Berkowitz, and Christopher Schnaars, "Big Money Not Just for Head Coaches," *USA Today*, December 10, 2015, pp. 1A-2A.

Survey Period: 2015

USAT02

"Top Team Payrolls," *USA Today*, September 28, 2016.

 Online: http://www.usatoday.com/sports/nhl/salaries/
            2014/team/all/
 Survey Period: 2014-2015

Note: Data were downloaded on September 28, 2016.

USAT03

Bob Nightengale, "Baseball Salaries: Defending Champion Royals Spread Wealth," *USA Today*, April 4, 2016, pp. 6C-7C.

 Survey Period: 2016

USAT04

Steve Berkowitz, et. al., "NCAAF Coaches," *USA Today*, October 26, 2016.

 Online: http://sports.usatoday.com/ncaa/salaries
 Survey Period: 2016

Note: Base salaries.

USAT05

Paul Myerberg, Steve Berkowitz and Christopher Schnaars, "Strength Coaches See Salaries Mushroom as Roles Expand," *USA Today*, December 8, 2016, pp. 1C, 4C.

 Survey Period: 2016

Note: Total cash compensation does not include bonuses, benefits, or perks.

USBLS

May 2015 National Occupational Employment and Wage Estimates, March 30, 2016.

 U.S. Department of Labor Statistics
 Division of Occupational Employment Statistics
 2 Massachusetts Avenue, NE, PSB Suite 2135
 Washington, DC 20212-0001
 Telephone: 202-691-6569
 Online: http://www.bls.gov/oes/tables.htm
 Survey Period: May 2015

USN01

Rick Newman, "The 10 Most Overpaid Jobs," *U.S. News and World Report*, March 21, 2013.

 Online: http://money.usnews.com
 Survey Period: 2013

Note: Median mid-career wage.

VAR01

Michael Schneider and Cynthia Littleton, "Salaries of TV's Top Talent Revealed," *Variety*, October 4, 2016.

 Online: http://www.variety.com
 Survey Period: 2016

Note: Average salary per episode of the top 25 highest paid actors and actresses in each category.

WABLS

Washington 2016 Occupational Employment and Wage Estimates, July 2016.

Employment Security Department
Labor Market and Economic Analysis Branch
P.O. Box 9046
Olympia, WA 98507-9046
Telephone: 360-407-2306
Fax: 360-438-4846
Online: https://fortress.wa.gov/esd/employmentdata/
reports-publications/
Contact: Paul Turek, Ph.D.
Email: lmpa@esd.wa.gov
Survey Period: March 2016

Note: All data are provided by the State Employment Security Administration to the Occupational Employment Statistics (OES) survey conducted by the U.S. Department of Labor, Bureau of Labor Statistics. May 2015 Occupational Employment and Wage Estimates have been adjusted to March 2016 using the Employment Cost Index.

WBM

Kerana Todorov, "2016 Salary Survey Report," *Wine Business Monthly*, October 2016, pp. 68-79.

Survey Period: February 1, 2016

Note: Salary data effective February 1, 2016.

WF01

Rick Bell, "By the Numbers," *Workforce*, October 2015, p. 11.

Survey Period: July 2015

WMBFN

"Government Employee Salary Database," *WMBF News*, December 16, 2016.

Online: http://www.wmbfnews.com/
Survey Period: 2017

Note: Salaries have been rounded to the nearest dollar. Actual salaries.

WSJ01

Sarah Nassauer, "Wal-Mart to Trim Staff," *The Wall Street Journal*, September 2, 2016, p. B3.

Survey Period: 2016

WSJ02

Alix Stuart, "Pensions Reduce CFO Pay by 1.5%," *The Wall Street Journal*, July 5, 2016, p. B6.

Survey Period: 2015

Note: Average median wage for Chief Financial Officers at S&P 500 companies who have held their position for the previous two years.

WSJ03

David Crook and Siemond Chan, "The Short Answer: How Economical Are Our National Parks?" *The Wall Street Journal*, August 25, 2016, p. B6.

Survey Period: 2016

WSJ04

Sarah E. Needleman, "Videogame Actors Strike Over Pay," *The Wall Street Journal*, October 24, 2016, p. B4.

Survey Period: 2016

Note: Average baseline rate for a four-hour session.

Appendix II

SALARY CONVERSION TABLE

Hour	Week	Month	Year	Hour	Week	Month	Year	Hour	Week	Month	Year	Hour	Week	Month	Year
2.00	80	346	4,157	4.10	164	710	8,521	6.20	248	1,074	12,886	8.30	332	1,438	17,251
2.05	82	355	4,261	4.15	166	719	8,625	6.25	250	1,083	12,990	8.35	334	1,446	17,355
2.10	84	364	4,365	4.20	168	727	8,729	6.30	252	1,091	13,094	8.40	336	1,455	17,459
2.15	86	372	4,469	4.25	170	736	8,833	6.35	254	1,100	13,198	8.45	338	1,464	17,562
2.20	88	381	4,572	4.30	172	745	8,937	6.40	256	1,108	13,302	8.50	340	1,472	17,666
2.25	90	390	4,676	4.35	174	753	9,041	6.45	258	1,117	13,406	8.55	342	1,481	17,770
2.30	92	398	4,780	4.40	176	762	9,145	6.50	260	1,126	13,510	8.60	344	1,490	17,874
2.35	94	407	4,884	4.45	178	771	9,249	6.55	262	1,134	13,614	8.65	346	1,498	17,978
2.40	96	416	4,988	4.50	180	779	9,353	6.60	264	1,143	13,717	8.70	348	1,507	18,082
2.45	98	424	5,092	4.55	182	788	9,457	6.65	266	1,152	13,821	8.75	350	1,516	18,186
2.50	100	433	5,196	4.60	184	797	9,561	6.70	268	1,160	13,925	8.80	352	1,524	18,290
2.55	102	442	5,300	4.65	186	805	9,665	6.75	270	1,169	14,029	8.85	354	1,533	18,394
2.60	104	450	5,404	4.70	188	814	9,768	6.80	272	1,178	14,133	8.90	356	1,541	18,498
2.65	106	459	5,508	4.75	190	823	9,872	6.85	274	1,186	14,237	8.95	358	1,550	18,602
2.70	108	468	5,612	4.80	192	831	9,976	6.90	276	1,195	14,341	9.00	360	1,559	18,706
2.75	110	476	5,716	4.85	194	840	10,080	6.95	278	1,204	14,445	9.05	362	1,567	18,810
2.80	112	485	5,820	4.90	196	849	10,184	7.00	280	1,212	14,549	9.10	364	1,576	18,913
2.85	114	494	5,923	4.95	198	857	10,288	7.05	282	1,221	14,653	9.15	366	1,585	19,017
2.90	116	502	6,027	5.00	200	866	10,392	7.10	284	1,230	14,757	9.20	368	1,593	19,121
2.95	118	511	6,131	5.05	202	875	10,496	7.15	286	1,238	14,861	9.25	370	1,602	19,225
3.00	120	520	6,235	5.10	204	883	10,600	7.20	288	1,247	14,964	9.30	372	1,611	19,329
3.05	122	528	6,339	5.15	206	892	10,704	7.25	290	1,256	15,068	9.35	374	1,619	19,433
3.10	124	537	6,443	5.20	208	901	10,808	7.30	292	1,264	15,172	9.40	376	1,628	19,537
3.15	126	546	6,547	5.25	210	909	10,912	7.35	294	1,273	15,276	9.45	378	1,637	19,641
3.20	128	554	6,651	5.30	212	918	11,016	7.40	296	1,282	15,380	9.50	380	1,645	19,745
3.25	130	563	6,755	5.35	214	927	11,119	7.45	298	1,290	15,484	9.55	382	1,654	19,849
3.30	132	572	6,859	5.40	216	935	11,223	7.50	300	1,299	15,588	9.60	384	1,663	19,953
3.35	134	580	6,963	5.45	218	944	11,327	7.55	302	1,308	15,692	9.65	386	1,671	20,057
3.40	136	589	7,067	5.50	220	953	11,431	7.60	304	1,316	15,796	9.70	388	1,680	20,160
3.45	138	598	7,170	5.55	222	961	11,535	7.65	306	1,325	15,900	9.75	390	1,689	20,264
3.50	140	606	7,274	5.60	224	970	11,639	7.70	308	1,334	16,004	9.80	392	1,697	20,368
3.55	142	615	7,378	5.65	226	979	11,743	7.75	310	1,342	16,108	9.85	394	1,706	20,472
3.60	144	624	7,482	5.70	228	987	11,847	7.80	312	1,351	16,212	9.90	396	1,715	20,576
3.65	146	632	7,586	5.75	230	996	11,951	7.85	314	1,360	16,315	9.95	398	1,723	20,680
3.70	148	641	7,690	5.80	232	1,005	12,055	7.90	316	1,368	16,419	10.00	400	1,732	20,784
3.75	150	649	7,794	5.85	234	1,013	12,159	7.95	318	1,377	16,523	10.05	402	1,741	20,888
3.80	152	658	7,898	5.90	236	1,022	12,263	8.00	320	1,386	16,627	10.10	404	1,749	20,992
3.85	154	667	8,002	5.95	238	1,031	12,366	8.05	322	1,394	16,731	10.15	406	1,758	21,096
3.90	156	675	8,106	6.00	240	1,039	12,470	8.10	324	1,403	16,835	10.20	408	1,767	21,200
3.95	158	684	8,210	6.05	242	1,048	12,574	8.15	326	1,412	16,939	10.25	410	1,775	21,304
4.00	160	693	8,314	6.10	244	1,057	12,678	8.20	328	1,420	17,043	10.30	412	1,784	21,408
4.05	162	701	8,418	6.15	246	1,065	12,782	8.25	330	1,429	17,147	10.35	414	1,793	21,511

Hour	Week	Month	Year	Hour	Week	Month	Year	Hour	Week	Month	Year	Hour	Week	Month	Year
10.40	416	1,801	21,615	13.20	528	2,286	27,435	16.00	640	2,771	33,254	18.80	752	3,256	39,074
10.45	418	1,810	21,719	13.25	530	2,295	27,539	16.05	642	2,780	33,358	18.85	754	3,265	39,178
10.50	420	1,819	21,823	13.30	532	2,304	27,643	16.10	644	2,789	33,462	18.90	756	3,273	39,282
10.55	422	1,827	21,927	13.35	534	2,312	27,747	16.15	646	2,797	33,566	18.95	758	3,282	39,386
10.60	424	1,836	22,031	13.40	536	2,321	27,851	16.20	648	2,806	33,670	19.00	760	3,291	39,490
10.65	426	1,845	22,135	13.45	538	2,330	27,954	16.25	650	2,815	33,774	19.05	762	3,299	39,594
10.70	428	1,853	22,239	13.50	540	2,338	28,058	16.30	652	2,823	33,878	19.10	764	3,308	39,697
10.75	430	1,862	22,343	13.55	542	2,347	28,162	16.35	654	2,832	33,982	19.15	766	3,317	39,801
10.80	432	1,871	22,447	13.60	544	2,356	28,266	16.40	656	2,840	34,086	19.20	768	3,325	39,905
10.85	434	1,879	22,551	13.65	546	2,364	28,370	16.45	658	2,849	34,190	19.25	770	3,334	40,009
10.90	436	1,888	22,655	13.70	548	2,373	28,474	16.50	660	2,858	34,294	19.30	772	3,343	40,113
10.95	438	1,897	22,758	13.75	550	2,382	28,578	16.55	662	2,866	34,398	19.35	774	3,351	40,217
11.00	440	1,905	22,862	13.80	552	2,390	28,682	16.60	664	2,875	34,501	19.40	776	3,360	40,321
11.05	442	1,914	22,966	13.85	554	2,399	28,786	16.65	666	2,884	34,605	19.45	778	3,369	40,425
11.10	444	1,923	23,070	13.90	556	2,407	28,890	16.70	668	2,892	34,709	19.50	780	3,377	40,529
11.15	446	1,931	23,174	13.95	558	2,416	28,994	16.75	670	2,901	34,813	19.55	782	3,386	40,633
11.20	448	1,940	23,278	14.00	560	2,425	29,098	16.80	672	2,910	34,917	19.60	784	3,395	40,737
11.25	450	1,949	23,382	14.05	562	2,433	29,202	16.85	674	2,918	35,021	19.65	786	3,403	40,841
11.30	452	1,957	23,486	14.10	564	2,442	29,305	16.90	676	2,927	35,125	19.70	788	3,412	40,944
11.35	454	1,966	23,590	14.15	566	2,451	29,409	16.95	678	2,936	35,229	19.75	790	3,421	41,048
11.40	456	1,974	23,694	14.20	568	2,459	29,513	17.00	680	2,944	35,333	19.80	792	3,429	41,152
11.45	458	1,983	23,798	14.25	570	2,468	29,617	17.05	682	2,953	35,437	19.85	794	3,438	41,256
11.50	460	1,992	23,902	14.30	572	2,477	29,721	17.10	684	2,962	35,541	19.90	796	3,447	41,360
11.55	462	2,000	24,006	14.35	574	2,485	29,825	17.15	686	2,970	35,645	19.95	798	3,455	41,464
11.60	464	2,009	24,109	14.40	576	2,494	29,929	17.20	688	2,979	35,748	20.00	800	3,464	41,568
11.65	466	2,018	24,213	14.45	578	2,503	30,033	17.25	690	2,988	35,852	20.05	802	3,473	41,672
11.70	468	2,026	24,317	14.50	580	2,511	30,137	17.30	692	2,996	35,956	20.10	804	3,481	41,776
11.75	470	2,035	24,421	14.55	582	2,520	30,241	17.35	694	3,005	36,060	20.15	806	3,490	41,880
11.80	472	2,044	24,525	14.60	584	2,529	30,345	17.40	696	3,014	36,164	20.20	808	3,499	41,984
11.85	474	2,052	24,629	14.65	586	2,537	30,449	17.45	698	3,022	36,268	20.25	810	3,507	42,088
11.90	476	2,061	24,733	14.70	588	2,546	30,552	17.50	700	3,031	36,372	20.30	812	3,516	42,192
11.95	478	2,070	24,837	14.75	590	2,555	30,656	17.55	702	3,040	36,476	20.35	814	3,525	42,295
12.00	480	2,078	24,941	14.80	592	2,563	30,760	17.60	704	3,048	36,580	20.40	816	3,533	42,399
12.05	482	2,087	25,045	14.85	594	2,572	30,864	17.65	706	3,057	36,684	20.45	818	3,542	42,503
12.10	484	2,096	25,149	14.90	596	2,581	30,968	17.70	708	3,066	36,788	20.50	820	3,551	42,607
12.15	486	2,104	25,253	14.95	598	2,589	31,072	17.75	710	3,074	36,892	20.55	822	3,559	42,711
12.20	488	2,113	25,356	15.00	600	2,598	31,176	17.80	712	3,083	36,996	20.60	824	3,568	42,815
12.25	490	2,122	25,460	15.05	602	2,607	31,280	17.85	714	3,092	37,099	20.65	826	3,577	42,919
12.30	492	2,130	25,564	15.10	604	2,615	31,384	17.90	716	3,100	37,203	20.70	828	3,585	43,023
12.35	494	2,139	25,668	15.15	606	2,624	31,488	17.95	718	3,109	37,307	20.75	830	3,594	43,127
12.40	496	2,148	25,772	15.20	608	2,633	31,592	18.00	720	3,118	37,411	20.80	832	3,603	43,231
12.45	498	2,156	25,876	15.25	610	2,641	31,696	18.05	722	3,126	37,515	20.85	834	3,611	43,335
12.50	500	2,165	25,980	15.30	612	2,650	31,800	18.10	724	3,135	37,619	20.90	836	3,620	43,439
12.55	502	2,174	26,084	15.35	614	2,659	31,903	18.15	726	3,144	37,723	20.95	838	3,629	43,542
12.60	504	2,182	26,188	15.40	616	2,667	32,007	18.20	728	3,152	37,827	21.00	840	3,637	43,646
12.65	506	2,191	26,292	15.45	618	2,676	32,111	18.25	730	3,161	37,931	21.05	842	3,646	43,750
12.70	508	2,200	26,396	15.50	620	2,685	32,215	18.30	732	3,170	38,035	21.10	844	3,655	43,854
12.75	510	2,208	26,500	15.55	622	2,693	32,319	18.35	734	3,178	38,139	21.15	846	3,663	43,958
12.80	512	2,217	26,604	15.60	624	2,702	32,423	18.40	736	3,187	38,243	21.20	848	3,672	44,062
12.85	514	2,226	26,707	15.65	626	2,711	32,527	18.45	738	3,196	38,346	21.25	850	3,680	44,166
12.90	516	2,234	26,811	15.70	628	2,719	32,631	18.50	740	3,204	38,450	21.30	852	3,689	44,270
12.95	518	2,243	26,915	15.75	630	2,728	32,735	18.55	742	3,213	38,554	21.35	854	3,698	44,374
13.00	520	2,252	27,019	15.80	632	2,737	32,839	18.60	744	3,222	38,658	21.40	856	3,706	44,478
13.05	522	2,260	27,123	15.85	634	2,745	32,943	18.65	746	3,230	38,762	21.45	858	3,715	44,582
13.10	524	2,269	27,227	15.90	636	2,754	33,047	18.70	748	3,239	38,866	21.50	860	3,724	44,686
13.15	526	2,278	27,331	15.95	638	2,763	33,150	18.75	750	3,248	38,970	21.55	862	3,732	44,790

Hour	Week	Month	Year	Hour	Week	Month	Year	Hour	Week	Month	Year	Hour	Week	Month	Year
21.60	864	3,741	44,893	24.40	976	4,226	50,713	27.20	1,088	4,711	56,532	30.00	1,200	5,196	62,352
21.65	866	3,750	44,997	24.45	978	4,235	50,817	27.25	1,090	4,720	56,636	30.05	1,202	5,205	62,456
21.70	868	3,758	45,101	24.50	980	4,243	50,921	27.30	1,092	4,728	56,740	30.10	1,204	5,213	62,560
21.75	870	3,767	45,205	24.55	982	4,252	51,025	27.35	1,094	4,737	56,844	30.15	1,206	5,222	62,664
21.80	872	3,776	45,309	24.60	984	4,261	51,129	27.40	1,096	4,746	56,948	30.20	1,208	5,231	62,768
21.85	874	3,784	45,413	24.65	986	4,269	51,233	27.45	1,098	4,754	57,052	30.25	1,210	5,239	62,872
21.90	876	3,793	45,517	24.70	988	4,278	51,336	27.50	1,100	4,763	57,156	30.30	1,212	5,248	62,976
21.95	878	3,802	45,621	24.75	990	4,287	51,440	27.55	1,102	4,772	57,260	30.35	1,214	5,257	63,079
22.00	880	3,810	45,725	24.80	992	4,295	51,544	27.60	1,104	4,780	57,364	30.40	1,216	5,265	63,183
22.05	882	3,819	45,829	24.85	994	4,304	51,648	27.65	1,106	4,789	57,468	30.45	1,218	5,274	63,287
22.10	884	3,828	45,933	24.90	996	4,313	51,752	27.70	1,108	4,798	57,572	30.50	1,220	5,283	63,391
22.15	886	3,836	46,037	24.95	998	4,321	51,856	27.75	1,110	4,806	57,676	30.55	1,222	5,291	63,495
22.20	888	3,845	46,140	25.00	1,000	4,330	51,960	27.80	1,112	4,815	57,780	30.60	1,224	5,300	63,599
22.25	890	3,854	46,244	25.05	1,002	4,339	52,064	27.85	1,114	4,824	57,883	30.65	1,226	5,309	63,703
22.30	892	3,862	46,348	25.10	1,004	4,347	52,168	27.90	1,116	4,832	57,987	30.70	1,228	5,317	63,807
22.35	894	3,871	46,452	25.15	1,006	4,356	52,272	27.95	1,118	4,841	58,091	30.75	1,230	5,326	63,911
22.40	896	3,880	46,556	25.20	1,008	4,365	52,376	28.00	1,120	4,850	58,195	30.80	1,232	5,335	64,015
22.45	898	3,888	46,660	25.25	1,010	4,373	52,480	28.05	1,122	4,858	58,299	30.85	1,234	5,343	64,119
22.50	900	3,897	46,764	25.30	1,012	4,382	52,584	28.10	1,124	4,867	58,403	30.90	1,236	5,352	64,223
22.55	902	3,906	46,868	25.35	1,014	4,391	52,687	28.15	1,126	4,876	58,507	30.95	1,238	5,361	64,326
22.60	904	3,914	46,972	25.40	1,016	4,399	52,791	28.20	1,128	4,884	58,611	31.00	1,240	5,369	64,430
22.65	906	3,923	47,076	25.45	1,018	4,408	52,895	28.25	1,130	4,893	58,715	31.05	1,242	5,378	64,534
22.70	908	3,932	47,180	25.50	1,020	4,417	52,999	28.30	1,132	4,902	58,819	31.10	1,244	5,387	64,638
22.75	910	3,940	47,284	25.55	1,022	4,425	53,103	28.35	1,134	4,910	58,923	31.15	1,246	5,395	64,742
22.80	912	3,949	47,388	25.60	1,024	4,434	53,207	28.40	1,136	4,919	59,027	31.20	1,248	5,404	64,846
22.85	914	3,958	47,491	25.65	1,026	4,443	53,311	28.45	1,138	4,928	59,130	31.25	1,250	5,412	64,950
22.90	916	3,966	47,595	25.70	1,028	4,451	53,415	28.50	1,140	4,936	59,234	31.30	1,252	5,421	65,054
22.95	918	3,975	47,699	25.75	1,030	4,460	53,519	28.55	1,142	4,945	59,338	31.35	1,254	5,430	65,158
23.00	920	3,984	47,803	25.80	1,032	4,469	53,623	28.60	1,144	4,954	59,442	31.40	1,256	5,438	65,262
23.05	922	3,992	47,907	25.85	1,034	4,477	53,727	28.65	1,146	4,962	59,546	31.45	1,258	5,447	65,366
23.10	924	4,001	48,011	25.90	1,036	4,486	53,831	28.70	1,148	4,971	59,650	31.50	1,260	5,456	65,470
23.15	926	4,010	48,115	25.95	1,038	4,495	53,934	28.75	1,150	4,979	59,754	31.55	1,262	5,464	65,574
23.20	928	4,018	48,219	26.00	1,040	4,503	54,038	28.80	1,152	4,988	59,858	31.60	1,264	5,473	65,677
23.25	930	4,027	48,323	26.05	1,042	4,512	54,142	28.85	1,154	4,997	59,962	31.65	1,266	5,482	65,781
23.30	932	4,036	48,427	26.10	1,044	4,521	54,246	28.90	1,156	5,005	60,066	31.70	1,268	5,490	65,885
23.35	934	4,044	48,531	26.15	1,046	4,529	54,350	28.95	1,158	5,014	60,170	31.75	1,270	5,499	65,989
23.40	936	4,053	48,635	26.20	1,048	4,538	54,454	29.00	1,160	5,023	60,274	31.80	1,272	5,508	66,093
23.45	938	4,062	48,738	26.25	1,050	4,546	54,558	29.05	1,162	5,031	60,378	31.85	1,274	5,516	66,197
23.50	940	4,070	48,842	26.30	1,052	4,555	54,662	29.10	1,164	5,040	60,481	31.90	1,276	5,525	66,301
23.55	942	4,079	48,946	26.35	1,054	4,564	54,766	29.15	1,166	5,049	60,585	31.95	1,278	5,534	66,405
23.60	944	4,088	49,050	26.40	1,056	4,572	54,870	29.20	1,168	5,057	60,689	32.00	1,280	5,542	66,509
23.65	946	4,096	49,154	26.45	1,058	4,581	54,974	29.25	1,170	5,066	60,793	32.05	1,282	5,551	66,613
23.70	948	4,105	49,258	26.50	1,060	4,590	55,078	29.30	1,172	5,075	60,897	32.10	1,284	5,560	66,717
23.75	950	4,113	49,362	26.55	1,062	4,598	55,182	29.35	1,174	5,083	61,001	32.15	1,286	5,568	66,821
23.80	952	4,122	49,466	26.60	1,064	4,607	55,285	29.40	1,176	5,092	61,105	32.20	1,288	5,577	66,924
23.85	954	4,131	49,570	26.65	1,066	4,616	55,389	29.45	1,178	5,101	61,209	32.25	1,290	5,586	67,028
23.90	956	4,139	49,674	26.70	1,068	4,624	55,493	29.50	1,180	5,109	61,313	32.30	1,292	5,594	67,132
23.95	958	4,148	49,778	26.75	1,070	4,633	55,597	29.55	1,182	5,118	61,417	32.35	1,294	5,603	67,236
24.00	960	4,157	49,882	26.80	1,072	4,642	55,701	29.60	1,184	5,127	61,521	32.40	1,296	5,612	67,340
24.05	962	4,165	49,986	26.85	1,074	4,650	55,805	29.65	1,186	5,135	61,625	32.45	1,298	5,620	67,444
24.10	964	4,174	50,089	26.90	1,076	4,659	55,909	29.70	1,188	5,144	61,728	32.50	1,300	5,629	67,548
24.15	966	4,183	50,193	26.95	1,078	4,668	56,013	29.75	1,190	5,153	61,832	32.55	1,302	5,638	67,652
24.20	968	4,191	50,297	27.00	1,080	4,676	56,117	29.80	1,192	5,161	61,936	32.60	1,304	5,646	67,756
24.25	970	4,200	50,401	27.05	1,082	4,685	56,221	29.85	1,194	5,170	62,040	32.65	1,306	5,655	67,860
24.30	972	4,209	50,505	27.10	1,084	4,694	56,325	29.90	1,196	5,179	62,144	32.70	1,308	5,664	67,964
24.35	974	4,217	50,609	27.15	1,086	4,702	56,429	29.95	1,198	5,187	62,248	32.75	1,310	5,672	68,068

Hour	Week	Month	Year	Hour	Week	Month	Year	Hour	Week	Month	Year	Hour	Week	Month	Year
32.80	1,312	5,681	68,172	35.60	1,424	6,166	73,991	38.40	1,536	6,651	79,811	41.20	1,648	7,136	85,630
32.85	1,314	5,690	68,275	35.65	1,426	6,175	74,095	38.45	1,538	6,660	79,914	41.25	1,650	7,144	85,734
32.90	1,316	5,698	68,379	35.70	1,428	6,183	74,199	38.50	1,540	6,668	80,018	41.30	1,652	7,153	85,838
32.95	1,318	5,707	68,483	35.75	1,430	6,192	74,303	38.55	1,542	6,677	80,122	41.35	1,654	7,162	85,942
33.00	1,320	5,716	68,587	35.80	1,432	6,201	74,407	38.60	1,544	6,686	80,226	41.40	1,656	7,170	86,046
33.05	1,322	5,724	68,691	35.85	1,434	6,209	74,511	38.65	1,546	6,694	80,330	41.45	1,658	7,179	86,150
33.10	1,324	5,733	68,795	35.90	1,436	6,218	74,615	38.70	1,548	6,703	80,434	41.50	1,660	7,188	86,254
33.15	1,326	5,742	68,899	35.95	1,438	6,227	74,718	38.75	1,550	6,711	80,538	41.55	1,662	7,196	86,358
33.20	1,328	5,750	69,003	36.00	1,440	6,235	74,822	38.80	1,552	6,720	80,642	41.60	1,664	7,205	86,461
33.25	1,330	5,759	69,107	36.05	1,442	6,244	74,926	38.85	1,554	6,729	80,746	41.65	1,666	7,214	86,565
33.30	1,332	5,768	69,211	36.10	1,444	6,253	75,030	38.90	1,556	6,737	80,850	41.70	1,668	7,222	86,669
33.35	1,334	5,776	69,315	36.15	1,446	6,261	75,134	38.95	1,558	6,746	80,954	41.75	1,670	7,231	86,773
33.40	1,336	5,785	69,419	36.20	1,448	6,270	75,238	39.00	1,560	6,755	81,058	41.80	1,672	7,240	86,877
33.45	1,338	5,794	69,522	36.25	1,450	6,278	75,342	39.05	1,562	6,763	81,162	41.85	1,674	7,248	86,981
33.50	1,340	5,802	69,626	36.30	1,452	6,287	75,446	39.10	1,564	6,772	81,265	41.90	1,676	7,257	87,085
33.55	1,342	5,811	69,730	36.35	1,454	6,296	75,550	39.15	1,566	6,781	81,369	41.95	1,678	7,266	87,189
33.60	1,344	5,820	69,834	36.40	1,456	6,304	75,654	39.20	1,568	6,789	81,473	42.00	1,680	7,274	87,293
33.65	1,346	5,828	69,938	36.45	1,458	6,313	75,758	39.25	1,570	6,798	81,577	42.05	1,682	7,283	87,397
33.70	1,348	5,837	70,042	36.50	1,460	6,322	75,862	39.30	1,572	6,807	81,681	42.10	1,684	7,292	87,501
33.75	1,350	5,845	70,146	36.55	1,462	6,330	75,966	39.35	1,574	6,815	81,785	42.15	1,686	7,300	87,605
33.80	1,352	5,854	70,250	36.60	1,464	6,339	76,069	39.40	1,576	6,824	81,889	42.20	1,688	7,309	87,708
33.85	1,354	5,863	70,354	36.65	1,466	6,348	76,173	39.45	1,578	6,833	81,993	42.25	1,690	7,318	87,812
33.90	1,356	5,871	70,458	36.70	1,468	6,356	76,277	39.50	1,580	6,841	82,097	42.30	1,692	7,326	87,916
33.95	1,358	5,880	70,562	36.75	1,470	6,365	76,381	39.55	1,582	6,850	82,201	42.35	1,694	7,335	88,020
34.00	1,360	5,889	70,666	36.80	1,472	6,374	76,485	39.60	1,584	6,859	82,305	42.40	1,696	7,344	88,124
34.05	1,362	5,897	70,770	36.85	1,474	6,382	76,589	39.65	1,586	6,867	82,409	42.45	1,698	7,352	88,228
34.10	1,364	5,906	70,873	36.90	1,476	6,391	76,693	39.70	1,588	6,876	82,512	42.50	1,700	7,361	88,332
34.15	1,366	5,915	70,977	36.95	1,478	6,400	76,797	39.75	1,590	6,885	82,616	42.55	1,702	7,370	88,436
34.20	1,368	5,923	71,081	37.00	1,480	6,408	76,901	39.80	1,592	6,893	82,720	42.60	1,704	7,378	88,540
34.25	1,370	5,932	71,185	37.05	1,482	6,417	77,005	39.85	1,594	6,902	82,824	42.65	1,706	7,387	88,644
34.30	1,372	5,941	71,289	37.10	1,484	6,426	77,109	39.90	1,596	6,911	82,928	42.70	1,708	7,396	88,748
34.35	1,374	5,949	71,393	37.15	1,486	6,434	77,213	39.95	1,598	6,919	83,032	42.75	1,710	7,404	88,852
34.40	1,376	5,958	71,497	37.20	1,488	6,443	77,316	40.00	1,600	6,928	83,136	42.80	1,712	7,413	88,956
34.45	1,378	5,967	71,601	37.25	1,490	6,452	77,420	40.05	1,602	6,937	83,240	42.85	1,714	7,422	89,059
34.50	1,380	5,975	71,705	37.30	1,492	6,460	77,524	40.10	1,604	6,945	83,344	42.90	1,716	7,430	89,163
34.55	1,382	5,984	71,809	37.35	1,494	6,469	77,628	40.15	1,606	6,954	83,448	42.95	1,718	7,439	89,267
34.60	1,384	5,993	71,913	37.40	1,496	6,478	77,732	40.20	1,608	6,963	83,552	43.00	1,720	7,448	89,371
34.65	1,386	6,001	72,017	37.45	1,498	6,486	77,836	40.25	1,610	6,971	83,656	43.05	1,722	7,456	89,475
34.70	1,388	6,010	72,120	37.50	1,500	6,495	77,940	40.30	1,612	6,980	83,760	43.10	1,724	7,465	89,579
34.75	1,390	6,019	72,224	37.55	1,502	6,504	78,044	40.35	1,614	6,989	83,863	43.15	1,726	7,474	89,683
34.80	1,392	6,027	72,328	37.60	1,504	6,512	78,148	40.40	1,616	6,997	83,967	43.20	1,728	7,482	89,787
34.85	1,394	6,036	72,432	37.65	1,506	6,521	78,252	40.45	1,618	7,006	84,071	43.25	1,730	7,491	89,891
34.90	1,396	6,045	72,536	37.70	1,508	6,530	78,356	40.50	1,620	7,015	84,175	43.30	1,732	7,500	89,995
34.95	1,398	6,053	72,640	37.75	1,510	6,538	78,460	40.55	1,622	7,023	84,279	43.35	1,734	7,508	90,099
35.00	1,400	6,062	72,744	37.80	1,512	6,547	78,564	40.60	1,624	7,032	84,383	43.40	1,736	7,517	90,203
35.05	1,402	6,071	72,848	37.85	1,514	6,556	78,667	40.65	1,626	7,041	84,487	43.45	1,738	7,526	90,306
35.10	1,404	6,079	72,952	37.90	1,516	6,564	78,771	40.70	1,628	7,049	84,591	43.50	1,740	7,534	90,410
35.15	1,406	6,088	73,056	37.95	1,518	6,573	78,875	40.75	1,630	7,058	84,695	43.55	1,742	7,543	90,514
35.20	1,408	6,097	73,160	38.00	1,520	6,582	78,979	40.80	1,632	7,067	84,799	43.60	1,744	7,552	90,618
35.25	1,410	6,105	73,264	38.05	1,522	6,590	79,083	40.85	1,634	7,075	84,903	43.65	1,746	7,560	90,722
35.30	1,412	6,114	73,368	38.10	1,524	6,599	79,187	40.90	1,636	7,084	85,007	43.70	1,748	7,569	90,826
35.35	1,414	6,123	73,471	38.15	1,526	6,608	79,291	40.95	1,638	7,093	85,110	43.75	1,750	7,577	90,930
35.40	1,416	6,131	73,575	38.20	1,528	6,616	79,395	41.00	1,640	7,101	85,214	43.80	1,752	7,586	91,034
35.45	1,418	6,140	73,679	38.25	1,530	6,625	79,499	41.05	1,642	7,110	85,318	43.85	1,754	7,595	91,138
35.50	1,420	6,149	73,783	38.30	1,532	6,634	79,603	41.10	1,644	7,119	85,422	43.90	1,756	7,603	91,242
35.55	1,422	6,157	73,887	38.35	1,534	6,642	79,707	41.15	1,646	7,127	85,526	43.95	1,758	7,612	91,346

Hour	Week	Month	Year	Hour	Week	Month	Year	Hour	Week	Month	Year	Hour	Week	Month	Year
44.00	1,760	7,621	91,450	46.80	1,872	8,106	97,269	49.60	1,984	8,591	103,089	52.40	2,096	9,076	108,908
44.05	1,762	7,629	91,554	46.85	1,874	8,114	97,373	49.65	1,986	8,599	103,193	52.45	2,098	9,084	109,012
44.10	1,764	7,638	91,657	46.90	1,876	8,123	97,477	49.70	1,988	8,608	103,296	52.50	2,100	9,093	109,116
44.15	1,766	7,647	91,761	46.95	1,878	8,132	97,581	49.75	1,990	8,617	103,400	52.55	2,102	9,102	109,220
44.20	1,768	7,655	91,865	47.00	1,880	8,140	97,685	49.80	1,992	8,625	103,504	52.60	2,104	9,110	109,324
44.25	1,770	7,664	91,969	47.05	1,882	8,149	97,789	49.85	1,994	8,634	103,608	52.65	2,106	9,119	109,428
44.30	1,772	7,673	92,073	47.10	1,884	8,158	97,893	49.90	1,996	8,643	103,712	52.70	2,108	9,128	109,532
44.35	1,774	7,681	92,177	47.15	1,886	8,166	97,997	49.95	1,998	8,651	103,816	52.75	2,110	9,136	109,636
44.40	1,776	7,690	92,281	47.20	1,888	8,175	98,100	50.00	2,000	8,660	103,920	52.80	2,112	9,145	109,740
44.45	1,778	7,699	92,385	47.25	1,890	8,184	98,204	50.05	2,002	8,669	104,024	52.85	2,114	9,154	109,843
44.50	1,780	7,707	92,489	47.30	1,892	8,192	98,308	50.10	2,004	8,677	104,128	52.90	2,116	9,162	109,947
44.55	1,782	7,716	92,593	47.35	1,894	8,201	98,412	50.15	2,006	8,686	104,232	52.95	2,118	9,171	110,051
44.60	1,784	7,725	92,697	47.40	1,896	8,210	98,516	50.20	2,008	8,695	104,336	53.00	2,120	9,180	110,155
44.65	1,786	7,733	92,801	47.45	1,898	8,218	98,620	50.25	2,010	8,703	104,440	53.05	2,122	9,188	110,259
44.70	1,788	7,742	92,904	47.50	1,900	8,227	98,724	50.30	2,012	8,712	104,544	53.10	2,124	9,197	110,363
44.75	1,790	7,751	93,008	47.55	1,902	8,236	98,828	50.35	2,014	8,721	104,647	53.15	2,126	9,206	110,467
44.80	1,792	7,759	93,112	47.60	1,904	8,244	98,932	50.40	2,016	8,729	104,751	53.20	2,128	9,214	110,571
44.85	1,794	7,768	93,216	47.65	1,906	8,253	99,036	50.45	2,018	8,738	104,855	53.25	2,130	9,223	110,675
44.90	1,796	7,777	93,320	47.70	1,908	8,262	99,140	50.50	2,020	8,747	104,959	53.30	2,132	9,232	110,779
44.95	1,798	7,785	93,424	47.75	1,910	8,270	99,244	50.55	2,022	8,755	105,063	53.35	2,134	9,240	110,883
45.00	1,800	7,794	93,528	47.80	1,912	8,279	99,348	50.60	2,024	8,764	105,167	53.40	2,136	9,249	110,987
45.05	1,802	7,803	93,632	47.85	1,914	8,288	99,451	50.65	2,026	8,773	105,271	53.45	2,138	9,258	111,090
45.10	1,804	7,811	93,736	47.90	1,916	8,296	99,555	50.70	2,028	8,781	105,375	53.50	2,140	9,266	111,194
45.15	1,806	7,820	93,840	47.95	1,918	8,305	99,659	50.75	2,030	8,790	105,479	53.55	2,142	9,275	111,298
45.20	1,808	7,829	93,944	48.00	1,920	8,314	99,763	50.80	2,032	8,799	105,583	53.60	2,144	9,284	111,402
45.25	1,810	7,837	94,048	48.05	1,922	8,322	99,867	50.85	2,034	8,807	105,687	53.65	2,146	9,292	111,506
45.30	1,812	7,846	94,152	48.10	1,924	8,331	99,971	50.90	2,036	8,816	105,791	53.70	2,148	9,301	111,610
45.35	1,814	7,855	94,255	48.15	1,926	8,340	100,075	50.95	2,038	8,825	105,894	53.75	2,150	9,309	111,714
45.40	1,816	7,863	94,359	48.20	1,928	8,348	100,179	51.00	2,040	8,833	105,998	53.80	2,152	9,318	111,818
45.45	1,818	7,872	94,463	48.25	1,930	8,357	100,283	51.05	2,042	8,842	106,102	53.85	2,154	9,327	111,922
45.50	1,820	7,881	94,567	48.30	1,932	8,366	100,387	51.10	2,044	8,851	106,206	53.90	2,156	9,335	112,026
45.55	1,822	7,889	94,671	48.35	1,934	8,374	100,491	51.15	2,046	8,859	106,310	53.95	2,158	9,344	112,130
45.60	1,824	7,898	94,775	48.40	1,936	8,383	100,595	51.20	2,048	8,868	106,414	54.00	2,160	9,353	112,234
45.65	1,826	7,907	94,879	48.45	1,938	8,392	100,698	51.25	2,050	8,876	106,518	54.05	2,162	9,361	112,338
45.70	1,828	7,915	94,983	48.50	1,940	8,400	100,802	51.30	2,052	8,885	106,622	54.10	2,164	9,370	112,441
45.75	1,830	7,924	95,087	48.55	1,942	8,409	100,906	51.35	2,054	8,894	106,726	54.15	2,166	9,379	112,545
45.80	1,832	7,933	95,191	48.60	1,944	8,418	101,010	51.40	2,056	8,902	106,830	54.20	2,168	9,387	112,649
45.85	1,834	7,941	95,295	48.65	1,946	8,426	101,114	51.45	2,058	8,911	106,934	54.25	2,170	9,396	112,753
45.90	1,836	7,950	95,399	48.70	1,948	8,435	101,218	51.50	2,060	8,920	107,038	54.30	2,172	9,405	112,857
45.95	1,838	7,959	95,502	48.75	1,950	8,443	101,322	51.55	2,062	8,928	107,142	54.35	2,174	9,413	112,961
46.00	1,840	7,967	95,606	48.80	1,952	8,452	101,426	51.60	2,064	8,937	107,245	54.40	2,176	9,411	113,070
46.05	1,842	7,976	95,710	48.85	1,954	8,461	101,530	51.65	2,066	8,946	107,349	54.45	2,178	9,420	113,174
46.10	1,844	7,985	95,814	48.90	1,956	8,469	101,634	51.70	2,068	8,954	107,453	54.50	2,180	9,429	113,278
46.15	1,846	7,993	95,918	48.95	1,958	8,478	101,738	51.75	2,070	8,963	107,557	54.55	2,182	9,437	113,382
46.20	1,848	8,002	96,022	49.00	1,960	8,487	101,842	51.80	2,072	8,972	107,661	54.60	2,184	9,446	113,486
46.25	1,850	8,010	96,126	49.05	1,962	8,495	101,946	51.85	2,074	8,980	107,765	54.65	2,186	9,454	113,590
46.30	1,852	8,019	96,230	49.10	1,964	8,504	102,049	51.90	2,076	8,989	107,869	54.70	2,188	9,463	113,694
46.35	1,854	8,028	96,334	49.15	1,966	8,513	102,153	51.95	2,078	8,998	107,973	54.75	2,190	9,472	113,798
46.40	1,856	8,036	96,438	49.20	1,968	8,521	102,257	52.00	2,080	9,006	108,077	54.80	2,192	9,480	113,902
46.45	1,858	8,045	96,542	49.25	1,970	8,530	102,361	52.05	2,082	9,015	108,181	54.85	2,194	9,489	114,006
46.50	1,860	8,054	96,646	49.30	1,972	8,539	102,465	52.10	2,084	9,024	108,285	54.90	2,196	9,498	114,110
46.55	1,862	8,062	96,750	49.35	1,974	8,547	102,569	52.15	2,086	9,032	108,389	54.95	2,198	9,506	114,214
46.60	1,864	8,071	96,853	49.40	1,976	8,556	102,673	52.20	2,088	9,041	108,492	55.00	2,200	9,515	114,318
46.65	1,866	8,080	96,957	49.45	1,978	8,565	102,777	52.25	2,090	9,050	108,596	55.05	2,202	9,524	114,421
46.70	1,868	8,088	97,061	49.50	1,980	8,573	102,881	52.30	2,092	9,058	108,700	55.10	2,204	9,532	114,525
46.75	1,870	8,097	97,165	49.55	1,982	8,582	102,985	52.35	2,094	9,067	108,804	55.15	2,206	9,541	114,629

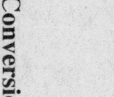

Salary Conversion Table

Hour	Week	Month	Year	Hour	Week	Month	Year	Hour	Week	Month	Year	Hour	Week	Month	Year
55.20	2,208	9,550	114,733	58.00	2,320	10,034	120,553	60.80	2,432	10,518	126,373	63.60	2,544	11,003	132,193
55.25	2,210	9,558	114,837	58.05	2,322	10,043	120,657	60.85	2,434	10,527	126,477	63.65	2,546	11,011	132,297
55.30	2,212	9,567	114,941	58.10	2,324	10,051	120,761	60.90	2,436	10,536	126,581	63.70	2,548	11,020	132,400
55.35	2,214	9,576	115,045	58.15	2,326	10,060	120,865	60.95	2,438	10,544	126,685	63.75	2,550	11,029	132,504
55.40	2,216	9,584	115,149	58.20	2,328	10,069	120,969	61.00	2,440	10,553	126,788	63.80	2,552	11,037	132,608
55.45	2,218	9,593	115,253	58.25	2,330	10,077	121,073	61.05	2,442	10,562	126,892	63.85	2,554	11,046	132,712
55.50	2,220	9,602	115,357	58.30	2,332	10,086	121,177	61.10	2,444	10,570	126,996	63.90	2,556	11,055	132,816
55.55	2,222	9,610	115,461	58.35	2,334	10,095	121,280	61.15	2,446	10,579	127,100	63.95	2,558	11,063	132,920
55.60	2,224	9,619	115,565	58.40	2,336	10,103	121,384	61.20	2,448	10,588	127,204	64.00	2,560	11,072	133,024
55.65	2,226	9,627	115,669	58.45	2,338	10,112	121,488	61.25	2,450	10,596	127,308	64.05	2,562	11,081	133,128
55.70	2,228	9,636	115,772	58.50	2,340	10,121	121,592	61.30	2,452	10,605	127,412	64.10	2,564	11,089	133,232
55.75	2,230	9,645	115,876	58.55	2,342	10,129	121,696	61.35	2,454	10,614	127,516	64.15	2,566	11,098	133,336
55.80	2,232	9,653	115,980	58.60	2,344	10,138	121,800	61.40	2,456	10,622	127,620	64.20	2,568	11,107	133,440
55.85	2,234	9,662	116,084	58.65	2,346	10,146	121,904	61.45	2,458	10,631	127,724	64.25	2,570	11,115	133,544
55.90	2,236	9,671	116,188	58.70	2,348	10,155	122,008	61.50	2,460	10,640	127,828	64.30	2,572	11,124	133,648
55.95	2,238	9,679	116,292	58.75	2,350	10,164	122,112	61.55	2,462	10,648	127,932	64.35	2,574	11,133	133,751
56.00	2,240	9,688	116,396	58.80	2,352	10,172	122,216	61.60	2,464	10,657	128,036	64.40	2,576	11,141	133,855
56.05	2,242	9,697	116,500	58.85	2,354	10,181	122,320	61.65	2,466	10,665	128,140	64.45	2,578	11,150	133,959
56.10	2,244	9,705	116,604	58.90	2,356	10,190	122,424	61.70	2,468	10,674	128,243	64.50	2,580	11,158	134,063
56.15	2,246	9,714	116,708	58.95	2,358	10,198	122,528	61.75	2,470	10,683	128,347	64.55	2,582	11,167	134,167
56.20	2,248	9,723	116,812	59.00	2,360	10,207	122,632	61.80	2,472	10,691	128,451	64.60	2,584	11,176	134,271
56.25	2,250	9,731	116,916	59.05	2,362	10,216	122,735	61.85	2,474	10,700	128,555	64.65	2,586	11,184	134,375
56.30	2,252	9,740	117,020	59.10	2,364	10,224	122,839	61.90	2,476	10,709	128,659	64.70	2,588	11,193	134,479
56.35	2,254	9,749	117,123	59.15	2,366	10,233	122,943	61.95	2,478	10,717	128,763	64.75	2,590	11,202	134,583
56.40	2,256	9,757	117,227	59.20	2,368	10,242	123,047	62.00	2,480	10,726	128,867	64.80	2,592	11,210	134,687
56.45	2,258	9,766	117,331	59.25	2,370	10,250	123,151	62.05	2,482	10,735	128,971	64.85	2,594	11,219	134,791
56.50	2,260	9,775	117,435	59.30	2,372	10,259	123,255	62.10	2,484	10,743	129,075	64.90	2,596	11,228	134,895
56.55	2,262	9,783	117,539	59.35	2,374	10,268	123,359	62.15	2,486	10,752	129,179	64.95	2,598	11,236	134,999
56.60	2,264	9,792	117,643	59.40	2,376	10,276	123,463	62.20	2,488	10,761	129,283	65.00	2,600	11,245	135,102
56.65	2,266	9,800	117,747	59.45	2,378	10,285	123,567	62.25	2,490	10,769	129,387	65.05	2,602	11,254	135,206
56.70	2,268	9,809	117,851	59.50	2,380	10,294	123,671	62.30	2,492	10,778	129,491	65.10	2,604	11,262	135,310
56.75	2,270	9,818	117,955	59.55	2,382	10,302	123,775	62.35	2,494	10,787	129,594	65.15	2,606	11,271	135,414
56.80	2,272	9,826	118,059	59.60	2,384	10,311	123,879	62.40	2,496	10,795	129,698	65.20	2,608	11,280	135,518
56.85	2,274	9,835	118,163	59.65	2,386	10,319	123,983	62.45	2,498	10,804	129,802	65.25	2,610	11,288	135,622
56.90	2,276	9,844	118,267	59.70	2,388	10,328	124,086	62.50	2,500	10,812	129,906	65.30	2,612	11,297	135,726
56.95	2,278	9,852	118,371	59.75	2,390	10,337	124,190	62.55	2,502	10,821	130,010	65.35	2,614	11,306	135,830
57.00	2,280	9,861	118,475	59.80	2,392	10,345	124,294	62.60	2,504	10,830	130,114	65.40	2,616	11,314	135,934
57.05	2,282	9,870	118,578	59.85	2,394	10,354	124,398	62.65	2,506	10,838	130,218	65.45	2,618	11,323	136,038
57.10	2,284	9,878	118,682	59.90	2,396	10,363	124,502	62.70	2,508	10,847	130,322	65.50	2,620	11,331	136,142
57.15	2,286	9,887	118,786	59.95	2,398	10,371	124,606	62.75	2,510	10,856	130,426	65.55	2,622	11,340	136,246
57.20	2,288	9,896	118,890	60.00	2,400	10,380	124,710	62.80	2,512	10,864	130,530	65.60	2,624	11,349	136,350
57.25	2,290	9,904	118,994	60.05	2,402	10,389	124,814	62.85	2,514	10,873	130,634	65.65	2,626	11,357	136,454
57.30	2,292	9,913	119,098	60.10	2,404	10,397	124,918	62.90	2,516	10,882	130,738	65.70	2,628	11,366	136,557
57.35	2,294	9,922	119,202	60.15	2,406	10,406	125,022	62.95	2,518	10,890	130,842	65.75	2,630	11,375	136,661
57.40	2,296	9,930	119,306	60.20	2,408	10,415	125,126	63.00	2,520	10,899	130,945	65.80	2,632	11,383	136,765
57.45	2,298	9,939	119,410	60.25	2,410	10,423	125,230	63.05	2,522	10,908	131,049	65.85	2,634	11,392	136,869
57.50	2,300	9,947	119,514	60.30	2,412	10,432	125,334	63.10	2,524	10,916	131,153	65.90	2,636	11,401	136,973
57.55	2,302	9,956	119,618	60.35	2,414	10,441	125,437	63.15	2,526	10,925	131,257	65.95	2,638	11,409	137,077
57.60	2,304	9,965	119,722	60.40	2,416	10,449	125,541	63.20	2,528	10,934	131,361	66.00	2,640	11,418	137,181
57.65	2,306	9,973	119,826	60.45	2,418	10,458	125,645	63.25	2,530	10,942	131,465	66.05	2,642	11,427	137,285
57.70	2,308	9,982	119,929	60.50	2,420	10,467	125,749	63.30	2,532	10,951	131,569	66.10	2,644	11,435	137,389
57.75	2,310	9,991	120,033	60.55	2,422	10,475	125,853	63.35	2,534	10,960	131,673	66.15	2,646	11,444	137,493
57.80	2,312	9,999	120,137	60.60	2,424	10,484	125,957	63.40	2,536	10,968	131,777	66.20	2,648	11,453	137,597
57.85	2,314	10,008	120,241	60.65	2,426	10,492	126,061	63.45	2,538	10,977	131,881	66.25	2,650	11,461	137,701
57.90	2,316	10,017	120,345	60.70	2,428	10,501	126,165	63.50	2,540	10,985	131,985	66.30	2,652	11,470	137,805
57.95	2,318	10,025	120,449	60.75	2,430	10,510	126,269	63.55	2,542	10,994	132,089	66.35	2,654	11,479	137,908

Hour	Week	Month	Year	Hour	Week	Month	Year	Hour	Week	Month	Year	Hour	Week	Month	Year
66.40	2,656	11,487	138,012	69.20	2,768	11,972	143,832	72.00	2,880	12,456	149,652	74.80	2,992	12,940	155,472
66.45	2,658	11,496	138,116	69.25	2,770	11,980	143,936	72.05	2,882	12,465	149,756	74.85	2,994	12,949	155,576
66.50	2,660	11,504	138,220	69.30	2,772	11,989	144,040	72.10	2,884	12,473	149,860	74.90	2,996	12,958	155,680
66.55	2,662	11,513	138,324	69.35	2,774	11,998	144,144	72.15	2,886	12,482	149,964	74.95	2,998	12,966	155,784
66.60	2,664	11,522	138,428	69.40	2,776	12,006	144,248	72.20	2,888	12,491	150,068	75.00	3,000	12,975	155,887
66.65	2,666	11,530	138,532	69.45	2,778	12,015	144,352	72.25	2,890	12,499	150,172	75.05	3,002	12,984	155,991
66.70	2,668	11,539	138,636	69.50	2,780	12,023	144,456	72.30	2,892	12,508	150,276	75.10	3,004	12,992	156,095
66.75	2,670	11,548	138,740	69.55	2,782	12,032	144,560	72.35	2,894	12,517	150,379	75.15	3,006	13,001	156,199
66.80	2,672	11,556	138,844	69.60	2,784	12,041	144,664	72.40	2,896	12,525	150,483	75.20	3,008	13,010	156,303
66.85	2,674	11,565	138,948	69.65	2,786	12,049	144,768	72.45	2,898	12,534	150,587	75.25	3,010	13,018	156,407
66.90	2,676	11,574	139,052	69.70	2,788	12,058	144,871	72.50	2,900	12,542	150,691	75.30	3,012	13,027	156,511
66.95	2,678	11,582	139,156	69.75	2,790	12,067	144,975	72.55	2,902	12,551	150,795	75.35	3,014	13,036	156,615
67.00	2,680	11,591	139,259	69.80	2,792	12,075	145,079	72.60	2,904	12,560	150,899	75.40	3,016	13,044	156,719
67.05	2,682	11,600	139,363	69.85	2,794	12,084	145,183	72.65	2,906	12,568	151,003	75.45	3,018	13,053	156,823
67.10	2,684	11,608	139,467	69.90	2,796	12,093	145,287	72.70	2,908	12,577	151,107	75.50	3,020	13,061	156,927
67.15	2,686	11,617	139,571	69.95	2,798	12,101	145,391	72.75	2,910	12,586	151,211	75.55	3,022	13,070	157,031
67.20	2,688	11,626	139,675	70.00	2,800	12,110	145,495	72.80	2,912	12,594	151,315	75.60	3,024	13,079	157,135
67.25	2,690	11,634	139,779	70.05	2,802	12,119	145,599	72.85	2,914	12,603	151,419	75.65	3,026	13,087	157,239
67.30	2,692	11,643	139,883	70.10	2,804	12,127	145,703	72.90	2,916	12,612	151,523	75.70	3,028	13,096	157,342
67.35	2,694	11,652	139,987	70.15	2,806	12,136	145,807	72.95	2,918	12,620	151,627	75.75	3,030	13,105	157,446
67.40	2,696	11,660	140,091	70.20	2,808	12,145	145,911	73.00	2,920	12,629	151,730	75.80	3,032	13,113	157,550
67.45	2,698	11,669	140,195	70.25	2,810	12,153	146,015	73.05	2,922	12,638	151,834	75.85	3,034	13,122	157,654
67.50	2,700	11,677	140,299	70.30	2,812	12,162	146,119	73.10	2,924	12,646	151,938	75.90	3,036	13,131	157,758
67.55	2,702	11,686	140,403	70.35	2,814	12,171	146,222	73.15	2,926	12,655	152,042	75.95	3,038	13,139	157,862
67.60	2,704	11,695	140,507	70.40	2,816	12,179	146,326	73.20	2,928	12,664	152,146	76.00	3,040	13,148	157,966
67.65	2,706	11,703	140,611	70.45	2,818	12,188	146,430	73.25	2,930	12,672	152,250	76.05	3,042	13,157	158,070
67.70	2,708	11,712	140,714	70.50	2,820	12,196	146,534	73.30	2,932	12,681	152,354	76.10	3,044	13,165	158,174
67.75	2,710	11,721	140,818	70.55	2,822	12,205	146,638	73.35	2,934	12,690	152,458	76.15	3,046	13,174	158,278
67.80	2,712	11,729	140,922	70.60	2,824	12,214	146,742	73.40	2,936	12,698	152,562	76.20	3,048	13,183	158,382
67.85	2,714	11,738	141,026	70.65	2,826	12,222	146,846	73.45	2,938	12,707	152,666	76.25	3,050	13,191	158,486
67.90	2,716	11,747	141,130	70.70	2,828	12,231	146,950	73.50	2,940	12,715	152,770	76.30	3,052	13,200	158,590
67.95	2,718	11,755	141,234	70.75	2,830	12,240	147,054	73.55	2,942	12,724	152,874	76.35	3,054	13,209	158,693
68.00	2,720	11,764	141,338	70.80	2,832	12,248	147,158	73.60	2,944	12,733	152,978	76.40	3,056	13,217	158,797
68.05	2,722	11,773	141,442	70.85	2,834	12,257	147,262	73.65	2,946	12,741	153,082	76.45	3,058	13,226	158,901
68.10	2,724	11,781	141,546	70.90	2,836	12,266	147,366	73.70	2,948	12,750	153,185	76.50	3,060	13,234	159,005
68.15	2,726	11,790	141,650	70.95	2,838	12,274	147,470	73.75	2,950	12,759	153,289	76.55	3,062	13,243	159,109
68.20	2,728	11,799	141,754	71.00	2,840	12,283	147,573	73.80	2,952	12,767	153,393	76.60	3,064	13,252	159,213
68.25	2,730	11,807	141,858	71.05	2,842	12,292	147,677	73.85	2,954	12,776	153,497	76.65	3,066	13,260	159,317
68.30	2,732	11,816	141,962	71.10	2,844	12,300	147,781	73.90	2,956	12,785	153,601	76.70	3,068	13,269	159,421
68.35	2,734	11,825	142,065	71.15	2,846	12,309	147,885	73.95	2,958	12,793	153,705	76.75	3,070	13,278	159,525
68.40	2,736	11,833	142,169	71.20	2,848	12,318	147,989	74.00	2,960	12,802	153,809	76.80	3,072	13,286	159,629
68.45	2,738	11,842	142,273	71.25	2,850	12,326	148,093	74.05	2,962	12,811	153,913	76.85	3,074	13,295	159,733
68.50	2,740	11,850	142,377	71.30	2,852	12,335	148,197	74.10	2,964	12,819	154,017	76.90	3,076	13,304	159,837
68.55	2,742	11,859	142,481	71.35	2,854	12,344	148,301	74.15	2,966	12,828	154,121	76.95	3,078	13,312	159,941
68.60	2,744	11,868	142,585	71.40	2,856	12,352	148,405	74.20	2,968	12,837	154,225	77.00	3,080	13,321	160,044
68.65	2,746	11,876	142,689	71.45	2,858	12,361	148,509	74.25	2,970	12,845	154,329	77.05	3,082	13,330	160,148
68.70	2,748	11,885	142,793	71.50	2,860	12,369	148,613	74.30	2,972	12,854	154,433	77.10	3,084	13,338	160,252
68.75	2,750	11,894	142,897	71.55	2,862	12,378	148,717	74.35	2,974	12,863	154,536	77.15	3,086	13,347	160,356
68.80	2,752	11,902	143,001	71.60	2,864	12,387	148,821	74.40	2,976	12,871	154,640	77.20	3,088	13,356	160,460
68.85	2,754	11,911	143,105	71.65	2,866	12,395	148,925	74.45	2,978	12,880	154,744	77.25	3,090	13,364	160,564
68.90	2,756	11,920	143,209	71.70	2,868	12,404	149,028	74.50	2,980	12,888	154,848	77.30	3,092	13,373	160,668
68.95	2,758	11,928	143,313	71.75	2,870	12,413	149,132	74.55	2,982	12,897	154,952	77.35	3,094	13,382	160,772
69.00	2,760	11,937	143,416	71.80	2,872	12,421	149,236	74.60	2,984	12,906	155,056	77.40	3,096	13,390	160,876
69.05	2,762	11,946	143,520	71.85	2,874	12,430	149,340	74.65	2,986	12,914	155,160	77.45	3,098	13,399	160,980
69.10	2,764	11,954	143,624	71.90	2,876	12,439	149,444	74.70	2,988	12,923	155,264	77.50	3,100	13,407	161,084
69.15	2,766	11,963	143,728	71.95	2,878	12,447	149,548	74.75	2,990	12,932	155,368	77.55	3,102	13,416	161,188

Hour	Week	Month	Year	Hour	Week	Month	Year	Hour	Week	Month	Year	Hour	Week	Month	Year
77.60	3,104	13,425	161,292	80.40	3,216	13,909	167,111	83.20	3,328	14,394	172,931	86.00	3,440	14,878	178,751
77.65	3,106	13,433	161,396	80.45	3,218	13,918	167,215	83.25	3,330	14,402	173,035	86.05	3,442	14,887	178,855
77.70	3,108	13,442	161,499	80.50	3,220	13,926	167,319	83.30	3,332	14,411	173,139	86.10	3,444	14,895	178,959
77.75	3,110	13,451	161,603	80.55	3,222	13,935	167,423	83.35	3,334	14,420	173,243	86.15	3,446	14,904	179,063
77.80	3,112	13,459	161,707	80.60	3,224	13,944	167,527	83.40	3,336	14,428	173,347	86.20	3,448	14,913	179,167
77.85	3,114	13,468	161,811	80.65	3,226	13,952	167,631	83.45	3,338	14,437	173,451	86.25	3,450	14,921	179,271
77.90	3,116	13,477	161,915	80.70	3,228	13,961	167,735	83.50	3,340	14,445	173,555	86.30	3,452	14,930	179,375
77.95	3,118	13,485	162,019	80.75	3,230	13,970	167,839	83.55	3,342	14,454	173,659	86.35	3,454	14,939	179,478
78.00	3,120	13,494	162,123	80.80	3,232	13,978	167,943	83.60	3,344	14,463	173,763	86.40	3,456	14,947	179,582
78.05	3,122	13,503	162,227	80.85	3,234	13,987	168,047	83.65	3,346	14,471	173,867	86.45	3,458	14,956	179,686
78.10	3,124	13,511	162,331	80.90	3,236	13,996	168,151	83.70	3,348	14,480	173,970	86.50	3,460	14,964	179,790
78.15	3,126	13,520	162,435	80.95	3,238	14,004	168,255	83.75	3,350	14,489	174,074	86.55	3,462	14,973	179,894
78.20	3,128	13,529	162,539	81.00	3,240	14,013	168,358	83.80	3,352	14,497	174,178	86.60	3,464	14,982	179,998
78.25	3,130	13,537	162,643	81.05	3,242	14,022	168,462	83.85	3,354	14,506	174,282	86.65	3,466	14,990	180,102
78.30	3,132	13,546	162,747	81.10	3,244	14,030	168,566	83.90	3,356	14,515	174,386	86.70	3,468	14,999	180,206
78.35	3,134	13,555	162,850	81.15	3,246	14,039	168,670	83.95	3,358	14,523	174,490	86.75	3,470	15,008	180,310
78.40	3,136	13,563	162,954	81.20	3,248	14,048	168,774	84.00	3,360	14,532	174,594	86.80	3,472	15,016	180,414
78.45	3,138	13,572	163,058	81.25	3,250	14,056	168,878	84.05	3,362	14,541	174,698	86.85	3,474	15,025	180,518
78.50	3,140	13,580	163,162	81.30	3,252	14,065	168,982	84.10	3,364	14,549	174,802	86.90	3,476	15,034	180,622
78.55	3,142	13,589	163,266	81.35	3,254	14,074	169,086	84.15	3,366	14,558	174,906	86.95	3,478	15,042	180,726
78.60	3,144	13,598	163,370	81.40	3,256	14,082	169,190	84.20	3,368	14,567	175,010	87.00	3,480	15,051	180,829
78.65	3,146	13,606	163,474	81.45	3,258	14,091	169,294	84.25	3,370	14,575	175,114	87.05	3,482	15,060	180,933
78.70	3,148	13,615	163,578	81.50	3,260	14,099	169,398	84.30	3,372	14,584	175,218	87.10	3,484	15,068	181,037
78.75	3,150	13,624	163,682	81.55	3,262	14,108	169,502	84.35	3,374	14,593	175,321	87.15	3,486	15,077	181,141
78.80	3,152	13,632	163,786	81.60	3,264	14,117	169,606	84.40	3,376	14,601	175,425	87.20	3,488	15,086	181,245
78.85	3,154	13,641	163,890	81.65	3,266	14,125	169,710	84.45	3,378	14,610	175,529	87.25	3,490	15,094	181,349
78.90	3,156	13,650	163,994	81.70	3,268	14,134	169,813	84.50	3,380	14,618	175,633	87.30	3,492	15,103	181,453
78.95	3,158	13,658	164,098	81.75	3,270	14,143	169,917	84.55	3,382	14,627	175,737	87.35	3,494	15,112	181,557
79.00	3,160	13,667	164,201	81.80	3,272	14,151	170,021	84.60	3,384	14,636	175,841	87.40	3,496	15,120	181,661
79.05	3,162	13,676	164,305	81.85	3,274	14,160	170,125	84.65	3,386	14,644	175,945	87.45	3,498	15,129	181,765
79.10	3,164	13,684	164,409	81.90	3,276	14,169	170,229	84.70	3,388	14,653	176,049	87.50	3,500	15,137	181,869
79.15	3,166	13,693	164,513	81.95	3,278	14,177	170,333	84.75	3,390	14,662	176,153	87.55	3,502	15,146	181,973
79.20	3,168	13,702	164,617	82.00	3,280	14,186	170,437	84.80	3,392	14,670	176,257	87.60	3,504	15,155	182,077
79.25	3,170	13,710	164,721	82.05	3,282	14,195	170,541	84.85	3,394	14,679	176,361	87.65	3,506	15,163	182,181
79.30	3,172	13,719	164,825	82.10	3,284	14,203	170,645	84.90	3,396	14,688	176,465	87.70	3,508	15,172	182,284
79.35	3,174	13,728	164,929	82.15	3,286	14,212	170,749	84.95	3,398	14,696	176,569	87.75	3,510	15,181	182,388
79.40	3,176	13,736	165,033	82.20	3,288	14,221	170,853	85.00	3,400	14,705	176,672	87.80	3,512	15,189	182,492
79.45	3,178	13,745	165,137	82.25	3,290	14,229	170,957	85.05	3,402	14,714	176,776	87.85	3,514	15,198	182,596
79.50	3,180	13,753	165,241	82.30	3,292	14,238	171,061	85.10	3,404	14,722	176,880	87.90	3,516	15,207	182,700
79.55	3,182	13,762	165,345	82.35	3,294	14,247	171,164	85.15	3,406	14,731	176,984	87.95	3,518	15,215	182,804
79.60	3,184	13,771	165,449	82.40	3,296	14,255	171,268	85.20	3,408	14,740	177,088	88.00	3,520	15,224	182,908
79.65	3,186	13,779	165,553	82.45	3,298	14,264	171,372	85.25	3,410	14,748	177,192	88.05	3,522	15,233	183,012
79.70	3,188	13,788	165,656	82.50	3,300	14,272	171,476	85.30	3,412	14,757	177,296	88.10	3,524	15,241	183,116
79.75	3,190	13,797	165,760	82.55	3,302	14,281	171,580	85.35	3,414	14,766	177,400	88.15	3,526	15,250	183,220
79.80	3,192	13,805	165,864	82.60	3,304	14,290	171,684	85.40	3,416	14,774	177,504	88.20	3,528	15,259	183,324
79.85	3,194	13,814	165,968	82.65	3,306	14,298	171,788	85.45	3,418	14,783	177,608	88.25	3,530	15,267	183,428
79.90	3,196	13,823	166,072	82.70	3,308	14,307	171,892	85.50	3,420	14,791	177,712	88.30	3,532	15,276	183,532
79.95	3,198	13,831	166,176	82.75	3,310	14,316	171,996	85.55	3,422	14,800	177,816	88.35	3,534	15,285	183,635
80.00	3,200	13,840	166,280	82.80	3,312	14,324	172,100	85.60	3,424	14,809	177,920	88.40	3,536	15,293	183,739
80.05	3,202	13,849	166,384	82.85	3,314	14,333	172,204	85.65	3,426	14,817	178,024	88.45	3,538	15,302	183,843
80.10	3,204	13,857	166,488	82.90	3,316	14,342	172,308	85.70	3,428	14,826	178,127	88.50	3,540	15,310	183,947
80.15	3,206	13,866	166,592	82.95	3,318	14,350	172,412	85.75	3,430	14,835	178,231	88.55	3,542	15,319	184,051
80.20	3,208	13,875	166,696	83.00	3,320	14,359	172,515	85.80	3,432	14,843	178,335	88.60	3,544	15,328	184,155
80.25	3,210	13,883	166,800	83.05	3,322	14,368	172,619	85.85	3,434	14,852	178,439	88.65	3,546	15,336	184,259
80.30	3,212	13,892	166,904	83.10	3,324	14,376	172,723	85.90	3,436	14,861	178,543	88.70	3,548	15,345	184,363
80.35	3,214	13,901	167,007	83.15	3,326	14,385	172,827	85.95	3,438	14,869	178,647	88.75	3,550	15,354	184,467

Hour	Week	Month	Year	Hour	Week	Month	Year	Hour	Week	Month	Year	Hour	Week	Month	Year
88.80	3,552	15,362	184,571	91.60	3,664	15,847	190,391	94.40	3,776	16,331	196,210	97.20	3,888	16,816	202,030
88.85	3,554	15,371	184,675	91.65	3,666	15,855	190,495	94.45	3,778	16,340	196,314	97.25	3,890	16,824	202,134
88.90	3,556	15,380	184,779	91.70	3,668	15,864	190,598	94.50	3,780	16,348	196,418	97.30	3,892	16,833	202,238
88.95	3,558	15,388	184,883	91.75	3,670	15,873	190,702	94.55	3,782	16,357	196,522	97.35	3,894	16,842	202,342
89.00	3,560	15,397	184,986	91.80	3,672	15,881	190,806	94.60	3,784	16,366	196,626	97.40	3,896	16,850	202,446
89.05	3,562	15,406	185,090	91.85	3,674	15,890	190,910	94.65	3,786	16,374	196,730	97.45	3,898	16,859	202,550
89.10	3,564	15,414	185,194	91.90	3,676	15,899	191,014	94.70	3,788	16,383	196,834	97.50	3,900	16,867	202,654
89.15	3,566	15,423	185,298	91.95	3,678	15,907	191,118	94.75	3,790	16,392	196,938	97.55	3,902	16,876	202,758
89.20	3,568	15,432	185,402	92.00	3,680	15,916	191,222	94.80	3,792	16,400	197,042	97.60	3,904	16,885	202,862
89.25	3,570	15,440	185,506	92.05	3,682	15,925	191,326	94.85	3,794	16,409	197,146	97.65	3,906	16,893	202,966
89.30	3,572	15,449	185,610	92.10	3,684	15,933	191,430	94.90	3,796	16,418	197,250	97.70	3,908	16,902	203,069
89.35	3,574	15,458	185,714	92.15	3,686	15,942	191,534	94.95	3,798	16,426	197,354	97.75	3,910	16,911	203,173
89.40	3,576	15,466	185,818	92.20	3,688	15,951	191,638	95.00	3,800	16,435	197,457	97.80	3,912	16,919	203,277
89.45	3,578	15,475	185,922	92.25	3,690	15,959	191,742	95.05	3,802	16,444	197,561	97.85	3,914	16,928	203,381
89.50	3,580	15,483	186,026	92.30	3,692	15,968	191,846	95.10	3,804	16,452	197,665	97.90	3,916	16,937	203,485
89.55	3,582	15,492	186,130	92.35	3,694	15,977	191,949	95.15	3,806	16,461	197,769	97.95	3,918	16,945	203,589
89.60	3,584	15,501	186,234	92.40	3,696	15,985	192,053	95.20	3,808	16,470	197,873	98.00	3,920	16,954	203,693
89.65	3,586	15,509	186,338	92.45	3,698	15,994	192,157	95.25	3,810	16,478	197,977	98.05	3,922	16,963	203,797
89.70	3,588	15,518	186,441	92.50	3,700	16,002	192,261	95.30	3,812	16,487	198,081	98.10	3,924	16,971	203,901
89.75	3,590	15,527	186,545	92.55	3,702	16,011	192,365	95.35	3,814	16,496	198,185	98.15	3,926	16,980	204,005
89.80	3,592	15,535	186,649	92.60	3,704	16,020	192,469	95.40	3,816	16,504	198,289	98.20	3,928	16,989	204,109
89.85	3,594	15,544	186,753	92.65	3,706	16,028	192,573	95.45	3,818	16,513	198,393	98.25	3,930	16,997	204,213
89.90	3,596	15,553	186,857	92.70	3,708	16,037	192,677	95.50	3,820	16,521	198,497	98.30	3,932	17,006	204,317
89.95	3,598	15,561	186,961	92.75	3,710	16,046	192,781	95.55	3,822	16,530	198,601	98.35	3,934	17,015	204,420
90.00	3,600	15,570	187,065	92.80	3,712	16,054	192,885	95.60	3,824	16,539	198,705	98.40	3,936	17,023	204,524
90.05	3,602	15,579	187,169	92.85	3,714	16,063	192,989	95.65	3,826	16,547	198,809	98.45	3,938	17,032	204,628
90.10	3,604	15,587	187,273	92.90	3,716	16,072	193,093	95.70	3,828	16,556	198,912	98.50	3,940	17,040	204,732
90.15	3,606	15,596	187,377	92.95	3,718	16,080	193,197	95.75	3,830	16,565	199,016	98.55	3,942	17,049	204,836
90.20	3,608	15,605	187,481	93.00	3,720	16,089	193,300	95.80	3,832	16,573	199,120	98.60	3,944	17,058	204,940
90.25	3,610	15,613	187,585	93.05	3,722	16,098	193,404	95.85	3,834	16,582	199,224	98.65	3,946	17,066	205,044
90.30	3,612	15,622	187,689	93.10	3,724	16,106	193,508	95.90	3,836	16,591	199,328	98.70	3,948	17,075	205,148
90.35	3,614	15,631	187,792	93.15	3,726	16,115	193,612	95.95	3,838	16,599	199,432	98.75	3,950	17,084	205,252
90.40	3,616	15,639	187,896	93.20	3,728	16,124	193,716	96.00	3,840	16,608	199,536	98.80	3,952	17,092	205,356
90.45	3,618	15,648	188,000	93.25	3,730	16,132	193,820	96.05	3,842	16,617	199,640	98.85	3,954	17,101	205,460
90.50	3,620	15,656	188,104	93.30	3,732	16,141	193,924	96.10	3,844	16,625	199,744	98.90	3,956	17,110	205,564
90.55	3,622	15,665	188,208	93.35	3,734	16,150	194,028	96.15	3,846	16,634	199,848	98.95	3,958	17,118	205,668
90.60	3,624	15,674	188,312	93.40	3,736	16,158	194,132	96.20	3,848	16,643	199,952	99.00	3,960	17,127	205,771
90.65	3,626	15,682	188,416	93.45	3,738	16,167	194,236	96.25	3,850	16,651	200,056	99.05	3,962	17,136	205,875
90.70	3,628	15,691	188,520	93.50	3,740	16,175	194,340	96.30	3,852	16,660	200,160	99.10	3,964	17,144	205,979
90.75	3,630	15,700	188,624	93.55	3,742	16,184	194,444	96.35	3,854	16,669	200,263	99.15	3,966	17,153	206,083
90.80	3,632	15,708	188,728	93.60	3,744	16,193	194,548	96.40	3,856	16,677	200,367	99.20	3,968	17,162	206,187
90.85	3,634	15,717	188,832	93.65	3,746	16,201	194,652	96.45	3,858	16,686	200,471	99.25	3,970	17,170	206,291
90.90	3,636	15,726	188,936	93.70	3,748	16,210	194,755	96.50	3,860	16,694	200,575	99.30	3,972	17,179	206,395
90.95	3,638	15,734	189,040	93.75	3,750	16,219	194,859	96.55	3,862	16,703	200,679	99.35	3,974	17,188	206,499
91.00	3,640	15,743	189,143	93.80	3,752	16,227	194,963	96.60	3,864	16,712	200,783	99.40	3,976	17,196	206,603
91.05	3,642	15,752	189,247	93.85	3,754	16,236	195,067	96.65	3,866	16,720	200,887	99.45	3,978	17,205	206,707
91.10	3,644	15,760	189,351	93.90	3,756	16,245	195,171	96.70	3,868	16,729	200,991	99.50	3,980	17,213	206,811
91.15	3,646	15,769	189,455	93.95	3,758	16,253	195,275	96.75	3,870	16,738	201,095	99.55	3,982	17,222	206,915
91.20	3,648	15,778	189,559	94.00	3,760	16,262	195,379	96.80	3,872	16,746	201,199	99.60	3,984	17,231	207,019
91.25	3,650	15,786	189,663	94.05	3,762	16,271	195,483	96.85	3,874	16,755	201,303	99.65	3,986	17,239	207,123
91.30	3,652	15,795	189,767	94.10	3,764	16,279	195,587	96.90	3,876	16,764	201,407	99.70	3,988	17,248	207,226
91.35	3,654	15,804	189,871	94.15	3,766	16,288	195,691	96.95	3,878	16,772	201,511	99.75	3,990	17,257	207,330
91.40	3,656	15,812	189,975	94.20	3,768	16,297	195,795	97.00	3,880	16,781	201,614	99.80	3,992	17,265	207,434
91.45	3,658	15,821	190,079	94.25	3,770	16,305	195,899	97.05	3,882	16,790	201,718	99.85	3,994	17,274	207,538
91.50	3,660	15,829	190,183	94.30	3,772	16,314	196,003	97.10	3,884	16,798	201,822	99.90	3,996	17,283	207,642
91.55	3,662	15,838	190,287	94.35	3,774	16,323	196,106	97.15	3,886	16,807	201,926	99.95	3,998	17,291	207,746

Hour	Week	Month	Year	Hour	Week	Month	Year	Hour	Week	Month	Year	Hour	Week	Month	Year
100.00	4,000	17,300	207,850	102.80	4,112	17,784	213,670	105.60	4,224	18,269	219,490	108.40	4,336	18,753	225,309
100.05	4,002	17,309	207,954	102.85	4,114	17,793	213,774	105.65	4,226	18,277	219,594	108.45	4,338	18,762	225,413
100.10	4,004	17,317	208,058	102.90	4,116	17,802	213,878	105.70	4,228	18,286	219,697	108.50	4,340	18,770	225,517
100.15	4,006	17,326	208,162	102.95	4,118	17,810	213,982	105.75	4,230	18,295	219,801	108.55	4,342	18,779	225,621
100.20	4,008	17,335	208,266	103.00	4,120	17,819	214,085	105.80	4,232	18,303	219,905	108.60	4,344	18,788	225,725
100.25	4,010	17,343	208,370	103.05	4,122	17,828	214,189	105.85	4,234	18,312	220,009	108.65	4,346	18,796	225,829
100.30	4,012	17,352	208,474	103.10	4,124	17,836	214,293	105.90	4,236	18,321	220,113	108.70	4,348	18,805	225,933
100.35	4,014	17,361	208,577	103.15	4,126	17,845	214,397	105.95	4,238	18,329	220,217	108.75	4,350	18,814	226,037
100.40	4,016	17,369	208,681	103.20	4,128	17,854	214,501	106.00	4,240	18,338	220,321	108.80	4,352	18,822	226,141
100.45	4,018	17,378	208,785	103.25	4,130	17,862	214,605	106.05	4,242	18,347	220,425	108.85	4,354	18,831	226,245
100.50	4,020	17,386	208,889	103.30	4,132	17,871	214,709	106.10	4,244	18,355	220,529	108.90	4,356	18,840	226,349
100.55	4,022	17,395	208,993	103.35	4,134	17,880	214,813	106.15	4,246	18,364	220,633	108.95	4,358	18,848	226,453
100.60	4,024	17,404	209,097	103.40	4,136	17,888	214,917	106.20	4,248	18,373	220,737	109.00	4,360	18,857	226,556
100.65	4,026	17,412	209,201	103.45	4,138	17,897	215,021	106.25	4,250	18,381	220,841	109.05	4,362	18,866	226,660
100.70	4,028	17,421	209,305	103.50	4,140	17,905	215,125	106.30	4,252	18,390	220,945	109.10	4,364	18,874	226,764
100.75	4,030	17,430	209,409	103.55	4,142	17,914	215,229	106.35	4,254	18,399	221,048	109.15	4,366	18,883	226,868
100.80	4,032	17,438	209,513	103.60	4,144	17,923	215,333	106.40	4,256	18,407	221,152	109.20	4,368	18,892	226,972
100.85	4,034	17,447	209,617	103.65	4,146	17,931	215,437	106.45	4,258	18,416	221,256	109.25	4,370	18,900	227,076
100.90	4,036	17,456	209,721	103.70	4,148	17,940	215,540	106.50	4,260	18,424	221,360	109.30	4,372	18,909	227,180
100.95	4,038	17,464	209,825	103.75	4,150	17,949	215,644	106.55	4,262	18,433	221,464	109.35	4,374	18,918	227,284
101.00	4,040	17,473	209,928	103.80	4,152	17,957	215,748	106.60	4,264	18,442	221,568	109.40	4,376	18,926	227,388
101.05	4,042	17,482	210,032	103.85	4,154	17,966	215,852	106.65	4,266	18,450	221,672	109.45	4,378	18,935	227,492
101.10	4,044	17,490	210,136	103.90	4,156	17,975	215,956	106.70	4,268	18,459	221,776	109.50	4,380	18,943	227,596
101.15	4,046	17,499	210,240	103.95	4,158	17,983	216,060	106.75	4,270	18,468	221,880	109.55	4,382	18,952	227,700
101.20	4,048	17,508	210,344	104.00	4,160	17,992	216,164	106.80	4,272	18,476	221,984	109.60	4,384	18,961	227,804
101.25	4,050	17,516	210,448	104.05	4,162	18,001	216,268	106.85	4,274	18,485	222,088	109.65	4,386	18,969	227,908
101.30	4,052	17,525	210,552	104.10	4,164	18,009	216,372	106.90	4,276	18,494	222,192	109.70	4,388	18,978	228,011
101.35	4,054	17,534	210,656	104.15	4,166	18,018	216,476	106.95	4,278	18,502	222,296	109.75	4,390	18,987	228,115
101.40	4,056	17,542	210,760	104.20	4,168	18,027	216,580	107.00	4,280	18,511	222,399	109.80	4,392	18,995	228,219
101.45	4,058	17,551	210,864	104.25	4,170	18,035	216,684	107.05	4,282	18,520	222,503	109.85	4,394	19,004	228,323
101.50	4,060	17,559	210,968	104.30	4,172	18,044	216,788	107.10	4,284	18,528	222,607	109.90	4,396	19,013	228,427
101.55	4,062	17,568	211,072	104.35	4,174	18,053	216,891	107.15	4,286	18,537	222,711	109.95	4,398	19,021	228,531
101.60	4,064	17,577	211,176	104.40	4,176	18,061	216,995	107.20	4,288	18,546	222,815	110.00	4,400	19,030	228,635
101.65	4,066	17,585	211,280	104.45	4,178	18,070	217,099	107.25	4,290	18,554	222,919	110.05	4,402	19,039	228,739
101.70	4,068	17,594	211,383	104.50	4,180	18,078	217,203	107.30	4,292	18,563	223,023	110.10	4,404	19,047	228,843
101.75	4,070	17,603	211,487	104.55	4,182	18,087	217,307	107.35	4,294	18,572	223,127	110.15	4,406	19,056	228,947
101.80	4,072	17,611	211,591	104.60	4,184	18,096	217,411	107.40	4,296	18,580	223,231	110.20	4,408	19,065	229,051
101.85	4,074	17,620	211,695	104.65	4,186	18,104	217,515	107.45	4,298	18,589	223,335	110.25	4,410	19,073	229,155
101.90	4,076	17,629	211,799	104.70	4,188	18,113	217,619	107.50	4,300	18,597	223,439	110.30	4,412	19,082	229,259
101.95	4,078	17,637	211,903	104.75	4,190	18,122	217,723	107.55	4,302	18,606	223,543	110.35	4,414	19,091	229,362
102.00	4,080	17,646	212,007	104.80	4,192	18,130	217,827	107.60	4,304	18,615	223,647	110.40	4,416	19,099	229,466
102.05	4,082	17,655	212,111	104.85	4,194	18,139	217,931	107.65	4,306	18,623	223,751	110.45	4,418	19,108	229,570
102.10	4,084	17,663	212,215	104.90	4,196	18,148	218,035	107.70	4,308	18,632	223,854	110.50	4,420	19,116	229,674
102.15	4,086	17,672	212,319	104.95	4,198	18,156	218,139	107.75	4,310	18,641	223,958	110.55	4,422	19,125	229,778
102.20	4,088	17,681	212,423	105.00	4,200	18,165	218,242	107.80	4,312	18,649	224,062	110.60	4,424	19,134	229,882
102.25	4,090	17,689	212,527	105.05	4,202	18,174	218,346	107.85	4,314	18,658	224,166	110.65	4,426	19,142	229,986
102.30	4,092	17,698	212,631	105.10	4,204	18,182	218,450	107.90	4,316	18,667	224,270	110.70	4,428	19,151	230,090
102.35	4,094	17,707	212,734	105.15	4,206	18,191	218,554	107.95	4,318	18,675	224,374	110.75	4,430	19,160	230,194
102.40	4,096	17,715	212,838	105.20	4,208	18,200	218,658	108.00	4,320	18,684	224,478	110.80	4,432	19,168	230,298
102.45	4,098	17,724	212,942	105.25	4,210	18,208	218,762	108.05	4,322	18,693	224,582	110.85	4,434	19,177	230,402
102.50	4,100	17,732	213,046	105.30	4,212	18,217	218,866	108.10	4,324	18,701	224,686	110.90	4,436	19,186	230,506
102.55	4,102	17,741	213,150	105.35	4,214	18,226	218,970	108.15	4,326	18,710	224,790	110.95	4,438	19,194	230,610
102.60	4,104	17,750	213,254	105.40	4,216	18,234	219,074	108.20	4,328	18,719	224,894	111.00	4,440	19,203	230,713
102.65	4,106	17,758	213,358	105.45	4,218	18,243	219,178	108.25	4,330	18,727	224,998	111.05	4,442	19,212	230,817
102.70	4,108	17,767	213,462	105.50	4,220	18,251	219,282	108.30	4,332	18,736	225,102	111.10	4,444	19,220	230,921
102.75	4,110	17,776	213,566	105.55	4,222	18,260	219,386	108.35	4,334	18,745	225,205	111.15	4,446	19,229	231,025

Hour	Week	Month	Year	Hour	Week	Month	Year	Hour	Week	Month	Year	Hour	Week	Month	Year
111.20	4,448	19,238	231,129	114.00	4,560	19,722	236,949	116.80	4,672	20,206	242,769	119.60	4,784	20,691	248,589
111.25	4,450	19,246	231,233	114.05	4,562	19,731	237,053	116.85	4,674	20,215	242,873	119.65	4,786	20,699	248,693
111.30	4,452	19,255	231,337	114.10	4,564	19,739	237,157	116.90	4,676	20,224	242,977	119.70	4,788	20,708	248,796
111.35	4,454	19,264	231,441	114.15	4,566	19,748	237,261	116.95	4,678	20,232	243,081	119.75	4,790	20,717	248,900
111.40	4,456	19,272	231,545	114.20	4,568	19,757	237,365	117.00	4,680	20,241	243,184	119.80	4,792	20,725	249,004
111.45	4,458	19,281	231,649	114.25	4,570	19,765	237,469	117.05	4,682	20,250	243,288	119.85	4,794	20,734	249,108
111.50	4,460	19,289	231,753	114.30	4,572	19,774	237,573	117.10	4,684	20,258	243,392	119.90	4,796	20,743	249,212
111.55	4,462	19,298	231,857	114.35	4,574	19,783	237,676	117.15	4,686	20,267	243,496	119.95	4,798	20,751	249,316
111.60	4,464	19,307	231,961	114.40	4,576	19,791	237,780	117.20	4,688	20,276	243,600	120.00	4,800	20,760	249,420
111.65	4,466	19,315	232,065	114.45	4,578	19,800	237,884	117.25	4,690	20,284	243,704	120.05	4,802	20,769	249,524
111.70	4,468	19,324	232,168	114.50	4,580	19,808	237,988	117.30	4,692	20,293	243,808	120.10	4,804	20,777	249,628
111.75	4,470	19,333	232,272	114.55	4,582	19,817	238,092	117.35	4,694	20,302	243,912	120.15	4,806	20,786	249,732
111.80	4,472	19,341	232,376	114.60	4,584	19,826	238,196	117.40	4,696	20,310	244,016	120.20	4,808	20,795	249,836
111.85	4,474	19,350	232,480	114.65	4,586	19,834	238,300	117.45	4,698	20,319	244,120	120.25	4,810	20,803	249,940
111.90	4,476	19,359	232,584	114.70	4,588	19,843	238,404	117.50	4,700	20,327	244,224	120.30	4,812	20,812	250,044
111.95	4,478	19,367	232,688	114.75	4,590	19,852	238,508	117.55	4,702	20,336	244,328	120.35	4,814	20,821	250,147
112.00	4,480	19,376	232,792	114.80	4,592	19,860	238,612	117.60	4,704	20,345	244,432	120.40	4,816	20,829	250,251
112.05	4,482	19,385	232,896	114.85	4,594	19,869	238,716	117.65	4,706	20,353	244,536	120.45	4,818	20,838	250,355
112.10	4,484	19,393	233,000	114.90	4,596	19,878	238,820	117.70	4,708	20,362	244,639	120.50	4,820	20,846	250,459
112.15	4,486	19,402	233,104	114.95	4,598	19,886	238,924	117.75	4,710	20,371	244,743	120.55	4,822	20,855	250,563
112.20	4,488	19,411	233,208	115.00	4,600	19,895	239,027	117.80	4,712	20,379	244,847	120.60	4,824	20,864	250,667
112.25	4,490	19,419	233,312	115.05	4,602	19,904	239,131	117.85	4,714	20,388	244,951	120.65	4,826	20,872	250,771
112.30	4,492	19,428	233,416	115.10	4,604	19,912	239,235	117.90	4,716	20,397	245,055	120.70	4,828	20,881	250,875
112.35	4,494	19,437	233,519	115.15	4,606	19,921	239,339	117.95	4,718	20,405	245,159	120.75	4,830	20,890	250,979
112.40	4,496	19,445	233,623	115.20	4,608	19,930	239,443	118.00	4,720	20,414	245,263	120.80	4,832	20,898	251,083
112.45	4,498	19,454	233,727	115.25	4,610	19,938	239,547	118.05	4,722	20,423	245,367	120.85	4,834	20,907	251,187
112.50	4,500	19,462	233,831	115.30	4,612	19,947	239,651	118.10	4,724	20,431	245,471	120.90	4,836	20,916	251,291
112.55	4,502	19,471	233,935	115.35	4,614	19,956	239,755	118.15	4,726	20,440	245,575	120.95	4,838	20,924	251,395
112.60	4,504	19,480	234,039	115.40	4,616	19,964	239,859	118.20	4,728	20,449	245,679	121.00	4,840	20,933	251,498
112.65	4,506	19,488	234,143	115.45	4,618	19,973	239,963	118.25	4,730	20,457	245,783	121.05	4,842	20,942	251,602
112.70	4,508	19,497	234,247	115.50	4,620	19,981	240,067	118.30	4,732	20,466	245,887	121.10	4,844	20,950	251,706
112.75	4,510	19,506	234,351	115.55	4,622	19,990	240,171	118.35	4,734	20,475	245,990	121.15	4,846	20,959	251,810
112.80	4,512	19,514	234,455	115.60	4,624	19,999	240,275	118.40	4,736	20,483	246,094	121.20	4,848	20,968	251,914
112.85	4,514	19,523	234,559	115.65	4,626	20,007	240,379	118.45	4,738	20,492	246,198	121.25	4,850	20,976	252,018
112.90	4,516	19,532	234,663	115.70	4,628	20,016	240,482	118.50	4,740	20,500	246,302	121.30	4,852	20,985	252,122
112.95	4,518	19,540	234,767	115.75	4,630	20,025	240,586	118.55	4,742	20,509	246,406	121.35	4,854	20,994	252,226
113.00	4,520	19,549	234,870	115.80	4,632	20,033	240,690	118.60	4,744	20,518	246,510	121.40	4,856	21,002	252,330
113.05	4,522	19,558	234,974	115.85	4,634	20,042	240,794	118.65	4,746	20,526	246,614	121.45	4,858	21,011	252,434
113.10	4,524	19,566	235,078	115.90	4,636	20,051	240,898	118.70	4,748	20,535	246,718	121.50	4,860	21,019	252,538
113.15	4,526	19,575	235,182	115.95	4,638	20,059	241,002	118.75	4,750	20,544	246,822	121.55	4,862	21,028	252,642
113.20	4,528	19,584	235,286	116.00	4,640	20,068	241,106	118.80	4,752	20,552	246,926	121.60	4,864	21,037	252,746
113.25	4,530	19,592	235,390	116.05	4,642	20,077	241,210	118.85	4,754	20,561	247,030	121.65	4,866	21,045	252,850
113.30	4,532	19,601	235,494	116.10	4,644	20,085	241,314	118.90	4,756	20,570	247,134	121.70	4,868	21,054	252,953
113.35	4,534	19,610	235,598	116.15	4,646	20,094	241,418	118.95	4,758	20,578	247,238	121.75	4,870	21,063	253,057
113.40	4,536	19,618	235,702	116.20	4,648	20,103	241,522	119.00	4,760	20,587	247,341	121.80	4,872	21,071	253,161
113.45	4,538	19,627	235,806	116.25	4,650	20,111	241,626	119.05	4,762	20,596	247,445	121.85	4,874	21,080	253,265
113.50	4,540	19,635	235,910	116.30	4,652	20,120	241,730	119.10	4,764	20,604	247,549	121.90	4,876	21,089	253,369
113.55	4,542	19,644	236,014	116.35	4,654	20,129	241,833	119.15	4,766	20,613	247,653	121.95	4,878	21,097	253,473
113.60	4,544	19,653	236,118	116.40	4,656	20,137	241,937	119.20	4,768	20,622	247,757	122.00	4,880	21,106	253,577
113.65	4,546	19,661	236,222	116.45	4,658	20,146	242,041	119.25	4,770	20,630	247,861	122.05	4,882	21,115	253,681
113.70	4,548	19,670	236,325	116.50	4,660	20,154	242,145	119.30	4,772	20,639	247,965	122.10	4,884	21,123	253,785
113.75	4,550	19,679	236,429	116.55	4,662	20,163	242,249	119.35	4,774	20,648	248,069	122.15	4,886	21,132	253,889
113.80	4,552	19,687	236,533	116.60	4,664	20,172	242,353	119.40	4,776	20,656	248,173	122.20	4,888	21,141	253,993
113.85	4,554	19,696	236,637	116.65	4,666	20,180	242,457	119.45	4,778	20,665	248,277	122.25	4,890	21,149	254,097
113.90	4,556	19,705	236,741	116.70	4,668	20,189	242,561	119.50	4,780	20,673	248,381	122.30	4,892	21,158	254,201
113.95	4,558	19,713	236,845	116.75	4,670	20,198	242,665	119.55	4,782	20,682	248,485	122.35	4,894	21,167	254,304

Hour	Week	Month	Year	Hour	Week	Month	Year	Hour	Week	Month	Year	Hour	Week	Month	Year
122.40	4,896	21,175	254,408	125.20	5,008	21,660	260,228	128.00	5,120	22,144	266,048	130.80	5,232	22,628	271,868
122.45	4,898	21,184	254,512	125.25	5,010	21,668	260,332	128.05	5,122	22,153	266,152	130.85	5,234	22,637	271,972
122.50	4,900	21,192	254,616	125.30	5,012	21,677	260,436	128.10	5,124	22,161	266,256	130.90	5,236	22,646	272,076
122.55	4,902	21,201	254,720	125.35	5,014	21,686	260,540	128.15	5,126	22,170	266,360	130.95	5,238	22,654	272,180
122.60	4,904	21,210	254,824	125.40	5,016	21,694	260,644	128.20	5,128	22,179	266,464	131.00	5,240	22,663	272,283
122.65	4,906	21,218	254,928	125.45	5,018	21,703	260,748	128.25	5,130	22,187	266,568	131.05	5,242	22,672	272,387
122.70	4,908	21,227	255,032	125.50	5,020	21,711	260,852	128.30	5,132	22,196	266,672	131.10	5,244	22,680	272,491
122.75	4,910	21,236	255,136	125.55	5,022	21,720	260,956	128.35	5,134	22,205	266,775	131.15	5,246	22,689	272,595
122.80	4,912	21,244	255,240	125.60	5,024	21,729	261,060	128.40	5,136	22,213	266,879	131.20	5,248	22,698	272,699
122.85	4,914	21,253	255,344	125.65	5,026	21,737	261,164	128.45	5,138	22,222	266,983	131.25	5,250	22,706	272,803
122.90	4,916	21,262	255,448	125.70	5,028	21,746	261,267	128.50	5,140	22,230	267,087	131.30	5,252	22,715	272,907
122.95	4,918	21,270	255,552	125.75	5,030	21,755	261,371	128.55	5,142	22,239	267,191	131.35	5,254	22,724	273,011
123.00	4,920	21,279	255,655	125.80	5,032	21,763	261,475	128.60	5,144	22,248	267,295	131.40	5,256	22,732	273,115
123.05	4,922	21,288	255,759	125.85	5,034	21,772	261,579	128.65	5,146	22,256	267,399	131.45	5,258	22,741	273,219
123.10	4,924	21,296	255,863	125.90	5,036	21,781	261,683	128.70	5,148	22,265	267,503	131.50	5,260	22,749	273,323
123.15	4,926	21,305	255,967	125.95	5,038	21,789	261,787	128.75	5,150	22,274	267,607	131.55	5,262	22,758	273,427
123.20	4,928	21,314	256,071	126.00	5,040	21,798	261,891	128.80	5,152	22,282	267,711	131.60	5,264	22,767	273,531
123.25	4,930	21,322	256,175	126.05	5,042	21,807	261,995	128.85	5,154	22,291	267,815	131.65	5,266	22,775	273,635
123.30	4,932	21,331	256,279	126.10	5,044	21,815	262,099	128.90	5,156	22,300	267,919	131.70	5,268	22,784	273,738
123.35	4,934	21,340	256,383	126.15	5,046	21,824	262,203	128.95	5,158	22,308	268,023	131.75	5,270	22,793	273,842
123.40	4,936	21,348	256,487	126.20	5,048	21,833	262,307	129.00	5,160	22,317	268,126	131.80	5,272	22,801	273,946
123.45	4,938	21,357	256,591	126.25	5,050	21,841	262,411	129.05	5,162	22,326	268,230	131.85	5,274	22,810	274,050
123.50	4,940	21,365	256,695	126.30	5,052	21,850	262,515	129.10	5,164	22,334	268,334	131.90	5,276	22,819	274,154
123.55	4,942	21,374	256,799	126.35	5,054	21,859	262,618	129.15	5,166	22,343	268,438	131.95	5,278	22,827	274,258
123.60	4,944	21,383	256,903	126.40	5,056	21,867	262,722	129.20	5,168	22,352	268,542	132.00	5,280	22,836	274,362
123.65	4,946	21,391	257,007	126.45	5,058	21,876	262,826	129.25	5,170	22,360	268,646	132.05	5,282	22,845	274,466
123.70	4,948	21,400	257,110	126.50	5,060	21,884	262,930	129.30	5,172	22,369	268,750	132.10	5,284	22,853	274,570
123.75	4,950	21,409	257,214	126.55	5,062	21,893	263,034	129.35	5,174	22,378	268,854	132.15	5,286	22,862	274,674
123.80	4,952	21,417	257,318	126.60	5,064	21,902	263,138	129.40	5,176	22,386	268,958	132.20	5,288	22,871	274,778
123.85	4,954	21,426	257,422	126.65	5,066	21,910	263,242	129.45	5,178	22,395	269,062	132.25	5,290	22,879	274,882
123.90	4,956	21,435	257,526	126.70	5,068	21,919	263,346	129.50	5,180	22,403	269,166	132.30	5,292	22,888	274,986
123.95	4,958	21,443	257,630	126.75	5,070	21,928	263,450	129.55	5,182	22,412	269,270	132.35	5,294	22,897	275,089
124.00	4,960	21,452	257,734	126.80	5,072	21,936	263,554	129.60	5,184	22,421	269,374	132.40	5,296	22,905	275,193
124.05	4,962	21,461	257,838	126.85	5,074	21,945	263,658	129.65	5,186	22,429	269,478	132.45	5,298	22,914	275,297
124.10	4,964	21,469	257,942	126.90	5,076	21,954	263,762	129.70	5,188	22,438	269,581	132.50	5,300	22,922	275,401
124.15	4,966	21,478	258,046	126.95	5,078	21,962	263,866	129.75	5,190	22,447	269,685	132.55	5,302	22,931	275,505
124.20	4,968	21,487	258,150	127.00	5,080	21,971	263,969	129.80	5,192	22,455	269,789	132.60	5,304	22,940	275,609
124.25	4,970	21,495	258,254	127.05	5,082	21,980	264,073	129.85	5,194	22,464	269,893	132.65	5,306	22,948	275,713
124.30	4,972	21,504	258,358	127.10	5,084	21,988	264,177	129.90	5,196	22,473	269,997	132.70	5,308	22,957	275,817
124.35	4,974	21,513	258,461	127.15	5,086	21,997	264,281	129.95	5,198	22,481	270,101	132.75	5,310	22,966	275,921
124.40	4,976	21,521	258,565	127.20	5,088	22,006	264,385	130.00	5,200	22,490	270,205	132.80	5,312	22,974	276,025
124.45	4,978	21,530	258,669	127.25	5,090	22,014	264,489	130.05	5,202	22,499	270,309	132.85	5,314	22,983	276,129
124.50	4,980	21,538	258,773	127.30	5,092	22,023	264,593	130.10	5,204	22,507	270,413	132.90	5,316	22,992	276,233
124.55	4,982	21,547	258,877	127.35	5,094	22,032	264,697	130.15	5,206	22,516	270,517	132.95	5,318	23,000	276,337
124.60	4,984	21,556	258,981	127.40	5,096	22,040	264,801	130.20	5,208	22,525	270,621	133.00	5,320	23,009	276,440
124.65	4,986	21,564	259,085	127.45	5,098	22,049	264,905	130.25	5,210	22,533	270,725	133.05	5,322	23,018	276,544
124.70	4,988	21,573	259,189	127.50	5,100	22,057	265,009	130.30	5,212	22,542	270,829	133.10	5,324	23,026	276,648
124.75	4,990	21,582	259,293	127.55	5,102	22,066	265,113	130.35	5,214	22,551	270,932	133.15	5,326	23,035	276,752
124.80	4,992	21,590	259,397	127.60	5,104	22,075	265,217	130.40	5,216	22,559	271,036	133.20	5,328	23,044	276,856
124.85	4,994	21,599	259,501	127.65	5,106	22,083	265,321	130.45	5,218	22,568	271,140	133.25	5,330	23,052	276,960
124.90	4,996	21,608	259,605	127.70	5,108	22,092	265,424	130.50	5,220	22,576	271,244	133.30	5,332	23,061	277,064
124.95	4,998	21,616	259,709	127.75	5,110	22,101	265,528	130.55	5,222	22,585	271,348	133.35	5,334	23,070	277,168
125.00	5,000	21,625	259,812	127.80	5,112	22,109	265,632	130.60	5,224	22,594	271,452	133.40	5,336	23,078	277,272
125.05	5,002	21,634	259,916	127.85	5,114	22,118	265,736	130.65	5,226	22,602	271,556	133.45	5,338	23,087	277,376
125.10	5,004	21,642	260,020	127.90	5,116	22,127	265,840	130.70	5,228	22,611	271,660	133.50	5,340	23,095	277,480
125.15	5,006	21,651	260,124	127.95	5,118	22,135	265,944	130.75	5,230	22,620	271,764	133.55	5,342	23,104	277,584

Hour	Week	Month	Year	Hour	Week	Month	Year	Hour	Week	Month	Year	Hour	Week	Month	Year
133.60	5,344	23,113	277,688	136.40	5,456	23,597	283,507	139.20	5,568	24,082	289,327	142.00	5,680	24,566	295,147
133.65	5,346	23,121	277,792	136.45	5,458	23,606	283,611	139.25	5,570	24,090	289,431	142.05	5,682	24,575	295,251
133.70	5,348	23,130	277,895	136.50	5,460	23,614	283,715	139.30	5,572	24,099	289,535	142.10	5,684	24,583	295,355
133.75	5,350	23,139	277,999	136.55	5,462	23,623	283,819	139.35	5,574	24,108	289,639	142.15	5,686	24,592	295,459
133.80	5,352	23,147	278,103	136.60	5,464	23,632	283,923	139.40	5,576	24,116	289,743	142.20	5,688	24,601	295,563
133.85	5,354	23,156	278,207	136.65	5,466	23,640	284,027	139.45	5,578	24,125	289,847	142.25	5,690	24,609	295,667
133.90	5,356	23,165	278,311	136.70	5,468	23,649	284,131	139.50	5,580	24,133	289,951	142.30	5,692	24,618	295,771
133.95	5,358	23,173	278,415	136.75	5,470	23,658	284,235	139.55	5,582	24,142	290,055	142.35	5,694	24,627	295,874
134.00	5,360	23,182	278,519	136.80	5,472	23,666	284,339	139.60	5,584	24,151	290,159	142.40	5,696	24,635	295,978
134.05	5,362	23,191	278,623	136.85	5,474	23,675	284,443	139.65	5,586	24,159	290,263	142.45	5,698	24,644	296,082
134.10	5,364	23,199	278,727	136.90	5,476	23,684	284,547	139.70	5,588	24,168	290,366	142.50	5,700	24,652	296,186
134.15	5,366	23,208	278,831	136.95	5,478	23,692	284,651	139.75	5,590	24,177	290,470	142.55	5,702	24,661	296,290
134.20	5,368	23,217	278,935	137.00	5,480	23,701	284,754	139.80	5,592	24,185	290,574	142.60	5,704	24,670	296,394
134.25	5,370	23,225	279,039	137.05	5,482	23,710	284,858	139.85	5,594	24,194	290,678	142.65	5,706	24,678	296,498
134.30	5,372	23,234	279,143	137.10	5,484	23,718	284,962	139.90	5,596	24,203	290,782	142.70	5,708	24,687	296,602
134.35	5,374	23,243	279,246	137.15	5,486	23,727	285,066	139.95	5,598	24,211	290,886	142.75	5,710	24,696	296,706
134.40	5,376	23,251	279,350	137.20	5,488	23,736	285,170	140.00	5,600	24,220	290,990	142.80	5,712	24,704	296,810
134.45	5,378	23,260	279,454	137.25	5,490	23,744	285,274	140.05	5,602	24,229	291,094	142.85	5,714	24,713	296,914
134.50	5,380	23,268	279,558	137.30	5,492	23,753	285,378	140.10	5,604	24,237	291,198	142.90	5,716	24,722	297,018
134.55	5,382	23,277	279,662	137.35	5,494	23,762	285,482	140.15	5,606	24,246	291,302	142.95	5,718	24,730	297,122
134.60	5,384	23,286	279,766	137.40	5,496	23,770	285,586	140.20	5,608	24,255	291,406	143.00	5,720	24,739	297,225
134.65	5,386	23,294	279,870	137.45	5,498	23,779	285,690	140.25	5,610	24,263	291,510	143.05	5,722	24,748	297,329
134.70	5,388	23,303	279,974	137.50	5,500	23,787	285,794	140.30	5,612	24,272	291,614	143.10	5,724	24,756	297,433
134.75	5,390	23,312	280,078	137.55	5,502	23,796	285,898	140.35	5,614	24,281	291,717	143.15	5,726	24,765	297,537
134.80	5,392	23,320	280,182	137.60	5,504	23,805	286,002	140.40	5,616	24,289	291,821	143.20	5,728	24,774	297,641
134.85	5,394	23,329	280,286	137.65	5,506	23,813	286,106	140.45	5,618	24,298	291,925	143.25	5,730	24,782	297,745
134.90	5,396	23,338	280,390	137.70	5,508	23,822	286,209	140.50	5,620	24,306	292,029	143.30	5,732	24,791	297,849
134.95	5,398	23,346	280,494	137.75	5,510	23,831	286,313	140.55	5,622	24,315	292,133	143.35	5,734	24,800	297,953
135.00	5,400	23,355	280,597	137.80	5,512	23,839	286,417	140.60	5,624	24,324	292,237	143.40	5,736	24,808	298,057
135.05	5,402	23,364	280,701	137.85	5,514	23,848	286,521	140.65	5,626	24,332	292,341	143.45	5,738	24,817	298,161
135.10	5,404	23,372	280,805	137.90	5,516	23,857	286,625	140.70	5,628	24,341	292,445	143.50	5,740	24,825	298,265
135.15	5,406	23,381	280,909	137.95	5,518	23,865	286,729	140.75	5,630	24,350	292,549	143.55	5,742	24,834	298,369
135.20	5,408	23,390	281,013	138.00	5,520	23,874	286,833	140.80	5,632	24,358	292,653	143.60	5,744	24,843	298,473
135.25	5,410	23,398	281,117	138.05	5,522	23,883	286,937	140.85	5,634	24,367	292,757	143.65	5,746	24,851	298,577
135.30	5,412	23,407	281,221	138.10	5,524	23,891	287,041	140.90	5,636	24,376	292,861	143.70	5,748	24,860	298,680
135.35	5,414	23,416	281,325	138.15	5,526	23,900	287,145	140.95	5,638	24,384	292,965	143.75	5,750	24,869	298,784
135.40	5,416	23,424	281,429	138.20	5,528	23,909	287,249	141.00	5,640	24,393	293,068	143.80	5,752	24,877	298,888
135.45	5,418	23,433	281,533	138.25	5,530	23,917	287,353	141.05	5,642	24,402	293,172	143.85	5,754	24,886	298,992
135.50	5,420	23,441	281,637	138.30	5,532	23,926	287,457	141.10	5,644	24,410	293,276	143.90	5,756	24,895	299,096
135.55	5,422	23,450	281,741	138.35	5,534	23,935	287,560	141.15	5,646	24,419	293,380	143.95	5,758	24,903	299,200
135.60	5,424	23,459	281,845	138.40	5,536	23,943	287,664	141.20	5,648	24,428	293,484	144.00	5,760	24,912	299,304
135.65	5,426	23,467	281,949	138.45	5,538	23,952	287,768	141.25	5,650	24,436	293,588	144.05	5,762	24,921	299,408
135.70	5,428	23,476	282,052	138.50	5,540	23,960	287,872	141.30	5,652	24,445	293,692	144.10	5,764	24,929	299,512
135.75	5,430	23,485	282,156	138.55	5,542	23,969	287,976	141.35	5,654	24,454	293,796	144.15	5,766	24,938	299,616
135.80	5,432	23,493	282,260	138.60	5,544	23,978	288,080	141.40	5,656	24,462	293,900	144.20	5,768	24,947	299,720
135.85	5,434	23,502	282,364	138.65	5,546	23,986	288,184	141.45	5,658	24,471	294,004	144.25	5,770	24,955	299,824
135.90	5,436	23,511	282,468	138.70	5,548	23,995	288,288	141.50	5,660	24,479	294,108	144.30	5,772	24,964	299,928
135.95	5,438	23,519	282,572	138.75	5,550	24,004	288,392	141.55	5,662	24,488	294,212	144.35	5,774	24,973	300,031
136.00	5,440	23,528	282,676	138.80	5,552	24,012	288,496	141.60	5,664	24,497	294,316	144.40	5,776	24,981	300,135
136.05	5,442	23,537	282,780	138.85	5,554	24,021	288,600	141.65	5,666	24,505	294,420	144.45	5,778	24,990	300,239
136.10	5,444	23,545	282,884	138.90	5,556	24,030	288,704	141.70	5,668	24,514	294,523	144.50	5,780	24,998	300,343
136.15	5,446	23,554	282,988	138.95	5,558	24,038	288,808	141.75	5,670	24,523	294,627	144.55	5,782	25,007	300,447
136.20	5,448	23,563	283,092	139.00	5,560	24,047	288,911	141.80	5,672	24,531	294,731	144.60	5,784	25,016	300,551
136.25	5,450	23,571	283,196	139.05	5,562	24,056	289,015	141.85	5,674	24,540	294,835	144.65	5,786	25,024	300,655
136.30	5,452	23,580	283,300	139.10	5,564	24,064	289,119	141.90	5,676	24,549	294,939	144.70	5,788	25,033	300,759
136.35	5,454	23,589	283,403	139.15	5,566	24,073	289,223	141.95	5,678	24,557	295,043	144.75	5,790	25,042	300,863

Hour	Week	Month	Year	Hour	Week	Month	Year	Hour	Week	Month	Year	Hour	Week	Month	Year
144.80	5,792	25,050	300,967	147.60	5,904	25,535	306,787	150.40	6,016	26,019	312,606	153.20	6,128	26,504	318,426
144.85	5,794	25,059	301,071	147.65	5,906	25,543	306,891	150.45	6,018	26,028	312,710	153.25	6,130	26,512	318,530
144.90	5,796	25,068	301,175	147.70	5,908	25,552	306,994	150.50	6,020	26,037	312,814	153.30	6,132	26,521	318,634
144.95	5,798	25,076	301,279	147.75	5,910	25,561	307,098	150.55	6,022	26,045	312,918	153.35	6,134	26,530	318,738
145.00	5,800	25,085	301,383	147.80	5,912	25,569	307,202	150.60	6,024	26,054	313,022	153.40	6,136	26,538	318,842
145.05	5,802	25,094	301,486	147.85	5,914	25,578	307,306	150.65	6,026	26,062	313,126	153.45	6,138	26,547	318,946
145.10	5,804	25,102	301,590	147.90	5,916	25,587	307,410	150.70	6,028	26,071	313,230	153.50	6,140	26,556	319,050
145.15	5,806	25,111	301,694	147.95	5,918	25,595	307,514	150.75	6,030	26,080	313,334	153.55	6,142	26,564	319,154
145.20	5,808	25,120	301,798	148.00	5,920	25,604	307,618	150.80	6,032	26,088	313,438	153.60	6,144	26,573	319,258
145.25	5,810	25,128	301,902	148.05	5,922	25,613	307,722	150.85	6,034	26,097	313,542	153.65	6,146	26,581	319,362
145.30	5,812	25,137	302,006	148.10	5,924	25,621	307,826	150.90	6,036	26,106	313,646	153.70	6,148	26,590	319,465
145.35	5,814	25,146	302,110	148.15	5,926	25,630	307,930	150.95	6,038	26,114	313,750	153.75	6,150	26,599	319,569
145.40	5,816	25,154	302,214	148.20	5,928	25,639	308,034	151.00	6,040	26,123	313,854	153.80	6,152	26,607	319,673
145.45	5,818	25,163	302,318	148.25	5,930	25,647	308,138	151.05	6,042	26,132	313,957	153.85	6,154	26,616	319,777
145.50	5,820	25,172	302,422	148.30	5,932	25,656	308,242	151.10	6,044	26,140	314,061	153.90	6,156	26,625	319,881
145.55	5,822	25,180	302,526	148.35	5,934	25,665	308,345	151.15	6,046	26,149	314,165	153.95	6,158	26,633	319,985
145.60	5,824	25,189	302,630	148.40	5,936	25,673	308,449	151.20	6,048	26,158	314,269	154.00	6,160	26,642	320,089
145.65	5,826	25,197	302,734	148.45	5,938	25,682	308,553	151.25	6,050	26,166	314,373	154.05	6,162	26,651	320,193
145.70	5,828	25,206	302,837	148.50	5,940	25,691	308,657	151.30	6,052	26,175	314,477	154.10	6,164	26,659	320,297
145.75	5,830	25,215	302,941	148.55	5,942	25,699	308,761	151.35	6,054	26,184	314,581	154.15	6,166	26,668	320,401
145.80	5,832	25,223	303,045	148.60	5,944	25,708	308,865	151.40	6,056	26,192	314,685	154.20	6,168	26,677	320,505
145.85	5,834	25,232	303,149	148.65	5,946	25,716	308,969	151.45	6,058	26,201	314,789	154.25	6,170	26,685	320,609
145.90	5,836	25,241	303,253	148.70	5,948	25,725	309,073	151.50	6,060	26,210	314,893	154.30	6,172	26,694	320,713
145.95	5,838	25,249	303,357	148.75	5,950	25,734	309,177	151.55	6,062	26,218	314,997	154.35	6,174	26,703	320,816
146.00	5,840	25,258	303,461	148.80	5,952	25,742	309,281	151.60	6,064	26,227	315,101	154.40	6,176	26,711	320,920
146.05	5,842	25,267	303,565	148.85	5,954	25,751	309,385	151.65	6,066	26,235	315,205	154.45	6,178	26,720	321,024
146.10	5,844	25,275	303,669	148.90	5,956	25,760	309,489	151.70	6,068	26,244	315,308	154.50	6,180	26,729	321,128
146.15	5,846	25,284	303,773	148.95	5,958	25,768	309,593	151.75	6,070	26,253	315,412	154.55	6,182	26,737	321,232
146.20	5,848	25,293	303,877	149.00	5,960	25,777	309,697	151.80	6,072	26,261	315,516	154.60	6,184	26,746	321,336
146.25	5,850	25,301	303,981	149.05	5,962	25,786	309,800	151.85	6,074	26,270	315,620	154.65	6,186	26,754	321,440
146.30	5,852	25,310	304,085	149.10	5,964	25,794	309,904	151.90	6,076	26,279	315,724	154.70	6,188	26,763	321,544
146.35	5,854	25,319	304,188	149.15	5,966	25,803	310,008	151.95	6,078	26,287	315,828	154.75	6,190	26,772	321,648
146.40	5,856	25,327	304,292	149.20	5,968	25,812	310,112	152.00	6,080	26,296	315,932	154.80	6,192	26,780	321,752
146.45	5,858	25,336	304,396	149.25	5,970	25,820	310,216	152.05	6,082	26,305	316,036	154.85	6,194	26,789	321,856
146.50	5,860	25,345	304,500	149.30	5,972	25,829	310,320	152.10	6,084	26,313	316,140	154.90	6,196	26,798	321,960
146.55	5,862	25,353	304,604	149.35	5,974	25,838	310,424	152.15	6,086	26,322	316,244	154.95	6,198	26,806	322,064
146.60	5,864	25,362	304,708	149.40	5,976	25,846	310,528	152.20	6,088	26,331	316,348	155.00	6,200	26,815	322,168
146.65	5,866	25,370	304,812	149.45	5,978	25,855	310,632	152.25	6,090	26,339	316,452	155.05	6,202	26,824	322,271
146.70	5,868	25,379	304,916	149.50	5,980	25,864	310,736	152.30	6,092	26,348	316,556	155.10	6,204	26,832	322,375
146.75	5,870	25,388	305,020	149.55	5,982	25,872	310,840	152.35	6,094	26,357	316,659	155.15	6,206	26,841	322,479
146.80	5,872	25,396	305,124	149.60	5,984	25,881	310,944	152.40	6,096	26,365	316,763	155.20	6,208	26,850	322,583
146.85	5,874	25,405	305,228	149.65	5,986	25,889	311,048	152.45	6,098	26,374	316,867	155.25	6,210	26,858	322,687
146.90	5,876	25,414	305,332	149.70	5,988	25,898	311,151	152.50	6,100	26,383	316,971	155.30	6,212	26,867	322,791
146.95	5,878	25,422	305,436	149.75	5,990	25,907	311,255	152.55	6,102	26,391	317,075	155.35	6,214	26,876	322,895
147.00	5,880	25,431	305,540	149.80	5,992	25,915	311,359	152.60	6,104	26,400	317,179	155.40	6,216	26,884	322,999
147.05	5,882	25,440	305,643	149.85	5,994	25,924	311,463	152.65	6,106	26,408	317,283	155.45	6,218	26,893	323,103
147.10	5,884	25,448	305,747	149.90	5,996	25,933	311,567	152.70	6,108	26,417	317,387	155.50	6,220	26,902	323,207
147.15	5,886	25,457	305,851	149.95	5,998	25,941	311,671	152.75	6,110	26,426	317,491	155.55	6,222	26,910	323,311
147.20	5,888	25,466	305,955	150.00	6,000	25,950	311,775	152.80	6,112	26,434	317,595	155.60	6,224	26,919	323,415
147.25	5,890	25,474	306,059	150.05	6,002	25,959	311,879	152.85	6,114	26,443	317,699	155.65	6,226	26,927	323,519
147.30	5,892	25,483	306,163	150.10	6,004	25,967	311,983	152.90	6,116	26,452	317,803	155.70	6,228	26,936	323,622
147.35	5,894	25,492	306,267	150.15	6,006	25,976	312,087	152.95	6,118	26,460	317,907	155.75	6,230	26,945	323,726
147.40	5,896	25,500	306,371	150.20	6,008	25,985	312,191	153.00	6,120	26,469	318,011	155.80	6,232	26,953	323,830
147.45	5,898	25,509	306,475	150.25	6,010	25,993	312,295	153.05	6,122	26,478	318,114	155.85	6,234	26,962	323,934
147.50	5,900	25,518	306,579	150.30	6,012	26,002	312,399	153.10	6,124	26,486	318,218	155.90	6,236	26,971	324,038
147.55	5,902	25,526	306,683	150.35	6,014	26,011	312,502	153.15	6,126	26,495	318,322	155.95	6,238	26,979	324,142

Hour	Week	Month	Year	Hour	Week	Month	Year	Hour	Week	Month	Year	Hour	Week	Month	Year
156.00	6,240	26,988	324,246	158.80	6,352	27,472	330,066	161.60	6,464	27,957	335,886	164.40	6,576	28,441	341,705
156.05	6,242	26,997	324,350	158.85	6,354	27,481	330,170	161.65	6,466	27,965	335,990	164.45	6,578	28,450	341,809
156.10	6,244	27,005	324,454	158.90	6,356	27,490	330,274	161.70	6,468	27,974	336,093	164.50	6,580	28,459	341,913
156.15	6,246	27,014	324,558	158.95	6,358	27,498	330,378	161.75	6,470	27,983	336,197	164.55	6,582	28,467	342,017
156.20	6,248	27,023	324,662	159.00	6,360	27,507	330,482	161.80	6,472	27,991	336,301	164.60	6,584	28,476	342,121
156.25	6,250	27,031	324,766	159.05	6,362	27,516	330,585	161.85	6,474	28,000	336,405	164.65	6,586	28,484	342,225
156.30	6,252	27,040	324,870	159.10	6,364	27,524	330,689	161.90	6,476	28,009	336,509	164.70	6,588	28,493	342,329
156.35	6,254	27,049	324,973	159.15	6,366	27,533	330,793	161.95	6,478	28,017	336,613	164.75	6,590	28,502	342,433
156.40	6,256	27,057	325,077	159.20	6,368	27,542	330,897	162.00	6,480	28,026	336,717	164.80	6,592	28,510	342,537
156.45	6,258	27,066	325,181	159.25	6,370	27,550	331,001	162.05	6,482	28,035	336,821	164.85	6,594	28,519	342,641
156.50	6,260	27,075	325,285	159.30	6,372	27,559	331,105	162.10	6,484	28,043	336,925	164.90	6,596	28,528	342,745
156.55	6,262	27,083	325,389	159.35	6,374	27,568	331,209	162.15	6,486	28,052	337,029	164.95	6,598	28,536	342,849
156.60	6,264	27,092	325,493	159.40	6,376	27,576	331,313	162.20	6,488	28,061	337,133	165.00	6,600	28,545	342,953
156.65	6,266	27,100	325,597	159.45	6,378	27,585	331,417	162.25	6,490	28,069	337,237	165.05	6,602	28,554	343,056
156.70	6,268	27,109	325,701	159.50	6,380	27,594	331,521	162.30	6,492	28,078	337,341	165.10	6,604	28,562	343,160
156.75	6,270	27,118	325,805	159.55	6,382	27,602	331,625	162.35	6,494	28,087	337,444	165.15	6,606	28,571	343,264
156.80	6,272	27,126	325,909	159.60	6,384	27,611	331,729	162.40	6,496	28,095	337,548	165.20	6,608	28,580	343,368
156.85	6,274	27,135	326,013	159.65	6,386	27,619	331,833	162.45	6,498	28,104	337,652	165.25	6,610	28,588	343,472
156.90	6,276	27,144	326,117	159.70	6,388	27,628	331,936	162.50	6,500	28,113	337,756	165.30	6,612	28,597	343,576
156.95	6,278	27,152	326,221	159.75	6,390	27,637	332,040	162.55	6,502	28,121	337,860	165.35	6,614	28,606	343,680
157.00	6,280	27,161	326,325	159.80	6,392	27,645	332,144	162.60	6,504	28,130	337,964	165.40	6,616	28,614	343,784
157.05	6,282	27,170	326,428	159.85	6,394	27,654	332,248	162.65	6,506	28,138	338,068	165.45	6,618	28,623	343,888
157.10	6,284	27,178	326,532	159.90	6,396	27,663	332,352	162.70	6,508	28,147	338,172	165.50	6,620	28,632	343,992
157.15	6,286	27,187	326,636	159.95	6,398	27,671	332,456	162.75	6,510	28,156	338,276	165.55	6,622	28,640	344,096
157.20	6,288	27,196	326,740	160.00	6,400	27,680	332,560	162.80	6,512	28,164	338,380	165.60	6,624	28,649	344,200
157.25	6,290	27,204	326,844	160.05	6,402	27,689	332,664	162.85	6,514	28,173	338,484	165.65	6,626	28,657	344,304
157.30	6,292	27,213	326,948	160.10	6,404	27,697	332,768	162.90	6,516	28,182	338,588	165.70	6,628	28,666	344,407
157.35	6,294	27,222	327,052	160.15	6,406	27,706	332,872	162.95	6,518	28,190	338,692	165.75	6,630	28,675	344,511
157.40	6,296	27,230	327,156	160.20	6,408	27,715	332,976	163.00	6,520	28,199	338,796	165.80	6,632	28,683	344,615
157.45	6,298	27,239	327,260	160.25	6,410	27,723	333,080	163.05	6,522	28,208	338,899	165.85	6,634	28,692	344,719
157.50	6,300	27,248	327,364	160.30	6,412	27,732	333,184	163.10	6,524	28,216	339,003	165.90	6,636	28,701	344,823
157.55	6,302	27,256	327,468	160.35	6,414	27,741	333,287	163.15	6,526	28,225	339,107	165.95	6,638	28,709	344,927
157.60	6,304	27,265	327,572	160.40	6,416	27,749	333,391	163.20	6,528	28,234	339,211	166.00	6,640	28,718	345,031
157.65	6,306	27,273	327,676	160.45	6,418	27,758	333,495	163.25	6,530	28,242	339,315	166.05	6,642	28,727	345,135
157.70	6,308	27,282	327,779	160.50	6,420	27,767	333,599	163.30	6,532	28,251	339,419	166.10	6,644	28,735	345,239
157.75	6,310	27,291	327,883	160.55	6,422	27,775	333,703	163.35	6,534	28,260	339,523	166.15	6,646	28,744	345,343
157.80	6,312	27,299	327,987	160.60	6,424	27,784	333,807	163.40	6,536	28,268	339,627	166.20	6,648	28,753	345,447
157.85	6,314	27,308	328,091	160.65	6,426	27,792	333,911	163.45	6,538	28,277	339,731	166.25	6,650	28,761	345,551
157.90	6,316	27,317	328,195	160.70	6,428	27,801	334,015	163.50	6,540	28,286	339,835	166.30	6,652	28,770	345,655
157.95	6,318	27,325	328,299	160.75	6,430	27,810	334,119	163.55	6,542	28,294	339,939	166.35	6,654	28,779	345,758
158.00	6,320	27,334	328,403	160.80	6,432	27,818	334,223	163.60	6,544	28,303	340,043	166.40	6,656	28,787	345,862
158.05	6,322	27,343	328,507	160.85	6,434	27,827	334,327	163.65	6,546	28,311	340,147	166.45	6,658	28,796	345,966
158.10	6,324	27,351	328,611	160.90	6,436	27,836	334,431	163.70	6,548	28,320	340,250	166.50	6,660	28,805	346,070
158.15	6,326	27,360	328,715	160.95	6,438	27,844	334,535	163.75	6,550	28,329	340,354	166.55	6,662	28,813	346,174
158.20	6,328	27,369	328,819	161.00	6,440	27,853	334,639	163.80	6,552	28,337	340,458	166.60	6,664	28,822	346,278
158.25	6,330	27,377	328,923	161.05	6,442	27,862	334,742	163.85	6,554	28,346	340,562	166.65	6,666	28,830	346,382
158.30	6,332	27,386	329,027	161.10	6,444	27,870	334,846	163.90	6,556	28,355	340,666	166.70	6,668	28,839	346,486
158.35	6,334	27,395	329,130	161.15	6,446	27,879	334,950	163.95	6,558	28,363	340,770	166.75	6,670	28,848	346,590
158.40	6,336	27,403	329,234	161.20	6,448	27,888	335,054	164.00	6,560	28,372	340,874	166.80	6,672	28,856	346,694
158.45	6,338	27,412	329,338	161.25	6,450	27,896	335,158	164.05	6,562	28,381	340,978	166.85	6,674	28,865	346,798
158.50	6,340	27,421	329,442	161.30	6,452	27,905	335,262	164.10	6,564	28,389	341,082	166.90	6,676	28,874	346,902
158.55	6,342	27,429	329,546	161.35	6,454	27,914	335,366	164.15	6,566	28,398	341,186	166.95	6,678	28,882	347,006
158.60	6,344	27,438	329,650	161.40	6,456	27,922	335,470	164.20	6,568	28,407	341,290	167.00	6,680	28,891	347,110
158.65	6,346	27,446	329,754	161.45	6,458	27,931	335,574	164.25	6,570	28,415	341,394	167.05	6,682	28,900	347,213
158.70	6,348	27,455	329,858	161.50	6,460	27,940	335,678	164.30	6,572	28,424	341,498	167.10	6,684	28,908	347,317
158.75	6,350	27,464	329,962	161.55	6,462	27,948	335,782	164.35	6,574	28,433	341,601	167.15	6,686	28,917	347,421

Hour	Week	Month	Year	Hour	Week	Month	Year	Hour	Week	Month	Year	Hour	Week	Month	Year
167.20	6,688	28,926	347,525	170.00	6,800	29,410	353,345	172.80	6,912	29,894	359,165	175.60	7,024	30,379	364,985
167.25	6,690	28,934	347,629	170.05	6,802	29,419	353,449	172.85	6,914	29,903	359,269	175.65	7,026	30,387	365,089
167.30	6,692	28,943	347,733	170.10	6,804	29,427	353,553	172.90	6,916	29,912	359,373	175.70	7,028	30,396	365,192
167.35	6,694	28,952	347,837	170.15	6,806	29,436	353,657	172.95	6,918	29,920	359,477	175.75	7,030	30,405	365,296
167.40	6,696	28,960	347,941	170.20	6,808	29,445	353,761	173.00	6,920	29,929	359,581	175.80	7,032	30,413	365,400
167.45	6,698	28,969	348,045	170.25	6,810	29,453	353,865	173.05	6,922	29,938	359,684	175.85	7,034	30,422	365,504
167.50	6,700	28,978	348,149	170.30	6,812	29,462	353,969	173.10	6,924	29,946	359,788	175.90	7,036	30,431	365,608
167.55	6,702	28,986	348,253	170.35	6,814	29,471	354,072	173.15	6,926	29,955	359,892	175.95	7,038	30,439	365,712
167.60	6,704	28,995	348,357	170.40	6,816	29,479	354,176	173.20	6,928	29,964	359,996	176.00	7,040	30,448	365,816
167.65	6,706	29,003	348,461	170.45	6,818	29,488	354,280	173.25	6,930	29,972	360,100	176.05	7,042	30,457	365,920
167.70	6,708	29,012	348,564	170.50	6,820	29,497	354,384	173.30	6,932	29,981	360,204	176.10	7,044	30,465	366,024
167.75	6,710	29,021	348,668	170.55	6,822	29,505	354,488	173.35	6,934	29,990	360,308	176.15	7,046	30,474	366,128
167.80	6,712	29,029	348,772	170.60	6,824	29,514	354,592	173.40	6,936	29,998	360,412	176.20	7,048	30,483	366,232
167.85	6,714	29,038	348,876	170.65	6,826	29,522	354,696	173.45	6,938	30,007	360,516	176.25	7,050	30,491	366,336
167.90	6,716	29,047	348,980	170.70	6,828	29,531	354,800	173.50	6,940	30,016	360,620	176.30	7,052	30,500	366,440
167.95	6,718	29,055	349,084	170.75	6,830	29,540	354,904	173.55	6,942	30,024	360,724	176.35	7,054	30,509	366,543
168.00	6,720	29,064	349,188	170.80	6,832	29,548	355,008	173.60	6,944	30,033	360,828	176.40	7,056	30,517	366,647
168.05	6,722	29,073	349,292	170.85	6,834	29,557	355,112	173.65	6,946	30,041	360,932	176.45	7,058	30,526	366,751
168.10	6,724	29,081	349,396	170.90	6,836	29,566	355,216	173.70	6,948	30,050	361,035	176.50	7,060	30,535	366,855
168.15	6,726	29,090	349,500	170.95	6,838	29,574	355,320	173.75	6,950	30,059	361,139	176.55	7,062	30,543	366,959
168.20	6,728	29,099	349,604	171.00	6,840	29,583	355,424	173.80	6,952	30,067	361,243	176.60	7,064	30,552	367,063
168.25	6,730	29,107	349,708	171.05	6,842	29,592	355,527	173.85	6,954	30,076	361,347	176.65	7,066	30,560	367,167
168.30	6,732	29,116	349,812	171.10	6,844	29,600	355,631	173.90	6,956	30,085	361,451	176.70	7,068	30,569	367,271
168.35	6,734	29,125	349,915	171.15	6,846	29,609	355,735	173.95	6,958	30,093	361,555	176.75	7,070	30,578	367,375
168.40	6,736	29,133	350,019	171.20	6,848	29,618	355,839	174.00	6,960	30,102	361,659	176.80	7,072	30,586	367,479
168.45	6,738	29,142	350,123	171.25	6,850	29,626	355,943	174.05	6,962	30,111	361,763	176.85	7,074	30,595	367,583
168.50	6,740	29,151	350,227	171.30	6,852	29,635	356,047	174.10	6,964	30,119	361,867	176.90	7,076	30,604	367,687
168.55	6,742	29,159	350,331	171.35	6,854	29,644	356,151	174.15	6,966	30,128	361,971	176.95	7,078	30,612	367,791
168.60	6,744	29,168	350,435	171.40	6,856	29,652	356,255	174.20	6,968	30,137	362,075	177.00	7,080	30,621	367,895
168.65	6,746	29,176	350,539	171.45	6,858	29,661	356,359	174.25	6,970	30,145	362,179	177.05	7,082	30,630	367,998
168.70	6,748	29,185	350,643	171.50	6,860	29,670	356,463	174.30	6,972	30,154	362,283	177.10	7,084	30,638	368,102
168.75	6,750	29,194	350,747	171.55	6,862	29,678	356,567	174.35	6,974	30,163	362,386	177.15	7,086	30,647	368,206
168.80	6,752	29,202	350,851	171.60	6,864	29,687	356,671	174.40	6,976	30,171	362,490	177.20	7,088	30,656	368,310
168.85	6,754	29,211	350,955	171.65	6,866	29,695	356,775	174.45	6,978	30,180	362,594	177.25	7,090	30,664	368,414
168.90	6,756	29,220	351,059	171.70	6,868	29,704	356,878	174.50	6,980	30,189	362,698	177.30	7,092	30,673	368,518
168.95	6,758	29,228	351,163	171.75	6,870	29,713	356,982	174.55	6,982	30,197	362,802	177.35	7,094	30,682	368,622
169.00	6,760	29,237	351,267	171.80	6,872	29,721	357,086	174.60	6,984	30,206	362,906	177.40	7,096	30,690	368,726
169.05	6,762	29,246	351,370	171.85	6,874	29,730	357,190	174.65	6,986	30,214	363,010	177.45	7,098	30,699	368,830
169.10	6,764	29,254	351,474	171.90	6,876	29,739	357,294	174.70	6,988	30,223	363,114	177.50	7,100	30,708	368,934
169.15	6,766	29,263	351,578	171.95	6,878	29,747	357,398	174.75	6,990	30,232	363,218	177.55	7,102	30,716	369,038
169.20	6,768	29,272	351,682	172.00	6,880	29,756	357,502	174.80	6,992	30,240	363,322	177.60	7,104	30,725	369,142
169.25	6,770	29,280	351,786	172.05	6,882	29,765	357,606	174.85	6,994	30,249	363,426	177.65	7,106	30,733	369,246
169.30	6,772	29,289	351,890	172.10	6,884	29,773	357,710	174.90	6,996	30,258	363,530	177.70	7,108	30,742	369,349
169.35	6,774	29,298	351,994	172.15	6,886	29,782	357,814	174.95	6,998	30,266	363,634	177.75	7,110	30,751	369,453
169.40	6,776	29,306	352,098	172.20	6,888	29,791	357,918	175.00	7,000	30,275	363,738	177.80	7,112	30,759	369,557
169.45	6,778	29,315	352,202	172.25	6,890	29,799	358,022	175.05	7,002	30,284	363,841	177.85	7,114	30,768	369,661
169.50	6,780	29,324	352,306	172.30	6,892	29,808	358,126	175.10	7,004	30,292	363,945	177.90	7,116	30,777	369,765
169.55	6,782	29,332	352,410	172.35	6,894	29,817	358,229	175.15	7,006	30,301	364,049	177.95	7,118	30,785	369,869
169.60	6,784	29,341	352,514	172.40	6,896	29,825	358,333	175.20	7,008	30,310	364,153	178.00	7,120	30,794	369,973
169.65	6,786	29,349	352,618	172.45	6,898	29,834	358,437	175.25	7,010	30,318	364,257	178.05	7,122	30,803	370,077
169.70	6,788	29,358	352,721	172.50	6,900	29,843	358,541	175.30	7,012	30,327	364,361	178.10	7,124	30,811	370,181
169.75	6,790	29,367	352,825	172.55	6,902	29,851	358,645	175.35	7,014	30,336	364,465	178.15	7,126	30,820	370,285
169.80	6,792	29,375	352,929	172.60	6,904	29,860	358,749	175.40	7,016	30,344	364,569	178.20	7,128	30,829	370,389
169.85	6,794	29,384	353,033	172.65	6,906	29,868	358,853	175.45	7,018	30,353	364,673	178.25	7,130	30,837	370,493
169.90	6,796	29,393	353,137	172.70	6,908	29,877	358,957	175.50	7,020	30,362	364,777	178.30	7,132	30,846	370,597
169.95	6,798	29,401	353,241	172.75	6,910	29,886	359,061	175.55	7,022	30,370	364,881	178.35	7,134	30,855	370,700

Hour	Week	Month	Year	Hour	Week	Month	Year	Hour	Week	Month	Year	Hour	Week	Month	Year
178.40	7,136	30,863	370,804	181.20	7,248	31,348	376,624	184.00	7,360	31,832	382,444	186.80	7,472	32,316	388,264
178.45	7,138	30,872	370,908	181.25	7,250	31,356	376,728	184.05	7,362	31,841	382,548	186.85	7,474	32,325	388,368
178.50	7,140	30,881	371,012	181.30	7,252	31,365	376,832	184.10	7,364	31,849	382,652	186.90	7,476	32,334	388,472
178.55	7,142	30,889	371,116	181.35	7,254	31,374	376,936	184.15	7,366	31,858	382,756	186.95	7,478	32,342	388,576
178.60	7,144	30,898	371,220	181.40	7,256	31,382	377,040	184.20	7,368	31,867	382,860	187.00	7,480	32,351	388,680
178.65	7,146	30,906	371,324	181.45	7,258	31,391	377,144	184.25	7,370	31,875	382,964	187.05	7,482	32,360	388,783
178.70	7,148	30,915	371,428	181.50	7,260	31,400	377,248	184.30	7,372	31,884	383,068	187.10	7,484	32,368	388,887
178.75	7,150	30,924	371,532	181.55	7,262	31,408	377,352	184.35	7,374	31,893	383,171	187.15	7,486	32,377	388,991
178.80	7,152	30,932	371,636	181.60	7,264	31,417	377,456	184.40	7,376	31,901	383,275	187.20	7,488	32,386	389,095
178.85	7,154	30,941	371,740	181.65	7,266	31,425	377,560	184.45	7,378	31,910	383,379	187.25	7,490	32,394	389,199
178.90	7,156	30,950	371,844	181.70	7,268	31,434	377,663	184.50	7,380	31,919	383,483	187.30	7,492	32,403	389,303
178.95	7,158	30,958	371,948	181.75	7,270	31,443	377,767	184.55	7,382	31,927	383,587	187.35	7,494	32,412	389,407
179.00	7,160	30,967	372,052	181.80	7,272	31,451	377,871	184.60	7,384	31,936	383,691	187.40	7,496	32,420	389,511
179.05	7,162	30,976	372,155	181.85	7,274	31,460	377,975	184.65	7,386	31,944	383,795	187.45	7,498	32,429	389,615
179.10	7,164	30,984	372,259	181.90	7,276	31,469	378,079	184.70	7,388	31,953	383,899	187.50	7,500	32,438	389,719
179.15	7,166	30,993	372,363	181.95	7,278	31,477	378,183	184.75	7,390	31,962	384,003	187.55	7,502	32,446	389,823
179.20	7,168	31,002	372,467	182.00	7,280	31,486	378,287	184.80	7,392	31,970	384,107	187.60	7,504	32,455	389,927
179.25	7,170	31,010	372,571	182.05	7,282	31,495	378,391	184.85	7,394	31,979	384,211	187.65	7,506	32,463	390,031
179.30	7,172	31,019	372,675	182.10	7,284	31,503	378,495	184.90	7,396	31,988	384,315	187.70	7,508	32,472	390,134
179.35	7,174	31,028	372,779	182.15	7,286	31,512	378,599	184.95	7,398	31,996	384,419	187.75	7,510	32,481	390,238
179.40	7,176	31,036	372,883	182.20	7,288	31,521	378,703	185.00	7,400	32,005	384,523	187.80	7,512	32,489	390,342
179.45	7,178	31,045	372,987	182.25	7,290	31,529	378,807	185.05	7,402	32,014	384,626	187.85	7,514	32,498	390,446
179.50	7,180	31,054	373,091	182.30	7,292	31,538	378,911	185.10	7,404	32,022	384,730	187.90	7,516	32,507	390,550
179.55	7,182	31,062	373,195	182.35	7,294	31,547	379,014	185.15	7,406	32,031	384,834	187.95	7,518	32,515	390,654
179.60	7,184	31,071	373,299	182.40	7,296	31,555	379,118	185.20	7,408	32,040	384,938	188.00	7,520	32,524	390,758
179.65	7,186	31,079	373,403	182.45	7,298	31,564	379,222	185.25	7,410	32,048	385,042	188.05	7,522	32,533	390,862
179.70	7,188	31,088	373,506	182.50	7,300	31,573	379,326	185.30	7,412	32,057	385,146	188.10	7,524	32,541	390,966
179.75	7,190	31,097	373,610	182.55	7,302	31,581	379,430	185.35	7,414	32,066	385,250	188.15	7,526	32,550	391,070
179.80	7,192	31,105	373,714	182.60	7,304	31,590	379,534	185.40	7,416	32,074	385,354	188.20	7,528	32,559	391,174
179.85	7,194	31,114	373,818	182.65	7,306	31,598	379,638	185.45	7,418	32,083	385,458	188.25	7,530	32,567	391,278
179.90	7,196	31,123	373,922	182.70	7,308	31,607	379,742	185.50	7,420	32,092	385,562	188.30	7,532	32,576	391,382
179.95	7,198	31,131	374,026	182.75	7,310	31,616	379,846	185.55	7,422	32,100	385,666	188.35	7,534	32,585	391,485
180.00	7,200	31,140	374,130	182.80	7,312	31,624	379,950	185.60	7,424	32,109	385,770	188.40	7,536	32,593	391,589
180.05	7,202	31,149	374,234	182.85	7,314	31,633	380,054	185.65	7,426	32,117	385,874	188.45	7,538	32,602	391,693
180.10	7,204	31,157	374,338	182.90	7,316	31,642	380,158	185.70	7,428	32,126	385,977	188.50	7,540	32,611	391,797
180.15	7,206	31,166	374,442	182.95	7,318	31,650	380,262	185.75	7,430	32,135	386,081	188.55	7,542	32,619	391,901
180.20	7,208	31,175	374,546	183.00	7,320	31,659	380,366	185.80	7,432	32,143	386,185	188.60	7,544	32,628	392,005
180.25	7,210	31,183	374,650	183.05	7,322	31,676	380,573	185.85	7,434	32,152	386,289	188.65	7,546	32,636	392,109
180.30	7,212	31,192	374,754	183.10	7,324	31,685	380,677	185.90	7,436	32,161	386,393	188.70	7,548	32,645	392,213
180.35	7,214	31,201	374,857	183.15	7,326	31,685	380,677	185.95	7,438	32,169	386,497	188.75	7,550	32,654	392,317
180.40	7,216	31,209	374,961	183.20	7,328	31,694	380,781	186.00	7,440	32,178	386,601	188.80	7,552	32,662	392,421
180.45	7,218	31,218	375,065	183.25	7,330	31,702	380,885	186.05	7,442	32,187	386,705	188.85	7,554	32,671	392,525
180.50	7,220	31,227	375,169	183.30	7,332	31,711	380,989	186.10	7,444	32,195	386,809	188.90	7,556	32,680	392,629
180.55	7,222	31,235	375,273	183.35	7,334	31,720	381,093	186.15	7,446	32,204	386,913	188.95	7,558	32,688	392,733
180.60	7,224	31,244	375,377	183.40	7,336	31,728	381,197	186.20	7,448	32,213	387,017	189.00	7,560	32,697	392,837
180.65	7,226	31,252	375,481	183.45	7,338	31,737	381,301	186.25	7,450	32,221	387,121	189.05	7,562	32,706	392,940
180.70	7,228	31,261	375,585	183.50	7,340	31,746	381,405	186.30	7,452	32,230	387,225	189.10	7,564	32,714	393,044
180.75	7,230	31,270	375,689	183.55	7,342	31,754	381,509	186.35	7,454	32,239	387,328	189.15	7,566	32,723	393,148
180.80	7,232	31,278	375,793	183.60	7,344	31,763	381,613	186.40	7,456	32,247	387,432	189.20	7,568	32,732	393,252
180.85	7,234	31,287	375,897	183.65	7,346	31,771	381,717	186.45	7,458	32,256	387,536	189.25	7,570	32,740	393,356
180.90	7,236	31,296	376,001	183.70	7,348	31,780	381,820	186.50	7,460	32,265	387,640	189.30	7,572	32,749	393,460
180.95	7,238	31,304	376,105	183.75	7,350	31,789	381,924	186.55	7,462	32,273	387,744	189.35	7,574	32,758	393,564
181.00	7,240	31,313	376,209	183.80	7,352	31,797	382,028	186.60	7,464	32,282	387,848	189.40	7,576	32,766	393,668
181.05	7,242	31,322	376,312	183.85	7,354	31,806	382,132	186.65	7,466	32,290	387,952	189.45	7,578	32,775	393,772
181.10	7,244	31,330	376,416	183.90	7,356	31,815	382,236	186.70	7,468	32,299	388,056	189.50	7,580	32,784	393,876
181.15	7,246	31,339	376,520	183.95	7,358	31,823	382,340	186.75	7,470	32,308	388,160	189.55	7,582	32,792	393,980

Salary Conversion Table

Hour	Week	Month	Year	Hour	Week	Month	Year	Hour	Week	Month	Year	Hour	Week	Month	Year
189.60	7,584	32,801	394,084	192.40	7,696	33,285	399,903	195.20	7,808	33,770	405,723	198.00	7,920	34,254	411,543
189.65	7,586	32,809	394,188	192.45	7,698	33,294	400,007	195.25	7,810	33,778	405,827	198.05	7,922	34,263	411,647
189.70	7,588	32,818	394,291	192.50	7,700	33,303	400,111	195.30	7,812	33,787	405,931	198.10	7,924	34,271	411,751
189.75	7,590	32,827	394,395	192.55	7,702	33,311	400,215	195.35	7,814	33,796	406,035	198.15	7,926	34,280	411,855
189.80	7,592	32,835	394,499	192.60	7,704	33,320	400,319	195.40	7,816	33,804	406,139	198.20	7,928	34,289	411,959
189.85	7,594	32,844	394,603	192.65	7,706	33,328	400,423	195.45	7,818	33,813	406,243	198.25	7,930	34,297	412,063
189.90	7,596	32,853	394,707	192.70	7,708	33,337	400,527	195.50	7,820	33,822	406,347	198.30	7,932	34,306	412,167
189.95	7,598	32,861	394,811	192.75	7,710	33,346	400,631	195.55	7,822	33,830	406,451	198.35	7,934	34,315	412,270
190.00	7,600	32,870	394,915	192.80	7,712	33,354	400,735	195.60	7,824	33,839	406,555	198.40	7,936	34,323	412,374
190.05	7,602	32,879	395,019	192.85	7,714	33,363	400,839	195.65	7,826	33,847	406,659	198.45	7,938	34,332	412,478
190.10	7,604	32,887	395,123	192.90	7,716	33,372	400,943	195.70	7,828	33,856	406,762	198.50	7,940	34,341	412,582
190.15	7,606	32,896	395,227	192.95	7,718	33,380	401,047	195.75	7,830	33,865	406,866	198.55	7,942	34,349	412,686
190.20	7,608	32,905	395,331	193.00	7,720	33,389	401,151	195.80	7,832	33,873	406,970	198.60	7,944	34,358	412,790
190.25	7,610	32,913	395,435	193.05	7,722	33,398	401,254	195.85	7,834	33,882	407,074	198.65	7,946	34,366	412,894
190.30	7,612	32,922	395,539	193.10	7,724	33,406	401,358	195.90	7,836	33,891	407,178	198.70	7,948	34,375	412,998
190.35	7,614	32,931	395,642	193.15	7,726	33,415	401,462	195.95	7,838	33,899	407,282	198.75	7,950	34,384	413,102
190.40	7,616	32,939	395,746	193.20	7,728	33,424	401,566	196.00	7,840	33,908	407,386	198.80	7,952	34,392	413,206
190.45	7,618	32,948	395,850	193.25	7,730	33,432	401,670	196.05	7,842	33,917	407,490	198.85	7,954	34,401	413,310
190.50	7,620	32,957	395,954	193.30	7,732	33,441	401,774	196.10	7,844	33,925	407,594	198.90	7,956	34,410	413,414
190.55	7,622	32,965	396,058	193.35	7,734	33,450	401,878	196.15	7,846	33,934	407,698	198.95	7,958	34,418	413,518
190.60	7,624	32,974	396,162	193.40	7,736	33,458	401,982	196.20	7,848	33,943	407,802	199.00	7,960	34,427	413,622
190.65	7,626	32,982	396,266	193.45	7,738	33,467	402,086	196.25	7,850	33,951	407,906	199.05	7,962	34,436	413,725
190.70	7,628	32,991	396,370	193.50	7,740	33,476	402,190	196.30	7,852	33,960	408,010	199.10	7,964	34,444	413,829
190.75	7,630	33,000	396,474	193.55	7,742	33,484	402,294	196.35	7,854	33,969	408,113	199.15	7,966	34,453	413,933
190.80	7,632	33,008	396,578	193.60	7,744	33,493	402,398	196.40	7,856	33,977	408,217	199.20	7,968	34,462	414,037
190.85	7,634	33,017	396,682	193.65	7,746	33,501	402,502	196.45	7,858	33,986	408,321	199.25	7,970	34,470	414,141
190.90	7,636	33,026	396,786	193.70	7,748	33,510	402,605	196.50	7,860	33,995	408,425	199.30	7,972	34,479	414,245
190.95	7,638	33,034	396,890	193.75	7,750	33,519	402,709	196.55	7,862	34,003	408,529	199.35	7,974	34,488	414,349
191.00	7,640	33,043	396,994	193.80	7,752	33,527	402,813	196.60	7,864	34,012	408,633	199.40	7,976	34,496	414,453
191.05	7,642	33,052	397,097	193.85	7,754	33,536	402,917	196.65	7,866	34,020	408,737	199.45	7,978	34,505	414,557
191.10	7,644	33,060	397,201	193.90	7,756	33,545	403,021	196.70	7,868	34,029	408,841	199.50	7,980	34,514	414,661
191.15	7,646	33,069	397,305	193.95	7,758	33,553	403,125	196.75	7,870	34,038	408,945	199.55	7,982	34,522	414,765
191.20	7,648	33,078	397,409	194.00	7,760	33,562	403,229	196.80	7,872	34,046	409,049	199.60	7,984	34,531	414,869
191.25	7,650	33,086	397,513	194.05	7,762	33,571	403,333	196.85	7,874	34,055	409,153	199.65	7,986	34,539	414,973
191.30	7,652	33,095	397,617	194.10	7,764	33,579	403,437	196.90	7,876	34,064	409,257	199.70	7,988	34,548	415,076
191.35	7,654	33,104	397,721	194.15	7,766	33,588	403,541	196.95	7,878	34,072	409,361	199.75	7,990	34,557	415,180
191.40	7,656	33,112	397,825	194.20	7,768	33,597	403,645	197.00	7,880	34,081	409,465	199.80	7,992	34,565	415,284
191.45	7,658	33,121	397,929	194.25	7,770	33,605	403,749	197.05	7,882	34,090	409,568	199.85	7,994	34,574	415,388
191.50	7,660	33,130	398,033	194.30	7,772	33,614	403,853	197.10	7,884	34,098	409,672	199.90	7,996	34,583	415,492
191.55	7,662	33,138	398,137	194.35	7,774	33,623	403,956	197.15	7,886	34,107	409,776	199.95	7,998	34,591	415,596
191.60	7,664	33,147	398,241	194.40	7,776	33,631	404,060	197.20	7,888	34,116	409,880	200.00	8,000	34,600	415,700
191.65	7,666	33,155	398,345	194.45	7,778	33,640	404,164	197.25	7,890	34,124	409,984	200.05	8,002	34,609	415,804
191.70	7,668	33,164	398,448	194.50	7,780	33,649	404,268	197.30	7,892	34,133	410,088	200.10	8,004	34,617	415,908
191.75	7,670	33,173	398,552	194.55	7,782	33,657	404,372	197.35	7,894	34,142	410,192	200.15	8,006	34,626	416,012
191.80	7,672	33,181	398,656	194.60	7,784	33,666	404,476	197.40	7,896	34,150	410,296	200.20	8,008	34,635	416,116
191.85	7,674	33,190	398,760	194.65	7,786	33,674	404,580	197.45	7,898	34,159	410,400	200.25	8,010	34,643	416,220
191.90	7,676	33,199	398,864	194.70	7,788	33,683	404,684	197.50	7,900	34,168	410,504	200.30	8,012	34,652	416,324
191.95	7,678	33,207	398,968	194.75	7,790	33,692	404,788	197.55	7,902	34,176	410,608	200.35	8,014	34,661	416,427
192.00	7,680	33,216	399,072	194.80	7,792	33,700	404,892	197.60	7,904	34,185	410,712	200.40	8,016	34,669	416,531
192.05	7,682	33,225	399,176	194.85	7,794	33,709	404,996	197.65	7,906	34,193	410,816	200.45	8,018	34,678	416,635
192.10	7,684	33,233	399,280	194.90	7,796	33,718	405,100	197.70	7,908	34,202	410,919	200.50	8,020	34,687	416,739
192.15	7,686	33,242	399,384	194.95	7,798	33,726	405,204	197.75	7,910	34,211	411,023	200.55	8,022	34,695	416,843
192.20	7,688	33,251	399,488	195.00	7,800	33,735	405,308	197.80	7,912	34,219	411,127	200.60	8,024	34,704	416,947
192.25	7,690	33,259	399,592	195.05	7,802	33,744	405,411	197.85	7,914	34,228	411,231	200.65	8,026	34,712	417,051
192.30	7,692	33,268	399,696	195.10	7,804	33,752	405,515	197.90	7,916	34,237	411,335	200.70	8,028	34,721	417,155
192.35	7,694	33,277	399,799	195.15	7,806	33,761	405,619	197.95	7,918	34,245	411,439	200.75	8,030	34,730	417,259

Appendix III

ABBREVIATIONS

Acronyms used to abbreviate data sources may be found in Appendix I.

A&P	Airframe and Powerplant		**HR**	High end range
AAGO	Associateship, American Guild of Organists		**ID**	Identification
ACA	Affordable Care Act		**IT**	Information Technology
ADA	Americans with Disabilities Act		**ITIL**	Infrastructure Technology Information Library
AE	Average entry wage		**J2EE**	Java 2, Enterprise Edition
AEX	Average experienced wage		**JROTC**	Junior Reserve Officer's Training Corps
ATC	Average total compensation		**K9**	Canine
AW	Average wage		**KGB**	Keep Georgia Beautiful
AWR	Average wage range		**LBGT**	Lesbian, Bisexual, Gay, and Transgender
AWS	Amazon Web Services		**LO**	Lowest wage paid
B	Biweekly		**LPA**	Locality Pay Area
B2B	Business to Business		**LR**	Low end range
CAD	Computer Aided Design		**M**	Monthly
CAGO	Collegue, American Guild of Organists		**MCC**	Median cash compensation
CAT	Computerized Axial Tomography		**ME**	Median entry wage
COBOL	Common Business-Oriented Language		**MSA**	Metropolitan Statistical Area
D	Daily		**MTC**	Median total compensation
DNA	Deoxyribonucleic Acid		**MW**	Median wage
DUI	Driving Under the Influence		**MWR**	Median wage range
E-911	Enhanced 911		**NECTA**	New England City and Town Area
EMS	Emergency Medical Services		**PAL**	Police Athletic League
ERP	Enterprise Resource Planning		**PMSA**	Primary Metropolitan Statistical Area
ESL	English as a Second Language		**S**	See annotated source
F&I	Finance and Insurance		**S&P**	Standard and Poor's
FAGO	Fellowship, American Guild of Organists		**SEO**	Search Engine Optimization
FBS	Football Bowl Subdivision		**SWAT**	Special Weapons and Tactics
FOIA	Freedom of Information Act		**TCC**	Total cash compensation
FQ	First quartile wage		**TQ**	Third quartile wage
FRIB	Facility for Rare Isotope Beams		**TV**	Television
GIS	Geographic Information System		**UH**	Utility Helicopter
H	Hourly		**UI**	User Interface
HANA	High Performance Analytical Appliance		**W**	Weekly
HI	Highest wage paid		**WIC**	Women, Infants, and Children
HIPAA	Health Insurance Portability and Accountability Act		**XML**	Extensible Markup Language
			Y	Yearly

Appendix IV

EMPLOYMENT BY OCCUPATION - 2014 AND 2024

This appendix displays data from the *National Industry-Occupational Matrix* prepared by the Department of Labor (DOL) from time to time. The data show employment by occupation for 2014 with DOL projections to 2024. The appendix is divided into three parts. The first part shows the occupations in alphabetical order using occupation titles as defined by DOL. The only exceptions are cases where the DOL refers to "All Other" followed by an occupation. These have been rendered by the name of the occupation, followed by the abbreviation 'nsk' to indicate 'not specified by kind.' The second arrangement shows occupations by 2014 employment, largest category first. The third sort is by rate of growth, 2014 to 2024, the fastest growing occupation shown first. Data were released in December 2015 and are referred to as the *National Employment Matrix*.

Alphabetical Order

Total Employment 2014	2024	% Change	Occupation	Total Employment 2014	2024	% Change	Occupation
1,332,700	1,475,100	10.7	Accountants and auditors	182,100	185,800	2.0	Architectural and engineering managers
69,400	76,100	9.6	Actors	9,100	9,900	9.4	Architecture teachers, postsecondary
24,600	29,000	18.1	Actuaries	6,900	7,400	6.8	Archivists
18,400	17,100	-6.8	Adhesive bonding machine operators and tenders	11,600	13,300	15.1	Area, ethnic, and cultural studies teachers, postsecondary
15,000	14,500	-3.6	Administrative law judges, adjudicators, and hearing officers	74,600	76,400	2.4	Art directors
287,300	310,800	8.2	Administrative services managers	120,700	133,700	10.8	Art, drama, and music teachers, postsecondary
77,500	83,000	7.1	Adult basic and secondary education and literacy teachers and instructors	13,400	13,500	0.4	Artists and related workers, nsk
				240,700	252,200	4.8	Assemblers and fabricators, nsk
31,000	32,400	4.7	Advertising and promotions managers	1,900	1,900	2.8	Astronomers
167,900	163,400	-2.7	Advertising sales agents	13,700	14,500	5.6	Athletes and sports competitors
11,400	11,800	3.6	Aerospace engineering and operations technicians	25,400	30,800	21.1	Athletic trainers
				11,800	12,900	9.2	Atmospheric and space scientists
72,500	70,800	-2.3	Aerospace engineers	13,200	14,300	8.7	Atmospheric, earth, marine, and space sciences teachers, postsecondary
19,700	20,200	2.5	Agents and business managers of artists, performers, and athletes	70,900	79,400	11.9	Audio and video equipment technicians
33,000	34,700	4.9	Agricultural and food science technicians	13,200	16,900	28.6	Audiologists
2,900	3,000	4.4	Agricultural engineers	10,000	10,800	7.9	Audio-visual and multimedia collections specialists
57,800	60,900	5.4	Agricultural equipment operators	105,800	117,600	11.1	Automotive and watercraft service attendants
14,200	14,100	-0.6	Agricultural inspectors	149,700	163,500	9.2	Automotive body and related repairers
12,100	12,800	6.0	Agricultural sciences teachers, postsecondary	19,300	20,800	7.8	Automotive glass installers and repairers
10,600	10,000	-5.7	Agricultural workers, nsk	739,900	779,000	5.3	Automotive service technicians and mechanics
24,500	22,400	-8.6	Air traffic controllers	17,400	17,500	0.4	Avionics technicians
5,800	5,800	0.5	Aircraft cargo handling supervisors	43,600	47,100	8.0	Baggage porters and bellhops
119,900	121,500	1.3	Aircraft mechanics and service technicians	17,300	18,100	4.7	Bailiffs
40,600	38,600	-4.9	Aircraft structure, surfaces, rigging, and systems assemblers	185,300	198,300	7.0	Bakers
				59,200	65,100	10.1	Barbers
7,200	7,500	3.9	Airfield operations specialists	580,900	640,900	10.3	Bartenders
75,700	76,500	1.1	Airline pilots, copilots, and flight engineers	10,800	13,200	21.7	Bicycle repairers
19,600	26,100	33.0	Ambulance drivers and attendants, except emergency medical technicians	350,400	330,900	-5.6	Bill and account collectors
				514,600	581,100	12.9	Billing and posting clerks
288,600	310,900	7.7	Amusement and recreation attendants	34,100	36,900	8.2	Biochemists and biophysicists
33,700	40,800	21.0	Anesthesiologists	64,300	74,800	16.2	Biological science teachers, postsecondary
7,000	6,900	-1.6	Animal breeders	36,400	36,200	-0.4	Biological scientists, nsk
15,000	15,900	5.8	Animal control workers	79,300	83,500	5.2	Biological technicians
2,900	3,200	7.3	Animal scientists	22,100	27,200	23.1	Biomedical engineers
36,800	40,900	11.1	Animal trainers	17,400	19,000	8.7	Boilermakers
7,700	8,000	3.8	Anthropologists and archeologists	1,760,300	1,611,500	-8.4	Bookkeeping, accounting, and auditing clerks
7,500	8,200	9.3	Anthropology and archeology teachers, postsecondary	78,100	92,600	18.6	Brickmasons and blockmasons
				3,500	3,400	-1.1	Bridge and lock tenders
85,800	92,500	7.9	Appraisers and assessors of real estate	5,100	4,500	-12.6	Broadcast news analysts
8,400	9,200	9.2	Arbitrators, mediators, and conciliators	30,100	28,200	-6.5	Broadcast technicians
112,600	120,400	6.9	Architects, except landscape and naval	57,200	62,400	9.0	Brokerage clerks
94,000	91,200	-3.0	Architectural and civil drafters	60,800	62,300	2.5	Budget analysts

Total Employment 2014	2024	% Change	Occupation
16,900	17,700	4.8	Building cleaning workers, nsk
263,900	295,500	12.0	Bus and truck mechanics and diesel engine specialists
497,300	524,900	5.6	Bus drivers, school or special client
167,800	177,600	5.9	Bus drivers, transit and intercity
998,000	1,046,000	4.8	Business operations specialists, nsk
106,800	116,200	8.8	Business teachers, postsecondary
139,000	146,000	5.0	Butchers and meat cutters
12,900	13,500	4.6	Buyers and purchasing agents, farm products
98,100	99,300	1.3	Cabinetmakers and bench carpenters
3,700	3,800	4.7	Camera and photographic equipment repairers
25,400	25,900	2.0	Camera operators, television, video, and motion picture
35,100	38,700	10.2	Captains, mates, and pilots of water vessels
52,000	63,500	22.2	Cardiovascular technologists and technicians
13,700	14,600	5.9	Career/technical education teachers, middle school
79,600	79,900	0.4	Career/technical education teachers, secondary school
78,800	84,300	7.0	Cargo and freight agents
945,400	1,005,800	6.4	Carpenters
45,300	45,100	-0.5	Carpet installers
12,300	15,900	29.3	Cartographers and photogrammetrists
3,424,200	3,491,100	2.0	Cashiers
155,200	175,500	13.1	Cement masons and concrete finishers
127,500	138,800	8.9	Chefs and head cooks
34,300	34,900	1.8	Chemical engineers
66,300	60,800	-8.3	Chemical equipment operators and tenders
38,100	34,600	-9.2	Chemical plant and system operators
66,500	67,700	1.9	Chemical technicians
26,600	30,700	15.4	Chemistry teachers, postsecondary
91,100	93,500	2.6	Chemists
343,400	339,400	-1.2	Chief executives
305,200	324,200	6.2	Child, family, and school social workers
1,260,600	1,329,900	5.5	Childcare workers
45,200	53,100	17.5	Chiropractors
7,100	7,500	6.3	Choreographers
74,000	77,600	4.8	Civil engineering technicians
281,400	305,000	8.4	Civil engineers
299,700	309,500	3.3	Claims adjusters, examiners, and investigators
346,900	380,000	9.5	Cleaners of vehicles and equipment
18,500	18,600	0.4	Cleaning, washing, and metal pickling equipment operators and tenders
244,200	258,000	5.6	Clergy
155,300	185,900	19.6	Clinical, counseling, and school psychologists
250,600	265,400	5.9	Coaches and scouts
97,700	97,000	-0.7	Coating, painting, and spraying machine setters, operators, and tenders
14,900	14,100	-5.7	Coil winders, tapers, and finishers
34,900	31,900	-8.7	Coin, vending, and amusement machine servicers and repairers
3,159,700	3,503,200	10.9	Combined food preparation and serving workers, including fast food
38,400	39,200	2.0	Commercial and industrial designers
4,400	6,000	36.9	Commercial divers
43,500	48,000	10.5	Commercial pilots
3,300	3,500	5.6	Communications equipment operators, nsk
36,000	39,500	9.7	Communications teachers, postsecondary
102,700	111,100	8.2	Community and social service specialists, nsk
54,300	62,400	14.9	Community health workers
16,900	18,000	6.5	Compensation and benefits managers
84,700	88,100	4.0	Compensation, benefits, and job analysis specialists
260,300	269,000	3.3	Compliance officers
25,600	28,300	10.7	Computer and information research scientists
348,500	402,200	15.4	Computer and information systems managers
77,700	80,100	3.1	Computer hardware engineers
146,200	158,900	8.7	Computer network architects

Total Employment 2014	2024	% Change	Occupation
181,000	194,600	7.5	Computer network support specialists
25,100	29,900	18.9	Computer numerically controlled machine tool programmers, metal and plastic
233,000	240,800	3.3	Computer occupations, nsk
61,100	49,500	-19.0	Computer operators
328,600	302,200	-8.0	Computer programmers
43,400	47,200	8.7	Computer science teachers, postsecondary
567,800	686,300	20.9	Computer systems analysts
585,900	661,000	12.8	Computer user support specialists
131,600	134,800	2.4	Computer, automated teller, and office machine repairers
148,800	174,800	17.5	Computer-controlled machine tool operators, metal and plastic
31,200	34,400	10.4	Concierges
21,100	22,500	6.9	Conservation scientists
101,200	109,200	8.0	Construction and building inspectors
35,400	37,800	6.9	Construction and related workers, nsk
1,159,100	1,306,500	12.7	Construction laborers
373,200	391,100	4.8	Construction managers
12,300	11,600	-5.3	Continuous mining machine operators
42,400	42,600	0.5	Control and valve installers and repairers, except mechanical door
39,700	39,600	-0.2	Conveyor operators and tenders
524,400	444,000	-15.3	Cooks, fast food
417,600	443,900	6.3	Cooks, institution and cafeteria
21,500	22,800	6.0	Cooks, nsk
35,900	36,200	0.6	Cooks, private household
1,109,700	1,268,700	14.3	Cooks, restaurant
181,600	172,300	-5.1	Cooks, short order
8,800	8,700	-0.6	Cooling and freezing equipment operators and tenders
457,600	474,700	3.7	Correctional officers and jailers
8,400	7,200	-14.7	Correspondence clerks
213,500	232,300	8.8	Cost estimators
6,200	6,700	8.8	Costume attendants
31,000	34,400	11.0	Counselors, nsk
442,100	458,500	3.7	Counter and rental clerks
481,200	510,000	6.0	Counter attendants, cafeteria, food concession, and coffee shop
92,900	97,700	5.2	Couriers and messengers
20,800	21,100	1.5	Court reporters
140,800	147,100	4.5	Court, municipal, and license clerks
10,600	10,600	0.6	Craft artists
45,500	49,000	7.6	Crane and tower operators
69,400	73,600	6.1	Credit analysts
46,100	43,300	-6.2	Credit authorizers, checkers, and clerks
32,600	37,600	15.5	Credit counselors
17,400	21,100	21.4	Criminal justice and law enforcement teachers, postsecondary
69,800	74,200	6.4	Crossing guards
30,200	27,900	-7.5	Crushing, grinding, and polishing machine setters, operators, and tenders
13,100	14,100	8.0	Curators
2,581,800	2,834,800	9.8	Customer service representatives
15,800	13,000	-17.5	Cutters and trimmers, hand
63,600	58,400	-8.1	Cutting and slicing machine setters, operators, and tenders
192,200	152,700	-20.6	Cutting, punching, and press machine setters, operators, and tenders, metal and plastic
13,000	13,600	4.8	Dancers
216,800	208,900	-3.7	Data entry keyers
120,000	133,400	11.1	Database administrators
93,000	101,300	8.9	Demonstrators and product promoters
318,800	377,400	18.4	Dental assistants
200,500	237,900	18.6	Dental hygienists
38,700	42,900	10.8	Dental laboratory technicians
129,000	152,300	18.0	Dentists, general
6,700	7,300	8.5	Dentists, nsk

Total Employment 2014	2024	% Change	Occupation
21,700	24,600	13.3	Derrick operators, oil and gas
8,900	9,500	6.2	Designers, nsk
14,800	11,700	-21.0	Desktop publishers
116,700	115,300	-1.2	Detectives and criminal investigators
60,700	76,700	26.4	Diagnostic medical sonographers
29,300	33,200	13.3	Dietetic technicians
66,700	77,600	16.4	Dietitians and nutritionists
415,300	440,700	6.1	Dining room and cafeteria attendants and bartender helpers
131,900	137,500	4.3	Directors, religious activities and education
507,400	487,900	-3.9	Dishwashers
199,500	208,200	4.4	Dispatchers, except police, fire, and ambulance
80,200	79,100	-1.4	Door-to-door sales workers, news and street vendors, and related workers
14,700	14,200	-3.4	Drafters, nsk
2,200	2,300	8.7	Dredge operators
17,800	14,100	-20.5	Drilling and boring machine tool setters, operators, and tenders, metal and plastic
445,300	466,100	4.7	Driver/sales workers
106,000	111,500	5.2	Drywall and ceiling tile installers
20,000	22,700	13.6	Earth drillers, except oil and gas
17,300	18,900	9.7	Economics teachers, postsecondary
21,500	22,700	5.7	Economists
117,200	111,000	-5.3	Editors
240,000	254,000	5.8	Education administrators, elementary and secondary school
37,800	39,300	4.0	Education administrators, nsk
175,100	190,300	8.7	Education administrators, postsecondary
64,000	68,200	6.6	Education administrators, preschool and childcare center/program
75,700	82,500	9.1	Education teachers, postsecondary
124,000	133,100	7.4	Education, training, and library workers, nsk
273,400	295,900	8.2	Educational, guidance, school, and vocational counselors
19,300	20,000	3.6	Electric motor, power tool, and related repairers
207,200	197,000	-4.9	Electrical and electronic equipment assemblers
30,100	31,700	5.4	Electrical and electronics drafters
139,400	136,600	-2.0	Electrical and electronics engineering technicians
14,800	15,400	4.4	Electrical and electronics installers and repairers, transportation equipment
67,800	67,800	0.1	Electrical and electronics repairers, commercial and industrial equipment
22,700	21,700	-4.5	Electrical and electronics repairers, powerhouse, substation, and relay
178,400	180,200	1.0	Electrical engineers
118,600	131,600	11.0	Electrical power-line installers and repairers
628,800	714,700	13.7	Electricians
47,200	44,700	-5.3	Electromechanical equipment assemblers
14,700	14,800	0.7	Electro-mechanical technicians
11,500	5,800	-50.0	Electronic equipment installers and repairers, motor vehicles
29,600	30,300	2.4	Electronic home entertainment equipment installers and repairers
137,400	135,500	-1.4	Electronics engineers, except computer
1,358,000	1,436,300	5.8	Elementary school teachers, except special education
20,700	23,400	13.0	Elevator installers and repairers
129,900	132,000	1.6	Eligibility interviewers, government programs
3,800	3,600	-6.1	Embalmers
10,500	11,200	6.2	Emergency management directors
241,200	299,600	24.2	Emergency medical technicians and paramedics
39,000	39,000	0.1	Engine and other machine assemblers
46,000	52,000	13.2	Engineering teachers, postsecondary
70,100	69,900	-0.2	Engineering technicians, except drafters, nsk

Total Employment 2014	2024	% Change	Occupation
136,900	142,300	4.0	Engineers, nsk
90,800	100,200	10.4	English language and literature teachers, postsecondary
30,000	32,100	6.8	Entertainers and performers, sports and related workers, nsk
16,900	19,800	17.1	Entertainment attendants and related workers, nsk
18,600	20,400	10.0	Environmental engineering technicians
55,100	62,000	12.4	Environmental engineers
36,200	39,600	9.5	Environmental science and protection technicians, including health
6,700	7,300	8.6	Environmental science teachers, postsecondary
94,600	104,800	10.7	Environmental scientists and specialists, including health
5,800	6,100	6.3	Epidemiologists
9,700	9,500	-2.7	Etchers and engravers
53,900	57,300	6.2	Excavating and loading machine and dragline operators
776,600	732,000	-5.7	Executive secretaries and executive administrative assistants
14,500	16,000	10.6	Exercise physiologists
8,100	8,400	3.9	Explosives workers, ordnance handling experts, and blasters
5,700	6,300	11.9	Extraction workers, nsk
73,400	55,500	-24.4	Extruding and drawing machine setters, operators, and tenders, metal and plastic
20,100	17,300	-14.1	Extruding and forming machine setters, operators, and tenders, synthetic and glass fibers
68,200	59,000	-13.6	Extruding, forming, pressing, and compacting machine setters, operators, and tenders
5,400	4,000	-26.0	Fabric and apparel patternmakers
800	700	-12.6	Fabric menders, except garment
8,200	6,800	-17.2	Fallers
139,800	154,100	10.2	Family and general practitioners
10,800	11,900	10.9	Farm and home management advisors
40,300	43,200	7.2	Farm equipment mechanics and service technicians
100	100	-8.9	Farm labor contractors
929,800	911,700	-1.9	Farmers, ranchers, and other agricultural managers
470,200	427,300	-9.1	Farmworkers and laborers, crop, nursery, and greenhouse
216,100	209,100	-3.2	Farmworkers, farm, ranch, and aquacultural animals
23,100	23,800	2.9	Fashion designers
24,400	26,400	8.0	Fence erectors
19,200	18,600	-3.3	Fiberglass laminators and fabricators
159,000	150,100	-5.6	File clerks
33,500	39,400	17.6	Film and video editors
277,600	310,000	11.7	Financial analysts
38,100	41,600	9.0	Financial clerks, nsk
38,200	42,000	9.7	Financial examiners
555,900	593,500	6.8	Financial managers
145,200	152,300	4.9	Financial specialists, nsk
26,300	27,100	3.1	Fine artists, including painters, sculptors, and illustrators
12,400	13,100	5.5	Fire inspectors and investigators
327,300	344,700	5.3	Firefighters
578,400	636,100	10.0	First-line supervisors of construction trades and extraction workers
47,600	49,100	3.1	First-line supervisors of correctional officers
47,100	43,300	-8.2	First-line supervisors of farming, fishing, and forestry workers
63,500	66,800	5.2	First-line supervisors of fire fighting and prevention workers
890,100	978,600	9.9	First-line supervisors of food preparation and serving workers

Total Employment 2014	2024	% Change	Occupation
173,100	176,900	2.2	First-line supervisors of helpers, laborers, and material movers, hand
247,900	262,800	6.0	First-line supervisors of housekeeping and janitorial workers
178,000	187,400	5.3	First-line supervisors of landscaping, lawn service, and groundskeeping workers
447,100	471,400	5.4	First-line supervisors of mechanics, installers, and repairers
430,700	451,000	4.7	First-line supervisors of non-retail sales workers
1,466,100	1,587,300	8.3	First-line supervisors of office and administrative support workers
255,800	283,800	10.9	First-line supervisors of personal service workers
108,100	112,700	4.2	First-line supervisors of police and detectives
606,900	588,200	-3.1	First-line supervisors of production and operating workers
68,700	71,900	4.6	First-line supervisors of protective service workers, nsk
1,537,800	1,605,400	4.4	First-line supervisors of retail sales workers
199,700	205,600	2.9	First-line supervisors of transportation and material-moving machine and vehicle operators
6,200	6,300	1.9	Fish and game wardens
28,400	28,200	-0.7	Fishing and hunting workers
279,100	302,500	8.4	Fitness trainers and aerobics instructors
97,900	100,100	2.2	Flight attendants
17,100	19,200	12.2	Floor layers, except carpet, wood, and hard tiles
7,900	8,400	6.2	Floor sanders and finishers
58,700	56,700	-3.4	Floral designers
18,500	18,700	0.7	Food and tobacco roasting, baking, and drying machine operators and tenders
122,500	122,000	-0.4	Food batchmakers
37,500	38,000	1.3	Food cooking machine operators and tenders
46,100	49,600	7.7	Food preparation and serving related workers, nsk
873,900	928,800	6.3	Food preparation workers
44,400	47,700	7.4	Food processing workers, nsk
15,400	16,000	3.5	Food scientists and technologists
253,100	287,000	13.4	Food servers, nonrestaurant
305,000	320,700	5.1	Food service managers
37,200	41,300	10.9	Foreign language and literature teachers, postsecondary
14,400	18,200	26.6	Forensic science technicians
32,600	30,800	-5.7	Forest and conservation technicians
14,000	14,600	4.2	Forest and conservation workers
1,700	2,000	13.1	Forest fire inspectors and prevention specialists
15,500	16,800	8.3	Foresters
2,300	2,400	6.8	Forestry and conservation science teachers, postsecondary
21,600	17,000	-21.5	Forging machine setters, operators, and tenders, metal and plastic
12,000	8,700	-27.7	Foundry mold and coremakers
73,400	80,300	9.3	Fundraisers
36,100	35,700	-1.2	Funeral attendants
29,300	30,300	3.3	Funeral service managers
20,900	18,900	-9.7	Furnace, kiln, oven, drier, and kettle operators and tenders
17,100	16,700	-2.4	Furniture finishers
11,500	11,900	3.4	Gaming and sports book writers and runners
11,300	11,900	5.0	Gaming cage workers
13,300	11,900	-10.9	Gaming change persons and booth cashiers
68,500	68,900	0.6	Gaming dealers
3,800	3,800	-0.6	Gaming managers
13,200	13,400	1.6	Gaming service workers, nsk
27,800	28,000	0.7	Gaming supervisors

Total Employment 2014	2024	% Change	Occupation
7,000	6,600	-7.0	Gaming surveillance officers and gaming investigators
5,100	5,300	3.4	Gas compressor and gas pumping station operators
16,700	16,100	-3.4	Gas plant operators
2,124,100	2,275,200	7.1	General and operations managers
2,400	3,100	28.8	Genetic counselors
1,400	1,400	-1.6	Geographers
5,400	5,900	7.9	Geography teachers, postsecondary
16,500	18,500	11.8	Geological and petroleum technicians
36,400	40,200	10.5	Geoscientists, except hydrologists and geographers
45,300	47,200	4.1	Glaziers
53,000	48,900	-7.8	Graders and sorters, agricultural products
159,200	169,100	6.2	Graduate teaching assistants
261,600	265,200	1.4	Graphic designers
29,900	27,300	-8.8	Grinding and polishing workers, hand
71,400	55,800	-21.9	Grinding, lapping, polishing, and buffing machine tool setters, operators, and tenders, metal and plastic
24,500	26,100	6.4	Grounds maintenance workers, nsk
597,200	655,600	9.8	Hairdressers, hairstylists, and cosmetologists
43,700	47,000	7.4	Hazardous materials removal workers
25,200	26,800	6.2	Health and safety engineers, except mining safety engineers and inspectors
50,100	56,100	12.0	Health diagnosing and treating practitioners, nsk
61,400	68,900	12.2	Health educators
210,400	250,400	19.0	Health specialties teachers, postsecondary
102,200	125,900	23.1	Health technologists and technicians, nsk
44,200	50,300	13.8	Healthcare practitioners and technical workers, nsk
160,100	191,000	19.3	Healthcare social workers
102,700	114,700	11.7	Healthcare support workers, nsk
5,900	7,500	27.2	Hearing aid specialists
21,300	17,200	-19.6	Heat treating equipment setters, operators, and tenders, metal and plastic
292,000	331,600	13.6	Heating, air conditioning, and refrigeration mechanics and installers
1,797,700	1,896,400	5.5	Heavy and tractor-trailer truck drivers
19,500	21,500	10.2	Helpers, construction trades, nsk
23,500	28,800	22.4	Helpers—brickmasons, blockmasons, stonemasons, and tile and marble setters
39,700	42,700	7.5	Helpers—carpenters
69,000	81,500	18.0	Helpers—electricians
25,800	29,000	12.6	Helpers—extraction workers
129,000	141,200	9.4	Helpers—installation, maintenance, and repair workers
11,900	13,100	10.5	Helpers—painters, paperhangers, plasterers, and stucco masons
52,400	59,400	13.4	Helpers—pipelayers, plumbers, pipefitters, and steamfitters
419,200	403,200	-3.8	Helpers—production workers
11,300	13,000	15.3	Helpers—roofers
151,300	158,600	4.8	Highway maintenance workers
3,500	3,500	1.7	Historians
29,200	32,100	10.0	History teachers, postsecondary
2,900	2,900	1.7	Hoist and winch operators
46,400	44,800	-3.4	Home appliance repairers
4,300	3,800	-11.6	Home economics teachers, postsecondary
913,500	1,261,900	38.1	Home health aides
376,400	393,200	4.4	Hosts and hostesses, restaurant, lounge, and coffee shop
243,200	265,100	9.0	Hotel, motel, and resort desk clerks
140,600	134,800	-4.1	Human resources assistants, except payroll and timekeeping
122,500	133,300	8.8	Human resources managers
482,000	503,900	4.6	Human resources specialists
7,000	7,500	6.9	Hydrologists

Total Employment 2014	2024	% Change	Occupation
66,500	63,500	-4.5	Industrial engineering technicians
241,100	243,200	0.9	Industrial engineers
332,200	391,900	18.0	Industrial machinery mechanics
173,400	167,000	-3.7	Industrial production managers
530,900	543,500	2.4	Industrial truck and tractor operators
2,000	2,300	19.1	Industrial-organizational psychologists
188,500	193,000	2.4	Information and record clerks, nsk
82,900	97,700	17.9	Information security analysts
496,600	495,500	-0.2	Inspectors, testers, sorters, samplers, and weighers
163,500	170,600	4.3	Installation, maintenance, and repair workers, nsk
151,100	161,600	7.0	Instructional coordinators
25,600	27,100	6.1	Insulation workers, floor, ceiling, and wall
30,100	35,900	19.4	Insulation workers, mechanical
15,500	15,400	-1.2	Insurance appraisers, auto damage
285,400	303,100	6.2	Insurance claims and policy processing clerks
466,100	509,500	9.3	Insurance sales agents
103,400	91,600	-11.4	Insurance underwriters
58,900	61,100	3.8	Interior designers
54,300	59,400	9.4	Internists, general
61,000	78,500	28.7	Interpreters and translators
198,000	208,300	5.2	Interviewers, except eligibility and loan
2,360,600	2,496,900	5.8	Janitors and cleaners, except maids and housekeeping cleaners
39,800	35,300	-11.3	Jewelers and precious stone and metal workers
29,700	29,900	0.6	Judges, magistrate judges, and magistrates
12,400	11,600	-6.3	Judicial law clerks
159,400	168,900	5.9	Kindergarten teachers, except special education
82,100	75,600	-7.8	Labor relations specialists
2,441,300	2,566,400	5.1	Laborers and freight, stock, and material movers, hand
22,500	23,700	5.5	Landscape architects
1,167,800	1,239,600	6.1	Landscaping and groundskeeping workers
42,900	34,300	-20.0	Lathe and turning machine tool setters, operators, and tenders, metal and plastic
208,200	212,000	1.8	Laundry and dry-cleaning workers
21,100	25,700	21.7	Law teachers, postsecondary
778,700	822,500	5.6	Lawyers
13,400	10,700	-20.1	Layout workers, metal and plastic
215,500	206,700	-4.1	Legal secretaries
52,600	52,400	-0.4	Legal support workers, nsk
58,300	57,900	-0.7	Legislators
143,100	145,700	1.9	Librarians
108,800	114,700	5.4	Library assistants, clerical
5,600	6,000	8.0	Library science teachers, postsecondary
101,800	107,100	5.2	Library technicians
719,900	837,200	16.3	Licensed practical and licensed vocational nurses
10,600	11,300	7.2	Life scientists, nsk
78,200	83,500	6.8	Life, physical, and social science technicians, nsk
141,300	150,800	6.7	Lifeguards, ski patrol, and other recreational protective service workers
884,700	911,900	3.1	Light truck or delivery services drivers
4,800	4,800	-0.1	Loading machine operators, underground mining
213,800	232,300	8.6	Loan interviewers and clerks
303,200	327,700	8.1	Loan officers
18,600	19,400	4.7	Locker room, coatroom, and dressing room attendants
20,900	17,800	-14.8	Locksmiths and safe repairers
40,400	39,500	-2.3	Locomotive engineers
1,700	500	-69.9	Locomotive firers
48,400	52,100	7.6	Lodging managers
3,700	3,700	-2.0	Log graders and scalers
37,300	37,100	-0.3	Logging equipment operators

Total Employment 2014	2024	% Change	Occupation
4,500	4,100	-7.5	Logging workers, nsk
130,400	132,900	1.9	Logisticians
104,200	100,700	-3.4	Machine feeders and offbearers
399,700	438,900	9.8	Machinists
33,600	37,100	10.3	Magnetic resonance imaging technologists
1,457,700	1,569,400	7.7	Maids and housekeeping cleaners
104,900	85,100	-18.8	Mail clerks and mail machine operators, except postal service
1,374,700	1,458,100	6.1	Maintenance and repair workers, general
91,200	98,700	8.2	Maintenance workers, machinery
3,600	4,300	19.2	Makeup artists, theatrical and performance
758,000	861,400	13.6	Management analysts
985,600	1,023,600	3.9	Managers, nsk
113,600	125,300	10.3	Manicurists and pedicurists
4,000	2,800	-30.0	Manufactured building and mobile home installers
8,300	9,000	8.9	Marine engineers and naval architects
495,500	587,800	18.6	Market research analysts and marketing specialists
194,300	212,500	9.4	Marketing managers
33,700	38,700	14.8	Marriage and family therapists
168,800	205,200	21.6	Massage therapists
23,600	24,700	4.4	Material moving workers, nsk
25,300	25,600	1.3	Materials engineers
7,300	7,500	2.7	Materials scientists
1,800	1,900	5.7	Mathematical science occupations, nsk
63,500	73,900	16.4	Mathematical science teachers, postsecondary
1,200	1,100	-12.6	Mathematical technicians
3,500	4,200	21.4	Mathematicians
152,400	152,300	-0.1	Meat, poultry, and fish cutters and trimmers
17,400	19,300	10.7	Mechanical door repairers
65,700	61,200	-6.8	Mechanical drafters
48,400	49,300	2.0	Mechanical engineering technicians
277,500	292,100	5.3	Mechanical engineers
19,400	18,700	-3.3	Media and communication equipment workers, nsk
33,500	37,000	10.3	Media and communication workers, nsk
163,400	192,400	17.8	Medical and clinical laboratory technicians
164,800	187,900	14.0	Medical and clinical laboratory technologists
333,000	389,300	16.9	Medical and health services managers
14,600	16,100	10.7	Medical appliance technicians
591,300	730,200	23.5	Medical assistants
52,000	59,300	14.0	Medical equipment preparers
48,000	50,900	6.1	Medical equipment repairers
188,600	217,600	15.4	Medical records and health information technicians
107,900	116,800	8.3	Medical scientists, except epidemiologists
527,600	635,800	20.5	Medical secretaries
70,000	67,800	-3.1	Medical transcriptionists
100,000	109,900	9.9	Meeting, convention, and event planners
117,800	140,000	18.9	Mental health and substance abuse social workers
134,500	160,900	19.6	Mental health counselors
120,800	124,100	2.8	Merchandise displayers and window trimmers
22,400	18,700	-16.6	Metal workers and plastic workers, nsk
21,200	20,200	-4.8	Metal-refining furnace operators and tenders
37,400	30,600	-18.0	Meter readers, utilities
22,400	23,200	3.5	Microbiologists
627,500	664,200	5.9	Middle school teachers, except special and career/technical education
22,400	17,800	-20.6	Milling and planing machine setters, operators, and tenders, metal and plastic
40,900	47,100	15.2	Millwrights
7,400	7,300	-1.8	Mine cutting and channeling machine operators
2,700	2,600	-2.2	Mine shuttle car operators
8,300	8,800	6.4	Mining and geological engineers, including mining safety engineers
2,600	2,600	0.3	Mining machine operators, nsk

Total Employment		%			Total Employment		%	
2014	2024	Change	Occupation		2014	2024	Change	Occupation
125,100	119,200	-4.7	Mixing and blending machine setters, operators, and tenders		91,900	82,000	-10.7	Paper goods machine setters, operators, and tenders
124,700	131,300	5.3	Mobile heavy equipment mechanics, except engines		6,400	6,600	2.4	Paperhangers
					279,500	300,800	7.6	Paralegals and legal assistants
6,200	4,900	-21.5	Model makers, metal and plastic		9,400	7,400	-20.8	Parking enforcement workers
2,600	2,600	-1.4	Model makers, wood		135,600	141,300	4.2	Parking lot attendants
5,800	5,800	-0.2	Models		234,700	251,500	7.2	Parts salespersons
41,400	38,900	-6.0	Molders, shapers, and casters, except metal and plastic		3,800	2,900	-23.4	Patternmakers, metal and plastic
					1,800	1,800	-0.3	Patternmakers, wood
129,500	97,200	-25.0	Molding, coremaking, and casting machine setters, operators, and tenders, metal and plastic		57,700	63,000	9.2	Paving, surfacing, and tamping equipment operators
					172,800	166,900	-3.4	Payroll and timekeeping clerks
31,100	33,200	6.7	Morticians, undertakers, and funeral directors		34,800	38,400	10.3	Pediatricians, general
6,700	5,500	-18.2	Motion picture projectionists		1,768,400	2,226,500	25.9	Personal care aides
62,000	67,300	8.6	Motor vehicle operators, nsk		93,200	99,100	6.3	Personal care and service workers, nsk
22,500	23,100	2.7	Motorboat mechanics and service technicians		249,400	323,200	29.6	Personal financial advisors
4,700	5,000	6.3	Motorboat operators		74,100	73,200	-1.2	Pest control workers
17,000	18,000	6.0	Motorcycle mechanics		36,400	37,800	3.8	Pesticide handlers, sprayers, and applicators, vegetation
64,400	68,300	6.0	Multimedia artists and animators					
99,800	97,300	-2.5	Multiple machine tool setters, operators, and tenders, metal and plastic		35,100	38,500	9.8	Petroleum engineers
					42,400	43,400	2.2	Petroleum pump system operators, refinery operators, and gaugers
11,300	11,900	5.2	Museum technicians and conservators					
82,100	84,700	3.2	Music directors and composers		297,100	306,200	3.1	Pharmacists
8,600	8,900	4.2	Musical instrument repairers and tuners		41,500	41,600	0.3	Pharmacy aides
173,300	179,300	3.5	Musicians and singers		372,500	407,200	9.3	Pharmacy technicians
55,100	56,900	3.3	Natural sciences managers		30,700	34,200	11.6	Philosophy and religion teachers, postsecondary
382,600	412,800	7.9	Network and computer systems administrators		112,700	140,800	24.9	Phlebotomists
52,900	48,600	-8.2	New accounts clerks		124,900	128,800	3.1	Photographers
204,800	226,400	10.6	Nonfarm animal caretakers		28,800	19,400	-32.9	Photographic process workers and processing machine operators
16,800	16,200	-4.0	Nuclear engineers					
20,700	21,000	1.5	Nuclear medicine technologists		28,500	28,800	1.0	Physical scientists, nsk
7,500	7,400	-0.9	Nuclear power reactor operators		50,000	69,500	39.0	Physical therapist aides
6,800	6,400	-5.1	Nuclear technicians		78,700	110,700	40.6	Physical therapist assistants
38,200	45,600	19.3	Nurse anesthetists		210,900	282,700	34.0	Physical therapists
5,300	6,600	24.6	Nurse midwives		94,400	123,200	30.4	Physician assistants
126,900	171,700	35.2	Nurse practitioners		347,200	398,800	14.9	Physicians and surgeons, nsk
1,492,100	1,754,100	17.6	Nursing assistants		18,100	19,500	7.9	Physicists
68,600	81,800	19.3	Nursing instructors and teachers, postsecondary		17,700	20,400	15.0	Physics teachers, postsecondary
					3,700	4,300	16.6	Pile-driver operators
24,400	28,700	17.6	Obstetricians and gynecologists		45,700	51,000	11.4	Pipelayers
70,300	73,100	4.0	Occupational health and safety specialists		11,900	11,500	-3.2	Plant and system operators, nsk
15,100	16,500	9.1	Occupational health and safety technicians		27,000	28,900	7.1	Plasterers and stucco masons
114,600	145,100	26.5	Occupational therapists		36,100	29,400	-18.4	Plating and coating machine setters, operators, and tenders, metal and plastic
8,800	11,600	30.6	Occupational therapy aides					
33,000	47,100	42.7	Occupational therapy assistants		425,000	474,100	11.5	Plumbers, pipefitters, and steamfitters
264,500	282,900	7.0	Office and administrative support workers, nsk		9,600	11,000	14.1	Podiatrists
3,062,500	3,158,200	3.1	Office clerks, general		680,000	714,200	5.0	Police and sheriff's patrol officers
69,600	58,000	-16.6	Office machine operators, except computer		102,000	99,000	-2.9	Police, fire, and ambulance dispatchers
363,400	400,600	10.2	Operating engineers and other construction equipment operators		21,600	23,700	9.7	Political science teachers, postsecondary
					6,200	6,000	-2.3	Political scientists
91,300	118,900	30.2	Operations research analysts		69,600	51,300	-26.2	Postal service clerks
30,200	33,200	9.8	Ophthalmic laboratory technicians		297,400	219,400	-26.2	Postal service mail carriers
37,000	46,100	24.7	Ophthalmic medical technicians		117,600	78,000	-33.7	Postal service mail sorters, processors, and processing machine operators
75,200	93,000	23.7	Opticians, dispensing					
40,600	51,600	27.0	Optometrists		17,300	12,800	-26.2	Postmasters and mail superintendents
6,800	8,000	17.9	Oral and maxillofacial surgeons		232,300	254,000	9.3	Postsecondary teachers, nsk
195,900	194,300	-0.8	Order clerks		9,800	7,200	-26.6	Pourers and casters, metal
53,000	58,800	10.9	Orderlies		11,400	10,800	-5.1	Power distributors and dispatchers
8,200	9,700	18.3	Orthodontists		41,100	38,400	-6.6	Power plant operators
8,300	10,100	22.6	Orthotists and prosthetists		12,800	13,000	1.4	Precision instrument and equipment repairers, nsk
32,300	33,800	4.8	Outdoor power equipment and other small engine mechanics					
					36,500	27,500	-24.6	Prepress technicians and workers
378,400	382,200	1.0	Packaging and filling machine operators and tenders		441,000	470,600	6.7	Preschool teachers, except special education
					51,500	48,100	-6.6	Pressers, textile, garment, and related materials
695,400	706,900	1.7	Packers and packagers, hand					
360,500	387,100	7.4	Painters, construction and maintenance		51,200	44,200	-13.7	Print binding and finishing workers
54,300	57,500	5.9	Painters, transportation equipment		173,000	151,400	-12.5	Printing press operators
17,500	17,200	-2.0	Painting, coating, and decorating workers		34,900	36,700	5.2	Private detectives and investigators

Total Employment		%	
2014	2024	Change	Occupation
91,700	95,000	3.6	Probation officers and correctional treatment specialists
72,300	66,300	-8.3	Procurement clerks
122,600	133,800	9.1	Producers and directors
236,200	244,000	3.3	Production workers, nsk
304,600	310,900	2.1	Production, planning, and expediting clerks
13,600	13,300	-2.4	Proofreaders and copy markers
313,800	339,100	8.1	Property, real estate, and community association managers
800	1,000	17.8	Prosthodontists
113,800	120,400	5.8	Protective service workers, nsk
77,300	81,400	5.3	Psychiatric aides
67,900	71,400	5.2	Psychiatric technicians
28,200	32,400	14.9	Psychiatrists
16,600	18,300	9.8	Psychologists, nsk
47,300	54,700	15.8	Psychology teachers, postsecondary
10,200	10,500	2.9	Public address system and other announcers
65,800	70,500	7.1	Public relations and fundraising managers
240,700	255,600	6.2	Public relations specialists
13,100	14,200	8.4	Pump operators, except wellhead pumpers
300,800	299,300	-0.5	Purchasing agents, except wholesale, retail, and farm products
73,000	73,700	1.0	Purchasing managers
16,600	18,900	14.0	Radiation therapists
42,300	36,300	-14.3	Radio and television announcers
1,200	1,200	-0.6	Radio operators
13,600	14,400	6.0	Radio, cellular, and tower equipment installers and repairs
197,000	214,200	8.7	Radiologic technologists
21,500	22,000	2.7	Rail car repairers
3,800	3,900	1.3	Rail transportation workers, nsk
4,000	4,100	1.5	Rail yard engineers, dinkey operators, and hostlers
22,100	21,700	-1.8	Railroad brake, signal, and switch operators
45,100	44,300	-1.9	Railroad conductors and yardmasters
15,600	17,000	9.3	Rail-track laying and maintenance equipment operators
83,900	85,400	1.8	Real estate brokers
337,400	346,800	2.8	Real estate sales agents
1,028,600	1,126,300	9.5	Receptionists and information clerks
22,100	24,300	10.1	Recreation and fitness studies teachers, postsecondary
379,300	418,300	10.3	Recreation workers
18,600	20,900	12.0	Recreational therapists
11,400	11,800	3.3	Recreational vehicle service technicians
1,800	1,800	0.7	Refractory materials repairers, except brickmasons
131,500	140,900	7.1	Refuse and recyclable material collectors
2,751,000	3,190,300	16.0	Registered nurses
120,100	130,900	9.0	Rehabilitation counselors
18,700	23,100	23.4	Reinforcing iron and rebar workers
55,900	58,500	4.7	Religious workers, nsk
49,300	45,100	-8.5	Reporters and correspondents
140,800	138,800	-1.4	Reservation and transportation ticket agents and travel clerks
103,700	117,900	13.6	Residential advisors
120,700	135,500	12.3	Respiratory therapists
10,700	8,700	-19.2	Respiratory therapy technicians
4,624,900	4,939,100	6.8	Retail salespersons
20,800	22,600	8.7	Riggers
3,700	3,900	6.9	Rock splitters, quarry
33,700	29,100	-13.5	Rolling machine setters, operators, and tenders, metal and plastic
6,000	5,300	-10.8	Roof bolters, mining
123,400	139,300	12.8	Roofers
27,700	31,200	12.7	Rotary drill operators, oil and gas
76,400	82,700	8.3	Roustabouts, oil and gas
28,300	30,900	9.1	Sailors and marine oilers

Total Employment		%	
2014	2024	Change	Occupation
103,000	114,000	10.7	Sales and related workers, nsk
69,900	74,900	7.0	Sales engineers
376,300	395,300	5.1	Sales managers
853,500	924,100	8.3	Sales representatives, services, nsk
1,453,100	1,546,500	6.4	Sales representatives, wholesale and manufacturing, except technical and scientific products
347,800	371,700	6.9	Sales representatives, wholesale and manufacturing, technical and scientific products
50,000	49,500	-1.1	Sawing machine setters, operators, and tenders, wood
961,600	1,017,500	5.8	Secondary school teachers, except special and career/technical education
2,457,000	2,521,100	2.6	Secretaries and administrative assistants, except legal, medical, and executive
341,500	374,000	9.5	Securities, commodities, and financial services sales agents
64,000	72,300	12.9	Security and fire alarm systems installers
1,095,400	1,150,900	5.1	Security guards
1,300	1,400	9.3	Segmental pavers
348,700	402,200	15.4	Self-enrichment education teachers
25,300	23,200	-8.3	Semiconductor processors
43,800	43,300	-1.3	Separating, filtering, clarifying, precipitating, and still machine setters, operators, and tenders
24,700	28,700	16.3	Septic tank servicers and sewer pipe cleaners
64,900	69,600	7.3	Service unit operators, oil, gas, and mining
13,300	14,200	6.8	Set and exhibit designers
12,000	10,800	-9.8	Sewers, hand
153,900	112,200	-27.1	Sewing machine operators
23,800	26,200	10.3	Shampooers
141,000	150,500	6.7	Sheet metal workers
10,300	11,100	7.5	Ship engineers
670,200	655,700	-2.2	Shipping, receiving, and traffic clerks
9,700	8,200	-15.1	Shoe and leather workers and repairers
3,500	2,500	-30.5	Shoe machine operators and tenders
9,500	9,500	-0.1	Signal and track switch repairers
55,000	61,600	12.1	Skincare specialists
86,400	85,900	-0.6	Slaughterers and meat packers
7,100	6,900	-3.2	Slot supervisors
138,500	151,700	9.5	Social and community service managers
386,600	430,800	11.4	Social and human service assistants
32,000	33,800	5.6	Social science research assistants
12,900	15,100	17.0	Social sciences teachers, postsecondary, nsk
35,600	34,900	-2.0	Social scientists and related workers, nsk
13,700	15,600	13.9	Social work teachers, postsecondary
66,400	68,900	3.8	Social workers, nsk
2,600	2,500	-0.7	Sociologists
20,700	23,900	15.3	Sociology teachers, postsecondary
718,400	853,700	18.8	Software developers, applications
395,600	447,000	13.0	Software developers, systems software
17,700	18,900	6.7	Soil and plant scientists
5,900	7,400	24.3	Solar photovoltaic installers
16,100	17,400	7.6	Sound engineering technicians
198,100	210,600	6.3	Special education teachers, kindergarten and elementary school
93,000	98,500	5.9	Special education teachers, middle school
40,400	43,300	7.2	Special education teachers, nsk
25,500	27,800	9.0	Special education teachers, preschool
134,000	141,900	5.9	Special education teachers, secondary school
135,400	164,300	21.3	Speech-language pathologists
39,100	39,700	1.4	Stationary engineers and boiler operators
16,600	14,800	-10.9	Statistical assistants
30,000	40,100	33.8	Statisticians
1,878,100	1,971,100	4.9	Stock clerks and order fillers
14,900	17,100	14.3	Stonemasons

Total Employment 2014	2024	% Change	Occupation
61,400	64,200	4.5	Structural iron and steel workers
79,200	80,800	2.0	Structural metal fabricators and fitters
94,900	116,200	22.3	Substance abuse and behavioral disorder counselors
12,000	12,500	4.7	Subway and streetcar operators
46,000	55,100	19.8	Surgeons
99,800	114,500	14.8	Surgical technologists
16,700	18,700	11.6	Survey researchers
57,300	52,900	-7.6	Surveying and mapping technicians
44,300	43,400	-2.0	Surveyors
112,400	75,400	-32.9	Switchboard operators, including answering service
40,500	37,000	-8.5	Tailors, dressmakers, and custom sewers
13,000	13,500	4.0	Tank car, truck, and ship loaders
21,000	22,100	5.2	Tapers
67,900	63,700	-6.2	Tax examiners and collectors, and revenue agents
90,400	91,800	1.6	Tax preparers
233,700	264,400	13.1	Taxi drivers and chauffeurs
1,234,100	1,312,800	6.4	Teacher assistants
982,500	1,049,000	6.8	Teachers and instructors, nsk
1,144,200	1,137,700	-0.6	Team assemblers
52,000	57,300	10.2	Technical writers
218,600	210,800	-3.6	Telecommunications equipment installers and repairers, except line installers
118,000	118,700	0.6	Telecommunications line installers and repairers
237,900	230,800	-3.0	Telemarketers
13,100	7,500	-42.4	Telephone operators
520,500	480,500	-7.7	Tellers
3,400	3,600	7.3	Terrazzo workers and finishers
11,700	8,900	-23.9	Textile bleaching and dyeing machine operators and tenders
14,300	10,600	-25.7	Textile cutting machine setters, operators, and tenders
27,900	20,600	-26.2	Textile knitting and weaving machine setters, operators, and tenders
26,000	20,300	-21.7	Textile winding, twisting, and drawing out machine setters, operators, and tenders
16,200	14,300	-11.8	Textile, apparel, and furnishings workers, nsk
24,700	30,500	23.6	Therapists, nsk
55,100	58,700	6.4	Tile and marble setters
1,700	1,600	-1.9	Timing device assemblers and adjusters
18,100	15,600	-13.6	Tire builders
105,500	109,900	4.1	Tire repairers and changers
71,100	70,800	-0.3	Title examiners, abstractors, and searchers
77,800	67,700	-13.0	Tool and die makers
11,500	9,500	-17.5	Tool grinders, filers, and sharpeners
43,500	45,700	5.1	Tour guides and escorts
6,800	7,200	6.3	Traffic technicians
32,900	35,200	7.0	Training and development managers
252,600	271,500	7.5	Training and development specialists
3,600	3,700	3.5	Transit and railroad police
16,500	17,600	6.4	Transportation attendants, except flight attendants
26,400	26,700	1.2	Transportation inspectors
46,600	42,400	-9.0	Transportation security screeners
40,200	41,600	3.3	Transportation workers, nsk
111,600	114,100	2.2	Transportation, storage, and distribution managers
74,100	65,400	-11.7	Travel agents
3,900	3,900	0.0	Travel guides
53,200	56,200	5.6	Tree trimmers and pruners
19,800	20,700	4.8	Umpires, referees, and other sports officials
42,200	40,400	-4.3	Upholsterers
38,000	40,400	6.3	Urban and regional planners
113,900	120,000	5.3	Ushers, lobby attendants, and ticket takers
78,300	85,200	8.9	Veterinarians

Total Employment 2014	2024	% Change	Occupation
73,400	80,000	9.0	Veterinary assistants and laboratory animal caretakers
95,600	113,600	18.7	Veterinary technologists and technicians
138,500	147,600	6.6	Vocational education teachers, postsecondary
2,465,100	2,534,000	2.8	Waiters and waitresses
2,700	2,000	-25.7	Watch repairers
117,000	124,000	6.0	Water and wastewater treatment plant and system operators
148,500	188,000	26.6	Web developers
71,300	71,200	-0.1	Weighers, measurers, checkers, and samplers, recordkeeping
397,900	412,300	3.6	Welders, cutters, solderers, and brazers
59,500	48,800	-18.0	Welding, soldering, and brazing machine setters, operators, and tenders
13,900	15,800	13.1	Wellhead pumpers
129,500	137,500	6.2	Wholesale and retail buyers, except farm products
4,400	9,200	108.0	Wind turbine service technicians
12,900	12,900	-0.3	Woodworkers, nsk
72,100	70,400	-2.4	Woodworking machine setters, operators, and tenders, except sawing
90,700	76,500	-15.7	Word processors and typists
136,500	139,700	2.3	Writers and authors
21,300	22,200	4.0	Zoologists and wildlife biologists

Employment Order - 2014

Total Employment 2014	2024	% Change	Occupation
4,624,900	4,939,100	6.8	Retail salespersons
3,424,200	3,491,100	2.0	Cashiers
3,159,700	3,503,200	10.9	Combined food preparation and serving workers, including fast food
3,062,500	3,158,200	3.1	Office clerks, general
2,751,000	3,190,300	16.0	Registered nurses
2,581,800	2,834,800	9.8	Customer service representatives
2,465,100	2,534,000	2.8	Waiters and waitresses
2,457,000	2,521,100	2.6	Secretaries and administrative assistants, except legal, medical, and executive
2,441,300	2,566,400	5.1	Laborers and freight, stock, and material movers, hand
2,360,600	2,496,900	5.8	Janitors and cleaners, except maids and housekeeping cleaners
2,124,100	2,275,200	7.1	General and operations managers
1,878,100	1,971,100	4.9	Stock clerks and order fillers
1,797,700	1,896,400	5.5	Heavy and tractor-trailer truck drivers
1,768,400	2,226,500	25.9	Personal care aides
1,760,300	1,611,500	-8.4	Bookkeeping, accounting, and auditing clerks
1,537,800	1,605,400	4.4	First-line supervisors of retail sales workers
1,492,100	1,754,100	17.6	Nursing assistants
1,466,100	1,587,300	8.3	First-line supervisors of office and administrative support workers
1,457,700	1,569,400	7.7	Maids and housekeeping cleaners
1,453,100	1,546,500	6.4	Sales representatives, wholesale and manufacturing, except technical and scientific products
1,374,700	1,458,100	6.1	Maintenance and repair workers, general
1,358,000	1,436,300	5.8	Elementary school teachers, except special education
1,332,700	1,475,100	10.7	Accountants and auditors
1,260,600	1,329,900	5.5	Childcare workers
1,234,100	1,312,800	6.4	Teacher assistants
1,167,800	1,239,600	6.1	Landscaping and groundskeeping workers
1,159,100	1,306,500	12.7	Construction laborers
1,144,200	1,137,700	-0.6	Team assemblers
1,109,700	1,268,700	14.3	Cooks, restaurant
1,095,400	1,150,900	5.1	Security guards
1,028,600	1,126,300	9.5	Receptionists and information clerks
998,000	1,046,000	4.8	Business operations specialists, nsk

Total Employment 2014	2024	% Change	Occupation
985,600	1,023,600	3.9	Managers, nsk
982,500	1,049,000	6.8	Teachers and instructors, nsk
961,600	1,017,500	5.8	Secondary school teachers, except special and career/technical education
945,400	1,005,800	6.4	Carpenters
929,800	911,700	-1.9	Farmers, ranchers, and other agricultural managers
913,500	1,261,900	38.1	Home health aides
890,100	978,600	9.9	First-line supervisors of food preparation and serving workers
884,700	911,900	3.1	Light truck or delivery services drivers
873,900	928,800	6.3	Food preparation workers
853,500	924,100	8.3	Sales representatives, services, nsk
778,700	822,500	5.6	Lawyers
776,600	732,000	-5.7	Executive secretaries and executive administrative assistants
758,000	861,400	13.6	Management analysts
739,900	779,000	5.3	Automotive service technicians and mechanics
719,900	837,200	16.3	Licensed practical and licensed vocational nurses
718,400	853,700	18.8	Software developers, applications
695,400	706,900	1.7	Packers and packagers, hand
680,000	714,200	5.0	Police and sheriff's patrol officers
670,200	655,700	-2.2	Shipping, receiving, and traffic clerks
628,800	714,700	13.7	Electricians
627,500	664,200	5.9	Middle school teachers, except special and career/technical education
606,900	588,200	-3.1	First-line supervisors of production and operating workers
597,200	655,600	9.8	Hairdressers, hairstylists, and cosmetologists
591,300	730,200	23.5	Medical assistants
585,900	661,000	12.8	Computer user support specialists
580,900	640,900	10.3	Bartenders
578,400	636,100	10.0	First-line supervisors of construction trades and extraction workers
567,800	686,300	20.9	Computer systems analysts
555,900	593,500	6.8	Financial managers
530,900	543,500	2.4	Industrial truck and tractor operators
527,600	635,800	20.5	Medical secretaries
524,400	444,000	-15.3	Cooks, fast food
520,500	480,500	-7.7	Tellers
514,600	581,100	12.9	Billing and posting clerks
507,400	487,900	-3.9	Dishwashers
497,300	524,900	5.6	Bus drivers, school or special client
496,600	495,500	-0.2	Inspectors, testers, sorters, samplers, and weighers
495,500	587,800	18.6	Market research analysts and marketing specialists
482,000	503,900	4.6	Human resources specialists
481,200	510,000	6.0	Counter attendants, cafeteria, food concession, and coffee shop
470,200	427,300	-9.1	Farmworkers and laborers, crop, nursery, and greenhouse
466,100	509,500	9.3	Insurance sales agents
457,600	474,700	3.7	Correctional officers and jailers
447,100	471,400	5.4	First-line supervisors of mechanics, installers, and repairers
445,300	466,100	4.7	Driver/sales workers
442,100	458,500	3.7	Counter and rental clerks
441,000	470,600	6.7	Preschool teachers, except special education
430,700	451,000	4.7	First-line supervisors of non-retail sales workers
425,000	474,100	11.5	Plumbers, pipefitters, and steamfitters
419,200	403,200	-3.8	Helpers—production workers
417,600	443,900	6.3	Cooks, institution and cafeteria
415,300	440,700	6.1	Dining room and cafeteria attendants and bartender helpers
399,700	438,900	9.8	Machinists
397,900	412,300	3.6	Welders, cutters, solderers, and brazers
395,600	447,000	13.0	Software developers, systems software
386,600	430,800	11.4	Social and human service assistants
382,600	412,800	7.9	Network and computer systems administrators
379,300	418,300	10.3	Recreation workers
378,400	382,200	1.0	Packaging and filling machine operators and tenders
376,400	393,200	4.4	Hosts and hostesses, restaurant, lounge, and coffee shop
376,300	395,300	5.1	Sales managers
373,200	391,100	4.8	Construction managers
372,500	407,200	9.3	Pharmacy technicians
363,400	400,600	10.2	Operating engineers and other construction equipment operators
360,500	387,100	7.4	Painters, construction and maintenance
350,400	330,900	-5.6	Bill and account collectors
348,700	402,200	15.4	Self-enrichment education teachers
348,500	402,200	15.4	Computer and information systems managers
347,800	371,700	6.9	Sales representatives, wholesale and manufacturing, technical and scientific products
347,200	398,800	14.9	Physicians and surgeons, nsk
346,900	380,000	9.5	Cleaners of vehicles and equipment
343,400	339,400	-1.2	Chief executives
341,500	374,000	9.5	Securities, commodities, and financial services sales agents
337,400	346,800	2.8	Real estate sales agents
333,000	389,300	16.9	Medical and health services managers
332,200	391,900	18.0	Industrial machinery mechanics
328,600	302,200	-8.0	Computer programmers
327,300	344,700	5.3	Firefighters
318,800	377,400	18.4	Dental assistants
313,800	339,100	8.1	Property, real estate, and community association managers
305,200	324,200	6.2	Child, family, and school social workers
305,000	320,700	5.1	Food service managers
304,600	310,900	2.1	Production, planning, and expediting clerks
303,200	327,700	8.1	Loan officers
300,800	299,300	-0.5	Purchasing agents, except wholesale, retail, and farm products
299,700	309,500	3.3	Claims adjusters, examiners, and investigators
297,400	219,400	-26.2	Postal service mail carriers
297,100	306,200	3.1	Pharmacists
292,000	331,600	13.6	Heating, air conditioning, and refrigeration mechanics and installers
288,600	310,900	7.7	Amusement and recreation attendants
287,300	310,800	8.2	Administrative services managers
285,400	303,100	6.2	Insurance claims and policy processing clerks
281,400	305,000	8.4	Civil engineers
279,500	300,800	7.6	Paralegals and legal assistants
279,100	302,500	8.4	Fitness trainers and aerobics instructors
277,600	310,000	11.7	Financial analysts
277,500	292,100	5.3	Mechanical engineers
273,400	295,900	8.2	Educational, guidance, school, and vocational counselors
264,500	282,900	7.0	Office and administrative support workers, nsk
263,900	295,500	12.0	Bus and truck mechanics and diesel engine specialists
261,600	265,200	1.4	Graphic designers
260,300	269,000	3.3	Compliance officers
255,800	283,800	10.9	First-line supervisors of personal service workers
253,100	287,000	13.4	Food servers, nonrestaurant
252,600	271,500	7.5	Training and development specialists
250,600	265,400	5.9	Coaches and scouts
249,400	323,200	29.6	Personal financial advisors
247,900	262,800	6.0	First-line supervisors of housekeeping and janitorial workers

Total Employment 2014	2024	% Change	Occupation
244,200	258,000	5.6	Clergy
243,200	265,100	9.0	Hotel, motel, and resort desk clerks
241,200	299,600	24.2	Emergency medical technicians and paramedics
241,100	243,200	0.9	Industrial engineers
240,700	252,200	4.8	Assemblers and fabricators, nsk
240,700	255,600	6.2	Public relations specialists
240,000	254,000	5.8	Education administrators, elementary and secondary school
237,900	230,800	-3.0	Telemarketers
236,200	244,000	3.3	Production workers, nsk
234,700	251,500	7.2	Parts salespersons
233,700	264,400	13.1	Taxi drivers and chauffeurs
233,000	240,800	3.3	Computer occupations, nsk
232,300	254,000	9.3	Postsecondary teachers, nsk
218,600	210,800	-3.6	Telecommunications equipment installers and repairers, except line installers
216,800	208,900	-3.7	Data entry keyers
216,100	209,100	-3.2	Farmworkers, farm, ranch, and aquacultural animals
215,500	206,700	-4.1	Legal secretaries
213,800	232,300	8.6	Loan interviewers and clerks
213,500	232,300	8.8	Cost estimators
210,900	282,700	34.0	Physical therapists
210,400	250,400	19.0	Health specialties teachers, postsecondary
208,200	212,000	1.8	Laundry and dry-cleaning workers
207,200	197,000	-4.9	Electrical and electronic equipment assemblers
204,800	226,400	10.6	Nonfarm animal caretakers
200,500	237,900	18.6	Dental hygienists
199,700	205,600	2.9	First-line supervisors of transportation and material-moving machine and vehicle operators
199,500	208,200	4.4	Dispatchers, except police, fire, and ambulance
198,100	210,600	6.3	Special education teachers, kindergarten and elementary school
198,000	208,300	5.2	Interviewers, except eligibility and loan
197,000	214,200	8.7	Radiologic technologists
195,900	194,300	-0.8	Order clerks
194,300	212,500	9.4	Marketing managers
192,200	152,700	-20.6	Cutting, punching, and press machine setters, operators, and tenders, metal and plastic
188,600	217,600	15.4	Medical records and health information technicians
188,500	193,000	2.4	Information and record clerks, nsk
185,300	198,300	7.0	Bakers
182,100	185,800	2.0	Architectural and engineering managers
181,600	172,300	-5.1	Cooks, short order
181,000	194,600	7.5	Computer network support specialists
178,400	180,200	1.0	Electrical engineers
178,000	187,400	5.3	First-line supervisors of landscaping, lawn service, and groundskeeping workers
175,100	190,300	8.7	Education administrators, postsecondary
173,400	167,000	-3.7	Industrial production managers
173,300	179,300	3.5	Musicians and singers
173,100	176,900	2.2	First-line supervisors of helpers, laborers, and material movers, hand
173,000	151,400	-12.5	Printing press operators
172,800	166,900	-3.4	Payroll and timekeeping clerks
168,800	205,200	21.6	Massage therapists
167,900	163,400	-2.7	Advertising sales agents
167,800	177,600	5.9	Bus drivers, transit and intercity
164,800	187,900	14.0	Medical and clinical laboratory technologists
163,500	170,600	4.3	Installation, maintenance, and repair workers, nsk
163,400	192,400	17.8	Medical and clinical laboratory technicians
160,100	191,000	19.3	Healthcare social workers
159,400	168,900	5.9	Kindergarten teachers, except special education

Total Employment 2014	2024	% Change	Occupation
159,200	169,100	6.2	Graduate teaching assistants
159,000	150,100	-5.6	File clerks
155,300	185,900	19.6	Clinical, counseling, and school psychologists
155,200	175,500	13.1	Cement masons and concrete finishers
153,900	112,200	-27.1	Sewing machine operators
152,400	152,300	-0.1	Meat, poultry, and fish cutters and trimmers
151,300	158,600	4.8	Highway maintenance workers
151,100	161,600	7.0	Instructional coordinators
149,700	163,500	9.2	Automotive body and related repairers
148,800	174,800	17.5	Computer-controlled machine tool operators, metal and plastic
148,500	188,000	26.6	Web developers
146,200	158,900	8.7	Computer network architects
145,200	152,300	4.9	Financial specialists, nsk
143,100	145,700	1.9	Librarians
141,300	150,800	6.7	Lifeguards, ski patrol, and other recreational protective service workers
141,000	150,500	6.7	Sheet metal workers
140,800	147,100	4.5	Court, municipal, and license clerks
140,800	138,800	-1.4	Reservation and transportation ticket agents and travel clerks
140,600	134,800	-4.1	Human resources assistants, except payroll and timekeeping
139,800	154,100	10.2	Family and general practitioners
139,400	136,600	-2.0	Electrical and electronics engineering technicians
139,000	146,000	5.0	Butchers and meat cutters
138,500	151,700	9.5	Social and community service managers
138,500	147,600	6.6	Vocational education teachers, postsecondary
137,400	135,500	-1.4	Electronics engineers, except computer
136,900	142,300	4.0	Engineers, nsk
136,500	139,700	2.3	Writers and authors
135,600	141,300	4.2	Parking lot attendants
135,400	164,300	21.3	Speech-language pathologists
134,500	160,900	19.6	Mental health counselors
134,000	141,900	5.9	Special education teachers, secondary school
131,900	137,500	4.3	Directors, religious activities and education
131,600	134,800	2.4	Computer, automated teller, and office machine repairers
131,500	140,900	7.1	Refuse and recyclable material collectors
130,400	132,900	1.9	Logisticians
129,900	132,000	1.6	Eligibility interviewers, government programs
129,500	97,200	-25.0	Molding, coremaking, and casting machine setters, operators, and tenders, metal and plastic
129,500	137,500	6.2	Wholesale and retail buyers, except farm products
129,000	152,300	18.0	Dentists, general
129,000	141,200	9.4	Helpers—installation, maintenance, and repair workers
127,500	138,800	8.9	Chefs and head cooks
126,900	171,700	35.2	Nurse practitioners
125,100	119,200	-4.7	Mixing and blending machine setters, operators, and tenders
124,900	128,800	3.1	Photographers
124,700	131,300	5.3	Mobile heavy equipment mechanics, except engines
124,000	133,100	7.4	Education, training, and library workers, nsk
123,400	139,300	12.8	Roofers
122,600	133,800	9.1	Producers and directors
122,500	122,000	-0.4	Food batchmakers
122,500	133,300	8.8	Human resources managers
120,800	124,100	2.8	Merchandise displayers and window trimmers
120,700	133,700	10.8	Art, drama, and music teachers, postsecondary
120,700	135,500	12.3	Respiratory therapists
120,100	130,900	9.0	Rehabilitation counselors
120,000	133,400	11.1	Database administrators
119,900	121,500	1.3	Aircraft mechanics and service technicians

Total Employment 2014	2024	% Change	Occupation
118,600	131,600	11.0	Electrical power-line installers and repairers
118,000	118,700	0.6	Telecommunications line installers and repairers
117,800	140,000	18.9	Mental health and substance abuse social workers
117,600	78,000	-33.7	Postal service mail sorters, processors, and processing machine operators
117,200	111,000	-5.3	Editors
117,000	124,000	6.0	Water and wastewater treatment plant and system operators
116,700	115,300	-1.2	Detectives and criminal investigators
114,600	145,100	26.5	Occupational therapists
113,900	120,000	5.3	Ushers, lobby attendants, and ticket takers
113,800	120,400	5.8	Protective service workers, nsk
113,600	125,300	10.3	Manicurists and pedicurists
112,700	140,800	24.9	Phlebotomists
112,600	120,400	6.9	Architects, except landscape and naval
112,400	75,400	-32.9	Switchboard operators, including answering service
111,600	114,100	2.2	Transportation, storage, and distribution managers
108,800	114,700	5.4	Library assistants, clerical
108,100	112,700	4.2	First-line supervisors of police and detectives
107,900	116,800	8.3	Medical scientists, except epidemiologists
106,800	116,200	8.8	Business teachers, postsecondary
106,000	111,500	5.2	Drywall and ceiling tile installers
105,800	117,600	11.1	Automotive and watercraft service attendants
105,500	109,900	4.1	Tire repairers and changers
104,900	85,100	-18.8	Mail clerks and mail machine operators, except postal service
104,200	100,700	-3.4	Machine feeders and offbearers
103,700	117,900	13.6	Residential advisors
103,400	91,600	-11.4	Insurance underwriters
103,000	114,000	10.7	Sales and related workers, nsk
102,700	111,100	8.2	Community and social service specialists, nsk
102,700	114,700	11.7	Healthcare support workers, nsk
102,200	125,900	23.1	Health technologists and technicians, nsk
102,000	99,000	-2.9	Police, fire, and ambulance dispatchers
101,800	107,100	5.2	Library technicians
101,200	109,200	8.0	Construction and building inspectors
100,000	109,900	9.9	Meeting, convention, and event planners
99,800	97,300	-2.5	Multiple machine tool setters, operators, and tenders, metal and plastic
99,800	114,500	14.8	Surgical technologists
98,100	99,300	1.3	Cabinetmakers and bench carpenters
97,900	100,100	2.2	Flight attendants
97,700	97,000	-0.7	Coating, painting, and spraying machine setters, operators, and tenders
95,600	113,600	18.7	Veterinary technologists and technicians
94,900	116,200	22.3	Substance abuse and behavioral disorder counselors
94,600	104,800	10.7	Environmental scientists and specialists, including health
94,400	123,200	30.4	Physician assistants
94,000	91,200	-3.0	Architectural and civil drafters
93,200	99,100	6.3	Personal care and service workers, nsk
93,000	101,300	8.9	Demonstrators and product promoters
93,000	98,500	5.9	Special education teachers, middle school
92,900	97,700	5.2	Couriers and messengers
91,900	82,000	-10.7	Paper goods machine setters, operators, and tenders
91,700	95,000	3.6	Probation officers and correctional treatment specialists
91,300	118,900	30.2	Operations research analysts
91,200	98,700	8.2	Maintenance workers, machinery
91,100	93,500	2.6	Chemists
90,800	100,200	10.4	English language and literature teachers, postsecondary
90,700	76,500	-15.7	Word processors and typists
90,400	91,800	1.6	Tax preparers
86,400	85,900	-0.6	Slaughterers and meat packers
85,800	92,500	7.9	Appraisers and assessors of real estate
84,700	88,100	4.0	Compensation, benefits, and job analysis specialists
83,900	85,400	1.8	Real estate brokers
82,900	97,700	17.9	Information security analysts
82,100	75,600	-7.8	Labor relations specialists
82,100	84,700	3.2	Music directors and composers
80,200	79,100	-1.4	Door-to-door sales workers, news and street vendors, and related workers
79,600	79,900	0.4	Career/technical education teachers, secondary school
79,300	83,500	5.2	Biological technicians
79,200	80,800	2.0	Structural metal fabricators and fitters
78,800	84,300	7.0	Cargo and freight agents
78,700	110,700	40.6	Physical therapist assistants
78,300	85,200	8.9	Veterinarians
78,200	83,500	6.8	Life, physical, and social science technicians, nsk
78,100	92,600	18.6	Brickmasons and blockmasons
77,800	67,700	-13.0	Tool and die makers
77,700	80,100	3.1	Computer hardware engineers
77,500	83,000	7.1	Adult basic and secondary education and literacy teachers and instructors
77,300	81,400	5.3	Psychiatric aides
76,400	82,700	8.3	Roustabouts, oil and gas
75,700	76,500	1.1	Airline pilots, copilots, and flight engineers
75,700	82,500	9.1	Education teachers, postsecondary
75,200	93,000	23.7	Opticians, dispensing
74,600	76,400	2.4	Art directors
74,100	73,200	-1.2	Pest control workers
74,100	65,400	-11.7	Travel agents
74,000	77,600	4.8	Civil engineering technicians
73,400	55,500	-24.4	Extruding and drawing machine setters, operators, and tenders, metal and plastic
73,400	80,300	9.3	Fundraisers
73,400	80,000	9.0	Veterinary assistants and laboratory animal caretakers
73,000	73,700	1.0	Purchasing managers
72,500	70,800	-2.3	Aerospace engineers
72,300	66,300	-8.3	Procurement clerks
72,100	70,400	-2.4	Woodworking machine setters, operators, and tenders, except sawing
71,400	55,800	-21.9	Grinding, lapping, polishing, and buffing machine tool setters, operators, and tenders, metal and plastic
71,300	71,200	-0.1	Weighers, measurers, checkers, and samplers, recordkeeping
71,100	70,800	-0.3	Title examiners, abstractors, and searchers
70,900	79,400	11.9	Audio and video equipment technicians
70,300	73,100	4.0	Occupational health and safety specialists
70,100	69,900	-0.2	Engineering technicians, except drafters, nsk
70,000	67,800	-3.1	Medical transcriptionists
69,900	74,900	7.0	Sales engineers
69,800	74,200	6.4	Crossing guards
69,600	58,000	-16.6	Office machine operators, except computer
69,600	51,300	-26.2	Postal service clerks
69,400	76,100	9.6	Actors
69,400	73,600	6.1	Credit analysts
69,000	81,500	18.0	Helpers—electricians
68,700	71,900	4.6	First-line supervisors of protective service workers, nsk
68,600	81,800	19.3	Nursing instructors and teachers, postsecondary
68,500	68,900	0.6	Gaming dealers
68,200	59,000	-13.6	Extruding, forming, pressing, and compacting machine setters, operators, and tenders

Total Employment		%	
2014	2024	Change	Occupation
67,900	71,400	5.2	Psychiatric technicians
67,900	63,700	-6.2	Tax examiners and collectors, and revenue agents
67,800	67,800	0.1	Electrical and electronics repairers, commercial and industrial equipment
66,700	77,600	16.4	Dietitians and nutritionists
66,500	67,700	1.9	Chemical technicians
66,500	63,500	-4.5	Industrial engineering technicians
66,400	68,900	3.8	Social workers, nsk
66,300	60,800	-8.3	Chemical equipment operators and tenders
65,800	70,500	7.1	Public relations and fundraising managers
65,700	61,200	-6.8	Mechanical drafters
64,900	69,600	7.3	Service unit operators, oil, gas, and mining
64,400	68,300	6.0	Multimedia artists and animators
64,300	74,800	16.2	Biological science teachers, postsecondary
64,000	68,200	6.6	Education administrators, preschool and childcare center/program
64,000	72,300	12.9	Security and fire alarm systems installers
63,600	58,400	-8.1	Cutting and slicing machine setters, operators, and tenders
63,500	66,800	5.2	First-line supervisors of fire fighting and prevention workers
63,500	73,900	16.4	Mathematical science teachers, postsecondary
62,000	67,300	8.6	Motor vehicle operators, nsk
61,400	68,900	12.2	Health educators
61,400	64,200	4.5	Structural iron and steel workers
61,100	49,500	-19.0	Computer operators
61,000	78,500	28.7	Interpreters and translators
60,800	62,300	2.5	Budget analysts
60,700	76,700	26.4	Diagnostic medical sonographers
59,500	48,800	-18.0	Welding, soldering, and brazing machine setters, operators, and tenders
59,200	65,100	10.1	Barbers
58,900	61,100	3.8	Interior designers
58,700	56,700	-3.4	Floral designers
58,300	57,900	-0.7	Legislators
57,800	60,900	5.4	Agricultural equipment operators
57,700	63,000	9.2	Paving, surfacing, and tamping equipment operators
57,300	52,900	-7.6	Surveying and mapping technicians
57,200	62,400	9.0	Brokerage clerks
55,900	58,500	4.7	Religious workers, nsk
55,100	62,000	12.4	Environmental engineers
55,100	56,900	3.3	Natural sciences managers
55,100	58,700	6.4	Tile and marble setters
55,000	61,600	12.1	Skincare specialists
54,300	62,400	14.9	Community health workers
54,300	59,400	9.4	Internists, general
54,300	57,500	5.9	Painters, transportation equipment
53,900	57,300	6.2	Excavating and loading machine and dragline operators
53,200	56,200	5.6	Tree trimmers and pruners
53,000	48,900	-7.8	Graders and sorters, agricultural products
53,000	58,800	10.9	Orderlies
52,900	48,600	-8.2	New accounts clerks
52,600	52,400	-0.4	Legal support workers, nsk
52,400	59,400	13.4	Helpers—pipelayers, plumbers, pipefitters, and steamfitters
52,000	63,500	22.2	Cardiovascular technologists and technicians
52,000	59,300	14.0	Medical equipment preparers
52,000	57,300	10.2	Technical writers
51,500	48,100	-6.6	Pressers, textile, garment, and related materials
51,200	44,200	-13.7	Print binding and finishing workers
50,100	56,100	12.0	Health diagnosing and treating practitioners, nsk
50,000	69,500	39.0	Physical therapist aides
50,000	49,500	-1.1	Sawing machine setters, operators, and tenders, wood

Total Employment		%	
2014	2024	Change	Occupation
49,300	45,100	-8.5	Reporters and correspondents
48,400	52,100	7.6	Lodging managers
48,400	49,300	2.0	Mechanical engineering technicians
48,000	50,900	6.1	Medical equipment repairers
47,600	49,100	3.1	First-line supervisors of correctional officers
47,300	54,700	15.8	Psychology teachers, postsecondary
47,200	44,700	-5.3	Electromechanical equipment assemblers
47,100	43,300	-8.2	First-line supervisors of farming, fishing, and forestry workers
46,600	42,400	-9.0	Transportation security screeners
46,400	44,800	-3.4	Home appliance repairers
46,100	43,300	-6.2	Credit authorizers, checkers, and clerks
46,100	49,600	7.7	Food preparation and serving related workers, nsk
46,000	52,000	13.2	Engineering teachers, postsecondary
46,000	55,100	19.8	Surgeons
45,700	51,000	11.4	Pipelayers
45,500	49,000	7.6	Crane and tower operators
45,300	45,100	-0.5	Carpet installers
45,300	47,200	4.1	Glaziers
45,200	53,100	17.5	Chiropractors
45,100	44,300	-1.9	Railroad conductors and yardmasters
44,400	47,700	7.4	Food processing workers, nsk
44,300	43,400	-2.0	Surveyors
44,200	50,300	13.8	Healthcare practitioners and technical workers, nsk
43,800	43,300	-1.3	Separating, filtering, clarifying, precipitating, and still machine setters, operators, and tenders
43,700	47,000	7.4	Hazardous materials removal workers
43,600	47,100	8.0	Baggage porters and bellhops
43,500	48,000	10.5	Commercial pilots
43,500	45,700	5.1	Tour guides and escorts
43,400	47,200	8.7	Computer science teachers, postsecondary
42,900	34,300	-20.0	Lathe and turning machine tool setters, operators, and tenders, metal and plastic
42,400	42,600	0.5	Control and valve installers and repairers, except mechanical door
42,400	43,400	2.2	Petroleum pump system operators, refinery operators, and gaugers
42,300	36,300	-14.3	Radio and television announcers
42,200	40,400	-4.3	Upholsterers
41,500	41,600	0.3	Pharmacy aides
41,400	38,900	-6.0	Molders, shapers, and casters, except metal and plastic
41,100	38,400	-6.6	Power plant operators
40,900	47,100	15.2	Millwrights
40,600	38,600	-4.9	Aircraft structure, surfaces, rigging, and systems assemblers
40,600	51,600	27.0	Optometrists
40,500	37,000	-8.5	Tailors, dressmakers, and custom sewers
40,400	39,500	-2.3	Locomotive engineers
40,400	43,300	7.2	Special education teachers, nsk
40,300	43,200	7.2	Farm equipment mechanics and service technicians
40,200	41,600	3.3	Transportation workers, nsk
39,800	35,300	-11.3	Jewelers and precious stone and metal workers
39,700	39,600	-0.2	Conveyor operators and tenders
39,700	42,700	7.5	Helpers—carpenters
39,100	39,700	1.4	Stationary engineers and boiler operators
39,000	39,000	0.1	Engine and other machine assemblers
38,700	42,900	10.8	Dental laboratory technicians
38,400	39,200	2.0	Commercial and industrial designers
38,200	42,000	9.7	Financial examiners
38,200	45,600	19.3	Nurse anesthetists
38,100	34,600	-9.2	Chemical plant and system operators
38,100	41,600	9.0	Financial clerks, nsk
38,000	40,400	6.3	Urban and regional planners

Total Employment 2014	2024	% Change	Occupation
37,800	39,300	4.0	Education administrators, nsk
37,500	38,000	1.3	Food cooking machine operators and tenders
37,400	30,600	-18.0	Meter readers, utilities
37,300	37,100	-0.3	Logging equipment operators
37,200	41,300	10.9	Foreign language and literature teachers, postsecondary
37,000	46,100	24.7	Ophthalmic medical technicians
36,800	40,900	11.1	Animal trainers
36,500	27,500	-24.6	Prepress technicians and workers
36,400	36,200	-0.4	Biological scientists, nsk
36,400	40,200	10.5	Geoscientists, except hydrologists and geographers
36,400	37,800	3.8	Pesticide handlers, sprayers, and applicators, vegetation
36,200	39,600	9.5	Environmental science and protection technicians, including health
36,100	35,700	-1.2	Funeral attendants
36,100	29,400	-18.4	Plating and coating machine setters, operators, and tenders, metal and plastic
36,000	39,500	9.7	Communications teachers, postsecondary
35,900	36,200	0.6	Cooks, private household
35,600	34,900	-2.0	Social scientists and related workers, nsk
35,400	37,800	6.9	Construction and related workers, nsk
35,100	38,700	10.2	Captains, mates, and pilots of water vessels
35,100	38,500	9.8	Petroleum engineers
34,900	31,900	-8.7	Coin, vending, and amusement machine servicers and repairers
34,900	36,700	5.2	Private detectives and investigators
34,800	38,400	10.3	Pediatricians, general
34,300	34,900	1.8	Chemical engineers
34,100	36,900	8.2	Biochemists and biophysicists
33,700	40,800	21.0	Anesthesiologists
33,700	38,700	14.8	Marriage and family therapists
33,700	29,100	-13.5	Rolling machine setters, operators, and tenders, metal and plastic
33,600	37,100	10.3	Magnetic resonance imaging technologists
33,500	39,400	17.6	Film and video editors
33,500	37,000	10.3	Media and communication workers, nsk
33,000	34,700	4.9	Agricultural and food science technicians
33,000	47,100	42.7	Occupational therapy assistants
32,900	35,200	7.0	Training and development managers
32,600	37,600	15.5	Credit counselors
32,600	30,800	-5.7	Forest and conservation technicians
32,300	33,800	4.8	Outdoor power equipment and other small engine mechanics
32,000	33,800	5.6	Social science research assistants
31,200	34,400	10.4	Concierges
31,100	33,200	6.7	Morticians, undertakers, and funeral directors
31,000	32,400	4.7	Advertising and promotions managers
31,000	34,400	11.0	Counselors, nsk
30,700	34,200	11.6	Philosophy and religion teachers, postsecondary
30,200	27,900	-7.5	Crushing, grinding, and polishing machine setters, operators, and tenders
30,200	33,200	9.8	Ophthalmic laboratory technicians
30,100	28,200	-6.5	Broadcast technicians
30,100	31,700	5.4	Electrical and electronics drafters
30,100	35,900	19.4	Insulation workers, mechanical
30,000	32,100	6.8	Entertainers and performers, sports and related workers, nsk
30,000	40,100	33.8	Statisticians
29,900	27,300	-8.8	Grinding and polishing workers, hand
29,700	29,900	0.6	Judges, magistrate judges, and magistrates
29,600	30,300	2.4	Electronic home entertainment equipment installers and repairers
29,300	33,200	13.3	Dietetic technicians
29,300	30,300	3.3	Funeral service managers
29,200	32,100	10.0	History teachers, postsecondary
28,800	19,400	-32.9	Photographic process workers and processing machine operators
28,500	28,800	1.0	Physical scientists, nsk
28,400	28,200	-0.7	Fishing and hunting workers
28,300	30,900	9.1	Sailors and marine oilers
28,200	32,400	14.9	Psychiatrists
27,900	20,600	-26.2	Textile knitting and weaving machine setters, operators, and tenders
27,800	28,000	0.7	Gaming supervisors
27,700	31,200	12.7	Rotary drill operators, oil and gas
27,000	28,900	7.1	Plasterers and stucco masons
26,600	30,700	15.4	Chemistry teachers, postsecondary
26,400	26,700	1.2	Transportation inspectors
26,300	27,100	3.1	Fine artists, including painters, sculptors, and illustrators
26,000	20,300	-21.7	Textile winding, twisting, and drawing out machine setters, operators, and tenders
25,800	29,000	12.6	Helpers—extraction workers
25,600	28,300	10.7	Computer and information research scientists
25,600	27,100	6.1	Insulation workers, floor, ceiling, and wall
25,500	27,800	9.0	Special education teachers, preschool
25,400	30,800	21.1	Athletic trainers
25,400	25,900	2.0	Camera operators, television, video, and motion picture
25,300	25,600	1.3	Materials engineers
25,300	23,200	-8.3	Semiconductor processors
25,200	26,800	6.2	Health and safety engineers, except mining safety engineers and inspectors
25,100	29,900	18.9	Computer numerically controlled machine tool programmers, metal and plastic
24,700	28,700	16.3	Septic tank servicers and sewer pipe cleaners
24,700	30,500	23.6	Therapists, nsk
24,600	29,000	18.1	Actuaries
24,500	22,400	-8.6	Air traffic controllers
24,500	26,100	6.4	Grounds maintenance workers, nsk
24,400	26,400	8.0	Fence erectors
24,400	28,700	17.6	Obstetricians and gynecologists
23,800	26,200	10.3	Shampooers
23,600	24,700	4.4	Material moving workers, nsk
23,500	28,800	22.4	Helpers—brickmasons, blockmasons, stonemasons, and tile and marble setters
23,100	23,800	2.9	Fashion designers
22,700	21,700	-4.5	Electrical and electronics repairers, powerhouse, substation, and relay
22,500	23,700	5.5	Landscape architects
22,500	23,100	2.7	Motorboat mechanics and service technicians
22,400	18,700	-16.6	Metal workers and plastic workers, nsk
22,400	23,200	3.5	Microbiologists
22,400	17,800	-20.6	Milling and planing machine setters, operators, and tenders, metal and plastic
22,100	27,200	23.1	Biomedical engineers
22,100	21,700	-1.8	Railroad brake, signal, and switch operators
22,100	24,300	10.1	Recreation and fitness studies teachers, postsecondary
21,700	24,600	13.3	Derrick operators, oil and gas
21,600	17,000	-21.5	Forging machine setters, operators, and tenders, metal and plastic
21,600	23,700	9.7	Political science teachers, postsecondary
21,500	22,800	6.0	Cooks, nsk
21,500	22,700	5.7	Economists
21,500	22,000	2.7	Rail car repairers
21,300	17,200	-19.6	Heat treating equipment setters, operators, and tenders, metal and plastic
21,300	22,200	4.0	Zoologists and wildlife biologists
21,200	20,200	-4.8	Metal-refining furnace operators and tenders
21,100	22,500	6.9	Conservation scientists
21,100	25,700	21.7	Law teachers, postsecondary
21,000	22,100	5.2	Tapers

Total Employment 2014	2024	% Change	Occupation
20,900	18,900	-9.7	Furnace, kiln, oven, drier, and kettle operators and tenders
20,900	17,800	-14.8	Locksmiths and safe repairers
20,800	21,100	1.5	Court reporters
20,800	22,600	8.7	Riggers
20,700	23,400	13.0	Elevator installers and repairers
20,700	21,000	1.5	Nuclear medicine technologists
20,700	23,900	15.3	Sociology teachers, postsecondary
20,100	17,300	-14.1	Extruding and forming machine setters, operators, and tenders, synthetic and glass fibers
20,000	22,700	13.6	Earth drillers, except oil and gas
19,800	20,700	4.8	Umpires, referees, and other sports officials
19,700	20,200	2.5	Agents and business managers of artists, performers, and athletes
19,600	26,100	33.0	Ambulance drivers and attendants, except emergency medical technicians
19,500	21,500	10.2	Helpers, construction trades, nsk
19,400	18,700	-3.3	Media and communication equipment workers, nsk
19,300	20,800	7.8	Automotive glass installers and repairers
19,300	20,000	3.6	Electric motor, power tool, and related repairers
19,200	18,600	-3.3	Fiberglass laminators and fabricators
18,700	23,100	23.4	Reinforcing iron and rebar workers
18,600	20,400	10.0	Environmental engineering technicians
18,600	19,400	4.7	Locker room, coatroom, and dressing room attendants
18,600	20,900	12.0	Recreational therapists
18,500	18,600	0.4	Cleaning, washing, and metal pickling equipment operators and tenders
18,500	18,700	0.7	Food and tobacco roasting, baking, and drying machine operators and tenders
18,400	17,100	-6.8	Adhesive bonding machine operators and tenders
18,100	19,500	7.9	Physicists
18,100	15,600	-13.6	Tire builders
17,800	14,100	-20.5	Drilling and boring machine tool setters, operators, and tenders, metal and plastic
17,700	20,400	15.0	Physics teachers, postsecondary
17,700	18,900	6.7	Soil and plant scientists
17,500	17,200	-2.0	Painting, coating, and decorating workers
17,400	17,500	0.4	Avionics technicians
17,400	19,000	8.7	Boilermakers
17,400	21,100	21.4	Criminal justice and law enforcement teachers, postsecondary
17,400	19,300	10.7	Mechanical door repairers
17,300	18,100	4.7	Bailiffs
17,300	18,900	9.7	Economics teachers, postsecondary
17,300	12,800	-26.2	Postmasters and mail superintendents
17,100	19,200	12.2	Floor layers, except carpet, wood, and hard tiles
17,100	16,700	-2.4	Furniture finishers
17,000	18,000	6.0	Motorcycle mechanics
16,900	17,700	4.8	Building cleaning workers, nsk
16,900	18,000	6.5	Compensation and benefits managers
16,900	19,800	17.1	Entertainment attendants and related workers, nsk
16,800	16,200	-4.0	Nuclear engineers
16,700	16,100	-3.4	Gas plant operators
16,700	18,700	11.6	Survey researchers
16,600	18,300	9.8	Psychologists, nsk
16,600	18,900	14.0	Radiation therapists
16,600	14,800	-10.9	Statistical assistants
16,500	18,500	11.8	Geological and petroleum technicians
16,500	17,600	6.4	Transportation attendants, except flight attendants
16,200	14,300	-11.8	Textile, apparel, and furnishings workers, nsk
16,100	17,400	7.6	Sound engineering technicians

Total Employment 2014	2024	% Change	Occupation
15,800	13,000	-17.5	Cutters and trimmers, hand
15,600	17,000	9.3	Rail-track laying and maintenance equipment operators
15,500	16,800	8.3	Foresters
15,500	15,400	-1.2	Insurance appraisers, auto damage
15,400	16,000	3.5	Food scientists and technologists
15,100	16,500	9.1	Occupational health and safety technicians
15,000	14,500	-3.6	Administrative law judges, adjudicators, and hearing officers
15,000	15,900	5.8	Animal control workers
14,900	14,100	-5.7	Coil winders, tapers, and finishers
14,900	17,100	14.3	Stonemasons
14,800	11,700	-21.0	Desktop publishers
14,800	15,400	4.4	Electrical and electronics installers and repairers, transportation equipment
14,700	14,200	-3.4	Drafters, nsk
14,700	14,800	0.7	Electro-mechanical technicians
14,600	16,100	10.7	Medical appliance technicians
14,500	16,000	10.6	Exercise physiologists
14,400	18,200	26.6	Forensic science technicians
14,300	10,600	-25.7	Textile cutting machine setters, operators, and tenders
14,200	14,100	-0.6	Agricultural inspectors
14,000	14,600	4.2	Forest and conservation workers
13,900	15,800	13.1	Wellhead pumpers
13,700	14,500	5.6	Athletes and sports competitors
13,700	14,600	5.9	Career/technical education teachers, middle school
13,700	15,600	13.9	Social work teachers, postsecondary
13,600	13,300	-2.4	Proofreaders and copy markers
13,600	14,400	6.0	Radio, cellular, and tower equipment installers and repairs
13,400	13,500	0.4	Artists and related workers, nsk
13,400	10,700	-20.1	Layout workers, metal and plastic
13,300	11,900	-10.9	Gaming change persons and booth cashiers
13,300	14,200	6.8	Set and exhibit designers
13,200	14,300	8.7	Atmospheric, earth, marine, and space sciences teachers, postsecondary
13,200	16,900	28.6	Audiologists
13,200	13,400	1.6	Gaming service workers, nsk
13,100	14,100	8.0	Curators
13,100	14,200	8.4	Pump operators, except wellhead pumpers
13,100	7,500	-42.4	Telephone operators
13,000	13,600	4.8	Dancers
13,000	13,500	4.0	Tank car, truck, and ship loaders
12,900	13,500	4.6	Buyers and purchasing agents, farm products
12,900	15,100	17.0	Social sciences teachers, postsecondary, nsk
12,900	12,900	-0.3	Woodworkers, nsk
12,800	13,000	1.4	Precision instrument and equipment repairers, nsk
12,400	13,100	5.5	Fire inspectors and investigators
12,400	11,600	-6.3	Judicial law clerks
12,300	15,900	29.3	Cartographers and photogrammetrists
12,300	11,600	-5.3	Continuous mining machine operators
12,100	12,800	6.0	Agricultural sciences teachers, postsecondary
12,000	8,700	-27.7	Foundry mold and coremakers
12,000	10,800	-9.8	Sewers, hand
12,000	12,500	4.7	Subway and streetcar operators
11,900	13,100	10.5	Helpers—painters, paperhangers, plasterers, and stucco masons
11,900	11,500	-3.2	Plant and system operators, nsk
11,800	12,900	9.2	Atmospheric and space scientists
11,700	8,900	-23.9	Textile bleaching and dyeing machine operators and tenders
11,600	13,300	15.1	Area, ethnic, and cultural studies teachers, postsecondary
11,500	5,800	-50.0	Electronic equipment installers and repairers, motor vehicles

Total Employment		%	
2014	2024	Change	Occupation
11,500	11,900	3.4	Gaming and sports book writers and runners
11,500	9,500	-17.5	Tool grinders, filers, and sharpeners
11,400	11,800	3.6	Aerospace engineering and operations technicians
11,400	10,800	-5.1	Power distributors and dispatchers
11,400	11,800	3.3	Recreational vehicle service technicians
11,300	11,900	5.0	Gaming cage workers
11,300	13,000	15.3	Helpers—roofers
11,300	11,900	5.2	Museum technicians and conservators
10,800	13,200	21.7	Bicycle repairers
10,800	11,900	10.9	Farm and home management advisors
10,700	8,700	-19.2	Respiratory therapy technicians
10,600	10,000	-5.7	Agricultural workers, nsk
10,600	10,600	0.6	Craft artists
10,600	11,300	7.2	Life scientists, nsk
10,500	11,200	6.2	Emergency management directors
10,300	11,100	7.5	Ship engineers
10,200	10,500	2.9	Public address system and other announcers
10,000	10,800	7.9	Audio-visual and multimedia collections specialists
9,800	7,200	-26.6	Pourers and casters, metal
9,700	9,500	-2.7	Etchers and engravers
9,700	8,200	-15.1	Shoe and leather workers and repairers
9,600	11,000	14.1	Podiatrists
9,500	9,500	-0.1	Signal and track switch repairers
9,400	7,400	-20.8	Parking enforcement workers
9,100	9,900	9.4	Architecture teachers, postsecondary
8,900	9,500	6.2	Designers, nsk
8,800	8,700	-0.6	Cooling and freezing equipment operators and tenders
8,800	11,600	30.6	Occupational therapy aides
8,600	8,900	4.2	Musical instrument repairers and tuners
8,400	9,200	9.2	Arbitrators, mediators, and conciliators
8,400	7,200	-14.7	Correspondence clerks
8,300	9,000	8.9	Marine engineers and naval architects
8,300	8,800	6.4	Mining and geological engineers, including mining safety engineers
8,300	10,100	22.6	Orthotists and prosthetists
8,200	6,800	-17.2	Fallers
8,200	9,700	18.3	Orthodontists
8,100	8,400	3.9	Explosives workers, ordnance handling experts, and blasters
7,900	8,400	6.2	Floor sanders and finishers
7,700	8,000	3.8	Anthropologists and archeologists
7,500	8,200	9.3	Anthropology and archeology teachers, postsecondary
7,500	7,400	-0.9	Nuclear power reactor operators
7,400	7,300	-1.8	Mine cutting and channeling machine operators
7,300	7,500	2.7	Materials scientists
7,200	7,500	3.9	Airfield operations specialists
7,100	7,500	6.3	Choreographers
7,100	6,900	-3.2	Slot supervisors
7,000	6,900	-1.6	Animal breeders
7,000	6,600	-7.0	Gaming surveillance officers and gaming investigators
7,000	7,500	6.9	Hydrologists
6,900	7,400	6.8	Archivists
6,800	6,400	-5.1	Nuclear technicians
6,800	8,000	17.9	Oral and maxillofacial surgeons
6,800	7,200	6.3	Traffic technicians
6,700	7,300	8.5	Dentists, nsk
6,700	7,300	8.6	Environmental science teachers, postsecondary
6,700	5,500	-18.2	Motion picture projectionists
6,400	6,600	2.4	Paperhangers
6,200	6,700	8.8	Costume attendants
6,200	6,300	1.9	Fish and game wardens
6,200	4,900	-21.5	Model makers, metal and plastic
6,200	6,000	-2.3	Political scientists

Total Employment		%	
2014	2024	Change	Occupation
6,000	5,300	-10.8	Roof bolters, mining
5,900	7,500	27.2	Hearing aid specialists
5,900	7,400	24.3	Solar photovoltaic installers
5,800	5,800	0.5	Aircraft cargo handling supervisors
5,800	6,100	6.3	Epidemiologists
5,800	5,800	-0.2	Models
5,700	6,300	11.9	Extraction workers, nsk
5,600	6,000	8.0	Library science teachers, postsecondary
5,400	4,000	-26.0	Fabric and apparel patternmakers
5,400	5,900	7.9	Geography teachers, postsecondary
5,300	6,600	24.6	Nurse midwives
5,100	4,500	-12.6	Broadcast news analysts
5,100	5,300	3.4	Gas compressor and gas pumping station operators
4,800	4,800	-0.1	Loading machine operators, underground mining
4,700	5,000	6.3	Motorboat operators
4,500	4,100	-7.5	Logging workers, nsk
4,400	6,000	36.9	Commercial divers
4,400	9,200	108.0	Wind turbine service technicians
4,300	3,800	-11.6	Home economics teachers, postsecondary
4,000	2,800	-30.0	Manufactured building and mobile home installers
4,000	4,100	1.5	Rail yard engineers, dinkey operators, and hostlers
3,900	3,900	0.0	Travel guides
3,800	3,600	-6.1	Embalmers
3,800	3,800	-0.6	Gaming managers
3,800	2,900	-23.4	Patternmakers, metal and plastic
3,800	3,900	1.3	Rail transportation workers, nsk
3,700	3,800	4.7	Camera and photographic equipment repairers
3,700	3,700	-2.0	Log graders and scalers
3,700	4,300	16.6	Pile-driver operators
3,700	3,900	6.9	Rock splitters, quarry
3,600	4,300	19.2	Makeup artists, theatrical and performance
3,600	3,700	3.5	Transit and railroad police
3,500	3,400	-1.1	Bridge and lock tenders
3,500	3,500	1.7	Historians
3,500	4,200	21.4	Mathematicians
3,500	2,500	-30.5	Shoe machine operators and tenders
3,400	3,600	7.3	Terrazzo workers and finishers
3,300	3,500	5.6	Communications equipment operators, nsk
2,900	3,000	4.4	Agricultural engineers
2,900	3,200	7.3	Animal scientists
2,900	2,900	1.7	Hoist and winch operators
2,700	2,600	-2.2	Mine shuttle car operators
2,700	2,000	-25.7	Watch repairers
2,600	2,600	0.3	Mining machine operators, nsk
2,600	2,600	-1.4	Model makers, wood
2,600	2,500	-0.7	Sociologists
2,400	3,100	28.8	Genetic counselors
2,300	2,400	6.8	Forestry and conservation science teachers, postsecondary
2,200	2,300	8.7	Dredge operators
2,000	2,300	19.1	Industrial-organizational psychologists
1,900	1,900	2.8	Astronomers
1,800	1,900	5.7	Mathematical science occupations, nsk
1,800	1,800	-0.3	Patternmakers, wood
1,800	1,800	0.7	Refractory materials repairers, except brickmasons
1,700	2,000	13.1	Forest fire inspectors and prevention specialists
1,700	500	-69.9	Locomotive firers
1,700	1,600	-1.9	Timing device assemblers and adjusters
1,400	1,400	-1.6	Geographers
1,300	1,400	9.3	Segmental pavers
1,200	1,100	-12.6	Mathematical technicians
1,200	1,200	-0.6	Radio operators

Employment by Occupation

Total Employment 2014	2024	% Change	Occupation
800	700	-12.6	Fabric menders, except garment
800	1,000	17.8	Prosthodontists
100	100	-8.9	Farm labor contractors

Growth/Decline Order - 2014 to 2024

Total Employment 2014	2024	% Change	Occupation
4,400	9,200	108.0	Wind turbine service technicians
33,000	47,100	42.7	Occupational therapy assistants
78,700	110,700	40.6	Physical therapist assistants
50,000	69,500	39.0	Physical therapist aides
913,500	1,261,900	38.1	Home health aides
4,400	6,000	36.9	Commercial divers
126,900	171,700	35.2	Nurse practitioners
210,900	282,500	34.0	Physical therapists
30,000	40,100	33.8	Statisticians
19,600	26,100	33.0	Ambulance drivers and attendants, except emergency medical technicians
8,800	11,600	30.6	Occupational therapy aides
94,400	123,200	30.4	Physician assistants
91,300	118,900	30.2	Operations research analysts
249,400	323,200	29.6	Personal financial advisors
12,300	15,900	29.3	Cartographers and photogrammetrists
2,400	3,100	28.8	Genetic counselors
61,000	78,500	28.7	Interpreters and translators
13,200	16,900	28.6	Audiologists
5,900	7,500	27.2	Hearing aid specialists
40,600	51,600	27.0	Optometrists
14,400	18,200	26.6	Forensic science technicians
148,500	188,000	26.6	Web developers
114,600	145,100	26.5	Occupational therapists
60,700	76,700	26.4	Diagnostic medical sonographers
1,768,400	2,226,500	25.9	Personal care aides
112,700	140,800	24.9	Phlebotomists
37,000	46,100	24.7	Ophthalmic medical technicians
5,300	6,600	24.6	Nurse midwives
5,900	7,400	24.3	Solar photovoltaic installers
241,200	299,600	24.2	Emergency medical technicians and paramedics
75,200	93,000	23.7	Opticians, dispensing
24,700	30,500	23.6	Therapists, nsk
591,300	730,200	23.5	Medical assistants
18,700	23,100	23.4	Reinforcing iron and rebar workers
22,100	27,200	23.1	Biomedical engineers
102,200	125,900	23.1	Health technologists and technicians, nsk
8,300	10,100	22.6	Orthotists and prosthetists
23,500	28,800	22.4	Helpers—brickmasons, blockmasons, stonemasons, and tile and marble setters
94,900	116,200	22.3	Substance abuse and behavioral disorder counselors
52,000	63,500	22.2	Cardiovascular technologists and technicians
10,800	13,200	21.7	Bicycle repairers
21,100	25,700	21.7	Law teachers, postsecondary
168,800	205,200	21.6	Massage therapists
17,400	21,100	21.4	Criminal justice and law enforcement teachers, postsecondary
3,500	4,200	21.4	Mathematicians
135,400	164,300	21.3	Speech-language pathologists
25,400	30,800	21.1	Athletic trainers
33,700	40,800	21.0	Anesthesiologists
567,800	686,300	20.9	Computer systems analysts
527,600	635,800	20.5	Medical secretaries
46,000	55,100	19.8	Surgeons
155,300	185,900	19.6	Clinical, counseling, and school psychologists
134,500	160,900	19.6	Mental health counselors
30,100	35,900	19.4	Insulation workers, mechanical
160,100	191,000	19.3	Healthcare social workers
38,200	45,600	19.3	Nurse anesthetists
68,600	81,800	19.3	Nursing instructors and teachers, postsecondary
3,600	4,300	19.2	Makeup artists, theatrical and performance
2,000	2,300	19.1	Industrial-organizational psychologists
210,400	250,400	19.0	Health specialties teachers, postsecondary
25,100	29,900	18.9	Computer numerically controlled machine tool programmers, metal and plastic
117,800	140,000	18.9	Mental health and substance abuse social workers
718,400	853,700	18.8	Software developers, applications
95,600	113,600	18.7	Veterinary technologists and technicians
78,100	92,600	18.6	Brickmasons and blockmasons
200,500	237,900	18.6	Dental hygienists
495,500	587,800	18.6	Market research analysts and marketing specialists
318,800	377,400	18.4	Dental assistants
8,200	9,700	18.3	Orthodontists
24,600	29,000	18.1	Actuaries
129,000	152,300	18.0	Dentists, general
69,000	81,500	18.0	Helpers—electricians
332,200	391,900	18.0	Industrial machinery mechanics
82,900	97,700	17.9	Information security analysts
6,800	8,000	17.9	Oral and maxillofacial surgeons
163,400	192,400	17.8	Medical and clinical laboratory technicians
800	1,000	17.8	Prosthodontists
33,500	39,400	17.6	Film and video editors
1,492,100	1,754,100	17.6	Nursing assistants
24,400	28,700	17.6	Obstetricians and gynecologists
45,200	53,100	17.5	Chiropractors
148,800	174,800	17.5	Computer-controlled machine tool operators, metal and plastic
16,900	19,800	17.1	Entertainment attendants and related workers, nsk
12,900	15,100	17.0	Social sciences teachers, postsecondary, nsk
333,000	389,300	16.9	Medical and health services managers
3,700	4,300	16.6	Pile-driver operators
66,700	77,600	16.4	Dietitians and nutritionists
63,500	73,900	16.4	Mathematical science teachers, postsecondary
719,900	837,200	16.3	Licensed practical and licensed vocational nurses
24,700	28,700	16.3	Septic tank servicers and sewer pipe cleaners
64,300	74,800	16.2	Biological science teachers, postsecondary
2,751,000	3,190,300	16.0	Registered nurses
47,300	54,700	15.8	Psychology teachers, postsecondary
32,600	37,600	15.5	Credit counselors
26,600	30,700	15.4	Chemistry teachers, postsecondary
348,500	402,200	15.4	Computer and information systems managers
188,600	217,600	15.4	Medical records and health information technicians
348,700	402,200	15.4	Self-enrichment education teachers
11,300	13,000	15.3	Helpers—roofers
20,700	23,900	15.3	Sociology teachers, postsecondary
40,900	47,100	15.2	Millwrights
11,600	13,300	15.1	Area, ethnic, and cultural studies teachers, postsecondary
17,700	20,400	15.0	Physics teachers, postsecondary
54,300	62,400	14.9	Community health workers
347,200	398,800	14.9	Physicians and surgeons, nsk
28,200	32,400	14.9	Psychiatrists
33,700	38,700	14.8	Marriage and family therapists
99,800	114,500	14.8	Surgical technologists
1,109,700	1,268,700	14.3	Cooks, restaurant
14,900	17,100	14.3	Stonemasons
9,600	11,000	14.1	Podiatrists
164,800	187,900	14.0	Medical and clinical laboratory technologists
52,000	59,300	14.0	Medical equipment preparers
16,600	18,900	14.0	Radiation therapists
13,700	15,600	13.9	Social work teachers, postsecondary
44,200	50,300	13.8	Healthcare practitioners and technical workers, nsk

Total Employment 2014	2024	% Change	Occupation
628,800	714,700	13.7	Electricians
20,000	22,700	13.6	Earth drillers, except oil and gas
292,000	331,600	13.6	Heating, air conditioning, and refrigeration mechanics and installers
758,000	861,400	13.6	Management analysts
103,700	117,900	13.6	Residential advisors
253,100	287,000	13.4	Food servers, nonrestaurant
52,400	59,400	13.4	Helpers—pipelayers, plumbers, pipefitters, and steamfitters
21,700	24,600	13.3	Derrick operators, oil and gas
29,300	33,200	13.3	Dietetic technicians
46,000	52,000	13.2	Engineering teachers, postsecondary
155,200	175,500	13.1	Cement masons and concrete finishers
1,700	2,000	13.1	Forest fire inspectors and prevention specialists
233,700	264,400	13.1	Taxi drivers and chauffeurs
13,900	15,800	13.1	Wellhead pumpers
20,700	23,400	13.0	Elevator installers and repairers
395,600	447,000	13.0	Software developers, systems software
514,600	581,100	12.9	Billing and posting clerks
64,000	72,300	12.9	Security and fire alarm systems installers
585,900	661,000	12.8	Computer user support specialists
123,400	139,300	12.8	Roofers
1,159,100	1,306,500	12.7	Construction laborers
27,700	31,200	12.7	Rotary drill operators, oil and gas
25,800	29,000	12.6	Helpers—extraction workers
55,100	62,000	12.4	Environmental engineers
120,700	135,500	12.3	Respiratory therapists
17,100	19,200	12.2	Floor layers, except carpet, wood, and hard tiles
61,400	68,900	12.2	Health educators
55,000	61,600	12.1	Skincare specialists
263,900	295,500	12.0	Bus and truck mechanics and diesel engine specialists
50,100	56,100	12.0	Health diagnosing and treating practitioners, nsk
18,600	20,900	12.0	Recreational therapists
70,900	79,400	11.9	Audio and video equipment technicians
5,700	6,300	11.9	Extraction workers, nsk
16,500	18,500	11.8	Geological and petroleum technicians
277,600	310,000	11.7	Financial analysts
102,700	114,700	11.7	Healthcare support workers, nsk
30,700	34,200	11.6	Philosophy and religion teachers, postsecondary
16,700	18,700	11.6	Survey researchers
425,000	474,100	11.5	Plumbers, pipefitters, and steamfitters
45,700	51,000	11.4	Pipelayers
386,600	430,800	11.4	Social and human service assistants
36,800	40,900	11.1	Animal trainers
105,800	117,600	11.1	Automotive and watercraft service attendants
120,000	133,400	11.1	Database administrators
31,000	34,400	11.0	Counselors, nsk
118,600	131,600	11.0	Electrical power-line installers and repairers
3,159,700	3,503,200	10.9	Combined food preparation and serving workers, including fast food
10,800	11,900	10.9	Farm and home management advisors
255,800	283,800	10.9	First-line supervisors of personal service workers
37,200	41,300	10.9	Foreign language and literature teachers, postsecondary
53,000	58,800	10.9	Orderlies
120,700	133,700	10.8	Art, drama, and music teachers, postsecondary
38,700	42,900	10.8	Dental laboratory technicians
1,332,700	1,475,100	10.7	Accountants and auditors
25,600	28,300	10.7	Computer and information research scientists
94,600	104,800	10.7	Environmental scientists and specialists, including health
17,400	19,300	10.7	Mechanical door repairers
14,600	16,100	10.7	Medical appliance technicians
103,000	114,000	10.7	Sales and related workers, nsk
14,500	16,000	10.6	Exercise physiologists
204,800	226,400	10.6	Nonfarm animal caretakers
43,500	48,000	10.5	Commercial pilots
36,400	40,200	10.5	Geoscientists, except hydrologists and geographers
11,900	13,100	10.5	Helpers—painters, paperhangers, plasterers, and stucco masons
31,200	34,400	10.4	Concierges
90,800	100,200	10.4	English language and literature teachers, postsecondary
580,900	640,900	10.3	Bartenders
33,600	37,100	10.3	Magnetic resonance imaging technologists
113,600	125,300	10.3	Manicurists and pedicurists
33,500	37,000	10.3	Media and communication workers, nsk
34,800	38,400	10.3	Pediatricians, general
379,300	418,300	10.3	Recreation workers
23,800	26,200	10.3	Shampooers
35,100	38,700	10.2	Captains, mates, and pilots of water vessels
139,800	154,100	10.2	Family and general practitioners
19,500	21,500	10.2	Helpers, construction trades, nsk
363,400	400,600	10.2	Operating engineers and other construction equipment operators
52,000	57,300	10.2	Technical writers
59,200	65,100	10.1	Barbers
22,100	24,300	10.1	Recreation and fitness studies teachers, postsecondary
18,600	20,400	10.0	Environmental engineering technicians
578,400	636,100	10.0	First-line supervisors of construction trades and extraction workers
29,200	32,100	10.0	History teachers, postsecondary
890,100	978,600	9.9	First-line supervisors of food preparation and serving workers
100,000	109,900	9.9	Meeting, convention, and event planners
2,581,800	2,834,800	9.8	Customer service representatives
597,200	655,600	9.8	Hairdressers, hairstylists, and cosmetologists
399,700	438,900	9.8	Machinists
30,200	33,200	9.8	Ophthalmic laboratory technicians
35,100	38,500	9.8	Petroleum engineers
16,600	18,300	9.8	Psychologists, nsk
36,000	39,500	9.7	Communications teachers, postsecondary
17,300	18,900	9.7	Economics teachers, postsecondary
38,200	42,000	9.7	Financial examiners
21,600	23,700	9.7	Political science teachers, postsecondary
69,400	76,100	9.6	Actors
346,900	380,000	9.5	Cleaners of vehicles and equipment
36,200	39,600	9.5	Environmental science and protection technicians, including health
1,028,600	1,126,300	9.5	Receptionists and information clerks
341,500	374,000	9.5	Securities, commodities, and financial services sales agents
138,500	151,700	9.5	Social and community service managers
9,100	9,900	9.4	Architecture teachers, postsecondary
129,000	141,200	9.4	Helpers—installation, maintenance, and repair workers
54,300	59,400	9.4	Internists, general
194,300	212,500	9.4	Marketing managers
7,500	8,200	9.3	Anthropology and archeology teachers, postsecondary
73,400	80,300	9.3	Fundraisers
466,100	509,500	9.3	Insurance sales agents
372,500	407,200	9.3	Pharmacy technicians
232,300	254,000	9.3	Postsecondary teachers, nsk
15,600	17,000	9.3	Rail-track laying and maintenance equipment operators
1,300	1,400	9.3	Segmental pavers
8,400	9,200	9.2	Arbitrators, mediators, and conciliators
11,800	12,900	9.2	Atmospheric and space scientists
149,700	163,500	9.2	Automotive body and related repairers

Total Employment 2014	2024	% Change	Occupation
57,700	63,000	9.2	Paving, surfacing, and tamping equipment operators
75,700	82,500	9.1	Education teachers, postsecondary
15,100	16,500	9.1	Occupational health and safety technicians
122,600	133,800	9.1	Producers and directors
28,300	30,900	9.1	Sailors and marine oilers
57,200	62,400	9.0	Brokerage clerks
38,100	41,600	9.0	Financial clerks, nsk
243,200	265,100	9.0	Hotel, motel, and resort desk clerks
120,100	130,900	9.0	Rehabilitation counselors
25,500	27,800	9.0	Special education teachers, preschool
73,400	80,000	9.0	Veterinary assistants and laboratory animal caretakers
127,500	138,800	8.9	Chefs and head cooks
93,000	101,300	8.9	Demonstrators and product promoters
8,300	9,000	8.9	Marine engineers and naval architects
78,300	85,200	8.9	Veterinarians
106,800	116,200	8.8	Business teachers, postsecondary
213,500	232,300	8.8	Cost estimators
6,200	6,700	8.8	Costume attendants
122,500	133,300	8.8	Human resources managers
13,200	14,300	8.7	Atmospheric, earth, marine, and space sciences teachers, postsecondary
17,400	19,000	8.7	Boilermakers
146,200	158,900	8.7	Computer network architects
43,400	47,200	8.7	Computer science teachers, postsecondary
2,200	2,300	8.7	Dredge operators
175,100	190,300	8.7	Education administrators, postsecondary
197,000	214,200	8.7	Radiologic technologists
20,800	22,600	8.7	Riggers
6,700	7,300	8.6	Environmental science teachers, postsecondary
213,800	232,300	8.6	Loan interviewers and clerks
62,000	67,300	8.6	Motor vehicle operators, nsk
6,700	7,300	8.5	Dentists, nsk
281,400	305,000	8.4	Civil engineers
279,100	302,500	8.4	Fitness trainers and aerobics instructors
13,100	14,200	8.4	Pump operators, except wellhead pumpers
1,466,100	1,587,300	8.3	First-line supervisors of office and administrative support workers
15,500	16,800	8.3	Foresters
107,900	116,800	8.3	Medical scientists, except epidemiologists
76,400	82,700	8.3	Roustabouts, oil and gas
853,500	924,100	8.3	Sales representatives, services, nsk
287,300	310,800	8.2	Administrative services managers
34,100	36,900	8.2	Biochemists and biophysicists
102,700	111,100	8.2	Community and social service specialists, nsk
273,400	295,900	8.2	Educational, guidance, school, and vocational counselors
91,200	98,700	8.2	Maintenance workers, machinery
303,200	327,700	8.1	Loan officers
313,800	339,100	8.1	Property, real estate, and community association managers
43,600	47,100	8.0	Baggage porters and bellhops
101,200	109,200	8.0	Construction and building inspectors
13,100	14,100	8.0	Curators
24,400	26,400	8.0	Fence erectors
5,600	6,000	8.0	Library science teachers, postsecondary
85,800	92,500	7.9	Appraisers and assessors of real estate
10,000	10,800	7.9	Audio-visual and multimedia collections specialists
5,400	5,900	7.9	Geography teachers, postsecondary
382,600	412,800	7.9	Network and computer systems administrators
18,100	19,500	7.9	Physicists
19,300	20,800	7.8	Automotive glass installers and repairers
288,600	310,900	7.7	Amusement and recreation attendants
46,100	49,600	7.7	Food preparation and serving related workers, nsk
1,457,700	1,569,400	7.7	Maids and housekeeping cleaners

Total Employment 2014	2024	% Change	Occupation
45,500	49,000	7.6	Crane and tower operators
48,400	52,100	7.6	Lodging managers
279,500	300,800	7.6	Paralegals and legal assistants
16,100	17,400	7.6	Sound engineering technicians
181,000	194,600	7.5	Computer network support specialists
39,700	42,700	7.5	Helpers—carpenters
10,300	11,100	7.5	Ship engineers
252,600	271,500	7.5	Training and development specialists
124,000	133,100	7.4	Education, training, and library workers, nsk
44,400	47,700	7.4	Food processing workers, nsk
43,700	47,000	7.4	Hazardous materials removal workers
360,500	387,100	7.4	Painters, construction and maintenance
2,900	3,200	7.3	Animal scientists
64,900	69,600	7.3	Service unit operators, oil, gas, and mining
3,400	3,600	7.3	Terrazzo workers and finishers
40,300	43,200	7.2	Farm equipment mechanics and service technicians
10,600	11,300	7.2	Life scientists, nsk
234,700	251,500	7.2	Parts salespersons
40,400	43,300	7.2	Special education teachers, nsk
77,500	83,000	7.1	Adult basic and secondary education and literacy teachers and instructors
2,124,100	2,275,200	7.1	General and operations managers
27,000	28,900	7.1	Plasterers and stucco masons
65,800	70,500	7.1	Public relations and fundraising managers
131,500	140,900	7.1	Refuse and recyclable material collectors
185,300	198,300	7.0	Bakers
78,800	84,300	7.0	Cargo and freight agents
151,100	161,600	7.0	Instructional coordinators
264,500	282,900	7.0	Office and administrative support workers, nsk
69,900	74,900	7.0	Sales engineers
32,900	35,200	7.0	Training and development managers
112,600	120,400	6.9	Architects, except landscape and naval
21,100	22,500	6.9	Conservation scientists
35,400	37,800	6.9	Construction and related workers, nsk
7,000	7,500	6.9	Hydrologists
3,700	3,900	6.9	Rock splitters, quarry
347,800	371,700	6.9	Sales representatives, wholesale and manufacturing, technical and scientific products
6,900	7,400	6.8	Archivists
30,000	32,100	6.8	Entertainers and performers, sports and related workers, nsk
555,900	593,500	6.8	Financial managers
2,300	2,400	6.8	Forestry and conservation science teachers, postsecondary
78,200	83,500	6.8	Life, physical, and social science technicians, nsk
4,624,900	4,939,100	6.8	Retail salespersons
13,300	14,200	6.8	Set and exhibit designers
982,500	1,049,000	6.8	Teachers and instructors, nsk
141,300	150,800	6.7	Lifeguards, ski patrol, and other recreational protective service workers
31,100	33,200	6.7	Morticians, undertakers, and funeral directors
441,000	470,600	6.7	Preschool teachers, except special education
141,000	150,500	6.7	Sheet metal workers
17,700	18,900	6.7	Soil and plant scientists
64,000	68,200	6.6	Education administrators, preschool and childcare center/program
138,500	147,600	6.6	Vocational education teachers, postsecondary
16,900	18,000	6.5	Compensation and benefits managers
945,400	1,005,800	6.4	Carpenters
69,800	74,200	6.4	Crossing guards
24,500	26,100	6.4	Grounds maintenance workers, nsk
8,300	8,800	6.4	Mining and geological engineers, including mining safety engineers
1,453,100	1,546,500	6.4	Sales representatives, wholesale and manufacturing, except technical and scientific products

Total Employment		%		Total Employment		%	
2014	2024	Change	Occupation	2014	2024	Change	Occupation
1,234,100	1,312,800	6.4	Teacher assistants	1,800	1,900	5.7	Mathematical science occupations, nsk
55,100	58,700	6.4	Tile and marble setters	13,700	14,500	5.6	Athletes and sports competitors
16,500	17,600	6.4	Transportation attendants, except flight	497,300	524,900	5.6	Bus drivers, school or special client
			attendants	244,200	258,000	5.6	Clergy
7,100	7,500	6.3	Choreographers	3,300	3,500	5.6	Communications equipment operators, nsk
417,600	443,900	6.3	Cooks, institution and cafeteria	778,700	822,500	5.6	Lawyers
5,800	6,100	6.3	Epidemiologists	32,000	33,800	5.6	Social science research assistants
873,900	928,800	6.3	Food preparation workers	53,200	56,200	5.6	Tree trimmers and pruners
4,700	5,000	6.3	Motorboat operators	1,260,600	1,329,900	5.5	Childcare workers
93,200	99,100	6.3	Personal care and service workers, nsk	12,400	13,100	5.5	Fire inspectors and investigators
198,100	210,600	6.3	Special education teachers, kindergarten and	1,797,700	1,896,400	5.5	Heavy and tractor-trailer truck drivers
			elementary school	22,500	23,700	5.5	Landscape architects
6,800	7,200	6.3	Traffic technicians	57,800	60,900	5.4	Agricultural equipment operators
38,000	40,400	6.3	Urban and regional planners	30,100	31,700	5.4	Electrical and electronics drafters
305,200	324,200	6.2	Child, family, and school social workers	447,100	471,400	5.4	First-line supervisors of mechanics, installers,
8,900	9,500	6.2	Designers, nsk				and repairers
10,500	11,200	6.2	Emergency management directors	108,800	114,700	5.4	Library assistants, clerical
53,900	57,300	6.2	Excavating and loading machine and dragline	739,900	779,000	5.3	Automotive service technicians and mechanics
			operators	327,300	344,700	5.3	Firefighters
7,900	8,400	6.2	Floor sanders and finishers	178,000	187,400	5.3	First-line supervisors of landscaping, lawn
159,200	169,100	6.2	Graduate teaching assistants				service, and groundskeeping workers
25,200	26,800	6.2	Health and safety engineers, except mining	277,500	292,100	5.3	Mechanical engineers
			safety engineers and inspectors	124,700	131,300	5.3	Mobile heavy equipment mechanics, except
285,400	303,100	6.2	Insurance claims and policy processing clerks				engines
240,700	255,600	6.2	Public relations specialists	77,300	81,400	5.3	Psychiatric aides
129,500	137,500	6.2	Wholesale and retail buyers, except farm	113,900	120,000	5.3	Ushers, lobby attendants, and ticket takers
			products	79,300	83,500	5.2	Biological technicians
69,400	73,600	6.1	Credit analysts	92,900	97,700	5.2	Couriers and messengers
415,300	440,700	6.1	Dining room and cafeteria attendants and	106,000	111,500	5.2	Drywall and ceiling tile installers
			bartender helpers	63,500	66,800	5.2	First-line supervisors of fire fighting and
25,600	27,100	6.1	Insulation workers, floor, ceiling, and wall				prevention workers
1,167,800	1,239,600	6.1	Landscaping and groundskeeping workers	198,000	208,300	5.2	Interviewers, except eligibility and loan
1,374,700	1,458,100	6.1	Maintenance and repair workers, general	101,800	107,100	5.2	Library technicians
48,000	50,900	6.1	Medical equipment repairers	11,300	11,900	5.2	Museum technicians and conservators
12,100	12,800	6.0	Agricultural sciences teachers, postsecondary	34,900	36,700	5.2	Private detectives and investigators
21,500	22,800	6.0	Cooks, nsk	67,900	71,400	5.2	Psychiatric technicians
481,200	510,000	6.0	Counter attendants, cafeteria, food concession,	21,000	22,100	5.2	Tapers
			and coffee shop	305,000	320,700	5.1	Food service managers
247,900	262,800	6.0	First-line supervisors of housekeeping and	2,441,300	2,566,400	5.1	Laborers and freight, stock, and material
			janitorial workers				movers, hand
17,000	18,000	6.0	Motorcycle mechanics	376,300	395,300	5.1	Sales managers
64,400	68,300	6.0	Multimedia artists and animators	1,095,400	1,150,900	5.1	Security guards
13,600	14,400	6.0	Radio, cellular, and tower equipment installers	43,500	45,700	5.1	Tour guides and escorts
			and repairs	139,000	146,000	5.0	Butchers and meat cutters
117,000	124,000	6.0	Water and wastewater treatment plant and	11,300	11,900	5.0	Gaming cage workers
			system operators	680,000	714,200	5.0	Police and sheriff's patrol officers
167,800	177,600	5.9	Bus drivers, transit and intercity	33,000	34,700	4.9	Agricultural and food science technicians
13,700	14,600	5.9	Career/technical education teachers, middle	145,200	152,300	4.9	Financial specialists, nsk
			school	1,878,100	1,971,100	4.9	Stock clerks and order fillers
250,600	265,400	5.9	Coaches and scouts	240,700	252,200	4.8	Assemblers and fabricators, nsk
159,400	168,900	5.9	Kindergarten teachers, except special	16,900	17,700	4.8	Building cleaning workers, nsk
			education	998,000	1,046,000	4.8	Business operations specialists, nsk
627,500	664,200	5.9	Middle school teachers, except special and	74,000	77,600	4.8	Civil engineering technicians
			career/technical education	373,200	391,100	4.8	Construction managers
54,300	57,500	5.9	Painters, transportation equipment	13,000	13,600	4.8	Dancers
93,000	98,500	5.9	Special education teachers, middle school	151,300	158,600	4.8	Highway maintenance workers
134,000	141,900	5.9	Special education teachers, secondary school	32,300	33,800	4.8	Outdoor power equipment and other small
15,000	15,900	5.8	Animal control workers				engine mechanics
240,000	254,000	5.8	Education administrators, elementary and	19,800	20,700	4.8	Umpires, referees, and other sports officials
			secondary school	31,000	32,400	4.7	Advertising and promotions managers
1,358,000	1,436,300	5.8	Elementary school teachers, except special	17,300	18,100	4.7	Bailiffs
			education	3,700	3,800	4.7	Camera and photographic equipment repairers
2,360,600	2,496,900	5.8	Janitors and cleaners, except maids and	445,300	466,100	4.7	Driver/sales workers
			housekeeping cleaners	430,700	451,000	4.7	First-line supervisors of non-retail sales
113,800	120,400	5.8	Protective service workers, nsk				workers
961,600	1,017,500	5.8	Secondary school teachers, except special and	18,600	19,400	4.7	Locker room, coatroom, and dressing room
			career/technical education				attendants
21,500	22,700	5.7	Economists	55,900	58,500	4.7	Religious workers, nsk

Total Employment 2014	2024	% Change	Occupation
12,000	12,500	4.7	Subway and streetcar operators
12,900	13,500	4.6	Buyers and purchasing agents, farm products
68,700	71,900	4.6	First-line supervisors of protective service workers, nsk
482,000	503,900	4.6	Human resources specialists
140,800	147,100	4.5	Court, municipal, and license clerks
61,400	64,200	4.5	Structural iron and steel workers
2,900	3,000	4.4	Agricultural engineers
199,500	208,200	4.4	Dispatchers, except police, fire, and ambulance
14,800	15,400	4.4	Electrical and electronics installers and repairers, transportation equipment
1,537,800	1,605,400	4.4	First-line supervisors of retail sales workers
376,400	393,200	4.4	Hosts and hostesses, restaurant, lounge, and coffee shop
23,600	24,700	4.4	Material moving workers, nsk
131,900	137,500	4.3	Directors, religious activities and education
163,500	170,600	4.3	Installation, maintenance, and repair workers, nsk
108,100	112,700	4.2	First-line supervisors of police and detectives
14,000	14,600	4.2	Forest and conservation workers
8,600	8,900	4.2	Musical instrument repairers and tuners
135,600	141,300	4.2	Parking lot attendants
45,300	47,200	4.1	Glaziers
105,500	109,900	4.1	Tire repairers and changers
84,700	88,100	4.0	Compensation, benefits, and job analysis specialists
37,800	39,300	4.0	Education administrators, nsk
136,900	142,300	4.0	Engineers, nsk
70,300	73,100	4.0	Occupational health and safety specialists
13,000	13,500	4.0	Tank car, truck, and ship loaders
21,300	22,200	4.0	Zoologists and wildlife biologists
7,200	7,500	3.9	Airfield operations specialists
8,100	8,400	3.9	Explosives workers, ordnance handling experts, and blasters
985,600	1,023,600	3.9	Managers, nsk
7,700	8,000	3.8	Anthropologists and archeologists
58,900	61,100	3.8	Interior designers
36,400	37,800	3.8	Pesticide handlers, sprayers, and applicators, vegetation
66,400	68,900	3.8	Social workers, nsk
457,600	474,700	3.7	Correctional officers and jailers
442,100	458,500	3.7	Counter and rental clerks
11,400	11,800	3.6	Aerospace engineering and operations technicians
19,300	20,000	3.6	Electric motor, power tool, and related repairers
91,700	95,000	3.6	Probation officers and correctional treatment specialists
397,900	412,300	3.6	Welders, cutters, solderers, and brazers
15,400	16,000	3.5	Food scientists and technologists
22,400	23,200	3.5	Microbiologists
173,300	179,300	3.5	Musicians and singers
3,600	3,700	3.5	Transit and railroad police
11,500	11,900	3.4	Gaming and sports book writers and runners
5,100	5,300	3.4	Gas compressor and gas pumping station operators
299,700	309,500	3.3	Claims adjusters, examiners, and investigators
260,300	269,000	3.3	Compliance officers
233,000	240,800	3.3	Computer occupations, nsk
29,300	30,300	3.3	Funeral service managers
55,100	56,900	3.3	Natural sciences managers
236,200	244,000	3.3	Production workers, nsk
11,400	11,800	3.3	Recreational vehicle service technicians
40,200	41,600	3.3	Transportation workers, nsk
82,100	84,700	3.2	Music directors and composers
77,700	80,100	3.1	Computer hardware engineers
26,300	27,100	3.1	Fine artists, including painters, sculptors, and illustrators

Total Employment 2014	2024	% Change	Occupation
47,600	49,100	3.1	First-line supervisors of correctional officers
884,700	911,900	3.1	Light truck or delivery services drivers
3,062,500	3,158,200	3.1	Office clerks, general
297,100	306,200	3.1	Pharmacists
124,900	128,800	3.1	Photographers
23,100	23,800	2.9	Fashion designers
199,700	205,600	2.9	First-line supervisors of transportation and material-moving machine and vehicle operators
10,200	10,500	2.9	Public address system and other announcers
1,900	1,900	2.8	Astronomers
120,800	124,100	2.8	Merchandise displayers and window trimmers
337,400	346,800	2.8	Real estate sales agents
2,465,100	2,534,000	2.8	Waiters and waitresses
7,300	7,500	2.7	Materials scientists
22,500	23,100	2.7	Motorboat mechanics and service technicians
21,500	22,000	2.7	Rail car repairers
91,100	93,500	2.6	Chemists
2,457,000	2,521,100	2.6	Secretaries and administrative assistants, except legal, medical, and executive
19,700	20,200	2.5	Agents and business managers of artists, performers, and athletes
60,800	62,300	2.5	Budget analysts
74,600	76,400	2.4	Art directors
131,600	134,800	2.4	Computer, automated teller, and office machine repairers
29,600	30,300	2.4	Electronic home entertainment equipment installers and repairers
530,900	543,500	2.4	Industrial truck and tractor operators
188,500	193,000	2.4	Information and record clerks, nsk
6,400	6,600	2.4	Paperhangers
136,500	139,700	2.3	Writers and authors
173,100	176,900	2.2	First-line supervisors of helpers, laborers, and material movers, hand
97,900	100,100	2.2	Flight attendants
42,400	43,400.	2.2	Petroleum pump system operators, refinery operators, and gaugers
111,600	114,100	2.2	Transportation, storage, and distribution managers
304,600	310,900	2.1	Production, planning, and expediting clerks
182,100	185,800	2.0	Architectural and engineering managers
25,400	25,900	2.0	Camera operators, television, video, and motion picture
3,424,200	3,491,100	2.0	Cashiers
38,400	39,200	2.0	Commercial and industrial designers
48,400	49,300	2.0	Mechanical engineering technicians
79,200	80,800	2.0	Structural metal fabricators and fitters
66,500	67,700	1.9	Chemical technicians
6,200	6,300	1.9	Fish and game wardens
143,100	145,700	1.9	Librarians
130,400	132,900	1.9	Logisticians
34,300	34,900	1.8	Chemical engineers
208,200	212,000	1.8	Laundry and dry-cleaning workers
83,900	85,400	1.8	Real estate brokers
3,500	3,500	1.7	Historians
2,900	2,900	1.7	Hoist and winch operators
695,400	706,900	1.7	Packers and packagers, hand
129,900	132,000	1.6	Eligibility interviewers, government programs
13,200	13,400	1.6	Gaming service workers, nsk
90,400	91,800	1.6	Tax preparers
20,800	21,100	1.5	Court reporters
20,700	21,000	1.5	Nuclear medicine technologists
4,000	4,100	1.5	Rail yard engineers, dinkey operators, and hostlers
261,600	265,200	1.4	Graphic designers
12,800	13,000	1.4	Precision instrument and equipment repairers, nsk
39,100	39,700	1.4	Stationary engineers and boiler operators

Total Employment		%		Total Employment		%	
2014	2024	Change	Occupation	2014	2024	Change	Occupation
119,900	121,500	1.3	Aircraft mechanics and service technicians	97,700	97,000	-0.7	Coating, painting, and spraying machine setters, operators, and tenders
98,100	99,300	1.3	Cabinetmakers and bench carpenters	28,400	28,200	-0.7	Fishing and hunting workers
37,500	38,000	1.3	Food cooking machine operators and tenders	58,300	57,900	-0.7	Legislators
25,300	25,600	1.3	Materials engineers	2,600	2,500	-0.7	Sociologists
3,800	3,900	1.3	Rail transportation workers, nsk	195,900	194,300	-0.8	Order clerks
26,400	26,700	1.2	Transportation inspectors	7,500	7,400	-0.9	Nuclear power reactor operators
75,700	76,500	1.1	Airline pilots, copilots, and flight engineers	3,500	3,400	-1.1	Bridge and lock tenders
178,400	180,200	1.0	Electrical engineers	50,000	49,500	-1.1	Sawing machine setters, operators, and tenders, wood
378,400	382,200	1.0	Packaging and filling machine operators and tenders	343,400	339,400	-1.2	Chief executives
28,500	28,800	1.0	Physical scientists, nsk	116,700	115,300	-1.2	Detectives and criminal investigators
73,000	73,700	1.0	Purchasing managers	36,100	35,700	-1.2	Funeral attendants
241,100	243,200	0.9	Industrial engineers	15,500	15,400	-1.2	Insurance appraisers, auto damage
14,700	14,800	0.7	Electro-mechanical technicians	74,100	73,200	-1.2	Pest control workers
18,500	18,700	0.7	Food and tobacco roasting, baking, and drying machine operators and tenders	43,800	43,300	-1.3	Separating, filtering, clarifying, precipitating, and still machine setters, operators, and tenders
27,800	28,000	0.7	Gaming supervisors				
1,800	1,800	0.7	Refractory materials repairers, except brickmasons	80,200	79,100	-1.4	Door-to-door sales workers, news and street vendors, and related workers
35,900	36,200	0.6	Cooks, private household	137,400	135,500	-1.4	Electronics engineers, except computer
10,600	10,600	0.6	Craft artists	2,600	2,600	-1.4	Model makers, wood
68,500	68,900	0.6	Gaming dealers	140,800	138,800	-1.4	Reservation and transportation ticket agents and travel clerks
29,700	29,900	0.6	Judges, magistrate judges, and magistrates				
118,000	118,700	0.6	Telecommunications line installers and repairers	7,000	6,900	-1.6	Animal breeders
				1,400	1,400	-1.6	Geographers
5,800	5,800	0.5	Aircraft cargo handling supervisors	7,400	7,300	-1.8	Mine cutting and channeling machine operators
42,400	42,600	0.5	Control and valve installers and repairers, except mechanical door	22,100	21,700	-1.8	Railroad brake, signal, and switch operators
13,400	13,500	0.4	Artists and related workers, nsk	929,800	911,700	-1.9	Farmers, ranchers, and other agricultural managers
17,400	17,500	0.4	Avionics technicians				
79,600	79,900	0.4	Career/technical education teachers, secondary school	45,100	44,300	-1.9	Railroad conductors and yardmasters
				1,700	1,600	-1.9	Timing device assemblers and adjusters
18,500	18,600	0.4	Cleaning, washing, and metal pickling equipment operators and tenders	139,400	136,600	-2.0	Electrical and electronics engineering technicians
2,600	2,600	0.3	Mining machine operators, nsk	3,700	3,700	-2.0	Log graders and scalers
41,500	41,600	0.3	Pharmacy aides	17,500	17,200	-2.0	Painting, coating, and decorating workers
67,800	67,800	0.1	Electrical and electronics repairers, commercial and industrial equipment	35,600	34,900	-2.0	Social scientists and related workers, nsk
				44,300	43,400	-2.0	Surveyors
39,000	39,000	0.1	Engine and other machine assemblers	2,700	2,600	-2.2	Mine shuttle car operators
3,900	3,900	0.0	Travel guides	670,200	655,700	-2.2	Shipping, receiving, and traffic clerks
4,800	4,800	-0.1	Loading machine operators, underground mining	72,500	70,800	-2.3	Aerospace engineers
				40,400	39,500	-2.3	Locomotive engineers
152,400	152,300	-0.1	Meat, poultry, and fish cutters and trimmers	6,200	6,000	-2.3	Political scientists
9,500	9,500	-0.1	Signal and track switch repairers	17,100	16,700	-2.4	Furniture finishers
71,300	71,200	-0.1	Weighers, measurers, checkers, and samplers, recordkeeping	13,600	13,300	-2.4	Proofreaders and copy markers
				72,100	70,400	-2.4	Woodworking machine setters, operators, and tenders, except sawing
39,700	39,600	-0.2	Conveyor operators and tenders				
70,100	69,900	-0.2	Engineering technicians, except drafters, nsk	99,800	97,300	-2.5	Multiple machine tool setters, operators, and tenders, metal and plastic
496,600	495,500	-0.2	Inspectors, testers, sorters, samplers, and weighers	167,900	163,400	-2.7	Advertising sales agents
5,800	5,800	-0.2	Models	9,700	9,500	-2.7	Etchers and engravers
37,300	37,100	-0.3	Logging equipment operators	102,000	99,000	-2.9	Police, fire, and ambulance dispatchers
1,800	1,800	-0.3	Patternmakers, wood	94,000	91,200	-3.0	Architectural and civil drafters
71,100	70,800	-0.3	Title examiners, abstractors, and searchers	237,900	230,800	-3.0	Telemarketers
12,900	12,900	-0.3	Woodworkers, nsk	606,900	588,200	-3.1	First-line supervisors of production and operating workers
36,400	36,200	-0.4	Biological scientists, nsk				
122,500	122,000	-0.4	Food batchmakers	70,000	67,800	-3.1	Medical transcriptionists
52,600	52,400	-0.4	Legal support workers, nsk	216,100	209,100	-3.2	Farmworkers, farm, ranch, and aquacultural animals
45,300	45,100	-0.5	Carpet installers				
300,800	299,300	-0.5	Purchasing agents, except wholesale, retail, and farm products	11,900	11,500	-3.2	Plant and system operators, nsk
				7,100	6,900	-3.2	Slot supervisors
14,200	14,100	-0.6	Agricultural inspectors	19,200	18,600	-3.3	Fiberglass laminators and fabricators
8,800	8,700	-0.6	Cooling and freezing equipment operators and tenders	19,400	18,700	-3.3	Media and communication equipment workers, nsk
3,800	3,800	-0.6	Gaming managers	14,700	14,200	-3.4	Drafters, nsk
1,200	1,200	-0.6	Radio operators	58,700	56,700	-3.4	Floral designers
86,400	85,900	-0.6	Slaughterers and meat packers	16,700	16,100	-3.4	Gas plant operators
1,144,200	1,137,700	-0.6	Team assemblers	46,400	44,800	-3.4	Home appliance repairers

Total Employment 2014	2024	% Change	Occupation
104,200	100,700	-3.4	Machine feeders and offbearers
172,800	166,900	-3.4	Payroll and timekeeping clerks
15,000	14,500	-3.6	Administrative law judges, adjudicators, and hearing officers
218,600	210,800	-3.6	Telecommunications equipment installers and repairers, except line installers
216,800	208,900	-3.7	Data entry keyers
173,400	167,000	-3.7	Industrial production managers
419,200	403,200	-3.8	Helpers—production workers
507,400	487,900	-3.9	Dishwashers
16,800	16,200	-4.0	Nuclear engineers
140,600	134,800	-4.1	Human resources assistants, except payroll and timekeeping
215,500	206,700	-4.1	Legal secretaries
42,200	40,400	-4.3	Upholsterers
22,700	21,700	-4.5	Electrical and electronics repairers, powerhouse, substation, and relay
66,500	63,500	-4.5	Industrial engineering technicians
125,100	119,200	-4.7	Mixing and blending machine setters, operators, and tenders
21,200	20,200	-4.8	Metal-refining furnace operators and tenders
40,600	38,600	-4.9	Aircraft structure, surfaces, rigging, and systems assemblers
207,200	197,000	-4.9	Electrical and electronic equipment assemblers
181,600	172,300	-5.1	Cooks, short order
6,800	6,400	-5.1	Nuclear technicians
11,400	10,800	-5.1	Power distributors and dispatchers
12,300	11,600	-5.3	Continuous mining machine operators
117,200	111,000	-5.3	Editors
47,200	44,700	-5.3	Electromechanical equipment assemblers
350,400	330,900	-5.6	Bill and account collectors
159,000	150,100	-5.6	File clerks
10,600	10,000	-5.7	Agricultural workers, nsk
14,900	14,100	-5.7	Coil winders, tapers, and finishers
776,600	732,000	-5.7	Executive secretaries and executive administrative assistants
32,600	30,800	-5.7	Forest and conservation technicians
41,400	38,900	-6.0	Molders, shapers, and casters, except metal and plastic
3,800	3,600	-6.1	Embalmers
46,100	43,300	-6.2	Credit authorizers, checkers, and clerks
67,900	63,700	-6.2	Tax examiners and collectors, and revenue agents
12,400	11,600	-6.3	Judicial law clerks
30,100	28,200	-6.5	Broadcast technicians
41,100	38,400	-6.6	Power plant operators
51,500	48,100	-6.6	Pressers, textile, garment, and related materials
18,400	17,100	-6.8	Adhesive bonding machine operators and tenders
65,700	61,200	-6.8	Mechanical drafters
7,000	6,600	-7.0	Gaming surveillance officers and gaming investigators
30,200	27,900	-7.5	Crushing, grinding, and polishing machine setters, operators, and tenders
4,500	4,100	-7.5	Logging workers, nsk
57,300	52,900	-7.6	Surveying and mapping technicians
520,500	480,500	-7.7	Tellers
53,000	48,900	-7.8	Graders and sorters, agricultural products
82,100	75,600	-7.8	Labor relations specialists
328,600	302,200	-8.0	Computer programmers
63,600	58,400	-8.1	Cutting and slicing machine setters, operators, and tenders
47,100	43,300	-8.2	First-line supervisors of farming, fishing, and forestry workers
52,900	48,600	-8.2	New accounts clerks
66,300	60,800	-8.3	Chemical equipment operators and tenders
72,300	66,300	-8.3	Procurement clerks

Total Employment 2014	2024	% Change	Occupation
25,300	23,200	-8.3	Semiconductor processors
1,760,300	1,611,500	-8.4	Bookkeeping, accounting, and auditing clerks
49,300	45,100	-8.5	Reporters and correspondents
40,500	37,000	-8.5	Tailors, dressmakers, and custom sewers
24,500	22,400	-8.6	Air traffic controllers
34,900	31,900	-8.7	Coin, vending, and amusement machine servicers and repairers
29,900	27,300	-8.8	Grinding and polishing workers, hand
100	100	-8.9	Farm labor contractors
46,600	42,400	-9.0	Transportation security screeners
470,200	427,300	-9.1	Farmworkers and laborers, crop, nursery, and greenhouse
38,100	34,600	-9.2	Chemical plant and system operators
20,900	18,900	-9.7	Furnace, kiln, oven, drier, and kettle operators and tenders
12,000	10,800	-9.8	Sewers, hand
91,900	82,000	-10.7	Paper goods machine setters, operators, and tenders
6,000	5,300	-10.8	Roof bolters, mining
13,300	11,900	-10.9	Gaming change persons and booth cashiers
16,600	14,800	-10.9	Statistical assistants
39,800	35,300	-11.3	Jewelers and precious stone and metal workers
103,400	91,600	-11.4	Insurance underwriters
4,300	3,800	-11.6	Home economics teachers, postsecondary
74,100	65,400	-11.7	Travel agents
16,200	14,300	-11.8	Textile, apparel, and furnishings workers, nsk
173,000	151,400	-12.5	Printing press operators
5,100	4,500	-12.6	Broadcast news analysts
800	700	-12.6	Fabric menders, except garment
1,200	1,100	-12.6	Mathematical technicians
77,800	67,700	-13.0	Tool and die makers
33,700	29,100	-13.5	Rolling machine setters, operators, and tenders, metal and plastic
68,200	59,000	-13.6	Extruding, forming, pressing, and compacting machine setters, operators, and tenders
18,100	15,600	-13.6	Tire builders
51,200	44,200	-13.7	Print binding and finishing workers
20,100	17,300	-14.1	Extruding and forming machine setters, operators, and tenders, synthetic and glass fibers
42,300	36,300	-14.3	Radio and television announcers
8,400	7,200	-14.7	Correspondence clerks
20,900	17,800	-14.8	Locksmiths and safe repairers
9,700	8,200	-15.1	Shoe and leather workers and repairers
524,400	444,000	-15.3	Cooks, fast food
90,700	76,500	-15.7	Word processors and typists
22,400	18,700	-16.6	Metal workers and plastic workers, nsk
69,600	58,000	-16.6	Office machine operators, except computer
8,200	6,800	-17.2	Fallers
15,800	13,000	-17.5	Cutters and trimmers, hand
11,500	9,500	-17.5	Tool grinders, filers, and sharpeners
37,400	30,600	-18.0	Meter readers, utilities
59,500	48,800	-18.0	Welding, soldering, and brazing machine setters, operators, and tenders
6,700	5,500	-18.2	Motion picture projectionists
36,100	29,400	-18.4	Plating and coating machine setters, operators, and tenders, metal and plastic
104,900	85,100	-18.8	Mail clerks and mail machine operators, except postal service
61,100	49,500	-19.0	Computer operators
10,700	8,700	-19.2	Respiratory therapy technicians
21,300	17,200	-19.6	Heat treating equipment setters, operators, and tenders, metal and plastic
42,900	34,300	-20.0	Lathe and turning machine tool setters, operators, and tenders, metal and plastic
13,400	10,700	-20.1	Layout workers, metal and plastic
17,800	14,100	-20.5	Drilling and boring machine tool setters, operators, and tenders, metal and plastic

Total Employment		%	
2014	2024	Change	Occupation
192,200	152,700	-20.6	Cutting, punching, and press machine setters, operators, and tenders, metal and plastic
22,400	17,800	-20.6	Milling and planing machine setters, operators, and tenders, metal and plastic
9,400	7,400	-20.8	Parking enforcement workers
14,800	11,700	-21.0	Desktop publishers
21,600	17,000	-21.5	Forging machine setters, operators, and tenders, metal and plastic
6,200	4,900	-21.5	Model makers, metal and plastic
26,000	20,300	-21.7	Textile winding, twisting, and drawing out machine setters, operators, and tenders
71,400	55,800	-21.9	Grinding, lapping, polishing, and buffing machine tool setters, operators, and tenders, metal and plastic
3,800	2,900	-23.4	Patternmakers, metal and plastic
11,700	8,900	-23.9	Textile bleaching and dyeing machine operators and tenders
73,400	55,500	-24.4	Extruding and drawing machine setters, operators, and tenders, metal and plastic
36,500	27,500	-24.6	Prepress technicians and workers
129,500	97,200	-25.0	Molding, coremaking, and casting machine setters, operators, and tenders, metal and plastic
14,300	10,600	-25.7	Textile cutting machine setters, operators, and tenders
2,700	2,000	-25.7	Watch repairers
5,400	4,000	-26.0	Fabric and apparel patternmakers
69,600	51,300	-26.2	Postal service clerks
297,400	219,400	-26.2	Postal service mail carriers
17,300	12,800	-26.2	Postmasters and mail superintendents
27,900	20,600	-26.2	Textile knitting and weaving machine setters, operators, and tenders
9,800	7,200	-26.6	Pourers and casters, metal
153,900	112,200	-27.1	Sewing machine operators
12,000	8,700	-27.7	Foundry mold and coremakers
4,000	2,800	-30.0	Manufactured building and mobile home installers
3,500	2,500	-30.5	Shoe machine operators and tenders
28,800	19,400	-32.9	Photographic process workers and processing machine operators
112,400	75,400	-32.9	Switchboard operators, including answering service
117,600	78,000	-33.7	Postal service mail sorters, processors, and processing machine operators
13,100	7,500	-42.4	Telephone operators
11,500	5,800	-50.0	Electronic equipment installers and repairers, motor vehicles
1,700	500	-69.9	Locomotive firers

JUN – – 2017